THE EXHAUSTIVE CONCORDANCE OF THE BIBLE:

SHOWING EVERY WORD OF THE TEXT OF THE COMMON ENGLISH VERSION OF THE CANONICAL BOOKS,

AND

EVERY OCCURRENCE OF EACH WORD IN REGULAR ORDER;

TOGETHER WITH A

KEY-WORD COMPARISON

OF SELECTED WORDS AND PHRASES IN THE KING JAMES VERSION

WITH

FIVE LEADING CONTEMPORARY TRANSLATIONS

ALSO BRIEF

DICTIONARIES OF THE HEBREW AND GREEK WORDS

OF THE ORIGINAL,

WITH REFERENCES TO THE ENGLISH WORDS:

BY

JAMES STRONG, S.T.D., LL.D.

ABINGDON
NASHVILLE

Library of Congress Cataloging in Publication Data

Strong, James, 1822-1894.
Strong's exhaustive concordance of the Bible, with key-word comparison of selected words and phrases in the King James version with five leading translations.

1. Bible—Concordances, English. 2. Hebrew language—Dictionaries—English. 3. Greek language, Biblical—Dictionaries—English. I. Title. II. Title: Exhaustive concordance of the Bible.
BS425.S8 1980 220.5'2 80-11952

ISBN 0-687-40030-9
ISBN 0-687-40031-7 (thumb-indexed)

PRINTED IN THE UNITED STATES OF AMERICA

First Edition Printed April, 1894
Thirty-eighth Printing 1980

GENERAL PREFACE

THIS work, as the title-page indicates, consists of several portions somewhat distinct but mutually related, all having reference to one great object, a thorough verbal index to the Holy Scriptures, as they exist in the three most important forms now known to British and American readers and scholars, namely, the partly Hebrew and partly Greek original text, and the "Authorized" and "Revised" English Versions. The basis of the whole work is the first and much the largest portion, to which this Preface more particularly applies. The design and use of the succeeding portions are explained in the Prefaces to them respectively.

The present work is entitled "The Exhaustive Concordance" to the text of the English Bible ordinarily in use, because it is the only one hitherto constructed that gives all the words of that book and all the passages where they are found; and in this respect no Concordance can ever be made more perfect.

In its preparation three great features have been constantly kept in view, *completeness*, *simplicity*, and *accuracy*. It is intended to be a permanent standard for purposes of reference: so full in its vocabulary and lists that every one consulting it will be sure to find a passage easily and quickly, by seeking it under any word whatever that it contains; so plain in its arrangement that a child cannot miss his way in using it; so correct in its citations, both numerical and verbal, that the most scholarly may implicitly depend upon it.* A mere comparison with other works of the kind hitherto produced, however useful they may have been in their place, will reveal the fact that none of them perfectly or adequately combines these advantages; and it will especially be evident that they all fall short in the most essential requisite, namely, completeness.

For this reason no preceding work of the kind has been taken as a basis for the present one; it is entirely independent of them all. The passages were collected directly from the sacred text, and they have been repeatedly compared with it, both in the manuscript and in type, in so careful and thorough a manner as to test satisfactorily their exhaustiveness and exactness. The comparatively few passages—chiefly unimportant particles, which have at last been found to have escaped all previous verification, are given in the ADDENDA at the close of this vocabulary.

By observing the subjoined Directions, in the associated use of the HEBREW and GREEK DICTIONARIES, the reader will have substantially a Concordance-Lexicon of the Authorized Version and the Hebrew Old Testament and the Greek New Testament.

---

*The most unsparing industry and scrupulous care have been exercised to weed out all errors, as the work was passing through the press, by means of varied and minute verification with the English and the original texts; but in a task so extended and of such intricacy and peculiar detail, the author cannot hope to have escaped all errata, whether typographical or clerical. He feels confident, however, that in the most essential part of the work, namely, the MAIN CONCORDANCE, which gives the means of readily finding any passage in the Common Version—the purpose for which a Concordance is usually consulted—this will rarely if ever be found defective. He will be thankful to any of his readers who will do him the favor of pointing out any errors that they may discover in it, with a view to their future correction.

DIRECTIONS AND EXPLANATIONS.

LOOK for the passage sought under any one of its words exactly as it is spelled in the Bible,* choosing for convenience' sake the most striking or significant word in the passage that you can recall.†

The leading word in each article is printed in *italic* letter in the several citations, and always abbreviated to its initial letter, followed by a suspended (technically "inverted") period-mark (·). No other italics are used in the quotations.

Phrases, groups or combinations of words (not printed as compounds in ordinary Bibles) will be found under each of their words separately. The chapter-headings and marginal notes of reference-Bibles and similar works are of course not included in the citations; but the *titles* to the Books, to the Psalms severally and the *subscriptions* to the Epistles are, as they represent parts of the original texts.

The following forty-seven unimportant words of very frequent occurrence are cited (in the APPENDIX) by reference to chapter and verse only, inasmuch as no person would think of searching out a text by means of them, and the quotation in full of the passages where they are found would be nearly tantamount to reprinting the entire Bible under each of them:

a	*as*	*for*	*him*	*is*	*not*	*out*	*that*	*them*	*to*	*us*	*with*
an	*be*	*from*	*his*	*it*	*O*	*shall*	*the*	*they*	*unto*	*was*	*ye*
and	*but*	*he*	*I*	*me*	*of*	*shalt*	*thee*	*thou*	*up*	*we*	*you*
are	*by*	*her*	*in*	*my*	*our*	*she*	*their*	*thy*	*upon*	*were*	

In the use of the *reference-column* appended to the passages, which is the key to the connection with the subsequent portions of the work, the following particulars will be sufficient to note here.

1. An *asterisk* (*) calls attention to the fact that in the text quoted the leading word is changed for some other in the Revised Version; while an *obelisk* (†)) shows that a change has been made by the British revisers only (English Revised Version 1881-85), and a *double obelisk* (‡) marks a change by the American revisers only (American Standard Version 1901). The nature of these changes were indicated in the COMPARATIVE CONCORDANCE. That section has now been replaced by the new KEY-WORD COMPARISON.

2. The appended *number* indicates that the leading word in the passage quoted is there the translation in the Authorized Version of the Hebrew or Greek word correspondingly numbered in the DICTIONARIES given in the latter portions of this work; upright numerals (1, 2, 3, etc.) being used for the Old Testament (that is, Heb. or Chald.), and sloping or "italic" ones (*1, 2, 3,* etc.) for the New Testament (that is, Greek). The lexical explanations may thus be found and used by any person, whether acquainted with the original languages or not. The absence of a number at the end of the passage shows that the word in question is not there the rendering of any particular term in the original, having either been supplied by the translators for the purpose of greater clearness (in which case in ordinary Bibles it is printed *in italics*), or being the representative merely of some inflectional *form* (auxiliary, preposition, adjunct, etc., or peculiar *idiom* of a Hebrew or Greek term (which in that case is to be sought under the principal associated word of the same passage).

The following abbreviations of the names of the several books of the Bible are uniformly employed, no two of them being designated by the same formula:

ABBREVIATIONS OF THE NAMES OF THE BOOKS OF THE BIBLE

Ge = Genesis.	Job = Job.	Hab = Habakkuk.	1Th = I. Thessalonians.
Ex " Exodus.	Ps " Psalms.	Zep " Zephaniah.	2Th " II. Thessalonians.
Le " Leviticus.	Pr " Proverbs.	Hag " Haggai.	1Ti " I. Timothy.
Nu " Numbers.	Ec " Ecclesiastes.	Zec " Zechariah.	2Ti " II. Timothy.
De " Deuteronomy.	Ca " Canticles.	Mal " Malachi.	Tit " Titus.
Jos " Joshua.	Isa " Isaiah.	M't " Matthew.	Ph'm " Philemon.
J'g " Judges.	Jer " Jeremiah.	M'r " Mark.	Heb " Hebrews.
Ru " Ruth.	La " Lamentations.	Lu " Luke.	Jas " James.
1Sa " I. Samuel.	Eze " Ezekiel.	Joh " John.	1Pe " I. Peter.
2Sa " II. Samuel.	Da " Daniel.	Ac " Acts.	2Pe " II. Peter
1Ki " I. Kings.	Ho " Hosea.	Ro " Romans.	1Jo " I. John.
2Ki " II. Kings.	Joe " Joel.	1Co " I. Corinthians.	2Jo " II. John.
1Ch " I. Chronicles.	Am " Amos.	2Co " II. Corinthians.	3Jo " III. John.
2Ch " II. Chronicles.	Ob " Obadiah.	Ga " Galatians.	Jude " Jude.
Ezr " Ezra.	Jon " Jonah.	Eph " Ephesians.	Re " Revelation.
Ne " Nehemiah.	Mic " Micah.	Ph'p " Philippians.	
Es " Esther.	Na " Nahum.	Col " Colossians.	

* The standard of verification employed is *"The Parallel Bible,"* minion (a large 8vo edition of the Oxford Press, England; impression of 1886), to which the spelling, punctuation, and use of (initial) capitals and hyphen have been rigidly conformed.

† From a failure to recollect a passage accurately, persons often search for it in a Concordance under some word which it really does not contain. If the reader does not find in this Concordance the passage sought for under the word which he has chosen for that purpose, he may be sure that such a mistake of his own is the reason. In that case he has only to look for it under some other word. If he can remember only one word of the passage, he could scarcely recognize or identify it, should he actually find it.

MAIN CONCORDANCE.

A.

2 See in the APPENDIX; also AN.

Aaron (a'-ur-un) See also AARON'S; AARONITES.
Ex 4:14 Is not A' the Levite thy brother? 175
27 the Lord said to A', Go into the "
28 Moses told A' all the words of the "
29 Moses and A' went and gathered "
30 A' spake all the words which the "
5: 1 afterward Moses and A' went in, "
4 Wherefore do ye, Moses and A', let "
20 they met Moses and A., who stood "
6:13 Lord spake unto Moses and unto A', "
20 and she bare him A' and Moses: "
23 A' took him Elisheba, daughter of "
26 These are that A' and Moses, to "
27 these are that Moses and A'. "
7: 1 and A' thy brother shall be thy "
2 and A' thy brother shall speak "
6 Moses and A' did as the Lord "
7 and A' fourscore and three years "
8 Lord spake unto Moses and unto A', "
9 then thou shalt say unto A', Take "
10 And Moses and A' went in unto "
10 and A' cast down his rod before "
19 Lord spake unto Moses, Say unto A', "
20 Moses and A' did so, as the Lord "
8: 5 Say unto A', Stretch forth thine "
6 A' stretched out his hand over the "
8 Pharaoh called for Moses and A', "
12 Moses and A' went out from "
16 Say unto A', Stretch out thy rod, "
17 for A' stretched out his hand with "
25 Pharaoh called for Moses and for A', "
9: 8 Lord said unto Moses and unto A', "
27 sent, and called for Moses and A', "
10: 3 Moses and A' came in unto "
8 Moses and A' were brought again "
16 Pharaoh called for Moses and A' in "
11:10 Moses and A' did all these wonders "
12: 1 the Lord spake unto Moses and A' "
28 Lord had commanded Moses and A', "
31 he called for Moses and A' by night, "
43 the Lord said unto Moses and A', "
50 the Lord commanded Moses and A', "
15:20 the prophetess, the sister of A', "
16: 2 murmured against Moses and A' "
6 Moses and A' said unto all the "
9 Moses spake unto A', Say unto all "
10 as A' spake unto the whole "
33 Moses said unto A', Take a pot, "
34 so A' laid it up before the "
17:10 and Moses, A', and Hur went up "
12 and A' and Hur stayed up his "
18:12 and A' came, and all the elders of "
19:24 thou shalt come up, thou, and A' "
24: 1 up unto the Lord thou and A', "
9 Then went up Moses, and A', "
14 and, behold, A' and Hur are with "
27:21 A' and his sons shall order it from "
28: 1 take thou unto thee A' thy "
1 in the priest's office, even A', "
2 shalt make holy garments for A' "
4 shall make holy garments for A' "
12 and A' shall bear their names "
29 A' shall bear the names of the "
30 and A' shall bear the judgment of "
35 And it shall be upon A' to minister "
38 that A' may bear the iniquity of "
41 thou shalt put them upon A' thy "
43 they shall be upon A', and upon "
29: 4 A' and his sons thou shalt bring "
5 and put upon A' the coat, and the "
9 shalt gird them with girdles, A' "
9 thou shalt consecrate A' and his "
10,15,19 A' and his sons shall put their "
20 upon the tip of the right ear of A', "
21 and sprinkle it upon A', and upon "
24 shalt put all in the hands of A', "
27 even of that which is for A', and "
29 the holy garments of A' shall be "
32 A' and his sons shall eat the flesh "
35 thus shalt thou do unto A', and to "
44 I will sanctify also both A' and "
30: 7 A' shall burn thereon sweet "
8 when A' lighteth the lamps at even, "
10 A' shall make an atonement upon "
19 For A' and his sons shall wash "
30 thou shalt anoint A' and his sons, "
31:10 and the holy garments for A' the "
32: 1 themselves together unto A', and "
2 A' said unto them, Break off the "
3 and brought them unto A'. "
5 when A' saw it he built an altar "
5 A' made proclamation, and said, "
21 Moses said unto A', What did this "

Ex 32:22 A' said, Let not the anger of my 175
25 (for A' had made them naked unto "
35 they made the calf, which A' made. "
34:30 when A' and all the children of "
31 A' and all the rulers of the "
35:19 the holy garments for A', the "
38:21 by the hand of Ithamar, son to A' "
39: 1 made the holy garments for A'; "
27 fine linen of woven work for A', "
41 and the holy garments for A' the "
40:12 thou shalt bring A' and his sons "
13 thou shalt put upon A' the holy "
31 Moses and A' and his sons washed "
Le 1: 7 the sons of A' the priest shall put "
3:13 the sons of A' shall sprinkle the "
6: 9 Command A' and his sons, saying, "
14 the sons of A' shall offer it before "
16 the remainder thereof shall A' "
18 males among the children of A' "
20 This is the offering of A' and of "
25 Speak unto A' and to his sons, "
7:10 and dry, shall all the sons of A' "
33 He among the sons of A', that "
34 and have given them unto A' the "
35 the portion of the anointing of A', "
8: 2 Take A' and his sons with him, "
6 Moses brought A' and his sons, "
14, 18 A' and his sons laid their hands "
22 the ram of consecration: and A' "
30 and sprinkled it upon A', and "
30 sanctified A', and his garments, "
31 Moses said unto A', and to his "
31 as I commanded, saying, A' and "
36 So A' and his sons did all things "
9: 1 the eighth day, that Moses called A' "
2 he said unto A', Take thee a young "
7 Moses said unto A', Go into the "
8 A' therefore went unto the altar, "
9 the sons of A' brought the blood "
21 And the right shoulder A' waved "
22 A' lifted up his right hand toward "
23 Moses and A' went into the "
10: 1 Nadab and Abihu, the sons of A', "
3 Moses said unto A', This is it that "
3 And A' held his peace. "
4 the sons of Uzziel the uncle of A', "
6 Moses said unto A' and unto "
8 the Lord spake unto A', saying, "
12 Moses spake unto A' and unto "
16 the sons of A' which were left "
19 A' said unto Moses, Behold, this "
11: 1 Lord spake unto Moses and to A', "
13: 1 the Lord spake unto Moses and A', "
2 then he shall be brought unto A' "
14:33 Lord spake unto Moses and unto A', "
15: 1 Lord spake unto Moses and to A', "
16: 1 the death of the two sons of A', "
2 Speak unto A' thy brother, that "
3 Thus shall A' come into the holy "
6 A' shall offer his bullock of the sin "
8 A' shall cast lots upon the two goats "
9 A' shall bring the goat upon which "
11 A' shall bring the bullock of the sin "
21 A' shall lay both his hands upon the "
23 A' shall come into the tabernacle "
17: 2 Speak unto A', and unto his sons, "
21: 1 unto the priests the sons of A', and "
17 Speak unto A', saying, Whosoever "
21 hath a blemish of the seed of A' the "
24 Moses told it unto A', and to his "
22: 2 Speak unto A' and to his sons, that "
4 What man soever of the seed of A' "
18 Speak unto A', and to his sons, and "
24: 3 Shall A' order it from the evening "
Nu 1: 3 thou and A' shall number them by "
17 Moses and A' took these men which "
44 which Moses and A' numbered, and "
2: 1 Lord spake unto Moses and unto A', "
3: 1 also are the generations of A' and "
2, 3 are the names of the sons of A' "
4 the priest's office in the sight of A' "
6 and present them before A' the "
9 thou shalt give the Levites unto A' "
10 thou shalt appoint A' and his sons "
32 Eleazar the son of A' the priest "
38 shall be Moses, and A' and his sons "
39 which Moses and A' numbered at "
48 is to be redeemed, unto A' and to "
51 that were redeemed unto A' and to "
4: 1 Lord spake unto Moses and unto A', "
5 when the camp setteth forward, A' "
15 when A' and his sons have made an "
16 the office of Eleazar the son of A' "
17 Lord spake unto Moses and unto A', "
19 A' and his sons shall go in, and "

Nu 4:27 At the appointment of A' and his 175
28, 33 hand of Ithamar the son of A' "
34 Moses and A' and the chief of the "
37 which Moses and A' did number "
41 whom Moses and A' did number "
45 whom Moses and A' numbered "
46 whom Moses and A' and the chief "
6:23 Speak unto A' and unto his sons, "
7: 8 the hand of Ithamar the son of A' "
8: 2 Speak unto A', and say unto him, "
3 A' did so; he lighted the lamps "
11 A' shall offer the Levites before the "
13 shalt set the Levites before A', and "
19 given the Levites as a gift to A' and "
20 And Moses, and A', and all the "
21 and A' offered them as an offering "
21 A' made an atonement for them "
22 of the congregation before A', and "
9: 6 came before Moses and before A' "
10: 8 the sons of A', the priests, shall "
12: 1 And Miriam and A' spake against "
4 suddenly unto Moses, and unto A', "
5 and called A' and Miriam: "
10 and A' looked upon Miriam, and, "
11 A' said unto Moses, Alas, my lord, "
13:26 and came to Moses, and to A', and "
14: 2 against Moses and against A': and "
5 Moses and A' fell on their faces "
26 Lord spake unto Moses and unto A', "
15:33 brought him unto Moses and A', "
16: 3 against Moses and against A', and "
11 and what is A', that ye murmur "
16 thou, and they, and A', to morrow: "
17 and A', each of you his censer. "
18 congregation with Moses and A'. "
20 Lord spake unto Moses and unto A', "
37 Speak unto Eleazar the son of A' "
40 which is not of the seed of A', come "
41, 42 against Moses and against A', "
43 And Moses and A' came before the "
46 Moses said unto A', Take a censer "
47 A' took as Moses commanded, and "
50 A' returned unto Moses unto the "
17: 6 the rod of A' was among their rods. "
8 the rod of A' for the house of Levi "
18: 1 the Lord said unto A', Thou and "
8 the Lord spake unto A', Behold, I "
20 the Lord spake unto A', Thou "
28 the Lord's heave offering to A' the "
19: 1 Lord spake unto Moses and unto A', "
20: 2 against Moses and against A'. "
6 And Moses and A' went from the "
8 thou and A' thy brother, and speak "
10 And Moses and A' gathered the "
12, 23 Lord spake unto Moses and A', "
24 A' shall be gathered unto his people "
25 Take A' and Eleazar his son, and "
26 strip A' of his garments, and put "
26 and A' shall be gathered unto his "
28 Moses stripped A' of his garments "
28 and A' died there in the top of the "
29 congregation saw that A' was dead, "
29 they mourned for A' thirty days "
25: 7 the son of Eleazar, the son of A' the "
11 the son of A' the priest, hath turned "
26: 1 and unto Eleazar the son of A' the "
9 and against A' in the company of "
59 and she bare unto Amram A' and "
60 And unto A' was born Nadab and "
64 a man of them whom Moses and A' "
27:13 as A' thy brother was gathered. "
33: 1 under the hand of Moses and A'. "
38 A' the priest went up into mount "
39 A' was a hundred and twenty and "
De 9:20 Lord was very angry with A' to "
20 and I prayed for A' also the "
10: 6 there A' died, and there he was "
32:50 as A' thy brother died in mount "
Jos 21: 4 and the children of A' the priest, "
10 Which the children of A', being of "
13 Thus they gave to the children of A' "
19 All the cities of the children of A', "
24: 5 I sent Moses also and A', and I "
33 And Eleazar the son of A' died; "
J'g 20:28 the son of A', stood before it in "
1Sa 12: 6 Lord that advanced Moses and A', "
8 then the Lord sent Moses and A', "
1Ch 6: 3 the children of Amram; A', and "
3 The sons also of A'; Nadab and "
49 But A' and his sons offered upon "
50 these are the sons of A'; Eleazar "
54 of the sons of A', of the families of "
57 And to the sons of A' they gave the "
15: 4 David assembled the children of A', "
23:13 of Amram; A' and Moses: and A' "

1Ch 23:28 office was to wait on the sons of A· 175
32 and the charge of the sons of A· "
24: 1 are the divisions of the sons of A· "
1 The sons of A·; Nadab and "
19 to their manner, under A· their "
31 their brethren the sons of A· in the "
2Ch 13: 9 the sons of A·, and the Levites, and "
10 unto the Lord, are the sons of A·, "
26:18 but to the priests the sons of A·, "
29:21 the priests the sons of A· to offer "
31:19 Also of the sons of A· the priests, "
35:14 because the priests the sons of A· "
14 and for the priests the sons of A·. "
Ezr 7: 5 Eleazar, the son of A· the chief "
Ne 10:38 the priest the son of A· shall be "
12:47 them unto the children of A·. "
Ps 77:20 flock by the hand of Moses and A·. "
99: 6 Moses and A· among his priests, "
105:26 He sent Moses his servant; and A· "
106:16 Moses also in the camp, and A· "
115:10 O house of A·, trust in the Lord: "
12 he will bless the house of A·. "
118: 3 Let the house of A· now say, that "
135:19 bless the Lord, O house of A·: "
Mic 6: 4 I sent before thee Moses, A·, and "
Lu 1: 5 wife was of the daughters of A·, *2*
Ac 7:40 Saying unto A·, Make us gods to "
Heb 5: 4 that is called of God, as was A·. "
7:11 not be called after the order of A·? "

Aaronites (*a'-ur-un-ites*)
1Ch 12:27 Jehoida was the leader of the A·, * 175
27:17 the son of Kemuel: of the A·, * "

Aaron's (*a'-ur-uns*)
Ex 6:25 Eleazar A· son took him one of the 175
7:12 but A· rod swallowed up their rods. "
28: 1 Eleazar and Ithamar, A· sons. "
3 that they may make A· garments "
30 and they shall be upon A· heart, "
38 And it shall be upon A· forehead "
40 for A· sons thou shalt make coats, "
29:26 of the ram of A· consecration, "
28 it shall be A· and his sons' by a * "
Le 1: 5 the priests, A· sons, shall bring "
8 the priests, A· sons, shall lay the "
11 the priests, A· sons, shall sprinkle "
2: 2 he shall bring it to A· sons the "
3, 10 of the meat offering shall be A· "
3: 2 A· sons the priests shall sprinkle "
5 A· sons shall burn it on the altar "
8 A· sons shall sprinkle the blood "
7:31 but the breast shall be A· and his "
8:12 the anointing oil upon A· head, "
13 Moses brought A· sons, and put "
23 put it upon the tip of A· right ear, "
24 he brought A· sons, and Moses "
27 he put all upon A· hands, and * "
9:12, 18 and A· sons presented unto him "
24: 9 it shall be A· and his sons'; and * "
Nu 17: 3 thou shalt write A· name upon "
10 Bring A· rod again before the * "
Ps 133: 2 upon the beard, even A· beard: "
Heb 9: 4 pot that had manna, and A· rod *2*

Abaddon (*ab-ad'-dun*)
Re 9:11 name in the Hebrew tongue is A·, *3*

Abagtha (*ab-ag'-thah*)
Es 1:10 Bigtha, and A·, Zethar, and Carcas, 5

Abana (*ab-ay'-nah*)
2Ki 5:12 Are not A· and Pharpar, rivers of * 71

Abarim (*ab'-ar-im*) See also IJE-ABARIM.
Nu 27:12 Get thee up into this mount A·, 5682
33:47 pitched in the mountains of A·, "
48 departed from the mountains of A·, "
De 32:49 get thee up into this mountain A·, "

abase See also ABASED; ABASING.
Job 40:11 every one that is proud, and a· 8213
Isa 31: 4 nor a· himself for the noise of 6031
Eze 21:26 is low, and a· him that is high. 8213
Da 4:37 that walk in pride he is able to a·. 8214

abased
M't 23:12 shall exalt himself shall be a·; *5013*
Lu 14:11 that exalteth himself shall be a·; * "
18:14 that exalteth himself shall be a·; * "
Ph'p 4:12 I know both how to be a·, and I *5013*

abasing
2Co 11: 7 a· myself that ye might be exalted, *5013*

abated
Ge 8: 3 and fifty days the waters were a·. *2637
8 him to see if the waters were a· 7043
11 nor knew that the waters were a· "
Le 27:18 shall be a· from thy estimation *1639
De 34: 7 not dim, nor his natural force a·. 5127
J'g 8: 3 their anger was a· towards him 7503

Abba (*ab'-bah*)
M'r 14:36 And he said, A·, Father, all things *5*
Ro 8:15 of adoption, whereby we cry, A·, "
Ga 4: 6 into your hearts, crying, A·, Father. "

Abbas See BARABBAS.

Abda (*ab'-dah*)
1Ki 4: 6 and Adoniram the son of A· 5653
Ne 11:17 and A· the son of Shammua, "

Abdeel (*ab'-de-el*)
Jer 36:26 and Shelemiah the son of A·, to 5655

Abdi (*ab'-di*)
1Ch 6:44 the son of Kishi, the son of A·, 5660
2Ch 29:12 Kish the son of A·, and Azariah "
Ezr 10:26 and Jehiel, and A·, and Jeremoth, "

Abdiel (*ab'-de-el*)
1Ch 5:15 Ahi the son of A·, the son of Guni, 5661

Abdon (*ab'-dun*)
Jos 21:30 Mishal with her suburbs, A· with 5658
J'g 12:13 And after him A· the son of "
15 And A· the son of Hillel the "
1Ch 6:74 Moshal with her suburbs, and A· "
8:23 Eliel and A·, and Zichri, and "
30 his firstborn son A·, and Zur, and "
9:36 A·, then Zur, and Kish, and Baal, "
2Ch 34:20 and A· the son of Micah, and "

Abed-nego (*ab-ed'-ne-go*)
Da 1: 7 Meshach; and to Azariah, of A·. 5664
2:49 Shadrach, Meshach, and A·, over 5665
3:12, 13, 14, 16, 19, 20, 22, 23, 26, 26, 28,
29, 30 Shadrach, Meshach, and A· "

Abel (*a'-bel*) See also ABEL-BETH-MAACHAH; ABEL-MAIM; ABEL-MEHOLAH; ABEL-MIZRAIM; ABEL-SHITTIM.
Ge 4: 2 bare his brother A·. And A· was 1893
4 And A·, he also brought of the "
4 the Lord had respect unto A· and "
8 Cain talked with A· his brother: "
8 that Cain rose up against A· his "
9 Lord said unto Cain, Where is A· "
25 me another seed instead of A·, "
1Sa 6:18 even unto the great stone of A·. * 59
2Sa 20:14 all the tribes of Israel unto A·, 62
15 they came and besieged him in A· "
18 They shall surely ask counsel at A·: 59
M't 23:35 from the blood of righteous A· unto *6*
Lu 11:51 From the blood of A· unto the "
Heb 11: 4 By faith A· offered unto God a more "
12:24 better things than that of A·. "

Abel-beth-maachah (*a"-bel-beth-ma'-a-kah*)
1Ki 15:20 and smote Ijon, and Dan, and A·, * 62
2Ki 15:29 and took Ijon, and A·, and * "

Abel-maim (*a"-bel-ma'-im*)
2Ch 16: 4 they smote Ijon, and Dan, and A·, 66

Abel-meholah (*a"-bel-me-ho'-lah*) See also MEHOLATHITE.
J'g 7:22 and to the border of A·, unto 65
1Ki 4:12 from Beth-shean to A·, even unto "
19:16 Elisha the son of Shaphat of A· "

Abel-mizraim (*a"-bel-miz'-ra-im*)
Ge 50:11 the name of it was called A·, which 67

Abel-shittim (*a"-bel-shit'-tim*)
Nu 33:49 from Beth-jesimoth even unto A· 63

Abez (*a'-bez*)
Jos 19:20 And Rabbith, and Kishion, and A·, * 77

abhor See also ABHORRED; ABHORREST; ABHORRETH; ABHORRING.
Le 26:11 and my soul shall not a· you. 1602
15 if your soul a· my judgments, so "
30 your idols, and my soul shall a· you. "
44 neither will I a· them, to destroy "
De 7:26 thou shalt utterly a· it; for it is a 8581
23: 7 Thou shalt not a· an Edomite; "
7 thou shalt not a· an Egyptian; "
1Sa 27:12 his people Israel utterly to a· him 887
Job 9:31 and mine own clothes shall a· me. 8581
30:10 They a· me, they flee far from me, "
42: 6 Wherefore I a· myself, and repent 3988
Ps 5: 6 the Lord will a· the bloody and *8581
119:163 I hate and a· lying: but thy "
Pr 24:24 the people curse, nations shall a· 2194
Jer 14:21 Do not a· us, for thy name's sake, 5006
Am 5:10 and they a· him that speaketh 8581
6: 8 I a· the excellency of Jacob, and 8374
Mic 3: 9 Israel, that a· judgment, and 8581
Ro 12: 9 A· that which is evil; cleave to *655*

abhorred
Ex 5:21 ye have made our savour to be a· 887
Le 20:23 things, and therefore I a· them. 6973
26:43 because their soul a· my statutes. 1602
De 32:19 when the Lord saw it, he a· them, 5006
1Sa 2:17 men a· the offering of the Lord. "
2Sa 16:21 shall hear that thou art a· of thy 887
1Ki 11:25 and he a· Israel, and reigned 6973
Job 19:19 All my inward friends a· me: *8581
Ps 22:24 he hath not despised nor a· the 8262
78:59 was wroth, and greatly a· Israel: 3988
89:38 thou hast cast off and a·, thou "
106:40 that he a· his own inheritance. 8581
Pro 22:14 he that is a· of the Lord shall fall 2194
La 2: 7 he hath a· his sanctuary, he hath 5010
Eze 16:25 hast made thy beauty to be a·, *8581
Zec 11: 8 and their soul also a· me. * 973

abhorrest
Isa 7:16 the land that thou a· shall be 6973
Ro 2:22 that a· idols, dost thou commit *948*

abhorreth
Job 33:20 So that his life a· bread, and 2092
Ps 10: 3 the covetous, whom the Lord a·. *5006
36: 4 that is not good; he a· not evil. 3988
107:18 Their soul a· all manner of meat; 8581
Isa 49: 7 to him whom the nation a·, to a "

abhorring
Isa 66:24 they shall be an a· unto all flesh. 1860

Abi (*a'-bi*) See also ABI-ALBON; ABI-EZER.
2Ki 18: 2 His mother's name also was A·, 21

Abia (*ab-i'-ah*) See also ABIAH; ABIJAH; ABIJAM.
1Ch 3:10 A· his son, Asa his son, * 29
M't 1: 7 Roboam begat A·; and A· begat * *7*
Lu 1: 5 Zacharias, of the course of A·: * "

Abiah (*ab-i'-ah*) See also ABIA.
1Sa 8: 2 and the name of his second, A·: * 29
1Ch 2:24 A· Hezron's wife bare him Ashur "
6:28 the firstborn Vashni, and A·. "
7: 8 Jerimoth, and A·, and Anathoth, * "

Abi-albon (*ab"-i-al'-bun*)
2Sa 23:31 A· the Arbathite, Azmaveth the 45

Abiasaph (*ab-i'-as-af*) See also EBI-ASAPH.
Ex 6:24 Assir, and Elkanah, and A·: 23

Abiathar (*ab-i'-uth-ur*) See also ABIATHAR'S.
1Sa 22:20 son of Ahitub, named A·, escaped, 54
21 And A· shewed David that Saul had "
22 David said unto A·, I knew it that "
23: 6 when A· the son of Ahimelech fled "
9 and he said to A· the priest, Bring "
30: 7 And David said to A· the priest, "
7 And A· brought thither the ephod "
2Sa 8:17 and Ahimelech the son of A·, were "
15:24 A· went up, until all the people "
27 and Jonathan the son of A·. "
29 Zadok therefore and A· carried the "
35 not there with thee Zadok and A· "
35 thou shalt tell it to Zadok and A· "
17:15 said Hushai unto Zadok and to A· "
19:11 king David sent to Zadok and to A· "
20:25 and Zadok and A· were the priests: "
1Ki 1: 7 the son of Zeruiah, and with A· "
19 sons of the king, and A· the priest, "
25 the captains of the host, and A· the "
42 Jonathan the son of A· the priest "
2:22 for him, and for A· the priest, "
26 unto A· the priest said the king, "
27 Solomon thrust out A· from being "
35 did the king put in the room of A·. "
4: 4 and Zadok and A· were the priests: "
1Ch 15:11 And David called for Zadok and A· "
18:16 and Abimelech the son of A·, were "
24: 6 priest, and Ahimelech the son of A·, "
27:34 the son of Benaiah, and A·: "
M'r 2:26 in the days of A· the high priest, *8*

Abiathar's (*ab-i'-uth-urs*)
2Sa 15:36 Zadok's son, and Jonathan A· 54

Abib (*a'-bib*) See also TEL-ABIB.
Ex 13: 4 day came ye out in the month A·. 24
23:15 time appointed of the month A·; "
34:18 in the time of the month A·: for in "
18 the month A· thou camest out from "
De 16: 1 Observe the month of A·, and keep "
1 in the month of A· the Lord thy God "

Abida (*ab'-id-ah*) See also ABIDAH.
1Ch 1:33 and Epher, and Henoch, and A·, 28

Abidah (*ab'-id-ah*) See also ABIDA.
Gen 25: 4 and Hanoch, and A·, and Eldaah, * 28

Abidan (*ab'-id-an*)
Nu 1:11 Of Benjamin; A· the son of Gideoni. 27
2:22 of the sons of Benjamin shall be A· "
7:60 On the ninth day A· the son of "
65 offering of A· the son of Gideoni. "
10:24 of the children Benjamin was A· "

abide See also ABIDETH; ABIDING; ABODE.
Ge 19: 2 we will a· in the street all night. 3885
22: 5 A· ye here with the ass; 3427
24:55 Let the damsel a· with us a few "
29:19 a· with me. "
44:33 let thy servant a· instead of the lad "
Ex 16:29 a· ye every man in his place, "
Le 8:35 Therefore shall ye a· at the door of "
19:13 shall not a· with thee all night 3885
Nu 22: 5 they a· over against me: 3427
31:19 a· without the camp seven days: *2583
23 Every thing that may a· the fire, 935
35:25 he shall a· in it unto the death of *3427
De 3:19 a· in your cities which I have "
Jos 18: 5 Judah shall a· in their coast on 5975
5 Joseph shall a· in their coasts on "
Ru 2: 8 a· here fast by my maidens: 1692
1Sa 1:22 and there a· for ever. 3427
5: 7 God of Israel shall not a· with us: "
19: 2 and a· in a secret place, and hide "
22: 5 A· not in the hold; "
23 A· thou with me, fear not: "
30:21 whom they had made also to a· at "
2Sa 11:11 the ark, and Israel, and Judah, a· "
15:19 return to thy place, and a· with "
16:18 with him will I a·. "
1Ki 8:13 a settled place for thee to a· in * "
2Ch 25:19 a· now at home; "
32:10 ye a· in the siege in Jerusalem? "
Job 24:13 nor a· in the paths thereof. "
38:40 and a· in the covert to lie in wait? "
39: 9 to serve thee, or a· by thy crib? 3885
Ps 15: 1 who shall a· in thy tabernacle? *1481
61: 4 I will a· in thy tabernacle "
7 He shall a· before God for ever: 3427
91: 1 shall a· under the shadow 3885
Pr 7:11 her feet a· not in her house: 7937
19:23 he that hath it shall a· satisfied; 3885
Ec 8:15 shall a· with him of his labour 3867
Jer 10:10 the nations shall not be able to a· 3557
42:10 If ye will still a· in this land, 3427
49:18 no man shall a· there, * "
33 there shall no man a· there, * "
50:40 so shall no man a· there, * "
Ho 3: 3 Thou shalt a· for me many days; "
4 children of Israel shall a· many "
11: 6 the sword shall a· on his cities, *2342
Joe 2:11 and who can a· it? 3557
Mic 5: 4 and they shall a·: 3427
Na 1: 6 who can a· in the fierceness of his 6965
Mal 3: 2 may a· the day of his coming? 3557
M't 10:11 and there a· till ye go thence. 3306
M'r 6:10 a· till ye depart from that place. "
Lu 9: 4 there a·, and thence depart. "
19: 5 for to-day I must a· at thy house. "
24:29 constrained him, saying, A· with "
Joh 12:46 believeth on me should not a· in "
14:16 that he may a· with you for ever: * "
15: 4 A· in me, and I in you. "

Joh 15:4 except it a· in the vine; 3306
4 no more can ye, except ye a· in me. "
6 If a man a· not in me, he is cast "
7 If ye a· in me, and my words a· in "
10 ye shall a· in my love; "
10 and a· in his love. "
Ac 15:34 it pleased Silas to a· there still. *1961
16:15 come into my house, and a· there. 3306
20:23 and afflictions a· me. "
27:31 Except these a· in the ship, "
Ro 11:23 if they a· not still in unbelief, *1961
1Co 3:14 any man's work a· which he hath 3306
7: 8 if they a· even as I. "
20 every man a· in the same calling "
24 every man,....therein a· with God. "
40 she is happier if she so a·, "
16: 6 And it may be that I will a·, yea, 3887
Ph'p 1:24 to a· in the flesh is more needful 1961
25 know that I shall a· and continue 3306
1Ti 1: 3 to a· still at Ephesus, *4357
1Jo 2:24 Let that therefore a· in you, 3306
27 ye shall a· in him. "
28 little children, a· in him; "

abideth
Nu 31:23 all that a· not the fire ye shall 935
2Sa 16: 3 he a· at Jerusalem: 3427
Job 39:28 She dwelleth and a· on the rock, ††3885
Ps 49:12 man being in honour a· not: "
55:19 even he that a· of old. 3427
119:90 established the earth, and it a·. 5975
125: 1 cannot be removed, but a· for ever. 3427
Pr 15:31 reproof of life a· among the wise. *3885
Ec 1: 4 the earth a· for ever. 5975
Jer 21: 9 He that a· in this city shall die 3427
Joh 3:36 the wrath of God a· on him. 3306
8:35 the servant a· not in the house for "
35 but the Son a· ever. "
12:24 ground and die, it a· alone: "
34 of the law that Christ a· for ever: "
15: 5 He that a· in me, and I in him, "
1Co 13:13 now a· faith, hope, charity, "
2Ti 2:13 he a· faithful: he cannot deny "
Heb 7: 3 a· a priest continually. "
1Pe 1:23 which liveth and a· for ever. "
1Jo 2: 6 He that saith he a· in him "
10 a· in the light, "
14 the word of God a· in you, "
17 doeth the will of God a· for ever. "
27 received of him a· in you, "
3: 6 Whosoever a· in him sinneth not: "
14 He that loveth not his brother a· in "
24 hereby we know that he a· in us, "
2Jo 1: 9 a· not in the doctrine of Christ, "
9 He that a· in the doctrine "

abiding
Nu 24: 2 he saw Israel a· in his tents *7931
J'g 16: 9 a· with her in the chamber. 3427
12 a· in the chamber. "
1Sa 26:19 driven me out this day from a· *5596
1Ch 29:15 there is none a·. 4723
Lu 2: 8 shepherds a· in the field, 63
Jo 5:38 ye have not his word a· in you: 3306
Ac 16:12 were in that city a· certain days. *1304
1Jo 3:15 no murderer hath eternal life a· 3306

Abiel (a'-be-el)
1Sa 9: 1 name was Kish, the son of A·, 22
14:51 father of Abner was the son of A·. "
1Ch 11:32 Hurai of the brooks of Gaash, A· "

Abiezer[1] or **Abi-ezer**[2] (ab-i-e'-zur) See also ABI-EZRITE; JEEZER.
Jos 17: 2 for the children of A·[1], and for the 44
J'g 6:34 and A·[2] was gathered after him. "
8: 2 better than the vintage of A·[2]? "
2Sa 23:27 A·[1] the Anethothite, Mebunnai the "
1Ch 7:18 Hammoleketh bare Ishod, and A·[1], "
11:28 Ikkesh the Tekoite, A·[2] the Antothite, "
27:12 captain for the ninth month was A·[1] "

Abi-ezrite (ab-i-ez'-rite) See also ABI-EZRITES.
J'g 6:11 that pertained unto Joash the A·: 33

Abi-ezrites (ab-i-ez'-rites)
J'g 6:24 it is yet in Ophrah of the A·. 33
8:32 his father, in Ophrah of the A·. "

Abigail (ab'-e-gal)
1Sa 25: 3 Nabal; and the name of his wife A·: 26
14 But one of the young men told A·, "
18 Then A· made haste, and took two "
23 when A· saw David, she hasted, "
32 David said to A·, Blessed be the Lord "
36 And A· came to Nabal; and, behold, "
39 David sent and communed with A·, "
40 servants of David were come to A· "
42 And A· hasted, and arose, and rode "
27: 3 A· the Carmelitess, Nabal's wife. "
30: 5 A· the wife of Nabal the Carmelite. "
2Sa 2: 2 and A· Nabal's wife the Carmelite. "
3: 3 A· the wife of Nabal the Carmelite; "
17:25 in to A· the daughter of Nahash, "
1Ch 2:16 Whose sisters were Zeruiah, and A·. "
17 and A· bare Amasa: and the father "
3: 1 the second Daniel, of A· the "

Abihail (ab-e-ha'-il)
Nu 3:35 of Merari was Zuriel the son of A·: 32
1Ch 2:29 name of the wife of Abishur was A·, "
5:14 These are the children of A· the son "
2Ch 11:18 and A· the daughter of Eliab the "
Es 2:15 the daughter of A· the uncle of "
9:29 Esther the queen, the daughter of A·, "

Abihu (a-bi'-hew)
Ex 6:23 and she bare him Nadab and A·, 30
24: 1 thou, and Aaron, Nadab, and A·, "
9 Moses, and Aaron, Nadab, and A·, "
28: 1 office, even Aaron, Nadab and A·, "
Le 10: 1 Nadab and A·, the sons of Aaron, "
Nu 3: 2 Nadab the firstborn, and A·, 30
4 Nadab and A· died before the Lord, "
26:60 unto Aaron was born Nadab, and A·, "
61 And Nadab and A· died, when they "
1Ch 6: 3 sons also of Aaron; Nadab, and A·, "
24: 1 The sons of Aaron; Nadab, and A·, "
2 But Nadab and A· died before their "

Abihud (a-bi'-hud)
1Ch 8: 3 Addar, and Gera, and A·, 31

Abijah (a-bi'-jah) See also ABIA; ABIJAM.
1Ki 14: 1 At that time A· the son of Jeroboam 29
1Ch 24:10 seventh to Hakkoz, the eighth to A·, "
2Ch 11:20 which bare him A·, and Attai, and "
22 Rehoboam made A· the son of "
12:16 and A· his son reigned in his stead. "
13: 1 year of king Jeroboam began A· to "
2 was war between A· and Jeroboam. "
3 And A· set the battle in array with "
4 A· stood up upon mount Zemaraim, "
15 Jeroboam and all Israel before A· "
17 And A· and his people slew them "
19 And A· pursued after Jeroboam, "
20 strength again in the days of A·: "
21 But A· waxed mighty, and married "
22 rest of the acts of A·, and his ways, "
14: 1 So A· slept with his fathers, "
29: 1 And his mother's name was A·, "
Ne 10: 7 Meshullam, A·, Mijamin, "
12: 4 Iddo, Ginnetho, A·, "
17 Of A·, Zichri; of Miniamin, of "

Abijam (a-bi'-jum) See also ABIJAH.
1Ki 14:31 And A· his son reigned in his stead. 38
15: 1 reigned A· over Judah. "
7 the rest of the acts of A·, and all "
7 was war between A· and Jeroboam. "
8 And A· slept with his fathers; and "

Abilene (ab-i-le'-ne)
Lu 3: 1 Lysanias the tetrarch of A·, 9

ability
Le 27: 8 according to his a· that vowed 5381
Ezr 2:69 They gave after their a· 3581
Ne 5: 8 We after our a· have redeemed 1767
Da 1: 4 such as had a· in them 3581
M't 25:15 according to his several a·; 1411
Ac 11:29 every man according to his a·, 2141
1Pe 4:11 as of the a· which God giveth; *2479

Abimael (a-bim'-ah-el)
Ge 10:28 And Obal, and A·, and Sheba, 39
1Ch 1:22 And Ebal, and A·, and Sheba, "

Abimelech (a-bim'-e-lek) See also ABIMELECH'S; AHIMELECH.
Ge 20: 2 and A· king of Gerar sent, and took 40
3 But God came to A· in a dream "
4 But A· had not come near her: "
8 A· rose early in the morning, "
9 Then A· called Abraham, and said "
10 A· said unto Abraham, What sawest "
14 And A· took sheep, and oxen, and "
15 A· said, Behold, my land is before "
17 and God healed A·, and his wife, "
18 all the wombs of the house of A·, "
21:22 that A· and Phichol the chief captain "
25 And Abraham reproved A· because "
26 A· said, I wot not who hath done "
27 and oxen, and gave them unto A·; "
29 A· said unto Abraham, What mean "
32 then A· rose up, and Phichol the "
26: 1 And Isaac went unto A· king of the "
8 A· king of the Philistines looked "
9 And A· called Isaac, and said, "
10 A· said, What is this thou hast done "
11 A· charged all his people, saying, "
16 And A· said unto Isaac, Go from us; "
26 Then A· went to him from Gerar, "
J'g 8:31 a son, whose name he called A·. "
9: 1 And A· the son of Jerubbaal went "
3 their hearts inclined to follow A·; "
4 A· hired vain and light persons, "
6 and went, and made A· king, "
16 in that ye have made A· king, "
18 made A·, the son of his maidservant, "
19 then rejoice ye in A·, and let him "
20 But if not, let fire come out from A·, "
20 the house of Millo, and devour A·. "
21 and dwelt there, for fear of A· his "
22 When A· had reigned three years "
23 God sent an evil spirit between A· "
23 dealt treacherously with A·: "
24 A· their brother, which slew them; "
25 way by them: and it was told A·. "
27 did eat and drink, and cursed A·. "
28 Who is A·, and who is Shechem, "
29 my hand! then would I remove A·. "
29 he said to A·, Increase thine army, "
31 he sent messengers unto A· privily, "
34 And A· rose up, and all the people "
35 And A· rose up, and the people that "
38 Who is A·, that we should serve him? "
39 of Shechem, and fought with A·. "
40 A· chased him, and he fled before "
41 And A· dwelt at Arumah: and Zebul "
42 out into the field; and they told A·. "
44 A·, and the company that was with "
45 And A· fought against the city all "
47 And it was told A·, that all the men "
48 A· gat him up to mount Zalmon, "
48 and A· took an axe in his hand, "
49 and followed A·, and put them to the "
50 went A· to Thebez, and encamped "
52 And A· came unto the tower, "
55 men of Israel saw that A· was dead, "
56 God rendered the wickedness of A·, "
10: 1 after A· there arose to defend Israel "
2Sa 11:21 smote A· the son of Jerubbesheth? "
1Ch 18:16 and A· the son of Abiathar, 40
Ps 34:*title* changed his behaviour before A·; "

Abimelech's (a-bim'-e-leks)
Ge 21:25 A· servants had violently taken 40
J'g 9:53 a piece of a millstone upon A· head, "

Abinadab (a-bin'-ah-dab)
1Sa 7: 1 and brought it into the house of A· 41
16: 8 Jesse called A·, and made him pass "
17:13 and next unto him A·, and the third "
31: 2 Philistines slew Jonathan, and A·, "
2Sa 6: 3 brought it out of the house of A· "
3 the sons of A·, drave the new cart. "
4 brought it out of the house of A· "
1Ki 4:11 son of A·, in all the region of Dor;* "
1Ch 2:13 begat his firstborn Eliab, and A· the "
8:33, 9:39 and Malchishua, and A·, "
10: 2 Philistines slew Jonathan, and A·, "
13: 7 in a new cart out of the house of A·: "

Abinoam (a-bin'-o-am)
J'g 4: 6 sent and called Barak the son of A· 42
12 that Barak the son of A· was gone "
5: 1 Deborah and Barak the son of A· "
12 thy captivity captive, thou son of A·. "

Abiram (a-bi'-rum)
Nu 16: 1 Dathan and A·, the sons of Eliab, 48
12 Moses sent to call Dathan and A·, "
24 tabernacle of Korah, Dathan, and A·. "
25 up and went unto Dathan and A·; "
27 tabernacle of Korah, Dathan, and A·, "
27 Dathan and A· came out, and stood "
26: 9 Eliab; Nemuel, and Dathan, and A·. "
9 Dathan and A·, which were famous "
De 11: 6 what he did unto Dathan and A·, "
1Ki 16:34 he laid the foundations thereof in A· "
Ps 106:17 and covered the company of A·. "

Abishag (ab'-e-shag)
1Ki 1: 3 and found A· a Shunammite, 49
15 and A· the Shunammite ministered "
2:17 give me A· the Shunammite to wife. "
21 she said, Let A· the Shunammite be "
22 dost thou ask A· the Shunammite "

Abishai (ab'-e-shahee)
1Sa 26: 6 and to A· the son of Zeruiah, 52
6 A· said, I will go down with thee. "
7 So David and A· came to the people "
8 said A· to David, God hath delivered "
9 David said to A·, Destroy him not: "
2Sa 2:18 sons of Zeruiah there, Joab, and A·, "
24 also and A· pursued after Abner: "
3:30 Joab and A· his brother slew Abner, "
10:10 he delivered into the hand of A· "
14 then fled they also before A·, "
16: 9 Then said A· the son of Zeruiah unto "
11 David said to A·, and to all his "
18: 2 a third part under the hand of A· "
5 the king commanded Joab and A· "
12 hearing the king charged thee and A· "
19:21 But A· the son of Zeruiah answered "
20: 6 David said to A·, Now shall Sheba "
10 So Joab and A· his brother pursued "
21:17 A· the son of Zeruiah succoured him, "
23:18 And A·, the brother of Joab, the son "
1Ch 2:16 the sons of Zeruiah; A·, and Joab, "
11:20 A· the brother of Joab, he was chief "
18:12 A· the son of Zeruiah slew of the "
19:11 he delivered unto the hand of A· "
15 likewise fled before A· his brother, "

Abishalom (a-bish'-ah-lum) See also ABSALOM.
1Ki 15: 2, 10 Maachah, the daughter of A·. 53

Abishua (a-bish'-u-ah)
1Ch 6: 4 begat Phinehas, Phinehas begat A·, 50
5 A· begat Bukki, and Bukki begat "
50 Phinehas his son, A· his son, "
8: 4 And A·, and Naaman, and Ahoah, "
Ezr 7: 5 The son of A·, the son of Phinehas, "

Abishur (ab'-e-shur)
1Ch 2:28 the sons of Shammai; Nadab and A· 51
29 name of the wife of A· was Abihail, "

Abital (ab'-e-tal)
2Sa 3: 4 the fifth, Shephatiah the son of A·; 37
1Ch 3: 3 The fifth, Shephatiah of A·: "

Abitub (ab'-e-tub)
1Ch 8:11 of Hushim he begat A·, and Elpaal. 36

Abiud (a-bi'-ud)
M't 1:13 Zorobabel begat A·; and A· begat 10

abjects
Ps 35:15 a· gathered themselves together 5222

able See also BLAMEABLE; CHANGEABLE; CHARGEABLE; COMFORTABLE; COMPARABLE; CONFORMABLE; CORRUPTIBLE; DAMNABLE; DECEIVABLENESS; DELECTABLE; DESIRABLE; DETESTABLE; DURABLE; ENABLED; FAVOURABLE; FORCIBLE; HONOURABLE; INCORRUPTIBLE; INCREDIBLE; INCURABLE; INEXCUSABLE; INFALLIBLE; LAMENTABLE; MISERABLE; MOVEABLE; PEACEABLE; POSSIBLE; PROFITABLE; QUENCHABLE; REBUKABLE; REPROVABLE; REASONABLE; SATIABLE; SEARCHABLE; VARIABLENESS.
Ge 13: 6 the land was not a· to bear them, 5375
15: 5 if thou be a· to number them: 3201
33:14 and the children be a· to endure, *7272
Ex 10: 5 one cannot be a· to see the earth: 3201
18:18 thou art not a· to perform it "
21 provide out of all the people a· 2428
23 then thou shalt be a· to endure, 3201
25 Moses chose a· men out of all 2428
40:35 Moses was not a· to enter into the 3201
Le 5: 7 be not a· to bring a lamb, *5060, 1767
11 he be not a· *5381
12: 8 be not a· to bring a lamb, *4672, 1767
14:22 such as he is a· to get; 5381

Le 31 such as he is a' to get, the one for 5381
32 whose hand is not a' to get that "
25:26 himself be a' to redeem it; * "
28 if he be not a' to restore it 4672, 1767
49 he be a', he may redeem himself. *5381
Nu 1: 3 all that are a' to go forth to war 3318
20, 22, 24, 26, 28, 30, 32, 34, 36, 38, 40,
42, 45 all that were a' to go forth to war "
11:14 I am not a' to bear all this people 3201
13:30 we are well a' to overcome it. "
31 not a' to go up against the people; "
14:16 the Lord was not a' to bring this "
22:11 I shall be a' to overcome them, "
37 am I not a' indeed to promote thee "
26: 2 all that are a' to go to war 3318
De 1: 9 am not a' to bear you myself alone: 3201
7:24 no man be a' to stand before thee, 3320
9:28 Lord was not a' to bring them 3201
11:25 no man be a' to stand before you: 3320
14:24 thou art not a' to carry it; 3201
16:17 man shall give as he is a', 4979, 3027
Jos 1: 5 There shall not any man be a' to 3320
14:12 I shall be a' to drive them out, *
23: 9 hath been a' to stand before you *5975
J'g 8: 3 what was I a' to do 3201
1Sa 6:20 Who is a' to stand before this holy "
17: 9 If he be a' to fight with me, "
33 Thou art not a' to go against this "
1Ki 3: 9 a' to judge this thy so great people? "
9:21 children of Israel also were not a' "
2Ki 3:21 all that were a' to put on armour, 2296
18:23 thou be a' on thy part to set riders 3201
29 he shall not be a' to deliver you "
1Ch 5:18 men a' to bear buckler and sword, 5375
9:13 a' men for the work of the service 2428
26: 8 a' men for strength for the service, "
29:14 that we should be a' to offer 6113, 3581
2Ch 2: 6 is a' to build him an house, " "
7: 7 a' to receive the burnt offerings, 3201
20: 6 that none is a' to withstand thee? "
37 they were not a' to go to Tarshish. 6113
25: 5 choice men, a' to go forth to war, "
9 Lord is a' to give thee much more "
32:13 any ways a' to deliver their lands 3201
14 your God should be a' to deliver "
15 was a' to deliver his people "
Ezr 10:13 we are not a' to stand without, 3581
Ne 4:10 we are not a' to build the wall. 3201
Job 41:10 who then is a' to stand before me? *
Ps 18:38 that they were not a' to rise: 3201
21:11 they are not a' to perform. "
36:12 shall not be a' to rise. "
40:12 I am not a' to look up; "
Pro 27: 4 who is a' to stand before envy? "
Ec 8:17 yet shall he not be a' to find it. 3201
Isa 36: 8 thou be a' on thy part to set riders "
14 he shall not be a' to deliver you. "
47:11 thou shalt not be a' to put it off: "
12 if so be thou shalt be a' to profit, "
Jer 10:10 the nations shall not be a' to abide "
11:11 they shall not be a' to escape; "
49:10 he shall not be a' to hide himself: "
La 1:14 I am not a' to rise up. "
Eze 7:19 their gold shall not be a' to deliver "
33:12 shall the righteous be a' to live "
46: 5 as he shall be a' to give, 4991, 3027
11 the lambs as he is a' to give, " "
Da 2:26 Art thou a' to make known unto 3546
3:17 God whom we serve is a' to deliver 3202
4:18 not a' to make known unto me the "
18 but thou art a'; for the spirit of 3546
37 walk in pride he is a' to abase. 3202
6:20 a' to deliver thee from the lions? "
Am 7:10 land is not a' to bear all his words. 3201
Zep 1:18 nor their gold shall be a' to deliver "
M't 3: 9 God is a' of these stones to raise 1410
9:28 Believe ye that I am a' to do this? "
10:28 but are not a' to kill the soul: "
28 fear him which is a' to destroy "
19:12 He that is a' to receive it, let him "
20:22 Are ye a' to drink of the cup that I "
22 They say unto him, We are a'. "
22:46 no man was a' to answer him "
26:61 am a' to destroy the temple of God, "
M'r 4:33 as they were a' to hear "
Lu 1:20 shalt be dumb, and not a' to speak, "
3: 8 God is a' of these stones to raise "
12:26 ye then be not a' to do that thing "
13:24 to enter in, and shall not be a'. 2480
14:29 is not a' to finish it, all that behold "
30 began to build, and was not a' to "
31 whether he be a' with ten 1415
21:15 not be a' to gainsay nor resist. 1410
Joh 10:29 no man is a' to pluck them out of "
21: 6 now they were not a' to draw it 2480
Ac 6:10 were not a' to resist the wisdom "
15:10 neither our fathers nor we were a' "
20:32 the word of his grace, which is a' 1410
25: 5 which among you are a', go down *1415
Ro 4:21 what he had promised, he was a' "
8:39 shall be a' to separate us from the 1410
11:23 God is a' to graff them in again. 1415
14: 4 for God is a' to make him stand. * "
15:14 a' also to admonish one another. 1410
1Co 3: 2 hitherto ye were not a' to bear it, "
2 neither yet now are ye a'. "
6: 5 not one that shall be a' to judge "
10:13 to be tempted above that ye are a'; "
13 that ye may be a' to bear it. "
2Co 1: 4 may be a' to comfort them which "
3: 6 hath made us a' ministers of the *2427
9: 8 God is a' to make all grace abound 1415
Eph 3:18 a' to comprehend with all saints *1840
20 Now unto him that is a' to do 1410
6:11 that ye may be a' to stand against "
13 that ye may be a' to withstand in "
Eph 6:16 ye shall be a' to quench all the 1410
Ph'p 3:21 he is a' even to subdue all things "
2Ti 1:12 persuaded that he is a' to keep 1415
2: 2 shall be a' to teach others also. 2425
3: 7 never a' to come to the knowledge 1410
15 scriptures, which are a' to make "
Tit 1: 9 he may be a' by sound doctrine 1415
Heb 2:18 he is a' to succour them that are 1410
5: 7 was a' to save him from death, "
7:25 Wherefore he is a' also to save "
11:19 that God was a' to raise him up, 1415
Jas 1:21 which is a' to save your souls. 1410
3: 2 a' also to bridle the whole body. 1415
4:12 lawgiver, who is a' to save and to 1410
2Pe 1:15 ye may be a' after my decease to 2192
Jude 24 Now unto him that is a' to keep 1410
Re 5: 3 was a' to open the book, neither "
6:17 who shall be a' to stand? "
13: 4 who is a' to make war with him? "
15: 8 was a' to enter into the temple, "

ably See ABOMINABLY; BLAMEABLY.

Abner (ab'-nur) See also ABNER'S.
1Sa 14:50 of the captain of his host was A'. 74
51 Ner the father of A' was the son of "
17:55 said unto A', the captain of the host, "
55 A', whose son is this youth? "
55 A' said, As thy soul liveth, O king, "
57 A' took him, and brought him "
20:25 and Jonathan arose, and A' sat by "
26: 5 and A' the son of Ner, the captain "
7 A' and the people lay round about "
14 David cried to the people, and to A' "
14 saying, Answerest thou not, A'? "
14 A' answered and said, Who art thou "
15 David said to A', Art not thou a "
2Sa 2: 8 A' the son of Ner, captain of Saul's "
12 A' the son of Ner, and the servants "
14 A' said to Joab, Let the young men "
17 A' was beaten, and the men of Israel, "
19 And Asahel pursued after A'; and "
19 nor to the left from following A'. "
20 A' looked behind him, and said, "
21 And A' said to him, Turn thee aside "
22 A' said again to Asahel, Turn thee "
23 A' with the hinder end of the spear "
24 also and Abishai pursued after A': "
25 themselves together after A', "
26 Then A' called to Joab, and said, "
29 A' and his men walked all that "
30 Joab returned from following A': "
3: 6 that A' made himself strong for the "
7 Ishbosheth said to A', Wherefore "
8 Then was A' very wroth for the "
9 So do God to A', and more also, "
11 And he could not answer A' a word "
12 And A' sent messengers to David "
16 Then said A' unto him, Go, return. "
17 And A' had communication with "
19 And A' also spake in the ears of "
19 A' went also to speak in the ears of "
20 So A' came to David to Hebron, "
20 David made A' and the men that "
21 A' said unto David, I will arise and "
21 David sent A' away; and he went in "
22 A' was not with David in Hebron; "
23 A' the son of Ner came to the king, "
24 behold, A' came unto thee; why is "
25 Thou knowest A' the son of Ner, "
26 he sent messengers after A', which "
27 when A' was returned to Hebron, "
28 for ever from the blood of A' the "
30 and Abishai his brother slew A', "
31 sackcloth, and mourn before A'. "
32 And they buried A' in Hebron: and "
32 voice, and wept at the grave of A'; "
33 the king lamented over A', and said, "
33 Died A' as a fool dieth? "
37 that it was not of the king to slay A' "
4: 1 Saul's son heard that A' was dead "
12 and buried it in the sepulchre of A' "
1Ki 2: 5 unto A' the son of Ner, and unto "
32 to wit, A' the son of Ner, captain of "
1Ch 26:28 Saul the son of Kish, and A' the son "
27:21 of Benjamin, Jaasiel the son of A': "

Abner's (ab'-nurs)
2Sa 2:31 of Benjamin, and of A' men, so that 74

aboard
Ac 21: 2 we went a', and set forth. 1910

abode See also ABODEST.
Ge 29:14 a' with him the space of a month, 3427
49:24 But his bow a' in strength, and "
Ex 24:16 glory of the Lord a' upon mount 7931
40:35 because the cloud a' thereon, "
Nu 9:17 the place where the cloud a', there "
18 as long as the cloud a' upon the "
20 a' in their tents, and according *2583
21 when the cloud a' from even *1961
22 the children of Israel a' in their *2583
11:35 unto Hazeroth; and a' at 1961
20: 1 and the people a' in Kadesh; 3427
22: 8 princes of Moab a' with Balaam. "
25: 1 And Israel a' in Shittim, and the "
De 1:46 So ye a' in Kadesh many days, "
46 according unto the days that ye a' "
3:29 So we a' in the valley over against "
9: 9 then I a' in the mount forty days "
Jos 2:22 and a' there three days, until the "
5: 8 they a' in their places in the camp, "
8: 9 and a' between Beth-el and Ai, "
J'g 5:17 Gilead a' beyond Jordan: 7931
17 and a' in his breaches. "
11:17 and Israel a' in Kadesh. 3427
19: 4 and he a' with him three days: "
20:47 a' in the rock Rimmon four months. "
J'g 21: 2 and a' there till even before God, *3427
1Sa 1:23 the woman a', and gave her son * "
7: 2 while the ark a' in Kirjath-jearim, "
13:16 a' in Gibeah of Benjamin: "
22: 6 Saul a' in Gibeah under a tree * "
23:14 David a' in the wilderness "
18 and David a' in the wood, "
25 and a' in the wilderness of Maon. "
25:13 two hundred a' by the stuff. "
26: 3 David a' in the wilderness, and he "
30:10 for two hundred a' behind, which *5975
2Sa 1: 1 David had a' two days in Ziklag; 3427
11:12 Uriah a' in Jerusalem that day, "
15: 8 while I a' in Geshur in Syria, "
1Ki 17:19 him up into a loft, where he a', "
2Ki 19:27 I know thy a', and thy going out, * "
Ezr 8:15 there a' we in tents three days: *2583
32 came to Jerusalem, and a' there 3427
Isa 37:28 I know thy a', and thy going out, * "
Jer 38:28 So Jeremiah a' in the court of the "
M't 17:22 while they a' in Galilee, Jesus 390
Lu 1:56 a' with her about three months, 3306
8:27 a' in any house, but in the tombs, "
21:37 he went out, and a' in the mount * 835
Joh 1:32 like a dove, and it a' upon him. 3306
39 saw where he dwelt, and a' with "
4:40 he a' there two days. "
7: 9 he a' still in Galilee. "
8:44 a' not in the truth, because there *2476
10:40 and there he a'. 3306
11: 6 a' two days still in the same place "
14:23 and make our a' with him. 3438
Ac 1:13 where a' both Peter, and James, *2650
12:19 Judæa to Cæsarea, and there a'. *1304
14: 3 Long time therefore a' they * "
28 a' long time with the disciples, * "
17:14 Silas and Timotheus a' there still. 5278
18: 3 he a' with them, and wrought: 3306
20: 3 And there a' three months. *4160
6 where we a' seven days. *1304
21: 7 saluted the brethren, and a' with 3306
8 one of the seven, and a' with him. "
Ga 1:18 see Peter, and a' with him fifteen *1961
2Ti 4:20 Erastus a' at Corinth: 3306

abodest
J'g 5:16 a' thou among the sheepfolds, to *3427

abolish See also ABOLISHED.
Isa 2:18 the idols he shall utterly a'. *2498

abolished
Isa 51: 6 my righteousness shall not be a'. 2865
Eze 6: 6 and your works may be a'. 4229
2Co 3:13 to the end of that which is a': *2673
Eph 2:15 Having a' in his flesh the enmity, "
2Ti 1:10 Christ, who hath a' death, "

abominable
Le 7:21 or any a' unclean thing, *8263
11:43 ye shall not make yourselves a' 8262
18:30 not any one of these a' customs, 8441
19: 7 it is a'; it shall not be accepted. *6292
20:25 ye shall not make your souls a' 8262
De 14: 3 Thou shalt not eat any a' thing. 8441
1Ch 21: 6 the king's word was a' to Joab. 8581
2Ch 15: 8 put away the a' idols out of all *8251
Job 15:16 How much more a' and filthy is 8581
Ps 14: 1 they have done a' works, "
53: 1 and have done a' iniquity: "
Isa 14:19 thy grave like an a' branch, "
65: 4 of a' things is in their vessels; 6292
Jer 16:18 detestable and a' things. *8441
44: 4 do not this a' thing that I hate. "
Eze 4:14 neither came there a' flesh into 6292
8:10 and a' beasts, and all the idols 8263
16:52 thou hast committed more a' than 8581
Mic 6:10 the scant measure that is a'? 2194
Na 3: 6 I will cast a' filth upon thee, 8251
Tit 1:16 him, being a', and disobedient, 947
1Pe 4: 3 banquetings, and a' idolatries: 111
Re 21: 8 unbelieving, and the a', and 948

abominably
1Ki 21:26 he did very a' in following idols, 8581

abomination See also ABOMINATIONS.
Ge 43:32 is an a' unto the Egyptians. 8441
46:34 every shepherd is an a' unto the "
Ex 8:26, 26 the a' of the Egyptians "
Le 7:18 it shall be an a', 6292
11:10 they shall be an a' unto you: 8263
11 be even an a' unto you; "
11 ye shall have their carcases in a'. 8262
12 that shall be an a' 8263
13 shall have in a' among the fowls; 8262
13 they are an a': 8263
20 an a' unto you. "
23 four feet, shall be an a' unto you. "
41 the earth shall be an a'; "
42 shall not eat; for they are an a'. "
18:22 with womankind: it is a'. 8441
20:13 of them have committed an a': "
De 7:25 for it is an a' to the Lord thy God. "
26 shalt thou bring an a' into thine "
12:31 for every a' to the Lord, which he "
13:14 such a' is wrought among you; "
17: 1 an a' unto the Lord "
4 such a' is wrought in Israel: "
18:12 these things are an a' unto the "
22: 5 all that do so are an a' unto the "
23:18 both these are an a' unto the Lord "
24: 4 that is a' before the Lord: "
25:16 unrighteously, are an a' unto "
27:15 molten image, an a' unto "
1Sa 13: 4 Israel also was had in a' 887
1Ki 11: 5 the a' of the Ammonites. 8251
7 the a' of Moab, "
7 the a' of the children of Ammon. "

2Ki 23:13 the a· of the Zidonians, and for 8251
13 Chemosh the a· of the Moabites, "
13 Milcom the a· of the children 8441
Ps 88: 8 thou hast made me an a· unto "
Pro 3:32 the froward is a· to the Lord: "
6:16 seven are an a· unto him: "
8: 7 and wickedness is an a· to my lips. "
11: 1 false balance is a· to the Lord: "
20 are of a froward heart are a· to "
12:22 Lying lips are a· to the Lord: "
13:19 it is a· to fools to depart from evil. "
15: 8 wicked is an a· to the Lord: "
9 way of the wicked is an a· unto the "
26 thoughts of the wicked are an a· to "
16: 5 proud in heart is an a· to "
12 a· to kings to commit wickedness: "
17:15 both are a· to the Lord. "
20:10 both of them are alike a· to the "
23 Divers weights are an a· unto "
21:27 sacrifice of the wicked is a·: "
24: 9 and the scorner is an a· to men. "
28: 9 even his prayer shall be a·. "
29:27 An unjust man is an a· to the just: "
27 is upright in the way is a· to the "
Isa 1:13 incense is an a· unto me; "
41:24 an a· is he that chooseth you. "
44:19 make the residue thereof an a·? "
66:17 eating swine's flesh, and the a·, 8263
Jer 2: 7 made mine heritage an a·. 8441
6:15 when they had committed a·? "
8:12 when they had committed a·? "
32:35 do this a·, to cause Judah to sin. "
Eze 16:50 were haughty, and committed a· "
18:12 the idols, hath committed a·, "
22:11 a· with his neighbour's wife; "
33:26 ye work a·, and ye defile every "
Da 11:31 place the a· that maketh desolate. 8251
12:11 the a· that maketh desolate set up, "
Mal 2:11 and an a· is committed in Israel 8441
M't 24:15 see the a· of desolation, 946
M'r 13:14 shall see the a· of desolation, "
Lu 16:15 is a· in the sight of God. "
Re 21:27 worketh a·, or maketh a lie: "

abominations
Le 18:26 not commit any of these a·; 8441
27 all these a· have the men of the "
29 shall commit any of these a·, "
De 18: 9 after the a· of these nations. "
12 and because of these a· the Lord "
20:18 you not to do after all their a·, "
29:17 have seen their a·, and their idols, 8251
32:16 a· provoked they him to anger. 8441
1Ki 14:24 all the a· of the nations "
2Ki 16: 3 according to the a· of the heathen, "
21: 2 after the a· of the heathen, "
11 Judah hath done these a·, "
23:24 the a· that were spied in the land 8251
2Ch 28: 3 after the a· of the heathen 8441
33: 2 like unto the a· of the heathen, "
34:33 Josiah took away all the a· out of "
36: 8 and his a· which he did, "
14 after all the a· of the heathen; "
Ezr 9: 1 according to their a·, "
11 with their a·, which have filled "
14 the people of these a·? "
Pro 26:25 for there are seven a· in his heart. "
Isa 66: 3 their soul delighteth in their a·. 8251
Jer 4: 1 put away thine a· out of my sight, "
7:10 delivered to do all these a·? 8441
30 have set their a· in the house 8251
13:27 whoredom, and thine a· on the "
32:34 they set their a· in the house, "
44:22 a· which ye have committed; 8441
Eze 5: 9 the like, because of all thine a·. "
11 and with all thine a·, therefore "
6: 9 have committed in all their a·. "
11 Alas for all the evil a· of the house "
7: 3 recompense upon thee all thine a·. "
4 a· shall be in the midst of thee: "
8 recompense thee for all thine a·. "
9 according to thy ways and thine a· "
20 made the images of their a· "
8: 6 a· that the house of Israel "
6, 13, 15 thou shalt see greater a· "
9 wicked a· that they do here. "
17 Judah that they commit the a· "
9: 4 that cry for all the a· that be done "
11:18 all the a· thereof from thence. "
21 detestable things and their a·, "
12:16 may declare all their a· among the "
14: 6 faces from all your a·. "
16: 2 cause Jerusalem to know her a·, "
22 in all thine a· and thy whoredoms "
36 with all the idols of thy a·, "
43 lewdness above all thine a·. "
47 nor done after their a·: "
51 thou hast multiplied thine a· more "
51 in all thine a· which thou hast done. "
58 borne thy lewdness and thine a·, "
18:13 hath done all these a·; "
24 doeth according to all the a· "
20: 4 cause them to know the a· of their "
7 Cast ye away every man the a· of 8251
8 cast away the a· of their eyes, "
30 commit ye whoredom after their a·? "
22: 2 thou shalt shew her all her a·. 8441
23:36 declare unto them their a·; "
33:29 desolate because of all their a· "
36:31 iniquities and for your a·. "
43: 8 defiled my holy name by their a· "
44: 6 suffice you of all your a·, "
7 because of all your a·. "
13 bear their shame, and their a· "
Da 9:27 the overspreading of a· he shall 8251
Ho 9:10 a· were according as they loved. * "
Zec 9: 7 and his a· from between his teeth: "

Re 17: 4 full of a· and filthiness of 946
5 mother of harlots and a· of the "

abound See also ABOUNDED; ABOUNDETH; ABOUNDING.
Pro 28:20 A faithful man shall a· with 7227
M't 24:12 because iniquity shall a·, *4129
Ro 5:20 the offence might a·. But where 4121
20 grace did much more a·: 5248
6: 1 that grace may a·? 4121
15:13 that ye may a· in hope, through 4052
2Co 1: 5 sufferings of Christ a· in us, so our "
8: 7 as ye a· in every thing, in faith, "
7 that ye a· in this grace also. "
9: 8 to make all grace a· toward you: "
8 may a· to every good work: "
Ph'p 1: 9 that your love may a· yet more "
4:12 and I know how to a·: "
12 both to a· and to suffer need. "
17 that may a· to your account. *4121
18 I have all and a·: 4052
1Th 3:12 make you to increase and a· in "
4: 1 so ye would a· more and more. "
2Pe 1: 8 if these things be in you, and a·, 4121

abounded
Ro 3: 7 hath more a· through my lie unto 4052
5:15 hath a· unto many. * "
20 But where sin a·, grace did much 4121
2Co 8: 2 a· unto the riches of their liberality 4052
Eph 1: 8 Wherein he hath a· toward us in* "

aboundeth
Pro 29:22 a furious man a· in transgression. 7227
2Co 1: 5 consolation also a· by Christ. 4052
2Th 1: 3 all toward each other a·; 4121

abounding
Pro 8:24 no fountains a· with water. 3513
1Co 15:58 always a· in the work of the Lord, 4052
Col 2: 7 a· therein with thanksgiving. "

about See also THEREABOUT; WHEREABOUT.
Ge 23:17 were in all the borders round a·,
35: 5 the cities that were round a· them,
37: 7 round a·, and made obeisance
38:24 came to pass a· three months after
39:11 it came to pass a· this time,
41:25 shewed Pharaoh what he is a· to
28 What God is a· to do he sheweth
42 and put a gold chain a· his neck; 5921
48 which was round a· every city,
42:24 he turned himself a· from them, *
46:34 servants' trade hath been a· *
Ex 7:24 the Egyptians digged round a·
9:18 to-morrow a· this time I will cause
13:18 God led the people a·, through 5437
16:13 the morning the dew lay round a·
19:12 bounds unto the people round a·,
23 Set bounds a· the mount, and 854
25:11 a crown of gold round a·.
24 thereto a crown of gold round a·.
25 border of an hand breadth round a·,
25 to the border thereof round a·.
27:17 All the pillars round a· the court
28:32 a binding of woven work round a·
33 round a· the hem thereof; and bells
33 of gold between them round a·:
34 upon the hem of the robe round a·.
29:16 sprinkle it round a· upon the altar.
20 the blood upon the altar round a·.
30: 3 the sides thereof round a·,
3 unto it a crown of gold round a·.
32:28 fell of the people that day a· three
37: 2 a crown of gold to it round a·.
11 thereunto a crown of gold round a·.
12 border of an handbreadth round a·;
12 for the border thereof round a·.
26 the sides thereof round a·,
26 unto it a crown of gold round a·.
38:16 the hangings of the court round a·
20 and of the court round a·,
31 the sockets of the court round a·,
31 all the pins of the court round a·.
39:23 with a band round a· the hole,
25 a· between the pomegranates;
26 round a· the hem of the robe
40: 8 shalt set up the court round a·,
33 he reared up the court round a· the
Le 1: 5 sprinkle the blood round a· upon
11 sprinkle his blood round a· upon
3: 2 the blood upon the altar round a·.
8 sprinkle the blood thereof round a·
13 thereof upon the altar round a·.
6: 5 Or all that a· which he hath sworn 5921
7: 2 sprinkle round a· upon the altar.
8:15 horns of the altar round a· with
19, 24 blood upon the altar round a·.
9:12 sprinkled round a· upon the altar.
18 sprinkled upon the altar round a·,
14:41 to be scraped within round a·,
16:18 the horns of the altar round a·.
25:31 which have no wall round a· them
44 the heathen that are round a· you;
Nu 1:50 encamp round a· the tabernacle.
53 the Levites shall pitch round a·
2: 2 far off a· the tabernacle of the 5439
3:26 by the altar round a·,
37 the pillars of the court round a·,
4: 4 tabernacle of the congregation, a·
14 wherewith they minister a· 5921
26 altar round a·, and their cords,
32 the pillars of the court round a·,
11: 8 people went a·, and gathered it, 7751
24 set them round a· the tabernacle.
31 the other side, round a· the camp.
32 for themselves round a· the camp.
16:24 up from a· the tabernacle of Korah, 5439
34 Israel that were round a· them fled

Nu 16:49 that died a· the matter of Korah. 5921
22: 4 lick up all that are round a· us,
32:33 the cities of the country round a·.
34:12 with the coasts thereof round a·.
35: 2 suburbs for the cities round a·
4 a thousand cubits round a·.
De 6:14 the people which are round a· you;
12:10 rest from all your enemies round a·.
13: 7 the people which are round a· you,
17:14 as all the nations that are a· me; 5439
21: 2 round a· him that is slain:
25:19 rest from all thine enemies round a·,
31:21 imagination which they go a·, ‡6213
32:10 he led him a·, he instructed him, 5437
Jos 2: 5 to pass a· the time of shutting of
3: 4 you and it, a· two thousand
4:13 A· forty thousand prepared for
6: 3 ye men of war, and go round a·
11 compassed the city, going a· it 5362
15 they rose early a· the dawning of *
7: 3 let a· two or three thousand men
4 up thither of the people a· three
5 men of Ai smote of them a· thirty
8:12 he took a· five thousand men, and
10:13 not to go down a· a whole day.
11: 6 to-morrow a· this time will I *
15:12 of the children of Judah round a·
16: 6 the border went a· eastward unto 5437
18:20 by the coasts thereof round a·,
19: 8 a· these cities to Baalath-beer,
21:11 the suburbs thereof round a· it.
42 with their suburbs round a· them:
44 the Lord gave them rest round a·,
23: 1 from all their enemies round a·,
J'g 2:12 the people that were round a· them,
14 hands of their enemies round a·,
3:29 they slew of Moab at that time a·
7:21 every man in his place round a·
8:10 with them, a· fifteen thousand men,
26 chains that were a· their camels'
9:49 of Shechem died also, a· a thousand
16:27 upon the roof a· three thousand
17: 2 silver that were taken from thee, a·
19:22 Belial, beset the house round a·,
20: 5 beset the house round a· upon me
29 set liers in wait round a· Gibeah.
31 in the field, a· thirty men of Israel.
39 the men of Israel a· thirty persons:
43 Benjamites round a·, and chased 3803
Ru 1: 4 and they dwelled there a· ten years.
19 all the city was moved a· them, 5921
2:17 and it was a· an ephah of barley.
1Sa 1:20 the time was come a· after Hannah
4: 2 in the field a· four thousand men.
20 And a· the time of her death
5: 8 of the God of Israel be carried a·, 5437
8 ark of the God of Israel a· thither. "
9 after they had carried it a·, "
10 brought a· the ark of the God of "
9:13 a· this time ye shall find him. *
16 To morrow a· this time I will send
22 which were a· thirty persons.
26 to pass a· the spring of the day,
13:15 present with him, a· six hundred
14: 2 with him were a· six hundred
14 was a· twenty men, within as it
21 from the country round a·,
15:12 set him up a place, and is gone a·, 5437
27 as Samuel turned a· to go away, "
17:42 when the Philistine looked a·, 5027
20:12 a· to morrow any time, or the
21: 5 kept from us a· these three days,
22: 2 with him a· four hundred men.
6 servants were standing a· him;) 5921
7 his servants that stood a· him, "
17 the footmen that stood a· him, "
23:13 David and his men, which were a·
26 his men round a· to take them.
25:13 there went up after David a· four
38 a· ten days after, that the Lord
26: 5 the people pitched round a· him.
7 Abner and the people lay round a·,
31: 9 land of the Philistines round a·,
2Sa 3:12 to bring a· all Israel unto thee. 5437
4: 5 and came a· the heat of the day to
5: 9 David built round a· from Millo
7: 1 Lord had given him rest round a·
14:20 To fetch a· this form of speech *5437
18:15 compassed a· and smote Absalom, "
20:26 Jairite was a chief ruler a· David.*
22: 6 sorrows of hell compassed me a·; 5437
12 made darkness pavilions round a·
24: 6 to Dan-jaan, and a· to Zidon, *5439
1Ki 2: 5 his girdle that was a· his loins,
15 howbeit the kingdom is turned a·, 5437
3: 1 the wall of Jerusalem round a·.
4:24 had peace on all sides round a·.
31 fame was in all nations round a·.
5: 3 for the wars which were a· him 5437
6: 5 built chambers round a·, against
5 the walls of the house round a·,
5 he made chambers round a·:
6 he made narrowed rests round a·,
29 the walls of the house round a·, 4524
7:12 the great court round a· was with
15 did compass either of them a·. 5437
18 two rows round a· upon the one
20 two hundred in rows round a·
23 it was round all a·, *
23 cubits did compass it round a·.
24 under the brim of it round a·
24 compassing the sea round a·:
36 and additions round a·.
8:14 And the king turned his face a·,
18:32 he made a trench a· the altar, 5439
35 the water ran round a· the altar:

1Ki 19: 2 of them by to morrow a' this time.
20: 6 unto thee to morrow a' this time,
22: 6 prophets together, a' four hundred
36 throughout the host a' the going
2Ki 1: 8 with a girdle of leather a' his loins.
3:25 the slingers went a' it, and smote 5437
4:16 A' this season, according to the *
6:14 and compassed the city a'. 5362
17 chariots of fire round a' Elisha.
7: 1 To morrow a' this time shall a
18 shall be to morrow a' this time in
8:21 which compassed him a', 413
11: 7 the house of the Lord a' the king. 413
8 shall compass the king round a',
11 in his hand, round a' the king, 5921
17:15 heathen that were round a' them,
23: 5 in the places round a' Jerusalem;
25: 1 built forts against it round a'.
4 were against the city round a':)
10 the walls of Jerusalem round a'.
17 upon the chapiter round a',
1Ch 4:33 villages that were round a' the
6:55 the suburbs thereof round a' it.
9:27 lodged round a' the house of God,
10: 9 land of the Philistines round a',
11: 8 he built the city round a',
8 even from Millo round a':
15:22 he instructed a' the song, because
18:17 the sons of David were chief a' the
22: 9 from all his enemies round a':
28:12 of all the chambers round a',
2Ch 2: 9 house which I am a' to build shall
4: 2 cubits did compass it round a'.
3 which did compass it round a':
3 compassing the sea round a'.
13:13 caused an ambushment to come a' 5437
14: 7 make a' them walls, and towers, "
14 smote all the cities round a' Gerar;
15:15 the Lord gave them rest round a'.
17: 9 went a' throughout all the cities 5437
10 lands that were round a' Judah,
18:31 they compassed a' him to fight:
34 a' the time of the sun going down
20:30 God gave him rest round a'.
23: 2 And they went a' in Judah, 5437
7 shall compass the king round a',
10 the temple, by the king round a'.
26: 6 built cities a' Ashdod, and *
33:14 compassed a' Ophel, and raised it
34: 6 with their mattocks round a'.
Ezr 1: 6 that were a' them strengthened 5439
10:15 Tikvah were employed a' this *5921
Ne 5:17 among the heathen that are a' us.
6:16 all the heathen that were a' us
12:28 plain country round a' Jerusalem,
29 had builded them villages round a'
13:21 them, Why lodge ye a' the wall? 5048
Job 1: 5 of their feasting were gone a', 5362
10 a' him, and a' his house, and a' 1157
8:17 roots are wrapped a' the heap, 5440
10: 8 fashioned me together round a';
11:18 yea, thou shalt dig a' thee, and 5439
16:13 archers compass me round a',
19:12 encamp round a' my tabernacle.
20:23 When he is a' to fill his belly, God
22:10 Therefore snares are round a'
29: 5 when my children were a' me; 5439
30:18 bindeth me a' as the collar of my 247
37:12 turned round a' by his counsels:
40:22 of the brook compass him a'.
41:14 his teeth are terrible round a'.
Ps 3: 6 themselves against me round a'.
7: 7 of the people compass thee a':
17: 9 enemies, who compass me a'.
18: 5 sorrows of hell compassed me a':
11 his pavilion round a' him were
27: 6 above mine enemies round a' me:
32: 7 shalt compass me a' with songs
10 mercy shall compass him a'.
34: 7 encampeth round a' them that
40:12 compassed me a': mine iniquities
44:13 derision to them that are round a'
48:12 Walk a' Zion, and go round 5439
12 Zion, and round a' her:
49: 5 of my heels shall compass me a'?
50: 3 very tempestuous round a' him.
55:10 Day and night they go a' it upon 5437
59: 6, 14 like a dog, and go round a' the city.
73: 6 pride compasseth them a' as a
76:11 let all that be round a' him bring
78:28 round a' their habitations.
79: 3 like water round a' Jerusalem;
4 to them that are round a' us.
88:17 They came round a' me daily like
17 they compassed me a' together.
89: 7 reverence of all them that are a' 5439
8 to thy faithfulness round a' thee?
97: 2 and darkness are round a' him:
3 burneth up his enemies round a'.
109: 3 They compassed me a' also with
118:10 All nations compassed me a':
11 me a'; yea, they compassed me a':
12 They compassed me a' like bees;
125: 2 As the mountains are round a'
2 so the Lord is round a' his people
128: 3 olive plants round a' thy table.
139:11 the night shall be light a' me. 1157
140: 9 of those that compass me a',
142: 7 righteous shall compass me a';
Pr 1: 9 thy head, and chains a' thy neck.
3: 3 bind them a' thy neck; write 5921
6:21 thine heart, and tie them a' thy "
20:19 He that goeth a' as a talebearer 1980
Ec 1: 6 and turneth a' unto the north;
6 it whirleth a' continually,
2:20 I went a' to cause my heart 5437

Ec 12: 5 the mourners go a' the streets: 5437
Ca 3: 2 I will rise now, and go a' the city "
3 The watchmen that go a' the city "
7 threescore valiant men are a' it, 5439
5: 7 watchmen that went a' the city 5437
7: 2 heap of wheat set a' with lilies. 5473
Isa 3:18 tinkling ornaments a' their feet, *
15: 8 cry is gone round a' the borders of
23:16 Take an harp, go a' the city, 5437
26:20 and shut thy doors a' thee: hide 1157
28:27 neither is a cart wheel turned a'
29: 3 will camp against thee round a',
42:25 it hath set him on fire round a',
49:18 Lift up thine eyes round a',
50:11 compass yourselves a' with sparks:
60: 4 Lift up thine eyes round a', and
Jer 1:15 all the walls thereof round a',
2:36 Why gaddest thou a' so much 235
4:17 are they against her round a';
6: 3 their tents against her round a':
12: 9 birds round a' are against her;
14:18 the prophet and the priest go a' 5503
17:26 from the places a' Jerusalem, 5439
21:14 shall devour all things round a' it.
25: 9 all these nations round a',
31:22 How long wilt thou go a', *2559
39 and shall compass a' to Goath.
32:44, 33:13 in the places a' Jerusalem, 5439
41:14 cast a' and returned, and went 5437
46: 5 fear was round a', saith the Lord. *
14 sword shall devour round a' thee.
48:17 ye that are a' him, bemoan him; 5439
39 a dismaying to all them a' him. "
49: 5 from all those that be a' thee; "
50:14 in array against Babylon round a':
15 Shout against her round a':
29 camp against it round a';
32 it shall devour all round a' him.
51: 2 they shall be against her round a'.
52: 4 built forts against it round a'.
7 were by the city round a':)
14 the walls of Jerusalem round a'.
22 upon the chapiters round a',
23 were an hundred round a'.
La 1:17 his adversaries should be round a'
2: 3 fire, which devoureth round a'.
22 solemn day my terrors round a', *
3: 7 hath hedged me a', that I cannot 1157
Eze 1: 4 a brightness was a' it, 5439
18 rings were full of eyes round a'
27 as the appearance of fire round a'
27 it had brightness round a'.
28 of the brightness round a'.
4: 2 battering rams against it round a'.
5: 2 and smite a' it with a knife: 5439
5, 6 countries that are round a' her.
7, 7 nations that are round a' you;
12 fall by the sword round a' thee;
14, 15 nations that are round a' thee,
6: 5 scatter your bones round a' your
13 among their idols round a' their
8:10 pourtrayed upon the wall round a'.
16 were a' five and twenty men, with
10:12 full of eyes round a', even the
11:12 the heathen that are round a' you.
12:14 all that are a' him to help him, 5439
16:10 I girded thee a' with fine linen,
37 I will even gather them round a' *
57 and all that are round a' her,
57 which despise thee round a'.
23:24 and shield and helmet round a':
27:11 were upon thy walls round a',
11 shields upon thy walls round a';
28:24 all that are round a' them,
26 despise them round a' them;
31: 4 rivers running round a' his plants,
32:22 his graves are a' him: 5439
23 her company is round a' her grave:
24 her multitude round a' her grave,
25, 26 her graves are round a' him:
34:26 places round a' my hill a blessing;
36: 4 of the heathen that are round a';
7 Surely the heathen that are a' you,5439
36 heathen that are left round a' you
37: 2 me to pass by them round a':
40: 5 the outside of the house round a',
14 unto the post of the court round a'
16 posts within the gate round a',
16 windows were round a' inward:
17 made for the court round a':
25 in the arches thereof round a',
29 round a': it was fifty cubits long,
30 the arches round a' were five and
33 in the arches thereof round a': it
36 the windows to it round a':
43 hand broad, fastened round a':
41: 5 round a' the house on every side.
6 for the side chambers round a',
7 a winding a' still upward to the *
7 the winding a' of the house went*
7 still upward round a' the house:
8 the height of the house round a':
10 twenty cubits round a' the house
11 five cubits round a'.
12 five cubits thick round a',
16 galleries round a' on their three
16 cieled with wood round a'
17 by all the wall round a'
19 through all the house round a'.
42:15 and measured it round a'.
16, 17 the measuring reed round a'.
19 He turned a' to the west side, and
20 had a wall round a', five hundred
43:12 limit thereof round a' shall be
13 the edge thereof round a' shall be
17 border a' it shall be half a cubit; 5439

Eze 43:17 bottom thereof shall be a cubit a';5439
20 and upon the border round a':
45: 1 in all the borders thereof round a'.
2 in breadth, square round a';
2 and fifty cubits round a'
46:23 a row of building round a' in them,
23 round a' them four,
23 under the rows round a'.
47: 2 led me a' the way without unto *5437
48:35 was round a' eighteen thousand
Da 5: 7 have a chain of gold a' his neck, 5922
16 a chain of gold a' thy neck, "
29 put a chain of gold a' his neck, "
31 kingdom, being a' threescore and
9:16 a reproach to all that are a' us. 5439
21 me a' the time of the evening
Ho 7: 2 own doings have beset them a'; 5437
11:12 Ephraim compassed me a' with
Joe 3:11 yourselves together round a':
12 to judge all the heathen round a'.
Am 3:11 even round a' the land;
Jon 2: 3 the floods compassed me a': all
5 The waters compassed me a', even
5 the depth closed me round a', the
5 weeds were wrapped a' my head.
6 with her bars was a' me for *1157
Na 3: 8 that had the waters round a' it,
Hab 1: 4 the wicked doth compass a' the
Zec 2: 5 unto her a wall of fire round a',
7: 7 cities thereof round a' her,
9: 8 And I will encamp a' mine house
12: 2 unto all the people round a',
6 devour all the people round a', "
14:14 wealth of all the heathen round a' "
M't 1:11 a' the time they were carried *1909
3: 4 girdle a' his loins; 4012
5 all the region round a' Jordan, 4066
4:23 And Jesus went a' all Galilee, 4013
8:18 Jesus saw great multitudes a' 4012
9:22 Jesus turned him a', and when *1994
35 Jesus went a' all the cities and 4013
14:21 were a' five thousand men, 5616
35 all that country round a', 4066
18: 6 millstone were hanged a' his neck, 1909
20: 3 he went out a' the third hour, 4012
5 Again he went out a' the sixth and "
6 And a' the eleventh hour he went "
9 were hired a' the eleventh hour, "
21:33 hedged it round a', and digged 4060
27:46 And a' the ninth hour Jesus cried 4012
M'r 1: 6 girdle of a skin a' his loins; "
28 all the region round a' Galilee. 4066
2: 2 not so much as a' the door: 4314
3: 5 when he had looked round a' on 4017
8 and they a' Tyre and Sidon, 4012
32 And the multitude sat a' him, "
34 And he looked round a' on them *2945
34 on them which sat a' him, 4012
4:10 they that were a' him "
5:13 they were a' two thousand;) and 5613
30 turned him a' in the press, and 1994
32 he looked round a' to see her 4017
6: 6 he went round a' the villages, 2945
36 into the country round a', and into "
44 were a' five thousand men. *5616
48 a' the fourth watch of the night 4012
55 that whole region round a', 4066
55 carry a' in beds those that were 4064
8: 9 had eaten were a' four thousand: 5613
33 But when he had turned a' and 1994
9: 8 when they had looked round a', 4017
14 he saw a great multitude a' them, 4012
42 millstone were hanged a' his neck,4012
10:23 Jesus looked round a', and saith 4017
11:11 and when he had looked round a' "
12: 1 and set an hedge a' it, 5418
14:51 cloth cast a' his naked body; 1909
15:17 thorns, and put it a' his head *4060
Lu 1:56 And Mary abode with her a' three 5616
65 on all that dwelt round a' them: 4037
2: 9 glory of the Lord shone round a' 4034
37 she was a widow of a' fourscore *5613
49 be a' my Father's business? *1722
3: 3 into all the country a' Jordan, 4066
23 began to be a' thirty years of age, 5616
4:14 through all the region round a'. 4066
37 place of the country round a'. "
6:10 looking round a' upon them all, 4017
7: 9 at him, and turned him a', *4762
17 all the region round a'. 4066
8:37 country of the Gadarenes round a' "
42 a' twelve years of age, and she lay 5613
9:12 and country round a', and lodge, 2945
14 were a' five thousand men. 5616
28 a' an eight days after these, "
10:40 Martha was cumbered a' much 4012
41 and troubled a' many things: "
12:35 Let your loins be girded a', and 4024
13: 8 till I shall dig a' it, and dung it: 4012
17: 2 hanged a' his neck, and he cast "
19:43 shall cast a trench a' thee, and 4016
22:41 withdrawn from them a' a stone's 5616
49 When they which were a' him 4012
59 a' the space of one hour after 5616
23:44 And it was a' the sixth hour, and "
24:13 Jerusalem a' threescore furlongs.*
Joh 1:39 for it was a' the tenth hour. 5613
3:25 and the Jews a' purifying. 4012
4: 6 well: and it was a' the sixth hour. 5616
6:10 in number a' five thousand. "
19 rowed a' five and twenty or thirty 5613
7:14 a' the midst of the feast Jesus *
19 Why go ye a' to kill me? *2212
20 who goeth a' to kill thee? * "
10:24 came the Jews round a' him, 2944
11:18 a' fifteen furlongs off; 5613

Joh 11:44 face was bound a· with a napkin. 4019
19:14 and a· the sixth hour: 5616
39 a· an hundred pound weight. "
20: 7 the napkin, that was a· his head, *1909
21:20 Then Peter, turning a·, seeth the 1994
Ac 1:15 together were a· an hundred and 5613
2:10 of Libya a· Cyrene, 2596
41 them a· three thousand souls. 5616
3: 3 seeing Peter and John a· to go 3195
4: 4 of the men was a· five thousand. 5616
5: 7 a· the space of three hours after, 5613
16 cities round a· unto Jerusalem, 4038
36 men, a· four hundred, joined 5616
9: 3 there shined round a· him a light 4015
29 they went a· to slay him. 2021
10: 3 a· the ninth hour of the day, 5616
9 to pray a· the sixth hour: 4012
38 went a· doing good, and healing 1330
11:19 persecution that arose a· Stephen 1909
12: 1 Now a· that time Herod the king 2596
8 Cast thy garment a· thee, and 4016
13:11 went a· seeking some to lead him 4013
18 a· the time of forty years suffered 5613
20 a· the space of four hundred and "
14: 6 the region that lieth round a·: 4066
20 the disciples stood round a· him, 2944
15: 2 the apostles and elders a· this 4012
18:14 when Paul was now a· to open his 3195
19: 7 all the men were a· twelve. 5616
23 no small stir a· that way. *4012
34 a· the space of two hours cried 5613
20: 3 as he was a· to sail into Syria, 3195
21:31 And as they went a· to kill him, *2212
22: 6 a· noon, suddenly there shone 4012
6 light round a· me. "
24: 6 Who also hath gone a· to profane *3985
25: 7 from Jerusalem stood round a·, 3936
15 A· whom, when I was at 4012
24 a· whom all the multitude of the "
26:13 shining round a· me and them 4034
21 and went a· to kill me. *3985
27:27 Adria, a· midnight the shipmen 2596
30 the shipmen were a· to flee out *2212
Ro 4:19 when he was a· an hundred years 4225
10: 3 and going a· to establish their *2212
15:19 from Jerusalem, and round a· 2945
1Co 9: 5 power to lead a· a sister, a wife, 4013
13 which minister a· holy things live
2Co 4:10 Always bearing a· in the body 4064
Eph 4:14 and carried a· with every wind of "
6:14 having your loins girt a· with *4024
1Ti 5:13 wandering a· from house to 4022
6: 4 doting a· questions and strifes of 4012
2Ti 2:14 that they strive not a· words to no
Tit 3: 9 strivings a· the law; for they are 3163
Heb 8: 5 he was a· to make the tabernacle: 3195
9: 4 overlaid round a· with gold, 3840
11:30 after they were compassed a· 2944
37 they wandered a· in sheepskins 4022
12: 1 we also are compassed a· with so 4029
13: 9 Be not carried a· with divers and *4064
Jas 3: 3 and we turn a· their whole body. 3329
4 yet are they turned a· with a very "
1Pe 5: 8 walketh a·, seeking whom he may 4043
Jude 1: 7 Gomorrha, and the cities a· them 4012
9 disputed a· the body of Moses,
12 carried a· of winds; trees whose *4064
Re 1:13 girt a· the paps with a golden 4024
4: 3 a rainbow round a· the throne, 2943
4 And round a· the throne were four "
6 and round a· the throne, were four "
8 six wings a· him; "
5:11 angels round a· the throne and "
7:11 all the angels stood round a· the "
8: 1 a· the space of half an hour. 5613
10: 4 their voices, I was a· to write: 3195
16:21 every stone a· the weight of a 5613
20: 9 the camp of the saints a·, 2944

above
Ge 1: 7 which were a· the firmament: 5921
20 a· the earth in the open "
3:14 cursed a· all cattle, and a· every "
6:16 in a cubit shalt thou finish it a·; *4605
7:17 and it was lift up a· the earth. 5921
27:39 and of the dew of heaven from a·; "
28:13 Lord stood a· it, and said, I am "
48:22 one portion a· thy brethren, which "
49:25 with blessings of heaven a·, "
26 prevailed a· the blessings of my "
Ex 18:11 dealt proudly he was a· them. * "
19: 5 treasure unto me a· all people: "
20: 4 of any thing that is in heaven a·, 4605
25:21 the mercy seat a· upon the ark; "
22 with thee from a· the mercy seat, 5921
26:14 a covering a· of badgers' skins. 4605
24 be coupled together a· the head *5921
28:27, 28 a· the curious girdle of the 4605
29:13 and the caul that is a· the liver, *5921
22 and the caul a· the liver, and the *
30:14 from twenty years old and a·, *4605
36:19 covering of badgers' skins a· that. "
39:20 a· the curious girdle of the ephod. "
21 it might be a· the curious girdle *5921
40:19 covering of the tent a· upon it; 4605
20 the mercy seat a· upon the ark: "
Le 3: 4 and the caul a· the liver, with *5921
10 flanks, and the caul a· the liver, * "
15 and the caul a· the liver, with * "
4: 9 flanks, and the caul a· the liver, * "
7: 4 and the caul that is a· the liver, *
8:16 inwards, and the caul a· the liver, *
25 and the caul a· the liver, and the *
9:10 a· the liver of the sin offering, *4480
19 kidneys, and the caul a· the liver: *5921
11:21 which have legs a· their feet, 4605
27: 7 from sixty years old and a·; *

Nu 3:49 of them that were over and a· 5921
4:25 is a· upon it, and the hanging for 4605
12: 3 Moses was very meek, a· all the
16: 3 lift ye up yourselves a· the 5921
De 4:39 he is God in heaven a·, 4605
5: 8 that is in heaven a·, or that is in "
7: 6 a· all people that are upon the face
14 Thou shalt be blessed a· all people:
10:15 even you a· all people, as it is this
14: 2 a· all the nations that are upon
17:20 his heart be not lifted up a· his
25: 3 and beat him a· these with many 5921
26:19 high a· all nations which he hath "
28: 1 set thee on high a· all nations of "
13 thou shalt be a· only, 4605
43 is within thee shall get up a· thee 5921
30: 5 and multiply thee a· thy fathers.
Jos 2:11 he is God in heaven a·, 4605
3:13 waters that come down from a·; "
16 waters which came down from a· "
J'g 5:24 Blessed a· women shall Jael the
24 blessed shall she be a· women in
1Sa 2:29 and honourest thy sons a· me, to
2Sa 22:17 He sent from a·, he took me; *4791
49 hast lifted me up on high a· them
1Ki 7: 3 covered with cedar a· upon the 4605
11 And a· were costly stones, "
20 had pomegranates also a·, "
25 the sea was set a· upon them, "
29 there was a base a·: "
31 within the chapiter and a· was ? "
8: 7 and the staves thereof a·. "
23 no God like thee, in heaven a·, "
14: 9 But hast done evil a· all that were
22 they had committed, a· all that
16:30 in the sight of the Lord a· all that
2Ki 21:11 hath done wickedly a· all that the
25:28 set his throne a· the throne of 5921
1Ch 5: 2 Judah prevailed a· his brethren,
16:25 he also is to be feared a· all gods. 5921
23:27 from twenty years old and a·: *4605
27: 6 a· the thirty: and in his course *5921
29: 3 house of my God, over and a· all 4605
11 and thou art exalted as head a· all.
2Ch 2: 5 for great is our God a· all gods.
4: 4 the sea was set a· upon them, 4605
5: 8 the staves thereof a·. "
11:21 daughter of Absalom a· all his
25: 5 from twenty years old and a·, *4605
34: 4 images, that were on high a· 5921
Ne 3:28 From a· the horse gate repaired
7: 2 man, and feared God a· many.
8: 5 (for he was a· all the people;) and 5921
9: 5 which is exalted a· all blessing
12:37 of the wall, a· the house of David, "
39 And from a· the gate of Ephraim, "
39 a· the old gate, and a· the fish * "
Es 2:17 king loved Esther a· all the women,
3: 1 and set his seat a· all the princes 5921
Job 3: 4 let not God regard it from a·, 4605
18:16 and a· shall his branch be cut off.
28:18 the price of wisdom is a· rubies.
31: 2 portion of God is there from a·? 4605
28 denied the God that is a·. "
Ps 8: 1 hast set thy glory a· the heavens. *5921
10: 5 judgments are far a· out of his 4791
18:16 He sent from a·, he took me, he * "
48 yea, thou liftest me up a· those
27: 6 lifted up a· mine enemies round 5921
45: 7 the oil of gladness a· thy fellows.
50: 4 call to the heavens from a·, 5921
57: 5 exalted, O God, a· the heavens; "
5, 11 let thy glory be a· all the earth.
11 exalted, O God, a· the heavens:
78:23 commanded the clouds from a·, 4605
95: 3 God, and a great king a· all gods. 5921
96: 4 praised: he is to be feared a· all "
97: 9 Lord, art high a· all the earth: "
9 thou art exalted far a· all gods.
99: 2 and he is high a· all the people.
103:11 as the heaven is high a· the earth,
104: 6 the water stood a· the mountains.
108: 4 thy mercy is great a· the heavens:
5 exalted, O God, a· the heavens:
5 and thy glory a· all the earth;
113: 4 the Lord is high a· all nations,
4 and his glory a· the heavens.
119:127 commandments a· gold; yea, a·
135: 5 and that our Lord is a· all gods.
136: 6 stretched out the earth a· the 5921
137: 6 prefer not Jerusalem a· my chief "
138: 2 magnified thy word a· all thy
144: 7 Send thine hand from a·; rid me, 4791
148: 4 ye waters that be a· the heavens "
13 glory is a· the earth and heaven.
Pr 8:28 established the clouds a·: 4605
15:24 The way of life is a· to the wise, * "
31:10 for her price is far a· rubies
Ec 2: 7 and small cattle a· all that were
3:19 a man hath no preeminence a· a 4480
Isa 2: 2 and shall be exalted a· the hills;
6: 2 A· it stood the seraphims: 4605
7:11 or in the height a·. "
14:13 a· the stars of God: "
14 I will ascend a· the heights of the 5921
45: 8 Drop down, ye heavens, from a·, 4605
Jer 4:28 the heavens a· be black: 4605
15: 8 increased to me a· the sand of the
17: 9 The heart is deceitful a· all things,
31:37 If heaven a· can be measured, 4605
35: 4 was a· the chamber of Maaseiah "
52:32 set his throne a· the throne of the "
La 1:13 From a· hath he sent fire into my *4791
Eze 1:22 stretched forth over their heads a·. 4605
26 And a· the firmament that was "
26 appearance of a man a· upon it. "

Eze 10: 1 firmament that was a· the head *5921
19 God of Israel was over them a·. 4605
11:22 God of Israel was over them a·. "
16:43 a· all thine abominations. 5921
29:15 itself any more a· the nations: for "
31: 5 his height was exalted a· all the "
37: 8 the skin covered them a·: 4605
41:17 To that a· the door, even unto the 5921
20 From the ground unto a· the door "
Da 6: 3 Daniel was preferred a· the 5922
11: 5 and he shall be strong a· him, and 5921
36 and magnify himself a· every god, "
37 for he shall magnify himself a· all. "
Am 2: 9 I destroyed his fruit from a·, 4605
Mic 4: 1 and it shall be exalted a· the hills;
Na 3:16 merchants a· the stars of heaven:
M't 10:24 The disciple is not a· his master, 5228
24 nor the servant a· his lord.
Lu 3:20 Added yet this a· all, that he †1909
6:40 The disciple is not a· his master: 5228
13: 2 sinners a· all the Galilæans, 3844
4 they were sinners a· all men that "
Joh 3:31 cometh from a· is a· all: 509
31 cometh from heaven is a· all. 1883
6:13 which remained over and a· *
8:23 are from beneath; I am from a·: 507
19:11 except it were given thee from a·: 509
Ac 2:19 I will shew wonders in heaven a·, 507
4:22 the man was a· forty years old, *4117
26:13 a· the brightness of the sun, 5228
Ro 10: 6 is, to bring Christ down from a·:) *
14: 5 one day a· another: 3844
1Co 4: 6 not to think of men a· that which *5228
10:13 to be tempted a· that ye are able; "
15: 6 seen of a· five hundred brethren 1883
2Co 1: 8 out of measure, a· strength, *5228
12: 2 a· fourteen years ago (whether in *4253
6 a· that which he seeth me to be, 5228
7 I should be exalted a· measure *
7 should be exalted a· measure. *
Ga 1:14 Jews' religion a· many my equals *5228
4:26 Jerusalem which is a· is free, 507
Eph 1:21 Far a· all principality, and power, 5231
3:20 exceeding abundantly a· all that 5228
4: 6 who is a· all, and through all, *1909
10 ascended up far a· all heavens, 5231
6:16 A· all, taking the shield of faith, *1909
Ph'p 2: 9 a name which is a· every name: 5228
Col 3: 1 seek those things which are a·, 507
2 Set your affections on things a·, "
14 a· all these things put on charity, 1909
2Th 2: 4 a· all that is called God, "
Ph'm 16 Not now as a servant, but a· a *5228
Heb 1: 9 the oil of gladness a· thy fellows. 3844
10: 8 A· when he said, Sacrifice and 511
Jas 1:17 every perfect gift is from a·, 509
3:15 descendeth not from a·, but is "
17 the wisdom that is from a· is first "
5:12 But a· all things, my brethren, 4253
1Pe 4: 8 a· all things have fervent charity "
3Jo 2 I wish a· all things that thou *4012

Abraham (a'-bra-ham) See also ABRAHAM'S; ABRAM.
Ge 17: 5 but thy name shall be A·; 85
9 God said unto A·, Thou shalt keep "
15 God said unto A·, As for Sarai thy "
17 A· fell upon his face, and laughed, "
18 A· said unto God, Oh that Ishmael "
22 and God went up from A·. "
23 And A· took Ishmael his son, and "
24 A· was ninety years old and nine, "
26 selfsame day was A· circumcised, "
18: 6 A· hastened into the tent unto "
7 A· ran unto the herd, and fetcht "
11 A· and Sarah were old and well "
13 the Lord said unto A·, Wherefore "
16 A· went with them to bring them "
17 Shall I hide from A· that thing "
18 Seeing that A· shall surely become "
19 that the Lord may bring upon A· "
22 but A· stood yet before the Lord. "
23 A· drew near, and said, Wilt thou "
27 A· answered and said, Behold now, "
33 as he had left communing with A·: "
33 and A· returned unto his place. "
19:27 A· gat up early in the morning to "
29 God remembered A·, and sent Lot "
20: 1 A· journeyed from thence toward "
2 A· said of Sarah his wife, She is my "
9 Abimelech called A·, and said unto "
10 Abimelech said unto A·, What "
11 A· said, Because I thought, surely "
14 gave them unto A·, and restored "
17 So A· prayed unto God: and God "
21: 2 and bare A· a son in his old age, "
3 A· called the name of his son that "
4 A· circumcised his son Isaac "
5 A· was an hundred years old, when "
7 Who would have said unto A·, that "
8 A· made a great feast the same day "
9 which she had born unto A·, "
10 she said unto A·, Cast out this "
12 God said unto A·, Let it not be "
14 A· rose up early in the morning, "
22 captain of his host spake unto A·, "
24 A· said, I will swear. "
25 A· reproved Abimelech because of a "
27 A· took sheep and oxen, and gave "
28 A· set seven ewe lambs of the flock "
29 Abimelech said unto A·, What mean "
33 A· planted a grove in Beer-sheba, "
34 A· sojourned in the Philistines' land 85
22: 1 that God did tempt A·, and said "
1 unto him, A·: and he said, Behold, "
3 A· rose up early in the morning, "
4 day A· lifted up his eyes, and saw "

Ge 22: 5 A· said unto his young men, Abide 85
6 A· took the wood of the burnt "
7 Isaac spake unto A· his father, and "
8 A· said, My son, God will provide "
9 A· built an altar there, and laid the "
10 A· stretched forth his hand, and "
11 him out of heaven, and said, A·, A·: "
13 A· lifted up his eyes, and looked, "
13 A· went and took the ram, and "
14 A· called the name of that place "
15 the angel of the Lord called unto A· "
19 So A· returned unto his young men, "
19 and A· dwelt at Beer-sheba. "
20 it was told A·, saying, Behold, "
23: 2 and A· came to mourn for Sarah, "
3 A· stood up from before his dead, "
5 the children of Heth answered A·, "
7 A· stood up, and bowed himself to "
10 Ephron the Hittite answered A· "
12 A· bowed down himself before the "
14 Ephron answered A·, saying unto "
16 And A· hearkened unto Ephron; "
16 A· weighed to Ephron the silver, "
18 Unto A· for a possession in the "
19 after this, A· buried Sarah his wife "
20 made sure unto A· for a possession "
24: 1 A· was old, and well stricken in age: "
1 Lord had blessed A· in all things. "
2 A· said unto his eldest servant of "
6 A· said unto him, Beware thou that "
9 put his hand under the thigh of A· "
12 O Lord God of my master A·, I pray "
12 shew kindness unto my master A· "
27 be the Lord God of my master A·, "
42 said, O Lord God of my master A·, "
48 the Lord God of my master A·, "
25: 1 Then again A· took a wife, and her "
5 A· gave all that he had unto Isaac "
6 concubines, which A· had, A· gave "
8 Then A· gave up the ghost, and died "
10 The field which A· purchased of the "
10 there was A· buried, and Sarah his "
11 the death of A·, that God blessed "
12 Sarah's handmaid, bare unto A·: "
19 A· begat Isaac: "
26: 1 famine that was in the days of A·. "
3 the oath which I sware unto A· "
5 Because that A· obeyed my voice, "
15 had digged in the days of A· "
18 they had digged in the days of A· "
18 stopped them after the death of A·: "
24 and said, I am the God of A· thy "
28: 4 And give thee the blessing of A·, "
4 a stranger, which God gave unto A·. "
13 I am the Lord God of A· thy father, "
31:42 the God of my father, the God of A·, "
53 The God of A·, and the God of Nahor, "
32: 9 Jacob said, O God of my father A·, "
35:12 the land which I gave A· and Isaac, "
27 which is Hebron, where A· and "
48:15 before whom my fathers A· and "
16 and the name of my fathers A· and "
49:30 which A· bought with the field of "
31 There they buried A· and Sarah his "
50:13 which A· bought with the field for a "
24 unto the land which he sware to A·, "
Ex 2:24 remembered his covenant with A·, "
3: 6 the God of thy father, the God of A·, "
15 God of your fathers, the God of A·, "
16 God of A·, of Isaac, and of Jacob, "
4: 5 God of their fathers, the God of A·, "
6: 3 I appeared unto A·, unto Isaac, and "
8 which I did sware to give it to A·, "
32:13 Remember A·, Isaac, and Israel, "
33: 1 the land which I sware unto A·, "
Le 26:42 also my convenant with A· will I "
Nu 32:11 see the land which I sware unto A·, "
De 1: 8 Lord sware unto your fathers, A·, "
6:10 he sware unto thy fathers, to A·, "
9: 5 Lord sware unto thy fathers, A·, "
27 Remember thy servants, A·, Isaac, "
29:13 hath sworn unto thy fathers, to A·, "
30:20 Lord sware unto thy fathers, to A·, "
34: 4 is the land which I sware unto A·, "
Jos 24: 2 even Terah, the father of A·, "
3 I took your father A· from the "
1Ki 18:36 came near, and said, Lord God of A·, "
2Ki 13:23 because of his covenant with A·, "
1Ch 1:27 Abram; the same is A·. "
28 The sons of A·; Isaac, and Ishmael. "
34 And A· begat Isaac. The sons of "
16:16 covenant which he made with A·, "
29:18 O Lord God of A·, Isaac, and of "
2Ch 20: 7 and gavest it to the seed of A· "
30: 6 again unto the Lord God of A·, "
Ne 9: 7 and gavest him the name of A·; "
Ps 47: 9 even the people of the God of A·: "
105: 6 O ye seed of A· his servant, "
9 Which covenant he made with A·, "
42 his holy promise, and A· "
Isa 29:22 saith the Lord, who redeemed A·, "
41: 8 the seed of A· my friend. "
51: 2 Look unto A· your father, and unto "
63:16 though A· be ignorant of us, "
Jer 33:26 to be rulers over the seed of A·, "
Eze 33:24 A· was one, and he inherited the "
Mic 7:20 truth to Jacob, and the mercy to A·, "
M't 1: 1 the son of David, the son of A·. 11
2 A· begat Isaac; and Isaac begat "
17 the generations from A· to David "
3: 9 We have A· to our father: "
9 to raise up children unto A·. "
8:11 shall sit down with A·, "
22:32 I am the God of A·, and the God of "
M'r 12:26 I am the God of A·, "
Lu 1:55 As he spake to our fathers, to A·, "
Lu 1:73 he sware to our father A·, 11
3: 8 We have A· to our father: "
8 to raise up children unto A·. "
34 which was the son of A·, "
13:16 this woman, being a daughter of A·, "
28 when ye shall see A·, and Isaac, "
16:23 and seeth A· afar off, "
24 Father A·, have mercy on me, "
25 But A· said, Son, remember that "
29 A· saith unto him, They have Moses "
30 Nay, father A·: but if one went "
19: 9 forsomuch as he also is a son of A·. "
Lu 20:37 he calleth the Lord the God of A·, "
Joh 8:39 answered and said unto him, A· is "
39 ye would do the works of A·. "
40 this did not A·. "
52 A· is dead, and the prophets; "
53 Art thou greater than our father A·, "
56 A· rejoiced to see my day: "
57 and hast thou seen A·? "
58 Before A· was, I am. "
Ac 3:13 The God of A·, and of Isaac, "
25 saying unto A·, And in thy seed "
7: 2 appeared unto our father A·, "
8 circumcision: and so A· begat "
16 the sepulchre that A· bought 11
17 which God had sworn to A·, "
32 God of thy fathers, the God of A·, "
13:26 children of the stock of A·, "
Ro 4: 1 A· our father, as pertaining "
2 if A· were justified by works, "
3 A· believed God, and it was counted "
9 faith was reckoned to A· for "
12 that faith of our father A·, "
13 not to A·, or to his seed, through "
16 which is of the faith of A·; "
9: 7 because they are the seed of A·, * "
11: 1 of the seed of A·, of the tribe of "
2Co 11:22 Are they the seed of A·? so am I. "
Ga 3: 6 Even as A· believed God, "
7 are the children of A·. "
8 preached before the gospel unto A·, "
9 blessed with faithful A·. "
14 the blessing of A· might come "
16 to A· and his seed were the "
18 God gave it to A· by promise. "
4:22 A· had two sons, the one by "
Heb 2:16 but he took on him the seed of A·. "
6:13 when God made promise to A·, "
7: 1 A· returning from the slaughter "
2 To whom also A· gave a tenth "
4 A· gave the tenth of the spoils. "
5 they come out of the loins of A·: "
6 received tithes of A·, "
9 payed tithes in A·. "
11: 8 By faith A·, when he was called to "
17 By faith A·, when he was tried, "
Jas 2:21 Was not A· our father justified by "
23 A· believed God, and it was imputed "
1Pe 3: 6 Sara obeyed A·, calling him lord: "

Abraham's (*a'-bra-hams*)
Ge 17:23 every male among the men of A· 85
20:18 because of Sarah A· wife. "
21:11 thing was very grievous in A· sight "
22:23 eight Milcah did bear to Nahor, A· "
24:15 son of Milcah, the wife of Nahor, A· "
34 And he said, I am A· servant. "
52 when A· servant heard their words, "
59 and her nurse, and A· servant, and "
25: 7 these are the days of the years of A· "
12 are the generations of Ishmael, A· "
19 are the generations of Isaac, A· "
26:24 multiply thy seed for my servant A· "
28: 9 the daughter of Ishmael A· "
1Ch 1:32 the sons of Keturah, A· concubine: "
Lu 16:22 carried by the angels into A· bosom: 11
Joh 8:33 We be A· seed, and were never in "
37 I know that ye are A· seed; "
39 If ye were A· children, ye would do "
Ga 3:29 then are ye A· seed, and heirs "

Abram (*a'-brum*) See also ABRAHAM; ABRAM'S.
Ge 11:26 lived seventy years, and begat A·, 87
27 Terah begat A·, Nahor, and Haran; "
29 And A· and Nahor took them wives: "
31 And Terah took A· his son, and Lot "
12: 1 the Lord had said unto A·, Get thee "
4 So A· departed, as the Lord had "
4 A· was seventy and five years old "
5 A· took Sarai his wife, and Lot "
6 A· passed through the land unto "
7 Lord appeared unto A·, and said, "
9 A· journeyed, going on still toward "
10 and A· went down into Egypt to "
14 when A· was come into Egypt, the "
16 And he entreated A· well for her "
18 Pharaoh called A·, and said, What "
13: 1 A· went up out of Egypt, he, and "
2 And A· was very rich in cattle, "
4 and there A· called on the name of "
5 Lot also, which went with A·, had "
8 A· said unto Lot, Let there be no "
12 A· dwelled in the land of Canaan, "
14 the Lord said unto A·, after that "
18 Then A· removed his tent, and "
14:13 one that had escaped, and told A· "
13 and these were confederate with A·. "
14 when A· heard that his brother was "
19 Blessed be A· of the most high God, "
21 the king of Sodom said unto A·, "
22 A· said to the king of Sodom, "
23 thou shouldest say, I have made A· "
15: 1 the word of the Lord came unto A· "
1 in a vision, saying, Fear not, A·: "
2 A· said, Lord God, what wilt thou "
3 A· said, Behold, to me thou hast "
Ge 15:11 came down upon the carcasses, A· 87
12 a deep sleep fell upon A·; "
13 he said unto A·, Know of a surety "
18 the Lord made a covenant with A·, "
16: 2 Sarai said unto A·, Behold now, the "
2 And A· hearkened to the voice of "
3 after A· had dwelt ten years in the "
3 and gave her to her husband A· "
5 Sarai said unto A·, My wrong be "
6 A· said unto Sarai, Behold, thy "
15 Hagar bare A· a son: and A· called "
16 A· was fourscore and six years old, "
16 when Hagar bare Ishmael to A·. "
17: 1 when A· was ninety years old and "
1 the Lord appeared to A·, "
3 A· fell on his face: and God talked "
5 thy name any more be called A·, "
1Ch 1:27 A·; the same is Abraham. "
Ne 9: 7 Lord the God, who didst choose A·, "

Abram's (*a'-brums*)
Ge 11:29 the name of A· wife was Sarai; 87
31 his daughter in law, his son A· wife; "
12:17 because of Sarai, A· wife. "
13: 7 a strife between the herdmen of A· "
14:12 they took Lot, A· brother's son, "
16: 1 Now Sarai, A· wife, bare him no "
3 And Sarai, A· wife, took Hagar her "

abroad
Ge 10:18 of the Canaanites spread a·. 5310
11: 4 lest we be scattered a· upon the 6527
8 the Lord scattered them a· from "
9 did the Lord scatter them a· "
15: 5 he brought him forth a·, and 2351
19:17 had brought them forth a·, "
28:14 and thou shalt spread a· to the 6555
Ex 5:12 So the people were scattered a· 6527
9:29 I will spread a· my hands unto 6566
33 from Pharaoh, and spread a· his "
12:46 carry forth aught of the flesh a· 2351
21:19 walk a· upon his staff, "
40:19 And he spread a· the tent over *6566
Le 13: 7 But if the scab spread much a· in 6581
12 And if a leprosy break out a· in 6524
22 And if it spread much a· in the 6581
27 if it be spread much a· in the "
14: 8 tarry a· out of his tent seven days.*2351
18: 9 at home, or born a·, "
Nu 11:32 they spread them all a· for 7849
De 23:10 then shall he go a· out of the 2351
12 whither thou shalt go forth a·: "
13 when thou wilt ease thyself a·, "
24:11 Thou shalt stand a·, and the * "
11 shall bring out the pledge a· * "
32:11 spreadeth a· her wings, taketh 6566
J'g 12: 9 daughters, whom he sent a·, 2351
9 took in thirty daughters from a· "
1Sa 9:26 he and Samuel, a·. "
30:16 they were spread a· upon all the 5203
2Sa 22:43 did spread them a·. 7554
1Ki 2:42 and walkest a· any whither, "
2Ki 4: 3 vessels a· of all thy neighbours, 2351
1Ch 13: 2 a· unto our brethren everywhere, 6555
14:13 themselves a· in the valley. *6584
2Ch 26: 8 Uzziah: and his name spread a· "
15 his name spread far a·; 7350
29:16 it out a· into the brook Kidron. 2351
31: 5 as the commandment came a·, 6555
Ne 1: 8 I will scatter you a· among the 6327
Es 1:17 deed of the queen shall come a· 3318
3: 8 is a certain people scattered a· 6340
Job 4:11 lion's whelps are scattered a·. 6504
15:23 wandereth a· for bread, saying, 5074
40:11 Cast a· the rage of thy wrath: *6327
Ps 41: 6 when he goeth a·, he telleth it. 2351
77:17 thine arrows also went a·. 1980
Pr 5:16 thy fountains be dispersed a·, 2351
Isa 24: 1 a· the inhabitants thereof. 6327
28:25 doth he not cast a· the fitches, "
44:24 spreadeth a· the earth by myself; 7554
Jer 6:11 pour it out upon the children a·, *2351
La 1:20 a· the sword bereaveth, at home "
Eze 34:21 till ye have scattered them a·; "
Zec 1:17 prosperity shall yet be spread a·; 6527
2: 6 spread you a· as the four winds 6566
M't 9:26 went a· into all that land. *1831
31 a· his fame in all that country. 1310
36 scattered a·, as sheep having no *4496
12:30 not with me scattereth a·. *4650
26:31 the flock shall be scattered a·. 1287
M'r 1:28 fame spread a· throughout all *1831
45 blaze a· the matter, insomuch that 1310
4:22 but that it should come a·. *1519, 5318
6:14 (for his name was spread a·:)* " 1096
Lu 1:65 these sayings were noised a· 1255
2:17 made known a· the saying *1232
5:15 more went there a fame a· of him: 1330
8:17 be known and come a·. *1519, 5318
Joh 11:52 of God that were scattered a·. 1287
21:23 went this saying a· among the *1831
Ac 2: 6 when this was noised a·, *1096, 5456
8: 1 all scattered a· throughout the 1289
4 they that were scattered a· went "
11:19 scattered a· upon the persecution "
Ro 5: 5 love of God is shed a· in our hearts 1632
16:19 your obedience is come a· unto all 864
2Co 9: 9 He hath dispersed a·; he hath 4650
1Th 1: 8 faith to God-ward is spread a·; *1831
Jas 1: 1 tribes which are scattered a·, *1290

Absalom (*ab'-sal-um*) See also ABISHALOM; ABSALOM'S.
2Sa 3: 3 the third, A· the son of Maacah 53
13: 1 that A· the son of David had a fair "
20 And A· her brother said unto her, "
22 And A· spake unto his brother "
22 Amnon neither good nor bad: for A· "

2Sa 13:23 A' had sheepshearers in Baal-hazor, 53
23 and A' invited all the king's "
24 And A' came to the king, and said, "
25 the king said to A', Nay, my son, "
26 Then said A', If not, I pray thee, "
27 A' pressed him, that he let Amnon "
28 Now A' had commanded his "
29 And the servants of A' did unto "
29 Amnon as A' had commanded. "
30 A' hath slain all the king's sons, "
32 by the appointment of A' this hath "
34 But A' fled. And the young man "
37 But A' fled, and went to Talmai, "
38 So A' fled, and went to Geshur, "
39 David longed to go forth unto A': "
14: 1 that the king's heart was toward A'. "
21 bring the young man A' again. "
23 went to Geshur, and brought A' to "
24 So A' returned to his own house, "
25 much praised as A' for his beauty: "
27 unto A' there were born three sons, "
28 A' dwelt two full years in Jerusalem, "
29 A' sent for Joab, to have sent him "
31 Then Joab arose, and came to A' "
32 A' answered Joab, Behold, I sent "
33 when he had called for A', he came "
33 the king: and the king kissed A'. "
15: 1 that A' prepared him chariots and "
2 And A' rose up early, and stood "
2 then A' called unto him, and said, "
3 A' said unto him, See, thy matters "
4 A' said moreover, Oh that I were "
6 on this manner did A' to all Israel "
6 so A' stole the hearts of the men of "
7 A' said unto the king, I pray thee, "
10 But A' sent spies throughout all the "
10 ye shall say, A' reigneth in Hebron. "
11 And with A' went two hundred men "
12 A' sent for Ahithophel the Gilonite, "
12 people increased continually with A' "
13 of the men of Israel are after A'. "
14 for we shall not else escape from A': "
31 is among the conspirators with A'. "
34 say unto A', I will be thy servant, "
37 came into the city, and A' came into "
16: 8 the kingdom into the hand of A' "
15 And A', and all the people the men "
16 David's friend, was come unto A', "
16 Hushai said unto A', God save the "
17 A' said to Hushai, Is this thy "
18 Hushai said unto A', Nay; but whom "
20 said A' to Ahithophel, Give counsel "
21 Ahithophel said unto A', Go in unto "
22 So they spread A' a tent upon the "
22 and A' went in unto his father's "
23 both with David and with A'. "
17: 1 Ahithophel said unto A', Let me "
4 And the saying pleased A' well, "
5 Then said A', Call now Hushai "
6 When Hushai was come to A', A' "
7 Hushai said unto A', The counsel "
9 among the people that follow A'. "
14 A' and all the men of Israel said, "
14 the Lord might bring evil upon A'. "
15 and thus did Ahithophel counsel A' "
18 a lad saw them, and told A': "
24 And A' passed over Jordan, he and "
25 A' made Amasa captain of the host "
26 Israel and A' pitched in the land of "
18: 5 with the young man, even with A'. "
5 the captains charge concerning A'. "
9 and A' met the servants of David. "
9 And A' rode upon a mule, "
10 Behold, I saw A' hanged in an oak. "
12 that none touch the young man A'. "
14 them through the heart of A', "
15 about and smote A', and slew him. "
17 they took A', and cast him into a "
18 Now, A' in his life time had taken "
29 said, Is the young man A' safe? "
32 Cushi, Is the young man A' safe? "
33 O my son A', my son, my son A'! "
33 died for thee, O A', my son, my son! "
19: 1 king weepeth and mourneth for A'. "
4 with a loud voice, O my son A', "
4 O A', my son, my son! "
6 I perceive, that if A' had lived, "
9 now he is fled out of the land for A'. "
10 And A', whom we anointed over us, "
20: 6 do us more harm than did A': "
1Ki 1: 6 and his mother bare him after A'. "
2: 7 I fled because of A' thy brother. "
28 though he turned not after A'. "
1Ch 3: 2 The third, A' the son of Maachah "
2Ch 11:20 took Maachah the daughter of A'; "
21 loved Maachah the daughter of A' "
Ps 3:*title* Psalm of David, when he fled from A' "

Absalom's (*ab'-sal-ums*)
2Sa 13: 4 I love Tamar, my brother A' sister, 53
20 desolate in her brother A' house. "
14:30 And A' servants set the field on fire. "
17:20 A' servants came to the woman "
18:18 it is called unto this day, A' place. "

absence
Lu 22: 6 in the a' of the multitude. *817*
Ph'p 2:12 now much more in my a', *666*

absent
Ge 31:49 when we are a' one from another. 5641
1Co 5: 3 For I verily, as a' in body, but *548*
2Co 5: 6 we are a' from the Lord: *1553*
8 rather to be a' from the body, "
9 that, whether present or a', "
10: 1 being a' am bold toward you: *548*
11 by letters when we are a', such "
13: 2 a' now I write to them "
2Co 13:10 write these things being a', *548*
Ph'p 1:27 come and see you, or else be a', "
Col 2: 5 though I be a' in the flesh, "

abstain
Ac 15:20 they a' from pollutions of idols, *567*
29 ye a' from meats offered to idols, "
1Th 4: 3 that ye should a' from fornication: "
5:22 A' from all appearance of evil. "
1Ti 4: 3 commanding to a' from meats, "
1Pe 2: 11 a' from fleshly lusts, which war "

abstinence
Ac 27:21 after long a' Paul stood forth in *776

abundance
De 28:47 for the a' of all things; 7230
33:19 they shall suck of the a' of the 8228
1Sa 1:16 out of the a' of my complaint 7230
2Sa 12:30 the spoil of the city in great a'. *7235
1Ki 1:19 and fat cattle and sheep in a', 7230
25 fat cattle and sheep in a', "
10:10 came no more such a' of spices "
27 as the sycomore trees .... for a'. "
18:41 there is a sound of a' of rain. 1995
1Ch 22: 3 David prepared iron in a' for the 7230
3 brass in a' without weight; "
4 Also cedar trees in a': 369, 4557
14 iron without weight; for it is in a': 7230
15 workmen with thee in a', "
29: 2 marble stones in a'. "
21 sacrifices in a' for all Israel: "
2Ch 1:15 as the sycomore trees .... for a'. "
2: 9 to prepare me timber in a': "
4:18 vessels in great a': "
9: 1 spices, and gold in a', "
9 of spices great a', and precious "
27 as the sycomore trees .... in a'. "
11:23 gave them victual in a'. "
14:15 sheep and camels in a', "
15: 9 fell to him out of Israel in a', "
17: 5 he had riches and honour in a'. "
18: 1 had riches and honour in a', "
2 killed sheep and oxen for him in a', "
20:25 found among them in a' both riches "
24:11 gathered money in a'. "
29:35 the burnt offerings were in a', "
31: 5 children of Israel brought in a' 7235
32: 5 made darts and shields in a'. 7230
29 flocks and herds in a': "
Ne 9:25 fruit trees in a': "
Es 1: 7 royal wine in a', according to the 7227
Job 22:11 and a' of waters cover thee. 8229
36:31 he giveth meat in a'. 4342
38:34 that a' of waters may cover 8229
Ps 37:11 delight themselves in the a' of 7230
52: 7 trusted in the a' of his riches, "
72: 7 a' of peace so long as the moon "
105:30 land brought forth frogs in a', *8317
Ec 5:10 he that loveth a' with increase: 1995
12 but the a' of the rich will not *7647
Isa 7:22 for the a' of milk that they shall 7230
15: 7 the a' they have gotten, 3502
47: 9 great a' of thine enchantments. 6109
60: 5 a' of the sea shall be converted 1995
66:11 with the a' of her glory. 2123
Jer 33: 6 reveal unto them the a' of peace 6283
Eze 16:49 and a' of idleness was in her *7962
26:10 By reason of the a' of his horses 8229
Zec 14:14 silver, and apparel, in great a'. 7230
M't 12:34 out of the a' of the heart the *4051*
13:12 and he shall have more a': *4052*
25:29 and he shall have a': "
M'r 12:44 did cast in of their a'; * "
Lu 6:45 of the a' of the heart his mouth *4051*
12:15 consisteth not in the a' of the *4052*
21: 4 these have of their a' cast in unto * "
Ro 5:17 they which receive a' of grace *4050*
2Co 8: 2 the a' of their joy and their deep "
14 your a' may be a supply for their *4051*
14 that their a' also may be a supply "
20 blame us in this a' which is **100*
12: 7 through the a' of the revelations, **5236*
Re 18: 3 the a' of her delicacies. **1411*

abundant
Ex 34: 6 and a' in goodness and truth, *7227
Isa 56:12 much more a'. *1419
Jer 51:13 many waters, a' in treasures, 7227
1Co 12:23 we bestow more a' honour; *4055*
23 have more a' comeliness. "
24 given more a' honour "
2Co 4:15 that the a' grace might through **4121*
7:15 his inward affection is more a' **4056*
9:12 is a' also by many thanksgivings **4052*
11:23 in labours more a', in stripes **4056*
Ph'p 1:26 may be more a' in Jesus Christ **4052*
1Ti 1:14 of our Lord was exceeding a' **5250*
1Pe 1: 3 according to his a' mercy hath **4183*

abundantly
Ge 1:20 Let the waters bring forth a' 8317
21 the waters brought forth a', "
8:17 they may breed a' in the earth, "
9: 7 bring forth a' in the earth, and "
Ex 1: 7 fruitful, and increased a', and "
8: 3 river shall bring forth frogs a', * "
Nu 20:11 the water came out a', 7227
1Ch 12:40 oxen, and sheep a': for there *7230
22: 5 David prepared a' before his "
8 Thou hast shed blood a', "
2Ch 31: 5 all things brought they in a'. "
Job 12: 6 whose hand God bringeth a'. "
36:28 distil upon man a'. 7227
Ps 36: 8 They shall be a' satisfied with 7301
65:10 waterest the ridges thereof a': "
132:15 I will a' bless her provision: 1288
145: 7 They shall a' utter the memory *5042
Ca 5: 1 drink, yea, drink a'. O beloved 7937
Isa 15: 3 every one shall howl, weeping a'. 3381
35: 2 it shall blossom a', and rejoice 6524
55: 7 for he will a' pardon. 7235
Jo 10:10 might have it more a'. *4053*
1Co 15:10 I laboured more a' than they all: *4054*
2Co 1:12 and more a' to you-ward. *4056*
2: 4 I have more a' unto you. "
10:15 according to our rule a', **1519, 4050*
12:15 the more a' I love you, the less I *4056*
Eph 3:20 able to do exceeding a' above *1537, 4053*
1Th 2:17 endeavoured the more a' to see **4056*
Tit 3: 6 Which he shed on us a' through **4146*
Heb 6:17 willing more a' to shew unto the *4054*
2Pe 1:11 shall be ministered unto you a' **4146*

abuse See also ABUSED; ABUSING.
1Sa 31: 4 thrust me through, and a' me. 5953
1Ch 10: 4 these uncircumcised come and a' "
1Co 9:18 I a' not my power in the gospel. **2710*

abused
J'g 19:25 they knew her, and a' her 5953

abusers
1Co 6: 9 a' of themselves with mankind, *733*

abusing
1Co 7:31 that use this world, as not a' it: *‡2710*

Accad (*ak'-kad*)
Ge 10:10 Babel, and Erech, and A', and 390

accept See also ACCEPTED; ACCEPTEST; ACCEPTETH; ACCEPTING.
Ge 32:20 peradventure he will a' of me. 5375
Ex 22:11 the owner of it shall a' thereof, 3947
Le 26:41 they then a' of the punishment 7521
43 they shall a' of the punishment "
De 33:11 a' the work of his hands: "
1Sa 26:19 me, let him a' an offering: 7306
2Sa 24:23 The Lord thy God a' thee. 7521
Job 13: 8 Will ye a' his person? will ye †‡5375
10 if ye do secretly a' persons. * "
32:21 Let me not, I pray you, a' any * "
42: 8 for him will I a': "
Ps 20: 3 a' thy burnt sacrifice; 1878
82: 2 a' the persons of the wicked? *5375
119:108 A', I beseech thee, the freewill 7521
Pr 18: 5 to a' the person of the wicked, 5375
Jer 14:10 the Lord doth not a' them; 7521
12 I will not a' them: "
Eze 20:40 there will I a' them, and there will "
41 will a' you with your sweet savour, "
43:27 I will a' you, saith the Lord God. 7521
Am 5:22 meat offerings, I will not a' them; "
Mal 1: 8 pleased with thee, or a' thy 5375
10 neither will I a' an offering at 7521
13 should I a' this of your hand? "
Ac 24: 3 We a' it always, and in all places, *588*

acceptable
Le 22:20 it shall not be a' for you. 7522
De 33:24 let him be a' to his brethren, "
Ps 19:14 be a' in thy sight, O Lord, "
69:13 is unto thee, O Lord, in an a' time: "
Pr 10:32 of the righteous know what is a': "
21: 3 justice and judgment is more a' 977
Ec 12:10 preacher sought to find out a' 2656
Isa 49: 8 In an a' time have I heard thee, 7522
58: 5 a fast, and an a' day to the Lord? "
61: 2 proclaim the a' year of the Lord, ‡ "
Jer 6:20 your burnt offerings are not a', "
Da 4:27 O king, let my counsel be a' unto 8232
Lu 4:19 To preach the a' year of the Lord. *1184*
Ro 12: 1 living sacrifice, holy, a' unto God, *2101*
2 and a', and perfect, will of God. "
14:18 a' to God, and approved of men. * "
15:16 up of the Gentiles might be a', *2144*
Eph 5:10 Proving what is a' unto the Lord. **2101*
Ph'p 4:18 a sweet smell, a sacrifice a', *1184*
1Ti 2: 3 this is good and a' in the sight of *587*
5: 4 good and a' before God. "
1Pe 2: 5 a' to God by Jesus Christ. *2144*
20 this is a' with God. *5485*

acceptably
Heb 12:28 serve God a' with reverence and **2102*

acceptance
Isa 60: 7 come up with a' on mine altar, 7522

acceptation
1Ti 1:15 worthy of all a', that *594*
4: 9 saying and worthy of all a'. "

accepted
Ge 4: 7 dost well, shalt thou not be a'? 7613
19:21 I have a' thee concerning this 5375
Ex 28:38 they may be a' before the Lord. 7522
Le 1: 4 and it shall be a' for him to make 7521
7:18 the third day, it shall not be a', "
10:19 been a' in the sight of the Lord? *3190
19: 7 is abominable; it shall not be a'. 7521
22:21 shall be perfect to be a'; 7522
23 for a vow it shall not be a'. 7521
25 they shall not be a' for you. "
27 it shall be a' for an offering made "
23:11 before the Lord, to be a' for you: 7522
1Sa 18: 5 and he was a' in the sight of all *3190
25:35 and have a' thy person. 5375
Es 10: 3 and a' of the multitude of his 7521
Job 42: 9 the Lord also a' Job. 5375
Isa 56: 7 their sacrifices shall be a' upon 7522
Jer 37:20 let my supplication .... be a' 5307
42: 2 Let .... our supplication be a' "
Lu 4:24 No prophet is a' in his own **1184*
Ac 10:35 worketh righteousness, is a' **1184*
Ro 15:31 may be a' of the saints; **2144*
2Co 5: 9 we may be a' of him. **2101*
6: 2 I have heard thee in a time a', **1184*
2 behold, now is the a' time; **2144*
8:12 it is a' according to that a man * "
17 For indeed he a' the exhortation; *1209*

2Co 11: 4 gospel, which ye have not a', *1209
Eph 1: 6 wherein he hath made us a' in *5487
acceptest
Lu 20:21 neither a' thou the person of any, 2983
accepteth
Job 34:19 him that a' not the persons of *5375
Ec 9: 7 God now a' thy works. *7521
Ho 8:13 the Lord a' them not; "
Ga 2: 6 God a' no man's person:) 2983
accepting
Heb 11:35 were tortured, not a' deliverance; 4327
access
Ro 5: 2 we have a' by faith into this grace 4318
Eph 2:18 we both have a' by one Spirit "
3:12 a' with confidence by the faith of "
Accho (ak'-ko)
J'g 1:31 drive out the inhabitants of A', 5910
accompanied
Ac 10:23 brethren from Joppa a' him. 4905
11:12 these six brethren a' me, 2064, 4862
20: 4 a' him into Asia Sopater of Berea; 4902
38 And they a' him unto the ship. *4311
accompany See also ACCOMPANIED; ACCOMPANYING.
Heb 6: 9 things that a' salvation, 2192
accompanying
2Sa 6: 4 a' the ark of God: *5973
accomplish See also ACCOMPLISHED, ACCOMPLISHING.
Le 22:21 to a' his vow, 6381
1Ki 5: 9 and thou shalt a' my desire, 6213
Job 14: 6 till he shall, a' as an hireling, 7521
Ps 64: 6 they a' a diligent search: *8552
Isa 55:11 it shall a' that which I please, 6213
Jer 44:25 ye will surely a' your vows, *6965
Eze 6:12 thus will I a' my fury upon them. 3615
7: 8 and a' mine anger upon thee: "
13:15 Thus will I a' my wrath upon the "
20: 8, 21 to a' my anger against them "
Da 9: 2 that he would a' seventy years in *4390
Lu 9:31 which he should a' at Jerusalem. 4137
accomplished
2Ch 36:22 word of the Lord ... might be a', 3615
Es 2:12 days of their purifications a', 4390
Job 15:32 It shall be a' before his time, "
Pr 13:19 The desire a' is sweet to the soul: 1961
Isa 40: 2 her warfare is a', that her 4390
Jer 25:12 when seventy years are a', that I * "
34 and of your dispersions are a'; * "
29:10 after seventy years be a' at "
39:16 and they shall be a' in that "
La 4:11 The Lord hath a' his fury; 3615
22 punishment of thine iniquity is a', 8552
Eze 4: 6 And when thou hast a' them, 3615
5:13 Thus shall mine anger be a', "
13 when I have a' my fury in them. "
Da 11:36 till the indignation be a': "
12: 7 and when he shall have a' to * "
Lu 1:23 days of his ministration were a', *4130
2: 6 the days were a' that she should * "
21 eight days were a' * "
22 when the days .... were a', * "
12:50 straitened till it be a'! 5055
18:31 the Son of man shall be a'. "
22:37 must yet be a' in me, * "
Joh 19:28 all things were now a', * "
Ac 21: 5 when we had a' those days, 1822
1Pe 5: 9 are a' in your brethren 2005
accomplishing
Heb 9: 6 a' the service of God. 2005
accomplishment
Ac 21:26 the a' of the days of purification, *1604
accord See also ACCORDING.
Le 25: 5 which groweth of its own a' *5599
Jos 9: 2 and with Israel, with one a'. 6310
Ac 1:14 continued with one a' in prayer 3661
2: 1 were all with one a' in one place.* "
46 daily with one a' in the temple, "
4:24 up their voice to God with one a', "
5:12 they were all with one a' in "
7:57 and ran upon him with one a', "
8: 6 the people with one a' gave heed "
12:10 opened to them of his own a': 844
20 but they came with one a' to him, 3661
15:25 being assembled with one a', to "
18:12 made insurrection with one a' "
19:29 rushed with one a' into the "
2Co 8:17 of his own a' he went unto you. 830
Ph'p 2: 2 love, being of one a', of one mind. 4861
according
Ge 18:10 return unto thee a' to the time *
25:13 by their names, a' to their
16 twelve princes a' to their nations.
27: 8 a' to that which I command thee.
30:34 I would it might be a' to thy word.
33:14 a' as the cattle that goeth before 7272
34:12 and I will give a' as ye shall say
36:40 the dukes that came of Esau, a'
43 a' to their habitations in the land
39:17 she spake unto him a' to these
40: 5 each man a' to the interpretation
41:11 we dreamed each man a' to the
12 to each man a' to his dream he
40 a' unto thy word shall all my 5921
54 dearth began to come, a' as
43: 7 we told him a' to the tenor of 5921
33 before him, the firstborn a' to his
33 and the youngest a' to his youth:
44: 2 he did a' to the word that Joseph
7 thy servants should do a' to this *
10 let it be a' unto your words:
Ge 45:21 a' to the commandment of 5921
47:12 with bread, a' to their families. 6310
49:28 every one a' to his blessing he 834
50: 6 and bury thy father, a' as he
12 sons did unto him a' as he 3651
Ex 6:16 the sons of Levi a' to their
17 Libni, and Shimi, a' to their
19 are the families of Levi a' to
25 of the fathers of the Levites a'
8:10 Be it a' to thy word: that thou
13 the Lord did a' to the word of
31 a' to the word of Moses; and he
12: 3 every man a lamb, a' to the
4 take it a' to the number of
4 every man a' to his eating shall 6310
21 a lamb a' to your families, and
25 the Lord will give you, a' as he
35 Israel did a' to the word of
16:16 every man a' to his eating, 6310
16 every man, a' to the number of
18, 21 every man a' to his eating. 6310
17: 1 a' to the commandment of the 5921
21:22 a' as the woman's husband will
31 a' to this judgment shall it be
22:17 he shall pay money a' to the
24: 4 twelve pillars, a' to the twelve tribes
25: 9 A' to all that I shew thee, after
35 a' to the six branches that *
26:30 a' to the fashion thereof which
28: 8 the same, a' to the work *
10 the rest on the other stone, a' to
21 a' to their names, like the 5921
21 with his name shall they be a' to*
29:35 a' to all things which I have
41 do thereto a' to the meat offering
41 and a' to the drink offering
30:37 not make to yourselves a' to the
31:11 a' to all that I have commanded
32:28 the children of Levi did a' to
36: 1 a' to all that the Lord had
37:21 a' to the six branches going out *
29 a' to the work of the apothecary.*
38:21 as it was counted, a' to the 5921
39: 5 the same, a' to the work thereof;*
14 the stones were a' to the names 5921
14 twelve, a' to their names, like the "
14 every one with his name, a' to the "
32 did a' to all that the Lord
42 A' to all that the Lord
40:16 Thus did Moses: a' to all that
Le 4: 3 do sin a' to the sin of the people;*
35 a' to the offerings made by fire *5921
5:10 burnt offering, a' to the manner:
12 a' to the offerings made by fire *5921
9:16 offered it a' to the manner.
10: 7 did a' to the word of Moses.
12: 2 a' to the days of the separation *
25:15 A' to the number of years after
15 a' unto the number of years of
16 A' to the multitude of years 6310
16 a' to the fewness of years thou
16 a' to the number of the years of *
50 price of his sale shall be a' unto
50 a' to the time of an hired servant
51 a' unto them he shall give again 6310
52 a' unto his years shall he give
26:21 more plagues upon you a' to
27: 8 a' to his ability that vowed "
16 thy estimation shall be a' to the "
17 year of jubile, a' to thy
18 a' to the years that remain, 5921,6310
25 estimations shall be a' to the
27 then he shall redeem it a' to
27 then it shall be sold a' to thy
Nu 1: 18, 20, 22, 24, 26, 28, 30, 32, 34, 36, 38,
40, 42 a' to the number of the names,
54 a' to all that the Lord commanded
2:10 the camp of Reuben a' to their
18 the camp of Ephraim a' to their
34 a' to all that the Lord commanded
34 after their families, a' to the 5921
3:16 Moses numbered them a' to the "
20 families of the Levites a' to the
22, 34 a' to the number of all the
51 Aaron and to his sons, a' to the 5921
4:31 a' to all their service in the
33 families of the sons of Merari, a'
37 a' to the commandment of the 5921
41 number a' to the commandment "
45 Moses and Aaron numbered a' to "
49 A' to the commandment of the "
49 Moses, every one a' to his service, "
49 and a' to his burden: thus were "
6:21 a' to the vow which he vowed, 6310
7: 5 every man a' to his service. "
7 a' to their service: "
8 a' unto their service, "
8: 4 a' unto the pattern which the
20 a' unto all that the Lord
9: 3 a' to all the rites of it, and a' to
5 a' to all that the Lord commanded
12 a' to all the ordinances of the
14 unto the Lord; a' to the
14 and a' to the manner thereof,
20 a' to the commandment of the *5921
20 and a' to the commandment of "
10:13 their journey a' to the
14 camp of the children of Judah a'
18 camp of Reuben set forward a'
22 of Ephraim set forward a' to
28 of the children of Israel a' to
14:17 be great, a' as thou hast spoken,
19 this people a' unto the greatness
20 I have pardoned a' to thy word:
29 all that were numbered of you, a'
15:12 A' to the number that ye shall
Nu 15:12 to every one a' to their number,
24 a' to the manner, and one kid of
17: 2 a rod a' to the house of their *
2 of all their princes a' to the house
6 for each prince one, a' to their
18:16 redeem, a' to thine estimation,
23:23 a' to this time it shall be said *
24: 2 saw Israel abiding in his tents a'
26:18 children of Gad a' to those that
22 families of Judah a' to those
25 families of Issachar a' to those
27 of the Zebulunites a' to those
37 of the sons of Ephraim a' to
43 of the Shuhamites, a' to those
47 of the sons of Asher a' to those
50 the families of Naphtali a' to
53 a' to the number of names.
54 be given a' to those that were 6310
55 a' to the names of the tribes of their
56 A' to the lot shall...possession 5921,6310
29: 6 a' unto their manner, for a sweet
18 shall be a' to their number, after
21, 24 a' to their number, after the
27 shall be a' to their number, after
30 a' to their number, after the
33 shall be a' to their number, after
37 a' to their number, after the
40 a' to all that the Lord commanded
30: 2 do a' to all that proceedeth out of
33: 2 Moses wrote their goings out a' to
2 these are their journeys a' to
54 a' to the tribes of your fathers ye
34:14 children of Reuben a' to the house
14 children of Gad a' to the house
35: 8 the Levites a' to his inheritance 6310
24 the revenger of blood a' to these 5921
36: 5 children of Israel a' to the word "
De 1: 3 a' unto all that the Lord had
30 a' to all that he did for you in
41 a' to all that the Lord our God
46 a' unto the days that ye abode
3:24 a' to thy works, and a' to thy
4:34 a' to all that the Lord your God
9:10 a' to all the words, which the Lord
10: 4 a' to the first writing, the ten
9 his inheritance, a' as the Lord thy
10 a' to the first time, forty days *
12:15 a' to the blessing of the Lord thy
16:10 a' as the Lord thy God hath
17 a' to the blessing of the Lord thy
17:10 shalt do a' to the sentence, 5921,6310
10 observe to do a' to all that they
11 A' to the sentence of the law 5921
11 and a' to the judgment which "
18:16 A' to all that thou desiredst of the
23:23 a' as thou hast vowed unto the
24: 8 a' to all that the priests the
25: 2 a' to his fault, by a certain 1767
26:13 a' to all thy commandments
14 and have done a' to all that thou
29:21 a' to all the curses of the
30: 2 a' to all that I command thee this
31: 5 a' unto all the commandments
32: 8 a' to the number of the children
34: 5 Moab, a' to the word of the Lord. 5921
Jos 1: 7 observe to do a' to all the law.
8 thou mayest observe to do a' to
17 A' as we hearkened unto Moses
2:21 A' unto your words, so be it.
4: 5 a' unto the number of the tribes
8 a' to the number of the tribes of
10 a' to all that Moses commanded
7:14 be brought a' to your tribes: *
14 shall come a' to the families *
8: 8 a' to the commandment of the
27 a' unto the word of the Lord
34 a' to all that is written in the
10:32, 35, 37 a' to all that he had done
11:23 a' to all that the Lord said unto
23 inheritance unto Israel a' to their
12: 7 Israel for a possession a' to their
13:15 children of Reuben inheritance a'
24 even unto the children of Gad a'
15:12 children of Judah round about a'
13 a' to the commandment of the 413
20 tribe of the children of Judah a'
16: 5 children of Ephraim a' to their
17: 4 a' to the commandment of the 413
18: 4 a' to the inheritance of them; 6310
10 the children of Israel a' to their
11 came up a' to their families:
20 round about, a' to their families.
21, 28 children of Benjamin a' to
19: 1, 8 children of Simeon a' to their
10, 16 children of Zebulun a' to their
17, 23 the children of Issachar a' to
24, 31 children of Asher a' to their
32, 39 the children of Naphtali a' to
40, 48 the children of Dan a' to their
50 A' to the word of the Lord they 5921
21:33 All the cities of the Gershonites a'
44 a' to all that he sware unto their
22: 9 a' to the word of the Lord by the 5921
24: 5 a' to that which I did among
J'g 8:35 a' to all the goodness which he
9:16 done unto him a' to the deserving
11:10 if we do not so a' to thy words.
36 to me a' to that which hath
39 who did with her a' to his vow
20:10 a' to all the folly that they have
21:23 wives, a' to their number, of them
Ru 3: 6 did a' to all that her mother in law
1Sa 2:35 that shall do a' to that which is in
6: 4 a' to the number of the lords of
18 a' to the number of all the cities
8: 8 A' to all the works which they

1Sa 13: 8 a· to the set time that Samuel had
14: 7 behold, I am with thee a· to thy
17: 23 spake a· to the same words:
23:20 come down a· to all the desire of
25: 9 they spake to Nabal a· to all those
30 a· to all the good that he hath
2Sa 3:39 reward the doer of evil a· to his
7:17 A· to all these words, and a· to all
21 sake, and a· to thine own heart,
22 a· to all that we have heard with
9:11 A· to all that my lord the king
14:20 a· to the wisdom of an angel of
22:21 the Lord rewarded me a· to my
21 a· to the cleanness of my hands
25 Lord hath recompensed me a· to
25 a· to my cleanness in his eye sight.
24:19 David, a· to the saying of Gad,
1Ki 2: 6 Do therefore a· to thy wisdom,
3: 6 a· as he walked before thee in
12 Behold, I have done a· to thy
4:28 every man a· to his charge.
5: 6 give hire for thy servants a· to all
10 cedar trees and fir trees a· to all
6: 3 a· to the breadth of the house; 5921,6440
38 and a· to all the fashion of it.
7: 9 a· to the measures of hewed
36 a· to the proportion of every one,
8:32 give him a· to his righteousness.
39 give to every man a· to his ways, 3605
43 and do a· to all that the stranger
56 rest unto his people Israel, a· to
9: 4 a· to all that I have commanded
11 with gold, a· to all his desire,)
11:37 and thou shalt reign a· to all that
12:24 returned to depart, a· to the word
13: 5 out from the altar, a· to the sign
26 slain him, a· to the word of the
14:18 a· to the word of the Lord, which
24 they did a· to all the abominations
15:29 destroyed him, a· unto the
16:12 Baasha, a· to the word of the Lord,
34 Segub, a· to the word of the Lord,
17: 1 a· to my word. 6310
5 did a· unto the word of the Lord:
15 a· to the saying of Elijah:
16 oil fail, a· to the word of the Lord,
18:31 a· to the number of the tribes of
20: 4 O king, a· to thy saying, I am thine,
21:26 following idols, a· to all things as
22:38 a· unto the word of the Lord
53 a· to all that his father had done.
2Ki 1:17 he died a· to the word of the Lord
2:22 a· to the saying of Elisha
4:16 About this season, a· to the time*
17 unto her, a· to the time of life. *
44 left thereof, a· to the word of the
5:14 a· to the saying of the man of God:
6:18 with blindness a· to the word of
7:16 barley for a shekel, a· to the word
9:26 ground, a· to the word of the Lord.
10:17 destroyed him, a· to the saying of
30 a· to all that was in mine heart,
11: 9 did a· to all things that Jehoiada
14: 3 he did a· to all things as Joash
6 a· unto that which is written in the
25 a· to the word of the Lord God of
15: 3 a· to all that his father Amaziah
34 a· to all that his father Uzziah
16: 3 fire, a· to the abominations of the
10 a· to all the workmanship thereof.
11 altar a· to all that king Ahaz had
16 the priest, a· to all that king Ahaz
17:13 a· to all the law which I
18: 3 a· to all that David his father did.
21: 8 they will observe to do a· to all
8 a· to all the law that my servant
22:13 to do a· unto all that which is
23:16 polluted it, a· to the word of the
19 a· to all the acts that he had done
25 might, a· to all the law of Moses;
32 a· to all that his fathers had done.
35 to give the money a· to the 5921
35 of every one a· to his taxation, to
37 a· to all that his fathers had done.
24: 2 destroy it, a· to the word of the
3 Manasseh, a· to all that he did;
9 sight of the Lord, a· to all that
19 a· to all that Jehoiakim had done.
1Ch 6:19 the families of the Levites a· to
32 waited on their office a· to their
49 a· to all that Moses the servant of
9: 9 brethren, a· to their generations,
11: 3 a· to the word of the Lord by
10 a· to the word of the Lord
12:23 of Saul to him, a· to the word of
15:15 a· to the word of the Lord.
16:40 a· to all that is written in the law
17:15 A· to all these words, and a· to all
17 regarded me a· to the estate of a
19 a· to thine own heart, hast thou
20 a· to all that we have heard with
23:11 reckoning, a· to their father's *
31 a· to the order commanded unto
24: 3 a· to their offices in their service.
4 sons of Ithamar a· to the house
19 a· to their manner, under Aaron,
25: 1 the number of the workmen a· to
2 prophesied a· to the order of the *5921
6 a· to the king's order to Asaph, * "
26:13 a· to the house of their fathers,
31 a· to the generations of his fathers.
28:15 a· to the use of every candlestick.
2Ch 3: 4 length of it was a· to the breadth 5921
8 the length whereof was a· to the
4: 7 gold a· to their form,
6:23 giving him a· to his righteousness.

2Ch 6:30 render unto every man a· unto all
33 a· to all that the stranger calleth to
7:17 and do a· to all that I have
18 a· as I have covenanted with
8:13 offering a· to the commandment
14 a· to the order of David his
17:14 numbers of them a· to the house
23: 8 a· to all things that Jehoiada the
24: 6 a· to the commandment of Moses *
25: 5 a· to the houses of their fathers,
26: 4 sight of the Lord, a· to all that
11 a· to the number of their account
27: 2 a· to all that his father Uzziah
29: 2 a· to all that David his father
15 came, a· to the commandment of
25 a· to the commandment of David,
30: 6 and Judah, and a· to the
16 a· to the law of Moses the man of
19 he be not cleansed a· to the
31: 2 every man a· to his service, 6310
16 their service in their charges a·
32:25 rendered not again a· to the
33: 8 a· to the whole law and the *
34:32 did a· to the covenant of God,
35: 4 a· to the writing of David king of
4 and a· to the writing of Solomon
5 the holy place a· to the divisions
6 may do a· to the word of the Lord
10 a· to the king's commandment.
13 with fire a· to the ordinance:
15 a· to the commandment of David,
16 a· to the commandment of king
26 a· to that which was written in the
Ezr 3: 4 a· to the custom, as the duty of
7 a· to the grant that they had of
6: 9 a· to the appointment of the
13 a· to that which Darius the king *6903
14 a· to the commandment of the 4481
14 and a· to the commandment of
17 twelve he goats, a· to the number
7: 6 a· to the hand of the Lord his God
9 to Jerusalem, a· to the good hand
14 a· to the law of thy God which is in
9: 1 doing a· to their abominations,
10: 3 a· to the counsel of my Lord, and
3 and let it be done a· to the law.
5 do a· to this word. And they sware,
8 come within three days, a· to the
Ne 2: 8 a· to the good hand of my God
5:12 should do a· to this promise.
13 people did a· to this promise.
19 a· to all that I have done for this*
6: 6 be their king, a· to these words.
7 reported to the king a· to these
14 a· to these their works, and on
8:18 a solemn assembly, a· unto the
9:27 a· to thy manifold mercies thou
28 didst thou deliver them a· to thy
12:24, 45 a· to the commandment of
13:22 and spare me a· to the greatness
24 but a· to the language of each
Es 1: 7 royal wine in abundance, a· to the
8 the drinking was a· to the law;
8 that they should do a· to every
15 we do unto the queen Vashti a·
21 did a· to the word of Memucan:
22 into every province a· to the writing
22 should be published a· to the
2:12 she had been twelve months, a· to
18 and gave gifts, a· to the state of
3:12 and there was written a· to all
12 every people of every province a·
4:16 king, which is not a· to the law:
17 and did a· to all that Esther had
8: 9 written a· to all that Mordecai
9 unto every province a· to the
9 Jews a· to their writing, and a· to
9:13 to do to morrow also a· unto this
27 a· to their writing, and a· to their
31 a· as Mordecai the Jew and
Job 1: 5 offered burnt offerings a· to the
20:18 a· to his substance shall the
33: 6 I am a· to thy wish in God's *
34:11 every man to find a· to his ways.
33 Should it be a· to thy mind? he *
36:27 they pour down rain a· to the *
42: 9 and did a· as the Lord commanded
Ps 7: 8 a· to my righteousness, and a· [*] to
17 I will praise the Lord a· to his
18:20 The Lord rewarded me a· to my
20 a· to the cleanness of my hands
24 hath the Lord recompensed me a·
24 a· to the cleanness of my hands
20: 4 Grant thee a· to thine own heart,*
25: 7 a· to thy mercy remember thou
28: 4 them a· to their deeds, and a· to
33:22 upon us, a· as we hope in thee.
35:24 Judge me, O Lord my God, a· to thy
48:10 A· to thy name, O God, so is thy *
51: 1 Have mercy upon me, O God, a· to
1 a· unto the multitude of thy
62:12 renderest to every man a· to his
69:16 turn unto me a· to the multitude
74: 5 A man was famous a· as he had *
78:72 So he fed them a· to the integrity
79:11 a· to the greatness of thy power
90:11 even a· to thy fear, so is thy
15 a· to the days wherein thou hast
103:10 rewarded us a· to our iniquities. *
106:45 and repented a· to the multitude
109:26 O Lord my God: O save me a· to
119: 9 taking heed thereto a· to thy word.
25 quicken thou me a· to thy word.
28 strengthen thou me a· unto thy
41 even thy salvation, a· to thy word.
58 merciful unto me a· to thy word.

Ps 119:65 O Lord, a· unto thy word.
76 be for my comfort, a· to thy word
91 this day a· to thine ordinances:
107 quicken me, O Lord, a· unto thy
116 Uphold me a· unto thy word, that
124 Deal with thy servant a· unto
149 hear my voice a· unto thy
149 quicken me a· to thy judgment.
154 and deliver me: quicken me a· to
156 quicken me a· to thy judgments.
159 quicken me, O Lord, a· to thy
169 me understanding a· to thy word.
150: 2 praise him a· to his excellent
Pr 12: 8 shall be commended a· to his 6310
24:12 render to every man a· to his
29 I will render to the man a· to
26: 4 Answer not a fool a· to his folly,
5 Answer a fool a· to his folly, lest
Ec 1: 6 and the wind returneth again a· *5921
8:14 a· to the work of the wicked;
14 a· to the work of the righteous:
Isa 8:20 if they speak not a· to this word,
9: 3 they joy before thee a· to the joy
10:26 a· to the slaughter of Midian at *
21:16 Within a year, a· to the years of
23:15 forgotten seventy years, a· to the
27: 7 or is he slain a· to the slaughter of
44:13 the figure of a man, a· to the
59:18 A· to their deeds, accordingly he 5921
63: 7 a· to all that the Lord hath "
7 he hath bestowed on them a· to
7 and a· to the multitude of his
Jer 2:28 for a· to the number of thy cities
3:15 And I will give you pastors a· to
11: 4 and do them, a· to all which I
13 For a· to the number of thy cities
13 and a· to the number of the
13: 2 girdle a· to the word of the Lord,
17:10 a· to his ways, and a· to the fruit
21: 2 the Lord will deal with us a· to
14 But I will punish you a· to the
25:14 recompense them a· to their
14 a· to the works of their own hands.
26:20 against this land a· to all the
27:12 to Zedekiah king of Judah a· to
31:32 Not a· to the covenant that I made
32: 8 a· to the word of the Lord, and
11 both that which was sealed a· to
19 to give every one a· to his ways,
19 and a· to the fruit of his doings:
35:10 and done a· to all that Jonadab
18 and done a· unto all that he hath
36: 8 did a· to all that Jeremiah the
38:27 a· to all these words that the king
40: 3 Lord hath brought it, and done a·
42: 4 a· to your words;
5 if we do not even a· to all things
20 and a· unto all that the Lord our
50:21 do a· to all that I have commanded
29 recompense her a· to her work;
29 a· to all that she hath done, do
52: 2 a· to all that Jehoiakim had done,
La 3:32 compassion a· to the multitude
64 a· to the work of their hands.
Eze 4: 4 a· to the number of the days
5 their iniquity, a· to the number of*
9 make thee bread thereof, a· to the
5: 7 have done a· to the judgments *
7: 3 and will judge thee a· to thy ways,
8 I will judge thee a· to thy ways,
9 I will recompense thee a· to thy
27 and a· to their deserts will I judge
8: 4 a· to the vision that I saw in the
14: 4 that cometh a· to the multitude
18:24 committeth iniquity, and doeth a·
30 every one a· to his ways, saith the
20:44 not a· to your wicked ways,
44 nor a· to your corrupt doings,
23:24 judge thee a· to their judgments.
24:14 a· to thy ways, and
14 a· to thy doings,
24 a· to all that he hath done shall
25:14 in Edom a· to mine anger and
14 a· to my fury;
35:11 do a· to thine anger, and
11 a· to thine envy
36:19 a· to their way and
19 a· to their doings I judged them.
39:24 A· to their uncleanness and
24 a· to their transgressions
40:24 and the arches thereof a· to these
28 measured the south gate a· to
29 and the arches thereof, a· to these
32 and he measured the gate a· to
33 the arches thereof, were a· to
35 the north gate, and measured it a·
42:11 both a· to their fashions, and
11 a· to their doors.
12 a· to the doors of the chambers
43: 3 a· to the appearance of the vision
3 even a· to the vision that I saw
44:24 judge it a· to my judgments:
45: 8 give to the house of Israel a· to
25 a· to the sin offering,
25 a· to the burnt offering,
25 and a· to the meat offering,
25 and a· to the oil.
46: 7 for the lambs a· as his hand shall
47:10 their fish shall be a· to their kinds,*
12 bring forth new fruit a· to his *
13 ye shall inherit the land a· to the
21 divide this land unto you a· to the
Da 4: 8 whose name was Belteshazzar, a·
35 and he doeth a· to his will in the
6: 8 a· to the law of the Medes and
12 is true, a· to the law of the Medes

Da 8: 4 but he did *a·* to his will, and
9:16 O Lord, *a·* to all thy righteousness,
11: 3 with great dominion, and do *a·*
4 to his posterity, nor *a·* to his
16 shall do *a·* to his own will, and
36 And the king shall do *a·* to his
Ho 3: 1 *a·* to the love of the Lord *
9:10 their abominations were *a·* as *
10: 1 *a·* to the multitude of his fruit he
1 *a·* to the goodness of his land
12: 2 *a·* to his ways; *a·* to his doings
13: 2 and idols *a·* to their own
6 *A·* to their pasture, so were they
Jon 3: 3 *a·* to the word of the Lord.
Mic 7:15 *A·* to the days of thy coming out *
Hab 3: 9 made quite naked, *a·* to the *
Hag 2: 5 *A·* to the word that I covenanted
Zec 1: 6 *a·* to our ways, and *a·* to our
5: 3 cut off as on this side *a·* to it; 3644
3 cut off as on that side *a·* to it.
Mal 2: 9 *a·* as ye have not kept my ways, 6310
M't 2:16 *a·* to the time which he had *2596*
9:29 *A·* to your faith be it unto you. "
16:27 he shall reward every man *a·* to "
25:15 to every man *a·* to his several "
M'r 7: 5 Why walk not thy disciples *a·* to "
Lu 1: 9 *A·* to the custom of the priest's "
38 be it unto me *a·* to thy word. "
2:22 *a·* to the law of Moses were "
24 *a·* to that which is said in the law "
29 in peace, *a·* to thy word: "
39 *a·* to the law of the Lord, "
5:14 and offer for thy cleansing, *a·* as "
12:47 neither did *a·* to his will, *4314*
23:56 *a·* to the commandment. *2596*
Joh 7:24 Judge not *a·* to the appearance, "
18:31 judge him *a·* to your law. "
Ac 2:30 *a·* to the flesh, he would raise up * "
4:35 unto every man *a·* as he had need. *2530*
7:44 should make it *a·* to the fashion *2596*
11:29 every man *a·* to his ability, *2531*
13:23 *a·* to his promise raised unto *2596*
22: 3 taught *a·* to the perfect manner "
12 a devout man *a·* to the law, "
24: 6 would have judged *a·* to our law. * "
Ro 1: 3 of the seed of David *a·* to the flesh; "
4 *a·* to the spirit of holiness, "
2: 2 the judgment of God is *a·* to truth "
6 to every man *a·* to his deeds: "
16 *a·* to my gospel. "
4:18 *a·* to that which was spoken, So "
8:27 *a·* to the will of God. "
28 *a·* to his purpose. "
9: 3 my kinsmen *a·* to the flesh: "
11 *a·* to election might stand, not of "
10: 2 have a zeal of God, but not *a·* to "
11: 5 *a·* to the election of grace. "
8 (*A·* as it is written, God hath given *2531*
12: 3 *a·* as God hath dealt to every
6 differing *a·* to the grace *2596*
6 *a·* to the proportion of faith; "
15: 5 *a·* to Christ Jesus: "
16:25 *a·* to my gospel, "
25 *a·* to the revelation of the mystery, "
26 *a·* to the commandment of the "
1Co 1:31 *a·* as it is written, He that glorieth, *2531*
3: 8 *a·* to his own labour. *2596*
10 *A·* to the grace of God which is "
15: 3 died for our sins *a·* to the "
4 *a·* to the scriptures: "
2Co 1:17 do I purpose *a·* to the flesh, "
4:13 *a·* as it is written, I believed, "
5:10 *a·* to that he hath done, *4314*
8:12 *a·* to that a man hath and not *a·* *2526*
9: 7 *a·* as he purposeth in his heart, *2531*
10: 2 as if we walked *a·* to the flesh. *2596*
13 but *a·* to the measure of the rule "
15 *a·* to our rule abundantly, "
11:15 and shall be *a·* to their works. "
13:10 *a·* to the power which the Lord "
Ga 1: 4 *a·* to the will of God and our Father: "
2:14 *a·* to the truth of the gospel, *4314*
3:29 heirs *a·* to the promise. *2596*
6:16 And as many as walk *a·* to this *
Eph 1: 4 *A·* as he hath chosen us in him *2531
5 *a·* to the good pleasure of his will, *2596*
7 *a·* to the riches of his grace; "
9 *a·* to his good pleasure "
11 *a·* to the purpose of him who "
19 *a·* to the working of his mighty "
2: 2 *a·* to the course of this world, "
2 *a·* to the prince of the power "
3: 7 *a·* to the gift of the grace of God "
11 *A·* to the eternal purpose which he "
16 *a·* to the riches of his glory, "
20 *a·* to the power that worketh in us, "
4: 7 grace *a·* to the measure of the "
16 *a·* to the effectual working "
22 *a·* to the deceitful lusts; * "
6: 5 *a·* to the flesh, with fear and "
Ph'p 1:20 *A·* to my earnest expectation and "
3:21 *A·* to the working whereby he is "
4:19 *a·* to his riches in glory by Christ "
Col 1:11 *a·* to his glorious power, "
25 *a·* to the dispensation of God "
29 striving *a·* to his working, "
3:22 obey in all thing your masters *a·* "
2Th 1:12 *a·* to the grace of our God "
1Ti 1:11 *A·* to the glorious gospel of the "
18 *a·* to the prophecies which went "
6: 3 which is *a·* to godliness; "
2Ti 1: 1 *a·* to the promise of life "
8 *a·* to the power of God; "
9 not *a·* to our works, but *a·* to his "
2: 8 *a·* to my gospel: "
4:14 Lord reward him *a·* to his works: "

Tit 1: 1 *a·* to the faith of God's elect, *2596*
3 *a·* to the commandment of God "
3: 5 but *a·* to his mercy he saved us, "
7 *a·* to the hope of eternal life. "
Heb 2: 4 *a·* to his own will? "
7: 5 tithes of the people *a·* to the law, "
8: 4 offer gifts *a·* to the law: "
5 *a·* to the pattern shewed to thee "
9 Not *a·* to the covenant that I made "
9:19 *a·* to the law, he took the blood "
Jas 2: 8 fulfil the royal law *a·* to the "
1Pe 1: 2 Elect *a·* to the foreknowledge of "
3 *a·* to his abundant mercy hath "
14 not fashioning yourselves *a·* to *2596*
17 judgeth *a·* to every man's work, "
3: 7 *a·* to knowledge, giving honour "
4: 6 judged *a·* to men in the flesh, "
6 but live *a·* to God in the spirit. "
19 that suffer *a·* to the will of God "
2Pe 1: 3 *A·* as his divine power hath given *5613*
2:22 *a·* to the true proverb, The dog is "
3:13 *a·* to his promise, look for new *2596*
15 *a·* to the wisdom given unto him "
1Jo 5:14 if we ask any thing *a·* to his will, "
Re 2:23 *a·* to your works. "
18: 6 double *a·* to her works: "
20:12, 13 *a·* to their works. "
21:17 *a·* to the measure of a man, that "
22:12 to give every man *a·* as his work *5613*

accordingly
Isa 59:18 *a·* he will repay, fury to his 5922

account See also ACCOUNTED; ACCOUNTING; ACCOUNTS.
2Ki 12: 4 of every one that passeth the *a·*, *
1Ch 27:24 was the number put in the *a·* of 4557
2Ch 26:11 number of their *a·* by the hand *6486
Job 33:13 he giveth not *a·* of any of his 6030
Ps 144: 3 son of man, that thou makest *a·* 2803
Ec 7:27 one by one, to find out the *a·*: 2808
M't 12:36 they shall give *a·* thereof in the *3056*
18:23 would take *a·* of his servants. * "
Lu 16: 2 give an *a·* of thy stewardship; "
Ac 19:40 whereby we may give an *a·* of this "
Ro 14:12 every one of us shall give *a·* of "
1Co 4: 1 Let a man so *a·* of us, as of the *3049*
Ph'p 4:17 fruit that may abound to your *a·*. *3056*
Ph'm 18 put that on mine *a·*; *1677*
Heb 13:17 as they that must give *a·*, *3056*
1Pe 4: 5 shall give *a·* to him that is ready "
2Pe 3:15 And *a·* that the longsuffering *2233*

accounted
De 2:11 Which also were *a·* giants, as the 2803
20 (That also was *a·* a land of giants: "
1Ki 10:21 it was nothing *a·* of in the days "
2Ch 9:20 of silver; it was not any thing *a·* "
Ps 22:30 it shall be *a·* to the Lord for a *5608
Isa 2:22 wherein is he to be *a·* of? 2803
M'r 10:42 they which are *a·* to rule over *1380*
Lu 20:35 which shall be *a·* worthy to *2661*
21:36 that ye may be *a·* worthy to * "
22:24 which of them should be *a·* the *1380*
Ro 8:36 we are *a·* as sheep for the *3049*
Ga 3: 6 it was *a·* to him for righteousness.* "

accounting
Heb 11:19 *A·* that God was able to raise *3049*

accounts
Da 6: 2 that the princes might give *a·* *2941

accursed
De 21:23 he that is hanged is *a·* of God;) 7045
Jos 6:17 the city shall be *a·*, *2764
18 keep yourselves from the *a·* * "
18 lest ye make yourselves *a·*, *2763
18 when ye take of the *a·* thing, and *2764
7: 1 a trespass in the *a·* thing: * "
1 took of the *a·* thing: * "
11 have even taken of the *a·* thing, * "
12 because they were *a·*: * "
12 except ye destroy the *a·* from * "
13 an *a·* thing in the midst of thee, * "
13 until ye take away the *a·* thing * "
15 taken with the *a·* thing shall be * "
22:20 commit a trespass in the *a·* thing,* "
1Ch 2: 7 who transgressed in the thing *a·*.* "
Isa 65:20 an hundred years old shall be *a·*. 7043
Ro 9: 3 that myself were *a·* from Christ *331*
1Co 12: 3 calleth Jesus *a·*: and that no man * "
Ga 1: 8 preached unto you, let him be *a·*. * "
9 have received, let him be *a·* * "

accusation
Ezr 4: 6 wrote they unto him an *a·* against 7855
M't 27:37 over his head his *a·* written, *156*
M'r 15:26 his *a·* was written over, "
Lu 6: 7 might find an *a·* against him. *2724*
19: 8 thing from any man by false *a·*, *4811*
Joh 18:29 What *a·* bring ye against this *2724*
Ac 25:18 they brought none *a·* of such * *156*
1Ti 5:19 receive not an *a·*, but before two *2724*
2Pe 2:11 bring not railing *a·* against them *2920*
Jude 9 a railing *a·*, but said, The Lord "

accuse See also ACCUSED; ACCUSETH; ACCUSING.
Pr 30:10 *A·* not a servant unto his master, *3960
M't 12:10 that they might *a·* him. *2723*
M'r 3: 2 sabbath day; that they might *a·* "
Lu 3:14 neither *a·* any falsely; and be †*4811*
11:54 his mouth, that they might *a·* †*2723*
23: 2 they began to *a·* him, "
14 whereof ye *a·* him: "
Joh 5:45 Do not think that I will *a·* you to "
8: 6 that they might have to *a·* him. "
Ac 24: 2 Tertullus began to *a·* him, "
8 these things, whereof we *a·* him. "
13 whereof they now *a·* me. "
25: 5 go down with me, and *a·* this man, "

Ac 25:11 whereof these *a·* me, no man may *2723*
28:19 ought to *a·* my nation of. "
1Pe 3:16 ashamed that falsely *a·* your *1908*

accused
Da 3: 8 Chaldeans came near, and *a·* *399, 7170
6:24 those men which had *a·* " "
M't 27:12 he was *a·* of the chief priests *2723*
M'r 15: 3 the chief priests *a·* him of many "
Lu 16: 1 the same was *a·* unto him that he *1225*
23:10 scribes stood and vehemently *a·* *2723*
Ac 22:30 wherefore he was *a·* of the Jews, "
23:28 the cause wherefore they *a·* him, *1458*
29 be *a·* of questions of their law, "
25:16 before that he which is *a·* have *2723*
26: 2 things whereof I am *a·* of the *1458*
7 king Agrippa, I am *a·* of the Jews. "
Tit 1: 6 children not *a·* of riot, or *1722, 2724*
Re 12:10 which *a·* them before our God *2723*

accuser See also ACCUSERS.
Re 12:10 for the *a·* of our brethren is cast *2725*

accusers
Joh 8:10 where are those thine *a·*? *2725*
Ac 23:30 gave commandment to his *a·* "
35 when thine *a·* are also come. "
24: 8 Commanding his *a·* to come unto * "
25:16 have the *a·* face to face, "
18 when the *a·* stood up, "
2Ti 3: 3 trucebreakers, false *a·*, *1228*
Tit 2: 3 not false *a·*, not given to much * "

accuseth
Joh 5:45 there is one that *a·* you, even *2723*

accusing
Ro 2:15 their thoughts the mean while *a·* *2723*

accustomed See also UNACCUSTOMED.
Jer 13:23 that are *a·* to do evil. 3928

Aceldama (*as-el'-dam-ah*)
Ac 1:19 *A·*, that is to say, The field of *184*

Achaia (*ak-ah'-yah*)
Ac 18:12 Gallio was the deputy of *A·*, *882*
27 to pass into *A·*, the brethren wrote, "
19:21 passed through Macedonia and *A·*, "
Ro 15:26 them of Macedonia and *A·* to make "
16: 5 who is the firstfruits of *A·* unto * "
1Co 16:15 firstfruits of *A·*, and that they have "
2Co 1: 1 saints which are in all *A·*: "
9: 2 *A·* was ready a year ago; "
11:10 of boasting in the regions of *A·*. "
1Th 1: 7 that believe in Macedonia and *A·*. "
8 not only in Macedonia and *A·*, but "

Achaicus (*ak-ah'-yah-cus*)
1Co 16:17 Fortunatus and *A·*: *883*
subscr. Stephanas, and Fortunatus, and *A·*.*

Achan (*a'-kan*) See also ACHAR.
Jos 7: 1 for *A·*, the son of Carmi, the son 5912
18 his household man by man; and *A·*, "
19 And Joshua said unto *A·*, My son, "
20 And *A·* answered Joshua, and said, "
24 and all Israel with him, took *A·* "
22:20 Did not *A·* the son of Zerah "

Achar (*a'-kar*) See also ACHAN.
1Ch 2: 7 And the sons of Carmi; *A·*, the 5917

Achaz (*a'-kaz*) See also AHAZ.
M't 1: 9 Joatham begat *A·*; *881*
9 and *A·* begat Ezekias; "

Achbor (*ak'-bor*)
Ge 36:38 and Baal-hanan the son of *A·* 5907
39 Baal-hanan the son of *A·* died, "
2Ki 22:12 And *A·* the son of Michaiah, and "
14 and *A·*, and Shaphan, and Asahiah, "
1Ch 1:49 Baal-hanan the son of *A·* reigned "
Jer 26:22 namely, Elnathan the son of *A·*, "
36:12 Elnathan the son of *A·*, and "

Achim (*a'-kim*)
M't 1:14 and Sadoc begat *A·*; *885*
14 and *A·* begat Eliud; "

Achish (*a'-kish*)
1Sa 21:10 and went to *A·* the king of Gath. 397
11 the servants of *A·* said unto him, "
12 was sore afraid of *A·* the king "
14 Then said *A·* unto his servants, "
27: 2 unto *A·*, the son of Maoch, king "
3 David dwelt with *A·* at Gath, "
5 David said unto *A·*, If I have "
6 *A·* gave him Ziklag that day: "
9 and returned, and came to *A·*. "
10 *A·* said, Whither have ye made "
12 *A·* believed David, saying, He hath "
28: 1 *A·* said unto David, Know thou "
2 David said to *A·*, Surely thou shalt "
2 *A·* said to David, Therefore will I "
29: 2 passed on in the rereward with *A·*. "
3 *A·* said unto the princes of the "
6 *A·* called David, and said unto him, "
8 David said unto *A·*, But what have I "
9 *A·* answered and said to David, "
1Ki 2:39 servants of Shimei ran away unto *A·* "
40 and went to Gath to *A·* to seek his "

Achmetha (*ak'-meth-ah*)
Ezr 6: 2 And there was found at *A·*, in the 307

Achor (*a'-kor*)
Jos 7:24 them unto the valley of *A·*. 5911
26 was called, The valley of *A·*, unto "
15: 7 toward Debir from the valley of *A·*, "
Isa 65:10 and the valley of *A·* a place for the "
Ho 2:15 and the valley of *A·* for a door of "

Achsa (*ak'-sah*) See also ACHSAH.
1Ch 2:49 the daughter of Caleb was *A·*. *5915

Achsah (*ak'-sah*) See also ACHSA.
Jos 15:16 him will I give *A·* my daughter 5915
17 and he gave him *A·* his daughter

J'g 1:12 and taketh it, to him will I give A' 5919
13 took it: and he gave him A' his "

Achshaph (*ak'-shaf*)
Jos 11: 1 of Shimron, and to the king of A', 407
12:20 the king of A', one; "
19:25 and Hali, and Beten, and A', "

Achzib (*ak'-zib*) See also CHEZIB.
Jos 15:44 Keilah, and A', and Mareshah; 392
19:29 at the sea from the coast to A': "
J'g 1:31 nor of A', nor of Helbah, "
Mic 1:14 the houses of A' shall be a lie "

acknowledge See also ACKNOWLEDGED; ACKNOWLEDGETH; ACKNOWLEDGING.
De 21:17 he shall a' the son of the hated 5234
33: 9 neither did he a' his brethren, "
Ps 51: 3 I a' my transgressions: 3045
Pr 3: 6 In all thy ways a' him, "
Isa 33:13 ye that are near, a' my might. "
61: 9 all that see them shall a' them, 5234
63:16 Israel a' us not: "
Jer 3:13 Only a' thine iniquity, 3045
14:20 We a', O Lord, our wickedness, "
24: 5 so will I a' them that are carried *5234
Da 11:39 a strange god, whom he shall a' * "
Ho 5:15 till they a' their offence, "
1Co 14:37 let him a' that the things that I *1921
16:18 therefore a' ye them that are such. "
2Co 1:13 than what ye read or a'; "
13 ye shall a' even to the end; "

acknowledged
Ge 38:26 And Judah a' them, 5234
Ps 32: 5 I a' my sin unto thee, and mine 3045
2Co 1:14 ye have a' us in part, *1922

acknowledgeth
1Joh 2:23 he that a' the Son hath the Father*

acknowledging
2Ti 2:25 repentance to the a' of the truth; *1922
Tit 1: 1 and the a' of the truth which is * "
Ph'm 6 by the a' of every good thing * "

acknowledgment
Col 2: 2 to the a' of the mystery of God, *1922

acquaint See also ACQUAINTED; ACQUAINTING.
Job 22:21 A' now thyself with him, 5532

acquaintance
2Ki 12: 5 it to them, every man of his a': 4378
7 receive no more money of your a', "
Job 19:13 and mine a' are verily estranged 3045
42:11 all they that had been of his a' "
Ps 31:11 a fear to mine a': "
55:13 my guide, and mine a'. * "
88: 8 Thou hast put away mine a' "
18 mine a' into darkness. "
Lu 2:44 among their kinsfolk and a'. 1110
23:49 all his a', and the women that "
Ac 24:23 he should forbid none of his a' *2398

acquainted
Ps 139: 3 and art a' with all my ways. 5532
Isa 53: 3 man of sorrows, and a' with grief: 3045

acquainting
Ec 2: 3 a' mine heart with wisdom; *5090

acquit
Job 10:14 thou wilt not a' me from mine 5352
Na 1: 3 will not at all a' the wicked: * "

Acrabbim See MAALEH-ACRABBIM.

acre See also ACRES.
1Sa 14:14 as it were an half a' of land, 4618

acres
Isa 5:10 ten a' of vineyard shall yield 6776

act See also ACTS; EXACT.
Isa 28:21 to pass his a', his strange a'. 5656
59: 6 a' of violence is in their hands. 6467
Joh 8: 4 taken in adultery, in the very a'. 1888

actions See also EXACTIONS.
1Sa 2: 3 by him a' are weighed. 5949

activity
Ge 47: 6 if thou knowest any men of a' *2428

acts
De 11: 3 his a', which he did in the midst *4639
7 seen all the great a' of the Lord * "
J'g 5:11 the righteous a' of the Lord, "
11 even the righteous a' "
1Sa 12: 7 all the righteous a' of the Lord, "
2Sa 23:20 who had done many a', he slew *6467
1Ki 10: 6 heard in mine own land of thy a' 1697
11:41 the rest of the a' of Solomon, "
41 in the book of the a' of Solomon? "
14:19 the rest of the a' of Jeroboam, how "
29 the rest of the a' of Rehoboam, and "
15: 7 the rest of the a' of Abijam, and "
23 rest of all the a' of Asa, and all his "
31 the rest of the a' of Nadab, and all "
16: 5 the rest of the a' of Baasha, and "
14 the rest of the a' of Elah, and all "
20 the rest of the a' of Zimri, and his "
27 the rest of the a' of Omri which he "
22:39 the rest of the a' of Ahab, and all "
45 the rest of the a' of Jehoshaphat, "
2Ki 1:18 the rest of the a' of Ahaziah which "
8:23 the rest of the a' of Joram, "
10:34 the rest of the a of Jehu, and all "
12:19 the rest of the a' of Joash, and all "
13: 8 the rest of the a' of Jehoahaz, "
12 the rest of the a' of Joash, "
14:15 the rest of the a' of Jehoash which "
18 the rest of the a' of Amaziah, "
28 the rest of the a' of Jeroboam, and "
15: 6 the rest of the a' of Azariah, "
11 the rest of the a' of Zachariah, "
15 the rest of the a' of Shallum, and "
2Ki 15:21 the rest of the a' of Menahem, 1697
26 the rest of the a' of Pekahiah, "
31 the rest of the a' of Pekah, "
36 the rest of the a' of Jotham, "
16:19 the rest of the a' of Ahaz "
20:20 the rest of the a' of Hezekiah, and "
21:17 the rest of the a' of Manasseh, and "
25 the rest of the a' of Amon which "
23:19 a' that he had done in Beth-el. 4640
28 the rest of the a' of Josiah, and all 1697
24: 5 the rest of the a' of Jehoiakim, "
1Ch 11:22 who had done many a'; *6467
29:29 Now the a' of David the king, first 1697
2Ch 9: 5 in mine own land of thine a', and "
29 the rest of the a' of Solomon, "
12:15 Now the a' of Rehoboam, first and "
13:22 the rest of the a' of Abijah, and "
16:11 behold, the a' of Asa, first and last, "
20:34 the rest of the a' of Jehoshaphat, "
25:26 the rest of the a' of Amaziah, first "
26:22 the rest of the a' of Uzziah, "
27: 7 the rest of the a' of Jotham, and "
28:26 Now the rest of his a' and of all his "
32:32 the rest of the a' of Hezekiah, and "
33:18 the rest of the a' of Manasseh, and "
35:26 the rest of the a' of Josiah, and his "
36: 8 the rest of the a' of Jehoiakim, "
Es 10: 2 all the a' of his power and of his 4640
Ps 103: 7 his a' unto the children of Israel.*5949
106: 2 Who can utter the mighty a' of "
145: 4 and shall declare thy mighty a'. "
6 the might of thy terrible a': "
12 to the sons of men his mighty a', "
150: 2 Praise him for his mighty a': "

Adadah (*ad'-ad-ah*)
Jos 15:22 Kinah, and Dimonah, and A', 5735

Adah (*a'-dah*)
Ge 4:19 the name of the one was A', 5711
20 and A' bare Jabal: he was the "
23 A' and Zillah, Hear my voice; "
36: 2 A' the daughter of Elon the "
4 And A' bare to Esau Eliphaz; "
10 Eliphaz the son of A' the wife of "
12 these were the sons of A' Esau's "
16 Edom: these were the sons of A'. "

Adaiah (*ad-a-i'-yah*)
2Ki 22: 1 was Jedidah, the daughter of A' 5718
1Ch 6:41 the son of Zerah, the son of A', "
8:21 A', and Beraiah, and Shimrath, "
9:12 and A' the son of Jeroham, the "
2Ch 23: 1 and Maaseiah the son of A', and "
Ezr 10:29 Malluch, and A', Jashub, and "
39 and Nathan, and A', "
Ne 11: 5 the son of Hazaiah, the son of A', "
12 and A' the son of Jeroham, the son "

Adalia (*ad-al-i'-yah*)
Es 9: 8 Poratha, and A', and Aridatha, 118

Adam (*ad'-um*) See also ADAM'S.
Ge 2:19 brought them unto A' to see what * 120
19 whatsoever A' called every living * "
20 A' gave names to all cattle, * "
20 but for A' there was not found an * "
21 a deep sleep to fall upon A', * 121
23 A' said, This is now bone of my * 120
3: 8 A' and his wife hid themselves * "
9 And the Lord God called unto A', * "
17 And unto A' he said, Because 121
20 A' called his wife's name Eve; * 120
21 Unto A' also and to his wife did the "
4: 1 And A' knew Eve his wife; * "
25 A' knew his wife again; "
5: 1 the book of the generations of A'. 121
2 called their name A', in the day 120
3 A' lived an hundred and thirty years, 121
4 And the days of A' after he had "
5 the days that A' lived "
De 32: 8 when he separated the sons A', * 120
Jos 3:16 very far from the city A', 121
1Ch 1: 1 A', Sheth, Enosh, "
Job 31:33 I covered my transgressions as A', "
Lu 3:38 which was the son of A', 76
Ro 5:14 death reigned from A' to Moses, "
1Co 15:22 as in A' all die, even so in Christ "
45 The first man A' was made a "
45 the last A' was made "
1Ti 2:13 For A' was first formed, "
14 And A' was not deceived, "
Jude 14 Enoch also, the seventh from A'. "

Adamah (*ad'-am-ah*)
Jos 19:36 And A', and Ramah, and Hazor, 128

adamant
Eze 3: 9 As an a' harder than flint 8068
Zec 7:12 made their hearts as an a' stone, "

adamant-stone See ADAMANT and STONE.

Adami (*ad'-am-i*)
Jos 19:33 from Allon to Zaanannim, and A', 129

Adam's (*ad'-ums*)
Ro 5:14 similitude of A' transgression, 76

Adan See NEBUZAR-ADAN.

Adar (*a'-dar*) See also ADDAR; ATAROTH-ADAR.
Jos 15: 3 and went up to A', and fetched a 146
Ezr 6:15 on the third day of the month A', 144
Es 3: 7 twelfth month, that is, the month A'. 143
13 which is the month A', "
8:12 month, which is the month A'. "
9: 1 that is the month A', "
15 fourteenth day also of the month A', "
17 thirteenth day of the month A'; "
21 fourteenth day of the month A', "

Adbeel (*ad'-be-el*)
Ge 25:13 and Kedar, and A', and Mibsam, 110
1Ch 1:29 then Kedar, and A', and Mibsam, "

add See also ADDED; ADDETH.
Ge 30:24 Lord shall a' to me another son. 3254
Le 5:16 shall a' the fifth part thereto, and "
6: 5 shall a' the fifth part more thereto, "
27:13 then he shall a' a fifth part "
15, 19 then he shall a' the fifth part "
27 and shall a' a fifth part "
31 he shall a' thereto the fifth part "
Nu 5: 7 a' unto it the fifth part thereof, "
35: 6 to them ye shall a' forty and two *5414
De 4: 2 Ye shall not a' unto the word 3254
12:32 thou shalt not a' thereto, nor "
19: 9 then shalt thou a' three cities "
29:19 to a' drunkenness to thirst: *5595
2Sa 24: 3 Now the Lord thy God a' unto the 3254
1Ki 12:11 I will a' to your yoke: "
14 heavy, and I will a' to your yoke: "
2Ki 20: 6 And I will a' unto thy days fifteen "
1Ch 22:14 thou mayest a' thereto. "
2Ch 10:14 I will a' thereto: my father "
28:13 ye intend to a' more to our sins "
Ps 69:27 A' iniquity unto their iniquity: 5414
Pr 3: 2 peace, shall they a' to thee. 3254
30: 6 A' thou not unto his words, lest he "
Isa 29: 1 a' ye year to year; 5595
30: 1 that they may a' sin to sin: "
38: 5 I will a' unto thy days fifteen 3254
M't 6:27 can a' one cubit unto his stature? 4369
Lu 12:25 can a' to his stature one cubit? "
Ph'p 1:16 to a' affliction to my bonds: *2018
2Pe 1: 5 a' to your faith virtue; *2023
Re 22:18 If any man shall a' unto these, 2007
18 God shall a' unto him the "

Addan (*ad'-dan*)
Ezr 2:59 Tel-harsa, Cherub, A', and Immer: 135

Addar (*ad'-dar*) See also ADAR; ATAROTH-ADDAR; HAZAR-ADDAR.
1Ch 8: 3 And the sons of Bela were, A', and 146

added
De 5:22 great voice: and he a' no more. 3254
1Sa 12:19 we have a' unto all our sins this "
Jer 36:32 there were a' besides unto them "
45: 3 Lord hath a' grief to my sorrow; "
Da 4:36 excellent majesty was a' unto me. 3255
M't 6:33 these things shall be a' unto you. 4369
Lu 3:20 A' yet this above all, that he shut "
12:31 these things shall be a' unto you. "
19:11 he a' and spake a parable, "
Ac 2:41 there were a' unto them about "
47 And the Lord a' to the church "
5:14 believers were the more a' to the "
11:24 much people was a' unto the Lord. "
Ga 2: 6 in conference a' nothing to me: * 4323
3:19 was a' because of transgressions, 4369

adder See also ADDERS'.
Ge 49:17 serpent by the way, an a' in the 8207
Ps 58: 4 the deaf a' that stoppeth her ear; 6620
91:13 shalt tread upon the lion and a: "
Pr 23:32 a serpent, and stingeth like an a'. 6848

adders'
Ps 140: 3 a' poison is under their lips. 5919

addeth
Job 34:37 he a' rebellion unto his sin, 3254
Pr 10:22 he a' no sorrow with it. "
16:23 a' learning to his lips. "
Ga 3:15 no man disannulleth, or a' 1928

Addi (*ad'-di*)
Lu 3:28 which was the son of A', which 78

addicted
1Co 16:15 they have a' themselves to the *5021

addition See also ADDITIONS.
1Ki 7:30 at the side of every a'. *3914

additions
1Ki 7:29 certain a' made of thin work. *3914
36 and a' round about. * "

Addon (*ad'-don*)
Ne 7:61 Tel-haresha, Cherub, A', and 114

Ader (*a'-dur*)
1Ch 8:15 And Zebadiah, and Arad, and A', *5738

Adiel (*a'-de-el*)
1Ch 4:36 and Asaiah, and A', and Jesimiel, 5717
9:12 and Maasiai the son of A', "
27:25 was Azmaveth the son of A': "

Adin (*a'-din*)
Ezr 2:15 The children of A', four hundred 5720
8: 6 Of the sons also of A'; Ebed the "
Ne 7:20 The children of A', six hundred "
10:16 Adonijah, Bigvai, A', "

Adina (*ad'-in-ah*)
1Ch 11:42 A' the son of Shiza the Reubenite, 5721

Adino (*ad'-in-o*)
2Sa 23: 8 the same was A' the Eznite: he 5722

Adithaim (*ad-ith-a'-im*)
Jos 15:36 Sharaim, and A', and Gederah, 5723

adjure See also ADJURED.
1Ki 22:16 How many times shall I a' thee 7650
2Ch 18:15 How many times shall I a' thee "
M't 26:63 I a' thee by the living God, 1844
M'r 5: 7 I a' thee by God, that thou 3726
Ac 19:13 We a' you by Jesus whom Paul "

adjured
Jos 6:26 Joshua a' them at that time, *7650
1Sa 14:24 for Saul had a' the people, 422

Adlai (*ad'-la-i*)
1Ch 27:29 was Shaphat the son of A': 5724

Admah (*ad'-mah*)
Ge 10:19 Sodom, and Gomorrah, and A'. 126
14: 2 of Gomorrah, Shinab king of A', "
8 of Gomorrah, and the king of A', "
De 29:23 A', and Zeboim, which the Lord "
Ho 11: 8 how shall I make thee as A'? "
Admatha (*ad'-math-ah*)
Es 1:14 Shethar, A', Tarshish, Meres, 133
administered
2Co 8:19 which is a' by us to the glory of *1247
20 abundance which is a' by us: * "
administration See also ADMINISTRATIONS.
2Co 9:12 For the a' of this service *1248
administrations
1Co 12: 5 are differences of a', but the *1248
admiration
Jude 16 having men's persons in a' *2296
Re 17: 6 her, I wondered with great a'. *2295
admired
2Th 1: 10 to be a' in all them that believe *2296
admonish See also ADMONISHED; ADMONISHING.
Ro 15:14 able also to a' one another. 3560
1Th 5:12 over you in the Lord, and a' you; "
2Th 3:15 but a' him as a brother. "
admonished
Ec 4:13 who will no more be a'. *2094
12:12 by these, my son, be a': "
Jer 42:19 know certainly that I have a' *5749
Ac 27: 9 already past, Paul a' them, 3867
Heb 8: 5 as Moses was a' of God when *5537
admonishing
Col 3:16 a' one another in psalms and 3560
admonition
1Co 10:11 they are written for our a', 3559
Eph 6: 4 the nurture and a' of the Lord. "
Tit 3:10 after the first and second a' reject; "
Adna (*ad'-nah*) See also ADNAH.
Ezr 10:30 A', and Chelal, Benaiah, Maaseiah, 5733
Ne 12:15 Of Harim, A'; of Meraioth, "
Adnah (*ad'-nah*) See also ADNA.
1Ch 12:20 fell to him of Manasseh, A', 5734
2Ch 17:14 A' the chief, and with him mighty "
ado
M'r 5:39 Why make ye this a', and weep? *2350
Adoni See ADONI-BEZEK; ADONI-ZEDEK.
Adoni-bezek (*ad''-on-i-be'-zek*)
J'g 1: 5 And they found A' in Bezek: 137
6 A' fled; and they pursued after him, "
7 A' said, Threescore and ten kings, "
Adonijah (*ad-on-i'-jah*) See also TOB-ADONIJAH.
2Sa 3: 4 the fourth, A' the son of Haggith; 138
1Ki 1: 5 A' the son of Haggith exalted "
7 and they following A' helped him. "
8 belonged to David, were not with A' "
9 And A' slew sheep and oxen and "
11 Hast thou not heard that A' the son "
13 why then doth A' reign? "
18 And now, behold, A' reigneth; "
24 hast thou said, A' shall reign after "
25 and say, God save king A'. "
41 And A' and all the guests that were "
42 and A' said unto him, Come in; "
43 Jonathan answered and said to A', "
49 guests that were with A' were afraid, "
50 A' feared because of Solomon, "
51 Behold, A' feareth king Solomon: "
2:13 And A' the son of Haggith came to "
19 to speak unto him for A'. "
21 the Shunammite be given to A' "
22 ask Abishag the Shunammite for A'? "
23 if A' have not spoken this word "
24 A' shall be put to death this day. "
28 for Joab had turned after A', "
1Ch 3: 2 the fourth, A' the son of Haggith: "
2Ch 17: 8 Jehonathan, and A', and Tobijah, "
Ne 10:16 A', Bigvai, Adin, "
Adonikam (*ad-on-i'-kam*)
Ezr 2:13 The children of A', six hundred 140
8:13 And of the last sons of A', whose "
Ne 7:18 The children of A', six hundred "
Adoniram (*ad-on-i'-ram*). See also ADORAM.
1Ki 4: 6 A' the son of Abda was over the 141
5:14 and A' was over the levy. "
Adoni-zedek (*ad''-on-i-ze'-dek*)
Jos 10: 1 when A' king of Jerusalem had 139
3 A' king of Jerusalem sent unto "
adoption
Ro 8:15 ye have received the Spirit of a', 5206
23 waiting for the a', to wit, the "
9: 4 to whom pertaineth the a', and "
Ga 4: 5 we might receive the a' of sons. "
Eph 1: 5 unto the a' of children by Jesus "
Adoraim (*ad-o-ra'-im*)
2Ch 11: 9 And A', and Lachish, and Azekah, 115
Adoram (*ad-o'-ram*). See also ADONIRAM.
2Sa 20:24 And A' was over the tribute: 151
1Ki 12:18 Then king Rehoboam sent A', "
adorn See also ADORNED; ADORNETH; ADORNING.
1Ti 2: 9 that women a' themselves in 2885
Tit 2:10 they may a' the doctrine of God "
adorned
Jer 31: 4 thou shalt again be a' with thy 5710
Lu 21: 5 how it was a' with goodly stones 2885
1Pe 3: 5 a' themselves, being in subjection "
Re 21: 2 as a bride a' for her husband. "
adorneth
Isa 61:10 a bride a' herself with her jewels. 5710

adorning
1Pe 3: 3 a' let it not be that outward a' 2889
Adrammelech (*a-dram'-mel-ek*)
2Ki 17:31 burnt their children in fire to A' 152
19:37 A' and Sharezer his sons smote "
Isa 37:38 A' and Sharezer his sons smote "
Adramyttium (*a-dram-mit'-te-um*)
Ac 27: 2 entering into a ship of A', 98
Adria (*a'-dre-ah*)
Ac 27:27 driven up and down in A', 99
Adriel (*a'-dre-el*)
1Sa 18:19 that she was given unto A' the 5741
2Sa 21: 8 whom she brought up for A' the "
Adullam (*a-dul'-lam*) See also ADULLAMITE.
Jos 12:15 of Libnah, one; the king of A', 5725
15:35 Jarmuth, and A', Socoh, and "
1Sa 22: 1 and escaped to the cave A': and "
2Sa 23:13 harvest time unto the cave of A': "
1Ch 11:15 rock to David, into the cave of A'; "
2Ch 11: 7 And Beth-zur, and Shoco, and A', "
Ne 11:30 Zanoah, A', and in their villages, "
Mic 1:15 he shall come unto A' the glory "
Adullamite (*a-dul'-lam-ite*)
Ge 38: 1 turned in to a certain A', whose 5726
12 he and his friend Hirah the A'. "
20 by the hand of his friend the A', "
adulterer See also ADULTERERS.
Le 20:10 the a' and the adulteress shall 5003
Job 24:15 the eye also of the a' waiteth for "
Isa 57: 3 the seed of the a' "
adulterers
Ps 50:18 hast been partaker with a'. 5003
Jer 9: 2 they be all a', "
23:10 the land is full of a'; "
Ho 7: 4 They are all a', "
Mal 3: 5 the sorcerers, and against the a', "
Lu 18:11 extortioners, unjust, a', 3432
1Co 6: 9 nor idolaters, nor a', "
Heb 13: 4 whoremongers and a' God will "
Jas 4: 4 Ye a' and adulteresses, * "
adulteress See also ADULTERESSES.
Le 20:10 adulterer and the a' shall surely 5003
Pr 6:26 and the a' will hunt for the 802, 376
Ho 3: 1 beloved of her friend, yet an a', 5003
Ro 7: 3 she shall be called an a': 3428
3 so that she is no a', "
adulteresses
Eze 23:45 after the manner of a', 5003
45 because they are a', "
Jas 4: 4 Ye adulterers and a', 3428
adulteries
Jer 13:27 I have seen thine a', 5004
Eze 23:43 her that was old in a', "
Ho 2: 2 out of her sight, and her a' 5005
M't 15:19 murders, a', fornications, 3430
M'r 7:21 evil thoughts, a', fornications, "
adulterous
Pr 30:20 such is the way of an a' woman; 5003
M't 12:39 An evil and a' generation seeketh 3428
16: 4 A wicked and a' generation "
M'r 8:38 in this a' and sinful generation; "
adultery See also ADULTERIES.
Ex 20:14 Thou shalt not commit a'. 5003
Le 20:10 the man that committeth a' "
10 he that committeth a' "
De 5:18 Neither shalt thou commit a'. "
Pr 6:32 committeth a' with a woman "
Jer 3: 8 backsliding Israel committed a' "
9 and committed a' with stones "
5: 7 they then committed a', and "
7: 9 ye steal, murder, and commit a', "
23:14 they commit a', and walk in lies: "
29:23 in Israel, and have committed a' "
Eze 16:32 a wife that committeth a', "
23:37 they have committed a', and blood "
37 their idols have they committed a', "
Ho 4: 2 stealing, and committing a', "
13 your spouses shall commit a'. "
14 when they commit a': "
M't 5:27 Thou shalt not commit a': 3431
28 hath committed a' with her "
32 causeth her to commit a': *3429
32 that is divorced committeth a'. "
19: 9 marry another, committeth a': "
9 is put away doth commit a'. "
18 Thou shalt not commit a', 3431
M'r 10:11 committeth a' against her. 3429
12 to another, she committeth a'. "
19 Do not commit a', 3431
Lu 16:18 marrieth another, committeth a': "
18 from her husband committeth a'. "
18:20 Do not commit a', Do not kill, "
Joh 8: 3 unto him a woman taken in a'; 3430
4 was taken in a', in the very act. 3431
Ro 2:22 should not commit a', "
22 dost thou commit a'? "
13: 9 Thou shalt not commit a', Thou "
Ga 5:19 A', fornication, uncleanness, *3430
Jas 2:11 Do not commit a', said also 3431
11 Now if thou commit no a', "
2Pe 2:14 Having eyes full of a', 3428
Re 2:22 and them that commit a' with her 3431
Adummim (*a-dum'-mim*)
Jos 15: 7 that is before the going up to A', 131
18:17 over against the going up of A', "
advanced
1Sa 12: 6 Lord that a' Moses and Aaron, *6213
Es 3: 1 and a' him, and set his seat above 5375
5:11 he had a' him above the princes "
10: 2 whereunto the king a' him, 1431

advantage See also ADVANTAGED; ADVANTAGETH.
Job 35: 3 thou saidst, What a' will it be 5532
Ro 3: 1 What a' then hath the Jew? 4053
2Co 2:11 Lest Satan should get an a' of us: 4122
Jude 16 in admiration because of a'. 5622
advantaged
Lu 9:25 For what is a man a', *5623
advantageth
1Co 15:32 what a' it me, if the dead rise *3786
adventure See also ADVENTURED; PERADVENTURE.
De 28:56 would not a' to set the sole of her 5254
Ac 19:31 not a' himself into the theatre. 1325
adventured
J'g 9:17 fought for you, and a' his life far, 7993
adversaries
Ex 23:22 and an adversary unto thine a'. 6696
De 32:27 a' should behave themselves 6862
43 render vengeance to his a', "
Jos 5:13 Art thou for us, or for our a'? "
1Sa 2:10 a' of the Lord shall be broken to *7378
2Sa 19:22 should this day be a' unto me? 7854
Ezr 4: 1 the a' of Judah and Benjamin 6862
Ne 4:11 And our a' said, They shall not "
Ps 38:20 render evil for good are mine a'; 7853
69:19 mine a' are all before thee. 6887
71:13 a' to my soul; 7853
81:14 turned my hand against their a'. 6862
89:42 hast set the right hand of his a'; "
109: 4 For my love they are my a': 7853
20 the reward of mine a' "
29 Let mine a' be clothed with "
Isa 1:24 I will ease me of mine a', 6862
9:11 shall set up the a' of Rezin against "
11:13 and the a' of Judah shall be cut *6887
59:18 he will repay, fury to his a', 6862
63:18 our a' have trodden down thy "
64: 2 make thy name known to thine a', "
Jer 30:16 devoured; and all thine a', "
46:10 avenge him of his a': "
50: 7 and their a' said, We offend not, "
La 1: 5 Her a' are the chief, * "
7 the a' saw her, and did mock "
17 his a' should be round about him: "
2:17 set up the horn of thine a'. "
Mic 5: 9 lifted up upon thine a', "
Na 1: 2 Lord will take vengeance on his a', "
Lu 13:17 all his a' were ashamed: 480
21:15 which all your a' shall not be able "
1Co 16: 9 unto me, and there are many a'. "
Ph'p 1:28 in nothing terrified by your a': "
Heb 10:27 which shall devour the a'. 5227
adversary See also ADVERSARIES.
Ex 23:22 and an a' unto thine adversaries. 6887
Nu 22:22 stood in the way for an a' against 7854
1Sa 1: 6 her a' also provoked her sore. *6869
29: 4 lest in the battle he be an a' 7854
1Ki 5: 4 is neither a' nor evil occurrent. "
11:14 the Lord stirred up an a' unto "
23 God stirred him up another a', "
25 he was an a' to Israel all the days "
Es 7: 6 The a' and enemy is this wicked 6862
Job 31:35 mine a' had written a book. 376, 7379
Ps 74:10 how long shall the a' reproach? 6862
Isa 50: 8 who is mine a'? 1166, 4941
La 1:10 The a' hath spread out his hand 6862
2: 4 with his right hand as an a', "
4:12 have believed that the a' and the "
Am 3:11 An a' there shall be even round "
M't 5:25 Agree with thine a' quickly, 476
25 at any time the a' deliver "
Lu 12:58 with thine a' to the magistrate, "
18: 3 saying, Avenge me of mine a'. "
1Ti 5:14 give none occasion to the a' 480
1Pe 5: 8 because your a' the devil, 476
adversities
1Sa 10:19 saved you out of all your a' *7451
Ps 31: 7 hast known my soul in a'; 6869
adversity See also ADVERSITIES.
2Sa 4: 9 redeemed my soul out of all a', 6869
2Ch 15: 6 God did vex them with all a'. "
Ps 10: 6 I shall never be in a'. 7451
35:15 But in mine a' they rejoiced, *6761
94:13 give him rest from the days of a', 7451
Pr 17:17 a brother is born for a'. 6869
24:10 If thou faint in the day of a', "
Ec 7:14 in the day of a' consider: 7451
Isa 30:20 the Lord give you the bread of a', 6862
Heb 13: 3 and them which suffer a', *2558
advertise
Nu 24:14 I will a' thee what this people 3289
Ru 4: 4 And I thought to a' thee, *1540, 241
advice
J'g 19:30 consider of it, take a', and speak *5779
20: 7 give here your a' and counsel. 1697
1Sa 25:33 blessed be thy a', and blessed be *2940
2Sa 19:43 that our a' should not be first had 1697
2Ch 10: 9 What a' give ye that we may *3289
14 answered them after the a' of *6098
25:17 Amaziah king of Judah took a', 3289
Pr 20:18 and with good a' make war. *8458
2Co 8:10 herein I give my a': for this is *1106
advise See also ADVISED.
2Sa 24:13 a', and see what answer I shall *3045
1Ki 12: 6 How do ye a' that I may answer *3289
1Ch 21:12 a' thyself what word I shall *7200
advised
Pr 13:10 with the well a' is wisdom. 3289
Ac 27:12 the more part a' to depart 1012, 5087
advisement
1Ch 12:19 the Philistines upon a' sent him 6098

advocate
1Jo 2: 1 a· with the Father, Jesus Christ *3875*

a-dying See DYING.

Æneas (*e'-ne-as*)
Ac 9:33 found a certain man named Æ·, *132*
34 And Peter said unto him, Æ·, "

Ænon (*e'-non*)
Joh 3:23 baptizing in Æ· near to Salim, *137*

afar
Ge 22: 4 Abraham.... saw the place a· off. 7350
37:18 when they saw him a· off, "
Ex 2: 4 his sister stood a· off, "
20:18 they removed, and stood a· off. "
21 the people stood a· off, and Moses "
24: 1 worship ye a· off. "
Ex 33: 7 pitched it without the camp, a· off 7368
Nu 9:10 in a journey a· off, 7350
1Sa 26:13 Stood on the top of a hill a· off; "
2Ki 2: 7 went, and stood to view a· off: "
Ezr 3:13 the noise was heard a· off. "
Ne 12:43 Jerusalem was heard even a· off. "
Job 2:12 they lifted up their eyes a· off, "
36: 3 I will fetch my knowledge from a·, "
25 man may behold it a· off. "
39:25 and he smelleth the battle a· off, "
29 her eyes behold a· off. "
Ps 10: 1 Why standest thou a· off, O Lord? "
38:11 my kinsmen stand a· off. "
65: 5 them that are a· off upon the sea: "
138: 6 the proud he knoweth a· off. 4801
139: 2 understandest my thought a· off. 7350
Pr 31:14 she bringeth her food from a·. 4801
Isa 23: 7 her own feet shall carry her a· off 7350
59:14 justice standeth a· off: "
66:19 isles a· off, that have not heard "
Jer 23:23 saith the Lord, and not a God a· "
30:10 I will save thee from a·, "
31:10 declare it in the isles a· off, 4801
46:27 I will save thee from a· off, 7350
51:50 remember the Lord a· off, "
Mic 4: 3 rebuke strong nations a· off; "
M't 26:58 Peter followed him a· off *3113*
27:55 women were there beholding a· "
M'r 5: 6 when he saw Jesus a· off, "
11:13 seeing a fig tree a· off "
14:54 Peter followed him a· off, "
15:40 women looking on a· off: "
Lu 16:23 and seeth Abraham a· off, "
17:12 lepers, which stood a· off: *4207*
18:13 the publican, standing a· off, *3113*
22:54 Peter followed a· off. "
23:49 stood a· off, beholding these "
Ac 2:39 and to all that are a· off, *3112*
Eph 2:17 peace to you which were a· off, * "
Heb 11:13 but having seen them a· off, *4207*
2Pe 1: 9 is blind, and cannot see a· off, *3467*
Re 18:10 Standing a· off for the fear of her *3113*
15 shall stand a· off for the fear of "
17 as many as trade by sea, stood a· "

affairs
1Ch 26:32 pertaining to God, and a· of the 1697
Ps 112: 5 he will guide his a· * "
Da 2:49 the a· of the province of Babylon: 5673
3:12 whom thou hast set over the a· of "
Eph 6:21 also may know my a·, *2596*
22 ye might know our a·, ††*4012*
Ph'p 1:27 I may hear of your a·, that ye * "
2Ti 2: 4 entangleth himself with the a· of *4230*

affect See also AFFECTED; AFFECTETH.
Ga 4:17 They zealously a· you, but not **2206*
17 that ye might a· them. "

affected
Ac 14: 2 and made their minds evil a· *2559*
Ga 4:18 be zealously a· always in a good **2206*

affecteth
La 3:51 Mine eye a· mine heart. 5953

affection See also AFFECTIONED; AFFECTIONS.
1Ch 29: 3 because I have set my a· to the 7521
Ro 1:31 without natural a·, implacable, *794*
2Co 7:15 his inward a· is more abundant *4698*
Col 3: 2 Set your a· on things above, **5426*
5 uncleanness, inordinate a·, **3806*
2Ti 3: 3 Without natural a·, trucebreakers, *794*

affectionately
1Th 2: 8 So being a· desirous of you, we *2442*

affectioned
Ro 12:10 Be kindly a· one to another *5387*

affections
Ro 1:26 God gave them up unto vile a·: **3806*
Ga 5:24 crucified the flesh with the a· **3804*

affinity
1Ki 3: 1 Solomon made a· with Pharaoh 2859
2Ch 18: 1 and joined a· with Ahab. "
Ezr 9:14 and join in a· with the people "

affirm See also AFFIRMED.
Ro 3: 8 and as some a· that we say,) *5346*
1Ti 1: 7 they say, nor whereof they a·. **1226*
Tit 3: 8 I will that thou a· constantly, "

affirmed
Lu 22:59 another confidently a·, saying, *1340*
Ac 12:15 she constantly a· that it was even "
25:19 whom Paul a· to be alive. *5335*

afflict See also AFFLICTED; AFFLICTEST.
Ge 15:13 they shall a· them four hundred 6031
31:50 If thou shalt a· my daughters, "
Ex 1:11 over them taskmasters to a· them "
22:22 Ye shall not a· any widow, "
23 If thou a· them in any wise, "
Le 16:29 ye shall a· your souls, "
31 you, and ye shall a· your souls, "
Le 23:27 ye shall a· your souls, and offer an 6031
32 ye shall a· your souls: in the ninth "
Nu 24:24 shall a· Asshur, and shall a· Eber, "
29: 7 and ye shall a· your souls: "
30:13 every binding oath to a· the soul, "
J'g 16: 5 that we may bind him to a· him: "
6 thou mightest be bound to a· thee. "
19 and she began to a· him, "
2Sa 7:10 shall the children of wickedness a· "
1Ki 11:39 I will for this a· the seed of David, "
2Ch 6:26 when thou dost a· them; "
Ezr 8:21 a· ourselves before our God, * "
Job 37:23 plenty of justice: he will not a·. "
Ps 44: 2 how thou didst a· the people, 7489
55:19 God shall hear, and a· them. *6031
89:22 nor the son of wickedness a· him. "
94: 5 and a· thine heritage. "
143:12 destroy all them that a· my soul: 6887
Isa 9: 1 afterward did more grievously a· *3513
51:23 into the hand of them that a· 3013
58: 5 a day for a man to a· his soul? 6031
64:12 hold thy peace, and a· us very sore?"
Jer 31:28 down, and to destroy, and to a·; 7489
La 3:33 For he doth not a· willingly 6031
Am 5:12 they a· the just, they take a bribe, 6887
6:14 and they shall a· you 3905
Na 1:12 I will a· thee no more. 6031
Zep 3:19 I will undo all that a· thee: "

afflicted
Ex 1:12 But the more they a· them, the 6031
Le 23:29 shall not be a· in that same day, "
Nu 11:11 Wherefore hast thou a· thy ††7489
De 26: 6 evil entreated us, and a· us, 6031
Ru 1:21 the Almighty hath a· me? 7489
2Sa 22:28 the a· people thou wilt save: 6041
1Ki 2:26 thou hast been a· in all 6031
26 wherein my father was a·. "
2Ki 17:20 all the seed of Israel, and a· them, "
Job 6:14 To him that is a· pity should be *4523
30:11 he hath loosed my cord, and a· 6031
34:28 and he heareth the cry of the a·. 6041
Ps 18:27 thou wilt save the a· people; "
22:24 abhorred the affliction of the a·; "
25:16 me; for I am desolate and a·. "
82: 3 do justice to the a· and needy. "
88: 7 hast a· me with all thy waves. 6031
15 I am a· and ready to die from my 6041
90:15 thou hast a· us, 6031
102:*title* A prayer of the a·, when he 6041
107:17 because of their iniquities, are a·. 6031
116:10 I was greatly a·: "
119:67 Before I was a· I went astray: "
71 good for me that I have been a·; "
75 thou in faithfulness hast a· me. "
107 I am a· very much: "
129: 1, 2 Many a time have they a· me 6887
140:12 maintain the cause of the a·, and 6041
Pr 15:15 All the days of the a· are evil: "
22:22 neither oppress the a· in the gate: "
26:28 hateth those that are a· by it; *1790
31: 5 the judgment of any of the a·. 6040
Isa 9: 1 lightly a· the land of Zebulun, *7043
49:13 and will have mercy upon his a·. 6041
51:21 Therefore hear now this, thou a·, "
53: 4 smitten of God, and a·. *6031
7 He was oppressed, and he was a·, † "
58: 3 wherefore have we a· our soul, "
10 satisfy the a· soul; "
60:14 The sons also of them that a· thee "
63: 9 In all their affliction he was a·, 6862
La 1: 4 priests sigh, her virgins are a·, 3013
5 for the Lord hath a· her for the "
12 wherewith the Lord hath a· me "
Mic 4: 6 her that I have a·; 7489
Na 1:12 Though I have a· thee, 6031
Zep 3:12 of thee an a· and poor people, 6041
M't 24: 9 they deliver you up to be a·, **2347*
2Co 1: 6 And whether we be a·, *2346*
1Ti 5:10 if she have relieved the a·, "
Heb 11:37 being destitute, a·, tormented; "
Jas 4: 9 Be a·, and mourn, and weep: *5003*
5:13 Is any among you a·? **2553*

afflictest
1Ki 8:35 their sin, when thou a· them: *6031

affliction See also AFFLICTIONS.
Ge 16:11 the Lord hath heard thy a·. 6040
29:32 the Lord hath looked upon my a·; "
31:42 God hath seen mine a· "
41:52 in the land of my a·. "
Ex 3: 7 surely seen the a· of my people "
17 bring you up out of the a· of Egypt "
4:31 he had looked upon their a·, "
De 16: 3 the bread of a·; "
26: 7 and looked on our a·, "
1Sa 1:11 look on the a· of thine handmaid, "
2Sa 16:12 the Lord will look on mine a·, *5869
1Ki 22:27 feed him with bread of a· 3905
27 and with water of a·, "
2Ki 14:26 the Lord saw the a· of Israel, 6040
2Ch 18:26 feed him with bread of a· 3905
26 and with water of a·, "
20: 9 and cry unto thee in our a·, 6869
33:12 when he was in a·, he besought *6887
Ne 1: 3 in great a· and reproach: 7451
9: 9 didst see the a· of our fathers *6040
Job 5: 6 a· cometh not forth of the dust, 205
10:15 see thou mine a·; 6040
30:16 days of a· have taken hold upon "
27 the days of a· prevented me. "
36: 8 in cords of a·; "
15 He delivereth the poor in his a·, 6040
21 hast thou chosen rather than a·. "
Ps 22:24 the a· of the afflicted; 6039
25:18 Look upon mine a· and my pain; 6040
44:24 our a· and our oppression? "
Ps 66:11 thou laidst a· upon our loins. *4157
88: 9 eye mourneth by reason of a·. 6040
106:44 he regarded their a·, *6862
107:10 bound in a· and iron; *6040
39 through oppression, a·, and *7451
41 he the poor on high from a·, 6040
119:50 my comfort in my a·: "
92 then have perished in mine a·. "
153 Consider mine a·, "
Isa 30:20 water of a·, yet shall not 3905
48:10 in the furnace of a·. 6040
63: 9 In all their a· he was afflicted, 6869
Jer 4:15 a· from mount Ephraim. * 205
15:11 of evil and in the time of a·. 6869
16:19 my refuge in the day of a·, "
30:15 Why criest thou for thine a·? *7667
48:16 and his a· hasteth fast. 7451
La 1: 3 gone into captivity because of a·, 6040
7 remembered in the days of her a· "
9 O Lord, behold my a·: "
3: 1 I am the man that hath seen a· "
19 Remembering mine a· and my "
Ho 5:15 in their a· they will seek me early. 6862
Am 6: 6 not grieved for the a· of Joseph. 7667
Ob 13 not have looked on their a· 7451
Jon 2: 2 reason of mine a· unto the Lord, 6869
Na 1: 9 a· shall not rise up the second time. "
Hab 3: 7 I saw the tents of Cushan in a·: 205
Zec 1:15 they helped forward the a·. 7451
8:10 out or came in because of the a·: *6862
10:11 pass through the sea with a·, 6869
M'r 4:17 when a· or persecution ariseth *2347*
13:19 in those days shall be a·, "
Ac 7:11 Egypt and Chanaan, and great a·: "
34 I have seen the a· of my people *2561*
2Co 2: 4 out of much a· and anguish of *2347*
4:17 light a·, which is but for a moment, "
8: 2 How that in a great trial of a· "
Ph'p 1:16 to add a· to my bonds: * "
4:14 ye did communicate with my a·. "
1Th 1: 6 the word in much a·, "
3: 7 our a· and distress by your faith: "
Heb 11:25 Choosing rather to suffer a· with **4797*
Jas 1:27 and widows in their a·, *2347*
5:10 an example of suffering a·, and **2552*

afflictions
Ps 34:19 Many are the a· of the righteous: 7451
132: 1 remember David, and all his a·: *6031
Ac 7:10 delivered him out of all his a·, *2347*
20:23 bonds and a· abide me. "
2Co 6: 4 in a·, in necessities, in distresses, "
Col 1:24 which is behind of the a· of Christ "
1Th 3: 3 man should be moved by these a·: "
2Ti 1: 8 partaker of the a· of the gospel **4777*
3:11 Persecutions, a·, which came **3804*
4: 5 a·, do the work of an evangelist, **2553*
Heb 10:32 endured a great fight of a·; **3804*
33 both by reproaches and a·; *2347*
1Pe 5: 9 the same a· are accomplished **3804*

affording
Ps 144:13 That our garners may be full, a· 6329

affright See also AFFRIGHTED.
2Ch 32:18 to a· them, and to trouble them; 3372

affrighted
De 7:21 Thou shalt not be a· at them: 6206
Job 18:20 that went before were a·. 270, 8178
39:22 He mocketh at fear, and is not a·; *2865
Isa 21: 4 fearfulness a· me: 1204
Jer 51:32 and the men of war are a·. 926
M'r 16: 5 white garment; and they were a·. **1568*
6 And he saith unto them, Be not a·: "
Lu 24:37 But they were terrified and a·, *1719*
Re 11:13 remnant were a·, and gave glory "

a-fishing See FISHING.

afoot
M'r 6:33 ran a· thither out of all cities, **3979*
Ac 20:13 minding himself to go a·. **3978*

afore See also AFOREHAND; AFORETIME; BEFORE.
2Ki 20: 4 came to pass, a· Isaiah was gone 3808
Ps 129: 6 which withereth a· it groweth up: 6924
Isa 18: 5 a· the harvest, when the bud is 6440
Eze 33:22 a· he that was escaped came; "
Ro 1: 2 had promised a· by his prophets *4279*
9:23 he had a· prepared unto glory. *4282*
Eph 3: 3 (as I wrote a· in few words, *4270*

aforehand
M'r 14: 8 she is come a· to anoint my body *4301*

aforetime
Ne 13: 5 a· they laid the meat offerings, 6440
Job 17: 6 a· I was as a tabret. †‡ "
Isa 52: 4 My people went down a· into *7223
Jer 30:20 Their children also shall be as a·, 6924
Da 6:10 his God, as he did a·. 4481,6928,1836
Joh 9:13 him that a· was blind. *4218*
Ro 15: 4 things were written a· were *4270*

afraid
Ge 3:10 I was a·, because I was naked; 3372
18:15 I laughed not; for she was a·. "
20: 8 and the men were sore a·. "
28:17 And he was a·, and said, "
31:31 Because I was a·: for I said, "
32: 7 Then Jacob was greatly a· and "
42:28 failed them, and they were a·, *2729
35 bundles of money, they were a·. 3372
43:18 And the men were a·, because "
Ex 3: 6 he was a· to look upon God. "
14:10 and they were sore a·; and the "
15:14 people shall hear, and be a·: *7264
34:30 they were a· to come nigh him. 3372
Le 26: 6 none shall make you a·: 2729
Nu 12: 8 then were ye not a· to speak 3372
22: 3 Moab was sore a· of the people, 1481

De 1:17 ye shall not be *a·* of the face of man; 1481
29 Dread not, neither be *a·* of them. 3372
2: 4 and they shall be *a·* of you: "
5: 5 ye were *a·* by reason of the fire, "
7:18 Thou shalt not be *a·* of them: but "
19 all the people of whom thou art *a·*. 3373
9:19 For I was *a·* of the anger and hot 3025
18:22 thou shalt not be *a·* of him. 1481
20: 1 be not *a·* of them: for the Lord 3372
28:10 and they shall be *a·* of thee. "
60 of Egypt, which thou wast *a·* of; 3025
31: 6 fear not, nor be *a·* of them: *6206
Jos 1: 9 not *a·*, neither be thou dismayed * "
9:24 we were sore *a·* of our lives 3372
11: 6 Be not *a·* because of them: "
J'g 7: 3 Whosoever is fearful and *a·*, *2730
Ru 3: 8 that the man was *a·*, and turned 2729
1Sa 4: 7 And the Philistines were *a·*, for 3372
7: 7 they were *a·* of the Philistines. "
17:11 were dismayed, and greatly *a·*. "
24 fled from him, and were sore *a·*. "
18:12 And Saul was *a·* of David, "
15 very wisely, he was *a·* of him. *1481
29 Saul was yet the more *a·* of David; 3372
21: 1 Ahimelech was *a·* at the meeting *2729
12 was sore *a·* of Achish the king of 3372
23: 3 we be *a·* here in Judah: 3373
28: 5 he was *a·*, and his heart 3372
13 the king said unto her, Be not *a·*: "
20 was sore *a·*, because of the words "
31: 4 would not; for he was sore *a·*. "
2Sa 1:14 How wast thou not *a·* to stretch "
6: 9 David was *a·* of the Lord that day, "
14:15 the people have made me *a·*: "
17: 2 and will make him *a·*: 2729
22: 5 of ungodly men made me *a·*; 1204
46 they shall be *a·* out of their close *2296
1Ki 1:49 that were with Adonijah were *a·*, *2729
2Ki 1:15 down with him: be not *a·* of him. 3372
10: 4 But they were exceedingly *a·*, "
19: 6 Be not *a·* of the words which thou "
25:26 they were *a·* of the Chaldees. "
1Ch 10: 4 would not; for he was sore *a·*. "
13:12 David was *a·* of God that day, "
21:30 he was *a·* because of the sword 1204
2Ch 20:15 Be not *a·* nor dismayed by reason *3372
32: 7 be not *a·* nor dismayed for the "
Ne 2: 2 Then I was very sore *a·*, "
4:14 Be not ye *a·* of them: "
6: 9 they all made us *a·*, saying, "
13 was he hired, that I should be *a·*, "
Es 7: 6 Haman was *a·* before the king 1204
Job 3:25 which I was *a·* of is come unto me. 3025
5:21 shalt thou be *a·* of destruction 3372
22 neither shalt thou be *a·* of the "
6:21 see my casting down, and are *a·*. "
9:28 I am *a·* of all my sorrows, I 3025
11:19 none shall make thee *a·*; 2729
13:11 not his excellency make you *a·*? 1204
21 let not thy dread make me *a·*. "
15:24 anguish shall make him *a·*; "
18:11 Terrors shall make him *a·* on every "
19:29 Be ye *a·* of the sword: 1481
21: 6 when I remember I am *a·*, *926
23:15 when I consider, I am *a·* of him. 6342
32: 6 wherefore I was *a·*, and durst *2119
33: 7 my terror shall not make thee *a·*, 1204
39:20 Canst thou make him *a·* as a *7493
41:25 the mighty are *a·*: 1481
Ps 3: 6 I will not be *a·* of ten thousands 3372
18: 4 floods of ungodly men made me *a·*. 1204
45 shall fade away, and be *a·* *2727
27: 1 of whom shall I be *a·*? 6342
49:16 Be not thou *a·* when one is made 3372
56: 3 time I am *a·*, I will trust in thee. "
11 not be *a·* what man can do unto me. "
65: 8 in the uttermost parts are *a·* at "
77:16 they were *a·*: the depths also 2342
83:15 make them *a·* with thy storm. *926
91: 5 Thou shalt not be *a·* for the 3372
112: 7 He shall not be *a·* of evil tidings: "
8 is established, he shall not be *a·*, "
119:120 I am *a·* of thy judgments. "
Pr 3:24 thou shalt not be *a·*: 6342
25 Be not *a·* of sudden fear, 3372
31:21 She is not *a·* of the snow for her "
Ec 12: 5 they shall be *a·* of that which is "
Isa 8:12 fear ye their fear, nor be *a·*. *6206
10:24 be not *a·* of the Assyrian: 3372
29 Ramah is *a·*; Gibeah of Saul is *2729
12: 2 I will trust, and not be *a·*: 6342
13: 8 And they shall be *a·*: pangs and *926
17: 2 none shall make them *a·*. 2729
19:16 and it shall be *a·* and fear because* "
17 mention thereof shall be *a·* in 6342
20: 5 they shall be *a·* and ashamed *2865
31: 4 he will not be *a·* of their voice, * "
9 princes shall be *a·* of the ensign,* "
33:14 The sinners in Zion are *a·*; 6342
37: 6 Be not *a·* of the words 3372
40: 9 lift it up, be not *a·*; "
41: 5 the ends of the earth were *a·*, *2729
44: 8 Fear ye not, neither be *a·*: 7297
51: 7 neither be ye *a·* of their revilings. *2865
12 that thou shouldest be *a·* of a man 3372
57:11 of whom hast thou been *a·* or 1672
Jer 1: 8 Be not *a·* of their faces: 3372
2:12 be horribly *a·*, be ye very desolate, 8175
10: 5 Be not *a·* of them; for they cannot 3372
26:21 he was *a·*, and fled, and went into "
30:10 none shall make him *a·*. 2729
36:16 heard all the words, they were *a·* *6342
24 Yet they were not *a·*, "
38:19 I am *a·* of the Jews 1672
39:17 of the men of whom thou art *a·*. 3025
41:18 *a·* of them, because of Ishmael 3372

Jer 42:11 Be not *a·* of the king of Babylon, 3372
11 of whom ye are *a·*; 3373
11 be not *a·* of him, saith the Lord 3372
16 the famine, whereof ye were *a·*, 1672
46:27 and none shall make him *a·*. 2729
Eze 2: 6 son of man, be not *a·* of them, 3372
6 neither be *a·* of their words, "
6 be not *a·* of their words, "
27:35 their kings shall be sore *a·*, 8175
30: 9 make the careless Ethiopians *a·*, 2729
32:10 their kings shall be horribly *a·* 8175
34:28 none shall make them *a·*. 2729
39:26 none made them *a·*. "
Da 4: 5 I saw a dream which made me *a·*, 1763
8:17 when he came, I was *a·*, *1204
Joe 2:22 Be not *a·*, ye beasts of the field: 3372
Am 3: 6 the people not be *a·*? 2729
Jon 1: 5 Then the mariners were *a·*, 3372
10 Then were the men exceedingly *a·*, "
Mic 4: 4 none shall make them *a·*: 2729
7:17 they shall be *a·* of the Lord *6342
Na 2:11 none made them *a·*? 2729
Hab 2:17 beasts, which made them *a·*, 2865
3: 2 heard thy speech, and was *a·*: 3372
Zep 3:13 none shall make them *a·*. 2729
Mal 2: 5 was *a·* before my name. *2865
M't 2:22 he was *a·* to go thither: *5399*
14:27 it is I; be not *a·*. "
30 the wind boisterous, he was *a·*; "
17: 6 fell on their face, and were sore *a·*. "
7 Arise, and be not *a·*. "
25:25 And I was *a·*, and went and hid "
28:10 Be not *a·*: go tell my brethren * "
M'r 5:15 his right mind: and they were *a·*. "
36 Be not *a·*, only believe. * "
6:50 it is I; be not *a·*. "
9: 6 to say; for they were sore *a·*. *1630*
32 and were *a·* to ask him. *5399*
10:32 and as they followed, they were *a·*. "
16: 8 any man; for they were *a·*. "
Lu 2: 9 and they were sore *a·*. "
8:25 And they being *a·* wondered, "
35 and they were *a·*. "
12: 4 Be not *a·* of them that kill the body, "
24: 5 as they were *a·*, and bowed down **1719*
Joh 6:19 unto the ship: and they were *a·*. *5399*
20 It is I; be not *a·*, "
14:27 be troubled, neither let it be *a·*. **1168*
19: 8 he was the more *a·*; *5399*
Ac 9:26 but they were all *a·* of him, "
10: 4 looked on him, he was *a·*, **1719*
18: 9 Be not *a·*, but speak, and hold *5399*
22: 9 saw indeed the light, and were *a·*; **1719*
29 and the chief captain also was *a·*, *5399*
Ro 13: 3 Wilt thou then not be *a·* of the "
4 if thou do that which is evil, be *a·*; "
Ga 4:11 I am *a·* of you, lest I have bestowed "
Heb 11:23 and they were not *a·* of the king's "
1Pe 3: 6 are not *a·* with any amazement. * "
14 and be not *a·* of their terror, * "
2Pe 2:10 they are not *a·* to speak evil of **5141*

afresh
Heb 6: 6 to themselves the Son of God *a·*. *388*

after See also AFTERNOON; AFTERWARD; HEREAFTER.
Ge 1:11 fruit tree yielding fruit *a.* his
12 herb yielding seed *a·* his kind,
12 seed was in itself, *a·* his kind;
21 *a·* their kind,
21 and every winged fowl *a·* his
24 the living creature *a·* his kind,
24 the beast of the earth *a·* his kind:
25 *a·* his kind, and cattle *a·* their
25 creepeth upon the earth *a·* his
4:17 *a·* the name of his son, Enoch.
5: 3 his own likeness, *a·* his image;
4 *a·* he had begotten Seth 310
7 *a·* he begat Enos "
10 *a·* he begat Cainan "
13 *a·* he begat Mahalaleel "
16 *a·* he begat Jared "
19 *a·* he begat Enoch eight hundred "
22 *a·* he begat Methuselah "
26 *a·* he begat Lamech "
30 *a·* he begat Noah "
6: 4 also *a·* that, when the sons of God "
20 fowls *a·* their kind, and of cattle *a·*
20 creeping thing of the earth *a·* his
7:10 it came to pass *a·* seven days,
14 beast *a·* his kind,
14 and all the cattle *a·*
14 *a·* his kind, and every fowl *a·* his
8: 3 *a·* the end of the hundred and
19 creepeth upon the earth, *a·* their
9: 9 with your seed *a·* you; 310
28 Noah lived *a·* the flood three "
10: 1 unto them were sons born *a·* the "
5 one *a·* his tongue, *a·* their families,
20, 31 *a·* their families, *a·* their
31 in their lands, *a·* their nations.
32 sons of Noah, *a·* their
32 divided in the earth *a·* the flood. 310
11:10 begat Arphaxad two years *a·* the "
11 Shem lived *a·* he begat Arphaxad "
13 Arphaxad lived *a·* he begat Salah "
15 Salah lived *a·* he begat Eber "
17 Eber lived *a·* he begat Peleg "
19 Peleg lived *a·* he begat Reu "
21 Reu lived *a·* he begat Serug "
23 Serug lived *a·* he begat Nahor "
25 Nahor lived after he begat Terah "
13:14 *a·* that Lot was separated from "
14:17 *a·* his return from the slaughter "
15: 1 *A·* these things the word of the "
16: 3 *a·* Abraham had dwelt ten years 7093

Ge 16:13 here looked *a·* him that seeth me? 310
17: 7 me and thee and thy seed *a·* thee "
7 God unto thee, and to the seed *a·* "
8 to thy seed *a·* thee. "
9 thy seed *a·* thee in their generations. "
10 between me and you and thy seed *a·* "
19 with his seed *a·* him. "
18: 5 *a·* that ye shall pass on: "
12 *A·* I am waxed old shall I have "
19 children and his household *a·* him, "
19: 6 shut the door *a·* him, "
22: 1, 20 it came to pass *a·* these things, "
23:19 And *a·* this, Abraham buried Sarah "
24:55 the least ten; *a·* that she shall go. "
67 Isaac was comforted *a·* his mother's "
25:11 it came to pass *a·* the death of "
26 And *a·* that came his brother out, "
26:18 the Philistines had stopped them *a·* "
18 he called their names *a·* the names
31:23 pursued *a·* him seven days' 310
30 thou sore longedst *a·* thy father's
36 thou hast so hotly pursued *a·* me? 310
32:29 that thou dost ask *a·* my name?
33: 2 Leah and her children *a·*, 314
7 *a·* came Joseph near and Rachel. 310
35: 5 did not pursue *a·* the sons of Jacob. "
12 thy seed *a·* thee will I give the land. "
36:40 to their families, *a·* their places,
37:17 Joseph went *a·* his brethren, 310
38:24 about three months *a·*, that it
39: 7 it came to pass *a·* these things, 310
19 *A·* this manner did thy servant
40: 1 it came to pass *a·* these things, 310
13 cup into his hand, *a·* the former
41: 3 seven other kine came up *a·* them 310
6 the east wind sprung up *a·* them. "
19 seven other kine came up *a·* them, "
23 the east wind, sprung up *a·* them: "
27 came up *a·* them are seven years; "
30 shall arise *a·* them seven years of "
44: 4 Up, follow *a·* the men; "
45:15 *a·* that his brethren talked with him, "
23 And to his father he sent *a·* this
48: 1 it came to pass *a·* these things, 310
4 give this land to thy seed *a·* thee "
6 which thou begettest *a·* them. "
6 shall be called *a·* the name of 5921
50:14 *a·* he had buried his father. 310
Ex 3:20 and *a·* that he will let you go. "
5:19 in evil case, *a·* it was said, *
7:25 seven days were fulfilled, *a·* that 310
10:14 neither *a·* them shall be such. "
11: 8 and *a·* that I will go out. "
14: 4 that he shall follow *a·* them; "
8 he pursued *a·* the children of Israel: "
9 the Egyptians pursued *a·* them, "
10 the Egyptians marched *a·* them; "
23 went in *a·* them to the midst of the "
28 that came into the sea *a·* them; "
15:20 all the women went out *a·* her with "
16: 1 *a·* their departing out of the land
17: 1 from the wilderness of Sin, *a·* *
18: 2 *a·* he had sent her back, 310
21: 9 shall deal with her *a·* the manner
23: 2 to decline *a·* many to wrest 310
24 nor serve them, nor do *a·* their
25:40 *a·* their pattern, which was
28:15 *a·* the work of the ephod thou *
43 his seed *a·* him. 310
29:29 Aaron shall be his sons' *a·* him, "
30:12 sum of the children of Israel *a·* *
13 half a shekel *a·* the shekel of the
24 five hundred shekels, *a·* the shekel
25 compound *a·* the art of the
32 ye make any other like it, *a·* *
35 a confection *a·* the art of the
32: 4 with a graving tool, *a·* he had *
33: 8 looked *a·* Moses, until he was gone 310
34:15 they go a whoring *a·* their gods, "
16 go a whoring *a·* their gods, and "
16 make thy sons go a whoring *a·* "
27 for *a·* the tenor of these words I 5921
37:19 Three bowls made *a·* the fashion *
38:24 shekels, *a·* the shekel of the
25 threescore and fifteen shekels, *a·*
26 *a·* the shekel of the sanctuary,
Le 5:15 *a·* the shekel of the sanctuary,
11:14 vulture, and the kite *a·* his kind;
15 Every raven *a·* his kind;
16 cuckow, and the hawk *a·* his kind,
19 the stork, the heron *a·* her kind,
22 *a·* his kind, and the bald locust *a·*
22 *a·* his kind, and the grasshopper *a·*
29 the mouse, and the tortoise *a·* his
13: 7 *a·* that he hath been seen of the 310
35 in the skin *a·* his cleansing; "
55 *a·* that it is washed; "
56 somewhat dark *a·* the washing of "
14: 8 *a·* that he shall come into the camp, "
43 *a·* that he hath taken away the "
43 and *a·* he hath scraped the house, "
43 and *a·* it is plaistered; "
48 *a·* the house was plaistered: "
15:28 and *a·* that she shall be clean. "
16: 1 *a·* the death of the two sons of "
17: 7 *a·* whom they have gone a whoring. "
18: 3 *A·* the doings of the land of Egypt,
3 *a·* the doings of the land of Canaan,
19:31 neither seek *a·* wizards, to be * 413
20: 5 all that go a whoring *a·* him, to * 413
6 the soul that turneth *a·* such as * 413
6 *a·* wizards, to go a whoring *a·* 310
23:15 from the morrow *a·* the sabbath,
16 unto the morrow *a·* the seventh
25:15 number of years *a·* the jubile 310
29 within a whole year *a·* it is sold;

Le 25:46 inheritance for your children a' 310
48 A' that he is sold he may be "
26:33 will draw out a sword a' you: "
27: 3 a' the shekel of the sanctuary.
18 if he sanctify his field a' the jubile, 310
Nu 1: 1 a' they were come out of the
2 a' their families, by the house of *
18 declared their pedigrees a' their
20 by their generations, a' their *
22 a' their families, by the house of *
24 of Gad, by their generations, a' *
26 of Judah, by their generations, a' *
28 Issachar, by their generations, a' *
30 Zebulun, by their generations, a' *
32 a' their families, by the house of *
34 Manasseh, by their generations, a' *
36 Benjamin, by their generations, a' *
38 of Dan, by their generations, a' *
40 of Asher, by their generations, a' *
42 throughout their generations, a' *
47 the Levites a' the tribe of their
2:34 every one a' their families, *
3:15 the children of Levi a' the house *
47 a' the shekel of the sanctuary
50 threescore and five shekels, a'
4: 2 a' their families, by the house of *
15 a' that, the sons of Kohath shall 310
29 number them a' their families, *
34 a' their families, and a' the house *
44 a' their families, were three *
46 a' their families, and a' the house *
6:19 a' the hair of his separation is 310
20 and a' that the Nazarite may drink "
21 so he must do a' the law of his 5921
7:13 bowl of seventy shekels, a' the
19 a' the shekel of the sanctuary;
25, 31, 37, 43, 49, 55, 61, 67, 73, 79 of
seventy shekels, a' the shekel of
85 and four hundred shekels, a' the
86 ten shekels apiece, a' the shekel
88 a' that it was anointed. 310
8:15 And a' that shall the Levites go "
22 And a' that went the Levites in "
9: 1 a' they were come out of the land
17 a' that the children of Israel 310
12:14 and a' that let her be received in "
13:25 searching of the land a' forty *7093
14:34 A' the number of the days in
15:13 do these things a' this manner, 3602
39 seek not a' your own heart and 310
39 and your own eyes, a' which "
16:29 visited a' the visitation of all men;
18:16 a' the shekel of the sanctuary,
25: 8 he went a' the man of Israel 310
13 shall have it, and his seed a' him, "
26: 1 it came to pass a' the plague,
12 sons of Simeon a' their families:
15 The children of Gad a' their
20 sons of Judah a' their families
23 Of the sons of Issachar a' their
26 sons of Zebulun a' their families:
28 sons of Joseph a' their families
35 are the sons of Ephraim a' their
37 These are the sons of Joseph a'
38 The sons of Benjamin a' their
41 are the sons of Benjamin a' their
42 These are the sons of Dan a' their
42 These are the families of Dan a'
44 Of the children of Asher a' their
48 sons of Naphtali a' their families:
57 numbered of the Levites a' their
27:21 for him a' the judgment of Urim *
28:24 A' this manner ye shall offer
26 offering unto the Lord, a' your *
29:18, 21, 24, 27, 30, 33, 37 number, a' the
30:15 make them void a' that he hath 310
32:15 if ye turn away from a' him, "
42 thereof, and called it Nobah, a' his
33: 3 on the morrow a' the passover
38 a' the children of Israel were
35:28 a' the death of the high priest 310
De 1: 4 A' he had slain Sihon the king of "
8 to their seed a' them. "
3:11 the breadth of it, a' the cubit of
14 and called them a' his own name, 5921
4:37 therefore he chose their seed a' 310
40 with thy children a' thee, "
45 a' they came forth out *
46 a' they were come forth out *
6:14 Ye shall not go a' other gods, 310
8:19 and walk a' other gods, and serve "
9: 4 a' that the Lord thy God hath
10:15 he chose their seed a' them, 310
11: 4 as they pursued a' you, "
28 to go a' other gods, which ye "
12: 8 Ye shall not do a' all the things
15, 20, 21 thy soul lusteth a',
25 with thy children a' thee, when 310
28 with thee, and with thy children a' "
30 following them, a' that they be "
30 thou enquire not a' their gods,
13: 2 Let us go a' other gods, 310
4 Ye shall walk a' the Lord your God, "
14:13 kite, and the vulture a' his kind,
14 And every raven a' his kind,
15 cuckow, and the hawk a' his kind,
18 stork, and the heron a' her kind,
14:26 whatsoever thy soul lusteth a', *
16:13 a' that thou hast gathered in thy
18: 9 learn to do a' the abominations
20:18 That they teach you not to do a'
21:13 a' that thou shalt go in unto her, 310
22: 2 thee until thy brother seek a' it,
24: 4 a' that she is defiled; 310
9 a' that ye were come forth out *
28:14 to go a' other gods to serve them. 310

De 29:22 that shall rise up a' you, 310
31:16 go a whoring a' the gods of the "
27 how much more a' my death? "
29 I know that a' my death ye will "
Jos 1: 1 Now a' the death of Moses "
2: 5 pursue a' them quickly; "
7 the men pursued a' them the way "
7 as soon as they which pursued a' "
3: 2 came to pass a' three days, 7097
3 remove from your place, and go a' 310
5: 4 a' they came out of Egypt.
12 a' they had eaten of the old corn
6: 9 and the rereward came a' the ark, 310
13 but the rereward came a' the ark of "
15 compassed the city a' the same
7:25 burned them with fire, a' they *
8: 6 (For they will come out a' us) 310
16 called together to pursue a' them: "
16 and they pursued a' Joshua, "
17 that went not out a' Israel: and "
17 left the city open, and pursued a'
9:16 a' they had made a league with 310
10:14 no day like that before it or a' it, "
19 stay ye not, but pursue a' your
13:23 of the children of Reuben a' their *
28 of the children of Gad a' their *
19:47 called Leshem, Dan, a' the name
20: 5 the avenger of blood pursue a' him, 310
22:27 and you, and our generations a' us, "
23: 1 it came to pass a long time a' "
24: 6 Egyptians pursued a' your fathers "
20 consume you, a' that he hath done "
29 it came to pass a' these things, "
J'g 1: 1 Now a' the death of Joshua "
6 fled; and they pursued a' him, "
2:10 arose another generation a' them, "
17 went a whoring a' other gods, "
3:22 the haft also went in a' the blade; "
28 he said unto them, Follow a' me: "
28 they went down a' him, "
31 And a' him was Shamgar the son "
4:14 ten thousand men a' him. "
16 Barak pursued a' the chariots, "
16 and a' the host, "
5:14 a' thee, Benjamin, among thy "
6:34 Abi-ezer was gathered a' him. "
35 who also was gathered a' him: "
7:23 pursued a' the Midianites. "
8: 5 I am pursuing a' Zebah and "
12 pursued a' them, and took the two "
27 went thither a whoring a' it: "
33 went a whoring a' Baalim, "
10: 1 a' Abimelech there arose to defend "
3 a' him arose Jair, a Gileadite, "
12: 8 a' him Ibzan of Beth-lehem judged "
11 a' him Elon, a Zebulonite, "
13 a' him Abdon the son of Hillel, "
13:11 Manoah arose, and went a' his wife, "
18 Why askest thou thus a' my
14: 8 a' a time he returned to take her,
15: 1 it came to pass within a while a'.
7 and a' that I will cease. 310
16:22 to grow again a' he was shaven. 834
18: 7 a' the manner of the Zidonians,
29 the name of the city Dan, a' the
19: 3 her husband arose, and went a' her, 310
20:45 pursued hard a' them unto Gidom, "
Ru 1:15 return thou a' thy sister in law. "
16 or to return from following a' thee: "
2: 2 glean ears of corn a' him in whose "
3 gleaned in the field a' the reapers: "
7 let me glean and gather a' the "
9 they do reap, and go thou a' them: "
2:18 to her that she had reserved a' she
4: 4 I am a' thee. And he said, I will 310
1Sa 1: 9 a' they had eaten in Shiloh,
9 and a' they had drunk.
20 a' Hannah had conceived, that *
5: 9 a' they had carried it about, 310
6:12 the lords of the Philistines went a' "
7: 2 house of Israel lamented a' the "
8: 3 but turned aside a' lucre, "
10: 5 A' that thou shalt come to the hill "
11: 5 Saul came a' the herd out of the * "
7 Whosoever cometh not forth a' Saul "
7 and a' Samuel, "
12:21 for then should ye go a' vain things, "
13: 4 called together a' Saul to Gilgal. "
14 the Lord hath sought him a man a'
14:12 armourbearer, Come up a' me: 310
13 his armourbearer a' him: "
13 his armourbearer slew a' him. "
22 they also followed hard a' them "
36 Let us go down a' the Philistines "
37 Shall I go down a' the Philistines? "
15:31 So Samuel turned again a' Saul; "
17:27 answered him a' this manner,
30 and spake a' the same manner:
30 him again a' the former manner.
35 I went out a' him, and smote him, 310
53 returned from chasing a' the "
18:30 a' they went forth, *167
20:37, 38 Jonathan cried a' the lad, 311
22:20 Abiathar, escaped, and fled a' 310
23:25 he pursued a' David in the "
28 Saul returned from pursuing a' "
24: 8 out of the cave, and cried a' Saul, "
14 A' whom is the king of Israel come "
14 a' whom dost thou pursue? "
14 a' a dead dog, a' a flea. "
21 not cut off my seed a' me, "
25:13 there went up a' David "
19 behold, I come a' you. "
38 about ten days a', that the Lord
42 damsels of hers that went a' her; * 7272
42 she went a' the messengers of 310

1Sa 26: 3 Saul came a' him into the 310
18 my lord thus pursue a' his servant? "
30: 8 Shall I pursue a' this troop? "
2Sa 1: 1 Now it came to pass a' the death "
6 horsemen followed hard a' him.
10 he could not live a' that he was 310
2: 1 it came to pass a' this, "
19 Asahel pursued a' Abner; "
24 Joab also and Abishai pursued a' "
25 gathered themselves together a' "
28 pursued a' Israel no more, "
3:26 he sent messengers a' Abner, "
5:13 a' he was come from Hebron: "
7:12 I will set up thy seed a' thee, "
8: 1 a' this it came to pass, "
10: 1 it came to pass a' this, "
11: 1 a' the year was expired, at the *
3 And David sent and enquired a'
12:28 city, and it be called a' my name. 5921
13: 1 it came to pass a' this, 310
17 bolt the door a' her. "
18 bolted the door a' her. "
23 a' two full years, that Absalom
14:26 head at two hundred shekels a'
15: 1 it came to pass a' this, 310
15: 7 it came to pass a' forty years, *7093
13 the men of Israel are a' Absalom. 310
16 and all his household a' him. 7272
17 went forth, and all the people a' "
18 six hundred men which came a' "
17: 1 I will arise and pursue a' David 310
6 saying, Ahithophel hath spoken a' "
6 shall we do a' his saying? if not; "
21 it came to pass, a' they were 310
18:16 returned from pursuing a' Israel: "
18 and he called the pillar a' his own 5921
22 let me, I pray thee, also run a' 310
20: 2 of Israel went up from a' David, * "
6 pursue a' him, lest he get him "
7 there went out a' him Joab's men, "
7 of Jerusalem, to pursue a' Sheba "
10 Abishai his brother pursued a' "
11 he that is for David, let him go a' * "
13 went on a' Joab, to pursue a' Sheba "
14 together, and went also a' him. "
21: 1 three years, year a' year; "
14 a' that God was intreated for the "
18 it came to pass a' this, "
23: 4 of the earth by clear shining a' rain.
9 And a' him was Eleazar the son 310
10 the people returned a' him only to "
11 And a' him was Shammah "
24:10 David's heart smote him a' that "
1Ki 1: 6 his mother bare him a' Absalom. "
13 Solomon thy son shall reign a' me, "
14 I also will come in a' thee, "
17 Solomon thy son shall reign a' me, "
20 throne of my lord the king a' him. "
24 Adonijah shall reign a' me, "
27 the throne of my lord the king a' "
30 shall reign a' me, and he shall sit "
35 Then ye shall come up a' him, "
40 all the people came up a' him, "
2:28 for Joab had turned a' Adonijah, "
28 though he turned not a' Absalom. "
3:12 neither a' thee shall any arise like "
18 And it came to pass the third day a'
6: 1 a' the children of Israel were
7:11 costly stones, a' the measures of *
31 the mouth thereof was round a'
37 A' this manner he made the ten
9:21 Their children that were left a' 310
11: 2 turn away your heart a' their gods: "
4 his wives turned away his heart a' "
5 Solomon went a' Ashtoreth "
5 a' Milcom the abomination of the "
6 went not fully a' the Lord, "
10 he should not go a' other gods: "
15 a' he had smitten every male in *
12:14 spake to them a' the counsel of
13:14 went a' the man of God, 310
23 a' he had eaten bread, and a' he "
31 it came to pass, a' he had buried "
33 A' this thing Jeroboam returned not "
15: 4 to set up his son a' him, and to "
16:24 a' the name of Shemer, owner of 5921
17: 7 a' a while, that the brook dried 7093
13 a' make for thee and for thy son. * 314
17 it came to pass a' these things, 310
18: 1 a' many days, that the word of the
19:11 and a' the wind an earthquake; 310
12 And a' the earthquake a fire; "
12 and a' the fire a still small voice. "
20 he left the oxen, and ran a' Elijah, "
21 Then he arose, and went a' Elijah, "
20:15 a' them he numbered all the people, "
21: 1 it came to pass a' these things, "
2Ki 1: 1 against Israel a' the death of Ahab. "
5:20 as the Lord liveth, I will run a' him, "
21 So Gehazi followed a' Naaman. "
21 Naaman saw him running a' him, "
6:24 it came to pass a' this, "
7:14 king sent a' the host of the Syrians, "
15 they went a' them unto Jordan: "
8: 2 a' the saying of the man of God: *
9:25 I and thou rode together a' Ahab 310
27 Jehu followed a' him, "
10:29 Jehu departed not from a' them, "
14:17 Joash king of Judah lived a' the "
19 they sent a' him to Lachish, "
22 a' that the king slept with his "
17:15 and went a' the heathen "
33 a' the manner of the nations
34 they do a' the former manners:
34 do they a' their statutes, or a' their
34 or a' the law and commandment

2Ki 17:40 they did a· their former manner.
18: 5 so that a· him was none like him 310
21: 2 a· the abominations of the heathen,
23: 3 to walk a· the Lord, 310
25 neither a· him arose there any like "
25: 5 the Chaldees pursued a· the king, "
1Ch 2:24 And a· that Hezron was dead "
5: 1 not to be reckoned a· the birthright.
25 went a whoring a· the gods 310
6:31 in the house of the Lord, a· that
7: 4 generations, a· the house of their
9 number of them, a· their genealogy
8: 8 a· he had sent them away; 4480
9:25 in their villages, were to come a· *
10: 2 hard a· Saul, and a· his sons; 310
11:12 And a· him was Eleazar the son "
14:14 said unto him, Go not up a· them; "
15:13 sought him not a· the due order. *
17:11 I will raise up thy seed a· thee, 310
18: 1 Now a· this it came to pass, "
19: 1 Now it came to pass a· this, "
20: 1 a· the year was expired, *6256
4 it came to pass a· this, that there 310
23:24 sons of Levi a· the house of their
24:30 Levites a· the house of their fathers.
27: 1 of Israel a· their number, to wit,
7 Zebadiah his son a· him: 310
34 And a· Ahithophel was Jehoiada "
28: 8 inheritance for your children a· you "
29:14 able to offer so willingly a· this sort?
21 Lord, on the morrow a· that day,
2Ch 1:12 there any a· thee have the like. 310
2:17 a· the numbering wherewith "
3: 3 length by cubits a· the first measure
4:20 burn a· the manner before the *
8: 8 who were left a· them in the land, 310
13 Even a· a certain rate every day, *
10: 5 again unto me a· three days.
14 answered them a· the advice of
11:16 And a· them out of all the tribes 310
20 And a· her he took Maachah "
13: 9 priests a· the manner of the nations
19 Abijah pursued a· Jeroboam, 310
18: 2 a· certain years he went down to 7093
19 one spake saying a· this manner, 3602
19 another saying a· that manner. "
20: 1 It came to pass a· this also, 310
35 And a· this did Jehoshaphat "
21:18 And a· all this the Lord smote him, "
19 a· the end of two years, his *
22: 4 his counsellors a· the death of his 310
5 He walked also a· their counsel,
23:21 a· that they had slain Athaliah *
24: 4 it came to pass a· this, 310
17 Now a· the death of Jehoiada "
25:14 it came to pass, a· that Amaziah "
15 sought a· the gods of the people,
20 they sought a· the gods of Edom,
25 lived a· the death of Joash son of 310
27 a· the time that Amaziah did *
27 sent to Lachish a· him, and slew 310
26: 2 a· that the king slept with his "
17 Azariah the priest went in a· him, "
28: 3 a· the abominations of the *
30:16 a· their manner, according to the
31: 2 a· their courses, every man 5921
32: 1 A· these things, and the 310
9 A· this did Sennacherib king of "
33:14 Now a· this he built a wall "
34: 3 he began to seek a· the God of
21 to do a· all that is written in this *
31 to walk a· the Lord, 310
35: 4 a· your courses, according to the
5 a· the division of the families of *
20 A· all this, when Josiah had 310
36:14 transgressed very much a· all the
Ezr 2:61 Gileadite, and was called a· their 5921
69 They gave a· their ability unto
3:10 praise the Lord, a· the ordinance 5921
5: 4 a· this manner, What are the
12 a· that our fathers had provoked 4481
7: 1 Now a· these things, 310
18 that do a· the will of your God.
25 And thou, Ezra, a· the wisdom of
9:10 what shall we say a· this? 310
13 And a· all that is come upon us "
10:16 chief of the fathers, a· the house of
Ne 3:16 A· him repaired Nehemiah 310
17 A· him repaired the Levites, "
18 A· him repaired their brethren, "
20 A· him Baruch the son of Zabbai "
21 A· him repaired Meremoth "
22 And a· him repaired the priests, "
23 A· him repaired Benjamin "
23 A· him repaired Azariah "
24 A· him repaired Binnui "
25 A· him Pedaiah the son of Parosh. "
27 A· them the Tekoites repaired "
29 A· them repaired Zadok "
29 A· him repaired also Shemaiah "
30 A· him repaired Hananiah "
30 A· him repaired Meshullam "
31 A· him repaired Malchiah "
4:13 I even set the people a· their
5: 8 We a· our ability, have redeemed 1767
6: 4 sent unto me four times a· this
4 and I answered them a· the same
7:63 and was called a· their name. 5921
9:28 But a· they had rest, they did
10:34 a· the houses of our fathers, *
11: 8 And a· him Gabbai, Sallai, 310
12:32 a· them went Hoshaiah, "
38 went over against them, and I a· "
13: 6 and a· certain days obtained I 7093
19 not be opened till a· the sabbath: 310
Es 1:22 to every people a· their language,

Es 2: 1 A· these things, when the wrath 310
12 a· that she had been twelve 7093
3: 1 A· these things did king Ahasuerus 310
12 to every people a· their language;
8: 9 thereof, and unto every people a·
9:26 they called these days Purim a· 5921
Job 3: 1 A· this opened Job his mouth, 310
10: 6 thou enquirest a· mine iniquity,
18:20 come a· him shall be astonied 314
19:26 though a· my skin worms destroy 310
21: 3 and a· that I have spoken, mock on. "
21 in his house a· him, "
33 and every man shall draw a· him, "
29:22 A· my words they spake not again; "
30: 5 (they cried a· them 5921
5 as a· a thief;)
31: 7 mine heart walked a· mine eyes, 310
37: 4 A· it a voice roareth: "
39: 8 he searcheth a· every green thing. "
10 will he harrow the valleys a· thee? "
41:32 He maketh a path to shine a· him; "
42: 7 a· the Lord had spoken these words "
16 A· this lived Job an hundred and "
Ps 4: 2 love vanity, and seek a· leasing?
10: 4 will not seek a· God: God is not *
16: 4 shall be multiplied that hasten a·*
27: 4 that will I seek a·; that I may
28: 4 give them a· the work of their
35: 4 put to shame that seek a· my
38:12 They also that seek a· my life
40:14 that seek a· my soul to destroy it;
42: 1 As the hart panteth a· the water 5921
1 so panteth my soul a· thee, O God. 413
49:11 they call their lands a· their own
17 his glory shall not descend a· him. 310
51 (title) a· he had gone in to Bath-sheba. 834
54: 3 and oppressors seek a· my soul;
63: 8 My soul followeth hard a· thee: 310
68:25 players on instruments followed a·; "
70: 2 confounded that seek a· my soul:
78:34 returned and enquired early a· *
86:14 violent men have sought a· my
103:10 not dealt with us a· our sins; nor
104:21 The young lions roar a· their prey,
110: 4 Thou art a priest for ever a· the 5921
119:40 I have longed a· thy precepts:
88 Quicken me a· thy lovingkindness;
150 nigh that follow a· mischief:
143: 6 my soul thirsteth a· thee, as a
144:12 as corner stones, polished a· the
Pr 2: 3 if thou criest a· knowledge, and
6:25 a· her beauty in thine heart;
7:22 He goeth a· her straightway, 310
15: 9 he loveth him that followeth a· *
20: 7 his children are blessed a· him. 310
25 and a· vows to make enquiry. "
21:21 that followeth a· righteousness
28:19 he that followeth a· vain persons
Ec 1:11 come with those that shall come a·. 314
2:12 man do that cometh a· the king? 310
18 unto the man that shall be a· me. "
3:22 bring him to see what shall be a· "
4:16 also that come a· shall not rejoice 314
6:12 who can tell a man what shall be a· 310
7:14 that man should find nothing a· "
9: 3 and a· that they go to the dead. "
10:14 what shall be a· him, "
11: 1 thou shalt find it a· many days.
12: 2 nor the clouds return a· the rain: 310
Ca 1: 4 Draw me, we will run a· thee: "
Isa 1:23 and followeth a· rewards:
5:17 lambs feed a· their manner, and *
10:24 against thee, a· the manner of
26 so shall he lift it up a· the manner
11: 3 not judge a· the sight of his eyes,
3 neither reprove a· the hearing of
23:15, 17 a· the end of seventy years
24:22 and a· many days shall they be
43:10 formed, neither shall there be a· 310
44:13 maketh it a· the figure of a man,
45:14 they shall come a· thee; 310
49:20 a· thou hast lost the other, shall *
51: 1 ye that follow a· righteousness,
65: 2 a· their own thoughts; 310
Jer 2: 2 when thou wentest a· me in the "
5 have walked a· vanity, "
8 walked a· things that do not profit. "
23 I have not gone a· Baalim? "
25 and a· them will I go. "
3: 7 a· she had done all these things, "
17 a· the imagination of their evil "
5: 8 morning: every one neighed a· 413
7: 6 neither walk a· other gods to 310
9 a· other gods whom ye know not; "
8: 2 a· whom they have walked, "
9:14 have walked a· the imagination "
14 of their own heart, and a· Baalim, "
16 I will send a sword a· them, "
22 as the handful a· the harvestman, "
11:10 they went a· other gods to serve "
12: 6 have called a multitude a· thee: "
15 a· that I have plucked them out "
13: 6 a· many days, that the Lord said 7093
9 A· this manner will I mar the 3602
10 walk a· other gods, to serve them, 310
16:11 have walked a· other gods, "
12 a· the imagination of his evil heart, "
16 a· will I send for many hunters, * "
18:12 we will walk a· our own devices, "
23:17 every one that walketh a· the *
24: 1 a· that Nebuchadrezzar king of 310
25: 6 go not a· other gods to serve them, "
26 of Sheshach shall drink a· them. "
28:12 a· that Hananiah the prophet had "
29: 2 (A· that Jeconiah the king, "
10 a· seventy years be accomplished 6310

Jer 30:17 Zion, whom no man seeketh a·.
18 palace shall remain a· the manner 5921
31:19 a· that I was turned, I repented; 310
19 and a· that I was instructed, "
33 A· those days, saith the Lord. "
32:18 into the bosom of their children a· "
39 of their children a· them: "
34: 8 a· that the king Zedekiah had "
35:15 go not a· other gods to serve them, "
36:27 a· that the king had burned the "
39: 5 the Chaldeans' army pursued a· "
40: 1 a· that Nebuzar-adan the captain "
41: 4 day a· he had slain Gedaliah, and
16 a· that he had slain Gedaliah 310
42: 7 a· ten days, that the word of the 7093
16 shall follow close a· you 310
49:37 I will send the sword a· them, "
50:21 waste and utterly destroy a· them, "
51:46 and a· that in another year shall "
52: 8 the Chaldeans pursued a· the king, "
Eze 5: 2, 12 I will draw out a sword a· them. "
6: 9 which go a whoring a· their idols:
7:27 I will do unto them a· their way,
9: 5 Go ye a· him through the city, 310
11:12 a· the manners of the heathen
21 whose heart walketh a· the heart
12:14 I will draw out the sword a· them. 310
16:23 came to pass a· all thy wickedness, "
47 walked a· their ways, nor done a· *
20:16 for their heart went a· their idols. 310
24 eyes were a· their fathers' idols. "
30 a· the manner of your fathers?
30 whoredom a· their abominations? 310
23:15 a· the manner of the Babylonians
30 thou hast gone a whoring a· the 310
45 shall judge them a· the manner of *
45 and a· the manner of women that *
48 may be taught not to do a· your
29:16 when they shall look a· them: 310
33:20 I will judge you every one a· his
31 heart goeth a· their covetousness. 310
34: 6 none did search or seek a· them.
36:11 I will settle you a· your old estates,
38: 8 A· many days thou shalt be
39:14 a· the end of seven months shall
26 A· that they have borne their *
40: 1 fourteenth year a· that the city was 310
1 the arches thereof were a· the
22 a· the measure of the gate that
24 A· that he brought me toward *
41:25 A· he measured the wall of the *
43:13 a· the cubits: The cubit is a cubit *
44:10 astray away from me a· their 310
26 And a· he is cleansed, "
45:11 the measure thereof shall be a· *
46:12 a· his going forth one shall shut 310
17 a· it shall return to the prince: *
19 A· he brought me through the *
48:31 be a· the names of the tribes of 5921
Da 2:39 And a· thee shall arise another 870
3:29 no other God that can deliver a· 1836
4:26 a· that thou shalt have known 1767
7: 6 A· this I beheld, and lo another, 870
7 A· this I saw in the night visions, "
24 and another shall rise a· them; 311
8: 1 a· that which appeared unto me at 310
9:26 And a· threescore and two weeks "
11:13 come a· certain years *7093
18 A· this shall he turn his face unto
23 And a· the league made with him
Ho 2: 5 I will go a· my lovers, 310
7 And she shall follow a· her lovers,
13 she went a· her lovers, 310
5: 8 a· thee, O Benjamin. * "
11 walked a· the commandment.
6: 2 A· two days will he revive us: in
7: 4 who ceaseth from raising a· he *
11:10 They shall walk a· the Lord: 310
12: 1 and followeth a· the east wind:
Joe 2: 2 neither shall be any more a· it, 310
Am 2: 4 a· the which their fathers have
7 pant a· the dust of the earth on 5921
4: 4 and your tithes a· three years: *
10 pestilence a· the manner of Egypt:
7: 1 growth a· the king's mowings. 310
Zec 2: 8 A· the glory hath he sent me unto "
6: 6 the white go forth a· them; "
7:14 the land was desolate a· them,
M't 1:12 a· they were brought to Babylon, 3326
3:11 but he that cometh a· me 3694
5: 6 they which do hunger and thirst a·
28 looketh on a woman to lust a· her
6: 9 A· this manner therefore pray ye: 3779
32 a· all these things do the Gentiles 1934
10:38 and followeth a· me, is not worthy 3694
12:39 generation seeketh a· a sign; 1934
15:12 were offended, a· they heard this *
23 for she crieth a· us. 3693
16: 4 generation seeketh a· a sign; 1934
24 If any man will come a· me, 3694
17: 1 a· six days Jesus taketh Peter, 3326
18:32 lord, a· that he had called him,
23: 3 but do not ye a· their works: 2596
24:29 Immediately a· the tribulation 3326
25:19 A· a long time the lord of those "
26: 2 Ye know that a· two days is the "
32 But a· I am risen again, I will go "
73 And a· a while came unto him "
27:31 a· that they had mocked him, *3753
53 of the graves a· his resurrection, 3326
63 A· three days I will rise again. "
M'r 1: 7 cometh one mightier than I a· me, 3694
14 a· that John was put in prison, 3326
17 Come ye a· me, 3694
20 and went a· him. "
36 that were with him followed a· 2614

M'r 2: 1 into Capernaum a· some days; 1223
4:28 a· that the full corn in the ear. *1534
8:12 Why doth this generation seek a· *1934
25 A· that he put his hands again *1534
31 and a· three days rise again. 3326
34 Whosoever will come a· me, 3694
9: 2 a· six days Jesus taketh with him 3326
12:34 no man a· that durst ask him 3765
13:24 a· that tribulation, the sun shall 3326
14: 1 A· two days was the feast of the "
28 But a· that I am risen, "
70 And a little a·, they that stood by "
16:12 A· that he appeared in another "
14 not them which had seen him a·
19 a· the Lord had spoken unto them, 3326
Lu 1:24 And a· those days his wife
59 a· the name of his father. 1909
2:27 a· the custom of the law, 2596
42 a· the custom of the feast.
46 a· three days they found him in 3326
5:27 a· these things he went forth,
6: 1 second sabbath a· the first, that *1207
7:11 it came to pass the day a·, *1836
9:23 If any man will come a· me, 3694
28 an eight days a· these sayings, 3326
10: 1 A· these things the Lord "
12: 4 a· that have no more that they "
5 which a· he hath killed hath power "
30 the nations of the world seek a·: 1934
13: 9 a· that thou shalt cut it *1519, 3195
14:27 and come a· me, cannot be my 3694
29 a· he hath laid the foundation, *
15: 4 and go a· that which is lost, until 1909
13 not many days a· the younger 3326
17:23 or, see there: go not a· them, *
19:14 and sent a messsage a· him, 3694
20:40 And a· that they durst not ask *2089
21: 8 go ye not therefore a· them. *3694
26 and for looking a· those things *4329
22:20 also the cup a· supper, 3326
58 a· a little while another saw him, "
59 about the space of one hour a·
23:26 that he might bear it a· Jesus. 3693
55 followed a·, and beheld the 2628
Joh 1:15 He that cometh a· me is preferred 3694
27 He it is, who coming a· me is "
30 A· me cometh a man which is "
35 the next day a·, John stood, *1887
2: 6 a· the manner of the purifying 2596
12 A· this he went down to 3326
3:22 A· these things came Jesus and "
4:43 Now a· two days he departed "
5: 1 A· this there was a feast of the "
4 first a· the troubling of the water * "
6: 1 A· these things Jesus went over "
23 a· that the Lord had given thanks:)
7: 1 A· these things Jesus walked in 3326
8:15 Ye judge a· the flesh; I judge no 2596
11: 7 a· that saith he to his disciples, 3326
11 and a· that he saith unto them, "
12:19 the world is gone a· him. 3694
13: 5 A· that he poureth water into a *1534
12 So a· he had washed their feet, *3753
27 a· the sop Satan entered into him. 3326
19:28 a· this, Jesus knowing that all "
38 a· this Joseph of Arimathæa, "
20:26 a· eight days again his disciples "
21: 1 A· these things Jesus shewed "
14 a· that he was risen from the dead.
Ac 1: 2 a· that he through the Holy Ghost
3 a· his passion by many infallible 3326
8 receive power, a· that the Holy *
3:24 those that follow a·, as many 2517
5: 4 and a· it was sold, was it not in
7 three hours a·, when his wife, not
37 A· this man rose up Judas of 3326
37 drew away much people a· him: 3694
7: 5 and to his seed a· him, 3326
7 and a· that shall they come forth,
36 a· that he had shewed wonders *
45 our fathers that came a· brought *3326
9:23 a· that many days were fulfilled, *5613
10:24 And the morrow a· they entered *3326
37 a· the baptism which John "
41 a· he rose from the dead. "
12: 4 intending a· Easter to bring him "
13:15 And a· the reading of the law "
20 And a· that he gave unto them "
22 a man a· mine own heart, 2596
25 there cometh one a· me, 3326
36 For David, a· he had served his
14:24 a· they had passed throughout *
15: 1 a· the manner of Moses, ye cannot
13 And a· they had held their peace, 3326
16 A· this I will return, and will "
17 men might seek after the Lord, 1567
23 they wrote letters by them a· this *
33 a· they had tarried there a space,
36 And some days a· Paul said unto 3326
16: 7 A· they were come to Mysia,
10 And a· he had seen the vision, *5613
17:27 if haply they might feel a· him,
18: 1 A· these things Paul departed 3326
18 And Paul a· this tarried there yet
23 a· he had spent some time there, *
19: 4 which should come a· him, 3326
21 A· these things were ended, 5613
21 A· I have been there, I must also 3326
20: 1 And a· the uproar was ceased,
6 a· the days of unleavened bread,
18 a· what manner I have been with 4459
29 a· my departing shall grievous 3326
30 to draw away disciples a· them. 3694
21: 1 it came to pass, that a· we were *5613
15 And a· those days we took up our 3326
21 neither to walk a· the customs.

Ac 21:36 multitude of the people followed a·,
22:29 a· he knew that he was a Roman, *
23: 3 to judge me a· the law, and *2596
25 a letter a· this manner: 4023
24: 1 a· five days Ananias the high 3326
10 Then Paul, a· that the governor *
14 a· the way which they call heresy, 2596
17 a· many years I came to bring 1223
24 And a· certain days, when Felix 3326
27 a· two years Porcius Festus came *4137
25: 1 a· three days he ascended from 3326
13 a· certain days king Agrippa and *1230
26 thee, O king Agrippa, that, a·
26: 5 that a· the most straitest sect of 2596
27:14 not long a· there arose against it
21 a· long abstinence Paul stood *5225
28: 6 a· they had looked a great while, *
11 a· three months we departed 3326
13 a· one day the south wind blew, "
17 a· three days Paul called the chief "
25 a· that Paul had spoken one word,
Ro 2: 5 a· thy hardness and impenitent 2596
3:11 none that seeketh a· God. 1567
5:14 had not sinned a· the similitude 1909
6:19 I speak a· the manner of men
7:22 I delight in the law of God a· the 2596
8: 1 walk not a· the flesh, but a· * "
4 walk not a· the flesh, but a· "
5 that are a· the flesh do mind the "
5 that are a· the Spirit the things of "
12 not to the flesh, to live a· the flesh. "
13 if ye live a· the flesh, ye shall die: "
9:30 followed not a· righteousness,
31 which followed a· the law of
10:20 unto them that asked not a· me. *1905
14:19 therefore follow a· the things 1377
1Co 1:21 for a· that in the wisdom of God *1894
22 and the Greeks seek a· wisdom:
26 wise men a· the flesh, 2596
7: 7 one a· this manner, and another a· 3779
40 so abide, a· my judgment: 2596
10: 6 we should not lust a· evil things, 1938
18 Behold Israel a· the flesh: 2596
11:25 A· the same manner also he *5615
12:28 a· that miracles, then gifts *1899
14: 1 Follow a· charity, and desire
15: 6 A· that, he was seen of above five *1899
7 A· that, he was seen of James; * "
32 If a· the manner of men I have 2596
2Co 5:16 know we no man a· the flesh: yea, "
16 we have known Christ a· the flesh, "
7: 9 made sorry a· a godly manner, "
11 ye sorrowed a· a godly sort, "
9:14 long a· you for the exceeding 1971
10: 3 we do not war a· the flesh: *2596
7 a· the outward appearance? * "
11:17 I speak it not a· the Lord, "
18 that many glory a· the flesh, "
Ga 1:11 which was preached of me is not a· "
18 Then a· three years I went up to "
2: 1 fourteen years a· I went up *1223
14 a· the manner of the Gentiles, *
3:15 I speak a· the manner of men; 2596
17 thirty years a·, cannot disannul, 3326
25 But a· that faith is come, we are *
4: 9 now, a· that ye have known God,
23 was born a· the flesh; 2596
29 he that was born a· the flesh "
29 persecuted him that was born a· "
Eph 1:11 all things a· the counsel of his own "
13 also trusted, a· that ye heard the *
13 whom also a· that ye believed, ye *
15 a· I heard of your faith in the *
4:24 a· God is created in righteousness 2596
Ph'p 1: 8 how greatly I long a· you all 1971
2:26 For he longed a· you all,
3:12 I follow a·, if that I may *
Col 2: 8 a· the tradition of men, 2596
8 a· the rudiments of the world, "
8 and not a· Christ. "
22 a· the commandments and "
3:10 a· the image of him that created "
1Th 2: 2 a· that we had suffered before, *
2Th 2: 9 whose coming is a· the working *2596
3: 6 and not a· the tradition "
1Ti 5:15 already turned aside a· Satan. 3694
24 some men they follow a·. 1872
6:10 while some coveted a·, they have
11 follow a· righteousness, godliness,
2Ti 4: 3 but a· their own lusts 2596
Tit 1: 1 the truth which is a· godliness; * "
4 own son a· the common faith: "
3: 4 a· that the kindness and love of *3753
10 a· the first and second admonition 3326
Heb 3: 5 which were to be spoken a·; *
4: 7 a· so long a time; *3326
11 a· the same example of unbelief. 1722
5: 6 a· the order of Melchisedec. 2596
10 an high priest a· the order of
6:15 a· he had patiently endured, he *
20 a· the order of Melchisedec. 2596
7: 2 a· that also king of Salem, *1899
11 rise a· the order of Melchisedec, 2596
11 be called a· the order of Aaron? "
15 a· the similitude of Melchisedec "
16 not a· the law of a carnal "
16 but a· the power of an "
17 a· the order of Melchisedec. "
21 a· the order of Melchisedec:) * "
8:10 a· those days, saith the Lord; 3326
9: 3 And a· the second veil,
17 a testament is of force a· men *
27 but a· this the judgment: 3326
10:12 a· he had offered one sacrifice *
15 for a· that he had said before, 3326
16 a· those days, saith the Lord, "

Heb 10:26 a· that we have received the 3326
32 a· ye were illuminated, ye endured
36 a· ye have done the will of God,
11: 8 which he should a· receive *3195
30 Jericho fell down, a· they were
12:10 chastened us a· their own *2596
Jas 3: 9 a· the similitude of God. "
1Pe 3: 5 a· this manner in the old time 3779
5:10 by Christ Jesus, a· that ye have
2Pe 1:15 ye may be able a· my decease 3326
2: 6 that a· should live ungodly; *3195
2:10 that walk a· the flesh in 3694
21 a· they have known it, to turn
3: 3 walking a· their own lusts, 2596
2Jo 6 we walk a· his commandments. "
3Jo 6 forward on their journey a· a * 516
Jude 7 and going a· strange flesh, *3694
11 and ran greedily a· the error of *
16 complainers, walking a· their 2596
18 who should walk a· their own "
Re 4: 1 A· this I looked, and, behold, 3326
7: 1 a· these things I saw four angels "
9 A· this I beheld, and, lo, "
11:11 And a· three days and an half "
12:15 as a flood a· the woman, 3694
13: 3 the world wondered a· the beast. "
15: 5 And a· that I looked, 3326
18: 1 a· these things I saw another angel "
14 the fruits that thy soul lusted a·
19: 1 a· these things I heard a great 3326
20: 3 a· that he must be loosed "

afternoon
J'g 19: 8 they tarried until a·, and *5186, 3117

afterward See also AFTERWARDS.
Ge 10:18 and a· were the families of the 310
15:14 a· shall they come out with 310, 3651
32:20 and a· I will see his face; " "
38:30 And a· came out his brother, 310
Ex 5: 1 a· Moses and Aaron went in, and "
34:32 a· all the children of Israel 310, 3651
Le 14:19 a· he shall kill the burnt offering: 310
36 a· the priest shall go in to see 310, 3651
16:26 a· come into the camp. " "
28 a· he shall come into the camp. " "
22: 7 and shall a· eat of the holy things; 310
Nu 5:26 a· shall cause the woman to drink "
12:16 a· the people removed from "
19: 7 a· he shall come into the camp, "
31: 2 a· shalt thou be gathered unto thy "
24 a· ye shall come into the camp. "
32:22 a· ye shall return, and be guiltless "
De 17: 7 a· the hands of all the people. 314
24:21 thou shalt not glean it a·: * 310
Jos 2:16 and a· may ye go your way. "
8:34 a· he read all the words of the 310, 3651
10:26 a· Joshua smote them, and " "
24: 5 and a· I brought you out. 310
J'g 1: 9 a· the children of Judah went down "
7:11 a· shall thine hands be strengthened "
16: 4 came to pass a·, that he loved 310, 3651
19: 5 and a· go your way. 310
1Sa 24: 5 a·, that David's heart smote 310, 3651
8 David also arose a·, and went " "
2Sa 3:28 a· when David heard it, he said, "
1Ch 2:21 a· Hezron went in to the daughter 310
2Ch 35:14 a· they made ready for themselves, "
Ezr 3: 5 a· offered the continual burnt 310, 3651
Ne 6:10 A· I came unto the house of *
Ps 73:24 and a· receive me to glory. 310
Isa 1:26 a· thou shalt be called, 310, 3651
9: 1 a· did more grievously afflict * 314
Jer 21: 7 a·, saith the Lord, I will 310, 3651
34:11 a· they turned, and caused * " "
46:26 a· it shall be inhabited, * " "
49: 6 a· I will bring again the " "
Eze 41: 1 A· he brought me to the temple, *
43: 1 A· he brought me to the gate,
47: 1 A· he brought me again unto the *
5 A· he measured a thousand;
Da 8:27 a· I rose up, and did the king's *
Ho 3: 5 A· shall the children of Israel 310
Joe 2:28 come to pass a·, that I will 310, 3651
Mat 4: 2 he was a· an hungred. 5305
21:29 but a· he repented, and went. "
32 ye had seen it, repented not a·, "
25:11 A· came also the other virgins, "
M'r 4:17 a·, when affliction or persecution *1534
16:14 A· he appeared unto the eleven 5305
Lu 4: 2 they were ended, he a· hungered. *
8: 1 it came to pass a·, that he went *2517
17: 8 a· thou shalt eat and drink? 3326, 5023
18: 4 but a· he said within himself, " "
Joh 5:14 A· Jesus findeth him in the
Ac 13:21 And a· they desired a king: 2547
1Co 15:23 a· they that are Christ's at his *1899
46 a· that which is spiritual. "
Heb 4: 8 would he not a· have spoken 3326, 5023
12:11 a· it yieldeth the peaceable fruit 5305
17 ye know how that a·, when he 3347
Jude 5 a· destroyed them that believed 1208

afterwards See also AFTERWARD.
Ge 30:21 And a· she bare a daughter, 310
Ex 11: 1 a· he will let you go hence: 310, 3651
De 13: 9 and a· the hand of all the people. 314
1Sa 9:13 a· they eat that be bidden. 310, 3651
Job 18: 2 and a· we will speak. 310
Pr 20:17 a· his mouth shall be filled with "
24:27 a· build thine house. "
28:23 rebuketh a man a· shall find * "
29:11 a wise man keepeth it in till a· * 268
Eze 11:24 A· the spirit took me up, and *
Joh 13:36 but thou shalt follow me a·. 5305
Ga 1:21 A· I came into the regions of *1899
3:23 which should a· be revealed.

Agabus (*ag'-ab-us*)
Ac 11:28 one of them named A'. 13
21:10 a certain prophet, named A'. "

Agag (*a'-gag*) See also AGAGITE.
Nu 24: 7 his king shall be higher than A', 90
1Sa 15: 8 took A' the king of the Amalekites "
9 But Saul and the people spared A', "
20 have brought A' the king of Amalek, "
32 Bring ye hither to me A' the king "
32 And A' came unto him delicately. "
32 A' said, Surely the bitterness of "
33 And Samuel hewed A' in pieces "

Agagite (*ag'-ag-ite*)
Es 3: 1, 10 the son of Hammedatha the A', 91
8: 3 away the mischief of Haman the A', "
5 the son of Hammedatha the A', "
9:24 the son of Hammedatha the A', "

again
Ge 4: 2 And she a' bare his brother Abel. 3254
25 And Adam knew his wife a': 5750
8:10 a' he sent forth the dove out of 3254
12 returned not a' unto him "
21 I will not a' curse the ground "
21 neither will I a' smite any more "
14:16 brought a' his brother Lot, and 7725
15:16 they shall come hither a': "
18:29 And he spake unto him yet a', 3254
19: 9 And they said a', This one fellow * "
22: 5 and worship, and come a' to you. 7725
24: 5 bring thy son a' unto the land "
6, 8 bring not my son thither a'. "
25: 1 Then a' Abraham took a wife, *3254
26:18 Isaac digged a' the wells of water, 7725
28:15 will bring thee a' into this land; "
21 I come a' to my father's house in "
29: 3 put the stone a' upon the well's "
33, 34, 35 conceived a', and bare a 5750
30: 7 conceived a', and bare Jacob a "
19 conceived a', and bare Jacob the "
31 I will a' feed and keep thy flock. 7725
35: 9 And God appeared unto Jacob a', 5750
37:14 and bring me word a'. 7725
22 to deliver him to his father a'. * "
38: 4 conceived a', and bare a son; and 5750
5 a' conceived, and bare a son; and "
26 he knew her a' no more. 3254
40:21 butler unto his butlership a'; 7725
42:24 and returned to them a', and * "
37 I will bring him to thee a'. "
43: 2 Go a', buy us a little food. "
12 the money that was brought a' * "
12 carry it a' in your hand; "
13 and arise, go a' unto the man: "
21 we have brought it a' in our hand. "
44: 8 money,...we brought a' unto thee "
25 Go a', and buy us a little food. "
46: 4 I will also surely bring thee up a': "
48:21 and bring you a' unto the land of 7725
50: 5 bury my father, and I will come a'. "
Ex 4: 7 Put thine hand into thy bosom a'. "
7 he put his hand into his bosom a'; "
7 it was turned a' as his other flesh. "
10: 8 Moses and Aaron were brought a' "
29 I will see thy face a' no more. 3254
14:13 ye shall see them a' no more "
26 may come a' upon the Egyptians, 7725
15:19 the Lord brought a' the waters "
21:19 If he rise a', and walk abroad "
23: 4 thou shalt surely bring it back a'. 7725
24:14 until we come a' unto you: "
33:11 And he turned a' into the camp: "
34:35 Moses put the vail upon his face a', "
Le 13: 6 look on him a' the seventh day: 8145
7 he shall be seen of the priest a': "
16 if the raw flesh turn a', 7725
14:39 shall come a' the seventh day, "
43 if the plague come a', and break "
20: 2 A', thou shalt say to the children*
24:20 so shall it be done to him a'. *
25:48 may be redeemed a'; one of his *
51 he shall give a' the price of his *7725
52 his years shall he give him a' * "
26:26 shall deliver you your bread a' "
Nu 11: 4 the children of Israel also wept a', "
12:14 after that let her be received in a'. "
17:10 Bring Aaron's rod a' before the *7725
22: 8 and I will bring you word a', as "
15 And Balak sent yet a' princes, 3254
25 and he smote her a'. "
34 thee, I will get me back a'. 7725
23:16 Go a' unto Balak, and say thus. * "
32:15 he will yet a' leave them in the 3254
33: 7 and turned a' unto Pi-hahiroth, *7725
35:32 come a' to dwell in the land, "
De 1:22 bring us word a' by what way "
25 and brought us word a', and said, "
5:30 Get you into your tents a'. * "
13:16 for ever; it shall not be built a'. 5750
15: 3 thou mayest exact it a': but that*
18:16 Let me not hear a' the voice of 3254
22: 1 shalt in any case bring them a' 7725
2 thou shalt restore it to him a'. "
4 surely help to lift them up a'. "
23:11 he shall come into the camp a'. *
24: 4 not take her a' to be his wife, *7725
13 shalt deliver him the pledge a' * "
19 thou shalt not go a' to fetch it: it "
20 shalt not go over the boughs a': 310
28:68 shall bring thee into Egypt a' 7725
68 Thou shalt see it no more a': and 3254
30: 9 will a' rejoice over thee for good, 7725
33:11 hate him, that they rise not a'. "
Jos 5: 2 and circumcise a' the children of 7725
8:21 then they turned a', and slew the "
14: 7 I brought him word a' as it was "
Jos 18: 4 and they shall come a' to me. *
8 describe it, and come a' to me, 7725
9 came a' to Joshua to the host of *
22:28 that we may say a', Behold the *
32 and brought them word a'. 7725
J'g 3:12 the children of Israel did evil a' 3254
19 turned a' from the quarries *7725
4: 1 the children of Israel a' did evil 3254
20 A' he said unto her, Stand in the *
6:18 I will tarry until thou come a'. 7725
8: 9 When I come a' in peace, I will "
33 the children of Israel turned a', "
9:37 And Gaal spake a' and said, 3254,5750
10: 6 the children of Israel did evil a' 3254
11: 8 we turn a' to thee now, that thou 7725
9 If ye bring me home a' to fight "
13 restore those lands a' peaceably. "
14 Jephthah sent messengers a' 3254,5750
13: 1 the children of Israel did evil a' 3254
8 thou didst send come a' unto us, 5750
9 the angel of God came a' unto the "
15:19 he had drunk, his spirit came a', 7725
16:22 hair of his head began to grow a'
19: 3 unto her, and to bring her a', 7725
7 therefore he lodged there a'. "
20:22 and set their battle a' in array in 3254
23 Shall I go up a' to battle "
25 ground of the children of Israel a'5750
28 Shall I yet a' go out to battle 3254
41 the men of Israel turned a', the *
48 the men of Israel turned a' 7725
21:14 Benjamin came a' at that time; * "
Ru 1:11 Naomi said, Turn a', my "
12 Turn a', my daughters, go your "
14 lifted up their voice, and wept a': 5750
21 Lord hath brought me home a' 7725
4: 3 Naomi, that is come a' out of the "
1Sa 3: 5 I called not; lie down a'. "
6 the Lord called yet a', Samuel. 3254
6 I called not, my son; lie down a'. 7725
8 And the Lord called Samuel a' the 3254
21 the Lord appeared a' in Shiloh: "
4: 5 so that the earth rang a'. "
5: 3 and set him in his place a'. 7725
11 and let it go a' to his own place, "
6:21 Philistines have brought a' the ark "
9: 8 the servant answered Saul a', 3254
15:25, 30 and turn a' with me, that 7725
31 So Samuel turned a' after Saul; "
16:10 A', Jesse made seven of his sons *
17:30 the people answered him a' after 7725
19: 8 And there was war a': and David 3254
15 Saul sent the messengers a' to "
21 And Saul sent messengers a' 3254
20:17 Jonathan caused David to swear a', "
23: 4 David enquired of the Lord yet a'. "
23 and come ye a' to me with the 7725
25:12 turned their way, and went a', * "
27: 4 he sought no more a' for him. 3254
29: 4 that he may go a' to his place *7725
30:12 when...his spirit came a' to him: "
2Sa 1: 9 He said unto me a', Stand, I pray *
2:22 And Abner said a' to Asahel, 3254,5750
3:11 not answer Abner a word a', * "
26 Abner, which brought him a' * "
34 all the people wept a' over him. 3254
5:22 the Philistines came up yet a'. "
6: 1 A', David gathered together all 5750
12:23 can I bring him back a'? "
14:13 the king doth not fetch home a' 7725
14 which cannot be gathered up a'; "
21 bring the young man Absalom a'. 7725
29 when he sent a' the second time, 5750
15: 8 Lord shall bring me a' indeed to 7725
25 he will bring me a', and shew me "
29 Abiathar carried the ark of God a' "
16:19 And a', whom should I serve? 8145
18:22 Then said Ahimaaz.... yet a' to 3254
19:24 until the day he came a' in peace. *
30 my lord the king is come a' in *7725
37 servant, I pray thee, turn back a', "
20:10 struck him not a', and he died. 8138
21:15 Philistines had yet war a' with 5750
18 was a' a battle with the Philistines "
19 there was a' a battle in Gob with "
22:38 not a' until I had consumed 7725
24: 1 And a' the anger of the Lord was 3254
1Ki 1:45 so that the city rang a'. This is "
2:30 Benaiah brought the king word a', 7725
41 Jerusalem to Gath, and was come a'. "
8:33 shall turn a' to thee, and confess "
34 and bring them a' unto the land "
12: 5 for three days, then come a' to me. "
12 Come to me a' the third day. "
20 that Jeroboam was come a', * "
21 to bring the kingdom a' to "
27 this people turn a' unto their lord "
27 go a' to Rehoboam king of Judah.* "
13: 4 he could not pull it in a' to him. "
6 my hand may be restored me a'. "
6 king's hand was restored him a', "
9 nor turn a' by the same way that* "
17 nor turn a' to go by the way that "
33 but made a'... priests of the high "
17:21 this child's soul come into him a'. "
22 soul of the child came into him a', "
18:37 hast turned their heart back a'. 322
43 And he said, Go a' seven times. 7725
19: 6 and drink, and laid him down a'. "
7 the angel of the Lord came a' the "
20 Go back a': for what have I done "
20: 5 the messengers came a', and said, "
9 departed, and brought him word a'. "
2Ki 1: 6 turn a' unto the king that sent you, "
11 A' also he sent unto him another "
13 sent a' a captain of the third fifty "
2Ki 2:18 when they came a' to him, (for he*7725
4:22 to the man of God, and come a'. "
29 salute thee, answer him not a': "
31 Wherefore he went a' to meet *7725
38 Elisha came a' to Gilgal: "
43 He said a', Give the people, *
5:10 thy flesh shall come a' to thee, 7725
14 his flesh came a' like unto the flesh "
26 when the man turned a' from his "
7: 8 came a', and entered into another*7725
9:18 he cometh not a'. "
20 even unto them, and cometh not a': "
36 Wherefore they came a', and told "
13:25 the son of Jehoahaz took a' "
19: 9 sent messengers a' unto Hezekiah, "
30 shall yet a' take root downward, 3254
20: 5 Turn again, and tell Hezekiah the 7725
21: 3 For he built up a' the high places "
22: 9 and brought the king word a', "
20 they brought the king word a'. "
24: 7 the king of Egypt came not a' any 3254
1Ch 13: 3 bring a' the ark of our God to us: 5437
14:13 Philistines yet a' spread 3254
14 Therefore David enquired a' of 5750
20: 5 was war a' with the Philistines; "
6 yet a' there was war at Gath, "
21:12 what word I shall bring a' to him *7725
27 put his sword a' into the sheath "
2Ch 6:25 bring them a' unto the land which "
10: 5 Come a' unto me after three days. "
12 Come a' to me on the third day. "
11: 1 bring the kingdom a' to Rehoboam. "
12:11 brought them a' into the guard "
13:20 did Jeroboam recover strength a' 5750
18:18 A' he said, Therefore hear the *
32 turned back a' from pursuing *7725
19: 4 he went out a' through the people "
20:27 to go a' to Jerusalem with joy; "
24:11 carried it to his place a'. "
19 to bring them a' unto the Lord; "
25:10 out of Ephraim, to go home a': "
28:11 and deliver the captives a', *
30: 6 a' unto the Lord God of Abraham, 7725
9 if ye turn a' unto the Lord, "
9 they shall come a' into this land: "
32:25 Hezekiah rendered not a' "
33: 3 For he built a' the high places "
13 a' to Jerusalem into his kingdom. "
34:16 brought the king word back a', 5750
28 So they brought the king word a'. 7725
Ezr 2: 1 a' unto Jerusalem and Judah, * "
4:13 the walls set up a', then will they *
16 if this city be builded a', and the *
6: 5 and brought a' unto the temple 1946
21 Israel, which were come a' out of 7725
9:14 we a' break thy commandments, "
Ne 7: 6 a' to Jerusalem and to Judah, * "
8:17 a' out of the captivity made booths, "
9:28 they did evil a' before thee: "
29 that thou mightest bring them a' "
13: 9 brought I a' the vessels of the "
21 if ye do so a', I will lay hands on 8138
Es 4:10 A' Esther spake unto Hatach, *
6:12 Mordecai came a' to the king's 7725
7: 2 the king said a' unto Esther on 1571
8: 3 Esther spake yet a' before the 3254
Job 2: 1 A' there was a day when the sons
6:29 not be iniquity; yea, return a', 5750
10: 9 wilt thou bring me into dust a'? 7725
16 and a' thou shewest thyself
12:14 down, and it cannot be built a':
23 nations, and straiteneth them a'. *
14: 7 cut down, that it will sprout a', 5750
14 If a man die, shall he live a'? all
20:15 and he shall vomit them up a':
29:22 After my words they spake not a'; 8138
34:15 man shall turn a' unto dust. 7725
Ps 18:37 neither did I turn a' till they were "
37:21 payeth not a': but the righteous 7999
60: 1 O turn thyself to us a'. 7725
68:22 I will bring a' from Bashan, "
22 I will bring my people a' "
71:20 shalt quicken me a', and shalt "
20 bring me up a' from the depths "
78:39 passeth away, and cometh not a'. "
80: 3 Turn us a', O God, and cause thy "
7 Turn us a', O God of hosts, "
19 Turn us a', O Lord God of hosts, "
85: 6 Wilt thou not revive us a': "
8 let them not turn a' to folly. "
104: 9 turn not a' to cover the earth. "
107:26 they go down a' to the depths:
39 A', they are minished and brought
126: 1 the Lord turned a' the captivity ‡
4 Turn a' our captivity, O Lord, 7725
6 shall doubtless come a' with
140:10 pits, that they rise not up a'.
Pr 2:19 that go unto her return a', 7725
3:28 thy neighbour, Go, and come a',
19:17 he hath given will he pay him a'. 7999
19 yet thou must do it a'. 3254
24 much as bring it to his mouth a'. 7725
23:35 I awake? I will seek it yet a'. 5750
24:16 seven times, and riseth up a':
26:15 grieveth him to bring it a' to his 7725
Ec 1: 6 the wind returneth a' according "
7 thither they return a'. "
3:20 the dust, and all turn to dust a'. *
4: 4 A', I considered all travail, and *
11 A', if two lie together, then they 1571
8:14 a', there be wicked men, to whom
Isa 7:10 the Lord spake a' unto Ahaz, 3254
8: 5 The Lord spake also unto me a', "
10:20 shall no more a' stay upon him "
11:11 the Lord shall set his hand a' "
24:20 it shall fall, and not rise a'. "

Isa 37:31 a· take root downward, and 3254
38: 8 I will bring a· the shadow of the *7725
46: 8 it a· to mind, O ye transgressors. "
49: 5 to bring Jacob a· to him, "
20 shall say a· in thine ears, The *5750
51:22 thou shalt no more drink it a·: "
52: 8 the Lord shall bring a· Zion. *7725
Jer 3: 1 man's, shall he return unto her a· 5750
1 yet return a· to me, saith the Lord. "
12:15 will bring them a·, every man to 7725
15:19 return, then will I bring thee a·, "
16:15 I will bring them a· into their land "
18: 4 so he made it a· another vessel, "
19:11 that cannot be made whole a·: 5750
23: 3 will bring them a· to their folds; 7725
24: 4 A· the word of the Lord came *
6 I will bring them a· to this land: 7725
25: 5 Turn ye a· now every one from * "
27:16 be brought a· from Babylon: "
28: 3 a· into this place all the vessels "
4 will bring a· to this place Jeconiah "
6 bring a· the vessels of the Lord's "
29:14 I will bring you a· into the place "
30: 3 bring a· the captivity of my people "
18 I will bring a· the captivity of 7725
31: 4 A· I will build thee, and thou shalt 5750
4 thou shalt a· be adorned with thy "
16 they shall come a· from the land 7725
17 that thy children shall come a· to "
21 turn a·, O virgin of Israel, turn a· "
23 I shall bring a· their captivity; "
32:15 vineyards shall be possessed a· 5750
37 will bring them a· unto this place, 7725
33:10 A· there shall be heard in this 5750
12 A· in this place, which is desolate "
13 of Judah, shall the flocks pass a· "
36:28 Take thee a· another roll, 7725
37: 8 the Chaldeans shall come a·, and "
41:16 whom he had brought a· from "
46:16 let us go a· to our own people, "
48:47 bring a· the captivity of Moab "
49: 6 I will bring a· the captivity of the "
39 will bring a· the captivity of Elam, "
50:19 And I will bring Israel a· to his "
La 3:40 our ways, and turn a· to the Lord. "
Eze 3:20 A·, When a righteous man doth "
4: 6 lie a· on thy right side, and thou 8145
5: 4 take of them a·, and cast them 5750
7: 7 sounding a· of the mountains. *1906
8: 6 turn thee yet a·, and thou shalt 5750
13 Turn thee yet a·, and thou shalt "
15 O son of man? turn thee yet a·, "
12:26 A· the word of the Lord came to
14:12 word of the Lord came a· to me, *
16: 1 A· the word of the Lord came
53 I shall bring a· their captivity, 7725
53 then will I bring a· the captivity *
18: 1 word of the Lord came unto me a·,
27 A·, when the wicked man turneth
21: 8 A· the word of the Lord came *
18 word of the Lord came unto me a·,
23: 1 word of the Lord came a· unto me,
24: 1 A· in the ninth year, in the tenth
25: 1 The word of the Lord came a· *
26:21 shalt thou never be found a·, 5750
27: 1 The word of the Lord came a·
28: 1 The word of the Lord came a·
20 A· the word of the Lord came *
29:14 bring a· the captivity of Egypt, 7725
30: 1 the word of the Lord came a· unto
33: 1 A· the word of the Lord came *
14 A·, when I say unto the wicked,
15 restore the pledge, give a· that he 7999
34: 4 neither have ye brought a· 7725
16 bring a· that which was driven "
37: 4 A· he said unto me, Prophesy
15 The word of the Lord came a·
39:25 bring a· the captivity of Jacob, 7725
27 When I have brought them a· "
47: 1 Afterward he brought me a· unto* "
4, 4 A· he measured a thousand,
Da 2: 7 They answered a· and said, *8579
9:25 the street shall be built a·, and 7725
10:18 there came a· and touched me 3254
Ho 1: 6 And she conceived a·, and bare a 5750
Joe 3: 1 bring a· the captivity of Judah, 7725
Am 7: 8 not a· pass by them any more: 3254
13 prophesy not a· any more at "
8: 2 not a· pass by them any more. "
14 shall fall, and never rise up a·. 5750
9:14 And I will bring a· the captivity 7725
Jon 2: 4 look a· toward thy holy temple. 3254
Mic 7:19 He will turn a·, he will have 7725
Zep 3:20 At that time will I bring you a·, *
Hag 2:20 a· the word of the Lord came *8145
Zec 2: 1 I lifted up mine eyes a·, and "
12 and shall choose Jerusalem a·. *5750
4: 1 that talked with me came a·, *7725
12 answered a·, and said unto him, *8145
8: 1 A· the word of the Lord of hosts *
15 a· have I thought in these days 7725
10: 6 will bring them a· to place them; "
9 with their children, and turn a·. "
10 bring them a· also out of the land "
12: 6 be inhabited a· in her own place, 5750
Mal 2:13 And this have ye done a·, 8145
M't 2: 8 bring me word a·, that I may * 518
4: 7 It is written a·, Thou shalt not 3825
8 A·, the devil taketh him up "
5:33 A·, ye have heard that it hath been "
7: 2 it shall be measured to you a·. * 488
6 and turn a· and rend you. *4762
11: 4 and shew John a· those things * 518
13:44 A·, the kingdom of heaven *3825
45, 47 A·, the kingdom of heaven "
16:21 and be raised a· the third day. *1453

M't 17: 9 until the son of man be risen a· * 450
23 third day he shall be raised a·. *1453
18:19 A· I say unto you, That if two of 3825
19:24 And a· I say unto you, It is easier "
20: 5 A· he went out about the sixth "
19 the third day he shall rise a·. *450
21:36 A·, he sent other servants more 3825
22: 1 spake unto them a· by parables, "
4 A·, he sent forth other servants, "
26:32 after I am risen a· I will go *1453
42 He went away a· the second time, 3825
43 came and found them asleep a·: "
44 went away a·, and prayed the "
52 Put up a· thy sword into his place, 654
72 And a· he denied with an oath, 3825
27: 3 brought a· the thirty pieces of *654
50 Jesus, when he had cried a· with 3825
63 After three days I will rise a·. 1453
M'r 2: 1 a· he entered into Capernaum 3825
13 he went forth a· by the seaside; "
3: 1 he entered a· into the synagogue; "
20 the multitude cometh together a·, "
4: 1 began a· to teach by the sea side: "
5:21 when Jesus was passed over a· by "
7:31 a·, departing from the coasts of "
8:13 entering into the ship a· departed "
25 he put his hands a· upon his eyes, "
31 after three days rise a·. 450
10: 1 resort unto him a·; and, as he 3825
1 was wont, he taught them a·. "
10 his disciples asked him a· of the "
24 But Jesus answereth a·, and saith "
32 he took a· the twelve, and began "
34 the third day he shall rise a·. 450
11:27 And they come a· to Jerusalem: 3825
12: 4 and a· he sent unto them another "
5 And a· he sent another; and him * "
13:16 is in the field not turn back a· *1994
14:39 a· he went away, and prayed, 3825
40 he found them asleep a·, "
61 A· the high priest asked him, "
69 a maid saw him a·, and began to "
70 he denied it a·. And a little after, "
70 they that stood by said a· to Peter, "
15: 4 And Pilate asked him a·, saying, "
12 Pilate answered and said a· unto "
13 And they cried out a·, Crucify him. "
Lu 2:34 and rising a· of many in Israel; †‡ 386
45 turned back a· to Jerusalem, *5290
4:20 he gave it a· to the minister, and * 591
6:30 thy goods ask them not a·. 523
34 to sinners, to receive as much a·. 618
35 lend, hoping for nothing a·; and * 560
38 measured to you a·. 488
8:37 the ship, and returned back a·. *5290
55 her spirit came a·, and she arose *1994
9: 8 of the old prophets was risen a·. 450
19 one of the old prophets is risen a·. "
39 him that he foameth a·, *3326
42 delivered him a· to his father. * 591
10: 6 if not, it shall turn to you a·. 344
17 the seventy returned a· with joy, *5290
35 when I come a·, I will repay thee. 1880
13:20 And a· he said, Whereunto shall 3825
14: 6 could not answer him a· to these 470
12 lest they also bid thee a·, and a 479
15:24 my son was dead, and is alive a·; 326
32 brother was dead, and is alive a·; "
17: 4 turn a· to thee, saying, I repent: 1994
18:33 the third day he shall rise a·. 450
20:11 a· he sent another servant: *4388
12 And a· he sent a third: and "
23:11 robe, and sent him a· to Pilate. * 375
20 willing to release Jesus, spake a· 3825
24: 7 crucified, and the third day rise a·. 450
Joh 1:35 A· the next day after John stood, 3825
3: 3 Except a man be born a·, he * 509
7 Ye must be born a·. "
4: 3 and departed a· into Galilee. 3825
13 of this water shall thirst a·: "
46 Jesus came a· into Cana of Galilee, "
54 This is a· the second miracle that "
6:15 he departed a· into a mountain "
39 should raise it up a· at the last * 450
8: 2 he came a· into the temple, 3825
8 a· he stooped down, and wrote "
12 Then spake Jesus a· unto them, "
21 Then said Jesus a· unto them, I go "
9:15 Then a· the Pharisees also asked "
17 They say unto the blind man a·, "
24 Then a· called they the man *1537, 1208
26 said they to him a·, What did he *3825
27 wherefore would you hear it a·? "
10: 7 Then said Jesus unto them a·, "
17 my life, that I might take it a·. "
18 and I have power to take it a·. "
19 a division therefore a· among the "
31 the Jews took up stones a· to stone "
39 Therefore they sought a· to take "
40 And went away a· beyond Jordan "
11: 7 Let us go into Judæa a·. "
8 and goest thou thither a·? "
23 unto her, Thy brother shall rise a·. 450
24 I know that he shall rise a· in the "
38 a· groaning in himself 3825
12:22 a· Andrew and Philip tell Jesus. * "
28 and will glorify it a·. "
39 because that Esaias said a·, "
13:12 and was set down a·, he said "
14: 3 I will come a·, and receive you "
28 I go away, and come a· unto you.*
16:16 and a·, a little while, and ye shall 3825
17, 19 and a·, a little while, and "
22 but I will see you a·, "
28 a·, I leave the world, and go to the "
18: 7 Then asked he them a·, Whom "

Joh 18:27 Peter then denied a·: 3825
33 into the judgment hall a·, * "
38 he went out a· unto the Jews, "
40 Then cried they all a·, saying, "
19: 4 Pilate therefore went forth a·, "
9 went a· into the judgment hall, "
37 And a· another scripture saith, "
20: 9 he must rise a· from the dead. 450
10 the disciples went away a· unto 3825
21 said Jesus to them a·, "
26 And after eight days a· his disciples "
21: 1 Jesus shewed himself a· to the "
16 He saith to him a· the second time, "
Ac 1: 6 this time restore a· the kingdom * 600
7:26 would have set them at one a·, 1515
39 their hearts turned back a· into *4762
10:15 the voice spake unto him a· the 3825
16 the vessel was received up a· into * "
11: 9 voice answered me a· from *1537, 1208
10 all were drawn up a· into heaven. 3825
13:33 he hath raised up Jesus a·; * 450
37 he, whom God raised a·, saw no *1453
14:21 they returned a· to Lystra, *5290
15:16 will build a· the tabernacle 456
16 I will build a· the ruins thereof, "
36 us go a· and visit our brethren *1994
17: 3 suffered, and risen a· from the 450
32 will hear thee a· of this matter. 3825
18:21 I will return a· unto you,
20:11 was come up a·, and had broken
21: 6 and they returned home a·. *5290
22:17 I was come a· to Jerusalem, * "
27:28 sounded a·, and found it fifteen 3825
Ro 4:25 raised a· for our justification. *1453
8:15 the spirit of bondage a· to fear; 3825
34 yea rather, that is risen a·, *1453
10: 7 bring up Christ a· from the dead.) * 321
11:23 is able to graff them in a·. 3825
35 shall be recompensed unto him a·? 467
15:10 a· he saith, Rejoice, ye Gentiles, 3825
11 a·, Praise the Lord, all ye Gentiles; "
12 And a·, Esaias saith, "
1Co 3:20 And a·, The Lord knoweth the "
7: 5 and come together a·, that Satan "
12:21 nor a· the head to the feet, I have "
15: 4 rose a· the third day according *1453
2Co 1:16 and to come a· out of Macedonia 3825
2: 1 not come a· to you in heaviness. "
3: 1 begin a· to commend ourselves? "
5:12 we commend not ourselves a· unto "
15 which died for them, and rose a·. 1453
10: 7 let him of himself think this a·, 3825
11:16 say a·, Let no man think me a fool; "
12:19 A·, think ye that we excuse * "
21 And lest, when I come a·, "
13: 2 come a·, I will not spare: 1519, 3588, "
Ga 1: 9 so say I now a·, if any man preach "
17 returned a· unto Damascus. "
2: 1 went up a· to Jerusalem "
18 For if I build a· the things which I "
4: 9 how turn ye a· to the weak "
9 ye desire a· to be in bondage? 3825, 509
19 of whom I travail in birth a· 3825
5: 1 not entangled a· with the yoke of "
3 For I testify a· to every man "
Ph'p 1:26 by my coming to you a·. "
2:28 when ye see him a·, ye may rejoice, "
4: 4 and a· I say, Rejoice. "
10 care of me hath flourished a·; * 330
16 ye sent once and a· unto my 1364
1Th 2:18 even I Paul, once and a·;
3: 9 can we render to God a· for you, 467
4:14 Jesus died and rose a·, even so 450
Tit 2: 9 in all things; not answering a·; * 483
Ph'm 12 Whom I have sent a·: thou * 375
Heb 1: 5 And a·, I will be to him a Father, 3825
6 And a·, when he bringeth in the "
2:13 And a·, I will put my trust in him. "
13 And a·, Behold I and the children "
4: 5 in this place a·, If they shall enter "
7 A·, he limiteth a certain day, "
5:12 ye have need that one teach you a· "
6: 1 not laying a· the foundation of "
6 to renew them a· unto repentance; "
10: 3 there is a remembrance a· made * 364
30 And a·, The Lord shall judge his 3825
11:35 their dead raised to life a·: * 386
13:20 that brought a· from the dead 321
Jas 5:18 he prayed a·, and the heaven gave 3825
1Pe 1: 3 which hath begotten us a· unto 313
23 Being born a·, not of corruptible "
2:23 he was reviled, reviled not a·; 486
2Pe 2:20 they are a· entangled therein, and 3825
22 dog is turned to his own vomit a·; 1994
1Jo 2: 8 A·, a new commandment I write 3825
Re 10: 8 from heaven spake unto me a·, "
11 prophesy a· before many peoples, "
19: 3 a· they said, Alleluia. *1208
20: 5 the rest of the dead lived not a· * 326

against

Ge 4: 8 Cain rose up a· Abel his brother, 413
14:15 And he divided himself a· them, 5921
15:10 laid each piece one a· another: 7125
16:12 a· every man,
12 and every man's hand a·
20: 6 withheld thee from sinning a· me:
21:16 sat her down over a· him a good 5048
16 she sat over a· him, and lifted up "
30: 2 anger was kindled a· Rachel: and
32:25 that he prevailed not a· him,
34:30 gather themselves together a· me, 5921
37:18 near unto them, they conspired a· 834
39: 9 this great wickedness, and sin a·
40: 2 Pharaoh was wroth a· two of his 5921
2 a· the chief of the butlers, and a· "
41:36 a· the seven years of famine, which

Ge 42:22 unto you, saying, Do not sin a· the
36 away: all these things are a· 5921
43:18 he may seek occasion a· us, and "
25 ready the present a· Joseph came 5704
44:18 and let not thine anger burn a·
50:20 ye thought evil a· me; but God 5921
Ex 1:10 unto our enemies, and fight a·
4:14 of the Lord was kindled a· Moses,
7:15 stand by the river's brink a· he *7125
8:12 he had brought a· Pharaoh. *
10:16 a· the Lord your God, and a· you.
11: 7 But a· any of the children of Israel
7 move his tongue, a· man or beast:
12:12 and a· all the gods of Egypt
14: 2 the sea, over a· Baal-zephon: *6440
5 of his servants was turned a· * 413
25 the Lord fighteth for them a·
27 the Egyptians fled a· it; 7125
15: 7 overthrown them that rose up a· 6965
24 the people murmured a· Moses, 5921
16: 2 Israel murmured a· Moses and "
7 heareth your murmurings a· the "
7 are we, that you murmur a· us? "
8 murmurings which ye murmur a· "
8 are not a· us, but a· the Lord. "
17: 3 the people murmured a· Moses, "
19:11 be ready a· the third day: for the
15 the people, Be ready a· the third
20:16 not bear false witness a· thy
23:29 beast of the field multiply a· thee. 5921
33 land, lest they make thee sin a·
25:27 Over a· the border shall the rings *5980
37 they may give light over a· 5676,6440
26:17 set in order one a· another: thus * 413
35 the candlestick over a· the table 5227
28:27 a· the other coupling thereof *5980
32:10 my wrath may wax hot a· them,
11 thy wrath wax hot a· thy people,
12 and repent of this evil a· thy
33 Whosoever hath sinned a· me,
37:14 Over a· the border were the rings, *5980
39:20 a· the other coupling thereof, * "
40:24 congregation, over a· the table, 5227
Le 4: 2 sin through ignorance a· any of *
2 do not to be done, and shall do a· *
13 have done somewhat a· any of *
14 which they have sinned a· it, is *5921
22 somewhat through ignorance a· *
27 a· any of the commandments *
5:19 certainly trespassed a· the Lord. *
6: 2 commit a trespass a· the Lord,
17:10 blood; I will even set my face a·
19:16 a· the blood of thy neighbour: 5921
18 nor bear any grudge a· the
20: 3 I will set my face a· that man,
5 a· that man, and a· his family,
6 even set my face a· that soul,
26:17 set my face a· you, and ye shall
40 trespass which they trespassed a·
Nu 5: 6 to do a trespass a· the Lord, and
7 give it unto him a· whom he *
12 and commit a trespass a· him,
13 and there be no witness a· her,
27 done trespass a· her husband,
8: 2 lamps shall give light over a· *4136,6440
3 therefore over a·...candlestick,* "
10: 9 to war in your land a· the enemy 5921
21 did set up the tabernacle a· they 5704
11:18 Sanctify yourselves a· to morrow,
33 Lord was kindled a· the people,
12: 1 Miriam and Aaron spake a· Moses
8 not afraid to speak a· my servant
13:31 be not able to go up a· the people; 413
14: 2 Israel murmured a· Moses and a· 5921
9 Only rebel not ye a· the Lord,
27 congregation, which murmur a· 5921
27 Israel, which they murmur a· me. "
29 upward, which have murmured a· "
35 gathered together a· me: in this "
36 congregation to murmur a· him, "
16: 3 gathered themselves together a· "
3 Moses and a· Aaron, and said "
11 company are gathered together a· "
11 what is Aaron, that ye murmur a· "
19 the congregation a· them unto "
38 these sinners a· their own souls,
41 children of Israel murmured a· 5921
41 Moses, and a· Aaron, saying, "
42 gathered a· Moses and a· Aaron, "
17: 5 whereby they murmur a· you. "
10 be kept for a token a· the rebels;
20: 2 together a· Moses and a· Aaron. 5921
18 lest I come out a· thee with the 7125
20 Edom came out a· him
24 rebelled a· my word at the water 4775
21: 1 then he fought a· Israel, and took
5 spake a· God, and a· Moses,
7 spoken a· the Lord, and a· thee;
23 out a· Israel into the wilderness: 7125
23 to Jahaz, and fought a· Israel.
26 who had fought a· the former king
33 the king of Bashan went out a· 7125
22: 5 they abide over a· me: 4136
22 in the way for an adversary a· him.
25 crushed Balaam's foot a· the wall: 413
34 thou stoodest in the way a· me: 7125
23:23 there is no enchantment a· Jacob,*
23 is there any divination a· Israel: *
24:10 And Balak's anger was kindled a· 413
25: 3 of the Lord was kindled a· Israel.
4 before the Lord a· the sun, *5048
26: 9 who strove a· Moses and a· Aaron 5921
9 when they strove a· the Lord: "
27: 3 a· the Lord in the company
14 ye rebelled a· my commandment
30: 9 bound their souls, shall stand a· 5921
Nu 31: 3 and let them go a· the Midianites, 5921
7 they warred a· the Midianites, as "
16 to commit trespass a· the Lord in
32:13 Lord's anger was kindled a· Israel,
23 ye have sinned a· the Lord: and
35:30 one witness shall not testify a·
De 1: 1 in the plain over a· the Red sea, 4136
26 rebelled a· the commandment of
41 We have sinned a· the Lord, we
43 a· the commandment of the Lord,
44 came out a· you, and chased you, 7125
2:15 the hand of the Lord was a· them,
19 over a· the children of Ammon, 4136
32 Sihon came out a· us, he and all 7125
3: 1 king of Bashan came out a· us, "
29 in the valley over a· Beth-peor. 4136
4:26 earth to witness a· you this day,
46 in the valley over a· Beth-peor, 4136
5:20 shalt thou bear false witness a·
6:15 Lord thy God be kindled a· thee,
7: 4 anger of the Lord be kindled a·
8:19 I testify a· you this day that ye
9: 7 have been rebellious a· the Lord. 5973
16 behold, ye had sinned a· the Lord
19 wherewith the Lord was wroth a· 5921
23 rebelled a· the commandment of
24 ye have been rebellious a· the Lord5973
11:17 Lord's wrath be kindled a· you,
30 in the champaign over a· Gilgal, 4136
15: 9 eye be evil a· thy poor brother,
9 and he cry unto the Lord a· thee, 5921
19:11 rise up a· him, and smite him "
15 One witness shall not rise up a·
16 a false witness rise up a· any man
16 testify a· him that which is wrong;
18 testified falsely a· his brother;
20: 1 to battle a· thine enemies, and 5921
3 approach this day unto battle a·
4 to fight for you a· your enemies, 5973
10 a city to fight a· it, then proclaim 5921
12 but will make war a· thee, then 5973
18 ye sin a· the Lord your God.
19 a long time, in making war a· it 5921
19 thereof by forcing an ax a· them: "
20 shalt build bulwarks a· the city "
21:10 forth to war a· thine enemies, "
22:14 give occasions of speech a· her, *
17 given occasions of speech a· her, *
26 a man riseth a· his neighbour, 5921
23: 4 they hired a· thee Balaam "
9 host goeth forth a· thine enemies, "
24:15 lest he cry a· thee unto the Lord, "
28: 7 enemies that rise up a· thee to "
7 shall come out a· thee one way, 413
25 shalt go out one way a· them, "
48 the Lord shall send a· thee, in
49 Lord shall bring a nation a· thee 5921
29: 7 the king of Bashan, came out a· 7125
20 jealousy shall smoke a· that man,
27 anger of the Lord was kindled a·
30:19 and earth to record this day a·
31:17 my anger shall be kindled a· them
19 a witness for me a· the children
21 this song shall testify a· them as *6440
26 may be there for a witness a· thee.
27 have been rebellious a· the Lord; 5973
28 and earth to record a· them.
32:49 of Moab that is over a· Jericho; 6440
51 Because ye trespassed a· me
33:11 the loins of them that rise a· him,
34: 1 Pisgah that is over a· Jericho. 6440
6 of Moab, over a· Beth-peor: 4136
Jos 1:18 doth rebel a· thy commandment,
3:16 passed over right a· Jericho. 5048
5:13 stood a man over a· him with his "
7: 1 anger of the Lord was kindled a·
13 Sanctify yourselves a· to morrow:
20 I have sinned a· the Lord God
8: 3 the people of war, to go up a· Ai: *
4 ye shall lie in wait a· the city, even
5 when they come out a· us, 7125
14 men of the city went out a· Israel "
14 that there were liers in ambush a·
22 issued out of the city a· them; 7125
33 over a·...Gerizim,...over a·...Ebal; *4136
9: 1 over a· Lebanon, * "
18 the congregation murmured a· 5921
10: 5 before Gibeon, and made war a· it. "
6 are gathered together a· us. 413
21 none moved his tongue a· any of
25 to all your enemies a· whom ye
29 him, unto Libnah, and fought a· 5973
31, 34 encamped a· it, and fought 5921
31, 34 encamped...and fought a· it;
36 unto Hebron; and they fought a· 5921
38 him, to Debir; and fought a· it: "
11: 5 of Merom, to fight a· Israel. *5973
7 people of war with him, a· them "
20 should come a· Israel in battle, 7125
18:17 a· the going up of Adummim, 5227
18 over a· Arabah northward, 4136
19:47 Dan went up to fight a· Leshem, 5973
22:11 over a· the land of Canaan, *4136
12 at Shiloh, to go up to war a· them.5921
16 committed a· the God of Israel,
16 might rebel this day a· the Lord?
18 seeing ye rebel to day a· the Lord,
19 not a· the Lord, nor rebel a· us,
22 or if in transgression a· the Lord,
29 God forbid that we should rebel a·
31 this trespass a· the Lord:
33 intend to go up a· them in battle, 5921
23:16 anger of the Lord be kindled a·
24: 9 Moab, arose and warred a· Israel,
11 the men of Jericho fought a· you,
22 Ye are witnesses a· yourselves
J'g 1: 1 a· the Canaanites first, to fight a·
3 we may fight a· the Canaanites;
5 in Bezek: and they fought a· him,
8 Judah had fought a· Jerusalem,
9 down to fight a· the Canaanites,
10 And Judah went a· the Canaanites 413
11 thence he went a· the inhabitants "
22 they also went up a· Beth-el:
2:14 anger of the Lord was hot a· Israel,
15 the hand of the Lord was a· them
20 anger of the Lord was hot a· Israel;
3: 8 anger of the Lord was hot a· Israel,
10 prevailed a· Chushan-rishathaim. 5921
12 Eglon the king of Moab a· Israel, "
4:24 and prevailed a· Jabin the king "
5:14 there a root of them a· Amalek; *
20 in their courses fought a· Sisera. 5973
23 to the help of the Lord a· the
6: 2 the hand of Midian prevailed a· 5921
3 east, even they came up a· them; "
4 And they encamped a· them, and "
31 Joash said unto all that stood a· "
32 Let Baal plead a· him, because he
39 Let not thine anger be hot a· me,
7: 2 Israel vaunt themselves a· me, 5921
22 the Lord set every man's sword a·
24 Come down a· the Midianites, 7125
9:18 risen up a· my father's house 5921
31 behold, they fortify the city a·
33 people that is with him come out a· 413
34 they laid wait a· Shechem in four 5921
43 he rose up a· them, and smote "
45 Abimelech fought a· the city all
50 encamped a· Thebez, and took it. 413
52 unto the tower, and fought a· it,
10: 7 anger of the Lord was hot a· Israel,
9 passed over Jordan to fight also a·
9 and a· Benjamin, and a· the house
10 Lord, saying, We have sinned a·
18 will begin to fight a· the children
11: 4 children of Ammon made war a· 5973
5 of Ammon made war a· Israel, "
8 fight a· the children of Ammon, *
9 again to fight a· the children *
12 come a· me to fight in my land? * 413
20 pitched in Jahaz, and fought a· 5973
25 a· Israel, or did he ever fight a·
27 I have not sinned a· thee,
27 thou doest me wrong to war a· me:
32 children of Ammon to fight a· them;
12: 3 over a· the children of Ammon, 413
3 unto me this day, to fight a· me?
14: 4 that he sought an occasion a· the
5 a young lion roared a· him. 7125
15:10 Why are ye come up a· us? And 5921
14 the Philistines shouted a· him: *7125
16: 5 what means we may prevail a·
18: 9 Arise, that we may go up a· them: 5921
19: 2 a· him, and went away from him
10 a· Jebus, which is Jerusalem; 5227
20: 5 the men of Gibeah rose a· me, 5921
9 Gibeah; we will go up by lot a· it; "
11 Israel were gathered a· the city, 413
14 to battle a· the children of Israel. 5973
18 shall go up first to the battle a·
19 in the morning, and encamped a· 5921
20 went out to battle a· Benjamin; 5973
20 array to fight a· them at Gibeah.
23 battle a· the children of Benjamin 5973
23 And the Lord said, Go up a· him.) 413
24 Israel came near a· the children "
25 Benjamin went forth a· them 7125
28 I yet again go out to battle a· 5973
30 Israel went up a· the children of 413
30 put themselves in array a· Gibeah, "
31 Benjamin went out a· the people 7125
34 came a· Gibeah ten thousand 5048
43 a· Gibeah toward the sunrising. 5227
Ru 1:13 hand of the Lord is gone out a· me.
21 the Lord hath testified a· me,
1Sa 2:25 If one man sin a· another, the
25 but if a man sin a· the Lord, who
3:12 In that day I will perform a· Eli 413
4: 1 Israel went out a· the Philistines 7125
2 put themselves in array a· Israel: "
7: 6 We have sinned a· the Lord.
7 the Philistines went up a· Israel. 413
10 Philistines drew near to battle a·
13 the hand of the Lord was a· the
9:14 Samuel came out a· them, †7125
11: 1 came up, and encamped a· 5921
12: 3 witness a· me before the Lord,
5 The Lord is witness a· you, and
9 and they fought a· them.
12 of the children of Ammon came a 5921
14 not rebel a· the commandment
15 but rebel a· the commandment
15 the hand of the Lord be a· you,
15 as it was a· your fathers.
23 that I should sin a· the Lord in
14: 5 northward over a· Michmash, *4136
5 southward over a· Gibeah. "
20 every man's sword was a· his
33 Behold, the people sin a· the Lord,
34 sin not a· the Lord in eating with
47 and fought a· all his enemies on
47 a· Moab, and a· the children of
47 a· Edom, and a· the kings of Zobah,
47 and a· the Philistines:
52 war a· the Philistines all the days 5921
15: 7 Shur, that is over a· Egypt. *6440
18 the Amalekites, and fight a· them
17: 2 battle in array a· the Philistines. 7125
9 if I prevail a· him, and kill him,
21 army a· army. 7125
28 Eliab's anger was kindled a· David,

1Sa 17:33 not able to go a· this Philistine 413
35 when he arose a· me, I caught him 5921
55 Saul saw David go forth a· the 7125
18:21 of the Philistines may be a· him.
19: 4 the king sin a· his servant, a· David;
4 because he hath not sinned a· thee,
5 wilt thou sin a· innocent blood,
20:30 Then Saul's anger was kindled a·
22: 8 all of you have conspired a· me, 5921
8 son hath stirred up my servant a· "
13 Why have ye conspired a· me, "
13 that he should rise up a· me, to 413
23: 1 the Philistines fight a· Keilah,
3 come to Keilah a· the armies of 413
9 secretly practised mischief a· 5921
28 pursuing after David, and went a· 7125
24: 6 to stretch forth mine hand a· him,
7 suffered them not to rise a· Saul. 413
10 not put forth mine hand a· my
11 I have not sinned a· thee; yet thou
25:17 evil is determined a· our master, 413
17 and a· all his household: for he is 5921
20 his men came down a· her; 7125
22, 34 light any that pisseth a· *
26: 9 stretch forth his hand a· the Lord's
11 I should stretch forth mine hand a·
19 Lord have stirred thee up a· me,
23 not stretch forth mine hand a· the
27:10 David said, A· the south of Judah,5921
10 a· the south of the Jerahmeelites, "
10 and a· the south of the Kenites. 413
28:15 the Philistines make war a· me,
29: 8 I may not go fight a· the enemies
30:23 delivered...company that came a· 5921
31: 1 the Philistines fought a· Israel:
3 And the battle went sore a· Saul, 413
2Sa 1:16 thy mouth hath testified a· thee,
3: 8 Am I a dog's head, which a· Judah *
5:23 come upon them over a· the 4136
6: 7 the Lord was kindled a· Uzzah;
8:10 he had fought a· Hadadezer,
10: 9 the front of the battle was a· him 413
9 put them in array a· the Syrians: 7125
10 in array a· the children of Ammon. "
13 unto the battle a· the Syrians:
17 set themselves in array a· David, 7125
11:23 Surely the men prevailed a· us, 5921
25 make thy battle more strong a· 413
12: 5 anger was greatly kindled a·
11 I will raise up evil a· thee out of 5921
13 I have sinned a· the Lord. And
26 Joab fought a· Rabbah of the
27 I have fought a· Rabbah, and have
28 encamp a· the city, and take it: 5921
29 and fought a· it, and took it.
14: 7 family is risen a· thine handmaid, 5921
13 thought such a thing a· the people "
16:13 on the hill's side over a· him, 5980
17:21 Ahithophel counselled a· you. 5921
18: 6 people went out into the field a· 7125
12 I not put forth mine hand a· the 413
13 should have wrought falsehood a·
13 wouldest have set thyself a· *5048
28 lifted up their hand a· my lord
31 this day of all them that rose up a· 5921
32 all that rise a· thee to do thee hurt, "
20:15 they cast up a bank a· the city, 413
21 hath lifted up his hand a· the king,
21: 5 and that devised a· us that we
15 and fought a· the Philistines: and
22:40 rose up a· me hast thou subdued
49 also... above them that rose up a·
23: 8 lift up his spear a· eight hundred, 5921
18 up his spear a· three hundred, "
24: 1 anger of the Lord was kindled a·
1 he moved David a· them to say,
4 the king's word prevailed a· Joab, 413
4 and a· the captains of the host. 5921
17 thine hand, I pray thee, be a· me,
17 and a· my father's house.
1Ki 2:23 have not spoken this word a· his
6: 5 a· the wall of the house he built 5921
5 a· the walls of the house round
10 And then he built chambers a· all 5921
7: 4 light was a· light in three ranks. * 413
5 light was a· light in three 4136,
20 over a· the belly which was by *5980
39 eastward over a· the south. *4136
8:31 any man trespass a· his neighbour,
33 because they have sinned a· thee,
35 rain, because they have sinned a·
44 go out to battle a· their enemy, 5921
46 If they sin a· thee, (for there is no
50 people that have sinned a· thee,
50 they have transgressed a· thee,
11:26, 27 he lifted up his hand a· the king.
12:19 So Israel rebelled a· the house of
21 to fight a· the house of Israel, to 5973
24 nor fight a· your brethren the
13: 2 And he cried a· the altar in the 5921
4 of God, which had cried a· the "
4 hand, which he put forth a· him, "
32 cried by the word of the Lord a· "
32 and a· all the houses of the high *
14:10 Jeroboam him that pisseth a· *
25 of Egypt came up a· Jerusalem: 5921
15:17 king of Israel went up a· Judah, "
20 of the hosts which he had a· "
27 of Issachar, conspired a· him; "
16: 1 Jehu the son of Hanani a· Baasha, "
7 the word of the Lord a· Baasha, 413
7 and a· his house, even for all "
9 his chariots, conspired a· him, 5921
11 a· a wall, neither of his kinsfolks, *
12 which he spake a· Baasha by Jehu 413
15 were encamped a· Gibbethon, 5921
1Ki 16:22 prevailed a· the people that
20: 1 besieged Samaria, and warred a·
12 themselves in array a· the city. 5921
22 king of Syria will come up a· thee. "
23 let us fight a· them in the plain,
25 we will fight a· them in the plain,
26 up to Aphek, to fight a· Israel. 5973
27 all present, and went a· them: 7125
29 they pitched one over a· the other 5227
21:10 before him, to bear witness a· him,
13 men of Belial witnessed a· him,
13 even a· Naboth, in the presence
21 off from Ahab him that pisseth a· *
22: 6 I go a· Ramoth-gilead to battle, 5921
15 shall we go a· Ramoth-gilead * 413
32 they turned aside to fight a· him: 5921
35 stayed up in his chariot a· the 5227
2Ki 1: 1 Then Moab rebelled a· Israel
3: 5 king of Moab rebelled a· the king
7 king of Moab hath rebelled a· me:
7 wilt thou go with me a· Moab 413
21 the kings were come up to fight a·
27 was great indignation a· Israel: 5921
5: 7 how he seeketh a quarrel a· me.
6: 8 king of Syria warred a· Israel,
7: 6 king of Israel hath hired a· us 5921
8:28 the war a· Hazael king of Syria 5973
29 Ramah, when he fought a· Hazael
9: 8 from Ahab him that pisseth a· *
14 son of Nimshi conspired a· Joram. 413
21 they went out a· Jehu, and met *7125
10: 9 I conspired a· my master, and 5921
12:17 went up, and fought a· Gath, and "
13: 3 anger of the Lord was kindled a·
12 his might wherewith he fought a· 5973
14:19 they made a conspiracy a· him 5921
15:10 the son of Jabesh conspired a· "
19 Pul the king of Assyria came a· "
25 conspired a· him, and smote him "
30 son of Elah made a conspiracy a· "
37 the Lord began to send a· Judah
16: 7 king of Israel, which rise up a· 5921
9 of Assyria went up a· Damascus 413
11 made it a· king Ahaz came from 5704
17: 3 A· him came up Shalmaneser 5921
7 children of Israel had sinned a·
9 things that were not right a· 5921
13 testified a· Israel, and a· Judah, *
15 which he testified a· them; and *
18: 7 rebelled a· the king of Assyria,
9 of Assyria came up a· Samaria, 5921
13 come up a· all the fenced cities "
17 with a great host a· Jerusalem. *
20 trust, that thou rebellest a· me?
25 come up without the Lord a· this 5921
25 Go up a· this land, and destroy it. "
19: 8 of Assyria warring a· Libnah: "
9 he is come out to fight a· thee: "
20 a· Sennacherib king of Assyria I 413
22 and a· whom hast thou exalted 5921
22 even a· the Holy One of Israel. "
27 coming in, and thy rage a· me. * 413
28 thy rage a· me and thy tumult * "
32 with shield, nor cast a bank a· 5921
21:23 servants of Amon conspired a· "
24 that had conspired a· king Amon; "
22:13 wrath of the Lord that is kindled a·
17 my wrath shall be kindled a· this
19 what I spake a· this place, 5921
19 and a· the inhabitants thereof, "
23:17 hast done a· the altar of Beth-el. "
26 his anger was kindled a· Judah,
29 went up a· the king of Assyria 5921
29 the king Josiah went a· him; 7125
24: 1 he turned and rebelled a· him.
2 sent a· him bands of the Chaldees,
2 sent them a· Judah to destroy it,
10 king of Babylon came a· *
11 came a· the city, and his servants *5921
20 Zedekiah rebelled a· the king of
25: 1 and all his host, a· Jerusalem, 5921
1 a· it; and they built forts a· it "
4 the Chaldees were a· the city "
1Ch 5:11 children of Gad dwelt over a· 5048
20 And they were helped a· them, 5921
25 transgressed a· the God of their
8:32 in Jerusalem, over a· them. 5048
9:38 brethren at Jerusalem, over a· "
10: 1 the Philistines fought a· Israel; 5921
3 And the battle went sore a· Saul, "
13 which he committed a· the Lord,
13 even a· the word of the Lord, *5921
11:11 up his spear a· three hundred "
20 up his spear a· three hundred, "
12:19 came with the Philistines a· Saul "
21 they helped David a· the band "
13:10 anger of the Lord was kindled a·
14: 8 heard of it, and went out a· them. 6640
10 Shall I go up a· the Philistines? 5921
14 them over a· the mulberry trees. 4136
18:10 he had fought a· Hadarezer,
19:10 the battle was set a· him before 413
10 put them in array a· the Syrians. 7125
11 set themselves in array a· the "
17 set the battle in array a· them. 413
17 the battle in array a· the Syrians, 7125
21: 1 And Satan stood up a· Israel, 5921
4 the king's word prevailed a· Joab. "
24:31 cast lots over a· their brethren *5980
31 over a· their younger brethren. * "
25: 8 they cast lots, ward a· ward, * "
26:12 having wards one a· another, * "
16 ward a· ward.
27:24 there fell wrath for it a· Israel; *5921
2Ch 4:10 east end, over a· the south. *4136
6:22 if a man sin a· his neighbour, and
2Ch 6:24 because they have sinned a· thee;
26 rain, because they have sinned a·
34 go out to war a· their enemies 5921
36 If they sin a· thee, (for there is no
39 people which have sinned a· thee.
8: 3 Hamath-zobah, and prevailed a· 5921
9:29 of Iddo the seer a· Jeroboam * "
10:19 Israel rebelled a· the house of
11: 1 were warriors, to fight a· Israel, 5973
4 shall not go up, nor fight a· your
4 returned from going a· Jeroboam. 413
12: 2 Shishak king of Egypt came up a· 5921
2 they had transgressed a· the Lord,
9 Shishak king of Egypt came up a· 5921
13: 3 also set the battle in array a· him 5973
6 up, and hath rebelled a· his lord. 5921
7 have strengthened themselves a· "
12 sounding trumpets to cry alarm a· "
12 fight ye not a· the Lord God 5973
14: 9 there came out a· them Zerah 413
10 Then Asa went out a· him, *6440
11 thy name we go a· this multitude. 5921
11 God; let not man prevail a· thee. 5973
16: 1 king of Israel came up a· Judah, 5921
4 captains of his armies a· the cities 413
17: 1 strengthened himself a· Israel. 5921
10 made no war a· Jehoshaphat. 5973
18:22 Lord hath spoken evil a· thee. *5921
34 up in his chariot a· the Syrians 5227
19:10 they trespass not a· the Lord, *
20: 1 came a· Jehoshaphat to battle. 5921
2 cometh a great multitude a· thee "
12 we have no might a· this great 6440
12 company that cometh a· us; 5921
16 To morrow go ye down a· them: "
17 to morrow go out a· them: 6440
22 ambushments a· the children of *5921
22 Seir, which were come a· Judah; "
23 a· the inhabitants of mount Seir, 5921
29 the Lord fought a· the enemies 5973
37 prophesied a· Jehoshaphat, 5921
21:16 the Lord stirred up a· Jehoram "
22: 5 king of Israel to war a· Hazael "
7 went out with Jehoram a· Jehu 413
24:19 the Lord; and they testified a·
21 conspired a· him, and stoned him 5921
23 the host of Syria came up a· him: "
24 executed judgment a· Joash. *
25 own servants conspired a· him 5921
26 are they that conspired a· him; "
25:10 anger was greatly kindled a·
15 anger of the Lord was kindled a·
27 they made a conspiracy a· him 5921
26: 6 and warred a· the Philistines,
7 God helped him a· the Philistines, 5921
7 and a· the Arabians that dwelt "
13 to help the king a· the enemy. "
16 transgressed a· the Lord his God,
27: 5 the Ammonites, and prevailed a· 5921
28:10 you, sins a· the Lord your God?
12 stood up a· them that came from 5921
13 we have offended a· the Lord
13 great, and there is fierce wrath a· 5921
19 and transgressed sore a· the Lord.
22 trespass yet more a· the Lord:
30: 7 trespassed a· the Lord God of
32: 1 into Judah, and encamped a· the 5921
2 purposed to fight a· Jerusalem, "
9 he himself laid siege a· Lachish, * "
16 his servants spake yet more a· the "
16 God, and a· his servant Hezekiah. "
17 Lord God of Israel, and to speak a· "
19 a· the God of Jerusalem, * 413
19 as a· the gods of the people *5921
33:24 And his servants conspired a· him, "
25 that had conspired a· king Amon; "
34:27 when thou heardest his words a· "
27 and a· the inhabitants thereof, "
35:20 king of Egypt came up to fight a·
20 and Josiah went out a· him. 7125
21 I come not a· thee this day, but 5921
21 a· the house wherewith I have 413
36: 6 A· him came up Nebuchadnezzar 5921
13 rebelled a· king Nebuchadnezzar,
16 the wrath of the Lord arose a· his
Ezr 4: 5 And hired counsellors a· them, 5921
6 a· the inhabitants of Judah "
8 wrote a letter a· Jerusalem unto 5922
19 made insurrection a· kings, "
7:23 should there be wrath a· the realm "
8:22 help us a· the enemy in the way:
22 wrath is a· all them that forsake 5921
10: 2 We have trespassed a· our God,
Ne 1: 6 which we have sinned a· thee:
7 have dealt very corruptly a· thee,
2:19 will ye rebel a· the king? 5921
3:10 even over a· his house. 5048
16 over a· the sepulchres of David, "
19 a· the going up to the armoury "
23 Benjamin and Hashub over a· "
25 over a· the turning of the wall, "
26 a· the water gate toward the east, "
27 over a· the great tower that lieth "
28 every one over a· his house. "
29 Zadok the son of Immer over a· "
31 over a· the gate Miphkad, "
4: 8 fight a· Jerusalem, and to hinder it.
9 a watch a· them day and night, 5921
5: 1 wives a· their brethren the Jews. 413
7 I set a great assembly a· them. 5921
6:12 pronounced this prophecy a· me: "
7: 3 every one to be over a· his house. 5048
9:10 that they dealt proudly a· 5921
26 disobedient, and rebelled a· thee,
26 prophets which testified a· them
29 And testifiedst a· them, that thou

Ne 9:29 commandments, but sinned *a·* thy
30 testifiedst *a·* them by thy spirit in
34 wherewith thou didst testify *a·* "
12: 9 were over *a·* them in the watches. 5048
24 brethren over *a·* them, to praise "
24 ward over *a·* ward. 5980
37 fountain gate, which was over *a·* *5048
38 that gave thanks went over *a·* *4136
13: 2 but hired Balaam *a·* them, that 5921
15 sabbath day: and I testified *a·*
21 Then I testified *a·* them, and said
27 transgress *a·* our God in marrying
Es 2: 1 and what was decreed *a·* her. 5921
3:14 they should be ready *a·* that day.
5: 1 over *a·* the king's house: 5227
1 over *a·* the gate of the house.
9 full of indignation *a·* Mordecai. 5921
6:13 thou shalt not prevail *a·* him, but
7: 7 determined *a·* him by the king. 413
8: 3 that he had devised *a·* the Jews. 5921
13 Jews should be ready *a·* that day
9:24 devised *a·* the Jews to destroy 5921
25 which he devised *a·* the Jews, "
Job 2: 3 although thou movedst me *a·* him,
6: 4 do set themselves in array *a·* me.
7:20 why hast thou set me as a mark *a·* *
8: 4 If thy children have sinned *a·* him,
9: 4 hath hardened himself *a·* him, 413
10:17 renewest thy witnesses *a·* me, 5048
17 changes and war are *a·* me. *5973
11: 5 speak, and open his lips *a·* thee; "
13:26 thou writest bitter things *a·* me, 5921
14:20 Thou prevailest for ever *a·* him,
15: 6 yea, thine own lips testify *a·* thee.
13 that thou turnest thy spirit *a·* God, 413
24 they shall prevail *a·* him, as a king
25 he stretcheth out his hand *a·* God, 413
25 strengtheneth himself *a·* the "
16: 4 I could heap up words *a·* you, and 5921
8 wrinkles, which is a witness *a·* me:
10 gathered themselves together *a·* 5921
17: 8 innocent shall stir up himself *a·* "
18: 9 the robber shall prevail *a·* him. * "
19: 5 ye will magnify yourselves *a·* "
5 and plead *a·* me my reproach: "
11 hath also kindled his wrath *a·* me, "
12 and raise up their way *a·* me, and "
18 I arose, and they spake *a·* me.
19 they whom I loved are turned *a·* me.
20:27 and the earth shall rise up *a·* him.
21:27 ye wrongfully imagine *a·* me. 5921
23: 6 *a·* me with his great power? *5978
24:13 They are of those that rebel *a·* the
27: 7 riseth up *a·* me as the unrighteous.
30:12 they raise up *a·* me the ways of 5921
21 thou opposest thyself *a·* me. *
31:21 up my hand *a·* the fatherless, 5921
38 If my land cry *a·* me, or that the "
32: 2 *a·* Job was his wrath kindled,
3 Also *a·* his three friends was his
14 hath not directed his words *a·* me: 413
33:10 he findeth occasions *a·* me, 5921
13 Why dost thou strive *a·* him? 413
34: 6 Should I lie *a·* my right? my *5921
29 done *a·* a nation, or *a·* a man only: * "
37 and multiplieth his words *a·* God.
35: 6 sinnest, what doest thou *a·* him?
38:23 reserved *a·* the time of trouble,
23 *a·* the day of battle and war?
39:16 She is hardened *a·* her young ‡
23 The quiver rattleth *a·* him, the 5921
42: 7 My wrath is kindled *a·* thee, and *a·*
Ps 2: 2 counsel together, *a·* the Lord, 5921
2 and *a·* his anointed, saying, "
3: 6 have set themselves *a·* me round "
5:10 for they have rebelled *a·* thee.
7:13 he ordaineth his arrows *a·* the *
10: 8 his eyes are privily set *a·* the poor.
13: 4 say, I have prevailed *a·* him;
15: 3 up a reproach *a·* his neighbour. 5921
5 taketh reward *a·* the innocent. "
17: 7 from those that rise up *a·* them.
18:39 under me those that rose up *a·* me.
48 rise up *a·* me: thou hast delivered
21:11 For they intended evil *a·* thee: 5921
12 thine arrows upon thy strings *a·* "
27: 3 host should encamp *a·* me, my "
3 though war should rise *a·* me, in "
12 false witnesses are risen up *a·* me,
31:13 they took counsel together *a·* me, 5921
18 proudly and contemptuously *a·*
34:16 the Lord is *a·* them that do evil,
35: 1 fight *a·* them that fight *a·* me.
3 way *a·* them that persecute me: 7125
15 gathered themselves together *a·* 5921
20 devise deceitful matters *a·* them "
21 mouth wide *a·* me, and said, Aha, "
26 that magnify themselves *a·* me.
36:11 Let not the foot of pride come *a·*
37: 1 envious *a·* the workers of iniquity.
12 The wicked plotteth *a·* the just,
38:16 they magnify themselves *a·* 5921
41: 4 my soul; for I have sinned *a·* thee.
7 hate me whisper together *a·* me: 5921
7 *a·* me do they devise my hurt. "
9 bread, hath lifted up his heel *a·* me. "
43: 1 plead my cause *a·* an ungodly
44: 5 tread them under that rise up *a·*
50: 7 O Israel, and I will testify *a·* thee: *
20 Thou sittest and speakest *a·* thy
51: 4 *A·* thee, thee only, have I sinned,
53: 5 the bones of him that encampeth *a·*
54: 3 strangers are risen up *a·* me, 5921
55:12 that did magnify himself *a·* me; "
18 peace from the battle that was *a·*
20 his hands *a·* such as be at peace

Ps 56: 2 for they be many that fight *a·* me,
5 their thoughts are *a·* me for evil. 5921
59: 1 me from them that rise up *a·* me.
3 the mighty are gathered *a·* me; 5921
62: 3 ye imagine mischief *a·* a man? * "
65: 3 Iniquities prevail *a·* me: as for
69:12 that sit in the gate speak *a·* me; *
71:10 mine enemies speak *a·* me; *
73: 9 set their mouth *a·* the heavens, *
15 I should offend *a·* the generation *
74: 1 smoke *a·* the sheep of thy pasture?
23 tumult of those that rise up *a·*
78:17 *a·* him by provoking the most High
19 Yea, they spake *a·* God; and said,
21 so a fire was kindled *a·* Jacob,
21 and anger also came up *a·* Israel;
79: 8 O remember not *a·* us former
80: 4 be angry *a·* the prayer of thy
81:14 my hand *a·* their adversaries. 5921
83: 3 have taken crafty counsel *a·* thy "
3 consulted *a·* thy hidden ones. "
5 they are confederate *a·* thee: "
86:14 O God, the proud are risen *a·* me, "
91:12 lest thou dash thy foot *a·* a stone.
92:11 the wicked that rise up *a·* me. 5921
94:16 rise up for me *a·* the evildoers? 5973
16 or who will stand up for me *a·* the "
21 *a·* the soul of the righteous, 5921
102: 8 are mad *a·* me are sworn *a·* me *
105:28 and they rebelled not *a·* his word.
106:26 he lifted up his hand *a·* them, *
40 the Lord kindled *a·* his people,
107:11 they rebelled *a·* the words of God,
109: 2 the deceitful are opened *a·* me: *5921
2 *a·* me with a lying tongue. *
3 and fought *a·* me without a cause.
20 them that speak evil *a·* my soul. 5921
119:11 heart, that I might not sin *a·* thee.
23 also did sit and speak *a·* me:
69 proud have forged a lie *a·* me: 5921
124: 2 our side, when men rose up *a·* us:
3 when their wrath was kindled *a·* us:
129: 2 yet they have not prevailed *a·* me.
137: 9 thy little ones *a·* the stones. 413
138: 7 stretch forth thine hand *a·* the 5921
139:20 they speak *a·* thee wickedly,
21 I grieved with those that rise up *a·*
Pr 3:29 Devise not evil *a·* thy neighbour, 5921
8:36 sinneth *a·* me wrongeth his own
14:35 his wrath is *a·* him that causeth
17:11 messenger shall be sent *a·* him.
19: 3 his heart fretteth *a·* the Lord. 5921
20: 2 to anger sinneth *a·* his own soul.
21:30 nor understanding nor counsel *a·* 5048
31 the horse is prepared *a·* the day
24: 1 Be not thou envious *a·* evil men,
15 *a·* the dwelling of the righteous;
28 Be not a witness *a·* thy neighbour
25:18 false witness *a·* his neighbour
Ec 4:12 And if one prevail *a·* him, two
7:14 God also hath set the one over *a·* *5980
8:11 sentence *a·* an evil work is not
9:14 great king *a·* it, and besieged it, 413
14 and built great bulwarks *a·* it: 5921
10: 4 spirit of the ruler rise up *a·* thee, "
Isa 1: 2 and they have rebelled *a·* me.
2: 4 nation shall not lift up sword *a·* 413
3: 5 shall behave himself proudly *a·*
5 and the base *a·* the honourable.
8 and their doings are *a·* the Lord, 413
9 countenance doth witness *a·* them;
5:25 the Lord kindled *a·* his people,
25 stretched forth his hand *a·* them, 5921
30 roar *a·* them like the roaring of "
7: 1 toward Jerusalem to war *a·* it, "
1 but could not prevail *a·* it. "
5 have taken evil counsel *a·* "
6 Let us go up *a·* Judah, and vex it,
9:11 the adversaries of Rezin *a·* him, 5921
21 they together shall be *a·* Judah. "
10: 6 send him *a·* an hypocritical nation,
6 and *a·* the people of my wrath 5921
15 Shall the ax boast itself *a·* him "
15 shall the saw magnify itself *a·* "
15 if the rod should shake itself *a·* *
24 and shall lift up his staff *a·* thee, 5921
32 shake his hand *a·* the mount of *
13:17 I will stir up the Medes *a·* them, 5921
14: 4 proverb *a·* the king of Babylon, "
8 no feller is come up *a·* us. "
22 For I will rise up *a·* them, "
19: 2 I will set the Egyptians *a·* the
2 fight every one *a·* his brother,
2 every one *a·* his neighbour; city *a·*
2 city, and kingdom *a·* kingdom.
17 which he hath determined *a·* it. 5921
20: 1 fought *a·* Ashdod, and took it;
23: 8 hath taken this counsel *a·* Tyre, 5921
11 *a·* the merchant city, to destroy * 413
25: 4 terrible ones is as a storm *a·* the
27: 4 set the briers and thorns *a·* me in
29: 3 I will camp *a·* thee round about, 5921
3 lay siege *a·* thee with a mount, "
3 and I will raise forts *a·* thee. "
7 of all the nations that fight *a·* "
7 fight *a·* her and her munition,
8 be, that fight *a·* mount Zion. 5921
31: 2 arise *a·* the house of the evildoers, "
2 and *a·* the help of them that work "
4 shepherds is called forth *a·* him, "
32: 6 and to utter error *a·* the Lord, to 413
36: 1 *a·* all the defenced cities of Judah, 5921
5 trust, that thou rebellest *a·* me?
10 Lord *a·* this land to destroy it? 5921
10 Go up *a·* this land, and destroy it. 413
37: 8 king of Assyria warring *a·* Libnah: 5921

Isa 37:21 *a·* Sennacherib king of Assyria: 413
23 *a·* whom hast thou exalted thy 5921
23 even *a·* the Holy One of Israel. 413
28 thy coming in, and thy rage *a·* me. "
29 Because thy rage *a·* me, and thy "
33 with shields, nor cast a bank *a·* it. 5921
41:11 incensed *a·* thee shall be ashamed
12 war *a·* thee shall be as nothing,
42:13 he shall prevail *a·* his enemies. 5921
24 Lord, he *a·* whom we have sinned?
43:27 teachers have transgressed *a·* me.
45:24 incensed *a·* him shall be ashamed.
54:15 *a·* thee shall fall for thy sake. 5921
17 is formed *a·* thee shall prosper; "
17 every tongue that shall rise *a·* thee
57: 4 *A·* whom do ye sport yourselves? 5921
4 *a·* whom make ye a wide mouth, "
59:12 and our sins testify *a·* us: for
13 and lying *a·* the Lord, *
19 shall lift up a standard *a·* him. *
63:10 enemy, and he fought *a·* them.
66:24 transgressed *a·* me: for their
Jer 1:15 and *a·* all the walls thereof round 5921
15 and *a·* all the cities of Judah. "
16 my judgments *a·* them touching "
18 brasen walls *a·* the whole land, "
18 *a·* the kings of Judah,
18 *a·* the princes
18 *a·* the priests thereof, and *a·* the
19 And they shall fight *a·* thee; but 413
19 not prevail *a·* thee; for I am with
2: 8 pastors also transgressed *a·* me,
29 ye all have transgressed *a·* me,
3:13 thou hast transgressed *a·* the Lord
25 have sinned *a·* the Lord our God,
4:12 also will I give sentence *a·* them.
16 *a·* Jerusalem, that watchers come 5921
16 their voice *a·* the cities of Judah. "
17 field, are they *a·* her round about; "
17 she hath been rebellious *a·* me,
5:11 dealt very treacherously *a·* me,
6: 3 pitch their tents *a·* her 5921
4 Prepare ye war *a·* her; arise, "
6 and cast a mount *a·* Jerusalem: "
23 set in array as men for war *a·* thee. "
8:14 drink, because we have sinned *a·*
18 I would comfort myself *a·* sorrow,
11:17 hath pronounced evil *a·* thee, 5921
17 they have done *a·* themselves *
19 they had devised devices *a·* me, 5921
12: 8 it crieth out *a·* me: therefore "
9 the birds round about are *a·* her; "
14 Lord *a·* all mine evil neighbours, "
13:14 I will dash them one *a·* another, 413
14: 7 though our iniquities testify *a·* us,
7 are many; we have sinned *a·* thee.
20 for we have sinned *a·* thee.
15: 6 will I stretch out my hand *a·* thee, 5921
8 brought upon them *a·* the mother "
20 and they shall fight *a·* thee, 413
20 they shall not prevail *a·* thee:
16:10 pronounced all this great evil *a·* 5921
10 committed *a·* the Lord our God?
18: 8 If that nation, *a·* whom I have *5921
11 *a·* you, and devise a device *a·* you: "
18 let us devise devices *a·* Jeremiah; "
23 all their counsel *a·* me to slay me: "
19:15 evil that I have pronounced *a·* it, "
20:10 and we shall prevail *a·* him,
21: 2 king of Babylon maketh war *a·* 5921
4 fight *a·* the king of Babylon, and *a·*
5 myself will fight *a·* you with an
10 I have set my face *a·* this city for *
13 I am *a·* thee, O inhabitant of the 413
13 Who shall come down *a·* us? or 5921
22: 7 I will prepare destroyers *a·* thee, "
23: 2 saith the Lord God of Israel *a·* the "
30 *a·* the prophets, saith the Lord. "
31 Behold, I am *a·* the prophets, saith "
32 *a·* them that prophesy false "
25: 9 my servant, and will bring them *a·* "
9 and *a·* the inhabitants thereof, "
9 *a·* all these nations round about, "
13 which I have pronounced *a·* it, "
13 Jeremiah hath prophesied *a·* all "
30 prophesy thou *a·* them all these 413
30 *a·* all the inhabitants of the earth. "
26: 9 were gathered *a·* Jeremiah * "
11 to die; for he hath prophesied *a·* "
12 sent me to prophesy *a·* this house "
12 and *a·* this city all the words that "
13 that he hath pronounced *a·* you. 5921
19 he had pronounced *a·* them? "
19 we procure great evil *a·* our souls. "
20 *a·* this city and *a·* this land "
27:13 Lord hath spoken *a·* the nation * 413
28: 8 *a·* many countries,
8 and *a·* great kingdoms, 5921
16 hast taught rebellion *a·* the Lord. 413
29:32 taught rebellion *a·* the Lord. 5921
31:20 since I spake *a·* him, I do
39 over *a·* it upon the hill Gareb, *5048
32:24 of the Chaldeans, that fight *a·* it, 5921
29 Chaldeans, that fight *a·* this city,
33: 8 whereby they have sinned *a·* me;
8 they have transgressed *a·* me.
34: 1, 7 fought *a·* Jerusalem, and *a·* all 5921
7 *a·* Lachish, and *a·* Azekah: for 413
22 they shall fight *a·* it, and take it, 5921
35:17 that I have pronounced *a·* them: "
36: 2 have spoken unto thee *a·* Israel, "
2 *a·* Judah, and *a·* all the nations, "
7 the Lord hath pronounced *a·* this 413
31 that I have pronounced *a·* them; "
37: 8 come again, and fight *a·* this 5921
10 of the Chaldeans that fight *a·* you,

Jer 37:18 have I offended a' thee, or a' thy
18 or a' this people, that ye have put
19 Babylon shall not come a' you, 5921
19 nor a' this land? "
38: 5 he that can do any thing a' you.
22 on, and have prevailed a' thee: *
39: 1 and all his army a' Jerusalem, 413
40: 3 because ye have sinned a' the Lord,
43: 3 son of Neriah setteth thee on a' us,
44: 7 this great evil a' your souls, 413
11 I will set my face a' you for evil,
23 because ye have sinned a' the Lord,
29 my words shall surely stand a' you 5921
46: 1 the prophet a' the Gentiles; * "
2 A' Egypt, *
2 a' the army of 5921
12 hath stumbled a' the mighty,
22 army, and come a' her with axes,
47: 1 the prophet a' the Philistines, * 413
7 charge a' Ashkelon, and a' the "
48: 1 A' Moab thus saith the Lord of *
2 they have devised evil a' it; 5921
26, 42 magnified himself a' the Lord "
49:14 ye together, and come a' her, "
19 a' the habitation of the strong: 413
20 Lord, that he hath taken a' Edom; "
20 hath purposed a' the inhabitants "
30 hath taken counsel a' you, 5921
30 hath conceived a purpose a' you. "
34 Jeremiah the prophet a' Elam * 413
50: 1 that the Lord spake a' Babylon * "
1 and a' the land of the Chaldeans * "
3 there cometh up a nation a' her, 5921
7 they have sinned a' the Lord,
9 come up a' Babylon an assembly 5921
9 set themselves in array a' her;
14 in array a' Babylon round about: 5921
14 for she hath sinned a' the Lord.
15 Shout a' her round about: she 5921
21 Go up a' the land of Merathaim, "
21 even a' it, "
21 and a' the inhabitants 413
24 thou hast striven a' the Lord.
26 a' her from the utmost border,
29 together the archers a' Babylon: 413
29 bend the bow, camp a' it round 5921
29 proud a' the Lord, a' the Holy One 413
31 I am a' thee, O thou most proud, "
42 a' thee, O daughter of Babylon. 5921
45 that he hath taken a' Babylon; 413
45 a' the land of the Chaldeans: "
51: 1 raise up a' Babylon, 5921
1 and a' them 413
1 midst of them that rise up a' me,*
2 they shall be a' her round about. 5921
3 A' him that bendeth let the * 413
3 a' him that lifteth himself up * "
5 sin a' the Holy One of Israel.
11 for his device is a' Babylon, to 5921
12 a' the inhabitants of Babylon. * 413
14 they shall lift up a shout a' thee. 5921
25 a' thee, O destroying mountain, 413
27 prepare the nations a' her, 5921
27 call together a' her the kingdoms "
27 appoint a captain a' her; cause "
28 Prepare a' her the nations with "
29 of the Lord shall be performed a' "
46 violence in the land, ruler a' ruler. "
60 that are written a' Babylon. * 413
62 thou hast spoken a' this place, * "
52: 3 that Zedekiah rebelled a' the king
4 a' Jerusalem, and pitched a' it, 5921
4 and built forts a' it round about. "
La 1:13 and it prevaileth a' them:
15 an assembly a' me to crush my 5921
18 rebelled a' his commandment:
2: 3 burned a' Jacob like a flaming *
16 opened their mouth a' thee: 5921
3: 3 Surely a' me is he turned; he
3 turneth his hand a' me all the *
5 He hath builded a' me, and 5921
46 have opened their mouths a' us.
60 all their imaginations a' me.
61 all their imaginations a' me; 5921
62 lips of those that rose up a' me,
62 their device a' me all the day. 5921
5:22 us; thou art very wroth a' us.
Eze 1:20 were lifted up over a' them: *5980
21 were lifted up over a' them: * "
2: 3 nation that hath rebelled a' me:
3 fathers have transgressed a' me,
3: 8 thy face strong a' their faces, 5980
8 forehead strong a' their foreheads. "
13 noise of the wheels over a' them, * "
4: 2 lay siege a' it, and build a fort 5921
2 a' it, and cast a mount a' it; "
2 set the camp also a' it, and set "
2 battering rams a' it round "
3 and set thy face a' it, and it shall* 413
3 and thou shalt lay siege a' it. 5921
7 and thou shalt prophesy a' it.
5: 8 Behold, I, even I, am a' thee, and "
6: 2 of Israel, and prophesy a' them, * 413
11: 4 prophesy a' them, prophesy, O 5921
13: 2 prophesy a' the prophets of Israel 413
8 I am a' you, saith the Lord God. "
17 a' the daughters of thy people, "
17 and prophesy thou a' them, 5921
20 Behold, I am a' your pillows, 413
14:13 land sinneth a' me by trespassing
15: 7 And I will set my face a' them;
7 Lord, when I set my face a' them.
16:37 gather them round about a' thee, 5921
40 also bring up a company a' thee, "
44 shall use this proverb a' thee, "
17:15 But he rebelled a' him in sending

Eze 17:20 that he hath trespassed a' me.
19: 8 Then the nations set a' him on 5921
20: 8 they rebelled a' me, and would
8 accomplish my anger a' them in
13 the house of Israel rebelled a' me
21 the children rebelled a' me:
21 to accomplish my anger a' them
27 have committed a trespass a' me.
38 and them that transgress a'
46 and prophesy a' the forest of the 413
21: 2 places, and prophesy a' the land "
3 Lord; Behold, I am a' thee, and "
4 a' all flesh from the south to "
15 of the sword a' all their gates, 5921
22 battering rams a' the gates, "
31 I will blow a' thee in the fire of * "
22: 3 idols a' herself to defile herself, "
23:22 I will raise up thy lovers a' thee, "
22 bring them a' thee on every side; "
24 shall come a' thee with chariots, "
24 of people, which shall set a' thee "
25 And I will set my jealousy a' thee,
24: 2 set himself a' Jerusalem this * 413
25: 2 set thy face a' the Ammonites, * "
2 and prophesy a' them; 5921
3 thou saidst, Aha, a' my sanctuary, 413
3 a' the land of Israel, when it was "
3 a' the house of Judah, when they "
6 all thy despite a' the land of Israel; "
12 Edom hath dealt a' the house of
26: 2 Tyrus hath said a' Jerusalem, 5921
3 Behold, I am a' thee, O Tyrus, "
3 many nations to come up a' thee, "
8 and he shall make a fort a' thee, "
8 a mount a' thee, and lift up the "
8 buckler a' thee. "
9 set engines of war a' thy walls,
27:30 their voice to be heard a' thee, *5921
28: 7 draw their swords a' the beauty of 5921
21 set thy face a' Zidon, * 413
21 and prophesy a' it, *5921
22 Behold, I am a' thee, O Zidon; "
29: 2 set thy face a' Pharaoh king of "
2 prophesy a' him, and a' all Egypt: "
3 I am a' thee, Pharaoh king of "
10 therefore I am a' thee, 413
10 and a' thy rivers, "
18 to serve a great service a' Tyrus: "
18 service that he had served a' it: 5921
20 labour wherewith he served a' it, *
30:22 I am a' Pharaoh king of Egypt, 413
33:30 of thy people still are talking a' *
34: 2 prophesy a' the shepherds of 5921
10 I am a' the shepherds; and I will 413
35: 2 set thy face a' mount Seir, 5921
2 and prophesy a' it, "
3 O mount Seir, I am a' thee, 413
3 stretch out mine hand a' thee, 5921
11 used out of thy hatred a' them;
12 spoken a' the mountains of Israel, 5921
13 mouth ye have boasted a' me, "
13 have multiplied your words a' me: "
36: 2 the enemy hath said a' you, "
5 a' the residue of the heathen, "
5 and a' all Idumea, "
38: 2 set thy face a' Gog, the land of * 413
2 and Tubal, and prophesy a' 5921
3 I am a' thee, O Gog, the chief 413
8 many people, a' the mountains *5921
16 come up a' my people of Israel, "
16 I will bring thee a' my land, "
17 that I would bring thee a' them? "
18 shall come a' the land of Israel, "
21 sword a' him throughout all my "
21 man's sword shall be a' his brother. "
22 will plead a' him with pestilence ‡
39: 1 thou son of man, prophesy a' Gog, 5921
1 the Lord God; Behold, I am a' thee, 413
23 because they trespassed a' me,
26 they have trespassed a' me,
40:13 and twenty cubits, door a' door. 5048
18 of the gates over a' the length *5980
23 over a' the gate toward the north, 5048
41:15 over a' the separate place which *6440
16 over a' the door, ceiled with wood 5048
42: 1 was over a' the separate place,
3 Over a' the twenty cubits which
3 court, and over a' the pavement 5048
7 without over a' the chambers, *5980
10 over a' the separate place, *6440
10 and over a' the building. "
44:12 I lifted up mine hand a' them, 5921
45: 6 over a' the oblation of the holy *5980
7 over a' one of the portions, * "
46: 9 but shall go forth over a' it. *5227
47:20 a man come over a' Hamath. 5704,
48:13 over a' the border of the priests *5980
15 a' five and twenty thousand, *5921, 6440
18 in length over a' the oblation *5980
18 it shall be over a' the oblation * "
21 a' the five and twenty * 413, 6440
21 a' the five and twenty *5921,
21 over a' the portions for the prince:*5980
Da 3:19 visage was changed a' Shadrach, 5922
29 a' the God of Shadrach, Meshach,
5: 5 over a' the candlestick upon the 6903
6 his knees smote one a' another.
23 up thyself a' the Lord of heaven; 5922
6: 4 occasion a' Daniel concerning
5 find any occasion a' this Daniel, 5922
5 find it a' him concerning the law
7:21 with the saints, and prevailed a'
25 great words a' the most High, 6655
8: 7 he was moved with choler a' him, 413
12 given him a' the daily sacrifice *5921
25 stand up a' the Prince of princes; "

Da 9: 7 that they have trespassed a' thee.
8 because we have sinned a'
9 though we have rebelled a' him;
11 because we have sinned a' him.
12 which he spake a' us, 5921
12 and a' our judges "
11: 2 stir up all a' the realm of Grecia.
7 and shall deal a' them, and shall
14 stand up a' the king of the south: 5921
16 cometh a' him shall do according 413
24 forecast his devices a' the strong 5921
25 his courage a' the king of the south "
25 they shall forecast devices a' him. "
28 shall be a' the holy covenant; "
30 of Chittim shall come a' him:
30 indignation a' the holy covenant: 5921
32 do wickedly a' the covenant shall
36 marvellous things a' the God 5921
40 come a' him like a whirlwind, "
Ho 4: 7 increased, so they sinned a' me:
5: 7 dealt treacherously a' the Lord:
6: 7 they dealt treacherously a' me.
7:13 they have transgressed a' me:
13 yet they have spoken lies a' me. 5921
14 and wine, and they rebel a' me.
15 do they imagine mischief a' me. 413
8: 1 an eagle a' the house of the Lord, 5921
1 covenant, and trespassed a' my law. "
5 mine anger is kindled a' them:
10: 9 Gibeah a' the children of iniquity 5921
10 people shall be gathered a' them,
13:16 for she hath rebelled a' her God:
Joe 3:19 violence a' the children of Judah, *
Am 1: 8 I will turn mine hand a' Ekron: 5921
3: 1 that the Lord hath spoken a' you, "
1 a' the whole family which I "
5: 1 up a' you, even a lamentation, * "
9 strengtheneth the spoiled a' the * "
9 shall come a' the fortress. * "
6:14 a' you a nation, O house of Israel, "
7: 9 will rise a' the house of Jeroboam "
10 Amos hath conspired a' thee in "
16 sayest, Prophesy not a' Israel, "
16 drop not thy word a' the house of "
Ob 1 and let us rise up a' her in battle. "
7 thee, and prevailed a' thee;
10 For thy violence a' thy brother *
Jon 1: 2 that great city, and cry a' it; 5921
13 and was tempestuous a' them.
Mic 1: 2 Lord God be witness a' you,
2: 3 a' this family do I devise an evil, 5921
4 shall one take up a parable a' you, "
3: 5 they even prepare war a' him. "
4: 3 shall not lift up a sword a' nation, 413
11 nations are gathered a' thee, 5921
5: 1 troops: he hath laid siege a' us: "
5 raise a' him seven shepherds, "
6: 3 have I wearied thee? testify a' me.
7: 6 daughter riseth up a' her mother,
6 in law a' her mother in law:
8 Rejoice not a' me, O mine enemy:
9 the Lord, because I have sinned a'
Na 1: 9 do ye imagine a' the Lord? 413
11 that imagineth evil a' the Lord, 5921
2: 4 one a' another in the broad ways: ‡
13 I am a' thee, saith the Lord of 413
3: 5 Behold, I am a' thee, saith the "
Hab 2: 6 parable a' him, 5921
6 and a taunting proverb a'
10 and hast sinned a' thy soul.
3: 8 the Lord displeased a' the rivers?
8 was thine anger a' the rivers?
8 was thy wrath a' the sea,
Zep 1:16 a' the fenced cities, 5921
16 and a' the high towers. "
17 they have sinned a' the Lord:
2: 5 the word of the Lord is a' you; 5921
8 themselves a' their border. "
10 themselves a' the people "
13 stretch out his hand a' the north, "
3:11 thou hast transgressed a' me:
Zec 1:12 a' which thou hast had indignation
7:10 evil a' his brother in your heart.
8:10 men every one a' his neighbour.
17 in your hearts a' his neighbour;
9:13 O Zion, a' thy sons, O Greece, 5921
10: 3 was kindled a' the shepherds, "
12: 2 both a' Judah * "
2 and a' Jerusalem. "
3 earth be gathered together a' it. "
7 magnify themselves a' Judah. * "
9 nations that come a' Jerusalem. "
13: 7 Awake, O sword, a' my shepherd, "
7 and a' the man that is my fellow, "
14: 2 nations a' Jerusalem to battle; 413
3 forth, and fight a' those nations,
12 that have fought a' Jerusalem; 5921
13 up a' the hand of his neighbour. "
16 of all the nations which came a' "
Mal 1: 4 The people a' whom the Lord
2:10 every man a' his brother,
14 a' whom thou hast dealt
15 a' the wife of his youth.
3: 5 a swift witness a' the sorcerers,
5 and a' the adulterers,
5 and a' false swearers,
5 and a' those that oppress
13 words have been stout a' me, 5921
13 have we spoken so much a' thee? "
M't 4: 6 thou dash thy foot a' a stone. 4314
5:11 all manner of evil a' you falsely, 2596
23 thy brother hath aught a' thee;
10: 1 them power a' unclean spirits, *
18 a' them and the Gentiles. *
21 shall rise up a' their parents, 1909
35 a man at variance a' his father. 2596

M't 10:35 and the daughter a· her mother, 2596
35 daughter in law a· her mother in "
12:14 held a council a· him, "
25 kingdom divided a· itself, "
25 city or house divided a· itself, "
26 he is divided a· himself; 1909
30 He that is not with me is a· me: 2596
31 the blasphemy a· the Holy Ghost
32 a word a· the Son of man, 2596
32 speaketh a· the Holy Ghost, "
16:18 gates of hell shall not prevail a· it. 2729
18:15 thy brother shall trespass a· thee, 1519
21 how oft shall my brother sin a· me, "
20:11 murmured a· the goodman of the 2596
24 indignation a· the two brethren. *4012
21: 2 Go into the village over a· you, 561
23:13 the kingdom of heaven a· men: 1715
24: 7 nation shall rise a· nation, 1909
7 and kingdom a· kingdom: "
26:55 are ye come out as a· a thief "
59 sought false witness a· Jesus, 2596
62 is it which these witness a· thee? 2649
27: 1 took counsel a· Jesus to put him 2596
13 many things they witness a· thee?
61 sitting over a· the sepulchre. 561
M'r 3: 6 counsel with the Herodians a· him, 2596
24 kingdom be divided a· itself, 1909
25 a house be divided a· itself, "
26 if Satan rise up a· himself, "
29 shall blaspheme a· the Holy Ghost 1519
6:11 feet for a testimony a· them. *
19 Herodias had a quarrel a· him,
9:40 he that is not a· us is on our part 2596
10:11 committeth adultery a· her. 1909
11: 2 way into the village over a· you: 2713
25 if ye have aught a· any: 2596
12:12 had spoken the parable a· them: 4314
41 Jesus sat over a· the treasury, 2713
13: 3 mount of Olives over a· the temple, "
8 nation shall rise a· nation, 1909
8 and kingdom a· kingdom: "
9 sake, for a testimony a· them. *
12 children shall rise up a· their 1909
14: 5 they murmured a· her. 1690
48 Are ye come out, as a· a thief, 1909
55 sought for witness a· Jesus to put 2596
56 bare false witness a· him, "
57 and bare false witness a· him, "
60 is it which these witness a· thee?
15: 4 many things they witness a· thee.*
39 which stood over a· him. 1537, 1727
Lu 2:34 which shall be spoken a·; 483
4:11 thou dash thy foot a· a stone. 4314
5:30 murmured a· his disciples, "
6: 7 might find an accusation a· him. *
49 a· which the stream did beat 4366
7:30 counsel of God a· themselves, *1519
8:26 Gadarenes, which is over a· Galilee. 495
9: 5 your feet for a testimony a· them. 1909
50 he that is not a· us is for us. 2596
10:11 on us, we do wipe off a· you:
11:17 Every kingdom divided a· itself, 1909
17 a house divided a· a house, "
18 Satan also be divided a· himself, "
23 he that is not with me is a· me: 2596
12:10 speak a word a· the Son of man, 1519
10 blasphemeth a· the Holy Ghost, "
52 three a· two, and two a· three. 1909
53 a· the son, "
53 and the son a· the father; "
53 the mother a· the daughter, "
53 and the daughter a· the mother; "
53 mother in law a· her daughter in "
53 daughter in law a· her mother in "
14:31 to make war a· another king, *
31 to meet him that cometh a· him 1909
15:18, 21 I have sinned a· heaven, 1519
17: 3 If thy brother trespass a· thee, * "
4 if he trespass a· thee seven times "
19:30 Go ye into the village over a· you; 2713
20:19 had spoken this parable a· them. 4314
21:10 Nation shall rise a· nation, 1909
10 and kingdom a· kingdom: "
22:52 Be ye come out, as a· a thief, "
53 ye stretched forth no hands a· me: "
65 blasphemously spake they a· him. 1519
Joh 12: 7 a· the day of my burying has she
13:18 lifted up his heel a· me. "
29 we have need of a· the feast; *
18:29 accusation bring ye a· this man? 2596
19:11 no power at all a· me,
12 himself a king speaketh a· Cæsar. 483
Ac 4:14 they could say nothing a· it. 471
26 gathered together a· the Lord, 2596
26 and a· his Christ. "
27 a truth a· thy holy child Jesus, 1909
5:39 ye be found even to fight a· God.
6: 1 of the Grecians a· the Hebrews, 4314
11 blasphemous words a· Moses, 1519
11 and a· God.
13 a· this holy place, 2596
8: 1 persecution a· the church 1909
9: 1 a· the disciples of the Lord, 1519
5 for thee to kick a· the pricks. *4314
29 and disputed a· the Grecians:
13:45 spake a· those things which * 483
50 raised persecution a· Paul 1909
51 dust of their feet a· them,
14: 2 evil affected a· the brethren. 2596
16:22 rose up together a· them:
18:12 insurrection with one accord a·
19:16 and prevailed a· them, 2596
36 these things cannot be spoken a·,* 368
38 have a matter a· any man, 4314
20:15 came the next day over a· Chios; 481
21:28 every where a· the people, 2596
Ac 22:24 wherefore they cried so a· him. 2019
23: 9 to him, let us not fight a· God. *
30 what they had a· him. 4314
24: 1 informed the governor a· Paul. 1718
19 if they had aught a· me. 4314
25: 2 informed him a· Paul, 2596
3 desired favour a· him, "
7 grievous complaints a· Paul, "
8 neither a· the law of the Jews, 1519
8 neither a· the temple, "
8 nor yet a· Cæsar, "
15 to have judgment a· him. 2596
16 concerning the crime laid a· him.
18 A· whom, when the accusers *4012
19 certain questions a· him of their 4314
27 the crimes laid a· him. 2596
26:10 to death, I gave my voice a· them. 2702
11 being exceedingly mad a· them, 1693
14 hard for thee to kick a· the pricks. 4314
27: 7 scarce were come over a· Cnidus, 2596
7 under Crete, over a· Salmone;
14 arose a· it a tempestuous wind, * "
28:17 committed nothing a· the people, 1727
19 when the Jews spake a· it, 483
22 every where it is spoken a·.
Ro 1:18 from heaven a· all ungodliness 1909
26 into that which is a· nature: 3844
2: 2 a· them which commit such 1909
5 wrath a· the day of wrath *1722
4:18 Who a· hope believed in hope, 3844
7:23 warring a· the law of my mind, 497
8: 7 carnal mind is enmity a· God: 1519
31 God be for us, who can be a· us? 2596
9:20 who art thou that repliest a· God? 470
11: 2 to God a· Israel, saying, 2596
18 Boast not a· the branches. *2620
1Co 4: 6 puffed up for one a· another. 2596
6: 1 having a matter a· another, 4314
18 sinneth a· his own body. 1519
8:12 ye sin so a· the brethren, "
12 ye sin a· Christ. "
9:17 if a· my will, a dispensation *210
2Co 10: 2 I think to be bold a· some, 1909
5 itself a· the knowledge of God, 2596
13: 8 we can do nothing a· the truth, "
Ga 3:21 law then a· the promises of God? "
5:17 the flesh lusteth a· the Spirit, "
17 and the Spirit a· the flesh: "
23 a· such there is no law. "
Eph 6:11 able to stand a· the wiles of the 4314
12 we wrestle not a· flesh and blood, "
12 but a· principalities, a· powers, "
12 a· the rulers of the darkness of "
12 a· spiritual wickedness in high "
Col 2:14 ordinances that was a· us, 2596
3:13 if any man have a quarrel a· any: 4314
19 be not bitter a· them.
1Ti 5:11 a· Christ, they will marry; 2691
19 A· an elder receive not an 2596
6:19 a good foundation a· the time to 1519
2Ti 1:12 committed unto him a· that day. "
Heb 12: 3 contradiction of sinners a· himself, "
4 unto blood, striving a· sin. 4314
Jas 2:13 and mercy rejoiceth a· judgment 2620
3:14 and lie not a· the truth. 2596
5: 9 Grudge not one a· another,
1Pe 2:11 which war a· the soul; 2596
12 they speak a· you as evildoers, 1909
3:12 the Lord is a· them that do evil. * "
2Pe 2:11 accusation a· them before the 2596
3: 7 reserved unto fire a· the day of 1519
3Jo 10 a· us with malicious words: 5396
Jude 9 bring a· him a railing accusation, 2018
15 ungodly sinners have spoken a· 2596
Re 2: 4 I have somewhat a· thee, "
14 I have a few things a· thee, "
16 will fight a· them with the sword 3326
20 I have a few things a· thee, 2596
11: 7 shall make war a· them, *3326
12: 7 his angels fought a· the dragon; *2596
13: 6 his mouth in blasphemy a· God, 4314
19:19 war a· him that sat on the horse, 3326
19 and a· his army. "

Agar (a'-gar) See also HAGAR.
Ga 4:24 gendereth to bondage, which is A·. 28
25 For this A· is mount Sinai

agate See also AGATES.
Ex 28:19 the third row a ligure, an a·, and 7618
39:12 And the third row a ligure, an a·,
Eze 27:16 fine linen, and coral, and a·. *3539

agates
Isa 54:12 I will make thy windows of a·, *3539

age See also AGED; AGES.
Ge 15:15 shalt be buried in a good old a·. 7872
18:11 well stricken in a·; and it ceased 3117
21: 2 bare Abraham a son in his old a·,
7 have born him a son in his old a·.
24: 1 was old, and well stricken in a·: 3117
25: 8 Abraham...died in a good old a·, 7872
37: 3 he was the son of his old a·:
44:20 child of his old a·, a little one;
47:28 whole a· of Jacob was an hundred *3117
48:10 the eyes of Israel were dim for a·, 2207
Nu 8:25 And from the a· of fifty years 1121
Jos 23: 1 waxed old and stricken in a·. *3117
2 I am old and stricken in a·: *
J'g 8:32 Gideon...died in a good old a·, 7872
Ru 4:15 and a nourisher of thine old a·: "
1Sa 2:33 shall die in the flower of their a·. 582
1Ki 14: 4 eyes were set by reason of his a·. 7869
15:23 in the time of his old a· he was
1Ch 23: 3 from the a· of thirty years and *1121
24 from the a· of twenty years and * "
29:28 died in a good old a·, full of days, 7872
2Ch 36:17 or him that stooped for a·: *3486
Job 5:26 come to thy grave in a full a·, 3624
8: 8 I pray thee, of the former a·, 1755
11:17 And thine a· shall be clearer *2465
30: 2 in whom old a· was perished? 3624
Ps 39: 5 mine a· is as nothing before thee: 2465
71: 9 me not off in the time of old a·;
92:14 still bring forth fruit in old a·; 7872
Isa 38:12 Mine a· is departed, and is ‡1755
46: 4 even to your old a· I am he; 2209
Zec 8: 4 his staff in his hand for very a·. 3117
M'r 5:42 she was of the a· of twelve years.*
Lu 1:36 also conceived a son in her old a·:
2:36 was of a great a·, and had lived 2250
3:23 about thirty years of a·, being (as
Joh 9:21 we know not: he is of a·; 2244
23 said his parents, He is of a·; "
1Co 7:36 she pass the flower of her a·, 5230
Heb 5:14 to them that are of full a·, *5046
11:11 when she was past a·, because she *2244

aged
2Sa 19:32 Barzillai was a very a· man, 2204
Job 12:20 away the understanding of the a·. *2205
15:10 the grayheaded and very a· men, 3453
29: 8 and the a· arose, and stood up. 2205
32: 9 neither do the a· understand "
Jer 6:11 a· with him that is full of days. "
Tit 2: 2 That the a· men be sober, grave, 4246
3 The a· women likewise, that they 4247
Ph'm 9 being such an one as Paul the a·, 4246

Agee (ag'-ee)
2Sa 23:11 him was Shammah the son of A· 89

ages
Eph 2: 7 That in the a· to come he might 165
3: 5 Which in other a· was not made *1074
21 throughout all a·, world without *
Col 1:26 hid from a· and from generations,* 165

ago See also AGONE.
1Sa 9:20 asses that were lost three days a·, 3117
2Ki 19:25 Hast thou not heard long a· how 7350
Ezr 5:11 was builded these many years a·, 6928
Isa 22:11 unto him that fashioned it long a·. 7350
37:26 Hast thou not heard long a·,
M't 11:21 repented long a· in sackcloth 3819
M'r 9:21 How long is it a· since this came *
Lu 10:13 they had a great while a· 3819
Ac 10:30 And Cornelius said, Four days a· 575
15: 7 how that a good while a· God made "
2Co 8:10 also to be forward a year a·. "
9: 2 that Achaia was ready a year a·; * "
12: 2 in Christ above fourteen years a·, 4253

agone See also AGO.
1Sa 30:13 because three days a· I fell sick. ‡

agony
Lu 22:44 being in an a· he prayed more 74

agree See also AGREED; AGREETH.
M't 5:25 A· with thine adversary quickly, 2132
18:19 That if two of you shall a· on 4856
20:13 didst not thou a· with me for a
M'r 14:59 neither so did their witness a· 2470
Ac 15:15 a· the words of the prophets; 4856
1Jo 5: 8 blood: and these three a· in one. 1526
Re 17:17 fulfil his will, and to a·, *4160, 3391, 1106

agreed
Am 3: 3 walk together, except they be a·? 3259
M't 20: 2 And when he had a· with the 4856
M'r 14:56 their witness a· not together. 2470
Joh 9:22 for the Jews had a· already, 4934
Ac 5: 9 How is it that ye have a· together 4856
40 And to him they a·: 3982
23:20 The Jews have a· to desire thee 4934
28:25 they a· not among themselves, 800

agreement
2Ki 18:31 an a· with me by a present, *
Isa 28:15 with hell are we at a·; 2374
18 and your a· with hell shall not 2380
36:16 Assyria, Make an a· with me by *
Da 11: 6 king of the north to make an a·: 4339
2Co 6:16 what a· hath the temple of God 4783

agreeth
M'r 14:70 and thy speech a· thereto. *3662
Lu 5:36 a· not with the old. *4856

Agrippa (ag-rip'-pah)
Ac 25:13 king A· and Bernice came 67
22 Then A· said unto Festus, "
23 when A· was come, "
24 And Festus said, King A·, "
26 specially before thee, O king A·, that "
26: 1 Then A· said unto Paul, "
2 I think myself happy, king A·, "
7 For which hope's sake, king A·, * "
19 Whereupon, O king A·, "
27 King A·, believest thou the prophets? "
28 Then A· said unto Paul, "
32 Then said A· unto Festus, "

aground
Ac 27:41 they ran the ship a·; 2027

ague
Le 26:16 consumption, and the burning a·, *6920

Agur (a'-gur)
Pr 30: 1 The words of A· the son of Jakeh, 94

ah See also AHA.
Ps 35:25 A·, so would we have it: let them * 253
Isa 1: 4 A· sinful nation, a people laden 1945
24 A·, I will ease me of mine "
Jer 1: 6 Then said I, A·, Lord God! behold, 162
4:10 A·, Lord God! surely thou hast "
14:13 A·, Lord God! behold, the prophets, "
22:18 A· my brother! or, A· sister! 1945
18 saying, A· Lord! or A· his glory! "

Jer 32:17 *A'* Lord God! behold, thou hast 162
34: 5 will lament thee, saying, *A'* lord! 1945
Eze 4:14 Then said I, *A'* Lord God! 162
9: 8 cried, and said, *A'* Lord God! "
11:13 and said, *A'* Lord God! "
20:49 Then said I, *A'* Lord God! "
21:15 *a'*! it is made bright, 253
M'r 15:29 *A'*, thou that destroyest the 3758

aha See also AH.
Ps 35:21 said, *A'*, *a'*, our eye hath seen it. 253
40:15 that say unto me, *A'*, *a'*. "
70: 3 of their shame that say, *A'*, *a'*. "
Isa 44:16 saith, *A'*, I am warm, "
Eze 25: 3 Because thou saidst, *A'*, against "
26: 2 *A'*, she is broken that was the gates "
36: 2 enemy hath said against you, *A'*, "

Ahab (*a'-hab*) See also AHAB'S.
1Ki 16:28 and *A'* his son reigned in his stead. 256
29 began *A'* the son of Omri to reign "
29 and *A'* the son of Omri reigned "
30 *A'* the son of Omri did evil "
33 *A'* made a grove; and *A'* did more "
17: 1 said unto *A'*, As the Lord God of "
18: 1 Go, shew thyself unto *A'*; and I will "
2 Elijah went to shew himself unto *A'*. "
3 *A'* called Obadiah, which was the "
5 *A'* said unto Obadiah, Go into the "
6 *A'* went one way by himself, and "
9 thy servant into the hand of *A'*, "
12 and so when I come and tell *A'*, "
16 So Obadiah went to meet *A'*, and "
16 and *A'* went to meet Elijah. "
17 it came to pass, when *A'* saw Elijah, "
17 that *A'* said unto him, Art thou he "
20 So *A'* sent unto all the children of "
41 Elijah said unto *A'*, Get thee up, eat "
42 So *A'* went up to eat and to drink. "
44 And he said, Go up, say unto *A'*, "
45 And *A'* rode, and went to Jezreel "
46 and ran before *A'* to the entrance "
19: 1 *A'* told Jezebel all that Elijah had "
20: 2 sent messengers to *A'* king of Israel. "
13 there came a prophet unto *A'*. "
14 *A'* said, By whom? And he said, "
34 Then said *A'*, I will send thee away "
21: 1 the palace of *A'* king of Samaria. 256
2 *A'* spake unto Naboth, saying, "
3 Naboth said to *A'*, The Lord forbid "
4 *A'* came into his house heavy and "
15 Jezebel said to *A'*, Arise, take "
16 *A'* heard that Naboth was dead, "
16 that *A'* rose up "
18 go down to meet *A'* king of Israel, "
20 *A'* said to Elijah, Hast thou found "
21 and will cut off from *A'* him "
24 Him that dieth of *A'* in the city "
25 But there was none like unto *A'*, "
27 to pass, when *A'* heard those words, "
29 Seest thou how *A'* humbleth himself "
22:20 Lord said, Who shall persuade *A'*, "
39 Now the rest of the acts of *A'*, "
40 So *A'* slept with his fathers; "
41 the fourth year of *A'* king of Israel. "
49 said Ahaziah the son of *A'* unto "
51 Ahaziah the son of *A'* began to reign "
2Ki 1: 1 against Israel after the death of *A'*. "
3: 1 Jehoram the son of *A'* began to reign "
5 it came to pass, when *A'* was dead, "
8:16 the fifth year of Joram the son of *A'* "
18 as did the house of *A'*: "
18 for the daughter of *A'* was his wife: "
25 twelfth year of Joram the son of *A'* "
27 walked in the way of the house of *A'*, "
27 as did the house of *A'*: for he was "
27 the son in law of the house of *A'*. "
28 he went with Joram the son of *A'* "
29 see Joram the son of *A'* in Jezreel, "
9: 7 thou shalt smite the house of *A'* "
8 the whole house of *A'* shall perish: "
8 and I will cut off from *A'* him "
9 I will make the house of *A'* like the "
25 I and thou rode together after *A'* "
29 year of Joram the son of *A'* "
10: 1 *A'* had seventy sons in Samaria. "
10 spake concerning the house of *A'*: "
11 all that remained of the house of *A'* "
17 he slew all that remained unto *A'* "
18 unto them, *A'* served Baal a little; "
30 and hast done unto the house of *A'* "
21: 3 and made a grove, as did *A'* "
13 and the plummet of the house of *A'*: "
2Ch 18: 1 and joined affinity with *A'*. "
2 certain years he went down to *A'* "
2 *A'* killed sheep and oxen for him "
3 *A'* king of Israel said unto "
19 Who shall entice *A'* king of Israel, "
21: 6 like as did the house of *A'*: "
6 he had the daughter of *A'* to wife: "
13 to the whoredoms of the house of *A'*, "
22: 3 in the ways of the house of *A'*: "
4 of the Lord like the house of *A'*: "
5 went with Jehoram the son of *A'* "
6 down to see Jehoram the son of *A'* "
7 anointed to cut off the house of *A'*. "
8 judgment upon the house of *A'*, "
Jer 29:21 of *A'* the son of Kolaiah, and of "
22 make thee like Zedekiah and like *A'*, "
Mic 6:16 all the works of the house of *A'*, "

Ahab's (*a'-habs*)
1Ki 21: 8 So she wrote letters in *A'* name, 256
2Ki 10: 1 them that brought up *A'* children, * "

Aharah (*a-har'-ah*) See also AHER; AHIRAM; EHI.
1Ch 8: 1 the second, and *A'* the third, 315

Aharhel (*a-har'-hel*)
1Ch 4: 8 families of *A'* the son of Harum, 316

Ahasai (*a-ha'-sa-i*)
Ne 11:13 the son Azareel, the son of *A'*, 273

Ahasbai (*a-has'-ba-i*)
2Sa 23:34 Eliphalet the son of *A'*, the son of 308

Ahasuerus (*a-has-u-e'-rus*) See also AHASUERUS'.
Ezr 4: 6 in the reign of *A'*, in the beginning 325
Es 1: 1 in the days of *A'*, "
1 (this is *A'* which reigned from India "
2 when the king *A'* sat on the throne "
9 house which belonged to king *A'*. "
10 in the presence of *A'* the king, "
15 the commandment of the king *A'* "
16 in all the provinces of the king *A'*. "
17 The king *A'* commanded Vashti "
19 Vashti come no more before king *A'*; "
2: 1 the wrath of king *A'* was appeased, "
12 turn was come to go in to king *A'*, "
16 So Esther was taken unto king *A'* "
21 sought to lay hand on the king *A'*. "
3: 1 After these things did king *A'* "
6 throughout the whole kingdom of *A'*, "
7 in the twelfth year of king *A'*, they "
8 Haman said unto king *A'*, There "
12 in the name of king *A'* was it "
6: 2 sought to lay hand on the king *A'*. "
7: 5 Then the king *A'* answered and "
8: 1 On that day did the king *A'* give "
7 Then the king *A'* said unto Esther "
12 day in all the provinces of king *A'*, "
9: 2 all the provinces of the king *A'*, "
20 the provinces of the king *A'*, both "
30 of the kingdom of *A'*, with words "
10: 1 the king *A'* laid a tribute upon the "
3 the Jew was next unto king *A'*, "
Da 9: 1 first year of Darius the son of *A'*, "

Ahasuerus' (*a-has-u-e'-rus*)
Es 8:10 he wrote in the king *A'* name, * 325

Ahava (*a-ha'-vah*) See also IVA.
Ezr 8:15 the river that runneth to *A'*; 163
21 a fast there, at the river of *A'*, "
31 we departed from the river of *A'* "

Ahaz (*a'-haz*) See also ACHAZ.
2Ki 15:38 *A'* his son reigned in his stead. 271
16: 1 *A'* the son of Jotham king of Judah "
2 Twenty years old was *A'* when he "
5 they besieged *A'*, but could not "
7 So *A'* sent messengers to "
8 *A'* took the silver and gold that was "
10 king *A'* went to Damascus to meet "
10 king *A'* sent to Urijah the priest "
11 king *A'* had sent from Damascus: "
11 priest made it against king *A'* came "
15 king *A'* commanded Urijah the "
16 to all that king *A'* commanded. "
17 *A'* cut off the borders of the bases, "
19 rest of the acts of *A'* which he did, "
20 *A'* slept with his fathers, and was "
17: 1 In the twelfth year of *A'* king of "
18: 1 of *A'* king of Judah began to reign. "
20:11 it had gone down in the dial of *A'*. "
23:12 the top of the upper chamber of *A'*, "
1Ch 3:13 *A'* his son, Hezekiah his son, "
8:35 and Melech, and Tarea, and *A'*. "
36 And *A'* begat Jehoiadah; and "
9:41 and Melech, and Tahrea, and *A'*. "
42 And *A'* begat Jarah; and Jarah 271
2Ch 27: 9 *A'* his son reigned in his stead. "
28: 1 *A'* was twenty years old when he "
16 At that time did king *A'* send unto "
19 brought Judah low because of *A'* "
21 *A'* took away a portion out of the "
22 against the Lord: this is that king *A'*. "
24 *A'* gathered together the vessels of "
27 And *A'* slept with his fathers, and "
29:19 all the vessels, which king *A'* in his "
Isa 1: 1 in the days of Uzziah, Jotham, *A'*, "
7: 1 the days of *A'* the son of Jotham, "
3 Go forth now to meet *A'*, thou, "
10 the Lord spake again unto *A'*, "
12 But *A'* said, I will not ask, "
14:28 that king *A'* died was this burden. "
38: 8 is gone down in the sun dial of *A'*, "
Ho 1: 1 *A'*, and Hezekiah, kings of Judah, "
Mic 1: 1 in the days of Jotham, *A'*, and "

Ahaziah (*a-haz-i'-ah*) See also AZARIAH; JEHOAHAZ.
1Ki 22:40 *A'* his son reigned in his stead. 274
49 Then said *A'* the son of Ahab unto "
51 *A'* the son of Ahab began to reign "
2Ki 1: 2 And *A'* fell down through a lattice "
18 rest of the acts of *A'* which he did, "
8:24 and *A'* his son reigned in his stead. "
25 did *A'* the son of Jehoram king of "
26 Two and twenty years old was *A'* "
29 *A'* the son of Jehoram king of Judah "
9:16 *A'* king of Judah was come down "
21 and *A'* king of Judah went out, "
23 his hands, and fled, and said to *A'*, "
23 There is treachery, O *A'*. "
27 when *A'* king of Judah saw this, "
29 began *A'* to reign over Judah. "
10:13 Jehu met with the brethren of *A'*, "
13 answered, We are the brethren of *A'*; "
11: 1 the mother of *A'* saw that her son "
2 daughter of king Joram, sister of *A'*, "
2 took Joash the son of *A'*, "
12:18 and *A'*, his fathers, kings of Judah, "
13: 1 twentieth year of Joash the son of *A'*, "
14:13 the son of Jehoash the son of *A'*, "
1Ch 3:11 Joram his son, *A'* his son, Joash "
2Ch 20:35 join himself with *A'* king of Israel, 274
37 thou hast joined thyself with *A'*, "
22: 1 made *A'* his youngest son king in "
1 So *A'* the son of Jehoram king of "
2 Forty and two years old was *A'* "
7 the destruction of *A'* was of God "
8 and the sons of the brethren of *A'*, "
8 that ministered to *A'*, "
9 he sought *A'*: and they caught him, "
9 So the house of *A'* had no power "
10 Athaliah the mother of *A'* saw that "
11 the king, took Joash the son of *A'*, "
11 (for she was the sister of *A'*,) hid "

Ahban (*ah'-ban*)
1Ch 2:29 and she bare him *A'*, and Molid. 257

Aher (*a'-hur*) See also AHARAH.
1Ch 7:12 Ir, and Hushim, the sons of *A'*. 313

Ahi (*a'-hi*).
1Ch 5:15 *A'* the son of Abdiel, the son of 277
7:34 *A'*, and Rohgah, Jehubbah, and "

Ahiah (*a-hi'-ah*) See also AHIJAH.
1Sa 14: 3 And *A'*, the son of Ahitub, 281
18 Saul said unto *A'*, Bring hither the "
1Ki 4: 3 Elihoreph and *A'*, the sons of "
1Ch 8: 7 And Naaman, and *A'*, and Gera, "

Ahiam (*a-hi'-am*)
2Sa 23:33 Shammah the Hararite, *A'* the 279
1Ch 11:35 *A'* the son of Sacar the Hararite, "

Ahian (*a-hi'-an*)
1Ch 7:19 the sons of Shemidah were, *A'*, 291

Ahiezer (*a-hi-e'-zer*)
Nu 1:12 *A'* the son of Ammishaddai. 295
2:25 of the children of Dan shall be *A'* "
7:66 On the tenth day *A'* the son of "
71 this was the offering of *A'* the son "
10:25 over his host was *A'* the son of "
1Ch 12: 3 The chief was *A'*, then Joash, the "

Ahihud (*a-hi'-hud*)
Nu 34:27 of Ashar, *A'* the son of Shelomi. 282
1Ch 8: 7 them, and begat Uzza, and *A'*. 284

Ahijah (*a-hi'-jah*) See also AHIAH; AHIMELECH.
1Ki 11:29 *A'* the Shilonite found him in * 281
30 *A'* caught the new garment that "
12:15 which the Lord spake by *A'* the "
14: 2 there is *A'* the prophet, which told "
4 and came to the house of *A'*. "
4 But *A'* could not see; for his eyes "
5 the Lord said unto *A'*, Behold, the "
6 when *A'* heard the sound of her feet, "
18 spake by the hand of his servant *A'* "
15:27 Baasha the son of *A'*, of the house "
29 which he spake by his servant *A'* "
33 began Baasha the son of *A'* to reign "
21:22 the house of Baasha the son of *A'*, "
2Ki 9: 9 the house of Baasha the son of *A'*: "
1Ch 2:25 Bunah, and Oren, and Ozem, and *A'*. "
11:36 Hepher the Mecherathite, *A'* the "
26:20 *A'* was over the treasures of the "
2Ch 9:29 and in the prophecy of *A'* the "
10:15 by the hand of *A'* the Shilonite to "
Ne 10:26 And *A'*, Hanan, Anan,

Ahikam (*a-hi'-kam*)
2Ki 22:12 Hilkiah the priest, and *A'* the son 296
14 So Hilkiah the priest, and *A'*, and "
25:22 he made Gedaliah the son of *A'*, "
2Ch 34:20 king commanded Hilkiah, and *A'* "
Jer 26:24 the hand of *A'* the son of Shaphan "
39:14 him unto Gedaliah the son of *A'* "
40: 5 back also to Gedaliah the son of *A'* "
6 Jeremiah unto Gedaliah the son of *A'* "
7 Gedaliah the son of *A'* governor "
9 the son of *A'* the son of Shaphan "
11 over them Gedaliah the son of *A'* "
14 the son of *A'* believed them not. "
16 the son of *A'* said unto Johanan the "
41: 1 came unto Gedaliah the son of *A'* "
2 and smote Gedaliah the son of *A'* "
6 Come to Gedaliah the son of *A'*. "
10 committed to Gedaliah the son of *A'*: "
16, 18 had slain Gedaliah the son of *A'*, "
43: 6 left with Gedaliah the son of *A'* "

Ahilud (*a-hi'-lud*)
2Sa 8:16 Jehoshaphat the son of *A'* was 286
20:24 Jehoshaphat the son of *A'* was "
1Ki 4: 3 Jehoshaphat the son of *A'*, the "
12 Baana the son of *A'*; to him "
1Ch 18:15 Jehoshaphat the son of *A'*, recorder. "

Ahimaaz (*a-him'-a-az*)
1Sa 14:50 was Ahinoam, the daughter of *A'*: 290
2Sa 15:27 *A'* thy son, and Jonathan the son "
36 *A'* Zadok's son, and Jonathan "
17:17 Jonathan and *A'* stayed by "
20 Where is *A'* and Jonathan? "
18:19 Then said *A'* the son of Zadok, Let "
22 Then said *A'* the son of Zadok yet "
23 *A'* ran by the way of the plain, "
27 foremost is like the running of *A'* "
28 *A'* called, and said unto the king, "
29 *A'* answered, When Joab sent the "
1Ki 4:15 *A'* was in Naphtali; he also took "
1Ch 6: 8 begat Zadok, and Zadok begat *A'*, "
9 *A'* begat Azariah, and Azariah "
53 Zadok his son, *A'* his son.

Ahiman (*a-hi'-man*)
Nu 13:22 where *A'*, Sheshai, and Talmai, 289
Jos 15:14 *A'*, and Talmai, the children of "
J'g 1:10 they slew Sheshai, and *A'*, and "
1Ch 9:17 Talmon, and *A'*, and their brethren: "

Ahimelech (*a-him'-el-ek*) See also AHIMELECH'S; ABIMELECH; AHIAH.
1Sa 21: 1 came David to Nob to *A'* the priest: 288
1 *A'* was afraid at the meeting of "
2 David said unto *A'* the priest, The "
8 David said unto *A'*, And is there "
22: 9 coming to Nob, to *A'* the son of "
11 Then the king sent to call *A'* the "
14 Then *A'* answered the king, and "
16 king said, Thou shalt surely die, *A'*, "
20 one of the sons of *A'* the son of "
23: 6 when Abiathar the son of *A'* fled "
26: 6 answered David and said to *A'* "
2Sa 8:17 Ahitub, and *A'*, the son of Abiathar, "
1Ch 24: 3 and *A'* of the sons of Ithamar, "
6 *A'* the son of Abiathar, and before "
31 David the king, and Zadok, and *A'*, "
Ps 52:*title* David is come to the house of *A'*.

Ahimelech's (*a-him'-el-eks*)
1Sa 30:7 to Abiathar the priest, *A'* son, * 288

Ahimoth (*a-hi'-moth*)
1Ch 6:25 sons of Elkanah; Amasai, and *A'*. 287

Ahinadab (*a-hin'-ad-ab*)
1Ki 4:14 *A'* the son of Iddo had Mahanaim: 292

Ahinoam (*a-hin'-o-am*)
1Sa 14:50 the name of Saul's wife was *A'*, 293
25:43 David also took *A'* of Jezreel; "
27: 3 *A'* the Jezreelitess, and Abigail "
30: 5 two wives were taken captives, *A'* "
2Sa 2: 2 *A'* the Jezreelitess, and Abigail "
3: 2 his firstborn was Amnon, of *A'* "
1Ch 3: 1 the firstborn Amnon, of *A'* the "

Ahio (*a-hi'-o*)
2Sa 6: 3 and Uzzah and *A'*, the sons of 283
4 and *A'* went before the ark. "
1Ch 8:14 And *A'*, Shashak, and Jeremoth, "
31 And Gedor, and *A'*, and Zacher. "
9:37 And Gedor, and *A'*, and Zechariah, "
13: 7 and Uzzah and *A'* drave the cart. "

Ahira (*a-hi'-rah*)
Nu 1:15 Of Naphtali; *A'* the son of Enan. 299
2:29 Naphtali shall be *A'* the son of Enan. "
7:78 the twelfth day *A'* the son of Enan, "
83 this was the offering of *A'* the son "
10:27 of the children of Naphtali was *A'* "

Ahiram (*a-hi'-rum*) See also AHARAH; AHIRAMITES.
Nu 26:38 *A'*, the family of the Ahiramites: 297

Ahiramites (*a-hi'-rum-ites*)
Nu 26:38 of Ahiram, the family of the *A'*: 298

Ahisamach (*a-his'-am-ak*)
Ex 31: 6 with him Aholiab, the son of *A'*, 294
35:34 both he, and Aholiab, the son of *A'*, "
38:23 with him was Aholiab, son of *A'*, "

Ahishahar (*a-hish'-a-har*)
1Ch 7:10 Zethan, and Tharshish, and *A'*. 300

Ahishar (*a-hi'-shar*)
1Ki 4: 6 And *A'* was over the household: 301

Ahithophel (*a-hith'-o-fel*)
2Sa 15:12 Absalom sent for *A'* the Gilonite, 302
31 *A'* is among the conspirators with "
31 the counsel of *A'* into foolishness. "
34 for me defeat the counsel of *A'*. "
16:15 to Jerusalem, and *A'* with him. "
20 said Absalom to *A'*, Give counsel "
21 *A'* said unto Absalom, Go in unto "
23 counsel of *A'*, which he counselled "
23 so was all the counsel of *A'* "
17: 1 *A'* said unto Absalom, Let me now "
6 *A'* hath spoken after this manner: "
7 The counsel that *A'* hath given is "
14 is better than the counsel of *A'*. "
14 to defeat the good counsel of *A'*, "
15 Thus and thus did *A'* counsel "
21 hath *A'* counselled against you. "
23 when *A'* saw that his counsel was "
23:34 Eliam the son of *A'* the Gilonite, "
1Ch 27:33 *A'* was the king's counsellor: "
34 after *A'* was Jehoida the son of "

Ahitub (*a-hi'-tub*)
1Sa 14: 3 Ahiah, the son of *A'*, I-chabod's 285
22: 9 to Ahimelech the son of *A'*. "
11 the son of *A'*, and all his father's "
12 Saul said, Hear now, thou son of *A'*. "
20 the sons of Ahimelech the son of *A'*, "
2Sa 8:17 Zadok the son of *A'*, and Ahimelech "
1Ch 6: 7 Amariah, and Amariah begat *A'*, "
8 And *A'* begat Zadok, and Zadok "
11 Amariah, and Amariah begat *A'*, "
12 *A'* begat Zadok, and Zadok begat "
52 Amariah his son, *A'* his son, "
9:11 *A'*, the ruler of the house of God; "
18:16 And Zadok the son of *A'*, and "
Ezr 7: 2 the son of Zadok, the son of *A'*, "
Ne 11:11 the son of *A'*, was the ruler of the "

Ahlab (*ah'-lab*)
J'g 1:31 of Zidon, nor of *A'*, nor of Achzib, 303

Ahlai (*ah'-lahee*)
1Ch 2:31 And the children of Sheshan; *A'*. 304
11:41 the Hittite, Zabad the son of *A'*, "

Ahoah (*a-ho'-ah*) See also AHOHITE.
1Ch 8: 4 Abishua, and Naaman, and *A'*, 265

Ahohite (*a-ho'-hite*)
2Sa 23: 9 Eleazar the son of Dodo the *A'* 1121,266
28 Zalmon the *A'*, Maharai the "
1Ch 11:12 Eleazar the son of Dodo, the *A'*, "
29 the Hushathite, Ilai the *A'*, "
27: 4 the second month was Dodai an *A'*, "

Aholah (*a-ho'-lah*)
Eze 23: 4 names of them were *A'* the elder, 170
4 were their names; Samaria is *A'*, "
5 *A'* played the harlot when she was "
36 Son of man, wilt thou judge *A'* "
44 so went they in unto *A'* and unto "

Aholiab (*a-ho'-lee-ab*)
Ex 31: 6 behold, I have given with him *A'*, 171
35:34 he may teach, both he, and *A'*, "
36: 1 Then wrought Bezaleel and *A'*, "
2 And Moses called Bezaleel and *A'*, "
38:23 And with him was *A'*, son of "

Aholibah (*a-hol'-ib-ah*)
Eze 23: 4 the elder, and *A'* her sister: 172
4 is Aholah, and Jerusalem *A'*. "
11 when her sister *A'* saw this, she "
22 Therefore, O *A'*, thus saith the Lord "
36 wilt thou judge Aholah and *A'*? "
44 and unto *A'*, the lewd women. "

Aholibamah (*a-hol''-ib-a'-mah*)
Ge 36: 2 and *A'* the daughter of Anah 173
5 And *A'* bare Jeush, and Jaalam, "
14 these were the sons of *A'*, the "
18 are the sons of *A'* Esau's wife; "
18 were the dukes that came of *A'* "
25 and *A'* the daughter of Anah. "
41 Duke *A'*, duke Elah, duke Pinon, "
1Ch 1:52 Duke *A'*, duke Elah, duke Pinon, "

Ahumai (*a-hoo'-mahee*)
1Ch 4: 2 and Jahath begat *A'*, and Lahad. 267

Ahuzam (*a-hoo'-zam*)
1Ch 4: 6 And Naarah bare him *A'*, and 275

Ahuzzath (*a-huz'-zath*)
Ge 26:26 *A'* one of his friends, and Phichol 276

Ai (*a'-i*) See also AIATH; AIJA; HAI.
Jos 7: 2 sent men from Jericho to *A'*, 5857
2 the men went up and viewed *A'*. "
3 thousand men go up and smite *A'*; "
4 and they fled before the men of *A'*. "
5 men of *A'* smote of them about "
8: 1 and arise, go up to *A'*: "
1 given into thy hand the king of *A'*, "
2 thou shalt do to *A'* and her king "
3 people of war, to go up against *A'*; "
9 and abode between Beth-el and *A'*, "
9 on the west side of *A'*: but Joshua "
10 of Israel, before the people to *A'*. "
11 pitched on the north side of *A'*: "
11 was a valley between them and *A'*. "
12 between Beth-el and *A'*, on the "
14 when the king of *A'* saw it, that "
16 the people that were in *A'* were *5892
17 there was not a man left in *A'* or 5857
18 that is in thy hand toward *A'*; "
20 the men of *A'* looked behind them, "
21 again, and slew the men of *A'*. "
23 And the king of *A'* they took alive, "
24 slaying all the inhabitants of *A'* in "
24 all the Israelites returned unto *A'*, "
25 thousand, even all the men of *A'*. "
26 destroyed all the inhabitants of *A'*. "
28 And Joshua burnt *A'*, and made it "
29 the king of *A'* he hanged on a tree "
9: 3 had done unto Jericho and to *A'*, "
10: 1 heard how Joshua had taken *A'*, "
1 her king, so he had done to *A'* and "
2 because it was greater than *A'*, "
12: 9 king of *A'*, which is beside Beth-el, "
Ezr 2:28 The men of Beth-el and *A'*, "
Ne 7:32 The men of Beth-el and *A'*, "
Jer 49: 3 Howl, O Heshbon, for *A'* is spoiled: "

Aiah (*a-i'-ah*) See also AJAH.
2Sa 3: 7 was Rizpah, the daughter of *A'*: 345
21: 8 sons of Rizpah the daughter of *A'*, "
10 Rizpah the daughter of *A'* took "
11 daughter of *A'*, the concubine of "
1Ch 1:40 the sons of Zibeon; *A'*, and Anah. "

Aiath (*a-i'-ath*) See also AI.
Isa 10:28 He is come to *A'*, he is passed to 5857

aided
J'g 9:24 which *a'* him in the killing *2388, 3027

Aija (*a-i'-jah*) See also AI.
Ne 11:31 Geba dwelt at Michmash, and *A'*, 5857

Aijalon (*a-ij'-el-on*) See also AJALON.
Jos 21:24 *A'* with her suburbs, Gath-rimmon 357
J'g 1:35 would dwell in mount Heres in *A'*, "
12:12 was buried in *A'* in the country of "
1Sa 14:31 that day from Michmash to *A'*: "
1Ch 6:69 And *A'* with her suburbs, and "
8:13 the fathers of the inhabitants of *A'*, "
2Ch 11:10 And Zorah, and *A'*, and Hebron, "

Aijeleth (*a-ij'-el-eth*)
Ps 22:*title* chief Musician upon *A'* Shahar, 365

ailed
Ps 114: 5 What *a'* thee, O thou sea, that *

aileth
Ge 21:17 said unto her, What *a'* thee, Hagar?
J'g 18:23 said unto Micah, What *a'* thee,
24 ye say unto me, What *a'* thee?
1Sa 11: 5 What *a'* the people that they weep?
2Sa 14: 5 king said unto her, What *a'* thee?
2Ki 6:28 king said unto her, What *a'* thee
Isa 22: 1 What *a'* thee now, that thou art

Ain (*a'-in*) See also EN.
Nu 34:11 to Riblah, on the east side of *A'*; 5871
Jos 15:32 *A'*, and Rimmon: all the cities are "
19: 7 *A'*, Remmon, and Ether, and "
21:16 *A'* with her suburbs, and Juttah "
1Ch 4:32 their villages were, Etam, and *A'*, "

air
Ge 1:26, 28 the fowl of the *a'*, and over 8064
30 every fowl of the *a'*, and to every "
2:19 the field, and every fowl of the *a'*; "
20 gave names...to the fowl of the *a'*, "
6: 7 fowls of the *a'*; for it repenteth me "
7: 3 Of fowls also of the *a'* by sevens, "
9: 2 upon every fowl of the *a'*, "
De 4:17 winged fowl that flieth in the *a'*, * "
28:26 all fowls of the *a'*, and unto the "
1Sa 17:44 thy flesh unto the fowls of the *a'*, "
46 carcases...unto the fowls of the *a'*, "
2Sa 21:10 the birds of the *a'* to rest on them "
1Ki 14:11 shall the fowls of the *a'* eat: "
16: 4 shall the fowls of the *a'* eat. "
21:24 field shall the fowls of the *a'* eat. "
Job 12: 7 fowls of the *a'*, and they shall tell "
28:21 kept close from the fowls of the *a'*. "
41:16 no *a'* can come between them. 7307
Ps 8: 8 The fowl of the *a'*, and the fish of 8064
Pr 30:19 The way of an eagle in the *a'*; "
Ec 10:20 bird of the *a'* shall carry the voice, "
M't 6:26 Behold the fowls of the *a'*: *3772
8:20 the birds of the *a'* have nests; * "
13:32 birds of the *a'* come and lodge in * "
M'r 4: 4 the fowls of the *a'* came and * "
32 fowls of the *a'* may lodge under * "
Lu 8: 5 the fowls of the *a'* devoured it. * "
9:58 and birds of the *a'* have nests; * "
13:19 the fowls of the *a'* lodged in the * "
Ac 10:12 things, and fowls of the *a'*. * "
11: 6 and fowls of the *a'*. * "
22:23 clothes, and threw dust into the *a'*, 109
1Co 9:26 not as one that beateth the *a'*: "
14: 9 for ye shall speak into the *a'*. "
Eph 2: 2 prince of the power of the *a'*, "
1Th 4:17 to meet the Lord in the *a'*: and "
Re 9: 2 the sun and the *a'* were darkened "
16:17 poured out his vial into the *a'*; "

Ajah (*a'-jah*) See also AIAH.
Ge 36:24 children of Zibeon; both *A'*, and * 345

Ajalon (*aj'-a-lon*) See also AIJALON.
Jos 10:12 thou, Moon, in the valley of *A'*. 357
19:42 Shaalabbin, and *A'*, and Jethlah, "
2Ch 28:18 had taken Beth-shemesh, and *A'*, "

Akan (*a'-kan*) See also JAAKAN; JAKAN.
Ge 36:27 Bilhan, and Zaavan, and *A'*. 6130

Akkub (*ak'-kub*)
1Ch 3:24 Pelaiah, and *A'*, and Johanan, 6126
9:17 Shallum, and *A'*, and Talmon, "
Ezr 2:42 of Talmon, the children of *A'*, the "
45 of Hagabah, the children of *A'*, "
Ne 7:45 the children of *A'*, the children of 6126
8: 7 Sherebiah, Jamin, *A'*, Shabbethai, "
11:19 Moreover the porters, *A'*, Talmon, "
12:25 Talmon, *A'*, were porters keeping "

Akrabbim (*ac-rab'-bim*) See also MAALEH-ACRABBIM.
Nu 34: 4 from the south to the ascent of *A'*, 6137
J'g 1:36 from the going up to *A'*, from the "

Al See AL-TASCHITH.

alabaster
M't 26: 7 having an *a'* box of very precious 211
M'r 14: 3 having an *a'* box of ointment "
Lu 7:37 brought an *a'* box of ointment, "

alabaster-box See ALABASTER and BOX.

Alameth (*al'-am-eth*)
1Ch 7: 8 and Abiah, and Anathoth, and *A'*. 5964

Alammelech (*a-lam'-mel-ek*)
Jos 19:26 *A'*, and Amad, and Mishael; 487

Alamoth (*al'-am-oth*)
1Ch 15:20 with psalteries on *A'*; 5961
Ps 46:*title* A Song upon *A'*. "

alarm
Nu 10: 5 When ye blow an *a'*, then the 8643
6 When ye blow an *a'* the second "
6 they shall blow an *a'* for their "
7 blow, ye shall not sound an *a'*. 7321
9 blow an *a'* with the trumpets; "
2Ch 13:12 with sounding trumpets to cry *a'* "
Jer 4:19 sound of the trumpet, the *a'*. of war. 8643
49: 2 I will cause an *a'* of war to be heard "
Joe 2: 1 sound an *a'* in my holy mountain: 7321
Zep 1:16 A day of the trumpet and *a'* 8643

alas
Nu 12:11 Aaron said unto Moses, *A'*, my, * 994
24:23 *A'*, who shall live when God doeth 188
Jos 7: 7 Joshua said, *A'*, O Lord 162
J'g 6:22 Gideon said, *A'*, O Lord God! "
11:35 *A'*, my daughter! thou hast "
1Ki 13:30 mourned over him, saying, *A'*, my 1945
2Ki 3:10 the king of Israel said, *A'*! 162
6: 5 *A'*, master! for it was borrowed. "
15 *A'*, my master! how shall we do? "
Jer 30: 7 *A'*! for that day is great, 1945
Eze 6:11 *A'* for all the evil abominations 253
Joe 1:15 *A'* for the day! for the day of the 162
Am 5:16 say in all the highways, *A'*! *a'*! 1930
Re 18:10 *A'*, *a'*, that great city Babylon, *3759
16 *A'*, *a'*, that great city, that was * "
19 *A'*, *a'*, that great city, wherein * "

albeit
Eze 13: 7 Lord saith it; *a'* I have not spoken?
Ph'm 19 *a'* I do not say to thee how thou *2443

Albon See ABI-ALBON.

Alemeth (*al-e'-meth*)
1Ch 6:60 and *A'* with her suburbs, and 5964
8:36 Jehoadah begat *A'*, and Azmaveth, "
9:42 Jarah begat *A'*, and Azmaveth.

Alexander (*al-ex-an'-dur*)
M'r 15:21 the father of *A'* and Rufus, *223*
Ac 4: 6 John, and *A'*, and as many as were "
19:33 they drew *A'* out of the multitude, "
33 *A'* beckoned with the hand,
1Ti 1:20 Of whom is Hymenæus and *A'*; "
2Ti 4:14 *A'* the coppersmith did me much "

Alexandria (*al-ex-an'-dree-ah*) See also ALEXANDRIANS.
Ac 18:24 Apollos, born at *A'*, an eloquent * *221*
27: 6 a ship of *A'* sailing into Italy; "
28:11 we departed in a ship of *A'*, "

Alexandrians (*al-ex-an'-dree-uns*)
Ac 6: 9 *A'*, and of them of Cilicia and of *221*

algum (*al'-gum*) See also ALMUG.
2Ch 2: 8 and *a'* trees, out of Lebanon: 418
9:10 *a'* trees and precious stones. "
11 king made of the *a'* trees terraces "

algum-trees See ALGUM and TREES.

Aliah (*a-li'-ah*) See also ALVAH.
1Ch 1:51 were; duke Timnah, duke *A'*, 5933

Alian (*a-li'-un*) See also ALVAN.
1Ch 1:40 of Shobal; *A'*, and Manahath, 5935

alien See also ALIENS.
Ex 18: 3 I have been an *a'* in a strange *1616
De 14:21 thou mayest sell it unto an *a'*: *5237
Job 19:15 I am an *a'* in their sight. "
Ps 69: 8 an *a'* unto my mother's children. "
Isa 61: 5 the *a'* shall be your ploughmen *5236

alienate See also ALIENATED.
Eze 48:14 nor *a'* the first fruits of the land: *5674

alienated
Eze 23:17 and her mind was *a'* from them. 3363
18 then my mind was *a'* from her, "
18 like as my mind was *a'* from her 5361
22 whom thy mind is *a'*, and I will "
28 them from whom thy mind is *a'*: "
Eph 4:18 being *a'* from the life of God *526*
Col 1:21 that were sometime *a'* and enemies "

aliens
La 5: 2 our houses to *a'*. 5237
Eph 2:12 being *a'* from the commonwealth * *526*
Heb 11:34 to flight the armies of the *a'*. *245*

alike
De 12:22 the clean shall eat of them *a'*. 3162
15:22 the clean person shall eat it *a'*, "
1Sa 30:24 they shall part *a'*. "
Job 21:26 They shall lie down *a'* in the dust, "
Ps 33:15 He fashioneth their hearts *a'*; * "
139:12 darkness and the light are both *a'* "
Pr 20:10 both of them are *a'* abomination 1571
27:15 and a contentious woman are *a'*. 7737
Ec 9: 2 All things come *a'* to all: 834
11: 6 whether they both shall be *a'* good. 259
Ro 14: 5 another esteemeth every day *a'*.

alive See also QUICK.
Ge 6:19 to keep them *a'* with thee; 2421
20 come unto thee, to keep them *a'*. "
7: 3 to keep seed *a'* upon the face of "
23 and Noah only remained *a'*, and *
12:12 but they will save thee *a'*. 2421
43: 7 Is your father yet *a'*? 2416
27 of whom ye spake? Is he yet *a'*? "
28 he is yet *a'*. "
45:26 told him, saying, Joseph is yet *a'*, "
28 Joseph my son is yet *a'*: "
46:30 because thou art yet *a'*. "
50:20 to save much people *a'*. 2421
Ex 1:17 but saved the men children *a'*. "
18 have saved the men children *a'*? "
22 every daughter ye shall save *a'*. "
4:18 see whether they be yet *a'*. 2416
22: 4 be certainly found in his hand *a'*, "
Le 10:16 sons of Aaron which were left *a'*, *
14: 4 cleansed two birds *a'* and clean, *2416
16:10 be presented *a'* before the Lord, "
26:36 And upon them that are left *a'* *
Nu 16:33 went down *a'* into the pit, and the 2416
21:35 until there was none left him *a'*: *8300
22:33 I had slain thee, and saved her *a'*. 2421
31:15 Have ye saved all the women *a'*? "
18 keep *a'* for yourselves. "
De 4: 4 *a'* every one of you this day. 2416
5: 3 who are all of us here *a'* this day. "
6:24 that he might preserve us *a'*, 2421
20:16 save *a'* nothing that breatheth: "
31:27 while I am yet *a'* with you this 2416
32:39 I kill, and I make *a'*; I wound, 2421
Jos 2:13 And that ye will save *a'* my father, "
6:25 Joshua saved Rahab the harlot *a'*, "
8:23 the king of Ai they took *a'*, 2416
14:10 the Lord hath kept me *a'*, 2421
J'g 8:19 if ye had saved them *a'*, I would "
21:14 which they had saved *a'* of the "
1Sa 2: 6 The Lord killeth, and maketh *a'*: "
15: 8 Agag the king of the Amalekites *a'*, 2416
27: 9 left neither man nor woman *a'*, 2421
11 saved neither man nor woman *a'*, "
2Sa 8: 2 with one full line to keep *a'*. "
12:18 while the child was yet *a'*, 2416
21 weep for the child, while it was *a'*; "
22 While the child was yet *a'*, I fasted "
18:14 while he was yet *a'* in the midst of "
1Ki 18: 5 to save the horses and mules *a'*, 2421
20:18 come out for peace, take them *a'*; 2416
18 be come out for war, take them *a'*. "
32 said, Is he yet *a'*? he is my brother. "
21:15 for Naboth is not *a'*, but dead. "
2Ki 5: 7 Am I God, to kill and to make *a'*, 2421
7: 4 if they save us *a'*, we shall live; "
12 catch them *a'*, and get into the 2416
2Ki 10:14 he said, Take them *a'*. 2416
14 And they took them *a'*, "
2Ch 25:12 other ten thousand left *a'* "
Ps 22:29 none can keep *a'* his own soul. 2421
30: 3 thou hast kept me *a'*, "
33:19 and to keep them *a'* in famine. "
41: 2 will preserve him, and keep him *a'*: "
Pr 1:12 swallow them up *a'* as the grave; 2416
Ec 4: 2 than the living which are yet *a'*. "
Jer 49:11 I will preserve them *a'*; 2421
Eze 7:13 although they were yet *a'*: 2416
13:18 save the souls *a'* that come unto 2421
19 save the souls *a'* that should not "
18:27 he shall save his soul *a'*. "
Da 5:19 whom he would he kept *a'*; 2418
M't 27:63 said, while he was yet *a'*, After *2198*
M'r 16:11 when they had heard that he was *a'*, "
Lu 15:24 my son was dead, and is *a'* again; *326*
32 brother was dead, and is *a'* again; "
24:23 angels, which said that he was *a'*. *2198*
Ac 1: 3 he shewed himself *a'* after his "
9:41 and widows, presented her *a'*. "
20:12 they brought the young man *a'*. "
25:19 whom Paul affirmed to be *a'*. "
Ro 6:11 dead indeed unto sin, but *a'* unto "
13 as those that are *a'* from the dead, "
7: 9 I was *a'* without the law once: "
1Co 15:22 so in Christ shall all be made *a'*. *2227*
1Th 4:15 we which are *a'* and remain *2198*
17 are *a'* and remain shall be caught "
Re 1:18 behold, I am *a'* for evermore, "
2: 8 which was dead, and is *a'*; * "
19:20 both were cast *a'* into a lake of fire "

all See also ALBEIT; ALMIGHTY; ALMOST; ALREADY; ALTOGETHER; ALTHOUGH; ALWAY.
Ge 1:26 the cattle, and over *a'* the earth, 3605
29 is upon the face of *a'* the earth, "
2: 1 finished, and *a'* the host of them. "
2 the seventh day from *a'* his work "
3 rested from *a'* his work which God "
20 *a'* cattle, and to the fowl of the air, "
3:14 thou art cursed above *a'* cattle, "
14 thou eat *a'* the days of thy life: "
17 eat of it *a'* the days of thy life; "
20 she was the mother of *a'* living. "
4:21 *a'* such as handle the harp and "
5: 5 *a'* the days that Adam lived were "
8 *a'* the days of Seth were "
11 *a'* the days of Enos were "
14 *a'* the days of Cainan were "
17 *a'* the days of Mahalaleel were "
20 *a'* the days of Jared were "
23 *a'* the days of Enoch were "
27 *a'* the days of Methuselah were "
31 *a'* the days of Lamech were "
6: 2 wives of *a'* which they chose. "
12 for *a'* flesh had corrupted his way "
13 of *a'* flesh is come before me; "
17 upon the earth, to destroy *a'* flesh, "
19 of *a'* flesh, two of every sort shalt "
21 unto thee of *a'* food that is eaten, "
22 according to *a'* that God "
7: 1 Come thou and *a'* thy house into "
3 keep seed alive upon the face of *a'* "
5 Noah did according unto *a'* that "
11 the same day were *a'* the fountains "
14 and *a'* the cattle after their kind, "
15 the ark, two and two of *a'* flesh, "
16 in male and female of *a'* flesh, "
19 *a'* the high hills, that were under "
21 And *a'* flesh died that moved upon "
22 *A'* in whose nostrils was the "
22 of *a'* that was in the dry land, died. "
8: 1 and *a'* the cattle that was with him "
17 of *a'* flesh, both of fowl, and of "
9: 2 fowl of the air, upon *a'* that moveth "
2 and upon *a'* the fishes of the sea; "
3 herb have I given you *a'* things. "
10 from *a'* that go out of the ark, to "
11 neither shall *a'* flesh be cut off any "
12 you and every living creature of *a'* "
15 become a flood to destroy *a'* flesh. "
16 and every living creature of *a'* flesh "
17 between me and *a'* flesh that is "
29 *a'* the days of Noah were "
10:21 Unto Shem also, the father of *a'* "
29 *a'* these were the sons of Joktan. "
11: 6 and they have *a'* one language; "
8 upon the face of *a'* the earth: "
9 the language of *a'* the earth: "
9 upon the face of *a'* the earth. "
12: 3 in thee shall *a'* families of the "
20 and his wife, and *a'* that he had. "
13:10 beheld *a'* the plain of Jordan, that "
11 chose him *a'* the plain of Jordan; "
15 *a'* the land which thou seest, to "
14: 3 *A'* these were joined together in "
7 and smote *a'* the country of the "
11 they took *a'* the goods of Sodom "
11 and *a'* their victuals, and went "
16 he brought back *a'* the goods, "
20 And he gave him tithes of *a'*. "
15:10 And he took unto him *a'* these, "
17:23 and *a'* that were born in his house, "
23 *a'* that were bought with his money, "
27 And *a'* the men of his house, born "
18:18 and all the nations of the earth "
25 Shall not the Judge of *a'* the earth "
26 then I will spare *a'* the place for "
28 wilt thou destroy *a'* the city for "
19: 2 tarry *a'* night, and wash your feet, 3885
2 we will abide in the street *a'* night. "
4 *a'* the people from every quarter: 3605
17 neither stay thou in *a'* the plain; "
25 *a'* the plain, and *a'* the inhabitants "
28 Gomorrah, and toward *a'* the land "
Ge 19:31 after the manner of *a'* the earth: 3605
20: 7 die, thou, and *a'* that are thine. "
8 called *a'* his servants, and told *a'* "
16 *a'* that are with thee, and with *a'* "
18 closed up *a'* the wombs of the "
21: 6 so that *a'* that hear will laugh * "
12 *a'* that Sarah hath said unto thee, "
24:54 with him, and tarried *a'* night; 3885
66 Isaac *a'* things that he had done. 3605
25: 4 *A'* these were the children of "
5 gave *a'* that he had unto Isaac. "
18 died in the presence of *a'* his "
25 *a'* over like an hairy garment; "
26: 3 seed, I will give *a'* these countries, "
4 unto thy seed *a'* these countries; "
4 *a'* the nations of the earth be "
11 Abimelech charged *a'* his people, "
15 For *a'* the wells which his father's "
27:33 I have eaten of *a'* before thou "
37 and *a'* his brethren have I given "
28:11 tarried there *a'* night, because 3885
14 in thy seed shall *a'* the families 3605
15 and will keep thee in *a'* places * "
22 *a'* that thou shalt give me I will "
29: 3 thither were *a'* the flocks gathered: "
8 until *a'* the flocks be gathered "
13 he told Laban *a'* these things. "
22 Laban gathered together *a'* the "
30:32 I will pass through *a'* thy flock "
32 from thence *a'* the speckled and * "
32 and *a'* the brown cattle among * "
35 and *a'* the she goats that were "
35 some white in it, and *a'* the brown "
40 *a'* the brown in the flock of Laban; "
31: 1 away *a'* that was our father's; "
1 father's hath he gotten *a'* this glory. "
6 know that with *a'* my power I have "
8 then *a'* the cattle bare speckled: "
8 bare *a'* the cattle ringstraked. "
12 eyes, and see, *a'* the rams which "
12 I have seen *a'* that Laban doeth "
16 For *a'* the riches which God hath "
18 carried away *a'* his cattle, and *a'* "
21 So he fled with *a'* that he had; and "
34 And Laban searched *a'* the tent, "
37 Whereas thou hast searched *a'* my "
37 what hast thou found of *a'* thy "
43 and *a'* that thou seest is mine. "
54 tarried *a'* night in the mount. 3885
32:10 of the least of *a'* the mercies, 3605
10 of *a'* the truth, which thou hast "
19 third, and *a'* that followed "
33: 8 What meanest thou by *a'* this "
13 them one day, *a'* the flock will die. "
34:19 was more honorable than *a'* the "
24 hearkened *a'* that went out of "
25 city boldly, and slew *a'* the males. "
29 *a'* their wealth, and *a'* their little "
29 and spoiled even *a'* that was in the "
35: 2 and to *a'* that were with him, "
4 unto Jacob *a'* the strange gods "
4 and *a'* their earrings which were * "
6 Beth-el, he and *a'* the people that 3605
36: 6 and *a'* the persons of his house, "
6 *a'* his beasts, and *a'* his substance, "
37: 3 loved Joseph more than *a'* his "
4 him more than *a'* his brethren, "
35 *a'* his sons and *a'* his daughters "
39: 3 made *a'* that he did to prosper "
4 and *a'* that he had he put into his "
5 and over *a'* that he had, that the "
5 blessing of the Lord was upon *a'* "
6 he left *a'* that he had in Joseph's "
8 and he hath committed *a'* that he "
22 to Joseph's hand *a'* the prisoners "
40:17 uppermost basket there was of *a'* "
20 that he made a feast unto *a'* his "
41: 8 he sent and called for *a'* the "
8 and *a'* the wise men thereof: and "
19 I never saw in *a'* the land of Egypt "
29 throughout *a'* the land of Egypt: "
30 *a'* the plenty shall be forgotten "
35 let them gather *a'* the food of "
37 and in the eyes of *a'* his servants. "
39 as God hath shewed thee *a'* this, "
40 word shall *a'* my people be ruled: "
41 I have set thee over *a'* the land "
43 ruler over *a'* the land of Egypt. "
44 his hand or foot in *a'* the land "
45 out over *a'* the land of Egypt. *
46 throughout *a'* the land of Egypt. 3605
48 And he gathered up *a'* the food of "
51 hath made me forget *a'* my toil, "
51 and *a'* my father's house. "
54 dearth was in *a'* lands; but in *a'* "
55 *a'* the land of Egypt was famished, "
55 said unto *a'* the Egyptians, Go "
56 was over *a'* the face of the earth: "
56 Joseph opened *a'* the storehouses, "
57 *a'* countries came into Egypt to "
57 famine was so sore in *a'* lands. "
42: 6 he it was that sold to *a'* the people "
11 We are *a'* one man's sons; we are "
17 And he put them *a'* together into 622
29 told him *a'* that befell unto them; 3605
36 *a'* these things are against me. "
45: 1 not refrain himself before *a'* them "
8 Pharaoh, and lord of *a'* his house, "
8 throughout *a'* the land of Egypt. "
9 hath made me lord of *a'* Egypt: "
10 thy herds, and *a'* that thou hast: "
11 *a'* that thou hast, come to poverty. "
13 tell my father of *a'* my glory in "
13 Egypt, and of *a'* that ye have seen; "
15 kissed *a'* his brethren, and wept "
26 the good of *a'* the land of Egypt "

Ge 45:22 To a· of them he gave each man 3605
26 governor over a· the land of Egypt. "
27 told him a· the words of Joseph, "
46: 1 And Israel took his journey with a· "
6 Jacob, and a· his seed with him: "
7 a· his seed brought he with him "
15 a· the souls of his sons and his "
22 Jacob: a· the souls were fourteen. "
25 Jacob: a· the souls were seven. "
26 A· the souls that came with Jacob "
26 a· the souls were threescore and "
27 a· the souls of the house of Jacob, "
32 their herds, and a· that they have. "
47: 1 a· that they have, are come out of "
12 and a· his father's household, with "
13 there was no bread in a· the land; "
13 a· the land of Canaan fainted *
14 Joseph gathered up a· the money 3605
15 a· the Egyptians came unto Joseph, "
17 for a· their cattle for that year. "
20 Joseph bought a· the land of Egypt "
48:15 God which fed me a· my life long "
16 which redeemed me from a· evil, 3605
49:28 A· these are the twelve tribes of "
50: 7 with him went up a· the servants "
7 a· the elders of the land of Egypt, "
8 a· the house of Joseph, and his "
14 a· that went up with him to bury "
15 a· the evil which we did unto him. "
Ex 1: 6 and a· his brethren, and a· that "
14 a· manner of service in the field: a· "
22 And Pharaoh charged a· his people, "
3:15 my memorial unto a· generations. "
4:21 a· those wonders before Pharaoh, 3605
28 Moses told Aaron a· the words of "
28 him, and a· the signs which he had "
29 gathered together a· the elders "
30 Aaron spake a· the words which "
5:12 throughout a· the land of Egypt "
23 hast thou delivered thy people at a·. "
6:29 of Egypt a· that I say unto thee. 3605
7: 2 speak a· that I command thee: "
19 ponds, and upon a· their pools of "
19 throughout a· the land of Egypt, "
20 a· the waters that were in the "
21 throughout a· the land of Egypt. "
24 And a· the Egyptians digged round "
8: 2 smite a· thy borders with frogs: "
4 people, and upon a· thy servants. "
24 and into a· the land of Egypt: "
9: 4 nothing die of a· that is the "
6 morrow, and a· the cattle of Egypt "
9 small dust in a· the land of Egypt, "
9 throughout a· the land of Egypt. "
11 and upon a· the Egyptians. "
14 a· my plagues upon thine heart, "
14 is none like me in a· the earth. "
16 declared throughout a· the earth. "
19 and a· that thou hast in the field; "
25 throughout a· the land of Egypt "
25 a· that was in the field, both man "
10: 6 and the houses of a· thy servants, "
6 houses of a· the Egyptians; "
12 even a· that the hail hath left. "
13 land a· that day, "
13 and a· that night; "
14 went up over a· the land of Egypt, "
14 rested in a· the coasts of Egypt: "
15 of the land, and a· the fruit of the "
15 through a· the land of Egypt. "
19 locust in a· the coasts of Egypt. "
22 darkness in a· the land of Egypt "
23 a· the children of Israel had light "
11: 5 And a· the firstborn in the land "
5 and a· the firstborn of beasts. "
6 throughout a· the land of Egypt, "
8 a· these thy servants shall come "
8 and a· the people that follow thee: "
10 a· these wonders before Pharaoh: "
12: 3 Speak ye unto a· the congregation "
9 nor sodden at a· with water, but "
12 smite a· the firstborn in the land 3605
12 against a· the gods of Egypt I will "
20 in a· your habitations shall ye eat "
21 Then Moses called for a· the elders "
29 the Lord smote a· the firstborn "
29 and a· the firstborn of cattle. "
30 a· his servants, "
30 and a· the Egyptians; "
41 a· the hosts of the Lord went out "
42 observed of a· the children of "
47 A· the congregation of Israel shall "
48 to the Lord, let a· his males be "
50 Thus did a· the children of Israel; "
13: 2 Sanctify unto me a· the firstborn, "
12 Lord a· that openeth the matrix, "
13 and a· the firstborn of man among "
15 that the Lord slew a· the firstborn "
15 sacrifice to the Lord a· that "
15 but a· the firstborn of my children "
14: 7 chosen chariots, and a· the chariots "
9 a· the horses and chariots of "
17 honour upon Pharaoh, and upon a· "
20 not near the other a· the night. "
21 to go back by a strong east wind a· "
23 the sea, even a· Pharaoh's horses, "
28 and a· the host of Pharaoh that "
15:15 a· the inhabitants of Canaan shall "
20 hand; and a· the women went out "
26 keep a· his statutes, I will put none "
16: 1 a· the congregation of the children "
6 said unto a· the children of Israel, "
9 a· the congregation of the children "
22 a· the rulers of the congregation "
17: 1 a· the congregation of the children "
18: 1 heard of a· that God had done

Ex 18: 8 a· that the Lord had done unto 3605
8 for Israel's sake, and a· the travail "
9 a· the goodness which the Lord "
11 the Lord is greater than a· gods: "
12 a· the elders of Israel, to eat "
14 saw a· that he did to the people, "
14 alone, and a· the people stand "
21 provide out of a· the people able "
22 let them judge the people at a· "
23 and a· this people shall also go "
24 and did a· that he had said. "
25 chose able men out of a· Israel, "
26 judged the people at a· seasons: "
19: 5 treasure unto me above a· people: "
5 for a· the earth is mine: "
7 before their faces a· these words "
8 a· the people answered together, "
8 A· that the Lord hath spoken we "
11 in the sight of a· the people upon "
16 so that a· the people that was in "
20: 1 And God spake a· these words, "
9 shalt thou labour, and do a· thy "
11 and earth, the sea, and a· that in "
18 a· the people saw the thunderings, "
24 in a· places where I record my * "
22: 9 For a· manner of trespass, * "
23 and they cry at a· unto me, I will "
26 If thou at a· take thy neighbour's "
23:13 in a· things that I have said unto 3605
17 a· thy males shall appear before "
22 his voice, and do a· that I speak; "
27 will destroy a· the people to whom "
27 and I will make a· thine enemies "
24: 3 a· the words of the Lord, "
3 and a· the judgments: "
3 a· the people answered with one "
3 A· the words which the Lord hath "
4 Moses wrote a· the words of the "
7 A· that the Lord hath said will we "
8 you concerning a· these words. "
25: 9 a· that I shew thee, after the "
9 the pattern of a· the instruments "
22 of a· things which I will give thee "
36 a· it shall be one beaten work of * "
39 he make it, with a· these vessels. "
26: 8 shall be a· of one measure, *
17 a· the boards of the tabernacle. 3605
27: 3 a· the vessels thereof thou shalt "
17 A· the pillars round about the "
19 A· the vessels of the tabernacle "
19 in a· the service thereof, "
19 and a· the pins thereof, "
19 and a· the pins of the court, "
28: 3 unto a· that are wise hearted, "
31 the robe of the ephod a· of blue. 3632
29:12 pour a· the blood beside the 3605
13 take a· the fat that covereth the "
24 put a· in the hands of Aaron, * "
35 a· things which I have commanded "
30:27 a· his vessels, and the candlestick "
28 burnt offering with a· his vessels, "
31: 3 and in a· manner of workmanship, "
5 a· manner of workmanship. "
6 hearts of a· that are wise hearted "
6 a· that I have commanded thee; "
7 a· the furniture of the tabernacle, "
8 candlestick with a· his furniture, "
9 offering with a· his furniture, "
11 a· that I have commanded thee "
32: 3 And a· the people brake off the "
13 a· this land that I have spoken of "
26 a· the sons of Levi gathered "
33: 8 that a· the people rose up, and "
10 a· the people saw the cloudy "
10 and a· the people rose up and "
16 and thy people, from a· the people "
19 a· my goodness pass before thee, "
34: 3 be seen throughout a· the mount; "
10 a· thy people I will do marvels, "
10 have not been done in a· the earth, "
10 a· the people among which thou "
19 A· that openeth the matrix is mine; "
20 A· the firstborn of thy sons thou "
23 a· your men-children appear "
30 a· the children of Israel saw Moses, "
31 Aaron and a· the rulers of the "
32 a· the children of Israel came nigh: "
32 commandment a· that the Lord "
35: 1 a· the congregation of the children "
4 spake unto a· the congregation "
10 a· that the Lord hath commanded; "
13 a· his vessels, and the shewbread, "
16 a· his vessels, the laver and his foot, "
20 a· the congregation of the children "
21 for a· his service, and for the holy "
22 and tablets, a· jewels of gold: "
25 And a· the women that were wise "
26 a· the women whose heart stirred "
29 them willing to bring for a· manner "
31 in a· manner of workmanship; "
35 to work a· manner of work, of the "
36: 1 a· manner of work for the service "
1 according to a· that the Lord had "
3 a· the offering, which the children "
4 a· the wise men, "
4 a· the work of the sanctuary, "
7 sufficient for a· the work to make "
9 the curtains were a· of one size. "
22 a· the boards of the tabernacle. "
37:22 a· of it was one beaten work of * "
24 it, and a· the vessels thereof. "
38: 3 made a· the vessels of the altar, "
3 a· the vessels thereof made he of "
16 A· the hangings of the court round "
17 a· the pillars of the court were "
20 a· the pins of the tabernacle, "

Ex 38:22 a· that the Lord commanded 3605
24 A· the gold that was occupied "
24 for the work in a· "
30 and a· the vessels of the altar, "
31 and a· the pins of the tabernacle, "
31 and a· the pins of the court "
39:22 ephod of woven work, a· of blue. 3632
32 was a· the work of the tabernacle 3605
32 according to a· that the Lord "
33 a· his furniture, his taches, his "
36 and a· the vessels thereof, and the "
37 a· the vessels thereof, and the oil "
39 his staves, and a· his vessels, "
40 a· the vessels of the service of the "
42 to a· that the Lord commanded "
42 of Israel made a· the work. "
43 Moses did look upon a· the work. "
40: 9 and a· that is therein, and shalt "
9 it, and a· the vessels thereof: "
10 burnt offering, and a· his vessels, "
16 a· that the Lord commanded him, "
36 Israel went onward in a· their "
38 the sight of a· the house of Israel, "
38 throughout a· their journeys. "
Le 1: 9 priest shall burn a· on the altar, * "
13 priest shall bring it a·, and burn * "
2: 2 with a· the frankincense thereof; "
13 with a· thine offerings thou shalt "
16 with a· the frankincense thereof: "
3: 3 and a· the fat that is upon the "
9 the inwards, and a· the fat that is "
14 a· the fat that is upon the inwards, "
16 savour: a· the fat is the Lord's. "
17 a· your dwellings, that ye eat "
4: 7 pour a· the blood of the bullock "
8 take off from it a· the fat of the "
8 a· the fat that is upon the inwards, "
11 and a· his flesh, with his head, "
18 pour out a· the blood at the bottom "
19 take a· his fat from him, and burn "
26 he shall burn a· his fat upon the "
30 pour out a· the blood thereof at "
31 shall take away a· the fat thereof, "
35 a· the fat thereof, as the fat of the "
6: 3 in any of a· these that a man doeth, "
5 Or a· that about which he hath * "
7 anything of a· that he hath done * "
9 upon the altar a· night unto the "
15 a· the frankincense which is upon "
18 A· the males among the children * "
29 A· the males among the priests * "
7: 3 shall offer of it a· the fat thereof; "
9 And a· the meat offering that is * "
9 and a· that is dressed in the "
10 oil, and dry, shall a· the sons of "
18 eaten at a· on the third day, it *
19 a· that be clean shall eat thereof. *3605
8: 3 gather thou a· the congregation "
10 a· that was therein, and sanctified "
11 anointed the altar and a· his vessels, "
16 he took a· the fat that was upon "
25 a· the fat that was upon the "
27 put a· upon Aaron's hands, and * "
36 sons did a· things which the Lord "
9: 5 a· the congregation drew near "
23 Lord appeared unto a· the people. "
24 when a· the people saw, they "
10: 3 and before a· the people I will be "
6 wrath come upon a· the people: "
11 children of Israel a· the statutes "
11: 2 eat among a· the beasts that are "
9 ye eat of a· that are in the waters: "
10 a· that have not fins and scales in "
10 of a· that move in the waters, "
20 A· fowls that creep, "
20 going upon a· four, "
21 thing, that goeth upon a· four, "
23 a· other flying creeping things, 3605
27 among a· manner of beasts "
27 that go on a· four, "
31 unclean to you among a· that 3605
34 Of a· meat which may be eaten, "
34 and a· drink that may be drunk "
42 whatsoever goeth upon a· four, "
42 feet among a· creeping things 3605
13:12 leprosy cover a· the skin of him "
13 leprosy have covered a· his flesh, "
46 A· the days wherein the plague "
14: 8 clothes, and shave off a· his hair, "
9 a· his hair off his head and his "
9 even a· his hair he shall shave off: "
36 a· that is in that house be not "
45 and a· the morter of the house; "
46 a· the while that it is shut up shall "
54 law for a· manner of plague of "
15:16 wash a· his flesh in water, and be "
24 And if any man lie with her at a·, *
24 a· the bed whereon he lieth shall *3605
25 of her separation; a· the days of "
26 whereon she lieth a· the days of "
16: 2 not at a· times into the holy place "
16 transgressions in a· their sins: "
17 for a· the congregation of Israel. "
21 a· the iniquities of the children "
21 a· their transgressions in a· their "
22 bear upon him a· their iniquities "
29 no work at a·, whether it be one * "
30 be clean from a· your sins before "
33 a· the people of the congregation. "
34 for a· their sins once a year. "
17: 2 and unto a· the children of Israel, "
14 For it is the life of a· flesh; the "
14 life of a· flesh is the blood thereof: "
18:24 in a· these the nations are defiled "
27 (For a· these abominations have "
19: 2 Speak unto a· the congregation of "

Le 19: 7 it be eaten at a' on the third day,
13 thee a' night until the morning.
20 not at a' redeemed, nor freedom
23 have planted a' manner of trees 3605
24 a' the fruit thereof shall be holy “
37 observe a' my statutes, “
37 and a' my judgments, “
20: 5 family, and will cut him off, and a' “
22 keep a' my statutes, “
22 and a' my judgments, “
23 for they committed a' these things, “
21:24 and unto a' the children of Israel. “
22: 3 a' your seed among your “
18 and unto a' the children of Israel, “
18 for a' his vows, * “
18 and for a' his freewill offerings, * “
23: 3 of the Lord in a' your dwellings. “
14 generations in a' your dwellings. “
21 in a' your dwellings throughout “
31 generations in a' your dwellings. “
38 beside a' your vows, “
38 beside a' your freewill offerings, “
42 a' that are Israelites born shall “
24:14 a' that heard him lay their hands “
14 let a' the congregation stone him. “
16 a' the congregation shall certainly “
25: 7 a' the increase thereof be meat. “
9 sound throughout a' your land. “
10 liberty throughout a' the land *
10 unto a' the inhabitants thereof: 3605
24 in a' the land of your possession “
26:14 not do a' these commandments; “
15 will not do a' my commandments, “
18 yet for a' this hearken unto me, *
27 not for a' this hearken unto me, “
44 yet for a' that, when they be in 1571
27: 9 a' that any man giveth of such 3605
10 shall at a' change beast for beast, “
13 But if he will at a' redeem it, *
25 a' thy estimations shall be 3605
28 unto the Lord of a' that he hath, “
30 a' the tithe of the land, whether of “
31 at a' redeem ought of his tithes, *
33 and if he change it at a', then “
Nu 1: 2 ye the sum of a' the congregation 3605
3 a' that are able to go forth to war “
18 assembled a' the congregation “
20, 22, 24, 26, 28, 30, 32, 34, 36, 38, 40,
42 a' that were able to go forth to war; “
45 were a' those that were numbered “
45 a' that were able to go forth to war “
46 Even a' they that were numbered “
50 over a' the vessels thereof, “
50 and over a' things “
50 tabernacle, and a' the vessels “
54 did according to a' that the Lord “
2: 9, 16 A' that were numbered in the “
24 A' that were numbered of the “
31 A' they that were numbered in the “
32 a' those that were numbered of the “
34 to a' that the Lord commanded “
3: 8 they shall keep a' the instruments “
12 of a' the firstborn that openeth the “
13 Because a' the firstborn are mine; “
13 I smote a' the firstborn in the land “
13 unto me a' the firstborn in Israel, “
22 to the number of a' the males, “
26 the cords of it for a' the service “
28 number of a' the males, from a “
31 hanging, and a' the service thereof. “
34 to the number of a' the males, “
36 a' the vessels thereof, “
36 and a' that serveth thereto, “
39 A' that were numbered of the “
39 a' the males from a month old and “
40 Number a' the firstborn of the “
41 a' the firstborn among the children “
41 a' the firstlings among the cattle “
42 a' the firstborn among the children “
43 And a' the firstborn males by the “
45 Levites instead of a' the firstborn “
4: 3 a' that enter into the host, to do “
9 snuffdishes, and a' the oil vessels “
10 put it and a' the vessels thereof “
12 a' the instruments of ministry, “
14 a' the vessels thereof, wherewith “
14 basons, a' the vessels of the altar; “
15 a' the vessels of the sanctuary, “
16 the oversight of a' the tabernacle, “
16 and of a' that therein is, “
23 a' that enter in to perform the “
26 a' the instruments of their “
26 and a' that is made for them: * “
27 a' the service of the sons of the “
27 in a' their burdens, “
27 and in a' their service: and ye “
27 them in charge a' their burdens. “
31 according to a' their service in the “
32 with a' their instruments, “
32 and with a' their service: “
33 according to a' their service, “
37, 41 a' that might do service in the “
46 A' those that were numbered of “
5: 9 offering of a' the holy things of the “
30 shall execute upon her a' this law. “
6: 4 A' the days of his separation “
5 A' the days of the vow of his “
6 A' the days that he separateth “
8 A' the days of his separation he is “
7: 1 a' the instruments thereof, “
1 both the altar and a' the vessels “
85 a' the silver vessels weighed “
86 a' the gold of the spoons was “
87 A' the oxen for the burnt offering “
88 And a' the oxen for the sacrifice of “
8: 7 and let them shave a' their flesh “

Nu 8:16 of the firstborn of a' the children 3605
17 For a' the firstborn of the children “
18 Levites for a' the firstborn of the “
20 Aaron, and a' the congregation “
20 unto a' that the Lord commanded “
9: 3 appointed season: according to a' “
3 according to a' the ceremonies “
5 to a' that the Lord commanded “
12 according to a' the ordinances of “
10: 3 a' the assembly shall assemble “
25 was the rereward of a' the camps “
11: 6 nothing at a', beside this manna, “
11 burden of a' this people upon me? “
12 Have I conceived a' this people? “
13 flesh to give unto a' this people? “
14 able to bear a' this people alone, “
22 a' the fish of the sea be gathered “
29 would God that a' the Lord's “
32 the people stood up a' that day, “
32 and a' that night, “
32 and a' the next day, “
32 they spread them a' abroad “
12: 3 above a' the men which were upon “
7 who is faithful in a' mine house. “
13: 3 a' those men were heads of the 3605
26 Aaron, and to a' the congregation “
26 and unto a' the congregation, “
32 a' the people that we saw in it are “
14: 1 a' the congregation lifted up their “
2 a' the children of Israel murmured “
5 their faces before a' the assembly “
7 spake unto a' the company of the “
10 a' the congregation bade stone “
10 before a' the children of Israel. “
11 me, for a' the signs which I have “
15 kill a' this people as one man, *
21 a' the earth shall be filled with 3605
22 Because a' those men which have “
35 do it unto a' this evil congregation “
36 a' the congregation to murmur “
39 these sayings unto a' the children “
15:13 A' that are born of the country “
23 a' that the Lord hath commanded “
24 a' the congregation shall offer one “
25 atonement for a' the congregation “
26 be forgiven a' the congregation “
26 a' the people were in ignorance. “
33 and unto a' the congregation. “
35 a' the congregation shall stone him “
36 a' the congregation brought him “
39 remember a' the commandments “
40 do a' my commandments, and be “
16: 3 a' the congregation are holy, “
5 Korah and unto a' his company, “
6 censers, Korah, and a' his company; “
10 a' thy brethren the sons of Levi “
11 and a' thy company are gathered “
16 Be thou and a' thy company before “
19 gathered a' the congregation “
19 appeared unto a' the congregation. “
22 the God of the spirits of a' flesh, “
22 wroth with a' the congregation? “
26 ye be consumed in a' their sins. “
28 Lord hath sent me to do a' these “
29 die the common death of a' men, “
29 after the visitation of a' men; “
30 a' that appertained unto them, “
31 an end of speaking a' these words, “
32 them up, and their houses, and a' “
32 unto Korah, and a' their goods. “
33 a' that appertained to them, went “
34 a' Israel that were round about “
41 a' the congregation of the children “
17: 2 their fathers, of a' their princes “
9 a' the rods from before the Lord “
9 unto a' the children of Israel: “
18: 3 the charge of a' the tabernacle: “
4 for a' the service of the tabernacle: “
8 offerings of a' the hallowed “
11 with a' the wave offerings of the “
12 A' the best of the oil, “
12 and a' the best of the wine, “
15 openeth the matrix in a' flesh, “
19 A' the heave offerings of the holy “
21 a' the tenth in Israel for an “
28 offering unto the Lord of a' your “
29 Out of a' your gifts ye shall offer “
29 offering of the Lord, of a' the best “
19:14 a' that come into the tent, * “
14 and a' that is in the tent, * “
18 the tent, and upon a' the vessels, “
20:14 Thou knowest a' the travel that “
27 in the sight of a' the congregation. “
29 when a' the congregation saw that “
29 for Aaron thirty days, even a' the “
21:23 Sihon gathered a' his people “
25 And Israel took a' these cities: “
25 in a' the cities of the Amorites, “
25 in Heshbon, and in a' “
26 taken a' his land out of his hand, “
33 he, and a' his people, to the battle “
34 into thy hand, and a' his people, “
35 and his sons, and a' his people, “
22: 2 the son of Zippor saw a' that Israel “
4 this company lick up a' that are “
38 any power at a' to say any thing? “
23: 6 sacrifice, he, and a' the princes 3605
13 of them, and shalt not see them a': “
25 Neither curse them at a', “
25 nor bless them at a'. “
26 A' that the Lord speaketh, that I 3605
24:17 destroy a' the children of Sheth. “
25: 4 Take a' the heads of the people, “
6 Moses, and in the sight of a' the “
26: 2 sum of a' the congregation of the “
2 a' that are able to go to war in “

Nu 26:43 A' the families of the Shuahmites, 3605
62 a' males from a month old and * “
27: 2 princes and a' the congregation, “
16 the God of the spirits of a' flesh, “
19 and before a' the congregation; “
20 upon him, that a' the congregation “
21 and a' the children of Israel with “
21 even a' the congregation. “
22 and before a' the congregation: “
29:40 to a' that the Lord commanded “
30: 4 her: then a' her vows shall stand, “
6 if she had at a' an husband, *
11 then a' her vows shall stand, 3605
14 establisheth a' her vows, “
14 or a' her bonds, “
31: 4 throughout a' the tribes of Israel, “
7 and they slew a' the males. * “
9 a' the women of Midian captives, *
9 a' their cattle, 3605
9 and a' their flocks, “
9 and a' their goods, “
10 And they burnt a' their cities “
10 a' their goodly castles, with fire. “
11 took a' the spoil, “
11 and a' the prey, both of men and “
13 a' the princes of the congregation, “
15 Have ye saved a' the women alive? “
18 a' the women children, that have “
20 And purify a' your raiment, * “
20 and a' that is made of skins, “
20 and a' work of goats' hair, “
20 and a' things made of wood. “
23 a' that abideth not the fire ye shall “
27 and between a' the congregation: “
30 flocks, of a' manner of beasts, “
35 and two thousand persons in a', “
51 of them, even a' wrought jewels. “
52 a' the gold of the offering that they “
32:13 forty years, until a' the generation, “
15 and ye shall destroy a' this people. “
21 go a' of you armed over Jordan *
26 a' our cattle, shall be there in the “
33: 3 in the sight of a' the Egyptians. “
4 Egyptians buried a' their firstborn, “
52 shall drive out a' the inhabitants “
52 and destroy a' their pictures, and “
52 destroy a' their molten images, “
52 pluck down a' their high places: “
35: 3 their goods, and for a' their beasts. “
7 a' the cities which ye shall give to “
29 generations in a' your dwellings. “
De 1: 1 a' Israel on this side Jordan “
3 unto a' that the Lord had given “
7 unto a' the places nigh thereunto, “
18 a' the things which ye should do. “
19 a' that great and terrible “
30 to a' that he did for you in Egypt “
31 son, in a' the way that ye went, “
41 to a' that the Lord our God “
2: 7 thee in a' the works of thy hand: “
14 until a' the generation of the men “
16 when a' the men of war were “
32 a' his people, to fight at Jahaz. “
33 and his sons, and a' his people. “
34 we took a' his cities at that time, “
36 Lord our God delivered a' unto us: “
3: 1 he and a' his people, to battle at “
2 and a' his people, and his land, “
3 king of Bashan, and a' his people: “
4 we took a' his cities at that time, “
4 a' the region of Argob, the kingdom “
5 A' these cities were fenced with “
7 But a' the cattle, and the spoil of “
10 A' the cities of the plain, “
10 and a' Gilead, and a' Bashan, “
13 the rest of Gilead, and a' Bashan, “
13 a' the region of Argob, “
13 with a' Bashan, “
14 Manasseh took a' the country of “
18 a' that are meet for the war. “
21 a' that the Lord your God hath “
21 the Lord do unto a' the kingdoms “
4: 3 a' the men that followed Baal-peor, “
6 which shall hear a' these statutes, “
7 in a' things that we call upon him * “
8 so righteous as a' this law, “
9 thy heart a' the days of thy life: “
10 may learn to fear me a' the days “
19 even a' the host of heaven, “
19 God hath divided unto a' nations “
29 with a' thy heart “
29 and with a' thy soul. “
30 and a' these things are come upon “
34 according to a' that the Lord “
49 a' the plain on this side Jordan “
5: 1 Moses called a' Israel, and said “
3 are a' of us here alive this day. “
13 shalt labour, and do a' thy work: “
22 a' your assembly in the mount “
23 even a' the heads of your tribes, “
26 For who is there of a' flesh, that “
27 hear a' that the Lord our God “
27 unto us a' that the Lord our God “
28 said a' that they have spoken. “
29 a' my commandments always, “
31 unto thee a' the commandments, “
33 walk in a' the ways which the “
6: 2 thy God, to keep a' his statutes “
2 son's son, a' the days of thy life; “
5 Lord thy God with a' thine heart, “
5 and with a' thy soul, “
5 and with a' thy might. “
11 And houses full of a' good things, “
19 To cast out a' thine enemies from “
22 and upon a' his household, “
24 commanded us to do a' these “

De 6:25 to do a· these commandments 3605
7: 6 above a· people that are upon the "
7 for ye were the fewest of a· people: "
14 shalt be blessed above a· people: "
15 take away from thee a· sickness, "
15 upon a· them that hate thee. "
16 consume a· the people which the "
18 unto Pharaoh, and unto a· Egypt; "
19 God do unto a· the people of whom "
8: 1 A· the commandments which I "
2 remember all the way which the "
13 multiplied, and a· that thou hast "
19 do at a· forget the Lord thy God, *
9:10 according to a· the words, 3605
18 of a· your sins which ye sinned, "
10:12 thy God, to walk in a· his ways, "
12 Lord thy God with a· thy heart "
12 and with a· thy soul, "
14 earth also, with a· that therein is. "
15 even you above a· people, as it is "
11: 3 of Egypt, and unto a· his land; "
6 and a· the substance that was in * "
6 in the midst of a· Israel: "
7 seen a· the great acts of the Lord "
8 ye keep a· the commandments "
13 to serve him with a· your heart "
13 and with a· your soul, "
22 keep a· these commandments "
22 your God, to walk in a· his ways, "
23 Lord drive out a· these nations "
25 you upon a· the land that ye shall "
32 to do a· the statutes and judgments "
12: 1 a· the days that ye live upon the "
2 shall utterly destroy a· the places, "
5 shall choose out of a· your tribes "
7 in a· that ye put your hand unto, "
8 a· the things that we do here this "
10 you rest from a· your enemies "
11 ye bring a· that I command you; "
11 a· your choice vows which ye vow "
14 shalt do a· that I command thee. "
15 kill and eat flesh in a· thy gates, "
18 before the Lord thy God in a· "
28 Observe and hear a· these words "
13: 3 God with a· your heart "
3 and with a· your soul. "
9 the hand of a· the people. "
11 a· Israel shall hear, and fear, "
15 it utterly, and a· that is therein, "
16 gather a· the spoil of it into the "
16 the city, and a· the spoil thereof "
18 to keep a· his commandments "
14: 2 above a· the nations that are "
9 eat of a· that are in the waters: "
9 a· that have fins and scales shall * "
11 Of a· clean birds ye shall eat. "
20 But of a· clean fowls ye may eat. "
22 tithe a· the increase of thy seed, "
28 bring forth a· the tithe of thine "
29 bless thee in a· the work of thine "
15: 5 to do a· these commandments "
10 God shall bless thee in a· thy works, "
10 in a· that thou puttest thine hand "
18 bless thee in a· that thou doest. "
19 A· the firstling males that come "
16: 3 of Egypt a· the days of thy life. "
4 seen with thee in a· thy coast "
4 remain a· night until the morning. 3885
15 bless thee in a· thine increase, 3605
15 and in a· the works of thine hands, "
16 shall a· thy males appear before "
18 thou make thee in a· thy gates, "
17: 7 the hands of a· the people. "
10 according to a· that they inform "
13 And a· the people shall hear, and "
14 a· the nations that are about me; "
19 read therein a· the days of his life: "
19 to keep a· the words of this law "
18: 1 Levites, and a· the tribe of Levi, "
5 chosen him out of a· thy tribes, "
6 any of thy gates out of a· Israel, "
6 come with a· the desire of his mind "
7 as a· his brethren the Levites do, "
12 For a· that do these things are * "
16 a· that thou desiredst of the Lord "
18 them a· that I shall command him. "
19: 8 a· the land which he promised "
9 keep a· these commandments to "
20:11 a· the people that is found therein "
14 a· that is in the city, "
14 even a· the spoil thereof, "
15 shalt thou do unto a· the cities "
18 to do after a· their abominations, "
21: 6 And a· the elders of that city, "
14 shalt not sell her at a· for money, "
17 double portion of a· that he hath. 3605
21 And a· the men of his city shall "
21 a· Israel shall hear, and fear. "
23 remain a· night upon the tree, 3885
22: 3 a· lost thing of thy brother's, *3605
5 for a· that do so are abomination * "
19, 29 not put her away a· his days. "
23: 6 prosperity a· thy days forever. "
20 God may bless thee in a· that "
24: 8 to a· that the priests the Levites "
19 God may bless thee in a· the work "
25:16 a· that do such things, "
16 and a· that do unrighteously, "
18 of thee, even a· that were feeble "
19 from a· thine enemies round about, "
26: 2 the first of a· the fruit of the earth, "
12 a· the tithes of thine increase "
13 to a· thy commandments which "
14 a· that thou hast commanded me. "
16 and do them with a· thine heart, "
16 and with a· thy soul. "

De 26:18 keep a· his commandments; 3605
19 a· nations which he hath made, "
27: 1 Keep a· the commandments which "
3 upon them a· the words of this law, "
8 the stones a· the words of this law "
9 the Levites spake unto a· Israel, "
14 and say unto a· the men of Israel "
15 And a· the people shall answer "
16, 17, 18, 19, 20, 21, 22, 23, 24, 25 And
a· the people shall say, Amen. "
26 confirmeth not a· the words of *
26 a· the people shall say, Amen. 3605
28: 1 and to do a· his commandments "
1 high above a· nations of the earth: "
2 a· these blessings shall come on "
8 in a· that thou settest thine hand "
10 a· people of the earth shall see "
12 bless a· the work of thine hand: "
15 to do a· his commandments "
15 a· these curses shall come upon "
20 vexation, and rebuke, in a· that "
25 into a· the kingdoms of the earth. "
26 shall be meat unto a· fowls of the "
32 longing for them a· the day long: "
33 a· thy labours, shall a nation which "
37 among a· nations whither the Lord "
40 olive trees throughout a· thy coasts, "
42 A· thy trees and fruit of thy land "
45 a· these curses shall come upon "
47 for the abundance of a· things; "
48 nakedness, and in want of a· things: "
52 shall besiege thee in a· thy gates, "
52 trustedst, throughout a· thy land: "
52 shall besiege thee in a· thy gates, "
52 throughout a· thy land, which the "
55 shall distress thee in a· thy gates. "
57 for want of a· things secretly in "
58 to do a· the words of this law "
60 upon thee a· the diseases of Egypt, "
64 shall scatter thee among a· people, "
29: 2 And Moses called unto a· Israel, "
2 Ye have seen a· that the Lord did "
2 and unto a· his servants, "
2 and unto a· his land; "
9 ye may prosper in a· that ye do. "
10 a· of you before the Lord your "
10 officers, with a· the men of Israel, "
20 a· the curses that are written in "
21 evil out of a· the tribes of Israel, "
21 a· the curses of the covenant that "
24 Even a· nations shall say, "
27 to bring upon it a· the curses that "
29 may do a· the words of this law. "
30: 1 when a· these things are come "
1 to mind among a· the nations, "
2 according to a· that I command "
2 with a· thine heart, "
2 and with a· thy soul; "
3 gather thee from a· the nations, "
6 Lord thy God with a· thine heart, "
6 and with a· thy soul, that thou "
7 God will put a· these curses upon "
8 and do a· his commandments "
10 turn unto the Lord thy God with a· "
10 thine heart, and with a· thy soul. "
31: 1 spake these words unto a· Israel. "
5 unto a· the commandments which "
7 sight of a· Israel, Be strong and "
9 and unto a· the elders of Israel. "
11 When a· Israel is come to appear "
11 thou shalt read this law before a· "
12 to do a· the words of this law: "
18 a· the evils which they shall have "
28 unto me a· the elders of your tribes, "
30 in the ears of a· the congregation "
32: 4 for a· his ways are judgment: "
27 and the Lord hath not done a· this. "
44 spake a· the words of this song, "
45 a· these words to a· Israel: "
46 hearts unto a· the words which I "
46 to do, a· the words of this law. "
33: 3 a· his saints are in thy hand: "
12 shall cover him a· the day long, "
34: 1 shewed him a· the land of Gilead, "
2 And a· Naphtali, and the land of "
2 Manasseh, and a· the land of Judah, "
11 In a· the signs and the wonders, "
11 to a· his servants, "
11 and to a· his land, "
12 And in a· that mighty hand, "
12 and in a· the great terror "
12 shewed in the sight of a· Israel. "
Jos 1: 2 Jordan, thou, and a· this people, "
4 a· the land of the Hittites, and "
5 before thee a· the days of thy life: "
7 do according to a· the law, which "
8 according to a· that is written "
14 a· the mighty men of valour, and "
16 A· that thou commandest us we "
17 hearkened unto Moses in a· things, "
18 words in a· that thou commandest "
2: 3 come to search out a· the country. "
9 that a· the inhabitants of the land "
13 my sisters, and a· that they have, "
18 and a· thy father's household, "
22 throughout a· the way, but found "
23 told him a· things that befell them: "
24 into our hands a· the land; "
24 a· the inhabitants of the country "
3: 1 he and a· the children of Israel, "
7 thee in the sight of a· Israel, "
11 covenant of the Lord of a· the earth "
13 the Lord, the Lord of a· the earth, "
15 a· his banks a· the time "
17 and a· the Israelites passed over "
17 a· the people were passed clean "

Jos 4: 1 when a· the people were clean 3605
10 according to a· that Moses "
11 when a· the people were clean "
14 Joshua in the sight of a· Israel; "
14 Moses, a· the days of his life. "
18 and flowed over a· his banks, as "
24 That a· the people of the earth "
5: 1 when a· the kings of the Amorites, "
1 a· the kings of the Canaanites, "
4 A· the people that came out of "
4 males, even a· the men of war, "
5 Now a· the people that came out "
5 but a· the people that were born "
6 years in the wilderness, till a· the "
8 done circumcising a· the people, "
6: 3 compass the city, a· ye men of war, "
5 trumpet, a· the people shall shout "
17 even it, and a· that are therein, "
17 a· that are with her in the house, "
19 But a· the silver, and gold, and "
21 destroyed a· that was in the city, "
22 the woman, and a· that she hath, "
23 her brethren, and a· that she had; "
23 brought out a· her kindred, and "
24 with fire, and a· that was therein: "
25 and a· that she had; and she "
27 noised throughout a· the country. "
7: 3 Let not a· the people go up; but "
3 make not a· the people to labour "
7 thou at a· brought this people over "
9 a· the inhabitants of the land 3605
15 with fire, he and a· that he hath: "
23 and unto a· the children of Israel, "
24 Joshua, and a· Israel with him, "
24 and his tent, and a· that he had: "
25 a· Israel stoned him with stones, "
8: 1 take a· the people of war with thee, "
3 arose, and a· the people of war, "
4 from the city, but be ye a· ready: "
5 and a· the people that are with me, "
11 And a· the people, even the people "
13 even a· the host that was on the "
14 to battle, he and a· his people, "
15 And Joshua and a· Israel made as "
16 And a· the people that were in Ai "
21 when Joshua and a· Israel saw "
24 slaying a· the inhabitants of Ai "
24 a· fallen on the edge of the sword, "
24 a· the Israelites returned unto Ai, "
25 that a· that fell that day, both of "
25 even a· the men of Ai. "
26 destroyed a· the inhabitants of Ai. "
33 And a· Israel, and their elders, "
34 he read a· the words of the law, "
34 a· that is written in the book of the "
35 word of a· that Moses commanded, "
35 a· the congregation of Israel, "
9: 1 when a· the kings which were on "
1 a· the coasts of the great sea over "
5 a· the bread of their provision "
9 of him, and a· that he did in Egypt, "
10 a· that he did to the two kings of "
11 our elders and a· the inhabitants "
18 And a· the congregation murmured "
21 of water unto a· the congregation; "
24 Moses to give you a· the land, "
24 a· the inhabitants of the land from "
10: 2 a· the men thereof were mighty. "
5 they and a· their hosts, and "
6 for a· the kings of the Amorites "
7 a· the people of war with him, "
7 and a· the mighty men "
9 and went up from Gilgal a· night. "
15 returned, and a· Israel with him, "
21 a· the people returned to the camp "
24 called for a· the men of Israel, "
25 the Lord do to a· your enemies "
28 them, and a· the souls that "
29 from Makkedah, and a· Israel "
30 and a· the souls that were therein; "
31 Libnah, and a· Israel with him, "
32 and a· the souls that were therein, "
32 according to a· that he had done "
34 unto Eglon, and a· Israel with him; "
35 and a· the souls that were therein, "
35 according to a· that he had done "
36 from Eglon, and a· Israel with him; "
37 thereof, and a· the cities thereof, "
37 and a· the souls that were therein; "
37 according to a· that he had done "
37 it utterly, and a· the souls "
38 and a· Israel with him, to Debir; "
39 thereof, and a· the cities thereof; "
39 a· the souls that were therein; "
40 So Joshua smote a· the country of "
40 of the springs, and a· their kings: "
40 utterly destroyed a· that breathed, "
41 and a· the country of Goshen, "
42 And a· these kings and their land "
43 returned, and a· Israel with him, "
11: 4 they and a· their hosts with them, "
5 a· these kings were met together, "
6 time will I deliver them up a· slain "
7 and a· the people of war with him, "
10 the head of a· those kingdoms. "
11 a· the souls that were therein with "
12 And a· the cities of those kings, "
12 and a· the kings "
14 And a· the spoil of these cities, "
15 of a· that the Lord commanded "
16 So Joshua took a· that land, "
16 and a· the south country, "
16 and a· the land of Goshen, "
17 under Mount Hermon: and a· "
18 a long time with a· those kings. "
19 Gibeon: a· other they took in battle. "

Jos 11:21 from *a* the mountains of Judah, 3605
21 *a* the mountains of Israel: "
23 *a* that the Lord said unto Moses; "
12: 1 Hermon, and *a* the plain on the "
5 and in *a* Bashan, unto the border "
24 one: *a* the kings thirty and one. "
13: 2 *a* the borders of the Philistines, "
2 and *a* Geshuri, "
4 *a* the land of the Canaanites, "
5 and *a* Lebanon, toward the "
6 *A* the inhabitants of the hill "
6 and *a* the Sidonians, then will I "
9 *a* the plain of Medeba unto Dibon; "
10 And *a* the cities of Sihon king of "
11 *a* mount Hermon, "
11 and *a* Bashan unto Salcah; "
12 *A* the kingdom of Og in Bashan, "
16 river, and *a* the plain by Medeba; "
17 *a* her cities that are in the plain; "
21 And *a* the cities of the plain, "
21 and *a* the kingdom of Sihon "
25 Jazer, and *a* the cities of Gilead, "
30 from Mahanaim, *a* Bashan, "
30 *a* the kingdom of Og king of "
30 *a* the towns of Jair, which are in "
15:32 and Rimmon: *a* the cities are "
46 *a* that lay near Ashdod, with their "
16: 9 *a* the cities with their villages. "
17:16 for us: and *a* the Canaanites "
19: 8 *a* the villages that were round "
20: 9 appointed for *a* the children of "
21:19 *A* the cities of the children of "
26 *A* the cities were ten with their "
33 *A* the cities of the Gershonites "
39 her suburbs; four cities in *a*. "
40 So *a* the cities for the children of "
41 *A* the cities of the Levites within "
42 them: thus were *a* these cities. "
43 Lord gave unto Israel *a* the land. "
44 according to *a* that he sware unto "
44 not a man of *a* their enemies "
44 Lord delivered *a* their enemies "
45 house of Israel; *a* came to pass. "
22: 2 *a* that Moses the servant of the "
2 in *a* that I commanded you: "
5 Lord your God, and to walk in *a* "
5 *a* your heart and with *a* your soul. "
14 *a* the tribes of Israel; *
20 wrath fell on *a* the congregation "
23: 1 unto Israel from *a* their enemies "
2 And Joshua called for *a* Israel, "
3 seen *a* that the Lord your God "
3 done unto *a* these nations because "
4 *a* the nations that I have cut off, "
6 do *a* that is written in the book of "
14 I am going the way of *a* the earth: "
14 know in *a* your hearts "
14 and in *a* your souls, that "
14 hath failed of *a* the good things "
14 concerning you; *a* are come to "
15 *a* good things are come upon you, "
15 Lord bring upon you *a* evil things, "
24: 1 Joshua gathered *a* the tribes of "
2 Joshua said unto *a* the people, "
3 throughout *a* the land of Canaan, "
17 and preserved us in *a* the way "
17 among *a* the people through whom "
18 out from before us *a* the people, "
27 Joshua said unto *a* the people, "
27 unto us; for it hath heard *a* the "
31 Israel served the Lord *a* the days "
31 and *a* the days of the elders that "
31 known *a* the works of the Lord, "
J'g 1:25 let go the man and *a* his family. "
2: 4 unto *a* the children of Israel, "
7 people served the Lord *a* the days "
7 and *a* the days of the elders that "
7 seen *a* the great works of the Lord, "
10 *a* that generation were gathered "
18 hand of their enemies *a* the days "
3: 1 not known *a* the wars of Canaan; "
3 and *a* the Canaanites, and the "
19 And *a* that stood by him went out "
29 ten thousand men, *a* lusty, *
29 *a* men of valour; and there *
4:13 gathered together *a* his chariots, "
13 *a* the people that were with him, "
15 and *a* his chariots, "
15 and *a* his host, with the "
16 *a* the host of Sisera fell upon the "
5:31 let *a* thine enemies perish, O Lord: "
6: 9 out of the hand of *a* that oppressed "
13 why then is *a* this befallen us? "
13 and where be *a* his "
31 unto *a* that stood against him, Will "
33 Then *a* the Midianites and the "
35 throughout *a* Manasseh; "
37 and it be dry upon *a* the earth "
39 upon *a* the ground let there be dew. "
40 there was dew on *a* the ground. "
7: 1 who is Gideon, and *a* the people "
6 but *a* the rest of the people bowed "
7 let *a* the other people go every "
8 he sent *a* the rest of Israel every "
12 and the Amalekites and *a* the "
14 hath God delivered Midian, and *a* "
18 a trumpet, I and *a* that are with "
18 also on every side of *a* the camp, "
21 and *a* the host ran, and cried, and "
22 fellow, even throughout *a* the host: "
23 of Asher, and out of *a* Manasseh, "
24 messengers throughout *a* mount "
24 *a* the men of Ephraim gathered "
8:10 *a* that were left of *a* the hosts of "
12 and discomfited *a* the host. "
27 Ophrah: and *a* Israel went thither "

J'g 8:34 out of the hands of *a* their enemies 3605
35 according to *a* the goodness which "
9: 1 with them, and with *a* the family "
2 pray you, in the ears of *a* the men "
2 that *a* the sons of Jerubbaal, "
3 the ears of *a* the men of Shechem "
3 *a* these words: and their hearts "
6 *a* the men of Shechem gathered "
6 and *a* the house of Millo, and went, "
14 said *a* the trees unto the bramble, "
25 they robbed *a* that came along "
34 rose up, and *a* the people that "
44 companies ran upon *a* the people "
45 fought against the city *a* that day; "
46 when *a* the men of the tower of "
47 *a* the men of the tower of Shechem "
48 he and *a* the people that were "
49 *a* the people likewise cut down "
49 *a* the men of the tower of Shechem "
51 thither fled *a* the men and women, "
51 and *a* they of the city, "
53 Abimelech's head, and *a* to brake *
57 *a* the evil of the men of Shechem 3605
10: 8 *a* the children of Israel "
18 over *a* the inhabitants of Gilead. "
11: 8 be our head over *a* the inhabitants "
11 Jephthah uttered *a* his words, "
20 but Sihon gathered *a* his people "
21 delivered Sihon and *a* his people "
21 so Israel possessed *a* the land of "
22 possessed *a* the coasts of the "
26 in *a* the cities that be along by the "
12: 4 Jephthah gathered together *a* the "
13:13 Of *a* that I said unto the woman "
14 *a* that I commanded her let her "
23 have shewed us *a* these things, "
14: 3 brethren, or among *a* my people, "
16: 2 wait for him *a* night in the gate of "
2 were quiet *a* the night, saying, "
3 went away with them, bar and *a*, 5973
17 that he told her *a* his heart, and 3605
18 that he had told her *a* his heart, "
18 he hath shewed me *a* his heart. "
27 *a* the lords of the Philistines were "
30 bowed himself with *a* his might; "
30 fell upon the lords, and upon *a* 3605
31 his brethren and *a* the house of "
18: 1 that day *a* their inheritance had *
31 *a* the time that the house of God 3605
19: 6 tarry *a* night, and let thine heart 3885
9 I pray you tarry *a* night: "
13 to lodge *a* night, in Gibeah, or in * "
20 howsoever let *a* thy wants lie 3605
25 *a* the night until the morning: "
29 sent her into *a* the coasts of Israel. "
30 that *a* that saw it said, There was "
20: 1 *a* the children of Israel went out, "
2 And the chief of *a* the people, "
2 even of *a* the tribes of Israel, "
6 sent her throughout *a* the country "
7 ye are *a* children of Israel; give "
8 *a* the people arose as one man, "
10 men of an hundred throughout *a* "
10 according to *a* the folly that they "
11 *a* the men of Israel were gathered "
12 through *a* the tribe of Benjamin, "
16 Among *a* this people there were "
17 sword: *a* these were men of war. "
25 men; *a* these drew the sword. "
26 Then *a* the children of Israel, "
26 and *a* the people, went up, "
33 And *a* the men of Israel rose up "
34 chosen men out of *a* Israel, and "
35 *a* these drew the sword. "
37 smote *a* the city with the edge of "
44 men; *a* these were men of valour. "
46 *a* which fell that day of Benjamin "
46 drew the sword; *a* these were men "
48 and *a* that came to hand: also "
48 they set on fire *a* the cities that "
21: 5 among *a* the tribes of Israel, "
Ru 1:19 that *a* the city was moved about "
2:11 fully been shewed me, *a* that thou "
21 they have ended *a* my harvest. "
3: 5 *A* that thou sayest unto me I will "
6 *a* that her mother in law bade her. "
11 do to thee *a* that thou requirest: "
11 for *a* the city of my people doth "
16 my daughter? And she told her *a* "
4: 7 confirm *a* things; a man plucked "
9 the elders, and unto *a* the people, "
9 this day, that I have bought *a* "
9 and *a* that was Chilion's "
11 *a* the people that were in the gate, "
1Sa 1: 4 Peninnah his wife, and to *a* her "
11 give him unto the Lord *a* the days "
21 man Elkanah, and *a* his house, "
2:14 *a* that the fleshhook brought up "
14 So they did in Shiloh unto *a* "
22 heard *a* that his sons did "
22 unto *a* Israel; "
23 evil dealings by *a* this people. "
28 choose him out of *a* the tribes of "
28 give unto the house of thy father *a* "
29 fat with the chiefest of *a* the "
2:32 *a* the wealth which God shall give "
33 grieve thine heart: and *a* the "
3:12 will perform against Eli *a* things "
17 hide anything from me of *a* the "
20 And *a* Israel from Dan even to "
4: 1 word of Samuel came to *a* Israel. "
5 into the camp, *a* Israel shouted "
8 that smote the Egyptians with *a* "
13 into the city, and told it, *a* the city "
5: 8 *a* the lords of the Philistines unto "
11 gathered together *a* the lords of "

1Sa 5:11 destruction throughout *a* the city; 3605
6: 4 for one plague was on you *a*, and "
18 according to the number of *a* the "
7: 2 *a* the house of Israel lamented "
3 Samuel spake unto *a* the house of "
3 unto the Lord with *a* your hearts, "
5 Gather *a* Israel to Mizpeh, and I "
13 against the Philistines *a* the days "
15 Samuel judged Israel *a* the days "
16 judged Israel in *a* those places. "
8: 4 *a* the elders of Israel gathered "
5 to judge us like *a* the nations. "
7 of the people in *a* that they say "
8 According to *a* the works which "
10 Samuel told *a* the words of the Lord "
20 we also may be like *a* the nations; "
21 And Samuel heard *a* the words of "
9: 6 *a* that he saith cometh surely to "
19 tell thee *a* that is in thine heart. "
20 on whom is *a* the desire of Israel? "
20 and on *a* thy father's house? "
21 least of *a* the families of the tribe "
10: 9 *a* those signs came to pass that "
11 when *a* that knew him beforetime "
18 Egyptians, and out of the hand of *a* "
19 saved you out of *a* your adversities "
20 had caused *a* the tribes of Israel "
24 And Samuel said to *a* the people, "
24 none like him among *a* the people? "
24 *a* the people shouted, and said, "
25 Samuel sent *a* the people away, "
11: 1 *a* the men of Jabesh said unto "
2 may thrust out *a* your right eyes, "
2 lay it for a reproach upon *a* Israel. "
3 send messengers unto *a* the coasts "
4 *a* the people lifted up their voices, "
7 throughout *a* the coasts of Israel "
10 *a* that seemeth good unto you. "
15 And *a* the people went to Gilgal; "
15 and *a* the men of Israel rejoiced "
12: 1 Samuel said unto *a* Israel, Behold, "
1 voice in *a* that ye said unto me, "
7 *a* the righteous acts of the Lord, "
18 *a* the people greatly feared the "
19 *a* the people said unto Samuel, "
19 added unto *a* our sins this evil, "
20 done *a* this wickedness: yet turn "
20 serve the Lord with *a* your heart; "
24 him in truth with *a* your heart. "
13: 4 And *a* Israel heard say that Saul "
7 and *a* the people followed him "
19 throughout *a* the land of Israel: "
20 *a* the Israelites went down to the "
14: 7 Do *a* that is in thine heart: turn "
15 the host, in the field; and among *a* "
20 Saul and *a* the people that were "
22 Likewise *a* the men of Israel "
25 And *a* they of the land came to a "
38 hither, *a* the chief of the people: "
39 *a* the people that answered him. "
40 unto *a* Israel, Be ye on one side, "
47 fought against *a* his enemies on "
52 against the Philistines *a* the days "
15: 3 and utterly destroy *a* that they "
6 to *a* the children of Israel, "
8 destroyed *a* the people with the "
9 the lambs, and *a* that was good, "
11 he cried unto the Lord *a* night. "
16:11 Jesse, Are here *a* thy children? 8552
17:11 and *a* Israel heard those words of 3605
19 and *a* the men of Israel, were "
24 And *a* the men of Israel, when "
46 *a* the earth may know that there "
47 And *a* this assembly shall know "
18: 5 in the sight of *a* the people, "
6 came out of *a* cities of Israel, "
14 behaved himself wisely in *a* his "
16 *a* Israel and Judah loved David, "
22 hath delight in thee and *a* his "
30 himself more wisely than *a* "
19: 1 to Jonathan his son, and to *a* "
5 a great salvation for *a* Israel: "
7 and Jonathan shewed him *a* those "
18 told him *a* that Saul had done to "
24 lay down naked *a* that day "
24 and *a* that night. "
20: 6 If thy father at *a* miss me, then
6 sacrifice there for *a* the family. 3605
22: 1 and *a* his father's house heard it, "
4 with him *a* the while that David "
6 in his hand, and *a* his servants "
7 make you *a* captains of thousands, "
8 That *a* of you have conspired "
11 Ahitub, and *a* his father's house, "
11 they came *a* of them to the king. "
14 so faithful among *a* thy servants "
15 nor to *a* the house of my father: "
15 servant knew nothing of *a* this, "
16 thou, and *a* thy father's house. "
22 the death of *a* the persons of "
23: 8 called *a* the people together to war, "
20 according to *a* the desire of thy "
23 knowledge of *a* the lurking places "
23 *a* the thousands of Judah. "
24: 2 three thousand chosen men out of *a* "
25: 1 *a* the Israelites were gathered "
6 peace be unto *a* that thou hast. "
7 them, *a* the while they were in "
9 Nabal according to *a* those words "
12 again, and came and told him *a* "
16 by night and day, *a* the while "
17 against our master, and against *a* "
21 have I kept *a* that this fellow "
21 was missed of *a* that pertained "
22 if I leave of *a* that pertain to him "
28 not been found in thee *a* thy days,

1Sa 25:30 according to a' the good that he 3605
26:12 for they were a' asleep; because "
24 deliver me out of a' tribulation. "
27:11 manner a' the while he dwelleth "
28: 3 dead, and a' Israel had lamented "
4 and Saul gathered a' Israel "
20 a' along on the earth, *4393
20 eaten no bread a' the day, 3605
20 nor a' the night. "
29: 1 gathered together a' their armies "
30: 6 soul of a' the people was grieved, "
8 them, and without fail recover a'.
16 spread abroad upon a' the earth, 3605
16 dancing, because of a' the great "
18 recovered a' that the Amalekites "
19 taken to them: David recovered a'. "
20 And David took a' the flocks and "
22 answered a' the wicked men and "
31 in Hebron, and to a' the places "
31: 6 armourbearer, and a' his men, "
12 A' the valiant men arose, "
12 and went a' night, and "
2Sa 1:11 them; and likewise a' the men that "
2: 9 Benjamin, and over a' Israel. "
28 and a' the people stood still, and "
29 and his men walked a' that night "
29 and went through a' Bithron, "
30 gathered a' the people together, "
32 Joab and his men went a' night, "
3:12 be with thee, to bring about a' "
18 out of the hand of a' their enemies. "
19 of David in Hebron a' that seemed "
21 will gather a' Israel unto my lord "
21 over a' that thine heart desireth. "
23 Joab and a' the host that was with "
25 and to know a' that thou doest. "
29 and on a' his father's house; "
31 and to a' the people that were "
32 of Abner; and a' the people wept. "
34 a' the people wept again over him. "
35 when a' the people came to cause "
36 a' the people took notice of it, "
36 whatsoever the king did pleased a' "
37 For a' the people and a' Israel "
4: 1 and a' the Israelites were troubled. "
7 away through the plain a' night. "
9 my soul out of a' adversity, "
5: 1 came a' the tribes of Israel to "
3 So a' the elders of Israel came to "
5 years over a' Israel and Judah. "
17 a' the Philistines came up to seek "
6: 1 a' the chosen men of Israel, "
2 arose, and went with a' the people "
5 and a' the house of Israel played "
5 on a' manner of instruments made "
11 Obed-edom, and a' his household. "
12 Obed-edom, and a' that pertaineth "
14 before the Lord with a' his might; "
15 a' the house of Israel brought up "
19 And he dealt among a' the people, "
19 So a' the people departed every "
21 and before a' his house, to appoint "
7: 1 round about from a' his enemies; "
3 Go, do a' that is in thine heart; "
7 a' the places wherein I have walked "
7 with a' the children of Israel "
9 a' thine enemies out of thy sight, "
11 to rest from a' thine enemies. "
17 According to a' these words, and "
21 thou done a' these great things, "
22 God beside thee, according to a' "
8: 4 houghed a' the chariot horses, "
9 smitten a' the host of Hadadezer, "
11 of a' nations which he subdued; "
14 throughout a' Edom put he "
14 garrisons, and a' they of Edom "
15 And David reigned over a' Israel; "
15 and justice unto a' his people. "
9: 7 a' the land of Saul thy father; "
9 a' that pertained to Saul "
9 and to a' his house. "
11 According to a' that my lord the "
12 And a' that dwelt in the house of "
10: 7 and a' the host of the mighty men. "
9 of a' the choice men of Israel, "
17 he gathered a' Israel together, "
19 a' the kings that were servants to "
11: 1 and his servants with him, and a' "
9 with a' the servants of his lord, "
18 a' the things concerning the war; "
22 shewed David a' that Joab had "
12:12 I will do this thing before a' Israel, "
16 and lay a' night upon the earth. 3885
29 And David gathered a' the people 3605
31 unto a' the cities of the children of "
31 David and a' the people returned "
13: 9 said, Have out a' men from me. "
21 king David heard of a' these things, "
23 Absalom invited a' the king's sons. "
25 Nay, my son, let us not a' now go, "
27 and a' the king's sons go with him. "
29 Then a' the king's sons arose, "
30 hath slain a' the king's sons, "
31 a' his servants stood by with their "
32 they have slain a' the young men "
33 that a' the king's sons are dead: "
36 and a' his servants wept very sore. "
14:19 hand of Joab with thee in a' this? "
19 put a' these words in the mouth "
20 to know a' things that are in the "
25 But in a' Israel there was none to "
15: 6 manner did Absalom to a' Israel "
10 sent spies throughout a' the tribes "
14 David said unto a' his servants "
16 went forth, and a' his household "
17 forth, and a' the people after him. "
2Sa 15:18 a' his servants passed on beside 3605
18 and a' the Cherethites, "
18 and a' the Pelethites, "
18 and a' the Gittites, six hundred "
22 passed over, and a' his men, "
22 and a' the little ones "
23 a' the country wept with a loud "
23 a' the people passed over: the king "
23 a' the people passed over, toward "
24 Zadok also, and a' the Levites "
24 a' the people had done passing out "
30 went barefoot: and a' the people "
16: 4 thine are a' that pertained unto "
6 and at a' the servants "
6 of king David: and a' the people "
6 and a' the mighty men "
8 a' the blood of the house of Saul, "
11 to Abishai, and to a' his servants, "
14 the king, and a' the people that "
15 and a' the people the men "
18 and a' the men of Israel, choose, "
21 a' Israel shall hear that thou art "
21 then shall the hands of a' that "
22 concubines in the sight of a' Israel. "
23 so was a' the counsel of Ahithophel "
17: 2 a' the people that are with him "
3 bring back a' the people unto thee: "
3 thou seekest is as if a' returned: "
3 so a' the people shall be in peace. "
4 pleased Absalom well, and a' the "
10 a' Israel knoweth that thy father "
11 a' Israel be generally gathered "
12 of a' the men that are with him "
13 a' Israel bring ropes to that city, "
14 and a' the men of Israel said, "
16 swallowed up, and a' the people "
22 arose, and a' the people that were "
24 Jordan, he and a' the men of Israel "
18: 4 by the gate side, and a' the people "
5 And a' the people heard when "
5 king gave a' the captains charge "
8 scattered over the face of a' the "
17 a' Israel fled every one to his tent. "
28 and said unto the king, A' is well. "
31 avenged thee this day of a' them 3605
32 a' that rise against thee to do "
19: 2 into mourning unto a' the people: "
5 day the faces of a' thy servants, "
6 had lived, and a' we had died "
7 worse unto thee than a' the evil "
8 unto a' the people, saying, Behold, "
8 a' the people came before the king: "
9 a' the people were at strife "
9 throughout a' the tribes of Israel, "
11 the speech of a' Israel is come "
14 the heart of a' the men of Judah, "
14 Return thou, and a' thy servants. "
20 the first this day of a' the house "
28 For a' of my father's house were "
30 Yea, let him take a', forasmuch "
39 a' the people went over Jordan. "
40 and a' the people of Judah "
41 behold, a' the men of Israel came to "
41 and a' David's men with him, "
42 a' the men of Judah answered "
42 we eaten at a' of the king's cost? "
20: 7 and a' the mighty men: 3605
12 saw that a' the people stood still, "
13 a' the people went on after Joab, "
14 through a' the tribes of Israel "
14 and to Beth-maachah, and a' the "
15 a' the people that were with Joab "
22 woman went unto a' the people in "
23 was over a' the host of Israel: "
21: 9 and they fell a' seven together, "
14 his father: and they performed a' 3605
22: 1 out of the hand of a' his enemies, "
23 a' his judgments were before me: "
31 Lord is tried: he is a buckler to a' "
23: 5 ordered in a' things, and sure: "
5 a' my salvation, and a' my desire, "
6 a' of them as thorns thrust away, "
39 Hittite: thirty and seven in a'. "
24: 2 now through a' the tribes of Israel, "
7 and to a' the cities of the Hivites, "
8 they had gone through a' the land, "
23 A' these things did Araunah, as a "
1Ki 1: 3 damsel throughout a' the coasts "
9 a' his brethren the king's sons, "
9 a' the men of Judah the king's "
19 hath called a' the sons of the king, "
20 the eyes of a' Israel are upon thee, "
25 called a' the king's sons, and the "
29 redeemed my soul out of a' distress, "
39 and a' the people said, God save "
40 a' the people came up after him, "
41, 49 a' the guests that were with "
2: 2 I go the way of a' the earth: be "
3 prosper in a' that thou doest, "
4 in truth with a' their heart "
4 and with a' their soul, "
15 that a' Israel set their faces on me, "
26 thou hast been afflicted in a' "
44 a' the wickedness which thine "
3:13 kings like unto thee a' thy days. "
15 made a feast to a' his servants. "
28 a' Israel heard of the judgment "
4: 1 Solomon was king over a' Israel. "
7 had twelve officers over a' Israel, "
10 Sochoh, and a' the land of Hepher: "
11 Abinadab, in a' the region of Dor: "
12 Taanach and Megiddo, and a' "
21 Solomon reigned over a' kingdoms "
21 Solomon a' the days of his life. "
24 a' the region on this side the river, "
24 a' the kings on this side the river: "
1Ki 4:24 peace on a' sides round about him. 3605
25 Beer-sheba, a' the days of Solomon. "
27 for king Solomon, and for a' "
30 excelled the wisdom of a' the "
30 and a' the wisdom of Egypt. "
31 For he was wiser than a' men; "
31 was in a' nations round about. "
34 of a' people to hear the wisdom "
34 Solomon, from a' kings of the earth, "
5: 6 servants according to a' that thou "
8 I will do a' thy desire concerning "
10 trees according to a' his desire. "
13 raised a levy out of a' Israel; "
6:10 chambers against a' the house, "
12 and keep a' my commandments "
18 a' was cedar; there was no stone "
22 with gold, until he had finished a' "
29 carved a' the walls of the house "
38 house finished throughout a' the "
38 according to a' the fashion of it. "
7: 1 thirteen years, and he finished a' "
5 a' the doors and posts were square, "
9 A' these were of costly stones, "
14 cunning to work a' works in brass. "
14 Solomon, and wrought a' his work. "
23 round a' about, and his height *
25 a' their hinder parts were 3605
33 and their spokes, were a' molten. "
37 a' of them had one casting, one "
40 made an end of doing a' the work "
45 and a' these vessels, which Hiram "
47 left a' the vessels unweighed, "
48 made a' the vessels that pertained "
51 a' the work that king Solomon "
8: 1 of Israel, and a' the heads of the "
2 a' the men of Israel assembled "
3 And a' the elders of Israel came, "
4 a' the holy vessels that were in the "
5 And king Solomon, and a' "
14 and blessed a' the congregation "
14 (and a' the congregation of Israel "
16 I chose no city out of a' the tribes "
22 of a' the congregation of Israel, "
23 before thee with a' their heart: "
38 any man, or by a' thy people Israel, "
39 hearts of a' the children of men;) "
40 thee a' the days that they live "
43 according to a' that the stranger "
43 that a' people of the earth may "
48 unto thee with a' their heart, "
48 and with a' their soul, in the land "
50 sinned against thee, and a' their "
52 unto them in a' that they call *
53 them from among a' the people of "
54 had made an end of praying a' "
55 a' the congregation of Israel "
56 people Israel, according to a' that "
56 hath not failed one word of a' "
58 unto him, to walk in a' his ways, "
59 of his people Israel at a' times, *
60 That a' the people of the earth 3605
62 the king, and a' Israel with him, "
63 king and a' the children of Israel "
65 held a feast, and a' Israel with him, "
66 a' the goodness that the Lord had "
9: 1 and a' Solomon's desire which he "
4 to do according to a' that I have "
6 at a' turn from following me, *
7 and a byword among a' people: 3605
9 brought upon them a' this evil. "
11 gold, according to a' his desire,) "
19 a' the cities of store that Solomon "
19 and in a' the land of his dominion. "
20 And a' the people that were left "
10: 2 him of a' that was in her heart. "
3 Solomon told her a' her questions: "
4 had seen a' Solomon's wisdom, "
13 the queen of Sheba a' her desire, "
15 and of a' the kings of Arabia, "
21 a' king Solomon's drinking vessels "
21 a' the vessels of the house "
23 exceeded a' the kings of the earth "
24 a' the earth sought to Solomon, "
29 so for a' the kings of the Hittites, "
11: 8 did he for a' his strange wives, "
13 will not rend away a' the kingdom; "
16 did Joab remain there with a' "
25 to Israel a' the days of Solomon, "
28 a' the charge of the house of "
32 out of a' the tribes of Israel:) "
34 prince a' the days of his life "
37 to a' that thy soul desireth, "
38 hearken unto a' that I command "
41 acts of Solomon, and a' that he did, "
42 reigned in Jerusalem over a' Israel "
12: 1 for a' Israel were come to Shechem "
3 and a' the congregation of Israel "
12 Jeroboam and a' the people came "
16 when a' Israel saw that the king "
18 a' Israel stoned him with stones, "
20 a' Israel heard that Jeroboam was "
20 and made him king over a' Israel: "
21 assembled a' the house of Judah, "
23 and unto a' the house of Judah "
13:11 came and told him a' the works "
32 altar in Beth-el, and against a' the "
14: 8 who followed me with a' his heart, "
9 evil above a' that were before thee: "
10 away dung, till it be a' gone. 8552
13 a' Israel shall mourn for him, 3605
18 buried him; and a' Israel mourned "
21 out of a' the tribes of Israel, "
22 a' that their fathers had done. "
24 according to a' the abominations "
26 house; he even took away a': "
26 he took away a' the shields of gold "

1Ki 14:29 Rehoboam, and *a'* that he did, 3605
30 Rehoboam and Jeroboam *a'* * "
15: 3 walked in *a'* the sins of his father, "
5 commanded him *a'* the days of his "
6 Jeroboam *a'* the days of his life. "
7 acts of Abijam, and *a'* that he did, "
12 *a'* the idols that his fathers "
14 perfect with the Lord *a'* his days. "
16 Asa and Baasha king of Israel *a'* "
18 Asa took *a'* the silver and the gold "
20 and *a'* Cinneroth, "
20 with *a'* the land of Naphtali. "
22 made a proclamation throughout *a'* "
23 The rest of *a'* the acts of Asa, "
23 and *a'* his might, "
23 and *a'* that he did, and the cities "
27 *a'* Israel laid siege to Gibbethon. "
29 smote *a'* the house of Jeroboam; "
31 acts of Nadab, and *a'* that he did, "
32 Asa and Baasha king of Israel *a'* "
33 son of Ahijah to reign over *a'* Israel "
16: 7 for *a'* the evil that he did in the "
11 he slew *a'* the house of Baasha: "
12 destroy *a'* the house of Baasha, "
13 For *a'* the sins of Baasha, and the "
14 the acts of Elah, and *a'* that he did, "
16 wherefore *a'* Israel made Omri, "
17 and *a'* Israel with him, and they "
25 did worse than *a'* that were before "
26 walked in *a'* the way of Jeroboam "
30 of the Lord above *a'* that were "
33 Lord God of Israel to anger than *a'* "
18: 5 land, unto *a'* fountains of water, "
5 and unto *a'* brooks: peradventure "
5 mules alive, that we lose not *a'* 3605
19 gather to me *a'* Israel unto mount "
20 Ahab sent unto *a'* the children of "
21 Elijah came unto *a'* the people, "
24 by fire, let him be God. And *a'* "
30 And Elijah said unto *a'* the people, "
30 *a'* the people came near unto him. "
36 done *a'* these things at thy word. "
39 And when *a'* the people saw it, "
19: 1 Ahab told Jezebel *a'* that Elijah "
1 how he had slain *a'* the prophets "
18 *a'* the knees which have not bowed "
20: 1 king of Syria gathered *a'* his host "
4 thy saying, I am thine, and *a'* that "
7 king of Israel called *a'* the elders "
8 And *a'* the elders "
8 and *a'* the people said, "
9 *A'* that thou didst send for thy "
10 for handfuls for *a'* the people that "
13 thou seen *a'* this great multitude? "
15 he numbered *a'* the people, "
15 even *a'* the children of Israel, being "
27 numbered, and were *a'* present, * "
28 I deliver *a'* this great multitude "
21:26 in following idols, according to *a'* 3605
22:10, 12 *a'* the prophets prophesied "
17 *a'* Israel scattered upon the hills, "
19 sitting on his throne, and *a'* the "
22 in the mouth of *a'* his prophets. "
23 *a'* these thy prophets, and the Lord "
28 said, If thou return at *a'* in peace, "
39 acts of Ahab, and *a'* that he did, 3605
39 and *a'* the cities that he built, "
43 in *a'* the ways of Asa his father; "
53 Lord God of Israel, according to *a'* "
2Ki 3: 6 time, and numbered *a'* Israel. "
19 every good tree, and stop *a'* wells "
21 And when *a'* the Moabites heard "
21 *a'* that were able to put on armour, "
25 they stopped *a'* the wells of water, "
25 and felled *a'* the good trees: "
4: 3 abroad of *a'* thy neighbours, "
4 shalt pour into *a'* those vessels, "
13 careful for us with *a'* this care; "
5:12 better than *a'* the waters of "
15 to the man of God, he and *a'* his "
15 there is no God in *a'* the earth, "
21 to meet him, and said, Is *a'* well? "
22 *A'* is well. My master hath sent "
6:24 king of Syria gathered *a'* his host, 3605
7:13 are as *a'* the multitude of Israel "
13 behold, I say, they are even as *a'* "
15 lo, *a'* the way was full of garments "
8: 4 *a'* the great things that Elisha "
6 Restore *a'* that was hers, "
6 and *a'* the fruits of the field "
21 Zair, and *a'* the chariots with him: "
23 acts of Joram, and *a'* that he did, "
9: 5 Jehu said, Unto which of *a'* of us? "
7 of *a'* the servants of the Lord, "
11 one said unto him, Is *a'* well? "
14 Ramoth-gilead, he and *a'* Israel, 3605
10: 5 will do *a'* that thou shalt bid us; "
9 to *a'* the people, Ye be righteous: "
11 Jehu slew *a'* that remained of the "
11 in Jezreel, and *a'* his great men, "
17 slew *a'* that remained unto Ahab "
18 gathered *a'* the people together, "
19 unto me *a'* the prophets of Baal, "
19 *a'* his servants, and *a'* his priests: "
21 And Jehu sent through *a'* Israel: "
21 and *a'* the worshippers of Baal "
22 vestments for *a'* the worshippers "
30 to *a'* that was in mine heart, thy "
31 with *a'* his heart: for he departed "
32 them in *a'* the coasts of Israel; "
33 eastward, *a'* the land of Gilead, "
34 acts of Jehu, and *a'* that he did, "
34 and *a'* his might, "
11: 1 arose and destroyed *a'* the seed "
7 *a'* you that go forth on the sabbath, "
9 *a'* things that Jehoiada the priest "

2Ki 11:14, 18, 19, 20 *a'* the people of the land 3605
12: 2 the sight of the Lord *a'* his days "
4 *A'* the money of the dedicated "
4 *a'* the money that cometh into any "
9 put therein *a'* the money "
12 of the house of the Lord, and for *a'* "
18 Jehoash king of Judah took *a'* the "
18 *a'* the gold that was found in the "
19 acts of Joash, and *a'* that he did, "
13: 3 the son of Hazael, *a'* their days. * "
8 of the acts of Jehoahaz, and *a'* "
11 he departed not from *a'* the sins of "
12 acts of Joash, and *a'* that he did, "
22 Israel *a'* the days of Jehoahaz. "
14: 3 according to *a'* things as Joash "
14 he took *a'* the gold and silver, "
14 and *a'* the vessels that were found "
21 And *a'* the people of Judah took "
24 he departed not from *a'* the sins "
28 acts of Jeroboam, and *a'* that he "
15: 3 *a'* that his father Amaziah had "
6 acts of Azariah, and *a'* that he did, "
16 smote Tiphsah, and *a'* that were "
16 him, therefore he smote it; and *a'* "
18 he departed not *a'* his days from "
20 of *a'* the mighty men of wealth, "
21 acts of Menahem, and *a'* that he "
26 of Pekahiah, and *a'* that he did, "
29 Gilead, and Galilee, *a'* the land of "
31 of the acts of Pekah, and *a'* that "
34 according to *a'* that his father "
36 acts of Jotham, and *a'* that he did, "
16:10 according to *a'* the workmanship "
11 according to *a'* that king Ahaz "
15 of *a'* the people of the land, "
15 *a'* the blood of the burnt offering, "
15 *a'* the blood of the sacrifice: and "
16 to *a'* that king Ahaz commanded. "
17: 5 came up throughout *a'* the land, "
9 them high places in *a'* their cities, "
11 incense in *a'* the high places, "
13 by *a'* the prophets, * "
13 and by *a'* the seers, saying, * "
13 to *a'* the law which I commanded "
16 *a'* the commandments of the Lord "
16 worshipped *a'* the host of heaven, "
20 Lord rejected *a'* the seed of Israel, "
22 of Israel walked in *a'* the sins "
23 by *a'* his servants the prophets. "
39 deliver you out of the hand of *a'* "
18: 3 to *a'* that David his father did. "
5 was none like him among *a'* the "
12 his covenant, and *a'* that Moses "
13 up against *a'* the fenced cities "
15 gave him *a'* the silver that was "
21 king of Egypt unto *a'* that trust on "
33 delivered at *a'* his land out of * "
35 *a'* the gods of the countries, 3605
19: 4 thy God will hear *a'* the words "
11 of Assyria have done to *a'* lands, "
15 thou alone, of *a'* the kingdoms "
19 of his hand, that *a'* the kingdoms "
24 sole of my feet have I dried up *a'* "
35 behold, they were *a'* dead corpses. "
20:13 *a'* the house of his precious things, "
13 *a'* the house of his armour, * "
13 *a'* that was found in his treasures: "
13 nor in *a'* his dominion, that "
15 *A'* the things that are in mine "
17 days come, that *a'* that is in thine "
20 acts of Hezekiah, and *a'* his might, "
21: 3 of Israel; and worshipped *a'* the "
5 altars for *a'* the host of heaven "
7 which I have chosen out of *a'* "
8 observe to do according to *a'* that "
8 *a'* the law that my servant Moses "
11 above *a'* that the Amorites "
14 and a spoil to *a'* their enemies; "
17 the acts of Manasseh, and *a'* that "
21 *a'* the way that his father walked "
24 of the land slew *a'* them that had "
22: 2 in *a'* the way of David his father, "
13 me, and for the people, and for *a'* "
13 *a'* that which is written concerning "
16 thereof, even *a'* the words "
17 me to anger with *a'* the works of "
20 shall not see *a'* the evil which I "
23: 1 unto him *a'* the elders of Judah "
2 and *a'* the men of Judah "
2 *a'* the inhabitants of Jerusalem "
2 the prophets, and *a'* the people, "
2 their ears *a'* the words of the book "
3 and his statutes with *a'* their heart "
3 and *a'* their soul, "
3 *a'* the people stood to the covenant. "
4 *a'* the vessels that were made for "
4 and for *a'* the host of heaven: "
5 and to *a'* the host of heaven. "
8 *a'* the priests out of the cities "
19 And *a'* the houses also of the high "
19 according to *a'* the acts that he had "
20 he slew *a'* the priests of the high "
21 king commanded *a'* the people, "
22 *a'* the days of the kings of Israel, "
24 and *a'* the abominations that were "
25 to the Lord with *a'* his heart, "
25 and with *a'* his soul, "
25 and with *a'* his might, "
25 according to *a'* the law of Moses; "
26 *a'* the provocations that Manasseh "
28 the acts of Josiah, and *a'* that he "
32 to *a'* that his fathers had done. "
37 sight of the Lord, according to *a'* "
24: 3 sins of Manasseh, according to *a'* "
5 of Jehoiakim, and *a'* that he did, "
7 *a'* that pertained to the king of "

2Ki 24:9 sight of the Lord, according to *a'* "
13 carried out thence *a'* the treasures "
13 cut in pieces *a'* the vessels of gold "
14 he carried away *a'* Jerusalem, "
14 *a'* the princes, and *a'* the mighty "
14 *a'* the craftsmen and smiths: "
16 And *a'* the men of might, even "
16 *a'* that were strong and apt for war, "
19 according to *a'* that Jehoiakim "
25: 1 and *a'* his host, against Jerusalem, "
4 and *a'* the men of war fled by night "
5 and *a'* his army were scattered "
9 and *a'* the houses of Jerusalem, "
10 And *a'* the army of the Chaldees, "
14 *a'* the vessels of brass wherewith "
16 *a'* these vessels was without weight. "
17 upon the chapiter round about, *a'* "
23 when *a'* the captains of the armies, "
26 *a'* the people, both small and great, "
29 continually before him, *a'* the days "
30 every day, *a'* the days of his life. "
1Ch 1:23 *A'* these were the sons of Joktan. "
33 *A'* these are the sons of Keturah. "
2: 4 *A'* the sons of Judah were five. "
6 and Dara: five of them in *a'*. "
23 *A'* these belonged to the sons of "
3: 9 These were *a'* the sons of David, "
4:27 did *a'* their family multiply, like "
33 *a'* their villages that were round "
5:10 *a'* the east land of Gilead. "
16 and in *a'* the suburbs of Sharon, "
17 *A'* these were reckoned by "
20 and *a'* that were with them: for "
6:48 appointed unto *a'* manner of "
49 *a'* the work of the place most holy, "
49 to *a'* that Moses the servant of God "
60 *A'* their cities throughout their "
7: 3 five: *a'* of them chief men. "
5 brethren among *a'* the families "
5 of might, reckoned in *a'* by their "
8 *A'* these are the sons of Becher. "
11 *A'* these the sons of Jediael, by "
40 *A'* these were the children of Asher, "
8:38 *A'* these were the sons of Azel. "
40 *A'* these are the sons of Benjamin. "
9: 1 So *a'* Israel were reckoned by "
9 *A'* these men were chief of the "
22 *A'* these which were chosen to be "
29 *a'* the instruments of the sanctuary, "
10: 6 and *a'* his house died together. "
7 *a'* the men of Israel that were in "
11 And when *a'* Jabesh-gilead "
11 heard *a'* that the Philistines had "
12 They arose, *a'* the valiant men, "
11: 1 Then *a'* Israel gathered themselves "
3 *a'* the elders of Israel to the king "
4 and *a'* Israel went to Jerusalem, "
10 him in his kingdom, and with *a'* "
12:15 when it had overflown *a'* his "
15 put to flight *a'* them of the valleys, "
21 they were *a'* mighty men of valour, "
32 and *a'* their brethren were at their "
33 war, with *a'* instruments of war, * "
37 tribe of Manasseh, with *a'* manner "
38 *A'* these men of war, that could "
38 make David king over *a'* Israel: "
38 *a'* the rest also of Israel were of "
13: 2 unto *a'* the congregation of Israel, "
2 that are left in *a'* the land of Israel, "
4 And *a'* the congregation said that "
4 right in the eyes of *a'* the people. "
5 David gathered *a'* Israel together, "
6 And David went up, and *a'* Israel, "
8 and *a'* Israel played before God "
8 with *a'* their might, and with "
14 house of Obed-edom, and *a'* that he "
14: 8 David was anointed king over *a'* "
8 *a'* the Philistines went up to seek "
17 of David went out into *a'* lands; "
17 the fear of him upon *a'* nations. "
15: 3 David gathered *a'* Israel together "
27 and *a'* the Levites that bare the ark, "
28 Thus *a'* Israel brought up the ark "
16: 9 talk ye of *a'* his wondrous works. "
14 his judgments are in *a'* the earth. "
23 Sing unto the Lord, *a'* the earth; "
24 works among *a'* nations. "
25 also is to be feared above *a'* gods. "
26 *a'* the gods of the people are idols: "
30 Fear before him, *a'* the earth: "
32 fields rejoice, and *a'* that is therein. "
36 And *a'* the people said, Amen, and "
40 according to *a'* that is written in "
43 And *a'* the people departed every "
17: 2 David, Do *a'* that is in thine heart; "
6 I have walked with *a'* Israel, spake "
8 *a'* thine enemies from before thee, "
10 I will subdue *a'* thine enemies. "
15 According to *a'* these words, and "
15 according to *a'* this vision, so did "
19 thine own heart, hast thou done *a'* "
19 known *a'* these great things. "
20 God beside thee, according to *a'* "
18: 4 houghed *a'* the chariot horses, "
9 David had smitten *a'* the host of "
10 him *a'* manner of vessels of gold "
11 he brought from *a'* these nations; "
13 *a'* the Edomites became David's "
14 So David reigned over *a'* Israel, "
14 and justice among *a'* his people. "
19: 8 and *a'* the host of the mighty men. "
10 chose out of *a'* the choice of Israel, "
17 told David; and he gathered *a'* "
20: 3 so dealt David with *a'* the cities of "
3 And David and *a'* the people "
21: 3 they not *a'* my lord's servants? "

1Ch 21: 4 and went throughout a' Israel, and 3605
5 people unto David. And a' they of "
12 throughout a' the coasts of Israel. "
23 for the meat offering; I give it a'. "
22: 5 of glory throughout a' countries: "
9 rest from a' his enemies round "
15 and a' manner of cunning men for "
17 also commanded a' the princes "
23: 2 together a' the princes of Israel, "
29 for a' manner of measure and size; "
31 And to offer a' burnt sacrifices "
25: 5 A' these were the sons of Heman "
6 A' these were under the hands of "
7 in the songs of the Lord, even a' "
26: 8 A' these of the sons of Obed-edom: "
11 a' the sons and brethren of Hosah "
26 and his brethren were over a' the "
28 And a' that Samuel the seer, and "
30 in a' the business of the Lord, and "
27: 1 a' the months of the year, of "
3 the chief of a' the captains of the "
31 A' these were the rulers of the "
28: 1 assembled a' the princes of Israel, "
1 the stewards over a' the substance "
1 and with a' the valiant men, unto "
4 of Israel chose me before a' the "
4 to make me king over a' Israel: "
5 And of a' my sons, (for the Lord "
8 sight of a' Israel the congregation "
8 seek for a' the commandments of "
9 mind: for the Lord searcheth a' "
9 understandeth a' the imaginations "
12 of a' that he had by the spirit, "
12 of a' the chambers round about, "
13 for a' the work of the service of the "
13 for a' the vessels of service in the "
14 of gold, for a' instruments "
14 of a' manner of service; * "
14 a' instruments of silver by weight, "
14 a' instruments of every kind of "
19 A' this, said David, the Lord made "
19 upon me, even a' the works of this "
20 thou hast finished a' the work "
21 they shall be with thee for a' the "
21 for a' manner of workmanship "
21 and a' the people will be wholly "
29: 1 king said unto a' the congregation, "
2 I have prepared with a' my might "
2 and a' manner of precious stones, "
3 of my God, over and above a' that "
5 for a' manner of work to be made "
10 Lord before a' the congregation: "
11 a' that is in the heaven and in the "
11 thou art exalted as head above a'. "
12 of thee, and thou reignest over a'; "
12 great, and to give strength unto a'. "
14 for a' things come of thee, and of "
15 sojourners, as were a' our fathers: "
16 a' this store that we have prepared "
16 of thine hand, and is a' thine own. "
17 willingly offered a' these things: "
19 statutes, and to do a' these things, "
20 David said to a' the congregation, "
20 a' the congregation blessed the "
21 in abundance for a' Israel: "
23 and a' Israel obeyed him. "
24 a' the princes, and the mighty men, "
24 a' the sons likewise of king David, "
25 exceedingly in the sight of a' Israel, "
26 son of Jesse reigned over a' Israel. "
30 With a' his reign and his might, "
30 a' the kingdoms of the countries. "
2Ch 1: 2 spake unto a' Israel, to the captains "
2 and to every governor in a' Israel, "
3 and a' the congregation with him, "
17 out horses for a' the kings of the "
2: 5 for great is our God above a' gods. "
17 Solomon numbered a' the strangers "
4: 4 and a' their hinder parts were "
16 a' their instruments, did Huram "
18 Solomon made a' these vessels in "
19 Solomon made a' the vessels that "
5: 1 a' the work that Solomon made "
1 a' the things that David his father *
1 and a' the instruments, put he 3605
2 elders of Israel, and a' the heads "
3 a' the men of Israel assembled "
4 And a' the elders of Israel came; "
5 a' the holy vessels that were in "
6 Solomon, and a' the congregation "
11 (for a' the priests that were present "
12 a' of them of Asaph, of Heman, of "
6: 3 a' the congregation of Israel stood. "
5 among a' the tribes of Israel to "
12 of the Lord in the presence of a' "
13 before a' the congregation of Israel, "
14 that walk before thee with a' "
29 or of a' thy people Israel, when "
30 man according unto a' his ways, "
33 to a' that the stranger calleth to "
33 that a' people of the earth may "
38 return to thee with a' their heart "
38 a' their soul in the land of their "
7: 3 when a' the children of Israel saw "
4 the king and a' the people offered "
5 the king and a' the people dedicated "
6 before them, and a' Israel stood. "
8 seven days, and a' Israel with him, "
11 a' that came into Solomon's heart "
17 a' that I have commanded thee, "
20 and a byword among a' nations. "
22 he brought a' this evil upon them. "
8: 4 a' the store cities, which he built "
6 a' the store cities that Solomon "
6 a' the chariot cities, and the cities "
6 a' that Solomon desired to build "

2Ch 8: 6 a' the land of his dominion. 3605
7 As for a' the people that were left "
16 Now a' the work of Solomon was "
9: 1 him of a' that was in her heart. "
2 Solomon told her a' her questions: "
12 the queen of Sheba a' her desire, "
14 And a' the kings of Arabia and "
20 a' the drinking vessels of king "
20 a' the vessels of the house of the "
22 Solomon passed a' the kings of "
23 a' the kings of the earth sought "
26 he reigned over a' the kings from "
28 out of Egypt, and out of a' lands. "
30 Jerusalem over a' Israel forty years. "
10: 1 a' Israel come to make him king. "
3 and a' Israel came and spake to "
12 a' the people came to Rehoboam "
16 when a' Israel saw that the king "
11: 3 and to a' Israel in Judah and "
13 the Levites that were in a' Israel "
13 to him out of a' their coasts. "
16 them out of a' the tribes of Israel "
21 of Absalom above a' his wives "
23 and dispersed of a' his children "
23 throughout a' the countries of "
12: 9 he took a': he carried away also "
13 chosen out of a' the tribes of Israel, "
13: 4 me, thou Jeroboam, and a' Israel; "
15 smote Jeroboam and a' Israel "
14: 5 away out of a' the cities of Judah "
8 a' these were mighty men of "
14 a' the cities round about Gerar; "
14 and they spoiled a' the cities; "
15: 2 Asa, and a' Judah and Benjamin; "
5 were upon a' the inhabitants "
6 did vex them with a' adversity. "
8 a' the land of Judah and Benjamin, "
9 gathered a' Judah and Benjamin, "
12 their fathers with a' their heart "
12 and with a' their soul; "
15 And a' Judah rejoiced at the oath: "
15 sworn with a' their heart, and "
17 of Asa was perfect a' his days. "
16: 6 Then Asa the king took a' Judah; "
17: 2 in a' the fenced cities of Judah, "
5 a' Judah brought to Jehoshaphat "
9 throughout a' the cities of Judah, "
10 Lord fell upon a' the kingdoms "
19 fenced cities throughout a' Judah. "
18: 9 a' the prophets prophesied before "
11 a' the prophets prophesied so, "
16 I did see a' Israel scattered upon "
18 sitting upon his throne, and a' the "
21 in the mouth of a' his prophets. "
27 And he said, Hearken, a' ye people. "
19: 5 judges in the land throughout a' "
11 you in a' the matters of the Lord; "
11 house of Judah, for a' the king's "
20: 3 a fast throughout a' Judah. "
4 Lord: even out of a' the cities of "
13 a' Judah stood before the Lord, "
15 he said, Hearken ye, a' Judah, "
18 his face to the ground: and a' "
29 of God was on a' the kingdoms, "
21: 2 a' these were the sons of "
4 slew a' his brethren with the sword, "
9 and a' his chariots with him: "
14 and thy wives, and a' thy goods: "
17 away a' the substance that was "
18 after a' this the Lord smote him "
22: 1 to the camp had slain a' the eldest. "
9 sought the Lord with a' his heart. "
10 destroyed a' the seed royal of the "
23: 2 Levites out of a' the cities of Judah, "
3 And a' the congregation made a "
5 a' the people shall be in the courts "
6 a' the people shall keep the watch "
8 and a' Judah did according to "
8 a' things that Jehoiada the priest "
10 he set a' the people, every man "
13 a' the people of the land rejoiced, "
16 between a' the people, and between "
17 a' the people went to the house of "
20 people, and a' the people of the "
21 a' the people of the land rejoiced: "
24: 2 the Lord a' the days of Jehoiada "
5 gather of a' Israel money to repair "
7 the house of God; and also a' the "
10 And a' the princes "
10 and a' the people rejoiced, "
14 continually a' the days of Jehoiada. "
23 destroyed a' the princes of the "
23 sent a' the spoil of them unto the "
25: 5 of their fathers, throughout a' "
7 not with Israel, to wit, with a' the "
12 the rock, that they a' were broken "
24 he took a' the gold and the silver, "
24 and a' the vessels that were found "
26: 1 a' the people of Judah took Uzziah, "
4 according to a' that his father "
14 prepared for them throughout a' "
20 a' the priests, looked upon him, "
27: 2 sight of the Lord, according to a' "
7 acts of Jotham, and a' his wars, "
28: 6 which were a' valiant men; "
14 princes and a' the congregation. "
15 clothed a' that were naked among "
15 carried a' the feeble of them upon "
23 the ruin of him, and of a' Israel. "
26 rest of his acts and of a' his ways, "
29: 2 according to a' that David his "
16 brought out a' the uncleanness "
18 cleansed a' the house of the Lord, "
18 offering, with a' the vessels thereof. "
18 table, with a' the vessels thereof: "
19 Moreover a' the vessels, which "

2Ch 29:24 make an atonement for a' Israel: 3605
24 should be made for a' Israel. "
28 a' the congregation worshipped, "
28 a' this continued until the burnt "
29 and a' that were present with him "
32 a' these were for a burnt offering "
34 not flay a' the burnt offerings: "
36 rejoiced, and a' the people, "
30: 1 sent to a' Israel and Judah, and "
2 counsel, and his princes, and a' "
4 the king and a' the congregation. "
5 proclamation throughout a' Israel, "
6 his princes throughout a' Israel "
14 a' the altars for incense took they "
22 spake comfortably unto a' the "
25 And a' the congregation of Judah, "
25 Levites, and a' the congregation "
31: 1 Now when a' this was finished, "
1 a' Israel that were present went "
1 out of a' Judah and Benjamin, "
1 they had utterly destroyed them a'. "
1 a' the children of Israel returned, 3605
5 and of a' the increase of the field; "
5 tithe of a' things brought they in "
18 genealogy of a' their little ones, "
18 through a' the congregation: "
19 to a' the males among the priests, "
19 and to a' that were reckoned by "
20 did Hezekiah throughout a' Judah, "
21 he did it with a' his heart, and "
32: 4 people together, who stopped a' "
5 built up a' the wall that was broken, "
7 for a' the multitude that is with "
9 Lachish, and a' his power with "
9 king of Judah, and unto a' Judah "
13 and my fathers have done unto a' "
14 among a' the gods of those nations "
21 off a' the mighty men of valour, "
22 and from the hand of a' other, "
23 magnified in the sight of a' nations "
27 for a' manner of pleasant jewels; "
28 and stalls for a' manner of beasts, "
30 Hezekiah prospered in a' his works. "
31 know a' that was in his heart. "
33 a' Judah and the inhabitants of "
33: 3 worshipped a' the host of heaven, "
5 altars for a' the host of heaven in "
7 before a' the tribes of Israel, "
8 a' that I have commanded them, "
14 captains of war in a' the fenced "
15 and a' the altars that he had built "
19 intreated of him, and a' his sins, "
22 unto a' the carved images, "
25 the people of the land slew a' them "
34: 7 and cut down a' the idols "
7 throughout a' the land of Israel, "
9 and of a' the remnant of Israel, "
9 and of a' Judah and Benjamin; "
12 a' that could skill of instruments "
13 of a' that wrought the work "
16 A' that was committed to thy "
21 a' that is written in this book. "
24 even a' the curses that are written "
25 with a' the works of their hands; "
28 eyes see a' the evil that I will "
29 gathered together a' the elders "
30 and a' the men of Judah, and the "
30 and the Levites, and a' the people, "
30 he read in their ears a' the words "
31 his statutes, with a' his heart, "
31 and with a' his soul, to perform "
32 a' that were present in Jerusalem "
33 took away a' the abominations "
33 out of a' the countries "
33 a' that were present in Israel "
33 And a' his days they departed not "
35: 3 the Levites that taught a' Israel, "
7 a' for the passover offerings, "
7 for a' that were present, "
13 them speedily among a' the people. "
16 So a' the service of the Lord was "
18 neither did a' the kings of Israel * "
18 the priests, and the Levites, and a' "
20 After a' this, when Josiah had "
24 a' Judah and Jerusalem mourned "
25 lamented for Josiah: and a' the "
36:14 Moreover a' the chief of the priests, "
14 much after a' the abominations of "
17 for age: he gave them a' into "
18 a' the vessels of the house of God, "
18 a' these he brought to Babylon. "
19 a' the palaces thereof with fire, "
19 destroyed a' the goodly vessels "
22 throughout a' his kingdom, "
23 A' the kingdoms of the earth hath "
23 there among you of a' his people? "
Ezra 1: 1 throughout a' his kingdom, and "
2 hath given me a' the kingdoms "
3 among you of a' his people? his "
5 with a' them whose spirit God had "
6 a' they that were about them "
6 things, beside a' that was willingly "
11 A' the vessels of gold and of silver "
11 A' these did Sheshbazzar bring up "
2:42 in a' an hundred thirty and nine. "
58 A' the Nethinims, and the children "
70 cities, and a' Israel in their cities. "
3: 5 new moons, and of a' the set feasts "
8 and a' they that were come out "
11 a' the people shouted with a great "
4: 5 their purpose, a' the days of Cyrus "
20 which have ruled over a' countries 3606
5: 7 Unto Darius the king, a' peace. "
6:12 destroy a' kings and people, "
17 for a sin offering for a' Israel, "
20 Levites were purified together, a' 3605

Ezra 6:20 and killed the passover for *a'* 3605
21 again out of captivity, and *a'* such "
7: 6 king granted him *a'* his request, "
13 that *a'* they of the people of Israel 3606
16 *a'* the silver and gold that thou "
16 find in *a'* the province of Babylon, "
21 decree to *a'* the treasurers which "
25 which may judge *a'* the people "
25 river, *a'* such as know the laws "
28 before *a'* the king's mighty princes. 3605
8:20 *a'* of them were expressed by "
21 for our little ones, and for *a'* our "
22 hand of our God is upon *a'* them "
22 power and his wrath is against *a'* "
25 lords, and *a'* Israel there present, "
34 *a'* the weight was written at that "
35 twelve bullocks for *a'* Israel, "
35 *a'* this was a burnt offering unto "
9:13 And after *a'* that is come upon us "
10: 3 our God to put away *a'* the wives, "
5 and *a'* Israel, to swear that they "
7 *a'* the children of the captivity, "
8 *a'* his substance should be "
9 *a'* the men of Judah and Benjamin "
9 *a'* the people sat in the street of "
12 *a'* the congregation answered and "
14 rulers of *a'* the congregation stand, "
14 and let *a'* them which have "
16 and *a'* of them by their names, "
17 made an end with *a'* the men that "
44 *A'* these had taken strange wives: "
Ne 4: 6 *a'* the wall was joined together "
8 And conspired *a'* of them together "
12 From *a'* places whence ye shall "
15 we returned *a'* of us to the wall, "
16 were behind *a'* the house of Judah. "
5:13 *a'* the congregation said, Amen, "
16 and *a'* my servants were gathered "
18 ten days store of *a'* sorts of wine: "
18 for *a'* this required not I the bread 5973
19 my God, for good, according to *a'* 3605
6: 9 For they *a'* made us afraid, saying, "
16 when *a'* our enemies heard thereof, "
16 *a'* the heathen that were about us "
7:60 *A'* the Nethinims, and the children "
73 and *a'* Israel, dwelt in their cities; "
8: 1 *a'* the people gathered themselves "
2 and *a'* that could hear with "
3 ears of *a'* the people were attentive "
5 book in the sight of *a'* the people; "
5 (for he was above *a'* the people;) "
5 it, *a'* the people stood up: "
6 And *a'* the people answered, Amen, "
9 taught the people, said unto *a'* the "
9 For *a'* the people wept, when they "
11 the Levites stilled *a'* the people, "
12 And *a'* the people went their way "
13 the chief of the fathers of *a'* "
15 and proclaim in *a'* their cities, and "
17 And *a'* the congregation of them "
9: 2 separated themselves from *a'* "
5 name, which is exalted above *a'* "
6 the heaven of heavens, with *a'* "
6 and *a'* things that are therein, "
6 the seas, and *a'* that is therein, "
6 preservest them *a'*; and the host "
10 wonders upon Pharaoh, and on *a'* "
10 and on *a'* the people of his land: "
25 possessed houses full of *a'* goods, "
32 covenant and mercy, let not *a'* "
32 our fathers, and on *a'* thy people, "
33 Howbeit thou art just in *a'* that is "
38 of *a'* this we make a sure covenant, "
10:28 and *a'* they that had separated "
29 *a'* the commandments of the Lord "
33 and for *a'* the work of the house "
35 and the firstfruits of *a'* fruit "
35 of *a'* trees, year by year, "
37 and the fruit of *a'* manner of trees, "
37 tithes in *a'* the cities of our tillage. "
11: 2 the people blessed *a'* the men, "
6 *A'* the sons of Perez that dwelt at "
18 *A'* the Levites in the holy city "
20 were in *a'* the cities of Judah, "
24 at the king's hand in *a'* matters "
12:27 the Levites out of *a'* their places, "
47 *a'* Israel in the days of Zerubbabel, "
13: 3 Israel *a'* the mixed multitude. "
6 *a'* this time was not I at Jerusalem: "
8 I cast forth *a'* the household stuff "
12 brought *a'* Judah the tithe of the "
15 grapes, and figs, and *a'* manner of "
16 and *a'* manner of ware, and sold "
18 *a'* this evil upon us, and upon this "
20 sellers of *a'* kind of ware lodged "
26 God made him king over *a'* Israel: "
27 unto you to do *a'* this great evil, "
30 cleansed I them from *a'* strangers, "
Es 1: 3 made a feast unto *a'* his princes "
5 feast unto *a'* the people that were "
8 had appointed to *a'* the officers "
13 the king's manner toward *a'* that "
16 but also to *a'* the princes, "
16 and to *a'* the people that are "
16 in *a'* the provinces of the king "
17 queen shall come abroad unto *a'* "
18 and Media say this day unto *a'* "
20 throughout *a'* his empire, "
20 *a'* the wives shall give to their "
22 into *a'* the king's provinces, "
2: 3 appoint officers in *a'* the provinces "
3 together *a'* the fair young virgins "
15 in the sight of *a'* them that looked "
17 loved Esther above *a'* the women, "
17 in his sight more than *a'* the "
18 a great feast unto *a'* his princes "

Es 3: 1 set his seat above *a'* the princes 3605
2 *a'* the king's servants, that were in "
6 sought to destroy *a'* the Jews that "
8 the people in *a'* the provinces of "
8 laws are diverse from *a'* people; * "
12 *a'* that Haman had commanded "
13 posts into *a'* the king's provinces, "
13 and to cause to perish, *a'* Jews, "
14 was published unto *a'* people, that "
4: 1 Mordecai perceived *a'* that was "
7 told him of *a'* that had happened "
11 *A'* the king's servants, and the "
13 house, more than *a'* the Jews. "
16 *a'* the Jews that are present in "
17 *a'* that Esther had commanded "
5:11 *a'* the things wherein the king had "
13 Yet *a'* this availeth me nothing, "
14 wife and *a'* his friends unto him, "
6:10 fail of *a'* that thou hast spoken. "
13 told Zeresh his wife and *a'* his "
8: 5 are in *a'* the king's provinces: "
9 to *a'* that Mordecai commanded "
11 perish, *a'* the power of the people "
12 Upon one day in *a'* the provinces "
13 was published unto *a'* people, "
9: 2 throughout *a'* the provinces of the "
2 the fear of them fell upon *a'* people. "
3 And *a'* the rulers of the provinces, "
4 throughout *a'* the provinces: "
5 the Jews smote *a'* their enemies "
20 things, and sent letters unto *a'* "
20 Jews that were in *a'* the provinces "
24 enemy of *a'* the Jews, had devised "
26 for *a'* the words of this letter, "
27 upon *a'* such as joined themselves "
29 the Jew, wrote with *a'* authority, "
30 sent the letters unto *a'* the Jews, "
10: 2 And *a'* the acts of his power and of "
3 and speaking peace to *a'* his seed. "
Job 1: 3 greatest of *a'* the men of the east. "
5 according to the number of them *a'*: "
10 *a'* that he hath on every side? "
11 and touch *a'* that he hath, and he "
12 *a'* that he hath is in thy power; "
22 In *a'* this Job sinned not, "
2: 4 yea, *a'* that a man hath will he give "
10 In *a'* this did not Job sin with his "
11 three friends heard of *a'* this evil "
4:14 which made *a'* my bones to shake. 7230
8:13 the paths of *a'* that forget God; 3605
9:28 I am afraid of *a'* my sorrows, "
12: 9 Who knoweth not in *a'* these that "
10 and the breath of *a'* mankind. "
13: 1 Lo, mine eye hath seen *a'* this, "
4 ye are *a'* physicians of no value. "
27 narrowly unto *a'* my paths; "
14:14 *a'* the days of my appointed time "
15:20 travaileth with pain *a'* his days, "
16: 2 miserable comforters are ye *a'*. "
7 made desolate *a'* my company. "
17: 7 dim by reason of sorrow, and *a'* my "
10 But as for you *a'*, do ye return, "
19:19 *A'* my inward friends abhorred me: "
20:26 *A'* darkness shall be hid in his "
24:24 taken out of the way as *a'* other, "
27: 3 *A'* the while my breath is in me,* "
12 *a'* ye yourselves have seen it; "
28: 3 and searcheth out *a'* perfection: * "
21 it is hid from the eyes of *a'* living: "
29:19 dew lay *a'* night upon my branch. 3885
30:23 the house appointed for *a'* living. 3605
31: 4 my ways, and count *a'* my steps? "
12 would root out *a'* mine increase. "
33: 1 and hearken to *a'* my words. "
11 in the stocks, he marketh *a'* my "
29 Lo, *a'* these things worketh God "
34:15 *A'* flesh shall perish together, "
19 they *a'* are the work of his hands. "
21 of man, and he seeth *a'* his goings. "
36:19 gold, nor *a'* the forces of strength. "
37: 7 every man; that *a'* men may know "
38: 7 *a'* the sons of God shouted for joy? "
18 earth? declare if thou knowest it *a'*. "
40:20 *a'* the beasts of the field play. "
41:34 He beholdeth *a'* high things: * "
34 over *a'* the children of pride. "
42:11 there unto him *a'* his brethren, "
11 and *a'* his sisters, "
11 and *a'* they that had been of "
11 and comforted him over *a'* the evil "
15 in *a'* the land were no women "
Ps 2:12 Blessed are *a'* they that put their "
3: 7 thou hast smitten *a'* mine enemies "
5: 5 thou hatest *a'* workers of iniquity. "
11 let *a'* those that put their trust in "
6: 6 *a'* the night make I my bed to * "
7 old because of *a'* mine enemies. "
8 from me, *a'* ye workers of iniquity; "
10 Let *a'* mine enemies be ashamed "
7: 1 from *a'* them that persecute me, "
8: 1 is thy name in *a'* the earth! "
6 hast put *a'* things under his feet: "
7 *A'* sheep and oxen, yea, and the "
9 is thy name in *a'* the earth! "
9: 1 forth *a'* thy marvellous works. "
14 that I may shew forth *a'* thy praise "
17 and *a'* the nations that forget God. "
10: 4 God is not in *a'* his thoughts. "
5 as for *a'* his enemies, he puffeth "
12: 3 Lord shall cut off *a'* flattering lips, "
14: 3 They are *a'* gone aside, "
3 they are *a'* together become * "
4 Have *a'* the workers of iniquity 3605
16: 3 in whom is *a'* my delight. "
18:*title* from the hand of *a'* his enemies, "
22 *a'* his judgments were before me, "

Ps 18:30 he is a buckler to *a'* those that 3605
19: 4 is gone out through *a'* the earth, "
20: 3 Remember *a'* thy offerings, and "
4 heart, and fulfil *a'* thy counsel. "
20: 5 the Lord fulfil *a'* thy petitions. "
21: 8 shall find out *a'* thine enemies: "
22: 7 *A'* they that see me laugh me to "
14 out like water, and *a'* my bones, "
17 I may tell *a'* my bones: they look "
23 praise him; *a'* ye the seed of Jacob, "
23 fear him, *a'* ye the seed of Israel. "
27 *A'* the ends of the world shall "
27 and *a'* the kindreds of the nations "
29 *A'* they that be fat upon earth "
29 *a'* they that go down to the dust "
23: 6 mercy shall follow me *a'* the days "
25: 5 on thee do I wait *a'* the day. "
10 *A'* the paths of the Lord are mercy "
18 and my pain; and forgive *a'* my "
22 O God, out of *a'* his troubles. "
26: 7 and tell of *a'* thy wondrous works. "
27: 4 in the house of the Lord *a'* the days "
31:11 reproach among *a'* mine enemies, "
23 O love the Lord, *a'* ye his saints: "
24 heart, *a'* ye that hope in the Lord. "
32: 3 through my roaring *a'* the day long. "
11 *a'* ye that are upright in heart. "
33: 4 Lord is right; and *a'* his works "
6 *a'* the host of them by the breath "
8 Let *a'* the earth fear the Lord: "
8 let *a'* the inhabitants of the world "
11 of his heart to *a'* generations. "
13 from heaven; he beholdeth *a'* the 3605
14 *a'* the inhabitants of the earth. "
15 hearts alike; he considereth *a'* "
34: 1 I will bless the Lord at *a'* times: "
4 delivered me from *a'* my fears. "
6 saved him out of *a'* his troubles. "
17 them out of *a'* their troubles. "
19 Lord delivereth him out of them *a'*. "
20 He keepeth *a'* his bones: not one "
35:10 *A'* my bones shall say, Lord, who "
28 and of thy praise *a'* the day long. "
38: 6 I go mourning *a'* the day long. "
9 Lord, *a'* my desire is before thee; "
12 imagine deceits *a'* the day long. "
39: 8 me from *a'* my transgressions: "
12 a sojourner, as *a'* my fathers "
40:16 Let *a'* those that seek thee rejoice "
41: 3 make *a'* his bed in his sickness. "
7 *A'* that hate me whisper together "
42: 7 *a'* thy waves and thy billows are "
44: 8 In God we boast *a'* the day long, "
17 *A'* this is come upon us; yet have "
22 sake are we killed *a'* the day long; "
45: 8 *A'* thy garments smell of myrrh, "
13 The king's daughter is *a'* glorious "
16 make princes in *a'* the earth. "
17 thy name to be remembered in *a'* "
47: 1 O clap your hands, *a'* ye people; "
2 is a great King over *a'* the earth. "
7 God is the King of *a'* the earth: "
49: 1 Hear this, *a'* ye people; "
1 give ear, *a'* ye inhabitants "
11 dwelling places to *a'* generations; "
50:11 *a'* the fowls of the mountains: 3605
51: 9 from my sins, and blot out *a'* mine "
52: 4 Thou lovest *a'* devouring words, "
54: 7 delivered me out of *a'* trouble: "
56: 5 *a'* their thoughts are against me "
57: 2 that performeth *a'* things for me. "
5, 11 glory be above *a'* the earth. 3605
59: 5 awake to visit *a'* the heathen: "
8 have *a'* the heathen in derision. "
62: 3 ye shall be slain *a'* of you: as a "
8 Trust in him at *a'* times; "
64: 8 *a'* that see them shall flee away. "
9 And *a'* men shall fear, and shall "
10 *a'* the upright in heart shall glory. "
65: 2 unto thee shall *a'* flesh come. "
5 of *a'* the ends of the earth, and "
66: 1 noise unto God, *a'* ye lands: "
4 *A'* the earth shall worship thee, "
16 Come and hear, *a'* ye that fear God, "
67: 2 saving health among *a'* nations. "
3, 5 let *a'* the people praise thee. "
7 and *a'* the ends of the earth shall "
69:19 adversaries are *a'* before thee. "
70: 4 Let *a'* those that seek thee rejoice "
71: 8 praise and with thy honour *a'* the "
15 salvation *a'* the day; for I know "
24 righteousness *a'* the day long: "
72: 5 throughout *a'* generations. "
11 *a'* kings shall fall down before 3605
11 *a'* nations shall serve him. "
17 in him: *a'* nations shall call "
73:14 For *a'* the day long have I been "
27 thou hast destroyed *a'* them that "
28 that I may declare *a'* thy works. "
74: 3 even *a'* that the enemy hath done "
8 burned up *a'* the synagogues of God "
17 set *a'* the borders of the earth: "
75: 3 *a'* the inhabitants thereof are "
8 *a'* the wicked of the earth shall "
10 *A'* the horns of the wicked also "
76: 9 to save *a'* the meek of the earth. "
11 your God: let *a'* that be round "
77:12 I will meditate also of *a'* thy work, "
78:14 *a'* the night with a light of fire. "
32 For *a'* this they sinned still, and "
38 and did not stir up *a'* his wrath. "
51 smote *a'* the firstborn in Egypt; "
79:13 forth thy praise to *a'* generations. "
80:12 so that *a'* they which pass by the 3605
82: 5 *a'* the foundations of the earth are "
6 *a'* of you are children of the most "

Ps 82: 8 for thou shalt inherit a· nations. 3605
83:11 a· their princes as Zebah, and as "
18 art the most high over a· the "
85: 2 thou hast covered a· their sin. "
3 hast taken away a· thy wrath: "
86: 5 unto a· them that call upon thee. "
9 A· nations whom thou hast made "
12 Lord my God, with a· my heart: * "
87: 2 than a· the dwellings of Jacob. "
7 be there: a· my springs are in thee. "
88: 7 afflicted me with a· thy waves. "
89: 1 thy faithfulness to a· generations. "
4 up thy throne to a· generations. "
7 of a· them that are about him. 3605
16 name shall they rejoice a· the day: "
40 hast broken down a· his hedges; "
41 A· that pass by the way spoil him: "
42 made a· his enemies to rejoice. "
47 hast thou made a· men in vain? "
50 reproach of a· the mighty people; "
90: 1 dwelling place in a· generations. "
9 a· our days are passed away in 3605
14 rejoice and be glad a· our days. "
92: 7 when a· the workers of iniquity do "
9 a· the workers of iniquity shall be "
94: 4 and a· the workers of iniquity boast "
15 a· the upright in heart shall follow "
95: 3 and a great King above a· gods. "
96: 1 sing unto the Lord, a· the earth. "
3 his wonders among a· people. "
4 he is to be feared above a· gods. "
5 a· the gods of the nations are idols: "
9 fear before him, a· the earth. "
12 be joyful, and a· that is therein: "
12 a· the trees of the wood rejoice "
97: 6 and a· the people see his glory. "
7 a· they that serve graven images, "
7 of idols: worship him, a· ye gods. "
9 art high above a· the earth: "
9 thou art exalted far above a· gods. "
98: 3 a· the ends of the earth have seen "
4 noise unto the Lord, a· the earth: "
99: 2 and he is high above a· the people. "
100: 1 noise unto the Lord, a· ye lands. "
5 truth endureth to a· generations. "
101: 8 destroy a· the wicked of the land; 3605
8 that I may cut off a· wicked doers "
102: 8 enemies reproach me a· the day; "
12 remembrance unto a· generations. "
15 a· the kings of the earth thy 3605
24 are throughout a· generations. "
26 but thou shalt endure: yea, a· of 3605
103: 1 a· that is within me, bless his holy "
2 and forget not a· his benefits: "
3 Who forgiveth a· thine iniquities; "
3 who healeth a· thy diseases; "
6 judgment for a· that are oppressed. "
19 and his kingdom ruleth over a·. "
21 Bless ye the Lord, a· ye his hosts; "
22 Bless the Lord, a· his works "
22 in a· places of his dominion: "
104:20 wherein a· the beasts of the forest "
24 in wisdom hast thou made them a·: "
27 These wait a· upon thee; that "
105: 2 talk ye of a· his wondrous works. "
21 of his house, and ruler of a· his "
31 flies, and lice in a· their coasts. "
35 eat up a· the herbs in their land, * "
36 also a· the firstborn in their land, "
36 the chief of a· their strength. "
106: 2 who can shew forth a· his praise? "
3 doeth righteousness at a· times. "
31 unto a· generations for evermore. "
46 a· those that carried them 3605
48 and let a· the people say, Amen. "
107:18 abhorreth a· manner of meat; "
42 a· iniquity shall stop her mouth. "
108: 5 and thy glory above a· the earth; "
109:11 extortioner catch a· that he hath; "
111: 2 Lord are great, sought out of a· "
7 a· his commandments are sure. "
10 a good understanding have a· "
113: 4 The Lord is high above a· nations, "
116:11 said in my haste, A· men are liars. "
12 unto the Lord for a· his benefits "
14 in the presence of a· his people. "
18 the Lord now in the presence of a· "
117: 1 O praise the Lord, a· ye nations: "
1 praise him, a· ye people. "
118:10 A· nations compassed me about: 3605
119: 6 unto a· thy commandments. "
13 With my lips have I declared a· "
14 as much as in a· riches. "
20 unto thy judgments at a· times. "
63 of a· them that fear thee, and of "
86 A· thy commandments are faithful: "
90 faithfulness is unto a· generations: "
91 for a· are thy servants. *3605
97 it is my meditation a· the day. "
99 than a· my teachers: for thy "
118 trodden down a· them that err "
119 a· the wicked of the earth like "
128 I esteem a· thy precepts "
128 concerning a· things to be right; "
151 a· thy commandments are truth. "
168 for a· my ways are before thee. "
172 for a· thy commandments are "
121: 7 shall preserve thee from a· evil: "
128: 5 Jerusalem a· the days of thy life. "
129: 5 Let them a· be confounded and "
130: 8 Israel from a· his iniquities. "
132: 1 David, and a· his afflictions: "
134: 1 Lord, a· ye servants of the Lord, "
135: 5 that our Lord is above a· gods. "
6 in the seas, and a· deep places. "
9 Pharaoh, and upon a· his servants. "

Ps 135:11 and a· the kingdoms of Canaan: 3605
13 O Lord, throughout a· generations. "
136:25 Who giveth food to a· flesh: for 3605
138: 4 A· the kings of the earth shall "
139: 3 art acquainted with a· my ways. "
16 book a· my members were written, "
143: 5 the days of old; I meditate on a· "
12 destroy a· them that afflict my soul: "
144:13 garners may be full, affording a· "
145: 9 The Lord is good to a·: and his 3605
9 mercies are over a· his works. "
10 A· thy works shall praise thee, O "
13 throughout a· generations. "
14 The Lord upholdeth a· that fall, 3605
14 raiseth up a· those that be bowed "
15 The eyes of a· wait upon thee; and "
17 Lord is righteous in a· his ways, "
17 and holy in a· his works. "
18 The Lord is nigh unto a· them that "
18 to a· that call upon him in truth. "
20 preserveth a· them that love him: "
20 but a· the wicked will he destroy. "
21 and let a· flesh bless his holy name "
146: 6 earth, the sea, and a· that therein "
10 God, O Zion, unto a· generations. "
147: 4 of the stars; he calleth them a· 3605
148: 2 Praise ye him, a· his angels: "
2 praise ye him, a· his hosts. "
3 praise him, a· ye stars of light. "
9 Mountains, and a· hills; "
9 fruitful trees, and a· cedars: "
10 Beasts, and a· cattle; creeping "
11 Kings of the earth, and a· people; "
11 princes, and a· judges of the earth: "
14 the praise of a· his saints; even of "
149: 9 written: this honour have a· "
Pr 1:13 shall find a· precious substance, "
14 us; let us a· have one purse: "
25 have set at nought a· my counsel, "
30 of my counsel: they despised a· "
3: 5 in the Lord with a· thine heart; "
6 In a· thy ways acknowledge him, "
9 and with the firstfruits of a· "
15 precious than rubies: and a· the* "
17 ways of pleasantness, and a· her "
4: 7 a· thy getting get understanding. "
22 find them, and health to a· their "
23 Keep thy heart with a· diligence; "
26 of thy feet, and let a· thy ways be "
5:14 I was almost in a· evil in the midst "
21 and he pondereth a· his goings. "
6:31 shall give a· the substance of his "
8: 8 A· the words of my mouth are in "
9 a· plain to him that understandeth, "
11 than rubies; and a· the things "
16 and nobles, even a· the judges of "
36 a· they that hate me love death. "
10:12 strifes: but love covereth a· sins. "
14:23 In a· labour there is profit: but "
15:15 A· the days of the afflicted are "
16: 2 A· the ways of a man are clean in "
4 hath made a· things for himself: * "
11 a· the weights of the bag are his "
17:17 A friend loveth at a· times, and a "
18: 1 intermeddleth with a· wisdom. "
19: 7 A· the brethren of the poor do hate "
20: 8 away a· evil with his eyes. "
27 candle of the Lord, searching a· "
21:26 He coveteth greedily a· the day "
22: 2 the Lord is the maker of them a·. "
23:17 fear of the Lord a· the day long. "
24: 4 a· precious and pleasant riches. "
31 it was a· grown over with thorns, "
26:10 great God that formed a· things "
28: 5 the Lord understand a· things "
29:11 A fool uttereth a· his mind: but a "
12 to lies, a· his servants are wicked. "
30:4 established a· the ends of the earth? "
27 king, yet go they forth a· of them "
31: 8 for the dumb in the cause of a· "
12 and not evil a· the days of her life. "
21 a· her household are clothed with "
29 but thou excellest them a·. "
Ec 1: 2 vanity of vanities; a· is vanity. "
3 What profit hath a man of a· his "
7 A· the rivers run into the sea; "
8 A· things are full of labour; man "
13 by wisdom concerning a· things "
14 I have seen a· the works that are "
14 a· is vanity and vexation of spirit. "
16 a· they that have been before me "
2: 3 heaven a· the days of their life. 4557
5 trees in them of a· kind of fruits: 3605
7 a· that were in Jerusalem before "
8 instruments, and that of a· sorts. * "
9 increased more than a· that were 3605
10 my heart rejoiced in a· my labour: "
10 was my portion of a· my labour. "
11 Then I looked on a· the works that "
11 a· was vanity and vexation of "
14 one event happeneth to them a·. "
16 days to come shall a· be forgotten. "
17 me: for a· is vanity and vexation "
18 I hated a· my labour which I had "
19 he have rule over a· my labour "
20 to despair of a· the labour which "
22 what hath man of a· his labour, "
23 For a· his days are sorrows, and "
3:13 enjoy the good of a· his labour, "
19 yea, they have a· one breath; so "
19 above a beast: for a· is vanity. "
20 A· go unto one place; "
20 a· are of the dust, "
20 and a· turn to dust again. "
4: 1 and considered a· the oppressions "
4 Again, I considered a· travail, and "

Ec 4: 8 is there no end of a· his labour; 3605
15 a· the living which walk under the "
16 There is no end of a· the people, "
16 of a· that have been before them: "
5: 9 the profit of the earth is for a·: "
16 that in a· points as he came, so "
17 A· his days also he eateth in "
18 to enjoy the good of a· his labour "
18 the sun a· the days of his life, 4557
6: 2 for his soul of a· that he desireth, 3605
6 no good: do not a· go to one place? "
7 A· the labour of man is for his "
12 a· the days of his vain life which 4557
7: 2 for that is the end of a· men; 3605
15 A· things have I seen in the days "
18 God shall come forth of them a·. "
21 heed unto a· words that are spoken; "
23 A· this have I proved by wisdom: "
28 among a· those have I not found. "
8: 9 A· this have I seen, and applied "
17 Then I beheld a· the work of God, "
9: 1 a· this I considered in my heart "
1 even to declare a· this, "
1 or hatred by a· that is before them. "
2 A· things come alike to a·: there "
3 This is an evil among a· things "
3 that there is one event unto a·: "
4 joined to a· the living there is hope: "
9 wife whom thou lovest a· the days "
9 a· the days of thy vanity: for that "
11 and chance happeneth to them a·. "
10:19 but money answereth a· things. "
11: 5 the works of God who maketh a·. "
8 many years, and rejoice in them a·; "
8 many. A· that cometh is vanity. "
9 that for a· these things God will "
12: 8 saith the preacher; a· is vanity. "
Ca 1:13 unto me; he shall lie a· night *3885
3: 6 with a· powders of the merchant? 3605
8 They a· hold swords, being expert "
4: 4 bucklers, a· shields of mighty men. "
7 Thou art a· fair, my love; there is "
10 thine ointments than a· spices! "
14 with a· trees of frankincense; "
14 aloes, with a· the chief spices: "
7:13 are a· manner of pleasant fruits, "
8: 7 a· the substance of his house for "
Isa 1:25 away thy dross, and take away a· "
2: 2 the hills; and a· nations shall flow "
13 upon a· the cedars of Lebanon, "
13 and upon a· the oaks of Bashan, "
2:14 And upon a· the high mountains, "
14 upon a· the hills that are lifted up "
16 And upon a· the ships of Tarshish, "
16 and upon a· pleasant pictures. "
4: 5 upon a· the glory shall be a defence. "
5:25 For a· this his anger is not turned "
28 are sharp, and a· their bows bent, "
7:19 come, and shall rest a· of them in "
19 of the rocks, and upon a· thorns, "
19 and upon a· bushes. "
24 a· the land shall become briers "
25 And on a· hills that shall be digged "
8: 7 king of Assyria, and a· his glory: "
7 come up over a· his channels, "
7 and go over a· his banks: "
9 give ear, a· ye of far countries: "
12 confederacy, to a· them to whom "
9: 9 And a· the people shall know, "
12 with open mouth. For a· this "
17 speaketh folly. For a· this his "
21 Judah. For a· this his anger is "
10: 4 For a· this his anger is not turned "
14 that are left, have I gathered a· "
23 in the midst of a· the land. "
11: 9 destroy in a· my holy mountain: "
12: 5 this is known in a· the earth. "
13: 7 Therefore shall a· hands be faint, "
14: 9 even a· the chief ones of the earth; "
9 thrones a· the kings of the nations. "
10 A· they shall speak and say unto "
18 A· the kings of the nations, "
18 even a· of them, lie in glory, "
26 stretched out upon a· the nations. "
15: 2 on a· their heads shall be baldness, "
16:14 be contemned, with a· that great "
18: 3 A· ye inhabitants of the world, "
6 a· the beasts of the earth shall "
19: 8 shall mourn, and a· they that cast "
10 a· that make sluices and ponds for "
21: 9 is fallen; and a· the graven images "
16 and a· the glory of Kedar shall fail: "
22: 3 A· thy rulers are fled together, "
3 a· that are found in thee are "
24 him a· the glory of his father's "
24 and the issue, a· vessels of small * "
24 the vessels of cups, even to a· the "
23: 9 to stain the pride of a· glory, "
9 a· the honourable of the earth. "
17 with a· the kingdoms of the world "
24: 7 a· the merryhearted do sigh. "
11 a· joy is darkened, the mirth of "
25: 6 hosts make unto a· people a feast "
7 covering cast over a· people, "
7 vail that is spread over a· nations. "
8 wipe away tears from off a· faces; "
8 shall he take away from off a· "
26:12 hast wrought a· our works in us. "
14 made a· their memory to perish. "
15 far unto a· the ends of the earth. "
27: 9 a· the fruit to take away his sin; "
9 maketh a· the stones of the altar "
28: 8 For a· tables are full of vomit and "
24 the plowman plow a· day to sow? * "
29: 7 of a· the nations that fight against "
7 even a· that fight against her and "

Isa 29: 8 so shall the multitude of a' the 3605
11 a' is become unto you as the words "
20 a' that watch for iniquity are cut "
30:18 blessed are a' they that wait for "
31: 3 fall down, and they a' shall fail "
32:13 upon a' the houses of joy in the "
20 are ye that sow beside a' waters, "
34: 1 let the earth hear, and a' that is *4393
1 and a' things that come forth of it. 3605
2 of the Lord is upon a' nations, "
2 and his fury upon a' their armies: "
4 And a' the host of heaven shall be "
4 and a' their host shall fall down, "
12 a' her princes shall be nothing. "
36: 1 Assyria came up against a' the "
6 of Egypt to a' that trust in him. "
20 among a' the gods of these lands, "
37:11 A' lands by destroying them "
16 of a' the kingdoms of the earth: "
17 hear a' the words of Sennacherib, "
18 have laid waste a' the nations, "
20 that a' the kingdoms of the earth "
25 a' the rivers of the besieged places. "
36 behold, they were a' dead corpses. "
38:13 so will he break a' my bones: "
15 a' my years in the bitterness of my "
16 men live, and in a' these things * "
17 cast a' my sins behind thy back. "
20 a' the days of our life in the house "
39: 2 and a' the house of his armour, "
2 a' that was found in his treasures: "
2 nor in a' his dominion, that "
4 A' that is in mine house have they "
6 that a' that is in thine house, "
40: 2 Lord's hand double for a' her sins. "
5 the Lord shall be revealed, and a' "
6 A' flesh is grass, "
6 and a' the goodliness thereof "
17 A' nations before him are as "
26 he calleth them a' by names by "
41:11 a' they that were incensed against "
29 they are a' vanity; their works "
42:10 to the sea, and a' that is therein; 4393
15 and hills, and dry up a' 3605
22 they are a' of them snared in holes, "
43: 9 Let a' the nations be gathered "
14 have brought down a' their nobles, "
44: 9 graven image are a' of them vanity; "
11 a' his fellows shall be ashamed: "
11 of men: let them a' be gathered "
24 the Lord that maketh a' things; "
28 my shepherd, and shall perform a' "
45: 7 I the Lord do a' these things. "
12 a' their host have I commanded. "
13 and I will direct a' his ways: "
16 a' of them: they shall go to "
22 ye saved, a' the ends of the earth: "
24 a' that are incensed against him "
25 shall a' seed of Israel be justified, "
46: 3 a' the remnant of the house of "
10 and I will do a' my pleasure: "
48: 6 Thou hast heard, see a' this; "
14 A' ye, assemble yourselves, and "
49: 9 pastures shall be in a' high places. "
11 I will make a' my mountains a "
18 a' these gather themselves "
18 surely clothe thee with them a'. "
26 a' flesh shall know that I the Lord "
50: 2 Is my hand shortened at a', that "
9 a' shall wax old as a garment; 3605
11 Behold, a' ye that kindle a fire, "
51: 3 Zion: he will comfort a' her "
18 to guide her among a' the sons "
20 fainted, they lie at the head of a' the "
52:10 bare his holy arm in the eyes of a' "
10 a' the ends of the earth shall see "
53: 6 A' we like sheep have gone astray; "
6 laid on him the iniquity of us a'. "
54:12 a' thy borders of pleasant stones. "
13 a' thy children shall be taught of "
55:12 a' the trees of the field shall clap "
56: 7 an house of prayer for a' people. "
9 A' ye beasts of the field, come to "
9 yea, a' ye beasts in the forest. "
10 they are a' ignorant, "
10 they are a' dumb dogs, "
11 they a' look to their own way, "
57:13 wind shall carry them a' away; "
58: 3 pleasure, and exact a' your labours. "
59:11 We roar a' like bears, and mourn "
60: 4 eyes round about, and see: a' they "
6 a' they from Sheba shall come: "
7 A' the flocks of Kedar shall be "
14 and a' they that despised thee "
21 people also shall be a' righteous: "
61: 2 our God; to comfort a' that mourn; "
9 a' that see them shall acknowledge "
11 spring forth before a' the nations. "
62: 2 and a' kings thy glory: "
63: 3 and I will stain a' my raiment. "
7 according to a' that the Lord "
9 In a' their affliction he was afflicted, "
9 carried them a' the days of old. "
64: 6 we are a' as an unclean thing, "
6 and a' our righteousnesses "
6 are as filthy rags; and we a' do "
8 we a' are the work of thy hand. "
9 beseech thee, we are a' thy people. "
11 and a' our pleasant things are laid "
65: 2 spread out my hands a' the day "
5 a fire that burneth a' the day. "
8 that I may not destroy them a'. "
25 destroy in a' my holy mountain, "
66: 2 For a' those things hath mine "
2 a' those things have been, saith "
10 glad with her, a' ye that love her: "

Isa 66:10 with her, a' ye that mourn for her: 3605
16 will the Lord plead with a' flesh: "
18 gather a' nations and tongues; "
20 a' your brethren for an offering "
20 out of a' nations upon horses, "
23 to another, shall a' flesh come "
24 shall be an abhorring unto a' flesh. "
Jer 1: 7 go to a' that I shall send thee, * "
14 upon a' the inhabitants of the land. "
15 I will call a' the families of the "
15 against a' the walls thereof round "
15 and against a' the cities of Judah. "
16 touching a' their wickedness, "
17 unto them a' that I command thee: "
2: 3 a' that devour him shall offend; "
4 the Lord, O house of Jacob, and a' "
24 a' they that seek her will not "
29 ye a' have transgressed against "
34 secret search, but upon a' these. "
3: 7 after she had done a' these things, "
8 when for a' the causes whereby * "
10 a' this her treacherous sister Judah "
17 a' the nations shall be gathered "
4:24 and a' the hills moved lightly. "
25 a' the birds of the heavens were "
26 and a' the cities thereof "
5:16 sepulchre, they are a' mighty men. "
19 our God a' these things unto us? "
6:15 nay, they were not at a' ashamed, "
28 They are a' grievous revolters, 3605
28 and iron; they are a' corrupters. "
7: 2 word of the Lord, a' ye of Judah, "
10 to do a' these abominations? "
13 ye have done a' these works, "
15 I have cast out a' your brethren, "
23 walk ye in a' the ways that I have "
25 even sent unto you a' my servants "
27 speak a' these words unto them; "
8: 2 and a' the host of heaven, whom "
3 rather than life by a' the residue "
3 which remain in a' the places "
12 they were not at a' ashamed, "
16 the land, and a' that is in it; the 4393
9: 2 for they be a' adulterers, an 3605
25 I will punish a' them which are "
26 a' that are in the utmost corners, "
26 for a' these nations are "
26 and a' the house of Israel are "
10: 7 a' the wise men of the nations, "
7 and in a' their kingdoms, there is "
9 are a' the work of cunning men. "
16 for he is the former of a' things; "
20 and a' my cords are broken: "
21 a' their flocks shall be scattered. "
11: 4 do them, according to a' which I "
6 Proclaim a' these words in the "
8 them a' the words of this covenant, "
12 at a' in the time of their trouble. "
12: 1 wherefore are a' they happy that 3605
9 assemble a' the beasts of the field, "
12 are come upon a' high places "
14 against a' mine evil neighbours, "
13:13 a' the inhabitants of this land, "
13 a' the inhabitants of Jerusalem, "
19 be carried away captive a' of it, "
14:22 for thou hast made a' these things. "
15: 4 to be removed into a' kingdoms of "
13 and that for a' thy sins, "
13 even in a' thy borders. "
16:10 shew this people a' these words, "
10 a' this great evil against us? "
15 from a' the lands whither he had "
17 mine eyes are upon a' their ways: "
17: 3 and a' thy treasures to the spoil, "
3 for sin, throughout a' thy borders. "
9 heart is deceitful above a' things, "
13 a' that forsake thee shall be "
19 and in a' the gates of Jerusalem; "
20 kings of Judah, and a' Judah, "
20 a' the inhabitants of Jerusalem, "
18:23 thou knowest a' their counsel "
19: 8 because of a' the plagues thereof. "
13 place of Tophet, because of a' the "
13 incense unto a' the host of heaven, "
14 house; and said to a' the people, "
15 and upon a' her towns "
15 a' the evil that I have pronounced "
20: 4 to thyself, and to a' thy friends: "
4 give a' Judah into the hand of the "
5 deliver a' the strength of this city, "
5 and a' the labours thereof, "
5 and a' the precious things thereof, "
5 a' the treasures of the kings of "
6 a' that dwell in thine house shall "
6 and a' thy friends, to whom thou "
10 A' my familiars watched for my "
21: 2 us according to a' his wondrous "
14 devour a' things round about it. "
22:20 for a' thy lovers are destroyed. "
22 wind shall eat up a' thy pastors, "
22 confounded for a' thy wickedness. "
23: 3 the remnant of my flock out of a' "
8 and from a' countries whither I "
9 a' my bones shake; I am like a "
14 are a' of them unto me as Sodom, "
15 gone forth into a' the land. "
32 shall not profit this people at a', "
24: 9 removed into a' the kingdoms of 3605
9 a' places whither I shall "
25: 1 Jeremiah concerning a' the people "
2 spake unto a' the people of Judah, "
2 a' the inhabitants of Jerusalem, "
4 you a' his servants the prophets, "
9 take a' the families of the north, "
9 a' these nations round about, "
13 that land a' my words which I "

Jer 25:13 even a' that is written in this book, 3605
13 prophesied against a' the nations. "
15 this fury at my hand, and cause a' "
17 and made a' the nations to drink, "
19 and his princes, and a' his people; "
20 And a' the mingled people, "
20 and a' the kings of the land of Uz, "
20 and a' the kings of the land of the "
22 And a' the kings of Tyrus, "
22 and a' the kings of Zidon, "
23 Buz, and a' that are in the utmost "
24 And a' the kings of Arabia, "
24 and a' the kings of the "
25 And a' the kings of Zimri, "
25 and a' the kings of Elam, "
25 and a' the kings of the Medes, "
26 And a' the kings of the north, far "
26 and a' the kingdoms of the world, "
29 upon a' the inhabitants of the "
30 thou against them a' these words, "
30 a' the inhabitants of the earth. "
31 he will plead with a' flesh; he will "
26: 2 speak unto a' the cities of Judah, "
2 a' the words that I command thee "
6 to a' the nations of the earth. "
7 and a' the people heard Jeremiah "
8 a' that the Lord had commanded "
8 him to speak unto a' the people, "
8 prophets and a' the people took "
9 And a' the people were gathered "
11 and to a' the people, saying, This "
12 spake Jeremiah unto a' the princes "
12 and to a' the people, "
12 a' the words that ye have heard. "
15 speak a' these words in your ears. "
16 the princes and a' the people unto "
17 elders of the land, and spake to a' "
18 to a' the people of Judah, saying, "
19 king of Judah and a' Judah "
19 put him at a' to death? "
20 to a' the words of Jeremiah: 3605
21 the king, with a' his mighty men, "
21 and a' the princes, heard his "
27: 6 given a' these lands into the hand "
12 king of Judah according to a' "
16 the priests and to a' this people, "
20 and a' the nobles of Judah and "
28: 1 the priests and of a' the people, "
3 a' the vessels of the Lord's house, "
4 with a' the captives of Judah, that "
5 in the presence of a' the people "
6 vessels of the Lord's house, and a' "
7 and in the ears of a' the people; "
11 in the presence of a' the people, "
11 from the neck of a' nations within "
14 upon the neck of a' these nations, "
29: 1 and to a' the people whom "
4 a' that are carried away captives, "
13 search for me with a' your heart. "
14 will gather you from a' the nations, "
14 from a' the places whither I have "
16 a' the people that dwelleth in this, "
18 to a' the kingdoms of the earth, "
18 among a' the nations whither I "
20 a' ye of the captivity, whom I have "
22 curse by a' the captivity of Judah "
25 in thy name unto a' the people "
25 the priest, and to a' the priests, "
31 to a' them of the captivity, saying, "
30: 2 Write thee a' the words that I have "
6 a' faces are turned into paleness? "
11 I make a full end of a' nations "
14 A' thy lovers have forgotten thee; "
16 Therefore a' they that devour thee "
16 a' thine adversaries, every one "
16 and a' that prey upon thee will I "
20 will punish a' that oppress them. "
31: 1 God of a' the families of Israel, "
12 shall not sorrow any more at a'. "
24 in a' the cities thereof together, 3605
34 for they shall a' know me, from "
37 I will also cast off a' the seed of "
37 Israel for a' that they have done, "
40 a' the fields unto the brook of "
32:12 before a' the Jews that sat in the "
19 a' the ways of the sons of men: "
23 of a' that thou commandest "
23 caused a' this evil to come upon "
27 I am the Lord, the God of a' flesh: "
32 a' the evil of the children of Israel "
37 gather them out of a' countries, "
42 brought a' this great evil upon this "
42 upon them a' the good that I "
33: 5 and for a' whose wickedness I "
8 cleanse them from a' their iniquity, "
8 I will pardon a' their iniquities, "
9 before a' the nations of the earth, "
9 which shall hear a' the good that "
9 tremble for a' the goodness "
9 a' the prosperity that I procure "
12 and in a' the cities thereof, shall "
34: 1 king of Babylon, and a' his army, "
1 and a' the kingdoms of the earth "
1 and a' the people, fought against "
1 and against a' the cities thereof, "
6 the prophet spake a' these words "
7 against a' the cities of Judah that "
8 a covenant with a' the people "
10 Now when a' the princes, "
10 a' the people, which had entered "
17 be removed into a' the kingdoms "
34:19 and a' the people of the land, "
35: 3 a' his sons, and the whole house "
7 a' your days ye shall dwell in tents; "
8 in a' that he hath charged us, "
8 no wine a' our days, we, our wives, "

Jer 35:10 according to a· that Jonadab our 3605
15 a· my servants the prophets, "
17 bring upon Judah and upon a· the "
17 Jerusalem a· the evil that I have "
18 and kept a· his precepts, "
18 and done according unto a· "
36: 2 and write therein a· the words "
2 and against a· the nations, "
3 of Judah will hear a· the evil "
4 from the mouth of Jeremiah a· the "
6 read them in the ears of a· Judah "
8 son of Neriah did according to a· "
9 to a· the people in Jerusalem, "
9 a· the people that came from the "
10 house, in the ears of a· the people. "
11 the book a· the words of the Lord, "
12 and, lo, a· the princes sat there, "
12 of Hananiah, and a· the princes. "
13 declared unto them a· the words "
14 Therefore a· the princes sent Jehudi "
16 when they had heard a· the words, "
16 surely tell the king of a· these words. "
17 didst thou write a· these words "
18 He pronounced a· these words "
20 a· the words in the ears of the king. "
21 and in the ears of a· the princes "
23 until a· the roll was consumed in "
24 servants that heard a· these words. "
28 and write in it a· the former words "
31 the men of Judah, a· the evil that "
32 mouth of Jeremiah a· the words "
37:21 a· the bread in the city was spent. "
38: 1 had spoken unto a· the people, "
4 and the hands of a· the people, "
9 a· that they have done to Jeremiah "
22 a· the women that are left in the "
23 they shall bring out a· thy wives "
27 came a· the princes unto Jeremiah, "
27 according to a· these words that "
39: 3 And a· the princes of the king "
3 with a· the residue of the princes "
4 saw them, and a· the men of war, "
6 king of Babylon slew a· the nobles "
13 a· the king of Babylon's princes; "
40: 1 among a· that were carried away "
4 behold, a· the land is before thee: "
7 when a· the captains of the forces "
11 a· the Jews that were in Moab, "
11 and that were in a· the countries, "
12 Even a· the Jews returned "
12 out of a· places whither they "
13 son of Kareah, and a· the captains "
15 a· the Jews which are gathered "
41: 3 Ishmael also slew a· the Jews that "
6 to meet them, weeping a· along "
9 had cast a· the dead bodies 3605
10 a· the residue of the people "
10 and a· the people that remained "
11 and a· the captains of the forces "
11 heard of a· the evil that Ishmael "
12 Then they took a· the men, "
13 a· the people which were with "
13 son of Kareah, and a· the captains "
14 So a· the people that Ishmael had "
16 son of Kareah, and a· the captains "
16 him, a· the remnant of the people "
42: 1 Then a· the captains of the forces, "
1 and a· the people from the least "
2 thy God, even for a· this remnant; "
5 if we do not even according to a· "
8 and a· the captains of the forces "
8 and a· the people from the least "
17 So shall it be with a· the men "
20 according unto a· that the Lord "
43: 1 end of speaking unto a· the people "
1 a· the words of the Lord their God, "
1 him to them, even a· these words, "
2 and a· the proud men, saying unto "
4 a· the captains of the forces, "
4 and a· the people, obeyed not "
5 son of Kareah, and a· the captains "
5 took a· the remnant of Judah, "
5 were returned from a· nations, "
44: 1 concerning a· the Jews which dwell "
2 a· the evil that I have brought "
2 and upon a· the cities of Judah; "
4 you a· my servants the prophets, "
8 a curse and a reproach among a· "
11 for evil, and to cut off a· Judah. "
12 and they shall a· be consumed, "
15 a· the men which knew that their "
15 other gods, and a· the women "
15 great multitude, even a· the people "
18 we have wanted a· things, "
20 Jeremiah said unto a· the people, "
20 to the women, and to a· the people "
24 Jeremiah said unto a· the people, "
24 a· the women, Hear the word "
24 of the Lord, a· Judah that are in "
26 a· Judah that dwell in the land of "
26 in a· the land of Egypt, saying, "
27 and a· the men of Judah that are "
28 and a· the remnant of Judah, "
45: 5 I will bring evil upon a· flesh, "
5 unto thee for a prey in a· places "
46:25 and a· them that trust in him: *
28 make a full end of a· the nations 3605
47: 2 the land, and a· that is therein; 4393
2 and a· the inhabitants of the land 3605
4 cometh to spoil a· the Philistines, "
48:17 A· ye that are about him, "
17 bemoan him; and a· ye that know "
24 a· the cities of the land of Moab, "
31 and I will cry out for a· Moab; "
37 a· the hands shall be cuttings, "
38 upon a· the housetops of Moab, "

Jer 48:39 and a dismaying to a· them about 3605
49: 5 from a· those that be about thee; "
13 and a· the cities thereof shall be "
17 shall hiss at a· the plagues thereof. "
26 a· the men of war shall be cut off "
29 a· their vessels, and their camels; "
32 I will scatter into a· winds them "
32 their calamity from a· sides * "
36 them toward a· those winds; "
50: 7 A· that found them have devoured "
10 a· that spoil her shall be satisfied, "
13 be astonished, and hiss at a· her "
14 a· ye that bend the bow, shoot at "
21 a· that I have commanded thee. "
27 Slay a· her bullocks; let them go "
29 the archers against Babylon: a· ye "
29 according to a· that she hath done, "
30 a· her men of war shall be cut off "
32 shall devour a· round about him. "
33 and a· that took them captives "
37 and upon a· the mingled people "
51: 3 young men; destroy ye utterly a· "
7 that made a· the earth drunken: "
19 for he is the former of a· things: "
24 to a· the inhabitants of Chaldea "
24 a· their evil that they have done "
25 which destroyest a· the earth: "
28 and a· the rulers thereof, "
28 and a· the land of his dominion. "
47 a· her slain shall fall in the midst "
48 and a· that is therein, shall sing "
49 shall fall the slain of a· the earth. "
52 through a· her land the wounded "
60 a book a· the evil that should come "
60 a· these words that are written "
61 and shalt read a· these words; "
52: 2 of the Lord, according to a· that "
4 a· his army, against Jerusalem, "
7 up, and a· the men of war fled, "
8 a· his army was scattered from "
10 slew also a· the princes of Judah "
13 and a· the houses of Jerusalem, "
13 a· the houses of the great men, "
14 And a· the army of the Chaldeans, "
14 down a· the walls of Jerusalem "
17 carried a· the brass . . . to Babylon. "
18 the bowls, and the spoons, and a· "
20 the brass of a· these vessels was "
22 chapiters round about, a· of brass. "
23 a· the pomegranates upon the "
30 a· the persons were four thousand "
33 before him a· the days of his life. "
34 until the day of his death, a· the "
La 1: 2 among a· her lovers she hath none "
2 a· her friends have dealt "
3 a· her persecutors overtook her "
4 a· her gates are desolate; her "
6 daughter of Zion a· her beauty is "
7 a· her pleasant things that she had "
8 a· that honoured her despise her, "
10 hath spread out his hand upon a· "
11 A· her people sigh, they seek bread; "
12 to you, a· ye that pass by? behold, "
13 me desolate and faint a· the day. "
15 trodden under foot a· my mighty "
18 hear, I pray you, a· people, "
21 a· mine enemies have heard of my "
22 a· their wickedness come before "
22 thou hast done unto me for a· my "
2: 2 The Lord hath swallowed up a· "
3 fierce anger a· the horn of Israel: "
4 and slew a· that were pleasant to "
5 hath swallowed up a· her palaces: "
15 A· that pass by clap their hands at "
16 A· thine enemies have opened their "
3: 3 he turneth his hand against me a· "
14 I was a derision to a· my people; "
14 and their song a· the day. "
34 feet a· the prisoners of the earth, "
46 A· our enemies have opened their "
60 Thou hast seen a· their vengeance "
60, 61 a· their imaginations against "
62 device against me a· the day. "
4:12 and a· the inhabitants of the world, "
Eze 3: 7 a· the house of Israel are impudent "
10 a· my words that I shall speak "
5: 4 forth into a· the house of Israel. "
9 because of a· thine abominations. "
10 will I scatter into a· the winds. "
11 with a· thy detestable things, "
11 and with a· thine abominations, "
12 third part into a· the winds, "
14 in the sight of a· that pass by. "
6: 6 In a· your dwellingplaces the "
9 in a· their abominations. "
11 Alas for a· the evil abominations "
13 in a· the tops of the mountains, "
13 sweet savour to a· their idols. "
14 in a· their habitations: and they "
7: 3 upon thee a· thine abominations. "
8 and will recompense thee for a· "
12 wrath is upon a· the multitude "
14 trumpet, even to make a· ready; "
14 battle: for my wrath is upon a· "
16 a· of them mourning, every one "
17 A· hands shall be feeble, "
17 and a· knees shall be weak "
18 shame shall be upon a· faces, "
18 and baldness upon a· their heads. "
8:10 a· the idols of the house of Israel, "
9: 4 cry for a· the abominations that "
8 destroy a· the residue of Israel "
11:15 and a· the house of Israel wholly, "
18 shall take away a· the detestable "
18 and a· the abominations thereof "
25 a· the things that the Lord had "

Eze 12:10 and a· the house of Israel that 3605
14 toward every wind a· that are "
14 to help him, and a· his bands; "
16 may declare a· their abominations "
19 be desolate from a· that is therein, 4393
19 of a· them that dwell therein. 3605
13:18 that sew pillows to a· armholes, "
14: 3 face: should I be enquired of at a· "
6 faces from a· your abominations. 3605
11 polluted any more with a· their "
22 concerning a· that I have brought "
23 cause a· that I have done in it, "
16: 4 thou wast not salted at a·,
4 nor swaddled at a·.
22 And in a· thine abominations and 3605
23 to pass after a· thy wickedness, "
30 seeing thou doest a· these things, "
33 They give gifts to a· whores: but "
33 givest thy gifts to a· thy lovers, "
36 a· the idols of thy abominations, "
37 I will gather a· thy lovers, with "
37 and a· them that thou hast loved, "
37 with a· them that thou hast hated; "
37 they may see a· thy nakedness. "
43 hast fretted me in a· these things; "
43 above a· thine abominations. "
47 more than they in a· thy ways. "
51 in a· thine abominations which "
54 a· that thou hast done, in that thou "
57 and a· that are round about her, "
63 toward thee for a· that thou "
17: 9 in a· the leaves of her spring, "
18 and hath done a· these things, he "
21 And a· his fugitives "
21 with a· his bands shall fall by the "
21 be scattered toward a· winds: * "
23 shall dwell a· fowl of every wing; "
24 And a· the trees of the field shall "
18: 4 Behold, a· souls are mine; as the "
13 not live: he hath done a· these "
14 that seeth a· his father's sins which "
19 kept a· my statutes, and hath "
21 will turn from a· his sins that he "
21 and keep a· my statutes, and do "
22 A· his transgressions that he * "
23 at a· that the wicked should die? *
24 according to a· the abominations 3605
24 A· his righteousness that he hath * "
28 and turneth away from a· "
30 from a· your transgressions; "
31 from you a· your transgressions, "
20: 6, 15 which is the glory of a· lands: "
26 to pass through the fire a· that "
28 high hill, and a· the thick trees, * "
31 pollute yourselves with a· your "
32 into your mind shall not be at a·.
40 there shall a· the house of Israel, 3605
40 a· of them in the land, serve me: "
40 oblations, with a· your holy things. "
43 your ways, and a· your doings, "
43 for a· your evils that ye have "
47 and a· faces from the south to the "
48 a· flesh shall see that I the Lord "
21: 4 a· flesh from the south to the north: "
5 That a· flesh may know that I "
7 melt, and a· hands shall be feeble, "
7 faint, and a· knees shall be weak "
12 be upon a· the princes of Israel: "
15 the sword against a· their gates, "
24 so that in a· your doings your sins "
22: 2 shalt shew her a· her abominations. "
4 and a mocking to a· countries. "
18 Israel is to me become dross: a· "
19 Because ye are a· become dross, "
23: 6 a· of them desirable young men, "
7 a· them that were the chosen men "
7 with a· on whom she doted: *3605
7 with a· their idols she defiled "
12 a· of them desirable young men. "
15 a· of them princes to look to, after "
23 and a· the Chaldeans, Pekod, and "
23 and a· the Assyrians with them: "
23 a· of them desirable young men, "
23 a· of them riding upon horses. "
29 shall take away a· thy labour, "
48 that a· women may be taught "
24:24 a· that he hath done shall ye do: "
25: 6 a· thy despite against the land of "
8 Judah is like unto a· the heathen; "
26:11 shall he tread down a· thy streets: "
16 Then a· the princes of the sea shall "
17 terror to be on a· that haunt it! "
27: 5 made a· thy ship boards of fir trees "
9 a· the ships of the sea with their "
12 of the multitude of a· kind of riches; "
18 for the multitude of a· riches; in "
21 Arabia, and a· the princes of Kedar, "
22 of a· spices, and with a· precious "
24 merchants in a· sorts of things, * "
27 and a· thy men of war, "
27 and in a· thy company "
29 And a· that handle the oar, "
29 the mariners, and a· the pilots "
34 and a· thy company in the midst "
35 A· the inhabitants of the isles "
28:18 earth in the sight of a· them that "
19 A· they that know thee among the "
24 of a· that are round about them, * "
26 judgments upon a· those that "
29: 2 against him, and against a· Egypt: "
4 and a· the fish of thy rivers shall "
5 wilderness, thee and a· the fish "
6 And a· the inhabitants of Egypt "
7 break, and rend a· their shoulder: "
30: 5 Lydia, and a· the mingled people, "
8 a· her helpers shall be destroyed. "

Eze 30:12 land waste, and *a'* that is therein, 4393
31: 4 unto *a'* the trees of the field. 3605
5 his height was exalted above *a'* the "
6 *A'* the fowls of heaven made their "
6 *a'* the beasts of the field bring "
6 his shadow dwelt *a'* great nations. "
9 so that *a'* the trees of Eden, "
12 in *a'* the valleys his branches are "
12 broken by *a'* the rivers of the land; "
12 *a'* the people of the earth are gone "
13 *a'* the fowls of the heaven remain, "
13 and *a'* the beasts of the field shall "
14 To the end that none of *a'* the trees "
14 *a'* that drink water: for "
14 they are *a'* delivered unto death, "
15 *a'* the trees of the field fainted for "
16 and *a'* the trees of Eden, "
16 *a'* that drink water, shall be "
18 is Pharaoh and *a'* his multitude, "
32: 4 cause *a'* the fowls of the heaven "
8 *A'* the bright lights of heaven "
12 terrible of the nations, *a'* of them: "
12 and *a'* the multitude thereof "
13 destroy also *a'* the beasts thereof "
15 smite *a'* them that dwell therein, "
16 Egypt, and for *a'* her multitude, "
20 draw her and *a'* her multitudes. "
22 is there and *a'* her company: "
22 *a'* of them slain, fallen by the "
23 round about her grave: *a'* of them "
24 Elam and *a'* her multitude round "
24 her grave, *a'* of them slain, fallen "
25 the slain with *a'* her multitude: "
25 are round about him: *a'* of them "
26 Tubal, and *a'* her multitude: "
26 *a'* of them uncircumcised, slain "
29 her kings, and *a'* her princes, "
30 princes of the north, *a'* of them, "
30 and *a'* the Zidonians, which are "
31 comforted over *a'* his multitude, "
31 Pharaoh and *a'* his army slain by "
32 Pharaoh and *a'* his multitude, "
33:13 iniquity, *a'* his righteousnesses * "
29 land most desolate because of *a'* "
34: 5 meat to *a'* the beasts of the field, "
6 through *a'* the mountains, "
6 was scattered upon *a'* the face "
12 and will deliver them out of *a'* "
13 and in *a'* the inhabited places of "
21 and pushed *a'* the diseased with "
35: 8 and in *a'* thy rivers, shall they fall "
12 I have heard *a'* thy blasphemies "
36: 5 and against *a'* Idumea, which have "
5 with the joy of *a'* their heart, "
10 multiply men upon you, *a'* the "
10 Israel, even *a'* of it: and the cities "
24 gather you out of *a'* countries, "
25 from *a'* your filthiness, "
25 and from *a'* your idols, "
29 you from *a'* your uncleannesses: "
33 you from *a'* your iniquities "
34 in the sight of *a'* that passed by. "
37:16 of Ephraim, and for *a'* the house "
22 one king shall be king to them *a'*: "
22 two kingdoms any more at *a'*: "
23 out of *a'* their dwellingplaces, 3650
24 they *a'* shall have one shepherd: "
38: 4 thee forth, and *a'* thine army, "
4 *a'* of them clothed "
4 with *a'* sorts of armour, * "
4 *a'* of them handling swords: "
5 *a'* of them with shield and helmet: "
6 Gomer, and *a'* his bands; "
6 north quarters, and *a'* his bands: "
7 prepare for thyself, thou, and *a'* "
8 they shall dwell safely *a'* of them. "
9 thou, and *a'* thy bands, and many "
11 *a'* of them dwelling without walls, "
13 Tarshish, with *a'* the young lions "
15 *a'* of them riding upon horses, "
20 and *a'* creeping things that creep "
20 *a'* the men that are upon the face "
21 him throughout *a'* my mountains, "
39: 4 mountains of Israel, thou, and *a'* "
11 bury Gog and *a'* his multitude: "
13 Yea, *a'* the people of the land shall "
18 *a'* of them fatlings of Bashan. "
20 men, and with *a'* men of war, "
21 and *a'* the heathen shall see my "
23 so fell they *a'* by the sword. "
26 and *a'* their trespasses whereby "
40: 4 upon *a'* that I shall shew thee; "
4 declare *a'* that thou seest to the "
41:17 and by *a'* the wall round about "
19 it was made through *a'* the house "
42:11 and *a'* their goings out were both "
43:11 ashamed of *a'* that they have done, "
11 and *a'* the forms thereof, "
11 and *a'* the ordinances thereof, "
11 and *a'* the forms thereof. "
11 and *a'* the laws thereof: "
11 and *a'* the ordinances thereof, "
44: 5 hear with thine ears *a'* that I say "
5 concerning *a'* the ordinances of "
5 *a'* the laws thereof; and mark well "
6 suffice you of *a'* your abominations, "
7 because of *a'* your abominations. "
14 for *a'* the service thereof, and "
14 for *a'* that shall be done therein. "
24 my statutes in *a'* mine assemblies; "
30 And the first of *a'* the firstfruits "
30 of *a'* things, and * "
30 every oblation of *a'*, of every sort "
45: 1 *a'* the borders thereof round about. "
16 *A'* the people of the land shall give "
17 *a'* solemnities of the house of Israel: "

Eze 45:22 and for *a'* the people of the land 3650
47:12 shall grow *a'* trees for meat, * "
48:13 *a'* the length shall be five and "
19 it out of *a'* the tribes of Israel. "
20 *A'* the oblation shall be five and "
Da 1: 4 skilful in *a'* wisdom, and cunning "
15 fatter in flesh than *a'* the children "
17 knowledge and skill in *a'* learning "
17 understanding in *a'* visions and "
19 among them *a'* was found none like "
20 And in *a'* matters of wisdom and * "
20 them ten times better than *a'* "
20 astrologers that were in *a'* his "
2:12 *a'* the wise men of Babylon. 3606
38 made thee ruler over them *a'*. "
39 shall bear rule over *a'* the earth. "
40 in pieces and subdueth *a'* things: "
40 and as iron that breaketh *a'* these, "
44 and consume *a'* these kingdoms, "
48 over *a'* the wise men of Babylon. "
3: 2, 3 *a'* the rulers of the provinces, "
5 dulcimer, and *a'* kinds of musick, "
7 *a'* the people heard the sound of "
7 and *a'* kinds of musick, *a'* the "
10 and *a'* kinds of musick, shall fall "
15 psaltery, and dulcimer, and *a'* "
4: 1 *a'* people, nations, and languages, "
1 that dwell in *a'* the earth; "
6 in *a'* the wise men of Babylon "
11 thereof to the end of *a'* the earth: "
12 and in it was meat for *a'*: "
12 *a'* flesh was fed of it. "
18 forasmuch as *a'* the wise men "
20 the sight thereof to *a'* the earth; "
21 much, and in it was meat for *a'*; "
28 *A'* this came upon the king "
35 And *a'* the inhabitants of the earth "
37 *a'* whose works are truth, "
5: 8 came in *a'* the king's wise men: "
19 *a'* people, nations, and languages, "
22 though thou knewest *a'* this; "
23 and whose are *a'* thy ways, "
6: 7 *A'* the presidents of the kingdom, "
24 and brake *a'* their bones in pieces "
25 *a'* people, nations, and languages, "
25 that dwell in *a'* the earth; "
7: 7 it was diverse from *a'* the beasts "
14 *a'* people, nations, and languages, "
16 and asked him the truth of *a'* this. "
19 was diverse from *a'* the others, "
23 shall be diverse from *a'* kingdoms, "
27 *a'* dominions shall serve and obey "
9: 6 and to *a'* the people of the land. 3605
7 and unto *a'* Israel, that are near, "
7 *a'* the countries whither thou hast "
11 *a'* Israel have transgressed thy law, "
13 Moses, *a'* this evil is come upon us: "
14 God is righteous in *a'* his works "
16 according to *a'* thy righteousness, "
16 a reproach to *a'* that are about us. "
10: 3 did I anoint myself at *a'*, "
11: 2 shall be far richer than they *a'*: 3605
2 up *a'* against the realm of Grecia. "
37 he shall magnify himself above *a'*. "
43 *a'* the precious things of Egypt: "
12: 7 *a'* these things shall be finished. "
Ho 2:11 also cause *a'* her mirth to cease, "
11 sabbaths, and *a'* her solemn feasts. "
5: 2 I have been a rebuker of them *a'*. "
7: 2 I remember *a'* their wickedness: "
4 They are *a'* adulterers, as an oven "
6 their baker sleepeth *a'* the night; "
7 They are *a'* hot as an oven, "
7 *a'* their kings are fallen: there is "
10 Lord their God, nor seek him for *a'* "
9: 4 *a'* that eat thereof shall be polluted: "
8 is a snare of a fowler in *a'* his "
15 *A'* their wickedness is in Gilgal: "
15 *a'* their princes are revolters. "
10:14 *a'* thy fortresses shall be spoiled, "
11: 7 most High, none at *a'* would exalt 3162
12: 8 in *a'* my labours they shall find 3605
13: 2 *a'* of it the work of the craftsmen: "
10 that may save thee in *a'* thy cities? "
15 the treasure of *a'* pleasant vessels. "
14: 2 Take away *a'* iniquity, and receive "
Joe 1: 2 ear, *a'* ye inhabitants of the land. "
5 and howl, *a'* ye drinkers of wine, "
12 even *a'* the trees of the field, "
13 come, lie *a'* night in sackcloth, 3885
14 and *a'* the inhabitants of the land 3605
19 the flame hath burned *a'* the trees "
2: 1 let *a'* the inhabitants of the land "
6 *a'* faces shall gather blackness. "
12 ye even to me with *a'* your heart, "
28 pour out my spirit upon *a'* flesh; "
3: 2 I will also gather *a'* nations, "
4 and *a'* the coasts of Palestine? "
9 let *a'* the men of war draw near; "
11 and come, *a'* ye heathen, and "
12 judge *a'* the heathen round about. "
18 *a'* the rivers of Judah shall flow "
Am 1:11 the sword, and did cast off *a'* pity, "
2: 3 and will slay *a'* the princes thereof 3605
3: 2 of *a'* the families of the earth: "
2 punish you for *a'* your iniquities. "
5 and have taken nothing at *a'*? "
4: 6 you cleanness of teeth in *a'* your 3605
6 want of bread in *a'* your places: "
5:16 Wailing shall be in *a'* streets; "
16 they shall say in *a'* the highways, "
17 in *a'* vineyards shall be wailing: "
6: 8 up the city with *a'* that is therein. 4393
7:10 land is not able to bear *a'* his 3605
8:10 *a'* your songs into lamentation; "
10 bring up sackcloth upon *a'* loins, "

Am 9: 1 cut them in the head, *a'* of them; 3605
5 *a'* that dwell therein shall mourn: "
9 house of Israel among *a'* nations, "
10 *A'* the sinners of my people shall "
12 and of *a'* the heathen, which are "
13 wine, and *a'* the hills shall melt. "
Ob 7 *A'* the men of thy confederacy have "
15 Lord is near upon *a'* the heathen: "
16 *a'* the heathen drink continually, "
Jon 2: 3 *a'* thy billows and thy waves "
Mic 1: 2 Hear, *a'* ye people; hearken, "
2 O earth, and *a'* that therein is: 4393
5 transgression of Jacob is *a'* this, 3605
7 And *a'* the graven images thereof "
7 and *a'* the hires thereof shall be "
7 and *a'* the idols thereof will I lay "
10 it not at Gath, weep ye not at *a'*:
2:12 assemble, O Jacob, *a'* of thee; 3605
3: 7 yea, they shall *a'* cover their lips; "
9 judgment, and pervert *a'* equity. "
4: 5 *a'* people will walk every one in the "
5: 9 and *a'* thine enemies shall be cut
11 throw down *a'* thy strong holds: 3605
6:16 are kept, and *a'* the works of the "
7: 2 among men: they *a'* lie in wait "
16 be confounded at *a'* their might: "
19 cast *a'* their sins into the depths "
Na 1: 3 will not at *a'* acquit the wicked: *
4 maketh it dry, and drieth up *a'* 3605
5 world, and *a'* that dwell therein. "
2: 9 out of *a'* the pleasant furniture. "
10 pain is in *a'* loins, "
10 faces of them *a'* gather blackness. "
3: 1 city! it is *a'* full of lies and "
7 that *a'* they that look upon thee "
10 pieces at the top of *a'* the streets: "
10 and *a'* her great men were bound "
12 *A'* thy strongholds shall be like fig "
19 *a'* that hear the bruit of thee shall "
Hab 1: 9 They shall come *a'* for violence: "
15 take up *a'* of them with the angle, "
2: 5 gathereth unto him *a'* nations, "
5 and heapeth unto him *a'* people: "
6 Shall not *a'* these take up a parable "
8 *a'* the remnant of the people shall "
8, 17 city, and of *a'* that dwell therein. "
19 no breath at *a'* in the midst of it. "
20 let *a'* the earth keep silence "
Zep 1: 2 *a'* things from off the land, "
4 hand upon Judah, and upon *a'* "
8 and *a'* such as are clothed with "
9 will I punish *a'* those that leap on "
11 *a'* the merchant people are cut "
11 down; *a'* they that bear "
18 a speedy riddance of *a'* them that "
2: 3 the Lord, *a'* ye meek of the earth, "
11 famish *a'* the gods of the earth; "
11 one from his place, even *a'* the "
14 in the midst of her, *a'* the beasts "
3: 7 and corrupted *a'* their doings. "
8 even *a'* my fierce anger: "
8 for *a'* the earth shall be devoured "
9 that they may *a'* call upon the name "
11 not be ashamed for *a'* thy doings, "
14 glad and rejoice with *a'* the heart, "
19 time I will undo *a'* that afflict thee: "
20 name and a praise among *a'* people "
Hag 1:11 upon *a'* the labour of the hands. "
12 with *a'* the remnant of the people, "
14 the spirit of *a'* the remnant of the "
2: 4 strong, *a'* ye people of the land, "
7 And I will shake *a'* nations, "
7 and the desire of *a'* nations "
17 hail in *a'* the labours of your hands; "
Zec 2:13 Be silent, O *a'* flesh, before the "
4: 2 and behold a candlestick *a'* of gold, "
5: 6 resemblance through *a'* the earth. "
6: 5 before the Lord of *a'* the earth. "
7: 5 unto *a'* the people of the land, "
5 years, did ye at *a'* fast unto me,
14 *a'* the nations whom they knew 3605
8:10 for I set *a'* men every one against "
12 of this people to possess *a'* "
17 for *a'* these are things that I hate, "
23 take hold out of *a'* languages of "
9: 1 of man, as of *a'* the tribes of Israel, "
10:11 *a'* the deeps of the river shall dry "
11:10 I had made with *a'* the people. "
12: 2 of trembling unto *a'* the people "
3 a burdensome stone for *a'* people: "
3 *a'* that burden themselves with it "
3 though *a'* the people of the earth "
6 devour *a'* the people round about, "
9 destroy *a'* the nations that come "
14 *A'* the families that remain, every "
13: 8 that in *a'* the land, saith the Lord, "
14: 2 *a'* nations against Jerusalem to "
5 come, and *a'* the saints with thee. "
9 shall be king over *a'* the earth: "
10 *A'* the land shall be turned as a "
12 the Lord will smite *a'* the people "
14 and the wealth of *a'* the heathen "
15 *a'* the beasts that shall be in these "
16 that is left of *a'* the nations which "
17 will not come up of *a'* the families "
19 and the punishment of *a'* nations 3605
21 the Lord of hosts: and *a'* they that "
Mal 2: 9 and base before *a'* the people, "
10 Have we not *a'* one father? hath "
3:10 *a'* the tithes into the storehouse, * "
12 *a'* nations shall call you blessed: "
4: 1 and *a'* the proud, yea, "
1 and *a'* that do wickedly, "
4 unto him in Horeb for *a'* Israel, "
M't 1:17 *a'* the generations from Abraham 3956
22 Now *a'* this was done, that it 3650

M't 2: 3 and a· Jerusalem with him. 3956
4 had gathered a· the chief priests "
16 and slew a· the children that were "
16 and in a· the coasts thereof, "
3: 5 to him Jerusalem, and a· Judæa, "
5 a· the region round about Jordan, "
15 us to fulfil a· righteousness. "
4: 8 and sheweth him a· the kingdoms "
9 A· these things will I give thee, "
23 Jesus went about a· Galilee, 3650
23 healing a· manner of sickness 3956
23 and a· manner of disease "
24 fame went throughout a· Syria: 3650
24 brought unto him a· sick people 3956
5:11 say a· manner of evil against you "
15 giveth light unto a· that are in "
18 till a· be fulfilled. "
34 Swear not at a·; neither by 3654
6:29 Solomon in a· his glory was not 3956
32 (For after a· these things do the 537
32 ye have need of a· these things. 3956
33 a· these things shall be added "
7:12 Therefore a· things whatsoever "
8:16 and healed a· that were sick: "
9:26 went abroad into a· that land. 3650
31 his fame in a· that country. "
35 Jesus went about a· the cities 3956
10: 1 and to heal a· manner of sickness, "
1 and a· manner of disease. "
22 ye shall be hated of a· men for my "
30 of your head are a· numbered. "
11:13 For a· the prophets and the law "
27 A· things are delivered unto me "
28 Come unto me, a· ye that labour "
12:15 and he healed them a·; "
23 And a· the people were amazed, "
31 A· manner of sin and blasphemy * "
13:32 indeed is the least of a· seeds: "
34 A· these things spake Jesus "
41 out of his kingdom a· things that "
44 and selleth a· that he hath, "
46 went and sold a· that he had, "
51 ye understood a· these things? "
56 sisters, are they not a· with us? "
56 hath this man a· these things? "
14:20 And they did a· eat, and were filled: "
35 they sent out into a· that country 3650
35 and brought unto him a· that 3956
15:37 And they did a· eat, and were "
17:11 first come, and restore a· things. "
18:25 and a· that he had, and payment "
26, and I will pay thee a·. "
26 with me, and I will pay thee a·. *
31 unto their lord a· that was done. 3956
32 I forgave thee a· that debt, "
34 till he should pay a· that was due "
19:11 A· men cannot receive this saying, "
20 A· these things have I kept from "
26 with God a· things are possible. "
27 we have forsaken a·, and followed "
20: 6 Why stand ye here a· the day idle? 3650
21: 4 A· this was done, that it might * "
10 a· the city was moved, saying, 3956
12 and cast out a· them that sold "
22 a· things, whatsoever ye shall ask "
26 for a· hold John as a prophet. "
37 of a· he sent unto them his son, *
22: 4 and a· things are ready: 3956
10 and gathered together a· as many "
27 And last of a· the woman died "
28 for they a· had her. "
37 the Lord thy God with a· thy heart, 3650
37 and with a· thy soul, "
37 and with a· thy mind. "
40 a· the law and the prophets. * "
23: 3 A· therefore whatsoever they bid 3956
5 But a· their works they do for to "
8 and a· ye are brethren. "
20 and by a· things thereon. "
27 and of a· uncleanness. "
35 may come a· the righteous blood "
36 A· these things shall come upon "
24: 2 See ye not a· these things? "
6 for a· these things must come to * "
8 A· these are the beginning of "
9 ye shall be hated of a· nations for "
14 in a· the world for a witness * 3650
14 unto a· nations; and then 3956
30 then shall a· the tribes of the "
33 when ye shall see a· these things, "
34 till a· these things be fulfilled. "
39 flood came, and took them a· away; 537
47 make him ruler over a· his goods. 3956
25: 5 they a· slumbered and slept. "
7 Then a· those virgins arose, "
31 and a· the holy angels with him, "
32 him shall be gathered a· nations: "
26: 1 Jesus had finished a· these "
27 saying, Drink ye a· of it; "
31 A· ye shall be offended because of "
33 Though a· men shall be offended "
35 Likewise also said a· the disciples. "
52 for a· they that take the sword "
56 But a· this was done, 3650
56 Then a· the disciples forsook him, 3956
59 and a· the council, sought false *3650
70 But he denied before them a·, 3956
27: 1 morning was come, a· the chief, "
22 They a· say unto him, Let him be "
25 Then answered a· the people, "
45 there was darkness over a· the land "
28: 9 Jesus met them, saying, A· hail. "
11 unto the chief priests a· the things 537
18 A· power is given unto me in 3956
19 and teach a· nations, baptising "
20 to observe a· things whatsoever "

M'r 1: 5 out unto him a· the land of Judæa, 3956
5 and were a· baptized of him * "
27 And they were a· amazed, "
28 throughout a· the region round 3650
32 brought unto him a· that were 3956
33 a· the city was gathered together 3650
37 A· men seek for thee. 3956
39 synagogues throughout a· Galilee, 3650
2:12 went forth before them a·; 3956
12 that they were a· amazed, "
13 and a· the multitude resorted "
3:28 A· sins shall be forgiven unto "
4:11 a· these things are done in "
13 then will ye know a· parables? "
31 is less than a· the seeds that be in "
32 becometh greater than a· herbs, "
34 expounded a· things to his disciples. "
5:12 And a· the devils besought him, * "
20 and a· men did marvel. "
26 and had spent a· that she had, "
33 and told him a· the truth. "
40 when he had put them a· out, 537
6:30 and told him a· things, both 3956
33 ran afoot thither out of a· cities, "
39 to make a· sit down by companies "
41 fishes divided he among them a·. "
42 And they did a· eat, "
50 For they a· saw him, and were "
7: 3 and a· the Jews, except they wash "
14 when he had called a· the people * "
19 purging a· meats? "
23 A· these evil things come from "
37 He hath done a· things well: "
9:12 and restoreth a· things; "
15 And straightway a· the people, "
23 a· things are possible to him that "
35 the same shall be last of a·, "
35 and servant of a·. "
10:20 a· these have I observed from my "
27 with God a· things are possible. "
28 Lo, we have left a·, and have "
44 chiefest, shall be servant of a·. "
11:11 looked round about upon a· things, "
17 of a· nations the house of prayer? "
18 a· the people were astonished at "
32 for a· men counted John, that he 537
12:22 last of a· the women died also. 3956
28 is the first commandment of a·? "
29 The first of a· the commandments * "
30 Lord thy God with a· thy heart, 3650
30 and with a· thy soul, * "
30 and with a· thy mind, "
30 and with a· thy strength: "
33 to love him with a· the heart, "
33 and with a· the understanding, "
33 and with a· the soul, * "
33 and with a· the strength, "
33 more than a· whole burnt offerings 3956
43 hath cast more in, than a· they "
44 For a· they did cast in of their "
44 did cast in a· that she had, "
44 even a· her living. 3650
13: 4 a· these things shall be fulfilled? 3956
10 be published among a· nations. "
13 hated of a· men for my name's sake: "
23 I have foretold you a· things. "
30 till a· these things be done. "
37 I say unto a·, Watch. "
14:23 and they a· drank of it. "
27 A· ye shall be offended because of "
29 Although a· shall be offended, "
31 Likewise also said they a·. "
36 a· things are possible unto thee; "
50 And they a· forsook him, and fled. "
53 were assembled a· the chief priests "
55 a· the council sought for witness *3650
64 a· condemned him to be guilty of 3956
16:15 Go ye into a· the world, 537

Lu 1: 3 perfect understanding of a· things 3956
6 walking in a· the commandments "
48 from henceforth a· generations "
63 And they marvelled a·. "
65 a· that dwelt round about them: "
65 and a· these sayings were noised "
65 a· the hill country of Judæa. 3650
66 And a· they that heard them 3956
71 from the hand of a· that hate us; "
75 before him, a· the days of our life. "
2: 1 that a· the world should be taxed. "
3 And a· went to be taxed, "
10 which shall be to a· people. "
18 a· they that heard it wondered "
19 But Mary kept a· these things, "
20 praising God for a· the things "
31 before the face of a· people; "
38 a· them that looked for redemption "
39 they had performed a· things 537
47 a· that heard him were astonished 3956
51 kept a· these sayings in her heart. "
3: 3 into a· the country about Jordan, "
6 And a· flesh shall see the salvation "
15 and a· men mused in their hearts "
16 answered, saying unto them a·, 537
19 a· the evils which Herod had done, 3956
20 Added yet this above a·, "
21 when a· the people were baptized, 537
4: 5 him a· the kingdoms of the world 3956
6 A· this power will I give thee, 537
7 worship me, a· shall be thine. 3956
13 had ended a· the temptation, * "
14 fame of him through a· the region 3650
15 being glorified of a·. 3956
20 a· them that were in the synagogue "
22 And a· bare him witness, "
25 famine was throughout a· the land; "
28 And a· they in the synagogue, "

Lu 4:36 And they were a· amazed, 3956
40 a· they that had any sick "
5: 5 we have toiled a· the night, 3650
9 and a· that were with him, 3956
11 they forsook a·, and followed him. 537
26 a· amazed, and they glorified God, "
28 left a·, rose up, and followed him. "
6:10 looking round about upon them a·, 3956
12 continued a· night in prayer to 1273
17 people out of a· Judæa 3956
19 and healed them a·. "
26 a· men shall speak well of you! "
7: 1 when he had ended a· his sayings "
16 there came a fear on a·: 537
17 went forth throughout a· Judæa. *3650
17 a· the region round about. 3956
18 shewed him of a· these things. "
29 and a· the people that heard him, "
35 wisdom is justified of a· her "
8:40 for they were a· waiting for him. "
43 a· her living upon physicians "
45 When a· denied, Peter and they "
47 declared unto him before a· the "
52 And a· wept and bewailed her: "
54 And he put them a· out, and took * "
9: 1 and authority over a· devils, "
7 heard of a· that was done by him: "
10 told him a· that they had done. *3745
13 buy meat for a· this people. 3956
15 did so, and made them a· sit down. 537
17 and were a· filled: 3956
23 he said to them a·, If any man will "
43 a· amazed at the mighty power of "
43 wondered every one at a· things, "
48 for he that is least among you a·, "
10:19 over a· the power of the enemy: "
22 A· things are delivered to me of "
27 Lord thy God with a· thy heart, 3650
27 and with a· thy soul, "
27 and with a· thy strength, "
27 and with a· thy mind; "
11:22 taketh from him a· his armour *3833
41 a· things are clean unto you. 3956
42 rue and a· manner of herbs, * "
50 That the blood of a· the prophets, "
12: 1 to say unto his disciples first of a·, "
7 hairs of your head are a· 3956
18 there will I bestow a· my fruits "
27 Solomon in a· his glory was not "
30 For a· these things do the nations "
31 and a· these things shall be added * "
41 this parable unto us, or even to a·? "
44 make him ruler over a· that he "
13: 2 sinners above a· the Galilæans, "
3 ye shall a· likewise perish. "
4 sinners above a· men "
5 ye shall a· likewise perish. "
17 a· his adversaries were ashamed: "
17 and a· the people rejoiced "
17 for a· the glorious things "
27 from me, a· ye workers of iniquity. "
28 a· the prophets, in the kingdom "
14:17 for a· things are now ready. "
18 And they a· with one consent "
29 a· that behold it begin to mock him, "
33 that forsaketh not a· that he hath, "
15: 1 a· the publicans and sinners "
13 younger son gathered a· together, 537
14 And when he had spent a·, 3956
31 and a· that I have is thine. "
16:14 covetous, heard a· these things: "
26 And beside a· this, between us "
17:10 ye shall have done a· those things "
27 flood came, and destroyed them a·. 537
29 heaven, and destroyed them a·. "
18:12 I give tithes of a· that I possess. 3956
21 A· these have I kept from my "
22 sell a· that thou hast, "
28 we have left a·, and followed thee * "
31 and a· things that are written "
43 a· the people, when they saw it, "
19: 7 they saw it, they a· murmured, 537
37 loud voice for a· the mighty works 3956
48 a· the people were very attentive 537
20: 6 a· the people will stone us: 3956
32 Last of a· the woman died also. * "
38 for a· live unto him. "
40 not ask him any question at a·. *
45 in the audience of a· the people 3956
21: 3 cast in more than they a·: "
4 a· these have of their abundance 537
4 cast in a· the living that she had. "
12 before a· these, they shall lay their "
15 which a· your adversaries shall 3956
17 hated of a· men for my name's sake: "
22 that a· things which are written "
24 led away captive into a· nations: "
29 Behold the fig tree, and a· the trees; "
32 not pass away, till a· be fulfilled. "
35 on a· them that dwell on the face "
36 to escape a· these things "
38 And a· the people came early "
22:70 Then said they a·, Art thou then "
23: 5 teaching throughout a· Jewry, 3650
18 they cried out a· at once, saying, 3829
44 darkness over a· the earth until * 3650
48 a· the people that came together 3956
49 And a· his acquaintance, "
24: 9 told a· these things unto the eleven, "
9 and to a· the rest. "
14 talked together of a· these things. "
19 before God and a· the people: "
21 beside a· this, to day is the third "
25 a· that the prophets have spoken: "
27 at Moses and a· the prophets, * "
27 unto them in a· the scriptures * "

Lu 24:44 that a' things must be fulfilled, 3956
47 a' nations, beginning at "
Joh 1: 3 A' things were made by him; "
7 a' men through him might believe. "
16 of his fulness have a' we received, "
2:15 drove them a' out of the temple, "
24 because he knew a' men, "
3:26 and a' men come to him. "
31 cometh from above is above a': "
31 cometh from heaven is above a'. "
35 given a' things into his hand. "
4:25 is come, he will tell us a' things. "
29 told me a' things that ever I did: "
39 He told me a' that ever I did. * "
45 seen a' the things that he did "
5:20 and sheweth him a' things "
22 committed a' judgment unto the "
23 a' men should honour the Son, "
28 a' that are in the graves shall "
6:37 A' that the Father giveth me shall "
39 of a' which he hath given me "
45 they shall be a' taught of God. "
7:21 done one work, and ye a' marvel. "
8: 2 and a' the people came unto him; "
10: 8 A' that ever came before me "
29 gave them me, is greater than a'; "
41 but a' things that John spake "
48 alone, a' men will believe on him: "
49 unto them, Ye know nothing at a', 3762
12:32 will draw a' men unto me. 3956
13: 3 the Father had given a' things "
10 ye are clean, but not a'. "
11 Ye are not a' clean. "
18 I speak not of you a': "
35 By this shall a' men know "
14:26 shall teach you a' things, and bring "
26 a' things to your remembrance, "
15:15 for a' things that I have heard "
21 a' these things will they do unto "
16:13 he will guide you into a' truth: "
15 A' things that the Father hath are "
30 that thou knowest a' things, "
17: 2 given him power over a' flesh, "
7 known that a' things whatsoever "
10 And a' mine are thine, "
21 That they a' may be one; "
18: 4 a' things that should come upon "
38 I find in him no fault at a'. *
40 Then cried they a' again, saying, *3956
19:11 have no power at a' against me, *3762
28 a' things were now accomplished. 3956
21:11 and for a' there were so many, "
17 Lord, thou knowest a' things; 3956
Ac 1: 1 of a' that Jesus began both to do "
8 and in a' Judæa, and in Samaria, "
14 These a' continued with one accord "
18 and a' his bowels gushed out. "
19 it was known unto a' the dwellers "
21 companied with us a' the time "
24 knowest the hearts of a' men, "
2: 1 a' with one accord in one place. 537
2 filled a' the house where they were 3650
4 were a' filled with the Holy Ghost, 537
7 And they were a' amazed 3956
7 a' these which speak Galilæans? "
12 And they were a' amazed, "
14 a' ye that dwell at Jerusalem, 537
17 out of my Spirit upon a' flesh: 3956
32 whereof we a' are witnesses. "
36 Therefore let a' the house of Israel "
39 and to a' that are afar off, "
44 a' that believed were together, "
44 and had a' things common; 537
45 and parted them to a' men, 3956
47 having favour with a' the people. 3650
3: 9 a' the people saw him walking 3956
11 a' the people ran together "
16 in the presence of you a'. "
18 by the mouth of a' his prophets, * "
21 times of restitution of a' things, "
21 the mouth of a' his holy prophets* "
22 a' things whatsoever he shall say "
24 and a' the prophets from Samuel "
25 shall a' the kindreds of the earth "
4:10 Be it known unto you a', "
10 and to a' the people of Israel, "
16 to a' them that dwell in Jerusalem; "
18 not to speak at a' nor teach in the 2527
21 for a' men glorified God for that 3956
23 reported a' that the chief priests 3745
24 the sea, and a' that in them is: 3956
29 with a' boldness they may speak "
31 were a' filled with the Holy Ghost, 537
32 they had a' things common. "
33 great grace was upon them a'. 3956
5: 5 and great fear came on a' "
11 And great fear came upon a' *3650
12 a' with one accord in Solomon's 537
17 and a' they that were with him, 3956
20 a' the words of this life. "
21 a' the senate of the children of "
23 found we shut with a' safety, "
34 in reputation among a' the people, "
36 and a', as many as obeyed him, "
37 a', even as many as obeyed him, "
6:15 a' that sat in the council, looking 537
7:10 delivered him out of a' his 3956
10 governor over Egypt and a' 3650
11 a dearth over a' the land of Egypt "
14 and a' his kindred, threescore 3956
22 in a' the wisdom of the Egyptians, "
50 my hands made a' these things? "
8: 1 and they were a' scattered abroad "
10 To whom they a' gave heed, "
27 had the charge of a' her treasure, "
37 thou believest with a' thine heart, *3650

Ac 8:40 he preached in a' the cities, 3956
9:14 to bind a' that call on thy name. "
21 a' that heard him were amazed, "
26 but they were a' afraid of him, "
31 churches rest throughout a' Judæa 3650
32 passed throughout a' quarters, 3956
35 And a' that dwelt at Lydda "
39 and a' the widows stood by him "
40 But Peter put them a' forth, "
42 was known throughout a' Joppa; 3650
10: 2 feared God with a' his house, 3956
8 declared a' these things unto them, 537
12 a' manner of fourfooted beasts of 3956
22 among a' the nation of the Jews, 3650
33 Now therefore are we a' here 3956
33 a' things that are commanded thee "
36 (he is Lord of a':) "
37 published throughout a' Judæa, 3650
38 a' that were oppressed of the devil; 3956
39 witnesses of a' things which he did "
41 Not to a' the people, but unto "
43 him give a' the prophets witness, "
44 the Holy Ghost fell on a' them "
11:10 a' were drawn up again into 537
14 thou and a' thy house shall be 3956
23 and exhorted them a', that with "
28 dearth throughout a' the world: 3650
12:11 a' the expectation of the people 3956
13:10 full of a' subtilty and a' mischief, "
10 thou enemy of a' righteousness, "
22 which shall fulfil a' my will. "
24 repentance to a' the people of "
29 fulfilled a' that was written of him, 537
39 And by him a' that believe *3956
39 are justified from a' things, "
49 throughout a' the region. 3650
14:15 and a' things that are therein: 3956
16 in times past suffered a' nations "
27 a' that God had done with them, 3745
15: 3 great joy unto a' the brethren. 3956
4 declared a' things that God had 3745
12 Then a' the multitude kept silence, 3956
17 a' the Gentiles, upon whom my name "
17 who doeth a' these things. * "
18 Known unto God are a' his works* "
16: 3 a' that his father was a Greek. 537
26 a' the doors were opened, and 3956
28 Do thyself no harm: for we are a' 537
32 to a' that were in his house. 3956
33 baptized, he and a' his, straightway. "
34 believing in God with a' his house. 3832
17: 5 and set a' the city on an uproar, *
7 a' do contrary to the decrees of 3956
11 the word with a' readiness "
15 to come to him with a' speed, 5613, 5033
21 a' the Athenians and strangers 3956
22 a' things ye are too superstitious. "
24 the world and a' things therein, "
25 to a' life, and breath, and a' things; "
26 of one blood a' nations of men * "
26 dwell on a' the face of the earth, "
30 commandeth a' men every where "
31 hath given assurance unto a' men, "
18: 2 Claudius had commanded a' Jews "
8 believed on the Lord with a' his 3650
17 a' the Greeks took Sosthenes, 3956
21 must by a' means keep this feast *3843
23 over a' the country of Galatia "
23 strengthening a' the disciples. 3956
19: 7 And a' the men were about twelve. "
10 that a' they which dwelt in Asia "
17 this was known to a' the Jews "
17 and fear fell on them a', "
19 and burned them before a' men: "
26 almost throughout a' Asia, "
27 whom a' Asia and the world 3650
34 a' with one voice about the space 3956
20:18 I have been with you at a' seasons, "
19 with a' humility of mind, "
25 I know that ye a', among whom "
26 pure from the blood of a' men. "
27 a' the counsel of God. * "
28 and to a' the flock, over the which "
32 a' them which are sanctified. "
35 I have shewed you a' things, "
36 and prayed with them a'. "
37 And they a' wept sore, "
38 Sorrowing most of a' for the words 3122
21: 5 they a' brought us on our way, 3956
18 and a' the elders were present. "
20 and they are a' zealous of the law: "
21 that thou teachest a' the Jews "
24 a' may know that those things, "
27 stirred up a' the people, and laid "
28 that teacheth a' men every where "
30 And a' the city was moved, 3650
31 a' Jerusalem was in an uproar. "
22: 3 as ye a' are this day. 3956
5 and a' the estate of the elders: "
10 it shall be told thee of a' things "
12 having a good report of a' the Jews "
15 shalt be his witness unto a' men "
30 and a' their council to appear, 3650
23: 1 I have lived in a' good conscience 3956
24: 3 always, and in a' places, 3837
3 most noble Felix, with a' 3956
5 of sedition among a' the Jews "
8 take knowledge of a' these things, "
14 believing a' things which are "
25: 8 have I offended any thing at a'. "
24 King Agrippa, and a' men which 3956
24 whom a' the multitude of the Jews "
26: 2 touching a' the things whereof "
3 to be expert in a' customs "
4 know a' the Jews; "
14 we were a' fallen to the earth, "

Ac 26:20 throughout a' the coasts of Judæa, 3956
29 but also a' that hear me this day, "
27:20 a' hope that we should be saved "
24 God hath given thee a' them "
33 besought them a' to take meat, 537
35 in presence of them a': 3956
36 Then were they a' of good cheer, "
37 we were in a' in the ship "
44 they escaped a' safe to land. "
28:30 and received a' that came in unto, "
31 with a' confidence, no man "
Ro 1: 5 to the faith among a' nations, for "
7 To a' that be in Rome, "
8 through Jesus Christ for you a', "
18 against a' ungodliness and "
29 filled with a' unrighteousness, "
3: 9 that they are a' under sin; "
12 They are a' gone out of the way, "
19 a' the world may become guilty "
22 by faith of Jesus Christ unto a' "
22 and upon a' them that believe * "
23 For a' have sinned, and come short "
4:11 might be the father of a' them that "
16 might be sure to a' the seed; "
16 who is the father of us a', "
5:12 and so death passed upon a' men, "
12 for that a' have sinned: "
18 upon a' men to condemnation; "
18 upon a' men unto justification of "
7: 8 in me a' manner of concupiscence. "
8:28 a' things work together for good "
32 delivered him up for us a', "
32 also freely give us a' things? "
36 we are killed a' the day long; 3650
37 Nay, in a' these things we are 3956
9: 5 who is over a', God blessed for ever. "
6 For they are not a' Israel, "
7 of Abraham, are they a' children: "
17 declared throughout a' the earth. "
10:12 same Lord over a' is rich "
12 unto a' that call upon him "
16 they have not a' obeyed the gospel. "
18 their sound went into a' the earth, "
21 A' day long I have stretched forth 3650
11:26 And so a' Israel shall be saved: 3956
32 concluded them a' in unbelief, "
32 that he might have mercy upon a'. "
36 and to him, are a' things: "
12: 4 and a' members have not the "
17 honest in the sight of a' men. "
18 live peaceably with a' men. "
13: 7 Render therefore to a' their dues: "
14: 2 that he may eat a' things: "
10 for we shall a' stand before the "
20 A' things indeed are pure; "
15:11 Praise the Lord, a' ye Gentiles; "
11 and laud him, a' ye people. "
13 fill you with a' joy and peace in "
14 filled with a' knowledge, "
33 the God of peace be with you a'. "
16: 4 but also a' the churches of the "
15 and a' the saints which are with "
19 is come abroad unto a' men. "
24 be with you a'. Amen. * "
26 made known to a' nations "
1Co 1: 2 with a' that in every place call "
5 in a' utterance, "
5 and in a' knowledge; "
10 that ye a' speak the same thing, "
2:10 the Spirit searcheth a' things, "
15 is spiritual judgeth a' things, "
3:21 For a' things are yours; "
22 or things to come; a' are yours; "
4:13 the offscouring of a' things unto "
6:12 A' things are lawful unto me, "
12 but a' things are not expedient: "
12 a' things are lawful for me, "
7: 7 For I would that a' men were "
17 And so ordain I in a' churches. "
8: 1 know that we a' have knowledge, "
6 of whom are a' things, and we in "
6 by whom are a' things, and we by "
9:12 but suffer a' things, lest we should "
19 though I be free from a' men, yet "
19 have I made myself servant unto a', "
22 I am made a' things to a' men, "
22 that I might by a' means save "
24 run in a race run a', but one "
25 is temperate in a' things. "
10: 1 how that a' our fathers were "
1 and a' passed through the sea; "
2 And were a' baptized unto Moses "
3 And did a' eat the same "
4 And did a' drink the same "
11 Now a' these things happened * "
17 for we are a' partakers of that one "
23 A' things are lawful for me, "
23 but a' things are not expedient: "
23 a' things are lawful for me, "
23 but a' things edify not. "
31 do a' to the glory of God. "
33 I please a' men in a' things, "
11: 2 that ye remember me in a' things, "
5 even a' one as if she were shaven. *
12 but a' things of God. 3956
18 For first of a' when ye come
12: 6 same God which worketh a' in a'. 3956
11 But a' these worketh that one "
12 and a' the members of that one "
13 are we a' baptized into one "
13 and have been a' made to drink "
19 And if they were a' one member, "
26 a' the members suffer with it; "
26 a' the members rejoice with it. "
29 Are a' apostles? are a' prophets? "
29 are a' teachers? are a' workers

1Co 12:30 Have a' the gifts of healing? 3956
30 do a' speak with tongues? "
30 do a' interpret? "
13: 2 and understand a' mysteries, "
2 and a' knowledge; "
2 and though I have a' faith, "
3 though I bestow a' my goods to "
7 Beareth a' things, believeth a' "
7 hopeth a' things, endureth a' "
14: 5 I would that ye a' spake with "
18 with tongues more than ye a': "
21 yet for a' that will they not hear *3779
23 and a' speak with tongues, 3956
24 But if a' prophesy, and there come "
24 convinced of a', he is judged of a': "
26 Let a' things be done unto "
31 For ye may a' prophesy one by one, "
31 that a' may learn, "
31 and a' may be comforted. "
33 as in a' churches of the saints. "
40 Let a' things be done decently and "
15: 3 delivered unto you first of a' "
7 then of a' the apostles. 3956
8 And last of a' he was seen of me "
10 more abundantly than they a': "
19 we are of a' men most miserable. "
22 For as in Adam a' die, "
22 in Christ shall a' be made alive. "
24 he shall have put down a' rule "
24 and a' authority and power. "
25 till he hath put a' enemies under "
27 hath put a' things under his feet. "
27 But when he saith a' things "
27 which did put a' things under him. "
28 And when a' things shall be "
28 him that put a' things under him, "
28 that God may be a' in a'. "
29 dead, if the dead rise not at a'? 3654
39 A' flesh is not the same flesh: 4561
51 We shall not a' sleep, *3956
51 but we shall a' be changed, * "
16:12 was not at a' to come at this time; 3843
14 Let a' your things be done with 3956
20 A' the brethren greet you. "
24 My love be with you a' in Christ "
2Co 1: 1 with a' the saints which are 3956
1 which are in a' Achaia: *3650
3 the God of a' comfort; 3956
4 in a' our tribulation, "
20 For a' the promises of God in *3745
2: 3 having confidence in you a', 3956
3 that my joy is the joy of you a'. "
5 I may not overcharge you a'. "
9 ye be obedient in a' things. "
3: 2 known and read of a' men: "
18 But we a', with open face "
4:15 For a' things are for your sakes. "
5:10 For we must a' appear before "
14 if one died for a', "
14 then were a' dead: "
15 And that he died for a', "
17 behold, a' things are become new.* "
18 And a' things are of God, "
6: 4 But in a' things approving * "
10 and yet possessing a' things. "
7: 1 from a' filthiness of the flesh "
4 joyful in a' our tribulation. "
11 In a' things ye have approved * "
13 was refreshed by you a'. "
14 but as we spake a' things to you "
15 the obedience of you a', "
16 confidence in you in a' things. * "
8: 7 and in a' diligence, "
18 throughout a' the churches; "
9: 8 God is able to make a' grace "
8 always having a' sufficiency in "
8 a' things, may abound to every * "
11 in everything to a' bountifulness, "
9:13 unto them, and unto a' men; "
10: 6 to revenge a' disobedience, "
11: 6 manifest among you in a' things.* "
9 and in a' things I have kept * "
28 the care of a' the churches. "
12:12 among you in a' patience, "
19 but we do a' things, dearly "
13: 2 and to a' other, that, if I come "
13 A' the saints salute you. "
14 Ghost, be with you a'. Amen. "
Ga 1: 2 And a' the brethren which are with "
2:14 said unto Peter before them a', "
3: 8 In thee shall a' nations be blessed. "
10 in a' things which are written "
22 hath concluded a' under sin, "
26 For ye are a' the children of God "
28 for ye are a' one in Christ Jesus. "
4: 1 though he be lord of a'; "
12 ye have not injured me at a'. *3762
26 which is the mother of us a'. *3956
5:14 For a' the law is fulfilled in one * "
6: 6 that teacheth in a' good things. "
10 let us do good unto a' men, "
Eph 1: 3 hath blessed us with a' spiritual * "
8 abounded toward us in a' wisdom "
10 gather together in one a' things "
11 who worketh a' things "
15 and love unto a' the saints, "
21 Far above a' principality, "
22 put a' things under his feet, "
22 to be the head over a' things "
23 of him that filleth a' in a'. "
2: 3 Among whom also we a' had our "
21 In whom a' the building * "
3: 8 less than the least of a' saints, "
9 and to make a' men see "
9 created a' things by Jesus Christ: "
18 to comprehend with a' saints "

Eph 3:19 with a' the fulness of God. 3956
20 above a' that we ask or think, "
21 throughout a' ages, world without "
4: 2 With a' lowliness and meekness, "
6 and Father of a', who is above a', "
6 and through a', and in you a'. "
10 up far above a' heavens, "
10 that he might fill a' things. "
13 Till we a' come in the unity of "
15 grow up into him in a' things, "
19 to work a' uncleanliness with "
31 Let a' bitterness, and wrath, "
31 put away from you, with a' malice: "
5: 3 and a' uncleanness, "
9 of the spirit is in a' goodness "
13 a' things that are reproved "
20 always for a' things unto God "
6:13 having done a', to stand. 537
16 Above a', taking the shield of *3956
16 to quench a' the fiery darts "
18 Praying always with a' prayer "
18 with a' perseverance and "
18 supplication for a' saints; "
21 make known to you a' things: "
24 Grace be with a' them that love "
Phil 1: 1 to a' the saints in Christ Jesus, "
4 you a' making request with joy, * "
7 to think this of you a', "
7 ye a' are partakers of my grace. "
8 I long after you a' in the bowels "
9 and in a' judgment; "
13 in a' the palace, *3650
13 and in a' other places, 3956
20 with a' boldness, as always, "
25 with you a' for your furtherance "
2:14 Do a' things without murmurings "
17 and rejoice with you a'. "
21 For a' seek their own, "
26 he longed after you a', "
29 with a' gladness; and hold such in "
3: 8 I count a' things but loss "
8 suffered the loss of a' things, "
21 to subdue a' things unto himself. "
4: 5 be known unto a' men. "
7 passeth a' understanding, "
12 everywhere and in a' things I am "
13 I can do a' things through Christ "
18 But I have a', and abound: "
19 shall supply a' your need * "
22 A' the saints salute you, "
23 Christ be with you a'. Amen. * "
Col 1: 4 which ye have to a' the saints, "
6 as it is in a' the world; "
9 knowledge of his will in a' wisdom "
10 unto a' pleasing, being fruitful in "
11 Strengthened with a' might, "
11 unto a' patience and "
16 by him were a' things created, "
16 a' things were created by him, "
17 he is before a' things, "
17 and by him a' things consist. "
18 that in a' things he might have "
19 in him should a' fulness dwell; "
20 to reconcile a' things unto himself; "
28 teaching every man in a' wisdom; "
2: 2 and unto a' riches of the full "
3 are hid a' the treasures of wisdom "
9 dwelleth a' the fulness of the "
10 the head of a' principality "
13 forgiven you a' trespasses; "
19 from which a' the body "
22 Which a' are to perish with the "
3: 8 put off a' these; anger, wrath, "
11 but Christ is a', and in a. "
14 And above a' these things "
16 dwell in you richly in a' wisdom; "
17 do a' in the name of the Lord "
20 obey your parents in a' things: "
22 obey in a' things your masters "
4: 7 A' my state shall Tychicus declare "
9 make known unto you a' things "
12 complete in a' the will of God. "
1Th 1: 2 to God always for you a', "
7 ensamples to a' that believe "
2:15 and are contrary to a' men: "
3: 7 in a' our affliction "
9 for a' the joy wherewith we joy "
12 and toward a' men, "
13 Jesus Christ with a' his saints. "
4: 6 is the avenger of a' such, "
10 ye do it toward a' the brethren "
10 which are in a' Macedonia: 3650
5: 5 Ye are a' the children of light, 3956
14 be patient toward a' men. "
15 among yourselves, and to a' men. "
21 Prove a' things; hold fast that "
22 Abstain from a' appearance of * "
26 Greet a' the brethren with an holy "
27 be read unto a' the holy brethren. "
2Th 1: 3 charity of every one of you a' "
4 faith in a' your persecutions "
10 admired in a' them that believe "
11 and fulfil a' the good pleasure * "
2: 4 above a' that is called God, "
9 with a' power and signs "
10 And with a' deceivableness "
12 That they a' might be damned "
3: 2 for a' men have not faith. "
11 disorderly, working not at a', but 3367
16 you peace always by a' means. 3956
16 The Lord be with you a'. "
18 Christ be with you a'. Amen. "
1Ti 1:15 worthy of a' acceptation, "
16 shew forth a' longsuffering, "
2: 1 that, first of a', supplications, "
1 be made for a' men; "

1Ti 2: 2 for a' that are in authority; 3956
2 peaceable life in a' godliness "
4 Who will have a' men to be saved, "
6 gave himself a ransom for a', "
11 in silence with a' subjection. "
3: 4 in subjection with a' gravity; "
11 faithful in a' things. "
4: 8 is profitable unto a' things, "
9 worthy of a' acceptation. "
10 who is the Saviour of a' men, "
15 thy profiting may appear to a'. "
5: 2 younger as sisters, with a' purity. "
20 rebuke before a', that others also "
6: 1 masters worthy of a' honour, "
10 money is the root of a' evil: "
13 who quickeneth a' things, "
17 richly a' things to enjoy; "
2Ti 1:15 a' they which are in Asia be "
2: 7 thee understanding in a' things. "
10 I endure a' things for the elect's "
24 but be gentle unto a' men, "
3: 9 shall be manifest unto a' men, "
11 out of them a' the Lord delivered "
12 Yea, and a' that will live godly "
16 A' scripture is given by * "
17 furnished unto a' good works. * "
4: 2 exhort with a' longsuffering "
5 watch thou in a' things, "
8 but unto a' them also that love "
16 but a' men forsook me: "
17 and that a' the Gentiles might "
21 and a' the brethren. "
Tit 1:15 Unto the pure a' things are pure: "
2: 7 In a' things shewing thyself "
9 to please them well in a' things; "
10 shewing a' good fidelity; "
10 of God our Saviour in a' things. "
11 hath appeared to a' men, "
14 might redeem us from a' iniquity, "
15 rebuke with a' authority. "
3: 2 shewing a' meekness unto a' men. "
15 A' that are with me salute thee. "
15 Grace be with you a'. "
Ph'm 5 and toward a' saints; "
Heb 1: 2 appointed heir of a' things, "
3 upholding a' things by the word "
6 And let a' the angels of God "
11 and they a' shall wax old "
14 Are they not a' ministering spirits, "
2: 8 hast put a' things in subjection "
8 he put a' in subjection under him, "
8 not yet a' things put under him. "
10 for whom are a' things, "
10 and by whom are a' things, "
11 sanctified are a' of one: "
15 a' their lifetime subject to bondage. "
17 in a' things it behoved him "
3: 2 Moses was faithful in a' his house. 3650
4 but he that built a' things is God. 3956
5 verily was faithful in a' his house, 3650
16 not a' that came out of Egypt 3956
4: 4 the seventh day from a' his works. "
13 but a' things are naked "
15 was in a' points tempted "
5: 9 unto a' them that obey him; "
6:16 is to them an end of a' strife. * "
7: 2 gave a tenth part of a'; "
7 And without a' contradiction * "
8: 5 a' things according to the pattern "
11 for a' shall know me, "
9: 3 which is called the Holiest of a'; *
8 that the way into the holiest of a' *
17 it is of no strength at a' while the *4219
19 every precept to a' the people 3956
19 both the book, and a' the people, "
21 and a' the vessels of the ministry. "
22 almost a' things are by the law "
10:10 body of Jesus Christ once for a'. 2178
11:13 These a' died in faith, not having 3956
39 these a', having obtained a good "
12: 8 whereof a' are partakers, "
14 Follow peace with a' men, "
23 to God the Judge of a', "
13: 4 marriage is honourable in a', "
18 a' things willing to live honestly. * "
24 Salute a' them that have the rule "
24 and a' the saints. "
25 Grace be with you a'. Amen. "
Jas 1: 2 count it a' joy when ye fall "
5 that giveth to a' men liberally, "
8 unstable in a' his ways. "
21 lay apart a' filthiness "
2:10 he is guilty of a'. "
3: 2 in many things we offend a'. 537
4:16 a' such rejoicing is evil. 3956
5:12 above a' things, my brethren, "
1Pe 1:15 holy in a' manner of conversation; "
24 For a' flesh is as grass, "
24 and a' the glory of man "
2: 1 laying aside a' malice, and a' guile, "
1 and a' evil speakings, "
17 Honour a' men. Love the "
18 masters with a' fear; "
3: 8 be ye a' of one mind, "
4: 7 the end of a' things is at hand: "
8 a' things have fervent charity "
11 God in a' things may be glorified "
5: 5 a' of you be subject one to another, "
7 Casting a' your care upon him; "
10 But the God of a' grace, "
14 Peace be with you a' that are in "
2Pe 1: 3 a' things that pertain unto life "
5 giving a' diligence, add to your "
3: 4 a' things continue as they were "
9 that a' should come to repentance. "
11 a' these things shall be dissolved, "

2Pe 3:16 As also in a' his epistles, 3956
1Jo 1: 5 and in him is no darkness at a'. 3762
7 cleanseth us from a' sin. 3956
9 us from a' unrighteousness. "
2:16 For a' that is in the world, "
19 that they were not a' of us. "
20 and ye know a' things. "
27 teacheth you of a' things, "
3:20 and knoweth a' things. "
5:17 A' unrighteousness is sin: "
2Jo 1 a' they that have known the truth; "
3Jo 2 I wish above a' things that thou "
12 hath good report of a' men, "
Jude 3 when I gave a' diligence "
15 judgment upon a', "
15 and to convince a' "
15 of a' their ungodly deeds "
15 and of a' their hard speeches "
Re 1: 2 and of a' things that he saw. 3745
7 a' kindreds of the earth shall wail 3956
2:23 and a' the churches shall know "
3:10 shall come upon a' the world, 3650
4:11 for thou hast created a' things, 3956
5: 6 sent forth into a' the earth. "
13 sea, and a' that are in them, "
7: 4 of a' the tribes of the children of * "
9 of a' nations, and kindreds, * "
11 a' the angels stood round about "
17 away a' tears from their eyes. * "
8: 3 with the prayers of a' saints "
7 and a' green grass was burnt up. "
11: 6 smite the earth with a' plagues, * "
12: 5 rule a' nations with a rod of iron: "
13: 3 a' the world wondered after the *3650
7 over a' kindreds, and tongues, *3956
8 And a' that dwell upon the earth "
12 a' the power of the first beast "
16 causeth a', both small and great, "
14: 8 because she made a' nations drink "
15: 4 for a' nations shall come and "
18: 3 a' nations have drunk of the wine "
12 and a' thyine wood, "
12 a' manner vessels of ivory, * "
12 and a' manner vessels of most * "
14 and a' things which were dainty "
14 shalt find them no more at a'. 3364
17 shipmaster, and a' the company *3956
19 rich a' that had ships in the sea "
21 and shall be found no more at a'. 3364
22 shall be heard no more at a' "
22 shall be heard no more at a' "
23 shall shine no more at a' in thee; "
23 shall be heard no more at a' in "
23 sorceries were a' nations deceived. 3956
24 a' that were slain upon the earth. "
19: 5 Praise our God, a' ye his servants, "
17 saying to a' the fowls that fly in "
18 flesh of a' men, both free and bond, "
21 a' the fowls were filled with their "
21: 4 God shall wipe away a' tears * "
5 Behold, I make a' things new. "
7 shall inherit a' things; * "
8 and a' liars, shall have their part "
19 with a' manner of precious stones. "
25 shall not be shut at a' by day: *3364
22:21 Lord Jesus Christ be with you a'. *3956

allege See ALLEGING.

alleging
Ac 17: 3 Opening and a', that Christ 3908

allegory
Ga 4:24 Which things are an a': for these 238

Alleluia (*al-le-loo'-yah*)
Re 19: 1 people in heaven, saying, A'; * 239
3 they said, A'. And her * "
4 the throne, saying, Amen; A'. * "
6 mighty thunderings, saying, A': * "

allied
Ne 13: 4 the priest,...was a' unto Tobiah: 7138

Allon (*al'-lon*) See also ALLON-BACHUTH; ELON.
Jos 19:33 Heleph, from A' to Zaanannim, * 438
1Ch 4:37 the son of Shiphi, the son of A', "

Allon-bachuth (*al''-lon-bak'-ooth*)
Ge 35: 8 and the name of it was called A'. 439

allow See also ALLOWED; ALLOWETH; ALLOWING; DISALLOW.
Lu 11:48 ye a' the deeds of your fathers: *4909
Ac 24:15 which they themselves also a', *4327
Ro 7:15 that which I do I a' not: *1097

allowance
2Ki 25:30 And his a' was a continual a' 737

allowed See also DISALLOWED.
1Th 2: 4 But as we were a' of God to be *1381

alloweth
Ro 14:22 in that thing which he a'. *1381

all-to (J'g 9:53) See ALL.

allure
Ho 2:14 I will a' her, and bring her into 6601
2Pe 2:18 a' through the lusts of the flesh, *1185

Almighty
Ge 17: 1 said unto him, I am the A' God; 7706
28: 3 And God A' bless thee, "
35:11 God said unto him, I am God A': "
43:14 God A' give you mercy "
48: 3 God A' appeared unto me at Luz "
49:25 and by the A', who shall bless thee "
Ex 6: 3 by the name of God A'. "
Nu 24: 4, 16 which saw the vision of the A', "
Ru 1:20 A' hath dealt very bitterly with me. "
21 and the A' hath afflicted me? "

Job 5:17 not thou the chastening of the A': 7706
6: 4 arrows of the A' are within me, "
14 he forsaketh the fear of the A'. "
8: 3 doth the A' pervert justice? "
5 make thy supplication to the A'; "
11: 7 find out the A' unto perfection? "
13: 3 Surely I would speak to the A', "
15:25 himself against the A'. "
21:15 What is the A', that we should "
20 shall drink of the wrath of the A'. "
22: 3 Is it any pleasure to the A', "
17 what can the A' do for them? "
23 If thou return to the A', "
25 the A' shall be thy defence, "
26 have thy delight in the A', "
23:16 and the A' troubleth me: "
24: 1 times are not hidden from the A', "
27: 2 the A', who hath vexed my soul; "
10 Will he delight himself in the A'? "
11 with the A' will I not conceal. "
13 they shall receive of the A'. "
29: 5 When the A' was yet with me, "
31: 2 inheritance of the A' from on high? "
35 that the A' would answer me, "
32: 8 inspiration of the A' giveth them "
33: 4 breath of the A' hath given me life. "
34:10 and from the A', that he should "
12 will the A' pervert judgment. "
35:13 neither will the A' regard it. "
37:23 the A', we cannot find him out: "
40: 2 he that contendeth with the A' "
Ps 68:14 When the A' scattered kings "
91: 1 under the shadow of the A'. "
Isa 13: 6 as a destruction from the A'. "
Eze 1:24 as the voice of the A', "
10: 5 the A' God when he speaketh. "
Joe 1:15 as a destruction from the A' "
2Co 6:18 saith the Lord A'. 3841
Re 1: 8 and which is to come, the A'. "
4: 8 Holy, holy, holy, Lord God A', "
11:17 O Lord God A', which art, and wast, "
15: 3 thy works, Lord God A'; "
16: 7 Lord God A', true and righteous "
14 that great day of God A'. "
19:15 and wrath of A' God. "
21:22 the Lord God A' and the Lamb are "

Almodad (*al-mo'-dad*)
Ge 10:26 Joktan begat A', and Sheleph, 486
1Ch 1:20 Joktan begat A', and Sheleph, "

Almon (*al'-mon*) See also ALMON-DIBLATHAIM.
Jos 21:18 A' with her suburbs; four cities. 5960

almond See also ALMONDS.
Ec 12: 5 the a' tree shall flourish, 8247
Jer 1:11 I see a rod of an a' tree. "

Almon-diblathaim (*al''-mon-dib-lath-a'-im*)
Nu 33:46 Dibon-gad, and encamped in A'. 5963
47 And they removed from A', and "

almonds
Ge 43:11 myrrh, nuts, and a': 8247
Ex 25:33 Three bowls made like unto a', *8246
33 bowls made like a' * "
34 four bowls made like unto a', * "
37:19 made after the fashion of a' * "
19 three bowls made like a' * "
20 four bowls made like a', * "
Nu 17: 8 blossoms, and yielded a'. 8247

almond-tree See ALMOND and TREE.

almost
Ex 17: 4 they be a' ready to stone me. 4592
Ps 73: 2 as for me my feet were a' gone; "
94:17 my soul had a' dwelt in silence. * "
119:87 had a' consumed me upon earth; "
Pr 5:14 I was a' in all evil * "
Ac 13:44 came a' the whole city together 4975
19:26 but a' throughout all Asia, "
21:27 the seven days were a' ended, 3195
26:28 A' thou persuadest me to be *1722, 3641
29 a', and altogether such as I * "
Heb 9:22 And a' all things are by the law 4975

alms See also ALMSDEEDS.
M't 6: 1 do not your a' before men, *1654
2 when thou doest thine a', "
3 when thou doest a', let not "
4 That thine a' may be in secret: "
Lu 11:41 give a' of such things as ye have; "
12:33 Sell that ye have, and give a'; "
Ac 3: 2 to ask a' of them that entered "
3 into the temple asked an a'. "
10 it was he which sat for a' "
10: 2 gave much a' to the people, "
4 prayers and thine a' are come up "
31 thine a' are had in remembrance "
24:17 I came to bring a' to my nation, "

almsdeeds
Ac 9:36 full of good works and a' which 1654

almug (*al'-mug*) See also ALGUM.
1Ki 10:11 great plenty of a' trees, 484
12 king made of the a' trees pillars "
12 there came no such a' trees, "

almug-trees See ALMUG and TREES.

aloes
Nu 24: 6 as the trees of lign a' which the 174
Ps 45: 8 garments smell of myrrh, and a', "
Pr 7:17 perfumed my bed with myrrh, a', "
Ca 4:14 a', with all the chief spices: "
Joh 19:39 brought a mixture of myrrh and a', 250

alone
Ge 2:18 good that the man should be a'; 905
32:24 And Jacob was left a'; and there "
42:38 brother is dead, and he is left a': * "
44:20 brother is dead, and he a' is left "

Ex 14:12 thee in Egypt, saying, Let us a', 2308
18:14 why sittest thou thyself a', 905
18 art not able to perform it thyself a'. "
24: 2 And Moses a' shall come near the "
32:10 Now therefore let me a', "
Le 13:46 shall dwell a'; without the camp 909
Nu 11:14 able to bear all this people a', 905
17 that thou bear it not thyself a', "
23: 9 the people shall dwell a', 909
De 1: 9 not able to bear you myself a': 905
12 How can I myself a' bear your "
9:14 me a', that I may destroy them, 7503
32:12 the Lord a' did lead him, 909
33:28 Israel then shall dwell in safety a': "
Jos 22:20 man perished not a' in his iniquity. 259
J'g 3:20 which he had for himself a'. 905
11:37 let me a' two months, 7503
1Sa 21: 1 Why art thou a', and no man with 905
2Sa 16:11 let him a', and let him curse; "
18:24 and behold a man running a'. 905
25 And the king said, If he be a', "
26 Behold another man running a'. "
1Ki 11:29 and they two were a' in the field: "
2Ki 4:27 Let her a'; for her soul is vexed 7503
19:15 thou art the God, even thou a', of 905
23:18 And he said, Let him a'; *
18 So they let his bones a', 4422
1Ch 29: 1 my son, whom a' God hath chosen, 259
Ezr 6: 7 the work of this house of God a'; 7662
Ne 9: 6 Thou, even thou, art Lord a'; 905
Es 3: 6 scorn to lay hands on Mordecai a'; "
Job 1:15, 16, 17, 19 am escaped a' to tell thee. "
7:16 let me a'; for my days are vanity. 2308
19 let me a' till I swallow down my 7503
9: 8 a' spreadeth out the heavens, 905
10:20 let me a', that I may take comfort 7896
13:13 Hold your peace, let me a', that I
15:19 whom a' the earth was given, 905
31:17 have eaten my morsel myself a', "
Ps 83:18 thou, whose name a' is Jehovah, "
102: 7 as a sparrow a' upon the housetop. 909
136: 4 him who a' doeth great wonders: 905
Pr 9:12 scornest, thou a' shalt bear it. "
Ec 4: 8 There is one a', and there is not a
10 him that is a' when he falleth; 259
11 but how can one be warm a'?
Isa 2:11, 17 Lord a' shall be exalted in that 905
5: 8 placed a' in the midst of the earth!
14:31 none shall be a' in his appointed * 909
37:16 thou art the God, even thou a', 905
44:24 stretcheth forth the heavens a'; "
49:21 Behold, I was left a'; these, where "
51: 2 I called him a', and blessed him, * 259
63: 3 I have trodden the winepress a'; 905
Jer 15:17 I sat a' because of thy hand: 909
49:31 which dwell a'. "
La 3:28 He sitteth a' and keepeth silence, 905
Da 10: 7 And I Daniel a' saw the vision: "
8 Therefore I was left a', and saw "
Ho 4:17 is joined to idols: let him a'.
8: 9 a wild ass a' by himself: 909
M't 4: 4 shall not live by bread a', 3441
14:23 he was there a'. "
15:14 Let them a': they be blind leaders 863
18:15 between thee and him a': 3441
M'r 1:24 Saying, Let us a'; what have we *1439
4:10 And when he was a', 2651
34 and when they were a', *2596, 2398
6:47 and he a' on the land. 3441
14: 6 Let her a'; why trouble ye her? 863
15:36 saying, Let a'; let us see whether* "
Lu 4: 4 not live by bread a', but by every 3441
34 Saying, Let us a'; what have we *1439
5:21 Who can forgive sins, but God a'? 3441
6: 4 but for the priests a'? "
9:18 as he was a' praying, ‡2651
36 Jesus was found a'. 3441
10:40 hath left me to serve a'? "
13: 8 Lord, let it a' this year also, 863
Joh 6:15 into a mountain himself a'. 3441
22 his disciples were gone away a'; "
8: 9 and Jesus was left a', "
16 for I am not a', but I and the "
29 the Father hath not left me a'; "
11:48 If we let him thus a', all men will 863
12: 7 Then said Jesus, Let her a': * "
24 and die, it abideth a': 3441
16:32 and shall leave me a': "
32 and yet I am not a', because the "
17:20 pray I for these a', but for *3440
Ac 5:38 from these men, and let them a': 1439
19:26 not a' at Ephesus, but almost 3440
Ro 4:23 for his sake a', that it was "
11: 3 and I am left a', and they seek 3441
Gal 6: 4 have rejoicing in himself a', "
1Th 3: 1 to be left at Athens a'; "
Heb 9: 7 went the high priest a' once every "
Jas 2:17 not works, is dead, being a'. *2596, 1438

along
Ex 2: 5 walked a' by the river's side;
9:23 the fire ran a' upon the ground; *
Nu 21:22 will go a' by the king's high way,*
34: 3 wilderness of Zin a' by the coast
De 2:27 I will go a' by the highway,
Jos 10:10 and chased them a' the way *
15: 3 and passed a' to Zin, *
3 and passed a' to Hezron,
6 a' by the north of Beth-arabah
10 a' unto the side of mount Jearim,
11 and passed a' to mount Baalah,
16: 2 and passeth a' unto the borders
17: 7 border went a' on the right hand
18:18 And passed a' toward the side to
19 And the border passed a' to the
19:13 And from thence passeth on a' the
J'g 7:12 of the east lay a' in the valley

J'g 7:13 it, that the tent lay a'.
9:25 robbed all that came a' that way
37 a' by the plain of Meonenim. *
11:18 went a' through the wilderness, *
26 cities that be a' by the coasts of
20:37 liers in wait drew themselves a',
1Sa 6:12 went a' the highway, lowing as 1980
28:20 Saul fell straightway all a' *4393, 6967
2Sa 3:16 went with her a' weeping *1980
16:13 Shimei went a' on the hill's side
2Ki 11:11 a' by the altar and the temple.
2Ch 23:10 a' by the altar and the temple,
Jer 41: 6 weeping all a' as he went: 1980

aloof
Ps 38:11 friends stand a' from my sore; 5048

Aloth (*a'-loth*) See also BEALOTH.
1Ki 4:16 Hushai was in Asher and in A': *1175

aloud
Gen 45: 2 And he wept a': 5414, 854, 6963
1Ki 18:27 Cry a': for he is a god; 6963, 1419
28 they cried a', and cut 1419, 3605
Ezr 3:12 many shouted a' for joy: 7311, 1419
Job 19: 7 I cry a', but there is no *7768
Ps 51:14 my tongue shall sing a' of thy 7442
55:17 will I pray, and cry a': and he *1993
59:16 yea, I will sing a' of thy mercy 7442
81: 1 Sing a' unto God our strength: "
132:16 her saints shall shout a' for joy. "
149: 5 let them sing a' upon their beds. * "
Isa 24:14 they shall cry a' from the sea. 6670
54: 1 break forth into singing and cry a',"
58: 1 Cry a', spare not, lift up thy voice 1627
Da 3: 4 Then an herald cried a', To you 2429
4:14 He cried a', and said thus, Hew "
5: 7 The king cried a' to bring in the "
Ho 5: 8 cry a' at Beth-aven, *7321
Mic 4: 9 thou cry out a'? is there no king 7452
M'r 15: 8 the multitude crying a' began to * 310

Alpha (*al'-fah*)
Re 1: 8 I am A' and Omega, the 1
11 I am A' and Omega, the first and * "
21: 6 I am A' and Omega, the beginning "
22:13 I am A' and Omega, the beginning "

Alphæus (*al-fe'-us*) See also CLEOPAS.
M't 10: 3 James the son of A', 256
M'r 2:14 Levi the son of A' sitting "
3:18 James the son of A', "
Lu 6:15 James the son of A', "
Ac 1:13 James the son of A', "

Alpheus See ALPHAEUS.

already
2Ch 28:13 offended against the Lord a', *
Ne 5: 5 are brought unto bondage a',
Ec 1:10 it hath been a' of old time, 3528
2:12 even that which hath been a' done. "
3:15 which is to be hath a' been; "
4: 2 the dead which are a' dead, "
6:10 which hath been is named a', * "
Mal 2: 2 I have cursed them a', because
M't 5:28 committed adultery with her a' 2235
17:12 Elias is come a', and they knew "
M'r 15:44 marvelled if he were a' dead: "
Lu 12:49 what will I, if it be a' kindled? "
Joh 3:18 believeth not is condemned a', "
4:35 they are white a' to harvest. "
9:22 for the Jews have agreed a', "
27 I have told you a', and ye did not * "
11:17 had lain in the grave four days a', "
19:33 saw that he was dead a', "
Ac 11:11 were three men a' come unto the *
27: 9 because the fast was now a' past, 2235
1Co 5: 3 have judged a', as though I were "
2Co 12:21 many which have sinned a', *4258
Ph'p 3:12 Not as though I had a' attained, 2235
12 either were a' perfect: "
16 whereto we have a' attained, let 5348
2Th 2: 7 mystery of iniquity doth a' work: 2235
1Ti 5:15 For some are a' turned aside "
2Ti 2:18 that the resurrection is past a'; "
1Jo 4: 3 even now a' is it in the world. "
Re 2:25 that which ye have a' hold fast *

also
Ge 1:16 rule the night: he made the stars a'.
2: 9 life a' in the midst of the garden,
3: 6 a' unto her husband with her; 1571
18 Thorns a' and thistles shall it "
21 Unto Adam a' and to his wife did *
22 and take a' of the tree of life, and 1571
4: 4 he a' brought of the firstlings of "
22 Zillah, she a' bare Tubal-cain, an "
26 to him also there was born a son; "
6: 3 for that he a' is flesh: 7683
4 the earth in those days; and a' 1571
11 The earth a' was corrupt before *
7: 3 Of fowls a' of the air by sevens, 1571
8: 2 The fountains a' of the deep and
8 A' he sent forth a dove from him,*
10:21 Unto Shem a', the father of all *1571
12:15 The princes a' of Pharaoh saw *
13: 5 And Lot a', which went with 1571
16 shall thy seed a' be numbered. "
14: 7 and a' the Amorites, that dwelt in "
16 a' brought again his brother Lot, "
16 and the women a', and the people. "
15:14 a' that nation, whom they shall "
16:13 Have I a' here looked after him * "
17:16 and give thee a son a' of her: "
18:12 pleasure, my lord being old a'? "
23 thou a' destroy the righteous * 637
24 wilt thou a' destroy and not spare * "
19:21 thee concerning this thing a', 1571
34 make him drink wine this night a'; "
35 father drink wine that night a': "
Ge 20: 4 thou slay a' a righteous nation? *1571
24:53 he gave a' to her brother and to
26:21 well, and strove for that a': 1571
27:31 he a' had made savoury meat, "
34 Bless me, even me a', O my father. "
38 a', O my father. And Esau lifted "
45 deprived a' of you both in one? * "
29:27 and we will give thee this a' for "
28 Rachel his daughter to wife a'. *
30 And he went in a' unto Rachel, 1571
30 a' Rachel more than Leah, and "
33 therefore given me this son a': "
30: 3 that I may a' have children by "
6 God hath judged me, and hath a' "
15 away my son's mandrakes a'? "
30 I provide for mine own house a'? "
31:15 sold us, and hath quite devoured a' "
32: 6 Esau, and a' he cometh to meet * "
18 lord Esau: and, behold, a' he is "
33: 7 Leah a' with her children came "
35:17 thou shalt have this son a'. * "
38:10 Lord: wherefore he slew him a'. "
11 Lest peradventure he die a', as his "
22 find her; and a' the men of the "
24 hath played the harlot; and a', * "
40:15 land of the Hebrews: and here a' "
16 unto Joseph, I a' was in my dream, 637
42:22 behold, a' his blood is required. 1571
43: 8 both we, and thou, and a' our "
13 Take a' your brother, and arise, "
44: 9 die, and we a' will be my lord's 1571
10 Now a' let it be according unto "
16 he a' with whom the cup is found. "
29 And if ye take this a' from me, "
45:20 A' regard not your stuff; for the
46: 4 will a' surely bring thee up again: 1571
34 until now, both we, and a' our * "
47: 3 both we, and a' our fathers. * "
18 lord a' hath our herds of cattle; * "
48:11 God hath shewed me a thy seed. 1571
19 he a' shall become a people, "
19 and he a' shall be great: "
50:18 his brethren a' went and fell down "
23 the children a' of Machir the son "
Ex 1:10 they join a' unto our enemies, "
2:19 and a' drew water enough for us,* "
3: 9 I have a' seen the oppression * "
4: 9 not believe a' these two signs, * "
14 And a', behold, he cometh forth "
6: 4 I have a' established my covenant "
5 I have a' heard the groaning of * "
7:11 Pharaoh a' called the wise men "
11 Egypt, they a' did in like manner "
23 did he set his heart to this a'. * "
8:32 hardened his heart at this time a', "
10:24 let your little ones a' go with you. "
25 Thou must give us a' sacrifices "
26 Our cattle a' shall go with us: "
12:32 A' take your flocks and your * "
32 and be gone; and bless me a'. "
38 multitude went up a' with them; * "
15: 4 a' are drowned in the Red sea. *
19:22 And let the priests a' which come 1571
21: 6 shall a' bring him to the door, *
29 owner a' shall be put to death. 1571
35 the dead ox a' shall divide. "
23: 9 A' thou shalt not oppress a *
24:11 a' they saw God, and eat and *
25:23 Thou shalt a' make a table of *
29:15 Thou shalt a' take one ram; and
22 A' thou shalt take of the ram the
44 sanctify a' both Aaron and his
30:18 shalt a' make a laver of brass,
18 foot a' of brass, to wash withal: *
23 thou a' unto thee principal spices,
31:13 Speak thou a' unto the children
33:12 thou hast a' found grace in my 1571
17 I will do this thing a' that thou "
35:14 The candlestick a' for the light, *
37:12 A' he made thereunto a border *
26 he made unto it a crown of *
Le 5: 2 he a' shall be unclean, and *
7:16 a' the remainder of it shall be *
8: 8 a' he put in the breastplate the *
9 a' upon the mitre, even upon his *
9: 4 A' a bullock and a ram for peace *
18 He slew a' the bullock and the ram
11:29 These a' shall be unclean unto *
40 he a' that beareth the carcase of
13:18 The flesh a', in which, even in *
38 If a man a' or a woman have in *
47 The garment a' that the plague
14: 9 a' he shall wash his flesh in water,*
15:18 The woman a' with whom man
20 every thing a' that she sitteth upon
18:19 A' thou shalt not approach unto
28 That the land spue not you out a'.
20:13 If a man a' lie with mankind, as *
27 A man a' or woman that hath a
22:12 priest's daughter a' be married *
23:27 A' on the tenth day of this seventh* 389
39 A' in the fifteenth day of the * "
26:16 I a' will do this unto you; I will 637
22 I will a' send wild beasts among *
24 Then will I a' walk contrary 637
28 contrary unto you a' in fury; * "
40 that a' they have walked contrary 637
41 that I a' have walked contrary "
42 my covenant with Jacob, and a' "
42 my covenant with Isaac, and a' "
43 The land a' shall be left of them, "
Nu 3: 1 These a' are generations of *
4:22 Take a' the sum of the sons of 1571
6:17 shall offer a' his meat offering,
9: 2 Let the children of Israel a' keep *
10:10 A' in the day of your gladness,
Nu 11: 4 children of Israel a' wept again, 1571
10 Moses a' was displeased. *
12: 2 hath he not spoken a' by us? 1571
15:15 a' for the stranger that sojourneth*
16:10 and seek ye the priesthood a'? 1571
17 thou a', and Aaron, each of you
34 Lest the earth swallow us up a'. *
18: 2 brethren a' of the tribe of Levi, 1571
3 neither they, nor ye a', die. * "
8 I a' have given thee the charge *
28 ye a' shall offer an heave offering 1571
20:11 drank, and their beasts a'. *
22:19 tarry ye a' here this night, *1571
33 surely now a' I had slain thee, "
24:12 Spake I not a' to thy messengers "
18 Seir a' shall be a possession for
24 and he a' shall perish for ever. 1571
25 and Balak a went his way. "
27:13 thou a' shall be gathered unto "
28:26 A' in the day of the firstfruits,
30: 3 If a woman a' vow a vow unto
31: 8 Balaam a' the son of Beor they
33: 4 a' the Lord executed judgments.
35: 2 give a' unto the Levites suburbs *
De 1:37 A' the Lord was angry with me 1571
2: 6 ye shall a' buy water of them
11 Which a' were accounted giants, 637
12 Horims a' dwelt in Seir beforetime;
20 (That a' was accounted a land of 637
3: 3 delivered into our hands Og a', 1571
17 The plain a', and Jordan, and
20 until they a' possess the land 1571
7:13 multiply thee: he will a' bless
8: 5 shalt a' consider in thine heart, *
9: 8 A' in Horeb ye provoked the
19 hearkened unto me at that time a'. 1571
20 I prayed for Aaron a' the same "
10:10 hearkened unto me at that time a', "
14 God, the earth a', with all that *
15:17 And a' unto thy maidservant 637
18: 4 The firstfruit a' of thy corn, *
20: 6 let him a' go and return unto *
23:12 Thou shalt have a place a'
26:13 a' have given them unto the 1571
28:51 which a' shall not leave thee
61 A' every sickness, and every 1571
29:15 a' with him that is not here with
31: 2 and come in: a' the Lord hath *
32:24 I will a' send the teeth of beasts *
25 the suckling a' with the man of *
33:28 a' his heavens shall drop down * 637
Jos 1:15 they a' have possessed the land 1571
2:12 ye will a' shew kindness unto my "
7:11 they have a' transgressed my * "
11 have a' stolen, and dissembled a', "
10:30 And the Lord delivered it a', "
39 as he had done a' to Libnah,
13: 3 the Ekronites; a' the Avites:
22 Balaam a' the son of Beor,
15:19 south land; give me a' springs of
17: 1 There was a' a lot for the tribe *
2 There was a' a lot for the rest *
9 the coast of Manasseh a' was on
19:30 Ummah a', and Aphek, and Rehob:
20: 1 The Lord a' spake unto Joshua, *
22: 7 them away a' unto the tents, *1571
24: 5 I sent Moses a' and Aaron,
18 will we a' serve the Lord; 1571
J'g 1:15 give me a' springs of water.
18 A' Judah took Gaza with the
22 they a' went up against Beth-el: 1571
2: 3 I a' said, I will not drive them "
10 And a' all that generation were "
21 I a' will not henceforth drive out "
3:22 the haft a' went in after the blade; "
31 and he a' delivered Israel. "
5: 4 the clouds a' dropped water. * "
15 even Issachar, and a' Barak: *3651
6:35 who a' was gathered after him: 1571
7:18 the trumpets a' on every side of "
8: 9 he spake a' unto the men of Penuel, "
22 and thy son, and thy son's son a': "
31 she a' bare him a son, whose name "
9: 2 remember a' that I am your bone "
19 and let him a' rejoice in you: 1571
49 of the tower of Shechem died a', "
10: 9 passed over Jordan to fight a' "
10 our God, and a' served Baalim. *
12 The Zidonians a', and the
15: 5 and a' the standing corn, with 5704
17: 2 and spakest of a' in mine ears, 1571
19:10 his concubine a' was with him.
16 which was a' of mount Ephraim; *
19 is bread and wine a' for me, 1571
20:48 a' they set on fire all the cities *
Ru 1: 5 Mahlon and Chilion died a' both *1571
12 to night, and should a' bear sons; * "
17 and more a', if ought but death 3541
2:16 let fall a' some of the handfuls 1571
21 He said unto me a', Thou shalt *
3:15 A' he said, Bring the vail that *
4: 5 thou must buy it a' of Ruth the *
1Sa 1: 6 adversary a' provoked her sore, *1571
28 a' I have lent him to the Lord; "
2:15 A' before they burnt the fat, * "
26 with the Lord, and a' with men. *
3:12 I begin, I will a' make an end. "
17 and more a', if thou hide 3541
4:17 been a' a great slaughter among 1571
17 two sons a', Hophni and Phinehas, "
8: 8 other goods, so do they a' unto thee. "
20 we a' may be like all the nations; "
10:11, 12 Is Saul a' among the prophets? "
26 And Saul a' went to Gibeah; "
12:14 a' the king that reigneth over you "
13: 4 Israel a' was had in abomination "

1Sa 14:15 they a' trembled, and the earth 1571
21 a' turned to be with the Israelites "
22 they a' followed hard after them "
44 answered, God do so and more a': 3541
15: 1 Samuel a' said unto Saul, *
23 a' rejected thee from being king.
29 a' the Strength of Israel will not 1571
17:38 a' he armed him with a coat of *
18: 5 and a' in the sight of Saul's 1571
19:11 Saul a' sent messengers unto *
20 of Saul, and they a' prophesied. 1571
21 third time, and they prophesied a'. "
22 Then went he a' to Ramah, "
23 the Spirit of God was upon him a', "
24 And he stripped off his clothes a', "
24 say, Is Saul a' among the prophets? "
20:15 But a' thou shalt not cut off thy
22:17 their hand a' is with David, 1571
23:17 that a' Saul my father knoweth.
25 Saul a' and his men went to seek *
24: 8 David a' arose afterward, and went
25:13 David a' girded on his sword: 1571
22 more a' do God unto the enemies 3541
43 David a' took Ahinoam of Jezreel; *
26:25 things, and a' shalt still prevail. *1571
28:19 the Lord will a' deliver Israel "
19 thy sons be with me: the Lord a' "
22 hearken thou a' unto the voice of "
30:21 a' to abide at the brook Besor:
2Sa 1: 4 many of the people a' are fallen 1571
4 and Jonathan his son are dead a'. "
18 (A' he bade them teach the *
2: 2 up thither, and his two wives a', 1571
6 I a' will requite you this kindness, "
7 and a' the house of Judah have "
24 Joab a' and Abishai pursued
3: 9 So do God to Abner, and more a', 3541
12 a', Make thy league with me, and,
19 Abner a' spake in the ears of 1571
19 a' to speak in the ears of David "
35 So do God to me, and more a', if I 3541
4: 2 (for Beeroth a' was reckoned to 1571
5: 2 A' in time past, when Saul was * "
15 Ibhar a', and Elishua, and *
18 The Philistines a' came and *
7:11 A' the Lord telleth thee that he *
19 spoken a' of thy servant's house 1571
8: 3 David smote also Hadadezer,
11 Which a' king David did dedicate
10:14 then fled they a' before Abishai, *
11:12 to Uriah, Tarry here to day a', 1571
17 and Uriah the Hittite died a'. "
21, 24 Uriah the Hittite is dead a'. "
12:13 The Lord a' hath put away thy sin; "
14 the child a' that is born unto thee "
13:36 king a' and all his servants wept "
14: 7 and we will destroy the heir a': "
15:19 Wherefore goest thou a' with us? "
19 art a stranger, and a' an exile. "
21 even there a' will thy servant be. "
23 the king a' himself passed over "
24 lo Zadok a', and all the Levites 1571
27 king said a' unto Zadok the priest, "
34 hitherto, so will I now also be *
17: 5 Call now Hushai the Archite a', 1571
10 he a' that is valiant, whose heart * "
18: 2 surely go forth with you myself a'. "
22 I pray thee, a' run after Cushi. "
26 said, He a' bringeth tidings. "
19:13 God do so to me, and more a', 3541
40 and a' half the people of Israel. 1571
43 we have a' more right in David "
20:14 together, and went a' after him. 637
26 Ira a' the Jairite was a chief ruler 1571
21:20 and he also was born to the giant. "
22:10 He bowed the heavens a', and came
20 brought me forth a' into a large
24 I was a' upright before him, and
36 Thou hast a' given me the shield
41 Thou hast a' given me the necks
44 a' hast delivered me from the
49 thou a' hast lifted me up on high *
23:20 he went down a' and slew a lion
1Ki 1: 6 and he a' was a very goodly man; 1571
14 I a' will come in after thee, and
22 Nathan the prophet a' came in. *
33 The king a' said unto them, Take *
46 a' Solomon sitteth on the throne 1571
48 And a' thus said the king, Blessed "
2: 5 Moreover thou knowest a' what "
22 ask for him the kingdom a';
23 God do so to me, and more a', 3541
3:13 I have a' given thee that which 1571
18 that this woman was delivered a': "
4:13 to him a' pertained the region of *
15 he a' took Basmath the daughter 1571
28 Barley a' and straw for the horses
33 he spake a' of beasts, and of fowl,
6:22 a' the whole altar that was by the
32 two doors a' were of olive tree;
33 So a' made he for the door of the
7: 2 built a' the house of the forest *
8 Solomon made a' an house for
20 two pillars had pomegranates a' 1571
31 and a' upon the mouth of it were *
8:24 thou spakest a' with thy mouth, *
9:21 the children of Israel a' were not *
10:11 And the navy a' of Hiram, that 1571
12 house, harps a' and psalteries
12:14 a' chastised you with whips, *
13: 5 altar a' was rent, and the ashes
11 them they told a' to their father.
18 I am a prophet a' as thou art; 1571
24 the lion a' stood by the carcase.
14:23 they a' built them high places, 1571
24 were a' sodomites in the land: "

1Ki 15:13 And a' Maachah his mother, 1571
16: 7 a' by the hand of the prophet * "
16 and hath a' slain the king: "
17:20 Lord my God, hast thou a' brought
18:35 he filled the trench a' with water. 1571
19: 2 the gods do to me, and more a', 3541
20: 3 thy wives a' and thy children,
10 more a', if the dust of Samaria 3541
21:19 killed, and a' taken possession? 1571
23 And of Jezebel a' spake the Lord, "
22:22 persuade him, and prevail a': "
2Ki 1:11 Again a' he sent unto him *
2:13 He took up a' the mantle of Elijah
14 and when he a' had smitten the
3:18 the Moabites a' into your hand.
5: 1 was a' a mighty man in valour,
6:31 God do so and more a' to me, if 3541
7: 4 if we sit still here, we die a'.
8 and carried thence a', and went
8: 1 and it shall a' come upon the land 1571
9:27 Smite him a' in the chariot.
10: 2 a fenced city a', and armour;
5 was over the city, the elders a',
11:17 between the king a' and the
13: 6 and there remained the grove a' 1571
16:14 he brought a' the brasen altar, *
17:19 A' Judah kept not the 1571
18: 2 His mother's name a' was Abi, *
21:11 made Judah a' to sin with idols: 1571
22:19 a' have heard thee, saith the Lord. "
23: 5 them a' that burned incense unto
19 the houses a' of the high places 1571
27 remove Judah a' out of my sight, "
24: 4 And a' for the innocent blood "
1Ch 1:14 The Jebusite a', and the Amorite, *
21 Hadoram a', and Uzal, and *
51 Hadad died a'. And the dukes of *
2: 9 The sons a' of Hezron, that were
26 Jerahmeel had a' another wife, *
49 She bare a' Shaaph the father of
3: 6 Ibhar a', and Elishama, and *
18 Malchiram a', and Pedaiah, and *
6: 3 The sons a' of Aaron; Nadab, *
48 Their brethren a' the Levites *
67 gave a' Gezer with her suburbs, *
79 Kedemoth a' with her suburbs, *
7:10 The sons a' of Jediael; Bilhan: *
12 Shuppim a', and Huppim,
25 Rephah was his son, a' Resheph, *
28 Shechem a' and the towns thereof,
8:13 Beriah a', and Shemia, who were *
18 Ishmerai a', and Jezliah, and *
32 these a' dwelt with their brethren 637
9:29 Some of them a' were appointed
38 they a' dwelt with their brethren 637
10:13 and a' for asking counsel of one 1571
11:10 These a' are the chief of the *
22 a' he went down and slew a lion
26 A' the valiant men of the armies
12:38 and all the rest a' of Israel were 1571
13: 2 and with them a' to the priests *
15:27 David a' had upon him an ephod *
16: 6 Benaiah a' and Jahaziel the *
30 the world a' shall be stable, that 637
38 Obed-edom a' the son of Jeduthun
17: 9 A' I will ordain a place for my *
17 a' spoken of thy servant's house *
18: 4 David a' houghed all the chariot *
11 Them a' king David dedicated 1571
20: 2 brought a' exceeding much spoil *
6 he a' was the son of the giant. 1571
21:23 lo, I give thee the oxen a' for *
22: 4 A' cedar trees in abundance: *
14 a' and stone have I prepared;
17 David a' commanded all the
23:26 And a' unto the Levites; they 1571
24:30 The sons a' of Mushi; Mahli, *
26: 6 A' unto Shemaiah his son were
10 A' Hosah, of the children of
27: 4 course was Mikloth a' the ruler: *
30 Over the camels a' was Obil *
32 A' Jonathan David's uncle was a
28:13 A' for the courses of the priests
14 silver a' for all instruments of *
15 and a' for the lamps thereof, *
17 A' pure gold for the fleshhooks, *
21 a' the princes and all the people
29: 9 David the king a' rejoiced with 1571
17 I know a', my God, that thou
2Ch 2: 8 Send me a' cedar trees, fir trees,
14 a' to grave any manner of graving,
3: 7 He overlaid a' the house,
12 the other wing was five cubits a',
15 A' he made before the house
4: 2 A' he made a molten sea of ten
6 He made a' ten lavers, and put
8 He made a' ten tables, and placed
14 He made a' bases, and lavers
16 The pots a', and the shovels,
19 the golden altar a', and the tables
5: 6 A' king Solomon, and a' the *
12 A' the Levites which were the
7: 6 the Levites a' with instruments
8 A' at the same time Solomon *
8: 5 A' he built Beth-horon the upper,
14 the porters a' by their courses at
9: 4 cupbearers a', and their apparel;
10 And the servants a' of Huram, 1571
12: 5 a' left you in the hand of Shishak.
9 he carried away a' the shields of
12 and a' in Judah things went well. *1571
13: 2 mother's name a' was Michaiah *
3 Jeroboam a' set the battle in *
11 the shewbread a' set they in order
14: 5 A' he took away out of all the
15 They smote a' the tents of cattle, 1571

2Ch 15:16 And a' concerning Maachah the 1571
17: 7 A' in the third year of his reign
11 A' some of the Philistines *
18:21 him, and thou shalt a' prevail: 1571
19:11 a' the Levites shall be officers
20: 1 It came to pass after this a', *
21: 4 divers a' of the princes of Israel. 1571
10 The same time a' did Libnah *
13 and a' hast slain thy brethren of 1571
17 king's house, and his sons a', "
22: 2 mother's name a' was Athaliah *
3 He a' walked in the ways of the 1571
5 He walked a' after their counsel, "
23:13 and sounded with trumpets, a' "
18 A' Jehoiada appointed the offices *
24: 1 his mother's name a' was Zibiah *
7 and a' all the dedicated things 1571
12 a' such as wrought iron and brass "
20 the Lord, he hath a' forsaken you.
25: 6 a' an hundred thousand mighty
24 the hostages a', and returned to
26: 3 mother's name a' was Jecoliah *
10 A' he built towers in the desert, *
10 husbandmen a', and vine *
20 yea, himself hasted a' to go out, 1571
27: 1 mother's name a' was Jerushah.
5 He fought a' with the king of the
28: 2 a' molten images for Baalim. 1571
4 sacrificed a' and burnt incense *
5 he was a' delivered into the hand
8 and took a' away much spoil 1571
18 Philistines a' had invaded the cities
18 Gimzo a' and the villages thereof:
29: 7 A' they have shut up the doors of 1571
22 they killed a' the lambs, and they
27 Lord began a' with the trumpets,
35 a' the burnt offerings were in 1571
30: 1 a' to Ephraim and Manasseh, "
12 A' in Judah the hand of God was "
31: 1 in Ephraim a' and Manasseh,
3 He appointed a' the king's portion
6 a' brought in the tithe of oxen and 1571
19 A' of the sons of Aaron the priests,
32: 5 A' he strengthened himself, and *
17 He wrote a' letters to rail on the
28 a' for the increase of corn, and
30 This same Hezekiah a' stopped
33: 4 A' he built altars in the house of *
6 a' he observed times, and used
19 His prayer a', and how God was
34:13 A' they were over the bearers of
27 I have even heard thee a', saith 1571
35: 9 Conaniah a', and Shemaiah and
36: 7 Nebuchadnezzar a' carried off the
13 And he a' rebelled against king 1571
22 all his kingdom, and put it a' in "
Ezr 1: 1 and put it a' in writing, saying, "
7 A' Cyrus the king brought forth
3: 4 They kept a' the feast of the *
7 gave money a' unto the masons,
4:20 mighty kings a' over Jerusalem,
5:10 We asked their names a', to 638
14 the vessels a' of gold and silver "
6: 5 And a' let the golden and silver "
11 A' I have made a decree, that
7:19 The vessels a' that are given thee *
24 A' we certify you, that touching
8: 6 Of the sons a' of Adin; Ebed the *
14 Of the sons a' of Bigvai; Uthai, *
16 a' for Joiarib, and for Elnathan,
20 A' of the Nethinims, whom *
27 A' twenty basons of gold, of a *
28 Lord; the vessels are holy a'; *
35 A' the children of those that had *
10: 4 we a' will be with thee: be of *
23 A' of the Levites; Jozabad, and *
24 Of the singers a'; Eliashib: and
28 Of the sons a' of Bebai; *
Ne 1: 3 wall of Jerusalem a' is broken down,
2: 6 me, (the queen a' sitting by him,)
18 as a' the king's words that he had 637
3: 3 sons of Hassenaah build, who a' *
8 unto him a' repaired Hananiah *
29 After him repaired a' Shemaiah *
5: 3 Some a' there were that said, We
4 There were a' that said, We have
9 A' I said, It is not good that ye do:
11 a' the hundredth part of the money,
13 A' I shook my lap, and said, So 1571
16 Yea, a' I continued in the work "
18 a' fowls were prepared for me,
6: 7 And thou hast a' appointed 1571
19 A' they reported his good deeds "
7:61 And ... went up a' from Tel-melah, *
8: 7 A' Jeshua, and Bani, and Sherebiah,
18 A' day by day, from the first day
9:13 down a' upon mount Sinai,
20 Thou gavest a' thy good spirit to
23 Their children a' multipliedst
37 a' they have dominion over our
10:32 A' we made ordinances for us,
36 A' the firstborn of our sons, and of
11: 1 the rest of the people a' cast lots,
15 A' of the Levites: Shemaiah the *
22 The overseer a' of the Levites at
31 The children a' of Benjamin from
12: 9 A' Bakbukiah and Unni, their
10 Joiakim a' begat Eliashib, and *
22 a' the priests, to the reign of
29 A' from the house of Gilgal, and
43 A' that day they offered great *
43 a' and the children rejoiced:
13:15 as a' wine, grapes, and figs, and 637
16 There dwelt men of Tyre a' therein,
22 O my God, concerning this a', 1571
23 a' saw I Jews that had married "

Es 1: 9 A' Vashti the queen made a feast 1571
16 wrong to the king only, but a'
2: 8 brought a' unto the king's house,*
3:11 given to thee, the people a', to do
4: 8 A' he gave him a copy of the
16 I a' and my maidens will fast 1571
5:12 am I invited unto her a' with "
7: 8 Will he force the queen a' before * "
9 Behold a', the gallows fifty cubits "
8: 8 Write ye a' for the Jews, as it
9:13 to do to morrow a' according unto 1571
15 together on the fourteenth day a' "
Job 1: 3 a' was seven thousand sheep,
6 and Satan came a' among them. 1571
16 speaking, there came a' another,
17 came a' another, and said, The
18 came a' another and said, Thy
2: 1 Satan came a' among them to 1571
5:25 Thou shalt know a' that thy seed
7: 1 a' like the days of an hireling? *
9:11 he passeth on a', but I perceive
20 am perfect, it shall a' prove me *
11:11 vain men: he seeth wickedness a';
19 A' thou shalt lie down, and none
12:15 a' he sendeth them out, and they *
13: 2 know, the same do I know a': 1571
16 He a' shall be my salvation: for an "
27 puttest my feet a' in the stocks,
14: 2 he fleeth a' as a shadow, and
16: 4 I a' could speak as ye do: if your 1571
12 he hath a' taken me by my neck, *
17 in mine hands: a' my prayer *
19 A' now, behold, my witness is in *1571
17: 6 He hath made me a' a byword of †
7 Mine eye a' is dim by reason of
9 The righteous a' shall hold on his*
19:11 He hath a' kindled his wrath
20: 9 The eye a' which saw him shall *
22:28 Thou shalt a' decree a thing, and
24:15 The eye a' of the adulterer waiteth
22 He draweth a' the mighty with his
30:11 they have a' let loose the bridle *
31 My harp a' is turned to mourning,*
31:28 This a' were an iniquity to be 1571
32: 3 A' against his three friends was
10 me; I a' will shew mine opinion. 637
17 said, I will answer a' my part, "
17 I a' will shew mine opinion. "
33: 6 I a' am formed out of the clay. 1571
19 He is chastened a' with pain upon
36: 1 Elihu a' proceeded, and said,
10 openeth a' their ear to discipline,
29 A' can any understand the * 637
33 the cattle concerning the vapour. "
37: 1 At this a' my heart trembleth, † "
11 A' by watering he wearieth the * "
39:30 young ones a' suck up blood:
40: 8 Wilt thou a' disannul my * 637
14 Then will I a' confess unto thee 1571
42: 9 them: the Lord a' accepted Job. *
10 a' the Lord gave Job twice as *
11 every man a' gave him a piece of
13 He had a' seven sons and three
Ps 1: 3 his leaf a' shall not wither; and
5:11 let them a' that love thy name
6: 3 My soul is a' sore vexed: but thou,
7:13 He hath a' prepared for him the
9: 9 The Lord a' will be a refuge for the
16: 7 a' instruct me in the night * 637
9 my flesh a' shall rest in hope. "
18: 7 the foundations a' of the hills
9 He bowed the heavens a', and came
13 Lord a' thundered in the heavens,
19 me forth a' into a large place;
23 I was a' upright before him, and I
35 Thou hast a' given me the shield
40 Thou hast a' given me the necks of
19:10 sweeter a' than honey and the
13 a' from presumptuous sins; 1571
26: 1 I have trusted a' in the Lord;
27: 7 have mercy a' upon me, and
28: 9 feed them a', and lift them up for
29: 6 maketh them a' to skip like a calf;
35: 3 Draw out a' the spear, and stop
37: 4 Delight thyself a' in the Lord; and
5 unto the Lord; trust a' in him;
38:10 mine eyes, it a' is gone from me. 1571
12 They a' that seek after my life
20 They a' that render evil for good
40: 2 me up a' out of an horrible pit, out
45:10 forget a' thine own people, and
52: 6 The righteous a' shall see, and
55:10 mischief a' and sorrow are in the
60: 7 Ephraim a' is the strength of mine
62:12 A' unto thee, O Lord, belongeth
65: 8 They a' that dwell in the
13 the valleys a' are covered over
13 they shout for joy, they a' sing. 637
68: 1 let them a' that hate him flee
8 the heavens a' dropped at the 637
18 yea, for the rebellious a', that the "
69:11 made sackcloth a' my garment; *
21 They gave me a' gall for my meat;
31 This a' shall please the Lord *
36 The seed a' of his servants shall
71:18 a' when I am old and greyheaded,*1571
19 Thy righteousness a', O God, is
22 I will a' praise thee with the 1571
24 My tongue a' shall talk of thy "
72: 8 have dominion a' from sea to sea,
12 the poor a', and him that hath no*
15 prayer a' shall be made for him *
74:16 day is thine, the night a' is thine: 637
75:10 horns of the wicked a' will I cut
76: 2 In Salem a' is his tabernacle,
77:12 I will meditate a' of all thy work,
Ps 77:16 the depths a' were troubled. 637
17 thine arrows a' went abroad. "
78:14 In the daytime a' he led them
16 brought streams a' out of the rock,
20 bread a'? can he provide flesh for 1571
21 anger a' came up against Israel; "
27 rained flesh a' upon them as dust,
46 He gave a' their increase unto the
48 gave up their cattle a' to the hail,
55 cast out the heathen a' before them,
62 his people over a' unto the sword;
70 He chose David a' his servant,
81:16 He should have fed them a' with the
83: 8 Assur a' is joined with them: 1571
84: 6 the rain a' filleth the pools. * "
89: 5 faithfulness a' in the congregation 637
11 heavens are thine, the earth a' is "
21 mine arm a' shall strengthen him. "
25 I will set his hand a' in the sea,
27 A' I will make him my firstborn, 637
29 His seed a' will I make to endure
43 Thou hast a' turned the edge of * 637
92:11 Mine eye a' shall see my desire
95: 4 the strength of the hills is his a'.
96:10 the world a' shall be established 637
99: 4 king's strength a' loveth judgment;
105:23 Israel a' came into Egypt;
33 smote their vines a' and their
36 He smote a' all the firstborn in
37 forth a' with silver and gold: *
106: 9 He rebuked the Red sea a', and it
16 They envied Moses a' in the camp,
27 their seed a' among the nations, *
28 joined themselves a' unto Baal-peor,
32 him a' at the waters of strife,
42 Their enemies a' oppressed them,
46 He made them a' to be pitied of
107:32 exalt him a' in the congregation
38 He blesseth them a', so that they
108: 8 Ephraim a' is the strength of mine
109: 3 compassed me about a' with words
10 seek their bread a' out of their *
25 I became a' a reproach unto them:
119: 3 They a' do no iniquity: They * 637
23 Princes a' did sit and speak 1571
24 Thy testimonies a' are my delight
41 Let thy mercies come a' unto me,
46 thy testimonies a' before kings,
48 My hands a' will I lift up unto
132:12 a' sit upon thy throne for evermore.1571
16 I will a' clothe her priests with
139:17 How precious a' are thy thoughts
141: 5 a' shall be in their calamities. *
145:19 he a' will hear their cry, and will
148: 6 He hath a' stablished them for
14 He a' exalteth the horn of his *
Pr 1:26 I a' will laugh at your calamity; 1571
4: 4 He taught me a', and said unto *
9: 2 she hath a' furnished her 637
11:25 shall be watered a' himself. 1571
17:26 A' to punish the just is not good, "
18: 3 cometh, then cometh a' contempt, "
9 He a' that is slothful in his work "
19: 2 A', that the soul be without "
21:13 his ears at the cry of the poor, he a' "
23:23 and sell it not; a' wisdom, *
28 She a' lieth in wait as for a prey, * 637
24:23 These things a' belong to the wise. 1571
25: 1 These are a' proverbs of Solomon, "
26: 4 according to his folly, lest thou a' "
28:16 wanteth understanding is a' a
30:31 A greyhound: an he goat a'; 176
31:15 She riseth a' while it is yet night,
28 her husband a', and he praiseth
Ec 1: 5 The sun a' ariseth, and the sun
17 that this a' is vexation of spirit. 1571
2: 1 and, behold, this a' is vanity. "
7 a' I had great possessions of great "
8 gathered me a' silver and gold, "
9 a' my wisdom remained with me. 637
14 perceived a' that one event *1571
15 in my heart, that this a' is vanity. "
19 under the sun. This is a' vanity. "
21 This a' is vanity and a great evil. "
23 rest in the night. This is a' vanity. "
24 This a' I saw, that it was from the "
26 This a' is vanity and vexation of "
3:11 a' he hath set the world in their "
13 a' that every man should eat and "
4: 4 This is a' vanity and vexation of "
8 a' vanity, yea, it is a sore travail "
14 a' he that is born in his kingdom * "
16 they a' that come after shall not * "
16 Surely this a' is vanity and vexation "
5: 7 there are a' divers vanities:
10 with increase: this is a' vanity. 1571
16 And this a' is a sore evil, that in "
17 his days a' he eateth in darkness, "
19 a' to whom God hath given riches "
6: 3 and a' that he have no burial; * "
9 this is a' vanity and vexation "
7: 6 of the fool: this a' is vanity. "
14 God a' hath set the one over * "
18 a' from this withdraw not thine "
21 A' take no heed unto all words "
22 a' thine own heart knoweth that "
8:10 had so done: this is a' vanity. "
14 I said that this a' is vanity. "
16 (for a' there is that neither day "
9: 3 a' the heart of the sons of men is "
6 A' their love, and their hatred, * "
12 For man a' knoweth not his time: "
13 wisdom have I seen a' under the "
10: 3 Yea a', when he that is a fool "
14 A fool a' is full of words: a man
11: 2 portion to seven, and a' to eight; *1571
Ec 12: 5 A' when they shall be afraid of *1571
Ca. 1:16 my beloved, yea, pleasant: a' 637
7: 8 of the boughs thereof: now a' *
Isa 2: 7 Their land a' is full of silver and
7 their land is a' full of horses,
8 Their land a' is full of idols;
5: 2 of it, and a' made a winepress 1571
6 I will a' command the clouds
6: 1 I saw a' the Lord sitting upon *
8 A' I heard the voice of the Lord,*
7:13 but will ye weary my God a'? 1571
20 and it shall a' consume the beard. "
8: 5 Lord spake a' unto me again, *
11: 6 The wolf a' shall dwell with the *
13 The envy a' of Ephraim shall
12: 2 he a' is become my salvation. *
13: 3 I have a' called my mighty ones *1571
16 Their children a' shall be dashed
18 bows a' shall dash the young *
14:10 Art thou a' become weak as we? 1571
13 I will sit a' upon the mount of *
23 I will a' make it a possession for
17: 3 The fortress a' shall cease from
19: 8 The fishers a' shall mourn, and
13 Noph are deceived; they have a' *
21:12 morning cometh, and a' the night: 1571
22: 9 Ye have seen a' the breaches of *
11 a' a ditch between the two walls
23:12 there a' shalt thou have no rest. *1571
24: 5 The earth a' is defiled under the
26:12 for thou a' hast wrought all our 1571
21 earth a' shall disclose her blood,
28: 7 they a' have erred through wine, ‡1571
17 Judgment a' will I lay to the line,*
29 a' cometh forth from the Lord 1571
29:19 The meek a' shall increase their
24 They a' that erred in spirit shall
30: 5 but a shame, and a' a reproach. 1571
22 defile a' the covering of thy graven
31: 2 Yet he a' is wise, and will bring 1571
5 defending a' he will deliver it; *
32: 4 The heart a' of the rash shall
7 instruments a' of the churl are evil:
33: 2 salvation a' in the time of trouble. 637
34: 3 Their slain a' shall be cast out,
11 the owl a' and the raven shall *
14 beasts of the desert shall a' meet*
14 the screech owl a' shall rest there, * 389
15 shall the vultures a' be gathered, * "
38:22 Hezekiah a' had said, what is the
40:24 and he shall a' blow upon them, *1571
44:19 a' I have baked bread upon the 637
45:16 be ashamed, and a' confounded, *1571
46:11 I will a' bring it to pass; 637
11 have purposed it, I will a' do it. "
48:12 I am the first, I a' am the last. "
13 Mine hand a' hath laid the * "
19 Thy seed a' had been as the sand,
21 clave the rock a', and the waters
49: 6 I will a' give thee for a light to
7 arise, princes a' shall worship, *
56: 6 A' the sons of the stranger, that
57: 8 Behind the doors a' and the posts*
15 with him a' that is of a contrite
18 I will lead him a', and restore
60:14 sons a' of them that afflicted thee*
16 Thou shalt a' suck the milk of
17 I will a' make thy officers peace,
21 people a' shall be all righteous:
62: 3 Thou shalt a' be a crown of glory
66: 4 I a' will choose their delusions, 1571
21 I will a' take of them for priests
Jer 1: 3 came a' in the days of Jehoiakim
2: 8 pastors a' transgressed against me,
16 A' the children of Noph and 1571
33 a' taught the wicked ones thy * "
34 A' in thy skirts is found the blood "
36 a' shalt be ashamed of Egypt, "
3: 6 Lord said a' unto me in the days *
8 but went and played the harlot a'. 1571
4:12 now a' will I give sentence against "
6:14 healed a' the hurt of the daughter
17 A' I set watchmen over you, *
7:27 thou shalt a' call unto them;
9:16 scatter them a' among the heathen,
10: 5 a' is it in them to do good. *1571
13:23 then may ye a' do good, that are "
14: 5 the hind a' calved in the field, "
16: 1 word of the Lord came a' unto me,
8 shalt not a' go into the house of *
19: 5 They have built a' the high places*
20: 1 who was a' chief governor in the*
23:14 I have seen a' in the prophets of
14 strengthen a' the hands of evildoers,*
25:14 serve themselves of them a': *1571
26:20 was a' a man that prophesied "
27: 6 the field have I given him a' to "
12 a' to Zedekiah king of Judah *
16 A' I spake to the priests and to
28:14 him the beasts of the field a'. 1571
29:24 Thus shalt thou a' speak to *
30:19 I will a' glorify them, and they *
20 children a' shall be as aforetime,
31:36 the seed of Israel a' shall cease 1571
37 a' cast off all the seed of Israel "
33:21 may a' my covenant be broken "
36: 6 and a' thou shalt read them in the "
39: 6 a' the king of Babylon slew all
40: 5 Go back a' to Gedaliah the son *
41: 3 Ishmael a' slew all the Jews that
43:13 He shall break a' the images of
46:21 A' her hired men are in the midst 1571
21 for they a' are turned back, "
48: 2 A' thou shalt be cut down, O "
7 treasures, thou shalt a' be taken: "
8 the valley a' shall perish, and the

Jer 48:26 Moab a' shall wallow in his vomit,*
26 and he a' shall be in derision. 1571
34 for the waters a' of Nimrim shall "
49:17 A' Edom shall be a desolation: *
50:24 for thee, and thou art a' taken, 1571
24 thou art found, and a' caught, "
51:22 With thee a' will I break in *
23 I will a' break in pieces with *
52:10 slew a' all the princes of Judah 1571
17 A' the pillars of brass that were *
18 the caldrons a', and the shovels,
22 The second pillar a' and the
25 took a' out of the city an eunuch, *
La 2: 9 her prophets a' find no vision *1571
3: 8 A' when I cry and shout, he * "
16 He hath a' broken my teeth with
4:21 cup a' shall pass through unto 1571
Eze 1: 5 A' out of the midst thereof came *
10 four a' had the face of an eagle.
3:13 I heard a' the noise of the wings *
21 a' thou hast delivered thy soul. *
4: 1 Thou a', son of man, take thee a
2 set the camp a' against it,
4 Lie thou a' upon thy left side, *
9 Take thou a' unto thee wheat,
11 shalt drink a' water by measure, *
5: 3 Thou shalt a' take thereof a few *
11 therefore will I a' diminish 1571
7: 2 A', thou son of man, thus saith *
18 They shall a' gird themselves
22 My face will I turn a' from them,
24 will a' make the pomp of the strong
8:13 He said a' unto me, Turn thee yet
18 Therefore will I a' deal in fury: 1571
9: 1 He cried a' in mine ears with a *
10 And as for me a', mine eye shall 1571
10:16 the same wheel a' turned not from "
17 these lifted up themselves a': *
19 the wheels a' were beside them, *
12: 1 word of the Lord a' came unto me,
13 My net a' will I spread upon him,
13:21 Your kerchiefs a' will I tear,
16:10 I clothed thee a' with broidered
11 I decked thee a' with ornaments,
17 Thou hast a' taken thy fair jewels
19 My meat a' which I gave thee,
24 That thou hast a' built unto thee
26 hast a' committed fornication
28 Thou hast played the whore a'
39 will a' give thee into their hand,
39 shall strip thee a' of thy clothes, *
40 They shall a' bring up a company
41 and thou a' shalt give no hire 1571
43 therefore I a' will recompense "
52 Thou a', which hast judged thy "
52 yea, be thou confounded a', "
17: 5 He took a' of the seed of the land,
7 There was a' another great eagle
13 a' taken the mighty of the land:
22 I will a' take of the highest branch
18: 4 so a' the soul of the son is mine:
19: 4 The nations a' heard of him;
20:15 Yet a' I lifted up my hand unto 1571
23 unto them a' in the wilderness, * "
25 I gave them a' statutes that were "
28 a' they made their sweet savour,
39 hereafter a', if ye will not hearken
21: 9 is sharpened, and a' furbished: 1571
17 will a' smite mine hands together, "
19 A', thou son of man, appoint thee
23:26 a' strip thee out of thy clothes,
35 bear thou a' thy lewdness and 1571
37 and have a' caused their sons, "
24: 3 set it on, and a' pour water "
5 of the flock, and burn a' the "
15 A' the word of the Lord came
25 A', thou son of man, shall it not *
25:13 I will a' stretch out mine hand *
26: 4 I will a' scrape her dust from her,
27:19 Dan a' and Javan going to and fro*
30: 6 They a' that uphold Egypt shall
10 a' make the multitude of Egypt
13 I will a' destroy the idols, and I
18 At Tehaphnehes a' the day shall
31:17 They a' went down into hell 1571
32: 6 a' water with thy blood the land
9 I will a' vex the hearts of many
13 I will destroy a' all the beasts
17 came to pass a' in the twelfth year,
33:30 A', thou son of man, the children*
36: 1 A', thou son of man, prophesy
26 A new heart a' will I give you,
29 I will a' save you from all your *
33 a' cause you to dwell in the cities,*
37:24 shall a' walk in my judgments,
27 tabernacle a' shall be with them:
38:10 It shall a' come to pass, that at *
39:16 And a' the name of the city shall 1571
40: 8 measured a' the porch of the gate
12 The space a' before the little *
14 He made a' posts of threescore
42 a' they laid the instruments *
41: 8 I saw a' the height of the house
14 A' the breadth of the face of the
43:21 take the bullock a' of the sin
25 shall a' prepare a young bullock,
44:30 shall a' give unto the priest the
45: 5 shall a' the Levites, the ministers*
47:20 side a' shall be the great sea *
Da 6:22 and a' before thee, O king, have I 638
7: 6 the beast had a' four heads;
8:25 And through his policy a' he shall *
25 shall a' stand up against the Prince
10: 6 His body a' was like the beryl,
11: 1 A' I in the first year of Darius *
8 a' carry captives into Egypt 1571
Da 11:14 a' the robbers of thy people shall
17 He shall a' set his face to enter *
22 be broken, yea, a' the prince of 1571
41 enter a' into the glorious land,
42 stretch forth his hand a' upon
Ho 2:11 will a' cause all her mirth to cease,
3: 3 man: so will I a' be for thee. 1571
4: 3 sea a' shall be taken away. "
5 and the prophet a' shall fall with "
6 hast rejected knowledge, I will a' "
6 law of thy God, I will a' forget thy 1571
5: 5 Judah a' shall fall with them. "
6:11 A', O Judah, he hath set an harvest"
7:11 Ephraim a' is like a silly dove *
8: 6 For from Israel was it a': the *
9:12 yea, woe a' to them when I 1571
10: 6 shall be a' carried unto Assyria "
8 The high places a' of Aven, the sin
11: 3 I taught Ephraim a' to go, *
12: 2 hath a' a controversy with Judah,
10 have a' spoken by the prophets,
Joe 1:12 tree, the palm tree a', and 1571
20 The beasts of the field cry a' "
2:12 Therefore a' now, saith the Lord,* "
29 And a' upon the servants and "
3: 2 I will a' gather all nations, and will *
6 The children a' of Judah and the
16 Lord a' shall roar out of Zion, *
Am 1: 5 break a' the bar of Damascus, *
2:10 A' I brought you up from the land
3:14 I will a' visit the altars of Beth-el:
4: 6 And I a' have given you cleanness 1571
7 And a' I have withholden the rain "
7: 6 This a' shall not be, saith the Lord
12 A' Amaziah said unto Amos,
9:14 they shall a' make gardens, and
Jon 4:11 and their left hand; and a' much
Mic 3: 3 Who a' eat the flesh of my people,
4:11 a' many nations are gathered *
5:13 graven images a' will I cut off, *
6:13 Therefore a' will I make thee sick 1571
7:12 In that day a' he shall come even*
Na 3:10 children a' were dashed in pieces 1571
11 Thou a' shalt be drunken: thou "
11 thou a' shalt seek strength "
Hab 1: 8 Their horses a' are swifter than
2: 5 Yea a', because he transgresseth * 637
15 him, and makest him drunken a', "
16 shame for glory: drink thou a', 1571
Zep 1: 4 I will a' stretch out mine hand *
9 In the same day a' will I punish *
13 they shall a' build houses, but *
2:12 Ye Ethiopians a', ye shall be 1571
3:12 I will a' leave in the midst of *
Zec 3: 7 thou shalt a' judge my house, 1571
7 and shalt a' keep my courts, "
4: 9 his hands shall a' finish it; and
8: 6 should it a' be marvellous in mine 1571
21 the Lord of hosts: I will go a'. "
9: 2 Hamath a' shall border thereby; "
5 Gaza a' shall see it, and be very
11 As for thee a', by the blood of thy 1571
10:10 bring them again a' out of the
11: 8 Three shepherds a' I cut off in *
8 lothed them, and their soul a' 1571
12: 7 The Lord a' shall save the tents of
13: 2 and a' I will cause the prophets 1571
14:14 Judah a' shall fight at Jerusalem; "
Mal 1:13 Ye said a', Behold, what a
2: 9 Therefore have I a' made you 1571
M't 2: 8 I may come and worship him a'. 2504
3:10 And now a' the ax is laid unto *2532
5:39 cheek, turn to him the other a'. "
40 thy coat, let him have thy cloke a'. "
6:14 heavenly Father will a' forgive you:"
21 is, there will your heart be a'. "
10: 4 Iscariot, who a' betrayed him. "
32 will I confess a' before my Father 2504
33 him will I a' deny before my Father"
12:45 be a' unto this wicked generation. 2532
13:22 He a' that received seed among *1161
23 which a' beareth fruit, and *1211
26 fruit, then appeared the tares a'. 2532
29 ye root up a' the wheat with them.* 260
15: 3 Why do ye a' transgress the 2532
16 ye a' yet without understanding? "
16: 1 a' with the Sadducees came, * "
18 And I say a' unto thee, That thou 1161
17:12 Likewise shall a' the Son of man 2532
18:33 not thou a' have had compassion "
35 shall my heavenly Father do a' "
19: 3 The Pharisees a' came unto him,* "
28 ye a' shall sit upon twelve thrones, "
20: 4 Go ye a' into the vineyard, and "
7 them, Go ye a' into the vineyard; "
21:21 but a' if ye shall say unto this *2579
24 I a' will ask you one thing, 2504
22:26 Likewise the second a', and the 2532
27 And last of all the woman died a'.* "
23:26 outside of them may be clean a'. "
28 Even so ye a' outwardly appear "
24:27 a' the coming of the Son of man * "
37 days of Noe were, so shall a' the * "
39 all away; so shall a' the coming * "
44 Therefore be ye a' ready: for in "
25:11 Afterward came a' the other "
17 two, he a' gained other two. "
22 He a' that had received two "
41 Then shall he say a' unto them "
44 Then shall they a' answer him, "
26:13 there shall a' this, that this "
35 Likewise a' said all the disciples. "
69 Thou a' wast with Jesus of Galilee. "
71 This fellow was a' with Jesus of "
73 Surely thou a' art one of them; "
27:44 The thieves a', which were "
M't 27:57 a' himself was Jesus' disciple: 2532
M'r 1:19 who a' were in the ship mending "
38 towns, that I may preach there a': 2546
2:15 publicans and sinners sat a' *2532
21 No man a' seweth a piece of new * "
26 and gave a' to them which were "
28 of man is Lord a' of the sabbath. * "
3:19 Iscariot, which a' betrayed him: "
4:36 And there were a' with him other *
5:16 and a' concerning the swine.
7:18 ye so without understanding a'? 2532
8: 7 to set them a' before them. "
34 unto him with his disciples a', *
38 of him a' shall the Son of man be 2532
11:25 that your Father a' which is in "
29 I will a' ask of you one question, *2504
12: 6 he sent him a' last unto them, *2532
22 last of all the woman died a'. "
14: 9 this a' that she hath done shall "
31 anywise. Likewise a' said they all. "
67 a' wast with Jesus of Nazareth. "
15:31 Likewise a' the chief priests "
40 There were a' women looking on "
41 (Who a', when he was in Galilee, * "
43 which a' waited for the kingdom of "
Lu 1: 3 It seemed good to me a', having 2504
35 therefore a' that holy thing which 2532
36 thy cousin Elizabeth, she hath a' "
2: 4 And Joseph a' went up from "
35 pierce through thy own soul a',) "
3: 9 And now a' the axe is laid unto * "
12 Then came a' publicans to be "
4:23 do a' here in thy country. "
41 And devils a' came out of many, "
43 kingdom of God to other cities a': "
5:10 And so was a' James, and John, "
36 he spake a' a parable unto them; "
39 No man a' having drunk old wine *"
6: 4 gave a' to them that were with "
5 the Son of man is Lord a' of the * "
6 a' on another sabbath, that he * "
13 whom a' he named apostles; "
14 Simon, (whom he a' named Peter,) "
16 Iscariot, which a' was the traitor.* "
29 on the one cheek offer a' the other; "
29 cloke forbid not to take thy coat a'. "
31 to you, do ye a' to them likewise. "
32 sinners a' love those that love * "
33 for sinners a' do even the same. * "
34 for sinners a' lend to sinners, * "
36 as your Father a' is merciful. * "
7: 8 I a' am a man set under authority, "
49 Who is this that forgiveth sins a'?* "
8:36 They a' which saw it told them "
9:61 another a' said, Lord, I will follow "
10: 1 Lord appointed other seventy a', "
39 Mary, which a' sat at Jesus' feet, "
11: 1 as John a' taught his disciples. "
4 for we a' forgive every one that is "
18 If Satan a' be divided against "
30 so shall a' the Son of man be to "
34 thy whole body a' is full of light; "
34 thy body a' is full of darkness. "
40 make that which is within a'. "
45 saying thou reproachest us a'? "
46 Woe unto you a', ye lawyers! "
49 a' said the wisdom of God, I will "
12: 8 A' I say unto you, Whosoever *1161
8 Son of man a' confess before the 2532
34 is, there will your heart be a'. "
40 Be ye therefore ready a': for the "
54 And he said a' to the people, "
13: 6 He spake a' this parable; *1161
8 Lord, let it alone this year a', 2532
14:12 said he a' to him that bade him, "
12 lest they a' bid thee again, "
26 and his own life a', he cannot be "
16: 1 he said a' unto his disciples, "
10 is least is faithful a' in much: "
10 in the least is unjust a' in much. "
14 And the Pharisees a', who were * "
22 the rich man a' died, and was "
28 lest they a' come into this place "
17:24 a' the Son of man be in his day. "
26 a' in the days of the Son of man. "
28 a' as it was in the days of Lot; * "
18:15 a' infants, that he would touch "
19: 9 as he a' is a son of Abraham. "
19 to him, Be thou a' over five cities. "
20: 3 I will a' ask you one thing; 2504
11 they beat him a', and entreated 2528
12 a third: and they wounded him a', 2532
31 and in like manner the seven a': "
32 Last of all the woman died a'. "
21: 2 a' a certain poor widow casting "
22:20 Likewise a' the cup after supper, * "
24 there was a' a strife among them, "
39 and his disciples a' followed "
56 said, This man was a' with him. "
58 Thou art a' of them. And Peter "
59 truth this fellow a' was with him: "
68 And if I a' ask you, ye will not "
23: 7 who himself a' was at Jerusalem "
27 of women, which a' bewailed and * "
32 And there were a' two other, "
35 the rulers a' with them derided "
36 And the soldiers a' mocked him, "
38 a superscription a' was written "
51 a' himself waited for the * "
55 And the women a', which came * "
24:22 certain women a' of our company* "
23 had a' seen a vision of angels, "
Joh 3:23 John a' was baptizing in Ænon "
5:18 said a' that God was his Father, "
19 soever he doeth, these a' doeth "
27 authority to execute judgment a',* "

Joh 6:24 disciples, they a' took shipping, *2532
36 That ye a' have seen me, and * "
67 the twelve, Will ye a' go away? "
7: 3 disciples a' may see the works "
10 then went he a' up unto the feast, "
47 the Pharisees, Are ye a' deceived? "
52 Art thou a' of Galilee? "
8:17 It is a' written in your law, that * "
19 should have known my Father a'. "
9:15 again the Pharisees a' asked him "
27 will ye a' be his disciples? "
40 said unto him, Are we blind a'? "
10:16 this fold: them a' I must bring, 2548
11:16 Let us a' go, that we may die 2532
33 a' weeping which came with her, "
52 that a' he should gather together "
12: 9 that they might see Lazarus a', "
10 that they might put Lazarus a' "
18 this cause the people a' met him, "
26 I am, there shall a' my servant be: "
42 the chief rulers a' many believed * "
13: 9 but a' my hands and my head. "
14 ye a' ought to wash one another's "
32 God shall a' glorify him in himself,* "
34 that ye a' love one another. "
14: 1 ye believe in God, believe a' in me. "
3 where I am, there ye may be a'. "
7 should have known my Father a': "
12 the works that I do shall he do a'; 2548
19 because I live, ye shall live a'. 2532
15:20 me, they will a' persecute you; "
20 saying, they will keep yours a'. "
23 hateth me hateth my Father a'. "
27 And ye a' shall bear witness, "
17: 1 that thy Son a' may glorify thee: "
18 have I a' sent them into the world. 2504
19 that they a' might be sanctified 2532
20 for these alone, but for them a' "
21 that they a' may be one in us: "
24 Father, I will that they a', whom 2548
18: 5 And Judas a', which betrayed him, 2532
17 Art not thou a' one of this man's "
25 not thou a' one of his disciples? "
19:23 soldier a part; and a' his coat: "
39 And there came a' Nicodemus, "
20: 8 Then went in a' that other disciple, "
21: 3 say unto him, We a' go with thee. "
20 a' leaned on his breast at supper, "
25 a' many other things which Jesus "
Ac 1: 3 To whom a' he shewed himself "
11 Which a' said, Ye men of Galilee, "
2:22 midst of you, as ye yourselves a' * "
26 moreover a' my flesh shall rest "
3:17 ye did it, as did a' your rulers. "
5: 2 part of the price, his wife a' being "
16 There came a' a multitude out of "
32 and so is a' the Holy Ghost, "
37 he a' perished; and all, even as 2548
7:45 Which a' our fathers that came 2532
8:13 Then Simon himself believed a': "
19 Give me a' this power, 2504
9:32 he came down a' to the saints 2532
10:26 I myself a' am a man. 2504
45 a' was poured out the gift of the 2532
11: 1 had a' received the word of God. "
18 God a' to the Gentiles granted "
30 Which a' they did, and sent it to "
12: 3 proceeded further to take Peter a'. "
13: 5 had a' John to their minister. "
9 Then Saul, (who a' is called Paul,) "
22 to whom a' he gave testimony, "
33 again; as it is a' written in the "
35 he saith a' in another psalm, "
14: 5 a' of the Jews with their rulers, * "
15 We a' are men of like passions "
15:27 shall a' tell you the same things "
32 Judas and Silas, being prophets a' "
35 Paul a' and Barnabas continued 1161
35 of the Lord, with many others a'. 2532
17: 6 upside down are come hither a'; * "
12 a' of honourable women which "
13 at Berea, they came thither a', 2546
28 as certain a' of your own poets *2532
28 For we are a' his offspring. "
19:17 to all the Jews and Greeks a' * "
19 them a' which used curious arts *1161
21 been there, I must a' see Rome. 2532
27 a' that the temple of the great "
20:30 A' of your own selves shall men * "
21:13 a' to die at Jerusalem for the "
16 with us a' certain of the disciples "
24 thou thyself a' walkest orderly, "
28 brought Greeks a' into the temple, "
22: 5 As a' the high priest doth bear "
5 from whom a' I received letters "
20 was shed, I a' was standing "
29 the chief captain a' was afraid, "
23:11 must thou bear witness a' at Rome. "
30 his accusers a' to say before thee "
33 presented Paul a' before him. "
35 when thine accusers are a' come. "
24: 6 a' hath gone about to profane * "
9 And the Jews a' assented, saying "
15 which they themselves a' allow, "
26 hoped a' that money *260, 1161, 2532
25:22 I would a' hear the man myself. 2532
24 both at Jerusalem, and a' here, "
26:10 Which thing I a' did in Jerusalem: 2532
26 before whom a' I speak freely: "
29 but a' all that hear me this day, "
27:10 lading and ship, but a' of our lives. "
12 part advised to depart thence a', *2547
36 and they a' took some meat. 2532
28: 9 So when this was done, others a', "
10 a' honoured us with many honours; "
Ro 1:13 have some fruit among you a', "

Ro 1:16 Jew first, and a' to the Greek. 2532
24 a' gave them up to uncleanness * "
27 And likewise a' the men, leaving "
2: 9 Jew first, and a' of the Gentile; "
10 good, to the Jew first, and a' "
12 law shall a' perish without law: "
15 conscience a' bearing witness, *4828
3: 7 yet am I a' judged as a sinner? 2504
29 of the Jews only? is he not a' of 2532
29 Yes, of the Gentiles a': "
4: 6 David a' describeth the blessedness "
9 or upon the uncircumcision a'? "
11 might be imputed unto them a': * "
12 who a' walk in the steps of that "
16 to that a' which is of the faith of "
21 he was able a' to perform. "
24 But for us a', to whom it shall be "
5: 3 but we glory in tribulations a': "
11 we a' joy in God through our Lord "
15 the offence, so a' is the free gift. "
6: 4 a' should walk in newness of life. "
5 we shall be a' in the likeness of "
8 believe that we shall a' live with "
11 reckon ye a' yourselves to be dead "
7: 4 ye a' are become dead to the law "
8:11 shall a' quicken your mortal bodies "
17 that we may be a' glorified "
21 creature itself a' shall be delivered "
23 not only they, but ourselves a', "
26 Spirit a' helpeth our infirmities: "
29 foreknow, he a' did predestinate "
30 he did predestinate, them he a' "
30 he called, them he a' justified: "
30 he justified, them he a' glorified. "
34 who a' maketh intercession for us. "
9: 1 a' bearing me witness in the Holy*4828
10 but when Rebecca a' had 2532
24 Jews only, but a' of the Gentiles? "
25 As he saith a' in Osee, I will call "
27 Esaias a' crieth concerning Israel,*1161
11: 1 For I a' am an Israelite, of the 2532
5 present time a' there is a remnant "
16 be holy, the lump is a' holy: "
21 heed lest he a' spare not thee. *3761
22 otherwise thou a' shalt be cut off. 2532
31 so have these a' now not believed, "
13: 5 wrath, but a' for conscience sake. "
6 for this cause pay ye tribute a': "
15: 7 receive ye one another, as Christ a' "
14 I myself a' am persuaded of you, "
14 that ye a' are full of goodness, * "
14 able a' to admonish one another. "
22 a' I have been much hindered "
27 their duty is a' to minister unto "
16: 2 of many, and of myself a'. * "
4 a' all the churches of the Gentiles. "
1Co 1: 8 Who shall a' confirm you unto "
16 And I baptized a' the household "
2:13 Which things a' we speak, not in "
4: 8 that we a' might reign with you. "
5:12 what have I to do to judge them a'* "
6:14 and will a' raise up us by his own* "
7: 3 a' the wife unto the husband. "
4 a' the husband hath not power of "
22 likewise a' he that is called, * "
34 difference a' between a wife and a "
40 I think a' that I have the Spirit 2504
9: 8 saith not the law the same a'? 2532
10: 6 evil things, as they a' lusted. 2548
9 as some of them a' tempted, *2532
10 as some of them a' murmured, * "
13 the temptation a' make a way to "
11: 1 even as I a' am of Christ. 2504
6 not covered, let her a' be shorn: 2532
12 so is the man a' by the woman; "
19 must be a' heresies among you, "
23 the Lord that which a' I delivered "
25 same manner a' he took the cup, "
12:12 are one body: so a' is Christ. "
13:12 I know even as a' I am known. "
14:15 pray with the understanding a': "
15 sing with the understanding a'. "
19 my voice I might teach others a', "
34 under obedience, as a' saith the "
15: 1 which a' ye have received, "
2 By which a' ye are saved, if ye "
3 of all that which I a' received, "
8 he was seen of me a', 2504
14 vain, and your faith is a' vain. 2532
18 they a' which are fallen asleep "
21 a' the resurrection of the dead. "
28 shall the Son a' himself be subject "
40 There are a' celestial bodies, "
42 a' is the resurrection of the dead. "
48 such are they a' that are earthy: "
48 such are they a' that are heavenly. "
49 a' bear the image of the heavenly, "
16: 4 And if it be meet that I go a', 2504
10 the work of the Lord, as I a' do. 2532
2Co 1: 5 consolation a' aboundeth by Christ. "
6 sufferings which we a' suffer: "
7 shall ye be a' of the consolation. "
11 Ye a' helping together by prayer "
14 As a' ye have acknowledged us in "
14 even as ye a' are ours in the day "
22 Who hath a' sealed us, and given "
2: 9 For to this end a' did I write, "
10 ye forgive any thing, I forgive a': "
3: 6 Who a' hath made us able "
4:10 that the life a' of Jesus might be "
11 for Jesus' sake, that the life a' "
13 we a' believe, and therefore speak; "
14 raise up us a' by Jesus, and shall "
5: 5 who a' hath given unto us the * "
11 and I trust a' are made manifest "
6: 1 beseech ye a' that ye receive not "

2Co 6:13 my children,) be ye a' enlarged. 2532
8: 6 so he would a' finish in you "
6 the same grace a'. "
7 see that ye abound in this grace a'. "
10 but a' to be forward a year ago. "
11 so there may be a performance a' "
14 abundance a' may be a supply for "
19 a' chosen of the churches to travel "
21 Lord, but a' in the sight of men. "
9: 6 sparingly shall reap a' sparingly; "
6 shall reap a' bountifully. "
12 abundant a' by many thanksgivings "
10:11 such will we be a' in deed when "
14 as far as to you a' in preaching * "
11:15 his ministers a' be transformed as "
18 after the flesh, I will glory a'. 2504
21 speak foolishly,) I am bold a'. "
13: 4 For we a' are weak in him, but we 2532
9 and this a' we wish, even your "
Ga 2: 1 and took Titus with me a'. "
10 which I a' was forward to do'. "
13 Barnabas a' was carried away * "
17 we ourselves a' are found sinners, "
5:21 as I have a' told you in time past,* "
25 Spirit, let us a' walk in the Spirit. "
6: 1 thyself, lest thou a' be tempted. "
7 man soweth, that shall he a' reap. "
Eph 1:11 In whom a' we have obtained an "
13 In whom ye a' trusted, after that "
13 in whom a' after that ye believed, "
15 I a', after I heard of your faith 2504
21 but a' in that which is to come: 2532
2: 3 a' we all had our conversation "
22 In whom ye a' are builded together "
4: 9 but that he a' descended first into "
10 is the same a' that ascended "
5: 2 in love, as Christ a' hath loved us, "
25 love your wives, even as Christ a' "
6: 9 that your Master a' is in heaven; * "
21 that ye a' may know my affairs, "
Ph'p 1:15 strife; and some a' of good will: "
20 now a' Christ shall be magnified "
29 but a' to suffer for his sake; "
2: 4 man a' on the things of others. "
5 you, which was a' in Christ Jesus: "
9 God a' hath highly exalted him, "
18 For the same cause a' do ye joy, "
19 that I a' may be of good comfort, 2504
27 not on him only, but on me a', 2532
3: 4 though I might a' have confidence* "
12 for which a' I am apprehended "
20 whence a' we look for the Saviour, "
4: 3 I intreat thee a', true yokefellow, "
3 with Clement a', and with other "
10 wherein ye were a' careful, but * "
15 Now ye Philippians know a', "
Col 1: 6 forth fruit, as it doth a' in you, "
7 As ye a' learned of Epaphras our * "
8 Who a' declared unto us your love "
9 For this cause we a', since the day "
29 Whereunto I a' labour, striving "
2:11 In whom a' ye are circumcised "
12 with him in baptism, wherein a' "
3: 4 ye a' appear with him in glory. "
7 the which ye a' walked some time, "
8 But now ye a' put off all these; "
13 Christ forgave you, so a' do ye. "
15 which a' ye are called in one body; "
4: 3 Withal praying a' for us, that God "
3 of Christ, for which I am a' "
16 that it be read a' in the church "
1Th 1: 5 a' in power, and in the Holy Ghost, "
8 but a' in every place your faith to* "
2: 8 of God only, but a' our own souls, "
10 Ye are witnesses, and God a', "
13 For this cause a' thank we God "
13 which effectually worketh a' in "
14 for ye a' have suffered like things "
3: 6 to see us, as we a' to see you: "
4: 6 as we a' have forewarned you and "
8 a' given unto us his holy Spirit. * "
14 so them a' which sleep in Jesus "
5:11 edify one another, even as a' ye do. "
24 that calleth you, who a' will do it. "
2Th 1: 5 of God, for which ye a' suffer: "
11 Wherefore a' we pray always for "
1Ti 2: 9 In like manner a', that women * "
3:10 And let these a' first be proved; "
5:13 but tattlers a' and busybodies, "
20 before all, that others a' may fear. "
25 Likewise a' the good works of "
6:12 life, whereunto thou art a' called, * "
2Ti 1: 5 I am persuaded that in thee a'. "
12 cause I a' suffer these things: "
2: 2 shall be able to teach others a'. "
5 if a man a' strive for masteries, "
10 they may a' obtain the salvation "
11 with him, we shall a' live with him: "
12 suffer, we shall a' reign with him: "
12 we deny him, he a' will deny us: 2548
20 but a' of wood and of earth; 2532
22 Flee a' youthful lusts: but follow *1161
3: 1 This know a', that in the last days "
8 so do these a' resist the truth: 2532
9 manifest unto all men, as theirs a' "
4: 8 them a' that love his appearing. "
15 Of whom be thou ware a'; for he "
Ph'm 21 thou wilt a' do more than I say. * "
22 withal prepare me a' a lodging: "
Heb 1: 2 by whom a' he made the worlds; "
2: 4 God a' bearing them witness, 4901
14 he a' himself likewise took part 2532
3: 2 as a' Moses was faithful in all his "
4:10 he a' hath ceased from his own "
5: 2 he himself a' is compassed with "
3 for the people, so a' for himself. "

Heb 5: 5 So a' Christ glorified not himself 2532
6 As he saith a' in another place, "
7: 2 a' Abraham gave a tenth part of "
2 and after that a' King of Salem, "
9 Levi a', who receiveth tithes, * "
12 necessity a change a' of the law. "
25 Wherefore he is able a' to save "
8: 3 this man have somewhat a' to offer. "
6 by how much a' he is the mediator "
9: 1 first covenant had a' ordinances * "
16 there must a' of necessity be the * "
10:15 the Holy Ghost a' is a witness 2532
11:11 Through faith a' Sara herself * "
19 from whence a' he received him "
32 of David a', and Samuel, and of * 5037
12: 1 seeing we a' are compassed about 2532
26 not the earth only, but a' heaven. "
13: 3 being yourselves a' in the body. "
12 Wherefore Jesus a', that he might "
Jas 1:11 so a' shall the rich man fade away "
2: 2 in a' a poor man in vile raiment; "
19 the devils a' believe, and tremble. "
25 Likewise a' was not Rahab the "
26 faith without works is dead a'. * "
3: 2 able a' to bridle the whole body. "
4 Behold a' the ships, which though "
5: 8 Be ye a' patient; stablish your "
1Pet 2: 5 Ye a', as lively stones, are built up "
6 Wherefore a' it is contained in * "
8 whereunto a' they were appointed. "
18 and gentle, but a' to the froward. "
21 because Christ a' suffered for us, "
3: 1 they a' may without the word * "
5 in the old time the holy women a', "
18 For Christ a' hath once suffered "
19 By which a' he went and preached "
21 even baptism doth a' now save us "
4: 6 preached a' to them that are dead, * "
13 may be glad a' with exceeding joy. "
5: 1 I exhort, who am a' an elder, and * "
1 and a' a partaker of the glory "
2Pet 1:19 We have a' a more sure word of * "
2: 1 But there were false prophets a' "
3:10 the earth a' and the works that * "
15 brother Paul a' according to the "
16 As a' in all his epistles, speaking "
16 as they do a' the other scriptures, "
17 things before, beware lest ye a' *4879
1Jo 1: 3 that ye a' may have fellowship 2532
2: 2 a' for the sins of the whole world. "
6 ought himself a' so to walk, "
23 the Son hath the Father a'. "
24 ye a' shall continue in the Son, "
3: 4 sin transgresseth a' the law: "
4:11 we ought a' to love one another "
21 loveth God love his brother a'. "
5: 1 him a' that is begotten of him. "
2Jo 1 but a' all they that have known the "
3Jo 12 and we a' bear record; and ye "
Jude 8 Likewise a' these filthy dreamers "
14 And Enoch a', the seventh from "
Re 1: 7 him, and they a' which pierced * "
9 I John, who a' am your brother, * "
2: 6 the Nicolaitanes, which I a' hate. 2504
15 So hast thou a' them that hold 2532
3:10 I a' will keep thee from the hour 2504
21 even as I a' overcame, and am set "
6:11 fellowservants a' and their 2532
11: 8 where a' our Lord was crucified. "
14:17 he a' having a sharp sickle. "

altar See also **ALTARS.**
Ge 8:20 Noah builded an a' unto the Lord 4196
20 offered burnt offerings on the a'. "
12: 7 there builded he an a' "
8 there he builded an a' "
13: 4 Unto the place of the a', "
18 built there an a' unto the Lord. "
22: 9 Abraham built an a' there, "
9 laid him on the a' "
26:25 he builded an a' there, "
33:20 And he erected there an a', "
35: 1 make there an a' unto God, "
3 I will make there an a' "
7 he built there an a', "
Ex 17:15 And Moses built an a', "
20:24 An a' of earth thou shalt make "
25 if thou wilt make me an a' of stone, "
26 go up by steps unto mine a', "
21:14 thou shalt take him from mine a', "
24: 4 builded an a' under the hill, "
6 the blood he sprinkled on the a'. "
27: 1 thou shalt make an a' "
1 the a' shall be foursquare: "
5 compass of the a' beneath, that "
5 may be even to the midst of the a'. "
6 thou shalt make staves for the a', "
7 be upon the two sides of the a', "
28:43 when they come near unto the a' "
29:12 put it upon the horns of the a' "
12 beside the bottom of the a'. "
13 burn them upon the a'. "
16 sprinkle it round about upon the a'. "
18 burn the whole ram upon the a': "
20 sprinkle the blood upon the a' "
21 the blood that is upon the a', "
25 burn them upon the a' "
36 thou shalt cleanse the a', "
37 an atonement for the a', and "
37 and it shall be an a' most holy: "
37 toucheth the a' shall be holy. "
38 thou shalt offer upon the a'; "
44 the congregation, and the a': "
30: 1 thou shalt make an a' to burn "
18 the congregation and the a', "
20 when they come near to the a' "

Ex 30:27 and the a' of incense, 4196
28 the a' of burnt offering "
31: 8 the a' of incense, "
9 the a' of burnt offering "
32: 5 he built an a' before it; "
35:15 the incense a', and his staves, "
16 The a' of burnt offering, "
37:25 he made the incense a' "
38: 1 he made the a' of burnt offering "
3 he made all the vessels of the a', "
4 he made for the a' a brasen grate "
7 the rings on the sides of the a', "
7 made the a' hollow with boards. * "
30 and the brasen a', 4196
30 all the vessels of the a', "
39:38 the golden a', and the anointing "
39 The brasen a', and his grate "
40: 5 thou shalt set the a' of gold "
6 the a' of the burnt offering "
7 of the congregation and the a', "
10 shalt anoint the a' of the burnt "
10 all his vessels, and sanctify the a': "
10 and it shall be an a' most holy. "
26 he put the golden a' in the tent "
29 he put the a' of burnt offering "
30 tent of the congregation and the a', "
32 they came near unto the a', "
33 about the tabernacle and the a', "
Le 1: 5 blood round about upon the a' "
7 shall put fire upon the a', "
8 the fire which is upon the a': "
9 the priest shall burn all on the a', "
11 kill it on the side of the a' "
11 blood round about upon the a'. "
12 the fire which is upon the a': "
13 burn it upon the a': "
15 the priest shall bring it unto the a', "
15 burn it on the a'; and the blood "
15 wrung out at the side of the a': "
16 cast it beside the a' "
17 the priest shall burn it upon the a', "
2: 2 burn the memorial of it upon the a', "
8 he shall bring it unto the a'. "
9 shall burn it upon the a': "
12 shall not be burnt on the a' "
3: 2 shall sprinkle the blood upon the a' "
5 shall burn it on the a' "
8 round about upon the a'. "
11 the priest shall burn it upon the a': "
13 upon the a' round about. "
16 priest shall burn them upon the a': "
4: 7 blood upon the horns of the a' "
7 the bullock at the bottom of the a' "
10 shall burn them upon the a' "
18 blood upon the horns of the a' "
18 the blood at the bottom of the a' "
19 burn it upon the a'. "
25 it upon the horns of the a' "
25 blood at the bottom of the a' "
26 burn all his fat upon the a', "
30 it upon the horns of the a' "
30 thereof at the bottom of the a'. "
31 shall burn it upon the a' "
34 it upon the horns of the a' "
34 thereof at the bottom of the a': "
35 shall burn them upon the a', "
5: 9 upon the side of the a'; "
9 out at the bottom of the a': "
12 burn it on the a', "
6: 9 the burning upon the a' "
9 the fire of the a' shall be burning "
10 with the burnt offering on the a', "
10 and he shall put them beside the a'. "
12 the fire upon the a' shall be "
13 shall ever be burning upon the a'; "
14 before the Lord, before the a'. "
15 shall burn it upon the a' "
7: 2 sprinkle round about upon the a'. "
5 priest shall burn them upon the a' "
31 shall burn the fat upon the a': "
8:11 he sprinkled thereof upon the a' "
11 and anointed the a' and all "
15 put it upon the horns of the a' "
15 and purified the a', and poured "
15 blood at the bottom of the a', "
16 Moses burnt it upon the a'. "
19 sprinkled the blood upon the a' "
21 burnt the whole ram upon the a': "
24 sprinkled the blood upon the a' "
28 burnt them on the a' "
30 the blood which was upon the a', "
9: 7 Go unto the a', "
8 Aaron therefore went unto the a', "
9 put it upon the horns of the a', "
9 the blood at the bottom of the a': 4196
10 he burnt upon the a'; "
12 sprinkled round about upon the a'. "
13 and he burnt them upon the a'. "
14 the burnt offering on the a'. "
17 burnt it upon the a', "
18 which he sprinkled upon the a' "
20 he burnt the fat upon the a': "
24 upon the a' the burnt offering "
10:12 eat it without leaven beside the a': "
14:20 the meat offering upon the a': "
16:12 burning coals of fire from off the a' "
18 he shall go out unto the a' "
18 put it upon the horns of the a' "
20 the a', he shall bring the live goat: "
25 shall he burn upon the a'. "
33 of the congregation, and for the a', "
17: 6 sprinkle the blood upon the a' "
11 to you upon the a' "
21:23 nor come nigh unto the a', "
22:22 offering by fire of them upon the a' "
Nu 3:26 by the a' round about, "

Nu 4:11 golden a' they shall spread a cloth 4196
13 take away the ashes from the a', "
14 all the vessels of the a', "
26 by the a' round about, "
5:25 offer it upon the a': "
26 and burn it upon the a', "
7: 1 both the a' and all the vessels "
10 offered for dedicating of the a' "
10 offered their offering before the a'. "
11 for the dedicating of the a', "
84 This was the dedication of the a', "
88 the dedication of the a', after that "
16:38, 39 plates for a covering of the a': "
46 put fire therein from off the a', "
18: 3 vessels of the sanctuary and the a', "
5 the charge of the a': "
7 for everything of the a', "
17 sprinkle their blood upon the a', "
23: 2 on every a' a bullock and a ram. "
4 upon every a' a bullock and a ram. "
14 bullock and a ram on every a', "
30 a bullock and a ram on every a'. "
De 12:27 upon the a' of the Lord thy God: "
27 shall be poured out upon the a' "
16:21 trees near unto the a' of the Lord "
26: 4 set it down before the a' "
27: 5 shalt thou build an a' "
5 an a' of stones: "
6 build the a' of the Lord thy God "
33:10 burnt sacrifice upon thine a'. "
Jos. 8:30 Then Joshua built an a' "
31 an a' of whole stones, "
9:27 and for the a' of the Lord, "
22:10 there an a' by Jordan, a great a' "
11 have built an a' over against "
16 in that ye have builded you an a', "
19 in building you an a' "
19 beside the a' of the Lord "
23 That we have built us an a' "
26 prepare to build us an a', "
28 Behold the pattern of the a' of "
29 to build an a' for burnt offerings, "
29 beside the a' of the Lord "
34 called the a' Ed: "
J'g 6:24 Then Gideon built an a' there "
25 throw down the a' of Baal "
26 and build an a' unto the Lord "
28 the a' of Baal was cast down, "
28 offered upon the a' that was built "
30 he hath cast down the a' of Baal, "
31 because one hath cast down his a'. "
32 because he hath thrown down his a'. "
13:20 toward heaven from off the a', "
20 in the flame of the a'. "
21: 4 built there an a', "
1 Sa 2:28 to offer upon mine a', "
33 I shall not cut off from mine a', "
7:17 and there he built an a' "
14:35 And Saul built an a' "
35 the same was the first a' "
2Sa 24:18 rear an a' unto the Lord "
21 to build an a' unto the Lord, "
25 David built there an a' "
1Ki 1:50 caught hold on the horns of the a'. "
51 on the horns of the a', saying, Let "
53 they brought him down from the a'. "
2:28 caught hold on the horns of the a'. "
29 behold, he is by the a'. "
3: 4 did Solomon offer upon that a'. "
6:20 and so covered the a' "
22 also the whole a' "
7:48 the a' of gold, and the table of gold, "
8:22 Solomon stood before the a' of the "
31 the oath come before thine a' "
54 he arose from before the a' "
64 the brasen a' that was before the "
9:25 upon the a' which he built "
25 he burnt incense upon the a' that "
12:32 he offered upon the a'. "
33 So he offered upon the a' which he "
33 he offered upon the a', and burnt "
13: 1 Jeroboam stood by the a' "
2 he cried against the a' in the word "
2 and said, O a', a', "
3 the a' shall be rent, "
4 which had cried against the a' in "
4 he put forth his hand from the a'. "
5 the a' also was rent, and "
5 the ashes poured out from the a', "
32 against the a' in Beth-el, "
16:32 he reared up an a' for Baal "
18:26 they leaped upon the a' "
30 he repaired the a' of the Lord "
32 And with the stones he built an a' "
32 he made a trench about the a', "
35 the water ran round about the a'; "
2Ki 11:11 by the a' and the temple. "
12: 9 set it beside the a', "
16:10 saw an a' that was at Damascus: "
10 the fashion of the a', "
11 And Urijah the priest built an a' "
12 the king saw the a': and "
12 the king approached to the a', "
13 his peace offerings, upon the a'. "
14 he brought also the brasen a', "
14 from between the a' "
14 put it on the north side of the a'. "
15 Upon the great a' burn "
15 and the brasen a' shall be for me "
18:22 Ye shall worship before this a' "
23: 9 came not up to the a' of the Lord "
15 the a' that was at Beth-el, "
15 both that a' and the high place "
16 burned them upon the a', "
17 hast done against the a' of Beth-el. "
1Ch 6:49 and his sons offered upon the a' "

1Ch 6:49 and on the *a* of incense, 4196
16:40 upon the *a* of the burnt offering "
21:18 set up an *a* unto the Lord "
22 that I may build an *a* "
26 built there an *a* unto the Lord "
26 fire upon the *a* of burnt offering. "
29 and the *a* of the burnt offering, "
22: 1 this is the *a* of the burnt offering "
28:18 And for the *a* of incense "
2Ch 1: 5 the brasen *a*, that Bezaleel "
6 went up thither to the brasen *a* "
4: 1 Moreover he made an *a* of brass, "
19 the golden *a* also, "
5:12 stood at the east end of the *a*, "
6:12 he stood before the *a* of the Lord "
22 and the oath come before thine *a* "
7: 7 brasen *a* which Solomon had made "
9 kept the dedication of the *a* seven "
8:12 on the *a* of the Lord, "
15: 8 renewed the *a* of the Lord, "
23:10 along by the *a* and the temple, "
26:16 incense upon the *a* of incense. "
19 from beside the incense *a*. "
29:18 the *a* of burnt offering, "
19 they are before the *a* of the Lord. "
21 to offer them on the *a* of the Lord. "
22 sprinkled it on the *a*: "
22 upon the *a*: they killed also the "
22 sprinkled the blood upon the *a*. "
24 their blood upon the *a*, "
27 the burnt offering upon the *a*. "
32:12 Ye shall worship before one *a*, "
33:16 he repaired the *a* of the Lord, "
35:16 to offer burnt offerings upon the *a* "
Ezr 3: 2 builded the *a* of the God of Israel, "
3 they set the *a* upon his bases; "
7:17 and offer them upon the *a* 4056
Ne 10:34 to burn upon the *a* of the Lord 4196
Ps 26: 6 so will I compass thine *a*, "
43: 4 Then will I go unto the *a* of God, "
51:19 they offer bullocks upon thine *a*. "
118:27 unto the horns of the *a*. "
Isa 6: 6 with the tongs from off the *a*: "
19:19 in that day shall there be an *a* "
27: 9 maketh all the stones of the *a* "
36: 7 Ye shall worship before this *a*? "
56: 7 accepted upon mine *a*; "
60: 7 with acceptance on mine *a*, "
La 2: 7 The Lord hath cast off his *a*, "
Eze 8: 5 at the gate of the *a* this image "
16 between the porch and the *a*, "
9: 2 stood beside the brasen *a*. "
40:46 the keepers of the charge of the *a*: "
47 the *a* that was before the house. "
41:22 The *a* of wood was three cubits "
43:13 measures of the *a* after the cubits: "
13 the higher place of the *a*. "
15 So the *a* shall be four cubits: 741
15 and from the *a* and upward "
16 And the *a* shall be twelve cubits "
18 are the ordinances of the *a* 4196
22 they shall cleanse the *a*, "
26 Seven days shall they purge the *a* "
27 your burnt offerings upon the *a*, "
45:19 four corners of the settle of the *a*, "
47: 1 at the south side of the *a*. "
Joel 1:13 howl, ye ministers of the *a*: "
2:17 weep between the porch and the *a*, "
Am 2: 8 laid to pledge by every *a*, "
3:14 the horns of the *a* shall be cut off, "
9: 1 the Lord standing upon the *a*: "
Zec 9:15 as the corners of the *a*. "
14:20 be like the bowls before the *a*. "
Mal 1: 7 offer polluted bread upon mine *a*; "
10 do ye kindle fire on mine *a* for "
2:13 covering the *a* of the Lord with "
M't 5:23 bring thy gift to the *a*, *2379*
24 thy gift before the *a*, "
23:18 shall swear by the *a*, "
19 the gift, or the *a* "
20 shall swear by the *a*, "
35 the temple and the *a*. "
Lu 1:11 of the *a* of incense. "
11:51 between the *a* and the temple: "
Ac 17:23 I found an *a* with this inscription, *1041*
1Co 9:13 and they which wait at the *a* *2379*
13 partakers with the *a*? "
10:18 partakers of the *a*? "
Heb 7:13 no man gave attendance at the *a*. "
13:10 We have an *a*, whereof "
Jas 2:21 offered Isaac his son upon the *a*? "
Re 6: 9 under the *a* the souls "
8: 3 stood at the *a*, having a golden "
3 of all saints upon the golden *a* "
5 filled it with fire of the *a*, "
9:13 horns of the golden *a* "
11: 1 the temple of God, and the *a*, "
14:18 another angel came out from the *a*, "
16: 7 I heard another out of the *a* say, "

altars
Ex 34:13 But ye shall destroy their *a*, 4196
Nu 3:31 the candlestick, and the *a*, "
23: 1 Build me here seven *a*, "
4 I have prepared seven *a*, "
14 and built seven *a*, "
29 Build me here seven *a*, and prepare "
De 7: 5 ye shall destroy their *a*, "
12: 3 ye shall overthrow their *a*, "
J'g 2: 2 ye shall throw down their *a*: "
1Ki 19:10, 14 thrown down thine *a*, "
2Ki 11:18 his *a* and his images "
18 the priest of Baal before the *a*. "
18:22 whose *a* Hezekiah hath taken "
21: 3 he reared up *a* for Baal, "
4 he built *a* in the house of the Lord, "
5 built *a* for all the host of heaven "
23:12 the *a* that were on the top 4196
12 the *a* which Manasseh had made "
20 that were there upon the *a*, "
2Ch 14: 3 he took away the *a* of the strange "
23:17 brake his *a* and his images "
17 the priest of Baal before the *a*. "
28:24 *a* in every corner of Jerusalem. "
30:14 they arose and took away the *a* "
14 the *a* for incense took they away, "
31: 1 the *a* out of all Judah 4196
32:12 away his high places and his *a*, "
33: 3 he reared up *a* for Baalim, "
4 Also he built *a* in the house "
5 built *a* for all the host of heaven "
15 all the *a* that he had built "
34: 4 they brake down the *a* of Baalim "
5 bones of the priests upon their *a*, "
7 when he had broken down the *a* "
Ps 84: 3 even thine *a*, O Lord of hosts, "
Isa 17: 8 he shall not look to the *a*, "
36: 7 whose *a* Hezekiah hath taken "
65: 3 burneth incense upon *a* of brick; *
Jer 11:13 set up *a* to that shameful thing, 4196
13 even *a* to burn incense unto Baal. "
17: 1 upon the horns of your *a*; "
2 their children remember their *a* "
Eze 6: 4 your *a* shall be desolate, "
5 your bones round about your *a*. "
6 that your *a* may be laid waste "
13 round about their *a*, "
Ho 8:11 Ephraim hath made many *a* to sin, "
11 *a* shall be unto him to sin. "
10: 1 he hath increased the *a*; "
2 he shall break down their *a*, "
8 shall come up on their *a*; "
12:11 their *a* are as heaps "
Am 3:14 I will also visit the *a* of Beth-el: "
Ro 11: 3 and digged down thine *a*; *2379*

Al-taschith (*al-tas'-kith*)
Ps 57:*title* To the chief Musician, *A*, 516
58:*title* chief Musician, *A*, Michtam of "
59:*title* *A*, Michtam of David; when Saul "
75:*title* Musician, *A*, A Psalm or Song "

alter See also ALTERED; ALTERETH.
Le 27:10 He shall not *a* it, nor change it, 2498
Ezr 6:11 that whosoever shall *a* this word, 8133
12 that shall put to their hand to *a* "
Ps 89:34 covenant will I not break, nor *a* 8138

altered
Es 1:19 it be not *a*, That Vashti come 5674
Lu 9:29 of his countenance was *a*, *1096, 2087*

altereth
Da 6: 8, 12 and Persians, which *a* not. 5709

although
Ex 13:17 *a* that was near; for God said, 3588
Jos 22:17 *a* there was a plague in the
2Sa 23: 5 *A* my house be not so with God; *3588
5 *a* he make it not to grow. "
1Ki 20: 5 *A* I have sent unto thee, saying, * "
Es 7: 4 held my tongue, *a* the enemy "
Job 2: 3 integrity, *a* thou movedst me "
5: 6 *A* affliction cometh not forth *3588
35:14 *A* thou sayest thou shalt *637, "
Jer 31:32 *a* I was an husband unto them,
Eze 7:13 is sold, *a* they were yet alive:
11:16 *A* I have cast them far off *3588
16 and *a* I have scattered them * 272
Hab 3:17 *A* the fig tree shall not blossom, * "
M'r 14:29 *A* all shall be offended, *2532, 1487*
Heb 4: 3 *a* the works were finished *2543*

all-to (J'g 9:53) See ALL; ALTOGETHER.

altogether
Ge 18:21 whether they have done *a* 3617
Ex 11: 1 thrust you out hence *a*.
19:18 And mount Sinai was *a* on a 3605
Nu 16:13 make thyself *a* a prince over us? *1571
23:11 behold, thou hast blest them *a*.
24:10 behold, thou hast *a* blessed them
30:14 her husband *a* hold his peace
De 16:20 which is *a* just shalt thou follow,
2Ch 12:12 he would not destroy him *a*: 3617
Es 4:14 For if thou *a* holdest thy peace
Job 13: 5 O that ye would *a* hold your
27:12 why then are ye thus *a* vain?
Ps 19: 9 are true and righteous *a*. 3162
39: 5 every man at his best state is *a* 3605
50:21 thoughtest that I was *a* such an
53: 3 they are *a* become filthy; *3162
62: 9 they are *a* lighter than vanity. * "
139: 4 lo, O Lord, thou knowest it *a*. 3605
Isa 10: 8 Are not my princes *a* kings? *3162
Jer 5: 5 these have *a* broken the yoke, * "
10: 8 they are *a* brutish and foolish: * 259
15:18 wilt thou be *a* unto me as a *
30:11 not leave thee *a* unpunished. *
49:12 that shall *a* go unpunished?
Joh 9:34 Thou wast *a* born in sins, *3650*
Ac 26:29 both almost, and *a* such as *1722, 4183*
1Co 5:10 Yet not *a* with the fornicators ‡*3843*
9:10 Or saith he it *a* for our sakes? ‡

Alush (*a'-lush*)
Nu 33:13 Dophkah, and encamped in *A*. 442
14 removed from *A*, and encamped "

Alvah (*al'-vah*) See also ALIAH.
Ge 36:40 names; duke Timnah, duke *A*, 5933

Alvan (*al'-van*) See also ALIAN.
Ge 36:23 children of Shobal were these; *A*, 5935

alway See also ALWAYS.
Ex 25:30 the table shewbread before me *a*. 8548
Nu 9:16 So it was *a*: the cloud covered it "
De 11: 1 his commandments, *a*. 3605, 3117
28:33 oppressed and crushed *a*: "
2Sa 9:10 shall eat bread *a* at my table. 8548
1Ki 11:36 have a light *a* before me 3605, 3117
2Ki 8:19 to give him *a* a light, " "
Job 7:16 I would not live *a*: 5769
Ps 9:18 needy shall not *a* be forgotten: 5331
119:112 heart to perform thy statutes *a*, *5769
Pr 28:14 Happy is the man that feareth *a*: 8548
M't 28:20 I am with you *a*, even unto *3956, 2250*
Joh 7: 6 but your time is *a* ready. *3842*
Ac 10: 2 the people, and prayed to God *a*. *1275*
Ro 11:10 bow down their back *a*. "
2Co 4:11 we which live are *a* delivered *104*
6:10 As sorrowful, yet *a* rejoicing; "
Ph'p 4: 4 Rejoice in the Lord *a*: "
Col 4: 6 Let your speech be *a* with grace, * "
1Th 2:16 to fill up their sins *a*: "
2Th 2:13 bound to give thanks *a* to God "
Tit 1:12 The Cretians are *a* liars, "
Heb 3:10 They do *a* err in their heart: "

always See also ALWAY.
Ge 6: 3 My spirit shall not *a* strive with *5769
Ex 27:20 to cause the lamp to burn *a*. *8548
28:38 it shall be *a* upon his forehead, "
De 5:29 all my commandments *a*, 3605, 3117
6:24 for our good *a*, " "
11:12 the Lord thy God are *a* upon it, 8548
14:23 to fear the Lord thy God *a*. 3605, 3117
1Ch 16:15 Be ye mindful *a* of his covenant; *5769
2Ch 18: 7 good unto me, but *a* evil: 3605, 3117
Job 27:10 will he *a* call upon God? * " 6256
32: 9 Great men are not *a* wise: *
Ps 10: 5 His ways are *a* grievous; *3605, 6256
16: 8 I have set the Lord *a* before me: 8548
103: 9 He will not *a* chide: 5331
Pr 5:19 be thou ravished *a* with her love. 8548
8:30 rejoicing *a* before him; 3605, 6256
Ec 9: 8 Let thy garments be *a* white; " "
Isa 57:16 neither will I be *a* wroth: 5331
Jer 20:17 her womb to be *a* great with me. 5769
Eze 38: 8 which have been *a* waste: *8548
M't 18:10 their angels do *a* behold the *1223, 3956*
26:11 ye have the poor *a* with you; *3842*
11 but me ye have not *a*. "
M'k 5: 5 *a*, night and day, he was in the *1275*
14: 7 ye have the poor with you *a*, *3842*
7 but me ye have not *a*. "
Lu 18: 1 that men ought *a* to pray, "
21:36 pray *a*, that ye may be *1722, 3956, 2540*
Joh 8:29 I do *a* those things that please *3842*
11:42 I knew that thou hearest me *a*: "
12: 8 the poor *a* ye have with you; "
8 but me ye have not *a*. "
18:20 whither the Jews *a* resort; * "
Ac 2:25 I foresaw the Lord *a* before *1223, 3956*
7:51 ye do *a* resist the Holy Ghost: *104*
24: 3 We accept it *a*, and in all places, **3839*
16 *a* a conscience void of offence **1275*
Ro 1: 9 mention of you *a* in my prayers; *3842*
1Co 1: 4 thank my God *a* on your behalf, "
15:58 *a* abounding in the work of the "
2Co 2:14 *a* causeth us to triumph in Christ, "
4:10 *A* bearing about in the body "
5: 6 Therefore we are *a* confident, * "
9: 8 that ye, *a* having all sufficiency "
Ga 4:18 affected *a* in a good thing, "
Eph 5:20 Giving thanks *a* for all things * "
6:18 Praying *a* with all **1722, 3956, 2540*
Ph'p 1: 4 *A* in every prayer of mine for you *3842*
20 with all boldness, as *a*, so now "
2:12 my beloved, as ye have *a* obeyed, "
Col 1: 3 praying *a* for you, "
4:12 *a* labouring fervently for you "
1Th 1: 2 We give thanks to God *a* for you "
3: 6 have good remembrance of us *a*, "
2Th 1: 3 bound to thank God *a* for you, * "
11 Wherefore also we pray *a* for you, "
3:16 you peace *a* by all means. **1223, 3956*
Ph'm 4 mention of thee *a* in my prayers, *3842*
Heb 9: 6 went *a* into the first tabernacle, **1275*
1Pe 3:15 be ready *a* to give an answer *104*
2Pe 1:12 *a* in remembrance of these things, "
15 these things *a* in remembrance. **1539*

am
Ge 4: 9 *A* I my brother's keeper?
15: 1 Fear not, Abram: I *a* thy shield,
7 I *a* the Lord that brought thee
17: 1 unto him, I *a* the Almighty God;
18:12 herself, saying, After I *a* waxed
13 surety bear a child, which *a* old?
27 speak unto the Lord, which *a* but
22: 1 and he said, Behold, here I *a*.
7 and he said, Here *a* I, my son.
11 Abraham: and he said, Here *a* I.
23: 4 I *a* a stranger and a sojourner
24:24 I *a* the daughter of Bethuel the
34 he said, I *a* Abraham's servant.
25:22 said, If it be so, why *a* I thus? *
30 for I *a* faint: therefore was his
32 Behold, I *a* at the point to die:
26:24 I *a* the God of Abraham thy father:
24 I *a* with thee, and will bless thee,
27: 1 said unto him, Behold, here *a* I.
2 Behold now, I *a* old, I know not
11 hairy man, and I *a* a smooth man:
18 Here *a* I; who art thou, my son?
19 his father, I *a* Esau thy firstborn;
24 son Esau? And he said, I *a*.
32 I *a* thy son, thy firstborn Esau.
46 said to Isaac, I *a* weary of my life,
28:13 said, I *a* the Lord God of Abraham
15 And, behold, I *a* with thee,
30: 2 and he said, *A* I in God's stead,
13 And Leah said, Happy *a* I,
31:11 Jacob: and I said, Here *a* I.
13 I *a* the God of Bethel, where thou

Ge 32:10 I a' not worthy of the least of all
10 and now I a' become two bands.
35:11 unto him, I a' God Almighty:
37:13 And he said to him, Here a' I.
38:25 whose these are, a' I with child:
41:44 I a' Pharaoh, and without thee
43:14 bereaved of my children, I a'
45: 3 said unto his brethren, I a' Joseph;
4 he said, I a' Joseph your brother,
46: 2 Jacob: and he said, Here a' I.
3 I a' God, the God of thy father:
49:29 a' to be gathered unto my people:
50:19 for a' I in the place of God?
Ex 3: 4 Moses. And he said, Here a' I.
6 he said, I a' the God of thy father,
8 I a' come down to deliver them
11 Who a' I, that I should go unto
14 said unto Moses, I A' that I A': 1961
14 Israel, I A' hath sent me unto you. "
19 I a' sure that the king of Egypt *
4:10 O Lord, I a' not eloquent,
10 but I a' slow of speech, and of a
6: 2 and said unto him, I a' the Lord:
6 children of Israel, I a' the Lord,
7 know that I a' the Lord your God,
8 you for a heritage: I a' the Lord.
12 me, who a' of uncircumcised lips?
29 unto Moses, saying, I a' the Lord:
30 Behold, I a' of uncircumcised lips,
7: 5 shall know that I a' the Lord,
17 shalt know that I a' the Lord:
8:22 I a' the Lord in the midst of the
9:29 As soon as I a' gone out of the city,
10: 2 know how that I a' the Lord.
12:12 execute judgment: I a' the Lord.
14: 4 may know that I a' the Lord.
18 that I a' the Lord, when I have
15:26 for I a' the Lord that healeth thee.
16:12 know that I a' the Lord your God.
18: 6 I thy father in law Jethro a' come
20: 2 I a' the Lord thy God, which have
5 for I the Lord thy God a' a jealous
22:27 that I will hear; for I a' gracious.
29:46 they shall know that I a' the Lord
46 dwell among them: I a' the Lord
31:13 a' the Lord that doth sanctify you.
Le 8:35 die not: for so I a' commanded.
10:13 by fire: for so I a' commanded.
11:44 For I a' the Lord your God:
44 and ye shall be holy; for I a' holy:
45 For I a' the Lord that bringeth you
45 therefore be holy, for I a' holy.
18: 2 unto them, I a' the Lord your God.
4 therein: I a' the Lord your God.
5 shall live in them: I a' the Lord.
6 their nakedness: I a' the Lord.
21 the name of thy God: I a' the Lord.
30 therein: I a' the Lord your God.
19: 2 for I the Lord your God a' holy.
3 sabbaths: I a' the Lord your God.
4 gods: I a' the Lord your God.
10 stranger: I a' the Lord your God.
12 the name of thy God: I a' the Lord.
14 shalt fear thy God: I a' the Lord.
16 of thy neighbour: I a' the Lord.
25 thereof: I a' the Lord your God.
30 my sanctuary: I a' the Lord.
31 by them: I a' the Lord your God.
32 and fear thy God: I a' the Lord.
34 of Egypt: I a' the Lord your God.
36 I a' the Lord your God, which
37 and do them: I a' the Lord.
20: 7 be ye holy: for I a' the Lord
8 I a' the Lord which sanctify you.
24 I a' the Lord your God, which have
26 for I the Lord a' holy, and have
21: 8 Lord, which sanctify you, a' holy.
12 God is upon him: I a' the Lord.
22: 2 they hallow unto me: I a' the Lord.
3 off from my presence: I a' the Lord.
8 himself therewith: I a' the Lord.
30 until the morrow: I a' the Lord.
31 and do them: I a' the Lord.
32 of Israel: I a' the Lord which
33 to be your God: I a' the Lord.
23:22 stranger: I a' the Lord your God.
43 Egypt: I a' the Lord your God.
24:22 country: for I a' the Lord your God.
25:17 thy God: for I a' the Lord your God.
38 I a' the Lord your God, which
55 Egypt: I am the Lord your God.
26: 1 unto it: for I a' the Lord your God.
2 my sanctuary: I a' the Lord.
13 I a' the Lord your God, which
44 them: for I a' the Lord their God.
45 might be their God: I a' the Lord.
Nu 3:13 mine shall they be: I a' the Lord.
41 Levites for me (I a' the Lord)
45 Levites shall be mine: I a' the Lord.
10:10 God: I a' the Lord your God.
11:14 I a' not able to bear all this people
21 The people among whom I a',
15:41 I a' the Lord your God, which
41 God: I a' the Lord your God.
18:20 I a' thy part and thine inheritance
22:30 A' not I thine ass, upon which thou
37 a' I not able indeed to promote
38 Lo, I a' come unto thee: have I now
De 1: 9 I a' not able to bear you myself
42 fight; for I a' not among you;
5: 6 I a' the Lord thy God, which
9 the Lord thy God a' a jealous God,
26: 3 that I a' come unto the country
29: 6 know that I a' the Lord your God.
31: 2 I a' an hundred and twenty years
27 while I a' yet alive with you this
De 32:39 even I, a' he, and there is no god
Jos 5:14 the host of the Lord a' I now come.
14:10 I a' this day fourscore and five
11 As yet I a' as strong this day as I
17:14 inherit, seeing I a' a great people,
23: 2 I a' old and stricken in age:
14 this day I a' going the way of all
J'g 4:19 little water to drink; for I a' thirsty.
6:10 unto you, I a' the Lord your God;
15 and I a' the least in my father's
8: 5 and I a' pursuing after Zebah
9: 2 I a' your bone and your flesh.
13:11 the woman? And he said, I a'.
17: 9 I a' a Levite of Beth-lehem-judah,
18: 4 hired me, and I a' his priest.
19:18 Ephraim; from thence a' I:
18 but I a' now going to the house
Ru 1:12 for I a' too old to have an husband.
2:10 of me, seeing I a' a stranger?
3: 9 answered, I a' Ruth thine handmaid:
12 true that I a' thy near kinsman:
4: 4 beside thee; and I a' after thee.
1Sa 1: 8 a' not I better to thee than ten sons?
15 I a' a woman of a sorrowful spirit:
26 I a' the woman that stood by thee
3: 4 and he answered, Here a' I.
5 and said, Here a' I; for thou
6, 8 went to Eli, and said, Here a' I;
16 son. And he answered, Here a' I.
4:16 Eli, I a' he that came out of the
9:19 Saul, and said, I a' the seer:
21 answered and said, A' not I
12: 2 and I a' old and grayheaded;
3 Behold, here I a': witness against
14: 7 I a' with thee according to thy
16: 2 I a' come to sacrifice to the Lord.
5 Peaceably: I a' come to sacrifice
17: 8 a' not I a Philistine, and ye
43 said unto David, A' I a dog,
58 I a' the son of thy servant Jesse
18:18 David said unto Saul, Who a' I?
23 that I a' a poor man, and
22:12 he answered, Here I a', my lord.
28:15 answered, I a' sore distressed;
30:13 said, I a' a young man of Egypt,
2Sa 1: 3 the camp of Israel a' I escaped.
7 me. And I answered, Here a' I.
8 him, I a' an Amalekite.
13 I a' the son of a stranger, an
26 I a' distressed for thee, my brother
2:20 Asahel? And he answered, I a'. *
3: 8 A' I a dog's head, which against
39 And I a' this day weak, though
7:18 he said, Who a' I, O Lord God?
9: 8 upon such a dead dog as I a'?
11: 5 David, and said, I a' with child.
14: 5 she answered, I a' indeed a widow
15 that I a' come to speak of this
32 Wherefore a' I come from Geshur?
15:26 behold, here a' I, let him do to me
19:20 I a' come the first this day of all
22 do not I know that I a' this day
35 I a' this day fourscore years old:
20:17 And he answered, I a' he. Then
19 I a' one of them that are peaceable
24:14 I a' in a great strait: let us fall
1Ki 3: 7 and I a' but a little child: I know
8:20 and I a' risen up in the room of
13:14 from Judah? And he said, I a'.
18 I a' a prophet also as thou art;
31 when I a' dead, then bury me in
14: 6 for I a' sent to thee with heavy
17:12 I a' gathering two sticks, that I
18: 8 And he answered him, I a': *
12 as soon as I a' gone from thee,
36 and that I a' thy servant, and that
19: 4 for I a' not better than my fathers.
10 and I, even I only, a' left; and
14 I only, a' left; and they seek my
20: 4 saying, I a' thine, and all that I
13 thou shalt know that I a' the Lord.
28 ye shall know that I a' the Lord
22: 4 I a' as thou art, my people as thy
34 of the host; for I a' wounded.
2Ki 2:10 see me when I a' taken from thee,
3: 7 I a' as thou art, my people as thy
5: 7 A' I God, to kill and to make alive,
16: 7 I a' thy servant and thy son: come
18:25 A' I now come up without the Lord
19:23 I a' come up to the height of the
21:12 I a' bringing such evil upon *
1Ch 17:16 Who a' I, O Lord God, and what is
21:13 I a' in a great strait: let me fall
29:14 But who a' I, and what is my people,
2Ch 2: 6 who a' I then, that I should build
9 the house which I a' about to build
6:10 for I a' risen up in the room of
10 a' set on the throne of Israel, *
18: 3 I a' as thou art, and my people as
33 of the host; for I a' wounded. *
35:23 me away; for I a' sore wounded.
Ezr 9: 6 God, I a' ashamed and blush to lift
Ne 6: 3 I a' doing a great work, so that I
11 there, that, being as I a', would *
Es 5:12 to morrow a' I invited unto her
Job 1:15 and I only a' escaped alone to tell
16 consumed them; and I only a'
17 the sword; and I only a' escaped
19 are dead; and I only a' escaped
7: 3 So a' I made to possess months of
4 and I a' full of tossings to and fro
8 eyes are upon me, and I a' not. *
12 A' I a sea, or a whale, that thou
20 so that I a' a burden to myself?
9:20 if I say, I a' perfect, it shall *
28 I a' afraid of all my sorrows, I know
Job 9:32 For he is not a man, as I a', that I
10: 7 Thou knowest that I a' not wicked;
15 I a' full of confusion: therefore *
11: 4 doctrine is pure, and I a' clean in
12: 3 I a' not inferior to you: yea, who 1961
4 I a' as one mocked of his neighbour,
13: 2 also: I a' not inferior unto you.
16: 6 though I forbear, what a' I eased?
19: 7 cry out of wrong, but I a' not heard:
10 and I a' gone: and mine hope hath
15 I a' an alien in their sight
20 and I a' escaped with the skin of
21: 6 I remember I a' afraid, and
23:15 Therefore a' I troubled at his
15 I consider, I a' afraid of him.
30: 9 And now a' I their song,
9 yea, I a' their byword.
19 and I a' become like dust and ashes.
29 I a' a brother to dragons, and a
32: 6 said, I a' young, and ye are very
18 For I a' full of matter, the spirit
33: 6 Behold, I a' according to thy wish
6 I also a' formed out of the clay.
9 I a' clean without transgression,
9 I a' innocent; neither is there
34: 5 For Job hath said, I a' righteous:
40: 4 Behold, I a' vile; what shall I
Ps 6: 2 for I a' weak: O Lord, heal me;
6 I a' weary with my groaning;
13: 4 trouble me rejoice when I a' moved.
17: 3 I a' purposed that my mouth shall
22: 2 the night season, and a' not silent.
6 But I a' a worm, and no man;
14 I a' poured out like water, and all
25:16 for I am desolate and afflicted.
28: 7 trusted in him, and I a' helped:
31: 9 O Lord, for I am in trouble:
12 I a' forgotten as a dead man out
12 I a' like a broken vessel.
22 I a' cut off from before thine eyes:
35: 3 say unto my soul, I a' thy salvation.
37:25 I have been young, and now a' old;
38: 6 I a' troubled;
6 I a' bowed down greatly; *
8 I a' feeble and sore broken:
17 For I a' ready to halt, and my
39: 4 that I may know how frail I a'.
10 I a' consumed by the blow of thine
39:12 for I a' a stranger with thee,
40:12 so that I a' not able to look up;
17 But I a' poor and needy:
46:10 Be still, and know that I a' God:
50: 7 I a' God, even thy God.
52: 8 But I a' like a green olive tree
56: 3 What time I a' afraid, I will trust
69: 2 I a' come into deep waters, where
3 I a' weary of my crying:
8 I a' become a stranger unto my
17 I a' in trouble: hear me speedily.
20 and I a' full of heaviness:
29 But I a' poor and sorrowful:
70: 5 But I a' poor and needy;
71: 7 I a' as a wonder unto many;
18 when I a' old and grayheaded,
73:23 Nevertheless I a' continually with
77: 4 I a' so troubled that I cannot
81:10 I a' the Lord thy God which
86: 1 hear me: for I a' poor and needy.
2 Preserve my soul; for I am holy:
88: 4 I a' counted with them that go
4 I a' as a man that hath no strength: 1961
8 I a' shut up, and I cannot come
15 I a' afflicted and ready to die from
15 I suffer thy terrors I a' distracted.
102: 2 in the day when I a' in trouble; *
6 I a' like a pelican of the wilderness: 1961
6 a' like an owl of the desert. "
7 I watch, and a' as a sparrow alone
11 and I a' withered like grass.
109:22 For I a' poor and needy,
23 I a' gone like the shadow when
23 I a' tossed up and down as the
116:16 truly I a' thy servant;
16 I a' thy servant,
119:19 I a' a stranger in the earth:
63 I a' a companion of all them
83 I a' become like a bottle in the
94 I a' thine, save me; for I have
107 I a' afflicted very much: quicken
120 fear of thee; and I a' afraid of
125 I a' thy servant; give me
141 I a' small and despised: yet do
120: 7 I a' for peace: but when I speak,
139:14 I a' fearfully and wonderfully
18 I awake, I a' still with thee.
142: 6 for I a' brought very low:
143:12 for I a' thy servant.
Pr 8:14 I a' understanding;
20: 9 I a' pure from my sin?
26:19 and saith, A' not I in sport?
30: 2 I a' more brutish than any man,
Ec 1:16 Lo, I a' come to great estate, *
Ca 1: 5 I a' black, but comely, O ye
6 not upon me, because I a' black,
2: 1 I a' the rose of Sharon, and the
5 for I a' sick of love.
16 My beloved is mine, and I a' his:
5: 1 I a' come into my garden, my
8 ye tell him, that I a' sick of love.
6: 3 I a' my beloved's, and my beloved
7:10 I a' my beloved's, and his desire
8:10 I a' a wall, and my breasts like
Isa 1:11 I a' full of the burnt offerings of
14 I a' weary to bear them.
6: 5 Woe is me! for I a' undone;
5 because I a' a man of unclean

Isa 6: 8 Then said I, Here a· I; send me.
10:13 by my wisdom; for I a· prudent: ‡
19:11 I a· the son of the wise, the son
21: 8 and I a· set in my ward whole
29:12 and he saith, I a· not learned.
33:24 inhabitant shall not say, I a· sick:
36:10 a· I now come up without the
37:24 of my chariots a· I come up
38:10 I a· deprived of the residue of my
14 O Lord, I a· oppressed; undertake
41: 4 the first, and with the last; I a· he.
10 Fear thou not; for I a· with thee:
10 be not dismayed; for I a· thy God:
42: 8 I a· the Lord; that is my name:
43: 3 For I a· the Lord thy God, the
5 Fear not; for I a· with thee:
10 and understand that I a· he:
11 I, even I, a· the Lord;
12 saith the Lord, that I a· God.
13 Yea, before the day was I a· he;
15 I a· the Lord, your Holy One,
25 I, even I, a· he that blotteth out
44: 5 One shall say, I a· the Lord's;
6 I a· the first,
6 and I a· the last;
16 and saith, Aha, I a· warm,
24 I a· the Lord that maketh all
45: 3 a· the God of Israel. ‡
5, 6, I a· the Lord, and there is
18 I a· the Lord; and there is none
22 I a· God, and there is none else.
46: 4 and even to your old age I a· he;
9 I a· God, and there is none else;
9 I a· God, and there is none like me,
47: 8 that sayest in thine heart, I a·.
10 I a·, and none else beside me,
48:12 I a· he; I a· the first,
12 I also a· the last.
16 the time that it was, there a· I:
17 I a· the Lord thy God which
49:21 lost my children, and a· desolate,
23 thou shalt know that I a· the Lord:
26 that I the Lord a· thy Saviour
51:12 even I, a· he that comforteth you:
15 But I a· the Lord thy God,
52: 6 in that day that I a· he that doth
56: 3 Behold, I a· a dry tree.
58: 9 and he shall say, Here I a·.
60:16 that I the Lord a· thy Saviour
65: 1 I a· sought of them that asked
1 I a· found of them that sought
5 for I a· holier than thou.
Jer 1: 6 I cannot speak: for I a· a child.
7 Say not, I a· a child:
8 I a· with thee to deliver thee,
19 I a· with thee, saith the Lord,
2:23 canst thou say, I a· not polluted,
35 sayest, Because I a· innocent,
3:12 for I a· merciful, saith the Lord,
14 for I a· married unto you:
4:19 I a· pained at my very heart;
6:11 I a· full of the fury of the Lord;
11 I a· weary with holding in:
8:21 daughter of my people a· I hurt;
21 I a· black; astonishment hath
9:24 that I a· the Lord which exercise
15: 6 I a· weary with repenting.
16 for I a· called by thy name,
20 I a· with thee to save thee and to
20: 7 I a· in derision daily, every one
21:13 I a· against thee, O inhabitant of
23: 9 I a· like a drunken man, and like
23 A· I a God at hand, saith the Lord,
30, 31 I a· against the prophets, saith
32 I a· against them that prophesy
24: 7 to know me, that I a· the Lord;
26:14 behold, I a· in your hand:
29:23 and a· a witness, saith the Lord.
30:11 For I a· with thee, saith the Lord,
31: 9 for I a· a father to Israel,
32:27 I a· the Lord, the God of all flesh:
36: 5 Baruch, saying, I a· shut up;
38:19 I a· afraid of the Jews that are
42:11 for I a· with you to save you,
46:28 for I a· with thee; for I will make
51:25 Behold, I a· against thee, O
La 1:11 for I a· become vile.
14 I a· not able to rise up.
20 I a· in distress: my bowels are
3: 1 I a· the man that hath seen
54 mine head; then I said, I a· cut off.
63 sitting down and rising up; I a·
Eze 5: 8 Behold, I, even I, a· against thee,
6: 7, 14 shall know that I a· the Lord.
10, 13 shall know that I a· the Lord,
7: 4 ye shall know that I a· the Lord.
9 ye shall know that I a· the Lord *
27 they shall know that I a· the Lord.
11:10, 12 shall know that I a· the Lord.
12:11 I a· your sign: like as I have done,
15, 16, 20 shall know that I a· the Lord.
25 for I a· the Lord: I will speak,
13: 8 I a· against you, saith the Lord
9, 14 shall know that I a· the Lord
20 Behold, I a· against your pillows,
21, 23 shall know that I a· the Lord.
14: 8 ye shall know that I a· the Lord.
15: 7 ye shall know that I a· the Lord,
16:62 thou shalt know that I a· the Lord:
63 when I a· pacified toward thee *
20: 5, 7 I a· the Lord your God.
12 I a· the Lord that sanctify them.
19 I a· the Lord your God; walk in
20 know that I a· the Lord your God.
26, 38, 42, 44 know that I a· the Lord,
21: 3 I a· against thee, and will draw

Eze 22:16 thou shalt know that I a· the Lord.
26 and I a· profaned among them.
23:49 shall know that I a· the Lord God.
24:24 shall know that I a· the Lord God.
27 they shall know that I a· the Lord.
25: 5 ye shall know that I a· the Lord.
7 thou shalt know that I a· the Lord.
11 they shall know that I a· the Lord.
17 shall know that I a· the Lord, when
26: 3 Behold, I a· against thee, O Tyrus,
6 they shall know that I a· the Lord.
27: 3 hast said, I a· of perfect beauty.
28: 2 thou hast said, I a· a God,
9 I a· God? but thou shalt be a man,
22 Behold, I a· against thee, O Zidon;
22 that I a· the Lord, when I shall have
23 shall know that I a· the Lord.
24 shall know that I a· the Lord God.
26 know that I a· the Lord their God.
29: 3 Behold, I a· against thee, Pharaoh
6 shall know that I a· the Lord,
9 they shall know that I a· the Lord:
10 Behold, therefore I a· against thee,
16 shall know that I a· the Lord God.
21 they shall know that I a· the Lord.
30: 8, 19 shall know that I a· the Lord.
22 Behold, I a· against Pharaoh
25, 26 shall know that I a· the Lord.
32:15 shall they know that I a· the Lord.
33:29 shall they know that I a· the Lord,
34:10 I a· against the shepherds; and I
27 they shall know that I a· the Lord,
30 I the Lord their God a· with them,
31 I a· your God, saith the Lord God.
35: 3 I a· against thee, and I will stretch
4 thou shalt know that I a· the Lord.
9 ye shall know that I a· the Lord.
12 shalt know that I a· the Lord, *
15 they shall know that I a· the Lord.
36: 9 For, behold, I a· for you, and I will
11 ye shall know that I a· the Lord.
23 shall know that I a· the Lord,
38 they shall know that I a· the Lord.
37: 6 ye shall know that I a· the Lord.
13 know that I a· the Lord, when
38: 3 I a· against thee, O Gog, the chief
23 they shall know that I a· the Lord.
39: 1 I a· against thee, O Gog, the chief
6 they shall know that I a· the Lord.
7 shall know that I a· the Lord,
22 Israel shall know that I a· the
27 and a· sanctified in them in the
28 shall they know that I a· the Lord,
44:28 I a· their inheritance: and ye shall
28 no possession in Israel: I a· their
Da 9:22 O Daniel, I a· now come forth to
23 and I a· come to shew thee; for
10:11 stand upright: for unto thee a· I
12 thy words were heard, and I a· come
14 Now I a· come to make thee
20 of Persia; and when I a· gone *
Ho 2: 2 neither a· I her husband: let her
11: 9 for I a· God, and not man; the
12: 8 Yet I a· become rich, I have found
9 And I that a· the Lord thy God
13: 4 Yet I a· the Lord thy God from the
14: 8 I a· like a green fir tree. From me
Joe 2:27 know that I a· in the midst of Israel,
27 and that I a· the Lord your God,
3:10 let the weak say, I a· strong.
17 ye know that I a· the Lord your
Am 2:13 Behold, I a· pressed under you, *
Jon 1: 9 I a· an Hebrew; and I fear the
2: 4 I a· cast out of thy sight; yet I will
Mic 3: 8 But truly I a· full of power by the
7: 1 for I a· as when they have gathered
Na 2:13 Behold, I a· against thee, saith the
3: 5 Behold, I a· against thee, saith the
Hab 2: 1 what I shall answer when I a· *
Zep 2:15 I a·, and there is none beside me:
Hag 1:13 saying, I a· with you, saith the
2: 4 for I a· with you, saith the Lord of
Zec 1:14 I a· jealous for Jerusalem and for
15 And I a· very sore displeased with
16 I a· returned to Jerusalem with
8: 3 I a· returned unto Zion, and will
10: 6 for I a· the Lord their God, and
11: 5 for I a· rich; and their own
13: 5 I a· no prophet,
5 I a· an husbandman;
Mal 1:14 for I a· a great king, saith
3: 6 For I a· the Lord, I change not; *
M't 3:11 whose shoes I a· not worthy to 1510
17 my beloved Son, in whom I a· well
5:17 Think not that I a· come to *
17 I a· not come to destroy, but to *
8: 8 I a· not worthy 1510
9 For I a· a man under authority, "
9:13 a· not come to call the righteous.*
28 Believe ye that I a· able to do this?
10:34 Think not that I a· come to send *
35 For I a· come to set a man at *
11:29 for I a· meek and lowly in heart: 1510
15:24 a· not sent but unto the lost sheep *
16:13 that I the Son of man a·? *1511
15 But whom say ye that I a· "
17: 5 my beloved Son, in whom I a· well
18:20 there a· I in the midst of them. 1510
20:15 Is thine eye evil, because I a· good? "
22, 23 with the baptism that I a· *
22:32 I a· the God of Abraham, and the 1510
24: 5 saying, I a· Christ; and shall "
26:32 But after I a· risen again, I will go
61 I a· able to destroy the temple of
27:24 I a· innocent of the blood of this 1510
43 for he said, I am the Son of God. "

M't 28:20 and, lo, I a· with you alway, even 1510
M'r 1: 7 whose shoes I a· not worthy to "
11 Son, in whom I a· well pleased.
8:27 Whom do men say that I a·? 1511
29 But whom say ye that I a·? And "
10:38 baptism that I a· baptized with?
39 baptism that I a· baptized withal
12:26 I a· the God of Abraham, and the
13: 6 in my name, saying, I a· Christ; 1510
14:28 But after that I a· risen, I will go
62 And Jesus said, I a·: and ye shall 1510
Lu 1:18 for I a· an old man, and my wife
19 I a· Gabriel, that stand in the 1510
19 and a· sent to speak unto thee, *
3:16 whose shoes I a· not worthy to 1510
22 Son, in thee I a· well pleased.
4:43 other cities also: for therefore a· *
5: 8 for I a· a sinful man, O Lord. 1510
7: 6 for I a· not worthy that thou "
8 For I also a· a man set under "
9:18 Whom say the people that I a·? 1511
20 But whom say ye that I a·? Peter "
12:49 I a· come to send fire on the earth;*
50 and how a· I straitened till it
51 Suppose ye that I a· come to give
15:19 And a· no more worthy to be called 1510
21 in thy sight, and a· no more worthy "
16: 3 I cannot dig; to beg I a· ashamed.
4 I a· resolved what to do,
4 that, when I a· put
24 cool my tongue; for I a· tormented
18:11 that I a· not as other men are, 1510
21: 8 saying, I a· Christ; and the time "
22:27 I a· among you as he that serveth. "
33 Lord, I a· ready to go with thee, "
58 And Peter said, Man, I a· not. "
70 he said unto them, Ye say that I a·. "
Joh 1:20 but confessed, I a· not the Christ. "
21 And he saith, I a· not. Art thou that "
23 I a· the voice of one crying in the
27 whose shoe's latchet I a· not 1510
31 therefore a· I come baptizing *
3:28 I a· not the Christ, 1510
28 but that I a· sent "
4: 9 me, which a· a woman of Samaria? 5607
26 I that speak to thee a· he. 1510
5: 7 but while I a· coming, another
43 I a· come in my father's name, and
6:35 said unto them, I a· the bread of 1510
41 I a· the bread which came down "
48 I a· that bread of life. "
51 I a· the living bread which came "
7:28 and ye know whence I a·: "
28 and I a· not come
29 But I know him: for I a· from him, 1510
33 Yet a little while a· I with you, "
34, 36 where I a·, thither ye cannot "
8:12 I a· the light of the world: he that "
16 for I a· not alone, but I and the "
18 I a· one that bear witness of myself, "
23 I a· from above: ye are of this "
23 I a· not of this world. "
24 believe not that I a· he, ye shall "
28 ye know that I a· he, and that I do "
58 Before Abraham was, I a·. "
9: 5 As long as I a· in the world, "
5 I a· the light of the world. "
9 He is like him: but he said, I a· he. "
39 For judgment I a· come into this *
10: 7 I a· the door of the sheep. 1510
9 I a· the door: by me if any man "
10 a· come that they might have life,*
11 I a· the good shepherd: the good 1510
14 I a· the good shepherd, and know "
14 and a· known of mine. *
36 because I said, I a· the Son of God?
11:15 And I a· glad for your sakes that I
25 I a· the resurrection, and the life: 1510
12:26 and where I a·, there shall also my "
46 I a· come a light into the world,
13:13 and ye say well; for so I a·. 1510
19 ye may believe that I a· he. "
33 yet a little while I a· with you. "
14: 3 that where I a·, there ye may be "
6 I a· the way, the truth, the life: "
10 that I a· in the Father, and the
11 Believe me that I a· in the Father,
20 that I a· in my Father, and ye in
15: 1 I a· the true vine, and my Father 1510
5 I a· the vine, ye are the branches: "
16:28 the Father, and a· come into the
32 and yet I a· not alone, because 1510
17:10 mine; and I a· glorified in them.
11 now I a· no more in the world 1510
14, 16 even as I a· not of the world. "
24 be with me where I a·; that they "
18: 5 Jesus saith unto them, I a· he. "
6 he said unto them, I a· he, they "
8 I have told you that I a· he: if "
17 man's disciples? He saith, I a· not."
25 He denied it, and said, I a· not. "
35 A· I a Jew? Thine own nation "
37 Thou sayest that I a· a king. "
19:21 but that he said, I a· King of the "
20:17 for I a· not yet ascended to my "
Ac 7:32 I a· the God of thy fathers, the "
34 and a· come down to deliver them.
9: 5 I a· Jesus whom thou persecutest: 1510
10 he said, Behold, I a· here, Lord.
10:21 Behold, I a· he whom ye seek: 1510
26 Stand up; I myself also a· a man.
13:25 Whom think ye that I a·? 1511
25 I a· not he. But, behold, there 1510
25 his feet I a· not worthy to loose. "
18: 6 I a· clean: from henceforth I will
10 For I a· with thee, and no man 1510

Ac 20:26 that I a' pure from the blood of
21:13 for I a' ready not to be bound only,
39 But Paul said, I a' a man which 1510
39 which a' a Jew of Tarsus, *
22: 3 I a' verily a man which a' a Jew * "
3 which a' a Jew, born in Tarsus, * "
8 I a' Jesus of Nazareth, whom thou 1510
23: 6 Men and brethren, I a' a Pharisee, "
6 of the dead I a' called in question.
24:21 I a' called in question by you this
26: 2 whereof I a' accused of the Jews.
6 And now I stand and a' judged *
7 sake, king Agrippa, I a' accused
15 I a' Jesus whom thou persecutest. 1510
25 I a' not mad, most noble Festus;
26 for I a' persuaded that none of
29 altogether such as I a', except 1510
27:23 the angel of God, whose I a', "
28:20 for the hope of Israel I a' bound
Ro 1:14 I a' debtor both to the Greeks, 1510
15 I a' ready to preach the gospel
16 For I a' not ashamed of the
3: 7 yet a' I also judged as a sinner?
7:14 but I a' carnal, sold under sin. 1510
24 O wretched man that I a'! who
8:38 For I a' persuaded, that neither
11: 1 For I also a' an Israelite, of the 1510
3 and I a' left alone, and they seek my
13 inasmuch as I a' the apostle of 1510
14:14 and a' persuaded by the Lord
15:14 I myself also a' persuaded of you,
29 And I a' sure that, when I come *
16:19 a' glad therefore on your behalf: *
1Co 1:12 one of you saith, I a' of Paul; 1510
3: 4 For while one saith, I a' of Paul; "
4 and another, I a' of Apollos;
4: 4 yet a' I not hereby justified: but
9: 1 A' I not an apostle? 1510
1 a' I not free? have I not seen "
2 yet doubtless I a' to you: for the
22 I a' made all things to all men,
10:30 by grace be a partaker, why a' I
11: 1 of me, even as I also a' of Christ.
12:15 Because I a' not the hand, 1510
15 I a' not of the body; "
16 Because I a' not the eye, "
16 I a' not of the body;
13: 1 I a' become as sounding brass,
2 have not charity, I a' nothing. 1510
12 I know even as also I a' known.
15: 9 For I a' the least of the apostles, 1510
9 that a' not meet "
10 the grace of God I a' what I a': * "
16:17 I a' glad of the coming of
2Co 7: 4 I a' filled with comfort,
4 I a' exceeding joyful *
14 to him of you, I a' not ashamed; *
10: 1 who in presence a' base among
1 being absent a' bold toward you:
2 may not be bold when I a' present
11: 2 For I a' jealous over you with *
21 (I speak foolishly,) I a' bold also.
22 Are they Hebrews? so a' I.
22 Are they Israelites? so a' I.
22 they the seed of Abraham? so a' I.
23 (I speak as a fool) I a' more;
29 I a' not weak? who is offended,
12:10 for when I a' weak, 1510
10 then a' I strong.
11 I a' become a fool in glorying;
11 for in nothing a' I behind the very
14 the third time I a' ready to come
13: 1 is the third time I a' coming to you
Ga 2:19 For I through the law a' dead *
20 I a' crucified with Christ: *
4:11 I a' afraid of you, lest I have
12 be as I a'; for I a' as ye are;
16 A' I therefore become your enemy,
18 and not only when I a' present
Eph 3: 8 who a' less than the least of all
6:20 For which I a' an ambassador
Ph'p 1:17 that I a' set for the defence
23 For I a' in a strait betwixt two,
3:12 a' apprehended of Christ Jesus. *
4:11 in whatsoever state I a', 1510
12 and in all things I a' instructed *
18 I a' full, having received of *
Col 1:23 I Paul a' made a minister; *
25 I a' made a minister, according *
2: 5 flesh, yet a' I with you in the 1510
4: 3 for which I a' also in bonds:
1Ti 1:15 to save sinners; of whom I a' 1510
2: 7 Whereunto I a' ordained a *
2Ti 1: 5 and I a' persuaded that in thee
11 Whereunto I a' appointed a *
12 nevertheless I a' not ashamed:
12 and a' persuaded that he is able
4: 6 For I a' now ready to be offered,
1Pe 1:16 Be ye holy; for I a' holy. 1510
5: 1 I exhort, who a' also an elder,
2Pe 1:13 so long as I a' in this tabernacle, 1510
17 son in whom I a' well pleased.
Rev 1: 8 I a' Alpha and Omega, the 1510
9 I John, who also a' your brother, *
11 I a' Alpha and Omega, the first * 1510
17 not; I a' the first and the last: "
18 I a' he that liveth, and was dead;* "
18 I a' alive for evermore, Amen; "
2:23 know that I a' he which searcheth "
3:17 Because thou sayest, I a' rich,
21 and a' set down with my Father *
18: 7 and a' no widow, and shall see 1510
19:10 I a' thy fellow servant, and of thy "
21: 6 I a' Alpha and Omega, the "
22: 9 for I a' thy fellowservant, and of. "
13 I a' Alpha and Omega, the
Rev 22:16 I a' the root and the offspring 1510

Amad (a'-mad)
Jos 19:26 and A', and Misheal; 6008

Amal (a'-mal)
1Ch 7:35 and Imna, and Shelesh, and A'. 6000

Amalek (am'-al-ek) See also AMALEKITE.
Ge 36:12 and she bare to Eliphaz A': 6002
16 Korah, duke Gatam, and duke A': "
Ex 17: 8 Then came A', and fought with "
9 men, and go out, fight with A': "
10 said to him, and fought with A': "
11 let down his hand, A' prevailed. "
13 And Joshua discomfited A' and "
14 put out the remembrance of A' "
16 the Lord will have war with A' "
Nu 24:20 And when he looked on A', he "
20 A' was the first of the nations; "
De 25:17 Remember what A' did unto thee "
19 blot out the remembrance of A' "
J'g 3:13 the children of Ammon and A', "
5:14 there a root of them against A'; "
1Sa 15: 2 that which A' did to Israel, how "
3 Now go, and smite A', and utterly "
5 And Saul came to a city of A', and "
20 have brought Agag the king of A', "
28:18 his fierce wrath upon A', "
2Sa 8:12 and of A', and of the spoil of "
1Ch 1:36 Gatam, Kenaz, and Timna, and A'. "
18:11 the Philistines, and from A'. "
Ps 83: 7 Gebal, and Ammon, and A'; "

Amalekite (am'-al-ek-ite) See also AMALEKITES.
1Sa 30:13 man of Egypt, servant to an A'; 6003
2Sa 1: 8 And I answered him, I am an A'. "
13 am the son of a stranger, an A'. "

Amalekites (am'-al-ek-ites)
Ge 14: 7 smote all the country of the A', 6003
Nu 13:29 A' dwell in the land of the south:* "
14:25 (Now the A' and the Canaanites * "
43 For the A' and the Canaanites * "
45 Then the A' came down, and the* "
J'g 6: 3 A', and the children of the east "
33 all the Midianites and the A' and "
7:12 A', and all the children of the east "
10:12 The Zidonians also, and the A', "
12:15 Ephraim, in the mount of the A'. "
1Sa 14:48 an host, and smote the A', and "
15: 6 get you down from among the A', "
6 departed from among the A'. "
7 Saul smote the A' from Havilah "
8 he took Agag the king of the A' "
15 have brought them from the A': "
18 utterly destroy the sinners the A', "
20 have utterly destroyed the A'. "
32 to me Agag the king of the A'. "
27: 8 and the Gezerites, and the A': "
30: 1 that the A' had invaded the south, "
18 all that the A' had carried away; "
2Sa 1: 1 from the slaughter of the A', and "
1Ch 4:43 And they smote the rest of the A' "

Amam (a'-mam)
Jos 15:26 A', and Shema, and Moladah, 538

Amana (am-a'-nah)
Ca 4: 8 look from the top of A', 549

Amariah (am-a-ri'-ah)
1Ch 6: 7 Meraioth begat A' 568
7 and A' begat Ahitub, "
11 Azariah begat A', "
11 and A' begat Ahitub, "
52 Meraioth his son, A' his son, "
23:19 Jeriah the first, A' the second, "
24:23 A' the second, Jahaziel the third, "
2Ch 19:11 A' the chief priest is over you "
31:15 Shemaiah, A', and Shecaniah, "
Ezr 7: 3 The son of A', the son of Azariah, "
10:42 Shallum, A', and Joseph. "
Ne 10: 3 Pashur, A', Malchijah, "
11: 4 son of A', the son of Shephatiah, "
12: 2 A', Malluch, Hattush, "
13 of A', Jehohanan; "
Zep 1: 1 the son of A', the son of Hizkiah, "

Amasa (am'-a-sah)
2Sa 17:25 Absalom made A' captain of the 6021
25 which A' was a man's son, "
19:13 And say ye to A', Art thou not "
20: 4 Then said the king to A', "
5 So A' went to assemble the men "
8 which is in Gibeon, A' went before "
9 And Joab said to A', Art thou "
9 And Joab took A' by the beard "
10 But A' took no heed to the sword "
12 And A' wallowed in blood in the "
12 he removed A' out of the highway "
1Ki 2: 5 and unto A' the son of Jether, "
32 and A' the son of Jether, captain "
1Ch 2:17 And Abigail bare A': "
17 and the father of A' was Jether "
2Ch 28:12 and A' the son of Hadlai, stood up "

Amasai (am'-as-ahee)
1Ch 6:25 of Elkanah; A', and Ahimoth. 6022
35 the son of Mahath, the son of A', "
12:18 Then the spirit came upon A, "
15:24 Nathaneel, and A', and Zechariah, "
2Ch 29:12 Levites arose, Mahath the son of A', "

Amashai (am'-ash-ahee)
Ne 11:13 and A' the son of Azareel, 6023

Amasiah (am-a-si'-ah)
2Ch 17:16 next him was A' the son of Zichri. 6007

amazed
Ex 15:15 the dukes of Edom shall be a'; ‡ 926
J'g 20:41 the men of Benjamin were a': ‡ "
Job 32:15 They were a', they answered no 2865
Isa 13: 8 they shall be a' one at another, 8539
Eze 32:10 will make many people a' at thee, 8074
M't 12:23 all the people were a', 1839
19:25 they were exceedingly a', *1605
M'r 1:27 And they were all a', 2284
2:12 insomuch that they were all a', 1839
6:51 they were sore a' in themselves, "
9:15 they beheld him, were greatly a', 1568
10:32 and they were a'; 2284
14:33 began to be sore a', 1568
16: 8 for they trembled and were a': *1611
Lu 2:48 they saw him, they were a': *1605
4:36 And they were all a', *1096, 2285
5:26 And they were all a', *1611, 2983
9:43 a' at the mighty power of God. *1605
Ac 2: 7 they were all a' and marvelled, 1839
12 were all a', and were in doubt, "
9:21 all that heard him were a'. "

amazement
Ac 3:10 filled with wonder and a' 1611
1Pe 3: 6 and are not afraid with any a'. *4423

Amaziah (am-a-zi'-ah)
2Ki 12:21 A' his son reigned in his stead. 558
13:12 wherewith he fought against A' "
14: 1 reigned A' the son of Joash "
8 A' sent messengers to Jehoash, "
9 the king of Israel sent to A', "
11 A' would not hear. Therefore "
11 he and A' king of Judah looked "
13 Jehoash king of Israel took A' "
15 and how he fought with A' king of "
17 A' the son of Joash king of Judah "
18 the rest of the acts of A', "
21 him king instead of his father A'. "
23 In the fifteenth year of A' the son "
15: 1 Azariah son of A' king of Judah "
3 to all that his father A' had done; "
1Ch 3:12 A' his son, Azariah his son, "
4:34 Jamlech, and Joshah the son of A', "
6:45 son of Hashabiah, the son of A', "
2Ch 24:27 A' his son reigned in his stead. "
25: 1 A' was twenty and five years old "
5 A' gathered Judah together, "
9 A' said to the man of God, "
10 Then A' separated them, to wit, "
11 A' strengthened himself, and led "
13 of the army which A' sent back, "
14 A' was come from the slaughter "
15 of the Lord was kindled against A', "
17 A' king of Judah took advice, "
18 Joash king of Judah sent to A' "
20 But A' would not hear; for it came "
21 both he and A' king of Judah, "
23 Joash the king of Israel took A' "
25 A' the son of Joash king of Judah "
26 the rest of the acts of A', "
27 the time that A' did turn away "
26: 1 king in the room of his father A' "
4 to all that his father A' did. "
Am 7:10 A' the priest of Beth-el sent to "
12 A' said unto Amos, O thou seer, "
14 answered Amos, and said to A', "

ambassador See also AMBASSADORS.
Pr 13:17 but a faithful a' is health. 6735
Jer 49:14 an a' is sent unto the heathen, "
Ob 1 an a' is sent among the heathen, "
Eph 6:20 For which I am an a' in bonds: 4243

ambassadors
Jos 9: 4 and made as if they had been a', 6735
2Ch 32:31 in the business of the a' of the 3887
35:21 he sent a' to him, 4397
Isa 18: 2 That sendeth a' by the sea, 6735
30: 4 and his a' came to Hanes. 4397
33: 7 the a' of peace shall weep bitterly. "
Eze 17:15 in sending his a' into Egypt, "
2Co 5:20 we are a' for Christ, 4243

ambassage
Lu 14:32 he sendeth an a', 4242

amber
Eze 1: 4 as the colour of a', ‡2830
27 I saw as the colour of a', ‡ "
8: 2 as the colour of a'. ‡ "

ambush See also AMBUSHES; AMBUSHMENT.
Jos 8: 2 lay thee an a' for the city 693
7 ye shall rise up from the a', "
9 they went to lie in a', * "
12 set them to lie in a' between "
14 liers in a' against him "
19 And the a' arose quickly "
21 saw that the a' had taken the city, "

ambushes
Jer 51:12 up the watchmen, prepare the a': 693

ambushment See also AMBUSHMENTS.
2Ch 13:13 Jeroboam caused an a' 3993
13 and the a' was behind them. "

ambushments
2Ch 20:22 the Lord set a' * 693

Amen
Nu 5:22 And the woman shall say, A', A'. 543
De 27:15, 16 people shall answer and say, A'.
17, 18, 19, 20, 21, 22, 23, 24, 25, 26 And
all the people shall say, A'. 543
1Ki 1:36 answered the king, and said, A': "
1Ch 16:36 And all the people said, A', "
Ne 5:13 all the congregation said, A', "
8: 6 the people answered, A', A', "
Ps 41:13 to everlasting. A', and A'. "
72:19 filled with his glory; A', and A'. "
89:52 for evermore. A', and A'. "
106:48 A'. Praise ye the Lord. "
Jer 28: 6 the prophet Jeremiah said, A': "
M't 6:13 and the glory, for ever. A'. * 281

M't 28:20 unto the end of the world. *A*·. * 281
M'k 16:20 the word with signs following. *A*·. "
Lu 24:53 praising and blessing God. *A*·. * "
Joh 21:25 books that should be written. *A*·. * "
Ro 1:25 Creator, who is blessed for ever. *A*·. "
9: 5 over all, God blessed for ever. *A*·. "
11:36 to whom be glory for ever. *A*·. "
15:33 God of peace be with you all. *A*·. "
16:20 Jesus Christ be with you. *A*·. * "
24 Jesus Christ be with you all. *A*·. * "
27 through Jesus Christ for ever. *A*·. "
1Co 14:16 unlearned say *A*· at thy giving of "
16:24 with you all in Christ Jesus. *A*·. "
2Co 1:20 yea, and in him *A*·, unto the glory "
13:14 Holy Ghost, be with you all. *A*·. * "
Ga 1: 5 be glory for ever and ever. *A*·. "
6:18 Christ be with your spirit. *A*·. "
Eph 3:21 all ages, world without end. *A*·. "
6:24 Jesus Christ in sincerity. *A*·. * "
Ph'p 4:20 be glory for ever and ever. *A*·. "
23 Jesus Christ be with you all. *A*·. * "
Col 4:18 my bonds. Grace be with you. *A*·. * "
1Th 5:28 of... Christ be with you. *A*·. * "
2Th 3:18 of...Christ be with you all. *A*·. * "
1Ti 1:17 and glory for ever and ever. *A*·. "
6:16 honour and power everlasting. *A*·. "
21 Grace be with thee. *A*·. * "
2Ti 4:18 be glory for ever and ever. *A*·. "
22 Grace be with you. *A*·. * "
Tit 3:15 Grace be with you all. *A*·. * "
Ph'm 25 Christ be with your spirit. *A*·. "
Heb 13:21 be glory for ever and ever. *A*·. "
25 Grace be with you all. *A*·. "
1Pe 4:11 dominion for ever and ever. *A*·. "
5:11 dominion for ever and ever. *A*·. "
14 all that are in Christ Jesus. *A*·. * "
2Pe 3:18 glory both now and for ever. *A*·. "
1Jo 5:21 keep yourselves from idols. *A*·. * "
2Jo 13 of thy elect sister greet thee. *A*·. * "
Jude 25 and power, both now and ever. *A*·. "
Re 1: 6 dominion for ever and ever. *A*·. "
7 wail because of him. Even so, *A*·. "
18 I am alive for evermore, *A*·; * "
3:14 These things saith the *A*·, "
5:14 And the four beasts said, *A*·. "
7:12 Saying, *A*·: Blessing, and glory, "
12 unto our God for ever and ever. *A*·. "
19: 4 Sat on the throne, saying, *A*·; "
22:20 *A*·. Even so, come, Lord Jesus. "
21 Jesus Christ be with you all. *A*·. "

amend See also AMENDS.
2Ch 34:10 to repair and *a*· the house: 2388
Jer 7: 3 *A*· your ways and your doings, 3190
5 if ye throughly *a*· your ways "
26:13 *a*· your ways and your doings, "
35:15 and *a*· your doings, "
Joh 4:52 hour when he began to *a*·. *2192, 2866*

amends
Le 5:16 he shall make *a*· for the harm *7999

amerce
De 22:19 shall *a*· him in an hundred shekels, 6064

amethyst
Ex 28:19 a ligure, an agate, and an *a*·. 306
39:12 a ligure, an agate, and an *a*·. "
Re 21:20 a jacinth; the twelfth, an *a*·. *271*

Ami (*a'-mi*)
Ezr 2:57 of Zebaim, the children of *A*·. 532

amiable
Ps 84: 1 How *a*· are thy tabernacles, 3039

Aminadab (*a-min'-a-dab*) See also AMMINADAB.
M't 1: 4 Aram begat *A*·; *284*
4 and *A*· begat Naasson; "
Lu 3:33 Which was the son of *A*·, "

amiss
2Ch 6:37 We have sinned, we have done *a*·, *5753
Da 3:29 speak anything *a*· against the God 7955
Lu 23:41 this man hath done nothing *a*·. *824*
Jas 4: 3 receive not, because ye ask *a*·, *2560*

Amittai (*a-mit'-tahee*)
2Ki 14:25 Jonah, the son of *A*·, the prophet, 573
Jon 1: 1 came unto Jonah the son of *A*·, "

Ammah (*am'-mah*) See also METHEG-AMMAH.
2Sa 2:24 they were come to the hill of *A*·. 522

Ammi (*am'-mi*) See also AMMI-NADIB; BEN-AMMI; LO-AMMI.
Ho 2: 1 Say ye unto your brethren, *A*·; 5971

Ammiel (*am'-me-el*) See also ELIAM.
Nu 13:12 of Dan, *A*· the son of Gemalli. 5988
2Sa 9: 4, 5 house of Machir, the son of *A*·, "
17:27 Machir the son of *A*· of Lo-debar, "
1Ch 3: 5 Bath-shua the daughter of *A*·: "
26: 5 *A*· the sixth, Issachar the seventh, "

Ammihud (*am-mi'-hud*)
Nu 1:10 Elishama the son of *A*·: 5989
2:18 shall be Elishama the son of *A*·. "
7:48 seventh day Elishama the son of *A*·, "
53 offering of Elishama the son of *A*·. "
10:22 host was Elishama the son of *A*·. "
34:20 Simeon, Shemuel the son of *A*·. "
28 Pedahel the son of *A*·. "
2Sa 13:37 went to Talmai, the son of *A*·. * "
1Ch 7:26 Laadan his son, *A*· his son, "
9: 4 Uthai the son of *A*·, the son of "

Amminadab (*am-min'-a-dab*) See also AMINADAB; AMMI-NADIB.
Ex 6:23 Elisheba, daughter of *A*·, sister 5992
Nu 1: 7 Nahshon the son of *A*·. "
2: 3 Nahshon the son of *A*· shall be "
7:12 the son of *A*·, of the tribe of Judah: "
7:17 offering of Nahshon the son of *A*·. 5992
10:14 his host was Nahshon the son of *A*·. "
Ru 4:19 begat Ram, and Ram begat *A*·, "
20 *A*· begat Nahshon, and Nahshon "
1Ch 2:10 Ram begat *A*·; "
10 and *A*· begat Nahshon, "
6:22 *A*· his son, Korah his son, "
15:10 *A*· the chief, and his brethren "
11 Shemaiah, and Eliel, and *A*·, "

Ammi-nadib (*am-min'-a-dib*) See also AMMINADAB.
Ca 6:12 made me like the chariots of *A*·. *5993

Ammishaddai (*am-mi-shad'-dahee*)
Nu 1:12 Of Dan; Ahiezer the son of *A*·. 5996
2:25 shall be Ahiezer the son of *A*·. "
7:66 tenth day Ahiezer the son of *A*·. "
71 offering of Ahiezer the son of *A*·. "
10:25 host was Ahiezer the son of *A*·. "

Ammizabad (*am-miz'-a-bad*)
1Ch 27: 6 in his course was *A*· his son. 5990

Ammon (*am'-mon*) See also AMMONITE.
Ge 19:38 the children of *A*· unto this day. 5983
Nu 21:24 even unto the children of *A*·: "
24 of the children of *A*· was strong. "
De 2:19 over against the children of *A*·, "
19 the children of *A*· any possession; "
37 of the children of *A*· thou camest "
3:11 in Rabbath of the children of *A*? "
16 is the border of the children of *A*·; "
Jos 12: 2 the border of the children of *A*·; "
13:10 the border of the children of *A*·; "
25 half the land of the children of *A*·, "
J'g 3:13 unto him the children of *A*· "
10: 6 and the gods of the children of *A*·, "
7 into the hands of the children of *A*·. "
9 children of *A*· passed over Jordan "
11 Amorites, from the children of *A*·, "
17 the children of *A*· were gathered "
18 to fight against the children of *A*? "
11: 4 children of *A*· made against Israel. "
5 when the children of *A*· made war "
6 we may fight with the children of *A*·. "
8, 9 against the children of *A*·, "
12 king of the children of *A*·, saying, "
13 king of the children of *A*· answered "
14 unto the king of the children of *A*·: "
15 nor the land of the children of *A*·: "
27 of Israel and the children of *A*·. "
28 the king of the children of *A*· "
29 passed over unto the children of *A*·. "
30 children of *A*· into mine hands, "
31 in peace from the children of *A*·, "
32 passed over unto the children of *A*· "
33 the children of *A*· were subdued "
36 enemies, even of the children of *A*·. "
12: 1 against the children of *A*·, "
2 great strife with the children of *A*·; "
3 over against the children of *A*·, "
1Sa 12:12 the king of the children of *A*· "
14:47 against the children of *A*·, "
2Sa 8:12 of Moab, and of the children of *A*·, "
10: 1 the king of the children of *A*· died, "
2 into the land of the children of *A*·. "
3 the princes of the children of *A*· "
6 when the children of *A*· saw that "
6 the children of *A*· sent and hired "
8 And the children of *A*· came out, "
10 array against the children of *A*·. "
11 if the children of *A*· be too strong "
14 when the children of *A*· saw that "
14 returned from the children of *A*·, "
19 feared to help the children of *A*· "
11: 1 they destroy the children of *A*·, "
12: 9 with the sword of the children of *A*·. "
26 of *A*·, and took the royal city. "
31 all the cities of the children of *A*·. "
17:27 of Rabbah of the children of *A*·, "
1Ki 11: 7 abomination of the children of *A*·. "
33 the god of the children of *A*·, "
2Ki 23:13 abomination of the children of *A*·. "
24: 2 and bands of the children of *A*·. "
1Ch 18:11 and from the children of *A*·, "
19: 1 the king of the children of *A*· died, "
2 into the land of the children of *A*· "
3 princes of the children of *A*· said "
6 of *A*· saw that they had made "
6 of *A*· sent a thousand talents of "
7 of *A*· gathered themselves together "
9 of *A*· came out, and put the battle "
11 array against the children of *A*·. "
12 of *A*· be too strong for thee, then "
15 of *A*· saw that the Syrians were "
19 the Syrians help the children of *A*· "
20: 1 of *A*·, and came and besieged "
3 all the cities of the children of *A*·. "
2Ch 20: 1 of *A*·, and with them other beside "
10 the children of *A*· and Moab, "
22 against the children of *A*·, "
23 children of *A*· and Moab stood up "
27: 5 of *A*· gave him the same year an "
5 So much did the children of *A*· pay "
Ne 13:23 married wives of Ashdod, of *A*·, "
Ps 83: 7 Gebal, and *A*·, and Amalek; "
Isa 11:14 the children of *A*· shall obey them. "
Jer 9:26 of *A*·, and Moab, and all that are "
25:21 and Moab, and the children of *A*·, "
49: 6 the captivity of the children of *A*·, "
Da 11:41 and the chief of the children of *A*·. "
Am 1:13 transgressions of the children of *A*·, "
Zep 2: 8 the revilings of the children of *A*·, "
9 of *A*· as Gomorrah, even the "

Ammonite (*am'-mon-ite*) See also AMMONITES; AMMONITESS.
De 23: 3 An *A*· or Moabite shall not enter 5984
1Sa 11: 1 the *A*· came up, and encamped 5984
2 Nahash the *A*· answered them, "
2Sa 23:37 Zelek the *A*·, Naharai the "
1Ch 11:39 Zelek the *A*·, Naharai the "
Ne 2:10 and Tobiah the servant, the *A*·, "
19 the *A*·, and Geshem the Arabian, "
4: 3 Now Tobiah the *A*· was by him, "
13: 1 the *A*· and the Moabite should not "

Ammonites (*am'-mon-ites*)
De 2:20 the *A*· call them Zamzummims; 5984
1Sa 11:11 slew the *A*· until the heat of the "
1Ki 11: 1 women of the Moabites, *A*·, "
5 Milcom the abomination of the *A*·. "
2Ch 20: 1 and with them other beside the *A*·, "
26: 8 the *A*· gave gifts to Uzziah: "
27: 5 fought also with the king of the *A*·,* "
Ezr 9: 1 the Perizzites, the Jebusites, the *A*·, "
Ne 4: 7 and the Arabians, and the *A*·, "
Jer 27: 3 to the king of the *A*·, and to the * "
40:11 among the *A*·, and in Edom, * "
14 Baalis the king of the *A*· hath * "
41:10 departed to go over to the *A*·. * "
15 eight men, and went to the *A*·. * "
49: 1 Concerning the *A*·, thus saith * "
2 to be heard in Rabbah of the *A*·; * "
Eze 21:20 come to Rabbath of the *A*·, *1121, "
28 concerning the *A*·, and * "
25: 2 set thy face against the *A*·, * "
3 unto the *A*·, Hear the word * "
5 *A*· a couchingplace for flocks;* "
10 men of the east with the *A*·, * "
10 *A*· may not be remembered * "

Ammonitess (*am'-mon-i-tess*)
1Ki 14:21 mother's name was Naamah an *A*·. 5984
31 was Naamah an *A*·. And Abijam "
2Ch 12:13 mother's name was Naamah an *A*·. "
24:26 Zabad the son of Shimeath, an *A*·. "

Amnon (*am'-non*) See also AMNON'S.
2Sa 3: 2 his firstborn was *A*·, of Ahinoam 550
13: 1 and *A*· the son of David loved her. "
2 *A*· was so vexed, that he fell sick "
2 *A*· thought it hard for him to do "
3 But *A*· had a friend whose name "
4 *A*· said unto him, I love Tamar, "
6 So *A*· lay down, and made himself "
6 *A*· said unto the king, I pray thee, "
9 *A*· said, Have out all men from me. "
10 *A*· said unto Tamar, Bring the "
10 them into the chamber to *A*· "
15 Then *A*· hated her exceedingly; "
15 *A*· said unto her, Arise, be gone. "
20 Hath *A*· thy brother been with thee? "
22 Absalom spake unto his brother *A*· "
22 for Absalom hated *A*·, because he "
26 I pray thee, Let my brother *A*· go "
27 he let *A*· and all the king's sons go "
28 and when I say unto you, Smite *A*·; "
29 did unto *A*· as Absalom had "
32 for *A*· only is dead: for by the "
33 *A*· only is dead. But Absalom fled. "
39 he was comforted concerning *A*·, "
1Ch 3: 1 the firstborn *A*·, of Ahinoam "
4:20 the sons of Shimon were, *A*·, and "

Amnon's (*am'-nons*)
2Sa 13: 7 Go now to thy brother *A*· house 550
8 So Tamar went to her brother *A*· "
28 when *A*· heart is merry with "

Amok (*a'-mok*)
Ne 12: 7 Sallu, *A*·, Hilkiah, Jedaiah. 5987
20 Of Sallai, Kallai: of *A*·, Eber; "

Amon (*a'-mon*)
1Ki 22:26 and carry him back unto *A*· the 526
2Ki 21:18 and *A*· his son reigned in his stead. "
19 *A*· was twenty and two years old "
23 the servants of *A*· conspired against "
24 that had conspired against king *A*·; "
25 the rest of the acts of *A*· which he "
1Ch 3:14 *A*· his son, Josiah his son. "
2Ch 18:25 carry him back to *A*· the governor "
33:20 and *A*· his son reigned in his stead. "
21 *A*· was two and twenty years old "
22 *A*· sacrificed unto all the carved "
23 but *A*· trespassed more and more. "
25 that had conspired against king *A*·; "
Ne 7:59 of Zebaim, the children of *A*·. "
Jer 1: 2 in the days of Josiah the son of *A*· "
25: 3 year of Josiah the son of *A*·, "
Zep 1: 1 the son of *A*·, king of Judah. "
M't 1:10 Manasses begat *A*·; *300*
10 and *A*· begat Josias; "

among See also AMONGST.
Ge 17:10 child *a*· you shall be circumcised.
12 shall be circumcised *a*· you, every
23 every male child *a*· the men of
23: 6 thou art a mighty prince *a*· us: 8432
10 Ephron dwelt *a*· the children of * "
24: 3 daughters of the Canaanites, *a*· 7130
30:32 all the brown cattle *a*· the sheep,
32 spotted and speckled *a*· the goats:
Ge 30:33 that is not speckled and spotted *a*·
33 and brown *a*· the sheep, that shall
35 and all the brown *a*· the sheep,
41 that they might conceive *a*· the rods.
34:22 if every male *a*· us be circumcised,
30 me to stink *a*· the inhabitants of ‡
30 *a*· the Canaanites and the
35: 2 strange gods that are *a*· you, 8432
36:30 Hori, *a*· their dukes in the land *
40:20 chief baker *a*· his servants. 8432
42: 5 of Israel came to buy corn *a*· those "
47: 6 knowest any men of activity *a*· them, "
Ex 2: 5 when she saw the ark *a*· the flags, 8432
7: 5 the children of Israel from *a*· them. "

Ex 9:20 the word of the Lord *a'* the servants
12:31 get you forth from *a'* my people, 8432
49 stranger that sojourneth *a'* you. "
13: 2 whatsoever openeth the womb *a'* thy
13 and all the firstborn of man *a'* thy
15:11 Who is like unto thee, O Lord, *a'*
17: 7 Is the Lord *a'* us, 7130
25: 8 that I may dwell *a'* them. 8432
28: 1 him, from *a'* the children of Israel, "
29:45 I will dwell *a'* the children of Israel, "
46 that I may dwell *a'* them: "
30:12 that there be no plague *a'* them, "
13 *a'* them that are numbered, *5921
14 Every one that passeth *a'* them * "
31:14 shall be cut off from *a'* his people. 7130
32:25 them naked unto their shame *a'*
34: 9 let my Lord, I pray thee, go *a'* us; *7130
10 the people *a'* which thou art "
19 and every firstling *a'* thy cattle, *
35: 5 Take ye from *a'* you an offering
10 And every wise hearted *a'* you shall
36: 8 *a'* them that wrought the work
Le 6:18 the males *a'* the children of Aaron
29 the males *a'* the priests shall eat
7: 6 Every male *a'* the priests shall eat
33 He *a'* the sons of Aaron, that
34 by a statute for ever from *a'* the *
11: 2 which ye shall eat *a'* all the beasts
3 and cheweth the cud, *a'* the beasts,
13 have in abomination *a'* the fowls; 4480
27 goeth upon his paws, *a'* all manner
29 shall be unclean unto you *a'* the
31 unclean to you *a'* all that creep:
42 or whatsoever hath more feet *a'* *
15:31 defile my tabernacle that is *a'* *8432
16:16 that remaineth *a'* them in the * 854
29 a stranger that sojourneth *a'* you:8432
17: 4 that man shall be cut off from *a'* 7130
8 strangers which sojourn *a'* you, 8432
9 that man shall be cut off from *a'* *
10 strangers that sojourn *a'* you, 8432
10 cut him off from *a'* his people. 7130
12 stranger that sojourneth *a'* you 8432
13 the strangers that sojourn *a'* you, "
18:26 stranger that sojourneth *a'* you: "
29 cut off from *a'* their people. 7130
19: 8 that soul shall be cut off from *a'* *
16 go up and down as a talebearer *a'*
34 be unto you as one born *a'* you, 854
20: 3 will cut him off from *a'* his people; 7130
5 cut him off,...from *a'* their people. "
6 cut him off from *a'* his people. "
14 there be no wickedness *a'* you. 8432
18 be cut off from *a'* their people. 7130
21: 1 defiled for the dead *a'* his people:
4 being a chief man *a'* his people, to
10 the high priest *a'* his brethren,
15 he profane his seed *a'* his people:
22: 3 all your seed *a'* your generations,*
32 hallowed *a'* the children of Israel: 8432
23:29 shall be cut off from *a'* his people.*
30 will I destroy from *a'* his people. 7130
24:10 went out *a'* the children of Israel: 8432
25:33 possession *a'* the children of "
45 strangers that do sojourn *a'* you, "
26:11 set my tabernacle *a'* you: 8432
12 I will walk *a'* you, "
22 send wild beasts *a'* you, which
25 I will send the pestilence *a'* you; 8432
33 I will scatter you *a'* the heathen,
38 And ye shall perish *a'* the heathen,
Nu 1:47 were not numbered *a'* them. 8432
49 them *a'* the children of Israel: "
2:33 numbered *a'* the children of Israel; "
3:12 from *a'* the children of Israel "
12 that openeth the matrix *a'*
41 firstborn *a'* the children of Israel;
41 the firstlings *a'* the cattle of the
45 *a'* the children of Israel, and the
4: 2 from *a'* the sons of Levi, 8432
18 Kohathites from *a'* the Levites: "
5:21 a curse and an oath *a'* thy people, "
27 a curse *a'* her people. 7130
8: 6, 14, 16, 19 *a'* the children of Israel, 8432
19 no plague *a'* the children of Israel,
9: 7 appointed season *a'* the children 8432
13 soul shall be cut off from *a'* his *
14 if a stranger shall sojourn *a'* you, 854
11: 1 the fire of the Lord burnt *a'* them,
3 because the fire of the Lord burnt *a'*
4 mixt multitude that was *a'* them 7130
20 the Lord which is *a'* you, "
21 The people, *a'* whom I am, "
12: 6 If there be a prophet *a'* you, I the
13: 2 send a man, every one a ruler *a'*
14:11 which I have shewed *a'* them? 7130
13 this people in thy might from *a'* "
14 thou Lord art *a'* this people, * "
42 the Lord is not *a'* you; "
15:14 whosoever be *a'* you in your 8432
23 Moses, and henceforward *a'* your *
26 stranger that sojourneth *a'* them; 8432
29 is born *a'* the children of Israel,
29 stranger that sojourneth *a'* them. 8432
30 cut off from *a'* his people. 7130
16: 3 and the Lord is *a'* them: 8432
21 Separate yourselves from *a'* this "
33 perished from *a'* the congregation. "
45 you up from *a'* this congregation, "
47 plague was begun *a'* the people: "
17: 6 rod of Aaron was *a'* their rods. 8432
18: 6 from *a'* the children of Israel: "
20 neither shalt thou have any part *a'* "
20 inheritance *a'* the children of Israel. "
23 that *a'* the children of Israel "
24 *A'* the children of Israel they "

Nu 19:10 stranger that sojourneth *a'* them, 8432
20 shall be cut off from *a'* the * "
21: 6 sent fiery serpents *a'* the people,
23: 9 not be reckoned *a'* the nations.
23:21 and the shout of a king is *a'* them.
25: 7 rose up from *a'* the congregation,*8432
11 was zealous for my sake *a'* them, "
14 a chief house *a'* the Simeonites.
26:62 numbered *a'* the children of Israel, 8432
62 them *a'* the children of Israel. "
64 But *a'* these there was not a man
27: 4 done away from *a'* his family, 8432
4 *a'* the brethren of our father. "
7 an inheritance *a'* their father's "
31:16 was a plague *a'* the congregation
17 kill every male *a'* the little ones,
32:30 they shall have possessions *a'* you 8432
33: 4 the Lord had smitten *a'* them:
54 by lot for an inheritance *a'* your *
35: 6 And *a'* the cities which ye shall * 854
15 and for the sojourner *a'* them: 8432
34 dwell *a'* the children of Israel. * "
De 1:13 understanding, and known *a'* *
15 tens, and officers *a'* your tribes. *
42 I am not *a'* you; 7130
2:14 wasted out from *a'* the host, * "
15 to destroy them from *a'* the host,* "
16 and dead from *a'* the people, "
4: 3 destroyed them from *a'* you. * "
27 shall scatter you *a'* the nations,
27 left few in number *a'* the heathen,
6:15 a jealous God *a'* you) *7130
7:14 male or female barren *a'* you,
14 or *a'* your cattle.
20 God will send the hornet *a'* them,
21 the Lord thy God is *a'* you, *7130
13: 1 If there arise *a'* you a prophet, * "
11 such wickedness as this is *a'* you. * "
13 Belial, are gone out from *a'* you, * "
14 abomination is wrought *a'* you; * "
14: 6 cheweth the cud *a'* the beasts, *
15: 4 there shall be no poor *a'* you; *
7 If there be *a'* you a poor man of *
16:11 and the widow, that are *a'* you, *7130
17: 2 If there be found *a'* you, * "
7 put the evil away from *a'* you. * "
15 one from *a'* thy brethren "
18: 2 no inheritance *a'* their brethren: "
10 not be found *a'* you any one *
18 a Prophet from *a'* their brethren, 7130
19:19 put the evil away from *a'* you. * "
20 no more any such evil *a'* you. * "
21: 9 of innocent blood from *a'* you, * "
11 seest *a'* the captives a beautiful
21 thou put evil away from *a'* you; *7130
22:21 thou put evil away from *a'* you. * "
24 put away evil from *a'* you. * "
23:10 If there be *a'* you any man, that
16 dwell with thee, even *a'* you, *7130
24: 7 put evil away from *a'* you. * "
26:11 the stranger that is *a'* you. * "
28:37 *a'* all nations whither the Lord
54 the man that is tender *a'* you,
56 tender and delicate woman *a'* you,
64 the Lord shall scatter thee *a'* all
65 *a'* these nations shalt thou find no
29:17 and gold, which were *a'* them:)
18 Lest there should be *a'* you man,
18 *a'* you a root that beareth gall
30: 1 them to mind *a'* all the nations,
31:16 whither they go to be *a'* them, 7130
17 because our God is not *a'* us? "
32:26 of them to cease from *a'* men:
34 and sealed up *a'* my treasures?
46 the words which I testify *a'* you
51 *a'* the children of Israel *8432
Jos 3: 5 the Lord will do wonders *a'* you. 7130
10 the living God is *a'* you, "
4: 6 That this may be a sign *a'* you, "
7:11 put it even *a'* their own stuff.
12 destroy the accursed from *a'* you. 7130
13 the accursed thing from *a'* you. "
21 When I saw *a'* the spoils a goodly
8: 9 lodged that night *a'* the people. 8432
33 as he that was born *a'* them; *
35 that were conversant *a'* them. 7130
9: 7 Peradventure ye dwell *a'* us; "
16 and that they dwelt *a'* them. "
22 when ye dwell *a'* us? "
10: 1 inhabitants of Gibeon....were *a'* "
13:13 the Maachathites dwell *a'* the * "
22 slay with the sword *a'* them that 413
14: 3 he gave none inheritance *a'* them. 8432
15 Arba was a great man *a'* the
15:13 a part *a'* the children of Judah, 8432
16: 9 the children of Ephraim were *a'* * "
10 the Canaanites dwell *a'* the *7130
17: 4 an inheritance *a'* our brethren. 8432
4 an inheritance *a'* the brethren "
6 had an inheritance *a'* his sons: "
9 cities of Ephraim are *a'* the cities "
18: 2 remained *a'* the children of Israel "
4 *a'* you three men of each tribe: *
7 the Levites have no part *a'* you; 7130
19:49 Joshua the son of Nun *a'* them: *8432
20: 4 a place, that he may dwell *a'* them. 5973
9 stranger that sojourneth *a'* them, 8432
22: 7 gave Joshua *a'* their brethren 5973
14 their fathers *a'* the thousands of
19 take possession *a'* us: 8432
31 perceive that the Lord is *a'* us, * "
23: 7 ye come not *a'* these nations,
7 remain *a'* you; neither make
12 even these that remain *a'* you, 854
24: 5 that which I did *a'* them: *7130
17 and *a'* all the people through

Jos 24:23 strange gods which are *a'* you, 7130
J'g 1:16 went and dwelt *a'* the people. * 854
29 Canaanites dwelt in Gezer *a'* them. 7130
30 the Canaanites dwelt *a'* them, "
32 Asherites dwelt *a'* the Canaanites, "
33 Naphtali....dwelt *a'* the Canaanites, "
3: 5 children of Israel dwelt *a'* the
5: 8 seen *a'* forty thousand in Israel?
9 offered themselves willingly *a'*
3 over the nobles *a'* the people: *
14 after thee, Benjamin, *a'* thy people;
16 abodest thou *a'* the sheepfolds, 996
10:16 away the strange gods from *a'* 7130
12: 4 Ephraim *a'* the Ephraimites, *8432
4 and *a'* the Manassites. * "
14: 3 *a'* the daughters of thy brethren,
3 or *a'* all my people, that thou
18: 1 unto them *a'* the tribes of Israel. 8432
25 Let not thy voice be heard *a'* us,
20:12 is this that is done *a'* you?
16 *A'* all this people there were
21: 5 there *a'* all the tribes of Israel
12 *a'* the inhabitants of Jabesh-gilead
Ru 2: 7 gather after the reapers *a'* the 996
15 Let her glean even *a'* the sheaves,
4:10 not cut off from *a'* his brethren, 5973
1Sa 2: 8 to set them *a'* princes, and to * "
4: 3 when it cometh *a'* us, it may 7130
17 a great slaughter *a'* the people,
6: 6 had wrought wonderfully *a'* them,
7: 3 Ashtaroth from *a'* you, 8432
9: 2 was not *a'* the children of Israel
22 place *a'* them that were bidden,
10:10 and he prophesied *a'* them. 8432
11 he prophesied *a'* the prophets, *5973
23 when he stood *a'* the people, 8432
14:15 *a'* all the people: the garrison,
30 much greater slaughter *a'* the
34 Saul said, Disperse yourselves *a'*
39 *a'* all the people that answered
15: 6 down from *a'* the Amalekites, 8432
6 departed from *a'* the Amalekites. "
33 thy mother be childless *a'* women.
16: 1 have provided me a king *a'* his sons.
17:12 man went *a'* men for an old man
19:24 Is Saul also *a'* the prophets?
22:14 *a'* all thy servants as David,
31: 9 the house of their idols, and *a'* * 854
2Sa 6:19 And he dealt *a'* all the people,
19 even *a'* the whole multitude
15:31 Ahithophel is *a'* the conspirators
16:20 Give counsel *a'* you what we *
17: 9 There is a slaughter *a'* the people
19:28 didst thou set thy servant *a'* them
22:50 unto thee, O Lord, *a'* the heathen,
23: 8 chief *a'* the captains; the same *
18 of Zeruiah, was chief *a'* three. *
18 and had the name *a'* three.
22 had the name *a'* three mighty men.
1Ki 3:13 *a'* the kings like unto thee all thy
5: 6 there is not *a'* us any that can
6:13 I will dwell *a'* the children of 8432
7:51 put *a'* the treasures of the house *
8:53 them from *a'* all the people of
9: 7 and a byword *a'* all people:
11:20 *a'* the sons of Pharaoh. 8432
14: 7 I exalted thee from *a'* the people, "
21: 9 a fast, and set Naboth on high *a'*
12 Naboth on high *a'* the people.
2Ki 4:13 I dwell *a'* mine own people. 8432
9: 2 arise up from *a'* his brethren, "
11: 2 stole him from *a'* the king's sons "
17:25, 26 the Lord sent lions *a'* them,
18: 5 after him was none like him *a'* all
35 *a'* all the gods of the countries,
20:15 there is nothing *a'* my treasures
23: 9 bread *a'* their brethren. 8432
1Ch 4:23 and those that dwelt *a'* plants *
7: 5 their brethren *a'* all the families
11:20 and had a name *a'* the three.
24 the name *a'* the three mighties.
25 he was honourable *a'* the thirty, *4480
12: 1 and they were *a'* the mighty men,
4 the Gibeonite, a mighty man *a'*
16: 8 known his deeds *a'* the people.
24 Declare his glory *a'* the heathen;
24 marvellous works *a'* all nations.
31 men say *a'* the nations, The Lord
18:14 judgment and justice *a'* all his *
21: 6 Benjamin counted he not *a'* them: 8432
23: 6 into courses *a'* the sons of Levi, *
24: 4 *A'* the sons of Eleazar there were *
4 eight *a'* the sons of Ithamar *
26:12 *A'* these were the divisions of *
12 even *a'* the chief men, having *
19 divisions of the porters *a'* the *
19 of Kore, and *a'* the sons of Merari.*
30 were officers *a'* them of Israel on *5921
31 *A'* the Hebronites was Jerijah *
31 even *a'* the Hebronites, according*
31 were found *a'* them mighty men
27: 6 who was mighty *a'* the thirty, *
28: 4 *a'* the sons of my father he liked
2Ch 5: 1 put he *a'* the treasures of the *
6: 5 I chose no city *a'* all the tribes *
7:13 I send pestilence *a'* my people;
20 and a byword *a'* all nations.
11:22 to be ruler *a'* his brethren:
20:25 they found *a'* them in abundance
22:11 stole him from *a'* the king's sons 8432
24:16 buried him in the city of David *a'* 5973
23 all the princes of the people from *a'*
26: 6 Ashdod, and *a'* the Philistines.
28:15 clothed all that were naked *a'*
31:19 to all the males *a'* the priests,
19 reckoned by genealogies *a'* the

2Ch 32:14 Who was there *a·* all the gods of
33:11 took Manasseh *a·* the thorns, *
19 they are written *a·* the sayings *5921
35:13 divided them speedily *a·* all the *
36:23 is there *a·* you of all his people?
Ezr 1: 3 is there *a·* you of all his people?
2:62 *a·* those that were reckoned
65 *a·* them two hundred singing *
10:18 And *a·* the sons of the priests
Ne 1: 8 scatter you abroad *a·* the nations:
4:11 we come in the midst *a·* them, *8432
5:17 unto us from *a·* the heathen that 4480
6: 6 It is reported *a·* the heathen,
7:64 *a·* those that were reckoned by
9:17 thy wonders thou didst *a·* them; 5973
10:34 we cast the lots *a·* the priests, *
11:17 the second *a·* his brethren,
13:26 yet *a·* many nations was there no
Es 1:19 and let it be written *a·* the laws of
3: 8 scattered abroad and dispersed *a·* 996
4: 3 was great mourning *a·* the Jews,
9:21 To stablish this *a·* them, *5921
28 should not fail from *a·* the Jews, 8432
10: 3 great *a·* the Jews, and accepted
Job 1: 6 Satan came also *a·* them. 8432
2: 1 came also *a·* them to present "
8 he sat down *a·* the ashes. "
15:19 no stranger passed *a·* them. "
17:10 cannot find one wise man *a·* you.
18:19 neither have son nor nephew *a·*
28:10 He cutteth out rivers *a·* the rocks;
30: 5 driven forth from *a·* men, *1460
7 *A·* the bushes they brayed; 996
33:23 one *a·* a thousand, to shew unto 4480
34: 4 know *a·* ourselves what is good. 996
37 he clappeth his hands *a·* us, "
36:14 and their life is *a·* the unclean.
39:25 He saith *a·* the trumpets, Ha, Ha;*1767
41: 6 part him *a·* the merchants? 996
42:15 inheritance *a·* their brethren. 8432
Ps 9:11 declare *a·* the people his doings.
12: 1 fail from *a·* the children of men.
18:49 unto thee, O Lord, *a·* the heathen,
21:10 seed from *a·* the children of men.
22:18 They part my garments *a·* them,
28 he is the governor *a·* the nations.*
31:11 a reproach *a·* all mine enemies, *
11 especially *a·* my neighbours, *
35:18 I will praise thee *a·* much people.
44:11 hast scattered us *a·* the heathen.
14 makest us a byword *a·* the heathen,
14 shaking of the head *a·* the people.
45: 9 were *a·* thy honourable women:
12 even the rich *a·* the people shall
46:10 I will be exalted *a·* the heathen,
55:15 in their dwellings, and *a·* them. *7130
57: 4 My soul is *a·* lions: and I lie 8432
4 even *a·* them that are set on fire,
9 praise thee, O Lord, *a·* the people:
9 will sing unto thee *a·* the nations.
67: 2 thy saving health *a·* all nations.
68:13 though ye have lien *a·* the pots, 996
17 the Lord is *a·* them, as in Sinai,
18 the Lord God might dwell *a·* them.*
25 *a·* them were the damsels *8432
74: 9 neither is their *a·* us any that 854
77:14 declared thy strength *a·* the people.
78:45 sent divers sorts of flies *a·* them,
49 by sending evil angels *a·* them. *
60 the tent which he placed *a·* men;
79:10 let him be known *a·* the heathen
80: 6 our enemies laugh *a·* themselves.
82: 1 mighty; he judgeth *a·* the gods. 8432
86: 8 *A·* the gods there is none like
88: 5 Free *a·* the dead, like the slain
89: 6 who *a·* the sons of the mighty can
94: 8 ye brutish *a·* the people: and ye
96: 3 Declare his glory *a·* the heathen,
3 his wonders *a·* all people.
10 Say *a·* the heathen that the Lord
99: 6 Moses and Aaron *a·* his priests,
6 and Samuel *a·* them that call
104:10 valleys, which run *a·* the hills. 996
12 which sing *a·* the branches.
105: 1 known his deeds *a·* the people.
27 they shewed his signs *a·* them,
37 one feeble person *a·* their tribes.
106:27 their seed also *a·* the nations,
35 were mingled *a·* the heathen, *
47 and gather us from *a·* the heathen,
108: 3 praise thee, O Lord, *a·* the people:
3 praises unto thee *a·* the nations.
109:30 yea, I will praise him *a·* the 8432
110: 6 He shall judge *a·* the heathen,
126: 2 then said they *a·* the heathen,
136:11 brought out Israel from *a·* them: 8432
Pr 1:14 Cast in thy lot *a·* us; let us all "
6:19 that soweth discord *a·* brethren. 996
7: 7 And beheld *a·* the simple ones,
7 I discerned *a·* the youths, a young
14: 9 *a·* the righteous there is favour. 996
15:31 reproof of life abideth *a·* the wise. 7130
17: 2 of the inheritance *a·* the brethren. 8432
23:20 Be not *a·* winebibbers; *a·* riotous
28 the transgressors *a·* men.
27:22 a mortar *a·* wheat with a pestle, 8432
30:14 earth, and the needy from *a·* men.
30 lion which is strongest *a·* beasts,
31:23 sitteth *a·* the elders of the land. 5973
Ec 6: 1 sun, and it is common *a·* men: *5921
7:28 one man *a·* a thousand have I
28 but a woman *a·* all those have I
9: 3 This is an evil *a·* all things that *
17 cry of him that ruleth *a·* fools.
Ca 1: 8 O thou fairest *a·* women, go thy
2: 2 As the lily *a·* thorns, 996

Ca 2: 2 so is my love *a·* the daughters. 996
3 As the apple tree *a·* the trees of
3 so is my beloved *a·* the sons. I sat 996
16 am his: he feedeth *a·* the lilies.
4: 2 twins, and none is barren *a·* them.
5 are twins, which feed *a·* the lilies.
5: 9 O thou fairest *a·* women? what is
10 the chiefest *a·* ten thousand.
6: 1 O thou fairest *a·* women?
3 is mine: he feedeth *a·* the lilies.
6 and there is not one barren *a·* them.
Isa 2: 4 he shall judge *a·* the nations, * 996
4: 3 written *a·* the living in Jerusalem:
5:27 be weary nor stumble *a·* them;
8:15 many *a·* them shall stumble, *
16 the testimony, seal the law *a·*
10:16 send *a·* his fat ones leanness;
12: 4 declare his doings *a·* the people,
24:13 midst of the land *a·* the people, 8432
29:14 to do a marvellous work *a·* this
19 and the poor *a·* men shall rejoice
33:14 Who *a·* us shall dwell with the
14 *a·* us shall dwell with everlasting
36:20 Who are they *a·* all the gods of these
39: 4 there is nothing *a·* my treasures
41:28 even *a·* them, and there was no
42:23 Who *a·* you will give ear to this?
43: 9 who *a·* them can declare this,
12 there was no strange god *a·* you:
44: 4 shall spring up as *a·* the grass, 996
14 himself *a·* the trees of the forest:
48:14 which *a·* them hath declared these
50:10 Who is *a·* you that feareth the
51:18 none to guide her *a·* all the sons
57: 6 *A·* the smooth stones of the stream
61: 9 shall be known *a·* the Gentiles,
9 and their offspring *a·* the people: 8432
65: 4 Which remain *a·* the graves,
66:19 And I will set a sign *a·* them,
19 declare my glory *a·* the Gentiles.
Jer 3:19 shall I put thee *a·* the children,
4: 3 ground, and sow not *a·* thorns. 413
5:26 For *a·* my people are found
6:15 they shall fall *a·* them that fall:
18 O congregation, what is *a·* them.
27 for a tower and a fortress *a·* my
8:12 *a·* them that fall: in the time of
17 send serpents, cockatrices, *a·* you,
9:16 scatter them also *a·* the heathen,
10: 7 *a·* all the wise men of the nations,
11: 9 conspiracy is found *a·* the men
9 *a·* the inhabitants of Jerusalem.
12:14 the house of Judah from *a·* them. 8432
14:22 *a·* the vanities of the Gentiles
18:13 Ask ye now *a·* the heathen,
24:10 and the pestilence, *a·* them, till
25:16 sword that I will send *a·* them. 996
27 sword which I will send *a·* you. "
29:18 *a·* all the nations whither I have
32 a man to dwell *a·* this people; 8432
31: 7 shout *a·* the chief of the nations:*
32:20 this day, and in Israel, and *a·*
37: 4 Jeremiah came in and went out *a·* 8432
10 remained but wounded men *a·*
39:14 so he dwelt *a·* the people. 8432
40: 1 bound in chains *a·* all that were "
5 dwell with him *a·* the people: "
6 dwelt with him *a·* the people that "
11 *a·* the Ammonites, and in Edom,
41: 8 But ten men were found *a·* them
8 slew them not *a·* their brethren. 8432
44: 8 a reproach *a·* all the nations of
46:18 as Tabor is *a·* the mountains,
48:27 was he found *a·* thieves?
49:15 small *a·* the heathen,
15 and despised *a·* men.
50: 2 Declare ye *a·* the nations,
23 a desolation *a·* the nations!
46 is moved, and the cry is heard *a·*
51:27 blow the trumpet *a·* the nations,
41 Babylon become an astonishment *a·*
La 1: 1 she that was great *a·* the nations,
1 and princess *a·* the provinces,
2 *a·* all her lovers she hath none to
3 she dwelleth *a·* the heathen,
17 as a menstruous woman *a·* them. 996
2: 9 her princes are *a·* the Gentiles:
4:15 wandered, they said *a·* the heathen,
20 we shall live *a·* the heathen.
Eze 1: 1 as I was *a·* the captives by the 8432
13 and down *a·* the living creatures; 996
2: 5 hath been a prophet *a·* them. 8432
6 and thou dost dwell *a·* scorpions: 413
3:15 astonished *a·* them seven days. 8432
25 thou shalt not go out *a·* them: "
4:13 eat their defiled bread *a·* the
5:14 and a reproach *a·* the nations
6: 8 escape the sword *a·* the nations,
9 shall remember me *a·* the nations
13 slain men shall be *a·* their idols 8432
9: 2 one man *a·* them was clothed * "
11: 1 *a·* whom I saw Jaazaniah the * "
9 will execute judgments *a·* you.
16 cast them far off *a·* the heathen,
16 scattered them *a·* the countries,
12:10 house of Israel that are *a·* them. 8432
12 the prince that is *a·* them "
15 I shall scatter them *a·* the nations,
16 their abominations *a·* the heathen
13:19 will ye pollute me *a·* my people 413
15: 2 which is *a·* the trees of the forest?
6 As the vine tree *a·* the trees of the
16:14 renown went forth *a·* the heathen
18:18 which is not good *a·* his people, 8432
19: 2 lioness: she lay down *a·* lions, 996
2 her whelps *a·* young lions. *8432

Eze 19: 6 he went up and down *a·* the lions, 8432
11 exalted *a·* the thick branches, 5921,996
20: 9 heathen, *a·* whom they were, 8432
23 would scatter them *a·* the heathen,
38 purge out from *a·* you the rebels,
22:15 scatter thee *a·* the heathen,
26 sabbaths, I am profaned *a·* them. 8432
30 And I sought for a man *a·* them,
23:10 she became famous *a·* women;
25:10 may not be remembered *a·*
27:24 of cedar, *a·* thy merchandise.
36 The merchants *a·* the people
28:19 they that know thee *a·* the people
25 house of Israel from the people *a·*
29:12 her cities *a·* the cities that are 8432
12 the Egyptians *a·* the nations,
30:23, 26 the Egyptians *a·* the nations
26 disperse them *a·* the countries; *
31: 3, 10 his top was *a·* the thick boughs, 996
14 their top *a·* the thick boughs, 413
18 glory and in greatness *a·* the trees
32: 9 bring thy destruction *a·* the nations,
21 The strong *a·* the mighty shall
33: 6 take any person from *a·* them,
33 that a prophet hath been *a·* them. 8432
34:12 the day that he is *a·* his sheep "
24 servant David a prince *a·* them "
35:11 will make myself known *a·* them,
36:19 I scattered them *a·* the heathen,
21 Israel had profaned *a·* the heathen,
22 ye have profaned *a·* the heathen,
23 great name, which was profaned *a·*
24 take you from *a·* the heathen,
30 reproach of famine *a·* the heathen.
37:21 the children of Israel from *a·* the 996
39: 6 a fire on Magog, and *a·* them *
21 I will set my glory *a·* the heathen,
28 them to be led into captivity *a·* 413
40:46 *a·* the sons of Levi, which come
44: 9 stranger that is *a·* the children 8432
47:22 strangers that sojourn *a·* you, "
22 which shall beget children *a·* you: "
22 country *a·* the children of Israel;
22 with you *a·* the tribes of Israel. 8432
Da 1: 6 Now *a·* these were of the children
19 and *a·* them all was found none
4:35 in the army of heaven, and *a·*
7: 8 there came up *a·* them another 997
11:24 shall scatter *a·* them the prey,
33 that understand *a·* the people
Ho 5: 9 *a·* the tribes of Israel have I made
7: 7 there is none *a·* them that
8 hath mixed himself *a·* the people;
8: 8 up: now shall they be *a·*
10 they have hired *a·* the nations,
9:17 shall be wanderers *a·* the nations.
10:14 shall a tumult arise *a·* thy people,
13:15 he be fruitful *a·* his brethren, 996
Joe 2:17 should they say *a·* the people,
19 you a reproach *a·* the heathen;
25 great army which I sent *a·*
3: 2 scattered *a·* the nations, and parted
9 Proclaim ye this *a·* the Gentiles;
Am 1: 1 Amos, who was *a·* the herdmen
2:16 that is courageous *a·* the mighty
4:10 I have sent *a·* you the pestilence
9: 9 the house of Israel *a·* all nations,
Ob 1 is sent *a·* the heathen,
2 made thee small *a·* the heathen:
4 thou set thy nest *a·* the stars, 996
Mic 3:11 Is not the Lord *a·* us? none *7130
4: 3 he shall judge *a·* many people, * 996
5: 2 Ephratah, though thou be little *a·*
8 Jacob shall be *a·* the Gentiles
8 people as a lion *a·* the beasts
8 young lion *a·* the flocks of sheep:
7: 2 and there is none upright *a·* men:
Na 3: 8 that was situate *a·* the rivers,
Hab 1: 5 Behold ye *a·* the heathen, and
Zep 3:20 praise *a·* all people of the earth,
Hag 2: 3 Who is left *a·* you that saw this
5 so my spirit remaineth *a·* you: 8432
Zec 1: 8 and he stood *a·* the myrtle trees 996
10 man that stood *a·* the myrtle trees "
11 Lord that stood *a·* the myrtle trees, "
3: 7 give the places *a·* these that "
7:14 a whirlwind *a·* all the nations 5921
8:13 ye were a curse *a·* the heathen,
10: 9 And I will sow them *a·* the people:
12: 6 like an hearth of fire *a·* the wood,
8 and he that is feeble *a·* them at that
14:13 from the Lord shall be *a·* them;
Mal 1:10 Who is there even *a·* you that
11 shall be great *a·* the Gentiles;
11 name shall be great *a·* the heathen,
14 name is dreadful *a·* the heathen.
M't 2: 6 not the least *a·* the princes of *1722*
4:23 manner of disease *a·* the people. "
9:35 and every disease *a·* the people. * "
11:11 *A·* them that are born of women "
12:11 What man shall there be *a·* you, **1537*
13: 7 and some fell *a·* thorns; and the **1909*
22 that received seed *a·* the thorns *1519*
25 sowed tares *a·* the wheat, *303, 3319*
32 it is the greatest *a·* herbs, *
49 the wicked from *a·* the just, *3319*
16: 7 they reasoned *a·* themselves, *1722*
8 why reason ye *a·* yourselves, "
20:26 But it shall not be so *a·* you: "
26 whosoever will be great *a·* you, "
27 whosoever will be chief *a·* you, "
21:38 they said *a·* themselves, This is "
23:11 But he that is greatest *a·* you shall
26: 5 there be an uproar *a·* the people. *1722*
27:35 parted my garments *a·* them,
56 *A·* which was Mary Magdalene, *1722*

M't 28:15 reported a' the Jews until this day 1722
M'r 1:27 they questioned a' themselves, 4814
4: 7 some fell a' thorns, and the thorns 1519
18 they which are sown a' thorns; "
5: 3 had his dwelling a' the tombs; *1722
6: 4 own country, and a' his own kin, "
41 two fishes divided he a' them all. "
8:16 they reasoned a' themselves, *4314
19 the five loaves a' five thousand, 1519
20 when the seven a' four thousand, "
9:33 that ye disputed a' yourselves *4314
34 they had disputed a' themselves, * "
10:26 saying a' themselves, Who then * "
43 so shall it not be a' you: 1722
43 whosoever will be great a' you, "
12: 7 husbandmen said a' themselves, 4314
13:10 first be published a' all nations. *1519
15:31 said a' themselves with the 4314
40 a' whom was Mary Magdelene, 1722
16: 3 they said a' themselves, Who 4314
Lu 1: 1 are most surely believed a' us, 1722
25 take away my reproach a' men. "
28 thee: blessed art thou a' women.* "
42 Blessed art thou a' women, "
2:44 a' their kinsfolk and acquaintance. "
4:36 amazed and spake a' themselves,*4314
7:16 a great prophet is risen up a' us; 1722
28 A' those that are born of women "
8: 7 some fell a' thorns: and *1722, 3319
14 that which fell a' thorns are they, 1519
9:46 there arose a reasoning a' them, 1722
48 that is least a' you all, the same "
10: 3 forth as lambs a' wolves. *1722, 3319
30 and fell a' thieves, which stripped 4045
36 unto him that fell a' the thieves? 1519
16:15 which is highly esteemed a' men 1722
19: 2 was the chief a' the publicans, "
39 the Pharisees from a' the multitude "
20:14 him they reasoned a' themselves *4314
22:17 this, and divide it a' yourselves: "
23 began to enquire a' themselves, 4314
24 was also a strife a' them, 1722
26 he that is greatest a' you, "
27 a' you as he that serveth. *1722, 3319
37 reckoned a' the transgressors: *3326
55 together, Peter sat down a' them.*3319
24: 5 seek ye the living a' the dead? 3326
47 in his name a' all nations, *1519
Joh 1:14 was made flesh, and dwelt a' 1722
26 there standeth one a' you, *1722, 5216
6: 9 what are they a' so many? 1519
43 them, Murmur not a' yourselves. 3326
52 therefore strove a' themselves, *4314
7:12 much murmuring a' the people 1722
35 said the the Jews a' themselves, 4314
35 unto the dispersed a' the Gentiles, "
43 was a division a' the people *1722
8: 7 He that is without sin a' you, "
9:16 And there was a division a' them. 1722
10:19 a' the Jews for these sayings. "
11:54 no more openly a' the Jews; "
56 they for Jesus, and spake a' *3326
12:19 therefore said a' themselves, 4314
20 Greeks a' them that came up to 1537
42 a' the chief rulers also many * "
15:24 I had not done a' them the works 1722
16:17 of his disciples a' themselves, *4314
19 Do ye enquire a' yourselves of 3326
19:24 said therefore a' themselves, *4314
24 parted my raiment a' them, and "
21:23 saying abroad a' the brethren, 1519
Ac 1:21 Lord Jesus went in and out a' us, 1909
2:22 of God a' you by miracles *1519
3:23 destroyed from a' the people. "
4:12 given a' men, whereby we must 1722
15 they conferred a' themselves, 4315
17 it spread no further a' the people, 1519
34 there any a' them that lacked: 1722
5:12 wonders wrought a' the people; "
34 in reputation a' all the people, * "
6: 3 a' you seven men of honest report,1537
8 wonders and miracles a' the 1722
10:22 of good report a' all the nation *5259
12:18 was no small stir a' the soldiers, 1722
13:26 whosoever a' you feareth God, "
14:14 ran in a' the people, crying out, 1519
15: 7 while ago God made choice a' us, 1722
12 had wrought a' the Gentiles by "
19 a' the Gentiles are turned to God. 575
22 Silas, chief men a' the brethren: 1722
17:33 Paul departed from a' them. 3319
34 a' the which was Dionysius the 1722
18:11 teaching the word of God a' them. "
20:25 a' whom I have gone preaching "
29 grievous wolves enter in a' you, 1519
32 an inheritance a' all them which 1722
21:19 wrought a' the Gentiles by his "
21 teachest all the Jews which are a' 2596
34 some another, a' the multitude: 1722
23:10 take him by force from a' 3319
24: 5 a mover of sedition a' all the Jews "
21 I cried standing a' them, 1722
25: 5 which a' you are able, go down "
6 And when he had tarried a' them "
26: 3 customs which are a' the Jews: 2596
4 a' mine own nation at Jerusalem, 1722
18 inheritance a' them which are "
27:22 no loss of any man's life a' you, 1537
28: 4 said a' themselves, No doubt *4314
25 when they agreed not a' themselves,"
29 and had great reasoning a' *1722
Ro 1: 5 obedience to the faith a' all nations, "
6 A' whom are ye also the called "
13 have some fruit a' you also, * "
13 even as a' other Gentiles. * "
2:24 the name of God is blasphemed a' * "
Ro 8:29 the firstborn a' many brethren. 1722
11:17 wert graffed in a' them, and with "
12: 3 to every man that is a' you, "
15: 9 confess to thee a' the Gentiles, "
16: 7 are of note a' the apostles, who "
1Co 1:10 that there be no divisions a' you; "
11 there are contentions a' you. "
2: 2 not to know any thing a' you, "
6 speak wisdom a' them that are "
3: 3 there is a' you envying, and strife, "
18 If any man a' you seemeth to be "
5: 1 there is fornication a' you, "
1 as named a' the Gentiles, "
2 might be taken away from a' you. 3319
13 put away from a' yourselves "
6: 5 there is not a wise man a' you? 1722
7 utterly a fault a' you, because * "
11:18 there be divisions a' you; "
19 there must be also heresies a' you, "
19 approved may be made manifest a' "
30 many are weak and sickly a' you, "
15:12 how say some a' you that there "
2Co 1:19 Jesus Christ who was preached a' "
6:17 come out from a' them, 3319
10: 1 who in presence am base a' you, 1722
12 comparing themselves a' *
11: 6 manifest a' you in all things. 1519
26 in perils a' false brethren; 1722
12:12 a' you in all patience, in signs, "
21 my God will humble me a' you, *4314
Ga 1:16 I might preach him a' the heathen;1722
2: 2 which I preach a' the Gentiles, "
3: 1 set forth, crucified a' you? * "
5 worketh miracles a' you, doeth he "
Eph 2: 3 A' whom also we all had our "
3: 8 I should preach a' the Gentiles * "
5: 3 not be once named a' you, "
Ph'p 2:15 a' whom ye shine as lights in the "
Col 1:27 mystery a' the Gentiles; which is "
4:16 when this epistle is read a' you, 3844
1Th 1: 5 men we are a' you for your sake. *1722
2: 7 But we were gentle a' you, *1722, 3319
10 we behaved ourselves a' you that * "
5:12 a' you, and are over you in the 1722
13 And be at peace a' yourselves. "
15 follow that which is good, both a' *1519
2Th 1:10 testimony a' you was believed) *1909
3: 7 not ourselves disorderly a' you; 1722
11 which walk a' you disorderly, "
2Ti 2: 2 heard of me a' many witnesses, 1223
Heb 5: 1 priest taken from a' men is 1537
Jas 1:26 If any man a' you seem to be *1722
3: 6 so is the tongue a' our members, "
13 endued with knowledge a' you? "
4: 1 come wars and fightings a' you? "
5:13 Is any a' you afflicted? let him pray. "
14 Is any sick a' you? "
1Pe 2:12 your conversation honest a' the "
4: 8 have fervent charity a' yourselves: 1519
5: 1 elders which are a' you I exhort, 1722
2 flock of God which is a' you, "
2Pe 2: 1 false prophets also a' the people, "
1 shall be false teachers a' you, "
8 righteous man dwelling a' them, "
3Jo 9 loveth to have the preeminence a' "
Jude 15 convince all that are ungodly a' * "
Re 2:13 who was slain a' you, where 3844
7:15 shall dwell a' them. *1909
14: 4 were redeemed from a' men,

amongst
Ge 3: 8 a' the trees of the garden. 8432
23: 9 possession of a buryingplace a' * "

Amorite (*am'-o-rite*) See also AMORITES.
Ge 10:16 And the Jebusite, and the A', 567
14:13 dwelt in the plain of Mamre the A', "
48:22 I took out of the hand of the A' "
Ex 33: 2 will drive out the Canaanite, the A', "
34:11 I drive out before thee the A', "
Nu 32:39 dispossessed the A' which was in it. "
De 2:24 given into thine hand Sihon the A', "
Jos 9: 1 Hittite, and the A', the Canaanite, "
11: 3 east and on the west, and to the A', "
1Ch 1:14 The Jebusite also, and the A', "
Eze 16: 3 thy father was an A', and thy "
45 was a Hittite, and your father an A'. "
Am 2: 9 destroyed I the A' before them, "
10 to possess the land of the A'. "

Amorites (*am'-o-rites*)
Ge 14: 7 and also the A', that dwelt in 567
15:16 iniquity of the A' is not yet full. * "
21 And the A' and the Canaanites, * "
Ex 3: 8 and the Hittites, and the A', * "
17 and the A', and the Perizzites, * "
13: 5 and the A', and the Hivites, * "
23:23 and bring thee in unto the A', * "
Nu 13:29 the A', dwell in the mountains: * "
21:13 cometh out of the coasts of the A': "
13 between Moab and the A'. "
21 unto Sihon king of the A', "
25 dwelt in all the cities of the A', "
26 city of Sihon the king of the A', "
29 captivity unto Sihon king of the A'. "
31 Israel dwelt in the land of the A'. "
32 drove out the A' that were there. "
34 didst unto Sihon king of the A', "
22: 2 all that Israel had done to the A'. "
32:33 the kingdom of Sihon king of the A', "
De 1: 4 had slain Sihon the king of the A', "
7 and go to the mount of the A', "
19 the way of the mountain of the A', "
20 come unto the mountain of the A', "
27 deliver us into the hand of the A', "
44 A', which dwell in that mountain, "
3: 2 of the A', which dwelt at Heshbon. "
8 the hand of the two kings of the A' "
De 3: 9 and the A' call it Shenir;) 567
4:46 in the land of Sihon king of the A', "
47 two kings of the A', which were on "
7: 1 and the Girgashites, and the A', * "
20:17 namely, the Hittites, and the A', * "
31: 4 to Sihon and to Og, kings of the A', "
Jos 2:10 ye did unto the two kings of the A', "
3:10 and the A', and the Jebusites, * "
5: 1 when all the kings of the A', "
7: 7 deliver us into the hand of the A', "
9:10 the two kings of the A', that were "
10: 5 Therefore the five kings of the A', "
6 all the kings of the A' that dwell "
12 when the Lord delivered up the A' "
12: 2 Sihon king of the A', who dwelt in "
8 the A', and the Canaanites, * "
13: 4 unto Aphek, to the borders of the A': "
10 Sihon king of the A', which reigned "
21 kingdom of Sihon king of the A', "
24: 8 brought you into the land of the A', "
11 fought against you, the A', * "
12 even the two kings of the A'; "
15 or the gods of the A', in whose land "
18 even the A' which dwelt in the land: "
J'g 1:34 the A' forced the children of Dan "
35 A' would dwell in mount Heres "
36 the coast of the A' was from the "
3: 5 the Canaanites, Hittites, and A', * "
6:10 fear not the gods of the A', "
10: 8 Jordan in the land of the A', "
11 the Egyptians, and from the A', "
11:19 Sihon king of the A', the king of "
21 A', the inhabitants of that country. "
22 possessed all the coasts of the A', "
23 of Israel hath dispossessed the A' "
1Sa 7:14 peace between Israel and the A'. "
2Sa 21: 2 but of the remnant of the A'; "
1Ki 4:19 the country of Sihon king of the A', "
9:20 the people that were left of the A', "
21:26 according to all things as did the A', "
2Ki 21:11 wickedly above all that the A' did, "
2Ch 8: 7 of the Hittites, and the A', "
Ezr 9: 1 Moabites, the Egyptians, and the A'. "
Ne 9: 8 the A', and the Perizzites, * "
Ps 135:11 Sihon king of the A', and Og "
136:19 Sihon king of the A': for his mercy "

Amos (*A'-mos*)
Am 1: 1 The words of A', who was among 5986
7: 8 And the Lord said unto me, A', "
10 saying, A' hath conspired against "
11 thus A' saith, Jeroboam shall die "
12 Amaziah said unto A', O thou seer, "
14 answered A', and said to Amaziah, "
8: 2 And he said, A', what seest thou? "
Lu 3:25 which was the son of A', 301

amounting
2Ch 3: 8 gold, a' to six hundred talents.

Amoz (*A'-moz*)
2Ki 19: 2 to Isaiah the prophet the son of A'. 531
20 the son of A' sent to Hezekiah, "
20: 1 the son of A' came to him, and said "
2Ch 26:22 did Isaiah the prophet, the son of A', "
32:20 the son of A', prayed and cried to "
32 Isaiah the prophet, the son of A', "
Isa 1: 1 The vision of Isaiah the son of A', "
2: 1 The word that Isaiah the son of A' "
13: 1 which Isaiah the son of A' did see. "
20: 2 the Lord by Isaiah the son of A', "
37: 2 Isaiah the prophet the son of A'. "
21 the son of A' sent unto Hezekiah, "
38: 1 son of A' came unto him, and said "

Amphipolis (*am-fip'-o-lis*)
Ac 17: 1 when they had passed through A' 295

Amplias (*am'-ple-as*)
Ro 16: 8 Greet A' my beloved in the Lord. *291

Amram (*am'-ram*) See also AMRAMITES; AMRAM'S; HEMDAN.
Ex 6:18 the sons of Kohath; A', and Izhar, 6019
20 And A' took him Jochebed, his "
20 and the years of the life of A' were "
Nu 3:19 of Kohath by their families; A', "
26:58 Korathites. And Kohath begat A'. "
59 and she bare unto A' Aaron, and "
1Ch 1:41 A', and Eshban, and Ithran, and 2566
6: 2 A', Izhar, and Hebron, and Uzziel. 6019
3 children of A'; Aaron and Moses, "
18 sons of Kohath were, A', and Izhar, "
23:12 sons of Kohath; A', Izhar, Hebron, "
13 sons of A'; Aaron and Moses: "
24:20 sons of A'; Shubael: of the sons "
Ezr 10:34 sons of Bani; Maadai, A', and Uel, "

Amramites (*am'-ram-ites*)
Nu 3:27 Kohath was the family of the A', 6020
1Ch 26:23 Of the A', and the Izharites, the "

Amram's (*am'-rams*)
Nu 26:59 name of A' wife was Jochebed, 6019

Amraphel (*am'-raf-el*)
Ge 14: 1 it came to pass in the days of A' 569
9 and A' king of Shinar, and Arioch "

Amzi (*am'-zi*)
1Ch 6:46 The son of A', the son of Bani, 557
Ne 11:12 the son of A', the son of Zechariah, "

an. See in the APPENDIX; also ANOTHER.

Anab (*a'-nab*)
Jos 11:21 from A', and from all the 6024
15:50 And A', and Eshtemoh, and Anim, "

Anah (*a'-nah*)
Ge 36: 2 Aholibamah, the daughter of A' 6034
14, 18 Aholibamah, the daughter of A', "
20 and Shobal, and Zibeon, and A', "
24 of Zibeon; both Ajah and A'; "

Ge 36:24 was that *A·* that found the mules 6034
25 And the children of *A·* were these; "
25 Aholibamah the daughter of *A·*. "
29 duke Shobal, duke Zibeon, duke *A·*, "
1Ch 1:38 and Zibeon, and *A·*, and Dishon, "
40 the sons of Zibeon; Aiah, and *A·*. "
41 The sons of *A·*; Dishon. And the "

Anaharath (*an-a-ha'-rath*)
Jos 19:19 Haphraim, and Shihon, and *A·*, 588

Anaiah (*an-a-i'-ah*)
Ne 8: 4 and Shema, and *A·*, and Urijah, 6043
10:22 Pelatiah, Hanan, *A·*, "

Anak (*a'-nak*) See also ANAKIMS.
Nu 13:22 and Talmai, the children of *A·*, 6061
28 we saw the children of *A·* there. "
33 we saw the giants, the sons of *A·*, "
De 9: 2 stand before the children of *A·*! "
Jos 15:13 the city of Arba the father of *A·*, "
14 drove thence the three sons of *A·*, "
14 and Talmai, the children of *A·*. "
21:11 the city of Arba the father of *A·*, "
J'g 1:20 expelled thence the three sons of *A·*. "

Anakims (*an'-ak-ims*)
De 1:28 seen the sons of the *A·* there. 6062
2:10 and many, and tall, as the *A·*; "
11 were accounted giants, as the *A·*; "
21 as the *A·*; but the Lord destroyed "
9: 2 and tall, the children of the *A·*, "
Jos 11:21 cut off the *A·* from the mountains, "
22 There was none of the *A·* left "
14:12 heardest in that day how the *A·* "
15 was a great man among the *A·*. "

Anamim (*an'-am-im*)
Ge 10:13 *A·*, and Lehabim, and Naphtuhim, 6047
1Ch 1:11 Mizraim begat Ludim, and *A·*, "

Anammelech (*a-nam'-mel-ek*)
2Ki 17:31 and *A·*, the gods of Sepharvaim. 6048

Anan (*a'-nan*)
Ne 10:26 And Ahijah, Hanan, *A·*, 6052

Anani (*an-a'-ni*)
1Ch 3:24 Johanan, and Dalaiah, and *A·*, 6054

Ananiah (*an-an-i'-ah*) See also ANANIAS.
Ne 3:23 son of Maaseiah, the son of *A·*, 6055
11:32 And at Anathoth, Nob, *A·*, "

Ananias (*an-an-i'-as*) See also ANANIAH.
Ac 5: 1 a certain man named *A·*, 367
3 But Peter said, *A·*, why hath Satan "
5 *A·* hearing these words fell down, "
9:10 disciple at Damascus, named *A·*; "
10 said the Lord in a vision, *A·*. "
12 a vision a man named *A·* coming "
13 Then *A·* answered, Lord, "
17 *A·* went his way, and entered into "
22:12 *A·*, a devout man according to the "
23: 2 the high priest *A·* commanded "
24: 1 after five days *A·* the high priest "

Anath (*a'-nath*) See also BETH-ANATH.
J'g 3:31 was Shamgar the son of *A·*, which 6067
5: 6 the days of Shamgar the son of *A·*, "

Anathema (*a-nath'-em-ah*)
1Co 16:22 let him be *A·* Maran-atha. 331

Anathoth (*an'-a-thoth*) See also ANETOTITHE.
Jos 21:18 *A·* with her suburbs, and Almon 6068
1Ki 2:26 Get thee to *A·*, unto thine own fields; "
1Ch 6:60 and *A·* with her suburbs. All their "
7: 8 and Abiah, and *A·*, and Alameth. "
Ezr 2:23 *A·*, an hundred twenty and eight. "
Ne 7:27 *A·*, an hundred twenty and eight. "
10:19 Hariph, *A·*, Nebai, "
11:32 And at *A·*, Nob, Ananiah, "
Isa 10:30 be heard unto Laish, O poor *A·*. "
Jer 1: 1 in *A·*, in the land of Benjamin: "
11:21 saith the Lord of the men of *A·*, "
23 will bring evil upon the men of *A·*, "
29:27 thou not reproved Jeremiah of *A·*, "
32: 7 Buy thee my field that is in *A·*: "
8 field, I pray thee, that is in *A·*, "
9 my uncle's son, that was in *A·*, "

ancestors
Le 26:45 remember the covenant of their *a·*, 7223

anchor See also ANCHORS.
Heb 6:19 hope we have as an *a·* of the soul, 45

anchors
Ac 27:29 they cast four *a·* out of the stern, 45
30 have cast *a·* out of the foreship
40 they had taken up the *a·*, 45

ancient See also ANCIENTS.
De 33:15 chief things of the *a·* mountains, 6924
J'g 5:21 that *a·* river, the river Kishon. 6917
2Ki 19:25 Hast thou not heard...of *a·* times 6924
1Ch 4:22 And these are *a·* things. 6267
Ezr 3:12 of the fathers, who were *a·* men, *2204
Job 12:12 With the *a·* is wisdom; *3453
Ps 77: 5 the years of *a·* times. 5769
Pr 22:28 Remove not the *a·* landmark, "
Isa 3: 2 and the prudent, and the *a·*, ‡2204
5 himself proudly against the *a·*, ‡ "
9:15 *a·* honourable, he is the head; ‡ "
19:11 son of the wise, the son of *a·* kings? 6924
23: 7 whose antiquity is of *a·* days? "
37:26 Hast thou not heard...of *a·* times, "
44: 7 since I appointed the *a·* people? 5769
45:21 hath declared this from *a·* time? 6924
46:10 *a·* times the things that are not "
47: 6 upon the *a·* hast thou very *2204
51: 9 *a·* days, in the generations of old. *6924
Jer 5:15 mighty nation, it is an *a·* nation, 5769
18:15 in their ways from the *a·* paths, "
Eze 9: 6 Then they began at the *a·* men ‡2204
36: 2 the *a·* high places are ours in 5769

Da 7: 9 *A·* of days did sit, whose garment *6268
13 came to the *A·* of days, * "
22 *A·* of days came, and judgment * "

ancients
1Sa 24:13 As saith the proverb of the *a·*, 6931
Ps 119:100 I understand more than the *a·*, *2204
Isa 3:14 enter into judgment with the *a·* * "
24:23 and before his *a·* gloriously. "
Jer 19: 1 and take of the *a·* of the people, * "
1 and of the *a·* of the priests; * "
Eze 7:26 priest, and counsel from the *a·*. ‡ "
8:11 seventy men of the *a·* of the ‡ "
12 the *a·* of the house of Israel do * "
27: 9 *a·* of Gebal and the wise men ‡ "

ancle See also ANCLES.
Ac 3: 7 feet and *a·* bones received strength. 4974

ancle-bones See ANCLE and BONES.

ancles
Eze 47: 3 the waters were to the *a·*. * 657

and See in the APPENDIX.

Andrew (*an'-drew*)
M't 4:18 Simon called Peter, and *A·* his 406
10: 2 called Peter, and *A·* his brother; "
M'k 1:16 Simon and *A·* his brother casting "
29 into the house of Simon and *A·*, "
3:18 *A·*, and Philip, and Bartholomew, "
13: 3 John and *A·* asked him privately, "
Lu 6:14 named Peter,) and *A·* his brother, "
Joh 1:40 *A·*, Simon Peter's brother. "
44 Bethsaida, the city of *A·* and Peter. "
6: 8 One of his disciples, *A·*, Simon "
12:22 Philip cometh and telleth *A·*: "
22 and again *A·* and Philip tell Jesus. "
Ac 1:13 *A·*, Philip, and Thomas, "

Andronicus (*an-dro-ni'-cus*)
Ro 16: 7 Salute *A·* and Junia, my kinsmen, 408

Anem (*a'-nem*) See also EN-GANNIM.
1Ch 6:73 suburbs, and *A·* with her suburbs: 6046

Aner (*a'-nur*)
Ge 14:13 of Eshcol, and brother of *A·*: 6063
24 the men which went with me, *A·*, "
1Ch 6:70 *A·* with her suburbs, and Bileam "

Anethothite (*an'-e-thoth-ite*) See also ANETOTHITE.
2Sa 23:27 Abiezer the *A·*, Mebunnai the 6069

Anetothite (*an'-e-toth-ite*) See also ANETHOTHITE; ANTOTHITE.
1Ch 27:12 Abiezer the *A·*, of the Benjamites: 6069

angel See also ANGEL'S; ANGELS; ARCHANGEL.
Ge 16: 7 the *a·* of the Lord found her by a 4397
9 the *a·* of the Lord said unto her, "
10 *a·* of the Lord said unto her, I will "
11 the *a·* of the Lord said unto her, "
21:17 the *a·* of God called to Hagar out "
22:11 the *a·* of the Lord called unto him "
15 *a·* of the Lord called unto Abraham "
24: 7 he shall send his *a·* before thee "
40 will send his *a·* with thee, "
31:11 the *a·* of God spake unto me in a "
48:16 The *A·* which redeemed me from "
Ex 3: 2 *a·* of the Lord appeared unto him, "
14:19 the *a·* of God, which went before "
23:20 Behold, I send an *A·* before thee, "
23 mine *A·* shall go before thee, "
32:34 mine *A·* shall go before thee: "
33: 2 I will send an *a·* before thee; "
Nu 20:16 he heard our voice, and sent an *a·*, "
22:22 the *a·* of the Lord stood in the way "
23 the ass saw the *a·* of the Lord "
24 the *a·* of the Lord stood in a path "
25 And when the ass saw the *a·* of the "
26 the *a·* of the Lord went further, "
27 the *a·* of the Lord, she fell down "
31 he saw the *a·* of the Lord standing "
32 the *a·* of the Lord said unto him, "
34 Balaam said unto the *a·* of the "
35 *a·* of the Lord said unto Balaam, "
J'g 2: 1 an *a·* of the Lord came up from "
4 when the *a·* of the Lord spake "
5:23 Meroz, said the *a·* of the Lord, "
6:11 there came an *a·* of the Lord, "
12 *a·* of the Lord appeared unto him, "
20 the *a·* of God said unto him, Take "
21 *a·* of the Lord put forth the end "
21 Then the *a·* of the Lord departed "
22 perceived that he was an *a·* "
22 I have seen an *a·* of the Lord "
13: 3 the *a·* of the Lord appeared unto "
6 like the countenance of an *a·* "
9 the *a·* of God came again unto the "
13, 16 the *a·* of the Lord said unto "
15, 17 Manoah said unto the *a·* of the "
16 Manoah knew not that he was an *a·* "
18 And the *a·* of the Lord said "
19 and the *a·* did wondrously; "
20 the *a·* of the Lord ascended in the 4397
21 *a·* of the Lord did no more appear "
21 Manoah knew that he was an *a·* "
1Sa 29: 9 good in my sight, as an *a·* of God: "
2Sa 14:17 *a·* of God, so is my lord the king 4397
20 to the wisdom of an *a·* of God, "
19:27 the king is as an *a·* of God: "
24:16 when the *a·* stretched out his hand "
16 to the *a·* that destroyed the people, "
16 *a·* of the Lord was by the threshing "
17 the *a·* that smote the people, "
1Ki 13:18 and an *a·* spake unto me by the "
19: 5 an *a·* touched him, and said unto "
7 the *a·* of the Lord came again "
2Ki 1: 3 the *a·* of the Lord said to Elijah "
15 the *a·* of the Lord said unto Elijah, "
19:35 the *a·* of the Lord went out, "

1Ch 21:12 and the *a·* of the Lord destroying 4397
15 God sent an *a·* unto Jerusalem "
15 *a·* that destroyed, It is enough, "
15 And the *a·* of the Lord stood by "
16 saw the *a·* of the Lord stand "
18 the *a·* of the Lord commanded "
20 Ornan turned back, and saw the *a·*; "
27 And the Lord commanded the *a·*; "
30 the sword of the *a·* of the Lord. "
2Ch 32:21 the Lord sent an *a·*, which cut off "
Ps 34: 7 The *a·* of the Lord encampeth "
35: 5 let the *a·* of the Lord chase them. "
6 let the *a·* of the Lord persecute "
Ec 5: 6 neither say thou before the *a·*, "
Isa 37:36 the *a·* of the Lord went forth, "
63: 9 the *a·* of his presence saved them: "
Da 3:28 who hath sent his *a·*, and delivered 4398
6:22 My God hath sent his *a·*, and hath "
Ho 12: 4 he had power over the *a·*, 4397
Zec 1: 9 the *a·* that talked with me "
11 they answered the *a·* of the Lord "
12 *a·* of the Lord answered and said, "
13 the Lord answered the *a·* that "
14 the *a·* that communed with me "
19 I said unto the *a·* that talked "
2: 3 *a·* that talked with me went forth, "
3 and another *a·* went out "
3: 1 the *a·* of the Lord, and Satan "
3 stood before the *a·*. "
5 And the *a·* of the Lord stood by. "
6 the *a·* of the Lord protested unto "
4: 1 *a·* that talked with me came again, "
4 spake to the *a·* that talked with "
5 *a·* that talked with me answered "
5: 5 *a·* that talked with me went forth, "
10 said I to the *a·* that talked with me, "
6: 4 I answered and said unto the *a·* "
5 the *a·* answered and said unto me, "
12: 8 as the *a·* of the Lord before them. "
M't 1:20 *a·* of the Lord appeared unto him 32
24 did as the *a·* of the Lord had bidden "
2:13 *a·* of the Lord appeareth to * "
19 behold, an *a·* of the Lord appeareth "
28: 2 for the *a·* of the Lord descended "
5 the *a·* answered and said unto the "
Lu 1:11 appeared unto him an *a·* of the Lord "
13 the *a·* said unto him, Fear not, "
18 Zacharias said unto the *a·*, "
19 the *a·* answering said unto him, "
26 the *a·* Gabriel was sent from God "
28 And the *a·* came in unto her, * "
30 *a·* said unto her, Fear not, Mary: "
34 Then said Mary unto the *a·*, "
35 the *a·* answered and said unto her, "
38 And the *a·* departed from her. "
2: 9 the *a·* of the Lord came upon them, "
10 the *a·* said unto them, Fear not: "
13 *a·* a multitude of the heavenly "
21 which was so named of the *a·* "
22:43 there appeared an *a·* unto him "
Joh 5: 4 *a·* went down at a certain season * "
12:29 others said, An *a·* spake to him. "
Ac 5:19 the *a·* of the Lord by night opened "
6:15 as it had been the face of an *a·*. "
7:30 an *a·* of the Lord in a flame "
35 the hand of the *a·* which appeared "
38 with the *a·* which spake to him "
8:26 *a·* of the Lord spake unto Philip, "
10: 3 an *a·* of God coming in to him, "
7 the *a·* which spake unto Cornelius "
22 warned from God by an holy *a·* "
11:13 how he had seen an *a·* in his house, "
12: 7 the *a·* of the Lord came upon him, "
8 the *a·* said unto him, Gird thyself, "
9 which was done by the *a·*; "
10 forthwith the *a·* departed "
11 the Lord hath sent his *a·*, "
15 said they, It is his *a·*. "
23 the *a·* of the Lord smote him, 32
23: 8 resurrection, neither *a·*, nor spirit: "
9 if a spirit or an *a·* hath spoken "
27:23 by me this night the *a·* of God, "
2Co 11:14 transformed into an *a·* of light. "
Ga 1: 8 we, or an *a·* from heaven, preach "
4:14 received me as an *a·* of God, "
Re 1: 1 he sent and signified it by his *a·* "
2: 1 the *a·* of the church of Ephesus "
8 the *a·* of the church in Smyrna "
12 to the *a·* of the church in Pergamos "
18 the *a·* of the church in Thyatira "
3: 1 unto the *a·* of the church in Sardis "
7 the *a·* of the church in Philadelphia "
14 unto the *a·* of the church of the "
5: 2 I saw a strong *a·* proclaiming "
7: 2 another *a·* ascending from the east, "
8: 3 *a·* came and stood at the altar, "
5 the *a·* took the censer, and filled it "
7 The first *a·* sounded, and there * "
8 the second *a·* sounded, and as it "
10 the third *a·* sounded, and there fell "
12 the fourth *a·* sounded, and the "
13 an *a·* flying through the midst * "
9: 1 the fifth *a·* sounded, and I saw "
11 which is the *a·* of the bottomless pit, "
13 and the sixth *a·* sounded, "
14 saying to the sixth *a·* which had the "
10: 1 And I saw another mighty *a·* come "
5 *a·* which I saw stand upon the sea "
7 of the voice of the seventh *a·*, "
8 open in the hand of the *a·* "
9 I went unto the *a·*, and said unto "
11: 1 and the *a·* stood, saying, Rise, * "
15 and the seventh *a·* sounded; "
14: 6 I saw another *a·* fly in the midst "
8 and there followed another *a·*, "
9 the third *a·* followed them. "

Re 14:15, 17 a' came out of the temple 32
18 another a' came out from the altar, "
19 a' thrust in his sickle into the earth, "
16: 3 the second a' poured out his vial * "
4 the third a' poured out his vial * "
5 I heard the a' of the waters say, "
8 the fourth a' poured out his vial * "
10 the fifth a' poured out his vial * "
12 the sixth a' poured out his vial * "
17 the seventh a' poured out his vial* "
17: 7 and the a' said unto me, "
18: 1 I saw another a' come down from "
21 a mighty a' took up a stone "
19:17 I saw an a' standing in the sun; "
20: 1 and I saw an a' come down "
21:17 measure of a man, that is, of the a'. "
22: 6 his a' to shew unto his servants "
8 before the feet of the a' "
16 have sent mine a' to testify unto "

angel's
Re 8: 4 before God out of the a' hand. 32
10:10 the little book out of the a' hand, "

angels See also ANGELS'.
Ge 19: 1 there came two a' to Sodom 4397
15 then the a' hastened Lot, "
28:12 the a' of God ascending "
32: 1 way, and the a' of God met him. "
Job 4:18 and his a' he charged with folly: "
Ps 8: 5 him a little lower than the a', * 430
68:17 thousand, even thousands of a': *8136
78:49 by sending evil a' among them. 4397
91:11 shall give his a' charge over thee, "
103:20 Bless the Lord, ye his a', "
104: 4 Who maketh his a' spirits; * "
148: 2 Praise ye him, all his a': "
M't 4: 6 He shall give his a' charge 32
11 a' came and ministered unto him. "
13:39 and the reapers are the a'. "
41 Son of man shall send forth his a', "
49 the a' shall come forth, and sever "
16:27 the glory of his Father with his a'; "
18:10 That in heaven their a' do always "
22:30 are as the a' of God in heaven. "
24:31 And he shall send his a' with a great "
36 no, not the a' of heaven, "
25:31 all the holy a' with him, "
41 prepared for the devil and his a': "
26:53 more than twelve legions of a'? "
M'r 1:13 and the a' ministered unto him. "
8:38 glory of his Father with the holy a'. "
12:25 are as the a' which are in heaven. "
13:27 then shall he send his a', "
32 not the a' which are in heaven, "
Lu 2:15 as the a' were gone away from "
4:10 He shall give his a' charge over thee, "
9:26 in his Father's, and of the holy a'. "
12: 8 confess before the a' of God: "
9 denied before the a' of God. "
15:10 in the presence of the a' of God "
16:22 carried by the a' into Abraham's "
20:36 for they are equal unto the a'; 2465
24:23 had also seen a vision of a', 32
Joh 1:51 the a' of God ascending and "
20:12 seeth two a' in white sitting, the "
Ac 7:53 the law by the disposition of a', "
Ro 8:38 nor life, nor a', nor principalities, "
1Co 4: 9 world, and to a', and to men. "
6: 3 Know ye not that we shall judge a'? "
11:10 on her head because of the a'. "
13: 1 the tongues of men and of a', "
Ga 3:19 and it was ordained by a' in the "
Col 2:18 humility and worshipping of a', "
2Th 1: 7 from heaven with his mighty a', "
1Ti 3:16 in the Spirit, seen of a', preached "
5:21 Jesus Christ, and the elect a', "
Heb 1: 4 made so much better than the a', "
5 unto which of the a' said he at "
6 let all the a' of God worship him. "
7 of the a' he saith, "
7 Who maketh his a' spirits, "
13 to which of the a' said he at any "
2: 2 if the word spoken by a' was "
5 unto the a' hath he not put in "
7 a little lower than the a'; "
9 made a little lower than the a' "
16 not on him the nature of a'; "
12:22 an innumerable company of a', "
13: 2 some have entertained a' unawares. "
1Pe 1:12 things the a' desire to look into. "
3:22 a' and authorities and powers being "
2Pe 2: 4 spared not the a' that sinned, "
11 Whereas a', which are greater "
Jude 6 a' which kept not their first estate, "
Re 1:20 the a' of the seven churches: "
3: 5 my Father, and before his a'. "
5:11 I heard the voice of many a' round "
7: 1 I saw four a' standing on the four "
2 with a loud voice to the four a', "
11 all the a' stood round about the "
8: 2 I saw the seven a' which stood "
6 a' which had the seven trumpets "
13 the trumpet of the three a', which "
9:14 Loose the four a' which are bound "
15 and the four a' were loosed, "
12: 7 Michael and his a' fought against "
7 and the dragon fought and his a', "
9 his a' were cast out with him. "
14:10 in the presence of the holy a', "
15: 1 seven a' having the seven last "
6 seven a' came out of the temple, "
7 gave unto the seven a' seven golden "
8 of the seven a' were fulfilled. "
16: 1 saying to the seven a', Go your "
17: 1 one of the seven a' which had the "
21: 9 unto me one of the seven a' which "
Re 21:12 at the gates twelve a', 32

angels'
Ps 78:25 Man did eat a' food: * 47

anger See also ANGERED.
Ge 27:45 Until thy brother's a' turn away * 639
30: 2 Jacob's a' was kindled against "
44:18 thine a' burn against thy servant: "
49: 6 in their a' they slew a man, "
7 Cursed be their a', for it was fierce; "
Ex 4:14 the a' of the Lord was kindled "
11: 8 out from Pharaoh in a great a'. "
32:19 Moses' a' waxed hot, and he cast "
22 Let not the a' of my lord wax hot; "
Nu 11: 1 heard it; and his a' was kindled; "
10 the a' of the Lord was kindled "
12: 9 a' of the Lord was kindled against "
22:22 God's a' was kindled because he "
27 Balaam's a' was kindled, and he "
24:10 Balak's a' was kindled against 639
25: 3 the a' of the Lord was kindled "
4 that the fierce a' of the Lord may "
32:10, 13 the Lord's a' was kindled "
14 to augment yet the fierce a' of the "
De 4:25 Lord thy God, to provoke him to a': 3707
6:15 lest the a' of the Lord thy God be 639
7: 4 will the a' of the Lord be kindled "
9:18 the Lord, to provoke him to a'. 3707
19 I was afraid of the a' and hot 639
13:17 turn from the fierceness of his a', "
29:20 a' of the Lord and his jealousy "
23 which the Lord overthrew in his a', "
24 meaneth the heat of this great a'? "
27 the a' of the Lord was kindled "
28 rooted them out of their land in a', "
31:17 Then my a' shall be kindled "
29 to provoke him to a' through the 3707
32:16 provoked they him to a'. "
21 they have provoked me to a' with "
21 I will provoke them to a' with a "
22 For a fire is kindled in mine a', 639
Jos 7: 1 the a' of the Lord was kindled "
26 turned from the fierceness of his a'. "
23:16 then shall the a' of the Lord be "
J'g 2:12 and provoked the Lord to a'. 3707
14 the a' of the Lord was hot against 639
20 And the a' of the Lord was hot "
3: 8 a' of the Lord was hot against Israel, "
6:39 Let not thine a' be hot against me, "
8: 3 their a' was abated toward him, 7307
9:30 son of Ebed, his a' was kindled. 639
10: 7 the a' of the Lord was hot against "
14:19 his a' was kindled, and he went up "
1Sa 11: 6 his a' was kindled greatly. "
17:28 Eliab's a' was kindled against "
20:30 Saul's a' was kindled against "
34 arose from the table in fierce a', "
2Sa 6: 7 the a' of the Lord was kindled "
12: 5 David's a' was greatly kindled "
24: 1 again the a' of the Lord was "
1Ki 14: 9 images, to provoke me to a', 3707
15 groves, provoking the Lord to a'. "
15:30 the Lord God of Israel to a'. "
16: 2 provoke me to a' with their sins; "
7 provoking him to a' with the work "
13 the Lord God of Israel to a' "
26 provoke the Lord God of Israel to a' "
33 Israel to a' than all the kings of "
21:22 thou hast provoked me to a', "
22:53 and provoked to a' the Lord God "
2Ki 13: 3 the a' of the Lord was kindled 639
17:11 things to provoke the Lord to a': 3707
17 the Lord, to provoke him to a'. "
21: 6 to provoke him to a'. "
15 provoked me to a', since the day "
22:17 that they might provoke me to a' "
23:19 made to provoke the Lord to a'. "
26 wherewith his a' was kindled 639
24:20 through the a' of the Lord it came "
1Ch 13:10 the a' of the Lord was kindled "
2Ch 25:10 wherefore their a' was greatly "
10 they returned home in great a'. "
15 the a' of the Lord was kindled "
28:25 and provoked to a' the Lord God 3707
33: 6 to provoke him to a'. "
34:25 that they might provoke me to a' "
Ne 4: 5 they have provoked thee to a' "
9:17 merciful, slow to a', and of great 639
Es 1:12 and his a' burned in him. 2534
Job 9: 5 which overturneth them in his a'. 639
13 God will not withdraw his a', "
18: 4 He teareth himself in his a': "
21:17 God distributeth sorrows in his a'. "
35:15 is not so, he hath visited in his a'; "
Ps 6: 1 O Lord, rebuke me not in thine a', "
7: 6 Arise, O Lord, in thine a', lift up "
21: 9 fiery oven in the time of thine a': 6440
27: 9 put not thy servant away in a': 639
30: 5 his a' endureth but a moment; "
37: 8 Cease from a', and forsake wrath: "
38: 3 in my flesh because of thine a'; *2195
56: 7 in thine a' cast down the people, 639
69:24 let thy wrathful a' take hold of "
74: 1 doth thine a' smoke against the "
77: 9 in a' shut up his tender mercies? "
78:21 a' also came up against Israel; "
38 many a time turned he his a' away, "
49 upon them the fierceness of his a', "
50 He made a way to his a'; "
58 For they provoked him to a' with 3707
85: 3 from the fierceness of thine a'. 639
4 cause thine a' toward us to cease. *3708
5 out thine a' to all generations? 639
90: 7 we are consumed by thine a', "
11 Who knoweth the power of thine a'? "
103: 8 gracious, slow to a', and plenteous "
Ps 106:29 Thus they provoked him to a' 3707
145: 8 slow to a', and of great mercy. 639
Pr 15: 1 grievous words stir up a'. "
18 that is slow to a' appeaseth strife. "
16:32 slow to a' is better than the mighty, "
19:11 discretion of a man deferreth his a'; "
20: 2 whoso provoketh him to a' sinneth 5674
21:14 A gift in secret pacifieth a': 639
22: 8 the rod of his a' shall fail. *5678
27: 4 is cruel, and a' is outrageous; 639
Ec 7: 9 a' resteth in the bosom of fools. 3708
Isa 1: 4 the Holy One of Israel unto a', *5006
5:25 the a' of the Lord kindled against 639
25 all this his a' is not turned away, "
7: 4 the fierce a' of Rezin with Syria, "
9:12 all this his a' is not turned away, "
17 his a' is not turned away, but his "
21 against Judah. For all this his a' "
10: 4 under the slain. For all this his a' "
5 O Assyrian, the rod of mine a', "
25 and mine a' in their destruction. "
12: 1 thine a' is turned away, and thou "
13: 3 called my mighty ones for mine a', "
9 both with wrath and fierce a', "
13 in the day of his fierce a'. "
14: 6 he that ruled the nations in a', "
30:27 from far burning with his a', "
30 with the indignation of his a', "
42:25 poured upon him the fury of his a', "
48: 9 name's sake will I defer mine a', "
63: 3 for I will tread them in mine a', "
6 tread down the people in mine a', "
65: 3 A people that provoketh me to a' *3707
66:15 to render his a' with fury, and his 639
Jer 2:35 surely his a' shall turn from me. "
3: 5 Will he reserve his a' forever? "
12 not cause mine a' to fall upon you: 6440
12 and I will not keep a' forever. "
4: 8 for the fierce a' of the Lord is not 639
26 presence of the Lord by his fierce a'. "
7:18 that they may provoke me to a'. 3707
19 Do they provoke me to a'? "
20 mine a' and my fury shall be poured 639
8:19 Why have they provoked me to a' 3707
10:24 not in thine a', lest thou bring me 639
11:17 to provoke me to a' in offering 3707
12:13 because of the fierce a' of the Lord. 639
15:14 for a fire is kindled in mine a', "
17: 4 have kindled a fire in mine a', "
18:23 with them in the time of thine a'. "
21: 5 a', and in fury, and in great wrath. "
23:20 The a' of the Lord shall not return, "
25: 6 provoke me not to a' with the 3707
7 that ye might provoke me to a' "
37 because of the fierce a' of the Lord. 639
38 because of his fierce a'. "
30:24 a' of the Lord shall not return, "
32:29 other gods, to provoke me to a'. 3707
30 provoked me to a' with the work "
31 to me as a provocation of mine a' 639
32 provoke me to a', they, their kings, 3707
37 I have driven them in mine a', 639
33: 5 whom I have slain in mine a', "
36: 7 for great is the a' and the fury "
42:18 As mine a' and my fury hath been "
44: 3 provoke me to a', in that they 3707
6 and mine a' was poured forth, 639
49:37 evil upon them, even my fierce a', "
51:45 from the fierce a' of the Lord. "
52: 3 through the a' of the Lord it came "
La 1:12 me in the day of his fierce a'. "
2: 1 with a cloud in his a', "
1 his footstool in the day of his a'! "
3 He hath cut off in his fierce a' "
6 of his a' the king and the priest. "
21 slain them in the day of thine a'; "
22 day of the Lord's a' none escaped "
3:43 covered with a', and persecuted us: "
66 Persecute and destroy them in a' "
4:11 he hath poured out his fierce a', "
16 a' of the Lord hath divided them; 6440
Eze 5:13 shall mine a' be accomplished, 639
15 in a' and in fury and in furious "
7: 3 I will send mine a' upon thee, "
8 accomplish mine a' upon thee: "
8:17 returned to provoke me to a': 3707
13:13 overflowing shower in mine a', 639
16:26 whoredoms, to provoke me to a'. 3707
20: 8 to accomplish my a' against them 639
21 to accomplish my a' against them "
22:20 so will I gather you in mine a' "
25:14 in Edom according to mine a' "
35:11 I will even do according to thine a', "
43: 8 I have consumed them in mine a'. "
Da 9:16 let thine a' and thy fury be turned "
11:20 neither in a', nor in battle. "
Ho 8: 5 mine a' is kindled against them: "
11: 9 execute the fierceness of mine a', "
12:14 provoked him to a' most bitterly: 3707
13:11 I gave thee a king in mine a', 639
14: 4 for mine a' is turned away from him. "
Joe 2:13 slow to a', and of great kindness, "
Am 1:11 his a' did tear perpetually, "
Jon 3: 9 turn away from his fierce a', "
4: 2 slow to a', and of great kindness, "
Mic 5:15 I will execute vengeance in a' "
7:18 he retaineth not his a' for ever, "
Na 1: 3 The Lord is slow to a', and great "
6 abide in the fierceness of his a'? "
Hab 3: 8 thine a' against the rivers? "
12 thou didst thresh the heathen in a'. "
Zep 2: 2 before the fierce a' of the Lord "
2 before the day of the Lord's a' come "
3 hid in the day of the Lord's a'. "
3: 8 even all my fierce a': "
Zec 10: 3 Mine a' was kindled against the "

M'r 3: 5 on them with a· being grieved 3709
Ro 10:19 by a foolish nation I will a· you. 3949
Eph 4:31 and wrath, and a·, and clamour, 3709
Col 3: 8 put off all these; a·, wrath, malice, "
21 provoke not your children to a· *

angered
Ps 106:32 a· him also at the waters of strife, 7107

angle
Isa 19: 8 they that cast a· into the brooks 2443
Hab 1:15 take up all of them with the a·, "

angry
Ge 18:30, 32 Oh let not the Lord be a·, and 2734
45: 5 grieved, nor a· with yourselves, "
Le 10:16 was a· with Eleazar and Ithamar, 7107
De 1:37 was a· with me for your sakes, 599
4:21 was a· with me for your sakes, "
9: 8 so that the Lord was a· with you "
20 the Lord was very a· with Aaron "
J'g 18:25 lest a· fellows run upon thee, 4751, 5315
2Sa 19:42 then be ye a· for this matter? 2734
1Ki 8:46 and thou be a· with them, and 599
11: 9 And the Lord was a· with Solomon, "
2Ki 17:18 the Lord was very a· with Israel, "
2Ch 6:36 be a· with them, and deliver them "
Ezr 9:14 wouldest not thou be a· with us "
Ne 5: 6 very a· when I heard their cry 2734
Ps 2:12 Kiss the Son, lest he be a·, and 599
7:11 God is a· with the wicked every *2194
76: 7 in thy sight when once thou art a·? 639
79: 5 wilt thou be a· for ever? shall thy 599
80: 4 how long wilt thou be a· against 6225
85: 5 Wilt thou be a· with us for ever? 599
Pr 14:17 that is soon a· dealeth foolishly: 639
21:19 a contentious and an a· woman. *3708
22:24 no friendship with an a· man; * 639
25:23 so doth an a· countenance a 2194
29:22 An a· man stirreth up strife, 639
Ec 5: 6 should God be a· at thy voice, 7107
7: 9 Be not hasty in thy spirit to be a·: 3707
Ca 1: 6 my mother's children were a· *2734
Isa 12: 1 though thou wast a· with me, 599
Eze 16:42 be quiet and will be no more a·. 3707
Da 2:12 the king was a· and very furious, 1149
Jon 4: 1 and he was very a·. 2734
4 Lord, Doest thou well to be a·? "
9 thou well to be a· for the gourd? "
9 I do well to be a·, even unto death. "
M't 5:22 whosoever is a· with his brother 3710
Lu 14:21 the master of the house being a· "
15:28 he was a·, and would not go in: "
Joh 7:23 are ye a· at me, because I have *5520
Eph 4:26 Be ye a·, and sin not: let not the 3710
Tit 1: 7 not soon a·, not given to wine, 3711
Re 11:18 nations were a·, and thy wrath *3710

anguish
Ge 42:21 we saw the a· of his soul, when *6869
Ex 6: 9 hearkened not...for a· of spirit, 7115
De 2:25 and be in a· because of thee. 2342
2Sa 1: 9 a· is come upon me, because my 7661
Job 7:11 I will speak in the a· of my spirit; 6862
15:24 and a· shall make him afraid; 4691
Ps 119:143 Trouble and a· have taken hold 4689
Pr 1:27 distress and a· cometh upon you. 6695
Isa 8:22 and darkness, dimness of a·; 6695
30: 6 the land of trouble and a·, "
Jer 4:31 the a· as of her that bringeth 6869
6:24 a· hath taken hold of us, "
49:24 a· and sorrows have taken her, "
50:43 a· took hold of him, and pangs as "
Joh 16:21 she remembereth no more the a·, 2347
Ro 2: 9 and a·, upon every soul of man 4730
2Co 2: 4 of much affliction and a· of heart 4928

an-hungered See HUNGERED.

Aniam (a'-ne-am)
1Ch 7:19 Shechem, and Likhi, and A·. 593

Anim (a'-nim)
Jos 15:50 And Anab, and Eshtemoh, and A·, 6044

anise
M't 23:23 tithe of mint, and a· and cummin, 432

ankle See ANCLE.

Anna (an'-nah)
Lu 2:36 there was one A·, a prophetess, 451

Annas (an'-nas)
Lu 3: 2 A· and Caiaphas being the high 452
Joh 18:13 led him away to A· first; "
24 A· had sent him bound unto "
Ac 4: 6 A· the high priest, and Caiaphas, "

annul See DISANNUL.

anoint See also ANOINTED; ANOINTEST; ANOINTING.
Ex 28:41 a· them, and consecrate them, 4886
29: 7 pour it upon his head, and a· him. "
36 and thou shalt a· it, to sanctify it. "
30:26 And thou shalt a· the tabernacle "
30 thou shalt a· Aaron and his sons, "
40: 9 a· the tabernacle, and all that is "
10 a· the altar of the burnt offering, "
11 thou shalt a· the laver and his foot, "
13 the holy garments, and a· him, "
15 And thou shalt a· them, "
15 as thou didst a· their father, "
Le 16:32 And the priest, whom he shall a·,* "
De 28:40 shalt not a· thyself with the oil; 5480
J'g 9: 8 trees went forth on a time to a· 4886
15 If in truth ye a· me king over you, "
Ru 3: 3 Wash thyself therefore, and a· 5480
1Sa 9:16 a· him to be captain over my 4886
15: 1 The Lord sent me to a· thee "
16: 3 shalt a· unto me him whom I name "
12 the Lord said, Arise, a· him: "
2Sa 14: 2 a· not thyself with oil, 5480
1Ki 1:34 and Nathan the prophet a· him 4886
19:15 a· Hazael to be king over Syria: "
16 the son of Nimshi shalt thou a· "
16 Elisha...shalt thou a· to be prophet "
Isa 21: 5 arise, ye princes, and a· the shield. "
Da 9:24 and to a· the most Holy. "
10: 3 neither did I a· myself at all, 5480
Am 6: 6 a· themselves with the chief 4886
Mic 6:15 thou shalt not a· thee with oil; 5480
M't 6:17 a· thine head, and wash thy face; 218
M'r 14: 8 to a· my body to the burying. *3462
16: 1 they might come and a· him. 218
Lu 7:46 My head with oil thou didst not a·: "
Re 3:18 a· thine eyes with eyesalve, that 1472

anointed See also ANOINTEDST.
Ex 29: 2 wafers unleavened a· with oil: 4886
29 a· therein, and to be consecrated 4888
Le 2: 4 unleavened wafers a· with oil. 4886
4: 3 If the priest that is a· do sin 4899
5 And the priest that is a· shall "
16 is a· shall bring of the bullock's "
6:20 the Lord in the day when he is a·; 4886
22 the priest of his sons that is a· in 4899
7:12 a· with oil, and cakes mingled 4886
36 in the day that he a· them, "
8:10 a· the tabernacle and all that was "
11 a· the altar and all his vessels, "
12 and a· him, to sanctify him. "
Nu 3: 3 of Aaron, the priests which were a·, "
6:15 wafers of unleavened bread a· "
7: 1 set up the tabernacle, and had a· it, "
1 vessels thereof, and had a· them, "
10 the altar in the day that it was a·, "
84 it was a·, by the princes of Israel; "
88 of the altar after that it was a·. "
35:25 which was a· with the holy oil. "
1Sa 2:10 and exalt the horn of his a·, 4899
35 shall walk before mine a· for ever. "
10: 1 Lord hath a· thee to be captain 4886
12: 3 before the Lord, and before his a·: 4899
5 his a· is witness this day, "
15:17 the Lord a· thee king over Israel? 4886
16: 6 Surely the Lord's a· is before him. 4899
13 a· him in the midst of his brethren. 4886
24: 6 unto my master, the Lord's a·, 4899
6 he is the a· of the Lord. "
10 he is the Lord's a·. "
26: 9 his hand against the Lord's a·, "
11 mine hand against the Lord's a·: "
16 kept your master, the Lord's a·. 4899
23 against the Lord's a·. "
2Sa 1:14 to destroy the Lord's a·? "
16 I have slain the Lord's a·. "
21 as though he had not been a· with "
2: 4 and there they a· David king 4886
7 house of Judah have a· me king "
3:39 this day weak, though a· king; "
5: 3 they a· David king over Israel. "
17 heard that they had a· David king "
12: 7 I a· thee king over Israel, "
20 earth and washed, and a· himself, 5480
19:10 Absalom, whom we a· over us, 4886
21 because he cursed the Lord's a·? 4899
22:51 sheweth mercy to his a·, "
23: 1 the a· of the God of Jacob, "
1Ki 1:39 the tabernacle, and a· Solomon. 4886
45 and Nathan...have a· him king "
5: 1 a· him king in the room of his "
2Ki 9: 3 I have a· thee king over Israel. "
6 have a· thee king over the people "
12 Thus saith the Lord, I have a· thee "
11:12 they made him king, and a· him; "
23:30 and a· him, and made him king "
1Ch 11: 3 they a· David king over Israel, "
14: 8 David was a· king over all Israel, "
16:22 Touch not mine a·, and do my 4899
29:22 and a· him unto the Lord 4886
2Ch 6:42 turn not away the face of thine a·: 4899
22: 7 a· to cut off the house of Ahab. 4886
23:11 Jehoiada and his sons a· him, "
28:15 to eat and to drink, and a· them, "
Ps 2: 2 the Lord, and against his a·, 4899
18:50 sheweth mercy to his a·, "
20: 6 the Lord saveth his a·; "
28: 8 he is the saving strength of his a·. "
45: 7 thy God, hath a· thee with the oil 4886
84: 9 look upon the face of thine a·. 4899
89:20 with my holy oil have I a· him: 4886
38 hast been wroth with thine a·. 4899
51 reproached the footsteps of thine a·. "
92:10 I shall be a· with fresh oil. 1101
105:15 Touch not mine a·, 4899
132:10 turn not away the face of thine a·. "
17 I have ordained a lamp for mine a·. "
Isa 45: 1 Thus saith the Lord to his a·, "
61: 1 the Lord hath a· me to preach 4886
La 4:20 a· of the Lord, was taken in their 4899
Eze 16: 9 and I a· thee with oil. 5480
28:14 art the a· cherub that covereth; 4473
Hab 3:13 for salvation with thine a·; 4899
Zec 4:14 the two a· ones, that stand †1121, 3323
M'r 6:13 a· with oil many that were sick, 218
Lu 4:18 hath a· me to preach the gospel 5548
7:38 a· them with the ointment. 218
46 hath a· my feet with ointment. "
Joh 9: 6 a· the eyes of the blind man 2025, 1909
11 made clay and a· mine eyes, 2025
11: 2 was that Mary which a· the Lord 218
12: 3 a· the feet of Jesus, and wiped "
Ac 4:27 child Jesus, whom thou hast a·, *5548
10:38 How God a· Jesus of Nazareth "
2Co 1:21 and hath a· us is God. "
Heb 1: 9 a· thee with the oil of gladness "

anointedst
Ge 31:13 Bethel, where thou a· the pillar, 4886

anointest
Ps 23: 5 thou a· my head with oil; my *1878

anointing
Ex 25: 6 spices for a· oil, and for sweet 4888
29: 7 Then shalt thou take the a· oil, "
21 and of the a· oil, and sprinkle it "
30:25 it shall be an holy a· oil. "
31 This shall be an holy a· oil unto "
31:11 And the a· oil, and sweet incense "
35: 8 the light, and spices for the a· oil, "
15 and his staves, and the a· oil, "
28 and for the a· oil, "
37:29 he made the holy a· oil, "
39:38 the golden altar and the a· oil, "
40: 9 thou shalt take the a· oil, "
15 a· shall surely be an everlasting "
Le 7:35 is the portion of the a· of Aaron, * "
35 and of the a· of his sons, * "
8: 2 and the a· oil, and a bullock for "
10 Moses took the a· oil, and anointed "
12 he poured of the a· oil upon "
30 Moses took the a· oil, "
10: 7 the a· oil of the Lord is upon you. "
21:10 whose head the a· oil was poured, "
12 the crown of the a· oil is of his "
Nu 4:16 daily meat offering, and the a· oil, "
18: 8 given them by reason of the a·, "
Isa 10:27 be destroyed because of the a·. *8081
Jas 5:14 a· him with oil in the name of the 218
1Jo 2:27 But the a· which ye have received 5545
27 same a· teacheth you of all things, "

anon
M't 13:20 and a· with joy receiveth it; *2117
M'r 1:30 a· they tell him of her. *2112

Anoth See BETH-ANOTH.

another See also ANOTHER'S.
Ge 4:25 appointed me a· seed instead of 312
11: 3 said one to a·, Go to, let us make 7453
15:10 laid each piece one against a·: * "
26:21 And they digged a· well, and 312
22 from thence, and digged a· well; "
29:19 I should give her to a· man: "
30:24 Lord shall add to me a· son. "
31:49 when we are absent one from a·. 7453
37: 9 he dreamed yet a· dream, 312
19 they said one to a·, Behold, this 250
42: 1 Why do ye look one upon a·? "
21 they said one to a·, We are verily 250
28 they were afraid, saying one to a·, "
43: 7 yet alive? have ye a· brother? and "
33 the men marvelled one at a·. 7453
Ex 10:23 They saw not one a·, neither rose 250
16:15 they said one to a·, it is manna: "
18:16 I judge between one and a·, *7453
21:10 If he take him a· wife, her food, 312
18 strive together, and one smite a· *7453
22: 5 shall feed in a· man's field; 312
9 which a· challengeth to be his, *
25:20 their faces shall look one to a·; 250
26: 3 coupled together one to a·; 269
3 curtains shall be coupled one to a·; "
4 uttermost edge of a· curtain; "
5 loops may take hold one of a·. * 269
17 set in order one against a·: "
19, 21, 25 and two sockets under a· 259
36:10 curtains one unto a·: and the "
10 curtains he coupled one unto a·. "
11 the uttermost side of a· curtain, *
12 the loops held one curtain to a·. 259
13 one unto a· with the taches: "
22 equally distant one from a·: "
24, 26 and two sockets under a· board "
37: 8 and a· cherub on the other end *
9 with their faces one to a·; 250
19 made like almonds in a· branch, * 259
Le 7:10 Aaron have, one as much as a·. 250
19:11 deal falsely, neither lie one to a·. 5997
20:10 adultery with a· man's wife, "
25:14 ye shall not oppress one a·: 250
17 not therefore oppress one a·; 5997
46 ye shall not rule one over a· with 250
26:37 they shall fall one upon a·, "
27:20 if he have sold the field to a· man, 312
Nu 5:19 with a· instead of thy husband, *
20 to a· instead of thy husband, *
29 when a wife goeth aside to a· *
8: 8 a· young bullock shalt thou take 8145
14: 4 they said one to a·, Let us make 250
24 because he had a· spirit with him, 312
23:13 with me unto a· place, "
27 I will bring thee unto a· place; "
Nu 36: 9 remove from one tribe to a· tribe; 312
De 4:34 midst of a· nation, by temptations, "
20: 5 the battle, and a· man dedicate it. 312
6 in the battle, and a· man eat of it. "
7 in the battle, and a· man take her. "
21:15 one beloved, and a· hated, * 259
24: 2 she may go and be a· man's wife. 312
25:11 men strive together one with a·, 250
28:30 a· man shall lie with her: 312
32 shall be given unto a· people, "
29:28 cast them into a· land, as it is this "
J'g 2:10 there arose a· generation after "
6:29 said one to a·, Who hath done this 7453
9:37 a· company come along by the * 259
10:18 princes of Gilead said one to a·, 7453
16: 7, 11 I be weak, and be as a· man. 259
Ru 2: 8 Go not to glean in a· field, 312
3:14 rose up before one could know a·. 7453
1Sa 2:25 If one man sin against a·, 376
10: 3 a· carrying three loaves of bread, 259
3 and a· carrying a bottle of wine: "
6 shalt be turned into a· man. 312
9 God gave him a· heart: "

1Sa 10:11 the people said one to a'. 7453
13:18 And a' company turned the way 259
18 and a' company turned to the way "
14:16 went on beating down one a'. *
17:30 he turned from him toward a'. 312
18: 7 And the women answered one a'
20:41 and they kissed one a'. 7453
41 and wept one with a'. "
21:11 did they not sing one to a' of him
29: 5 sang one to a' in dances, saying,
2Sa 11:25 devoureth one as well as a': 2090
18:20 thou shalt bear tidings a' day: 312
26 the watchman saw a' man running "
26 Behold a' man running alone.
1Ki 6:27 and their wings touched one a' 3671
7: 8 had a' court within the porch, * 312
11:23 God stirred him up a' adversary,
13:10 So he went a' way, and returned 312
14: 5 shall feign herself to be a' woman.5234
6 why feignest thou thyself to be a'? "
18: 6 Obadiah went a' way by himself. 259
20:37 Then he found a' man, and said, 312
21: 6 I will give thee a' vineyard for it:
22:20 one said on this manner, and a' 2088
2Ki 1:11 he sent unto him a' captain of fifty 312
3:23 they have smitten one a': *7453
7: 3 said one to a', why sit we here
6 they said one to a', Lo, the king 250
8 entered into a' tent, and carried 312
9 Then they said one to a', We do 7453
10:21 Baal was full from one end to a'.
14: 8 let us look one a' in the face.
11 looked one a' in the face at
21:16 filled Jerusalem from one end to a';
1Ch 2:26 Jerahmeel had also a' wife, 312
16:20 from one kingdom to a' people; "
17: 5 and from one tabernacle to a'.
24: 5 divided by lot, one sort with a';
26:12 having wards one against a', * 251
2Ch 18:19 and a' saying after that manner. 2088
20:23 every one helped to destroy a'. 7453
25:17 Come, let us see one a' in the face.
21 and they saw one a' in the face,
32: 5 a' wall without, and repaired * 312
Ezr 4:21 a' commandment shall be given *
9:11 end to a' with their uncleanness.
Ne 3:19 a' piece over against the going 8145
21 the son of Koz a' piece, "
24 the son of Henadad a' piece, "
27 the Tekoites repaired a' piece, "
30 the sixth son of Zalaph, a' piece. "
4:19 upon the wall, one far from a'. 250
9: 3 and a' fourth part they confessed.
Es 1: 7 vessels being diverse one from a',)
19 give her royal estate unto a' 7468
4:14 arise to the Jews from a' place; 312
9:19 and of sending portions one to a'. 7453
22 one to a', and gifts to the poor.
Job 1:16 came also a', and said, The fire 2088
17 also a', and said, The Chaldeans "
18 yet speaking, there came also a', "
13: 9 as one man mocketh a', do ye *
19:27 eyes shall behold, and not a'; ‡2114
21:25 And a' dieth in the bitterness of 2088
31: 8 let me sow, and let a' eat; 312
10 let my wife grind unto a', "
41:16 One is so near to a', that no air 259
17 They are joined one to a', they 250
Ps 16: 4 that hasten after a' god: 312
75: 7 down one, and setteth up a'. 2088
105:13 they went from one nation to a', *
13 from one kingdom to a' people; 312
109: 8 let a' take his office.
145: 4 shall praise thy works to a', and
Pr 25: 9 discover not a secret to a': 312
27: 2 Let a' man praise thee, and not 2114
Ec 1: 4 away, and a' generation cometh:
4:10 for he hath not a' to help him up. 8145
8: 9 wherein one man ruleth over a'
Ca 5: 9 beloved more than a' beloved, O
9 a' beloved, that thou dost so
Isa 3: 5 every one by a', and every one by
6: 3 And one cried unto a', and said, 2088
13: 8 they shall be amazed one at a'; 7453
28:11 with stammering lips and a' tongue 312
42: 8 my glory will I not give to a', "
44: 5 and a' shall call himself by 2088
5 and a' shall subscribe with his
48:11 I will not give my glory unto a'. 312
57: 8 thou hast discovered thyself to a'
65:15 call his servants by a' name: 312
22 not build, and a' inhabit; "
22 they shall not plant, and a' eat: "
66:23 that from one new moon to a', shall
23 and from one sabbath to a', shall
Jer 3: 1 become a' man's, shall he return 312
13:14 I will dash them one against a', 250
18: 4 so he made it again a' vessel, 312
14 come from a' place be forsaken? *2114
22:26 into a' country, where ye were not 312
25:26 far and near, one with a', 250
36:28 Take thee again a' roll, and write 312
32 Then took Jeremiah a' roll, "
46:16 many to fall, yea, one fell upon a': 7453
51:31 One post shall run to meet a',
31 and one messenger to meet a',
46 one year, and after that in a' year
Eze 1: 9 Their wings were joined one to a'; 269
11 of every one were joined one to a', 376
3:13 creatures that touched one a', 269
4: 8 not turn thee from one side to a',
17 astonied one with a', and consume 250
10: 9 by one cherub, and a' wheel by 259
9 a' cherub: and the appearance
12: 3 remove from thy place to a' place 312
15: 7 and a' fire shall devour them; *

Eze 17: 7 There was also a' great eagle 259
19: 5 she took a' of her whelps
22:11 a' hath lewdly defiled his daughter 376
11 a' in thee hath humbled his sister, "
24:23 mourn one toward a'. 250
33:30 and speak one to a', every one to 259
37:16 then take a' stick, and write upon "
17 join them one to a' into one stick; "
40:13 little chamber to the roof of a': *
26, 49 one on this side, and a' on that 259
41: 6 one over a', and thirty in order;
11 the north, and a' door toward the 259
47:14 shall inherit it, one as well as a': 250
Da 2:39 arise a' kingdom inferior to thee, 317
39 and a' third kingdom of brass,
43 they shall not cleave one to a', 1836
5: 6 his knees smote one against a'. 1668
17 to thyself, give thy rewards to a'; 321
7: 3 diverse one from a'. 1668
5 And behold a' beast, a second, like 317
6 I beheld, and lo a', like a leopard, "
8 came up among them a' little horn, "
24 and a' shall rise after them; 321
8:13 a' saint said unto that certain 259
Ho 3: 3 thou shalt not be for a' man: *
4: 4 let no man strive, nor reprove a': * 376
Joe 1: 3 their children a' generation. 312
2: 8 Neither shall one thrust a'; 250
Am 4: 7 caused it not to rain upon a' city: 259
Na 2: 4 against a' in the broad ways: ‡8264
Zec 2: 3 a' angel went out to meet him, 312
8:21 inhabitants of one city shall go to a',259
11: 9 rest eat every one the flesh of a'. 7468
Mal 3:16 they .... spake often one to a': 7453
M't 2:12 into their own country a' way. 243
8: 9 and to a', Come, and he cometh; "
21 And a' of his disciples said unto 2087
10:23 you in this city, flee ye into a': * 243
11: 3 should come, or do we look for a'? 2087
13:24, 31 A' parable put he forth unto 243
33 A' parable spake he unto them; "
19: 9 for fornication, and shall marry a', "
21:33 Hear a' parable: There was a "
35 and killed a', and stoned a'. 3739
22: 5 his farm, a' to his merchandise:
24: 2 left here one stone upon a', that
10 shall betray one a', 240
10 and shall hate one a'. "
25:15 to a' two, and to a' one; to every 3739
32 he shall separate them one from a',240
26:71 into the porch, a' maid saw him, 243
27:38 right hand, and a' on the left. * 1520
M'r 4:41 exceedingly, and said one to a', 240
9:10 questioning one with a' what the *1438
50 and have peace one with a'. 240
10:11 put away his wife, and marry a', 243
12 her husband, and be married to a', "
12: 4 he sent unto them a' servant; "
5 he sent a'; and him they killed, "
13: 2 not be left one stone upon a',
14:19 one, Is it I? and a' said, Is it I? * 243
58 will build a' made without hands.
16:12 appeared in a' form unto two of 2087
Lu 2:15 the shepherds said one to a', 240
6: 6 came to pass also on a' sabbath, 2087
11 with a' what they might do to Jesus. 240
7: 8 and to a', Come, and he cometh; 243
19, 20 should come? or look we for a'? "
32 marketplace, and calling one to a', 240
8:25 wondered, saying one to a', What "
9:56 And they went to a' village. 2087
59 And he said unto a', Follow me. "
61 a' also said, Lord, I will follow "
12: 1 that they trode one upon a', 240
14:19 a' said, I have bought five yoke of 2087
20 a' said, I have married a wife, "
31 to make war against a' king, "
16: 7 said he to a', And how much owest "
12 faithful in that which is a' man's,* 245
18 marrieth a', committeth adultery: 2087
19:20 a' came, saying, Lord, behold, "
44 in thee one stone upon a';
20:11 he sent a' servant: and they beat 2087
21: 6 not be left one stone upon a',
22:58 a' saw him, and said, Thou art also 2087
59 a' confidently affirmed, saying, 243
24:17 these that ye have one to a', as ye 240
32 they said one to a', Did not our "
Joh 4:33 said the disciples one to a', "
37 true, One soweth, and a' reapeth. 243
5: 7 while I am coming, a' steppeth "
32 There is a' that beareth witness "
43 a' shall come in his own name, "
44 which receive honor one of a', 240
13:22 disciples looked one on a', doubting "
34 give unto you, That ye love one a'; "
34 loved you, that ye also love one a'. "
35 if ye have love one to a'. "
14:16 he shall give you a' Comforter, 243
15:12 love one a', as I have loved you. 240
17 command you, that love one a'. "
18:15 Peter followed Jesus, and so did a' 243
19:37 a' scripture saith, They shall 2087
21:18 and a' shall gird thee, and carry 243
Ac 1:20 His bishoprick let a' take. 2087
2: 7 marvelled, saying one to a', * 240
12 were in doubt, saying one to a', 243
7:18 a' king arose, which knew not 2087
26 why do ye wrong one to a'? 240
10:28 or come unto one of a' nation; 246
12:17 departed and went into a' place. 2087
13:35 Wherefore he saith also in a' psalm, "
17: 7 that there is a' king, one Jesus. "
19:32 cried one thing, and some a': 243
38 deputies: let them implead one a'. 240
21: 6 we had taken our leave one of a', * "

Ac 21:34 some cried one thing, some a', 243
Ro 1:27 burned in their lust one toward a'; 240
2: 1 wherein thou judgest a', thou 2087
15 accusing or else excusing one a';) * 240
21 Thou therefore which teachest a', 2087
7: 3 she be married to a' man, "
3 though she be married to a' man. "
4 that ye should be married to a', "
23 But I see a' law in my members, * "
9:21 one vessel unto honour, and a' 3739
12: 5 every one members one of a'. 240
10 one to a' with brotherly love; "
10 in honour preferring one a'; "
16 Be of the same mind one toward a'. "
13: 8 but to love one a': for he that "
8 loveth a' hath fulfilled the law. *2087
14: 2 a', who is weak, eateth herbs. *3739
4 that judgest a' man's servant? 245
5 esteemeth one day above a': "
5 a' esteemeth every day alike. 3739
13 therefore judge one a' any more: 240
19 things wherewith one may edify a'. "
15: 5 to be likeminded one toward a' "
7 Wherefore receive ye one a', "
14 able also to admonish one a'. "
20 build upon a' man's foundation: 245
16:16 Salute one a' with an holy kiss. 240
1Co 3: 4 and a', I am of Apollos; are ye not 2087
10 the foundation, and a' buildeth 243
4: 6 be puffed up for one against a'. *2087
7 maketh thee to differ from a'? *
6: 1 you, having a matter against a', *2087
7 because ye go to law one with a'. 1438
7: 7 one after this manner, and a' 3588
10:29 judged of a' man's conscience? 243
11:21 one is hungry, and a' is drunken. 3739
33 together to eat, tarry one for a'. 240
12: 8 to a' the word of knowledge by 243
9 To a' faith by the same Spirit; 2087
9 to a' the gifts of healing by the 243
10 to a' the working of miracles; "
10 to a' prophecy; "
10 to a' discerning of spirits; "
10 to a' divers kinds of tongues; 2087
10 to a' the interpretation of tongues: 243
25 have the same care one for a'. 240
14:30 If anything be revealed to a' that 243
15:39 a' flesh of beasts, "
39 a' of fishes, and a' of birds. "
40 glory of the terrestrial is a'. 2087
41 sun, and a' glory of the moon, 243
41 moon, and a' glory of the stars: "
41 star differeth from a' star in glory.
16:20 Greet ye one a' with an holy kiss. 240
2Co 10:16 not to boast in a' man's line of * 245
11: 4 a' Jesus, whom we have not 243
4 or if ye receive a' spirit, *2087
4 or a' gospel, which ye have not * "
13:12 Greet one a' with a holy kiss. 240
Ga 1: 6 grace of Christ unto a' gospel: *2087
7 Which is not a'; but there be 243
5:13 the flesh, but by love serve one a'. 240
15 if ye bite and devour one a', take "
15 that ye be not consumed one of a'. "
26 provoking one a', envying one a'. "
6: 4 in himself alone, and not in a'. *2087
Eph 4: 2 forbearing one a' in love; 240
25 for we are members one of a'. "
32 be kind one to a', tenderhearted, "
32 tenderhearted, forgiving one a', *1438
5:21 Submitting yourselves one to a' in 240
Col 3: 9 Lie not one to a', seeing that ye "
13 Forbearing one a', 240
13 and forgiving one a', *1438
16 admonishing one a' in psalms
1Th 3:12 abound in love one toward a', 240
4: 9 are taught of God to love one a'. "
18 comfort one a' with these words. "
5:11 edify one a', even as also ye do. 1520
1Ti 5:21 without preferring one before a', *4299
Tit 3: 3 envy, hateful, and hating one a'. 240
Heb 3:13 exhort one a' daily, while it is 1438
4: 8 afterward have spoken of a' day. 243
5: 6 As he saith also in a' place, 2087
7:11 that a' priest should rise "
13 pertaineth to a' tribe, "
15 there ariseth a' priest, "
10:24 let us consider one a' to provoke 240
25 but exhorting one a': and so "
Jas 2:25 and had sent them out a' way? 2087
4:11 Speak not evil one of a', brethren. 240
12 who art thou that judgest a'? *2087
5: 9 Grudge not one against a', 240
16 Confess your faults one to a', "
16 and pray one for a', that ye may be "
1Pe 1:22 love one a' with a pure heart "
3: 8 having compassion one of a', *4835
4: 9 Use hospitality one to a' without 240
10 minister the same one to a', *1438
5: 5 Yea, all of you be subject one to a', 240
14 Greet ye one a' with a kiss of "
1Jo 1: 7 we have fellowship one with a', "
3:11 that we should love one a'. "
23 love one a', as he gave us "
4: 7 Beloved, let us love one a': "
11 us, we ought also to love one a'. "
12 If we love one a', God dwelleth in "
2Jo 5 beginning, that we love one a'. "
Re 6: 4 there went out a' horse that was 243
4 they should kill one a': 240
7: 2 And I saw a' angel ascending 243
8: 3 And a' angel came and stood "
10: 1 I saw a' mighty angel come "
11:10 and shall send gifts one to a'; 240
12: 3 And there appeared a' wonder in 243
13:11 And I beheld a' beast coming "

Re 14: 6 And I saw a· angel fly in the 243
8 And there followed a· angel, "
15, 17 a· angel came out of the temple "
18 a· angel came out from the altar, "
15: 1 And I saw a· sign in heaven, great "
16: 7 And I heard a· out of the altar * "
18: 1 a· angel come down from heaven. "
4 And I heard a· voice from heaven, "
20:12 and a· book was opened, which "

another's
Ge 11: 7 not understand one a· speech. 7453
Ex 21:35 if one man's ox hurt a·, that he die; "
Joh 13:14 ye also ought to wash one a· feet. 240
1Co 10:24 but every man a· wealth. *2087
Ga 6: 2 Bear ye one a· burdens, and so 240

answer See also ANSWERED; ANSWEREST; ANSWERETH; ANSWERING; ANSWERS.
Ge 30:33 shall my righteousness a· for me 6030
41:16 God shall give Pharaoh an a· of "
45: 3 his brethren could not a· him; "
De 20:11 if it make thee a· of peace, "
21: 7 And they shall a· and say, "
25: 9 shall a· and say, So shall it be done "
27:15 the people shall a· and say, Amen. "
Jos 4: 7 Then ye shall a· them, That the * 559
J'g 5:29 yea, she returned a· to herself, "
1Sa 2:16 then he would a· him, Nay; * "
20:10 if thy father a· thee roughly? 6030
2Sa 3:11 he could not a· Abner a word 7725
24:13 see what a· I shall return to him 1697
1Ki 9: 9 And they shall a·, Because they 559
12: 6 do ye advise, that I may a· 7725, 1697
7 and wilt serve them, and a· them, 6030
9 that we may a· this people, 7725, 1697
18:29 neither voice, nor any to a·, 6030
2Ki 4:29 if any salute thee, a· him not "
18:36 commandment was, saying, A· "
2Ch 10: 6 to return a· to this people? 1697
9 we may return a· to this people, "
10 Thus shalt thou a· the people * 559
Ezr 4:17 sent the king an a· unto Rehum 6600
5: 5 then they returned a· by letter 8421
11 And thus they returned us a·, 6600
Ne 5: 8 peace, and found nothing to a·. *1696
Es 4:13 commanded to a· Esther, *7725
15 bade them return Mordecai this a·,
Job 5: 1 if there be any that will a· thee; 6030
9: 3 cannot a· him one of a thousand. "
14 How much less shall I a· him, "
15 would I not a·, but I would make "
32 I should a· him, and we should "
13:22 Then call thou, and I will a·: "
22 let me speak, and a· thou me. 7725
14:15 Thou shalt call, and I will a· thee: 6030
19:16 servant, and he gave me no a·; "
20: 2 do my thoughts cause me to a·, 7725
3 understanding causeth me to a·. *6030
23: 5 the words which he would a· me, "
31:14 when he visiteth, what shall I a· 7725
35 that the Almighty would a· me, 6030
32: 1 these three men ceased to a· Job, "
3 they had found no a·, and yet had 4617
5 saw that there was no a· "
14 will I a· him with your speeches. 7725
17 I said, I will a· also my part, 6030
20 I will open my lips and a·. "
33: 5 If thou canst a· me, set thy 7725
12 I will a· thee, that God is greater 6030
32 If thou hast any thing to say, a· 7725
35: 4 I will a· thee and thy 7725,4405
12 there they cry, but none giveth a·, 6030
38: 3 demand of thee, and a· thou me. *3045
40: 2 he that reproveth God, let him a· 6030
4 vile; what shall I a· thee? 7725
5 have I spoken; but I will not a·: 6030
Ps 27: 7 mercy also upon me, and a· me. "
65: 5 wilt thou a· us, O God "
86: 7 call upon thee: for thou wilt a· me. "
91:15 call upon me, and I will a· him: "
102: 2 the day when I call a· me speedily. "
108: 6 with thy right hand, and a· me. "
119:42 to a· him that reproacheth me: "
143: 1 in thy faithfulness a· me, and in "
Pr 1:28 call upon me, but I will not a·; "
15: 1 A soft a· turneth away wrath: 4617
23 hath joy by the a· of his mouth: "
28 of the righteous studieth to a·: 6030
16: 1 a· of the tongue, is from the Lord 4617
22:21 mightest a· the words of truth *7725
24:26 his lips that giveth a right a·. 7725,1697
26: 4 A· not a fool according to his 6030
5 A· a fool according to his folly, "
27:11 a· him that reproacheth me. 7725, 1697
29:19 he understand he will not a·. *4617
Ca 5: 6 called him, but he gave me no a· 6030
Isa 14:32 shall one then a· the messengers "
30:19 he shall hear it, he will a· thee. "
36:21 was, saying, A· him not. "
41:28 I asked of them, could a· 7725
46: 7 yet can he not a·, nor save him 6030
50: 2 I called, was there none to a·? "
58: 9 thou call, and the Lord shall a·; "
65:12 when I called, ye did not answer; "
24 before they call, I will a·; "
66: 4 when I called, none did a·; "
Jer 5:19 then shalt thou a· them, Like as * 559
7:27 they will not a· thee. 6030
22: 9 Then they shall a·, Because they 559
33: 3 Call unto me, and I will a· thee, 6030
42: 4 the Lord shall a· you, "
44:20 which had given him that a·, "
Eze 14: 4 I the Lord will a· him that cometh "
7 I the Lord will a· him by myself: "
21: 7 thou shalt a·, For the tidings; * 559
Da 3:16 careful to a· thee in this matter, 8421
Joe 2:19 Yea, the Lord will a· and say *6030
Mic 3: 7 for there is no a· of God. 4617
Hab 2: 1 what I shall a· when I am 7725
11 beam out of the timber shall a· 6030
Zec 13: 6 Then he shall a·, Those with 559
M't 22:46 no man was able to a· him a word, 611
25:37 Then shall the righteous a· him, "
40 King shall a· and say unto them, "
44 Then shall they also a· him, "
45 Then shall he a· them, "
M'k 11:29 ask of you one question, and a· me, "
30 from heaven, or of men? a· me. "
14:40 wist they what to a· him. "
Lu 11: 7 shall a· and say, Trouble me not: 611
12:11 how or what thing ye shall a·, 626
13:25 he shall a· and say unto you, 611
14: 6 could not a· him again to these 470
20: 3 ask you one thing; and a· me: *2036
26 they marvelled at his a·, and held 612
21:14 meditate before what ye shall a·: 626
22:68 ye will not a· me, nor let me go. 611
Joh 1:22 give an a· to them that sent us. 612
19: 9 Jesus gave him no a·. "
Ac 24:10 more cheerfully a· for myself: * 626
25:16 have licence to a· for himself * 627
26: 2 a· for myself this day before thee * 626
Ro 11: 4 what saith the a· of God unto him? 5538
1Co 9: 3 a· to them that do examine me * 627
2Co 5:12 somewhat to a· them which glory
Col 4: 6 how ye ought to a· every man. 611
2Ti 4:16 first a· no man stood with me, * 627
1Pe 3:15 a· to every man that asketh you "
21 a· of a good conscience toward *1906

answerable
Ex 38:18 a· to the hangings of the court. 5980

answered See also ANSWEREDST.
Ge 18:27 And Abraham a· and said, 6030
23: 5 the children of Heth a· Abraham, "
10 and Ephron the Hittite a· Abraham "
14 and Ephron a· Abraham, saying "
24:50 Laban and Bethuel a· and said, "
27:37 And Isaac a· and said unto Esau, "
39 And Isaac his father a· and said "
31:14 And Rachel and Leah a· and said "
31, 36 Jacob a· and said to Laban, "
43 And Laban a· and said unto Jacob, "
34:13 And the sons of Jacob a· Shechem "
35: 3 unto God, who a· me in the day of "
40:18 And Joseph a· and said, This is "
41:16 And Joseph a· Pharaoh, saying, "
42:22 And Reuben a· them, saying, "
43:28 they a·, Thy servant our father is* 559
Ex 4: 1 Moses a· and said, But, behold, 6030
15:21 And Miriam a· them, "
19: 8 And all the people a· together, "
19 and God a· him by a voice. "
24: 3 and all the people a· with one voice, "
Nu 11:28 And Joshua the son of Nun,...a· "
22:18 And Balaam a· and said unto the "
23:12 and he a· and said, "
26 But Balaam a· and said unto Balak, "
32:31 And the children of Gad...a·, "
De 1:14 And ye a· me, and said, "
41 Then ye a· and said unto me, "
Jos 1:16 And they a· Joshua, saying, "
2:14 men a· her, Our life for yours, * 559
7:20 And Achan a· Joshua, 6030
9:24 And they a· Joshua, "
15:19 Who a·, Give me a blessing; * 559
17:15 Joshua a· them, If thou be a great* "
22:21 the half tribe of Manasseh a·, 6030
24:16 the people a· and said, God forbid "
J'g 5:29 Her wise ladies a· her, "
7:14 And his fellow a· and said, "
8: 8 and the men of Penuel a· him "
8 as the men of Succoth had a· him. "
18 they a·, As thou art, so were they; 559
25 they a·, We will willingly give them. "
11:13 of Ammon a· unto the messengers "
15: 6 they a·, Samson, the son in law * "
10 And they a·, To bind Samson 6030
18:14 a· the five men that went to spy 6030
19:28 and let us be going. But none a·. "
20: 4 And the Levite...a· and said, "
Ru 2: 4 they a· him, The Lord bless thee. 559
6 And the servant...a· and said, 6030
11 And Boaz a· and said unto her, "
3: 9 she a·, I am Ruth thine handmaid; 559
1Sa 1:15 Hannah a· and said, No, my lord, 6030
17 Then Eli a· and said, Go in peace: "
3: 4 and he a·, Here am I. * 559
6 And he a·, I called not, my son; "
10 Then Samuel a·, Speak; for thy * "
16 And he a·, Here am I. * "
4:17 And the messenger a· and said, 6030
20 she a· not, neither did she regard it. "
5: 8 And they a·, Let the ark of the God 559
6: 4 They a·, Five golden emerods, "
9: 8 the servant a· Saul again, 6030
12 and they a· them, and said, "
19 And Samuel a· Saul, and said, "
21 And Saul a·, and said, "
10:12 And one of the same place a· "
22 the Lord a·, Behold, he hath hid 559
11: 2 Nahash the Ammonite a· them, * "
12: 5 And they a·, He is witness. "
14:12 men of the garrison a· Jonathan 6030
28 Then a· one of the people, "
37 he a· him not that day. "
39 among all the people that a· him. "
44 Saul a·, God do so and more: * 559
16:18 Then a· one of the servants, 6030
17:27 people a· him after this manner, 559
30 the people a· him again after 7725, 1697
58 David a·, I am the son of thy servant 559
1Sa 18: 7 the women a· one another as *6030
19:17 Michal a· Saul, He said unto me, 559
20:28 And Jonathan a· Saul, David 6030
32 And Jonathan a· Saul his father, "
21: 4 And the priest a· David, "
5 And David a· the priest, "
22: 9 Then a· Doeg the Edomite, "
12 And he a·, Here I am, my lord. 559
14 Then Ahimelech a· the king, 6030
23: 4 the Lord a· him and said, Arise, "
25:10 And Nabal a· David's servants, "
26: 6 a· David and said to Ahimelech "
14 Abner a· and said, Who art thou "
22 David a· and said, Behold the king's "
28: 6 the Lord a· him not, neither by "
15 Saul a·, I am sore distressed; "
29: 9 And Achish a· and said to David, "
30: 8 And he a· him, Pursue: 559
22 Then a· all the wicked men 6030
2Sa 1: 4 And he a·, That the people are fled 559
7 And I a·, Here am I. "
8 I a· him, I am an Amalekite. "
13 he a·, I am the son of a stranger, "
2:20 Art thou Ashel? And he a·, I am. "
4: 9 David a· Rechab and Baanah his 6030
9: 6 And he a·, Behold thy servant! 559
13:12 she a· him, Nay, my brother, "
32 And Jonadab,...David's brother, a· 6030
14: 5 she a·, I am indeed a widow woman, 559
18 king a· and said unto the woman, 6030
19 And the woman a· and said, "
32 Absalom a· Joab, Behold, I sent 559
15:21 And Ittai a· the king, and said, 6030
18: 3 people a·, Thou shalt not go * 559
29 And Ahimaaz a·, When Joab sent "
32 Cushi a·, The enemies of my lord "
19:21 But Abishai the son of Zeruiah a· 6030
26 he a·, My lord, O king, my servant 559
38 the king a·, Chimham shall go over "
42 men of Judah a· the men of Israel, 6030
43 men of Israel a· the men of Judah, "
20:17 he a·, I am he. Then she said 559
17 And he a·, I do hear. "
20 And Joab a· and said, Far be it, 6030
21: 1 And the Lord a·, It is for Saul, * 559
5 And they a· the king, The man * "
22:42 the Lord, but he a· them not. 6030
1Ki 1:28 Then king David a· and said, "
36 And Benaiah...a· the king, "
43 Jonathan a· and said to Adonijah, "
2:22 And king Solomon a· and said "
30 Thus said Joab, and thus he a· me. "
3:27 Then the king a· and said, "
11:22 he a·, Nothing: howbeit let me go 559
12:13 the king a· the people roughly, 6030
16 people a· the king, saying, 7725, 1697
13: 6 king a· and said unto the man of 6030
18: 8 And he a· him, I am: 559
18 he a·, I have not troubled Israel; "
21 the people a· him not a word. 6030
24 people a· and said, It is well spoken. "
26 was no voice, nor any that a·. "
20: 4 And the king of Israel a· and "
11 a· and said, Tell him, Let not him "
14 And he a·, Thou. 559
21: 6 a·, I will not give thee my vineyard. "
20 And he a·, I have found thee: "
22:15 he a· him, Go, and prosper: "
2Ki 1: 8 they a· him, He was a hairy man, "
10 Elijah a· and said to the captain 6030
11 And he a· and said unto him, "
12 And Elijah a· and said unto them, "
2: 5 And he a·, Yea, I know it; hold 559
3: 8 a·, The way through the wilderness "
11 of the king of Israel's servants a· 6030
4:13 she a·, I dwell among mine own 559
14 Gehazi a·, Verily she hath no child, "
26 the child? And she a·, It is well. "
6: 2 And he a·, Go ye. "
3 thy servants. And he a·, I will go. "
16 And he a·, Fear not: for they that "
22 he a·, Thou shalt not smite them: "
28 she a·, This woman said unto me, "
7: 2 king leaned a· the man of God, 6030
13 one of his servants a· and said, "
19 And that lord a· the man of God, "
8:12 he a·, Because I know the evil 559
13 Elisha a·, The Lord hath shewed "
14 And he a·, He told me that thou "
9:19 And Jehu a·, What hast thou to do "
22 And he a·, What peace, so long as "
10:13 And they a·, We are the brethren "
15 And Jehonadab a·, It is. If it be, "
18:36 and a· him not a word: 6030
20:10 Hezekiah a·, It is a light thing 559
15 And Hezekiah a·, All the things "
1Ch 12:17 David went out.... and a· and 6030
21: 3 And Joab a·, The Lord make his * 559
26 he a· him from heaven by fire 6030
28 the Lord had answered him in "
2Ch 2:11 the king of Tyre a· in writing, 559
7:22 And it shall be a·, Because they * "
10:13 And the king a· them roughly; 6030
14 And a· them after the advice of *1697
16 when.... the people a· the king, 7725
18: 3 And he a· him, I am as thou art, 559
25: 9 the man of God a·, The Lord is able "
29:31 Then Hezekiah a· and said, 6030
31:10 priest of the house of Zadok a· 559
34:15 Hilkiah a· and said to Shaphan 6030
23 she a· them, Thus saith the Lord * 559
Ezr 10: 2 sons of Elam, a· and said unto 6030
12 all the congregation a· and said "
Ne 2:20 Then a· I them, and said unto 7725,1697
6: 4 I a· them after the same manner. 7725
8: 6 all the people a·, Amen, Amen. 6030

Es 1:16 And Memucan a' before the king 559
5: 4 Esther a', If it seem good unto * "
7 Then a' Esther, and said, My 6039
6: 7 And Haman a' the king, For the * 559
7: 3 Esther the queen a' and said, 6030
5 the king Ahasuerus a' and said * 559
Job 1: 7, 9 Satan a' the Lord and said, 6030
2: 2, 4 Satan a' the Lord, and said, "
4: 1 Eliphaz the Temanite a' and said, "
6: 1 But Job a' and said, "
8: 1 Then a' Bildad the Shuhite, "
9: 1 Then Job a' and said, "
16 If I had called, and he had a' me; "
11: 1 a' Zophar the Naamathite, "
2 not the multitude of words be a'? "
12: 1 And Job a' and said, "
15: 1 Then a' Eliphaz the Temanite, "
16: 1 Then Job a' and said. "
18: 1 Then a' Bildad the Shuhite, "
19: 1 Then Job a' and said, "
20: 1 Then a' Zophar the Naamathite, "
21: 1 But Job a' and said, "
22: 1 Then Eliphaz the Temanite a' "
23: 1 Then Job a' and said, "
25: 1 Then a' Bildad the Shuhite. "
26: 1 But Job a' and said, "
32: 6 the son of Barachel the Buzite a' "
12 convinced Job, or that a' his words: "
15 were amazed they a' no more: * "
16 stood still, and a' no more, * "
34: 1 Furthermore Elihu a' and said, "
38: 1 Lord a' Job out of the whirlwind, "
40: 1 Moreover the Lord a' Job, "
3 Then Job a' the Lord, and said, "
6 Then a' the Lord unto Job "
42: 1 Then Job a' the Lord, "
Ps 18:41 the Lord, but he a' them not. "
81: 7 I a' thee in the secret place of "
99: 6 upon the Lord, and he a' them. "
118: 5 Lord a' me, and set me in a large "
Isa 6:11 And he a', Until the cities 559
21: 9 he a' and said, Babylon is fallen, 6030
36:21 peace, and a' him not a word: "
39: 4 Hezekiah a', All that is in mine 559
Jer 7:13 I called you, but ye a' not; 6030
11: 5 Then a' I, and said, so be it, O Lord. "
23:35 What hath the Lord a'? "
37 What hath the Lord a' thee? "
35:17 unto them, but they have not a'. "
36:18 Then Baruch a' them, 559
44:15 all the men.... a' Jeremiah, 6030
Eze 24:20 I a' them, The word of the Lord * 559
37: 3 I a', O Lord God, thou knowest. "
Da 2: 5 king a' and said to the Chaldeans, 6032
7 a' again and said, Let the king tell "
8 a' and said, I know of certainty "
10 Chaldeans a' before the king, and "
14 a' with counsel and wisdom to *8421
15 He a' and said to Arioch 6032
20 Daniel a' and said, Blessed be the "
26 The king a' and said to Daniel, "
27 a' in the presence of the king, "
47 The king a' unto Daniel, "
3:16 a' and said to the king, "
24 They a' and said unto the king, "
25 He a' and said, Lo, I see four men "
4:19 Belteshazzar a' and said, My lord, "
5:17 Daniel a' and said before the king, "
6:12 king a' and said, The thing is true, "
13 a' they and said before the king, "
Am 7:14 a' Amos, and said to Amaziah, 6030
Mic 6: 5 Balaam the son of Beor a' him, "
Hab 2: 2 And the Lord a' me, and said, "
Hag 2:12 And the priests a' and said, No. "
13 the priests a' and said, It shall be "
14 Then a' Haggai, and said, "
Zec 1:10 the man that stood.... a' and said, "
11 And they a' the angel of the Lord "
12 Then the angel of the Lord a' "
13 And the Lord a' the angel "
19 And he a' me, These are the horns 559
3: 4 And he a' and spake 6030
4: 4 So I a' and spake to the angel "
5 the angel that talked with me a' "
6 Then he a' and spake unto me, "
11 Then a' I, and said unto him, "
12 And I a' again, and said unto him, "
13 And he a' me and said, 559
5: 2 And I a', I see a flying roll; "
6: 4 Then I a' and said unto the angel 6030
5 the angel a' and said unto me, "
M't 4: 4 he a' and said, It is written, 611
8: 8 The centurion a' and said, Lord, "
11: 4 Jesus a' and said unto them, "
25 At that time Jesus a' and said, "
12:38 scribes and of the Pharisees a', "
39 he a' and said unto them, "
48 he a' and said unto him that told "
13:11, 37 He a' and said unto them, "
14:28 Peter a' him and said, Lord, "
15: 3 he a' and said unto them, "
13 he a' and said, Every plant, "
15 Then a' Peter and said unto him, "
23 he a' her not a word. "
24 he a' and said, I am not sent "
26 he a' and said, It is not meet "
28 Then Jesus a' and said unto her, "
16: 2 He a' and said unto them, "
16 Simon Peter a' and said, "
17 Jesus a' and said unto him, "
17: 4 Then a' Peter, and said unto "
11 Jesus a' and said unto them, "
17 Then Jesus a' and said, O faithless "
19: 4 he a' and said unto them, "
27 Then a' Peter and said unto him, "
20:13 he a' one of them, and said, "
M't 20:22 Jesus a' and said, Ye know 611
21:21, 24 Jesus a' and said unto them, "
27 they a' Jesus, and said, We cannot "
29 He a' and said, I will not: "
30 he a' and said, I go, sir: "
22: 1 Jesus a' and spake unto them again "
29 Jesus a' and said unto them, "
24: 4 Jesus a' and said unto them, "
25: 9 the wise a', saying, Not so; "
12 he a' and said, Verily I say unto "
26 His lord a' and said unto him, "
26:23 he a' and said, He that dippeth his "
25 which betrayed him, a' and said, "
33 Peter a' and said unto him, "
63 the high priest a' and said unto * "
66 a' and said, He is guilty of death. "
27:12 priests and elders, he a' nothing. "
14 he a' him to never a word; * "
21 The governor a' and said unto them, "
25 Then a' all the people, and said, "
28: 5 the angel a' and said unto the "
M'k 3:33 he a' them, saying, Who is my * "
5: 9 he a', saying, My name is Legion:* "
6:37 He a' and said unto them, "
7: 6 He a' and said unto them, * "
28 she a' and said unto him, "
8: 4 his disciples a' him, "
28 they a', John the Baptist: * "
9: 5 Peter a' and said to Jesus, * "
12 he a' and told them, Elias verily * "
17 one of the multitude a' and said, "
38 John a' him, saying, Master, * "
10: 3 he a' and said unto them, "
5 Jesus a' and said unto them, * "
20 he a' and said unto him, Master, * "
29 Jesus a' and said, Verily I say * "
51 Jesus a' and said unto him, "
11:14 Jesus a' and said unto it, "
29 Jesus a' and said unto them, * "
33 they a' and said unto Jesus, We "
12:28 perceiving that he had a' them well, "
29 Jesus a' him, The first of all the "
34 saw that he a' discreetly, "
35 Jesus a' and said, while he taught "
14:20 he a' and said unto them, * "
48 Jesus a' and said unto them, "
61 held his peace and a' nothing. "
15: 3 many things: but he a' nothing. * "
5 Jesus yet a' nothing; so that Pilate "
9 Pilate a' them, saying, "
12 Pilate a' and said again unto them "
Lu 1:35 the angel a' and said unto her, "
60 his mother a' and said, "
3:16 John a', saying unto them all, "
4: 4 Jesus a' him, saying, "
8 Jesus a' and said unto him, "
7:43 Simon a' and said, I suppose that "
8:21 he a' and said unto them, "
50 he a' him, saying, Fear not: "
9:49 John a' and said, Master, we saw "
10:28 unto him, Thou hast a' right: "
41 Jesus a' and said unto her, "
11:45 Then a' one of the lawyers, and * "
13:14 the ruler of the synagogue a' "
15 The Lord then a' him, and said, "
14: 5 a' them, saying, Which of you * "
17:20 he a' them and said, "
37 they a' and said unto him, "
19:40 he a' and said unto them, * "
20: 3 he a' and said unto them, "
7 they a', that they could not tell "
24 They a' and said, Cæsar's. * "
22:51 Jesus a' and said, Suffer ye thus "
23: 3 he a' him and said, Thou sayest it. "
9 he a' him nothing. "
Jo 1:21 thou that prophet? And he a', No. "
26 John a' them, saying, I baptize "
48 Jesus a' and said unto him, "
49 Nathanael a' and saith "
50 Jesus a' and said unto him, "
2:18 Then a' the Jews and said "
19 Jesus a' and said unto them, "
3: 3 Jesus a' and said unto him, "
5 Jesus a', Verily, verily, "
9 Nicodemus a' and said "
10 Jesus a' and said unto him, Art "
27 John a' and said, A man can "
4:10, 13 Jesus a' and said unto her, "
17 a' and said, I have no husband. "
5: 7 The impotent man a' "
11 He a' them, He that made me "
17 Jesus a' them, My Father worketh "
19 Then a' Jesus and said unto them, "
6: 7 Philip a' him, Two hundred "
26 Jesus a' them and said, "
29 Jesus a' and said unto them, "
43 Jesus therefore a' and said "
68 Then Simon Peter a' him, "
70 Jesus a' them, Have not I chosen "
7:16 Jesus a' them, and said, "
20 The people a' and said, "
21 Jesus a' and said unto them, "
46 The officers a', Never man "
47 Then a' them the Pharisees, "
52 They a' and said unto him, "
8:14 Jesus a' and said unto them, "
19 Jesus a', Ye neither know me, "
33 a' him, We be Abraham's seed, "
34 Jesus a' them, Verily, "
39 They a' and said unto him, "
48 Then a' the Jews, and said "
49 Jesus a', I have not a devil; "
54 Jesus a', If I honour myself, my "
9: 3 Jesus a', Neither hath this man "
11 He a' and said, A man that is "
20 His parents a' them "
Jo 9:25 He a' and said, Whether he be a 611
27 He a' them, I have told "
30 The man a' and said unto them, "
34 They a' and said unto him, "
36 He a' and said, Who is he, "
10:25 Jesus a' them, I told you, and ye "
32 Jesus a' them, Many good works "
33 The Jews a' him, saying, "
34 Jesus a' them, Is it not "
11: 9 Jesus a', Are there not twelve "
12:23 Jesus a' them, saying, "
30 Jesus a' and said, This voice "
34 The people a' him, We have heard "
13: 7 Jesus a' and said unto him, "
8 Jesus a' him, If I wash thee not, "
26 Jesus a', He it is, to whom * "
36 Jesus a' him, Whither I go, "
38 Jesus a' him, Wilt thou lay * "
14:23 Jesus a' and said unto him, "
16:31 Jesus a' them, Do ye now believe? "
18: 5 They a' him, Jesus of Nazareth. "
8 Jesus a', I have told you that I am "
20 Jesus a' him, I spake openly to "
23 Jesus a' him, If I have spoken evil, "
30 They a' and said unto him, "
34 Jesus a' him, Sayest thou this "
35 Pilate a', Am I a Jew? "
36 Jesus a', My kingdom is not of "
37 Jesus a', Thou sayest that I am "
19: 7 The Jews a' him, We have a law, "
11 Jesus a', Thou couldest have no "
15 chief priests a', We have no king "
22 Pilate a', What I have written, "
20:28 Thomas a' and said unto "
21: 5 They a' him, No. "
Ac 3:12 he a' unto the people, ye men of "
4:19 Peter and John a' and said unto "
5: 8 Peter a' unto her, Tell me "
29 and the other apostles a' and said, "
8:24 Then a' Simon, and said, Pray ye, "
34 the eunuch a' Philip, and said, "
37 he a' and said, I believe * "
9:13 Ananias a', Lord, I have heard "
10:46 magnify God. Then a' Peter, "
11: 9 the voice a' me again from heaven, "
15:13 James a', saying, Men, "
19:15 the evil spirit a' and said, "
21:13 Then Paul a', What mean ye to "
22: 8 I a', Who art thou, Lord? "
28 chief captain a', With a great sum "
24:10 answered, Forasmuch as I know "
25 trembled, and a', Go thy way "
25: 4 Festus a', that Paul should be "
8 While he a' for himself, * 626
9 a' Paul, and said, Wilt thou go up 611
12 a', Hast thou appealed unto "
16 whom I a', It is not the manner "
26: 1 the hand, and a' for himself: * 626
Re 7:13 one of the elders a', saying unto 611

answeredst
Ps 99: 8 Thou a' them, O Lord our God: 6030
138: 3 the day when I cried thou a' me, "

answerest
1Sa 26:14 A' thou not, Abner? 6030
Job 16: 3 emboldeneth thee that thou a'? "
M't 26:62 unto him, A' thou nothing? 611
M'r 14:60 saying, A' thou nothing? "
15: 4 him, saying, a' thou nothing? "
Joh 18:22 A' thou the high priest so? "

answereth
1Sa 28:15 and a' me no more, neither by 6030
1Ki 18:24 the God that a' by fire, let him "
Job 12: 4 upon God, and he a' him: "
Pr 18:13 He that a' a matter before *7725
23 intreaties; but the rich a' roughly. 6030
27:19 As in water face a' to face, so
Ec 5:20 God a' him in the joy of his 6030
10:19 but money a' all things. "
M'r 8:29 And Peter a' and saith unto 611
9:19 He a' him, and saith, O faithless "
Lu 3:11 He a' and saith unto them, * "
Ga 4:25 and a' to Jerusalem which now is, 4960

answering
M't 3:15 Jesus a' said unto him, 611
M'r 11:22 And Jesus a' saith unto them, * "
33 Jesus a' saith unto them, * "
12:17 Jesus a' said unto them, * "
24 Jesus a' said unto them, * "
13: 2 Jesus a' said unto him, * "
5 Jesus a' them, began to say, * "
15: 2 he a' said unto him, Thou sayest it. "
Lu 1:19 the angel a' said unto him, "
4:12 Jesus a' said unto him, "
5: 5 Simon a' said unto him, Master, * "
22 a' said unto them, What reason * "
31 Jesus a' said unto them, "
6: 3 Jesus a' them said, Have ye not "
7:22 Then Jesus a' said unto * "
40 Jesus a' said unto him, "
9:19 They a' said, John the Baptist; "
20 Peter a' said, The Christ of God. "
41 Jesus a' said, O faithless "
10:27 he a' said, Thou shalt love the "
30 And Jesus a' said, A certain man *5274
13: 2 Jesus a' said unto them, * 611
8 he a' said unto him, Lord, "
14: 3 Jesus a' spake unto the lawyers "
15:29 he a' said to his father, * "
17:17 Jesus a' said, Were there not ten "
20:34 Jesus a' said unto them, * "
39 certain of the scribes a' said, "
23:40 the other a' rebuked him, * "
24:18 Cleopas, a' said unto him, "
Tit 2: 9 well in a' things; not a' again; * 488

answers
Job 21:34 *a'* there remaineth falsehood? 8666
34:36 of his *a'* for wicked men. * "
Lu 2:47 at his understanding and *a'*. *612*

ant See also ANTS.
Pro 6: 6 Go to the *a'*, thou sluggard; 5244

antichrist See also ANTICHRISTS.
1Jo 2:18 ye have heard that *a'* shall come, *500*
22 He is *a'*, that denieth the Father "
4: 3 this is that spirit of *a'*, whereof "
2Jo 7 This is a deceiver and an *a'*. "

antichrists
1Jo 2:18 come, even now are there many *a'*; *500*

Antioch (*an'-te-ok*)
Ac 6: 5 and Nicolas a proselyte of *A'*: *491*
11:19 far as Phenice, and Cyprus, and *A'*, *490*
20 when they were come to *A'*, "
22 that he should go as far as *A'*. "
26 brought him unto *A'*. "
26 were called Christians first in *A'*. "
27 from Jerusalem unto *A'*. "
13: 1 in the church that was at *A'* "
14 they came to *A'* in Pisidia, "
14:19 certain Jews from *A'* and Iconium, "
21 Iconium, and *A'*, "
26 and thence sailed to *A'*, "
15:22 men of their own company to *A'* "
23 Gentiles in *A'* and Syria "
30 were dismissed, they came to *A'*: "
35 Barnabas continued in *A'*, teaching "
18:22 the church, he went down to *A'*. "
Ga 2:11 when Peter was come to *A'*, "
2Ti 3:11 which came unto me at *A'*, "

Antipas (*an'-tip-as*)
Re 2:13 *A'* was my faithful martyr, *498*

Antipatris (*an-tip'-at-ris*)
Ac 23:31 and brought him by night to *A'*. *494*

antiquity
Isa 23: 7 whose *a'* is of ancient days? 6927

Antothijah (*an-to-thi'-jah*)
1Ch 8:24 And Hananiah, and Elam, and *A'*, 6070

Antothite (*an'-to-thite*) See also ANETOTHITE.
1Ch 11:28 the Tekoite, Abi-ezer the *A'*, *6069
12: 3 and Berachah, and Jehu the *A'*, * "

ants
Pr 30:25 The *a'* are a people not strong, 5244

Anub (*a'-nub*)
1Ch 4: 8 And Coz begat *A'*, and Zobebah, 6036

anvil
Isa 41: 7 hammer him that smote the *a'*, 6471

any
Ge 3: 1 was more subtil than *a'* beast 3605
4:15 a mark upon Cain, lest *a'* finding "
8:12 not again unto him *a'* more. 5750
21 not again curse the ground *a'* more "
21 again smite *a'* more every thing "
9:11 shall all flesh be cut off *a'* more "
11 there *a'* more be a flood to destroy "
14:23 not take *a'* thing that is thine, *3605
17: 5 name *a'* more be called Abram, 5750
12 bought with money of *a'* stranger, 3605
18:14 Is *a'* thing too hard for the Lord? "
19:12 Hast thou here *a'* besides? 4310
22 I cannot do *a'* thing till thou be
22:12 neither do thou *a'* thing unto 3972
24:16 neither had *a'* man known her:
30:31 Thou shalt not give me *a'* thing: * 3972
31:14 there yet *a'* portion or inheritance
35:10 shall not be called *a'* more Jacob, 5750
36:31 reigned *a'* king over the children of
39: 9 neither hath he kept back *a'* thing 3972
23 *a'* thing that was under his hand; "
42:16 be proved, whether there be *a'* *
47: 6 if thou knowest *a'* men of activity
Ex 8:29 Pharaoh deal deceitfully *a'* more 3254
9:29 shall there be *a'* more hail; 5750
10:23 neither rose *a'* from his place 376
11: 6 nor shall be like it *a'* more. 3254
7 against *a'* of the children of Israel 3605
16:24 neither was there *a'* worm
20: 4 unto thee *a'* graven image, *
4 or *a'* likeness of *3605
4 *a'* thing that is in heaven above
10 in it thou shalt not do *a'* work, 3605
17 *a'* thing that is thy neighbour's. "
21:23 And if *a'* mischief follow, then
22: 9 or for *a'* manner of lost thing, 3605
10 or *a'* beast, to keep; and it die, "
20 He that sacrificeth unto *a'* god,
22 Ye shall not afflict *a'* widow, 3605
23 If thou afflict them in *a'* wise,
31 neither shall ye eat *a'* flesh that
24:14 if *a'* man have *a'* matters to do, *
30:32 neither shall ye make *a'* other
33 Whosoever compoundeth *a'* like it,
33 whosoever putteth *a'* of it upon
31:14 whosoever doeth *a'* work therein, 3605
15 doeth *a'* work in the sabbath day, "
32:24 Whosoever hath *a'* gold,
34: 3 neither let *a'* man be seen
10 done in all the earth, nor in *a'* 3605
24 neither shall *a'* man desire thy
35:24 found shittim wood for *a'* work of 3605
33 to make *a'* manner of cunning * "
35 even of them that do *a'* work,
36: 6 man nor woman make *a'* more 5750
Le 1: 2 If *a'* man of you bring an offering
2: 1 when *a'* will offer a meat offering 5315
11 burn no leaven, nor *a'* honey, in 3605
11 *a'* offering of the Lord made by *
4: 2 sin through ignorance against *a'* 3605

Le 4: 2 be done, and shall do against *a'* 259
13 have done somewhat against *a'* of "
22 through ignorance against *a'* of "
27 if *a'* one of the common people sin 5315
27 he doeth somewhat against *a'* of 259
5: 2 if a soul touch *a'* unclean thing, 3605
11 he put *a'* frankincense thereon:
17 sin, and commit *a'* of these things 259
6: 3 *a'* of all these that a man doeth, "
7 shall be forgiven him for *a'* thing * "
27 of the blood thereof upon *a'*
30 offering, whereof *a'* of the blood
7: 8 *a'* man's burnt offering, even the
15 not leave *a'* of it until the morning.
18 if *a'* of the flesh of the sacrifice of
19 that toucheth *a'* unclean thing 3605
21 that shall touch *a'* unclean thing, "
21 or *a'* unclean beast, *
21 or *a'* abominable unclean 3605
26 of beast, in *a'* of your dwellings. "
27 he that eateth *a'* manner of blood, "
11:10 of *a'* living thing which is in the * "
32 And upon whatsoever *a'* of them,
32 whether it be *a'* vessel of wood, 3605
33 vessel, whereinto *a'* of them "
35 whereupon *a'* part of their carcase
37 And if *a'* part of their carcase *
37 fall upon *a'* sowing seed *3605
38 if *a'* water be put upon the seed, *
38 *a'* part of their carcase fall *
39 if *a'* beast, of which he may eat,
43 abominable with *a'* creeping 3605
44 defile yourselves with *a'* manner "
13:24 Or if there be *a'* flesh, in the skin *
48 or in *a'* thing made of skin; 3605
49 the work, or in *a'* thing of skin; "
51 in *a'* work that is made of skin; * "
52 or in linen, or *a'* thing of skin, "
53 in the woof, or in *a'* thing of skin; "
57 or in *a'* thing of skin; it is a "
59 or *a'* thing of skins, to pronounce "
15: 2 When *a'* man hath a running issue 376
6 he that sitteth on *a'* thing
10 whosoever toucheth *a'* thing that, 3605
10 he that beareth *a'* of those things *
16 if *a'* man's seed of copulation go
22 whosoever toucheth *a'* thing that 3605
23 or on *a'* thing whereon she sitteth,
24 And if *a'* man lie with her at all,
17:10 that eateth *a'* manner of blood; 3605
12 shall eat blood, neither shall *a'*
13 catcheth *a'* beast or fowl that may
18: 6 shall approach to *a'* that is near 376
21 not let *a'* of thy seed pass through
23 lie with *a'* beast to defile thyself 3605
23 neither shall *a'* woman stand before
24 yourselves in *a'* of these things: 3605
26 commit *a'* of these abominations; * "
26 *a'* of your own nations, nor *a'* "
29 commit *a'* of these abominations; 3605
30 not *a'* one of these abominable
19:17 in *a'* wise rebuke thy neighbour, *
18 nor bear *a'* grudge against the
26 not eat *a'* thing with the blood:
28 not make *a'* cuttings in your flesh
28 nor print *a'* marks upon you:
20: 2 giveth *a'* of his seed unto Molech; *
4 people of the land do *a'* ways hide
16 a woman approach unto *a'* beast, 3605
25 by *a'* manner of living thing that "
21: 5 nor make *a'* cuttings in their flesh.
9 the daughter of *a'* priest, if she 376
11 shall he go into *a'* dead body, 3605
17 that hath *a'* blemish, let him not *
18 a flat nose, or *a'* thing superfluous,
22: 4 toucheth *a'* thing that is unclean 3605
5 toucheth *a'* creeping thing, "
6 soul which hath touched *a'* such
11 priest buy *a'* soul with his money,
23 that hath *a'* thing superfluous or
24 neither shall ye make *a'* offering *
25 bread of your God of *a'* of these; 3605
23:22 gather *a'* gleaning of thy harvest: *
30 soul it be that doeth *a'* work 3605
24:17 he that killeth *a'* man shall surely
25:25 if *a'* of his kin come to redeem it, *
32 the Levites redeem at *a'* time. 5769
49 *a'* that is nigh of kin unto him of
26: 1 neither shall ye set up *a'* image of
27: 9 all that *a'* man giveth of such
11 And if it be *a'* unclean beast, 3605
19 sanctified the field will in *a'* wise*
20 it shall not be redeemed *a'* more.
Nu 4:15 they shall not touch *a'* holy thing.*
5: 6 man or woman shall commit *a'* sin 3605
10 whatsoever *a'* man giveth the priest,
12 If *a'* man's wife go aside, and 376
6: 3 shall he drink *a'* liquor of grapes, 3605
9 if *a'* man die very suddenly by him,
9:10 If *a'* man of you or of your posterity 376
12 morning, nor break any bone of *
14:23 shall *a'* of them that provoked me 3605
15:27 if *a'* soul sin through ignorance, * 259
17:13 Whosoever cometh *a'* thing near *
18: 5 wrath *a'* more upon the children *
20 thou have *a'* part among them:
19:11, 13 toucheth the dead body of *a'* 3605
20: 5 neither is there *a'* water to drink.
19 without doing *a'* thing else, go
21: 5 bread, neither is there *a'* water; *
9 serpent had bitten *a'* man,
22:38 I now *a'* power...to say *a'* thing?
23:23 there *a'* divination against Israel:
29: 7 souls: ye shall not do *a'* work *3605
30: 5 not *a'* of her vows, or of her * "
15 shall *a'* ways make them void *

Nu 31:19 whosoever hath killed *a'* person,
19 whosoever hath touched *a'* slain,
35:11 killeth *a'* person at unawares.
15 Every one that killeth *a'* person
22 or have cast upon him *a'* thing 3605
23 Or with *a'* stone, wherewith a man "
26 if the slayer shall at *a'* time come
30 killeth *a'* person, the murderer
30 shall not testify against *a'* person
36: 3 be married to *a'* of the sons of the 259
8 possesseth an inheritance in *a'*
De 2:19 children of Ammon *a'* possession; *
37 unto *a'* place of the river Jabbok, *3605
4:16 graven image, the similitude of *a'* "
17 The likeness of *a'* beast that is "
17 the likeness of *a'* winged fowl "
18 likeness of *a'* thing that creepeth "
18 likeness of *a'* fish that is in the "
23 likeness of *a'* thing, which the Lord "
25 graven image, or the likeness of *a'* "
32 there hath been *a'* such thing as
5: 8 *a'* graven image, or *a'* likeness *3605
8 of *a'* thing that is in heaven above,
14 thou shalt not do *a'* work, thou, 3605
14 nor *a'* of thy cattle, nor thy "
21 or *a'* thing that is thy neighbour's. "
25 voice of the Lord our God *a'* more
7: 7 more in number than *a'* people; 3605
8: 9 thou shalt not lack *a'* thing in it; "
12:17 nor *a'* of thy vows which thou
13:11 do no more *a'* such wickedness 1697
14: 1 nor make *a'* baldness between
3 shalt not eat *a'* abominable thing. 3605
21 shall not eat of *a'* thing that dieth "
15: 7 brethren within *a'* of thy gates 259
21 if there be *a'* blemish therein, as
21 or have *a'* ill blemish, thou shalt 3605
16: 4 shall there *a'* thing of the flesh,
5 passover within *a'* of thy gates, 259
21 thee a grove of *a'* trees near 3605
22 shalt thou set thee up *a'* image; *
17: 1 the Lord thy God *a'* bullock, *
1 or *a'* evilfavouredness: for that 3605
2 among you, within *a'* of thy gates 259
3 moon, or *a'* of the host of heaven, 3605
15 in *a'* wise set him king over thee, ‡
18: 6 a Levite come from *a'* of thy gates 259
10 not be found among you *a'* one
16 let me see this great fire *a'* more,
19:11 if *a'* man hate his neighbour, and
15 against a man for *a'* iniquity, or 3605
15 for *a'* sin, in *a'* sin that he sinneth: "
16 witness rise up against *a'* man to
20 commit no more *a'* such evil 1697
21:23 in *a'* wise bury him that day *
22: 1 shalt in *a'* case bring them again *
6 before thee in the way in *a'* tree, 3605
7 shalt in *a'* wise let the dam go, ‡
8 house, if *a'* man fall from thence.
13 If *a'* man take a wife, and go in
23:10 among you *a'* man, that is not clean
18 of the Lord thy God for *a'* vow: 3605
19 usury of *a'* thing that is lent "
24 shalt not put *a'* in thy vessel.
24: 5 he be charged with *a'* business: 3605
7 found stealing *a'* of his brethren 5315
10 dost lend thy brother *a'* thing, 3972
13 In *a'* case thou shalt deliver him *
26:14 taken away ought thereof for *a'* *
27: 5 not lift up *a'* iron tool upon them.*
15 Cursed be the man that maketh *a'* *
21 with *a'* manner of beast. And all 3605
28:14 go aside from any of the words "
55 not give to *a'* of them of the flesh 259
29:23 nor *a'* grass groweth therein, like 3605
30: 4 If *a'* of thine be driven out unto
31:13 have not known *a'* thing, may *
32:28 there *a'* understanding in them. *
39 neither is there *a'* that can deliver *
Jos 1: 5 There shall not *a'* man be able
2:11 remain *a'* more courage in *a'* man,
19 our head, if *a'* hand be upon him.
5: 1 spirit in them *a'* more, because
12 children of Israel manna *a'* more;
6:10 shout, nor make *a'* noise with *
10 neither shall *a'* word proceed out
18 And ye, in *a'* wise keep yourselves
7:12 neither will I be with you *a'* more,
8:31 no man hath lift up *a'* iron:
10:21 against *a'* of the children of Israel.
11:11 there was not *a'* left to breathe: *3605
14 them neither left they *a'* "
13:33 Moses gave not *a'* inheritance: * "
20: 3 that killeth *a'* person unawares
9 killeth *a'* person at unawares
21:45 failed not ought of *a'* good thing 3605
23:12 Else if ye do in *a'* wise go back,
13 God will no more drive out *a'* of *
J'g 2:14 could not *a'* longer stand before
21 drive out *a'* from before them
4:20 when *a'* man doth come...and say,
20 Is there *a'* man here? that thou
11:25 art thou *a'* thing better than Balak
13: 4 and eat not *a'* unclean thing: 3605
7 neither eat *a'* unclean thing: for "
14 She may not eat of *a'* thing that "
14 nor eat *a'* unclean thing: all "
16:17 weak, and be like *a'* other man.
18: 7 put them to shame in *a'* thing;
7 and had no business with *a'* man.
10 there is no want of *a'* thing that 3605
28 had no business with *a'* man; and
19:19 there is no want of *a'* thing: 3605
20: 8 not *a'* of us go to his tent, neither 376
8 we *a'* of us turn into his house.
21: 1 shall not *a'* of us give his daughter "

J'g 21:12 a' male: and they brought them *
Ru 1:11 with me? are there yet a' more *
2:22 meet thee not in a' other field.
1Sa 2: 2 is there a' rock like our God.
13 when a' man offered sacrifice, 3605
16 if a' man said unto him, Let them *
3:17 if thou hide a' thing from me of
5: 5 a' that come into Dagon's house, 3605
6: 3 in a' wise return him a trespass
9: 2 was higher than a' of the people. 3605
10:23 higher than a' of the people from "
12: 3 of whose hand I received a' bribe*
4 thou taken ought of a' man's hand.
13:22 nor spear found in the hand of a' 3605
14:24 the man that eateth a' food until
24 none of the people tasted a' food. *3605
28 Cursed be the man that eateth a' *
52 Saul saw a' strong man, or a' 3605
18:25 The king desireth not a' dowry,
20:12 my father about to morrow a' *
26 Saul spake not a' thing that day: 3972
39 the lad knew not a' thing: "
21: 2 Let no man know a' thing of the
22:15 let not the king impute a' thing 3605
25:15 neither missed we a' thing, 3972
22 to him by the morning light a' *
34 Nabal by the morning light a' *
27: 1 to seek me a' more *
1 in a' coast of Israel: *3605
30: 2 slew not a', either great or small, 376
12 bread, nor drunk a' water,
19 nor a' thing that they had taken 3605
2Sa 2: 1 up into a' of the cities of Judah? 259
28 more, neither fought they a' more.
7: 6 I have not dwelt in a' house *
7 with a' of the tribes of Israel, 259
10 of wickedness afflict them a' more,
22 neither is there a' God beside thee,
9: 1 Is there yet a' that is left of the
3 not yet a' of the house of Saul, 376
10:19 help the children of Ammon a' more.
13: 2 hard for him to do a' thing to her. 3972
14:10 he shall not touch thee a' more.
11 revengers of blood to destroy a',
14 doth God respect a' person: *
32 and if there be a' iniquity in me, *
15: 2 a' man that had a controversy 3605
4 every man which hath a' suit or
5 when a' man came nigh to him
11 and they knew not a' thing. 3605
19:22 there a' man be put to death
28 therefore have I yet to cry a' more
29 Why speakest thou a' more of thy
35 can I hear a' more the voice of
42 or hath he given us a' gift?
21: 4 shalt thou kill a' man in Israel.
5 in a' of the coasts of Israel, 3605
1Ki 1: 6 had not displeased him at a' time
2:36 go not forth thence a' whither.
2:42 and walkest abroad a' whither,
3:12 neither after thee shall a' arise.
13 shall not be a' among the kings 376
5: 6 there is not among us a' that can
6: 7 nor ax nor a' tool of iron heard 3605
8:31 If a' man trespass against his *
38 supplication soever be made by a' 3605
10: 3 all her questions: there was not a'
20 not the like made in a' kingdom. 3605
11:22 howbeit let me go in a' wise.
15: 5 turned not aside from a' thing 3605
17 he might not suffer a' to go out
21 not to Jeroboam a' that breathed, 3605
18:26 was no voice, nor a' that answered.
29 neither voice, nor a' to answer,
29 nor a' that regarded.
20:33 diligently observe whether a' *
39 if by a' means he be missing,
2Ki 2:21 there shall not be from thence a' more
4: 2 handmaid hath not a' thing 3605
29 if thou meet a' man, salute him
29 if a' salute thee, answer him not 376
6:33 I wait for the Lord a' longer?
10: 5 we will not make a' king: 376
14 forty men; neither left he a' of "
24 a' of the men whom I have brought
12: 4 that cometh into a' man's heart
5 a' breach shall be found. 376
14:26 for there was not a' shut up, *
26 nor a' left, *
26 nor a' helper for Israel. *
18: 5 nor a' that were before him. *
33 Hath a' of the gods of the nations 376
21: 8 the feet of Israel move a' more
23:25 after him arose there a' like him.
24: 7 of Egypt came not again a' more
1Ch 1:43 before a' king reigned over the
17: 6 word to a' of the judges of Israel, 259
9 of wickedness waste them a' more,
20 neither is there a' God beside thee,
19:19 help the children of Ammon a' more.
23:26 nor a' vessels of it for the service *3605
26:28 whosoever had dedicated a' thing,
27: 1 that served the king in a' matter 3605
28:21 skilful man, for a' manner of "
29:25 as had not been on a' king "
2Ch 1:12 there a' after thee have the like.
2:14 to grave a' manner of graving, 3605
6: 5 neither chose I a' man to be a ruler
29 soever shall be made of a' man, 3605
8:15 concerning a' matter, or "
9: 9 neither was there a' such spice
19 not the like made in a' kingdom. 3605
20 it was not a' thing accounted of *3972
23:19 which was unclean in a' thing 3605
32:13 a' ways able to deliver their lands
15 no god of a' nation or kingdom, 3605

2Ch 33: 8 I a' more remove the foot of Israel
34:13 work in a' manner of service: *3605
Ezr 1: 4 whosoever remaineth in a' place "
7:24 a' of the priests and Levites, 3606
Ne 2:12 neither told I a' man what my God
12 at Jerusalem: neither was there a'
5:16 wall, neither bought we a' land:
10:31 the land bring ware or a' victuals
Job 4:20 for ever without a' regarding it.
5: 1 there be a' that will answer thee;
4 neither is there a' to deliver them.
6: 6 a' taste in the white of an egg?
7:10 shall his place know him a' more.
8:12 it withered before a' other herb. 3605
9:33 is there a' daysman betwixt us, *
10:22 shadow of death, without a' order,
15:11 there a' secret thing with thee? *
16:17 for a' injustice in mine hands: *
18:19 people, nor a' remaining in his
20: 9 his place a' more behold him.
21:22 Shall a' teach God knowledge?
22: 3 Is it a' pleasure to the Almighty,
25: 3 Is there a' number of his armies?
31: 7 a' blot hath cleaved to mine hands;
19 a' perish for want of clothing,
19 or a' poor without covering; *
32:21 pray you, accept a' man's person,
33:13 not account of a' of his matters. 3605
27 upon men, and if a' say, I *
32 [*In most editions*] hast a' thing to say.
34:27 would not consider a' of his ways: 3605
31 I will not offend a' more:
36: 5 is mighty, and despiseth not a':
29 can a' understand the spreadings
37:24 respecteth not a' that are wise of 3605
Ps 4: 6 say, Who will shew us a' good?
14: 2 there were a' that did understand,
33:17 deliver a' by his great strength.
34:10 shall not want a' good thing. 3605
37: 8 fret not thyself in a' wise to do *
38: 3 neither is there a' rest in my bones
49: 7 by a' means redeem his brother,
53: 2 there were a' that did understand,
59: 5 to a' wicked transgressors. 3605
74: 9 signs: there is no more a' prophet:
9 is there a' among us that knoweth
81: 9 thou worship a' strange God.
86: 8 neither are there a' works like
91:10 neither shall a' plague come nigh
109:12 be a' to favour his fatherless
115:17 a' that go down into silence. 3605
119:133 let not a' iniquity have dominion "
135:17 neither is their a' breath in their
139:24 if there be a' wicked way in me,
141: 4 Incline not my heart to a' evil
146: 2 my God while I have a' being.
147:20 hath not dealt so with a' nation: 3605
Pr 1:17 is spread in the sight of a' bird. "
6:35 He will not regard a' ransom; "
14:34 but sin is a reproach to a' people.
28:17 violence to the blood of a' person
30: 2 I am more brutish than a' man,
30 and turneth not away from a'. 3605
31: 5 the judgment of a' of the afflicted. "
Ec 1:10 Is there a' thing whereof it may *
11 shall there be a' remembrance
2:10 withheld not my heart from a' 3605
3:14 nothing can be put to it, nor a'
5: 2 heart be hasty to utter a' thing
6: 5 not seen the sun, nor known a' *
9: 5 but the dead know not a' thing, 3972
5 they a' more a reward; for the
6 have they a' more a portion ever
6 a' thing that is done under the 3605
Isa 1: 5 should ye be stricken a' more? *
2: 4 shall they learn war a' more.
7 there a' end of their treasures;
7 is their a' end of their chariots;
19:15 shall their be a' work for Egypt,
26:18 have not wrought a' deliverance
27: 3 lest a' hurt it, I will keep it night
30:20 removed into a corner a' more,
33:20 a' of the cords thereof be broken. 3605
35: 9 nor a' ravenous beast shall
36:18 Hath a' of the gods of the 376
51:18 neither is there a' that taketh her
52:14 was so marred more than a' man,
53: 9 neither was a' deceit in his mouth.
54: 4 of thy widowhood a' more. *
56: 2 his hand from doing a' evil. 3605
59: 4 nor a' pleadeth for truth: *
62: 4 land a' more be termed Desolate:
Jer 3:16 neither shall that be done a' more.
17 neither shall they walk a' more
5: 1 there be a' that executeth judgment.
9: 4 and trust ye not in a' brother: 3605
10:20 to stretch forth my tent a' more,
14:22 Are there a' among the vanities
17:22 neither do ye a' work, but 3605
18:18 not give heed to a' of his words.
20: 9 nor speak a' more in his name.
22:11 shall not return thither a' more:
30 and ruling a' more in Judah.
23:24 Can a' hide himself in secret 376
31:12 they shall not sorrow a' more at all.
40 nor thrown down a' more for ever.
32:27 is there a' thing too hard for me? 3605
33:26 I will not take a' of his seed *
34:10 serve themselves of them a' more
35: 7 nor plant vineyard, nor have a':
36:24 nor a' of his servants that heard 3605
37:17 Is there a' word from the Lord?
38: 5 he that can do a' thing against you.
42:21 voice of the Lord your God, nor a' 3605
44:26 more be named in the mouth of a' "
48: 9 without a' to dwell therein.

Jer 49:33 nor a' son of man dwell in it.
50:40 shall a' son of man dwell therein.
51:43 neither doth a' son of man pass
44 shall not flow together a' more
La 1:12 and see if there be a' sorrow like
3:49 down, and ceaseth not, without a'
Eze 5: 9 whereunto I will not do a' more
11 spare, neither will I have a' pity. *
7:11 multitude, nor of a' of theirs: *1991
13 neither shall a' strengthen himself 376
9: 6 a' man upon whom is the mark; 3605
12:24 shall be no more a' vain vision
28 my words be prolonged a' more, 3605
14:11 polluted a' more with all their "
15: 3 be taken thereof to do a' work?
3 of it to hang a' vessel thereon? 3605
4 burned. Is it meet for a' work?
5 shall it be meet yet for a' work,
16: 5 thee, to do a' of these unto thee, 259
41 also shalt give no hire a' more.
63 never open thy mouth a' more.
18: 3 ye shall not have occasion a' more
7 And hath not oppressed a', but 376
8 neither hath taken a' increase,
10 the like to a' one of these things,
11 that doeth not a' of those duties, 3605
16 Neither hath oppressed a', hath 376
23 Have I a' pleasure at all that the
21: 5 it shall not return a' more.
23:27 nor remember Egypt a' more.
24:13 purged from thy filthiness a' more,
27:36 terror, and never shalt be a' more.
28:19 and never shalt thou be a' more.
24 nor a' grieving thorn of all that *
29:15 itself a' more above the nations:
31: 8 nor a' tree in the garden of God 3605
32:13 foot of man trouble them a' more,
33: 6 come, and take a' person from
34:10 shepherds feed themselves a' more;
29 the shame of the heathen a' more.
36:14 neither bereave thy nations a' more,
15 in thee the shame of the heathen a'
15 reproach of the people a' more,
37:22 into two kingdoms a' more
23 they defile themselves a' more
23 with a' of their transgressions: 3605
39: 7 pollute my holy name a' more:
10 cut down a' out of the forests;
15 when a' seeth a man's bone, then
28 have left none of them a' more
29 hide my face a' more from them:
44: 9 sanctuary, of a' stranger that 3605
13 come near to a' of my holy things, "
18 with a' thing that causeth sweat.
21 Neither shall a' priest drink wine, 3605
31 of a' thing that is dead of itself, "
46:16 give a gift unto a' of his sons, 376
Da 2:10 asked such things at a' magician, 3606
30 for a' wisdom that I have more
30 than a' living, but for their sakes 3606
3:28 not serve nor worship a' god, "
29 which speak a' thing amiss
6: 4 was there a' error or fault found 3606
5 We shall not find a' occasion "
7 ask a petition of a' God or man "
12 that shall ask a petition of a' God 3606
8: 4 before him, neither was there a'
11:15 neither shall there be a' strength
37 nor regard a' god: for he shall 3605
Ho 13:10 where is a' other that may save *
14: 3 neither will we say a' more to the
8 have I to do a' more with idols?
Joe 2: 2 neither shall be a' more after it,
3:17 pass through her a' more.
Am 6:10 Is there yet a' with thee? and he
7: 8 I will not pass by them a' more:
13 not again a' more at Beth-el:
8: 2 not again pass by them a' more.
7 never forget a' of their works. 3605
Ob 18 a' remaining of the house of Esau;
Jon 3: 7 herd nor flock, taste a' thing: 3792
Mic 4: 3 shall they learn war a' more.
Zep 3:15 thou shalt not see evil a' more.
Hag 2:12 or wine, or oil, or a' meat, shall 3605
13 by a dead body touch a' of these, "
Zec 8:10 nor a' hire for beast;
10 neither was there a' peace
9: 8 shall pass through them a' more:
13: 3 when a' shall yet prophesy, then 376
Mal 2:13 regardeth not the offering a' more,
M't 4: 6 lest at a' time thou dash thy foot *3379
5:25 at a' time the adversary deliver * "
40 if a' man will sue thee at the law,
11:27 knoweth a' man the Father, *5100*
12:19 shall a' man hear his voice in "
13:15 lest at a' time they should see **3379*
19 When a' one heareth the word *3956*
16:24 If a' man will come after me, let *1536*
18:19 agree on earth as touching a' *3956*
21: 3 if a' man say ought unto you, *5100*
22:16 neither carest thou for a' man: *3762*
46 a' man from that day forth *5100*
46 forth ask him a' more questions. *3765*
24:17 take a' thing out of his house: *5100*
23 if a' man shall say unto you, "
M'r 1:44 See thou say nothing to a' man: *3367*
4:12 a' time they should be converted, **3379*
22 neither was a' thing kept secret, *5100*
23 If a' man have ears to hear, let *1536*
5: 4 neither could a' man tame him. **3762*
35 thou the Master a' further? *2089*
7:16 If a' man have ears to hear, let **1536*
8:26 nor tell it to a' in the town. **5100*
9: 8 they saw no man a' more, save *3765*
22 if thou canst do a' thing, have *1536*
30 that a' man should know it. *5100*

M'r 9:35 If a' man desire to be first, the 1536
11: 3 And if a' man say unto you, Why "
13 he might find a' thing thereon: "
16 suffer that a' man should carry "
16 carry a' vessel through the * "
25 if ye have ought against a': * "
12:21 and died, neither left he a' seed: *
34 that durst ask him a' question.
13: 5 heed lest a' man deceive you: *5100
15 take a' thing out of his house: "
21 if a' man shall say to you, Lo, "
14:31 I will not deny thee in a' wise. *3364
63 need we a' further witnesses? *2089
15:44 whether he had been a' while dead.
16: 8 said they a' thing to *3762
8 to a' man; for they were afraid. "
18 and if they drink a' deadly thing, 5100
Lu 3:14 man, neither accuse a' falsely;
4:11 lest at a' time thou dash thy foot *3379
8:17 neither a' thing hid, that shall not
27 neither abode in a' house, but in
43 neither could be healed of a', 3762
9:23 If a' man will come after me, let 5100
36 in those days a' of those things 3762
10:19 shall by a' means hurt you. 3364
11:11 son shall ask bread of a' of you *5100
14: 8 art bidden of a' man to a wedding, "
26 a' man come to me, and hate not 1536
15:29 neither transgressed I at a' time *3763
19: 8 taken a' thing from *5100
8 a' man by false accusation, I 1536
31 if a' man ask you, Why do ye 5100
20:21 acceptest thou the person of a',
27 deny that there is a' resurrection; *3361
28 If a' man's brother die, having a *5100
36 Neither can they die a' more: 2089
40 not ask him a' question at all 3762
21:34 lest at a' time your hearts *3379
22:16 I will not a' more eat thereof, *3765
35 lacked ye a' thing? And they 5100
71 What need we a' further witness? *2089
24:41 them, Have ye here a' meat? *5100
Joh 1: 3 not a' thing made that was made. 1520
18 No man hath seen God at a' time; 4455
46 there a' good thing come out of 5100
2:25 that a' should testify of man: "
4:33 Hath a' man brought him ought 3387
5:37 neither heard his voice at a' time, 4455
6:46 Not that a' man hath seen the 5100
51 if a' man eat of this bread, he shall "
7: 4 no man that doeth a' thing in secret, "
17 If a' man will do his will, he shall "
37 If a' man thirst, let him come unto "
48 Have a' of the rulers or of the 3387
51 Doth our law judge a' man, *3588
8:33 were never in bondage to a' man: 3762
9:22 if a' man did confess that he was 5100
31 if a' man be a worshipper of God, "
32 that a' man opened the eyes of "
10: 9 if a' man enter in, he shall be saved, "
28 neither shall a' man pluck them * "
11: 9 If a' man walk in the day, he * "
57 if a' man knew where he were, "
12:26 If a' man serve me, let him follow "
26 if a' man serve me, him will my "
47 And if a' man hear my words, "
14:14 If ye shall ask a' thing in my name, "
16:30 that a' man should ask thee: "
18:31 for us to put a' man to death: 3762
21: 5 Children, have ye a' meat? *3387
Ac 4:12 is there salvation in a' other: *3762
32 neither said a' of them that *1520
34 there a' among them that lacked: 5100
9: 2 that if he found a' of this way, "
10:14 I have never eaten a' thing that 3956
28 I should not call a' man common 3367
47 Can a' man forbid water, that 5100
11: 8 common or unclean hath at a' time *3763
13:15 brethren, if ye have a' word of 5150
17:25 as though he needed a' thing, 5100
19: 2 whether there be a' Holy Ghost. *
38 have a matter against a' man, 5100
39 if ye enquire a' thing concerning "
24:12 the temple disputing with a' man, "
20 have found a' evil doing in me, *1536
25: 5 if there be a' wickedness in him. "
8 have I offended a' thing at all. *5100
11 committed a' thing worthy of death, "
16 to deliver a' man to die, before "
17 without a' delay on the morrow *3362
24 he ought not to live a' longer. 3370
27:12 if by a' means they might attain 4458
22 shall be no loss of a' man's life 3762
34 hair fall from the head of a' of you. "
42 lest a' of them should swim out, 5100
28:21 neither a' of the brethren that "
21 or spake a' harm of thee. "
Ro 1:10 if by a' means now at length I 4458
6: 2 to sin, live a' longer therein? 2089
8: 9 if a' man have not the Spirit of 5100
33 lay a' thing to the charge of God's
39 nor depth, nor a' other creature, 5100
9:11 having done a' good or evil, * "
11:14 If by a' means I may provoke 4458
13: 8 Owe no man a' thing, but to love 3367
9 there be a' other commandment, 1536
14:13 judge one another a' more: 3370
14 esteemeth a' thing to be unclean, 5100
21 nor a' thing whereby thy brother 3362
15:18 dare to speak of a' of those things 5100
1Co 1:15 Lest a' should say that I had 3387
16 not whether I baptized a' other. 1536
2: 2 not to know a' thing among you, 5100
3: 7 neither is he that planteth a' thing, "
12 a' man build upon this foundation "
14 If a' man's work abide which he 1536

1Co 3:15 If a' man's work shall be burned, 1536
17 If a' man defile the temple of God, "
18 If a' man among you seemeth to "
5:11 if a' man that is called a brother 5100
6: 1 Dare a' of you, having a matter "
12 brought under the power of a'. "
7:12 If a' brother hath a wife that 1536
18 a' man called being circumcised? 5100
18 Is a' called in uncircumcision? "
36 But if a' man think that he "
8: 2 if a' man think that he knoweth a' "
3 But if a' man love God, the same "
9 lest by a' means this liberty of 3381
10 For if a' man see thee which hast *5100
9: 7 a warfare a' time at his own *4218
15 a' man should make my glorying 5100
27 lest that by a' means, when I 3381
10:19 that the idol is a' thing, or that 5100
19 in sacrifice to idols is a' thing? "
27 If a' of them that believe not bid * "
28 But if a' man say unto you, "
11:16 if a' man seem to be contentious, "
34 if a' man hunger, let him eat at "
14:27 If a' man speak in an unknown "
30 If a' thing be revealed to another *
35 And if they will learn a' thing, 5100
37 If a' man think himself to be a 1536
38 But if a' man be ignorant, let him "
16:22 If a'man love not the Lord Jesus "
2Co 1: 4 them which are in a' trouble, 3956
2: 5 But if a' have caused grief, he 5100
10 To whom ye forgive a' thing, "
10 if I forgave a' thing, to whom I 1536
3: 5 to think a' thing as of ourselves; 5100
5:17 Therefore if a' man be in Christ, 1536
6: 3 Giving no offence in a' thing, 3367
7:14 if I have boasted a' thing to him 1536
8:23 Whether a' do enquire of Titus,
10: 7 If a' man trust to himself that he 5100
11: 3 But I fear, lest by a' means, as 3381
21 Howbeit whereinsoever a' is bold, 5100
12: 6 lest a' man should think of me "
17 a' of them whom I sent unto you? "
Ga 1: 8 heaven, preach a' other gospel
9 If a' man preach a' other gospel 1536
2: 2 lest by a' means I should run, 3381
5: 6 neither circumcision availeth a' 5100
6:15 neither circumcision availeth a' "
Eph 2: 9 lest a' man should boast. * "
5: 5 an idolater, hath a' inheritance
27 or wrinkle, or a' such thing; 5100
6: 8 whatsoever good thing a' man *1538
Ph'p 2: 1 therefore a' consolation in Christ, 1536
1 if a' comfort of love, "
1 if a' fellowship of the Spirit, "
1 if a' bowels and mercies, "
3: 4 If a' other man thinketh that he "
11 If by a' means I might attain unto 4458
15 if in a' thing ye be otherwise 1536
4: 8 a' virtue, and if there be a' praise, "
Col 2: 4 lest a' man should beguile you *3387
8 Beware lest a' man spoil you "
23 not in a' honor to the satisfying 5100
3:13 if a' man have a quarrel against a': "
1Th 1: 8 we need not to speak a' thing.
2: 5 at a' time used we flattering words, 4218
9 not be chargeable unto a' of you, 5100
4: 6 defraud his brother in a' matter: *
5:15 render evil for evil unto a' man; 5100
2Th 2: 3 man deceive you by a' means: 3367
3: 8 we eat a' man's bread for nought; 5100
8 not be chargeable to a' of you: "
10 that if a' would not work, neither 1536
14 And if a' man obey not our word 5100
1Ti 1:10 if there be a' other thing that is 1536
5: 4 But if a' widow have children 1536
8 But if a' provide not for his own, "
16 If a' man or woman that believeth 1536
6: 3 If a' man teach otherwise, and "
Tit 1: 6 If a' be blameless, the husband * "
Heb 1: 5 of the angels said he at a' time, 4218
13 said he at a' time, Sit on my right "
2: 1 lest at a' time we should let them *3379
3:12 there be in a' of you an evil heart 5100
13 lest a' of you be hardened through "
4: 1 a' of you should seem to come * "
11 a' man fall after the same * "
12 sharper than a' twoedged sword, 3956
13 Neither is there a' creature that *
10:38 shall live by faith: but if a' man *
12:15 lest a' man fail of the grace of God; 5100
15 lest a' root of bitterness springing "
16 Lest there be a' fornicator, or "
19 not be spoken to them a' more: *2089
Jas 1: 5 If a' of you lack wisdom, let him 5100
7 shall receive a' thing of the Lord. "
13 neither tempteth he a' man: *3762
23 if a' man be a hearer of the word, 1536
26 If a' man among you seem to be "
3: 2 If a' man offend not in word, "
5:12 neither by a' other oath: but let 5100
13 Is a' among you afflicted? let him "
13 Is a' merry? let him sing psalms. "
14 Is a' sick among you? let him call "
19 if a' of you do err from the truth, 1536
1Pe 3: 1 if a' obey not the word, they also 5100
6 not afraid with a' amazement. 1536
4:11 If a' man speak, let him speak "
11 if a' man minister, let him do it "
16 if a' man suffer as a Christian, *
2Pe 1:20 of the scripture is of a' private
3: 9 not willing that a' should perish, 5100
1Jo 2: 1 if a' man sin, we have an advocate "
15 If a' man love the world, the love "
27 ye need not that a' man teach you: "
4:12 No man hath seen God at a' time. 4455

1Jo 5:14 if we ask a' thing according to his 5100
16 If a' man see his brother sin a sin 1530
2Jo 10 If there come a' unto you, and "
Re 3:20 if a' man hear my voice, and open "
7: 1 nor on the sea, nor on a' tree. 3956
16 hunger no more, neither thirst a' 2089
16 sun light on them, nor a' heat. 3956
9: 4 neither a' green thing, "
4 neither a' tree; "
11: 5 And if a' man will hurt them, fire 1536
5 if a' man will hurt them, he must "
12: 8 place found a' more in heaven. 2089
13: 9 If a' man have an ear, let him hear. 1536
14: 9 If a' man worship the beast and "
18:11 buyeth their merchandise a' more: 3765
22 shall be found a' more in thee; 2089
21: 4 shall there be a' more pain: "
27 into it a' thing that defileth, 3956
22:18 If a' man shall add unto these 5100
19 if a' man shall take away from the "

any-man See ANY and MAN.

any-one See ANY and ONE.

anything See also ANY and THING.
Job 33:32 [*In some editions*] If thou hast a' to say.

any-wise See ANY and WISE.

apace
2Sa 18:25 And he came a', and drew near.
Ps 68:12 Kings of armies did flee a': *
Jer 46: 5 their mighty ones... are fled a',

apart
Ex 13:12 thou shalt set a' unto the Lord 5674
Le 15:19 she shall be put a' seven days: *5079
18:19 as long as she is put a' for her * "
Ps 4: 3 the Lord hath set a' him that is 6395
Eze 22:10 they humbled her that was set a' *5079
Zec 12:12 land shall mourn, every family a'; 905
12 the family of the house of David a', "
12 and their wives a'; "
12 family of the house of Nathan a'; "
12 and their wives a'; "
13 The family of.... Levi a', "
13 and their wives a'; "
13 the family of Shimei a', "
13 and their wives a'; "
14 every family a', "
14 and their wives a'. "
M't 14:13 into a desert place a': 2596, 2398
23 into a mountain a' to pray: " "
17: 1 into an high mountain a', " "
19 the disciples to Jesus a', " "
20:17 took the twelve disciples a' in " "
M'r 6:31 ye yourselves a' into a desert " "
9: 2 mountain a' by themselves: " "
Jas 1:21 Wherefore lay a' all filthiness * 659

ape See APES.

Apelles (*a-pel'-leze*)
Ro 16:10 Salute A' approved in Christ. 559

apes
1Ki 10:22 ivory, and a', and peacocks. 6971
2Ch 9:21 ivory, and a', and peacocks. "

Apharsachites (*a-far'-sak-ites*) See also APHARSATHCHITES.
Ezr 5: 6 and his companions the A', which 671
6: 6 and your companions the A', which "

Apharsathchites (*a-far'-sath-kites*) See also APHARSACHITES; APHARSITES.
Ezr 4: 9 Dinaites, the A', the Tarpelites, 671

Apharsites (*a-far'-sites*) See also APHARSATHCHITES.
Ezr 4: 9 Tarpelites, the A', the Archevites, 670

Aphek (*a'-fek*) See also APHIK.
Jos 12:18 The king of A', one; the king of 663
13: 4 unto A', to the borders of the "
19:30 Ummah also, and A', and Rehob: "
1Sa 4: 1 and the Philistines pitched in A'. "
29: 1 together all their armies to A': "
1Ki 20:26 up to A', to fight against Israel. "
30 the rest fled to A', into the city; "
2Ki 13:17 thou shalt smite the Syrians in A'. "

Aphekah (*af-e'-kah*)
Jos 15:53 Janum, and Beth-tappuah, and A', 664

Aphiah (*af-i'-ah*)
1Sa 9: 1 son of A', a Benjamite, a mighty 647

Aphik (*a'-fik*) See also APHEK.
J'g 1:31 nor of A', nor of Rehob: 663

Aphrah (*af'-rah*) See also BETH-LEAPHRAH; OPHRAH.
Mic 1:10 house of A' roll thyself in the dust. 1036

Aphses (*af'-seze*)
1Ch 24:15 Hezir, the eighteenth to A', *6483

apiece
Nu 3:47 take five shekels a' by the poll,
7:86 ten shekels a', after the shekel
17: 6 their princes gave him a rod a', *
1Ki 7:15 eighteen cubits high a': 5982, 259
Eze 10:21 Every one had four faces apiece, ‡ "
41:24 and the doors had two leaves a',
Lu 9: 3 money, neither have two coats a'.* 303
Joh 2: 6 containing two or three firkins a'. "

Apollonia (*ap-ol-lo'-ne-ah*)
Ac 17: 1 through Amphipolis and A', 624

Apollos (*ap-ol'-los*)
Ac 18:24 a certain Jew named A', 625
19: 1 while A' was at Corinth,

1Co 1:12 and I of A·; and I of Cephas; 625
3: 4 another, I am of A·; are ye not "
5 Who then is Paul, and who is A·, "
6 A· watered; but God gave the "
22 Whether Paul, or A·, or Cephas, "
4: 6 and to A· for your sakes; "
16:12 touching our brother A·, "
Tit 3:13 Bring Zenas the lawyer and A· "

Apollyon (*ap-ol'-le-on*)
Re 9:11 Greek tongue hath this name A·. 623

apostle See also APOSTLES.
Ro 1: 1 called to be an a·, separated unto 652
11:13 as I am the a· of the Gentiles, "
1Co 1: 1 called to be an a· of Jesus Christ "
9: 1 Am I not an a·? am I not free? "
2 If I be not an a· unto others, "
15: 9 not meet to be called an a·, "
2Co 1: 1 Paul, an a· of Jesus Christ by the "
12:12 the signs of an a· were wrought "
Ga 1: 1 Paul, an a·, (not of men, neither by "
Eph 1: 1 Paul, an a· of Jesus Christ "
Col 1: 1 Paul, an a· of Jesus Christ by the "
1Ti 1: 1 Paul, an a· of Jesus Christ by the "
2: 7 am ordained a preacher, and an a·, "
2Ti 1: 1 Paul, an a· of Jesus Christ "
11 appointed a preacher, and an a·, "
Tit 1: 1 an a· of Jesus Christ, according to "
Heb 3: 1 consider the A· and High Priest "
1Pe 1: 1 Peter, an a· of Jesus Christ, to the "
2Pe 1: 1 a servant and an a· of Jesus "

apostles See also APOSTLES'.
M't 10: 2 names of the twelve a· are these; 652
M'r 6:30 the a· gathered themselves together "
Lu 6:13 whom also he named a·; "
9:10 the a·, when they were returned, "
11:49 I will send them prophets and a·, "
17: 5 the a· said unto the Lord, "
22:14 the twelve a· with him. "
24:10 told these things unto the a·. "
Ac 1: 2 commandments unto the a· whom "
26 numbered with the eleven a·. "
2:37 Peter, and to the rest of the a·, "
43 and signs were done by the a·. "
4:33 the a· witness of the resurrection "
36 by the a· was surnamed Barnabas, "
5:12 hands of the a· were many signs "
18 laid their hands on the a·, "
29 Peter and the other a· answered "
34 to put the a· forth a little space; * "
40 called the a·, and beaten them, "
6: 6 Whom they set before the a·: "
8: 1 Judæa and Samaria, except the a·. "
14 the a· which were at Jerusalem "
9:27 him and brought him to the a·, "
11: 1 a· and brethren that were in Judæa, "
14: 4 with the Jews, and part with the a·. "
14 when the a·, Barnabas and Paul, "
15: 2 unto the a· and elders about this "
4 of the a· and elders, and they "
6 the a· and elders came together "
22 Then pleased it the a· and elders, "
23 The a· and elders and brethren "
33 the brethren unto the a·. *
16: 4 were ordained of the a· and elders 652
Ro 16: 7 who are of note among the a·, "
1Co 4: 9 God hath set forth us the a· last, "
9: 5 as well as other a·, and as the "
12:28 first a·, secondarily prophets, "
29 Are all a·? are all prophets? "
15: 7 of James; then of all the a·. "
9 I am the least of the a·, that am "
2Co 11: 5 a whit behind the very chiefest a· "
13 are false a·, deceitful workers, 5570
13 themselves into the a· of Christ. 652
12:11 the very chiefest a·, though I be "
Ga 1:17 to them which were a· before me; "
19 other of the a· saw I none, "
Eph 2:20 foundation of the a· and prophets, "
3: 5 revealed unto his holy a· "
4:11 gave some, a·; and some, prophets; "
1Th 2: 6 burdensome, as the a· of Christ. "
2Pe 3: 2 the a· of the Lord and Saviour: "
Jude 17 before of the a· of our Lord Jesus "
Re 2: 2 them which say they are a·, "
18:20 ye holy a· and prophets; "
21:14 names of the twelve a· of the Lamb. "

apostles'
Ac 2:42 in the a· doctrine and fellowship, 652
4:35 laid them down at the a· feet: "
37 the money, and laid it at the a· feet. "
5: 2 part, and laid it at the a· feet. "
8:18 through laying on of the a· hands "

apostleship
Ac 1:25 take part of this ministry and a·, 651
Ro 1: 5 received grace and a·, for obedience "
1Co 9: 2 seal of mine a· are ye in the Lord. "
Ga 2: 8 to the a· of the circumcision, "

apothecaries See also APOTHECARIES'.
Ne 3: 8 Hananiah the son of one of the a·, ‡7543

apothecaries'
2Ch 16:14 spices prepared by the a· art: ‡4842

apothecary See also APOTHECARIES.
Ex 30:25 compound after the art of the a·: *7543
35 confection after the art of the a·, * "
37:29 according to the work of the a·. * "
Ec 10: 1 the ointment of the a· "

Appaim (*ap'-pa-im*)
1Ch 2:30 the sons of Nadab; Seled, and A·: 649
31 the sons of A·; Ishi. And the sons "

apparel See also APPARELLED.
J'g 17:10 and a suit of a·, and thy victuals. 899
1Sa 27: 9 the camels, and the a·, "
2Sa 1:24 ornaments of gold upon your a·. 3830
12:20 himself, and changed his a·, 8071
14: 2 put on now mourning a·, 899
1Ki 10: 5 his ministers, and their a·, 4403
2Ch 9: 4 his ministers, and their a·; his "
4 cupbearers also, and their a·; "
Ezr 3:10 they set the priests in their a·; 3847
Es 5: 1 that Esther put on her royal a·, "
6: 8 Let the royal a· be brought 3830
9 let this a· and horse be delivered "
10 take the a· and the horse, "
11 Then took Haman the a· "
8:15 in royal a· of blue and white, "
Isa 3:22 The changeable suits of a·, *4254
4: 1 own bread, and wear our own a·: 8071
63: 1 this that is glorious in his a·, 3830
2 Wherefore art thou red in thine a·, "
Eze 27:24 in chests of rich a·, bound with 1264
Zep 1: 8 as are clothed with strange a·. 4403
Zec 14:14 gold, and silver, and a·, 899
Ac 1:10 men stood by them in white a·; 2066
12:21 Herod, arrayed in royal a·, "
20:33 no man's silver, or gold, or a·. 2441
1Ti 2: 9 adorn themselves in modest a·, 2689
Jas 2: 2 gold ring, in goodly a·, *2066
1Pe 3: 3 of gold or of putting on of a·; 2440

apparelled
2Sa 13:18 daughters that were virgins a·. 3847
Lu 7:25 they which are gorgeously a·, 2441

apparently
Nu 12: 8 speak mouth to mouth, even a·, *4758

appeal See also APPEALED.
Ac 25:11 I a· unto Cæsar. 1941
28:19 constrained to a· unto Cæsar; "

appealed
Ac 25:12 Hast thou a· unto Cæsar? 1941
21 when Paul had a· to be reserved "
25 himself hath a· to Augustus, "
26:32 if he had not a· unto Cæsar. "

appear See also APPEARED; APPEARETH; APPEARING.
Ge 1: 9 let the dry land a·: and it was so. 7200
30:37 made the white a· which was in 4286
Ex 23:15 none shall a· before me empty:) 7200
17 all thy males shall a· before "
34:20 none shall a· before me empty. "
23 menchildren a· before the Lord "
24 to a· before the Lord thy God "
Le 9: 4 to day the Lord will a· unto you. * "
6 glory of the Lord shall a· unto you. "
13:57 if it a· still in the garment, "
16: 2 I will a· in the cloud upon the "
De 16:16 males a· before the Lord thy God "
16 they shall not a·...empty: "
31:11 Israel is come to a· before the Lord "
J'g 13:21 angel of the Lord did no more a· "
1Sa 1:22 that he may a· before the Lord, "
2:27 Did I plainly a· unto the house of*1540
2Ch 1: 7 night did God a· unto Solomon, 7200
Ps 42: 2 shall I come and a· before God? "
90:16 thy work a· unto thy servants, "
102:16 he shall a· in his glory. * "
Ca 2:12 The flowers a· on the earth; "
4: 1 goats, that a· from mount Gilead. *1570
6: 5 of goats that a· from Gilead. "
7:12 whether the tender grape a·, *6524
Isa 1:12 When ye come to a· before me, 7200
66: 5 but he shall a· to your joy, and * "
Jer 13:26 that thy shame may a·. "
Eze 21:24 so that...your sins do a·; "
M't 6:16 they may a· unto men to fast. *5316
18 thou a· not unto men to fast. * "
23:27 which indeed a· beautiful outward, "
28 ye also outwardly a· righteous "
24:30 shall a· the sign of the Son of man "
Lu 11:44 are as graves which a· not, 82
19:11 of God should immediately a·. 398
Ac 22:30 and all their council to a·, *2064
26:16 in the which I will a· unto thee; 3700
Ro 7:13 But sin, that it might a· sin, *5316
2Co 5:10 all a· before the judgment seat *5319
7:12 sight of God might a· unto you. "
13: 7 not that we should a· approved, 5316
Col 3: 4 Christ, who is our life, shall a·, *5319
4 then shall ye also a· with him in * "
1Ti 4:15 that thy profiting may a·. 5318, 5600
Heb 9:24 a· in the presence of God for us. 1718
28 them that look for him shall he a· 3700
11: 3 not made of things which do a·. 5316
1Pe 4:18 the ungodly and the sinner a·? "
5: 4 when the chief Shepherd shall a·,*5319
1Jo 2:28 when he shall a·, we may have * "
3: 2 doth not yet a· what we shall be: * "
2 when he shall a·, we shall be like* "
Re 3:18 of thy nakedness do not a·: "

appearance See also APPEARANCES.
Nu 9:15 as it were the a· of fire, 4758
16 and the a· of fire by night. "
1Sa 16: 7 man looketh on the outward a·, 5869
Eze 1: 5 this was their a·; they had the 4758
13 their a· was like burning coals "
13 and like the a· of lamps: "
14 as the a· of a flash of lightning. "
16 The a· of the wheels "
16 and their a· and their work "
26 as the a· of a sapphire "
26 as the a· of a man above it. "
27 as the a· of fire round about "
Eze 1:27 the a· of his loins even upward, 4758
27 the a· of his loins even downward, "
27 as it were the a· of fire, "
28 a· of the bow that is in the cloud "
28 a· of the brightness round about. "
28 This was the a· of the likeness "
8: 2 a likeness as the a· of fire: "
2 from the a· of his loins "
2 as the a· of brightness, as the "
10: 1 the a· of the likeness of a throne. "
9 and the a· of the wheels "
40: 3 whose a· was like the a· of brass, "
41:21 of the one as the a· of the other. "
42:11 like the a· of the chambers "
43: 3 according to the a· of the vision, "
Da 8:15 as the a· of a man. "
10: 6 his face as the a· of lightning, "
18 like the a· of a man, and he "
Joe 2: 4 a· of them is as the a· of horses; "
Joh 7:24 Judge not according to the a·, 3799
2Co 5:12 glory in a·, and not in heart. 4383
10: 7 on things after the outward a·? * "
1Th 5:22 Abstain from all a· of evil. *1491

appearances
Eze 10:10 And as for their a·, they four had 4758
22 Chebar, their a· and themselves: "

appeared
Ge 12: 7 And the Lord a· unto Abram, 7200
7 unto the Lord, who a· unto him. "
17: 1 And when...the Lord a· to Abram, "
18: 1 And the Lord a· unto him in the "
26: 2 And the Lord a· unto him, "
24 a· unto him the same night, "
35: 1 God, that a· unto thee when thou "
7 because there God a· unto him, *1540
9 And God a· unto Jacob again, 7200
48: 3 God Almighty a· unto me at Luz "
Ex 3: 2 And the angel of the Lord a· "
16 The Lord God of your fathers,...a· "
4: 1 The Lord hath not a· unto thee. "
5 God of Jacob, hath a· unto thee. "
6: 3 And I a· unto Abraham, "
14:27 strength when the morning a·; 6437
16:10 glory of the Lord a· in the cloud. 7200
Le 9:23 and the glory of the Lord a· unto "
Nu 14:10 the glory of the Lord a· in the "
16:19 Lord a· unto all the congregation. "
42 and the glory of the Lord a·. "
20: 6 the glory of the Lord a· unto them. "
De 31:15 And the Lord a· in the tabernacle "
J'g 6:12 the angel of the Lord a· unto him, "
13: 3 a· unto the woman, and said unto "
10 the man hath a· unto me, "
1Sa 3:21 the Lord a· again in Shiloh: "
2Sa 22:16 And the channels of the sea a·, "
1Ki 3: 5 In Gibeon the Lord a· to Solomon "
9: 2 the Lord a· to Solomon the second "
2 as he had a· unto him at Gibeon. "
11: 9 Lord God of Israel, which had a· "
2Ki 2:11 behold, there a· a chariot of fire. "
2Ch 3: 1 where the Lord a· unto David 7200
7:12 the Lord a· to Solomon by night, "
Ne 4:21 of the morning till the stars a·. 3318
Jer 31: 3 The Lord hath a· of old 7200
Eze 10: 1 there a· over them as it were a "
8 And there a· in the cherubims "
19:11 and she a· in her height * "
Da 1:15 countenances a· fairer and fatter "
8: 1 a· unto me,... after that which a· "
M't 1:20 behold, the angel of the Lord a· 5316
2: 7 what time the star a·. "
13:26 then a· the tares also. "
17: 3 a· unto them Moses and Elias 3700
27:53 into the holy city, and a· unto 1718
M'k 9: 4 a· unto them Elias with Moses: 3700
16: 9 he a· first to Mary Magdalene, 5316
12 a· in another form unto two of *5319
14 Afterward he a· unto the eleven * "
Lu 1:11 there a· unto him an angel 3700
9: 8 of some, that Elias had a·; 5316
31 Who a· in glory, and spake of his 3700
22:43 And there a· an angel unto him "
24:34 and hath a· to Simon. "
Ac 2: 3 there a· unto them cloven tongues "
7: 2 God of glory a· unto our father "
30 there a· to him in the wilderness. "
35 angel which a· to him in the bush. "
9:17 Jesus, that a· unto thee in the way "
16: 9 a vision a· to Paul in the night; "
26:16 I a· unto thee for this purpose, "
27:20 nor stars in many days a·, *2014
Tit 2:11 salvation hath a· to all men, "
3: 4 of God our Saviour toward man a·, "
Heb 9:26 hath he a· to put away sin by *5319
Re 12: 1 a· a great wonder in heaven, *3700
3 a· another wonder in heaven; * "

appeareth
Le 13:14 when raw flesh a· in him, 7200
43 a· in the skin of the flesh; *4758
De 2:30 into thy hands, as a· this day. *
Ps 84: 7 every one of them in Zion a· 7200
Pr 27:25 The hay a·, and the tender grass *1540
Jer 6: 1 evil a· out of the north, *8259
Mal 3: 2 who shall stand when he a·? 7200
M't 2:13 angel of the Lord a· to Joseph in 5316
19 a· in a dream to Joseph in Egypt, "
Jas 4:14 a vapour, that a· for a little time, "

appearing
1Ti 6:14 the a· of our Lord Jesus Christ: 2015
2Ti 1:10 the a· of our Saviour Jesus Christ, "
4: 1 at his a· and his kingdom; "
8 them also that love his a·. "

Tit 2:13 the glorious a' of the great God 2015
1Pe 1: 7 glory at the a' of Jesus Christ: * 602

appease See also APPEASED; APPEASETH.
Ge 32:20 will a' him with the present 3722, 6440

appeased
Es 2: 1 wrath of king Ahasuerus was a', *7918
Ac 19:35 the townclerk had a' the people, *2687

appeaseth
Pr 15:18 he that is slow to anger a' strife. 8252

appertain See also APPERTAINED; APPERTAINETH; PURTENANCE.
Nu 16:30 with all that a' unto them,
Jer 10: 7 for to thee doth it a': 2969

appertained
Nu 16:32 all the men that a' unto Korah,
33 they, and all that a' to them,
Ne 2: 8 palace which a' to the house, *

appertaineth
Le 6: 5 it unto him to whom it a',
2Ch 26:18 It a' not unto thee, Uzziah *

appetite
Job 38:39 or fill the a' of the young lions, 2416
Pr 23: 2 if thou be a man given to a'. 5315
Ec 6: 7 the a' is not filled.
Isa 29: 8 he is faint, and his soul hath a': 8264

Apphia (af'-fee-ah)
Ph'm 2 to our beloved A', and Archippus 682

Appii (ap'-pe-i)
Ac 28:15 to meet us as far as A' forum, * 675

Appii-forum See APPII and FORUM.

apple See also APPLES.
De 32:10 he kept him as the a' of his eye. 380
Ps 17: 8 Keep me as the a' of the eye, 380, 1323
Pr 7: 2 my law as the a' of thine eye. 380
Ca 2: 3 as the a' tree among the trees 8598
8: 5 I raised thee up under the a' tree: "
La 2:18 not the a' of thine eye cease. 1323
Joe 1:12 palm tree also, and the a' tree, 8598
Zec 2: 8 toucheth the a' of his eye. 892

apples
Pr 25:11 A word fitly spoken is like a' of 8598
Ca 2: 5 flagons, comfort me with a': "
7: 8 the smell of thy nose like a'; "

apple-tree See APPLE and TREE.

applied
Ec 7:25 I a' mine heart to know, and *5437
8: 9 and a' my heart unto every work 5414
16 I a' mine heart to know wisdom, "

apply See also APPLIED.
Ps 90:12 may a' our hearts unto wisdom. * 935
Pr 2: 2 a' thine heart to understanding; 5186
22:17 a' thine heart unto my 7896
23:12 A' thine heart unto instruction, 935

appoint See also APPOINTED; APPOINTETH; APPOINTING; DISAPPOINT.
Ge 30:28 A' me thy wages, and I will give 5344
41:34 him a' officers over the land, 6485
Ex 21:13 then I will a' thee a place, 7760
30:16 and shalt a' it for the service of 5414
Le 26:16 I will even a' over you terror, 6485
Nu 1:50 thou shalt a' the Levites over "
3:10 And thou shalt a' Aaron "
4:19 and a' them every one to his 7760
27 ye shall a' unto them in charge 6485
35: 6 ye shall a' for the manslayer, *5414
11 Then ye shall a' you cities to be 7136
Jos 20: 2 A' out for you cities of refuge, *5414
1Sa 8:11 and a' them for himself, for his 7760
12 And he will a' him captains "
2Sa 6:21 to a' me ruler over the people 6680
7:10 I will a' a place for my people 7760
15:15 my lord the king shall a'. * 977
1Ki 5: 6 all that thou shalt a': * 559
9 the place that thou shalt a' me, 7971
1Ch 15:16 the Levites to a' their brethren 5975
Ne 7: 3 a' watches of the inhabitants
Es 2: 3 And let the king a' officers 6485
Job 14:13 thou wouldest a' me a set time, 7896
Isa 26: 1 salvation will God a' for walls
61: 3 To a' unto them that mourn in 7760
Jer 15: 3 I will a' over them four kinds, 6485
49:19 that I may a' over her?
19 who will a' me the time? 3259
50:44 man, that I may a' over her? 6485
44 and who will a' me the time? 3259
51:27 a' a captain against her; 6485
Eze 21:19 son of man, a' thee two ways, 7760
20 A' a way, that the sword may "
22 to a' captains, and to open the * "
22 to a' battering rams against the "
45: 6 ye shall a' the possession of the 5414
Ho 1:11 and a' themselves one head, 7760
M't 24:51 and a' him his portion with 5087
Lu 12:46 and will a' him his portion with "
22:29 I a' unto you a kingdom, as my 1303
Ac 6: 3 we may a' over this business. 2525

appointed See also DISAPPOINTED.
Ge 4:25 said she, hath a' me another seed 7896
18:14 At the time a' I will return *4150
24:14 hast a' for thy servant Isaac; 3198
44 woman whom the Lord hath a' "
Ex 9: 5 And the Lord a' a set time, 7760
23:15 the time a' of the month Abib; 4150
Nu 9: 2 keep the passover at his a' season. "
3 ye shall keep it in his a' season: "
7 in his a' season among the children "
13 of the Lord in his a' season, "
Jos 8:14 at a time a', before the plain; 4150
20: 7 And they a' Kedesh in Galilee *6942
9 These were the cities a' for all 4152
J'g 18:11 men a' with weapons of war. *2296
16 the six hundred men a' * "
17 men that were a' with weapons * "
20:38 there was an a' sign between 4150
1Sa 13: 8 set time that Samuel had a': "
11 camest not within the days a', 4150
19:20 Samuel standing as a' over *5324
20:35 field at the time a' with David, 4150
21: 2 I have a' my servants to such 3045
25:30 and shall have a' thee ruler over 6680
29: 4 his place which thou hast a' him, 6485
2Sa 17:14 Lord had a' to defeat the good *6680
20: 5 the set time which he had a' him, 3259
24:15 the morning even to the time a': 4150
1Ki 1:35 I have a' him to be ruler 6680
11:18 a' him victuals, and gave him 559
12:12 as the king had a', saying, *1696
20:42 whom I a' to utter destruction, *2764
2Ki 7:17 king a' the lord on whose hand 6485
8: 6 king a' unto her a certain officer, 5414
10:24 Jehu a' fourscore men without, *7760
11:18 And the priest a' officers over the "
18:14 the king of Assyria a' unto
1Ch 6:48 Levites were a' unto all manner 5414
49 and were a' for all the work *
9:29 were a' to oversee the vessels, 4487
15:17 So the Levites a' Heman 5975
19 And Ethan, were a' to sound
16: 4 And he a' certain of the Levites 5414
2Ch 8:14 And he a', according to the order 5975
20:21 he a' singers unto the Lord,
23:18 Jehoiada a' the officers of the 7760
31: 2 And Hezekiah a' the courses 5975
3 He a' also the king's portion
33: 8 which I have a' for your fathers; 5975
34:22 king had a', went to Huldah *
Ezr 3: 8 and a' the Levites, from twenty 5975
8:20 David and the princes had a' *5414
10:14 come at a' times, and with them 2163
Ne 5:14 I was a' to be their governor 6680
6: 7 thou hast also a' prophets to 5975
7: 1 singers and the Levites were a', 6485
9:17 in their rebellion a' a captain 5414
10:34 at times a' year by year 2163
12:31 and a' two great companies 5975
44 were some a' over the chambers 6485
13:30 and a' the wards of the priests 5975
31 for the wood offering, at times a', 2163
Es 1: 8 king had a' to all the officers 3245
2:15 the keeper of the women, a'. 559
4: 5 whom he had a' to attend 5975
9:27 and according to their a' time
31 days of Purim in their times a',
Job 7: 1 a' time to man upon the earth? *6635
3 wearisome nights are a' to me. 4487
14: 5 thou hast a' his bounds that he 6213
14 days of my a' time will I wait, *6635
20:29 the heritage a' unto him by God. 561
23:14 the thing that is a' for me: 2706
30:23 the house a' for all living. 4150
Ps 44:11 given us like sheep a' for meat;
78: 5 a' a law in Israel, which he 7760
79:11 preserve thou those that are a' 1121
81: 3 in the new moon, in the time a', *3677
102:20 loose those that are a' to death; 1121
104:19 He a' the moon for seasons: 6213
Pr 7:20 will come home at the day a'. *3677
8:29 when he a' the foundations of *2710
31: 8 all such as are a' to destruction. *1121
Isa 1:14 new moons and your a' feasts 4150
14:31 shall be alone in his a' times. 4151
28:25 wheat and the a' barley 5567
44: 7 since I a' the ancient people? ‡7760
Jer 5:24 reserveth unto us the a' weeks 2708
8: 7 the stork...knoweth her a' times; 4150
33:25 if I have not a' the ordinances 7760
46:17 he hath passed the time a'. 4150
47: 7 there hath he a' it. 3259
Eze 4: 6 have a' thee each day for a year. 5414
36: 5 have a' my land into their "
43:21 he shall burn it in the a' place 4662
Da 1: 5 And the king a' them a daily 4487
10 who hath a' your meat, and "
8:19 at the time a' the end shall be. 4150
10: 1 but the time a' was long: *6635
11:27 the end shall be at the time a'. 4150
29 At the time a' he shall return, "
35 it is yet for a time a'. "
Mic 6: 9 the rod, and who hath a' it. 3259
Hab 2: 3 the vision is yet for an a' time, 4150
M't 26:19 disciples did as Jesus had a' them; 4929
27:10 as the Lord a' me.
28:16 where Jesus had a' them. 5021
Lu 3:13 than that which is a' you. 1299
10: 1 the Lord a' other seventy also, 322
22:29 as my Father hath a' unto me; 1303
Ac 1:23 a' two, Joseph called Barsabas, *2476
7:44 as he had a', speaking unto Moses, 1299
17:26 determined the times before a', 4384
31 Because he hath a' a day, 2476
20:13 for so he had a', minding himself 1299
22:10 which are a' for thee to do. 5021
28:23 And when they had a' him a day,
1Co 4: 9 as it were a' to death; *1935
Ga 4: 2 until the time a' of the father. 4287
1Th 3: 3 know that we are a' thereunto. 2749
5: 9 God hath not a' us to wrath, 5087
2Ti 1:11 Whereunto I am a' a preacher, "
Tit 1: 5 as I had a' thee: *1299
Heb 1: 2 he hath a' heir of all things, 5087
3: 2 faithful to him that a' him, 4160
9:27 as it is a' unto men once to die, 606
1Pe 2: 8 whereunto also they were a'. 5087

appointeth See also DISAPPOINTETH.
Da 5:21 he a' over it whomsoever he will. *6966

appointment
Nu 4:27 At the a' of Aaron and his sons *6310
2Sa 13:32 by the a' of Absalom this hath "
Ezr 6: 9 according to the a' of the priests *3983
Job 2:11 for they had made an a' together 3259

apprehend See also APPREHENDED.
2Co 11:32 desirous to a' me: *4084
Ph'p 3:12 if that I may a' that for which ‡2638

apprehended
Ac 12: 4 when he had a' him, *4084
Ph'p 3:12 for which also I am a' of Christ ‡2638
13 I count not myself to have a': ‡ "

approach See also APPROACHED; APPROACHETH; APPROACHING.
Le 18: 6 None of you shall a' to any that 7126
14 thou shalt not a' to his wife: "
19 thou shalt not a' unto a woman "
20:16 if a woman a' unto any beast, "
21:17 let him not a' to offer the bread "
18 hath a blemish, he shall not a': "
Nu 4:19 they a' unto the most holy things: 5066
De 20: 2 that the priest shall a' and speak "
3 Israel, ye a' this day unto battle *7126
31:14 thy days a' that thou must die: "
Jos 8: 5 people that are with me will a' "
Job 40:19 make his sword to a' unto him. ‡5066
Ps 65: 4 thou choosest and causest to a' 7126
Jer 30:21 and he shall a' unto me: 5066
21 engaged his heart to a' unto me? "
Eze 42:13 the priests that a' unto the Lord *7138
14 shall a' to those things which are 7126
43:19 the Levites.... which a' unto me, *7138
1Ti 6:16 in the light which no man can a' * 676

approached
2Sa 11:20 Wherefore a' ye so nigh unto the *5066
2Ki 16:12 and the king a' to the altar, *7126

approacheth
Lu 12:33 where no thief a', neither moth *1448

approaching
Isa 58: 2 they take delight in a' to God. *7132
Heb 10:25 the more, as ye see the day a'. 1448

approve See also APPROVED; APPROVEST; APPROVETH; APPROVING.
Ps 49:13 their posterity a' their sayings. 7520
1Co 16: 3 whosoever ye shall a' by... letters 1381
Ph'p 1:10 may a' things that are excellent; "

approved
Ac 2:22 a man a' of God among you by 584
Ro 14:18 acceptable to God, and a' of men. 1384
16:10 Salute Apelles a' in Christ. "
1Co 11:19 which... a' may be made manifest "
2Co 7:11 ye have a' yourselves to be clear 4921
10:18 he that commendeth himself is a', 1384
13: 7 not that we should appear a', "
2Ti 2:15 Study to shew thyself a' unto God, "

approvest
Ro 2:18 a' the things that are more 1381

approveth
La 3:36 in his cause, the Lord a' not. 7200

approving
2Co 6: 4 a' ourselves as the ministers of *4921

appurtenance See PURTENANCE.

aprons
Ge 3: 7 together, and made themselves a'. 2290
Ac 19:12 handkerchiefs or a', and the 4612

apt
2Ki 24:16 all that were strong and a' for war, 6213
1Ch 7:40 that were a' to the war and to *
1Ti 3: 2 given to hospitality, a' to teach; 1317
2Ti 2:24 unto all men, a' to teach, patient, "

Aquila (ac'-quil-ah)
Ac 18: 2 a certain Jew named A', born in 207
18 with him Priscilla and A'; "
26 when A' and Priscilla had heard, "
Ro 16: 3 Greet Priscilla and A' my helpers "
1Co 16:19 A' and Priscilla salute you much "
2Ti 4:19 Salute Prisca and A', "

Ar (ar)
Nu 21:15 goeth down to the dwelling of A', 6144
28 it hath consumed A' of Moab, "
De 2: 9 I have given A' unto the children "
18 Thou art to pass over through A', "
29 the Moabites which dwell in A', "
Isa 15: 1 in the night A' of Moab is laid "

Ara (a'-rah)
1Ch 7:38 Jephunneh, and Pispah, and A'. 690

Arab (a'-rab) See also ARBITE.
Jos 15:52 A', and Dumah, and Eshean, 694

Arabah (ar'-ab-ah) See also BETH-ARABAH.
Jos 18:18 over against A' northward, 6160
18 and went down unto A': "

Arabia (a-ra'-be-ah) See also ARABIAN.
1Ki 10:15 of all the kings of A', and of the *6152
2Ch 9:14 all the kings of A' and governors "
Isa 21:13 The burden upon A'. In the forest "
13 In the forest in A' shall ye lodge, "
Jer 25:24 And all the kings of A', and all "
Eze 27:21 A', and all the princes of Kedar, "
Ga 1:17 I went into A', and returned 688
4:25 this Agar is mount Sinai in A'. "

Arabian (a-ra'-be-un) See also ARABIANS.
Ne 2:19 and Geshem the A', heard it, they 6163
6: 1 Geshem the A', and the rest of "
Isa 13:20 neither shall the A' pitch tent "
Jer 3: 2 thou sat for them, as the A' in the "

Arabians (a-ra'-be-uns)
2Ch 17:11 and the A' brought him flocks, 6163
21:16 of the Philistines, and of the A', "
22: 1 band of men that came with the A', "
26: 7 the A' that dwelt in Gur-baal, "
Ne 4: 7 and the A', and the Ammonites, "
Ac 2:11 Cretes and A', we do hear them 690

Arad (a'-rad)
Nu 21: 1 And when king A' the Canaanite, 6166
33:40 A' the Canaanite, which dwelt in "
Jos 12:14 Hormah, one; the king of A', one; "
J'g 1:16 which lieth in the south of A'; "
1Ch 8:15 And Zebadiah, and A', and Ader, "

Arah (a'-rah)
1Ch 7:39 the sons of Ulla; A', and Haniel, 733
Ezr 2: 5 A', seven hundred seventy and five. "
Ne 6:18 in law of Shechaniah the son of A'; "
7:10 the children of A', six hundred "

Aram (a'-ram) See also ARAMITESS; ARAM-NAHARAIM; ARAM-ZOBAH; BETH-ARAM; PADAN-ARAM; SYRIA.
Ge 10:22 and Arphaxad, and Lud, and A'. 758
23 the children of A'; Uz, and Hul, "
22:21 and Kemuel the father of A', "
Nu 23: 7 of Moab that brought me from A', "
1Ch 1:17 Arphaxad, and Lud, and A', and Uz, "
2:23 he took Geshur, and A', with the "
7:34 Rohgah, Jehubbah, and A'. "
M't 1: 3 Esrom begat A'; 689
4 A' begat Aminadab; "
Lu 3:33 which was the son of A', * "

Aramitess (a'-ram-i-tes) See also SYRIAN.
1Ch 7:14 his concubine the A' bare Machir 761

Aram-naharaim (a''-ram-na-ha-ra'-im) See also MESOPOTAMIA.
Ps 60:*title* when he strove with A' 763

Aram-zobah (a''-ram-zo'-bah)
Ps 60:*title* and with A', 760

Aran (a'-ran) See also BETH-ARAN.
Ge 36:28 of Dishan are these; Uz and A'. 765
1Ch 1:42 The sons of Dishan; Uz and A'. "

Ararat (ar'-ar-at) See also ARMENIA.
Ge 8: 4 upon the mountains of A'. 780
Jer 51:27 against her the kingdoms of A', "

Araunah (a-raw'-nah) See also ORNAN.
2Sa 24:16 threshingplace of A' the Jebusite. 728
18 threshingfloor of A' the Jebusite. "
20 A' looked, and saw the king and "
20 A' went out, and bowed himself "
21 A' said, Wherefore is my lord "
22 A' said unto David, Let my lord "
23 All these things did A', as a king, "
23 A' said unto the king, The Lord "
24 the king said unto A', Nay, but I "

Arba (ar'-bah) See also ARBAH; ARBATHITE; ARBITE; KIRJATH-ARBA.
Jos 14:15 which A' was a great man among
15:13 even the city of A' the father of 704
21:11 they gave them the city of A' "

Arbah (ar'-bah) See also ARBA.
Ge 35:27 the city of A', which is Hebron, 704

Arbathite (ar'-bath-ite)
2Sa 23:31 Abi-albon the A', Azmaveth the 6164
1Ch 11:32 brooks of Gaash, Abiel the A', "

Arbel See BETH-ARBEL.

Arbite (ar'-bite)
2Sa 23:35 the Carmelite, Paarai the A', 701

arch See ARCHANGEL; ARCHES.

archangel
1Th 4:16 with the voice of the a', 743
Jude 9 Michael the a', when contending "

Archelaus (ar-ke-la'-us)
M't 2:22 heard that A' did reign in Judæa 745

archer See also ARCHERS.
Ge 21:20 he grew...and became an a'. 7198
Jer 51: 3 let the a' bend his bow, 1869

archers
Ge 49:23 a' have sorely grieved him, 1167, 2671
J'g 5:11 are delivered from the noise of a' 2686
1Sa 31: 3 the a' hit him; and he 3384, 376, 7198
3 sore wounded of the a'. 3384
1Ch 8:40 mighty men of valour, a', 1869, 7198
10: 3 the a' hit him, 3384,
3 he was wounded of the a'. 3384
2Ch 35:23 the a' shot at king Josiah; "
Job 16:13 His a' compass me round about, 7228
Isa 21:17 the residue of the number of a', 7198
22: 3 they are bound by the a'; "
Jer 50:29 Call together the a' against 7228

arches
Eze 40:16 about, and likewise to the a': 361
21 posts thereof and the a' thereof "
22 their windows, and their a', "
24 and the a' thereof according to "
25 windows in it and in the a' thereof "
26 the a' thereof were before them: "
29 and the posts thereof, and the a' "
29 the a' thereof round about: it was "
30 a' round about were five and twenty "
31 a' thereof were toward the outer "
33 a' thereof, were according to these "
33 windows therein and in the a' "
34 the a' thereof were toward the "
36 and the a' thereof, and the windows "

Archevites (ar'-ke-vites)
Ezr 4: 9 the Apharsites, the A', the 756

Archi (ar'-kee) See also ARCHITE.
Jos 16: 2 along unto the borders of A' * 757

Archippus (ar-kip'-pus)
Col 4:17 say to A', Take heed to the 751
Ph'm 2 A' our fellowsoldier, "

Archite (ar'-kite) See also ARCHI.
2Sa 15:32 Hushai the A' came to meet him 757
16:16 Hushai the A', David's friend, "
17: 5 Call now Hushai the A' also, "
14 counsel of Hushai the A' is better "
1Ch 27:33 Hushai the A' was the king's "

Arcturus (ark-tu'-rus)
Job 9: 9 maketh A', Orion, and Pleiades, *5906
38:32 thou guide A' with his sons? * "

Ard (ard) See also ARDITES.
Ge 46:21 Muppim, and Huppim, and A'. 714
Nu 26:40 sons of Bela were A' and Naaman: "
40 of A', the family of the Ardites: "

Ardites (ar'-dites)
Nu 26:40 of Ard, the family of the A': 716

Ardon (ar'-don)
1Ch 2:18 Jesher, and Shobab, and A'. 715

are See in the APPENDIX.

Areli (a-re'-li) See also ARELITES.
Ge 46:16 Ezbon, Eri, and Arodi, and A'. 692
Nu 26:17 of A', the family of the Arelites. "

Arelites (a-re'-lites) See also ARELI.
Nu 26:17 of Areli, the family of the A'. 692

Areopagite (a-re-op'-a-jite)
Ac 17:34 which was Dionysius, the A', 698

Areopagus (a-re-op'-a-gus) See also AREOPAGITE; MARS'-HILL.
Ac 17:19 took him, and brought him unto A', 697

Aretas (ar'-e-tas)
2Co 11:32 under A' the king kept the city 702

Argob (ar'-gob)
De 3: 4 all the region of A', the kingdom 709
13 the region of A', with all Bashan, "
14 Manasseh took all the country of A' "
1Ki 4:13 him also pertained the region of A', "
2Ki 15:25 with A' and Arieh, and with him "

arguing
Job 6:25 what doth your a' reprove? ‡3198

arguments
Job 23: 4 fill my mouth with a'. 8433

Aridai (a-rid'-a-i)
Es 9: 9 Parmashta, and Arisai, and A', 742

Aridatha (a-rid'-a-thah)
Es 9: 8 Poratha, and Adalia, and A', 743

Arieh (a-ri'-eh)
2Ki 15:25 with Argob and A', and with him 745

Ariel (a'-re-el) See also JERUSALEM.
Ezr 8:16 Then sent I for Eliezer, for A', for 740
Isa 29: 1 Woe to A', to A', the city where "
2 Yet I will distress A', and there "
2 it shall be unto me as A'. "
7 the nations that fight against A', "

aright
Ps 50:23 that ordereth his conversation a'
78: 8 that set not their heart a', 3559
Pr 15: 2 of the wise useth knowledge a': 3190
23:31 the cup, when it moveth itself a'. *4339
Jer 8: 6 heard, but they spake not a': 3651

Arim See KIRJATH-ARIM.

Arimathæa (ar-im-ath-e'-ah)
M't 27:57 there came a rich man of A', 707
M'r 15:43 Joseph of A', an honourable "
Lu 23:51 A', a city of the Jews: "
Joh 19:38 Joseph of A', being a disciple of "

Arioch (a'-re-ok)
Ge 14: 1 A' king of Ellasar, Chedorlaomer 746
9 and A' king of Ellasar; four kings "
Da 2:14 A' the captain of the king's guard, "
15 He answered and said to A' "
15 A' made the thing known to Daniel. "
24 Therefore Daniel went in unto A', "
25 Then A' brought in Daniel before "

Arisai (a-ris'-a-i)
Es 9: 9 Parmashta, and A', and Aridai, 747

arise See also ARISETH; ARISING; AROSE.
Ge 13:17 A', walk through the land 6965
19:15 A', take thy wife, and thy two "
21:18 A', lift up the lad, and hold him in "
27:19 a', I pray thee, sit and eat of my "
31 Let my father a', and eat of his "
43 a', flee thou to Laban my brother "
28: 2 A', go to Padan-aram, to the home "
31:13 a', get thee out from this land, "
35: 1 A', go up to Beth-el, and dwell "
3 And let us a', and go up to Bethel; "
41:30 And there shall a' after them "
43: 8 with me, and we will a' and go; "
13 Take also your brother, and a', "
De 9:12 A', get thee down quickly from "
10:11 A', take thy journey before the "
13: 1 If there a' among you a prophet, "
17: 8 there a' a matter too hard for thee "
8 then shalt thou a', and get thee 6965
Jos 1: 2 therefore a', go over this Jordan, "
8: 1 and a', go up to Ai: see, I have "
J'g 5:12 a', Barak, and lead thy captivity "
7: 9 A', get thee down unto the host; "
15 A'; for the Lord hath delivered "
18: 9 A', that we may go up against "
20:40 when the flame began to a' up 5927

1Sa 9: 3 and a', go seek the asses. 6965
16:12 A', anoint him: for this is he. "
23: 4 A', go down to Keilah; "
2Sa 2:14 Let the young men now a', and "
14 And Joab said, Let them a'. "
3:21 Abner said unto David, I will a' "
11:20 if so be that the king's wrath a', 5927
13:15 Ammon said unto her, A', be 6965
15:14 A', and let us flee; "
17: 1 I will a' and pursue after David "
21 A', and pass quickly over the "
19: 7 Now therefore a', go forth, "
22:39 them, that they could not a': "
1Ki 3:12 after thee shall any a' like thee. "
14: 2 A', I pray thee, and disguise "
12 A' thou therefore, get thee to thine "
17: 9 A', get thee to Zarephath, "
19: 5 said unto him, A' and eat. "
7 A' and eat; because the journey is "
21: 7 a', and eat bread, and let thine "
15 A', take possession of the "
18 A', go down to meet Ahab king of "
2Ki 1: 3 A', go up to meet the messengers "
8: 1 A', and go thou and thine "
9: 2 a' up from among his brethren "
1Ch 22:16 A' therefore, and be doing, "
19 a' therefore, and build ye the "
2Ch 6:41 Now therefore a', O Lord God, "
Ezr 10: 4 A'; for this matter belongeth unto "
Ne 2:20 we his servants will a' and build: "
Es 1:18 a' too much contempt and wrath. "
4:14 and deliverance a' to the Jews 5975
Job 7: 4 When shall I a', and the night 6965
25: 3 upon whom doth not his light a'? "
Ps 3: 7 A', O Lord; save me, O my God: "
7: 6 A', O Lord, in thine anger, "
9:19 A', O Lord; let not man prevail: "
10:12 A', O Lord; O God, lift up thine "
12: 5 now will I a', saith the Lord; "
17:13 A', O Lord, disappoint him, "
44:23 why sleepest thou, O Lord? a', 6974
26 A' for our help, and redeem us *6965
68: 1 Let God a', let his enemies be "
74:22 A', O God, plead thine own cause: "
78: 6 who should a' and declare them to "
82: 8 A', O God, judge the earth: "
88:10 shall the dead a' and praise thee? "
89: 9 when the waves thereof a', thou 7721
102:13 Thou shalt a', and have mercy 6965
109:28 they a', let them be ashamed; "
132: 8 A', O Lord, into thy rest; "
Pr 6: 9 when wilt thou a' out of thy sleep? "
31:28 children a' up, and call her *6965
Ca 2:13 A', my love, my fair one, and "
Isa 21: 5 a', ye princes, and anoint the * "
23:12 a', pass over to Chittim; "
26:19 with my dead body shall they a'. "
31: 2 but will a' against the house of "
49: 7 Kings shall see and a', "
52: 2 a', and sit down, O Jerusalem: "
60: 1 A', shine; for thy light is come, "
2 but the Lord shall a' upon thee, 2224
Jer 1:17 gird up thy loins, and a', 6965
2:27 they will say, A', and save us. "
28 let them a', if they can save thee "
6: 4 a', and let us go up at noon. "
5 A', and let us go by night, "
8: 4 Shall they fall, and not a'? * "
13: 4 and a', go to Euphrates, and hide "
6 A', go to Euphrates, and take the "
18: 2 A', and go down to the potter's "
31: 6 A' ye, and let us go up to Zion "
46:16 A', and let us go again to our own "
49:28 A' ye, go up to Kedar, "
31 A', get you up unto the wealthy "
La 2:19 A', cry out in the night: "
Eze 3:22 A', go forth into the plain, "
Da 2:39 And after thee shall a' another 6966
7: 5 A', devour much flesh. "
17 which shall a' out of the earth. "
24 ten kings that shall arise: "
Ho 10:14 a tumult a' among thy people 6965
Am 7: 2, 5 by whom shall Jacob a'? for * "
Ob 1 A' ye, and let us rise up against "
Jon 1: 2 A', go to Nineveh, that great city, "
6 a', call upon thy God, "
3: 2 A', go unto Nineveh, "
4: 8 when the sun did a', *2224
Mic 2:10 A' ye, and depart, for this is not 6965
4:13 A' and thresh, O daughter of "
6: 1 A', contend thou before the "
7: 8 enemy: when I fall, I shall a'; "
Hab 2:19 A', it shall teach! Behold, it is 5782
Mal 4: 2 shall the Sun of righteousness a' 2224
M't 2:13 A', and take the young child 1453
20 A', and take the young child "
9: 5 or to say, A', and walk? "
6 A', take up thy bed, and go unto "
17: 7 said, A', and be not afraid. "
24:24 For there shall a' false Christs, "
M'r 2: 9 or to say, A', and take up thy bed, "
11 unto thee, A', and take up thy bed, "
5:41 Damsel, I say unto thee, a', "
Lu 5:24 I say unto thee, A', and take up thy "
7:14 Young man, I say unto thee, A'. "
8:54 called, saying, Maid, a'. "
15:18 I will a' and go to my father, 450
17:19 he said unto him, A', go thy way: "
24:38 why do thoughts a' in your hearts? 305
Joh 14:31 even so I do. A', let us go hence. 1453
Ac 8:26 A', and go toward the south 450
9: 6 A', and go into the city, and it * "
11 A', and go into the street which "
34 a', and make thy bed. And he "
40 him to the body said, Tabitha, a'. "
10:20 A' therefore, and get thee down, "

Ac 11: 7 A', Peter; slay and eat. * 450
12: 7 raised him up, saying, A' up "
20:30 of your own selves, shall men a'. "
22:10 me, A', and go unto Damascus; "
16 a', and be baptized, and wash away "
Eph 5:14 a' from the dead, and Christ shall "
2Pe 1:19 the day star a' in your hearts: 393

ariseth
1Ki 18:44 a' a little cloud out of the sea, 5927
Ps 104:22 sun a', they gather themselves 2224
112: 4 Unto the upright there a' light "
Ec 1: 5 The sun also a', and the sun "
Isa 2:19, 21 when he a' to shake terribly 6965
Nah 3:17 when the sun a' they flee away 2224
M't 13:21 tribulation or persecution a' 1096
M'r 4:17 affliction or persecution a' for "
Joh 7:52 for out of Galilee a' no prophet. 1453
He 7:15 there a' another priest, 450

arising
Es 7: 7 the king a' from the banquet of *6965

Aristarchus (*ar-is-tar'-cus*)
Ac 19:29 having caught Gaius and A', 708
20: 4 Thessalonians, A' and Secundus; "
27: 2 A', a Macedonian of Thessalonica, "
Col 4:10 A' my fellowprisoner saluteth you, "
Ph'm 24 Marcus, A', Demas, "

Aristobulus' (*a-ris-to-bu'-lus*)
Ro 16:10 them which are of A' household. 711

ark
Ge 6:14 Make thee an a' of gopher wood; 8392
14 rooms shalt thou make in the a', "
15 the length of the a' shall be three "
16 window shalt thou make to the a', "
16 the door of the a' shalt thou set "
18 thou shalt come into the a', "
19 shalt thou bring into the a', "
7: 1 thou and all thy house into the a'; "
7 sons' wives with him, into the a', "
9 and two unto Noah into the a', "
13 of his sons with them, into the a'; "
15 went in unto Noah into the a', "
17 increased, and bare up the a', "
18 the a' went upon the face of the "
23 that were with him in the a'. "
8: 1 cattle that was with him in the a': "
4 the a' rested in the seventh month, "
6 Noah opened the window of the a' "
9 she returned unto him into the a', "
9 pulled her in unto him into the a'. "
10 sent forth the dove out of the a'; "
13 removed the covering of the a', "
16 Go forth of the a', "
19 went forth out of the a'. "
9:10 from all that go out of the a', "
18 that went forth of the a', "
Ex 2: 3 she took for him an a' of bulrushes, "
5 she saw the a' among the flags, "
25:10 shall make an a' of shittim wood: 727
14 into the rings by the sides of the a', "
14 the a' may be borne with them. "
15 shall be in the rings of the a': "
16 shalt put into the a' the testimony "
21 the mercy seat above upon the a'; "
21 and in the a' thou shalt put "
22 are upon the a' of the testimony "
26:33 within the vail the a' of the "
34 upon the a' of the testimony in the "
30: 6 that is by the a' of the testimony, "
26 therewith, and the a' of the "
31: 7 the a' of the testimony, and the "
35:12 The a', and the staves thereof, "
37: 1 Bezaleel made the a' of shittim "
5 the sides of the a', to bear the a'. "
39:35 The a' of the testimony, and the "
40: 3 therein the a' of the testimony, "
3 and cover the a' with the vail. "
5 before the a' of the testimony, "
20 put the testimony into the a', "
20 and set the staves on the a', "
20 the mercy seat above upon the a': "
21 brought the a' into the tabernacle, "
21 covered the a' of the testimony; "
Le 16: 2 which is upon the a'; "
Nu 3:31 the charge shall be the a', and the "
4: 5 cover the a' of testimony with it: "
7:89 mercy seat that was upon the a' "
10:33 and the a' of the covenant of the "
35 when the a' set forward, "
14:44 nevertheless the a' of the covenant "
De 10:1 make thee an a' of wood. "
2 thou shalt put them in the a'. "
3 made an a' of shittim wood, "
5 put the tables into the a' which "
8 to bear the a' of the covenant "
31: 9 the sons of Levi which bear the a' "
25 which bare the a' of the covenant "
26 the side of the a' of the covenant "
Jos 3: 3 When ye see the a' of the covenant "
6 Take up the a' of the covenant, "
6 they took up the a' of the covenant, "
8 that bear the a' of the covenant, "
11 Behold, the a' of the covenant "
13 that bear the a' of the Lord, "
14 the priests bearing the a' "
15 as they that bare the a' were come "
15 the priests that bare the a' were "
17 the priests that bare the a' of the "
4: 5 Pass over before the a' of the Lord "
7 before the a' of the covenant "
9 which bare the a' of the covenant "
10 the priests which bare the a' stood "
11 that the a' of the Lord passed over, "
16 command the priests that bear the a' "

Jos 4:18 when the priests that bare the a' 727
6: 4 priests shall bear before the a' "
6 Take up the a' of the covenant, "
6 before the a' of the Lord. "
8 and the a' of the covenant of "
9 the rereward came after the a', "
11 the a' of the Lord compassed the "
12 the priests took up the a' of the "
13 a' of the Lord went on continually, "
13 but the rereward came after the a' "
7: 6 before the a' of the Lord "
8:33 judges, stood on this side the a' "
33 which bare the a' of the covenant "
Ju 20:27 the a' of the covenant of God was "
1Sa 3: 3 where the a' of God was, "
4: 3 Let us fetch the a' of the "
4 bring from thence the a' of "
4 there with the a' of the covenant "
5 when the a' of the covenant "
6 that the a' of the Lord was come "
11 And the a' of God was taken; "
13 his heart trembled for the a' of God. "
17 and the a' of God is taken. "
18 he made mention of the a' of God, "
19 that the a' of God was taken, "
21 because the a' of God was taken, "
22 for the a' of God is taken. "
5: 1 the Philistines took the a' of God, "
2 When the Philistines took the a' "
3 before the a' of the Lord. "
7 The a' of the God of Israel "
8 What shall we do with the a' of "
8 Let the a' of the God of Israel be "
8 And they carried the a' of the God "
10 Therefore they sent the a' of God "
10 as the a' of God came to Ekron, "
10 They have brought about the a' of "
11 Send away the a' of the God of "
6: 1 a' of the Lord was in the country "
2 What shall we do to the a' of "
3 If ye send away the a' of "
8 take the a' of the Lord, "
11 they laid the a' of the Lord upon "
13 saw the a', and rejoiced to see it. "
15 the Levites took down the a' of "
18 whereon they set down the a' of "
19 because they had looked into the a' "
21 Philistines have brought again the a' "
7: 1 fetched up the a' of the Lord, "
1 Eleazar his son to keep the a' of "
2 the a' abode in Kirjath-jearim, "
14:18 Bring hither the a' of God. "
18 For the a' of God was at that time "
2Sa 6: 2 bring up from thence the a' of God, "
3 they set the a' of God upon a new "
4 accompanying the a' of God: "
4 and Ahio went before the a'. "
6 put forth his hand to the a' of God, "
7 there he died by the a' of God. "
9 How shall the a' of the Lord "
10 David would not remove the a' of "
11 the a' of the Lord continued "
12 because of the a' of God. "
12 went and brought up the a' of "
13 when they that bare the a' of "
15 brought up the a' of the Lord "
16 as the a' of the Lord came into the "
17 they brought in the a' of the Lord, "
7: 2 but the a' of God dwelleth within "
11:11 The a', and Israel, and Judah, "
15:24 the a' of the covenant of God: "
24 and they set down the a' of God; "
25 Carry back the a' of God into the "
29 carried the a' of God again to "
1Ki 2:26 because thou barest the a' of "
3:15 stood before the a' of the covenant "
6:19 set there the a' of the covenant "
8: 1 bring up the a' of the covenant "
3 the priests took up the a'. "
4 they brought up the a' of the Lord, "
5 with him before the a', "
6 the priests brought in the a' of the "
7 two wings over the place of the a', "
7 and the cherubims covered the a' "
9 nothing in the a' save the two "
21 I have set there a place for the a', "
1Ch 6:31 after that the a' had rest. "
13: 3 let us bring again the a' of our God "
5 bring the a' of God from "
6 to bring up thence the a' of God "
7 they carried the a' of God in a new "
9 put forth his hand to hold the a'; "
10 because he put his hand to the a': "
12 How shall I bring the a' of "
13 David brought not the a' "
14 the a' of God remained "
15: 1 prepared a place for the a' of God, "
2 None ought to carry the a' of God "
2 the Lord chosen to carry the a' of "
3, 14 to bring up the a' of the Lord "
12 may bring up the a' of the Lord "
15 the Levites bare the a' of God "
23, 24 doorkeepers for the a'. "
24 with the trumpets before the a' of "
25 bring up the a' of the covenant "
23 helped the Levites that bare the a' "
27 the Levites that bare the a', "
28 Thus all Israel brought up the a' "
29 the a' of the covenant of the Lord "
16: 1 they brought the a' of God, "
4 Levites to minister before the a' "
6 before the a' of the covenant "
37 he left there before the a' of the "
37 minister before the a' continually, "
17: 1 the a' of the covenant of the Lord "
22:19 to bring the a' of the covenant "

1Ch 28: 2 an house of rest for the a' of 727
18 covered the a' of the covenant "
2Ch 1: 4 But the a' of God had David "
5: 2 to bring up the a' of the covenant "
4 the Levites took up the a'. "
5 they brought up the a', "
6 assembled unto him before the a', "
7 the priests brought in the a' "
8 their wings over the place of the a', "
8 and the cherubims covered the a' "
9 drew out the staves of the a', *
9 were seen from the a' before the 727
10 nothing in the a' save the two "
6:11 in it have I put the a', "
41 and the a' of thy strength: "
8:11 the a' of the Lord hath come. "
35: 3 Put the holy a' in the house "
Ps 132: 8 thou, and the a' of thy strength. "
Jer 3:16 The a' of the covenant of the Lord: "
M't 24:38 day that Noe entered into the a', 2787
Lu 17:27 Noe entered into the a', and the "
Heb 9: 4 censer, and the a' of the covenant "
11: 7 prepared an a' to the saving of "
1Pe 3:20 while the a' was a preparing "
Re 11:19 was seen in his temple the a' of "

Arkite (*ar'-kite*)
Ge 10:17 Hivite, and the A', and the Sinite, 6208
1Ch 1:15 and the A', and the Sinite, "

arm See also ARMED; ARMHOLES; ARMS.
Ex 6: 6 you with a stretched out a', 2220
15:16 by the greatness of thine a' "
Nu 31: 3 A' some of yourselves unto the 2502
De 4:34 and by a stretched out a', and by 2220
5:15 hand and by a stretched out a': "
7:19 and the stretched out a', "
9:29 and by thy stretched out a'. "
11: 2 hand, and his stretched out a', "
26: 8 and with an outstretched a', "
33:20 teareth the a' with the crown of "
1Sa 2:31 that I will cut off thine a', and "
31 the a' of thy father's house, "
2Sa 1:10 the bracelet that was on his a', "
1Ki 8:42 and of thy stretched out a';) "
2Ki 17:36 great power and a stretched out a', "
2Ch 6:32 and thy stretched out a'; "
32: 8 With him is an a' of flesh; "
Job 26: 2 the a' that hath no strength? "
31:22 a' fall from my shoulder blade, *3802
22 mine a' be broken from the bone. 248
35: 9 by reason of the a' of the mighty. 2220
38:15 and the high a' shall be broken. "
40: 9 Hast thou an a' like God? "
Ps 10:15 Break thou the a' of the wicked "
44: 3 neither did their own a' save them: "
3 but thy right hand, and thine a', "
77:15 with thine a' redeemed thy people, "
89:10 thine enemies with thy strong a'. "
13 Thou hast a mighty a': "
21 mine a' also shall strengthen him. "
98: 1 a', hath gotten him the victory. "
136:12 and with a stretched out a':) "
Ca 8: 6 as a seal upon thine a': "
Isa 9:20 every man the flesh of his own a': "
17: 5 and reapeth the ears with his a'; "
30:30 shew the lighting down of his a', "
33: 2 be thou their a' every morning, "
40:10 and his a' shall rule for him: "
11 shall gather the lambs with his a', "
48:14 his a' shall be on the Chaldeans. "
51: 5 on mine a' shall they trust. "
9 put on strength, O a' of the Lord; "
52:10 Lord hath made bare his holy a' "
53: 1 to whom is the a' of the Lord "
59:16 his a' brought salvation unto him; "
62: 8 and by the a' of his strength, "
63: 5 own a' brought salvation unto me; "
12 Moses with his glorious a', dividing "
Jer 17: 5 and maketh flesh his a', "
21: 5 and with a strong a', "
27: 5 and by my outstretched a', "
32:17 great power and stretched out a', "
21 and with a stretched out a', 248
48:25 his a' is broken, saith the Lord. 2220
Eze 4: 7 and thine a' shall be uncovered, "
20:33 with a stretched out a', and with "
34 hand, and with a stretched out a', "
30:21 I have broken the a' of Pharaoh "
31:17 and they that were his a', "
Da 11: 6 not retain the power of the a'; "
6 neither shall he stand, nor his a': "
Zec 11:17 the sword shall be upon his a', "
17 his a' shall be clean dried up, "
Lu 1:51 hath shewed strength with his a'; 1023
Joh 12:38 to whom hath the a' of the Lord "
Ac 13:17 with an high a' brought he them "
1Pe 4: 1 a' yourselves likewise with the 3695

Armageddon (*ar-mag-ed'-don*)
Re 16:16 in the Hebrew tongue A'. * 717

armed
Ge 14:14 when...he a' his trained servants,*7324
Nu 31: 5 twelve thousand a' for war. 2502
32:17 we ourselves will go ready a' "
20 if ye will go a' before the Lord * "
21 go all of you a' over Jordan "
27 every man a' for war, "
29 every man a' to battle, "
30 they will not pass over with you a', "
32 will pass over a' before the Lord "
De 3:18 pass over a' before your brethren "
Jos 1:14 pass before your brethren a', 2571
4:12 Manasseh, passed over a' before "
6: 7 that is a' pass on before the ark 2502
9 the a' men went before the priests "
13 the a' men went before them: but "

J'g 7:11 the *a·* men that were in the host. 2571
1Sa 17: 5 he was *a·* with a coat of mail; *3847
38 Saul *a·* David with his armour, * "
38 also he *a·* him with a coat of mail.* "
1Ch 12: 2 They were *a·* with bows, 5401
23 that were ready *a·* to the war, 2502
24 ready *a·* to the war. "
2Ch 17:17 *a·* men with bow and shield 5401
28:14 the *a·* men left the captives and 2502
Job 39:21 he goeth on to meet the *a·* men. 5402
Ps 78: 9 The children of Ephraim, being *a·*, 5401
Pr 6:11 and thy want as an *a·* man. 4043
24:34 and thy want as an *a·* man. "
Isa 15: 4 *a·* soldiers of Moab shall cry out 2502
Lu 11:21 strong man *a·* keepeth his palace. *3528*

Armenia (*ar-me'-ne-ah*) See also ARARAT.
2Ki 19:37 they escaped into the land of *A·*: * 780
Isa 37:38 they escaped into the land of *A·*: * "

armholes
Jer 38:12 rotten rags under thine *a·* 679, 3027
Eze 13:18 sew pillows to all *a·*, * "

armies
Ex 6:26 from...Egypt according to their *a·*.*6635
7: 4 forth mine *a·*, and my people * "
12:17 your *a·* out of the land of Egypt: * "
51 of the land of Egypt by their *a·*. * "
Nu 1: 3 number them by their *a·*. * "
2: 3 pitch throughout their *a·*: and * "
9 throughout their *a·*. These shall * "
10 of Reuben according to their *a·*: * "
16 throughout their *a·*. And they * "
18 of Ephraim according to their *a·*:* "
24 throughout their *a·*. And they * "
25 on the north side by their *a·*: * "
10:14, 18 according to their *a·*: and * "
22 according to his *a·*; and over his *6635
28 of Israel according to their *a·*, * "
33: 1 their *a·* under the hand of Moses * "
De 20: 9 make captains of the *a·* to lead * "
1Sa 17: 1 together their *a·* to battle, 4264
8 and cried unto the *a·* of Israel, 4634
10 I defy the *a·* of Israel this day; "
23 out of the *a·* of the Philistines, *4630
26 defy the *a·* of the living God? 4634
36 defied the *a·* of the living God. "
45 the God of the *a·* of Israel, "
23: 3 against the *a·* of the Philistines? "
28: 1 the Philistines gathered their *a·* *4264
29: 1 together all their *a·* to Aphek: * "
2Ki 25:23 the captains of the *a·*, they and *2428
26 captains of the *a·*, arose, and * "
1Ch 11:26 the valiant men of the *a·* were, "
2Ch 16: 4 of his *a·* against the cities "
Job 25: 3 Is there any number of his *a·*? 1416
Ps 44: 9 goest not forth with our *a·*. *6635
60:10 didst not go out with our *a·*? * "
68:12 Kings of *a·* did flee apace: and * "
Ca 6:13 As it were the company of two *a·*.*4264
Isa 34: 2 his fury upon all their *a·*: he *6635
M't 22: 7 he sent forth his *a·*, and destroyed *4753*
Lu 21:20 Jerusalem compassed with *a·*, *4760*
Heb 11:34 turned to flight the *a·* of the aliens. *3925*
Re 19:14 And the *a·* which were in heaven *4753*
19 and their *a·*, gathered together "

Armoni (*ar-mo'-ni*)
2Sa 21: 8 unto Saul, *A·* and Mephibosheth; 764

armour See also ARMOURBEARER.
1Sa 14: 1 the young man that bare his *a·*, 3627
6 that bare his *a·*, Come, and let us "
17:38 Saul armed David with his *a·*, *4055
39 girded his sword upon his *a·*, "
54 he put his *a·* in his tent. 3627
31: 9 his head, and stripped off his *a·*, "
10 his *a·* in the house of Ashtaroth: "
2Sa 2:21 take thee his *a·*. But Asahel would 2488
18:15 young men that bare Joab's *a·* 3627
1Ki 10:25 garments, and *a·*, and spices, 5402
22:38 they washed his *a·*; according *2185
2Ki 3:21 all that were able to put on *a·*, 2290
10: 2 horses, a fenced city also, and *a·*; 5402
20:13 of his *a·*, and all that was found 3627
1Ch 10: 9 they took his head, and his *a·*, "
10 his *a·* in the house of their gods, "
Isa 22: 8 the *a·* of the house of the forest. 5402
39: 2 the house of his *a·*, and all that 3627
Eze 38: 4 clothed with all sorts of *a·*, even "
Lu 11:22 him all his *a·* wherein he trusted, *3833*
Ro 13:12 let us put on the *a·* of light. *3696*
2Co 6: 7 by the *a·* of righteousness on the "
Eph 6:11 Put on the whole *a·* of God, that *3833*
13 take unto you the whole *a·* of God, "

armourbearer
J'g 9:54 the young man his *a·*, 5375, 3627
1Sa 14: 7 his *a·* said unto him, "
12 Jonathan and his *a·*, and said, "
12 Jonathan said unto his *a·*, "
13 and his *a·* after him: "
13 and his *a·* slew after him. "
14 Jonathan and his *a·* made, "
17 Jonathan and his *a·* were not "
16:21 he became his *a·*. "
31: 4 Then said Saul unto his *a·*, "
4 his *a·* would not; for he was "
5 *a·* saw that Saul was dead, "
6 Saul died,...and his *a·*, and "
2Sa 23:37 *a·* to Joab the son of Zeruiah, * "
1Ch 10: 4 Then said Saul to his *a·*, "
4 his *a·* would not; "
5 his *a·* saw that Saul was dead, "
11:39 *a·* of Joab the son of Zeruiah, "

armoury
Ne 3:19 going up to the *a·* at the turning 5402
Ca 4: 4 builded for an *a·*, whereon there 8530
Jer 50:25 The Lord hath opened his *a·*. 214

arms
Ge 49:24 the *a·* of his hands were made 2220
De 33:27 underneath are the everlasting *a·*: "
J'g 15:14 the cords that were upon his *a·* "
16:12 he brake them from off his *a·* like "
2Sa 22:35 bow of steel is broken by mine *a·*. "
2Ki 9:24 smote Jehoram between his *a·*, * "
Job 22: 9 the *a·* of the fatherless have been "
Ps 18:34 bow of steel is broken by mine *a·*. "
37:17 For the *a·* of the wicked shall be "
Pr 31:17 strength, and strengtheneth her *a·*. "
Isa 44:12 it with the strength of his *a·*: * "
49:22 bring thy sons in their *a·*, and thy *2684
51: 5 mine *a·* shall judge the people: 2220
Eze 13:20 I will tear them from your *a·*, "
30:22 of Egypt, and will break his *a·*, "
24 I will strengthen the *a·* of the king "
24 but I will break Pharaoh's *a·*, "
25 I will strengthen the *a·* of the king "
25 the *a·* of Pharaoh shall fall down: "
Da 2:32 his breast and his *a·* of silver, 1872
10: 6 his *a·* and his feet like in colour 2220
11:15 and the *a·* of the south shall not "
22 with the *a·* of a flood shall they be "
31 And *a·* shall stand on his part, "
Ho 7:15 bound and strengthened their *a·*, "
11: 3 taking them by their *a·*; but they "
M'r 9:36 when he had taken him in his *a·*, *1723*
10:16 he took them up in his *a·*, put his "
Lu 2:28 took he him up in his *a·*, *43*

army See also ARMIES.
Ge 26:26 the chief captain of his *a·*. *6635
Ex 14: 9 and his horsemen, and his *a·*, 2428
De 11: 4 what he did unto the *a·* of Egypt, "
J'g 4: 7 Sisera, the captain of Jabin's *a·*, 6635
8: 6 should give bread unto thine *a·*? "
9:29 Increase thine *a·*, and come out. "
1Sa 4: 2 they slew of the *a·* in the field 4634
12 a man of Benjamin out of the *a·*, "
16 I am he that came out of the *a·*, "
16 I fled to day out of the *a·*. "
17:21 battle in array, *a·* against *a·*. "
22 and ran into the *a·*, and came and "
48 David hasted, and ran toward the *a·* "
1Ki 20:19 and the *a·* which followed them. 2428
25 number thee an *a·*, "
25 like the *a·* that thou hast lost, "
2Ki 25: 5 the *a·* of the Chaldees pursued "
5 all his *a·* were scattered from him. "
10 And all the *a·* of the Chaldees, "
1Ch 20: 1 Joab led forth the power of the *a·*, 6635
27:34 the general of the king's *a·* * "
2Ch 13: 3 in array with an *a·* of valiant 2428
14: 8 Asa had an *a·* of men that bare "
20:21 they went out before the *a·*, 2502
24:24 *a·* of the Syrians came with a 2428
25: 7 let not the *a·* of Israel go with 6635
9 I have given to the *a·* of Israel? 1416
10 the *a·* that was come to him out of "
13 But the soldiers of the *a·* which "
26:13 under their hand was an *a·*, 2426, 6635
Ne 2: 9 had sent captains of the *a·* 2428
4: 2 the *a·* of Samaria, and said, What "
Job 29:25 dwelt as a king in the *a·*, 1416
Ca 6: 4, 10 terrible as an *a·* with banners. "
Isa 36: 2 king Hezekiah with a great *a·*. 2426
43:17 horse, the *a·* and the power; 2428
Jer 32: 2 Babylon's *a·* besieged Jerusalem: "
34: 1 king of Babylon, and all his *a·*, "
7 the king of Babylon's *a·* fought "
21 hand of the king of Babylon's *a·*, "
35:11 for fear of the *a·* of the Chaldeans, "
11 for fear of the *a·* of the Syrians: "
37: 5 Pharaoh's *a·* was come forth out "
7 Pharaoh's *a·*, which is come "
10 ye had smitten the whole *a·* of "
11 when the *a·* of the Chaldeans was "
11 for fear of Pharaoh's *a·*, "
38: 3 the king of Babylon's *a·*, "
39: 1 all his *a·* against Jerusalem, "
5 Chaldeans' *a·* pursued after them, "
46: 2 against the *a·* of Pharaoh-necho "
22 they shall march with an *a·*, "
52: 4 he and all his *a·*, against Jerusalem, "
8 *a·* of the Chaldeans pursued after "
8 all his *a·* was scattered from him. "
14 all the *a·* of the Chaldeans, "
Eze 17:17 Pharaoh with his mighty *a·* "
27:10 Lud and Phut were in thine *a·*, "
11 The men of Arvad with thine *a·* "
29:18 caused his *a·* to serve a great service "
18 yet had he no wages, nor his *a·*, "
19 and it shall be the wages for his *a·*. "
32:31 Pharaoh and all his *a·* slain by "
37:10 an exceeding great *a·*. "
38: 4 all thine *a·*, horses and horsemen, "
15 a great company, and a mighty *a·*: "
Da 3:20 mighty men that were in his *a·* 2429
4:35 according to his will in the *a·* of "
11: 7 which shall come with an *a·*, 2428
13 after certain years with a great *a·* "
25 of the south with a great *a·*; "
25 with a very great and mighty *a·*; "
26 and his *a·* shall overflow: "
Joe 2:11 shall utter his voice before his *a·*: "
20 far off from you the northern *a·*, "
25 my great *a·* which I sent among 2428
Zec 9: 8 mine house because of the *a·*, 4675
Ac 23:27 then came I with an *a·*, and *4753*
Re 9:16 number of the *a·* of the horsemen * "
19:19 sat on the horse, and against his *a·*. "

Arnan (*ar'-nan*)
1Ch 3:21 the sons of *A·*, the sons of Obadiah 770

Arnon (*ar'-non*)
Nu 21:13 and pitched on the other side of *A·*, 769
21:13 for *A·* is the border of Moab, 769
14 Red sea, and in the brooks of *A·*, "
24 possessed his land from *A·* unto "
26 land out of his hand, even unto *A·*. "
28 the lords of the high places of *A·*. "
22:36 Moab, which is in the border of *A·*, "
De 2:24 and pass over the river *A·*: "
36 is by the brink of the river of *A·*, "
3: 8 river of *A·* unto mount Hermon; "
12 Aroer, which is by the river *A·*, "
16 from Gilead even unto the river *A·* "
4:48 is by the bank of the river *A·*, "
Jos 12: 1 rising of the sun, from the river *A·* "
2 is upon the bank of the river *A·*, "
13: 9 is upon the bank of the river *A·*, "
16 the river *A·*, and the city that is "
J'g 11:13 from *A·* even unto Jabbok, and "
18 and pitched on the other side of *A·*, "
18 for *A·* was the border of Moab. "
22 from *A·* even unto Jabbok, and "
26 that be along by the coasts of *A·*, "
2Ki 10:33 by the river *A·*, even Gilead and "
Isa 16: 2 of Moab shall be at the fords of *A·*. "
Jer 48:20 tell ye it in *A·*, that Moab is spoiled, "

Arod (*a'-rod*) See also ARODITES.
Nu 26:17 *A·*, the family of the Arodites: 720

Arodi (*ar'-o-di*) See also ARODITES.
Ge 46:16 Ezbon, Eri, and *A·*, and Areli. 722

Arodites (*a'-ro-dites*) See also ARODI.
Nu 26:17 Of Arod, the family of the *A·*: 722

Aroer (*ar'-o-ur*) See also AROERITE.
Nu 32:34 built Dibon, and Ataroth, and *A·*, 6177
De 2:36 From *A·*, which is by the brink of "
3:12 we possessed at that time, from *A·*, "
4:48 From *A·*, which is by the bank of "
Jos 12: 2 in Heshbon, and ruled from *A·*, "
13: 9 From *A·*, that is upon the bank "
16 And their coast was from *A·*, that "
25 unto *A·* that is before Rabbah; "
J'g 11:26 towns, and in *A·* and her towns, "
33 And he smote them from *A·*, even "
1Sa 30:28 And to them which were in *A·*, "
2Sa 24: 5 over Jordan, and pitched in *A·*, "
2Ki 10:33 from *A·*, which is by the river "
1Ch 5: 8 the son of Joel, who dwelt in *A·*, "
Isa 17: 2 The cities of *A·* are forsaken; "
Jer 48:19 O inhabitant of *A·*, stand by the "

Aroerite (*ar'-o-ur-ite*)
1Ch 11:44 Jehiel the sons of Hothan the *A·*, 6200

arose
Ge 19:15 when the morning *a·*, then the 5927
33 she lay down, nor when she *a·*. 6965
35 and the younger *a·*, and lay with "
35 she lay down, nor when she *a·*. "
24:10 he *a·*, and went to Mesopotamia, "
61 And Rebekah *a·*, and her damsels, "
37: 7 my sheaf *a·*, and also stood upright; "
38:19 And she *a·*, and went away, "
Ex 1: 8 there *a·* up a new king over Egypt, "
De 34:10 there *a·* not a prophet since in * "
Jos 8: 3 So Joshua *a·*, and all the people "
19 the ambush *a·* quickly out of their "
18: 8 And the men *a·*, and went away: "
24: 9 *a·* and warred against Israel, "
J'g 2:10 *a·* another generation after them, "
3:20 And he *a·* out of his seat. "
4: 9 Deborah *a·*, and went with Barak "
5: 7 until that I Deborah *a·*, "
7 that I *a·* a mother in Israel. "
6:28 when the men of the city *a·* early 7925
8:21 And Gideon *a·*, and slew Zebah 6965
10: 1 after Abimelech there *a·* to defend "
3 And after him *a·* Jair, a Gileadite, "
13:11 And Manoah *a·*, and went after "
16: 3 Samson lay till midnight, and *a·* at "
19: 3 her husband *a·*, and went after her, "
5 they *a·* early in the morning, 7925
8 And he *a·* early in the morning on "
20: 8 And all the people *a·* as one man, 6965
18 And the children of Israel *a·*, "
Ru 1: 6 she *a·* with her daughters in law, "
1Sa 3: 6 And Samuel *a·* and went to Eli, "
8 And he *a·* and went to Eli, "
5: 3 And when they of Ashdod *a·* early 7925
4 when they *a·* early on the morrow "
9:26 And they *a·* early: and it came "
26 Saul *a·*, and they went out both 6965
13:15 Samuel *a·*, and gat him up from "
17:35 he *a·* against me, I caught him "
48 came to pass, when the Philistine *a·*, "
52 the men of Israel and of Judah *a·*, "
18:27 Wherefore David *a·* and went, "
20:25 Jonathan *a·*, and Abner sat by * "
34 *a·* from the table in fierce anger, "
41 soon as the lad was gone, David *a·* "
42 And he *a·* and departed: "
21:10 And David *a·*, and fled that day "
23:13 David...*a·* and departed out of "
16 And Jonathan Saul's son *a·*, "
24 *a·*, and went to Ziph before Saul: "
24: 4 Then David *a·*, and cut off the skirt "
8 David also *a·* afterward, and went "
25: 1 And David *a·*, and went down to "
41 And she *a·*, and bowed herself "
42 Abigail hasted, and *a·*, and "
26: 2 Then Saul *a·*, and went down "
5 David *a·*, and came to the place "
27: 2 David *a·*, and he passed over with "
28:23 hearkened unto their voice. So he *a·* "
31:12 All the valiant men *a·*, "
2Sa 2:15 Then there *a·* and went over by "
6: 2 And David *a·*, and went with all "
11: 2 that David *a·* from off his bed, "
12:17 And the elders of his house *a·*, "

2Sa 12:20 Then David a· from the earth, 6965
13:29 Then all the king's sons a·, "
31 the king a·, and tare his garments, "
14:23 So Joab a·, and went to Geshur, "
31 Then Joab a·, and came to Absalom "
15: 9 So he a·, and went to Hebron. "
17:22 Then David a·, and all the people "
23 he saddled his ass, and a·, "
19: 8 the king a·, and sat in the gate. "
23:10 He a·, and smote the Philistines "
1Ki 1:50 and a·, and went, and caught hold "
2:40 Shimei a·, and saddled his ass, "
3:20 And she a· at midnight, "
8:54 he a· from before the altar of the "
11:18 And they a· out of Midian, "
40 Jeroboam a·, and fled into Egypt, "
14: 4 Jeroboam's wife did so, and a·, "
17 Jeroboam's wife a·, and departed, "
17:10 So he a· and went to Zarephath. "
19: 3 And when he saw that, he a·, "
8 And he a·, and did eat and drink, "
21 Then he a·, and went after Elijah, "
2Ki 1:15 he a·, and went down with him "
4:30 And he a·, and followed her. "
7: 7 they a· and fled in the twilight, "
12 And the king a· in the night, "
8: 2 woman a·, and did after the saying "
9: 6 he a·, and went into the house; "
10:12 And he a· and departed, "
11: 1 she a· and destroyed all the seed "
12:20 servants a·, and made a conspiracy, "
19:35 they a· early in the morning, 7925
23:25 after him a· there any like him. 6965
25:26 the captains of the armies, a·, "
1Ch 10:12 They a·, all the valiant men, "
20: 4 a· war at Gezer with the 5975
2Ch 22:10 she a· and destroyed all the seed 6965
29:12 Then the Levites a·, Mahath the "
30:14 they a· and took away the altars "
27 Then the priests the Levites a· "
36:16 the wrath of the Lord a· against 5927
Ezr 9: 5 I a· up from my heaviness; 6965
10: 5 a· Ezra, and made the chief priest, "
Ne 2:12 And I a· in the night, "
Es 8: 4 Esther a·, and stood before the "
Job 1:20 Then Job a·, and rent his mantle, "
19:18 I a·, and they spake against me. * "
29: 8 the aged a·, and stood up. * "
Ps 76: 9 When God a· to judgment, "
Ec 1: 5 hasteth to his place where he a·. *2224
Isa 37:36 when they a· early in the morning,*7925
Jer 41: 2 a· Ishmael the son of Nethaniah, 6965
Eze 3:23 Then I a·, and went forth into the "
Da 6:19 king a· very early in the morning, 6966
Jon 3: 3 Jonah a·, and went unto Nineveh, 6965
6 and he a· from his throne, "
M't 2:14 he a· he took the young child and 1453
21 he a·, and took the young child "
8:15 she a·, and ministered unto them. "
24 there a· a great tempest in the sea, 1096
26 he a·, and rebuked the winds 1453
9: 7 he a·, and departed to his house. "
9 And he a·, and followed him. 450
19 Jesus a·, and followed him, 1453
25 her by the hand, and the maid a·. "
25: 7 all those virgins a·, and trimmed "
26:62 the high priest a·, and said * 450
27:52 of the saints which slept a·, *1453
M'r 2:12 immediately he a·, took up the bed, "
14 And he a· and followed him. 450
4:37 there a· a great storm of wind, *1096
39 he a·, and rebuked the wind, *1326
5:42 the damsel a·, and walked; * 450
7:24 he a·, and went into the borders "
9:27 lifted him up; and he a·. "
10: 1 he a· from thence, and cometh "
14:57 a· certain, and bare false witness, * "
Lu 1:39 And Mary a· in those days, and "
4:38 he a· out of the synagogue, * "
39 she a· and ministered unto them. * "
6: 8 he a· and stood forth. "
48 a·, the stream beat vehemently 1096
8:24 he a·, and rebuked the wind *1453
55 again, and she a· straightway: * 450
9:46 there a· a reasoning among them, 1525
15:14 a· a mighty famine in that land; 1096
20 he a·, and came to his father. 450
23: 1 the whole multitude of them a·, * "
24:12 a· Peter, and ran unto the sepulchre; "
Joh 3:25 there a· a question between some 1096
6:18 sea a· by reason of a great wind *1326
11:29 she a· quickly, and came unto him. 1453
Ac 5: 6 the young men a·, wound him 450
6: 1 a· a murmuring of the Grecians 1096
9 there a· certain of the synagogue, 450
7:18 king a·, which knew not Joseph. "
8:27 he a· and went: and, behold, a "
9: 8 Saul a· from the earth; and when 1453
18 a·, and was baptized. 450
34 thy bed. And he a· immediately. "
39 Then Peter a· and went with them. "
11:19 persecution that a· about Stephen 1096
19:23 same time there a· no small stir, "
23: 7 there a· a dissension between the "
9 a· a great cry: and the scribes "
9 of the Pharisees' part a·, and * 450
10 when there a· a great dissension 1096
27:14 a· against it a tempestuous wind * 906
Re 9: 2 there a· a smoke out of the pit, * 305

Arpad (*ar'-pad*) See also Arphad.
2Ki 18:34 the gods of Hamath, and of A·? 774
19:13 of Hamath, and the king of A·, "
Isa 10: 9 not Hamath as A·? is not Samaria "
Jer 49:23 Hamath is confounded, and A·: "

Arphad (*ar'-fad*) See also Arpad.
Isa 36:19 are the gods of Hamath and A·? * 774
37:13 of Hamath, and the king of A·, * "
Arphaxad (*ar-fax'-ad*)
Ge 10:22 Elam, and Asshur, and A·, and * 775
24 A· begat Salah; and Salah begat * "
11:10 begat A· two years after the flood: * "
11 Shem lived after he begat A· five * "
12 A· lived five and thirty years, * "
13 A· lived after he begat Salah four * "
1Ch 1:17 A·, and Lud, and Aram, * "
18 A· begat Shelah, and Shelah * "
24 Shem, A·, Shelah, * "
Lu 3:36 which was the son of A·, 742
array See also arrayed.
J'g 20:20 men of Israel put themselves in a· 6186
22 battle again in a· in the place "
22 where they put themselves in a· "
30 themselves in a· against Gibeah, "
33 themselves in a· at Baal-tamar: "
1Sa 4: 2 Philistines put themselves in a· "
17: 2 and set the battle in a· "
8 come out to set your battle in a·? "
21 Philistines had put the battle in a·, "
2Sa 10: 8 put the battle in a· at the entering "
9 and put them in a· against the "
10 that he might put them in a· "
17 the Syrians set themselves in a· "
1Ki 20:12 his servants, Set yourselves in a·. "
12 themselves in a· against the city. "
1Ch 19: 9 and put the battle in array 6186
10 and put them in a· against the "
11 they set themselves in a· against "
17 set the battle in a· against them. "
17 when David had put the battle in a· "
2Ch 13: 3 And Abijah set the battle in a· * 631
3 Jeroboam also set the battle in a· 6186
14:10 set the battle in a· in the valley "
Es 6: 9 a· the man withal whom the king 3847
Job 6: 4 set themselves in a· against me. 6186
40:10 a· thyself with glory and beauty. 3847
Isa 22: 7 set themselves in a· at the gate. 7896
Jer 6:23 they ride upon horses, set in a· 6186
43:12 and he shall a· himself with the 5844
50: 9 and they shall set themselves in a· 6186
14 yourselves in a· against Babylon "
42 put in a·, like a man to the battle, "
Joe 2: 5 a strong people set in battle a·. "
1Ti 2: 9 or gold, or pearls, or costly a·; *2441
arrayed
Ge 41:42 a· him in vestures of fine linen, 3847
2Ch 5:12 a· in white linen, having cymbals "
28:15 and a· them, and shod them). "
Es 6:11 a· Mordecai, and brought him on "
M't 6:29 was not a· like one of these. 4016
Lu 12:27 was not a· like one of these. "
23:11 a· him in a gorgeous robe, and "
Ac 12:21 Herod, a· in royal apparel, 1746
Re 7:13 these which are a· in white robes? 4016
17: 4 And the woman was a· in purple "
19: 8 she should be a· in fine linen, * "
arrived
Lu 8:26 a· at the country of the Gadarenes, 2668
Ac 20:15 and the next day we a· at Samos, *3846
arrogancy
1Sa 2: 3 not a· come out of your mouth: 6277
Pr 8:13 pride, and a·, and the evil way, 1347
Isa 13:11 the a· of the proud to cease, "
Jer 48:29 his a·, and his pride, "
arrow See also arrows.
1Sa 20:36 he shot an a· beyond him. 2678
37 was come to the place of the a· "
37 is not the a· beyond thee? "
2Ki 9:24 the a· went out at his heart, "
13:17 The a· of the Lord's deliverance, 2671
17 and the a· of deliverance "
19:32 nor shoot an a· there, "
Job 41:28 a· cannot make him flee: 1121, 7198
Ps 11: 2 they make ready their a· 2671
64: 7 God shall shoot at them with an a·; "
91: 5 for the a· that flieth by day; "
Pr 25:18 a sword, and a sharp a·. "
Isa 37:33 nor shoot an arrow there, "
Jer 9: 8 Their tongue is as an a·; "
La 3:12 set me as a mark for the a·. "
Zec 9:14 his a· shall go forth "
arrows
Nu 24: 8 pierce them through with his a·. 2671
De 32:23 I will spend mine a· upon them. "
42 make mine a· drunk with blood, "
1Sa 20:20 I will shoot three a· on the side "
21 Go, find out the a·. "
21 the a· are on this side of thee, "
22 the a· are beyond thee; "
36 find out now the a· which I shoot. "
38 Jonathan's lad gathered up the a·, 2678
2Sa 22:15 he sent out a·, and scattered them; 2671
2Ki 13:15 Take bow and a·. "
15 And he took unto him bow and a·. "
18 he said, Take the a·. "
1Ch 12: 2 in hurling stones and shooting a· "
2Ch 26:15 to shoot a· and great stones "
Job 6: 4 For the a· of the Almighty are "
Ps 7:13 he ordaineth his a· against the "
18:14 Yea, he sent out his arrows, "
21:12 ready thine a· upon thy strings *
38: 2 For thine a· stick fast in me, 2671
45: 5 Thine a· are sharp in the heart "
57: 4 whose teeth are spears and a·, "
58: 7 bendeth his bow to shoot his a·, "
64: 3 bend their bows to shoot their a·, "
76: 3 brake he the a· of the bow, 7565
77:17 thine a· also went abroad. 2687

Ps 120: 4 Sharp a· of the mighty, 2671
127: 4 As a· are in the hand of a mighty "
144: 6 shoot out thine a·, and destroy "
Pr 26:18 casteth firebrands, a·, and death, "
Isa 5:28 Whose a· are sharp, "
7:24 With a· and with bows shall men "
Jer 50: 9 their a· shall be as of a mighty "
14 shoot at her, spare no a·: "
51:11 Make bright the a·; "
La 3:13 hath caused the a· of his quiver *1121
Eze 5:16 send upon them the evil a· of 2671
21:21 he made his a· bright, he "
39: 3 and will cause thine a· to fall "
9 the bows and the a·, and the "
Hab 3:11 at the light of thine a· they went, "
art See also arts.
Ge 3: 9 and said unto him, Where a· thou?
14 thou a· cursed above all cattle,
19 for dust thou a·, and unto dust
4: 6 unto Cain, Why a· thou wroth?
11 now a· thou cursed from the earth,
12:11 a· a fair woman to look upon:
13 I pray thee, thou a· my sister:
13:14 look from the place where thou a·
16:11 Behold, thou a· with child, and
17: 8 land wherein thou a· a stranger, *
20: 3 Behold, thou a· but a dead man,
23: 6 Thou a· a mighty prince among us:
24:23 And said, Whose daughter a· thou?
47 and said, Whose daughter a· thou?
60 Thou a· our sister; be thou the *
26:16 thou a· much mightier than we.
29 a· now the blessed of the Lord.
27:18 Here am I; who a· thou, my son?
24 A· thou my very son Esau? And he
32 said unto him, Who a· thou?
28: 4 land wherein thou a· a stranger, *
29:14 thou a· my bone and my flesh.
15 Because thou a· my brother,
32:17 thee, saying, Whose a· thou?
39: 9 thee, because thou a· his wife:
41:39 so discreet and wise as thou a·: *
44:18 for thou a· even as Pharaoh.
45:19 Now thou a· commanded, this do
46:30 face, because thou a· yet alive.
47: 8 unto Jacob, How old a· thou? *
49: 3 Reuben, thou a· my firstborn, my
8 thou a· he whom thy brethren *
9 thou a· gone up: he stooped
Ex 4:25 a bloody husband a· thou to me!
26 said, A bloody husband thou a·,
18:18 thou a· not able to perform it
30:25, 35 the a· of the apothecary: 4640
33: 3 for thou a· a stiffnecked people:
34:10 the people among which thou a·
Le 27:12 valuest it, who a· the priest *
Nu 14:14 thou Lord a· among this people
14 that thou Lord a· seen face to face,
21:29 thou a· undone, O people of
De 2:18 Thou a· to pass over through Ar,
4:30 When thou a· in tribulation,
38 and mightier than thou a·, *
7: 6 For thou a· an holy people unto
19 people of whom thou a· afraid.
8:10 thou hast eaten and a· full, *
12 and a· full, and hast built goodly
9: 1 a· to pass over Jordan this day,
6 for thou a· a stiffnecked people.
14: 2 For thou a· an holy people unto the
21 a· an holy people unto the Lord
24 that thou a· not able to carry it;
17:14 When thou a· come unto the land
18: 9 a· come into the land which the
26: 1 when thou a· come in unto the
27: 3 law, when thou a· passed over,
9 a· become the people of the Lord
28:10 the earth shall see that thou a·
32:15 thou a· waxen fat,
15 thou a· grown thick,
15 thou a· covered with fatness;
18 that begat thee thou a· unmindful,
33:29 Happy a· thou, O Israel: who is
Jos 5:13 A· thou for us, or for our
13: 1 Thou a· old and stricken in years,
17:17 saying, Thou a· a great people,
J'g 8:18 As thou a·, so were they;
11: 2 a· the son of a strange woman.
12 thou a· come against me to fight
25 a· thou any thing better than Balak
35 a· one of them that trouble me:
12: 5 unto him, A· thou an Ephraimite?
13: 3 Behold now, thou a· barren, and
11 A· thou the man that spakest
Ru 2: 9 when thou a· athirst, go unto the
11 and a· come unto a people which
12 wings thou a· come to trust.
3: 9 And he said, Who a· thou?
9 for thou a· a near kinsman
11 that thou a· a virtuous woman.
16 said, Who a· thou, my daughter?
1Sa 8: 5 unto him, Behold, thou a· old,
10: 2 thou a· departed from me to day,
5 thou a· come thither to the city,
17:28 for thou a· come down that thou
33 Thou a· not able to go against
33 for thou a· but a youth, and he
58 Whose son a· thou, thou young
19: 3 father in the field where thou a·,
21: 1 Why a· thou alone, and no man
24:17 Thou a· more righteous than I:
26:14 Who a· thou that criest to the king?
15 Abner, A· not thou a valiant man?
28:12 deceived me? for thou a· Saul.
29: 9 that thou a· good in my sight,
30:13 thou? and whence a· thou?

2Sa 1: 8 he said unto me, Who a· thou?
13 that told him, Whence a· thou?
2:20 and said, A· thou Asahel? *
7:22 Wherefore thou a· great, O Lord
24 thou, Lord, a· become their God.
28 O Lord God, thou a· that God, *
9: 2 king said unto him, A· thou Ziba?
12: 7 Nathan said to David, Thou a·
13: 4 he said unto him, Why a· thou,
15: 2 Of what city a· thou? and he said,
19 for thou art a stranger, and also
27 A· not thou a seer? return into
16: 8 thou a· taken in thy mischief,
8 because thou a· a bloody man.
21 shall hear that thou a· abhorred
18: 3 thou a· worth ten thousand of us:
19:13 A· thou not of my bone, and of my
20: 9 A· thou in health, my brother? *
17 the woman said, A· thou Joab?
22:29 For thou a· my lamp, O Lord:
1Ki 1:42 for thou a· a valiant man, and
2: 9 for thou a· a wise man, and
6:12 concerning this house which thou a·
13:14 A· thou the man of God that
18 I am a prophet also as thou a·:
17:18 a· thou come unto me to call my
24 I know that thou a· a man of God,
18: 7 A· thou that my lord Elijah? *
17 A· thou he that troubleth Israel?*
36 this day that thou a· God in Israel,
37 know that thou a· the Lord God,
20:36 as soon as thou a· departed from
22: 4 I am as thou a·, my people as thy
2Ki 1: 4 bed on which thou a· gone up,
6 on which thou a· gone up, but
16 off that bed on which thou a· gone
3: 7 I am as thou a·, my people as thy
4: 4 And when thou a· come in, thou *
19:15 thou a· the God, even thou alone,
19 know that thou a· the Lord God,
1Ch 17:26 And now, Lord, thou a· God, and
29:11 and thou a· exalted as head above
2Ch 14:11 O Lord, thou a· our God; let not
16:14 prepared by the apothecaries' a·: 4640
18: 3 I am as thou a·, and my people as
20: 6 of our fathers, a· not thou God in
7 A· not thou our God, who didst *
25:16 A· thou made of the king's *
Ezr 7:14 as thou a· sent to the king, and of
9:15 of Israel: thou a· righteous:
Ne 2: 2 sad, seeing thou a· not sick?
9: 6 Thou, even thou, a· Lord alone;
7 Thou a· the Lord the God, who
8 thy words; for thou a· righteous:
17 but thou a· a God ready to pardon,
31 a· a gracious and merciful God.
33 thou a· just in all that is brought
Es 4:14 knoweth whether thou a· come
Job 4: 5 thee, and thou a· troubled.
15: 7 A· thou the first man that was
17:14 Thou a· my father;
14 to the worm, Thou a· my
22: 3 Almighty, that thou a· righteous?
30:21 Thou a· become cruel to me: with
31:24 fine gold, thou a· my confidence;
33:12 Behold, in this thou a· not just;
34:18 say to a king, Thou a· wicked?
35: 8 may hurt a man as thou a·; and
Ps 2: 7 Thou a· my son; this day have I
3: 3 But thou, O Lord, art a shield
5: 4 For thou a· not a God that hath
8: 4 man, that thou a· mindful of him?
10:14 a· the helper of the fatherless. *
16: 2 Thou a· my Lord: my goodness
22: 1 why a· thou so far from helping
3 But thou a· holy, O thou that
9 But thou a· he that took me out
10 thou a· my God from my mother's
23: 4 fear no evil; for thou a· with me;
25: 5 thou a· the God of my salvation;
31: 3 thou a· my rock and my fortress;
4 for me: for thou a· my strength.
14 O Lord: I said, Thou a· my God.
32: 7 Thou a· my hiding place; thou
40:17 thou a· my help and my deliverer;
42: 5 Why a· thou cast down, O my
5 why a· thou disquieted in me?
11 Why a· thou cast down, O my
11 why a· thou disquieted within me?
43: 2 For thou a· the God of my strength,
5 Why a· thou cast down, O my soul?
5 why a· thou disquieted within me?
44: 4 Thou a· my King, O God:
45: 2 Thou a· fairer than the children
63: 1 O God, thou a· my God; early will
65: 5 who a· the confidence of all the
66: 3 How terrible a· thou in thy works:
68:35 thou a· terrible out of thy holy
70: 5 thou a· my help and my deliverer;
71: 3 thou a· my rock and my fortress.
5 thou a· my hope, O Lord God;
5 thou a· my trust from my youth.
6 thou a· he that took me out of
7 but thou a· my strong refuge.
76: 4 Thou a· more glorious and excellent
7 Thou, even thou, a· to be feared:
7 sight when once thou a· angry?
77:14 Thou a· the God that doest
83:18 Jehovah, a· the most high over
86: 5 For thou, Lord, a· good, and
10 For thou a· great, and doest
10 thou a· God alone.
15 Lord, a· a God full of compassion,
89:17 thou a· the glory of their strength:
26 Thou a· my father, my God, and
90: 2 to everlasting thou a· God.

Ps 92: 8 But thou, Lord, a· most high
93: 2 of old: thou a· from everlasting.
97: 9 Lord, a· high above all the earth:
9 thou a· exalted far above all gods.
102:27 But thou a· the same, and thy
104: 1 God, thou a· very great; thou a·
110: 4 Thou a· a priest for ever after the
118:21 and a· become my salvation.
28 Thou a· my God, I will praise thee;
28 thou a· my God, I will exalt thee.
119:12 Blessed a· thou, O Lord: teach
57 Thou a· my portion, O Lord: *
68 Thou a· good, and doest good;
114 Thou a· my hiding place and my
137 Righteous a· thou, O Lord, and
151 Thou a· near, O Lord; and all thy
137: 8 Babylon who a· to be destroyed;
139: 3 a· acquainted with all my ways.
8 up into heaven, thou a· there:
8 bed in hell, behold, thou a· there:
140: 6 unto the Lord, Thou a· my God:
142: 5 Thou a· my refuge and my portion
143:10 for thou a· my God: thy spirit is
Pr 6: 2 Thou a· snared with the words of
2 thou a· taken with the words of
3 when thou a· come into the hand
7: 4 Thou a· my sister,
24:24 the wicked, Thou a· righteous;
Ec 10:17 Blessed a· thou, O land, when
Ca 1:15 Behold, thou a· fair, my love;
15 behold, thou a· fair;
16 Behold, thou a· fair, my beloved,
2:14 that a· in the clefts of the rock,
4: 1 Behold, thou a· fair, my love;
1 behold, thou a· fair;
7 Thou a· all fair, my love;
6: 4 Thou a· beautiful, O my love,
7: 6 How fair and how pleasant a· thou,
Isa 14: 8 saying, Since thou a· laid
10 A· thou also become weak as we?
10 a· thou become like unto us?
12 How a· thou fallen from heaven,
12 how a· thou cut down to the ground,
19 thou a· cast out of thy grave like
31 whole Palestina, a· dissolved:
22: 1 thou a· wholly gone up to the
2 Thou that a· full of stirs,
25: 1 O Lord, thou a· my God;
26:15 hast increased the nation: thou a·
37:16 thou a· the God, even thou alone,
20 may know that thou a· the Lord,
41: 8 But thou, Israel, a· my servant, *
9 unto thee, Thou a· my servant;
43: 1 thee by thy name; thou a· mine.
44:17 Deliver me; for thou a· my God.
21 for thou a· my servant;
21 formed thee; thou a· my servant:
45:15 thou a· a God that hidest thyself,
47: 8 thou that a· given to pleasures,
13 Thou a· wearied in the multitude
48: 4 I knew that thou a· obstinate,
49: 3 Thou a· my servant, O Israel,
51: 9 A· thou not it that hath cut Rahab,
10 A· thou not it which hath dried
12 who a· thou that thou shouldest
16 and say unto Zion, Thou a· my
57: 8 thyself to another than me, and a·
10 Thou a· wearied in the greatness*
63: 2 Wherefore a· thou red in thine
16 Doubtless thou a· our father,
16 thou, O Lord, a· our father
64: 5 behold, thou a· wroth; for we *
8 But now, O Lord, thou a· our
Jer 2:21 wholly a right seed: how then a·
23 thou a· a swift dromedary
27 Thou a· my father;
3: 4 My father, thou a· the guide of
22 for thou a· the Lord our God.
4:30 And when thou a· spoiled, what
10: 6 thou a· great, and thy name is
12: 1 Righteous a· thou, O Lord, when I
2 thou a· near in their mouth, and
14: 9 O Lord, a· in the midst of us, and
22 A· not thou he, O Lord our God?
15: 6 saith the Lord, thou a· gone
17:14 and I shall be saved: for thou a·
17 Be not a terror unto me: thou a·
20: 7 thou a· stronger than I, and hast
22: 6 Thou a· Gilead unto me, and the
31:18 for thou a· the Lord my God.
39:17 the hand of men of whom thou a·
49:12 and a· thou he that shall
50:24 and thou a· also taken, O
24 was not aware: thou a· found,
51:20 Thou a· my battle ax and
La 5:22 hast utterly rejected us; thou a·
Eze 3: 5 For thou a· not sent to a people
16: 7 and thou a· come to excellent *
34 therefore thou a· contrary.
45 Thou a· thy mother's daughter,
45 children; and thou a· the sister
54 in that thou a· a comfort unto
22: 4 Thou a· become guilty in thy
4 and a· come even unto thy years:
5 which a· infamous and much *
24 Thou a· the land that is not
23:30 and because thou a· polluted
26:17 How a· thou destroyed, that wast
27: 3 Tyrus, O thou that a· situate *
3 which a· a merchant of the
28: 2 yet thou a· a man, and not God,
3 Behold, thou a· wiser than
14 Thou a· the anointed cherub
31: 2 his multitude; whom a· thou
18 To whom a· thou thus like in
32: 2 Thou a· like a young lion of the *

Eze 32: 2 and thou a· as a whale in the
33:32 And lo, thou a· unto them as a
38:13 A· thou come to take a spoil?
17 A· thou he of whom I have
40: 4 unto thee a· thou brought hither:
Dan 2:26 A· thou able to make known 383
37 Thou, O king, a· a king of kings:
38 Thou a· this head of gold.
4:18 but thou a· able; for the spirit
22 It is thou, O king, that a· grown
5:13 A· thou that Daniel,
13 which a· of the children of the
27 Tekel; Thou a· weighed in the
27 and a· found wanting.
9:23 for thou a· greatly beloved:
Ho 2:23 Thou a· my people; and they
23 Thou a· my God.
Ob 2 the heathen: thou a· greatly
5 by night, (how a· thou cut off!)
Jon 1: 8 and of what people a· thou?
4: 2 that thou a· a gracious God, and
Mic 2: 7 O thou that a· named the house *
Na 1:14 make thy grave; for thou a· vile.
3: 8 A· thou better than populous No,
Hab 1:12 A· thou not from everlasting,
13 Thou a· of purer eyes than to
Zec 4: 7 Who a· thou, O great mountain?
M't 2: 6 in the land of Juda, a· not 1488
5:25 whiles thou a· in the way with "
6: 9 Our Father which a· in heaven,
8:29 a· thou come hither to torment
11: 3 A· thou he that should come, or 1488
23 thou, Capernaum, which a· *
14:33 Of a truth thou a· the Son of God. 1488
16:14 Some say that thou a· John the *
16 Thou a· the Christ, the Son of 1488
17 Blessed a· thou, Simon Bar-jona; "
18 That thou a· Peter, "
23 thou a· an offence unto me: "
22:16 we know that thou a· true, and "
25:24 that thou a· an hard man, "
26:50 him, Friend, wherefore a· thou
73 Surely thou also a· one of them; 1488
27:11 A· thou the king of the Jews? "
M'r 1:11 Thou a· my beloved Son, in
24 A· thou come to destroy us?
24 who thou a·, the Holy One of God. 1488
3:11 saying, Thou a· the Son of God. "
8:29 saith unto him, Thou a· the "
12:14 we know that thou a· true, and "
34 Thou a· not far from the "
14:61 A· thou the Christ, the Son of the "
70 Surely thou a· one of them: * "
15: 2 Pilate asked him, A· thou the "
Lu 1:28 Hail, thou that a· highly favoured,
28 blessed a· thou among women. *
42 Blessed a· thou among women,
3:22 Thou a· my beloved Son; 1488
4:34 a· thou come to destroy us?
34 I know thee who thou a·: 1488
41 Thou a· Christ the Son of God. "
7:19, 20 A· thou he that should come? "
10:15 Capernaum, which a· exalted to *
41 Martha, Martha, thou a· careful
11: 2 Our Father which a· in heaven, *
12:58 thou a· in the way, give diligence*
13:12 thou a· loosed from thine infirmity.
14: 8 a· bidden of any man to a wedding,
10 when thou a· bidden, go and sit
15:31 Son, thou a· ever with me, 1488
16:25 comforted, and thou a· tormented.
19:21 because thou a· an austere man;
22:32 and when thou a· converted, *
58 Thou a· also of them. And Peter 1488
67 A· thou the Christ? tell us. "
70 A· thou then the Son of God? "
23: 3 A· thou the king of the Jews? "
40 a· in the same condemnation? "
24:18 A· thou only a stranger in *
Joh 1:19 to ask him, Who a· thou? 1488
21 A· thou Elias? And he saith, I "
21 A· thou that prophet? And he "
22 Who a· thou? that we may give "
42 Thou a· Simon the son of Jona: "
49 thou a· the Son of God; "
49 thou a· the king of Israel "
3: 2 we know that thou a· a teacher
10 A· thou a master of Israel, 1488
4:12 A· thou greater than our father "
19 I perceive that thou a· a prophet. "
5:14 Behold, thou a· made whole:
6:69 that thou a· that Christ, the Son 1488
7:52 A· thou also of Galilee? "
8:25 Who a· thou? And Jesus saith "
48 that thou a· a Samaritan, and hast "
53 A· thou greater than our father "
57 Thou a· not yet fifty years old, 2192
9:28 Thou a· his disciple; but we are 1488
11:27 I believe that thou a· the Christ, "
17:21 as thou, Father, a· in me, and I in
18:17 A· not thou also one of this man's 1488
25 A· not thou also one of his "
33 A· thou the king of the Jews? "
37 A· thou a king then? Jesus "
19: 9 Whence a· thou? But Jesus gave "
12 thou a· not Cæsar's friend: "
21:12 Who a· thou? knowing that it was "
Ac 4:24 Lord, thou a· God, which hast *
8:23 thou a· in the gall of bitterness,
9: 5 Who a· thou, Lord? And the Lord 1488
10:33 hast well done that thou a· come.
12:15 Thou a· mad. But she constantly
13:33 Thou a· my Son, this day have I 1488
17:29 graven by a· and man's device. 5078
21:22 they will hear that thou a· come.
38 A· not thou that Egyptian, which 1488

Ac 22: 8 Who *a'* thou, Lord? And he said 1488
27 Tell me, *a'* thou a Roman? "
26: 1 said unto Paul, Thou *a'* permitted
15 Who *a'* thou, Lord? And he said, 1488
24 Paul, thou *a'* beside thyself;
Ro 2: 1 Therefore thou *a'* inexcusable, 1488
1 whosoever thou *a'* that judgest:
17 Behold, thou *a'* called a Jew, *
19 And *a'* confident
19 that thou thyself *a'* a guide
3: 4 overcome when thou *a'* judged. *
9:20 who *a'* thou that repliest against 1488
14: 4 Who *a'* thou that judgest another "
1Co 7:21 *A'* thou called being a servant? *
27 *A'* thou bound unto a wife?
27 *A'* thou loosed from a wife?
Ga 4: 7 thou *a'* no more a servant, 1488
1Ti 6:12 whereunto thou *a'* also called, *
Heb 1: 5 Thou *a'* my Son, this day have I 1488
12 but thou *a'* the same, and thy "
2: 6 man that thou *a'* mindful of him?
5: 5 Thou *a'* my Son, to day have I 1488
6 Thou *a'* a priest for ever after the
7:17, 21 Thou *a'* a priest for ever after
Jas 2:11 *a'* become a transgressor of the
4:11 *a'* not a doer of the law, but a 1488
12 Who *a'* thou that judgest another? "
Re 2: 5 from whence thou *a'* fallen,
9 and poverty, (but thou *a'* rich) 1488
3: 1 name that thou livest and *a'* dead. "
15 that thou *a'* neither cold nor hot: "
16 So then because thou *a'* lukewarm, "
17 knowest not that thou *a'* wretched, "
4:11 Thou *a'* worthy, O Lord, to receive "
5: 9 Thou *a'* worthy to take the book, "
11:17 O Lord God Almighty which *a'*, 5607
17 and wast, and *a'* to come; *
15: 4 thou only *a'* holy: for all nations
16: 5 Thou *a'* righteous, O Lord, 1488
5 which *a'*, and wast, and 5607

Artaxerxes (*ar-tax-erx'-ees*) See also ARTAXERXES'.
Ezr 4: 7 in the days of *A'*, wrote Bishlam, 783
7 unto *A'* king of Persia; and the "
8 to *A'* the king in this sort: "
11 they sent unto him, even unto *A'* "
6:14 and Darius, and *A'* king of Persia. "
7: 1 in the reign of *A'* king of Persia, "
7 in the seventh year of *A'* the king. "
11 that the king *A'* gave unto Ezra "
12 *A'*, king of kings, unto Ezra the "
21 And I, even I *A'* the king, "
8: 1 in the reign of *A'*, the king, "
Ne 2: 1 in the twentieth year of *A'* the king, "
5:14 the two and thirtieth year of *A'* "
13: 6 in the two and thirtieth year of *A'* "

Artaxerxes' (*ar-tax-erx'-eez*)
Ezr 4:23 the copy of king *A'* letter was read 783

Artemas (*ar'-te-mas*)
Tit 3:12 When I shall send *A'* unto thee, 734

artificer See also ARTIFICERS.
Ge 4:22 an instructer of every *a'* *2794
Isa 3: 3 and the cunning *a'*, and the 2796

artificers
1Ch 29: 5 by the hands of *a'*. 2796
2Ch 34:11 Even to the *a'* and builders * "

artillery
1Sa 20:40 Jonathan gave his *a'* unto his lad, *3627

arts
Ac 19:19 them also which used curious *a'* 4021

Aruboth (*ar'-u-both*)
1Ki 4:10 The son of Hesed, in *A'*; to him 700

Arumah (*a-ru'-mah*)
J'g 9:41 And Abimelech dwelt at *A'*: 725

Arvad (*ar'-vad*) See also ARVADITE.
Eze 27: 8 The inhabitants of Zidon and *A'* 719
11 The men of *A'* with thine army "

Arvadite (*ar'-vad-ite*)
Ge 10:18 And the *A'*, and the Zemarite, 721
1Ch 1:16 And the *A'*, and the Zemarite, "

Arza (*ar'-zah*)
1Ki 16: 9 himself drunk in the house of *A'* 777

as See in the APPENDIX; also FORASMUCH; INASMUCH.

Asa (*a'-sah*) See also ASA'S.
1Ki 15: 8 and *A'* his son reigned in his stead. 609
9 of Israel reigned *A'* over Judah. "
11 And *A'* did that which was right "
13 *A'* destroyed her idol, and burnt it "
16 was war between *A'* and Baasha "
17 any to go out or come in to *A'* "
18 *A'* took all the silver and the gold "
18 king *A'* sent them to Ben-hadad, "
20 Ben-hadad hearkened unto king *A'*, "
22 Then king *A'* made a proclamation "
22 and king *A'* built with them Geba "
23 The rest of all the acts of *A'*, "
24 And *A'* slept with his fathers, "
25 over Israel in the second year of *A'* "
28 Even in the third year of *A'* king of "
32 was war between *A'* and Baasha "
33 In the third year of *A'* king of "
16: 8 In the twenty and sixth year of *A'* "
10, 15 twenty and seventh year of *A'* "
23 In the thirty and first year of *A'* "
29 in the thirty and eighth year of *A'* "
22:41 the son of *A'* began to reign "
43 he walked in all the ways of *A'* his "
46 in the days of his father *A'*, "
1Ch 3:10 Abia his son, *A'* his son, "
9:16 and Berechiah, the son of *A'*, "
2Ch 14: 1 and *A'* his son reigned in his stead. "
2Ch 14: 2 *A'* did that which was good and 609
8 *A'* had an army of men that bare "
10 Then *A'* went out against him, "
11 *A'* cried unto the Lord his God, "
12 smote the Ethiopians before *A'*, "
13 And *A'* and the people that were "
15: 2 And he went out to meet *A'*, and "
2 Hear ye me, *A'*, and all Judah "
8 when *A'* heard these words, and "
10 fifteenth year of the reign of *A'*. "
16 Maachah the mother of *A'* the king, "
16 *A'* cut down her idol, and stamped "
17 of *A'* was perfect all his days. "
19 year of the reign of *A'*. "
16: 1 year of the reign of *A'*, Baasha "
1 or come in to *A'* king of Judah. "
2 Then *A'* brought out silver and gold "
4 Ben-hadad hearkened unto king *A'*, "
6 Then *A'* the king took all Judah; "
7 time Hanani the seer came to *A'* "
10 Then *A'* was wroth with the seer, "
10 *A'* oppressed some of the people "
11 the acts of *A'*, first and last, lo, "
12 *A'* in the thirty and ninth year "
13 *A'* slept with his fathers, and died "
17: 2 which *A'* his father had taken. "
20:32 walked in the way of *A'* his father, "
21:12 the ways of *A'* king of Judah, "
Jer 41: 9 which *A'* the king had made for "
M't 1: 7 and Abia begat *A'*; 760
8 and *A'* begat Josaphat; "

Asahel (*as'-a-hel*)
2Sa 2:18 there, Joab, Abishai, and *A'*: "
18 *A'* was as light of foot as a wild 6214
19 And *A'* pursued after Abner; and "
20 him, and said, Art thou *A'*? "
21 But *A'* would not turn aside from "
22 And Abner said again to *A'*, Turn "
23 where *A'* fell down and died "
30 servants nineteen men and *A'*. "
32 And they took up *A'*, and buried "
3:27 for the blood of *A'* his brother. "
30 slain their brother *A'* at Gibeon "
23:24 *A'* the brother of Joab was one "
1Ch 2:16 Abishai, and Joab, and *A'*, three. "
11:26 were, *A'* the brother of Joab, "
27: 7 for the fourth month, was *A'* the "
2Ch 17: 8 and Zebadiah, and *A'*, and "
31:13 and Nahath, and *A'*, and Jerimoth, "
Ezr 10:15 Only Jonathan the son of *A'*, and "

Asahiah (*as-a-hi'-ah*) See also ASAIAH.
2Ki 22:12 and *A'* a servant of the king's, 6222
14 and *A'*, went unto Huldah the "

Asaiah (*as-a'-yah*) See also ASAHIAH.
1Ch 4:36 and *A'*, and Adiel, and Jesimiel, 6222
6:30 Haggiah his son, *A'* his son. "
9: 5 *A'* the first born, and his sons. "
15: 6 sons of Merari; *A'* the chief, "
11 Uriel, *A'*, and Joel, Shemaiah, "
2Ch 34:20 the scribe, and *A'* a servant of "

Asaph (*a'-saf*) See also ASAPH'S.
2Ki 18:18 Joah the son of *A'* the recorder. 623
37 the son of *A'* the recorder, to "
1Ch 6:39 And his brother *A'*, who stood on "
39 right hand, even *A'* the son of "
9:15 the son of Zichri, the son of *A'*; "
15:17 *A'* the son of Berechiah; "
19 singers, Heman, *A'*, and Ethan, "
16: 5 *A'* the chief, and next to him "
5 *A'* made a sound with cymbals; "
7 the hand of *A'* and his brethren. "
37 *A'* and his brethren, to minister "
25: 1 to the service of the sons of *A'*, "
2 Of the sons of *A'*; Zaccur, and "
2 the sons of *A'* under the "
2 under the hands of *A'*, "
6 according to the king's order to *A'*, "
9 the first lot came forth for *A'* "
26: 1 son of Kore, of the sons of *A'*. "
2Ch 5:12 all of them of *A'*, of Heman, "
20:14 a Levite of the sons of *A'*, came "
29:13 of the sons of *A'*; Zechariah, and "
30 words of David, and of *A'* the seer. "
35:15 the sons of *A'* were in their place, "
15 commandment of David, and *A'*, "
Ezr 2:41 the children of *A'*, an hundred "
3:10 the sons of *A'* with cymbals, "
Ne 2: 8 *A'* the keeper of the king's forest, "
7:44 The singers: the children of *A'*, "
11:17 the son of *A'*, was the principal "
22 Of the sons of *A'*, the singers were "
12:35 the son of Zaccur, the son of *A'*: "
12:46 the days of David and *A'* of old "
Ps 50:*title* A Psalm of *A'*. The mighty God, "
73:*title* A Psalm of *A'*. Truly God is good "
74:*title* Maschil of *A'*. O God, why hast "
75:*title* A Psalm or Song of *A'*. Unto thee, "
76:*title* A Psalm or Song of *A'*. In Judah "
77:*title* A Psalm of *A'*. I cried unto God "
78:*title* Maschil of *A'*. Give ear, O my "
79:*title* A Psalm of *A'*. O God, the "
80:*title* A Psalm of *A'*. Give ear, O "
81:*title* A Psalm of *A'*. Sing aloud "
82:*title* A Psalm of *A'*. God standeth in "
83:*title* A Song or Psalm of *A'*. Keep not "
Isa 36:22 Joah, the son of *A'*, the recorder, "

Asaph's (*a'-safs*)
Isa 36: 3 the scribe, and Joah, *A'* son, * 623

Asareel (*a-sar'e-el*)
1Ch 4:16 Ziph, and Ziphah, Tiria, and *A'*. 840

Asarelah (*as-a-re'-lah*) See also JESHARELAH.
1Ch 25: 2 Joseph, and Nethaniah, and *A'*. 841

Asa's (*a'-sahz*)
1Ki 15:14 nevertheless *A'* heart was perfect* 609

ascend See also ASCENDED; ASCENDETH; ASCENDING.
Jos 6: 5 and the people shall *a'* up *5927
Ps 24: 3 Who shall *a'* into the hill of the "
135: 7 He causeth the vapours to *a'* "
139: 8 If I *a'* up into heaven, "
Isa 14:13 I will *a'* into heaven, "
14 I will *a'* above the heights of the "
Jer 10:13 and he causeth the vapours to *a'* "
51:16 and he causeth the vapours to *a'* "
Eze 38: 9 Thou shalt *a'* and come like a "
Joh 6:62 ye shall see the Son of man *a'* up * 305
20:17 I *a'* unto my Father, and your "
Ro 10: 6 Who shall *a'* into heaven? "
Re 17: 8 shall *a'* out of the bottomless pit,* "

ascended
Ex 19:18 and the smoke thereof *a'* 5927
Nu 13:22 And they *a'* by the south, * "
Jos 8:20 the smoke of the city *a'* up "
21 the smoke of the city *a'*, "
10: 7 So Joshua *a'* from Gilgal, * "
15: 3 and *a'* up on the south side * "
J'g 13:20 that the angel of the Lord *a'* in "
20:40 flame of the city *a'* up to heaven,* "
Ps 68:18 Thou hast *a'* on high, "
Pr 30: 4 Who hath *a'* up into heaven, "
Joh 3:13 no man hath *a'* up to heaven, 305
20:17 for I am not yet *a'* to my Father: "
Ac 2:34 David is not *a'* into the heavens: "
25: 1 *a'* from Cæsarea to Jerusalem ** "
Eph 4: 8 When he *a'* up on high, "
9 (Now that he *a'*, what is it "
10 is the same also that *a'* up "
Re 8: 4 *a'* up before God out of the angel's "
11:12 they *a'* up to heaven in a cloud; * "

ascendeth
Re 11: 7 that *a'* out of the bottomless pit * 305
14:11 their torment *a'* up for ever * "

ascending
Ge 28:12 angels of God *a'* and descending 5927
1Sa 28:13 I saw gods *a'* out of the earth. * "
Lu 19:28 went before, *a'* up to Jerusalem. * 305
Joh 1:51 the angels of God *a'* and "
Re 7: 2 another angel *a'* from the east, * "

ascent
Nu 34: 4 to the *a'* of Akrbabim, 4608
2S 15:30 up by the *a'* of mount Olivet, "
1Ki 10: 5 and his *a'* by which he went up 5930
2Ch 9: 4 and his *a'* by which he went up 5944

ascribe See also ASCRIBED.
De 32: 3 *a'* ye greatness unto our God. 3051
Job 36: 3 *a'* righteousness to my Maker. 5414
Ps 68:34 *A'* ye strength unto God: "

ascribed
1Sa 18: 8 They have *a'* unto David 5414
8 to me they have *a'* but thousands: "

Asenath (*as'-e-nath*)
Ge 41:45 and he gave him to wife *A'* the 621
50 *A'* the daughter of Poti-pherah "
46:20 Manasseh and Ephraim, which *A'* "

Aser (*a'-sur*) See also ASHER.
Lu 2:36 of the tribe of *A'*: 768
Re 7: 6 Of the tribe of *A'* were sealed "

ash
Isa 44:14 he planteth an *a'*, and the rain * 766

ashamed
Ge 2:25 and were not *a'*. 954
Nu 12:14 should she not be *a'* seven days? 3637
J'g 3:25 they tarried till they were *a'*: 954
2Sa 10: 5 because the men were greatly *a'*: 3637
19: 3 as people being *a'* steal away "
2Ki 2:17 they urged him till he was *a'*, 954
8:11 until he was *a'*: and the man of "
1Ch 19: 5 the men were greatly *a'*. 3637
2Ch 30:15 and the Levites were *a'*, * "
Ezr 8:22 I was *a'* to require of the king 954
9: 6 I am *a'* and blush to lift up my face "
Job 6:20 they came thither, and were *a'*. *2659
11: 3 shall no man make thee *a'*? 3637
19: 3 ye are not *a'* that ye make 954
Ps 6:10 Let all mine enemies be *a'* ‡ "
10 them return and be *a'* suddenly. ‡ "
25: 2 I trust in thee: let me not be *a'*, ‡ 954
3 let none that wait on thee be *a'*: ‡ "
3 let them be *a'* which transgress ‡ "
20 let me not be *a'*; for I put ‡ "
31: 1 let me never be *a'*: ‡ "
17 Let me not be *a'*, O Lord; ‡ "
17 let the wicked be *a'*, ‡ "
34: 5 their faces were not *a'*. *2659
35:26 be *a'* and brought to confusion ‡ 954
37:19 shall not be *a'* in the evil time: ‡ "
40:14 Let them be *a'* and confounded ‡ "
69: 6 them that wait on thee,...be *a'* ‡ "
70: 2 Let them be *a'* and confounded ‡ "
74:21 let not the oppressed return *a'*: 3637
86:17 may see it, and be *a'*: ‡ 954
109:28 them be *a'*; but let thy servant ‡ "
119: 6 Then shall I not be *a'*, ‡ "
46 and will not be *a'*. ‡ "
78 Let the proud be *a'*; ‡ "
80 that I be not *a'*. ‡ "
116 let me not be *a'* of my hope. ‡ "
127: 5 they shall not be *a'*, ‡ "
Pr 12: 4 she that maketh *a'* is as rottenness ‡ "
Isa 1:29 For they shall be *a'* of the oaks ‡ "
20: 5 shall be afraid and *a'* of Ethiopia ‡ "
23: 4 Be thou *a'*, O Zidon: ‡ "
24:23 and the sun *a'*, ‡ "
26:11 be *a'* for their envy at the people; ‡ "

Isa 29:22 Jacob shall not now be *a*·, ‡ 954
30: 5 They were all *a*· of a people ‡ "
33: 9 Lebanon is *a*· and hewn down: 2659
41:11 shall be *a*· and confounded: ‡ 954
42:17 they shall be greatly *a*·, ‡ "
44: 9 that they may be *a*·. ‡ "
11 all his fellows shall be *a*·: ‡ "
11 they shall be *a*· together. ‡ "
45:16 shall be *a*·, and also confounded, ‡ "
17 shall not be *a*· nor confounded ‡ "
24 incensed against him shall be *a*·. ‡ "
49:23 shall not be *a*· that wait for me. ‡ "
50: 7 that I shall not be *a*·. ‡ "
54: 4 for thou shalt not be *a*·: ‡ "
65:13 but ye shall be *a*·: ‡ "
66: 5 they shall be *a*·. ‡ "
Jer 2:26 the thief is *a*· when he is found, ‡1322
26 so is the house of Israel *a*·; 954
36 thou also shalt be *a*· of Egypt, "
36 as thou wast *a*· of Assyria. "
3: 3 thou refusedst to be *a*·. 3637
6:15 Were they *a*· when they had ‡ 954
15 they were not at all *a*·, ‡ "
8: 9 The wise men are *a*·, ‡ "
12 Were they *a*· when they "
12 at all *a*·, neither could they blush: "
12:13 they shall be *a*· of your enemies ‡ "
14: 3 they were *a*· and confounded, ‡ "
4 the plowmen were *a*·, ‡ "
15: 9 hath been *a*· and confounded, ‡ "
17:13 all that forsake thee shall be *a*·, ‡ "
20:11 they shall be greatly *a*·; ‡ "
22:22 surely then shalt thou be *a*· ‡ "
31:19 I was *a*·, yea, even confounded ‡ "
48:13 And Moab shall be *a*· of Chemosh, "
13 house of Israel was *a*· of Beth-el "
50:12 she that bare you shall be *a*·: ‡2659
Eze 16:27 of the Philistines, which are *a*· 3637
61 remember thy ways, and be *a*·, "
32:30 they are *a*· of their might; 954
36:32 be *a*· and confounded for your own "
43:10 they may be *a*· of their iniquities: 3637
11 if they be *a*· of all that "
Ho 4:19 and they shall be *a*· ‡ 954
10: 6 Israel shall be *a*· of his own counsel. "
Joe 1:11 Be ye *a*·, O ye husbandmen; "
2:26, 27 My people shall never be *a*·. ‡ "
Mic 3: 7 the seers be *a*·, and the diviners ‡ "
Zep 3:11 In that day shalt thou not be *a*· ‡ "
Zec 9: 5 her expectation shall be *a*·; ‡ "
13: 4 the prophets shall be *a*· every one ‡ "
M'r 8:38 therefore shall be *a*· of me *1870*
38 shall the Son of man be *a*·, "
Lu 9:26 whosoever shall be *a*· of me "
26 of him shall the Son of man be *a*·. "
13:17 all his adversaries were *a*·: **2617*
16: 3 I cannot dig; to beg I am *a*·. *153*
Ro 1:16 am not *a*· of the gospel of Christ: *1870*
5: 5 hope maketh not *a*·; because **2617*
6:21 whereof ye are now *a*·? *1870*
9:33 believeth on him shall not be *a*. **2617*
10:11 on him shall not be *a*·. * "
2Co 7:14 I am not *a*·; * "
9: 4 we...should be *a*· in this same * "
10: 8 destruction, I should not be *a*·: * *153*
Ph'p 1:20 in nothing I shall be *a*·, "
2Th 3:14 with him, that he may be *a*·. *1788*
2Ti 1: 8 thou therefore *a*· of the testimony *1870*
12 nevertheless I am not *a*·: "
16 and was not *a*· of my chain: "
2:15 workman that needeth not to be *a*·, *422*
Tit 2: 8 the contrary part may be *a*·, *1788*
Heb 2:11 is not *a*· to call them brethren, *1870*
11:16 is not *a*· to be called their God: * "
1Pe 3:16 as of evildoers, they may be *a*· **2617*
4:16 a Christian, let him not be *a*·; *153*
1Jo 2:28 not be *a*· before him.

Ashan (*a'-shan*) See also COR-ASHAN.
Jos 15:42 Libnah, and Ether, and *A*·, 6228
19: 7 Ain, Remmon, and Ether, and *A*·; "
1Ch 4:32 Rimmon, and Tochen, and *A*·, five "
6:59 And *A*· with her suburbs, and "

Ashbea (*ash'-be-ah*)
1Ch 4:21 of the house of *A*·, 791

Ashbel (*ash'-bel*) See also ASHBELITES.
Ge 46:21 Becher, and *A*·, Gera, and Naaman, 788
Nu 26:38 of *A*·, the family of the Ashbelites: "
1Ch 8: 1 Bela his firstborn, *A*· the second, "

Ashbelites (*ash'-bel-ites*)
Nu 26:38 of Ashbel, the family of the *A*·: 789

Ashchenaz (*ash'-ke-naz*) See also ASHKENAZ.
1Ch 1: 6 sons of Gomer; *A*·, and Riphath, 813
Jer 51:27 kingdoms of Ararat, Minni, and *A*·; "

Ashdod (*ash'-dod*) See also ASHDODITES; AZOTUS.
Jos 11:22 only in Gaza, in Gath, and in *A*·, 795
15:46 lay near *A*·, with their villages: "
47 *A*· with her towns and her villages; "
1Sa 5: 1 brought it from Eben-ezer unto *A*·. "
3 of *A*· rose early on the morrow, "
5 the threshold of Dagon in *A*· "
6 was heavy upon them of *A*·, and "
6 even *A*· and the coasts thereof. "
7 when the men of *A*· saw that it "
6:17 for *A*· one, for Gaza one, for "
2Ch 26: 6 of *A*·, and built cities about *A*·, "
Ne 13:23 Jews that had married wives of *A*·, "
24 spake half in the speech of *A*·, "
Isa 20: 1 year that Tartan came unto *A*·, "
1 and fought against *A*·, and took it; "
Jer 25:20 and Ekron, and the remnant of *A*·, "
Am 1: 8 cut off the inhabitant from *A*·, "
3: 9 Publish in the palaces at *A*·, "
Zep 2: 4 shall drive out *A*· at the noonday. "
Zec 9: 6 And a bastard shall dwell in *A*·. "

Ashdodites (*ash'-dod-ites*) See also ASHDOTHITES.
Ne 4: 7 and the *A*·, heard that the walls 796

Ashdoth See ASHDOTH-PISGAH.

Ashdothites (*ash'-doth-ites*) See also ASHDODITES.
Jos. 13: 3 *A*·, the Eshkalonites, the Gittites, 796

Ashdoth-pisgah (*ash''-doth-piz'-gah*)
De 3:17 salt sea, under *A*· eastward. *798, 6449
Jos 12: 3 from the south, under *A*·: * "
13:20 And Beth-peor, and *A*·, and * "

Asher (*ash'-ur*) See also ASER; ASHERITES.
Ge 30:13 and she called his name *A*·. 836
35:26 Leah's handmaid; Gad, and *A*·: "
46:17 sons of *A*·; Jimnah, and Ishuah, "
49:20 Out of *A*· his bread shall be fat, "
Ex 1: 4 Dan, and Naphtali, Gad, and *A*·. "
Nu 1:13 Of *A*·; Pagiel the son of Ocran. "
40 children of *A*·, by their generations, "
41 of the tribe of *A*·, were forty and "
2:27 by him shall be the tribe of *A*·: "
27 captain of the children of *A*· shall "
7:72 prince of the children of *A*·, offered: "
10:26 tribe of the children of *A*· was "
13:13 of *A*·, Sethur the son of Michael. "
26:44 children of *A*· after their families: "
46 of the daughter of *A*· was Sarah. "
47 are the families of the sons of *A*· "
34:27 of *A*·, Ahihud the son of Shelomi. "
De 27:13 Reuben, Gad, and *A*·, and Zebulun, "
33:24 of *A*· he said, Let *A*· be blessed "
Jos 17: 7 coast of Manasseh was from *A*· to "
10 met together in *A*· on the north, "
11 Manasseh had in Issachar and in *A*· "
19:24 tribe of the children of *A*· according "
31 of the tribe of the children of *A*· "
34 reacheth to *A*· on the west side, "
21: 6 out of the tribe of *A*·, and out of "
30 of *A*·, Mishal with her suburbs, "
J'g 1:31 did *A*· drive out the inhabitants of "
5:17 *A*· continued on the sea shore, "
6:35 and he sent messengers unto *A*·, "
7:23 of *A*·, and out of all Manasseh, "
1Ki 4:16 son of Hushai was in *A*· and in "
1Ch 2: 2 Benjamin, Naphtali, Gad, and *A*·. "
6:62 out of the tribe of *A*·, and out of "
74 of *A*·; Mashal with her suburbs, "
7:30 sons of *A*·; Imnah, and Isuah, "
40 All these were the children of *A*·, "
12:36 of *A*·, such as went forth to battle, "
2Ch 30:11 divers of *A*· and Manasseh "
Eze 48: 2 the west side, a portion for *A*·. "
3 border of *A*·, from the east side, "
34 gate of *A*·, one gate of Naphtali. "

Asherites (*ash'-ur-ites*)
J'g 1:32 *A*· dwelt among the Canaanites, 843

ashes
Ge 18:27 which am but dust and *a*·: 665
Ex 9: 8 you handfuls of *a*· of the furnace, 6368
10 And they took *a*· of the furnace, "
27:3 pans to receive his *a*·, 1878
Le 1:16 by the place of the *a*·: 1880
4:12 where the *a*· are poured out, and "
12 where the *a*· are poured out shall "
6:10 take up the *a*· "
11 carry forth the *a*· "
Nu 4:13 And they shall take away the *a*· 1878
19: 9 the *a*· of the heifer, 665
10 he that gathereth the *a*· of "
17 they shall take of the *a*· of the 6083
2Sa 13:19 Tamar put *a*· on her head, 665
1Ki 13: 3 the *a*· that are upon it 1880
5 the *a*· poured out from the altar, * "
20:38 disguised himself with *a*· upon * 665
41 took the *a*· away from his face; "
2Ki 23: 4 the *a*· of them unto Beth-el. 6083
Es 4: 1 put on sackcloth with *a*·, 665
3 many lay in sackcloth and *a*·. "
Job 2: 8 he sat down among the *a*·. "
13:12 remembrances are like unto *a*·, "
30:19 I am become like dust and *a*·. "
42: 6 repent in dust and *a*·. "
Ps 102: 9 For I have eaten *a*· like bread, "
147:16 he scattereth the hoarfrost like *a*·. "
Isa 44:20 He feedeth on *a*·: "
58: 5 spread sackcloth and *a*· under him? "
61: 3 to give unto them beauty for *a*·, "
Jer 6:26 wallow thyself in *a*·: "
25:34 and wallow yourselves in the *a*·, ye "
31:40 and of the *a*·, and all the fields 1880
La 3:16 he hath covered me with *a*·. 665
Eze 27:30 wallow themselves in the *a*·: "
28:18 I will bring thee to *a*· "
Da 9: 3 with fasting, and sackcloth, and *a*·: "
Jon 3: 6 and sat in *a*·. "
Mal 4: 3 for they shall be *a*· "
M't 11:21 long ago in sackcloth and *a*·. 4700
Lu 10:13 sitting in sackcloth and *a*·. "
Heb 9:13 the *a*· of an heifer sprinkling the "
2Pe 2: 6 Sodom and Gomorrha into *a*· 5077

Ashima (*ash'-im-ah*)
2Ki 17:30 and the men of Hamath made *A*·, 807

Ashkelon (*ash'-ke-lon*) See also ASKELON; ESHKALONITES.
J'g 14:19 and he went down to *A*·, and slew 831
Jer 25:20 *A*·, and Azzah, and Ekron, "
47: 5 *A*· is cut off with the remnant "
7 *A*·, and against the sea shore? "
Am 1: 8 that holdeth the sceptre from *A*·, "
Zep 2: 4 Gaza shall be forsaken, and *A*· "
7 houses of *A*· shall they lie down "
Zec 9: 5 *A*· shall see it, and fear; "
5 and *A*· shall not be inhabited. "

Ashkenaz (*ash'-ke-naz*) See also ASHCHENAZ.
Ge 10: 3 sons of Gomer; *A*·, and Riphath, 813

Ashnah (*ash'-nah*)
Jos 15:33 Eshtaol, and Zoreah, and *A*·, 823
43 Jiphtah, and *A*·, and Nezib, "

Ashpenaz (*ash'-pe-naz*)
Da 1: 3 the king spake unto *A*· the master 828

Ashriel (*ash'-re-el*) See also ASRIEL.
1Ch 7:14 of Manasseh; *A*·, whom she bare: 845

Ashtaroth (*ash'-ta-roth*), See also ASHTERATHITE; ASHTEROTH; ASTORETH; ASTAROTH; BEESHTERAH.
Jos 9:10 king of Bashan, which was at *A*·. 6252
12: 4 that dwelt at *A*· and at Edrei, "
13:12 Og in Bashan, which reigned in *A*· "
31 half Gilead, and *A*·, and Edrei, "
J'g 2:13 the Lord, and served Baal and *A*·. "
10: 6 served Baalim, and *A*·, and the "
1Sa 7: 3 put away the strange gods and *A*· "
4 Israel did put away Baalim and *A*·, "
12:10 and have served Baalim and *A*·: "
31:10 put his armour in the house of *A*·; "
1Ch 6:71 and *A*· with her suburbs: "

Asherathite (*ash'-ter-a-thite*)
1Ch 11:44 Uzzia the *A*·, Shama and Jehiel 6254

Ashteroth (*ash'-te-roth*) See also ASHTAROTH.
Ge 14: 5 and smote the Rephaims in *A*· *6255

Ashteroth-Karnaim See ASHTEROTH and KARNAIM.

Ashtoreth (*ash'-to-reth*) See also ASHTAROTH.
1Ki 11: 5 Solomon went after *A*· the 6252
33 *A*· the goddess of the Sidonians, "
2Ki 23:13 for *A*· the abomination of the "

Ashur (*ash'-ur*) See also ASHURITES; ASSHUR; ASSUR; ASSYRIA.
1Ch 2:24 Hezron's wife bare him *A*· the 804
4: 5 *A*· the father of Tekoa had two "

Ashurites (*ash'-ur-ites*) See also ASSHURIM.
2Sa 2: 9 over the *A*·, and over Jezreel, 843
Eze 27: 6 the *A*· have made thy benches * "

Ashvath (*ash'-vath*)
1Ch 7:33 and *A*·. These are the children 6220

Asia (*a'-she-ah*)
Ac 2: 9 Pontus, and *A*·, *773*
6: 9 them of Cilicia, and of *A*·, "
16: 6 to preach the word in *A*·, "
19:10 all they which dwelt in *A*· "
22 stayed in *A*· for a season. "
26 but almost throughout all *A*·, "
27 all *A*· and the world worshippeth. "
31 certain of the chief of *A*·, ‡ *775*
20: 4 accompanied him into *A*· *773*
4 of *A*·, Tychicus and Trophimus. "
16 would not spend the time in *A*·: "
18 that I came into *A*·, "
21:27 the Jews which were of *A*·, "
24:18 certain Jews from *A*· "
27: 2 by the coasts of *A*·; "
1Co 16:19 The churches of *A*· salute you. "
2Co 1: 8 which came to us in *A*·, "
2Ti 1:15 all they which are in *A*· "
1Pe 1: 1 *A*· and Bithynia, "
Re 1: 4 seven churches which are in *A*·: "
11 seven churches which are in *A*·; * "

aside
Ex 3: 3 I will now turn *a*·, and see this
4 the Lord saw that he turned *a*·
32: 8 They have turned *a*· quickly out
Nu 5:12 If any man's wife go *a*·, 7847
19 if thou hast not gone *a*· "
20 if thou hast gone *a*· "
29 when a wife goeth *a*· "
22:23 and the ass turned *a*· 5186
De 5:32 ye shall not turn *a*· to the right
9:12 they are quickly turned *a*· out of
16 ye had turned *a*· quickly out of
11:16 ye turn *a*·, and serve other gods,
28 but turn *a*· out of the way
17:20 that he turn not *a*· from the
28:14 thou shalt not go *a*· from any 5493
31:29 corrupt yourselves, and turn *a*·
Jos 23: 6 that ye turn not *a*· therefrom
J'g 14: 8 he turned *a*· to see the carcase
19:12 We will not turn *a*· hither into
15 And they turned *a*· thither, to go
Ru 4: 1 Ho, such a one! turn *a*·, sit down
1 And he turned *a*·, and sat down,
1Sa 6:12 turned not *a*· to the right hand
8: 3 but turned *a*· after lucre, 5186
12:20 turn not *a*· from following the
21 turn ye not *a*·: for then
2Sa 2:21 Turn thee *a*· to thy right hand, or 5186
21 But Asahel would not turn *a*·
22 Turn thee *a*· from following me:
23 Howbeit he refused to turn *a*·:
3:27 And when...Joab took him *a*· in 5186
6:10 but David carried it *a*·
18:30 Turn *a*·, and stand here. 5437
30 And he turned *a*·, and stood still.
1Ki 15:45 turned not *a*· from any thing
20:39 behold, a man turned *a*·,
22:32 And they turned *a*· to fight
43 he turned not *a*· from it,
2Ki 4: 4 thou shalt set *a*· that which is 5265
22: 2 turned not *a*· to the right hand 5493
1Ch 13:13 but carried it *a*· into the house of 5186
Job 6:18 paths of their way are turned *a*·; 3943
Ps 14: 3 They are all gone *a*·, 5493
40: 4 nor such as turn *a*· to lies. 7847
78:57 were turned *a*· like a deceitful 2015
101: 3 the work of them that turn *a*·: 7750

Ps 125: 5 As for such as turn a· unto their 5186
Ca 1: 7 should I be as one that turneth a·*5844
6: 1 whither is thy beloved turned a·?*6437
Isa 10: 2 To turn a· the needy from 5186
29:21 and turn a· the just for a thing of "
30:11 turn a· out of the path, "
44:20 heart hath turned him a·, "
Jer 14: 8 a wayfaring man that turneth a· "
15: 5 who shall go a· to ask how thou 5493
La 3:11 He hath turned a· my ways, "
35 To turn a· the right of a man 5186
Am 2: 7 and turn a· the way of the meek: "
5:12 they turn a· the poor "
Mal 3: 5 and that turn a· the stranger "
M't 2:22 he turned a· into the parts of * 402
M'r 7: 8 laying a· the commandment of * 863
33 a· from the multitude, 2596, 2398
Lu 9:10 and went a· privately *5298
Joh 13: 4 and laid a· his garments; 5087
Ac 4:15 commanded them to go a· out of 565
23:19 went with him a· privately, and 402
26:31 when they were gone a·, they * "
1Ti 1: 6 turned a· unto vain jangling; 1824
5:15 some are already turned a· after "
Heb 12: 1 let us lay a· every weight, and 659
1Pe 2: 1 Wherefore laying a· all malice, * "

Asiel (a'-se'-el).
1Ch 4:35 of Seraiah, the son of A·, 6221

ask See also ASKED; ASKEST; ASKETH; ASKING.
Ge 32:29 thou dost a· after my name? 7592
34:12 A· me never so much dowry and "
Nu 27:21 who shall a· counsel for him *7592
De 4:32 a· now of the days that are past, "
32 a· from the one side of heaven * "
13:14 enquire, and make search, and a· 7592
32: 7 a· thy father, and he will shew "
Jos 4: 6 your children a· their fathers "
21 When your children shall a· "
15:18 she moved him to a· of her "
J'g 1:14 she moved him to a· of her "
18: 5 A· counsel, we pray thee, of God, "
1Sa 12:19 our sins this evil, to a· us a king. "
25: 8 A· thy young men, and they will "
28:16 Wherefore then dost thou a· of me, "
2Sa 14:18 thee, the thing that I shall a· thee. "
20:18 shall surely a· counsel at Abel; "
1Ki 2:16 I a· one petition of thee, "
20 the king said unto her, A· on, my "
22 why dost thou a· Abishag "
22 a· for him the kingdom also; "
3: 5 A· what I shall give thee. "
14: 5 cometh to a· a thing of thee for *1875
2Ki 2: 9 A· what I shall do for thee, 7592
2Ch 1: 7 A· what I shall give thee. "
20: 4 to a· help of the Lord: *1245
Job 12: 7 a· now the beasts, and they shall 7592
Ps 2: 8 A· of me, and I shall give thee "
Isa 7:11 A· thee a sign of the Lord "
11 a· it either in the depth, or in the "
12 Ahaz said, I will not a·, "
45:11 A· me of things to come "
58: 2 a· of me the ordinances of justice; "
Jer 6:16 and a· for the old paths, "
15: 5 who shall go aside to a· how thou "
18:13 A· ye now among the heathen, "
23:33 prophet, or a priest, shall a· thee, "
30: 6 A· ye now, and see "
38:14 I will a· thee a thing; "
48:19 a· him that fleeth, "
50: 5 They shall a· the way to Zion * "
La 4: 4 the young children a· bread, "
Da 6: 7 whosoever shall a· a petition of 1156
12 every man that shall a· a petition* "
Ho 4:12 My people a· counsel at their 7592
Hag 2:11 A· now the priests concerning "
Zec 10: 1 A· ye of the Lord rain "
M't 6: 8 have need of, before ye a· him. 154
7: 7 A·, and it shall be given you; "
9 if his son a· bread, will he give "
10 Or if he a· a fish, will he give him "
11 good things to them that a· him? "
14: 7 give her whatsoever she would a·. "
18:19 any thing that they shall a·, "
20:22 said, Ye know not what ye a·. "
21:22 whatsoever ye shall a· in prayer "
24 I also will a· you one thing, 2065
22:46 a· him any more questions. 1905
27:20 that they should a· Barabbas, 154
M'r 6:22 A· of me whatsoever thou wilt; "
23 Whatsoever thou shalt a· of me, "
24 unto her mother, What shall I a·? "
9:32 saying, and were afraid to a· him. 1905
10:38 Ye know not what ye a·: 154
11:29 I will also a· of you one question, 1905
12:34 And no man after that durst a· "
Lu 6: 9 I will a· you one thing; Is it "
30 away thy goods a· them not 523
9:45 they feared to a· him of that 2065
11: 9 A·, and it shall be given you; 154
11 If a son shall a· bread of any "
11 if he a· a fish will he for a fish * "
12 Or if he shall a· an egg, will 154
13 Holy Spirit to them that a· him? "
12:48 of him they will a· the more. "
19:31 if any man a· you, 2065
20: 3 I will also a· you one thing; "
40 they durst not a· him any 1905
22:68 And if I also a· you, 2065
Joh 1:19 from Jerusalem to a· him, Who "
9:21 he is of age; a· him: he shall "
23 his parents, He is of age; a· him. "
11:22 whatsoever thou wilt a· of God, 154
13:24 that he should a· who it should *4441
14:13 whatsoever ye shall a· in my 154
14 If ye shall a· any thing in my "
Joh 15: 7 abide in you, ye shall a· what * 154
16 whatsoever ye shall a· of the "
16:19 they were desirous to a· him, 2065
23 ye shall a· me nothing. "
23 Whatsoever ye shall a· the 154
24 a·, and ye shall receive, that your "
26 At that day ye shall a· in my name: "
30 that any man should a· thee: 2065
18:21 Why askest thou me? a· them 1905
21:12 none of the disciples durst a· *1833
Ac 3: 2 to a· alms of them that entered 154
10:29 I a· therefore for what intent 4441
1Co 14:35 let them a· their husbands at 1905
Eph 3:20 above all that we a· or think, 154
Jas 1: 5 you lack wisdom, let him a· of "
6 But let him a· in faith, nothing "
4: 2 ye have not, because ye a· not. "
3 Ye a·, and receive not, because "
3 ye a· amiss, that ye may "
1Jo 3:22 whatsoever we a·, we receive "
5:14 if we a· any thing according to his "
15 we a·, we know that we have the "
16 not unto death, he shall a·, and "

asked
Ge 24:47 And I a· her, and said, 7592
26: 7 the men of the place a· him of "
32:29 And Jacob a· him, "
37:15 and the man a· him, "
38:21 Then he a· the men of that place, "
40: 7 And he a· Pharaoh's officers "
43: 7 The man a· us straitly "
27 And he a· them of their welfare, "
44:19 My lord a· his servants, "
Ex 18: 7 they a· each other of their welfare; "
Jos 9:14 a· not counsel at the mouth of the "
19:50 gave him the city which he a·, "
J'g 1: 1 that the children of Israel a· "
5:25 a· water, and she gave him milk; "
6:29 And when they enquired and a·, 1245
13: 6 I a· him not whence he was, 7592
20:18 and a· counsel of God, "
23 and a· counsel of the Lord, "
1Sa 1:17 thy petition that thou hast a· "
20 I have a· him of the Lord. "
27 my petition which I a· of him: "
8:10 the people that a· of him a king. "
14:37 And Saul a· counsel of God, "
19:22 and he a· and said, "
20: 6 David earnestly a· leave "
28 a· leave of me to go to Beth-lehem: "
1Ki 3:10 Solomon had a· this thing. "
11 Because thou hast a· this thing, "
11 hast not a· for thyself long life; "
11 neither hast a· riches for thyself, "
11 hast a· the life of thine enemies; "
11 hast a· for thyself understanding "
13 thee that which thou hast not a·, "
10:13 whatsoever she a·, "
2Ki 2:10 Thou hast a· a hard thing: "
8: 6 when the king a· the woman, "
2Ch 1:11 thou hast not a· riches, "
11 neither yet hast a· long life; "
11 hast a· wisdom and knowledge "
9:12 all her desire, whatsoever she a·, "
Ezr 5: 9 Then a· we those elders, 7593
10 We a· their names also, "
Ne 1: 2 and I a· them concerning the Jews 7592
Job 21:29 Have ye not a· them that go by "
Ps 21: 4 He a· life of thee, "
105:40 The people a·, and he brought "
Isa 30: 2 have not a· at my mouth; "
41:28 when I a· of them, could answer * "
65: 1 I am sought of them that a· not "
Jer 36:17 they a· Baruch, "
37:17 the king a· him secretly in his "
38:27 the princes unto Jeremiah, and a· "
Da 2:10 a· such things at any magician, 7593
7:16 and a· him the truth of all this. 1156
M't 12:10 they a· him, saying, 1905
16:13 he a· his disciples, saying, Whom 2065
17:10 his disciples a· him, saying, 1905
22:23 is no resurrection, and a· him, "
35 them, which was a lawyer, a· him "
41 gathered together, Jesus a· them, "
27:11 and the governor a· him, saying, "
M'r 4:10 about him with the twelve a· of 2065
5: 9 And he a· him, What is thy name? 1905
6:25 unto the king, and a·, saying, 154
7: 5 Pharisees and scribes a· him, *1905
8: 5 he a· them, How many loaves "
23 he a· him if he saw ought. "
27 by the way he a· his disciples, "
9:11 And they a· him saying, Why say "
16 And he a· the scribes, What "
21 And he a· his father, How long is it "
28 his disciples a· him privately, Why "
33 being in the house he a· them, "
10: 2 Pharisees came to him, and a· him, "
10 disciples a· him again of the same "
17 and a· him, Good Master, what "
12:18 no resurrection; and they a· him, "
28 a· him, Which is the first "
13: 3 John and Andrew a· him privately, "
14:60 the midst, and a· Jesus, saying, "
61 Again the high priest a· him, and "
15: 2 And Pilate a· him, Art thou the "
4 And Pilate a· him again, saying, "
44 he a· him whether he had been "
Lu 1:63 he a· for a writing table, and wrote, 154
3:10 And the people a· him, saying, 1905
8: 9 And his disciples a· him, saying, "
30 And Jesus a· him, saying, What is "
9:18 and he a· them, saying, Whom say "
15:26 and a· what these things meant. *4441
18:18 a certain ruler a· him, saying, 1905
36 pass by, he a· what it meant. *4441
Lu 18:40 he was come near, he a· him, 1905
20:21 they a· him, saying, Master, we "
27 any resurrection; and they a· him, "
21: 7 And they a· him, saying, Master, "
22:64 and a· him, saying, Prophesy, who "
23: 3 And Pilate a· him, saying, Art "
6 he a· whether the man were a "
Joh 1:21 And they a· him, What then? 2065
25 they a· him, and said "
4:10 thou wouldest have a· of him, 154
5:12 Then a· they him, What man is 2065
9: 2 his disciples a· him, "
15 the Pharisees also a· him, "
19 a· them, saying, Is this your son, "
16:24 have ye a· nothing in my name: 154
18: 7 Then a· he them again, Whom 1905
19 The high priest then a· Jesus of 2065
Ac 1: 6 they a· of him, saying, Lord, wilt 1905
3: 3 to go into the temple a· an alms. 2065
4: 7 they a·, By what power, or by *4441
5:27 and the high priest a· them, 1905
10:18 and a· whether Simon, 4441
23:19 aside privately, and a· him, 2065
34 he a· of what province he was. 1905
25:20 I a· him whether he would go 3004
Ro 10:20 unto them that a· not after me. 1905

Askelon (as'-ke-lon) See also ASHKELON.
J'g 1:18 and A· with the coast thereof, 831
1Sa 6:17 for Gaza one, for A· one, for Gath "
2Sa 1:20 publish it not in the streets of A·; "

askest
J'g 13:18 Why a· thou thus after my name, 7592
Joh 4: 9 being a Jew, a· drink of me, 154
18:21 Why a· thou me? ask them which 1905

asketh
Ge 32:17 my brother meeteth thee, and a· 7592
Ex 13:14 when thy son a· thee "
De 6:20 thy son a· thee in time to come, "
Mic 7: 3 hands earnestly, the prince a·, "
3 and the judge a· for a reward; * "
M't 5:42 Give to him that a· thee, and 154
7: 8 every one that a· receiveth; "
Lu 6:30 Give to every man that a· of thee; "
11:10 every one that a· receiveth; "
Joh 16: 5 none of you a· me, 2065
1Pe 3:15 every man that a· you a reason 154

asking
1Sa 12:17 in a· you a king. 7592
1Ch 10:13 for a· counsel of one that had a * "
Ps 78:18 tempted God in their heart by a· "
Lu 2:46 them, and a· them questions. 1905
Joh 8: 7 So when they continued a· him, 2065
1Co 10:25 a· no question for conscience sake: 350
27 eat, a· no question for conscience "

asleep
J'g 4:21 he was fast a· and weary. *7290
1Sa 26:12 for they were all a·; 3463
Ca 7: 9 those that are a· to speak. "
Jon 1: 5 and he lay, and was fast a·. 7290
M't 8:24 but he was a·. 2518
26:40 and findeth them a·, * "
43 came and found them a· again: * "
M'k 4:38 a· on a pillow: and they awake "
14:40 he found them a· again, * "
Lu 8:23 as they sailed he fell a·: 879
Ac 7:60 when he had said this, he fell a·. 2837
1Co 15: 6 but some are fallen a·. "
18 also which are fallen a· in Christ "
1Th 4:13 concerning them which are a·, "
15 not prevent them which are a·. "
2Pe 3: 4 since the fathers fell a·, all things "

Asnah (as'-nah)
Ezr 2:50 The children of A·, the children 619

Asnapper (as-nap'-pur)
Ezr 4:10 great and noble A· brought over, 620

asp See also ASPS.
Isa 11: 8 shall play on the hole of the a·, 6620

Aspatha (as'-pa-thah)
Es 9: 7 and Dalphon, and A·, 630

asps
De 32:33 and the cruel venom of a·. 6620
Job 20:14 the gall of a· within him. "
16 He shall suck the poison of a·: "
Ro 3:13 poison of a· is under their lips: 785

Asriel (as'-re-el) See also ASHRIEL; ASRIELITES.
Nu 26:31 of A·, the family of the Asrielites: 844
Jos 17: 2 and for the children of A·, "

Asrielites (as'-re-el-ites)
Nu 26:31 of Asriel, the family of the A·: 845

ass See also ASS'S; ASSES.
Ge 22: 3 saddled his a·, and took two of 2543
5 Abide ye here with the a·; "
42:27 give his a· provender in the inn, "
44:13 laded every man his a·, "
49:14 Issachar is a strong a· couching "
Ex 4:20 set them upon an a·, "
13:13 every firstling of an a· thou shalt "
20:17 nor his ox, nor his a·, nor anything "
21:33 an ox or an a· fall therein; "
22: 4 whether it be ox, or a·, or sheep; "
9 for ox, for a·, for sheep, "
10 deliver unto his neighbour an a·, "
23: 4 thine enemy's ox or his a· going "
5 If thou see the a· of him that "
12 thine ox and thine a· may rest, "
34:20 firstling of an a· thou shalt redeem "
Nu 16:15 I have not taken one a· from them, "
22:21 and saddled his a·, and went with 860
22 Now he was riding upon his a·, "
23 the a· saw the angel of the Lord "
23 the a· turned aside out of the way "

Nu 22:23 Balaam smote the *a*, to turn her 860
25, 27 the *a* saw the angel of the Lord, "
27 he smote the *a* with a staff. "
28 Lord opened the mouth of the *a*, "
29 Balaam said unto the *a*, "
30 the *a* said unto Balaam, "
30 Am not I thine *a*, "
32 hast thou smitten thine *a* "
33 And the *a* saw me, and turned "
De 5:14 nor thine ox, nor thine *a*, 2543
21 his ox, or his *a*, or any thing "
22: 3 shalt thou do with his *a*; "
4 see thy brother's *a* or his ox fall "
10 plow with an ox and an *a* together "
28:31 thine *a* shall be violently taken "
Jos 6:21 ox, and sheep, and *a*, with the "
15:18 she lighted off her *a*; "
J'g 1:14 she lighted from off her *a*; "
6: 4 neither sheep, nor ox, nor *a*. "
10: 4 sons that rode on thirty *a* colts, 5895
12:14 threescore and ten *a* colts: "
15:15 found a new jawbone of an *a*, 2543
16 With the jawbone of an *a*, "
16 upon heaps, with the jaw of an *a* "
19:28 the man took her up upon an *a*, "
1Sa 12: 3 or whose *a* have I taken? "
15: 3 ox and sheep, camel and *a*. "
16:20 Jesse took an *a* laden with bread, "
25:20 she rode on the *a*, * "
23 hasted, and lighted off the *a*, * "
42 arose, and rode upon an *a*, "
2Sa 17:23 he saddled his *a*, and arose, "
19:26 I will saddle me an *a*, "
1Ki 2:40 Shimei arose, and saddled his *a*, "
13:13 Saddle me the *a*. "
13 So they saddled him the *a*: "
23 that he saddled for him the *a*, "
24 cast in the way, and the *a* stood by "
27 Saddle me the *a*. "
28 and the *a* and the lion standing "
28 the carcase, nor torn the *a*. "
29 laid it upon the *a*, "
2Ki 4:24 Then she saddled an *a*, 860
Job 6: 5 Doth the wild *a* bray 6501
24: 3 away the *a* of the fatherless, 2543
39: 5 hath sent out the wild *a* free? 6501
5 loosed the bands of the wild *a*? 6171
Pr 26: 3 a bridle for the *a*, 2543
Isa 1: 3 and the *a* his master's crib: "
32:20 the feet of the ox and the *a*. "
Jer 2:24 A wild *a* used to the wilderness, 6501
22:19 buried with the burial of an *a*, 2543
Hos 8: 9 a wild *a* alone by himself: 6501
Zec 9: 9 lowly, and riding upon an *a*, 2543
9 and upon a colt the foal of an *a*. 860
14:15 mule, of the camel, and of the *a*, 2543
M't 21: 2 ye shall find an *a* tied, *3688*
5 meek, and sitting upon an *a*, "
5 and a colt the foal of an *a*. *5268*
7 And brought the *a*, and the colt, *3688*
Lu 13:15 loose his ox or his *a* from the stall," "
14: 5 Which of you shall have an *a* or "
Joh 12:14 when he had found a young *a*, *3678*
2Pe 2:16 *a* speaking with man's voice *5268*

assault See also ASSAULTED.
Es 8:11 the people...that would *a* them, 6696
Ac 14: 5 when there was an *a* made **3730*

assaulted
Ac 17: 5 *a* the house of Jason, and sought *2186*

assay See also ASSAYED; ASSAYING.
Job 4: 2 If we *a* to commune with thee, 5254

assayed
De 4:34 hath God *a* to go and take him 5254
1Sa 17:39 and he *a* to go; for he had not 2974
Ac 9:26 *a* to join himself to the disciples: *3987*
16: 7 they *a* to go into Bithynia: *3985*

assaying
Heb 11:29 Egyptians *a* to do were *3984, 2983*

ass-colts See ASS and COLTS.

assemble See also ASSEMBLED; ASSEMBLING.
Nu 10: 3 shall *a* themselves to thee *3259
2Sa 20: 4 *A* me the men of Judah *2199
5 went to *a* the men of Judah: * "
Isa 11:12 shall *a* the outcasts of Israel, 622
45:20 *A* yourselves and come; 6908
48:14 All ye, *a* yourselves, and hear; "
Jer 4: 5 and say, *A* yourselves, and let us 622
8:14 do we sit still? *a* yourselves, "
12: 9 *a* all the beasts of the field, "
21: 4 and I will *a* them into the midst * "
Eze 11:17 and *a* you out of the countries "
39:17 *A* yourselves, and come; 6908
Da 11:10 *a* a multitude of great forces: 622
Ho 7:14 they *a* themselves for corn 1481
Joe 2:16 Gather the people,...*a* the elders, 6908
3:11 *A* yourselves, and come, all ye *5789
Am 3: 9 *A* yourselves upon the mountains 622
Mic 2:12 surely *a*, O Jacob, all of thee; "
4: 6 will I *a* her that halteth, "
Zep 3: 8 that I may *a* the kingdoms, 6908

assembled
Ex 38: 8 *a* at the door of the tabernacle †‡6633
Nu 1:18 they *a* all the congregation 6950
Jos 18: 1 congregation...*a* together at "
J'g 10:17 of Israel *a* themselves together, 622
1Sa 2:22 *a* at the door of the tabernacle *6633
14:20 all the people...*a* themselves, *2199
1Ki 8: 1 Solomon *a* the elders of Israel, 6950
2 *a* themselves unto king Solomon "
5 that were *a* unto him, 3259
12:21 he *a* all the house of Judah, 6950
1Ch 15: 4 David *a* the children of Aaron, * 622
28: 1 David *a* all the princes of Israel, 6950
2Ch 5: 2 Solomon *a* the elders of Israel, 6950
3 all the men of Israel *a* themselves "
6 were *a* unto him before the ark, 3259
20:26 they *a* themselves in the valley 6950
30:13 *a* at Jerusalem much people, 622
Ezr 9: 4 Then were *a* unto me every one "
10: 1 there *a* unto him...a very great *6908
Ne 9: 1 the children of Israel were *a* 622
Es 9:18 that were at Shushan *a* together 6950
Ps 48: 4 kings were *a*, they passed by 3259
Isa 43: 9 and let the people be *a*: 622
Jer 5: 7 and *a* themselves by troops 1413
Eze 38: 7 company that are *a* unto thee, 6950
Da 6: 6 presidents and princes *a* together 7284
11 these men *a*, and found Daniel "
15 Then these men *a* unto the king, "
M't 26: 3 *a* together the chief priests, **4863*
57 scribes and the elders were *a*. * "
28:12 they were *a* with the elders, "
M'r 14:53 were *a* all the chief priests, **4905*
Joh 20:19 where the disciples were *a* **4863*
Ac 1: 4 And being *a* together with them, *4871*
4:31 when they were *a* together; **4863*
11:26 *a* themselves with the church, * "
15:25 being *a* with one accord, **1096*

assemblies
Ps 86:14 and the *a* of violent men *5712
Ec 12:11 fastened by the masters of *a*, 627
Isa 1:13 calling of *a*, I cannot away with; 4744
4: 5 her *a*, a cloud of smoke by day, "
Eze 44:24 my statutes in all mine *a*; *4150
Am 5:21 not smell in your solemn *a*. 6116

assembling
Ex 38: 8 glasses of the women *a*, †‡6633
Heb 10:25 the *a* of ourselves together, *‡1997*

assembly See also ASSEMBLIES.
Ge 49: 6 into their secret; unto their *a*, 6951
Ex 12: 6 *a* of the congregation of Israel "
16: 3 kill this whole *a* with hunger. "
Le 4:13 be hid from the eyes of the *a*, "
8: 4 the *a* was gathered together *5712
23:36 it is a solemn *a*; 6116
Nu 8: 9 thou shalt gather the whole *a* *5712
10: 2 the calling of the *a*, and for the * "
3 *a* shall assemble themselves to * "
14: 5 on their faces before all the *a* 6951
16: 2 princes of the *a*, famous *5712
20: 6 went from the presence of the *a* 6951
8 gather thou the *a* together, *5712
29:35 ye shall have a solemn *a*: 6116
De 5:22 the Lord spake unto all your *a* 6951
9:10 fire in the day of the *a*. "
10: 4 of the fire, in the day of the *a* "
16: 8 a solemn *a* to the Lord thy God: 6116
18:16 Horeb in the day of the *a*, 6951
J'g 20: 2 themselves in the *a* of the people, "
21: 8 from Jabesh-gilead to the *a*. "
1Sa 17:47 this *a* shall know that the Lord "
2Ki 10:20 Proclaim a solemn *a* for Baal. 6116
2Ch 7: 9 they made a solemn *a*: "
30:23 the whole *a* took counsel *6951
Ne 5: 7 And I set a great *a* against them. 6952
8:18 the eighth day was a solemn *a*, 6116
Ps 22:16 *a* of the wicked have inclosed me: 5712
89: 7 to be feared in the *a* of the saints, *5475
107:32 and praise him in the *a* of the *4186
111: 1 in the *a* of the upright, *5475
Pr 5:14 midst of the congregation and *a*. 5712
Jer 6:11 the *a* of young men together: 5475
9: 2 an *a* of treacherous men. 6116
15:17 I sat not in the *a* of the mockers, 5475
26:17 spake to all the *a* of the people, 6951
50: 9 Babylon an *a* of great nations, "
La 1:15 he hath called an *a* against me, 4150
2: 6 destroyed his places of the *a*: "
Eze 13: 9 not be in the *a* of my people, *5475
23:24 and with an *a* of people, 6951
Joe 1:14 call a solemn *a*, gather the elders 6116
2:15 sanctify a fast, call a solemn *a*: "
Zep 3:18 are sorrowful for the solemn *a*, 4150
Ac 19:32 for the *a* was confused; *1577*
39 determined in a lawful *a*. "
41 thus spoken, he dismissed the *a*. "
Heb 12:23 *a* and church of the firstborn, *3831*
Jas 2: 2 there come unto your *a* a man **4864*

assent See also ASSENTED.
2Ch 18:12 good to the king with one *a*; *6310

assented
Ac 24: 9 And the Jews also *a*, saying **4934*

ass's
Ge 49:11 his *a* colt unto the choice vine; 860
2Ki 6:25 an *a* head was sold for fourscore 2543
Job 11:12 man be born like a wild *a* colt. 6501
Joh 12:15 King cometh, sitting on an *a* colt. *3688*

asses
Ge 12:16 he *a*, and menservants, 2543
16 and maidservants, and she *a*, 860
24:35 maidservants, and camels, and *a*: 2543
30:43 menservants, and camels, and *a*. "
32: 5 I have oxen, and *a*, flocks, "
15 twenty she *a*, and ten foals. 860
34:28 their oxen, and their *a*, 2543
36:24 as he fed the *a* of Zibeon "
42:26 they laded their *a* with the corn, "
43:18 take us for bondmen, and our *a*. "
24 he gave their *a* provender. "
44: 3 sent away, they and their *a*. "
45:23 ten *a* laden with the good things "
23 she *a* laden with corn and bread 860
47:17 herds, and for the *a*: 2543
Ex 9: 3 upon the horses, upon the *a*, "
Nu 31:28 of the beeves, and of the *a*, "
30 of the *a*, and of the flocks, "
Nu 31:34 threescore and one thousand *a*, 2543
39 And the *a* were thirty thousand "
45 thousand *a* and five hundred, "
Jos 7:24 his oxen, and his *a*, "
9: 4 took old sacks upon their *a*, "
J'g 5:10 speak, ye that ride on white *a*, 860
19: 3 with him, and a couple of *a*: 2543
10 with him two *a* saddled, "
19 straw and provender for our *a*; "
21 gave provender unto the *a*: "
1Sa 8:16 goodliest young men, and your *a*, "
9: 3 *a* of Kish, Saul's father were lost. 860
3 arise, go seek the *a*. "
5 leave caring for the *a*, "
20 And as for thine *a* that were lost "
10: 2 The *a* which thou wentest to seek "
2 hath left the care of the *a*, "
14 And he said, To seek the *a*: "
16 plainly that the *a* were found. "
22:19 oxen, and *a*, and sheep, 2543
25:18 laid them on *a*. "
27: 9 oxen, and the *a*, and the camels, "
2Sa 16: 1 with a couple of *a* saddled, "
2 The *a* be for the king's household "
2Ki 4:22 the young men, and one of the *a*, 860
7: 7 their horses, and their *a*, 2543
10 horses tied, and *a* tied, "
1Ch 5:21 and of *a* two thousand, "
12:40 brought bread on *a*, "
27:30 and over the *a* was Jehdeiah 860
2Ch 28:15 all the feeble of them upon *a*, 2543
Ezr 2:67 *a*, six thousand seven hundred "
Ne 7:69 seven hundred and twenty *a*. "
13:15 bringing in sheaves, and lading *a*; "
Job 1: 3 five hundred she *a*, 860
14 and the *a* feeding beside them "
24: 5 as wild *a* in the desert, 6501
42:12 a thousand she *a*. 860
Ps 104:11 the wild *a* quench their thirst. 6501
Isa 21: 7 a chariot of *a*, and a chariot of 2543
30: 6 upon the shoulders of young *a*, 5895
24 the young *a* that ear the ground "
32:14 joy of wild *a*, a pasture of flocks; 6501
Jer 14: 6 *a* did stand in the high places, "
Eze 23:20 whose flesh is as the flesh of *a*, 2543
Da 5:21 his dwelling was with the wild *a*: 6167

Asshur (*ash'-ur*) See also ASHUR; ASSUR; ASSYRIA.
Ge 10:11 Out of that land went forth *A*, *804
22 Elam, and *A*, and Arphaxad, and "
Nu 24:22 *A* shall carry thee away captive. "
24 afflict *A*, and shall afflict Eber, "
1Ch 1:17 The sons of Shem; Elam, and *A*, "
Eze 27:23 the merchants of Sheba, *A*, and "
32:22 *A* is there and all her company: "
Hos 14: 3 *A* shall not save us; we will not "

Asshurim (*ash'-u-rim*) See also ASHURITES.
Ge 25: 3 the sons of Dedan were *A*, and 805

assigned
Ge 47:22 priests had a portion *a* them *
Jos 20: 8 they *a* Bezer in the wilderness 5414
2Sa 11:16 that he *a* Uriah unto a place

Assir (*as'-sur*)
Ex 6:24 *A*, and Elkanah, and Abiasaph: 617
1Ch 3:17 Jeconiah; *A*, Salathiel his son, * "
6:22 Korah his son, *A* his son, "
23 Ebiasaph his son, and *A* his son, "
37 The son of Tahath, the son of *A*, "

assist
Ro 16: 2 and that ye *a* her in whatsoever *3936*

associate
Isa 8: 9 *A* yourselves, O ye people, *7489

Assos (*as'-sos*)
Ac 20:13 sailed unto *A*, there intending to *789*
14 he met with us at *A*. "

assuage See ASSWAGE.

Assur (*as'-sur*) See also ASSHUR.
Ezr 4: 2 days of Esar-haddon king of *A*, * 804
Ps 83: 8 *A* also is joined with them: they* "

assurance
De 28:66 shalt have none *a* of thy life: 539
Isa 32:17 quietness and *a* for ever. * 983
Ac 17:31 he hath given *a* unto all men, *4102*
Col 2: 2 of the full *a* of understanding, *4136*
1Th 1: 5 and in much *a*; as ye know "
He 6:11 the full *a* of hope unto the end: * "
10:22 in full *a* of faith, having our * "

assure See also ASSURED.
1Jo 3:19 and shall *a* our hearts before him. *3982*

assured
Le 27:19 and it shall be *a* to him. 6966
Jer 14:13 *a* peace in this place. 571
2Ti 3:14 and hast been *a* of, *4104*

assuredly
1Sa 28: 1 know thou *a*, that thou shalt go 3045
1Ki 1:13 *A* Solomon thy son shall reign 3588
17, 30 saying, *A* Solomon thy son
Jer 32:41 *a* with my whole heart 571
38:17 wilt *a* go forth unto the king *3318
49:12 of the cup have *a* drunken; 8354
Ac 2:36 house of Israel know *a*, *806*
16:10 *a* gathering that the Lord had **4822*

asswage See ASSWAGED.
Job 16: 5 my lips should *a* your grief *2820

asswaged
Ge 8: 1 and the waters *a*; *7918
Job 16: 6 my grief is not *a*: *2820

Assyria (*as-sir'-e-ah*) See also ASSHUR; ASSYRIAN.
Ge 2:14 which goeth toward the east of *A*·. 804
25:18 Egypt, as thou goest toward *A*·: "
2Ki 15:19 Pul the king of *A*· came against "
20 of silver, to give to the king of *A*·. "
20 So the king of *A*· turned back, "
29 came Tiglath-pileser king of *A*·, "
29 and carried them captive to *A*·. "
16: 7 to Tiglath-pileser king of *A*·, "
8 for a present to the king of *A*·. "
9 the king of *A*· hearkened unto him: "
9 of *A*· went up against Damascus, "
10 to meet Tiglath-pileser king of *A*·, "
18 of the Lord for the king of *A*·. "
17: 3 came up Shalmaneser king of *A*·; "
4 the king of *A*· found conspiracy "
4 brought no present to the king of *A*·," "
4 therefore the king of *A*· shut him up," "
5 Then the king of *A*· came up "
6 the king of *A*· took Samaria, "
6 and carried Israel away into *A*·, "
23 away out of their own land to *A*· "
24 the king of *A*· brought men from "
26 they spake to the king of *A*·, "
27 Then the king of *A*· commanded, "
18: 7 he rebelled against the king of *A*·, "
9 Shalmaneser king of *A*· came up "
11 And the king of *A*· did carry away "
11 did carry away Israel unto *A*·, "
13 did Sennacherib king of *A*· come "
14 sent to the king of *A*· to Lachish, "
14 king of *A*· appointed unto Hezekiah "
16 and gave it to the king of *A*·. "
17 the king of *A*· sent Tartan and "
19 the great king, the king of *A*·, "
23 pledges to my lord the king of *A*·, "
28 of the great king, the king of *A*·: "
30 into the hand of the king of *A*·. "
31 for thus saith the king of *A*·, "
33 out of the hand of the king of *A*·? "
19: 4 whom the king of *A*· his master "
6 the servants of the king of *A*· have "
8 and found the king of *A*· warring "
10 into the hand of the king of *A*·. "
11 what the kings of *A*· have done "
17 the kings of *A*· have destroyed the "
20 against Sennacherib king of *A*· I "
32 Lord concerning the king of *A*·, "
36 Sennacherib king of *A*· departed, "
20: 6 out of the hand of the king of *A*·; "
23:29 went up against the king of *A*· "
1Ch 5: 6 whom Tilgath-pilneser king of *A*· "
26 up the spirit of Pul king of *A*·, "
26 spirit of Tilgath-pilneser king of *A*·," "
2Ch 28:16 Ahaz send unto the kings of *A*· to "
20 Tilgath-pilneser king of *A*· came "
21 and gave it unto the king of *A*·: "
30: 6 out of the hand of the kings of *A*·. "
32: 1 Sennacherib king of *A*· came, "
4 Why should the kings of *A*· come, "
7 nor dismayed for the king of *A*·, "
9 did Sennacherib king of *A*· send "
10 Thus saith Sennacherib king of *A*·, "
11 out of the hand of the king of *A*·? "
21 in the camp of the king of *A*·. "
22 hand of Sennacherib the king of *A*·, "
33:11 of the host of the king of *A*·, "
Ezr 6:22 turned the heart of the king of *A*· "
Ne 9:32 since the time of the kings of *A*· "
Isa 7:17 from Judah; even the king of *A*·. "
18 the bee that is in the land of *A*·. "
20 beyond the river, by the king of *A*·. "
8: 4 taken away before the king of *A*·. "
7 the king of *A*·, and all his glory: "
10:12 of the stout heart of the king of *A*·, "
11:11 which shall be left, from *A*·, and "
16 which shall be left, from *A*·; like as "
19:23 a highway out of Egypt to *A*·, "
23 and the Egyptian into *A*·, and the "
24 the third with Egypt and with *A*·, "
25 and *A*· the work of my hands, "
20: 1 Sargon the king of *A*· sent him,) "
4 So shall the king of *A*· lead away "
6 be delivered from the king of *A*·: "
27:13 ready to perish in the land of *A*·, "
36: 1 that Sennacherib king of *A*· came "
2 the king of *A*· sent Rabshakeh "
4 the king of *A*·, What confidence "
8 thee, to my master the king of *A*·, "
13 of the great king, the king of *A*·. "
15 into the hand of the king of *A*·. "
16 for thus saith the king of *A*·, "
18 out of the hand of the king of *A*·? "
37: 4 whom the king of *A*· his master hath "
6 the servants of the king of *A*· have "
8 and found the king of *A*· warring "
10 into the hand of the king of *A*·. "
11 what the kings of *A*· have done "
18 the kings of *A*· have laid waste all "
21 me against Sennacherib king of *A*·: "
33 Lord concerning the king of *A*·, "
37 Sennacherib king of *A*· departed, "
38: 6 out of the hand of the king of *A*·: "
Jer 2:18 hast thou to do in the way of *A*·, "
36 Egypt, as thou wast ashamed of *A*·. "
50:17 the king of *A*· hath devoured him; "
18 as I have punished the king of *A*·. "
Eze 23: 7 that were the chosen men of *A*·, "
Ho 7:11 they called to Egypt, they go of *A*·. "
8: 9 For they are gone up to *A*·, a wild "
9: 3 they shall eat unclean things in *A*·. "
10: 6 It shall be also carried unto *A*· "
11:11 as a dove out of the land of *A*·: "
Mic 5: 6 they shall waste the land of *A*· "
7:12 shall come even to thee from *A*·, "
Na 3:18 shepherds slumber, O king of *A*·: 804
Zep 2:13 against the north, and destroy *A*·; "
Zec 10:10 Egypt, and gather them out of *A*·; "
11 pride of *A*· shall be brought down, "

Assyrian (*as-sir'-e'-un*) See also ASSYRIANS.
Isa 10: 5 O *A*·, the rod of mine anger, 804
24 in Zion, be not afraid of the *A*·: "
14:25 I will break the *A*· in my land, "
19:23 and the *A*· shall come into Egypt, "
23:13 till the *A*· founded it for them that "
30:31 shall the *A*· be beaten down, "
31: 8 shall the *A*· fall with the sword, "
52: 4 *A*· oppressed them without cause. "
Eze 31: 3 the *A*· was a cedar in Lebanon with "
Ho 5:13 then went Ephraim to the *A*·, * "
11: 5 but the *A*· shall be his king, "
Mic 5: 5 the *A*· shall come into our land: "
6 thus shall he deliver us from the *A*·," "

Assyrians (*as-sir'-e-uns*)
2Ki 19:35 and smote in the camp of the *A*· 804
Isa 19:23 shall serve with the *A*·. "
37:36 and smote in the camp of the *A*· "
La 5: 6 and to the *A*·, to be satisfied with "
Eze 16:28 the whore also with the *A*·, 1121, "
23: 5 her lovers, on the *A*· her neighbours, "
9 into the hand of the *A*·, upon 1121, "
12 upon the *A*· her neighbours, "
23 and Koa, and all the *A*· with them: "
Ho 12: 1 do make a covenant with the *A*·, * "

Astaroth (*as'-ta-roth*) See also ASHTAROTH.
De 1: 4 king of Bashan, which dwelt at *A*· 6252

astonied See also ASTONISHED.
Ezr 9: 3 of my beard, and sat down *a*·. ‡8074
4 sat *a*· until the evening sacrifice. ‡ "
Job 17: 8 upright men shall be *a*· at this, ‡ "
18:20 that come after him shall be *a*· ‡ "
Isa 52:14 As many were *a*· at thee; ‡ "
Jer 14: 9 shouldest thou be as a man *a*·, ‡1724
Eze 4:17 *a*· one with another, and ‡8074
Da 3:24 Nebuchadnezzar the king was *a*·, ‡8429
4:19 Daniel,....was *a*· for one hour. ‡8075
5: 9 in him, and his lords were *a*·. *7672

astonished See also ASTONIED.
Le 26:32 and your enemies...shall be *a*· 8074
1Ki 9: 8 passeth by it shall be *a*·, "
Job 21: 5 Mark me, and be *a*·, and lay your "
26:11 and are *a*· at his reproof. 8539
Jer 2:12 Be *a*·, O ye heavens, at this, 8074
4: 9 and the priests shall be *a*·, "
18:16 that passeth thereby shall be *a*·, "
19: 8 that passeth thereby shall be *a*· "
49:17 that goeth by it shall be *a*·, "
50:13 that goeth by Babylon shall be *a*·, "
Eze 3:15 remained there *a*· among them * "
26:16 every moment, and be *a*· at thee. "
27:35 inhabitants of the isles shall be *a*· "
28:19 the people shall be *a*· at thee: "
Da 8:27 and I was *a*· at the vision, "
M't 7:28 the people were *a*· at his doctrine: *1605*
13:54 insomuch that they were *a*·, "
22:33 they were *a*· at his doctrine. "
M'r 1:22 they were *a*· at his doctrine: "
5:42 *a*· with a great astonishment. **1839*
6: 2 many hearing him were *a*·, *1605*
7:37 were beyond measure *a*·, "
10:24 disciples were *a*· at his words. **2284*
26 they were *a*· out of measure, *1605*
11:18 the people was *a*· at his doctrine. "
Lu 2:47 were *a*· at his understanding **1839*
4:32 they were *a*· at his doctrine: *1605*
5: 9 For he was *a*·, and all that **4023, 2285*
8:56 her parents were *a*·: **1839*
24:22 made us *a*·, which were early * "
Ac 9: 6 And he trembling and *a*· said, **2284*
10:45 were *a*·, as many as came with **1839*
12:16 saw him, they were *a*·. * "
13:12 *a*· at the doctrine of the Lord. *1605*

astonishment
De 28:28 and *a*· of heart: 8541
37 thou shalt become an *a*·, 8047
2Ch 7:21 shall be an *a*· to every one *8074
29: 8 to trouble, to *a*·, and to hissing, 8047
Ps 60: 3 made us to drink the wine of *a*·. *8653
Jer 8:21 *a*· hath taken hold on me. 8047
25: 9 make them an *a*·, and an hissing, "
11 desolation, and an *a*·; "
18 a desolation, an *a*·, an hissing, "
29:18 a curse, and an *a*·, "
42:18 execration, and an *a*·, "
44:12 an *a*·, and a curse, "
22 desolation, and an *a*·, "
51:37 an *a*·, and an hissing, "
41 Babylon become an *a*·. * "
Eze 4:16 water by measure, and with *a*·: 8078
5:15 instruction and an *a*· 8047
12:19 and drink their water with *a*·, 8078
23:33 with the cup of *a*· and desolation, 8047
Zec 12: 4 smite every horse with *a*·, 8541
M'r 5:42 astonished with a great *a*·. **1611*

astray
Ex 23: 4 enemy's ox or his ass going *a*·, 8582
De 22: 1 not see thy brother's ox...go *a*·, 5080
Ps 58: 3 they go *a*· as soon as they be born, 8582
119:67 Before I was afflicted I went *a*·: 7683
176 I have gone *a*· like a lost sheep; 8582
Pr 5:23 of his folly he shall go *a*·. 7686
7:25 go not *a*· in her paths. 8582
28:10 causeth the righteous to go *a*· 7686
Isa 53: 6 All we like sheep have gone *a*·; 8582
Jer 50: 6 have caused them to go *a*·, "
Eze 14:11 Israel may go no more *a*· from me, "
44:10 when Israel went *a*·, "
10 which went *a*· away from me "
Eze 44:15 the children of Israel went *a*·, 8582
48:11 which went not *a*· "
11 when the children of Israel went *a*·, "
11 as the Levites went *a*·. "
M't 18:12 and one of them be gone *a*·, *4105*
12 and seeketh that which is gone *a*·? "
13 ninety and nine which went not *a*·. "
1Pe 2:25 ye were as sheep going *a*·; "
2Pe 2:15 and are gone *a*·, following the way "

astrologer See also ASTROLOGERS.
Da 2:10 things at any magician, or *a*·, * 826

astrologers.
Isa 47:13 now the *a*·, the stargazers, 1895, 8064
Da 1:20 *a*· that were in all his realm, * 825
2: 2 the magicians, and the *a*·, * "
27 cannot the wise men, the *a*·, * 826
4: 7 came in the magicians, the *a*·, * "
5: 7 cried aloud to bring in the *a*·, * "
11 master of the magicians, *a*·, * "
15 the *a*·, have been brought in * "

asunder
Le 1:17 shall not divide it *a*·:
5: 8 his neck, but shall not divide it *a*·:
Nu 16:31 the ground clave *a*· that was
2Ki 2:11 and parted them both *a*·; 996
Job 16:12 but he hath broken me *a*·: he hath
13 about, he cleaveth my reins *a*·,
Ps 2: 3 Let us break their bands *a*·, and
129: 4 he hath cut *a*· the cords of the
Jer 50:23 hammer of the whole earth cut *a*·
Eze 30:16 No shall be rent *a*·, *
Hab 3: 6 and drove *a*· the nations;
Zec 11:10 and cut it *a*·, that I might break
14 Then I cut *a*· mine other staff,
M't 19: 6 together, let not man put *a*·. *5563*
24:51 shall cut him *a*·, and appoint him *1371*
M'r 5: 4 had been plucked *a*· by him, *1288*
10: 9 let not man put *a*·. *5563*
Ac 1:18 he burst *a*· in the midst, *2997*
15:39 they departed *a*· one from the *673*
Heb 4:12 even to the dividing *a*· of soul and *
11:37 they were sawn *a*·, were tempted, *4249*

Asuppim
1Ch 26:15 to his sons, the house of *A*·. * 624
17 and toward *A*· two and two. * "

Asyncritus (*a-sin'-cri-tus*).
Ro 16:14 Salute *A*·, Phlegon, Hermas, *799*

at See also THEREAT.
Ge 3:24 and he placed *a*· the east of the
4: 7 doest not well, sin lieth *a*· the
6: 6 and it grieved him *a*· his heart. 413
8: 6 And it came to pass *a*· the end of
9: 5 *a*· the hand of every beast will I
5 require it, and *a*· the hand of man;
5 *a*· the hand of every man's brother
13: 3 where his tent had been *a*· the
4 he had made there *a*· the first:
14:17 *a*· the valley of Shaveh, which is 413
17:21 unto thee *a*· this set time in the
18:14 *A*· the time appointed I will
19: 1 angels to Sodom *a*· even; and Lot
6 And lot went out *a*· the door unto*
11 that were *a*· the door of the house
20:13 *a*· every place whither we shall 413
21: 2 *a*· the set time of which God had
22 And it came to pass *a*· that time,
32 Thus they made a covenant *a*·
22:19 and Abraham dwelt *a*· Beer-sheba.
23:10 that went in *a*· the gate of his city,
18 that went in *a*· the gate of his city,
24:11 by a well of water *a*· the time of
21 And the man wondering *a*· her *
30 stood by the camels *a*· the well. 5921
55 with us a few days, *a*· the least ten; 176
57 damsel, and inquire *a*· her mouth.
63 in the field *a*· the eventide:
25:32 Behold, I am *a*· the point to die:
26: 8 looked out *a*· a window, and 1157
27:41 for my father are *a*· hand; 7126
28:19 city was called Luz *a*· the first.
31:10 And it came to pass *a*· the time
33:10 receive my present *a*· my hand:
19 tent, *a*· the hand of the children
38: 1 it came to pass *a*· that time, that
5 and he was *a*· Chezib, when she
11 Remain a widow *a*· thy father's *
41: 1 it came to pass *a*· the end of two
21 ill favored, as *a*· the beginning.
43:16 shall dine with me *a*· noon.
18 in our sacks *a*· the first time
19 communed with him *a*· the door
20 came indeed down *a*· the first time
25 against Joseph came *a*· noon:
33 men marvelled one *a*· another. * 413
44:12 began *a*· the eldest, and left *a*· the
45: 3 they were troubled *a*· his presence.
48: 3 appeared unto me *a*· Luz in the
49:13 Zebulun shall dwell *a*· the haven
19 but he shall overcome *a*· the last.*
23 and shot *a*· him, and hated him:
27 the prey, and *a*· night he shall
Ex 2: 5 wash herself *a*· the river; and her 5921
4:25 of her son, and cast it *a*· his feet,
5:23 thou delivered the people *a*· all.
8:32 hardened his heart *a*· this time *
9:14 For I will *a*· this time send all my*
12: 9 raw, nor sodden *a*· all with water,
18 fourteenth day of the month, *a*· even,
18 twentieth day of the month *a*· even.
22 shall go out *a*· the door of his *
29 *a*· midnight the Lord smote all
41 it came to pass *a*· the end of the
16: 6 *A*· even, then ye shall know that

Ex 16:12 A' even ye shall eat flesh, and in 996
13 it came to pass, that a' ever the
18: 5 he encamped a' the mount of God:
22 judge the people a' all seasons:
26 judged the people a' all seasons:
19:15 third day: come not a' your wives.* 413
17 and they stood a' the nether part
22:23 in any wise, and they cry a' all
26 If thou a' all take thy neighbour's
28: 7 joined a' the two edges thereof; * 413
14 chains of pure gold a' the ends; *
22 chains a' the ends of wreathen *
29:39 lamb thou shalt offer a' even: 996
41 thou shalt offer a' even, and shalt "
42 a' the door of the tabernacle of
30: 8 Aaron lighteth the lamps a' even, 996
32: 4 received them a' their hand, and
33: 8 stood every man a' his tent door,
9 stood a' the door of the tabernacle,
10 stand a' the tabernacle door:
34:22 of ingathering a' the year's end,
35:15 for the door a' the entering in of
36:29 together a' the head thereof, * 413
38: 8 assembled a' the door of the
39:15 breastplate chains a' the ends, *
40: 8 up the hanging a' the court gate.*
28 set up the hanging a' the door of*
Le 1: 3 voluntary will a' the door of the 413
15 shall be wrung out a' the side of *5921
3: 2 of the offering, and kill it a' the
4: 7 of the bullock a' the bottom of the 413
7 which is a' the door of the
18 pour out all the blood a' the 413
18 a' the door of the tabernacle of the
25 a' the bottom of the altar of burnt 413
30 thereof a' the bottom of the altar. "
34 the blood thereof a' the bottom "
5: 9 wrung out a' the bottom of the "
6:20 and half thereof a' night. *
7:18 be eaten a' all on the third *
8:15 blood a' the bottom of the altar, 413
31 Boil the flesh a' the door of the
33 your consecration be a' an end: *3117
9: 9 the blood a' the bottom of the 413
13: 5 plague in his sight be a' a stay,
37 if the scall be in his sight a' a stay,
14:11 before the Lord, a' the door of the
15:24 man lie with her a' all, and her *
16: 2 come not a' all times into the holy
7 before the Lord a' the door of the
29 do no work a' all, whether it be *
17: 6 of the Lord a' the door of the
18: 9 be born a' home, or born abroad,
19: 5 ye shall offer it a' your will.
7 if it be eaten a' all on the third day,
20 not a' all redeemed, nor freedom
22:19 Ye shall offer a' your own will a *
29 Lord, offer it a' your own will. *
23: 5 the first month a' even is the 996
32 ninth day of the month a' even,
25:32 the Levites redeem a' any time.
26:32 therein shall be astonished a' it. 5921
27:10 if he shall a' all change beast for
13 But if he will a' all redeem it, *
16 shall be valued a' fifty shekels
31 And if a man will a' all redeem *
33 if he change it a' all, then both it
Nu 3:39 numbered a' the commandment 5921
4:27 A' the appointment of Aaron "
6: 6 he shall come a' no dead body. * "
18 a' the door of the tabernacle of
9: 2 the passover a' his appointed *
3 day of this month, a' even, 996
5 first month a' even in the "
11 a' even they shall keep it, and eat "
15 and a' even there was upon the
18 A' the commandment of the Lord 5921
18 a' the commandment of the Lord "
23 A' the commandment of the Lord "
23 a' the commandment of the Lord "
23 of the Lord, a' the commandment "
10: 3 themselves to the a' the door of 413
11: 6 there is nothing a' all besides this
20 until it come out a' your nostrils,
13:30 Let us go up a' once, and possess
16:34 round about them, fled a' the cry
19:19 and shall be clean a' even.
20:24 against my word a' the water
21:11 both, and pitched a' Ije-abarim,
15 And a' the stream of the brooks *
30 We have shot a' them; Heshbon is
33 his people, to the battle a' Edrei.
34 Amorites, which dwelt a' Heshbon.
22: 4 king of the Moabites a' that time.
20 came unto Balaam a' night, and
38 I now any power a' all to say any
23:25 them a' all, nor bless them a' all.
24: 1 he went not, as a' other times, to
27:14 to sanctify me a' the water before
21 go out, and a' his word they shall 5921
28: 4 lamb shalt thou offer a' even; 996
8 lamb shalt thou offer a' even; "
30: 4 father shall hold his peace a' her;
6 And if she had a' all a husband, *
7 it, and held his peace a' her
11 and held his peace a' her, and
30:14 altogether hold his peace a' her
14 because he held his peace a' her,
31:12 the camp a' the plains of Moab, 413
33:14 and encamped a' Rephidim, *
16 pitched a' Kibroth-hattaavah. *
17 and encamped a' Hazeroth. *
19 and pitched a' Rimmon-parez. *
21 Libnah, and pitched a' Rissah. *
26 and encamped a' Tahath. *
27 Tahath, and pitched a' Tarah. *

Nu 33:30 and encamped a' Moseroth. *
32 and encamped a' Hor-hagidgod, *
34 and encamped a' Ebronah. *
35 and encamped a' Ezion-gaber. *
38 a' the commandment of the Lord, 5921
34: 5 goings out of it shall be a' the sea.
9 out of it shall be a' Hazar-enan:
12 out of it shall be a' the salt sea:
35:11 killeth any person a' unawares.
20 or hurl a' him by laying of wait,
26 the slayer shall a' any time come
De 1: 4 dwelt a' Astaroth in Edrei: *
9 And I spake unto you a' that time,
16 I charged your judges a' that time,
18 I commanded you a' that time
2:32 all his people, to fight a' Jahaz.
34 we took all his cities a' that time,
3: 2 Amorites, which dwelt a' Heshbon.
4 we took all his cities a' that time,
8 took a' that time out of the hand
12 which we possessed a' that time,
18 a' that time, saying, The Lord
21 I commanded Joshua a' that time,
23 I besought the Lord a' that time,
4:14 Lord commanded me a' that time
46 Amorites, who dwelt a' Heshbon,
5: 5 the Lord and you a' that time,
6:24 us alive, as it is a' this day.
7:21 shalt not be affrighted a' them: 6440
22 not consume them a' once, 4118
8:16 do thee good a' thy latter end;
19 if thou do a' all forget the Lord *
9:11 it came to pass a' the end of
18 before the Lord, as a' the first,
19 hearkened unto me a' that time *
22 And a' Taberah, and a' Massah,
22 and a' Kibroth-hattaavah,
25 as I fell down a' the first; *
10: 1 A' that time the Lord said unto
8 A' that time the Lord separated
10 hearkened unto me a' that time *
14:28 A' the end of three years thou
15: 1 A' the end of every seven years
9 the year of release is a' hand; 7126
16: 4 sacrificedst the first day a' even,
6 But a' the place which the Lord 413
6 a' even, a' the going down of the
6 a' the season that thou camest
17: 6 A' the mouth of two witnesses, 5921
6 but a' the mouth of one witness "
19:15 a' the mouth of two witnesses, "
15 a' the mouth of three witnesses, "
21:14 shalt not sell her a' all for money,
23:24 thy fill a' thine own pleasure;
24: 5 shall be free a' home one year,
15 A' his day thou shalt give him *
28:29 thou shalt grope a' noonday,
67 and a' even thou shalt say,
31:10 A' the end of every seven years,
32:35 day of their calamity is a' hand, 7138
51 a' the waters of Meribah-kadesh,
33: 3 and they sat down a' thy feet;
8 whom thou didst prove a' Massah,5921
8 and with whom thou didst strive a'
Jos 5: 2 A' that time the Lord said unto
3 the children of Israel a' the hill 413
10 a' even in the plains of Jericho.
6:16 came to pass a' the seventh time,
26 Joshua adjured them a' that time,
7: 7 hast thou a' all brought this people
8: 5 out against us, as a' the first,
6 flee before us, as a' the first:
14 his people, a' a time appointed,
29 cast it a' the entering in of the 413
9: 6 Joshua unto the camp a' Gilgal,
10 Bashan, which was a' Ashtaroth.
14 counsel a' the mouth of the Lord.
16 to pass a' the end of three days
10:10 with a great slaughter a' Gibeon,
16 themselves in a cave a' Makkedah.
17 found hid in a cave a' Makkedah.
21 the camp to Joshua a' Makkedah.
27 it came to pass a' the time of the
42 land did Joshua take a' one time,
11: 5 pitched together a' the waters of 413
10 Joshua a' that time turned back,
21 And a' that time came Joshua,
12: 4 that dwelt a' Ashtaroth and a'
15: 4 out of that coast were a' the sea:
5 of the sea a' the uttermost part 5704
7 out thereof were a' En-rogel: 413
8 westward, which is a' the end of
11 out of the border were a' the sea.
63 children of Judah a' Jerusalem
16: 3 goings out thereof are a' the sea.
7 to Jericho, and went out a' Jordan.
8 out thereof were a' the sea.
17: 9 the outgoings of it were a' the sea:
18: 1 Israel assembled together a' Shiloh,
9 to Joshua to the host a' Shiloh.
12 out thereof were a' the wilderness
14 out thereof were a' Kirjath-baal, 413
19 a' the north bay of the salt sea
19 a' the south end of Jordan:
19:22 of their border were a' Jordan:
29 are a' the sea from the coast to
33 outgoings thereof were a' Jordan:
51 a' the door of the tabernacle
20: 4 stand a' the entering of the gate
9 killeth any person a' unawares *
21: 2 they spake unto them a' Shiloh
3 a' the commandment of the * 413
22:11 a' the passage of the children of *
12 themselves together a' Shiloh,
J'g 3: 2 a' the least such as before knew 7535
29 slew of Moab a' that time about

J'g 4: 4 she judged Israel a' that time.
10 ten thousand men a' his feet:
5:27 A' her feet he bowed, he fell, he 996
27 a' her feet he bowed, he fell: where
28 Sisera looked out a' a window, *1157
7:25 slew a' the winepress of Zeeb,
8:18 were they whom ye slew a' Tabor?
9: 5 unto his father's house a' Ophrah,
41 Abimelech dwelt a' Arumah:
11:39 it came to pass a' the end of two
12: 2 my people were a' great strife
6 him a' the passages of Jordan: 413
6 there fell a' that time of the
10 and was buried a' Beth-lehem.
13:23 a meat offering a' our hands,
23 as a' this time have told us such
25 began to move him a' times
14: 4 for a' that time the Philistines had
16: 3 midnight, and arose a' midnight,
20 I will go out as a' other times
28 I may be a' once avenged of the
30 dead which he slew a' his death
18:27 a people that were a' quiet and *
29 of the city was Laish a' the first.
19:16 his work out of the field a' even,
22 beat a' the door, and spake to 5921
26 fell down a' the door of the man's
27 was fallen down a' the door
20:15 were numbered a' that time *
16 one could sling a stone a' an hair 413
30 against Gibeah, as a' other times.
31 and kill, as a' other times, in the
32 down before us, as a' the first.
21:14 Benjamin came again a' that time;
22 not give unto them a' this time, *
24 of Israel departed thence a' that
Ru 2:14 A' mealtime come thou hither,
3: 7 he went to lie down a' the end of
8 And it came to pass a' midnight,
8 behold, a woman lay a' his feet.
10 latter end than a' the beginning,
14 And she lay a' his feet until the
1Sa 2:22 women that assembled a' the door
29 ye a' my sacrifice and a' mine
3: 2 pass a' that time, when Eli was
10 and called as a' other times,
11 in Israel, a' which both the ears
6:10 and shut up their calves a' home:
9: 8 I have here a' hand the fourth *
10: 2 the border of Benjamin a' Zezah;
13:11 themselves together a' Michmash;
14:18 the ark of God was a' that time
16: 4 of the town trembled a' his *
17: 1 were gathered together a' Shocoh,
15 his father's sheep a' Beth-lehem.
18:10 with his hand, as a' other times: *
19 it came to pass a' the time when
19:19 David is a' Naioth in Ramah.
22 they be a' Naioth in Ramah.
20: 5 fail to sit with the king a' meat:
5 field unto the third day a' even.
6 If thy father a' all miss me,
16 a' the hand of David's enemies.
20 thereof, as though I shot a' a mark.
25 upon his seat, as a' other times,
33 Saul cast a javelin a' him to smite 5921
35 went out into the field a' the time
21: 1 was afraid a' the meeting of *
4 themselves a' least from women.* 389
22: 8, 13 to lie in wait, as a' this day?
14 in law, and goeth a' thy bidding, * 413
23:29 dwelt in strong holds a' En-gedi.*
25: 1 buried him in his house a' Ramah.
24 And fell a' his feet, and said, 5921
26: 7 stuck in the ground a' his bolster:
8 spear even to the earth a' once,
11 the spear that is a' his bolster,
16 of water that was a' his bolster.
27: 3 David dwelt with Achish a' Gath,
28: 7 hath a familiar spirit a' En-dor.
30: 8 David enquired a' the Lord, *
21 also to abide a' the brook Besor:
31:13 them under a tree a' Jabesh, *
2Sa 2:32 they came to Hebron a' break of
3:30 slain their brother Asahel a'
32 and wept a' the grave of Abner;
4: 5 who lay on a bed a' noon.
6: 4 which was a' Gibeah, *
8: 3 to recover his border a' the river
9: 7 shalt eat bread a' my table 5921
10 eat bread alway a' my table. "
11 he shall eat a' my table, as one "
13 did eat continually a' the king's "
10: 5 the king said, Tarry a' Jericho
8 battle in array a' the entering in
11: 1 the year was expired, a' the time
1 But David tarried still a'
9 But Uriah slept a' the door of the
13 and a' even he went out to lie
13: 5 see it, and eat it a' her hand.
6 sight, that I may eat a' her hand.
14:26 for it was a' every year's end
26 the hair of his head a' two
15: 8 while I abode a' Geshur in Syria,
14 that were a' Jerusalem, Arise,
16: 3 he abideth a' Jerusalem: for he
6 And he cast stones a' David,
6 and a' all the servants of the
13 threw stones a' him, and cast 5980
23 as if a man had inquired a' the
17: 7 given is not good a' this time. *
9 of them be overthrown a' the
19: 9 And all the people were a' strife
28 them that did eat a' thine own
32 of sustenance while he lay a'
42 have we eaten a' all of the king's

2Sa 20: 3 David came to his house a'
8 When they were a' the great 5973
18 surely ask counsel a' Abel: and
21:18 with the Philistines a' Gob:
22:16 a' the rebuking of the Lord, *
16 a' the blast of the
23: 8 whom he slew a' one time.
24: 8 they came to Jerusalem a' the
24 I will surely buy it of thee a' a
1Ki 1: 6 had not displeased him a' any time
2: 7 of those that eat a' thy table: for
8 came down to meet me a' Jordan,
26 but I will not a' this time put thee
39 And it came to pass a' the end of
3:20 And she arose a' midnight, and
5:14 Lebanon, and two months a' home;
7:30 undersetters molten, a' the side of
8: 2 unto king Solomon a' the feast
9 which Moses put there a' Horeb,
59 cause of his people Israel a' all *
61 keep his commandments as a' this
65 And a' that time Solomon held a
9: 2 had appeared unto him a' Gibeon.
6 But if ye shall a' all turn from *
8 And a' this house, which is high,*
10 And it came to pass a' the end of
10:22 For the king had a' sea a navy of
26 and with the king at Jerusalem.
28 received the linen yarn a' a price.
11:29 And it came to pass a' that time
12:27 house of the Lord a' Jerusalem.
13:20 it came to pass as they sat a' the 413
14: 1 A' that time Abijah the son of
6 as she came in a' the door, that he
15:18 king of Syria, that dwelt a'
27 Baasha smote him a' Gibbethon,
18:19 which eat a' Jezebel's table.
27 And it came to pass a' noon, that
36 it came to pass a' the time of the
36 I have done all these things a' thy
44 And it came to pass a' the seventh
19: 6 and a cruse of water a' his head.
20: 9 to thy servant a' the first I will do:
16 And they went out a' noon. But
22 a' the return of the year the king
26 And it came to pass a' the return
22: 5 I pray thee, a' the word of the Lord
20 go up and fall a' Ramoth-gilead?
28 if thou return a' all in peace, the
34 drew a bow a' a venture, and smote
35 died a' even: and the blood ran
48 ships were broken a' Ezion-geber.
2Ki 2: 3 prophets that were a' Beth-el came
5 prophets that were a' Jericho came
15 were to view a' Jericho, saw him,
18 he tarried a' Jericho,) he said unto,
4:17 and bare a son a' that season that
37 fell a' his feet, and bowed herself 5921
5: 9 stood a' the door of the house of
20 not receiving a' his hands that
6:32 and hold him fast a' the door: is *
7: 3 four leprous men a' the entering
8: 3 came to pass a' the seven years'
22 Then Libna revolted a' the same
29 the Syrians had given him a' Ramah,
9: 7 servants of the Lord, a' the hand
24 the arrow went out a' his heart,
27 they did so a' the going up to Gur,
30 and looked out a' a window. 1157
31 And as Jehu entered in a' the gate,
10: 8 Lay ye them in two heaps a' the
12 as he was a' the shearing house
14 slew them a' the pit of the shearing
11: 6 shall be a' the gate of Sur; and a
6 a' the gate behind the guard:
12: 4 money that every man is set a', *
13:20 invaded the land a' the coming in
14:10 glory of this, and tarry a' home:
11 looked one another in the face a'
13 son of Ahaziah, a' Beth-shemesh,
20 and he was buried a' Jerusalem
16: 6 A' that time Rezin king of Syria
10 an altar that was a' Damascus:
17:25 And so it was a' the beginning of
18:10 And a' the end of three years they
16 A' that time did Hezekiah cut off
33 gods of the nations delivered a' *
19:21 hath shaken her head a' thee.
36 returned, and dwelt a' Nineveh.
20:12 A' that time Berodach-baladan,
23: 6 burned it a' the brook Kidron,
8 left hand a' the gate of the city.
11 given to the sun, a' the entering in
15 altar that was a' Beth-el, and the
29 he slew him a' Megiddo, when he
33 put him in bands a' Riblah in the
24: 3 Surely a' the commandment of 5921
10 A' that time the servants of
25:21 slew them a' Riblah in the land
25 the Chaldees that were with him a'
1Ch 2:55 the scribes which dwelt a' Jabez;
4:28 And they dwelt a' Beer-sheba,
29 a' Bilhah, and a' Ezem, and a' Tolad,
30 And a' Bethuel, and a' Hormah,
30 Hormah, and a' Ziklag,
31 And a' Beth-marcaboth, and
31 a' Beth-birei, and a' Shaaraim.
8:29 a' Gibeon dwelt the father of *
9:34 their generations: these dwelt a'
38 with their brethren a' Jerusalem,*
11:11 three hundred slain by him a' one
13 He was with David a' Pas-dammim,
16 Philistines' garrison was then a' *
17 Bethlehem, that is a' the gate! *
12:22 For a' that time day by day there
32 their brethren were a' their 5921

1Ch 13: 3 inquired not a' it in the days of *
14: 3 David took more wives a'
15:13 because ye did it not a' the first,
29 daughter of Saul looking out a' a 1157
16:33 wood sing out a' the presence of *
17: 9 them any more, as a' the beginning,
19: 5 Tarry a' Jericho until your beards
20: 1 year was expired, a' the time that
1 But David tarried a' Jerusalem.
4 that there arose war a' Gezer
4 a' which time Sibbechai the *
6 was war a' Gath, where was a man
21:19 David went up a' the saying of Gad,
28 A' that time when David saw that
29 a' that season in the high place a'
23:30 praise the Lord, and likewise a'
26:18 A' Parbar westward, *
18 four a' the causeway,
18 and two a' Parbar.
31 mighty men of valour a' Jazer of
28: 7 my judgments, as a' this day.
21 the people will be wholly a' thy
2Ch 1: 3 high place that was a' Gibeon;
4 pitched a tent for it a' Jerusalem.
6 which was a' the tabernacle of
13 the high place that was a' Gibeon
14 and with the king a' Jerusalem.
15 silver and gold a' Jerusalem *
16 received the linen yarn a' a price.
3: 1 to build the house of the Lord a'
5:10 which Moses put therein a' Horeb,
12 stood a' the east end of the altar,
7: 8 Also a' the same time Solomon
8: 1 to pass a' the end of twenty years,
14 also by their courses a' every gate:
17 to Eloth, a' the sea side in the *5921
9: 1 Solomon with hard questions a'
25 and with the king a' Jerusalem.
13:18 of Israel were brought under a'
14:10 in the valley of Zephathah a'
15:10 gathered themselves together a'
15 all Judah rejoiced a' the oath: 5921
16 and burned it a' the brook Kidron.
16: 2 king of Syria, that dwelt a'
7 And a' that time Hanani the seer
18: 4 Enquire, I pray thee, a' the word
9 sat in a void place a' the entering
19 go up and fall a' Ramoth-gilead?
33 a certain man drew a bow a' a
19: 4 Jehoshaphat dwelt a' Jerusalem:
20:16 ye shall find them a' the end of
22: 5 against Hazael king of Syria a'
6 that were given him a' Ramah,
6 Ahab a' Jezreel, because he was *
23: 5 part shall be a' the king's house;
5 part a' the gate of the foundation:
13 the king stood a' his pillar *5921
13 a' the entering in, and the princes
19 porters a' the gates of the house 5921
24: 8 And a' the king's commandment*
8 and set it without a' the gate of
11 came to pass, that a' what time
21 and stoned him with stones a' the
23 came to pass a' the end of the year,
25:19 abide now a' home; why shouldest
21 king of Judah, a' Beth-shemesh,
23 son of Jehoahaz, a' Beth-shemesh,
26: 9 built towers in Jerusalem a' the 5921
9 and a' the valley gate, and a' "
28:16 A' that time did king Ahaz send
30: 1 house of the Lord a' Jerusalem,
3 could not keep it a' that time,
5 Lord God of Israel a' Jerusalem:
13 there assembled a' Jerusalem
21 that were present a' Jerusalem
31:13 brother, a' the commandment *
32: 9 all Judah that were a' Jerusalem,
33 did honour him a' his death.
33:14 to the entering in a' the fish gate,
35:15 the porters waited a' every gate;
17 kept the passover a' that time,
23 the archers shot a' king Josiah;
36: 3 put him down a' Jerusalem,
7 put them in his temple a' Babylon.
Ezr 1: 2 him a house a' Jerusalem, *
2:68 the Lord which is a' Jerusalem, *
3: 8 unto the house of God a' Jerusalem,
4:10, 11 the river, and a' such a time. *
17 Peace, and a' such a time.
24 of God which is a' Jerusalem.
5: 2 of God which is a' Jerusalem:
3 A' the same time came to them
17 which is there a' Babylon,
17 this house of God a' Jerusalem,
6: 2 there was found a' Achmetha,
3 the house of God a' Jerusalem,
5 the temple which is a' Jerusalem,
9 priests which are a' Jerusalem,
12 of God which is a' Jerusalem.
17 a' the dedication of this house of
18 of God, which is a' Jerusalem;
7:12 perfect peace, and a' such a time.*
8:17 the chief a' the place Casiphia,
17 Nethinims, a' the place Casiphia,
21 a fast there, a' the river 5921
29 a' Jerusalem, in the chambers
34 weight was written a' that time.
9: 4 trembled a' the words of the God
5 a' the evening sacrifice I arose up
10: 3 that tremble a' the commandment
14 in our cities come a' appointed
Ne 2:12 in my heart to do a' Jerusalem: *
3:19 armoury a' the turning of the wall.
4:22 Likewise a' the same time said I
5:17 there were a' my table an 5921
6: 1 a' that time I had not set up the *5704

Ne 6: 7 to preach of thee a' Jerusalem,
7: 5 of them which came up a' the first,
9:37 over our cattle, a' their pleasure,
10:34 a' times appointed year by year,
11: 1 the people dwelt a' Jerusalem: *
2 to dwell a' Jerusalem. *
4 And a' Jerusalem dwelt certain *
6 of Perez that dwelt a' Jerusalem *
22 overseer of the Levites a' Jerusalem
24 of Judah, was a' the king's hand
25 dwelt a' Kirjath-arba, and in the *
25 and a' Dibon, and in the villages *
25 a' Jekabzeel, and in the villages *
26 And a' Jeshua, and a' Moladah, *
26 and a' Beth-phelet, *
27 a' Hazar-shual, and a' *
28 And a' Ziklag, and a' Mekonah, *
29 a' En-rimmon, and a' Zareah, *
29 and a' Jarmuth, *
30 a' Lachish, and the fields *
30 a' Azekah, and in the villages *
31 dwelt a' Michmash, and Aija,
32 And a' Anathoth, Nob, Ananiah,
12:25 a' the thresholds of the gates.
27 And a' the dedication of the wall
37 a' the fountain gate, which was *5921
37 David, a' the going up of the wall,
44 a' that time were some appointed *
13: 6 this time was not I a' Jerusalem:
19 my servants set I a' the gates, *5921
31 wood offering, a' times appointed,
Es 1:12 come a' the king's commandment,
4: 8 a' Shushan to destroy them, *
14 thou holdest thy peace a' this time,
5: 6 said unto Esther a' the banquet
13 the Jew sitting a' the king's gate.
6:10 Jew, that sitteth a' the king's gate:
7: 2 second day a' the banquet of wine,
3 my life be given me a' my petition,
3 and my people a' my request:
8: 3 fell down a' his feet, and besought 6440
9 king's scribes called a' that time
14 the decree was given a' Shushan *
9:14 decree was given a' Shushan; *
15 three hundred men a' Shushan; *
18 the Jews that were a' Shushan *
Job 2:10 receive good a' the hand of God,
3:13 have slept: then had I been a' rest,
17 and there the weary be a' rest.
5:22 A' destruction and famine thou
23 beasts of the field shall be a' peace
9:23 laugh a' the trial of the innocent
12: 5 thought of him that is a' ease.
15:12 and what do thy eyes wink a', *
23 of darkness is ready a' his hand.
16: 4 and shake mine head a' you.
12 I was a' ease, but he hath broken
17: 8 men shall be astonied a' this, †5921
18:12 destruction shall be ready a' his *
20 shall be astonied a' his day, 5921
19:25 he shall stand a' the latter day
21:12 rejoice a' the sound of the organ.
23 being wholly a' ease and quiet.
22:21 thyself with him, and be a' peace
23:15 am I troubled a' his presence:
26:11 and are astonished a' his reproof.
27:23 Men shall clap their hands a' him, 5921
29:21 and kept silence a' my counsel. *3926
31: 9 lain wait a' my neighbour's door; 5921
29 rejoiced a' the destruction of him
34:20 shall be troubled a' midnight,
37: 1 A' this also my heart trembleth
39:22 He mocketh a' fear, and is not
27 eagle mount up a' thy command, 5291
41: 9 down even a' the sight of him?
26 sword of him that layeth a' him
29 laugheth a' the shaking of a spear.
Ps 7: 4 him that was a' peace with me;
9: 3 fall and perish a' thy presence.
10: 5 his enemies, he puffeth a' them.
11: 2 may privily shoot a' the upright
12: 5 from him that puffeth a' him.
16: 8 because he is a' my right hand, I
11 a' thy right hand there are *
18:12 A' the brightness that was before
15 a' thy rebuke, O Lord,
15 a' the blast of the breath
25:13 His soul shall dwell a' ease;
30:*title* Psalm and Song a' the dedication
4 give thanks a' the remembrance *
34: 1 I will bless the Lord a' all times:
35: 8 come upon him a' unawares;
26 together that rejoice a' mine hurt:
37:13 The Lord shall laugh a' him:
39: 5 verily every man a' his best state
12 hold not thy peace a' my tears: 413
42: 7 Deep calleth unto deep a' the noise
52: 6 fear, and shall laugh a' him: 5921
55: 6 would I fly away, and be a' rest.
17 and morning, and a' noon, will I
20 such as be a' peace with him.
59: 6 They return a' evening: they make
8 thou, O Lord, shalt laugh a' them;
14 And a' evening let them return:
62: 8 Trust in him a' all times;
64: 4 shoot in secret a' the perfect:
4 suddenly do they shoot a' him,
7 God shall shoot a' them with an
65: 8 parts are afraid a' thy tokens:
68: 2 perish a' the presence of God,
8 dropped a' the presence of God:
8 even Sinai itself was moved a' the
12 she that tarried a' home divided
29 of thy temple a' Jerusalem 5921
73: 3 For I was envious a' the foolish,
74: 6 the carved work thereof a' once ††3162

Ps 76: 6 *A'* thy rebuke, O God of Jacob,
80:16 *a'* the rebuke of thy countenance.
81: 7 I proved thee *a'* the waters of 5291
83: 9 Jabin, *a'* the brook of Kison:
10 which perished *a'* En-dor: they
91: 6 destruction that wasteth *a'* noonday.
7 A thousand shall fall *a'* thy side,
7 and ten thousand *a'* thy right hand;
97: 5 The hills melted like wax *a'* the
5 *a'* the presence of the Lord of the
12 give thanks *a'* the remembrance *
99: 5 and worship *a'* his footstool;
9 and worship *a'* his holy hill;
104: 7 *A'* thy rebuke they fled; 4480
7 *a'* the voice of thy "
105:22 To bind his princes *a'* his pleasure;
106: 3 doeth righteousness *a'* all times.
7 but provoked him *a'* the sea, 5921
7 even *a'* the Red sea. "
32 angered him also *a'* the waters of "
107:27 man, and are *a'* their wit's end.
109: 6 let Satan stand *a'* his right hand. 5921
31 he shall stand *a'* the right hand
110: 1 Sit thou *a'* my right hand, until I
5 Lord *a'* thy right hand shall 5921
114: 7 earth, *a'* the presence of the Lord,
7 *a'* the presence of the God of Jacob;
118:13 Thou hast thrust sore *a'* me that
119:20 unto thy judgments *a'* all times.
45 And I will walk *a'* liberty: for I
62 *A'* midnight I will rise to give
162 I rejoice *a'* thy word, as one that 5921
123: 4 scorning of those that are *a'* ease,
Ps 132: 6 Lo, we heard of it *a'* Ephratah: *
7 we will worship *a'* his footstool.
135:21 Zion, which dwelleth *a'* Jerusalem.
141: 7 are scattered *a'* the grave's mouth,
Pr 1:23 Turn you *a'* my reproof:
25 set *a'* nought all my counsel, 6544
26 also will laugh *a'* your calamity;*
4:19 know not *a'* what they stumble.
5:11 and thou mourn *a'* the last,
19 her breasts satisfy thee *a'* all times;
7: 6 For *a'* the window of my house I
12 and lieth in wait *a'* every corner. 681
19 For the goodman is not *a'* home,
20 come home *a'* the day appointed.
8: 3 She crieth *a'* the gates, *3027
3 *a'* the entry of the city, "
3 *a'* the coming in *a'* the doors:
34 watching daily *a'* my gates, 5921
34 waiting *a'* the posts of my doors.
9:14 sitteth *a'* the door of her house,
14: 9 Fools make a mock *a'* sin:
19 *a'* the gates of the righteous. 5921
16: 7 enemies to be *a'* peace with him.
17: 5 and he that is glad *a'* calamities
17 A friend loveth *a'* all times,
20:21 be gotten hastily *a'* the beginning;
21:13 his ears *a'* the cry of the poor,
23:30 They that tarry long *a'* the wine; 5921
32 *A'* the last it biteth like a serpent,
24:19 be thou envious *a'* the wicked;
28:18 in his ways shall fall *a'* once.
29:21 become his son *a'* the length.
30:17 eye that mocketh *a'* his father,
Ec 5: 6 should God be angry *a'* thy voice, 5921
8 marvel not *a'* the matter:
10: 2 man's heart is *a'* his right hand;
2 but a fool's heart *a'* his left.
12: 4 rise up *a'* the voice of the bird,
6 be broken *a'* the fountain, 5921
6 wheel broken *a'* the cistern. 413
Ca 1: 7 makest thy flock to rest *a'* noon:
12 While the king sitteth *a'* his table,
2: 9 he looketh forth *a'* the windows, 4480
7:13 and *a'* our gates are all manner 5921
8:11 had a vineyard *a'* Baal-hamon;
Isa 1:12 hath required this *a'* your hand,
26 restore thy judges as *a'* the first,
26 counsellors as *a'* the beginning:
6: 4 door moved *a'* the voice of him
7: 3 *a'* the end of the conduit of the 413
23 vines *a'* a thousand silverlings,
9: 1 *a'* the first he lightly afflicted *
10:26 of Midian *a'* the rock of Oreb:
28 *a'* Michmash he hath laid up his
29 taken up their lodging *a'* Geba;
32 shall remain *a'* Nob that day:
13: 6 for the day of the Lord is *a'* hand: 7138
8 shall be amazed one *a'* another; 413
14: 7 The whole earth is *a'* rest,
8 Yea, the fir trees rejoice *a'* thee,
9 thee to meet thee *a'* thy coming:
16: 2 of Moab shall be *a'* the fords
4 for the extortioner is *a'* an end, *
17: 7 *A'* that day shall a man look to *
14 behold *a'* eveningtide trouble;
19: 1 idols of Egypt shall be moved *a'*
19 *a'* the border thereof to the Lord. 681
20: 2 *A'* the same time spake the Lord
21: 3 down *a'* the hearing of it; *
3 I was dismayed *a'* the seeing of *
22: 7 shall set themselves in array *a'*
23: 5 *a'* the report concerning Egypt, *
5 pained *a'* the report of Tyre.
26:11 for their envy *a'* the people; *
27:13 in the holy mount *a'* Jerusalem.
28:15 with hell are we *a'* agreement;
29: 5 it shall be *a'* an instant suddenly
30: 2 and have not asked *a'* my mouth;
4 For his princes were *a'* Zoan,
13 cometh suddenly *a'* an instant.
17 shall flee *a'* the rebuke of one; 6440
17 *a'* the rebuke of five shall ye flee: "
19 dwell in Zion *a'* Jerusalem:

Isa 30:19 gracious unto thee *a'* the voice
32: 9 Rise up, ye women that are *a'* ease;
11 Tremble, ye women that are *a'* ease;
33: 3 *A'* the noise of the tumult the
3 *a'* the lifting up of thyself the
37:22 hath shaken her head *a'* thee.
37 and dwelt *a'* Nineveh.
39: 1 *A'* that time Merodach-baladan,
42:14 destroy and devour *a'* once. *3162
47:14 shall not be a coal to warm *a'*,
50: 2 Is my hand shortened *a'* all,
2 *a'* my rebuke I dry up the sea,
51:17 drank *a'* the hand of the Lord
20 lie *a'* the head of all the streets,
52:14 As many were astonied *a'* thee;
15 shall shut their mouths *a'* him:
59:10 we stumble *a'* noon day as in the
60: 4 shall be nursed *a'* thy side. *5921
14 down *a'* the soles of thy feet; 5921
64: 1 might flow down *a'* thy
2 may tremble *a'* thy presence!
3 flowed down *a'* thy presence.
66: 2 and trembleth *a'* my word. 5921
5 ye that tremble *a'* his word; 413
8 shall a nation be born *a'* once?
Jer 1:15 every one his throne *a'* the entering
17 be not dismayed *a'* their faces,
2:12 O ye heavens, *a'* this, 5921
24 up the wind *a'* her pleasure; *
3:17 *A'* that time they shall call
4: 9 shall come to pass *a'* that day,
11 *A'* that time shall it be said to this
19 I am pained *a'* my very heart;
26 down *a'* the presence of the Lord,
5:22 ye not tremble *a'* my presence,
6: 4 arise, and let us go up *a'* noon.
15 they were not *a'* all ashamed,
15 *a'* the time that I visit them they
7: 2 that enter in *a'* these gates to
12 where I set my name *a'* the first,
8: 1 *A'* that time, saith the Lord,
12 they were not *a'* all ashamed,
16 whole land trembled *a'* the sound
10: 2 dismayed *a'* the signs of heaven;
2 heathen are dismayed *a'* them.
10 *a'* his wrath the earth shall
18 of the land *a'* this once,
11:12 they shall not save them *a'* all
15: 8 young men a spoiler *a'* noonday;
17:11 and *a'* his end shall be a fool.
27 in *a'* the gates of Jerusalem
18: 7 *A'* what instant I shall speak
9 And *a'* what instant I shall speak
20:16 and the shouting *a'* noontide:
23:23 Am I a God *a'* hand, saith the
32 profit this people *a'* all, saith the
25:15 winecup of this fury *a'* my hand,
17 I took the cup *a'* the Lord's hand,
28 to take the cup *a'* thine hand
33 the Lord shall be *a'* that day from
26:19 Judah put him *a'* all to death?
27:18 *a'* Jerusalem, go not to Babylon.
29:10 years be accomplished *a'* Babylon*
25 the people that are *a'* Jerusalem,
31: 1 *A'* the same time, saith the Lord,
12 shall not sorrow any more *a'* all.
32:20 thee a name, as *a'* this day; 5704
33: 7 build them, as *a'* the first.
11 of the land, as *a'* the first, saith
15 In those days, and *a'* that time,
34: 8 people which were *a'* Jerusalem,
14 *A'* the end of seven years let ye go
16 whom he had set *a'* liberty *
16 *a'* their pleasure, to return
35:11 so we dwell *a'* Jerusalem.
36:10 court, *a'* the entry of the new
17 write all these things *a'* his mouth?
27 wrote *a'* the mouth of Jeremiah
39:10 and fields *a'* the same time.
40:10 I will dwell *a'* Mizpah, to serve
41: 3 even with Gedaliah, *a'* Mizpah,
43: 9 *a'* the entry of Pharaoh's house in
44: 1 which dwell *a'* Migdol,
1 and *a'* Tahpanhes, and *a'* Noph,
6 and desolate, as *a'* this day. *
22 an inhabitant as *a'* this day. *
23 happened unto you, as *a'* this *
45: 1 words in a book *a'* the mouth of
46:27 and be in rest and *a'* ease, and
47: 3 *A'* the noise of the stamping of
3 *a'* the rushing of his chariots,
3 and *a'* the rumbling of his wheels,
48:11 Moab hath been *a'* ease from his
41 hearts in Moab *a'* that day shall
49:17 hiss *a'* all the plagues thereof. 5921
21 The earth is moved *a'* the noise
21 *a'* the cry the noise thereof was *
22 *a'* that day shall the heart of the
50:11 ye are grown fat as the heifer *a'* *
13 and hiss *a'* all her plagues. 5921
14 shoot *a'* her, spare no arrows: 413
46 *A'* the noise of the taking of
51:31 that his city is taken *a'* one end, *
49 so *a'* Babylon shall fall the slain
La 1: 7 and did mock *a'* her sabbaths. 5921
20 sword bereaveth, *a'* home there
2:15 pass by clap their hands *a'* thee; 5921
15 wag their head *a'* the daughter "
3:56 ear *a'* my breathing, *a'* my cry.
Eze 2: 6 nor be dismayed *a'* their looks,
3: 9 neither be dismayed *a'* their looks,
15 of the captivity *a'* Tel-abib, that
16 came to pass *a'* the end of seven
17 hear the word *a'* my mouth,
18, 20 blood will I require *a'* thine hand.
8: 5 northward *a'* the gate of the *

Eze 8:16 *a'* the door of the temple of the
9: 6 and begin *a'* my sanctuary.
6 Then they began *a'* the ancient
10:19 and every one stood *a'* the door
11: 1 behold *a'* the door of the gate
12: 4 go forth *a'* even in their sight
23 The days are *a'* hand, and the 7126
14: 3 be enquired of *a'* all by them?
16: 4 thou wast not salted *a'* all,
4 nor swaddled *a'* all.
25 place *a'* every head of the way, 413
46 that dwell *a'* thy left hand: 5921
46 that dwelleth *a'* thy right hand,
57 as *a'* the time of thy reproach of
18:23 *a'* all that the wicked should die?*
20:32 into your mind shall not be *a'* all,
21:19 choose it *a'* the head of the way
21 of Babylon stood *a'* the parting 413
21 *a'* the head of the two ways, to
22 *A'* his right hand was the *
22:13 mine hand *a'* thy dishonest gain 413
13 made, and *a'* thy blood which 5921
23:42 voice of a multitude being *a'* ease
24:18 and *a'* even my wife died; and I
26:10 shake *a'* the noise of the horsemen,
15 not the isle shake *a'* the sound of
16 shall tremble *a'* every moment, *
16 and be astonished *a'* thee.
18 shall be troubled *a'* thy departure.
27: 3 situate *a'* the entry of the sea 5921
28 shake *a'* the sound of the cry of thy
35 isles shall be astonished *a'* thee, 5921
36 the people shall hiss *a'* thee; "
28:19 people shall be astonished *a'* thee: "
29: 7 all their loins to be *a'* a stand.
13 God; *A'* the end of forty years
30:18 *A'* Tehaphnehes also the day
31:16 to shake *a'* the sound of his fall,
32:10 make many people amazed *a'* thee,5921
10 shall tremble *a'* every moment,
33: 6 require *a'* the watchman's hand.
7 shalt hear the word *a'* my mouth,
8 blood will I require *a'* thine hand.
34:10 require my flock *a'* their hand,
35:15 didst rejoice *a'* the inheritance *
36: 8 for they are *a'* hand to come. 7126
11 you than *a'* your beginnings:
37:22 into two kingdoms any more *a'* all:
38:10 *a'* the same time shall things *
11 I will go to them that are *a'* rest,
18 it come to pass *a'* the same time *
20 shall shake *a'* my presence, and
39:20 shall be filled *a'* my table with 5921
40:40 And *a'* the side without, as one * 413
40 which was *a'* the porch of the *
44 which was *a'* the side of the north 413
44 one *a'* the side of the east gate "
41:12 the separate place *a'* the end
44:11 having charge *a'* the gates of 413
17 they enter in *a'* the gates of the "
25 they shall come *a'* no dead person "
46: 2 he shall worship *a'* the threshold 5921
3 shall worship *a'* the door of
19 which was *a'* the side of the gate, 5921
47: 1 *a'* the south side of the altar *
7 *a'* the bank of the river were * 413
48:28 *a'* the south side southward, "
32 *a'* the east side four thousand
33 *a'* the south side four thousand
34 *A'* the west side four thousand
Da 1: 5 that *a'* the end thereof they might
15 And *a'* the end of ten days their
18 Now *a'* the end of the days that
2:10 such things *a'* any magician, *
3: 5 That *a'* what time ye hear the sound
7 Therefore *a'* that time, when all
8 Wherefore *a'* that time certain
15 that *a'* what time ye hear the
4: 4 was *a'* rest in mine house, and
8 But *a'* the last Daniel came in 5705
29 *A'* the end of twelve months he
34 And *a'* the end of the days I
36 *A'* the same time my reason
5: 3 of God which was *a'* Jerusalem;
6:24 they came *a'* the bottom of the
8: 1 appeared unto me *a'* the first.
2 I was *a'* Shushan in the palace, *
17 for *a'* the time of the end shall be*
19 for *a'* the time appointed the end*
27 I was astonished *a'* the vision, 5921
9: 7 *a'* this day; to the men of Judah,
15 as *a'* this day; we have sinned,
21 in the vision *a'* the beginning,
23 *A'* the beginning of thy supplications
10: 3 did I anoint myself *a'* all, till
11:27 lies *a'* one table; but it shall not 5921
27 yet the end shall be *a'* the time
29 *A'* the time appointed he shall
40 And *a'* the time of the end shall
40 king of the south push *a'* him: *
43 Ethiopians shall be *a'* his steps.
12: 1 And *a'* that time Michael stand
1 and *a'* that time thy people shall
13 stand in thy lot *a'* the end of
Ho 1: 5 come to pass *a'* that day, that
2:16 And it shall be *a'* that day, saith
4:12 My people ask counsel *a'* their
5: 8 cry aloud *a'* Beth-aven, after thee,
9:10 in the fig tree *a'* her first time;
11: 7 none *a'* all would exalt him. 3162
Joe 1:15 the Lord is *a'* hand, and as a 7138
2: 1 cometh, for it is nigh *a'* hand;
9 shall enter in *a'* the windows like 1157
Am 3: 5 and have taken nothing *a'* all?
9 Publish in the palaces *a'* Ashdod,
4: 3 ye shall go out *a'* the breaches,

Am 4: 3 every cow *a*' that which is before
4 transgress; *a*' Gilgal multiply
6: 1 to them that are *a*' ease in Zion,
7:13 not again any more *a*' Beth-el:
8: 9 the sun to go down *a*' noon, and
Ob 7 the men that were *a*' peace with
Mic 1:10 Declare ye it not *a*' Gath, *
10 weep ye not *a*' all: in the house
3: 4 his face from them *a*' that time,
7:16 and be confounded *a*' all their *
Na 1: 3 will not *a*' all acquit the wicked: *
5 The mountains quake *a*' him, and
5 and the earth is burned *a*' his
3:10 dashed in pieces *a*' the top of
Hab 1:10 And they shall scoff *a*' the kings,
2: 3 but *a*' the end it shall speak. *
5 neither keepeth *a*' home, who
19 there is no breath *a*' all in the
3: 5 coals went forth *a*' his feet.
11 *a*' the light of thine arrows they
11 *a*' the shining of thy glittering
16 my lips quivered *a*' the voice:
Zep 1: 7 Hold thy peace *a*' the presence
7 the day of the Lord is *a*' hand;
12 shall come to pass *a*' that time,
2: 4 out of Ashdod *a*' the noon day,
3:19 *a*' that time I will undo all
20 *A*' that time will I bring you
Zec 1:11 earth sitteth still, and is *a*' rest.
15 the heathen that are *a*' ease:
3: 1 Satan standing *a*' his right hand 5921
8 for they are men wondered *a*':
7: 5 did ye *a*' all fast unto me, even
11:13 I was prised *a*' of them. And I
12: 8 feeble among them *a*' that day
14: 7 *a*' evening time it shall be light.
14 shall also fight *a*' Jerusalem; *
Mal 1:10 accept an offering *a*' your hand.
13 ye have snuffed *a*' it, saith the
2: 7 should seek the law *a*' his mouth:
8 many to stumble *a*' the law;
13 it with good will *a*' your hand.
M't 3: 2 kingdom of heaven is *a*' hand. 1448
4: 6 lest *a*' any time thou dash thy *3379
17 kingdom of heaven is *a*' hand. 1448
5:25 lest *a*' any time the adversary 3379
34 Swear not *a*' all; 3654
40 any man will sue thee *a*' the law *2919
7:13 Enter ye in *a*' the strait gate *1223
28 were astonished *a*' his doctrine: 1909
8: 6 my servant lieth *a*' home *1722
9: 9 sitting *a*' the receipt of custom; 1909
10 as Jesus sat *a*' meat in the house, 345
10: 7 kingdom of heaven is *a*' hand. 1448
35 am come to set a man *a*' variance 1369
11:22 Tyre and Sidon *a*' the day of *1722
25 *A*' that time Jesus answered and "
12: 1 *A*' that time Jesus went on the "
41 repented *a*' the preaching of 1519
13:15 lest *a*' any time they should see *3379
49 So shall it be *a*' the end of the *1722
14: 1 *A*' that time Herod the tetrarch "
9 them which sat *a*' meat with him 4873
15:17 whatsoever entereth in *a*' the 1519
30 and cast them *a*' Jesus' feet; 3844
18: 1 *A*' the same time came the *1722
29 fell down *a*' his feet *1519
19: 4 *a*' the beginning made them male * 575
22:33 were astonished *a*' his doctrine. 1909
23: 6 the uppermost rooms *a*' feasts, 1722
24 which strain *a*' a gnat, and *1368
24:33 it is near, even *a*' the doors. 1909
41 shall be grinding *a*' the mill; 1722
25: 6 *a*' midnight there was a cry made,
27 and then *a*' my coming I should
26: 7 it on his head, as he sat *a*' meat. 345
18 My time is *a*' hand; I will keep 1451
18 *a*' thy house with my disciples. 4314
45 the hour is *a*' hand, and the Son 1448
46 he is *a*' hand that doth betray me. "
60 *A*' the last came two false *
27:15 Now *a*' that feast the governor 2596
M'r 1:15 the kingdom of God is *a*' hand: 1448
22 were astonished *a*' his doctrine: 1909
32 And *a*' even, when the sun did set,
33 gathered together *a*' the door. 4314
2:14 Alphaeus sitting *a*' the 1909
15 Jesus sat *a*' meat in his house, 2621
4:12 lest *a*' any time they should be *3379
5:22 he saw him, he fall *a*' his feet. 4314
23 lieth *a*' the point of death:
6: 3 And they were offended *a*' him. *1722
7:25 and came and fell *a*' his feet. 4314
9:12 many things, and be set *a*' nought. 1847
10:22 And he was sad *a*' that saying, 1909
24 disciples were astonished *a*' his "
11: 1 Bethany, *a*' the mount of Olives, 4314
18 the people was astonished *a*' his 1909
12: 2 And *a*' the season he sent to the
4 and *a*' him they cast stones, and *
17 And they marvelled *a*' him. 1909
39 the uppermost rooms *a*' feasts. 1722
13:29 is nigh, even *a*' the doors. 1909
35 of the house cometh, *a*' even, *
35 *a*' midnight, or *a*' the cockcrowing,
14: 3 as he sat *a*' meat, there came a 2621
42 that betrayeth me is *a*' hand. 1448
54 and warmed himself *a*' the fire. *4314
15: 6 Now *a*' that feast he released 2596
34 *a*' the ninth hour Jesus cried
16: 2 sepulchre *a*' the rising of the sun.*
14 the eleven as they sat *a*' meat, 345
Lu 1:10 praying without *a*' the time of
14 many shall rejoice *a*' his birth. 1909
29 she was troubled *a*' this saying,
2:18 wondered *a*' those things which 4012

Lu 2:33 marvelled *a*' those things which 1909
41 Jerusalem every year *a*' the feast
47 astonished *a*' his understanding "
4:11 up, lest *a*' any time thou dash *3379
18 to set *a*' liberty them that are 1722
22 wondered *a*' the gracious words 1909
32 were astonished *a*' his doctrine; "
5: 5 nevertheless *a*' thy word I will let "
8 he fell down *a*' Jesus' knees, 4363
9 were with him, *a*' the draught 1909
27 Levi, sitting *a*' the receipt of "
7: 9 he marvelled *a*' him, and turned
37 knew that Jesus sat *a*' meat in 345
38 stood *a*' his feet behind him 3844
49 they that sat *a*' meat with him 345
8:19 could not come *a*' him for the 1519
26 they arrived *a*' the country of "
35 sitting *a*' the feet of Jesus, 3844
41 and fell down *a*' Jesus' feet, and "
9:31 should accomplish *a*' Jerusalem 1722
9:43 amazed *a*' the mighty power of 1909
43 wondered every one *a*' all things "
61 farewell, which are *a*' home *
61 home *a*' my house. 1519
10:14 Tyre and Sidon *a*' the judgment, *1722
32 when he was *a*' the place, came 2596
39 which also sat *a*' Jesus' feet, and 3844
11: 5 shall go unto him *a*' midnight, 3317
32 they repented *a*' the preaching of 1519
12:40 Son of man cometh *a*' an hour *
46 not for him, and *a*' an hour when *1722
13: 1 There were present *a*' that season "
24 to enter in *a*' the strait gate: *1223
25 and to knock *a*' the door, saying,
14:10 of them that sit *a*' meat with thee. 4873
14 recompensed *a*' the resurrection *1722
15 them that sat *a*' meat with him 4873
17 sent his servant *a*' supper time
15:29 neither transgressed I *a*' any *3763
16:20 which was laid *a*' his gate, full of 4314
17:16 fell down on his face *a*' his feet, 3844
19: 5 to day I must abide *a*' thy house. 1722
23 bank, that *a*' my coming I might
29 Bethany, *a*' the mount called 4314
30 in the which *a*' your entering ye *1531
37 even now *a*' the descent of the 4314
42 even thou, *a*' least in this thy day, *1065
20:10 *a*' the season he sent a servant to 1722
26 and they marvelled *a*' his answer, 1909
37 Moses shewed *a*' the bush, when * "
40 not ask him any question *a*' all, *
46 and the chief rooms *a*' feasts; 1722
21:30 that summer is now nigh *a*' hand. *1451
31 kingdom of God is nigh *a*' hand. * "
34 to yourselves, lest *a*' any time *3379
37 *a*' night he went out, and abode *3571
22:27 he that sitteth *a*' meat, or he that 345
27 is not he that sitteth *a*' meat? "
30 eat and drink *a*' my table in my 1909
40 And when he was *a*' the place, he
23: 7 to Herod, who himself also was *a*' 1722
7 Jerusalem *a*' that time. * "
11 men of war set him *a*' nought, and 1848
12 they were *a*' enmity between 1722
17 release one unto them *a*' the *2596
18 cried all *a*' once, saying, Away *3826
24:12 wondering in himself *a*' that
22 which were early *a*' the sepulchre; 1909
27 And beginning *a*' Moses and all * 575
30 as he sat *a*' meat with them, he *2625
47 nations, beginning *a*' Jerusalem. * 575
Joh 1:18 No man hath seen God *a*' any 4455
2:10 Every man *a*' the beginning doth *4412
13 the Jews' passover was *a*' hand, 1451
23 was in Jerusalem *a*' the passover, 1722
4:21 nor yet *a*' Jerusalem, worship the* "
45 seen all the things that he did *a*' * "
45 Jerusalem *a*' the feast: for they "
46 whose son was sick *a*' Capernaum. "
47 for he was *a*' the point of death. 3195
52 Yesterday *a*' the seventh hour the
53 knew that it was *a*' the same hour, 1722
5: 2 Now there is *a*' Jerusalem by the * "
4 an angel went down *a*' a certain *2596
28 Marvel not *a*' this: for the hour is
37 his voice *a*' any time, nor seen his 4455
6:21 ship was *a*' the land whither they 1909
39 raise it up again *a*' the last day. 1722
40 I will raise him up *a*' the last day.
41 Jews then murmured *a*' him, *4012
44 raise him up *a*' the last day. *
54 I will raise him up *a*' the last day.
61 his disciples murmured *a*' it, he 4012
7: 2 Jews' feast of tabernacles was *a*' 1451
11 Jews sought him *a*' the feast, and 1722
23 are ye angry *a*' me, because I have*
8: 7 let him first cast a stone *a*' her. 1909
9 beginning *a*' the eldest, even unto* 575
59 took they up stones to cast *a*' him: 1909
10:22 And it was *a*' Jerusalem the feast 1722
40 place where John *a*' first baptized;
11:24 in the resurrection at the last day. 1722
32 she fell down *a*' his feet, saying 1519
49 Ye know nothing *a*' all, 3762
55 Jews' passover was nigh *a*' hand: 1451
12: 2 one of them that sat *a*' the table 4873
16 understood not his disciples *a*' the 4412
20 came up to worship *a*' the feast: 1722
13:28 Now no man *a*' the table knew for 345
14:20 *A*' that day ye shall know that I *1722
16: 4 not unto you *a*' the beginning, *1537
26 *A*' that day ye shall ask in my *1722
18:16 Peter stood *a*' the door without. 4314
38 I find no fault in him *a*' all.
39 release unto you one *a*' the 1722
19:11 couldest have no power *a*' all *

Joh 19:39 Nicodemus, which *a*' the first
42 the sepulchre was nigh *a*' hand. 1451
20:11 Mary stood without *a*' the 4314
12 one *a*' the head, and the other *a*' "
19 Then the same day *a*' evening, *
21: 1 disciples *a*' the sea of Tiberias; 1909
20 leaned on his breast *a*' supper, 1722
Ac 1: 6 wilt thou *a*' this time restore "
19 all the dwellers *a*' Jerusalem;
2: 5 were dwelling *a*' Jerusalem Jews, 1722
14 all ye that dwell *a*' Jerusalem, be
3: 1 into the temple *a*' the hour of 1909
2 whom they laid daily *a*' the gate 4314
10 for alms *a*' the Beautiful gate of 1909
10 amazement *a*' that which had "
12 why marvel ye *a*' this? or why "
4: 6 gathered together *a*' Jerusalem. *1519
11 which was set *a*' nought of you 1848
18 not to speak *a*' all nor teach in 2527
35 laid them down *a*' the apostles' 3844
37 and laid it *a*' the apostles' feet. "
5: 2 and laid it *a*' the apostles' feet. "
9 thy husband are *a*' the door, and 1909
10 down straightway *a*' his feet, and 3844
15 *a*' the least the shadow of Peter 2579
7:13 *a*' the second time Joseph was 1722
26 would have set them *a*' one again, 1519
29 Then fled Moses *a*' this saying, 1722
31 Moses saw it, he wondered *a*' the
58 laid down their clothes *a*' a young 3844
8: 1 And *a*' that time there was a *1722
1 church which was *a*' Jerusalem; * "
14 apostles which were *a*' Jerusalem "
35 and began *a*' the same scripture, * 575
40 But Philip was found *a*' Azotus: 1519
9:10 a certain disciple *a*' Damascus, 1722
13 done to thy saints *a*' Jerusalem: "
19 disciples which were *a*' Damascus. "
22 Jews which dwelt *a*' Damascus, "
27 preached boldly *a*' Damascus in "
28 in and going out *a*' Jerusalem, "
32 the saints which dwelt *a*' Lydda.
35 all that dwelt *a*' Lydda and Saron,
36 Now there was *a*' Joppa a certain 1722
10:11 sheet knit *a*' the four corners, *
25 down *a*' his feet, and worshipped 1909
30 *a*' the ninth hour I prayed in my *
11: 8 unclean hath *a*' any time entered *3763
15 them, as on us *a*' the beginning. 1722
12:13 Peter knocked *a*' the door of the
13: 1 church that was *a*' Antioch 1722
5 when they were *a*' Salamis, they "
12 being astonished *a*' the doctrine 1909
27 they that dwell *a*' Jerusalem, and *1722
14: 8 sat a certain man *a*' Lystra, "
15:14 declared how God *a*' the first did *
16: 2 brethren that were *a*' Lystra and 1722
4 elders which were *a*' Jerusalem. "
25 And *a*' midnight Paul and Silas *2596
17:13 God was preached of Paul *a*' 1722
16 Paul waited for them *a*' Athens, "
30 this ignorance God winked *a*'; *
18:22 when he had landed *a*' Cæsarea, 1519
24 Apollos, born *a*' Alexandria, an *
19: 1 Apollos was *a*' Corinth, Paul 1722
17 Greeks also dwelling *a*' Ephesus;
26 not alone *a*' Ephesus, but almost
27 our craft is in danger to be set *a*' *1519
20: 5 before tarried for us *a*' Troas. 1722
14 when he met with us *a*' Assos, 1519
15 we arrived *a*' Samos, and *1519
15 tarried *a*' Trogyllium; and the *1722
16 *a*' Jerusalem the day of Pentecost. 1519
18 have been with you *a*' all seasons,*
21: 3 into Syria, and landed *a*' Tyre: 1519
11 So shall the Jews *a*' Jerusalem 1722
13 but also to die *a*' Jerusalem for 1519
24 and be *a*' charges with them, that 1159
22: 3 brought up in this city *a*' the feet 3844
23:11 thou bear witness also *a*' Rome. 1519
23 two hundred, *a*' the third hour of 575
25: 4 should be kept *a*' Cæsarea, and 1722
8 have I offended any thing *a*' all.
10 I stand *a*' Cæsar's judgment seat, *1909
15 About whom, when I was *a*' 1519
23 men of the city, *a*' Festus'
24 both *a*' Jerusalem, and also here, 1722
26: 4 which was *a*' the first among * 575
4 nation *a*' Jerusalem, know all the 1722
13 *A*' midday, O king, I saw in the
20 and *a*' Jerusalem, and throughout
32 might have been set *a*' liberty, if 630
27: 3 the next day we touched *a*' Sidon. 1519
28:12 And landing *a*' Syracuse, we
Ro 1:10 if by any means now *a*' length I 4218
15 gospel to you that are *a*' Rome *1722
3:26 To declare, I say, *a*' this time his "
4:20 He staggered not *a*' the promise *1519
8:34 who is even *a*' the right hand of 1722
9: 9 *A*' this time will I come, and *2596
32 stumbled *a*' that stumblingstone;
11: 5 Even so then *a*' this present time 1722
13:12 spent, the day is *a*' hand: let us 1448
14:10 set *a*' nought thy brother? for 1848
15:26 saints which are *a*' Jerusalem. 1722
16: 1 servant of the church *a*' Cenchrea: "
1Co 1: 2 which is *a*' Corinth, to them that "
7:39 she is *a*' liberty to be married to *1657
8:10 sit *a*' meat in the idol's temple, 2621
9: 7 time *a*' his own charges? who *4218
13 and they which wait *a*' the altar *
11:34 let him eat *a*' home; that ye come 1722
14:16 say Amen *a*' thy giving of thanks, 1909
27 or *a*' the most by three, and that
35 their husbands *a*' home: for it is 1722
15: 6 five hundred brethren *a*' once; 2178

1Co 15:23 that are Christ's a· his coming. 1722
29 if the dead rise not a· all? why 3654
32 fought with beasts a· Ephesus, 1722
52 twinkling of an eye a· the last "
16: 8 But I will tarry a· Ephesus until "
12 but his will was not a· all 3843
12 to come a· this time; *3568
2Co 1: 1 which is a· Corinth, with all the 1722
4:18 While we look not a· the things 4648
18 but a· the things which are not "
5: 6 whilst we are a· home in the 1722
8:14 that now a· this time your "
Ga 4:12 ye have not injured me a· all. *3762
13 the gospel unto you a· the first.
Eph 1: 1 saints which are a· Ephesus, 1722
20 and set him a· his own right "
2:12 That a· that time ye were "
3:13 faint not a· my tribulations "
Ph'p 1: 1 Christ Jesus which are a· Philippi. "
2:10 That a· the name of Jesus every *
4: 5 to all men. The Lord is a· hand. 1451
10 that now a· the last your care of 4218
Col 1: 2 brethren in Christ which are a· 1722
2: 1 for them a· Laodicea, and for "
1Th 2: 2 know, a· Philippi we were bold "
5 For neither a· any time used we 4218
19 our Lord Jesus a· his coming? 1722
3: 1 good to be left a· Athens alone; "
13 even our Father, a· the coming of "
5:13 And be a· peace among yourselves."
2Th 2: 2 the day of Christ is a· hand. †1764
3:11 disorderly, working not a· all, 3367
1Ti 1: 3 to abide still a· Ephesus, when 1722
5: 4 to show piety a· home, and to *
2Ti 1:18 ministered unto me a· Ephesus, 1722
2:26 captive by him a· his will. *1519
3:11 a· Antioch, a· Iconium, a· Lystra; 1722
4: 1 and the dead a· his appearing *2596
6 of my departure is a· hand. *2186
8 shall give me a· that day: 1722
13 left a· Troas with Carpus, when "
16 A· my first answer no man stood "
20 Erastus abode a· Corinth: "
20 have I left a· Miletum sick. "
Tit 2: 5 keepers a· home, good, obedient 3626
Heb 1: 1 God, who a· sundry times and in *
5, 13 the angels said he a· any time, 4218
2: 1 lest a· any time we should let *3379
3 which a· the first began to be
7:13 man gave attendance a· the altar.
9:17 no strength a· all while the *3379
12: 2 and is set down a· the right hand 1722
13:23 brother Timothy is set a· liberty; 630
Jas 3:11 send forth a· the same place *1537
1Pe 1: 7 and glory a· the appearing 1722
13 unto you a· the revelation of "
2: 8 which stumble a· the word, being
4: 7 is a· hand: be ye therefore 1448
17 begin a· the house of God: and if 575
17 it first begin a· us, what shall the "
5:13 that is a· Babylon, elected 1722
1Jo 1: 5 and in him is no darkness a· all. 3762
2:28 before him a· his coming. 1722
4:12 man hath seen God a· any time. 4455
Re 1: 3 therein: for the time is a· hand. 1451
17 saw him, I fell a· his feet as dead. 4314
3:20 Behold I stand a· the door, and 1909
8: 3 and stood a· the altar, having "
18:14 shalt find them no more a· all.
21 shall be found no more a· all
22 shall be heard no more a· all in
22 shall be heard no more a· all in
23 shall shine no more a· all in thee:
23 shall be heard no more a· all in thee:
19: 2 blood of his servants a· her hand. 1537
10 And I fell a· his feet to worship *1715
21:12 twelve gates, and a· the gates 1909
25 not be shut a· all by day; for *
22:10 this book; for the time is a· hand. 1451

Atad (a'-tad) See also ABEL-MIZRAIM.
Ge 50:10 came to the threshingfloor of A·, 329
11 saw the mourning in the floor of A·, "

Atarah (at'-a-rah)
1Ch 2:26 another wife, whose name was A·; 5851

Ataroth (at'-a-roth) See also ATAROTH-ADAR; ATROTH.
Nu 32: 3 A·, and Dibon, and Jazer, 5852
34 of Gad built Dibon, and A·, "
Jos 16: 2 unto the borders of Archi to A·, "
7 went down from Janohah to A·, "
1Ch 2:54 A·, the house of Joab, and half * "

Ataroth-adar (at''-a-roth-a'-dar) See also ATAROTH-ADDAR.
Jos 18:13 the border descended to A·, 5853

Ataroth-addar (at''-a-roth-ad'-dar) See also ATAROTH-ADAR.
Jos 16: 5 on the east side was A·, unto 5853

ate
Ps 106:28 and a· the sacrifices of the dead. 398
Da 10: 3 I a· no pleasant bread, neither "
Re 10:10 of the angel's hand, and a· it up; 2719

Ater (a'-tur)
Ezr 2:16 The children of A· of Hezekiah, 333
42 the children of A·, the children of "
Ne 7:21 The children of A· of Hezekiah, "
45 of Shallum, the children of A·, "
10:17 A·, Hizkijah, Azzur, "

Atha See MARAN-ATHA.

Athach (a'-thak)
1Sa 30:30 and to them which were in A·, 6269

Athaiah (ath-a-i'-ah)
Ne 11: 4 of Judah; A· the son of Uzziah, 6265

Athaliah (ath-a-li'-ah)
2Ki 8:26 and his mother's name was A·, 6271
11: 1 And when A·, the mother of "
2 from A·, so that he was not slain. "
3 And A· did reign over the land. "
13 when A· heard the noise of the "
14 and A· rent her clothes, and cried "
20 and they slew A· with the sword "
1Ch 8:26 and Shehariah, and A·, "
2Ch 22: 2 was A· the daughter of Omri. "
10 when A· the mother of Ahaziah "
11 hid him from A·, so that she slew "
12 house of God in six years: and A· "
23:12 Now when A· heard the noise 6271
13 A· rent her clothes, and said, "
21 they had slain A· with the sword. "
24: 7 sons of A·, that wicked woman, "
Ezr 8: 7 of Elam; Jeshaiah the son of A·, "

Athenians (a-the'-ne-uns)
Ac 17:21 (For all the A· and strangers 117

Athens (ath'-ens) See also ATHENIANS.
Ac 17:15 brought him unto A·: 116
16 while Paul waited for them at A·, "
22 Ye men of A·, I perceive 117
18: 1 Paul departed from A·, 116
1Th 3: 1 it good to be left at A· alone; "
subscr. Thessalonians was written from A·."
2Th *subscr.* Thessalonians was written from A·"

athirst
J'g 15:18 he was sore a·, and called on the 6770
Ru 2: 9 thou art a·, go unto the vessels,
M't 25:44 saw we thee an hungered, or a·, 1372
Re 21: 6 I will give to him that is a· "
22:17 let him that is a· come. "

Athlai (ath'-lahee)
Ezr 10:28 Hananiah, Zabbai, and A·. 6270

atonement See also ATONEMENTS:
Ex 29:33 wherewith the a· was made, 3722
36 a bullock for a sin offering for a·: 3725
36 when thou hast made an a· for it, 3722
37 shalt make an a· for the altar, "
30:10 shall make an a· upon the horns "
10 once in the year shall he make a· "
15 to make a· for your souls. "
16 take the a· money of the children 3725
16 to make an a· for your souls. 3722
32:30 I shall make an a· for your sin. "
Le 1: 4 to make a· for him. "
4:20 priest shall make an a· for them, "
26 and the priest shall make an a· "
31 priest shall make an a· for him, "
35 shall make an a· for his sin "
5: 6, 10, 13 shall make an a· for him "
16 the priest shall make an a· "
18 an a· for him concerning his "
6: 7 an a· for him before the Lord: "
7: 7 the priest that maketh a· "
8:34 to make an a· for you. "
9: 7 and make an a· for thyself, "
7 and make an a· for them; "
10:17 make a· for them before the Lord? "
12: 7 and make an a· for her; "
8 priest shall make an a· for her, "
14:18 and the priest shall make an a· "
19 and make an a· for him "
20 and the priest shall make an a· "
21, 29 to make an a· for him, "
31 and the priest shall make an a· "
53 and make an a· for the house: "
15:15, 30 the priest shall make an a· for "
16: 6 and make an a· for himself, "
10 to make an a· with him, "
11 and shall make an a· for himself, "
16 shall make an a· for the holy place, "
17 to make an a· in the holy place, "
17 and have made an a· for himself, "
18 and make an a· for it; "
24 and make an a· for himself, "
27 blood was brought in to make a· "
30 the priest make an a· for you, "
32 And the priest,...shall make the a·, "
33 make an a· for the holy sanctuary, "
33 shall make an a· for the tabernacle "
33 and he shall make an a· for the "
34 an a· for the children of Israel. "
17:11 to make an a· for your souls: "
11 the blood that maketh an a· for "
19:22 the priest shall make an a· for "
23:27 there shall be a day of a·: 3725
28 it is a day of a·, "
28 to make an a· for you 3722
25: 9 the day of a· shall ye make the 3725
Nu 5: 8 the ram of the a·, "
8 an a· shall be made for him. 3722
6:11 and make an a· for him, "
8:12 to make an a· for the Levites. "
19 and to make an a· for the children "
21 and Aaron made an a· "
15:25 And the priest shall make an a· "
28 shall make an a· for the soul "
28 to make an a· for him; "
16:46 and make an a· for them: "
47 and made an a· for the people. "
25:13 an a· for the children of Israel. "
28:22 sin offering, to make an a· for you. "
30 the goats, to make an a· for you. "
29: 5 offering to make an a· for you: "
11 the sin offering of a·, 3725
31:50 to make an a· for our souls 3722
2Sa 21: 3 wherewith shall I make the a·, "
1Ch 6:49 and to make an a· for Israel, "
2Ch 29:24 to make an a· for all Israel: "
Ne 10:33 to make an a· for Israel, "
Ro 5:11 we have now received the a·. 2643

atonements
Ex 30:10 the sin offering of a·: *3725

Atroth (a'-troth) See also ATAROTH.
Nu 32:35 And A·, Shophan, and Jaazer, 5855

Attai (at'-tahee)
1Ch 2:35 to wife, and she bare him A·. 6262
36 And A· begat Nathan, and Nathan "
12:11 A· the sixth, Eliel the seventh, "
2Ch 11:20 which bare him Abijah, and A·, "

attain See also ATTAINED.
Ps 139: 6 it is high, I cannot a· unto it.
Pr 1: 5 a man of understanding shall a· 7069
Eze 46: 7 as his hand shall a· unto, *5381
Ho 8: 5 will it be ere they a· to innocency?3201
Ac 27:12 means they might a· to Phenice, *2658
Ph'p 3:11 I might a· unto the resurrection "

attained
Ge 47: 9 not a· unto the days of the years 5381
2Sa 23:19 he a· not unto the first three: 935
23 he a· not to the first "
1Ch 11:21 howbeit he a· not to the first three. "
25 but a· not to the first three. "
Ro 9:30 have a· to righteousness, 2638
31 not a· to the law of righteousness.*5348
Ph'p 3:12 Not as though I had already a·, *2983
16 whereto we have already a·, 5348
1Ti 4: 6 whereunto thou hast a·. *3877

Attalia (at-ta-li'-ah)
Ac 14:25 they went down into A·: 825

attend
Es 4: 5 he had appointed to a· upon her, 6440
Ps 17: 1 a· unto my cry, give ear unto my 7181
55: 2 A· unto me, and hear me: "
61: 1 a· unto my prayer. "
86: 6 a· to the voice of my supplications.*"
142: 6 A· unto my cry; for I am brought "
Pr 4: 1 and a· to know understanding. "
20 My son, a· to my words; "
5: 1 My son, a· unto my wisdom, "
7:24 and a· to the words of my mouth. "
1Co 7:35 that ye may a· upon the Lord 2145

attendance
1Ki 10: 5 and the a· of his ministers, 4612
2Ch 9: 4 and the a· of his ministers, "
1Ti 4:13 Till I come, give a· to reading, *4337
Heb 7:13 no man gave a· at the altar. "

attended
Job 32:12 Yea, I a· unto you, and, behold, 995
Ps 66:19 hath a· to the voice of my prayer. 7181
Ac 16:14 she a· unto the things which were*4337

attending
Ro 13: 6 a· continually upon this very thing. 4342

attent
2Ch 6:40 thine ears be a· unto the prayer 7183
7:15 mine ears a· unto the prayer "

attentive
Ne 1: 6 let now thine ear be a·, 7183
11 now thine ear be a· to the prayer "
8: 3 were a· unto the book of the law. "
Ps 130: 2 let thine ears be a· to the voice 7183
Lu 19:48 were very attentive to hear him.* 1582

attentively
Job 37: 2 Hear a· the noise of his voice, †‡8085

attire See also ATTIRED.
Pr 7:10 the a· of an harlot, 7897
Jer 2:32 her ornaments, or a bride her a·? 7196
Eze 23:15 in dyed a· upon their heads, 2871

attired
Le 16: 4 the linen mitre shall he be a·: 6801

audience
Ge 23:10 in the a· of the children of Heth, 241
13 in the a· of the people of the land, "
16 named in the a· of the sons of Heth, "
Ex 24: 7 read in the a· of the people: "
1Sa 25:24 in thine a·, and hear the words * "
1Ch 28: 8 and in the a· of our God, "
Ne 13: 1 in the a· of the people; "
Lu 7: 1 sayings in the a· of the people, * 189
20:45 in the a· of all the people he said * 191
Ac 13:16 ye that fear God, give a·. * "
15:12 and gave a· to Barnabas and * "
22:22 they gave him a· unto this word, "

aught See NAUGHT; OUGHT.

augment
Nu 32:14 to a· yet the fierce anger of the 5595

Augustus (aw-gus'-tus) See also AUGUSTUS'; CÆSAR.
Lu 2: 1 a decree from Cæsar A·, 828
Ac 25:21 reserved unto the hearing of A·, * "
25 himself hath appealed to A·, * "

Augustus' (aw-gus'-tus)
Ac 27: 1 a centurion of A· band. * 828

aul
Ex 21: 6 bore his ear through with an a·; 4836
De 15:17 Then thou shalt take an a·, "

aunt
Le 18:14 she is thine a·. 1733

austere
Lu 19:21 because thou art an a· man: 840
22 that I was an a· man, "

author
1Co 14:33 God is not the a· of confusion, but*
Heb 5: 9 became the a· of eternal salvation 159
12: 2 the a· and finisher of our faith; 747

authorities
1Pe 3:22 a· and powers being made subject 1849

authority See also AUTHORITIES.
Es 9:29 Mordecai the Jew....with all a'. 8633
Pr 29: 2 When the righteous are in a', the*7235
M't 7:29 taught them as one having a'. 1849
8: 9 For I am a man under a', "
20:25 that are great exercise a' upon 2715
21:23 what a' doest thou these things? 1849
23 and who gave thee this a'? "
24, 27 by what a' I do these things. "
M'r 1:22 as one that had a', "
27 for with a' commandeth he even "
10:42 their great ones exercise a' upon 2715
11:28 what a' doest thou these things? 1849
28 and who gave thee this a' "
29, 33 by what a' I do these things. "
13:34 gave a' to his servants, "
Lu 4:36 with a' and power he commandeth "
7: 8 am a man set under a', "
9: 1 gave them power and a' over all "
19:17 have thou a' over ten cities. "
20: 2 what a' doest thou these things? "
2 who is he that gave thee this a'? "
8 by what a' I do these things. "
20 power and a' of the governor. "
22:25 that exercise a' upon them are 1850
Joh 5:27 hath given him a' to execute 1849
Ac 8:27 eunuch of great a' under Candace 1413
9:14 he hath a' from the chief priests 1849
26:10 having received a' from the chief "
12 went to Damascus with a' and "
1Co 15:24 all rule and all a' and power. "
2Co 10: 8 somewhat more of our a', "
1Ti 2: 2 and for all that are in a'; *5247
12 nor to usurp a' over the man, but* 831
Tit 2:15 exhort, and rebuke with all a'. 2003
Re 13: 2 power, and his seat, and great a'. 1849

Ava (a'-vah) See also IVAH.
2Ki 17:24 and from Cuthah, and from A', 5755

availeth
Es 5:13 all this a' me nothing, 7737
Ga 5: 6 neither circumcision a' any thing, 2480
6:15 neither circumcision a' any thing,* "
Jas 5:16 prayer of a righteous man a' much. "

Aven See also BETH-AVEN.
Eze 30:17 young men of A' and of Pi-beseth 206
Ho 10: 8 high places also of A', the sin of "
Am 1: 5 inhabitant from the plain of A', "

avenge See also AVENGED; AVENGETH; AVENGING.
Le 19:18 Thou shalt not a', nor bear any *5358
26:25 a sword...that shall a' the quarrel* "
Nu 31: 2 A' the children of Israel of 5358, 5360
3 and a' the Lord of Midian. *5414, "
De 32:43 will a' the blood of his servants, 5358
1Sa 24:12 and the Lord a' me of thee: "
2Ki 9: 7 I may a' the blood of my servants "
Es 8:13 to a' themselves on their enemies. "
Isa 1:24 and a' me of mine enemies: "
Jer 46:10 he may a' him of his adversaries: "
Ho 1: 4 and I will a' the blood of Jezreel 6485
Lu 18: 3 saying, A' me of mine adversary. 1556
5 I will a' her, lest by her continual "
7 not God a' his own elect, 4160, 3588, 1557
8 he will a' them speedily. "
Ro 12:19 Dearly beloved, a' not yourselves, 1556
Re 6:10 dost thou not judge and a' our "

avenged
Ge 4:24 If Cain shall be a' sevenfold, 5358
Jos 10:13 the people had a' themselves "
J'd 15: 7 yet will I be a' of you, "
16:28 that I may be at once a' of the "
1Sa 14:24 that I may be a' on mine enemies. "
18:25 to be a' of the king's enemies. "
25:31 or that my Lord hath a' himself: 3467
2Sa 4: 8 the Lord hath a' my lord 5414, 5360
18:19 hath a' him of his enemies. 8199
31 Lord hath a' thee this day of all "
Jer 5: 9, 29 shall not my soul be a' on such 5358
9: 9 shall not my soul be a' on such "
Ac 7:24 a' him that was oppressed, * 4160, 1557
Re 18:20 God hath a' you on her. 2919, 3588, 2917
19: 2 hath a' the blood of his servants 1556

avenger
Nu 35:12 for refuge from the a'; that the 1350
De 19: 6 Lest the a' of the blood pursue the "
12 into the hand of the a' of blood, "
Jos 20: 3 your refuge from the a' of blood. "
5 if the a' of blood pursue after him, "
9 by the hand of the a' of blood, "
Ps 8: 2 still the enemy and the a'. 5358
44:16 by reason of the enemy and a'. "
1Th 4: 6 the Lord is the a' of all such, 1558

avengeth
2Sa 22:48 It is God that a' me, *5414, 5360
Ps 18:47 It is God that a' me, * " "

avenging
J'g 5: 2 Praise ye the Lord for the a'*6544, 6546
1Sa 25:26 from a' thyself with thine own 3467
33 from a' myself with mine own "

averse
Mic 2: 8 by securely as men a' from war. 7725

Avim (a'-vim) See also AVIMS; AVITES.
Jos 18:23 And A', and Parah, and Ophrah, 5761

Avims (a'-vims) See also AVIM.
De 2:23 And the A' which dwelt in *5757

Avites (a'-vites) See also AVIM.
Jos 13: 3 and the Ekronites; also the A': *5757
2Ki 17:31 the A' made Nibhaz and Tartak,

Avith (a'-vith)
Ge 36:35 and the name of his city was A'. 5762
1Ch 1:46 and the name of his city was A'.

avoid See also AVOIDED; AVOIDING.
Pr 4:15 A' it, pass not by it, turn from it, 6544
Ro 16:17 which ye have learned; and a' *1578
1Co 7: 2 Nevertheless, to a' fornication, *1223
2Ti 2:23 and unlearned questions a', *3868
Tit 3: 9 But a' foolish questions, and *4026

avoided See also AVOID.
1Sa 18:11 And David a' out of his presence 5437

avoiding
2Co 8:20 A' this, that no man should 4724
1Ti 6:20 a' profane and vain babblings, *1624

avouched
De 26:17 Thou hast a' the Lord this day to 559
18 the Lord hath a' thee this day "

await
Ac 9:24 laying a' was known of Saul. *1917

awake See also AWAKED; AWAKEST; AWAKETH; AWAKING; AWOKE.
J'g 5:12 A', a', Deborah: a', a', utter a 5782
Job 8: 6 surely now he would a' for thee, "
14:12 they shall not a', nor be raised 6974
Ps 7: 6 and a' for me to the judgment 5782
17:15 I shall be satisfied, when I a', with 6974
35:23 Stir up thyself, and a' to my "
44:23 A', why sleepest thou, O Lord? 5782
57: 8 A' up, my glory, "
8 a', psaltery and harp: "
8 I myself will a' early. "
59: 4 a' to help me, and behold. "
5 a' to visit all the heathen: *6974
108: 2 A', psaltery and harp: 5782
2 I myself will a' early. "
139:18 when I a', I am still with thee. 6974
Pr 23:35 when shall I a'? I will seek it yet "
Ca 2: 7 nor a' my love, till he please. 5782
3: 5 not up, nor a' my love, till he * "
4:16 A', O north wind; and come, "
8: 4 ye stir not up, nor a' my love, * "
Isa 26:19 A' and sing, ye that dwell in dust: 6974
51: 9 A', a', put on strength, O arm of 5782
9 the Lord; a', as in the ancient "
17 A', a'; stand up, O Jerusalem, "
52: 1 A', a'; put on thy strength, "
Da 12: 2 in the dust of the earth shall a', 6974
Joe 1: 5 A', ye drunkards, and weep; "
Hab 2: 7 and a' that shall vex thee, "
19 him that saith to the wood, A'; "
Zec 13: 7 A', O sword, against my shepherd, 5782
M'r 4:38 they a' him, and say unto him, 1326
Lu 9:32 when they were a', they saw his 1235
Joh 11:11 that I may a' him out of sleep. 1852
Ro 13:11 is high time to a' out of sleep: 1453
1Co 15:34 A' to righteousness, and sin not; 1594
Eph 5:14 A' thou that sleepest, and arise 1453

awaked See also AWOKE.
Ge 28:16 And Jacob a' out of his sleep, 3364
J'g 16:14 And he a' out of his sleep, "
1Sa 26:12 saw it, nor knew it, neither a': *6974
1Ki 18:27 he sleepeth, and must be a'. 3364
2Ki 4:31 The child is not a'. 6974
Ps 3: 5 I a'; for the Lord sustained me. "
78:65 the Lord a' as one out of sleep, 3364
Jer 31:26 Upon this I a', and beheld; 6974

awakest
Ps 73:20 when thou a', thou shalt despise 5782
Pr 6:22 when thou a', it shall talk with 6974

awaketh
Ps 73:20 As a dream when one a'; 6974
Isa 29: 8 but he a', and his soul is empty: "
8 but he a', and, behold, he is faint, "

awaking
Ac 16:27 a' out of his sleep, and *1096, 1853

aware See also WARE.
Ca 6:12 Or ever I was a', my soul made 3045
Jer 50:24 thou wast not a': thou art found, "
M't 24:50 in an hour that he is not a' of, *1097
Lu 11:44 over them are not a' of them. *1492
12:46 and at an hour when he is not a', *1097

away See also CASTAWAY.
Ge 12:20 and they sent him a', and his wife,*
15:11 carcasses, Abram drove them a'.
18: 3 favour in thy sight, pass not a',
21:14 and the child, and sent her a':
25 servants had violently taken a'.
24:54 said, Send me a' unto my master.
56 send me a' that I may go to my
59 they sent a' Rebekah, their sister,
25: 6 gifts, and sent them a' from Isaac
26:27 me, and have sent me a' from you?
29 and have sent thee a' in peace:
31 Isaac sent them a', and they
27:35 and hath taken a' thy blessing.
36 times: he took a' my birthright:
36 now he hath taken a' my blessing.
44 until thy brother's fury turn a';
45 Until thy brother's anger turn a'
28: 5 And Isaac sent a' Jacob: and he
6 and sent him a' to Padan-aram,
30:15 take a' my son's mandrakes also?
23 Lord hath taken a' my reproach:
25 said unto Laban, Send me a',
31: 1 taken a' all that was our father's;
9 taken a' the cattle of your father,
18 And he carried a' all his cattle,
20 And Jacob stole a' unawares
26 stolen a' unawares to me,
26 and carried a' my daughters,
27 didst thou flee a' secretly,
27 and steal a' from me; and
27 that I might have sent thee a'
42 hadst sent me a' now empty.
35: 2 Put a' the strange gods that are
Ge 38:19 and she arose, and went a', and
40:15 I was stolen a' out of the land
42:36 and ye will take Benjamin a':
43:14 may send a' your other brother *
44: 3 the men were sent a', they and
45:24 So he sent his brethren a', and
Ex 2: 9 Take this child a', and nurse it
17 came and drove them a':
8: 8 may take a' the frogs from me,
28 not go very far a': intreat for me.
10:17 take a' from me this death only.
19 which took a' the locusts, and *
12:15 first day ye shall put a' leaven
28 the children of Israel went a', *
13:19 up my bones a' hence with you.
22 He took not a' the pillar of the *
14:11 hast thou taken us a' to die in the
15:15 of Canaan shall melt a'.
18:18 Thou wilt surely wear a', both
19:24 the Lord said unto him, A', get * 3212
22:10 die, or be hurt, or driven a',
23:25 I will take sickness a' from the
33:23 And I will take a' mine hand,
Lev 1:16 he shall pluck a' his crop with his
3: 4, 10, 15 kidneys, it shall he take a',
4: 9 the kidneys, it shall he take a',
31 a' all the fat thereof,
31 as the fat is taken a'
35 shall take a' all the fat thereof,
35 the fat of the lamb is taken a'
6: 2 or in a thing taken a' by violence,*
4 that which he took violently a', *
7: 4 the kidneys, it shall he take a':
14:40 that they take a' the stones *
43 that he hath taken a' the stones, *
25:25 sold a' some of his possession, *
26:39 that are left of you shall pine a'
39 of their fathers shall they pine a'
44 I will not cast them a', neither *
Nu 4:13 take a' the ashes from the altar,
11: 6 But now our soul is dried a':
14:43 ye are turned a' from the Lord, * 310
17:10 quite take a' their murmurings *
20:21 wherefore Israel turned a' from
21: 7 he take a' the serpents from us.
24:22 Asshur shall carry thee a' captive.
25: 4 anger of the Lord may be turned a'
11 hath turned my wrath a' from
27: 4 name of our father be done a' 1639
32:15 For if ye turn a' from after him,
36: 4 their inheritance be taken a' from
De 7: 4 turn a' thy son from following me,
15 take a' from thee all sickness,
13: 5 to turn you a' from the Lord *
5 So shalt thou put the evil a' 1197
10 he hath sought to thrust thee a'
15:13 shalt not let him go a' empty:
16 thee, I will not go a' from thee; *3318
18 sendest him a' free from thee; *
17: 7 put the evil a' from among you. 1197
12 shalt put a' the evil from Israel. "
17 that his heart turn not a':
19:13 put a' the guilt of innocent blood 1197
19 put the evil a' from among you. "
21: 9 put a' the guilt of innocent blood "
21 thou put evil a' from among you; "
22:19 may not put her a' all his days.
21 thou put evil a' from among you. 1197
22 shalt thou put a' evil from Israel. "
24 thou put a' evil from among you. "
29 may not put her a' all his days.
23:14 in thee, and turn a' from thee.
24: 4 husband, which sent her a',
7 shalt put evil a' from among you. 1197
26:13 brought a' the hallowed things "
14 have I taken a' aught thereof "
28:26 and no man shall fray them a'.
31 ass shall be violently taken a'
29:18 heart turneth a' this day from
30:17 But if thine heart turn a', so that
17 not hear, but shalt be drawn a',
Jos 2:21 And she sent them a', and they
5: 9 day have I rolled a' the reproach
7:13 ye take a' the accursed thing
8: 3 and sent them a' by night.
16 Joshua, and were drawn a' from
18: 8 the men arose, and went a': *
22: 6 blessed them, and sent them a':
7 when Joshua sent them a' also
16 to turn a' this day from following
18 ye must turn a' this day from
24:14 a' the gods which your fathers 5493
23 therefore put a', said he, the
J'g 3:18 sent a' the people that bare the
4:15 chariot, and fled a' on his feet
17 Howbeit Sisera fled a' on his feet
5:21 river of Kishon swept them a',
8:21 and took a' the ornaments *
9:21 And Jotham ran a', and fled,
10:16 And they put a' the strange gods 5493
11:13 Because Israel took a' my land,
15 took not a' the land of Moab,
38 he sent her a' for two months:
15:17 cast a' the jawbone out of his hand,
16: 3 posts, and went a' with them, *5265
14 went a' with the pin of the beam,
18:24 taken a' my gods which I made,
24 ye are gone a': and what have I
19: 2 went a' from him unto her
20:13 and put a' evil from Israel. 1197
31 and were drawn a' from the city;
1Sa 1:14 put a' thy wine from thee. 5493
5:11 Send a' the ark of the God of Israel,
6: 3 send a' the ark of the God of Israel,
8 by the side thereof; and send it a',
7: 3 then put a' the strange gods 5493

1Sa 7: 4 the children of Israel did put a· 5493
9:26 Up, that I may send thee a·.
10:25 And Samuel sent all the people a·
14:16 behold, the multitude melted a·,
15:27 as Samuel turned about to go a·
17:26 taketh a· the reproach from Israel?
19:10 slipped a· out of Saul's presence.
17 me so, and sent a· mine enemy. *
20:13 shew it thee, and send thee a·,
22 for the Lord hath sent thee a·.
29 let me get a·, I pray thee, and see 4422
21: 6 in the day when it was taken a·.
23: 5 and brought a· their cattle,
26 haste to get a· for fear of Saul; 3212
24:19 will he let him go well a·? 1870
25:10 break a· every man from his
26:12 and gat them a·, and no man 3212
27: 9 alive, and took a· the sheep,
28: 3 had put a· those that had familiar 5493
25 rose up, and went a· that night.
30: 2 but carried them a·, and went on*
18 the Amalekites had carried a·: *
22 that they may lead them a·,
2Sa 1:21 of the mighty is vilely cast a·,
3:21 And David sent Abner a·; and he
23 and he hath sent him a·, and he is
24 thou hast sent him a·, and he is
4: 7 gat them a· through the plain *3212
11 and take you a· from the earth?
5: 6 Except thou take a· the blind and 5493
7:15 But my mercy shall not depart a·*
15 Saul, whom I put a· before thee, 5493
10: 4 their buttocks, and sent them a·,
12:13 Lord also hath put a· thy sin; 5674
13:16 this evil in sending me a· is *
17:18 went both of them a· quickly,
18: 3 for if we flee a·, they will not care
9 that was under him went a·.
19: 3 as people being ashamed steal a·
41 the men of Judah stolen thee a·,
22:46 Strangers shall fade a·, and they
23: 6 as thorns thrust a·, because they 5074
9 the men of Israel were gone a·:
24:10 take a· the iniquity of thy 5674
1Ki 2:31 thou mayest take a· the innocent 5493
39 the servants of Shimei ran a·
8:46 that they carry them a· captives 7617
48 which led them a· captive, "
66 eighth day he sent the people a·:
11: 2 surely they will turn a· your heart
3 and his wives turned a· his heart.
4 that his wives turned a· his heart
13 I will not rend a· all the kingdom;
14: 8 the kingdom a· from the house
10 take a· the remnant of the house
10 as a man taketh a· dung, till it
26 he took a· the treasures of the
26 he even took a· all:
26 and he took a· all the shields
15:12 he took a· the sodomites out of
22 took a· the stones of Ramah,
16: 3 I will take a· the posterity of
19: 4 now, O Lord, take a· my life;
10, 14 they seek my life, to take it a·.
20: 6 it in their hand, and take it a·.
24 Take the kings a·, every man out
34 I will send thee a· with this *
34 with him, and sent him a·. *
41 took the ashes a· from his face; 5493
21: 4 and turned a· his face, and would
21 and will take a· thy posterity,
22:43 the high places were not taken a·; 5493
2Ki 2: 3, 5 Lord will take a· thy master
9 before I be taken a· from thee. *
3: 2 he put a· the image of Baal that 5493
4:27 came near to thrust her a·.
5: 2 had brought a· captive out of
11 and went a·, and said, Behold,
12 he turned and went a· in a rage.
6:23 he sent them a·, and they went
32 hath sent to take a· mine head?
7:15 the Syrians had cast a· in their
12: 3 high places were not taken a·: 5493
18 and he went a· from Jerusalem.
14: 4 the high places were not taken a·: 5493
17: 6 and carried Israel a· into Assyria, 1540
11 Lord carried a· before them; "
23 So was Israel carried a· out of "
28 had carried a· from Samaria "
33 the nations whom they carried a· "
18:11 king of Assyria did carry a· Israel "
22 altars Hezekiah hath taken a·, 5493
24 How then wilt thou turn a· the
32 take you a· to a land like your own
20:18 thou shalt beget, shall they take a·;
23:11 he took a· the horses that the 7673
19 Josiah took a·, and did to them 5493
24 did Josiah put a·, that he might 1197
34 and took Jehoahaz a·: and he
24:14 And he carried a· all Jerusalem, 1540
15 And he carried a· Jehoiachin to
25:11 the fugitives that fell a· to the
11 the captain of the guard carry a·. 1540
14 they ministered, took they a·.
15 the captain of the guard took a·.
21 So Judah was carried a· out of 1540
1Ch 5: 6 king of Assyria carried a· captive: "
21 And they took a· their cattle; 7617
26 and he carried them a·, even the 1540
6:15 carried a· Judah and Jerusalem "
7:21 came down to take a· their cattle
8: 8 after he had sent them a·;
13 who drove a· the inhabitants of *1272
9: 1 were carried a· to Babylon for 1540
10:12 and took a· the body of Saul,
12:19 upon advisement sent him a·,

1Ch 14:14 turn a· from them, and come upon
17:13 not take my mercy a· from him, 5493
19: 4 their buttocks, and sent them a·.
21: 8 thee, do a· the iniquity of thy 5674
2Ch 6:36 they carry them a· captives unto 7617
42 O Lord God, turn not a· the face
7:10 sent the people a· into their tents,
19 But if ye turn a·, and forsake my
9:12 and went a· to her own land, *
12: 9 took a· the treasures of the house
9 he carried a· also the shields of
14: 3 took a· the altars of the strange 5493
5 took a· out of all the cities of "
13 they carried a· very much spoil.
15 and carried a· sheep and camels 7617
15: 8 and put a· the abominable idols 5674
17 the high places were not taken a· 5493
16: 6 and they carried a· the stones of
17: 6 he took a· the high places and 5493
19: 3 thou hast taken a· the groves out 1197
20:25 came to take a· the spoil of them, *
25 more than they could carry a·:
33 high places were not taken a·: 5493
21:17 carried a· all the substance 7617
25:12 children of Judah carry a· captive,
27 Amaziah did turn a· from following
28: 5 and carried a· a great multitude 7617
8 children of Israel carried a· captive
8 and took also a· much spoil
17 and smitten Judah, and carried a·
21 Ahaz took a· a portion out of the
29: 6 have turned a· their faces from the
10 his fierce wrath may turn a· from
19 king Ahaz in his reign did cast a·
30: 8 his wrath may turn a· from you.
9 not turn a· his face from you,
14 they arose and took a· the altars 5493
14 the altars for incense took they a· "
32:12 Hezekiah taken a· his high places "
33:15 And he took a· the strange gods, "
34:33 took a· all the abominations "
35:23 Have me a·; for I am sore 5674
36:20 sword carried he a· to Babylon; 1540
Ezr 2: 1 those which had been carried a·, 1473
1 the king of Babylon had carried a·1540
5:12 carried the people a· into Babylon.1541
8:35 of those that had been carried a·,*1473
9: 4 of those that had been carried a·;* "
10: 3 our God to put a· all the wives, 3318
6 of them that had been carried a·.*1473
8 of those that had been carried a·.* "
19 that they would put a· their wives;3318
Ne 7: 6 had been carried a·, whom 1473
6 the king of Babylon had carried a·,1546
Es 2: 6 been carried a· from Jerusalem "
6 captivity which had been carried a· "
6 the king of Babylon had carried a·. "
4: 4 take a· his sackcloth from him: *5493
8: 3 with tears to put a· the mischief 5674
Job 1:15 fell upon them, and took them a·;
17 and have carried them a·,
21 and the Lord hath taken a·;
4:21 excellency which is in them go a·? 5265
6:15 streams of brooks they pass a·;
7: 9 is consumed and vanisheth a·:
21 and take a· mine iniquity? 5674
8: 4 he have cast them a· for their *
20 God will not cast a· a perfect man,
9:12 Behold, he taketh a·, who can *2862
25 they flee a·, they see no good.
26 are passed a· as the swift ships:
34 Let him take his rod a· from me, 5493
11:14 put it far a·, and let not wickedness
16 it as waters that pass a·:
12:17 He leadeth counsellors a· spoiled,
19 He leadeth princes a· spoiled,
20 He removeth a· the speech of the*
20 taketh a· the understanding of
24 He taketh a· the heart of the chief 5493
14:10 But man dieth, and wasteth a·: ‡
19 thou washest a· the things which
20 countenance, and sendest him a·.
15:12 doth thine heart carry thee a·?
30 breath of his mouth shall he go a·.
20: 8 He shall fly a· as a dream, and
8 he shall be chased a· as a vision
19 taken a· an house which he 1497
28 his goods shall flow a· in the day
21:18 as chaff that the storm carrieth a·.1589
22: 9 Thou hast sent widows a· empty,
23 thou shalt put a· iniquity far from 7368
24: 2 they violently take a· flocks, and
3 drive a· the ass of the fatherless,
10 take a· the sheaf from the hungry;*
27: 2 who hath taken a· my judgment; 5493
8 when God taketh a· his soul? 7953
20 stealeth him a· in the night.
21 the east wind carrieth him a·,
28: 4 up, they are gone a· from men. *
30:12 they push a· my feet, and they *
15 my welfare passeth a· as a cloud.
32:22 Maker would soon take me a·.
33:21 His flesh is consumed a·, that
34: 5 God hath taken a· my judgment. 5493
20 be troubled at midnight, and pass a·:
20 and the mighty shall be taken a· 5493
36:18 lest he take thee a· with his ‡5496
Ps 1: 4 the chaff which the wind driveth a·.
2: 3 and cast a· their cords from us.
18:22 I did not put a· his statutes from 5493
45 The strangers shall fade a·,
27: 9 put not thy servant a· in anger: 5186
28: 3 Draw me not a· with the wicked,
31:13 They devised to take a· my life.
34:*title* Abimelech; who drove him a·,
37:20 into smoke shall they consume a·.

Ps 37:36 Yet he passed a·, and, lo, he was *
39:10 Remove thy stroke a· from me:
11 makest his beauty to consume a·
48: 5 were troubled, and hasted a·.
49:17 he dieth he shall carry nothing a·:
51:11 Cast me not a· from thy presence;
52: 5 he shall take thee a·, and pluck 2846
55: 6 for then would I fly a·, and be at
58: 7 Let them melt a· as waters which
8 let every one of them pass a·:
9 he shall take them a· as with a
64: 8 all that see them shall flee a·. *
65: 3 thou shalt purge them a·. ‡
66:20 hath not turned a· my prayer,
68: 2 As smoke is driven a·,
2 so drive them a·:
69: 4 restored that which I took not a·. 1497
78:38 turned his anger a·, and did not
39 a wind that passeth a·, and cometh
79: 9 and purge a· our sins, for thy ‡
85: 3 Thou hast taken a· all thy wrath:
88: 8 hast put a· mine acquaintance *7368
90: 5 carriest them a· as with a flood;
9 For all our days are passed a· in
10 it is soon cut off, and we fly a·.
102:24 O my God, take me not a· in the
104: 7 voice of thy thunder they hasted a·.
29 takest a· their breath, they die,
106:23 to turn a· his wrath, lest he should
112:10 gnash with his teeth, and melt a·:
119:37 Turn a· mine eyes from beholding
39 Turn a· my reproach which I fear:
119 Thou puttest a· all the wicked of
132:10 David's sake turn not a· the face
137: 3 carried us a· captive required *
144: 4 are as a shadow that passeth a·.
Pro 1:19 taketh a· the life of the owners
32 the turning a· of the simple shall*
4:15 turn from it, and pass a·. *
16 and their sleep is taken a·, unless 1497
24 Put a· from thee a froward mouth,5493
6:33 reproach shall not be wiped a·.
10: 3 casteth a· the substance of the 1920
14:32 is driven a· in his wickedness: *
15: 1 A soft answer turneth a· wrath:
19:26 and chaseth a· his mother,
20: 8 throne of judgment scattereth a·
30 blueness of a wound cleanseth a·
22:27 why should he take a· the bed
23: 5 they fly a· as an eagle toward *
24:18 he turn a· his wrath from him.
25: 4 Take a· the dross from the silver, 1898
5 Take a· the wicked from before "
10 and thine infamy turn not a·.
20 taketh a· a garment in cold *5710
23 The north wind driveth a· rain: *
28: 9 turneth a· his ear from hearing the
29: 8 but wise men turn a· wrath.
30:30 and turneth not a· for any;
Ec 1: 4 One generation passeth a·, *
3: 5 A time to cast a· stones, and a
6 to keep, and a time to cast a·;
5:15 he may carry a· in his hand.
11:10 and put a· evil from thy flesh: 5493
Ca 2:10, 13 love, my fair one, and come a·.
17 day break, and the shadows flee a·,
4: 6 day break, and the shadows flee a·,
5: 7 keepers of the walls took a· my veil
6: 5 Turn a· thine eyes from me,
Isa 1: 4 they are gone a· backward. *
13 of assemblies, I cannot a· with;
16 put a· the evil of your doings 5493
25 and purely purge a· thy dross,
25 and take a· all thy tin: 5493
3: 1 the Lord of hosts doth take a· from "
18 the Lord will take a· the bravery "
4: 1 to take a· our reproach.
4 Lord shall have washed a· the filth
5: 5 I will take a· the hedge thereof, 5493
23 take a· the righteousness of the "
24 because they have cast a· the law
25 all this his anger is not turned a·,
29 shall carry it a· safe, and none shall
6: 7 and thine iniquity is taken a·, 5493
12 the Lord have removed men far a·,
8: 4 spoil of Samaria shall be taken a·
9:12, 17, 21 his anger is not turned a·,
10: 2 to take a· the right from the poor 1497
4 all this his anger is not turned a·,
27 his burden shall be taken a· from *5493
12: 1 thine anger is turned a·, and thou
15: 6 for the hay is withered a·,
7 carry a· to the brook of the willows.
16:10 And gladness is taken a·, and joy
17: 1 Damascus is taken a· from being 5493
18: 5 a· and cut down the branches. *
19: 6 they shall turn the rivers far a·;
7 be driven a·, and be no more.
20: 4 shall the king of Assyria lead a·
22: 4 Therefore said I, Look a· from me;
17 Behold, the Lord will carry thee a·
24: 4 The earth mourneth and fadeth a·,
4 world languisheth and fadeth a·,
25: 8 Lord God will wipe a· tears from
8 of his people shall he take a· 5493
27: 9 is all the fruit to take a· his sin; "
28:17 shall sweep a· the refuge of lies,
29: 5 shall be as chaff that passeth a·:
30:22 them a· as a menstruous cloth; 2219
31: 7 shall cast a· his idols of silver, 3988
35:10 sorrow and sighing shall flee a·.
36: 7 altars Hezekiah hath taken a·, 5493
9 How then wilt thou turn a· the face
17 I come and take you a· to a land
39: 7 thou shalt beget, shall they take a·;
40:24 shall take them a· as stubble.

Isa 41: 9 chosen thee, and not cast thee a'.
16 and the wind shall carry them a',
49:19 swallowed thee up shall be far a'.
25 of the mighty shall be taken a'.
50: 1 whom I have put a'?
1 transgressions is your mother put a'.
5 neither turned a' back.
51: 6 heavens shall vanish a' like smoke,
11 sorrow and mourning shall flee a'.
52: 5 my people is taken a' for nought?
57: 1 and merciful men are taken a',
1 that the righteousness is taken a'
13 the wind shall carry them all a';
58: 9 If thou take a' from the midst of 5493
13 If thou turn a' thy foot from the
59:13 and departing a' from our God,
14 judgment is turned a' backward,
64: 6 like the wind, have taken us a'.
Jer 1: 3 carrying a' of Jerusalem captive
2:24 her occasion who can turn her a'?
3: 1 They say, If a man put a' his wife,
8 committed adultery I had put her a',
19 and shalt not turn a' from me
4: 1 put a' thine abominations 5493
4 take a' the foreskins of your heart, "
5:10 take a' her battlements; "
25 Your iniquities have turned a' these
6: 4 unto us! for the day goeth a', *
29 for the wicked are not plucked a'.
7:29 and cast it a', and take up a
33 and none shall fray them a'.
8: 4 shall he turn a', and not return?
13 I have given them shall pass a'
13:17 Lord's flock is carried a' captive. *
19 Judah shall be carried a' captive
19 shall be wholly carried a' captive.
24 that passeth a' by the wind of the
15:15 me not a' in thy longsuffering:
16: 5 for I have taken a' my peace from
18:20 to turn a' thy wrath from them.
22:10 weep sore for him that goeth a':
23: 2 and driven them a', and have not
24: 1 Babylon had carried a' captive
5 are carried a' captive of Judah,
27:20 he carried a' captive Jeconiah
28: 3 king of Babylon took a' from this
6 and all that is carried a' captive, *
29: 1 which were carried a' captives, *
1 carried a' captive from Jerusalem
4 all that are carried a' captives, *
4 to be carried a' from Jerusalem
7 you to be carried a' captives,
14 and I will turn a' your captivity, *
14 I caused you to be carried a'
32:40 I will turn a' from them, to do
33:26 will I cast a' the seed of Jacob,
37:13 Thou fallest a' to the Chaldeans.
14 I fall not a' to the Chaldeans.
38:22 mire, and they are turned a' back.
39: 9 carried a' captive into Babylon
9 the city, and those that fell a',
40: 1 carried a' captive of Jerusalem *
1 carried a' captive unto Babylon.
7 not carried a' captive to Babylon;
41:10 carried a' captive all the residue
10 carried them a' captive, and
14 people that Ishmael had carried a'
43: 3 carry us a' captives into Babylon.
12 carry them a' captives: and he
46: 5 turned a' back? and their mighty *
6 Let not the swift flee a', nor the
15 Why are thy valiant men swept a'?
21 and are fled a' together: they did
48: 9 may flee and get a': for the cities 3318
49:19 suddenly make him run a' from
29 their flocks shall they take a':
50: 6 they have turned them a' on the
17 the lions have driven him a':
44 suddenly run a' from her; and
51:50 go a', stand not still: remember *
52:15 guard carried a' captive certain
15 and those that fell a', that
18 they ministered, took they a'.
19 took the captain of the guard a'.
27 Judah was carried a' captive
28 whom Nebuchadrezzar carried a'
29 carried a' captive from Jerusalem
30 the captain of the guard carried a'
La 2: 6 violently taken a' his tabernacle,
14 to turn a' thy captivity; but have *
4: 9 for these pine a', stricken through
15 when they fled a' and wandered,
22 more carry thee a' into captivity:
Eze 3:14 spirit lifted me up, and took me a',
4:17 and consume a' for their iniquity.
11:18 take a' all the detestable things 5493
14: 6 and turn a' your faces from all
16: 9 I thoroughly washed a' thy blood
50 I took them a' as I saw good. 5493
18:24 But when the righteous turneth a'
26 a righteous man turneth a' from
27 when the wicked man turneth a'
28 he considereth, and turneth a'
31 Cast a' from you all your
20: 7 ye a' every man the abominations
8 they did not every man cast a' the
23:25 take a' thy nose and thine ears; 5493
26 clothes, and take a' thy fair jewels.
29 and shall take a' all thy labour,
24:16 Son of man, behold, I take a' from
23 shall pine a' for your iniquities,
26:16 and lay a' their robes, and put off *5493
30: 4 they shall take a' her multitude,
33: 4 and take him a', his blood shall
6 he is taken a' in his iniquity; but
10 we pine a' in them, how should
Eze 34: 4 again that which was driven a',
16 that which was driven a', and will
36:26 I will take a' the stony heart out 5493
38:13 to carry a' silver and gold,
13 to take a' cattle and goods,
43: 9 let them put a' their whoredom, 7368
44:10 are gone a' far from me, when *
10 a' from me after their idols; *
22 nor her that is put a': but they
45: 9 take a' your exactions from my 7311
Da 1:16 Thus Melzar took a' the portion
2:35 carried them a', that no place was
4:14 the beasts get a' from under it, 5111
7:12 had their dominion taken a': 5709
14 which shall not pass a', and his "
26 they shall take a' his dominion, "
8:11 the daily sacrifice was taken a', 7311
9:16 fury be turned a' from thy city
11:12 hath taken a' the multitude, his *
31 shall take a' the daily sacrifice, 5493
44 and utterly to make a' many. 2763
12:11 be taken a', and the abomination 5493
Ho 1: 6 I will utterly take them a'. *
2: 2 therefore put a' her whoredoms 5493
9 and take a' my corn in the time *
17 I will take a' the names of Baalim 5493
4: 3 the sea also shall be taken a'.
11 and new wine take a' the heart.
5:14 I, even I, will tear and go a';
14 I will take a', and none shall *
6: 4 as the early dew it goeth a'.
9:11 their glory shall fly a' like a bird,
17 God will cast them a', because
13: 3 the early dew that passeth a', as
11 and took him a' in my wrath.
14: 2 Take a' all iniquity, and receive us
4 mine anger is turned a' from him.
Joe 1: 7 and cast it a'; the branches thereof
12 joy is withered a' from the sons of
Am 1: 3 I will not turn a' the punishment
6 not turn a' the punishment thereof;
6 because they carried a' captive
9, 11, 13 I will not turn a' the
2: 1, 4, 6 I will not turn a' the
16 the mighty shall flee a' naked in
4: 2 he will take you a' with hooks,
10 and have taken a' your horses; 7628
5:23 Take thou a' from me the noise 5493
6: 3 Ye that put far a' the evil day, 5077
7:11 surely be led a' captive out of
12 flee thee a' into the land of Judah,
9: 1 shall not flee a', and he that
Ob 11 strangers carried a' captive his
Jon 3: 9 and turn a' from his fierce anger,
Mic 1:11 Pass ye a', thou inhabitant of
2: 2 and take them a'; so they oppress 7726
4 turning a' he hath divided our *
9 have ye taken a' my glory for ever.
Na 2: 2 hath turned a' the excellency *
7 Huzzab shall be led a' captive, she 1540
8 yet they shall flee a'. Stand, stand,
3:10 Yet was she carried a', she went 1473
16 cankerworm spoileth, and fleeth a'.
17 the sun ariseth they flee a', and
Zep 2: 7 visit them, and turn a' their *
3:11 then I will take a' out of the 5493
15 The Lord hath taken a' thy "
Zec 3: 4 Take a' the filthy garments from* "
7:11 and pulled a' the shoulder, and
9: 7 And I will take a' his blood out 5493
10:11 sceptre of Egypt shall depart a'.
14:12 Their flesh shall consume a' while
12 their eyes shall consume a' in
12 and their tongue shall consume a'
Mal 2: 3 one shall take you a' with it.
6 and did turn many a' from iniquity.
16 saith that he hateth putting a':
3: 7 are gone a' from mine ordinances, 5493
M't 1:11 they were carried a' to Babylon: 3350
17 carrying a' into Babylon are "
17 from the carrying a' into Babylon "
19 was minded to put her a' privily. 630
5:31 Whosoever shall put a' his wife, "
32 whosoever shall put a' his wife, "
40 and take a' thy coat,
42 turn not thou a'. 654
8:31 suffer us to go a' into the herd of 565
13: 6 they had no root, they withered a'.
12 him shall be taken a' even that 142
19 and catcheth a' that which was 726
36 Then Jesus sent the multitude a',* 863
48 but cast the bad a'. 1854
14:15 send the multitude a', 630
22 while he sent the multitudes a'. "
23 he had sent the multitudes a', "
15:23 saying, Send her a'; for she crieth "
32 I will not send them a' fasting, "
39 And he sent a' the multitude, "
19: 3 for a man to put a' his wife "
7 and to put her a'? "
8 suffered you to put a' your wives: "
9 Whosoever shall put a' his wife, "
9 whoso marrieth her which is put a' "
22 he went a' sorrowful; for he had 565
21:19 presently the fig tree withered a'.
20 soon is the fig tree withered a'!
22:13 and take him a', and cast him into* 142
24:35 Heaven and earth shall pass a', 3928
35 but my word shall not pass a'.
39 flood came, and took them all a'; 142
25:29 shall be taken a' even that which
46 these shall go a' into everlasting 565
26:42 He went a' again the second time,
42 cup may not pass a' from me, 3928
44 and went a' again, and prayed 565
57 led him a' to Caiaphas the 520
M't 27: 2 they led him a', and delivered him 520
31 and led him a' to crucify him.
64 and steal him a', and say unto the
28:13 and stole him a' while we slept.
16 the eleven disciples went a' into *
M'r 1:43 and forthwith sent him a'; *1544
2:20 bridegroom shall be taken a' from 522
21 taketh a' from the old, and the * 142
4: 6 it had no root, it withered a'.
15 and taketh a' the word that was 142
36 when they had sent a' the * 863
5:10 not send them a' out of the 649
6:36 Send them a', that they may go 630
45 while he sent a' the people. "
46 he had sent them a', he departed * 657
8: 3 if I send them a' fasting to their 630
9 thousand: and he sent them a'. "
26 And he sent him a' to his house, 649
9:18 with his teeth, and pineth a': and I
10: 2 for a man to put a' his wife? 630
4 divorcement, and to put her a'. "
11 Whosoever shall put a' his wife, "
12 woman shall put a' her husband, "
22 and went a' grieved: for he had 565
50 And he, casting a' his garment, 577
11:21 which thou cursedst is withered a'.
12: 3 and sent him a' empty. 649
4 and sent him a' shamefully * "
13:31 Heaven and earth shall pass a': 3928
31 but my words shall not pass a'. "
14:36 take a' this cup from me: *3911
39 And again he went a', and prayed, 565
44 take him, and lead him a' safely. 520
53 And they led Jesus a' to the high "
15: 1 and carried him a', and delivered 667
16 soldiers led him a' into the hall, 520
16: 3 Who shall roll a' the stone from 617
4 that the stone was rolled a': for it* "
Lu 1:25 to take a' my reproach among 851
53 the rich he hath sent empty a'. 1821
2:15 the angels were gone a' from them 565
5:35 shall be taken a' from them, and 851
6:29 that taketh a' thy cloke forbid not 142
30 that taketh a' thy goods ask "
8: 6 it withered a', because it lacked
12 and taketh a' the word out of 142
13 and in time of temptation fall a'. 868
38 but Jesus sent him a', saying, 630
9:12 when the day began to wear a',
12 Send the multitude a', that they 630
25 lose himself, or be cast a'? *2210
10:42 which shall not be taken a' from 851
11:52 taken a' the key of knowledge:
13:15 and lead him a' to watering? 520
16: 3 for my lord taketh a' from me the 851
18 Whosoever putteth a' his wife, and 630
18 a' from her husband committeth "
17:31 not come down to take it a': and
19:26 he hath shall be taken a' from him.
20:10 beat him, and sent him a' empty. 1821
11 shamefully, and sent him a' empty."
21:24 and shall be led a' captive into *
32 generation shall not pass a', till
33 earth shall pass a': but
33 my words shall not pass a'.
23:18 saying, A' with this man, and
26 And as they led him a', they laid 520
24: 2 stone rolled a' from the sepulchre. 617
Joh 1:29 taketh a' the sin of the world.
4: 8 his disciples were gone a' unto the 565
5:13 Jesus had conveyed himself a', a 1593
6:22 his disciples were gone a' alone; 565
67 unto the twelve, Will ye also go a'? 5217
10:40 And went a' again beyond Jordan 565
11:39 Take ye a' the stone. Martha, the
41 Then they took a' the stone from
48 come and take a' both our place
12:11 the Jews went a', and believed on 5217
14:28 I go a' and come again unto you. "
15: 2 he taketh a': and every branch
16: 7 is expedient for you that I go a': 565
7 if I go not a', the Comforter will "
18:13 And led him a' to Annas first; 520
19:15 A' with him, a' with him, crucify 142
16 took Jesus, and led him a'. * 520
31 and that they might be taken a'.
38 that he might take a' the body of
20: 1 stone taken a' from the sepulchre.
2 They have taken a' the Lord out of
10 disciples went a' again unto their 565
13 they have taken a' my Lord, and I
15 and I will take him a'.
Ac 3:26 in turning a' every one of you from 654
5:37 drew a' much people after him: 868
7:27 him a', saying, Who made thee 683
43 will carry you a' beyond Babylon. 3351
8:33 his judgment was taken a': and
39 the Lord caught a' Philip, that the 726
10:23 morrow Peter went a' with them, *1831
13: 3 hands on them, they sent them a'. 630
8 seeking to turn a' the deputy *1294
17:10 immediately sent a' Paul and Silas 1599
14 the brethren sent a' Paul to go as *1821
19:26 turned a' much people, saying, 3179
20: 6 And we sailed a' from Philippi 1602
30 to draw a' disciples after them. 645
21:36 followed after, crying, A' with him. 142
22:16 wash a' thy sins, calling on the 628
22 A' with such a fellow from the 142
24: 7 great violence took him a' out of * 520
27:20 should be saved was then taken a'. 4014
Ro 11: 1 Hath God cast a' his people? * 683
2 God hath not cast a' his people * "
15 For if the casting a' of them be 580
26 and shall turn a' ungodliness from 654
27 when I shall take a' their sins. 851

1Co 5: 2 might be taken a' from among you.
13 Therefore put a' from among 1808
7:11 not the husband put a' his wife. * 863
12 let him not put her a'. * "
31 fashion of this world passeth a'.
12: 2 carried a' unto these dumb idols, 520
13: 8 be knowledge, it shall vanish a'. 2673
10 which is in part shall be done a'. "
11 when I became a man, I put a' "
2Co 3: 7 which glory was to be done a': "
11 For of that which is done a' was "
14 vail untaken a' in the reading 343
14 which vail is done a' in Christ. 2673
16 the vail shall be taken a'. 4014
5:17 old things are passed a'; behold,
Ga 2:13 Barnabas also was carried a' with 4879
Eph 4:25 Wherefore putting a' lying, speak 659
31 evil speaking, be put a' from you,
Col 1:23 be not moved a' from the hope of 3334
2Th 2: 3 except there come a falling a' first, 646
1Ti 1:19 some having put a' concerning * 683
2Ti 1:15 are in Asia be turned a' from me; 654
3: 5 power thereof: from such turn a'. 665
6 women laden with sins, led a'
4:4 And they shall turn a' their ears 654
Heb 6: 6 they shall fall a', to renew them 3895
8:13 waxeth old, is ready to vanish a'.
9:26 a' sin by the sacrifice of himself. 115
10: 4 should take a' sins. 851
9 He taketh a' the first, that he may 337
11 which can never take a' sins: 4014
35 Cast not a' therefore your 577
12:25 we turn a' from him that speaketh 654
Jas 1:10 of the grass he shall pass a'.
11 the rich man fade a' in his ways.
14 he is drawn a' of his own lust,
4:14 little time, and then vanisheth a'.
1Pe 1: 4 undefiled, and that fadeth not a',
24 the flower thereof falleth a': *1601
3:21 (not the putting a' of the filth of the 595
5: 4 crown of glory that fadeth not a'.
2Pe 3:10 heavens shall pass a' with a great
17 a' with the error of the wicked, 4879
1Jo 2:17 the world passeth a', and the lust
3: 5 manifested to take a' our sins;
Re 7:17 God shall wipe a' all tears from 1813
12:15 her to be carried a' of the flood.
16:20 And every island fled a', and the
17: 3 So he carried me a' in the spirit 667
20:11 the earth and the heaven fled a';
21: 1 first earth were passed a'; and
4 God shall wipe a' all tears from 1813
4 the former things are passed a'. 565
10 he carried me a' in the spirit to a 667
22:19 if any man shall take a' from the 851
19 God shall take a' his part out of the "

awe
Ps 4: 4 Stand in a', and sin not: 7264
33: 8 of the world stand in a' 1481
119:161 heart standeth in a' of thy word. 6342

awhile See WHILE.

awl See AUL.

awoke See also AWAKED.
Ge 9:24 And Noah a' from his wine, 3364
41: 4 and fat kine. So Pharaoh a'. "
7 and Pharaoh a', and, behold, it "
21 as at the beginning. So I a'. "
J'g 16:20 And he a' out of his sleep, "
1Ki 3:15 And Solomon a'; and, behold, it "
M't 8:25 a' him, saying, Lord, save us: 1453
Lu 8:24 they came to him, and a' him, 1326

ax See also AXE.
De 19: 5 with the a' to cut down the tree, 1631
20:19 by forcing an a' against them:
J'g 9:48 Abimelech took an a' in his hand, 7134
1Sa 13:20 to sharpen every man...his a',
1Ki 6: 7 neither hammer nor a' nor any 1631
2Ki 6: 5 the a' head fell into the water: 1270
Isa 10:15 Shall the a' boast itself 1631
Jer 10: 3 of the workman, with the a'. 4621
51:20 Thou art my battle a' and 4661
M't 3:10 now also the a' is laid unto the 513

axe See also AXES. [*Most editions have* AX.]
Lu 3: 9 now also the a' is laid unto the 513

axes
1Sa 13:21 for the forks, and for the a', 7134
2Sa 12:31 and under a' of iron, 4037
1Ch 20: 3 with harrows of iron, and with a'. 4050
Ps 74: 5 he had lifted up a' upon the thick 7134
6 with a' and hammers. *3781
Jer 46:22 and come against her with a', 7134
Eze 26: 9 with his a' he shall break down 2719

ax-head See AXE and HEAD.

axletrees
1Ki 7:32 and the a' of the wheels 3027
33 their a', and their naves, "

ay See NAY.

Azal (*a'-zal*)
Zec 14: 5 mountains shall reach unto A': 682

Azaliah (*az-a-li'-ah*)
2Ki 22: 3 king sent Shaphan the son of A', 683
2Ch 34: 8 the son of A', and Maaseiah "

Azaniah (*az-a-ni'-ah*)
Ne 10: 9 both Jeshua the son of A', 245

Azarael (*a-zar'-a-el*) See also AZAREEL.
Ne 12:36 his brethren, Shemaiah, and A', 5832

Azareel (*a-zar'-e-el*) See also AZARAEL.
1Ch 12: 6 and A', and Joezer, and 5832
25:18 The eleventh to A', he, his sons, "
27:22 Of Dan, A' the son of Jeroham. "
Ezr 10:41 A', and Shelemiah, Shemariah, "
Ne 11:13 and Amashai the son of A', the son "

Azariah (*az-a-ri'-ah*) See also AHAZIAH.
1Ki 4: 2 A' the son of Zadok the priest, 5838
5 And A' the son of Nathan was "
2Ki 14:21 all the people of Judah took A', "
15: 1 began A' son of Amaziah king of "
6 And the rest of the acts of A', and "
7 So A' slept with his fathers; and "
8 In the thirty and eighth year of A' "
17 In the nine and thirtieth year of A' "
23 In the fiftieth year of A' king of "
27 In the two and fiftieth year of A' "
1Ch 2: 8 And the sons of Ethan; A'. "
38 begat Jehu, and Jehu begat A', "
39 And A' begat Helez, and Helez "
3:12 Amaziah his son, A' his son, "
6: 9 And Ahimaaz begat A', "
9 And A' begat Johanan, "
10 And Johanan begat A', (he it is "
11 And A' begat Amariah, and "
13 and Hilkiah begat A', "
14 and A' begat Seraiah, and "
36 the son of Joel, the son of A', "
9:11 And A' the son of Hilkiah, the son "
2Ch 15: 1 the Spirit of God came upon A' "
21: 2 the sons of Jehoshaphat, A', and "
2 Zechariah, and A', and Michael, "
22: 6 And A' the son of Jehoram king "
23: 1 A' the son of Jeroham, and "
1 A' the son of Obed, and Maaseiah "
26:17 A' the priest went in after him, "
20 And A' the chief priest, and all "
28:12 A' the son of Johanan, Berechiah "
29:12 Amasai, and Joel the son of A', "
12 and A' the son of Jehalelel: "
31:10 And A' the chief priest of the "
13 and A' the ruler of the house of "
Ezr 7: 1 the son of Seraiah, the son of A', 5838
3 The son of Amariah, the son of A', "
Ne 3:23 After him repaired A' the son of "
24 from the house of A' unto the "
7: 7 Nehemiah, A', Raamiah, "
8: 7 Kelita, A', Jozabad, Hanan, "
10: 2 Seraiah, A', Jeremiah, "
12:33 And A', Ezra, and Meshullam, "
Jer 43: 2 spake A' the son of Hoshaiah, "
Da 1: 6 Daniel, Hananiah, Mishael, and A': "
7 and to A', of Abed-nego. "
11 Daniel, Hananiah, Mishael, and A', "
19 and A': therefore stood they "
2:17 Mishael, and A', his companions: 5839

Azaz (*a'-zaz*)
1Ch 5: 8 And Bela the son of A', the son of 5811

Azaziah (*az-a-zi'-ah*)
1Ch 15:21 A', with harps on the Sheminith 5812
27:20 Ephraim, Hoshea the son of A': 5812
2Ch 31:13 And Jehiel, and A', and Nahath, "

Azbuk (*az'-buk*)
Ne 3:16 Nehemiah the son of A', the ruler 5802

Azekah (*a-ze'-kah*)
Jos 10:10 and smote them to A', and unto 5825
11 from heaven upon them unto A', "
15:35 and Adullam, Socoh, and A', "
1Sa 17: 1 pitched between Shochoh and A', "
2Ch 11: 9 Adoraim, and Lachish, and A', "
Ne 11:30 and the fields thereof, at A', "
Jer 34: 7 against Lachish, and against A': "

Azel (*a'-zel*) See also JAAZIEL.
1Ch 8:37 Eleasah his son, A' his son: 682
38 A' had six sons, whose names are "
38 All these were the sons of A'. "
9:43 Eleasah his son, A' his son. "
44 A' had six sons, whose names are "
44 these were the sons of A'. "

Azem (*a'-zem*) See also EZEM.
Jos 15:29 Baalah, and Iim, and A', 6107
19: 3 Hazar-shual, and Balah, and A', "

Azgad (*az'-gad*)
Ezr 2:12 The children of A', a thousand 5803
8:12 And of the sons of A'; Johanan "
Ne 7:17 The children of A', two thousand "
10:15 Bunni, A', Bebai, "

Aziel (*a'-ze-el*)
1Ch 15:20 And Zechariah, and A', and 5815

Aziza (*a-zi'-zah*)
Ezr 10:27 and Jeremoth, and Zabad, and A'. 5819

Azmaveth (*az-ma'-veth*) See also BETH-AZMAVETH.
2Sa 23:31 Abi-albon the Arbathite, A' the 5820
1Ch 8:36 Jehoadah begat Alemeth, and A', "
9:42 and Jarah begat Alemeth, and A', "
11:33 A' the Baharumite, Eliahba "
12: 3 Jeziel, and Pelet, the sons of A'; "
27:25 over the king's treasures was A' "
Ezr 2:24 The children of A', forty and two. "
Ne 12:29 out of the fields of Geba and A': "

Azmon (*az'-mon*) See also HESHMON.
Nu 34: 4 Hazar-addar, and pass on to A': 6111
5 shall fetch a compass from A' "
Jos 15: 4 From thence it passed toward A', "

Aznoth-tabor (*az''-noth-ta'-bor*)
Jos 19:34 the coast turneth westward to A', 243

Azor (*a'-zor*)
M't 1:13 and Eliakim begat A'; 107
14 And A' begat Sadoc; "

Azotus (*a-zo'-tus*) See also ASHDOD.
Ac 8:40 But Philip was found at A': 108

Azriel (*az'-re-el*)
1Ch 5:24 and Ishi, and Eliel, and A', 5837
27:19 Naphtali, Jerimoth the son of A': "
Jer 36:26 and Seraiah the son of A', and "

Azrikam (*az'-ri-kam*)
1Ch 3:23 Elioenai, and Hezekiah, and A', 5840
8:38 whose names are these, A', "
9:14 son of A', the son of Hashabiah, "
44 sons, whose names are these, A', "
2Ch 28: 7 A', the governor of the house, "
Ne 11:15 the son of Hashub, the son of A', "

Azubah (*a-zu'-bah*)
1Ki 22:42 And his mother's name was A', 5806
1Ch 2:18 son of Hezron begat children of A' "
19 And when A' was dead, Caleb "
2Ch 20:31 And his mother's name was A' "

Azur (*a'-zur*) See also AZZUR.
Jer 28: 1 that Hananiah the son of A' the 5809
Eze 11: 1 I saw Jaazaniah the son of A', "

Azzah (*az'-zah*) See also GAZA.
De 2:23 dwelt in Hazerim, even unto A', *5804
1Ki 4:24 from Tiphsah even to A', over all * "
Jer 25:20 and Ashkelon, and A', and * "

Azzan (*az'-zan*)
Nu 34:26 Paltiel the son of A'. 5821

Azzur (*az'-zur*) See also AZUR.
Ne 10:17 Ater, Hizkijah, A', 5809

B.

Baal (*ba'-al*) See also BAAL-BERITH; BAALE; BAAL-GAD; BAAL-HAMON; BAAL-HANAN; BAAL-HAZOR; BAAL-HERMON; BAALIM; BAAL-MEON; BAAL-PEOR; BAAL-PERAZIM; BAAL'S; BAAL-SHALISHA; BAAL-TAMAR; BAAL-ZEBUB; BAAL-ZEPHON; BAMOTH-BAAL; GUR-BAAL; BEL; KIRJATH-BAAL; MERIB-BAAL.
Nu 22:41 up into the high places of B', 1168
J'g 2:13 Lord, and served B' and Ashtaroth. "
6:25 and throw down the altar of B' "
28 the altar of B' was cast down, "
30 hath cast down the altar of B', "
31 Will ye plead for B'? will ye save "
32 Let B' plead against him, because "
1Ki 16:31 and served B', and worshipped "
32 he reared up an altar for B' "
32 in the house of B', "
18:19 the prophets of B' four hundred "
21 but if B', then follow him. "
25 Elijah said unto the prophets of B', "
26 and called on the name of B' "
26 saying, O B', hear us. "
40 them, Take the prophets of B'; "
19:18 which have not bowed unto B', "
22:53 For he served B', and worshipped "
2Ki 3: 2 for he put away the image of B' 1168
10:18 unto them, Ahab served B' a little; "
19 unto me all the prophets of B', "
19 have a great sacrifice to do to B'; "
19 destroy the worshippers of B'. "
20 Proclaim a solemn assembly for B'. "
21 all the worshippers of B' came, "
21 they came into the house of B'; "
21 and the house of B' was full "
22 for all the worshippers of B'. "
23 into the house of B', "
23 said unto the worshippers of B', "
23 but the worshippers of B' only. "
25 went to the city of the house of B'. "
26 the images out of the house of B', "
27 they brake down the image of B', "
27 and brake down the house of B', "
28 Jehu destroyed B' out of Israel. "
11:18 the land went into the house of B', "
18 and slew Mattan the priest of B' "
17:16 the host of heaven, and served B'. "
21: 3 and he reared up altars for B', "
23: 4 the vessels that were made for B', "
5 also that burned incense unto B', "
1Ch 4:33 about the same cities, unto B'. "
5: 5 Reaia his son, B' his son, 1168
8:30 and Kish, and B', and Nadab, "
9:36 Kish, and B', and Ner, and Nadab, "
2Ch 23:17 the people went to the house of B', "
17 and slew Mattan the priest of B' "
Jer 2: 8 the prophets prophesied by B', "
7: 9 falsely, and burn incense unto B', "
11:13 altars to burn incense unto B'. "
17 anger in offering incense unto B'. "
12:16 taught my people to swear by B'; "
19: 5 built also the high places of B', "
5 fire for burnt offerings unto B', "
23:13 they prophesied in B', and caused "
27 have forgotten my name for B'. "
32:29 they have offered incense unto B', "
35 they build the high places of B', "
Ho 2: 8 gold, which they prepared for B'. "
13: 1 when he offended in B', he died. "
Zep 1: 4 I will cut off the remnant of B' "
Ro 11: 4 bowed the knee to the image of B'. 896

Baalah (*ba'-al-ah*) See also BAALE; BALEH; BILHAH; KIRJATH-BAAL.
Jos 15: 9 and the border was drawn to B', 1173
10 the border compassed from B' "

Jos 15:11 and passed along to mount B'. 1173
29 B', and Iim, and Azem, "
1Ch 13: 6 went up, and all Israel, to B', "

Baalath (ba'-al-ath) See also BAALATH-BEER.
Jos 19:44 Eltekeh, and Gibbethon, and B', 1191
1Ki 9:18 B', and Tadmor in the wilderness, "
2Ch 8: 6 B', and all the store cities "

Baalath-beer (ba''-al-ath-be'-ur)
Jos 19: 8 round about these cities to B', 1192

Baal-berith (ba''-al-be'-rith)
J'g 8:33 and made B' their god, 1170
9: 4 of silver out of the house of B', "

Baale (ba'-al-eh)
2Sa 6: 2 people that were with him from B' 1184

Baal-gad (ba''-al-gad')
Jos 11:17 even unto B' in the valley of 1171
12: 7 the west, from B' in the valley "
13: 5 from B' under mount Hermon "

Baal-hamon (ba''-al-ha'-mon)
Ca 8:11 Solomon had a vineyard at B'; 1174

Baal-hanan (ba''-al-ha'-nan)
Ge 36:38 B' the son of Achbor reigned 1177
39 And B' the son of Achbor died, "
1Ch 1:49 when Shaul was dead, B' the son "
50 when B' was dead, Hadad reigned "
27:28 the low plains was B' the Gederite: "

Baal-hazor (ba''-al-ha'-zor) See also HAZOR.
2Sa 13:23 Absalom had sheepshearers in B', 1178

Baal-hermon (ba''-al-her'-mon)
J'g 3: 3 from mount B' unto the entering 1179
1Ch 5:23 from Bashan unto B' and Senir, "

Baali (ba'-al-i)
Hos 2:16 and shalt call me no more B'. 1180

Baalim (ba'-al-im) See also BAAL.
J'g 2:11 sight of the Lord, and served B': 1168
3: 7 and served B' and the groves. "
8:33 went a whoring after B', and made "
10: 6 and served B', and Ashtaroth, "
10 our God, and also served B'. "
1Sa 7: 4 children of Israel did put away B' "
12:10 have served B' and Ashtaroth: "
1Ki 18:18 and thou hast followed B'. "
2Ch 17: 3 David, and sought not unto B'; "
24: 7 Lord did they bestow upon B'. "
28: 2 made also molten images for B'. "
33: 3 and he reared up altars for B', "
34: 4 they brake down the altars of B' "
Jer 2:23 polluted, I have not gone after B'? "
9:14 after B', which their fathers "
Ho 2:13 I will visit upon her the days of B', "
17 I will take away the names of B' "
11: 2 sacrificed unto B', and burned "

Baalis (ba'-al-is)
Jer 40:14 B' the king of the Ammonites 1185

Baal-meon (ba''-al-me'-on) See also BETH-BAAL-MEON.
Nu 32:38 Nebo, and B', (their names being 1186
1Ch 5: 8 even unto Nebo and B': "
Eze 25: 9 Beth-jeshimoth, B', and "

Baal-peor (ba''-al-pe'-or) See also PEOR.
Nu 25: 3 Israel joined himself unto B': 1187
5 his men that were joined unto B'. "
De 4: 3 what the Lord did because of B': "
3 for all the men that followed B', "
Ps 106:28 joined themselves also unto B', "
Ho 9:10 they went to B', and separated "

Baal-perazim (ba''-al-per'-a-zim)
2Sa 5:20 David came to B', and David 1188
20 called the name of that place B'. "
1Ch 14:11 So they came up to B'; and David "
11 called the name of that place B'. "

Baal's (ba'-als)
1Ki 18:22 but B' prophets are four hundred 1168

Baal-shalisha (ba''-al-shal'-i-shah)
2Ki 4:42 there came a man from B', 1190

Baal-tamar (ba''-al-ta'-mar)
J'g 20:33 put themselves in array at B': 1193

Baal-zebub (ba''-al-ze'-bub) See also BEELZEBUB.
2Ki 1: 2 Go, enquire of B' the god of Ekron 1176
3 that ye go to enquire of B' the god "
6 that thou sendest to enquire of B' "
16 sent messengers to enquire of B' "

Baal-zephon (ba''-al-ze'-fon)
Ex 14: 2 and the sea, over against B': 1189
9 beside Pi-hahiroth, before B'. "
Nu 33: 7 Pi-hahiroth, which is before B': "

Baana (ba'-an-ah) See also BAANAH.
1Ki 4:12 B' the son of Ahilud; to him 1195
Ne 3: 4 repaired Zadok the son of B'. "

Baanah (ba'-an-ah) See also BAANA.
2Sa 4: 2 the name of the one was B', 1195
5 Rechab and B', went, and came "
6 Rechab and B' his brother "
9 David answered Rechab and B' "
23:29 Heleb the son of B, a Netophathite, "
1Ki 4:16 B' the son of Hushai was in Asher "
1Ch 11:30 Netophathite, Heled the son of B' "
Ezr 2: 2 Mizpar, Bigvai, Rehum, B'. "
Ne 7: 7 Mispereth, Bigvai, Nehum, B'. "
10:27 Malluch, Harim, B'. "

Baara (ba'-ar-ah)
1Ch 8: 8 Hushim and B' were his wives. 1199

Baaseiah (ba-as-i'-ah)
1Ch 6:40 the son of B', the son of Malchiah, 1202

Baasha (ba'-ash-ah)
1Ki 15:16 was war between Asa and B' 1201
17 B' king of Israel went up against "
1Ki 15:19 and break thy league with B' 1201
21 to pass, when B' heard thereof, "
22 wherewith B' had builded; "
27 B' the son of Ahijah, of the house "
27 and B' smote him at Gibbethon, "
28 did B' slay him, and reigned "
32 was war between Asa and B' "
33 began B' the son of Ahijah to reign "
16: 1 the son of Hanani against B', "
3 will take away the posterity of B', "
4 Him that dieth of B' in the city "
5 Now the rest of the acts of B', "
6 B' slept with his fathers, and was "
7 the word of the Lord against B', "
8 Elah the son of B' to reign "
11 that he slew all the house of B': "
12 Zimri destroy all the house of B', "
12 which he spake against B' by Jehu "
13 all the sins of B', and the sins of "
21:22 like the house of B', the son of "
2Ki 9: 9 like the house of B' the son of "
2Ch 16: 1 B' king of Israel came up against "
3 go, break thy league with B' king "
5 it came to pass, when B' heard it, "
6 wherewith B' was building; "
Jer 41: 9 king had made for fear of B' "

babbler
Ec 10:11 and a b' is no better. *1167, 3956
Ac 17:18 said, What will this b' say? 4691

babbling See also BABBLINGS.
Pr 23:29 who hath b'? who hath wounds *7879

babblings
1Ti 6:20 avoiding profane and vain b', 2757
2Ti 2:16 shun profane and vain b': for "

babe See also BABES.
Ex 2: 6 behold, the b' wept. 5288
Lu 1:41 the b' leaped in her womb; 1025
44 the b' leaped in my womb for joy. "
2:12 the b' wrapt in swaddling clothes, "
16 Mary, and Joseph, and the b' lying "
Heb 5:13 of righteousness: for he is a b'. 3516

Babel (ba'-bel) See also BABYLON.
Ge 10:10 beginning of his kingdom was B', 894
11: 9 is the name of it called B'; "

babes
Ps 8: 2 of the mouth of b' and sucklings 5768
17:14 rest of their substance to their b'. "
Isa 3: 4 and b' shall rule over them. 8586
M't 11:25 hast revealed them unto b'. 3516
21:16 Out of the mouth of b' "
Lu 10:21 hast revealed them unto b': "
Ro 2:20 teacher of b', which hast the form "
1Co 3: 1 as unto b' in Christ. "
1Pe 2: 2 As newborn b', desire the sincere 1025

Babylon (bab'-il-un) See also BABEL; BABYLONIANS; BABYLONISH; BABYLON'S; CHALDEA; SHESHACH.
2Ki 17:24 of Assyria brought men from B', 894
30 men of B' made Succoth-benoth, "
20:12 son of Baladan, king of B', sent "
14 from a far country, even from B'. "
17 this day, shall be carried unto B': "
18 in the palace of the king of B'. "
24: 1 king of B' came up, and Jehoiakim "
7 the king of B' had taken from "
10 of B' came up against Jerusalem, "
11 king of B' came against the city, "
12 Judah went out to the king of B', "
12 king of B' took him in the eighth "
15 he carried away Jehoiachin to B', "
15 into captivity from Jerusalem to B'. "
16 king of B' brought captive to B'. "
17 the king of B' made Mattaniah his "
20 rebelled against the king of B'. "
25: 1 of B' came, he, and all his host, "
6 him up to the king of B' to Riblah; "
7 of brass, and carried him to B'. "
8 of king Nebuchadnezzar king of B', "
8 a servant of the king of B', unto "
11 that fell away to the king of B', "
13 carried the brass of them to B'. "
20 them to the king of B' to Riblah: "
21 king of B' smote them, and slew "
22 Nebuchadnezzar king of B' had "
23 of B' had made Gedaliah governor, "
24 the land, and serve the king of B'; "
27 Evil-merodach king of B' in the "
28 kings that were with him in B'; "
1Ch 9: 1 away to B' for their transgression. "
2Ch 32:31 ambassadors of the princes of B', "
33:11 with fetters, and carried him to B'. "
36: 6 up Nebuchadnezzar king of B', "
6 him in fetters, to carry him to B'. "
7 of the house of the Lord to B', "
7 put them in his temple at B'. "
10 brought him to B', with the goodly "
18 all these he brought to B'. "
20 the sword carried he away to B'; "
Ezr 1:11 up from B' unto Jerusalem. "
2: 1 of B' had carried away unto B', "
5:12 the king of B', the Chaldean, who 895
12 carried the people away into B'. "
13 first year of Cyrus the king of B' "
14 brought them into the temple of B', "
14 king take out of the temple of B', "
17 treasure house, which is there at B', "
6: 1 the treasures were laid up in B', "
5 and brought unto B', be restored, "
7: 6 This Ezra went up from B'; and 894
9 began he to go up from B', and on "
16 canst find in all the province of B', 895
8: 1 that went up with me from B', 894
Ne 7: 6 the king of B' had carried away, "
Ne 13: 6 of Artaxerxes king of B' came I 894
Es 2: 6 the king of B' had carried away. "
Ps 87: 4 make mention of Rahab and B' "
137: 1 the rivers of B', there we sat down, "
8 O daughter of B', who art to be "
Isa 13: 1 The burden of B', which Isaiah "
19 And B', the glory of kingdoms, "
14: 4 this proverb against the king of B', "
22 and cut off from B' the name, "
21: 9 and said, B' is fallen, is fallen; "
39: 1 king of B', sent letters and a "
3 far country unto me, even from B'. "
6 this day, shall be carried to B': "
7 in the palace of the king of B'. "
43:14 For your sake I have sent to B', "
47: 1 O virgin daughter of B', sit on the "
48:14 he will do his pleasure on B', "
20 Go ye forth of B', flee ye from the "
Jer 20: 4 into the hand of the king of B', "
4 he shall carry them captive into B', "
5 take them, and carry them to B'. "
6 and thou shalt come to B', and "
21: 2 Nebuchadrezzar king of B' "
4 ye fight against the king of B', "
7 of Nebuchadrezzar king of B', "
10 into the hand of the king of B', "
22:25 king of B', and into the hand of the "
24: 1 king of B' had carried away "
1 and had brought them to B'. "
25: 1 of Nebuchadrezzar king of B'; "
9 the king of B', my servant, and "
11 serve the king of B' seventy years. "
12 I will punish the king of B', "
27: 6 the king of B', my servant; and "
8 the king of B', and that will not "
8 under the yoke of the king of B', "
9 Ye shall not serve the king of B': "
11, 12 under the yoke of the king of B', "
13 that will not serve the king of B'? "
14 Ye shall not serve the king of B': "
16 shortly be brought again from B': "
17 serve the king of B', and live: "
18 and at Jerusalem, go not to B'. "
20 Nebuchadnezzar king of B' took "
20 from Jerusalem to B', and all the "
22 They shall be carried to B', "
28: 2 broken the yoke of the king of B'. "
3 Nebuchadnezzar king of B' took "
3 and carried them to B': "
4 of Judah, that went into B', "
4 break the yoke of the king of B'. "
6 captive, from B' into this place. "
11 king of B' from the neck of all "
14 serve Nebuchadnezzar king of B': "
29: 1 away captive from Jerusalem to B'; "
3 king of Judah sent unto B' "
3 to Nebuchadnezzar king of B') "
4 away from Jerusalem unto B'; "
10 years be accomplished at B' "
15 hath raised us up prophets in B'; "
20 I have sent from Jerusalem to B': "
21 king of B'; and he shall slay them "
22 of Judah which are in B', saying, "
22 the king of B' roasted in the fire; "
28 therefore he sent unto us in B', "
32: 3 the king of B', and he shall take it; "
4 of the king of B', and shall speak "
5 he shall lead Zedekiah to B', "
28 Nebuchadrezzar king of B', "
36 of the king of B' by the sword, "
34: 1 king of B', and all his army, "
2 the king of B', and he shall burn it "
3 behold the eyes of the king of B', "
3 to mouth, and thou shalt go to B'. "
35:11 Nebuchadrezzar king of B' came up "
36:29 king of B' shall certainly come. "
37: 1 Nebuchadrezzar king of B' made "
17 into the hand of the king of B'. "
19 The king of B' shall not come "
38:23 by the hand of the king of B': "
39: 1 came Nebuchadrezzar king of B' "
3 princes of the king of B' came in, "
3 of the princes of the king of B'. "
5 up to Nebuchadnezzar king of B' "
6 Then the king of B' slew the sons "
6 the king of B' slew all the nobles "
7 with chains, to carry him to B'. "
9 guard carried away captive into B' "
11 king of B' gave charge concerning "
40: 1 were carried away captive unto B'. "
4 unto thee to come with me into B', "
4 unto thee to come with me into B', "
5 whom the king of B' hath made "
7 the king of B' had made Gedaliah "
7 not carried away captive to B'; "
9 and serve the king of B', and it "
11 the king of B' had left a remnant "
41: 2 and slew him, whom the king of B' "
18 Ahikam, whom the king of B' made "
42:11 Be not afraid of the king of B', "
43: 3 and carry us away captives into B'. "
10 Nebuchadrezzar the king of B', "
44:30 king of B', his enemy, and that "
46: 2 king of B' smote in the fourth year "
13 Nebuchadrezzar king of B' should "
26 hand of Nebuchadrezzar king of B', "
49:28 which Nebuchadrezzar king of B' "
30 king of B' hath taken counsel "
50: 1 that the Lord spake against B' "
2 B' is taken, Bel is confounded, "
8 Remove out of the midst of B', "
9 and cause to come up against B' "
13 goeth by B' shall be astonished, "
14 Put yourselves in array against B' "
16 Cut off the sower from B', "
17 king of B' hath broken his bones. "

Jer 50:18 I will punish the king of B' and 894
23 how is B' become a desolation "
24 and thou art also taken, O B', "
28 and escape out of the land of B', "
29 together the archers against B': "
34 and disquiet the inhabitants of B'. "
35 and upon the inhabitants of B', "
42 against thee, O daughter of B'. "
43 king of B' hath heard the report, "
45 that he hath taken against B'; "
46 At the noise of the taking of B' "
51: 1 Behold, I will raise up against B', "
2 and will send unto B' fanners, "
6 Flee out of the midst of B', "
7 B' hath been a golden cup "
8 B' is suddenly fallen and destroyed: "
9 We would have healed B', but she "
11 for his device is against B', "
12 the standard upon the walls of B', "
12 spake against the inhabitants of B'. "
24 I will render unto B' and to all "
29 shall be performed against B', "
29 make the land of B' a desolation "
30 mighty men of B' have forborn "
31 shew the king of B' that his city "
33 of B' is like a threshing floor, "
34 the king of B' hath devoured me, "
35 and to my flesh be upon B', "
37 B' shall become heaps, a dwelling "
41 how is B' become an astonishment "
42 The sea is come up upon B': "
44 I will punish Bel in B', "
44 yea, the wall of B' shall fall. "
47 upon the graven images of B': "
48 that is therein, shall sing for B': "
49 As B' hath caused the slain of "
49 so at B' shall fall the slain of all "
53 B' should mount up to heaven, "
54 A sound of a cry cometh from B', "
55 Because the Lord hath spoiled B', "
56 is come upon her, even upon B', "
58 walls of B' shall be utterly broken, "
59 B' in the fourth year of his reign. "
60 evil that should come upon B', "
60 words that are written against B'. "
61 When thou comest to B', and shalt "
64 Thus shall B' sink, and shall not "
52: 3 rebelled against the king of B'. "
4 king of B' came, he and all his "
9 carried him up unto the king of B' "
10 king of B' slew the sons of Zedekiah "
11 the king of B' bound him in chains, "
11 and carried him to B', "
12 year of Nebuchadrezzar king of B', "
12 which served the king of B', into "
15 that fell to the king of B', "
17 carried all the brass of them to B'. "
26 them to the king of B' to Riblah. "
27 the king of B' smote them, and "
31 Evil-merodach king of B', in the "
32 of the kings that were with him in B', "
34 diet given him of the king of B', "
Eze 12:13 I will bring him to B' to the land "
17:12 tell them, Behold, the king of B' "
12 and led them with him to B'; "
16 in the midst of B' he shall die. "
20 I will bring him to B', and will "
19: 9 and brought him to the king of B': "
21:19 the sword of the king of B' may "
21 the king of B' stood at the parting "
24: 2 the king of B' set himself against "
26: 7 Nebuchadrezzar king of B', a king "
29:18 of man, Nebuchadrezzar king of B' "
19 unto Nebuchadrezzar king of B'; "
30:10 of Nebuchadrezzar king of B'. "
24 the arms of the king of B', "
25 the king of B', and the arms of "
25 of the king of B', and he shall "
32:11 The sword of the king of B' "
Da 1: 1 Nebuchadnezzar king of B' "
2:12 to destroy all the wise men of B'. 895
14 to slay the wise men of B': "
18 with the rest of the wise men of B'. "
24 to destroy the wise men of B': "
24 Destroy not the wise men of B': "
48 ruler over the whole province of B', "
48 over all the wise men of B'. "
49 the affairs of the province of B': "
3: 1 of Dura, in the province of B'. "
12 the affairs of the province of B', "
30 Abed-nego, in the province of B'. "
4: 6 to bring in all the wise men of B' "
29 in the palace of the kingdom of B'. "
30 Is not this great B', that I have "
5: 7 and said to the wise men of B', "
7: 1 first year of Belshazzar king of B' "
Mic 4:10 and thou shalt go even to B'; 894
Zec 2: 7 with the daughter of B'. "
6:10 which are come from B', "
M't 1:11 they were carried away to B': *897*
12 after they were brought to B', "
17 the carrying away into B' "
17 carrying away into B' unto Christ "
Ac 7:43 carry you away beyond B'. "
1Pe 5:13 The church that is at B', "
Re 14: 8 B' is fallen, is fallen, "
16:19 great B' came in remembrance "
17: 5 B' the great, the mother of "
18: 2 B' the great is fallen, "
10 that great city B', that mighty city! "
21 great city B' be thrown down, "

Babylonians (*bab-il-o'-ne-ans*) See also CHALDEANS.
Ezr 4: 9 the B', the Susanchites, the 896
Eze 23:15 manner of the B' of Chaldea, 1121,894
23:17 the B' came to her into the 1121,894
23 The B', and all the Chaldeans, " "

Babylonish (*bab-il-o'-nish*) See also BABYLONIANS.
Jos 7:21 spoils a goodly B' garment, 8152

Babylon's (*bab'-il-ons*)
Jer 32: 2 the king of B' army besieged 894
34: 7 When the king of B' army fought "
21 the hand of the king of B' army, "
38: 3 of B' army, which shall take it. "
17 go forth unto the king of B' princes, "
18 to the king of B' princes, then shall "
22 forth to the king of B' princes, "
39:13 and all the king of B' princes; * "

Baca (*ba'-cah*)
Ps 84: 6 passing through the valley of B' *1056

Bachrites (*bak'-rites*)
Nu 26:35 of Becher, the family of the B': 1076

Bachuth See ALLON-BACHUTH.

back See also BACKBITERS; BACKBITETH; BACKBITING; BACKBONE; BACKS; BACKSIDE; BACKSLIDER; BACKSLIDING; BACKWARD; HORSEBACK.
Ge 14:16 And he brought b' all the goods, 7725
19: 9 they said, Stand b'. 1973
26 his wife looked b' from behind "
38:29 as he drew b' his hand, 7725
39: 9 neither hath he kept b' anything 2820
Ex 14:21 Lord caused the sea to go b' by a *
18: 2 after he had sent her b', *
23: 4 surely bring it b' to him again. 7725
33:23 thou shalt see my b' parts: 268
Nu 9: 7 wherefore are we kept b', 1639
13:26 and brought b' word unto them, 7725
22:34 thee, I will get me b' again. "
24:11 hath kept thee b' from honour. 4513
De 23:13 and shalt turn b' and cover that 7725
Jos 8:20 wilderness turned b' upon the 2015
26 Joshua drew not his hand b', 7725
11:10 And Joshua at that time turned b', "
23:12 if ye do in any wise go b', "
J'g 11:35 the Lord, and I cannot go b'. "
18:26 he turned and went b' unto his "
Ru 1:15 is gone b' unto her people, "
2: 6 Moabitish damsel that came b' "
1Sa 10: 9 he had turned his b' to go from 7926
15:11 he is turned b' from following me, 7725
25:34 hath kept me b' from hurting *4513
2Sa 1:22 the bow of Jonathan turned not b', 268
12:23 can I bring him b' again? I 7725
15:20 and take b' thy brethren: mercy "
25 Carry b' the ark of God into the "
17: 3 I will bring b' all the people unto "
18:16 Joab held b' the people. 2820
19:10 a word of bringing the king b'? 7725
11 to bring the king b' to his house? "
12 ye the last to bring b' the king? "
37 I pray thee, turn b' again, "
43 first had in bringing b' our king? "
1Ki 13:18 Bring him b' with thee into thine "
19 So he went b' with him, and did eat "
20 the prophet that brought him b': "
22 But camest b', and hast eaten "
23 prophet whom he had brought b'. "
26 prophet that brought him b' from "
29 upon the ass, and brought it b': "
14: 9 hast cast me behind thy b': 1458
28 and brought them b' into the 7725
18:37 hast turned their heart b' again. 322
19:20 Go b' again: for what have I done 7725
21 And he returned b' from him, * "
22:26 and carry him b' unto Amon the "
33 they turned b' from pursuing him. "
2Ki 1: 5 the messengers turned b' unto * "
5 Why are ye now turned b'? * "
2:13 and went b', and stood by the bank "
24 And he turned b', and looked on * 310
8:29 king Joram went b' to be healed *7725
15:20 So the king of Assyria turned b', "
19:28 and I will turn thee b' by the way "
20: 9 ten degrees, or go b' ten degrees? "
1Ch 21:20 And Ornan turned b', and saw the "
2Ch 13:14 when Judah looked b', behold, 6437
18:25 and carry him b' to Amon the 7725
32 turned b' again from pursuing "
19: 4 and brought them b' unto the Lord "
25:13 the army which Amaziah sent b', "
34:16 brought the king word b' again, * "
Ne 2:15 viewed the wall, and turned b', and "
Job 23:12 I gone b' from the commandment 4185
26: 9 He holdeth b' the face of his *
33:18 He keepeth b' his soul from the 2820
30 To bring b' his soul from the pit, 7725
34:27 they turned b' from him, and *5493
39:22 neither turneth he b' from the 7725
Ps. 9: 3 enemies are turned b', they shall 268
14: 7 the Lord bringeth b' the captivity 7725
19:13 Keep b' thy servant also from 2820
21:12 make them turn their b', when 7926
35: 4 let them be turned b' and brought 268
44:10 makest us to turn b' from the "
18 Our heart is not turned b', neither "
53: 3 Every one of them is gone b': 5472
6 God bringeth b' the captivity of 7725
56: 9 then shall mine enemies turn b': 268
70: 3 Let them be turned b' for a 7725
78: 9 turned b' in the day of battle. 2015
41 Yea, they turned b' and tempted *7725
57 But turned b', and dealt 5472
80:18 will not we go b' from thee: "
85: 1 hast brought b' the captivity of 7725
114: 3 and fled: Jordan was driven b'. 268
5 Jordan, that thou wast driven b'? "
129: 3 plowed upon my b': they made 1354
5 all be confounded and turned b' * 268
Pr. 10:13 a rod is for the b' of him that is 1458
19:29 and stripes for the b' of fools. "
26: 3 a rod for the fool's b'. "
Isa 14:27 out, and who shall turn it b'? 7725
31: 2 will not call b' his words: but 5493
37:29 and I will turn thee b' by the way 7725
38:17 cast all my sins behind thy b'. 1458
42:17 They shall be turned b', they shall 268
43: 6 and to the south, Keep not b': 3607
50: 5 neither turned away b. * 268
6 I gave my b' to the smiters, and 1458
Jer 2:27 have turned their b' unto me, 6203
4: 8 of the Lord is not turned b' 7725
28 neither will I turn b' from it. "
6: 9 turn b' thine hand as a grape * "
8: 5 of Jerusalem slidden b' by a "
11:10 They are turned b' to the "
18:17 shew them the b', and not the *6203
21: 4 I will turn b' the weapons of war 5437
32:33 they have turned unto me the b', 6203
38:22 and they are turned away b'. 268
40: 5 he was not yet gone b', he said, 7725
5 Go b' also to Gedaliah the son of "
42: 4 I will keep nothing b' from you. 4513
46: 5 dismayed and turned away b'? * 268
5 are fled apace, and look not b': 3437
21 also are turned b', and are fled "
47: 3 fathers shall not look b' to their "
48:10 he that keepeth b' his sword from 4513
39 hath Moab turned the b' with 6203
49: 8 Flee ye, turn b', dwell deep, 6437
La 1:13 he hath turned me b': he hath 268
2: 3 he hath drawn b' his right hand "
Eze 23:35 me behind thy b', therefore bear 1458
24:14 I will not go b', neither will I 6544
38: 4 And I will turn thee b', *7725
8 the land that is brought b' from "
39: 2 I will turn thee b', and leave but * "
44: 1 Then he brought me b' the way of "
Da 7: 6 which had upon the b' of it four 1355
Ho 4:16 Israel slideth b' as a backsliding *5637
Na 2: 8 they cry; but none shall look b'. 6437
Zep 1: 6 them that are turned b' from the 5253
3:20 when I turn b' your captivity *7725
M't 24:18 return b' to take his clothes. *3694*
28: 2 came and rolled b' the stone * *617*
M'r 13:16 that is in the field not turn b' "
Lu 2:45 turned b' again to Jerusalem, *5290*
8:37 the ship, and returned b' again. "
9:62 looking b', is fit for the kingdom *3694*
17:15 turned b', and with a loud voice *5290*
31 let him likewise not return b'. *3694*
Joh 6:66 many of his disciples went b', "
20:14 turned herself b', and saw Jesus "
Ac 5: 2 And kept b' part of the price, *3557*
3 to keep b' part of the price of the "
7:39 hearts turned b' again into Egypt, *4762*
20:20 how I kept b' nothing that was *5288*
Ro 11:10 and bow down their b' alway. *3577*
Heb 10:38 but if any man draw b', my soul *5288*
39 we are not of them who draw b' *5289*
Jas 5: 4 is of you kept b' by fraud, *650*

backbiters
Ro 1:30 B', haters of God, despiteful, *2637*

backbiteth
Ps 15: 3 He that b' not with his tongue, *7270

backbiting See also BACKBITINGS.
Pr 25:23 angry countenance a b' tongue. 5643

backbitings
2Co 12:20 strifes, b', whisperings, *2636*

backbone
Le 3: 9 it shall he take off hard by the b'; 6096

backed See BACKT.

backs
Ex 23:27 all thine enemies turn their b' 6203
Jos 7: 8 when Israel turneth their b' "
12 their b' before their enemies, "
J'g 20:42 Therefore they turned their b' "
2Ch 29: 6 of the Lord, and turned their b'. 6203
Ne 9: 26 cast thy law behind their b', *1458
Eze 8:16 with their b' toward the temple 268
10:12 and their b', and their hands, 1354

backside
Ex 3: 1 flock to the b' of the desert, and * 310
26:12 over the b' of the tabernacle. * 268
Re 5: 1 book written within and on the b'. *3693*

backslider
Pr 14:14 The b' in heart shall be filled 5472

backsliding See also BACKSLIDINGS.
Jer 3: 6 that which b' Israel hath done? 4878
8 b' Israel committed adultery "
11 The b' Israel hath justified herself "
12 Return, thou b' Israel, saith the "
14 Turn, O b' children, saith the 7726
22 Return, ye b' children, and I will "
8: 5 slidden back by a perpetual b'? 4878
31:22 O thou b' daughter? 7728
49: 4 thy flowing valley, O b' daughter? "
Ho 4:16 Israel slideth back as a b' heifer: *5637
11: 7 my people are bent to b' from me: 4878
14: 4 I will heal their b', "

backslidings
Jer 2:19 and thy b' shall reprove thee: 4878
3:22 and I will heal your b'. "
5: 6 their b' are increased. "
14: 7 our b' are many; "

backward
Ge 9:23 both their shoulders, and went b', 322
23 and their faces were b', and they "
49:17 so that his rider shall fall b'. 268
1Sa 4:18 he fell from off the seat b' 322
2Ki 20:10 shadow return b' ten degrees. "

2Ki 20:11 brought the shadow ten degrees b', 322
Job 23: 8 and b', but I cannot perceive 268
Ps 40:14 them be driven b' and put to shame "
70: 2 be turned b', and put to confusion, "
Isa 1: 4 unto anger, they are gone away b'. "
28:13 that they might go, and fall b', "
38: 8 sun dial of Ahaz, ten degrees b'. 322
44:25 that turneth wise men b', 268
59:14 judgment is turned away b', "
Jer 7:24 went b', and not forward. "
15: 6 saith the Lord, thou art gone b': "
La 1: 8 she sigheth, and turneth b'. "
Joh 18: 6 they went b', and fell to *1519, 3588, 3694*

bad See also WORSE; WORST.
Ge 24:50 cannot speak unto thee b' or good. 7451
31:24, 29 not to Jacob either good or b'. "
Le 27:10 nor change it, a good for a b', "
10 or a b' for a good: and if he "
12 value it, whether it be good or b': "
14 estimate it, whether it be good or b', "
33 not search whether it be good or b', "
Nu 13:19 whether it be good or b'; and what "
24:13 good or b' of mine own mind; "
2Sa 13:22 brother Amnon neither good nor b': "
14:17 the king to discern good and b': "
1Ki 3: 9 discern between good and b': * "
Ezr 4:12 the rebellious and the b' city, 873
Jer 24: 2 not be eaten, they were so b'. 7451
M't 13:48 into vessels, but cast the b' away. *4550*
22:10 as they found, both b' and good: *4190*
2Co 5:10 done, whether it be good or b'. *2556*

bade See also BADEST; FORBAD.
Ge 43:17 did as Joseph b'; and the man 559
Ex 16:24 up till the morning, as Moses b': 6680
Nu 14:10 congregation b' stone them with 559
Jos 11: 9 unto them as the Lord b' him: "
Ru 3: 6 all that her mother in law b' her. 6680
1Sa 24:10 and some b' me kill thee: but 559
2Sa 1:18 b' them teach the children of Judah "
14:19 thy servant Joab, he b' me, and 6680
2Ch 10:12 the king b', saying, Come again 1696
Es 4:15 Then Esther b' them return 559
M't 16:12 they how that he b' them not *2036*
Lu 14: 9 And he that b' thee and him come *2564*
10 when he that b' thee cometh, he "
12 said he also to him that b' him, "
16 made a great supper, and b' many: "
Ac 11:12 the spirit b' me go with them, *2036*
18:21 b' them farewell, saying, I must * *657*
22:24 b' that he should be examined **2036*

badest
Ge 27:19 done according as thou b' me: 1696

badgers'
Ex 25: 5 b' skins, and shittim wood, *8476
26:14 a covering above of b' skins. * "
35: 7 dyed red, and b' skins, and * "
23 red skins of rams, and b' skins, * "
36:19 a covering of b' skins above that * "
39:34 the covering of b' skins, * "
Nu 4: 6 the covering of b' skins, * "
8 with a covering of b' skins, * "
10 within a covering of b' skins, * "
11 with a covering of b' skins, * "
12 a covering of b' skins, and shall * "
14 upon it a covering of b' skins, * "
25 the covering of the b skins * "
Eze 16:10 shod thee with b' skin, * "

badger-skin See BADGERS' and SKIN.

badness
Ge 41:19 in all the land of Egypt for b': 7455

bag See also BAGS.
De 25:13 not have in thy b' divers weights, 3599
1Sa 17:40 in a shepherd's b' which he had, 3627
49 David put his hand in his b', "
Job 14:17 transgression is sealed up in a b', 6872
Pr 7:20 taken a b' of money with him, "
16:11 weights of the b' are his work. 3599
Isa 46: 6 They lavish gold out of the b', "
Mic 6:11 with the b' of deceitful weights? "
Hag 1: 6 to put it into a b' with holes. 6872
Joh 12: 6 he was a thief, and had the b', *1101*
13:29 thought, because Judas had the b', "

bags
2Ki 5:23 two talents of silver in two b', 2754
12:10 they put up in b', and told the 6696
Lu 12:33 provide yourselves b' which wax * *905*

Bah See HEPHZI-BAH.

Baharumite (*ba-ha'-rum-ite*) See also BARHUMITE.
1Ch 11:33 Azmaveth the B', Eliahba the 978

Bahurim (*ba-hu'-rim*) See also BAHARUMITE.
2Sa 3:16 along weeping behind her to B'. 980
16: 5 And when king David came to B' "
17:18 and came to a man's house in B', "
19:16 a Benjamite, which was of B', "
1Ki 2: 8 a Benjamite of B', which cursed "

Bajith (*ba'-jith*)
Isa 15: 2 is gone up to B', and to Dibon, 1006

Bakbakkar (*bak-bak'-kar*)
1Ch 9:15 B', Heresh, and Galal, and 1230

Bakbuk (*bak'-buk*)
Ezr 2:51 The children of B', the children 1227
Ne 7:53 The children of B', the children "

Bakbukiah (*bak-buk-i'-ah*)
Ne 11:17 B' the second among his brethren, 1229
12: 9 B' and Unni, their brethren, "
25 Mattaniah, and B', Obadiah, "

bake See also BAKED; BAKEMEATS; BAKEN; BAKETH.
Ge 19: 3 did b' unleavened bread, and they 644
Ex 16:23 b' that which ye will b' "
Le 24: 5 and b' twelve cakes thereof: 644
26:26 ten women shall b' your bread in "
1Sa 28:24 did b' unleavened bread thereof: "
2Sa 13: 8 in his sight, and did b' the cakes. 1310
Eze 4:12 thou shalt b' it with dung that 5746
46:20 they shall b' the meat offering; 644

baked See also BAKEN.
Ex 12:39 And they b' unleavened cakes 644
Nu 11: 8 b' it in pans, and made cakes *1310
1Ch 23:29 and for that which is b' in the pan, "
Isa 44:19 I have b' bread upon the coals 644

bakemeats
Ge 40:17 of b' for Pharaoh; 3978, 4639, 644

baken See also BAKED.
Le 2: 4 a meat offering b' in the oven, 644
5 be a meat offering b' in a pan, *
7 offering b' in the frying pan, *
6:17 It shall not be b' with leaven. 644
21 when it is b', thou shalt *7246
21 the b' pieces of the meat offering 8601
7: 9 all the meat offering that is b' 644
23:17 they shall be b' with leaven; "
1Ki 19: 6 there was a cake b' on the coals, "

baketh
Isa 44:15 he kindleth it, and b' bread; 644

baker See also BAKERS.
Ge 40: 1 and his b' had offended their lord 644
5 and the b' of the king of Egypt, "
16 When the chief b' saw that the "
20 of the chief b' among his servants. "
22 But he hanged the chief b': "
41:10 both me and the chief b': "
Ho 7: 4 as an oven heated by the b', "
6 their b' sleepeth all the night; "

bakers See also BAKERS'.
Ge 40: 2 against the chief of the b'. 644
1Sa 8:13 and to be cooks, and to be b'. "

bakers'
Jer 37:21 piece of bread out of the b' street. 644

Balaam (*ba'-la-am*) See also BALAAM'S.
Nu 22: 5 therefore unto B' the son of Beor 1109
7 and they came unto B', and spake "
8 princes of Moab abode with B'. "
9 And God came unto B', and said, "
10 And B' said unto God, Balak the "
12 God said unto B', Thou shalt not "
13 B' rose up in the morning, and said "
14 said, B' refuseth to come with us. "
16 they came to B', and said to him, "
18 B' answered and said unto the "
20 And God came unto B' at night, "
21 And B' rose up in the morning, "
23 and B' smote the ass, to turn her "
27 fell down under B': and Balaam's "
28 she said unto B', What have I done "
29 And B' said unto the ass, Because "
30 ass said unto B', Am not I thine "
31 the Lord opened the eyes of B', "
34 B' said unto the angel of the Lord, "
35 angel of the Lord said unto B', Go "
35 B' went with the princes of Balak. "
36 Balak heard that B' was come, "
37 And Balak said unto B', Did I not "
38 B' said unto Balak, Lo, I am come "
39 B' went with Balak, and they came "
40 sent to B', and to the princes "
41 Balak took B', and brought him "
23: 1 And B' said unto Balak, Build me "
2 Balak did as B' had spoken; "
2 Balak and B' offered on every altar "
3 B' said unto Balak, Stand by thy "
4 And God met B': and he said unto "
11 Balak said unto B', What hast thou "
16 the Lord met B', and put a word "
25 Balak said unto B', Neither curse "
26 B' answered and said unto Balak. "
27 Balak said unto B', Come, I pray "
28 brought B' unto the top of Peor, "
29 B' said unto Balak, Build me here "
30 And Balak did as B' had said. "
24: 1 B' saw that it pleased the Lord "
2 And B' lifted up his eyes, and he "
3 and said, B' the son of Beor "
10 anger was kindled against B', "
10 Balak said unto B', I called thee "
12 B' said unto Balak, Spake I not "
15 said, B' the son of Beor hath said, "
25 B' rose up, and went and returned "
31: 8 B' also the son of Beor they slew "
16 through the counsel of B', "
De 23: 4 they hired against thee B' the son "
5 God would not hearken unto B'; "
Jos 13:22 B' also the son of Beor, the "
24: 9 sent and called B' the son of Beor "
10 But I would not hearken unto B'; "
Ne 13: 2 water, but hired B' against them, "
Mic 6: 5 what B' the son of Beor answered "
2Pe 2:15 following the way of B' the son of *903*
Jude 11 the error of B' for reward) "
Re 2:14 doctrine of B', who taught Balac "

Balaam's (*ba'-la-ams*)
Nu 22:25 and crushed B' foot against 1109
27 and B' anger was kindled, "
23: 5 the Lord put a word in B' mouth, "

Balac (*ba'-lak*) See also BALAK.
Re 2:14 taught B' to cast a stumblingblock *904*

Baladan (*bal'-adan*) See also BERODACH-BALADAN; MERODACH-BALADAN.
2Ki 20:12 the son of B', king of Babylon, 1081
Isa 39: 1 Merodach-baladan, the son of B', "

Balah (*ba'-lah*) See also BAALAH.
Jos 19: 3 Hazar-shual, and B', and Azem, 1088

Balak (*ba'-lak*) See also BALAC; BALAK'S.
Nu 22: 2 B' the son of Zippor saw all that 1111
4 B' the son of Zippor was king of "
7 spake unto him the words of B'. "
10 B' the son of Zippor, king of "
13 and said unto the princes of B', "
14 went unto B', and said, Balaam "
15 And B' sent yet again princes, "
16 Thus saith B' the son of Zippor, "
18 unto the servants of B', "
18 If B' would give me "
35 went with the princes of B'. "
36 B' heard that Balaam was come, "
37 B' said unto Balaam, Did I not "
38 Balaam said unto B', Lo, I am "
39 Balaam went with B', and they "
40 And B' offered oxen and sheep, "
41 B' took Balaam, and brought him "
23: 1 Balaam said unto B', Build me "
2 B' did as Balaam had spoken; "
2 B' and Balaam offered on every "
3 Balaam said unto B', Stand by thy "
5 Return unto B', and thus thou "
7 and said, B' the king of Moab "
11 B' said unto Balaam, What hast "
13 B' said unto him, Come, I pray "
15 said unto B', Stand here by thy "
16 Go again unto B', and say thus. "
17 B' said unto him, What hath the "
18 and said, Rise up, B', and hear; "
25 And B' said unto Balaam, "
26 and said unto B', Told not I thee, "
27 B' said unto Balaam, Come, I pray "
28 B' brought Balaam unto the top "
29 Balaam said unto B', Build me "
30 B' did as Balaam had said, "
24:10 B' said unto Balaam, I called thee "
12 Balaam said unto B', Spake I not "
13 If B' would give me his house "
25 to his place: and B' also went "
Jos 24: 9 Then B' the son of Zippor, king of "
J'g 11:25 art thou anything better than B' "
Mic 6: 5 what B' king of Moab consulted, "

Balak's (*ba'-laks*)
Nu 24:10 And B' anger was kindled against 1111

balance See also BALANCES; BALANCINGS.
Job 31: 6 Let me be weighed in an even b', 3976
Ps 62: 9 to be laid in the b', they are * "
Pr 11: 1 false b' is abomination to the "
16:11 just weight and b' are the Lord's: "
20:23 and a false b' is not good. "
Isa 40:12 and the hills in a b'? "
15 count as the small dust of the b': "
46: 6 weigh silver in the b' and hire a 7070

balances
Le 19:36 Just b', just weights, a just 3976
Job 6: 2 my calamity laid in the b' together! "
Jer 32:10 weighed him the money in the b'. "
Eze 5: 1 then take thee b' to weigh, and "
45:10 Ye shall have just b', "
Da 5:27 Thou art weighed in the b', 3977
Ho 12: 7 the b' of deceit are in his hand: 3976
Am 8: 5 falsifying the b' by deceit? "
Mic 6:11 pure with the wicked b', "
Re 6: 5 had a pair of b' in his hand. *

balancings
Job 37:16 thou know the b' of the clouds, 4657

bald
Le 11:22 the b' locust after his kind, and 5556
13:40 he is b'; yet is he clean. 7142
41 he is forehead b': yet is he clean. 1371
42 if there be in the b' head, 7146
42 or b' forehead, a white 1372
42 leprosy sprung up in his b' head, 7146
42 head or his b' forehead. 1372
43 be white reddish in his b' head, 7146
43 or in her bald forehead, 1372
2Ki 2:23 b' head; go up, thou b' head. 7142
Jer 16: 6 make themselves b' for them: 7139
48:37 every head shall be b', and every 7144
Eze 27:31 themselves utterly b' for thee, 7139
29:18 every head was made b', and every "
Mic 1:16 Make thee b', and poll thee for thy "

bald-head See BALD and HEAD.

bald-locust See BALD and LOCUST.

baldness
Le 21: 5 They shall not make b' upon their 7144
De 14: 1 nor make any b' between your "
Isa 3:24 instead of well set hair b'; "
15: 2 on all their heads shall be b', "
22:12 to mourning, and to b', "
Jer 47: 5 B' is come upon Gaza; "
Eze 7:18 b' upon all their heads. "
Am 8:10 b' upon every head; and I will "
Mic 1:16 enlarge thy b' as the eagle; "

ball
Isa 22:18 and toss thee like a b' into a 1754

balm See also EMBALM.
Ge 37:25 spicery and b' and myrrh, going 6875
43:11 a little b', and a little honey, "
Jer 8:22 Is there no b' in Gilead; "
46:11 Go up into Gilead, and take b', "
51: 8 take b' for her pain, if so be she "
Eze 27:17 and honey, and oil, and b'. "

Bamah (*ba'-mah*) See also BAMOTH.
Eze 20:29 thereof is called B' unto this day. 1117

Bamoth (*ba'-moth*) See also BAMOTH-BAAL.
Nu 21:19 from Nahaliel to B': 1120
20 And from B' in the valley, that is "

Bamoth-baal (*ba''-moth-ba'-al*)
Jos 13:17 Dibon, and B', and 1120

band See also BANDED; BANDS; SWADDLING BAND.
Ex 39:23 a b' round about the hole, that it *8193
1Sa 10:26 him a b' of men, whose hearts *2428
1Ki 11:24 captain over a b', when David *1416
2Ki 13:21 they spied a b' of men; and they "
1Ch 12:18 made them captains of the b'. "
21 David against the b' of the "
2Ch 22: 1 the b' of men that came with the "
Ezr 8:22 the king a b' of soldiers and 2428
Job 39:10 unicorn with his b' in the furrow? 5688
Da 4:15 even with a b' of iron and brass, 613
23 in the earth, even with a b' of iron "
M't 27:27 gathered unto him the whole b' 4686
M'r 15:16 they call together the whole b'. "
Joh 18: 3 having received a b' of men and "
12 Then the b' and the captain and "
Ac 10: 1 of the b' called the Italian b', "
21:31 chief captain of the b', that all "
27: 1 Julius, a centurion of Augustus' b'. "

banded
Ac 23:12 of the Jews b' together, *4160, 4963

bands See also HEADBANDS.
Ge 32: 7 herds, and the camels, into two b';*4264
10 and now I am become two b'. * "
Le 26:13 have broken the b' of your yoke, *4133
J'g 15:14 his b' loosed from off his hands. 612
2Sa 4: 2 two men that were captains of b': 1416
2Ki 6:23 So the b' of Syria came no more "
13:20 And the b' of the Moabites invaded "
23:33 Pharaoh-nechoh put him in b' at 631
24: 2 against him b' of the Chaldees, 1416
2 and b' of the Syrians, "
2 and b' of the Moabites, "
2 and b' of the children of Ammon, "
1Ch 7: 4 were b' of soldiers for war, "
12:23 of the b. that were ready armed *7218
2Ch 26:11 went out to war by b', according 1416
Job 1:17 Chaldeans made out three b', and 7218
38:31 Pleiades, or loose the b' of Orion? 4189
39: 5 hath loosed the b' of the wild ass? 4147
Ps 2: 3 break their b' asunder, and cast "
73: 4 there are no b' in their death: 2784
107:14 and break their b' in sunder. 4147
119:61 The b' of the wicked have robbed *2256
Pr 30:27 go they forth all of them by b'; 2683
Ec 7:26 and nets, and her hands as b': 612
Isa 28:22 lest your b' be made strong: 4147
52: 2 loose thyself from the b' of thy "
58: 6 loose the bands of wickedness, to*2784
Jer 2:20 thy yoke, and burst thy b'; 4147
Eze 3:25 they shall put b' upon thee, and 5688
4: 8 I will lay b. upon thee, and thou "
12:14 to help him, and all his b'; 102
17:21 with all his b' shall fall by the "
34:27 have broken the b' of their yoke, *4133
38: 6 Gomer, and all his b'; * 102
6 the north quarters, and all his b': * "
9 the land, thou, and all thy b', * "
22 upon him, upon his b', * "
39: 4 of Israel, thou, and all thy b', * "
Ho 11: 4 of a man, with b' of love: 5688
Zec 11: 7 Beauty, the other I called B'; 2256
14 asunder mine other staff, even B', "
Lu 8:29 he brake the b', and was driven 1199
Ac 16:26 and every one's b' were loosed. "
22:30 he loosed him from his b', and * "
27:40 loosed the rudder b', and hoised 2202
Col 2:19 the body by joints and b' having 4886

Bani (ba'-ni)
2Sa 23:36 Nathan of Zobah, B' the Gadite, 1137
1Ch 6:46 The son of B', the son of Shamer, "
9: 4 the son of B', of the children of "
Ezr 2:10 The children of B', six hundred "
10:29 sons of B'; Meshullam, and "
34 Of the sons of B'; Maadai, Amram, "
38 And B', and Binnui, and Shimei, "
Ne 3:17 Rehum the son of B'. Next "
8: 7 Jeshua, and B', and Sherebiah, "
9: 4 Levites, Jeshua, and B', Kadmiel, "
4 B', and Chenani, and cried "
5 and Kadmiel, B', Hashabniah, "
10:13 Hodijah, B', Beninu. "
14 Pahath-moab, Elam, Zatthu, B', "
11:22 Uzzi the son of B', the son of "

banished
2Sa 14:13 doth not fetch home again his b'. *5080
14 that his b' be not expelled "

banishment
Ezr 7:26 it be unto death, or to b', 8331
La 2:14 false burdens and causes of b'. 4065

bank See also BANKS.
Ge 41:17 I stood upon the b' of the river: *8193
De 4:48 is by the b' of the river Arnon, * "
Jos 12: 2 upon the b' of the river Arnon, * "
13: 9 is upon the b' of the river Arnon, * "
16 is on the b' of the river Arnon, * "
2Sa 20:15 cast up a b' against the city, *5550
2Ki 2:13 and stood by the b' of Jordan; 8193
19:32 shield, nor cast a b' against it. *5550
Isa 37:33 shields, nor cast a b' against it. * "
Eze 47: 7 at the b' of the river were very 8193
12 by the river upon the b' thereof, "
Da 12: 5 this side of the b' of the river, * "
5 other on that side of the b' of * "
Lu 19:23 money into the b', that at my 5132

banks
Jos 3:15 overfloweth all his b' all the time 1415
4:18 flowed over all his b', as they did "
1Ch 12:15 it had overflown all his b'; 1428
Isa 8: 7 channels, and go over all his b': 1415
Da 8:16 man's voice between the b' of Ulai,

banner See also BANNERS.
Ps 60: 4 given a b' to them that fear 5251
Ca 2: 4 and his b' over me was love. 1714
Isa 13: 2 Lift ye up a b' upon the high *5251

banners
Ps 20: 5 set up our b': the Lord fulfil all 1713
Ca 6: 4 terrible as an army with b'. "
10 and terrible as an army with b'? "

banquet See also BANQUETING.
Es 5: 4 Haman come this day unto the b' 4960
5 the king and Haman came to the b' "
6 said unto Esther at the b' of wine, "
8 the king and Haman come to the b' "
12 come in with the king unto the b' "
14 merrily with the king unto the b'. "
6:14 hasted to bring Haman unto the b' "
7: 1 the king and Haman came to 8354
2 Esther on the second day at the b' 4960
7 the king arising from the b' of "
8 into the place of the b' of wine; "
Job 41: 6 Shall the companions make a b' *3738
Da 5:10 his lord, came into the b' house: 4961
Am 6: 7 the b' of them that stretched *4797

banqueting See also BANQUETINGS.
Ca 2: 4 He brought me to the b' house, 3196

banquetings
1Pe 4: 3 b', and abominable idolatries: *4224

baptism See also BAPTISMS.
M't 3: 7 and Sadducees come to his b', 908
20:22 the b' that I am baptized with? * "
23 be baptized with the b' that I am * "
21:25 The b' of John, whence was it? "
M'r 1: 4 preach the b' of repentance for "
10:38 the b' that I am baptized with? "
39 with the b' that I am baptized "
11:30 The b' of John, was it from heaven, "
Lu 3: 3 preaching the b' of repentance "
7:29 being baptized with the b' of John. "
12:50 I have a b' to be baptized with, "
20: 4 The b' of John, was it from heaven, "
Ac 1:22 Beginning from the b' of John, "
10:37 after the b' which John preached; "
13:24 the b' of repentance to all the people "
18:25 Lord, knowing only the b' of John. "
19: 3 And they said, Unto John's b'. "
4 with the b' of repentance, saying "
Ro 6: 4 buried with him by b' into death: "
Eph 4: 5 One Lord, one faith, one b', "
Col 2:12 Buried with him in b', wherein "
1Pe 3:21 even b' doth also now save us "

baptisms
Heb 6: 2 Of the doctrine of b', and of laying 909

Baptist (bap'-tist) See also BAPTIST'S.
M't 3: 1 In those days came John the B', 910
11:11 risen a greater than John the B': "
12 from the days of John the B' until "
14: 2 This is John the B'; he is risen "
16:14 Some say that thou art John the B': "
17:13 he spake unto them of John the B'. "
M'r 6:14 That John the B' was risen from 907
24 she said, The head of John the B'. 910
25 a charger the head of John the B'. "
8:28 they answered, John the B': "
Lu 7:20 John B' hath sent us unto thee, "
28 greater prophet than John the B':* "
33 John the B' came neither eating "
9:19 answering said, John the B'; "

Baptist's (bap'-tists)
M't 14: 8 Give me here John B' head in * 910

baptize See also BAPTIZED; BAPTIZEST; BAPTIZETH; BAPTIZING.
M't 3:11 I indeed b' you with water 907
11 he shall b' you with the Holy Ghost, "
M'r 1: 4 John did b' in the wilderness, "
8 he shall b' you with the Holy Ghost "
Lu 3:16 I indeed b' you with water; "
16 he shall b' you with the Holy Ghost "
Joh 1:26 saying, I b' with water: but "
33 he that sent me to b' with water, "
1Co 1:17 Christ sent me not to b', but to "

baptized
M't 3: 6 And were b' of him in Jordan, 907
13 Jordan unto John, to be b' of him. "
14 I have need to be b' of thee, and "
16 Jesus, when he was b', went up "
20:22 I shall drink of, and to be b', "
22 the baptism that I am b' with? "
23 and be b' with the baptism "
23 that I am b' with: "
M'r 1: 5 all b' of him in the river of Jordan, "
8 I indeed have b' you with water: "
9 and was b' of John in Jordan. "
10:38 and be b' with the baptism "
38 that I am b' with? "
39 and with the baptism that I am b' "
39 withal shall ye be b': "
16:16 believeth and is b' shall be saved; "
Lu 3: 7 came forth to be b' of him, "
12 Then came also publicans to be b', "
21 when all the people were b', it came "
21 that Jesus also being b', "
7:29 being b' with the baptism of John. "
30 themselves, being not b' of him. "
12:50 I have a baptism to be b' with; "
Joh 3:22 there he tarried with them, and b'. "
23 and they came, and were b'. "
4: 1 Jesus made and b' more disciples* "
2 (Though Jesus himself b' not, "
10:40 place where John at first b'; "
Ac 1: 5 John truly b' with water; "
1: 5 ye shall be b' with the Holy Ghost 907
2:38 Repent, and be b' every one of you "
41 gladly received his word were b': "
8:12 were b', both men and women. "
13 he was b', he continued with Philip, "
16 only they were b' in the name "
36 what doth hinder me to be b'? "
38 and the eunuch; and he b' him. "
9:18 forthwith, and arose, and was b'. "
10:47 water, that these should not be b', "
48 commanded them to be b' in the "
11:16 John indeed b' with water; "
16 ye shall be b' with the Holy Ghost. "
16:15 when she was b', and her household, "
33 was b', he and all his, straightway. "
18: 8 hearing believed, and were b'. "
19: 3 Unto what then were ye b'? "
4 John verily b' with the baptism of "
5 heard this, they were b' in the name "
22:16 and be b', and wash away thy sins, "
Ro 6: 3 of us as were b' into Jesus Christ "
3 were b' into his death? "
1Co 1:13 or were ye b' in the name of Paul? "
14 I thank God that I b' none of you, "
15 say that I had b' in mine own name. "
16 I b' also the household of Stephanas: "
16 I know not whether I b' any other. "
10: 2 were all b' unto Moses in the cloud "
12:13 For by one Spirit are we all b' into "
15:29 they do which are b' for the dead, "
29 why are they then b' for the dead? "
Ga 3:27 as have been b' into Christ have put "

baptizest
Joh 1:25 said unto him, Why b' thou then, 907

baptizeth
Joh 1:33 is he which b' with the Holy Ghost. 907
3:26 behold, the same b', and all men "

baptizing
M't 28:19 b' them in the name of the Father, 907
Joh 1:28 Jordan, where John was b'. "
31 therefore am I come b' with water. "
3:23 John also was b' in Ænon "

bar See also BARS.
Ex 26:28 And the middle b' in the midst of 1280
36:33 he made the middle b' to shoot "
Nu 4:10 skins, and shall put it upon a b'. *4132
12 skins, and shall put them on a b':* "
J'g 16: 3 away with them, b' and all, and 1280
Ne 7: 3 them shut the doors, and b' them: 270
Am 1: 5 break also the b' of Damascus, 1280

Bar See BARABBAS; BAR-JESUS; BAR-JONAH; BARNABAS; BARSABAS; BARTHOLOMEW; BARTIMAEUS.

Barabbas (ba-rab'-bas)
M't 27:16 a notable prisoner, called B'. 912
17 B', or Jesus which is called Christ? "
20 should ask B', and destroy Jesus. "
21 release unto you? They said, B'. "
26 Then released he B' unto them: "
M'r 15: 7 And there was one named B', "
11 that he should rather release B' "
15 released B' unto them, and delivered "
Lu 23:18 this man, and release unto us B': "
Joh 18:40 Not this man, but B'. "
40 Now B' was a robber. "

Barachel (bar'-ak-el)
Job 32: 2 the wrath of Elihu the son of B' 1292
6 Elihu the son of B' the Buzite "

Barachias (bar'-ak-i'-as)
M't 23:35 Zacharias son of B', whom ye slew 914

Barah See BETH-BARAH.

Barak (ba'-rak)
J'g 4: 6 and called B' the son of Abinoam 1301
8 B' said unto her, If thou wilt go "
9 and went with B' to Kedesh. "
10 B' called Zebulun and Naphtali to "
12 they shewed Sisera that B' the son "
14 Deborah said unto B', Up; for this "
14 B' went down from mount Tabor, "
15 the edge of the sword before B'; "
16 But B' pursued after the chariots, "
22 behold, as B' pursued Sisera, "
5: 1 Then sang Deborah and B' the son "
12 arise, B', and lead thy captivity "
15 even Issachar, and also B': he was "
Heb 11:32 to tell of Gedeon, and of B', 913

barbarian See also BARBARIANS; BARBAROUS.
1Co 14:11 unto him that speaketh a b', 915
11 that speaketh shall be a b' unto me. "
Col 3:11 B', Scythian, bond nor free: "

barbarians
Ac 28: 4 when the b' saw the venomous 915
Ro 1:14 to the Greeks, and to the B'; "

barbarous
Ac 28: 2 the b' people shewed us no little * 915

barbed
Job 41: 7 thou fill his skin with b' irons? 7905

barber's
Eze 5: 1 sharp knife, take thee a b' rasor, 1532

bare See also BAREFOOT; BAREST; FORBARE.
Ge 4: 1 she conceived, and b' Cain, and 3205
2 she again b' his brother Abel. "
17 she conceived, and b' Enoch: "
20 Adah b' Jabal: he was the father "
22 And Zillah, she also b' Tubal-cain, "
25 b' a son, and called his name Seth; "
6: 4 and they b' children to them, "
7:17 increased, and b' up the ark, 5375
16: 1 Abram's wife, b' him no children: 3205

Ge 16:15 And Hagar b' Abram a son: and 3205
15 his son's name, which Hagar b', "
16 when Hagar b' Ishmael to Abram. "
19:37 the firstborn b' a son, and called "
38 And the younger, she also b' a son. "
20:17 maidservants; and they b' children. "
21: 2 Sarah conceived, and b' Abraham a "
3 whom Sarah b' to him, Isaac. "
22:24 she b' also Tebah, and Gaham, "
24:24 Milcah, which she b' unto Nahor. "
36 wife b' a son to my master "
47 son, whom Milcah b' unto him: "
25: 2 she b' him Zimran, and Jokshan, "
12 handmaid, b' unto Abraham: "
26 threescore years old when she b' "
29:32 And Leah conceived, and b' a son, "
33, 34, 35 conceived again, and b' a "
30: 1 saw that she b' Jacob no children, "
5 conceived, and b' Jacob a son. "
7 maid conceived again, and b' Jacob "
10 Zilpah Leah's maid b' Jacob a son. "
12 Leah's maid b' Jacob a second "
17 she conceived, and b' Jacob a fifth "
19 again, and b' Jacob the sixth son. "
21 And afterwards she b' a daughter, "
23 And she conceived, and b' a son; "
31: 8 then all the cattle b' speckled: "
8 then b' all the cattle ringstraked. "
39 I b' the loss of it; of my hand 2398
34: 1 which she b' unto Jacob, went 3205
36: 4 Adah b' to Esau Eliphaz; "
4 and Bashemath b' Reuel; "
5 Aholibamah b' Jeush, and Jaalam, "
12 and she b' to Eliphaz Amalek: "
14 she b' to Esau Jeush, and Jaalam, "
38: 3 And she conceived, and b' a son; "
4 she conceived again, and b' a son; "
5 yet again conceived, and b' a son; "
5 was at Chezib, when she b' him. "
41:50 Poti-pherah priest of On b' unto "
44:27 Ye know that my wife b' me two "
46:15 she b' unto Jacob in Padan-aram, "
18 and these she b' unto Jacob, "
20 priest of On b' unto him. "
25 and she b' these unto Jacob: "
Ex 2: 2 the woman conceived, and b' a son: "
22 And she b' him a son, and he called "
6:20 and she b' him Aaron and Moses: "
23 and she b' him Nadab, and Abihu, "
25 and she b' him Phinehas: these are "
19: 4 and how I b' you on eagles' wings, 5375
Le 13:45 and his head b', and he shall put *6544
55 whether it be b' within or *7146
Nu 13:23 and they b' it between two 5375
26:59 her mother b' to Levi in Egypt: *3205
59 and she b' unto Amram Aaron "
De 1:31 how that the Lord thy God b' thee, 5375
31: 9 the sons of Levi, which b' the ark "
25 the Levites, which b' the ark "
Jos 3:15 they that b' the ark were come "
15 and the feet of the priests that b' "
17 the priests that b' the ark "
4: 9 which b' the ark of the covenant "
10 the priest which b' the ark stood "
18 when the priests that b' the ark "
8:33 the Levites, which b' the ark "
J'g 3:18 the people that b' the present. "
8:31 she also b' him a son, whose 3205
11: 2 And Gilead's wife b' him sons; "
13: 2 his wife was barren, and b' not. "
24 And the woman b' a son, "
Ru 4:12 Pharez whom Tamar b' unto "
13 her conception and she b' a son. "
1Sa 1:20 Hannah had conceived that she b' "
2:21 she conceived, and b' three sons "
14: 1 unto the young man that b' his 5375
6 the young man that b' his armour, "
17:41 man that b' the shield went before "
2Sa 6:13 they that b' the ark of the Lord. "
11:27 became his wife, and b' him a 3205
12:15 the child that Uriah's wife b' "
24 and she b' a son, and he called "
18:15 ten young men that b' Joab's 5375
21: 8 Aiah, whom she b' unto Saul, 3205
1Ki 1: 6 his mother b' him after Absalom.* "
5:15 and ten thousand that b' burdens, 5375
9:23 five hundred and fifty which b' 7287
10: 2 camels that b' spices, and very 5375
11:20 the sister of Tahpenes b' him 3205
14:28 the guard b' them, and brought 5375
2Ki 4:17 the woman conceived, and b' a son 3205
5:23 and they b' them before him. 5375
1Ch 1:32 she b' Zimran, and Jokshan, 3205
2: 4 Tamar, his daughter in law, b' him "
17 Abigail b' Amasa; and the father "
19 Ephrath, which b' him Hur. "
21 and she b' him Segub. "
24 then Abiah Hezron's wife b' him "
29 and she b' him Ahban, and Molid. "
35 servant to wife; and she b' him "
46 Ephah, Caleb's concubine, b' "
48 Maachah, Caleb's concubine, b' "
49 she b' also Shaaph the father "
4: 6 And Naarah b' him Ahuzam, and "
9 saying, Because I b' him with "
17 and she b' Miriam, and Shammai, 2029
18 And his wife Jehudijah b' Jered 3205
7:14 Ashriel, whom she b': but his "
14 concubine the Aramitess b' Machir "
16 Maachah the wife of Machir b' a "
18 his sister Hammoleketh b' Ishod, "
23 she conceived, and b' a son, and he "
12:24 children of Judah that b' shield 5375
15:15 children of the Levites b' the ark "
26 the Levites that b' the ark of the "
27 and all the Levites that b' the ark, "

2Ch 8:10 two hundred and fifty, that b' rule 7287
9: 1 camels that b' spices and gold in 5375
11:19 Which b' him children; Jeush, 3205
20 which b' him Abijah, and Attai, "
14: 8 an army of men that b' targets 5375
8 out of Benjamin, that b' shields "
Ne 4:17 and they that b' burdens, with the "
5:15 even their servants b' rule 7980
Pr 17:25 and bitterness to her that b' him. 3205
23:25 she that b' thee shall rejoice. "
Ca 6: 9 is the choice one of her that b' her. "
8: 5 brought thee forth that b' thee. * "
Isa 8: 3 she conceived, and b' a son. "
22: 6 Elam b' the quiver with chariots 5375
32:11 strip you, and make you b', and 6209
47: 2 make b' the leg, uncover the *2834
51: 2 father, unto Sarah that b' you: 2342
52:10 Lord hath made b' his holy arm 2834
53:12 and he b' the sin of many, and 5375
63: 9 and he b' them, and carried them 5190
Jer 13:22 discovered, and thy heels made b'. *2554
16: 3 concerning their mothers that b' 3205
20:14 day wherein my mother b' me be "
22:26 out, and thy mother that b' thee, "
49:10 I have made Esau b', I have 2834
50:12 she that b' you shall be ashamed: 3205
Eze 12: 7 I b' it upon my shoulder in their 5375
16: 7 whereas thou wast naked and b'. 6181
22 when thou wast naked and b', "
39 jewels, and leave thee naked and b'. "
19:11 the sceptres of them that b' rule, 4910
23: 4 and they b' sons and daughters. 3205
29 shall leave thee naked and b': 6181
37 their sons, whom they b' unto me, 3205
Ho 1: 3 which conceived, and b' him a son. "
6 she conceived again, and b' him a "
8 she conceived, and b' a son. "
Joe 1: 7 he hath made clean b', and cast it 2834
M't 8:17 our infirmities, and b' our 941
M'k 14:56 For many b' false witness against 5576
57 and b' false witness against him, "
Lu 4:22 all b' him witness, and wondered 3140
7:14 they that b' him stood still. * 941
8: 8 and sprang up, and b' fruit an *4160
11:27 Blessed is the womb that b' thee, 941
23:29 and the wombs that never b', 1080
Joh 1:15 John b' witness of him, and cried, 3140
32 And John b' record, saying, I saw "
34 I saw, and b' record that this * "
2: 8 of the feast. And they b' it. 5342
5:33 and he b' witness unto the truth. *3140
12: 6 had the bag, and b' what was put * 941
17 from the dead, b' record. 3140
19:35 he that saw it b' record, and his "
Ac 15: 8 b' them witness, giving them the "
1Co 15:37 body that shall be, but b' grain, 1131
1Pe 2:24 who his own self b' our sins in his 399
Re 1: 2 Who b' record of the word of God, 3140
22: 2 which b' twelve manner of fruits, *4160

barefoot
2Sa 15:30 head covered, and he went b': 3182
Isa 20: 2 he did so, walking naked and b'. "
3 Isaiah hath walked naked and b' "
4 young and old, naked and b', "

barest
1Ki 2:26 because thou b' the ark of the 5375
Isa 63:19 thou never b' rule over them: 4910
Joh 3:26 to whom thou b' witness, behold, *3140

Barhumite (*bar'-hu-mite*) See also BAHARUMITE.
2Sa 23:31 Azmaveth the B', 1273

Bariah (*ba-ri'-ah*)
1Ch 3:22 Hattush, and Igeal, and B', and 1282

Bar-jesus (*bar-je'-sus*) See also ELYMAS.
Ac 13: 6 a Jew, whose name was B': 919

Bar-jona (*bar-jo'-nah*) See also SIMON.
M't 16:17 Blessed art thou, Simon B': 920

bark See also BARKED.
Isa 56:10 all dumb dogs, they cannot b'; 5024

barked
Joe 1: 7 and b' my fig tree: he hath *7111

Barkos (*bar'-cos*)
Ezr 2:53 The children of B', the children 1302
Ne 7:55 The children of B', "

barley
Ex 9:31 the flax and the b' was smitten: 8184
31 for the b' was in the ear, "
Le 27:16 an homer of b' seed shall be valued "
Nu 5:15 tenth part of an ephah of b' meal; "
De 8: 8 A land of wheat, and b', and vines, "
J'g 7:13 and, lo, a cake of b' bread tumbled "
Ru 1:22 in the beginning of b' harvest. "
2:17 and it was about an ephah of b'. "
23 to glean unto the end of b' harvest "
3: 2 he winnoweth b' to-night in the "
15 he measured six measures of b', "
17 six measures of b' gave he me; "
2Sa 14:30 he hath b' there; go and set it on "
17:28 wheat, and b', and flour "
21: 9 beginning of b' harvest. "
1Ki 4:28 B' also and straw for the horses "
2Ki 4:42 twenty loaves of b', and full ears "
7: 1 two measures of b' for a shekel, "
16 two measures of b' for a shekel, "
18 saying, Two measures of b' for a "
1Ch 11:13 parcel of ground full of b'; "
2Ch 2:10 twenty thousand measures of b', "
15 and the b', the oil, and the wine, "
27: 5 of wheat, and ten thousand of b'. "
Job 31:40 cockle instead of b'. The words "
Isa 28:25 and the appointed b' and the rie "
Jer 41: 8 of wheat, and of b', and of oil, "
Eze 4: 9 unto thee wheat, and b', and beans, "
12 thou shalt eat it as b' cakes, "

Eze 13:19 for handfuls of b', and for pieces 8184
45:13 part of an ephah of an homer of b': "
Ho 3: 2 and for an homer of b', "
2 and an half homer of b': "
Joe 1:11 for the wheat and for the b'; "
Joh 6: 9 which hath five b' loaves and two 2916
13 the fragments of the five b' loaves, "
Re 6: 6 three measures of b' for a penny; 2915

barn See also BARNFLOOR; BARNS.
Job 39:12 seed, and gather it into thy b'? *1637
Hag 2:19 Is the seed yet in the b'? 4035
M't 13:30 but gather the wheat into my b'. 596
Lu 12:24 neither have storehouse nor b'; "

Barnabas (*bar'-na-bas*) See also JOSES.
Ac 4:36 by the apostles was surnamed B', 921
9:27 But B' took him and brought him "
11:22 and they sent forth B', that he "
25 Then departed B' to Tarsus, * "
30 it to the elders by the hands of B' "
12:25 And B' and Saul returned from "
13: 1 as B', and Simeon that was called "
2 Separate me B' and Saul for the "
7 called for B' and Saul, and desired "
43 proselytes followed Paul and B'; "
46 Then Paul and B' waxed bold, "
50 persecution against Paul and B', "
14:12 And they called B', Jupiter; "
14 when the apostles, B' and Paul, "
20 he departed with B' to Derbe. "
15: 2 When therefore Paul and B' had "
2 they determined that Paul and B', "
12 and gave audience to B' and Paul, "
22 to Antioch with Paul and B'; "
25 with our beloved B' and Paul, "
35 also and B' continued in Antioch, "
36 some days after, Paul said unto B', "
37 B' determined to take with them "
39 and so B' took Mark, and sailed "
1Co 9: 6 Or I only and B', have not we "
Ga 2: 1 up again to Jerusalem with B', "
9 gave to me and B' the right hands "
13 that B' also was carried away "
Co 4:10 and Marcus, sister's son to B', "

Barnea (*bar'-ne-ah*) See also KADESH-BARNEA.

barnfloor
2Ki 6:27 the b', or out of the winepress? *1637

barns
Pr 3:10 shall thy b' be filled with plenty, 618
Joe 1:17 the b' are broken down; 4460
M't 6:26 do they reap, nor gather into b'; 596
Lu 12:18 I will pull down my b', and build "

barrel See also BARRELS.
1Ki 17:12 a handful of meal in a b', and a ‡3537
14 The b' of meal shall not waste, ‡ "
16 the barrel of meal wasted not, ‡ "

barrels
1Ki 18:33 Fill four b' with water, and pour ‡3537

barren
Ge 11:30 Sarai was b'; she had no child. 6135
25:21 for his wife, because she was b': "
29:31 but Rachel was b'. "
Ex 23:26 nothing cast their young, nor be b', "
De 7:14 shall not be male or female b' "
J'g 13: 2 his wife was b', and bare not. "
3 Behold now, thou art b', "
1Sa 2: 5 so that the b' hath born seven; "
2Ki 2:19 is naught, and the ground b'. *7921
21 any more death or b' land. * "
Job 24:21 He evil entreateth the b' that 6135
39: 6 and the b' land his dwellings. *4420
Ps 113: 9 maketh the b' woman to keep 6135
Pr 30:16 The grave; and the b' womb; 6115
Ca 4: 2 and none is b' among them. *7909
6: 6 there is not one b' among them. * "
Isa 54: 1 Sing, O b', thou that didst not 6135
Joe 2:20 him into a land b' and desolate, 6723
Lu 1: 7 because that Elisabeth was b', 4723
36 month with her, who was called b'. "
23:29 Blessed are the b', and the wombs "
Ga 4:27 Rejoice, thou b' that bearest not; "
2Pe 1: 8 neither be b' nor unfruitful in the* 692

barrenness
Ps 107:34 A fruitful land into b', for the *4420

bars
Ex 26:26 shalt make b' of shittim wood; 1280
27 b' for the boards of the other side "
27 b' for the boards of the side of "
29 rings of gold for places for the b': "
29 thou shalt overlay the b' with gold. "
35:11 his b', his pillars, and his sockets; "
36:31 And he made b' of shittim wood; "
32 five b' for the boards of the other "
32 b' for the boards of the tabernacle "
34 rings of gold to be places for the b', "
34 and overlaid the b' with gold. "
39:33 his b', and his pillars, and his "
40:18 put in the b' thereof, and reared up "
Nu 3:36 and the b' thereof, and the pillars "
4:31 boards of the tabernacle, and the b' "
De 3: 5 with high walls, gates, and b'; "
1Sa 23: 7 a town that hath gates and b'. "
1Ki 4:13 cities with walls and brasen b': "
2Ch 8: 5 cities, with walls, gates, and b'; "
14: 7 walls, and towers, gates, and b', "
Ne 3: 3 locks thereof, and the b' thereof. "
6 and the b' thereof. "
13 and the b' thereof, and a thousand "
14 and the b' thereof. "
15 and the b' thereof, and the wall of "
Job 17:16 shall go down to the b' of the pit, 905
38:10 place, and set b' and doors, 1280
40:18 his bones are like b' of iron. 4300

Ps 107:16 and cut the b' of iron in sunder. 1280
147:13 strengthened the b' of thy gates: "
Pr 18:19 are like the b' of a castle. "
Isa 45: 2 and cut in sunder the b' of iron: "
Jer 49:31 which have neither gates nor b', "
51:30 dwellingplaces; her b' are broken. "
La 2: 9 hath destroyed and broken her b': "
Eze 38:11 having neither b' nor gates, "
Jon 2: 6 the earth with her b' was about me "
Na 3:13 the fire shall devour thy b'. "

Barsabas (*bar'-sab-as*) See also JOSEPH; JUDAS: JUSTUS.
Ac 1:23 B', who was surnamed Justus, 923
15:22 namely, Judas surnamed B', "

Bartholomew (*bar-thol'-o-mew*) See also NATHANAEL.
M't 10: 3 Philip, and B'; Thomas, 918
M'k 3:18 Philip, and B', and Matthew, "
Lu 6:14 Philip and B', "
Ac 1:13 Philip, and Thomas, B', "

Bartimæus (*bar-ti-me'-us*)
M'k 10:46 blind B', the son of Timæus, sat 924

Baruch (*ba'-rook*)
Ne 3:20 After him B' the son of Zabbai 1263
10: 6 Daniel, Ginnethon, B', "
11: 5 Maaseiah the son of B', the son of "
Jer 32:12 evidence of the purchase unto B' "
13 And I charged B' before them, "
16 evidence of the purchase unto B' "
36: 4 Then Jeremiah called B' the son of "
4 and B' wrote from the mouth of "
5 Jeremiah commanded B', saying, "
8 B' the son of Neriah did according "
10 Then read B' in the book the words "
13 when B' read the book in the ears "
14 unto B', saying, Take in thine "
14 B' the son of Neriah took the roll "
15 So B' read it in their ears. "
16 and said unto B', We will surely "
17 they asked B', saying, Tell us now, "
18 B' answered them, He pronounced "
19 Then said the princes unto B', Go, "
26 to take B' the scribe and Jeremiah "
27 and the words which B' wrote at "
32 gave it to B' the scribe, the son "
43: 3 B' the son of Neriah setteth thee "
6 Jeremiah the prophet, and B' the "
45: 1 the prophet spake unto B' "
2 the God of Israel, unto thee, O B'; "

Barzillai (*bar-zil'-la-i*)
2Sa 17:27 and B' the Gileadite of Rogelim, 1271
19:31 B' the Gileadite came down from "
32 Now B' was a very aged man, "
33 the king said unto B', Come thou "
34 B' said unto the king, How long "
39 king kissed B', and blessed him; "
21: 8 brought up for Adriel the son of B' "
1Ki 2: 7 shew kindness unto the sons of B' "
Ezr 2:61 children of Koz, the children of B'; "
61 took a wife of the daughters of B' "
Ne 7:63 the children of B', which took "
63 one of the daughters of B' "

base See also ABASE; BASER; BASES; BASEST: DEBASE.
2Sa 6:22 will be b' in mine own sight: 8217
1Ki 7:27 cubits was the length of one b'. 4350
29 upon the ledges there was a b' *3653
30 every b' had four brasen wheels, 4350
31 work of the b', a cubit and a *3653
32 axletrees...were joined to the b': 4350
34 the four corners of one b': "
34 undersetters were of the very b' "
35 in the top of the b' was there a "
35 and on the top of the b' the ledges "
Job 30: 8 yea, children of b' men: 1097, 8034
Isa 3: 5 the b' against the honourable. 7034
Eze 17:14 That the kingdom might be b', 8217
29:14 they shall be there a b' kingdom. "
Zec 5:11 and set there upon her own b'. *4369
Mal 2: 9 and b' before all the people, 8217
1Co 1:28 And b' things of the world, 36
2Co 10: 1 who in presence am b' among *5011

baser
Ac 17: 5 lewd fellows of the b' sort, * 60

bases
1Ki 7:27 And he made ten b' of brass; 4350
28 the work of the b' was on this "
37 this manner he made the ten b': "
38 upon every one of the ten b' one "
39 he put five b' on the right side of "
43 And the ten b', "
43 and ten lavers on the b'; "
2Ki 16:17 Ahaz cut off the borders of the b'. "
25:13 and the b', and the brasen sea "
16 the b' which Solomon had made "
2Ch 4:14 He made also b', "
14 and lavers made he upon the b'; "
Ezr 3: 3 they set the altar upon his b'; * "
Jer 27:19 concerning the b', and concerning 4369
52:17 and the b', and the brasen sea 4350
20 bulls that were under the b'. "

basest
Eze 29:15 shall be the b' of the kingdoms; 8217
Da 4:17 setteth up over it the b' of men. *8215

Bashan (*ba'-shan*) See also BASHAN-HAVOTH-JAIR.
Nu 21:33 and went up by the way of B': 1316
33 and Og the king of B' went out "
32:33 the kingdom of Og king of B', "
De 1: 4 and Og the king of B', which dwelt "
3: 1 up the way to B': "
1 and Og the king of B' came out "
De 3: 3 our hands Og also, the king of B', 1316
4 Argob, the kingdom of Og in B'. "
10 all Gilead, and all B', unto Salchah "
10 cities of the kingdom of Og in B'. "
11 For only Og king of B' remained "
13 And the rest of Gilead, and all B', "
13 all the region of Argob, with all B', "
4:43 Golan in B', of the Manassites. "
47 and the land of Og king of B', "
29: 7 Heshbon, and Og the king of B', "
32:14 and rams of the breed of B', "
33:22 lion's whelp: he shall leap from B'. "
Jos 9:10 and to Og king of B', which was at "
12: 4 And the coast of Og king of B', "
5 and in Salcah, and in all B', "
13:11 and all mount Hermon, and all B' "
12 All the kingdom of Og in B', "
30 coast was from Mahanaim, all B', "
30 all the kingdom of Og king of B', "
30 the towns of Jair, which are in B', "
31 cities of the kingdom of Og in B', "
17: 1 therefore he had Gilead and B'. "
5 besides the land of Gilead and B', "
20: 8 tribe of Gad, and Golan in B' out "
21: 6 half tribe of Manasseh in B', "
27 of Manasseh they gave Golan in B' "
22: 7 Moses had given possession in B': "
1Ki 4:13 the region of Argob, which is in B', "
19 Amorites, and of Og king of B'; "
2Ki 10:33 river Arnon, even Gilead and B'. "
1Ch 5:11 them, in the land of B' unto Salcah: "
12 Jaanai, and Shaphat in B'. "
16 dwelt in Gilead in B', and in her "
23 they increased from B' unto "
6:62 the tribe of Manasseh in B', "
71 Golan in B' with her suburbs, "
Ne 9:22 and the land of Og king of B'. "
Ps 22:12 bulls of B' have beset me round. "
68:15 The hill of God is as the hill of B'; "
15 a high hill as the hill of B'. "
22 I will bring again from B', I will "
135:11 Amorites, and Og king of B', "
136:20 Og the king of B': for his mercy "
Isa 2:13 up, and upon all the oaks of B', "
33: 9 Sharon is like a wilderness; and B' "
Jer 22:20 cry; and lift up thy voice in B', "
50:19 feed on Carmel and B', and his "
Eze 27: 6 of B' have they made thine oars; "
39:18 bullocks, all of them fatlings of B'. "
Am 4: 1 Hear this word, ye kine of B', that "
Mic 7:14 let them feed in B' and Gilead, "
Na 1: 4 B' languisheth, and Carmel, "
Zec 11: 2 howl, O ye oaks of B'; for the "

Bashan-havoth-jair (*ba''-shan-ha''-voth-ja'-ur*)
De 3:14 own name, B', unto this day. *1316, 2334

Bashemath (*bash'-e-math*) See also BASMATH.
Ge 26:34 and B' the daughter of Elon 1315
36: 3 B' Ishmael's daughter, sister of "
4 Esau Eliphaz; and B' bare Reuel; "
10 the son of B' the wife of Esau. "
13 were the sons of B' Esau's wife. "
17 are the sons of B' Esau's wife. "

basin See BASON.

basket See also BASKETS.
Ge 40:17 And in the uppermost b' there 5536
17 birds did eat them out of the b' "
Ex 29: 3 thou shalt put them into one b', "
3 and bring them in the b', "
23 wafer out of the b' of unleavened "
32 and the bread that is in the b', "
Le 8: 2 and a b' of unleavened bread; "
26 out of the b' of unleavened bread, "
31 that is in the b' of consecrations, "
Nu 6:15 And a b' of unleavened bread, "
17 with the b' of unleavened bread: "
19 one unleavened cake out of the b', "
De 26: 2 shalt put it in a b', and shalt go 2935
4 the priest shall take the b' out of "
28: 5 Blessed shall be thy b' and thy "
17 Cursed shall be thy b' and thy "
J'g 6:19 the flesh he put in a b', and he 5536
Jer 24: 2 One b' had very good figs, 1731
2 other b' had very naughty figs, "
Am 8: 1 behold a b' of summer fruit. 3619
2 And I said, A b' of summer fruit. "
Ac 9:25 let him down by the wall in a b'. 4711
2Co 11:33 in a b' was I let down by the wall, 4553

baskets
Ge 40:16 I had three white b' on my head: 5536
18 The three b' are three days: "
2Ki 10: 7 put their heads in b', and sent 1731
Jer 6: 9 as a grapegatherer into the b'. 5552
24: 1 two b' of figs were set before the 1736
M't 14:20 that remained twelve b' full. 2894
15:37 meat that was left seven b' full. 4711
16: 9 and how many b' ye took up? 2894
10 and how many b' ye took up? 4711
M'r 6:43 twelve b' full of the fragments, *2894
8: 8 meat that was left seven b'. 4711
19 how many b' full of fragments 2894
20 how many b' full of fragments *4711
Lu 9:17 remained to them twelve b'. 2894
Joh 6:13 and filled twelve b' with the "

Basmath (*bas'-math*) See also BASHEMATH.
1Ki 4:15 took B' the daughter of Solomon 1315

bason See also BASONS.
Ex 12:22 in the blood that is in the b', 5592
22 with the blood that is in the b'; "
1Ch 28:17 gave gold by weight for every b'; *3713
17 silver by weight for every b' of * "
Joh 13: 5 that he poureth water into a b', 3537

basons
Ex 24: 6 half of the blood, and put it in b'; 101
Ex 27: 3 ashes, and his shovels, and his b', 4219
38: 3 the shovels, and the b', and the "
Nu 4:14 the shovels, and the b', all the "
2Sa 17:28 beds, and b', and earthen vessels, 5592
1Ki 7:40 the shovels, and the b'. So Hiram 4219
45 and the b': and all these vessels, "
50 the snuffers, and the b', and the "
2Ki 12:13 bowls of silver, snuffers, b', "
1Ch 28:17 for the golden b' he gave gold by *3713
2Ch 4: 8 he made an hundred b' of gold. 4219
11 pots, and the shovels, and the b'. "
22 the snuffers, and the b', and the "
Ezr 1:10 Thirty b' of gold, *3713
10 silver b' of a second sort * "
8:27 Also twenty b' of gold, of a * "
Ne 7:70 thousand drams of gold, fifty b' 4219
Jer 52:19 the b', and the firepans, and the 5592

bastard See also BASTARDS.
De 23: 2 A b' shall not enter into the 4464
Zec 9: 6 and a b' shall dwell in Ashdod, "

bastards
Heb 12: 8 then are ye b', and not sons. 3541

bat See also BATS.
Le 11:19 kind, and the lapwing, and the b'. 5847
De 14:18 the lapwing, and the b'. "

bath See also BATHS.
Isa 5:10 of vineyard shall yield one b', 1324
Eze 45:10 a just ephah, and a just b'. "
11 the b' shall be of one measure, "
11 that the b' may contain "
14 the b' of oil, ye shall "
14 offer the tenth part of a b' "

Bath See BATH-RABBIM; BATH-SHEBA; BATH-SHUA.

bathe See also BATHED.
Le 15: 5 and b' himself in water, and be 7364
6 wash his clothes, and b' himself "
7 b' himself in water, and be unclean "
8 wash his clothes, and b' himself "
10 b' himself in water, and be unclean "
11 wash his clothes, and b' himself "
13 and b' his flesh in running water, "
18 shall both b' themselves in water "
21 wash his clothes, and b' himself "
22 b' himself in water, and be unclean "
27 wash his clothes, and b' himself "
16:26 b' his flesh in water, and afterward "
28 clothes, and b' his flesh in water, "
17:15 b' himself in water, and be unclean "
16 nor b' his flesh; "
Nu 19: 7 he shall b' his flesh in water, "
8 b' his flesh in water, and shall be "
19 clothes, and b' himself in water, "

bathed
Isa 34: 5 my sword shall be b' in heaven: *7301

Bath-rabbim (*bath-rab'-bim*)
Ca 7: 4 Heshbon, by the gate of B': thy 1337

baths
1Ki 7:26 it contained two thousand b'. 1324
38 one laver contained forty b': "
2Ch 2:10 twenty thousand b' of wine, "
10 and twenty thousand b' of oil. "
4: 5 received and held three thousand b'. "
Ezr 7:22 and to an hundred b' of wine, 1325
22 and to an hundred b' of oil, 1324
Eze 45:14 an homer of ten b'; "
14 for ten b' are an homer. "

Bath-sheba (*bath'-she-bah*) See also BATH-SHUA.
2Sa 11: 3 one said, Is not this B', the 1339
12:24 David comforted B' his wife, "
1Ki 1:11 Nathan spake unto B' the "
15 And B' went in unto the king "
16 And B' bowed, and did obeisance "
28 answered and said, Call me B'. "
31 Then B' bowed with her face to "
2:13 came to B' the mother of Solomon. "
18 And B' said, Well; I will speak "
19 B' therefore went unto king "
Ps 51:*title* him, after he had gone in to B'.

Bath-shua (*bath'-shu-ah*) See also BATH-SHEBA.
1Ch 3: 5 Solomon, four, of B' the daughter 1340

bats
Isa 2:20 to the moles and to the b'; 5847

battered
2Sa 20:15 b' the wall, to throw it down. 7843

battering
Eze 4: 2 set b' rams against it
21:22 appoint b' rams against the gates,

battering-ram See BATTERING and RAM.

battle See also BATTLES.
Ge 14: 8 they joined b' with them in the 4421
Nu 21:33 all his people, to the b' at Edrei. "
31:14 which came from the b'. *6635, 4421
21 men of war which went to the b'. 4421
27 upon them, who went out to b', 6635
28 men of war which went out to b': "
32:27 before the Lord to b', as my lord 4421
29 man armed to b', before the Lord, "
De 2: 9 neither contend with them in b': "
24 and contend with him in b'. "
3: 1 and all his people, to b' at Edrei. "
20: 1 When thou goest out to b' against "
2 ye are come nigh unto the b', "
3 ye approach this day unto b' "
5, 6 his house, lest he die in the b', "
7 lest he die in the b', and another "
29: 7 came out against us unto b', "
Jos 4:13 unto b', to the plains of Jericho. "
8:14 went out against Israel to b', "
11:19 of Gibeon: all other they took in b'. "
20 should come against Israel in b', "

Jos 22:33 to go up against them in b', to *6635
J'g 8:13 the son of Joash returned from b' 4421
20:14 unto Gibeah, to go out to b' "
18 of us shall go up first to the b' "
20 the men of Israel went out to b' "
22 and set their b' again in array "
23 Shall I go up again to b' "
28 Shall I yet again go out to b' "
34 of all Israel, and the b' was sore: "
39 the men of Israel retired in the b', "
39 as in the first b'. "
42 but the b' overtook them; and "
1Sa 4: 1 out against the Philistines to b', "
2 they joined b', Israel was smitten "
7:10 the Philistines drew near to b' "
13:22 So it came to pass in the day of b', "
14:20 themselves, and they came to the b': "
22 followed hard after them in the b'. "
23 the b' passed over unto Beth-aven. "
17: 1 together their armies to b', "
2 and set the b' in array against "
8 come out to set your b' in array? "
13 went and followed Saul to the b': "
13 three sons that went to the b' "
20 the fight, and shouted for the b'. "
21 had put the b' in array, "
28 that thou mightest see the b'. 4421
47 for the b' is the Lord's, and he "
26:10 he shall descend into b', and perish. "
28: 1 thou shalt go out with me to b', *4264
29: 4 not go down with us to b', 4421
4 lest in the b' he be an adversary "
9 He shall not go up with us to the b'. "
30:24 part is that goeth down to the b': "
31: 3 the b' went sore against Saul, "
2Sa 1: 4 the people are fled from the b', "
25 fallen in the midst of the b'! "
2:17 there was a very sore b' that day; "
3:30 brother Asahel at Gibeon in the b'. "
10: 8 put the b' in array at the entering "
9 Joab saw that the front of the b' "
13 unto the b' against the Syrians: "
11: 1 the time when kings go forth to b', "
15 in the forefront of the hottest b', 4421
25 make thy b' more strong against "
17:11 go to b' in thine own person. 7128
18: 6 b' was in the wood of Ephraim; 4421
8 the b' was there scattered "
19: 3 steal away when they flee in b'. "
10 anointed over us, is dead in b'. "
21:17 go no more out with us to b', "
18 that there was again a b' with the * "
19 there was again a b' in Gob * "
20 And there was yet a b' in Gath, * "
22:40 girded me with strength to b': "
23: 9 gathered together to b', and the "
1Ki 8:44 go out to b' against their enemy, "
20:14 Who shall order the b'? And he "
29 the seventh day the b' was joined: "
39 went out into the midst of the b'; "
22: 4 Wilt thou go with me to b' "
6 I go against Ramoth-gilead to b', "
15 go against Ramoth-gilead to b', "
30 enter into the b'; but put thou on "
30 himself, and went into the b'. "
35 the b' increased that day: and the "
2Ki 3: 7 go with me against Moab to b'? "
26 the king of Moab saw that the b' "
1Ch 5:20 they cried to God in the b', and he "
7:11 fit to go out for war and b'. * "
40 were apt to the war and to b' * "
10: 3 the b' went sore against Saul, "
11:13 were gathered together to b', "
12: 8 men of war fit for the b', that * "
19 Philistines against Saul to b': "
33 Zebulun, such as went forth to b', *6635
36 of Asher, such as went forth to b', * "
37 of instruments of war for the b', 4421
14:15 then thou shalt go out to b': "
19: 7 from their cities, and came to b'. "
9 came out, and put the b' in array "
10 Joab saw that the b' was set "
14 before the Syrians unto the b'; "
17 set the b' in array against them. "
17 David had put the b' in array 4421
20: 1 the time that kings go out to b', "
2Ch 13: 3 Abijah set the b' in array with an 4421
3 Jeroboam also set the b' in array "
14 the b' was before and behind: "
14:10 set the b' in array in the valley "
18: 5 we go to Ramoth-gilead to b', "
14 shall we go to Ramoth-gilead to b', "
29 myself, and will go to the b'; "
29 himself, and they went to the b'. "
34 And the b' increased that day: "
20: 1 came against Jehoshaphat to b'. "
15 for the b' is not yours, but God's. "
17 shall not need to fight in this b': "
25: 8 will go, do it, be strong for the b': 4421
13 they should not go with him to b', "
Job 15:24 him, as a king ready to the b'. 3593
38:23 against the day of b' and war? 7128
39:25 he smelleth the b' afar off, 4421
41: 8 remember the b', do no more. "
Ps 18:39 me with strength unto the b': "
24: 8 mighty, the Lord mighty in b'. 4421
55:18 my soul in peace from the b' 7128
76: 3 shield, and the sword, and the b'. 4421
78: 9 turned back in the day of b'. 7128
89:43 not made him to stand in the b'. 4421
140: 7 covered my head in the day of b'. 5402
Pr 21:31 is prepared against the day of b': 4421
Ec 9:11 nor the b' to the strong, neither "
Isa 9: 5 For every b' of the warrior is *5430
13: 4 mustereth the host of the b'. 4421
22: 2 with the sword, nor dead in b'. "
Isa 27: 4 and thorns against me in b'? 4421
28: 6 strength to them that turn the b' "
42:25 the strength of b': and it hath set "
Jer 8: 6 as the horse rusheth into the b'. "
18:21 men be slain by the sword in b'. "
46: 3 and shield, and draw near to b'. "
49:14 against her, and rise up to the b'. "
50:22 A sound of b' is in the land, "
42 like a man to the b', against thee, "
51:20 Thou art my b' axe and weapons 4661
Eze 7:14 none goeth to the b': for my 4421
13: 5 to stand in the b' in the day "
Da 11:20 neither in anger, nor in b'. "
25 stirred up to b' with a very great "
Hos 1: 7 by bow, nor by sword, nor by b', "
2:18 the bow and the sword and the b' "
10: 9 b' in Gibeah against the children "
14 spoiled Beth-arbel in the day of b': "
Joe 2: 5 a strong people set in b' array. "
Am 1:14 with shouting in the day of b', "
Ob 1 let us rise up against her in b'. "
Zec 9:10 and the b' bow shall be cut off: "
10: 3 them as his goodly horse in the b'. "
4 out of him the b' bow, out of him "
5 down their enemies...in the b': "
14: 2 nations against Jerusalem to b'; "
3 when he fought in the day of b'. 7128
1Co 14: 8 shall prepare himself to the b'? *4171
Rev 9: 7 horses prepared unto b'; and on * "
9 of many horses running to b'. * "
16:14 to the b' of that great day of God * "
20: 8 to gather them together to b': * "

battle-axe See BATTLE and AX.

battle-bow See BATTLE and BOW.

battlement See also BATTLEMENTS.
De 22: 8 thou shalt make a b' for thy roof, 4624

battlements
Jer 5:10 take away her b'; for they are *5189

battles
1Sa 8:20 go out before us, and fight our b'. 4421
18:17 fight the Lord's battles. For Saul "
25:28 my lord fighteth the b' of the Lord, "
1Ch 26:27 spoils won in b' did they dedicate "
2Ch 32: 8 and to fight our b'. And the people "
Isa 30:32 and in b' of shaking will he fight "

Bavai (*bav'-a-i*)
Ne 3:18 B' the son of Henadad, the ruler 942

bay
Jos 15: 2 the b' that looketh southward: 3956
5 the b' of the sea at the uttermost "
18:19 the north b' of the salt sea "
Ps 37:35 himself like a green b' tree. * 249
Zec 6: 3 fourth chariot grisled and b' horses. 554
7 And the b' went forth, and sought "

bay-tree See BAY and TREE.

Baz See MAHER-SHALAL-HASH-BAZ.

Bazlith (*baz'-lith*) See also BAZLUTH.
Ne 7:54 the children of B', the children 1213

Bazluth (*baz'-luth*) See also BAZLITH.
Ezr 2:52 the children of B', the children 1213

bdellium (*del'-le-um*)
Ge 2:12 there is b' and the onyx stone. 916
Nu 11: 7 colour thereof as the colour of b'. "

be See in the APPENDIX; also ALBEIT; AM; ARE; ART; BECOME; BEEN; BEING; HOWBEIT; IS; WAS; WERE; WERT.

beacon
Isa 30:17 left as a b' upon the top of a 8650

Bealiah (*be-a-li'-ah*)
1Ch 12: 5 Eluzai, and Jerimoth, and B', 1183

Bealoth (*be'-a-loth*) See also ALOTH.
Jos 15:24 Ziph, and Telem, and B' 1175

beam See also BEAMS.
J'g 16:14 went away with the pin of the b', 708
1Sa 17: 7 of his spear was like a weaver's b'; 4500
2Sa 21:19 whose spear was like a weaver's b'. "
1Ki 7: 6 the thick b' were before them. *5646
2Ki 6: 2 take thence every man a b', and 6982
5 as one was felling a b', the axe head "
1Ch 11:23 was a spear like a weaver's b'; 4500
20: 5 spear staff was like a weaver's b'. "
Hab 2:11 b' out of the timber shall answer 3714
M't 7: 3 considerest not the b' that is in 1385
4 behold, a b' is in thine own eye? "
5 cast out the b' out of thine own eye; "
Lu 6:41 perceivest not the b' that is in "
42 beholdest not the b' that is in "
42 cast out first the b' out of thine "

beams
1Ki 6: 6 that the b' should not be fastened
9 covered the house with b' and 1356
36 stone, and a row of cedar b'. 3773
7: 2 with cedar b' upon the pillars. "
3 with cedar above upon the b', 6763
12 a row of cedar b', both for the 3773
2Ch 3: 7 the b', the posts, and the walls 6982
Ne 2: 8 give me timber to make b' for the 7136
3: 3 who also laid the b' thereof, and "
6 they laid the b' thereof, and set up "
Ps 104: 3 Who layeth the b' of his chambers "
Ca 1:17 The b' of our house are cedar, 6982

beans
2Sa 17:28 flour, and parched corn, and b'. 6321
Eze 4: 9 barley, and b', and lentiles, "

bear See also BARE; BEAREST; BEARETH; BEARING; BEARS; FORBEAR.
Ge 4:13 is greater than I can b'. 5375
13: 6 the land was not able to b' them. "
16:11 art with child, and shalt b' a son. 3205
Ge 17:17 Sarah, that is ninety years old, b'? 3205
19 Sarah thy wife shall b' thee a son "
21 Sarah shall b' unto thee at this set "
18:13 Shall I of a surety b' a child, "
22:23 these eight Milcah did b' to Nahor, "
30: 3 and she shall b' upon my knees, "
36: 7 were strangers could not b' them 5375
43: 9 then let me b' the blame forever: 2398
44:32 then I shall b' the blame to my "
49:15 and bowed his shoulder to b', 5445
Ex 18:22 shall b' the burden with thee. 5375
20:16 Thou shalt not b' false witness. 6030
25:27 places of the staves to b' the table. 5375
27: 7 the two sides of the altar, to b' it. * "
28:12 and Aaron shall b' their names "
29 And Aaron shall b' the names "
30 and Aaron shall b' the judgment "
38 that Aaron may b' the iniquity "
43 that they b' not iniquity, and die: "
30: 4 for the staves to b' it withal. "
37: 5 the sides of the ark, to b' the ark. "
14 for the staves to b' the table. "
15 them with gold, to b' the table. "
27 for the staves to b' it withal. "
38: 7 sides of the altar, to b' it withal; "
Le 5: 1 it, then he shall b' his iniquity. "
17 guilty, and shall b' his iniquity. "
7:18 eateth of it shall b' his iniquity. "
10:17 b' the iniquity of the congregation, "
12: 5 But if she b' a maid child, 3205
16:22 And the goat shall b' upon him 5375
17:16 flesh; then he shall b' his iniquity. "
19: 8 every one that eateth it shall b' his "
18 nor b' any grudge against the 5201
20:17 nakedness; he shall b' his 5375
19 they shall b' their iniquity. "
20 they shall b' their sin; they shall "
22: 9 lest they b' sin for it, and die "
16 Or suffer them to b' the iniquity "
24:15 curseth his God shall b' his sin. "
Nu 1:50 they shall b' the tabernacle, and "
4:15 sons of Kohath shall come to b' it: "
25 And they shall b' the curtains of "
5:31 this woman shall b' her iniquity. "
7: 9 should b' upon their shoulders. * "
9:13 season, that man shall b' his sin. "
11:14 I am not able to b' all this people "
17 shall b' the burden of the people "
17 that thou b' it not thyself alone. "
14:27 how long shall I b' with this evil
33 years, and b' your whoredoms, *5375
34 shall ye b' your iniquities, even "
18: 1 b' the iniquity of the sanctuary: "
1 b' the iniquity of your priesthood. "
22 congregation, lest they b' sin, and "
23 and they shall b' their iniquity: "
32 ye shall b' no sin by reason of it, "
30:15 them; then he shall b' her iniquity. "
De 1: 9 I am not able to b' you myself "
12 I myself alone b' your cumbrance, "
31 as a man doth b' his son, in all "
5:20 Neither shalt thou b' false witness 6030
10: 8 to b' the ark of the covenant of 5375
28:57 her children which she shall b': 3205
Jos 3: 8 command the priests that b' the 5375
13 feet of the priests that b' the ark "
4:16 the priests that b' the ark of the "
6: 4 seven priests shall b' before the "
6 let seven priests b' seven trumpets "
J'g 13: 3 thou shalt conceive, and b' a son. 3205
5, 7 shalt conceive, and b' a son; "
Ru 1:12 to-night, and should also b' sons; "
1Sa 17:34 there came a lion, and a b', 1677
36 slew both the lion and the b': "
37 out of the paw of the b', he will "
2Sa 17: 8 as a b' robbed of her whelps 1677
18:19 and b' the king tidings, how that 1319
20 Thou shalt not b' tidings this * "
20 thou shalt b' tidings another day: "
20 thou shalt b' no tidings, because "
1Ki 3:21 it was not my son, which I did b'. 3205
21:10 before him, to b' witness against 5749
2Ki 18:14 thou puttest on me will I b'. 5375
19:30 root downward, and b' fruit 6213
1Ch 5:18 men able to b' buckler and sword, 5375
2Ch 2: 2 ten thousand men to b' burdens, 5445
Es 1:22 every man should b' rule in his 8323
Ps 75: 3 dissolved: I b' up the pillars of *8505
89:50 how I do b' in my bosom the 5375
91:12 shall b' thee up in their hands, "
Pr 9:12 scornest, thou alone shalt b' it. "
12:24 The hand of the diligent shall b' 4910
17:12 Let a b' robbed of her whelps 1677
18:14 but a wounded spirit who can b'? 5375
28:15 roaring lion, and a ranging b'; 1677
30:21 and for four which it cannot b': 5375
Ca 4: 2 whereof every one b' twins, and *8382
Isa 1:14 unto me; I am weary to b' ‡5375
7:14 virgin shall conceive, and b' a son, 3205
11: 7 the cow and the b' shall feed; 1677
37:31 downward, and b' fruit upward: 6213
46: 4 I have made, and I will b'; 5375
7 They b' him upon the shoulder, "
52:11 ye clean, that b' the vessels of the "
53:11 for he shall b' their iniquities. 5445
Jer 5:31 the priests b' rule 7287
10:19 this is a grief, and I must b' it. 5375
17:21 b' no burden on the sabbath day, "
27 not to b' a burden, even entering "
29: 6 they may b' sons and daughters; 3205
31:19 I did b' the reproach of my youth. 5375
44:22 that the Lord could no longer b', "
La 3:10 He was unto me as a b' lying in 1677
27 good for a man that he b' the yoke 5375
Eze 4: 4 upon it thou shalt b' their iniquity. "
5 so shalt thou b' the iniquity of the "

Eze 4: 6 thou shalt b' the iniquity of the 5375
12: 6 In their sight shalt thou b' it upon "
12 prince that is among them shall b' "
14:10 And they shall b' the punishment "
16:52 b' thine own shame for thy sins "
52 confounded also, and b' thy shame, "
54 thou mayest b' thine own shame, "
17: 8 and that it might b' fruit, "
23 bring forth boughs, and b' fruit, 6213
18:19 doth not the son b' the iniquity 5375
20 The son shall not b' the iniquity "
20 neither shall the father b' "
23:35 b' thou also thy lewdness and thy "
49 ye shall b' the sins of your idols: "
32:30 b' their shame with them that go "
34:29 neither b' the shame of the "
36: 7 they shall b' their shame. "
15 neither shalt thou b' the reproach "
44:10 they shall even b' their iniquity. "
12 and they shall b' their iniquity, "
13 and they shall b' their shame, "
46:20 they b' them not out into the *3318
Da 2:39 which shall b' rule over all the 7981
7: 5 beast, a second, like to a b', 1678
Ho 9:16 dried up, they shall b' no fruit: 6213
13: 8 I will meet them as a b' that is 1677
Am 5:19 from a lion, and a b' met him; "
7:10 land is not able to b' all his words. 3557
Mic 6:16 ye shall b' the reproach of my 5375
7: 9 I will b' the indignation of the "
Zep 1:11 they that b' silver are cut off. *5187
Hag 2:12 If one b' holy flesh in the skirt 5375
Zec 5:10 Whither do these b' the ephah? 3212
6:13 he shall b' the glory, and sit and 5375
M't 3:11 whose shoes I am not worthy to b': 941
4: 6 their hands they shall b' thee up, 142
19:18 Thou shalt not b' false witness, 5576
27:32 him they compelled to b' his cross. 142
M'r 10:19 Do not b' false witness, Defraud 5576
15:21 Alexander and Rufus, to b' his 142
Lu 1:13 wife Elisabeth shall b' thee a son, 1080
4:11 their hands they shall b' thee up, 142
11:48 Truly ye b' witness that ye allow *3140
13: 9 And if it b' fruit, well: and if not, 4160
14:27 whosoever doth not b' his cross, 941
18: 7 though he b' long with them? *3114
20 Do not b' false witness, Honour 5576
23:26 that he might b' it after Jesus. 5342
Joh 1: 7 to b' witness of the Light, that all 3140
8 to b' witness of that Light. "
2: 8 b' unto the governor of the feast. 5342
3:28 yourselves b' me witness, that I 3140
5:31 If I b' witness of myself, my witness "
36 works that I do, b' witness of me, "
8:14 Though I b' record of myself, "
18 I am one that b' witness of myself, "
10:25 Father's name, they b' witness of "
15: 4 the branch cannot b' fruit of itself, 5342
8 that ye b' much fruit; so shall ye "
27 ye also shall b' witness, because 3140
16:12 but ye cannot b' them now. 941
18:23 b' witness of the evil: but if well, 3140
37 I should b' witness unto the truth, "
Ac 9:15 to b' my name before the Gentiles, 941
15:10 our fathers nor we were able to b'? "
18:14 would that I should b' with you: 430
22: 5 doth b' me witness, and all the 3140
23:11 must thou b' witness also at Rome. "
27:15 could not b' up in the wind, * 503
Ro 10: 2 For I b' them record that they 3140
13: 9 Thou shalt not b' false witness, *5576
15: 1 to b' the infirmities of the weak, 941
1Co 3: 2 ye were not able to b' it, "
10:13 that ye may be able to b' it. *5297
15:49 also b' the image of the heavenly. 5409
2Co 8: 3 I b' record, yea, and beyond their 3140
11: 1 b' with me a little in my folly: 430
1 and indeed b' with me. "
4 ye might well b' with him. "
Ga 4:15 for I b' you record, that, if it had 3140
5:10 shall b' his judgment, whosoever 941
6: 2 B' ye one another's burdens, "
5 every man shall b' his own burden. "
17 for I b' in my body the marks of "
Col 4:13 For I b' him record, that he hath 3140
1Ti 5:14 woman marry, b' children, 5041
Heb 9:28 offered to b' the sins of many; 399
Jas 3:12 my brethren, b' olive berries? *4160
1Jo 1: 2 and b' witness and shew unto you 3140
5: 7 three that b' record in heaven, * "
8 three that b' witness in earth, the "
3Jo 12 yea, and we also b' record; "
Re 2: 2 canst not b' them which are evil: 941
13: 2 his feet were as the feet of a b', 715

beard See also BEARDS.
Le 13:29 plague upon the head or the b'; 2206
30 a leprosy upon the head or b'. "
14: 9 head and his b' and his eyebrows, "
19:27 thou mar the corners of thy b'. "
21: 5 shave off the corner of their b'. "
1Sa 17:35 him by his b', and smote him "
21:13 his spittle fall down upon his b'. "
2Sa 19:24 his feet, nor trimmed his b', 8222
20: 9 And Joab took Amasa by the b' 2206
Ezr 9: 3 of my b', and sat down astonied "
Ps 133: 2 that ran down upon the b', "
2 even Aaron's b': that went down "
Isa 7:20 and it shall also consume the b'. "
15: 2 be baldness, and every b' cut off. "
Jer 48:37 shall be bald and every b' clipped: "
Eze 5: 1 upon thine head and upon thy b': "

beards
2Sa 10: 4 shaved off the one half of their b', 2206
5 at Jericho until your b' be grown, "
1Ch 19: 5 Jericho until your b' be grown, "

Jer 41: 5 b' shaven, and their clothes rent, 2206

bearer See ARMOURBEARER; BEARERS; CUPBEARER; STANDARDBEARER; TALEBEARER.

bearers
2Ch 2:18 of them to be b' of burdens, *5449
34:13 they were over the b' of burdens, "
Ne 4:10 of the b' of burdens is decayed, "

bearest
J'g 13: 3 thou art barren and b' not: 3205
Ps 106: 4 the favour that thou b' unto thy
Joh 8:13 Thou b' record of thyself; thy 3140
Ro 11:18 thou b' not the root, but the root 941
Ga 4:27 Rejoice, thou barren that b' not; 5088

beareth See also FORBEARETH.
Le 11:25 whosoever b' ought of the 5375
28 he that b' the carcase of them "
40 he also that b' the carcase of it "
15:10 and he that b' any of those things "
Nu 11:12 a nursing father b' the sucking * "
De 25: 6 the firstborn which she b' shall 3205
29:18 a root that b' gall and wormwood; 6509
23 is not sown, nor b', nor any grass 6779
32:11 b' them on her wings: *5375
Job 16: 8 rising up in me b' witness *6030
24:21 entreateth the barren that b' not: 3205
Pr 25:18 A man that b' false witness 6030
29: 2 but when the wicked b' rule, 4910
Ca 6: 6 every one b' twins, and there is *8382
Joe 2:22 tree that b' her fruit, the fig tree 5375
M't 13:23 also b' fruit, and bringeth forth, 2592
Joh 5:32 another that b' witness of me: 3140
8:18 that sent me b' witness of me. "
15: 2 branch in me that b' not fruit 5342
2 branch that b' fruit, he purgeth it, "
Ro 8:16 The Spirit itself b' witness with 4828
13: 4 for he b' not the sword in vain: 5409
1Co 13: 7 B' all things, believeth all things, 4722
Heb 6: 8 that which b' thorns and briers 1627
1Jo 5: 6 it is the Spirit that b' witness, 3140

bearing See also CHILDBEARING; FORBEARING.
Ge 1:29 given you every herb b' seed, *2232
16: 2 Lord hath restrained me from b': 3205
29:35 his name Judah; and left b'. "
30: 9 Leah saw that she had left b', "
37:25 b' spicery and balm and myrrh, 5375
Nu 10:17 set forward, b' the tabernacle. * "
21 set forward, b' the sanctuary: "
Jos 3: 3 the priests the Levites b' it, "
14 priests b' the ark of the covenant * "
6: 8 seven priests b' the seven trumpets "
13 seven priests b' seven trumpets "
1Sa 17: 7 one b' a shield went before him. * "
2Sa 15:24 b' the ark of the covenant of God: "
Ps 126: 6 b' precious seed, shall doubtless "
M'r 14:13 a man b' a pitcher of water: 941
Lu 22:10 meet you, b' a pitcher of water; "
Joh 19:17 b' his cross went forth "
Ro 2:15 conscience also b' witness, and 4828
9: 1 conscience also b' me witness "
2Co 4:10 Always b' about in the body the 4064
Heb 2: 4 God also b' them witness both 4901
13:13 without the camp, b' his reproach. 5342

bears
2Ki 2:24 forth two she b' out of the wood, 1677
Isa 59:11 We roar all like b', and mourn "

beast See also BEAST'S; BEASTS.
Ge 1:24 and b' of the earth after his kind: 2416
25 God made the b' of the earth "
30 And to every b' of the earth, "
2:19 God formed every b' of the field, "
20 every b' of the field; but for Adam "
3: 1 subtil than any b' of the field "
14 above every b' of the field; "
6: 7 man, and b', and the creeping 929
7: 2 Of every clean b' thou shalt take "
14 every b' after his kind, and all the 2416
21 of b', and of every creeping thing "
8:19 Every b', every creeping thing, and "
20 clean b', and of every clean fowl, 929
9: 2 be upon every b' of the earth, 2416
5 hand of every b' will I require it, "
10 every b' of the earth with you; "
10 to every b' of the earth. "
34:23 every b' of theirs be ours? * 929
37:20 Some evil b' hath devoured him: 2416
33 an evil b' hath devoured him; "
Ex 8:17 became lice in man, and in b'; 929
18 were lice upon man, and upon b'. "
9: 9 blains upon man, and upon b', "
10 blains upon man, and upon b'. "
19 every man and b' which shall be "
22 man, and upon b', and upon every "
25 was in the field, both man and b'; "
11: 7 his tongue, against man or b': "
12:12 land of Egypt, both man and b'; "
13: 2 of man and of b': it is mine. "
12 cometh of a b' which thou hast; "
15 of man, and the firstborn of b': "
19:13 whether it be b' or man, "
21:34 them; and the dead b' shall be his. "
22: 5 shall put in his b', and shall feed 1165
10 or an ox, or a sheep, or any b', 929
19 lieth with a b' shall surely "
23:29 the b' of the field multiply against 2416
Le 5: 2 the carcase of an unclean b', "
7:21 unclean b', or any abominable 929
24 fat of the b' that dieth of itself *5038
25 whosoever eateth the fat of the b', 929
26 or of b', in any of your dwellings. "
11:26 every b' which divideth the hoof, "
39 if any b', of which ye may eat, die; "
47 between the b' that may be eaten *2416
47 the b' that may not be eaten. * "

Le 17:13 hunteth and catcheth any b' 2416
18:23 Neither shalt thou lie with any b' 929
23 shall any woman stand before a b' "
20:15 And if a man lie with a b', "
15 and ye shall slay the b'. "
16 if a woman approach unto any b', "
16 kill the woman and the b': "
25 make your souls abominable by b', "
24:18 that killeth a b' shall make it 5315,929
18 good; b' for b'. *5315
21 that killeth a b', he shall restore it. 929
25: 7 cattle, and for the b' that are *2416
27: 9 And if it be a b', whereof men 929
10 if he shall at all change b' for b', "
11 if it be any unclean b', of which "
11 present the b' before the priest: "
27 if it be an unclean b', "
28 of man and b', and of the field "
Nu 3:13 firstborn in Israel, both man and b': "
8:17 Israel are mine, both man and b': "
31:26 man and of b', thou, and Eleazar "
47 of man and of b', and gave them "
De 4:17 likeness of any b'...on the earth, "
14: 6 And every b' that parteth the hoof, "
27:21 that lieth with any manner of b'. "
J'g 20:48 the men of every city, as the b', * "
2Ki 14: 9 passed by a wild b' that was in 2416
2Ch 25:18 passed by a wild b' that was in "
Ne 2:12 neither was there any b' with me, 929
12 save the b' that I rode upon. "
14 for the b' that was under me to pass. "
Job 39:15 that the wild b' may break them. 2416
Ps 36: 6 thou preservest man and b'. 929
50:10 every b' of the forest is mine, 2416
73:22 I was as a b' before thee. 929
80:13 wild b' of the field doth devour it. *2123
104:11 give drink to every b' of the field: 2416
135: 8 of Egypt, both of man and b'. 929
147: 9 He giveth to the b' his food, "
Pr 12:10 regardeth the life of his b': "
Ec 3:19 hath no preeminence above a b': "
21 the spirit of the b' that goeth "
Isa 35: 9 nor any ravenous b' shall go up 2416
43:20 The b' of the field shall honour * "
46: 1 they are a burden to the weary b'. "
63:14 As a b' goeth down into the valley,* 929
Jer 7:20 upon man, and upon b', and upon "
9:10 the fowl of the heavens and the b' "
21: 6 of this city, both man and b': "
27: 5 the b' that are upon the ground, "
31:27 of man, and with the seed of b'. "
32:43 desolate without man or b'; "
33:10 without man and without b', "
10 without inhabitant, and without b', "
12 without man and without b', "
36:29 to cease from thence man and b'? "
50: 3 shall depart, both man and b'. "
51:62 neither man nor b', but that it shall "
Eze 14:13 will cut off man and b' from it: "
17 so that I cut off man and b' "
19 to cut off from it man and b': "
21 the famine, and the noisome b', *2416
21 to cut off from it man and b'? 929
25:13 and will cut off man and b' "
29: 8 cut off man and b' out of thee. "
11 nor foot of b' shall pass through it, "
34: 8 meat to every b' of the field, *2416
28 neither shall the b' of the land "
36:11 multiply upon you man and b'; 929
39:17 to every b' of the field, Assemble 2416
44:31 or torn, whether it be fowl or b'. 929
Da 7: 5 And behold another b', a second, 2423
6 the b' had also four heads; "
7 I beheld a fourth b', dreadful and "
11 I beheld even till the b' was slain, "
19 know the truth of the fourth b', "
23 The fourth b' shall be the fourth "
Ho 13: 8 the wild b' shall tear them. 2416
Jon 3: 7 Let neither man nor b', herd nor 929
8 But let man and b' be covered "
Mic 1:13 bind the chariot to the swift b': *7409
Zep 1: 3 I will consume man and b'; 929
Zec 8:10 no hire for man, nor any hire for b'; "
Lu 10:34 and set him on his own b', and 2934
Ac 28: 4 the venomous b' hang on his hand, 2342
5 shook off the beast into the fire, "
Heb 12:20 And if so much as a b' touch the "
Re 4: 7 the first b' was like a lion, *2226
7 and the second b' like a calf, * "
7 third b' had a face as a man * "
7 and the fourth b' was like a * "
6: 3 I heard the second b' say, * "
5 I heard the third b' say, Come * "
7 the voice of the fourth b' say, * "
11: 7 the b' that ascendeth out of the 2342
13: 1 saw a beast rise up out of the sea, "
2 the b' which I saw was like "
3 the world wondered after the b'. "
4 power unto the b': and they "
4 worshipped the b', saying, "
4 Who is like unto the b'? "
11 I beheld another b' coming up "
12 all the power of the first b' before "
12 therein to worship the first b', "
14 to do in the sight of the b'; "
14 should make an image to the b', "
15 unto the image of the b', that the "
15 image of the b' should both speak, "
15 worship the image of the b' "
17 or the name of the b', or the "
18 count the number of the b': "
14: 9 If any man worship the b' and his "
11 who worship the b' and his image "
15: 2 the victory over the b', and over "
16: 2 the mark of the b', and upon them "
10 his vial upon the seat of the b';

Re 16:13 and out of the mouth of the *b'*. *2342*
17: 3 upon a scarlet coloured *b'*, "
7 of the *b'* that carrieth her, which "
8 The *b'* that thou sawest was "
8 the *b'* that was, and is not, "
11 And the *b'* that was and is not, "
12 as kings one hour with the *b'*. "
13 power and strength unto the *b'*. "
16 which thou sawest upon the *b'*, "
17 give their kingdom unto the *b'*, "
19:19 And I saw the *b'*, and the kings "
20 And the *b'* was taken, "
20 had received the mark of the *b'*, "
20: 4 had not worshipped the *b'*, "
10 where the *b'* and the false prophet "

beast's
Da 4:16 and let a *b'* heart be given unto 2423

beasts
Ge 7: 2 of *b'* that are not clean by two, 929
8 Of clean *b'*, and of *b'* that are not "
31:39 That which was torn of *b'* I 2966
36: 6 and all his *b'*, and all his 929
45:17 lade your *b'*, and go, get you 1165
Ex 11: 5 and all the firstborn of *b'*. * 929
22:31 flesh that is torn of *b'* in the field; 2966
23:11 what they leave the *b'* of the field*2416
Le 7:24 fat of that which is torn with *b'*, 2966
11: 2 These are the *b'* which ye shall *2416
2 among all the *b'* that are on * 929
3 cheweth the cud, among the *b'*, "
27 among all manner of *b'* that go 2416
46 This is the law of the *b'*, and of * 929
17:15 or that which was torn with *b'*, 2966
20:25 between clean *b'* and unclean, * 929
22: 8 or is torn with *b'*, he shall not eat 2966
26: 6 I will rid evil *b'* out of the land, 2416
22 I will also send wild *b'* among * "
27:26 Only the firstling of the *b'*, 929
Nu 18:15 whether it be of men or *b'*, * "
15 the firstling of unclean *b'* shalt "
20: 8 congregation and their *b'* drink. *1165
11 drank, and their beasts also. * "
31:11 prey, both of men and of *b'*. * 929
30 of all manner of *b'* and give * "
35: 3 their goods, and for all their *b'*. 2416
De 7:22 lest the *b'* of the field increase "
14: 4 These are the *b'* which ye shall 929
6 cheweth the cud among the *b'*, "
28:26 and unto the *b'* of the earth, "
32:24 I will also send the teeth of *b'* upon "
1Sa 17:44 of the air, and to the *b'* of the field. "
46 and to the wild *b'* of the earth; 2416
2Sa 21:10 nor the *b'* of the field by night. "
1Ki 4:33 he spake also of *b'*, and of fowl, 929
18: 5 that we lose not all the *b'*. "
2Ki 3:17 and your cattle, and your *b'*. "
2Ch 32:28 stalls for all manner of *b'*, "
Ezr 1: 4 with goods, and with *b'*, beside "
6 with goods, and with *b'*, and with "
Job 5:22 shalt thou be afraid of the *b'* of 2416
23 and the *b'* of the field shall be at "
12: 7 But ask now the *b'*, and they shall 929
18: 3 Wherefore are we counted as *b'*, "
35:11 teacheth us more than the *b'* of "
37: 8 Then the *b'* go into dens, and 2416
40:20 where all the *b'* of the field play. "
Ps 8: 7 oxen, yea, and the *b'* of the field; 929
49:12 he is like the *b'* that perish. "
20 is like the *b'* that perish. "
50:11 the wild *b'* of the field are mine. 2123
79: 2 saints unto the *b'* of the earth. 2416
104:20 all the *b'* of the forest do creep "
25 both small and great *b'*. "
148:10 *B'*, and all cattle; creeping things, "
Pr 9: 2 She hath killed her *b'*; she hath 2874
30:30 lion which is strongest among *b'*, 929
Ec 3:18 see that they themselves are *b'*. "
19 the sons of men befalleth *b'*; "
Isa 1:11 the fat of fed *b'*; and I delight 4806
13:21 wild *b'* of the desert shall lie 6728
22 wild *b'* of the islands shall cry * 338
18: 6 and to the *b'* of the earth: 929
6 the *b'* of the earth shall winter "
30: 6 The burden of the beasts of the "
34:14 The wild *b'* of the desert shall 6728
14 with the wild *b'* of the island, * 338
40:16 nor the *b'* thereof sufficient for a 2416
46: 1 their idols were upon the *b'*, "
56: 9 ye *b'* of the field, come to devour, "
9 all ye *b'* in the forest. "
66:20 upon mules, and upon swift *b'*, 3753
Jer 7:33 and for the *b'* of the earth; 929
12: 4 the *b'* are consumed, and the birds; "
9 assemble all the *b'* of the field, 2416
15: 3 the *b'* of the earth, to devour 929
16: 4 and for the *b'* of the earth. "
19: 7 for the *b'* of the earth. "
27: 6 the *b'* of the field have I given him 2416
28:14 given him the *b'* of the field also. "
34:20 heaven, and to the *b'* of the earth. 929
50:39 Therefore the wild *b'* of the 6728
39 with the wild *b'* of the islands * 338
Eze 5:17 send upon you famine and evil *b'*, 2416
8:10 and abominable *b'*, and all the 929
14:15 cause noisome *b'* to pass through 2416
15 pass through because of the *b'*: "
29: 5 for meat to the *b'* of the field "
31: 6 under his branches did all the *b'* of "
13 all the *b'* of the field shall be upon "
32: 4 I will fill the *b'* of the whole earth "
13 destroy also all the *b'* thereof 929
13 nor the hoofs of *b'* trouble them. "
33:27 will I give to the *b'* to be devoured, 2416
34: 5 became meat to all the *b'* of the "
25 the evil *b'* to cease out of the land: "
Eze 38:20 and the *b'* of the field, and all 2416
39: 4 and to the *b'* of the field, to be "
Da 2:38 the *b'* of the field and the fowls 2423
4:12 the *b'* of the field had shadow "
14 let the *b'* get away from under it, "
15 let his portion be with the *b'* "
21 under which the *b'* of the field dwelt, "
23 let his portion be with the *b'* of "
25 dwelling shall be with the *b'* of the "
32 shall be with the *b'* of the field: "
5:21 his heart was made like the *b'*, "
7: 3 four great *b'* came up from the sea, "
7 from all the *b'* that were before it; "
12 concerning the rest of the *b'*, "
17 These great *b'*, which are four, "
8: 4 no *b'* might stand before him, 2416
Ho 2:12 the *b'* of the field shall eat them. "
18 a covenant for them with the *b'* of "
4: 3 with the *b'* of the field, and with "
Joe 1:18 How do the *b'* groan! the herds of 929
20 The *b'* of the field cry also "
2:22 Be not afraid, ye *b'* of the field: "
Am 5:22 the peace offerings of your fat *b'*. 4806
Mic 5: 8 a lion among the *b'* of the forest, 929
Hab 2:17 the spoil of *b'*, which made them "
Zep 2:14 of her, all the *b'* of the nations: 2416
15 a place for *b'* to lie down in! "
Zec 14:15 all the *b'* that shall be in these 929
M'k 1:13 was with the wild *b'*; and the *2342*
Ac 7:42 have ye offered to me slain *b'* *4968*
10:12 all manner of fourfooted *b'* *5074*
12 of the earth, and wild *b'*, **2342*
11: 6 and saw fourfooted *b'* of the earth, *5074*
6 and wild *b'*, and creeping things, *2342*
23:24 And provide them *b'*, that they *2934*
Ro 1:23 fourfooted *b'*, and creeping things. *5074*
1Co 15:32 I have fought with *b'* at Ephesus, *2341*
39 another flesh of *b'*, another of *2934*
Tit 1:12 alway liars, evil *b'*, slow bellies. *2342*
Heb 13:11 of those *b'*, whose blood is brought *2226*
Jas 3: 7 Every kind of *b'*, and of birds, *2342*
2Pe 2:12 as natural brute *b'*, made to be **2226*
Jude 10 they know naturally, as brute *b'*, * "
Re 4: 6 were four *b'* full of eyes * "
8 And the four *b'* had each of them * "
9 those *b'* give glory and honour * "
5: 6 of the throne and of the four *b'*, * "
8 the four *b'* and four and twenty * "
11 round about the throne and the *b'*, * "
14 And the four *b'* said, Amen. * "
6: 1 one of the four *b'* saying, Come * "
6 voice in the midst of the four *b'* * "
8 death, and with the *b'* of the earth. *2342*
7:11 about the elders and the four *b'*, **2226*
14: 3 before the four *b'*, and the elders: * "
15: 7 one of the four *b'* gave unto the * "
18:13 and *b'*, and sheep, and horses, **2934*
19: 4 elders and the four *b'* fell down **2226*

beat See also BEATEN; BEATEST; BEATETH; BEATING.
Ex 30:36 shalt *b'* some of it very small, 7833
39: 3 did *b'* the gold into thin plates, 7554
Nu 11: 8 it in mills, or *b'* it in a mortar, 1743
De 25: 3 and *b'* him above these with 5221
J'g 8:17 he *b'* down the tower of Penuel, *5422
9:45 and *b'* down the city, and sowed "
19:22 *b'* at the door, and spake to the *1849
Ru 2:17 and *b'* out that she had gleaned: 2251
2Sa 22:43 Then did I *b'* them as small as 7833
2Ki 3:25 they *b'* down the cities, and on 2040
13:25 Three times did Joash *b'* him, *5221
23:12 did the king *b'* down, and brake *5422
Ps 18:42 did I *b'* them small as the dust 7833
89:23 *b'* down his foes before his face, 3807
Pr 23:14 Thou shalt *b'* him with the rod, 5221
Isa 2: 4 *b'* their swords into plowshares, 3807
3:15 ye *b'* my people to pieces, and *1792
27:12 Lord shall *b'* off from the channel *2251
41:15 and *b'* them small, and shalt make 1854
Joe 3:10 *B'* your plowshares into swords, 3807
Jon 4: 8 the sun *b'* upon the head of Jonah, 5221
Mic 4: 3 *b'* their swords into plowshares, 3807
13 shalt *b'* in pieces many people: 1854
M't 7:25 winds blew, and *b'* upon that *4363*
27 *b'* upon that house; and it fell: **4350*
21:35 took his servants, and *b'* one, *1194*
M'k 4:37 and the waves *b'* into the ship, *1911*
12: 3 they caught him, and *b'* him, *1194*
Lu 6:48 stream *b'* vehemently upon that **4366*
49 against which the stream did *b'* * "
12:45 shall begin to *b'* the menservants *5180*
20:10 the husbandmen *b'* him, and *1194*
11 servant: and they *b'* him also, "
Ac 16:22 and commanded to *b'* them. *4463*
18:17 *b'* him before the judgment seat. *5180*
22:19 and *b'* in every synagogue *1194*

beaten
Ex 5:14 had set over them, were *b'*, 5221
16 and, behold, thy servants are *b'*; "
Ex 25:18 of *b'* work shalt thou make them, 4749
31 of *b'* work shall the candlestick "
36 one *b'* work of pure gold. "
27:20 pure oil olive *b'* for the light, 3795
29:40 fourth part of an hin of *b'* oil; "
37: 7 of gold, *b'* out of one piece 4749
17 *b'* work made he the candlestick; "
22 it was one *b'* work of pure gold. "
Le 2:14 even corn *b'* out of full ears. *1643
16 of the *b'* corn thereof, and part * "
16:12 full of sweet incense *b'* small, 1851
24: 2 pure oil olive *b'* for the light, 3795
Nu 8: 4 the candlestick was of *b'* gold, 4749
4 the flowers thereof, was *b'* work: "
28: 5 fourth part of an hin of *b'* oil. 3795
De 25: 2 the wicked man be worthy to be *b'*, 5221
De 25: 2 and to be *b'* before his face, 5221
Jos 8:15 made as if they were *b'* before 5060
2Sa 2:17 and Abner was *b'*, and the men 5062
1Ki 10:16 two hundred targets of *b'* gold: 7820
17 three hundred shields of *b'* gold; "
2Ch 2:10 measures of *b'* wheat, 4347
9:15 two hundred targets of *b'* gold: 7820
15 hundred shekels of *b'* gold "
16 three hundred shields made he of *b'* "
34: 7 *b'* the graven images into powder, *3807
Pr 23:35 they have *b'* me, and I felt it not: 1986
Isa 27: 9 chalkstones that are *b'* in sunder, 5310
28:27 the fitches are *b'* out with a staff, 2251
30:31 shall the Assyrian be *b'* down, *2865
Jer 46: 5 and their mighty ones are *b'* down, 3807
Mic 1: 7 images thereof shall be *b'* to pieces, "
M'r 13: 9 in the synagogues ye shall be *b'*: *1194*
Lu 12:47 shall be *b'* with many stripes. "
48 shall be *b'* with few stripes. "
Ac 5:40 called the apostles, and *b'* them, * "
16:37 have *b'* us openly uncondemned "
2Co 11:25 Thrice was I *b'* with rods, once *4463*

beatest
De 24:20 When thou *b'* thine olive tree, 2251
Pr 23:13 if thou *b'* him with the rod, *5221

beateth
1Co 9:26 not as one that *b'* the air: **1194*

beating
1Sa 14:16 went on *b'* down one another. *1986
M'r 12: 5 others; *b'* some, and killing some. *1194*
Ac 21:32 the soldiers, they left *b'* of Paul. *5180*

beauties
Ps 110: 3 in the *b'* of holiness from the ‡1926

beautiful
Ge 29:17 Rachel was *b'* and well 3303, 8389
De 21:11 among the captives a *b'* woman, "
1Sa 16:12 withal of a *b'* countenance, 3303
25: 3 and of a *b'* countenance: "
2Sa 11: 2 was very *b'* to look upon. 2896
Es 2: 7 the maid was fair and *b'*; 2896, 4758
Ps 48: 2 *B'* for situation, the joy of the 3303
Ec 3:11 made every thing *b'* in his time: "
Ca 6: 4 Thou art *b'*, O my love, "
7: 1 How *b'* are thy feet with shoes, "
Isa 4: 2 shall the branch of the Lord be *b'* 6643
52: 1 put on thy *b'* garments, O 8597
7 How *b'* upon the mountains are 4998
64:11 Our holy and our *b'* house, 8597
Jer 13:20 was given thee, thy *b'* flock? "
48:17 strong staff broken, and the *b'* rod! "
Eze 16:12 a *b'* crown upon thine head. "
13 thou wast exceeding *b'*, and thou 3303
23:42 *b'* crowns upon their heads. 8597
M't 23:27 which indeed appear *b'* outward, *5611*
Ac 3: 2 the temple which is called *B'*, "
10 sat for alms at the *B'* gate "
Ro 10:15 How *b'* are the feet of them that "

beautify
Ezr 7:27 to *b'* the house of the Lord 6286
Ps 149: 4 he will *b'* the meek with salvation, "
Isa 60:13 to *b'* the place of my sanctuary; "

beauty See also BEAUTIES.
Ex 28: 2 thy brother, for glory and for *b'*. 8597
40 for them, for glory and for *b'*. "
2Sa 1:19 The *b'* of Israel is slain upon thy *6643
14:25 praised as Absalom for his *b'*: 3303
1Ch 16:29 the Lord in the *b'* of holiness. 1927
2Ch 3: 6 house with precious stones for *b'*: 8597
20:21 should praise the *b'* of holiness, 1927
Es 1:11 the people and the princes her *b'*: 3308
Job 40:10 array thyself with glory and *b'*. *1926
Ps 27: 4 to behold the *b'* of the Lord, 5278
29: 2 the Lord in the *b'* of holiness. 1927
39:11 makest his *b'* to consume away 2530
45:11 the king greatly desire thy *b'*: 3308
49:14 and their *b'* shall consume in the 6736
50: 2 out of Zion, the perfection of *b'*, 3308
90:17 let the *b'* of the Lord our God ‡5278
96: 6 and *b'* are in his sanctuary. 8597
9 the Lord in the *b'* of holiness: 1927
Pr 6:25 Lust not after her *b'* in thine 3308
20:29 *b'* of old men is the gray head. 1926
31:30 Favour is deceitful, and *b'* is vain: 3308
Isa 3:24 burning instead of *b'*. "
13:19 the *b'* of the Chaldees' excellency, 8597
28: 1 glorious *b'* is a fading flower, "
4 glorious *b'*, which is on the head "
5 of glory, and for a diadem of *b'*, "
33:17 eyes shall see the king in his *b'*: 3308
44:13 according to the *b'* of a man; 8597
53: 2 no *b'* that we should desire him. 4758
61: 3 to give unto them *b'* for ashes, *6287
La 1: 6 her *b'* is departed: her princes *1926
2: 1 the *b'* of Israel, and remembered 8597
15 the perfection of *b'*, The joy of 3308
Eze 7:20 As for the *b'* of his ornament, 6643
16:14 among the heathen for thy *b'*: 3308
15 thou didst trust in thine own *b'*, "
25 hast made thy *b'* to be abhorred, "
27: 3 thou hast said, I am of perfect *b'*. "
4 thy builders have perfected thy *b'*. "
11 they have made thy *b'* perfect. "
28: 7 against the *b'* of thy wisdom, "
12 full of wisdom, and perfect in *b'*. "
17 was lifted up because of thy *b'*, "
31: 8 God was like unto him in his *b'*. "
32:19 Whom dost thou pass in *b'*? 5276
Ho 14: 6 his *b'* shall be as the olive tree, 1935
Zec 9:17 goodness, how great is his *b'*! 3308
11: 7 the one I called *B'*, and the other 5278
10 I took my staff, even *B'*, and cut "

Bebai (*beb'-a-i*)
Ezr 2:11 The children of *B'*, six hundred 893

Ezr 8:11 And of the sons of B˙; 893
11 Zechariah the son of B˙, "
10:28 the sons also of B˙; Jehohanan, "
Ne 7:16 The children of B˙, six hundred "
10:15 Bunni, Azgad, B˙, "

became See also BECAMEST.
Ge 2: 7 of life; and man b˙ a living soul. 1961
10 parted, and b˙ into four heads. "
6: 4 the same b˙ mighty men which * "
19:26 and she b˙ a pillar of salt. 1961
20:12 my mother; and she b˙ my wife. "
24:67 Rebekah, and she b˙ his wife; "
26:13 and grew until he b˙ very great: 1431
44:32 thy servant b˙ surety for the lad 6148
47:20 them: so the land b˙ Pharaoh's. 1961
26 only, which b˙ not Pharaoh's. "
49:15 and b˙ a servant unto tribute. "
Ex 2:10 daughter, and he b˙ her son. "
4: 3 it b˙ a serpent; and Moses fled "
4 and it b˙ a rod in his hand: "
7:10 his servants, and it b˙ a serpent. "
12 his rod, and they b˙ serpents: "
8:17 it b˙ lice in man, and in beast; * "
17 all the dust of the land b˙ lice "
9:10 and it b˙ a boil breaking forth "
24 land of Egypt since it b˙ a nation. "
36:13 so it b˙ one tabernacle. * "
Nu 12:10 Miriam b˙ leprous, white as * "
26:10 and fifty men: and they b˙ a sign. 1961
De 26: 5 b˙ there a nation, great, mighty, "
Jos 7: 5 hearts of the people melted, and b˙ "
14:14 therefore b˙ the inheritance "
24:32 and it b˙ the inheritance of the "
J'g 1:30 among them, and b˙ tributaries. "
33 and of Beth-anath b˙ tributaries "
35 so that they b˙ tributaries. "
8:27 thing b˙ a snare unto Gideon, "
15:14 b˙ as flax that was burnt with fire, "
17: 5 one of his sons, who b˙ his priest. "
12 and the young man b˙ his priest, "
Ru 4:16 laid it in her bosom, and b˙ nurse "
1Sa 10:12 b˙ a proverb, Is Saul also among "
16:21 and he b˙ his armourbearer. "
18:29 b˙ David's enemy continually. * "
22: 2 and he b˙ a captain over them: "
25:37 and he b˙ as a stone. "
42 messengers of David, and b˙ "
2Sa 2:25 and b˙ one troop, and stood on "
4: 4 he fell, and b˙ lame. And his 6452
8: 2 the Moabites b˙ David's servants, 1961
6 the Syrians b˙ servants to David, "
14 they of Edom b˙ David's servants. "
11:27 she b˙ his wife, and bare him a son. "
1Ki 11:24 and b˙ captain over a band, when "
12:30 And this thing b˙ a sin: for the "
13: 6 again, and b˙ as it was before. "
33 and he b˙ one of the priests of the * "
34 this thing b˙ sin unto the house "
2Ki 17: 3 and Hoshea b˙ his servant, "
15 and b˙ vain, and went after 1891
24: 1 and Jehoiakim b˙ his servant 1961
1Ch 18: 2 the Moabites b˙ David's servants, "
6 the Syrians b˙ David's servants, "
13 the Edomites b˙ David's servants. "
19:19 with David, and b˙ his servants: *5647
2Ch 27: 6 So Jotham b˙ mighty, because he 2388
Ne 9:25 and were filled, and b˙ fat, 8080
Es 8:17 people of the land b˙ Jews; 3054
Ps 69:11 my garment; and I b˙ a proverb 1961
83:10 perished at Endor: they b˙ as dung "
109:25 I b˙ also a reproach unto them: * "
Jer 51:30 they b˙ as women: they have * "
Eze 17: 6 b˙ a spreading vine of low stature, "
6 b˙ a vine, and brought forth "
19: 3 whelps: it b˙ a young lion, "
6 he b˙ a young lion, and learned "
23:10 she b˙ famous among women; "
31: 5 and his branches b˙ long because 748
34: 5 they b˙ meat to all the beasts 1961
8 b˙ a prey, and my flock b˙ "
36: 4 are forsaken, which b˙ a prey "
Da 2:35 b˙ like the chaff of the summer 1934
35 image b˙ a great mountain, "
8: 4 according to his will, and b˙ great. *1431
10:15 toward the ground, and I b˙ dumb.* 481
Ob 12 in the day that he b˙ a stranger; *5235
M't 28: 4 keepers did shake, and b˙ as dead *1096*
M'r 9: 3 his raiment b˙ shining, exceeding "
Ac 10:10 he b˙ very hungry, and would have "
Ro 1:21 but b˙ vain in their imaginations, *3154*
22 to be wise, they b˙ fools, *3471*
6:18 b˙ the servants of righteousness. *1402*
1Co 9:20 unto the Jews I b˙ as a Jew, *1096*
22 To the weak b˙ I as weak, "
13:11 when I b˙ a man, I put away * "
2Co 8: 9 yet for your sakes he b˙ poor, *4433*
Ph'p 2: 8 and b˙ obedient unto death, even *1096*
1Th 1: 6 ye b˙ followers of us, and of the "
2:14 ye, brethren, b˙ followers of the "
Heb 2:10 For it b˙ him, for whom are all *4241*
5: 9 b˙ the author of eternal salvation *1096*
7:26 an high priest b˙ us, who is holy, *4241*
10:33 whilst ye b˙ companions of them *1096*
11: 7 b˙ heir of the righteousness which "
Re 6:12 sun b˙ black as sackcloth of hair, "
12 and the moon b˙ as blood; "
8: 8 third part of the sea b˙ blood; "
11 of the waters b˙ wormwood; *1096, 1519*
16: 3 it b˙ as the blood of a dead man: *1096*
4 of waters; and they b˙ blood. "

becamest
1Ch 17:22 and thou, Lord, b˙ their God. 1961
Eze 16: 8 and thou b˙ mine. "

because
Ge 2: 3 b˙ that in it he had rested 3588
2:23 called Woman, b˙ she was taken 3588
3:10 I was afraid, b˙ I was naked; "
14 B˙ thou hast done this, thou art "
17 he said, B˙ thou hast hearkened "
20 B˙ she was the mother of all living. "
5:29 b˙ of the ground which the Lord 4480
7: 7 b˙ of the waters of the flood. 6440
11: 9 it is called Babel; b˙ the Lord did 3588
12:13 my soul shall live b˙ of thee. 1558
17 plagues b˙ of Sarai Abram's 5921, 1697
16:11 his name Ishmael; b˙ the Lord 3588
18:20 the Lord said, B˙ the cry of Sodom "
20 Gomorrah is great, and b˙ their "
19:13 destroy this place, b˙ the cry of "
20:11 Abraham said, B˙ I thought, "
18 b˙ of Sarah Abraham's wife. 5921, 1697
21:11 Abraham's sight b˙ of his * 182
12 in thy sight b˙ of the lad, 5921
12 and b˙ of thy bondwoman; "
13 make a nation, b˙ he is thy seed 3588
25 reproved Abimelech b˙ of a 5921, 182
22:16 b˙ thou hast done this thing, 3282, 834
18 b˙ thou hast obeyed my voice. 6118, "
25:21 for his wife, b˙ she was barren: 3588
28 loved Esau, b˙ he did eat of his "
26: 5 B˙ that Abraham obeyed my 6118
7 for Rebekah; b˙ she was fair 3588
9 B˙ I said, Lest I die for her. "
26:20 b˙ they strove with him. 3588
27:20 he said, B˙ the Lord thy God "
23 And he discerned him not, b˙ "
41 Esau hated Jacob b˙ of the 5921
46 weary of my life b˙ of the 6440
28:11 tarried there all night, b˙ the sun 3588
29:15 B˙ thou art my brother, "
33 And said, B˙ the Lord hath heard "
34 be joined unto me, b˙ I have born "
30:18 my hire, b˙ I have given my hand 834
20 dwell with me, b˙ I have born him 3588
31:30 be gone, b˙ thou sore longedst "
31 said to Laban, B˙ I was afraid: "
32:32 b˙ he touched the hollow of Jacob's "
33:11 b˙ God hath dealt graciously "
11 and b˙ I have enough. "
34: 7 very wroth, b˙ he had wrought "
13 said, B˙ he had defiled Dinah 834
19 to do the thing, b˙ he had delight 3588
27 spoiled the city, b˙ they had 834
35: 7 El-beth-el: b˙ there God appeared 3588
36: 7 could not bear them b˙ of their 6440
37: 3 b˙ he was the son of his old age 3588
38:15 an harlot; b˙ she had covered * "
26 more righteous than I; b˙ that I * "
39: 9 b˙ thou art his wife: how then can 834
23 b˙ the Lord was with him, "
41:32 b˙ the thing is established by God, 3588
57 to buy corn; b˙ that the famine "
43:18 afraid, b˙ they were brought "
18 B˙ of the money that was 5921, 1697
32 b˙ the Egyptians might not eat 3588
46:30 seen thy face, b˙ thou art yet * "
47:20 sold every man his field, b˙ the "
49: 4 b˙ thou wentest up to thy "
Ex 1:12 were grieved b˙ of the children of 6440
19 B˙ the Hebrew women are not as 3588
21 b˙ the midwives feared God "
2:10 B˙ I drew him out of the water "
4:26 bloody husband thou art, b˙ of the "
5:21 and judge; b˙ ye have made our 834
8:12 b˙ of the frogs which he had *5921, 1697
9:11 not stand before Moses b˙ of the 6440
12:39 not leavened; b˙ they were 3588
13: 8 b˙ of that which the Lord did 5668
14:11 said unto Moses, B˙ there were no 1115
17: 7 b˙ of the chiding of the children 5921
7 and b˙ they tempted the Lord, "
16 he said, B˙ the Lord hath *3588
18:15 B˙ the people come unto me "
19:18 b˙ the Lord descended upon 6440, 834
29:33 not eat thereof, b˙ they are holy. 3588
34 shall not be eaten, b˙ it is holy. "
32:35 plagued the people, b˙ they 5921, 834
40:35 b˙ the cloud abode thereon, 3588
Le 6: 4 it shall be, b˙ he hath sinned, * "
9 burnt offering, b˙ of the burning *5921
10:13 b˙ it is thy due, and thy son's 3588
11: 4 as the camel, b˙ he cheweth the "
5 and the coney, b˙ he cheweth the "
6 and the hare, b˙ he cheweth the "
14:48 the house clean, b˙ the plague "
15: 2 b˙ of his issue he is unclean "
16:16 b˙ of the uncleanness of the "
16 and b˙ of their transgressions "
19: 8 shall bear his iniquity, b˙ he 3588
20 not be put to death, b˙ she was not "
20: 3 b˙ he hath given of his seed "
21:23 b˙ he hath a blemish; "
22: 7 b˙ it is his food "
25 b˙ their corruption is in them "
26:10 bring forth the old b˙ of the new. 6440
35 it shall rest; b˙ it did not rest *854, 834
43 b˙, even b˙ they despised my *3282
43 judgments, and b˙ their soul * "
Nu 3:13 B˙ all the firstborn are mine; *3588
6: 7 b˙ the consecration of his God "
12 shall be lost, b˙ his separation "
7: 9 he gave none: b˙ the service "
9: 13 b˙ he brought not the offering "
11: 3 Taberah: b˙ the fire of the Lord "
14 this people alone, b˙ it is too "
20 b˙ that ye have despised the Lord 3282
34 Kibroth-hattaavah: b˙ there they 3588
12: 1 against Moses b˙ of the 5921, 182
13:24 b˙ of the cluster of grapes "
14:16 B˙ the Lord was not able to 1115
22 B˙ all those men which have 3588
Nu 14:24 b˙ he had another spirit with him, 6118
43 b˙ ye are turned away 3588, 5921, 3651
15:31 B˙ he hath despised the word 3588
34 put him in ward, b˙ it was not "
19:13 b˙ the water of separation "
20 b˙ he hath defiled the sanctuary "
20:12 unto Moses and Aaron, B˙ ye 3282
13 b˙ the children of Israel strove 834
24 b˙ ye rebelled against my 5921, 834
21: 4 much discouraged b˙ of the way. "
22: 3 of the people, b˙ they were many: 3588
3 b˙ of the children of Israel. 6440
22 God's anger was kindled b˙ he 3588
29 unto the ass, B˙ thou hast "
32 b˙ thy way is perverse before me: "
25:13 b˙ he was zealous for his God, 8478, 834
26:62 b˙ there was no inheritance 3588
27: 4 his family, b˙ he hath no son? "
30: 5 forgive her, b˙ her father "
14 b˙ he held his peace at her "
32:11 b˙ they have not wholly followed "
17 b˙ of the inhabitants of the land. 6440
19 b˙ our inheritance is fallen 3588
35:28 B˙ he should have remained "
De 1:27 and said, B˙ the Lord hated "
36 b˙ he hath wholly followed the 3282, 834
2: 5 b˙ I have given Mount Seir 3588
9 for a possession; b˙ I have given "
19 any possession; b˙ I have given it "
25 and be in anguish b˙ of thee. 6440
4: 3 the Lord did b˙ of Baal-peor: "
37 And b˙ he loved thy fathers, 8478, 3588
7: 7 nor choose you, b˙ ye were more "
8 But b˙ the Lord loved you, 3588
8 b˙ he would keep the oath which he
8:20 b˙ ye would not be obedient unto 6118
12:20 I will eat flesh, b˙ thy soul 3588
13: 5 put to death; b˙ he hath spoken "
10 that he die; b˙ he hath sought to "
14: 8 the swine, b˙ it divideth the hoof. "
29 the Levite, (b˙ he hath no part "
15: 2 b˙ it is called the Lord's release. "
10 b˙ that for this thing the Lord "
16 b˙ he loveth thee and thine house, "
16 b˙ he is well with thee; "
16:15 b˙ the Lord thy God shall bless "
18:12 and b˙ of these abominations 1558
19: 6 b˙ the way is long, and slay him; 3588
20: 3 neither be ye terrified b˙ of them; *6440
21:14 b˙ thou hast humbled her. 8478, 834
22:19 b˙ he hath brought up an evil 3588
21 b˙ she hath wrought folly "
24 damsel, b˙ she cried not, 5921, 1697, 843
24 man, b˙ he hath humbled " " "
29 his wife; b˙ he hath humbled 8478, 834
23: 4 B˙ they met you not 5921, 1697, 834
5 blessing unto thee, b˙ the Lord 3588
7 b˙ thou wast a stranger "
24: 1 no favour in his eyes, b˙ he hath "
27:20 b˙ he hath uncovered his "
28:20 b˙ of the wickedness of thy doings, 6440
45 destroyed; b˙ thou hearkenedst 3588
47 B˙ thou servedst not the Lord 8478, 834
55 b˙ he hath nothing left him "
62 b˙ thou wouldst not obey 3588
29:25 say, B˙ they have forsaken 5921, 834
31:29 b˙ ye will do evil in the sight 3588
32: 3 B˙ I will publish the name * "
19 abhorred them, b˙ of the provoking "
47 vain thing for you; b˙ it is your 3588
51 B˙ ye trespassed against me 5921, 834
33:21 part for himself, b˙ there, in a *3588
Jos 2: 9 inhabitants of the land faint b˙ of *6440
11 more courage in any man, b˙ of "
24 the country do faint b˙ of us. * "
5: 1 them any more, b˙ of the children "
6 were consumed, b˙ they obeyed 834
7 b˙ they had not circumcised 3588
6: 1 up b˙ of the children of Israel: 6440
17 b˙ she hid the messengers 3588
25 unto this day; b˙ she hid the "
7:12 before their enemies, b˙ they were "
15 b˙ he hath transgressed the "
15 b˙ he hath wrought folly in Israel. "
9: 9 thy servants are come b˙ of the "
18 smote them not, b˙ the princes 3588
20 be upon us, b˙ of the oath which 5921
24 B˙ it was certainly told thy 3588
24 sore afraid of our lives b˙ of you, 6440
10: 2 feared greatly, b˙ Gibeon was a 3588
2 b˙ it was greater than Ai, "
42 b˙ the Lord God...fought for Israel "
11: 6 Be not afraid b˙ of them: 6440
14: 9 for ever, b˙ thou hast wholly 3588
14 unto this day, b˙ that he wholly 3282
17: 1 b˙ he was a man of war, 3588
6 B˙ the daughters of Manasseh "
20: 5 b˙ he smote his neighbour "
22:31 b˙ ye have not committed this 834
23: 3 done unto all these nations b˙ of 6440
J'g 1:19 b˙ they had chariots 3588
2:18 b˙ of their groanings by reason of 6440
20 he said, B˙ that this people hath 3282
3:12 against Israel, b˙ they had 5921, 3588
5:23 b˙ they came not to the help of the "
6: 2 against Israel: and b˙ of the 6440
6 impoverished, b˙ of the Midianites; "
7 cried unto the Lord b˙ of the 5921, 182
22 for b˙ I have seen an angel *5921, 3651
27 so it was, b˙ he feared his father's 834
30 he may die: b˙ he hath cast down 3588
30 and b˙ he hath cut down the grove "
31 plead for himself, b˙ one hath cast "
32 against him, b˙ he hath thrown "
8:20 he feared, b˙ he was yet a youth. "
24 b˙ they were Ishmaelites. "

J'g 9:18 b' he is your brother;) 3588
10:10 sinned against thee, both b' we "
11:13 B' Israel took away my land, "
12: 4 smote Ephraim, b' they said, "
13:22 surely die, b' we have seen God. "
14:17 told her, b' she lay sore upon him "
15: 6 b' he had taken his wife, "
18:28 no deliverer, b' it was far "
20:36 b' they trusted to the liers in wait "
21:15 b' that the Lord had made a breach "
22 b' we reserved not to each man "
1Sa 1: 6 make her fret, b' the Lord had "
20 B' I have asked him of the Lord. "
2: 1 b' I rejoice in thy salvation. "
25 b' the Lord would slay them. "
3:13 b' his sons made themselves "
4:21 b' the ark of God was taken, 413
21 and b' of her father in law "
6:19 b' they had looked into the ark 3588
19 people lamented, b' the Lord had "
8:18 b' of your king which ye shall 6440
9:13 until he come, b' he doth bless 3588
16 my people, b' their cry is come "
10: 1 it not b' the Lord hath anointed * "
12:10 sinned, b' we have forsaken "
22 b' it hath pleased the Lord "
13:11 B' I saw that the people "
14 b' thou hast not kept "
14:29 enlightened, b' I tasted a little "
15:23 B' thou hast rejected the word 3282
16: 7 b' I have refused him: 3588
17:32 no man's heart fail b' of him; 5921
18: 3 b' he loved him as his own "
12 afraid of David, b' the Lord 3588
16 loved David, b' he went out * "
19: 4 b' he hath not sinned against thee, "
4 and b' his works have been "
20:17 swear again, b' he loved him. *
18 missed, b' thy seat will be empty. 3588
34 b' his father had done him shame. "
21: 8 with me, b' the king's business "
22:17 b' their hand also is with David, "
17 and b' they knew when he fled, "
24: 5 smote him, b' he had cut off 5921, 834
25:28 b' my lord fighteth the battles 3588
26:12 all asleep; b' a deep sleep from the "
16 worthy to die, b' ye have not kept 834
21 b' my soul was precious 8478, "
28:18 b' thou obeyedst not the voice of "
20 b' of the words of Samuel: "
30: 6 stoning him, b' the soul of all 3588
13 left me, b' three days agone I fell "
16 b' of all the great spoil "
22 said, B' they went not with us, 3282
2Sa 1: 9 b' my life is yet whole in me. 3588
10 slew him, b' I was sure that he "
12 b' they were fallen by the sword. "
2: 6 b' ye have done this thing. 834
3:11 a word again, b' he feared him. "
30 b' he had slain their brother 5921, 834
6: 8 displeased, b' the Lord had " "
12 b' of the ark of God. 5668
8:10 bless him, b' he had fought 5921, 834
10: 5 b' the men were greatly *3588
12: 6 b' he did this thing, 6118, 834
6 and b' he had no pity. 5921, "
10 b' thou hast despised me, 6118, 3588
14 b' by this deed thou hast given "
25 name Jedidiah, b' of the Lord. *5668
13:22 b' he had forced his 5921, 1697, 834
14:15 it is b' the people have made me 3588
26 he polled it: b' the hair was heavy "
16: 8 b' thou art a bloody man. "
10 let him curse, b' the Lord hath said "
18:20 bear no tidings, b' the king's 3588, 5921
19:21 b' he cursed the Lord's anointed? 3588
26 b' thy servant is lame. "
42 B' the king is near of kin "
21: 1 b' he slew the Gibeonites. 5921, 834
7 b' of the Lord's oath 5921
22: 8 shook, b' he was wroth. 3588
20 delivered me, b' he delighted in "
23: 6 thrust away, b' they cannot be * "
1Ki 1:50 Adonijah feared b' of Solomon, 6440
2: 7 I fled b' of Absalom thy brother. * "
26 b' thou bearest the ark of the Lord 3588
26 and b' thou hast been afflicted "
3: 2 b' there was no house built "
11 B' thou hast asked this thing, 3282
19 died in the night; b' she overlaid 834
7:47 b' they were exceeding many:
8:11 stand to minister b' of the cloud: *6440
33 b' they have sinned against thee, 834
35 no rain, b' they have sinned 3588
64 b' the brasen altar that was 3588
9: 9 B' they forsook the Lord 5921, 834
10: 9 B' the Lord loved Israel for ever,
11: 9 b' his heart was turned 3588
33 B' that they have forsaken 3282, 834
34 b' he kept my commandments "
14:13 b' in him there is found some 3282
15 b' they have made their groves, 834
16 b' of the sins of Jeroboam, who 1558
15: 5 B' David did that which was right 834
13 from being queen, b' she had made "
30 B' of the sins of Jeroboam *5921
16: 7 and b' he killed him. 834
17: 7 up, b' there had been no rain 3588
19: 7 Arise and eat; b' the journey is too "
14 b' the children of Israel have * "
20:28 B' the Syrians have said, 3282, 834
36 B' thou hast not obeyed the " "
42 B' thou hast let go out of thy 3282
21: 2 garden of herbs, b' it is near 3588
4 displeased b' of the word which 5921
6 B' I spake unto Naboth 3588

1Ki 23:20 found thee: b' thou hast sold 3282
29 b' he humbleth himself 3282, 3588
2Ki 1: 3 Is it not b' there is not a God
6 Is it not b' there is not a God in
16 is it not b' there is no God in Israel,
17 king of Judah, b' he had no son. 3588
5: 1 honourable, b' by him the Lord "
8:12 answered, b' I know the evil that "
29 b' he was sick. "
9:14 b' of Hazael king of Syria. 6440
10:30 unto Jehu, B' thou hast done 3282, 834
13: 4 b' the king of Syria oppressed *3588
23 b' of his covenant with Abraham, 4616
15:16 b' they opened not to him, 3588
17:26 slay them, b' they know not 834
18:12 B' they obeyed not the voice 3282, 834
19:28 B' thy rage against me 3282
21:11 B' Manasseh king of Judah 3282, 834
15 B' they have done that "
22: 7 into their hand, b' they dealt *3588
13 kindled against us, b' our 3282, 834
17 B' they have forsaken me, 8478, "
19 B' thine heart was tender, 3282
23:26 against Judah, b' of all the 5921
1Ch 1:19 Peleg; b' in his days the earth *3588
4: 9 saying, b' I bare him with sorrow. "
41 b' there was pasture there "
5: 9 b' their cattle were multiplied "
20 intreated of them; b' they put "
22 many slain, b' the war was of God. "
7:21 b' they came down to take "
23 Beriah, b' it went evil with his "
9:27 b' the charge was upon them, "
12: 1 close b' of Saul the son of Kish: 6440
13:10 b' he put his hand to the ark: 5921, 834
11 displeased, b' the Lord had made 3588
14: 2 b' of his people Israel. *5668
15:13 For b' ye did it not at the first, 3588
22 b' he was skilful. "
16:33 b' he cometh to judge the earth. * "
41 thanks to the Lord, b' his mercy "
18:10 congratulate him, b' he had 5921, 834
19: 2 b' his father showed kindness 3588
21: 8 b' I have done this thing: * 834
30 b' of the sword of the angel 6440
22: 8 unto my name, b' thou hast shed 3588
23:28 B' their office was to wait * "
27:23 b' the Lord had said "
24 finished not, b' there fell wrath *
28: 3 b' thou hast been a man of war, 3588
29: 3 b' I have set my affection to the "
9 b' with perfect heart 3588
2Ch 1:11 to Solomon, B' this was in 3282, 834
2:11 B' the Lord hath loved his people,
6:24 b' they have sinned against 3588
26 no rain, b' they have sinned "
7: 2 b' the glory of the Lord "
6 praise the Lord, b' his mercy * "
7 peace offerings, b' the brasen "
22 B' they forsook the Lord God 3282, 834
8:11 b' the places are holy, 3588
9: 8 b' thy God loved Israel,
12: 2 against Jerusalem, b' they had 3588
5 to Jerusalem b' of Shishak, 6448
14 did evil, b' he prepared not 3588
13:18 b' they relied upon the Lord "
14: 6 b' the Lord had given him "
7 b' we have sought the Lord "
15:16 b' she had made an idol 834
16: 7 B' thou hast relied on the king
8 yet, because thou didst rely on
10 rage with him b' of this thing. 5921
17: 3 b' he walked in the first 3588
20:37 B' thou hast joined thyself
21: 3 Jehoram; b' he was the firstborn 3588
7 b' of the covenant 3282
10 his hand; b' he had forsaken 3588
12 B' thou hast not walked 8478, 834
22: 6 in Jezreel b' of the wounds *3588
6 b' he was sick. "
9 B', said they, he is the son * "
24:16 the kings, b' he had done good "
20 b' ye have forsaken the Lord, "
24 their hand, b' they had forsaken "
25:16 thee, b' thou hast done this, "
20 b' they sought after the gods "
26:20 to go out, b' the Lord had smitten "
27: 6 became mighty, b' he prepared "
28: 6 b' they had forsaken the Lord "
9 Behold, b' the Lord God "
19 brought Judah low b' of Ahaz 5668
23 he said, B' the gods of the kings 3588
30: 3 at that time, b' the priests had "
34:21 poured out upon us, b' our 3282, 834
25 B' they have forsaken me, 8478, "
27 B' thine heart was tender, 3282
35:14 for the priests: b' the priests 3588
36:15 b' he had compassion on his "
Ezr 3: 3 was upon them b' of the people "
11 thanks unto the Lord; b' he is *3588
11 the Lord, b' the foundation 5921
4:14 Now b' we have 3606, 6903, 1768
8:22 b' we had spoken unto the king 3588
9: 4 b' of the transgression of those 5921
15 cannot stand before thee b' of this. "
10: 6 he mourned b' of the transgression "
9 of God, trembling b' of this matter, "
Ne 4: 9 against them day and night, b' of 6440
5: 3 buy corn, b' of the dearth.
9 fear of our God, b' of the reproach
15 So did not I, b' of the fear of God. 6440
18 b' the bondage was heavy upon 3588
8:12 great mirth, b' they had
9:37 thou hast set over us b' of our
38 And b' of all this we make *
13: 2 B' they met not the children 3588

Ne 13:29 b' they have defiled the 5921
Es 1:15 b' she hath not performed 5921, 834
8: 7 upon the gallows, b' he laid " "
9: 3 helped the Jews; b' the fear of 3588
Job 3:10 B' it shut not up the doors "
6:20 were confounded b' they had "
11:16 B' thou shalt forget thy misery, * "
18 shalt be secure, b' there is hope; "
15:27 B' he covereth his face "
17:12 the light is short b' of darkness. *6440
18:15 in his tabernacle, b' it is none *
20:19 B' he hath oppressed *3588
19 b' he hath violently taken away *
23:17 B' I was not cut off 3588
29:12 B' I delivered the poor that cried, "
30:11 B' he hath loosed my cord, *3588
31:25 I rejoiced b' my wealth was great, "
25 and b' mine hand had gotten much; "
32: 1 answer Job, b' he was righteous "
2 his wrath kindled, b' he justified 5921
3 b' they had found no answer, 5921, 834
4 Job had spoken, b' they were 3588
34:27 B' they turned back 834, 5921, 3651
36 unto the end b' of his answers 5921
35:12 b' of the pride of evil men. 6440
15 But now, b' it is not so, 3588
36:18 B' there is wrath, ‡ "
38:21 thou it, b' thou wast then born? * "
21 b' the number of thy days is *
39:11 trust him, b' his strength 3588
17 B' God hath deprived her of
Ps 5: 8 in thy righteousness b' of mine 4616
11 shout for joy, b' thou defendest
6: 7 Mine eye is consumed b' of grief;
7 it waxeth old b' of all mine
7: 6 lift up thyself b' of the rage *
8: 2 strength b' of thine enemies, 4616
13: 6 b' he hath dealt bountifully 3588
14: 6 counsel of the poor, b' the Lord "
16: 8 b' he is at my right hand, "
18: 7 shaken, b' he was wroth. "
19 he delivered me, b' he delighted "
27:11 plain path, b' of mine enemies. 4616
28: 5 B' they regard not the works 3588
6 Blessed be the Lord, b' he hath
31:10 my strength faileth b' of mine
33:21 rejoice in him, b' we have 3588
37: 1 Fret not thyself b' of evil doers,
7 fret not thyself b' of him who
7 his way, b' of the man
40 save them, b' they trust 3588
38: 3 b' of thine anger; neither is 6440
3 any rest in my bones b' of my sin. "
5 corrupt b' of my foolishness. "
20 b' I follow the thing that good is. 8478
39: 9 not my mouth; b' thou didst it. 3588
41:11 favourest me, b' mine enemy
42: 9 go I mourning b' of the oppression
43: 2 mourning b' of the oppression
44: 3 b' thou hadst a favour unto them. 3588
45: 4 b' of truth and meekness 5921, 1697
48:11 be glad, b' of thy judgments. 4616
52: 9 forever, b' thou hast done it: 3588
53: 5 put them to shame, b' God
55: 3 B' of the voice of the enemy,
3 b' of the oppression of the wicked: 6440
19 B' they have no change, * 834
59: 9 B' of his strength will I wait †
60: 4 may be displayed b' of the truth. 6440
8 triumph thou b' of me. 5921
63: 3 B' thy loving kindness is better *3588
7 B' thou hast been my help, * "
68:29 B' of thy temple at Jerusalem
69: 7 B' for thy sake I have borne 3588
18 deliver me b' of mine enemies. 4616
78:22 B' they believed not in God, 3588
86:17 b' thou, Lord, hast holpen me,
91: 9 B' thou hast made the Lord, * "
14 B' he hath set his love upon me, "
14 set him on high, b' he hath known "
97: 8 Judah rejoiced b' of thy 4616
102:10 B' of thine indignation and thy 6440
106:33 B' they provoked his spirit, 3588
107:11 B' they rebelled against the "
17 b' of their transgression, 1870
17 b' of their iniquities, are afflicted
26 their soul is melted b' of trouble.
30 glad b' they are quiet; 3588
109:16 B' that he remembered not to 3282
21 b' thy mercy is good, 3588
116: 1 b' he hath heard my voice "
2 B' he hath inclined his ear "
118: 1 b' his mercy endureth for ever. * "
119:56 I had, b' I kept thy precepts. "
62 give thanks unto thee b' of thy 5921
74 b' I have hoped in thy word. 3588
100 than the ancients, b' I keep
136 down mine eyes, b' they keep 5921
139 consumed me, b' mine enemies 3588
158 was grieved; b' they kept not 834
164 praise thee b' of thy righteous 5921
122: 9 B' of the house of the Lord *4616
Pr 1:24 B' I have called, and ye refused; 3282
21: 7 destroy them; b' they refuse 3588
22:22 Rob not the poor, b' he is poor:
24:13 eat honey, b' it is good; * "
19 Fret not thyself b' of evil men,
Ec 2:17 I hated life; b' the work 3588
18 b' I should leave it *
4: 9 Two are better than one; b' they 834
5:20 b' God answereth him in the joy 3588
8: 6 B' to every purpose there is *3588
11 B' sentence against an evil work 834
13 as a shadow; b' he feareth not "
15 mirth, b' a man hath no better "
17 b' though a man labor to seek it "

Ec 10:15 b' he knoweth not how to go * 834
12: 3 grinders cease b' they are few, 3588
5 shall fail: b' man goeth to his "
9 moreover, b' the preacher was wise, "
Ca 1: 3 B' of the savour of thy good *
6 not upon me, b' I am black,
6 b' the sun hath looked upon me:
3: 8 upon his thigh b' of fear
Isa 2: 6 b' they be replenished 3588
3: 8 Judah is fallen: b' their tongue "
16 B' the daughters of Zion 3282, 3588
5:13 into captivity, b' they have no *
24 b' they have cast away the law, 3588
6: 5 I am undone; b' I am a man "
7: 5 B' Syria, Ephraim, and the 3282, 3588
24 men come thither; b' all the land "
8:20 it is b' there is no light * 834
10:27 destroyed b' of the anointing. ‡6440
14:20 with them in burial, b' thou hast 3588
29 Palestina, b' the rod of him "
15: 1 B' in the night Ar of Moab * "
1 b' in the night Kir of Moab * "
17: 9 left b' of the children of Israel: *6440
10 B' thou hast forgotten the God *3588
19:16 b' of the shaking of the hand 6440
17 b' of the counsel of the Lord of "
20 b' of the oppressors, and he shall "
22: 4 comfort me, b' of the spoiling *5921
24: 5 b' they have transgressed 3588
26: 3 b' he trusteth in thee. "
28:15 B' ye have said, "
28 is bruised; b' he will not ever * "
30:12 B' ye despise this word, 3282
31: 1 b' they are many; and in 3588
1 b' they are very strong; "
32:14 B' the palaces shall be forsaken;* "
37:29 B' thy rage against me, 3282
40: 7 fadeth: b' the spirit of the Lord 3588
43:20 b' I give waters in the wilderness, "
48: 4 B' I knew that thou art obstinate, "
49: 7 shall worship, b' of the Lord 4616
50: 2 fish stinketh, b' there is no water, "
51:13 b' of the fury of the oppressor, 6440
53: 9 b' he had done no violence, *5921
53:12 b' he hath poured out his 8478, 834
55: 5 run unto thee b' of the Lord 4616
60: 5 be enlarged; b' the abundance 3588
9 Holy One of Israel, b' he hath "
61: 1 b' the Lord hath anointed me 3282
64: 7 us, b' of our iniquities. *3027
65:12 down to the slaughter: b' when I 3282
16 b' the former troubles are 3588
16 forgotten, and b' they are hid "
66: 4 fears upon them; b' when I 3282
Jer 2:35 B' I am innocent, *3588
35 plead with thee, b' thou sayest, 5921
4: 4 b' of the evil of your doings. 6440
17 b' she hath been rebellious. 3588
18 b' it is bitter, b' it reacheth * "
19 hold my peace, b' thou hast "
28 b' I have spoken it, 5921, 3588
31 soul is wearied b' of murderers. *
5: 6 in pieces: b' their transgressions 3588
14 B' ye speak this word, behold, 3282
6:19 b' they have not 3588, 5921, 1697
30 them, b' the Lord hath rejected 3588
7:13 now, b' ye have done all these 3282
8:14 gall to drink, b' we have sinned 3588
19 daughter of my people b' of them *
9:10 lamentation, b' they are burned 3588
13 saith, B' they have forsaken 5921
19 confounded, b' we have forsaken 3588
19 b' our dwellings have cast "
10: 5 be borne, b' they cannot go, "
12: 4 b' they said, He shall not see "
11 made desolate, b' no man "
13 b' of the fierce anger of the Lord. "
13:17 b' the Lord's flock is carried 3588
25 saith the Lord; b' thou hast 834
14: 4 B' the ground is chapt, 5668
5 forsook it, b' there was no grass. 3588
6 did fail, b' there was no grass. "
16 b' of the famine and the sword; 6440
15: 4 b' of Manasseh the son of 1558
17 I sat alone b' of thy hand: 6440
16:11 say unto them, B' your fathers 5921, 834
18 sin doubled; b' they have defiled 5921
17:13 b' they have forsaken the Lord, 3588
18:15 B' my people hath forgotten * "
19: 4 B' they have forsaken me, 3282, 834
8 hiss b' of all the plagues 5921
13 Tophet, b' of all the houses *3605
15 it, b' they have hardened 3588
20: 8 violence and spoil; b' the word "
17 B' he slew me not 834
21:12 b' of the evil of your doings. 6440
22: 9 B' they have forsaken 5921, 834
15 reign, b' thou closest thyself 3588
23: 9 is broken b' of the prophets; *
9 b' of the Lord, and b' of the 6440
10 b' of swearing the land mourneth; "
38 B' ye say this word, The burden 3282
25: 8 B' ye have not heard 3282, 834
16 b' of the sword that I will send 6440
27 b' of the sword which I will send "
37 b' of the fierce anger of the Lord. "
38 b' of the fierceness of the oppressor, "
38 and b' of his fierce anger. "
26: 3 b' of the evil of their doings. "
28:16 shalt die, b' thou hast taught 3588
29:15 B' ye have said, * "
29:19 B' they have not hearkened 8478, 834
23 B' they have committed 3282, 834
25 saying, B' thou hast sent " "
31 B' that Shemaiah hath " "
32 b' he hath taught rebellion 3588

Jer 30:14, 15 b' thy sins were increased.
17 b' they called thee an Outcast, 3588
31:15 comforted for her children, b' they "
19 even confounded, b' I did bear "
32:24 against it, b' of the sword, 6440
32 B' of all the evil of the children 5921
35:16 B' the sons of Jonadab *3588
17 against them: b' I have spoken 3282
18 B' ye have obeyed 3282, 834
40: 3 b' ye have sinned against 3588
41: 9 b' of Gedaliah, was it which Asa *3027
18 B' of the Chaldeans: for they 6440
18 b' Ishmael the son of Nethaniah 3588
44: 3 B' of their wickedness which they 6440
22 b' of the evil of your doings, "
22 and b' of the abominations "
23 B' ye have burned incense, 6440, 834
23 and b' ye have sinned against "
46:15 stood not, b' the Lord did 3588
21 did not stand, b' the day * "
23 be searched; b' they are more "
47: 4 B' of the day that cometh 5921
48: 7 For b' thou hast trusted 3588, 3282
36 b' the riches that he hath *5921, 3651
42 being a people, b' he hath 3588, 5921
45 of Heshbon b' of the force: *
50: 7 not, b' they have sinned 8471, 834
11 B' ye are glad, b' ye rejoiced, 3588
11 b' ye are grown fat as the heifer "
13 B' of the wrath of the Lord "
24 caught, b' thou hast striven 3588
51:11 destroy it; b' it is the vengeance * "
51 are confounded, b' we have heard "
55 B' the Lord hath spoiled * "
56 B' the spoiler is come * "
La 1: 3 gone into captivity b' of affliction,
3 and b' of great servitude:
4 do mourn, b' none come
8 despise her, b' they have seen 3588
16 down with water, b' the comforter "
16 desolate, b' the enemy prevailed. "
2:11 b' the children and the sucklings
3:22 not consumed, b' his compassions 3588
28 keepeth silence, b' he hath borne "
51 affecteth mine heart b' of all
5: 9 b' of the sword of the wilderness. 6440
10 b' of the terrible famine.
18 B' of the mountain of Zion, *5921
Eze 3:20 he shall die; b' thou hast not 3588
21 surely live, b' he is warned; "
5: 7 B' ye multiplied more 3282
9 b' of all thine abominations, "
11 Surely, b' thou hast defiled "
6: 9 captives, b' I am broken * 834
7:19 b' it is the stumbling block 3588
12:19 b' of the violence of all them
13: 8 B' ye have spoken vanity, and 3282
10 B', even b' they have seduced my "
22 B' with lies ye have made the "
14: 5 b' they are all estranged 834
15 pass through b' of the beasts: 6440
15: 8 desolate, b' they have committed 3282
16:15 the harlot b' of thy renown, 5921
28 b' thou wast unsatiable; yea, 1115
36 B' thy filthiness was poured 3282
43 B' thou hast not remembered 3282, 834
63 b' of thy shame, when I am 6440
18:18 b' he cruelly oppressed, 3588
28 B' he considereth, "
20:16 B' they despised my judgments 3282
24 B' they had not executed "
21: 7 For the tidings; b' it cometh: 3588
13 B' it is a trial, * "
24 B' ye have made your iniquity 3282
24 do appear; b', I say, ye are come "
28 to consume b' of the glittering: *4616
22:19 B' ye are all become dross, 3282
23:30 unto thee, b' thou hast gone *
30 and b' thou art polluted 5921, 834
35 B' thou hast forgotten me, 3282
45 b' they are adulteresses, 3588
24:13 lewdness: b' I have purged thee, 3282
25: 3 B' thou saidst, Aha,
6 B' thou hast clapped thine hands "
8 B' that Moab and Seir do say, "
12 B' that Edom hath dealt "
15 B' the Philistines have dealt "
26: 2 Son of man, b' that Tyrus 3282
28: 2 B' thine heart is lifted up,
5 heart is lifted up b' of thy riches:
6 B' thou hast set thine heart 3282
17 was lifted up b' of thy beauty,
29: 6 am the Lord, b' they have been 3282
9 am the Lord: b' he hath said, "
20 served against it, b' they wrought 834
31: 5 became long b' of the multitude *
10 B' thou hast lifted up thyself 3282, 834
33:29 most desolate b' of all their 5921
34: 5 scattered, b' there is no shepherd:
8 surely b' my flock became *3282
8 b' there was no shepherd,
21 B' ye have thrust with side 3282
35:10 B' thou hast said, "
15 of Israel, b' it was desolate, 5921, 834
36: 2 B' the enemy hath said 3282
3 B' they have made you desolate, * "
6 and in my fury, b' ye have borne "
13 B' they say unto you, "
39:23 iniquity: b' they trespassed 5921, 834
44: 2 enter in by it; b' the Lord, *3588
7 b' of all your abominations. * 413
12 B' they ministered unto them 3282, 834
47: 9 of fish, b' these waters shall *3588
12 b' their waters they issued
Da 2: 8 b' ye see the thing is 3606, 6903, 1768
3:22 Therefore b' the king's 4481, 1768

Da 3:29 b' there is no other God 3606, 6903, 1768
4: 9 b' I know that the spirit 1768
6: 3 b' an excellent spirit 3606, 6903, 1768
23 upon him, b' he believed 1768
7:11 b' of the voice of the great words 4481
9: 7 driven them, b' of their trespass
8 to our fathers, b' we have sinned 834
11 b' we have sinned *3588
16 b' for our sins, "
11:35 b' it is yet for a time 3588, 5750
Ho 4: 1 of the land, b' there is no truth, 3588
6 knowledge, b' thou hast rejected "
10 increase: b' they have left 3588
13 and elms, b' the shadow 3588
19 ashamed b' of their sacrifices.
5: 1 is toward you, b' ye have been *3588
11 in judgment, b' he willingly "
7:13 destruction unto them! b' they * "
8: 1 b' they have transgressed 3282
11 B' Ephraim hath made 3588
9: 6 they are gone b' of destruction: *
17 cast them away, b' they did not 3588
10: 3 king b' we feared not the Lord, * "
5 shall fear b' of the calves
5 thereof, b' it is departed from it. 3588
13 b' thou didst trust in thy way, * "
15 b' of your great wickedness: 6440
11: 5 be his king, b' they refused 3588
6 them, b' of their own counsels.
Joe 1: 5 of wine, b' of the new wine; 5921
11 b' the harvest of the field *3588
12 withered: b' joy is withered away* "
18 perplexed, b' they have no pasture; "
2:20 come up, b' he hath done great "
3: 5 B' ye have taken my silver * 834
19 b' they have shed innocent blood
Am 1: 3 b' they have threshed Gilead 5921
6 b' they carried away captive the "
9 b' they delivered up the whole "
11 punishment thereof; b' he did "
13 b' they have ripped up the women "
2: 1 b' he burned the bones of the king "
4 b' they have despised the law "
6 b' they sold the righteous "
4:12 b' I will do this unto thee, 6118, 3588
Jon 1:10 presence of the Lord, b' he had told "
Mic 2: 1 practise it, b' it is in the power "
10 is not your rest: b' it is polluted, 5668
6:13 thee desolate b' of thy sins. 5921
7: 9 b' I have sinned against him, 3588
13 be desolate b' of them that dwell 5921
17 and shall fear b' of thee.
18 anger for ever, b' he delighteth 3588
Na 3: 4 B' of the multitude of the
11 seek strength b' of the enemy.
Hab 1:16 b' by them their portion is fat, 3588
2: 3 wait for it; b' it will surely come, "
5 b' he transgresseth by wine, "
17 them afraid, b' of men's blood,
Zep 1:17 blind men, b' they have sinned 3588
2:10 pride, b' they have reproached
3:11 haughty b' of my holy mountain *
Hag 1: 9 B' of mine house that is waste, 3282
Zec 8:10 or came in b' of the affliction: 4480
9: 8 about mine house b' of the army, *
8 b' of him that passeth by, *
8 and b' of him that returneth: *
10: 2 troubled, b' there was no shepherd. 3588
5 fight, b' the Lord is with them,
11: 2 fallen; b' the mighty are spoiled: 834
Mal 2: 2 b' ye do not lay it to heart. 3588
14 B' the Lord hath been 5921, "
M't 2:18 not be comforted, b' they are not. 3754
5:36 b' thou canst not make one hair * "
7:14 B' strait is the gate, and narrow * "
9:36 b' they fainted, and were "
11:20 were done, b' they repented not: "
25 b' thou hast hid these things * "
12:41 b' they repented at the * "
13: 5 b' they had no deepness of earth: 1223
6 b' they had no root, they withered 1223
11 B' it is given unto you to know 3754
13 b' they seeing see not; "
21 ariseth b' of the word, 1223
58 works there b' of their unbelief. "
14: 5 b' they counted him as a prophet. 3754
15:32 b' they continue with me now "
16: 7 It is b' we have taken no bread. * "
8 b' ye have brought no bread? "
17:20 unto them, B' of your unbelief: 1223
18: 7 unto the world b' of offences! 575
32 that debt, b' thou desiredst me: 1893
19: 8 b' of the hardness of your hearts *4314
20: 7 B' no man hath hired us, 3754
15 thine eye evil, b' I am good? "
31 b' they should hold their peace: *2443
21:46 b' they took him for a prophet. 1894
23:29 b' ye build the tombs of the *3754
24:12 b' iniquity shall abound, the 1223
26:31 be offended b' of me this night: *1722
33 shall be offended b' of thee, yet "
27: 6 b' it is the price of blood. *1893
19 this day in a dream b' of him. 1223
M'r 1:34 devils to speak, b' they knew him. 3754
3: 9 wait on him b' of the multitude, 1223
30 B' they said, He hath an unclean 3754
4: 5 b' it had no depth of earth: 1223
6 b' it had no root, it withered away. "
29 sickle, b' the harvest is come. 3754
5: 4 B' that he had been often bound 1223
6: 6 he marvelled b' of their unbelief. "
34 b' they were as sheep not having 3754
7:19 B' it entereth not into his heart, "
8: 2 b' they have now been with me "
16 It is b' we have no bread. * "
17 reason ye, b' ye have no bread? "

M'r 9:38 forbad him, *b*· he followeth not us. *3754*
41 *b*· ye belong to Christ, verily I say "
11:18 *b*· all the people was astonished * "
12:24 err, *b*· ye know not the scriptures,* "
14:27 be offended *b*· of me this night: *1722
15:42 *b*· it was the preparation, that is, *1893*
16:14 *b*· they believed not them which *3754*
Lu 1: 7 *b*· that Elisabeth was barren, *2530*
20 *b*· thou believest not my *473, 3759*
2: 4 (*b*· he was of the house and lineage *1223*
7 *b*· there was no room for them in *1360*
4:18 *b*· he hath anointed me to *3739, 1752*
5:19 bring him in *b*· of the multitude, *1223*
8: 6 away, *b*· it lacked moisture. "
30 *b*· many devils were entered into *3754
9: 7 *b*· that it was said of some, that *1223*
49 *b*· he followeth not with us. *3754*
53 *b*· his face was as though "
10:20 *b*· your names are written in * "
11: 8 give him, *b*· he is his friend, *1223*
8 *b*· of his importunity he will rise "
18 *b*· ye say that I cast out *3754*
12:17 *b*· I have no room where to "
13: 2 *b*· they suffered such things? "
14 *b*· that Jesus had healed on "
15:27 *b*· he hath received him safe "
16: 8 steward, *b*· he had done wisely: "
17: 9 *b*· he did the things that were "
18: 5 Yet *b*· this widow troubleth me, *1223*
19: 3 *b*· he was little of stature. *3754*
11 *b*· he was nigh to Jerusalem, *1223*
11 *b*· they thought that the kingdom "
17 *b*· thou hast been faithful in a *3754*
21 *b*· thou art an austere man: thou "
31 *B*· the Lord hath need of him. * "
44 *b*· thou knewest not the time *473, 3739*
23: 8 *b*· he had heard many things of *1223*
Joh 1:50 *B*· I said unto thee, I saw thee *3754*
2:24 unto them, *b*· he knew all men, *1223
3:18 *b*· he hath not believed in the *3754*
19 *b*· their deeds were evil. *1063
23 *b*· there was much water there: *3754*
29 *b*· of the bridegroom's voice: *1223*
4:41 more believed *b*· of his own word; "
42 we believe, not *b*· of thy saying: "
5:16 *b*· he had done these things *3754*
18 *b*· he not only had broken the "
27 *b*· he is the Son of man. "
30 *b*· I seek not mine own will, "
6: 2 *b*· they saw his miracles which he "
26 not *b*· ye saw the miracles, but "
26 *b*· ye did eat of the loaves, "
41 *b*· he said, I am the bread which "
7: 1 *b*· the Jews sought to kill him. "
7 but me it hateth, *b*· I testify of "
22 (not *b*· it is of Moses, but of the "
23 are ye angry at me *b*· I have "
30 *b*· his hour was not yet come. "
39 *b*· that Jesus was not yet glorified. "
43 a division among the people *b*· of *1223*
8:22 *b*· he saith, Whither I go, ye *3754*
37 *b*· my word hath no place in you. "
43 *b*· ye cannot hear my word. "
44 *b*· there is no truth in him. "
45 And *b*· I tell you the truth, "
47 them not, *b*· ye are not of God. "
9:16 *b*· he keepeth not the sabbath "
22 *b*· they feared the Jews: for the "
10:13 fleeth, *b*· he is an hireling, "
17 *b*· I lay down my life, that I might "
26 *b*· ye are not of my sheep, as *1063*
33 and *b*· that thou, being a man, *3754*
36 *b*· I said, I am the son of God? "
11: 9 *b*· he seeth the light of this world. "
10 *b*· there is no light in him. "
42 *b*· of the people which stand by *1223*
12: 6 but *b*· he was a thief, and had *3754*
11 *B*· that by reason of him many "
30 This voice came not *b*· of me, *1223*
39 *b*· that Esaias said again, *3754*
42 *b*· of the Pharisees they did not *1223*
13:29 *b*· Judas had the bag, that Jesus *1893*
14:12 *b*· I go unto my Father. *3754*
17 *b*· it seeth him not, neither * "
19 *b*· I live, ye shall live also. "
28 *b*· I said, I go unto the Father: "
15:19 but *b*· ye are not of the world, "
21 *b*· they know not him that sent me. "
27 *b*· ye have been with me from "
16: 3 *b*· they have not known the Father, "
4 beginning, *b*· I was with you. "
6 But *b*· I have said these things "
9 *b*· they believe not on me; "
10 *b*· I go to my Father, and ye see "
11 *b*· the prince of this world is "
16 see me, *b*· I go to the Father. "
17 *B*· I go to the Father? "
21 *b*· her hour is come: but as soon "
27 *b*· ye have loved me, and have "
32 *b*· the Father is with me. "
17:14 *b*· they are not of the world, even "
19: 7 *b*· he made himself the Son of God. "
31 *b*· it was the preparation, that the *1893*
42 *b*· of the Jews' preparation day; *1223*
20:13 *B*· they have taken away my Lord, *3754*
29 Thomas, *b*· thou hast seen me, "
21:17 Peter was grieved *b*· he said unto "
Ac 2: 6 *b*· that every man heard them "
24 *b*· it was not possible that he *2530*
27 *B*· thou wilt not leave my soul *3754*
4:21 punish them, *b*· of the people: *1223*
6: 1 *b*· their widows were neglected. *3754*
8:11 *b*· that of long time he had *1223*
20 *b*· thou hast thought that the *3754*
10:45 *b*· that on the Gentiles also "
12: 3 And *b*· he saw it pleased the Jews,* "

Ac 12:20 *b*· their country was nourished *1223*
23 smote him, *b*· he gave not God *473, 3739*
13:27 *b*· they knew him not. "
14:12 Mercurius, *b*· he was the chief *1894*
16: 3 circumcised him *b*· of the Jews *1223*
17:18 *b*· he preached unto them Jesus, *3754*
31 *B*· he hath appointed a day, in *1360
18: 2 *b*· that Claudius had commanded *1223*
3 *b*· he was of the same craft, "
20:16 *b*· he would not spend the *3704
22:29 Roman, and *b*· he had bound him. *3754*
30 the morrow, *b*· he would have *
24:11 *B*· that thou mayest understand, *
25:20 And *b*· I doubted of such *
26: 2 Agrippa, *b*· I shall answer *
3 Especially *b*· I know thee
27: 4 *b*· the winds were contrary. *1223*
9 *b*· the fast was now already past, "
12 And *b*· the haven was not "
28: 2 *b*· of the present rain, *1223*
2 and *b*· of the cold. "
18 *b*· there was no cause of death in "
20 *b*· that for the hope of Israel *1063*
Ro 1:19 *B*· that which may be known of *1360*
21 *B*· that, when they knew God, "
3: 2 chiefly, *b*· that unto them were *3754
4:15 *B*· the law worketh wrath: for *1063*
5: 5 *b*· the love of God is shed abroad *3754*
6:15 *b*· we are not under the law, "
19 *b*· of the infirmity of your flesh: *1223*
8: 7 *B*· the carnal mind is enmity *1360*
10 body is dead *b*· of sin; but the *1223*
10 Spirit is life *b*· of righteousness. "
21 *b*· the creature itself also shall be *3754
27 *b*· he maketh intercession for the "
9: 7 Neither, *b*· they are the seed "
28 *b*· a short work will the Lord * "
32 *B*· they sought it not by faith, "
11:20 Well; *b*· of unbelief they were *
14:23 if he eat, *b*· he eateth not of faith: *3754*
15:15 *b*· of the grace that is given to me *1223*
1Co 1:25 *B*· the foolishness of God is wiser *3754*
2:14 *b*· they are spiritually discerned. "
3:13 *b*· it shall be revealed by fire; "
6: 7 *b*· ye go to law one with another. * "
11:10 power on her head *b*· of the angels. *1223*
12:15 *B*· I am not the hand, I am not of *3754*
16 *B*· I am not the eye, I am not of "
15: 9 *b*· I persecuted the church of God. *1360*
15 *b*· we have testified of God that *3754*
2Co 2:13 my spirit, *b*· I found not Titus "
5:14 *b*· we thus judge, "
7:13 *b*· his spirit was refreshed by you *3754*
11: 7 *b*· I have preached to you the "
11 Wherefore? *b*· I love you not? "
Ga 2: 4 that *b*· of false brethren unawares *1223*
11 *b*· he was to be blamed. *3754*
3:19 It was added *b*· of transgressions, *5484*
4: 6 And *b*· ye are sons, God hath *3754*
16 your enemy, *b*· I tell you the truth? "
Eph 4:18 *b*· of the blindness of their heart: *1223*
5: 6 for *b*· of these things cometh "
16 the time, *b*· the days are evil. *3754*
Ph'p 1: 7 *b*· I have you in my heart; *1223*
2:26 *b*· that ye had heard that he *1360*
30 *B*· for the work of Christ he was *3754*
4:17 Not *b*· I desire a gift: but I desire * "
1Th 2: 8 *b*· ye were dear unto us. *1360*
9 night and day, *b*· we would not *4314*
13 *b*·, when ye received the word *3754
4: 6 *b*· that the Lord is the avenger *1360*
2Th 1: 3 *b*· that your faith groweth *3754*
10 (*b*· our testimony among you was "
2:10 that perish; *b*· they received *473, 3739*
13 *b*· God hath from the beginning *3754
3: 9 Not *b*· we have not power, "
1Ti 1:13 *b*· I did it ignorantly in unbelief. "
4:10 *b*· we trust in the living God, "
5:12 *b*· they have cast off their first "
6: 2 despise them, *b*· they are brethren; "
2 *b*· they are faithful and beloved, "
Ph'm 7 *b*· the bowels of the saints are "
Heb 3:19 could not enter in *b*· of unbelief. *1223*
6 entered not in *b*· of unbelief: "
6:13 *b*· he could swear by no greater, *1893
7:23 many priests, *b*· they were not *1223*
24 this man, *b*· he continueth "
8: 9 *b*· they continued not in my *3754
10: 2 *b*· that the worshippers once *1223*
11: 5 not found, *b*· God had translated *1360*
11 *b*· she judged him faithful who *1893
23 *b*· they saw he was a proper *1360*
Jas 1:10 *b*· as the flower of the grass *3754*
4: 2 ye have not, *b*· ye ask not. *1223*
3 and receive not, *b*· ye ask amiss. *1360*
1Pe 1:16 *B*· it is written, Be ye holy; "
2:21 *b*· Christ also suffered us, leaving *3754*
5: 8 *b*· your adversary the devil, as a * "
1Jo 2: 8 *b*· the darkness is past, and the "
11 *b*· that darkness hath blinded his "
12 *b*· your sins are forgiven "
13 *b*· ye have known him that is "
13 *b*· ye have overcome the wicked "
13 *b*· ye have known the Father. "
14 *b*· ye have known him that is from "
14 young men, *b*· ye are strong, "
21 *b*· ye know not the truth, "
21 but *b*· ye know it, "
3: 1 us not, *b*· it knew him not. "
9 cannot sin, *b*· he is born of God. "
12 *B*· his own works were evil, and "
14 *b*· we love the brethren. He that "
16 *b*· he laid down his life for us: "
22 *b*· we keep his commandments, "
4: 1 *b*· many false prophets are gone "
4 *b*· greater is he that is in you, "

1Jo 4: 9 *b*· that God sent his only begotten *3754*
13 *b*· he hath given us of his Spirit. "
17 *b*· as he is, so are we in this world. "
18 *b*· fear hath torment. He that "
19 We love him, *b*· he first loved us. "
5: 6 beareth witness, *b*· the Spirit is "
10 *b*· he believeth not the record "
3Jo 7 *B*· that for his name's sake *1063*
Jude 16 in admiration *b*· of advantage. *5484
Re 1: 7 shall wail *b*· of him. Even so, *1909
2: 4 *b*· thou hast left thy first love. *3754
14 *b*· thou hast there them that hold "
20 *b*· thou sufferest that woman * "
3:10 *B*· thou hast kept the word of my "
16 So then *b*· thou art lukewarm, "
17 *B*· thou sayest, I am rich, "
5: 4 *b*· no man was found worthy to "
8:11 *b*· they were made bitter. "
11:10 *b*· these two prophets tormented "
17 *b*· thou hast taken to thee "
12:12 great wrath, *b*· he knoweth *
14: 8 *b*· she made all the nations drink *3754
16: 5 *b*· thou hast judged thus. "
11 *b*· of their pains and their sores, *1537*
21 *b*· of the plague of the hail; "

Becher (*be'-ker*) See also BACHRITES.
Ge 46:21 Belah, and *B*·, and Ashbel, Gera, **1071**
Nu 26:35 of *B*·, the family of the Bachrites: "
1Ch 7: 6 Bela, and *B*·, and Jediael, three. "
8 the sons of *B*·; Zemira, and Joash, "
8 All these are the sons of *B*·. "

Bechorath (*be-ko'-rath*)
1Sa 9: 1 Zeror, the son of *B*·, the son of **1064**

beckoned
Lu 1:22 he *b*· unto them, and remained *1269
5: 7 they *b*· unto their partners, *2656*
Joh 13:24 Peter therefore *b*· to him, that *3506*
Ac 19:33 Alexander *b*· with the hand, and *2678*
21:40 *b*· with the hand unto the people. "
24:10 after that the governor had *b*· *3506*

beckoning
Ac 12:17 *b*· unto them with the hand *2678*
13:16 and *b*· with his hand, said "

become See also BECAME; BECOMETH.
Ge 3:22 Behold, the man is *b*· as one of us, **1961**
9:15 the waters shall no more *b*· a "
18:18 Abraham shall surely *b*· a great "
24:35 and he is *b*· great: and he hath **1431**
32:10 and now I am *b*· two bands. **1961**
34:16 with you, and we will *b*· one "
37:20 We shall see what will *b*· of his "
48:19 he also shall *b*· a people, and he "
19 shall *b*· a multitude of nations. "
Ex 4: 9 of the river shall *b*· blood upon "
7: 9 and it shall *b*· a serpent. "
19 water, that they may *b*· blood; "
8:16 that it may *b*· lice throughout all "
9: 9 And it shall *b*· small dust in all "
15: 2 and he is *b*· my salvation: he is "
6 *b*· glorious in power: thy right * **142**
23:29 lest the land *b*· desolate, and the **1961**
32: 1, 23 we wot not what is *b*· of him. "
Le 19:29 and the land *b*· full of wickedness. **4390**
Nu 5:24 shall enter into her, and *b*· bitter. "
27 and *b*· bitter, and her belly shall "
De 27: 9 thou art *b*· the people of the Lord **1961**
28:37 thou shalt *b*· an astonishment, "
Jos 9:13 *b*· old by reason of the very long **1086**
J'g 16:17 and I shall *b*· weak, and be like **2470**
1Sa 28:16 from thee, and is *b*· thine enemy? **1961**
2Sa 7:24 and thou, Lord, art *b*· their God. * "
1Ki 2:15 about, and is *b*· my brother's; "
14: 3 he shall tell thee what shall *b*· of "
2Ki 21:14 they shall *b*· a prey and a spoil "
22:19 that they should *b*· a desolation "
Es 2:11 what should *b*· of her. **6213**
Job 7: 5 skin is broken, and *b*· loathsome. ***3988**
15:28 which are ready to *b*· heaps. "
21: 7 do the wicked live, *b*· old, **6275**
30:19 and I am *b*· like dust and ashes. **4911**
21 Thou art *b*· cruel to me: with ***2015**
Ps 14: 3 they are all together *b*· filthy: **444**
28: 1 I *b*· like them that go down into **4911**
53: 3 they are altogether *b*· filthy; **444**
62:10 *b*· not vain in robbery: if riches **1891**
69: 8 I am *b*· a stranger unto my **1961**
22 Let their table *b*· a snare before "
22 for their welfare, let it *b*· a trap. "
79: 4 *b*· a reproach to our neighbours, **1961**
109: 7 and let his prayer *b*· sin. * "
118:14 and song, and is *b*· my salvation. "
21 heard me, and art *b*· my salvation. "
22 is *b*· the head stone of the corner. "
119:83 For I am *b*· like a bottle in the "
Isa 1:21 the faithful city *b*· an harlot! "
22 Thy silver is *b*· dross, thy wine "
7:24 land shall *b*· briers and thorns. * "
12: 2 he also is *b*· my salvation. "
14:10 Art thou also *b*· weak as we? **2470**
10 art thou *b*· like unto us? **4911**
19:11 of Pharaoh is *b*· brutish: **1197**
13 The princes of Zoan are *b*· fools, **2973**
29:11 And the vision of all is *b*· unto **1961**
34: 9 thereof shall *b*· burning pitch. "
35: 7 parched ground shall *b*· a pool, "
59: 6 Their webs shall not *b*· garments, "
60:22 A little one shall *b*· a thousand, "
Jer 2: 5 after vanity, and are *b*· vain? **1891**
3: 1 from him, and *b*· another man's, **1961**
5:13 And the prophets shall *b*· wind, "
27 they are *b*· great, and waxen rich. **6238**
7:11 *b*· a den of robbers in your eyes: **1961**
10:21 the pastors are *b*· brutish, and **1197**
22: 5 this house shall *b*· a desolation. **1961**

Jer 26:18 and Jerusalem shall b' heaps, 1961
49:13 Bozrah shall b' a desolation, "
50:23 how is Babylon b' a desolation "
37 and they shall b' as women: "
51:37 And Babylon shall b' heaps, "
41 is Babylon b' an astonishment "
La 1: 1 how is she b' as a widow! she "
1 provinces, how is she b' tributary! "
2 with her, they are b' her enemies. "
6 her princes are b' like harts that "
11 and consider; for I am b' vile. "
4: 1 How is the gold b' dim! how is 6004
3 daughter of my people is b' cruel, "
8 is withered, it is b' like a stick. 1961
Eze 22: 4 Thou art b' guilty in thy blood 816
18 Israel is to me b' dross: all they 1961
19 Because ye are all b' dross, "
26: 5 it shall b' a spoil to the nations. "
36:35 land that was desolate is b' like * "
35 and ruined cities are b' fenced, "
37:17 they shall b' one in thine hand. 1961
Da 4:22 that art grown and b' strong: 8631
9:16 people are b' a reproach to all
11:23 come up, and shall b' strong 6105
Ho 12: 8 Ephraim said, Yet I am b' rich, 6238
13:15 and his spring shall b' dry, and his
16 Samaria shall b' desolate; * 816
Jon 4: 5 see what would b' of the city. 1961
Mic 3:12 Jerusalem shall b' heaps, and "
Zep 1:13 their goods shall b' a booty, and "
2:15 is she b' a desolation, a place for "
Zec 4: 7 Zerubbabel thou shalt b' a plain:
M't 18: 3 converted, and b' as little children, *1096*
21:42 is b' the head of the corner. *1096, 1519*
M'r 1:17 make you to b' fishers of men. *1096*
12:10 is b' the head of the corner: *1096, 1519*
Lu 20:17 is b' the head of the corner?* "
Joh 1:12 he power to b' the sons of God, *1096*
Ac 4:11 is b' the head of the corner: *1096, 1519*
7:40 we wot not what is b' of him. *1096*
12:18 the soldiers, what was b' of Peter. "
Ro 3:12 they are together b' unprofitable; *889*
19 world may b' guilty before God. *1096*
4:18 he might b' the father of many "
6:22 and b' servants to God, ye have *1402*
7: 4 ye also are b' dead to the law *2289*
13 might b' exceeding sinful. *1096*
1Co 3:18 b' a fool, that he may be wise. "
7:18 let him not b' uncircumcised. *1986*
8: 9 b' a stumblingblock to them that *1096*
13: 1 I am b' as sounding brass, or a "
15:20 b' the firstfruits of them that slept.* "
2Co 5:17 behold, all things are b' new. "
12:11 I am b' a fool in glorying; "
Ga 4:16 Am I therefore b' your enemy, "
5: 4 Christ is b' of no effect unto you, *2673*
Ti 2: 1 things which b' sound doctrine: *4241*
Ph'm 6 thy faith may b' effectual by *1096*
Heb 5:12 are b' such as have need of milk, "
Jas 2: 4 are b' judges of evil thoughts? "
11 art b' a transgressor of the law. "
Re 11:15 The kingdoms of this world are b' "
18: 2 is b' the habitation of devils, and "

becometh
Ps 93: 5 holiness b' thine house, O Lord, 4998
Pr 10: 4 He b' poor that dealeth with a
17: 7 Excellent speech b' not a fool: 5000
18 b' surety in the presence of his 6148
Ec 4:14 is born in his kingdom b' poor.
M't 3:15 for thus it b' us to fulfil all *4241*
13:22 the word, and he b' unfruitful. *1096*
32 among herbs, and b' a tree, "
M'r 4:19 the word, and it b' unfruitful. "
32 b' greater than all herbs, "
Ro 16: 2 her in the Lord, as b' saints, * *516*
Eph 5: 3 named among you, as b' saints: *4241*
Ph'p 1:27 be as it b' the gospel of Christ: * *516*
1Ti 2:10 b' women professing godliness) "
Tit 2: 3 be in behaviour as b' holiness, *2412*

bed See also BEDS; BEDCHAMBER; BEDSTEAD.
Ge 48: 2 himself, and sat upon the b'. 4296
49: 4 thou wentest up to thy father's b';4904
33 gathered up his feet into the b'. 4296
Ex 8: 3 bedchamber, and upon thy b', "
21:18 he die not, but keepeth his b': 4904
Le 15: 4 Every b', whereon he lieth that "
5 whosoever toucheth his b' shall "
21 whosoever toucheth her b' shall "
23 if it be on her b', or on any "
24 all the b' whereon he lieth shall be "
26 Every b' whereon she lieth all the "
26 her as the b' of her separation: "
1Sa 19:13 an image, and laid it in the b', 4296
15 Bring him up to me in the b', "
16 there was an image in the b', "
28:23 the earth, and sat upon the b'. "
2Sa 4: 5 who lay on a b' at noon. *4904
7 lay on his b' in his bedchamber, 4296
11 in his own house upon his b'? 4904
11: 2 David arose from off his b', "
13 he went out to lie on his b' "
13: 5 Lay thee down on thy b', and "
1Ki 1:47 king bowed himself upon the b'. "
17:19 and laid him upon his own b'. 4296
21: 4 he laid him down upon his b', "
2Ki 1: 4 that b' on which thou art gone up, "
6 shalt not come down from that b' "
16 shalt not come down off that b' "
4:10 let us set for him there a b', "
21 him on the b' of the man of God, "
32 was dead, and laid upon his b'. "
1Ch 5: 1 he defiled his father's b', his *3326
2Ch 16:14 laid him in the b' which was 4904
24:25 slew him on his b', and he died: 4296

Es 7: 8 Haman was fallen upon the b' *4296
Job 7:13 My b' shall comfort me, my couch 6210
17:13 made my b' in the darkness. *3326
33:15 men, in slumberings upon the b'; 4904
19 also with pain upon his b', "
Ps 4: 4 with your own heart upon your b', "
6: 6 the night make I my b' to swim; 4296
36: 4 He deviseth mischief upon his b'; 4904
41: 3 strengthen him upon the b' of *6210
3 make all his b' in his sickness. 4904
63: 6 I remember thee upon my b', 3326
132: 3 my house, nor go up into my b';6210, "
139: 8 if I make my b' in hell, behold, 3331
Pr 7:16 decked my b' with coverings *6210
17 perfumed my b' with myrrh, 4904
22:27 why should he take away thy b' "
26:14 So doth the slothful upon his b'. 4296
Ca 1:16 pleasant: also our b' is green. *6210
3: 1 By night on my b' I sought him 4904
7 his b', which is Solomon's; *4296
5:13 His cheeks are as a b' of spices, 6170
Isa 28:20 the b' is shorter than that a man 4702
57: 7 mountain hast thou set thy b': 4904
8 thou hast enlarged thy b', "
8 their b' where thou sawest it. "
Eze 23:17 came to her into the b' of love, "
41 And satest upon a stately b', *4296
32:25 They have set her a b' in the 4904
Da 2:28 visions of thy head upon thy b', 4903
29 came into thy mind upon thy b', "
4: 5 and the thoughts upon my b' "
10 the visions of mine head in my b'; "
13 the visions of my head upon my b', "
7: 1 visions of his head upon his b': "
Am 3:12 in Samaria in the corner of a b', 4296
M't 9: 2 sick of the palsy, lying on a b': *2825*
6 take up thy b', and go unto thine "
M'r 2: 4 they let down the b' wherein *2895*
9 Arise, and take up thy b', "
11 Arise, and take up thy b', and go "
12 he arose, took up the b', and went "
4:21 under a bushel, or under a b'? *2825*
7:30 and her daughter laid upon the b'. "
Lu 5:18 men brought in a b' a man which "
8:16 putteth it under a b'; but setteth "
11: 7 my children are with me in b'; *2845*
17:34 there shall be two men in one b'; *2825*
Joh 5: 8 Rise, take up thy b', and walk. *2895*
9 and took up his b', and walked: "
10 lawful for thee to carry thy b'. "
11 unto me, Take up thy b', and walk. "
12 Take up thy bed, and walk? "
Ac 9:33 Æneas, which had kept his b' "
34 arise, and make thy b'. And he *4766*
Heb 13: 4 b' undefiled: but whoremongers *2845*
Re 2:22 Behold, I will cast her into a b', *2825*

Bedad (*be'-dad*)
Ge 36:35 and Hadad the son of B', who 911
1Ch 1:46 Hadad the son of B', which smote "

Bedan (*be'-dan*)
1Sa 12:11 the Lord sent Jerubbaal, and B', 917
1Ch 7:17 sons of Ulam; B'. These were "

bedchamber
Ex 8: 3 into thy b', and upon thy bed, 2315, 4904
2Sa 4: 7 he lay on his bed in his b', "
2Ki 6:12 that thou speakest in thy b'. "
11: 2 in the b' from Athalia, *4296
2Ch 22:11 put him and his nurse in a b'. "
Ec 10:20 curse not the rich in thy b': "

Bedeiah (*be-de'-yah*)
Ezr 10:35 Benaiah, B', Chelluh, 912

bed's
Ge 47:31 bowed himself upon the b' head. 4296

beds
2Sa 17:28 b', and basons, and earthen 4904
Es 1: 6 the b' were of gold and silver, *4296
Ps 149: 5 let them sing aloud upon their b'. 4904
Ca 6: 2 to the b' of spices, to feed in 6170
Isa 57: 2 they shall rest in their b', each 4904
Ho 7:14 they howled upon their b': "
Am 6: 4 That lie upon b' of ivory, 4296
Mic 2: 1 and work evil upon their b'! 4904
M'r 6:55 and began to carry about in b' *2895*
Ac 5:15 and laid them on b' and couches, *2825*

bedstead
De 3:11 his b' was a b' of iron; 6210

bee See also BEES.
Isa 7:18 and for the b' that is in the land 1682

Beeliada (*be-e-li'-ad-ah*)
1Ch 14: 7 Elishama, and B', and Eliphalet. 1182

Beelzebub (*be-el'-ze-bub*) See also BAAL-ZEBUB.
M't 10:25 called the master of the house B', *954*
12:24 but by B' the prince of the devils. "
27 And if I by B' cast out devils, "
M'r 3:22 said, He hath B', and by the prince "
Lu 11:15 He casteth out devils through B' "
18 I cast out devils through B'. "
19 And if I by B' cast out devils, "

been
Ge 13: 3 place where his tent had b' at the 1961
26: 8 when he had b' there a long time, "
31: 5 God of my father hath b' with me. 1961
38 twenty years have I b' with thee; "
41 have I b' twenty years in thy house: "
42 the fear of Isaac, had b' with me, 1961
38:26 She hath b' more righteous than *
45: 6 hath the famine b' in the land:
46:34 servants' trade hath b' about 1961
47: 9 days of the years of my life b' "
Ex 2:22 b' a stranger in a strange land. "
9:18 such as hath not b' in Egypt "

Ex 14:12 had b' better for us to serve the *
18: 3 have b' an alien in a strange land: 1961
21:29 it hath b' testified to his owner,
34:10 such as have not b' done in all
Le 10:19 should it have b' accepted
13: 7 he hath b' seen of the priest *
De 2: 7 Lord thy God hath b' with thee;
4:32 there hath b' any such thing as 1961
32 or hath b' heard like it?
9: 7 b' rebellious against the Lord. 1961
24 b' rebellious against the Lord from "
15:18 b' worth a double hired servant *
21: 3 which hath not b' wrought with,
31:27 b' rebellious against the Lord; 1961
Jos 7: 7 would to God we had b' content,
9: 4 as if they had b' ambassadors,
10:27 cave wherein they had b' hid, *
23: 9 no man hath b' able to stand *
J'g 16: 8 withs which had not b' dried,
17 for I have b' a Nazarite unto God
Ru 2:11 It hath fully been shewed me,
1Sa 1:13 Eli thought she had b' drunken.
4: 7 not b' such a thing heretofore. 1961
9 Hebrews, as they have b' to you:
17 hath b' also a great slaughter 1961
9:24 hath it b' kept for thee
14:29 how mine eyes have b' enlightened,
30 b' now a much greater slaughter
38 wherein this sin hath b' this 1961
15:21 should have b' utterly destroyed, *
18:19 daughter should have b' given
19: 4 have b' to thee-ward very good:
20:13 as he hath b' with my father. 1961
21: 5 women have b' kept from us
25:28 evil hath not b' found in thee *
34 there had not b' left unto Nabal
29: 3 which hath b' with me these days, 1961
6 Lord liveth, thou hast b' upright,
8 so long as I have b' with thee 1961
2Sa 1:21 he had not b' anointed *
26 pleasant hast thou b' unto me:
12: 8 and if that had b' too little, I
13:20 Amnon thy brother b' with thee? 1961
32 this hath b' determined "
14:32 it had b' good for me *
32 to have b' there still. *
15:34 as I have b' thy father's servant 1961
1Ki 1:37 As the Lord hath b' with my lord "
2:26 because thou hast b' afflicted *
14: 8 hast not b' as my servant David, 1961
16:31 as if it had b' a light thing for him
17: 7 because there had b' no rain in *1961
19:10, 14 have b' very jealous for the Lord
2Ki 4:13 Behold, thou hast b' careful for us
1Ch 17: 8 And I have b' with thee 1961
28: 3 thou hast b' a man of war,
29:25 majesty as had not b' on any king 1961
2Ch 1:12 kings have had that have b' before
15: 3 a long season Israel hath b' without
23: 9 shields, that had b' king David's,
Ezr 2: 1 those which had b' carried away,
4:18 hath b' plainly read before me.
19 and search hath b' made,
19 sedition have b' made therein.
20 There have b' mighty kings also 1934
5:16 now hath it b' in building,
8:35 of those that had b' carried away,*
9: 2 princes and rulers hath b' chief 1961
4 those that had b' carried away: *
7 our fathers have we b' in a great
7 and our priests, b' delivered
8 grace hath b' showed from the Lord
10: 6 of them that had b' carried away.*
8 those that had b' carried away. *
Ne 2: 1 I had not b' beforetime sad in 1961
5:15 governors that had b' before me *
7: 6 of those that had b' carried away,
13:10 portions of the Levites had not b'
Es 2: 6 Who had b' carried away
6 which had b' carried away
12 that she had b' twelve months, 1961
4:11 I have not b' called to come
6: 3 honour and dignity hath b' done
7: 4 if we had b' sold for bondmen
Job 3:13 have lain still and b' quiet,
13 have slept: then had I b' at rest.
16 untimely birth I had not b; 1961
10:19 I should have b' as though "
19 as though I had not b'; "
19 I should have b' carried from
22: 9 arms of the fatherless have b' broken.
31: 9 If mine heart have b' deceived
27 my heart hath b' secretly enticed,
38:17 Have the gates of death b' opened
42:11 that had b' of his acquaintance
Ps 25: 6 for they have b' ever of old.
27: 9 thou hast b' my help: leave me 1961
35:14 as though he had b' my friend
37:25 I have b' young, and now am old; 1961
42: 3 My tears have b' my meat day and "
50: 8 to have b' continually before, *
18 hast b' partakers with adulterers.
59:16 hast b' my defence and refuge in 1961
60: 1 thou hast b' displeased;
61: 3 thou hast b' a shelter for me, 1961
63: 7 Because thou hast b' my help,
69:22 which should have b' for their
73:14 all the day long have I b' plagued,1961
85: 1 Lord, thou hast b' favourable unto
89:38 hast b' wroth with thine anointed.
90: 1 thou hast b' our dwelling place in 1961
94:17 Unless the Lord had b' my help
115:12 The Lord hath b' mindful of us:
119:54 Thy statutes have b' my songs 1961
71 good for me that I have b' afflicted;

Ps 119:92 Unless thy law had b' my delights,
124: 1, 2 If it had not b' the Lord who 1961
143: 3 as those that have b' long dead.
Pr 7:26 many strong men have b' slain *
Ec 1: 9 The thing that hath b', it is that 1961
10 it hath b' already of old time, "
16 than all they that have b' before * "
2:12 which hath b' already done.
3:15 that which hath b' is now; 1961
15 that which is to be hath already b'; "
4: 3 which hath not yet b', "
16 of all that have b' before them: * "
6:10 which hath b' is named already. "
Isa 1: 6 they have not b' closed,
9 we should have b' as Sodom, 1961
9 should have b' like unto Gomorrah.
5: 4 What could have b' done more
17:10 hast not b' mindful of the rock of
23:16 harlot that hast b' forgotten;
25: 4 hast b' a strength to the poor, 1961
26:17 so have we b' in thy sight, O Lord. "
18 We have b' with child,
18 we have b' in pain,
30:24 which hath b' winnowed
38: 9 king of Judah, when he had b' sick,
39: 1 he had heard that he had b' sick,
40:21 hath it not b' told you
43: 4 thou hast b' honourable, and I
22 thou hast b' weary of me, O Israel.
48:18 then had thy peace b' as a river, 1961
19 Thy seed also had b' as the sand,
19 name should not have b' cut off *
49:21 these, where had they b'? *
52:15 which had not b' told them
57:11 And of whom hast thou b' afraid
60:15 thou hast b' forsaken and hated, 1961
66: 2 and all those things have b', * "
Jer 2:31 Have I b' a wilderness unto Israel? "
3: 2 where thou hast not b' lien with.
3 the showers have b' withholden,
3 and there hath b' no latter rain; 1961
4:17 she hath b' rebellious against me,
20:17 mother might have b' my grave, 1961
22:21 b' thy manner since thy youth,
28: 8 prophets that have b' before me 1961
32:31 city hath b' to me as a provocation "
42:18 and my fury hath b' poured
43: 5 whither they had b' driven,
44:18 and have b' consumed by the sword
48:11 Moab hath b' at ease from his youth,
50: 6 My people hath been lost sheep: 1961
29 hath b' proud against the Lord,
51: 5 For Israel hath not b' forsaken, *
7 Babylon hath b' a golden cup in
Eze 2: 5 hath b' a prophet among them. 1961
4:14 my soul hath not b' polluted:
10:10 as if a wheel had b' in the midst 1961
11:17 where ye have b' scattered, and
20:41 wherein ye have b' scattered;
43 wherein ye have b' defiled;
22:13 blood which hath b' in the midst 1961
28:13 Thou hast b' in Eden the garden * "
29: 6 because they have b' a staff of reed "
33:33 that a prophet hath b' among them. "
34:12 where they have b' scattered
38: 8 which have b' always waste: 1961
Da 5:15 have b' brought in before me,
9:12 whole heaven hath not b' done
12 as hath b' done upon Jerusalem.
Hos 5: 1 because ye have b' a snare on 1961
2 though I have b' a rebuker of *
Joe 1: 2 Hath this b' in your days, 1961
2: 2 there hath not b' ever the like, "
Ob 1:16 be as though they had not b'. "
Mic 5: 2 goings forth have b' from of old,
Zep 3:19 they have b' put to shame.
Zec 1: 2 The Lord hath b' sore displeased
Mal 1: 9 this hath b' by your means: 1961
2: 9 but have b' partial in the law.
14 the Lord hath b' witness between
3:13 Your words have b' stout against
M't 1: 6 that had b' the wife of Urias; *
5:31 It hath b' said, *
33 heard that it hath b' said *
38 that it hath b' said, *
43 have heard that it hath b' said, *
11:21 had b' done in Tyre
23 which have b' done in thee,
23 had b' done in Sodom,
13:35 which have b' kept secret *
23:30 b' in the days of our fathers, 2258
30 we would not have b' partakers "
25:21, 23 thou hast b' faithful over a few "
26: 9 might have b' sold for much,
24 it had b' good for that man 2258
24 if he had not b' born.
M'r 5: 4 he had b' often bound
4 chains had b' plucked asunder
18 he that had b' possessed
6:49 they supposed he had b' a spirit, 1511
8: 2 they have now b' with me three 4357
14: 5 It might have b' sold
5 and have b' given to the poor.
21 if he had never b' born.
15:44 whether he had b' any while dead.
16:10 told them that had b' with him, 1096
11 and had b' seen of her, believed
Lu 1: 4 wherein thou hast b' instructed. *
70 which have b' since the world
2:44 supposing him to have b' in the 1511
4:16 where he had b' brought up:
7:10 the servant whole that had b' sick.
8: 2 which had b' healed of evil spirits
10:13 mighty works had b' done
13 which have b' done in you, *
11 ye have not b' faithful in the 1096

Lu 16:12 And if ye have not b' faithful in 1096
19:17 because thou hast b' faithful * "
24:21 trusted that it had b' he which *2076
Joh 5: 6 that he had b' now a long time 2192
9:18 that he had b' blind, and received 2258
11:21, 32 if thou hadst b' here, my
39 for he hath b' dead four days. 2076
12: 1 which had b' dead, whom he *
38 arm of the Lord b' revealed?
14: 9 Have I b' so long time with you, 1510
15:27 because ye have b' with me from 2075
Ac 1:16 must needs have b' fulfilled, *
4:13 that they had b' with Jesus. 2258
16 miracle hath b' done by them
5:26 lest they should have b' stoned,
6:15 it had b' the face of an angel.
7:52 ye have b' now the betrayers 1096
9:18 from his eyes as it had b' scales: *
10:11 as it had b' a great sheet knit *
11: 5 as it had b' a great sheet, let *
13: 1 which had b' brought up *
46 should first have b' spoken *
14:19 city, supposing he had b' dead. *
26 whence they had b' recommended
15: 7 there had b' much disputing, 1096
16:27 that the prisoners had b' fled. *
19:21 After I have b' there, I must also 1096
20:18 what manner I have b' with you * "
23:10 Paul should have b' pulled *
27 and should have b' killed *
24:10 that thou hast b' of many years 5607
19 ought to have b' here before thee, 3918
26 that money should have b' given *
25:14 they had b' there many days, *1304
26:32 This man might have b' set *1096
Ro 6: 5 For if we have b' planted
9:29 we have b' as Sodoma, *1096
29 and b' made like unto Gomorrha.
11:34 or who hath b' his counsellor? 1096
15:22 I have b' much hindered *
27 Gentiles have b' made partakers
16: 2 hath b' a succourer of many, 1096
1Co 1:11 it hath b' declared unto me of you,
12:13 and have b' all made to drink *
2Co 11: 6 but we have b' throughly made
21 as though we had b' weak.
25 a night and a day I have been in 4160
12:11 I ought to have b' commended
Gal 3: 1 Christ had b' evidently set forth, *
21 if there had b' a law given
21 should have b' by the law. 2258
27 as have b' baptized into Christ *
4:15 if it had b' possible, ye would *
5:13 ye have b' called unto liberty; *
Eph 3: 9 of the world had b' hid in God,
4:21 heard him, and have b' taught
Col 1:26 which hath b' hid from ages
2: 7 as ye have b' taught,
4:11 which have b' a comfort unto me. 1096
1Th 2: 6 when we might have b' ‡
2Th 2:15 which ye have b' taught, *
1Ti 5: 9 having b' the wife of one man, 1096
2Ti 3:14 learned and hast b' assured of,
Tit 1: 9 word as he hath b' taught,
Heb 8: 7 first covenant had b' faultless, 2258
7 no place have b' sought for the
11:15 if they had b' mindful,
13: 9 them that hath b' occupied
Ja 3: 7 and hath b' tamed of mankind:
5: 5 pleasures on the earth, and b' *
2Pe 2:21 For it had b' better for them *2258
1Jo 2:19 for if they had b' of us, they
Re 5: 6 stood a lamb as it had b' slain,
17: 2 of the earth have b' made drunk *

Beer (*be'-ur*) See also BAALATH-BEER; BEER-ELIM; BEER-LAHAI-ROI; BEER-SHEBA.
Nu 21:16 from thence they went to *B'*: 876
J'g 9:21 ran away, and fled, and went to *B'*, "

Beera (*be-e'-rah*)
1Ch 7:37 Shilshah, and Ithran, and *B'*. 878

Beerah (*be-e'-rah*)
1Ch 5: 6 *B'* his son, when Tilgath-pilneser 880

Beer-elim (*be''-ur-e'-lim*)
Isa 15: 8 and the howling thereof unto *B'*. 879

Beeri (*be-e'-ri*)
Ge 26:34 the daughter of *B'* the Hittite, 882
Ho 1: 1 Hosea, the son of *B'*, in the days "

Beer-lahai-roi (*be'''-ur-la''-hahe-ro'-e*)
Ge 16:14 Wherefore the well was called *B'*; 883

Beeroth (*be-e'-roth*) See also BEEROTHITE.
De 10: 6 took their journey from *B'* of 881
Jos 9:17 and *B'*, and Kirjath-jearim. "
18:25 Gibeon, and Ramah, and *B'*, "
2Sa 4: 2 *B'* also was reckoned to Benjamin: "
Eze 2:25 Kirjath-arim, Chephirah, and *B'*, "
Neh 7:29 Kirjath-jearim, Chephirah, and *B'*, "

Beerothite (*be-er'-o-thite*) See also BEEROTHITES; BEROTHITE.
2Sa 4: 2 the sons of Rimmon a *B'*, of the 886
5 Rimmon the *B'*, Rechab and "
9 brother, the sons of Rimmon the *B'*, "
23:37 Nahari the *B'*, armourbearer

Beerothites (*be-er'-o-thites*)
2Sa 4: 3 the *B'* fled to Gittaim, and were 886

Beer-sheba (*be-ur'-she-bah*)
Ge 21:14 wandered in the wilderness of *B'*. 884
31 Wherefore he called that place *B'*; "
32 Thus they made a covenant at *B'*: "
33 Abraham planted a grove in *B'*, "
22:19 up and went together to *B'*; and "
19 Abraham dwelt at *B'*. "
26:23 he went up from thence to *B'*. "
33 therefore the name of the city is *B'* "

Ge 28:10 Jacob went out from *B'*, and went 884
46: 1 came to *B'*, and offered sacrifices. "
5 rose up from *B'*: and the sons "
Jos 15:28 Hazar-shual, and *B'*, and "
19: 2 they had in their inheritance *B'*, "
J'g 20: 1 as one man, from Dan even to *B'*, "
1Sa 3:20 all Israel from Dan even to *B'*, "
8: 2 they were judges in *B'*. "
2Sa 3:10 over Judah, from Dan even to *B'*. "
17:11 from Dan even to *B'*, as the sand "
24: 2 of Israel, from Dan even to *B'*, "
7 to the south of Judah even to *B'*. "
15 from Dan even to *B'*, seventy "
1Ki 4:25 even to *B'*, all the days of Solomon. "
19: 3 went for his life, and came to *B'*, "
2Ki 12: 1 his mother's name was Zibiah of *B'*. "
23: 8 from Geba to *B'*, and brake down "
1Ch 4:28 they dwelt at *B'*, and Moladah, "
21: 2 number Israel from *B'* even to Dan; "
2Ch 19: 4 people from *B'* to mount Ephraim, "
24: 1 name also was Zibiah of *B'*. "
30: 5 all Israel, from *B'* even to Dan, "
Ne 11:27 at *B'*, and in the villages thereof, "
30 from *B'* unto the valley of Hinnom. "
Am 5: 5 into Gilgal, and pass not to *B'*: "
8:14 manner of *B'* liveth; even they shall "

bees
De 1:44 you, as *b'* do, and destroyed you 1682
J'g 14: 8 of *b'* and honey in the carcase "
Ps 118:12 They compassed me about like *b'*; "

Beesh-terah (*be-esh'-te-rah*) See also ASHTAROTH.
Jos 21:27 and *B'* with her suburbs; two 1203

beetle
Le 11:22 the *b'* after his kind, and the *2728

beeves
Le 22:19 blemish, of the *b'*, of the sheep, 1241
21 a freewill offering in *b'* or sheep, * "
Nu 31:28 of persons, and of the *b'*, "
30 of the persons, of the *b'*, "
33 threescore and twelve thousand *b'*, "
38 And the *b'* were thirty and six "
44 And thirty and six thousand *b'*, "

befall See also BEFALLEN; BEFALLETH; BEFELL.
Ge 42: 4 peradventure mischief *b'* him. 7122
38 if mischief *b'* him by the way "
44:29 mischief *b'* him, ye shall bring 7136
49: 1 tell you that which shall *b'* you 7122
De 31:17 evils and troubles shall *b'* them; *4672
29 will *b'* you in the latter days; 7122
Ps 91:10 There shall be no evil *b'* thee, 579
Da 10:14 what shall *b'* thy people 7136
Ac 20:22 the things that shall *b'* me. 4876

befallen
Le 10:19 and such things have *b'* me: 7122
Nu 20:14 travel that hath *b'* us: 4672
De 31:21 many evils and troubles are *b'* * "
J'g 6:13 why then is all this *b'* us? "
1Sa 20:26 Something hath *b'* him, he is not 4745
Es 6:13 every thing that had *b'* him. 7136
M't 8:33 *b'* to the possessed of the devils. 4876

befalleth
Ec 3:19 *b'* the sons of men *b'* beasts; 4745
19 even one thing *b'* them: "

befell
Ge 42:29 told him all that *b'* unto them; *7136
Jos 2:23 told him all things that *b'* them: *4672
2Sa 19: 7 evil that *b'* thee from thy youth * 935
M'r 5:16 *b'* to him that was possessed 1096
Ac 20:19 and temptations, which *b'* me by 4819

before See also AFORE; BEFOREHAND; BEFORETIME.
Ge 2: 5 *b'* it was in the earth, and every *2962
5 herb of the field *b'* it grew: * "
6:11 earth also was corrupt *b'* God; 6440
13 flesh is come *b'* me; for the earth "
7: 1 thee have I seen righteous *b'* me "
10: 9 was a mighty hunter *b'* the Lord: "
9 the mighty hunter *b'* the Lord. "
11:28 died *b'* his father Terah *5921, "
12:15 saw her, and commended her *b'* * 413
13: 9 Is not the whole land *b'* thee? 6440
10 *b'* the Lord destroyed Sodom "
13 sinners *b'* the Lord exceedingly. *
17: 1 walk *b'* me, and be thou perfect. 6440
18 that Ishmael might live *b'* thee! "
18: 8 and set it *b'* them; and he stood "
22 Abraham stood yet *b'* the Lord. "
19: 4 But *b'* they lay down, the men of 2962
13 great *b'* the face of the Lord; 854
27 where he stood *b'* the Lord: 854, 6440
20:15 my land is *b'* thee: dwell where it "
23: 3 stood up from *b'* his dead, 5921, "
12 bowed down himself *b'* the "
17 Machpelah, which was *b'* Mamre, "
19 field of Machpelah *b'* Mamre: 5921, "
24: 7 he shall send his angel *b'* thee, "
33 there was set meat *b'* him to eat: "
40 The Lord, *b'* whom I walk, will send "
45 *b'* I had done speaking in mine 2962
51 Behold, Rebekah is *b'* thee, 6440
25: 9 Hittite, which is *b'* Mamre; 5921, "
18 that is *b'* Egypt, as thou goest "
27: 4 my soul may bless thee *b'* I die. 2962
7 bless thee *b'* the Lord *b'* my 6440
10 he may bless thee *b'* his death. "
33 have eaten of all *b'* thou camest, 2962
29:26 give the younger *b'* the firstborn. 6440
30:30 which thou hadst *b'* I came. "
33 for my hire *b'* thy face; "
38 pilled *b'* the flocks in the gutters *5227
39 the flocks conceived *b'* the rods, 413
41 the rods *b'* the eyes of the cattle "
31: 2 was not toward him as *b'*. *8543, 8032

Ge 31: 5 it is not toward me as b'; *8543, 8032
32 b' our brethren discern thou 5048
35 I cannot rise up b' thee; 6440
37 set it here b' my brethren 5048
32: 3 sent messengers b' him to Esau 6440
16 Pass over b' me, and put a space "
17 and whose are these b' thee? "
20 with the present that goeth b' me, "
21 went the present over b' him:5921, "
33: 3 he passed over b' them, and bowed "
12 and I will go b' thee. 5048
14 thee, pass over b' his servant: 6440
14 as the cattle that goeth b' me "
18 and pitched his tent b' the city. 854, "
34:10 and the land shall be b' you; "
36:31 b' there reigned any king over the "
37:18 afar off, even b' he came near 2962
40: 9 a vine was b' me; 6440
41:43 cried b' him, Bow the knee: "
46 stood b' Pharaoh king of Egypt. "
50 born two sons b' the years 2962
42: 6 bowed down themselves b' him *
24 and bound him b' their eyes. "
43: 9 and set him b' thee, then let me 6440
14 give you mercy b' the man, "
15 to Egypt, and stood b' Joseph. "
33 And they sat b' him, the firstborn "
34 messes unto them from b' him: "
44:14 they fell b' him on the ground. "
45: 1 Joseph could not refrain himself b' "
5 did send me b' you to preserve 6440
7 God sent me b' you to preserve "
28 I will go and see him b' I die. 2962
46:28 sent Judah b' him unto Joseph, 6440
47: 6 The land of Egypt is b' thee; "
7 set him b' Pharaoh, and Jacob "
10 and went out b' Pharaoh. * "
19 shall we die b' thine eyes, "
48: 5 b' I came unto thee into Egypt, 5704
15 said, God, b' whom my fathers 6440
20 and he set Ephraim b' Manasseh. "
49: 8 shall bow down b' thee. "
30 Machpelah, which is b' Mamre5921,6440
50:13 of Ephron the Hittite, b' Mamre." "
16 father did command b' he died, "
18 went and fell down b' his face; "
Ex 4: 3 and Moses fled from b' it. 6440
21 do all those wonders b' Pharaoh, "
6:12 Moses spake b' the Lord, saying, "
30 Moses said b' the Lord, Behold, "
7: 9 thy rod, and cast it b' Pharaoh, "
10 cast down his rod b' Pharaoh, "
10 and b' his servants, "
8:20 morning, and stand b' Pharaoh; "
26 of the Egyptians b' their eyes, "
9:10 furnace and stood b' Pharaoh; 6440
11 magicians could not stand b' Moses "
13 morning, and stand b' Pharaoh, "
10: 1 shew these my signs b' him: *7130
3 refuse to humble thyself b' me? 6440
10 look to it; for evil is b' you. "
14 b' them there were no such "
11:10 did all these wonders b' Pharaoh: "
12:34 their dough b' it was leavened, 2962
13:21 the Lord went b' them by day 6440
22 fire by night, from b' the people. "
14: 2 encamp b' Pi-hahiroth, between "
2 b' it shall ye encamp by the sea. 5226
9 Pi-hahiroth, b' Baal-zephon. 6440
19 angel of God, which went b' the "
19 pillar of cloud went from b' their "
16: 9 Come near b' the Lord: for he "
33 lay it up b' the Lord, to be kept "
34 laid it up b' the Testimony, to be "
17: 5 Go on b' the people, and take "
6 I will stand b' thee there upon the "
18:12 bread with Moses' father-in-law b' "
19: 2 there Israel camped b' the mount. 5048
7 and laid b' their faces "
20: 3 shalt have no other gods b' me.5921,6440
20 his fear may be b' your faces, 5921
21: 1 judgments which thou shalt set b' 6440
22: 9 parties shall come b' the judges; 5703
23:15 none shall appear b' me empty: 6440
17 males shall appear b' the Lord413, "
20 I send an Angel b' thee to keep "
23 mine Angel shall go b' thee, "
27 I will send my fear b' thee, and "
28 I will send hornets b' thee, which "
28 and the Hittite, from b' thee, "
29 not drive them out from b' thee "
30 I will drive them out from b' thee, "
31 thou shalt drive them out b' thee. "
25:30 the table shewbread b' me alway "
27:21 without the vail, which is b' the 5921
21 evening to morning b' the Lord: 6440
28:12 shall bear their names b' the Lord "
25 of the ephod b' it, *434,4136, "
29 for a memorial b' the Lord "
30 when he goeth in b' the Lord: "
30 his heart b' the Lord continually. "
35 unto the holy place b' the Lord, "
38 they may be accepted b' the Lord. "
29:10 to be brought b' the tabernacle "
11 kill the bullock b' the Lord, "
23 unleavened bread that is b' the "
24 a wave offering b' the Lord. "
25 for a sweet savour b' the Lord: "
26 a wave offering b' the Lord: "
42 the congregation b' the Lord: "
30: 6 b' the vail that is by the ark of "
6 the testimony, b' the mercy seat "
8 incense b' the Lord throughout "
16 children of Israel b' the Lord, "
36 b' the testimony in the tabernacle "

Ex 32: 1 make us gods, which shall go b' us; 6440
5 he built an altar b' it; and Aaron "
23 shall go b' us: for as for this "
34 behold, mine Angel shall go b' thee: "
33: 2 I will send an angel b' thee; "
19 my goodness pass b' thee, and5921, "
19 the name of the Lord b' thee; "
34: 3 nor herds feed b' that mount. 413, 4136
6 the Lord passed by b' him, 5921, 6440
10 a covenant: b' all thy people 5048
11 I drive out b' thee the Amorite, 6440
20 none shall appear b' me empty. "
23 your menchildren appear b' the "
24 I will cast out the nations b' thee, "
24 go up to appear b' the Lord 413, "
34 when Moses went in b' the Lord "
39:18 of the ephod, b' it. *413, 4136, "
40: 5 b' the ark of the testimony, "
6 b' the door of the tabernacle "
23 in order upon it b' the Lord; "
25 he lighted the lamps b' the Lord; "
26 b' the vail: "
Le 1: 3 of the congregation b' the Lord. "
5 shall kill the bullock b' the Lord: "
11 the altar northward b' the Lord: "
3: 1 it without blemish b' the Lord. "
7 shall he offer it b' the Lord. "
8 and kill it b' the tabernacle "
12 then shall he offer it b' the Lord. "
13 kill it b' the tabernacle "
4: 4 the congregation b' the Lord; "
4 kill the bullock b' the Lord. "
6 blood seven times b' the Lord, "
6 b' the vail of the sanctuary "
7 incense b' the Lord, which is in "
14 bring him b' the tabernacle of the "
15 head of the bullock b' the Lord: "
15 bullock shall be killed b' the Lord. "
17 sprinkle it seven times b' the Lord, "
17 even b' the vail. "
18 the altar which is b' the Lord, "
24 kill the burnt offering b' the Lord: "
6: 7 an atonement for him b' the Lord: "
14 offer it b' the Lord, b' the altar. "
25 shall be killed b' the Lord: "
7:30 for a wave offering b' the Lord. "
8:26 bread that was b' the Lord, "
27 them for a wave offering b' the "
29 it for a wave offering b' the Lord: "
9: 2 blemish, and offer them b' the Lord. "
4 offerings, to sacrifice b' the Lord; "
5 b' the tabernacle of the 413, "
5 near and stood b' the Lord. "
21 for a wave offering b' the Lord; "
24 there came a fire out from b' "
10: 1 offered strange fire b' the Lord, "
2 them, and they died b' the Lord. "
3 b' all the people I will be 5921, "
4 near, carry your brethren from b' "
15 for a wave offering b' the Lord; "
17 atonement for them b' the Lord? "
19 their burnt offering b' the Lord; "
12: 7 Who shall offer it b' the Lord, "
14:11 clean, and those things, b' the Lord, "
12 for a wave offering b' the Lord: "
16 his finger seven times b' the Lord: "
18 an atonement for him b' the Lord. "
23 of the congregation, b' the Lord. "
24 for a wave offering b' the Lord: "
27 left hand seven times b' the Lord: "
29 an atonement for him b' the Lord. "
31 is to be cleansed b' the Lord. "
36 they empty the house, b' the priest2962
15:14 come b' the Lord unto the door 6440
15 him b' the Lord for his issue. "
30 an atonement for her b' the Lord "
16: 1 they offered b' the Lord, and died; "
2 the vail b' the mercy seat, 413, "
7 present them b' the Lord at the "
10 be presented alive b' the Lord, "
12 from off the altar b' the Lord, "
13 incense upon the fire b' the Lord, "
14 eastward; and b' the mercy seat "
15 seat, and b' the mercy seat: "
18 that is b' the Lord, and make "
30 from all your sins b' the Lord. "
17: 4 b' the tabernacle of the "
18:23 neither shall any woman stand b' "
24 defiled which I cast out b' you: * "
27 which were b' you, and the land "
28 the nations that were b' you. "
30 which were committed b' you, "
19:14 put a stumblingblock b' the blind, "
22 trespass offering b' the Lord for "
32 shalt rise up b' the hoary head, "
20:23 nation, which I cast out b' you: "
23:11 wave the sheaf b' the Lord, "
20 for a wave offering b' the Lord, "
28 for you b' the Lord your God. "
40 rejoice b' the Lord your God "
24: 3 morning b' the Lord continually: "
4 pure candlestick b' the Lord "
6 upon the pure table b' the Lord. "
8 in order b' the Lord continually, "
26: 7 they shall fall b' you by the sword. "
8 your enemies shall fall b' you "
17 ye shall be slain b' your enemies: "
37 as it were b' a sword, when none "
37 no power to stand b' your enemies. "
27: 8 shall present himself b' the priest, "
11 present the beast b' the priest: "
Nu 3: 4 died b' the Lord, when they offered "
4 strange fire b' the Lord, "
6 present them b' Aaron the priest, "
7 b' the tabernacle of the "

Nu 3:38 b' the tabernacle toward the east, 6440
38 even b' the tabernacle of the "
5:16 near, and set her b' the Lord: "
18 set the woman b' the Lord, and "
25 wave the offering b' the Lord, "
30 the woman b' the Lord, "
6:12 days that were b' shall be lost, *7223
16 priest shall bring them b' the Lord, 6440
20 for a wave offering b' the Lord: "
7: 3 brought their offering b' the Lord, "
3 brought them b' the tabernacle. "
10 offered their offering b' the altar. "
8: 9 b' the tabernacle of the "
10 bring the Levites b' the Lord: "
11 shall offer the Levites b' the Lord "
13 set the Levites b' Aaron, and b' "
21 them as an offering b' the Lord; "
22 congregation b' Aaron, and b' his "
9: 6 they came b' Moses and b' Aaron "
10: 9 b' the Lord your God, and ye shall "
10 memorial b' your God: I am the "
33 the Lord went b' them in the three "
35 let them that hate thee flee b' thee. "
11: 6 beside this manna, b' our eyes. *
20 and have wept b' him, saying, 6440
13:22 Hebron was built seven years b' "
30 Caleb stilled the people b' Moses, 413
14: 5 Aaron fell on their faces b' all 6440
10 of the congregation b' all the * 413
14 thou goest b' them, by day time 6440
37 died by the plague b' the Lord. "
42 be not smitten b' your enemies. "
43 the Canaanites are there b' you, "
15:15 shall the stranger be b' the Lord. "
25 their sin offering b' the Lord for "
28 sinneth by ignorance b' the Lord, "
16: 2 they rose up b' Moses, with certain "
7 in them b' the Lord to morrow: "
9 b' the congregation to minister "
16 b' the Lord, thou, and they, "
17 bring ye b' the Lord every man "
38 for they offered them b' the Lord, "
40 near to offer incense b' the Lord; "
43 Moses and Aaron came b' the *413, "
17: 4 b' the testimony, where I will meet "
7 laid up the rods b' the Lord "
9 the rods from b' the Lord unto all "
10 again b' the testimony, to be kept "
18: 2 minister b' the tabernacle of "
19 for ever b' the Lord unto thee "
19: 3 one shall slay her b' his face: "
4 blood directly b' the tabernacle * "
20: 3 our brethren died b' the Lord! "
8 speak ye unto the rock b' their eyes; "
9 Moses took the rod from b' the 6440
10 congregation together b'...rock,413, "
21:11 wilderness which is b' Moab,5921, "
22:32 thy way is perverse b' me: 5048
25: 4 hang them up b' the Lord against *
6 Who were weeping b' the door *
26:61 offered strange fire b' the Lord. 6440
27: 2 And they stood b' Moses, "
2 and b' Eleazar the priest, "
2 and b' the princes "
5 brought their cause b' the Lord. "
14 sanctify me at the water b' their "
17 Which may go out b' them, 6440
17 and which may go in b' them, "
19 b' Eleazar the priest, and b' all "
21 And he shall stand b' Eleazar the "
21 of Urim b' the Lord: "
22 b' Eleazar the priest, and b' all "
31:50 atonement for our souls b' the Lord. "
54 children of Israel b' the Lord. "
32: 4 smote b' the congregation of Israel, "
17 b' the children of Israel, until we "
20 armed b' the Lord to war, "
21 over Jordan b' the Lord, until he "
21 driven out his enemies from b' him, "
22 the land be subdued b' the Lord: 6440
22 guiltless b' the Lord, and b' Israel;*
22 be your possession b' the Lord. 6440
27 b' the Lord to battle, as my lord "
29 to battle, b' the Lord, "
29 the land shall be subdued b' you; "
32 pass over armed b' the Lord "
33: 7 b' Baal-zephon: 5921, "
7 and they pitched b' Migdol. "
8 they departed from b' Pi-hahiroth, "
47 the mountains of Abarim, b' Nebo. "
52 inhabitants of the land from b' you, "
55 the inhabitants of the land from b' "
35:12 until he stand b' the congregation "
36: 1 and spake b' Moses, and b' the "
De 1: 8 I have set the land b' you: "
21 thy God hath set the land b' thee: "
22 We will send men b' us, and they "
30 your God which goeth b' you, "
30 did for you in Egypt b' your eyes; "
33 Who went in the way b' you, 6440
38 son of Nun, which standeth b' thee, "
42 lest ye be smitten b' your enemies. "
45 ye returned and wept b' the Lord; "
2:12 had destroyed them from b' them, "
21 the Lord destroyed them b' them; "
22 destroyed the Horims from b' them; "
31 to give Sihon and his land b' thee: "
33 Lord our God delivered him b' us; "
3:18 pass over armed b' your brethren "
28 he shall go over b' this people, "
4: 8 this law, which I set b' you "
10 thou stoodest b' the Lord thy God "
32 which were b' thee, since the day "
34 did for you in Egypt b' your eyes? "
38 To drive out nations from b' thee 6440

De 4:44 Moses set b' the children of Israel: 6440
5: 7 have none other gods b' me. 5921, "
6:19 all thine enemies from b' thee, "
22 all his household, b' our eyes: "
25 b' the Lord our God, as he hath 6440
7: 1 hath cast out many nations b' thee, "
2 God shall deliver them b' thee; "
22 put out those nations b' thee little "
24 no man be able to stand b' thee, "
8:20 the Lord destroyeth b' your face, "
9: 2 Who can stand b' the children of 6440
3 is he which goeth over b' thee; "
3 shall bring them down b' thy face: "
4 cast them out from b' thee, 6440
4 drive them out from b' thee. "
5 doth drive them out from b' thee, "
17 and brake them b' your eyes. "
18 And I fell down b' the Lord, 6440
25 Thus I fell down b' the Lord "
10: 8 of the Lord, to stand b' the Lord "
11 take thy journey b' the people, "
11:23 all these nations from b' you, "
25 no man be able to stand b' you: "
26 I set b' you this day a blessing "
32 which I set b' you this day. "
12: 7 there ye shall eat b' the Lord "
12 And ye shall rejoice b' the Lord "
18 thou must eat them b' the Lord "
18 thou shalt rejoice b' the Lord "
29 cut off the nations from b' thee, "
30 that they be destroyed from b' thee; "
14:23 thou shalt eat b' the Lord thy God, "
26 thou shalt eat there b' the Lord "
15:20 Thou shalt eat it b' the Lord "
16:11 thou shalt rejoice b' the Lord "
16 all thy males appear b' the Lord 854, "
16 they shall not appear b' the Lord "
17:12 to minister there b' the Lord 854
18 that which is b' the priests 6440
18: 7 which stand there b' the Lord. "
12 drive them out from b' thee. "
19:17 shall stand b' the Lord, "
17 b' the priests and the judges, "
21:16 firstborn b' the son of the hated, "
22: 6 a bird's nest chance to be b' thee "
17 cloth b' the elders of the city. "
23:14 to give up thine enemies b' thee; "
24: 4 that is abomination b' the Lord: "
13 unto thee b' the Lord thy God. "
25: 2 to be beaten b' his face, "
26: 4 b' the altar of the Lord thy God. 6440
5 shalt speak and say b' the Lord "
10 set it b' the Lord thy God, "
10 and worship b' the Lord thy God: "
13 shalt say b' the Lord thy God, "
27: 7 and rejoice b' the Lord thy God. "
28: 7 thee to be smitten b' thy face: "
7 and flee b' thee seven ways. 6440
25 to be smitten b' thine enemies: "
25 and flee seven ways b' them: "
31 ox shall be slain b' thine eyes, "
31 taken away from b' thy face, "
66 life shall hang in doubt b' thee; 5048
29: 2 all that the Lord did b' your eyes "
10 all of you b' the Lord your God; 6440
15 this day b' the Lord our God, "
30: 1 curse, which I have set b' thee, "
15 I have set b' thee this day "
19 I have set b' you life and death, "
31: 3 he will go over b' thee, and he will "
3 destroy these nations from b' thee, "
3 Joshua, he shall go over b' thee, "
5 shall give them up b' your face, "
8 he it is that doth go b' thee; 6440
11 is come to appear b' the Lord 854, "
11 read this law b' all Israel 5048
21 now, b' I have brought them 2962
32:52 thou shalt see the land b' thee; 5048
33: 1 the children of Israel b' his death. 6440
10 shall put incense b' thee, and 639
27 thrust out the enemy from b' thee; 6440
Jos 1: 5 any man be able to stand b' thee "
14 ye shall pass b' your brethren "
2: 8 And b' they were laid down, 2962
3: 1 lodged there b' they passed over. "
6 and pass over b' the people. 6440
6 covenant, and went b' the people. "
10 without fail drive out from b' you "
11 the earth passeth over b' you "
14 of the covenant b' the people; "
4: 5 Pass over b' the ark of the Lord "
7 b' the ark of the covenant "
12 armed b' the children of Israel, "
13 passed over b' the Lord unto "
18 all his banks, as they did b'. *8543, 8032
23 the waters of Jordan from b' you, 6440
23 which he dried up from b' us, "
5: 1 from b' the children of Israel, "
6: 4 seven priests shall bear b' the ark "
5 up every man straight b' him. 5048
6 horns b' the ark of the Lord. 6440
7 pass on b' the ark of the Lord. "
8 horns passed on b' the Lord, "
9 the armed men went b' the priests "
13 rams' horns b' the ark of the Lord "
13 the armed men went b' them; "
20 every man straight b' him, 5048
26 Cursed be the man b' the Lord. 6440
7: 4 they fled b' the men of Ai. "
5 b' the gate even unto Shebarim, "
6 upon his face b' the ark "
8 their backs b' their enemies! "
12 could not stand b' their enemies, "
12 but turned their backs b' their "
13 canst not stand b' thine enemies, "
23 and laid them out b' the Lord. "

Jos 8: 5 first, that we will flee b' them, 6440
6 They flee b' us, as at the first: "
6 therefore we will flee b' them. "
10 of Israel, b' the people to Ai. "
11 drew nigh, and came b' the city, 5048
14 a time appointed, b' the plain; 6440
15 made as if they were beaten b' "
33 and on that side b' the priests 5048
33 had commanded b', that they †7223
35 which Joshua read not b' all 5048
9:24 of the land from b' you, 6440
10: 5 and encamped b' Gibeon: *5921
8 not a man of them stand b' thee. 6440
10 Lord discomfited them b' Israel, "
11 as they fled from b' Israel, "
12 Amorites b' the children of Israel, "
14 no day like that b' it or after it, "
11: 6 deliver them up all slain b' Israel: "
13: 3 Sihor, which is b' Egypt, 5921, "
6 drive out from b' the children "
25 Aroer that is b' Rabbah; 5921, "
14:15 of Hebron b' was Kirjath-arba; * "
15: 7 b' the going up to Adummim, *5227
8 that lieth b' the valley 5921, 6440
15 of Debir b' was Kirjath-sepher. * "
17: 4 came near b' Eleazar the priest, "
4 and b' Joshua the son of Nun, "
4 and b' the princes, "
7 that lieth b' Shechem; 5921 "
18: 1 the land was subdued b' them. "
6 cast lots for you here b' the Lord "
8 for you b' the Lord in Shiloh. "
10 for them in Shiloh b' the Lord: "
14 hill that lieth b' Beth-horon 5921, "
16 b' the valley of the son of " "
19:11 the river that is b' Jokneam; " "
46 the border b' Japho. *4136
51 by lot in Shiloh b' the Lord, 6440
20: 6 he stand b' the congregation "
9 he stood b' the congregation. "
21:44 of all their enemies b' them; "
22:27 do the service of the Lord b' him "
29 Lord our God that is b' his "
23: 5 shall expel them from b' you, "
9 Lord hath driven out from b' you "
9 hath been able to stand b' you "
13 any of these nations from b' you; * "
24: 1 they presented themselves b' God. "
8 I destroyed them from b' you. "
12 I sent the hornet b' you, which "
12 drave them out from b' you, "
18 the Lord drave out from b' us "
J'g 1:10 now the name of Hebron b' was * "
11 and the name of Debir b' * "
23 the name of the city b' was Luz.) * "
2: 3 not drive them out from b' you; "
14 any longer stand b' their enemies. "
21 drive out any from b' them of the "
3: 2 such as b' knew nothing thereof; * "
27 from the mount, and he b' them. "
4:14 not the Lord gone out b' thee? "
15 the edge of the sword b' Barak; "
23 Canaan b' the children of Israel. "
5: 5 mountains melted from b' the * "
5 even that Sinai from b' the Lord * "
6: 9 drave them out from b' you, "
18 my present, and set it b' thee. "
7:24 take b' them the waters "
8:13 from battle b' the sun was up, *4608
28 Midian subdued b' the children 6440
9:39 Gaal went out b' the men of "
40 chased him and he fled b' him, "
11: 9 the Lord deliver them b' me, "
11 Jephthah uttered all his words b' "
23 from b' his people Israel, "
24 God shall drive out from b' us, "
33 subdued b' the children of Israel. "
12: 5 of Jordan b' the Ephraimites: * "
14:16 Sampson's wife wept b' him, 5921
17 she wept b' him the seven days, "
18 seventh day b' the sun went down, 2962
16: 3 of an hill that is b' Hebron. 5921, 6440
20 as at other times b', and shake *6471
18: 6 b' the Lord is your way wherein 5227
21 cattle and the carriage b' them. 6440
20:23 and wept b' the Lord until even, "
26 and sat there b' the Lord, "
26 and peace offerings b' the Lord. "
28 Aaron, stood b' it in those days,) "
32 They are smitten down b' us, "
35 the Lord smote Benjamin b' Israel: "
39 they are smitten down b' us, "
42 turned their backs b' the men of "
21: 2 abode there till even b' God, "
Ru 3:14 she rose up b' one could know 2958
4: 4 Buy it b' the inhabitants, 5048
4 and b' the elders of my people. "
1Sa 1:12 continued praying b' the Lord, 6440
15 poured out my soul b' the Lord. "
19 and worshipped b' the Lord, "
22 that he may appear b' the Lord, 854, "
2:11 the Lord b' Eli the priest. " "
15 b' they burnt the fat, the priest's 2962
17 was very great b' the Lord: 854, 6440
18 Samuel ministered b' the "
21 child Samuel grew b' the Lord. 5973
28 incense, to wear an ephod b' me? 6440
30 of thy father, should walk b' me "
35 he shall walk b' mine anointed "
3: 1 ministered unto the Lord b' "
4: 2 was smitten b' the Philistines: "
3 us to day b' the Philistines? "
17 Israel is fled b' the Philistines, "
5: 3 to the earth b' the ark of the Lord. "
4 ground b' the ark of the Lord; "
6:20 is able to stand b' this holy Lord "

1Sa 7: 6 drew water; and poured it out b' 6440
10 and they were smitten b' Israel. "
8:11 some shall run b' his chariots. "
20 may judge us, and go out b' us, "
9:12 He is; behold, he is b' you: "
13 find him, b' he go up to the high 2962
15 a day b' Saul came, saying, 6440
19 go up b' me unto the high place; "
24 and set it b' Saul. And Samuel "
24 is left! set it b' thee, and eat: "
27 Bid the servant pass on b' us, "
10: 5 and a pipe, and a harp, b' them; "
8 shalt go down b' me to Gilgal; "
19 present yourselves b' the Lord "
25 book, and laid it up b' the Lord. "
11:15 they made Saul king b' the Lord "
15 of peace offerings b' the Lord; "
12: 2 the king walketh b' you: and I am "
2 I have walked b' you from my "
3 witness against me b' the Lord, 5048
3 the Lord, and b' his anointed: "
7 may reason with you b' the Lord 6440
16 the Lord will do b' your eyes. "
14:13 him: and they fell b' Jonathan; 6440
21 the Philistines b' that time, *865
15:30 thee, b' the elders of my people, 5048
30 and b' Israel, and turn again "
33 hewed Agag in pieces b' the Lord, 6440
16: 6 the Lord's anointed is b' him. 5048
8 made him pass b' Samuel. 6440
10 made seven of his sons to pass b' "
16 thy servants, which are b' thee, "
21 came to Saul, and stood b' him: "
22 Let David, I pray thee, stand b' me; "
17: 7 one bearing a shield went b' him. "
31 they rehearsed them b' Saul: "
41 that bare the shield went b' him. "
57 brought him b' Saul with the head "
18:13 out and came in b' the people. "
16 he went out and came in b' them. "
19:24 prophesied b' Samuel in like "
20: 1 and came and said b' Jonathan, "
1 what is my sin b' thy father, "
21: 6 was taken from b' the Lord, "
7 that day, detained b' the Lord; "
13 he changed his behaviour b' them, 5869
22: 4 he brought them b' the king 854, 6440
23:18 made a covenant b' the Lord: "
24 arose and went to Ziph b' Saul: "
25:19 Go on b' me; behold, I come after "
23 fell b' David on her face, 639
26: 1 which is b' Jeshimon? 5921, 6440
3 which is b' Jeshimon, by the " "
19 cursed be they b' the Lord; "
20 fall to the earth b' the face of the *5048
28:22 me set a morsel of bread b' thee; 6440
25 And she brought it b' Saul, "
25 and b' his servants; "
30:20 they drave b' those other cattle, "
31: 1 Israel fled from b' the Philistines, "
2Sa 2:14 men now arise, and play b' us. "
17 of Israel, b' the servants of David. "
24 Ammah, that lieth b' Giah 5921, 6440
3:28 are guiltless b' the Lord 5973
31 sackcloth, and mourn b' Abner. 6440
34 as a man falleth b' wicked men, "
5: 3 with them in Hebron b' the Lord: "
20 forth upon mine enemies b' me, "
24 the Lord go out b' thee, to smite "
6: 4 and Ahio went b' the ark. "
5 played b' the Lord on all manner "
14 David danced b' the Lord with all "
16 leaping and dancing b' the Lord; "
17 and peace offerings b' the Lord. "
21 It was b' the Lord, which chose * "
21 which chose me b' thy father * "
21 and b' all his house, "
21 therefore will I play b' the Lord. 6440
7:15 Saul, whom I put away b' thee. "
16 be established forever b' thee: "
18 and sat b' the Lord, and he said, "
23 for thy land, b' thy people, "
26 David be established b' thee. "
29 it may continue for ever b' thee: "
10: 6 that they stank b' David, * "
9 was against him b' and behind, 6440
13 the Syrians: and they fled b' him. "
14 fled they also b' Abishai, and "
15 were smitten b' Israel, they "
16 host of Hadarezer went b' them. * "
18 And the Syrians fled b' Israel; "
19 they were smitten b' Israel, they "
11:13 he did eat and drink b' him; "
12:11 I will take thy wives b' thine eyes, "
12 I will do this thing b' all Israel, 5048
12 and b' the sun. "
20 they set bread b' him, "
13: 9 pan and poured them out b' him; 6440
14:33 face to the ground b' the king: "
15: 1 and fifty men to run b' him. "
18 from Gath, passed...b' the king. 5921, "
18: 7 the people of Israel were slain b' "
28 upon his face b' the king, "
19: 8 all the people came b' the king: 6440
13 captain of the host b' me "
17 went over Jordan b' the king. * "
18 fell down b' the king, as he was "
20: 8 in Gibeon, Amasa went b' them. * "
21: 9 them in the hill b' the Lord: "
22:13 Through the brightness b' him 5048
23 his judgments were b' me: "
24 I was also upright b' him, *
24:13 wilt thou flee three months b' 6440
20 and bowed himself b' the king "
1Ki 1: 2 let her stand b' the king, and let 6440
5 and fifty men to run b' him. "

1Ki 1:23 when he was come in *b'* the king, 6440
25 behold, they eat and drink *b'* him, "
28 king's presence, and stood *b'* the "
32 And they came *b'* the king. "
2: 4 heed to their way, to walk *b'* me "
26 the ark of the Lord God *b'* David "
45 shall be established *b'* the Lord "
3: 6 according as he walked *b'* thee "
12 there was none like thee *b'* thee, "
15 stood *b'* the ark of the covenant "
16 unto the king, and stood *b'* him. "
22 Thus they spake *b'* the king. "
24 they brought a sword *b'* the king. "
6: 3 *b'* the temple of the house, 5921, "
3 was the breadth thereof *b'* "
7 ready *b'* it was brought thither: *4551
17 the temple *b'* it, was forty cubits 3942
21 *b'* the oracle; and he overlaid it 6440
7: 6 the porch was *b'* them: and the 5921, "
6 and the thick beam were *b'* them "
49 left, *b'* the oracle, with the "
8: 5 *b'* the ark, sacrificing sheep and "
8 in the holy place *b'* the oracle, 5921, "
22 stood *b'* the altar of the Lord "
23 thy servants that walk *b'* thee "
25 that they walk *b'* me as thou "
25 hast walked *b'* me. "
28 servant prayeth *b'* thee to day: "
31 come *b'* thine altar in this house: "
33 people Israel be smitten down *b'* "
50 *b'* them who carried them captive, "
54 from *b'* the altar of the Lord, "
59 made supplication *b'* the Lord, "
62 Israel with him offered sacrifice *b'* "
64 that was *b'* the house of the Lord: "
64 brasen altar that was *b'* the Lord "
65 *b'* the Lord our God, seven days "
9: 3 that thou hast made *b'* me: "
4 if thou wilt walk *b'* me, as David "
6 statutes which I have set *b'* you, "
25 the altar that was *b'* the Lord. "
10: 8 which stand continually *b'* thee, "
11: 7 the hill that is *b'* Jerusalem, 5921, "
36 a light alway *b'* me in Jerusalem, "
12: 6 men, that stood *b'* Solomon 854, "
8 him, and which stood *b'* him: "
30 people went to worship *b'* the one, "
13: 6 again, and became as it was *b'*. 7223
14: 9 evil above all that were *b'* thee: 6440
24 cast out *b'* the children of Israel. "
15: 3 father which he had done *b'* him: "
16:25 worse than all that were *b'* him. "
30 above all that were *b'* him. "
33 kings of Israel that were *b'* him. "
17: 1 of Israel liveth, *b'* whom I stand, "
3 Cherith, that is *b'* Jordan. 5921, "
5 Cherith, that is *b'* Jordan. "
18:15 liveth, *b'* whom I stand, I will "
46 ran *b'* Ahab to the entrance "
19:11 stand upon the mount *b'* the Lord. "
11 in pieces the rocks *b'* the Lord; "
19 with twelve yoke of oxen *b'* him, "
20:27 Israel pitched *b'* them like 5048
21:10 sons of Belial, *b'* him, to bear "
13 and sat *b'* him: "
26 cast out *b'* the children of Israel. 6440
29 how Ahab humbleth himself *b'* me? "
29 he humbleth himself *b'* me, "
22:10 the prophets prophesied *b'* them. "
21 came forth a spirit, and stood *b'* "
2Ki 1:13 and fell on his knees *b'* Elijah, 5048
2: 9 do for thee, *b'* I be taken away 2962
15 themselves to the ground *b'* him. "
3:14 *b'* whom I stand, surely, were it 6440
24 so that they fled *b'* them: "
4:12 had called her, she stood *b'* him. "
31 Gehazi passed on *b'* them, and laid "
38 the prophets were sitting *b'* him: "
43 I set this *b'* an hundred men? "
44 So he set it *b'* them, and they "
5:15 and came, and stood *b'* him: "
16 the Lord liveth, *b'* whom I stand, "
23 and they bare them *b'* him. "
25 and stood *b'* his master. 413
6:22 set bread and water *b'* them, 6440
32 the king sent a man from *b'* him: "
8: 9 and came and stood *b'* him, and "
10: 4 Behold, two kings stood not *b'* him: "
11:18 the priest of Baal *b'* the altars. "
14:12 was put to the worse *b'* Israel; "
15:10 and smote him *b'* the people, 6905
16: 3 cast out from *b'* the children 6440
14 altar, which was *b'* the Lord, "
17: 2 kings of Israel that were *b'* him. "
8 out from *b'* the children of Israel, "
11 the Lord carried away *b'* them; "
18: 5 Judah, nor any that were *b'* him. "
22 Ye shall worship *b'* this altar in "
19:14 Lord, and spread it *b'* the Lord. "
15 Hezekiah prayed *b'* the Lord, "
26 corn blasted *b'* it be grown up. "
32 nor come *b'* it with shield, nor 6924
20: 3 I have walked *b'* thee in truth 6440
21: 2 cast out *b'* the children of Israel. "
9 destroyed *b'* the children of Israel. "
11 Amorites did, which were *b'* him, "
22:10 And Shaphan read it *b'* the king. "
19 hast humbled thyself *b'* the Lord, "
19 rent thy clothes, and wept *b'* me; "
23: 3 made a covenant *b'* the Lord, "
13 that were *b'* Jerusalem, 5921, "
25 unto him was there no king *b'* him, "
25: 7 sons of Zedekiah *b'* his eyes, "
29 did eat bread continually *b'* him 6440
1Ch 1:43 of Edom *b'* any king reigned over "
5:25 land whom God destroyed *b'* them. "

1Ch 6:32 they ministered *b'* the dwelling 6440
10: 1 Israel fled from *b'* the Philistines, "
11: 3 with them in Hebron *b'* the Lord; "
13 people fled from *b'* the Philistines. "
13: 8 David and all Israel played *b'* God "
10 the ark: and there he died *b'* God. "
14:15 God is gone forth *b'* thee to smite "
15:24 the trumpets *b'* the ark of God: "
16: 1 and peace offerings *b'* God. "
4 to minister *b'* the ark of the Lord, "
6 *b'* the ark of the covenant of God. "
29 an offering, and come *b'* him: "
30 Fear *b'* him, all the earth: the "
37 there *b'* the ark of the covenant "
37 to minister *b'* the ark continually, "
39 *b'* the tabernacle of the Lord "
17: 8 off all thine enemies from *b'* thee, "
13 it from him that was *b'* thee: "
16 the king came and sat *b'* the Lord, "
21 out nations from *b'* thy people, "
24 thy servant be established *b'* thee. "
25 found in his heart to pray *b'* thee. "
27 that it may be *b'* thee for ever: "
19: 7 who came and pitched *b'* Medeba. "
9 the battle in array *b'* the gate *
10 was set against him *b'* and behind, 6440
14 *b'* the Syrians unto the battle; "
14 and they fled *b'* him. "
15 likewise fled *b'* Abishai his brother, "
16 put to the worse *b'* Israel, "
16 host of Hadarezer went *b'* them. "
18 Syrians fled *b'* Israel; and David "
19 put to the worse *b'* Israel, they "
21:12 to be destroyed *b'* thy foes, while "
30 not go *b'* it to enquire of God: "
22: 5 prepared abundantly *b'* his death. "
18 the land is subdued *b'* the Lord, "
18 and *b'* his people. "
23:13 to burn incense *b'* the Lord, to "
31 unto them continually *b'* the Lord: "
24: 2 and Abihu died *b'* their father, "
6 wrote them *b'* the king, *
6 and *b'* the chief of the fathers *
28: 4 chose me *b'* all the house *
29:10 the Lord *b'* all the congregation: 5869
15 strangers *b'* thee, and sojourners 6440
22 And did eat and drink *b'* the Lord "
25 been on any king *b'* him in Israel. "
2Ch 1: 5 *b'* the tabernacle of the Lord: "
6 to the brasen altar *b'* the Lord, "
10 go out and come in *b'* this people: "
12 have had that have been *b'* thee, "
13 from *b'* the tabernacle of the "
2: 4 and to burn *b'* him sweet incense, "
6 save only to burn sacrifice *b'* him? "
3:15 he made *b'* the house two pillars "
17 up the pillars *b'* the temple, 5921, "
4:20 after the manner *b'* the oracle, "
5: 6 assembled unto him *b'* the ark, "
9 seen from the ark *b'* the oracle; 5921, "
6:12 he stood *b'* the altar of the Lord "
13 down upon his knees *b'* all 5048
14 thy servants, that walk *b'* thee 6440
16 my law as thou hast walked *b'* me. "
19 which thy servant prayeth *b'* thee: "
22 come *b'* thine altar in this house; "
24 be put to the worse *b'* the enemy, "
24 and make supplication *b'* thee "
36 deliver them over *b'* their enemies, * "
7: 4 offered sacrifices *b'* the Lord. "
6 priests sounded trumpets *b'* them, 5048
7 was *b'* the house of the Lord: 6440
17 if thou wilt walk *b'* me, as David "
19 which I have set *b'* you, "
8:12 which he had built *b'* the porch, "
14 and minister *b'* the priests, 5048
9: 7 which stand continually *b'* thee, 6440
11 and there were none such seen *b'* "
10: 6 men that had stood *b'* Solomon "
8 up with him, that stood *b'* him. "
13:13 they were *b'* Judah, and the "
14 the battle was *b'* and behind: "
15 Jeroboam and all Israel *b'* Abijah "
16 children of Israel fled *b'* Judah: "
14: 5 the kingdom was quiet *b'* him. "
7 while the land is yet *b'* us; "
12 the Lord smote the Ethiopians *b'* "
12 Asa, and *b'* Judah; "
13 they were destroyed *b'* the Lord, "
13 and *b'* his host; "
15: 8 that was *b'* the porch of the Lord. "
18: 9 the prophets prophesied *b'* them. "
20 and stood *b'* the Lord, and said, "
19: 2 wrath upon thee from *b'* the Lord. "
11 the Levites shall be officers *b'* you. "
20: 5 *b'* the new court, "
7 *b'* thy people Israel, and gavest "
9 we stand *b'* this house, and in thy "
13 and all Judah stood *b'* the Lord, "
16 brook, *b'* the wilderness of Jeruel. "
18 of Jerusalem fell *b'* the Lord, "
21 as they went out *b'* the army, "
23:17 slew Mattan the priest of Baal *b'* "
24:14 the rest of the money *b'* the king "
25: 8 shall make thee fall *b'* the enemy: "
14 and bowed himself down *b'* them, "
22 was put to the worse *b'* Israel, "
26:19 forehead *b'* the priests in the "
27: 6 he prepared his ways *b'* the Lord "
28: 3 cast out *b'* the children of Israel. "
9 he went out *b'* the host that came * "
14 *b'* the princes and all the "
29:11 hath chosen you to stand *b'* him, "
19 they are *b'* the altar of the Lord. "
23 *b'* the king and the congregation, "
30: 9 *b'* them that lead them captive, "

2Ch 31:20 and truth *b'* the Lord his God. 6440
32:12 Ye shall worship *b'* one altar, and "
33: 2 cast out *b'* the children of Israel. "
7 which I have chosen *b'* all the *
9 destroyed *b'* the children of 6440
12 himself greatly *b'* the God 854, "
19 graven images, *b'* he was humbled: "
23 humbled not himself *b'* the Lord, "
34:18 And Shaphan read it *b'* the king. "
24 have read *b'* the king of Judah: "
27 thou didst humble thyself *b'* God, "
27 humbledst thyself *b'* me, and didst "
27 rend thy clothes, and weep *b'* me; "
31 and made a covenant *b'* the Lord, "
36:12 humbled not himself *b'* Jeremiah "
Ezr 3:12 this house was laid *b'* their eyes, "
4:18 us hath been plainly read *b'* me. 6925
23 letter was read *b'* Rehum, "
7:19 vessels. . . deliver thou *b'* the God "
28 extended mercy unto me *b'* the 6440
28 *b'* all the king's mighty princes. "
8:21 might afflict ourselves *b'* our God, "
29 weigh them *b'* the chief of the "
9:15 we are *b'* thee in our trespasses: "
15 for we cannot stand *b'* thee "
10: 1 himself down *b'* the house of God, "
6 Ezra rose up from *b'* the house of "
Neh 1: 4 and prayed *b'* the God of heaven, "
6 I pray *b'* thee now, day and night, "
2: 1 the king, that wine was *b'* him: "
13 valley, even *b'* the dragon well, *413, "
4: 2 spake *b'* his brethren and the "
5 sin be blotted out from *b'* thee: "
5 to anger *b'* the builders. 5048
5:15 governors that had been *b'* me 6440
6:19 reported his good deeds *b'* me, "
8: 1 street that was *b'* the water gate; "
2 law *b'* the congregation both of "
3 he read therein *b'* the street "
3 that was *b'* the water gate "
3 *b'* the men and the women, and *5048
9: 8 foundest his heart faithful *b'* thee, 6440
11 thou didst divide the sea *b'* them, "
24 and thou subduedst *b'* them the "
28 rest, they did evil again *b'* thee: "
32 all the trouble seem little *b'* thee, "
35 land which thou gavest *b'* them, "
12:36 God, and Ezra the scribe *b'* them. "
13: 4 And *b'* this, Eliashib the priest, "
19 began to be dark *b'* the sabbath, "
Est 1: 3 princes of the provinces, being *b'* "
11 bring Vashti the queen *b'* the king "
16 Memucan answered *b'* the king "
17 the queen to be brought in *b'* him, "
19 That Vashti come no more *b'* king "
2:11 walked every day *b'* the court "
23 book of the chronicles *b'* the king. "
3: 7 the lot *b'* Haman from day to day, "
4: 2 And came even *b'* the king's gate: "
6 which was *b'* the king's gate. "
8 to make request *b'* him for her "
6: 1 And they were read *b'* the king. "
9 and proclaim *b'* him, Thus shall "
11 of the city, and proclaimed *b'* him, "
13 *b'* whom thou hast begun to fall, "
13 but shalt surely fall *b'* him. "
7: 6 afraid *b'* the king and the queen. "
8 queen also *b'* me in the house? 5973
9 chamberlains, said *b'* the king, 6440
8: 1 And Mordecai came *b'* the king; "
3 Esther spake yet again *b'* the king, "
4 Esther arose, and stood *b'* the "
5 the thing seem right *b'* the king, "
9:11 palace was brought *b'* the king. "
25 when Esther came *b'* the king, "
Job 1: 6 present themselves *b'* the Lord, 5921
2: 1 present themselves *b'* the Lord, "
3:24 my sighing cometh *b'* I eat, and 6440
4:15 Then a spirit passed *b'* my face; 5921
16 an image was *b'* mine eyes, 5048
19 dust, which are crushed *b'* the 6440
8:12 it withereth *b'* any other herb. "
16 He is green *b'* the sun, and his "
10:21 *B'* I go whence I shall not return, 2962
13:15 maintain mine own ways *b'* 413, 6440
16 an hypocrite shall not come *b'* him. "
15: 4 and restrainest prayer *b'* God. "
7 or wast thou made *b'* the hills? "
32 It shall be accomplished *b'* his 3808
18:20 they that went *b'* were affrighted. 6931
21: 8 and their offspring *b'* their eyes. "
18 They are as stubble *b'* the wind, 6440
33 as there are innumerable *b'* him. "
23: 4 I would order my cause *b'* him, "
17 I was not cut off *b'* the darkness, "
30:11 have also let loose the bridle *b'* me. "
33: 5 set thy words in order *b'* me, "
35:14 judgment is *b'* him; therefore "
41:10 who then is able to stand *b'* me? "
22 sorrow is turned into joy *b'* him. "
42:10 twice as much as he had *b'* "
11 had been of his acquaintance *b'*, 6440
Ps 5: 8 make thy way straight *b'* my face. "
16: 8 set the Lord always *b'* me: 5048
18: 6 and my cry came *b'* him, even 6440
12 brightness that was *b'* him 5048
22 his judgments were *b'* me, "
23 I was also upright *b'* him, *5973
42 small as the dust *b'* the 5921, 6440
22:27 the nations shall worship *b'* thee. "
29 down to the dust shall bow *b'* him: "
23: 5 Thou preparest a table *b'* me in "
26: 3 thy loving kindness is *b'* mine 5048
31:19 that trust in thee *b'* the sons of "
22 I am cut off from *b'* thine eyes: "
34:*title* his behaviour *b'* Abimelech: 6440

Ps 35: 5 Let them be as chaff b' the wind: 6440
36: 1 no fear of God b' his eyes, 5048
38: 9 Lord, all my desire is b' thee; "
17 my sorrow is continually b' me. "
39: 1 while the wicked is b' me. "
5 mine age is nothing b' thee: "
13 I may recover strength b' I go 2962
41:12 settest me b' thy face for ever. "
42: 2 shall I come and appear b' God? 6440
44:15 confusion is continually b' me, 5048
50: 3 a fire shall devour b' him, and it 6440
8 to have been continually b' me. 5048
21 set them in order b' thine eyes.
51: 3 my sin is ever b' me. 5048
52: 9 for it is good b' thy saints. * "
54: 3 they have not set God b' them. "
56:13 that I may walk b' God in the 6440
57: 6 they have digged a pit b' me, "
58: 9 B' your pots can feel the thorns, 2962
61: 7 He shall abide b' God for ever: 6440
62: 8 people, pour out your heart b' him: "
68: 1 also that hate him flee b' him. "
2 as wax melteth b' the fire, so let "
3 let them rejoice b' God: yea, let "
4 his name Jah, and rejoice b' him. "
7 thou wentest forth b' thy people, "
25 The singers went b', the players 6924
69:22 table become a snare b' them: 6440
72: 9 the wilderness shall bow b' him; "
11 all kings shall fall down b' him,
73:22 I was a beast b' thee. 5973
78:55 cast out the heathen also b' them, 6440
79:11 sighing of the prisoner come b' thee; "
80: 2 B' Ephraim and Benjamin and "
9 Thou preparedst room b' it, "
83:13 as the stubble b' the wind. "
84: 7 of them in Zion appeareth b' God. 413
85:13 Righteousness shall go b' him; 6440
86: 9 and worship b' thee, O Lord; "
14 have not set thee b' them. 5048
88: 1 I have cried day and night b' thee: "
2 Let my prayer come b' thee: *6440
89:14 mercy and truth shall go b' thy "
23 will beat down his foes b' his face,
90: 2 B' the mountains were brought 2962
8 hast set our iniquities b' thee, 5048
95: 2 Let us come b' his presence with 6924
6 us kneel b' the Lord our maker. 6440
96: 6 Honour and majesty are b' him: "
9 fear b' him, all the earth. "
13 B' the Lord: for he cometh, for he "
97: 3 A fire goeth b' him, and burneth "
98: 6 make a joyful noise b' the Lord, "
9 B' the Lord; for he cometh "
100: 2 come b' his presence with singing.
102: title poureth out his complaint b' the 6440
28 seed shall be established b' thee. "
105:17 He sent a man b' them, even "
106:23 Moses his chosen stood b' him "
109:15 them be b' the Lord continually, 5048
116: 9 I will walk b' the Lord in the land 6440
119:30 thy judgments have I laid b' me.
46 of thy testimonies also b' kings, 5048
67 B' I was afflicted I went astray: 2962
168 all my ways are b' thee. 5048
169 Let my cry come near b' thee, 6440
170 Let my supplication come b' thee: "
138: 1 b' the gods will I sing praise 5048
139: 5 Thou hast beset me behind and b', 6924
141: 2 Let my prayer be set forth b' thee 6440
3 a watch, O Lord, b' my mouth
142: 2 poured out my complaint b' him; 6440
2 I shewed b' him my trouble. "
147:17 who can stand b' his cold? "
Pr 4:25 eyelids look straight b' thee. 5048
5:21 ways of man are b' the eyes of 5227
8:22 of his way, b' his works of old. 6924
25 B' the mountains were settled, 2962
25 b' the hills was I brought forth: 6440
30 delight, rejoicing always b' him; "
14:19 The evil bow b' the good; and the "
15:33 wisdom; and b' honour is humility. "
16:18 Pride goeth b' destruction, "
18 and an haughty spirit b' a fall. "
17:14 off contention, b' it be meddled "
24 Wisdom is b' him that hath 854.
18:12 B' destruction the heart of man is "
12 and b' honour is humility. "
13 that answereth a matter b' he 2962
16 and bringeth him b' great men. 6440
22:29 he shall stand b' kings; "
29 he shall not stand b' mean men. "
23: 1 consider diligently what is b' thee: "
25: 5 Take away the wicked from b' the "
26 man falling down b' the wicked "
26:26 shewed b' the whole congregation. "
27: 4 but who is able to stand b' envy? 6440
30: 7 deny me them not b' I die: 2962
Ec 1:10 of old time, which was b' us. 6440
16 all they that have been b' me "
2: 7 all that were in Jerusalem b' me: "
9 more than all that were b' me "
26 to him that is good b' God. * "
3:14 that men should fear b' him. "
4:16 of all that have been b' them: * "
5: 2 hasty to utter any thing b' God: "
6 neither say thou b' the angel, that "
6: 8 knoweth to walk b' the living? 5048
7:17 shouldest thou die b' thy time? 3808
8:12 that fear God, which fear b' him: 6440
13 he feareth not b' God. "
9: 1 or hatred by all that is b' them. "
Ca 8:12 vineyard, which is mine, is b' me: "
Isa 1:12 When ye come to appear b' me, "
16 of your doings from b' mine eyes; 5048
7:16 For b' the child shall know 2962

Isa 8: 4 b' the child shall have knowledge 2962
4 taken away b' the king of Assyria. 6440
9: 3 they joy b' thee according to the "
12 Syrians b', and the Philistines 6924
13:16 be dashed to pieces b' their eyes; "
17:13 the chaff off the mountains b' the 6440
13 and like a rolling thing b' the "
14 b' the morning he is not. 2962
23:18 them that dwell b' the Lord, to eat 6440
24:23 b' his ancients gloriously. 5048
28: 4 as the hasty fruit b' the summer; 2962
30: 8 Now go, write it b' them 854
11 of Israel to cease from b' us. 6440
36: 7 Ye shall worship b' this altar? "
37:14 Lord, and spread it b' the Lord. "
27 as corn blasted b' it be grown up. "
33 come b' it with shields, nor cast 6924
38: 3 I have walked b' thee in truth 6440
40:10 with him, and his work b' him. "
41: 1 Keep silence b' me, 413
2 gave the nations b' him, 6440
42: 9 b' they spring forth I tell you 2962
16 will make darkness light b' them, 6440
43:10 b' me there was no God "
13 b' the day was I am he; *
45: 1 to subdue nations b' him; and I 6440
1 open b' him the two leaved gates; "
2 I will go b' thee, and make the "
47:14 nor fire to sit b' it. 5048
48: 5 b' it came to pass I shewed 2962
7 even b' the day when thou 6440
19 cut off nor destroyed from b' me. "
49:16 thy walls are continually b' me. 5048
52:12 will go b' you; and the God 6440
53: 2 grow up b' him as a tender "
7 sheep b' her shearers is dumb, so "
55:12 the hills shall break forth b' you "
57:16 should fail b' me, and the souls "
58: 8 thy righteousness, shall go b' thee; "
59:12 are multiplied b' thee, 5048
61:11 to spring forth b' all the nations. "
62:11 is with him and his work b' him. 6440
63:12 arm, dividing the water b' them, "
65: 6 it is written b' me: I will not keep "
12 but did evil b' mine eyes, and did *
24 that b' they call, I will answer; 2962
66: 4 did evil b' mine eyes, and chose *
7 B' she travailed, she brought 2962
7 b' her pain came,
22 remain b' me,...so shall your seed 6440
23 all flesh come to worship b' me, "
Jer 1: 5 B' I formed thee in the belly I 2962
5 and b' thou camest forth "
17 lest I confound thee b' them. 6440
2:22 is marked b' me, saith the Lord "
6: 7 b' me continually is grief 5921, "
21 lay stumblingblocks b' this people, 413
7:10 and stand b' me in this house, 6440
8: 2 spread them b' the sun, "
9:13 my law which I set b' them, 6440
13:16 b' he cause darkness, and 2962
16 b' your feet stumble "
15: 1 Moses and Samuel stood b' me, 6440
9 to the sword b' their enemies, "
19 shalt stand b' me: and if thou "
17:16 of my lips was right b' thee. 5227, "
18:17 with an east wind b' the enemy; "
20 I stood b' thee to speak good for "
23 let them be overthrown b' thee; "
19: 7 fall by the sword b' their enemies, "
21: 8 I set b' you the way of life, "
24: 1 two baskets of figs were set b' the "
26: 4 my law, which I have set b' you, "
28: 8 prophets that have been b' me "
8 and b' thee of old prophesied "
29:21 he shall slay them b' your eyes; "
30:20 shall be established b' me, 6440
31:36 ordinances depart from b' me, "
36 being a nation b' me for ever. "
32:12 b' all the Jews that sat in the 5869
13 charged Baruch b' them, saying, "
30 Judah have only done evil b' me * "
31 should remove it from b' my face, 5921
33: 9 an honour b' all the nations "
18 the Levites want a man b' me 6440
24 should be no more a nation b' them. "
34: 5 former kings which were b' thee, "
15 ye had made a covenant b' me "
18 which they had made b' me, "
35: 5 I set b' the sons of the house "
19 not want a man to stand b' me "
36: 7 their supplication b' the Lord, "
9 proclaimed a fast b' the Lord to all "
22 fire on the hearth burning b' him. "
37:20 I pray thee, be accepted b' thee; "
38:10 out of the dungeon, b' he die. 2962
26 my supplication b' the king, 6440
39: 6 Zedekiah in Riblah b' his eyes: "
16 accomplished in that day b' thee. 6440
40: 4 behold, all the land is b' thee: "
42: 2 supplication be accepted b' thee, "
9 present your supplication b' him; "
44:10 statutes, that I set b' you and b' "
49:19 shepherd that will stand b' me? "
37 to be dismayed b' their enemies, "
37 and b' them that seek their life: "
50: 8 as the he goats b' the flocks. "
44 shepherd that will stand b' me? "
52:10 sons of Zedekiah b' his eyes: "
33 did continually eat bread b' him 6440
La 1: 5 gone into captivity b' the enemy. "
6 without strength b' the pursuer. "
22 all their wickedness come b' thee; "
2: 3 right hand from b' the enemy, "
19 water b' the face of the Lord: 5227
3:35 man b' the face of the most High, 5048

Eze 2:10 he spread it b' me; and it was 6440
3:20 I lay a stumbling block b' him, "
4: 1 thee a tile, and lay it b' thee, "
6: 4 will cast down your slain men b' "
5 children of Israel b' their idols; "
8: 1 the elders of Judah sat b' me, "
11 stood b' them seventy men of the "
9: 6 men which were b' the house. "
14: 1 of Israel unto me, and sat b' me. "
3 their iniquity b' their face: 5227
4 his iniquity b' his face, and cometh "
7 his iniquity b' his face, "
16:18 oil and mine incense b' them. 6440
19 hast even set it b' them for a sweet "
50 committed abomination b' me: "
57 B' thy wickedness was discovered, 2962
20: 1 inquire of the Lord, and sat b' me. 6440
9 not be polluted b' the heathen, *5869
14 that it should not be polluted b' * "
41 sanctified in you b' the heathen. * "
21: 6 with bitterness sigh b' their eyes. "
22:30 stand in the gap b' me for the 6440
23:24 and I will set judgment b' them. * "
41 bed, and a table prepared b' it, "
28: 9 thou yet say b' him that slayeth "
17 I will lay thee b' kings, that they "
30:24 and he shall groan b' him with "
32:10 brandish my sword b' them; 5921, "
33:31 they sit b' thee as my people, "
36:17 their way was b' me as the "
23 sanctified in you b' their eyes.
37:20 be in thine hand b' their eyes.
38:16 in thee, O Gog, b' their eyes.
40:12 space also b' the little chambers 6440
22 the arches thereof were b' them. "
26 the arches thereof were b' them: "
47 the altar that was b' the house. "
41: 4 twenty cubits, b' the temple: 413, "
12 b' the separate place at the end " "
22 is the table that is b' the Lord. "
42: 2 B' the length of an hundred 413, "
4 And b' the chambers was a walk "
8 b' the temple was an hundred 5921, "
11 And the way b' them was like "
12 directly b' the wall toward the east, "
13 which are b' the separate place, 413, "
43:24 thou shalt offer them b' the Lord, "
44: 3 sit in it to eat bread b' the Lord; "
4 of the north gate b' the house: 413, "
11 shall stand b' them to minister "
12 they ministered unto them b' their "
15 they shall stand b' me to offer "
22 or a widow that had a priest b'. *
45: 7 b' the oblation of the holy *413, 6440
7 b' the possession of the city, * "
46: 3 gate b' the Lord in the sabbaths "
9 shall come b' the Lord in the "
Da 1: 5 they might stand b' the king. "
13 countenances be looked upon b' "
18 them in b' Nebuchadnezzar. "
19 therefore stood they b' the king. "
2: 2 they came and stood b' the king. "
9 corrupt words to speak b' me, 6925
10 Chaldeans answered b' the king, "
11 other that can shew it b' the king, "
24 bring me in b' the king, and I will "
25 brought in Daniel b' the king "
31 brightness was excellent, stood b' 6903
36 interpretation thereof b' the king. 6925
3: 3 and they stood b' the image 6903
13 brought these men b' the king. 6925
4: 6 the wise men of Babylon b' me, "
7 and I told the dream b' them; "
8 at...last Daniel came in b' me. 5922, "
8 and b' him I told the dream, "
5: 1 and drank wine b' the thousand. 6903
13 Daniel brought in b' the king, 6925
15 have been brought in b' me, "
17 answered and said b' the king, "
19 trembled and feared b' him: 4481, "
23 the vessels of his house b' thee, "
6:10 and gave thanks b' his God, "
11 making supplication b' his God. "
12 and spake b' the king concerning "
13 and said b' the king, That Daniel "
18 of musick brought b' him; "
22 b' him innocency was found in "
22 and also b' thee, "
26 and fear b' the God of Daniel: 4481, "
7: 7 from all the beasts that were b' it; "
8 b' whom there were three "
10 and came forth from b' him: "
10 times ten thousand stood b' him: "
13 and they brought him near b' him. "
20 up, and b' whom three fell; 4481, "
8: 3 there stood b' the river a ram 6440
4 no beasts might stand b' him, "
6 had seen standing b' the river, "
7 power in the ram to stand b' him, "
15 stood b' me as the appearance 5048
9:10 his laws, which he set b' us by 6440
13 prayer b' the Lord our God, *854, "
18 present our supplications b' thee "
20 supplication b' the Lord my God "
10:12 and to chasten thyself b' thy God, "
11:16 will, and none shall stand b' him: "
22 they be overflown from b' him, "
Ho 7: 2 them about; they are b' my face. 5048
Joe 1:16 Is not the meat cut off b' our eyes, "
2: 3 A fire devoureth b' them; 6440
3 as the garden of Eden b' them, "
6 B' their face the people shall be *
10 The earth shall quake b' them; 6440
11 Lord shall utter his voice b' his "
31 b' the great and the terrible day "
Am 1: 1 two years b' the earthquake. "

Am 2: 9 destroyed I the Amorite b' them, 6440
4: 3 at that which is b' her; 5084
9: 4 go into captivity b' their enemies, 6440
Jon 1: 2 their wickedness is come up b' me. "
2 Therefore I fled b' unto Tarshish *6924
Mi 1: 4 as wax b' the fire, and as the 6440
2:13 The breaker is come up b' them: "
13 and their king shall pass b' them, "
6: 1 contend thou b' the mountains, 854
4 I sent b' thee Moses, Aaron, and 6440
6 Wherewith shall I come b' the 6924
6 and bow myself b' the high God? "
6 shall I come b' him with burnt 6924
Na 1: 6 Who can stand b' his indignation? 6440
2: 1 in pieces is come up b' thy face: 5921
Hab 1: 3 spoiling and violence are b' me: 5048
2:20 let all the earth keep silence b' 6440
3: 5 B' him went the pestilence, and "
Zep 3:20 turn back your captivity b' your "
Hag 1:12 the people did fear b' the Lord. 6440
2:14 so is this nation b' me, saith the "
15 b' a stone was laid upon a stone 2962
Zec 2:13 Be silent, O all flesh, b' the Lord: 6440
3: 1 standing b' the angel of the Lord. "
3 garments, and stood b' the angel. "
4 those that stood b' him, saying, "
8 and thy fellows that sit b' thee: "
9 stone that I have laid b' Joshua; "
4: 7 b' Zerubbabel thou shalt become "
6: 5 from standing b' the Lord 5921
7: 2 their men, to pray b' the Lord,*854, 6440
8:10 b' these days there was no hire "
21, 22 speedily to pray b' the Lord,*854, "
12: 8 the angel of the Lord b' them. "
14: 4 the mount of Olives, which is b'5921, "
5 as ye fled from b' the earthquake "
20 shall be like the bowls b' the altar. "
Mal 2: 5 me, and was afraid b' my name. * "
9 and base b' all the people, "
3: 1 he shall prepare the way b' me: 6440
11 vine cast her fruit b' the time "
14 mournfully b' the Lord of hosts? 6440
16 remembrance was written b' him "
4: 5 b' the coming of the great and 6440
M't 1:18 b' they came together, 4250, 2228
2: 9 went b' them, till it came and 4254
5:12 the prophets which were b' you. 4253
16 Let your light so shine b' men, 1715
24 Leave there thy gift b' the altar, "
6: 1 do not your alms b' men, "
2 do not sound a trumpet b' thee, "
8 ye have need of, b' ye ask him. 4253
7: 6 cast ye your pearls b' swine, 1715
8:29 hither to torment us b' the time? 4253
10:18 b' governors and kings for my 1909
32 shall confess me b' men, him will 1715
32 I confess also b' my Father "
33 shall deny me b' men, "
33 him will I also deny b' my "
11:10 I send my messenger b' thy face, 4253
10 shall prepare thy way b' thee. 1715
14: 6 of Herodias danced b' them, *3319
8 she, being b' instructed of her *4264
22 to go b' him unto the other side, 4254
17: 2 was transfigured b' them: and his 1715
21: 9 the multitudes that went b', 4254
31 go into the kingdom of God b' you. "
24:25 I have told you b'. *4280
38 in the days that were b' the flood 4253
25:32 b' him shall be gathered all 1715
26:32 I will go b' you into Galilee. 4254
34 That this night, b' the cock crow, 4250
70 he denied b' them all, saying, 1715
75 B' the cock crow, thou shalt deny 4250
27:11 Jesus stood b' the governor: 1715
24 washed his hands b' the multitude, 561
29 and they bowed the knee b' him, 1715
28: 7 he goeth b' you into Galilee; 4254
M'k 1: 2 I send my messenger b' thy face, 4253
2 shall prepare thy way b' thee. *1715
35 rising up a great while b' day, 1773
2:12 bed, and went forth b' them all; 1726
3:11 they saw him, fell down b' him, 4363
5:33 came and fell down b' him, "
6:41 to his disciples to set b' them; 3908
45 to go to the other side b' unto 4254
8: 6 to his disciples to set b' them; 3908
6 they did set them b' the people. "
7 commanded to set them also b' "
9: 2 and he was transfigured b' them. 1715
10:32 Jesus went b' them: and they 4254
11: 9 And they that went b', and they "
13: 9 b' rulers and kings for my sake, 1909
14:28 I will go b' you into Galilee. 4254
30 night, b' the cock crow twice, 4250, 2228
72 B' the cock crow twice, thou shalt 4250
15:42 that is, the day b' the sabbath, 4315
16: 7 that he goeth b' you into Galilee: 4254
Lu 1: 6 they were both righteous b' God, 1799
8 b' God in the order of his course, 1725
17 shall go b' him in the spirit and 1799
75 In holiness and righteousness b' "
76 shalt go b' the face of the Lord 4253
2:21 b' he was conceived in the womb. "
26 b' he had seen the Lord's 4250, 2228
31 b' the face of all people; 2596
5:18 him in, and to lay him b' him. 1799
19 his couch into the midst b' Jesus. 1715
25 he rose up b' them, and took up 1799
7:27 I send my messenger b' thy face, 4253
27 shall prepare thy way b' thee. 1715
8:28 and fell down b' him, and with a 4363
47 and falling down b' him, 4363
47 unto him b' all the people for *1799
9:16 to set b' the multitude. 3908
52 and sent messengers b' his face: 4253
Lu 10: 1 two and two b' his face into every 4253
8 such things as are set b' you: 3908
11: 6 and I have nothing to set b' him? "
38 he had not first washed b' dinner. 4253
12: 6 one of them is forgotten b' God? *1799
8 shall confess me b' men, 1715
8 also confess b' the angels of God: "
9 he that denieth me b' men shall *1799
9 be denied b' the angels of God. * "
14: 2 there was a certain man b' him 1715
15:18 against heaven, and b' thee, *1799
16:15 which justify yourselves b' men; * "
18:39 they which went b' rebuked him, 4254
19: 4 he ran b', and climbed up 1715
27 bring hither, and slay them b' me. "
28 had thus spoken, he went b', "
20:26 his words b' the people: and they 1726
21:12 But b' all these, they shall lay 4253
12 brought b' kings and rulers for 1909
14 meditate b' what ye shall answer: *4304
36 to stand b' the Son of man. 1715
22:15 this passover with you b' I suffer: 4253
34 b' that thou shalt thrice *4250, 2228
47 one of the twelve, went b' them, 4281
61 B' the cock crow, thou shalt 4250
23:12 for b' they were at enmity 4391
14 having examined him b' you, 1799
53 wherein never man b' was laid. *3764
24:19 word b' God and all the people: 1726
43 did eat b' them. 1799
Joh 1:15 after me is preferred b' me: 1715
15 for he was b' me. 4413
27 after me is preferred b' me, *1715
30 a man which is preferred b' me; "
30 for he was b' me. 4413
48 B' that Philip called thee, when 4253
3:28 but that I am sent b' him. 1715
5: 7 another steppeth down b' me. 4253
6:62 ascend up where he was b'? 4386
7:51 man, b' it hear him, *3362, 4386
8:58 unto you, B' Abraham was, I am. 4250
9: 8 they which b' had seen him *4386
10: 4 he goeth b' them, and the sheep 1715
8 that ever came b' me are thieves 4253
11:55 up to Jerusalem b' the passover, "
12: 1 Jesus six days b' the passover "
37 done so many miracles b' them, 1715
13: 1 Now b' the feast of the passover, 4253
19 Now I tell you b' it come, that, "
14:29 I have told you b' it come to pass, 4250
15:18 hated me b' it hated you. 4412
17: 5 I had with thee b' the world 4253
24 b' the foundation of the world. "
Ac 1:16 by the mouth of David spake b' 4277
2:20 b' that great and notable 4250, 2228
25 the Lord always b' my face, 1799
31 He seeing this b' spake of the *4275
3:18 which God b' had showed *4293
20 which b' was preached unto you: *4296
4:10 man stand here b' you whole. 1799
28 counsel determined b' to be done. *4309
5:23 standing without b' the doors: *4253
27 set them b' the counsel: and the 1722
36 b' these days rose up Theudas, 4253
6: 6 Whom they set b' the apostles: 1799
7: 2 b' he dwelt in Charran, 4250, 2228
40 Make us gods to go b' us: for as 4313
45 God drave out b' the face of our 575
46 Who found favour b' God, *1799
52 which shewed b' the coming 4293
8:32 like a lamb dumb b' his shearer, 1726
9:15 to bear my name b' the Gentiles, 1799
10: 4 come up for a memorial b' God. "
17 stood b' the gate, 1909
30 stood b' me in bright clothing, 1799
33 are we all here present b' God * "
41 unto witnesses chosen b' of God, 4401
12: 6 and the keepers b' the door kept 4253
14 told how Peter stood b' the gate. "
13:24 b' his coming the baptism 4253, 4383
14:13 Jupiter, which was b' their city, 4253
16:29 and fell down b' Paul and Silas, 4363
34 he set meat b' them, 3908
17:26 hath determined the times b' *4384
18:17 beat him b' the judgment seat. 1715
19: 9 that way b' the multitude, 1799
19 burned them b' all men: and * "
20: 5 going b' tarried for us at Troas. 4281
13 And we went b' to ship, and "
21:29 (For they had seen b' with him 4308
38 which b' these days madest 4253
22:30 Paul down, and set him b' them. 1519
23: 1 in all good conscience b' God "
30 to say b' thee what they had 1909
33 presented Paul also b' him. "
24:19 to have been here b' thee, and 1909
20 while I stood b' the council, "
25: 9 judge of these things b' me? "
16 b' that he which is accused have 4250
26 brought him forth b' you, 1909
26 and specially b' thee, O king "
26: 2 for myself this day b' thee "
26 b' whom also I speak freely: *4314
27:24 thou must be brought b' Cæsar: 3936
Ro 2:13 of the law are just b' God, 3844
3: 9 b' proved both Jews and Gentiles, 4256
18 no fear of God b' their eyes. 561
19 world may become guilty b' God. *
4: 2 but not b' God. *4314
17 b' him whom he believed, even 2713
9:29 as Esaias said b', Except the Lord 4280
14:10 all stand b' the judgment seat 3936
22 have it to thyself b' God. Happy 1799
16: 7 who also were in Christ b' me. 4253
1Co 2: 7 God ordained b' the world unto "
4: 5 judge nothing b' the time, "
1Co 6: 1 go to law b' the unjust, 1909
1 and not b' the saints? "
6 and that b' the unbelievers. "
10:27 whatsoever is set b' you, eat, 3908
11:21 taketh b' other his own supper: 4301
2Co 1:15 was minded to come unto you b', ‡4386
5:10 b' the judgment seat of Christ; 1715
7: 3 I have said b', that ye are in our 4280
14 which I made b' Titus, is found 1909
8:10 who have begun b', not only to *4278
24 and b' the churches, the *1519, 4383
9: 5 that they would go b' unto you, 4281
5 whereof ye had notice b', that *4293
12:19 we speak b' God in Christ: *2714
13: 2 I told you b', and foretell you, *4280
Gal 1: 9 As we said b', so say I now again, 4280
17 which were apostles b' me; 4253
20 you, behold, b' God, I lie not. 1799
2:12 b' that certain came from James, 4253
14 I said unto Peter b' them all, 1715
3: 1 b' whose eyes Jesus Christ hath 2596
8 b' the gospel unto Abraham, *4283
17 that was confirmed b' of God *4300
23 But b' faith came, 4253
5:21 of the which I tell you b', as I *4302
Eph 1: 4 us in him b' the foundation 4253
4 and without blame b' him in love: 2714
2:10 which God hath b' ordained that *4282
Ph'p 3:13 unto those things which are b', 1715
Col 1: 5 heard b' in the word of the truth 4257
17 he is b' all things, and by him 4253
1Th 2: 2 after that we had suffered b', 4310
3: 4 you b' that we should suffer *4302
9 joy for your sakes b' our God; 1715
13 unblameable in holiness b' God, "
1Ti 1:13 Who was b' a blasphemer, and a 4386
18 to the prophecies which went b' ‡4254
5: 4 that is good and acceptable b' *1799
19 but b' two or three witnesses. *1909
20 Them that sin rebuke b' all, *1799
21 I charge thee b' God, and the * "
21 preferring one b' another, *4299
24 going b' to judgment; and some 4254
6:12 profession b' many witnesses. *1799
13 and b' Christ Jesus, *
13 b' Pontius Pilate witnessed 1909
2Ti 1: 9 Christ Jesus b' the world began, 4253
2:14 charging them b' the Lord *1799
4: 1 therefore b' God, and the Lord * "
21 thy diligence to come b' winter. 4253
Ti 1: 2 promised b' the world began; "
Heb 6:18 lay hold upon the hope set b' us: 4295
7:18 of the commandment going b' *4254
10:15 after that he had said b', *4280
11: 5 b' his translation he had this 4253
12: 1 the race that is set b' us, 4295
2 for the joy that was set b' him "
Jas 1:27 b' God and the Father is this, 3844
2: 6 you b' the judgment seats? 1519
5: 9 the judge standeth b' the door. 4253
1Pe 1:20 b' the foundation of the world, "
2Pe 2:11 against them b' the Lord. 3844
3: 2 which were spoken b' by the holy 4280
17 seeing ye know these things b', *4267
1Jo 2:28 be ashamed b' him at his coming. 575
3:19 shall assure our hearts b' him. 1715
3Jo 6 of thy charity b' the church: 1799
Jude 4 who were b' of old ordained to †‡4270
17 were spoken b' of the apostles 4280
24 faultless b' the presence of his 2714
Re 1: 4 spirits which are b' his throne; 1799
2:14 a stumblingblock b' the children "
3: 2 found thy works perfect b' God. "
5 b' my Father, and b' his angels. "
8 I have set b' thee an open door, "
9 to come and worship b' thy feet, "
4: 5 of fire burning b' the throne, "
6 b' the throne there was a sea "
6 beasts full of eyes b' and behind. 1715
10 elders fall down b' him that sat 1799
10 and cast their crowns b' the throne, "
5: 8 elders fell down b' the Lamb, "
7: 9 b' the throne, and b' the Lamb, "
11 fell b' the throne on their faces, "
15 are they b' throne of God, "
8: 2 seven angels which stood b' God; "
3 altar which was b' the throne. "
4 ascended up b' God out of the "
9:13 golden altar which is b' God, "
10:11 prophesy again b' many peoples, *1909
11: 4 standing b' the God of the earth. 1799
16 which sat b' God on their seats, "
12: 4 the dragon stood b' the woman "
10 accused them b' our God day and "
13:12 power of the first beast b' him, * "
14: 3 b' the throne, and b' the four "
5 without fault b' the throne of God.* "
15: 4 shall come and worship b' thee; "
16:19 came in remembrance b' God, * "
19:20 that wrought miracles b' him, * "
20:12 small and great, stand b' God; "
22: 8 b' the feet of the angel which 1715

beforehand See also AFOREHAND.
M'r 13:11 take no thought b' what ye shall 4305
2Co 9: 5 and make up b' your bounty, 4294
1Ti 5:24 Some men's sins are open b', *4271
25 works of some are manifest b'; "
1Pe 1:11 testified b' the sufferings of Christ, 4303

beforetime See also AFORETIME.
De 2:12 The Horims also dwelt in Seir b';*6440
Jos 11:10 for Hazor b' was the head of all "
20: 5 and hated him not b'. 8543, 8032
1Sa 9: 9 (B' in Israel, when a man 6440
9 a Prophet was b' called a Seer.) "
10:11 when all that knew him b' 865, 8032

2Sa 7:10 afflict them any more, or *b·* *7223
2Ki 13: 5 dwelt in their tents, as *b·*. 8543, 8032
Ne 2: 1 Now I had not been *b·* sad
Isa 41:26 and *b·*, that we may say, He is 6440
Ac 8: 9 called Simon, which *b·* in the same *4391*

beg See also BEGGED; BEGGING.
Ps 109:10 be continually vagabonds, and *b·*: 7592
Pr 20: 4 therefore shall he *b·* in the harvest, "
Lu 16: 3 cannot dig; to *b·* I am ashamed. *1871*

began
Ge 4:26 then *b·* men to call upon the name 2490
6: 1 when men *b·* to multiply on the "
9:20 And Noah *b·* to be an husbandman, "
10: 8 *b·* to be a mighty one in the earth. "
41:54 seven years of dearth *b·* to come, "
44:12 he searched, and *b·* at the eldest, "
Nu 25: 1 people *b·* to commit whoredom "
De 1: 5 *b·* Moses to declare this law, 2974
J'g 13:25 the Spirit of the Lord *b·* to move 2490
16:19 and she *b·* to afflict him, and his "
22 the hair of his head *b·* to grow "
19:25 when the day *b·* to spring, they 5927
20:31 they *b·* to smite of the people, 2490
39 Benjamin *b·* to smite and kill "
40 when the flame *b·* to arise up out "
1Sa 3: 2 his eyes *b·* to wax dim, that he * "
2Sa 2:10 old when he *b·* to reign over Israel,
5: 4 years old when he *b·* to reign,
1Ki 6: 1 *b·* to build the house of the Lord.
14:21 when he *b·* to reign, and he
15:25 son of Jeroboam *b·* to reign over
33 *b·* Baasha the son of Ahijah to
16: 8 *b·* Elah the son of Baasha to reign
11 when he *b·* to reign, as soon as
23 *b·* Omri to reign over Israel,
29 *b·* Ahab the son of Omri to reign
22:41 son of Asa *b·* to reign over Judah
42 when he *b·* to reign; and he
51 the son of Ahab *b·* to reign over
2Ki 3: 1 the son of Ahab *b·* to reign over
8:16 king of Judah *b·* to reign.
17 when he *b·* to reign; and he
26 when he *b·* to reign; and he
9:29 *b·* Ahaziah to reign over Judah.
10:32 the Lord *b·* to cut Israel short: 2490
11:21 Jehoash when he *b·* to reign.
12: 1 Jehoash *b·* to reign; and forty
13: 1 the son of Jehu *b·* to reign
10 *b·* Jehoash the son of Jehoahaz
14: 2 when he *b·* to reign, and reigned
23 Joash king of Israel *b·* to reign
15: 1 *b·* Azariah son of Amaziah king
2 old was he when he *b·* to reign,
13 the son of Jabesh *b·* to reign
17 *b·* Menahem the son of Gadi to reign
23 the son of Menahem *b·* to reign
27 the son of Remaliah *b·* to reign
32 *b·* Jotham the son of Uzziah king
33 old was he when he *b·* to reign.
37 In those days the Lord *b·* to send 2490
16: 1 Jotham king of Judah *b·* to reign.
2 Ahaz when he *b·* to reign, and
17: 1 *b·* Hoshea the son of Elah to reign
18: 1 of Ahaz king of Judah *b·* to reign.
2 when he *b·* to reign; and he
21: 1 years old when he *b·* to reign,
19 twenty and two years old when he *b·*
22: 1 years old when he *b·* to reign,
23:31 years old when he *b·* to reign,
36 twenty and five years old when he *b·*
24: 8 years old when he *b·* to reign,
18 twenty and one years old when he *b·*
25:27 in the year that he *b·* to reign did
1Ch 1:10 *b·* to be mighty upon the earth. 2490
27:24 the son of Zeruiah *b·* to number, "
2Ch 3: 1 Solomon *b·* to build the house "
2 And he *b·* to build in the second "
12:13 years old when he *b·* to reign,
13: 1 *b·* Abijah to reign over Judah.
20:22 when they *b·* to sing and to praise, 2490
31 years old when he *b·* to reign,
21: 5 years old when he *b·* to reign,
20 years old was he when he *b·* to
22: 2 was Ahaziah when he *b·* to reign,
24: 1 seven years old when he *b·* to reign,
25: 1 years old when he *b·* to reign,
26: 3 was Uzziah when he *b·* to reign,
27: 1 twenty and five years old when he *b·*
8 years old when he *b·* to reign,
28: 1 years old when he *b·* to reign,
29: 1 Hezekiah *b·* to reign when he was
17 Now they *b·* on the first day of 2490
27 when the burnt offering *b·*, "
27 the song of the Lord *b·* "
31: 7 they *b·* to lay the foundation of "
10 Since the people *b·* to bring the "
21 And in every work that he *b·* "
33: 1 twelve years old when he *b·* to
21 years old when he *b·* to reign,
34: 1 eight years old when he *b·* to reign,
3 *b·* to seek after the God of David 2490
3 in the twelfth year he *b·* to purge "
36: 2 twenty and three years old when he *b·*
5 twenty and five years old when he *b·*
9 eight years old when he *b·* to reign,
11 one and twenty years old when he *b·*
Ezr 3: 6 *b·* they to offer burnt offerings 2490
8 *b·* Zerubbabel the son of Shealtiel "
" 5: 2 and *b·* to build the house of God 8271
7: 9 of the first month *b·* he to go up 3246
Ne 4: 7 that the breaches *b·* to be stopped, 2490
13:19 gates of Jerusalem *b·* to be dark 6751
Jer 52: 1 years old when he *b·* to reign,
Eze 9: 6 Then they *b·* at the ancient men 2490
Jon 3: 4 Jonah *b·* to enter into the city "
M't 4:17 Jesus *b·* to preach, and to say, *756*
11: 7 Jesus *b·* to say unto the multitudes "
20 Then *b·* he to upbraid the cities "
12: 1 *b·* to pluck the ears of corn, and to "
16:21 *b·* Jesus to shew unto his disciples, "
22 *b·* to rebuke him, saying, Be it far "
26:22 *b·* every one of them to say unto "
37 *b·* to be sorrowful and very heavy. "
74 Then *b·* he to curse and to swear, "
28: 1 as it *b·* to dawn toward the first *2020*
M'r 1:45 *b·* to publish it much, and to *756*
2:23 his disciples *b·*, as they went, "
4: 1 he *b·* again to teach by the sea side: "
5:17 they *b·* to pray him to depart "
20 *b·* to publish in Decapolis how great "
6: 2 he *b·* to teach in the synagogue: "
7 *b·* to send them forth by two and "
34 he *b·* to teach them many things. "
55 *b·* to carry about in beds those "
8:11 *b·* to question with him, seeking "
31 he *b·* to teach them, that the Son of "
32 Peter took him, and *b·* to rebuke "
10:28 Then Peter *b·* to say unto him, "
32 *b·* to tell them what things should "
41 they *b·* to be much displeased "
47 he *b·* to cry out, and say, Jesus, "
11:15 *b·* to cast out them that sold and "
12: 1 *b·* to speak unto them by parables. "
13: 5 Jesus answering them *b·* to say, "
14:19 they *b·* to be sorrowful, and to "
33 *b·* to be sore amazed, and to be "
65 some *b·* to spit on him, and to cover "
69 *b·* to say to them that stood by, "
71 he *b·* to curse and to swear, saying, "
15: 8 crying aloud, *b·* to desire him to do "
18 *b·* to salute him, Hail, king of the "
Lu 1:70 have been since the world *b·*: ‡
3:23 Jesus himself *b·* to be about thirty *756*
4:21 he *b·* to say unto them, This day "
5: 7 the ships, so that they *b·* to sink.
21 scribes and the Pharisees *b·* to *756*
7:15 he that was dead sat up, and *b·* to "
24 he *b·* to speak unto the people "
38 *b·* to wash his feet with tears, and "
49 *b·* to say within themselves, Who is "
9:12 when the day *b·* to wear away, then "
11:29 gathered thick together, he *b·* to "
53 scribes and the Pharisees *b·* to "
12: 1 he *b·* to say unto his disciples first "
14:18 with one consent *b·* to make excuse. "
30 Saying, This man *b·* to build, and "
15:14 famine in that land, and he *b·* to be "
24 And they *b·* to be merry. "
19:37 multitude of the disciples *b·* to "
45 *b·* to cast out them that sold "
20: 9 Then *b·* he to speak to the people "
22:23 they *b·* to enquire among themselves "
23: 2 they *b·* to accuse him, saying, "
Joh 4:52 when he *b·* to amend. And they *2192*
9:32 Since the world *b·* was it not heard
13: 5 *b·* to wash the disciples' feet, and *756*
Ac 1: 1 all that Jesus *b·* both to do and "
2: 4 *b·* to speak with other tongues, as "
3:21 holy prophets since the world *b·*. ‡
8:35 *b·* at the same scripture, and * *756*
10:37 *b·* from Galilee, after the baptism "
11:15 as I *b·* to speak, the Holy Ghost fell "
18:26 he *b·* to speak boldly in the "
24: 2 Tertullus *b·* to accuse him, saying, "
27:35 when he had broken it, he *b·* to eat "
Ro 16:25 kept secret since the world *b·*, *
2Ti 1: 9 Christ Jesus before the world *b·*; *
Tit 1: 2 promised before the world *b·*. *
Heb 2: 3 which at the first *b·* to be *746, 2983*

begat
Ge 4:18 Irad *b·* Mehujael: 3205
18 and Mehujael *b·* Methusael: "
18 and Methusael *b·* Lamech. "
5: 3 and *b·* a son in his own likeness, "
4 and he *b·* sons and daughters: "
6 an hundred and five years, and *b·* "
7 Seth lived after he *b·* Enos eight "
7 and seven years, and *b·* sons and "
9 Enos lived ninety years, and *b·* "
10 Enos lived after he *b·* Cainan eight "
10 fifteen years, and *b·* sons and "
12 Cainan lived seventy years, and *b·* "
13 And Cainan lived after he *b·* "
13 forty years, and *b·* sons and "
15 lived sixty and five years and *b·* "
16 Mahalaleel lived after he *b·* Jared "
16 and thirty years, and *b·* sons and "
18 sixty and two years, and he *b·* "
19 And Jared lived after he *b·* Enoch "
19 hundred years, and *b·* sons and "
21 lived sixty and five years, and *b·* "
22 walked with God after he *b·* "
22 three hundred years, and *b·* sons "
25 eighty and seven years, and *b·* "
26 And Methuselah lived after he *b·* "
26 and two years, and *b·* sons and "
28 eighty and two years, and *b·* a son: "
30 And Lamech lived after he *b·* Noah "
30 and five years, and *b·* sons and "
32 Noah *b·* Shem, Ham, and Japheth. "
6:10 Noah *b·* three sons, Shem, Ham, "
10: 8 Cush *b·* Nimrod: he began to be "
13 Mizraim *b·* Ludim, and Anamim, "
15 Canaan *b·* Sidon his firstborn "
24 Arphaxad *b·* Salah; "
24 and Salah *b·* Eber "
26 Joktan *b·* Almodad, and Sheleph, "
11:10 and *b·* Arphaxad two years after "
11 Shem lived after he *b·* Arphaxad "
11 five hundred years, and *b·* sons and "
Ge 11:12 and thirty years, and *b·* Salah: 3205
13 Arphaxad lived after he *b·* Salah "
13 and three years, and *b·* sons and "
14 lived thirty years, and *b·* Eber; "
15 Salah lived after he *b·* Eber four "
15 hundred and three years, and *b·* "
16 four and thirty years, and *b·* Peleg: "
17 Eber lived after he *b·* Peleg four "
17 hundred and thirty years, and *b·* "
18 Peleg lived thirty years, and *b·* "
19 Peleg lived after he *b·* Reu two "
19 hundred and nine years, and *b·* "
20 two and thirty years, and *b·* Serug: "
21 Reu lived after he *b·* Serug two "
21 hundred and seven years, and *b·* "
22 lived thirty years, and *b·* Nahor: "
23 Serug lived after he *b·* Nahor two "
23 Nahor two hundred years, and *b·* "
24 nine and twenty years, and *b·* "
25 Nahor lived after he *b·* Terah an "
25 and nineteen years, and *b·* sons "
26 Terah lived seventy years, and *b·* "
27 Terah *b·* Abram, Nahor, and "
27 Haran; and Haran *b·* Lot. "
22:23 Bethuel *b·* Rebekah: these eight "
25: 3 Jokshan *b·* Sheba, and Dedan. "
19 Abraham *b·* Isaac: "
Le 25:45 with you, which they *b·* in your "
Nu 26:29 Machir *b·* Gilead: of Gilead come*
58 Kohath *b·* Amram. "
De 32:18 the Rock that *b·* thee thou art "
J'g 11: 1 an harlot: and Gilead *b·* Jephthah. "
Ru 4:18 Pharez *b·* Hezron, "
19 Hezron *b·* Ram, and Ram *b·* "
20 Amminadab *b·* Nahshon, "
20 and Nahshon *b·* Salmon, "
21 Salmon *b·* Boaz, and Boaz *b·* Obed, "
22 Obed *b·* Jesse, and Jesse *b·* David. "
1Ch 1:10 Cush *b·* Nimrod: he began to be "
11 Mizraim *b·* Ludim, and Anamim, "
13 Canaan *b·* Zidon his firstborn, "
18 Arphaxad *b·* Shelah, "
18 and Shelah *b·* Eber. "
20 Joktan *b·* Almodad, and Sheleph, "
34 Abraham *b·* Isaac. The sons of "
2:10 Ram *b·* Amminadab; "
10 and Amminadab *b·* Nahshon, "
11 Nahshon *b·* Salma, and Salma *b·* "
12 Boaz *b·* Obed, and Obed *b·* Jesse, "
13 Jesse *b·* his firstborn Eliab, "
18 Caleb, the son of Hezron *b·* "
20 Hur *b·* Uri, and Uri *b·* Bezaleel, "
22 Segub *b·* Jair, who had three "
36 Attai *b·* Nathan, and Nathan *b·* "
37 Zabad *b·* Ephlal, and Ephlal *b·* "
38 Obed *b·* Jehu, and Jehu *b·* Azariah, "
39 Azariah *b·* Helez, and Helez *b·* "
40 Eleasah *b·* Sisamai, and Sisamai *b·* "
41 Shallum *b·* Jekamiah, "
41 and Jekamiah *b·* Elishama, "
44 Shema *b·* Raham, the father of "
44 Jorkoam: and Rekem *b·* Shammai. "
46 Haran *b·* Gazez. "
4: 2 Reaiah the son of Shobal *b·* Jahath; "
2 and Jahath *b·* Ahumai, "
8 Coz *b·* Anub, and Zobebah, "
11 Chelub the brother of Shuah *b·* "
12 Eshton *b·* Beth-rapha, and Paseah, "
14 Meonothai *b·* Ophrah: "
14 and Seraiah *b·* Joab, "
6: 4 Eleazar *b·* Phinehas, "
4 Phinehas *b·* Abishua, "
5 And Abishua *b·* Bukki, "
5 and Bukki *b·* Uzzi, "
6 And Uzzi *b·* Zerahiah, "
6 and Zerahiah *b·* Meraioth, "
7 Meraioth *b·* Amariah, "
7 and Amariah *b·* Ahitub, "
8 And Ahitub *b·* Zadok, "
8 and Zadok *b·* Ahimaaz, "
9 And Ahimaaz *b·* Azariah, "
9 and Azariah *b·* Johanan, "
10 And Johanan *b·* Azariah (he it is "
11 And Azariah *b·* Amariah, "
11 and Amariah *b·* Ahitub, "
12 And Ahitub *b·* Zadok, "
12 and Zadok *b·* Shallum, "
13 And Shallum *b·* Hilkiah, "
13 and Hilkiah *b·* Azariah, "
14 And Azariah *b·* Seraiah, "
14 and Seraiah *b·* Jehozadak, "
7:32 Heber *b·* Japhlet, and Shomer, "
8: 1 Benjamin *b·* Belah his firstborn, "
7 removed them, and *b·* Uzza, and "
8 Shaharaim *b·* children in the "
9 And he *b·* of Hodesh his wife, "
11 of Hushim he *b·* Abitub, and "
32 Mikloth *b·* Shimeah. And these "
33 Ner *b·* Kish, and Kish *b·* Saul, "
33 and Saul *b·* Jonathan, "
34 Merib-baal *b·* Micah. "
36 Ahaz *b·* Jehoadah; and "
36 Jehoadah *b·* Alemeth, and "
36 and Zimri *b·* Moza, "
37 Moza *b·* Binea: Rapha was his son, "
9:38 Mikloth *b·* Shimeam. And they also "
39 Ner *b·* Kish; and Kish *b·* Saul; "
39 and Saul *b·* Jonathan, "
40 was Merib-baal: Merib-baal *b·* "
42 Ahaz *b·* Jarah; and "
42 Jarah *b·* Alemeth, and Azmaveth, "
42 and Zimri *b·* Moza, "
43 Moza *b·* Binea; and Rephaiah his "
14: 3 and David *b·* more sons and "
2Ch 11:21 and *b·* twenty and eight sons, "
13:21 and *b·* twenty and two sons, "

2Ch 24: 3 and he b' sons and daughters. 3205
Ne 12:10 Jeshua b' Joiakim, "
10 Joiakim also b' Eliashib, "
10 and Eliashib b' Joiada, "
11 Joiada b' Jonathan, "
11 and Jonathan b' Jaddua. "
Pr 23:22 unto thy father that b' thee, "
Jer 16: 3 their fathers that b' them in this "
Da 11: 6 brought her, and he that b' her, "
Zec 13: 3 father and his mother that b' him "
3 father and his mother that b' him "
M't 1: 2 Abraham b' Isaac; 1080
2 and Isaac b' Jacob; "
2 and Jacob b' Judas "
3 Judas b' Phares and Zara of "
3 and Phares b' Esrom; "
3 and Esrom b' Aram; "
4 Aram b' Aminadab; "
4 and Aminadab b' Naasson; "
4 and Naasson b' Salmon; "
5 Salmon b' Booz of Rachab; "
5 and Booz b' Obed of Ruth; "
5 and Obed b' Jesse; "
6 Jesse b' David the king; and "
6 David the king b' Solomon "
7 Solomon b' Roboam; "
7 and Roboam b' Abia; "
7 and Abia b' Asa; "
8 Asa b' Josaphat; "
8 and Josaphat b' Joram; "
8 and Joram b' Ozias; "
9 Ozias b' Joatham; "
9 and Joatham b' Achaz; "
9 and Achaz b' Ezekias; "
10 Ezekias b' Manasses; "
10 and Manasses b' Amon; "
10 and Amon b' Josias; "
11 Josias b' Jechonias and his "
12 Jechonias b' Salathiel; "
12 and Salathiel b' Zorobabel; "
13 Zorobabel b' Abiud; "
13 and Abiud b' Eliakim; "
13 and Eliakim b' Azor; "
14 Azor b' Sadoc; "
14 and Sadoc b' Achim; "
14 and Achim b' Eliud; "
15 Eliud b' Eleazar; "
15 and Eleazar b' Matthan; "
15 and Matthan b' Jacob; "
16 Jacob b' Joseph the husband of "
Ac 7: 8 Abraham b' Isaac, and circumcised "
8 Isaac b' Jacob; and Jacob b' the "
29 Madian, where he b' two sons. 1080
Jas 1:18 own will b' he us with the word * 616
1Jo 5: 1 every one that loveth him that b' 1080

beget See also BEGAT; BEGETTEST; BEGETTETH; BEGOTTEN.
Ge 17:20 twelve princes shall he b', 3205
De 4:25 When thou shalt b' children, "
28:41 Thou shalt b' sons and daughters, "
2Ki 20:18 which thou shalt b', shall they "
Ec 6: 3 If a man b' a hundred children, "
Isa 39: 7 from thee, which thou shalt b', "
Jer 29: 6 Take ye wives, and b' sons and "
Eze 18:10 If he b' a son that is a robber, "
14 if he b' a son, that seeth all "
47:22 which shall b' children among you: "

begettest
Ge 48: 6 issue, which thou b' after them, 3205
Isa 45:10 unto his father, What b' thou? "

begetteth
Pr 17:21 He that b' a fool doeth it to his 3205
23:24 and he that b' a wise child shall "
Ec 5:14 he b' a son, and there is nothing "

beggar
1Sa 2: 8 up the b' from the dunghill, * 34
Lu 16:20 was a certain b' named Lazarus, 4434
22 that the b' died, and was carried "

beggarly
Ga 4: 9 to the weak and b' elements, 4434

begged
M't 27:58 Pilate, and b' the body of Jesus. * 154
Lu 23:52 Pilate, and b' the body of Jesus. * "
Joh 9: 8 Is not this he that sat and b'? 4319

begging
Ps 37:25 forsaken, nor his and b' bread. 1245
M'r 10:46 sat by the highway side b'. *4319
Lu 18:35 man sat by the wayside b': "

begin See also BEGAN; BEGINNEST; BEGINNING; BEGUN.
Ge 11: 6 this they b' to do: and now 2490
De 2:24 b' to possess it, and contend "
25 will I b' to put the dread of thee "
31 his land before thee: b' to possess, "
16: 9 b' to number the seven weeks "
Jos 3: 7 This day will I b' to magnify thee "
J'g 10:18 What man is he that will b' "
13: 5 he shall b' to deliver Israel "
1Sa 3:12 I b', I will also make an end. * "
22:15 Did I then b' to enquire of God * "
2Ki 8:25 Jehoram king of Judah b' to reign. "
Ne 11:17 to b' the thanksgiving in prayer: 8462
Jer 25:29 I b' to bring evil on the city 2490
Eze 9: 6 and b' at my sanctuary. "
M't 24:49 b' to smite his fellowservants, 756
Lu 3: 8 b' not to say within yourselves, "
12:45 shall b' to beat the menservants "
13:25 ye b' to stand without, and to knock "
26 Then shall ye b' to say, We have "
14: 9 thou b' with shame to take the "
29 behold it b' to mock him, "
21:28 these things b' to come to pass, "
23:30 they b' to say to the mountains, "
2Co 3: 1 Do we b' again to commend * 756
1Pe 4:17 must b' at the house of God: "
17 and if it first b' at us, what shall "
Re 10: 7 he shall b' to sound, the mystery *3195

beginnest
De 16: 9 from such time as thou b' to put 2490

beginning See also BEGINNINGS.
Ge 1: 1 In the b' God created the heaven 7225
10:10 the b' of his kingdom was Babel, "
13: 3 his tent had been at the b', 8462
41:21 still ill favoured, as at the b'. "
49: 3 might, and the b' of my strength, 7225
Ex 12: 2 the b' of months: it shall be the 7218
De 11:12 for the b' of the year even unto the 7225
21:17 for he is the b' of his strength; "
32:42 b' of revenges upon the enemy. *7218
J'g 7:19 in the b' of the middle watch; "
Ru 1:22 Beth-lehem in the b' of barley 8462
3:10 in the latter end than at the b'. 7223
2Sa 21: 9 in the b' of barley harvest. 8462
10 from the b' of harvest until water "
2Ki 17:25 was at the b' of their dwelling "
1Ch 17: 9 them any more, as at the b', *7223
Ezr 4: 6 Ahasuerus, in the b' of his reign, 8462
Job 8: 7 Though thy b' was small, yet thy 7225
42:12 end of Job more than his b': "
Ps 111:10 of the Lord is the b' of wisdom: "
119:160 is true from the b': and every *7218
Pr 1: 7 the b' of knowledge: but fools 7225
8:22 possessed me in the b' of his "
23 up from everlasting, from the b', 7218
9:10 fear of the Lord is the b' of 8462
17:14 The b' of strife is as when 7225
20:21 hastily at the b'; but the end 7223
Ec 3:11 that God maketh from the b' 7218
7: 8 end of a thing than the b' thereof: 7225
10:13 The b' of the words of his mouth 8462
Isa 1:26 thy counsellors as at the b': * "
18: 2 terrible from their b' hitherto; a 1931
7 a people terrible from their b' "
40:21 you from the b'? have ye not 7218
41: 4 the generations from the b'? "
26 Who hath declared from the b', "
46:10 Declaring the end from the b', 7225
48: 3 the former things from the b'; * 227
5 I have even from the b' declared * "
7 now, and not from the b'; even * "
16 not spoken in secret from the b'; 7218
64: 4 For since the b' of the world men *5769
Jer 17:12 glorious high throne from the b' 7223
26: 1 the b' of the reign of 7225
27: 1 the b' of the reign of Jehoiakim "
28: 1 in the b' of the reign of Zedekiah "
49:34 Elam in the b' of the reign "
La 2:19 in the b' of the watches pour out 7218
Eze 40: 1 in the b' of the year of our "
Da 9:21 seen in the vision at the b', 8462
23 At the b' of my supplications "
Ho 1: 2 The b' of the word of the Lord * "
Am 7: 1 poured grasshoppers in the b' of "
Mic 1:13 the b of the sin to the daughter 7225
M't 14:30 b' to sink, he cried, saying, 756
19: 4 which made them at the b' 746
8 from the b' it was not so. "
20: 8 b' from the last unto the first. 756
24: 8 these are the b' of sorrows. 746
21 since the b' of the world to this "
M'r 1: 1 The b' of the gospel of Jesus "
10: 6 from the b' of the creation "
13:19 such as was not from the b' "
Lu 1: 2 from the b' were eyewitnesses, "
23: 5 b' from Galilee to this place. 756
24:27 b' at Moses and all the prophets, "
47 among all nations, b' at Jerusalem. "
Joh 1: 1 In the b' was the Word, and the 746
2 The same was in the b' with God. "
2:10 man at the b' doth set forth *4412
11 This b' of miracles did Jesus 746
6:64 Jesus knew from the b' who "
8: 9 b' at the eldest, even unto the last: 756
25 I said unto you from the b'. 746
44 was a murderer from the b', "
15:27 ye have been with me from the b'. "
16: 4 not unto you at the b', because I "
Ac 1:22 B' from the baptism of John, 756
11: 4 rehearsed the matter from the b',* "
15 fell on them, as on us at the b'. 746
15:18 his works from the b' of the ‡
26: 5 Which knew me from the b', * 509
Eph 3: 9 which from the b' of the world * "
Ph'p 4:15 that in the b' of the gospel, 746
Col 1:18 who is the b', the firstborn "
2Th 2:13 God hath from the b' chosen you "
Heb 1:10 Thou, Lord, in the b' hast laid "
3:14 if we hold the b' of our confidence "
7: 3 having neither b' of days, nor end "
2Pe 2:20 is worse with them than the b'. *4413
3: 4 were from the b' of the creation. 746
1Jo 1: 1 That which was from the b', "
2: 7 which ye had from the b'. "
7 ye have heard from the b'. * "
13 him that is from the b'. "
14 known him that is from the b'. "
24 which ye have heard from the b'. "
24 ye have heard from the b' "
3: 8 the devil sinneth from the b'. "
11 that ye heard from the b', "
2Jo 5 which we had from the b', "
6 as ye have heard from the b', "
Re 1: 8 the b' and the ending, * "
3:14 the b' of the creation of God; "
21: 6 the b' and the end. I will "
22:13 Alpha and Omega, the b' and the "

beginnings
Nu 10:10 and in the b' of your months, 7218
28:11 And in the b' of your months 7218
Eze 36:11 better unto you than at your b': 7221
M'k 13: 8 these are the b' of sorrows. * 746

begotten See also FIRSTBEGOTTEN.
Ge 5: 4 days of Adam after he had b' Seth *3205
Le 18:11 b' of thy father, she is thy sister, 4138
Nu 11:12 I b' them, that thou shouldest *3205
De 23: 8 The children that are b' of them * "
J'g 8:30 and ten sons of his body b': 3318
Job 38:28 who hath b' the drops of dew? 3205
Ps 2: 7 my son; this day have I b' thee. "
Isa 49:21 Who hath b' me these, seeing I "
Hos 5: 7 for they have b' strange children: * "
Joh 1:14 as of the only b' of the Father,) 3439
18 the only b' Son, which is "
3:16 his only b' Son, that whosoever "
18 name of the only b' Son of God. "
Ac 13:33 my Son, this day have I b' thee. 1080
1Co 4:15 I have b' you through the gospel.* "
Ph'm 10 whom I have b' in my bonds: "
Heb 1: 5 my Son, this day have I b' thee? "
5: 5 my Son, to day have I b' thee. "
11:17 offered up his only b' son, 3439
1Pe 1: 3 b' us again unto a lively hope * 313
1Jo 4: 9 God sent his only b' Son 3439
5: 1 loveth him also that is b' of him. 1080
18 but he that is b' of God keepeth "
Re 1: 5 first b' of the dead, and the prince *4416

beguile See also BEGUILED; BEGUILING.
Col 2: 4 lest any man should b' you with *3884
18 Let no man b' you of your reward *2603

beguiled
Ge 3:13 The serpent b' me, and I did eat. 5377
29:25 wherefore then hast thou b' me? 7411
Nu 25:18 they have b' you in the matter of 5230
Jos 9:22 Wherefore have ye b' us, saying, 7411
2Co 11: 3 as the serpent b' Eve through his 1818

beguiling
2Pe 2:14 b' unstable souls: an heart they *1185

begun
Nu 16:46 from the Lord; the plague is b'. 2490
47 plague was b' among the people: "
De 2:31 I have b' to give Sihon and his "
3:24 thou hast b' to shew thy servant "
Es 6:13 before whom thou hast b' to fall, "
9:23 undertook to do as they had b', "
M't 18:24 when he had b' to reckon, one was 756
2Co 8: 6 that as he had b', so he would also *4278
10 who have b' before, not only to do,* "
Ga 3: 3 having b' in the Spirit, are ye now 1728
Ph'p 1: 6 that he which hath b' a good * "
1Ti 5:11 when they have b' to wax wanton *2691

behalf
Ex 27:21 on the b' of the children of Israel. 854
2Sa 3:12 messengers to David on his b', 8478
2Ch 16: 9 to shew himself strong in the b' 5973
Job 36: 2 I have yet to speak on God's b'.
Da 11:18 but a prince for his own b' shall *
Ro 16:19 I am glad therefore on your b': *1909
1Co 1: 4 thank my God always on your b', *4012
2Co 1:11 may be given by many on our b'. 5228
5:12 you occasion to glory on our b', "
8:24 and of our boasting on your b'. "
9: 3 you should be in vain in this b'; *3313
Ph'p 1:29 it is given in the b' of Christ, 5228
1Pe 4:16 let him glorify God on this b'. *3313

behave See also BEHAVED; BEHAVETH.
De 32:27 lest their adversaries should b' ††5234
1Ch 19:13 and let us b' ourselves valiantly *2388
Ps 101: 2 I will b' myself wisely in a perfect 7919
Isa 3: 5 the child shall b' himself proudly 7292
1Co 13: 5 Doth not b' itself unseemly, 807
1Ti 3:15 to b' thyself in the house of God, 390

behaved
1Sa 18: 5 sent him, and b' himself wisely: 7919
14 David b' himself wisely in all his "
15 saw that he b' himself very wisely, "
30 David b' himself more wisely than "
Ps 35:14 I b' myself as though he had been 1980
131: 2 I have b' and quieted myself *7737
Mic 3: 4 as they have b' themselves ill *7489
1Th 2:10 unblameably we b' ourselves 1096
2Th 3: 7 for we b' not ourselves disorderly 812

behaveth
1Co 7:36 think that he b' himself uncomely 807

behaviour
1Sa 21:13 he changed his b' before them, 2940
Ps 34: *title* when he changed his b' before "
1Ti 3: 2 vigilant, sober, of good b', *2887
Tit 2: 3 that they be in b' as becometh *2688

beheaded
De 21: 6 the heifer that is b' in the valley: *6202
2Sa 4: 7 and slew him, and b' him, 5493, 7218
M't 14:10 he sent, and b' John in the prison, 607
M'k 6:16 It is John, whom I b': "
27 he went and b' him in the prison. "
Lu 9: 9 Herod said, John have I b': "
Re 20: 4 the souls of them that were b' 3990

beheld
Ge 12:14 the Egyptians b' the woman that 7200
13:10 and b' all the plain of Jordan, "
19:28 and b', and, lo, the smoke of "
31: 2 And Jacob b' the countenance "
48: 8 And Israel b' Joseph's sons, "
Nu 21: 9 when he b' the serpent of brass, *5027
23:21 He hath not b' iniquity in Jacob, "
J'g 16:27 men and women, that b' 7200
1Sa 26: 5 and David b' the place where Saul "
1Ch 21:15 the Lord b', and he repented him "
Job 31:26 If I b' the sun when it shined, "
Ps 119:158 I b' the transgressors, and was "
142: 4 and b', but there was no man * "

Pr 7: 7 And *b*' among the simple ones, 7200
Ec 8:17 Then I *b*' all the work of God, "
Isa 41:28 For I *b*', and there was no man; * "
Jer 4:23 I *b*' the earth, and, lo, it was "
24 I *b*' the mountains, and, lo, they "
25 I *b*', and, lo, there was no man, "
26 I *b*', and, lo, the fruitful place "
31:26 I awaked, and *b*'; and my sleep "
Eze 1:15 Now as I *b*' the living creatures, 7200
8: 2 Then I *b*', and lo a likeness as the "
37: 8 when I *b*', lo, the sinews and the "
Da 7: 4 *b*' till the wings thereof were 2370,934
6 *b*', and lo another, like a leopard," "
9 *b*' till the thrones were cast down," "
11 I *b*' then because of the voice "
11 I *b*' even till the beast was slain," "
21 I *b*', and the same horn made war" "
Hab 3: 6 he *b*', and drove asunder the 7200
M't 19:26 *b*' them, and said unto them, *1689
M'k 9:15 the people, when they *b*' him, *1492
12:41 *b*' how the people cast money 2334
15:47 mother of Joses *b*' where he was "
Lu 10:18 I *b*' Satan as lightning fall from "
19:41 *b*' the city, and wept over it, *1492
20:17 *b*' them, and said, What is this *1689
22:56 a certain maid *b*' him as he sat *1492
23:55 *b*' the sepulchre, and how his 2300
24:12 he *b*' the linen clothes laid by * 991
Joh 1:14 we *b*' his glory, the glory as of 2300
42 when Jesus *b*' him, he said, *1689
Ac 1: 9 while they *b*', he was taken up; * 991
17:23 passed by, and *b*' your devotions, * 333
Re 5: 6 I *b*', and, lo, in the midst of the *1492
11 I *b*', and I heard the voice of * "
6: 5 And I *b*', and lo a black horse; * "
12 *b*' when he had opened the sixth * "
7: 9 After this I *b*', and, lo, a great * "
8:13 I *b*', and heard an angel flying * "
11:12 and their enemies *b*' them. 2334
13:11 I *b*' another beast coming up out *1492

behemoth (*be'-he-moth*)
Job 40:15 Behold now *b*', which I made 930

behind
Ge 18:10 in the tent door, which was *b*' him. 310
19:17 look not *b*' thee, neither stay thou "
26 his wife looked back from *b*' him, "
22:13 *b*' him a ram, caught in a thicket "
32:18 and, behold, also he is *b*' us. "
20 Behold, thy servant Jacob is *b*' us. "
Ex 10:26 there shall not an hoof be left *b*'; "
11: 5 the maidservant that is *b*' the mill; 310
14:19 removed and went *b*' them; and the "
19 before their face, and stood *b*' them: "
Le 25:51 If there be yet many years *b*', *
Nu 3:23 pitch *b*' the tabernacle westward. 310
De 25:18 even all that were feeble *b*' thee, "
Jos 8: 2 lay thee an ambush for the city *b*' "
4 *b*' the city: go not very far from "
14 in ambush against him *b*' the city. "
20 when the men of Ai looked *b*' them, "
J'g 18:12 behold, it is *b*' Kirjath-jearim. "
20:40 the Benjamites looked *b*' them, "
1Sa 21: 9 wrapped in a cloth *b*' the ephod: "
24: 8 when Saul looked *b*' him, David "
30: 9 those that were left *b*' stayed. 3498
10 for two hundred abode *b*', which 5975
2Sa 1: 7 when he looked *b*' him, he saw 310
2:20 Then Abner looked *b*' him, "
23 the spear came out *b*' him; and he "
3:16 weeping *b*' her to Bahurim. * "
5:23 fetch a compass *b*' them, and come "
10: 9 was against him before and *b*', 268
13:34 by the way of the hill side *b*' him. 310
1Ki 10:19 top of the throne was round *b*': "
14: 9 and hast cast me *b*' thy back: "
2Ki 6:32 sound of his master's feet *b*' him? "
9:18, 19 do with peace? turn thee *b*' me. "
11: 6 third part at the gate *b*' the guard: "
1Ch 19:10 was set against him before and *b*', 268
2Ch 13:13 an ambushment to come about *b*' 310
13 the ambushment was *b*' them. "
14 the battle was before and *b*': 268
Ne 4:13 in the lower places *b*' the wall, 310
16 the rulers were *b*' all the house "
9:26 cast thy law *b*' their backs, and slew "
Ps 50:17 and castest my words *b*' thee. "
139: 5 Thou hast beset me *b*' and before, 268
Ca 2: 9 he standeth *b*' our wall, he looketh 310
Isa 9:12 before, and the Philistines *b*'; 268
30:21 Ears shall hear a word *b*', 310
38:17 hast cast all my sins *b*' thy back. "
57: 8 *B*' the doors also and the posts "
66:17 *b*' one tree in the midst, eating "
Eze 3:12 I heard *b*' me a voice of a great "
23:35 and cast me *b*' thy back, therefore "
41:15 separate place which was *b*' it, * "
Joe 2: 3 and *b*' them a flame burneth: "
3 and *b*' them a desolate wilderness; "
14 leave a blessing *b*' him; even a "
Zec 1: 8 and *b*' him were there red horses, "
M't 9:20 came *b*' him, and touched the hem 3693
16:23 Get thee *b*' me, Satan: thou art 3694
M'k 5:27 came in the press *b*', and touched 3693
8:33 Get thee *b*' me, Satan: for thou 3694
12:19 brother die, and leave his wife *b*', 2641
Lu 2:43 Jesus tarried *b*' in Jerusalem; 5278
4: 8 Get thee *b*' me, Satan: for it is *3694
7:38 And stood at his feet *b*' him "
8:44 Came *b*' him, and touched the 3693
1Co 1: 7 So that ye come *b*' in no gift; 5302
2Co 11: 5 I suppose I was not a whit *b*' the "
12:11 for in nothing am I *b*' the very "
Ph'p 3:13 those things which are *b*', 3694
Col 1:24 that which is *b*' of the afflictions *5303
Re 1:10 and heard *b*' me a great voice, 3694

Re 4: 6 beasts full of eyes before and *b*'. 3693

behold See also BEHELD; BEHOLDEST; BEHOLDETH; BEHOLDING.
Ge 1:29 God said, *B*', I have given you 2009
31 had made, and, *b*', it was very good. "
3:22 *B*', the man is become as one of 2005
4:14 *B*', thou hast driven me out this "
6:12 the earth, and, *b*', it was corrupt; 2009
13 *b*', I will destroy them with the 2005
17 And, *b*', I, even I, do bring a flood "
8:13 *b*', the face of the ground was dry. 2009
9: 9 And I, *b*', I establish my covenant 2005
11: 6 the Lord said, *B*', the people is "
12:11 *B*' now, I know that thou art 2009
19 therefore *b*' thy wife, take her, "
15: 3 *B*', to me thou hast given no seed: 2005
4 And, *b*', the word of the Lord came 2009
17 the sun went down, *b*' a smoking "
16: 2 *B*' now, the Lord hath restrained "
6 *B*', thy maid is in thy hand; do to "
11 *B*', thou art with child, and shalt "
14 *b*', it is between Kadesh and Bered. "
17: 4 As for me, *b*', my covenant is "
20 have heard thee: *B*', I have blessed "
18: 9 And he said, *B*', in the tent. "
27, 31 *B*' now, I have taken upon me "
19: 2 *B*' now, my lords, turn in, I pray "
8 *B*' now, I have two daughters "
19 *B*' now, thy servant hath found "
20 *B*' now, this city is near to flee "
34 *B*', I lay yesternight with my 2005
20: 3 *B*', thou art but a dead man, 2009
15 said, *B*', my land is before thee: "
16 unto Sarah he said, *B*', I have, "
16 *b*', he is to thee a covering of the "
22: 1 And he said, *B*', here I am. * "
24:51 *B*', Rebekah is before thee, take "
63 and, *b*', the camels were coming. "
25:24 were fulfilled, *b*', there were "
32 *B*', I am at the point to die: "
26: 8 *b*', Isaac was sporting with "
9 *B*', of a surety she is thy wife: "
27: 1 he said unto him, *B*', here I am. * "
2 And he said, *B*' now, I am "
6 saying, *B*', I heard thy father "
11 *B*', Esau my brother is a 2005
36 and, *b*', now he hath taken away 2009
37 *B*', I have made him thy lord, 2005
39 *B*', thy dwelling shall be the 2009
42 *B*', thy brother Esau, as touching "
28:12 he dreamed, and *b*' a ladder set "
12 *b*' the angels of God ascending "
13 And, *b*', the Lord stood above it, "
15 And, *b*', I am with thee, and will "
29: 2 he looked, and *b*' a well in the field, "
6 and, *b*', Rachel his daughter "
25 in the morning, *b*', it was Leah: "
30: 3 she said, *B*' my maid Bilhah, go in "
34 *B*', I would it might be according 2005
31: 2 and, *b*', it was not toward him as 2009
10 and, *b*', the rams which leaped "
51 *B*' this heap, and *b*' this pillar, "
32:18 unto my lord Esau: and, *b*', also "
20 *B*', thy servant Jacob is behind us. "
33: 1 and, *b*', Esau came, and with him "
34:21 for the land, *b*', it is large enough "
37: 7 For, *b*', we were binding sheaves "
7 and, *b*', your sheaves stood round "
9 *B*', I have dreamed a dream more; "
9 and, *b*' the sun and the moon and "
15 *b*', he was wandering in the field: "
19 another, *B*', this dreamer cometh. "
25 and, *b*', a company of Ishmeelites "
38:13 *B*' thy father in law goeth up to "
23 *b*', I sent this kid, and thou hast "
24 and also, *b*', she is with child "
27 that, *b*', twins were in her womb. "
29 *b*', his brother came out: and she "
39: 8 *B*', my master wotteth not what 2005
40: 6 and looked upon them, and, *b*', 2009
9 In my dream, *b*', a vine was before "
16 and, *b*', I had three white baskets "
41: 1 that Pharaoh dreamed: and, *b*', "
2 And, *b*', there came up out of the "
3 And, *b*', seven other kine came up "
5 and, *b*', seven ears of corn came "
6 *b*', seven thin ears and blasted "
7 Pharaoh awoke, and, *b*', it was a "
17 In my dream, *b*', I stood upon the 2005
18 *b*', there came up out of the river 2009
19 *b*', seven other kine came up after "
22 *b*', seven ears came up in one stalk, "
23 *b*', seven ears, withered, thin, and "
29 *B*', there came seven years of great "
42: 2 *B*', I have heard that there is corn "
13 *b*', the youngest is this day with "
22 *b*', also his blood is required. "
27 for, *b*', it was in his sack's mouth. "
35 *b*', every man's bundle of money "
43:21 we opened our sacks, and, *b*', "
44: 8 *B*', the money, which we found 2005
16 *B*', we are my lord's servants, 2009
45:12 And, *b*', your eyes see, and the "
47: 1 *b*', they are in the land of Goshen. "
48: 1 *B*', thy father is sick: and he took "
2 *B*', thy son Joseph cometh unto "
4 *B*', I will make thee fruitful, and 2005
21 *B*', I die; but God shall be with 2009
50:18 they said, *B*', we be thy servants. "
Ex 2:13 *b*', two men of the Hebrews "
3: 2 looked, and, *b*', the bush burned "
9 *b*', the cry of the children of Israel "
13 *B*', when I come unto the children "
4: 1 But, *b*', they will not believe me, 2005
6 *b*', his hand was leprous as snow. 2009
7 *b*', it was turned again as his "

Ex 4:14 *b*', he cometh forth to meet thee: 2009
23 *b*', I will slay thy son, even thy "
5: 5 *B*', the people of the land now are 2005
16 and, *b*', thy servants are beaten; 2009
6:12 *B*', the children of Israel have 2005
30 Moses said before the Lord, *B*', "
7:16 *b*', hitherto thou wouldest not 2009
17 know that I am the Lord: *b*', "
8: 2 if thou refuse to let them go, *b*', I "
21 thou wilt not let my people go, *b*', 2005
29 *B*', I go out from thee, 2009
9: 7 *b*', there was not one of the cattle "
18 *B*', to morrow about this time 2005
10: 4 let my people go, *b*', to morrow "
14:10 and, *b*', the Egyptians marched 2009
17 And I, *b*', I will harden 2005
16: 4 *B*', I will rain bread "
10 *b*', the glory of the Lord 2009
14 *b*', upon the face of the wilderness "
17: 6 *B*', I will stand before thee 2005
23:20 *B*', I send an Angel before thee, 2009
24: 8 *B*' the blood of the covenant, "
14 *b*', Aaron and Hur are with you: "
31: 6 *b*', I have given with him Aholiab, "
32: 9 and, *b*', it is a stiffnecked people: "
34 *b*', mine Angel shall go before thee: "
33:21 said, *B*', there is a place by me, "
34:10 he said, *B*', I make a covenant: "
11 *b*', I drive out before thee the 2005
30 *b*', the skin of his face shone; 2009
Le 10:16 and, *b*', it was burnt: "
18 *B*', the blood of it was not brought 2005
19 *B*', this day have they offered "
13: 5 *b*', if the plague in his sight 2009
6 *b*', if the plague be somewhat "
8 *b*', the scab spreadeth in the skin, "
10 *b*', if the rising be white "
13 *b*', if the leprosy have covered "
17 *b*', if the plague be turned "
20 *b*', if it be in sight lower than "
21 *b*', there be no white hairs "
25 *b*', if the hair in the bright "
26 *b*', there be no white hair "
30 *b*', if it be in sight deeper "
31 *b*', it be not in sight deeper "
32 *b*', if the scall spread not, "
34 *b*', if the scall be not spread "
36 *b*', if the scall be spread "
39 *b*', if the bright spots in the skin "
53 *b*', the plague be not spread "
55 *b*', if the plague have not changed "
56 *b*', the plague be somewhat "
14: 3 *b*', if the plague of leprosy "
37 *b*', if the plague be in the walls "
39, 44 *b*', if the plague be spread "
48 *b*', the plague hath not spread "
25:20 *b*', we shall not sow, 2005
Nu 3:12 *b*', I have taken the Levites 2009
12: 8 similitude of the Lord shall he *b*': 5027
10 *b*', Miriam became leprous, 2009
10 *b*', she was leprous. "
16:42 *b*', the cloud covered it "
47 *b*', the plague was begun "
17: 8 *b*', the rod of Aaron for the house "
12 *B*', we die, we perish, 2005
18: 6 *b*', I have taken your brethren 2009
21 *b*', I have given the children "
20:16 *b*', we are in Kadesh, "
22:11 *B*', there is a people come out "
32 *b*', I went out to withstand "
23: 9 him, and from the hills I *b*' him: 7789
11 *b*', thou hast blessed them 2009
17 *b*', he stood by his burnt * "
20 *B*', I have received commandment "
24 *B*', the people shall rise up 2005
24:14 *b*', I go unto my people: "
17 I shall *b*' him, but not nigh: 7789
25: 6 *b*', one of the children of Israel 2009
12 *B*', I give unto him my covenant 2005
31:16 *B*', these caused the children "
32: 1 *b*', the place was a place 2009
14 *b*', ye are risen up "
23 *b*', ye have sinned "
De 1: 8 *B*', I have set the land before you: 7200
10 *b*', ye are this day as the stars 2009
21 *B*', the Lord thy God hath set 7200
2:24 *b*', I have given into thine hand "
31 *B*', I have begun to give Sihon "
3:11 *b*', his bedstead was a bedstead 2009
27 and *b*' it with thine eyes: 7200
4: 5 *B*', I have taught you statutes "
5:24 *B*', the Lord our God hath shewed 2005
9:16 I looked, and, *b*', ye had sinned 2009
10:14 *B*', the heaven and the heaven 2005
11:26 *B*', I set before you this day a 7200
13:14 *b*', if it be truth, 2009
17: 4 *b*', if it be true, "
19:18 *b*', if the witness be a false "
26:10 *b*', I have brought the firstfruits "
31:14 *B*', thy days approach 2005
16 *B*', thou shalt sleep with thy 2009
27 *b*', while I am yet alive 2005
32:49 and *b*' the land of Canaan, which 7200
Jos 2: 2 *B*', there came men in hither 2009
18 *B*', when we come into the land, "
3:11 *b*', the ark of the covenant "
5:13 *b*', there stood a man "
7:21 *b*', they are hid in the earth "
22 *b*', it was hid in his tent, "
8: 4 *B*', ye shall lie in wait against the 7200
20 *b*', the smoke of the city 2009
9:12 *b*', it is dry, "
13 *b*', they be rent: "
25 And now, *b*', we are in thine hand: 2005
14:10 *b*', the Lord hath kept me 2009
22:11 *B*', the children of Reuben "

Jos 22:28 *B*' the pattern of the altar 7200
23: 4 *B*', I have divided unto you by lot "
14 And, *b*', this day I am going 2009
24:27 *B*', this stone shall be a witness "
J'g 1: 2 *b*', I have delivered the land "
3:24 *b*', the doors of the parlour were "
25 and, *b*', he opened not "
25 and, *b*', their lord was fallen "
4:22 And, *b*', as Barak pursued "
22 *b*', Sisera lay dead, "
6:15 *b*', my family is poor "
28 *b*', the altar of Baal was cast "
37 *B*', I will put a fleece of wool "
7:13 *b*', there was a man "
13 *B*', I dreamed a dream, "
17 and, *b*', when I come "
8:15 said, *B*', Zebah and Zalmunna "
9:31 saying, *B*', Gaal the son of Obed "
31 *b*', they fortify the city "
33 *b*', when he and the people "
36 *B*', there come people "
43 *b*', the people were come "
11:34 *b*', his daughter came out "
13: 3 *B*' now, thou art barren, "
7 *B*', thou shalt conceive, "
10 *B*', the man hath appeared "
14: 5 and, *b*', a young lion roared "
8 *b*', there was a swarm of bees "
16 *B*', I have not told it "
16:10 *B*', thou hast mocked me "
17: 2 *b*', the silver is with me; "
18: 9 and, *b*', it is very good: "
12 *b*', it is behind Kirjath-jearim. "
19: 9 *B*', now the day draweth "
9 *b*', the day groweth to an end, "
16 And, *b*', there came an old man "
22 *b*', the men of the city, "
24 *B*', here is my daughter "
27 *b*', the woman his concubine "
20: 7 *B*', ye are all children "
40 *b*', the flame of the city "
21: 8 *b*', there came none to the camp "
9 *b*', there were none of the "
19 *B*', there is a feast of the Lord "
21 *b*', if the daughters of Shiloh "
Ru 1:15 *B*', thy sister in law "
2: 4 *b*', Boaz came from Beth-lehem "
3: 2 *B*', he winnoweth barley "
8 *b*', a woman lay at his feet. "
4: 1 *b*', the kinsman of whom Boaz "
1Sa 2:31 *B*', the days come, that I will cut "
3:11 to Samuel, *B*', I will do a thing in "
5: 3, 4 *b*', Dagon was fallen upon his "
8: 5 *B*', thou art old, "
9: 6 *B*' now, there is in this city "
7 *b*', if we go, what shall we bring "
8 *B*', I have here at hand "
12 He is; *b*', he is before you: "
14 *b*', Samuel came out against "
17 *B*' the man whom I spake "
24 *B*' that which is left! "
10: 8 *b*', I will come down unto thee, "
10 *b*', a company of prophets "
11 *b*', he prophesied among "
22 *B*', he hath hid himself "
11: 5 *b*', Saul came after the herd "
12: 1 *B*', I have hearkened unto your "
2 *b*', the king walketh before you: "
2 *b*', my sons are with you: "
13 Now therefore *b*' the king "
13 And, *b*', the Lord hath set "
18:10 *b*', Samuel came; "
14: 7 *b*', I am with thee according 2005
8 *B*', we will pass over unto these 2009
11 *B*', the Hebrews come forth "
16 *b*', the multitude melted "
17 *b*', Jonathan and his "
20 *b*', every man's sword "
26 *b*', the honey dropped; "
33 *B*', the people sin against "
16:11 and, *b*', he keepeth the sheep. "
15 *B*' now, an evil spirit from God "
18 *B*', I have seen a son of Jesse, the "
17:23 *b*', there came up the champion, "
18:17 *B*' my elder daughter "
22 *B*', the king hath delight "
19:16 *b*', there was an image "
22 *B*', they be at Naioth in Ramah. "
20: 2 *b*', my father will do nothing "
5 *B*', to morrow is the new moon, "
12 *b*', if there be good toward "
21 And, *b*', I will send a lad, "
21 *B*', the arrows are on this side "
22 *B*', the arrows are beyond "
23 *b*', the Lord be between "
21: 9 *b*', it is here wrapped in a cloth "
23: 1 *B*', the Philistines fight against "
3 *B*', we be afraid here "
24: 1 *B*', David is in the wilderness "
4 *B*', the day of which the Lord said "
4 *B*', I will deliver thine enemy "
9 *B*', David seeketh thy hurt? "
10 *B*', this day thine eyes have seen "
20 now, *b*', I know well that "
25:14 *B*', David sent messengers "
19 *b*', I come after you. 2005
20 and, *b*', David and his men 2009
36 *b*', he held a feast in his "
41 *B*', let thine handmaid "
26: 7 *b*', Saul lay sleeping within "
21 *b*', I have played the fool, "
22 *B*' the king's spear! "
24 *b*', as thy life was much "
28: 7 *B*', there is a woman "
9 *B*', thou knowest what Saul "
21 *B*', thine handmaid hath "

1Sa 30: 3 *b*', it was burned with fire; 2009
16 *b*', they were spread abroad "
26 *B*' a present for you "
2Sa 1: 2 *b*', a man came out "
6 *b*', Saul leaned upon his spear "
18 *b*', it is written in the book "
3:12 *b*', my hand shall be with "
22 *b*', the servants of David "
24 *b*', Abner came unto thee; "
4: 8 *B*' the head of Ish-bosheth "
10 *B*', Saul is dead, "
5: 1 *B*', we are thy bone and thy flesh. 2005
9: 4 *B*', he is in the house 2009
6 answered, *B*' thy servant! "
12:11 *B*', I will raise up evil 2005
18 *B*', while the child was yet alive, 2009
13:24 *B*' now, thy servant hath "
34 *b*', there came much people "
35 *B*', the king's sons come; "
36 *B*', the king's sons came, "
14: 7 And, *b*', the whole family "
21 *B*' now, I have done this thing, "
32 *B*', I sent unto thee, "
15:15 *B*', thy servants are ready "
26 *b*', here am I, let him do 2005
32 *b*', Hushai, the Archite 2009
36 *B*', they have there with them "
16: 1 *b*', Ziba, the servant of "
3 *B*', he abideth at Jerusalem: "
4 *B*', thine are all that pertained "
5 *b*', thence came out a man "
8 *b*', thou art taken in thy "
11 *B*', my son, which came "
17: 9 *B*', he is hid now "
18:11 *b*', thou sawest him, "
24 and *b*' a man running "
26 *B*' another man running "
31 And, *b*', Cushi came; "
19: 1 *B*', the king weepeth "
8 *B*', the king doth sit "
20 therefore, *b*', I am come "
37 But *b*' thy servant Chimham; "
41 And, *b*', all the men of Israel "
20:21 *B*', his head shall be thrown "
24:22 *b*', here be oxen for burnt 7200
1Ki 1:14 *B*', while thou yet talkest 2009
18 *b*', Adonijah reigneth; "
23 *B*' Nathan the prophet. "
25 *b*', they eat and drink "
42 *b*', Jonathan the son of Abiathar "
51 *B*', Adonijah feareth king "
2: 8 *b*', thou hast with thee "
29 *b*', he is by the altar. "
39 *B*', thy servants be in Gath. "
3:12 *B*', I have done according "
15 *b*', it was a dream. "
21 *b*', it was dead: "
21 *b*', it was not my son, "
5: 5 And, *b*', I purpose to build 2005
8:27 *b*' the heaven and heaven of 2009
10: 7 *b*', the half was not told me: "
11:22 *b*', thou seekest to go "
31 *B*', I will rend the kingdom 2005
12:28 *b*' thy gods, O Israel, 2009
13: 1 *b*', there came a man of God "
2 *B*', a child shall be born "
3 *B*', the altar shall be rent, "
25 *b*', men passed by "
14: 2 *b*', there is Ahijah "
5 *B*' the wife of Jeroboam "
10 *b*', I will bring evil upon 2005
19 *b*', they are written in the book 2009
15:19 *b*', I have sent unto thee "
16: 3 *B*', I will take away the posterity 2005
17: 9 *b*', I have commanded 2009
10 *b*', the widow woman was "
12 *b*', I am gathering two sticks, 2005
18: 7 *b*', Elijah met him: 2009
8, 11, 14 *B*', Elijah is here: "
44 *B*', there ariseth a little cloud "
19: 5 *b*', then an angel touched "
6 *b*', there was a cake baken "
9 *b*', the word of the Lord came "
11 And, *b*', the Lord passed by, "
13 *b*', there came a voice "
20:13 *b*', there came a prophet "
13 *b*', I will deliver it 2005
31 *B*' now, we have heard 2009
36 *b*', as soon as thou art "
39 *b*', a man turned aside, "
21:18 *b*', he is in the vineyard "
21 *B*', I will bring evil upon thee, 2005
22:13 *B*' now, the words of the prophet 2009
23 *b*' now the Lord hath put a lying "
25 *B*', thou shalt see in that "
2Ki 1: 9 *b*', he sat on the top of an hill. "
14 *B*', there came fire down from "
2:11 *b*', there appeared a chariot "
16 *B*' now, there be with thy servants "
19 *B*', I pray thee, the situation "
3:20 *b*', there came water by the way "
4: 9 *B*' now, I perceive that this "
13 *B*', thou hast been careful "
25 *B*', yonder is that Shunammite: "
32 *b*', the child was dead, "
5: 6 *b*', I have therewith sent "
11 *B*', I thought, He will surely "
15 *B*', now I know that there is "
20 *B*', my master hath spared "
22 *B*', even now there be come "
6: 1 *B*' now, the place where "
13 *B*', he is in Dothan. "
15 *b*', an host compassed the city "
17 *b*', the mountain was full "
20 *b*', they were in the midst "
25 *b*', they besieged it. "

2Ki 6:30 *b*', he had sackcloth within 2009
33 *b*', the messenger came down "
33 *B*', this evil is of the Lord; "
7: 2 *B*', if the Lord would make "
2 *B*', thou shalt see it with thine "
5 *b*', there was no man there. "
10 *b*', there was no man there, "
13 (*b*', they are as all the multitude "
13 *b*', I say they are even as all "
19 Now, *b*', if the Lord should make "
19 *B*', thou shalt see it "
8: 5 *b*', the woman, whose son "
9: 5 *b*', the captains of the host "
10: 4 *B*', two kings stood not "
9 *b*', I conspired against my "
11:14 when she looked, *b*', the king stood "
13:21 *b*', they spied a band of men; "
15:11, 15 *b*', they are written in the book "
26, 31 *b*', they are written in the book "
17:26 and, *b*', they slay them, "
18:21 *b*', thou trustest upon the staff "
19: 7 *B*', I will send a blast upon him, 2005
9 *B*', he is come out to fight 2009
11 *B*', thou hast heard what "
35 *b*', they were all dead corpses. "
20: 5 *b*', I will heal thee: 2005
17 *B*', the days come, that all 2009
21:12 *B*', I am bringing such evil "
22:16 *B*', I will bring evil upon 2005
20 *B*' therefore, I will gather thee "
1Ch 9: 1 *b*', they were written in the book 2009
11: 1 *B*', we are thy bone and thy flesh. "
25 *b*', he was honourable among "
22: 9 *B*', a son shall be born to thee, "
14 *b*', in my trouble I have "
28:21 *b*', the courses of the priests "
29:29 *b*', they are written in the book "
2Ch 2: 4 *B*', I build an house "
8 *b*', my servants shall be "
10 *b*', I will give to thy servants, "
6:18 *b*', heaven and the heaven of "
9: 6 *b*', the one half of the greatness "
13:12 *b*', God himself is with us "
14 looked back, *b*', the battle was "
16: 3 *b*', I have sent thee silver "
11 *b*', the acts of Asa, "
18:12 *B*', the words of the prophets "
22 *b*', the Lord hath put a lying "
24 *B*', thou shalt see on that day "
19:11 *b*', Amariah the chief priest "
20: 2 *b*', they be in Hazazon-tamar, "
10 *b*', the children of Ammon "
11 *B*', I say, how they reward us, "
16 *b*', they come up by the cliff "
24 *b*', they were dead bodies "
34 *b*', they are written in the book "
21:14 *B*', with a great plague will the "
23: 3 *B*', the king's son shall reign, "
13 and, *b*', the king stood at his pillar "
24:27 *b*', they are written in the story "
25:26 *b*', are they not written in the "
26:20 *b*', he was leprous in his forehead "
28: 9 *B*', because the Lord God of your "
26 *b*', they are written in the book "
29:19 *b*', they are before the altar "
32:32 *b*', they are written in the vision "
33:18 *b*', they are written in the book "
19 *b*', they are written among "
34:24 *B*', I will bring evil upon this 2005
28 *B*', I will gather thee to thy fathers "
35:25 and, *b*', they are written in the 2009
27 *b*', they are written in the book "
36: 8 *b*', they are written in the book "
Ezr 9:15 *b*', we are before thee in our 2005
Ne 9:36 *B*', we are servants this day, 2009
36 *b*', we are servants in it: "
Es 6: 5 *B*', Haman standeth "
7: 9 *B*' also, the gallows fifty cubits "
8: 7 *B*', I have given Esther the house "
Job 1:12 *B*', all that he hath is in thy "
19 *b*', there came a great wind "
2: 6 *B*', he is in thine hand; "
4: 3 *B*', thou hast instructed many, "
18 *B*', he put no trust in his 2005
5:17 *B*', happy is the man whom 2009
8:19 *B*', this is the joy of his way, 2005
20 *B*', God will not cast away "
9:12 *B*', he taketh away, who can hinder "
12:14 *B*', he breaketh down, "
15 *B*', he withholdeth the waters, "
13:18 *B*' now, I have ordered my 2009
15:15 *B*', he putteth no trust in his 2005
16:19 *b*', my witness is in heaven, 2009
19: 7 *B*', I cry out of wrong, 2005
27 and mine eyes shall *b*', 7200
20: 9 shall his place any more *b*' him. 7789
21:27 *B*', I know your thoughts, 2005
22:12 and *b*' the height of the stars, 7200
23: 8 *B*', I go forward, 2005
9 but I cannot *b*' him: he hideth 2372
24: 5 *B*', as wild asses in the desert 2005
25: 5 *B*' even to the moon, "
27:12 *B*', all ye yourselves have seen "
28:28 *B*', the fear of the Lord, "
31:35 *b*', my desire is, * "
32:11 *B*', I waited for your words; "
12 *b*', there was none of you 2009
19 *B*', my belly is as wine "
33: 2 *B*', now I have opened my mouth, "
6 *B*', I am according to thy wish 2005
7 *B*', my terror shall not make 2009
10 *B*', he findeth occasions 2005
12 *B*', in this thou art not just: "
34:29 who then can *b*' him? whether it 7789
35: 5 and *b*' the clouds which are higher "
36: 5 *B*', God is mighty, 2005

Job 36:22 *B*˙, God exalteth by his power: 2005
24 his work, which men *b*˙. *7891
25 man may see it; man may *b*˙ it *5027
26 *B*˙, God is great, and we know 2005
30 *B*˙, he spreadeth his light "
39:29 her eyes *b*˙ afar off. 5027
40: 4 *B*˙, I am vile; 2005
11 and *b*˙ every one that is proud, *7200
15 *B*˙ now behemoth, which I made 2009
23 *B*˙, he drinketh up a river, 2005
41: 9 *B*˙, the hope of him is in vain: "
Ps 7:14 *B*˙, he travaileth with iniquity, 2009
11: 4 his eyes *b*˙, his eyelids try, the 2372
7 his countenance doth *b*˙ the "
17: 2 let thine eyes *b*˙ the things that * "
15 will *b*˙ thy face in righteousness: "
27: 4 to *b*˙ the beauty of the Lord, and "
33:18 *B*˙, the eye of the Lord is upon 2009
37:37 and *b*˙ the upright: for the end of 7200
39: 5 *B*˙, thou hast made my days 2009
46: 8 come, *b*˙ the works of the Lord, 2372
51: 5 *B*˙, I was shapen in iniquity; 2005
6 *B*˙, thou desirest truth in the "
54: 4 *B*˙, God is mine helper: 2009
59: 4 awake to help me, and *b*˙, 7200
7 *B*˙, they belch out with their 2009
66: 7 power forever; his eyes *b*˙ the *6822
73:12 *B*˙, these are the ungodly, 2009
15 *B*˙, I should offend against "
78:20 *B*˙, he smote the rock, 2005
80:14 look down from heaven, and *b*˙, 7200
84: 9 *B*˙, O God our shield, and look "
87: 4 *B*˙ Philistia, and Tyre, with 2009
91: 8 with thine eyes shalt thou *b*˙ and 5027
102:19 from heaven did the Lord *b*˙ the "
113: 6 to *b*˙ the things that are in 7200
119:18 that I may *b*˙ wondrous things 5027
40 *B*˙, I have longed after thy 2009
121: 4 *B*˙, he that keepeth Israel shall "
123: 2 *B*˙, as the eyes of servants look "
128: 4 *B*˙, that thus shall the man be "
133: 1 *B*˙, how good and how pleasant "
134: 1 *B*˙, bless ye the Lord, all ye "
139: 8 *b*˙, thou art there. "
Pr 1:23 *B*˙, I will pour out my spirit unto "
7:10 *b*˙, there met him a woman "
11:31 *B*˙, the righteous shall be 2005
23:33 Thine eyes shall *b*˙ strange 7200
24:12 *B*˙, we knew it not; 2005
Ec 1:14 *b*˙, all is vanity and vexation of 2009
2: 1 *b*˙, this also is vanity. "
11 *b*˙, all was vanity and vexation of "
12 I turned myself to *b*˙ wisdom, 7200
4: 1 *B*˙ the tears of such as were 2009
5:18 *B*˙ that which I have seen: good "
7:27 *B*˙, this have I found, saith the 7200
11: 7 it is for the eyes to *b*˙ the sun: "
Ca 1:15 *B*˙, thou art fair, my love; 2009
15 *b*˙, thou art fair; "
16 *B*˙, thou art fair, my beloved, "
2: 8 *b*˙, he cometh leaping upon the "
9 *b*˙, he standeth behind our wall, "
3: 7 *B*˙ his bed, "
11 and *b*˙ king Solomon with the 7200
4: 1 *B*˙, thou art fair, my love; 2009
1 *b*˙, thou art fair; "
Isa 3: 1 *B*˙, the Lord, the Lord of hosts, "
5: 7 but *b*˙ oppression; "
7 but *b*˙ a cry. "
26 *b*˙, they shall come with speed "
30 *b*˙ darkness and sorrow, "
7:14 *B*˙, a virgin shall conceive, "
8: 7 *b*˙, the Lord bringeth up "
18 *B*˙, I and the children whom "
22 and *b*˙ trouble and darkness, "
10:33 *B*˙, the Lord, the Lord of hosts, "
12: 2 *B*˙, God is my salvation; "
13: 9 *B*˙, the day of the Lord cometh, "
17 *B*˙, I will stir up the Medes against 2005
17: 1 *B*˙, Damascus is taken 2009
14 and *b*˙ at eventide trouble; "
19: 1 *B*˙, the Lord rideth upon a swift "
20: 6 *B*˙, such is our expectation, "
21: 9 *b*˙, here cometh a chariot of men "
22:13 and *b*˙ joy and gladness, "
17 *B*˙, the Lord will carry thee "
23:13 *B*˙, the land of the Chaldeans; 2005
24: 1 *B*˙, the Lord maketh the earth 2009
26:10 will not *b*˙ the majesty of the 7200
21 *b*˙, the Lord cometh out of his 2009
28: 2 *B*˙, the Lord hath a mighty and "
16 *B*˙, I lay in Zion for a foundation 2005
29: 8 *b*˙, he eateth; but he awaketh, 2009
8 *b*˙, he drinketh; but he awaketh, "
8 *b*˙, he is faint, and his soul hath "
14 *b*˙, I will proceed to do a marvelous 2005
30:27 *B*˙, the name of the Lord cometh 2009
32: 1 *B*˙, a king shall reign in 2005
33: 7 *B*˙, their valiant ones shall cry "
17 they shall *b*˙ the land that is very 7200
34: 5 *B*˙, it shall come down upon 2009
35: 4 *b*˙, your God will come with "
37: 7 *B*˙, I will send a blast upon 2005
11 *B*˙, thou hast heard what 2009
36 *b*˙, they were all dead corpses. "
38: 5 *b*˙, I will add unto thy days 2005
8 *B*˙, I will bring again the shadow "
11 I shall *b*˙ man no more with the 7200
17 *B*˙, for peace I had great 2009
39: 6 *B*˙, the days come, "
40: 9 *B*˙ your God! "
10 *B*˙, the Lord God will come with "
10 *b*˙, his reward is with him, "
15 *B*˙, the nations as a drop of a 2005
15 *b*˙, he taketh up the isles as a "
26 and *b*˙ who hath created these *7200

Isa 41:11 *B*˙, all they that were incensed 2005
15 *B*˙, I will make thee a new sharp 2009
23 be dismayed, and *b*˙ it together. 7200
24 *B*˙, ye are of nothing, and your 2005
27 shall say to Zion, *B*˙, *b*˙ them: 2009
29 *B*˙, they are all vanity; 2005
42: 1 *B*˙ my servant, whom I uphold; "
9 *B*˙, the former things are come 2009
43:19 *B*˙, I will do a new thing; 2005
44:11 *B*˙, all his fellows shall be "
47:14 *B*˙, they shall be as stubble; 2009
48: 7 *B*˙, I knew them. "
10 *B*˙, I have refined thee, "
49:12 *B*˙, these shall come from far: * "
16 *B*˙, I have graven thee upon 2005
18 thine eyes round about, and *b*˙: 7200
21 *B*˙, I was left alone; 2005
22 *B*˙, I will lift up mine hand, 2009
50: 1 *B*˙, for your iniquities have 2005
2 *b*˙, at my rebuke I dry up the "
9 *B*˙, the Lord God will help me; "
11 *B*˙, all ye that kindle a fire, "
51:22 *B*˙, I have taken out of 2009
52: 6 *b*˙, it is I. "
13 *B*˙, my servant shall deal "
54:11 *b*˙, I will lay thy stones with "
15 *B*˙, they shall surely gather 2005
16 *B*˙, I have created the smith "
55: 4 *B*˙, I have given him for "
5 *B*˙, thou shalt call a nation "
56: 3 *B*˙, I am a dry tree. "
58: 3 *B*˙, in the day of your fast "
4 *B*˙, ye fast for strife and debate, "
59: 1 *B*˙, the Lord's hand is not "
9 But *b*˙ obscurity; 2009
60: 2 *b*˙, the darkness shall cover "
62:11 *B*˙, the Lord hath proclaimed "
11 *B*˙, thy salvation cometh: "
11 *b*˙, his reward is with him, 2009
63:15 Look down from heaven, and *b*˙ 7200
64: 5 *b*˙, thou art wroth; 2005
9 *b*˙, see, we beseech thee, we are all "
65: 1 I said *B*˙ me, *b*˙ me, unto a 2009
6 *B*˙, it is written before me: "
13 *B*˙, my servants shall eat, "
13 *b*˙, my servants shall drink, "
13 *b*˙, my servants shall rejoice, "
14 *B*˙, my servants shall sing for "
17 *B*˙, I create new heavens and a new 2005
18 *b*˙, I create Jerusalem a rejoicing, "
66:12 *B*˙, I will extend peace to her "
15 *b*˙, the Lord will come with fire, 2009
Jer 1: 6 *B*˙, I cannot speak: "
9 *B*˙, I have put my words in thy "
18 *b*˙, I have made thee this day "
2:35 *B*˙, I will plead with thee, 2005
3: 5 *B*˙, thou hast spoken and done 2009
22 *B*˙, we come unto thee; 2005
4:13 *B*˙, he shall come up as clouds, 2009
16 *b*˙, publish against Jerusalem, "
5:14 *b*˙, I will make my words in 2005
6:10 *b*˙, their ear is uncircumcised, and 2009
10 *b*˙, the word of the Lord is unto "
19 *b*˙, I will bring evil upon this "
21 *B*˙, I will lay stumblingblocks 2005
22 *B*˙, a people cometh from the 2009
7: 8 *B*˙, ye trust in lying words, "
11 *B*˙, even I have seen it, "
20 *B*˙, mine anger and my fury "
32 *b*˙, the days come, "
8:15 and *b*˙ trouble! "
17 *b*˙, I will send serpents, 2005
19 *B*˙ the voice of the cry of the 2009
9: 7 *B*˙, I will melt them, and try them; 2005
15 *B*˙, I will feed them, even this "
25 *B*˙, the days come, saith the Lord, 2009
10:18 *B*˙, I will sling out the inhabitants 2005
22 *B*˙, the noise of the bruit is come, 2009
11:11 *B*˙, I will bring evil upon them, 2005
22 *B*˙, I will punish them: "
12:14 *B*˙, I will pluck them out of their "
13: 7 *b*˙, the girdle was marred, 2009
13 *B*˙, I will fill all the inhabitants of 2005
20 Lift up your eyes, and *b*˙ them 7200
14:13 *b*˙, the prophets say unto them, 2009
18 *B*˙ the slain with the sword! "
18 then *b*˙ them that are sick with "
19 and *b*˙ trouble! "
16: 9 *B*˙, I will cause to cease out of 2005
12 for, *b*˙, ye walk every one after 2009
14 *b*˙, the days come, saith the Lord, "
16 *B*˙, I will send for many fishers, 2005
21 *b*˙, I will this once cause them "
17:15 *B*˙, they say unto me, 2009
18: 3 and, *b*˙, he wrought a work "
6 *B*˙, as the clay is in the potter's "
11 *B*˙, I frame evil against you, "
19: 3 *B*˙, I will bring evil upon this place, 2005
6 *b*˙, the days come. 2009
15 *B*˙, I will bring upon this city 2005
20: 4 *B*˙, I will make thee a terror to "
4 thine eyes shall *b*˙ it: and I will 7200
21: 4 *B*˙, I will turn back the weapons 2005
8 *B*˙, I set before you the way "
13 *B*˙, I am against thee, "
23: 2 *b*˙, I will visit upon you the evil "
5, 7 *B*˙, the days come, 2009
15 *B*˙, I will feed them...wormwood, 2005
19 *B*˙, a whirlwind of the Lord 2009
30, 31 *B*˙, I am against the prophets, 2005
32 *B*˙, I am against them that "
39 *b*˙, I, even I, will utterly forget "
24: 1 *b*˙, two baskets of figs were 2009
25: 9 *B*˙, I will send and take all 2005
32 *B*˙, evil shall go forth from 2009
26:14 *b*˙, I am in your hand: 2005

Jer 27:16 *B*˙, the vessels of the Lord's house 2009
28:16 *B*˙, I will cast thee from off 2005
29:17 *B*˙, I will send upon them the "
32 *B*˙, I will furnish Shemaiah the "
32 neither shall he *b*˙ the good that 7200
30:18 *B*˙, I will bring again the captivity 2005
23 *B*˙, the whirlwind of the Lord 2009
31: 8 *B*˙, I will bring them from the north 2005
27, 31, 38 *B*˙, the days come, 2009
32: 3 *B*˙, I will give this city into 2005
4 and his eyes shall *b*˙ his eyes; 7200
7 *B*˙, Hanameel the son of Shallum 2009
17 *b*˙, thou hast made the heaven "
24 *B*˙ the mounts, they are come "
24 *B*˙, thou seest it. "
27 *B*˙, I am the Lord, "
28 *B*˙, I will give this city into 2005
37 *B*˙, I will gather them out of "
33: 6 *B*˙, I will bring it health and "
14 *B*˙, the days come, 2009
34: 2 *B*˙, I will give this city into the 2005
3 thine eyes shall *b*˙ the eyes of 7200
17 *B*˙, I proclaim a liberty for you, 2005
22 *B*˙, I will command, "
35:17 *B*˙, I will bring upon Judah "
37: 7 *B*˙, Pharaoh's army, "
38: 5 *B*˙, he is in your hand: 2009
22 *B*˙, all the women that are left "
39:16 *b*˙, I will bring my words upon 2005
40: 4 *b*˙, I loose thee this day from the 2009
4 *b*˙, all the land is before thee: 7200
10 *b*˙, I will dwell at Mizpah, 2005
42: 2 of many, as thine eyes do *b*˙ us) 7200
4 *b*˙, I will pray unto the Lord 2005
43:10 *B*˙, I will send and take "
44: 2 *b*˙, this day they are a desolation, 2009
11 *B*˙, I will set my face against 2005
26 *B*˙, I have sworn by my great "
27 *B*˙, I will watch over them "
30 *B*˙, I will give Pharaoh-hophra "
45: 4 *B*˙, that which I have built 2009
5 *b*˙, I will bring evil upon all 2005
46:25 *B*˙, I will punish the multitude "
27 *b*˙, I will save thee from afar * "
47: 2 *B*˙, waters rise up out of the 2009
48:12 *b*˙, the days come, "
40 *B*˙, he shall fly as an eagle, "
49: 2 *b*˙, the days come, "
5 *B*˙, I will bring a fear upon thee, 2005
12 *B*˙, they whose judgment was 2009
22 *B*˙, he shall come up and fly "
35 *B*˙, I will break the bow of Elam, 2005
50:12 *b*˙, the hindermost of the nations 2009
18 *B*˙, I will punish the king of 2005
31 *B*˙, I am against thee, "
44 *B*˙, he shall come up like a 2009
51: 1 *B*˙, I will raise up against 2005
25 *B*˙, I am against thee, "
36 *B*˙, I will plead thy cause, "
47 *b*˙, the days come, that I will do 2009
52 *b*˙, the days come, saith the Lord, "
La 1: 9 O Lord, *b*˙ my affliction: for the 7200
12 *b*˙, and see if there be any sorrow 5027
18 all people, and *b*˙ my sorrow: 7200
20 *B*˙, O Lord: for I am in distress: "
2:20 *B*˙, O Lord, and consider to whom "
3:50 Till the Lord look down, and *b*˙ "
63 *B*˙ their sitting down, and their 5027
5: 1 consider, and *b*˙ our reproach. 7200
Eze 1: 4 And I looked, and, *b*˙, a whirlwind 2009
15 the living creatures, *b*˙, one wheel "
2: 9 And when I looked, *b*˙, an hand "
3: 8 *B*˙, I have made thy face strong "
23 *b*˙, the glory of the Lord stood there, "
25 *b*˙, they shall put bands upon "
4: 8 *b*˙, I will lay bands upon "
14 *b*˙, my soul hath not been "
16 *b*˙, I will break the staff of bread 2005
5: 8 *B*˙, I, even I, am against "
6: 3 *B*˙, I, even I, will bring a sword "
7: 5 an only evil, *b*˙, is come. 2009
6 *b*˙, it is come. "
10 *B*˙ the day, *b*˙, it is come: "
8: 4 *b*˙, the glory of the God of Israel "
5 and *b*˙ northward at the gate "
7 *b*˙ a hole in the wall. "
8 *b*˙ a door. "
9 and *b*˙ the wicked abominations *7200
10 and *b*˙ every form of creeping 2009
14 *b*˙, there sat women weeping "
16 *b*˙, at the door of the temple "
9: 2 and, *b*˙, six men came from the "
11 and, *b*˙, the man clothed with "
10: 1 and, *b*˙, in the firmament "
9 *b*˙ the four wheels by the "
11: 1 and *b*˙ at the door of the gate "
12:27 *b*˙, they of the house of Israel say, "
13: 8 *b*˙, I am against you, 2005
20 *B*˙, I am against your pillows, "
14:22 *b*˙, therein shall be left a 2009
22 *b*˙, they shall come forth unto you, "
15: 4 *B*˙, it is cast into the fire for fuel; "
5 *B*˙, when it was whole, "
16: 8 *b*˙, thy time was the time of love; "
27 *B*˙, therefore I have stretched out "
37 *B*˙, therefore I will gather all thy 2005
43 *b*˙, therefore I also will recompense 1887
44 *B*˙, every one that useth proverbs 2009
49 *B*˙, this was the iniquity of thy "
17: 7 *b*˙, this vine did bend her "
10 *b*˙, being planted, "
12 *B*˙, the king of Babylon is come "
18: 4 *B*˙, all souls are mine; 2005
20:47 *B*˙, I will kindle fire in thee, "
21: 3 *B*˙, I am against thee, "
7 *B*˙, it cometh, and shall be brought 2009

Eze 22: 6 B', the princes of Israel, 2009
13 B', therefore I have smitten "
19 b', therefore I will gather you 2005
23:22 B', I will raise up thy lovers "
28 B', I will deliver thee into the "
24:16 b', I take away from thee the "
21 B', I will profane my sanctuary, "
25: 4 B', therefore I will deliver thee to "
7 B', therefore I will stretch out "
8 B', the house of Judah is like 2009
9 b', I will open the side of Moab 2005
16 B', I will stretch out mine "
26: 3 B', I am against thee, "
7 B', I will bring upon Tyrus "
28: 3 B', thou art wiser than Daniel; 2009
7 B', therefore I will bring strangers 2005
17 kings, that they may b' thee. 7200
18 the sight of all them that b' thee. "
22 B', I am against thee, 2005
29: 3 B', I am against thee, "
8 B', I will bring a sword upon "
10 B', therefore I am against thee, "
19 B', I will give the land of "
30:22 B', I am against Pharaoh "
31: 3 B', the Assyrian was a cedar 2009
34:10 B', I am against the shepherds; 2005
11 B', I, even I, will both search my "
17 B', I judge between cattle and "
20 B', I, even I, will judge between "
35: 3 B', O mount Seir, I am against "
36: 6 B', I have spoken in my jealousy "
9 b', I am for you, and I will "
37: 2 b', there were very many in 2009
5 B', I will cause breath to enter "
11 b', they say, Our bones are "
12 B', O my people, I will open "
19 B', I will take the stick of Joseph, "
21 B', I will take the children "
38: 3 B', I am against thee, 2005
39: 1 B', I am against thee, "
8 B', it is come, and it is done, 2009
40: 3 b', there was a man, "
4 Son of man, b' with thine eyes, 7200
5 and b' a wall on the outside 2009
24 and b' a gate toward the south: "
43: 2 b', the glory of the God of Israel "
5 b', the glory of the Lord filled "
12 B', this is the law of the house. "
44: 4 and, b', the glory of the Lord filled "
5 and b' with thine eyes, and hear 7200
46:19 b', there was a place on the two 2009
21 b', in every corner of the court "
47: 1 b', waters issued out from "
2 b', there ran out waters "
7 b', at the bank of the river "
Da 2:31 king, sawest, and b' a great image. 431
4:10 b' a tree in the midst of the earth, "
13 and, b', a watcher and a holy "
7: 2 b', the four winds of the heaven 718
5 And b' another beast, a second, "
7 and b' a fourth beast, dreadful and "
8 and, b', there came up among 431
8 and, b', in this horn were eyes like "
13 and, b', one like the Son of man 718
8: 3 b', there stood before the river 2009
5 b', an he goat came from "
15 b', there stood before me "
19 B', I will make thee know 2005
9:18 thine eyes, and b' our desolations, 7200
10: 5 b' a certain man clothed in linen, 2009
10 b', an hand touched me, "
16 b', one like the similitude of the "
11: 2 b', there shall stand up yet three "
12: 5 and b', there stood other two, "
Ho 2: 6 b' I will hedge up thy way 2005
14 b', I will allure her, 2009
Joe 2:19 B', I will send you corn, 2005
3: 7 B', I will raise them out of "
Am 2:13 B', I am pressed under you, 2009
3: 9 and b' the great tumults in 7200
6:14 b', I will raise up against you, 2005
7: 1 b', he formed grasshoppers 2009
4 b', the Lord God called to contend "
7 b', the Lord stood upon a wall "
8 B', I will set a plumbline 2005
8: 1 and b' a basket of summer fruit. 2009
11 B', the days come, "
9: 8 B', the eyes of the Lord God "
13 B', the days come, "
Ob 2 B', I have made thee small "
Mic 1: 3 b', the Lord cometh forth out of "
2: 3 B', against this family do I 2005
7: 9 and I shall b' his righteousness. 7200
10 mine eyes shall b' her: now shall "
Na 1:15 B' upon the mountains the 2209
2:13 B', I am against thee, 2205
3: 5 B', I am against thee, "
13 B', thy people in the midst of 2009
Hab 1: 3 and cause me to b' grievance? *5027
5 B' ye among the heathen, and 7200
13 art of purer eyes than to b' evil, "
2: 4 B', his soul which is lifted up 2009
13 B', is it not of the Lord of hosts "
19 B', it is laid over with gold and "
Zep 3:19 B', at that time I will undo all 2005
Zec 1: 8 and b' a man riding upon 2009
11 b', all the earth sitteth still, "
18 and b' four horns. "
2: 1 and b' a man with a measuring "
3 b', the angel that talked with me "
9 b', I will shake mine hand upon 2005
3: 4 B', I have caused thine iniquity 7200
8 b', I will bring forth my servant 2005
9 For b' the stone that I have laid 2009
9 b', I will engrave the graving 2005
4: 2 and b' a candlestick all of gold, "

Zec 5: 1 and b' a flying roll. 2009
7 b', there was lifted up a talent "
9 b', there came out two women, "
6: 1 b', there came four chariots out "
8 B', these that go towards the 7200
12 B', the man whose name is The 2009
8: 7 B', I will save my people 2005
9: 4 B', the Lord will cast her out, 2009
9 b', thy king cometh unto thee: "
12: 2 B', I will make Jerusalem a "
14: 1 B', the day of the Lord cometh, "
Mal 1:13 B', what a weariness is it! "
2: 3 B', I will corrupt your seed, 2005
3: 1 B', I will send my messenger, "
1 b', he shall come, 2009
4: 1 For, b', the day cometh, "
5 B', I will send you Elijah the "
M't 1:20 b', the angel of the Lord appeared 2400
23 B', a virgin shall be with child, "
2: 1 b' there came wise men from the "
13 b', the angel of the Lord appeareth "
19 was dead, b', an angel of the Lord "
4:11 leaveth him, and, b', angels came "
6:26 B' the fowls of the air: for they 1689
7: 4 b', a beam is in thine own eye? *2400
8: 2 And, b', there came a leper "
24 b', there arose a great tempest "
29 and, b', they cried out, saying, "
32 b', the whole herd of swine ran "
34 And, b', the whole city came out "
9: 2 And, b', they brought to him "
3 And, b', certain of the scribes "
10 b', many publicans and sinners "
18 b', there came a certain ruler, "
20 b', a woman, which was diseased "
32 b', they brought to him a dumb "
10:16 B', I send you forth as sheep "
11: 8 b', they that wear soft clothing "
10 B', I send my messenger before "
19 B' a man gluttonous, and a "
12: 2 B', thy disciples do that which is "
10 And, b', there was a man "
18 B' my servant, whom I have "
41 b', a greater than Jonas is here. "
42 b', a greater than Solomon is here. "
46 b', his mother and his brethren "
47 B', thy mother and thy brethren "
49 B', my mother and my brethren! "
13: 3 B', a sower went forth to sow; "
15:22 b', a woman of Canaan came out "
17: 3 And, b', there appeared unto them "
5 b', a bright cloud overshadowed "
5 and b' a voice out of the cloud, "
18:10 do always b' the face of my Father 991
19:16 b', one came and said unto him, 2400
27 B', we have forsaken all, and * "
20:18 B', we go up to Jerusalem; and "
30 And, b', two blind men sitting "
21: 5 B', thy King cometh unto thee, "
22: 4 B', I have prepared my dinner: "
23:34 Wherefore, b', I send unto you "
38 B', your house is left unto you "
24:25 B', I have told you before. "
26 b', he is in the desert; go not "
26 b', he is in the secret chambers; "
25: 6 B', the bridegroom cometh; go ye "
20 b', I have gained beside them *2396
22 b', I have gained two other * "
26:45 b', the hour is at hand, and the 2400
46 b', he is at hand that doth betray "
51 And, b', one of them which were "
65 b', now ye have heard his 2396
27:51 b', the veil of the temple was rent 2400
28: 2 b', there was a great earthquake: "
7 and, b', he goeth before you into * "
9 b', Jesus met them, saying, All hail. "
11 were going, b', some of the watch "
M'r 1: 2 B', I send my messenger before "
2:24 B', why do they on the sabbath 2396
3:32 B', thy mother and thy brethren "
34 B' my mother and my brethren! 2396
4: 3 B', there went out a sower to sow: 2400
5:22 b', there cometh one of the rulers* "
10:33 saying, B', we go up to Jerusalem, "
11:21 b', the fig tree which thou 2396
13:23 b', I have foretold you all things. 2400
14:41 b', the Son of man is betrayed "
15: 4 b' how many things they witness 2396
35 heard it, said, B', he calleth Elias. 2400
16: 6 b' the place where they laid him. 2396
Lu 1:20 And, b', thou shalt be dumb, 2400
31 And, b', thou shalt conceive in thy "
36 And, b', thy cousin Elisabeth, she "
38 B' the handmaid of the Lord; "
48 for, b', from henceforth all "
2:10 for, b', I bring you good tidings of "
25 b', there was a man in Jerusalem, "
34 B', this child is set for the fall "
48 b', thy father and I have sought "
5:12 city, b' a man full of leprosy: "
18 And, b', men brought in a bed "
6:23 for, b', your reward is great "
7:12 b', there was a dead man carried "
25 B', they which are gorgeously "
27 B', I send my messenger before "
34 B' a gluttonous man, and a "
37 And, b', a woman in the city, "
8:41 And, b', there came a man named "
9:30 And, b', there talked with him two "
38 And, b', a man of the company "
10: 3 b', I send you forth as lambs 2400
19 B', I give unto you power to tread "
25 And, b', a certain lawyer stood up, "
11:31 and, b', a greater than Solomon "
32 and, b', a greater than Jonas "
41 and, b', all things are clean "

Lu 13: 7 B', these three years I come 2400
11 And, b', there was a woman which "
30 And, b', there are last which shall "
32 B', I cast out devils, and I do cures "
35 B', your house is left unto you "
14: 2 And, b', there was a certain man "
29 all that b' it begin to mock him, 2334
17:21 for, b', the kingdom of God *2400
18:31 B', we go up to Jerusalem, and all "
19: 2 And, b', there was a man named "
8 B', Lord, the half of my goods "
20 b', here is thy pound, which I have "
21: 6 As for these things which ye b', 2334
29 B' the fig tree, and all the trees; 1492
22:10 B', when ye are entered into the 2400
21 b', the hand of him that betrayeth "
31 b', Satan hath desired to have you, "
38 Lord, b', here are two swords. "
47 b' a multitude, and he that was "
23:14 and, b', I, having examined him "
29 For, b', the days are coming, in "
50 And, b', there was a man named "
24: 4 b', two men stood by them in "
13 b', two of them went that same "
39 B' my hands and my feet, that it *1492
49 And, b', I send the promise of 2400
Joh 1:29 B' the Lamb of God, which taketh 2396
36 B' the Lamb of God! "
47 B' an Israelite indeed, in whom "
3:26 b', the same baptizeth, and all "
4:35 b', I say unto you, Lift up your 2400
5:14 B', thou art made whole: sin no 2396
11: 3 Lord, b', he whom thou lovest is "
36 the Jews, B' how he loved him! "
12:15 b', thy King cometh, sitting on an 2400
19 b', the world is gone after him. *2396
16:32 B', the hour cometh, yea, is now 2400
17:24 that they may b' my glory, which 2334
18:21 unto them: b' they know what I 2396
19: 4 B', I bring him forth to you, that "
5 Pilate saith unto them, B' the "
14 unto the Jews, B' your king! "
26 unto his mother, Woman, b' thy 2400
27 B' thy mother! And from that "
20:27 hither thy finger, and b' my *2396
Ac 1:10 b', two men stood by them in 2400
2: 7 B', are not all these which speak "
4:29 now, Lord, b' their threatenings: *1896
5: 9 b', the feet of them which have 2400
25 B', the men whom ye put in prison "
28 and, b', ye have filled Jerusalem "
7:31 and as he drew near to b' it, 2657
32 Moses trembled and durst not b'. "
56 B', I see the heavens opened, 2400
8:27 and, b', a man of Ethiopia, an "
9:10 And he said, B', I am here, Lord. "
11 Saul, of Tarsus: for, b', he "
10:17 b', the men which were sent from "
19 B', three men seek thee. "
21 B', I am he whom ye seek: what "
30 and, b', a man stood before me in "
11:11 And, b', immediately there were "
12: 7 And, b', the angel of the Lord "
13:11 And now, b', the hand of the Lord "
25 But, b', there cometh one after me, "
41 B', ye despisers, and wonder, 1492
16: 1 and, b', a certain disciple was 2400
20:22 And now, b', I go bound in the "
25 b', I know that ye all, "
Ro 2:17 B', thou art called a Jew, and *2396
9:33 B', I lay in Sion a stumblingstone 2400
11:22 B' therefore the goodness and 1492
1Co 10:18 B' Israel after the flesh: are not 991
15:51 B', I shew you a mystery: We 2400
2Co 3: 7 Israel could not stedfastly b' the * 816
5:17 b', all things are become new. 2400
6: 2 b', now is the accepted time; "
2 b', now is the day of salvation.) "
9 and, b', we live; as chastened, "
7:11 For b' this selfsame thing that ye "
12:14 B', the third time I am ready to "
Ga 1:20 unto you, b', before God, I lie not. "
5: 2 B', I Paul say unto you, that if ye 2396
Heb 2:13 B' I and the children which God 2400
8: 8 B', the days come, saith the Lord, "
Jas 3: 3 B', we put bits in the horses' * "
4 B' also the ships, which though "
5 B', how great a matter a little fire "
5: 4 B', the hire of the labourers who "
7 B', the husbandman waiteth for "
9 b', the judge standeth before the "
11 B', we count them happy which "
1Pe 2: 6 B', I lay in Sion a chief corner "
12 good works, which they shall b', 2029
3: 2 they b' your chaste conversation * "
1Jo 3: 1 B', what manner of love the 1492
Jude 14 B', the Lord cometh with ten 2400
Re 1: 7 B', he cometh with clouds; and "
18 and, b', I am alive for evermore, "
2:10 b', the devil shall cast some of you "
22 B', I will cast her into a bed, and "
3: 8 b', I have set before thee an open "
9 B', I will make them of the "
9 b', I will make them to come and "
11 B', I come quickly: hold that * "
20 B', I stand at the door and knock: "
4: 1 and, b', a door was opened in "
2 and, b', a throne was set in heaven, "
5: 5 b', the Lion of the tribe of Juda, "
6: 2 And I saw, and b' a white horse: "
8 And I looked, and b' a pale horse: "
9:12 and, b', there come two woes more "
11:14 and, b', the third woe cometh "
12: 3 and b' a great red dragon, having "
14:14 And I looked, and b' a white cloud, "
15: 5 b', the temple of the tabernacle "

Re 16:15 B', I come as a thief. Blessed 2400
17: 8 when they b' the beast that was 991
19:11 opened, and b' a white horse; 2400
21: 3 B', the tabernacle of God is with "
5 said, B', I make all things new. "
22: 7 B', I come quickly: blessed is he "
12 And, b', I come quickly; and my "

beholdest
Ps 10:14 thou b' mischief and spite, to 5027
M't 7: 3 why b' thou the mote that is in thy 991
Lu 6:41 And why b' thou the mote that is "
42 when thou thyself b' not the beam "

beholdeth
Job 24:18 b' not the way of the vineyards. *6437
41:34 He b' all high things: he is a 7200
Ps 33:13 heaven; he b' all the sons of men. "
Jas 1:24 For he b' himself, and goeth his 2657

beholding
Ps 119:37 Turn away mine eyes from b' 7200
Pr 15: 3 every place, b' the evil and the *6822
Ec 5:11 the b' of them with their eyes? 7200
M't 27:55 women were there b' afar off, 2334
M'k 10:21 Jesus b' him loved him, and said *1689
Lu 23:35 the people stood b'. And the 2334
48 b' the things which were done, * "
49 stood afar off b' these things, *3708
Ac 4:14 b' the man which was healed * 991
8:13 b' the miracles and signs which 2334
14: 9 who stedfastly b' him and * 816
23: 1 Paul, earnestly b' the council, * "
2Co 3:18 b' as in a glass the glory of the †2734
Col 2: 5 joying and b' your order, and the 991
Jas 1:23 like unto a man b' his natural 2657

behoved
Lu 24:46 thus it b' Christ to suffer, and *1163
Heb 2:17 in all things it b' him to be made 3784

being
Ge 18:12 I have pleasure, my lord b' old
19:16 the Lord b' merciful unto him:
21: 4 Isaac b' eight days old, as God *
24:27 I b' in the way, the Lord led me *
34:30 and I b' few in number, they shall
35:29 gathered unto his people, b' old *
37: 2 Joseph, b' seventeen years old,
50:26 So Joseph died, b' an hundred and
Ex 12:34 their kneadingtroughs b' bound
13:15 all that openeth the matrix, b'
22:14 the owner thereof b' not with it,
28:16 it shall be b' doubled; a span *
32:18 of them that cry for b' overcome:
39: 9 a span the breadth thereof, b'
Le 21: 4 b' a chief man among his people.
24: 8 b' taken from the children of *
Nu 1:44 princes of Israel, b' twelve men:
22:24 of the vineyards, a wall b' on the
30: 3 bond, b' in her father's house in
16 b' yet in her youth in her father's
31:32 And the booty, b' the rest of the *
32:38 Baal-meon, (their names b'
De 3:13 and all Bashan, b' the kingdom *
17: 8 b' matters of controversy within
22:24 because she cried not, b' in the
32:31 even our enemies themselves b' *
Jos 9:23 of you be freed from b' bondmen,*
21:10 of Aaron, b' of the family of the *
24:29 died, b' an hundred and ten years
J'g 2: 8 servant of the Lord died, b' an
9: 5 Jerubbaal, b' threescore and ten
1Sa 2:18 ministered before the Lord, b' a
15:23 also rejected thee from b' king.
26 hath rejected thee from b' king
26:13 a great space b' between them:
2Sa 8:13 salt, b' eighteen thousand men. *
13: 4 Why art thou, b' the king's son, *
14 but b' stronger than she, forced
19: 3 as people b' ashamed steal away*
21:16 he b' girded with a new sword,
1Ki 1:41 noise of the city, b' in an uproar?
2:27 thrust out Abiathar from b' priest 1961
11:17 Hadad b' yet a little child,
15:13 her he removed from b' queen,
16: 7 in b' like the house of Jeroboam; 1961
20:15 of Israel, b' seven thousand.
2Ki 8:16 Jehoshaphat b' then king of Judah,
10: 6 king's sons, b' seventy persons,
12:11 gave the money, b' told, into the *
1Ch 9:19 fathers, b' over the host of the *
24: 6 household b' taken for Eleazar,
2Ch 5:12 b' arrayed in white linen, *
13: 3 thousand chosen men, b' mighty *
15:16 he removed her from b' queen,
21:20 and departed without b' desired.
26:21 in a several house, b' a leper;
Ezr 6:11 down from his house, and b' *
10:19 and b' guilty, they offered a ram
Ne 6:11 and who is there, that, b' as I am,
Es 1: 3 of the provinces, b' before him:
3:15 out, b' hastened by the king's *
8:14 b' hastened and pressed on by
Job 4: 7 who ever perished, b' innocent?
21:23 b' wholly at ease and quiet,
42:17 Job died, b' old and full of days,
Ps 49:12 man b' in honour abideth not: †
65: 6 the mountains; b' girded with
69: 4 would destroy me, b' mine enemies
78: 9 children of Ephraim, b' armed,
38 But he, b' full of compassion,
83: 4 cut them off from b' a nation;
104:33 to my God while I have my b'. 5750
107:10 b' bound in affliction and iron;
139:16 substance, yet b' unperfect; *
146: 2 unto my God while I have any b'. 5750
Pr 3:26 shall keep thy foot from b' taken.
29: 1 that b' often reproved hardeneth

Ca 3: 8 hold swords, b' expert in war: *
10 midst thereof b' paved with love,
Isa 3:26 and she b' desolate shall set *
17: 1 is taken away from b' a city,
40:13 b' his counseller hath taught him?
65:20 b' a hundred years old shall be
Jer 2:25 Withhold thy foot from b' unshod,
12:11 b' desolate it mourneth unto me;
17:16 not hastened from b' a pastor
31:36 shall cease from b' a nation 1961
34: 9 his maidservant b' a Hebrew
40: 1 taken him b' bound in chains
48: 2 us cut it off from b' a nation.
42 Moab shall be destroyed from b' a
Eze 17:10 Yea, behold, b' planted, shall it
23:42 voice of the multitude b' at ease
48:22 b' in the midst of that which is
Da 3:27 king's counsellers, b' gathered
5:31 b' about threescore and two
6:10 and his windows b' open in his *
8:22 Now that b' broken, whereas
9:21 b' caused to fly swiftly, touched
M't 1:19 Joseph her husband, b' a just 5607
23 Emmanuel, which b' interpreted
24 Joseph b' raised from sleep did *
2:12 b' warned of God in a dream
22 go thither: notwithstanding, b'
7:11 If ye then, b' evil, know 5607
12:34 ye, b' evil, speak good things "
14: 8 b' before instructed of her mother,
M'r 3: 5 with anger, b' grieved for the
5:41 which is, b' interpreted,
8: 1 the multitude b' very great, *5607
9:33 b' in the house he asked them, *1096
14: 3 b' in Bethany in the house of *5607
15:22 Golgotha, which is, b' interpreted,
34 which is, b' interpreted, My God,
Lu 1:74 that we, b' delivered out of the
2: 5 wife, b' great with child. 5607
3: 1 Pontius Pilate b' governor of
1 Herod b' tetrarch of Galilee,
2 and Caiaphas b' the high priest, *1909
19 b' reproved by him for Herodias
21 that Jesus also b' baptized, *
23 thirty years of age, b' (as was 5607
4: 1 Jesus b' full of the Holy Ghost
2 B' forty days tempted of the devil.
15 taught in their synagogues, b'
7:29 justified God, b' baptized with
30 themselves, b' not baptized of
8:25 And they b' afraid wondered,
11:13 If ye then, b' evil, know how to 5225
13:16 this woman, b' a daughter of 5607
14:21 master of the house b' angry said
16:23 lift up his eyes, b' in torments, 5225
20:36 children of God, b' the children 5607
21:12 b' brought before kings and rulers
22: 3 Iscariot, b' of the number 5607
44 And b' in an agony he prayed 1096
Joh 1:38 is to say, b' interpreted, Master,)
41 which is, b' interpreted, the Christ.
4: 6 Jesus therefore, b' wearied with
9 How is it that thou, b' a Jew, 5607
5:13 a multitude b' in that place, "
6:71 betray him, b' one of the twelve, "
7:50 Jesus by night, b' one of them,) "
8: 9 b' convicted by their own
10:33 that thou, b' a man, makest 5607
11:49 Caiaphas, b' the high priest that "
51 but b' high priest that year, "
13: 2 And supper b' ended, the devil *
14:25 you, b' yet present with you. *
18:26 high priest, b' his kinsman 5607
19:38 Joseph of Arimathæa, b' a disciple "
20:19 evening, b' the first day of the week,
26 came Jesus, the doors b' shut,
Ac 1: 3 b' seen of them forty days,
4 And, b' assembled together with
2:23 b' delivered by the determinate
30 Therefore b' a prophet, and 5225
33 Therefore b' by the right hand
3: 1 of prayer, b' the ninth hour.
4: 2 B' grieved that they taught the
23 And b' let go, they went to their
36 (which is, b' interpreted, The son
5: 2 his wife also b' privy to it, and
7:55 b' full of the Holy Ghost, 5225
13: 4 b' sent forth by the Holy Ghost,
12 b' astonished at the doctrine of
14: 8 in his feet, b' a cripple from *5225
15: 3 And b' brought on their way
21 b' read in the synagogues every
25 good unto us, b' assembled with *
32 b' prophets also themselves, 5607
40 chose Silas, and departed, b'
16:20 These men, b' Jews, do 5225
21 neither to observe, b' Romans. 5605
37 openly uncondemned, b' Romans,*5225
17:28 and move, and have our b'; 2070
18:25 and b' fervent in the spirit,
19:40 there b' no cause whereby we 5225
20: 9 b' fallen into a deep sleep:
22:11 see for the glory of that light, b'
26:11 and b' exceedingly mad against
27: 2 Macedonian of Thessalonica, b' 5607
18 And we b' exceedingly tossed *
Ro 1:20 b' understood by the things
29 B' filled with all unrighteousness,
2:18 b' instructed out of the law;
3:21 b' witnessed by the law and the
24 B' justified freely by his grace
4:11 he had yet b' uncircumcised: *
12 he had b' yet uncircumcised. *
19 And b' not weak in faith, he *
21 And b' fully persuaded that, what
5: 1 Therefore b' justified by faith.

Ro 5: 9 then, b' now justified by his
10 much more, b' reconciled,
6: 9 that Christ b' raised from the dead
18 B' then made free from sin, ye
22 But now b' made free from sin,
7: 6 b' dead wherein we were held;
9:11 (For the children b' not yet born,
10: 3 b' ignorant of God's righteousness
11:17 thou, b' a wild olive tree, 5607
12: 5 So we, b' many, are one body
15:16 b' sanctified by the Holy Ghost.
1Co 4:12 b' reviled, we bless;
12 b' persecuted, we suffer it:
13 B' defamed, we intreat: we are
7:18 any man called b' circumcised?
21 Art thou called b' a servant?
22 b' a servant, is the Lord's
22 b' free is Christ's servant.
8: 7 conscience b' weak is defiled. 5607
9:21 (b' not without law to God, "
10:17 we b' many are one bread, *
12:12 of that one body, b' many 5607
2Co 5: 3 If so be that b' clothed we shall
4 tabernacle do groan, b' burdened:
8:17 b' more forward, of his own 5225
9:11 B' enriched in every thing to all
10: 1 but b' absent am bold toward
11: 9 myself from b' burdensome
12:16 nevertheless, b' crafty, I caught 5225
13: 2 and b' absent now I write to
10 these things b' absent, *
10 lest b' present I should use *
Gal 1:14 b' more exceedingly zealous of 5225
2: 3 who was with me, b' a Greek, 5607
14 if thou, b' a Jew, livest after 5225
3:13 the curse of the law, b' made *
Eph 1:11 inheritance, b' predestinated *
18 understanding b' enlightened; *
2:11 that ye b' in time past Gentiles *
12 b' aliens from the commonwealth
20 Jesus Christ himself b' the chief 5607
3:17 b' rooted and grounded in love,
4:18 b' alienated from the life of God 5607
19 Who b' past feeling have given
Ph'p 1: 6 B' confident of this very thing,
11 B' filled with the fruits of
2: 2 the same love, b' of one accord,
6 Who, b' in the form of God, ‡5225
8 And b' found in fashion as a man,
3:10 b' made conformable unto his *
Col 1:10 b' fruitful in every good work,
2: 2 might be comforted, b' knit
13 And you, b' dead in your sins 5607
1Th 2: 8 So b' desirous of you, we were
17 But we, brethren, b' taken from
1Ti 2:14 but the woman b' deceived
3: 6 novice, lest b' lifted up with
10 office of a deacon, b' found 5607
2Ti 1: 4 b' mindful of thy tears, that I
3:13 worse, deceiving and b' deceived.
Tit 1:16 they deny him, b' abominable, 5607
3: 7 That b' justified by his grace,
11 sinneth, b' condemned of himself. 5607
Ph'm 9 b' such a one as Paul the aged, "
Heb 1: 3 Who b' the brightness of his glory,
4 B' made so much better than *
2:18 b' tempted, he is able to succour
4: 1 fear, lest, a promise b' left
2 not b' mixed with faith in them †‡
5: 9 And b' made perfect, he became
7: 2 first b' by interpretation King
12 For the priesthood b' changed,
9:11 Christ b' come an high priest of
11: 4 and by it he b' dead yet speaketh.
7 Noah, b' warned of God of things
37 and goatskins; b' destitute,
13: 3 as b' yourselves also in the body. 5607
Jas 1:25 he b' not a forgetful hearer, but 1096
2:17 hath not works, is dead, b' alone.
1Pe 1: 7 your faith, b' much more precious 1096
23 B' born again, not of corruptible *
2: 8 stumble at the word, b' disobedient:
24 that we, b' dead to sins, should live
3: 5 b' in subjection unto their own
7 as b' heirs together of the grace of
18 bring us to God, b' put to death
22 b' made subject unto him.
5: 3 as b' lords over God's heritage,
3 but b' ensamples to the flock. *1096
2Pe 3: 6 was, b' overflowed with water,
12 heavens b' on fire shall be dissolved,
17 b' led away with the error
Re 1:12 b' turned, I saw seven golden
12: 2 And she b' with child cried, *2192
14: 4 b' the firstfruits unto God and *

bekah (be'-kah)
Ex 38:26 A b' for every man, that is, 1235

Bel (bel) See also BAAL.
Isa 46: 1 B' boweth down, Nebo stoopeth, 1078
Jer 50: 2 Babylon is taken, B' is confounded, "
51:44 I will punish B' in Babylon, and "

Bela (be'-lah) See also BELAH; BELAITES.
Ge 14: 2 and the king of B', which is Zoar. 1106
8 the king of B' (the same is Zoar;) "
36:32 And B' the son of Beor reigned in "
33 And B' died, and Jobab the son of "
Nu 26:38 of B', the family of the Belaites: "
40 sons of B' were Ard and Naaman: "
1Ch 1:43 B' the son of Beor: and the name "
44 And when B' was dead, Jobab the "
5: 8 And B' the son of Azaz, the son of "
7: 6 sons of Benjamin; B', and Becher, "
7 the sons of B'; Ezbon, and Uzzi, "
8: 1 Benjamin begat B' his firstborn, "
3 sons of B' were, Addar, and Gera, "

Belah (*be'-lah*) See also BELA.
Ge 46:21 sons of Benjamin were B', and 1106

Belaites (*be'-lah-ites*)
Nu 26:38 the family of the B': of Ashbel. 1108

belch
Ps 59: 7 they b' out with their mouth: 5042

Belial (*be'-le-al*)
De 13:13 the children of B', are gone out *1100
J'g 19:22 certain sons of B', beset the ‡ "
20:13 the children of B', which are in ‡ "
1Sa 1:16 handmaid for a daughter of B': ‡ "
2:12 the sons of Eli were sons of B'; ‡ "
10:27 But the children of B' said, How ‡ "
25:17 for he is such a son of B', that a ‡ "
25 pray thee, regard this man of B', ‡ "
30:22 men of B', of those that went ‡ "
2Sa 16: 7 man, and thou man of B': ‡ "
20: 1 there a man of B', whose name ‡ "
23: 6 the sons of of B' shall be all of * "
1Ki 21:10 set two men, sons of B', before ‡ "
13 came in two men, children of B', ‡ "
13 the men of B' witnessed against ‡ "
2Ch 13: 7 him vain men, the children of B', ‡ "
2Co 6:15 what concord hath Christ with B'? 955

belied
Jer 5:12 They have b' the Lord, and said, *3584

belief See also UNBELIEF.
2Th 2:13 of the Spirit and b' of the truth: 4102

believe See also BELIEVED; BELIEVEST; BELIEVETH; BELIEVING.
Ex 4: 1 they will not b' me, nor hearken 539
5 That they may b' that the Lord "
8 if they will not b' thee, neither "
8 that they will b' the voice of the "
9 if they will not b' also these two "
19: 9 with thee, and b' thee for ever. * "
Nu 14:11 how long will it be ere they b' me, "
De 1:32 ye did not b' the Lord your God, "
2Ki 17:14 that did not b' in the Lord their * "
2Ch 20:20 B' in the Lord your God, so shall "
20 b' his prophets, so shall ye prosper. "
32:15 on this manner, neither yet b' him: "
Job 9:16 I not b' that he had hearkened "
39:12 Wilt thou b' him, that he will * "
Pr 26:25 When he speaketh fair, b' him not: "
Isa 7: 9 If ye will not b', surely ye shall not "
43:10 that ye may know and b' me, and "
Jer 12: 6 b' them not, though they speak "
Hab 1: 5 ye will not b', though it be told "
M't 9:28 B' ye that I am able to do this? 4100
18: 6 little ones which b' in me, it were "
21:25 Why did ye not then b' him? "
32 afterwards, that ye might b' him. "
24:23 here is Christ, or there, b' it not. "
26 in the secret chambers; b' it not. "
27:42 and we will b' him. * "
M'r 1:15 repent ye, and b' the gospel. *4100, 1722
5:36 Be not afraid, only b'. 4100
9:23 If thou canst b', all things are * "
24 Lord, I b'; help thou mine "
42 little ones that b' in me, "
11:23 but shall b' that those things which "
24 b' that ye receive them, and ye "
31 say, Why then did ye not b' him? "
13:21 or, lo, he is there; b' him not: "
15:32 that we may see and b'. And they "
16:17 signs shall follow them that b'; "
Lu 8:12 lest they should b' and be saved. "
13 which for a while b', and in time "
50 b' only, and she shall be made "
22:67 ye will not b': "
24:25 fools, and slow of heart to b' 4100, 1909
Joh 1: 7 all men through him might b'. 4100
12 even to them that b' on his name: "
3:12 and ye b' not, "
12 how shall ye b', if I tell you of "
4:21 Woman, b' me, the hour cometh, "
42 Now we b', not because of thy "
48 signs and wonders, ye will not b'. "
5:38 whom he hath sent, him ye b' not. "
44 How can ye b', which receive "
47 But if ye b' not his writings, "
47 how shall ye b' my words? "
6:29 ye b' on him whom he hath sent. "
30 that we may see, and b' thee? "
36 ye also have seen me, and b' not. "
64 there are some of you that b' not. "
69 And we b' and are sure that thou "
7: 5 neither did his brethren b' in him. "
39 which they that b' on him should "
8:24 if ye b' not that I am he, ye shall "
45 I tell you the truth, ye b' me not. "
46 the truth, why do ye not b' me? "
9:18 the Jews did not b' concerning "
35 Dost thou b' on the Son of God? "
36 he, Lord, that I might b' on him? "
38 Lord, I b'. And he worshipped "
10:26 But ye b' not, because ye are not "
37 the works of my Father, b' me not. "
38 though ye b' not me, "
38 b' the works: that ye may know, "
38 and b', that the Father * "
11:15 to the intent ye may b'; nevertheless "
27 I b' that thou art the Christ, the * "
40 thou wouldest b', thou shouldest * "
42 by I said it, that they may b' that "
48 thus alone, all men will b' on him: "
12:36 b' in the light, that ye may be "
39 Therefore they could not b', "
47 man hear my words, and b' not, "
13:19 come to pass, ye may b' that I am he. "
14: 1 ye b' in God, b' also in me. "
11 B' me that I am in the Father, "
11 else b' me for the very works' sake. "
Joh 14:29 it is come to pass, ye might b'. 4100
16: 9 because they b' not on me; "
30 by this we b' that thou camest "
31 answered them, Do ye now b'? "
17:20 for them also which shall b' on me "
21 that the world may b' that thou "
19:35 he saith true, that ye might b'. "
20:25 my hand into his side, I will not b'. "
31 might b' that Jesus is the Christ, "
Ac 8:37 I b' that Jesus Christ is the Son of "
13:39 by him all that b' are justified * "
41 which ye shall in no wise b', "
15: 7 hear the word of the gospel, and b'. "
11 But we b' that through the grace "
16:31 B' on the Lord Jesus Christ, and "
19: 4 that they should b' on him which "
21:20 of Jews there are which b'; * "
25 touching the Gentiles which b', * "
27:25 for I b' God, that it shall be even "
Ro 3: 3 For what if some did not b'? * 569
22 unto all and upon all them that b': 4100
4:11 be the father of all them that b', "
24 if we b' on him that raised up "
6: 8 we b' that we shall also live with "
10: 9 shalt b' in thine heart that God "
14 not believed? and how shall they b' "
15:31 them that do not b' in Judæa; * 544
1Co 1:21 preaching to save them that b'. 4100
10:27 If any of them that b' not bid you 571
11:18 and I partly b' it. 4100
14:22 not to them that b', "
22 but to them that b' not: * 571
22 serveth not for them that b' not, * "
22 but for them which b'. 4100
2Co 4: 4 minds of them which b' not, * 571
13 spoken; we also b', and therefore 4100
Ga 3:22 might be given to them that b'. "
Eph 1:19 to us-ward who b', according to "
Ph'p 1:29 not only to b' on him, but also to "
1Th 1: 7 were ensamples to all that b' "
2:10 ourselves among you that b': "
13 worketh also in you that b'. "
4:14 if we b' that Jesus died and rose "
2Th 1:10 be admired in all them that b' * "
2:11 delusion, that they should b' a lie: "
1Ti 1:16 should hereafter b' on him to life "
4: 3 them which b' and know the truth. 4103
10 all men, specially of those that b'. "
2Ti 2:13 If we b' not, yet he abideth * 569
Heb 10:39 of them that b' to the saving *4102
11: 6 must b' that he is, and that he is 4100
Jas 2:19 the devils also b', and tremble. "
1Pe 1:21 Who by him do b' in God, that * "
2: 7 Unto you therefore which b' he is "
1Jo 3:23 That we should b' on the name of "
4: 1 Beloved, b' not every spirit, but "
5:13 unto you that b' on the name of * "
13 ye may b' on the name of the Son "

believed
Ge 15: 6 And he b' in the Lord; and he 539
45:26 Jacob's heart fainted, for he b' "
Ex 4:31 And the people b': and when they "
14:31 and b' the Lord, and his servant "
Nu 20:12 Because ye b' me not, to sanctify "
De 9:23 and ye b' him not, nor hearkened "
1Sa 27:12 And Achish b' David, saying, He "
1Ki 10: 7 Howbeit I b' not the words, until "
2Ch 9: 6 Howbeit I b' not their words, until "
Job 29:24 I laughed on them, they b' it not; "
Ps 27:13 unless I had b' to see the goodness "
78:22 Because they b' not in God, and "
32 b' not for his wondrous works. "
106:12 Then b' they his words; they sang "
24 pleasant land they b' not his word: "
116:10 I b', therefore have I spoken: I * "
119:66 for I have b' thy commandments. "
Isa 53: 1 Who hath b' our report? and to "
Jer 40:14 the son of Ahikam, b' them not. "
La 4:12 of the world, would not have b' that "
Da 6:23 upon him, because he b' in his * 540
Jon 3: 5 So the people of Nineveh b' God, 539
M't 8:13 and as thou hast b', so be it 4100
21:32 and ye b' him not: but the "
32 publicans and the harlots b' him: "
M'r 16:11 and had been seen of her, b' not. * 569
13 unto the residue: neither b' they 4100
14 because they b' not them which "
Lu 1: 1 things which are most surely b' *4135
45 blessed is she that b': for there 4100
20: 5 say, Why then b' ye him not? * "
24:11 idle tales, and they b' them not. * 569
41 while they yet b' not for joy, and * "
Joh 2:11 his disciples b' on him. 4100
22 and they b' the scripture, and the "
23 many b' in his name, when they "
3:18 already, because he hath not b' "
4:39 of the Samaritans of that city b' on "
41 many more b' because of his own "
50 the man b' the word that Jesus had "
53 himself b', and his whole house. "
5:46 had ye b' Moses, "
46 ye would have b' me. * "
6:64 who they were that b' not, and who "
7:31 And many of the people b' on him, "
48 or of the Pharisees b' on him? "
8:30 spake these words, many b' on "
31 to those Jews which b' on him, "
10:25 ye b' not: the works that I do * "
42 And many b' on him there. "
11:45 things which Jesus did, b' on him "
12:11 of the Jews went away, and b' on "
37 before them, yet they b' not on him: "
38 Lord, who hath b' our report? "
42 chief rulers also many b' on him; "
16:27 have b' that I came out from God. "
17: 8 and they have b' that thou didst "
Joh 20: 8 the sepulchre, and he saw, and b'. 4100
29 thou hast b': blessed are they "
29 have not seen, and yet have b'. "
Ac 2:44 And all that b' were together, "
4: 4 of them which heard the word b'; "
32 of them that b' were of one heart "
8:12 But when they b' Philip preaching "
13 Then Simon himself b' also: "
9:26 and b' not that he was a disciple. * "
42 Joppa; and many b' in the Lord. "
10:45 they of the circumcision which b' 4103
11:17 who b' on the Lord Jesus Christ; 4100
21 a great number b', and turned "
13:12 when he saw what was done, b', "
48 as were ordained to eternal life b'. "
14: 1 Jews and also of the Greeks b'. "
23 them to the Lord, on whom they b'. "
15: 5 of the Pharisees which b', saying, "
16: 1 which was a Jewess, and b'; 4103
17: 4 And some of them b', and *3982
5 the Jews which b' not, moved * 544
12 Therefore many of them b'; also 4100
34 certain men clave unto him, and b': "
18: 8 b' on the Lord with all his house; "
8 of the Corinthians hearing b', "
27 helped them much which had b' "
19: 2 received the Holy Ghost since ye b'? "
9 divers were hardened, and b' not,* 544
18 And many that b' came, and 4100
22:19 every synagogue them that b' on "
27:11 the centurion b' the master and *3982
28:24 And some b' the things which "
24 were spoken, and some b' not. "
Ro 4: 3 Abraham b' God, and it was *569, 4100
17 before him whom he b', even God, "
18 who against hope b' in hope, "
10:14 on him in whom they have not b'? "
16 saith, Lord, who hath b' our report? "
11:30 ye in times past have not b' God, * 544
31 so have these also now not b', "
13:11 salvation nearer than when we b'.*4100
1Co 3: 5 ministers by whom ye b', even as "
15: 2 unless ye have b' in vain. "
11 or they, so we preach, and so ye b'. "
2Co 4:13 I b', and therefore have I spoken; "
Ga 2:16 even we have b' in Jesus Christ, "
3: 6 as Abraham b' God, and it was "
Eph. 1:13 in whom also after that ye b', "
2Th 1:10 our testimony among you was b') "
2:12 who b' not the truth, but had "
1Ti 3:16 b' on in the world, received up into "
2Ti 1:12 I know whom I have b', and am "
Tit 3: 8 that they which have b' in God "
Heb 3:18 his rest, but to them that b' not? * 544
4: 3 which have b' do enter into rest. 4100
11:31 perished not with them that b' * 544
Jas 2:23 Abraham b' God, and it was 4100
1Jo 4:16 we have known and b' the love "
Jude 5 destroyed them that b' not. "

believers See also UNBELIEVERS.
Ac 5:14 And b' were the more added 4100
1Ti 4:12 be thou an example of the b', in *4103

believest
Lu 1:20 because thou b' not my words, *4100
Joh 1:50 thee under the fig tree, b' thou? "
11:26 in me shall never die. B' thou "
14:10 B' thou not that I am in the "
Ac 8:37 If thou b' with all thine heart, * "
26:27 King Agrippa, b' thou the prophets? "
27 I know that thou b'. "
Jas 2:19 Thou b' that there is one God; "

believeth
Job 15:22 He b' not that he shall return 539
39:24 neither b' he that it is the sound "
Pr 14:15 The simple b' every word: "
Isa 28:16 he that b' shall not make haste. "
M'r 9:23 are possible to him that b'. *4100
16:16 He that b' and is baptized shall "
16 he that b' not shall be damned. * 569
Joh 3:15, 16 whosoever b' in him should 4100
18 He that b' on him is not "
18 but he that b' not is condemned "
36 He that b' on the Son hath "
36 that b' not the Son shall not see * 544
5:24 and b' on him that sent me, 4100
6:35 he that b' on me shall never thirst. "
40 and b' on him, may have "
47 He that b' on me hath everlasting "
7:38 He that b' on me, as the scripture "
11:25 He that b' in me, though he were "
26 and b' in me shall never die. "
12:44 He that b' on me, b' not on me, but "
46 that whosoever b' on me should not "
14:12 He that b' on me, the works that I "
Ac 10:43 whosoever b' in him shall receive "
Ro 1:16 unto salvation to every one that b'; "
3:26 justifier of him which b' in * 1537, 4102
4: 5 but b' on him that justifieth the 4100
9:33 whosoever b' on him shall not be "
10: 4 righteousness to every one that b'. "
10 For with the heart man b' unto "
11 Whosoever b' on him shall not be "
14: 2 For one b' that he may eat all "
1Co 7:12 hath a wife, that b' not, and she * 571
13 hath an husband that b' not, and * "
13: 7 b' all things, hopeth all things, 4100
14:24 there come in one that b' not, or 571
2Co 6:15 hath he that b' with an infidel? *4103
1Ti 5:16 If any man or woman that b' "
1Pe 2: 6 and he that b' on him shall not be 4100
1Jo 5: 1 Whosoever b' that Jesus is the "
5 he that b' that Jesus is the Son "
10 He that b' on the Son of God "
10 he that b' not God hath made "
10 because he b' not the record * "

believing See also UNBELIEVING.
M't 21:22 ye shall ask in prayer, b', ye shall 4100
Joh 20:27 and be not faithless, but b'. 4103
31 and that b' ye might have life 4100
Ac 16:34 rejoiced, b' in God with all his "
24:14 b' all things which are written "
Ro 15:13 you with all joy and peace in b', "
1Ti 6: 2 And they that have b' masters, 4103
1Pe 1: 8 yet b', ye rejoice with joy 4100
bell See also BELLS.
Ex 28:34 b' and a pomegranate, 6472
34 a golden b' "
39:26 A b' and a pomegranate, a b' "
bellies
Tit 1:12 always liars, evil beasts, slow b'. *1064
bellow See also BELLOWS.
Jer 50:11 as the heifer at grass, and b' as *6670
bellows
Jer 6:29 The b' are burned, the lead is 4647
bells
Ex 28:33 and b' of gold between them 6472
39:25 b' of pure gold, and put the b' "
Zec 14:20 there be upon the b' of the horses, 4698
belly See also BELLIES.
Ge 3:14 upon thy b' shalt thou go, and 1512
Le 11:42 goeth upon the b', and whatsoever "
Nu 5:21 thy thigh to rot, and thy b' to ‡ 990
22 to make thy b' to swell, and thy ‡ "
27 her b' shall swell, and her thigh ‡ "
25: 8 and the woman through her b'. ‡6897
J'g 3:21 thrust it into his b': ‡ 990
22 not draw the dagger out of his b';‡ "
1Ki 7:20 over against the b' which was by "
Job 3:11 ghost when I came out of the b'? ‡ "
15: 2 and fill his b' with the east wind? "
35 vanity, and their b' prepareth "
20:15 God shall cast them out of his b'. "
20 shall not feel quietness in his b', * "
23 he is about to fill his b', God "
32:19 b' is as wine which hath no vent;‡ "
40:16 his force is in the navel of his b'. "
Ps 17:14 whose b' thou fillest with thy hid "
22:10 art my God from my mother's b'. ‡ "
31: 9 grief, yea, my soul and my b'. * "
44:25 to the dust, our b' cleaveth unto ‡ "
Pr 13:25 but the b' of the wicked shall want. "
18: 8 the innermost parts of the b'. ‡ "
20 A man's b' shall be satisfied with "
20:27 all the inward parts of the b'. ‡ "
30 stripes the inward parts of the b'.‡ "
26:22 into the innermost parts of the b'. "
Ca 5:14 his b' is as bright ivory, overlaid *4578
7: 2 thy b' is like an heap of wheat set ‡ 990
Isa 46: 3 borne by me from the b', which ‡ "
Jer 1: 5 Before I formed thee in the b' I "
51:34 he hath filled his b' with my *3770
Eze 3: 3 cause thy b' to eat, and fill thy 990
Da 2:32 arms of silver, his b' and his 4577
Jon 1:17 in the b' of the fish three days 4578
2: 1 Lord his God out of the fish's b'. "
2 out of the b' of hell cried I, and 990
Hab 3:16 my b' trembled; my lips quivered ‡ "
M't 12:40 three nights in the whale's b'; 2836
15:17 in at the mouth goeth into the b', "
M'r 7:19 but into the b', and goeth out into "
Lu 15:16 he would fain have filled his b' † "
Joh 7:38 out of his b' shall flow rivers of † "
Ro 16:18 Jesus Christ, but their own b'; "
1Co 6:13 Meats for the b', "
13 and the b' for meats: "
Ph'p 3:19 whose God is their b', and whose "
Re 10: 9 it shall make thy b' bitter, but it "
10 as I had eaten it, my b' was bitter. "
belong See also BELONGED; BELONGETH; BELONGEST; BELONGING.
Ge 40: 8 Do not interpretations b' to God?
Le 27:24 the possession of the land did b'. *
Nu 1:50 and over all things that b' to it: *
De 29:29 The secret things b' unto the Lord
29 things which are revealed b' unto
Ps 47: 9 shields of the earth b' unto God
68:20 the Lord b' the issues from death.
Pr 24:23 These things also b' to the wise. *
Da 9: 9 To the Lord our God b' mercies
M'r 9:41 because ye b' to Christ, verily I *1510
Lu 19:42 things which b' unto thy peace!
1Co 7:32 careth for the things that b' to
belonged
Jos 17: 8 b' to the children of Ephraim;
1Sa 21: 7 the herdmen that b' to Saul.
1Ki 1: 8 mighty men which b' to David,
15:27 which b' to the Philistines;
16:15 which b' to the Philistines.
2Ki 14:28 and Hamath, which b' to Judah,
1Ch 2:23 these b' to the sons of Machir *
13: 6 Kirjath-jearim, which b' to Judah,
2Ch 26:23 the burial which b' to the kings;
Es 1: 9 house which b' to king Ahasuerus
2: 9 things as b' to her, and seven *4490
Lu 23: 7 he b' unto Herod's jurisdiction, *1510
belongest
1Sa 30:13 unto him, To whom b' thou?
belongeth
Nu 8:24 This is it that b' unto the Levites:
De 32:35 To me b' vengeance, and *
J'g 19:14 by Gibeah, which b' to Benjamin.
20: 4 into Gibeah that b' to Benjamin,
1Sa 17: 1 at Shochoh, which b' to Judah,
30:14 the coast which b' to Judah, and
1Ki 17: 9 Zarephath, which b' to Zidon,
19: 3 Beer-sheba, which b' to Judah,
2Ki 14:11 Beth-shemesh, which b' to Judah.
2Ch 25:21 Beth-shemesh, which b' to Judah.
Ezr 10: 4 for this matter b' unto thee:
Ps 3: 8 Salvation b' unto the Lord: thy
62:11 heard this; that power b' unto God.
12 unto thee, O Lord, b' mercy: for thou
94: 1 O Lord God, to whom vengeance b';
1 O God, to whom vengeance b', shew
Da 9: 7 O Lord, righteousness b' unto thee,
8 O Lord, to us b' confusion of face,
Heb 5:14 But strong meat b' to them that *1510
10:30 Vengeance b' unto me, I will
belonging
Nu 7: 9 service of the sanctuary b' unto *
Ru 2: 3 a part of the field b' unto Boaz
1Sa 6:18 of the Philistines b' to the five lords,
Pr 26:17 with strife b' not to him, is like
Lu 9:10 desert place b' to the city called *
beloved See also BELOVED'S; WELL BELOVED.
De 21:15 wives, one b', and another hated, 157
15 both the b' and the hated; "
16 not make the son of the b' firstborn "
33:12 The b' of the Lord shall dwell in 3039
Neh 13:26 was b' of his God, and God made 157
Ps 60: 5 That thy b' may be delivered; 3039
108: 6 That thy b' may be delivered: "
127: 2 for so he giveth his b' sleep. "
Pr 4: 3 only b' in the sight of my mother.
Ca 1:14 My b' is unto me as a cluster 1730
16 Behold, thou art fair, my b', 157
2: 3 so is my b' among the sons. 1730
8 The voice of my b'! behold, he "
9 My b' is like a roe or a young hart: "
10 My b' spake, and said unto me, "
16 My b' is mine, and I am his: "
17 turn, my b', and be thou like a roe "
4:16 b' come into his garden, and eat "
5: 1 yea, drink abundantly, O b'. "
2 the voice of my b' that knocketh, "
4 My b' put in his hand by the hole "
5 rose up to open to my b'; and my "
6 to my b'; but my b' had withdrawn "
8 if ye find my b', that ye tell him, "
9 thy b' more than another b', O thou "
9 thy b' more than another b', that thou "
10 my b' is white and ruddy, the "
16 This is my b', and this is my friend, "
6: 1 Whither is thy b' gone, O thou "
1 whither is thy b' turned aside? "
2 My b' is gone down into his garden, "
3 my beloved's, and my b' is mine: "
7: 9 the best wine for my b' that goeth, "
11 come my b', let us go forth "
13 I have laid up for thee, O my b'. "
8: 5 the wilderness, leaning upon her b'? "
14 Make haste, my b', and be thou like "
Isa 5: 1 to my wellbeloved a song of my b' "
Jer 11:15 hath my b' to do in mine house, 3039
12: 7 dearly b' of my soul into the hand 3033
Da 9:23 greatly b': therefore understand 2530
10:11 a man greatly b', understand the "
19 said, O man greatly b', fear not: "
Ho 3: 1 yet, love a woman b of her friend, 157
9:16 even the b' fruit of their womb. 4261
M't 3:17 saying, This is my b' Son, in whom 27
12:18 I have chosen; my b' in whom, "
17: 5 which said, This is my b' Son, "
M'r 1:11 Thou art my b' Son, in whom "
9: 7 saying, This is my b' Son: hear him. "
Lu 3:22 which said, Thou art my b' Son; "
9:35 saying, This is my b' Son: hear * "
20:13 shall I do? I will send my b' son: "
Ac 15:25 chosen men unto you with our b' "
Ro 1: 7 To all that be in Rome, b' of God, "
9:25 and her b', which was not b'. 25
11:28 touching the election, they are b' 27
12:19 Dearly b', avenge not yourselves, "
16: 8 Greet Amplias my b' in the Lord. "
9 helper in Christ, and Stachys my b'. "
12 Salute the b' Persis, which laboured "
1Co 4:14 but as my b' sons I warn you. "
17 who is my b' son, and faithful in the "
10:14 my dearly b', flee from idolatry. "
15:58 Therefore, my b' brethren, be ye "
2Co 7: 1 dearly b', let us cleanse ourselves "
12:19 we do all things, dearly b', for your "
Eph 1: 6 he hath made us accepted in the b'. 25
6:21 a b' brother and faithful minister 27
Ph'p 2:12 Wherefore, my b', as ye have "
4: 1 brethren dearly b' and longed for, "
1 stand fast in the Lord, my dearly b'. "
Col 3:12 as the elect of God, holy and b', 25
4: 7 declare unto you, who is a b' brother 27
9 Onesimus, a faithful and b' brother, "
14 Luke, the b' physician, and Demas, "
1Th 1: 4 Knowing, brethren b', your election 25
2Th 2:13 for you, brethren b' of the Lord, "
1Ti 6: 2 because they are faithful and b', 27
2Ti 1: 2 To Timothy, my dearly b' son: "
Ph'm 1 unto Philemon our dearly b', and "
2 to our b' Apphia, and Archippus * "
16 but above a servant, a brother b', "
Heb 6: 9 b', we are persuaded better things "
Jas 1:16 Do not err, my b' brethren. "
19 Wherefore, my b' brethren, let every "
2: 5 Hearken, my b' brethren, Hath not "
1Pe 2:11 b', I beseech you as strangers "
4:12 B', think it not strange concerning "
2Pe 1:17 This is my b' Son, in whom I am "
3: 1 This second epistle, b', I now write "
8 But, b', be not ignorant of this "
14 Wherefore, b', seeing that ye look "
15 our b' brother Paul also according "
17 Ye therefore, b', seeing ye know "
1Jo 3: 2 B', now are we the sons of God, "
21 B', if our heart condemn us not, "
1Jo 4: 1 B', believe not every spirit, but try 27
7 B', let us love one another: for love "
11 B', if God so loved us, we ought also "
3Jo 2 B', I wish above all things that "
5 B', thou doest faithfully whatsoever "
11 B', follow not that which is evil, "
Jude 3 B', when I gave all diligence to "
17 b', remember ye the words which "
20 But ye, b', building up yourselves "
Re 20: 9 of the saints about, and the b' city: 25
beloved's
Ca 6: 3 my b', and my beloved is mine: 1730
7:10 I am my b', and his desire is "
Belshazzar (*bel-shaz'-ar*)
Da 5: 1 B' the king made a great feast to 1113
2 B', whiles he tasted the wine, "
9 was king B' greatly troubled, and "
22 B', hast not humbled thine heart, "
29 B', and they clothed Daniel "
30 B' the king of the Chaldeans slain. "
7: 1 B' king of Babylon Daniel had "
8: 1 B' a vision appeared unto me, "
Belteshazzar (*bel-te-shaz'-ar*) See also DANIEL.
Da 1: 7 gave unto Daniel the name of B'; 1095
2:26 to Daniel, whose name was B', 1096
4: 8 in before me, whose name was B', "
9 O B', master of the magicians, "
18 B', declare the interpretation "
19 whose name was B', was astonied "
19 and said, B', let not the dream, "
19 B' answered and said, My lord, "
5:12 Daniel, whom the king named B': "
10: 1 Daniel, whose name was called B';1095
bemoan See also BEMOANED; BEMOANING.
Jer 15: 5 who shall b' thee? or who shall go 5110
16: 5 neither go to lament nor b' them: "
22:10 ye not for the dead, neither b' him: "
48:17 All ye that are about him, b' him; "
Na 3: 7 is laid waste: who will b' her? "
bemoaned
Job 42:11 and they b' him, and comforted 5110
bemoaning
Jer 31:18 heard Ephraim b' himself thus; 5110
Ben (*ben*) See also BEN-AMMI; BEN-HADAD; BEN-HAIL; BEN-HANAN; BEN-ONI; BEN-ZOHETH.
1Ch 15:18 second degree, Zechariah, B', and 1122
Ben-ammi (*ben-am'-mi*)
Ge 19:38 bare a son, and called his name B':1151
Benaiah (*ben-ay'-ah*)
2Sa 8:18 And B' the son of Jehoiada was 1141
20:23 and B' the son of Jehoiada was "
23:20 B' the son of Jehoiada, the son of "
22 These things did B' the son of "
30 B' the Pirathonite, Hiddai of the "
1Ki 1: 8 priest, and B' the son of Jehoiada, "
10 Nathan the prophet, and B', "
26 and Zadok the priest, and B' the "
32 and B' the son of Jehoiada. "
36 B' the son of Jehoiada answered "
38 and Nathan the prophet, and B' "
44 B' the son of Jehoiada, and the "
2:25 Solomon sent by the hand of B' "
29 sent B' the son of Jehoiada, "
30 And B' came to the tabernacle "
30 B' brought the king word again, "
34 B' the son of Jehoiada went up, "
35 king put B' the son of Jehoiada "
46 So the king commanded B' the son "
4: 4 B' the son of Jehoiada was over "
1Ch 4:36 and Adiel, and Jesimiel, and B', "
11:22 B' the son of Jehoiada, the son of "
24 These things did B' the son of "
31 of Benjamin, B' the Pirathonite, "
15:18 Eliab, and B', and Maaseiah, "
20 and Eliab, and Maaseiah, and B', "
24 Zechariah, and B', and Eliezer, "
16: 5 and Eliab, and B', and Obed-edom: "
6 B' also and Jahaziel the priests "
18:17 And B' the son of Jehoiada was "
27: 5 for the third month was B' the son "
6 This is that B', who was mighty "
14 month was B' the Pirathonite, "
34 was Jehoiada the son of B', "
2Ch 20:14 of Zechariah, the son of B', the "
31:13 Mahath, and B', were overseers "
Ezr 10:25 Eleazar, and Malchijah, and B'. "
30 Chelal, B', Maaseiah, Mattaniah, "
35 B', Bedeiah, Chelluh, "
43 Zebina, Jadau, and Joel, B'. "
Eze 11: 1 and Pelatiah the son of B', "
13 that Pelatiah the son of B' died. "
benches
Eze 27: 6 made thy b' of ivory, brought out 7175
bend See also BENDETH; BENDING; BENT.
Ps 11: 2 the wicked b' their bow, they 1869
64: 3 b' their bows to shoot their * "
Jer 9: 3 they b' their tongues like their "
46: 9 Lydians, that handle and b' the "
50:14 all ye that b' the bow, "
29 Babylon: all ye that b' the bow, "
51: 3 bendeth let the archer b' his bow, "
Eze 17: 7 vine did b' her roots toward him, 3719
bendeth
Ps 58: 7 he b' his bow to shoot his arrows,*1869
Jer 51: 3 Against him that b' let the archer * "
bending
Isa 60:14 thee shall come b' unto thee; 7817
Bene See BENE-BERAH; BENE-JAAKAN.

beneath
Ge 35: 8 and she was buried *b'* Beth-el. *8478
Ex 20: 4 or that is in the earth *b'*, or that "
26:24 they shall be coupled together *b'*, 4295
27: 5 under the compass of the altar *b'*, "
28:33 And *b'* upon the hem of it thou *
32:19 and brake them *b'* the mount. 8478
36:29 they were coupled *b'*, and coupled 4295
38: 4 thereof, *b'* unto the midst of it. "
De 4:18 that is in the waters *b'* the earth: *8478
39 upon the earth *b'*: there is none "
5: 8 or that is in the earth *b'*, "
8 or that is in the waters *b'* * "
28:13 above only, thou shalt not be *b'*; 4295
33:13 and for the deep that coucheth *b'*, 8478
Jos 2:11 in heaven above, and in earth *b'*. "
J'g 7: 8 the host of Midian was *b'* him "
1Ki 4:12 which is by Zartanah *b'* Jezreel, "
7:29 and *b'* the lions and oxen were "
8:23 in heaven above, or on earth *b'*, "
Job 18:16 His roots shall be dried up *b'*, and "
Pr 15:24 that he may depart from hell *b'*. 4295
Isa 14: 9 Hell from *b'* is moved for thee to 8478
51: 6 and look upon the earth *b'*: "
Jer 31:37 of the earth searched out *b'*, 4295
Am 2: 9 from above, and his roots from *b'*. 8478
M'k 14:66 And as Peter was *b'* in the palace, *2736*
Joh 8:23 Ye are from *b'*; I am from above: "
Ac 2:19 and signs in the earth *b'*; blood, "

Bene-berak (*be''-ne-be'-rak*)
Jos 19:45 Jehud, and *B'*, and Gath-rimmon, 1138

benefactors
Lu 22:25 authority upon them are called *b'*. *2110*

benefit See also BENEFITS.
2Ch 32:25 according to the *b'* done unto 1576
Jer 18:10 wherewith I said I would *b'* them. 3190
2Co 1:15 that ye might have a second *b'*; *5485*
1Ti 6: 2 and beloved, partakers of the *b'*. *2108*
Ph'm 14 that thy *b'* should not be as it * *18*

benefits
Ps 68:19 who daily loadeth us with *b'*, *
103: 2 and forget not all his *b'*: 1576
116:12 Lord for all his *b'* toward me? 8408

Bene-jaakan (*be''-ne-ja'-a-kan*)
Nu 33:31 from Moseroth, and pitched in *B'*. 1142
32 removed from *B'*, and encamped "

benevolence
1Co 7: 3 render unto the wife due *b'*: **2133*

Ben-hadad (*ben'-ha-dad*)
1Ki 15:18 and king Asa sent them to *B'*, 1131
20 So *B'* hearkened unto king Asa, "
20: 1 And *B'* the king of Syria gathered "
2 said unto him, Thus saith *B'*, "
5 Thus speaketh *B'*, saying, "
9 unto the messengers of *B'*, Tell "
10 And *B'* sent unto him, and said, "
12 when *B'* heard this message, "
16 *B'* was drinking himself drunk 1130
17 and *B'* sent out, and they told him, "
20 and *B'* the king of Syria escaped "
26 the year, that *B'* numbered the "
30 And *B'* fled, and came into the city, "
32 thy servant *B'* saith, I pray thee, "
33 and they said, Thy brother *B'*. "
33 Then *B'* came forth to him; "
34 And *B'* said unto him, "
2Ki 6:24 after this, that *B'* king of Syria 1130
8: 7 and *B'* the king of Syria was sick; "
9 and said, Thy son *B'* king of Syria "
13: 3 the hand of *B'* the son of Hazael, "
24 and *B'* his son reigned in his stead. "
25 of the hand of *B'* the son of Hazael "
2Ch 16: 2 and sent to *B'* king of Syria, that "
4 And *B'* hearkened unto king Asa, "
Jer 49:27 shall consume the palaces of *B'*. "
Am 1: 4 shall devour the palaces of *B'*. "

Ben-hail (*ben-ha'-il*)
2Ch 17: 7 sent to his princes, even to *B'*, 1134

Ben-hanan (*ben-ha'-nan*)
1Ch 4: 20 Amnon, and Rinnah, *B'*, and 1135

Beninu (*ben'-i-nu*)
Ne 10:13 Hodijah, Bani, *B'*. 1148

Benjamin (*ben'-ja-min*) See also BENJAMIN'S; BENJAMITE.
Ge 35:18 but his father called him *B'*. 1144
24 sons of Rachel; Joseph, and *B'*: "
42: 4 *B'*, Joseph's brother, Jacob sent "
36 and ye will take *B'* away: "
43:14 away your other brother, and *B'*. "
15 money in their hand, and *B'*; "
16 Joseph saw *B'* with them, he said "
29 saw his brother *B'*, his mother's "
45:12 and the eyes of my brother *B'*, "
14 and wept; and *B'* wept upon "
22 But to *B'* he gave three hundred "
46:19 Jacob's wife; Joseph, and *B'*. "
21 sons of *B'* were Belah, and Becher, "
49:27 *B'* shall ravin as a wolf: in the "
Ex 1: 3 Issachar, Zebulun, and *B'*, "
Nu 1:11 Of *B'*; Abidan the son of Gideoni. "
36 Of the children of *B'*, by their "
37 even of the tribe of *B'*, were thirty "
2:22 Then the tribe of *B'*: "
22 the captain of the sons of *B'*, "
7:60 prince of the children of *B'*, offered: "
10:24 the children of *B'* was Abidan the "
13: 9 Of the tribe of *B'*, Palti the son of "
26:38 The sons of *B'* after their families: "
41 *B'* after their families: and they "
34:21 Of the tribe of *B'*, Elidad the son "
De 27:12 and Issachar, and Joseph, and *B'*: "
33:12 And of *B'* he said, The beloved of "
Jos 18:11 children of *B'* came up according 1144
20 children of *B*, by the coasts "
21 *B'* according to their families were "
28 inheritance of the children of *B'* "
21: 4 of the tribe of *B'*, thirteen cities. "
17 of *B'*, Gibeon with her suburbs, "
J'g 1:21 *B'* did not drive out the Jebusites "
21 of *B'* in Jerusalem unto this day. "
5:14 after thee, *B'*, among thy people; "
10: 9 against Judah, and against *B'*, "
19:14 by Gibeah, which belongeth to *B'*. "
20: 3 children of *B'* heard that the "
4 belongeth to *B'*, I and my "
10 come to Gibeah of *B'*, according to "
12 men through all the tribe of *B'*, "
13 *B'* would not hearken to the voice "
14 children of *B'* gathered themselves "
15 of *B'* were numbered at that time "
17 Israel, beside *B'*, were numbered "
18 against the children of *B'*? "
20 went out to battle against *B'*; "
21 of *B'* came forth out of Gibeah, "
23 of *B'* my brother? And the Lord "
24 near against the children of *B'* "
25 *B'* went forth against them out of "
28 against the children of *B'* my "
30 against the children of *B'* on the "
31 *B'* went out against the people, "
32 *B'* said, They are smitten down "
35 the Lord smote *B'* before Israel: "
36 So the children of *B'* saw that they "
39 in the battle, *B'* began to smite "
41 the men of *B'* were amazed: "
44 fell of *B'* eighteen thousand men; "
46 fell that day of *B'* were twenty and "
48 upon the children of *B'*, and smote "
21: 1 give his daughter unto *B'* to wife. "
6 Israel repented them for *B'* their "
13 speak to the children of *B'* that "
14 And *B'* came again at that time; "
15 repented them for *B'*, because the "
16 women are destroyed out of *B'*? "
17 that be escaped of *B'*, that a tribe "
18 be he that giveth a wife to *B'*. "
20 commanded the children of *B'*, "
21 Shiloh, and go to the land of *B'*. "
23 children of *B'* did so, and took "
1Sa 4:12 ran a man of *B'* out of the army, "
9: 1 a man of *B'*, whose name was Kish, "
16 man out of the land of *B'*, and thou "
21 the families of the tribe of *B'*? "
10: 2 in the border of *B'* at Zelzah; "
20 near, the tribe of *B'* was taken. "
21 tribe of *B'* to come near by their "
13: 2 with Jonathan in Gibeah of *B'*: "
15 up from Gilgal unto Gibeah of *B'*. "
16 with them, abode in Gibeah of *B'*: "
14:16 watchmen of Saul in Gibeah of *B'* "
2Sa 2: 9 and over Ephraim, and over *B'*, "
15 went over by number twelve of *B'*, "
25 children of *B'* gathered themselves "
31 of David had smitten of *B'*, and "
3:19 Abner also spake in the ears of *B'*: "
19 good to the whole house of *B'*. "
4: 2 Beerothite, of the children of *B'*: "
2 Beeroth also was reckoned to *B'*: "
19:17 thousand men of *B'* with him, "
21:14 in the country of *B'* in Zelah, "
23:29 of Gibeah of the children of *B'*, "
1Ki 4:18 Shimei the son of Elah, in *B'*: "
12:21 Judah, with the tribe of *B'*, an "
23 unto all the house of Judah and *B'*, "
15:22 Asa built with them Geba of *B'*, "
1Ch 2: 2 Dan, Joseph, and *B'*, Naphtali, "
6:60 And out of the tribe of *B'*; Geba "
65 children of *B'*, these cities, which "
7: 6 The sons of *B'*; Bela, and Becher, "
10 Jeush, and *B'*, and Ehud, and "
8: 1 Now *B'* begat Bela his firstborn, "
40 All these are of the sons of *B'*. "
9: 3 children of *B'*, and of the children "
7 And of the sons of *B'*; Sallu the "
11:31 to the children of *B'*, Benaiah "
12: 2 even of Saul's brethren of *B'*. "
16 came of the children of *B'* and "
29 children of *B'*, the kindred of "
21: 6 But Levi and *B'* counted he not "
27:21 of *B'*, Jaasiel the son of Abner: "
2Ch 11: 1 house of Judah and *B'* an hundred "
3 all Israel in Judah and *B'*, saying, "
10 which are in Judah and in *B'* "
12 having Judah and *B'* on his side. "
23 all the countries of Judah and *B'*, "
14: 8 and out of *B'*, that bare shields "
15: 2 ye me, Asa, and all Judah and *B'*; "
8 land of Judah and *B'*, and out of "
9 gathered all Judah and *B'*, and "
17:17 And of *B'*; Eliada a mighty man "
25: 5 throughout all Judah and *B'*: "
31: 1 the altars out of all Judah and *B'*, "
34: 9 and all Judah and *B'*; and they "
32 were present in Jerusalem and *B'* "
Ezr 1: 5 fathers of Judah and *B'*, and the "
4: 1 adversaries of Judah and *B'* heard "
10: 9 men of Judah and *B'* gathered "
32 *B'*, Malluch, and Shemariah. "
Ne 3:23 After him repaired *B'* and Hashub "
11: 4 of Judah, and of the children of *B'*. "
7 All these are the sons of *B'*; Sallu "
31 The children also of *B'* from Geba "
36 were divisions in Judah, and in *B'*. "
12:34 Judah, and *B'*, and Shemaiah, "
Ps 68:27 There is little *B'* with their ruler, "
80: 2 Before Ephraim and *B'* and "
Jer 1: 1 in Anathoth in the land of *B'*: "
6: 1 O ye children of *B'*, gather "
Jer 17:26 and from the land of *B'*, 1144
20: 2 that were in the high gate of *B'*, "
32: 8 which is in the country of *B'*: "
44 take witnesses in the land of *B'*, "
33:13 and in the land of *B'*, and in the "
37:12 to go into the land of *B'*, to "
13 was in the gate of *B'*, a captain of "
38: 7 king then sitting in the gate of *B'*; "
Eze 48:22 of Judah and the border of *B'*, "
23 west side, *B'* shall have a portion. "
24 by the border of *B'*, from the east "
32 one gate of Joseph, one gate of *B'*, "
Hos 5: 8 at Beth-aven, after thee, O *B'*. "
Ob 19 Samaria; and *B'* shall possess "
Ac 13:21 a man of the tribe of *B'*, by the *958*
Ro 11: 1 of Abraham, of the tribe of *B'*. "
Ph'p 3: 5 of the tribe of *B'*, an Hebrew of "
Re 7: 8 Of the tribe of *B'* were sealed "

Benjamin's (*ben'-ja-mins*)
Ge 43:34 but *B'* mess was five times so 1144
44:12 the cup was found in *B'* sack. "
45:14 he fell upon his brother *B'* neck, "
Zec 14:10 inhabited in her place, from *B'* "

Benjamite (*ben'-ja-mite*) See also BENJAMITES.
J'g 3:15 Ehud the son of Gera, a *B'*, a man 1145
1Sa 9: 1 the son of Aphiah, a *B'*, a mighty "
21 Am not I a *B'*, of the smallest of "
2Sa 16:11 much more now may this *B'* do it? "
19:16 Shimei the son of Gera, a *B'*, "
20: 1 Sheba, the son of Bichri, a *B'*: "
1Ki 2: 8 the son of Gera, a *B'* of Bahurim, "
Es 2: 5 Shimei, the son of Kish, a *B'*; "
Ps 7:*title* the words of Cush the *B'*. "

Benjamites (*ben'-ja-mites*)
J'g 19:16 but the men of the place were *B'*. 1145
20:35 Israel destroyed of the *B'* that * "
36 Israel gave place to the *B'*, "
40 pillars of smoke, the *B'* looked "
43 thus they inclosed the *B'* round "
1Sa 9: 4 passed through the land of the *B'*, "
22: 7 Hear now, ye *B'*; will the son of "
1Ch 27:12 Abiezer the Anetothite, of the *B'*: "

Beno (*be'-no*)
1Ch 24:26 Mushi: the sons of Jaaziah; *B'*. 1121
27 *B'*, and Shoham, and Zaccur, and "

Benob See ISBI-BENOB.

Ben-oni (*ben-o'-ni*)
Ge 35:18 she called his name *B'*: but his 1126

Benoth See ISHBI-BENOTH.

bent
Ps 7:12 he hath *b'* his bow, and made it 1869
37:14 and have *b'* their bow, to cast "
Isa 5:28 all their bows *b'*, their horses' "
21:15 drawn sword, and from the *b'* bow, "
La 2: 4 He hath *b'* his bow like an enemy: "
3:12 He hath *b'* his bow, and set me as "
Ho 11: 7 my people are *b'* to backsliding 8511
Zec 9:13 When I have *b'* Judah for me, 1869

Ben-zoheth (*ben-zo'-heth*)
1Ch 4:20 sons of Ishi were, Zoheth, and *B'*. 1132

Beon (*be'-on*)
Nu 32: 3 and Shebam, and Nebo, and *B'*, 1194

Beor (*be'-or*)
Ge 36:32 And Bela the son of *B'* reigned in 1160
Nu 22: 5 Balaam the son of *B'* to Pethor, "
24: 3 Balaam the son of *B'* hath said, "
15 the son of *B'* hath said, and the "
31: 8 Balaam also the son of *B'* they "
De 23: 4 against thee Balaam the son of *B'* "
Jos 13:22 Balaam also the son of *B'*, the "
24: 9 called Balaam the son of *B'* to "
1Ch 1:43 Bela the son of *B'*: and the name "
Mic 6: 5 Balaam the son of *B'* answered "

Bera (*be'-rah*)
Ge 14: 2 these made war with *B'* king of 1298

Berachah (*ber'-a-kah*)
1Ch 12: 3 Azmaveth; and *B'*, and Jehu the 1294
2Ch 20:26 themselves in the valley of *B'*; "
26 was called, The valley of *B'*, "

Berachiah (*ber-a-ki'-ah*) See also BERECHIAH.
1Ch 6:39 even Asaph the son of *B'*, the son 1296

Beraiah (*ber-a-i'-ah*)
1Ch 8:21 Adaiah, and *B'*, and Shimrath, 1256

Berea (*be-re'-a*)
Ac 17:10 Paul and Silas by night unto *B'*: *960*
13 was preached of Paul at *B'*, they "
20: 4 him into Asia Sopater of *B'*; "

bereave See also BEREAVED; BEREAVETH.
Ec 4: 8 I labour and *b'* my soul of good? *2637
Jer 15: 7 I will *b'* them of children, I will 7921
Eze 5:17 beasts, and they shall *b'* thee: "
36:12 no more henceforth *b'* them of "
14 neither *b'* thy nations any 3782, (7921)
Ho 9:12 yet will I *b'* them, that there shall 7921

bereaved
Ge 42:36 Me have ye *b'* of my children: 7921
43:14 I be *b'* of my children, I am *b'*. "
Jer 18:21 wives be *b'* of their children, *7909
Eze 36:13 up men, and hast *b'* thy nations; *7921
Ho 13: 8 as a bear that is *b'* of her whelps, 7909

bereaveth
La 1:20 abroad the sword *b'*, at home 7921

Berechiah (*ber-e-ki'-ah*) See also BERACHIAH.
1Ch 3:20 and Ohel, and *B'*, and Hasadiah, 1296
9:16 *B'* the son of Asa, the son of "
15:17 his brethren, Asaph the son of *B'*; "
23 *B'* and Elkanah were doorkeepers "
2Ch 28:12 *B'* the son of Meshillemoth, and "

Ne 3: 4 Meshullam the son of B', the son 1296
30 son of B' over against his chamber. "
6:18 of Meshullam the son of B'. "
Zec 1: 1, 7 the son of B', the son of Iddo "

Bered (*be'-red*)
Ge 16:14 it is between Kadesh and B'. 1260
1Ch 7:20 Shuthelah, and B' his son, and

Beri (*be'-ri*) See also BERITES.
1Ch 7:36 Shual, and B', and Imrah, 1275

Beriah (*be-ri'-ah*) See also BERIITES.
Ge 46:17 and B', and Serah their sister: 1283
17 sons of B'; Heber, and Malchiel. "
Nu 26:44 Jesuites: of B', the family of the "
45 Of the sons of B': of Heber, the "
1Ch 7:23 he called his name B', because it "
30 and B', and Serah their sister. "
31 sons of B'; Heber, and Malchiel, "
8:13 B' also, and Shema, who were "
16 Ispah, and Joha, the sons of B'; "
23:10 Jahath, Zina, and Jeush, and B'. "
11 Jeush and B' had not many sons; "

Beriites (*be-ri'-ites*)
Nu 26:44 of Beriah, the family of the B'. 1284

Berites (*be'-rites*)
2Sa 20:14 to Beth-maachah, and all the B': 1276

Berith (*be'-rith*) See also BAAL-BERITH.
J'g 9:46 hold of the house of the god B'. 1286

Bernice (*bur-ni'-see*)
Ac 25:13 and B' came unto Cæsarea to 959
23 come, and B', with great pomp, "
26:30 B', and they that sat with them: "

Berodach-baladan (*ber-o''-dak-bal'-ad-an*) See also MERODACH-BALADAN.
2Ki 20:12 At that time B', the son of 1255

Berœa See BEREA.

Berothah (*ber-o'-thah*) See also BEROTHAI; BEROTHITE.
Eze 47:16 Hamath, B', Sibraim, 1268

Berothai (*ber'-o-thahee*) See also BEROTHAH.
2Sa 8: 8 and from B', cities of Hadadezer, 1268

Berothite (*be'-ro-thite*) See also BEEROTHITE.
1Ch 11:39 Naharai the B', the armourbearer 1307

berries
Isa 17: 6 two or three b' in the top of the 1620
Jas 3:12 tree, by brethren, bear olive b'? *1636

beryl (*ber'-il*)
Ex 28:20 the fourth row a b', and an onyx, 8658
39:13 a b', an onyx, and a jasper: they "
Ca 5:14 are as gold rings set with the b': "
Eze 1:16 was like unto the colour of a b': "
10: 9 was as the colour of a b' stone. "
28:13 topaz, and the diamond, the b', "
Da 10: 6 His body also was like the b', "
Re 21:20 seventh, chrysolyte; the eighth, b'; 969

Besai (*be'-sahee*)
Ezr 2:49 of Paseah, the children of B', 1153
Ne 7:52 of B', the children of Meunim, "

beseech See also BESEECHING; BESOUGHT.
Ex 3:18 and now let us go, we b' thee, *4994
33:18 I b' thee, shew me thy glory. * "
Nu 12:11 I b' thee, lay not the sin upon us, * "
13 Heal her now, O God, I b' thee. "
14:17 And now, I b' thee, let the power * "
19 Pardon, I b' thee, the iniquity * "
1Sa 23:11 I b' thee, tell thy servant. "
2Sa 13:24 let the king, I b' thee, and his * "
16: 4 I humbly b' thee that I may find * "
24:10 and now I b' thee, O Lord, take 4994
2Ki 19:19 I b' thee, save thou us out of his "
20: 3 I b' thee, O Lord, remember now 577
1Ch 21: 8 I b' thee, do away the iniquity 4994
2Ch 6:40 Now, my God, let, I b' thee, "
Ne 1: 5 And said, I b' thee, O Lord God 577
8 Remember, I b' thee, the word 4994
11 O Lord, I b' thee, let now thine ear 577
Job 10: 9 Remember, I b' thee, that thou 4994
42: 4 Hear, I b' thee, and I will speak: "
Ps 80:14 Return, we b' thee, O God of hosts: "
116: 4 O Lord, I b' thee, deliver my soul. 577
118:25 Save now, I b' thee, O Lord: "
25 O Lord, I b' thee, send now "
119:108 Accept, I b' thee, the freewill 4994
Isa 38: 3 Remember now, O Lord, I b' thee, 577
64: 9 we b' thee, we are all thy people. 4994
Jer 38: 4 We b' thee, let this man be put to * "
20 Obey, I beseech thee, the voice of "
42: 2 we b' thee, our supplication be * "
Da 1:12 Prove thy servants, I b' thee, ten "
9:16 I b' thee, let thine anger and thy * "
Am 7: 2 God, forgive, I b' thee: by whom "
5 O Lord God, cease, I b' thee : by "
Jon 1:14 We b' thee, O Lord, we b' thee, 577
4: 3 take, I b' thee, my life from me: 4994
Mal 1: 9 b' God that he...be gracious *2470, 6440
M'r 7:32 b' him to put his hand upon him. 3870
Lu 8:28 high? I b' thee, torment me not. 1189
9:38 I b' thee, look upon my son: "
Ac 21:39 I b' thee, suffer me to speak unto "
26: 3 I b' thee to hear me patiently. "
Ro 12: 1 I b' you therefore, brethren, by 3870
15:30 Now I b' you, brethren, for the "
16:17 Now I b' you, brethren, mark "
1Co 1:10 Now I b' you, brethren, by the 3870
4:16 Wherefore I b' you, be ye followers "
16:15 I b' you, brethren, (ye know the "
2Co 2: 8 Wherefore I b' you that ye would "
5:20 as though God did b' you by us: * "
6: 1 him, b' you also that ye receive * "
10: 1 I Paul myself b' you by the * "
2 I b' you, that I may not be bold 1189
Ga 4:12 Brethren, I b' you. be as I am:
Eph 4: 1 b' you that ye walk worthy of the 3870
Ph'p 4: 2 I b' Euodias, and b' Syntyche, * "
1Th 4: 1 we b' you, brethren, and exhort 2065
10 but we b' you, brethren, that ye *3870
5:12 And we b' you, brethren, to know 2065
2Th 2: 1 Now we b' you, brethren, by the "
Ph'm 9 for love's sake I rather b' thee, 3870
10 I b' thee for my son Onesimus, "
Heb 13:19 But I b' you the rather to do this,* "
22 I b' you, brethren, suffer the * "
1Pe 2:11 beloved, I b' you as strangers "
2Jo 5 now I b' thee, lady, not as though 2065

beseeching
M't 8: 5 unto him a centurion, b' him, 3870
M'r 1:40 there came a leper to him, b' him, "
Lu 7: 3 b' him that he would come and *2065

beset
J'g 19:22 Belial, b' the house round about, 5437
20: 5 and b' the house round about "
Ps 22:12 of Bashan have b' me round. 3803
139: 5 hast b' me behind and before, 6696
Ho 7: 2 own doings have b' them about; 5437
Heb 12: 1 the sin which doth so easily b' us, 2139

Beseth See PI-BESETH.

beside See also BESIDES.
Ge 26: 1 b' the first famine that was in 905
31:50 take other wives b' my daughters, 5921
Ex 12:37 that were men, b' children. 905
14: 9 the sea, b' Pi-hahiroth, before 5921
29:12 blood b' the bottom of the altar. * 413
Le 1:16 cast it b' the altar on the east part, 681
6:10 he shall put them b' the altar. "
9:17 b' the burnt sacrifice of the * 905
10:12 eat it without leaven b' the altar: 681
18:18 b' the other in her life time. 5921
23:38 B' the sabbaths of the Lord, 905
38 and b' your gifts, "
38 and b' all your vows, "
38 and b' all your freewill offerings, "
Nu 5: 8 b' the ram of the atonement, * "
20 lain with thee b' thine husband: 1107
6:21 b' that that his hand shall get: 905
11: 6 at all, b' this manna, before our *1115
16:49 b' them that died about the * 905
24: 6 and as cedar trees b' the waters. 5921
28:10 b' the continual burnt offering, "
15 shall be offered, b' the continual "
23 Ye shall offer these b' the burnt 905
24 it shall be offered b' the continual 5921
31 shall offer them b' the continual 905
29: 6 B' the burnt offering of the month, "
11 b' the sin offering of atonement, "
34, 38 b' the continual burnt offering, "
39 b' your vows, and your freewill "
31: 8 b' the rest of them that were *5921
De 3: 5 b' unwalled towns a great many. 905
4:35 is God; there is none else b' him. "
11:30 Gilgal, b' the plains of Moreh? 681
18: 8 to eat, b' that which cometh 905
19: 9 more for thee, b' these three; 5921
29: 1 the land of Moab, b' the covenant 905
Jos 3:16 city Adam, that is b' Zaretan: 6654
7: 2 to Ai, which is b' Beth-aven, on 5973
12: 9 of Ai, which is b' Beth-el, one; 6654
13: 4 Mearah that is b' the Sidonians, *
17: 5 b' the land of Gilead 905
22:19 building you an altar b' the altar *1107
29 or for sacrifices, b' the altar of * 905
J'g 6:37 it be dry upon all the earth b' *
7: 1 and pitched b' the well of Harod: 5921
8:26 shekels of gold; b' ornaments, 905
26 b' the chains that were about "
11:34 and she was his only child; b' her
20:15 drew sword, b' the inhabitants 905
17 the men of Israel, b' Benjamin, "
36 wait which they had set b' Gibeah.* 413
Ru 2:14 she sat b' the reapers: and he 6654
4: 4 there is none to redeem it b' thee; 2108
1Sa 2: 2 for there is none b' thee: neither 1115
4: 1 battle, and pitched b' Ebenezer: 5921
19: 3 go out and stand b' my father 3027
2Sa 7:22 neither is there any God b' thee, 2108
13:23 Baal-hazor, which is b' Ephraim: 5973
15: 2 stood b' the way of the gate: 5921, 3027
18 his servants passed on b' him;"
1Ki 3:20 my son from b' me, while thine 681
4:23 sheep, b' harts, and roebucks, 905
5:16 B' the chief of Solomon's officers*
9:26 Ezion-geber, which is b' Eloth, 854
10:13 asked, b' that which Solomon 905
15 B' that he had of the merchantmen "
19 two lions stood b' the stays. 681
11:25 b' the mischief that Hadad did: 854
13:31 lay my bones b' his bones: 681
2Ki 11:20 the sword b' the king's house. *
12: 9 set it b' the altar, on the right 681
21:16 b' his sin wherewith he made 905
1Ch 3: 9 sons of David, b' the sons
17:20 neither is there any God b' 2108
2Ch 9:12 b' that which she had brought 905
14 B' that which chapmen and "
17:19 waited on the king, b' those
20: 1 them other b' the Ammonites, *
26:19 Lord, from b' the incense altar. 5921
31:16 B' their genealogy of males, 905
Ezr 1: 4 beasts, b' the freewill offering 5973
6 b' all that was willingly 905, 5921
2:65 B' their servants and their 905
Ne 5:15 wine, b' forty shekels of silver; 310
17 fifty of the Jews and rulers, b'
7:67 B' their manservants and their 905
8: 4 b' him stood Mattithiah, and 681
Job 1:14 the asses feeding b' them: 5921, 3027
Ps 23: 2 leadeth me b' the still waters. 5921
73:25 upon earth that I desire b' thee. 5973
Ca 1: 8 thy kids b' the shepherds' tents. 5921
Isa 26:13 our God, other lords b' thee 2108
32:20 Blessed are ye that sow b' all 5921
43:11 and b' me there is no saviour. 1107
44: 6 and b' me there is no God. "
8 Is there a God b' me? yea, there "
45: 5 else, there is no God b' me: 2108
6 west, that there is none b' me. 1107
21 no God else b' me; "
21 there is none b' me. 2108
47: 8 I am, and none else b' me; 657
10 I am, and none else b' me. "
56: 8 others to him, b' those that
64: 4 the eye seen, O God, b' thee, 2108
Jer 36:21 princes which stood b' the king. 5921
Eze 9: 2 and stood b' the brasen altar. 681
10: 6 went in, and stood b' the wheels. "
16 turned not from b' them. "
19 the wheels also were b' them, 5980
11:22 wings, and the wheels b' them; "
32:13 beasts thereof from b' the great 5921
Da 11: 4 even for others b' those. 905
Ho 13: 4 for there is no saviour b' me. 1115
Zep 2:15 there is none b' me: how is she 657
M't 14:21 men, b' women and children. 5565
15:38 b' women and children.
25:20 I have gained b' them five *1909
22 gained two other talents b' them.* "
M'r 3:21 for they said, He is b' himself. 1839
Lu 16:26 b' all this, between us and you 1909
24:21 and b' all this, to day 4862
Ac 26:24 Paul, thou art b' thyself; *3105
2Co 5:13 whether we be b' ourselves, 1839
11:28 B' those things that are without. 5565
2Pe 1: 5 And b' this, giving all *846

besides
Ge 19:12 Lot, Hast thou here any b'? 5750
46:26 b' Jacob's sons' wives, all the 905
Le 7:13 B' the cakes, he shall offer for *5921
1Ki 22: 7 not here a prophet of the Lord b', 5750
2Ch 18: 6 here a prophet of the Lord b', "
Jer 36:32 and there were added b' unto "
1Co 1:16 b', I know not whether I 3063
Ph'm 19 unto me even thine own self b'. 4359

besiege See also BESIEGED.
De 20:12 thee, then thou shalt b' it: 6696
19 When thou shalt b' a city a long "
28:52 And he shall b' thee in all thy 6887
52 b' thee in all thy gates "
1Sa 23: 8 to b' David and his men. 6696
1Ki 8:37 if their enemy b' them in the 6887
2Ki 24:11 city, and his servants did b' *6696
2Ch 6:28 if their enemies b' them in the "
Isa 21: 2 Go up, O Elam: b', O Media; "
Jer 21: 4 the Chaldeans, which b' you, "
9 to the Chaldeans that b' you, "

besieged
2Sa 11: 1 of Ammon, and b' Rabbah. 6696
20:15 And they came and b' him "
1Ki 16:17 with him, and they b' Tirzah. "
20: 1 and he went up and b' Samaria, "
2Ki 6:24 and went up, and b' Samaria. "
25 and, behold, they b' it, until "
16: 5 they b' Ahaz, but could not "
17: 5 Samaria, and b' it three years. "
18: 9 came up against Samaria, and b' it."
19:24 up all the rivers of b' places. *4693
24:10 and the city was b'. 935, 4692
25: 2 And the city was b' unto the "
1Ch 20: 1 and came and b' Rabbah. 6696
Ec 9:14 and b' it, and built great 5437
Isa 1: 8 of cucumbers, as a b' city. 5341
37:25 all the rivers of the b' places. *4693
Jer 32: 2 the king of Babylon's army b' 6696
37: 5 the Chaldeans that b' Jerusalem "
39: 1 against Jerusalem, and they b' it. "
52: 5 city was b' unto the eleventh 935, 4692
Eze 4: 3 it shall be b', and thou shalt "
6:12 he that remaineth and is b' shall 5341
Da 1: 1 unto Jerusalem, and b' it. 6696

Besodeiah (*bes-o-di'-ah*)
Ne 3: 6 and Meshullam the son of B'; 1152

besom
Isa 14:23 it with the b' of destruction, 4292

Besor (*be'-sor*)
1Sa 30: 9 and came to the brook B', 1308
10 could not go over the brook B'. "
21 also to abide at the brook B': "

besought
Ge 42:21 when he b' us, and we would not 2603
Ex 32:11 And Moses b' the Lord his God, 2470
De 3:23 And I b' the Lord at that time, 2603
2Sa 12:16 David therefore b' God for the 1245
1Ki 13: 6 And the man of God b' the Lord, *2470
2Ki 1:13 knees before Elijah, and b' him, 2603
13: 4 And Jehoahaz b' the Lord, and 2470
2Ch 33:12 he b' the Lord his God, "
Ezr 8:23 fasted and b' our God for this: 1245
Es 8: 3 and b' him with tears to put 2603
Jer 26:19 fear the Lord, and b' the Lord, *2470
M't 8:31 the devils b' him, saying, If thou 3870
34 they b' him that he would depart "
14:36 And b' him that they might only "
15:23 his disciples came and b' him, 2065
18:29 b' him, saying, Have patience 3870
M'r 5:10 And he b' him much that he "
12 And all the devils b' him, saying, "
23 And b' him greatly, saying, "
6:56 streets, and b' him that they "
7:26 and she b' him that he would 2065
8:22 him, and b' him to touch him. 3870
Lu 4:38 and they b' him for her. 2065
5:12 Jesus fell on his face, and b' 1189

Lu 7: 4 they *b'* him instantly, saying, 3870
8:31 And they *b'* him that he would * "
32 and they *b'* him that he would "
37 *b'* him to depart from them; *2065
38 *b'* him that he might be with *1189
41 *b'* him that he would come into 3870
9:40 I *b'* thy disciples to cast him out; 1189
11:37 certain Pharisee *b'* him to dine *2065
Joh 4:40 they *b'* him that he would tarry "
47 *b'* him that he would come down, "
19:31 *b'* Pilate that their legs might * "
38 *b'* Pilate that he might take * "
Ac 13:42 the Gentiles *b'* that these words 3870
16:15 she *b'* us, saying, If ye have "
39 And they came and *b'* them, "
21:12 *b'* him not to go up to Jerusalem. "
25: 2 him against Paul, and *b'* him, "
27:33 Paul *b'* them all to take meat, "
2Co 12: 8 I *b'* the Lord thrice, that it might "
1Ti 1: 3 As I *b'* thee to abide still at * "

best
Ge 43:11 take of the *b'* fruits in the land in *2173
47: 6 in the *b'* of the land make thy 4315
11 Egypt, in the *b'* of the land, in the "
Ex 22: 5 of the *b'* of his own field, and of "
5 the *b'* of his own vineyard, "
Nu 18:12 All the *b'* of the oil, 2459
12 and all the *b'* of the wine, "
29 of all the *b'* thereof, even the "
30 when ye have heaved the *b'* "
32 ye have heaved from it the *b'* of it: "
36: 6 to whom they think *b'*; 2896
De 23:16 where it liketh him *b'*: thou "
1Sa 8:14 your oliveyards, even the *b'* of "
15: 9 the *b'* of the sheep, and of the 4315
15 for the people spared the *b'* of the "
2Sa 18: 4 What seemeth you *b'* I will do. 3190
1Ki 10:18 and overlaid it with the *b'* gold. *6338
2Ki 10: 3 Look even out the *b'* and meetest 2896
Es 2: 9 her maids unto the *b'* place of the "
Ps 39: 5 man at his *b'* state is altogether 5324
Ca 7: 9 roof of thy mouth like the *b'* wine 2896
Eze 31:16 the choice and *b'* of Lebanon, "
Mic 7: 4 the *b'* of them is as a brier: the "
Lu 15:22 Bring forth the *b'* robe, and put 4413
1Co 12:31 but covet earnestly the *b'* gifts: *2909

bestead
Isa 8:21 shall pass through it, hardly *b'* ‡

bestir
2Sa 5:24 then thou shalt *b'* thyself: for 2782

bestow See also BESTOWED.
Ex 32:29 he may *b'* upon you a blessing 5414
De 14:26 And thou shalt *b'* that money for "
2Ch 24: 7 of the Lord did they *b'* upon 6213
Ezr 7:20 thou shalt have occasion to *b'*, 5415
20 *b'* it out of the king's treasure "
Lu 12:17 I have no more room where to *b'* 4863
18 there will I *b'* all my fruits and my "
1Co 12:23 upon these we *b'* more abundant 4060
13: 3 And though I *b'* all my goods to 5595

bestowed
1Ki 10:26 horsemen, whom he *b'* in the 3240
2Ki 5:24 their hand, and *b'* them in the 6485
12:15 the money to be *b'* on workmen: *5414
1Ch 29:25 *b'* upon him such royal majesty "
2Ch 9:25 whom he *b'* in the chariot cities, 3240
Isa 63: 7 to all that the Lord hath *b'* on us, 1580
7 he hath *b'* on them according "
Joh 4:38 whereon ye *b'* no labour: other *2872
Ro 16: 6 Mary, who *b'* much labour on us. "
1Co 15:10 his grace which was *b'* upon me "
2Co 1:11 that for the gift *b'* upon us by the "
8: 1 grace of God *b'* on the churches *1325
Ga 4:11 lest I have *b'* upon you labour in 2872
1Jo 3: 1 of love the Father hath *b'* on us. 1325

Betah (*be'-tah*)
2Sa 8: 8 And from *B'*, and from Berothai, 984

Beten (*be'-ten*)
Jos 19:25 and Hali, and *B'*, and Achshaph, 991

Beth See also BETH-ANATH; BETH-ANOTH; BETHANY; BETH-ARABAH; BETH-ARAM; BETH-ARBEL; BETH-AVEN; BETH-AZMAVETH; BETH-BAAL-MEON; BETH-BARAH; BETH-BIREI; BETH-CAR; BETH-DAGON; BETH-DIB-LATHAIM; BETH-EL; BETH-EMEK; BETHESDA; BETH-EZEL; BETH-GADER; BETH-GAMUL; BETH-HACCEREM; BETH-LEHEM; BETH-HARAN; BETH-HOGLAH; BETH-HORON; BETH-JESHIMOTH; BETH-LEBAOTH; BETH-MAACHAH; BETH-MARCABOTH; BETH-MEON; BETH-NIMZAH; BETH-PALET; BETH-PAZZEZ; BETH-PEOR; BETHPHAGE; BETH-RAPHA; BETH-REHOB; BETHSAIDA; BETH-SHAW; BETH-SHEMESH; BETH-SHITTAH; BETH-TAPPUAH; BETH-ZUR.

Bethabara (*beth-ab'-ar-ah*) See also BETH-BARAH.
Joh 1:28 These things were done in *B'* * 962

Beth-anath (*beth'-a-nath*)
Jos 19:38 Harem, and *B'*, and 1043
J'g 1:33 nor the inhabitants of *B'*; but he "
33 Beth-shemesh, and of *B'* became "

Beth-anoth (*beth'-a-noth*)
Jos 15:59 Maarath, and *B'*, and Eltekon; 1042

Bethany (*beth'-a-ny*)
M't 21:17 and went out of the city into *B'*; 963
26: 6 Now when Jesus was in *B'*, in the "
M'k 11: 1 unto Bethphage and *B'*, at the "
11 he went out unto *B'* with the "
12 when they were come from *B'*, he "
14: 3 And being in *B'* in the house of "
Lu 19:29 come nigh to Bethphage and *B'*, "
24:50 he led them out as far as to *B'*, 963
Joh 11: 1 named Lazarus, of *B'*, the town "
18 Now *B'* was nigh unto Jerusalem, "
12: 1 before the passover came to *B'*, "

Beth-arabah (*beth-ar'-ab-ah*)
Jos 15: 6 passed along by the north of *B'*; 1026
61 In the wilderness, *B'*, Middin, and "
18:22 *B'*, and Zemaraim, and Beth-el, "

Beth-aram (*beth'-a-ram*)
Jos 13:27 And in the valley, *B'*, and 1027

Beth-arbel (*beth-ar'-bel*)
Ho 10:14 Shalman spoiled *B'* in the day of 1009

Beth-aven (*beth-a'-ven*)
Jos 7: 2 to Ai, which is beside *B'*, on the 1007
18:12 were at the wilderness of *B'*. "
1Sa 13: 5 in Michmash, eastward from *B'*. "
14:23 and the battle passed over unto *B'*. "
Ho 4:15 neither go ye up to *B'*, nor swear, "
5: 8 cry aloud at *B'*, after thee, O "
10: 5 because of the calves of *B'*: "

Beth-azmaveth (*beth-az'-maveth*) See also AZMAVETH.
Ne 7:28 The men of *B'*, forty and two. 1041

Beth-baal-meon (*beth-ba"-al-me'-on*) See also BAAL-MEON.
Jos 13:17 Dibon, and Bamoth-baal, and *B'*, 1010

Beth-barah (*beth-ba'-rah*) See also BETHABARA
J'g 7:24 before them the waters unto *B'* 1012
24 and took the waters unto *B'* and "

Beth-birei (*beth-bir-e-i*) See also BETH-LEBAOTH.
1Ch 4:31 Hazar-susim, and at *B'*, and at 1011

Beth-car (*beth'-car*)
1Sa 7:11 them, until they came under *B'*. 1033

Beth-dagon (*beth-da'-gon*)
Jos 15:41 And Gederoth, *B'*, and Naamah, 1016
19:27 toward the sunrising to *B'*, "

Beth-diblathaim (*beth-dib-lath-a'-im*)
Jer 48:22 and upon Nebo, and upon *B'*, 1015

Beth-el (*beth'-el*) See also BETHELITE; EL-BETH-EL; LUZ.
Ge 12: 8 a mountain on the east of *B'*, 1008
8 pitched his tent, having *B'* on the "
13: 3 from the south even to *B'*, "
3 beginning, between *B'* and Hai; "
28:19 called the name of that place *B'*: "
31:13 I am the God of *B'*, where thou "
35: 1 unto Jacob, Arise, go up to *B'*, "
3 let us arise, and go up to *B'*; "
6 in the land of Canaan, that is, *B'*, "
8 she was buried beneath *B'* under "
15 where God spake with him, *B'*. "
16 they journeyed from *B'*; and "
Jos 7: 2 Beth-aven, on the east side of *B'*, "
8: 9 and abode between *B'* and Ai, "
12 lie in ambush between *B'* and Ai, "
17 was not man left in Ai or *B'*, "
12: 9 king of Ai, which is beside *B'*. "
16 the king of *B'*, one; "
16: 1 from Jericho throughout mount *B'*, "
2 And goeth out from *B'* to Luz, "
18:13 to the side of Luz, which is *B'*, "
22 Zemaraim, and *B'*, "
J'g 1:22 they also went up against *B'*: "
23 house of Joseph sent to descry *B'*. "
4: 5 between Ramah and *B'* in mount "
21:19 which is on the north side of *B'*, "
19 the highway that goeth up from *B'* "
1Sa 7:16 from year to year in circuit to *B'*, "
10: 3 three men going up to God to *B'*, "
13: 2 in Michmash and in mount *B'*, "
30:27 To them which were in *B'*, and "
1Ki 12:29 he set the one in *B'*, and the other "
32 So did he in *B'*, sacrificing unto "
32 and he placed in *B'* the priests of "
33 altar which he had made in *B'* "
13: 1 by the word of the Lord unto *B'*: "
4 had cried against the altar in *B'*, "
10 by the way that he came to *B'*. "
11 there dwelt an old prophet in *B'*; "
11 of God had done that day in *B'*: "
32 the Lord against the altar in *B'*, "
2Ki 2: 2 for the Lord hath sent me to *B'*. "
2 So they went down to *B'*. "
3 of the prophets that were at *B'* "
23 he went up from thence unto *B'*: "
10:29 the golden calves that were in *B'*, "
17:28 came and dwelt in *B'*, and taught "
23: 4 carried the ashes of them unto *B'*. "
15 Moreover the altar that was at *B'*, "
17 hast done against the altar of *B'*. "
19 all the acts that he had done in *B'*. "
1Ch 7:28 *B'* and the towns thereof, and "
2Ch 13:19 *B'* with the towns thereof, and "
Ezr 2:28 men of *B'* and Ai, two hundred "
Ne 7:32 The men of *B'* and Ai, a hundred "
11:31 and Aiji, and *B'*, and in their "
Jer 48:13 house of Israel was ashamed of *B'* "
Ho 10:15 So shall *B'* do unto you because "
12: 4 he found him in *B'*, and there "
Am 3:14 I will also visit the altars of *B'*: "
4: 4 Come to *B'*, and transgress; at "
5: 5 But seek not *B'*, nor enter into "
5 captivity, and *B'* shall come to "
6 there be none to quench it in *B'*. "
7:10 Then Amaziah the priest of *B'* "
13 prophesy not again any more at *B'*: "

Beth-elite (*beth'-el-ite*)
1Ki 16:34 did Hiel the *B'* build Jericho: 1017

Beth-emek (*beth-e'-mek*)
Jos 19:27 toward the north side of *B'*, 1025

Bether (*be'-thur*)
Ca 2:17 hart upon the mountains of *B'*. 1336

Bethesda (*beth-ez'-dah*)
Joh 5: 2 is called in the Hebrew tongue *B'*, 964

Beth-ezel (*beth-e'-zel*)
Mic 1:11 not forth in the mourning of *B'*; 1018

Beth-gader (*beth-ga'-der*) See also GEDER.
1Ch 2:51 Hareph the father of *B'*. 1013

Beth-gamul (*beth-ga'-mul*)
Jer 48:23 upon *B'*, and upon Beth-meon, 1014

Beth-haccerem (*beth-hak'-se-rem*)
Ne 3:14 Rechab, the ruler of part of *B'*; 1021
Jer 6: 1 and set up a sign of fire in *B'*: "

Beth-hanan See ELON-BETH-HANAN.

Beth-haran (*beth-ha'-ran*) See also ELON-BETH-HARAN.
Nu 32:36 Beth-nimrah, and *B'*, fenced 1028

Beth-hogla (*beth-hog'-lah*) See also BETH-HOGLAH.
Jos 15: 6 went up to *B'*, and passed 1031

Beth-hoglah (*beth-hog'-lah*) See also BETH-HOGLA.
Jos 18:19 along to the side of *B'* northward: 1031
21 Jericho, and *B'*, and the valley of "

Beth-horon (*beth-ho'-ron*)
Jos 10:10 the way that goeth up to *B'*, 1032
11 and were in the going down to *B'*, "
16: 3 the coast of *B'* the nether, and "
5 Ataroth-addar, unto *B'* the upper; "
18:13 on the south side of the nether *B'*. "
14 hill that lieth before *B'* southward; "
21:22 *B'* with her suburbs; four cities. "
1Sa 13:18 company turned the way to *B'*: "
1Ki 9:17 built Gezer, and *B'* the nether, "
1Ch 6:68 *B'* with her suburbs, "
7:24 Sherah, who built *B'* the nether, "
2Ch 8: 5 Also he built *B'* the upper, and "
5 *B'* the nether, fenced cities, "
25:13 from Samaria even unto *B'*, and "

bethink
1Ki 8:47 *b'* themselves in the 7725, 413, 3820
2Ch 6:37 *b'* themselves in the "

Beth-jesimoth (*beth-jes'-im-oth*) See also BETH-JESHIMOTH.
Nu 33:49 from *B'* even unto Abel-shittim 1020

Beth-jeshimoth (*beth-jesh'-im-oth*) See also BETH-JESIMOTH.
Jos 12: 3 sea on the east, the way to *B'*; 1020
13:20 Ashdoth-pisgah, and *B'*, "
Eze 25: 9 of the country, *B'*, Baal-meon, "

Beth-lebaoth (*beth-leb'-a-oth*) See also BETH-BISEI.
Jos 19: 6 And *B'*, and Sharuhen; thirteen 1034

Beth-lehem (*beth'-le-hem*) See also BETH-LEHEMITE; BETH-LEHEM-JUDAH.
Ge 35:19 the way to Ephrath, which is *B'*. 1035
48: 7 way of Ephrath; the same is *B'*. "
Jos 19:15 Shimron, and Idalah, and *B'*: "
J'g 12: 8 after him Ibzan of *B'* judged Israel. "
10 died Ibzan, and was buried at *B'*. "
Ru 1:19 two went until they came to *B'*. "
19 they were come to *B'*, that all "
22 came to *B'* in the beginning of "
2: 4 Boaz came from *B'*, and said "
4:11 in Ephratah, and be famous in *B'*: "
1Sa 16: 4 and came to *B'*. And the elders "
17:15 to feed his father's sheep at *B'*. "
20: 6 that he might run to *B'* his city: "
28 asked leave of me to go to *B'*: "
2Sa 2:32 of his father, which was in *B'*. "
23:14 of the Philistines was then in *B'*. "
15 the water of the well of *B'*, which "
16 drew water out of the well of *B'*, "
24 Elhanan the son of Dodo of *B'*, "
1Ch 2:51 the father of *B'*, Hareph the "
54 Salma; *B'*, and the Netophathites, "
4: 4 of Ephratah, the father of *B'*. "
11:16 Philistines' garrison was then at *B'*. "
17 the well of *B'*, that is at the gate! "
18 drew water out of the well of *B'*, "
26 Elhanan the son of Dodo of *B'*, "
2Ch 11: 6 He built even *B'*, and Etam, and "
Ezr 2:21 children of *B'*, an hundred twenty "
Ne 7:26 The men of *B'* and Netophah, "
Jer 41:17 of Chimham, which is by *B'*, to go "
Mic 5: 2 thou, *B'* Ephratah, though thou "
M't 2: 1 Jesus was born in *B'* of Judæa 965
5 In *B'* of Judæa: for thus it is "
6 And thou *B'*, in the land of Juda, "
8 And he sent them to *B'*, and said, "
16 all the children that were in *B'*, "
Lu 2: 4 city of David, which is called *B'*; "
15 Let us now go even unto *B'*, and see "
Joh 7:42 and out of the town of *B'*, where "

Beth-lehemite (*beth'-le-hem-ite*)
1Sa 16: 1 I will send thee to Jesse the *B'*, 1022
18 I have seen a son of Jesse the *B'*, "
17:58 the son of thy servant Jesse the *B'*. "
2Sa 21:19 the son of Jaare-oregim, a *B'*, "

Beth-lehem-judah (*beth"-le-hem-ju'-dah*)
J'g 17: 7 there was a young man out of *B'* 1035
8 from *B'* to sojourn where he could "
9 I am a Levite of *B'*, and I "
19: 1 to him a concubine out of *B'*. "
2 unto her father's house to *B'*, "
18 We are passing from *B'* toward "
18 and I went to *B'*, but I "
Ru 1: 1 a certain man of *B'* went to "
2 and Chilion, Ephrathites of *B'*. "
1Sa 17:12 son of that Ephrathite of *B'*, "

Beth-maachah (*beth-ma'-a-kah*) See also ABEL-BETH-MAACHAH.
2Sa 20:14 unto Abel, and to *B'*, and all 1038
15 and besieged him in Abel of *B'*, "

Beth-marcaboth (*beth-mar'-cab-oth*)
Jos 19: 5 Ziklag, and *B'*, and Hazar-susah, 1024
1Ch 4:31 at *B'*, and Hazar-susim, and at "

Beth-meon (*beth-me'-on*) See also BETH-BAAL-MEON.
Jer 48:23 upon Beth-gamul, and upon *B'*, 1010

Beth-nimrah (*beth-nim'-rah*) See also NIMRAH.
Nu 32:36 *B'*, and Beth-haran, fenced cities: 1039
Jos 13:27 in the valley, Beth-aram, and *B'*, "

Beth-palet (*beth-pa'-let*) See also BETH-PELET.
Jos 15:27 and Heshmon, and *B'*, 1046

Beth-pazzez (*beth-paz'-zez*)
Jos 19:21 and En-haddah, and *B'*; 1048

Beth-peor (*beth-pe'-or*)
De 3:29 in the valley over against *B'*. 1047
4:46 against *B'*, in the land of Sihon "
34: 6 the land of Moab, over against *B'*: "
Jos 13:20 And *B'*, and Ashdoth-pisgah, and "

Bethphage (*beth'-fa-je*)
M't 21: 1 were come to *B'*, unto the mount *967*
M'r 11: 1 Jerusalem, unto *B'* and Bethany, "
Lu 19:29 was come nigh to *B'* and Bethany, "

Beth-phelet (*beth'-fe-let*) See also BETH-PALET.
Ne 11:26 and at Moladah, and at *B'*, 1046

Beth-rapha (*beth'-ra-fah*)
1Ch 4:12 And Eshton begat *B'*, and 1051

Beth-rehob (*beth'-re-hob*)
J'g 18:28 was in the valley that lieth by *B'*. 1050
2Sa 10: 6 sent and hired the Syrians of *B'*, "

Bethsaida (*beth-sa'-dah*)
M't 11:21 woe unto thee, *B'*! for if the *966*
M'r 6:45 go to the other side before unto *B'*, "
8:22 And he cometh to *B'*; and they "
Lu 9:10 belonging to the city called *B'*. "
10:13 woe unto thee, *B'*! for if the mighty "
Joh 1:44 Now Philip was of *B'*, the city of "
12:21 therefore to Philip, which was of *B'* "

Beth-shan (*beth'-shan*) See also BETH-SHEAN.
1Sa 31:10 his body to the wall of *B'*. 1052
12 of his sons from the wall of *B'*, "
2Sa 21:12 stolen them from the street of *B'*, "

Beth-shean (*beth-she'-an*) See also BETH-SHAN.
Jos 17:11 *B'* and her towns, and Ibleam 1052
16 both they who are of *B'* and her "
J'g 1:27 drive out the inhabitants of *B'* "
1Ki 4:12 and all *B'*, which is by Zartanah "
12 Jezreel, from *B'* to Abel-meholah, "
1Ch 7:29 children of Manasseh, *B'* and her "

Beth-shemesh (*beth'-she-mesh*) See also BETH-SHEMITE.
Jos 15:10 and went down to *B'*, and passed 1053
19:22 to Tabor, and Shahazimah, and *B'*; "
38 Horem, and Beth-anath, and *B'*; "
21:16 Juttah with her suburbs, and *B'* "
J'g 1:33 drive out the inhabitants of *B'*, "
33 the inhabitants of *B'* and of "
1Sa 6: 9 by the way of his own coast to *B'*, "
12 the straight way to the way of *B'*, "
12 after them unto the border of *B'*. "
13 they of *B'* were reaping their "
15 the men of *B'* offered burnt "
19 smote the men of *B'*, because they "
20 And the men of *B'* said, Who is "
1Ki 4: 9 Makaz, and in Shaalbim, and *B'*, "
2Ki 14:11 looked one another in the face at *B'*, "
13 the son of Ahaziah, at *B'*, and "
1Ch 6:59 Ashan with her suburbs, and *B'* "
2Ch 25:21 Amaziah king of Judah, at *B'*, "
23 the son of Jehoahaz, at *B'*, and "
28:18 Judah, and had taken *B'*, and "
Jer 43:13 break also the images of *B'*, that is "

Beth-shemite (*beth'-shem-ite*)
1Sa 6:14 the field of Joshua, a *B'*, and 1030
18 day in the field of Joshua, the *B'*. "

Beth-shittah (*beth-shit'-tah*)
J'g 7:22 and the host fled to *B'* in 1029

Beth-tappuah (*beth-tap'-pu-ah*)
Jos 15:53 And Janum, and *B'*, and Aphekah, 1054

Bethuel (*beth-u'-el*) See also BETHUL.
Ge 22:22 and Pildash, and Jidlaph, and *B'*. 1328
23 And *B'* begat Rebekah: these "
24:15 who was born to *B'*, son of Milcah, "
24 I am the daughter of *B'* the son of "
47 And she said, The daughter of *B'*, "
50 Then Laban and *B'* answered and "
25:20 daughter of *B'* the Syrian of "
28: 2 to the house of *B'* thy mother's "
5 unto Laban, son of *B'* the Syrian, "
1Ch 4:30 And at *B'*, and at Hormah, and at "

Bethul (*beth'-ul*) See also BETHUEL.
Jos 19: 4 And Eltolad, and *B'*, and Hormah, 1329

Beth-zur (*beth'-zur*)
Jos 15:58 Halhul, *B'*, and Gedor, 1049
1Ch 2:45 and Maon was the father of *B'*. "
2Ch 11: 7 And *B'*, and Shoco, and Adullam, "
Ne 3:16 the ruler of the half part of *B'*, "

betimes
Ge 26:31 and they rose up *b'* in the 7925
2Ch 36:15 rising up *b'*, and sending; * "
Job 8: 5 thou wouldest seek unto God *b'*, *7836
24: 5 rising *b'* for a prey: the * "
Pr 13:24 loveth him chasteneth him *b'*. "

Betonim (*bet'-o-nim*)
Jos 13:26 unto Ramath-mizpeh, and *B'*; 993

betray See also BETRAYED; BETRAYEST; BETRAYETH; BEWRAY.
1Ch 12:17 but if ye be come to *b'* me to 7411
M't 24:10 and shall *b'* one another, and **3860*
26:16 he sought opportunity to *b'* him. * "
21 one of you shall *b'* me. "
23 in the dish, the same shall *b'* me. "
46 he is at hand that doth *b'* me. * "
M'r 13:12 the brother shall *b'* the brother * "
14:10 the chief priests, to *b'* him unto * "
11 he might conveniently *b'* him. * "
18 eateth with me shall *b'* me. "
Lu 22: 4 how he might *b'* him unto them. * "
6 sought opportunity to *b'* him * "
Joh 6:64 not, and who should *b'* him. "
71 he it was that should *b'* him, being "
12: 4 Simon's son, which should *b'* him, "
13: 2 Iscariot, Simon's son, to *b'* him; "
11 For he knew who should *b'* him; "
21 you, that one of you shall *b'* me. "

betrayed
M't 10: 4 Judas Iscariot, who also *b'* him. *3860*
17:22 The Son of man shall be *b'* into * "
20:18 The Son of man shall be *b'* unto * "
26: 2 Son of man is *b'* to be crucified. * "
24 by whom the Son of man is *b'*! "
25 Then Judas, which *b'* him, "
45 Son of man is *b'* into the hands of "
48 Now he that *b'* him gave them a "
27: 3 Then Judas, which had *b'* him, "
4 I have sinned in that I have *b'* "
M'r 3:19 Judas Iscariot, which also *b'* him: "
14:21 by whom the Son of man is *b'*! "
41 the Son of man is *b'* into the hands "
44 And he that *b'* him had given them "
Lu 21:16 And ye shall be *b'* both by * "
22:22 unto that man by whom he is *b'*! "
Joh 18: 2 And Judas also, which *b'* him, "
5 Judas also, which *b'* him, stood "
1Co 11:23 night in which he was *b'* took "

betrayers
Ac 7:52 ye have been now the *b'* and *4273*

betrayest
Lu 22:48 *b'* thou the Son of man with a *3860*

betrayeth See also BEWRAYETH.
M'r 14:42 lo, he that *b'* me is at hand. *3860*
Lu 22:21 the hand of him that *b'* me is with "
Joh 21:20 Lord, which is he that *b'* thee? "

betroth See also BETROTHED.
De 28:30 Thou shalt *b'* a wife, and another 781
Ho 2:19 And I will *b'* thee unto me for ever; "
19 yea, I will *b'* thee unto me in "
20 I will even *b'* thee unto me in "

betrothed
Ex 21: 8 who hath *b'* her to himself, *3259
9 And if he have *b'* her unto his * "
22:16 maid that is not *b'*, and lie with 781
Le 19:20 that is a bondmaid, *b'* to an 2778
De 20: 7 that hath *b'* a wife, and hath not 781
22:23 that is a virgin be *b'* unto an "
25 But if a man find a *b'* damsel in the "
27 the *b'* damsel cried, and there was "
28 which is not *b'*, and lay hold on her, "

better See also BETTERED.
Ge 29:19 *b'* that I give her to thee, than 2896
Ex 14:12 been *b'* for us to serve the "
Nu 14: 3 not *b'* for us to return into Egypt? "
J'g 8: 2 the grapes of Ephraim *b'* than the "
9: 2 Whether is *b'* for you, either that "
11:25 now art thou any thing *b'* than "
18:19 is it *b'* for thee to be a priest unto "
Ru 4:15 which is *b'* to thee than seven sons, "
1Sa 1: 8 am not I *b'* to thee than ten sons? "
15:22 Behold, to obey is *b'* than sacrifice, "
28 neighbour of thine, that is *b'* than "
27: 1 nothing *b'* for me than that I "
2Sa 17:14 *b'* than the counsel of Ahithophel. "
18: 3 *b'* that thou succour us out of the "
1Ki 1:47 God make the name of Solomon *b'* 3190
2:32 more righteous and *b'* than he, 2896
19: 4 for I am not *b'* than my fathers. "
21: 2 I will give thee for it a *b'* vineyard "
2Ki 5:12 *b'* than all the waters of Israel? "
2Ch 21:13 which were *b'* than thyself: "
Es 1:19 estate unto another that is *b'* than "
Ps 37:16 *b'* than the riches of many wicked. "
63: 3 loving kindness is *b'* than life, my "
69:31 This also shall please the Lord *b'* 3190
84:10 a day in thy courts is *b'* than a 2896
118: 8, 9 *b'* to trust in the Lord than to "
119:72 the law of thy mouth is *b'* unto me "
Pr 3:14 *b'* than the merchandise of silver, "
8:11 For wisdom is *b'* than rubies; "
19 My fruit is *b'* than gold, yea, "
12: 9 is *b'* than he that honoureth "
15:16 *B'* is little with the fear of the "
17 *B'* is a dinner of herbs where love "
16: 8 *B'* is a little with righteousness "
16 how much *b'* is it to get wisdom "
19 *B'* it is to be of an humble spirit "
32 slow to anger is *b'* than the mighty "
17: 1 *B'* is a dry morsel, and quietness "
19: 1 *B'* is the poor that walketh in his "
22 and a poor man is *b'* than a liar. "
21: 9 *b'* to dwell in a corner of the "
19 *b'* to dwell in the wilderness, "
25: 7 *b'* it is that it be said unto thee, "
24 It is *b'* to dwell in the corner "
27: 5 Open rebuke is *b'* than secret love. "
10 *b'* is a neighbour that is near than "
28: 6 *B'* is the poor that walketh in his "
Ec 2:24 nothing *b'* for a man, than that he "
3:22 I perceive that there is nothing *b'*, 2896
4: 3 Yea, *b'* is he than both they, which "
6 *B'* is an handful with quietness, "
9 Two are *b'* than one; because they "
13 *B'* is a poor and a wise child than "
5: 5 *B'* is it that thou shouldest not "
6: 3 an untimely birth is *b'* than he. "
9 *B'* is the sight of the eyes than the "
11 what is man the *b'*? 3148
7: 1 A good name is *b'* than 2896
2 *b'* to go to the house of mourning, "
3 Sorrow is *b'* than laughter: for by "
3 countenance the heart is made *b'*. *3190
5 *b'* to hear the rebuke of the wise, 2896
8 *B'* is the end of a thing than the "
8 spirit is *b'* than the proud in spirit. "
10 cause that the former days were *b'* "
8:15 hath no *b'* thing under the sun, "
9: 4 a living dog is *b'* than a dead lion. "
16 said I, Wisdom is *b'* than strength: "
18 Wisdom is *b'* than weapons of war: "
10:11 and a babbler is no *b'*. *3504
Ca 1: 2 for thy love is *b'* than wine. 2896
4:10 how much *b'* is thy love than wine! "
Isa 56: 5 *b'* than of sons and of daughters: "
La 4: 9 *b'* than they that be slain with "
Eze 36:11 will do *b'* unto you than at your "
Da 1:20 ten times *b'* than all the magicians 3027
Ho 2: 7 then it was *b'* with me than now. 2896
Am 6: 2 be they *b'* than these kingdoms? "
Jon 4: 3, 8 it is *b'* for me to die than to live. "
Na 3: 8 Art thou *b'* than populous No, 3190
M't 6:26 Are ye not much *b'* than they? **1308*
12:12 then is a man *b'* than a sheep? * "
18: 6 it were *b'* for him that a millstone **4851*
8, 9 it is *b'* for thee to enter into life **2570*
M'r 9:42 is *b'* for him that a millstone *2570, 3123*
43 it is *b'* for thee to enter into life **2570*
45 it is *b'* for thee to enter halt * "
47 it is *b'* for thee to enter into the "
Lu 5:39 for he saith, The old is *b'*. **5543*
12:24 more are ye *b'* than the fowls? **1308*
17: 2 were *b'* for him that a millstone *3081*
Ro 3: 9 What then? are we *b'* than they? *†4284*
1Co 7: 9 it is *b'* to marry than to burn. *2909*
38 her not in marriage doeth *b'*. *2573*
8: 8 neither, if we eat, are we the *b'*; *4052*
9:15 it were *b'* for me to die, **2570, 3123*
11:17 not for the *b'*, but for the worse. *2909*
Ph'p 1:23 to be with Christ; which is far *b'*: "
2: 3 esteem other *b'* than themselves. *5242*
Heb 1: 4 made so much *b'* than the angels, *2909*
6: 9 we are persuaded *b'* things of you, "
7: 7 the less is blessed of the *b'*. "
19 but the bringing in of a *b'* hope "
22 made a surety of a *b'* testament. "
8: 6 the mediator of a *b'* covenant, "
6 was established upon *b'* promises. "
9:23 with *b'* sacrifices than these. "
10:34 in heaven a *b'* and an enduring "
11:16 But now they desire a *b'* country, "
35 they might obtain a *b'* resurrection: "
40 provided some *b'* thing for us, "
12:24 *b'* things than that of Abel. "
1Pe 3:17 it is *b'*, if the will of God be so, "
2Pe 2:21 For it had been *b'* for them not to "

bettered
M'r 5:26 nothing *b'*, but rather grew worse, *5623*

between See also BETWIXT.
Ge 3:15 enmity *b'* thee and the woman, 996
15 and *b'* thy seed and her seed; "
9:12 covenant which I make *b'* me and "
13 a covenant *b'* me and the earth. "
15 covenant, which is *b'* me and you "
16 covenant *b'* God and every living "
17 which I have established *b'* me and "
10:12 And Resen *b'* Nineveh, and Calah "
13: 3 the beginning, *b'* Beth-el and Hai; "
7 there was a strife *b'* the herdmen "
8 *b'* me and thee, and *b'* my "
15:17 lamp that passed *b'* those pieces. "
16: 5 the Lord judge *b'* me and thee. "
14 behold, it is *b'* Kadesh and Bered. "
17: 2 make my covenant *b'* me and thee, "
7 establish my covenant *b'* me and "
10 *b'* me and you and thy seed after "
20: 1 and dwelled *b'* Kadesh and Shur, "
31:44 be for a witness *b'* me and thee. "
48 said, This heap is a witness *b'* me "
49 The Lord watch *b'* me and thee, "
48:12 them out from *b'* his knees, 5973
49:10 nor a lawgiver from *b'* his feet, 996
14 is a strong ass couching down *b'* two "
Ex 8:23 I will put a division *b'* my people "
11: 7 a difference *b'* the Egyptians and "
13: 9 and for a memorial *b'* thine eyes, "
16 and for frontlets *b'* thine eyes: "
14: 2 *b'* Migdol and the sea, over against "
20 came *b'* the camp of the Egyptians "
16: 1 the wilderness of Sin, which is *b'* "
18:16 and I judge *b'* one and another, "
22:11 an oath of the Lord be *b'* them both, "
25:22 from *b'* the two cherubim which "
26:33 vail shall divide unto you *b'* the holy "
28:33 bells of gold *b'* them round about: 8432
30:18 thou shalt put it *b'* the tabernacle 996
31:13 for it is a sign *b'* me and you "
17 It is a sign *b'* me and the children of "
39:25 put the bells *b'* the pomegranates 8432
25 round about *b'* the pomegranates; "
40: 7 thou shalt set the laver *b'* the tent 996
30 laver *b'* the tent of the congregation "
Le 10:10 that ye may put difference *b'* holy "
10 and *b'* unclean and clean; "
11:47 make a difference *b'* the unclean "

Le 11:47 and b' the beast that may be eaten 996
20:25 therefore put difference b' clean "
25 and unclean, and b' unclean fowls "
26:46 which the Lord made b' him and "
Nu 7:89 from b' the two cherubim: "
11:33 the flesh was yet b' their teeth, "
13:23 and they bare it b' two upon a staff; "
16:48 stood b' the dead and the living; "
21:13 is the border of Moab, b' Moab "
26:56 thereof be divided b' many and few. "
30:16 b' a man and his wife, "
16 b' the father and his daughter, "
31:27 prey into two parts; b' them that "
27 and b' all the congregation. * "
35:24 congregation shall judge b' the "
De 1: 1 plain over against the Red sea, b' "
16 Hear the causes b' your brethren, "
16 and judge righteously b' "
39 had no knowledge b' good and evil, *
5: 5 (I stood b' the Lord and you at 996
6: 8 shall be as frontlets b' thine eyes. "
11:18 may be as frontlets b' your eyes. "
14: 1 baldness b' your eyes for the dead. "
17: 8 b' blood and blood, b' plea and plea, "
8 and b' stroke and stroke, "
19:17 men, b' whom the controversy is, "
25: 1 If there be a controversy b' men, 996
28:57 young one that cometh out from b' "
33:12 he shall dwell b' his shoulders. "
Jos 3: 4 there shall be a space b' you and it, "
8: 9 to lie in ambush, and abode b' "
11 there was a valley b' them and Ai. "
12 to lie in ambush b' Beth-el and Ai. "
18:11 coast of their lot came forth b' the "
22:25 Lord hath made Jordan a border b' "
27 But that it may be a witness b' us, "
28 but it is a witness b' us and "
34 witness b' us that the Lord is God. "
24: 7 darkness b' you and the Egyptians, "
J'g 4: 5 b' Ramah and Beth-el in mount "
17 there was peace b' Jabin the king "
9:23 God sent an evil spirit b' Abimelech "
11:10 The Lord be witness b' us, if we do "
27 the Judge be judge this day b' the "
13:25 camp of Dan b' Zorah and Eshtaol. "
15: 4 firebrand in the midst b' two tails. "
16:25 and they set him b' the pillars. "
20:38 there was an appointed sign b' the 5973
1Sa 4: 4 which dwelleth b' the cherubim: *
7:12 Samuel took a stone, and set it b' 996
14 was peace b' Israel and the Amorites. "
14: 4 And b' the passages, by which "
42 And Saul said, Cast lots b' me and "
17: 1 pitched b' Shochoh and Azekah, "
3 and there was a valley b' them. "
6 a target of brass b' his shoulders. "
20: 3 there is but a step b' me and death. "
23 the Lord be b' thee and me for ever. "
42 b' me and thee, and b' my seed "
24:12 The Lord judge b' me and thee, "
15 therefore be judge, and judge b' "
26:13 a great space being b' them: "
2Sa 3: 1 was long war b' the house of Saul "
6 there was war b' the house of Saul "
6: 2 that dwelleth b' the cherubim. *
18: 9 up b' the heaven and the earth; 996
24 And David sat b' the two gates: "
19:35 can I discern b' good and evil? "
21: 7 the Lord's oath that was b' them, b' "
1Ki 3: 9 I may discern b' good and bad: "
5:12 peace b' Hiram and Solomon; "
7:28 the borders were b' the ledges: "
29 b' the ledges were lions, oxen, "
46 in the clay ground b' Succoth "
14:30 war b' Rehoboam and Jeroboam "
15: 6 war b' Rehoboam and Jeroboam all "
7 was war b' Abijam and Jeroboam. "
16 was war b' Asa and Baasha king of "
19 There is a league b' me and thee, "
19 and b' my father and thy father: "
32 was war b' Asa and Baasha king of "
18: 6 divided the land b' them to pass "
21 How long halt ye b' two opinions? 5921
42 and put his face b' his knees, 996
22: 1 without war b' Syria and Israel. "
34 smote the king of Israel b' the joints "
2Ki 9:24 and smote Jehoram b' his arms, "
11:17 made a covenant b' the Lord "
17 b' the king also and the people. "
16:14 from b' the altar and the house of "
19:15 God of Israel, which dwellest b' the *
25: 4 the way of the gate b' two walls, 996
1Ch 13: 6 that dwelleth b' the cherubim, *
21:16 angel of the Lord stand b' the earth 996
2Ch 4:17 in the clay ground b' Succoth and "
12:15 wars b' Rehoboam and Jeroboam "
13: 2 And there was war b' Abijah and 996
16: 3 There is a league b' me and thee, "
3 was b' my father and thy father: "
18:33 and smote the king of Israel b' "
19:10 b' blood and blood, b' law and "
23:16 Jehoiada made a covenant b' him, "
16 and b' all the people, * "
16 and b' the king, that they should * "
Ne 3:32 And b' the going up of the corner "
Job 41:16 that no air can come b' them. "
Ps 80: 1 that dwellest b' the cherubim, *
99: 1 he sitteth b' the cherubim: *
Pr 18:18 cease, and parteth b' the mighty. 996
Isa 22:11 Ye made also a ditch b' the "
37:16 God of Israel, that dwellest b' *
59: 2 b' you and your God, and your 996
Jer 7: 5 b' a man and his neighbour; "
34:18 and passed b' the parts thereof, "
19 passed b' the parts of the calf; "
42: 5 faithful witness b' us, if we do *
Jer 52: 7 way of the gate b' the two walls, 996
La 1: 3 persecutors overtook her b' the *
Eze 4: 3 a wall of iron b' thee and the city: "
8: 3 lifted me up b' the earth and the "
16 b' the porch and the altar, "
10: 2 Go in b' the wheels, even under "
2 coals of fire from b' the cherubim "
6 fire from b' the wheels, from b' the "
7 his hand from b' the cherubim "
7 that was b' the cherubim, "
18: 8 executed true judgment b' man "
20:12 to be a sign b' me and them, that "
20 and they shall be a sign b' "
22:26 difference b' the holy and profane, "
26 they shewed difference b' the "
34:17 I judge b' cattle and cattle, "
17 b' the rams and the he goats. *
20 will judge b' the fat cattle and 996
20 b' the lean cattle. *
22 I will judge b' cattle and cattle. "
40: 7 and b' the little chambers were "
41:10 b' the chambers was the wideness "
18 so that a palmtree was b' a cherub "
42:20 a separation b' the sanctuary "
43: 8 and the wall b' me and them, they "
44:23 difference b' the holy and profane, "
23 cause them to discern b' the "
47:16 which is b' the border of Damascus "
48:22 b' the border of Judah and the "
Da 7: 5 three ribs in the mouth of it b' the 997
8: 5 goat had a notable horn b' his eyes. 996
16 a man's voice b' the banks of Ulai, "
21 the great horn that is b' his eyes "
11:45 the tabernacles of his palace b' "
Ho 2: 2 her adulteries from b' her breasts; "
Joe 2:17 weep b' the porch and the altar, "
Jon 4:11 persons that cannot discern b' "
Zec 5: 9 lifted up the ephah b' the earth "
6: 1 out from b' two mountains; "
13 counsel of peace shall be b' them "
9: 7 his abominations from b' his teeth: "
11:14 brotherhood b' Judah and Israel. "
Mal 2:14 Lord hath been witness b' thee "
3:18 shall ye return, and discern b' the "
18 the wicked, b' him that serveth "
M't 18:15 his fault b' thee and him alone: 3342
23:35 b' the temple and the altar. "
Lu 11:51 b' the altar and the temple: "
16:26 b' us and you there is a great gulf "
23:12 were at enmity b' themselves. 4314
Joh 3:25 b' some of John's disciples *1537, 3326
Ac 12: 6 was sleeping b' two soldiers, 3342
15: 9 no difference b' us and them, "
39 contention was so sharp b' them, *
23: 7 dissension b' the Pharisees and "
26:31 they talked b' themselves, *4314
Ro 1:24 dishonour their own bodies b' *1722
10:12 there is no difference b' the Jew "
1Co 6: 5 able to judge b' his brethren? 303, 3319
7:34 There is difference also b' a wife 3307
Eph 2:14 middle wall of partition b' us; *
1Ti 2: 5 one God, and one mediator b' God

betwixt See also BETWEEN.
Ge 17:11 token of the covenant b' me and 996
23:15 what is that b' me and thee? "
26:28 an oath b' us, even b' us and thee, "
30:36 And he set three days' journey b' "
31:37 that they may judge b' us both. "
50 God is witness b' me and thee. "
51 which I have cast b' me and thee; "
53 God of their father, judge b' us. "
32:16 put a space b' drove and drove. "
Job 9:33 is there any daysman b' us, that "
36:32 by the cloud that cometh b'. *6293
Ca 1:13 he shall lie all night b' my breasts. 996
Isa 5: 3 pray you, b' me and my vineyard. "
Jer 39: 4 the gate b' the two walls: and he "
Ph'p 1:23 I am in a strait b' two, having 1537

Beulah (*be-u'-lah*)
Isa 62: 4 and thy land B': for the Lord 1166

bewail See also BEWAILED; BEWAILETH.
Le 10: 6 the whole house of Israel, b' 1058
De 21:13 and b' her father and her mother "
J'g 11:37 and b' my virginity, I and my "
Isa 16: 9 I will b' with the weeping * "
2Co 12:21 and that I shall b' many which *3996
Re 18: 9 shall b' her, and lament for her, *2799

bewailed
J'g 11:38 companions, and b' her virginity 1058
Lu 8:52 And all wept, and b' her: but he 2875
23:27 which also b' and lamented "

bewaileth
Jer 4:31 daughter of Zion, that b' herself, *3306

beware
Ge 24: 6 B' thou that thou bring not my 8104
Ex 23:21 B' of him, and obey his voice, * "
De 6:12 Then b' lest thou forget the Lord, "
8:11 B' that thou forget not the Lord "
15: 9 B' that there be not a thought in "
J'g 13: 4 Now therefore b', I pray thee, "
13 I said unto the woman let her b'. "
2Sa 18:12 B' that none touch the young man "
2Ki 6: 9 B' that thou pass not such a place; "
Job 36:18 Because there is wrath, b' lest ‡
Pr 19:25 a scorner, and the simple will b': *6191
Isa 36:18 B' lest Hezekiah persuade you,
M't 7:15 B' of false prophets, which come 4337
10:17 But b' of men: for they will "
16: 6 Take heed and b' of the leaven "
11 that ye should b' of the leaven "
12 not b' of the leaven of bread, but "
M'k 8:15 Take heed, b' of the leaven of the 991
12:38 B' of the scribes, which love to go "
Lu 12: 1 B' ye of the leaven of the 4337
15 heed, and b' of covetousness: *5442
20:46 B' of the scribes, which desire 4337
Ac 13:40 B' therefore, lest that come 991
Ph'p 3: 2 B' of dogs, b' of evil workers, "
2 b' of the concision. "
Col 2: 8 B' lest any man spoil you * "
2Pe 3:17 ye know these things before, b' 5442

bewitched
Ac 8: 9 b' the people of Samaria, giving *1839
11 he had b' them with sorceries. * "
Ga 3: 1 foolish Galatians, who hath b' * 940

bewray See also BETRAY; BEWRAYETH.
Isa 16: 3 the outcasts; b' not him that ‡1540

bewrayeth See also BETRAYETH.
Pr 27:16 of his right hand, which b' itself. *7121
29:24 heareth cursing, and b' it not. *5046
M't 26:73 for thy speech b' thee. 1212, 4160

beyond
Ge 35:21 spread his tent b' the tower of 1973
50:10 of Atad, which is b' Jordan, 5676
11 called Abel-Mizraim, which is b' "
Le 15:25 run b' the time of her separation; 5921
Nu 22:18 I cannot go b' the word of the 5674
24:13 go b' the commandment of the "
De 3:20 God hath given them b' Jordan: 5676
25 the good land that is b' Jordan, "
30:13 Neither is it b' the sea, that thou "
Jos 9:10 the Amorites, that were b' Jordan, "
13: 8 Moses gave them, b' Jordan "
18: 7 received their inheritance b' "
J'g 3:26 and passed b' the quarries, and 5674
5:17 Gilead abode b' Jordan: and why 5676
1Sa 20:22 the arrows are b' thee; go thy 1973
36 lad ran, he shot an arrow b' him. 5674
37 and said, Is not the arrow b' thee? 1973
2Sa 10:16 the Syrians that were b' the river: 5676
1Ki 4:12 even unto the place that is b' "
14:15 shall scatter them b' the river, "
1Ch 19:16 the Syrians that were b' the river: "
2Ch 20: 2 from b' the sea on this side Syria; "
Ezr 4:17 and unto the rest b' the river, 5675
20 have ruled over all countries b' "
6: 6 therefore, Tatnai, governor b' the "
6 which are b' the river, be ye far "
8 even of the tribute b' the river, "
7:21 treasurers which are b' the river, "
25 the people that are b' the river, all "
Ne 2: 7 to the governors b' the river, that 5676
9 came to the governors b' the river, "
12:38 b' the tower of the furnaces *5921
Isa 7:20 by them b' the river, by the king 5676
9: 1 b' Jordan, in Galilee of the nations. "
18:1 which is b' the rivers of Ethiopia: "
Jer 22:19 and cast forth b' the gates of 1973
25:22 the isles which are b' the sea, 5676
Am 5:27 you to go into captivity b' 1973
Zep 3:10 From b' the rivers of Ethiopia 5676
M't 4:15 the way of the sea, b' Jordan, 4008
25 Judæa, and from b' Jordan. "
19: 1 the coasts of Judæa b' Jordan; "
M'r 3: 8 Idumæa, and from b' Jordan; "
6:51 in themselves b' measure, *1537, 4053
7:37 And were b' measure astonished, 5249
Joh 1:28 in Bethabara b' Jordan, where 4008
3:26 he that was with thee b' Jordan, "
10:40 went away again b' Jordan into "
Ac 7:43 I will carry you away b' Babylon. 1900
2Co 8: 3 yea, and b' their power they 5228
10:14 we stretch not ourselves b' our *5239
16 the gospel in the regions b' you, 5238
Gal 1:13 b' measure I persecuted 2596, 5236
1Th 4: 6 no man go b' and defraud *5233

Bezai (*be'-zahee*)
Ezr 2:17 The children of B', three 1209
Ne 7:23 children of B', three hundred "
10:18 Hodijah, Hashum, B', "

Bezaleel (*be-zal'-e-el*)
Ex 31: 2 I have called by name B' the son 1212
35:30 the Lord hath called by name B' "
36: 1 Then wrought B' and Aholiab, "
2 Moses called B' and Aholiab, "
37: 1 B' made the ark of shittim wood: "
38:22 B' the son of Uri, the son of Hur, "
1Ch 2:20 Hur begat Uri, and Uri begat B'. "
2Ch 1: 5 Moreover the brasen altar, that B' "
Ezr 10:30 Mattaniah, B', and Binnui, and "

Bezek (*be'-zek*) See also ADONI-BEZEK.
J'g 1: 4 they slew of them in B' ten 966
5 And they found Adoni-bezek in B': "
1Sa 11: 8 And when he numbered them in B', "

Bezer (*be'-zer*)
De 4:43 Namely, B' in the wilderness, 1221
Jos 20: 8 assigned B' in the wilderness "
21:36 Reuben, B' with her suburbs * "
1Ch 6:78 B' in the wilderness with her "
7:37 B', and Hod, and Shamma, and "

bibber See WINEBIBBER.

Bichri (*bik'-ri*)
2Sa 20: 1 the son of B', a Benjamite: 1075
2 Sheba the son of B': but the men "
6 Sheba the son of B' do us more "
7 pursue after Sheba the son of B'. "
10 pursued after Sheba the son of B'. "
13 pursue after Sheba the son of B'. "
21 Sheba the son of B' by name, "
22 the head of Sheba the son of B', "

bid See also BADE; BIDDEN; BIDDING; FORBID.
Nu 15:38 and b' them that they make them 559
Jos 6:10 until the day I b' you shout; "
1Sa 9:27 B' the servant pass on before us, "

2Sa 2:26 long shall it be then, ere thou b' 559
2Ki 4:24 riding for me, except I b' thee. "
5:13 if the prophet had b' thee do 1696
10: 5 will do all that thou shalt b' us; 559
Jo 3: 2 the preaching that I b' thee. 1696
Zep 1: 7 prepared a sacrifice, he hath b' *6942
M't 14:28 b' me come unto thee on the *2753*
22: 9 ye shall find, b' to the marriage. *2564*
23: 3 therefore whatsoever they b' you *2036*
Lu 9:61 let me first go b' them farewell, *657*
10:40 b' her therefore that she help me. *2036*
14:12 lest they also b' thee again, and *479*
1Co 10:27 any of them that believe not b' *2564*
2Jo 10 house, neither b' him God speed: **3004*

bidden See also FORBIDDEN.
1Sa 9:13 afterwards they eat that be b'. 7121
22 among them that were b', which "
2Sa 16:11 for the Lord hath b' him. 559
M't 1:24 angel of the Lord had b' him, **4367*
22: 3 to call them that were b' *2564*
4 Tell them which are b', Behold, I "
8 which were b' were not worthy. "
Lu 7:39 the Pharisee which had b' him "
14: 7 a parable to those which were b', "
8 When thou art b' of any man "
8 man than thou be b' of him; "
10 when thou art b', go and sit down "
17 to say to them that were b', "
24 none of those men which were b' "

biddeth See also FORBIDDETH.
2Jo 11 For he that b' him God speed **3004*

bidding See also FORBIDDING.
1Sa 22:14 and goeth at thy b', and is *4928

Bidkar (*bid'-kar*)
2Ki 9:25 said Jehu to B' his captain, 920

bier
2Sa 3:31 king David himself followed the b'.4296
Lu 7:14 And he came and touched the b': *4673*

Bigtha (*big'-thah*)
Es 1:10 Harbona, B', and Abagtha, 903

Bigthan (*big'-than*) See also BIGTHANA.
Es 2:21 king's chamberlains, B' and 904

Bigthana (*big'-than-ah*) See also BIGTHAN.
Es 6: 2 Mordecai had told of B' and 904

Bigvai (*big'-vahee*)
Ezr 2: 2 Mizpar, B', Rehum, Baanah. 902
14 The children of B', two thousand "
8:14 Of the sons also of B'; Uthai, and "
Ne 7: 7 Bilshan, Mispereth, B', Nehum, "
19 The children of B', two thousand "
10:16 Adonijah, B', Adin, "

Bildad (*bil'-dad*)
Job 2:11 B' the Shuhite, and Zophar 1085
8: 1 Then answered B' the Shuhite, "
18: 1 B' the Shuhite, and said, "
25: 1 B' the Shuhite, and said, "
42: 9 Temanite and B' the Shuhite "

Bileam (*bil'-e-am*) See also IBLEAM.
1Ch 6:70 suburbs, and B' with her suburbs,1109

Bilgah (*bil'-gah*)
1Ch 24:14 The fifteenth to B', the 1083
Ne 12: 5 Miamin, Maadiah, B', "
18 Of B', Shammua; of Shemaiah, "

Bilgai (*bil'-gahee*)
Ne 10: 8 Maaziah, B', Shemaiah: these 1084

Bilhah (*bil'-hah*) See also BALAH.
Ge 29:29 B' his handmaid to be her 1090
30: 3 Behold my maid B', go in unto "
4 gave him B' her handmaid to "
5 And B' conceived, and bare "
7 And B' Rachel's maid conceived "
35:22 went and lay with B' his father's "
25 And the sons of B', Rachel's "
37: 2 the lad was with the sons of B', "
46:25 These are the sons of B', which "
1Ch 4:29 And at B', and at Ezem, and at "
7:13 and Shallum, the sons of B'. "

Bilhan (*bil'-han*)
Ge 36:27 B', and Zaavan, and Akan. 1092
1Ch 1:42 Ezer; B', and Zavan, and Jakan. "
7:10 The sons also of Jediael; B': "
10 and the sons of B'; Jeush, "

bill
De 24: 1 write her a b' of divorcement, 5612
3 and write her a b' of divorcement, "
Isa 50: 1 Where is the b' of your mother's "
Jer 3: 8 and given her a b' of divorce; "
M'r 10: 4 to write a b' of divorcement, *975*
Lu 16: 6, 7 he said unto him, Take thy b', **1121*

billows
Ps 42: 7 all thy waves and thy b' are 1530
Jon 2: 3 all thy b' and thy waves passed 4867

Bilshan (*bil'-shan*)
Ezr 2: 2 Reelaiah, Mordecai, B', Mizpar, 1114
Ne 7: 7 Nahamani, Mordecai, B', "

Bimhal (*bim'-hal*)
1Ch 7:33 Pasach, and B', and Ashvath. 1118

bind See also BINDETH; BINDING; BOUND.
Ex 28:28 they shall b' the breastplate 7405
39:21 And they did b' the breastplate "
Nu 30: 2 swear an oath to b' his soul 631
3 Lord, and b' herself by a bond, * "
De 6: 8 thou shalt b' them for a sign 7194
11:18 and b' them for a sign upon * "
14:25 b' up the money in thine hand, 6887
Jos 2:18 thou shalt b' this line of scarlet 7194
J'g 15:10 To b' Samson are we come up, 631
12 We are come down to b' thee, "
J'g 15:13 but we will b' thee fast, and 631
16: 5 that we may b' him to afflict him: "
7 they b' me with seven green withs "
11 If they b' me fast with new ropes "
Job 31:36 and b' it as a crown to me. 6029
38:31 Canst thou b' the sweet 7194
39:10 Canst thou b' the unicorn with "
40:13 and b' their faces in secret. 2280
41: 5 or wilt thou b' him for thy 7194
Ps 105:22 To b' his princes at his pleasure; 631
118:27 b' the sacrifice with cords, even "
149: 8 To b' their kings with chains, "
Pro 3: 3 b' them about thy neck; write 7194
6:21 B' them continually upon thine "
7: 3 B' them upon thy fingers, write "
Isa 8:16 B' up the testimony, seal the law 6887
49:18 and b' them on thee, as a bride *7194
61: 1 to b' up the brokenhearted, 2280
Jer 51:63 thou shalt b' a stone to it, and 7164
Eze 3:25 and shall b' thee with them, and 631
5: 3 and b' them in thy skirts. 6887
24:17 b' the tire of thine head upon 2280
30:21 to put a roller to b' it, to make "
34:16 b' up that which was broken, "
Da 3:20 were in his army to b' Shadrach, 3729
Ho 6: 1 smitten, and he will b' us up. 2280
10:10 when they shall b' themselves *631
Mic 1:13 b' the chariot to the swift beast: 7573
M't 12:29 except he first b' the strong man? *1210*
13:30 b' them in bundles to burn them: "
16:19 whatsoever thou shalt b' on earth "
18:18 shall b' on earth shall be bound in "
22:13 B' him hand and foot, and take "
23: 4 For they b' heavy burdens and *1195*
M'r 3:27 he will first b' the strong man; *1210*
5: 3 no man could b' him, no, not with "
Ac 9:14 to b' all that call on thy name. "
12: 8 thyself, and b' on thy sandals. *5265*
21:11 the Jews at Jerusalem b' the man *1210*

bindeth
Job 5:18 for he maketh sore, and b' up: 2280
26: 8 He b' up the waters in his thick 6887
28:11 b' the floods from overflowing; 2280
30:18 it b' me about as the collar of my 247
36:13 they cry not when he b' them. 631
Ps 129: 7 nor he that b' sheaves his bosom. 6014
147: 3 in heart, and b' up their wounds. 2280
Pr 26: 8 As he that b' a stone in a sling, †6887
Isa 30:26 that the Lord b' up the breach 2280

binding
Ge 37: 7 For, behold, we were b' sheaves 481
49:11 B' his foal unto the vine, and his 631
Ex 28:32 it shall have a b' of woven work 8193
Nu 30:13 every b' oath to afflict the soul, 632
Ac 22: 4 b' and delivering into prisons *1195*

Binea (*bin'-e-ah*)
1Ch 8:37 Moza begat B': Rapha was his 1150
9:43 Moza begat B'; and Rephaiah "

Binnui (*bin'-nu-ee*)
Ezr 8:33 Noadiah the son of B', Levites; 1131
10:30 Mattaniah, Bezaleel, and B', and "
38 And Bani, and B', Shimei, "
Ne 3:24 After him repaired B' the son of "
7:15 The children of B', six hundred "
10: 9 the son of Azaniah, B' of the sons "
12: 8 Moreover the Levites: Jeshua, B', "

bird See also BIRD'S; BIRDS.
Ge 7:14 his kind, every b' of every sort. 6833
Le 14: 6 As for the living b', he shall take "
6 the living b' in the blood of the b' "
7 and shall let the living b' loose "
51 and the scarlet, and the living b', "
51 them in the blood of the slain b', "
52 the house with the blood of the b', "
52 living b', and with the cedar wood, "
53 But he shall let go the living b' "
Job 41: 5 thou play with him as with a b'? "
Ps 11: 1 Flee as a b' to your mountain? "
124: 7 b' out of the snare of the fowlers: "
Pr 1:17 spread in the sight of any b'. 1167, 3671
6: 5 a b' from the hand of the fowler. 6833
7:23 as a b' hasteth to the snare, and "
26: 2 As the b' by wandering, as the * "
27: 8 As a b' that wandereth from "
Ec 10:20 b' of the air shall carry the voice, 5775
12: 4 the voice of the b', and all the 6833
Isa 16: 2 wandering b' cast out of the nest,*5775
46:11 a ravenous b' from the east, 5861
Jer 12: 9 heritage is unto me as a speckled b', "
La 3:52 enemies chased me sore, like a b', 6833
Ho 9:11 their glory shall fly away like a b', 5775
11:11 shall tremble as a b' out of Egypt, 6833
Am 3: 5 Can a b' fall in a snare upon the "
Re 18: 2 of every unclean and hateful b'. *3732*

bird's
De 22: 6 b' nest chance to be before thee 6833

birds See also BIRDS'.
Ge 15:10 another: but the b' divided he not. 6833
40:17 and the b' did eat them out of the 5775
19 b' shall eat thy flesh from off thee. "
Le 14: 4 cleansed two b' alive and clean, 6833
5 that one of the b' be killed "
49 take to cleanse the house two b', "
50 and he shall kill the one of the b' "
De 14:11 Of all clean b' ye shall eat. "
2Sa 21:10 neither the b' of the air to rest 5775
Ps 104:17 Where the b' make their nests: 6833
Ec 9:12 and as the b' that are caught in "
Ca 2:12 time of the singing of b' is come,
Isa 31: 5 As b' flying, so will the Lord of 6833
Jer 4:25 the b' of the heavens were fled. 5775
5:27 As a cage is full of b', so are their "
12: 4 beasts are consumed, and the b': "
Jer 12: 9 as a speckled bird, the b' round 5861
Eze 39: 4 give thee unto the ravenous b' 6833
M't 8:20 and the b' of the air have nests; *4071*
13:32 so that the b' of the air come "
Lu 9:58 holes, and b' of the air have nests; "
Ro 1:23 like to corruptible man, and to b', "
1Co 15:39 of fishes, and another of b'. *4421*
Jas 3: 7 every kind of beasts, and of b', *4071*

birds'
Da 4:33 and his nails like b' claws. 6853

Birei See BETH-BIREI.

Birsha (*bur'-shah*)
Ge 14: 2 and with B' king of Gomorrah, 1306

birth See also BIRTHDAY; BIRTHRIGHT.
Ex 28:10 other stone, according to their b'. 8435
2Ki 19: 3 for the children are come to the b', 4866
Job 3:16 untimely b' I had not been; 5309
Ps 58: 8 like the untimely b' of a woman, "
Ec 6: 3 an untimely b' is better than he. "
7: 1 of death than the day of one's b'. 3205
Isa 37: 3 the children are come to the b', 4866
66: 9 I bring to the b', and not cause 7665
Eze 16: 3 Thy b' and thy nativity is of the 4351
Ho 9:11 from the b', and from the womb, 3205
M't 1:18 the b' of Jesus Christ was on this *1083*
Lu 1:14 and many shall rejoice at his b'. "
Joh 9: 1 man which was blind from his b'. *1079*
Ga 4:19 I travail in b' again until Christ **5605*
Re 12: 2 cried, travailing in b', and pained "

birthday
Ge 40:20 which was Pharaoh's b', 3117, 3205
M't 14: 6 when Herod's b' was kept, the *1077*
M'r 6:21 Herod on his b' made a supper "

birthright
Ge 25:31 said, Sell me this day thy b'. 1062
32 what profit shall this b' do to me? "
33 and he sold his b' unto Jacob. "
34 way; thus Esau despised his b'. "
27:36 he took away my b'; and, behold, "
43:33 the firstborn according to his b', "
1Ch 5: 1 his b' was given unto the sons "
1 is not to be reckoned after the b'. "
2 ruler; but the b' was Joseph's:) "
Heb 12:16 for one morsel of meat sold his b'. *4415*

Birzavith (*bur'-za-vith*)
1Ch 7:31 Malchiel, who is the father of B'. 1269

Bishlam (*bish'-lam*)
Ezr 4: 7 days of Artaxerxes, wrote B', 1312

bishop See also BISHOPRICK; BISHOPS.
1Ti 3: 1 If a man desire the office of a b', *1984*
2 A b' then must be blameless, the *1985*
2Ti *subscr.* Timotheus, ordained the first b'* "
Tit 1: 7 For a b' must be blameless, as the "
subscr. Titus, ordained the first b' of * "
1Pe 2:25 Shepherd and B' of your souls. "

bishoprick
Ac 1:20 therein: and his b' let another **1984*

bishops
Ph'p 1: 1 Philippi, with the b' and deacons: *1985*

bit See also BITS
Nu 21: 6 people, and they b' the people; 5391
Ps 32: 9 be held in with b' and bridle, 4964
Am 5:19 on the wall, and a serpent b' him. 5391

bite See also BACKBITE; BIT; BITETH; BITTEN.
Ec 10: 8 an hedge, a serpent shall b' him. 5391
11 will b' without enchantment; "
Jer 8:17 be charmed, and they shall b' you, "
Am 9: 3 the serpent, and he shall b' them: "
Mic 3: 5 that b' with their teeth, and cry, "
Hab 2: 7 up suddenly that shall b' thee, "
Ga 5:15 if ye b' and devour one another, *1143*

biteth See also BACKBITETH.
Ge 49:17 the path, that b' the horse heels, 5391
Pr 23:32 it b' like a serpent, and stingeth "

Bithiah (*bith-i'-ah*)
1Ch 4:18 the sons of B' the daughter of 1332

Bithron (*bith'-ron*)
2Sa 2:29 went through all B', and they 1338

Bithynia (*bith-in'-e-ah*)
Ac 16: 7 Mysia, they assayed to go into B': *978*
1Pe 1: 1 Galatia, Cappadocia, Asia, and B', "

bits
Jas 3: 3 we put b' in the horses' mouths, **5469*

bitten See also HUNGERBITTEN.
Nu 21: 8 every one that is b', when he 5391
9 if a serpent had b' any man, when "

bitter
Ge 27:34 with a great and exceeding b' cry, 4751
Ex 1:14 made their lives b' with hard 4843
12: 8 with b' herbs they shall eat it. 4844
15:23 waters of Marah, for they were b': 4751
Nu 5:18 b' water that causeth the curse: * "
19 be thou free from this b' water * "
23 blot them out with the b' water: * "
24 drink the b' water that causeth * "
24 enter into her, and become b', "
27 into her, and become b', and her "
9:11 unleavened bread and b' herbs. 4844
De 32:24 heat, and with b' destruction: 4815
32 of gall, their clusters are b': 4846
2Ki 14:26 of Israel, that it was very b': 4784
Es 4: 1 cried with a loud and a b' cry; 4751
Job 3:20 and life unto the b' in soul; "
13:26 thou writest b' things against me, 4846
23: 2 Even to day is my complaint b': *4805
Ps 64: 3 to shoot their arrows, even b' 4751
Pr 5: 4 her end is b' as wormwood, sharp "
27: 7 to the hungry soul every b' thing "

Ec 7:26 more b' than death the woman, 4751
Isa 5:20 put b' for sweet, and sweet for b'!
24: 9 strong drink shall be b' to them 4843
Jer 2:19 it is an evil thing and b', that thou 4751
4:18 is thy wickedness, because it is b', "
6:26 an only son, most b' lamentation: 8563
31:15 in Ramah, lamentation, and 8563
Eze 27:31 bitterness of heart and b' wailing. 4751
Am 8:10 and the end thereof as a b' day. 4751
Hab 1: 6 Chaldeans, that b' and hasty
Col 3:19 wives, and be not b' against them. 4087
Jas 3:11 same place sweet water and b'? 4089
14 if ye have b' envying and strife "
Re 8:11 waters, because they were made b'. 4087
10: 9 it shall make thy belly b', but it "
10 I had eaten it, my belly was b'. "

bitterly
J'g 5:23 curse ye b' the inhabitants thereof; 779
Ru 1:20 Almighty hath dealt very b' with 4843
Isa 22: 4 I will weep b', labor not to comfort "
33: 7 of peace shall weep b'. 4751
Eze 27:30 and shall cry b', and shall cast up "
Ho 12:14 provoked him to anger most b': 8563
Zep 1:14 the mighty man shall cry there b'. 4751
M't 26:75 And he went out, and wept b'. 4090
Lu 22:62 Peter went out, and wept b'. "

bittern
Isa 14:23 make it a possession for the b', *7090
34:11 cormorant and the b' shall * "
Zep 2:14 cormorant and the b' shall lodge * "

bitterness
1Sa 1:10 she was in b' of soul, and prayed 4751
15:32 said, Surely the b' of death is past. "
2Sa 2:26 that it will be b' in the latter end? "
Job 7:11 I will complain in the b' of my "
9:18 breath, but filleth me with b'. 4472
10: 1 I will speak in the b' of my soul. 4751
21:25 another dieth in the b' of his soul, "
Pr 14:10 The heart knoweth his own b'; "
17:25 father, and b' to her that bare 4470
Isa 38:15 my years in the b' of my soul. 4751
17 Behold, for peace I had great b': 4843
La 1: 4 are afflicted, and she is in b'. "
3:15 He hath filled me with b', 4844
Eze 3:14 took me away, and I went in b', 4751
21: 6 and with b' sigh before their eyes. 4814
27:31 they shall weep for thee with b' 4751
Zec 12:10 and shall be in b' for him, 4843
10 as one that is in b' "
Ac 8:23 thou art in the gall of b', and in 4088
Ro 3:14 mouth is full of cursing and b': "
Eph 4:31 Let all b', and wrath, and anger, "
Heb 12:15 lest any root of b' springing up "

Bizjothjah (*biz-joth'-jah*)
Jos 15:28 and Beer-sheba, and B', 964

Biztha (*biz'-thah*)
Es 1:10 he commanded Mehuman, B', 968

black See BLACKER; BLACKISH.
Le 13:31 that there is no b' hair in it; 7838
37 there is b' hair grown up therein; "
1Ki 18:45 heaven was b' with clouds and 6937
Es 1: 6 of red, and blue, and white, and b', 5508
Job 30:30 My skin is b' upon me, and my 7835
Pr 7: 9 in the evening, in the b' and ††380
Ca 1: 5 I am b', but comely, O ye 7838
6 not upon me, because I am b', *7840
5:11 his locks are bushy, and b' as a 7838
Jer 4:28 and the heavens above be b': 6937
8:21 I am b'; astonishment hath taken "
14: 2 they are b' unto the ground; and "
La 5:10 Our skin was b' like an oven 3648
Zec 6: 2 in the second chariot b' horses; 7838
6 The b' horses which are therein "
M't 5:36 not make one hair white or b'. 3189
Re 6: 5 And I beheld, and lo a b' horse; "
12 sun became b' as sackcloth of "

blacker
La 4: 8 Their visage is b' than a coal; 2821

blackish
Job 6:16 Which are b' by reason of the ice, *6937

blackness
Job 3: 5 let the b' of the day terrify it. *3650
Isa 50: 3 I clothe the heavens with b', 6940
Joe 2: 6 pained: all faces shall gather b'. *6289
Na 2:10 the faces of them all gather b'. * "
Heb 12:18 nor unto b', and darkness, and 1105
Jude 13 to whom is reserved the b' of 2217

blade
J'g 3:22 the haft also went in after the b'; 3851
22 and the fat closed upon the b', "
Job 31:22 arm fall from my shoulder b', 7929
M't 13:26 But when the b' was sprung up, 5528
M'k 4:28 first the b', then the ear, after that "

blains
Ex 9: 9 be a boil breaking forth with b' 76
10 a boil breaking forth with b' "

blame See also BLAMED; BLAMELESS; UNBLAMEABLE.
Ge 43: 9 then let me bear the b' for ever: 2398
44:32 then I shall bear the b' to my "
2Co 8:20 that no man should b' us in this 3469
Eph 1: 4 be holy and without b' * 299

blamed
2Co 6: 3 that the ministry be not b': 3469
Ga 2:11 the face, because he was to be b'. *2607

blameless
Ge 44:10 my servant; and ye shall be b'. 5355
Jos 2:17 We will be b' of this thine oath * "
J'g 15: 3 Now shall I be more b' than the 5352
M't 12: 5 profane the sabbath, and are b'? * 338
Lu 1: 6 and ordinances of the Lord b'. 273
1Co 1: 8 that ye may be b' in the day of * 410
Ph'p 2:15 that ye may be b' and harmless, 273
3: 6 which is in the law, b'. "
1Th 5:23 be preserved b' unto the coming * 274
1Ti 3: 2 a bishop then must be b', the * 483
10 office of a deacon, being found b'. 410
5: 7 in charge, that they may be b'. * 483
Tit 1: 6 if any be b', the husband of one 410
7 For a bishop must be b', as the "
2Pe 3:14 in peace, without spot, and b'. * 298

blaspheme See also BLASPHEMED; BLASPHEMEST; BLASPHEMETH; BLASPHEMING.
2Sa 12:14 the enemies of the Lord to b', 5006
1Ki 21:10 Thou didst b' God and the king. *1288
13 Naboth did b' God and the king. * "
Ps 74:10 shall the enemy b' thy name for 5006
M'r 3:28 wherewith soever they shall b': 987
29 he that shall b' against the Holy "
Ac 26:11 and compelled them to b'; "
1Ti 1:20 that they may learn not to b'. "
Jas 2: 7 Do not they b' that worthy name "
Re 13: 6 to b' his name, and his tabernacle, "

blasphemed
Le 24:11 Israelitish woman's son b' the 5344
2Ki 19: 6 of the king of Assyria have b' me. 1442
22 hast thou reproached and b'? "
Ps 74:18 the foolish people have b' thy 5006
Isa 37: 6 of the king of Assyria have b' me. 1442
23 hast thou reproached and b'? "
52: 5 name continually every day is b'. 5006
65: 7 upon the mountains, and b' me 2778
Eze 20:27 in this your fathers have b' me, 1442
Ac 18: 6 they opposed themselves, and b', 987
Ro 2:24 the name of God is b' among the "
1Ti 6: 1 God and his doctrine be not b'. "
Tit 2: 5 that the word of God be not b'. "
Re 16: 9 heat, and b' the name of God, "
11 b' the God of heaven because of "
21 men b' God because of the plague "

blasphemer See also BLASPHEMERS.
1Ti 1:13 Who was before a b', and a 989

blasphemers
Ac 19:37 churches, nor yet b' of your 987
2Ti 3: 2 covetous, boasters, proud, b', * 989

blasphemest
Joh 10:36 Thou b'; because I said, I am the 987

blasphemeth
Le 24:16 he that b' the name of the Lord, 5344
16 when he b' the name of the Lord, "
Ps 44:16 of him that reproacheth and b'; 1442
M't 9: 3 within themselves, This man b'. 987
Lu 12:10 unto him that b' against the Holy "

blasphemies
Eze 35:12 I have heard all thy b' which thou 5007
M't 15:19 thefts, false witness, b': * 988
M'r 2: 7 Why doth this man thus speak b'? * "
3:28 b' wherewith soever they shall "
Lu 5:21 Who is this which speaketh b'? "
Re 13: 5 mouth speaking great things and b'; "

blaspheming
Ac 13:45 by Paul, contradicting and b'. * 987

blasphemous
Ac 6:11 we have heard him speak b' words 989
13 ceaseth not to speak b' words * "

blasphemously
Lu 22:65 things b' spake they against him. * 987

blasphemy See also BLASPHEMIES.
2Ki 19: 3 of trouble, and of rebuke, and b': *5007
Isa 37: 3 trouble, and of rebuke, and of b': * "
M't 12:31 All manner of sin and b' shall be 988
31 the b' against the Holy Ghost "
26:65 clothes, saying, He hath spoken b'; 987
65 behold, now ye have heard his b'. 988
M'r 7:22 an evil eye, b', pride, foolishness: * "
14:64 Ye have heard the b': what think "
Joh 10:33 for b'; and because that thou, "
Col 3: 8 anger, wrath, malice, b', filthy * "
Re 2: 9 I know the b' of them which say "
13: 1 and upon his heads the name of b'. "
6 And he opened his mouth in b' * "
17: 3 full of names of b', having seven "

blast See also BLASTED; BLASTING.
Ex 15: 8 And with the b' of thy nostrils 7307
Jos 6: 5 when they make a long b' with the
2Sa 22:16 at the b' of the breath of his 5397
2Ki 19: 7 I will send a b' upon him, and he *7307
Job 4: 9 By the b' of God they perish, and *5397
Ps 18:15 at the b' of the breath of thy "
Isa 25: 4 when the b' of the terrible ones 7307
37: 7 I will send a b' upon him, and he * "

blasted
Ge 41: 6 seven thin ears and b' with the 7710
23 seven ears, withered, thin, and b' "
27 seven empty ears b' with the east "
2Ki 19:26 and as corn b' before it be grown 7711
Isa 37:27 and as corn b' before it be grown *7709

blasting
De 28:22 sword, and with b', and with 7711
1Ki 8:37 famine, if there be pestilence, b', "
2Ch 6:28 if there be b', or mildew, locusts, "
Am 4: 9 I have smitten you with b' and "
Hag 2:17 I smote you with b' and with "

Blastus (*blas'-tus*)
Ac 12:20 and having made B' the king's 986

blaze
M'r 1:45 and to b' abroad the matter, *1310

bleating See also BLEATINGS.
1Sa 15:14 What meaneth then this b' of the 6963

bleatings
J'g 5:16 to hear the b' of the flocks? *8292

blemish See also BLEMISHES.
Ex 12: 5 Your lamb shall be without b', a 8549
29: 1 and two rams without b', "
Le 1: 3 let him offer a male without b': "
10 he shall bring it a male without b'. "
3: 1 he shall offer it without b' before "
6 he shall offer it without b'. "
4: 3 a young bullock without b' unto "
23 of the goats, a male without b': "
28 goats, a female without b', for his "
32 shall bring it a female without b'. "
5:15 a ram without b' out of the flocks, "
18 he shall bring a ram without b' "
6: 6 a ram without b' out of the flock, "
9: 2 for a burnt offering without b', and "
3 of the first year, without b', for a "
14:10 shall take two he lambs without b', "
10 lamb of the first year without b', "
21:17 generations that hath any b', 3971
18 man he be that hath a b', "
20 or that hath a b' in his eye, or be 8400
21 No man that hath a b' of the seed 3971
21 he hath a b'; he shall not come "
23 the altar, because he hath a b'; "
22:19 your own will a male without b', 8549
20 whatsoever hath a b', that shall 3971
21 there shall be no b' therein. "
23:12 An he lamb without b' of the first 8549
18 seven lambs without b' of the first "
24:19 and if a man cause a b' in his 3971
20 as he hath caused a b' in a "
Nu 6:14 lamb of the first year without b' 8549
14 lamb of the first year without b' "
14 and one ram without b' for peace "
19: 2 without spot, wherein is no b', 3971
28:19 they shall be unto you without b': 8549
31 (they shall be unto you without b') "
29: 2 lambs of the first year without b': "
8 they shall be unto you without b': "
13 year; they shall be without b': "
20 lambs of the first year without b'; "
23, 29, 32, 36 the first year without b': "
De 15:21 be any b' therein, as if it be lame, 3971
21 or blind, or have any ill b', "
17: 1 bullock, or sheep, wherein is b', "
2Sa 14:25 head there was no b' in him. "
Eze 43:22 offer a kid of the goats without b' 8549
23 a young bullock without b', and "
23 a ram out of the flock without b'. "
25 a ram out of the flock, without b'. "
45:18 take a young bullock without b', "
23 seven rams without b' daily the "
46: 4 six lambs without b', "
4 and a ram without b'. "
6 a young bullock without b', and "
6 a ram: they shall be without b'. "
13 lamb of the first year without b': "
Da 1: 4 Children in whom was no b', but 3971
Eph 5:27 it should be holy and without b'. 299
1Pe 1:19 as of a lamb without b' and without "

blemishes
Le 22:25 corruption in them, and b' be in *3971
2Pe 2:13 Spots they are and b', sporting 3470

bless See also BLESSED; BLESSEST; BLESSETH; BLESSING.
Ge 12: 2 and I will b' thee, and make thy 1288
3 And I will b' them that b' thee, "
17:16 And I will b' her, and give thee a "
16 son also of her: yea, I will b' her, "
22:17 in blessing I will b' thee, and in "
26: 3 be with thee, and will b' thee; for "
24 for I am with thee, and will b' thee, "
27: 4 that my soul may b' thee before I "
7 and b' thee before the Lord before "
10 he may eat, and that he may b' thee "
19 venison, that thy soul may b' me. "
25 venison, that my soul may b' thee. "
31 venison, that thy soul may b' me. "
34 B' me, even me also, O my father. "
38 b' me, even me also, O my father. "
28: 3 God Almighty b' thee, and make "
32:26 let thee go, except thou b' me. "
48: 9 thee, unto me, and I will b' them. "
16 me from all evil, b' the lads; "
20 In thee shall Israel b', saying, God "
49:25 the Almighty, who shall b' thee "
Ex 12:32 said, and be gone; and b' me also. "
20:24 come unto thee, and I will b' thee. "
23:25 and he shall b' thy bread, and thy "
Nu 6:23 on this wise ye shall b' the children "
24 The Lord b' thee, and keep thee: "
27 children of Israel; and I will b' "
23:20 have received commandment to b': "
25 Neither curse them at all, nor b' "
24: 1 it pleased the Lord to b' Israel, he "
De 1:11 and b' you, as he hath promised "
7:13 will love thee, and b' thee, and "
13 he will also b' the fruit of thy "
8:10 then thou shalt b' the Lord thy "
10: 8 unto him, and to b' in his name, "
14:29 the Lord thy God may b' thee in all "
15: 4 the Lord shall greatly b' thee in "
10 thy God shall b' thee in all thy "
18 thy God shall b' thee in all that "
16:15 the Lord thy God shall b' thee in "
21: 5 unto him, and to b' in the name of "
23:20 the Lord thy God may b' thee in all "
24:13 sleep in his own raiment, and b' "
19 thy God may b' thee in all the work "
26:15 from heaven, and b' thy people "
27:12 upon mount Gerizim to b' the "
28: 8 and he shall b' thee in the land "
12 and to b' all the work of thine "

De 29:19 that he b' himself in his heart, 1288
30:16 and the Lord thy God shall b' "
33:11 B', Lord, his substance, and accept "
Jos 8:33 that they should b' the people of "
J'g 5: 9 among the people. B' ye the Lord. "
Ru 2: 4 answered him, The Lord b' thee. "
1Sa 9:13 because he doth b' the sacrifice; "
2Sa 6:20 Then David returned to b' his "
7:29 let it please thee to b' the house of "
8:10 to salute him, and to b' him, "
21: 3 that ye may b' the inheritance of "
1Ki 1:47 servants came to b' our lord king "
1Ch 4:10 Oh that thou wouldest b' me "
16:43 house: and David returned to b' "
17:27 to b' the house of thy servant, that "
23:13 minister unto him, and to b' in his "
29:20 the congregation, Now b' the Lord "
Ne 9: 5 b' the Lord your God for ever and "
Ps 5:12 For thou, Lord, wilt b' the "
16: 7 I will b' the Lord, who hath given "
26:12 in the congregations will I b' the "
28: 9 Save thy people, and b' thine "
29:11 the Lord will b' his people with "
34: 1 I will b' the Lord at all times: his "
62: 4 they b' with their mouth, but they "
63: 4 Thus will I b' thee while I live: "
66: 8 O b' our God, ye people, and make "
67: 1 God be merciful unto us and b' us; "
6 God, even our own God, shall b' us. "
7 God shall b' us; and all the ends of "
68:26 B' ye God in the congregations, "
96: 2 Sing unto the Lord, b' his name; "
100: 4 be thankful unto him, and b' his "
103: 1 B' the Lord, O my soul, and all "
1 that is within me, b' his holy "
2 B' the Lord, O my soul, and 1288
20 B' the Lord, ye his angels, that "
21 B' ye the Lord, all ye his hosts; ye "
22 B' the Lord, all his works in all "
22 places of his dominion; b' the Lord, "
104: 1 B' the Lord, O my soul. O Lord, "
35 B' thou the Lord, O my soul. "
109:28 Let them curse, but b' thou: when "
115:12 he will b' us; he will b' the house "
12 of Israel; he will b' the house of "
13 He will b' them that fear the Lord, "
18 But we will b' the Lord from this "
128: 5 The Lord shall b' thee out of Zion: "
129: 8 upon you: we b' you in the name "
132:15 I will abundantly b' her provision: "
134: 1 b' ye the Lord, all ye servants of "
2 in the sanctuary, and b' the Lord. "
3 heaven and earth b' thee out of "
135:19 B' the Lord, O house of Israel: "
19 b' the Lord, O house of Aaron: "
20 B' the Lord, O house of Levi: "
20 ye that fear the Lord, b' the Lord. "
145: 1 and I will b' thy name for ever "
2 Every day will I b' thee; and I will "
10 Lord; and thy saints shall b' thee. "
21 and let all flesh b' his holy name "
Pr 30:11 and doth not b' their mother. "
Isa 19:25 Whom the Lord of hosts shall b', * "
65:16 shall b' himself in the God of truth; "
Jer 4: 2 and the nations shall b' themselves "
31:23 The Lord b' thee, O habitation of "
Hag 2:19 forth: from this day will I b' you. "
M't 5:44 b' them that curse you, do good *2127
Lu 6:28 B' them that curse you, and pray "
Ac 3:26 sent him to b' you, in turning "
Ro 12:14 B' them which persecute you: b', "
1Co 4:12 being reviled, we b'; being "
10:16 The cup of blessing which we b', "
14:16 Else, when thou shalt b' with the "
Heb 6:14 Surely blessing I will b' thee, and "
Jas 3: 9 Therewith b' we God, even the "

blessed

Ge 1:22 And God b' them, saying, 1288
28 God b' them, and God said unto "
2: 3 And God b' the seventh day, and "
5: 2 created he them; and b' them, "
9: 1 And God b' Noah and his sons, "
26 B' be the Lord God of Shem; "
12: 3 shall all families of the earth be b'. "
14:19 And he b' him, and said, "
19 B' be Abram of the most high "
20 And b' the most high God, which "
17:20 Behold, I have b' him, and will "
18:18 the nations of the earth shall be b' "
22:18 all the nations of the earth be b'; "
24: 1 and the Lord had b' Abraham in "
27 B' be the Lord God of my master "
31 Come in, thou b' of the Lord; "
35 Lord hath b' my master greatly; "
48 and b' the Lord God of my master "
60 And they b' Rebekah, and said unto "
25:11 Abraham, that God b' his son Isaac; "
26: 4 the nations of the earth be b'; "
12 hundredfold: and the Lord b' him. "
29 thou art now the b' of the Lord. "
27:23 brother Esau's hands: so he b' him. "
27 and b' him, and said, See, the smell "
27 of a field which the Lord hath b': "
29 and b' be he that blesseth thee. "
33 thou camest, and have b' him? "
33 yea, and he shall be b'. "
41 wherewith his father b' him: "
28: 1 Isaac called Jacob, and b' him, "
6 Esau saw that Isaac had b' Jacob, "
6 and that as he b' him he gave him "
14 all the families of the earth be b'. "
30:13 for the daughters will call me b': * 833
27 that the Lord hath b' me for thy 1288
30 and the Lord hath b' thee since my "
31:55 and b' them: and Laban departed, "
32:29 my name? And he b' him there. "
Ge 35: 9 out of Padan-aram, and b' him. 1288
39: 5 the Lord b' the Egyptian's house "
47: 7 Pharaoh: and Jacob b' Pharaoh. "
10 Jacob b' Pharaoh, and went out "
48: 3 in the land of Canaan, and b' me, "
15 And he b' Joseph, and said, God, "
20 And he b' them that day, saying, "
49:28 spake unto them, and b' them; "
28 according to his blessing he b' them. "
Ex 18:10 Jethro said, B' be the Lord, "
20:11 the Lord b' the sabbath day, and "
39:43 they done it: and Moses b' them. "
Le 9:22 toward the people, and b' them, "
23 and came out, and b' the people: "
Nu 22: 6 that he whom thou blessest is b', "
12 curse the people: for they are b'. "
23:11 thou hast b' them altogether. "
20 he hath b'; and I cannot reverse it. "
24: 9 B' is he that blesseth thee, and "
10 thou hast altogether b' them these "
De 2: 7 the Lord thy God hath b' thee in "
7:14 Thou shalt be b' above all people: "
12: 7 the Lord thy God hath b' thee. "
14:24 the Lord thy God hath b' thee: * "
15:14 the Lord thy God hath b' thee "
16:10 the Lord thy God hath b' thee: * "
28: 3 B' shalt thou be in the city, "
3 and b' shalt thou be in the field. "
4 B' shall be the fruit of thy body, "
5 B' shall be thy basket and thy "
6 B' shalt thou be when thou comest "
6 and b' shalt thou be when thou "
33: 1 Moses the man of God b' the "
13 B' of the Lord be his land, for "
20 B' be he that enlargeth Gad: he "
24 Let Asher be b' with children; "
Jos 14:13 And Joshua b' him, and gave unto "
17:14 forasmuch as the Lord hath b' me "
22: 6 So Joshua b' them, and sent them "
7 unto their tents, then he b' them, "
33 and the children of Israel b' God, "
24:10 Balaam; therefore he b' you still: "
J'g 5:24 B' above women shall Jael the wife "
24 b' shall she be above women "
13:24 child grew, and the Lord b' him. "
17: 2 B' be thou of the Lord, my son. "
Ru 2:19 b' be he that did take knowledge "
20 B' be he of the Lord, who hath not "
3:10 B' be thou of the Lord, my "
4:14 B' be the Lord, which hath not "
1Sa 2:20 And Eli b' Elkanah and his wife, "
15:13 B' be thou of the Lord: I have "
23:21 B' be ye of the Lord; for ye have "
25:32 B' be the Lord God of Israel, "
33 And b' be thy advice, "
33 and b' be thou, which hast kept. "
39 B' be the Lord, that hath pleaded "
26:25 B' be thou, my son David: thou "
2Sa 2: 5 B' be ye of the Lord, that ye have "
6:11 and the Lord b' Obed-edom, and "
12 The Lord hath b' the house of "
18 he b' the people in the name of the "
7:29 house of thy servant be b' forever. "
13:25 he would not go, but b' him. "
18:28 B' be the Lord thy God, which hath "
19:39 king kissed Barzillai, and b' him; "
22:47 the Lord liveth; and b' be my rock; "
1Ki 1:48 B' be the Lord God of Israel, "
2:45 and king Solomon shall be b', "
5: 7 B' be the Lord this day, which "
8:14 and b' all the congregation of "
15 B' be the Lord God of Israel, which "
55 stood, and b' all the congregation "
56 B' be the Lord, that hath given "
66 and they b' the king, and went "
10: 9 B' be the Lord thy God, which "
1Ch 13:14 And the Lord b' the house of "
16: 2 he b' the people in the name of the "
36 B' be the Lord God of Israel for "
17:27 O Lord, and it shall be b' for ever. "
26: 5 the eighth: for God b' him. "
29:10 Wherefore David b' the Lord "
10 B' be thou, Lord God of Israel our "
20 all the congregation b' the Lord "
2Ch 2:12 B' be the Lord God of Israel, that "
6: 3 and b' the whole congregation of "
4 B' be the Lord God of Israel, who "
9: 8 B' be the Lord thy God, which "
20:26 for there they b' the Lord: "
30:27 Levites arose and b' the people: "
31: 8 they b' the Lord, and his people "
10 for the Lord hath b' his people; "
Ezr 7:27 B' be the Lord God of our fathers, "
Ne 8: 6 Ezra b' the Lord, the great God. "
9: 5 and b' be thy glorious name, which "
11: 2 And the people b' all the men, "
Job 1:10 hast b' the work of his hands, "
21 b' be the name of the Lord. "
29:11 the ear heard me, then it b' me; 833
31:20 If his loins have not b' me, and if 1288
42:12 So the Lord b' the latter end of "
Ps 1: 1 B' is the man that walketh not 835
2:12 B' are all they that put their "
18:46 Lord liveth; and b' be my rock; 1288
21: 6 hast made him most b' for ever: 1293
28: 6 B' be the Lord, because he hath 1288
31:21 B' be the Lord: for he hath "
32: 1 B' is he whose transgression is 835
2 B' is the man unto whom the Lord "
33:12 B' is the nation whose God is the "
34: 8 b' is the man that trusteth in him. "
37:22 For such as be b' of him shall 1288
26 and lendeth; and his seed is b'. 1293
40: 4 B' is that man that maketh the 835
41: 1 B' is he that considereth the poor: "
2 and he shall be b' upon the earth: 833
Ps 41:13 B' be the Lord God of Israel 1288
45: 2 therefore God hath b' thee for ever. "
49:18 while he lived he b' his soul: and "
65: 4 B' is the man whom thou choosest, 835
66:20 B' be God, which hath not turned 1288
68:19 B' be the Lord, who daily loadeth "
35 power unto his people. B' be God. "
72:17 sun: and men shall be b' in him: "
17 him: all nations shall call him b'. * 833
18 B' be the Lord God, the God of 1288
19 b' be his glorious name for ever: "
84: 4 B' are they that dwell in thy house: 835
5 B' is the man whose strength is in "
12 B' is the man that trusteth in thee. "
89:15 B' is the people that know the "
52 B' be the Lord for evermore. 1288
94:12 B' is the man whom thou 835
106: 3 B' are they that keep judgment, "
48 B' be the Lord God of Israel from 1288
112: 1 B' is the man that feareth the Lord, 835
2 of the upright shall be b'. 1288
113: 2 B' be the name of the Lord from "
115:15 Ye are b' of the Lord which made "
118:26 B' be he that cometh in the name "
26 we have b' you out of the house of "
119: 1 B' are the undefiled in the way, 835
2 B' are they that keep his "
12 B' art thou, O Lord: teach me 1288
124: 6 B' be the Lord, who hath not "
128: 1 B' is every one that feareth the 835
4 thus shall the man be b' that 1288
135:21 B' be the Lord out of Zion, which "
144: 1 B' be the Lord my strength, "
147:13 he hath b' thy children within "
Pr 5:18 Let thy fountain be b': and rejoice "
8:32 for b' are they that keep my ways. 835
34 B' is the man that heareth me, "
10: 7 The memory of the just is b': but 1293
20: 7 his children are b' after him. 835
21 the end thereof shall not be b'. 1288
22: 9 hath a bountiful eye shall be b'; "
31:28 children arise up, and call her b'; 833
Ec 10:17 B' art thou, O land, when thy * 835
Ca 6: 9 daughters saw her, and b' her; 833
Isa 19:25 B' be Egypt my people, 1288
30:18 b' are all they that wait for him. 835
32:20 B' are ye that sow beside all "
51: 2 I called him alone, and b' him, 1288
56: 2 B' is the man that doeth this, 835
61: 9 the seed which the Lord hath b'. 1288
65:23 the seed of the b' of the Lord, "
66: 3 incense, as if he b' an idol. * "
Jer 17: 7 B' is the man that trusteth in the "
20:14 wherein my mother bare me be b'. "
Eze 3:12 B' be the glory of the Lord from "
Da 2:19 Then Daniel b' the God of heaven. 1289
20 B' be the name of God forever "
3:28 B' be the God of Shadrach, "
4:34 I b' the most High, and I praised "
12:12 B' is he that waiteth, and cometh 835
Zec 11: 5 that sell them say, B' be the Lord; 1288
Mal 3:12 And all nations shall call you b': * 833
M't 5: 3 B' are the poor in spirit: 3107
4 B' are they that mourn: for they "
5 B' are the meek: for they shall "
6 B' are they which do hunger and "
7 B' are the merciful: for they shall "
8 B' are the pure in heart: for they "
9 B' are the peacemakers: for they "
10 B' are they which are persecuted "
11 B' are ye, when men shall revile "
11: 6 And b' is he, whosoever shall not "
13:16 But b' are your eyes, for they see: "
14:19 he b', and brake, and gave 2127
16:17 said unto him, B' art thou, Simon 3107
21: 9 B' is he that cometh in the name 2127
23:39 B' is he that cometh in the name "
24:46 B' is that servant, whom his lord 3107
25:34 ye b' of my Father, inherit the 2127
26:26 b' it, and brake it, and gave it to "
M'k 6:41 he looked up to heaven, and b', "
8: 7 and he b', and commanded to set "
10:16 hands upon them, and b' them. "
11: 9 B' is he that cometh in the name "
10 B' be the kingdom of our father "
14:22 and b', and brake it, and gave to "
61 thou the Christ, the Son of the B'? 2128
Lu 1:28 thee: b' art thou among women, *2127
42 B' art thou among women, "
42 and b' is the fruit of thy womb. "
45 b' is she that believed: for there 3107
48 all generations shall call me b'. 3106
68 B' be the Lord God of Israel; 2128
2:28 him up in his arms, and b' God, 2127
34 And Simeon b' them, and said "
6:20 disciples, and said, B' be ye poor: 3107
21 B' are ye that hunger now: for ye "
21 B' are ye that weep now: for ye "
22 B' are ye, when men shall hate "
7:23 And b' is he, whosoever shall not "
9:16 he b' them, and brake, and gave 2127
10:23 B' are the eyes which see the 3107
11:27 B' is the womb that bare thee, "
28 Yea rather, b' are they that hear "
12:37 B' are those servants, whom the "
38 b' are those servants. "
43 B' is that servant, whom his lord "
13:35 B' is he that cometh in the name 2127
14:14 thou shalt be b'; for they cannot 3107
15 B' is he that shall eat bread in "
19:38 B' be the king that cometh 2127
23:29 they shall say, B' are the barren, 3107
24:30 took bread, and b' it, and brake, 2127
50 he lifted up his hands, and b' them. "
51 while he b' them, he was parted "
Joh 12:13 B' is the King of Israel that "

Joh 20:29 *b*' are they that have not seen. 3107
Ac 3:25 all the kindreds of the earth be *b*'. 1757
20:35 more *b*' to give than to receive. 3107
Ro 1:25 the Creator, who is *b*' for ever. 2128
4: 7 *B*' are they whose iniquities are 3107
8 *B*' is the man to whom the Lord "
9: 5 who is over all, God *b*' for ever. 2128
2Co 1: 3 *B*' be God, even the Father of our 2128
11:31 Jesus Christ, which is *b*' for "
Ga 3: 8 In thee shall all nations be *b*'. 1757
9 are *b*' with faithful Abraham. 2127
Eph 1: 3 *B*' be the God and Father of our 2128
3 *b*' us with all spiritual blessings 2127
1Ti 1:11 the glorious gospel of the *b*' God, 3107
6:15 *b*' and only Potentate, the King "
Tit 2:13 Looking for that *b*' hope, and the "
Heb 7: 1 slaughter of the kings, and *b*' him; 2127
6 *b*' him that had the promises. "
7 contradiction the less is *b*' of "
11:20 By faith Isaac *b*' Jacob and Esau "
21 Jacob, when he was a dying, *b*' "
Jas 1:12 *B*' is the man that endureth 3107
25 this man shall be *b*' in his deed. "
1Pe 1: 3 *B*' be the God and Father of our 2128
Re 1: 3 *B*' is he that readeth, and they 3107
14:13 *B*' are the dead which die in the "
16:15 *B*' is he that watcheth, and "
19: 9 *B*' are they which are called "
20: 6 *B*' and holy is he that hath part "
22: 7 *b*' is he that keepeth the sayings "
14 *B*' are they that do his "

blessedness
Ro 4: 6 also describeth the *b*' of the man, 3108
9 Cometh this *b*' then upon the * "
Ga 4:15 Where is then the *b*' ye spake of? * "

blessest
Nu 22: 6 that he, whom thou *b*' is blessed, 1288
1Ch 17:27 for thou *b*', O Lord, and it shall * "
Ps 65:10 it soft with showers: thou *b*' the "

blesseth
Ge 27:29 and blessed be he that *b*' thee. 1288
Nu 24: 9 Blessed is he that *b*' thee, and "
De 15: 6 the Lord thy God *b*' thee, as he * "
Ps 10: 3 *b*' the covetous, whom the Lord * "
107:38 He *b*' them also, so that they are "
Pr 3:33 but he *b*' the habitation of the just. "
27:14 that *b*' his friend with a loud voice, "
Isa 65:16 That he who *b*' himself in the earth "

blessing See also BLESSINGS.
Ge 12: 2 great; and thou shalt be a *b*': 1293
22:17 That in *b*' I will bless thee, and in 1288
27:12 a curse upon me, and not a *b*'. 1293
30 Isaac had made an end of *b*' "
35 and hath taken away thy *b*'. "
36 hath taken away my *b*'. And he "
36 Hast thou not reserved a *b*' "
38 Hast thou but one *b*', my father? "
41 because of the *b*' wherewith his "
28: 4 and give thee the *b*' of Abraham, * "
33:11 Take, I pray thee, my *b*' that is * "
39: 5 the *b*' of the Lord was upon all "
49:28 every one according to his *b*' he "
Ex 32:29 he may bestow upon you a *b*' "
Le 25:21 I will command my *b*' upon you "
De 11:26 you this day a *b*' and a curse; "
27 A *b*', if ye obey the commandments "
29 thou shalt put the *b*' upon mount "
12:15 according to the *b*' of the Lord "
16:17 according to the *b*' of the Lord "
23: 5 thy God turned the curse into a *b*' "
28: 8 The Lord shall command the *b*' "
30: 1 the *b*' and the curse, which I have "
19 life and death, *b*' and cursing: "
33: 1 this is the *b*' wherewith Moses "
7 And this is the *b*' of Judah: "
16 *b*' come upon the head of Joseph, "
23 and full with the *b*' of the Lord: 1293
Jos 15:19 Who answered, Give me a *b*'; "
J'g 1:15 Give me a *b*': for thou hast given "
1Sa 25:27 now this *b*' with thine handmaid * "
2Sa 7:29 and with thy *b*' let the house of "
2Ki 5:15 thee, take a *b*' of thy servant. * "
Ne 9: 5 is exalted above all *b*' and praise. "
13: 2 God turned the curse into a *b*'. "
Job 29:13 *b*' of him that was ready to perish "
Ps 3: 8 thy *b*' is upon thy people. "
24: 5 shall receive the *b*' from the Lord, "
109:17 as he delighted not in *b*', so let it "
129: 8 The *b*' of the Lord be upon you: "
133: 3 there the Lord commanded the *b*', "
Pr 10:22 The *b*' of the Lord, it maketh rich, "
11:11 By the *b*' of the upright the city is "
26 but *b*' shall be upon the head of "
24:25 a good *b*' shall come upon them. "
Isa 19:24 even a *b*' in the midst of the land: "
44: 3 and my *b*' upon thine offspring: "
65: 8 Destroy it not; for a *b*' is in it: "
Eze 34:26 places round about my hill a *b*'; "
26 there shall be showers of *b*'. "
44:30 that he may cause the *b*' to rest "
Joe 2:14 repent, and leave a *b*' behind him; "
Zec 8:13 I save you, and ye shall be a *b*': "
Mal 3:10 pour you out a *b*', that there shall "
Lu 24:53 in the temple, praising and *b*' God. 2127
Ro 15:29 the fulness of the *b*' of the gospel 2129
1Co 10:16 The cup of *b*' which we bless, "
Ga 3:14 the *b*' of Abraham might come "
Heb 6: 7 is dressed, receiveth *b*' from God: "
14 Saying, Surely *b*' I will bless thee, "
12:17 would have inherited the *b*', "
Jas 3:10 mouth proceedeth *b*' and cursing. "
1Pe 3: 9 but contrariwise *b*'; "
9 that ye should inherit a *b*' "
Re 5:12 and honour, and glory, and *b*'. "
5:13 *B*', and honour, and glory, 2129
7:12 *B*', and glory, and wisdom, "

blessings
Ge 49:25 bless thee with *b*' of heaven above, 1293
25 *b*' of the deep that lieth under, "
25 *b*' of the breasts, and of the womb: "
26 The *b*' of thy father have prevailed "
26 above the *b*' of my progenitors "
De 28: 2 all these *b*' shall come on thee, "
Jos 8:34 the *b*' and cursings, according to * "
Ps 21: 3 preventest with the *b*' of goodness: "
Pr 10: 6 *B*' are upon the head of the just: "
28:20 faithful man shall abound with *b*': "
Mal 2: 2 I will curse your *b*': yea, I have "
Eph 1: 3 with all spiritual *b*' in heavenly *2129

blew
Jos 6: 8 Lord, and *b*' with the trumpets: 8628
9 priests that *b*' with the trumpets, "
13 went on continually, and *b*' with "
16 the priests *b*' with the trumpets, "
20 people shouted when the priests *b*' "
J'g 3:27 he *b*' a trumpet in the mountain "
6:34 upon Gideon, and he *b*' a trumpet; "
7:19 they *b*' the trumpets, and brake "
20 three companies *b*' the trumpets, "
22 three hundred *b*' the trumpets, "
1Sa 13: 3 *b*' the trumpet throughout all the "
2Sa 2:28 So Joab *b*' a trumpet, and all "
18:16 And Joab *b*' the trumpet, and the "
20: 1 and he *b*' a trumpet, and said, "
22 And he *b*' a trumpet, and they "
1Ki 1:39 And they *b*' the trumpet; and all "
2Ki 9:13 of the stairs, and *b*' with trumpets, "
11:14 rejoiced, and *b*' with trumpets: "
M't 7:25 winds *b*', and beat upon that 4154
27 *b*', and beat upon that house; "
Joh 6:18 by reason of a great wind that *b*'. "
Ac 27:13 south wind *b*' softly, supposing 5285
28:13 one day the south wind *b*', and *1920

blind See also BLINDED; BLINDETH; BLINDFOLDED.
Ex 4:11 or deaf, or the seeing, or the *b*'? 5787
Le 19:14 a stumblingblock before the *b*', "
21:18 a *b*' man, or a lame, or he that "
22:22 *B*', or broken, or maimed, or 5788
De 15:21 it be lame, or *b*', or have any ill 5787
16:19 a gift doth *b*' the eyes of the wise, 5786
27:18 he that maketh the *b*' to wander 5787
28:29 *b*' gropeth in darkness, and thou "
1Sa 12: 3 bribe to *b*' mine eyes therewith? 5956
2Sa 5: 6 take away the *b*' and the lame, 5787
8 *b*', that are hated of David's soul, "
8 The *b*' and the lame shall not come "
Job 29:15 I was eyes to the *b*', and feet was I "
Ps 146: 8 Lord openeth the eyes of the *b*': "
Isa 29:18 the *b*' shall see out of obscurity, "
35: 5 eyes of the *b*' shall be opened, "
42: 7 open the *b*' eyes, to bring out the "
16 bring the *b*' by a way that they "
18 Hear, ye deaf; and look, ye *b*', that "
19 Who is *b*', but my servant? or deaf "
19 who is *b*' as he that is perfect, and "
19 *b*' as the Lord's servant? "
43: 8 forth the *b*' people that have eyes, "
56:10 His watchmen are *b*': they are all "
59:10 for the wall like the *b*', and we "
Jer 31: 8 and with them the *b*' and the lame, "
La 4:14 wandered as *b*' men in the streets, "
Zep 1:17 walk like *b*' men, because they "
Mal 1: 8 the *b*' for sacrifice, is it not evil? "
M't 9:27 two *b*' men followed him, crying, 5185
9:28 the house, the *b*' men came to him: "
11: 5 The *b*' receive their sight, and the "
12:22 one possessed with a devil, *b*', "
22 that the *b*' and dumb both spake * "
15:14 Let them alone: they be *b*' "
14 leaders of the *b*'. And * "
14 if the *b*' lead the *b*', "
30 lame, *b*', dumb, maimed, and many "
31 lame to walk, and the *b*' to see: "
20:30 And, behold, two *b*' men sitting by "
21:14 the *b*' and the lame came to him "
23:16 Woe unto you, ye blind guides, "
17, 19 Ye fools and *b*': for whether is "
24 Ye *b*' guides, which strain at a "
26 Thou *b*' Pharisee, cleanse first that "
M'r 8:22 and they bring a *b*' man unto him, "
23 he took the *b*' man by the hand, "
10:46 *b*' Bartimæus, the son of Timæus, "
49 they call the *b*' man, saying unto "
51 The *b*' man said unto him, Lord, "
Lu 4:18 and recovering of sight to the *b*', "
6:39 Can the *b*' lead the *b*'? "
7:21 many that were *b*' he gave sight. "
22 how that the *b*' see, the lame walk, "
14:13 the maimed, the lame, the *b*': "
21 maimed, and the halt, and the *b*'. "
18:35 a certain *b*' man sat by the way side "
Joh 5: 3 *b*', halt, withered, waiting for the "
9: 1 which was *b*' from his birth. "
2 his parents, that he was born *b*'? "
6 anointed the eyes of the *b*' man * "
8 had seen him that he was *b*', * "
13 him that aforetime was *b*'. "
17 They say unto the *b*' man again, "
18 he had been *b*', and received his "
19 your son, who ye say was born *b*'? "
20 and that he was born *b*': "
24 called they the man that was *b*', "
25 whereas I was *b*', now I see. "
32 the eyes of one that was born *b*'. "
39 they which see might be made *b*'. "
40 and said unto him, Are we *b*' also? "
41 If ye were *b*', ye should have no "
10:21 a devil open the eyes of the *b*'? "
Joh 11:37 opened the eyes of the *b*', have 5185
Ac 13:11 shalt be *b*', not seeing the sun "
Ro 2:19 thou thyself art a guide of the *b*', "
2Pe 1: 9 he that lacketh these things is *b*', "
Re 3:17 and poor, and *b*', and naked: "

blinded
Joh 12:40 He hath *b*' their eyes, and 5186
Ro 11: 7 obtained it, and the rest were *b*' *4456
2Co 3:14 But their minds were *b*': for until * "
4: 4 of this world hath *b*' the minds 5186
1Jo 2:11 that darkness hath *b*' his eyes. "

blindeth
Ex 23: 8 *b*' the wise, and perverteth the 5786

blindfolded
Lu 22:64 And when they had *b*' him, they 4028

blindness
Ge 19:11 at the door of the house with *b*', 5575
De 28:28 smite thee with madness, and *b*', 5788
2Ki 6:18 this people, I pray thee, with *b*'. 5575
18 And he smote them with *b*' "
Zec 12: 4 every horse of the people with *b*'. 5788
Ro 11:25 *b*' in part is happened to Israel, *4457
Eph 4:18 because of the *b*' of their heart: * "

block See also STUMBLINGBLOCK.
Isa 57:14 take up the stumbling *b*' out of 4383

blood See also BLOODGUILTINESS; BLOODTHIRSTY.
Ge 4:10 of thy brother's *b*' crieth unto me 1818
11 thy brother's *b*' from thy hand; "
9: 4 thereof, which is the *b*' thereof, "
5 surely your *b*' of your lives will "
6 sheddeth man's *b*',...his *b*' be shed: "
37:22 Shed no *b*', but cast him into "
26 our brother, and conceal his *b*'? "
31 goats, and dipped the coat in the *b*'; "
42:22 behold, also his *b*' is required. "
49:11 and his clothes in the *b*' of grapes: "
Ex 4: 9 become *b*' upon the dry land. "
7:17 and they shall be turned to *b*'. "
19 that they may become *b*'; "
19 and that there may be *b*' "
20 in the river were turned to *b*'. "
21 *b*' throughout all the land of Egypt. "
12: 7 shall take of the *b*', and strike it "
13 the *b*' shall be to you for a token "
13 when I see the *b*', I will pass over "
22 dip it in the *b*' that is in the bason, "
22 the *b*' that is in the bason; "
23 he seeth the *b*' upon the lintel, "
22: 2 shall no *b*' be shed for him. * "
3 there shall be *b*' shed for him; * "
23:18 not offer the *b*' of my sacrifice "
24: 6 took half of the *b*' and put it "
6 half of the *b*' he sprinkled on "
8 Moses took the *b*', and sprinkled "
8 Behold the *b*' of the covenant, "
29:12 thou shalt take the *b*' of "
12 pour all the *b*' beside the bottom "
16 shalt take his *b*' and sprinkle it "
20 kill the ram, and take of his *b*', "
20 sprinkle the *b*' upon the altar "
21 shalt take of the *b*' that is upon "
30:10 with the *b*' of the sin offering "
34:25 not offer the *b*' of my sacrifice "
Le 1: 5 bring the *b*', and sprinkle the *b*' "
11 sprinkle his *b*' round about upon "
15 the *b*' thereof shall be wrung out "
3: 2 sprinkle the *b*' upon the altar "
8 sons shall sprinkle the *b*' thereof "
13 Aaron shall sprinkle the *b*' thereof "
17 that ye eat neither fat nor *b*'. "
4: 5 shall take of the bullock's *b*', and "
6 dip his finger in the *b*', and "
6 sprinkle of the *b*' seven times "
7 some of the *b*' upon the horns "
7 pour all the *b*' of the bullock "
16 shall bring of the bullock's *b*' "
17 dip his finger in some of the *b*', "
18 And he shall put some of the *b*' "
18 pour out all the *b*' at the bottom "
25 the priest shall take of the *b*' of "
25 shall pour out his *b*' at the bottom "
30 shall take of the *b*' thereof "
30 shall pour out all the *b*' thereof "
34 priest shall take of the *b*' of the "
34 shall pour out all the *b*' thereof "
5: 9 he shall sprinkle of the *b*' of the "
9 the rest of the *b*' shall be wrung out "
6:27 is sprinkled of the *b*' thereof "
30 whereof any of the *b*' is brought "
7: 2 the *b*' thereof shall he sprinkle "
14 the priest's that sprinkleth the *b*' of "
26 ye shall eat no manner of *b*', "
27 that eateth any manner of *b*', "
33 the *b*' of the peace offerings, "
8:15 Moses took the *b*', and put it upon "
15 poured the *b*' at the bottom of the "
19 Moses sprinkled the *b*' upon the "
23 and Moses took of the *b*' of it, and "
24 Moses put of the *b*' upon the tip of "
24 the *b*' upon the altar round about. "
30 the *b*' which was upon the altar, "
9: 9 brought the *b*' unto him: and he "
9 dipped his finger in the *b*', "
9 poured out the *b*' at the bottom of "
12, 18 sons presented unto him the *b*', "
10:18 Behold, the *b*' of it was not brought "
12: 4 shall then continue in the *b*' of her "
5 shall continue in the *b*' of her "
7 cleansed from the issue of her *b*'. "
14: 6 the living bird in the *b*' of the "
14 the *b*' of the trespass offering, "
17 upon the *b*' of the trespass offering: "
25 some of the *b*' of the trespass "
28 upon the place of the *b*' of the "

Le 14:51 dip them in the b' of the slain 1818
52 the house with the b' of the bird, "
15:19 her issue in her flesh be b', "
25 if a woman have an issue of her b' "
16:14 shall take of the b' of the bullock, "
14 shall he sprinkle of the b' "
15 bring his b' within the vail, "
15 and do with that b' as he did "
15 with the b' of the bullock, "
18 take of the b' of the bullock, "
18 and of the b' of the goat, "
19 And he shall sprinkle of the b' "
27 whose b' was brought in to make "
17: 4 b' shall be imputed unto that man; "
4 he hath shed b'; and that man "
6 the priest shall sprinkle the b' "
10 that eateth any manner of b'; "
10 against that soul that eateth b', "
11 the life of the flesh is in the b': "
11 the b' that maketh an atonement "
12 No soul of you shall eat b', "
12 that sojourneth among you eat b'. "
13 shall even pour out the b' thereof, "
14 the b' of it is for the life thereof: "
14 Ye shall eat the b' of no manner "
14 the life of all flesh is the b' thereof: "
19:16 against the b' of thy neighbour: "
26 shall not eat anything with the b': "
20: 9 his b' shall be upon him. "
11 their b' shall be upon them. "
12 wrought confusion; their b' shall "
13 their b' shall be upon them. "
16 put to death; their b' shall be "
18 uncovered the fountain of her b': "
27 their b' shall be upon them. "
Nu 18:17 thou shalt sprinkle their b' upon "
19: 4 take of her b' with his finger, "
4 and sprinkle of her b' "
5 her skin, and her flesh, and her b', "
23:24 prey, and drink the b' of the slain "
35:19 The revenger of b' himself shall "
21 the revenger of b' shall slay "
24 the slayer and the revenger of b' "
25 of the hand of the revenger of b', "
27 And the revenger of b' find him "
27 the revenger of b' kill the slayer; "
27 he shall not be guilty of b': "
33 for b' it defileth the land: and the "
33 cannot be cleansed of the b' "
33 but by the b' of him that shed it. "
De 12:16 Only ye shall not eat the b'; "
23 sure that thou eat not the b': "
23 for the b' is the life; "
27 the flesh, and the b', upon the "
27 and the b' of thy sacrifices shall "
15:23 thou shalt not eat the b' thereof; "
17: 8 between b' and b', between plea "
19: 6 Lest the avenger of the b' pursue "
10 That innocent b' be not shed in "
10 and so b' be upon thee. "
12 into the hand of the avenger of b', "
13 of innocent b' from Israel, "
21: 7 Our hands have not shed this b', "
8 lay not innocent b' unto thy people "
8 And the b' shall be forgiven them. "
9 put away the guilt of innocent b' "
22: 8 that thou bring not b' upon "
32:14 drink the pure b' of the grape. "
42 make mine arrows drunk with b', "
42 and that with the b' of the slain "
43 will avenge the b' of his servants, "
Jos 2:19 his b' shall be upon his head, "
19 his b' shall be on our head, if any "
20: 3 refuge from the avenger of b'. "
5 if the avenger of b' pursue after "
9 by the hand of the avenger of b', "
J'g 9:24 their b' be laid upon Abimelech "
1Sa 14:32 people did eat them with the b'. "
33 Lord, in that they eat with the b'. "
34 the Lord in eating with the b'. "
19: 5 wilt thou sin against innocent b', "
25:26 thee from coming to shed b', *
31 either that thou hast shed b' "
33 this day from coming to shed b'.* "
26:20 let not my b' fall to the earth "
2Sa 1:16 Thy b' be upon thy head; "
22 From the b' of the slain, "
3:27 that he died, for the b' of Asahel "
28 from the b' of Abner the son "
4:11 therefore now require his b' "
14:11 the revengers of b' to destroy "
16: 8 all the b' of the house of Saul, "
20:12 Amasa wallowed in b' in the "
23:17 the b' of the men that went in "
1Ki 2: 5 shed the b' of war in peace, "
5 put the b' of war upon his girdle "
9 thou down to the grave with b'. "
31 take away the innocent b', which "
32 the Lord shall return his b' "
33 Their b' shall therefore return "
37 thy b' shall be upon thine own "
18:28 lancets, till the b' gushed out "
21:19 dogs licked the b' of Naboth "
19 shall dogs lick thy b', "
22:35 and the b' ran out of the wound "
38 and the dogs licked up his b'; "
2Ki 3:22 on the other side as red as b': "
23 they said, This is b': the kings "
9: 7 avenge the b' of my servants "
7 and the b' of all the servants "
26 seen yesterday the b' of Naboth, "
26 and the b' of his sons, "
33 and some of her b' was sprinkled "
16:13 sprinkled the b' of his peace "
15 all the b' of the burnt offering, "
15 and all the b' of the sacrifice: "

2Ki 21:16 shed innocent b' very much, 1818
24: 4 for the innocent b' that he shed: "
4 filled Jerusalem with innocent b'; "
1Ch 11:19 shall I drink the b' of these men "
22: 8 Thou hast shed b' abundantly, "
8 thou hast shed much b' upon the "
28: 3 man of war, and hast shed b'. "
2Ch 19:10 between b' and b', between law "
24:25 conspired against him for the b' "
29:22 the priests received the b', and "
22 sprinkled the b' upon the altar: "
22 lambs, and they sprinkled the b' "
24 reconciliation with their b' upon "
30:16 the priests sprinkled the b', which "
35:11 the priests sprinkled the b' from "
Job 16:18 O earth, cover not thou my b', 1818
39:30 Her young ones also suck up b': "
Ps 9:12 he maketh inquisition for b', "
16: 4 their drink offerings of b' will I "
30: 9 What profit is their in my b', when "
50:13 of bulls, or drink the b' of goats? "
58:10 his feet in the b' of the wicked. "
68:23 dipped in the b' of thine enemies, "
72:14 precious shall their b' be in his "
78:44 had turned their rivers into b'; "
79: 3 Their b' have they shed like water "
10 revenging of the b' of thy servants "
94:21 and condemn the innocent b'. "
105:29 turned their waters into b', and "
106:38 shed innocent b', even "
38 even the b' of their sons "
38 the land was polluted with b'. "
Pr 1:11 let us lay wait for b', let us look "
16 evil, and make haste to shed b'. "
18 they lay wait for their own b'; "
6:17 and hands that shed innocent b', "
12: 6 to lie in wait for b': but the mouth "
28:17 violence to the b' of any person "
30:33 of the nose bringeth forth b': "
Isa 1:11 delight not in the b' of bullocks, "
15 hear: your hands are full of b'. "
4: 4 have purged the b' of Jerusalem "
9: 5 noise, and garments rolled in b'; "
15: 9 of Dimon shall be full of b': "
26:21 the earth also shall disclose her b', "
33:15 his ears from hearing of b', "
34: 3 shall be melted with their b'. "
6 sword of the Lord is filled with b', "
6 with the b' of lambs and goats, "
7 their land shall be soaked with b', "
49:26 be drunken with their own b', "
59: 3 your hands are defiled with b', "
7 make haste to shed innocent b': "
63: 3 their b' shall be sprinkled upon *5332
66: 3 as if he offered swine's b'; he that 1818
Jer 2:34 skirts is found the b' of the souls "
7: 6 shed not innocent b' in this place, "
18:21 pour out their b' by the force *
19: 4 this place with the b' of innocents; 1818
22: 3 neither shed innocent b' in this "
17 and for to shed innocent b', and "
26:15 shall surely bring innocent b' upon "
46:10 and made drunk with their b': "
48:10 keepeth back his sword from b'. "
51:35 and my b' upon the inhabitants of "
Lam 4:13 that have shed the b' of the just "
14 polluted themselves with b', so "
Eze 3:18, 20 but his b' will I require at thine "
5:17 pestilence and b' shall pass "
9: 9 the land is full of b', and the city "
14:19 and pour out my fury upon it in b', "
16: 6 polluted in thine own b', I said "
6 when thou wast in thy b', Live; "
6 thee when thou wast in thy b', "
9 washed away thy b' from thee, and "
22 bare, and wast polluted in thy b'. "
36 and by the b' of thy children, "
38 that break wedlock and shed b' "
38 will give thee b' in fury and "
18:10 that is a robber, a shedder of b', "
13 surely die; his b' shall be upon him. "
19:10 Thy mother is like a vine in thy b', "
21:32 thy b' shall be in the midst of the "
22: 3 The city sheddeth b' in the midst of "
4 Thou art become guilty in thy b' "
6 in thee to their power to shed b'. "
9 are men that carry tales to shed b': "
12 have they taken gifts to shed b'; "
13 at thy b' which hath been in the "
27 to shed b', and to destroy souls, "
23:37 and b' is in their hands, and with "
45 the manner of women that shed b'; "
45 are adulteresses, and b' is in their "
24: 7 For her b' is in the midst of her; "
8 I have set her b' upon the top of a "
28:23 her pestilence, and b' into her "
32: 6 I will also water with thy b' the "
33: 4 his b' shall be upon his own head. "
5 warning; his b' shall be upon him. "
6 but his b' will I require at the "
8 but his b' will I require at thine "
25 Ye eat with the b', and lift up your "
25 toward your idols, and shed b': "
35: 6 shed the b' of the children of *
6 I will prepare thee unto b', 1818
6 and b' shall pursue thee: sith "
6 thou hast not hated b', even b' shall "
36:18 the b' that they had shed upon the "
38:22 him with pestilence and with b'; ‡
39:17 that ye may eat flesh, and drink b'. "
18 and drink the b' of the princes of "
19 and drink b' till ye be drunken, of "
43:18 thereon, and to sprinkle b' thereon. "
20 thou shalt take of the b' thereof, "
44: 7 my bread, the fat and the b', and "
15 offer unto me the fat and the b', "

Eze 45:19 the priest shall take of the b' of the 1818
Ho 1: 4 I will avenge the b' of Jezreel upon "
4: 2 they break out, and b' toucheth b'. "
6: 8 iniquity, and is polluted with b'. "
12:14 therefore shall he leave his b' upon "
Joe 2:30 b', and fire, and pillars of smoke. "
31 darkness, and the moon into b', "
3:19 they have shed innocent b' in their "
21 For I will cleanse their b' that I "
Jon 1:14 and lay not upon us innocent b': "
Mic 3:10 They build up Zion with b', and "
7: 2 they all lie in wait for b'; they "
Hab 2: 8 because of men's b', and for the "
12 him that buildeth a town with b', "
17 them afraid, because of men's b', "
Zep 1:17 and their b' shall be poured out as "
Zec 9: 7 I will take away his b' out of his "
11 by the b' of thy covenant I have "
M't 9:20 diseased with an issue of b' twelve 131
16:17 for flesh and b' hath not revealed 129
23:30 with them in the b' of the prophets. "
35 the righteous b' shed upon the "
35 from the b' of righteous Abel "
35 unto the b' of Zacharias son of "
26:28 for this is my b' of the new "
27: 4 I have betrayed the innocent b'. "
6 because it is the price of b'. "
8 was called, The field of b', unto this "
24 I am innocent of the b' of this just "
25 His b' be on us, and on our children. "
M'r 5:25 which had an issue of b' twelve "
29 the fountain of her b' was dried up; "
14:24 This is my b' of the new testament, "
Lu 8:43 having an issue of b' twelve years, "
44 and immediately her issue of b' "
11:50 the b' of all the prophets, which "
51 From the b' of Abel "
51 unto the b' of Zacharias, "
13: 1 whose b' Pilate had mingled with "
22:20 new testament in my b', which is "
44 great drops of b' falling down to "
Joh 1:13 Which were born, not of b', nor of "
6:53 Son of man, and drink his b', he "
54 eateth my flesh, and drinketh my b', "
55 is meat indeed, and my b' is drink "
56 eateth my flesh, and drinketh my b', "
19:34 forthwith came there out b' and "
Ac 1:19 that is to say, The field of b'. "
2:19 b', and fire, and vapour of smoke: "
20 into darkness, and the moon into b', "
5:28 intend to bring this man's b' upon "
15:20 from things strangled, and from b'. "
29 offered to idols, and from b', and "
17:26 hath made of one b' all nations of *
18: 6 Your b' be upon your own heads; I "
20:26 that I am pure from the b' of all "
28 hath purchased with his own b'. "
21:25 from b', and from strangled, and "
22:20 the b' of thy martyr Stephen was "
Ro 3:15 Their feet are swift to shed b': "
25 through faith in his b', to declare "
5: 9 then, being now justified by his b', "
1Co 10:16 the communion of the b' of Christ? "
11:25 the new testament in my b': "
27 of the body and b' of the Lord. "
15:50 that flesh and b' cannot inherit the "
Ga 1:16 I conferred not with flesh and b': "
Eph 1: 7 have redemption through his b', the "
2:13 are made nigh by the b' of Christ. "
6:12 wrestle not against flesh and b', "
Col 1:14 redemption through his b', even "
20 made peace through the b' of his "
Heb 2:14 partakers of flesh and b', he also "
9: 7 once every year, not without b', "
12 neither by the b' of goats and "
12 calves, but by his own b' he "
13 For if the b' of bulls and of goats, "
14 How much more shall the b' of "
18 testament was dedicated without b'. "
19 he took the b' of calves and of "
20 Saying, this is the b' of the "
21 sprinkled with b' both the "
22 are by the law purged with b'; and "
22 without shedding of b' is no 130
25 the holy place every year with b' of 129
10: 4 that the b' of bulls and of goats "
19 to enter into the holiest by the b' of "
29 and hath counted the b' of the "
11:28 passover, and the sprinkling of b', "
12: 4 not yet resisted unto b', striving "
24 to the b' of sprinkling, that "
13:11 those beasts, whose b' is brought "
12 sanctify the people with his own b', "
20 through the b' of the everlasting "
1Pe 1: 2 sprinkling of the b' of Jesus Christ: "
19 with the precious b' of Christ, as of "
1Jo 1: 7 the b' of Jesus Christ his Son "
5: 6 water and b', even Jesus Christ; "
6 by water only, but by water and b'. "
8 spirit, and the water, and the b': "
Re 1: 5 us from our sins in his own b', "
5: 9 redeemed us to God by thy b' out of "
6: 10 thou not judge and avenge our b' "
12 of hair, and the moon became as b'; "
7:14 them white in the b' of the Lamb. "
8: 7 hail and fire mingled with b', and "
8 third part of the sea became b'; "
11: 6 over waters to turn them to b', and "
12:11 by the b' of the Lamb, and by the "
14:20 the city, and b' came out of the "
16: 3 it became as the b' of a dead man: "
4 of waters; and they became b'. "
6 shed the b' of saints and prophets, "
6 thou hast given them b' to drink; "
17: 6 drunken with the b' of the saints, "
6 and with the b' of the martyrs of "

Re 18:24 And in her was found the b· of 129
19: 2 avenged the b· of his servants at "
13 clothed with a vesture dipped in b·: "

bloodguiltiness
Ps 51:14 Deliver me from b·, O God, 1818

bloodthirsty
Pro 29:10 The b· hate the upright: but 582, 1818

bloody
Ex 4:25 Surely a b· husband art thou to *1818
26 A b· husband thou art because of* "
2Sa 16: 7 come out, thou b· man, and thou * "
8 because thou art a b· man. * "
21: 1 for Saul, and for his b· house, "
Ps 5: 6 Lord will abhor the b· and * "
26: 9 with sinners, nor my life with b· * "
55:23 b· and deceitful men shall not * "
59: 2 iniquity, and save me from b· * "
139:19 depart from me therefore, ye b· * "
Eze 7:23 the land is full of b· crimes, and "
22: 2 wilt thou judge the b· city? yea, "
24: 6 Woe to the b· city, to the pot "
9 Woe to the b· city! I will even "
Nah 3: 1 Woe to the b· city! it is all full "
Ac 28: 8 lay sick of a fever and of a b· flux: *1420

bloomed See also BLOSSOMED.
Nu 17: 8 and b· blossoms, and yielded 6692

blossom See also BLOSSOMED; BLOSSOMS.
Nu 17: 5 whom I shall choose, shall b·: *6524
Isa 5:24 and their b· shall go up as dust: 6525
27: 6 Israel shall b· and bud, and fill 6692
35: 1 shall rejoice, and b· as the rose. 6524
2 It shall b· abundantly, and rejoice "
Hab 3:17 Although the fig tree shall not b·, "

blossomed See all BLOOMED.
Eze 7:10 rod hath b·, pride hath budded. 6692

blossoms
Ge 40:10 it budded, and her b· shot forth; 5322
Nu 17: 8 and bloomed b·, and yielded 6731

blot See also BLOTTED; BLOTTETH; BLOTTING.
Ex 32:32 b· me, I pray thee, out of thy book 4229
33 him will I b· out of my book. "
Nu 5:23 and he shall b· them out with the "
De 9:14 and b· out their name from under "
25:19 b· out the remembrance of Amalek "
29:20 the Lord shall b· out his name "
2Ki 14:27 he would b· out the name of Israel "
Job 31: 7 if any b· hath cleaved to mine *3971
Ps 51: 1 mercies b· out my transgressions. 4229
9 sins, and b· out all mine iniquities. "
Pr 9: 7 wicked man getteth himself a b·. 3971
Jer 18:23 neither b· out their sin from thy 4229
Re 3: 5 I will not b· out his name out of 1813

blotted
Ne 4: 5 let not their sin be b· out from 4229
Ps 69:28 Let them be b· out of the book "
109:13 following let their name be b· out. "
14 the sin of his mother be b· out. "
Isa 44:22 b· out, as a thick cloud, thy "
Ac 3:19 your sins may be b· out, when 1813

blotteth
Isa 43:25 he that b· out thy transgressions 4229

blotting
Col 2:14 B· out the handwriting of * 1813

blow See also BLEW; BLOWETH; BLOWING; BLOWN.
Ex 15:10 Thou didst b· with thy wind, the 5398
Nu 10: 3 when they shall b· with them, 8628
4 they b· but with one trumpet, "
5 When ye b· an alarm, then the "
6 When ye b· an alarm the second "
6 they shall b· an alarm for their "
7 ye shall b·, but ye shall not sound "
8 Aaron, the priests, shall b· with "
9 then ye shall b· an alarm with *7321
10 ye shall b· with the trumpets over 8628
31: 6 the trumpets to b· in his hand. *8643
Jos 6: 4 priests shall b· with the trumpets. 8628
J'g 7:18 When I b· with the trumpet, I "
18 with me, then b· ye the trumpets "
20 trumpets in their right hands to b· "
1Ki 1:34 and b· ye with the trumpet, and "
1Ch 15:24 did b· with the trumpets before 2690
Ps 39:10 I am consumed by the b· of thine 8409
78:26 He caused an east wind to b· in 5265
81: 3 B· up the trumpet in the new 8628
147:18 he causeth his wind to b·, and 5380
Ca 4:16 b· upon my garden, that the 6315
Isa 40:24 he shall also b· upon them, and *5398
Jer 4: 5 B· ye the trumpet in the land: 8628
6: 1 b· the trumpet in Tekoa, and set "
14:17 breach, with a very grievous b·. *4347
51:27 b· the trumpet among the nations, 8628
Eze 21:31 I will b· against thee in the fire 6315
22:20 to b· the fire upon it, to melt it; 5301
21 I will gather you, and b· upon "
33: 3 upon the land, he b· the trumpet, 8628
6 b· not the trumpet, and the "
Ho 5: 8 B· ye the cornet in Gibeah, and "
Joe 2: 1 B· ye the trumpet in Zion, "
15 B· the trumpet in Zion, sanctify "
Hag 1: 9 brought it home, I did b· upon it. 5301
Zec 9:14 Lord God shall b· the trumpet, 8628
Lu 12:55 when ye see the south wind b·, 4154
Re 7: 1 wind should not b· on the earth, "

bloweth
Isa 18: 3 when he b· a trumpet, hear ye. 8628
40: 7 the spirit of the Lord b· upon it: 5380
54:16 the smith that b· the coals in the 5301
Joh 3: 8 the wind b· where it listeth, 4154

blowing
Le 23:24 a memorial of b· of trumpets, 8643
Nu 29: 1 a day of b· the trumpets unto you. 8643
Jos 6: 9, 13 on and b· with the trumpets. 8628

blown
Job 20:26 a fire not b· shall consume him; 5301
Isa 27:13 the great trumpet shall be b·, 8628
Eze 7:14 They have b· the trumpet, even "
Am 3: 6 Shall a trumpet be b· in the city, "

blue
Ex 25: 4 And b·, and purple, and scarlet, 8504
26: 1 twined linen, and b·, and purple, "
4 thou shalt make loops of b· upon "
31 shalt make a vail of b·, and purple, "
36 for the door of the tent, of b·, "
27:16 an hanging of twenty cubits, of b·, "
28: 5 shall take gold, and b·, and purple, "
6 make the ephod of gold, of b·, "
8 even of gold, of b·, and purple, "
15 thou shalt make it; of gold, of b·, "
28 the ephod with a lace of b·, that it "
31 the robe of the ephod all of b·. "
33 shalt make pomegranates of b·, "
37 thou shalt put it on a b· lace, that "
35: 6 And b·, and purple, and scarlet, "
23 man with whom was found b·, "
25 spun, both of b·, and of purple, "
35 and of the embroiderer, in b·, "
36: 8 twined linen, and b·, and purple, "
11 he made loops of b· on the edge "
35 he made a vail of b·, and purple, "
37 for the tabernacle door of b·, "
38:18 the court was needlework, of b·, "
23 embroiderer in b·, and in purple, "
39: 1 of the b·, and purple, and scarlet, "
2 the ephod of gold, b·, and purple, "
3 it into wires, to work it in the b·, "
5 thereof; of gold, b·, and purple, "
8 of gold, b·, and purple, and scarlet, "
21 the ephod with a lace of b·, that it "
22 ephod of woven work, all of b·. "
24 of the robe pomegranates of b·, "
29 twined linen, and b·, and purple, "
31 they tied unto it a lace of b·, to "
Nu 4: 6 spread over it a cloth wholly of b·, "
7 they shall spread a cloth of b·, "
9 they shall take a cloth of b·, and "
11 spread a cloth of b·, and cover it "
12 and put them in a cloth of b·, "
15:38 of the borders a ribband of b·: "
2Ch 2: 7 in purple, and crimson, and b·, "
14 in b·, and in fine linen, and in "
3:14 he made the vail of b·, and purple, "
Es 1: 6 white, green, and b·, hangings, "
6 b·, and white, and black, marble. *8336
8:15 the king in royal apparel of b· 8504
Jer 10: 9 b· and purple is their clothing: "
Eze 23: 6 were clothed with b·, captains "
27: 7 b· and purple from the isles "
24 in b· clothes, and broidered work, "

blueness
Pr 20:30 b· of a wound cleanseth away *2250

blunt
Ec 10:10 If the iron be b·, and he do not 6949

blush
Ezr 9: 6 I am ashamed and b· to lift 3637
Jer 6:15 ashamed, neither could they b·: "
8:12 neither could they b·: therefore "

Boanerges (*bo-an-er'-jees*)
M'r 3:17 he surnamed them B·, which is, 993

boar
Ps 80:13 b· out of the wood doth waste it, 2386

board See also ABOARD; BOARDS.
Ex 26:16 cubits shall be the length of a b·, 7175
16 half shall be the breadth of one b· "
17 tenons shall there be in one b·, "
19 under one b· for his two tenons, "
19 two sockets under another b· for "
21, 25 two sockets under one b·, and "
21, 25 two sockets under another b·. "
36:21 b· was ten cubits, "
21 and the breadth of a b· one cubit "
22 One b· had two tenons, equally "
24 two sockets under one b· for his "
24 two sockets under another b· for "
26 two sockets under one b·, and "
26 two sockets under another b·. "
30 of silver, under every b· two sockets. "

boards
Ex 26:15 shalt make b· for the tabernacle 7175
17 for all the b· of the tabernacle. "
18 make the b· for the tabernacle, "
18 twenty b· on the south side "
19 of silver under the twenty b·; "
20 north side there shall be twenty b·. "
22 westward thou shalt make six b·. "
23 two b· shalt thou make for the "
25 And they shall be eight b·, and "
26 for the b· of the one side of the "
27 five bars for the b· of the other "
27 five bars for the b· of the side of "
28 in the midst of the b· shall reach "
29 overlay the b· with gold, and make "
27: 8 with b· shalt thou make it: as *3871
35:11 his b·, his bars, his pillars, and 7175
36:20 he made b· for the tabernacle of "
22 for all the b· of the tabernacle. "
23 he made b· for the tabernacle; "
23 twenty b· for the south side "
24 he made under the twenty b·; "
25 north corner, he made twenty b·, "
27 westward he made six b·. "
28 two b· made he for the corners of "
30 and there were eight b·; and their "
31 for the b· of the one side of the "
Ex 36:32 five bars for the b· of the other 7175
32 bars for the b· of the tabernacle, "
33 middle bar to shoot through the b· "
34 And he overlaid the b· with gold, "
38: 7 made the altar hollow with b·. *3871
39:33 his furniture, his taches, his b·, 7175
40:18 set up the b· thereof, and put in "
Nu 3:36 the b· of the tabernacle, and the "
4:31 the b· of the tabernacle, and the "
1Ki 6: 9 the house with beams and b· of *7713
15 walls of the house within with b· 6763
16 and the walls with b· of cedar: "
Ca 8: 9 we will inclose her with b· of 3871
Eze 27: 5 thy ship b· of fir trees of Senir: "
Ac 27:44 And the rest, some on b·, and *4548

boast See also BOASTED; BOASTEST; BOASTETH; BOASTING.
1Ki 20:11 that girdeth on his harness b· 1984
2Ch 25:19 thine heart lifteth thee up to b·: 3513
Ps 34: 2 My soul shall make her b· in the 1984
44: 8 In God we b· all the day long, "
49: 6 trust in their wealth, and b· "
94: 4 workers of iniquity b· themselves? 559
97: 7 images, that b· themselves of 1984
Pr 27: 1 B· not thyself of to morrow; for "
Isa 10:15 Shall the ax b· itself against him 6286
61: 6 their glory shall ye b· yourselves. 3235
Ro 2:17 law, and makest thy b· of God, *2744
23 Thou that makest thy b· of the * "
11:18 B· not against the branches. But *2620
18 if thou b·, thou bearest not *
2Co 9: 2 for which I b· of you to them of *2744
10: 8 though I should b· somewhat * "
13 we will not b· of things without * "
16 not to b· in another man's line * "
11:16 me, that I may b· myself a little. * "
Eph 2: 9 of works, lest any man should b·. * "

boasted
Eze 35:13 with your mouth ye have b· *1431
2Co 7:14 I have b· any thing to him of *2744

boasters
Ro 1:30 despiteful, proud, b·, inventors * 213
2Ti 3: 2 covetous, b·, proud, blasphemers, * "

boastest
Ps 52: 1 Why b· thou thyself in mischief, 1984

boasteth
Ps 10: 3 wicked b· of his heart's desire, 1984
Pr 20:14 he is gone his way, then he b·. "
25:14 Whoso b· himself of a false gift "
Jas 3: 5 little member, and b· great 3166

boasting See also BOASTINGS.
Ac 5:36 Theudas, b· himself to be *3004
Ro 3:27 Where is b· then? It is excluded. *2746
2Co 7:14 even so our b·, which I made * "
8:24 love, and of our b· on your behalf. * "
9: 3 lest our b· of you should be in *2745
4 in this same confident b·. *2746
10:15 Not b· of things without our *2744
11:10 no man shall stop me of this b· *2746
17 in this confidence of b·. * "

boastings
Jas 4:16 now ye rejoice in your b·: all * 212

boat See also BOATS.
2Sa 19:18 And there went over a ferry b· 5679
Joh 6:22 that there was none other b· there, 4142
22 with his disciples into the b·, "
Ac 27:16 much work to come by the b·: 4627
30 when they had let down the b· "
32 cut off the ropes of the b·, and "

boats
Joh 6:23 (Howbeit there came other b· 4142

Boaz (*bo'-az*) See also Booz.
Ru 2: 1 Elimelech; and his name was B·. 1162
3 of the field belonging unto B·, "
4 behold, B· came from Bethlehem, "
5 Then said B· unto his servant "
8 Then said B· unto Ruth, Hearest "
11 B· answered and said unto her, "
14 B· said unto her, At mealtime "
15 B· commanded his young men, "
19 with whom I wrought to day is B·. "
23 she kept fast by the maidens of B· "
3: 2 now is not B· of our kindred, "
7 when B· had eaten and drunk, "
4: 1 Then went B· up to the gate, "
1 behold, the kinsman of whom B· "
5 Then said B·, What day thou "
8 the kinsman said unto B·, Buy it "
9 And B· said unto the elders, and "
13 So B· took Ruth, and she was his "
21 Salmon begat B·, and B· begat "
1Ki 7:21 and called the name thereof B·. "
1Ch 2:11 begat Salma, and Salma begat B·. "
12 B· begat Obed, and Obed begat "
2Ch 3:17 the name of that on the left B·. "

Bocheru (*bok'-er-u*)
1Ch 8:38 these, Azrikam, B·, and Ishmael, 1074
9:44 B·, and Ishmael, and Sheariah, "

Bochim (*bo'-kim*)
J'g 2: 1 came up from Gilgal to B·, and 1066
5 called the name of that place B·: "

bodies
Ge 47:18 lord, but our b·, and our lands: 1472
1Sa 31:12 body of Saul and the b· of his "
1Ch 10:12 away the body of Saul, and the b· 1480
2Ch 20:24 they were dead b· fallen to the 6297
25 riches with the dead b·, and "
Ne 9:37 they have dominion over our b·, 1472
Job 13:12 ashes, your b· to b· of clay. *1354
Ps 79: 2 The dead b· of thy servants have 5038
110: 6 fill the places with the dead b·, 1472

Jer 31:40 the whole valley of the dead b'. 6297
33: 5 the dead b' of men, whom I have "
34:20 and their dead b' shall be for 5038
41: 9 the dead b' of the men, whom he 6297
Eze 1:11 another, and two covered their b'. 1472
23 covered on that side, their b'. "
Da 3:27 upon whose b' the fire had no 1655
28 and yielded their b', that they "
Am 8: 3 there shall be many dead b' in 6297
M't 27:52 and many b' of the saints which 4983
Joh 19:31 the b' should not remain upon "
Ro 1:24 to dishonour their own b' between "
8:11 shall also quicken your mortal b' "
12: 1 that ye present your b' a living "
1Co 6:15 that your b' are the members of "
15:40 also celestial b', and b' terrestrial: "
Eph 5:28 to love their wives as their own b'. "
Heb 10:22 and our b' washed with pure * "
13:11 For the b' of those beasts, whose "
Re 11: 8 And their dead b' shall lie in the 4430
9 shall see their dead b' three days "
9 shall not suffer their dead b' to be "

bodily
Lu 3:22 Holy Ghost descended in a b' 4984
2Co 10:10 but his b' presence is weak, and 4983
Col 2: 9 all the fulness of the Godhead b'. 4985
1Ti 4: 8 For b' exercise profiteth little: 4984

body See also BODIES; BODY'S; BUSYBODY; SOMEBODY.
Ex 24:10 and as it were the b' of heaven in *6106
Le 21:11 any dead b', nor defile himself 5315
Nu 6: 6 Lord he shall come at no dead b'. "
9: 6 defiled by the dead b' of a man, "
7 we are defiled by the dead b' of a "
10 unclean by reason of a dead b', "
19:11 He that toucheth the dead b' of "
13 Whosoever toucheth the dead b' of "
16 or a dead b', or a bone of a man, "
De 21:23 His b' shall not remain all 5038
28: 4 Blessed shall be the fruit of thy b', 990
11 in goods, in the fruit of thy b', "
18 Cursed shall be the fruit of thy b', "
53 shalt eat the fruit of thine own b', "
30: 9 in the fruit of thy b', and in the "
J'g 8:30 threescore and ten sons of his b' 3409
1Sa 31:10 they fastened his b' to the wall of 1472
12 took the b' of Saul and the bodies "
2Ki 8: 5 he had restored a dead b' to life, * "
1Ch 10:12 took away the b' of Saul, and the 1480
Job 19:17 children's sake of mine own b'. †† 990
26 worms destroy this b', yet in †
20:25 drawn, and cometh out of the b'; 1465
Ps 132:11 fruit of thy b', will I set upon 990
Pr 5:11 when thy flesh and thy b' are 7607
Isa 10:18 both soul and b': and they shall 1320
26:19 with my dead b' shall they arise. *5038
51:23 thou hast laid thy b' as the *1460
Jer 26:23 and cast his dead b' into the 5038
36:30 and his dead b' shall be cast out "
La 4: 7 they were more ruddy in b' than 6106
Eze 10:12 And their whole b', and their 1320
Da 4:33 his b' was wet with the dew of 1655
5:21 his b' was wet with the dew of "
7:11 and his b' destroyed, and given to "
15 in my spirit in the midst of my b', 5085
10: 6 His b' also was like the beryl, 1472
Mic 6: 7 the fruit of my b' for the sin of 990
Hag 2:13 unclean by a dead b' touch any 5315
M't 5:29 not that thy whole b' should be 4983
30 that thy whole b' should be cast "
6:22 The light of the b' is the eye: if "
22 thy whole b' shall be full of light. "
23 thy whole b' shall be full of "
25 nor yet for your b', what ye shall "
25 more than meat, and the b' than "
10:28 fear not them which kill the b', "
28 able to destroy both soul and b' in "
14:12 came, and took up the b', and * "
26:12 hath poured this ointment on my b', "
26 and said, Take, eat; this is my b'. "
27:58 begged the b' of Jesus. Then "
58 Pilate commanded the b' to be * "
59 when Joseph had taken the b', "
M'r 5:29 and she felt in her b' that she was "
14: 8 aforehand to anoint my b' to the "
22 and said, Take, eat: this is my b. "
51 cloth cast about his naked b'; "
15:43 unto Pilate, and craved the b' of "
45 of the centurion, he gave the b' * "
Lu 11:34 The light of the b' is the eye: "
34 is single, thy whole b' also is full "
34 evil, thy b' also is full of darkness. "
36 If thy whole b' therefore be full of "
12: 4 not afraid of them that kill the b', "
22 neither for the b', what ye shall "
23 than meat, and the b' is more "
17:37 Wheresoever the b' is, thither will "
22:19 This is my b' which is given for "
23:52 unto Pilate, and begged the b' of "
55 sepulchre, and how his b' was laid, "
24: 3 and found not the b' of the Lord "
23 when they found not his b', they "
Joh 2:21 he spake of the temple of his b'. "
19:38 that he might take away the b' of "
38 came therefore, and took the b' "
40 Then took they the b' of Jesus, "
20:12 the feet, where the b' of Jesus had "
Ac 9:40 and turning him to the b' said, "
19:12 So that from his b' were brought 5559
Ro 4:19 he considered not his own b' now 4983
6: 6 the b' of sin might be destroyed, "
12 reign in your mortal b', that ye "
7: 4 dead to the law by the b' of Christ; "
24 shall deliver me from the b' of this "
8:10 the b' is dead because of sin; but "
Ro 8:13 do mortify the deeds of the b', ye 4983
23 to wit, the redemption of our b'. "
12: 4 we have many members in one b', "
5 being many, are one b' in Christ, "
1Co 5: 3 For I verily, as absent in b', but "
6:13 Now the b' is not for fornication, "
13 and the Lord for the b'. "
16 is joined to an harlot is one b'? "
18 that a man doeth is without the b'; "
18 sinneth against his own b'. "
19 your b' is the temple of the Holy "
20 therefore glorify God in your b', "
7: 4 wife hath not power of her own b', "
4 hath not power of his own b': "
34 she may be holy both in b' and in "
9:27 But I keep under my b', and bring "
10:16 is it not the communion of the b' "
17 many are one bread, and one b': "
11:24 Take, eat: this is my b', which is "
27 shall be guilty of the b' and blood "
29 not discerning the Lord's b'. "
12:12 For as the b' is one, and hath many "
12 the members of that one b', being "
12 are one b': so also is Christ. "
13 are we all baptized into one b', "
14 For the b' is not one member, but "
15 I am not of the b'; is it "
15 therefore not of the b'? "
16 I am not of the b'; is it "
16 therefore not of the b'? "
17 If the whole b' were an eye, where "
18 every one of them in the b', as it "
19 all one member, where were the b'? "
20 many members, yet but one b'. "
22 those members of the b' which "
23 And those members of the b' "
24 but God hath tempered the b' "
25 should be no schism in the b'; "
27 Now ye are the b' of Christ, and "
13: 3 though I give my b' to be burned, "
15:35 and with what b' do they come? "
37 thou sowest not that b' that shall "
38 But God giveth it a b' as it hath "
38 him, and to every seed his own b'. "
44 It is sown a natural b'; "
44 it is raised a spiritual b'. "
44 There is a natural b', "
44 and there is a spiritual b'. "
2Co 4:10 bearing about in the b' the dying "
10 might be made manifest in our b'. "
5: 6 whilst we are at home in the b', we "
8 rather to be absent from the b', "
10 receive the things done in his b', "
12: 2 the b', I cannot tell; "
2 or whether out of the b', "
3 in the b', or out of the b', I cannot "
Gal 6:17 I bear in my b' the marks of the "
Eph 1:23 Which is his b', the fulness of him "
2:16 unto God in one b' by the cross, "
3: 6 fellow heirs, and of the same b', 4954
4: 4 There is one b', and one Spirit, 4983
12 ministry, for the edifying of the b' "
16 From whom the whole b' fitly "
16 maketh increase of the b' unto "
5:23 and he is the saviour of the b'. "
30 For we are members of his b', of "
Php 1:20 Christ shall be magnified in my b', "
3:21 Who shall change our vile b', that "
21 like unto his glorious b', according "
Col 1:18 And he is the head of the b', the "
22 In the b' of his flesh through "
2:11 putting off the b' of the sins of the "
17 of things to come; but the b' is of "
19 from which all the b' by joints and "
23 humility, and neglecting of the b'; "
3:15 which also ye are called in one b'; "
1Th 5:23 and b' be preserved blameless "
Heb 10: 5 but a b' hast thou prepared me: "
10 through the offering of the b' of "
13: 3 as being yourselves also in the b'. "
Jas 2:16 things which are needful to the b'; "
26 as the b' without the spirit is dead, "
3: 2 able also to bridle the whole b'. "
3 and to turn about their whole b'. "
6 that it defileth the whole b', and "
1Pe 2:24 bare our sins in his own b' on the "
Jude 9 he disputed about the b' of Moses, "

body's
Col 1:24 in my flesh for his b' sake, which 4983

Bohan (*Bo'-han*).
Jos 15: 6 border went up to the stone of B' 932
18:17 and descended to the stone of B' "

boil See also BOILED; BOILING; BOILS.
Ex 9: 9 a b' breaking forth with blains 7822
10 and it became a b' breaking forth "
11 because of the boils; for the b' * "
Le 8:31 B' the flesh at the door of the 1310
13:18 in the skin thereof, was a b', and 7822
19 in the place of the b' there be a "
20 of leprosy broken out of the b'. "
23 it is a burning b'; and the priest "
2Ki 20: 7 And they took and laid it on the b', "
Job 41:31 He maketh the deep to b' like a 7570
Isa 38:21 lay it for a plaister upon the b', 7822
64: 2 the fire causeth the waters to b', 1158
Eze 24: 5 make it b' well, and let them 7570
46:20 the priests shall b' the trespass 1310
24 the places of them that b', where * "
24 the ministers of the house shall b' "

boiled
1Ki 19:21 b' their flesh with the instruments 1310
2Ki 6:29 So we b' my son, and did eat him: "
Job 30:27 My bowels b', and rested not: *7570

boiling
Eze 46:23 and it was made with b' places 4018

boiling-places See BOILING and PLACES.

boils
Ex 9:11 before Moses because of the b'; 7822
Job 2: 7 smote Job with sore b' from the "

boisterous
M't 14:30 when he saw the wind b', he was *2478

bold See also EMBOLDENED.
Pr 28: 1 but the righteous are b' as a lion. 982
Ac 13:46 Paul and Barnabas waxed b', *3955
Ro 10:20 Esaias is very b', and saith, I was 662
2Co 10: 1 being absent am b' toward you: *2292
2 that I may not be b' when I am * "
2 wherewith I think to be b' against 5111
11:21 whereinsoever any is b', (I speak "
21 foolishly,) I am b' also. "
Ph'p 1:14 much more b' to speak the word "
1Th 2: 2 we were b' in our God to speak 3955
Ph'm 8 I might be much b' in Christ *3954

boldly
Ge 34:25 came upon the city b', and slew * 983
M'r 15:43 and went in b' unto Pilate, and 5111
Joh 7:26 But, lo, he speaketh b', and they *3954
Ac 9:27 he had preached b' at Damascus 3955
29 spake b' in the name of the Lord "
14: 3 speaking b' in the Lord, which "
18:26 to speak b' in the synagogue: "
19: 8 spake b' for the space of three "
Ro 15:15 I have written the more b' unto 5112
Eph 6:19 may open my mouth b', to make *3954
20 may speak b', as I ought to speak. 3955
Heb 4:16 Let us therefore come b' unto *3954
13: 6 So that we may b' say, The Lord *2292

boldness
Ec 8: 1 the b' of his face shall be changed. *5797
Ac 4:13 they saw the b' of Peter and John, 3954
29 all b' they may speak thy word, "
31 they spake the word of God with b'. "
2Co 7: 4 Great is my b' of speech toward "
Eph 3:12 In whom we have b' and access "
Ph'p 1:20 but that with all b', as always, "
1Ti 3:13 great b' in the faith which is in "
Heb 10:19 b' to enter into the holiest by the "
1Jo 4:17 have b' in the day of judgment: "

bolled
Ex 9:31 in the ear, and the flax was b'. 1392

bolster
1Sa 19:13, 16 pillow of goats' hair for his b', *4763
26: 7 stuck in the ground at his b': * "
11 the spear that is at his b', and * "
12 the cruse of water from Saul's b';* "
16 cruse of water that was at his b'.* "

bolt See also BOLTED; THUNDERBOLTS.
2Sa 13:17 woman out from me, and b' the 5274

bolted
2Sa 13:18 out, and b' the door after her. 5274

bond See also BONDMAID; BONDMAN; BONDSERVANT; BONDSERVICE; BONDWOMAN; BOUND.
Nu 30: 2 an oath to bind his soul with a b'; 632
3 bind herself by a b', being in her "
4 and her b' wherewith she hath "
4 every b' wherewith she hath bound "
10 bound her soul by a b' with an oath; "
11 and every b' wherewith she bound "
12 or concerning the b' of her soul, "
Job 12:18 He looseth the b' of kings, and 4148
Eze 20:37 I will bring you into the b' of the 4562
Lu 13:16 be loosed from this b' on the 1199
Ac 8:23 bitterness, and in the b' of 4886
1Co 12:13 whether we be b' or free; and 1401
Ga 3:28 there is neither b' nor free, there "
Eph 4: 3 of the Spirit in the b' of peace. 4886
6: 8 Lord, whether he be b' or free. 1401
Col 3:11 Barbarian, Scythian, b' nor free: * "
14 which is the b' of perfectness. 4886
Re 13:16 rich and poor, free and b', to 1401
19:18 flesh of all men, both free and b', "

bondage
Ex 1:14 their lives bitter with hard b', *5656
2:23 sighed by reason of the b', "
23 up unto God by reason of the b'. "
6: 5 whom the Egyptians keep in b'; 5647
6 and I will rid you out of their b', 5656
9 anguish of spirit, and for cruel b'. "
13: 3 out of the house of b'; for by 5650
14 from Egypt, from the house of b': "
20: 2 of Egypt, out of the house of b'. "
De 5: 6 of Egypt, from the house of b'. "
6:12 of Egypt, from the house of b'. "
8:14 of Egypt, from the house of b'; "
13: 5 you out of the house of b', "
10 of Egypt, from the house of b'. "
26: 6 us, and laid upon us hard b': 5656
Jos 24:17 from the house of b', and which 5650
J'g 6: 8 you forth out ot the house of b'; "
Ezr 9: 8 give us a little reviving in our b'. 5659
9 hath not forsaken us in our b', "
Ne 5: 5 we bring into b' our sons and our 3533
5 our daughters are brought unto b' "
18 because the b' was heavy upon 5656
9:17 a captain to return to their b': 5659
Isa 14: 3 the hard b' wherein thou wast *5656
Joh 8:33 and were never in b' to any man: 1398
Ac 7: 6 they should bring them into b', 1402
7 to whom they shall be in b' will 1398
Ro 8:15 received the spirit of b' again to 1397
21 shall be delivered from the b' of "
1Co 7:15 a sister is not under b' in such 1402
2Co 11:20 if a man bring you into b', 2615
Ga 2: 4 that they might bring us into b': 2615
4: 3 were in b' under the elements of 1402
9 ye desire again to be in b'? 1398
24 which gendereth to b', which is 1397

Ga 4:25 and is in b' with her children. 1398
5: 1 again with the yoke of b'. 1397
Heb 2:15 all their lifetime subject to b'. "
2Pe 2:19 of the same is he brought in b'. 1402

bondmaid See also BONDMAIDS.
Le 19:20 is a b', betrothed to an husband, 8198
Ga 4:22 two sons, the one by a b', the *3814

bondmaids
Le 25:44 Both thy bondmen, and thy b', 519
44 them shall ye buy bondmen and b'. "

bondman See also BONDMEN.
Ge 44:33 instead of the lad a b' to my lord; 5650
De 15:15 remember that thou wast a b' in "
16:12 remember that thou wast a b' in "
24:18 thou wast a b' in Egypt, and the "
22 a b' in the land of Egypt: "
Re 6:15 every b', and every free man, hid 1401

bondmen
Ge 43:18 and take us for b', and our asses. 5650
44: 9 and we also will be my lord's b'. "
Le 25:42 Egypt: they shall not be sold as b'. "
44 Both thy b', and thy bondmaids, "
44 of them shall ye buy b' and "
46 they shall be your b' for ever: 5647
26:13 that ye should not be their b'; 5650
De 6:21 We were Pharaoh's b' in Egypt; "
7: 8 you out of the house of b', * "
28:68 be sold unto your enemies for b' "
Jos 9:23 none of you be freed from being b', "
1Ki 9:22 Israel did Solomon make no b': * "
2Ki 4: 1 unto him my two sons to be b'. "
2Ch 28:10 of Judah and Jerusalem for b' "
Ezr 9: 9 For we were b'; yet our God hath "
Es 7: 4 But if we had been sold for b' "
Jer 34:13 of Egypt, out of the house of b'. * "

bonds
Nu 30: 5 or of her b' wherewith she 632
7 and her b' wherewith she bound "
14 or all her b', which are upon her: "
Ps 116:16 handmaid:...hast loosed my b'. ‡4147
Jer 5: 5 broken the yoke, and burst the b'.* "
27: 2 Make thee b' and yokes, and put * "
30: 8 burst thy b', and strangers shall * "
Na 1:13 and will burst thy b' in sunder. ‡ "
Ac 20:23 saying that b' and afflictions 1199
23:29 charge worthy of death or of b'. "
25:14 a certain man left in b' by Felix: *1198
26:29 such as I am, except these b'. 1199
31 nothing worthy of death or of b'. "
Eph 6:20 which I am an ambassador in b': * 254
Ph'p 1: 7 as both in my b', and in the 1199
13 So that my b' in Christ are "
14 waxing confident by my b', are "
16 to add affliction to my b': * "
Col 4: 3 for which I am also in b': 1210
18 Remember my b'. Grace be with 1199
2Ti 2: 9 as an evil doer, even unto b'; "
Ph'm 10 whom I have begotten in my b': "
13 have ministered unto me in the b' "
Heb 10:34 had compassion of me in my b', "
11:36 moreover of b' and imprisonment: "
13: 3 Remember them that are in b', 1198

bondservant
Le 25:39 compel him to serve as a b': 5656, 5650

bondservice
1Ki 9:21 Solomon levy a tribute of b' *5647

bondwoman See also BONDWOMEN.
Ge 21:10 Cast out this b' and her son: for 519
10 the son of this b' shall not be heir "
12 because of thy b'; in all that Sarah "
13 the son of the b' will I make a "
Gal 4:23 he who was of the b' was born *3814
30 Cast out the b' and her son: * "
30 for the son of the b' shall not be * "
31 children of the b', but of the free. * "

bondwomen
De 28:68 for bondmen and b', and no man 8198
2Ch 28:10 for bondmen and b' unto you: "
Es 7: 4 bondmen and b', I had held my "

bone See BONES; JAWBONE.
Ge 2:23 This is now b' of my bones, and 6106
29:14 thou art my b' and my flesh. "
Ex 12:46 neither shall ye break a b' thereof. "
Nu 9:12 nor break any b' of it: "
19:16 a dead body, or a b' of a man, "
18 him that touched a b', or one slain, "
J'g 9: 2 that I am your b' and your flesh. "
2Sa 5: 1 Behold, we are thy b' and thy flesh. "
19:13 Art thou not of my b', and of my "
1Ch 11: 1 Behold, we are thy b' and thy flesh. "
Job 2: 5 touch his b' and his flesh, and he "
19:20 My b' cleaveth to my skin and to "
31:22 mine arm be broken from the b'. 7070
Ps 3: 7 all mine enemies upon the cheek b'; "
Eze 37: 7 bones came together, b' to his b'. 6106
39:15 when any seeth a man's b', then "
Joh 19:36 A b' of him shall not be broken. 3747

bones
Ge 2:23 bone of my b', and flesh of my 6106
50:25 shall carry up my b' from hence. "
Ex 13:19 took the b' of Joseph with him: "
19 ye shall carry up my b' away hence "
Nu 24: 8 break their b', and pierce them "
Jos 24:32 b' of Joseph, which the children "
J'g 19:29 divided her, together with her b', "
1Sa 31:13 took their b', and buried them "
2Sa 19:12 ye are my b' and my flesh: * "
21:12 went and took the b' of Saul "
12 and the b' of Jonathan "
13 b' of Saul and the b' of Jonathan "
13 the b' of them that were hanged. "
14 the b' of Saul and Jonathan "

1Ki 13: 2 men's b' shall be burnt upon thee. 6106
31 buried; lay my b' beside his b': "
2Ki 13:21 and touched the b' of Elisha, "
23:14 their places with the b' of men. "
16 took the b' out of the sepulchres, "
18 let no man move his b'. So they let "
18 his b' alone, with the b' of the "
20 men's b' upon them, and returned "
1Ch 10:12 buried their b' under the oak in "
2Ch 34: 5 b' of the priests upon their altars, "
Job 4:14 which made all my b' to shake. "
10:11 fenced me with b' and sinews. "
20:11 His b' are full of the sin of his "
21:24 his b' are moistened with marrow. "
30:17 My b' are pierced in me in the "
30 and my b' are burned with heat. "
33:19 of his b' with strong pain: "
21 b' that were not seen stick out. "
40:18 b' are as strong as pieces of "
18 his b' are like bars of iron. 1634
Ps 6: 2 heal me; for my b' are vexed. 6106
22:14 all my b' are out of joint: "
17 all my b': they look and stare "
31:10 and my b' are consumed. "
32: 3 b' waxed old through my roaring "
34:20 He keepeth all his b': not one of "
35:10 All my b' shall say, Lord, who is "
38: 3 neither is there any rest in my b' "
42:10 with a sword in my b', "
51: 8 the b' which thou hast broken "
53: 5 God hath scattered the b' of him "
102: 3 my b' are burned as an hearth. "
5 my b' cleave to my skin. "
109:18 water, and like oil into his b'. "
141: 7 Our b' are scattered at the grave's "
Pr 3: 8 thy navel, and marrow to thy b'. "
12: 4 is as rottenness in his b'. "
14:30 but envy the rottenness of the b'. "
15:30 a good report maketh the b' fat. "
16:24 to the soul and health to the b'. "
17:22 a broken spirit drieth the b'. 1634
25:15 a soft tongue breaketh the b'. "
Ec 11: 5 how the b' do grow in the womb 6106
Isa 38:13 lion, so will he break all my b': "
58:11 drought and make fat thy b': "
66:14 and your b' shall flourish like an "
Jer 8: 1 the b' of the kings of Judah, "
1 and the b' of his princes, "
1 and the b' of the priests, "
1 and the b' of the prophets, "
1 and the b' of the inhabitants "
20: 9 as a burning fire shut up in my b', "
23: 9 all my b' shake; I am like a "
50:17 king of Babylon hath broken his b'. "
La 1:13 he sent fire into my b', and it "
3: 4 made old; he hath broken my b'. "
4: 8 their skin cleaveth to their b'; "
Eze 6: 5 scatter your b' round about your "
24: 4 fill it with the choice b'. "
5 burn also the b' under it, "
5 let them seethe the b' of it "
10 it well, and let the b' be burned. "
32:27 iniquities shall be upon their b', "
37: 1 the valley which was full of b', "
3 Son of man, can these b' live? "
4 upon these b', and say unto them, "
4 O ye dry b', hear the word "
5 saith the Lord God unto these b'; "
7 b' came together bone to his bone. "
11 these b' are the whole house of "
11 Our b' are dried, and our hope is "
Da 6:24 and brake all their b' in pieces or 1635
Am 2: 1 burned the b' of the king of Edom 6106
6:10 to bring out the b' out of the house, "
Mic 3: 2 their flesh from off their b'; "
3 they break their b', and chop them "
Hab 3:16 rottenness entered into my b', and "
Zep 3: 3 gnaw not the b' till the morrow. *1633
M't 23:27 full of dead men's b', and of all 3747
Lu 24:39 hath not flesh and b', as ye see "
Ac 3: 7 feet and ancle b' received 4974
Eph 5:30 body, of his flesh, and of his b'. *3747
Heb 11:22 commandment concerning his b'. "

bonnets
Ex 28:40 and b' shalt thou make for them. *4021
29: 9 put the b' on them: and the * "
39:28 goodly b' of fine linen, and linen * "
Le 8:13 put b' upon them; as the Lord * "
Isa 3:20 The b', and the ornaments of the *6287
Eze 44:18 They shall have linen b' upon * "

book See also BOOKS.
Ge 5: 1 This is the b' of the generations of 5612
Ex 17:14 Write this for a memorial in a b', "
24: 7 he took the b' of the covenant, and "
32:32 blot me, I pray thee, out of thy b' "
33 me, him will I blot out of my b'. "
Nu 5:23 shall write these curses in a b', "
21:14 it is said in the b' of the wars of "
De 17:18 him a copy of this law in a b' out "
28:58 this law that are written in this b', "
61 which is not written in the b' of "
29:20 curses that are written in this b' "
21 that are written in this b' of the "
27 curses that are written in this b': "
30:10 statutes which are written in this b' "
31:24 the words of this law in a b', "
26 Take this b' of the law and put it "
Jos 1: 8 This b' of the law shall not depart "
8:31 it is written in the b' of the law "
34 all that is written in the b' of the "
10:13 Is not this written in the b' of "
18: 9 by cities into seven parts in a b', "
23: 6 all that is written in the b' of the "
24:26 wrote these words in the b' of the "
1Sa 10:25 wrote it in a b', and laid it up "

2Sa 1:18 behold, it is written in the b' of 5612
1Ki 11:41 they not written in the b' of the "
14:19 b' of the chronicles of...Israel? "
29 b' of the chronicles of...Judah? "
15: 7,23 b' of the chronicles of...Judah? "
31 b' of the chronicles of...Israel? "
16: 5, 14, 20, 27 b' of the...of Israel? "
22:39 b' of the chronicles of...Israel? "
45 b' of the chronicles of...Judah? "
2Ki 1:18 b' of the chronicles of...Israel? "
8:23 b' of the chronicles of...Judah? "
10:34 b' of the chronicles of...Israel? "
12:19 b' of the chronicles of...Judah? "
13: 8 b' of the chronicles of...Israel? "
12 are they not written in the b' of the "
14: 6 which is written in the b' of the law "
15 b' of the chronicles of...Israel? "
18 b' of the chronicles of...Judah? "
28 b' of the chronicles of...Israel? "
15: 6, 11, 15, 21, 26, 31, 36 in the b' of the chronicles of the kings of Judah? "
16:19 b' of the chronicles of...Judah? "
20:20 b' of the chronicles of...Judah? "
21: 17, 25 b' of the chronicles of...Judah? "
22: 8 I have found the b' of the law in "
8 Hilkiah gave the b' to Shaphan "
10 the priest hath delivered me a b'. "
11 king had heard the words of the b' "
13 concerning the words of this b' "
13 hearkened unto the words of this b', "
16 all the words of the b' which the "
23: 2 all the words of the b' of the "
3 that were written in this b'. "
21 written in the b' of this covenant. "
24 law which were written in the b' "
28 written in the b' of the chronicles "
24: 5 did, are they not written in the b' "
1Ch 9: 1 were written in the b' of the kings "
29:29 behold, they are written in the b' *1697
29 in the b' of Nathan the prophet, * "
29 and in the b' of Gad the seer, * "
2Ch 9:29 in the b' of Nathan the prophet, * "
12:15 in the b' of Shemaiah the * "
16:11 are written in the b' of the kings 5612
17: 9 had the b' of the law of the Lord "
20:34 in the b' of Jehu the son of *1697
34 who is mentioned in the b' of the 5612
24:27 in the story of the b' of the kings. "
25: 4 in the law in the b' of Moses, "
26 in the b' of the kings of Judah and "
27: 7 they are written in the b' of the "
28:26 in the b' of the kings of Judah and "
32:32 in the b' of the kings of Judah and "
33:18 written in the b' of the kings of *1697
34:14 Hilkiah the priest found a b' of 5612
15 I have found the b' of the law in "
15 And Hilkiah delivered the b' to "
16 Shaphan carried the b' to the king, "
18 the priest hath given me a b'. "
21 concerning the words of the b' "
21 after all that is written in this b'. "
24 curses that are written in the b' "
30 all the words of the b' of the "
31 which are written in this b'. "
35:12 as it is written in the b' of Moses. "
27 in the b' of the kings of Israel "
36: 8 they are written in the b' of the "
Ezr 4:15 search may be made in the b' of 5609
15 so shalt thou find it in the b' of the "
6:18 as it is written in the b' of Moses. "
Neh 8: 1 bring the b' of the law of Moses, 5612
3 people were attentive unto the b' "
5 And Ezra opened the b' in the "
8 they read in the b' in the law of "
18 last day, he read in the b' of the "
9: 3 read in the b' of the law of the "
12:23 written in the b' of the chronicles, "
13: 1 they read in the b' of Moses in the "
Es 2:23 written in the b' of the chronicles "
6: 1 he commanded to bring the b' of "
9:32 Purim; and it was written in the b'. "
10: 2 in the b' of the chronicles of the "
Job 19:23 oh that they were printed in a b'! "
31:35 mine adversary had written a b'.* "
Ps 40: 7 in the volume of the b' it is "
56: 8 thy bottle: are they not in thy b'? "
69:28 Let them be blotted out of the b' of "
139:16 in thy b' all my members were "
Isa 29:11 the words of a b' that is sealed, "
12 And the b' is delivered to him that "
18 the deaf hear the words of the b', "
30: 8 and note it in a b', that it may be "
34:16 Seek ye out of the b' of the Lord "
Jer 25:13 even all that is written in this b', "
30: 2 I have spoken unto thee in a b'. "
32:12 subscribed the b' of the purchase,* "
36: 2 Take thee a roll of a b', and write "
4 unto him, upon a roll of a b'. "
8 reading in the b' the words of the "
10 Then read Baruch in the b' the "
11 out of the b' all the words of the "
13 Baruch read the b' in the ears of "
18 I wrote them with ink in the b'. "
32 all the words of the b' which "
45: 1 he had written these words in a b' "
51:60 Jeremiah wrote in a b' all the evil "
63 made an end of reading this b', "
Eze 2: 9 and, lo, a roll of a b' was therein; "
Da 12: 1 shall be found written in the b'. "
4 shut up the words, and seal the b', "
Na 1: 1 The b' of the vision of Nahum the "
Mal 3:16 and a b' of remembrance was "
M't 1: 1 The b' of the generation of Jesus 976
M'r 12:26 have ye not read in the b' of Moses, "
Lu 3: 4 As it is written in the b' of the "
4:17 delivered unto him the b' of the 97[illegible]

Lu 4:17 And when he had opened the b', he 975
20 he closed the b', and he gave it "
20:42 David himself saith in the b' of 976
Joh 20:30 which are not written in this b': 975
Ac 1:20 For it is written in the b' of 976
7:42 as it is written in the b' of the "
Gal 3:10 things which are written in the b' 975
Ph 4: 3 whose names are in the b' of life. 976
Heb 9:19 sprinkled both the b', and all the 975
10: 7 (in the volume of the b' it is "
Rev 1:11 What thou seest, write in a b', and "
3: 5 blot out his name out of the b' of 976
5: 1 on the throne a b' written within 975
2 Who is worthy to open the b', and "
3 was able to open the b', neither to "
4 worthy to open and to read the b', "
5 hath prevailed to open the b', and "
7 he came and took the b' out of the "
8 when he had taken the b', the four "
9 Thou art worthy to take the b', and "
10: 2 he had in his hand a little b' open: 974
8 Go and take the little b' which "
9 said unto him, Give me the little b'. "
10 I took the little b' out of the "
13: 8 not written in the b' of life of the 976
17: 8 names were not written in the b' "
20:12 and another b' was opened, "
12 which is the b' of life: "
15 was not found written in the b' 976
21:27 written in the Lamb's b' of life. 975
22: 7 sayings of the prophecy of this b'. "
9 which keep the sayings of this b': "
10 sayings of the prophecy of this b': "
18 words of the prophecy of this b', "
18 plagues that are written in this b': "
19 take away from the words of the b' 976
19 take away his part out of the b' of * "
19 things which are written in this b'. 975

books
Ec 12:12 making many b' there is no end; 5612
Dan 7:10 judgment was set, and the b' 5609
9: 2 I Daniel understood by b' the 5612
Joh 21:25 could not contain the b' that 975
Ac 19:19 brought their b' together, and 976
2Ti 4:13 bring with thee, and the b', but 975
Re 20:12 the b' were opened: and another "
12 which were written in the b', "

booth See also BOOTHS.
Job 27:18 and as a b' that the keeper 5521
Jon 4: 5 and there made him a b', and sat "

booths
Ge 33:17 made b' for his cattle: therefore 5521
Le 23:42 Ye shall dwell in b' seven days; "
42 are Israelites born shall dwell in b': "
43 children of Israel to dwell in b', "
Ne 8:14 children of Israel should dwell in b' "
15 branches of thick trees, to make b', "
16 made themselves b', every one "
17 again out of the captivity made b', "
17 and sat under the b': "

booties
Hab 2: 7 thou shalt be for b' unto them? 4933

booty See also BOOTIES.
Nu 31:32 the b', being the rest of the prey 4455
Jer 49:32 their camels shall be a b', and 957
Zep 1:13 their goods shall become a b', *4933

booz (*Bo'-oz*). See also BOAZ.
M't 1: 5 And Salmon begat B' of Rachab; 1003
5 and B' begat Obed of Ruth; "
Lu 3:32 which was the son of B', which "

border See also BORDERS.
Ge 10:19 the b' of the Canaanites was 1366
49:13 and his b' shall be unto Zidon. 3411
Ex 19:12 or touch the b' of it: whosoever 7097
25:25 make unto it a b' of an hand 4526
25 a golden crown to the b' thereof "
27 Over against the b' shall the "
28:26 breastplate in the b' thereof, *8193
37:12 made thereunto a b' of an hand 4526
12 a crown of gold for the b' thereof "
14 Over against the b' were the rings, "
39:19 b' of it, which was on the *8193
Nu 20:16 a city in the uttermost of thy b': 1366
21 passage through his b': "
21:13 for Arnon is the b' of Moab, "
15 and lieth upon the b' of Moab. "
23 Israel to pass through his b': "
24 the b' of the children of Ammon "
22:36 which is in the b' of Arnon, "
33:44 in Ije-abarim, in the b' of Moab. "
34: 3 and your south b' shall be "
4 And your b' shall turn from "
5 the b' shall fetch a compass from "
6 And as for the western b', ye "
6 even have the great sea for a b': "
6 this shall be your west b'. "
7 And this shall be your north b': "
8 shall point out your b' unto the * "
8 the goings forth of the b' shall be 1366
9 the b' shall go on to Ziphron, "
9 this shall be your north b'. "
10 ye shall point out your east b' "
11 the b' shall descend, and shall "
12 the b' shall go down to Jordan, "
35:26 the b' of the city of his refuge, "
De 3:16 the b' even unto the river Jabbok "
16 the b' of the children of Ammon; "
12:20 God shall enlarge thy b', as he "
Jos 4:19 in the east b' of Jericho. 7097
12: 2 is the b' of the children of Ammon 1366
5 unto the b' of the Geshurites "
5 the b' of Sihon king of Heshbon. "
13:10 the b' of the children of Ammon; "
11 and the b' of the Geshurites and "

Jos 13:23 the b' of the children of Reuben 1366
23 Jordan, and the b' thereof. "
26 Mahanaim unto the b' of Debir; "
27 Jordan and his b', even unto the "
15: 1 to the b' of Edom the wilderness "
2 their south b' was from the shore "
5 And the east b' was the salt sea, "
5 And their b' in the north quarter "
6 the b' went up to Beth-hogla, "
6 b' went up to the stone of Bohan "
7 And the b' went up toward Debir "
7 the b' passed toward the waters of "
8 the b' went up by the valley of "
8 and the b' went up to the top of "
9 the b' was drawn from the top "
9 and the b' was drawn to Baalah, "
10 the b' compassed from Baalah "
11 b' went out unto the side of Ekron "
11 and the b' was drawn to Shicron, "
11 goings out of the b' were at the "
12 the west b' was to the great sea, "
47 the great sea, and the b' thereof. "
16: 5 the b' of the children of Ephraim "
5 even the b' of their inheritance "
6 And the b' went out toward the "
6 the b' went about eastward "
8 The b' went out from Tappuah "
17: 7 b' went along on the right hand "
8 Tappuah on the b' of Manasseh "
10 the sea is his b'; and they met "
18:12 And their b' on the north side "
12 b' went up to the side of Jericho "
13 the b' went over from thence "
13 the b' descended to Ataroth-adar, "
14 the b' was drawn thence, and "
15 b' went out on the west, "
16 the b' came down to the end of "
19 b' passed along to the side of "
19 outgoings of the b' were at the "
20 Jordan was the b' of it on the 1379
19:10 the b' of their inheritance was 1366
11 their b' went up toward the sea, "
12 unto the b' of Chisloth-tabor, "
14 the b' compasseth it on the north "
18 their b' was toward Jezreel, "
22 outgoings of their b' were at "
25 their b' was Helkath, and Hali, "
46 Rakkon, with the b' before Japho. "
22:25 the Lord hath made Jordan a b' "
24:30 in the b' of his inheritance in "
J'g 2: 9 in the b' of his inheritance in "
7:22 to the b' of Abel-meholah, 8193
11:18 within the b' of Moab: 1366
18 for Arnon was the b' of Moab. "
1Sa 6:12 them unto the b' of Beth-shemesh. "
10: 2 in the b' of Benjamin at Zelzah; "
13:18 the way of the b' that looketh to "
2Sa 8: 3 to recover his b' at the river *3027
1Ki 4:21 and unto the b' of Egypt: 1366
2Ki 3:21 and upward, and stood in the b'. "
2Ch 9:26 Philistines, and to the b' of Egypt. "
Ps 78:54 he brought them to the b' of his "
Pr 15:25 will establish the b' of the widow. "
Isa 19:19 at the b' thereof to the Lord. "
37:24 into the height of his b', and the *7093
Jer 31:17 shall come again to their own b'. 1366
50:26 from the utmost b', open her 7093
Eze 11:10 will judge you in the b' of Israel; 1366
11 I will judge you in the b' of Israel: "
29:10 even unto the b' of Ethiopia. "
43:13 and the b' thereof by the edge "
17 and the b' about it shall be half "
20 and upon the b' round about: "
45: 7 the west b' unto the east b'. "
47:13 This shall be the b', whereby ye "
15 this shall be the b' of the land "
16 between the b' of Damascus "
16 and the b' of Hamath; "
17 the b' from the sea shall be "
17 Hazar-enan, the b' of Damascus, "
17 northward, and the b' of Hamath. "
18 from the b' unto the east sea. "
20 the great sea from the b', till a "
48: 1 the b' of Damascus northward, "
2 by the b' of Dan, from the east side "
3 the b' of Asher, from the east side "
4 b' of Naphtali, from the east side "
5 b' of Manasseh, from the east side "
6 b' of Ephraim, from the east side "
7 b' of Reuben, from the east side "
8 b' of Judah, from the east side "
12 by the b' of the Levites. "
13 against the b' of the priests "
21 the oblation toward the east b', "
21 thousand toward the west b', "
22 between the b' of Judah "
22 and the b' of Benjamin, "
24 b' of Benjamin, from the east side "
25 b' of Simeon, from the east side "
26 b' of Issachar, from the east side "
27 b' of Zebulun, from the east side "
28 b' of Gad, at the south side "
28 the b' shall be even from Tamar "
Joe 3: 6 remove them far from their b'. "
Am 1:13 that they might enlarge their b': "
6: 2 or their b' greater than your b'? "
Ob 7 have brought thee even to the b': "
Zep 2: 8 themselves against their b'. "
Zec 9: 2 Hamath also shall b' thereby; 1379
Mal 1: 4 The b' of wickedness, and, The 1366
5 magnified from the b' of Israel. "
M'r 6:56 were but the b' of his garment: 2899
Lu 8:44 touched the b' of his garment; "

borders
Ge 23:17 in all the b' round about, were *1366
47:21 from one end of the b' of Egypt * "

Ex 8: 2 I will smite all thy b' with frogs: 1366
16:35 unto the b' of the land of Canaan. 7097
34:24 before thee, and enlarge thy b': 1366
Nu 15:38 in the b' of their garments 3671
38 the fringe of the b' a ribband * "
20:17 until we have passed thy b'. *1366
21:22 until we be passed thy b'. * "
35:27 him without the b' of the city of * "
Jos 11: 2 and in the b' of Dor on the west, *5299
13: 2 all the b' of the Philistines, *1552
3 unto the b' of Ekron northward, *1366
4 Aphek, to the b' of the Amorites: * "
16: 2 unto the b' of Archi to Ataroth, * "
22:10 came unto the b' of Jordan, that *1552
11 the b' of Jordan, at the passage * "
1Ki 7:28 they had b', and ‡4526
28 the b' were between the ledges: "
29 on the b' that were between the ‡ "
31 with their b', foursquare ‡ "
32 under the b' were four wheels; ‡ "
35 the b' thereof were of the same. ‡ "
36 b' thereof, he graved cherubim, ‡ "
2Ki 16:17 Ahaz cut off the b' of the bases, ‡ "
18: 8 the b' thereof, from the tower 1366
19:23 into the lodgings of his b', *7093
1Ch 5:16 suburbs of Sharon, upon their b'. 8444
7:29 b' of the children of Manasseh, 3027
Ps 74:17 hast set all the b' of the earth: 1367
147:14 maketh peace in thy b', and filleth 1366
Ca 1:11 b' of gold with studs of silver. *8447
Isa 15: 8 gone round about the b' of Moab; 1366
54:12 and all thy b' of pleasant stones. * "
60:18 nor destruction within thy b'; "
Jer 15:13 all thy sins, even in all thy b'. "
17: 3 for sin, throughout all thy b'. "
Eze 27: 4 Thy b' are in the midst of the seas, "
45: 1 holy in all the b' thereof round "
Mic 5: 6 when he treadeth within our b'. * "
M't 4:13 the b' of Zabulon and Nephthalim: 3725
23: 5 enlarge the b' of their garments, 2899
M'r 7:24 into the b' of Tyre and Sidon, 3181

bore See also BARE; BORED.
Ex 21: 6 master shall b' his ear through 7527
Job 41: 2 b' his jaw through with a thorn? *5344

bored
2Ki 12: 9 and b' a hole in the lid of it, 5344

born See also BORNE; FIRSTBORN; FORBORN; NEWBORN.
Ge 4:18 And unto Enoch was b' Irad: 3205
26 to him also there was b' a son; "
6: 1 and daughters were b' unto them, "
10: 1 them were sons b' after the flood. "
21 even to him were children b'. "
25 unto Eber were b' two sons: the "
14:14 b' in his own house, three 3211
15: 3 one b' in my house is mine heir. 1121
17:12 he that is b' in the house, or 3211
13 He that is b' in thy house, and "
17 Shall a child be b' unto him that 3205
23 all that were b' in his house, 3211
27 men of his house, b' in the house, * "
21: 3 his son that was b' unto him, whom 3205
5 his son Isaac was b' unto him. "
7 I have b' him a son in his old age.* "
9 which she had b' unto Abraham, * "
22:20 she hath also b' children unto "
24:15 was b' to Bethuel, son of Milcah, "
29:34 because I have b' him three sons:* "
30:20 I have b' him six sons: and she * "
25 Rachel had b' Joseph, that Jacob * "
31:43 children which they have b'? * "
35:26 were b' to him in Padan-aram. "
36: 5 b' unto him in the land of Canaan. "
41:50 And unto Joseph were b' two sons "
46:20 land of Egypt were b' Manasseh "
22 of Rachel, which were b' to Jacob: "
27 which were b' him in Egypt, were "
48: 5 Manasseh, which were b' unto thee "
Ex 1:22 Every son that is b' ye shall cast 3209
12:19 be a stranger, or b' in the land. 249
48 be as one that is b' in the land. "
21: 4 have b' him sons or daughters; *3205
Le 12: 2 and b' a man child, then she * "
7 law for her that hath b' a male * "
18: 9 whether she be b' at home, 4138
9 or b' abroad, "
19:34 unto you as one b' among you, * 249
22:11 and he that is b' in his house: 3211
23:42 all that are Israelites b' shall * 249
24:16 as he that is b' in the land, when * "
Nu 9:14 him that was b' in the land. "
15:13 All that are b' of the country "
29 him that is b' among the children * "
30 be b' in the land, or a stranger, * "
26:60 unto Aaron was b' Nadab and 3205
De 21:15 and they have b' him children, * "
Jos 5: 5 the people that were b' in the 3209
8:33 as he that was b' among them; * 249
J'g 13: 8 do unto the child that shall be b'. 3205
18:29 father, who was b' unto Israel: "
Ru 4:15 than seven sons, hath b' him. * "
17 There is a son b' to Naomi; * "
1Sa 2: 5 so that the barren hath b' seven;* "
4:20 Fear not, for thou hast b' a son. * "
2Sa 3: 2 unto David were sons b' in Hebron: "
5 These were b' to David in Hebron. "
5:13 sons and daughters b' to David. "
14 names of those that were b' unto 3209
12:14 the child also that is b' unto thee "
14:27 Absalom there were b' three sons, 3205
21:20 and he also was b' to the giant, "
22 four were b' to the giant in Gath, "
1Ki 13: 2 be b' unto the house of David, "
1Ch 1:19 And unto Eber were b' two sons: "
2: 3 which three were b' unto him of "

1Ch 2: 9 of Hezron, that were b' unto him: 3205
3: 1 which were b' unto him in Hebron: "
4 six were b' unto him in Hebron; "
5 were b' unto him in Jerusalem; "
7:21 of Gath that were b' in that land "
20: 8 were b' unto the giant in Gath; "
22: 9 a son shall be b' to thee, who shall "
26: 6 Shemaiah his son were sons b', "
Ezr 10: 3 such as are b' of them, according "
Job 1: 2 there were b' unto him seven sons "
3: 3 the day perish wherein I was b', "
5: 7 man is b' unto trouble, as the "
11:12 man be b' like a wild ass's colt. "
14: 1 Man that is b' of a woman is of "
15: 7 Art thou the first man that was b'? "
14 he which is b' of a woman, that he "
25: 4 he be clean that is b' of a woman? "
38:21 thou it, because thou wast then b'? "
Ps 22:31 a people that shall be b', that he "
58: 3 go astray as soon as they be b', 990
78: 6 the children which should be b'; 3205
87: 4 Ethiopia; this man was b' there. "
5 that man was b' in her: and the "
6 people, that this man was b' there. "
Pr 17:17 and a brother is b' for adversity. "
Ec 2: 7 and had servants b' in my house; 1121
3: 2 A time to be b', and a time to die; 3205
4:14 is b' in his kingdom becometh "
Isa 9: 6 unto us a child is b', unto us a son "
66: 8 shall a nation be b' at once? for as "
Jer 16: 3 daughters that are b' in this place, "
20:14 be the day wherein I was b': "
15 A man child is b' unto thee; "
22:26 country, where ye were not b'; "
Eze 16: 4 in the day thou wast b' thy "
5 in the day that thou wast b'. "
47:22 shall be unto you as b' in the * 249
Ho 2: 3 her as in the day that she was b'. 3205
M't 1:16 of whom was b' Jesus, who is *1080*
2: 1 when Jesus was b' in Bethlehem "
2 is he that is b' King of the Jews? *5088*
4 of them where Christ should be b'. *1080*
11:11 Among them that are b' of women *1084*
19:12 so b' from their mother's womb: *1080*
26:24 that man if he had not been b'. "
M'r 14:21 that man if he had never been b'. "
Lu 1:35 that holy thing which shall be b' * "
2:11 For unto you is b' this day in the *5088*
7:28 Among those that are b' of women *1084*
Joh 1:13 Which were b', not of blood, nor *1080*
3: 3 Except a man be b' again, he "
4 can a man be b' when he is old? "
4 into his mother's womb, and be b'? "
5 Except a man be b' of water and "
6 which is b' of the flesh is flesh; "
6 which is b' of the Spirit is spirit. "
7 unto thee, Ye must be b' again. "
8 every one that is b' of the Spirit. "
8:41 We be not b' of fornication; we "
9: 2 or his parents, that he was b' blind? "
19 your son, who ye say was b' blind? "
20 our son, and that he was b' blind: "
32 the eyes of one that was b' blind. "
34 Thou wast altogether b' in sins, "
16:21 joy that a man is b' into the world. "
18:37 To this end was I b', and for this "
Ac 2: 8 own tongue, wherein we were b'? "
7:20 In which time Moses was b', and "
18: 2 Aquila, b' in Pontus, lately come *1085*
24 named Apollos, b' at Alexandria, * "
22: 3 which am a Jew, b' in Tarsus, *1080*
28 Paul said, But I was free b'. "
Ro 9:11 (For the children being not yet b', "
1Co 15: 8 also, as of one b' out of due time. *1626*
Ga 4:23 bondwoman was b' after the flesh; *1080*
29 he that was b' after the flesh "
29 him that was b' after the Spirit, "
Heb 11:23 By faith Moses, when he was b', *1080*
1Pe 1:23 b' again not of corruptible seed, * *313*
1Jo 2:29 doeth righteousness is b' of him. *1080*
3: 9 Whosoever is b' of God doth not * "
9 sin, because he is b' of God. "
4: 7 every one that loveth is b' of God,* "
5: 1 Jesus is the Christ is b' of God: * "
4 For whatsoever is b' of God * "
18 whosoever is b' of God sinneth not;* "
Re 12: 4 her child as soon as it was b'. *5088*

borne See also BORN.
Ex 25:14 the ark may be b' with them. *5375
28 the table may be b' with them. "
J'g 16:29 and on which it was b' up, *5564
Job 34:31 I have b' chastisement, I will not 5375
Ps 55:12 then I could have b' it: neither "
69: 7 I have b' reproach; shame hath "
Isa 46: 3 are b' by me from the belly, 6006
53: 4 Surely he hath b' our griefs, 5375
66:12 ye shall be b' upon her sides, "
Jer 10: 5 they must needs be b', because "
15: 9 that hath b' seven languisheth: 3205
10 thou hast b' me a man of strife "
La 3:28 because he hath b' it upon him. *5190
5: 7 and we have b' their iniquities. 5445
Eze 16:20 daughters, whom thou hast b' 3205
58 Thou hast b' thy lewdness 5375
32:24, 25 yet have they b' their shame * "
36: 6 ye have b' the shame of the "
39:26 that they have b' their shame, "
Am 5:26 b' the tabernacle of your Moloch "
M't 20:12 which have b' the burden and heat *941*
23: 4 burdens and grievous to be b', *1418*
M'k 2: 3 the palsy, which was b' of four. *142*
Lu 11:46 with burdens grievous to be b', *1418*
Joh 5:37 hath sent me, hath b' witness of me.
20:15 Sir, if thou have b' him hence, *941*
Ac 21:35 that he was b' of the soldiers "
1Co 15:49 have b' the image of the earthy, *5409*

3Jo 6 have b' witness of thy charity *
Re 2: 3 And hast b', and hast patience, * *941*

borrow See also BORROWED; BORROWETH.
Ex 3:22 woman shall b' of her neighbour,*7592
11: 2 every man b' of his neighbour, * "
22:14 borrow ought of his neighbour, "
De 15: 6 nations, but thou shalt not b'; 5670
28:12 nations, and thou shalt not b'. 3867
2Ki 4: 3 b' thee vessels abroad of all thy 7592
3 even empty vessels; b' not a few. "
M't 5:42 from him that would b' of thee *1155*

borrowed
Ex 12:35 they b' of the Egyptians jewels *7592
2Ki 6: 5 Alas, master! for it was b'. "
Ne 5: 4 We have b' money for the king's 3867

borrower
Pr 22: 7 the b' is servant to the lender. 3867
Isa 24: 2 so with the b'; as with the taker "

borroweth
Ps 37:21 The wicked b', and payeth not 3867

Boscath (*bos'-cath*) See also BOSKETH.
2Ki 22: 1 the daughter of Adaiah of B'. *1218

Bosketh See ISH-BOSKETH.

bosom
Ge 16: 5 I have given my maid into thy b'; 2436
Ex 4: 6 Put now thine hand into thy b'. "
6 And he put his hand into his b': "
7 Put thine hand into thy b' again. "
7 he put his hand into his b' again; "
7 and plucked it out of his b', "
Nu 11:12 Carry them in thy b', as a nursing "
De 13: 6 or the wife of thy b', or thy friend, "
28:54 toward the wife of his b', "
56 evil toward the husband of her b', "
Ru 4:16 laid it in her b', and became nurse "
2Sa 12: 3 lay in his b', and was unto him "
8 thy master's wives into thy b', "
1Ki 1: 2 let her lie in thy b', that my lord "
3:20 and laid it in her b', and laid her "
20 and laid her dead child in my b'. "
17:19 he took him out of her b', "
Job 31:33 by hiding mine iniquity in my b': 2243
Ps 35:13 prayer returned into mine own b'. 2436
74:11 hand? pluck it out of thy b'. "
79:12 sevenfold into their b' their "
89:50 I do bear in my b' the reproach of "
129: 7 he that bindeth sheaves his b'. 2683
Pr 5:20 and embrace the b' of a stranger? 2436
6:27 Can a man take fire in his b', and "
17:23 man taketh a gift out of the b' to "
19:24 man hideth his hand in his b', *6747
21:14 a reward in the b' strong wrath. 2436
26:15 slothful hideth his hand in his b';*6747
Ec 7: 9 anger resteth in the b' of fools. 2436
Isa 40:11 and carry them in his b', and shall "
65: 6 even recompense into their b', "
7 their former work into their b'. "
Jer 32:18 into the b' of their children after "
La 2:12 poured out into their mother's b'. "
Mic 7: 5 from her that lieth in thy b'. "
Lu 6:38 shall men give into your b'. *2859*
16:22 by the angels into Abraham's b': "
23 afar off, and Lazarus in his b'. "
Joh 1:18 which is in the b' of the Father, "
13:23 leaning on Jesus' b' one of his "

bosor (*bo'-sor*)
2Pe 2:15 Balaam the son of B', who loved * *1007*

bosses
Job 15:26 upon the thick b' of his bucklers: 1354

botch
De 28:27 smite thee with the b' of Egypt, *7822
35 with a sore b' that cannot be * "

both
Ge 2:25 they were b' naked, the man and 8147
3: 7 the eyes of them b' were opened, "
6: 7 b' man, and beast, and the "
7:21 upon the earth, b' of fowl, and of "
23 upon the face of the ground, b' "
8:17 all flesh, b' of fowl, and of cattle, "
9:23 laid it upon b' their shoulders, 8147
19: 4 b' old and young, all the people
11 with blindness, b' small and great:
36 b' the daughters of Lot with child 8147
21:27 b' of them made a covenant. * "
31 and there they sware b' of them. "
22: 6 they went b' of them together. "
8 so they went b' of them together. "
24:25 We have b' straw and provender 1571
27:45 deprived also of you b' in one day?8147
31:37 they may judge betwixt us b'. "
36:24 children of Zibeon; b' Ajah, and *
40: 5 dreamed a dream b' of them, 8147
41:10 b' me and the chief baker: *
42:35 when b' they and their father *
43: 8 live, and not die, b' we, and thou, 1571
44: 9 it be found, b' let him die, *
16 my lord's servants, b' we, and he 1571
46:34 now, b' we, and also our fathers: "
47: 3 b' we, and also our fathers. "
19 we die before thine eyes, b' we "
48:13 Joseph took them b', Ephraim in 8147
50: 9 went up with him b' chariots 1571
Ex 5:14 making brick b' yesterday and to "
8: 4 the frogs shall come up b' on thee, "
12:31 forth from among my people, b' 1571
13: 2 b' of man and of beast: it is mine.
15 of Egypt, b' the firstborn of man,
18:18 surely wear away, b' thou, and 1571
22: 9 the cause of b' parties shall come 8147
11 the Lord be between them b', "
26:24 thus shall it be for them b'; "
29:44 sanctify also b' Aaron and his *

Ex 32:15 tables were written on b' their 8147
35:22 b' men and women, as many as
25 that which they had spun, b' of *
34 may teach, b' he, and Aholiab,
36:29 thus he did to b' of them in 8147
29 of them in b' the corners. * "
37:26 overlaid it with pure gold, b' the *
Le 6:28 brasen pot, it shall be b' scoured,*
8:11 b' the laver and his foot, *
9: 3 and a lamb, b' of the first year,
15:18 shall b' bathe themselves in water,
16:21 And Aaron shall lay b' his hands 8147
17:15 he shall b' wash his clothes, *
20:11 b' of them shall surely be put to 8147
12 daughter in law, b' of them shall "
13 b' of them have committed an "
14 burnt with fire, b' he and they;
18 and b' of them shall be cut off 8147
21:22 eat the bread of his God, b' of the
22:28 kill it and her young b' in one
25:41 shall he depart from thee, b' he *
44 B' thy bondmen, and thy *
54 go out in the year of jubile, b' *
27:28 b' of man and beast, and of the *
33 then b' it and the change thereof
Nu 3:13 b' man and beast: mine shall they
5: 3 B' male and female shall ye put
7: 1 b' the altar and all the vessels *
13 b' of them were full of fine flour 8147
19, 25, 31, 37, 43, 49, 55, 61, 67, 73, 79
b' of them full of fine flour "
8:17 of Israel are mine, b' man and
9:14 ordinance, b' for the stranger,
12: 5 Aaron and Miriam, and they b' 8147
15:15 One ordinance shall be b' for you *
29 b' for him that is born among *
16:11 For which cause b' thou and all *
25: 8 thrust b' of them through, 8147
27:21 his word they shall come in, b' he,
31:11 and all the prey, b' of men and of
19 any slain, purify b' yourselves *
26 prey that was taken, b' of man
28 of five hundred, b' of the persons,
47 portion of fifty, b' of man and
35:15 be a refuge, b' for the children *
De 19:17 Then b' the men, between whom 8147
21:15 b' the beloved, and the hated; "
22:22 then they shall b' of them die,*1571,8147
22 b' the man that lay with the *
24 bring them b' out unto the gate 8147
23:18 for even b' these are abomination "
30:19 life, that b' thou and thy seed *
32:25 shall destroy b' the young man 1571
Jos 6:21 all that was in the city, b' man
8:25 fell that day, b' of men and women,
14:11 war, b' to go out, and to come in.*
17:16 b' they who are of Beth-shean
J'g 5:30 colours of needlework on b' sides,
6: 5 for b' they and their camels were
8:22 Rule thou over us, b' thou, and 1571
10:10 against thee, b' because we have*
15: 5 and burnt up b' the shocks,
19: 6 did eat and drink b' of them 8147
8 afternoon, and they did eat b' of "
19 there is b' straw and provender 1571
Ru 1: 5 Mahlon and Chilion died also b' 8147
1Sa 2:26 was in favour b' with the Lord, 1571
34 one day they shall die b' of them. 8147
3:11 b' the ears of every one that "
5: 4 b' the palms of his hands were cut "
9 smote the men of the city, b' small
9:26 they went out b' of them, he and 8147
12:14 then shall b' ye and also the king 1571
25 be consumed, b' ye and your king. "
14:11 b' of them discovered themselves 8147
15: 3 spare them not; but slay b' man
17:36 Thy servant slew b' the lion and 1571
20:11 they went out b' of them into the 8174
42 we have sworn b' of us in the name "
22:19 b' men and women, children and
25: 6 Peace be b' to thee, and peace be
16 wall unto us b' by night and day, 1571
43 were also b' of them his wives. 8147
26:25 thou shalt b' do great things, 1571
2Sa 8:18 the son of Jehoiada was over b' *
9:13 and was lame on b' his feet. 8147
15:25 shew me b' it, and his habitation:
16:23 of Ahithophel b' with David 1571
17:18 went b' of them away quickly, 8147
1Ki 3:13 thou hast not asked, b' riches, 1571
6: 5 b' of the temple and of the oracle:
15 b' the floor of the house, and the *
16 b' the floor and the walls with *
25 b' the cherubims were of one 8147
7:12 b' for the inner court of the
50 hinges of gold, b' for the doors
2Ki 2:11 parted them b' asunder; and 8147
3:17 that ye may drink, b' ye, and your
6:15 host compassed the city b' with *
17:41 served their graven images, b' *1571
21:12 of it, b' his ears shall tingle. 8147
23: 2 all the people, b' small and great:
15 b' that altar and the high place 1571
25:26 people, b' small and great, and the
1Ch 12: 2 and could use b' the right hand
15 b' toward the east, and toward
15:12 sanctify yourselves, b' ye and
16: 3 one of Israel, b' man and woman,
23:29 B' for the shewbread, and for *
28:15 by weight, b' for the candlestick, *
29:12 B' riches and honour come of thee,
2Ch 22:25 abundance b' riches with the dead
24:16 done good in Israel, b' toward *
25:21 face, b' he and Amaziah king *
26:10 cattle, b' in the low country, *
27: 5 of Ammon pay unto him, b' the *

2Ch 31:17 B' to the genealogy of the priests *
32:26 pride of his heart, b' he and the
Ezr 3: 5 burnt offering, b' of the new *
6: 9 have need of, b' young bullocks, *
Ne 1: 6 b' I and my father's house have *
4:16 half of them held b' the spears, *
8: 2 congregation b' of men and *
10: 9 And the Levites: b' Jeshua the *
12:27 gladness, b' with thanksgivings,
28 b' out of the plain country round
45 b' the singers and the porters *
Es 1: 5 the palace, b' unto great and small,
20 husbands honour, b' to great and
2:23 therefore they were b' hanged on 8147
3:13 to perish, all Jews, b' young and
8:11 them, b' little ones and women, *
9:20 the king Ahasuerus, b' nigh, and
Job 9:33 might lay his hand upon us b'. 8147
15:10 With us are b' the greyheaded 1571
Ps 4: 8 I will b' lay me down in peace, 3162
49: 2 B' low and high, rich and poor, 1571
58: 9 whirlwind, b' living, and in his *
64: 6 b' the inward thought of every *
76: 6 O God of Jacob, b' the chariot
104:25 innumerable, b' small and great
115:13 that fear the Lord, b' small and
135: 8 the firstborn of Egypt, b' of man
139:12 darkness and the light are b' alike
148:12 B' young men and maidens; old
Pr 17:15 they b' are abomination 8147
20:10 b' of them are alike abomination "
12 the Lord hath made even b' of them."
24:22 who knoweth the ruin of them b'? "
26:10 formed all things b' rewardeth *
27: 3 wrath is heavier than them b' 8147
29:13 the Lord lighteneth b' their eyes. "
Ec 4: 3 better is he than b' they, which "
6 than b' the hands full with *
8: 5 a wise man's heart discerneth b' *
11: 6 whether they b' shall be alike 8147
Isa 1:31 they shall b' burn together, and "
7:16 shall be forsaken of b' her * "
8:14 to b' the houses of Israel, for a gin "
10:18 fruitful field, b' soul and body:
13: 9 Lord cometh, cruel b' with *
18: 5 he shall b' cut off the sprigs *
38:15 What shall I say? he hath b'
44:12 with the tongs b' worketh it in *
Jer 5:24 that giveth rain, b' the former and
9:10 b' the fowl of the heavens and the
14:18 yea, b' the prophet and the priest 1571
16: 6 B' the great and the small shall
21: 6 of this city, b' man and beast:
23:11 For b' prophet and priest are 1571
26: 5 sent unto you, b' rising up early *
28: 8 prophesied b' against many *
31:13 b' young men and old together *
32:11 purchase, b' that which was
14 of the purchase, b' which is
36:16 were afraid b' one and other, and * 413
44:25 wives have b' spoken with your
46:12 the mighty, and they are fallen b' 8147
50: 3 they shall depart, b' man and
51:12 for the Lord hath b' devised and 1571
46 a rumor shall b' come one year, *
La 3:26 good that a man should b' hope *
Eze 9: 6 young, b' maids, and little *
14:22 that shall be brought forth, b' sons
15: 4 the fire devoureth b' the ends of 8147
21:19 b' twain shall come forth out of "
23:13 defiled, that they took b' one way, 8147
29 b' thy lewdness and thy whoredoms.
34:11 I, will b' search my sheep, and *
39: 9 b' the shields and the bucklers,
42:11 their goings out were b' according
Da 8:13 to give b' the sanctuary and the
11:27 And b' these kings' hearts shall 8147
Mic 5: 8 he go through, b' treadeth down *
7: 3 they may do evil with b' hands *
Na 3: 3 horseman lifteth up b' the bright *
Zep 2:14 b' the cormorant and the bittern 1571
Zec 6:13 of peace shall be between them b'. 8147
12: 2 siege b' against Judah and *1571
M't 9:17 new bottles, and b' are preserved. 297
10:28 to destroy b' soul and body in 2532
12:22 blind and dumb b' spake and *
13:30 Let b' grow together until the 297
15:14 blind, b' shall fall into the ditch. "
22:10 many as they found, b' bad 5037
M'r 6:30 him all things, b' what they had * "
7:37 he maketh b' the deaf to hear, * "
Lu 1: 6 they were b' righteous before God, 297
7 they b' were now well stricken in "
2:46 doctors, b' hearing them and 2532
5: 7 they came, and filled b' the ships, 297
36 then b' the new maketh a rent, *2532
38 into new bottles; and b' are * 297
6:39 shall they not b' fall into the ditch? "
7:42 to pay, he frankly forgave them b'. "
21:16 shall be betrayed b' by parents *2532
22:33 thee, b' into prison, and to death. "
Joh 2: 2 And b' Jesus was called, and his "
4:36 that b' he that soweth and he * "
7:28 Ye b' know me, and ye know "
9:37 Thou hast b' seen him, and it is "
11:48 take away b' our place and nation. "
57 Now b' the chief priests and the * "
12:28 saying, I have b' glorified it, and "
15:24 they b' seen and hated b' me and "
20: 4 So they ran b' together: and the 1417
Ac 1: 1 Jesus began b' to do and teach, 5037
8 b' in Jerusalem, and in all Judæa, "
13 b' Peter, and James, and John, "
2:29 patriarch David, that he is b' 2532
36 have crucified, b' Lord and Christ. "
4:27 b' Herod, and Pontius Pilate, 5037
Ac 5:14 to the Lord, multitudes b' of men 5037
8:12 they were baptized, b' men and "
38 and they went down b' into the 297
38 b' Philip and the eunuch; and he 5037
10:39 b' in the land of the Jews, and in "
14: 1 that they went b' together into
1 b' of the Jews and also of the 5037
5 b' of the Gentiles, and also of the "
19:10 Lord Jesus, b' Jews and Greeks. "
20:21 b' to the Jews, and also to the "
21:12 b' we, and they of that place, "
22: 4 delivering into prisons b' men and "
23: 8 but the Pharisees confess b'. 297
24:15 of the dead, b' of the just and 5037
25:24 b' at Jerusalem, and also here, "
26:16 a witness b' of these things which "
22 witnessing b' to small and great, "
29 hear me this day, were b' *2532
28:23 b' out of the law of Moses, and out 5037
Ro 1:12 by the mutual faith b' of you and "
14 b' to the Greeks, and to the "
14 b' to the wise, and to the unwise. "
3: 9 b' Jews and Gentiles, that they "
11:33 the riches b' of the wisdom and 2532
14: 9 For to this end Christ b' died, * "
9 be Lord b' of the dead and living. "
1Co 1: 2 Jesus Christ our Lord, b' theirs *5037
24 b' Jews and Greeks, Christ the "
4: 5 Lord come, who b' will bring to 2532
11 we b' hunger, and thirst, and are "
6:13 God shall destroy b' it and them. "
14 And God hath b' raised up the "
7:29 it remaineth, that b' they that "
34 that she may be holy b' in body "
2Co 9:10 to the sower b' minister bread * "
Eph 1:10 b' which are in heaven, and *5037
2:14 our peace, who hath made b' one, 297
16 he might reconcile b' unto God "
18 through him we b' have access "
Ph'p 1: 7 inasmuch as b' in my bonds, and 5037
2:13 God which worketh in you b' to 2532
4: 9 things which ye have b' learned, "
12 I know b' how to be abased, and * "
12 b' to be full and to be hungry, b' "
1Th 2:15 Who b' killed the Lord Jesus, and "
5:15 is good, b' among yourselves, * "
1Ti 4:10 For therefore we b' labour and * "
16 shalt b' save thyself, and them "
Tit 1: 9 able by sound doctrine b' to exhort "
Ph'm 16 thee, b' in the flesh, and in the "
Heb 2: 4 b' with signs and wonders, and 5037
11 For b' he that sanctifieth and they "
5: 1 that he may offer b' gifts and "
14 exercised to discern b' good and * "
6:19 an anchor of the soul, b' sure and "
9: 9 offered b' gifts and sacrifices, "
19 sprinkled b' the book, and all the "
21 he sprinkled with blood b' the *2532
10:33 b' by reproaches and afflictions; 5037
11:21 blessed b' the sons of Joseph; *1538
Jas 3:12 so can no fountain b' yield salt *
2Pe 3: 1 in b' which I stir up your pure
18 To him be glory b' now and for 2532
2Jo 9 he hath b' the Father and the Son. "
Jude 25 dominion and power, b' now and *
Re 13:15 image of the beast should b' speak, "
16 And he causeth all, b' small and
19: 5 ye that fear him, b' small and *
18 all men, b' free and bond, 5037
18 b' small and great. *2532
20 These b' were cast alive into a *1417

bottle See also BOTTLES.
Ge 21:14 took bread, and a b' of water, 2573
15 the water was spent in the b', and "
19 filled the b' with water, and gave "
J'g 4:19 she opened a b' of milk, and gave 4997
1Sa 1:24 one ephah of flour, and a b' of 5035
10: 3 another carrying a b' of wine:
16:20 and a b' of wine, and a kid, and 4997
2Sa 16: 1 summer fruits, and a b' of wine. 5035
Ps 56: 8 put thou my tears into thy b': 4997
119:83 am become like a b' in the smoke; "
Jer 13:12 Every b' shall be filled with wine: 5035
12 not certainly know that every b' "
19: 1 get a potter's earthen b', and take 1228
10 Then shalt thou break the b' in "
Hab 2:15 that puttest thy b' to him, and *2573

bottles
Jos 9: 4 and wine b', old, and rent, and *4997
13 these b' of wine, which we filled, * "
1Sa 25:18 two b' of wine, and five sheep 5035
Job 32:19 it is ready to burst like new b'. 178
38:37 or who can stay the b' of heaven, 5035
Jer 48:12 his vessels, and break their b'. "
Ho 7: 5 have made him sick with b' of *2573
M't 9:17 put new wine into old b': * 779
17 else the b' break, and the wine * "
17 runneth out, and the b' perish: * "
17 put new wine into new b', * "
M'r 2:22 putteth new wine into old b': * "
22 new wine doth burst the b', * "
22 spilled, and the b' will be * "
22 wine must be put into new b', * "
Lu 5:37 putteth new wine into old b'; * "
37 new wine will burst the b', and * "
37 spilled, and the b' shall perish. * "
38 wine must be put into new b'; * "

bottom See also BOTTOMLESS; BOTTOMS.
Ex 15: 5 they sank into the b' as a stone. 4688
29:12 blood beside the b' of the altar. *3247
Le 4: 7 blood of the bullock at the b' of * "
18 blood at the b' of the altar of the * "
25 pour out his blood at the b' of the* "
30 thereof at the b' of the altar. * "
34 thereof at the b' of the altar: * "
Le 5: 9 blood shall be wrung out at the b' *3247
8:15 the blood at the b' of the altar. * "
9: 9 poured out the blood at the b' of * "
Job 36:30 and covereth the b' of the sea. 8328
Ca 3:10 b' thereof of gold, the covering 7507
Eze 43:13 even the b' shall be a cubit, and 2436
14 And from the b' upon the ground "
17 and the b' thereof shall be a cubit "
Dan 6:24 or ever they came at the b' of the 773
Am 9: 3 in the b' of the sea, thence will I 7172
Zec 1: 8 myrtle trees that were in the b'; 4699
M't 27:51 from the top to the b'; and the 2736
M'k 15:38 in twain from the top to the b'. "

bottoms
Jon 2: 6 I went down to the b' of the 7095

bottomless
Rev 9: 1 was given the key of the b' pit. * 12
2 And he opened the b' pit; * "
11 the angel of the b' pit, whose * "
11: 7 that ascendeth out of the b' pit * "
17: 8 and shall ascend out of the b' pit, * "
20: 1 having the key of the b' pit and a * "
3 cast him into the b' pit, and shut * "

bough See also BOUGHS.
Ge 49:22 Joseph is a fruitful b', 1121
22 even a fruitful b' by a well; "
J'g 9:48 and cut down a b' from the trees, 7754
49 cut down every man his b', and "
Isa 10:33 the Lord of hosts, shall lop the b' 6288
17: 6 the top of the uppermost b', four 534
9 strong cities be as a forsaken b', *2793

boughs
Le 23:40 the b' of goodly trees, branches *6529
40 and the b' of thick trees, and 6057
De 24:20 thou shalt not go over the b' 6288
2Sa 18: 9 the thick b' of a great oak, and 7730
Job 14: 9 will bud, and bring forth b' like 7105
Ps 80:10 and the b' thereof were like the 6057
11 She sent out her b' unto the sea, *7105
Ca 7: 8 I will take hold of the b' thereof: *5577
Isa 27:11 When the b' thereof are 7105
Eze 17:23 it shall bring forth b', and bear 6057
31: 3 his top was among the thick b'. 5688
5 his b' were multiplied, and his 5634
6 heaven made their nests in his b', 5589
8 the fir trees were not like his b', "
10 up his top among the thick b', 5688
12 his b' are broken by all the rivers 6288
14 up their top among the thick b', 5688
Da 4:12 of the heaven dwelt in the b' *6056

bought
Ge 17:12 or b' with money of any stranger, 4736
13 and he that is b' with thy money, "
23 all that were b' with his money, "
27 b' with money of the stranger, "
33:19 And he b' a parcel of a field, 7069
39: 1 b' him of the hands of the "
47:14 for the corn which they b': 7666
20 And Joseph b' all the land of 7069
22 Only the land of the priests b' he "
23 Behold, I have b' you this day and "
49:30 which Abraham b' with the field "
50:13 which Abraham b' with the field "
Ex 12:44 man's servant that is b' for 4736
Le 25:28 hand of him that hath b' it until 7069
30 to him that b' it throughout his "
50 him that b' him from the year "
51 of the money that he was b' for. 4736
27:22 field which he hath b', which is "
24 unto him of whom it was b', even 7069
De 32: 6 he thy father that hath b' thee? "
Jos 24:32 which Jacob b' of the sons of "
Ru 4: 9 that I have b' all that was "
2Sa 12: 3 which he had b' and nourished up: "
24:24 So David b' the threshingfloor and "
1Ki 16:24 And he b' the hill Samaria of "
Ne 5:16 of this wall, neither b' we any "
Isa 43:24 Thou hast b' me no sweet cane "
Jer 32: 9 And I b' the field of Hanameel my "
43 And fields shall be b' in this land, "
Ho 3: 2 So I b' her to me for fifteen pieces 3739
M't 13:46 and sold all that he had, and b' it. 59
21:12 sold and b' in the temple, and "
27: 7 b' with them the potter's field, to "
M'r 11:15 cast out them that sold and b' in "
15:46 he b' fine linen, and took him "
16: 1 had b' sweet spices, that they "
Lu 14:18 I have b' a piece of ground, and I "
19 I have b' five yoke of oxen, and I go "
17:28 they did eat, they drank, they b', "
19:45 that sold therein, and them that b'; "
Ac 7:16 Abraham b' for a sum of money of 5608
1Co 6:20 For ye are b' with a price: 59
7:23 Ye are b' with a price; be not ye "
2Pe 2: 1 denying the Lord that b' them, and "

bound See also BOUNDS.
Ge 22: 9 and b' Isaac his son, and laid 6123
38:28 and b' upon his hand a scarlet 7194
39:20 where the king's prisoners were b': 631
40: 3 the place where Joseph was b'. "
5 Egypt, which were b' in the prison. "
42:19 let one of your brethren be b' in "
24 Simeon, and b' him before their "
44:30 seeing that his life is b' up in the 7194
49:26 the utmost b' of the everlasting 8379
Ex 12:34 their kneadingtroughs being b' 6887
Le 8: 7 and b' it unto him therewith. 640
Nu 19:15 vessel, which hath no covering b' 6616
30: 4 her bond wherein she hath b' her 631
4 wherewith she hath b' her soul, "
5 bonds wherewith she hath b' her "
6 out of her lips, wherewith she b' "
7 wherewith she b' her soul shall "
8 wherewith she b' her soul, of none "

Nu 30: 9 have b' their souls, shall stand 631
10 house, or b' her soul by a bond "
11 every bond wherewith she b' her "
Jos 2:21 and she b' the scarlet line in the 7194
9: 4 wine bottles, old, and rent, and b' 6887
J'g 15:13 they b' him with two new cords, 631
16: 6 wherewith thou mightest be b' to "
8 not been dried, and she b' him "
10 thee, wherewith thou mightest be b'. "
13 me wherewith thou mightest be b'. "
21 and b' him with fetters of brass; "
1Sa 25:29 the soul of my lord shall be b' in 6887
2Sa 3:34 Thy hands were not b', nor thy 631
2Ki 5:23 and b' two talents of silver in two 6887
17: 4 of Assyria shut him up, and b' him 631
25: 7 and b' him with fetters of brass, "
2Ch 33:11 and b' him with fetters, and "
36: 6 and b' him in fetters, to carry him "
Job 36: 8 if they be b' in fetters, and be "
38:20 to the b' thereof, and that thou 1366
Ps 68: 6 bringeth out those which are b' * 615
104: 9 Thou hast set a b' that they may 1366
107:10 shadow of death, being b' in 615
Pr 22:15 Foolishness is b' in the heart of a 7194
30: 4 who hath b' the waters in a 6887
Isa 1: 6 have not been closed, neither b' 2280
22: 3 they are b' by the archers: 631
3 all that are found in thee are b' "
61: 1 of the prison to them that are b'; "
Jer 5:22 the b' of the sea by a perpetual 1366
30:13 thy cause, that thou mayest be b' 4205
39: 7 and b' him with chains to carry 631
40: 1 being b' in chains among all that "
52:11 and the king of Babylon b' him "
La 1:14 yoke of my transgressions is b' by 8244
Eze 27:24 apparel, b' with cords, and made 2280
30:21 it shall not be b' up to be healed, "
34: 4 neither have ye b' up that which "
Da 3:21 Then these men were b' in their 3729
23 fell down b' into the midst of the "
24 Did not we cast three men b' into "
Ho 4:19 The wind hath b' her up in her *6887
5:10 them that remove the b': *1366
7:15 I have b' and strengthened their *3256
13:12 The iniquity of Ephraim is b' up; 6887
Na 3:10 and all her great men were b' in 7576
M't 14: 3 laid hold on John, and b' him, 1210
16:19 on earth shall be b' in heaven: "
18:18 on earth shall be b' in heaven; "
27: 2 when they had b' him, they led him "
M'k 5: 4 had been often b' with fetters and "
6:17 laid hold upon John, and b' him in "
15: 1 and b' Jesus, and carried him "
7 Barabbas, which lay b' with them "
Lu 8:29 he was kept b' with chains and in 1196
10:34 And went to him, and b' up his 2611
13:16 whom Satan hath b', lo, these 1210
Joh 11:44 b' hand and foot with "
44 his face was b' about with a 4019
18:12 the Jews took Jesus and b' him, 1210
24 Now Annas had sent him b' unto "
Ac 9: 2, 21 he might bring them b' unto "
12: 6 b' with two chains: and the "
20:22 I go b' in the spirit unto "
21:11 b' his own hands and feet, and "
13 I am ready not to be b' only, but "
33 commanded him to be b' with * "
22: 5 b' unto Jerusalem, for to be "
25 as they b' him with thongs, Paul *4385
29 a Roman, and because he had b' 1210
23:12 and b' themselves under a curse, 332
14 b' ourselves under a great curse, "
21 have b' themselves with an oath, "
24:27 the Jews a pleasure, left Paul b'. *1210
28:20 hope of Israel I am b' with this 4029
Ro 7: 2 which hath an husband is b' by 1210
1Co 7:27 Art thou b' unto a wife? seek not "
39 The wife is b' by the law as long as "
2Th 1: 3 We are b' to thank God always 3784
2:13 we are b' to give thanks alway "
2Ti 2: 9 but the word of God is not b'. 1210
He 13: 3 them that are in bonds, as b' 4887
Re 9:14 Loose the four angels which are b' 1210
20: 2 Satan, and b' him a thousand "

bounds
Ex 19:12 thou shalt set b' unto the people 1379
23 Set b' about the mount, and "
23:31 set thy b' from the Red sea even *1366
De 32: 8 he set the b' of the people 1367
Job 14: 5 hast appointed his b' that he 2706
26:10 waters with b', until the day * "
Isa 10:13 removed the b' of the people, 1367
Ac 17:26 and the b' of their habitation; 3734

bountiful
Pr 22: 9 hath a b' eye shall be blessed; 2896
Isa 32: 5 nor the churl said to be b'. 7771

bountifully
Ps 13: 6 he hath dealt b' with me. 1580
116: 7 the Lord hath dealt b' with thee. "
119:17 Deal b' with thy servant, that I "
142: 7 thou shalt deal b' with me. "
2Co 9: 6 which soweth b' shall reap also b'. 2129

bountifulness
2Co 9:11 thing to all b', which causeth * 572

bounty
1Ki 10:13 Solomon gave her of his royal b'. 3027
2Co 9: 5 your b', whereof ye had notice 2129
5 might be ready, as a matter of b', "

bow See also BOWED; BOWETH; BOWING; BOWMEN; BOWS; BOWSHOT.
Ge 9:13 I do set my b' in the cloud, and it 7198
14 the b' shall be seen in the cloud: "
16 And the b' shall be in the cloud; "
27: 3 thy weapons, thy quiver and thy b', "
27:29 and nations b' down to thee: 7812
29 thy mother's sons b' down to thee: "
37:10 come to b' down ourselves to thee "
41:43 cried before him, B' the knee: 86
48:22 with my sword and with my b'. 7198
49: 8 children shall b' down before thee. 7812
24 his b' abode in strength, and the 7198
Ex 11: 8 and b' down themselves unto me, 7812
20: 5 Thou shalt not b' down thyself "
23:24 Thou shalt not b' down to their "
Le 26: 1 in your land, to b' down unto it: "
De 5: 9 Thou shalt not b' down thyself "
Jos 23: 7 nor b' yourselves unto them: "
24:12 with thy sword, nor with thy b'. 7198
J'g 2:19 them, and to b' down unto them; 7812
1Sa 18: 4 and to his b', and to his girdle. 7198
2Sa 1:18 of Judah the use of the b': "
22 the b' of Jonathan turned not back, "
22:35 a b' of steel is broken by mine "
1Ki 22:34 certain man drew a b' at a venture, "
2Ki 5:18 b' myself in the house of Rimmon: 7812
18 when I b' down myself in the "
6:22 with thy sword and with thy b'? 7198
9:24 drew a b' with his full strength, "
13:15 said unto him, Take b' and arrows. "
15 he took unto him b' and arrows. "
16 Put thine hand upon the b'. And "
17:35 other gods, nor b' yourselves to 7812
19:16 Lord, b' down thine ear and *5186
1Ch 5:18 to shoot with b', and skilful in 7198
12: 2 arrows out of a b', even of Saul's "
2Ch 17:17 armed men with b' and shield "
18:33 certain man drew a b' at a venture, "
Job 20:24 the b' of steel shall strike him "
29:20 my b' was renewed in my hand. "
31:10 and let others b' down upon her. 3766
39: 3 They b' themselves, they bring "
Ps 7:12 bent his b', and made it ready. 7198
11: 2 bend their b', they make ready "
18:34 a b' of steel is broken by mine "
22:29 go down to the dust shall b' 3766
31: 2 B' down thine ear to me; deliver 5186
37:14 have bent their b', to cast down 7198
44: 6 I will not trust in my b', neither "
46: 9 he breaketh the b', and cutteth "
58: 7 bendeth his b' to shoot his arrows, *
72: 9 wilderness shall b' before him; 3766
76: 3 the arrows of the b', the shield, 7198
78:57 turned aside like a deceitful b'. "
86: 1 B' down thine ear, O Lord, hear 5186
95: 6 let us worship and b' down: 3766
144: 5 B' thy heavens, O Lord, and 5186
Pr 5: 1 b' thine ear to my understanding:* "
14:19 The evil b' before the good; and 7817
22:17 B' down thine ear, and hear the *5186
Ec 12: 3 strong men shall b' themselves, 5791
Isa 10: 4 Without me they shall b' down 3766
21:15 sword, and from the bent b', 7198
41: 2 and as driven stubble to his b'. "
45:23 unto me every knee shall b', every 3766
46: 2 stoop, they b' down together; "
49:23 b' down to thee with their face 7812
51:23 B' down, that we may go over: "
58: 5 b' down his head as a bulrush, 3721
60:14 shall b' themselves down at the 7812
65:12 all b' down to the slaughter: 3766
66:19 Pul, and Lud, that draw the b', 7198
Jer 6:23 shall lay hold on b' and spear; "
9: 3 bend their tongues like their b' "
46: 9 that handle and bend the b'. "
49:35 I will break the b' of Elam, the "
50:14 all ye that bend the b', shoot at "
29 all ye that bend the b', camp "
42 shall hold the b' and the lance: "
51: 3 bendeth his b', and against him "
La 2: 4 hath bent his b' like an enemy: "
3:12 He hath bent his b', and set me as "
Eze 1:28 As the appearance of the b' that is "
39: 3 smite thy b' out of thy left hand, "
Ho 1: 5 I will break the b' of Israel "
7 not save them by b', nor by sword, "
2:18 and I will break the b' and the "
7:16 they are like a deceitful b': "
Am 2:15 he stand that handleth the b'; "
Mic 6: 6 b' myself before the high God? 3721
Hab 3: 6 the perpetual hills did b': 7817
9 Thy b' was made quite naked, 7198
Zec 9:10 and the battle b' shall be cut off: "
13 filled the b' with Ephraim, and "
10: 4 out of him the battle b', out of "
Ro 11:10 and b' down their back alway. *4781
14:11 every knee shall b' to me, and 2578
Eph 3:14 I b' my knees unto the Father "
Ph'p 2:10 of Jesus every knee should b', "
Re 6: 2 he that sat on him had a b'; 5115

bowed
Ge 18: 2 and b' himself toward the ground, 7812
19: 1 b' himself with his face toward "
23: 7 and b' himself to the people 7812
12 b' down himself before the people "
24:26 the man b' down his head, and 6915
48 b' down my head, and worshipped "
33: 3 and b' himself to the ground 7812
6 children, and they b' themselves. "
7 came near, and b' themselves: "
7 and Rachel, and they b' themselves. "
42: 6 and b' down themselves before "
43:26 and b' themselves to him to the * "
28 And they b' down their heads, 6915
47:31 Israel b' himself upon the bed's 7812
48:12 b' himself with his face to the "
49:15 and b' his shoulder to bear, and 5186
Ex 4:31 b' their heads and worshipped. 6915
12:27 b' the head and worshipped. "
34: 8 Moses made haste, and b' his head "
Nu 22:31 he b' down his head, and fell flat "
25: 2 eat, and b' down to their gods. 7812
Jos 23:16 gods, and b' yourselves to them; * "
J'g 2:12 and b' themselves unto them, and "
17 and b' themselves unto them: "
5:27 he b', he fell, he lay down: 3766
27 at her feet he b', he fell: "
27 where he b', there he fell "
7: 6 people b' down upon their knees "
16:30 he b' himself with all his might; 5186
Ru 2:10 and b' herself to the ground, and 7812
1Sa 4:19 she b' herself and travailed: for 3766
20:41 and b' himself three times: 7812
24: 8 face to the earth, and b' himself. * "
25:23 and b' herself to the ground, "
41 b' herself on her face to the earth, "
28:14 to the ground, and b' himself. * "
2Sa 9: 8 And he b' himself, and said, * "
14:22 b' himself, and thanked the king:* "
33 the king, and b' himself on his face "
18:21 And Cushi b' himself unto Joab, "
19:14 And he b' the heart of all the men 5186
22:10 He b' the heavens also, and "
24:20 b' himself before the king on his 7812
1Ki 1:16 Bath-sheba b', and did obeisance 6915
23 he b' himself before the king 7812
31 Bath-sheba b' with her face to the 6915
47 the king b' himself upon the bed. 7812
53 and b' himself to king Solomon: * "
2:19 to meet her, and b' himself unto "
19:18 which have not b' unto Baal, 3766
2Ki 2:15 and b' themselves to the ground 7812
4:37 and b' herself to the ground, "
1Ch 21:21 b' himself to David with his face "
29:20 and b' down their heads, and 6915
2Ch 7: 3 the house, they b' themselves 3766
20:18 Jehoshaphat b' his head with his 6915
25:14 b' down himself before them, and 7812
29:29 present with him b' themselves 3766
30 b' their heads and worshipped. 6915
Ne 8: 6 b' their heads, and worshipped "
Es 3: 2 b', and reverenced Haman: 3766
2 Mordecai b' not, nor did him "
5 Haman saw that Mordecai b' not, "
Ps 18: 9 He b' the heavens also, and 5186
35:14 I b' down heavily, as one that 7817
38: 6 b' down greatly; I go mourning "
44:25 our soul is b' down to the dust: 7743
57: 6 my soul is b' down: they have 3721
145:14 all those that be b' down. "
146: 8 raiseth them that are b' down: "
Isa 2:11 of men shall be b' down, 7817
17 loftiness of man shall be b' down, "
21: 3 I was b' down at hearing of it; *5791
M't 27:29 and they b' the knee before him, *1120
Lu 13:11 was b' together, and could in no 4794
24: 5 afraid, and b' down their faces 2827
Joh 19:30 b' his head, and gave up the ghost. "
Ro 11: 4 have not b' the knee to the image 2578

bowels
Ge 15: 4 of thine own b' shall be thine 4578
25:23 shall be separated from thy b'; "
43:30 his b' did yearn upon his brother: 7358
Nu 5:22 the curse shall go into thy b', 4578
2Sa 7:12 which shall proceed out of thy b', "
16:11 which came forth of my b', "
20:10 and shed out his b' to the ground, "
1Ki 3:26 her b' yearned upon her son, 7358
2Ch 21:15 of thy b', until thy b' fall out by 4578
18 the Lord smote him in his b' with "
19 his b' fell out by reason of his "
32:21 they that came forth of his own b' "
Job 20:14 his meat in his b' is turned, it is "
30:27 My b' boiled, and rested not: "
Ps 22:14 it is melted in the midst of my b'. "
71: 6 took me out of my mother's b': "
109:18 into his b' like water, and like *7130
Ca 5: 4 and my b' were moved for him. *4578
Isa 16:11 my b' shall sound like an harp for "
48:19 the offspring of thy b' like the "
49: 1 from the b' of my mother hath "
63:15 the sounding of my b' and of thy "
Jer 4:19 My b', my b'! I am pained at my "
31:20 my b' are troubled for him; "
La 1:20 my b' are troubled; mine heart "
2:11 my b' are troubled, my liver is "
Eze 3: 3 and fill thy b' with this roll that "
7:19 their souls, neither fill their b': "
Ac 1:18 and all his b' gushed out. 4698
2Co 6:12 are straightened in your own b'. * "
Ph'p 1: 8 you all in the b' of Jesus Christ. * "
2: 1 Spirit, if any b' and mercies, * "
Col 3:12 b' of mercies, kindness, * "
Ph'm 7 the b' of the saints are refreshed * "
12 receive him, that is, mine own b': * "
20 refresh my b' in the Lord. * "
1Jo 3:17 shutteth up his b' of compassion * "

boweth
J'g 7: 5 every one that b' down upon 3766
Isa 2: 9 And the mean man b' down, *7817
46: 1 Bel b' down, Nebo stoopeth, 3766

bowing
Ge 24:52 worshipped the Lord, b' *
Ps 17:11 have set their eyes b' down *5186
62: 3 as a b' wall shall ye be, and as a †5186
M'r 15:19 b' their knees worshipped him. 5087

bowl See also BOWLS.
Nu 7:13, 19, 25, 31, 37, 43, 49, 55, 61, 67, 73,
79 one silver b' of seventy shekels, 4219
85 and thirty shekels, each b' seventy: "
J'g 6:38 of the fleece, a b' full of water. 5602
Ec 12: 6 or the golden b' be broken, 1543
Zec 4: 2 with a b' upon the top of it, and his "
3 upon the right side of the b', "

bowls
Ex 25:29 covers thereof, and b' thereof, 4518
31 his branches, his b', his knops, *1375
33 Three b' made like unto almonds,* "
33 three b' made like almonds in * "
34 four b' made like unto almonds, * "
37:16 his spoons, and his b', and his 4518
17 his branch, his b', his knops, *1375
19 Three b' made after the fashion * "
19 and three b' made like almonds * "
20 in the candlestick were four b' * "
Nu 4: 7 the spoons, and the b', and 4518
7:84 twelve silver b', twelve spoons 4219
1Ki 7:41 the two b' of the chapiters that 1543
41 the two b' of the chapiters which "
42 cover the two b' of the chapiters "
50 And the b', and the snuffers, *5592
2Ki 12:13 house of the Lord b' of silver, * "
25:15 firepans, and the b', and such *4219
1Ch 28:17 for the fleshhooks, and the b', * "
Jer 52:18 the snuffers, and the b', and the * "
19 the firepans, and the b', and the "
Am 6: 6 That drink wine in b', and anoint "
Zec 9:15 they shall be filled like b', and as "
14:20 shall be like b' before the altar. "

bowmen
Jer 4:29 of the horsemen and b'; 7411, 7198

bows
1Sa 2: 4 b' of the mighty men are broken, 7198
1Ch 12: 2 They were armed with b', "
2Ch 14: 8 bare shields and drew b', "
26:14 helmets, and habergeons, and b', "
Ne 4:13 swords, their spears, and their b'. "
16 spears, the shields, and the b', "
Ps 37:15 and their b' shall be broken. "
64: 3 and bend their b' to shoot their *
78: 9 being armed, and carrying b', 7198
Isa 5:28 all their b' bent, their horses "
7:24 With arrows and with b' shall "
13:18 Their b' also shall dash the young "
Jer 51:56 every one of their b' is broken: "

bowshot
Ge 21:16 way off, as it were a b': 2909, 7198

box
2Ki 9: 1 take this b' of oil in thine hand, *6378
3 Then take the b' of oil, and pour* "
Isa 41:19 pine, and the b' tree together: 8391
60:13 and the b' together, to beautify "
M't 26: 7 having an alabaster b' of very * 211
M'r 14: 3 having an alabaster b' of * "
3 she brake the b', and poured it * "
Lu 7:37 brought an alabaster b' of * "

box-tree See BOX and TREE.

boy See also BOYS.
Joe 3: 3 given a b' for an harlot, and 3206

boys
Ge 25:27 And the b' grew: and Esau was 5288
Zec 8: 5 b' and girls playing in the streets 3206

Bozez (bo'-zez)
1Sa 14: 4 and the name of the one was B', 949

Bozkath (boz'-kath) See also BOSCATH.
Jos 15:39 Lachish, and B', and Eglon, 1218

Boznai See SHETHAR-BOZNAI.

Bozrah (boz'-rah)
Ge 36:33 the son of Zerah of B' reigned 1224
1Ch 1:44 Jobab the son of Zerah of B', "
Isa 34: 6 the Lord hath a sacrifice in B', "
63: 1 with dyed garments from B'? "
Jer 48:24 And upon Kerioth, and upon B', "
49:13 that B' shall become a desolation, "
22 and spread his wings over B': "
Am 1:12 shall devour the palaces of B'. "
Mic 2:12 them together as the sheep of B'. "

bracelet See also BRACELETS.
2Sa 1:10 and the b' that was on his arm, 685

bracelets
Ge 24:22 two b' for her hands of ten 6781
30 b' upon his sister's hands, "
47 and the b' upon her hands. "
38:18 Thy signet, and thy b', and thy *6616
25 the signet, and b', and staff. * "
Ex 35:22 brought b', and earrings, and *2397
Nu 31:50 jewels of gold, chains, and b', 6781
Isa 3:19 The chains, and the b', and the 8285
Eze 16:11 I put b' upon thy hands, 6781
23:42 b' upon their hands, and "

braided See BROIDED.

brake See also BRAKEST.
Ex 9:25 b' every tree of the field. 7665
32: 3 people b' off the golden earrings 6561
19 and b' them beneath the mount. 7665
De 9:17 and b' them before your eyes. "
J'g 7:19 the trumpets, and b' the pitchers 5310
20 the trumpets, and b' the pitchers, 7665
9:53 head, and all to b' his skull. 7533
16: 9 And he b' the withs, as a thread 5423
12 he b' them from off his arms "
1Sa 4:18 and his neck b', and he died: 7665
2Sa 23:16 three mighty men b' through 1234
1Ki 19:11 and b' in pieces the rocks before 7665
2Ki 10:27 they b' down the image of Baal, 5422
27 and b' down the house of Baal, "
11:18 house of Baal, and b' it down; "
18 his images b' they in pieces 7665
14:13 b' down the wall of Jerusalem 6555
18: 4 and b' the images, and cut down 7665
4 b' in pieces the brasen serpent 3807
23: 7 And he b' down the houses of 5422
8 and b' down the high places "
12 and b' them down from thence, *7323
14 And he b' in pieces the images, 7665
2Ki 23:15 the high place he b' down, and 5422
25:10 b' down the walls of Jerusalem "
1Ch 11:18 And the three b' through the host 1234
2Ch 14: 3 and b' down the images, and cut 7665
21:17 and b' into it, and carried away 1234
23:17 the house of Baal, and b' it down, 5422
17 and b' his altars and his images 7665
25:23 b' down the wall of Jerusalem 6555
26: 6 and b' down the wall of Gath, "
31: 1 and b' the images in pieces, 7665
34: 4 they b' down the altars of Baalim 5422
4 images, he b' in pieces, 7665
36:19 b' down the wall of Jerusalem, 5422
Job 29:17 I b' the jaws of the wicked, 7665
38: 8 when it b' forth, as if it had 1518
10 b' up for it my decreed place, †‡7665
Ps 76: 3 b' he the arrows of the bow, "
105:16 he b' the whole staff of bread. "
33 and b' the trees of their coasts. "
106:29 inventions: and the plague b' in 6555
107:14 and b' their bands in sunder. 5423
Jer 28:10 off...Jeremiah's neck, and b' it. 7665
31:32 my covenant they b', although 6565
39: 8 b' down the walls of Jerusalem. 5422
52:14 b' down all the walls of Jerusalem "
17 the Chaldeans b', and carried *7665
Eze 17:16 whose covenant he b', even with 6565
Da 2: 1 and his sleep b' from him. 1961
34 and clay, and b' them to pieces. 1855
45 that it b' in pieces the iron, "
6:24 and b' all their bones in pieces "
7: 7 it devoured and b' in pieces, "
19 which devoured, b' in pieces, "
8: 7 the ram, and b' his two horns: 7665
M't 14:19 he blessed, and b', and gave 2806
15:36 and gave thanks, and b' them, "
26:26 bread, and blessed it, and b' "
M'r 6:41 and b' the loaves, and gave them 2622
8: 6 and gave thanks, and b', and 2806
19 When I b' the five loaves among "
14: 3 and she b' the box, and poured 4937
22 took bread, and blessed, and b' 2806
Lu 5: 6 of fishes: and their net b'. *1284
8:29 he b' the bands, and was * "
9:16 he blessed them, and b', and 2622
22:19 and gave thanks, and b' it, 2806
24:30 and blessed it, and b', and gave ‡ "
Joh 19:32 and b' the legs of the first, and of 2608
33 already, they b' not his legs: "
1Co 11:24 he b' it, and said, Take, eat: 2806

brakest
Ex 34: 1 the first tables, which thou b'. 7665
De 10: 2 the first tables which thou b', "
Ps 74:13 thou b' the heads of the dragons "
14 Thou b' the heads of leviathan 7533
Eze 29: 7 they leaned upon thee, thou b', 7665

bramble See also BRAMBLES.
J'g 9:14 said all the trees unto the b', 329
15 the b' said unto the trees, If in "
15 let fire come out of the b', and "
Lu 6:44 of a b' bush gather they grapes. 942

brambles
Isa 34:13 nettles and b' in the fortresses *2336

branch See also BRANCHES.
Ex 25:33 in one b'; and three bowls made 7070
33 like almonds in the other b', "
37:17 his shaft, and his b', his bowls, * "
19 fashion of the almonds in one b', "
19 made like almonds in another b', "
Nu 13:23 cut down from thence a b' with 2156
Job 8:16 b' shooteth forth in his garden. *3127
14: 7 tender b' thereof will not cease. "
15:32 and his b' shall not be green. 3712
18:16 above shall his b' be cut off. 7105
29:19 dew lay all night upon my b'. "
Ps 80:15 the b' that thou madest strong 1121
Pr 11:28 righteous shall flourish as a b'. *5929
Isa 4: 2 day shall the b' of the Lord 6780
9:14 head and tail, b' and rush, *3712
11: 1 B' shall grow out of his roots: 5342
14:19 like an abominable b', and as the "
17: 9 bough, and an uppermost b', * 534
19:15 the head or tail, b' or rush, may *3712
25: 5 the b' of the terrible ones shall *2158
60:21 the b' of my planting, the work of 5342
Jer 23: 5 raise unto David a righteous B', 6780
33:15 at that time, will I cause the B' of "
Eze 8:17 and, lo, they put the b' to their 2156
15: 2 a b' which is among the trees of "
17: 3 and took the highest b' of the *6788
22 the highest b' of the high cedar. * "
Da 11: 7 out of a b' of her roots shall *5342
Zec 3: 8 bring forth my servant the B'. 6780
6:12 the man whose name is The B': "
Mal 4: 1 leave them neither root nor b'. 6057
M't 24:32 When his b' is yet tender, and 2798
M'k 13:28 When her b' is yet tender, and "
Joh 15: 2 Every b' in me that beareth not 2814
2 and every b' that beareth fruit. "
4 As the b' cannot bear fruit of 2814
6 he is cast forth as a b', and is "

branches
Ge 40:10 And in the vine were three b': 8299
12 The three b' are three days: "
49:22 a well; whose b' run over the 1121
Ex 25:31 his shaft, and his b', his bowls, *7070
32 six b' shall come out of the sides "
32 three b' of the candlestick out of "
32 and three b' of the candlestick "
33 so in the six b' that come out of "
35 a knop under two b' of the same, "
35 and a knop under two b' of the "
35 a knop under two b' of the same, "
35 according to the six b' "
Ex 25:36 and their b' shall be of the same: 7070
37:18 six b' going out of the sides "
18 three b' of the candlestick out of "
18 three b' of the candlestick out of "
19 so throughout the six b' going out "
21 a knop under two b' of the same, "
21 a knop under two b' of the same, "
21 a knop under two b' of the same, "
21 according to the six b' going out of "
22 Their knops and their b' were of "
Le 23:40 b' of palm trees, and the boughs 3709
Ne 8:15 and fetch olive b', and pine b', 5929
15 and myrtle b', and palm b', "
15 and b' of thick trees, "
Job 15:30 the flame shall dry up his b', and 3127
Ps 80:11 unto the sea, and her b' unto the* "
104:12 which sing among the b'. 6073
Isa 16: 8 her b' are stretched out, they 7976
17: 6 in the outmost fruitful b' thereof, 5585
18: 5 take away and cut down the b'. 5189
27:10 lie down, and consume the b' 5585
Jer 11:16 it, and the b' of it are broken. 1808
Eze 17: 6 whose b' turned toward him, and "
6 brought forth b', and shot forth 905
7 and shot forth her b' toward him, 1808
8 that it might bring forth b', and 6057
23 the shadow of the b' thereof shall 1808
19:10 fruitful and full of b' by reason 6058
11 was exalted among the thick b', *5688
11 with the multitude of her b'. 1808
14 fire is gone out of a rod of her b' 905
31: 3 a cedar in Lebanon with fair b', 6057
5 his b' became long because of the 6288
6 under his b' did all the beasts "
7 greatness, in the length of his b': 1808
8 chestnut trees were not like his b'; 6288
9 fair by the multitude of his b': 1808
12 in all the valleys his b' are fallen, "
13 of the field shall be upon his b': 6288
36: 8 ye shall shoot forth your b', and 6057
Da 4:14 cut off his b', shake off his leaves, 6056
14 under it, and the fowls from his b': "
21 and upon whose b' the fowls of "
Ho 11: 6 consume his b', and devour them,* 905
14: 6 His b' shall spread, and his 3127
Joe 1: 7 the b' thereof are made white. 8299
Na 2: 2 out, and marred their vine b'. 2156
Zec 4:12 these two olive b' which through 7641
M't 13:32 come and lodge in the b' thereof. 2798
21: 8 others cut down b' from the trees, "
M'r 4:32 shooteth out great b'; so that "
11: 8 others cut down b' off the trees, 4746
Lu 13:19 fowls of the air lodged in the b' 2798
Joh 12:13 Took b' of palm trees, and went 902
15: 5 I am the vine, ye are the b': 2814
Ro 11:16 if the root be holy so are the b'. 2798
17 if some of the b' be broken off, "
18 Boast not against the b'. But if "
19 The b' were broken off, that I "
21 if God spared not the natural b', "
24 these, which be the natural b', be "

brand See also BRANDS; FIREBRAND.
Zec 3: 2 is not this a b' plucked out of the 181

brandish
Eze 32:10 I shall b' my sword before them; 5774

brands See also FIREBRANDS.
J'g 15: 5 when he had set the b' on fire, he 3940

brasen
Ex 27: 4 make four b' rings in the four 5178
35:16 burnt offering with his b' grate, * "
38: 4 he made for the altar a b' grate * "
10 their b' sockets twenty; the * "
30 and the b' altar, and the b' grate "
39:39 b' altar, and his grate of brass, "
Le 6:28 sodden in a b' pot, it shall be both "
Nu 16:39 the priest took the b' censers, "
1Ki 4:13 great cities walls and b' bars: "
7:30 every base had four b' wheels, "
8:64 b' altar that was before the Lord "
14:27 made in their stead b' shields, * "
2Ki 16:14 he brought also the b' altar, "
15 the b' altar shall be for me to "
17 down the sea from off the b' oxen "
18: 4 brake in pieces the b' serpent that "
25:13 the b' sea that was in the house of "
1Ch 18: 8 wherewith Solomon made the b' "
2Ch 1: 5 Moreover the b' altar, that Bezaleel "
6 the b' altar before the Lord, which "
6:13 Solomon had made a b' scaffold, "
7: 7 b' altar which Solomon had made "
Jer 1:18 an iron pillar, and b' walls "
15:20 unto this people a fenced b' wall: "
52:17 the b' sea that was in the house of "
20 twelve b' bulls that were under the "
Eze 9: 2 and stood beside the b' altar. "
M'r 7: 4 of cups, and pots, b' vessels, 5473

brass
Ge 4:22 of every artificer in b' and iron: 5178
Ex 25: 3 of them; gold, and silver, and b', "
26:11 thou shalt make fifty taches of b', "
37 cast five sockets of b' for them. "
27: 2 and thou shalt overlay it with b'. "
3 thereof thou shalt make of b'. "
4 for it a grate of network of b'; "
6 wood, and overlay them with b'. "
10 their twenty sockets shall be of b'; "
11 and their twenty sockets of b'; "
17 of silver, and their sockets of b'. "
18 twined linen, and their sockets of b'. "
19 the pins of the court, shall be of b'. "
30:18 Thou shalt also make a laver of b', "
18 and his foot also of b', "
31: 4 in gold, and in silver, and in b', "
35: 5 the Lord; gold, and silver, and b', "

Ex 35:24 an offering of silver and b' 5178
32 in gold, and in silver, and in b', "
36:18 he made fifty taches of b' to couple "
38 but their five sockets were of b'. "
38: 2 same: and he overlaid it with b'. "
3 the vessels thereof made he of b'. "
5 the four ends of the grate of b', "
6 wood, and overlaid them with b'. "
8 he made the laver of b', "
8 and the foot of it of b', "
11 and their sockets of b' twenty; "
17 sockets for the pillars were of b'; "
19 four, and their sockets of b' four; "
20 court round about, were of b'. "
29 And the b' of the offering was "
39:39 brasen altar, and his grate of b'. "
Le 26:19 as iron, and your earth as b': 5154
Nu 21: 9 Moses made a serpent of b', and 5178
9 when he beheld the serpent of b'. "
31:22 the gold, and the silver, the b', "
De 8: 9 of whose hills thou mayest dig b'. "
28:23 that is over thy head shall be b'. "
33:25 Thy shoes shall be iron and b'; "
Jos 6:19 vessels of b' and iron, are "
24 the vessels of b' and of iron, they "
22: 8 with gold, and with b', and with "
J'g 16:21 bound him with fetters of b'; and "
1Sa 17: 5 had an helmet of b' upon his head, "
5 was five thousand shekels of b'. "
6 had greaves of b' upon his legs, "
6 and a target of b' between his "
38 an helmet of b' upon his head; "
2Sa 8: 8 David took exceeding much b'. "
10 vessels of gold, and vessels of b': "
21:16 three hundred shekels of b' in "
1Ki 7:14 a man of Tyre, a worker in b': "
14 cunning to work all works in b'. "
15 he cast two pillars of b', of "
16 two chapiters of molten b', to set "
27 he made ten bases of b'; four "
30 brasen wheels, and plates of b': "
38 Then made he ten lavers of b': "
45 of the Lord, were of bright b'. "
47 the weight of the b' found out. "
2Ki 25: 7 bound him with fetters of b', and* "
13 pillars of b' that were in the house "
13 carried the b' of them to Babylon. "
14 all the vessels of b' wherewith "
16 b' of all these vessels was without "
17 and the chapiter upon it was b': "
17 the chapiter round about, all of b': "
1Ch 15:19 to sound with cymbals of b'; "
18: 8 brought David very much b', "
8 the pillars, and the vessels of b'. "
10 vessels of gold and silver and b'. "
22: 3 b' in abundance without weight; "
14 and of b' and iron without weight; "
16 the gold, the silver, and the b', "
29: 2 the b' for things of b', the iron for "
7 of b' eighteen thousand talents, "
2Ch 2: 7 in silver, and in b', and in iron, "
14 in gold, and in silver, and in b', "
4: 1 made an altar of b', twenty cubits "
9 overlaid the doors of them with b'. "
16 house of the Lord, of bright b'. "
18 the weight of the b' could not be "
12:10 king Reoboham made shields of b' "
24:12 also such as wrought iron and b' "
Job 6:12 of stones? or is my flesh of b'? 5153
28: 2 b' is molten out of the stone. 5154
40:18 bones are as strong pieces of b'; "
41:27 as straw, and b' as rotten wood. "
Ps 107:16 he hath broken the gates of b', 5178
Isa 45: 2 break in pieces the gates of b', 5154
48: 4 is an iron sinew, and thy brow b'. "
60:17 For b' I will bring gold, and for 5178
17 bring silver, and for wood b', "
Jer 6:28 they are b' and iron; they are all "
52:17 Also the pillars of b' that were in "
17 and carried all the b' of them to "
18 of b' wherewith they ministered, "
20 the b' of all these vessels was "
22 a chapiter of b' was upon it; and "
22 the chapiters round about, all of b'. "
Eze 1: 7 like the colour of burnished b'. "
22:18 all they are b', and tin, and iron, "
20 they gather silver, and b', and iron, "
24:11 that the b' of it may be hot, and "
27:13 persons of men and vessels of b' "
40: 3 was like the appearance of b', "
Da 2:32 his belly and his thighs of b', 5174
35 the clay, the b', the silver, and "
39 another third kingdom of b', "
45 the iron, the b', the clay, the "
4:15, 23 with a band of iron and b', "
5: 4 gods of gold, and of silver, of b', "
23 the gods of silver, and gold, of b', "
7:19 were of iron, and his nails of b'; "
10: 6 feet like in colour to polished b'. 5178
Mic 4:13 I will make thy hoofs b': and 5154
Zec 6: 1 mountains were mountains of b'. 5178
M't 10: 9 nor silver, nor b' in your purses, *5475*
1Co 13: 1 I am become as sounding b', "
Re 1:15 and his feet like unto fine b', as *5474*
2:18 and his feet are like fine brass; "
9:20 idols of gold, and silver, and b', *5470*
18:12 and of b', and iron, and marble, *5475*

bravery
Isa 3:18 b' of their tinkling ornaments ‡8597

brawler See also BRAWLERS.
1Ti 3: 3 patient, not a b', not covetous; * *269*

brawlers
Tit 3: 2 evil of no man, to be no b', but * *269*

brawling
Pr 21: 9 with a b' woman in a wide house. *4090
25:24 with a b' woman in a wide house. *4090

bray See also BRAYED.
Job 6: 5 Doth the wild ass b' when he 5101
Pr 27:22 shouldest b' a fool in a mortar 3806

brayed
Job 30: 7 Among the bushes they b'; *5101

brazen See BRASEN.

breach See also BREACHES; BREAKING.
Ge 38:29 this b' be upon thee: therefore 6556
Le 24:20 B' for b', eye for eye, tooth for 7667
Nu 14:34 ye shall know my b' of promise. *8569
J'g 21:15 made a b' in the tribes of Israel. 6556
2Sa 5:20 before me, as the b' of waters. "
6: 8 Lord had made a b' upon Uzzah:* "
2Ki 12: 5 wheresoever any b' shall be found. 919
1Ch 13:11 Lord had made a b' upon Uzzah: *6556
15:13 our God made a b' upon us, 6555
Ne 6: 1 there was no b' left therein; 6556
Job 16:14 He breaketh me with b' upon b', "
Ps 106:23 chosen stood before him in the b', "
Pr 15: 4 therein is a b' in the spirit. *7667
Isa 7: 6 let us make a b' therein for us, 1234
30:13 as a b' ready to fall, swelling out 6556
26 bindeth up the b' of his people, *7667
58:12 repairer of the b', the restorer 6556
Jer 14:17 people is broken with a great b', 7667
La 2:13 thy b' is great like the sea: "
Eze 26:10 into a city wherein is made a b'. 1234

breaches
J'g 5:17 seashore, and abode in his b'. *4664
1Ki 11:27 repaired the b' of the city of *6556
2Ki 12: 5 them repair the b' of the house, 919
6 not repaired the b' of the house. "
7 repair ye not the b' of the house? "
7 deliver it for the b' of the house. "
8 to repair the b' of the house. "
12 stone to repair the b' of the house "
22: 5 Lord, to repair the b' of the house, "
Ne 4: 7 the b' began to be stopped, then 6555
Ps 60: 2 heal the b' thereof; for it shaketh. 7667
Isa 22: 9 b' of the city of David, that they 1233
Am 4: 3 And ye shall go out at the b', 6556
6:11 smite the great house with b', 7447
9:11 and close up the b' thereof; 6556

bread See also SHEWBREAD.
Ge 3:19 sweat of thy face shalt thou eat b', 3899
14:18 Salem brought forth b' and wine: "
18: 5 I will fetch a morsel of b', "
19: 3 and did bake unleavened b', "
21:14 and took b', and a bottle of water, 3899
25:34 Jacob gave Esau b' and pottage "
27:17 gave the savoury meat and the b', "
28:20 and will give me b' to eat, "
31:54 called his brethren to eat b': "
54 and they did eat b', "
37:25 they sat down to eat b': and they "
39: 6 save the b' which he did eat. "
41:54 all the land of Egypt there was b'. "
55 the people cried to Pharaoh for b': "
43:25 they heard that they should eat b' "
31 himself, and said, Set on b'. "
32 the Egyptians might not eat b' "
45:23 laden with corn and b' and meat "
47:12 with b', according to their "
13 And there was no b' in all the land; "
15 unto Joseph, and said, Give us b': "
17 Joseph gave them b' in exchange "
17 fed them with b' for all their cattle "
19 buy us and our land for b', and we "
49:20 Out of Asher his b' shall be fat, "
Ex 2:20 call him, that he may eat b'. "
12: 8 roast with fire, and unleavened b'; "
15 shall ye eat unleavened b'; "
15 whosoever eateth leavened b' "
17 observe the feast of unleavened b'; "
18 ye shall eat unleavened b', until "
20 shall ye eat unleavened b'. "
13: 3 shall no leavened b' be eaten. "
6 thou shalt eat unleavened b', "
7 Unleavened b' shall be eaten "
7 there shall no leavened b' be seen "
16: 3 when we did eat b' to the full; 3899
4 I will rain b' from heaven for you; "
8 and in the morning b' to the full; "
12 morning ye shall be filled with b'; "
15 the b' which the Lord hath given "
22 they gathered twice as much b', "
29 on the sixth day the b' of two days; "
32 the b' wherewith I have fed you "
18:12 to eat b' with Moses' father in law "
23:15 the feast of unleavened b': "
15 (thou shalt eat unleavened b' "
18 of my sacrifice with leavened b'; "
25 shall bless thy b', and thy water; 3899
29: 2 And unleavened b', and cakes "
23 loaf of b', and one cake of oiled b', "
23 basket of the unleavened b' that is "
32 the b' that is in the basket, by the 3899
34 of the b', remain until the morning, "
34:18 The feast of unleavened b' shalt "
18 (thou shalt eat unleavened b', "
28 he did neither eat b', nor drink 3899
40:23 he set the b' in order upon it "
Le 6:16 with unleavened b' shall it be *
7:13 leavened b' with the sacrifice of 3899
8: 2 and a basket of unleavened b'; "
26 the basket of unleavened b', that "
26 a cake of oiled b', and one wafer, "
31 the b' that is in the basket of 3899
32 of the b' shall ye burn with fire. "
21: 6 by fire, and the b' of their God, "
8 for he offereth the b' of thy God: "
17 approach to offer the b' of his God. "
21 nigh to offer the b' of his God.
22 He shall eat the b' of his God, 3899
22:25 the b' of your God of any of these; "
23: 6 the feast of unleavened b' unto "
6 ye must eat unleavened b'. "
14 ye shall eat neither b', nor 3899
18 offer with the b' seven lambs "
20 the b' of the firstfruits for a wave "
24: 7 may be on the b' for a memorial, "
26: 5 ye shall eat your b' to the full, "
26 the staff of your b', "
26 ten women shall bake your b' "
26 and they shall deliver you your b' "
Nu 4: 7 the continual b' shall be thereon: "
6:15 a basket of unleavened b', cakes "
15 wafers of unleavened b' anointed *
17 the basket of unleavened b': "
9:11 eat it with unleavened b' and bitter "
14: 9 they are b' for us: their defence 3899
15:19 when ye eat of the b' of the land, "
21: 5 for there is no b', neither is there "
5 our soul loatheth this light b'. "
28: 2 my b' for my sacrifices made by "
17 shall unleavened b' be eaten. "
De 8: 3 man doth not live by b' only, 3899
9 A land wherein thou shalt eat b' "
9: 9 I neither did eat b' nor drink "
18 I did neither eat b', nor drink "
16: 3 shalt eat no leavened b' with it; "
3 shalt thou eat unleavened b' "
3 even the b' of affliction; for thou 3899
4 there shall be no leavened b' *
8 thou shalt eat unleavened b': "
16 the feast of unleavened b', and in "
23: 4 they met you not with b' and with 3899
29: 6 Ye have not eaten b', neither have "
Jos 9: 5 all the b' of their provision was "
12 This our b' we took hot for our "
J'g 7:13 and, lo, a cake of barley b' "
8: 5 Give, I pray you, loaves of b' "
6 should give b' unto thine army? "
15 we should give b' unto thy men "
13:16 detain me, I will not eat of thy b': "
19: 5 thine heart with a morsel of b', "
19 there is b' and wine also for me, "
Ru 1: 6 visited his people in giving them b'. "
2:14 eat of the b', and dip thy "
1Sa 2: 5 hired out themselves for b'; "
36 and a morsel of b', and shall say, "
36 that I may eat a piece of b'. "
9: 7 the b' is spent in our vessels, "
10: 3 another carrying three loaves of b', "
4 and give thee two loaves of b'; "
16:20 an ass laden with b', and a bottle "
21: 3 give me five loaves of b' in mine "
4 no common b' under mine hand, "
4 but there is hallowed b': "
5 the b' is in a manner common, *
6 the priest gave him hallowed b': "
6 b' there but the shewbread, 3899
6 to put hot b' in the day when it "
22:13 in that thou hast given him b', "
25:11 Shall I then take my b', and my "
28:20 he had eaten no b' all the day, "
22 let me set a morsel of b' before "
24 did bake unleavened b' thereof: "
30:11 to David, and gave him b', and he 3899
12 for he had eaten no b', nor drunk "
2Sa 3:29 on the sword, or that lacketh b'. "
35 if I taste b', or ought else, till the "
6:19 to every one a cake of b', and a "
9: 7 thou shalt eat b' at my table "
10 thy master's son shall eat b' always "
12:17 neither did he eat b' with them. "
20 they set b' before him, and he did "
21 dead, thou didst rise and eat b'. "
16: 1 two hundred loaves of b', and an "
2 b' and summer fruit for the young "
1Ki 13: 8 neither will I eat b' nor drink "
9 Eat no b', nor drink water, nor "
15 Come home with me, and eat b'. "
16 neither will I eat b' nor drink "
17 Thou shalt eat no b', nor drink "
18 he may eat b' and drink water. "
19 went back with him, and did eat b' "
22 hast eaten b' and drunk water in "
22 Eat no b', and drink no water; "
23 after he had eaten b', and after he "
17: 6 ravens brought him b' and flesh "
6 and b' and flesh in the evening; "
11 me, I pray thee, a morsel of b' "
18: 4 and fed them with b' and water.) "
13 and fed them with b' and water? "
21: 4 away his face, and would eat no b'. "
5 so sad that thou eatest no b'? "
7 arise, and eat b', and let thine "
22:27 feed him with b' of affliction and "
2Ki 4: 8 and she constrained him to eat b'. "
8 he turned in thither to eat b'. "
42 b' of the firstfruits, twenty loaves "
6:22 set b' and water before them, that "
18:32 a land of b' and vineyards, a land "
23: 9 they did eat of the unleavened b' "
25: 3 there was no b' for the people of 3899
29 he did eat b' continually before "
1Ch 12:40 b' on asses, and on camels, and "
16: 3 to every one a loaf of b', and a "
2Ch 8:13 in the feast of unleavened b', and
18:26 feed him with b' of affliction and 3899
30:13 the feast of unleavened b' in the "
21 feast of unleavened b' seven days "
35:17 feast of unleavened b' seven days. "
Ezr 6:22 feast of unleavened b' seven days "
Ne 5:14 brethren have not eaten the b' of "
15 had taken of them b' and wine, "
18 the b' of the governor, because

Ne 9:15 And gavest them b' from heaven 3899
13: 2 not the children of Israel with b' "
Job 15:23 wandereth abroad for b', saying, "
22: 7 thou hast withholden b' from the "
27:14 shall not be satisfied with b'. "
28: 5 for the earth, out of it cometh b': "
33:20 his life abhorreth b', and his soul "
42:11 and did eat b' with him in his "
Ps 14: 4 up my people as they eat b', and "
37:25 forsaken, nor his seed begging b'. "
41: 9 which did eat of my b', hath lifted "
53: 4 eat up my people as they eat b': "
78:20 he give b' also? can he provide "
80: 5 feedest them with the b' of tears; "
102: 4 grass; so that I forget to eat my b'. "
9 I have eaten ashes like b', and "
104:15 and b' which strengtheneth man's "
105:16 he brake the whole staff of b'. "
40 and satisfied them with the b' of "
109:10 and beg: let them seek their b' also
127: 2 to eat the b' of sorrows: for so 3899
132:15 I will satisfy her poor with b'. "
Pr 4:17 they eat the b' of wickedness, and "
6:26 a man is brought to a piece of b': "
9: 5 Come, eat of my b', and drink of "
17 are sweet, and b' eaten in secret is "
12: 9 honoureth himself, and lacketh b'. "
11 his land shall be satisfied with b': "
20:13 and thou shalt be satisfied with b'. "
17 B' of deceit is sweet to a man; "
22: 9 for he giveth of his b' to the poor. "
23: 6 the b' of him that hath an evil eye, "
25:21 enemy be hungry, give him b' to "
28:19 his land shall have plenty of b': "
21 For a piece of b' that man will "
31:27 and eateth not the b' of idleness. "
Ec 9: 7 eat thy b' with joy, and drink "
11 neither yet b' to the wise, nor "
11: 1 Cast thy b' upon the waters: for "
Isa 3: 1 the whole stay of b', and the whole "
7 house is neither b' nor clothing: "
4: 1 We will eat our own b', and wear "
21:14 they prevented with their b' him "
28:28 B' corn is bruised; because he "
30:20 the b' of adversity, and the water "
23 and b' of the increase of the earth, "
33:16 of rocks: b' shall be given him; "
36:17 wine, a land of b' and vineyards. "
44:15 he kindleth it and baketh b'; yea, "
19 I have baked b' upon the coals "
51:14 pit, nor that his b' should fail. "
55: 2 money for that which is not b'? "
10 seed to the sower, and b' to the "
58: 7 to deal thy b' to the hungry, and "
Jer 5:17 eat up thine harvest, and thy b', "
37:21 give him daily a piece of b' out of "
21 the bakers' street, until all the b' "
38: 9 for there is no more b' in the city. "
41: 1 they did eat b' together in Mizpah. "
42:14 nor have hunger of b'; and there "
52: 6 there was no b' for the people of "
33 did continually eat b' before him "
La 1:11 All her people sigh, they seek b'; "
4: 4 the young children ask b', and no "
5: 6 Assyrians, to be satisfied with b'. "
9 We gat our b' with the peril of "
Eze 4: 9 make thee b' thereof, according "
13 their defiled b' among the Gentiles, "
15 thou shalt prepare thy b' "
16 I will break the staff of b' in "
16 and they shall eat b' by weight, "
17 That they may want b' and water, "
5:16 and will break your staff of b': "
12:18 of man, eat thy b' with quaking, "
19 shall eat their b' with carefulness, "
13:19 of barley and for pieces of b', "
14:13 will break the staff of the b' "
16:49 fulness of b', and abundance of "
18: 7 given his b' to the hungry, and "
16 hath given his b' to the hungry, "
24:17 thy lips, and eat not the b' of men. "
22 your lips, nor eat the b' of men. "
44: 3 sit in it to eat b' before the Lord; "
7 when ye offer my b', the fat and "
45:21 days; unleavened b' shall be eaten. "
Da 10: 3 I ate no pleasant b', neither 3899
Ho 2: 5 give me my b' and my water, "
9: 4 unto them as the b' of mourners; "
4 their b' for their soul shall not "
Am 4: 6 and want of b' in all your places: "
7:12 and there eat b', and prophesy "
8:11 not a famine of b', nor a thirst for "
Ob 7 they that eat thy b' have laid a "
Hag 2:12 and with his skirt do touch b', "
Mal 1: 7 Ye offer polluted b' upon mine "
M't 4: 3 that these stones be made b'. 740
4 Man shall not live by b' alone, "
6:11 Give us this day our daily b'. "
7: 9 whom if his son ask b', will he *
15: 2 not their hands, when they eat b'. "
26 not meet to take the children's b', "
33 should we have so much b' in *
16: 5 they had forgotten to take b'. "
7 It is because we have taken no b'. "
8 because ye have brought no b'? "
11 not to you concerning b', that "
12 not beware of the leaven of b', but "
26:17 the feast of unleavened b' the "
26 Jesus took b', and blessed it, and 740
M'r 3:20 could not so much as eat b'. "
6: 8 no scrip, no b', no money in their "
36 villages, and buy themselves b': *
37 two hundred pennyworth of b', "
7: 2 saw some of his disciples eat b' "
5 but eat b' with unwashen hands? "
27 not meet to take the children's b', "
M'r 8: 4 satisfy these men with b' here in 740
14 disciples had forgotten to take b', "
16 saying, It is because we have no b'. "
17 reason ye, because ye have no b'? "
14: 1 the passover, and of unleavened b': "
12 the first day of unleavened b', "
22 Jesus took b', and blessed, and 740
Lu 4: 3 this stone that it be made b'. "
4 man shall not live by b' alone, but "
7:33 neither eating b' nor drinking "
9: 3 scrip, neither b', neither money; "
11: 3 Give us day by day our daily b'. "
11 If a son shall ask b' of any of you* "
14: 1 to eat b' on the sabbath day, that "
15 he that shall eat b' in the kingdom "
15:17 servants of my father's have b' "
22: 1 Now the feast of unleavened b' drew
7 came the day of unleavened b', "
19 he took b', and gave thanks, and 740
24:30 he took b', and blessed it, and "
35 known of them in breaking of b'. "
Joh 6: 5 Whence shall we buy b', that these "
7 Two hundred pennyworth of b' "
23 place where they did eat b', after "
31 He gave them b' from heaven to "
32 Moses gave you not that b' from "
32 my Father giveth you the true b' "
33 For the b' of God is he which "
34 Lord, evermore give us this b'. "
35 I am the b' of life: he that cometh "
41 I am the b' which came down from "
48 I am that b' of life. "
50 This is the b' which cometh down "
51 I am the living b' which came "
51 if any man eat of this b', he shall "
51 the b' that I will give is my flesh, "
58 This is that b' which came down "
58 he that eateth of this b' shall live "
13:18 He that eateth b' with me hath "
21: 9 there, and fish laid thereon, and b'. "
13 Jesus then cometh, and taketh b' "
Ac 2:42 in breaking of b', and in prayers. "
46 breaking b' from house to house, "
12: 3 were the days of unleavened b'.) "
20: 6 after the days of unleavened b', "
7 came together to break b', Paul 740
11 had broken b', and eaten, and "
27:35 he took b', and gave thanks to God "
1Co 5: 8 unleavened b' of sincerity and "
10:16 The b' which we break, is it not 740
17 we being many are one b', and "
17 are all partakers of that one b'. "
11:23 which he was betrayed took b': "
26 as often as ye eat this b', and drink "
27 whosoever shall eat this b', and "
28 so let him eat of that b', and drink "
2Co 9:10 minister b' for your food, and *
2Th 3: 8 Neither did we eat any man's b' *
12 they work, and eat their own b'. "

breadth See also HANDBREADTH.
Ge 6:15 the b' of it fifty cubits, and the 7341
13:17 the length of it and in the b' of it; "
Ex 25:10 a cubit and a half the b' thereof, "
17 and a cubit and a half the b' "
23 a cubit the b' thereof, and a cubit "
25 border of an hand b' round *2948
26: 2 and the b' of one curtain four 7341
8 shall be thirty cubits, and the b' "
16 cubit and a half shall be the b' of "
27:12 And for the b' of the court on the "
13 And the b' of the court on the "
18 and the b' fifty every where, and "
28:16 and a span shall be the b' thereof. "
30: 2 a cubit the b' thereof; four "
36: 9 and the b' of one curtain four "
15 four cubits was the b' of one "
21 the b' of a board one cubit and a "
37: 1 a cubit and a half the b' of it, and "
6 and one cubit and a half the b' "
10 a cubit the b' thereof, and a cubit "
25 the b' of it a cubit; it was four "
38: 1 five cubits the b' thereof; it was "
18 length, and the height in the b' "
39: 9 thereof, and span the b' thereof, "
De 2: 5 so much as a foot b': *4096
3:11 four cubits the b' of it, after the 7341
J'g 20:16 could sling stones at an hair b'. *
1Ki 6: 2 the b' thereof twenty cubits, and 7341
3 according to the b' of the house; "
3 the b' thereof before the house. "
20 in length, and twenty cubits in b', "
7: 2 the b' thereof fifty cubits, and the "
6 fifty cubits, and the b' thereof "
26 And it was an hand b' thick, *2947
27 four cubits the b' thereof, and 7341
2Ch 3: 3 threescore cubits, and the b' "
4 the b' of the house, twenty cubits, "
8 was according to the b' of the "
8 twenty cubits, and the b' thereof "
4: 1 twenty cubits the b' thereof, and "
Ezr 6: 3 and the b' thereof threescore 6613
Job 37:10 and the b' of the waters is 7341
38:18 Hast thou perceived the b' of the 7338
Isa 8: 8 shall fill the b' of thy land, O 7341
Eze 40: 5 by the cubit and an hand b': *2948
5 he measured the b' of the *7341
11 the b' of the entry of the gate, ten "
13 the b' was five and twenty cubits, "
19 the b' from the forefront of "
20 the length thereof and the b' "
21 25, 36 and the b' five and twenty "
48 and the b' of the gate was three "
49 twenty cubits, and the b' eleven "
41: 1 other side, which was the b' of the "
2 And the b' of the door was ten "
2 forty cubits; and the b', twenty "
Eze 41: 3 and the b' of the door, seven 7341
4 and the b', twenty cubits, before "
5 and the b' of every side chamber, "
7 therefore the b' of the house was "
11 and the b' of the place that was "
14 Also the b' of the face of the house "
42: 2 north door, and the b' was fifty "
4 a walk of ten cubits b' inward, "
43:13 cubit is a cubit and an hand b': *2948
13 and the b' a cubit, and the border 7341
14 shall be two cubits, and the b' "
14 shall be four cubits, and the b' "
45: 1 and the b' shall be ten thousand. "
2 five hundred in b', square round "
3 and the b' of ten thousand: and "
5 the ten thousand of b', shall also "
48: 8 and twenty thousand reeds in b', "
9 length, and of ten thousand in b'. "
10 the west ten thousand in b', "
10 the east ten thousand in b', "
13 and ten thousand in b': all the "
13 twenty thousand, and the b' ten "
15 in the b' over against the five "
Da 3: 1 threescore cubits, and the b' 6613
Hab 1: 6 through the b' of the land, to 4800
Zec 2: 2 to see what is the b' thereof, and 7341
5: 2 twenty cubits, and the b' thereof "
Eph 3:18 what is the b', and length, and 4114
Re 20: 9 they went up on the b' of the "
21:16 the length is as large as the b': "
16 and the b' and the height of it are "

break See also BRAKE; BREAKEST; BREAKETH; BREAKING; BROKEN.
Ge 19: 9 even Lot, came near to b' the 7665
27:40 that thou shalt b' his yoke from *6561
Ex 12:46 neither shall ye b' a bone 7665
13:13 then thou shalt b' his neck: and 6202
19:21 lest they b' through unto the 2040
22 lest the Lord b' forth upon them. 6555
24 the people b' through to come up 2040
24 lest he b' forth upon them. 6555
22: 6 If fire b' out, and catch in thorns, 3318
23:24 overthrow them, and quite b' 7665
32: 2 B' off the golden earrings, which 6561
24 hath any gold, let them b' it off. "
34:13 b' their images, and cut down *7665
20 him not, then shalt thou b' his 6202
Le 11:33 shall be unclean; and ye shall b' 7665
13:12 if a leprosy b' out abroad in the 6524
14:43 and b' out in the house, after that "
45 And he shall b' down the house, 5422
26:15 but that ye b' my covenant: 6565
19 I will b' the pride of your power; 7665
44 to b' my covenant with them: for 6565
Nu 9:12 of it unto the morning, nor b' 7665
24: 8 shall b' their bones, and pierce 1633
30: 2 he shall not b' his word, he shall 2490
De 7: 5 b' down their images, and cut *7665
12: 3 and b' their pillars, and burn *7665
31:16 and b' my covenant which I have 6565
20 provoke me, and b' my covenant. "
J'g 2: 1 I will never b' my covenant with "
8: 9 again in peace, I will b' down this 5422
1Sa 25:10 servants now a days that b' away 6555
2Sa 2:32 they came to Hebron at b' of day.* 215
1Ki 15:19 and b' thy league with Baasha 6565
2Ki 3:26 that drew swords, to b' through 1234
25:13 did the Chaldees b' in pieces, and 7665
2Ch 16: 3 go, b' thy league with Baasha 6565
Ezr 9:14 Should we again b' thy "
Ne 4: 3 he shall even b' down their "
Job 13:25 Wilt thou b' a leaf driven to and *6206
19: 2 vex my soul, and b' me in pieces 1792
34:24 He shall b' in pieces mighty *7489
39:15 that the wild beast may b' them. *1758
Ps 2: 3 Let us b' their bands asunder, 5423
9 Thou shalt b' them with a rod of 7489
10:15 B' thou the arm of the wicked 7665
58: 6 B' their teeth, O God, in their 2040
6 b' out the great teeth of the 5422
72: 4 shall b' in pieces the oppressor. 1792
74: 6 But now they b' down the carved 1986
89:31 If they b' my statutes, and keep 2490
34 My covenant will I not b', nor "
94: 5 They b' in pieces thy people, 1792
141: 5 shall not b' my head: forget my *5106
Ec 3: 3 a time to b' down, and a time to 6555
Ca 2:17 Until the day b', and the *6315
4: 6 day b', and the shadows flee * "
Isa 5: 5 and b' down the wall thereof, 6555
14: 7 and is quiet: they b' forth into 6476
25 That I will b' the Assyrian in my 7665
28:24 doth he open and b' the clods of ‡7702
28 nor b' it with the wheel of his *2000
30:14 And he shall b' it as the breaking 7665
35: 6 in the wilderness shall waters b' 1234
38:13 as a lion, so will he b' all my 7665
42: 3 A bruised reed shall he not b', "
44:23 b' forth into singing, ye 6476
45: 2 I will b' in pieces the gates of 7665
49:13 and b' forth into singing, O 6476
52: 9 B' forth into joy, sing together, "
54: 1 b' forth into singing, and cry "
3 thou shalt b' forth on the right *6555
55:12 mountains and the hills shall b' 6476
58: 6 go free, and that ye b' every yoke? 5423
8 Then shall thy light b' forth as 1234
Jer 1:14 an evil shall b' forth upon all the 6605
4: 3 B' up your fallow ground, and 5214
14:21 remember, b' not thy covenant 6565
15:12 Shall iron b' the northern iron 7489
19:10 Then shalt thou b' the bottle in 7665
11 Even so will I b' this people and "
28: 4 I will b' the yoke of the king of "
11 Even so will I b' the yoke of "

Jer 30: 8 I will b' his yoke from off thy 7665
31:28 to pluck up, and to b' down, 5422
33:20 If ye can b' my covenant of the 6565
43:13 He shall b' also the images of 7665
45: 4 which I have built will I b' down, 2040
48:12 empty his vessels, and b' their 5310
49:35 I will b' the bow of Elam, the 7665
51:20 for with thee will I b' in pieces 5310
21 And with thee will I b' in pieces "
21 rider; and with thee will I b' in "
22 With thee also will I b' in pieces "
22 and with thee will I b' in pieces old "
22 and with thee will I b' in pieces "
23 I will also b' in pieces with thee "
23 and with thee will I b' in pieces "
23 And with thee will I b' in pieces "
Eze 4:16 I will b' the staff of bread in 7665
5:16 and will b' your staff of bread: "
13:14 So will I b' down the wall that ye 2040
14:13 and will b' the staff of the bread 7665
16:38 women that b' wedlock and shed 5003
39 shall b' down thy high places: 5422
17:15 or shall he b' the covenant, and 6565
23:34 thou shalt b' the sherds thereof, *1633
26: 4 Tyrus, and b' down her towers: 2040
9 he shall b' down thy towers. 5422
12 and they shall b' down thy walls, 2040
29: 7 thou didst b', and rend all their 7533
30:18 when I shall b' there the yokes of 7665
22 and will b' his arms, the strong "
24 but I will b' Pharaoh's arms, and "
Da 2:40 all these shall it b' in pieces 1854
44 it shall b' in pieces and consume "
4:27 b' off thy sins by righteousness, 6562
7:23 shall tread it down, and b' it in 1854
Ho 1: 5 that I will b' the bow of Israel in 7665
2:18 I will b' the bow and the sword "
4: 2 they b' out, and blood toucheth 6555
10: 2 he shall b' down their altars, he *6202
11 shall plow, and Jacob shall b' his 7702
12 mercy; b' up your fallow ground: 5214
Joe 2: 7 and they shall not b' their ranks: 5670
Am 1: 5 I will b' also the bar of Damascus, 7665
5: 6 lest he b' out like fire in the 6743
Mic 3: 3 they b' their bones, and chop 6476
Na 1:13 now will I b' his yoke from off 7665
Zec 11:10 that I might b' my covenant 6565
14 that I might b' the brotherhood "
M't 5:19 shall b' one of these least 3089
6:19 where thieves b' through and 1358
20 where thieves do not b' through "
9:17 else the bottles b', and the wine *4486
12:20 A bruised reed shall he not b', 2608
Ac 20: 7 came together to b' bread, Paul 2806
11 a long while, even to b' of day, 827
21:13 What mean ye to weep and to b' *4919
1Co 10:16 The bread which we b', is it not 2806
Ga 4:27 b' forth and cry, thou that 4486

breaker See also COVENANTBREAKERS; TRUCEBREAKERS.
Mic 2:13 The b' is come up before them: 6555
Ro 2:25 but if thou be a b' of the law, *3848

breakest
Ps 48: 7 Thou b' the ships of Tarshish 7665

breaketh
Ge 32:26 he said, Let me go, for the day b'. 5927
Job 9:17 he b' me with a tempest, and 7779
12:14 Behold, he breaketh down, and it 2040
16:14 He b' me with breach upon 6555
28: 4 The flood b' out from the "
Ps 29: 5 The voice of the Lord b' the 7665
5 yea, the Lord b' the cedars "
46: 9 he b' the bow, and cutteth the "
119:20 My soul b' for the longing that it 1638
Pr 25:15 and a soft tongue b' the bone. 7665
Ec 10: 8 whoso b' an hedge, a serpent 6555
Isa 59: 5 is crushed b' out into a viper. 1234
Jer 19:11 as one b' a potter's vessel, that 7665
23:29 like a hammer that b' the rock in 6327
La 4: 4 ask bread, and no man b' it unto 6566
Da 2:40 forasmuch as iron b' in pieces 1855
40 as iron that b' all these, shall it *7940

breaking See also BREACH; BREAKINGS.
Ge 32:24 a man with him until the b' of 5927
Ex 9: 9 a boil b' forth with blains upon 6524
10 it became a boil b' forth with "
22: 2 If a thief be found b' up, and be 4290
1Ch 14:11 like the b' forth of waters: *6556
Job 30:14 me as a wide b' in of waters: * "
Ps 144:14 that there be no b' in, nor going "
Isa 22: 5 b' down the walls, and of crying 6979
30:13 whose b' cometh suddenly at an 7667
14 as the b' of the potters' vessel "
Eze 16:59 despised the oath in b' the 6565
17:18 by b' the covenant, when, lo, he "
21: 6 with the b' of thy loins; and 7670
Ho 13:13 in the place of the b' forth of 4866
Lu 24:35 known of them in b' of bread. 2800
Ac 2:42 in b' of bread, and in prayers. "
46 and b' bread from house to house, 2806
Ro 2:23 b' the law dishonourest thou *3847

breakings
Job 41:25 by reason of b' they purify *7667

breast See also BREASTPLATE; BREASTS.
Ex 29:26 thou shalt take the b' of the 2373
27 sanctify the b' of the wave "
Le 7:30 the fat with the b', it shall he "
30 that the b' may be waved "
31 but the b' shall be Aaron's and his "
34 the wave b' and the heave "
8:29 Moses took the b', and waved it "
10:14 the wave b' and heave shoulder "
15 heave shoulder and the wave b' "
Nu 6:20 priest, with the wave b' and heave "
Nu 18:18 as the wave b' and as the right 2373
Job 24: 9 pluck the fatherless from the b', 7699
Isa 60:16 shalt suck the b' of kings; and "
La 4: 3 the sea monsters draw out the b', "
Da 2:32 his b' and his arms of silver, his 2306
Lu 18:13 but smote upon his b', saying, 4738
Joh 13:25 He then lying on Jesus' b' saith "
21:20 which also leaned on his b' at "

breastplate See also BREASTPLATES.
Ex 25: 7 be set in the ephod, and in the b'. 2833
28: 4 they shall make; a b', and an "
15 shalt make the b' of judgment "
22 make upon the b' chains at the "
23 make upon the b' two rings of "
23 two rings on the two ends of the b'. "
24 which are on the ends of the b'. "
26 two ends of the b' in the border "
28 they shall bind the b' by the rings "
28 that the b' be not loosed from the "
29 the children of Israel in the b' of "
30 put in the b' of judgment the "
29: 5 the ephod, and the b', and gird "
35: 9 set for the ephod, and for the b'. "
27 set, for the ephod, and for the b'; "
39: 8 he made the b' of cunning work, "
9 they made the b' double: "
15 upon the b' chains at the ends, "
16 rings in the two ends of the b'. "
17 two rings on the ends of the b'. "
19 put them on the two ends of the b'. "
21 bind the b' by his rings unto the "
21 that the b' might not be loosed "
Le 8: 8 he put the b' upon him: "
8 also he put in the b' the Urim "
Isa 59:17 put on righteousness as a b', 8302
Eph 6:14 having on the b' of righteousness; 2382
1Th 5: 8 putting on the b' of faith and love; "

breastplates
Re 9: 9 b', as it were b' of iron; 2382
17 b' of fire, and of jacinth, and "

breasts
Ge 49:25 blessings of the b', and of the 7699
Le 9:20 they put the fat upon the b', and 2373
21 the b' and the right shoulder "
Job 3:12 or why the b' that I should suck? 7699
21:24 His b' are full of milk, and his 5845
Ps 22: 9 when I was upon my mother's b'. 7699
Pr 5:19 let her b' satisfy thee at all times; 1717
Ca 1:13 shall lie all night betwixt my b'. 7699
4: 5 Thy two b' are like two young roes "
7: 3 thy two b' are like two young roes "
7 and thy b' to clusters of grapes. "
8 thy b' shall be as clusters of the "
8: 1 that sucked the b' of my mother! "
8 little sister, and she hath no b': "
10 and my b' like towers: then was "
Isa 28: 9 the milk, and drawn from the b'. "
66:11 satisfied with the b' of her "
Eze 16: 7 thy b' are fashioned, and thine "
23: 3 there were their b' pressed, and "
8 bruised the b' of her virginity. ††1717
34 and pluck off thine own b': 7699
Ho 2: 2 adulteries from between her b'; "
9:14 miscarrying womb and dry b'. "
Joe 2:16 and those that suck the b': "
Na 2: 7 of doves, tabering upon their b'. 3824
Lu 23:48 smote their b', and returned. 4738
Re 15: 6 their b' girded with golden girdles. "

breath
Ge 2: 7 into his nostrils the b' of life; 5397
6:17 wherein is the b' of life, from 7307
7:15 flesh, wherein is the b' of life. "
22 in whose nostrils was the b' of life, 5397
2Sa 22:16 at the blast of the b' of his nostrils. 7307
1Ki 17:17 that there was no b' left in him. 5397
Job 4: 9 and by the b' of his nostrils are *7307
9:18 will not suffer me to take my b'. "
12:10 and the b' of all mankind. "
15:30 by the b' of his mouth shall he go "
17: 1 My b' is corrupt, my days are * "
19:17 My b' is strange to my wife, "
27: 3 while my b' is in me, and the *5397
33: 4 and the b' of the Almighty hath "
34:14 unto himself his spirit and his b'; "
37:10 By the b' of God frost is given: "
41:21 His b' kindleth coals, and a flame 5315
Ps 18:15 the blast of the b' of thy nostrils. 7307
33: 6 the host of them by the b' of his "
104:29 thou takest away their b', they "
135:17 neither is there any b' in their "
146: 4 His b' goeth forth, he returneth "
150: 6 every thing that hath b' praise 5397
Ec 3:19 yea, they have all one b'; so that 7307
Isa 2:22 from man, whose b' is in his 5397
11: 4 and with the b' of his lips shall 7307
30:28 And his b', as an overflowing "
33 the b' of the Lord, like a stream 5397
33:11 your b', as fire, shall devour you. 7307
42: 5 he that giveth b' unto the people 5397
Jer 10:14 falsehood, and there is no b' in 7307
51:17 falsehood, and there is no b' in "
La 4:20 b' of our nostrils, the anointed "
Eze 37: 5 I will cause b' to enter into you, "
6 and put b' in you, and ye shall "
8 but there was no b' in them. "
9 the four winds, O b', and breathe "
10 the b' came into them, and they "
Da 5:23 God in whose hand thy b' is, and 5396
10:17 me, neither is there b' left in me. 5397
Hab 2:19 there is no b' at all in the midst 7307
Ac 17:25 he giveth to all life, and b', and 4157

breathe See also BREATHED; BREATHEST; BREATHING.
Jos 11:11 there was not any left to b': and *5397
Jos 11:14 them, neither left they any to b'. *5397
Ps 27:12 me, and such as b' out cruelty. 3307
Eze 37: 9 and b' upon these slain, that 5301

breathed
Ge 2: 7 and b' into his nostrils the breath 5301
Jos 10:40 utterly destroyed all that b', as 5397
1Ki 15:29 left not to Jeroboam any that b', "
Joh 20:22 said this, he b' on them, and said 1720

breatheth
De 20:16 shalt save alive nothing that b': 5397

breathing
La 3:56 hide not thine ear at my b', at 7309
Ac 9: 1 Saul, yet b' out threatenings and 1709

bred
Ex 16:20 morning, and it b' worms, and 7311

breeches
Ex 28:42 thou shalt make them linen b' to 4370
39:28 and linen b' of fine twined linen, "
Le 6:10 and his linen b' shall he put upon "
16: 4 and he shall have the linen b' upon "
Eze 44:18 and shall have linen b' upon their "

breed See also BRED; BREEDING.
Ge 8:17 that they may b' abundantly in 8317
De 32:14 rams of the b' of Bashan, and 1121

breeding
Zep 2: 9 the b' of nettles, and salt pits, *4476

brethren See also BRETHREN'S; BROTHERS'.
Ge 9:22 his father, and told his two b' 251
25 of servants shall he be unto his b'. "
13: 8 and thy herdmen; for we be b'. "
16:12 dwell in the presence of his b'. "
19: 7 pray you, b', do not so wickedly. "
24:27 to the house of my master's b'. "
25:18 died in the presence of all his b'. "
27:29 be lord over thy b', and let thy "
37 all his b' have I given to him for "
29: 4 unto them, My b', whence be ye? "
31:23 he took his b' with him, and "
25 Laban with his b' pitched in the "
32 before our b' discern thou what "
37 it here before my b' and thy b', "
46 Jacob said unto his b', Gather "
54 called his b' to eat bread: and they "
34:11 unto her father and unto her b', "
25 Simeon and Levi, Dinah's b', took "
37: 2 feeding the flock with his b'; and "
4 his b' saw that their father loved "
4 him more than all his b', "
5 a dream, and he told it his b': "
8 his b' said to him, Shalt thou "
9 another dream, and told it his b', "
10 told it to his father, and to his b': "
10 Shall I and thy mother and thy b' "
11 his b' envied him; but his father "
12 his b' went to feed their father's "
13 Do not thy b' feed the flock in "
14 whether it be well with thy b', "
16 he said, I seek my b': tell me, I pray "
17 Joseph went after his b', and found "
23 when Joseph was come unto his b', "
26 Judah said unto his b', What profit "
27 our flesh: and his b' were content. "
30 he returned unto his b', and said, "
38: 1 Judah went down from his b', and "
11 peradventure he die also, as his b' "
42: 3 Joseph's ten b' went down to buy "
4 not with his b'; for he said, Lest "
6 Joseph's b' came, and bowed "
7 Joseph saw his b', and he knew "
8 Joseph knew his b', but they knew "
13 Thy servants are twelve b', the "
19 let one of your b' be bound in the "
28 he said unto his b', My money is "
32 We be twelve b', sons of our father; "
33 leave one of your b' here with me, "
44:14 Judah and his b' came to Joseph's "
33 and let the lad go up with his b'. "
45: 1 made himself known unto his b'. "
3 Joseph said unto his b', I am "
3 And his b' could not answer him; "
4 Joseph said unto his b', Come "
15 Moreover he kissed all his b', and "
15 after that his b' talked with him. "
16 Joseph's b' are come: and it "
17 Say unto thy b', This do ye; lade "
24 So he sent his b' away, and they "
46:31 Joseph said unto his b', and unto "
31 My b', and my father's house, "
47: 1 My father and my b', and their "
2 he took some of his b', even five "
3 Pharaoh said unto his b', What is "
5 saying, Thy father and thy b' are "
6 make thy father and b' to dwell; "
11 placed his father and his b', and "
12 nourished his father, and his b', "
48: 6 the name of their b' in their "
22 to thee one portion above thy b', "
49: 5 Simeon and Levi are b'; "
8 art he whom thy b' shall praise: "
26 him that was separate from his b'. "
50: 8 the house of Joseph, and his b', "
14 returned into Egypt, he, and his b', "
15 when Joseph's b' saw that their "
17 trespass of thy b', and their sin "
18 his b' also went and fell down "
24 And Joseph said unto his b', "
Ex 1: 6 And Joseph died, and all his b', "
2:11 that he went out unto his b', "
11 smiting an Hebrew, one of his b'. "
4:18 unto my b' which are in Egypt, "
Le 10: 4 carry your b' from before the "
6 but let your b', the whole house of "
21:10 the high priest among his b', "

Le 25:46 over your b' the children of Israel, 251
48 one of his b' may redeem him: "
Nu 8:26 with their b' in the tabernacle "
16:10 thy b' the sons of Levi with thee: "
18: 2 thy b' also of the tribe of Levi, "
6 I have taken your b' the Levites "
20: 3 when our b' died before the Lord! "
25: 6 brought unto his b' a Midianitish "
27: 4 possession among the b' of our "
7 among their father's b', and thou "
9 give his inheritance unto his b'. "
10 if he have no b', then ye shall give "
10 his inheritance unto his father's b'. "
11 if his father have no b', then ye "
32: 6 Shall your b' go to war, and shall "
De 1:16 Hear the causes between your b', "
28 our b' have discouraged our heart, "
2: 4 pass through the coast of your b' "
8 when we passed by from our b' "
3:18 pass over armed before your b' "
20 Lord have given rest unto your b', "
10: 9 no part nor inheritance with his b'; "
15: 7 a poor man of one of thy b' within "
17:15 from among thy b' shalt thou set "
20 heart be not lifted up above his b', "
18: 2 no inheritance among their b': "
7 as all his b' the Levites do, which "
15 from the midst of thee, of thy b', "
18 a Prophet from among their b', "
24: 7 any of his b' of the children of "
14 whether he be of thy b', or of "
25: 5 If b' dwell together, and one of "
33: 9 neither did he acknowledge his b', "
16 him that was separated from his b'. "
24 let him be acceptable to his b', "
Jos 1:14 ye shall pass before your b' armed, "
15 Until the Lord have given your b' "
2:13 father, and my mother, and my b', "
18 and thy b', and all thy father's "
6:23 father, and her mother, and her b', "
14: 8 Nevertheless my b' that went up "
17: 4 us an inheritance among our b'. "
4 among the b' of their father. "
22: 3 Ye have not left your b' these many "
4 God hath given rest unto your b', "
7 gave Joshua among their b' on "
8 spoil of your enemies with your b'. "
J'g 8:19 They were my b', even the sons of "
9: 1 to Shechem unto his mother's b', "
3 his mother's b' spake of him in "
5 slew his b' the sons of Jerubbaal, "
24 aided him in the killing of his b'. "
26 son of Ebed came with his b', "
31 and his b' be come to Shechem; "
41 Zebul thrust out Gaal and his b', "
56 his father, in slaying his seventy b': "
11: 3 Jepthah fled from his b', and dwelt "
14: 3 among the daughters of thy b', "
16:31 Then his b' and all the house "
18: 8 they came unto their b' to Zorah "
8 and their b' said unto them, "
14 said unto their b', Do ye know "
19:23 said unto them, Nay, my b', nay, "
20:13 hearken to the voice of their b' "
21:22 their b' come unto us to complain, "
Ru 4:10 not cut off from among his b', "
1Sa 16:13 anointed him in the midst of his b': "
17:17 Take now for thy b' an ephah of "
17 and run to the camp to thy b'; "
18 look how thy b' fare, and take their "
22 and came and saluted his b'. "
20:29 I pray thee, and see my b'. "
22: 1 his b' and all his father's house "
30:23 Ye shall not do so, my b', with that "
2Sa 2:26 return from following their b'? "
3: 8 to his b', and to his friends, "
15:20 take back thy b': mercy and truth "
19:12 Ye are my b', ye are my bones "
41 Why have our b' the men of Judah "
1Ki 1: 9 called all his b' the king's sons, "
12:24 nor fight against your b' the "
2Ki 9: 2 him arise up from among his b', "
10:13 Jehu met with the b' of Ahaziah "
13 We are the b' of Ahaziah; and we "
23: 9 unleavened bread among their b'. "
1Ch 4: 9 was more honourable than his b': "
27 but his b' had not many children, "
5: 2 Judah prevailed above his b', "
7 And his b' by their families, "
13 And their b' of the house of their "
6:44 And their b' the sons of Merari "
48 Their b' also the Levites were "
7: 5 And their b' among all the families "
22 and his b' came to comfort him. "
8:32 dwelt with their b' in Jerusalem, "
9: 6 sons of Zerah; Jeuel, and their b', "
9 And their b', according to their "
13 And their b', heads of the house of "
17 Talmon, and Ahiman, and their b': "
19 the son of Korah, and his b', "
25 And their b', which were in their "
32 other of their b', of the sons of the "
38 And they also dwelt with their b' at "
38 Jerusalem, over against their b'. "
12: 2 even of Saul's b' of Benjamin. "
32 b' were at their commandment. "
39 for their b' had prepared for them. "
13: 2 let us send abroad unto our b' "
15: 5 and his b' an hundred and twenty: "
6 and his b' two hundred and twenty: "
7 and his b' an hundred and thirty: "
8 the chief, and his b' two hundred: "
9 the chief, and his b' fourscore: "
10 and his b' an hundred and twelve. "
12 both ye and your b', that ye may "
16 appoint their b' to be the singers "

1Ch 15:17 the son of Joel, and of his b', 251
17 of the sons of Merari their b', "
18 with them their b' of the second "
16: 7 into the hand of Asaph and his b'. "
37 Asaph and his b', to minister before "
38 Obed-edom with their b', "
39 Zadok the priest, and his b' "
23:22 and their b' the sons of Kish "
32 charge of the sons of Aaron their b', "
24:31 cast lots over against their b' the "
31 over against their younger b'. * "
25: 7 their b' that were instructed in "
9 with his b' and sons were twelve: "
10, 11, 12, 13, 14, 15, 16, 17, 18, 19, 20, "
21, 22, 23, 24, 25, 26, 27, 28, 29, 30, 31, "
his sons, and his b', were twelve: "
26: 7 whose b' were strong men, Elihu, "
8 they and their sons, and their b', "
9 Meshelemiah had sons and b', "
11 all the sons and b' of Hosah were "
25 And his b' by Eliezer; Rehabiah "
26 Shelomith and his b' were over "
28 the hand of Shelomith, and of his b'. "
30 Hashabiah and his b', men of "
32 And his b', men of valour, were "
27:18 Elihu, one of the b' of David: "
28: 2 Hear me, my b', and my people: "
2Ch 5:12 with their sons and their b', being "
11: 4 go up, nor fight against your b': "
22 chief, to be ruler among his b': "
19:10 shall come to you of your b' that "
10 come upon you, and upon your b': "
21: 2 he had b' the sons of Jehoshaphat, "
4 slew all his b' with the sword, "
13 hast slain thy b' of thy father's "
22: 8 the sons of the b' of Ahaziah, "
28: 8 carried away captive of their b' "
11 ye have taken captive of your b': "
15 the city of palm trees, to their b': "
29:15 they gathered their b', and "
34 their b' the Levites did help "
30: 7 and like your b', which trespassed "
9 your b' and your children shall "
31:15 to give to their b' by courses, "
35: 5 families of the fathers of your b' "
6 prepare your b', that they may "
9 Shemaiah and Nethaneel, his b', "
15 for their b' the Levites prepared "
Ezr 3: 2 his b' the priests, and Zerubbabel "
2 the son of Shealtiel, and his b', "
8 their b' the priests and the Levites, "
9 Jeshua with his sons and his b', "
9 their sons and their b' the Levites. "
6:20 for their b' the priests, and for "
7:18 seem good to thee, and to thy b', 252
8:17 to his b' the Nethinims at the place 251
18 with his sons and his b', "
19 sons of Merari, his b' and their "
24 and ten of their b' with them, "
10:18 the son of Jozadak, and his b': "
Ne 1: 2 That Hanani, one of my b', came, "
3: 1 with his b' the priests, and they "
18 After him repaired their b', "
4: 2 he spake before his b' and the "
14 fight for your b', your sons, and "
23 So neither I, nor my b', nor my "
5: 1 wives against their b' the Jews. "
5 our flesh is as the flesh of our b', "
8 have redeemed our b' the Jews, "
8 and will ye even sell your b'? "
10 I likewise, and my b', and my "
14 and my b' have not eaten the bread "
10:10 And their b', Shebaniah, Hodijah, "
29 They clave to their b', their nobles, "
11:12 And their b' that did the work of "
13 And his b', chief of the fathers, "
14 And their b', mighty men of valour, "
17 Bakbukiah the second among his b', "
19 and their b' that kept the gates, "
12: 7 of their b' in the days of Jeshua. "
8 the thanksgiving, he and his b'. "
9 Bakbukiah and Unni, their b', "
24 with their b' over against them, "
36 his b', Shemaiah, and Azarael, "
13:13 was to distribute unto their b'. "
Es 10: 3 accepted of the multitude of his b', "
Job 6:15 My b' have dealt deceitfully as a "
19:13 He hath put my b' far from me, "
42:11 came there unto him all his b', "
15 them inheritance among their b'. "
Ps 22:22 will declare thy name unto my b': "
69: 8 become a stranger unto my b', "
122: 8 For my b' and companions' sakes, "
133: 1 is for b' to dwell together in unity! "
Pr 6:19 he that soweth discord among b'. "
17: 2 of the inheritance among the b'. "
19: 7 All the b' of the poor do hate him: "
Isa 66: 5 Your b' that hated you, that cast "
20 they shall bring all your b' for an "
Jer 7:15 I have cast out all your b', "
12: 6 For even thy b', and the house of "
29:16 of your b' that are not gone forth "
35: 3 son of Habaziniah, and his b', "
41: 8 and slew them not among their b'. "
49:10 and his b', and his neighbours, "
Eze 11:15 Son of man, thy b', even thy "
15 even thy b', the men of thy kindred, "
Hos 2: 1 Say ye unto your b', Ammi; and to "
13:15 he be fruitful among his b', "
Mic 5: 3 the remnant of his b' shall return "
M't 1: 2 and Jacob begat Judas and his b'; 80
11 Josias begat Jechonias and his b', "
4:18 by the sea of Galilee, saw two b', "
21 he saw other two b', James the son "
5:47 if ye salute your b' only, what do ye "
12:46 his mother and his b' stood without. "

M't 12:47 thy mother and thy b' that stand 80
48 my mother? and who are my b'? "
49 said, Behold my mother and my b'! "
13:55 b', James, and Joses, and Simon, "
19:29 b', or sisters, or father, or mother, "
20:24 with indignation against the two b'. "
22:25 there were with us seven b': and "
23: 8 even Christ; and all ye are b'. "
25:40 the least of these my b', ye have "
28:10 tell my b' that they go into Galilee, "
M'k 3:31 came then his b' and his mother, "
32 and thy b' without seek for thee. "
33 Who is my mother, or my b'? "
34 Behold my mother and my b'! "
10:29 left house, or b', or sisters, "
30 and b', and sisters, and mothers, "
12:20 Now there were seven b': and the "
Lu 8:19 his mother, and his b', and could "
20 Thy mother and thy b' stand "
21 My mother and my b' are these "
14:12 not thy friends, nor thy b', neither "
26 children, and b', and sisters, yea, "
16:28 I have five b'; that he may testify "
18:29 parents, or b', or wife, or children, "
20:29 There were therefore seven b': "
21:16 by parents, and b', and kinsfolks, "
22:32 art converted, strengthen thy b'. "
Joh 2:12 his mother, and his b', and his "
7: 3 His b' therefore said unto him, "
5 neither did his b' believe in him. "
10 But when his b' were gone up, "
20:17 go to my b', and say unto them, "
21:23 saying abroad among the b', "
Ac 1:14 mother of Jesus, and with his b'. "
16 Men and b', this scripture must "
2:29 Men and b', let me freely speak "
37 Men and b', what shall we do? "
3:17 b', I wot that through ignorance "
22 unto you of your b', like unto me; "
6: 3 Wherefore, b', look ye out among "
7: 2 said, Men, b', and fathers, hearken; "
13 Joseph was made known to his b'; "
23 visit his b' the children of Israel. "
25 his b' would have understood "
26 saying, Sirs, ye are b'; why do ye "
37 unto you of your b', like unto me; "
9:30 Which when the b' knew, they "
10:23 b' from Joppa accompanied him. "
11: 1 apostles and b' that were in Judæa "
12 these six b' accompanied me, "
29 send relief unto the b' which dwelt "
12:17 things unto James, and to the b'. "
13:15 saying, Ye men and b', if ye have "
26 Men and b', children of the stock of "
38 unto you therefore, men and b', "
14: 2 minds evil affected against the b'. "
15: 1 from Judæa taught the b', "
3 caused great joy unto all the b'. "
7 and said unto them, Men and b', "
13 Men and b', hearken unto me: "
22 and Silas, chief men among the b': "
23 The apostles and elders and b' "
23 send greeting unto the b' "
32 exhorted the b' with many words "
33 peace from the b' unto the apostles. "
36 and visit our b' in every city where "
40 being recommended by the b' unto "
16: 2 b' that were at Lystra and Iconium. "
40 and when they had seen the b', "
17: 6 they drew Jason and certain b' "
10 the b' immediately sent away Paul "
14 the b' sent away Paul to go as it "
18:18 took his leave of the b', and sailed "
27 b' wrote, exhorting the disciples "
20:32 now, b', I commend you to God, * "
21: 7 saluted the b', and abode with them "
17 the b' received us gladly. "
22: 1 Men, b', and fathers, hear ye my "
5 I received letters unto the b', "
23: 1 Men and b', I have lived in all good "
5 I wist not, b', that he was the high "
6 Men and b', I am a Pharisee, "
28:14 we found b', and were desired to "
15 when the b' heard of us, they came "
17 Men and b', though I have committed "
21 any of the b' that came shewed or "
Ro 1:13 you ignorant, b', that oftentimes I "
7: 1 Know ye not, b', (for I speak to them "
4 my b', ye also are become dead to "
8:12 Therefore, b', we are debtors, "
29 be the firstborn among many b'. "
9: 3 accursed from Christ for my b', * "
10: 1 B', my heart's desire and prayer to "
11:25 not, b', that ye should be ignorant "
12: 1 I beseech you therefore, b', by the "
15:14 persuaded of you, my b', that ye "
15 b', I have written the more * "
30 Now I beseech you, b', for the Lord "
16:14 and the b' which are with them. "
17 I beseech you, b', mark them which "
1Co 1:10 I beseech you, b', by the name of "
11 declared unto me of you, my b', "
26 ye see your calling, b', how that not "
2: 1 I, b', when I came to you, came not "
3: 1 I, b', could not speak unto you as "
4: 6 these things, b', I have in a figure "
6: 5 be able to judge between his b'? "
8 and defraud, and that your b'. "
7:24 B', let every man, wherein he is "
29 But this I say, b', the time is short: "
8:12 ye sin so against the b', and wound "
9: 5 the b' of the Lord, and Cephas? "
10: 1 b', I would not that ye should be "
11: 2 praise you, b', that ye remember * "
33 Wherefore, my b', when ye come "
12: 1 Now concerning spiritual gifts, b', "

1Co 14: 6 *b*', if I come unto you speaking 80
20 *B*', be not children in "
26 How is it then, *b*'? when ye come "
39 Wherefore, *b*', covet to prophesy, "
15: 1 Moreover, *b*', I declare unto you "
6 of above five hundred *b*' at once; "
50 this I say, *b*', that flesh and blood "
58 Therefore, my beloved *b*', be ye "
16:11 me: for I look for him with the *b*'. "
12 him to come unto you with the *b*': "
15 beseech you, *b*', (ye know the house "
20 All the *b*' greet you. Greet ye one "
2Co 1: 8 *b*', have you ignorant of our trouble "
8: 1 Moreover, *b*', we do you to wit of "
23 or our *b*' be enquired of, they are "
9: 3 Yet have I sent the *b*', lest our "
5 necessary to exhort the *b*', that "
11: 9 the *b*' which came from Macedonia "
26 the sea, in perils among false *b*'; *5569*
13:11 Finally, *b*', farewell. Be perfect, 80
Ga 1: 2 And all the *b*' which are with me, "
11 I certify you, *b*', that the gospel "
2: 4 that because of false *b*' unawares *5569*
3:15 *B*', I speak after the manner of men; *80*
4:12 *B*', I beseech you, be as I am; for I "
28 Now we, *b*', as Isaac was, are the "
31 So then, *b*', we are not children of "
5:11 I, *b*', if I yet preach circumcision, "
13 *b*', ye have been called unto liberty; "
6: 1 *B*', if a man be overtaken in a fault, "
18 *B*', the grace of our Lord Jesus "
Eph 6:10 Finally, my *b*', be strong in the *
23 Peace be to the *b*', and love with "
Ph'p 1:12 ye should understand, *b*', that the "
14 many of the *b*' in the Lord, waxing "
3: 1 Finally, my *b*', rejoice in the Lord. "
13 *B*', I count not myself to have "
17 *B*', be followers together of me, "
4: 1 my *b*' dearly beloved and longed "
8 Finally, *b*', whatsoever things are "
21 The *b*' which are with me greet you. "
Col 1: 2 saints and faithful *b*' in Christ "
4:15 Salute the *b*' which are in Laodicea, "
1Th 1: 4 Knowing, *b*' beloved, your election "
2: 1 yourselves, *b*', know our entrance "
9 ye remember, *b*', our labour and "
14 For ye, *b*', became followers of the "
17 we, *b*', being taken from you for a "
3: 7 Therefore, *b*', we were comforted "
4: 1 we beseech you, *b*', and exhort you "
10 toward all the *b*' which are in all "
10 we beseech you, *b*', that ye increase "
13 not have you to be ignorant, *b*', "
5: 1 the times and the seasons, *b*', ye "
4 ye, *b*', are not in darkness, that "
12 we beseech you, *b*', to know them "
14 we exhort you, *b*', warn them that "
25 *B*', pray for us. "
26 Greet all the *b*' with an holy kiss. "
27 epistle be read unto all the holy *b*'. "
2Th 1: 3 thank God always for you, *b*', as it "
2: 1 we beseech you, *b*', by the coming "
13 for you, *b*' beloved of the Lord, "
15 Therefore, *b*', stand fast, and hold "
3: 1 Finally, *b*', pray for us, that the "
6 we command you, *b*', in the name "
13 ye, *b*' be not weary in well doing. "
1Ti 4: 6 put the *b*' in remembrance of these "
5: 1 father; and the younger men as *b*'; "
6: 2 despise then, because they are *b*'; "
2Ti 4:21 Linus, and Claudia, and all the *b*'. "
Heb 2:11 he is not ashamed to call them *b*', "
12 I will declare thy name unto my *b*', "
17 made like unto his *b*', that he "
3: 1 Wherefore, holy *b*', partakers of "
12 Take heed, *b*', lest there be in any "
7: 5 that is, of their *b*', though they "
10:19 Having therefore, *b*', boldness to "
13:22 I beseech you, *b*', suffer the word "
Jas 1: 2 My *b*', count it all joy when ye fall "
16 Do not err, my beloved *b*'. "
19 Wherefore, my beloved *b*', let every "
2: 1 My *b*', have not the faith of our "
5 Hearken, my beloved *b*', Hath not "
14 What doth it profit, my *b*', though "
3: 1 My *b*', be not many masters, "
10 My *b*', these things ought not so to "
12 Can the fig tree, my *b*', bear olive "
4:11 Speak not evil one of another, *b*'. "
5: 7 Be patient therefore, *b*', unto the "
9 Grudge not one against another, *b*'. "
10 Take, my *b*', the prophets, who "
12 above all things, my *b*', swear not "
19 *B*', if any of you do err from the "
1Pe 1:22 unto unfeigned love of the *b*', see *5360*
3: 8 love as *b*', be pitiful, be courteous: *5361*
5: 9 accomplished in your *b*' that are *81*
2Pe 1:10 the rather, *b*', give diligence to *80*
1Jo 2: 7 *B*', I write no new commandment * "
3:13 Marvel not, my *b*', if the world "
14 because we love the *b*'. He that "
16 to lay down our lives for the *b*'. "
3Jo 3 when the *b*' came and testified of "
5 thou doest to the *b*', and to "
10 he himself receive the *b*', and "
Re 6:11 fellowservants also and their *b*', "
12:10 the accuser of our *b*' is cast down, "
19:10 of thy *b*' that have the testimony "
22: 9 of thy *b*' the prophets, and of them "

brethren's See also BROTHERS'.
De 20: 8 lest his *b*' heart faint as well as 251

bribe See also BRIBES.
1Sa 12: 3 hand have I received any *b*' *3724
Am 5:12 they take a *b*', and they turn aside "

bribery
Job 15:34 consume the tabernacles of *b*'. 7810

bribes
1Sa 8: 3 aside after lucre, and took *b*', 7810
Ps 26:10 and their right hand is full of *b*'. "
Isa 33:15 his hands from holding of *b*', "

brick See also BRICKKILN; BRICKS.
Ge 11: 3 Go to, let us make *b*', and burn 3835
3 they had *b*' for stone, and slime 3843
Ex 1:14 in morter, and in *b*', and in all "
5: 7 give the people straw to make *b*', 3835
14 fulfilled your task in making *b*' "
16 and they say to us, Make *b*': and 3843
Isa 65: 3 burneth incense upon altars of *b*';* "

brickkiln
2Sa 12:31 made them pass through the *b*': 4404
Jer 43: 9 the clay in the *b*', which is at the * "
Na 3:14 morter, make strong the *b*'. "

bricks
Ex 5: 8 the tale of the *b*', which they did 3843
18 yet shall ye deliver the tale of *b*'. "
19 from your *b*' of your daily task. "
Isa 9:10 The *b*' are fallen down, but we will "

bride See also BRIDECHAMBER; BRIDEGROOM.
Isa 49:18 bind them on thee, as a *b*' doeth. 3618
61:10 a *b*' adorneth herself with jewels. "
62: 5 bridegroom rejoiceth over the *b*', "
Jer 2:32 maid forget her ornaments, or a *b*' "
7:34 bridegroom, and the voice of the *b*': "
16: 9 and the voice of the *b*'. "
25:10 the voice of the *b*', the sound of "
33:11 the voice of the *b*', the voice of "
Joe 2:16 and the *b*' out of her closet. "
Joh 3:29 that hath the *b*' is the bridegroom: *3565*
Re 18:23 of the *b*' shall be heard no more "
21: 2 prepared as a *b*' adorned for her "
9 shew thee the *b*', the Lamb's wife. "
22:17 the Spirit and the *b*' say, Come. "

bridechamber
M't 9:15 Can the children of the *b*' mourn, *3567*
M'r 2:19 Can the children of the *b*' fast, "
Lu 5:34 make the children of the *b*' fast, "

bridegroom See also BRIDEGROOM'S.
Ps 19: 5 a *b*' coming out of his chamber, 2860
Isa 61:10 as a *b*' decketh himself with "
62: 5 the *b*' rejoiceth over the bride, so "
Jer 7:34 the voice of the *b*', and the voice "
16: 9 of gladness, the voice of the *b*', "
25:10 the voice of the *b*', and the voice "
33:11 the voice of the *b*', and the voice "
Joe 2:16 let the *b*' go forth of his chamber, "
M't 9:15 as long as the *b*' is with them? *3566*
15 when the *b*' shall be taken from "
25: 1 and went forth to meet the *b*'. "
5 While the *b*' tarried, they all "
6 Behold, the *b*' cometh; go ye out "
10 they went to buy, the *b*' came; "
M'r 2:19 while the *b*' is with them? "
19 as long as they have the *b*' "
20 when the *b*' shall be taken away "
Lu 5:34 fast, while the *b*' is with them? "
35 come, when the *b*' shall be taken "
Joh 2: 9 governor of the feast called the *b*', "
3:29 that hath the bride is the *b*': "
29 but the friend of the *b*', "
Re 18:23 and the voice of the *b*' and of the "

bridegroom's
Joh 3:29 greatly because of the *b*' voice: *3566*

bridle See also BRIDLES; BRIDLETH.
2Ki 19:28 my *b*' in thy lips, and I will turn 4964
Job 30:11 they have also let loose the *b*' 7448
41:13 come to him with his double *b*'? "
Ps 32: 9 must be held in with bit and *b*', "
39: 1 I will keep my mouth with a *b*', 4269
Pr 26: 3 a *b*' for the ass, and a rod for the 4964
Isa 30:28 be a *b*' in the jaws of the people, 7448
37:29 in thy nose, and my *b*' in thy lips, 4964
Jas 3: 2 able also to *b*' the whole body. *5469*

bridles
Re 14:20 even unto the horse *b*', by the *5469*

bridleth
Jas 1:26 *b*' not his tongue, but deceiveth *5468*

briefly
Ro 13: 9 *b*' comprehended in this saying, * *346*
1Pe 5:12 I have written *b*', exhorting *1223, 3641*

brier See also BRIERS.
Isa 55:13 instead of the *b*' shall come up 5636
Eze 28:24 shall be no more a pricking *b*' 5544
Mic 7: 4 The best of them is as a *b*': the 2312

briers
J'g 8: 7 of the wilderness and with *b*'. 1303
16 thorns of the wilderness, and *b*', "
Isa 5: 6 but there shall come up *b*' and 8068
7:23 it shall even be for *b*' and thorns. "
24 all the land shall become *b*' and "
25 come thither the fear of *b*' and "
9:18 it shall devour the *b*' and thorns, "
10:17 and devour his thorns and his *b*' "
27: 4 who would set the *b*' and thorns "
32:13 shall come up thorns and *b*'; "
Eze 2: 6 *b*' and thorns be with thee, and 5621
Heb 6: 8 which beareth thorns and *b*' **5146*

brigandine See also BRIGANDINES.
Jer 51: 3 that lifteth himself up in his *b*': *5630

brigandines
Jer 46: 4 the spears, and put on the *b*'. 5630

bright
Le 13: 2 a rising, a scab, or *b*' spot, and it 934
4 If the *b*' spot be white in the skin "
19 or a *b*' spot, white, and somewhat "
23 if the *b*' spot stay in his place, and 934
24 have a white *b*' spot, somewhat "
25 the hair in the *b*' spot be turned "
26 no white hair in the *b*' spot, and it "
28 if the *b*' spot stay in his place, and "
38 in the skin of their flesh *b*' spots, "
38 even white *b*' spots; "
39 the *b*' spots in the skin of their "
14:56 and for a scab, and for a *b*' spot: "
1Ki 7:45 of the Lord, were of *b*' brass. *4803
2Ch 4:16 for the house of the Lord of *b*' 4838
Job 37:11 he scattereth his *b*' cloud: * 216
21 now men see not the *b*' light 925
Ca 5:14 his belly is as *b*' ivory overlaid *6247
Jer 51:11 Make *b*' the arrows; gather the *1305
Eze 1:13 and the fire was *b*', and out of 5051
21:15 ah! it is made *b*', it is wrapped *1300
21 he made his arrows *b*', he *7043
27:19 *b*' iron, cassia, and calamus, 6219
32: 8 All the *b*' lights of heaven will I 3974
Na 3: 3 both the *b*' sword and the *3851
Zec 10: 1 so the Lord shall make *b*' clouds, 2385
M't 17: 5 behold, a *b*' cloud overshadowed *5460*
Lu 11:36 as when the *b*' shining of a candle *796*
Ac 10:30 stood before me in *b*' clothing, *2986*
Re 22:16 and the *b*' and morning star. "

brightness
2Sa 22:13 Through the *b*' before him were 5051
Job 31:26 shined, or the moon walking in *b*'; 3368
Ps 18:12 At the *b*' that was before him his 5051
Isa 59: 9 for *b*', but we walk in darkness. 5054
60: 3 and kings to the *b*' of thy rising. 5051
19 neither for *b*' shall the moon give "
62: 1 righteousness thereof go forth as *b*' "
Eze 1: 4 and a *b*' was about it, and out of "
27 of fire, and it had *b*' round about. "
28 the appearance of the *b*' round "
8: 2 as the appearance of *b*', as the 2096
10: 4 the court was full of the *b*' of the 5051
28: 7 wisdom, they shall defile thy *b*'. 3314
17 thy wisdom by reason of thy *b*': "
Da 2:31 This great image, whose *b*' was 2122
4:36 mine honour and *b*' returned "
12: 3 shall shine as the *b*' of the 2096
Am 5:20 even very dark, and no *b*' in it? 5051
Hab 3: 4 And his *b*' was as the light; "
Ac 26:13 light from heaven, above the *b*' of *2987*
2Th 2: 8 with the *b*' of his coming: **2015*
Heb 1: 3 Who being the *b*' of his glory * *541*

brim See also BRIMSTONE.
Jos 3:15 were dipped in the *b*' of the *7097
1Ki 7:23 ten cubits from the one *b*' to the 8193
24 under the *b*' of it round about "
26 and the *b*' thereof was wrought "
26 like the *b*' of a cup, "
2Ch 4: 2 from *b*' to *b*', round in compass, "
5 and the *b*' of it like the work "
5 like the work of the *b*' of a cup, "
Joh 2: 7 And they filled them up to the *b*'. *507*

brimstone
Ge 19:24 Sodom and upon Gomorrah *b*' 1614
De 29:23 the whole land thereof is *b*', and "
Job 18:15 *b*' shall be scattered upon his "
Ps 11: 6 he shall rain snares, fire and *b*', "
Isa 30:33 like a stream of *b*', doth kindle it. "
34: 9 the dust thereof into *b*', and the "
Eze 38:22 and great hail stones, fire and *b*'. "
Lu 17:29 fire and *b*' from heaven, and *2303*
Rev 9:17 of fire, and of jacinth, and *b*', *2306*
17 issued fire and smoke and *b*'. *2303*
18 the smoke, and by the *b*', which "
14:10 with fire and *b*' in the presence of "
19:20 a lake of fire burning with *b*'. "
20:10 the lake of fire and *b*', where the "
21: 8 lake which burneth with fire and *b*': "

bring See also BRINGEST; BRINGETH; BRINGING; BROUGHT.
Ge 1:11 Let the earth *b*' forth grass, the *1876
20 the waters *b*' forth abundantly 8317
24 Let the earth *b*' forth the living 3318
3:16 in sorrow thou shalt *b*' forth 3205
18 also and thistles shall it *b*' forth 6779
6:17 do *b*' a flood of waters upon the 935
19 two of every sort shalt thou *b*' into "
8:17 *B*' forth with thee every living 3318
9: 7 *b*' forth abundantly in the earth 8317
14 when I *b*' a cloud over the earth, 6049
18:16 went with them to *b*' them on the 7971
19 the Lord may *b*' upon Abraham 935
19: 5 *b*' them out unto us, that we may 3318
8 let me, I pray thee, *b*' them out "
12 hast in the city, *b*' them out of "
24: 5 must I needs *b*' thy son again 7725
6 Beware thou that thou *b*' not my "
8 my oath: only *b*' not my son "
27: 4 and *b*' it to me, that I may eat; 935
5 to hunt for venison, and to *b*' it. "
7 *B*' me venison, and make me "
10 And thou shalt *b*' it to thy father, "
12 and I shall *b*' a curse upon me, and "
25 *B*' it near to me, and I will eat of 5066
28:15 and will *b*' thee again into this 7725
37:14 well with the flocks; and *b*' me "
38:24 *B*' her forth, and let her be burnt. 3318
40:14 and *b*' me out of this house: "
41:32 and God will shortly *b*' it to pass. 6213
42:20 *b*' your youngest brother unto 935
34 And *b*' your youngest brother "
37 Slay my two sons, if I *b*' him not "
37 and I will *b*' him to thee again. 7725
38 then shall ye *b*' down my gray 3381
43: 7 know that he would say, *B*' your "
9 if I *b*' him not unto thee, and set 935
16 *B*' these men home, and slay, and

Ge 44:21 *B'* him down unto me, that I may 3381
29 ye shall *b'* down my gray hairs "
31 and thy servants shall *b'* down "
32 If I *b'* him not unto thee, then I 935
45:13 ye shall haste and *b'* down my 3381
19 and for your wives, and *b'* your 5375
46: 4 and I will also surely *b'* thee up 5927
48: 9 *B'* them, I pray thee, unto me, 3947
21 and *b'* you again unto the land of 7725
50:20 to *b'* to pass, as it is this day, to 6213
24 and *b'* you out of this land into 5927
Ex 3: 8 and to *b'* them up out of that "
10 that thou mayest *b'* forth my 3318
11 I should *b'* forth the children of "
17 I will *b'* you up out of the 5927
6: 6 and I will *b'* you out from under 3318
8 And I will *b'* you in unto the land, 935
13 to *b'* the children of Israel out of "
26 *B'* out the children of Israel from 3318
27 to *b'* out the children of Israel "
7: 4 and *b'* forth mine armies, and my "
5 and *b'* out the children of Israel "
8: 3 And the river shall *b'* forth *8317
18 enchantments to *b'* forth lice, 3318
10: 4 to morrow will I *b'* the locusts 935
11: 1 Yet will I *b'* one plague more upon "
12:51 the Lord did *b'* the children of 3318
13: 5 the Lord shall *b'* thee into the 935
11 shall be when the Lord shall *b'* "
15:17 Thou shalt *b'* them in, and plant "
16: 5 prepare that which they *b'* in; "
18:19 that thou mayest *b'* the causes "
22 they shall *b'* unto thee, but "
21: 6 Then his master shall *b'* him 5066
6 the judges; he shall also *b'* him "
22:13 let him *b'* it for witness, and he 935
23: 4 thou shalt surely *b'* it back to 7725
19 thou shalt *b'* into the house of the 935
20 and to *b'* thee into the place which "
23 and *b'* thee in unto the Amorites, "
25: 2 that they *b'* me an offering: *3947
26:33 that thou mayest *b'* in thither 935
27:20 that they *b'* thee pure oil olive 3947
29: 3 and *b'* them in the basket, with 7126
4 Aaron and his sons thou shalt *b'* "
8 thou shalt *b'* his sons, and put "
32: 2 your daughters, and *b'* them unto 935
12 For mischief did he *b'* them out, 3318
33:12 *B'* up this people: and thou hast 5927
34:26 firstfruits of thy land thou shalt *b'* 935
35: 5 let him *b'* it, an offering "
29 made them willing to *b'* for all "
36: 5 The people *b'* much more than "
40: 4 And thou shalt *b'* in the table, "
4 thou shalt *b'* in the candlestick, "
12 And thou shalt *b'* Aaron and his 7126
14 thou shalt *b'* his sons, and "
Le 1: 2 If any man of you *b'* an offering * "
2 unto the Lord, ye shall *b'* your * "
5 the priests, Aaron's sons, shall *b'* * "
10 he shall *b'* it a male without * "
13 and the priest shall *b'* it all, and * "
14 he shall *b'* his offering of turtle * "
15 And the priest shall *b'* it unto * "
2: 2 And he shall *b'* it to Aaron's sons 935
4 if thou *b'* an oblation of a meat *7126
8 thou shalt *b'* the meat offering 935
8 priest, he shall *b'* it unto the 5066
11 meat offering, which ye shall *b'* *7126
4: 3 then let him *b'* for his sin, * "
4 And he shall *b'* the bullock unto 935
5 and *b'* it to the tabernacle of the "
14 and *b'* him before the tabernacle "
16 priest that is anointed shall *b'* of "
23 he shall *b'* his offering, a kid of "
28 then he shall *b'* his offering, a "
32 if he *b'* a lamb for a sin offering, "
32 shall *b'* it a female without blemish "
5: 6 And he shall *b'* his trespass "
7 And if he be not able to *b'* a lamb, 5060
7 then he shall *b'* for his trespass, 935
Le 5: 8 he shall *b'* them unto the priest, "
11 not able to *b'* two turtledoves, 5381
11 sinned shall *b'* for his offering 935
12 Then shall he *b'* it to the priest, "
15 *b'* for his trespass unto the Lord "
18 And he shall *b'* a ram without "
6: 6 he shall *b'* his trespass offering "
21 it is baken, thou shalt *b'* it in: "
7:29 shall *b'* his oblation unto the "
30 His own hands shall *b'* the "
30 he *b'*, that the breast may be "
10:15 the wave breast shall they *b'* "
12: 6 she shall *b'* a lamb of the first "
8 if she not be able to *b'* a lamb, *4672
8 then she shall *b'* two turtles, *3947
14:23 And he shall *b'* them on the 935
15:29 and *b'* them unto the priest, "
16: 9 And Aaron shall *b'* the goat *7126
11 And Aaron shall *b'* the bullock * "
12 small, and *b'* it within the vail: 935
15 and *b'* his blood within the vail, "
20 altar, he shall *b'* the live goat: *7126
17: 5 may *b'* their sacrifices, which 935
5 even that they may *b'* them unto "
18: 3 whither I *b'* you, shall ye not do: "
19:21 he shall *b'* his trespass offering "
20:22 whither I *b'* you to dwell therein, "
23:10 then ye shall *b'* a sheaf of the "
17 Ye shall *b'* out of your habitations "
24: 2 that they *b'* unto thee pure oil 3947
14 *B'* forth him that hath cursed 3318
23 they should *b'* forth him that * "
25:21 and it shall *b'* forth fruit for three 6213
26:10 and *b'* forth the old because of 3318
21 I will *b'* seven times more 3254

Le 26:25 And I will *b'* a sword upon you, 935
31 and *b'* your sanctuaries unto *8074
32 *b'* the land into desolation: "
27: 9 *b'* an offering unto the Lord, *7126
Nu 3: 6 *B'* the tribe of Levi near, and * "
5: 9 *b'* unto the priest, shall be his. * "
15 *b'* his wife unto the priest, 935
15 and he shall *b'* her offering "
16 And the priest shall *b'* her near, 7126
6:10 he shall *b'* two turtles, or two 935
12 and shall *b'* a lamb of the first "
16 *b'* them before the Lord, *7126
8: 9, 10 And thou shalt *b'* the Levites * "
11:16 and *b'* them unto the tabernacle 3947
13:20 and *b'* of the fruit of the land. "
14: 8 then he will *b'* us into the land, 935
16 was not able to *b'* this people "
24 him will I *b'* into the land "
31 them will I *b'* in, and they shall "
37 that did *b'* up the evil report 3318
15: 4 his offering unto the Lord *b'* *7126
9 shall he *b'* with a bullock * "
10 thou shalt *b'* for a drink offering * "
18 into the land whither I *b'* you, 935
25 they shall *b'* their offering, a * "
27 then he shall *b'* a she goat of *7126
16: 9 to *b'* you near to himself to do "
17 and *b'* ye before the Lord every "
17:10 *B'* Aaron's rod again before the *7725
18: 2 *b'* thou with thee, that they may 7126
13 they shall *b'* unto the Lord, 935
15 which they *b'* unto the Lord, *7126
19: 2 that they *b'* thee a red heifer 3947
3 *b'* her forth without the camp, 3318
20: 5 to *b'* us in unto this evil place? 935
8 and thou shalt *b'* forth to them 3318
12 therefore ye shall not *b'* this 935
25 and *b'* them up unto mount Hor: 5927
22: 8 I will *b'* you word again, as the 7725
23:27 I will *b'* thee unto another place;* 3947
27:17 which may *b'* them in; that the 935
28:26 when ye *b'* a new meat offering *7126
32: 5 and *b'* us not over Jordan. 5674
De 1:17 *b'* it unto me, and I will hear it. 7126
22 and *b'* us word again by what 7725
4:38 to *b'* thee in, to give thee their 935
6:23 that he might *b'* us in, to give us "
7: 1 shall *b'* thee into the land "
26 Neither shalt thou *b'* an "
9: 3 *b'* them down before thy face: 3665
28 to *b'* them into the land which 935
12: 6 And thither ye shall *b'* your "
11 thither ye shall *b'* all that I "
14:28 thou shalt *b'* forth all the tithe 3318
17: 5 Then shalt thou *b'* forth that man "
21: 4 elders of that city shall *b'* down 2381
12 Then thou shalt *b'* her home 935
19 and *b'* him out unto the elders 3318
22: 1 any case *b'* them again unto 7725
2 shalt *b'* it unto thine own house, 622
8 that thou *b'* not blood upon 7760
14 and *b'* up an evil name upon her, 3318
15 and *b'* forth the tokens of the "
21 Then they shall *b'* out the damsel "
24 Then ye shall *b'* them both out "
23:18 Thou shalt not *b'* the hire of a 935
24:11 shall *b'* out the pledge abroad 3318
26: 2 which thou shalt *b'* of thy land 935
28:36 The Lord shall *b'* thee, and thy 3212
49 shall *b'* a nation against thee 5375
60 *b'* upon thee all the diseases 7725
61 them will the Lord *b'* upon thee, 5927
63 and to *b'* you to nought; and ye *8045
68 shall *b'* thee into Egypt again 7725
29:27 to *b'* upon it all the curses that 935
30: 5 And the Lord thy God will *b'* thee "
12 us to heaven, and *b'* it unto us, 3947
13 the sea for us, and *b'* it unto us, "
31:23 for thou shalt *b'* the children 935
33: 7 and *b'* him unto his people: "
Jos 2: 3 *B'* forth the men that are come 3318
18 *b'* thy father, and thy mother, * 622
6:22 and *b'* out thence the woman, 3318
10:22 and *b'* out those five kings "
18: 6 and *b'* the description hither 935
23:15 so shall the Lord *b'* upon you "
J'g 6:13 Did not the Lord *b'* us up 5927
18 and *b'* forth my present, and 3318
30 *B'* out thy son, that he may die: "
7: 4 *b'* them down unto the water, 338
11: 9 If ye *b'* me home again to fight 7725
19: 3 unto her, and to *b'* her again, "
22 *B'* forth the man that came into 3318
24 I will *b'* out now, and humble ye "
Ru 3:15 *B'* the vail that thou hast upon 3051
1Sa 1:22 and then I will *b'* him, that he 935
4: 4 might *b'* from thence the ark *5375
6: 7 *b'* their calves home from them: 7725
9: 7 what shall we *b'* the man? 935
7 not a present to *b'* to the man "
23 *B'* the portion which I gave thee, 5414
11:12 *b'* the men, that we may put them "
13: 9 *B'* hither a burnt offering to me, 5066
14:18 *B'* hither the ark of God. For the "
34 *B'* me hither every man his ox, "
15:32 *B'* ye hither to me Agag the king "
16:17 well, and *b'* him to me. 935
19:15 *B'* him up to me in the bed, 5927
20: 8 why shouldest thou *b'* me to thy 935
23: 9 priest, *B'* hither the ephod. 5066
27:11 to *b'* tidings to Gath, saying, 935
28: 8 and *b'* me him up, whom I shall 5927
11 Whom shall I *b'* up unto thee? "
11 And he said, *B'* me up Samuel. "
15 disquieted me, to *b'* me up? "
30: 7 *b'* me hither the ephod, 5066

1Sa 30:15 Canst thou *b'* me down to this 3381
15 and I will *b'* thee down to this "
2Sa 2: 3 were with him did David *b'* up, 5927
3:12 to *b'* about all Israel unto thee. 5437
13 except thou first *b'* Michal 935
6: 2 to *b'* up from thence the ark 5927
9:10 and thou shalt *b'* in the fruits, 935
12:23 can I *b'* him back again? I shall 7725
13:10 *B'* the meat into the chamber, 935
14:10 *b'* him to me, and he shall not "
21 *b'* the young man Absalom 7725
15: 8 shall *b'* me again indeed to "
14 and *b'* evil upon us, and smite *5080
25 he will *b'* me again, and shew 7725
17: 3 I will *b'* back all the people unto "
13 then shall all Israel *b'* ropes 5375
14 that the Lord might *b'* evil 935
19:11 the last to *b'* the king back 7725
12 the last to *b'* back the king? "
22:28 that thou mayest *b'* them down. 8213
1Ki 1:33 and *b'* him down to Gihon: 3381
2: 9 head *b'* thou down to the grave "
3:24 king said, *B'* me a sword. *3947
5: 9 My servants shall *b'* them down 3381
8: 1 that they might *b'* up the ark 5927
4 priests and the Levites *b'* up. "
32 to *b'* his way upon his head; 5414
34 and *b'* them again unto the land 7725
10:29 did they *b'* them out by their 3318
12:21 to *b'* the kingdom again to 7725
13:18 *B'* him back with thee unto thine "
14:10 I will *b'* evil upon the house of 935
17:11 *B'* me, I pray thee, a morsel of 3947
13 and *b'* it unto me, and after 3318
20:33 Go ye, *b'* him. Then Ben-hadad 3947
21:21 I will *b'* evil upon thee, and will 935
29 I will not *b'* evil in his days: "
29 son's days will I *b'* evil upon his "
2Ki 2:20 *B'* me a new cruse, and put salt 3947
3:15 *b'* me a minstrel. And it came to "
4: 6 unto her son, *B'* me yet a vessel. 5066
41 Then *b'* meal. And he cast it 3947
6:19 and I will *b'* you to the man 3212
10:22 *B'* forth vestments for all the 3318
12: 4 *b'* into the house of the Lord, 935
19: 3 there is not strength to *b'* forth. 3205
22:16 I will *b'* evil upon this place, 935
20 which I will *b'* upon this place. "
23: 4 to *b'* forth out of the temple 3318
1Ch 9:28 that they should *b'* them in *935, 3318
13: 3 And let us *b'* again the ark of our 5437
5 to *b'* the ark of God from 935
6 to *b'* up thence the ark of God 5927
12 How shall I *b'* the ark of God 935
15: 3 to *b'* up the ark of the Lord unto 5927
12 that ye may *b'* up the ark of the "
14 sanctified themselves to *b'* up the "
25 to *b'* up the ark of the covenant of "
16:29 *b'* an offering, and come before 5375
21: 2 and *b'* the number of them to me, 935
12 what word I shall *b'* again *7725
22:19 to *b'* the ark of the covenant of the 935
2Ch 2:16 and we will *b'* it to thee in floats "
5: 2 to *b'* up the ark of the covenant 5927
5 did the priests and the Levites *b'* "
6:25 and *b'* them again unto the land 7725
11: 1 that he might *b'* the kingdom "
24: 6 required of the Levites to *b'* in 935
9 to *b'* in to the Lord the collection "
19 to *b'* them again unto the Lord; 7725
28:13 Ye shall not *b'* in the captives 935
29:31 *b'* sacrifices and thank offerings "
31:10 Since the people began to *b'* the "
34:24 I will *b'* evil upon this place, and "
28 all the evil that I will *b'* upon this "
Ezr 1: 8 did Cyrus king of Persia *b'* forth 3318
11 All these did Sheshbazzar *b'* up 5927
3: 7 to *b'* cedar trees from Lebanon to 935
8:17 they should *b'* unto us ministers "
30 to *b'* them to Jerusalem unto the "
Ne 1: 9 and will *b'* them unto the place "
5: 5 we *b'* into bondage our sons and 3533
8: 1 to *b'* the book of the law of Moses, 935
9:29 that thou mightest *b'* them again 7725
10:31 the people of the land *b'* ware 935
34 to *b'* it into the house of our God, "
35 And to *b'* the firstfruits of our "
36 to *b'* to the house of our God, "
37 we should *b'* the firstfruits of our "
38 the Levites shall *b'* up the tithe 5927
39 *b'* the offering of the corn, of the 935
11: 1 *b'* one of ten to dwell in Jerusalem "
12:27 to *b'* them to Jerusalem, to keep "
13:18 and did not our God *b'* all this "
18 *b'* more wrath upon Israel by "
Es 1:11 To *b'* Vashti the queen before the "
3: 9 business to *b'* it into the king's "
6: 1 to *b'* the book of records of the "
9 *b'* him on horseback through *7392
14 hasted to *b'* Haman unto the 935
Job 6:22 Did I say, *B'* unto me? or, Give *3051
10: 9 and wilt thou *b'* me into dust 7725
14: 4 Who can *b'* a clean thing out of 5414
9 will bud, and *b'* forth boughs *6213
15:35 They conceive mischief, and *b'* 3205
18:14 and it shall *b'* him to the king of *6805
30:23 thou wilt *b'* me to death, and the 7725
33:30 To *b'* back his soul from the pit, "
38:32 Canst thou *b'* forth Mazzaroth *3318
39: 1 when the wild goats of the rock *b'* 3205
2 thou the time when they *b'* "
3 They bow themselves, they *b'* 6398
12 he will *b'* home thy seed, and 7725
40:12 and *b'* him low; and tread down 3665
20 the mountains *b'* him forth food, 5375
Ps 18:27 afflicted; but wilt *b'* down high 8213

Ps 25:17 O b' thou me out of my distresses. 3318
37: 5 him; and he shall b' it to pass. 6213
6 shall b' forth thy righteousness *3318
38:*title* A Psalm of David, to b' to 2142
43: 3 let them b' me unto thy holy hill, 935
55:23 thou, O God, shalt b' them down 3381
59:11 and b' them down, O Lord our "
60: 9 Who will b' me into the strong 2986
68:22 I will b' again from Bashan, 7725
22 I will b' my people again "
29 Jerusalem shall kings b' presents 2986
70:*title* A Psalm of David, to b' to 2142
71:20 b' me up again from the depths 5927
72: 3 The mountains shall b' peace to 5375
10 Tarshish and of the isles shall b' 7725
76:11 all that be round about him b' 2986
81: 2 and b' hither the timbrel, the 5414
92:14 They shall still b' forth fruit in 5107
94:23 And he shall b' upon them their 7725
96: 8 b' an offering, and come into his 5375
104:14 that he may b' forth food out of 3318
108:10 Who will b' me into the strong 2986
142: 7 B' my soul out of prison, that I 3318
143:11 sake b' my soul out of trouble. "
144:13 our sheep may b' forth thousands 503
Pr 4: 8 she shall b' thee to honour, when 3513
19:24 will not so much as b' it to his 7725
26:15 him to b' it again to his mouth. "
27: 1 knowest not what a day may b' 3205
29: 8 Scornful men b' a city into a *6315
23 A man's pride shall b' him low: 8213
Ec 3:22 for who shall b' him to see what 935
11: 9 God will b' thee into judgment. "
12:14 God shall b' every work into "
Ca 8: 2 I would lead thee, and b' thee "
11 was to b' a thousand pieces of "
Isa 1:13 B' no more vain oblations; incense "
5: 2 he looked that it should b' forth 6213
4 when I looked that it should b' "
7:17 The Lord shall b' upon thee, and 935
14: 2 and b' them to their place: and "
15: 9 I will b' more upon Dimon, lions 7896
23: 4 I travail not, nor b' forth 3205
4 up young men, nor b' up virgins. 7311
9 to b' into contempt all the 7034
25: 5 Thou shalt b' down the noise *3665
11 and he shall b' down their pride 8213
12 of thy walls shall he b' down, 7817
12 lay low, and b' to the ground, 5060
28:21 and b' to pass his act, his strange 5647
31: 2 and will b' evil, and will not call 935
33:11 ye shall b' forth stubble: your 3205
37: 3 and there is not strength to b' "
38: 8 I will b' again the shadow of the 7725
41:21 b' forth your strong reasons, 5066
22 Let them b' them forth, and shew "
42: 1 he shall b' forth judgment to the 3318
3 he shall b' forth judgment unto "
7 to b' out the prisoners from the "
16 And I will b' the blind by a way 3212
43: 5 I will b' thy seed from the east, 935
6 b' my sons from far, and my "
8 B' forth the blind people that 3318
9 let them b' forth their witnesses, 5414
45: 8 and let them b' forth salvation, 6509
21 Tell ye, and b' them near; yea, 5066
46: 8 b' it again to mind, O ye 7725
11 I will also b' it to pass; I have 935
13 I b' near my righteousness; it 7126
49: 5 to b' Jacob again to him, Though 7725
22 and they shall b' thy sons in their 935
52: 8 the Lord shall b' again Zion. *7725
55:10 and maketh it b' forth and bud 3205
56: 7 Even them will I b' to my holy 935
58: 7 that thou b' the poor that are cast "
59: 4 they conceive mischief, and b' 3205
60: 6 they shall b' gold and incense; 5375
9 to b' thy sons from far, their 935
11 that men may b' unto thee the "
17 For brass I will b' gold, "
17 and for iron I will b' silver, "
63: 6 and I will b' down their strength *3381
65: 9 And I will b' forth a seed out of 3318
23 in vain, nor b' forth for trouble; 3205
66: 4 will b' their fears upon them; 935
8 Shall the earth be made to b' *2342
9 Shall I b' to the birth, 7665
9 and not cause to b' forth? 3205
9 shall I cause to b' forth, and "
20 And they shall b' all your brethren 935
20 as the children of Israel b' an "
Jer 3:14 family, and I will b' you to Zion: "
4: 6 for I will b' evil from the north, "
5:15 I will b' a nation upon you from "
6:19 I will b' evil upon this people, "
8: 1 they shall b' out the bones of the 3318
10:24 anger, lest thou b' me to nothing. "
11: 8 therefore I will b' upon them all 935
11 I will b' evil upon them, which "
23 for I will b' evil upon the men of "
12: 2 they grow, yea, they b' forth 6213
15 and will b' them again, every 7725
15:19 then will I b' thee again, and thou "
16:15 and I will b' them again into their "
17:18 b' upon them the day of evil, and 935
21 sabbath day, nor b' it in by the "
24 to b' in no burden through the "
18:22 when thou shalt b' a troop suddenly "
19: 3 I will b' evil upon this place, the "
15 I will b' upon this city and upon all "
23: 3 and will b' them again to their 7725
12 for I will b' evil upon them, even 935
40 I will b' an everlasting reproach 5414
24: 6 And I will b' them again to this 7725
25: 9 and will b' them against this 935
13 And I will b' upon that land all "

Jer 25:29 I begin to b' evil on the city *
26:15 ye shall surely b' innocent blood 5414
27:11 But the nations that b' their neck 935
12 B' your necks under the yoke of "
22 will I b' them up, and restore 5927
28: 3 will I b' again into this place all 7725
4 will b' again to this place Jeconiah "
6 to b' again the vessels of the "
29:14 and I will b' you again into the "
30: 3 that I will b' again the captivity * "
18 I will b' again the captivity of * "
31: 8 I will b' them from the north 935
23 I shall b' again their captivity 7725
32 b' them out of the land of Egypt; 3318
32:37 and I will b' them again unto 7725
42 so will I b' upon them all the 935
33: 6 I will b' it health and cure, and 4608
11 of them that shall b' the sacrifice 935
35: 2 and b' them into the house of the "
17 I will b' upon Judah and upon all "
36:31 and I will b' upon them, and upon "
38:23 they shall b' out all thy wives 4672
39:16 I will b' my words upon this city 935
41: 5 b' them to the house of the Lord. "
42:17 the evil that I will b' upon them. "
45: 5 I will b' evil upon all flesh, saith "
48:44 for I will b' upon it, even upon "
47 Yet will I b' again the captivity 7725
49: 5 I will b' a fear upon thee, saith 935
6 I will b' again the captivity of 7725
8 I will b' the calamity of Esau 935
16 I will b' thee down from thence, 3381
32 I will b' their calamity from all 935
36 And upon Elam will I b' the four "
37 and I will b' evil upon them, even "
39 I will b' again the captivity of 7725
50:19 And I will b' Israel again to his "
51:40 I will b' them down like lambs to 3381
44 I will b' forth out of his mouth 3318
64 the evil that I will b' upon her: 935
La 1:21 thou wilt b' the day that thou hast "
Eze 5:17 I will b' the sword upon thee. 935
6: 3 will b' a sword upon you, and I "
7:24 Wherefore I will b' the worst of "
11: 7 I will b' you forth out of the *3318
8 I will b' a sword upon you, saith 935
9 And I will b' you out of the midst 3318
12: 4 Then shalt thou b' forth thy stuff "
13 and I will b' him to Babylon to the 935
13:14 and b' it down to the ground, so 5060
14:17 Or if I b' a sword upon that land, 935
16:40 They shall also b' up a company 5927
53 When I shall b' again their *7725
53 then will I b' again the captivity *
17: 8 that it might b' forth branches, 6213
20 and I will b' him to Babylon, and 935
23 and it shall b' forth boughs, and 5375
20: 6 to b' them forth of the land of 3318
15 I would not b' them into the land 935
34 I will b' you out from the people, 3318
35 I will b' you into the wilderness 935
37 and I will b' you into the bond of "
38 I will b' them forth out of the 3318
41 when I b' you out from the people, "
42 when I shall b' you into the land 935
21:29 to b' thee upon the necks of them *5414
23:22 and I will b' them against thee on 935
46 I will b' up a company upon 5927
24: 6 b' it out piece by piece; let no lot 3318
26: 7 b' upon Tyrus Nebuchadrezzar 935
19 when I shall b' up the deep upon 5927
20 When I shall b' thee down with 3381
28: 7 I will b' strangers upon thee, the 935
8 They shall b' thee down to the 3381
18 therefore will I b' forth a fire *3318
18 and I will b' thee to ashes upon *5414
29: 4 I will b' thee up out of the midst 5927
8 I will b' a sword upon thee, and 935
14 And I will b' again the captivity 7725
31: 6 did all the beasts of the field b' 3205
32: 3 and they shall b' thee up in my 5927
9 when I shall b' thy destruction 935
33: 2 When I b' the sword upon a land, "
34:13 will b' them out from the people, 3318
13 and will b' them to their own land, 935
16 and b' again that which was 7725
36:11 they shall increase and b' fruit: *6509
24 and will b' you into your own land. 935
37: 6 and will b' up flesh upon you, 5927
12 your graves, and b' you into the 935
21 every side, and b' them into their "
38: 4 and I will b' thee forth, and all 3318
16 and I will b' thee against my land, 935
17 I would b' thee against them? "
39: 2 b' thee upon the mountains of "
25 Now will I b' again the captivity 7725
47:12 it shall b' forth...fruit according 1069
Da 1: 3 that he should b' certain of the 935
18 he should b' them in, then the * "
2:24 b' me in before the king, and I 5924
3:13 his rage and fury commanded to b' 858
4: 6 made I a decree to b' in all the 5924
5: 2 commanded to b' the golden and 858
7 The king cried aloud to b' in the 5924
9:24 b' in everlasting righteousness, 935
Ho 2:14 and b' her into the wilderness, 1980
7:12 I will b' them down as the fowls 3381
9:12 Though they b' up their children, 1431
13 Ephraim shall b' forth his 3318
16 though they b' forth, yet will I 3205
Joe 3: 1 I shall b' again the captivity of 7725
2 and will b' them down into the 3381
Am 3:11 and he shall b' down thy strength "
4: 1 masters, B', and let us drink. 935
4 and b' your sacrifices every "
6:10 to b' out the bones out of the 3318

Am 8:10 and I will b' up sackcloth upon 5927
9: 2 heaven, thence will I b' them 3381
14 And I will b' again the captivity 7725
Ob 3 Who shall b' me down to the 3381
4 thence will I b' thee down, saith "
Jon 1:13 the men rowed hard to b' it to *7725
Mic 1:15 Yet will I b' an heir unto thee, 935
4:10 and labour to b' forth, O daughter 1518
7: 9 he will b' me forth to the light, 3318
Zep 1:17 And I will b' distress upon men, "
2: 2 Before the decree b' forth, 3205
3: 5 doth he b' his judgment to 5414
10 dispersed, shall b' mine offering. 2986
20 At that time will I b' you again, 935
Hag 1: 6 and b' in little; yet eat, but ye "
8 Go up to the mountain, and b' wood, "
Zec 3: 8 I will b' forth my servant the "
4: 7 he shall b' forth the headstone 3318
5: 4 I will b' it forth, saith the Lord of * "
8: 8 And I will b' them, and they shall 935
10: 6 and I will b' them again to place 7725
10 I will b' them again also out of "
10 I will b' them into the land of 935
13: 9 And I will b' the third part "
Mal 3:10 B' ye all the tithes into the "
M't 1:21 And she shall b' forth a son, and *5088*
23 And shall b' forth a son, and they "
2: 8 b' me word again, that I may *518*
13 until I b' thee word: for Herod **2036*
3: 8 B' forth therefore fruits meet for *4160*
5:23 if thou b' thy gift to the altar, *4374*
7:18 A good tree cannot b' forth evil *4160*
18 a corrupt tree b' forth good fruit. "
14:18 He said, B' them hither to me. *5342*
17:17 suffer you? b' him hither to me. "
21: 2 loose them, and b' them unto me. *71*
28: 8 did run to b' his disciples word. *518*
M'k 4:20 b' forth fruit, some thirtyfold, **2592*
7:32 And they b' unto him one that *5342*
8:22 and they b' a blind man unto him, "
9:19 shall I suffer you? b' him unto me. "
11: 2 never man sat; loose him, and b' *71*
12:15 tempt ye me? b' me a penny, *5342*
15:22 And they b' him unto the place "
Lu 1:31 and b' forth a son, and shall call *5088*
2:10 I b' you good tidings of great joy, *2097*
3: 8 B' forth therefore fruits worthy *4160*
5:18 sought means to b' him in, and to *1533*
19 they might b' him in because of "
6:43 neither doth a corrupt tree b' *4160*
8:14 pleasures of this life, and b' no *5062*
15 keep it, and b' forth fruit with *2592*
9:41 suffer you? B' thy son hither. *4317*
12:11 when they b' you unto the *4374*
14:21 b' in hither the poor, and the *1521*
15:22 B' forth the best robe, and put it *1627*
23 b' hither the fatted calf, and kill *5342*
19:27 reign over them, b' hither, and *71*
30 sat: loose him, and b' him hither. "
Joh 10:16 this fold: them also I must b', "
14:26 shall teach you all things, and b' *5179*
15: 2 that it may b' forth more fruit. **5342*
16 that ye should go and b' forth * "
18:29 What accusation b' ye against "
19: 4 Behold, I b' him forth to you, *71*
21:10 B' of the fish which ye have now *5342*
Ac 5:28 and intend to b' this man's blood *1863*
7: 6 they should b' them into bondage, *1402*
9: 2 he might b' them bound unto *71*
21 he might b' them bound unto the "
12: 4 after Easter to b' him forth to the *321*
17: 5 and sought to b' them out to the *71*
22: 5 to b' them which were there bound "
23:10 them, and to b' him into the castle. "
15 b' him down unto you to morrow *2609*
17 B' this young man unto the chief *520*
18 to b' this young man unto thee, *71*
20 that thou wouldest b' down Paul *2609*
24 and b' him safe unto Felix the *1295*
24:17 I came to b' alms to my nation, *4160*
Ro 7: 4 we should b' forth fruit unto God. *2592*
5 to b' forth fruit unto death. "
10: 6 (that is, to b' Christ down from *2609*
7 to b' up Christ again from the *321*
15 and b' glad tidings of good things! *2097*
1Co 1:19 b' to nothing the understanding † *114*
28 to b' to nought things that are: *2673*
4: 5 who both will b' to light the *5461*
17 b' you into remembrance of my * *363*
9:27 under my body, and b' it into *1396*
16: 3 them will I send to b' your * *667*
6 ye may b' me on my journey **4311*
2Co 11:20 if any man b' you into bondage, **2615*
Ga 2: 4 they might b' us into bondage: "
3:24 schoolmaster to b' us unto Christ, "
Eph 6: 4 b' them up in the nurture and **1625*
1Th 4:14 in Jesus will God b' with him. *71*
2Ti 4:11 Take Mark, and b' him with thee: "
13 b' with thee, and the books, but *5342*
Tit 3:13 B' Zenas the lawyer and Apollos **4311*
1Pe 3:18 that he might b' us to God, being *4317*
2Pe 2: 1 who privily shall b' in damnable *3919*
1 and b' upon themselves swift **1863*
11 b' not railing accusation against *5342*
2Jo 10 and b' not this doctrine, receive * "
3Jo 6 thou b' forward on their journey **4311*
Jude 9 durst not b' against him a railing *2018*
Re 21:24 do b' their glory and honour into *5342*
26 shall b' the glory and honour of "

bringers
2Ki 10: 5 and the b' up of the children, * 539

bringest
1Ki 1:42 art a valiant man, and b' good 1319
Job 14: 3 b' me into judgment with thee? 935
Isa 40: 9 O Zion, that b' good tidings, get *1319

Isa 40: 9 O Jerusalem, that b' good *1319
Ac 17:20 thou b' certain strange things to 1533

bringeth
Ex 6: 7 b' you out from under the 3318
Le 11:45 I am the Lord that b' you up *5927
17: 4 b' it not unto the door of the * 935
9 b' it not unto the door of the "
De 8: 7 the Lord thy God b' thee into a "
14:22 the field b' forth year by year. *3318
1Sa 2: 6 he b' down to the grave, 3381
6 to the grave, and b' up. 5927
7 rich: he b' low, and lifteth up. 8213
2Sa 18:26 He also b' tidings. 1319
22:48 and that b' down the people 3381
49 And that b' me forth from mine 3318
Job 12: 6 into whose hand God b' 935
22 and b' out to light the shadow of ‡3318
19:29 for wrath b' the punishments
28:11 that is hid b' he forth to light. 3318
Ps 1: 3 b' forth his fruit in his season; 5414
14: 7 when the Lord b' back the 7725
33:10 The Lord b' the counsel of the 6331
37: 7 of the man who b' wicked 6213
53: 6 When God b' back the captivity 7725
68: 6 he b' out those which are bound 3318
107:28 he b' them out of their distresses. "
30 b' them unto their desired haven. 5148
135: 7 b' the wind out of his treasuries. 3318
Pr 10:31 The mouth of the just b' forth 5107
16:30 moving his lips he b' evil to pass. 3615
18:16 and b' him before great men. 5148
19:26 causeth shame, and b' reproach. 2659
20:26 and b' the wheel over them. 7725
21:27 he b' it with a wicked mind? 935
29:15 himself b' his mother to shame. *
21 He that delicately b' up his *6445
25 The fear of man b' a snare: but 5414
30:33 churning of milk b' forth butter. 3318
33 wringing of the nose b' forth "
33 forcing of wrath b' forth strife. "
31:14 ships; she b' her food from afar. 935
Ec 2: 6 the wood that b' forth trees: *6779
Isa 8: 7 the Lord b' up upon them the 5927
26: 5 he b' down them that dwell on *7817
5 ground; he b' it even to the dust. 5060
40:23 That b' the princes to nothing; 5414
26 that b' out their host by number: 3318
41:27 to Jerusalem one that b' good 1319
43:17 Which b' forth the chariot and 3318
52: 7 the feet of him that b' good 1319
7 peace; that b' good tidings "
54:16 b' forth an instrument for his 3318
61:11 as the earth b' forth her bud, "
Jer 4:31 her that b' forth her first child, 1069
10:13 and b' forth the wind out of his 3318
51:16 and b' forth the wind out of his "
Eze 29:16 which b' their iniquity to *2142
Ho 10: 1 he b' forth fruit unto himself: *7737
Na 1:15 feet of him that b' good tidings, 1319
Hag 1:11 that which the ground b' forth, 3318
M't 3:10 tree which b' not forth good fruit 4160
7:17 good tree b' forth good fruit; "
17 but a corrupt tree b' forth evil "
19 tree that b' not forth good fruit is "
12:35 of the heart b' forth good things: 1544
35 evil treasure b' forth evil things. "
13:23 and b' forth some an hundredfold, 4160
52 b' forth out of his treasure things 1544
17: 1 b' them up into an high mountain 399
M'k 4:28 earth b' forth fruit of herself; *2592
Lu 3: 9 which b' not forth good fruit is 4160
6:43 b' not forth corrupt fruit; neither "
45 b' forth that which is good; 4393
45 an evil b' forth that which is evil: "
Joh 12:24 if it die, it b' forth much fruit. *5342
15: 5 the same b' forth much fruit: * "
Col 1: 6 and b' forth fruit, as it doth also 2592
Tit 2:11 grace of God that b' salvation 4992
Heb 1: 6 when he b' in the firstbegotten 1521
6: 7 b' forth herbs meet for them by 5088
Jas 1:15 when lust hath conceived, it b' * 616
15 when it is finished, b' forth death. 5088

bringing
Ex 12:42 for b' them out from the land of 3318
36: 6 people were restrained from b'. 935
Nu 5:15 b' iniquity to remembrance. 2142
14:36 by b' up a slander upon the land, 3318
2Sa 19:10 speak ye not a word of b' the king 7725
43 be first had in b' back our king? "
1Ki 10:22 b' gold, and silver, ivory, and 5375
2Ki 21:12 am b' such evil upon Jerusalem * 935
2Ch 9:21 the ships of Tarshish b' gold, and 5375
Ne 13:15 b' in sheaves, and lading asses; 935
Ps 126: 6 rejoicing, b' his sheaves with him. 5375
Jer 17:26 b' burnt offerings, and sacrifices, 935
26 and b' sacrifices of praise unto the "
Eze 20: 9 b' them forth out of the land of 3318
Da 9:12 by b' upon us a great evil: 935
M't 21:43 a nation b' forth the fruits thereof. 4160
M'k 2: 3 b' one sick of the palsy, which was 5342
Lu 24: 1 b' the spices which they had "
Ac 5:16 unto Jerusalem, b' sick folks, and "
Ro 7:23 b' me into captivity to the law of 163
2Co 10: 5 b' into captivity every thought to "
Heb 2:10 b' many sons unto glory, to make 71
7:19 the b' in of a better hope did; 1898
2Pe 2: 5 b' in the flood upon the world 1863

brink
Ge 41: 3 kine upon the b' of the river. 8193
Ex 2: 3 in the flags by the river's b'. "
7:15 stand by the river's b' against he "
De 2:36 is by the b' of the river Arnon, * "
Jos 3: 8 When ye are come to the b' of 7097
Eze 47: 6 to return to the b' of the river. *8193

broad See also ABROAD; BROADER.
Ex 27: 1 five cubits long, and five cubits b'; 7341
Nu 16:38 let them make them b' plates for *7555
39 and they were made b' plates for *7554
1Ki 6: 6 chamber was five cubits b', 7341
6 and the middle was six cubits b', "
6 and the third was seven cubits b': "
2Ch 6:13 five cubits long, and five cubits b', "
Ne 3: 8 Jerusalem unto the b' wall. 7342
12:38 furnaces even unto the b' wall; "
Job 36:16 out of the strait into a b' place, 7338
Ps 119:96 commandment is exceeding b'. 7342
Ca 3: 2 in the streets, and in the b' ways 7339
Isa 33:21 of b' rivers and streams; 7338, 3027
Jer 5: 1 seek in the b' places thereof, if ye 7339
51:58 The b' walls of Babylon shall be 7342
Eze 40: 6 the gate, which was one reed b'; 7341
6 the other threshold...one reed b'. "
7 one reed long, and one reed b'; "
29 and five and twenty cubits b'. "
30 cubits long, and five cubits b'. "
33 and five and twenty cubits b'. "
42 and a cubit and a half b', and one "
43 hooks, an hand b', fastened *
47 and an hundred cubits b', four 7341
41: 1 six cubits b' on the one side, "
1 six cubits b' on the other side, "
12 the west was seventy cubits b'; "
42:11 long as they, and as b' as they: *7342
20 and five hundred b', to make a *7341
43:16 twelve cubits long, twelve b', * "
17 cubits long and fourteen b' in the "
45: 6 of the city five thousand b', "
46:22 forty cubits long and thirty b': "
Na 2: 4 against another in the b' ways: 7339
M't 7:13 b' is the way, that leadeth to 2149
23: 5 they make b' their phylacteries, 4115

broader
Job 11: 9 the earth, and b' than the sea. 7342

broided See also BROIDERED.
1Ti 2: 9 not with b' hair, or gold, or *4117

broidered
Ex 28: 4 a b' coat, a mitre, and a girdle: *8665
Eze 16:10 I clothed thee also with b' work, 7553
13 fine linen, and silk, and b' work; "
18 tookest thy b' garments, and "
26:16 and put off their b' garments: "
27: 7 linen with b' work from Egypt "
16 b' work, and fine linen, and coral, "
24 blue clothes, and b' work, and in "

broiled
Lu 24:42 they gave him a piece of a b' fish, 3702

broke See BRAKE.

broken See also BROKENFOOTED; BROKENHANDED; BROKENHEARTED.
Ge 7:11 fountains of the great deep b' up, 1234
17:14 he hath b' my covenant. 6565
38:29 How hast thou b' forth? this *6555
Le 6:28 wherein it is sodden shall be b': 7665
11:35 they shall be b' down: for they 5422
13:20 a plague of leprosy b' out of the *6524
25 a leprosy b' out of the burning: * "
15:12 which hath the issue, shall be b': 7665
21:20 scabbed, or hath his stones b'; 4790
22:22 Blind, or b', or maimed, or having 7665
24 bruised, or crushed, or b', or cut; 5423
26:13 I have b' the bands of your yoke, 7665
26 I have b' the staff of your bread, * "
Nu 15:31 and hath b' his commandment, 6565
J'g 5:22 Then were the horsehoofs b' by *1986
16: 9 as a thread of tow is b' when it 5423
1Sa 2: 4 bows of the mighty men are b', 2844
10 shall be b' to pieces; out of 2865
2Sa 5:20 hath b' forth upon mine enemies 6555
22:35 a bow of steel is b' by mine arms. *5181
1Ki 18:30 altar of the Lord that was b' 2040
22:48 the ships were b' at Ezion-geber. 7665
2Ki 11: 6 the house, that it be not b' down. *4535
25: 4 And the city was b' up, and all *1234
1Ch 14:11 God hath b' in upon mine enemies 6555
2Ch 20:37 the Lord hath b' thy works. * "
37 And the ships were b', that they 7665
24: 7 that wicked woman, had b' up 6555
25:12 that they all were b' in pieces. 1234
32: 5 the wall that was b', and raised *6555
33: 3 his father had b' down, and he 5422
34: 7 when he had b' down the altars * "
Ne 1: 3 wall of Jerusalem also is b' down, 6555
2:13 of Jerusalem, which were b' down, "
Job 4:10 teeth of the young lions, are b'. 5421
7: 5 my skin is b', and become *7280
16:12 but he hath b' me asunder: *6565
17:11 my purposes are b' off, even the 5423
22: 9 of the fatherless have been b'. 1792
24:20 wickedness shall be b' as a tree. 7665
31:22 mine arm be b' from the bone. "
38:15 and the high arm shall be b'. "
Ps 3: 7 hast b' the teeth of the ungodly. "
18:34 a bow of steel is b' by mine arms. *5181
31:12 of mind: I am like a b' vessel. 6
34:18 unto them that are of a b' heart; 7665
20 his bones: not one of them is b'. "
37:15 and their bows shall be b'. "
17 the arms of the wicked shall be b' "
38: 8 I am feeble and sore b': I have *1794
44:19 Though thou hast sore b' us in "
51: 8 the bones which thou hast b' may "
17 sacrifices of God are a b' spirit: 7665
17 a b' and a contrite heart, "
55:20 him: he hath b' his covenant. *2490
60: 2 earth to tremble; thou hast b' it: *6480
69:20 Reproach hath b' my heart; 7665
80:12 thou then b' down her hedges, 6555
89:10 Thou hast b' Rahab in pieces, 1792
Ps 89:40 thou hast b' down all his hedges; 6555
107:16 he hath b' the gates of brass, 7665
109:16 might even slay the b' in heart. 5218
124: 7 snare is b', and we are escaped. 7665
147: 3 He healeth the b' in heart, "
Pr 3:20 knowledge the depths are b' up, 1234
6:15 suddenly shall he be b' without 7665
15:13 sorrow of the heart the spirit is b'. 5218
17:22 but a b' spirit drieth the bones. "
24:31 stone wall thereof was b' down. 2040
25:19 is like a b' tooth, and a foot out 7465
28 is like a city that is b' down, 6555
Ec 4:12 a threefold cord is not quickly b'. 5423
12: 6 or the golden bowl be b', 7533
6 the pitcher be b' at the fountain, 7665
6 or the wheel b' at the cistern. 7533
Isa 5:27 the latchet of their shoes be b': 5423
7: 8 five years shall Ephraim be b', 2844
8: 9 people, and ye shall be b' in pieces; "
9 be b' in pieces; gird yourselves, "
9 and ye shall be b' in pieces. "
15 shall stumble, and fall, and be b', 7665
9: 4 hast b' the yoke of his burden, 2865
14: 5 hath b' the staff of the wicked, 7665
29 rod of him that smote thee is b': "
16: 8 the heathen have b' down the 1986
19:10 they shall be b' in the purposes 1792
21: 9 images of her gods he hath b' 7665
22:10 and the houses have ye b' down *5422
24: 5 b' the everlasting covenant. 6565
10 The city of confusion is b' down: 7665
19 The earth is utterly b' down, 7489
27:11 withered, they shall be b' off: 7665
28:13 and fall backward, and be b', "
30:14 potter's vessel that is b' in pieces 3807
33: 8 he hath b' the covenant, he hath 6565
20 any of the cords thereof be b'. 5423
36: 6 staff of this b' reed, on Egypt; *7533
Jer 2:13 b' cisterns, that can hold no 7665
16 have b' the crown of thy head. 7462
20 I have b' thy yoke, and burst thy 7665
4:26 all the cities thereof were b' down 5422
5: 5 have altogether b' the yoke, 7665
10:20 all my cords are b': my children 5423
11:10 of Judah have b' my covenant 6565
16 it, and the branches of it are b'. 7489
14:17 virgin daughter of my people is b' *7665
22:28 man Coniah a despised b' idol? 5310
23: 9 Mine heart within me is b' 7665
28: 2 b' the yoke of the king of Babylon. "
12 had b' the yoke from off the neck "
13 Thou hast b' the yokes of wood; "
33:21 Then may also my covenant be b' 6565
37:11 the army of the Chaldeans was b' *5927
39: 2 the month, the city was b' up. *1234
48:17 How is the strong staff b', and 7665
20 for it is b' down: howl and cry; 2865
25 his arm is b', saith the Lord. 7665
38 I have b' Moab like a vessel "
39 howl, saying, How is it b' down! 2865
50: 2 Merodach is b' in pieces; her *2844
2 her images are b' in pieces. *2865
17 king of Babylon hath b' his bones *6105
23 whole earth cut asunder and b'! 7665
51:30 dwelling places; her bars are b'. "
56 every one of their bows is b': 2865
58 of Babylon shall be utterly b', *6209
52: 7 Then the city was b' up, and all *1234
La 2: 9 destroyed and b' her bars: 7665
3: 4 made old; he hath b' my bones. "
16 b' my teeth with gravel stones, 1638
Eze 6: 4 and your images shall be b': 7665
6 and your idols may be b' and "
9 I am b' with their whorish heart, "
17:19 and my covenant that he hath b', 6331
19:12 her strong rods were b' and 6561
26: 2 b' that was the gates of the people: 7665
27:26 the east wind hath b' thee in the "
34 thou shalt be b' by the seas in "
30: 4 her foundations shall be b' 2040
21 I have b' the arm of Pharaoh 7665
22 strong, and that which was b'; "
31:12 and his boughs are b' by all the "
32:28 thou shalt be b' in the midst of "
34: 4 ye bound up that which was b', "
16 will bind up that which was b', "
27 have b' the bands of their yoke, "
44: 7 and they have b' my covenant 6565
Da 2:35 silver, and the gold, b' to pieces 1854
42 be partly strong, and partly b'. 8406
8: 8 strong, the great horn was b'; 7665
22 Now that being b', whereas "
25 but he shall be b' without hand. "
11: 4 his kingdom shall be b', and shall "
22 and shall be b'; yea, also the prince "
Ho 5:11 Ephraim is oppressed and b' *7533
8: 6 Samaria shall be b' in pieces. 7616
Joe 1:17 the barns are b' down; for the 2040
Jon 1: 4 that the ship was like to be b'. 7665
Mic 2:13 they have b' up, and have passed 6555
Zec 11:11 And it was b' in that day: and so 6565
16 nor heal that that is b', nor feed 7665
M't 15:37 they took up of the b' meat that 2801
21:44 fall on this stone shall be b': 4917
24:43 suffered his house to be b' up. 1358
M'r 2: 4 when they had b' it up, they let 1846
5: 4 and the fetters b' in pieces: 4937
8: 8 they took up the b' meat that 2801
Lu 12:39 suffered his house to be b' 1358
20:18 fall upon that stone shall be b'; 4917
Joh 5:18 he not only had b' the sabbath, 3089
7:23 law of Moses should not be b'; "
10:35 and the scripture cannot be b'; "
19:31 that their legs might be b', 2608
36 A bone of him shall not be b'. 4937
21:11 many, yet was not the net b'. 4977

Ac 13:43 when the congregation was b' *3089
20:11 and had b' bread, and eaten, 2806
27:35 when he had b' it, he began to
41 the hinder part was b' with the *3089
44 some on b' pieces of the ship. *
Ro 11:17 some of the branches be b' off, 1575
19 The branches were b' off, that I "
20 because of unbelief they were b' off, "
1Co 11:24 is my body, which is b' for you: *2806
Eph 2:14 hath b' down the middle wall 3089
Re 2:27 of the potter shall they be b' 4937

brokenfooted
Le 21:19 Or a man that is b', 7667, 7272

brokenhanded
Le 21:19 that is brokenfooted, or b', 7667, 3027

brokenhearted
Isa 61: 1 bind up the b', to proclaim 7665, 3820
Lu 4:18 hath sent me to heal the b', *4937, 2588

brood
Lu 13:34 as a hen doth gather her b' 3555

brook See also BROOKS.
Ge 32:23 and sent them over the b', *5158
Le 23:40 willows of the b'; and ye shall "
Nu 13:23 they came unto the b' of Eschol, * "
24 The place was called the b' * "
De 2:13 you over the b' Zered. "
13 And we went over the b' Zered. "
14 until we were come over the b' "
9:21 I cast the dust thereof into the b' "
1Sa 17:40 five smooth stones out of the b', "
30: 9 and came to the b' Besor, where "
10 could not go over the b' Besor. "
21 to abide at the b' Besor: and they "
2Sa 15:23 himself passed over the b' Kidron, "
17:20 They be gone over the b' of water. 4323
1Ki 2:37 out and passest over the b' Kidron, 5158
15:13 and burnt it by the b' Kidron. "
17: 3 hide thyself by the b' Cherith, "
4 thou shalt drink of the b'; "
5 and dwelt by the b' Cherith, that "
6 evening; and he drank of the b'. "
7 the b' dried up, because there "
18:40 brought them down to the b' "
2Ki 23: 6 unto the b' Kidron, and "
6 burned it at the b' Kidron, "
12 dust of them into the b' Kidron. "
2Ch 15:16 and burnt it at the b' Kidron. "
20:16 at the end of the b', before * "
29:16 abroad into the b' Kidron. "
30:14 cast them into the b' Kidron. "
32: 4 the b' that ran through the midst "
Ne 2:15 went I up in the night by the b', "
Job 6:15 have dealt deceitfully as a b', "
40:22 willows of the b' compass him "
Ps 83: 9 as to Jabin, at the b' of Kison: * "
110: 7 He shall drink of the b' in the way: "
Pr 18: 4 of wisdom as a flowing b'. "
Isa 15: 7 away to the b' of the willows. "
Jer 31:40 the fields unto the b' of Kidron, "
Joh 18: 1 over the b' Cedron, where was 5493

brooks
Nu 21:14 in the b' of Arnon, *5158
15 the stream of the b' that goeth * "
De 8: 7 good land, a land of b' of water, "
2Sa 23:30 Hiddai of the b' of Gaash, "
1Ki 18: 5 and unto all b': peradventure "
1Ch 11:32 Hurai of the b' of Gaash, "
Job 6:15 and as a stream of b' they pass "
20:17 the b' of honey and butter. * "
22:24 of Ophir as the stones of the b'. "
Ps 42: 1 hart panteth after the water b' 650
Isa 19: 6 and the b' of defence shall be *2975
7 the paper reeds by the b', * "
7 by the mouth of the b', * "
7 and everything sown by the b', * "
8 they that cast angle into the b' * "

broth
J'g 6:19 and he put the b' in a pot, and 4839
20 this rock, and pour out the b'. "
Isa 65: 4 and b' of abominable things 6564

brother See also BRETHREN; BROTHERHOOD; BROTHER'S; BROTHERS'.
Ge 4: 2 And she again bare his b' Abel. 251
8 And Cain talked with Abel his b': "
8 Cain rose up against Abel his b', "
9 Where is Abel thy b'? "
9: 5 at the hand of every man's b' "
10:21 the b' of Japheth the elder, even "
14:13 b' of Eschol, and b' of Aner: "
14 Abram heard that his b' was taken "
16 also brought his b' Lot, and his "
20: 5 she herself said, He is my b': "
13 come, say of me, He is my b'. "
16 Behold, I have given thy b' "
22:20 born children unto thy b' Nahor; "
21 Huz his firstborn, and Buz his b', "
23 did bear to Nahor, Abraham's b'. "
24:15 the wife of Nahor, Abraham's b', "
29 Rebekah had a b', and his name "
53 he gave also to her b' and to her "
55 her b' and her mother said, Let the "
25:26 after that came his b' out, and his "
27: 6 thy father speak unto Esau thy b', "
11 Esau my b' is a hairy man, and "
23 as his b' Esau's hands: so he "
30 Esau his b' came in from his "
35 Thy b' came with subtilty, "
40 thou live, and shalt serve thy b'; "
41 then will I slay my b' Jacob. "
42 Behold, thy b' Esau, as touching "
43 flee thou to Laban my b' to Haran; "
28: 2 daughters of Laban thy mother's b'. "
5 the Syrian, the b' of Rebekah, "

Ge 29:10 daughter of Laban his mother's b', 251
10 sheep of Laban his mother's b', "
10 the flock of Laban his mother's b'. "
12 Rachel that he was her father's b', "
15 Because thou art my b', "
32: 3 before him to Esau his b' "
6 We came to thy b' Esau, and also "
11 from the hand of my b', from the "
13 hand a present for Esau his b'; "
17 When Esau my b' meeteth thee, "
33: 3 until he came near to his b'. "
9 Esau said, I have enough, my b'; "
35: 1 from the face of Esau thy b'. "
7 he fled from the face of his b'. "
36: 6 from the face of his b' Jacob. "
37:26 is it if we slay our b', and conceal "
27 for he is our b' and our flesh: "
38: 8 her, and raise up seed to thy b'. "
9 that he should give seed to his b'. "
29 behold, his b' came out: and she "
30 afterward came out his b', that "
42: 4 But Benjamin, Joseph's b', "
15 except your youngest b' come "
16 let him fetch your b', and ye shall "
20 bring your youngest b' unto me; "
21 guilty concerning our b', in that "
42:34 bring your youngest b' unto me: "
34 I deliver you your b', and ye shall "
38 his b' is dead, and he is left alone: "
43: 3 face, except your b' be with you. "
4 If thou wilt send our b' with us, we "
5 face, except your b' be with you. "
6 the man whether ye had yet a b'? "
7 have ye another b'? and we told "
7 he would say, Bring your b' down? "
13 Take also your b', and arise, and "
14 he may send away your other b', "
29 saw his b' Benjamin, his mother's "
29 Is this your younger b', of whom "
30 his bowels did yearn upon his b': "
44:19 saying, Have ye a father, or a b'? "
20 and his b' is dead, and he alone is "
23 Except your youngest b' come "
26 if our youngest b' be with us, then "
26 except our youngest b' be with us. "
45: 4 he said, I am Joseph your b', whom "
12 the eyes of my b' Benjamin, that "
14 fell upon his b' Benjamin's neck, "
48:19 younger b' shall be greater than he, "
Ex 4:14 Is not Aaron the Levite thy b'? "
7: 1 Aaron thy b' shall be thy prophet. "
2 thy b' shall speak unto Pharoah, "
28: 1 take thou unto thee Aaron thy b', "
2, 4 holy garments for Aaron thy b', "
41 put them upon Aaron thy b', and "
32:27 slay every man his b', and every "
29 man upon his son, and upon his b'; "
Le 16: 2 Speak unto Aaron thy b', that he "
18:14 the nakedness of thy father's b', "
19:17 Thou shalt not hate thy b' in thine "
21: 2 for his daughter, and for his b', "
25:25 If thy b' be waxen poor, and hath "
25 he redeem that which his b' sold. "
35 if thy b' be waxen poor, and fallen "
36 God; that thy b' may live with thee. "
39 if thy b' that dwelleth by thee be "
47 b' that dwelleth by him wax poor, "
Nu 6: 7 for his b', or for his sister, when "
20: 8 thou, and Aaron thy b', and speak "
14 Thus saith thy b' Israel, Thou "
27:13 as Aaron thy b' was gathered, "
36: 2 our b' unto his daughters. "
De 1:16 between every man and his b', and "
13: 6 If thy b', the son of thy mother, or "
15: 2 of his neighbour, or of his b'; "
3 that which is thine with thy b' "
7 shut thine hand from thy poor b': "
9 eye be evil against thy poor b', and "
11 open thine hand wide unto thy b', "
12 if thy b', an Hebrew man, or an "
17:15 over thee, which is not thy b'. "
19:18 hath testified falsely against his b'; "
19 thought to have done unto his b': "
22: 1 case bring them again unto thy b'. "
2 if thy b' be not nigh unto thee, or if "
2 until thy b' seek after it, and thou "
23: 7 an Edomite; for he is thy b': "
19 not lend upon usury to thy b'; "
20 unto thy b' thou shalt not lend upon "
24:10 When thou dost lend thy b' *7453
25: 3 thy b' should seem vile unto thee. 251
5 husband's b' shall go in unto her, 2993
5 the duty of an husband's b' 2992
6 shall succeed in the name of his b' 251
7 My husband's b' refuseth to raise 2993
7 his b' a name in Israel, he will not 251
7 the duty of my husband's b'. 2992
28:54 his eye shall be evil toward his b', 251
32:50 Aaron thy b' died in mount Hor, "
Jos 15:17 son of Kenaz, the b' of Caleb, took "
J'g 1: 3 And Judah said unto Simeon his b', "
13 son of Kenaz, Caleb's younger b', "
17 Judah went with Simeon his b', "
3: 9 son of Kenaz, Caleb's younger b'. "
9: 3 for they said, He is our b'. "
18 Shechem, because he is your b'; "
21 there, for fear of Abimelech his b'. "
24 upon Abimelech their b', which "
20:23 the children of Benjamin my b'? "
28 of Benjamin my b', or shall I cease? "
21: 6 repented them for Benjamin their b', "
Ru 4: 3 which was our b' Elimelech's: "
1Sa 14: 3 the son of Ahitub, I-chabod's b', "
17:28 Eliab his eldest b' heard when he "
20:29 my b', he hath commanded me to "
26: 6 the son of Zeruiah, b' to Joab, "

2Sa 1:26 distressed for thee, my b' Jonathan: 251
2:22 I hold up my face to Joab thy b'? "
27 every one from following his b'. "
3:27 died, for the blood of Asahel his b'. "
30 Joab and Abishai his b' slew Abner, "
30 because he had slain their b' "
4: 6 Rechab and Baanah his b' escaped. "
9 answered Rechab and Baanah his b', "
10:10 into the hand of Abishai his b', "
13: 3 the son of Shimeah David's b': "
4 Tamar, my b' Absalom's sister. "
7 Go now to thy b' Amnon's house, "
8 Tamar went to her b' Amnon's "
10 into the chamber to Amnon her b'. "
12 she answered him, Nay, my b', do "
20 Absalom her b' said unto her, Hath "
20 Amnon thy b' been with thee? "
20 peace, my sister: he is thy b'; "
20 desolate in her b' Absalom's house. "
22 Absalom spake unto his b' Amnon *
26 thee, let my b' Amnon go with us. 251
32 the son of Shimeah David's b', "
14: 7 Deliver him that smote his b', that "
7 life of his b' whom he slew; "
18: 2 the son of Zeruiah, Joab's b', and "
20: 9 said, Art thou in health, my b'? "
10 Abishai his b' pursued after Sheba "
21:19 slew the b' of Goliath the Gittite, *
21 Shimeah the b' of David slew him. 251
23:18 Abishai, the b' of Joab, the son of "
24 Asahel the b' of Joab was one of "
1Ki 1:10 and Solomon his b', he called not. "
2: 7 I fled because of Absalom thy b'. "
21 be given to Adonijah thy b' to wife. "
22 for he is mine elder b'; even for "
9:13 which thou hast given me, my b'? "
13:30 over him, saying, Alas, my b'! "
20:32 said, Is he yet alive? he is my b'. "
33 Thy b' Ben-hadad. Then he said, "
2Ki 24:17 made Mattaniah his father's b' king "
1Ch 2:32 sons of Jada the b' of Shammai; "
42 sons of Caleb the b' of Jerahmeel "
4:11 Chelub the b' of Shuah begat Mehir, "
6:39 And his b' Asaph, who stood on "
7:16 the name of his b' was Sheresh; "
35 the sons of his b' Helem; Zophah, "
8:39 the sons of Eshek his b' were, Ulam "
11:20 Abishai the b' of Joab, he was chief "
26 Asahel the b' of Joab, Elhanan "
38 Joel the b' of Nathan, Mibhar the "
45 Shimei, and Joha his b', the Tizite, "
19:11 unto the hand of Abishai his b', "
15 fled before Abishai his b', and "
20: 5 Jair slew Lahmi the b' of Goliath "
7 son of Shimea David's b' slew him. "
24:25 The b' of Michah was Isshiah: of 1730
26:22 Zetham, and Joel his b', which 251
27: 7 Asahel the b' of Joab, and Zebadiah "
2Ch 31:12 and Shimei his b' was the next. "
13 Cononiah and Shimei his b', at the "
36: 4 Eliakim his b' king over Judah "
4 Necho took Jehoahaz his b', and "
10 Zedekiah his b' king over Judah "
Ne 5: 7 Ye exact usury, every one of his b'. "
7: 2 That I gave my b' Hanani, and "
Job 22: 6 hast taken a pledge from thy b' "
30:29 I am a b' to dragons, and a "
Ps 35:14 though he had been my friend or b': "
49: 7 can by any means redeem his b', "
50:20 sittest and speakest against thy b'; "
Pr 17:17 times, and a b' is born for adversity. "
18: 9 is b' to him that is a great waster. "
19 A b' offended is harder to be won "
24 friend that sticketh closer than a b'. "
27:10 that is near than a b' far off. "
Ec 4: 8 yea, he hath neither child nor b': "
Ca 8: 1 O that thou wert as my b', that "
Isa 3: 6 a man shall take hold of his b' of "
9:19 the fire: no man shall spare his b'. "
19: 2 fight every one against his b', and "
41: 6 every one said to his b', Be of good "
Jer 9: 4 trust ye not in any b': for "
4 every b' will utterly supplant, "
22:18 saying, Ah my b'! or, Ah sister! "
23:35 every one to his b', What hath the "
31:34 every man his b', saying, Know the "
34: 9 of them, to wit, of a Jew his b'. "
14 ye go every man his b' an Hebrew, "
17 liberty, every one to his b', "
Eze 18:18 spoiled his b' by violence, and did "
33:30 every one to his b', saying, Come, "
38:21 man's sword shall be against his b'. "
44:25 for son, or for daughter, for b', or "
Ho 12: 3 He took his b' by the heel in the "
Am 1:11 because he did pursue his b' with "
Ob 10 thy violence against thy b' Jacob, "
12 have looked on the day of thy b' "
Mic 7: 2 hunt every man his b' with a net. "
Hag 2:22 every one by the sword of his b'. "
Zec 7: 9 compassions every man to his b': "
10 evil against his b' in your heart. "
Mal 1: 2 Was not Esau Jacob's b'? saith "
2:10 every man against his b', "
M't 4:18 called Peter, and Andrew his b', 80
21 of Zebedee, and John his b', "
5:22 whosoever is angry with his b' "
22 whosoever shall say to his b', Raca, "
23 thy b' hath ought against thee; "
24 first be reconciled to thy b', and "
7: 4 wilt thou say to thy b', Let me "
10: 2 called Peter, and Andrew his b'; "
2 son of Zebedee, and John his b'; "
21 b' shall deliver up the b' to death, "
12:50 the same is my b', and sister, and "
14: 3 Herodias' sake, his b' Philip's wife. "
17: 1 James, and John his b', and "

M't 18:15 thy b' shall trespass against thee, 80
15 hear thee, thou hast gained thy b'. "
21 how oft shall my b' sin against me, "
35 every one his b' their trespasses. "
22:24 his b' shall marry his wife, "
24 and raise up seed unto his b'. "
25 no issue, left his wife unto his b': "
M'r 1:16 saw Simon and Andrew his b' "
19 the son of Zebedee and John his b'. "
3:17 and John the b' of James; and he "
35 will of God, the same is my b', and "
5:37 James, and John the b' of James. "
6: 3 son of Mary, the b' of James, and "
17 Herodias' sake, his b' Philip's wife: "
12:19 If a man's b' die, and leave his wife "
19 that his b' should take his wife, "
19 and raise up seed unto his b'. "
13:12 the b' shall betray the b' to death, "
Lu 3: 1 and his b' Philip tetrarch of Ituræa "
19 for Herodias his b' Philip's wife, * "
6:14 named Peter,) and Andrew his b', "
16 And Judas the b' of James, and * "
42 say to thy b', B', let me pull out the 80
12:13 Master, speak to my b', that he "
15:27 said unto him, Thy b' is come; "
32 for this thy b' was dead, and is alive "
17: 3 If thy b' trespass against thee, "
20:28 If any man's b' die, having a wife, "
28 that his b' should take his wife, "
28 and raise up seed unto his b'. "
Joh 1:40 was Andrew, Simon Peter's b'. "
41 findeth his own b' Simon, and saith "
6: 8 Andrew, Simon Peter's b', saith "
11: 2 hair, whose b' Lazarus was sick.) "
19 to comfort them concerning their b'. "
21 hadst been here, my b' had not died. "
23 unto her, Thy b' shall rise again. "
32 hadst been here, my b' had not died. "
Ac 1:13 Zelotes, and Judas the b' of James.* "
9:17 said, B' Saul, the Lord, even Jesus, 80
12: 2 he killed James the b' of John with "
21:20 Thou seest, b', how many thousands "
22:13 unto me, B' Saul, receive thy sight. "
Ro 14:10 why dost thou judge thy b'? or why "
10 dost thou set at nought thy b'? "
15 if thy b' be grieved with thy meat, "
21 thing whereby thy b' stumbleth, "
16:23 city saluteth you, and Quartus a b'. "
1Co 1: 1 will of God, and Sosthenes our b', "
5:11 that is called a b' be a fornicator, "
6: 6 b' goeth to law with b', and that "
7:12 If any b' hath a wife that "
15 A b' or a sister is not under "
8:11 shall the weak b' perish, for "
13 meat make my b' to offend, "
13 lest I make my b' to offend. "
16:12 As touching our b' Apollos, "
2Co 1: 1 will of God, and Timothy our b', "
2:13 I found not Titus my b': but "
8:18 have sent with him the b', whose "
22 have sent with them our b', "
12:18 Titus, and with him I sent a b'. "
Ga 1:19 none, save James the Lord's b'. "
Eph 6:21 a beloved b' and faithful minister "
Ph'p 2:25 send to you Epaphroditus, my b', "
Col 1: 1 will of God, and Timotheus our b', "
4: 7 you, who is a beloved b', and a "
9 a faithful and beloved b', who is "
1Th 3: 2 sent Timotheus, our b', and "
4: 6 and defraud his b' in any matter: "
2Th 3: 6 from every b' that walketh "
15 but admonish him as a b'. "
Ph'm 1 Timothy our b'; unto Philemon "
7 the saints are refreshed by thee, b'. "
16 above a servant, a b' beloved, "
20 Yea, b', let me have "
Heb 8:11 neighbour, and every man his b', "
13:23 Know ye that our b' Timothy "
Jas 1: 9 Let the b' of low degree rejoice "
2:15 If a b' or sister be naked, and "
4:11 evil of his b', and judgeth his b', "
1Pe 5:12 a faithful b' unto you, as I suppose, "
2Pe 3:15 as our beloved b' Paul also "
1Jo 2: 9 in the light, and hateth his b', "
10 He that loveth his b' abideth in the "
11 he that hateth his b' is in darkness, "
3:10 neither he that loveth not his b'. "
12 wicked one, and slew his b'. "
14 loveth not his b' abideth in death.* "
15 Whosoever hateth his b' is a "
17 seeth his b' have need, and "
4:20 hateth his b', he is a liar: for he "
20 that loveth not his b' whom he "
21 who loveth God, love his b' also. "
5:16 any man see his b' sin a sin which "
Jude 1 of Jesus Christ, and b' of James, "
Re 1: 9 I John who also am your b', and "

brotherhood
Zec 11:14 the b' between Judah and Israel. 264
1Pe 2:17 Love the b'. Fear God. Honour 81

brotherly
Am 1: 9 remembered not the b' covenant: 251
Ro 12:10 one to another with b' love; *5360
1Th 4: 9 But as touching b' love ye need * "
Heb 13: 1 Let b' love continue. "
2Pe 1: 7 godliness b' kindness; and to b' † "

brother's
Ge 4: 9 I know not: Am I my b' keeper? 251
10 the voice of thy b' blood crieth "
11 her mouth to receive thy b' blood "
21 And his b' name was Jubal: "
10:25 and his b' name was Joktan. "
12: 5 Sarah his wife, and Lot his b' son, "
14:12 And they took Lot, Abram's b' son, "
24:48 to take my master's b' daughter "
27:44 until thy b' fury turn away; 251
45 Until thy b' anger turn away "
38: 8 in unto thy b' wife, and marry her, "
9 he went in unto his b' wife, that he "
Le 18:16 the nakedness of thy b' wife: "
16 it is thy b' nakedness. "
20:21 if a man shall take his b' wife, "
21 hath uncovered his b' nakedness; "
De 22: 1 Thou shalt not see thy b' ox "
3 with all lost thing of thy b', "
4 Thou shalt not see thy b' ass or "
25: 7 like not to take his b' wife, 2994
7 then let his b' wife go up to the "
9 Then shall his b' wife come unto "
9 will not build up his b' house 251
1Ki 2:15 turned about, and is become my b': "
1Ch 1:19 and his b' name was Joktan. "
Job 1:13 drinking wine in their eldest b' "
18 wine in their eldest b' house: "
Pr 27:10 neither go into thy b' house in "
M't 7: 3 the mote that is in thy b' eye, 80
5 out the mote out of thy b' eye. "
M'r 6:18 lawful for thee to have thy b' wife, "
Lu 6:41 mote that is in thy b' eye, "
42 out the mote that is in thy b' eye. "
Ro 14:13 an occasion to fall in his b' way. "
1Jo 3:12 were evil, and his b' righteous. "

brothers' See also BRETHREN'S.
Nu 36:11 unto their father's b' sons: 1730

brought See also BROUGHTEST.
Ge 1:12 And the earth b' forth grass, 3318
21 the waters b' forth abundantly, 8317
2:19 and b' them unto Adam to see 935
22 and b' her unto the man. "
4: 3 that Cain b' of the fruit of the "
4 he also b' of the firstlings of his "
14:16 b' back all the goods, and also 7725
16 b' again his brother Lot, "
18 king of Salem b' forth bread and 3318
15: 5 And he b' him forth abroad, and "
7 I am the Lord that b' thee out of "
19:16 and they b' him forth, and set him "
17 when they had b' them forth "
20: 9 thou hast b' on me and on my 935
24:53 And the servant b' forth jewels 3318
67 And Isaac b' her into his mother 935
26:10 and thou shouldest have b' "
27:14 and b' them to his mother: "
20 the Lord thy God b' it to me. *7136
25 And he b' it near to him, and 5066
25 he b' him wine, and he drank. 935
31 and b' it unto his father, and "
33 hath taken venison, and b' it me, "
29:13 and b' him to his house. "
23 and b' her to him; and he went "
30:14 and b' them unto his mother Leah. "
39 and b' forth cattle ringstraked, 3205
31:39 I b' not unto thee; I bear the loss 935
33:11 I pray thee, my blessing that is b' "
37: 2 and Joseph b' unto his father "
28 and they b' Joseph into Egypt. "
32 and they b' it to their father; "
38:25 When she was b' forth, she sent 3318
39: 1 Joseph was b' down to Egypt; 3381
1 which had b' him down thither. "
14 he hath b' in an Hebrew unto us 935
17 which thou hast b' unto us, "
40:10 thereof b' forth ripe grapes: 1310
41:14 b' him hastily out of the dungeon: 7323
47 the earth b' forth by handfuls. 6213
43: 2 which they had b' out of Egypt, 935
12 the money that was b' again *7725
17 and the man b' the men into 935
18 they were b' into Joseph's house; "
18 at the first time are we b' in; "
21 have b' it again in our hand. 7725
22 other money have we b' down 3381
23 And he b' Simeon out unto them. 3318
24 b' the men into Joseph's house, 935
26 they b' him the present "
44: 8 we b' again unto thee out of the 7725
46: 7 seed b' he with him into Egypt. 935
32 they have b' their flocks, and "
47: 7 And Joseph b' in Jacob his father, "
14 and Joseph b' the money into "
17 they b' their cattle unto Joseph: "
48:10 And he b' them near unto him; 5066
12 And Joseph b' them out from 3318
13 hand, and b' them near unto him. 5066
50:23 were b' up upon Joseph's knees. *3205
Ex 2:10 b' him unto Pharaoh's daughter, 935
3:12 When thou hast b' forth the 3318
8: 7 and b' up frogs upon the land 5927
12 the frogs which he had b' against 7760
9:19 be b' home, the hail shall come 622
10: 8 And Moses and Aaron were b' 7725
13 the Lord b' an east wind upon 5090
13 the east wind b' the locusts. 5375
12:17 day have I b' your armies out 3318
39 the dough which they b' forth "
13: 3 Lord b' you out from this place: "
9 hand hath the Lord b' thee out "
14 the Lord b' us out from Egypt, "
16 the Lord b' us forth out of Egypt. "
15:19 b' again the waters of the sea 7725
22 So Moses b' Israel from the Red *5265
26 I have b' upon the Egyptians: *7760
16: 3 ye have b' us forth into this 3318
6 the Lord hath b' you out from "
32 when I brought you forth from "
17: 3 thou hast b' us up out of Egypt, 5927
18: 1 had b' Israel out of Egypt; 3318
26 the hard causes they b' unto 935
19: 4 and b' you unto myself. "
17 And Moses b' forth the people 3318
Ex 20: 2 have b' thee out of the land of 3318
22: 8 master of the house shall be b' *7126
29:10 shalt cause a bullock to be b' * "
46 that b' them forth out of the land 3318
32: 1 the man that b' us up out of the 5927
3 ears, and b' them unto Aaron. 935
4 gods, O Israel, which b' thee up 5927
6 and b' peace offerings; and the 5066
8 Israel, which have b' thee up 5927
11 b' forth out of the land of Egypt 3318
21 hast b' so great a sin upon them? 935
23 the man that b' us up out of the 5927
33: 1 thou hast b' up out of the land "
35:21 they b' the Lord's offering to the 935
22 b' bracelets, and earrings, and rings, "
23 rams, and badgers' skins, b' them. "
24 b' the Lord's offering: and every "
24 for any work of the service, b' it. "
25 and b' that which they had spun, "
27 the rulers b' onyx stones, and "
29 Israel b' a willing offering "
36: 3 Israel had b' for the work of the "
3 they b' yet unto him free offerings "
39:33 And they b' the tabernacle unto "
40:21 he b' the ark into the tabernacle, "
Le 6:30 whereof any of the blood is b' into 935
8: 6 And Moses b' Aaron and his 7126
13 And Moses b' Aaron's sons, and "
14 And he b' the bullock for the sin 5066
18 And he b' the ram for the *7126
22 And he b' the other ram, the * "
24 And he b' Aaron's sons, and "
9: 5 And they b' that which Moses 3947
9 And the sons of Aaron b' the *7126
15 And he b' the people's offering, * "
16 And he b' the burnt offering, * "
17 And he b' the meat offering, * "
10:18 the blood of it was not b' in 935
13: 2 then he shall be b' unto Aaron "
9 in a man, then he shall be b' unto "
14: 2 He shall be b' unto the priest: "
16:27 whose blood was b' in to make "
19:36 which b' you out of the land of 3318
22:27 or a sheep, or a goat, is b' forth, 3205
33 That b' you out of the land of 3318
23:14 that ye have b' an offering unto 935
15 the day that ye b' the sheaf of "
43 when I b' them out of the land of 3318
24:11 And they b' him unto Moses: (and 935
25:38 which b' you forth out of the land 3318
42 which I b' forth out of the land of "
55 whom I b' forth out of the land of "
26:13 which b' you forth out of the land "
41 and have b' them into the land of 935
45 whom I b' forth out of the land 3318
Nu 6:13 he shall be b' unto the door of 935
7: 3 And they b' their offering before "
3 and they b' them before the *7126
9:13 he b' not the offering of the Lord * "
11:31 and b' quails from the sea, and 1468
12:15 not till Miriam was b' in again. 622
13:23 and they b' of the pomegranates, "
26 and b' back word unto them, and 7725
32 And they b' up an evil report of 3318
14: 3 wherefore hath the Lord b' us * 935
15:33 him gathering sticks b' him 7126
36 And all the congregation b' him 3318
41 which b' you out of the land of "
16:10 And he hath b' thee near to him, 7126
13 thou hast b' us up out of a land 5927
14 thou hast not b' us into a land 935
17: 8 and b' forth buds, and bloomed *3318
9 And Moses b' out all the rods "
20: 4 And why have ye b' up the 935
16 hath b' us forth out of Egypt: 3318
21: 5 Wherefore have ye b' us up out 5927
22:41 and b' him up into the high "
23: 7 Balak the king of Moab hath b' 5148
14 And he b' him into the field of *3947
22 God b' them out of Egypt; he *3318
28 And Balak b' Balaam unto the *3947
24: 8 God b' him forth out of Egypt; *3318
25: 6 and b' unto his brethren a 7126
27: 5 And Moses b' their cause before "
31:12 And they b' the captives, and the 935
50 We have therefore b' an oblation 7126
54 and b' it into the tabernacle of 935
32:17 until we have b' them unto their "
De 1:25 in their hands, and b' it down 3381
25 unto us, and b' us word again, 7725
27 he has b' us forth out of the land 3318
4:20 hath taken you, and b' you forth "
37 and b' thee out in his sight with "
5: 6 which b' thee out of the land of "
15 the Lord thy God b' thee out "
6:10 Lord thy God shall have b' thee * 935
12 which b' thee forth out of the 3318
21 and the Lord b' us out of Egypt "
23 he b' us out from thence, that he "
7: 8 b' you out with a mighty hand, "
19 the Lord thy God b' thee out: "
8:14 which b' thee forth out of the land "
15 who b' thee forth water out of the "
9: 4 hath b' me in to possess this land: 935
12 people which thou hast b' forth 3318
26 which thou hast b' forth out of "
28 he hath b' them out to slay them "
11:29 hath b' thee in unto the land * 935
13: 5 which b' you out of the land of 3318
10 which b' thee out of the land of "
16: 1 the Lord thy God b' thee forth out "
20: 1 God is with thee, which b' thee 5927
22:19 he hath b' up an evil name upon 3318
26: 8 And the Lord b' us forth out of "
9 And he hath b' us into this place, 935
10 I have b' the firstfruits of the land, "

De 26:13 I have b' away the hallowed *1197
29:25 when he b' them forth out of the 3318
31:20 For when I shall have b' them 935
21 before I have b' them into the land "
33:14 precious fruits b' forth by the sun,*
Jos 2: 6 she had b' them up to the roof 5927
6:23 and b' out Rahab, and her father, 3318
23 they b' out all her kindred, and "
7: 7 hast thou at all b' this people 5674
14 ye shall be b' according to your 7126
16 and b' Israel by their tribes; and "
17 And he b' the family of Judah; "
17 he b' the family of the Zarhites * "
18 And he b' his household man by "
23 and b' them unto Joshua, and 935
24 and they b' them unto the valley 5927
8:23 took alive, and b' him to Joshua. 7126
10:23 and b' forth those five kings unto 3318
24 when they b' out those kings unto "
14: 7 and I b' him word again as it was 7725
22:32 of Israel, and b' them word again. "
24: 5 them: and afterward I b' you out. 3318
6 And I b' your fathers out of Egypt: "
7 and b' the sea upon them, and 935
8 And I b' you into the land of the "
17 he it is that b' us up and our 5927
32 which the children of Israel b' up "
J'g 1: 7 And they b' him to Jerusalem, 935
2: 1 and have b' you unto the land "
12 b' them out of the land of Egypt, 3318
3:17 he b' the present unto Eglon 7126
5:25 she b' forth butter in a lordly dish. "
6: 8 I b' you up from Egypt, and 5927
8 b' you forth out of the house of 3318
19 b' it out unto him under the oak, "
7: 5 So he b' down the people unto the 3381
25 and b' the heads of Oreb and Zeeb 935
11:35 thou hast b' me very low, and 3766
14:11 that they b' thirty companions to 3947
15:13 and b' him up from the rock. 5927
16: 8 the lords of the Philistines b' up "
18 her, and b' money in their hand. "
21 b' him down to Gaza, and bound 3381
31 and b' him up, and buried him 5927
18: 3 unto him, Who b' thee hither? 935
19: 3 b' him into her father's house: "
21 So he b' him into his house, and "
25 took his concubine, and b' her 3318
21:12 and they b' them unto the camp 935
Ru 1:21 the Lord hath b' me home again 7725
2:18 and she b' forth, and gave to her 3318
1Sa 1:24 and b' him unto the house of the 935
25 a bullock, and b' the child to Eli. "
2:14 all that the fleshhook b' up the 5927
19 and b' it to him from year to year, "
5: 1 and b' it from Eben-ezer unto 935
2 they b' it into the house of Dagon, "
10 They have b' about the ark of the 5437
6:21 Philistines have b' again the ark 7725
7: 1 b' it into the house of Abinadab 935
8: 8 that I b' them up out of Egypt 5927
9:22 and b' them into the parlour, and 935
10:18 I b' up Israel out of Egypt, and 5927
27 him, and b' him no presents. 935
12: 6 that b' your fathers up out of the 5927
8 b' forth your fathers out of Egypt, 3318
14:34 the people b' every man his ox 5066
15:15 Saul said, They have b' them from 935
20 have b' Agag the king of Amalek, "
16:12 he sent, and b' him in. Now he "
17:54 and b' it to Jerusalem; but he put "
57 b' him before Saul with the head "
18:27 David b' their foreskins, and they "
19: 7 And Jonathan b' David to Saul, "
20: 8 b' thy servant into a covenant of "
21: 8 I have neither b' my sword nor *3947
14 then have ye b' him to me? 935
15 b' this fellow to play the mad man "
22: 4 he b' them before the king of 5148
23: 5 b' away their cattle, and smote 5090
25:27 which thine handmaid hath b' 935
35 which she had b' him, and said "
28:25 she b' it before Saul, and before 5066
30: 7 Abiathar b' thither the ephod to "
11 b' him to David, and gave him 3947
16 And when he had b' him down, 3381
2Sa 1:10 have b' them hither unto my Lord. 935
2: 8 and b' him over to Mahanaim; 5674
3:22 b' in a great spoil with them: 935
26 messengers after Abner, which b' 7725
4: 8 b' the head of Ish-bosheth unto 935
10 thinking to have b' good tidings, 1319
6: 3, 4 b' it out of the house of Abinadab5375
12 David went and b' up the ark 5927
15 b' up the ark of the Lord with "
17 they b' in the ark of the Lord, 935
7: 6 I b' up the children of Israel out 5927
18 that thou hast b' me hitherto? 935
8: 2 became David's servants, and b' 5375
6 servants to David, and b' gifts. "
7 of Hadadezer, and b' them to 935
10 Joram b' with him vessels of 1961
10:16 and b' out the Syrians that were 3318
12:30 he b' forth the spoil of the city in "
31 And he b' forth the people that "
13:10 and b' them into the chamber to 935
11 when she had b' them unto him to 5066
18 Then his servant b' her out, and 3318
14:23 went to Geshur, and b' Absalom to 935
17:28 B' beds, and basons, and earthen 5066
19:41 and have b' the king, and his 5674
21: 8 whom she b' up for Adriel the son*3205
13 And he b' up from thence the 5927
22:20 He b' me forth also into a large 3318
23:16 and b' it to David: nevertheless 935
1Ki 1: 3 Shunammite, and b' her to the "

1Ki 1:38 king David's mule, and b' him 3212
53 and they b' him down from the 3381
2:30 And Benaiah b' the king word 7725
40 and b' his servants from Gath. 935
3: 1 and b' her into the city of David, "
24 And they b' a sword before the "
4:21 they b' presents, and served 5066
28 dromedaries b' they unto the 935
5:17 and they b' great stones, costly *5265
6: 7 made ready before it was b' *4551
7:51 And Solomon b' in the things 935
8: 4 And they b' up the ark of the 5927
6 And the priests b' in the ark of 935
16 the day that I b' forth my people 3318
21 when he b' them out of the land "
9: 9 who b' forth their fathers out of "
9 therefore hath the Lord b' upon 935
28 twenty talents, and b' it to king "
10:11 that b' gold from Ophir, 5375
11 b' in from Ophir great plenty 935
25 they b' every man his present, "
28 And Solomon had horses b' out 4161
12:28 gods, O Israel, which b' thee up 5927
13:20 unto the prophet that b' him 7725
23 the prophet whom he had b' back. "
26 And when the prophet that b' him "
29 it upon the ass, and b' it back: "
14:28 and b' them back into the guard "
15:15 And he b' in the things which 935
17: 6 the ravens b' him bread and flesh "
20 hast thou also b' evil upon the "
23 b' him down out of the chamber 3381
18:40 and Elijah b' them down to the "
20: 9 the messengers departed, and b' 7725
39 and b' a man unto me, and said, 935
22:37 and was b' to Samaria; and they "
2Ki 2:20 salt therein. And they b' it to 3947
4: 5 who b' the vessels to her; and 5066
20 and b' him to his mother, he sat 935
42 and b' the man of God bread of "
5: 2 and had b' away captive out of 7617
6 And he b' the letter to the king 935
20 at his hands that which he b': "
10: 1 them that b' up Ahab's children, 539
6 of the city, which b' them up. 1431
8 They have b' the heads of the 935
22 And he b' them forth vestments. 3318
24 any of the men whom I have b' * 935
26 And they b' forth the images out 3318
11: 4 b' them to him into the house of 935
12 And he b' forth the king's son, 3318
19 and they b' down the king from 3381
12: 4 that is b' into the house of the 935
9 money that was b' into the house "
13 that was b' into the house of the "
16 money was not b' into the house "
14:20 And they b' him on horses: and 5375
16:14 And he b' also the brasen altar, 7126
17: 4 and b' no present to the king of *5927
7 Lord their God, which had b' "
24 And the king of Assyria b' men 935
27 whom ye b' from thence; and let 1540
36 But the Lord, who b' you up out 5927
19:25 now have I b' it to pass, that 935
20:11 and he b' the shadow ten degrees 7725
20 and b' water into the city, are 935
22: 4 the silver which is b' into the house "
9 and b' the king word again, and 7725
20 And they b' the king word again. "
23: 6 And he b' out the grove from the 3318
8 And he b' all the priests out of the 935
30 and b' him to Jerusalem, and "
24:16 the king of Babylon b' captive to "
25: 6 So they took the king, and b' *5927
7 b' them to the king of Babylon 3212
1Ch 5:26 and b' them unto Halah, and 935
10:12 and b' them to Jabesh, and buried "
11:18 and b' it to David: but David "
19 jeopardy of their lives they b' it. "
12:40 b' bread on asses, and on camels, "
13:13 David b' not the ark home to *5493
14:17 and the Lord b' the fear of him 5414
15:28 Thus all Israel b' up the ark of 5927
16: 1 So they b' the ark of God, and set 935
17: 5 since the day that I b' up Israel 5927
16 that thou hast b' me hitherto? 935
18: 2, 6 David's servants, and b' gifts. 5375
7 servants of Hadarezer, and b' them 935
8 b' David very much brass, *3947
11 silver and the gold that he b' *5375
20: 2 he b' also exceeding much spoil 3318
3 he b' out the people that were in "
22: 4 they of Tyre b' much cedar wood 935
2Ch 1: 4 the ark of God had David b' up 5927
16 And Solomon had horses b' out of 4161
17 b' forth out of Egypt a chariot 3318
17 and so b' they out horses for all * "
5: 1 and Solomon b' in all the things 935
5 And they b' up the ark, and the 5927
7 And the priests b' in the ark of the 935
6: 5 Since the day that I b' forth my 3318
7:22 of their fathers, which b' them "
22 hath he b' all this evil upon them. 935
8:11 Solomon b' up the daughter of 5927
18 gold, and b' them to king Solomon. 935
9:10 which b' gold from Ophir, b' algum "
12 which she had b' unto the king. "
14 which chapmen and merchants b'. "
14 b' gold and silver to Solomon. "
24 they b' every man his present, "
28 And they b' unto Solomon horses 3318
10: 8 that were b' up with him, that *1431
10 the young men that were b' up * "
12:11 and b' them again into the guard 7725
13:18 the children of Israel were b' 3665
15:11 of the spoil which they had b', 935

2Ch 15:18 And he b' into the house of God 935
16: 2 Then Asa b' out silver and gold 3318
17: 5 and all Judah b' to Jehoshaphat 5414
11 the Philistines b' Jehoshaphat 935
11 the Arabians b' him flocks, seven "
19: 4 and b' them back unto the Lord 7725
22: 9 and b' him to Jehu: and when 935
23:11 Then they b' out the king's son, 3318
14 Then Jehoiada the priest b' out "
20 and b' down the king from the 3381
24:10 and b' in, and cast into the chest, 935
11 at what time the chest was b' unto "
14 they b' the rest of the money "
25:12 and b' them unto the top of the "
14 that he b' the gods of the children "
23 and b' him to Jerusalem, and "
28 And they b' him upon horses, and 5375
28: 5 captives, and b' them to Damascus.935
8 and b' the spoil to Samaria. "
15 and b' them to Jericho, the "
19 the Lord b' Judah low because 3665
27 they b' him not into the sepulchres 935
29: 4 And he b' in the priests and the "
16 and b' out all the uncleanness 3318
21 And they b' seven bullocks, and 935
23 And they b' forth the he goats 5066
31 the congregation b' in sacrifices 935
32 which the congregation b', was "
30:15 and b' in the burnt offerings into "
31: 5 children of Israel b' in abundance* "
5 all things b' they in abundantly. "
6 they also b' in the tithe of oxen "
12 And b' in the offerings and the "
32:23 many b' gifts unto the Lord to "
30 b' it straight down to the west 3474
33:11 Wherefore the Lord b' upon them 935
13 and b' him again to Jerusalem 7725
34: 9 the money that was b' into the 935
14 they b' out the money 3318
14 that was b' into the 935
16 b' the king word back again, 7725
28 So they b' the king word again. "
35:24 and they b' him to Jerusalem, 3212
36:10 and b' him to Babylon, with the 935
17 Therefore he b' upon them the 5927
18 all these he b' to Babylon. 935
Ezr 1: 7 the king b' forth the vessels of the 3318
7 which Nebuchadnezzar had b' "
11 were b' up from Babylon unto 5927
4: 2 of Assur, which b' us up hither. "
10 and noble Asnapper b' over, and 1541
5:14 and b' them into the temple of 2987
6: 5 and b' unto Babylon, be restored, "
5 and b' again unto the temple 1946
8:18 they b' us a man of understanding, 935
Ne 4:15 and God had b' their counsel 6565
5: 5 daughters are b' unto bondage 3533
8: 2 And Ezra the priest b' the law 935
16 went forth, and b' them, and made "
9:18 This is thy God that b' thee up 5927
33 in all that is b' upon us; for * 935
12:31 Then I b' up the princes of 5927
13: 9 and thither b' I again the vessels 7725
12 Then b' all Judah the tithe of the 935
15 which they b' into Jerusalem "
16 which b' fish, and all manner of "
19 there should no burden be b' in "
Es 1:17 Vashti the queen to be b' in before "
2: 7 And he b' up Hadassah, that is, 539
8 that Esther was b' also unto the *3947
20 like as when she was b' up with 539
6: 8 Let the royal apparel be b' which 935
11 b' him on horseback through *7392
9:11 palace was b' before the king. 935
Job 4:12 a thing was secretly b' to me, 1589
10:18 Wherefore then hast thou b' me 3318
14:21 and they are b' low, but he 6819
21:30 they shall be b' forth to the day *2986
32 Yet shall he be b' to the grave, * "
24:24 are gone and b' low; they are *4355
31:18 he was b' up with me, as with a *1431
42:11 evil the Lord had b' upon him: 935
Ps 7:14 mischief, and b' forth falsehood. 3205
18:19 He b' me forth also into a large 3318
20: 8 They are b' down and fallen: *3766
22:15 thou hast b' me into the dust 8239
30: 3 thou hast b' up my soul from 5927
35: 4 turned back and b' to confusion *2659
26 be ashamed and b' to confusion * "
40: 2 He b' me up also out of an 5927
45:14 She shall be b' unto the king *2986
14 that follow her shall be b' unto 935
15 and rejoicing shall they be b': *2986
71:24 for they are b' unto shame, *2659
73:19 How are they b' into desolation, *
78:16 b' streams also out of the rock, 3318
26 his power he b' in the south wind.*5090
54 And he b' them to the border of 935
71 he b' him to feed Jacob his people, "
79: 8 us: for we are b' very low. 1809
80: 8 Thou hast b' a vine out of Egypt: 5265
81:10 Lord thy God, which b' thee out 5927
85: 1 b' back the captivity of Jacob. 7725
89:40 hast b' his strong holds to ruin. 7760
90: 2 Before the mountains were b' 3205
105:30 b' forth frogs in abundance, *8317
37 He b' them forth also with silver 3318
40 and he b' quails, and satisfied 935
43 And he b' forth his people with 3318
106:42 and they were b' into subjection 3665
43 and were b' low for their iniquity. 4355
107:12 Therefore he b' down their heart 3665
14 He b' them out of darkness and 3318
39 they are minished and b' low *7817
116: 6 I was b' low, and he helped me. 1809
136:11 b' out Israel from among them: 3318

Ps 142: 6 for I am b' very low: deliver me 1809
Pr 6:26 a man is b' to a piece of bread:
8:24 no depths, I was b' forth; when 2342
25 before the hills was I b' forth: "
30 as one b' up with him: and I * 539
Ec 12: 4 of music shall be b' low; 7817
Ca 1: 4 the king hath b' me into his 935
2: 4 He b' me to the banqueting house, "
3: 4 b' him into my mother's house, "
8: 5 there thy mother b' thee forth: *2254
5 she b' thee forth that bare thee. * "
Isa 1: 2 nourished and b' up children, 7311
2:12 lifted up; and he shall be b' low: 8213
5: 2 grapes, and it b' forth wild grapes.6213
4 grapes, b' it forth wild grapes? "
15 the mean man shall be b' down, *7817
14:11 Thy pomp is b' down to the 3381
15 thou shalt be b' down to hell, "
15: 1 is laid waste, and b' to silence; 1820
1 is laid waste, and b' to silence; "
18: 7 shall the present be b' unto 2986
21:14 land of Tema b' water to him 857
23:13 thereof; and he b' it to ruin. *7760
25: 5 the terrible ones shall be b' low. 6030
26:18 have as it were b' forth wind; 3205
29: 4 And thou shalt be b' down, 8213
20 the terrible one is b' to nought, 656
37:26 now have I b' it to pass, that thou 935
43:14 have b' down all their nobles, *3381
23 Thou hast not b' me the small 935
45:10 What hast thou b' forth? *2342
48:15 I have b' him, and he shall make 935
49:21 who hath b' up these? Behold, 1431
51:18 the sons whom she hath b' forth; 3205
18 the sons that she hath b' up. 1431
53: 7 is b' as a lamb to the slaughter, *2986
59:16 therefore his arm b' salvation 3467
60:11 and that their kings may be b'. *5090
62: 9 they that have b' it together *6908
63: 5 mine own arm b' salvation unto 3467
11 Where is he that b' them up out 5927
66: 7 Before she travailed, she b' forth; 3205
8 she b' forth her children. "
Jer 2: 6 where is the Lord that b' us up 5927
7 b' you into a plentiful country, 935
27 Thou hast b' me forth: for they 3205
7:22 the day that I b' them out of the 3318
10: 9 Silver spread into plates is b' 935
11: 4 the day that I b' them forth out 3318
7 in the day that I b' them up 5927
19 ox that is b' to the slaughter; *2986
15: 8 I have b' upon them against 935
16:14, 15 liveth, that b' up the children 5927
20: 3 that Pashur b' forth Jeremiah 3318
15 man who b' tidings to my father, 1319
23: 7, 8 The Lord liveth, which b' up 5927
24: 1 and had b' them to Babylon. 935
26:23 and b' him unto Jehoiakim, the "
27:16 shortly be b' again from Babylon:7725
32:21 And hast b' forth thy people 3318
42 Like as I have b' all this great 935
34:11 and b' them into subjection for 3533
13 the day that I b' them forth out 3318
16 and b' them into subjection, 3533
35: 4 And I b' them into the house 935
37:14 and b' him to the princes. "
38:22 b' forth to the king of Babylon's 3318
39: 5 they b' him up to Nebuchadnezzar 5927
40: 3 Now the Lord hath b' it, and done 935
41:16 whom he had b' again from 7725
44: 2 all the evil that I have b' upon 935
50:25 and hath b' forth the weapons 3318
51:10 The Lord hath b' forth our "
52:26 b' them to the king of Babylon 3212
31 and b' him forth out of prison, 3318
La 2: 2 hath b' them down to the ground: 5060
22 that I have swaddled and b' up 7235
3: 2 led me, and b' me into darkness, *3212
4: 5 they that were b' up in scarlet 539
Eze 8: 3 and b' me in the visions of God 935
7 he b' me to the door of the court; "
14 Then he b' me to the door of the "
16 And he b' me into the inner court "
11: 1 and b' me unto the east gate "
24 and b' me in a vision by the Spirit "
12: 7 I b' forth my stuff by day, 3318
7 I b' it forth in the twilight, "
14:22 remnant that shall be b' forth, * "
22 the evil that I have b' upon 935
22 all that I have b' upon it. "
17: 6 a vine, and b' forth branches, 5375
24 I the Lord have b' down the high 8213
19: 3 she b' up one of her whelps: 5927
4 and they b' him with chains 935
9 b' him to the king of Babylon: "
9 they b' him into holds, "
20:10 and b' them into the wilderness. 3318
14 in whose sight I b' them out. "
22 in whose sight I b' them forth. "
28 I had b' them into the land, 935
21: 7 cometh, and shall be b' to pass, *1961
23: 8 her whoredoms b' from Egypt: *
27 whoredom b' from the land of
42 the common sort were b' 935
27: 6 b' out of the isles of Chittim.
15 they b' thee for a present 7725
26 Thy rowers have b' thee into 935
29: 5 thou shalt not be b' together, 622
30:11 shall be b' to destroy the land: 935
31:18 thou be b' down with the trees 3381
34: 4 have ye b' again that which 7725
37:13 b' you up out of your graves, *5927
38: 8 the land that is b' back from the 7725
8 it is b' forth out of the nations, 3318
39:27 b' them again from the people, 7725
40: 1 was upon me, and b' me thither 935
Eze 40: 2 In the visions of God b' he me 935
3 And he b' me thither, and, "
4 art thou b' hither: declare all "
17 Then b' he me into the outward "
24 that he b' me toward the south, 3212
28 And he b' me to the inner court 935
32 And he b' me into the inner court "
35 And he b' me to the north gate, "
48 And he b' me to the porch of the "
49 cubits; and he b' me by the steps *
41: 1 Afterward he b' me to the temple, 935
42: 1 Then he b' me forth into the 3318
1 and he b' me into the chamber 935
15 he b' me forth toward the gate 3318
43: 1 Afterward he b' me to the gate 3212
5 and b' me into the inner court; 935
44: 1 Then he b' me back the way of 7725
4 Then b' he me the way of the 935
7 that ye have b' into my sanctuary "
46:19 After he b' me through the entry, "
21 Then he b' me forth into the 3318
47: 1 Afterward he b' me again unto 7725
2 Then b' he me out of the way of 3318
3 he b' me through the waters; *5674
4 and b' me through the waters; * "
4 b' me through; the waters were "
6 b' me, and caused me to return 3212
8 b' forth into the sea, the waters *3318
Da 1: 2 b' the vessels into the treasure 935
9 God had b' Daniel into favour *5414
18 then the prince of the eunuchs b' 935
2:25 Then Arioch b' in Daniel 5954
3:13 b' these men before the king. 858
5: 3 Then they b' the golden vessels "
13 was Daniel b' in before the king. 5954
13 king my father b' out of Jewry? 858
15 been b' in before me, that they 5954
23 and they have b' the vessels of 858
6:16 and they b' Daniel, and cast him "
17 And a stone was b', and laid "
18 b' before him: and his sleep 5954
24 and they b' those men which 858
7:13 and they b' him near before him. 7127
9:14 upon the evil, and b' it upon us: 935
15 that hast b' thy people forth out 3318
11: 6 and they that b' her, and he that 935
Ho 12:13 the Lord b' Israel out of Egypt, 5927
Am 2:10 I b' you up from the land of "
3: 1 I b' up from the land of Egypt, "
9: 7 Have not I b' up Israel out of the "
Ob 7 of thy confederacy have b' thee 7971
Jon 2: 6 yet hast thou b' up my life 5927
Mic 5: 3 which travaileth hath b' forth: 3205
6: 4 I b' thee up out of the land of 5927
Na 2: 7 she shall be b' up, and her maids "
Hag 1: 9 and when ye b' it home, I did 935
2:19 the olive tree, hath not b' forth: 5375
Zec 10:11 of Assyria shall be b' down, 3381
Mal 1:13 and ye b' that which was torn, 935
13 thus ye b' an offering: should I "
M't 1:12 after they were b' to Babylon, *3350
25 b' forth her firstborn son: 5088
4:24 they b' unto him all sick people 4374
8:16 they b' unto him many that were "
9: 2 b' to him a man sick of the palsy, "
32 they b' to him a dumb man "
10:18 ye shall be b' before governors 71
11:23 heaven, shalt be b' down to hell: *2601
12:22 Then was b' unto him one 4374
25 is b' to desolation; and every city 2049
13: 8 unto good ground, and b' forth *1325
26 and b' forth fruit, then appeared 4160
14:11 his head was b' in a charger, 5342
11 and she b' it to her mother. "
35 and b' unto him all that were 4374
16: 8 because ye have b' no bread? *2989
17:16 And I b' him to thy disciples, 4374
18:24 one was b' unto him, which owed "
19:13 these b' unto him little children "
21: 7 And b' the ass, and the colt, 71
22:19 And they b' unto him a penny. 4374
25:20 came and b' other five talents, "
27: 3 b' again the thirty pieces of 654
M'r 1:32 they b' unto him all that were 5342
4: 8 and b' forth, some thirty, and
21 b' to be put under a bushel, 2064
29 when the fruit is b' forth, *3860
6:27 commanded his head to be b': 5342
28 And b' his head in a charger, "
9:17 I have b' unto thee my son, "
20 And they b' him unto him: and "
10:13 they b' young children to him, ‡4374
13 disciples rebuked those that b' * "
11: 7 And they b' the colt to Jesus, 71
12:16 And they b' it. And he saith 5342
13: 9 ye shall be b' before rulers and *2476
Lu 1:57 delivered; and she b' forth a son. 1080
2: 7 she b' forth her firstborn son, 5088
22 they b' him to Jerusalem to 321
27 when the parents b' in the child 1521
3: 5 mountain and hill shall be b' low; 5013
4: 9 And he b' him to Jerusalem, and * 71
16 Nazareth, where he had been b' up: 5142
40 divers diseases b' them unto him; 71
5:11 they had b' their ships to land, 2609
18 And, behold, men b' in a bed 5342
7:37 b' an alabaster box of ointment, 2865
10:34 b' him to an inn, and took care 71
11:17 against itself is b' to desolation; 2049
12:16 of a certain rich man b' forth 2164
18:15 they b' unto him also infants, ‡4374
40 commanded him to be b' unto him: 71
19:35 And they b' him to Jesus: and "
21:12 being b' before kings and rulers * "
22:54 b' him into the high priest's 1521
23:14 Ye have b' this man unto me, 4374
Joh 1:42 And he b' him to Jesus. And 71
4:33 any man b' him ought to eat? 5342
7:45 Why have ye not b' him? 71
8: 3 the scribes and Pharisees b' * "
9:13 They b' to the Pharisees him "
18:16 kept the door, and b' in Peter, 1521
19:13 he b' Jesus forth, and sat down 71
39 b' a mixture of myrrh and aloes, 5342
Ac 4:34 and b' the prices of the things "
37 and b' the money, and laid it at "
5: 2 and b' a certain part, and laid it "
15 b' forth the sick into the streets, *1627
19 b' them forth, and said, 1806
21 to the prison to have them b'. 71
26 officers and b' them without "
27 And when they had b' them, "
36 scattered, and b' to nought. *1096
6:12 and caught him, and b' him 71
7:36 He b' them out, after that *1806
40 Moses, which b' us out of the "
45 b' in with Jesus into the 1521
9: 8 hand, and b' him to Damascus. "
27 took him, and b' him to the 71
30 they b' him down to Cæsarea, 2609
39 b' him into the upper chamber: 321
11:26 when he had found him, he b' him 71
12: 6 Herod would have b' him forth, *4254
17 Lord had b' him out of the prison. 1806
13: 1 which had been b' up with *4939
17 b' he them out of it. *1806
14:13 b' oxen and garlands unto the 5342
15: 3 And being b' on their way by 4311
16:16 which b' her masters much gain 3930
20 And b' them to the magistrates, *4317
30 And b' them out, and said, Sirs, 4254
34 he had b' them into his house, 321
39 b' them out, and desired them 1806
17:15 conducted Paul b' him unto Athens: 71
19 him, and b' him unto Areopagus, "
18:12 against Paul, and b' him to the "
19:12 his body were b' unto the sick *2018
19 b' their books together, and 4851
24 b' no small gain unto the 3930
37 b' hither these men, which are 71
20:12 they b' the young man alive, and "
21: 5 and they all b' us on our way, 4311
16 b' with them one Mnason of 71
28 b' Greeks also into the temple, 1521
29 that Paul had b' into the temple.) "
22: 3 yet b' up in this city at the feet 397
24 him to be b' into the castle, 71
30 b' Paul down, and set him before 2609
23:18 and b' him to the chief captain, 71
28 I b' him forth into their council: 2609
31 and b' him by night to Antipatris. 71
25: 6 seat commanded Paul to be b'. "
17 commanded the man to be b' forth. "
18 they b' none accusation of such 2018
23 commandment Paul was b' forth. 71
26 Wherefore I have b' him forth 4254
27:24 thou must be b' before Cæsar *3936
Ro 15:24 to be b' on my way thitherward 4311
1Co 6:12 not be b' under the power of any. 1850
15:54 then shall be b' to pass the *1096
2Co 1:16 b' on my way toward Judæa. *4311
Ga 2: 4 false brethren unawares b' in, 3920
1Th 3: 6 b' us good tidings of your faith 2097
1Ti 5:10 if she have b' up children, if she 5044
6: 7 we b' nothing into this world, 1533
2Ti 1:10 and hath b' life and immortality 5461
subscr. when Paul was b' before Nero 3936
Heb 13:11 b' into the sanctuary by the high 1533
20 that b' again from the dead our 321
Jas 5:18 and the earth b' forth her fruit. 985
1Pe 1:13 be b' unto you at the revelation 5342
2Pe 2:19 of the same is he b' in bondage. 1402
Re 12: 5 And she b' forth a man child, *5088
13 which b' forth the man child. "

broughtest
Ex 32: 7 thy people, which thou b' out of 5927
Nu 14:13 thou b' up this people in thy "
De 9:28 land whence thou b' us out say, 3318
29 which thou b' out by thy mighty "
2Sa 5: 2 that leddest out and b' in Israel: 935
1Ki 8:51 thou b' forth out of Egypt, from 3318
53 thou b' our fathers out of Egypt, "
1Ch 11: 2 and b' in Israel: and the Lord 935
Ne 9: 7 and b' him forth out of Ur of the 3318
15 b' forth water for them out of "
23 and b' them into the land, 935
Ps 66:11 Thou b' us into the net; thou "
12 thou b' us out into a wealthy place.3318

brow See also EYEBROW.
Isa 48: 4 an iron sinew, and thy b' brass; 4696
Lu 4:29 and led him unto the b' of the hill 3790

brown
Ge 30:32 the b' cattle among the sheep, *2345
33 b' among the sheep, that shall * "
35 all the b' among the sheep, and * "
40 all the b' in the flock of Laban; "

bruise See also BRUISED; BRUISES; BRUISING.
Ge 3:15 it shall b' thy head, 7779
15 and thou shalt b' his heel. "
Isa 28:28 cart, nor b' it with his horsemen. *1854
53:10 Yet it pleased the Lord to b' him; 1792
Jer 30:12 Thy b' is incurable, and thy *7667
Da 2:40 shall it break in pieces and b'. *7490
Na 3:19 no healing of thy b'; thy wound *7667
Ro 16:20 b' Satan under your feet shortly. 4937

bruised
Le 22:24 unto the Lord that which is b', 4600
2Ki 18:21 the staff of this b' reed, even 7533
Isa 28:28 Bread corn is b'; because he *1854
42: 3 A b' reed shall he not break, and 7533

Isa 53: 5 he was b' for our iniquities: the 1792
Eze 23: 3 they b' the teats of their virginity. ‡6213
8 b' the breasts of her virginity, ‡ "
M't 12:20 A b' reed shall he not break, and 4937
Lu 4:18 to set at liberty them that are b', 2352

bruises
Isa 1: 6 and b', and putrifying sores: 2250

bruising
Eze 23:21 in b' thy teats by the Egyptians ‡6213
Lu 9:39 b' him, hardly departeth from 4937

bruit
Jer 10:22 the noise of the b' is come, and †‡8052
Na 3:19 that hear the b' of thee shall ‡8088

brute
2Pe 2:12 these, as natural b' beasts, made * 249
Jude 10 know naturally, as b' beasts, in * "

brutish
Ps 49:10 the fool and the b' person perish, 1197
92: 6 A b' man knoweth not; neither "
94: 8 ye b' among the people: and ye "
Pr 12: 1 but he that hateth reproof is b'. "
30: 2 Surely I am more b' than any "
Isa 19:11 of Pharaoh is become b': "
Jer 10: 8 they are altogether b' and foolish: "
14 Every man is b' in his knowledge: "
21 the pastors are become b', and "
51:17 Every man is b' by his knowledge; "
Eze 21:31 into the hand of b' men, and skilful "

buck See ROEBUCK.

bucket See also BUCKETS.
Isa 40:15 the nations are as a drop of a b', 1805

buckets
Nu 24: 7 pour the water out of his b', and 1805

buckler See also BUCKLERS.
2Sa 22:31 a b' to all them that trust in him. *4043
1Ch 5:18 men able to bear b' and sword, "
12: 8 that could handle shield and b'. *7420
Ps 18: 2 my b', and the horn of my *4043
30 he is a b' to all those that trust * "
35: 2 Take hold of shield and b', and 6793
91: 4 truth shall be thy shield and b'. 5507
Pr 2: 7 a b' to them that walk uprightly. *4043
Jer 46: 3 Order ye the b' and shield, and "
Eze 23:24 set against thee b' and shield 6793
26: 8 and lift up the b' against thee. "

bucklers
2Ch 23: 9 spears, and b', and shields, that 4043
Job 15:26 upon the thick bosses of his b': "
Ca 4: 4 there hang a thousand b', all "
Eze 38: 4 company with b' and shields, *6793
39: 9 the shields and the b', the bows "

bud See also BUDDED; BUDS.
Job 14: 9 the scent of water it will b', and 6524
38:27 to cause the b' of the tender herb *4161
Ps 132:17 I make the horn of David to b': 6779
Ca 7:12 the pomegranates b' forth: there *5132
Isa 18: 5 when the b' is perfect, and the *6525
27: 6 Israel shall blossom and b', and 6524
55:10 maketh it bring forth and b', that 6779
61:11 the earth bringeth forth her b', "
Eze 16: 7 to multiply as the b' of the field, ‡ "
29:21 of the house of Israel to b' forth, "
Ho 8: 7 the b' shall yield no meal: if so * "

budded
Ge 40:10 it was as though it b', and her 6524
Nu 17: 8 Aaron for the house of Levi was b', "
Ca 6:11 and the pomegranates b'. *5132
Eze 7:10 hath blossomed, pride hath b'. 6524
Heb 9: 4 Aaron's rod that b', and the tables 985

buds
Nu 17: 8 was budded, and brought forth b', 6525

buffet See also BUFFETED.
M'r 14:65 to cover his face, and to b' him, 2852
2Co 12: 7 messenger of Satan to b' me, lest "

buffeted
M't 26:67 they spit in his face and b' him; *2852
1Co 4:11 and are b', and have no certain "
1Pe 2:20 when ye be b' for your faults, ye "

build See also BUILDED; BUILDEST; BUILDETH; BUILDING; BUILT.
Ge 11: 4 Go to, let us b' us a city and 1129
8 and they left off to b' the city. "
Ex 20:25 thou shalt not b' it of hewn stone: "
Nu 23: 1, 29 B' me here seven altars, and "
32:16 We will b' sheepfolds here for our "
24 B' you cities for your little ones, "
De 20:20 and thou shalt b' bulwarks against "
25: 9 will not b' up his brother's house. "
27: 5 there shalt thou b' an altar unto "
6 Thou shalt b' the altar of the Lord "
28:30 thou shalt b' an house, and thou "
Jos 22:26 Let us now prepare to b' us an "
29 to b' an altar for burnt offerings, "
J'g 6:26 And b' an altar unto the Lord "
Ru 4:11 two did b' the house of Israel: "
1Sa 2:35 and I will b' him a sure house; "
2Sa 7: 5 Shalt thou b' me an house for me "
7 Why b' ye not me an house of * "
13 shall b' an house for my name, "
27 saying, I will b' thee an house: "
24:21 to b' an altar unto the Lord, that "
1Ki 2:36 B' thee an house in Jerusalem "
5: 3 my father could not b' an house "
5 behold, I purpose to b' an house "
5 shall b' an house unto my name. "
18 timber and stones to b' the house. "
6: 1 that he began to b' the house of "
8:16 tribes of Israel to b' an house, "
17 David my father to b' an house "
18 to b' an house unto my name, thou "
1Ki 8:19 thou shalt not b' the house; but 1129
19 shall b' the house unto my name. "
9:15 to b' the house of the Lord, and "
19 which Solomon desired to b' in "
24 built for her: then did he b' Millo. "
11: 7 Then did Solomon b' an high place "
38 and b' thee a sure house, "
16:34 did Hiel the Beth-elite b' Jericho: "
1Ch 14: 1 carpenters, to b' him an house. "
17: 4 Thou shalt not b' me an house "
10 the Lord will b' thee an house. "
12 He shall b' me an house, and I will "
25 that thou wilt b' him an house: "
21:22 that I may b' an altar therein unto "
22: 2 stones to b' the house of God. "
6 him to b' an house for the Lord "
7 it was in my mind to b' an house "
8 thou shalt not b' an house unto "
10 shall b' an house for my name; "
11 b' the house of the Lord thy God, "
19 and b' the sanctuary of the Lord "
28: 2 in mine heart to b' an house of "
3 Thou shalt not b' an house for my "
6 shall b' my house and my courts, "
10 to b' an house for the sanctuary: "
29:16 to b' thee an house for thine holy "
19 and to b' the palace, for the which "
2Ch 2: 1 Solomon determined to b' an house "
3 send him cedars to b' him an "
4 Behold, I b' an house to the name "
5 the house which I b' is great: for "
6 who is able to b' him an house, "
6 that I should b' him an house, "
9 the house which I am about to b' "
12 that might b' an house for the Lord, "
3: 1 Solomon began to b' the house "
2 And he began to b' in the second "
6: 5 to b' an house in, that my name "
7 David my father to b' an house "
8 heart to b' an house for my name, "
9 thou shalt not b' the house; but "
9 he shall b' the house for my name. "
8: 6 desired to b' in Jerusalem, "
14: 7 Let us b' these cities, and make "
35: 3 son of David king of Israel did b'; "
36:23 to b' him an house in Jerusalem, "
Ezr 1: 2 to b' him an house at Jerusalem, "
3 and b' the house of the Lord God "
5 to b' the house of the Lord which "
4: 2 Let us b' with you: for we seek "
3 to b' an house unto our God; "
3 but we ourselves together will b' "
5: 2 and began to b' the house of God 1124
3 Who hath commanded you to b' "
9 commanded you to b' this house, "
13 made a decree to b' this house of "
17 was made of Cyrus the king to b' "
6: 7 the elders of the Jews b' this house "
Ne 2: 5 sepulchres, that I may b' it. 1129
17 let us b' up the wall of Jerusalem, "
18 Let us rise up and b'. So they "
20 we his servants will arise and b': "
3: 3 did the sons of Hassenaah b', who "
4: 3 Even that which they b', if a fox "
10 that we are not able to b' the wall. "
Ps 28: 5 destroy them, and not b' them up. "
51:18 b' thou the walls of Jerusalem. "
69:35 and will b' the cities of Judah: "
89: 4 b' up thy throne to all generations. "
102:16 the Lord shall b' up Zion, he shall* "
127: 1 Except the Lord b' the house, they "
147: 2 The Lord doth b' up Jerusalem: "
Pr 24:27 and afterwards b' thine house. "
Ec 3: 3 break down, and a time to b' up; "
Ca 8: 9 will b' upon her a palace of silver: "
Isa 9:10 but we will b' with hewn stones: "
45:13 he shall b' my city, and he shall "
58:12 they that shall be of thee shall b' "
60:10 the sons of strangers shall b' up "
61: 4 And they shall b' the old wastes, "
65:21 shall b' houses, and inhabit them; "
22 shall not b', and another inhabit; "
66: 1 where is the house that ye b' unto "
Jer 1:10 to throw down, to b', and to plant. "
18: 9 concerning a kingdom, to b' and "
22:14 I will b' me a wide house and large "
24: 6 I will b' them, and not pull them "
29: 5, 28 B' ye houses, and dwell in them; "
31: 4 Again I will b' thee, and thou shalt "
28 so will I watch over them, to b', "
33: 7 and will b' them, as at the first. "
35: 7 Neither shall ye b' house, nor sow "
9 Nor to b' houses for us to dwell in: "
42:10 then will I b' you, and not pull you "
Eze 4: 2 and b' a fort against it, and cast a "
11: 3 let us b' houses: this city is the "
21:22 to cast a mount, and to b' a fort. "
28:26 and shall b' houses, and plant "
36:36 that I the Lord b' the ruined "
Da 9:25 to restore and to b' Jerusalem "
Am 9:11 I will b' it as in the days of old: "
14 and they shall b' the waste cities, "
Mic 3:10 They b' up Zion with blood, and "
Zep 1:13 they shall also b' houses, but not "
Hag 1: 8 and b' the house; and I will take "
Zec 5:11 To b' it an house in the land of "
6:12 and he shall b' the temple of the "
13 Even he shall b' the temple of "
15 and b' in the temple of the Lord, "
9: 3 Tyrus did b' herself a strong hold, "
Mal 1: 4 return and b' the desolate places; "
4 shall b', but I will throw down; "
M't 16:18 upon this rock I will b' my 3618
23:29 because ye b' the tombs of the "
26:61 God, and to b' it in three days. "
M'r 14:58 within three days I will b' another "
Lu 11:47 b' the sepulchres of the prophets, 3618
48 them, and ye b' their sepulchres. "
12:18 I will pull down my barns, and b' "
14:28 intending to b' a tower, sitteth "
30 This man began to b', and was not "
Ac 7:49 what house will ye b' me? saith "
15:16 b' again the tabernacle of David, 456
16 I will b' again the ruins thereof, "
20:32 to b' you up, and to give you an 2026
Ro 15:20 lest I should b' upon another 3618
1Co 3:12 Now if any man b' upon this 2026
Gal 2:18 if I b' again the things which I 3618

builded See also BUILDEDST; BUILT.
Ge 4:17 and he b' a city, and called the 1129
8:20 Noah b' an altar unto the Lord; "
10:11 and b' Nineveh, and the city "
11: 5 which the children of men b'. "
12: 7 there b' he an altar unto the Lord, "
8 and there he b' an altar unto the "
26:25 And he b' an altar there, and "
Ex 24: 4 and b' an altar under the hill, "
Nu 32:38 unto the cities which they b'. "
Jos 22:16 in that ye have b' you an altar, "
1Ki 8:27 less this house that I have b'? "
43 this house, which I have b', is * "
15:22 thereof, wherewith Baasha had b'; "
2Ki 23:13 Solomon the king of Israel had b' "
1Ch 22: 5 to be b' for the Lord must be "
Ezr 3: 2 and b' the altar of the God of Israel, "
4: 1 children of the captivity b' the "
13 if this city be b', and the walls set 1124
16 if this city be b' again, and the "
21 and that this city be not b', until "
5: 8 which is b' with great stones, "
11 b' these many years ago, which "
11 which a great king of Israel b' and "
15 let the house of God be b' in this "
6: 3 Let the house be b', the place "
14 And the elders of the Jews b', "
14 And they b', and finished it, "
Ne 3: 1 and they b' the sheep gate; 1129
2 And next unto him b' the men "
2 And next to him b' Zaccur "
4: 1 heard that we b' the wall, he was "
17 They which b' on the wall, and "
18 girded by his side, and so b'. "
6: 1 heard that I had b' the wall, and "
7: 4 and the houses were not b'. "
12:29 the singers had b' them villages "
Job 20:19 away an house which he b' not; * "
Ps 122: 3 Jerusalem is b' as a city that is "
Pr 9: 1 Wisdom hath b' her house, she "
24: 3 Through wisdom is an house b'; "
Ec 2: 4 I b' me houses; I planted me "
Ca 4: 4 tower of David b' for an armoury, "
Jer 30:18 and the city shall be b' upon "
La 3: 5 He hath b' against me, and "
Eze 36:10 and the wastes shall be b': "
33 cities, and the wastes shall be b'. "
Lu 17:28 they sold, they planted, they b'; 3618
Eph 2:22 In whom ye also are b' together 4925
Heb 3: 3 as he who hath b' the house hath 2680
4 every house is b' by some man; "

buildedst
De 6:10 goodly cities, which thou b' not, 1129

builder See also BUILDERS; MASTERBUILDER.
Heb 11:10 whose b' and maker is God. 5079

builders
1Ki 5:18 Solomon's b' and Hiram's b' 1129
2Ki 12:11 to the carpenters and b', that "
22: 6 Unto carpenters, and b', and "
2Ch 34:11 to the artificers and b' gave they it, "
Ezr 3:10 when the b' laid the foundation "
Ne 4: 5 thee to anger before the b'. "
18 For the b', every one had his "
Ps 118:22 the stone which the b' refused "
Eze 27: 4 thy b' have perfected thy beauty. "
M't 21:42 The stone which the b' rejected, 3618
M'r 12:10 The stone which the b' rejected "
Lu 20:17 The stone which the b' rejected, "
Ac 4:11 which was set at nought of you b', "
1Pe 2: 7 the stone which the b' disallowed, "

buildest
De 22: 8 When thou b' a new house, 1129
Neh 6: 6 which cause thou b' the wall, "
Eze 16:31 In that thou b' thine eminent "
M't 27:40 temple and b' it in three days, 3618
M'r 15:29 temple, and b' it in three days, "

buildeth
Jos 6:26 and b' this city Jericho: he shall 1129
Job 27:18 he b' his house as a moth, and "
Pr 14: 1 Every wise woman b' her house: "
Jer 22:13 Woe unto him that b' his house "
Ho 8:14 and b' temples; and Judah "
Am 9: 6 that b' his stories in the heaven, "
Hab 2:12 Woe to him that b' a town with "
1Co 3:10 foundation, and another b' 2026
10 take heed how he b' thereupon. "

building See also BUILDINGS.
Jos 22:19 in b' you an altar beside the 1129
1Ki 3: 1 made an end of b' his own house, "
6: 7 when it was in b', was built of "
7 in the house, while it was in b'. "
12 which thou art in b', if thou wilt "
38 So was he seven years in b' it. "
7: 1 Solomon was b' his own house "
9: 1 Solomon had finished the b' of "
15:21 that he left off b' of Ramah, "
1Ch 28: 2 and had made ready for the b': "
2Ch 3: 3 for the b' of the house of God. "
16: 5 that he left off b' of Ramah, "
6 wherewith Baasha was b'; and * "
Ezr 4: 4 Judah, and troubled them in b', "

Ezr 4:12 b· the rebellious and the bad 1124
5: 4 of the men that make this b·? 1147
16 even until now hath it been in b·. 1124
6: 8 for the b· of this house of God: "
Ec 10:18 By much slothfulness the b· *4746
Eze 17:17 and b· forts, to cut off many 1129
40: 5 the breadth of the b·, one reed; 1146
41:12 Now the b· that was before the "
12 broad; and the wall of the b· "
13 and the b·, with the walls thereof, 1140
15 the length of the b· over against 1146
42: 1 before the b· toward the north. "
5 and than the middlemost of the b·. "
42: 6 therefore the b· was straitened *
10 place, and over against the b·. 1146
46:23 there was a row of b· round about
Joh 2:20 was this temple in b·, and wilt 3618
1Co 3: 9 husbandry, ye are God's b·. 3619
2Co 5: 1 we have a b· of God, an house "
Eph 2:21 In whom all the b· fitly framed "
Heb 9:11 that is to say, not of this b·; *2937
Jude 20 b· up yourselves on your most 2026
Re 21:18 the b· of the wall of it was of 1739

buildings
M't 24: 1 to shew him the b· of the temple. 3619
M'r 13: 1 stones and what b· are here! "
2 him, Seest thou these great b·? "

built See also BUILDED.
Ge 13:18 b· there an altar unto the Lord. 1129
22: 9 and Abraham b· an altar there, "
33:17 and b· him an house, and made "
35: 7 And he b· there an altar, "
Ex 1:11 b· for Pharaoh treasure cities, "
17:15 And Moses b· an altar, and called "
32: 5 he b· an altar before it; and Aaron "
Nu 13:22 Hebron was b· seven years before "
21:27 let the city of Sihon be b· and "
23:14 and b· seven altars, and offered "
32:34 And the children of Gad b· Dibon, "
37 the children of Reuben b· Heshbon, "
De 8:12 and hast b· goodly houses, and "
13:16 for ever; it shall not be b· again. "
20: 5 that hath b· a new house, and "
Jos 8:30 Joshua b· an altar unto the Lord "
19:50 Ephraim: and he b· the city, "
22:10 tribe of Manasseh b· there an altar "
11 b· an altar over against the land "
23 That we have b· us an altar to "
24:13 cities which ye b· not, and ye "
J'g 1:26 and b· a city, and called the name "
6:24 Then Gideon b· an altar there "
28 offered upon the altar that was b·. "
18:28 And they b· a city, and dwelt "
21: 4 and b· there an altar, and offered "
1Sa 7:17 there he b· an altar unto the Lord. "
14:35 And Saul b· an altar unto the Lord: "
35 same was the first altar that he b· "
2Sa 5: 9 And David b· round about from "
11 and they b· David an house. "
24:25 And David b· there an altar unto "
1Ki 3: 2 b· unto the name of the Lord, "
6: 2 the house which king Solomon b· "
5 against the wall of the house he b· "
7 was b· of stone made ready before "
9 So he b· the house, and finished it; "
10 And then he b· chambers against "
14 So Solomon b· the house, and "
15 And he b· the walls of the house "
16 And he b· twenty cubits on the "
16 with boards of cedar: he even b· "
36 And he b· the inner court with "
7: 2 He b· also the house of the forest "
8:13 I have surely b· thee an house to "
20 promised, and have b· an house "
44 house that I have b· for thy name: "
48 and the house which I have b·: "
9: 3 thou hast b·, to put my name "
10 Solomon had b· the two houses, "
17 And Solomon b· Gezer, and "
24 house which Solomon had b· for "
25 altar which he b· unto the Lord, "
10: 4 and the house that he had b·, "
11:27 Solomon b· Millo, and repaired the "
38 a sure house, as I b· for David, "
12:25 Then Jeroboam b· Shechem in "
25 out from thence, and b· Penuel. "
14:23 they also b· them high places, "
15:17 up against Judah, and b· Ramah, "
22 and king Asa b· with them Geba "
23 the cities which he b·, are they "
16:24 and b· on the hill, and called "
24 the name of the city which he b·, "
32 Baal, which he had b· in Samaria. "
18:32 And with the stones he b· an altar "
22:39 made, and all the cities that he b·, "
2Ki 14:22 He b· Elath, and restored it to "
15:35 He b· the higher gate of the house "
16:11 And Urijah the priest b· an altar "
18 that they had b· in the house, and "
17: 9 and they b· them high places in all "
21: 3 he b· up again the high places "
4 And he b· altars in the house of "
5 And he b· altars for all the host of "
25: 1 they b· forts against it round about. "
1Ch 6:10 that Solomon b· in Jerusalem:) "
32 until Solomon had b· the house of "
7:24 who b· Beth-horon the nether, and "
8:12 who b· Ono,and Lod, with the towns "
11: 8 And he b· the city round about, "
17: 6 Why have ye not b· me an house "
21:26 And David b· there an altar unto "
22:19 the house that is to be b· to the "
2Ch 6: 2 I have b· an house of habitation "
10 and have b· the house for the name "
18 less this house which I have b·! * "
2Ch 6:33 this house which I have b· is called 1129
34 which I have b· for thy name; "
38 toward the house which I have b· "
8: 1 Solomon had b· the house of the "
2 Solomon b· them, and caused the "
4 he b· Tadmor in the wilderness, "
4 store cities, which he b· in Hamath. "
5 Also he b· Beth-horon the upper, "
11 house that he had b· for her: "
12 which he had b· before the porch, "
9: 3 and the house that he had b·, "
11: 5 b· cities for defence in Judah. "
6 He b· even Beth-lehem, and Etam, "
14: 6 And he b· fenced cities in Judah: "
7 So they b· and prospered. "
16: 1 and b· Ramah, to the intent that "
6 he b· therewith Geba and Mizpah. "
17:12 he b· in Judah castles, and cities "
20: 8 b· thee a sanctuary therein for thy "
26: 2 He b· Eloth, and restored it to "
6 and b· cities about Ashdod, and "
9 Uzziah b· towers in Jerusalem at "
10 Also he b· towers in the desert, "
27: 3 He b· the high gate of the house of "
3 and on the wall of Ophel he b· "
4 he b· cities in the mountains of "
4 and in the forests he b· castles "
32: 5 and b· up all the wall that was "
33: 3 For he b· again the high places "
4 Also he b· altars in the house of "
5 And he b· altars for all the host of "
14 after this he b· a wall without the "
15 all the altars that he had b· in the "
19 places wherein he b· high places, "
Ne 3:13 they b· it, and set up the doors "
14 he b· it, and set up the doors "
15 he b· it, and covered it, and set up "
4: 6 So b· we the wall; and all the wall "
7: 1 when the wall was b·, and I had set "
Job 3:14 b· desolate places for themselves; "
12:14 down, and it cannot be b· again: "
22:23 thou shalt be b· up, thou shalt put "
Ps 78:69 b· his sanctuary like high palaces, "
89: 2 Mercy shall be b· up for ever: thy "
Ec 9:14 and b· great bulwarks against it: "
Isa 5: 2 and b· a tower in the midst of it, "
25: 2 to be no city; it shall never be b·. "
44:26 Ye shall be b·, and I will raise up "
28 Thou shalt be b·; and to the "
Jer 7:31 And they have b· the high places "
12:16 then shall they be b· in the midst "
19: 5 They have b· also the high places "
31: 4 thou shalt be b·, O virgin of Israel: "
38 the city shall be b· to the Lord "
32:35 And they b· the high places of Baal, "
45: 4 which I have b· will I break down, "
52: 4 and b· forts against it round about. "
Eze 13:10 one b· up a wall, and, lo, others "
16:24 also b· unto thee an eminent place, "
25 Thou hast b· thy high place at "
26:14 thou shalt be b· no more: for I the "
Da 4:30 I have b· for the house of the 1124
9:25 the street shall be b· again, 1129
Am 5:11 ye have b· houses of hewn stone, "
Mic 7:11 the day that thy walls are to be b·, "
Hag 1: 2 that the Lord's house should be b·. "
Zec 1:16 my house shall be b· in it, saith "
8: 9 laid, that the temple might be b·. "
M't 7:24 which b· his house upon a rock: 3618
26 which b· his house upon the sand: "
21:33 winepress in it, and b· a tower, "
M'r 12: 1 and b· a tower, and let it out to "
Lu 4:29 whereon their city was b·, that "
6:48 a man which b· an house, and * "
49 a man that . . . b· an house upon "
7: 5 and he hath b· us a synagogue. * "
Ac 7:47 But Solomon b· him an house. "
1Co 3:14 abide which he hath b· thereupon, 2026
Eph 2:20 And are b· upon the foundation "
Col 2: 7 Rooted and b· up in him, and "
Heb 3: 4 but he that b· all things is God. 2680
1Pe 2: 5 are b· up a spiritual house, 3618

Bukki (*buk'-ki*)
Nu 34:22 of Dan, B· the son of Jogli. 1231
1Ch 6: 5 Abishua begat B·, and B· begat "
51 B· his son, Uzzi his son, Zerahiah "
Ezr 7: 4 the son of Uzzi, the son of B·, "

Bukkiah (*buk-ki'-ah*)
1Ch 25: 4 B·, Mattaniah, Uzziel, Shebuel, 1232
13 The sixth to B·, he, his sons, and "

Bul (*bul*)
1Ki 6:38 in the month B·, which is the 945

bull See also BULLS; BULRUSH.
Job 21:10 Their b· gendereth, and faileth 7794
Isa 51:20 as a wild b· in a net: they are *8377

bullock See also BULLOCK'S; BULLOCKS.
Ex 29: 1 Take one young b·, and two rams 6499
3 with the b· and the two rams. "
10 thou shalt cause a b· to be brought "
10 hands upon the head of the b·. "
11 shalt kill the b· before the Lord, "
12 take of the blood of the b·, and "
14 the flesh of the b·, and his skin, "
36 And thou shalt offer every day a b· "
Le 1: 5 kill tho b· before the Lord. 1121, 1241
4: 3 a young b· without blemish unto 6499
4 he shall bring the b· unto the door "
4 the bullock's head, and kill the b· "
7 the blood of the b· at the bottom "
8 fat of the b· for the sin offering; "
10 from the b· of the sacrifice of *7794
11 skin of the b·, and all his flesh, 6499
12 Even the whole b· shall he carry "
14 congregation shall offer a young b· "
Le 4:15 upon the head of the b· before the 6499
15 Lord: and the b· shall be killed "
20 And he shall do with the b· "
20 as he did with the b· for "
21 he shall carry forth the b· without "
21 burn him as he burned the first b·: "
8: 2 a b· for the sin offering, and two "
14 the b· for the sin offering: and "
14 hands upon the head of the b· for "
17 the b·, and his hide, his flesh, and "
9: 4 Also a b· and a ram for peace *7794
18 He slew also the b· and the ram * "
19 the fat of the b· and of the ram, * "
16: 3 a young b· for a sin offering, and 6499
6 shall offer his b· of the sin offering, "
11 Aaron shall bring the b· of the "
11 shall kill the b· of the sin offering "
14 take of the blood of the b·, and "
15 as he did with the blood of the b·, "
18 and shall take of the blood of the b·, "
27 the b· for the sin offering, and "
22:23 Either a b· or a lamb, that hath 7794
27 When a b·, or a sheep, or a goat, "
23:18 and one young b·, and two rams: 6499
Nu 7:15, 21, 27, 33, 39, 45, 51, 57, 63, 69, 75, 81
One young b·, one ram, one lamb "
8: 8 Then let them take a young b· with "
8 another young b· shalt thou take "
15: 8 when thou preparest a b· for 1121, 1241
9 with a b· a meat offering of "
11 Thus shall it be done for one b·, 7794
24 offer one young b· for a burnt 6499
23: 2 offered on every altar a b· and a "
4 offered upon every altar a b· and "
14, 30 offered a b· and a ram on every "
28:12 mingled with oil, for one b·; "
14 half an hin of wine unto a b·, and "
20 tenth deals shall ye offer for a b·, "
28 three tenth deals unto one b·, two "
29: 2 one young b·, one ram, and seven "
3 three tenth deals for a b·, and two "
8 for a sweet savour; one young b·, "
9 three tenth deals to a b·, and two "
14 deals unto every b· of the thirteen "
36 one b·, one ram, seven lambs of "
37 for the b·, for the ram, and for the "
De 15:19 the firstling of thy b·, nor shear *7794
17: 1 any b·, or sheep, wherein is * "
33:17 like the firstling of his b·, and his "
J'g 6:25 Take thy father's young b·, 6499
25 even the second b· of seven years "
26 and take the second b·, and offer "
28 the second b· was offered upon the "
1Sa 1:25 And they slew a b·, and brought "
1Ki 18:23 and let them choose one b· for "
23 and I will dress the other b·, "
25 Choose you one b· for yourselves, "
26 they took the b· which was given "
33 and cut the b· in pieces; and laid "
2Ch 13: 9 consecrate himself with a young b· "
Ps 50: 9 I will take no b· out of thy house, "
69:31 or b· that hath horns and hoofs. "
Isa 65:25 lion shall eat straw like the b·: *1241
Jer 31:18 a b· unaccustomed to the yoke: *5695
Eze 43:19 a young b· for a sin offering. 6499
21 take the b· also of the sin offering, "
22 as they did cleanse it with the b·. "
23 offer a young b· without blemish, "
25 they shall also prepare a young b·, "
45:18 take a young b· without blemish, "
22 for all the people of the land a b· "
24 an ephah for a b·, and an ephah "
46: 6 a young b· without blemish, "
7 an ephah for a b·, and an ephah "
11 shall be an ephah to a b·, and an "

bullock's
Le 4: 4 his hand upon the b· head, *6499
5 shall take of the b· blood, * "
16 anointed, shall bring of the b· * "

bullocks
Nu 7:87 were twelve b·, the rams twelve, 6499
88 were twenty and four b·, the rams "
8:12 upon the heads of the b·: "
23:29 prepare me here seven b· and "
28:11 unto the Lord; two young b·, "
19 two young b·, and one ram, "
27 unto the Lord; two young b·, "
29:13 thirteen young b·, two rams, "
14 every bullock of the thirteen b·, "
17 ye shall offer twelve young b·, "
18 their drink offerings for the b·, "
20 the third day eleven b·, two rams, "
21 for the b·, for the rams, and for "
23 on the fourth day ten b·, two rams, "
24 drink offerings for the b·, for the "
26 And on the fifth day nine b·, two "
27 offerings for the b·, for the rams, "
29 on the sixth day eight b·, two "
30 b·, for the rams, and for the lambs, "
32 And on the seventh day seven b·, "
33 and their drink offerings for the b·, "
1Sa 1:24 him up with her, with three b·, "
1Ki 18:23 them therefore give us two b·; "
1Ch 15:26 they offered seven b·, and seven "
29:21 a thousand b·, a thousand rams, "
2Ch 29:21 they brought seven b·, and seven "
22 they killed the b·, and the priests 1241
32 threescore and ten b·, an hundred "
30:24 thousand b· and seven thousand 6499
24 to the congregation a thousand b· "
35: 7 three thousand b·: these were 1241
Ezr 6: 9 both young b·, and rams, and 8450
17 an hundred b·, two hundred rams, "
7:17 buy speedily with this money b·, "
8:35 twelve b· for all Israel, ninety 6499

Job 42: 8 take unto you now seven b' and 6499
Ps 51:19 then shall they offer b' upon thine "
66:15 I will offer b' with goats. 1241
Isa 1:11 I delight not in the blood of b', 6499
34: 7 and the b' with the bulls; and "
Jer 46:21 in the midst of her like fatted b':*5695
50:27 Slay all her b'; let them go down 6499
Eze 39:18 of lambs, and of goats, of b', all of "
45:23 seven b' and seven rams without "
Hos 12:11 they sacrifice b' in Gilgal; yea, 7794

bulls
Ge 32:15 forty kine, and ten b', twenty 6499
Ps 22:12 Many b' have compassed me: "
12 strong b' of Bashan have beset me "
50:13 Will I eat the flesh of b', or drink 47
68:30 the multitude of the b', with the "
Isa 34: 7 the bullocks with the b'; and their "
Jer 50:11 heifer at grass, and bellow as b':* "
52:20 and twelve brasen b' that were 1241
Heb 9:13 if the blood of b' and of goats, 5022
10: 4 not possible that the blood of b' "

bulrush See also BULRUSHES.
Isa 58: 5 bow down his head as a b', * 100

bulrushes
Ex 2: 3 took for him an ark of b', 1573
Isa 18: 2 in vessels of b' upon the waters, * "

bulwarks
De 20:20 shalt build b' against the city 4692
2Ch 26:15 be on the towers and upon the b',*6438
Ps 48:13 Mark ye well her b', consider her 2430
Ec 9:14 and built great b' against it: 4685
Isa 26: 1 will God appoint for walls and b'. 2426

Bunah (*boo'-nah*)
1Ch 2:25 Ram the firstborn, and B', and 946

bunch See also BUNCHES.
Ex 12:22 ye shall take a b' of hyssop, and 92

bunches
2Sa 16: 1 an hundred b' of raisins, and an *6778
1Ch 12:40 cakes of figs, and b' of raisins, * "
Isa 30: 6 upon the b' of camels, to a ‡1707

bundle See also BUNDLES.
Ge 42:35 every man's b' of money was in 6872
1Sa 25:29 bound in the b' of life with the "
Ca 1:13 A b' of myrrh is my wellbeloved "
Ac 28: 3 gathered a b' of sticks, and laid 4128

bundles
Ge 42:35 their father saw the b' of money, 6872
M't 13:30 bind them in b' to burn them: 1197

Bunni (*bun'-ni*)
Ne 9: 4 Shebaniah, B', Sherebiah, Bani, 1137
10:15 B', Azgad, Bebai, "
11:15 son of Hashabiah, the son of B'; "

burden See also BURDENED; BURDENS; BURDENSOME.
Ex 18:22 they shall bear the b' with thee.
23: 5 lying under his b', and wouldest 4853
Nu 4:15 the b' of the sons of Kohath in the "
19 one to his service and to his b': "
31 And this is the charge of their b', "
32 of the charge of their b'. "
47 service of the b' in the tabernacle* "
49 according to his b': thus were they "
11:11 the b' of all this people upon me? "
17 they shall bear the b' of the people "
De 1:12 and your b', and your strife? "
2Sa 15:33 then thou shalt be a b' unto me: "
19:35 should thy servant be yet a b' "
2Ki 5:17 servant two mules' b' of earth? "
8: 9 forty camels' b', and came and "
9:25 the Lord laid this b' upon him; "
2Ch 35: 3 not be a b' upon your shoulders: "
Ne 13:19 there should no b' be brought in "
Job 7:20 so that I am a b' to myself? "
Ps 38: 4 as an heavy b' they are too heavy "
55:22 Cast thy b' upon the Lord, and he 3053
81: 6 removed his shoulder from the b':5449
Ec 12: 5 and the grasshopper shall be a b',5445
Isa 9: 4 broken the yoke of his b', and the 5448
10:27 his b' shall be taken away from off "
13: 1 The b' of Babylon, which Isaiah 4853
14:25 and his b' depart from off their 5448
28 that king Ahaz died was this b'. 4853
15: 1 The b' of Moab. Because in the "
17: 1 The b' of Damascus. Behold, "
19: 1 The b' of Egypt. Behold, the Lord "
21: 1 The b' of the desert of the sea. "
11 The b' of Dumah. He calleth to "
13 The b' upon Arabia. In the forest "
22: 1 The b' of the valley of vision. "
25 fall; and the b' that was upon it "
23: 1 The b' of Tyre. Howl, ye ships "
30: 6 The b' of the beasts of the south: "
27 the b' thereof is heavy: his lips *4858
46: 1 they are a b' to the weary beast. 4853
2 they could not deliver the b', but "
Jer 17:21 bear no b' on the sabbath day, "
22 Neither carry forth a b' out of "
24 to bring in no b' through the gates "
27 not to bear a b', even entering in at "
23:33 saying, What is the b' of the Lord? "
33 then say unto them, What b'? "
34 that shall say, The b' of the Lord, "
36 And the b' of the Lord shall ye "
36 every man's word shall be his b': "
38 ye say, The b' of the Lord; "
38 this word, The b' of the Lord, "
38 shall not say, The b' of the Lord; "
Eze 12:10 This b' concerneth the prince "
Ho 8:10 for the b' of the king of princes. "
Na 1: 1 The b' of Nineveh. The book of "
Hab 1: 1 b' which Habakkuk the prophet "
Zep 3:18 whom the reproach of it was a b'. 4864

Zec 9: 1 The b' of the word of the Lord in 4853
12: 1 The b' of the word of the Lord "
3 all that b' themselves with it 6006
Mal 1: 1 The b' of the word of the Lord to 4853
M't 11:30 yoke is easy, and my b' is light. 5413
20:12 which have borne the b' and heat 922
Ac 15:28 upon you no greater b' than these "
21: 3 the ship was to unlade her b'. 1117
2Co 12:16 I did not b' you: nevertheless, 2599
Ga 6: 5 every man shall bear his own b'. 5413
Re 2:24 will put upon you none other b'. 922

burdened
2Co 5: 4 do groan, being b': not for that 916
8:13 other men be eased, and ye b': *2347

burdens
Ge 49:14 crouching down between two b': *4942
Ex 1:11 to afflict them with their b'. 5450
2:11 looked on their b': and he spied "
5: 4 their works? get you unto your b'. "
5 ye make them rest from their b'. "
6: 6 from under the b' of the Egyptians, "
7 bringeth you out from under the b' "
Nu 4:24 Gershonites, to serve, and for b': 4853
27 the Gershonites, in all their b', * "
27 unto them in charge all their b'. * "
1Ki 5:15 and ten thousand that bare b', 5449
2Ch 2: 2 ten thousand men to bear b', "
18 to be bearers of b', and fourscore "
24:27 the greatness of the b' laid upon 4853
34:13 over the bearers of b', and were 5449
Ne 4:10 The strength of the bearers of b' "
17 and they that bare b', with those 5447
13:15 all manner of b', which they 4853
Isa 58: 6 to undo the heavy b', and to * 92
La 2:14 false b' and causes of banishment. 4864
Am 5:11 ye take from him b' of wheat: * "
M't 23: 4 For they bind heavy b' and 5413
Lu 11:46 with b' grievous to be borne, and "
46 ye yourselves touch not the b' "
Ga 6: 2 Bear ye one another's b', and 922

burdensome
Zec 12: 3 will I make Jerusalem a b' stone 4614
2Co 11: 9 kept myself from being b' unto 4
12:13 I myself was not b' to you? *2655
14 I will not be b' to you: for I seek* "
1Th 2: 6 we might have been b', as the ‡1722,922

burial
2Ch 26:23 in the field of the b' which 6900
Ec 6: 3 good, and also that ye have no b'; "
Isa 14:20 not be joined with them in b', "
Jer 22:19 with the b' of an ass, drawn and "
M't 26:12 my body, she did it for my b'. 1779
Ac 8: 2 men carried Stephen to his b', *

buried
Ge 15:15 thou shalt be b' in a good old age. 6912
23:19 Abraham b' Sarah his wife in the "
25: 9 his sons Isaac and Ishmael b' him "
10 there was Abraham b', and Sarah "
35: 8 nurse died, and she was b' "
19 Rachel died, and was b' in the "
29 his sons Esau and Jacob b' him. "
48: 7 and I b' her there in the way of "
49:31 There they b' Abraham and Sarah "
31 there they b' Isaac and Rebekah "
31 and there I b' Leah. "
50:13 and b' him in the cave of the field "
14 after he had b' his father. "
Nu 11:34 because there they b' the people "
20: 1 Miriam died there, and was b' "
33: 4 For the Egyptians b' all their * "
De 10: 6 Aaron died, and there he was b'; "
34: 6 And he b' him in a valley in the "
Jos 24:30 And they b' him in the border of "
32 b' they in Shechem, in a parcel "
33 and they b' him in a hill that "
J'g 2: 9 And they b' him in the border of "
8:32 died in a good old age, and was b' "
10: 2 and died, and was b' in Shamir. "
5 Jair died, and was b' in Camon. "
12: 7 the Gileadite, and was b' in one of "
10 Ibzan, and was b' at Beth-lehem. "
12 died, and was b' in Aijalon "
15 died, and was b' in Pirathon in "
16:31 b' him between Zorah and Eshtaol "
Ru 1:17 and there will I be b': the Lord "
1Sa 25: 1 and b' him in his house at Ramah. "
28: 3 and b' him in Ramah, even in "
31:13 b' them under a tree at Jabesh, "
2Sa 2: 4 Jabesh-gilead were they that b' "
5 even unto Saul, and have b' him. "
32 and b' him in the sepulchre of his "
3:32 And they b' Abner in Hebron: "
4:12 head of Ish-bosheth, and b' it "
17:23 and was b' in the sepulchre of his "
19:37 be b' by the grave of my father * "
21:14 and Jonathan his son b' they 6912
1Ki 2:10 slept with his fathers, and was b' "
34 and he was b' in his own house "
11:43 slept with his fathers, and was b' "
13:31 after he had b' him, that he spake "
31 wherein the man of God is b'; "
14:18 And they b' him; and all Israel "
31 slept with his fathers, and was b' "
15: 8 they b' him in the city of David: "
24 slept with his fathers, and was b' "
16: 6, 28 with his fathers, and was b' "
22:37 and they b' the king in Samaria. "
50 slept with his fathers, and was b' "
2Ki 8:24 slept with his fathers, and was b' "
9:28 and b' him in his sepulchre with "
10:35 fathers: and they b' him in "
12:21 and they b' him with his fathers "
13: 9 and they b' him in Samaria: and "
13 and Joash was b' in Samaria with "

2Ki 13:20 And Elisha died, and they b' him. 6912
14:16 slept with his fathers, and was b' "
20 and he was b' at Jerusalem with "
15: 7 and they b' him with his fathers "
38 slept with his fathers, and was b' "
16:20 slept with his fathers, and was b' "
21:18 slept with his fathers, and was b' "
26 And he was b' in his sepulchre "
23:30 And b' him in his own sepulchre. "
1Ch 10:12 and b' their bones under the oak "
2Ch 9:31 and he was b' in the city of David "
12:16 slept with his fathers, and was b' "
14: 1 they b' him in the city of David: "
16:14 b' him in his own sepulchres, "
21: 1 slept with his fathers, and was b' "
20 Howbeit they b' him in the city of "
22: 9 they had slain him, they b' him: "
24:16 they b' him in the city of David "
25 and they b' him in the city of David, "
25 they b' him not in the sepulchres "
25:28 and b' him with his fathers in the "
26:23 b' him with his fathers in the field "
27: 9 they b' him in the city of David: "
28:27 and they b' him in the city, even "
32:33 and they b' him in the chiefest of "
33:20 and they b' him in his own house: "
35:24 and was b' in one of the sepulchres "
Job 27:15 remain of him shall be b' in death: "
Ec 8:10 And so I saw the wicked b', who "
Jer 8: 2 shall not be gathered, nor be b'; "
16: 4 lamented; neither shall they be b'; "
6 they shall not be b', neither shall "
20: 6 thou shalt die, and shalt be b' "
22:19 He shall be b' with the burial of an "
25:33 lamented, neither gathered, nor b'; "
Eze 39:15 till the buriers have b' it in the "
M't 14:12 and b' it, and went and told Jesus. 2290
Lu 16:22 rich man also died, and was b'; "
Ac 2:29 he is both dead and b', and his "
5: 6 and carried him out, and b' him. "
9 the feet of them which have b' thy "
10 carrying her forth, b' her by her "
Ro 6: 4 we are b' with him by baptism 4916
1Co 15: 4 And that he was b', and that he 2290
Col 2:12 B' with him in baptism, wherein 4916

buriers
Eze 39:15 till the b' have buried it in the 6912

burn See also BURNED; BURNETH; BURNING; BURNT.
Ge 11: 3 let us make brick, and b' them 8313
44:18 let not thine anger b' against thy 2734
Ex 12:10 until the morning ye shall b' with 8313
27:20 light, to cause the lamp to b' 5927
29:13 them, and b' them upon the altar. 6999
14 his dung, shalt thou b' with fire 8313
18 And thou shalt b' the whole ram 6999
25 and b' them upon the altar for a "
34 then thou shalt b' the remainder 8313
30: 1 make an altar to b' incense upon: 4729
7 And Aaron shall b' thereon sweet 6999
7 lamps, he shall b' incense upon it. "
8 at even, he shall b' incense upon "
20 to b' offering made by fire unto "
Le 1: 9 the priest shall b' all on the altar, "
13 and b' it upon the altar: it is a "
15 b' it on the altar; and the blood "
17 the priest shall b' it upon the altar. "
2: 2 the priest shall b' the memorial * "
9 and shall b' it upon the altar: "
11 ye shall b' no leaven, nor any "
16 the priest shall b' the memorial of "
3: 5 And Aaron's sons shall b' it on the "
11 And the priest shall b' it upon the "
16 And the priest shall b' them upon "
4:10 and the priest shall b' them upon "
12 are poured out, and b' him on the 8313
19 from him, and b' it upon the altar. 6999
21 bullock without the camp, and b' 8313
26 he shall b' all his fat upon the 6999
31 and the priest shall b' it upon the "
35 and the priest shall b' them upon "
5:12 and b' it on the altar, according "
6:12 and the priest shall b' wood on it 1197
12 and he shall b' thereon the fat 6999
15 and shall b' it upon the altar "
7: 5 the priest shall b' them upon the "
31 And the priest shall b' the fat "
8:32 of the bread shall ye b' with fire. 8313
13:52 He shall therefore b' that garment, "
55 thou shalt b' it in the fire; "
57 thou shalt b' that wherein the "
16:25 offering shall he b' upon the altar. 6999
27 and they shall b' in the fire their 8313
17: 6 and b' the fat for a sweet savour 6999
24: 2 cause the lamps to b' continually. 5927
Nu 5:26 and b' it upon the altar, and 6999
18:17 shalt b' their fat for an offering "
19: 5 And one shall b' the heifer in his 8313
5 blood, with her dung, shall he b': "
De 5:23 the mountain did b' with fire,) 1197
7: 5 b' their graven images with fire. 8313
25 images of their gods shall ye b' "
12: 3 b' their groves with fire; and ye "
13:16 and shalt b' with fire the city, "
32:22 and shall b' unto the lowest hell, *3344
Jos 11: 6 and b' their chariots with fire. 8313
13 Hazor only; that did Joshua b'. "
J'g 9:52 the door of the tower to b' it "
12: 1 we will b' thine house upon thee "
14:15 lest we b' thee and thy father's "
1Sa 2:16 Let them not fail to b' the fat 6999
28 to b' incense, to wear an ephod "
1Ki 13: 1 stood by the altar to b' incense. "
2 the high places that b' incense "
2Ki 16:15 Upon the great altar b' the morning "

2Ki 18: 4 children of Israel did b' incense 6699
23: 5 ordained to b' incense in the "
1Ch 23:13 to b' incense before the Lord, "
2Ch 2: 4 to b' before him sweet incense, "
6 save only to b' sacrifice before "
4:20 that they should b' after the 1197
13:11 And they b' unto the Lord 6999
11 to b' every evening: for we keep 1197
26:16 the temple of the Lord to b' 6999
18 to b' incense unto the Lord, "
18 that are consecrated to b' incense: "
19 a censer in his hand to b' incense: "
28:25 places to b' incense unto other "
29:11 unto him, and b' incense. "
32:12 altar, and b' incense upon it? "
Ne 10:34 to b' upon the altar of the Lord 1197
Ps 79: 5 shall thy jealousy b' like fire? "
89:46 shall thy wrath b' like fire? "
Isa 1:31 and they shall both b' together, "
10:17 and it shall b' and devour his "
27: 4 I would b' them together. 6702
40:16 Lebanon is not sufficient to b', 1197
44:15 shall it be for a man to b': for he "
47:14 the fire shall b' them; they shall 8313
Jer 4: 4 and b' that none can quench it, 1197
7: 9 and b' incense unto Baal, and 6999
20 and it shall b',and shall not be 1197
31 b' their sons and their daughters 8313
11:13 altars to b' incense unto Baal. 6999
15:14 anger, which shall b' upon you. 3344
17: 4 anger, which shall b' for ever. "
19: 5 to b' their sons with fire for 8313
21:10 and he shall b' it with fire. "
12 and b' that none can quench it, 1197
32:29 and b' it with the houses, upon 8313
34: 2 and he shall b' it with fire: "
5 so shall they b' odours for thee; * "
22 and b' it with fire: and I will "
36:25 that he would not b' the roll: "
37: 8 and take it, and b' it with fire. "
10 and b' this city with fire. "
38:18 and they shall b' it with fire, "
43:12 and he shall b' them, and carry "
13 the Egyptians shall he b' with fire. "
44: 3 in that they went to b' incense, 6999
5 to b' no incense unto other gods. "
17 to b' incense unto the queen of "
18 since we left off to b' incense "
25 b' incense to the queen of heaven, "
Eze 5: 2 Thou shalt b' with fire a third 1197
4 and b' them in the fire; for 8313
16:41 And they shall b' thine houses "
23:47 and b' up their houses with fire. "
24: 5 b' also the bones under it, and *1754
11 may be hot, and may b', and 2787
39: 9 set on fire and b' the weapons, 5400
9 and they shall b' them with fire 1197
10 shall b' the weapons with fire: * "
43:21 and he shall b' it in the appointed 8313
Ho 4:13 b' incense upon the hills, 6999
Na 2:13 and I will b' her chariots in the 1197
Hab 1:16 and b' incense unto their drag; 6999
Mal 4: 1 that shall b' as an oven; and all 1197
1 and the day that cometh shall b' 3857
M't 3:12 but he will b' up the chaff with *2618*
13:30 bind them in bundles to b' "
Lu 1: 9 his lot was to b' incense when *2370*
3:17 but the chaff he will b' with fire *2618*
24:32 Did not our heart b' within us, *2545*
1Co 7: 9 it is better to marry than to b'. *4448*
2Co 11:29 who is offended, and I b' not? "
Re 17:16 and b' her with fire. **2618*

burned See also BURNT.
Ex 3: 2 the bush b' with fire, and the 1197
Le 4:21 him as he b' the first bullock: 8313
8:16 and Moses b' it upon the altar. 6999
De 4:11 the mountain b' with fire unto 1197
9:15 and the mount b' with fire: "
Jos 7:25 and b' them with fire, after 8313
11:13 Israel b' none of them, save Hazor "
1Sa 30: 1 Ziklag, and b' it with fire; "
3 behold, it was b' with fire; and "
14 Caleb; and we b' Ziklag with fire. "
2Sa 5:21 and David and his men b' them. *5375
23: 7 they shall be utterly b' with fire 8313
2Ki 10:26 the house of Baal, and b' them. "
15:35 b' incense still in the high places. 6999
22:17 have b' incense unto other gods, "
23: 4 he b' them without Jerusalem 8313
5 also that b' incense unto Baal, 6999
6 and b' it at the brook Kidron, 8313
8 where the priest had b' incense, 6999
11 and b' the chariots of the sun 8313
15 to powder, and b' the grove. "
16 and b' them upon the altar, "
20 and b' men's bones upon them, "
1Ch 14:12 and they were b' with fire. "
2Ch 25:14 them, b' incense unto them. 6999
29: 7 have not b' incense nor offered "
34:25 have b' incense unto other gods, "
Neh 1: 3 gates thereof are b' with fire. 3341
2:17 and the gates thereof are b' with "
4: 2 heaps of rubbish which are b'? 8313
Es 1:12 wroth, and his anger b' in him. 1197
Job 1:16 and hath b' up the sheep, "
30:30 and my bones are b' with heat. 2787
Ps 39: 3 while I was musing the fire b': 1197
74: 8 have b' up all the synagogues 8313
80:16 It is b' with fire, it is cut down: "
102: 3 and my bones are b' as an hearth. 2787
106:18 the flame b' up the wicked. 3857
Pr 6:27 and his clothes not be b'? 8313
28 hot coals, and his feet not be b'? *3554
Isa 1: 7 your cities are b' with fire: your 8313
24: 6 inhabitants of the earth are b'. 2787
33:12 as thorns cut up shall they be b' 3341
42:25 and it b' him, yet he laid it not 1197
43: 2 thou shalt not be b'; neither 3554
44:19 I have b' part of it in the fire; 8314
64:11 is b' up with fire: and all our 8316
65: 7 b' incense upon the mountains, 6999
Jer 1:16 have b' incense unto other gods, "
2:15 cities are b' without inhabitant. 3341
6:29 The bellows are b', the lead is *2787
9:10 they are b' up, so that none can 3341
12 the land perisheth and is b' up "
18:15 they have b' incense to vanity, 6999
19: 4 b' incense in it unto other gods, "
13 they have b' incense unto all the "
36:27 after that the king had b' the roll. 8313
28 the king of Judah hath b'. "
29 Thou hast b' this roll, saying, "
32 Jehoiakim king of Judah had b' "
38:17 this city shall not be b' with fire; "
23 cause this city to be b' with fire. "
39: 8 the Chaldeans b' the king's house, "
44:15 wives had b' incense unto other 6999
19 b' incense to the queen of heaven, "
21 that ye b' in the cities of Judah, "
23 Because ye have b' incense, and "
49: 2 her daughters shall be b' with fire:3341
51:30 they have b' her dwellingplaces; * "
32 the reeds they have b' with fire, 8313
58 high gates shall be b' with fire; 3341
52:13 And b' the house of the Lord, 8313
13 of the great men, b' he with fire. "
La 2: 3 he b' against Jacob like a flaming 1197
Eze 15: 4 of it, and the midst of it is b'. 2787
5 fire hath devoured it, and it is b'? "
20:47 the south to the north shall be b' *6866
24:10 it well, and let the bones be b'. 2787
Ho 2:13 wherein she b' incense to them, 6999
11: 2 and b' incense to graven images. "
Joe 1:19 the flame hath b' all the trees of 3857
Am 2: 1 b' the bones of the king of Edom 8313
Mic 1: 7 the hires thereof shall be b' with "
Na 1: 5 the earth is b' at his presence, 5375
M't 13:40 the tares are gathered and b' in *2618*
22: 7 murderers, and b' up their city. *1714*
Joh 15: 6 into the fire, and they are b'. *2545*
Ac 19:19 and b' them before all men: and *2618*
Ro 1:27 b' in their lust one toward *1572*
1Co 3:15 If any man's work shall be b', he *2618*
13: 3 I give my body to be b', and have *2545*
Heb 6: 8 cursing, whose end is to be b'. *2740*
12:18 and that b' with fire, nor unto *2545*
13:11 high priest for sin, are b' without *2618*
2Pe 3:10 works that are therein shall be b' "
Re 1:15 as if they b' in a furnace; and his **4448*
18: 8 she shall be utterly b' with fire: *2618*

burneth
Le 13:24 that b' have a white bright spot, *4348
16:28 And he that b' them shall wash 8313
Nu 19: 8 And he that b' her shall wash his "
Ps 46: 9 he b' the chariot in the fire. "
83:14 As the fire b' a wood, and as the 1197
97: 3 A fire goeth before him, and b' up 3857
Isa 9:18 For wickedness b' as a fire: it shall 1197
44:16 He b' part thereof in the fire; 8313
62: 1 thereof as a lamp that b'. 1197
64: 2 As when the melting fire b', the *6919
65: 3 b' incense upon altars of brick; *6999
5 nose, a fire that b' all the day. 3344
66: 3 he that b' incense, as if he 2142
Jer 48:35 and him that b' incense to his gods.6999
Ho 7: 6 in the morning it b' as a flaming 1197
Joe 2: 3 behind them a flame b': the land 3857
Am 6:10 that b' him, to bring out the bones 5635
Re 21: 8 in the lake which b' with fire and *2545*

burning See also BURNINGS.
Ge 15:17 a b' lamp that passed between * 784
Ex 21:25 B' for b', wound for wound, 3555
Le 6: 9 because of the b' upon the altar *4169
9 the fire of the altar shall be b' in 3344
12 the fire upon the altar shall be b' "
13 The fire shall ever be b' upon "
10: 6 b' which the Lord hath kindled. 8316
13:23 it is a b' boil; and the priest *6867
24 skin thereof there is a hot b', 4348
25 a leprosy broken out of the b': "
28 a rising of the b', and the priest "
28 it is an inflammation of the b'. "
16:12 shall take a censer full of b' coals* 784
26:16 consumption, and the b' ague, *6920
Nu 16:37 take up the censers out of the b', 8316
19: 6 cast it into the midst of the b' of "
De 28:22 and with an extreme b', and with *2746
29:23 brimstone, and salt, and b', that 8316
32:24 devoured with b' heat, and with "
2Ch 16:14 they made a very great b' for him. 8316
21:19 his people made no b' for him, "
19 like the b' of his fathers. "
Job 41:19 Out of his mouth go b' lamps, 3940
Ps 140:10 Let b' coals fall upon them: let 784
Pr 16:27 in his lips there is as a b' fire. *6867
26:21 As coals are to b' coals, and *1513
23 B' lips and a wicked heart are *1814
Isa 3:24 and b' instead of beauty. *3587
4: 4 and by the spirit of b'. 1197
9: 5 but this shall be with b' and fuel 8316
10:16 kindle a b' like the b' of a fire. 3350
30:27 b' with his anger, and the burden 1197
34: 9 land thereof shall become b' pitch. "
Jer 20: 9 was in mine heart as a b' fire * "
36:22 fire on the hearth b' before him. "
44: 8 b' incense unto other gods in 6999
Eze 1:13 like b' coals of fire, and like the 1197
Da 3: 6 into the midst of a b' fiery furnace.3345
11 should be cast into the midst of a b' "
15 same hour into the midst of a b' "
17 able to deliver us from the b' fiery 3345
20 cast them into the b' fiery furnace. "
21, 23 the midst of the b' fiery furnace. "
26 to the mouth of the b' fiery furnace, "
7: 9 flame, and his wheels as b' fire. 1815
11 and given to the b' flame. *3346
Am 4:11 firebrand plucked out of the b': 8316
Hab 3: 5 b' coals went forth at his feet. *7565
Lu 12:35 girded about, and your lights b'; **2545*
Joh 5:35 He was a b' and a shining light: * "
Jas 1:11 no sooner risen with a b' heat, **2742*
Re 4: 5 lamps of fire b' before the throne, *2545*
8: 8 a great mountain b' with fire was "
10 b' as it were a lamp, and it fell "
18: 9 they shall see the smoke of her b', *4451*
18 saw the smoke of her b', saying, "
19:20 a lake of fire b' with brimstone. **2545*

burnings
Isa 33:12 people shall be as the b' of lime: 4955
14 us shall dwell with everlasting b'? 4168
Jer 34: 5 and with the b' of thy fathers, 4955

burnished
Eze 1: 7 like the colour of b' brass. 7044

burnt See also BURNED.
Ge 8:20 offered b' offerings on the altar. 5930
22: 2 offer him there for a b' offering "
3 clave the wood for the b' offering, "
6 took the wood of the b' offering, "
7 where is the lamb for a b' offering? "
8 himself a lamb for a b' offering: "
13 offered him up for a b' offering "
38:24 Bring her forth, and let her be b'. 8313
Ex 3: 3 sight, why the bush is not b'. 1197
10:25 b' offerings, that we may sacrifice 5930
18:12 father in law, took a b' offering "
20:24 sacrifice thereon thy b' offerings, "
24: 5 of Israel, which offered b' offerings, "
29:18 it is a b' offering unto the Lord: "
25 upon the altar for a b' offering, "
42 continual b' offering throughout "
30: 9 nor b' sacrifice, nor meat offering; "
28 of b' offering with all his vessels, "
31: 9 of b' offering with all his furniture, "
32: 6 offered b' offerings, and brought "
20 and b' it in the fire, and ground 8313
35:16 of b' offering, with his brasen 5930
38: 1 he made the altar of b' offering "
40: 6 shalt set the altar of the b' offering "
10 anoint the altar of the b' offering, "
27 And he b' sweet incense thereon; 6999
29 he put the altar of b' offering by 5930
29 and offered upon it the b' offering "
Le 1: 3 If his offering be a b' sacrifice of "
4 upon the head of the b' offering; "
6 shall flay the b' offering, and cut "
9 on the altar, to be a b' sacrifice, "
10 or of the goats, for a b' sacrifice; "
13 a b' sacrifice, an offering made by "
14 the b' sacrifice for his offering to "
17 it is a b' sacrifice, an offering "
2:12 they shall not be b' on the altar *5927
3: 5 upon the b' sacrifice, which is 5930
4: 7 of the altar of the b' offering, "
10 upon the altar of the b' offering. "
12 are poured out shall he be b'. 8313
18 the altar of the b' offering, which 5930
24 kill the b' offering before the Lord: "
25 horns of the altar of b' offering, "
25 bottom of the altar of b' offering. "
29 in the place of the b' offering. "
30 horns of the altar of b' offering, "
33 where they kill the b' offering. "
34 altar of b' offering, and shall pour "
5: 7 and the other for a b' offering. "
10 offer the second for a b' offering, "
6: 9 the law of the b' offering: "
9 It is the b' offering, because of "
10 with the b' offering on the altar, "
12 lay the b' offering in order upon it; 6999
22 the Lord; it shall be wholly b'. "
23 shall be wholly b': it shall not "
25 place where the b' offering is killed 5930
30 eaten: it shall be b' in the fire. 8313
7: 2 where they kill the b' offering 5930
8 offereth any man's b' offering, "
8 himself the skin of the b' offering "
17 the third day shall be b' with fire. 8313
19 it shall be b' with fire: and as for "
37 This is the law of the b' offering, 5930
8:17 he b' with fire without the camp; 8313
18 the ram for the b' offering: 5930
20 b' the head, and the pieces, and 6999
21 Moses b' the whole ram upon the "
21 a b' sacrifice for a sweet savour, 5930
28 from off their hands, and b' them 6999
28 on the altar upon the b' offering: 5930
9: 2 a ram for a b' offering, without "
3 without blemish, for a b' offering; "
7 sin offering, and thy b' offering, "
10 sin offering, he b' upon the altar; "
11 he b' with fire without the camp. 8313
12 he slew the b' offering; and 5930
13 presented the b' offering unto him, "
13 and he b' them upon the altar. 6999
14 inwards and the legs, and b' them "
14 upon the b' offering on the 5930
16 the b' offering, and offered it "
17 and b' it upon the altar, 6999
17 the b' sacrifice of the morning. 5930
20 and he b' the fat upon the altar: 6999
22 sin offering, and the b' offering, 5930
24 upon the altar the b' offering "
10:16 it was b': and he was angry with 8313
19 sin offering and their b' offering 5930
12: 6 of the first year for a b' offering, "

Le 12: 8 the one for the *b'* offering, and the 5930
13:52 leprosy; it shall be *b'* in the fire. 8313
14:13 sin offering and the *b'* offering, in 5930
19 he shall kill the *b'* offering: "
20 the priest shall offer the *b'* offering "
22 and the other a *b'* offering. "
31 and the other for a *b'* offering, "
15:15 and the other for a *b'* offering; "
30 and the other for a *b'* offering 5930
16: 3 a ram for a *b'* offering. "
5 and one ram for a *b'* offering. "
24 and offer his *b'* offering, and the "
24 *b'* offering of the people, "
17: 8 offereth a *b'* offering or sacrifice, "
19: 6 it shall be *b'* in the fire. 8313
20:14 they shall be *b'* with fire, both he "
21: 9 she shall be *b'* with fire. "
22:18 unto the Lord for a *b'* offering; 5930
23:12 for a *b'* offering unto the Lord. "
18 a *b'* offering unto the Lord, "
37 a *b'* offering, and a meat offering, "
Nu 6:11 the other for a *b'* offering, "
14 without blemish for a *b'* offering, "
16 sin offering, and his *b'* offering: "
7:15, 21, 27, 33, 39, 45, 51, 57, 63, 69, 75,
81 the first year, for a *b'* offering: "
87 the oxen for the *b'* offering "
8:12 for a *b'* offering, unto the Lord, "
10:10 over your *b'* offerings, and over "
11: 1 fire of the Lord *b'* among them, 1197
3 the fire of the Lord *b'* among them. "
15: 3 a *b'* offering, or a sacrifice 5930
5 with the *b'* offering or sacrifice, "
8 a bullock for a *b'* offering, "
24 one young bullock for a *b'* offering, "
16:39 they that were *b'* had offered; 8313
19:17 take of the ashes of the *b'* heifer *8316
23: 3 Stand by thy *b'* offering, and I 5930
6 he stood by his *b'* sacrifice, "
15 Stand here by thy *b'* offering, "
17 he stood by his *b'* offering, and "
28: 3 by day, for a continual *b'* offering. "
6 a continual *b'* offering, which was "
10 the *b'* offering of every Sabbath, "
10 beside the continual *b'* offering, "
11 ye shall offer a *b'* offering unto "
13 a *b'* offering of a sweet savour, "
14 the *b'* offering of every month "
15 the continual *b'* offering, and his "
19 for a *b'* offering unto the Lord; "
23 the *b'* offering in the morning, "
23 is for a continual *b'* offering. "
24 the continual *b'* offering, and his "
27 ye shall offer the *b'* offering for a "
31 beside the continual *b'* offering, "
29: 2 ye shall offer a *b'* offering for a "
6 Beside the *b'* offering of the month, "
6 and the daily *b'* offering, "
8 a *b'* offering unto the Lord "
11 and the continual *b'* offering, "
13 And ye shall offer a *b'* offering, "
16, 19, 22, 28, 31, 34 beside the continual *b'* offering, "
36 ye shall offer a *b'* offering, "
38 *b'* offering, and his meat offering, "
39 for your *b'* offerings, and for your "
31:10 they *b'* all their cities wherein 8313
De 9:21 and *b'* it with fire, and stamped it, "
12: 6 ye shall bring your *b'* offerings, 5930
11 *b'* offerings, and your sacrifices, "
13 thou offer not thy *b'* offerings "
14, 27 thou shalt offer thy *b'* offerings, "
31 daughters they have *b'* in the fire *8313
27: 6 shalt offer *b'* offerings thereon 5930
32:24 They shall be *b'* with hunger, *4198
33:10 whole *b'* sacrifice upon thine altar. 3632
Jos 6:24 they *b'* the city with fire, and 8313
7:15 the accursed thing shall be *b'* "
8:28 And Joshua *b'* Ai, and made it "
31 they offered thereon *b'* offerings 5930
11: 9 and *b'* their chariots with fire. 8313
11 and he *b'* Hazor with fire. "
22:23 to offer thereon *b'* offering 5930
26 not for *b'* offering, nor for sacrifice: "
27 before him with our *b'* offerings, "
28 *b'* offerings, nor for sacrifices; "
29 to build an altar for *b'* offerings, "
J'g 6:26 and offer a *b'* sacrifice with the "
11:31 will offer it up for a *b'* offering. "
13:16 if thou wilt offer a *b'* offering, "
23 not have received a *b'* offering "
15: 5 and *b'* up both the shocks, and 1197
6 *b'* her and her father with fire. 8313
14 as flax that was *b'* with fire, 1197
18:27 sword, and *b'* the city with fire. 8313
20:26 and offered *b'* offerings and 5930
21: 4 and offered *b'* offerings and "
1Sa 2:15 before they *b'* the fat, the priest's 6999
6:14 a *b'* offering unto the Lord. 5930
15 Beth-shemesh offered *b'* offerings "
7: 9 a *b'* offering wholly unto the Lord: "
10 *b'* offering, the Philistines drew "
10: 8 unto thee, to offer *b'* offerings, "
13: 9 Bring hither a *b'* offering to me, "
9 And he offered the *b'* offering. "
10 an end of offering the *b'* offering, "
12 therefore, and offered a *b'* offering. "
15:22 as great delight in *b'* offerings "
31:12 Jabesh, and *b'* them there. 8313
2Sa 6:17 and David offered *b'* offerings 5930
18 an end of offering *b'* offerings "
24:22 here be oxen for *b'* sacrifice: "
24 neither will I offer *b'* offerings "
25 the Lord, and offered *b'* offerings "
1Ki 3: 3 and *b'* incense in high places. 6999
4 a thousand *b'* offerings did 5930
1Ki 3:15 and offered up *b'* offerings, 5930
8:64 there he offered *b'* offerings, "
64 too little to receive the *b'* offerings. "
9:16 and *b'* it with fire, and slain 8313
25 did Solomon offer *b'* offerings 5930
25 and he *b'* incense upon the altar *6999
11: 8 which *b'* incense and sacrificed "
12:33 upon the altar, and *b'* incense. * "
13: 2 bones shall be *b'* upon thee. *8313
15:13 her idol, and *b'* it by the brook "
16:18 and *b'* the king's house over him "
18:33 pour it on the *b'* sacrifice, and 5930
38 fell, and consumed the *b'* sacrifice. "
22:43 the people offered and *b'* incense 6999
2Ki 1:14 and *b'* up the two captains of * 398
3:27 and offered him for a *b'* offering 5930
5:17 neither *b'* offering nor sacrifice "
10:24 to offer sacrifices and *b'* offerings, "
25 an end of offering the *b'* offering, "
12: 3 sacrificed and *b'* incense in the 6999
14: 4 *b'* incense on the high places. "
15: 4 people sacrificed and *b'* incense "
16: 4 And he sacrificed and *b'* incense "
13 And he *b'* [6999] his *b'* offering and 5930
15 the morning *b'* offering, and the "
15 the king's *b'* sacrifice, and his "
15 the *b'* offering of all the people "
15 the blood of the *b'* offering, "
17:11 And there they *b'* incense in all 6999
31 Sepharvites *b'* their children 8313
25: 9 And he *b'* the house of the Lord, "
9 every great man's house *b'* he "
1Ch 6:49 the altar of the *b'* offering, and 5930
16: 1 they offered *b'* sacrifices and "
2 end of offering the *b'* offerings "
40 To offer *b'* offerings unto the Lord "
40 the altar of the *b'* offering "
21:23 the oxen also for *b'* offerings, "
24 nor offer *b'* offerings without cost. "
26 offered *b'* offerings and peace "
26 by fire upon the altar of *b'* offering. "
29 the altar of the *b'* offering, "
22: 1 is the altar of the *b'* offering "
23:31 offer all *b'* sacrifices unto the Lord "
29:21 offered *b'* offerings unto the Lord, "
2Ch 1: 6 offered a thousand *b'* offerings "
2: 4 and for the *b'* offerings morning "
4: 6 as they offered for the *b'* offering "
7: 1 and consumed the *b'* offering "
7 there he offered *b'* offerings, "
7 to receive the *b'* offerings, "
8:12 Solomon offered *b'* offerings "
13:11 *b'* sacrifices and sweet incense: "
15:16 and *b'* it at the brook Kidron. 8313
23:18 the *b'* offerings of the Lord, as it 5930
24:14 they offered *b'* offerings in the "
28: 3 he *b'* incense in the valley of the 6999
3 and *b'* his children in the fire, 1197
4 and *b'* incense in the high place, 6999
29: 7 nor offered *b'* offerings in the 5930
18 the altar of *b'* offering, with all "
24 the *b'* offering and the sin "
27 offer the *b'* offering upon the altar. "
27 And when the *b'* offering began, "
28 until the *b'* offering was finished. "
31 as were of a free heart *b'* offerings. "
32 the number of the *b'* offerings, "
32 for a *b'* offering to the Lord. "
34 could not flay all the *b'* offerings: "
35 the *b'* offerings were in abundance, "
35 drink offerings for every *b'* offering. "
30:15 brought in the *b'* offerings unto "
31: 2 priests and Levites for *b'* offerings 5930
3 his substance for the *b'* offerings, "
3 morning and evening *b'* offerings, "
3 the *b'* offerings for the sabbaths, "
34: 5 he *b'* the bones of the priests, 8313
35:12 they removed the *b'* offerings, 5930
14 in offering of *b'* offerings "
16 to offer *b'* offerings upon the altar "
36:19 And they *b'* the house of God, 8313
19 and *b'* all the palaces thereof "
Ezr 3: 2 to offer *b'* offerings thereon, 5930
3 they offered *b'* offerings thereon "
3 *b'* offerings morning and evening. "
4 and offered the daily *b'* offerings "
5 offered the continual *b'* offering, "
6 to offer *b'* offerings unto the Lord. "
6: 9 for the *b'* offerings of the God of 5928
8:35 *b'* offerings unto the God of Israel, 5930
35 a *b'* offering unto the Lord. "
Ne 10:33 and for the continual *b'* offering, "
Job 1: 5 and offered *b'* offerings according "
42: 8 up for yourselves a *b'* offering; "
Ps 20: 3 and accept thy *b'* sacrifice; "
40: 6 *b'* offering and sin offering hast "
50: 8 thy sacrifices or thy *b'* offerings, "
51:16 thou delightest not in *b'* offering. "
19 *b'* offering and whole *b'* offering: "
66:13 go into thy house with *b'* offerings: "
15 I will offer unto thee *b'* sacrifices "
Isa 1:11 I am full of the *b'* offerings of "
40:16 thereof sufficient for a *b'* offering. "
43:23 the small cattle of thy *b'* offerings; "
56: 7 *b'* offerings and their sacrifices "
61: 8 I hate robbery for *b'* offering; * "
Jer 6:20 your *b'* offerings are not acceptable, "
7:21 Put your *b'* offerings unto your "
22 concerning *b'* offerings or "
14:12 when they offer *b'* offering and "
17:26 bringing *b'* offerings, and sacrifices, "
19: 5 burn their sons with fire for *b'* "
33:18 before me to offer *b'* offerings, "
51:25 will make thee a *b'* mountain. 8316
Eze 40:38 they washed the *b'* offering. 5930
39 to slay thereon the *b'* offering "
Eze 40:42 of hewn stone for the *b'* offering, 5930
42 they slew the *b'* offering, and "
43:18 to offer *b'* offerings thereon, "
24 for a *b'* offering unto the Lord. "
27 priests shall make your *b'* offerings "
44:11 they shall slay the *b'* offering "
45:15 and for a *b'* offering, and for "
17 prince's part to give *b'* offerings, "
17 meat offering, and the *b'* offering, "
23 a *b'* offering to the Lord, seven "
25 according to the *b'* offering, "
46: 2 priests shall prepare his *b'* offering "
4 And the *b'* offering that the prince "
12 prepare a voluntary *b'* offering "
12 he shall prepare his *b'* offering "
13 a *b'* offering unto the Lord of "
15 for a continual *b'* offering. "
Ho 6: 6 of God more than *b'* offerings. "
Am 5:22 ye offer me *b'* offerings and your "
Mic 6: 6 come before him with *b'* offerings, "
M'r 12:33 more than all whole *b'* offerings *3646*
Heb 10: 6 In *b'* offerings and sacrifices for "
8 and *b'* offerings and offering for "
Re 8: 7 the third part of trees was *b'* up, *2618*
7 and all green grass was *b'* up. "

burnt-offering See BURNT and OFFERING.

burnt-sacrifice See BURNT and SACRIFICE.

burst See also BURSTING.
Job 32:19 it is ready to *b'* like new bottles. 1234
Pr 3:10 and thy presses shall *b'* out *6555
Jer 2:20 thy yoke, and *b'* thy bands; 5423
5: 5 broken the yoke, and *b'* the bonds. "
30: 8 and will *b'* thy bonds, and "
Na 1:13 and will *b'* thy bonds in sunder. "
M'r 2:22 doth *b'* the bottles, and the wine *4486*
Lu 5:37 new wine will *b'* the bottles, "
Ac 1:18 he *b'* asunder in the midst, *2997*

bursting
Isa 30:14 shall not be found in the *b'* of it *4386

bury See also BURIED; BURYING.
Ge 23: 4 I may *b'* my dead out of my sight. 6912
6 of our sepulchres *b'* thy dead; "
6 but that thou mayest *b'* thy dead. "
8 mind that I should *b'* my dead "
11 people give I it thee; *b'* thy dead. "
13 me, and I will *b'* my dead there. "
15 and thee: *b'* therefore thy dead. "
47:29 *b'* me not, I pray thee, in Egypt: "
30 and *b'* me in their buryingplace. "
49:29 *b'* me with my fathers in the "
50: 5 Canaan, there shalt thou *b'* me. "
5 and *b'* my father, and I will come "
6 Go up, and *b'* thy father, according "
7 Joseph went up to *b'* his father: "
14 went up with him to *b'* his father, "
De 21:23 shalt in any wise *b'* him that day; "
1Ki 2:31 and fall upon him, and *b'* him; "
11:15 host was gone up to *b'* the slain, "
13:29 the city, to mourn and to *b'* him. "
31 When I am dead, then *b'* me in "
14:13 shall mourn for him, and *b'* him: "
2Ki 9:10 and there shall be none to *b'* her. "
34 and *b'* her: for she is the king's "
35 they went to *b'* her: but they "
Ps 79: 3 and there was none to *b'* them. "
Jer 7:32 for they shall *b'* in Tophet, "
14:16 they shall have none to *b'* them, "
19:11 they shall *b'* them in Tophet, "
11 till there be no place to *b'*. "
Eze 39:11 and there shall they *b'* Gog and "
13 all the people of the land shall *b'* "
14 to *b'* with the passengers those "
Ho 9: 6 them up, Memphis shall *b'* them: "
M't 8:21 me first to go and *b'* my father. *2290*
22 and let the dead *b'* their dead. "
27: 7 potter's field, to *b'* strangers in. *5027*
Lu 9:59 me first to go and *b'* my father. *2290*
60 Let the dead *b'* their dead: "
Joh 19:40 the manner of the Jews is to *b'*. 1779

burying See also BURYINGPLACE.
2Ki 13:21 as they were *b'* a man, that, 6912
Eze 39:12 house of Israel be *b'* of them, "
M'r 14: 8 to anoint my body to the *b'*. *1780*
Joh 12: 7 against the day of my *b'* hath she "

buryingplace
Ge 23: 4 give me a possession of a *b'* 6913
9 possession of a *b'* amongst you. "
20 possession of a *b'* by the sons "
47:30 bury me in their *b'*. And he said, "
49:30 Hittite for a possession of a *b'*. "
50:13 for a possession of a *b'* of Ephron "
J'g 16:31 in the *b'* of Manoah his father. "

bush See also BUSHES.
Ex 3: 2 fire out of the midst of a *b'*: 5572
2 behold, the *b'* burned with fire, "
2 and the *b'* was not consumed. "
3 sight, why the *b'* is not burnt. "
4 him out of the midst of the *b'*. "
De 33:16 will of him that dwelt in the *b'*: "
M'r 12:26 how in the *b'* God spake unto him, *942*
Lu 6:44 of a bramble *b'* gather they grapes. "
20:37 even Moses shewed at the *b'*, "
Ac 7:30 Lord in a flame of fire in a *b'*. "
35 which appeared to him in the *b'*. "

bushel
M't 5:15 a candle, and put it under a *b'*, *3426*
M'r 4:21 brought to be put under a *b'*, "
Lu 11:33 neither under a *b'*, but on a "

bushes
Job 30: 4 Who cut up mallows by the *b'*, 7880
7 Among the *b'* they brayed; under "
Isa 7:19 all thorns, and upon all *b'*. *5097

bushy
Ca 5:11 his locks are b', and black as a 8534
busied
2Ch 35:14 priests the sons of Aaron were b'
business
Ge 39:11 went into the house to do his b'; *4399
De 24: 5 shall he be charged with any b': 1697
Jos 2:14 yours, if ye utter not this our b'. "
20 if thou utter this our b', then we "
J'g 18: 7 and had no b' with any man. * "
28 they had no b' with any man; * "
1Sa 20:19 when the b' was in hand, 4639
21: 2 hath commanded me a b', and 1697
2 man know any thing of the b' "
8 the king's b' required haste. "
1Ch 26:29 his sons were for the outward b' 4399
30 westward in all the b' of the Lord, "
2Ch 13:10 the Levites wait upon their b': * "
17:13 much b' in the cities of Judah: * "
32:31 in the b' of the ambassadors of "
Ne 11:16 outward b' of the house of God. 4399
22 over the b' of the house of God. "
13:30 Levites, every one in his b'; * "
Es 3 : 9 that have the charge of the b', "
Ps 107:23 ships, that do b' in great waters; "
Pr 22:29 thou a man diligent in his b'? "
Ec 5: 3 through the multitude of b'; 6045
8:16 the b' that is done upon the earth: "
Da 8:27 rose up, and did the king's b'; 4399
Lu 2:49 must be about my Father's b'? *
Ac 6: 3 we may appoint over this b'. 5532
Ro 12:11 Not slothful in b'; fervent in *4710
16: 2 in whatsoever b' she hath need of *4229
1Th 4:11 to do your own b', and to work 2398
busy See also BUSIED; BUSYBODY.
1Ki 20:40 servant was b' here and there, 6213
busybodies
2Th 3:11 working not at all, but are b'. 4020
1Ti 5:13 but tattlers also and b', speaking 4021
busybody See also BUSYBODIES.
1Pe 4:15 or as a b' in other men's matters. * 244
but See in the APPENDIX; also SACKBUT.
butler See also BUTLERS; BUTLERSHIP.
Ge 40: 1 the b' of the king of Egypt and 4945
5 the b' and the baker of the king of "
9 chief b' told his dream to Joseph, "
13 manner when thou wast his b'. "
20 lifted up the head of the chief b' "
21 he restored the chief b' unto his "
23 Yet did not the chief b' remember "
41: 9 spake the chief b' unto Pharaoh, "
butlers
Ge 40: 2 against the chief of the b', and 4945
butlership
Ge 40:21 the chief butler unto his b' 4945
butter
Ge 18: 8 he took b', and milk, and the calf 2529
De 32:14 B' of kine, and milk of sheep, "
J'g 5:25 brought forth b' in a lordly dish. "
2Sa 17:29 honey, and b', and sheep, and "
Job 20:17 floods, the brooks of honey and b'. "
29: 6 When I washed my steps with b', "
Ps 55:21 his mouth were smoother than b', 4260
Pr 30:33 of milk bringeth forth b', and the 2529
Isa 7:15 B' and honey shall he eat, that he "
22 they shall give, he shall eat b': "
22 for b' and honey shall every one "
buttocks
2Sa 10: 4 in the middle, even to their b', 8357
1Ch 19: 4 in the midst hard by their b', 4667
Isa 20: 4 with their b' uncovered, to the 8357
buy See also BUYEST; BUYETH; BOUGHT.
Ge 41:57 Egypt to Joseph for to b' corn; 7666
42: 2 b' for us from thence; that we "
3 went down to b' corn in Egypt. "
5 the sons of Israel came to b' corn "
7 From the land of Canaan to b' food. "
10 to b' food are thy servants come. "
43: 2 Go again, b' us a little food. "
4 we will go down and b' thee food: "
20 down at the first time to b' food: "
22 money have we brought...to b' "
44:25 Go again, and b' us a little food. "
47:19 b' us and our land for bread, 7069
Ex 21: 2 If thou b' an Hebrew servant, "
Le 22:11 But if the priest b' any soul with "
25:15 thou shalt b' of thy neighbour, "
44 of them shall ye b' bondmen "
45 of them shall ye b', and of their "
De 2: 6 shall b' meat of them for money, *7666
6 ye shall also b' water of them for 3739
28:68 bondwomen, and no man shall b' 7069
Ru 4: 4 B' it before the inhabitants, "
5 b' it also of Ruth the Moabitess, "
8 said unto Boaz, B' it for thee. "
2Sa 24:21 To b' the threshingfloor of thee to "
24 will surely b' it of thee at a price: "
2Ki 12:12 to b' timber and hewed stone * "
22: 6 and to b' timber and hewn stone * "
1Ch 21:24 I will verily b' it for the full price: "
2Ch 34:11 to b' hewn stone, and timber for "
Ezr 7:17 b' speedily with this money 7066
Ne 5: 3 that we might b' corn, because *3947
10:31 not b' it of them on the sabbath, "
Pr 23:23 B' the truth, and sell it not; 7069
Isa 55: 1 come ye, b', and eat; 7666
1 yea, come, b' wine and milk "
Jer 32: 7 B' thee my field that is in 7069
7 of redemption is thine to b' it. "
Jer 32: 8 B' my field, I pray thee, that is in 7069
8 is thine; b' it for thyself. "
25 B' thee the field for money, and "
44 Men shall b' fields for money, "
Am 8: 6 That we may b' the poor for silver, "
M't 14:15 villages, and b' themselves victuals. 59
25: 9 that sell, and b' for yourselves. "
10 while they went to b', the "
M'k 6:36 villages, and b' themselves bread: "
37 b' two hundred pennyworth of bread, "
Lu 9:13 go and b' meat for all this people. "
22:36 let him sell his garment, and b' one. "
Joh 4: 8 away unto the city to b' meat.) "
6: 5 Whence shall we b' bread, that "
13:29 B' those things that we have need "
1Co 7:30 they that b', as though they "
Jas 4:13 and b' and sell, and get gain: *1710
Re 3:18 I counsel thee to b' of me gold 59
13:17 that no man might b' or sell, "
buyer
Pr 20:14 it is naught, saith the b': but 7069
Isa 24: 2 as with the b', so with the seller; "
Eze 7:12 let not the b' rejoice, nor the seller "
buyest
Le 25:14 b' ought of thy neighbour's hand, *7069
Ru 4: 5 What day thou b' the field of the "
buyeth
Pr 31:16 She considereth a field, and b' it: 3947
M't 13:44 all that he hath, and b' that field. 59
Re 18:11 for no man b' their merchandise "
Buz (*buz*)
Ge 22:21 his firstborn, and B' his brother, 938
1Ch 5:14 the son of Jahdo, the son of B'; "
Jer 25:23 Dedan, and Tema, and B', "
Buzi (*boo'-zi*) See also BUZITE.
Eze 1: 3 Ezekiel the priest, the son of B', 941
Buzite (*boo'-zite*)
Job 32: 2 of Barachel the B', of the kindred 940
6 Elihu the son of Barachel the B' "
by See in the APPENDIX; also BYWAYS; BYWORD; HEREBY; THEREBY; WHEREBY.
by-and-by See BY and AND.
byways
J'g 5: 6 travellers walked through b'. 734, 6128
byword
De 28:37 a b', among all nations whither 8148
1Ki 9: 7 and a b' among all people: "
2Ch 7:20 and a b' among all nations. "
Job 17: 6 made me also a b' of the people; 4914
30: 9 their song, yea, I am their b'. 4405
Ps 44:14 us a b' among the heathen, 4912

C.

cab
2Ki 6:25 fourth part of a c' of dove's dung 6894
Cabbon (*cab'-bon*)
Jos 15:40 C', and Lahmam, and Kithlish, 3522
cabins
Jer 37:16 into the c', and Jeremiah *2588
Cabul (*ca'-bul*)
Jos 19:27 goeth out to C' on the left hand, 3521
1Ki 9:13 he called them the land of C' "
Cæsar (*se'-zur*) See also CÆSAR'S.
M't 22:17 to give tribute unto C', or not? 2541
21 unto C' the things which are "
M'r 12:14 to give tribute to C', or not? "
17 C' the things that are Cæsar's, "
Lu 2: 1 a decree from C' Augustus, "
3: 1 the reign of Tiberius C', Pontius "
20:22 to give tribute unto C', or no? "
25 C' the things which be Cæsar's, "
23: 2 forbidding to give tribute to C', "
Joh 19:12 himself a king speaketh against C'. "
15 answered, We have no king but C'. "
Ac 11:28 pass in the days of Claudius C'. * "
17: 7 contrary to the decrees of C', "
25: 8 nor yet against C', have I offended "
11 unto them. I appeal unto C'. "
12 Hast thou appealed unto C'? "
12 unto C' shalt thou go. "
21 be kept till I might send him to C'. "
26:32 if he had not appealed unto C'. "
27:24 thou must be brought before C': "
28:19 constrained to appeal unto C'; "
Cæsar Augustus See CÆSAR and AUGUSTUS.
Cæsarea (*ses-a-re'-ah*)
M't 16:13 into the coasts of C' Philippi, 2542
M'k 8:27 into the towns of C' Philippi: "
Ac 8:40 all the cities, till he came to C'. "
9:30 they brought him down to C', "
10: 1 certain man in C' called Cornelius, "
24 morrow after they entered into C'. "
11:11 I was, sent from C' unto me. "
12:19 went down from Judæa to C', "
18:22 he had landed at C', and gone up, "
21: 8 came unto C': and we entered "
16 of the disciples of C', and brought "
23:23 soldiers to go to C', "
33 they came to C', and delivered "
25: 1 ascended from C' to Jerusalem. "
4 that Paul should be kept at C', "
6 ten days, he went down unto C'; "
13 Bernice came unto C' to salute "
Cæsarea-Philippi See CÆSAREA and PHILIPPI.
Cæsar's (*se'-zurs*)
M't 22:21 They say unto him, C'. Then 2541
21 Cæsar the things which are C'; "
M'k 12:16 And they said unto him, C'. "
17 to Cæsar the things that are C', "
Lu 20:24 They answered and said, C'. "
25 unto Cæsar the things which be C', "
Jo 19:12 thou art not C' friend: whosoever "
Ac 25:10 I stand at C' judgment seat, "
Ph'p 4:22 they that are of C' household. "
cage
Jer 5:27 As a c' is full of birds, so are their 3619
Re 18: 2 a c' of every unclean and hateful *5438
Caiaphas (*cah'-ya-fus*)
M't 26: 3 high priest, who was called C', 2533
57 led him away to C' the high priest, "
Lu 3: 2 Annas and C' being the high "
Joh 11:49 And one of them, named C', "
18:13 he was father in law to C', "
14 C' was he, which gave counsel to "
24 Annas had sent him bound unto C' "
28 Then led they Jesus from C' unto "
Ac 4: 6 Annas the high priest, and C', "
Cain See also TUBAL-CAIN.
Ge 4: 1 and she conceived, and bare C', 7014
2 but C' was a tiller of the ground. "
3 pass, that C' brought of the fruit "
5 unto C' and to his offering he had "
5 And C' was very wroth, and his "
6 And the Lord said unto C', Why "
8 C' talked with Abel his brother: "
8 C' rose up against Abel his "
9 And the Lord said unto C', Where "
13 And C' said unto the Lord, "
15 Therefore whosoever slayeth C', "
15 And the Lord set a mark upon C', "
16 C' went out from the presence of "
17 And C' knew his wife; and she "
24 If C' shall be avenged seven fold, "
25 instead of Abel, whom C' slew. "
Jos 15:57 C', Gibeah, and Timnah; ten cities "
Heb 11: 4 a more excellent sacrifice than C', 2535
1Jo 3:12 Not as C', who was of that wicked "
Jude 11 gone in the way of C', and ran "
Cainan (*ca'-nun*) See also KENAN.
Ge 5: 9 lived ninety years, and begat C': *7018
10 Enos lived after he begat C' * "
12 C' lived seventy years, and * "
13 C' lived after he begat * "
Ge 5:14 the days of C' were nine hundred *7018
Lu 3:36, 37 Which was the son of C', 2536
cake See also CAKES.
Ex 29:23 and one c' of oiled bread, and one 2471
Le 8:26 he took one unleavened c', "
26 and a c' of oiled bread, "
24: 5 two tenth deals shall be in one c'. "
Nu 6:19 unleavened c' out of the basket, "
15:20 Ye shall offer up a c' of the first "
J'g 7:13 a c' of barley bread tumbled into 6742
1Sa 30:12 gave him a piece of a c' of figs, 1690
2Sa 6:19 to every one a c' of bread, and a 2471
1Ki 17:12 I have not a c', but an handful of 4580
13 make me thereof a little c' first, 5692
19: 6 there was a c' baken on the coals, "
Hos 7: 8 Ephraim is a c' not turned. "
cakes
Ge 18: 6 it, and make c' upon the hearth. 5692
Ex 12:39 baked unleavened c' of the dough "
29: 2 bread, and c' unleavened 2471
Le 2: 4 unleavened c' of fine flour "
7:12 unleavened c' mingled with oil, "
12 with oil, and c', mingled with oil, "
13 Besides the c', he shall offer for "
24: 5 bake twelve c' thereof: two tenth "
Nu 6:15 c' of fine flour mingled with oil, "
11: 8 baked it in pans, and make c' of it: 5692
Jos 5:11 unleavened c', and parched corn 4682
J'g 6:19 unleavened c' of an ephah of flour: "
20, 21 flesh and the unleavened c'. "
1Sa 25:18 two hundred c' of figs, and laid 1690
2Sa 13: 6 make me a couple of c' in my sight, 3834
8 made c' in his sight, 3823
8 and did bake the c'. 3834
10 Tamar took the c' which she had "
1Ch 12:40 meal, c' of figs, and bunches of 1690
23:29 for the unleavened c', and the *7550
Jer 7:18 make c' to the queen of heaven, 3561
44:19 we make her c' to worship her, "
Eze 4:12 And thou shalt eat it as barley c', 5692
Calah (*ca'-lah*)
Ge 10:11 and the city Rehoboth, and C', 3625
12 Resen between Nineveh and C': "
calamities
Ps 57: 1 refuge, until these c' be overpast. 1942
141: 5 prayer also shall be in their c'. *7451
Pr 17: 5 he that is glad at c' shall not be * 343
calamity See also CALAMITIES.
De 32:35 the day of their c' is at hand, and 343
2Sa 22:19 prevented me in the day of my c':

Job 6: 2 and my c· laid in the balances 1942
30:13 they set forward my c·, they have "
Ps 18:18 prevented me in the day of my c·: 343
Pr 1:26 I also will laugh at your c·; I will "
6:15 shall his c· come suddenly; "
19:13 foolish son is the c· of his father: 1942
24:22 For their c· shall rise suddenly; 343
27:10 brother's house in the day of thy c·: "
Jer 18:17 the face, in the day of their c·. "
46:21 the day of their c· was come upon "
48:16 The c· of Moab is near to come, "
49: 8 will bring the c· of Esau upon him, "
32 bring their c· from all sides thereof, "
Eze 35: 5 the sword in the time of their c·, "
Ob 13 in the day of their c·; yea, thou "
13 their affliction in the day of their c·, "
13 substance in the day of their c·; "

calamus (*cal'-a-mus*)
Ex 30:23 of sweet c· two hundred and fifty 7070
Ca 4:14 and saffron; c· and cinnamon, "
Eze 27:19 cassia, and c·, were in thy market. "

Calcol (*cal'-col*) See also CHALCOL.
1Ch 2: 6 and Heman, and C· and Dara: 3633

caldron See also CALDRONS.
1Sa 2:14 the pan, or kettle, or c·, or pot; 7037
Job 41:20 as out of a seething pot or c·. * 100
Eze 11: 3 city is the c·, and we be the flesh. 5518
7 this city is the c·: but I will bring "
11 This city shall not be your c·, "
Mic 3: 3 the pot, and as flesh within the c·. 7037

caldrons
2Ch 35:13 sod they in pots, and in c·, and in 1731
Jer 52:18 The c· also, and the shovels, *5518
19 the c·, and the candlesticks, * "

Caleb (*ca'-leb*) See also CALEB'S; CALEB-EPHRATAH; CHELLUBAI.
Nu 13: 6 Judah, C· the son of Jephunneh. 3612
30 C· stilled the people before Moses, "
14: 6 Joshua the son of Nun, and C· the "
24 But my servant C·, because he had "
30 to make you dwell therein, save C· "
38 Joshua, the son of Nun, and C· the "
26:65 was not left a man of them, save C· "
32:12 Save C· the son of Jephunneh "
34:19 Judah, C· the son of Jephunneh. "
De 1:36 Save C· the son of Jephunneh; "
Jos 14: 6 C· the son of Jephunneh the "
13 blessed him, and gave unto C· "
14 became the inheritance of C· "
15:13 unto C· the son of Jephunneh he "
14 C· drove thence the three sons of "
16 And C· said, He that smiteth "
17 Kenaz, the brother of C·, took: "
18 C· said unto her, What wouldest "
21:12 villages thereof, gave they to C· "
J'g 1:12 And C· said, He that smiteth "
14 C· said unto her, What wilt thou? "
15 And C· gave her the upper springs "
20 they gave Hebron unto C·, as "
1Sa 25: 3 and he was of the house of C·. "
30:14 Judah, and upon the south of C·; "
1Ch 2:18 And C· the son of Hezron begat "
19 Azubah was dead, C· took unto "
42 Now the sons of C· the brother of "
49 and the daughter of C· was Achsa. "
50 These were the sons of C· the son "
4:15 sons of C· the son of Jephunneh; "
6:56 villages thereof, they gave to C· "

Caleb-ephratah (*ca''-leb-ef'-ra-tah*)
1Ch 2:24 after that Hezron was dead in C·, 3613

Caleb's (*ca'-lebs*)
J'g 1:13 son of Kenaz, C· younger brother, 3612
3: 9 son of Kenaz, C· younger brother. "
1Ch 2:46 Ephah, C· concubine, bare Haran, "
48 Maachah, C· concubine, bare "

calf See also CALF'S; CALVES.
Ge 18: 7 fetcht a c· tender and good, 1121, 1241
8 the c· which he had dressed, " "
Ex 32: 4 after he had made it a molten c·: 5695
8 they have made them a molten c·, "
19 he saw the c·, and the dancing: "
20 took the c· which they had made, "
24 fire, and there came out this c·. "
35 made the c·, which Aaron made "
Le 9: 2 a young c· for a sin offering, "
3 a c· and a lamb, both of the first "
8 slew the c· of the sin offering, "
De 9:16 and had made you a molten c·: "
21 the c· which ye had made, and "
1Sa 28:24 woman had a fat c· in the house; "
Ne 9:18 They had made them a molten c·, "
Job 21:10 cow calveth, and casteth not her c·.
Ps 29: 6 maketh them also to skip like a c·; 5695
106:19 They made a c· in Horeb, and "
Isa 11: 6 and the c· and the young lion and "
27:10 wilderness: there shall the c· feed, "
Jer 34:18 when they cut the c· in twain, and "
19 passed between the parts of the c·; "
Ho 8: 5 Thy c·, O Samaria, hath cast thee "
6 the c· of Samaria shall be broken "
Lu 15:23 bring hither the fatted c·, and kill 3448
27 thy father hath killed the fatted c·, "
30 hast killed for him the fatted c·. "
Ac 7:41 they made a c· in those days, and 3447
Re 4: 7 the second beast like a c·, and the 3448

calf's
Eze 1: 7 feet was like the sole of a c· foot: 5695

calkers
Eze 27: 9 thereof were in thee thy c·: 2388, 919
27 mariners, and thy pilots, thy c·, " "

call See also CALLED; CALLEST; CALLETH; CALLING; RECALL.
Ge 2:19 to see what he would c· them: 7121
4:26 began men to c· upon the name "
16:11 shalt c· his name Ishmael; "
17:15 thou shalt not c· her name Sarai, "
19 and thou shalt c· his name Isaac: "
24:57 We will c· the damsel, and enquire "
30:13 the daughters will c· me blessed: 833
46:33 when Pharaoh shall c· you, and 7121
Ex 2: 7 Shall I go and c· to thee a nurse "
20 c· him, that he may eat bread. "
34:15 c· thee, and thou eat of his sacrifice; "
Nu 16:12 Moses sent to c· Dathan and "
22: 5 of his people, to c· him, saying, "
20 If the men come to c· thee, rise "
37 earnestly send unto thee to c· thee? "
De 2:11 but the Moabites c· them Emims. "
20 Ammonites c· them Zamzummims; "
3: 9 Hermon the Sidonians c· Sirion; "
9 and the Amorites c· it Shenir;) "
4: 7 things that we c· upon him for? "
26 I c· heaven and earth to witness 5749
25: 8 the elders of his city shall c· him, 7121
30: 1 thou shalt c· them to mind among 7725
19 I c· heaven and earth to record 5749
31:14 c· Joshua, and present yourselves 7121
28 and c· heaven and earth to record 5749
33:19 c· the people unto the mountain; 7121
J'g 12: 1 didst not c· us to go with thee? "
16:25 C· for Samson, that he may make "
21:13 and to c· peaceably unto them. * "
Ru 1:20 C· me not Naomi, c· me Mara: for "
21 why then c· ye me Naomi, seeing "
1Sa 3: 6 Here am I; for thou didst c· me. * "
8 for thou didst c· me. And Eli * "
9 if he c· thee, that thou shalt say, "
12:17 I will c· unto the Lord, and he "
16: 3 And c· Jesse to the sacrifice, and I "
22:11 Then the king sent to c· Ahimelech "
2Sa 17: 5 C· now Hushai the Archite also, "
22: 4 I will c· on the Lord, who is worthy "
1Ki 1:28 C· me Bath-sheba. And she came "
32 C· me Zadok the priest, and Nathan "
8:52 in all that they c· for unto thee. * "
17:18 to c· my sin to remembrance, and *2142
18:24 c· ye on the name of your gods, 7121
24 I will c· on the name of the Lord: "
25 and c· on the name of your gods, "
22:13 messenger that was gone to c· "
2Ki 4:12 C· this Shunammite. And when he "
15 And he said, C· her. And when he "
36 and said, C· this Shunammite. "
5:11 c· on the name of the Lord his "
10:19 c· unto me all the prophets of Baal, "
1Ch 16: 8 c· upon his name, make known his "
2Ch 18:12 messenger that went to c· Micaiah "
Job 5: 1 C· now, if there be any that will "
13:22 Then c· thou, and I will answer: "
14:15 Thou shalt c·, and I will answer "
27:10 will he always c· upon God? "
Ps 4: 1 Hear me when I c·, O God of my "
3 the Lord will hear when I c· unto "
14: 4 bread, and c· not upon the Lord. "
18: 3 I will c· upon the Lord, who is "
20: 9 let the king hear us when we c·. "
49:11 c· their lands after their own names. "
50: 4 shall c· to the heavens from above, "
15 c· upon me in the day of trouble: "
55:16 I will c· upon God; and the Lord "
72:17 all nations shall c· him blessed. 833
77: 6 I c· to remembrance my song in 2142
80:18 and we will c· upon thy name. 7121
86: 5 unto all them that c· upon thee. "
7 In the day of my trouble I will c· "
91:15 He shall c· upon me, and I will "
99: 6 among them that c· upon his name; "
102: 2 day when I c· answer me speedily. "
105: 1 c· upon his name: make known his "
116:13 and c· upon the name of the Lord. "
17 will c· upon the name of the Lord. "
145:18 unto all them that c· upon him, "
18 to all that c· upon him "
Pr 1:28 Then shall they c· upon me, but I "
7: 4 c· understanding thy kinswoman: "
8: 4 Unto thee, O men, I c·; and my "
9:15 To c· passengers who go right on "
31:28 arise up, and c· her blessed; 833
Isa 5:20 that c· evil good, and good evil; 559
7:14 and shall c· his name Immanuel. 7121
8: 3 C· his name Maher-shalal-hash-baz. "
12: 4 Praise the Lord, c· upon his name, "
22:12 Lord God of hosts c· to weeping, "
20 that I will c· my servant Eliakim "
31: 2 will not c· back his words: but 5493
34:12 They shall c· the nobles thereof 7121
41:25 shall he c· upon my name: and * "
44: 5 c· himself by the name of Jacob; "
7 who, as I, shall c·, and shall "
45: 3 the Lord, which c· thee by thy name, "
48: 2 they c· themselves of the holy city, "
13 when I c· unto them, they stand "
55: 5 c· a nation that thou knowest not, "
6 c· ye upon him while he is near: "
58: 5 wilt thou c· this a fast, and an "
9 thou c·, and the Lord shall answer; "
13 and c· the sabbath a delight, the "
60:14 shall c· thee, The city of the Lord, "
18 thou shalt c· thy walls Salvation, "
61: 6 c· you the Ministers of our God: "
62:12 they shall c· them, The holy people, "
65:15 c· his servants by another name: "
24 and before they c·, I will answer; "
Jer 1:15 I will c· all the families of the "
3:17 c· Jerusalem the throne of the Lord; "
19 Thou shalt c· me, My father; and "
Jer 6:30 Reprobate silver shall men c· 7121
7:27 thou shalt also c· unto them; but "
9:17 and c· for the mourning women, "
10:25 families that c· not on thy name: "
25:29 I will call for a sword upon all the "
29:12 Then shall ye c· upon me, and ye "
33: 3 C· unto me, and I will answer "
50:29 C· together the archers against 8085
51:27 c· together against her the "
La 2:15 city that men c· The perfection of 559
Eze 21:23 c· to remembrance the iniquity, *2142
36:29 and I will c· for the corn, and will 7121
38:21 And I will c· for a sword against "
39:11 shall c· it The valley of Hamon-gog. "
Da 2: 2 commanded to c· the magicians, "
Ho 1: 4 C· his name Jezreel: for yet a "
6 C· her name Lo-ruhamah: for I "
9 C· his name Lo-ammi: for ye are "
2:16 thou shalt c· me Ishi; "
16 and shalt c· me no more Baali. "
7:11 they c· to Egypt, they go to Assyria. "
Joe 1:14 c· a solemn assembly, gather the "
2:15 a fast, c· a solemn assembly: "
32 whosoever shall c· on the name of "
32 remnant whom the Lord shall c·. "
Am 5:16 and they shall c· the husbandman "
Jon 1: 6 arise, c· upon thy God, if so be "
Zep 3: 9 all c· upon the name of the Lord, "
Zec 3:10 ye c· every man his neighbour "
13: 9 they shall c· on my name, and I "
Mal 1: 4 c· them, The border of wickedness, "
3:12 all nations shall c· you blessed: 833
15 now we c· the proud happy; yea, "
M't 1:21 thou shalt c· his name Jesus: 2564
23 shall call his name Emmanuel, "
9:13 I am not come to c· the righteous, "
20: 8 C· the labourers, and give them "
22: 3 to c· them that were bidden "
43 doth David in spirit c· him Lord, "
45 If David then c· him Lord, how is "
23: 9 And c· no man your father upon "
M'r 2:17 came not to c· the righteous, but "
10:49 they c· the blind man, saying unto 5455
15:12 whom ye c· the King of the Jews? 3004
16 and they c· together the whole 4779
Lu 1:13 thou shalt c· his name John. 2564
31 son, and shalt c· his name Jesus. "
48 generations shall c· me blessed. 3106
5:32 I came not to c· the righteous, 2564
6:46 And why c· ye me, Lord, Lord, "
14:12 c· not thy friends, nor thy brethren, 5455
13 when thou makest a feast, c· the *2564
Joh 4:16 Go, c· thy husband, and come 5455
13:13 Ye c· me Master and Lord: and ye "
15:15 Henceforth I c· you not servants; 3004
Ac 2:21 whosoever shall c· on the name of 1941
39 many as the Lord our God shall c·. 4341
9:14 to bind all that c· on thy name. 1941
10: 5 to Joppa, and c· for one Simon *3343
15 that c· not thou common. *2840
28 I should not c· any man common 3004
32 c· hither Simon, whose surname 3333
11: 9 that c· not thou common. *2840
13 and c· for Simon, whose surname *3343
19:13 c· over them which had evil *3687
24:14 c· heresy, so worship I the God 3004
25 season, I will c· for thee. 3333
Ro 9:25 I will c· them my people which 2564
10:12 rich unto all that c· upon him. 1941
13 whosoever shall c· upon the name "
14 How then shall they c· on him in "
1Co 1: 2 in every place c· upon the name "
2Co 1:23 I c· God for a record upon my "
2Ti 1: 5 When I c· to remembrance the *2983
2:22 with them that c· on the Lord 1941
He 2:11 not ashamed to c· them brethren, 2564
10:32 c· to remembrance the former days, 363
Jas 5:14 c· for the elders of the church; 4341
1Pe 1:17 And if ye c· on the Father, who 1941

called See also CALLEDST.
Ge 1: 5 And God c· the light Day, 7121
5 and the darkness he c· Night. "
8 God c· the firmament Heaven. "
10 and God c· the dry land Earth; "
10 together of the waters c· he Seas: "
2:19 Adam c· every living creature, "
23 she shall be c· Woman, because "
3: 9 And the Lord God c· unto Adam, "
20 and Adam c· his wife's name Eve; "
4:17 c· the name of the city, after the "
25 and c· his name Seth: "
26 and he c· his name Enos: "
5: 2 and c· their name Adam, "
3 his image; and c· his name Seth: "
29 And he c· his name Noah, "
11: 9 therefore is the name of it c· Babel; "
12: 8 and c· upon the name of the Lord. "
18 And Pharoah c· Abram, and said, "
13: 4 Abram c· on the name of the Lord. "
16:13 And she c· the name of the Lord "
14 the well was c· Beer-lahai-roi; "
15 Abram c· his son's name, which "
17: 5 thy name any more be c· Abram, "
19: 5 And they c· unto Lot, and said "
22 the name of the city was c· Zoar. "
37 and c· his name Moab: "
38 and c· his name Ben-ammi: "
20: 8 and c· all his servants, and told all "
9 Then Abimelech c· Abraham, and "
21: 3 And Abraham c· the name of his "
12 in Isaac shall thy seed be c·. "
17 the angel of God c· to Hagar "
31 he c· that place Beer-sheba; "
33 c· there on the name of the Lord, "
22:11 angel of the Lord c· unto him out "
14 Abraham c· the name of that place "

Ge 22:15 angel of the Lord c' unto Abraham 7121
24:58 And they c' Rebekah, and said "
25:25 and they c' his name Esau. "
26 and his name was c' Jacob: "
30 therefore was his name c' Edom. "
26: 9 And Abimelech c' Isaac, and said, "
18 he c' their names after the names "
18 by which his father had c' them. "
20 he c' the name of the well Esek; "
21 and he c' the name of it Sitnah. "
22 and he c' the name of it Rehoboth; "
25 and c' upon the name of the Lord, "
33 and he c' it Shebah: "
27: 1 he called Esau his eldest son, and "
42 she sent and c' Jacob "
28: 1 Isaac c' Jacob, and blessed him, "
19 c' the name of that place Beth-el: "
19 the name of that city was c' Luz *
29:32 and she c' his name Reuben: 7121
33 and she c' his name Simeon. "
34 therefore was his name c' Levi. "
35 she c' his name Judah; "
30: 6 therefore c' she his name Dan. "
8 and she c' his name Naphtali. "
11 and she c' his name Gad. "
13 and she c' his name Asher. "
18 and she c' his name Issachar. "
20 and she c' his name Zebulun. "
21 and c' her name Dinah. "
24 And she c' his name Joseph; "
31: 4 Jacob sent and c' Rachel and Leah "
47 And Laban c' it Jegar-sahadutha: "
47 Jacob c' it Galeed. "
31:48 was the name of it c' Galeed; "
54 and c' his brethren to eat bread: "
32: 2 and he c' the name of that place "
28 name shall be c' no more Jacob, 559
30 c' the name of the place Peniel: 7121
33:17 name of the place is c' Succoth. "
20 and c' it El-elohe-Israel. "
35: 7 and c' the place El-Beth-el: "
8 name of it was c' Allon-bachuth. "
10 shall not be c' any more Jacob, "
10 and he c' his name Israel. "
15 And Jacob c' the name of the place "
18 that she c' his name Ben-oni: "
18 his father c' him Benjamin. "
38: 3 and he c' his name Er. "
4 and she c' his name Onan. "
5 and c' his name Shelah: "
29 therefore his name was c' Pharez. "
30 and his name was c' Zarah. "
39:14 she c' unto the men of her house, "
41: 8 and c' for all the magicians "
14 Pharaoh sent and c' Joseph, "
45 And Pharaoh c' Joseph's name "
51 c' the name of the firstborn "
52 of the second c' he Ephraim: "
47:29 and he c' his son Joseph, "
48: 6 c' after the name of their brethren "
49: 1 And Jacob c' unto his sons, "
50:11 name of it was c' Abel-mizraim, "
Ex 1:18 king of Egypt c' for the midwives, "
2: 8 went and c' the child's mother. "
10 And she c' his name Moses: "
22 and he c' his name Gershom: "
3: 4 God c' unto him out of the midst * "
7:11 Pharaoh also c' the wise men "
8: 8 Pharaoh c' for Moses and Aaron, "
25 c' for Moses and for Aaron, "
9:27 Pharaoh sent, and c' for Moses "
10:16 Pharaoh c' for Moses and Aaron "
24 And Pharaoh c' unto Moses, "
12:21 Then Moses c' for all the elders "
31 And he c' for Moses and Aaron "
15:23 the name of it was c' Marah. "
16:31 c' the name thereof Manna: "
17: 7 c' the name of the place Massah, "
15 c' the name of it Jehovah-nissi: "
19: 3 c' unto him out of the mountain, "
7 Moses came and c' for the elders "
20 and the Lord c' Moses up "
24:16 the seventh day he c' unto Moses "
31: 2 I have c' by name Bezaleel "
33: 7 and c' it the Tabernacle of the "
34:31 Moses c' unto them; and Aaron "
35:30 the Lord hath c' by name Bezaleel "
36: 2 c' Bezaleel and Aholiab, "
Le 1: 1 And the Lord c' unto Moses, "
9: 1 Moses c' Aaron and his sons, "
10: 4 Moses c' Mishael and Elzaphan, "
Nu 11: 3 c' the name of the place Taberah: "
34 And he c' the name of that place "
12: 5 and c' Aaron and Miriam: "
13:16 And Moses c' Oshea the son of Nun "
24 The place was c' the brook Eshcol, "
21: 3 c' the name of the place Hormah. "
24:10 I c' thee to curse mine enemies, "
25: 2 c' the people unto the sacrifices "
32:41 and c' them Havoth-jair. "
42 c' it Nobah, after his own name. "
De 3:13 which was c' the land of giants. "
14 and c' them after his own name, "
5: 1 c' all Israel, and said unto them, "
15: 2 because it is c' the Lord's release.* "
25:10 And his name shall be c' in Israel, "
28:10 art c' by the name of the Lord; "
29: 2 And Moses c' unto all Israel, "
31: 7 And Moses c' unto Joshua, "
Jos 4: 4 Then Joshua c' the twelve men, "
5: 9 the name of the place is c' Gilgal "
6: 6 the son of Nun c' the priests, "
7:26 place was c', The valley of Achor, "
8:16 c' together to pursue after them: 2199
9:22 And Joshua c' for them, 7121
10:24 Joshua c' for all the men of Israel, "

Jos 19:47 c' Leshem, Dan, after the name 7121
22: 1 Then Joshua c' the Reubenites, "
34 and the children of Gad c' the altar "
23: 2 And Joshua c' for all Israel, "
24: 1 and c' for the elders of Israel, "
9 sent and c' Balaam the son of Beor "
J'g 1:17 name of the city was c' Hormah. "
26 and c' the name thereof Luz: "
2: 5 c' the name of that place Bochim: "
4: 6 c' Barak the son of Abinoam "
10 Barak c' Zebulun and Naphtali 2199
6:24 and c' it Jehovah-shalom: 7121
32 on that day he c' him Jerubbaal, "
8:31 son, whose name he c' Abimelech. 7760
9:54 he c' hastily unto the young man 7121
10: 4 cities, which are c' Havoth-jair "
12: 2 I c' you, ye delivered me not 2199
13:24 and c' his name Samson: 7121
14:15 have ye c' us to take that we have? "
15:17 and c' that place Ramath-lehi. "
18 and c' on the Lord, and said, "
19 c' the name thereof En-hakkore, "
16:18 c' for the lords of the Philistines, "
19 and she c' for a man, and she "
25 c' for Samson out of the prison "
28 And Samson c' unto the Lord, "
18:12 they c' that place Mahaneh-dan "
29 they c' the name of the city Dan, "
Ru 4:17 and they c' his name Obed: "
1Sa 1:20 a son, and c' his name Samuel, "
3: 4 That the Lord c' Samuel: "
5 he said, I c' not; lie down again. "
6 the Lord c' yet again, Samuel. "
6 I c' not, my son; lie down again. "
8 Lord c' Samuel again the third "
8 that the Lord had c' the child. "
10 the Lord came, and stood, and c' "
16 Then Eli c' Samuel, and said, "
6: 2 the Philistines c' for the priests "
7:12 and c' the name of it Eben-ezer, "
9: 9 he that is now c' a Prophet was "
9 beforetime c' a Seer.) 7121
26 c' Saul to the top of the house, "
10:17 And Samuel c' the people together 6817
12:18 So Samuel c' unto the Lord; 7121
13: 4 were c' together after Saul, *6817
16: 5 and c' them to the sacrifice. 7121
8 Then Jesse c' Abinadab, and "
19: 7 And Jonathan c' David, and "
23: 8 Saul c' all the people together *8085
28 c' that place Sela-hammahlekoth. 7121
28:15 I have c' thee, that thou mayest "
29: 6 Then Achish c' David, and said "
2Sa 1: 7 he saw me, and c' unto me. "
15 David c' one of the young men, "
2:16 place was c' Helkath-hazzurim, "
26 Then Abner c' to Joab, and said, "
5: 9 and c' it the city of David. "
20 he c' the name of that place "
6: 2 whose name is c' by the name of "
8 and he c' the name of the place "
9: 2 when they had c' him unto David, "
9 king c' to Ziba, Saul's servant, "
11:13 David had c' him, he did eat "
12:24 and he c' his name Solomon: "
25 and he c' his name Jedidiah, "
28 and it be c' after my name. "
13:17 Then he c' his servant that "
14:33 he had c' for Absalom, he came "
15: 2 Absalom c' unto him, and said, "
11 out of Jerusalem, that were c'; * "
18:18 c' the pillar after his own name: "
18 and it is c' unto this day, "
26 the watchman c' unto the porter, "
28 Ahimaaz c', and said unto the king, "
21: 2 And the king c' the Gibeonites, "
22: 7 In my distress I c' upon the Lord, "
1Ki 1: 9 c' all his brethren the king's sons, "
10 Solomon his brother, he c' not. "
19 and hath c' all the sons of the king, "
19 Solomon thy servant hath he not c'. "
25 and hath c' all the king's sons, "
26 servant Solomon, hath he not c'. "
2:36 the king sent and c' for Shimei, "
42 sent and c' for Shimei, and said "
7:21 and c' the name thereof Jachin: "
21 and c' the name thereof Boaz. "
8:43 have builded, is c' by thy name. "
9:13 And he c' them the land of Cabul "
12: 3 and c' him. And Jeroboam "
20 and c' him unto the congregation, "
16:24 and c' the name of the city "
17:10 he c' to her, and said, Fetch me, "
11 he c' to her, and said, Bring me, "
18: 3 And Ahab c' Obadiah, which was "
26 and c' on the name of Baal "
20: 7 the king of Israel c' all the elders "
22: 9 the king of Israel c' an officer, "
2Ki 3:10 that the Lord hath c' these three "
13 for the Lord hath c' these three "
4:12 had c' her, she stood before him. "
15 had c' her, she stood in the door. "
22 And she c' unto her husband, "
36 And he c' Gehazi, and said, Call "
36 this Shunammite. So he c' her. "
6:11 and he c' his servants, and said "
7:10 they came and c' unto the porter "
11 c' the porters; and they told "
8: 1 for the Lord hath c' for a famine; "
9: 1 the prophet c' one of the children "
12: 7 Jehoash c' for Jehoiada the priest, "
14: 7 and c' the name of it Joktheel "
18: 4 and he c' it Nehushtan. "
18 when they had c' to the king, "
1Ch 4: 9 c' his name Jabez, saying, "
10 And Jabez c' on the God of Israel, "

1Ch 6:65 which are c' by their names. *7121
7:16 and she c' his name Peresh; "
23 he c' his name Beriah, because "
11: 7 they c' it the city of David. "
13: 6 cherubims, whose name is c' on it. "
11 that place is c' Perez-uzza "
14:11 they c' the name of that place "
15:11 David c' for Zadok and Abiathar "
21:26 and c' upon the Lord; "
22: 6 Then he c' for Solomon his son, "
2Ch 3:17 and c' the name of that on the "
6:33 I have built is c' by thy name. "
7:14 people, which are c' by my name, "
10: 3 And they sent and c' him. "
18: 8 Israel c' for one of his officers, "
20:26 the name of the same place was c', "
24: 6 And the king c' for Jehoiada "
Ezr 2:61 and was c' after their name: "
Ne 5:12 Then I c' the priests, and took "
7:63 and was c' after their name. "
Es 2:14 that she were c' by name. "
3:12 scribes c' on the thirteenth day "
4: 5 Then c' Esther for Hatach, "
11 who is not c', there is one law "
11 I have not been c' to come in "
5:10 and c' for his friends, and * 935
8: 9 king's scribes c' at that time 7121
9:26 they c' these days Purim after "
Job 1: 4 and c' for their three sisters to eat "
9:16 I had c', and he had answered me; "
19:16 I c' my servant, and he gave me * "
42:14 c' the name of the first, Jemima; "
Ps 17: 6 I have c' upon thee, for thou "
18: 6 In my distress I c' upon the Lord, "
31:17 O Lord; for I have c' upon thee: "
50: 1 Lord hath spoken and c' the earth "
53: 4 they have not c' upon God. * "
79: 6 kingdoms that have not c' upon "
88: 9 Lord, I have c' daily upon thee, "
99: 6 they c' upon the Lord, and he "
105:16 c' for a famine upon the land, "
116: 4 c' I upon the name of the Lord; "
118: 5 I c' upon the Lord in distress: the "
Pr 1:24 I have c', and ye refused; I have "
16:21 wise in heart shall be c' prudent: "
24: 8 be c' a mischievous person. * "
Ca 5: 6 c' him, but he gave me no answer. "
Isa 1:26 c', The city of righteousness, "
4: 1 only let us be c' by thy name, "
3 c' holy, even every one that is 559
9: 6 his name shall be c' Wonderful, 7121
13: 3 I have also c' my mighty ones "
19:18 be c', The city of destruction, 559
31: 4 multitude of shepherds is c' forth 7121
32: 5 person shall be no more c' liberal, "
35: 8 it shall be c' The way of holiness; "
41: 2 man from the east, c' him "
9 c' thee from the chief men thereof, "
42: 6 I the Lord have c' thee "
43: 1 I have c' thee by thy name; "
7 every one that is c' by my name: "
22 thou hast not c' upon me, O Jacob, "
45: 4 I have even c' thee by thy name: "
47: 1 thou shalt no more be c' tender "
5 be c', The lady of kingdoms. "
48: 1 which are c' by the name of Israel, "
8 and wast c' a transgressor "
12 O Jacob and Israel, my c'; I am he; "
15 yea, I have c' him: I have "
49: 1 The Lord hath c' me from the "
50: 2 I c', was there none to answer? "
51: 2 I c' him alone, and blessed him, "
54: 5 of the whole earth shall he be c'. "
6 the Lord hath c' thee as a woman "
56: 7 mine house shall be c' an house of "
58:12 and thou shalt be c', The repairer "
61: 3 might be c' trees of righteousness, "
62: 2 thou shalt be c' by a new name, "
4 thou shalt be c' Hephzi-bah, and "
12 thou shalt be c', Sought out, "
63:19 they were not c' by thy name. "
65: 1 a nation that was not c' by my "
12 when I c', ye did not answer; "
66: 4 when I c', none did answer; "
Jer 7:10 in this house, which is c' by my "
11 Is this house, which is c' by my "
13 I c' you, but ye answered not; "
14 this house, which is c' by my name, "
30 the house which is c' by my name, "
32 it shall no more be c' Tophet, 559
11:16 The Lord c' thy name, A green 7121
12: 6 they have c' a multitude after * "
14: 9 we are c' by thy name; leave us "
15:16 I am c' by thy name, O Lord God "
19: 6 place shall no more be c' Tophet, "
20: 3 Lord hath not c' thy name Pashur, "
23: 6 he shall be c', The Lord our "
25:29 the city which is c' by my name, "
30:17 they c' thee an Outcast, saying, "
32:34 house, which is c' by my name, "
33:16 name wherewith she shall be c', "
34:15 house which is c' by my name: "
35:17 and I have c' unto them, but they "
36: 4 Then Jeremiah c' Baruch the "
42: 8 Then c' he Johanan the son of "
La 1:15 he hath c' an assembly against me "
19 I c' for my lovers, but they "
21 bring the day that thou hast c'. * "
2:22 Thou hast c' as in a solemn day "
3:55 I c' upon thy name, O Lord, "
57 in the day that I c' upon thee: "
Eze 9: 3 he c' to the man clothed with linen, "
20:29 And the name thereof is c' Bamah "
Da 5:12 now let Daniel be c', and he will 7123
8:16 which c', and said, Gabriel, make 7121
9:18 the city which is c' by thy name: "

Da 9:19 thy people are c' by thy name. 7121
10: 1 whose name was c' Belteshazzar: "
Ho 11: 1 c' my son out of Egypt. "
2 As they c' them, so they went "
7 though they c' them to the most "
Am 7: 4 Lord God c' to contend by fire, "
9:12 heathen, which are c' by my name, "
Hag 1:11 And I c' for a drought upon the "
Zec 8: 3 Jerusalem shall be c' a city of "
11: 7 the one I c' Beauty, "
7 and the other I c' Bands; "
M't 1:16 born Jesus, who is c' Christ. 3004
25 and he c' his name Jesus. 2564
2: 7 privily c' the wise men, enquired "
15 Out of Egypt have I c' my son. "
23 and dwelt in a city c' Nazareth: *3004
23 He shall be c' a Nazarene. 2564
4:18 Simon c' Peter, and Andrew his 3004
21 mending their nets; and he c' 2564
5: 9 they shall be c' the children of God. "
19 he shall be c' the least in the "
19 the same shall be c' great in the "
10: 1 And when he had c' unto him his 4341
2 The first, Simon, who is c' Peter, 3004
25 If they have c' the master of the 2564
13:55 is not his mother c' Mary? and 3004
15:10 And he c' the multitude, and said 4341
32 Then Jesus c' his disciples unto "
18: 2 Jesus c' a little child unto him, "
32 after that he had c' him, said "
20:16 for many be c', but few chosen. *2822
25 But Jesus c' them unto him, and 4341
32 Jesus stood still, and c' them, 5455
21:13 My house shall be c' the house of 2564
22:14 many are c', but few are chosen. 2822
23: 7 and to be c' of men, Rabbi, Rabbi. 2564
8 be not ye c' Rabbi: for one is your "
10 Neither be ye c' masters: for one "
25:14 c' his own servants, and delivered "
26: 3 high priest, who was c' Caiaphas, 3004
14 Then one of the twelve, c' Judas "
36 unto a place c' Gethsemane, and "
27: 8 that field was c', The field of 2564
16 a notable prisoner, c' Barabbas. 3004
17 or Jesus which is c' Christ? "
22 do then with Jesus which is c' "
33 unto a place c' Golgotha, that is "
M'r 1:20 straightway he c' them: and they 2564
3:23 And he c' them unto him, and said 4341
6: 7 And he c' unto him the twelve, "
7:14 when he had c' all the people unto "
8: 1 Jesus c' his disciples unto him, "
34 when he had c' the people unto "
9:35 and c' the twelve, and saith unto 5455
10:42 But Jesus c' them to him, and 4341
49 and commanded him to be c'. *5455
11:17 My house shall be c' of all nations 2564
12:43 he c' unto him his disciples, and 4341
14:72 Peter c' to mind the word that 363
15:16 into the hall, c' Prætorium; *3739, 2076
Lu 1:32 shall be c' the Son of the Highest: 2564
35 shall be c' the Son of God. "
36 with her, who was c' barren. "
59 and they c' him Zacharias, after "
60 Not so, but he shall be c' John. "
61 kindred that is c' by this name. "
62 father, how he would have him c'. "
76 shalt be c' the prophet of the "
2: 4 David, which is c' Bethlehem; "
21 his name was c' Jesus, which was "
23 shall be c' holy to the Lord;) "
6:13 he c' unto him his disciples: 4377
15 and Simon c' Zelotes, 2564
7:11 he went into a city c' Nain; "
8: 2 Mary c' Magdalene, out of whom "
54 and c', saying, Maid, arise. 5455
9: 1 c' his twelve disciples together, 4779
10 belonging to the city c' Bethsaida. 2564
10:39 she had a sister c' Mary, which "
13:12 he c' her to him, 4377
15:19 no more worthy to be c' thy son: 2564
21 no more worthy to be c' thy son. "
26 he c' one of the servants, and 4341
16: 2 And he c' him, and said unto 5455
5 So he c' every one of his lord's *4341
18:16 But Jesus c' them unto him, "
19:13 And he c' his ten servants, and 2564
15 these servants to be c' unto him, 5455
29 the mount c' the mount of Olives, 2564
21:37 that is c' the mount of Olives. "
22: 1 which is c' the Passover. 3004
25 upon them are c' benefactors. 2564
47 he that was c' Judas, one of the 3004
23:13 when he had c' together the 4779
33 to the place which is c' Calvary, 2564
24:13 to a village c' Emmaus, which *3686
Joh 1:42 thou shalt be c' Cephas, which 2564
48 Before that Philip c' thee, when 5455
2: 2 Jesus was c', and his disciples, *2564
9 governor of the feast c' the 5455
4: 5 of Samaria, which is c' Sychar, 3004
25 Messias cometh, which is c' Christ: "
5: 2 which is c' in the Hebrew tongue 1951
9:11 A man that is c' Jesus made clay, 3004
18 until they c' the parents of him 5455
24 Then again c' they the man that "
10:35 If he c' them gods, unto whom 2036
11:16 Thomas, which is c' Didymus, 3004
28 and c' Mary her sister secretly, 5455
54 into a city c' Ephraim, and there 3004
12:17 when he c' Lazarus out of his 5455
15:15 but I have c' you friends; 2046
18:33 c' Jesus, and said unto him, Art 5455
19:13 in a place that is c' the Pavement, 3004
17 a place c' the place of a skull, "
17 is c' in the Hebrew Golgotha: "
Joh 20:24 one of the twelve, c' Didymus, 3004
21: 2 and Thomas c' Didymus, and "
Ac 1:12 from the mount c' Olivet, which 2564
19 insomuch as that field is c' in "
23 Joseph c' Barsabas, who was "
3: 2 gate of the temple which is c' 3004
11 the porch that is c' Solomon's, 2564
4:18 they c' them, and commanded "
5:21 and c' the council together, and 4779
40 when they had c' the apostles, 4341
6: 2 Then the twelve c' the multitude "
9 of the synagogue, which is c' 3004
7:14 and c' his father Jacob to him, 3333
8: 9 a certain man, c' Simon, which *3686
9:11 the street which is c' Straight, 2564
11 for one c' Saul, of Tarsus: for *3686
21 them which c' on his name in 1941
36 by interpretation is c' Dorcas: 3004
41 when he had c' the saints and *5455
10: 1 man in Cæsarea c' Cornelius, *3686
1 of the band c' the Italian band, 2564
7 c' two of his household servants, 5455
18 And c', and asked whether Simon, "
23 Then c' he them in, and lodged 1528
24 and had c' together his kinsmen 4779
11:26 the disciples were c' Christians 5537
13: 1 and Simeon that was c' Niger, 2564
2 work whereunto I have c' them. 4341
7 who c' for Barnabas and Saul, "
9 Then Saul, (who also is c' Paul,) "
14:12 they c' Barnabas, Jupiter; and 2564
15:17 upon whom my name is c', 1941
16:10 that the Lord had c' us for to 4341
29 Then he c' for a light, and 154
19:25 Whom he c' together with the *4867
40 we are in danger to be c' in *1458
20: 1 Paul c' unto him the disciples, *4341
17 and c' the elders of the church. 3333
23: 6 I am c' in question. 2919
17 c' one of the centurions unto him, 4341
18 Paul the prisoner c' me unto him, "
23 he c' unto him two centurions, "
24: 2 when he was c' forth, Tertullus 2564
21 I am c' in question by you this 2919
27: 8 which is c' The fair havens; 3004
14 tempestuous wind, c' Euroclydon. 2564
16 a certain island which is c' Clauda, "
28: 1 knew that the island was c' Melita. "
17 Paul c' the chief of the Jews 4779
20 have I c' for you, to see you, *3870
Ro 1: 1 c' to be an apostle, separated 2822
6 are ye also the c' of Jesus Christ: "
7 c' to be saints: grace to you "
2:17 Behold, thou art c' a Jew, and *2028
7: 3 she shall be c' an adulteress: 5537
8:28 to them who are the c' according 2822
30 them he also c': and whom he c', 2564
9: 7 In Isaac shall thy seed be c'. "
24 Even us, whom he hath c', not of "
26 there shall they be c' the children "
1Co 1: 1 c' to be an apostle of Jesus Christ 2822
2 in Christ Jesus, c' to be saints, "
9 by whom ye were c' unto the 2564
24 But unto them which are c', both 2822
26 mighty, not many noble, are c': "
5:11 if any man that is c' a brother *3687
7:15 but God hath c' us to peace. 2564
17 as the Lord hath c' every one, so "
18 Is any man c' being circumcised? "
18 Is any c' in uncircumcision? let "
20 same calling wherein he was c'. "
21 Art thou c' being a servant? care "
22 For he that is c' in the Lord, being "
22 he that is c', being free, is "
24 wherein he is c', therein abide "
8: 5 though there be that are c' gods, 3004
15: 9 am not meet to be c' an apostle, 2564
Ga 1: 6 from him that c' you into the "
15 and c' me by his grace, "
5:13 ye have been c' unto liberty; "
Eph 2:11 c' Uncircumcision by that 3004
11 that which is c' the Circumcision "
4: 1 wherewith ye are c', 2564
4 even as ye are c' in one hope "
Col 3:15 to the which also ye are c' "
4:11 Jesus, which is c' Justus, who are 3004
1Th 2:12 worthy of God, who hath c' you *2564
4: 7 hath not c' us unto uncleanness, "
2Th 2: 4 himself above all that is c' God, 3004
14 he c' you by our gospel, to the 2564
1Ti 6:12 life, whereunto thou art also c', "
20 of science falsely so c': 5581
2Ti 1: 9 and c' us with an holy calling, 2564
Heb 3:13 while it is c' To day; lest any "
5: 4 but he that is c' of God, as was "
10 C' of God an high priest after *4316
7:11 not be c' after the order of Aaron? *3004
9: 2 which is c' the sanctuary. "
3 tabernacle which is c' the Holiest "
15 are c' might receive the promise 2564
11: 8 Abraham, when he was c' to go "
16 not ashamed to be c' their God: 1941
18 in Isaac shall thy seed be c': 2564
24 refused to be c' the son of 3004
Jas 2: 7 name by the which ye are c'? 1941
23 he was c' the Friend of God. 2564
1Pe 1:15 as he which hath c' you is holy "
2: 9 who hath c' you out of darkness "
21 hereunto were ye c': because "
3: 9 that ye are thereunto c', that ye "
5:10 the God of all grace, who hath c' * "
2Pe 1: 3 of him that hath c' us to glory "
1Jo 3: 1 we should be c' the sons of God: "
Jude 1 preserved in Jesus Christ, and c' 2822
Re 1: 9 was in the isle that is c' Patmos, 2564
8:11 name of the star is c' Wormwood: 3004
Re 11: 8 spiritually is c' Sodom and Egypt, 2564
12: 9 serpent, c' the Devil, and Satan, "
16:16 c' in the Hebrew tongue "
17:14 they that are with him are c', 2822
19: 9 which are c' unto the marriage *2564
11 him was c' Faithful and True, "
13 his name is c' The Word of God. "

calledst
J'g 8: 1 that thou c' us not, when thou 7121
1Sa 3: 5 for thou c' me. And he said, I "
Ps 81: 7 c' in trouble, and I delivered thee; "
Eze 23:21 Thus thou c' to remembrance the 6485

callest
M't 19:17 Why c' thou me good? there is *3004
M'k 10:18 unto him, Why c' thou me good? "
Lu 18:19 Why c' thou me good? none is "

calleth
1Ki 8:43 that the stranger c' to thee for: 7121
2Ch 6:33 that the stranger c' to thee for; "
Job 12: 4 c' upon God, and he answereth * "
Ps 42: 7 Deep c' unto deep at the noise "
147: 4 he c' them all by their names. * "
Pro 18: 6 and his mouth c' for strokes. "
Isa 21:11 He c' to me out of Seir, Watchman, "
40:26 he c' them all by names by the "
59: 4 None c' for justice, nor any * "
64: 7 there is none that c' upon thy "
Hos 7: 7 there is none among them that c' "
Am 5: 8 that c' for the waters of the sea, "
9: 6 he that c' for the waters of the sea, "
M't 27:47 that, said, This man c' for Elias. 5455
M'r 3:13 and c' unto him whom he would: 4341
10:49 of good comfort, rise; he c' thee. 5455
12:37 therefore himself c' him Lord; 3004
15:35 heard it, said, Behold, he c' Elias. 5455
Lu 15: 6 home, he c' together his friends 4779
9 c' her friends and her neighbours "
20:37 c' the Lord the God of Abraham, 3004
44 David therefore c' him Lord, how 2564
Joh 10: 3 and he c' his own sheep by name, "
11:28 The Master is come, and c' for thee. 5455
Ro 4:17 c' those things which be not as 2564
9:11 not of works, but of him that c';) "
1Co 12: 3 c' Jesus accursed: and that no *3004
Gal 5: 8 cometh not of him that c' you. 2564
1Th 5:24 Faithful is he that c' you, who "
Re 2:20 which c' herself a prophetess, to 3004

calling
Nu 10: 2 for the c' of the assembly, and for 4744
Isa 1:13 the c' of assemblies, I cannot 7121
41: 4 c' the generations from the "
46:11 C' a ravenous bird from the east, "
Eze 23:19 in c' to remembrance the days of *2142
M't 11:16 and c' unto their fellows, *4377
M'r 3:31 without, sent unto him, c' him. 5455
11:21 Peter c' to remembrance saith 363
15:44 and c' unto him the centurion, he 4341
Lu 7:19 And John c' unto him two of his "
32 c' one to another, and saying, *4377
Ac 7:59 stoned Stephen, c' upon God, and 1941
22:16 sins, c' on the name of the Lord. "
Ro 11:29 gifts and c' of God are without 2821
1Co 1:26 For ye see your c', brethren, how "
7:20 abide in the same c' wherein he "
Eph 1:18 what is the hope of his c', and "
4: 4 are called in one hope of your c'; "
Ph'p 3:14 for the prize of the high c' of "
2Th 1:11 would count you worthy of this c', "
2Ti 1: 9 us, and called us with an holy c', "
Heb 3: 1 partakers of the heavenly c', "
1Pe 3: 6 Even as Sara obeyed Abraham, c' 2564
2Pe 1:10 give diligence to make your c' 2821

calm
Ps 107:29 He maketh the storm a c', so that 1827
Jon 1:11 unto thee, that the sea may be c' 8367
12 so shall the sea be c' unto you: "
M't 8:26 the sea; and there was a great c'. 1055
M'k 4:39 ceased, and there was a great c'. "
Lu 8:24 they ceased, and there was a c'. "

Calneh (*cal'-neh*) See also CALNO; CANNEH.
Ge 10:10 and Erech, and Accad, and C'. 3641
Am 6: 2 Pass ye unto C'; and "

Calno (*cal'-no*) See also CALNEH.
Isa 10: 9 Is not C' as Carchemish? is not 3641

Calvary (*cal'-va-ry*)
Lu 23:33 which is called C', there they *2898

calve See also CALVED; CALVETH.
Job 39: 1 thou mark when the hinds do c'? 2342
Ps 29: 9 the Lord maketh the hinds to c', "

calved
Jer 14: 5 the hind also c' in the field, and *3205

calves
1Sa 6: 7 bring their c' home from them: 1121
10 and shut up their c' at home: "
14:32 took sheep, and oxen, and c', 1121, 1241
1Ki 12:28 made two c' of gold, and said 5695
32 unto the c' that he had made: "
2Ki 10:29 golden c' that were in Beth-el, "
17:16 them molten images, even two c', "
2Ch 11:15 and for the c' which he had made. "
13: 8 there are with you golden c', which "
Ps 68:30 with the c' of the people, till "
Hos 10: 5 shall fear because of the c' of 5697
13: 2 the men that sacrifice kiss the c'. "
14: 2 so will we render the c' of our lips. *6499
Am 6: 4 the c' out of the midst of the stall; 5695
Mic 6: 6 offerings, with c' of a year old? "
Mal 4: 2 and grow up as c' of the stall. "
Heb 9:12 by the blood of goats and c', but 3448
19 took the blood of c' and of goats, "

calveth
Job 21:10 their cow c', and casteth not her 6403

came See also BECAME; CAMEST; OVERCAME.
Ge 4: 3 *c*· to pass, that Cain brought of 1961
8 *c*· to pass, when they were in the "
6: 1 *c*· to pass, when men began to "
4 sons of God *c*· in unto the daughters 935
7:10 *c*· to pass after seven days, that 1961
8: 6 it *c*· to pass at the end of forty "
11 And the dove *c*· in to him in the 935
13 it *c*· to pass in the six hundredth 1961
10:14 (out of whom *c*· Philistim,) and *3318
11: 2 it *c*· to pass, as they journeyed 1961
5 the Lord *c*· down to see the city 3381
31 and they *c*· unto Haran, and 935
12: 5 and into the land of Canaan they *c*·. "
11 it *c*· to pass, when he was come 1961
14 *c*· to pass, that, when Abram was "
13:18 *c*· and dwelt in the plain of Mamre, 935
14: 1 *c*· to pass in the days of Amraphel 1961
5 fourteenth year *c*· Chedorlaomer, 935
7 and *c*· to En-mishpat, which is "
13 there *c*· one that had escaped, "
15: 1 word of the Lord *c*· unto Abram 1961
4 the word of the Lord *c*· unto him, "
11 when the fowls *c*· down upon the 3381
17 And it *c*· to pass, that, when the 1961
19: 1 And there *c*· two angels to Sodom 935
5 Where are the men which *c*· in to "
8 *c*· they under the shadow * "
9 This one fellow *c*· in to sojourn "
9 Lot, and *c*· near to break the door. 5066
17 *c*· to pass, when they had brought 1961
29 it *c*· to pass, when God destroyed "
34 *c*· to pass on the morrow, that the "
20: 3 God *c*· to Abimelech in a dream 935
13 *c*· to pass when God caused me 1961
21:22 And it *c*· to pass at that time, that "
22: 1 *c*· to pass after these things, that "
9 they *c*· to the place which God had 935
20 it *c*· to pass after these things, 1961
23: 2 Abraham *c*· to mourn for Sarah, 935
24:15 it *c*· to pass, before he had done 1961
15 behold, Rebekah *c*· out, who was 3318
16 and filled her pitcher, and *c*· up. 5927
22 it *c*· to pass, as the camels had 1961
30 it *c*· to pass, when he saw the "
30 that he *c*· unto the man; and, 935
32 And the man *c*· into the house: "
42 And I *c*· this day unto the well, "
45 Rebekah *c*· forth with her pitcher 3318
52 *c*· to pass, that when Abraham's 1961
62 Isaac *c*· from the way of the well 935
25:11 it *c*· to pass after the death of 1961
25 And the first *c*· out red, all over 3318
26 after that *c*· his brother out, 3318
29 and Esau *c*· from the field, 935
26: 8 And it *c*· to pass, when he had 1961
32 And it *c*· to pass the same day, "
32 that Isaac's servants *c*·, and told 935
27: 1 And it *c*· to pass, that when Isaac 1961
18 And he *c*· unto his father and 935
27 And he *c*· near, and kissed him: 5066
30 And it *c*· to pass, as soon as 1961
30 that Esau his brother *c*· in from 935
35 Thy brother *c*· with subtilty, "
29: 1 on his journey, and *c*· into the 3212
9 Rachel *c*· with her father's sheep: 935
10 And it *c*· to pass, when Jacob 1961
13 And it *c*· to pass, when Laban "
23 And it *c*· to pass in the evening, "
25 it *c*· to pass, that in the morning, "
30:16 And Jacob *c*· out of the field in 935
25 And it *c*· to pass, when Rachel 1961
30 little which thou hadst before I *c*·, "
38 when the flocks *c*· to drink, 935
38 when they *c*· to drink. "
41 And it *c*· to pass, whensoever 1961
31:10 And it *c*· to pass at the time that "
24 And God *c*· to Laban...in a dream 935
32: 6 We *c*· to thy brother Esau, "
13 took of that which *c*· to his hand * "
33: 1 Esau *c*·, and with him four hundred "
3 until he *c*· near to his brother. 5066
6 Then the handmaidens *c*· near, "
7 Leah also with her children *c*· near, "
7 after *c*· Joseph near and Rachel, "
18 And Jacob *c*· to Shalem, a city of 935
18 when he *c*· from Padan-aram; "
34: 7 *c*· out of the field when they heard "
20 And Hamor and Shechem his son *c*· "
25 And it *c*· to pass on the third day, 1961
25 and *c*· upon the city boldly, 935
27 The sons of Jacob *c*· upon the slain, "
35: 6 So Jacob *c*· to Luz, which is in the "
9 when he *c*· out of Padan-aram, and "
22 And it *c*· to pass when Israel dwelt 1961
27 Jacob *c*· unto Isaac his father 935
36:16 dukes that *c*· of Eliphaz in the "
17 these are the dukes that *c*· of Reuel "
18 the dukes that *c*· of Aholibamah "
29 the dukes that *c*· of the Horites; "
40 names of the dukes that *c*· of Esau, "
37:14 Hebron, and he *c*· to Shechem. 935
18 before he *c*· near unto them, 7126
23 And it *c*· to pass, when Joseph 1961
25 a company of Ishmeelites *c*· 935
38: 1 it *c*· to pass at that time, 1961
9 and it *c*· to pass, when he "
18 and *c*· in unto her, and she 935
24 it *c*· to pass about three months 1961
27 And it *c*· to pass in the time of "
28 it *c*· to pass, when she travailed, 1961
28 thread, saying, This *c*· out first. 3318
29 And it *c*· to pass, as he drew back 1961
29 behold, his brother *c*· out: and 3318
30 afterward *c*· out his brother, "

Ge 39: 5 And it *c*· to pass from the time 1961
7 And it *c*· to pass after these things, "
10 And it *c*· to pass, as she spake "
11 And it *c*· to pass about this time, "
13 And it *c*· to pass, when she saw "
14 he *c*· in unto me to lie with me, 935
15 And it *c*· to pass, when he heard 1961
16 by her, until his lord *c*· home. 935
17 us, *c*· in unto me to mock me: "
18 And it *c*· to pass, as I lifted 1961
19 And it *c*· to pass, when his master "
40: 1 it *c*· to pass after these things, "
6 And Joseph *c*· in unto them 935
20 And it *c*· to pass the third day, 1961
41: 1 And it *c*· to pass at the end of "
2 there *c*· up out of the river seven 5927
3 seven other kine *c*· up after them "
5 seven ears of corn *c*· up upon "
8 And it *c*· to pass in the morning 1961
13 And it *c*· to pass, as he interpreted "
14 raiment, and *c*· in unto Pharaoh. 935
18 there *c*· up out of the river seven 5927
19 seven other kine *c*· up after them, "
22 seven ears *c*· up in one stalk, "
27 ill favoured kine that *c*· up "
50 sons before the years of famine *c*·. 935
57 all countries *c*· into Egypt to "
42: 5 And the sons of Israel *c*· to buy "
6 and Joseph's brethren *c*·, and "
29 they *c*· unto Jacob their father, "
35 And it *c*· to pass as they emptied 1961
43: 2 And it *c*· to pass, when they had "
19 And they *c*· near to the steward 5066
20 we *c*· indeed down at the first 3381
21 And it *c*· to pass, when we 1961
21 when we *c*· to the inn, that we 935
25 against Joseph *c*· at noon: for they "
26 And when Joseph *c*· home, they "
44:14 And Judah and his brethren *c*· "
18 Then Judah *c*· near unto him, 5066
24 And it *c*· to pass when we 1961
24 when we *c*· up unto thy servant 5927
45: 4 And they *c*· near. And he said, 5066
25 and *c*· into the land of Canaan 935
46: 1 and *c*· to Beer-sheba, and offered "
6 and *c*· into Egypt, Jacob, and all "
8 of the children of Israel, which *c*· "
26 All the souls that *c*· with Jacob "
26 which *c*· out of his loins, 3318
27 which *c*· into Egypt, were 935
28 they *c*· into the land of Goshen. "
47: 1 Then Joseph *c*· and told Pharaoh,* "
15 the Egyptians *c*· unto Joseph, "
18 they *c*· unto him the second year, "
48: 1 And it *c*· to pass after these 1961
5 before I *c*· unto thee into Egypt, 935
7 for me, when I *c*· from Padan, "
50:10 And they *c*· to the threshingfloor "
Ex 1: 1 of Israel, which *c*· into Egypt; "
1 and his household *c*· with Jacob. "
5 all the souls that *c*· out of the 3318
21 And it *c*· to pass, because the 1961
2: 5 And the daughter of Pharaoh *c*· 3381
11 And it *c*· to pass in those days, 1961
16 and they *c*· and drew water, 935
17 And the shepherds *c*· and drove "
18 And when they *c*· to Reuel their "
23 And it *c*· to pass in process of 1961
23 and their cry *c*· up unto God 5927
3: 1 and *c*· to the mountain of God, 935
4:24 And it *c*· to pass by the way in 1961
5:15 officers of the children of Israel *c*· 935
20 as they *c*· forth from Pharaoh: 3318
23 For since I *c*· to Pharaoh to speak 935
6:28 And it *c*· to pass on the day when 1961
8: 6 and the frogs *c*· up, and covered 5927
24 and there *c*· a grievous swarm 935
10: 3 And Moses and Aaron *c*· in unto * "
12:29 it *c*· to pass, that at midnight 1961
41 And it *c*· to pass at the end of the "
41 the selfsame day it *c*· to pass, "
51 And it *c*· to pass the selfsame day, "
13: 3 ye *c*· out from Egypt, out of the 3318
4 *c*· ye out in the month Abib. * "
8 when I *c*· forth out of Egypt. "
15, 17 it *c*· to pass, when Pharaoh 1961
14:20 And it *c*· between the camp of 935
20 the one *c*· not near the other 7126
24 it *c*· to pass, that in the morning 1961
28 that *c*· into the sea after them; * 935
15:23 And when they *c*· to Marah, "
27 And they *c*· to Elim, where were "
16: 1 Israel *c*· unto the wilderness of "
10 And it *c*· to pass, as Aaron spake 1961
13 And it *c*· to pass, that at even "
13 that at even the quails *c*· up, 5927
22 *c*· to pass, that on the sixth day 1961
22 the rulers of the congregation *c*· 935
27 And it *c*· to pass, that there 1961
35 until they *c*· to a land inhabited; 935
35 until they *c*· unto the borders "
17: 8 Then *c*· Amalek, and fought with "
11 And it *c*· to pass, when Moses 1961
18: 5 Jethro, Moses' father in law, *c*· 935
7 welfare; and they *c*· into the tent. "
12 and Aaron *c*·, and all the elders "
13 it *c*· to pass on the morrow, 1961
19: 1 day *c*· they into the wilderness 935
7 Moses *c*· and called for the elders "
16 And it *c*· to pass on the third day 1961
20 Lord *c*· down upon mount Sinai, 3381
21: 3 If he *c*· in by himself, he shall * 935
22:15 hired thing, it *c*· for his hire. "
24: 3 And Moses *c*· and told the people "
32:19 *c*·[1961] to pass, as soon as he *c*· nigh 7126

Ex 32:24 fire, and there *c*· out this calf. 3318
30 And it *c*· to pass on the morrow, 1961
33: 7 *c*· to pass, that every one which "
8 And it *c*· to pass, when Moses "
9 And it *c*· to pass, as Moses entered "
34:29 And it *c*· to pass, when Moses "
29 Moses *c*· down from mount Sinai 3381
29 when he *c*· down from the mount, "
32 all the children of Israel *c*· nigh: 5066
34 took the vail off, until he *c*· out. 3318
34 And he *c*· out, and spake unto "
35:21 And they *c*·, every one whose 935
22 And they *c*·, both men and women, "
36: 4 sanctuary, *c*· every man from his "
40:17 it *c*· to pass in the first month 1961
32 when they *c*· near unto the altar, 7126
Le 9:22 and *c*· down from offering of the 3381
23 *c*· out, and blessed the people: 3318
24 And there *c*· a fire out from before "
Nu 4:47 every one that *c*· to do the service* 935
7: 1 And it *c*· to pass on the day that 1961
9: 6 *c*· before Moses and before Aaron 7126
10:11 it *c*· to pass on the twentieth day 1961
21 the tabernacle against they *c*·. 935
35 And it *c*· to pass when the ark 1961
11:20 Why *c*· we forth out of Egypt? 3318
25 And the Lord *c*· down in a cloud, 3381
25 and it *c*· to pass, that, when the 1961
12: 4 And they three *c*· out. 3318
5 And the Lord *c*· down in the pillar 3381
5 Miriam: and they both *c*· forth. 3318
13:22 the south, and *c*· unto Hebron; 935
23 they *c*· unto the brook of Eshcol, "
26 they went and *c*· to Moses, and to "
27 We *c*· unto the land whither thou "
14:45 Amalekites *c*· down, and the 3381
16:27 Dathan and Abiram *c*· out, and 3318
31 And it *c*· to pass, as he had made 1961
35 there *c*· out a fire from the Lord, 3318
42 *c*· to pass, when the congregation 1961
43 And Moses and Aaron *c*· before 935
17: 8 it *c*· to pass, that on the morrow 1961
19: 2 and upon which never *c*· yoke. 5927
20: 1 Then *c*· the children of Israel, even 935
11 and the water *c*· out abundantly, 3318
20 And Edom *c*· out against him with "
22 Kadesh, and *c*· unto Mount Hor. 935
28 Eleazar *c*· down from the mount. 3381
21: 1 heard tell that Israel *c*· by the way 935
7 Therefore the people *c*· to Moses, "
9 and it *c*· to pass, that if a serpent 1961
23 and he *c*· to Jahaz, and fought 935
22: 7 they *c*· unto Balaam, and spake "
9 And God *c*· unto Balaam, and said, "
16 And they *c*· to Balaam, and said to "
20 And God *c*· unto Balaam at night, "
39 and they *c*· unto Kirjath-huzoth, "
41 And it *c*· to pass on the morrow, 1961
23:17 And when he *c*· to him, behold, he 935
24: 2 the spirit of God *c*· upon him. 1961
25: 6 one of the children of Israel *c*· 935
26: 1 And it *c*· to pass after the plague, 1961
27: 1 *c*· the daughters of Zelophehad, *7126
31:14 hundreds, which *c*· from the battle. 935
48 of hundreds, *c*· near unto Moses: 7126
32: 2 Reuben *c*· and spake unto Moses, 935
11 none of the men that *c*· up out of 5927
16 they *c*· near unto him, and said, 5066
33: 9 from Marah, and *c*· unto Elim: 935
36: 1 of the sons of Joseph, *c*· near, and 7126
De 1: 3 it *c*· to pass in the fortieth year, 1961
19 and we *c*· to Kadesh-barnea. 935
22 And ye *c*· near unto me every one 7126
24 and *c*· unto the valley of Eshcol, 935
31 ye went, until ye *c*· into this place. "
44 *c*· out against you, and chased 3318
2:14 which we *c*· from Kadesh-barnea, 1980
16 it *c*· to pass, when all the men 1961
23 which *c*· forth out of Caphtor, 3318
32 Then Sihon *c*· out against us, he "
3: 1 king of Bashan *c*· out against us, "
4:11 And ye *c*· near and stood under 7126
45 after they *c*· forth out of Egypt, 3318
5:23 *c*· to pass, when ye heard the voice 1961
23 that ye *c*· near unto me, even all 7126
9: 7 until ye *c*· unto this place, ye have 935
11 *c*· to pass at the end of forty days 1961
15 So I turned and *c*· down from the 3381
10: 5 I turned myself and *c*· down from "
11: 5 until ye *c*· into this place; 935
10 from whence ye *c*· out, where 3318
22:14 took this woman, and when I *c*· 7126
23: 4 when ye *c*· forth out of Egypt; 3318
29: 7 And when ye *c*· unto this place, 935
7 Og the king of Bashan, *c*· out 3318
16 how we *c*· through the nations 5674
31:24 And it *c*· to pass, when Moses 1961
32:17 to new gods that *c*· newly up, 935
44 And Moses *c*· and spake all the "
33: 2 The Lord *c*· from Sinai, and "
2 and he *c*· with ten thousands of 857
21 *c*· with the heads of the people, he "
Jos 1: 1 it *c*· to pass, that the Lord spake 1961
2: 1 and *c*· into an harlot's house, 935
2 there *c*· men in hither to night of "
4 There *c*· men unto me, but I "
5 it *c*· to pass about the time of 1961
8 *c*· up unto them upon the roof; 5927
10 when ye *c*· out of Egypt; and 3318
22 *c*· unto the mountain, and abode 935
23 and *c*· to Joshua the son of Nun, "
3: 1 *c*· to Jordan, he and all the "
2 And it *c*· to pass after three 1961
14 And it *c*· to pass, when the people "
16 waters which *c*· down from 3381

Jos 3:16 those that c' down toward the sea*3381
4: 1, 11 it c' to pass, when all the people 1961
18 it c' to pass, when the priests "
19 the people c' up out of Jordan on 5927
22 Israel c' over this Jordan on dry 5674
5: 1 it c' to pass, when all the kings 1961
4 the people that c' out of Egypt, 3318
4 the way, after they c' out of Egypt. "
5 all the people that c' out were "
5 as they c' forth out of Egypt, "
6 c' out of Egypt, were consumed, * "
8 it c' to pass, when they had done 1961
13 And it c' to pass, when Joshua was "
6: 1 none went out, and none c' in. 935
8 c' to pass, when Joshua had *1961
9 the rereward c' after the ark, *1980
11 and they c' into the camp, and 935
13 the rereward c' after the ark of 1980
15 it c' to pass on the seventh day, 1961
16 it c' to pass at the seventh time, "
20 c' to pass, when the people heard "
8:11 c' before the city, and pitched 935
14 it c' to pass, when the king of Ai 1961
24 And it c' to pass, when Israel "
9: 1 it c' to pass, when all the kings "
12 we c' forth to go unto you; but 3318
16 it c' to pass, at the end of three 1961
17 c' unto their cities on the third 935
10: 1 it c' to pass, when Adoni-zedec 1961
9 Joshua therefore c' unto them 935
11 And it c' to pass, as they fled 1961
20 And it c' to pass, when Joshua "
24 it c' to pass, when they brought "
24 they c' near, and put their feet 7126
27 And it c' to pass at the time of 1961
33 king of Gezer c' up to help 5927
11: 1 c' to pass, when Jabin king of 1961
5 they c' and pitched together at 935
7 So Joshua c', and all the people of "
21 And at that time c' Joshua, and "
14: 6 Then the children of Judah c' *5066
15:18 And it c' to pass, as she 1961
18 as she c' unto him, that she 935
16: 7 and c' to Jericho, and went out 6293
17: 4 they c' near before Eleazar the 7126
13 it c' to pass, when the children of 1961
18: 9 and c' again to Joshua to the host 935
11 the children of Benjamin c' up 5927
11 the coast of their lot c' forth *3318
16 And the border c' down to the *3381
19: 1 the second lot c' forth to Simeon, 3318
10 And the third lot c' up for the 5927
17 And the fourth lot c' out to 3318
24 the fifth lot c' out for the tribe "
32 The sixth lot c' out to the children "
40 And the seventh lot c' out for the "
21: 1 c' near the heads of the fathers 5066
4 the lot c' out for the families of 3318
45 the house of Israel; all c' to pass. 935
22:10 And when they c' unto the borders "
15 they c' unto the children of Reuben, "
23: 1 it c' to pass a long time after that 1961
24: 6 and ye c' unto the sea; and the 935
11 and c' unto Jericho: and the men "
29 it c' to pass after these things, 1961
J'g 1: 1 after the death of Joshua it c' to "
14 And it c' to pass, when she "
14 when she c' to him, that she 935
28 c' to pass, when Israel was strong, 1961
2: 1 an angel of the Lord c' up from 5927
4 it c' to pass, when the angel of the 1961
19 c' to pass, when the judge was "
3:10 the Spirit of the Lord c' upon him, "
20 Ehud c' unto him; and he was 935
22 of his belly: and the dirt c' out. 3318
24 his servants c'; and when they 935
27 it c' to pass, when he was come, 1961
4: 5 and the children of Israel c' up to 5927
22 Jael c' out to meet him, and said 3318
22 and when he c' into her tent, 935
5:14 out of Machir c' down governors, 3381
19 The kings c' and fought, then 935
23 because they c' not to the help of "
6: 3 that the Midianites c' up, and 5927
3 east, even they c' up against them; "
5 they c' up with their cattle and "
5 and they c' as grasshoppers 935
7 it c' to pass, when the children of 1961
11 And there c' an angel of the Lord, 935
25 And it c' to pass the same night, 1961
34 Spirit of the Lord c' upon Gideon, 3847
35 and they c' up to meet them. 5927
7: 9 And it c' to pass the same night, 1961
13 and c' unto a tent, and smote it 935
19 were with him, c' unto the outside "
8: 4 Gideon c' to Jordan, and passed "
15 And he c' unto the men of Succoth, "
33 it c' to pass, as soon as Gideon 1961
9:25 they robbed all that c' along that 5674
26 And Gaal the son of Ebed c' with 935
42 And it c' to pass on the morrow, 1961
52 And Abimelech c' unto the tower, 935
57 and upon them c' the curse of "
11: 4 c' to pass in process of time, that 1961
13 when they c' up out of Egypt, 5927
16 when Israel c' up from Egypt, "
16 the Red sea, and c' to Kadesh; 935
18 c' by the east side of the land of "
18 c' not within the border of Moab: "
29 Spirit of the Lord c' upon 1961
34 Jephthah c' to Mizpeh unto his 935
34 his daughter c' out to meet him 3318
35 it c' to pass, when he saw her, 1961
39 c' to pass at the end of two months, "
13: 6 woman c' and told her husband, 935
6 A man of God c' unto me, "
J'g 13: 9 the angel of God c' again unto the 935
10 that c' unto me the other day. "
11 c' to the man, and said unto him, "
20 it c' to pass, when the flame went 1961
14: 2 And he c' up, and told his father 5927
5 c' to the vineyards of Timnath: 935
6 Spirit of the Lord c' mightily 6743
9 and c' to his father and mother, 1980
11 it c' to pass, when they saw him, 1961
14 Out of the eater c' forth meat, 3318
14 out of the strong c' forth sweetness. "
15, 17 c' to pass on the seventh day, 1961
19 Spirit of the Lord c' upon him, 6743
15: 1 it c' to pass, within a while after, 1961
6 the Philistines c' up, and burnt 5927
14 he c' unto Lehi, the Philistines 935
14 Spirit of the Lord c' mightily 6743 "
17 c' to pass, when he had made an 1961
19 there c' water thereout; and when 3318
19 spirit c' again, and he revived: 7725
16: 4 it c' to pass afterward, that he 1961
5 lords of the Philistines c' up unto 5927
16 c' to pass, when she pressed him 1961
18 lords of the Philistines c' up unto 5927
25 it c' to pass, when their hearts 1961
31 the house of his father c' down, 3381
17: 8 he c' to mount Ephraim to the 935
18: 2 when they c' to mount Ephraim, "
7 c' to Laish, and saw the people "
8 they c' unto their brethren to Zorah "
13 and c' unto the house of Micah. "
15 c' to the house of the young man "
17 c' in thither, and took the graven "
27 and c' unto Laish, unto a people "
19: 1 And it c' to pass on those days, 1961
5 it c' to pass on the fourth day, "
10 and c' over against Jebus, which 935
16 there c' an old man from his work "
22 the man that c' into thine house, "
26 Then c' the woman in the dawning "
30 day that the children of Israel c' 5927
20: 4 I c' into Gibeah that belongeth to 935
21 the children of Benjamin c' forth 3318
24 And the children of Israel c' near 7126
26 c' unto the house of God, and wept, 935
33 c' forth out of their places, even *1518
34 there c' against Gibeah ten 935
42 them which c' out of the cities "
48 all that c' to hand: also they set *4672
48 all the cities that they c' to. * "
21: 2 the people c' to the house of God, 935
4 And it c' to pass on the morrow, 1961
5 c' not up with the congregation 5927
5 him that c' not up to the Lord "
8 c' not up to Mizpeh to the Lord? "
8 there c' none to the camp from 935
14 Benjamin c' again at that time; *7725
Ru 1: 1 it c' to pass in the days when 1961
2 they c' into the country of Moab, 935
19 until they c' to Beth-lehem. And it "
19 And it c' to pass, when they were 1961
22 until they c' to Beth-lehem in the 935
2: 3 she went, and c', and gleaned in "
4 Boaz c' from Beth-lehem, and said "
6 the Moabitish damsel that c' back 7725
7 among the sheaves: so she c', 935
3: 7 she c' softly, and uncovered his "
8 it c' to pass at midnight, that the 1961
14 that a woman c' into the floor. 935
16 when she c' to her mother in law, "
4: 1 of whom Boaz spake c' by; unto 5674
1Sa 1:12 c' to pass, as she continued 1961
19 and c' to their house to Ramah: 935
20 it c' to pass, when the time was 1961
2:13 sacrifice, the priest's servant c', 935
14 all the Israelites that c' thither. "
15 the priest's servant c', and said "
19 when she c' up with her husband 5927
27 there c' a man of God unto Eli, 935
3: 2 And it c' to pass at that time, 1961
10 the Lord c', and stood, and called 935
4: 1 the word of Samuel c' to all Israel. 1961
5 ark of the covenant of the Lord c' 935
12 and c' to Shiloh the same day with "
13 when he c', lo, Eli sat upon a seat "
13 when the man c' into the city, "
14 the man c' in hastily, and told Eli. "
16 I am he that c' out of the army, "
18 c' to pass, when he made mention 1961
19 for her pains c' upon her. 2015
5:10 it c' to pass, as the ark of God 1961
10 as the ark of God c' to Ekron, 935
6:14 the cart c' into the field of Joshua, "
7: 1 And the men of Kirjath-jearim c', "
2 it c' to pass, while the ark abode 1961
11 them, until they c' under Beth-car.
13 c' no more into the coast of Israel: 935
8: 1 c' to pass, when Samuel was old, 1961
4 and c' to Samuel unto Ramah, 935
9:12 for he c' to day to the city; for * "
14 Samuel c' out against them, for 3318
15 a day before Saul c', saying, 935
26 c' to pass about the spring of the 1961
10: 9 all those signs c' to pass that day. 935
10 when they c' thither to the hill, "
10 the Spirit of God c' upon him, 6743
11 c' to pass, when all that knew 1961
13 made an end of prophesying, he c' 935
14 were no where, we c' to Samuel. "
11: 1 Then Nahash the Ammonite c' up, 5927
4 Then c' the messengers to Gibeah 935
5 Saul c' after the herd out of the "
6 the Spirit of God c' upon Saul *6743
7 and they c' out with one consent. 3318
9 the messengers that c', Thus shall 935
9 the messengers c' and shewed it "
1Sa 11:11 they c' into the midst of the 935
11 and it c' to pass that they which 1961
12:12 Ammon c' against you, ye said 935
13: 5 c' up and pitched in Michmash, 5927
8 Samuel c' not to Gilgal: and the 935
10 it c' to pass, that as soon as he 1961
10 behold, Samuel c'; and Saul went 935
17 the spoilers c' out of the camp 3318
22 it c' to pass in the day of battle, 1961
14: 1 Now it c' to pass upon a day, * "
19 it c' to pass, while Saul talked "
20 they c' to the battle: and, behold, 935
25 all they of the land c' to a wood; "
15: 2 way, when he c' up from Egypt. 5927
5 And Saul c' to a city of Amalek, 935
6 when they c' up out of Egypt. 5927
10 c' the word of the Lord unto 1961
12 Saul c' to Carmel, and, behold, 935
13 Samuel c' to Saul: and Saul said "
32 And Agag c' unto him delicately. 1980
35 Samuel c' no more to see Saul
16: 4 spake, and c' to Beth-lehem. 935
6 c' to pass, when they were come, 1961
13 Spirit of the Lord c' upon David 6743
21 David c' to Saul, and stood before 935
23 it c' to pass, when the evil spirit 1961
17:20 he c' to the trench, as the host 935
22 and c' and saluted his brethren. "
23 there c' up the champion, the 5927
34 and there c' a lion, and a bear, 935
41 the Philistine c' on and drew 3212
48 it c' to pass, when the Philistine 1961
48 and c' and drew nigh to meet 3212
18: 1 c' to pass, when he had made 1961
6 And it c' to pass as they "
6 as they c', when David was 935
6 the women c' out of all cities 3318
10 And it c' to pass on the morrow, 1961
10 spirit from God c' upon Saul, 6473
13 out and c' in before the people. 935
16 he went out and c' in before them. "
19 c' to pass at the time when Merab 1961
30 it c' to pass, after they went forth, "
19:18 c' to Samuel to Ramah, and told 935
22 c' to a great well that is in Sechu: "
23 until he c' to Naioth in Ramah. "
20: 1 and c' and said before Jonathan, "
27 it c' to pass on the morrow, 1961
35 And it c' to pass in the morning, "
38 the arrows, and c' to his master. 935
21: 1 c' David to Nob to Ahimelech "
5 these three days, since I c' out, 3318
22: 5 and c' into the forest of Hareth. 935
11 they c' all of them to the king. "
23: 6 it c' to pass, when Abiathar 1961
6 c' down with an ephod in his 3381
19 Then c' up the Ziphites to Saul 5927
25 wherefore he c' down into a rock, 3381
27 there c' a messenger unto Saul, 935
24: 1 c' to pass, when Saul was 1961
3 he c' to the sheepcotes by the way, 935
5 c' to pass afterward, that David 1961
16 And it c' to pass, when David "
25: 9 when David's young men c', they 935
12 went again, and c' and told him all "
20 c' down by the covert of the hill, 3381
20 and his men c' down against her; "
36 Abigail c' to Nabal; and, behold, 935
37 But it c' to pass in the morning, 1916
38 it c' to pass about ten days after, "
26: 1 And the Ziphites c' unto Saul to 935
3 he saw that Saul c' after him into "
5 and c' to the place where Saul had "
7 David and Abishai c' to the people "
15 for there c' one of the people in to "
27: 9 and returned, and c' to Achish. "
28: 1 And it c' to pass in those days, 1961
4 and c' and pitched in Shunem: 935
8 they c' to the woman by night: "
21 And the woman c' unto Saul, "
30: 1 And it c' to pass, when David 1961
3 David and his men c' to the city, 935
9 and c' to the brook Besor, where "
12 when he had eaten, his spirit c' 7725
21 David c' to the two hundred men, 935
21 when David c' near to the people, 5066
23 the company that c' against us 935
26 when David c' to Ziklag, he sent "
31: 7 Philistines c' and dwelt in them. "
8 And it c' to pass on the morrow, 1691
8 Philistines c' to strip the slain, 935
12 c' to Jabesh, and burnt them "
2Sa 1: 1 c' to pass after the death of Saul, 1961
2 It c' even to pass on the third day, "
2 a man c' out of the camp from Saul 935
2 when he c' to David, that he fell to "
2: 1 And it c' to pass after this, that 1961
4 the men of Judah c', and there 935
23 that the spear c' out behind 3318
23 that as many as c' to the place 935
29 and they c' to Mahanaim. "
32 they c' to Hebron at break of day "
3: 6 it c' to pass, while there was war 1961
20 So Abner c' to David to Hebron, 935
22 Joab c' from pursuing a troop, "
23 Abner the son of Ner c' to the king, "
24 Then Joab c' to the king, and said, "
24 behold, Abner c' unto thee; why is "
25 he c' to deceive thee, and to know "
35 all the people c' to cause David to "
4: 4 when the tidings c' of Saul and "
4 c' to pass, as she made haste to 1961
5 c' about the heat of the day to the 935
6 And they c' thither into the midst "
7 For when they c' into the house, "
5: 1 c' all the tribes of Israel to David "

2Sa 5: 3 the elders of Israel c' to the king 935
17 Philistines c' up to seek David; *5927
18 Philistines also c' and spread * 935
20 And David c' to Baal-perazim, "
22 Philistines c' up yet again, and 5927
6: 6 they c' to Nachon's threshingfloor, 935
16 the ark of the Lord c' into the city "
20 daughter of Saul c' out to meet 3318
7: 1 it c' to pass, when the king sat in 1961
4 c' to pass that night, that the "
4 word of the Lord c' unto Nathan, "
8: 1 c' to pass, that David smote the "
5 Syrians of Damascus c' to succour 935
10: 1 And it c' to pass after this, that 1961
2 David's servants c' into the land 935
8 the children of Ammon c' out, 3318
14 of Ammon, and c' to Jerusalem. 935
16 and they c' to Helam; and Shobach "
17 over Jordan, and c' to Helam. "
11: 1 And it c' to pass, after the year 1961
2 it c' to pass in an evening tide, "
4 and she c' in unto him, and he lay 935
14 And it c' to pass in the morning 1961
16 it c' to pass, when Joab observed "
22 and c' and shewed David all that 935
23 and c' out unto us into the field, 3318
12: 1 he c' unto him, and said unto him, 935
4 And there c' a traveller unto the "
18 it c' to pass on the seventh day, 1961
20 and c' into the house of the Lord, 935
20 then he c' to his own house; "
13: 1 c' to pass after this, that Absalom 1961
23 it c' to pass after two full years, "
24 Absalom c' to the king, 935
30 And it c' to pass, while they were 1961
30 that tidings c' to David, saying, 935
34 there c' much people by the way 1980
36 it c' to pass, as soon as he had 1961
36 behold, the king's sons c', 935
14:31 and c' to Absalom unto his house, "
33 Joab c' to the king, and told him: "
33 called for Absalom, he c' to the "
15: 1 c' to pass after this, that 1961
2 c' to the king for judgment, * 935
5 when any man c' nigh to him to 7126
6 all Israel that c' to the king for 935
7 And it c' to pass after forty years, 1961
13 there c' a messenger to David, 935
18 six hundred men which c' after 935
32 it c' to pass, that when David 1961
32 Hushai the Archite c' to meet him "
37 Hushai David's friend c' into the 935
37 Absalom c' into Jerusalem. "
16: 5 when king David c' to Bahurim, "
5 behold, thence c' out a man 3318
5 he c' forth, and cursed still as he "
5 and cursed still as he c'. "
11 my son, which c' forth of my "
14 the people that were with him, c' 935
15 the men of Israel, c' to Jerusalem, "
16 it c' to pass, when Hushai the 1961
17:18 c' to a man's house in Bahurim, 935
20 And when Absalom's servants c' "
21 c' to pass, after they were 1961
21 that they c' up out of the well, 5927
24 Then David c' to Mahanaim. 935
27 And it c' to pass, when David 1961
18: 4 all the people c' out by hundreds *3318
25 And he c' apace, and drew near. 3212
31 And, behold, Cushi c'; and Cushi 935
19: 5 Joab c' into the house to the king, "
8 all the people c' before the king: "
15 king returned, and c' to Jordan. "
15 And Judah c' to Gilgal, "
16 c' down with the men of Judah 3381
24 the son of Saul c' down to meet "
24 until the day he c' again in peace. 935
25 And it c' to pass, when he was 1961
31 Gileadite c' down from Rogelim, 3381
41 all the men of Israel c' to the king, 935
20: 3 David c' to his house at Jerusalem; "
12 every one that c' by him stood still. "
15 they c' and besieged him in Abel "
21:18 c' to pass after this, that there 1961
22:10 bowed the heavens also, and c' 3381
23:13 c' to David in the harvest time 935
24: 6 Then they c' to Gilead, and to the "
6 and they c' to Dan-jaan, "
7 And c' to the stronghold of Tyre, "
8 all the land, they c' to Jerusalem "
11 the word of the Lord c' unto the 1961
13 So Gad c' to David, and told him, 935
18 And Gad c' that day to David, "
1Ki 1:22 Nathan the prophet also c' in. "
28 And she c' into the king's presence, "
32 And they c' before the king. "
40 all the people c' up after him, 5927
42 Abiathar the priest c': and 935
47 the king's servants c' to bless our "
53 he c' and bowed himself to king 7126
2: 7 they c' to me when I fled because 935
8 he c' down to meet me at Jordan, 3381
13 son of Haggith c' to Bathsheba 935
28 Then tidings c' to Joab: for Joab "
30 And Benaiah c' to the tabernacle "
39 c' to pass at the end of three 1961
3:15 And he c' to Jerusalem, and stood 935
16 Then c' there two women, that "
18 And it c' to pass the third day 1961
4:27 that c' unto king Solomon's table, 7131
34 And there c' of all people to hear 935
5: 7 it c' to pass, when Hiram heard 1961
6: 1 it c' to pass in the four hundred "
11 word of the Lord c' to Solomon, "
7:14 And he c' to king Solomon, 935
8: 3 And all the elders of Israel c' "

1Ki 8: 9 they c' out of the land of Egypt. 3318
10 c' to pass, when the priests were 1961
9: 1 And it c' to pass, when Solomon "
10 c' to pass at the end of twenty "
12 And Hiram c' out from Tyre 3318
24 Pharaoh's daughter c' up out of 5927
28 And they c' to Ophir, and fetched 935
10: 1 c' to prove him with hard questions. "
2 And she c' to Jerusalem with a "
7 believed not the words, until I c', "
10 c' no more such abundance of spices "
12 there c' no such almug trees, "
14 gold that c' to Solomon in one year "
22 once in three years c' the navy of "
29 And a chariot c' up and went out 5927
11: 4 c' to pass, when Solomon was old, 1961
15 c' to pass, when David was in "
18 and c' to Paran: and they took 935
18 out of Paran, and they c' to Egypt, "
29 it c' to pass at that time when 1961
12: 2 And it c' to pass, when Jeroboam "
3 all the congregation of Israel c', 935
12 Jeroboam and all the people c' to "
20 And it c' to pass, when all Israel 1961
22 word of God c' unto Shemaiah "
13: 1 there c' a man of God out of Judah 935
4 it c' to pass, when king Jeroboam 1961
10 returned not by the way that he c' 935
11 and his sons c' and told him all "
12 God went, which c' from Judah. "
20 c' to pass, as they sat at the table, 1961
20 the word of the Lord c' unto the "
21 that c' from Judah, saying, 935
23 c' to pass, after he had eaten 1961
25 and they c' and told it in the city 935
29 and the old prophet c' to the city, "
31 c' to pass, after he had buried 1961
14: 4 and c' to the house of Ahijah. 935
6 as she c' in at the door, that he "
17 and departed, and c' to Tirzah: "
17 c' to the threshold of the door, "
25 And it c' to pass in the fifth year 1961
25 of Egypt c' up against Jerusalem: 5927
15:21 it c' to pass, when Baasha heard 1961
29 it c' to pass, when he reigned, "
16: 1 the word of the Lord c' to Jehu "
7 Jehu the son of Hanani c' the "
11 c' to pass, when he began to reign, "
18 c' to pass, when Zimri saw that "
31 c' to pass, as if it had been a light "
17: 2 the word of the Lord c' unto him, "
7 And it c' to pass after a while, that "
8 word of the Lord c' unto him, "
10 when he c' to the gate of the city, 935
17 it c' to pass after these things, 1961
22 soul of the child c' into him again, 7725
18: 1 it c' to pass after many days, 1961
1 the word of the Lord c' to Elijah "
17 c' to pass, when Ahab saw Elijah, "
21 And Elijah c' unto all the people, 5066
27 it c' to pass at noon, that Elijah 1961
29 c' to pass, when midday was past,* "
30 all the people c' near unto him. 5066
31 word of the Lord c', saying, Israel 1961
36 And it c' to pass at the time of the "
36 that Elijah the prophet c' near, 5066
44 c' to pass at the seventh time, 1961
45 it c' to pass in the mean while, "
19: 3 and c' to Beer-sheba, which 935
4 c' and sat down under a juniper "
7 the angel of the Lord c' again 7725
9 And he c' thither unto a cave, 935
9 behold, the word of the Lord c' to "
20: 5 the messengers c' again, and said, 7725
12 c' to pass, when Benhadad heard 1961
13 there c' a prophet unto Ahab king 5066
19 the princes of the provinces c' *3318
22 the prophet c' to the king of Israel, 5066
26 c' to pass at the return of the year, 1961
28 there c' a man of God, and spake 5066
30 Ben-hadad fled, and c' into the 935
32 c' to the king of Israel, and said, "
33 Then Ben-hadad c' forth to him; 3318
43 and displeased, and c' to Samaria. 935
21: 1 it c' to pass after these things, 1961
4 Ahab c' into his house heavy and 935
5 But Jezebel his wife c' to him, and "
13 there c' in two men, children of "
15 c' to pass, when Jezebel heard 1961
16 And it c' to pass, when Ahab heard "
17 word of the Lord c' to Elijah "
27 And it c' to pass, when Ahab heard "
28 the word of the Lord c' to Elijah "
22: 2 it c' to pass in the third year, "
2 the king of Judah c' down 3381
15 So he c' to the king. And the * 935
21 there c' forth a spirit, and stood 3318
32, 33 it c' to pass, when the captains 1961
2Ki 1: 6 There c' a man up to meet us, 5927
7 manner of man was he which c' "
10 there c' down fire from heaven, 3381
12 fire of God c' down from heaven, "
13 c' and fell on his knees before 935
14 there c' fire down from heaven, 3381
2: 1 c' to pass, when the Lord would 1961
3 that were at Beth-el c' forth 3318
4 leave thee. So they c' to Jericho. 935
5 that were at Jericho c' to Elisha, *5066
9 it c' to pass, when they were 1961
11 c' to pass, as they still went on, "
15 they c' to meet him, and bowed 935
18 when they c' again to him, (for he 7725
23 there c' forth little children out 3318
24 there c' forth two she bears out "
3: 5 it c' to pass, when Ahab was dead, 1961
15 it c' to pass, when the minstrel "

2Ki 3:15 the hand of the Lord c' upon him. 1961
20 c' to pass in the morning, when "
20 there c' water by the way of Edom, 935
24 when they c' to the camp of Israel, "
4: 6 it c' to pass, when the vessels 1961
7 Then she c' and told the man of 935
11 that he c' thither, and he turned "
25 went, and c' unto the man of God "
25 it c' to pass, when the man of God 1961
27 when she c' to the man of God to 935
27 Gehazi c' near to thrust her away. 5066
38 Elisha c' again to Gilgal: and 7725
39 c' and shred them into the pot of 935
40 it c' to pass, as they were eating 1961
42 there c' a man from Baal-shalisha, 935
5: 7 it c' to pass, when the king of 1961
9 So Naaman c' with his horses 935
13 his servants c' near, and spake 5066
14 his flesh c' again like unto the 7725
15 and c', and stood before him: 935
24 And when he c' to the tower, he "
6: 4 when they c' to Jordan, they cut "
14 they c' by night, and compassed "
18 when they c' down to him, Elisha 3381
20 it c' to pass, when they were come 1961
23 the bands of Syria c' no more into 935
24 c' to pass after this, that 1961
30 it c' to pass, when the king heard "
32 ere the messenger c' to him, he 935
33 behold, the messenger c' down 3381
7: 8 when these lepers c' to the * 935
8 c' again, and entered into 7725
10 they c', and called unto the porter 935
10 We c' to the camp of the Syrians, "
17 when the king c' down to him. 3381
18 it c' to pass as the man of God 1961
8: 3 c' to pass at the seven years' end, "
5 it c' to pass, as he was telling the "
7 And Elisha c' to Damascus; and 935
9 c' and stood before him, and said, "
14 and c' to his master; who said to "
15 it c' to pass on the morrow, that 1961
9: 5 when he c', behold, the captains of 935
11 Jehu c' forth to the servants of 3318
11 wherefore c' this mad fellow to 935
17 spied the company of Jehu as he c', "
18 The messenger c' to them, but he "
19 on horseback, which c' to them, "
20 He c' even unto them, and cometh "
22 c' to pass, when Joram saw Jehu, 1961
36 Wherefore they c' again, and told 7725
10: 7 And it c' to pass, when the letter 1961
7 when the letter c' to them, 935
8 And there c' a messenger, and told "
9 it c' to pass in the morning, that 1961
12 and departed, and c' to Samaria. *1980
17 And when he c' to Samaria, he slew 935
21 and all the worshippers of Baal c', "
21 not a man left that c' not. "
21 And they c' into the house of Baal; "
25 it c' to pass, as soon as he had 1961
11: 9 and c' to Jehoiada the priest, 935
13 she c' to the people into the temple "
16 way by the which the horses c' *3996
19 and c' by the way of the gate of 935
12:10 scribe and the high priest c' up, 5927
13:14 Joash the king of Israel c' down 3381
21 it c' to pass, as they were burying 1961
14: 5 c' to pass, as soon as the kingdom "
13 and c' to Jerusalem, and brake 935
15:12 And so it c' to pass. 1961
14 and c' to Samaria, and smote 935
19 of Assyria c' against the land: "
29 c' Tiglath-pileser king of Assyria, "
16: 5 son of Remaliah king of Israel c' 5927
6 the Syrians c' to Elath, and dwelt 935
11 against king Ahaz c' from Damascus. "
17: 3 Against him c' up Shalmaneser 5927
5 Then the king of Assyria c' up "
28 had carried away from Samaria c'. 935
18: 1 it c' to pass in the third year of 1961
9 it c' to pass in the fourth year of "
9 Shalmaneser king of Assyria c' up 5927
17 and c' to Jerusalem. And when 935
17 they were come up, they c' and 935
18 there c' out to them Eliakim the 3318
37 Then c' Eliakim the son of Hilkiah, 935
19: 1 it c' to pass, when king Hezekiah 1961
5 So the servants of king Hezekiah c' 935
33 By the way that he c', by the same "
35 c' to pass that night, that the 1961
37 And it c' to pass, as he was "
20: 1 prophet Isaiah the son of Amoz c' 935
4 c' to pass, afore Isaiah was gone 1961
4 word of the Lord c' to him, saying, "
14 Then c' Isaiah the prophet unto 935
14 from whence c' they unto thee? "
21:15 the day their fathers c' forth out 3318
22: 3 it c' to pass in the eighteenth year 1961
9 Shaphan the scribe c' to the king, 935
11 c' to pass, when the king had 1961
23: 9 the priests of the high places c' 5927
17 which c' from Judah, and 935
18 prophet that c' out of Samaria. "
34 he c' to Egypt, and died there. "
24: 1 king of Babylon c' up, and 5927
3 c' this upon Judah, to remove 1961
7 And the king of Egypt c' not 3318
10 king of Babylon c' up against 5927
11 Nebuchadnezzar king of Babylon c' 935
20 c' to pass in Jerusalem and *1961
25: 1 it c' to pass in the ninth year of "
1 king of Babylon c', he, and all 935
8 king of Babylon, c' Nebuzar-adan, "
23 there c' to Gedaliah, to Mizpah, "
25 c' to pass in the seventh month, 1961

2Ki 25:25 c', and ten men with him, and 935
26 and c' to Egypt: for they were "
27 it c' to pass in the seven and 1961
1Ch 1:12 (of whom c' the Philistines,) and 3318
2:53 of them c' the Zareathites, and "
55 the Kenites that c' of Hemath, the 935
4:41 And these written by name c' in "
5: 2 and of him c' the chief ruler; but "
7:21 because they c' down to take away 3381
22 and his brethren c' to comfort him. 935
10: 7 the Philistines c' and dwelt in "
8 it c' to pass on the morrow, 1961
8 when the Philistines c' to strip the 935
11: 3 Therefore c' all the elders of Israel "
12: 1 these are they that c' to David "
16 And there c' of the children of "
18 the spirit c' upon Amasai, who 3847
19 when he c' with the Philistines 935
22 there c' to David to help him, "
23 c' to David to Hebron, to turn the "
38 c' with a perfect heart to Hebron, "
13: 9 they c' unto the threshingfloor "
14: 9 the Philistines c' and spread * "
11 So they c' up to Baal-perazim; 5927
15:26 c' to pass, when God helped the 1961
29 And it c' to pass, as the ark of the "
29 ark of the covenant of the Lord c' 935
17: 1 it c' to pass, as David sat in his 1961
3 And it c' to pass the same night, "
16 And David the king c' and sat * 935
18: 1 it c' to pass, that David smote the 1961
5 Syrians of Damascus c' to help 935
19: 1 c' to pass after this, that Nahash 1961
2 So the servants of David c' into 935
7 who c' and pitched before Medeba. "
7 from their cities, and c' to battle. "
9 the children of Ammon c' out, 3318
15 city. Then Joab c' to Jerusalem. 935
17 and c' upon them, and set the "
20: 1 it c' to pass, that after the year 1961
1 and c' and besieged Rabbah. 935
4 And it c' to pass after this, that 1961
21: 4 all Israel, and c' to Jerusalem. 935
11 So Gad c' to David, and said unto "
21 And as David c' to Ornan, Ornan "
22: 8 But the word of the Lord c' to me, 1961
24: 7 the first lot c' forth to Jehoiarib, 3318
28 Mahli c' Eleazar, who had no son *
25: 9 the first lot c' forth for Asaph 3318
26:14 lots; and his lot c' out northward. "
16 Hosah the lot c' forth westward, *
27: 1 which c' in and went out month 935
2Ch 1:13 Solomon c' from his journey to "
5: 4 And all the elders of Israel c'; "
10 children of Israel, when they c' out 3318
11 And it c' to pass, when the priests 1961
13 It c' even to pass, as the trumpeters "
7: 1 the fire c' down from heaven, and 3381
3 Israel saw how the fire c' down, "
11 all that c' into Solomon's heart to 935
8: 1 it c' to pass at the end of twenty 1961
9: 1 she c' to prove Solomon with hard 935
6 believed not their words, until I c' "
13 Now the weight of gold that c' to "
21 c' the ships of Tarshish bringing "
10: 2 And it c' to pass, when Jeroboam 1961
3 So Jeroboam and all Israel c' and 935
12 So Jeroboam and all the people c' "
11: 2 word of the Lord c' to Shemaiah 1961
14 and c' to Judah and Jerusalem: 3212
16 c' to Jerusalem, to sacrifice unto 935
12: 1 it c' to pass, when Rehoboam had 1961
2 it c' to pass, that in the fifth year "
2 Shishak king of Egypt c' up 5927
3 that c' with him out of Egypt; 935
4 to Judah, and c' to Jerusalem. "
5 Then c' Shemaiah, the prophet to "
7 word of the Lord c' to Shemaiah, 1961
9 So Shishak king of Egypt c' up 5927
11 the guard c' and fetched them, 935
13:15 of Judah shouted, it c' to pass, 1961
14: 9 there c' out against them Zerah 3318
9 chariots; and c' unto Mareshah. 935
14 the fear of the Lord c' upon them: 1961
15: 1 the Spirit of God c' upon Azariah "
5 nor to him that c' in, but great 935
16: 1 Baasha king of Israel c' up *5927
5 it c' to pass, when Baasha heard 1961
7 Hanani the seer c' to Asa king of 935
18:20 Then there c' out a spirit, and 3318
23 the son of Chenaanah c' near, 5066
31 it c' to pass, when the captains of 1961
32 For it c' to pass, that, when the "
20: 1 c' to pass after this also, that the "
1 Ammonites c' against Jehoshaphat 935
2 c' some that told Jehoshaphat, "
4 of Judah they c' to seek the Lord. "
10 invade, when they c' out of the land, "
14 Asaph, c' the Spirit of the Lord 1961
24 Judah c' toward the watch tower 935
25 when Jehoshaphat and his people c' "
28 And they c' to Jerusalem with "
21:12 And there c' a writing to him from "
17 And they c' up into Judah, and 5927
19 c' to pass, that in process of time, 1961
22: 1 the band of men that c' with the 935
8 c' to pass, that, when Jehu was 1961
23: 2 Israel, and they c' to Jerusalem. 935
12 and praising the king, she c' to "
20 they c' through the high gate into "
24: 4 it c' to pass after this, that Joash 1961
11 it c' to pass, that at what time * "
11 high priest's officer c' and emptied 935
17 c' the princes of Judah, and made "
18 c' upon Judah and Jerusalem 1961
20 the Spirit of God c' upon Zechariah 3847

2Ch 24:23 it c' to pass at the end of the year, 1961
23 host of Syria c' up against him: 5927
23 and they c' to Judah 935
24 c' with a small company of men, "
25: 3 it c' to pass, when the kingdom 1961
7 But there c' a man of God to him, 935
14 it c' to pass, after that Amaziah 1961
16 it c' to pass, as he talked with "
20 would not hear; for it c' of *
28: 9 went out before the host that c' to 935
12 against them that c' from the war. "
20 Tilgath-pilneser king of Assyria c' "
29:15 sanctified themselves, and c', * "
17 c' they to the porch of the Lord: "
30:11 themselves, and c' to Jerusalem. "
25 all the congregation that c' out of "
25 and the strangers that c' "
27 their prayer c' up to his holy "
31: 5 as the commandment c' abroad, 6555
8 Hezekiah and the princes c' and 935
32: 1 Sennacherib king of Assyria c', and "
21 they that c' forth of his own bowels 3329
26 the wrath of the Lord c' not upon 935
34: 9 And when they c' to Hilkiah the "
19 And it c' to pass, when the king 1961
35:20 Necho king of Egypt c' up to fight *5927
22 c' to fight in the valley of Megiddo. 935
36: 6 c' up Nebuchadnezzar king of 5927
Ezr 2: 1 and c' again unto Jerusalem and *7725
2 Which c' with Zerubbabel: Jeshua, 935
68 they c' to the house of the Lord "
4: 2 Then they c' to Zerubbabel, and *5066
12 the Jews which c' up from thee 5559
5: 3 At the same time c' to them Tatni, 858
5 till the matter c' to Darius: and *1946
16 Then c' the same Sheshbazzar, 858
7: 8 c' to Jerusalem in the fifth month, 935
9 c' he to Jerusalem, according to "
8:32 And we c' to Jerusalem, and abode "
9: 1 the princes c' to me, saying, *5066
10: 6 he c' thither, he did eat no bread, 3212
Ne 1: 1 it c' to pass in the month Chisleu, 1961
2 Hanani, one of my brethren, c', he 935
4 it c' to pass, when I heard these 1961
2: 1 it c' to pass in the month Nisan "
9 Then I c' to the governors beyond 935
11 So I c' to Jerusalem, and was there "
4: 1, 7 c' to pass, that when Sanballat, 1961
12 it c' to pass, that when the Jews "
12 the Jews which dwelt by them c' 935
15 it c' to pass, when our enemies 1961
16 And it c' to pass from that time "
5:17 beside those that c' unto us from 935
6: 1 Now it c' to pass, when Sanballat, 1961
10 I c' unto the house of Shemaiah * 935
16 it c' to pass, that when all our 1961
17 the letters of Tobiah c' unto them. 935
7: 1 It c' to pass, when the wall was 1961
5 the genealogy of them which c' up 5927
6 and c' again to Jerusalem and *7725
7 Who c' with Zerubbabel, Jeshua, 935
73 when the seventh month c', the *5060
13: 3 c' to pass, when they had heard 1961
6 c' I unto the king, and after * 935
7 I c' to Jerusalem, and understood "
19 it c' to pass, that when the gates 1961
21 c' they no more on the sabbath. 935
Es 1: 1 Now it c' to pass in the days of 1961
17 in before him, but she c' not. 935
2: 8 So it c' to pass, when the king's 1961
13 Then thus c' every maiden unto 935
14 she c' in unto the king no more, "
3: 4 Now it c' to pass, when they 1961
4: 2 c' even before the king's gate: 935
3 commandment and his decree c', 5060
4 maids and her chamberlains c' 935
9 And Hatach c' and told Esther "
5: 1 it c' to pass on the third day 1961
5 So the king and Haman c' to the 935
10 and when he c' home, he sent * "
6: 6 So Haman c' in. And the king "
12 Mordecai c' again to the king's 7725
14 c' the king's chamberlains, 935
7: 1 king and Haman c' to banquet "
8: 1 Mordecai c' before the king; "
17 commandment and his decree c', 5060
9:25 when Esther c' before the king, 935
Job 1: 6 a day when the sons of God c' "
6 and Satan c' also among them. "
14 there c' a messenger unto Job, "
16, 17, 18 c' also another, and said, "
19 there c' a great wind from the "
21 c' I out of my mother's womb, 3318
2: 1 a day when the sons of God c' 935
1 and Satan c' also among them "
11 c' every one from his own place; "
3:11 when I c' out of the belly? ‡3318
26 was I quiet; yet trouble c'. * 935
4:14 Fear c' upon me, and trembling, 7122
6:20 they c' thither, and were ashamed. 935
26: 4 and whose spirit c' from thee? 3318
29:13 was ready to perish c' upon me: 935
30:14 They c' upon me as a wide * 857
26 then evil c' unto me: and when I 935
26 waited for light, there c' darkness. "
38:29 Out of whose womb c' the ice? 3318
42:11 Then c' there unto him all his 935
Ps 18: 6 and my cry c' before him, even "
9 the heavens also, and c' down: 3381
27: 2 c' upon me to eat up my flesh, 7126
51:*title* when Nathan the prophet c' 935
52:*title* when Doeg the Edomite c' and "
54:*title* when the Ziphims c' and said "
78:21 anger also c' up against Israel; *5927
31 The wrath of God c' upon them, * "
88:17 They c' round about me daily 5437

Ps 105:19 Until the time that his word c': * 935
23 Israel also c' into Egypt; and "
31 and there c' divers sorts of flies, "
34 He spake, and the locusts c', "
Pr 7:15 Therefore c' I forth to meet thee, 3318
Ec 5:15 he c' forth of his mother's "
15 shall he return to go as he c', 935
16 in all points as he c', so shall he go: "
9:14 there c' a great king against it, "
Ca 4: 2 which c' up from the washing; *5927
Isa 7: 1 And it c' to pass in the day of 1961
11:16 in the days that he c' up out of 5927
20: 1 that Tartan c' unto Ashdod, 935
30: 4 his ambassadors c' to Hanes. *5060
36: 1 Now it c' to pass in the fourteenth 1961
1 Sennacherib king of Assyria c' up 5927
3 Then c' forth unto him Eliakim, 3318
22 Then c' Eliakim, the son of 935
37: 1 c' to pass, when king Hezekiah 1961
5 servants of king Hezekiah c' to 935
34 By the way that he c', by the same "
38 c' to pass, as he was worshipping 1961
38: 1 the son of Amoz c' unto him, 935
4 Then c' the word of the Lord to 1961
39: 3 Then c' Isaiah the prophet unto 935
3 from whence c' they unto thee? "
41: 5 were afraid, drew near, and c'. 857
48: 3 suddenly, and they c' to pass. 935
5 before it c' to pass I shewed it "
50: 2 when I c', was there no man? "
66: 7 before her pain c', she was "
Jer 1: 2 word of the Lord c' in the days 1961
3 c' also in the day of Jehoiakim "
4 word of the Lord c' unto me, "
11 the word of the Lord c' unto me "
13 word of the Lord c' unto me the "
2: 1 word of the Lord c' to me, "
3: 9 it c' to pass through the lightness "
7: 1 The word that c' to Jeremiah from "
25 day that your fathers c' forth 3318
31 neither c' it into my heart. 5927
8:15 looked for peace, but no good c'; "
11: 1 The word that c' to Jeremiah 1961
13: 3 And the word of the Lord c' unto "
6 it c' to pass after many days, "
8 the word of the Lord c' unto me, "
14: 1 c' to Jeremiah concerning the "
3 they c' to the pits, and found no * 935
16: 1 The word of the Lord c' also unto 1961
17:16 that which c' out of my lips was 4161
18: 1 The word which c' to Jeremiah 1961
5 Then the word of the Lord c' to "
19: 5 neither c' it into my mind: 5927
14 Then c' Jeremiah from Tophet, 935
20: 3 And it c' to pass on the morrow, 1961
18 Wherefore c' I forth out of the 3318
21: 1 the word which c' unto Jeremiah 1961
24: 4 the word of the Lord c' unto me, "
25: 1 The word that c' to Jeremiah "
26: 1 Judah c' this word from the Lord, "
8 Now it c' to pass, when Jeremiah "
10 they c' up from the king's house 5927
27: 1 came this word unto Jeremiah 1961
28: 1 And it c' to pass the same year, "
12 word of the Lord c' unto Jeremiah "
29:30 Then c' the word of the Lord unto "
30: 1 The word that c' to Jeremiah from "
32: 1 The word that c' to Jeremiah from "
6 The word of the Lord c' unto me, "
8 Hanameel mine uncle's son c' to 935
23 And they c' in, and possessed it; "
26 Then c' the word of the Lord unto 1961
35 neither c' it into my mind, that 5927
33: 1 word of the Lord c' unto Jeremiah 1961
19 word of the Lord c' unto Jeremiah, "
23 word of the Lord c' to Jeremiah, "
34: 1 The word which c' unto Jeremiah "
8 This is the word that c' unto "
12 word of the Lord c' to Jeremiah "
35: 1 The word which c' unto Jeremiah "
11 But it c' to pass, when "
11 king of Babylon c' up into the land, 5927
12 Then c' the word of the Lord 1961
36: 1 And it c' to pass in the fourth "
1 c' unto Jeremiah from the Lord, "
9 And it c' to pass in the fifth year "
9 to all the people that c' from the 935
14 in his hand, and c' unto them. "
16 Now it c' to pass when they had 1961
23 it c' to pass, that when Jehudi "
27 word of the Lord c' to Jeremiah, "
37: 4 Jeremiah c' in and went out 935
6 Then c' the word of the Lord 1961
11 it c' to pass, that when the army "
38:27 c' all the princes unto Jeremiah, 935
39: 1 c' Nebuchadrezzar king of Babylon "
3 of the king of Babylon c' in, "
4 it c' to pass, that when Zedekiah 1961
15 c' unto Jeremiah, while he was "
40: 1 The word that c' to Jeremiah "
8 Then they c' to Gedaliah to 935
12 and c' to the land of Judah, to "
13 fields, c' to Gedaliah to Mizpah, "
41: 1 it c' to pass in the seventh month, 1961
1 c' unto Gedaliah the son of Ahikam 935
4 it c' to pass the second day after 1961
5 there c' certain from Shechem, 935
6 and it c' to pass, as he met them, 1961
7 when they c' into the midst of 935
13 Now it c' to pass, that when all 1961
42: 1 even unto the greatest, c' near, 5066
7 And it c' to pass after ten days, 1961
7 that the word of the Lord c' unto "
43: 1 it c' to pass, that when Jeremiah "
7 they c' into the land of Egypt: 935
7 the Lord: thus c' they even to "

Jer 43: 8 Then c' the word of the Lord 1961
44: 1 The word that c' to Jeremiah "
21 and c' it not into his mind? 5927
46: 1 The word of the Lord which c' to 1961
47: 1 word of the Lord that c' to "
49:34 of the Lord that c' to Jeremiah "
52: 3 anger of the Lord it c' to pass * "
4 it c' to pass in the ninth year of "
4 Nebuchadrezzar king of Babylon c',935
12 c' Nebuzar-adan, captain of the "
31 And it c' to pass in the seven 1961
La 1: 9 end; therefore she c' down *3381
Eze 1: 1 it c' to pass in the thirtieth year 1961
3 word of the Lord c' expressly "
4 whirlwind c' out of the north, 935
5 the midst thereof c' the likeness "
3:15 Then I c' to them of the captivity 935
16 it c' to pass at the end of seven 1961
16 of the Lord c' unto me, saying, "
4:14 neither c' there abominable 935
6: 1 the word of the Lord c' unto me, 1961
7: 1 the word of the Lord c' unto me, "
8: 1 And it c' to pass in the sixth "
9: 2 six men c' from the way of the 935
8 it c' to pass, while they were 1961
10: 6 it c' to pass, that when he had "
11:13 it c' to pass, when I prophesied, "
14 the word of the Lord c' unto me, "
12: 1 The word of the Lord also c' unto "
8 in the morning c' the word of the "
17 word of the Lord c' to me, saying, "
21 word of the Lord c' unto me, "
26 word of the Lord c' to me, saying, "
13: 1 word of the Lord c' unto me, "
14: 1 Then c' certain of the elders of 935
2 word of the Lord c' unto me, 1961
12 word of the Lord c' again to me, "
15: 1 word of the Lord c' unto me, "
16: 1 the word of the Lord c' unto me, "
23 c' to pass after all thy * "
17: 1 word of the Lord c' unto me, "
3 c' unto Lebanon, and took the 935
11 word of the Lord c' unto me. 1961
18: 1 word of the Lord c' unto me again, "
20: 1 it c' to pass in the seventh year, "
1 certain of the elders of Israel c' 935
2 Then c' the word of the Lord 1961
45 of the Lord c' unto me, saying, "
21: 1 word of the Lord c' unto me, "
8 the word of the Lord c' unto me, "
18 word of the Lord c' unto me again, "
22: 1, 17, 23 word of the Lord c' unto me, "
23: 1 word of the Lord c' again unto me, "
17 And the Babylonians c' to her into 935
39 then they c' the same day into "
40 lo, they c': for whom thou didst "
24: 1, 15, 20 word of the Lord c' unto 1961
25: 1 word of the Lord c' again unto me, "
26: 1 it c' to pass in the eleventh year, "
1 of the Lord c' unto me, saying, "
27: 1 word of the Lord c' again unto me, "
28: 1 The word of the Lord c' again "
11 Moreover the word of the Lord c' "
20 word of the Lord c' unto me, "
29: 1 of the Lord c' unto me, saying, "
17 And it c' to pass in the seven and "
17 the word of the Lord c' unto me, "
30: 1 word of the Lord c' again unto "
20 it c' to pass in the eleventh year, "
20 the word of the Lord c' unto me, "
31: 1 it c' to pass in the eleventh year, "
1 the word of the Lord c' unto me, "
32: 1 it c' to pass in the twelfth year, "
1 the word of the Lord c' unto me, "
17 c' to pass also in the twelfth year, "
17 of the Lord c' unto me, saying, "
33: 1 word of the Lord c' unto me, "
21 it c' to pass in the twelfth year of "
21 c' unto me, saying, The city is 935
22 afore he that was escaped c'; and "
22 until he c' to me in the morning; "
25 the word of the Lord c' unto me, 1961
34: 1 the word of the Lord c' unto me, "
35: 1 the word of the Lord c' unto me, "
36:16 the word of the Lord c' unto me, "
37: 7 the bones c' together, bone to his 7126
8 the sinews and the flesh c' up 5927
10 the breath c' into them, and they 935
15 The word of the Lord c' again 1961
38: 1 the word of the Lord c' unto me, "
40: 6 Then c' he unto the gate which 935
43: 2 the glory of the God of Israel c' "
3 when I c' to destroy the city: and "
4 the glory of the Lord c' into the "
46: 9 whereby he c' in, but shall go forth "
47: 1 the waters c' down from under 3381
Da 1: 1 c' Nebuchadnezzar king of 935
2: 2 they c' and stood before the king. "
29 O king, thy thoughts c' into thy 5559
3: 8 at that time certain Chaldeans c' 7127
26 Nebuchadnezzar c' near to the "
26 c' forth of the midst of the fire. 5312
4: 7 Then c' in the magicians, the 5954
8 But at the last Daniel c' in before "
13 an holy one c' down from heaven; 5182
28 All this c' upon the king 4291
5: 5 In the same hour c' forth fingers 5312
8 Then c' in all the king's wise men: 5954
10 c' into the banquet house: and "
6:12 Then they c' near, and spake 7127
20 when he c' to the den, he cried "
24 they c' at the bottom of the den. 4291
7: 3 great beasts c' up from the sea, 5559
8 there c' up among them another "
10 A fiery stream issued and c' forth 5312
13 one like the Son of man c' 858, 1934

Da 7:13 and c' to the Ancient of days, 4291
16 I c' near unto one of them that 7127
20 and of the other which c' up, 5559
22 Until the Ancient of days c', and 858
22 time c' that the saints possessed 4291
8: 2 c' to pass, when I saw, that I *1961
3 other, and the higher c' up last. 5927
5 an he goat c' from the west on 935
6 c' to the ram that had two horns, "
8 for it c' up four notable ones 5927
9 one of them c' forth a little horn, 3318
15 c' to pass, when I, even I Daniel, 1961
17 So he c' near where I stood: 935
17 and when he c', I was afraid, "
9: 2 word of the Lord c' to Jeremiah 1961
23 the commandment came forth, *3318
10: 3 neither c' flesh nor wine in my 935
13 c' to help me; and I remained "
18 there c' again and touched *
Ho 1: 1 word of the Lord that c' unto 1961
2:15 c' up out of the land of Egypt. 5927
Joe 1: 1 word of the Lord that c' to Joel 1961
Am 6: 1 to whom the house of Israel c'! 935
7: 2 it c' to pass, that when they had 1961
Ob 5 If thieves c' to thee, if robbers 935
5 if the grapegatherers c' to thee, "
Jon 1: 1 word of the Lord c' unto Jonah 1961
6 So the shipmaster c' to him, and 7126
2: 7 and my prayer c' in unto thee, 935
3: 1 word of the Lord c' unto Jonah 1961
6 word c' unto the king of Nineveh, *5060
4: 8 it c' to pass, when the sun did 1961
10 c' up in a night, and perished "
Mic 1: 1 word of the Lord that c' to Micah "
11 inhabitant of Zaanan c' not forth *3318
12 evil c' down from the Lord unto *3381
Hab 3: 3 God c' from Teman, and the 935
14 they c' out as a whirlwind to "
Zep 1: 1 which c' unto Zephaniah the son 1961
Hag 1: 1, 3 c' the word of the Lord by "
9 for much, and, lo, it c' to little; "
14 they c' and did work in the house 935
2: 1 c' the word of the Lord by the 1961
5 when ye c' out of Egypt, so my 3318
10 in the second year of Darius, c' 1961
16 when one c' to an heap of twenty 935
16 when one c' to the pressfat for to "
20 word of the Lord c' unto Haggai 1961
Zec 1: 1 year of Darius, c' the word of "
7 Darius, c' the word of the Lord "
4: 1 angel that talked with me c' again, 7725
8 the word of the Lord c' unto me, 1961
5: 9 there c' out two women, and the 3318
6: 1 there c' four chariots out from "
9 And the word of the Lord c' unto 1961
7: 1 And it c' to pass in the fourth year "
1 word of the Lord c' unto Zechariah "
4 Then c' the word of the Lord of "
8 word of the Lord c' unto Zechariah, "
12 therefore c' a great wrath from "
8: 1 word of the Lord of hosts c' to me, "
10 to him that went out or c' in 935
18 word of the Lord of hosts c' unto 1961
10: 4 Out of him c' forth the corner, *3318
14:16 which c' against Jerusalem shall 935
M't 1:18 before they c' together, she was 4905
2: 1 behold, there came wise men 3854
9 till it c' and stood over where the 2064
21 and c' into the land of Israel. "
23 he c' and dwelt in a city called "
3: 1 those days c' John the Baptist. *3854
4: 3 when the tempter c' to him, 4334
11 angels c' and ministered unto him. "
13 he c' and dwelt in Capernaum, 2064
5: 1 was set, his disciples c' unto him: 4334
7:25, 27 the floods c', and the winds 2064
28 it c' to pass, when Jesus had 1096
8: 2 there c' a leper and worshipped 2064
5 there c' unto him a centurion, 4334
19 a certain scribe c', and said unto "
25 his disciples c' to him, and awoke "
34 whole city c' out to meet Jesus: 1831
9: 1 over, and c' into his own city. 2064
10 it c' to pass, as Jesus sat at meat 1096
10 sinners c' and sat down with him 2064
14 c' to him the disciples of John, *4334
18 there c' a certain ruler, and 2064
20 c' behind him, and touched the 4334
23 when Jesus c' unto the ruler's 2064
28 the blind men c' to him: and Jesus 4334
10:34 I c' not to send peace, but a sword. 2064
11: 1 it c' to pass, when Jesus had made 1096
18 For John c' neither eating nor 2064
19 The Son of man c' eating and "
12:42 she c' from the uttermost parts "
44 from whence I c' out; and when 1831
13: 4 fowls c' and devoured them up: 2064
10 disciples c', and said unto him, 4334
25 his enemy c' and sowed tares 2064
27 c' and said unto him, Sir, didst 4334
36 his disciples c' unto him, saying, "
53 it c' to pass, that when Jesus had 1096
14:12 disciples c', and took up the body, 4334
15 his disciples c' to him, saying, "
33 c' and worshipped him, saying, *2064
34 when they were gone over, they c' "
15: 1 Then c' to Jesus scribes and *4334
12 Then c' his disciples, and said "
22 a woman of Canaan c' out of the 1831
23 his disciples c' and besought him, 4334
25 Then c' she and worshipped him, 2064
29 c' nigh unto the sea of Galilee; "
30 great multitudes c' unto him, 4334
39 and c' into the coasts of Magdala. 2064
16: 1 the Sadducees c', and tempting 4334
13 When Jesus c' into the coasts 2064

M't 17: 7 Jesus c' and touched them, and 4334
9 they c' down from the mountain, *2597
14 there c' to him a certain man, 4334
19 c' the disciples to Jesus apart, "
24 c' to Peter, and said, Doth not "
18: 1 time c' the disciples unto Jesus, "
21 Then c' Peter to him, and said, "
31 and c' and told unto their lord 2064
19: 1 it c' to pass, that when Jesus had 1096
1 and c' into the coasts of Judæa 2064
3 The Pharisees also c' unto him, 4334
16 And, behold, one c' and said unto "
20: 9 when they c' that were hired 2064
10 when the first c', they supposed "
20 Then c' to him the mother of 4334
28 c' not to be ministered unto, 2064
21:14 the blind and the lame c' to him 4334
19 he c' to it, and found nothing 2064
23 the elders of the people c' unto 4334
28 and he c' to the first, and said, "
30 And he c' to the second, and said "
32 For John c' unto you in the way 2064
22:11 when the king c' in to see the 1525
23 same day c' to him the Sadducees, 4334
24: 1 and his disciples c' to him for to "
3 Olives, the disciples c' unto him "
39 until the flood c', and took them 2064
25:10 went to buy, the bridegroom c'; "
11 Afterward c' also the other * "
20 c' and brought other five talents, 4334
22 c' and said, Lord, thou deliveredst "
24 c' and said, Lord, I knew thee "
36 in prison, and ye c' unto me. 2064
39 or in prison, and c' unto thee? "
26: 1 it c' to pass, when Jesus had 1096
7 There c' unto him a woman 4334
17 the disciples c' to Jesus, saying, "
43 he c' and found them asleep 2064
47 one of the twelve, c', and with "
49 he c' to Jesus, and said, Hail, 4334
50 Then c' they, and laid hands on "
60 though many false witnesses c', "
60 At the last c' two false witnesses, "
69 a damsel c' unto him, saying, "
73 c' unto him they that stood by, "
27:32 as they c' out, they found a man 1831
53 c' out of the graves after his * "
57 there c' a rich man of Arimathæa, 2064
62 priests and Pharisees c' together *4863
28: 1 c' Mary Magdalene and the other 2064
2 and c' and rolled back the stone 4334
9 they c' and held him by the feet, "
11 c' into the city, and shewed unto 2064
13 c' by night, and stole him away "
18 Jesus c' and spake unto them, 4334
M'r 1: 9 it c' to pass in those days, that 1096
9 Jesus c' from Nazareth 2064
11 And there c' a voice from heaven, 1096
14 Jesus c' into Galilee, preaching 2064
26 with a loud voice, he c' out of him. 1831
31 he c' and took her by the hand, 4334
38 also: for therefore c' I forth. 1831
40 c' a leper to him, beseeching *2064
45 they c' to him from every quarter. "
2:15 it c' to pass, that, as Jesus sat at 1096
17 I c' not to call the righteous, but 2064
23 it c' to pass, that he went through 1096
3: 8 what great things he did, c' unto 2064
13 whom he would: and they c' * 565
22 And the scribes which c' down 2597
31 There c' then his brethren and *2064
4: 4 it c' to pass, as he sowed, some 1096
4 and the fowls of the air c' 2064
5: 1 they c' over unto the other side of "
27 c' in the press behind, and touched "
33 c' and fell down before him, and "
35 c' from the ruler of the * "
6: 1 and c' into his own country; and * "
22 daughter of the said Herodias c' 1525
25 c' in straightway with haste unto "
29 his disciples heard of it, they c' 2064
33 outwent them, and c' together *4905
34 Jesus, when he c' out, saw much 1831
35 his disciples c' unto him, and said, 4334
53 when they had passed over, they c' 2064
7: 1 c' together unto him the Pharisees, *4863
1 certain of the scribes, which c' *2064
25 him, and c' and fell at his feet: "
31 he c' unto the sea of Galilee, "
8: 3 for divers of them c' from far. *2240
10 c' into the parts of Dalmanutha. 2064
11 the Pharisees c' forth, and began 1831
9: 7 a voice c' out of the cloud, saying, 2064
9 they c' down from the mountain, *2597
14 when he c' to his disciples, he 2064
21 is it ago since this c' unto him? *1096
25 the people c' running together, 1998
26 rent him sore, and c' out of him: 1831
33 And he c' to Capernaum: and 2064
10: 2 the Pharisees c' to him, and asked 4334
17 there c' one running, and kneeled *4370
45 c' not to be ministered unto, but 2064
46 they c' to Jericho: and as he * "
50 garment, rose, and c' to Jesus. "
11: 1 when they c' nigh to Jerusalem, *1448
13 he c', if haply he might find 2064
13 thereon: and when he c' to it, "
12:28 And one of the scribes c', and 4334
42 There c' a certain poor widow, and 2064
14: 3 c' a woman having an alabaster "
16 and c' into the city, and found as "
32 And they c' to a place which was * "
15:41 many other women which c' up 4872
43 for the kingdom of God, c', *2064
16: 2 they c' unto the sepulchre at the * "
Lu 1: 8 c' to pass, that while he executed 1096

Lu 1:22 when he c' out, he could not 1831
23 it c' to pass, that, as soon as the 1096
28 the angel c' in unto her, and said, 1525
41 c' to pass, that, when Elisabeth 1096
57 Now Elisabeth's full time c' that *4130
59 c' to pass, that on the eighth day 1096
59 they c' to circumcise the child; 2064
65 fear c' on all that dwelt round 1096
2: 1 it c' to pass in those days, that "
9 the angel of the Lord c' upon *2186
15 it c' to pass, as the angels were 1096
16 they c' with haste, and found 2064
27 he c' by the Spirit into the temple: "
46 it c' to pass, that after three days 1096
51 c' to Nazareth, and was subject 2064
3: 2 the word of God c' unto John the 1096
3 he c' into all the country about 2064
7 to the multitude that c' forth to *1607
12 c' also publicans to be baptized, 2064
21 it c' to pass, that Jesus also being 1096
22 a voice c' from heaven, which said, "
4:16 he c' to Nazareth, where he had 2064
31 c' down to Capernaum, a city of 2718
35 c' out of him, and hurt him not. 1831
41 devils also c' out of many, crying "
42 c' unto him, and stayed him, that 2064
5: 1 c' to pass, that, as the people 1096
7 they c', and filled both the ships, 2064
12 it c' to pass, when he was in a 1096
15 great multitudes c' together to 4905
17 it c' to pass on a certain day, as 1096
32 I c' not to call the righteous, but *2064
6: 1 c' to pass on the second sabbath 1096
6 it c' to pass also on another "
12 And it c' to pass in those days, "
17 he c' down with them, and stood 2597
17 which c' to hear him, and to be 2064
7: 4 when they c' to Jesus, they 3854
11 it c' to pass the day after, that he 1096
12 when he c' nigh to the gate of the *1448
14 And he c' and touched the bier: 4334
16 And there c' a fear on all: and *2983
33 For John the Baptist c' neither *2064
45 since the time I c' in hath not 1525
8: 1 it c' to pass afterward, that he 1096
19 c' to him his mother and his 3854
22 it c' to pass on a certain day, that 1096
23 there c' down a storm of wind on 2597
24 And they c' to him, and awoke him, 4334
35 c' to Jesus, and found the man, 2064
40 c' to pass, that, when Jesus was *1096
41 there c' a man named Jairus, and 2064
44 C' behind him, and touched the 4334
47 was not hid, she c' trembling, 2064
51 when he c' into the house, he 1525
55 her spirit c' again, and she arose *1994
9:12 then c' the twelve, and said unto 4334
18 c' to pass, as he was alone 1096
28 it c' to pass about an eight days "
33 it c' to pass, as they departed "
34 c' a cloud, and overshadowed "
35 there c' a voice out of the cloud, "
37 it c' to pass, that on the next day, "
51 c' to pass, when the time was come "
57 c' to pass, that, as they went in * "
10:31 by chance there c' down a certain *2597
32 c' and looked on him, and passed *2064
33 as he journeyed, c' where he was: "
38 Now it c' to pass, as they went, *1096
40 and c' to him, and said, Lord, 2186
11: 1 c' to pass, that, as he was praying 1096
14 it c' to pass, when the devil was "
24 unto my house whence I c' out. 1831
27 c' to pass, as he spake these 1096
31 c' from the utmost parts of the 2064
13: 6 he c' and sought fruit thereon, "
31 The same day there c' certain of 4334
14: 1 c' to pass, as he went into the 1096
21 So that servant c', and shewed 3854
15:17 And when he c' to himself, he 2064
20 he arose, and c' to his father. "
25 c' and drew nigh to the house, he "
28 therefore c' his father out, and 1831
16:21 the dogs c' and licked his sores. 2064
22 it c' to pass that the beggar died, 1096
17:11 it c' to pass, as he went to "
14 it c' to pass, that, as they went, "
27 and the flood c', and destroyed 2064
18: 3 she c' unto him, saying, Avenge "
35 c' to pass, that as he was come 1096
19: 5 when Jesus c' to the place, he 2064
6 And he made haste, and c' down, 2597
15 it c' to pass, that when he was 1096
16 Then c' the first, saying, Lord, 3854
18 And the second c', saying, Lord, 2064
20 another c' saying, Lord, behold, "
29 c' to pass, when he was come nigh 1096
20: 1 c' to pass, that on one of those "
1 chief priests and the scribes c' 2186
27 c' to him certain of the Sadducees, 4334
21:38 And all the people c' early in the 3719
22: 7 c' the day of unleavened bread, 2064
39 c' out, and went, as he was wont, 1831
66 priests and the scribes c' together, *4863
23:48 all the people that c' together to 4836
55 which c' with him from Galilee, *4905
24: 1 very early in the morning, they c' 2064
4 it c' to pass, as they were much 1096
15 it c' to pass, that, while they "
23 found not his body, they c', saying, 2064
30 c' to pass, as he sat at meat with 1096
51 it c' to pass, while he blessed "
Joh 1: 7 The same c' for a witness, to bear 2064
11 He c' unto his own, and his own "
17 grace and truth c' by Jesus Christ. 1096
39 They c' and saw where he dwelt, 2064
Joh 3: 2 The same c' to Jesus by night, and 2064
13 but he that c' down from heaven, *2597
22 After these things c' Jesus and 2064
23 and they c', and were baptized. 3854
26 c' unto John, and said unto him, 2064
4:27 upon this c' his disciples, and "
30 out of the city, and c' unto him. "
46 So Jesus c' again into Cana of "
6:23 (Howbeit there c' other boats from "
24 shipping, and c' to Capernaum, "
38 For I c' down from heaven, not to *2597
41 I am the bread which c' down from "
42 I c' down from heaven? "
51 bread which c' down from heaven: "
58 This is that bread which c' down "
7:45 Then c' the officers to the chief 2064
50 (he that c' to Jesus by night, "
8: 2 early in the morning he c' again 3854
2 the people c' unto him; 2064
14 for I know whence I c', and "
42 I proceeded forth and c' from 2240
42 neither c' I of myself, *2064
9: 7 therefore, and washed, and c' "
10: 8 All that ever c' before me are "
24 c' the Jews round about him, 2944
35 unto whom the word of God c', 1096
11:17 Then when Jesus c', he found that 2064
19 many of the Jews c' to Martha * "
29 arose quickly, and c' unto him. * "
33 Jews also weeping which c' with 4905
44 he that was dead c' forth, bound 1831
45 of the Jews which c' to Mary, 2064
12: 1 before the passover c' to Bethany, "
9 they c' not for Jesus' sake only, "
20 Greeks among them that c' up to * 305
21 The same c' therefore to Philip, 4334
27 for this cause c' I unto this hour. 2064
28 Then c' there a voice from heaven, "
30 This voice c' not because of me, *1096
47 for I c' not to judge the world, 2064
16:27 believed that I c' out from God. 1831
28 I c' forth from the Father, and am "
17: 8 that I c' out from thee, and they "
18:37 for this cause c' I into the world, *2064
19: 5 then c' Jesus forth, wearing the 1831
32 Then c' the soldiers, and 2064
33 But when they c' to Jesus, "
34 forthwith c' there out blood and 1831
38 He c' therefore, and took the body 2064
39 And there c' also Nicodemus, "
39 at the first c' to Jesus by night, "
20: 3 disciple, and c' to the sepulchre. * "
4 Peter, and c' first to the sepulchre. "
8 which c' first to the sepulchre, "
18 Mary Magdalene c' and told the "
19 c' Jesus and stood in the midst, "
24 was not with them when Jesus c'. "
26 c' Jesus, the doors being shut, "
21: 8 other disciples c' in a little ship; "
Ac 2: 2 suddenly there c' a sound from 1096
6 multitude c' together, and were 4905
43 And fear c' upon every soul: 1096
4: 1 and the Sadducees, c' upon them, 2186
5 it c' to pass on the morrow, that 1096
5: 5 great fear c' on all them that "
7 knowing what was done, c' in. 1525
10 young men c' in, and found "
11 great fear c' upon all the church, 1096
16 There c' also a multitude out of 4905
21 But the high priest c', and they 3854
22 But when the officers c', and found "
25 Then c' one and told them, saying, "
6:12 c' upon him, and caught him, 2186
7: 4 Then c' he out of the land of the 1831
11 c' a dearth over all the land of 2064
23 it c' into his heart to visit his 305
31 the voice of the Lord c' unto him, 1096
45 also our fathers that c' after *1237
8: 7 c' out of many that were possessed 1831
36 they c' unto a certain water: 2064
40 the cities, till he c' to Cæsarea. "
9: 3 journeyed, he c' near Damascus: *1096
21 and c' hither for that intent, that 2064
32 it c' to pass, as Peter passed 1096
32 he c' down also to the saints 2718
37 it c' to pass in those days, that 1096
43 it c' to pass, that he tarried many "
10:13 there c' a voice to him, Rise, "
29 Therefore c' I unto you without 2064
45 as many as c' with Peter, because 4905
11: 5 four corners; and it c' even to me: 2064
22 tidings of these things c' unto the 191
23 Who, when he c', and had seen *3854
26 it c' to pass, that a whole year 1096
27 c' prophets from Jerusalem unto 2718
28 which c' to pass in the days of 1096
12: 7 angel of the Lord c' upon him, *2186
10 they c' unto the iron gate that 2064
12 c' to the house of Mary the mother "
13 a damsel c' to hearken, named 4334
20 they c' with one accord to him, 3918
13:13 they c' to Perga in Pamphylia: 2064
14 they c' to Antioch in Pisidia, 3854
31 of them which c' up with him 4872
44 c' almost the whole city together *4863
51 them, and c' unto Iconium. 2064
14: 1 it c' to pass in Iconium, that they 1096
19 there c' thither certain Jews 1904
20 he rose up, and c' into the city: 1525
24 Pisidia, they c' to Pamphylia. 2064
15: 1 men which c' down from Judæa 2718
6 apostles and elders c' together *4863
30 dismissed, they c' to Antioch: 2064
16: 1 Then c' he to Derbe and Lystra: 2658
8 passing by Mysia c' down to Troas. 2597
11 we c' with a straight course to *2113
Ac 16:16 it c' to pass, as he went to prayer, 1096
18 And he c' out the same hour. 1831
29 and c' trembling, and fell down *1096
39 they c' and besought them, 2064
17: 1 they c' to Thessalonica, where "
13 they c' thither also, and stirred up "
18: 1 from Athens, and c' to Corinth; "
2 from Rome:) and c' unto them. 4334
19 he c' to Ephesus, and left them 2658
24 mighty in the scriptures, c' to "
19: 1 it c' to pass, that, while Apollos 1096
1 the upper coasts c' to Ephesus: 2064
6 the Holy Ghost c' on them; "
18 that believed c', and confessed, "
20: 2 exhortation, he c' into Greece, "
6 c' unto them to Troas in five days; "
7 when the disciples c' together to *4863
14 took him in, and c' to Mitylene. 2064
15 c' the next day over against Chios; "
15 and the next day we c' to Miletus. 2658
18 first day that I c' into Asia, *1910
21: 1 it c' to pass, that after we were 1096
1 we c' with a straight course unto 2064
7 we c' to Ptolemais, and saluted *2658
8 departed, and c' unto Cæsarea: 2064
10 there c' down from Judæa a 2718
31 tidings c' unto the chief captain of 305
33 Then the chief captain c' near, 1448
35 when he c' upon the stairs, so it 1096
22: 6 it c' to pass, that, as I made my "
11 with me, I c' into Damascus. 2064
13 C' unto me, and stood, and said "
17 And it c' to pass, that, when I 1096
27 Then the chief captain c', and 4334
23:14 And they c' to the chief priests "
27 c' I with an army, and rescued 2186
33 Who, when they c' to Cæsarea, 1525
24: 7 chief captain Lysias c' upon us, *3928
17 I c' to bring alms to my nation, 3854
24 Felix c' with his wife Drusilla, "
27 Porcius Festus c' into Felix' 2983, 1240
25: 7 the Jews which c' down from 2597
13 Agrippa and Bernice c' unto *2658
27: 5 we c' to Myra, a city of Lycia. 2718
8 hardly passing it, c' unto a place 2064
44 so it c' to pass, that they escaped 1096
28: 3 c' a viper out of the heat, 1831
8 it c' to pass, that the father of *1096
9 in the island, c', and were healed: 4334
13 c' to Rhegium: and after one day *2658
13 and we c' the next day to Puteoli: 2064
15 they c' to meet us as far as Appii 1831
16 when we c' to Rome, the *2064
17 it c' to pass, that after three days 1096
21 any of the brethren that c' *3854
23 c' many to him into his lodging; 2240
30 received all that c' in unto him, *1531
Ro 5:18 one judgment c' upon all men to
18 the free gift c' upon all men unto
7: 9 but when the commandment c', 2064
9: 5 concerning the flesh Christ c', *
1Co 2: 1 I, brethren, when I c' to you, 2064
1 c' not with excellency of speech "
14:36 c' the word of God out from you? *1831
36 or c' it unto you only? 2658
15:21 since by man c' death, by man c' also
2Co 1: 8 trouble which c' to us in Asia, *1096
23 I c' not as yet unto Corinth. *2064
2: 3 lest, when I c', I should have "
12 when I c' to Troas to preach "
11: 9 brethren which c' from Macedonia "
Gal 1:21 I c' into the regions of Syria and "
2: 4 who c' in privily to spy out our 3922
12 before that certain c' from James, 2064
3:23 But before faith c', we were kept "
Eph 2:17 And c' and preached peace to you "
1Th 1: 5 our gospel c' not unto you in 1096
3: 4 even as it c' to pass, and ye know. "
6 now when Timotheus c' from you 2064
1Ti 1:15 Christ Jesus c' into the world to "
2Ti 3:11 afflictions, which c' unto me at *1096
Heb 3:16 not all that c' out of Egypt 1831
11:15 from whence they c' out, they * "
2Pe 1:17 when there c' such a voice to him ‡5342
18 this voice which c' from heaven * "
21 the prophecy c' not in old time "
1Jo 5: 6 he that c' by water and blood, 2064
3Jo 3 the brethren c' and testified of the "
Re 5: 7 And he c' and took the book out "
7:13 in white robes? and whence c' "
14 These are they which c' out of * "
8: 3 angel c' and stood at the altar, "
4 smoke of the incense, which c' *
9: 3 there c' out of the smoke locusts 1831
14:15 another angel c' out of the temple, "
17 And another angel c' out of the "
18 angel c' out from the altar, "
20 blood c' out of the winepress, "
15: 6 seven angels c' out of the temple, "
16:17 c' a great voice out of the temple "
19 Babylon c' in remembrance *3415
17: 1 there c' one of the seven angels 2064
19: 5 And a voice c' out of the throne, 1831
20: 9 and fire c' down from God out of 2597
21: 9 c' unto me one of the seven angels 2064

came to pass See CAME and PASS.

camel See also CAMEL'S; CAMELS.
Ge 24:64 saw Isaac, she lighted off the c'. 1581
Le 11: 4 c', because he cheweth the cud, "
De 14: 7 the c', and the hare, and the "
1Sa 15: 3 suckling, ox and sheep, c' and ass. "
Zec 14:15 of the mule, of the c', "
M't 19:24 easier for a c' to go through the 2574
23:24 at a gnat, and swallow a c'. "
M'k 10:25 easier for a c' to go through the "

Lu 18:25 easier for a c· to go through a 2574
camel's
Ge 31:34 put them in the c· furniture, and 1581
M't 3: 4 his raiment of c· hair, and a 2574
M'k 1: 6 clothed with c· hair, and with a "
camels See also CAMELS'.
Ge 12:16 and she asses, and c·. 1581
24:10 took ten c· of the c· of his master, "
11 he made his c· to kneel down "
14 I will give thy c· drink also: let "
19 draw water for thy c· also, until "
20 water, and drew for all his c·. "
22 as the c· had done drinking, that "
30 he stood by the c· at the well. "
31 the house, and room for the c·. "
32 and he ungirded his c·, and gave "
32 and provender for the c·, "
35 maidservants, and c·, and asses. "
44 I will also draw for thy c·: let the "
46 I will give thy c· drink also: so I "
46 and she made the c· drink "
61 they rode upon the c·, and "
63 and, behold, the c· were coming. "
30:43 menservants, and c·, and asses. "
31:17 set his sons and his wives upon c·; "
32: 7 herds, and the c·, into two bands; "
15 Thirty milch c· with their colts, "
37:25 came from Gilead with their c· "
Ex 9: 3 upon the asses, upon the c·, upon "
J'g 6: 5 both they and their c· were "
7:12 and their c· were without number, "
1Sa 27: 9 the asses, and the c·, and the "
30:17 young men, which rode upon c·, "
1Ki 10: 2 with c· that bare spices, and very "
1Ch 5:21 cattle; of their c· fifty thousand, "
12:40 bread on asses, and on c·, and on "
27:30 Over the c· also was Obil the "
2Ch 9: 1 company, and c· that bare spices, "
14:15 carried away sheep and c· in "
Ezr 2:67 Their c·, four hundred thirty and "
Ne 7:69 c·, four hundred thirty and five: "
Es 8:10 c·, and young dromedaries: * 327
14 rode upon mules and c· went out,* "
Job 1: 3 three thousand c·, and five 1581
17 fell upon the c·, and have carried "
42:12 six thousand c·, and a thousand "
Isa 21: 7 of asses, and a chariot of c·; "
30: 6 treasures upon the bunches of c·, "
60: 6 The multitude of c· shall cover "
Jer 49:29 and all their vessels, and their c·; "
32 And their c· shall be a booty, and "
Eze 25: 5 make Rabbah a stable for c·, and "
camels'
J'g 8:21 that were on their c· necks. 1581
26 chains that were about their c· "
2Ki 8: 9 of Damascus, forty c· burden, "
camest See also BECAMEST.
Ge 16: 8 whence c· thou? and whither wilt 935
24: 5 the land from whence thou c·? 3318
27:33 eaten of all before thou c·, and 935
Ex 23:15 in it thou c· out from Egypt: 3318
34:18 Abib thou c· out from Egypt. "
Nu 22:37 wherefore c· thou not unto me? 1980
De 2:37 children of Ammon thou c· not, 7126
16: 3 for thou c· forth out of the land of 3318
3 when thou c· forth out of the land "
6 season that thou c· forth out of "
1Sa 13:11 thou c· not within the days 935
17:28 Why c· thou down hither? and *3381
2Sa 11:10 C· thou not from thy journey? * 935
15:20 Whereas thou c· but yesterday, "
1Ki 13: 9 by the same way that thou c·. 1980
14 man of God that c· from Judah? 935
17 to go by the way that thou c·. 1980
22 But c· back, and hast eaten bread 7725
2Ki 19:28 back by the way by which thou c·. 935
Ne 9:13 Thou c· down also upon mount 3381
Isa 37:29 back by the way by which thou c·. 935
64: 3 thou c· down, the mountains 3381
Jer 1: 5 before thou c· forth out of the 3318
Eze 32: 2 thou c· forth with thy rivers, and *1518
M't 22:12 Friend, how c· thou in hither 1525
Joh 6:25 him, Rabbi, when c· thou hither? 1096
16:30 that thou c· forth from God. 1831
Ac 9:17 in the way as thou c·, hath sent 2064
Camon *(ca'-mon)*
J'g 10: 5 Jair died, and was buried in C·. 7056
camp See also CAMPED; CAMPS; ENCAMP.
Ex 14:19 which went before the c· of Israel, 4264
20 between the c· of the Egyptians "
20 and the c· of Israel; "
16:13 quails came up, and covered the c·: "
19:16 people that was in the c· trembled. "
17 all the people out of the c· to meet "
29:14 burn with fire without the c·: "
32:17 There is a noise of war in the c·. "
19 as he came nigh unto the c·, that "
26 stood in the gate of the c·, and "
27 gate to gate throughout the c·, "
33: 7 without the c·, afar off from the c·, "
7 which was without the c·. "
11 he turned again into the c·: but "
36: 6 proclaimed throughout the c·, "
Le 4:12 he carry forth without the c· unto "
21 forth the bullock without the c·, "
6:11 the ashes without the c· unto a "
8:17 he burnt with fire without the c·; "
9:11 he burnt with fire without the c·. "
10: 4 before the sanctuary out of the c·. "
5 their coats out of the c·; as Moses "
13:46 without the c· shall his habitation "
14: 3 shall go forth out of the c·; and "
8 come into the c·, and shall tarry "
16:26 and afterward come into the c·. "
Le 16:27 carry forth without the c·; and 4264
28 afterward he shall come into the c·. "
17: 3 lamb, or goat, in the c·, or that "
3 killeth it out of the c·, "
24:10 strove together in the c·; "
14 that hath cursed without the c·; "
23 had cursed out of the c·, and "
Nu 1:52 every man by his own c·, and "
2: 3 standard of the c· of Judah pitch "
9 All that were numbered in the c· "
10 the standard of the c· of Reuben "
16 All that were numbered in the c· "
17 with the c· of the Levites "
17 in the midst of the c·: "
18 standard of the c· of Ephraim "
24 that were numbered of the c· of "
25 The standard of the c· of Dan "
31 that were numbered in the c· of "
4: 5 when the c· setteth forward, "
15 as the c· is to set forward; "
5: 2 put out of the c· every leper, "
3 without the c· shall ye put them; "
4 and put them out without the c·: "
10:14 standard of the c· of the children "
18 standard of the c· of Reuben set "
22 c· of the children of Ephraim set "
25 the c· of the children of Dan set "
34 when they went out of the c·. "
11: 1 in the uttermost parts of the c·. "
9 dew fell upon the c· in the night, "
26 remained two of the men in the c·, "
26 and they prophesied in the c·. "
27 and Medad do prophesy in the c·. "
30 Moses gat him into the c·, "
31 let them fall by the c·, as it were "
31 the other side, round about the c·, "
32 themselves round about the c·. "
12:14 let her be shut out from the c· "
15 Miriam was shut out from the c· "
14:44 Moses departed not out of the c·. "
15:35 him with stones without the c·. "
36 brought him without the c·, and "
19: 3 bring her forth without the c·, and "
7 afterward he shall come into the c·, "
9 without the c· in a clean place, "
31:12 unto the c· at the plains of Moab, "
13 forth to meet them without the c·. "
19 do ye abide without the c· seven "
24 afterward ye shall come into the c·. "
De 23:10 shall he go abroad out of the c·, "
10 he shall not come within the c·: "
11 he shall come into the c· again. "
12 have a place also without the c·, "
14 God walketh in the midst of thy c·, "
14 therefore shall thy c· be holy: "
29:11 thy stranger that is in thy c·, * "
Jos 5: 8 abode in their places in the c·, till "
6:11 into the c·, and lodged in the c·. "
14 returned into the c·: so they did "
18 make the c· of Israel a curse, and "
23 left them without the c· of Israel. "
9: 6 to Joshua unto the c· at Gilgal, "
10: 6 sent unto Joshua to the c· to Gilgal, "
15 and all Israel with him, unto the c· "
21 all the people returned to the c· to "
43 with him, unto the c· to Gilgal. "
J'g 7:17 I come to the outside of the c·, "
18 also on every side of all the c·, "
19 came unto the outside of the c· "
21 in his place round about the c·: "
13:25 him at times in the c· of Dan * "
21: 8 there came none to the c· from "
12 brought them unto the c· to Shiloh, "
1Sa 4: 3 the people were come into the c·, "
5 of the Lord came into the c·, "
6 noise of this great shout in the c· "
6 of the Lord was come into the c·. "
7 they said, God is come into the c·. "
13:17 out of the c· of the Philistines "
14:21 went up with them into the c· "
17: 4 out of the c· of the Philistines, "
17 run to the c· to thy brethren; "
26: 6 down with me to Saul to the c·? "
2Sa 1: 2 a man came out of the c· from "
3 Out of the c· of Israel am I "
1Ki 16:16 king over Israel that day in the c·. "
2Ki 3:24 when they came to the c· of Israel, "
6: 8 and such a place shall be my c·. 8466
7: 5 to go unto the c· of the Syrians: 4264
5 to the uttermost part of the c· "
7 even the c· as it was, and fled "
8 to the uttermost part of the c·, "
10 We came to the c· of the Syrians, "
12 are they gone out of the c· to hide "
19:35 smote in the c· of the Assyrians "
2Ch 22: 1 came with the Arabians to the c· "
32:21 the leaders and captains in the c· "
Ps 78:28 let it fall in the midst of their c·, "
106:16 They envied Moses also in the c·, "
Isa 29: 3 And I will c· against thee round ‡2583
37:36 smote in the c· of the Assyrians 4264
Jer 50:29 c· against it round about; and ‡2583
Eze 4: 2 set the c· also against it, and set *4264
Joe 2:11 for his c· is very great: for he is "
Na 3:17 c· in the hedges in the cold day, ‡2583
Heb 13:11 sin, are burned without the c·. 3925
13 unto him without the c·, bearing "
Re 20: 9 compassed the c· of the saints "
camped
Ex 19: 2 and there Israel c· before the ‡2583
camphire
Ca 1:14 a cluster of c· in the vineyards *3724
4:13 c·, with spikenard, * "
camps
Nu 2:32 that were numbered of the c· 4264
Nu 5: 3 that they defile not their c·, in *4264
10: 2 for the journeying of the c·. "
5 then the c· that lie on the east "
6 then the c· that lie on the south "
25 the rereward of all the c· "
Am 4:10 the stink of your c· to come up "
can See also CANNOT; CANST.
Ge 4:13 punishment is greater than I c·
13:16 c· number the dust of the 3201
31:43 and what c· I do this day unto
39: 9 then c· I do this great wickedness,
41:15 is none that c· interpret it:
38 C· we find such a one as this is?
44: 1 as much as they c· carry, 3201
15 a man as I c· certainly divine?
Ex 4:14 I know that he c· speak well.
5:11 you straw where ye c· find it:
Le 14:30 pigeons such as he c· get; *
Nu 23:10 Who c· count the dust of Jacob,
De 3:24 c· do according to thy works,
7:17 how c· I dispossess them? 3201
9: 2 Who c· stand before the children
31: 2 I c· no more go out and 3201
32:39 that c· deliver out of my hand.
J'g 14:12 if ye c· certainly declare it me
1Sa 9: 6 peradventure he c· shew us our
16: 2 Samuel said, How c· I go?
17 me now a man that c· play well,
18: 8 and what c· he have more but
26: 9 c· stretch forth his hand against
28: 2 know what thy servant c· do. *
2Sa 7:20 And what c· David say more unto
12:22 Who c· tell whether God will *
23 c· I bring him back again? 3201
14:19 none c· turn to the right hand
15:36 me every thing that ye c· hear. *
19:35 c· I discern between good and evil?
35 c· thy servant taste what I eat
35 c· I hear any more the voice of
1Ch 17:18 What c· David speak more to thee
2Ch 1:10 who c· judge this thy people,
2: 7 and that c· skill to grave with the
8 I know that thy servants c·
Es 8: 6 c· I endure to see the evil 3201
6 people? or how c· I endure to "
Job 3:22 when they c· find the grave?
4: 2 but who c· withhold himself 3201
6: 6 C· that which is unsavoury be
8:11 C· the rush grow up without mire?
11 c· the flag grow without water?
9:12 taketh away, who c· hinder him?
10: 7 there is none that c· deliver out
11:10 together, then who c· hinder him?
12:14 man, and there c· be no opening.
14: 4 Who c· bring a clean thing out of
15: 3 wherewith he c· do no good?
22: 2 C· a man be profitable unto God,
13 doth God know? c· he judge
17 and what c· the Almighty do for
23:13 one mind and who c· turn him?
25: 4 How then c· man be justified with
4 how c· he be clean that is born of
26:14 of his power who c· understand?
34:29 who then c· make trouble?
29 his face, who then c· behold him?
36:23 or who c· say, Thou hast wrought
26 neither c· the number of his *
29 c· any understand the spreadings
38:37 c· number the clouds in wisdom?
37 who c· stay the bottles of heaven,
40:14 thine own right hand c· save thee.
19 he that made him c· make his ‡
23 he trusteth that he c· draw *
41:13 Who c· discover the face of his *
13 who c· come to him with his double
14 c· open the doors of his face?
16 that no air c· come between
42: 2 that no thought c· be withholden
Ps 11: 3 destroyed, what c· the righteous
19:12 Who c· understand his errors?
22:29 none c· keep alive his own soul. *
40: 5 they are more than c· be numbered.
49: 7 None of them c· by any means
56: 4 fear what flesh c· do unto me.
11 not be afraid what man c· do unto
58: 9 Before your pots c· feel the thorns,
78:19 C· God furnish a table in 3201
20 c· he give bread also?
20 c· he provide flesh * "
89: 6 who in the heaven c· be compared
6 sons of the mighty c· be likened
106: 2 Who c· utter the mighty acts
2 who c· shew forth all his praise?*
118: 6 fear: what c· man do unto me?
147:17 who c· stand before his cold?
Pr 6:27 C· a man take fire in his bosom,
28 C· one go upon hot coals, and his
18:14 but a wounded spirit who c· bear?
20: 6 but a faithful man who c· find?
9 Who c· say, I have made my heart
24 how c· a man then understand
26:16 seven men that c· render a reason.
31:10 Who c· find a virtuous woman?
Ec 2:12 for what c· the man do that
25 For who c· eat,
25 or who else c· hasten hereunto,
3:11 no man c· find out the work *
14 nothing c· be put to it, nor
4:11 but how c· one be warm alone?
6:12 for who c· tell a man what shall
7:13 who c· make that straight, 3201
24 who c· find it out?
8: 7 for who c· tell him when it shall
10:14 be after him, who c· tell him?
Ca 8: 7 neither c· the floods drown it:
Isa 28:20 shorter than a man c· stretch

Isa 28:20 narrower than that he c· wrap
43: 9 among them c· declare this,
13 that c· deliver out of my hand:
46: 7 unto him, yet c· he not answer,
49:15 C· a woman forget her sucking
56:11 greedy dogs which c· never have 3045
Jer 2:13 cisterns, that c· hold no water.
24 occasion who c· turn her away?
28 if they c· save thee in the time of
32 C· a maid forget her ornaments,
4: 4 and burn that none c· quench it,
5: 1 if ye c· find a man, if there be any
22 yet c· they not prevail;
22 yet c· they not pass over it? 3201
13:23 C· the Ethiopian change his skin,
14:22 the Gentiles that c· cause rain?
22 or c· the heavens give showers?
17: 9 desperately wicked; who c· know
21:12 and burn that none c· quench it,
23:24 C· any hide himself in secret
31:37 If heaven above c· be measured,
33:20 If ye c· break my covenant of the
38: 5 king is not he that c· do 3201
47: 7 How c· it be quiet, seeing the *
La 2:13 like the sea: who c· heal thee?
Eze 22:14 C· thine heart endure, or c· thine
28: 3 no secret that they c· hide from ‡
33:32 c· play well on an instrument:
37: 3 c· these bones live? And I
Da 2: 9 know that ye c· shew me the
10 upon the earth that c· shew the 3202
11 none other that c· shew it before
3:29 God that c· deliver after this *3202
4:35 none c· stay his hand,
10:17 c· the servant of this my lord 3201
Joel 2:11 terrible; and who c· abide it?
Am 3: 3 C· two walk together, except *
5 C· a bird fall in a snare upon the
8 hath spoken, who c· but prophesy?
Jon 3: 9 Who c· tell if God will turn and *
Mic 3:11 none evil c· come upon us. *
5: 8 in pieces, and none c· deliver. *
Na 1: 6 Who c· stand before his indignation?
6 and who c· abide in the fierceness
M't 6:24 No man c· serve two masters: 1410
27 Which of you by taking thought c· "
7:18 neither c· a corrupt tree bring "
9:15 C· the children of the 1410
12:29 Or else how c· one enter into a 1410
34 how c· ye, being evil, speak good "
16: 3 ye c· discern the face of the sky; *1097
3 but c· ye not discern the signs of *1410
19:25 saying, Who then c· be saved? "
23:33 how c· ye escape the damnation *
27:65 way, make it as sure as ye c·. 1492
M'k 2: 7 who c· forgive sins but God only? 1410
19 C· the children of the "
3:23 How c· Satan cast out Satan? "
27 No man c· enter into a strong "
7:15 entering into him c· defile him: "
8: 4 From whence c· a man satisfy * "
9: 3 no fuller on earth c· white them. "
29 This kind c· come forth by nothing, "
39 name, that c· lightly speak evil * "
10:26 themselves, Who then c· be saved? "
38 know not what ye ask: c· ye * "
39 And they said unto him, We c·. * "
Lu 5:21 Who c· forgive sins, but God alone? "
34 C· ye make the children of the "
6:39 C· the blind lead the blind? "
12: 4 have no more that they c· do. "
25 thought c· add to his stature 1410
56 ye c· discern the face of the sky *1492
16:13 No servant c· serve two masters: 1410
26 neither c· they pass to us, that *
18:26 it said, Who then c· be saved? 1410
20:36 Neither c· they die any more: "
Joh 1:46 C· there any good thing come out "
3: 2 for no man c· do these miracles "
4 How c· a man be born when he is "
4 c· he enter the second time into "
9 unto him, How c· these things be? "
27 A man c· receive nothing except it "
5:19 The Son c· do nothing of himself, "
30 I c· of mine own self do nothing: "
44 How c· ye believe, which received "
6:44 No man c· come to me, except the "
52 How c· this man give us his flesh "
60 an hard saying; who c· hear it? "
65 that no man c· come unto me, "
9: 4 cometh, when no man c· work. "
16 How c· a man that is a sinner do "
10:21 C· a devil open the eyes of the "
14: 5 and how c· we know the way? "
15: 4 no more c· ye, except ye abide in me. "
5 for without me ye c· do nothing. 1410
Ac 8:31 How c· I, except some man should "
10:47 C· any man forbid water, that "
24:13 Neither c· they prove the things "
Ro 8: 7 law of God, neither indeed c· be. "
31 If God be for us, who c· be against
1Co 2:14 neither c· he know them, for *1410
3:11 other foundation c· no man lay "
12: 3 no man c· say that Jesus is the "
2Co 13: 8 we c· do nothing against the truth, "
Ph'p 4:13 I c· do all things through Christ 2480
1Th 3: 9 what thanks c· we render to God 1410
1Ti 6: 7 is certain we c· carry nothing out. "
16 light which no man c· approach *
16 no man hath seen, nor c· see: 1410
Heb 5: 2 Who c· have compassion on the "
10: 1 very image of the things, c· never "
11 the same sacrifices, which c· never "
Jas 2:14 not works? C· faith save him? "
3: 8 But the tongue c· no man tame; "
12 C· the fig tree, my brethren, bear "
Jas 3:12 so c· no fountain both yield salt
1Jo 4:20 how c· he love God whom he *1410
Re 3: 8 open door, and no man c· shut it: "
9:20 neither c· see, nor hear, nor walk: "

Cana (*ca'-nah*)
Joh 2: 1 in C· of Galilee; and the mother 2580
11 did Jesus in C· of Galilee, "
4:46 Jesus came again into C· of "
21: 2 Nathanael of C· in Galilee, "

Canaan (*ca'-na-an*) See also CANAANITE.
Ge 9:18 and Ham is the father of C·. 3667
22 Ham, the father of C·, saw the "
25 And he said, Cursed be C·; "
26 God of Shem; and C· shall be his "
27 tents of Shem; and C· shall be his "
10: 6 and Mizraim, and Phut, and C·. "
15 And C· begat Sidon his firstborn, "
11:31 Chaldees, to go into the land of C·; "
12: 5 forth to go into the land of C·; "
5 into the land of C· they came. "
13:12 Abram dwelt in the land of C·, "
16: 3 dwelt ten years in the land of C·, "
17: 8 the land of C·, for an everlasting "
23: 2 same is Hebron in the land of C·: "
19 same is Hebron in the land of C·. "
28: 1 take a wife of the daughters of C·. "
6 take a wife of the daughters of C·; "
8 daughters of C· pleased not Isaac "
31:18 Isaac his father in the land of C·. "
33:18 which is in the land of C·, "
35: 6 to Luz, which is in the land of C·, "
36: 2 his wives of the daughters of C·; "
5 born unto him in the land of C·. "
6 which he had got in the land of C·; "
37: 1 was a stranger, in the land of C·. "
42: 5 the famine was in the land of C·. "
7 From the land of C· to buy food. "
13 sons of one man in the land of C·; "
29 their father unto the land of C·, "
32 with our father in the land of C·. "
44: 8 unto thee out of the land of C·: "
45:17 go, get you unto the land of C·; "
25 came into the land of C· unto "
46: 6 they had gotten in the land of C·, "
12 Er and Onan died in the land of C·. "
31 which were in the land of C·, "
47: 1 are come out of the land of C·; "
4 famine is sore in the land of C·: "
13 the land of C· fainted by reason "
14 of Egypt, and in the land of C·, "
15 in the land of C·, all the Egyptians "
48: 3 at Luz in the land of C·, "
7 Rachel died by me in the land of C· "
49:30 is before Mamre, in the land of C·, "
50: 5 digged for me in the land of C·, "
13 carried him into the land of C·, "
Ex 6: 4 them, to give them the land of C·, "
15:15 inhabitants of C· shall melt away. "
16:35 unto the borders of the land of C·. "
Le 14:34 come into the land of C·, which "
18: 3 the doings of the land of C·, "
25:38 to give you the land of C·, and "
Nu 13: 2 they may search the land of C·, "
17 them to spy out the land of C·, "
26:19 Onan died in the land of C·. "
32:30 among you in the land of C·. "
32 before the Lord into the land of C·, "
33:40 in the south in the land of C·, "
51 over Jordan into the land of C·; "
34: 2 When ye come into the land of C·; "
2 land of C· with the coasts thereof:) "
29 children of Israel in the land of C·. "
35:10 over Jordan into the land of C·; "
14 shall ye give in the land of C·, "
De 32:49 the land of C·, which I give "
Jos 5:12 the fruit of the land of C· that "
14: 1 of Israel inherited the land of C·, "
21: 2 at Shiloh in the land of C·, saying, "
22: 9 Shiloh, which is in the land of C·, "
10 Jordan, that are in the land of C·, "
11 an altar over against the land of C·, "
32 unto the land of C·, to the children "
24: 3 throughout all the land of C·, "
J'g 3: 1 had not known all the wars of C·; "
4: 2 the hand of Jabin the king of C·, "
23 on that day Jabin the king of C·, "
24 against Jabin the king of C·, "
24 had destroyed Jabin king of C·. "
5:19 fought the kings of C· in Taanach "
21:12 to Shiloh, which is in the land of C·. "
1Ch 1: 8 Cush, and Mizraim, Put, and C·. "
13 And C· begat Zidon his firstborn, "
16:18 Unto thee will I give the land of C·, "
Ps 105:11 Unto thee will I give the land of C·, "
106:38 they sacrificed unto the idols of C·: "
135:11 and all the kingdoms of C·: "
Isa 19:18 speak the language of C·, and "
Eze 16: 3 thy nativity is of the land of C·; "
29 thy fornication in the land of C· "
Zep 2: 5 O C·, the land of the Philistines, "
M't 15:22 behold, a woman of C· came out 5478

Canaanite (*ca'-na-an-ite*) See also CANAANITES; CANAANITESS; CANAANITISH; ZELOTES.
Ge 12: 6 And the C· was then in the land. 3669
13: 7 the C· and the Perizzite dwelled "
38: 2 certain C·, whose name was Shuah; "
Ex 23:28 shall drive out the Hivite, the C·, "
33: 2 and I will drive out the C·, "
34:11 before thee the Amorite, and the C·, "
Nu 21: 1 king Arad the C·, which dwelt in "
33:40 king Arad the C·, which dwelt in "
Jos 9: 1 Hittite, and the Amorite, the C·, "
11: 3 the C· on the east and on the west, "
13: 3 which is counted to the C·: "
Zec 14:21 the C· in the house of the Lord "
M't 10: 4 Simon the C·, and Judas Iscariot, *2581
M'r 3:18 Thaddæus, and Simon the C·, * "

Canaanites (*ca'-na-an-ites*)
Ge 10:18 families of the C· spread abroad *3669
19 border of the C· was from Sidon, * "
15:21 And the Amorites, and the C·, * "
24: 3 my son of the daughters of the C·, * "
37 my son of the daughters of the C·, * "
34:30 among the C·, and the Perizzites: "
50:11 the C·, saw the mourning in the "
Ex 3: 8 place of the C·, and the Hittites, * "
17 land of the C·, and the Hittites, * "
13: 5, 11 thee into the land of the C·, * "
23:23 C·, the Hivites, and the Jebusites; * "
Nu 13:29 and the C· dwell by the sea, * "
14:25 and the C· dwelt in the valley. * "
43 the C· are there before you, * "
45 the C· which dwelt in that hill, * "
21: 3 and delivered up the C·; and they "
De 1: 7 sea side, to the land of the C·, "
7: 1 and the Amorites, and the C·, "
11:30 goeth down in the land of the C·, "
20:17 and the Amorites, the C·, * "
Jos 3:10 drive out from before you the C·, * "
5: 1 the kings of the C·, which were "
7: 9 the C· and all the inhabitants "
12: 8 the Amorites, and the C·, * "
13: 4 the south, all the land of the C·, "
16:10 And they drove not out the C· "
10 the C· dwell among the Ephraimites "
17:12 the C· would dwell in that land. "
13 that they put the C· to tribute; "
16 all the C· that dwell in the land "
18 for thou shalt drive out the C·, "
24:11 and the Perizzites, and the C·, * "
J'g 1: 1 shall go up for us against the C· "
3 that we may fight against the C·; "
4 and the Lord delivered the C· "
5 slew the C· and the Perizzites. "
9 went down to fight against the C·, "
10 went against the C· that dwelt "
17 they slew the C· that inhabited "
27 the C· would dwell in that land. "
28 that they put the C· to tribute, "
29 did Ephraim drive out the C· "
29 the C· dwelt in Gezer among them. "
30 but the C· dwelt among them, "
32 the Asherites dwelt among the C·, "
33 but he dwelt among the C·, "
3: 3 the Philistines, and all the C·, "
5 of Israel dwelt among the C·, "
2Sa 24: 7 of the Hivites, and of the C·: "
1Ki 9:16 slain the C· that dwelt in the city, "
Ezr 9: 1 their abominations, even of the C·, "
Ne 9: 8 him to give the land of the C· * "
24 inhabitants of the land, the C·, "
Ob 20 Israel shall possess that of the C·, "

Canaanitess (*ca'-na-an-ite-ess*)
1Ch 2: 3 of the daughter of Shua the C·. 3669

Canaanitish (*ca'-na-an-i-tish*)
Ge 46:10 Shaul the son of a C· woman. 3669
Ex 6:15 Shaul the son of a C· woman. "

Candace (*can'-da-see*)
Ac 8:27 under C· queen of the Ethiopians, 2582

candle See also CANDLES; CANDLESTICK.
Job 18: 6 and his c· shall be put out *5216
21:17 is the c· of the wicked put out! * "
29: 3 When his c· shined upon my * "
Ps 18:28 For thou wilt light my c·: * "
Pr 20:27 the c· of the Lord, searching * "
24:20 c· of the wicked shall be put out. * "
31:18 her c· goeth not out by night. * "
Jer 25:10 and the light of the c·. ‡ "
M't 5:15 men light a c·, and put it under *3088
M'r 4:21 Is a c· brought to be put under * "
Lu 8:16 when he hath lighted a c·, * "
11:33 when he hath lighted a c·, * "
36 the bright shining of a c· doth * "
15: 8 doth not light a c·, and sweep * "
Re 18:23 And the light of a c· shall shine * "
22: 5 they need no c·, neither light of * "

candles
Zep 1:12 I will search Jerusalem with c·. 5216

candlestick See also CANDLESTICKS.
Ex 25:31 thou shalt make a c· of pure gold: 4501
31 beaten work shall the c· be made: "
32 branches of the c· out of the one "
32 branches of the c· out of the other "
33 branches that come out of the c·. "
34 And in the c· shall be four bowls "
35 branches that proceed out of the c·. "
26:35 the c· over against the table "
30:27 the c· and his vessels, and the "
31: 8 the pure c· with all his furniture, "
35:14 The c· also for the light, "
37:17 he made the c· of pure gold: "
17 of beaten work made he the c·; "
18 c· out of the one side thereof, "
18 and three branches of the c· "
19 six branches going out of the c·. "
20 And in the c· were four bowls "
39:37 The pure c·, with the lamps "
40: 4 thou shalt bring in the c·, "
24 he put the c· in the tent of the "
Le 24: 4 the lamps upon the pure c· "
Nu 3:31 c·, and the altars, and the vessels "
4: 9 and cover the c· of the light, "
8: 2 give light over against the c·. "
3 over against the c·, as the Lord "
4 work of the c· was of beaten gold, "
4 Moses, so he made the c·. "
2Ki 4:10 a table, a stool, and a c·: "
1Ch 28:15 by weight for every c·, and for the "

1Ch 28:15 the *c*, and also for the lamps 4501
15 according to the use of every *c*. "
2Ch 13:11 and the *c* of gold with the lamps "
Da 5: 5 and wrote over against the *c* 5043
Zec 4: 2 a *c* all of gold, with a bowl 4501
11 upon the right side of the *c* "
M't 5:15 but on a *c*; and it giveth light *3087
M'r 4:21 abed? and not to be set on a *c*? * "
Lu 8:16 but setteth it on a *c*, that they * "
11:33 but on a *c*, that they which * "
Heb 9: 2 wherein was the *c*, and the table, "
Re 2: 5 remove thy *c* out of his place, "

candlesticks
1Ki 7:49 the *c* of pure gold, five on the 4501
1Ch 28:15 the weight for the *c* of gold, and "
15 and for the *c* of silver by weight, "
2Ch 4: 7 he made ten *c* of gold according "
20 the *c* with their lamps, that they "
Jer 52:19 the *c*, and the spoons, and the "
Re 1:12 turned, I saw seven golden *c*; 3087
13 in the midst of the seven *c* one "
20 hand, and the seven golden *c*. "
20 and the seven *c* which thou sawest "
2: 1 the midst of the seven golden *c*; "
11: 4 and the two *c* standing before the "

cane
Isa 43:24 Thou hast bought me no sweet *c* 7070
Jer 6:20 Sheba, and the sweet *c* from a far "

canker See also CANKERED; CANKERWORM.
2Ti 2:17 their word will eat as doth a *c*: *1044

cankered
Jas 5: 3 Your gold and silver is *c*; and *2728

cankerworm
Joe 1: 4 hath the *c* eaten; 3218
4 and that which the *c* hath left "
2:25 the *c*, and the caterpillar, and the "
Na 3:15 it shall eat thee up like the *c*: "
15 make thyself many as the *c*, "
16 the *c* spoileth, and fleeth away. "

Canneh (*can'-neh*) See also CALNEH.
Eze 27:23 *C*, and Eden, the merchants of 3656

cannot
Ge 19:19 I *c* escape to the mountain, 3808, 3201
22 I *c* do any thing till thou be " "
24:50 we *c* speak unto thee bad or " "
29: 8 We *c*, until all the flocks be " "
31:35 I *c* rise up before thee: for " "
32:12 the sand of the sea, which *c* be 3808
34:14 We *c* do this thing, to give 3808, 3201
38:22 and said, I *c* find her; and also *3808
43:22 *c* tell who put our money * "
44:22 The lad *c* leave his father: 3808, 3201
26 *c* go down: if our youngest " "
Ex 10: 5 one *c* be able to see the earth: *3808
19:23 people *c* come up to mount 3808, 3201
Nu 22:18 I *c* go beyond the word of " "
23:20 he hath blessed; and I *c* reverse 3808
24:13 I *c* go beyond the 3808, 3201
35:33 and the land *c* be cleansed of *3308
De 28:35 a sore botch that *c* be *3808, 3201
Jos 24:19 Ye *c* serve the Lord: for he is " "
J'g 11:35 mouth unto the Lord, and I *c* " "
14:13 if ye *c* declare it me, then " "
Ru 4: 6 I *c* redeem it for myself, lest " "
6 my right to thyself; for I *c* " "
1Sa 12:21 things, which *c* profit nor deliver: 3308
17:39 I *c* go with these; for I 3808
55 As thy soul liveth, O king, I *c* tell. 518
25:17 that a man *c* speak to him.
2Sa 5: 6 thinking, David *c* come in hither. 3808
14:14 which *c* be gathered up again: "
23: 6 they *c* be taken with hands: "
1Ki 3: 8 that *c* be numbered nor counted "
8:27 heaven of heavens *c* contain "
18:12 tell Ahab, and he *c* find thee, "
2Ch 2: 6 heaven of heavens *c* contain him? "
6:18 heaven of heavens *c* contain "
24:20 of the Lord, that ye *c* prosper? "
Ezr 9:15 we *c* stand before thee because "
Ne 6: 3 so that I *c* come down: 369
Job 5:12 their hands *c* perform their 3808, 3201
6:30 *c* my taste discern perverse things? 3808
9: 3 *c* answer him one of a thousand. "
12:14 *c* be built again: he shutteth "
14: 5 appointed his bounds that he *c* "
17:10 *c* find one wise man among you * "
23: 8 backward, but I *c* perceive him: "
9 doth work, but I *c* behold him: "
9 the right hand, that I *c* see him: "
28:15 It *c* be gotten for gold, neither "
16 It *c* be valued with the gold of "
17 gold and the crystal *c* equal it: "
31:31 of his flesh! we *c* be satisfied. * "
33:21 that it *c* be seen; and his bones "
36:18 then a great ransom *c* deliver * "
37: 5 which we *c* comprehend. 408
19 we *c* order our speech by reason 3808
23 Almighty, we *c* find him out: "
41:17 stick together, that they *c* be "
23 in themselves; they *c* be moved. 1077
26 him *c* hold: the spear, the dart, 1097
28 The arrow *c* make him flee: 3808
Ps 40: 5 they *c* be reckoned up in order 408
77: 4 I am so troubled that I *c* speak. 3808
93: 1 is stablished, that it *c* be moved. 1077
125: 1 mount Zion, which *c* be removed, 3808
139: 6 for me; it is high, I *c* attain 3808, 3201
Pr 30:21 and for four which it *c* bear: "
Ec 1: 8 man *c* utter it: the eye is not "
15 crooked *c* be made straight: "
15 that which is wanting *c* be "
8:17 man *c* find out the work that "
10:14 a man *c* tell what shall be; *3045

Ca 8: 7 Many waters *c* quench love, 3808, 3201
Isa 1:13 the calling of assemblies, I *c* " "
29:11 and he saith, I *c*; for it is " "
38:18 For the grave *c* praise thee, 3808
18 go down into the pit *c* hope for "
44:18 shut their eyes, that they *c* see; "
18 and their hearts, that they *c* "
20 that he *c* deliver his soul, nor 3808
45:20 and pray unto a god that *c* save. "
50: 2 hand shortened at all, that it *c* "
56:10 all dumb dogs, they *c* bark; 3808, 3201
11 shepherds that *c* understand: " 3045
57:20 troubled sea, when it *c* rest, " 3201
59: 1 is not shortened, that it *c* save; 3808
1 his ear heavy, that it *c* hear: "
14 and equity *c* enter. 3808, 3201
Jer 1: 6 Ah, Lord God! behold, I *c* speak: ‡3808
4:19 noise in me; I *c* hold my peace, "
6:10 they *c* hearken: behold, 3808, 3201
7: 8 trust in lying words, that *c* profit. 1115
10: 5 needs be borne, because they *c* go 3808
5 for they *c* do evil, neither also "
14: 9 as a mighty man that *c* 3808, 3201
18: 6 of Israel, *c* I do with you as " "
19:11 vessel, that *c* be made whole " "
24: 3 that *c* be eaten, they are so evil. 3808
8 evils figs, which *c* be eaten, they "
29:17 them like vile figs, that *c* be "
33:22 host of heaven *c* be numbered, "
36: 5 am shut up; I *c* go into 3808, 3201
46:23 Lord, though it *c* be searched; 3808
49:23 on the sea; it *c* be quiet. 3808, 3201
La 3: 7 I *c* get out: he hath made my 3808
4:18 that we *c* go in our streets: "
Da 2:27 *c* the wise men, the 3809, *3202
Ho 1:10 sea, which *c* be measured nor 3808
Jon 4:11 that *c* discern between their "
Hab 2: 5 and *c* be satisfied, but gathereth "
M't 5:14 city that is set on an hill *c* be 3756, 1410
6:24 Ye *c* serve God and mammon. " "
7:18 A good tree *c* bring forth evil " "
19:11 All men *c* receive this saying, 3756
21:27 We *c* tell. And he said unto 3756, 1492
26:53 Thinkest thou that I *c* now " 1410
27:42 saved others; himself he *c* " "
M'k 2:19 bridegroom with them, they *c* " "
3:24 itself, that kingdom *c* stand. " "
25 itself, that house *c* stand. * " "
26 he *c* stand, but hath an end. " "
7:18 it *c* defile him; " "
11:33 *c* tell. And Jesus answering " 1492
15:31 others; himself he *c* save. " 1410
Lu 11: 7 in bed; I *c* rise and give thee. 3756, "
13:33 it *c* be that a prophet perish " 1735
14:14 for they *c* recompense thee: " *2192
20 wife, and therefore I *c* come. " 1410
26 life also, he *c* be my disciple. " "
27 after me, *c* be my disciple. " "
33 he hath, he *c* be my disciple. " "
16: 3 I *c* dig; to beg I am ashamed. " *2480
13 Ye *c* serve God and mammon. " 1410
26 pass from hence to you *c*; *3361, "
Joh 3: 3 *c* see the kingdom of God. 3756 "
5 *c* enter into the kingdom of " "
7: 7 world *c* hate you; but me it " "
34, 36 I am, thither ye *c* come. " "
8:14 ye *c* tell whence I come, *3756, 1492
21 whither I go, ye *c* come. " 1410
22 Whither I go, ye *c* come. " "
43 because ye *c* hear my word. " "
10:35 the scripture *c* be broken; " "
13:33 Whither I go, ye *c* come; so " "
37 why *c* I follow thee now? I " "
14:17 whom the world *c* receive, " "
15: 4 As the branch *c* bear fruit of " "
16:12 but ye *c* bear them now. " "
18 we *c* tell what he saith. " 1492
Ac 4:16 Jerusalem; and we *c* deny " 1410
20 we *c* but speak the things " "
5:39 ye *c* overthrow it lest; haply * * "
15: 1 of Moses, ye *c* be saved. " "
19:36 these things *c* be spoken against, 368
27:31 in the ship, ye *c* be saved. 3756, 1410
Ro 8: 8 are in the flesh *c* please God. " "
26 groanings which *c* be uttered. 215
1Co 7: 9 But if they *c* contain, let them *3756
10:21 *c* drink the cup of the Lord, 3756, 1410
21 ye *c* be partakers of the " "
12:21 the eye *c* say unto the hand, I " "
15:50 flesh and blood *c* inherit the " "
2Co 12: 2 I *c* tell; or whether out * " 1492
2 of the body, I *c* tell: * * "
3 the body, I *c* tell: God * * "
Ga 3:17 *c* disannul, that it should make *3756
5:17 ye *c* do the things that ye would. *3361
1Ti 5:25 that are otherwise *c* be hid. 3756, 1410
2Ti 2:13 abideth faithful: he *c* deny " "
Tit 1: 2 which God, that *c* lie, promised 893
2: 8 speech, that *c* be condemned; 176
He 4:15 priest which *c* be touched 3361, 1410
9: 5 of which we *c* now speak 3756, 1410
12:27 things which *c* be shaken may *3361
28 a kingdom which *c* be moved, 761
Jas 1:13 for God *c* be tempted with evil, 551
4: 2 desire to have, and *c* obtain: 3756, 1410
2Pe 1: 9 is blind, and *c* see afar off, and *3467
2:14 that *c* cease from sin; beguiling 180
1Jo 3: 9 he *c* sin, because he is born 3756, 1410

canst
Ge 41:15 that thou *c* understand a dream to
Ex 33:20 And he said, Thou *c* not see 3201
De 28:27 the itch, whereof thou *c* not
Jos 7:13 thou *c* not stand before
J'g 16:15 unto him, How *c* thou say, I love
1Sa 30:15 David said to him, *C* thou bring *
2Ki 8: 1 sojourn wheresoever thou *c* sojourn:

Ezr 7:16 silver and gold that thou *c* find *
Job 11: 7 *C* thou by searching find out God?
7 *c* thou find out the Almighty unto
8 is as high as heaven; what *c* thou do?
8 deeper than hell; what *c* thou know?
22:11 Or darkness, that thou *c* not see;
33: 5 If thou *c* answer me, set thy 3201
38:31 *C* thou bind the sweet influences of
32 *C* thou bring forth Mazzaroth in his
32 or *c* thou guide Arcturus with his
33 *c* thou set the dominion thereof in
34 *C* thou lift up thy voice to the clouds,
35 *C* thou send lightnings, that they
39: 1 or *c* thou mark when the hinds do
2 *C* thou number the months that they
10 *C* thou bind the unicorn with his
20 *C* thou make him afraid as a *
40: 9 or *c* thou thunder with a voice *
41: 1 *C* thou draw out leviathan with an
2 *C* thou put an hook into his nose?
7 *C* thou fill his skin with barbed
42: 2 I know that thou *c* do every 3201
Pr 3:15 and all the things thou *c* desire are
5: 6 ways are moveable, that thou *c* *
30: 4 is his son's name, if thou *c* tell? *
Isa 33:19 deeper speech than thou *c* perceive;
19 tongue, that thou *c* not understand
Jer 12: 5 how *c* thou contend with horses?
Eze 3: 6 words thou *c* not understand.
Da 5:16 that thou *c* make interpretations, 3202
16 doubts: now if thou *c* read "
Hab 1:13 and *c* not look on iniquity: 3201
M't 5:36 because thou *c* not make 1410
8: 2 thou *c* make me clean. "
M'r 1:40 If thou wilt, thou *c* make me "
9:22 but if thou *c* do any thing, have "
23 If thou *c* believe, all things are "
Lu 5:12 if thou wilt, thou *c* make me clean. "
6:42 how *c* thou say to thy brother, "
Joh 3: 8 but *c* not tell whence it cometh, *1492
13:36 Whither I go, thou *c* not follow 1410
Ac 21:37 Who said, *C* thou speak Greek? *1097
Re 2: 2 and how thou *c* not bear them 1410

Capernaum (*ca-pur'-na-um*)
M't 4:13 he came and dwelt in *C*, which is 2584
8: 5 when Jesus was entered into *C*, "
11:23 And thou, *C*, which art exalted "
17:24 were come to *C*, they that "
M'r 1:21 they went into *C*; and straightway "
2: 1 he entered into *C* after some days; "
9:33 he came to *C*: and being in the "
Lu 4:23 have heard done in *C*, do also here "
31 And came down to *C*, a city of "
7: 1 of the people, he entered into *C*. "
10:15 And thou, *C*, which art exalted to "
Joh 2:12 After this he went down to *C*, "
4:46 whose son was sick at *C*. "
6:17 and went over the sea toward *C*. "
24 came to *C*, seeking for Jesus. "
59 synagogue, as he taught in *C*. "

Caphthorim (*caf'-tho-rim*) See also CAPHTORIM.
1Ch 1:12 came the Philistines,) and *C*. 3732

Caphtor (*caf'-tor*) See also CAPHTORIM.
De 2:23 which came forth out of *C*, 3731
Jer 47: 4 the remnant of the country of *C*. "
Am 9: 7 the Philistines from *C*, and the "

Caphtorim (*caf'-to-rim*) See also CAPHTHORIM; CAPHTORIMS.
Ge 10:14 came Philistim,) and *C*. 3732

Caphtorims (*caf'-to-rims*) See also CAPHTORIM.
De 2:23 the *C*, which came forth out of 3732

capital See CHAPITER.

Cappadocia (*cap-pa-do'-she-ah*)
Ac 2: 9 and *C*, in Pontus, and Asia, 2587
1Pe 1: 1 Galatia, *C*, Asia, and Bithynia, "

captain See also CAPTAINS.
Ge 21:22 *c* of his host spake unto 8269
32 Phichol, the chief *c* of his host, "
26:26 Phichol, the chief *c* of his army. "
37:36 Pharaoh's, and *c* of the guard. "
39: 1 *c* of the guard, an Egyptian, "
40: 3 the house of the *c* of the guard, "
4 *c* of the guard charged Joseph "
41:10 *c* of the guard's house, both me "
12 Hebrew, servant to the *c* of the "
Nu 2: 3 be *c* of the children of Judah. *5387
5 be *c* of the children of Issachar. * "
7 be *c* of the children of Zebulun. * "
10 the *c* of the children of Reuben * "
12 the *c* of the children of Simeon * "
14 the *c* of the sons of Gad shall be * "
18 the *c* of the sons of Ephraim * "
20 *c* of the children of Manasseh * "
22 the *c* of the sons of Benjamin * "
25 the *c* of the children of Dan * "
27 the *c* of the children of Asher * "
29 the *c* of the children of Naphtali * "
14: 4 Let us make a *c*, and let us 7218
Jos 5:14 but as *c* of the host of the Lord ‡8269
15 *c* of the Lord's host said unto ‡ "
J'g 4: 2 the *c* of whose host was Sisera, "
7 the *c* of Jabin's army, with his "
11: 6 and be our *c*, that we may fight *7101
11 made him head and *c* over them:* "
1Sa 9:16 to be *c* over my people Israel, *5057
10: 1 thee to be *c* over his inheritance? * "
12: 9 *c* of the host of Hazor, and into 8269
13:14 to be *c* over his people, because *5057
14:50 the name of the *c* of his host was 8269
17:18 unto the *c* of their thousand, "
55 the *c* of the host, Abner, whose "
18:13 made him his *c* over a thousand; "
22: 2 he became a *c* over them: and "

1Sa 26: 5 Abner the son of Ner, the c' of his 8269
2Sa 2: 8 Abner the son of Ner, c' of Saul's "
5: 2 and thou shalt be a c' over Israel.*5057
8 soul, he shall be chief and c'. *
10:16 Shobach, the c' of the host of 8269
18 Shobach, the c' of their host, who "
17:25 And Absalom made Amasa c' *5921
19:13 c' of the host before me 8269
23:19 therefore he was their c': howbeit "
24: 2 Joab the c' of the host, which was "
1Ki 1:19 Joab the c' of the host: but "
2:32 c' of the host of Israel, and Amasa "
32 Jether, c' of the host of Judah. "
11:15 Joab the c' of the host was gone up "
21 Joab the c' of the host was dead, "
24 became c' over a band, when "
16: 9 c' of half his chariots, conspired "
16 Omri, the c' of the host, king over "
2Ki 1: 9 unto him a c' of fifty with his fifty. "
10 said to the c' of fifty, If I be a man "
11 unto him another c' of fifty "
12 a c' of the third fifty with his "
13 And the third c' of fifty went up, "
4:13 the c' of the host? And she "
5: 1 c' of the host of the king of Syria, "
9: 5 I have an errand to thee, O c'. "
5 all us? And he said, To thee, O c'. "
25 Then said Jehu to Bidkah his c', 7991
15:25 Pekah, the son of Remaliah, a c' "
18:24 one c' of the least of my master's 6346
20: 5 Hezekiah the c' of my people, *5057
25: 8 Nebuzar-adan, c' of the guard, 7227
10 were with the c' of the guard, "
11 Nebuzar-adan the c' of the guard "
12 But the c' of the guard left of the "
15 in silver, the c' of the guard took "
18 the c' of the guard took Seraiah "
20 c' of the guard took these, and "
1Ch 11: 6 first shall be the chief and c'. 8269
21 than the two; for he was their c': "
42 a c' of the Reubenites, and *7218
19:16 the c' of the host of Hadarezer 8269
18 killed Shophach the c' of the host. "
27: 5 The third c' of the host for the "
7 The fourth c' for the fourth month
8 fifth c' for the fifth month was 8269
9 The sixth c' for the sixth month
10 The seventh c' for the seventh
11 The eighth c' for the eighth month
12 The ninth c' for the ninth month
13 The tenth c' for the tenth month
14 The eleventh c' for the eleventh
15 The twelfth c' for the twelfth
2Ch 13:12 himself is with us for our c', *7218
17:15 Jehohanan the c', and with him 8269
Ne 9:17 in their rebellion appointed a c' 7218
Isa 3: 3 c' of fifty, and the honourable 8269
36: 9 one c' of the least of my master's 6346
Jer 37:13 a c' of the ward was there, 1167
39: 9 the c' of the guard carried away 7227
10 the c' of the guard left of the poor "
11 Nebuzar-adan, the c' of the guard, "
13 the c' of the guard sent, "
40: 1 after that Nebuzar-adan the c' of "
2 c' of the guard took Jeremiah, "
5 the c' of the guard gave him "
41:10 Nebuzar-adan the c' of the guard "
43: 6 person that Nebuzar-adan the c' "
51:27 appoint a c' against her; cause *2951
52:12 Nebuzar-adan, c' of the guard, 7227
14 that were with the c' of the guard, "
15 the c' of the guard carried away "
16 the c' of the guard left certain "
19 took the c' of the guard away. "
24 the c' of the guard took Seraiah "
26 Nebuzar-adan the c' of the guard "
30 the c' of the guard carried away "
Da 2:14 the c' of the king's guard, which 7229
15 said to Arioch the king's c', Why 7990
Joh 18:12 band and the c' and officers *5506
Ac 4: 1 and the c' of the temple, and the 4755
5:24 and the c' of the temple and the "
26 went the c' with the officers, "
21:31 tidings came unto the chief c' 5506
32 the chief c' and the soldiers, "
33 Then the chief c' came near, "
37 he said unto the chief c', May I "
22:24 The chief c' commanded him to "
26 he went and told the chief c', "
27 Then the chief c' came, and said "
28 And the chief c' answered, With a "
29 the chief c' also was afraid, after "
23:10 the chief c', fearing lest Paul "
15 signify to the chief c' that he "
17 this young man unto the chief c': "
18 and brought him to the chief c', "
19 chief c' took him by the hand, "
22 chief c' then let the young man "
24: 7 But the chief c' Lysias came * "
22 When Lysias the chief c' shall "
28:16 delivered the prisoners to the c' *4759
Heb 2:10 make the c' of their salvation * 747

captains
Ex 14: 7 and c' over every one of them. 7991
15: 4 his chosen c' also are drowned "
Nu 31:14 the c' over thousands, 8269
14 and c' over hundreds, "
48 the c' of thousands, "
48 and c' of hundreds, "
52 of the c' of thousands, "
52 and of the c' of hundreds, "
54 c' of thousands and of hundreds, "
De 1:15 c' over thousands, "
15 and c' over hundreds, "
15 and c' over fifties, "
15 and c' over tens. "
De 20: 9 c' of the armies to lead the 8269
29:10 your c' of your tribes, your *7218
Jos 10:24 unto the c' of the men of war *7101
1Sa 8:12 c' over thousands, 8269
12 and c' over fifties; "
22: 7 make you all c' of thousands, "
7 and c' of hundreds; "
2Sa 4: 2 two men that were c' of bands: "
18: 1 c' of thousands "
1 and c' of hundreds "
5 the king gave all the c' charge "
23: 8 chief among the c'; the same 7991
24: 4 against the c' of the host. 8269
4 and the c' of the host went out "
1Ki 1:25 and the c' of the host, and "
2: 5 two c' of the hosts of Israel, unto "
9:22 his princes, and his c', and rulers 7991
15:20 the c. of the hosts which he had 8269
20:24 and put c' in their rooms: 6346
22:31 thirty and two c' that had rule 8269
32 the c' of the chariots saw "
33 the c' of the chariots perceived "
2Ki 1:14 the two c' of the former fifties "
8:21 the c' of the chariots: and the "
9: 5 the c' of the host were sitting; "
10:25 said to the guard and to the c', 7991
25 guard and the c' cast them out, "
11: 4 with the c' and the guard, *3746
9 the c' over the hundreds did 8269
10 to the c' over hundreds did the "
15 the c' of the hundreds, and "
19 the c', and the guard, and all *3746
25:23 all the c' of the armies, 8269
26 and the c' of the armies, "
1Ch 4:42 having for their c' Pelatiah, 7218
11:11 chief of the c': he lifted up *7991
15 three of the thirty c' went down *7218
12:14 the sons of Gad, c' of the host: "
18 chief of the c', and he said, *7991
18 and made them c' of the band. 7218
20 c' of the thousands that were "
21 and were c' of the host. 8269
28 father's house twenty and two c'. "
34 of Naphtali a thousand c', and "
13: 1 c' of thousands and hundreds, "
15:25 and the c' over thousands, went "
25: 1 and the c' of the host separated "
26:26 the c' over thousands and "
26 hundreds, and the c' of the host, "
27: 1 c' of thousands and hundreds, "
3 the chief of all the c' of the host "
28: 1 and the c' of the companies that "
1 and the c' over the thousands, "
1 and c' over the hundreds, "
29: 6 c' of thousands and of hundreds, "
2Ch 1: 2 c' of thousands and of hundreds, "
8: 9 and chief of his c', 7991
9 and c' of his chariots *8269
11:11 strong holds, and put c' in them, 5057
16: 4 the c' of his armies against the 8269
17:14 the c' of thousands; Adnah the "
18:30 Syria had commanded the c' of "
31 when the c' of the chariots saw "
32 the c' of the chariots perceived "
21: 9 and the c' of the chariots. "
23: 1 took the c' of hundreds, Azariah "
9 to the c' of hundreds spears, "
14 the priest brought out the c' of "
20 he took the c' of hundreds, and "
25: 5 c' over thousands, "
5 and c' over hundreds, "
26:11 Hananiah, one of the king's c'. "
32: 6 set c' of war over the people, "
21 the leaders and c' in the camp "
33:11 the c' of the host of the king "
14 c' of war in all the fenced cities "
Ne 2: 9 king had sent c' of the army "
Job 39:25 the thunder of the c', and the "
Jer 13:21 hast taught them to be c', †‡ 441
40: 7 Now when all the c' of the 8269
13 and all the c' of the forces that "
41:11, 13, 16 all the c' of the forces that "
42: 1 Then all the c' of the forces, and "
8 all the c' of the forces which were "
43: 4 all the c' of the forces, and all "
5 and all the c' of the forces, took "
51:23 will I break in pieces c' and *6346
28 the Medes, the c' thereof, and * "
57 her c', and her rulers, and her * "
Eze 21:22 to appoint c', to open the mouth *3733
23: 6 c' and rulers, all of them *6346
12 c' and rulers clothed most * "
23 desirable young men, c' and * "
Da 3: 2 and the c', the judges, the *6347
3 the governors, and c', the judges,* "
27 c', and the king's counsellers, * "
6: 7 counsellers, and the c', have * "
Na 3:17 locusts, and thy c' as the great *2951
M'r 6:21 a supper to his lords, high c', 5506
Lu 22: 4 with the chief priest and c', 4755
52 and c' of the temple, and the "
Ac 25:23 with the chief c', and principal 5506
Rev 6:15 the rich men, and the chief c', "
19:18 of kings, and the flesh of c', "

captive See also CAPTIVES.
Ge 14:14 that his brother was taken c', 7617
34:29 their wives took they c', and "
Ex 12:29 the firstborn of the c' that was 7628
Nu 24:22 Asshur shall carry thee away c'. 7617
De 21:10 and thou hast taken them c', "
J'g 5:12 and lead thy captivity c', thou son "
1Ki 8:48 enemies, which led them away c', "
50 who carried them c', that they "
2Ki 5: 2 and had brought away c' out of "
6:22 those whom thou hast taken c' "
15:29 and carried them c' to Assyria. 1540
16: 9 and carried the people of it c' to 1540
24:16 king of Babylon brought c' to 1473
1Ch 5: 6 king of Assyria carried away c': 1540
2Ch 6:37 whither they are carried c', and 7617
25:12 children of Judah carry away c', * "
28: 8 carried away c' of their brethren "
11 again, which ye have taken c' "
30: 9 them that lead them c', so that "
Ps 68:18 thou hast led captivity c': thou ‡ "
137: 3 that carried us away c' required "
Isa 49:21 am desolate, a c', and removing *1473
24 the mighty, or the lawful c' *7628
51:14 The c' exile hasteneth that he 6808
52: 2 thy neck, O c' daughter of Zion. 7628
Jer 1: 3 carrying away of Jerusalem c' 1540
13:17 Lord's flock is carried away c'. 7617
19 shall be carried away c' all of it, 1540
19 it shall be wholly carried away c'. "
20: 4 and he shall carry them c' into "
22:12 they have led him c', and shall * "
24: 1 had carried away c' Jeconiah the "
5 are carried away c' of Judah, 1546
27:20 he carried away c' Jeconiah the 1540
28: 6 all that is carried away c', from *1473
29: 1 carried away c' from Jerusalem "
14 caused you to be carried away c'. 1540
39: 9 carried away c' into Babylon the "
40: 1 all that were carried away c' of *1546
1 which were carried away c' unto 1540
7 not carried away c' to Babylon; "
41:10 Then Ishmael carried away c' 7617
10 carried them away c', and "
14 Ishmael had carried away c' from "
52:15 carried away c' certain of the 1540
27 Thus Judah was carried away c'. "
28 Nebuchadrezzar carried away c': "
29 he carried away c' from Jerusalem "
30 carried away c' of the Jews seven 1540
Am 1: 6 they carried away c' the whole "
6: 7 therefore now shall they go c' with "
7 with the first that go c', "
7:11 Israel shall surely be led away c' "
Ob 11 the strangers carried away c' *7617
Na 2: 7 Huzzab shall be led away c', *1540
Lu 21:24 shall be led away c' into all 163
Eph 4: 8 upon high, he led captivity c', and 162
2Ti 2:26 who are taken c' by him at his 2221
3: 6 lead c' silly women laden with 162

captives
Ge 31:26 away my daughters, as c' taken 7617
Nu 31: 9 took all the women of Midian c', * "
12 they brought the c', and the prey, 7628
19 purify both yourselves and your c' "
De 21:11 And seest among the c' a 7633
32:42 blood of the slain and of the c', "
1Sa 30: 2 And had taken the women c', *7617
3 their daughters, were taken c'. "
5 David's two wives were taken c', "
1Ki 8:46 they carry them away c' unto * "
47 whither they were carried c', * "
47 of them that carried them c', * "
2Ki 24:14 ten thousand c', and all the 1540
2Ch 6:36 they carry them away c' unto a *7617
38 they have carried them c', and * "
28: 5 a great multitude of them c', 7633
11 deliver the c' again, which ye "
13 Ye shall not bring in the c' hither: "
14 the armed men left the c' and the "
15 by name rose up, and took the c', "
17 Judah, and carried away c'. 7628
Ps 106:46 of all those that carried them c'. 7617
Isa 14: 2 and they shall take them c', * "
2 whose c' they were; and they shall "
20: 4 the Ethiopians c', young and old,*1546
45:13 and he shall let go my c', not * "
49:25 the c' of the mighty shall be 7628
61: 1 to proclaim liberty to the c', and "
Jer 28: 4 with all the c' of Judah, that went1546
29: 1 which were carried away c', *1473
4 all that are carried away c', * "
7 caused you to be carried away c',*1540
43: 3 death, and carry us away c' into "
12 and carry them away c': and he 7617
48:46 thy sons are taken c', and *7628
46 and thy daughters c'. *7633
50:33 and all that took them c' held 7617
Eze 1: 1 as I was among the c' by the 1473
6: 9 they shall be carried c', because 7617
16:53 captivity of thy c' in the midst of 7628
Da 2:25 found a man of the c' of *1123, 1547
11: 8 shall also carry c' into Egypt *7628
Lu 4:18 to preach deliverance to the c'. 164

captivity
Nu 21:29 and his daughters, into c' 7628
De 21:13 the raiment of her c' from off 7633
28:41 them; for they shall go into c'. 7628
30: 3 the Lord thy God will turn thy c', 7622
J'g 5:12 and lead thy c' captive, thou son 7628
18:30 Dan until the day of the c' of the 1546
2Ki 24:15 carried he into c' from Jerusalem 1473
25:27 thirtieth year of the c' of 1546
1Ch 5:22 dwelt in their steads until the c'. 1473
6:15 And Jehozadak went into c', "
2Ch 6:37 the land of their c', saying, We 7633
38 in the land of their c', whither "
29: 9 daughters and our wives are in c' 7628
Ezr 1:11 bring up with them of the c' that 1473
2: 1 that went up out of the c', 7628
3: 8 that were come out of the c' unto "
4: 1 that the children of the c' 1473
6:16 the rest of the children of the c', 1547
19 And the children of the c' kept 1473
20 all the children of the c', and for "
21 were come again out of the c', and all "
8:35 which were come out of the c', 7628

Ezr 9: 7 to the sword, to c', and to a spoil, 7628
10: 7 all the children of the c', that 1473
16 the children of the c' did so. And "
Ne 1: 2 escaped, which were left of the c', 7628
3 remnant that are left of the c' "
4: 4 them for a prey in the land of c': 7633
7: 6 went up out of the c', of those 7628
8:17 come again out of the c' made "
Es 2: 6 from Jerusalem with the c', *1473
Job 42:10 Lord turned the c' of Job when 7622
Ps 14: 7 Lord bringeth back the c' of his "
53: 6 God bringeth back the c' of his "
68:18 high, thou hast led c' captive: ‡7628
78:61 delivered his strength into c', and "
85: 1 brought back the c' of Jacob. 7622
126: 1 the Lord turned again the c' of ‡ "
4 Turn again our c', O Lord, as the "
Isa 5:13 my people are gone into c', 1540
22:17 thee away with a mighty c', *2925
46: 2 but themselves are gone into c'. 7628
Jer 15: 2 such as are for the c', to the c'. "
20: 6 in thine house, shall go into c': "
22:22 and thy lovers shall go into c': "
29:14 and I will turn away your c', 7622
16 not gone forth with you into c'; 1473
20 word of the Lord, all ye of the c', "
22 a curse by all the c' of Judah *1546
28 This c' is long: build ye houses, "
31 Send to all them of the c', saying, 1473
30: 3 I will bring again the c' of my 7622
10 seed from the land of their c'; 7628
16 every one of them, shall go into c';7633
18 will bring again the c' of Jacob's 7622
31:23 when I shall bring again their c'; "
32:44 I will cause their c' to return, "
33: 7 I will cause the c' of Judah and the "
7 and the c' of Israel to return, "
11 I will cause to return the c' of the "
26 I will cause their c' to return, and "
43:11 and such as are for c' to c'; 7628
46:19 furnish thyself to go into c': 1473
27 seed from the land of their c'; 7633
48: 7 Chemosh shall go forth into c' 1473
11 neither hath he gone into c': "
47 Yet will I bring again the c' of 7622
49: 3 their king shall go into c', and 1473
6 I will bring again the c' of the 7622
39 I will bring again the c' of Elam, "
52:31 and thirtieth year of the c' of 1546
La 1: 3 Judah is gone into c' because 1540
5 her children are gone into c' 7628
18 my young men are gone into c'. "
2:14 to turn away thy c'; but have 7622
4:22 more carry thee away into c': 1540
Eze 1: 2 fifth year of king Jehoiachin's c', 1546
3:11 get thee to them of the c', unto 1473
15 I came to them of the c' at "
11:24 God into Chaldea, to them of the c'. "
25 Then I spake unto them of the c' "
12: 4 as they that go forth into c'. * "
7 as stuff for c', and in the even * "
11 they shall remove and go into c'. "
16:53 I shall bring again their c', 7622
53 the c' of Sodom and her daughters, "
53 and the c' of Samaria and her "
53 the c' of thy captives in the midst "
25: 3 Judah, when they went into c'; 1473
29:14 And I will bring again the c' of 7622
30:17 and these cities shall go into c'. 7628
18 her daughters shall go into c'. "
33:21 the twelfth year of our c', in the 1546
39:23 Israel went into c' for their 1540
25 will I bring again the c' of Jacob, 7622
28 them to be led into c' among the 1473
40: 1 year of our c', in the beginning 1546
Da 5:13 art of the children of the c' of 1547
6:13 which is of the children of the c' "
11:33 the sword, and by flame, by c', 7628
Ho 6:11 when I returned the c' of my 7622
Joe 3: 1 shall bring again the c' of Judah, "
Am 1: 5 people of Syria shall go into c' 1540
6 carried away captive the whole c',*1546
9 they delivered up the whole c' to* "
15 their king shall go into c', he 1473
5: 5 Gilgal shall surely go into c', and 1540
27 will I cause you to go into c' "
7:17 Israel shall surely go into c' * "
9: 4 though they go into c' before 7628
14 I will bring again the c' of my 7622
Ob 20 And the c' of this host of the ‡1546
20 and the c' of Jerusalem, which ‡ "
Mic 1:16 for they are gone into c' from 1540
Na 3:10 she went into c': her young 7628
Hab 1: 9 they shall gather the c' as the * "
Zep 2: 7 them, and turn away their c'. 7622
3:20 when I turn back your c' before "
Zec 6:10 Take of them of the c', even of 1473
14: 2 of the city shall go forth into c', "
Ro 7:23 bringing me into c' to the law of 163
2Co 10: 5 bringing into c' every thought to "
Eph 4: 8 he led c' captive, and gave gifts 161
Re 13:10 that leadeth into c' shall go into c': "

Car See BETH-CAR.

carbuncle See also CARBUNCLES.
Ex 28:17 topaz, and a c': this shall be the 1304
39:10 was a sardius, a topaz, and a c': "
Eze 28:13 emerald, and the c', and gold: "

carbuncles
Isa 54:12 and thy gates of c', and all thy 68, 688

Carcas *(car'-cas)*
Es 1:10 Abagtha, Zethar, and C'. 3752

carcase See also CARCASES.
Le 5: 2 a c' of an unclean beast, 5038
5: 2 or a c' of unclean cattle, 5038
2 the c' of unclean creeping things, "
11: 8 and their c' shall ye not touch; * "
24 whosoever toucheth the c' of them "
25 beareth ought of the c' of them "
27 whoso toucheth their c' shall be "
28 he that beareth the c' of them "
35 any part of their c' falleth "
36 that which toucheth their c' shall "
37 if any part of their c' fall upon any "
38 any part of their c' fall thereon, "
39 he that toucheth the c' thereof "
40 he that eateth of the c' of it shall "
40 he also that beareth the c' of it "
De 14: 8 flesh, nor touch their dead c'. * "
28:26 thy c' shall be meat unto all fowls "
Jos 8:29 they should take his c' down from "
J'g 14: 8 aside to see the c' of the lion: 4658
8 and honey in the c' of the lion. *1472
9 honey out of the c' of the lion. * "
1Ki 13:22 thy c' shall not come unto the 5038
24 his c' was cast in the way, "
24 the lion also stood by the c'. "
25 and saw the c' cast in the way, "
25 and the lion standing by the c': "
28 and found his c' cast in the way, "
28 ass and the lion standing by the c': "
28 the lion had not eaten the c', "
29 prophet took up the c' of the man "
30 he laid his c' in his own grave; "
2Ki 9:37 the c' of Jezebel shall be as dung "
Isa 14:19 as a c' trodden under feet. 6297
M't 24:28 For wheresoever the c' is, there 4430

carcases
Ge 15:11 the fowls came down upon the c', 6297
Le 11:11 shall have their c' in abomination. 5038
26:30 cast your c' upon the c' of your 6297
Nu 14:29 Your c' shall fall in this wilderness; "
32 for you, your c', they shall fall "
33 your c' be wasted in the wilderness. "
1Sa 17:46 the c' of the host of the Philistines "
Isa 5:25 their c' were torn in the midst of 5038
34: 3 stink shall come up out of their c', 6297
66:24 upon the c' of the men that have "
Jer 7:33 the c' of this people shall be meat 5038
9:22 the c' of men shall fall as dung "
16: 4 their c' shall be meat for the fowls "
18 with the c' of their detestable "
19: 7 their c' will I give to be meat for "
Eze 6: 5 dead c' of the children of Israel 6297
43: 7 nor by the c' of their kings in "
9 the c' of their kings, far from me, "
Na 3: 3 slain, and a great number of c'; "
Heb 3:17 whose c' fell in the wilderness? 2966

carcass See CARCASE.

Carchemish *(car'-ke-mish)* See also CHARCHEMISH.
Isa 10: 9 Is not Calno as C'? is not Hamath 3751
Jer 46: 2 was by the river Euphrates in C', "

care See also CARED; CAREFUL; CARELESS; CARES; CAREST; CARETH; CARING.
1Sa 10: 2 hath left the c' of the asses, ‡1697
2Sa 18: 3 they will not c' for us; 7760, 3820
3 of us die, will they c' for us: " "
2Ki 4:13 been careful for us with all this c';2731
Jer 49:31 nation, that dwelleth without c', 983
Eze 4:16 eat bread by weight, and with c'; *1674
M't 13:22 the c' of this world, and the 3308
Lu 10:34 to an inn, and took c' of him. 1959
35 Take c' of him; and whatsoever "
40 Lord, dost thou not c' that my 3199
1Co 7:21 being a servant? c' not for it; "
9: 9 Doth God take c' for oxen? * "
12:25 the same c' one for another. 3309
2Co 7:12 or c' for you in the sight of God 4710
8:16 earnest c' into the heart of Titus "
11:28 daily, the c' of all the churches. *3308
Ph'p 2:20 will naturally c' for your state. 3309
4:10 your c' of me hath flourished *5426
1Ti 3: 5 shall he take c' of the church of 1959
1Pe 5: 7 Casting all your c' upon him; *3308

Careah *(ca-re'-ah)* See also KAREAH.
2Ki 25:23 and Johanan the son of C'. 7143

cared
Ps 142: 4 failed me; no man c' for my soul. *1875
Joh 12: 6 not that he c' for the poor; 3199
Ac 18:17 Gallio c' for none of those things. "

careful
2Ki 4:13 thou hast been c' for us with all 2729
Jer 17: 8 not be c' in the year of drought, 1672
Da 3:16 we are not c' to answer thee in *2818
Lu 10:41 Martha, thou art c' and troubled *3309
Ph'p 4: 6 Be c' for nothing; but in "
10 wherein ye were also c', but ye *5426
Tit 3: 8 be c' to maintain good works. 5431

carefully
De 15: 5 Only if thou c' hearken unto the *8085
Mic 1:12 inhabitant of Maroth waited c' *2470
Ph'p 2:28 sent him therefore the more c', *4708
Heb 12:17 though he sought it c' with tears.*1567

carefulness
Eze 12:18 water with trembling and with c'; 1674
19 eat their bread with c', and drink "
1Co 7:32 But I would have you without c'. * 275
2Co 7:11 sort, what c' it wrought in you, *4710

careless
J'g 18: 7 how they dwelt c', after the * 983
Isa 32: 9 ye c' daughters; give ear unto my 982
10 ye be troubled, ye c' women: for "
32:11 at ease; be troubled, ye c' ones: 982
Eze 30: 9 to make the c' Ethiopians afraid, 983

carelessly
Isa 47: 8 that dwellest c', that sayest in 983
Eze 39: 6 and among them that dwell c' in * "
Zep 2:15 is the rejoicing city that dwelt c'. "

cares
M'r 4:19 the c' of this world, and the 3308
Lu 8:14 are choked with c' and riches and "
21:34 and c' of this life, and so that day "

carest
M't 22:16 neither c' thou for any man: for 3199
M'r 4:38 Master, c' thou not that we perish? "
12:14 thou art true, and c' for no man: "

careth
De 11:12 which the Lord thy God c' for: 1875
Joh 10:13 hireling, and c' not for the sheep. 3199
1Co 7:32 He that is unmarried c' for the *3309
33 he that is married c' for the * "
34 unmarried woman c' for the * "
34 married c' for the things of the * "
1Pe 5: 7 upon him, for he c' for you. 3199

caring
1Sa 9: 5 lest my father leave c' for the asses,

Carmel *(car'-mel)* See also CARMELITE.
Jos 12:22 the king of Jokneam of C', one; 3760
15:55 Maon, C', and Ziph, and Juttah, "
19:26 Misheal; and reacheth to C' "
1Sa 15:12 Samuel, saying, Saul came to C', "
25: 2 whose possessions were in C'; "
2 he was shearing his sheep in C'. "
5 Get you up to C', and go to Nabal, "
7 them, all the while they were in C'. "
40 of David were come to Abigail to C', "
1Ki 18:19 to me all Israel unto mount C', "
20 prophets together unto mount C'. "
42 Elijah went up to the top of C'; "
2Ki 2:25 he went from thence to mount C', "
4:25 unto the man of God to mount C'. "
19:23 and into the forest of his C'. * "
2Ch 26:10 in the mountains, and in C': * "
Ca 7: 5 Thine head upon thee is like C', "
Isa 33: 9 and C' shake off their fruits. "
35: 2 the excellency of C' and Sharon, "
37:24 border, and the forests of his C'. * "
Jer 46:18 and as C' by the sea, so shall he "
50:19 he shall feed on C' and Bashan, "
Am 1: 2 shall mourn, and the top of C' "
9: 3 hide themselves in the top of C', "
Mic 7:14 in the wood, in the midst of C': "
Na 1: 4 Bashan languisheth, and C', and "

Carmelite *(car'-mel-ite)* See also CARMELITESS.
1Sa 30: 5 Abigail the wife of Nabal the C'. 3761
2Sa 2: 2 and Abigail Nabal's wife the C'. "
3: 3 Abigail the wife of Nabal the C'; "
23:35 Hezrai the C', Paarai the Arbite, "
1Ch 11:37 Hezro the C', Naarai the son of "

Carmelitess *(car'-mel-i-tess)*
1Sa 27: 3 and Abigail the C', Nabal's wife. 3762
1Ch 3: 1 second Daniel, of Abigail the C': "

Carmi *(car'-mi)* See also CARMITES.
Ge 46: 9 and Phallu, and Hezron, and C'. 3756
Ex 6:14 Hanoch, and Pallu, Hezron, and C': "
Nu 26: 6 Hezronites: of C', the family of "
Jos 7: 1 for Achan, the son of C', the son "
18 by man; and Achan, the son of C', "
1Ch 2: 7 And the sons of C'; Achar, the "
4: 1 of Judah; Pharez, Hezron, and C', "
5: 3 Hanoch, and Pallu, Hezron, and C'. "

Carmites *(car'-mites)*
Nu 26: 6 of Carmi, the family of the C'. 3757

carnal
Ro 7:14 but I am c', sold under sin. 4559
8: 7 Because the c' mind is enmity *4561
15:27 to minister unto them in c' things.4559
1Co 3: 1 but as unto c', even as unto "
3 For ye are yet c': for whereas "
3 are ye not c', and walk as men? "
4 I am of Apollos; are ye not c'? * "
9:11 if we shall reap your c' things? "
2Co 10: 4 weapons of our warfare are not c',* "
He 7:16 the law of a c' commandment, "
9:10 and c' ordinances, imposed on 4561

carnally
Le 18:20 thou shalt not lie c' with thy 7903, 2233
19:20 whosoever lieth c' with a 7902, "
Nu 5:13 And a man lie with her c', and " "
Ro 8: 6 to be c' minded is death; but to *4561

carpenter See also CARPENTER'S; CARPENTERS.
Isa 41: 7 the c' encouraged the goldsmith, 2796
44:13 The c' stretched out his rule;2796, 6086
M'r 6: 3 Is not this the c', the son of 5045

carpenter's
M't 13:55 Is not this the c' son? is not his 5045

carpenters
2Sa 5:11 c', and masons: and they 2796, 6086
2Ki 12:11 they laid it out to the c' and "
22: 6 Unto c', and builders, and 2796
1Ch 14: 1 with masons and c', to build 2796, 6086
2Ch 24:12 and hired masons and c' to repair 2796
Ezr 3: 7 unto the masons, and to the c'; "
Jer 24: 1 with the c' and smiths, from * "
29: 2 and the c', and the smiths, * "
Zec 1:20 And the Lord shewed me four c'. * "

Carpus *(car'-pus)*
2Ti 4:13 cloak that I left at Troas with C'. 2591

carriage See also CARRIAGES.
J'g 18:21 the cattle and the c' before them.*3520
1Sa 17:22 David left his c' in the hand *3627
22 the hand of the keeper of the c'. * "

carriages
Isa 10:28 Michmash he hath laid up his c': *3627
46: 1 your c' were heavy loaden; *5385
Ac 21:15 we took up our c', and went up * 643

carried
Ge 31:18 And he c' away all his cattle, 5090
26 and c' away my daughters, "
46: 5 of Israel c' Jacob their father, 5375
50:13 For his sons c' him into the land "
Le 10: 5 and c' them in their coats out of "
Jos 4: 8 and c' them over with them 5674
J'g 16: 3 c' them up to the top of an hill 5927
1Sa 5: 8 ark of the God of Israel be c' 5437
8 c' the ark of the God of Israel "
9 so, that, after they had c' it about, "
30: 2 or small, but c' them away, 5090
18 the Amalekites had c' away: *3947
2Sa 6:10 David c' it aside into the house 5186
15:29 and Abiathar c' the ark of God 7725
1Ki 8:47 whither they were c' captives, 7617
47 of them that c' them captives, "
50 before them who c' them captive, "
17:19 and c' him up into a loft, 5927
21:13 c' him forth out of the city, 3318
2Ki 7: 8 and c' thence silver, and gold, 5375
8 and c' thence also, and went "
9:28 c' him in a chariot to Jerusalem, 7392
15:29 and c' them captive to Assyria. 1540
16: 9 and c' the people of it captive "
17: 6 and c' Israel away into Assyria, "
11 the Lord c' away before them; "
23 So was Israel c' away out of their "
28 had c' away from Samaria "
33 whom they c' away from thence. * "
20:17 shall be c' unto Babylon: 5375
23: 4 c' the ashes of them unto Beth-el. "
30 his servants c' him in a chariot 7392
24:13 he c' out thence all the treasures 3318
14 And he c' away all Jerusalem, 1540
15 And he c' away Jehoiachin "
15 those c' he into captivity from 1980
25: 7 of brass, and c' him to Babylon. 935
13 c' the brass of them to Babylon. 5375
21 So Judah was c' away 1540
1Ch 5: 6 king of Assyria c' away captive: "
26 of Assyria, and he c' them away, "
6:15 when the Lord c' away Judah "
9: 1 were c' away to Babylon "
13: 7 And they c' the ark of God 7392
13 but c' it aside into the house of 5186
2Ch 6:37 whither they are c' captive, 7617
38 they have c' them captives, "
12: 9 he c' away also the shields *3947
14:13 they c' away very much spoil. 5375
15 and c' away sheep and camels 7617
16: 6 they c' away the stones of Ramah, 5375
21:17 and c' away all the substance 7617
24:11 it, and c' it to his place again. 7725
28: 5 and they smote him, and c' away 7617
8 c' away captive of their brethren "
15 and c' all the feeble of them 5095
17 Judah, and c' away captives. 7617
33:11 fetters, and c' him to Babylon. 3212
34:16 Shaphan c' the book to the king, 935
36: 4 brother, and c' him to Egypt. "
7 Nebuchadnezzar also c' of the "
20 sword c' he away to Babylon; 1473
Ezr 2: 1 of those which had been c' away, 1540
1 king of Babylon had c' away "
5:12 c' the people away into Babylon. 1541
8:35 those that had been c' away, *1473
9: 4 those that had been c' away; * "
10: 6 them that had been c' away. * "
8 those that had been c' away. * "
Ne 7: 6 of those that had been c' away, "
6 king of Babylon had c' away, 1540
Es 2: 6 been c' away from Jerusalem "
6 captivity which had been c' away "
6 king of Babylon had c' away. "
Job 1:17 and have c' them away, yea, *3947
5:13 of the froward is c' headlong. 4116
10:19 I should have been c' from the 2986
Ps 46: 2 though the mountains be c' into *4131
106:46 those that c' them captives. 7617
137: 3 they that c' us away captive * "
Isa 39: 6 shall be c' to Babylon: nothing 5375
46: 3 are c' from the womb: "
49:22 thy daughters shall be c' upon "
53: 4 our grief, and c' our sorrows: 5445
63: 9 and c' them all the days of old. 5375
Jer 13:17 Lord's flock is c' away captive. *7617
19 shall be c' away captive all of 1540
19 shall be wholly c' away captive. "
24: 1 had c' away captive Jeconiah "
5 them that are c' away captive. *1546
27:20 he c' away captive Jeconiah the "
22 They shall be c' to Babylon, 935
28: 3 this place, and c' them to Babylon: "
6 all that is c' away captive, *1473
29: 1 which were c' away captives, * "
1 Nebuchadnezzar had c' away 1540
4 all that are c' away captives, *1473
4 whom I have caused to be c' away 1540
7 caused you to be c' away captives, "
14 caused you to be c' away captive. "
39: 9 the guard c' away captive into "
40: 1 c' away captive of Jerusalem *1546
1 which were c' away captive unto 1540
7 that were not c' away captive "
41:10 Then Ishmael c' away captive 7617
10 c' them away captive, and "
Jer 41:14 Ishmael had c' away captive 7617
52: 9 they took the king and c' him up 5927
11 and c' him to Babylon, and put 935
15 the captain of the guard c' away 1540
17 and c' all the brass of them to 5375
27 Thus Judah was c' away captive 1540
28 whom Nebuchadrezzar c' away "
29 Nebuchadrezzar he c' away "
Eze 6: 9 they shall be c' captives, 7617
17: 4 and c' it into a land of traffick; 935
37: 1 and c' me out in the spirit 3318
Da 1: 2 he c' into the land of Shinar 935
2:35 and the wind c' them away, 5376
Ho 10: 6 It shall be also c' unto Assyria 2986
12: 1 and oil is c' into Egypt. "
Joe 3: 5 have c' into your temples 935
Am 1: 6 because they c' away captive 1540
Ob 11 the strangers c' away captive 7617
Na 3:10 Yet was she c' away, she went 1473
M't 1:11 the time they were c' away 3350
M'r 15: 1 bound Jesus, and c' him away, 667
Lu 7:12 there was a dead man c' out, 1580
16:22 was c' by the angels into 667
24:51 them, and c' up into heaven. 399
Ac 3: 2 from his mother's womb was c', 941
5: 6 up, and c' him out, and buried 1627
7:16 And were c' over into Sychem, 3346
8: 2 c' Stephen to his burial, *4792
21:34 him to be c' into the castle. * 71
1Co 12: 2 c' away unto these dumb idols, * 520
Ga 2:13 Barnabas also was c' away with 4879
Eph 4:14 and c' about with every wind 4064
Heb 13: 9 Be not c' about with divers "
2Pe 2:17 that are c' with a tempest; *1643
Jude 12 without water, c' about of winds; 4064
Re 12:15 her to be c' away of the flood. 4216
17: 3 So he c' me away in the spirit 667
21:10 c' me away in the spirit to a great "

carriest
Ps 90: 5 c' them away as with a flood; 2229

carrieth
Job 21:18 chaff that the storm c' away. 1589
27:21 The east wind c' him away, 5375
Re 17: 7 and of the beast that c' her, 941

carry See also CARRIED; CARRIEST; CARRIETH; CARRYING.
Ge 37:25 going to c' it down to Egypt. 3381
42:19 go ye, c' corn for the famine of 935
43:11 and c' down the man a present, 3381
12 sacks, c' it again in your hand; 7725
44: 1 as much as they can c', and put 5375
45:27 which Joseph had sent to c' him, "
46: 5 which Pharaoh had sent to c' him. "
47:30 and thou shalt c' me out of Egypt, "
50:25 shall c' up my bones from hence. 5927
Ex 12:46 thou shalt not c' forth aught of 3318
13:19 ye shall c' up my bones away 5927
14:11 us, to c' us forth out of Egypt? *3318
33:15 with me, c' us not up hence. 5927
Le 4:12 whole bullock shall he c' forth 3318
21 And he shall c' forth the bullock "
6:11 c' forth the ashes without the "
10: 4 c' your brethren from before the 5375
14:45 and he shall c' them forth out of 3318
16:27 shall one c' forth without the * "
Nu 11:12 C' them in thy bosom, as a 5375
24:22 Asshur shall c' thee away captive. 7617
De 14:24 so that thou art not able to c' it; 5375
28:38 Thou shalt c' much seed out 3318
Jos 4: 3 ye shall c' them over with you, 5674
1Sa 17:18 And c' these ten cheeses unto * 935
20:40 him, Go, c' them to the city. "
2Sa 15:25 C' back the ark of God into the 7725
19:18 to c' over the king's household, *5674
1Ki 8:46 c' them away captives unto the 7617
18:12 the Spirit of the Lord shall c' thee 5375
21:10 And then c' him out and stone 3318
22:26 and c' him back unto Amon 7725
34 Turn thine hand, and c' me out 3318
2Ki 4:19 C' him to his mother. 5375
9: 2 and c' him to an inner chamber; 935
17:27 C' thither one of the priests 1980
18:11 the king of Assyria did c' away *1540
25:11 the captain of the guard c' away. "
1Ch 10: 9 to c' tidings unto their idols, and 1319
15: 2 None ought to c' the ark of God 5375
2 the Lord chosen to c' the ark "
23:26 shall no more c' the tabernacle, *5375
2Ch 2:16 shalt c' it up to Jerusalem. 5927
6:36 enemies, and they c' them away 7617
18:25 Micaiah, and c' him back to Amon 7725
33 mayest c' me out of the host; 3318
20:25 more than they could c' away; 4853
25:12 the children of Judah c' away 7617
29: 5 and c' forth the filthiness out of 3318
16 And the Levites took it, to c' it "
36: 6 in fetters, to c' him to Babylon. 3212
Ezr 5:15 go, c' them into the temple that *5182
7:15 And to c' the silver and gold, 2987
Job 15:12 Why doth thine heart c' thee 3947
Ps 49:17 he shall c' nothing away: his glory "
Ec 5:15 he may c' away in his hand. 3212
10:20 a bird of the air shall c' the voice "
Isa 5:29 the prey, and shall c' it away 6403
15: 7 laid up, shall they c' away to the 5375
22:17 the Lord will c' thee away with a 2904
23: 7 her own feet shall c' her afar off 2986
30: 6 they will c' their riches upon the 5375
40:11 and c' them in his bosom, and "
41:16 and the wind shall c' them away, "
46: 4 to hoar hairs will I c' you: I have 5445
4 even I will c', and will deliver you. "
7 c' him, and set him in his place, "
57:13 the wind shall c' them all away; 5375
Jer 17:22 Neither c' forth a burden out of 3318
20: 4 shall c' them captive into Babylon, 1540
5 them, and c' them to Babylon. 935
39: 7 with chains, to c' him to Babylon. "
14 Shaphan, that he should c' him 3318
43: 3 c' us away captives into Babylon. 1540
12 and c' them away captives: and 7617
La 4:22 he will no more c' thee away 1540
Eze 12: 5 their sight, and c' out thereby. 3318
6 and c' it forth in the twilight: "
12 the wall to c' out thereby: "
22: 9 In thee are men that c' tales to *7400
38:13 to c' away silver and gold, to 5375
Da 11: 8 And shall also c' captives into 935
M'r 6:55 to c' about in beds those that 4064
11:16 any man should c' any vessel 1308
Lu 10: 4 C' neither purse, nor scrip, nor 941
Joh 5:10 it is not lawful for thee to c' thy * 142
21:18 shall gird thee, and c' thee whither 5342
Ac 5: 9 at the door, and shall c' thee out. 1627
7:43 c' you away beyond Babylon. 3351
1Ti 6: 7 is certain we can c' nothing out. 1627

carrying See also MISCARRYING.
1Sa 10: 3 one c' three kids, and another 5375
3 another c' three loaves of bread, "
3 and another c' a bottle of wine: "
Ps 78: 9 c' bows, turned back in the day 7411
Jer 1: 3 c' away of Jerusalem captive 1540
M't 1:17 from David until the c' away 3350
17 from the c' away into Babylon "
Ac 5:10 c' her forth, buried her by her *1627

Carshena (*car-she'-nah*)
Es 1:14 And the next unto him was C'. 3771

cart
1Sa 6: 7 Now therefore make a new c', 5699
7 tie the kine to the c', and bring "
8 the Lord, and lay it upon the c'; "
10 milch kine, and tied them to the c'; "
11 the ark of the Lord upon the c', "
14 And the c' came into the field of "
14 they clave the wood of the c', and "
2Sa 6: 3 set the ark of God upon a new c', "
3 of Abinadab, drave the new c'. "
1Ch 13: 7 carried the ark of God in a new c' "
7 And Uzza and Ahio drave the c'. "
Isa 5:18 and sin as it were with a c' rope: "
28:27 neither is a c' wheel turned about "
28 break it with the wheel of his c', "
Am 2:13 as a c' is pressed that is full of "

carved
J'g 18:18 fetched the c' image, the ephod, *6459
1Ki 6:18 the house within was c' with 4734
29 he c' all the walls of the house 7049
29 c' figures of cherubims and palm 6603
32 and he c' upon them carvings of 7049
35 And he c' thereon cherubims "
35 with gold fitted upon the c' work. *2707
2Ch 33: 7 he set a c' image, the idol which *6459
22 sacrificed unto all the c' images *6456
34: 3 the c' images, and the molten * "
4 the groves, and the c' images, * "
Ps 74: 6 now they break down the c' work 6603
Pr 7:16 with c' works, with fine linen of *2405

carving See also CARVINGS.
Ex 31: 5 and in c' of timber, to work in all 2799
35:33 and in c' of wood, to make any "

carvings
1Ki 6:32 c' of cherubims and palm trees 4734

case See also CASES.
Ex 5:19 did see that they were in evil c', "
De 19: 4 this is the c' of the slayer, which 1697
22: 1 thou shalt in any c' bring them *7725
24:13 In any c' thou shalt deliver him * "
Ps 144:15 that people, that is in such a c': 3602
M't 5:20 ye shall in no c' enter into the *3364
19:10 If the c' of the man be so with his 156
Joh 5: 6 a long time in that c', he saith unto

casement
Pro 7: 6 I looked through my c', * 822

cases
1Co 7:15 is not under bondage in such c':

Casiphia (*cas-if'-e-ah*)
Ezr 8:17 Iddo the chief at the place C', 3708
17 the Nethinims, at the place C', "

Casluhim (*cas'-loo-him*)
Ge 10:14 and C', (out of whom came 3695
1Ch 1:12 and C', (of whom came the "

cassia
Ex 30:24 And of c' five hundred shekels, 6916
Ps 45: 8 smell of myrrh, and aloes, and c', 7102
Eze 27:19 bright iron, c', and calamus, 6916

cast See also CASTAWAY; CASTEDST; CASTEST; CASTETH; CASTING; FORECAST; OUTCAST.
Ge 21:10 C' out this bondwoman and her 1644
15 and she c' the child under one of 7993
31:38 she goats have not c' their young, 7921
51 behold this pillar, which I have c' *3384
37:20 him, and c' him into some pit, 7993
22 c' him into this pit that is in the "
24 took him, and c' him into a pit: "
39: 7 master's wife c' her eyes upon 5375
Ex 1:22 is born ye shall c' into the river, 7993
4: 3 And he said, C' it on the ground. "
3 And he c' it on the ground, "
25 and c' it at his feet, and said, 5060
7: 9 Take thy rod, and c' it before 7993

Ex 7:10 and Aaron c' down his rod before 7993
12 For they c' down every man his "
10:19 locusts, and c' them into the Red *8628
15: 4 his host hath he c' into the sea: 3384
25 when he had c' into the waters, 7993
22:31 ye shall c' it to the dogs. "
23:26 shall nothing c' their young, 7921
25:12 thou shalt c' four rings of gold 3332
26:37 thou shalt c' five sockets of brass "
32:19 he c' the tables out of his hands, 7993
24 then I c' it into the fire, and "
34:24 I will c' out the nations before 3423
36:36 and he c' for them four sockets of 3332
37: 3, 13 he c' for it four rings of gold, "
38: 5 he c' four rings for the four ends "
27 hundred talents of silver were c' * "
Le 1:16 and c' it beside the altar on the 7993
14:40 and they shall c' them into an "
16: 8 Aaron shall c' lots upon the two 5414
18:24 nations are defiled which I c' out 7971
20:23 nation, which I c' out before you: "
26:30 and c' your carcases upon the 5414
44 I will not c' them away, neither *3988
Nu 19: 6 and c' it into the midst of the 7993
35:22 or have c' upon him any thing * "
23 and c' it upon him, that he die, 5307
De 6:19 To c' out all thine enemies from *1920
7: 1 hath c' out many nations before 5394
9: 4 Lord thy God hath c' them out *1920
17 and c' them out of my two hands, 7993
21 and I c' the dust thereof into the "
28:40 for thine olive shall c' his fruit. 5394
29:28 and c' them into another land, as 7993
Jos 8:29 and c' it at the entering of the "
10:11 the Lord c' down great stones "
27 and c' them into the cave "
13:12 Moses smite, and c' them out. *3423
18: 6 that I may c' lots for you here 3384
8 that I may here c' lots for you 7993
10 And Joshua c' lots for them "
J'g 6:28 the altar of Baal was c' down, *5422
30 he hath c' down the altar of Baal,* "
31 because one hath c' down his * "
8:25 and did c' therein every man the 7993
9:53 a certain woman c' a piece of "
15:17 that he c' away the jawbone out "
1Sa 14:42 C' lots between me and Jonathan 5307
18:11 And Saul c' the javelin; for he 2904
20:33 And Saul c' a javelin at him to "
2Sa 1:21 of the mighty is vilely c' away, 1602
11:21 did not a woman c' a piece of a 7993
16: 6 And he c' stones at David, and at 5619
13 threw stones at him, and c' dust. 6080
18:17 and c' him into a great pit in 7993
20:12 and c' a cloth upon him, "
15 c' up a bank against the city, 8210
22 Bichri, and c' it out to Joab. *7993
1Ki 7:15 For he c' two pillars of brass, *6696
24 knops were c' in two rows, 3332
in two rows, when it was c'. 3333
46 plain of Jordan did the king c' 3332
9: 7 name, will I c' out of my sight; 7971
13:24 his carcase was c' in the way, 7993
25 passed by, and saw the carcase c' "
28 he went and found his carcase c' "
14: 9 and hast c' me behind thy back: "
24 the nations which the Lord c' *3423
18:42 c' himself down upon the earth, *1457
19:19 and c' his mantle upon him. 7993
21:26 whom the Lord c' out before the 3423
2Ki 2:16 and c' him upon some mountain 7993
21 and c' the salt in there, and said, "
3:25 c' every man his stone, and "
4:41 And he c' it into the pot; "
6: 6 and c' it in thither; and the iron "
7:15 Syrians had c' away in their haste. "
9:25 c' him in the portion of the field "
26 c' him into the plat of ground, "
10:25 and the captain c' them out, "
13:21 c' the man into the sepulchre "
23 neither c' he them from his "
16: 3 whom the Lord c' out from 3423
17: 8 c' out from before the children "
20 had c' them out of his sight. 7993
19:18 have c' their gods into the fire: 5414
32 shield, nor c' a bank against it. 8210
21: 2 heathen, whom the Lord c' out 3423
23: 6 and c' the powder thereof upon 7993
12 and c' the dust of them into the "
27 will c' off this city Jerusalem 3988
24:20 until he had c' them out from 7993
1Ch 24:31 These likewise c' lots over 5307
25: 8 And they c' lots, hard against "
26:13 And they c' lots, as well the small "
14 they c' lots; and his lot came out "
28: 9 thou forsake him, he will c' thee 2186
2Ch 4: 3 rows of oxen were c'. 3332
3 when it was c'. 4166
17 plain of Jordan did the king c' 3332
7:20 will I c' out of my sight, and 7993
11:14 and his sons had c' them off 2186
13: 9 Have ye not c' out the priests *5080
20:11 to come to c' us out of thy 1644
24:10 in, and c' into the chest, 7993
25: 8 power to help, and to c' down. 3782
12 and c' them down from the top of 7993
26:14 and bows, and slings to c' stones.* "
28: 3 whom the Lord had c' out 3423
29:19 king Ahaz in his reign did c' 2186
30:14 and c' them into the brook 7993
33: 2 whom the Lord had c' out before 3423
15 and c' them out of the city. 7993
Neh 1: 9 there were of you c' out unto *5080
6:16 they were much c' down in their 5307
9:26 and c' thy law behind their backs, 7993
10:34 we c' the lots among the priests, 5307

Neh 11: 1 the rest of the people also c' lots, 5307
13: 8 therefore I c' forth all the 7993
Es 3: 7 they c' Pur, that is, the lot, 5307
9:24 and had c' Pur, that is, the lot, "
Job 8: 4 and he have c' them away for their *7971
20 God will not c' away a perfect 3988
15:33 and shall c' off his flower as the 7993
18: 7 his own counsel shall c' him down. "
8 he is c' into a net by his own 7971
20:15 God shall c' them out of his belly. 3423
23 God shall c' the fury of his wrath 7971
22:29 When men are c' down, then thou 8213
27:22 For God shall c' upon him, and *7993
29:24 my countenance they c' not down. 5307
30:19 He hath c' me into the mire, 3384
39: 3 ones, they c' out their sorrows. 7971
40:11 C' abroad the rage of thy wrath: *6327
41: 9 shall not one be c' down even 2904
Ps 2: 3 and c' away their cords from us. 7993
5:10 c' them out in the multitude *5080
17:13 disappoint him, c' him down: 3766
18:42 I did c' them out as the dirt 7324
22:10 I was c' upon thee from the womb: 7993
18 and c' lots upon my vesture. 5307
36:12 they are c' down, and shall not *1760
37:14 to c' down the poor and needy, 5307
24 he shall not be utterly c' down: 2904
42: 5 Why art thou c' down, O my soul? 7817
6 my soul is c' down within me: "
11 Why art thou c' down, O my soul? "
43: 2 why dost thou c' me off? 2186
5 Why art thou c' down, O my soul? 7817
44: 2 the people, and c' them out. *7971
9 But thou hast c' off, and put us 2186
23 arise, c' us not off for ever. "
51:11 C' me not away from thy presence; 7993
55: 3 they c' iniquity upon me, and in 4131
22 C' thy burden upon the Lord, 7993
56: 7 in thine anger c' down the people, 3381
60: 1 O God, thou hast c' us off, thou 2186
8 over Edom will I c' out my shoe: 7993
10 O God, which hadst c' us off? 2186
62: 4 They only consult to c' him down *5080
71: 9 C' me not off in the time of old 7993
74: 1 hast thou c' us off for ever? 2186
7 have c' fire into thy sanctuary, *7971
76: 6 the chariot and horse are c' into 7290
77: 7 Will the Lord c' off for ever? 2186
78:49 He c' upon them the fierceness 7971
55 He c' out the heathen also *1644
80: 8 thou hast c' out the heathen, "
89:38 thou hast c' off and abhorred, 2186
44 c' his throne down to the ground. 4048
94:14 Lord will not c' off his people, 5203
102:10 lifted me up, and c' me down. 7993
108: 9 over Edom will I c' out my shoe; "
11 O God, who hast c' us off? 2186
140:10 let them be c' into the fire; 5307
144: 6 C' forth lightning, and scatter 1299
Pr 1:14 C' in thy lot among us; let us all 5307
7:26 she hath c' down many wounded: "
16:33 The lot is c' into the lap; but 2904
22:10 C' out the scorner, and contention 1644
Ec 3: 5 A time to c' away stones, and a 7993
6 and a time to c' away; "
11: 1 C' thy bread upon the waters: 7971
Isa 2:20 a man shall c' his idols of silver, *7993
5:24 because they have c' away the *3988
6:13 when they c' their leaves: *7995
14:19 thou art c' out of thy grave 7993
16: 2 wandering bird c' out of the nest, *7971
19: 8 all they that c' angle into the 7993
25: 7 the covering c' over all people, 3874
26:19 the earth shall c' out the dead. 5307
28: 2 shall c' down to the earth with 3240
25 doth he not c' abroad the fitches, 6327
25 and c' in the principal wheat *7760
30:22 gold: thou shalt c' them away 2219
31: 7 every man shall c' away his idols 3988
34: 3 Their slain also shall be c' out, 7993
17 he hath c' the lot for them, 5307
37:19 have c' their gods into the fire: 5414
33 nor c' a bank against it. 8210
38:17 c' all my sins behind thy back. 7993
41: 9 chosen thee, and not c' thee away. 3988
57:14 C' ye up, c' ye up, prepare the 5549
20 whose waters c' up mire and 1644
58: 7 poor that are c' out to thy house? 4788
62:10 c' up, c' up the highway; 5549
66: 5 c' you out for my name's sake, 5077
Jer 6: 6 c' a mount against Jerusalem: 8210
15 I visit them they shall be c' down, 3782
7:15 I will c' you out of my sight, 7993
15 I have c' out all your brethren, "
29 O Jerusalem, and c' it away, "
8:12 visitation, they shall be c' down, 3782
9:19 our dwellings have c' us out. 7993
14:16 shall be c' out in the streets of "
15: 1 people: c' them out of my sight, 7971
16:13 Therefore will I c' you out of 2904
18:15 in paths, in a way not c' up; 5549
22: 7 cedars, and c' them into the fire.
19 burial of an ass, drawn and c' forth 7993
26 And I will c' thee out, and thy 2904
28 wherefore are they c' out, he and 7993
28 and are c' into a land which 2904
23:39 your fathers, and c' you out of *
26:23 and c' his dead body into the 7993
28:16 will c' thee from off the face of *7971
31:37 also c' off all the seed of Israel 3988
33:24 he hath even c' them off? "
26 I will c' away the seed of Jacob, "
36:23 and c' it into the fire that was 7993
30 his dead body shall be c' out in "
38: 6 and c' him into the dungeon "
9 whom they have c' into the "

Jer 38:11 took thence old c' clouts and old 5499
12 Put now these old c' clouts and "
41: 7 and c' them into the midst of the "
9 Ishmael had c' all the dead 7993
14 from Mizpah c' about and †5437
50:26 c' her up as heaps, and destroy 5549
51:34 my delicates, he hath c' me out. 1740
63 and c' it into the midst of 7993
52: 3 till he had c' them out from his "
La 2: 1 c' down from heaven unto the "
7 The Lord hath c' off his altar, he 2186
10 they have c' up dust upon their 5927
3:31 the Lord will not c' off for ever: 2186
53 and c' a stone upon me. 3034
Eze 4: 2 against it, and c' a mount against 8210
5: 4 and c' them into the midst of the 7993
6: 4 and I will c' down your slain 5307
7:19 They shall c' their silver in the 7993
11:16 I have c' them far off among the *7368
15: 4 Behold, it is c' into the fire for 5414
16: 5 but thou wast c' out in the open 7993
18:31 C' away from you all your "
19:12 in fury, she was c' down to the "
20: 7 C' ye away every man the "
8 they did not every man c' away "
21:22 to c' a mount, and to build a fort. 8210
23:35 forgotten me, and c' me behind 7993
26: 8 and c' a mount against thee, 8210
27:30 shall c' up dust upon their heads, 5927
28:16 therefore I will c' thee as profane 2490
17 I will c' thee to the ground, I will 7993
31:16 when I c' him down to hell with 3381
32: 4 I will c' thee forth upon the open 2904
18 of Egypt, and c' them down, even 3381
36: 5 to c' it out for a prey. 4054
43:24 and the priests shall c' salt upon 7993
Da 3: 6 shall the same hour be c' into 7412
11 he should be c' into the midst of "
15 ye shall be c' the same hour into "
20 and to c' them into the burning "
21 and were c' into the midst of the "
24 Did not we c' three men bound "
6: 7 he shall be c' into the den of lions. "
12 shall be c' into the den of lions? "
16 they brought Daniel, and c' him "
24 they c' them into the den of lions, "
7: 9 till the thrones were c' down, * "
8: 7 but he c' him down to the 7993
10 and it c' down some of the host 5307
11 the place of his sanctuary was c' 7993
12 and it c' down the truth to the "
11:12 and he shall c' down many ten 5307
15 and c' up a mount, and take the 8210
Ho 8: 3 Israel hath c' off the thing that 2186
5 Thy calf, O Samaria, hath c' thee "
9:17 My God will c' them away, 3988
14: 5 and c' forth his roots as Lebanon. 5221
Joe 1: 7 made it clean bare, and c' it away; 7993
3: 3 they have c' lots for my people; 3032
Am 1:11 and did c' off all pity, and his 7843
4: 3 and ye shall c' them into the 7993
8: 3 they shall c' them forth with "
8 and it shall be c' out and *1644
Ob 11 and c' lots upon Jerusalem, 3032
Jon 1: 5 and c' forth the wares that were 2904
7 Come, and let us c' lots, that we 5307
7 So they c' lots, and the lot fell "
12 and c' me forth into the sea; 2904
15 and c' him forth into the sea: "
2: 3 For thou hadst c' me into the 7993
4 I said, I am c' out of thy sight; 1644
Mic 2: 5 none that shall c' a cord by lot 7993
9 women of my people have ye c' 1644
4: 7 and her that was c' far off a 1972
7:19 and thou wilt c' all their sins 7993
Na 3: 6 And I will c' abominable filth "
10 they c' lots for her honourable 3032
Zep 3:15 thy judgments, he hath c' out 6437
Zec 1:21 c' out the horns of the Gentiles, 3034
5: 8 And he c' it into the midst of the 7993
8 and he c' the weight of lead upon "
9: 4 the Lord will c' her out, and he *3423
10: 6 though I had not c' them off: 2186
11:13 C' it unto the potter: a goodly 7993
13 and c' them to the potter in the "
Mal 3:11 shall your vine c' her fruit before 7921
M't 3:10 hewn down, and c' into the fire. *906*
4: 6 the Son of God, c' thyself down: "
12 had heard that John was c' into **3860*
5:13 good for nothing, but to be c' out, *906*
25 to the officer, and thou be c' into "
29 pluck it out, and c' it from thee: "
29 thy whole body should be c' into "
30 cut it off, and c' it from thee: "
30 that thy whole body should be c' * "
6:30 and to morrow is c' into the oven. "
7: 5 first c' out the beam out of thine *1544*
5 see clearly to c' out the mote out "
6 neither c' ye your pearls before *906*
19 hewn down, and c' into the fire. "
22 in thy name have c' out devils? *1544*
8:12 shall be c' out into outer darkness; "
16 he c' out the spirits with his word, "
31 saying, If thou c' us out, suffer us "
9:33 when the devil was c' out, the "
10: 1 unclean spirits, to c' them out, "
8 lepers, raise the dead, c' out devils: "
12:24 doth not c' out devils, but by "
26 if Satan c' out Satan, he is divided "
27 And if I by Beelzebub c' out devils, "
27 do your children c' them out? "
28 if I c' out devils by the Spirit "
13:42 shall c' them into a furnace of fire: *906*
47 like unto a net, that was c' into the "
48 good into vessels, but c' the bad "
50 shall c' them into the furnace of "

M't 15:17 and is c' out into the draught? 1544
26 children's bread, and to c' it to 906
30 and c' them down at Jesus' feet; 4496
17:19 Why could not we c' him out? 1544
27 go thou to the sea, and c' an hook, 906
18: 8 cut them off, and c' them from thee: "
8 feet to be c' into everlasting fire. "
9 pluck it out, and c' it from thee: "
9 having two eyes to be c' into hell "
30 went and c' him into prison, till he "
21:12 c' out all that sold and bought 1544
21 and be thou c' into the sea; 906
39 they caught him, and c' him out 1544
22:13 and c' him into outer darkness; * "
25:30 And c' ye the unprofitable servant "
27: 5 And he c' down the pieces of 4496
35 upon my vesture did they c' lots. * 906
44 him, c' the same in his teeth. 3679
M'k 1:34 and c' out many devils; and 1544
39 throughout all Galilee, and c' out "
3:15 sicknesses, and to c' out devils: "
23 How can Satan c' out Satan? "
4:26 a man should c' seed into the 906
6:13 they c' out many devils, and 1544
7:26 he would c' forth the devil out of "
27 children's bread, and to c' it unto 906
9:18 that they should c' him out; 1544
22 it hath c' him into the fire, 906
28 Why could not we c' him out? 1544
42 his neck, and he were c' into the 906
45 two feet to be c' into hell, into the "
47 two eyes to be c' into hell fire: "
11: 7 and c' their garments on him; 1911
15 and began to c' out them that 1544
23 removed, and be thou c' into the 906
12: 4 at him they c' stones, and *3036
8 killed him, and c' him out of the *1544
41 people c' money into the treasury: 906
41 and many that were rich c' in "
43 this poor widow hath c' more in, "
43 than all they which have c' into "
44 they did c' in of their abundance, "
44 but she of her want did c' in all "
14:51 having a linen cloth c' about his 4016
16: 9 out of whom he had c' seven 1544
17 In my name shall they c' out "
Lu 1:29 c' in her mind what manner of 1260
3: 9 is hewn down, and c' into the fire. 906
4: 9 Son of God, c' thyself down from "
29 that they might c' him down *2630
6:22 shall reproach you, and c' out 1544
42 c' out first the beam out of thine "
9:25 and lose himself, or be c' away? *2210
40 I besought thy disciples to c' him 1544
11:18 ye say that I c' out devils through "
19 if I by Beelzebub c' out devils, "
19 by whom do your sons c' them out? "
20 if I with the finger of God c' out "
12: 5 hath power to c' into hell; yea, I 1685
28 and to morrow is c' into the oven; 906
58 and the officer c' thee into prison. "
13:19 a man took, and c' into his garden; "
32 Behold, I c' out devils, and I do 1544
14:35 for the dunghill; but men c' it out. 906
17: 2 about his neck, and he c' into *4496
19:35 they c' their garments upon the *1977
43 thine enemies shall c' a trench 4016
45 began to c' out them that sold 1544
20:12 wounded him also, and c' him out. "
15 c' him out of the vineyard, and "
21: 3 this poor widow hath c' in more 906
4 of their abundance c' in unto the "
4 but she of her penury hath c' in "
22:41 from them about a stone's c', 1000
23:19 for murder, was c' into prison. 906
25 and murder was c' into prison, "
34 parted his raiment, and c' lots. "
Joh 3:24 John was not yet c' into prison. "
6:37 to me I will in no wise c' out. 1544
8: 7 let him first c' a stone at her. 906
59 took they up stones to c' at him: "
9:34 teach us? And they c' him out. 1544
35 heard that they had c' him out; "
12:31 the prince of this world be c' out. "
15: 6 he is c' forth as a branch, and is 906
6 c' them into the fire, and they are "
19:24 Let us not rend it, but c' lots for it, 2975
24 and for my vesture they did c' lots. 906
21: 6 C' the net on the right side of the "
6 They c' therefore, and now they "
7 and did c' himself into the sea. "
Ac 7:19 they c' out their young 4160, 1570
21 when he was c' out, Pharaoh's 1620
58 c' him out of the city, and stoned 1544
12: 8 C' thy garment about thee, and 4016
16:23 they c' them into prison, charging 906
37 have c' us into prison; and now do "
22:23 they cried out, and c' off their *4496
27:19 we c' out with our own hands the "
26 we must be c' upon a certain 1601
29 they c' four anchors out of the *4496
30 as though they would have c' *1614
38 and c' out the wheat into the sea. *1544
43 should c' themselves first into the 641
Ro 11: 1 Hath God c' away his people? 683
2 God hath not c' away his people "
13:12 let us therefore c' off the works of 656
1Co 7:35 not that I may c' a snare upon you, 1911
2Co 4: 9 but not forsaken; c' down, but *2598
7: 6 comforteth those that are c' down, *5011
Ga 4:30 C' out the bondwoman and her 1544
1Ti 5:12 they have c' off their first faith. * 114
Heb 10:35 C' not away therefore your 577
2Pe 2: 4 but c' them down to hell, and 5020
Re 2:10 the devil shall c' some of you into 906
14 Balac to c' a stumblingblock "
Re 2:22 Behold, I will c' her into a bed, 906
4:10 and c' their crowns before the "
8: 5 c' it into the earth: and there were "
7 they were c' upon the earth: and "
8 burning with fire was c' into the "
12: 4 stars of heaven, and did c' them to "
9 the great dragon was c' out, that "
9 he was c' out into the earth, "
9 and his angels were c' out with "
10 accuser of our brethren is c' down, 2598
13 dragon saw that he was c' unto 906
15 the serpent c' out of his mouth "
16 the dragon c' out of his mouth. "
14:19 c' it into the great winepress of "
18:19 they c' dust on their heads, and "
21 millstone, and c' it into the sea, "
19:20 These both were c' alive into a "
20: 3 c' him into the bottomless pit, and "
10 was c' into the lake of fire and "
14 death and hell were c' into the "
15 was c' into the lake of fire. "

castaway
1Co 9:27 to others, I myself should be a c'. *96

castedst
Ps 73:18 c' them down into destruction. *5307

castest
Job 15: 4 thou c' off fear, and restrainest *6565
Ps 50:17 instruction, and c' my words 7993
88:14 Lord, why c' thou off my soul? 2186

casteth
Job 21:10 their cow calveth, and c' not her 7921
Ps 147: 6 he c' the wicked down to the *8213
17 He c' forth his ice like morsels: 7993
Pr 10: 3 but he c' away the substance of *1920
19:15 Slothfulness c' into a deep sleep; 5307
21:22 and c' down the strength of the *3381
26:18 who c' firebrands, arrows, and 3384
Isa 40:19 with gold, and c' silver chains. 6884
Jer 6: 7 As a fountain c' out her waters, 6979
7 so she c' out her wickedness: "
M't 9:34 He c' out devils through the prince 1544
M'r 3:22 prince of the devils c' he out devils. "
Lu 11:15 He c' out devils through Beelzebub "
1Jo 4:18 perfect love c' out fear: because 906
3Jo 10 and c' them out of the church. 1544
Re 6:13 as a fig tree c' her untimely figs, 906

casting
2Sa 8: 2 c' them down to the ground; *7901
1Ki 7:37 all of them had one c', one 4165
Ezr 10: 1 c' himself down before the house 5307
Job 6:21 ye see my c' down, and are afraid.*2866
Ps 74: 7 sanctuary, have they defiled by c'*
89:39 his crown by c' it to the ground. *
Eze 17:17 by c' up mounts, and building 8210
Mic 6:14 and thy c' down shall be in the *3445
M't 4:18 c' a net into the sea: for they were 906
27:35 parted his garments, c' lots: that "
M'r 1:16 Andrew his brother c' a net into "
9:38 we saw one c' out devils in thy 1544
10:50 he, c' away his garment, rose, and 577
15:24 parted his garments, c' lots upon 906
Lu 9:49 we saw one c' out devils in thy 1544
11:14 he was c' out a devil, and it was "
21: 1 the rich men c' their gifts into the 906
2 a certain poor widow c' in thither "
Ro 11:15 For if the c' away of them be the 580
2Co 10: 5 C' down imaginations, and every 2507
1Pe 5: 7 C' all your care upon him; for he 1977

castle See also CASTLES.
1Ch 11: 5 David took the c' of Zion, which *4686
7 David dwelt in the c'; therefore *4679
Pr 18:19 contentions are like the bars of a c'.759
Ac 21:34 him to be carried into the c'. 3925
37 Paul was to be led into the c', he "
22:24 to be brought into the c', and bade "
23:10 and to bring him into the c'. "
16 he went and entered into the c', "
32 and returned to the c': "

castles
Ge 25:16 by their towns, and by their c'; *2918
Nu 31:10 they dwelt, and all their goodly c'.* "
1Ch 6:54 places throughout their c' * "
27:25 in the villages, and in the c', 4026
2Ch 17:12 he built in Judah c', and cities 1003
27: 4 and in the forests he built c' and "

Castor (*cas'-tor*)
Ac 28:11 whose sign was C' and Pollux. *1359

catch See also CATCHETH; CAUGHT.
Ex 22: 6 If fire break out, and c' in 4672
J'g 21:21 and c' you every man his wife of 2414
1Ki 20:33 from him, and did hastily c' it: 2480
2Ki 7:12 we shall c' them alive, and get *8610
Ps 10: 9 in wait to c' the poor: he doth c' 2414
35: 8 let his net that he hath hid c' 3920
109:11 Let the extortioner c' all that he 5367
Jer 5:26 snares; they set a trap, they c' 3920
Eze 19: 3 it learned to c' the prey; it 2963
6 and learned to c' the prey, and "
Hab 1:15 they c' them in their net, and 1641
M'r 12:13 of the Herodians, to c' him in his 64
Lu 5:10 henceforth thou shalt c' men. 2221
11:54 seeking to c' something out of his 2340

catcheth
Le 17:13 which hunteth and c' any beast *6679
M't 13:19 cometh the wicked one, and c' * 726
Joh 10:12 the wolf c' them, and scattereth "

caterpillar See CATERPILLER.

caterpiller See also CATERPILLERS.
1Ki 8:37 if there be c'; if their enemy 2625
Ps 78:46 their increase unto the c', and "
Isa 33: 4 the gathering of the c': as the "
Joe 1: 4 cankerworm hath left hath the c' 2625
2:25 cankerworm, and the c', and the "

caterpillers
2Ch 6:28 mildew, locusts, or c'; if their *2625
Ps 105:34 the locusts came, and c', and †‡3218
Jer 51:14 fill thee with men, as with c': * "
27 horses to come up as the rough c'. "

cattle
Ge 1:24 c', and creeping thing, and beast 929
25 c' after their kind, and every thing "
26 and over the c', and over all the "
2:20 Adam gave names to all c', and to "
3:14 thou art cursed above all c', and "
4:20 in tents, and of such as have c'. 4735
6:20 c' after their kind, of every 929
7:14 all the c' after their kind, and every "
21 of fowl, and of c', and of beast, and "
23 both man, and c', and the creeping "
8: 1 all the c' that was with him in the "
17 of fowl, and of c', and of every "
9:10 of the fowl, of the c', and of every "
13: 2 Abram was very rich in c', in 4735
7 between the herdmen of Abram's c' "
7 and the herdmen of Lot's c': "
29: 7 neither is it time that the c' should "
30:29 I have served thee, and how thy c' "
32 all the speckled and spotted c', *7716
32 and all the brown c' among the "
39 and brought forth c' ringstraked, *6629
40 and put them not unto Laban's c'.* "
41 the stronger c' did conceive, that * "
41 the rods before the eyes of the c' * "
42 when the c' were feeble, he put * "
43 had much c', and maidservants, * "
31: 8 all the c' bare speckled: and if * "
8 then bare all the c' ringstraked. * "
9 the c' of your father, and given *4735
10 the time that the c' conceived, *6629
10 the rams which leaped upon the c'* "
12 the rams which leap upon the c' * "
18 carried away all his c', and all 4735
18 the c' of his getting, which he had "
41 and six years for thy c': and *6629
43 and these c' are my c', and all *4735
33:14 according as the c' that goeth 4399
17 house, and made booths for his c':4735
34: 5 his sons were with his c' in the "
23 Shall not their c' and their "
36: 6 his c', and all his beasts, and all "
7 bear them because of their c'. "
46: 6 And they took their c', and their "
32 their trade hath been to feed c'; "
34 trade hath been about c' from our "
47: 6 then make them rulers over my c'. "
16 Joseph said, Give your c'; and I "
16 will give you for your c', "
17 they brought their c' unto Joseph: "
17 and for the c' of the herds, and for* "
17 bread for all their c' for that year. "
18 hath our herds of c'; there is not 929
Ex 9: 3 hand of the Lord is upon thy c' 4735
4 sever between the c' of Israel "
4 and the c' of Egypt: and there shall "
6 all the c' of Egypt died: "
6 but of the c' of the children of "
7 not one of the c' of the Israelites "
19 now, and gather thy c', and all "
20 his servants and his c' flee into the "
21 his servants and his c' in the field. "
10:26 Our c' also shall go with us; there "
12:29 and all the firstborn of c'. 929
38 and herds, even very much c'. 4735
17: 3 kill us and our children and our c' "
20:10 thy maidservant nor thy c', nor 929
34:19 firstling among thy c', whether 4735
Le 1: 2 bring your offering of the c', even 929
5: 2 or a carcase of unclean c', or the "
19:19 Thou shalt not let thy c' gender "
25: 7 And for thy c', and for the beast "
26:22 and destroy your c', and make you "
Nu 3:41 the c' of the Levites, instead of all "
41 all the firstlings among the c' of the "
45 c' of the Levites instead of their c'; "
20: 4 that we and our c' should die 1165
19 I and my c' drink of thy water, 4735
31: 9 the spoil of all their c', and all 929
32: 1 had a very great multitude of c': 4735
1 the place was a place for c'; "
4 Israel, is a land for c', "
4 and thy servants have c'; "
16 sheepfolds here for our c', and "
26 and all our c', shall be there in the 929
35: 3 shall be for their c', and for their "
De 2:35 Only the c' we took for a prey "
3: 7 But all the c', and the spoil of the "
19 your little ones, and your c', 4735
19 (for I know that ye have much c',) "
5:14 nor any of thy c', nor thy stranger 929
7:14 among you, or among your c'. "
11:15 send grass in thy fields for thy c', "
13:15 and the c' thereof, with the edge of "
20:14 the little ones, and the c', and all "
28: 4 the fruit of thy c', the increase of "
11 thy body, and in the fruit of thy c', "
51 he shall eat the fruit of thy c', and "
30: 9 in the fruit of thy c', and in the "
Jos 1:14 your little ones, and your c', shall 4735
8: 2 the c' thereof, shall ye take 929
27 Only the c' and the spoil of that "
11:14 these cities, and the c', the children "
14: 4 with their suburbs for their c' and 4735
21: 2 the suburbs thereof for our c'. 929
22: 8 with very much c', with silver, 4735
J'g 6: 5 came up with their c', and their "
18:21 the little ones and the c' and the "

1Sa 23: 5 and brought away their c', and 4735
30:20 before those other c', and said, "
1Ki 1: 9 slew sheep and oxen and fat c' *4806
19 hath slain oxen and fat c' and * "
25 fat c' in abundance, and hath * "
2Ki 3: 9 for the c' that followed them. * 929
17 ye, and your c', and your beasts. 4735
1Ch 5: 9 because their c' were multiplied in "
21 they took away their c'; of their 929
7:21 came down to take away their c'. "
2Ch 14:15 also the tents of c', and carried "
26:10 for he had much c', both in the "
35: 8 small c', and three hundred oxen.
9 offerings five thousand small c', and
Ne 9:37 over our bodies, and over our c', 929
10:36 of our c', as it is written in the "
Job 36:33 the c' also concerning the vapour. 4735
Ps 50:10 the c' upon a thousand hills. 929
78:48 He gave up their c' also to the 1165
104:14 the grass to grow for the c', and 929
107:38 and suffereth not their c' to decrease."
148:10 Beasts, and all c'; creeping "
Ec 2: 7 possessions of great and small c' *4735
Isa 7:25 for the treading of lesser c'. *7716
30:23 thy c' feed in large pastures. 4735
43:23 small c' of thy burnt offerings; 7716
46: 1 upon the beasts, and upon the c': 929
Jer 9:10 can men hear the voice of the c'; 4735
49:32 multitude of their c' a spoil: and 4734
Eze 34:17 between c' and c', between the 7716
20 I, will judge between the fat c' "
20 and between the lean c'. "
22 I will judge between c' and c'. "
38:12 nations, which have gotten c' and 4735
13 to take away c' and goods, "
Joe 1:18 the herds of c' are perplexed, 1241
Jon 4:11 left hand; and also much c'? 929
Hag 1:11 upon men, and upon c', and upon "
Zec 2: 4 for the multitude of men and c' "
13: 5 to keep c' from my youth. *7069
Lu 17: 7 a servant plowing or feeding c', *4165
Joh 4:12 and his children, and his c'? 2353

caught
Ge 22:13 ram c' in a thicket by his horns: 270
39:12 And she c' him by his garment, 8610
Ex 4: 4 put forth his hand, and c' it, *2388
Nu 31:32 which the men of war had c', * 962
J'g 1: 6 pursued after him, and c' him, 270
8:14 And c' a young man of the men 3920
15: 4 went and c' three hundred foxes, "
21:23 whom they c': and they went *1497
1Sa 17:35 he arose against me, I c' him 2388
2Sa 2:16 And they c' every one his fellow "
18: 9 and his head c' hold of the oak, "
1Ki 1:50 and c' hold on the horns of the "
51 he hath c' hold on the horns of * 270
2:28 and c' hold on the horns of the 2388
11:30 And Ahijah c' the new garment *8610
2Ki 4:27 she c' him by the feet: but 2388
2Ch 22: 9 sought Ahaziah: and they c' him, 3920
Pr 7:13 So she c' him, and kissed him, 2388
Ec 9:12 birds that are c' in the snare; 270
Jer 50:24 thou art found, and also c', 8610
M't 14:31 c' him, and said unto him, *1949
21:39 they c' him, and cast him out *2983
M'r 12: 3 And they c' him and beat him, "
Lu 8:29 For oftentimes it had c' him: *4884
Joh 21: 3 and that night they c' nothing. *4084
10 the fish which we have now c'. "
Ac 6:12 c' him, and brought him to the *4884
8:39 Spirit of the Lord c' away Philip, 726
16:19 they c' Paul and Silas, and drew *1949
19:29 c' Gaius and Aristarchus, men *4884
26:21 the Jews c' me in the temple, *4815
27:15 And when the ship was c', 4884
2Co 12: 2 one c' up to the third heaven. 726
4 he was c' up into paradise, "
16 being crafty, I c' you with guile. 2983
1Th 4:17 shall be c' up together with 726
Re 12: 5 her child was c' up unto God, "

caul See also CAULS.
Ex 29:13 the c' that is above the liver, 3508
22 and the c' above the liver, "
Le 3: 4 c' above the liver, with the kidneys,"
10 and the c' above the liver, "
15 c' above the liver, with the kidneys,"
4: 9 c' above the liver, with the kidneys,"
7: 4 and the c' that is above the liver, "
8:16 and the c' above the liver, and "
25 the c' above the liver, and the two "
9:10 and the c' above the liver of the "
19 and the c' above the liver: "
Ho 13: 8 and will rend the c' of their heart,5458

cauls
Isa 3:18 about their feet, and their c', 7636

cause See also CAUSED; CAUSES; CAUSEST; CAUSETH; CAUSING; CAUSELESS; CAUSEWAY.
Ge 7: 4 I will c' it to rain upon the earth
45: 1 C' every man to go out from me.
Ex 8: 5 and c' frogs to come up upon
9:16 And in very deed for this c' have I 5668
18 I will c' it to rain a very grievous
21:19 shall c' him to be thoroughly healed.
22: 5 c' a field or vineyard to be eaten.
9 the c' of both parties shall come 1697
23: 2 speak in a c' to decline after 7379
3 countenance a poor man in his c'. "
6 the judgment of thy poor in his c'. "
27:20 to c' the lamp to burn always.
29:10 shalt c' a bullock to be brought
Le 14:41 he shall c' the house to be scraped
19:29 to c' her to be a whore; lest the *
24: 2 the light, to c' the lamps to burn

Le 24:19 c' a blemish in his neighbor: 5414
25: 9 Then shalt thou c' the trumpet *
26:16 the eyes, and c' sorrow of heart: *
Nu 5:24 he shall c' the woman to drink *
26 shall c' the woman to drink the *
16: 5 and will c' him to come near
5 will he c' to come near unto him.
11 which c' both thou and all thy *3651
27: 5 brought their c' before the Lord. 4941
7 and thou shalt c' the inheritance
8 then ye shall c' his inheritance
28: 7 shalt thou c' the strong wine *
35:30 any person to c' him to die. *
De 1:17 the c' that is too hard for you, 1697
38 he shall c' Israel to inherit it.
3:28 he shall c' them to inherit the land
12:11 choose to c' his name to dwell
17:16 nor c' the people to return to Egypt,
24: 4 thou shalt not c' the land to sin,
25: 2 the judge shall c' him to lie down,
28: 7 shall c' thine enemies that rise 5414
25 shall c' thee to be smitten before "
31: 7 thou shalt c' them to inherit it.
Jos 5: 4 the c' why Joshua did circumcise: 1697
20: 4 his c' in the ears of the elders
23: 7 nor c' to swear by them,
1Sa 17:29 now done? Is there not a c'? 1697
19: 5 blood, to slay David without a c? 2600
24:15 plead my c', and deliver me out 7379
25:39 pleaded the c' of my reproach "
28: 9 for my life to c' me to die?
2Sa 3:35 to c' David to eat meat while it
13:13 whither shall I c' my shame *
16 said unto him, There is no c': *
15: 4 suit or c' might come unto me, 4941
1Ki 1:33 and c' Solomon my son to ride
5: 9 c' them to be discharged there,
8:31 laid upon him to c' him to swear,
45 supplication, and maintain their c'.4941
49 place, and maintain their c', "
59 maintain the c' of his servant, "
59 and the c' of his people Israel "
11:27 the c' that he lifted up his hand 1697
12:15 the c' was from the Lord, *5438
2Ki 19: 7 c' him to fall by the sword
1Ch 21: 3 he be a c' of trespass to Israel?
2Ch 6:35 supplication, and maintain their c'.4941
39 maintain their c', and forgive "
10:15 for the c' was of God, that the *5252
19:10 And what c' soever shall come *7379
32:20 And for this c' Hezekiah the *
Ezr 4:15 which c' was this city destroyed.
21 to c' these men to cease,
5: 5 they could not c' them to cease, *
Ne 4:11 slay them, and c' the work to cease.
6: 6 for which c' thou buildest the wall,
13:26 did outlandish women c' to sin.
Es 3:13 and to c' to perish, all Jews,
5: 5 C' Haman to make haste,
8:11 to slay, and to c' to perish, all the
Job 2: 3 him, to destroy him without c'. 2600
5: 8 unto God would I commit my c': 1700
6:24 and c' me to understand wherein
9:17 multiplieth my wounds without c'. 2600
13:18 I have ordered my c'; I know 4941
20: 2 do my thoughts c' me to answer, *
23: 4 I would order my c' before him, 4941
24: 7 They c' the naked to lodge *
10 They c' him to go naked *
29:16 and the c' which I knew not I 7379
31:13 If I did despise the c' of my 4941
34:11 c' every man to find according to
28 So that they c' the cry of the *
38:26 To c' it to rain on the earth,
27 and to c' the bud of the tender
Ps 7: 4 delivered him that without c' is 7387
9: 4 maintained my right and my c'; 1779
10:17 their heart, thou wilt c' thine ear
25: 3 which transgress without c'. 7387
35: 1 Plead my c', O Lord, with them *
7 For without c' have they hid for 2600
7 in a pit, which without c' they "
19 the eye that hate me without a c'. "
23 my judgment, even unto my c', 7379
27 glad, that favour my righteous c':
43: 1 plead my c' against an ungodly 7379
67: 1 bless us; and c' his face to shine
69: 4 that hate me without a c' are 2600
71: 2 and c' me to escape: incline *
74:22 Arise, O God, plead thine own c': 7379
76: 8 Thou didst c' judgment to be
80: 3 and c' thy face to shine; and we
7 of hosts, and c' thy face to shine;
9 and didst c' it to take deep root, *
19 God of hosts, c' thy face to shine;
85: 4 and c' thine anger toward us to
109: 3 fought against me without a c'. 2600
119:78 perversely with me without a c': 8267
154 Plead my c', and deliver me: 7379
161 persecuted me without a c': 2600
140:12 Lord will maintain the c' of the 1779
143: 8 C' me to hear thy lovingkindness
8 c' me to know the way wherein
Pr 1:11 for the innocent without c': 2600
3:30 Strive not with a man without c', "
4:16 away, unless they c' some to fall.
8:21 That I may c' those that love me
18:17 He that is first in his own c' 7379
22:23 the Lord will plead their c', and "
23:11 mighty; he shall plead their c' "
29 who hath wounds without c'? 2600
24:28 against thy neighbour without c'; "
25: 9 Debate thy c' with thy neighbour 7379
29: 7 The righteous considereth the c' 1779
31: 8 dumb in the c' of all such as are *
9 and plead the c' of the poor and *

Ec 2:20 to c' my heart to despair of all
5: 6 Suffer not thy mouth to c' thy
7:10 What is the c' that the former 1961
10: 1 c' the ointment of the apothecary
Ca 8: 2 I would c' thee to drink of spiced
13 hearken to thy voice: c' me to
Isa 1:23 neither doth the c' of the widow 7379
3:12 they which lead thee c' thee to
9:16 leaders of this people c' them to
10:30 c' it to be heard unto Laish, O *
13:10 moon shall not c' her light to
11 and I will c' the arrogancy of the
27: 6 He shall c' them that come of *
28:12 ye may c' the weary to rest; *
30:11 c' the Holy One of Israel to cease
30 And the Lord shall c' his glorious
32: 6 he will c' the drink of the thirsty
37: 7 and I will c' him to fall by the
41:21 Produce your c', saith the Lord; 7379
42: 2 nor c' his voice to be heard in the
49: 8 the earth, to c' to inherit the *
51:22 thy God that pleadeth the c' of
52: 4 oppressed them without c'. 657
58:14 and I will c' thee to ride upon *
61:11 the Lord God will c' righteousness
66: 9 to the birth, and not c' to bring
9 shall I c' to bring forth, and shut
Jer 3:12 and I will not c' mine anger to *
5:28 judge not the c', the c' of the 1779
7: 3 and I will c' you to dwell in this
7 Then will I c' you to dwell in this
34 Then will I c' to cease from the
11:20 unto thee have I revealed my c'. 7379
13:16 before he c' darkness, and before
14:22 of the Gentiles that can c' rain?
15: 4 And I will c' them to be removed 5414
11 c' the enemy to entreat thee well
16: 9 Behold, I will c' to cease out of
21 I will this once c' them to know,
21 I will c' them to know mine hand
17: 4 and I will c' thee to serve thine
18: 2 and there I will c' thee to hear
19: 7 and I will c' them to fall by the
9 And I will c' them to eat the flesh
20:12 unto thee have I opened my c'. 7379
22:16 He judged the c' of the poor and 1779
23:27 which think to c' my people to
32 and c' my people to err by their
25:15 and c' all the nations, to whom I
29: 8 to your dreams which ye c' to be
30: 3 and I will c' them to return to
13 none to plead thy c', that thou 1779
21 and I will c' him to draw near,
31: 2 when I went to c' him to rest.
9 I will c' them to walk by the
32:35 c' their sons and their daughters 4616
35 abomination, to c' Judah to sin.
37 this place, and I will c' them to
44 I will c' their captivity to return,
33: 7 And I will c' the captivity of
11 I will c' to return the captivity of
15 c' the Branch of righteousness
26 I will c' their captivity to return,
34:22 the Lord, and c' them to return
36:29 and shall c' to cease from thence
37:20 that thou c' me not to return to
38:23 thou shalt c' this city to be
26 that he would not c' me to return
42:12 and c' you to return to your own
48:12 that shall c' him to wander, and *
35 Moreover I will c' to cease in
49: 2 that I will c' an alarm of war to
37 For I will c' Elam to be dismayed
50: 9 I will raise and c' to come up
34 he shall throughly plead their c', 7379
51:27 c' the horses to come up as the
36 I will plead thy c', and take 7379
La 3:32 though he c' grief, yet will he
36 To subvert a man in his c', the 7379
52 me sore, like a bird, without c'. 2600
59 seen my wrong: judge thou my c'. 4941
Eze 3: 3 c' thy belly to eat, and fill thy bowels
5: 1 and c' it to pass upon thine head
13 I will c' my fury to rest upon †
9: 1 C' them that have charge over the
14:15 If I c' noisome beasts to pass through
23 that I have not done without c' all 2600
16: 2 c' Jerusalem to know her
21 c' them to pass through the fire *
41 and I will c' thee to cease from
20: 4 c' them to know the abominations
37 I will c' you to pass under the rod,
21:17 and I will c' my fury to rest: †
30 Shall I c' it to return into his sheath?
23:48 Thus will I c' lewdness to cease out of
24: 8 That it might c' fury to come up to
26 to c' thee to hear it with thine ears?
25: 7 and I will c' thee to perish out of the
26: 3 and will c' many nations to come up
13 And I will c' the noise of thy songs to
17 inhabitants, which c' their terror *5414
27:30 shall c' their voice to be heard
29: 4 I will c' the fish of thy rivers to stick
14 will c' them to return into the land
21 I c' the horn of the house of Israel
30:13 I will c' their images to cease out of
22 and I will c' the sword to fall out of
32: 4 will c' all the fowls of the heaven to
12 will I c' thy multitude to fall, the
14 c' their rivers to run like oil, saith the
34:10 c' them to cease from feeding the
15 I will c' them to lie down, saith the
25 and will c' the evil beasts to cease out
26 I will c' the shower to come down in
36:12 Yea, I will c' men to walk upon
15 Neither will I c' men to hear in *

Eze 36:15 neither shalt thou c' thy nations to fall
27 and c' you to walk in my statutes,
33 I will also c' you to dwell in the cities,
37: 5 Behold, I will c' breath to enter into
12 open your graves, and c' you to come
39: 2 will c' thee to come up from the
3 and will c' thine arrows to fall out of
44:23 and c' them to discern between the
30 he may c' the blessing to rest in
Da 2:12 For this c' the king 3606, 6903, 1836
8:25 also he shall c' craft to prosper in
9:17 and c' thy face to shine upon thy
27 shall c' the sacrifice and the oblation
11:18 shall c' the reproach offered by him
18 his own reproach he shall c' it to cease;
39 he shall c' them to rule over many,
Ho 1: 4 will c' to cease the kingdom of the
2:11 I will also c' all her mirth to cease,
Joe 2:23 he will c' to come down for you the*
3:11 c' thy mighty ones to come down,
Am 5:27 Therefore will I c' you to go into
6: 3 and c' the seat of violence to come
8: 9 I will c' the sun to go down at noon,
Jon 1: 7 may know for whose c' this evil is 7945
8 for whose c' this evil is upon us? 834
Mic 7: 9 until he plead my c', and execute 7379
Hab 1: 3 and c' me to behold grievance? *
Zec 8:12 and I will c' the remnant of this
13: 2 I will c' the prophets and the unclean
M't 5:22 with his brother without a c' *1500
32 saving for the c' of fornication 3056
10:21 and c' them to be put to death. 2289
19: 3 put away his wife for every c'? 156
5 For this c' shall a man leave father 1752
M'r 10: 7 For this c' shall a man leave his "
13:12 shall c' them to be put to death. 2289
Lu 8:47 for what c' she had touched him, 156
21:16 some of you shall they c' to be put 2289
23:22 I have found no c' of death in him: 158
Joh 12:18 For this c' the people also met him, 1223
27 for this c' came I unto this hour. "
15:25 law, They hated me without a c'. 1432
18:37 this c' came I into the world, *
Ac 10:21 what is the c' wherefore ye are 156
13:28 though they found no c' of death "
19:40 there being no c' whereby we may 158
23:28 when I would have known the c' 156
25:14 Festus declared Paul's c' *3588, 2596
28:18 there was no c' of death in me. 156
20 For this c' therefore have I called "
Ro 1:26 For this c' God gave them 1223
13: 6 For for this c' pay ye tribute "
15: 9 For this c' I will confess to *
22 For which c' also I have been *1352
16:17 mark them which c' divisions *4160
1Co 4:17 For this c' have I sent unto 1223
11:10 For this c' ought the woman "
30 For this c' many are weak "
2Co 4:16 For which c' we faint not; but *1352
5:13 we be sober, it is for your c'. *
7:12 not for his c' that had done the 1752
12 nor for his c' that suffered wrong, "
Eph 3: 1 For this c' I Paul, the prisoner of 5484
14 For this c' I bow my knees unto "
5:31 For this c' shall a man leave his 873
Ph'p 2:18 For the same c' also do ye joy, * 846
Col 1: 9 For this c' we also, since 1223, 5124
4:16 c' that it be read also in the 4160
1Th 2:13 For this c' also thank we God 1223
3: 5 For this c', when I could no longer "
2Th 2:11 for this c' God shall send them "
1Ti 1:16 Howbeit for this c' I obtained "
2Ti 1:12 For the which c' I also suffer 156
Tit 1: 5 For this c' left I thee in Crete, 5484
Heb 2:11 for which c' he is not ashamed to 156
9:15 for this c' he is the mediator 1223
1Pe 4: 6 for this c' was the gospel *
Re 12:15 he might c' her to be carried 4160
13:15 and c' that as many as would not "

caused
Ge 2: 5 the Lord God had not c' it to rain
21 And the Lord God c' a deep sleep to
20:13 when God c' me to wander from my
41:52 God hath c' me to be fruitful
Ex 14:21 and the Lord c' the sea to go
36: 6 and they c' it to be proclaimed
Le 24:20 as he hath c' a blemish in a man 5414
Nu 31:16 Behold, these c' the children of 1961
De 34: 4 I have c' thee to see it with
J'g 16:19 she c' him to shave off the se.... *
1Sa 10:20 when Samuel had c' all the tribes*
21 When he had c' the tribe of Benjamin*
20:17 Jonathan c' David to swear again,
2Sa 7:11 and have c' thee to rest from all *
1Ki 1:38 and c' Solomon to ride upon king
44 and they have c' him to ride upon
2:19 and c' a seat to be set for the king's
20:33 he c' him to come up into the chariot.
2Ki 17:17 And they c' their sons and their
2Ch 8: 2 and c' the children of Israel to dwell
13:13 Jeroboam c' an ambushment to come
21:11 c' the inhabitants of Jerusalem *
33: 6 he c' his children to pass through the
Ezr 6:12 God that hath c' his name to dwell
Ne 8: 7 c' the people to understand the law:
8 and c' them to understand the *
Es 5:14 and he c' the gallows to be made.
Job 29:13 I c' the widow's heart to sing for joy.
31:16 have c' the eyes of the widow to fail;
39 have c' the owners thereof to lose
37:15 and c' the light of his cloud to *
38:12 c' the dayspring to know his place;
Ps 66:12 Thou hast c' men to ride over our
78:13 the sea, and c' them to pass through;
16 and c' waters to run down like rivers.
26 He c' an east wind to blow

Ps 119:49 upon which thou hast c' me to *
Pr 7:21 With her much fair speech she c' *
Isa 19:14 and they have c' Egypt to err
43:23 I have not c' thee to serve with † ‡
48:21 he c' the waters to flow out of the rock
63:14 the Spirit of the Lord c' him to rest:
Jer 12:14 I have c' my people Israel to inherit;
13:11 so have I c' to cleave unto me
15: 8 I have c' him to fall upon it
18:15 they have c' them to stumble in ‡
23:13 and c' my people Israel to err.
22 had c' my people to hear my words,
29: 4 whom I have c' to be carried away
7 I have c' you to be carried away
14 I c' you to be carried away captive.
32:23 therefore thou hast c' all this evil to
34:11 c' the servants and the handmaids,
16 c' every man his servant, and every
48: 4 little ones have c' a cry to be heard.
33 I have c' wine to fail from the
50: 6 shepherds have c' them to go astray,
51:49 As Babylon hath c' the slain
La 2: 6 c' the solemn feasts and sabbaths to
17 he hath c' thine enemy to rejoice
3:13 He hath c' the arrows of his quiver
Eze 3: 2 mouth, and he c' me to eat that roll.
16: 7 I have c' thee to multiply as the 5414
20:10 Wherefore I c' them to go forth out of
26 in that they c' to pass through the fire
22: 4 and thou hast c' thy days to draw near,
23:37 c' their sons, whom they bare unto me,
24:13 have c' my fury to rest upon thee, †
29:18 king of Babylon c' his army to serve
31:15 down to the grave I c' a mourning:
15 and I c' Lebanon to mourn for him,
32:23 c' terror in the land of the living. 5414
24 which c' their terror in the land "
25 their terror was c' in the land "
26 they c' their terror in the land of "
32 I have c' my terror in the land "
37: 2 And c' me to pass by them round
39:28 which c' them to be led into captivity
44:12 c' the house of Israel to fall into *
46:21 and c' me to pass by the four corners
47: 6 and c' me to return to the brink
Da 9:21 being c' to fly swiftly, touched me
Ho 4:12 hath c' them to err, and they have
Am 2: 4 and their lies c' them to err, after the
4: 7 and I c' it to rain upon one city,
7 c' it not to rain upon another city:
Jon 3: 7 And he c' it to be proclaimed and *
Zec 3: 4 c' thine iniquity to pass from thee,
Mal 2: 8 ye have c' many to stumble at the law;
Joh 11:37 eyes of the blind, have c' that 4160
Ac 15: 3 they c' great joy unto all the
2Co 2: 5 if any have c' grief, he hath not 3076

causeless
1Sa 25:31 that thou hast shed blood c', 2600
Pr 26: 2 by flying, so the curse c' shall

causes
Ex 18:19 that thou mayest bring the c' 1697
26 hard c' they brought unto Moses, "
De 1:16 Hear the c' between your brethren,
Jer 3: 8 I saw, when for all the c' whereby *182
La 2:14 for thee false burdens and c' of
3:58 O Lord, thou hast pleaded the c' 7379
Ac 26:21 For these c' the Jews caught me *1752

causest
Job 30:22 thou c' me to ride upon it, and
Ps 65: 4 man whom thou choosest, and c' to

causeth
Nu 5:18 the bitter water that c' the curse:
19 free from this bitter water that c'
22 this water that c' the curse shall go
24 the bitter water that c' the curse:
24 and the water that c' the curse
27 that the water that c' the curse shall
Job 12:24 c' them to wander in a wilderness
20: 3 my understanding c' me to answer.*
37:13 He c' it to come, whether for *
Ps 104:14 He c' the grass to grow for the cattle,
107:40 c' them to wander in the wilderness,
135: 7 He c' the vapours to ascend from the
147:18 he c' his wind to blow, and the
Pr 10: 5 in harvest is a son that c' shame.
10 winketh with the eye c' sorrow: 5414
14:35 wrath is against him that c' shame.
17: 2 have rule over a son that c' shame,
18:18 The lot c' contentions to cease,
19:26 a son that c' shame, and bringeth
27 hear the instruction that c' to err *
28:10 c' the righteous to go astray in an
Isa 61:11 the garden c' the things that are
64: 2 fire burneth, the fire c' the waters to
Jer 10:13 and he c' the vapours to ascend from
51:16 in the heavens; and he c' the vapours
Eze 26: 3 as the sea c' his waves to come up.
44:18 gird themselves with anything that c'
M't 5:32 c' her to commit adultery: and *4160
2Co 2:14 c' us to triumph in Christ, and *2358
9:11 c' through us thanksgiving to *2716
Re 13:12 beast before him, and c' the *4160
16 he c' all, both small and great,

causeway
1Ch 26:16 by the c' of the going up, ward 4546
18 four at the c', and two at Parbar. "

causing
Ca 7: 9 c' the lips of those that are asleep *
Isa 30:28 in the jaws of the people, c' them to
Jer 29:10 in c' you to return to this place.
33:12 of shepherds, c' their flocks to lie

cave See also CAVES; CAVES.
Ge 19:30 and he dwelt in a c', he and his two 4631

Ge 23: 9 That he may give me the c' of 4631
11 the field give I thee, and the c' "
17 field, and the c' which was therein, "
19 in the c' of the field of Machpelah "
20 field, and the c' that is therein, "
25: 9 buried him in the c' of Machpelah. "
49:29 in the c' that is in the field of "
30 In the c' that is in the field of "
32 purchase of the field and of the c' "
50:13 buried him in the c' of the field "
Jos 10:16 hid themselves in a c' at "
17 five kings are found hid in a c' "
18 stones upon the mouth of the c', "
22 Open the mouth of the c', and "
22 five kings unto me out of the c'. "
23 five kings unto him out of the c', "
27 cast them into the c' wherein they "
1Sa 22: 1 and escaped to the c' Adullam: "
24: 3 where was a c'; and Saul went in "
3 remained in the sides of the c'. "
7 Saul rose up out of the c', and "
8 went out of the c', and cried after "
10 to day into mine hand in the c': "
2Sa 23:13 in the harvest time unto the c' "
1Ki 18: 4 hid them by fifty in a c', and fed "
13 Lord's prophets by fifty in a c', "
19: 9 he came thither unto a c', and "
1Ch 11:15 into the c' of Adullam; and the "
Ps 57 *title* he fled from Saul in the c'. "
142 *title* A Prayer when he was in the c'. "
Joh 11:38 It was a c', and a stone lay upon 4693

cave's
Jos 10:27 laid great stones in the c' *4631

caves
J'g 6: 2 in the mountains, and c', and 4631
1Sa 13: 6 people did hide themselves in c', "
Job 30: 6 cliffs of the valleys, in c' of the *2356
Isa 2:19 into the c' of the earth, for fear 4247
Eze 33:27 in the forts and in the c' shall die 4631
Heb 11:38 mountains, and in dens and c' 3692

cease See also CEASED; CEASETH; CEASING.
Ge 8:22 and day and night shall not c'. 7673
Ex 9:29 the thunder shall c', neither shall 2308
Nu 8:25 years they shall c' waiting upon 7725
11:25 they prophesied, and did not c'. *3254
17: 5 and I will make to c' from me the 7918
De 15:11 For the poor shall never c' out of 2308
32:26 the remembrance of them to c' 7673
Jos 22:25 children make our children c' "
J'g 15: 7 of you, and after that I will c'. 2308
20:28 or shall I c'? And the Lord said, "
1Sa 7: 8 C' not to cry unto the Lord our 2790
2Ch 16: 5 of Ramah, and let his work c'. 7673
Ezr 4:21 to cause these men to c', 989
23 and made them to c' by force and "
5: 5 they could not cause them to c', "
Ne 4:11 them, and cause the work to c'. 7673
6: 3 why should the work c', whilst I "
Job 3:17 the wicked c' from troubling; 2308
10:20 c' then, and let me alone, that I "
14: 7 tender branch thereof will not c'. "
Ps 37: 8 C' from anger, and forsake 7503
46: 9 He maketh wars to c' unto the 7673
85: 4 cause thine anger toward us to c'. 6565
89:44 Thou hast made his glory to c', 7673
Pr 18:18 The lot causeth contentions to c', "
19:27 C', my son, to hear the instruction 2308
20: 3 It is an honour for a man to c' *7674
22:10 yea, strife and reproach shall c'. 7673
23: 4 c' from thine own wisdom. 2308
Ec 12: 3 and the grinders c' because they 988
Isa 1:16 before mine eyes; c' to do evil; 2308
2:22 C' ye from man, whose breath is "
10:25 and the indignation shall c', *3615
13:11 the arrogancy of the proud to c', 7673
16:10 their vintage shouting to c'. "
17: 3 The fortress also shall c' from "
21: 2 sighing thereof have I made to c'. "
30:11 cause the Holy One of Israel to c' "
33: 1 when thou shalt c' to spoil, thou 8552
Jer 7:34 Then will I cause to c' from the 7673
14:17 and day, and let them not c': 1820
16: 9 I will cause to c' out of this place 7673
17: 8 drought, neither shall c' from 4185
31:36 the seed of Israel also shall c' 7673
36:29 and shall cause to c' from thence "
48:35 I will cause to c' in Moab, saith "
La 2:18 let not the apple of thine eye c'. 1826
Eze 6: 6 your idols may be broken and c', 7673
7:24 the pomp of the strong to c'; "
12:23 I will make this proverb to c', "
16:41 and I will cause thee to c' from "
23:27 will I make thy lewdness to c' "
48 Thus will I cause lewdness to c' "
26:13 cause the noise of thy songs to c'; "
30:10 make the multitude of Egypt to c' "
13 I will cause their images to c', "
18 the pomp of her strength shall c' "
33:28 the pomp of her strength shall c'; "
34:10 and cause them to c' from feeding "
25 and will cause the evil beasts to c' "
Da 9:27 sacrifice and the oblation to c', "
11:18 reproach offered by him to c'; "
Ho 1: 4 and will cause to c' the kingdom "
2:11 will also cause all her mirth to c', "
Am 7: 5 O Lord God, c', I beseech thee: 2308
Ac 13:10 wilt thou not c' to pervert the 3973
1Co 13: 8 there be tongues, they shall c'; "
Eph 1:16 C' not to give thanks for you, "
Col 1: 9 do not c' to pray for you, and to "
2Pe 2:14 that cannot c' from sin; beguiling 180

ceased
Ge 18:11 it c' to be with Sarah after the 2308
Ex 9:33 and the thunders and hail c', 2308
34 hail and the thunders were c', "

Jos 5:12 and the manna c' on the morrow 7673
J'g 2:19 c' not from their own doings, 5307
5: 7 the villages c', they c' in Israel, 2308
1Sa 2: 5 they that were hungry c': so that "
25: 9 in the name of David, and c'. 5117
Ezr 4:24 Then c' the work of the house of 989
24 So it c' unto the second year 1934, "
Job 32: 1 these three men c' to answer Job,7673
Ps 35:15 they did tear me, and c' not: 1826
77: 2 my sore ran in the night, and c' *6313
Isa 14: 4 How hath the oppressor c'! 7673
4 the golden city c'! "
La 5:14 The elders have c' from the gate, "
15 The joy of our heart is c'; our "
Jon 1:15 and the sea c' from her raging. 5975
M't 14:32 come into the ship, the wind c'. 2869
M'r 4:39 the wind c', and there was a great "
6:51 the wind c': and they were sore "
Lu 7:45 came in hath not c' to kiss my feet. 1257
8:24 they c', and there was a calm. 3973
11: 1 when he c', one of his disciples "
Ac 5:42 they c' not to teach and preach "
20: 1 And after the uproar was c', Paul "
31 I c' not to warn every one night "
21:14 not be persuaded, we c', saying, 2270
Ga 5:11 then is the offence of the cross c'.*2673
Heb 4:10 he also hath c' from his own *2664
10: 2 would they not have c' to be 3973
1Pe 4: 1 suffered in the flesh hath c' from "

ceaseth
Ps 12: 1 Help, Lord; for the godly man c'; 1584
49: 8 is precious, and it c' for ever:) † ‡2308
Pr 26:20 there is no talebearer, the strife c'. 8367
Isa 16: 4 the spoiler c', the oppressors are 3615
24: 8 The mirth of tabrets c', the noise 7673
8 endeth, the joy of the harp c'. "
33: 8 lie waste, the wayfaring man c': "
La 3:49 eye trickleth down, and c' not, 1820
Ho 7: 4 who c' from raising after he hath 7673
Ac 6:13 This man c' not to speak 3973

ceasing
1Sa 12:23 the Lord in c' to pray for you: 2308
Ac 12: 5 prayer was made without c' of *1618
Ro 1: 9 that without c' I make mention of* 89
1Th 1: 3 Remembering without c' your "
2:13 also thank we God without c', "
5:17 Pray without c'. "
2Ti 1: 3 without c' I have remembrance * 83

cedar See also CEDARS.
Le 14: 4 c' wood, and scarlet, and hyssop: 730
6 the c' wood, and the scarlet, and "
49 two birds, and c' wood, and scarlet, "
51 he shall take the c' wood, and the "
52 the c' wood, and with the hyssop, "
Nu 19: 6 the priest shall take c' wood, "
24: 6 and as c' trees beside the waters. "
2Sa 5:11 c' trees, and carpenters, and "
7: 2 I dwell in an house of c', but the "
7 build ye not me an house of c'? "
1Ki 4:33 from the c' tree that is in Lebanon "
5: 6 hew me c' trees out of Lebanon; "
8 concerning timber of c', and "
10 Hiram gave Solomon c' trees and fir "
6: 9 house with beams and boards of c'. "
10 on the house with timber of c'. "
15 the house within with boards of c'. "
16 and the walls with boards of c': "
18 c' of the house within was carved "
18 was c'; there was no stone seen. "
20 covered the altar which was of c'. "
36 hewed stone, and a row of c' beams. "
7: 2 upon four rows of c' pillars, "
2 with c' beams upon the pillars. "
3 And it was covered with c' above "
7 covered with c' from one side of "
12 a row of c' beams, both for the inner "
9:11 furnished Solomon with c' trees "
2Ki 14: 9 sent to the c' that was in Lebanon, "
19:23 and will cut down the tall c' trees* "
1Ch 22: 4 Also c' trees in abundance: for the "
4 they of Tyre brought much c' wood "
2Ch 1:15 c' trees made he as the sycomore * "
2: 8 Send me also c' trees, fir trees, and "
9:27 in Jerusalem as stones, and c' * "
25:18 was in Lebanon sent to the c' that "
Ezr 3: 7 to bring c' trees from Lebanon "
Job 40:17 He moveth his tail like a c': the "
Ps 92:12 he shall grow like a c' in Lebanon. "
Ca 1:17 The beams of our house are c', * "
8: 9 we will inclose her with boards of c'. "
Isa 41:19 plant in the wilderness the c', the "
Jer 22:14 cieled with c', and painted with "
15 thou closest thyself in c'? did not "
Eze 17: 3 took the highest branch of the c': "
22 the highest branch of the high c', "
23 be a goodly c': and under it shall "
27:24 bound with cords, and made of c', 729
31: 3 the Assyrian was a c' in Lebanon 730
Zep 2:14 for he shall uncover the c' work. 731
Zec 11: 2 for the c' is fallen; because the 730

cedars
J'g 9:15 and devour the c' of Lebanon. 730
1Ki 7:11 measures of hewed stones, and c'.* "
10:27 c' made he to be as the sycomore * "
1Ch 14: 1 timber of c', with masons and * "
17: 1 I dwell in an house of c', but the * "
6 ye not built me an house of c'? * "
2Ch 2: 3 send him c' to build him an house "
Ps 29: 5 the Lord breaketh the c'; yea, "
5 the Lord breaketh the c' of "
80:10 thereof were like the goodly c'. "
104:16 c' of Lebanon, which he hath "
148: 9 all hills; fruitful trees, and all c': "
Ca 5:15 as Lebanon, excellent as the c', "
Isa 2:13 upon all the c' of Lebanon, that 730
9:10 but we will change them into c', "
14: 8 the c' of Lebanon, saying, Since "
37:24 cut down the tall c' thereof, and "
44:14 He heweth him down c', and taketh "
Jer 22: 7 shall cut down thy choice c', and "
23 that makest thy nest in the c', how "
Eze 27: 5 they have taken c' from Lebanon to "
31: 8 The c' in the garden of God could "
Am 2: 9 like the height of the c', and he "
Zec 11: 1 that the fire may devour thy c'. "

cedar-tree See CEDAR and TREE.

cedar-wood See CEDAR and WOOD.

Cedron (*se'-drun*) See also KIDRON.
Joh 18: 1 over the brook C', where was a 2748

ceiled See CIELED.

ceiling See CIELING.

celebrate
Le 23:32 even, shall ye c' your sabbath. *7673
41 shall c' it in the seventh month. *2287
Isa 38:18 praise thee, death can not c' thee:1984

celestial
1Co 15:40 There are also c' bodies, and 2032
40 but the glory of the c' is one, "

cellars
1Ch 27:27 for the wine c' was Zabdi the 214
28 and over the c' of oil was Joash: "

Cenchrea (*sen'-kre-ah*)
Ac 18:18 having shorn his head in C': 2747
Ro 16: 1 of the church which is at C': "
subscr. servant of the church at C'.* "

censer See also CENSERS.
Le 10: 1 took either of them his c', and put 4289
16:12 shall take a c' full of burning coals "
Nu 16:17 take every man his c', and put "
17 before the Lord every man his c', "
17 and Aaron, each of you his c'. "
18 took every man his c', and put fire "
46 Take a c', and put fire therein "
2Ch 26:19 a c' in his hand to burn incense: 4730
Eze 8:11 with every man his c' in his hand; "
Heb 9: 4 Which had the golden c', and the 2369
Re 8: 3 at the altar, having a golden c'; 3031
5 took the c', and filled it with fire "

censers
Nu 4:14 the c', the fleshhooks, and the *4289
16: 6 This do; Take you c', Korah, and "
17 two hundred and fifty c'; thou "
37 take up the c' out of the burning, "
38 The c' of these sinners against their "
39 the priest took the brasen c', "
1Ki 7:50 spoons, and the c' of pure gold; * "
2Ch 4:22 spoons, and the c' of pure gold: * "

centurion (*sen-too'-ree-un*) See also CENTURION'S; CENTURIONS.
M't 8: 5 unto him a c', beseeching him, 1543
8 The c' answered and said, Lord, "
13 Jesus said unto the c', Go thy way; "
27:54 c', and they that were with him, "
M'r 15:39 c', which stood over against him, 2760
44 calling unto him the c', he asked "
45 when he knew it of the c', he gave "
Lu 7: 6 the c' sent friends to him, saying 1543
23:47 when the c' saw what was done, "
Ac 10: 1 c' of the band called the Italian "
22 they said, Cornelius the c', a just "
22:25 Paul said unto the c' that stood by, "
26 When the c' heard that, he went "
24:23 commanded a c' to keep Paul, "
27: 1 Julius, a c' of Augustus' band. "
6 there the c' found a ship of "
11 the c' believed the master and the "
31 Paul said to the c' and to the "
43 the c', willing to save Paul, kept "
28:16 the c' delivered the prisoners to * "

centurion's (*sen-too'-ree-uns*)
Lu 7: 2 a certain c' servant, who was dear 1543

centurions (*sen-too'-ree-uns*).
Ac 21:32 immediately took soldiers and c', 1543
23:17 Paul called one of the c' unto him, "
23 he called unto him two c', saying, "

Cephas (*se'-fas*) See also PETER.
Joh 1:42 thou shalt be called C', which is 2786
1Co 1:12 and I of Apollos; and I of C'; "
3:22 Whether Paul, or Apollos, or C', "
9: 5 as the brethren of the Lord, and C'? "
15: 5 he was seen of C', then of the "
Ga 2: 9 And when James, C', and John, "

ceremonies
Nu 9: 3 all the c' thereof, shall ye keep it. *4941

certain See also UNCERTAIN.
Ge 28:11 And he lighted upon a c' place, "
37:15 And a c' man found him, and "
38: 1 turned in to a c' Adullamite, 376
2 there a daughter of a c' Canaanite, "
Ex 16: 4 gather a c' rate every day, that I *1697
Nu 9: 6 there were c' men, who were "
16: 2 with c' of the children of Israel, 582
De 13:13 C' men, the children of Belial, "
14 thing c', that such abomination 3559
17: 4 behold, it be true, and the thing c', "
25: 2 to his fault, by a c' number. "
J'g 9:53 a c' woman cast a piece of a 259
13: 2 a c' man of Zorah, of the family of "
19: 1 there was a c' Levite sojourning 376
22 men of the city, c' sons of Belial, 582
Ru 1: 1 And a c' man of Beth-lehem-judah "
1Sa 1: 1 a c' man of Ramathaim-zophim, 259
21: 7 a c' man of the servants of Saul "
2Sa 18:10 a c' man saw it, and told Joab, 259
1Ki 2:37 thou shalt know for c' that thou 3045
42 Know for a c', on the day thou "
7:29 c' additions made of thin work. *
11:17 Hadad fled, he and c' Edomites 582
20:35 c' man of the sons of the prophets 259
22:34 And a c' man drew a bow at a "
2Ki 4: 1 Now there cried a c' woman of the 259
8: 6 unto her a c' officer, saying, "
1Ch 9:28 And c' of them had the charge "
16: 4 he appointed c' of the Levites to "
19: 5 Then there went c', and told David "
2Ch 8:13 Even after a c' rate every day, *1697
18: 2 And after c' years he went down "
33 And a c' man drew a bow at a "
28:12 c' of the heads of the children of 582
Ezr 10:16 c' chief of the fathers, after the "
Ne 1: 2 came, he and c' men of Judah; "
4 and wept, and mourned c' days, "
11: 4 And at Jerusalem dwelt c' of the "
23 that a c' portion should be for *
12:35 and c' of the priests' sons with "
13: 6 after c' days obtained I leave of "
25 smote c' of them, and plucked off 582
Es 2: 5 c' Jew whose name was Mordecai, 376
3: 8 There is a c' people scattered 259
Jer 26:15 for c', that if ye put me to death, 3045
17 rose up c' of the elders of the land, 582
22 and c' men with him into Egypt, "
41: 5 there came c' from Shechem ‡ 582
52:15 away captive c' of the poor of the *
16 of the guard left c' of the poor *
Eze 14: 1 came c' of the elders of Israel 582
20: 1 c' of the elders of Israel came to "
Da 1: 3 bring c' of the children of Israel, "
2:45 and the dream is c', and the 3330
3: 8 that time c' Chaldeans came near, 1400
12 There are c' Jews whom thou hast "
8:13 another saint said unto that c' 6422
27 Daniel fainted, and was sick c' days; "
10: 5 behold a c' man clothed in linen, * 259
11:13 come after c' years with a great *6256
M't 8:19 a c' scribe came, and said unto *1520
9: 3 And, behold, c' of the scribes said 5100
18 behold, there came a c' ruler, "
12:38 Then c' of the scribes and of the 5100
17:14 came to him a c' man, kneeling *
18:23 heaven likened unto a c' king, 444
20:20 and desiring a c' thing of him. 5100
21:28 A c' man had two sons; and he *
33 There was a c' householder, *444, 5100
22: 2 of heaven is like unto a c' king, 444
M'r 2: 6 But there were c' of the scribes 5100
5:25 a c' woman, which had an issue * "
35 c' which said, Thy daughter is * "
7: 1 and c' of the scribes, which came 5100
25 c' woman, whose young daughter *
11: 5 And c' of them that stood there 5100
12: 1 A c' man planted a vineyard, *
13 send unto him c' of the Pharisees 5100
42 there came a c' poor widow, and *1520
14:51 followed him a c' young man, 5100
57 And there arose c', and bear false "
Lu 1: 5 a c' priest named Zacharias, of the "
5:12 when he was in a c' city, behold *1520
17 it came to pass on a c' day, as he "
6: 2 And c' of the Pharisees said unto 5100
7: 2 And a c' centurion's servant, who "
41 There was a c' creditor which had "
8: 2 c' women, which had been healed "
20 And it was told him by c' which "
22 it came to pass on a c' day, that *1520
27 c' man, which had devils long time, 5100
9:57 a c' man said unto him, Lord, I "
10:25 a c' lawyer stood up, and tempted "
30 A c' man went down from "
31 came down a c' priest that way: "
33 a c' Samaritan, as he journeyed, "
38 he entered into a c' village: "
38 and a c' woman named Martha "
11: 1 as he was praying in a c' place, "
27 a c' woman of the company lifted "
37 a c' Pharisee besought him to * "
12:16 ground of a c' rich man brought "
13: 6 A c' man had a fig tree planted "
31 there came c' of the Pharisees, "
14: 2 there was a c' man before him "
16 A c' man made a great supper, "
15:11 A c' man had two sons: "
16: 1 There was a c' rich man, which "
19 a c' rich man, which was clothed "
20 was a c' beggar named Lazarus, "
17:12 as he entered into a c' village, "
18: 9 c' which trusted in themselves "
18 And a c' ruler asked him, saying, "
35 a c' blind man sat by the wayside "
19:12 A c' nobleman went into a far "
20: 9 A c' man planted a vineyard, * "
27 came to him c' of the Sadducees "
39 c' of the scribes answering said, "
21: 2 saw also a c' poor widow casting "
22:56 a c' maid beheld him as he sat "
23:19 for a c' sedition made in the city, "
24: 1 prepared, and c' others with them.* "
22 Yea, and c' women also of our 5100
24 c' of them which were with us "
Joh 4:46 there was a c' nobleman, whose "
5: 4 angel went down at a c' season *
5 And a c' man was there, which 5100
11: 1 Now a c' man was sick, named "
12:20 there were c' Greeks among them "
Ac 3: 2 And a c' man lame from his "
5: 1 But a c' man named Ananias, "
2 brought a c' part, and laid it at "
6: 9 there arose c' of the synagogue, "
8: 9 there was a c' man, called Simon, "
36 way, they came unto a c' water: "

Ac 9:10 was a c' disciple at Damascus, 5100
19 Then was Saul c' days with the "
33 And there he found a c' man "
36 at Joppa a c' disciple named "
10: 1 a c' man in Cæsarea called "
11 a c' vessel descending unto him, "
23 and c' brethren from Joppa "
48 prayed they him to tarry c' days. "
11: 5 A c' vessel descend, as it had been "
12: 1 his hands to vex c' of the church. "
13: 1 c' prophets and teachers; * "
6 a c' sorcerer, a false prophet, "
14: 8 And there sat a c' man at Lystra, "
19 And there came thither c' Jews *
15: 1 And c' men which came down 5100
2 Barnabas, and c' other of them, "
5 up c' of the sect of the Pharisees "
24 that c' which went out from us "
16: 1 a c' disciple was there, named * "
1 Timotheus, the son of a c' woman,* "
12 were in that city abiding c' days. "
14 a c' woman named Lydia, a seller "
16 a c' damsel possessed with a spirit "
17: 5 took unto them c' lewd fellows of "
6 they drew Jason and c' brethren "
18 c' philosophers of the Epicureans, "
20 thou bringest c' strange things "
28 c' also of your own poets have said "
34 c' men clave unto him, and "
18: 2 a c' Jew named Aquila, born in "
7 entered into a c' man's house, "
24 And a c' Jew named Apollos, born "
19: 1 Ephesus: and finding c' disciples, "
13 Then c' of the vagabond Jews, "
24 a c' man named Demetrius, a "
31 And c' of the chief of Asia, which "
20: 9 a window a c' young man named "
21:10 a c' prophet, named Agabus. "
16 also c' of the disciples of Cæsarea, "
23:12 c' of the Jews banded together, 5100
17 for he hath a c' thing to tell him. * "
24: 1 with a c' orator named Tertullus,* "
18 Whereupon c' Jews from Asia "
24 And after c' days, when Felix "
25:13 c' days king Agrippa and Bernice "
14 is a c' man left in bonds by Felix: "
19 had c' questions against him of "
26 Of whom I have no c' thing to 804
27: 1 Paul and c' other prisoners 5100
16 running under a c' island which * "
26 we must be cast upon a c' island. "
39 they discovered a c' creek "
Ro 15:26 a c' contribution for the poor "
1Co 4:11 and have no c' dwellingplace; 790
Ga 2:12 before that c' came from James, 5100
1Ti 6: 7 it is c' we can carry nothing out. *1212
Heb 2: 6 But one in a c' place testified, *4225
4: 4 spake in a c' place of the seventh * "
7 Again, he limiteth a c' day, saying 5100
10:27 c' fearful looking for of judgment "
Jude 4 For there are c' men crept in "

certainly See also UNCERTAINLY.
Ge 26:28 We saw c' that the Lord was with*
43: 7 could we c' know that he would *
44:15 such a man as I can c' divine? *
50:15 will c' requite us all the evil *
Ex 3:12 he said, C' I will be with thee; 3588
22: 4 If the theft be c' found in his *
Le 5:19 hath c' trespassed against the Lord.
24:16 the congregation shall c' stone him:
Jos 9:24 Because it was c' told thy
J'g 14:12 if ye can c' declare it me within *
1Sa 20: 3 Thy father c' knoweth that I *
9 if I knew c' that evil were *
23:10 thy servant hath c' heard *
25:28 the Lord will c' make my lord a sure
1Ki 1:30 even so will I c' do this day. *
2Ki 8:10 him, Thou mayest c' recover: *
2Ch 18:27 If thou c' return in peace, *
Pr 23: 5 riches c' make themselves wings; *
Jer 8: 8 Lo, c' in vain made he it; 403
13:12 Do we not c' know that every †
25:28 Lord of hosts; Ye shall c' drink. *
36:29 king of Babylon shall c' come
40:14 Dost thou c' know that Baalis *
42:19 know c' that I have admonished you
22 Now therefore know c' that ye shall
44:17 we will c' do whatsoever thing goeth
La 2:16 c' this is the day that we looked 389
Da 11:10 one shall c' come, and overflow, *
13 c' come after certain years *
Lu 23:47 C' this was a righteous man. 3689

certainty
Jos 23:13 Know for a c' that the Lord your God
1Sa 23:23 come ye again to me with the c', 3559
Pr 22:21 the c' of the words of truth; that 7189
Da 2: 8 I know of c' that ye would gain 3330
Lu 1: 4 know the c' of those things, 803
Ac 21:34 not know the c' for the tumult, 804
22:30 he would have known the c' "

certified
Ezr 4:14 have we sent and c' the king; 3046
Es 2:22 and Esther c' the king thereof in * 559

certify See also CERTIFIED.
2Sa 15:28 come word from you to c' me. 5046
Ezr 4:16 We c' the king that, if this city 3046
5:10 asked their names also, to c' thee, "
7:24 Also we c' you that touching any "
Ga 1:11 But I c' you, brethren, that the *1107

Cesar See CÆSAR.

Cesarea See CÆSAREA.

Chabod See I-CHABOD.

chafed
2Sa 17: 8 be c' in their minds, as a bear 4751

chaff
Job 21:18 c' that the storm carrieth away. 4671
Ps 1: 4 c' which the wind driveth away. "
35: 5 Let them be as c' before the wind: "
Isa 5:24 and the flame consumeth the c', *2842
17:13 chased as the c' of the mountains 4671
29: 5 the terrible ones shall be as c' "
33:11 Ye shall conceive c', ye shall 2842
41:15 and shalt make the hills as c'. 4671
Jer 23:28 What is the c' to the wheat? *8401
Da 2:35 like the c' of the summer 5784
Ho 13: 3 as the c' that is driven with the 4671
Zep 2: 2 before the day pass as the c', "
M't 3:12 burn up the c' with unquenchable 892
Lu 3:17 the c' he will burn with fire "

chain See also CHAINS.
Ge 41:42 put a gold c' about his neck; 7242
1Ki 7:17 wreaths of c' work, for the 8333
Ps 73: 6 compasseth them about as a c'; 6059
Ca 4: 9 eyes, with one c' of thy neck. 6060
La 3: 7 he hath made my c' heavy. 5178
Eze 7:23 Make a c': for the land is full of 7569
16:11 thy hands, and a c' on thy neck. 7242
Da 5: 7 have a c' of gold about his neck, 2002
16 have a c' of gold about thy neck, "
29 put a c' of gold about his neck, "
Ac 28:20 of Israel I am bound with this c'. 254
2Ti 1:16 and was not ashamed of my c': "
Re 20: 1 pit and a great c' in his hand. "

chains
Ex 28:14 two c' of pure gold at the ends; 8333
14 the wreathen c' to the ouches. "
22 upon the breastplate c' at the ends 8331
24 thou shalt put the two wreathen c' 5688
39:15 upon the breastplate c' at the ends, 8333
17 c' of gold in the two rings 5688
18 the two wreathen c' they fastened "
Nu 31:50 of gold, c', and bracelets, rings, 685
J'g 8:26 c' that were about their camels' 6060
1Ki 6:21 made a partition by the c' of gold 7569
2Ch 3: 5 and set thereon palm trees and c'.8333
16 And he made c', as in the oracle, "
16 and put them on the c'. "
Ps 68: 6 those which are bound with c': *3574
149: 8 To bind their kings with c', 2131
Pr 1: 9 thy head, and c' about thy neck. 6060
Ca 1:10 jewels, thy neck with c' of gold. *2737
Isa 3:19 The c', and the bracelets, and the *5188
40:19 with gold, and casteth silver c'. 7569
45:14 in c' they shall come over, 2131
Jer 39: 7 and bound him with c', to carry *5178
40: 1 being bound in c' among all that 246
4 I loose thee this day from the c' "
52:11 king of Babylon bound him in c', *5178
Eze 19: 4 brought him with c' unto the land *2397
9 put him in ward in c', and * "
Na 3:10 her great men were bound in c'. 2131
M'r 5: 3 could bind him, no, not with c': * 254
4 often bound with fetters and c', "
4 the c' had been plucked asunder "
Lu 8:29 he was kept bound with c' and in "
Ac 12: 6 two soldiers, bound with two c': "
7 And his c' fell off from his hands. "
21:33 him to be bound with two c'; "
2Pe 2: 4 delivered them into c' of darkness, 4577
Jude 6 hath reserved in everlasting c' *1199

chain-work See CHAIN and WORK.

chalcedony (*kal-sed'-o-nee*)
Re 21:19 the third, a c'; the fourth, 5472

Chalcol (*kal'-kol*) See also CALCOL.
1Ki 4:31 the Ezrahite, and Heman, and C', 3633

Chaldæans (*kal-de'-uns*) See also CHALDEANS.
Ac 7: 4 out of the land of the C', 5466

Chaldea (*kal-de'-ah*) See also BABYLON; CHALDEAN.
Jer 50:10 And C' shall be a spoil: all that 3778
51:24 the inhabitants of C' all their evil "
35 blood upon the inhabitants of C', "
Eze 11:24 vision by the Spirit of God into C', "
16:29 in the land of Canaan unto C'; "
23:15 manner of the Babylonians of C', "
16 messengers unto them into C'. "

Chaldean (*kal-de'-un*) See also BABYLONIAN; CHALDEANS; CHALDEANS'.
Ezr 5:12 the C', who destroyed this house, 3777
Da 2:10 any magician, or astrologer, or C'. "

Chaldeans (*kal-de'-uns*) See also BABYLONIANS; CHALDÆANS; CHALDEANS'; CHALDEES.
Job 1:17 The C' made out three bands, 3778
Isa 23:13 Behold the land of the C'; this "
43:14 nobles, and the C', whose cry is in "
47: 1 no throne, O daughter of the C': "
5 darkness, O daughter of the C': "
48:14 and his arm shall be on the C'. "
20 flee ye from the C', with a voice of "
Jer 21: 4 and against the C', which besiege "
9 out, and falleth to the C' that "
22:25 and into the hand of the C'. "
24: 5 the land of the C' for their good. "
25:12 iniquity, and the land of the C', "
32: 4 escape out of the hand of the C', "
5 though ye fight with the C', "
24, 25 is given into the hand of the C', "
28 this city into the hand of the C', "
29 the C', that fight against the city, "
43 is given into the hand of the C'. "
33: 5 They come to fight with the C', "
35:11 for fear of the army of the C', "
37: 5 the C' that besieged Jerusalem "
8 the C' shall come again, and fight "
Jer 37: 9 The C' shall surely depart from us:3778
10 smitten the whole army of the C' "
11 the army of the C' was broken up "
13 saying, Thou fallest away to the C'. "
14 is false: I fall not away to the C'. "
38: 2 goeth forth to the C' shall live, "
18 be given into the hand of the C', "
19 the Jews that are fallen to the C', "
23 wives and thy children to the C': "
39: 8 And the C' burned the king's house, "
40: 9 saying, Fear not to serve the C': "
10 dwell at Mizpah, to serve the C', "
41: 3 and the C' that were found there, "
18 Because of the C': for they were "
43: 3 deliver us into the hand of the C', "
50: 1 and against the land of the C' "
8 go forth out of the land of the C', "
25 God of hosts in the land of the C'. "
35 A sword is upon the C', saith the "
45 purposed against the land of the C': "
51: 4 shall fall in the land of the C', "
54 destruction from the land of the C': "
52: 7 C' were by the city round about:) "
8 of the C' pursued after the king, 3779
14 the C', that were with the captain "
17 C' brake, and carried all the brass "
Eze 1: 3 land of the C' by the river Chebar; "
12:13 to Babylon to the land of the C'; "
23:14 images of the C' pourtrayed with "
23 The Babylonians, and all the C', "
Da 1: 4 learning and the tongue of the C'. "
2: 2 C', for to shew the king his dreams. "
4 Then spake the C' to the king "
5 king answered and said to the C', "
10 C' answered before the king, "
3: 8 at that time certain C' came near, "
4: 7 magicians, the astrologers, the C', "
5: 7 to bring in the astrologers, the C', "
11 astrologers, C', and soothsayers; "
30 Belshazzar the king of the C' slain. "
9: 1 king over the realm of the C'; 3778
Hab 1: 6 For, lo, I raise up the C', that "

Chaldeans' (*kal-de'uns*) See also CHALDEES.
Jer 39: 5 the C' army pursued after them, *3778

Chaldees (*kal'-dees*) See also CHALDEES'.
Ge 11:28 of his nativity, in Ur of the C'. 3778
31 forth with them from Ur of the C', "
15: 7 brought thee out of Ur of the C', "
2Ki 24: 2 sent against him bands of the C', * "
25: 4 the C' were against the city round * "
5 of the C' pursued after the king, * "
10 And all the army of the C', that "
13 C' break in pieces, and carried * "
24 to be the servants of the C': * "
25 Jews and the C' that were with * "
26 for they were afraid of the C'. * "
2Ch 36:17 upon them the king of the C', * "
Ne 9: 7 him forth out of Ur of the C', "

Chaldees' (*kal-'dees*) See also CHALDEANS.
Isa 13:19 the beauty of the C' excellency, *3778

chalkstones
Isa 27: 9 of the altar as c' that are beaten 68, 1615

challengeth
Ex 22: 9 which another c' to be his, * 559

chamber See also BEDCHAMBER; CHAMBERING; CHAMBERLAIN; CHAMBERS; GUESTCHAMBER.
Ge 43:30 he entered into his c', 2315
J'g 3:24 covereth his feet in his summer c'. "
15: 1 I will go in to my wife into the c'. "
16: 9 wait, abiding with her in the c'. * "
12 were liers in wait abiding in the c'. "
2Sa 13:10 Bring the meat into the c', that I "
10 brought them into the c' to "
18:33 the c' over the gate, and wept: 5944
1Ki 1:15 in unto the king into the c': 2315
6: 6 The nethermost c' was five cubits *3326
8 The door for the middle c' was *6763
8 into the middle c', and out of the *
14:28 them back into the guard c'. 8372
17:23 brought him down out of the c' 5944
20:30 into the city, into an inner c'. 2315
22:25 when thou shalt go into an inner c' "
2Ki 1: 2 through a lattice in his upper c' 5944
4:10 Let us make a little c', I pray thee, "
11 he turned into the c', and lay "
9: 2 and carry him to an inner c'; 2315
23:11 the c' of Nathan-melech the 3957
12 the upper c' of Ahaz, which the 5944
2Ch 12:11 them again into the guard c'. 8372
18:24 thou shalt go into an inner c' 2315
Ezr 10: 6 c' of Johanan the son of Eliashib: 3957
Ne 3:30 Berechiah over against his c'. 5393
13: 4 of the c' of the house of our God, *3957
5 had prepared for him a great c', "
7 a c' in the courts of the house 5393
8 stuff of Tobiah out of the c'. 3957
Ps 19: 5 bridegroom coming out of his c', 2646
Ca 3: 4 the c' of her that conceived me. 2315
Jer 35: 4 the c' of the sons of Hanan, 3957
4 by the c' of the princes, which "
4 was above the c' of Maaseiah "
36:10 in the c' of Gemariah the son of "
12 king's house, into the scribe's c': "
20 in the c' of Elishama the scribe, "
21 it out of Elishama the scribe's c'. "
Eze 40: 7 every little c' was one reed long, *8372
13 from the roof of one little c' to * "
45 This c', whose prospect is toward 3957
46 c' whose prospect is toward the "
41: 5 and the breadth of every side c', 6763
7 from the lowest c' to the highest "
9 which was for the side c' without,*6763
42: 1 into the c' that was over against 3957
Da 6:10 windows being open in his c' 5952

Joe 2:16 the bridegroom go forth of his c', 2315
Ac 9:37 they laid her in an upper c'. *5253*
39 they brought him into the upper c': "
20: 8 were many lights in the upper c', "

chambering
Ro 13:13 not in c' and wantonness, nor in *2845*

chamberlain See also CHAMBERLAINS.
2Ki 23:11 chamber of Nathan-melech the c', 5631
Es 2: 3 custody of Hege the king's c', "
14 of Shaashgaz, the king's c', which "
15 Hegai the king's c', the keeper of "
Ac 12:20 Blastus the king's c' *1909, 3588, 2846*
Ro 16:23 Erastus the c' of the city saluteth *3623*

chamberlains
Es 1:10 the seven c' that served in the 5631
12 king's commandment by his c': "
15 of the king Ahasuerus by the c'? "
2:21 two of the king's c', Bigthan and "
4: 4 maids and her c' came and told it "
5 for Hatach, one of the king's c', "
6: 2 two of the king's c', the keepers of "
14 came the king's c', and hasted "
7: 9 Harbonah, one of the c', said "

chambers
1Ki 6: 5 built c' round about, against the *3326
5 of the oracle: and he made c' *6763
10 he built c' against all the house *3326
1Ch 9:26 were over the c' and treasuries 3957
33 Levites, who remaining in the c' "
23:28 in the courts, and in the c', and in "
28:11 and of the upper c' thereof, and *5944
12 all the c' round about, of the 3957
2Ch 3: 9 he overlaid the upper c' with gold. 5944
31:11 to prepare c' in the house of the 3957
Ezr 8:29 the c' of the house of the Lord. "
Ne 10:37 to the c' of the house of our God; "
38 the c', into the treasure house. "
39 the c', where are the vessels of the "
12:44 the c' for the treasures, for the 5393
13: 9 and they cleansed the c': 3957
Job 9: 9 Pleiades, and the c' of the south. 2315
Ps 104: 3 Who layeth the beams of his c' 5944
13 He watereth the hills from his c': "
105:30 abundance, in the c' of their 2315
Pr 7:27 going down to the c' of death. "
24: 4 by knowledge shall the c' be filled "
Ca 1: 4 king hath brought me into his c': "
Isa 26:20 people, enter thou into thy c', and "
Jer 22:13 and his c' by wrong; 5944
14 a wide house and large c', and "
35: 2 into one of the c', and give them 3957
Eze 8:12 man in the c' of his imagery? 2315
21:14 which entereth into their privy c'. "
40: 7 between the little c' were five *8372
10 the little c' of the gate eastward * "
12 The space also before the little c' * "
12 the little c' were six cubits on * "
16 narrow windows to the little c', * "
17 there were c', and a pavement 3957
17 thirty c' were upon the pavement. "
21 And the little c' thereof were *8372
29 And the little c' thereof, and the * "
33 the little c' thereof, and the posts * "
36 The little c' thereof, the posts * "
38 the c' and the entries thereof 3957
44 the c' of the singers in the inner "
41: 6 the side c' were three, one over 6763
6 house for the side c' round about, "
7 upward to the side c': for the "
8 the foundations of the side c' were "
9 the place of the side c' that were "
10 And between the c' was the 3957
11 the doors of the side c' were 6763
26 and upon the side c' of the house, "
42: 4 before the c' was a walk of ten 3957
5 Now the upper c' were shorter: "
7 over against the c', toward the "
7 court on the forepart of the c', "
8 For the length of the c' that were "
9 from under these c' was the entry "
10 The c' were in the thickness of "
11 the appearance of the c' which "
12 according to the doors of the c "
13 The north c' and the south c', "
13 separate place, they be holy c', "
44:19 in the holy c', and they shall put "
45: 5 for a possession for twenty c'. "
46:19 into the holy c' of the priests, "
M't 24:26 behold, he is in the secret c'; *5009*

chameleon *(ca-me'-le-un)*
Le 11:30 ferret, and the c', and the lizard, 3581

chamois *(sham'-my)*
De 14: 5 and the wild ox, and the c'. 2169

champaign *(sham-pane')*
De 11:30 in the c' over against Gilgal, *6160

champion
1Sa 17: 4 went out a c' out of the camp 376, 1143
23 the c', the Philistine of Gath, "
51 when the Philistines saw their c' 1368

Chanaan *(ka'-na-un)* See also CANAAN.
Ac 7:11 over all the land of Egypt and C', *5477*
13:19 seven nations in the land of C', "

chance See also CHANCETH.
De 22: 6 If a bird's nest c' to be before thee 7122
1Sa 6: 9 it was a c' that happened to us. 4745
2Sa 1: 6 I happened by c' upon mount 7122
Ec 9:11 time and c' happeneth to them 6294
Lu 10:31 by c' there came down a certain *4795*
1Co 15:37 grain, it may c' of wheat, *5177*

chancellor
Ezr 4: 8 Rehum the c', and Shimshai 1169, 2942
4: 9 Then wrote Rehum the c', 1169, 2942
17 an answer unto Rehum the c', " "

chanceth
De 23:10 by reason of uncleanness that c' 4745

change See also CHANGEABLE; CHANGED; CHANGES; CHANGEST; CHANGETH; CHANGING; EXCHANGE.
Ge 35: 2 be clean, and c' your garments: 2498
Le 27:10 nor c' it, a good for a bad, or a 4171
10 and if he shall at all c' "
33 neither shall he c' it: "
33 and if he c' it at all, "
33 and the c' thereof shall be holy; *8545
J'g 14:12, 13 and thirty c' of garments: *2487
19 gave c' of garments unto them * "
Job 14:14 time will I wait, till my c' come. * "
17:12 They c' the night into day: and 7760
Ps 102:26 as a vesture shalt thou c' them, 2498
Pr 24:21 with them that are given to c': 8138
Isa 9:10 but we will c' them into cedars. ‡2498
Jer 2:36 about so much to c' thy way? 8138
13:23 Can the Ethiopian c' his skin, or 2015
Da 7:25 and think to c' times and laws: 8133
Ho 4: 7 will I c' their glory into shame. 4171
Hab 1:11 Then shall his mind c', and he *2498
Zec 3: 4 clothe thee with c' of raiment. *4254
Mal 3: 6 I am the Lord, I c' not; therefore 8138
Ac 6:14 shall c' the customs which Moses *236*
Ro 1:26 their women did c' the natural **3337*
Ga 4:20 with you now, and to c' my voice; *236*
Ph'p 3:21 Who shall c' our vile body, that it *3345*
Heb 7:12 of necessity a c' also of the law. *3331*

changeable See also UNCHANGEABLE.
Isa 3:22 The c' suits of apparel, and the *4254

changed
Ge 31: 7 and c' my wages ten times; but 2498
41 thou hast c' my wages ten times. "
41:14 c' his raiment, and came in unto "
Le 13:16 turn again, and be c' unto white, 2015
55 the plague have not c' his colour, "
Nu 32:38 (their names being c',) and 5437
1Sa 21:13 he c' his behaviour before them, 8138
2Sa 12:20 c' his apparel, and came into the 2498
2Ki 24:17 and c' his name to Zedekiah. 5437
25:29 c' his prison garments: and he 8132
Job 30:18 of my disease is my raiment c': *2664
Ps 34 *title* when he c' his behaviour 8138
102:26 and they shall be c': 2498
106:20 Thus they c' their glory into the 4171
Ec 8: 1 boldness of his face shall be c'. 8132
Isa 24: 5 have transgressed the laws, c' the 2498
Jer 2:11 Hath a nation c' their gods, 4171
11 my people have c' their glory for "
48:11 in him, and his scent is not c'. "
52:33 And c' his prison garments: and 8138
La 4: 1 how is the most fine gold c'! 8132
Eze 5: 6 And she had c' my judgments *4171
Da 2: 9 before me, till the time be c': 8133
3:19 the form of his visage was c' "
27 neither were their coats c', nor "
28 and have c' the king's word, and "
4:16 Let his heart be c' from man's, and "
5: 6 the king's countenance was c', and "
9 his countenance was c' in him, "
10 nor let thy countenance be c': "
6: 8 that it be not c', according to the "
15 the king establisheth may be c'. "
17 might not be c' concerning Daniel. "
7:28 my countenance c' in me: but I "
Mic 2: 4 hath c' the portion of my people: 4171
Ac 28: 6 they c' their minds, and said that *3328*
Ro 1:23 c' the glory of the uncorruptible *236*
25 Who c' the truth of God into a **3337*
1Co 15:51 all sleep, but we shall all be c', *236*
52 incorruptible, and we shall be c'. "
2Co 3:18 are c' into the same image from **3339*
Heb 1:12 them up, and they shall be c': *236*
7:12 priesthood being c', there is made *3346*

changers See also CHANGERS'; MONEYCHANGERS.
Joh 2:14 doves, and the c' of money sitting: *2773*

changers'
Joh 2:15 poured out the c' money, and *2855*

changes
Ge 45:22 he gave each man c' of raiment; 2487
22 of silver, and five c' of raiment. "
2Ki 5: 5 of gold, and ten c' of raiment. "
22 of silver, and two c' of garments. "
23 two bags, with two c' of garments, "
Job 10:17 me; c' and war are against me. "
Ps 55:19 Because they have no c', therefore "

changest
Job 14:20 thou c' his countenance, and 8138

changeth
Ps 15: 4 to his own hurt, and c' not. 4171
Da 2:21 he c' the times and the seasons: 8133

changing
Ru 4: 7 redeeming and concerning c', 8545

channel See also CHANNELS.
Isa 27:12 from the c' of the river unto the *7641

channels
2Sa 22:16 the c' of the sea appeared, the 650
Ps 18:15 Then the c' of waters were seen, "
Isa 8: 7 he shall come up over all his c', "

chant
Am 6: 5 That c' to the sound of the viol, *6527

chapel
Am 7:13 it is the king's c', and it is the 4720

chapiter See also CHAPITERS.
1Ki 7:16 the height of the one c' was five ‡3805
16 and the height of the other c' ‡ "
17 seven for the one c', ‡ "
17 and seven for the other c'. ‡3805
18 and so he did for the other c'. ‡ "
20 round about upon the other c'. ‡ "
31 the mouth of it within the c' and ‡ "
2Ki 25:17 and the c' upon it was brass: ‡ "
17 the height of the c' three cubits; ‡ "
17 the pomegranates upon the c' ‡ "
2Ch 3:15 the c' that was on the top of each ‡6858
Jer 52:22 And a c' of brass was upon it; ‡3805
22 and the height of one c' was five ‡ "

chapiters
Ex 36:38 he overlaid their c' and their ‡7218
38:17 overlaying of their c' of silver; ‡ "
19 their c' and their fillets of silver. ‡ "
28 overlaid their c', and filleted ‡ "
1Ki 7:16 he made two c' of molten brass, ‡3805
17 the c' which were upon the top ‡ "
18 the c' that were upon the top, ‡ "
19 the c' that were upon the top of ‡ "
20 And the c' upon the two pillars ‡ "
41 the two bowls of the c' that were ‡ "
41 to cover the two bowls of the c' ‡ "
42 the two bowls of the c' that were ‡ "
2Ch 4:12 the c' which were on the top ‡ "
12 cover the two pommels of the c' ‡ "
13 c' which were upon the pillars. ‡ "
Jer 52:22 and pomegranates upon the c' †‡ "

chapmen
2Ch 9:14 c' and merchants brought. ‡582, 8446

chapped See CHAPT.

chapt
Jer 14: 4 Because the ground is c', for 2865

Charashim *(car'-a-shim)*
1Ch 4:14 of C'; for they were craftsmen. 2798

Charchemish *(car'-ke-mish)* See also CARCHEMISH.
2Ch 35:20 to fight against C' by Euphrates: 3751

charge See also CHARGEABLE; CHARGED; CHARGES; CHARGEST; CHARGING; OVERCHARGE.
Ge 26: 5 obeyed my voice, and kept my c', 4931
28: 6 he blessed him he gave him a c', 6680
Ex 6:13 gave them a c' unto the children 5749
19:21 c' the people, lest they break 5749
Le 8:35 keep the c' of the Lord, that ye 4931
Nu 1:53 Levites shall keep the c' of the "
3: 7 they shall keep his c', and the "
7 c' of the whole congregation "
8 the c' of the children of Israel, "
25 And the c' of the sons of Gershon "
28 keeping the c' of the sanctuary. "
31 And their c' shall be the ark, "
32 that keep the c' of the sanctuary. "
36 the custody and c' of the sons "
38 keeping the c' of the sanctuary for "
38 the c' of the children of Israel; "
4:27 unto them in c' all their burdens. "
28 their c' shall be under the hand of "
31 this is the c' of their burden, "
32 instruments of the c' of their burden. "
5:19 the priest shall c' her by an oath, *7650
21 the priest shall c' the woman * "
8:26 congregation, to keep the c', and 4931
26 the Levites touching their c'. "
9:19 the children of Israel kept the c' "
23 they kept the c' of the Lord, "
18: 3 shall keep thy c', and the c' of "
4 keep the c' of the tabernacle of "
5 keep the c' of the sanctuary, "
5 and the c' of the altar: "
8 I also have given thee the c' of "
27:19 and give him a c' in their sight. 6680
23 and gave him a c', as the Lord "
31:30 keep the c' of the tabernacle of 4931
47 kept the c' of the tabernacle of "
49 which are under our c', and 3027
De 3:28 c' Joshua, and encourage him, 6680
11: 1 keep his c', and his statutes, 4931
21: 8 unto thy people of Israel's c'. 7130
31:14 that I may give him a c'. 6680
23 gave Joshua the son of Nun a c', "
Jos 22: 3 kept the c' of the commandment 4931
2Sa 14: 8 I will give c' concerning thee. 6680
18: 5 the king gave all the captains c' "
1Ki 2: 3 keep the c' of the Lord thy God, 4931
4:28 every man according to his c'. 4941
11:28 the c' of the house of Joseph. *5447
2Ki 7:17 hand he leaned to have the c' 5921
1Ch 9:27 because the c' was upon them, 4931
28 And certain of them had the c' 5921
22:12 give thee c' concerning Israel, 6680
23:32 the c' of the tabernacle of the 4931
32 and the c' of the holy place, "
32 and the c' of the sons of Aaron. "
2Ch 13:11 for we keep the c' of the Lord "
30:17 Levites had the c' of the killing 5921
Ne 7: 2 the palace, c' over Jerusalem: 6680
10:32 to c' ourselves yearly with the 5414
Es 3: 9 that have the c' of the business, 6213
4: 8 to c' her that she should go in 6680
Job 34:13 Who hath given him a c' over 6485
Ps 35:11 to my c' things that I knew not. *7592
91:11 shall give his angels c' over thee, 6680
Ca 2: 7 I c' you, O ye daughters of *7650
3: 5 I c' you, O ye daughters of * "
5: 8 I c' you, O daughters of * "
9 beloved, that thou dost so c' us? * "
8: 4 I c' you, O daughters of * "
Isa 10: 6 of my wrath will I give him a c', 6680
Jer 39:11 King of Babylon gave c' concerning "
47: 7 the Lord had given it a c' against "
52:25 which had the c' of the men *6496
Eze 9: 1 them that have c' over the city 6486
40:45 keepers of the c' of the house. 4931

Eze 40:46 the keepers of the c' of the altar: 4931
44: 8 kept the c' of mine holy things: "
8 but ye have set keepers of my c' "
11 c' at the gates of the house, *6486
14 keepers of the c' of the house, 4931
15 kept a c' of my sanctuary when "
16 me, and they shall keep my c'. "
48:11 which have kept my c', which "
Zec 3: 7 keep my c', then thou shalt also "
M't 4: 6 give his angels c' concerning 1781
M'r 9:25 I c' thee, come out of him, and *2004
Lu 4:10 shall give his angels c' over thee, 1781
Ac 7:60 Lord, lay not this sin to their c'. 2476
8:27 who had the c' of all her treasure,*1909
16:24 Who, having received such a c', 3852
23:29 to have nothing laid to his c' 1462
Ro 8:33 shall lay anything to the c' of 1458, 2596
1Co 9:18 the gospel of Christ without c', 77
1Th 5:27 I c' you by the Lord that this *3726
1Ti 1: 3 that thou mightest c' some that 3853
18 This c' I commit unto thee, son 3852
5: 7 And these things give in c', that 3853
21 I c' thee before God, and the Lord 1263
6:13 I give thee c' in the sight of God, 3853
17 C' them that are rich in this world, "
2Ti 4: 1 I c' thee therefore before God, 1263
16 it may not be laid to their c'. *3049

chargeable
2Sa 13:25 now go, lest we be c' unto thee. *3513
Ne 5:15 before me were c' unto the people, "
2Co 11: 9 I was c' to no man: for that *2655
1Th 2: 9 not be c' unto any of you, *1912
2Th 3: 8 that we might not be c' to any * "

charged See also CHARGEDST; OVERCHARGED.
Ge 26:11 And Abimelech c' all his people, 6680
28: 1 and c' him, and said unto him, "
40: 4 the captain of the guard c' Joseph 6485
49:29 he c' them, and said unto them, 6680
Ex 1:22 Pharaoh c' all his people, saying, "
De 1:16 I c' your judges at that time, "
24: 5 be c' with any business: 5674, 5921
27:11 Moses c' the people the same day, 6680
Jos 18: 8 and Joshua c' them that went "
22: 5 Moses the servant of the Lord c' "
Ru 2: 9 have I not c' the young men "
1Sa 14:27 father c' the people with the oath:7650
28 straitly c' the people with an oath, "
2Sa 11:19 And c' the messenger, saying, 6680
18:12 c' thee and Abishai and Ittai, "
1Ki 2: 1 he c' Solomon his son, saying, "
43 that I have c' thee with? "
13: 9 For so was it c' me by the word "
2Ki 17:15 the Lord had c' them, that they "
35 had made a covenant, and c' them, "
1Ch 22: 6 and c' him to build an house 6680
13 c' Moses with concerning Israel: "
2Ch 19: 9 c' them, saying, Thus shall ye do "
36:23 hath c' me to build him an house 6485
Ezr 1: 2 and he hath c' me to build him "
Ne 13:19 c' that they should not be opened * 559
Es 2:10 Mordecai had c' her that she 6680
20 Mordecai had c' her: for Esther "
Job 1:22 sinned not, nor c' God foolishly. 5414
4:18 and his angels he c' with folly: *7760
Jer 32:13 And I c' Baruch before them, 6680
35: 8 he hath c' us, to drink no wine "
M't 9:30 Jesus straitly c' them, saying, 1690
12:16 And c' them that they should not 2008
16:20 Then c' he his disciples that they 1291
17: 9 Jesus c' them, saying, Tell the *1781
M'r 1:43 he straitly c' him, and forthwith 1690
3:12 straitly c' them that they should 2008
5:43 he c' them straitly that no man 1291
7:36 c' them that they should tell no "
36 but the more he c' them, "
8:15 he c' them, saying, Take heed, "
30 he c' them that they should tell 2008
9: 9 c' them they should tell no man 1291
10:48 And many c' him that he should *2008
Lu 5:14 And he c' him to tell no man: 3853
8:56 but he c' them that they should "
9:21 straitly c' them, and commanded 2008
Ac 23:22 c' him, See thou tell no man *3853
1Th 2:11 c' every one of you, as a father *3143
1Ti 5:16 and let not the church be c'; * 916

chargedst
Ex 19:23 thou c' us, saying, Set bounds *5749

charger See also CHARGERS.
Nu 7:13 And his offering was one silver c', ‡7086
19 for his offering one silver c', ‡ "
25, 31, 37, 43, 49, 55, 61, 67, 73 79,
His offering was one silver c', ‡7086
85 c' of silver weighing an hundred ‡ "
M't 14: 8 here John Baptist's head in a c'. 4094
11 was brought in a c', and given to "
M'r 6:25 by and by in a c' the head of John "
28 brought his head in a c', and gave "

chargers
Nu 7:84 c' of silver, twelve silver bowls, ‡7086
Ezr 1: 9 thirty c' of gold, and a thousand 105
9 c' of silver, nine and twenty. "

charges
2Ch 8:14 the Levites to their c', to praise 4931
31:16 service in their c' according to "
17 in their c' by their courses; "
35: 2 And he set the priests in their c', "
Ac 21:24 c' with them, that they may shave 1159
1Co 9: 7 warfare any time at his own c'? 3800

chargest
2Sa 3: 8 thou c' me to day with a fault 6485

charging
Ac 16:23 c' the jailor to keep them safely: 3853
2Ti 2:14 c' them before the Lord that they 1263

chariot See also CHARIOTS.
Ge 41:43 made him to ride in the second c' 4818
46:29 Joseph made ready his c', and "
Ex 14: 6 ready his c', and took his people 7393
25 their c' wheels, that they drave 4818
J'g 4:15 Sisera lighted down off his c', and "
5:28 Why is his c' so long in coming? 7393
2Sa 8: 4 David houghed all the c' horses, "
1Ki 7:33 like the work of a c' wheel: 4818
10:29 c' came up and went out of Egypt "
12:18 speed to get him up to his c', "
18:44 say unto Ahab, Prepare thy c', "
20:25 horse for horse, and c' for c': 7393
33 caused him to come up into the c'. 4818
22:34 he said unto the driver of his c', 7395
35 the king was stayed up in his c' 4818
35 wound into the midst of the c'. 7393
38 the c' in the pool of Samaria; "
2Ki 2:11 appeared a c' of fire, and horses "
12 c' of Israel, and the horsemen * "
5: 9 with his horses and with his c', * "
21 down from the c' to meet him, 4818
26 again from his c' to meet thee? "
7:14 took therefore two c' horses; *7393
9:16 Jehu rode in a c', and went to Jezreel; "
21 And his c' was made ready. 7393
21 of Judah went out, each in his c', "
24 heart, and he sunk down in his c'. "
27 and said, Smite him also in the c'. 4818
28 carried him in a c' to Jerusalem, "
10:15 took him up to him into the c'. 4818
16 So they made him ride in his c'. 7393
13:14 c' of Israel, and the horsemen * "
23:30 servants carried him in a c' dead "
1Ch 18:4 also houghed all the c' horses, 7393
28:18 c' of the cherubims, that spread 4818
2Ch 1:14 which he placed in the c' cities, 7393
17 brought forth out of Egypt a c' 4818
8: 6 all the c' cities, and the cities * 7393
9:25 in the c' cities, and with the king "
10:18 speed to get him up to his c', 4818
18:33 to his c' man, Turn thine hand, 7395
34 Israel stayed himself up in his c' 4818
35:24 therefore took him out of that c', "
24 him in the second c' that he had; 7393
Ps 46: 9 he burneth the c' in the fire. 5699
76: 6 the c' and horse are cast into 7393
104: 3 who maketh the clouds his c': 7398
Ca 3: 9 King Solomon made himself a c' * 668
Isa 21: 7 a c' with a couple of horsemen, *7393
7 a c' of asses, and a c' of camels; * "
9 behold, here cometh a c' of men, * "
43:17 bringeth forth the c' and horse, "
Jer 51:21 thee will I break in pieces the c' "
Mic 1:13 bind the c' to the swift beast: 4818
Zec 6: 2 In the first c' were red horses; "
2 and in the second c' black horses; "
3 in the third c' white horses; "
3 in the fourth c' grisled and bay "
9:10 will cut off the c' from Ephraim, 7393
Ac 8:28 and sitting in his c' read Esaias 716
29 Go near, and join thyself to this c'. "
38 he commanded the c' to stand still: "

chariot-cities See CHARIOT and CITIES.

chariot-horses See CHARIOT and HORSES.

chariot-man See CHARIOT and MAN.

chariots
Ge 50: 9 there went up with him both c' 7393
Ex 14: 7 he took six hundred chosen c', "
7 and all the c' of Egypt, "
9 c' of Pharaoh, and his horsemen, "
17 upon all his host, upon his c', "
18 his c', and upon his horsemen. "
23 even all Pharaoh's horses, his c', "
26 the Egyptians, upon their c', "
28 returned, and covered the c', "
15: 4 Pharaoh's c' and his host hath he 4818
19 of Pharaoh went in with his c' 7393
De 11: 4 unto their horses, and to their c'; "
20: 1 seest horses, and c', and a people "
Jos 11: 4 with horses and c' very many. "
6 and burn their c' with fire. 4818
9 and burnt their c' with fire. "
17:16 have c' of iron, both they who are 7393
18 have iron c', and though they "
24: 6 c' and horsemen unto the Red sea. "
J'g 1:19 because they had c' of iron. "
4: 3 he had nine hundred c' of iron; "
7 Jabin's army, with his c' and his "
13 Sisera gathered together all his c', "
13 even nine hundred c' of iron, "
15 discomfited Sisera, and all his c', "
16 Barak pursued after the c', and "
5:28 why tarry the wheels of his c'? 4818
1Sa 8:11 them for himself, for his c', "
11 and some shall run before his c'. "
12 war, and instruments of his c'. 7393
13: 5 with Israel, thirty thousand c', "
2Sa 1: 6 c' and horsemen followed hard "
8: 4 took from him a thousand c', *
4 of them for an hundred c'. 7393
10:18 of seven hundred c' of the Syrians, "
15: 1 prepared him c' and horses, *4818
1Ki 1: 5 prepared him c' and horsemen, 7393
4:26 stalls of horses for his c', 4817
9:19 cities for his c', and cities for his 7393
22 his captains, and rulers of his c', "
10:26 Solomon gathered together c' "
26 a thousand and four hundred c', "
26 he bestowed in the cities for c', * "
16: 9 Zimri, captain of half his c', "
20: 1 with him, and horses, and c': "
21 and c', and slew the Syrians "
22:31 captains that had rule over his c', "
1Ki 22:32 captains of the c' saw Jehosaphat,7393
33 the captains of the c' perceived "
2Ki 6:14 sent he thither horses, and c', "
15 the city both with horses and c'. "
17 mountain was full of horses and c' "
7: 6 noise of c', and a noise of horses, "
8:21 went over to Zair, and all the c' "
21 of the c': and the people fled "
10: 2 there are with you c' and horses, "
13: 7 but fifty horsemen, and ten c', "
18:24 put thy trust on Egypt for c' "
19:23 the multitude of my c' I am come "
23:11 burned the c' of the sun with fire. "
1Ch 18: 4 c', and seven thousand horsemen, "
4 reserved of them an hundred c'. "
19: 6 hire them c' and horsemen out of "
7 hired thirty and two thousand c', "
18 thousand men which fought in c', "
2Ch 1:14 gathered c' and horsemen: "
14 a thousand and four hundred c', "
8: 9 captains of his c' and horsemen. "
9:25 thousand stalls for horses and c', 4818
12: 3 twelve hundred c', and threescore 7393
14: 9 and three hundred c'; and came 4818
16: 8 with very many c' and horsemen? 7393
18:30 of the c' that were with him, "
31 when the captains of the c' saw "
32 the captains of the c' perceived "
21: 9 princes, and all his c' with him: "
9 him in, and the captains of the c'. "
Ps 20: 7 trust in c', and some in horses: "
68:17 c' of God are twenty thousand, "
Ca 1: 9 company of horses in Pharaoh's c'. "
6:12 my soul made me like the c' of 4818
Isa 2: 7 neither is there any end of their c': "
22: 6 Elam bare the quiver with c' of 7393
7 choicest valleys shall be full of c', "
18 c' of thy glory shall be the shame 4818
31: 1 trust in c', because they are 7393
36: 9 and put thy trust on Egypt for c' "
37:24 By the multitude of my c' am I "
66:15 with his c' like a whirlwind, to 4818
20 upon horses, and in c', and in 7393
Jer 4:13 his c' shall be as a whirlwind: 4818
17:25 riding in c' and on horses, they, 7393
22: 4 David, riding in c' and on horses, "
46: 9 rage, ye c'; and let the mighty "
47: 3 the rushing of his c', and at the "
50:37 upon their c', and upon all the "
Eze 23:24 come against thee with c', 2021
26: 7 with horses, and with c', and 7393
10 of the wheels, and of the c', when "
27:20 in precious clothes for c'. *7396
39:20 with horses and c', with mighty 7393
Da 11:40 with c', and with horsemen, and "
Joe 2: 5 Like the noise of c' on the tops of 4818
Mic 5:10 I will destroy thy c': "
Na 2: 3 c' shall be with flaming torches 7393
4 The c' shall rage in the streets, "
13 I will burn her c' in the smoke, "
3: 2 horses, and of the jumping c'. 4818
Hab 3: 8 thine horses and thy c' of "
Hag 2:22 I will overthrow the c', and those "
Zec 6: 1 came four c' out from between "
Re 9: 9 as the sound of c' of many horses 716
18:13 and horses, and c', and slaves, 4480

charitably
Ro 14:15 meat, now walkest thou not c'.*2596, 26

charity
1 Cor 8: 1 Knowledge puffeth up, but c' * 26
13: 1 of angels, and have not c', I am * "
2 mountains, and have not c', * "
3 to be burned, and have not c'. * "
4 C' suffereth long, and is kind; * "
4 c' envieth not; c' vaunteth not * "
8 C' never faileth: but whether * "
13 now abideth faith, hope, c', these * "
13 the greatest of these is c'. * "
14: 1 Follow after c', and desire * "
16:14 all your things be done with c'. * "
Col 3:14 above all these things put on c', * "
1 Th 3: 6 good tidings of your faith and c', * "
2 Th 1: 3 the c' of every one of you all * "
1 Ti 1: 5 commandment is c' out of a * "
2:15 in faith and c' and holiness with * "
4:12 in conversation, in c', in spirit, in * "
2 Ti 2:22 follow righteousness, faith, c', * "
3:10 faith, longsuffering, c', patience, * "
Tit 2: 2 temperate, sound in faith, in c', * "
1 Pe 4: 8 fervent c' among yourselves: * "
8 for c' shall cover the multitude * "
5:14 ye one another with a kiss of c'. * "
2 Pe 1: 7 and to brotherly kindness c'. * "
3 Jo 6 have borne witness of thy c' * "
Jude 12 spots in your feasts of c', when * "
Re 2:19 I know thy works, and c', and * "

charmed
Jer 8:17 which will not be c', and they 3908

charmer See also CHARMERS.
De 18:11 Or a c', or a consulter with 2266, 2267

charmers
Ps 58: 5 hearken to the voice of c', 3907
Isa 19: 3 seek to the idols, and to the c', 328

charming
Ps 58: 5 to the voice of charmers, c' 2266, 2267

Charran (car'-ran) See also HARAN.
Ac 7: 2 before he dwelt in C', 5488
4 and dwelt in C': and from thence, "

chase See also CHASED; CHASETH; CHASING.
Le 26: 7 And ye shall c' your enemies, and 7291
8 And five of you shall c' an hundred, "
36 the sound of a shaken leaf shall c' "
De 32:30 How should one c' a thousand, "

Jos 23:10 man of you shall c· a thousand: 7291
Ps 35: 5 and let the angel of the Lord c· *1760

chased
De 1:44 came out against you, and c· you, 7291
Jos 7: 5 for they c· them from before the "
8:24 the wilderness wherein they c· * "
10:10 and c· them along the way that "
11: 8 and c· them unto great Zidon, "
J'g 9:40 And Abimelech c· him, and he "
20:43 c· them, and trode them down "
Ne 13:28 Horonite: therefore I c· him from 1272
Job 18:18 into darkness, and c· out of the 5074
20: 8 he shall be c· away as a vision of "
Isa 13:14 it shall be as the c· roe, and as a 5080
17:13 and shall be c· as the chaff of the 7291
La 3:52 Mine enemies c· me sore, like a 6679

chaseth
Pr 19:26 c· away his mother, is a son that 1272

chasing
1 Sa 17:53 of Israel returned from c· after 1814

chaste
2 Co 11: 2 present you as a c· virgin to * *53*
Tit 2: 5 discreet, c·, keepers at home, "
1 Pe 3: 2 they behold your c· conversation "

chasten See also CHASTENED; CHASTENEST; CHASTENETH; CHASTENING; CHASTISE.
2 Sa 7:14 I will c· him with the rod of men, 3198
Ps 6: 1 neither c· me in thy hot 3256
38: 1 c· me in thy hot displeasure. "
Pr 19:18 C· thy son while there is hope, "
Da 10:12 and to c· thyself before thy God, *6031
Re 3:19 many as I love, I rebuke and c·: *3811*

chastened
De 21:18 when they have c· him, will not *3256
Job 33:19 He is c· also with pain upon his 3198
Ps 69:10 When I wept, and c· my soul
73:14 have I been plagued, and c· every 8433
118:18 The Lord hath c· me sore: but he 3256
1 Co 11:32 we are c· of the Lord, that we *3811*
2 Co 6: 9 as c·, and not killed; "
Heb 12:10 for a few days c· us after their own "

chastenest
Ps 94:12 Blessed is the man whom thou c·, 3256

chasteneth
De 8: 5 as a man c· his son, so 3256
5 the Lord thy God c· thee. "
Pr 13:24 he that loveth him c· him 4148
Heb 12: 6 For whom the Lord loveth he c·, *3811*
7 son is he whom the father c· not? "

chastening
Job 5:17 therefore despise not thou the c· 4148
Pr 3:11 despise not the c· of the Lord; "
Isa 26:16 a prayer when thy c· was upon
Heb 12: 5 despise not thou the c· of the *3809*
7 If ye endure c·, God dealeth with "
11 Now no c· for the present "

chastise See also CHASTEN; CHASTISED; CHASTISETH.
Le 26:28 and I, even I, will c· you seven 3256
De 22:18 city shall take that man and c· "
1 Ki 12:11 but I will c· you with scorpions. "
14 with whips, but I will c· you with "
2Ch 10:11, 14 I will c· you with scorpions. "
Hos 7:12 I will c· them, as their 3256
10:10 in my desire that I should c· "
Lu 23:16 I will therefore c· him, and release *3811*
22 I will therefore c· him, and let him "

chastised
1K 12:11 my father hath c· you with whips, 3256
14 my father also c· you with whips, "
2Ch 10:11 my father c· you with whips, but "
14 will add thereto: my father c· you "
Jer 31:18 Thou hast c· me, and I was c·, "

chastisement
De 11: 2 not seen the c· of the Lord your 4148
Job 34:31 I have borne c·, I will not offend
Isa 53: 5 the c· of our peace was upon 4148
Jer 30:14 the c· of a cruel one, for the "
Heb 12: 8 But if ye be without c·, whereof *3809*

chastiseth
Ps 94:10 He that c· the heathen, shall not 3256

chatter
Isa 38:14 so did I c·: I did mourn as a 6850

Chebar (*ke'-bar*)
Eze 1: 1 the captives by the river of C·, 3529
3 the Chaldeans by the river C·; "
3:15 that dwelt by the river of C·, "
23 which I saw by the river of C·: "
10:15 that I saw by the river of C·. "
20 God of Israel by the river of C·; "
22 which I saw by the river of C·, "
43: 3 vision that I saw by the river C·; "

check
Job 20: 3 heard the c· of my reproach, *4148

checker
1Ki 7:17 nets of c· work, and wreaths of 7639

checker-work See CHECKER and WORK.

Chedorlaomer (*ked''-or-la'-o-mer*)
Ge 14: 1 C· king of Elam, and Tidal king 3540
4 Twelve years they served C·, and "
5 in the fourteenth year came C·, "
9 With C· the king of Elam, and "
17 his return from the slaughter of C·. "

cheek See also CHEEKS.
1Ki 22:24 and smote Micaiah on the c·, and 3895
2Ch 18:23 and smote Micaiah upon the c·, "
Job 16:10 they have smitten me upon the c· "
Ps 3: 7 all mine enemies upon the c· bone; "
La 3:30 He giveth his c· to him that "
Joe 1: 6 hath the c· teeth of a great lion. *4973
Mic 5: 1 Israel with a rod upon the c·. 3895
M't 5:39 smite thee upon thy right c·, *4600*
Lu 6:29 smiteth thee upon the one c· "

cheek-bone See CHEEK and BONE.

cheeks
De 18: 3 the shoulder, and the two c·, 3895
Ca 1:10 Thy c· are comely with rows of "
5:13 His c· are as a bed of spices, as "
Isa 50: 6 and my c· to them that plucked "
La 1: 2 and her tears are on her c·: "

cheek-teeth See CHEEK and TEETH.

cheer See also CHEERETH; CHEERFUL.
De 24: 5 and shall c· up his wife which he 8055
Ec 11: 9 and let thy heart c· thee in the 3190
M't 9: 2 be of good c·; thy sins be forgiven *2293*
14:27 Be of good c·; it is I; be not afraid. "
M'r 6:50 saith unto them, Be of good c·; it "
Joh 16:33 but be of good c·; I have overcome "
Ac 23:11 Be of good c·, Paul: for as thou "
27:22 I exhort you to be of good c·: for *2114*
25 Wherefore, sirs, be of good c·: "
36 Then were they all of good c·, "

cheereth
J'g 9:13 which c· God and man, and go to 8055

cheerful
Pr 15:13 A merry heart maketh a c· 3190
Zec 8:19 gladness, and c· feasts; therefore 2896
9:17 shall make the young men c·, *5107
2Co 9: 7 for God loveth a c· giver. *2431*

cheerfully
Ac 24:10 the more c· answer for myself: *2115*

cheerfulness
Ro 12: 8 he that sheweth mercy, with c·. *2432*

cheese See also CHEESES.
2Sa 17:29 sheep, and c· of kine, for David, 8194
Job 10:10 as milk, and curdled me like c·? 1385

cheeses
1Sa 17:18 carry these ten c· unto the 2757, 2461

Chelal (*ke'-lal*)
Ezr 10:30 Adna, and C·, Benaiah, Maaseiah, 3636

Chelluh (*kel'-loo*)
Ezr 10:35 Benaiah, Bedeiah, C·, 3622

Chelub (*ke'-lub*)
1Ch 4:11 And C· the brother of Shuah 3620
27:26 the ground was Ezri the son of C·. "

Chelubai (*ke-loo'-bahee*) See also CALEB.
1Ch 2: 9 Jerahmeel, and Ram, and C·. 3621

Chemarims (*kem'-a-rims*)
Zep 1: 4 name of the C· with the priests; 3649

Chemosh (*ke'-mosh*)
Nu 21:29 thou art undone, O people of C·: 3645
J'g 11:24 that which C· thy god giveth "
1Ki 11: 7 Solomon build an high place for C·, "
33 C· the god of the Moabites, and "
2Ki 23:13 C· the abomination of the Moabites, "
Jer 48: 7 and C· shall go forth into captivity "
13 Moab shall be ashamed of C·, as "
46 O Moab! the people of C· perisheth: "

Chenaanah (*ke-na'-a-nah*)
1Ki 22:11 C· made him horns of iron: 3668
24 C· went near, and smote Micaiah "
1Ch 7:10 Benjamin, and Ehud, and C·, "
2Ch 18:10 C· had made him horns of iron, "
23 Zedekiah the son of C· came near, "

Chenani (*ken'-a-ni*)
Ne 9: 4 Bani, and C·, and cried with 3662

Chenaniah (*ken-a-ni'-ah*) See also CONONIAH.
1Ch 15:22 And C·, chief of the Levites, was 3663
27 and C· the master of the song "
26:29 C· and his sons were for the "

Chephar-haammonai (*ke''-far-ha-am'-mo-nahee*)
Jos 18:24 And C·, and Ophni, and Gaba; 3726

Chephirah (*ke-fi'-rah*)
Jos 9:17 their cities were Gibeon, and C·, 3716
18:26 Mizpeh, and C·, and Mozah, "
Ezr 2:25 Kirjath-arim, C·, and Beeroth, "
Ne 7:29 of Kirjath-jearim, C·, and Beeroth, "

Cheran (*ke'-ran*)
Ge 36:26 and Eshban, and Ithran, and C·. 3763
1Ch 1:41 and Eshban, and Ithran, and C·. "

Cherethims (*ker'-e-thims*) See also CHERETHITES.
Eze 25:16 I will cut off the C·, and destroy *3774

Cherethites (*ker'-e-thites*) See also CHERETHIMS.
1Sa 30:14 invasion upon the south of the C·. 3774
2Sa 8:18 both the C· and the Pelethites; "
15:18 all the C·, and all the Pelethites, "
20: 7 and the C·, and the Pelethites, "
23 was over the C· and over "
1Ki 1:38 and the C·, and the Pelethites, 3746
44 and the C·, and the Pelethites, 3774
1Ch 18:17 was over the C· and the Pelethites; "
Zep 2: 5 the nation of the C·! the word of "

cherish See also CHERISHED.
1Ki 1: 2 let her c· him, and let her lie in 5532

cherished
1Ki 1: 4 was very fair, and c· the king, 5532

cherisheth
Eph 5:29 but nourisheth and c· it, even *2282*
1Th 2: 7 even as a nurse c· her children: "

Cherith (*ke'-rith*)
1Ki 17: 3 and hide thyself by the brook C·, 3747
5 went and dwelt by the brook C·. "

Cherub (*ke'-rub*)
Ezr 2:59 up from Tel-melah, Tel-harsa, C·, 3743
Ne 7:61 from Tel-melah, Tel-haresha, C·, "

cherub (*cher'-ub*) See also CHERUBIMS.
Ex 25:19 one c· on the one end, 3742
19 and the other c· on the other end: "
37: 8 One c· on the end on this side, "
8 and another c· on the other "
2Sa 22:11 he rode upon a c·, and did fly: "
1Ki 6:24 the one wing of the c·, and five "
24 cubits the other wing of the c·: "
25 the other c· was ten cubits: both "
26 height of the one c· was ten cubits, "
26 and so was it of the other c·. "
27 of the other c· touched the wall; "
2Ch 3:11 one wing of the one c· was five
11 to the wing of the other c·. 3742
12 one wing of the other c· was five "
12 joining to the wing of the other c·. "
Ps 18:10 he rode upon a c·, and did fly: "
Eze 9: 3 was gone up from the c·, "
10: 2 under the c·, and fill thine hand "
4 went up from the c·, and stood "
7 one c· stretched forth his hand "
9 one wheel by one c·, and another "
9 another wheel by another c·: "
14 the first face was the face of a c·, "
28:14 Thou art the anointed c· that "
16 I will destroy thee, O covering c·, "
41:18 between a c· and a c·; and "
18 every c· had two faces; "

cherubims (*cher'-u-bims*) See also CHERUBIMS'.
Ge 3:24 of the garden of Eden C·, and *3742
Ex 25:18 thou shalt make two c· of gold, * "
19 mercy seat shall ye make the c· * "
20 c· shall stretch forth their wings * "
20 seat shall the faces of the c· * "
22 between the two c· which are * "
26: 1 c· of cunning work shalt thou * "
31 work: with c· shall it be made: * "
36: 8 c· of cunning work made he * "
35 c· made he it of cunning work. * "
37: 7 he made two c· of gold, beaten * "
8 the mercy seat made he the c· * "
9 the c· spread out their wings on * "
9 seatward were the faces of the c·. * "
Nu 7:89 from between the two c·: * "
1Sa 4: 4 which dwelleth between the c·: * "
2Sa 6: 2 that dwelleth between the c·. * "
1Ki 6:23 oracle he made two c· of olive * "
25 the c· were of one measure and * "
27 set the c· within the inner house: * "
27 stretched forth the wings of the c·, * "
28 And he overlaid the c· with gold. * "
29 about with carved figures of c· * "
32 carvings of c· and palm trees * "
32 spread gold upon the c·, and upon * "
35 carved thereon c· and palm trees * "
7:29 ledges were lions, oxen, and c·: * "
36 graved c·, lions, and palm trees, * "
8: 6 even under the wings of the c·. * "
7 c· spread forth their two wings * "
7 ark, and the c· covered the ark * "
2Ki 19:15 which dwellest between the c·, * "
1Ch 13: 6 that dwelleth between the c·, * "
28:18 the chariot of the c·, that spread * "
2Ch 3: 7 gold; and graved c· on the walls. * "
10 he made two c· of image work, * "
11 wings of the c· were twenty * "
13 The wings of these c· spread * "
14 linen, and wrought c· thereon. * "
5: 7 even under the wings of the c·: * "
8 the c· spread forth their wings * "
8 c· covered the ark and the staves * "
Ps 80: 1 that dwellest between the c·, * "
99: 1 he sitteth between the c·; let * "
Isa 37:16 that dwellest between the c·, * "
Eze 10: 1 head of the c· there appeared * "
2 coals of fire from between the c·, * "
3 c· stood on the right side of the * "
6 the wheels, from between the c·; * "
7 from between the c· unto the fire * "
7 the fire that was between the c·, * "
8 there appeared in the c· the form * "
9 behold the four wheels by the c·, * "
15 the c· were lifted up. This is the * "
16 when the c· went, the wheels * "
16 them: and when the c· lifted * "
18 house, and stood over the c·. * "
19 the c· lifted up their wings, and * "
20 and I knew that they were the c·. * "
11:22 the c· lift up their wings, and the * "
41:18 was made with c· and palm trees, * "
20 door were c· and palm trees * "
25 c· and palm trees, like as were * "
Heb 9: 5 c· of glory shadowing the *5502*

cherubims'
Eze 10: 5 sound of the c· wings was heard *3742

Chesalon (*kes'-a-lon*)
Jos 15:10 of mount Jearim, which is C·, 3693

Chesed (*ke'-sed*)
Ge 22:22 And C·, and Hazo, and Pildash, 3777

Chesil (*ke'-sil*)
Jos 15:30 And Eltolad, and C·, and Hormah, 3686

chesnut
Ge 30:37 and of the hazel and c· tree *6196
Eze 31: 8 and the c· trees were not like * "

chesnut-tree See CHESNUT and TREE.

chest See also CHESTS.
2Ki 12: 9 Jehoiada the priest took a c·, and 727
10 much money in the c·, that the "
2Ch 24: 8 made a c·, and set it without at the "
10 cast into the c·, until they had "
11 c· was brought unto the king's "
11 came and emptied the c·, and took "

chestnut See CHESNUT.

chests
Eze 27:24 in c' of rich apparel, bound with 1595
Chesulloth (*ke-sul'-loth*) See also CHISLOTH-TABOR.
Jos 19:18 was toward Jezreel, and C' 3694
chew See also CHEWED; CHEWETH.
Le 11: 4 shall ye not eat of them that c' 5927
De 14: 7 of them that c' the cud, or of them "
7 c' the cud, but divide not the hoof; "
chewed
Nu 11:33 between their teeth, ere it was c', 3772
cheweth
Le 11: 3 and c' the cud, among the beasts, 5927
4 he c' the cud, but divideth not the "
5 the coney, because he c' the cud, "
6 because he c' the cud, but divideth "
7 he c' not the cud; he is unclean 1641
26 not clovenfooted, nor c' the cud, 5927
De 14: 6 and c' the cud among the beasts, "
8 yet c' not the cud, it is unclean "
Chezib (*ke'-zib*) See also ACHZIB; CHOZEBA.
Ge 38: 5 he was at C', when she bare him. 3580
chickens
M't 23:37 as a hen gathereth her c' under 3556
chid See CHODE.
chide See also CHIDING; CHODE.
Ex 17: 2 Wherefore the people did c' with *7378
2 Why c' ye with me? wherefore * "
J'g 8: 1 they did c' with him sharply. "
Ps 103: 9 He will not always c': neither will "
chided See CHODE.
chiding
Ex 17: 7 of the c' of the children of Israel, *7379
Chidon (*ki'-don*) See also NACHON.
1Ch 13: 9 unto the threshingfloor of C', 3592
chief See also CHIEFEST.
Ge 21:22 Phichol the c' captain of his host *
32 Phichol the c' captain of his host,*
26:26 Phichol the c' captain of his army.*
40: 2 against the c' of the butlers, 8269
2 and against the c' of the bakers. "
9 c' butler told his dream to Joseph, "
16 When the c' baker saw that the "
20 of the c' butler and of the c' baker "
21 he restored the c' butler unto his "
22 he hanged the c' baker: as Joseph "
23 Yet did not the c' butler remember "
41: 9 spake the c' butler unto Pharaoh, "
10 house, both me and the c' baker: "
Le 21: 4 a c' man among his people, to 1167
Nu 3:24 the c' of the house of the father *5387
30 the c' of the house of the father * "
32 be c' over the c' of the Levites, * "
35 And the c' of the house of the * "
4:34 and the c' of the congregation * "
46 and the c' of Israel numbered, * "
25:14 prince of a c' house among the * 1
15 and of a c' house in Midian. "
31:26 c' fathers of the congregation: *7218
32:28 the c' fathers of the tribes of the * "
36: 1 the c' fathers of the families of * "
1 c' fathers of the children of * "
De 1:15 I took the c' of your tribes, wise "
33:15 for the c' things of the ancient "
Jos 22:14 c' house a prince throughout all * 1
J'g 20: 2 c' of all the people, even of all *6438
1Sa 14:38 Draw ye near thither, all the c' of * "
15:21 c' of the things which should 7225
2Sa 5: 8 of David's soul, he shall be c'. *
8:18 and David's sons were c' rulers. *3548
20:26 was a c' ruler about David. "
23: 8 c' among the captains; the same 7218
13 three of the thirty c' went down, "
18 of Zeruiah, was c' among three. "
1Ki 5:16 Beside the c' of Solomon's officers 8269
8: 1 c' of the fathers of the children *5387
9:23 the c' of the officers that were 8269
14:27 c' of the guard, which kept the "
2Ki 25:18 guard took Seraiah the c' priest, 7218
1Ch 5: 2 and of him came the c' ruler; *5057
7 the c', Jeiel, and Zechariah, 7218
12 Joel the c', and Shapham the "
15 c' of the house of their fathers. "
7: 3 Isheah, five: all of them c' men. "
40 men of valour, c' of the princes. "
8:28 by their generations, c' men. "
9: 9 these men were c' of the fathers * "
17 brethren: Shallum was the c'; "
26 four c' porters, were in their set 1368
33 c' of the fathers of the Levites, *7218
34 c' fathers of the Levites were * "
34 c' throughout their generations; "
11: 6 the Jebusites first shall be c' "
6 Zeruiah went first up, and was c'. "
10 c' of the mighty men whom David "
11 Hachmonite, the c' of the captains: "
20 of Joab, he was c' of the three: "
12: 3 The c' was Ahiezer, then Joash, "
18 Amasai, who was c' of the captains," "
15: 5 the sons of Kohath; Uriel the c', 8269
6 the sons of Merari; Asaiah the c', "
7 the sons of Gershom; Joel the c', "
8 of Elizaphan; Shemaiah the c', "
9 the sons of Hebron; Eliel the c', "
10 sons of Uzziel; Amminadab the c', "
12 c' of the fathers of the Levites: *7218
16 spake to the c' of the Levites 8269
22 Chenaniah, c' of the Levites, was "
16: 5 Asaph the c', and next to him 7218
18:17 sons of David were c' about the 7223
23: 8 the c' was Jehiel, and Zetham, 7218
9 the c' of the fathers of Laadan. * "
1Ch 23:11 Jahath was the c', and Zizah the 7218
16 of Gershom, Shebuel was the c'. "
17 of Eliezer were, Rehabiah the c'. "
18 sons of Izhar; Shelomith the c'. "
24 c' of the fathers, as they were * "
24: 4 more c' men found of the sons of "
4 were sixteen c' men of the house * "
6 and before the c' of the fathers * "
31 c' of the fathers of the priests * "
26:10 Simri the c', (for though he was "
10 yet his father made him the c';) "
12 even among the c' men, having "
21 c' fathers, even of Laadan the * "
26 the c' fathers, the captains over * "
31 Jerijah the c', even among the "
32 two thousand and seven hundred c' * "
27: 1 the c' fathers and captains of * "
3 Of the children of Perez was the c' * "
5 Benaiah the son of Jehoiada, a c' * "
29: 6 the c' of the fathers and princes *8269
22 to be the c' governor, and Zadok *5057
2Ch 1: 2 all Israel, the c' of the fathers. *7218
5: 2 c' of the fathers of the children *5387
8: 9 c' of his captains, and captains of 8269
10 c' of king Solomon's officers, "
11:22 c', to be ruler among his brethren: 7218
12:10 the c' of the guard, that kept the *8269
17:14 Aduah the c', and with him * "
19: 8 of the c' of the fathers of Israel, *7218
11 Amariah the c' priest is over you "
23: 2 the c' of the fathers of Israel, * "
24: 6 king called for Jehoiada the c', "
26:12 c' of the fathers of the mighty * "
20 the c' priest, and all the priests, "
31:10 Azariah the c' priest of the house "
35: 9 and Jozabad, c' of the Levites, *8269
36:14 c' of the priests, and the people * "
Ezr 1: 5 the c' of the fathers of Judah *7218
2:68 some of the c' of the fathers, "
3:12 and c' of the fathers, who were * "
4: 2 the c' of the fathers, and said * "
3 of the c' of the fathers of Israel, * "
5:10 men that were the c' of them. *7217
7: 5 the son of Aaron the c' priest: 7218
28 Israel c' men to go up with me. "
8: 1 are now the c' of their fathers, * "
16 and for Meshullam, c' men; "
17 Iddo the c' at the place Casiphia, "
24 twelve of the c' of the priests, *8269
29 c' of the priests and the Levites, * "
29 and c' of the fathers of Israel, * "
9: 2 hath been c' in this trespass. 7223
10: 5 Ezra, and made the c' priests, *8269
16 c' of the fathers, after the house *7218
Ne 7:70 some of the c' of the fathers * "
71 the c' of the fathers gave to the * "
8:13 c' of the fathers of all the people, * "
10:14 The c' of the people; Parosh, "
11: 3 the c' of the province that dwelt "
13 his brethren, c' of the fathers, "
16 of the c' of the Levites, had the "
12: 7 These were the c' of the priests "
12 the c' of the fathers: of Seraiah, * "
22 were recorded c' of the fathers: * "
23 sons of Levi, the c' of the fathers, * "
24 the c' of the Levites: Hashabiah, * "
46 old there were c' of the singers, "
Job 12:24 the c' of the people of the earth, * "
29:25 I chose out their way, and sat c', "
40:19 the c' of the ways of God: 7225
Ps 4:*title* To the c' Musician on Neginoth, 5329
5:*title* the c' Musician upon Nehiloth, "
6:*title* To the c' Musician on Neginoth "
8:*title* To the c' Musician upon Gittith, "
9:*title* c' Musician upon Muth-labben, 5329
11:*title* c' Musician, A Psalm of David. "
12:*title* the c' Musician upon Sheminith, "
13:*title* c' Musician, A Psalm of David. "
14:*title* c' Musician, A Psalm of David. "
18:*title* c' Musician, A Psalm of David. "
19:*title* c' Musician, A Psalm of David. "
20:*title* c' Musician, A Psalm of David. "
21:*title* c' Musician, A Psalm of David. "
22:*title* c' Musician upon Aijeleth "
31:*title* c' Musician, A Psalm of David. "
36:*title* c' Musician, A Psalm of David "
39:*title* c' Musician, even to Jeduthun, "
40:*title* c' Musician, A Psalm of David. "
41:*title* c' Musician, A Psalm of David. "
42:*title* the c' Musician, Maschil, for the "
44:*title* To the c' Musician for the sons "
45:*title* c' Musician upon Shoshannim, "
46:*title* To the c' Musician for the sons "
47:*title* To the c' Musician, A Psalm for "
49:*title* To the c' Musician, A Psalm for "
51:*title* c' Musician, A Psalm of David, "
52:*title* c' Musician, Maschil, A Psalm of "
53:*title* the c' Musician upon Mahalath, "
54:*title* To the c' Musician on Neginoth, "
55:*title* To the c' Musician on Neginoth, "
56:*title* To the c' Musician upon "
57:*title* To the c' Musician, Al-taschith, "
58:*title* To the c' Musician, Al-taschith, "
59:*title* To the c' Musician, Al-taschith, "
60:*title* c' Musician upon Shushan-eduth, "
61:*title* the c' Musician upon Neginah, "
62:*title* To the c' Musician, to Jeduthun, "
64:*title* c' Musician, A Psalm of David. "
65:*title* c' Musician, A Psalm and Song "
66:*title* c' Musician, A Song or Psalm. "
67:*title* To the c' Musician on Neginoth, "
68:*title* c' Musician, A Psalm or Song of "
69:*title* c' Musician upon Shoshannim, "
70:*title* c' Musician, A Psalm of David, "
75:*title* To the c' Musician, Al-taschith, "
76:*title* To the c' Musician on Neginoth, "
Ps 77:*title* To the c' Musician, to Jeduthun, 5329
78:51 the c' of their strength in the 7225
80:*title* To the c' Musician upon 5329
81:*title* To the c' Musician upon Gittith, "
84:*title* To the c' Musician upon Gittith, "
85:*title* To the c' Musician, A Psalm for "
88:*title* the c' Musician upon Mahalath "
105:36 land, the c' of all their strength. 7225
109:*title* c' Musician, A Psalm of David. 5329
137: 6 not Jerusalem above my c' joy. 7218
139:*title* c' Musician, A Psalm of David. 5329
140:*title* c' musician, A Psalm of David. "
Pr 1:21 in the c' place of concourse, 7218
16:28 a whisperer separateth c' friends. 441
Ca 4:14 and aloes, with all the c' spices: 7218
Isa 14: 9 even all the c' ones of the earth; 6260
41: 9 thee from the c' men thereof, * 678
Jer 13:21 them to be captains, and as c' *7218
20: 1 c' governor in the house of the 5057
31: 7 among the c' of the nations: 7218
49:35 of Elam, the c' of their might. 7225
52:24 guard took Seraiah the c' priest, 7218
La 1: 5 Her adversaries are the c', her "
Eze 27:22 in thy fairs with c' of all spices, "
38: 2 c' prince of Meshech and Tubal, * "
3 I am against thee, O Gog, the c' "
39: 1 c' prince of Meshech and Tubal: * "
Da 2:48 and c' of the governors over all 7229
10:13 lo, Michael, one of the c' princes, 7223
11:41 the c' of the children of Ammon. 7225
Am 6: 1 which are named c' of the nations, "
6 themselves with the c' ointments: "
Hab 3:19 to the c' singer on my stringed 5329
M't 2: 4 all the c' priests and scribes 749
16:21 elders and c' priests and scribes, "
20:18 be betrayed unto the c' priests "
27 whosoever will be c' among you, *4413
21:15 when the c' priests and scribes 749
23 the c' priests and the elders of the "
45 the c' priests and Pharisees had "
23: 6 the c' seats in the synagogues, 4410
26: 3 assembled together the c' priests, 749
14 Iscariot, went unto the c' priests, "
47 from the c' priests and elders "
59 Now the c' priests, and elders, "
27: 1 c' priests and elders of the people "
3 silver to the c' priests and elders, "
6 the c' priests took the silver pieces, "
12 he was accused of the c' priests "
20 the c' priests and elders persuaded "
41 also the c' priests mocking him, "
62 the c' priests and Pharisees came "
28:11 shewed unto the c' priests all the "
M'r 6:21 captains, and c' estates of Galilee: 4413
8:31 of the c' priests, and scribes, 749
10:33 be delivered unto the c' priests, "
11:18 the scribes and c' priests heard it, "
27 there come to him the c' priests, "
12:39 the c' seats in the synagogues, 4410
14: 1 the c' priests and the scribes 749
10 went unto the c' priests, to betray "
43 from the c' priests and the scribes "
53 all the c' priests and the elders "
55 the c' priests and all the council "
15: 1 the c' priests held a consultation "
3 c' priests accused him of many "
10 the c' priests had delivered him for "
11 the c' priests moved the people, "
31 also the c' priests mocking said "
Lu 9:22 c' priests and scribes, and be slain, "
11:15 devils through Beelzebub the c' * 758
14: 1 house of one of the c' Pharisees * "
7 how they chose out the c' rooms; 4411
19: 2 was the c' among the publicans, 754
47 the c' priests and the scribes 749
47 and the c' of the people sought *4413
20: 1 the c' priests and the scribes came 749
19 the c' priests and the scribes the "
46 and the c' rooms at feasts; 4411
22: 2 the c' priests and scribes sought 749
4 communed with the c' priests "
26 that is c', as he that doth serve. 2233
52 Jesus said unto the c' priests, 749
66 the c' priests and the scribes came "
23: 4 said Pilate to the c' priests and to "
10 the c' priests and scribes stood "
13 together the c' priests and the "
23 of them and of the c' priests * "
24:20 how the c' priests and our rulers "
Joh 7:32 the Pharisees and the c' priests "
45 came the officers to the c' priests "
11:47 the c' priests and the Pharisees "
57 both the c' priests and the Pharisees "
12:10 c' priests consulted that they might "
42 Nevertheless among the c' rulers * 758
18: 3 from the c' priests and Pharisees, 749
35 Thine own nation and the c' priests "
19: 6 c' priests therefore and officers "
15 The c' priests answered, We have "
21 Then said the c' priests of the Jews "
Ac 4:23 the c' priests and elders had said "
5:24 c' priests heard these things "
9:14 authority from the c' priests to "
21 them bound unto the c' priests? "
13:50 and the c' men of the city, 4413
14:12 because he was the c' speaker. 2233
15:22 c' men among the brethren: "
16:12 c' city of that part of Macedonia, *4413
17: 4 and of the c' women not a few. "
18: 8 the c' ruler of the synagogues, * 752
17 the c' ruler of the synagogue, * "
19:14 a Jew, and c' of the priests, * 749
31 and certain of the c' of Asia, †‡ 775
21:31 unto the c' captain of the band, 5506
32 when they saw the c' captain and "
33 Then the c' captain came near, "

Ac 21:37 he said unto the c' captain, May 5506
22:24 The c' captain commanded him "
26 he went and told the c' captain, "
27 Then the c' captain came, and said "
28 And the c' captain answered, With "
29 and the c' captain also was afraid, "
30 commanded the c' priests and all 749
23:10 the c' captain, fearing lest Paul 5506
14 came to the c' priests and elders, 749
15 signify to the c' captain that he 5506
17 this young man to the c' captain: "
18 brought him to the c' captain, "
19 Then the c' captain took him by "
22 the c' captain then let the young "
24: 7 But the c' captain Lysias came * "
22 When Lysias the c' captain shall "
25: 2 the c' of the Jews informed him *4413
15 the c' priests and the elders of 749
23 with the c' captains, and principal 5506
26:10 authority from the c' priests; 749
12 commission from the c' priests, "
28: 7 of the c' man of the island, 4413
17 Paul called the c' of the Jews "
Eph 2:20 himself being the c' corner stone; 204
1Ti 1:15 to save sinners; of whom I am c'. 4413
1Pe 2: 6 I lay in Sion a c' corner stone, 204
5: 4 when the c' Shepherd shall appear, 750
Re 6:15 c' captains, and the mighty men, 5506

chiefest
1Sa 2:29 with the c' of all the offerings 7225
9:22 in the c' place among them that 7218
21: 7 Edomite, the c' of the herdmen 47
2Ch 32:33 they buried him in the c' of the *4608
Ca 5:10 ruddy, the c' among ten thousand. 1713
M'r 10:44 the c', shall be servant of all. *4413
2Co 11: 5 behind the very c' apostles. 5228, 3029
12:11 behind the very c' apostles. "
1Ti *subscr.* which is the c' city *3390

chiefly
Ro 3: 2 c', because that unto them were *4412
Ph'p 4:22 c' they that are of Cæsar's *3122
2Pe 2:10 c' them that walk after the flesh "

chief-priest See CHIEF and PRIEST.

child See also CHILDBEARING; CHILDHOOD; CHILDLESS; CHILDREN; CHILD'S.
Ge 11:30 Sarai was barren; she had no c'. 2056
16:11 her, Behold, thou art with c', 2030
17:10 Every man c' among you shall *
12 every man c' in your generations, *
14 the uncircumcised man c' whose *
19:36 both the daughters of Lot with c' 2029
21: 8 the c' grew, and was weaned: 3206
14 and the c', and sent her away: "
15 cast the c' under one of the shrubs. "
16 Let me not see the death of the c'. "
37:30 The c' is not; and I, whither shall "
38:24 she is with c' by whoredom. 2030
25 am I with c': and she said, "
42:22 Do not sin against the c'; 3206
44:20 and a c' of his old age, a little one; "
Ex 2: 2 saw him that he was a goodly c', "
3 and put the c' therein; and she 3206
6 had opened it, she saw the c': "
7 women, that she may nurse the c' "
9 Take this c' away, and nurse it "
9 the woman took the c', and nursed "
10 And the c' grew, and she brought "
21:22 hurt a woman with c', so that her 2030
22:22 afflict any widow, or fatherless c'. "
Le 12: 2 and born a man c': then she shall "
5 if she bear a maid c', then she "
22:13 and have no c', and is returned 2233
Nu 11:12 father beareth the sucking c', "
De 25: 5 and have no c', the wife of the *1121
Jud 11:34 she was his only c'; beside her he 3173
13: 5 for the c' shall be a Nazarite unto 5288
7 the c' shall be Nazarite to God "
8 what we shall do unto the c' that "
12 How shall we order the c', and "
24 and the c' grew, and the Lord "
Ru 4:16 Naomi took the c', and laid it in 3206
1Sa 1:11 unto thine handmaid a man c', 2233
22 I will not go up until the c' be 5288
24 in Shiloh: and the c' was young, "
25 and brought the c' to Eli. "
27 For this c' I prayed; and the "
2:11 the c' did minister unto the Lord "
18 before the Lord, being a c', "
21 c' Samuel grew before the Lord. "
26 And the c' Samuel grew on, and "
3: 1 And the c' Samuel ministered "
8 that the Lord had called the c'. "
4:19 Phinehas' wife, was with c', near 2030
21 she named the c' I-chabod, 5288
2Sa 6:23 the daughter of Saul had no c' 3206
11: 5 told David, and said, I am with c'. 2030
12:14 the c' also that is born unto thee 1121
15 And the Lord struck the c' that 3206
16 therefore besought God for the c'; 5288
18 the seventh day, that the c' died. 3206
18 to tell him that the c' was dead: "
18 while the c' was yet alive, we "
18 if we tell him that the c' is dead? "
19 David perceived that the c' was "
19 unto his servants, Is the c' dead? "
21 thou didst fast and weep for the c', "
21 when the c' was dead, thou didst "
22 While the c' was yet alive, I fasted "
22 gracious to me, that the c' may live? "
1Ki 3: 7 I am but a little c': I know not 5288
17 and I was delivered of a c' with her 3205
19 this woman's c' died in the night; 1121
20 and laid her dead c' in my bosom. "
21 in the morning to give my c' suck. "
1Ki 3:25 Divide the living c' in two, and 3206
26 the woman whose the living c' was 1121
26 O my Lord, give her the living c', 3205
27 Give her the living c', and in no "
11:17 Egypt; Hadad being yet a little c'. 5288
13: 2 a c' shall be born unto the house 1121
14: 3 what shall become of the c'. 5288
12 enter into the city, the c' shall die. 3206
17 threshold of the door, the c' died; 5288
17:21 he stretched himself upon the c' 3206
22 the soul of the c' came into him "
23 Elijah took the c', and brought "
2Ki 4:14 Verily she hath no c', and her *1121
18 when the c' was grown, it fell on 3206
26 is it well with the c'? And she "
29 my staff upon the face of the c'. 5288
30 the mother of the c' said, As the "
31 laid the staff on the face of the c'; "
31 him, saying, The c' is not awaked. "
32 the c' was dead and laid upon his "
34 he went up, and lay upon the c', 3206
34 stretched himself upon the c'; *
34 the flesh of the c' waxed warm. 3206
35 the c' sneezed seven times, 5288
35 and the c' opened his eyes. "
5:14 like unto the flesh of a little c', "
8:12 and rip up their women with c'. 2030
15:16 women therein that were with c' "
Job 3: 3 said, There is a man c' conceived.
Ps 131: 2 c' that is weaned of his mother:
2 my soul is even as a weaned c'.
Pr 20:11 a c' is known by his doings, 5288
22: 6 Train up a c' in the way he "
15 is bound in the heart of a c'; "
23:13 Withhold not correction from the c': "
24 he that begetteth a wise c' shall
29:15 but a c' left to himself bringeth 5288
21 his servant from a c' shall have 5290
Ec 4: 8 he hath neither c' nor brother: *1121
13 Better is a poor and a wise c' *3206
15 the second c' that shall stand up * "
10:16 O land, when thy king is a c', 5288
11: 5 in the womb of her that is with c': 4392
Isa 3: 5 the c' shall behave himself 5288
7:16 before the c' shall know to refuse "
8: 4 the c' shall have knowledge to cry, "
9: 6 unto us a c' is born, unto us a 3206
10:19 shall be few, that a c' may write 5288
11: 6 and a little c' shall lead them. "
8 the sucking c' shall play on the
8 and the weaned c' shall put his
26:17 Like as a woman with c', that 2030
18 We have been with c', we have 2029
49:15 a woman forget her sucking c',
54: 1 that didst not travail with c':
65:20 the c' shall die an hundred years 5288
66: 7 she was delivered of a man c'.
Jer 1: 6 I cannot speak: for I am a c'. 5288
7 Say not, I am a c': for thou shalt "
4:31 that bringeth forth her first c',
20:15 A man c' is born unto thee; 1121
30: 6 a man doth travail with c'? 3205
31: 8 the lame, the woman with c' 2030
8 and her that travaileth with c' 3205
20 dear son? Is he a pleasant c'? 3206
44: 7 off from you man and woman, c' *5768
La 4: 4 The tongue of the sucking c'
Hos 11: 1 When Israel was a c', then I 5288
13:16 women with c' shall be ripped up. 2030
Am 1:13 have ripped up the women with c' "
M't 1:18 with c' of the Holy Ghost. 1722, 1064, 2192
23 a virgin shall be with c', " "
2: 8 search diligently for the young c'; 3813
9 stood over where the young c' was. "
11 they saw the young c' with Mary "
13 Arise, and take the young c' and "
13 Herod will seek the young c' to "
14 took the young c' and his mother "
20 Arise, and take the young c' and "
21 took the young c' and his mother, "
10:21 and the father the c': and the 5043
17:18 c' was cured from that very hour. *3816
18: 2 And Jesus called a little c' unto 3813
4 humble himself as this little c', "
5 whoso shall receive one such little c' "
23:15 twofold more the c' of hell than *5207
24:19 them that are with c', 1722, 1064, 2192
M'r 9:21 unto him? And he said, Of a c'. 3812
24 straightway the father of the c' 3813
36 And he took a c', and set him in "
10:15 the kingdom of God as a little c', "
13:17 them that are with c', 1722, 1064, 2192
Lu 1: 7 And they had no c', because that 5043
59 they came to circumcise the c'; 3813
66 What manner of c' shall this be! "
76 And thou, c', shalt be called the "
80 the c' grew, and waxed strong "
2: 5 wife, being great with c'. 1471
17 was told them concerning this c'. 3813
21 for the circumcising of the c', * "
27 parents brought in the c' Jesus, "
34 Behold, this c' is set for the fall
40 And the c' grew, and waxed strong 3813
43 the c' Jesus tarried behind *3816
9:38 my son: for he is mine only c'. 3439
42 and healed the c', and delivered *3816
47 their heart, took a c', and set him 3813
48 Whosoever shall receive this c' "
18:17 the kingdom of God as a little c' "
21:23 them that are with c', 1722, 1064, 2192
Joh 4:49 Sir, come down ere my c' die. 3813
16:21 soon as she is delivered of the c',
Ac 4:27 against thy holy c' Jesus, whom *3816
30 by the name of thy holy c' Jesus. * "
7: 5 him, when as yet he had no c'. 5043
13:10 thou c' of the devil, thou enemy *5207
1Co 13:11 When I was a c', I spake as a c', 3516
11 I understood as a c', "
11 I thought as a c': "
Gal 4: 1 the heir, as long as he is a c', "
1Th 5: 3 upon a woman with c'; 1722, 1064, 2192
2Ti 3:15 from a c' thou hast known the *1025
Heb 11:11 and was delivered of a c' when 5088
23 they saw he was a proper c'; 3813
Re 12: 2 And she being with c' 1722, 1064, 2192
4 to devour her c' as soon as it 5043
5 she brought forth a man c', who 5207
5 her c' was caught up unto God, 5043
13 which brought forth the man c'.

childbearing
1Ti 2:15 she shall be saved in c', if they 5042

childhood
1Sa 12: 2 walked before you from my c' *5271
Ec 11:10 evil from thy flesh: for c' and *3208

childish
1Co 13:11 a man, I put away c' things. 3516

childless
Ge 15: 2 wilt thou give me, seeing I go c', 6185
Le 20:20 bear their sins; they shall die c'. "
21 nakedness; they shall be c'. "
1Sa 15:33 thy sword hath made women c', 7921
33 so shall thy mother be c' "
Jer 22:30 Write ye this man c', a man that 6185
Lu 20:30 took her to wife, and he died c'. 815

children See also CHILDREN'S.
Ge 3:16 sorrow thou shalt bring forth c'; 1121
6: 4 and they bare c' to them, the same
10:21 c' of Eber, the brother of Japheth 1121
21 the elder, even to him were c' born.
22 c' of Shem; Elam, and Asshur, *1121
23 And the c' of Aram; Uz, and Hul, * "
11: 5 which the c' of men builded. "
16: 1 Sarai Abram's wife bare him no c':
2 that I may obtain c' by her. 1129
18:19 he will command his c' and his 1121
19:38 the father of the c' of Ammon "
20:17 maidservants; and they bare c'.
21: 7 Sarah should have given c' suck? 1121
22:20 also born c' unto thy brother
23: 5 c' of Heth answered Abraham, "
7 the land, even to the c' of Heth. "
10 dwelt among the c' of Heth: "
10 in the audience of the c' of Heth, "
18 in the presence of the c' of Heth, "
25: 4 these were the c' of Keturah. "
22 c' struggled together within her;
30: 1 she bare Jacob no c', Rachel
1 Give me c', or else I die. 1121
3 that I may also have c' by her. 1129
26 Give me my wives and my c', 3206
31:43 and these c' are my c', and these 1121
43 their c' which they have born? "
32:11 me, and the mother with the c'. "
32 Therefore the c' of Israel eat not "
33: 1 the c' unto Leah, and unto Rachel, 3206
2 handmaids and their c' foremost, "
2 and Leah and her c' after, "
5 and saw the women and the c'; "
5 The c' which God hath graciously "
6 came near, they and their c', "
7 Leah also with her c' came near, "
13 knoweth that the c' are tender, "
14 and the c' be able to endure, "
19 at the hand of the c' of Hamor, 1121
36:21 the c' of Seir in the land of Edom. "
22 c' of Lotan were Hori and Hemam; "
23 the c' of Shobal were these; Alvan, "
24 c' of Zibeon; both Ajah, and Anah: "
25 the c' of Anah were these; Dishon, "
26 c' of Dishon; Hemdan, and Eshban, "
27 c' of Ezer are these; Bilhan and "
28 c' of Dishan are these; Uz, and "
31 any king over the c' of Israel. "
37: 3 loved Joseph more than all his c', "
42:36 bereaved of my c': Joseph is not,
43:14 If I be bereaved of my c', I am
45:10 and thy c', and thy children's c', 1121
21 the c' of Israel did so: and Joseph* "
46: 8 the names of the c' of Israel, "
49: 8 thy father's c' shall bow down * "
32 therein was from the c' of Heth. "
50:23 saw Ephraim's c' of the third "
23 c' also of Machir the son of Manasseh "
25 took an oath of the c' of Israel, "
Ex 1: 1 are the names of the c' of Israel, * "
7 And the c' of Israel were fruitful, "
9 people of the c' of Israel are more "
12 grieved because of the c' of Israel. "
13 the c' of Israel to serve with rigour: "
17 but saved the men c' alive. 3206
18 have saved the men c' alive? "
2: 6 This is one of the Hebrews' c'. "
23 the c' of Israel sighed by reason 1121
25 God looked upon the c' of Israel, "
3: 9 the cry of the c' of Israel is come "
10 the c' of Israel out of Egypt. "
11 I should bring forth the c' of Israel "
13 come unto the c' of Israel, "
14 thou say unto the c' of Israel, I AM "
15 thou say unto the c' of Israel, The "
4:29 all the elders of the c' of Israel: "
31 Lord had visited the c' of Israel, "
5:14 the officers of the c' of Israel, "
15 the c' of Israel came and cried "
19 And the officers of the c' of Israel "
6: 5 the groaning of the c' of Israel, "
6 say unto the c' of Israel, I am the "
9 Moses spake so unto the c' of "
11 let the c' of Israel go out of his land. "
12 c' of Israel have not hearkened

Ex 6:13 a charge unto the c' of Israel, 1121
13 to bring the c' of Israel out of the "
26 the c' of Israel from the land of "
27 out the c' of Israel from Egypt: "
7: 2 send the c' of Israel out of his land. "
4 and my people the c' of Israel, out "
5 bring out the c' of Israel from "
9: 6 cattle of the c' of Israel died not "
26 Goshen, where the c' of Israel were, "
35 would he let the c' of Israel go; "
10:20 would not let the c' of Israel go. "
23 all the c' of Israel had light in their "
11: 7 against any of the c' of Israel shall "
10 would not let the c' of Israel go "
12:26 when your c' shall say unto you, "
27 over the houses of the c' of Israel "
28 the c' of Israel went away, "
31 both ye and the c' of Israel; "
35 And the c' of Israel did according "
37 the c' of Israel journeyed from "
37 on foot that were men, beside c'. 2945
40 the sojourning of the c' of Israel, 1121
42 of all the c' of Israel in their "
50 Thus did all the c' of Israel; "
51 the Lord did bring the c' of Israel "
13: 2 among the c' of Israel, both of "
13 the firstborn of man among thy c'* "
15 the firstborn of my c' I redeem. * "
18 the c' of Israel went up harnessed "
19 had straitly sworn the c' of Israel, "
14: 2 Speak unto the c' of Israel, that "
3 Pharaoh will say of the c' of Israel, "
8 pursued after the c' of Israel: and "
8 the c' of Israel went out with an "
10 the c' of Israel lifted up their eyes, "
10 c' of Israel cried out unto the Lord "
15 c' of Israel, that they go forward: "
16 c' of Israel shall go on dry ground "
22 the c' of Israel went into the midst "
29 But the c' of Israel walked upon "
15: 1 sang Moses and the c' of Israel this "
19 but the c' of Israel went on dry "
16: 1 congregation of the c' of Israel "
2 the c' of Israel murmured against "
3 the c' of Israel said unto them, "
6 Aaron said unto all the c' of Israel, "
9 the c' of Israel, Come near before "
10 the c' of Israel, that they looked "
12 the murmurings of the c' of Israel: "
15 when the c' of Israel saw it, "
17 the c' of Israel did so, and gathered, "
35 And the c' of Israel did eat manna "
17: 1 congregation of the c' of Israel "
3 kill us and our c' and our cattle "
7 the chiding of the c' of Israel, "
19: 1 when the c' of Israel were gone "
3 and tell the c' of Israel; "
6 shalt speak unto the c' of Israel. "
20: 5 the fathers upon the c' unto "
22 shalt say unto the c' of Israel, "
21: 4 the wife and her c' shall be her 3206
5 my master, my wife, and my c'; 1121
22:24 widows, and your c' fatherless. "
24: 5 sent young men of the c' of Israel, "
11 upon the nobles of the c' of Israel "
17 mount in the eyes of the c' of Israel. "
25: 2 Speak unto the c' of Israel, that "
22 commandment unto the c' of Israel. "
27:20 shalt command the c' of Israel, "
21 on the behalf of the c' of Israel, "
28: 1 among the c' of Israel, that he "
9 them the names of the c' of Israel: "
11 with the names of the c' of Israel: "
12 stones of memorial unto the c' of "
21 the c' of Israel, twelve, according "
29 the c' of Israel in the breastplate "
30 the judgment of the c' of Israel "
38 which the c' of Israel shall hallow "
29:28 for ever from the c' of Israel: "
28 offering from the c' of Israel "
43 I will meet with the c' of Israel, "
45 I will dwell among the c' of Israel, "
30:12 takest the sum of the c' of Israel "
16 atonement money of the c' of Israel, "
16 memorial unto the c' of Israel "
31 speak unto the c' of Israel, saying, "
31:13 thou also unto the c' of Israel, "
16 c' of Israel shall keep the sabbath, "
17 between me and the c' of Israel "
32:20 made the c' of Israel drink of it. "
28 the c' of Levi did according to * "
33: 5 Moses, Say unto the c' of Israel, "
6 c' of Israel stripped themselves "
34: 7 the fathers upon the c', and upon
7 the children's c', unto the third *
23 shall all your men c' appear
30 all the c' of Israel saw Moses, 1121
32 all the c' of Israel came nigh: "
34 spake unto the c' of Israel that "
35 c' of Israel saw the face of Moses, "
35: 1 of the c' of Israel together, and said "
4 congregation of the c' of Israel, "
20 the c' of Israel departed from the "
29 The c' of Israel brought a willing "
30 Moses said unto the c' Israel, "
36: 3 the c' of Israel had brought for "
39: 6 graven, with the names of the c' of "
7 for a memorial to the c' of Israel; "
14 names of the c' of Israel, twelve, "
32 the c' of Israel did according to "
42 the c' of Israel made all the work. "
40:36 the c' of Israel went onward in all "
Le 1: 2 Speak unto the c' of Israel, and say "
4: 2 Speak unto the c' of Israel, saying, "
6:18 among the c' of Aaron shall eat "
7:23 29 Speak unto the c' of Israel. "
Le 7:34 have I taken of the c' of Israel 1121
34 ever from among the c' of Israel. "
36 be given them of the c' of Israel, "
38 he commanded the c' of Israel "
9: 3 the c' of Israel thou shalt speak, "
10:11 ye may teach the c' of Israel all "
14 peace offerings of the c' of Israel. "
11: 2 unto the c' of Israel, saying, These "
12: 2 unto the c' of Israel, saying, If a "
15: 2 Speak unto the c' of Israel, and say "
31 shall ye separate the c' of Israel "
16: 5 congregation of the c' of Israel two "
16 of the uncleanness of the c' of Israel, "
19 from the uncleanness of the c' of "
21 the iniquities of the c' of Israel, "
34 an atonement for the c' of Israel "
17: 2 sons, and unto all the c' of Israel, "
5 the c' of Israel may bring their "
12 I said unto the c' of Israel, "
13 whatsoever man there be of the c' "
14 therefore I said unto the c' of "
18: 2 c' of Israel, and say unto them, I "
19: 2 c' of Israel, and say unto them, Ye "
18 against the c' of thy people, "
20: 2 say to the c' of Israel, Whosoever "
2 he be of the c' of Israel, or of the "
21:24 sons, and unto all the c' of Israel. "
22: 2 the holy things of the c' of Israel, "
3 c' of Israel hallow unto the Lord, "
15 the holy things of the c' of Israel, "
18 and unto all the c' of Israel, "
32 hallowed among the c' of Israel: "
23: 2, 10 unto the c' of Israel, and say "
24, 34 Speak unto the c' of Israel, "
43 the c' of Israel to dwell in booths, "
44 Moses declared unto the c' of "
24: 2 the c' of Israel, that they bring "
8 being taken from the c' of Israel "
10 Egyptian, went out among the c' of "
15 speak unto the c' of Israel, saying, "
23 Moses spake to the c' of Israel, "
23 the c' of Israel did as the Lord "
25: 2 Speak unto the c' of Israel, and say "
33 their possession among the c' of "
41 both he and his c' with him, and "
45 c' of the strangers that do sojourn "
46 inheritance for your c' after you, "
46 over your brethren the c' of Israel, "
54 both he, and his c' with him. "
55 me the c' of Israel are servants; "
26:22 which shall rob you of your c', "
46 him and the c' of Israel in mount 1121
27: 2 c' of Israel, and say unto them, "
34 for the c' of Israel in mount Sinai. "
Nu 1: 2 congregation of the c' of Israel, "
10 Of the c' of Joseph; of Ephraim; "
20 c' of Reuben, Israel's eldest son, "
22 c' of Simeon, by their generations, "
24 c' of Gad, by their generations, "
26 Of the c' of Judah, by their "
28 Of the c' of Issachar, by their "
30 Of the c' of Zebulun, by their "
32 Of the c' of Joseph, namely, "
32 Of the c' of Ephraim, by their "
34 Of the c' of Manasseh, by their "
36 Of the c' of Benjamin, by their "
38 Of the c' of Dan, "
40 Of the c' of Asher, by their "
42 Of the c' of Naphtali, throughout "
45 were numbered of the c' of Israel, "
49 of them among the c' of Israel: "
52 c' of Israel shall pitch their tents, "
53 upon the congregation of the c' of "
54 the c' of Israel did according to all "
2: 2 man of the c' of Israel shall pitch "
3 shall be captain of the c' of Judah. "
5 be captain of the c' of Issachar. "
7 be captain of the c' of Zebulun. "
10 and the captain of the c' of Reuben "
12 captain of the c' of Simeon shall be "
20 the captain of the c' of Manasseh "
25 captain of the c' of Dan shall be "
27 captain of the c' of Asher shall be "
29 the captain of the c' of Naphtali "
32 were numbered of the c' of Israel "
33 numbered among the c' of Israel; "
34 the c' of Israel did according to all "
3: 4 and they had no c': and Eleazar "
8 the charge of the c' of Israel, to do "
9 unto him out of the c' of Israel. "
12 from among the c' of Israel instead "
12 the matrix among the c' of Israel: "
15 the c' of Levi after the house of "
38 for the charge of the c' of Israel; "
40 of the males of the c' of Israel "
41 firstborn among the c' of Israel; "
41 among the cattle of the c' of Israel "
42 firstborn among the c' of Israel. "
45 firstborn among the c' of Israel, "
46 the firstborn of the c' of Israel, "
50 the c' of Israel took he the money; "
5: 2 Command the c' of Israel, that they "
4 the c' of Israel did so, and put "
4 unto Moses, so did the c' of Israel. "
6 Speak unto the c' of Israel, When "
9 the holy things of the c' of Israel, "
12 unto the c' of Israel, and say "
6: 2 unto the c' of Israel, and say "
23 wise ye shall bless the c' of Israel, "
27 put my name upon the c' of Israel; "
7:24 prince of the c' of Zebulun, did "
30 prince of the c' of Reuben, did offer: "
36 prince of the c' of Simeon, did offer: "
42 prince of the c' of Gad, offered; "
48 prince of the c' of Ephraim, offered: "
54 prince of the c' of Manasseh: "
Nu 7:60 prince of the c' of Benjamin, 1121
66 prince of the c' of Dan, offered: "
72 prince of the c' of Asher, offered: "
78 prince of the c' of Naphtali, offered: "
8: 6 the Levites from among the c' of "
9 whole assembly of the c' of Israel "
10 c' of Israel shall put their hands "
11 for an offering of the c' of Israel, "
14 the Levites from among the c' of "
16 me from among the c' of Israel; "
16 of the firstborn of all the c' of "
17 For all the firstborn of the c' of "
18 for all the firstborn of the c' of "
19 sons from among the c' of Israel, "
19 do the service of the c' of Israel in "
19 an atonement for the c' of Israel: "
19 no plague among the c' of Israel, "
19 when the c' of Israel come nigh "
20 congregation of the c' of Israel, "
20 so did the c' of Israel unto them. "
9: 2 c' of Israel also keep the passover "
4 Moses spake unto the c' of Israel, "
5 Moses, so did the c' of Israel. "
7 season among the c' of Israel? "
10 unto the c' of Israel, saying, If any "
17 after that the c' of Israel journeyed: "
17 the c' of Israel pitched their tents. "
18 the Lord the c' of Israel journeyed, "
19 then the c' of Israel kept the charge "
22 c' of Israel abode in their tents, "
10:12 c' of Israel took their journeys "
14 of the camp of the c' of Judah "
15 the tribe of the c' of Issachar was "
16 the tribe of the c' of Zebulun was "
19 the c' of Simeon was Shelumiel "
20 of the c' of Gad was Eliasaph the "
22 of the camp of the c' of Ephraim "
23 of the tribe of the c' of Manasseh "
24 of the tribe of the c' of Benjamin "
25 the camp of the c' of Dan set "
26 the tribe of the c' of Asher was "
27 tribe of the c' of Naphtali was "
28 these were the journeyings of the c' "
11: 4 and the c' of Israel also wept "
13: 2 which I give unto the c' of Israel: "
3 men were heads of the c' of Israel. "
22 and Talmai, the c' of Anak, were. 3211
24 which the c' of Israel cut down 1121
26 c' of Israel, unto the wilderness of "
28 moreover we saw the c' of Anak 3211
32 had searched unto the c' of Israel, 1121
14: 2 c' of Israel murmured against "
3 our wives and our c' should be a *2945
5 congregation of the c' of Israel. 1121
7 all the company of the c' of Israel, "
10 before all the c' of Israel. "
18 iniquity of the fathers upon the c' "
27 heard the murmurings of the c' of "
33 c' shall wander in the wilderness "
39 sayings unto all the c' of Israel: "
15: 2, 18 Speak unto the c' of Israel, and "
25, 26 congregation of the c' of Israel, "
29 that is born among the c' of Israel, "
32 c' of Israel were in the wilderness, "
38 Speak unto the c' of Israel, and say "
16: 2 with certain of the c' of Israel, "
27 and their sons, and their little c'. *2945
38 be a sign unto the c' of Israel. 1121
40 To be a memorial unto the c' of "
41 all the congregation of the c' of "
17: 2 Speak unto the c' of Israel, and take "
5 me the murmurings of the c' of "
6 spake unto the c' of Israel, and "
9 before the Lord unto all the c' of "
12 the c' of Israel spake unto Moses, "
18: 5 any more upon the c' of Israel. "
6 the Levites from among the c' of "
8 hallowed things of the c' of Israel; "
11 wave offering of the c' of Israel: "
19 the c' of Israel offer unto the Lord, "
20 inheritance among the c' of Israel. "
21 behold, I have given the c' of Levi "
22 Neither must the c' of Israel "
23 among the c' of Israel they have no "
24 But the tithes of the c' of Israel, "
24 Among the c' of Israel they shall "
26 When ye take of the c' of Israel "
28 which ye receive of the c' of Israel; "
32 the holy things of the c' of Israel, "
19: 2 Speak unto the c' of Israel, that they "
9 of the c' of Israel for a water of "
10 it shall be unto the c' of Israel, "
20: 1 Then came the c' of Israel, even "
12 in the eyes of the c' of Israel, "
13 because the c' of Israel strove with "
19 the c' of Israel said unto him, "
22 And the c' of Israel, even the "
24 I have given unto the c' of Israel, "
21:10 the c' of Israel set forward, and "
24 even unto the c' of Ammon: for "
24 the border of the c' of Ammon "
22: 1 And the c' of Israel set forward, "
3 was distressed because of the c' of "
5 the land of the c' of his people, "
24:17 and destroy all the c' of Sheth. * "
25: 6 one of the c' of Israel came and "
6 the c' of Israel, who were weeping "
8 plague was stayed from the c' of "
11 wrath away from the c' of Israel, "
11 I consumed not the c' of Israel "
13 an atonement for the c' of Israel. "
26: 2 the congregation of the c' of Israel, "
4 Moses and the c' of Israel, which * "
5 c' of Reuben; Hanoch, of whom * "
11 Notwithstanding the c' of Korah * "
15 The c' of Gad after their families: * "

Nu 26:18 are the families of the c' of Gad *1121
44 c' of Asher after their families: * "
51 the numbered of the c' of Israel, "
62 numbered among the c' of Israel, "
62 given them among the c' of Israel. "
63 the c' of Israel in the plains of Moab "
64 they numbered the c' of Israel in "
27: 8 shalt speak unto the c' of Israel, "
11 c' of Israel a statute of judgment, "
12 I have given unto the c' of Israel. "
20 the c' of Israel may be obedient. "
21 and all the c' of Israel with him, "
28: 2 Command the c' of Israel, and say "
29:40 And Moses told the c' of Israel "
30: 1 concerning the c' of Israel, saying, "
31: 2 Avenge the c' of Israel of the "
9 the c' of Israel took all the women "
12 unto the c' of Israel, unto the camp "
16 Behold, these caused the c' of "
18 But all the women c', that have 2945
30 42 And of the c' of Israel's half, 1121
47 even of the c' of Israel's half, Moses "
54 for a memorial for the c' of Israel "
32: 1 Now the c' of Reuben and the "
1 and the c' of Gad had a very "
2 c' of Gad and the c' of Reuben came "
6 Moses said unto the c' of Gad and "
6 of Gad and to the c' of Reuben, "
7 the heart of the c' of Israel from "
9 the heart of the c' of Israel, that "
17 ready armed before the c' of Israel, "
18 until the c' of Israel have inherited "
25 the c' of Gad and the c' of Reuben "
28 of the tribes of the c' of Israel: "
29 If the c' of Gad and the c' of Reuben "
31 the c' of Gad and the c' of Reuben "
33 even to the c' of Gad, and to the "
33 and to the c' of Reuben, "
34 And the c' of Gad built Dibon, "
37 the c' of Reuben built Heshbon, "
39 c' of Machir the son of Manasseh "
33: 1 are the journeys of the c' of Israel, "
3 the c' of Israel went out with an "
5 c' of Israel removed from Rameses, "
38 after the c' of Israel were come "
40 of the coming of the c' of Israel. "
51 Speak unto the c' of Israel, and "
34: 2 Command the c' of Israel, and "
13 Moses commanded the c' of Israel, "
14 for the tribe of the c' of Reuben "
14 and the tribe of the c' of Gad "
20 And of the tribe of the c' of Simeon, "
22 prince of the tribe of the c' of Dan, "
23 The prince of the c' of Joseph, "
23 of the tribe of the c' of Manasseh, "
24 of the tribe of the c' of Ephraim, "
25 of the tribe of the c' of Zebulun, "
26 of the tribe of the c' of Issachar, "
27 of the tribe of the c' of Asher, "
28 of the tribe of the c' of Naphtali, "
29 inheritance unto the c' of Israel "
35: 2 Command the c' of Israel, that they "
8 the possession of the c' of Israel: "
10 Speak unto the c' of Israel, and "
15 a refuge, both for the c' of Israel, "
34 Lord dwell among the c' of Israel. "
36: 1 families of the c' of Gilead, the son "
1 chief fathers of the c' of Israel: "
2 for an inheritance by lot to the c' of "
3 the other tribes of the c' of Israel, "
4 the jubile of the c' of Israel shall "
5 Moses commanded the c' of Israel "
7 the inheritance of the c' of Israel "
7 every one of the c' of Israel shall "
8 any tribe of the c' of Israel, shall "
8 that the c' of Israel may enjoy "
9 the tribes of the c' of Israel shall "
13 hand of Moses unto the c' of Israel "
De 1: 3 Moses spake unto the c' of Israel, "
36 and to his c', because he hath "
39 and your c', which in that day had "
2: 4 your brethren the c' of Esau, "
8 from our brethren the c' of Esau, "
9 unto the c' of Lot for a possession. "
12 the c' of Esau succeeded them, "
19 nigh over against the c' of Ammon, "
19 the land of the c' of Ammon any "
19 unto the c' of Lot for a possession. "
22 As he did to the c' of Esau, which "
29 the c' of Esau which dwell in Seir, "
37 the c' of Ammon thou camest not, "
3: 6 men, women, and c', of every city. 2945
11 in Rabbath of the c' of Ammon? 1121
16 is the border of the c' of Ammon; "
18 your brethren the c' of Israel, all "
4:10 and that they may teach their c'. "
25 shalt beget c', and children's c', "
40 with thee, and with thy c' after "
44 Moses set before the c' of Israel: "
45 Moses spake unto the c' of Israel, "
46 whom Moses and the c' of Israel "
5: 9 iniquity of the fathers upon the c' "
29 them, and with their c' for ever! "
6: 7 teach them diligently unto thy c', "
9: 2 and tall, the c' of the Anakims, * "
2 can stand before the c' of Anak! * "
10: 6 the c' of Israel took their journey "
6 from Beeroth of the c' of Jaakan * "
11: 2 for I speak not with your c' which "
19 ye shall teach them your c', "
21 the days of your c', in the land "
12:25 thy c' after thee, when thou shalt "
28 well with thee, and with thy c' "
13:13 Certain men, the c' of Belial, are * "
14: 1 are the c' of the Lord your God: "
17:20 and his c', in the midst of Israel. "

De 21:15 hated, and they have born him c', 1121
23: 8 The c' that are begotten of them "
24: 7 of his brethren of the c' of Israel, "
16 shall not be put to death for the c', "
16 neither shall the c' be put to death "
28:54 remnant of his c' which he shall "
55 flesh of his c' whom he shall eat: "
57 toward her c' which she shall bear: "
29: 1 with the c' of Israel in the land "
22 the generation to come of your c' "
29 unto us and to our c' for ever, "
30: 2 thee this day, thou and thy c', "
31:12 men, and women, and c', *2945
13 And that their c', which have not 1121
19 and teach it the c' of Israel: "
19 for me against the c' of Israel. "
22 and taught it the c' of Israel. "
23 thou shalt bring the c' of Israel "
32: 5 their spot is not the spot of his c': "
8 according to the number of the c' "
20 generation, c' in whom is no faith. "
46 command your c' to observe to do, "
49 which I give unto the c' of Israel "
51 among the c' of Israel at the waters, "
51 in the midst of the c' of Israel. "
52 land which I give the c' of Israel. "
33: 1 blessed the c' of Israel before his "
9 his brethren, nor knew his own c': "
24 Let Asher be blessed with c'; "
34: 8 the c' of Israel wept for Moses "
9 c' of Israel hearkened unto him, "
Jos 1: 2 to them, even to the c' of Israel. "
2: 2 men in hither to night of the c' of "
3: 1 he and all the c' of Israel, and "
9 Joshua said unto the c' of Israel, "
4: 4 he had prepared of the c' of Israel, "
5 of the tribes of the c' of Israel: "
6 your c' ask their fathers in time "
7 a memorial unto the c' of Israel "
8 the c' of Israel did so as Joshua "
8 of the tribes of the c' of Israel, "
12 And the c' of Reuben, and the "
12 of Reuben, and the c' of Gad, "
12 over armed before the c' of Israel, "
21 he spake unto the c' of Israel, "
21 saying, When your c' shall ask "
22 ye shall let your c' know, saying, "
5: 1 Jordan from before the c' of Israel, "
1 more, because of the c' of Israel. "
2 circumcise again the c' of Israel "
3 circumcised the c' of Israel at the "
6 the c' of Israel walked forty years "
7 And their c', whom he raised up "
10 c' of Israel encamped in Gilgal, "
12 neither had the c' of Israel manna "
6: 1 shut up because of the c' of Israel: "
7: 1 c' of Israel committed a trespass "
1 kindled against the c' of Israel. "
12 the c' of Israel could not stand "
23 unto all the c' of Israel, and laid "
8:31 Lord commanded the c' of Israel, "
32 in the presence of the c' of Israel. "
9:17 the c' of Israel journeyed, and "
18 the c' of Israel smote them not, "
26 out of the hand of the c' of Israel, "
10: 4 peace with Joshua and with the c' "
11 the c' of Israel slew with the sword. "
12 Amorites before the c' of Israel, "
20 the c' of Israel had made an end "
21 against any of the c' of Israel. "
11:14 the c' of Israel took for a prey "
19 made peace with the c' of Israel, "
22 Anakims left in the land of the c' "
12: 1 which the c' of Israel smote, "
2 the border of the c' of Ammon; "
6 Lord and the c' of Israel smite: "
7 Joshua and the c' of Israel smote "
13: 6 will I drive out from before the c' "
10 the border of the c' of Ammon; "
13 the c' of Israel expelled not the "
15 the tribe of the c' of Reuben "
22 soothsayer, did the c' of Israel slay "
23 the border of the c' of Reuben "
23 inheritance of the c' of Reuben "
24 unto the c' of Gad according to "
25 the land of the c' of Ammon, "
28 the inheritance of the c' of Gad "
29 half tribe of the c' of Manasseh "
31 unto the c' of Machir the son of "
31 the one half of the c' of Machir "
14: 1 which the c' of Israel inherited "
1 of the tribes of the c' of Israel, "
4 the c' of Joseph were two tribes, "
5 Moses, so the c' of Israel did, "
6 Then the c' of Judah came unto "
10 while the c' of Israel wandered *
15: 1 the tribe of the c' of Judah 1121
12 the coast of the c' of Judah "
13 gave a part among the c' of Judah, "
14 and Talmai, the c' of Anak. 3211
20 inheritance of the ... c' of Judah 1121
21 cities of the tribe of the c' of Judah "
63 the c' of Judah could not drive "
63 Jebusites dwell with the c' of Judah "
16: 1 the lot of the c' of Joseph fell "
4 So the c' of Joseph, Manasseh "
5 the border of the c' of Ephraim "
8 of the tribe of the c' of Ephraim "
9 separate cities for the c' of Ephraim "
9 inheritance of the c' of Manasseh, "
17: 2 c' of Manasseh by their families; "
2 for the c' of Abiezer, "
2 and for the c' of Helek, "
2 and for the c' of Asriel, "
2 and for the c' of Shechem, "
2 and for the c' of Hepher, "

Jos 17: 2 and for the c' of Shemida: 1121
2 these were the male c' of Manasseh "
8 belonged to the c' of Ephraim; "
12 the c' of Manasseh could not drive "
13 when the c' of Israel were waxen "
14 c' of Joseph spake unto Joshua, "
16 the c' of Joseph said, The hill "
18: 1 c' of Israel assembled together "
2 remained among the c' of Israel "
3 Joshua said unto the c' of Israel, "
10 the land unto the c' of Israel "
11 the tribe of the c' of Benjamin "
11 between the c' of Judah and the "
11 of Judah and the c' of Joseph. "
14 a city of the c' of Judah: "
20 the c' of Benjamin, by the coasts "
21 of the tribe of the c' of Benjamin "
28 inheritance of the c' of Benjamin "
19: 1 c' of Simeon according to their "
1 the inheritance of the c' of Judah. "
8 of the tribe of the c' of Simeon "
9 the portion of the c' of Judah was "
9 the inheritance of the c' of Simeon: "
9 for the part of the c' of Judah was "
9 therefore the c' of Simeon had "
10 came up for the c' of Zebulun "
16 inheritance of the c' of Zebulun "
17 Issachar, for the c' of Issachar "
23 the tribe of the c' of Issachar "
24 the c' of Asher according to their "
31 the tribe of the c' of Asher "
32 came out to the c' of Naphtali, "
32 even for the c' of Naphtali "
39 the tribe of the c' of Naphtali "
40 out for the tribe of the c' of Dan "
47 the coast of the c' of Dan went out "
47 c' of Dan went up to fight against "
48 the c' of Dan according to their "
49 c' of Israel gave an inheritance "
51 of the tribes of the c' of Israel, "
20: 2 Speak to the c' of Israel, saying, "
9 appointed for all the c' of Israel, "
21: 1 of the tribes of the c' of Israel; "
3 c' of Israel gave unto the Levites "
4 the c' of Aaron the priest, which "
5 And the rest of the c' of Kohath "
6 And the c' of Gershon had by lot "
7 The c' of Merari by their families "
8 the c' of Israel gave by lot unto "
9 out of the tribe of the c' of Judah, "
9 out of the tribe of the c' of Simeon, "
10 Which the c' of Aaron, being of "
10 of the c' of Levi, had: for theirs "
13 Thus they gave to the c' of Aaron "
19 the cities of the c' of Aaron, "
20 families of the c' of Kohath, the "
20 which remained of the c' of Kohath, "
26 the c' of Kohath that remained. "
27 And unto the c' of Gershon, of the "
34 families of the c' of Merari, the "
40 the c' of Merari by their families, "
41 the possession of the c' of Israel "
22: 9 And the c' of Reuben "
9 and the c' of Gad and the half "
9 and departed from the c' of Israel "
10 the c' of Reuben and the c' of Gad "
11 And the c' of Israel heard say, "
11 Behold the c' of Reuben "
11 and the c' of Gad and the half "
11 at the passage of the c' of Israel. "
12 when the c' of Israel heard of it, "
12 congregation of the c' of Israel "
13 And the c' of Israel sent unto "
13 sent unto the c' of Reuben, "
13 of Reuben, and to the c' of Gad, "
15 they came unto the c' of Reuben, "
15 of Reuben, and to the c' of Gad, "
21 Then the c' of Reuben and the "
21 and the c' of Gad and the half "
24 your c' might speak unto our c', "
25 ye c' of Reuben and c' of Gad; ye "
25 so shall your c' make our c' cease "
27 your c' may not say to our c' in time "
30 that the c' of Reuben and the "
30 of Reuben and the c' of Gad "
30 and the c' of Manasseh spake, "
31 priest said unto the c' of Reuben, "
31 and to the c' of Gad, "
31 and to the c' of Manasseh, This "
31 ye have delivered the c' of Israel "
32 returned from the c' of Reuben, "
32 and from the c' of Gad, "
32 to the c' of Israel, and brought "
33 the thing pleased the c' of Israel; "
33 and the c' of Israel blessed God, "
33 the c' of Reuben and Gad dwelt. "
34 And the c' of Reuben and "
34 the c' of Gad called the altar Ed: "
24: 4 Jacob and his c' went down into "
32 which the c' of Israel brought up "
32 the inheritance of the c' of Joseph. "
J'g 1: 1 the c' of Israel asked the Lord, "
8 Now the c' of Judah had fought "
9 afterward the c' of Judah went "
16 And the c' of the Kenite, Moses' "
16 the c' of Judah into the wilderness "
21 And the c' of Benjamin did not "
21 dwell with the c' of Benjamin "
34 the Amorites forced the c' of Dan "
2: 4 words unto all the c' of Israel, "
6 the c' of Israel went every man "
11 the c' of Israel did evil in the sight "
3: 2 the generations of the c' of Israel "
5 the c' of Israel dwelt among the "
7 And the c' of Israel did evil "
8 and the c' of Israel served "

J'g 3: 9 And when the c' of Israel cried 1121
9 up a deliverer to the c' of Israel. "
12 the c' of Israel did evil again "
13 gathered unto him the c' of Ammon "
14 c' of Israel served Eglon the king "
15 c' of Israel cried unto the Lord, "
15 the c' of Israel sent a present unto "
27 c' of Israel went down with him "
4: 1 the c' of Israel again did evil "
3 c' of Israel cried unto the Lord: "
3 oppressed the c' of Israel. "
5 the c' of Israel came up to her "
6 men of the c' of Naphtali and of "
6 and of the c' of Zebulun? "
11 the c' of Hobab the father in law "
23 of Canaan before the c' of Israel. "
24 hand of the c' of Israel prospered, "
6: 1 c' of Israel did evil in the sight of "
2 c' of Israel made them the dens "
3 and the c' of the east, even they "
6 c' of Israel cried unto the Lord. "
7 when the c' of Israel cried unto "
8 sent a prophet unto the c' of Israel, "
33 and the c' of the east were gathered "
7:12 the c' of the east lay along "
8:10 the hosts of the c' of the east: "
18 one resembled the c' of a king. "
28 subdued before the c' of Israel, "
33 the c' of Israel turned again, and "
34 c' of Israel remembered not the "
10: 6 the c' of Israel did evil again "
6 the gods of the c' of Ammon, "
7 the hands of the c' of Ammon. "
8 and oppressed the c' of Israel: "
8 the c' of Israel that were on the "
9 c' of Ammon passed over Jordan "
10 the c' of Israel cried unto the Lord, "
11 Lord said unto the c' of Israel, "
11 Amorites, from the c' of Ammon, "
15 the c' of Israel said unto the Lord, "
17 the c' of Ammon were gathered "
17 c' of Israel assembled themselves "
18 to fight against the c' of Ammon? "
11: 4 that the c' of Ammon made war "
5 the c' of Ammon made war against "
6 may fight with the c' of Ammon. "
8 and fight against the c' of Ammon, "
9 to fight against the c' of Ammon, "
12 king of the c' of Ammon, saying, "
13 king of the c' of Ammon answered "
14 unto the king of the c' of Ammon: "
15 nor the land of the c' of Ammon: "
27 c' of Israel and the c' of Ammon. "
28 of the c' of Ammon hearkened not "
29 passed over unto the c' of Ammon. "
30 the c' of Ammon into mine hands, "
31 in peace from the c' of Ammon, "
32 passed over unto the c' of Ammon "
33 Thus the c' of Ammon were subdued "
33 before the c' of Israel. "
36 enemies, even of the c' of Ammon. "
12: 1 to fight against the c' of Ammon, "
2 great strife with the c' of Ammon; "
3 the c' of Ammon, and the Lord "
13: 1 the c' of Israel did evil again "
14:16 a riddle unto the c' of my people, "
17 the riddle to the c' of her people. "
18: 2 the c' of Dan sent of their family "
16 were of the c' of Dan, stood by "
22 and overtook the c' of Dan. "
23 they cried unto the c' of Dan. "
25 c' of Dan said unto him, Let not "
26 the c' of Dan went their way: "
30 the c' of Dan set up the graven "
19:12 that is not of the c' of Israel; "
30 the day that the c' of Israel came "
20: 1 Then all the c' of Israel went out, "
3 the c' of Benjamin heard that the "
3 c' of Israel were gone up to Mizpeh.) "
3 Then said the c' of Israel, "
7 Behold, ye are all c' of Israel; "
13 c' of Belial, which are in Gibeah, * "
13 c' of Benjamin would not hearken * "
13 of their brethren the c' of Israel: "
14 But the c' of Benjamin gathered "
14 to battle against the c' of Israel. "
15 the c' of Benjamin were numbered "
18 the c' of Israel arose, and went up "
18 battle against the c' of Benjamin? "
19 the c' of Israel rose up in the "
21 the c' of Benjamin came forth "
23 the c' of Israel went up and wept "
23 against the c' of Benjamin my "
24 the c' of Israel came near against "
24 the c' of Benjamin the second day. "
25 to the ground of the c' of Israel "
26 the c' of Israel, and all the people, "
27 c' of Israel enquired of the Lord, "
28 the c' of Benjamin my brother, "
30 c' of Israel went up against the "
30 c' of Benjamin on the third day, "
31 c' of Benjamin went out against "
32 the c' of Benjamin said, They are "
32 the c' of Israel said, Let us flee, "
35 the c' of Israel destroyed of the "
48 So the c' of Benjamin saw that "
48 again upon the c' of Benjamin, "
21: 5 the c' of Israel said, Who is there "
6 the c' of Israel repented them for "
10 sword with the women and the c'. *2945
13 to speak to the c' of Benjamin 1121
18 c' of Israel have sworn, saying, "
20 commanded the c' of Benjamin, "
23 the c' of Benjamin did so, and "
24 the c' of Israel departed thence "
1Sa 1: 2 and Peninnah had c', 3206

1Sa 1: 3 but Hannah had no c'. 3206
2: 5 hath many c' is waxed feeble. 1121
28 made by fire of the c' of Israel? "
7: 4 c' of Israel did put away Baalim "
6 judged the c' of Israel in Mizpeh. "
7 Philistines heard that the c' of "
7 And when the c' of Israel heard it, "
8 the c' of Israel said to Samuel, "
9: 2 was not among the c' of Israel "
10:18 And said unto the c' of Israel, "
10:27 the c' of Belial said, How shall * "
11: 8 the c' of Israel were three hundred "
12:12 the king of the c' of Ammon "
14:18 at that time with the c' of Israel. "
47 and against the c' of Ammon, "
15: 6 kindness to all the c' of Israel, "
16:11 unto Jesse, Are here all thy c'? 5288
17:53 c' of Israel returned from chasing 1121
22:19 and women, c' and sucklings, 5768
26:19 the c' of men, cursed be they 1121
30:22 to every man his wife and his c', "
2Sa 1:18 bade them teach the c' of Judah "
2:25 the c' of Benjamin gathered "
4: 2 Beerothite, of the c' of Benjamin: "
7: 6 up the c' of Israel out of Egypt, "
7 walked with all the c' of Israel "
10 the c' of wickedness afflict them "
7:14 with the stripes of the c' of men: "
8:12 c' of Ammon, and of the Philistines, "
10: 1 the king of the c' of Ammon died, "
2 into the land of the c' of Ammon. "
3 the c' of Ammon said unto Hanun "
6 when the c' of Ammon saw that "
6 the c' of Ammon sent and hired "
8 the c' of Ammon came out, and "
10 in array against the c' of Ammon. "
11 if the c' of Ammon be too strong "
14 c' of Ammon saw that the Syrians "
14 returned from the c' of Ammon, "
19 feared to help the c' of Ammon "
11: 1 they destroyed the c' of Ammon, "
12: 3 together with him, and with his c'; "
9 the sword of the c' of Ammon. "
26 Rabbah of the c' of Ammon, "
31 all the cities of the c' of Ammon. "
17:27 of Rabbah of the c' of Ammon, "
21: 2 were not of the c' of Israel, "
2 c' of Israel had sworn unto them: "
2 zeal to the c' of Israel and Judah.) "
23:29 of Gibeah of the c' of Benjamin, "
1Ki 2: 4 If thy c' take heed to their way, "
4:30 the wisdom of all the c' of the east "
6: 1 the c' of Israel were come out of "
13 I will dwell among the c' of Israel, "
8: 1 of the fathers of the c' of Israel, "
9 a covenant with the c' of Israel, "
25 that thy c' take heed to their way, "
39 the hearts of all the c' of men; "
63 and all the c' of Israel dedicated "
9: 6 from following me, ye or your c', "
20 which were not of the c' of Israel, "
21 Their c' that were left after them in "
21 in the land, whom the c' of Israel "
22 the c' of Israel did Solomon make "
11: 2 Lord said unto the c' of Israel, "
7 abomination of the c' of Ammon. "
33 the god of the c' of Ammon, "
12:17 But as for the c' of Israel which "
24 your brethren the c' of Israel: "
33 a feast unto the c' of Israel: "
14:24 cast out before the c' of Israel. "
18:20 Ahab sent unto all the c' of Israel, "
19:10 the c' of Israel have forsaken thy "
14 because the c' of Israel have "
20: 3 thy wives also and thy c', even the "
5 thy gold, and thy wives, and thy c'; "
7 me for my wives, and for my c', "
15 c' of Israel, being seven thousand, "
27 the c' of Israel were numbered, "
27 c' of Israel pitched before them "
29 the c' of Israel slew of the Syrians "
21:13 came in two men, c' of Belial, †‡ "
26 cast out before the c' of Israel. "
2Ki 2:23 came forth little c' out of the city, ‡5288
24 and tare forty and two c' of them. ‡3206
4: 7 live thou and thy c' of the rest. *1121
8:12 wilt do unto the c' of Israel: * "
12 and wilt dash their c', and rip *6768
19 him alway a light, and to his c', 1121
9: 1 one of the c' of the prophets, * "
10: 1 them that brought up Ahab's c', *
5 and the bringers up of the c'
13 down to salute the c' of the king 1121
13 and the c' of the queen. "
30 thy c' of the fourth generation * "
13: 5 the c' of Israel dwelt in their tents, "
14: 6 But the c' of the murderers he "
6 shall not be put to death for the c', "
6 nor the c' be put to death for the "
16: 3 Lord cast out from before the c' "
17: 7 that the c' of Israel had sinned "
8 the Lord cast out from before the c' "
9 the c' of Israel did secretly those "
22 c' of Israel walked in all the sins "
24 Samaria instead of the c' of Israel: "
31 Sepharvites burnt their c' in fire "
34 Lord commanded the c' of Jacob, "
41 their c', and their children's c': "
18: 4 the c' of Israel did burn incense "
19: 3 for the c' are come to the birth, "
12 and the c' of Eden which were in "
21: 2 cast out before the c' of Israel. "
9 destroyed before the c' of Israel. "
23: 6 the graves of the c' of the people. * "
10 in the valley of the c' of Hinnom, "
13 abomination of the c' of Ammon, "

2Ki 24: 2 bands of the c' of Ammon, and 1121
1Ch 1:43 king reigned over the c' of Israel; "
2:10 Nahshon, prince of the c' of Judah; "
18 Caleb the son of Hezron begat c'
30 Appaim: but Seled died without c'. 1121
31 And the c' of Sheshan; Ahlai. * "
32 and Jether died without c'. "
4:27 his brethren had not many c', "
27 multiply, like to the c' of Judah. "
5:11 And the c' of Gad dwelt over * "
14 These are the c' of Abihail the * "
23 c' of the half tribe of Manasseh "
6: 3 c' of Amram; Aaron, and Moses, "
33 are they that waited with their c'.* "
64 the c' of Israel gave to the Levites "
65 the tribe of the c' of Judah, and "
65 of the tribe of the c' of Simeon, "
65 of the tribe of the c' of Benjamin, "
77 Unto the rest of the c' of Merari * "
7:12 and Huppim, the c' of Ir, and * "
29 the borders of the c' of Manasseh, "
29 dwelt the c' of Joseph the son of "
33 These are the c' of Japhlet. "
40 All these were the c' of Asher, "
8: 8 And Shaharaim begat c' in the "
9: 3 dwelt of the c' of Judah, 1121
3 and of the c' of Benjamin, "
3 and of the c' of Ephraim, "
4 the c' of Pharez the son of Judah. "
18 in the companies of the c' of Levi. "
23 and their c' had the oversight "
11:31 Gibeah, that pertained to the c' of "
12:16 there came of the c' of Benjamin "
24 The c' of Judah that bare shield "
25 Of the c' of Simeon, mighty men "
26 Of the c' of Levi four thousand "
29 And of the c' of Benjamin, the "
30 the c' of Ephraim twenty thousand "
32 of the c' of Issachar, which were "
14: 4 these are the names of his c' 3205
15: 4 David assembled the c' of Aaron, *1121
15 the c' of the Levites bare the ark "
16:13 ye c' of Jacob, his chosen ones. "
17: 9 neither shall the c' of wickedness "
18:11 Moab, and from the c' of Ammon, "
19: 1 king of the c' of Ammon died, "
2 into the land of the c' of Ammon "
3 the princes of the c' of Ammon "
6 when the c' of Ammon saw that "
6 the c' of Ammon sent a thousand "
7 And the c' of Ammon gathered "
9 the c' of Ammon came out, and put "
11 in array against the c' of Ammon. "
12 if the c' of Ammon be too strong "
15 c' of Ammon saw that the Syrians "
19 the Syrians help the c' of Ammon "
20: 1 the country of the c' of Ammon, "
3 all the cities of the c' of Ammon. "
4 that was of the c' of the giant: *3211
24: 2 before their father, and had no c': 1121
26:10 Hosah, of the c' of Merari, had "
27: 1 the c' of Israel after their number, "
3 Of the c' of Perez was the chief "
10 the Pelonite, of the c' of Ephraim: "
14 Pirathonite, of the c' of Ephraim: "
20 Of the c' of Ephraim, Hoshea the "
28: 8 inheritance for your c' after you "
2Ch 5: 2 of the fathers of the c' of Israel, "
10 a covenant with the c' of Israel, "
6:11 that he made with the c' of Israel. "
16 yet so that thy c' take heed to "
30 knowest the hearts of the c' of men:) "
7: 3 all the c' of Israel saw how the fire "
8: 2 caused the c' of Israel to dwell "
8 of their c', who were left after "
8 whom the c' of Israel consumed "
9 of the c' of Israel did Solomon "
10:17 as for the c' of Israel that dwelt "
18 and the c' of Israel stoned him "
11:19 Which bare him c'; Jeush, and * "
23 wisely, and dispersed of all his c'.* "
13: 7 unto him vain men, the c' of Belial,* "
12 O c' of Israel, fight ye not against "
16 the c' of Israel fled before Judah: "
18 the c' of Israel were brought "
18 the c' of Judah prevailed, because "
20: 1 c' of Moab, and the c' of Ammon, "
10 the c' of Ammon and Moab and "
13 little ones, their wives, and their c'. "
19 of the c' of the Kohathites, "
19 and of the c' of the Korhites, "
22 against the c' of Ammon, Moab, "
23 the c' of Ammon and Moab stood "
21:14 people, and thy c', and thy wives, "
25: 4 But he slew not their c', but did "
4 The fathers shall not die for the c', "
4 neither shall the c' die for the "
7 to wit, with all the c' of Ephraim. "
11 of the c' of Seir ten thousand. "
12 the c' of Judah carry away captive, "
14 brought the gods of the c' of Seir, "
27: 5 the c' of Ammon gave him the "
5 So much did the c' of Ammon pay "
28: 3 burnt his c' in the fire, after the "
3 had cast out before the c' of Israel. "
8 c' of Israel carried away captive "
10 to keep under the c' of Judah "
12 the heads of the c' of Ephraim, "
30: 6 Ye c' of Israel, turn again unto "
9 your brethren and your c' shall "
21 the c' of Israel that were present "
31: 1 Then all the c' of Israel returned, "
5 c' of Israel brought in abundance "
6 And concerning the c' of Israel "
33: 2 had cast out before the c' of Israel. "
6 caused his c' to pass through the "

2Ch 33: 9 Lord had destroyed before the c' of 1121
34:33 that pertained to the c' of Israel, "
35:17 the c' of Israel that were present "
Ezr 2: 1 Now these are the c' of the province "
3 c' of Parosh, two thousand an "
4 c' of Shephatiah, three hundred "
5 c' of Arah, seven hundred seventy "
6 The c' of Pahath-moab, of the "
6 of the c' of Jeshua and Joab, two "
7 The c' of Elam, a thousand two "
8 The c' of Zattu, nine hundred forty "
9 The c' of Zaccai, seven hundred and "
10 The c' of Bani, six hundred forty "
11 The c' of Bebai, six hundred twenty "
12 The c' of Azgad, a thousand two "
13 The c' of Adonikam, six hundred "
14 The c' of Bigvai, two thousand fifty "
15 The c' of Adin, four hundred fifty "
16 The c' of Ater of Hezekiah, ninety "
17 The c' of Bezai, three hundred "
18 The c' of Jorah, an hundred and "
19 The c' of Hashum, two hundred "
20 The c' of Gibbar, ninety and five. "
21 The c' of Beth-lehem, an hundred "
24 The c' of Azmaveth, forty and two. "
25 The c' of Kirjath-arim, Chephirah, "
26 The c' of Ramah and Gaba, six "
29 The c' of Nebo, fifty and two. "
30 The c' of Magbish, an hundred fifty "
31 The c' of the other Elam, a thousand "
32 The c' of Harim, three hundred and "
33 The c' of Lod, Hadid, and Ono, seven "
34 The c' of Jericho, three hundred "
35 The c' of Senaah, three thousand "
36 The priests: the c' of Jedaiah, of "
37 The c' of Immer, a thousand fifty "
38 The c' of Pashur, a thousand two "
39 The c' of Harim, a thousand and "
40 The c' of Jeshua and Kadmiel, "
40 of the c' of Hodaviah, seventy "
41 The singers: the c' of Asaph, an "
42 The c' of the porters: the "
42 the c' of Shallum, the c' of Ater, "
42 the c' of Talmon, the c' of Akkub, "
42 the c' of Hatita, the c' of Shobai, "
43 the c' of Ziha, the c' of Hasupha, "
43 the c' of Tabbaoth, in all an "
44 The c' of Keros, the c' of Siaha, "
44 the c' of Padon, "
45 The c' of Lebanah, "
45 the c' of Hagabah, "
45 the c' of Akkub, "
46 The c' of Hagab, the c' of Shalmai, "
46 the c' of Hanan, "
47 The c' of Giddel, the c' of Gahar, "
47 the c' of Reaiah, "
48 The c' of Rezin, the c' of Nekoda, "
48 the c' of Gazzam, "
49 The c' of Uzza, the c' of Paseah, "
49 the c' of Besai, "
50 The c' of Asnah, the c' of Mehunim, "
50 the c' of Nephusim, "
51 The c' of Bakbuk, the c' of Hakupha, "
51 the c' of Harhur, "
52 The c' of Bazluth, the c' of Mehida, "
52 the c' of Harsha, "
53 The c' of Barkos, the c' of Sisera, "
53 the c' of Thamah, "
54 The c' of Neziah, the c' of Hatipha, "
55 The c' of Solomon's servants: "
55 the c' of Sotai, the c' of Sophereth, "
55 the c' of Peruda, "
56 The c' of Jaalah, the c' of Darkon, "
56 the c' of Giddel, "
57 The c' of Shephatiah, "
57 the c' of Hattil, "
57 the c' of Pochereth of Zebaim, "
57 the c' of Ami. "
58 and the c' of Solomon's servants, "
60 The c' of Delaiah, the c' of Tobiah, "
60 the c' of Nekoda, "
61 And of the c' of the priests: "
61 the c' of Habaiah, the c' of Koz, "
61 the c' of Barzillai; "
3: 1 and the c' of Israel were in the "
4: 1 heard that the c' of the captivity "
6:16 And the c' of Israel, the priests, "
16 the rest of the c' of the captivity, "
19 the c' of the captivity kept the "
20 for all the c' of the captivity, and "
21 And the c' of Israel, which were "
7: 7 went up some of the c' of Israel, "
8:35 c' of those that had been carried "
9:12 an inheritance to your c' forever. "
10: 1 of men and women and c': 3206
7 unto all the c' of the captivity, 1121
16 the c' of the captivity did so. "
44 and wives by whom they had c'. "
Ne 1: 6 for the c' of Israel thy servants, "
6 confess the sins of the c' of Israel, "
2:10 seek the welfare of the c' of Israel. "
5: 5 our c' as their c': and, lo, we bring "
7: 6 These are the c' of the province, "
8 The c' of Parosh, two thousand "
9 The c' of Shephatiah, three "
10 The c' of Arah, six hundred fifty "
11 The c' of Pahath-moab, of the "
11 c' of Jeshua and Joab, "
12 The c' of Elam, a thousand two "
13 The c' of Zatu, eight hundred "
14 The c' of Zaccai, seven hundred "
15 The c' of Binnui, six hundred "
16 The c' of Bebai, six hundred "
17 The c' of Azgad, two thousand "
18 The c' of Adonikam, six hundred "
19 The c' of Bigvai, two thousand "

Ne 7:20 The c' of Adin, six hundred fifty 1121
21 The c' of Ater of Hezekiah, ninety "
22 The c' of Hashum, three hundred "
23 The c' of Bezai, three hundred "
24 The c' of Hariph, an hundred "
25 The c' of Gibeon, ninety and five. "
34 The c' of the other Elam, "
35 The c' of Harim, three hundred "
36 The c' of Jericho, three hundred "
37 The c' of Lod, Hadid, and Ono, "
38 The c' of Senaah, three thousand "
39 the c' of Jedaiah, of the house of "
40 The c' of Immer, a thousand "
41 The c' of Pashur, a thousand "
42 The c' of Harim, a thousand "
43 the c' of Jeshua of Kadmiel, and "
43 of the c' of Hodevah, seventy and "
44 the c' of Asaph, an hundred forty "
45 the c' of Shallum, the c' of Ater, "
45 the c' of Talmon, the c' of Akkub, "
45 the c' of Hatita, the c' of Shobai, "
46 the c' of Ziha, the c' of Hashupha, "
46 the c' of Tabbaoth, "
47 The c' of Keros, the c' of Sia, "
47 the c' of Padon, "
48 The c' of Lebana, the c' of Hagaba, "
48 the c' of Shalmai, "
49 The c' of Hanan, the c' of Giddel, "
49 the c' of Gahar, "
50 The c' of Reaiah, the c' of Rezin, "
50 the c' of Nekoda, "
51 The c' of Gazzam, the c' of Uzza, "
51 the c' of Phaseah, "
52 The c' of Besai, the c' of Meunim, "
52 the c' of Nephishesim, "
53 The c' of Bakbuk, the c' of Hakupha, "
53 the c' of Harhur, "
54 The c' of Bazlith, the c' of Mehida, "
54 the c' of Harsha, "
55 The c' of Barkos, the c' of Sisera, "
55 the c' of Tamah, "
56 The c' of Neziah, the c' of Hatipha, "
57 The c' of Solomon's servants: "
57 the c' of Sotai, the c' of Sophereth, "
57 the c' of Perida, "
58 The c' of Jaala, the c' of Darkon, "
58 the c' of Giddel, "
59 The c' of Shephatiah, "
59 the c' of Hattil, "
59 the c' of Pochereth of Zebaim, "
59 the c' of Amon. "
60 and the c' of Solomon's servants, "
62 The c' of Delaiah, the c' of Tobiah, "
62 the c' of Nekoda, "
63 the c' of Habaiah, the c' of Koz, "
63 the c' of Barzillai, "
73 the c' of Israel were in their cities, "
8:14 the c' of Israel should dwell in "
17 had not the c' of Israel done so. "
9: 1 the c' of Israel were assembled "
23 Their c' also multipliedst thou "
24 c' went in and possessed the land, "
10:39 the c' of Israel and the c' of Levi "
11: 3 and the c' of Solomon's servants. "
4 certain of the c' of Judah, and of the "
4 c' of Benjamin. Of the c' of Judah; "
4 of Mahalaleel, of the c' of Perez; "
24 c' of Zerah the son of Judah, "
25 c' of Judah dwelt at Kirjath-arba, "
31 c' also of Benjamin from Geba "
12:43 the wives also and the c' rejoiced: 3206
47 them unto the c' of Aaron. *1121
13: 2 they met not the c' of Israel "
16 sabbath unto the c' of Judah, "
24 their c' spake half in the speech "
Es 3:13 and old, little c' and women, 2945
5:11 and the multitude of his c', 1121
Job 5: 4 His c' are far from safety, and "
8: 4 If thy c' have sinned against him, "
17: 5 even the eyes of his c' shall fail. "
19:18 young c' despised me; I arose, "
20:10 His c' shall seek to please the poor, 1121
21:11 like a flock, and their c' dance. 3206
19 layeth up his iniquity for his c': 1121
24: 5 food for them and for their c'. 5288
27:14 If his c' be multiplied, it is for 1121
29: 5 my c' were about me; 5288
30: 8 c' of fools, yea, c' of base men: 1121
41:34 a king over all the c' of pride. * "
Ps 11: 4 his eyelids try, the c' of men. "
12: 1 fail from among the c' of men. "
14: 2 from heaven upon the c' of men, to "
17:14 are full of c', and leave the rest * "
21:10 seed from among the c' of men. "
34:11 Come, ye c', hearken unto me: "
36: 7 the c' of men put their trust "
45: 2 art fairer than the c' of men: "
16 of thy fathers shall be thy c', "
53: 2 from heaven upon the c' of men, to "
66: 5 in his doing toward the c' of men. "
69: 8 and an alien unto my mother's c'. "
72: 4 he shall save the c' of the needy, "
73:15 against the generation of thy c'. "
78: 4 will not hide them from their c', "
5 make them known to their c': "
6 the c' which should be born; "
6 and declare them to their c': "
9 The c' of Ephraim, being armed, "
82: 6 of you are c' of the most High. * "
83: 8 they have holpen the c' of Lot. "
89:30 If his c' forsake my law, and walk "
90: 3 and sayest, Return, ye c' of men. "
16 and thy glory unto their c'. "
102:28 c' of thy servants shall continue, "
103: 7 his acts unto the c' of Israel. "
13 Like as a father pitieth his c', so "

Ps 103:17 righteousness unto children's c'; 1121
105: 6 ye c' of Jacob his chosen. "
107: 8, 15, 21, 31 works to the c' of men! "
109: 9 Let his c' be fatherless, and his wife "
10 Let his c' be continually vagabonds, "
12 be any to favour his fatherless c'. "
113: 9 and to be a joyful mother of c'. 1121
115:14 more and more, you and your c'. "
16 earth hath he given to the c' of men. "
127: 3 Lo, c' are an heritage of the Lord: "
4 so are the c' of the youth. "
128: 3 thy c' like olive plants round about "
6 thou shalt see thy children's c', "
132:12 If thy c' will keep my covenant "
12 c' shall also sit upon the throne "
137: 7 c' of Edom in the day of Jerusalem; "
144: 7 from the hand of strange c'; * "
11 me from the hand of strange c', * "
147:13 he hath blessed thy c' within thee. "
148:12 and maidens; old men, and c': 5288
14 even of the c' of Israel, a people 1121
149: 2 c' of Zion be joyful in their king. "
Pr 4: 1 Hear, ye c', the instruction of a * "
5: 7 Hear me now therefore, O ye c', * "
7:24 unto me now therefore, O ye c', * "
8:32 hearken unto me, O ye c': "
13:22 an inheritance to his children's c': "
14:26 his c' shall have a place of refuge. "
15:11 the hearts of the c' of men? "
17: 6 Children's c' are the crown of old "
6 and the glory of c' are their fathers. "
20: 7 his c' are blessed after him. "
31:28 her c' arise up and call her blessed; "
Ec 6: 3 If a man beget an hundred c', "
Ca 1: 6 mother's c' were angry with me; *1121
Isa 1: 2 I have nourished and brought up c', "
4 c' that are corrupters: they have "
2: 6 themselves in the c' of strangers, 3206
3: 4 I will give c' to be their princes, 5288
12 people, c' are their oppressors, 5768
8:18 c' whom the Lord hath given me 3206
11:14 the c' of Ammon shall obey them. 1121
13:16 c' also shall be dashed to pieces *5768
18 their eye shall not spare c'. 1121
14:21 Prepare slaughter for his c' for "
17: 3 be as the glory of the c' of Israel, "
9 left because of the c' of Israel: "
21:17 the mighty men of the c' of Kedar, "
23: 4 nor bring forth c', neither do I *
27:12 one by one, O ye c' of Israel. 1121
29:23 he seeth his c', the work of mine 3206
30: 1 the rebellious c', saith the Lord, 1121
9 lying c', that will not hear the "
31: 6 c' of Israel have deeply revolted. "
37: 3 for the c' are come to the birth, "
12 and the c' of Eden which were in "
38:19 the c' shall make known thy truth. "
47: 8 neither shall I know the loss of c': "
9 day, the loss of c', and widowhood:
49:17 Thy c' shall make haste; thy 1121
20 The c' which thou shalt have,
21 I have lost my c', and am desolate,
25 and I will save thy c'. 1121
54: 1 for more are the c' of the desolate "
1 than the c' of the married wife, "
13 thy c' shall be taught of the Lord; "
13 great shall be the peace of thy c'. "
57: 4 are ye not c' of transgression, 3206
5 slaying c' in the valleys under the "
63: 8 my people, c' that will not lie: 1121
66: 8 travailed, she brought forth her c'. "
20 the c' of Israel bring an offering "
Jer 2: 9 your children's c' will I plead. "
16 the c' of Noph and Tahapanes "
30 In vain have I smitten your c'; "
3:14 O backsliding c', saith the Lord; "
19 shall I put thee among the c', "
21 supplications of the c' of Israel: "
22 Return, ye backsliding c', and I "
4:22 are sottish c', and they have none "
5: 7 thy c' have forsaken me, and sworn "
6: 1 O ye c' of Benjamin, gather "
11 pour it out upon the c' abroad, 5768
7:18 c' gather wood, and the fathers 1121
30 c' of Judah have done evil in my "
9:21 to cut off the c' from without, and 5768
26 and Edom, and the c' of Ammon, 1121
10:20 my c' are gone forth of me, and "
15: 7 will bereave them of c', I will destroy "
16:14 the c' of Israel out of the land of 1121
15 that brought up the c' of Israel "
17: 2 their c' remember their altars "
19 in the gate of the c' of the people, "
18:21 deliver up their c' to the famine, "
21 wives be bereaved of their c', *
23: 7 brought up the c' of Israel out of 1121
25:21 Moab, and the c' of Ammon, "
30:20 Their c' also shall be as aforetime, "
31:15 Rahel weeping for her c' refused "
15 to be comforted for her c', "
17 Lord, that thy c' shall come again "
32:18 the bosom of their c' after them: "
30 For the c' of Israel and the "
30 c' of Judah have done evil before "
30 c' of Israel have only provoked me "
32 c' of Israel and of the c' of Judah, "
39 them, and of their c' after them: "
38:23 wives and thy c' to the Chaldeans: "
40: 7 men, and women, and c', and of 2945
41:16 women, and the c', and the eunuchs, "
43: 6 and c', and the king's daughters, "
47: 3 shall not look back to their c' 1121
49: 6 the captivity of the c' of Ammon, "
11 Leave thy fatherless c', I will preserve
50: 4 the c' of Israel shall come, 1121
4 they and the c' of Judah together "

Jer 50:33 The c' of Israel and the c' of Judah 1121
La 1: 5 her c' are gone into captivity *5768
16 my c' are desolate, because the 1121
2:11 the c' and the sucklings swoon 5768
19 the life of thy young c', that faint
20 their fruit, and c' of a span long? 5768
3:33 nor grieve the c' of men. 1121
4: 4 young c' ask bread, and no man 5768
10 women have sodden their own c': 3206
5:13 and the c' fell under the wood. 5288
Eze 2: 3 I send thee to the c' of Israel, 1121
4 are impudent c' and stiffhearted. "
3:11 captivity, unto the c' of thy people, "
4:13 c' of Israel eat their defiled bread "
6: 5 dead carcases of the c' of Israel "
9: 6 maids, and little c', and women: 2945
16:21 hast slain my c', and delivered 1121
36 blood of thy c', which thou didst "
45 lotheth her husband and her c'; "
45 lothed their husbands and their c': "
20:18 unto their c' in the wilderness, "
21 the c' rebelled against me: they "
23:39 had slain their c' to their idols, "
31:14 in the midst of the c' of men, "
33: 2 man, speak to the c' of thy people, "
12 man, say unto the c' of thy people, "
17 Yet the c' of thy people say, The "
30 c' of thy people still are talking "
35: 5 shed the blood of the c' of Israel "
37:16 the c' of Israel his companions: "
18 the c' of thy people shall speak "
21 take the c' of Israel from among "
25 their c', and their children's c' "
43: 7 in the midst of the c' of Israel "
44: 9 any stranger that is among the c' "
15 c' of Israel went astray from me, "
47:22 shall beget the c' among you: "
22 country among the c' of Israel; "
48:11 when the c' of Israel went astray, "
Da 1: 3 bring certain of the c' of Israel, "
4 C' in whom was no blemish, but *3206
6 c' of Judah, Daniel, Hananiah, 1121
10 the c' which are of your sort? *3206
13 countenance of the c' that eat * "
15 the c' which did eat the portion * "
17 for these four c', God gave them * "
2:38 wheresoever the c' of men dwell, 1123
5:13 which art of the c' of the captivity "
6:13 Daniel, which is of the c' of the "
24 the den of lions, them, their c', "
11:41 and the chief of the c' of Ammon. 1121
12: 1 standeth for the c' of thy people: "
Ho 1: 2 and c' of whoredoms: 3206
10 number of the c' of Israel shall be 1121
11 the c' of Judah and the c' of Israel "
2: 4 will not have mercy upon her c'; "
4 for they be the c' of whoredoms. "
3: 1 toward the c' of Israel, who look to "
4 c' of Israel shall abide many days "
5 shall the c' of Israel return, "
4: 1 word of the Lord, ye c' of Israel: "
6 I will also forget thy c'. "
5: 7 for they have begotten strange c': "
9:12 Though they bring up their c', "
13 Ephraim shall bring forth his c' "
10: 9 Gibeah against the c' of iniquity "
14 was dashed in pieces upon her c'. "
11:10 the c' shall tremble from the west. "
13:13 place of the breaking forth of c'. "
Joe 1: 3 Tell ye your c' of it, and "
3 let your c' tell their c', "
3 and their c' another generation. "
2:16 gather the c', and those that suck 5768
23 Be glad then, ye c' of Zion, and 1121
3: 6 The c' also of Judah and the "
6 c' of Jerusalem have ye sold unto "
8 into the hand of the c' of Judah, "
16 the strength of the c' of Israel. "
19 violence against the c' of Judah, "
Am 1:13 transgressions of the c' of Ammon, "
2:11 not even thus, O ye c' of Israel? "
3: 1 spoken against you, O c' of Israel, "
12 so shall the c' of Israel be taken "
4: 5 ye c' of Israel, saith the Lord God. "
9: 7 Are ye not as c' of the Ethiopians "
7 unto me, O c' of Israel? "
Ob 12 have rejoiced over the c' of Judah "
20 host of the c' of Israel shall possess "
Mic 1:16 and poll thee for thy delicate c'; "
2: 9 c' have ye taken away my glory 5768
5: 3 shall return unto the c' of Israel. 1121
Na 3:10 young c' also were dashed in pieces 5768
Zep 1: 8 the princes, and the king's c', *1121
2: 8 the revilings of the c' of Ammon, "
9 the c' of Ammon as Gomorrah, "
Zec 10: 7 their c' shall see it, and be glad; "
9 they shall live with their c', and "
Mal 4: 6 the heart of the fathers to the c', "
6 the heart of the c' to their fathers, "
M't 2:16 and slew all the c' that were in 3816
18 Rachel weeping for her c', and 5043
3: 9 to raise up c' unto Abraham. "
5: 9 they shall be called the c' of God. *5207
45 That ye may be the c' of your * "
7:11 to give good gifts unto your c', 5043
8:12 But the c' of the kingdom shall be *5207
9:15 Can the c' of the bridechamber * "
10:21 and the c' shall rise up against 5043
11:16 It is like unto c' sitting in the 3808
19 But wisdom is justified of her c'. *5043
12:27 by whom do your c' cast them *5207
13:38 seed are the c' of the kingdom; * "
38 tares are the c' of the wicked * "
14:21 men, beside women and c'. 3813
15:38 men, beside women and c'. "
M't 17:25 of their own c', or of strangers? *5207
26 saith unto him, Then are the c' * "
18: 3 and become as little c', ye shall 3813
25 him to be sold, and his wife, and c', 5043
19:13 brought unto him little c', that 3813
14 Jesus said, Suffer little c', and forbid "
29 or c', or lands, for my name's 5043
20:20 him the mother of Zebedee's c' *5207
21:15 and the c' crying in the temple, 3816
22:24 If a man die, having no c', his 5043
23:31 that ye are the c' of them which *5207
37 would I have gathered thy c' 5043
27: 9 they of the c' of Israel did value; 5207
25 His blood be on us, and on our c'. 5043
56 and the mother of Zebedee's c'. *5207
M'r 2:19 Can the c' of the bridechamber * "
7:27 said unto her, Let the c' first be 5043
9:37 receive one of such c' in my 3813
10:13 And they brought young c' to "
14 Suffer the little c' to come unto "
24 C', how hard is it for them that 5043
29 or wife, or c', or lands, for my "
30 mothers, and c', and lands, with "
12:19 and leave no c', that his brother * "
13:12 and c' shall rise up against their "
Lu 1:16 many of the c' of Israel shall he 5207
17 the hearts of the fathers to the c', 5043
3: 8 to raise up c' unto Abraham. "
5:34 Can ye make the c' of the *5207
6:35 ye shall be the c' of the Highest: * "
7:32 like unto c' sitting in the 3813
35 wisdom is justified of all her c'. 5043
11: 7 my c' are with me in bed; I cannot 3813
13 to give good gifts unto your c': 5043
13:34 have gathered thy c' together, as "
14:26 c', and brethren, and sisters, yea, "
16: 8 for the c' of this world are *5207
8 wiser than the c' of light. "
18:16 Suffer little c' to come unto me, 3813
29 or wife, or c', for the kingdom of 5043
19:44 and thy c' within thee; and they "
20:28 he died without c', that his *815
29 took a wife, and died without c'. * "
31 and they left no c', and died. 5043
34 The c' of this world marry, and *5207
36 and are the c' of God, being * "
36 the c' of the resurrection. * "
23:28 for yourselves, and for your c'. 5043
Joh 4:12 drank thereof himself, and his c', *5207
8:39 If ye were Abraham's c', ye would 5043
11:52 c' of God that were scattered "
12:36 that ye may be the c' of light. *5207
13:33 Little c', yet a little while I am 5040
21: 5 Jesus saith unto them, C', have ye 3813
Ac 2:39 is unto you, and to your c', 5043
3:25 Ye are the c' of the prophets, *5207
5:21 all the senate of the c' of Israel, "
7:19 they cast out their young c', to *1025
23 visit his brethren the c' of Israel. 5207
37 which said unto the c' of Israel, "
9:15 Gentiles, and kings, and the c' of "
10:36 God sent unto the c' of Israel, "
13:26 c' of the stock of Abraham, "
33 fulfilled the same unto us their c', 5043
21: 5 on our way, with wives and c', "
21 ought not to circumcise their c', "
Ro 8:16 spirit, that we are the c' of God: "
17 And if c', then heirs; heirs of God, "
21 the glorious liberty of the c' of God. "
9: 7 seed of Abraham, are they all c': "
8 They which are the c' of the flesh, "
8 these are not the c' of God: "
8 the c' of the promise are counted "
11 (For the c' being not yet born, "
26 be called the c' of the living God. *5207
27 the number of the c' of Israel be "
1Co 7:14 else were your c' unclean; but 5043
14:20 be not c' in understanding, 3813
20 howbeit in malice be ye c', but *3515
2Co 3: 7 so that the c' of Israel could not 5207
13 that the c' of Israel could not "
6:13 (I speak as unto my c',) be ye also 5043
12:14 the c' ought not to lay up for the "
14 but the parents for the c'. "
Ga 3: 7 the same are the c' of Abraham. *5207
26 ye are all the c' of God by faith * "
4: 3 when we were c', were in 3516
19 My little c', of whom I travail 5040
25 and is in bondage with her c'. 5043
27 the desolate hath many more c' "
28 as Isaac was, are the c' of promise. "
31 we are not c' of the bondwoman, "
Eph 1: 5 us unto the adoption of c' by *5206
2: 2 worketh in the c' of disobedience: *5207
3 were by nature the c' of wrath, 5043
4:14 be no more c', tossed to and fro, 3516
5: 1 followers of God, as dear c'; 5043
6 God upon the c' of disobedience. *5207
8 in the Lord: walk as c' of light: 5043
6: 1 C', obey your parents in the Lord: "
4 provoke not your c' to wrath, "
Col 3: 6 cometh on the c' of disobedience: *5207
20 C', obey your parents in all 5043
21 provoke not your c' to anger, "
1Th 2: 7 even as a nurse cherisheth her c': "
11 as a father doth his c', "
5: 5 Ye are all the c' of light, *5207
5 and the c' of the day: "
1Ti 3: 4 having his c' in subjection with 5043
12 ruling their c' and their own "
5: 4 But if any widow have c' or "
10 if she have brought up c', if she 5044
14 younger women marry, bear c', 5041
Tit 1: 6 having faithful c', not accused of 5043
2: 4 their husbands, to love their c', 5388
Heb 2:13 Behold I and the c' which God 3813
14 then as the c' are partakers "
11:22 of the departing of the c' of Israel; 5027
12: 5 speaketh unto you as unto c'. * "
1Pet 1:14 As obedient c', not fashioning 5043
2Pet 2:14 with covetous practices; cursed c': "
1Jo 2: 1 My little c', these things write I 5040
12 I write unto you, little c', because "
13 I write unto you, little c', because 3813
18 Little c', it is the last time: and "
28 And now, little c', abide in him; 5040
3: 7 Little c', let no man deceive you: "
10 In this the c' of God are manifest, 5043
10 and the c' of the devil: "
18 My little c', let us not love in 5040
4: 4 Ye are of God, little c', and have "
5: 2 know that we love the c' of God, 5043
21 Little c', keep yourselves from 5040
2Jo 1 unto the elect lady and her c', 5043
4 that I found of thy c' walking in "
13 The c' of thy elect sister greet "
3Jo 4 joy I have to hear that my c' walk "
Re 2:14 before the c' of Israel, to eat 5207
23 And I will kill her c' with death; 5043
7: 4 of all the tribes of the c' of Israel. 5207
21:12 the twelve tribes of the c' of Israel: "

children of Israel See CHILDREN and ISRAEL.

children of men See CHILDREN and MEN.

children's
Ge 31:16 father, that is ours, and our c': 1121
45:10 thy c' children, and thy flocks, and "
Ex 9: 4 die of all that is the c' of Israel. * "
34: 7 the c' children, unto the third "
Jos 14: 9 inheritance, and thy c' for ever, * "
2Ki 17:41 children, and their c' children: "
Job 19:17 I entreated for the c' sake of * "
Ps 103:17 righteousness unto c' children; "
128: 6 see thy c' children, and peace "
Pro 13:22 leaveth an inheritance to his c' "
17: 6 C' children are the crown of old men; "
Jer 2: 9 and with your c' children will "
31:29 and the c' teeth are set on edge. "
Eze 18: 2 the c' teeth are set on edge? "
37:25 their c' children for ever: and my "
M't 15:26 It is not meet to take the c' bread, 5043
M'r 7:27 it is not meet to take the c' bread, "
28 the table eat of the c' crumbs. 3813

child's
Ex 2: 8 went and called the c' mother. 3206
1Ki 17:21 let this c' soul come into him again. "
Job 33:25 flesh shall be fresher than a c': 5290
M't 2:20 which sought the young c' life. 3813

Chileab (*kil'-e-ab*) See also DANIEL.
2Sa 3: 3 And his second, C', of Abigail the 3609

Chilion (*kil'-e-on*) See also CHILION'S.
Ru 1: 2 of his two sons Mahlon and C', 3630
5 And Mahlon and C' died also "

Chilion's (*kil'-e-ons*)
Ru 4: 9 Elimelech's, and all that was C' 3630

Chilmad (*kil'-mad*)
Eze 27:23 of Sheba, Asshur, and C'. 3638

Chimham (*kim'-ham*)
2Sa 19:37 But behold thy servant C'; let 3643
38 the king answered, C' shall go "
40 and C' went on with him: and all "
Jer 41:17 and dwelt in the habitation of C', "

chimney
Hos 13: 3 and as the smoke out of the c'. 699

Chinnereth (*kin'-ne-reth*) See also CHINNEROTH; CINNEROTH; GENNESARET.
Nu 34:11 the side of the sea of C' eastward: 3672
Deu 3:17 C' even unto the sea of the plain, "
Jos 13:27 even unto the edge of the sea of C'. "
19:35 and Hammath, Rakkath, and C', "

Chinneroth (*kin'-ne-roth*) See also CHINNERETH.
Jos 11: 2 and the plains south of C', 3672
12: 3 from the plain to the sea of C' "

Chios (*ki'-os*)
Ac 20:15 the next day over against C'; 5508

Chisleu (*kis'-lew*)
Ne 1: 1 month C', in the twentieth year, 3691
Zec 7: 1 of the ninth month, even in C'; "

Chislon (*kis'-lon*)
Nu 34:21 Benjamin, Elidad the son of C' 3692

Chisloth-tabor (*kis''-loth-ta'-bor*) See also CHESULLOTH.
Jos 19:12 sunrising unto the border of C'. 3696

Chittim (*kit'-tim*) See also KITTIM.
Nu 24:24 shall come from the coast of C'. 3794
Isa 23: 1 from the land of C' it is revealed "
12 pass over to C'; there also shalt "
Jer 2:10 For pass over the isles of C', "
Eze 27: 6 brought out of the isles of C'. "
Da 11:30 ships of C' shall come against him: "

Chiun (*ki'-un*) See also REMPHAN.
Am 5:26 tabernacle of your Moloch and C' 3594

Chloe (*clo'-e*)
1Co 1:11 which are of the house of C', 5514

chode
Ge 31:36 was wroth, and c' with Laban: 7378
Nu 20: 3 And the people c' with Moses, * "

choice See also CHOICEST.
Ge 23: 6 c' of our sepulchres bury thy dead; 4005
49:11 his ass's colt unto the c' vine; 8321

De 12:11 your c' vows which ye vow unto 4005
1Sa 9: 2 a c' young man, and a goodly: * 970
2Sa 10: 9 chose of all the c' men of Israel, 977
2Ki 3:19 fenced city, and every c' city, 4005
19:23 and the c' fir trees thereof: "
1Ch 7:40 c' and mighty men of valour, 1305
19:10 all the c' of Israel, and put them 970
2Ch 25: 5 three hundred thousand c' men, * "
Ne 5:18 one ox and six c' sheep; also 1305
Pr 8:10 knowledge rather than c' gold. 977
19 and my revenue than c' silver. "
10:20 tongue of the just is as c' silver: "
Ca 6: 9 is the c' one of her that bare her. 1249
Isa 37:24 the c' fir trees thereof: and I will 4005
Jer 22: 7 shall cut down thy c' cedars, "
Eze 24: 4 shoulder, fill it with the c' bones. "
5 Take the c' of the flock, and burn "
31:16 Eden, the c' and best of Lebanon, "
Ac 15: 7 God made c' among us, that the *1586*

choicest
Isa 5: 2 planted it with the c' vine, 8321
22: 7 c' valleys shall be full of chariots, 4005

choke See also CHOKED.
M't 13:22 deceitfulness of riches, c' the *4846*
M'r 4:19 entering in, c' the word, and it "

choked
M't 13: 7 thorns sprung up, and c' them: *638*
M'r 4: 7 c' it, and it yielded no fruit. *4846*
5:13 and were c' in the sea. *4155*
Lu 8: 7 sprang up with it, and c' it. *638*
14 and are c' with cares and riches *4846*
33 place into the lake, and were c'. ‡ *638*

choler (*col'-ur*)
Dan 8: 7 was moved with c' against him, 4843
11:11 the south shall be moved with c', "

choose See also CHOOSEST; CHOOSETH; CHOOSING; CHOSE; CHOSEN.
Ex 17: 9 C' us out men, and go out, 977
Nu 16: 7 the man whom the Lord doth c', "
17: 5 the man's rod, whom I shall c', "
De 7: 7 nor c' you, because ye were more "
12: 5 the Lord your God shall c' out "
11 God shall c' to cause his name "
14 the place which the Lord shall c' "
18 which the Lord thy God shall c', "
26 the place which the Lord shall c': "
14:23 the place which he shall c' to "
24 which the Lord thy God shall c', "
25 which the Lord thy God shall c': "
15:20 the place which the Lord shall c', "
16: 2 the place which the Lord shall c' "
6 which the Lord thy God shall c' "
7 which the Lord thy God shall c': "
15 the place which the Lord shall c': "
16 in the place which he shall c'; "
17: 8 which the Lord thy God shall c'; "
10 which the Lord shall c' shall shew "
15 whom the Lord thy God shall c': "
18: 6 the place which the Lord shall c'; "
23:16 that place which he shall c' in one "
26: 2 God shall c' to place his name "
30:19 therefore c' life, that both "
31:11 in the place which he shall c', "
Jos 9:27 in the place which he should c'. "
24:15 c' you this day whom ye will serve; "
1Sa 2:28 did I c' him out of all the tribes "
17: 8 c' you a man for you, and let 1262
2Sa 16:18 and all the men of Israel, c', * 977
17: 1 Let me now c' out twelve thousand "
21: 6 of Saul, whom the Lord did c'. * 972
24:12 c' thee one of them, that I may do 977
1Ki 14:21 which the Lord did c' out of all * "
18:23 and let them c' one bullock for "
25 C' you one bullock for yourselves, "
1Ch 21:10 c' thee one of them, that I may "
11 Thus saith the Lord, C' thee *6901
Ne 9: 7 the God, who didst c' Abram, 977
Job 9:14 and c' out my words to reason "
34: 4 Let us c' to us judgment: let us "
33 thou refuse, or whether thou c'; "
Ps 25:12 teach in the way that he shall c'. "
47: 4 He shall c' our inheritance for us, "
Pr 1:29 did not c' the fear of the Lord: "
3:31 oppressor, and c' none of his ways. "
Isa 7:15, 16 refuse the evil, and c' the good, "
14: 1 and will yet c' Israel, and set them "
49: 7 of Israel, and he shall c' thee. * "
56: 4 and c' the things that please me, "
65:12 c' that wherein I delighted not. "
66: 4 I also will c' their delusions, "
Eze 21:19 c' thou a place, c' it at the head *1254
Zec 1:17 Zion, and shall yet c' Jerusalem. 977
2:12 and shall c' Jerusalem again. "
Phil 1:22 yet what I shall c' I wot not. *138*

choosest
Job 15: 5 thou c' the tongue of the crafty. 977
Ps 65: 4 Blessed is the man whom thou c', "

chooseth
Job 7:15 So that my soul c' strangling, 977
Isa 40:20 he hath no oblation c' a tree that "
41:24 an abomination is he that c' you. "

choosing
Heb 11:25 C' rather to suffer affliction with *138*

chop
Mic 3: 3 their bones, and c' them in pieces, 6566

Chor-ashan (*cor-a'-shan*)
1Sa 30:30 and to them which were in C', 3565

Chorazin (*co-ra'-zin*)
M't 11:21 Woe unto thee, C'! woe unto *5523*
Lu 10:13 Woe unto thee, C'! woe unto "

chose
Ge 6: 2 them wives of all which they c'. 977
13:11 Lot c' him all the plain of Jordan; "
Ex 18:25 Moses c' able men out of all Israel, "
De 4:37 therefore he c' their seed after them, "
10:15 and he c' their seed after them, "
Jos 8: 3 Joshua c' out thirty thousand "
J'g 5: 8 They c' new gods; then was war in "
1Sa 13: 2 Saul c' him three thousand men "
17:40 and c' him five smooth stones out "
2Sa 6:21 which c' me before thy father, "
10: 9 behind, he c' of all the choice men "
1Ki 8:16 I c' no city out of all the tribes of "
16 but I c' David to be over my people "
11:34 David my servant's sake whom I c', "
1Ch 19:10 c' out of all the choice of Israel, "
28: 4 the Lord God of Israel c' me before "
2Ch 6: 5 I c' no city among all the tribes "
5 neither c' I any man to be a ruler "
Job 29:25 I c' out their way, and sat chief, "
Ps 78:67 and c' not the tribe of Ephraim: "
68 But c' the tribe of Judah, the "
70 He c' David also his servant, "
Isa 66: 4 and c' that in which I delighted not. "
Eze 20: 5 In the day when I c' Israel, "
Lu 6:13 of them he c' twelve, whom also *1586*
14: 7 they c' out the chief rooms; saying "
Ac 6: 5 they c' Stephen, a man full of faith "
13:17 c' our fathers, and exalted the "
15:40 And Paul c' Silas, and departed, *1951*

chosen
Ex 14: 7 he took six hundred c' chariots, 970
15: 4 his c' captains also are drowned 4005
Nu 16: 5 even him whom he hath c' will * 977
De 7: 6 the Lord thy God hath c' thee to be "
12:21 which the Lord thy God hath c' * "
14: 2 the Lord hath c' thee to be a "
16:11 the Lord thy God hath c' to place* "
18: 5 For the Lord thy God hath c' him "
21: 5 Lord thy God hath c' to minister "
Jos 24:22 that ye have c' you the Lord to "
J'g 10:14 cry unto the gods which ye have c'; "
20:15 numbered seven hundred c' men. 970
16 there were seven hundred c' men "
34 ten thousand c' men out of all "
1Sa 8:18 your king which ye shall have c' 977
10:24 See ye him whom the Lord hath c', "
12:13 the king whom ye have c', and "
16: 8, 9 Neither hath the Lord c' this. "
10 Jesse, The Lord hath not c' these. "
20:30 that thou hast c' the son of Jesse "
24: 2 Saul took three thousand c' men 970
26: 2 having three thousand c' men of "
2Sa 6: 1 together all the c' men of Israel, "
1Ki 3: 8 thy people which thou hast c', 977
8:44 toward the city which thou hast c', "
48 the city which thou hast c', and the "
11:13 Jerusalem's sake which I have c'. "
32 sake, the city which I have c' out of "
36 Jerusalem, the city which I have c' "
12:21 hundred and fourscore thousand c' 970
2Ki 21: 7 which I have c' out of all tribes 977
23:27 Jerusalem, which I have c', and the "
1Ch 9:22 c' to be porters in the gates 1305
15: 2 them hath the Lord c' to carry the 977
16:13 ye children of Jacob, his c' ones. 972
41 the rest that were c', who were 1305
28: 4 he hath c' Judah to be the ruler; 977
5 he hath c' Solomon my son to sit "
6 I have c' him to be my son, and I "
10 heed now; for the Lord hath c' thee "
29: 1 whom alone God hath c', is yet "
2Ch 6: 6 But I have c' Jerusalem, that my "
6 and have c' David to be over my "
34 toward this city which thou hast c', "
38 toward the city which thou hast c', "
7:12 and have c' this place to myself for "
16 For now have I c' and sanctified "
11: 1 fourscore thousand c' men which 970
12:13 which the Lord had c' out of all 977
13: 3 four hundred thousand c' men: 970
3 eight hundred thousand c' men, "
17 five hundred thousand c' men. "
29:11 Lord hath c' you to stand before 977
33: 7 which I have c' before all the tribes "
Ne 1: 9 the place that I have c' to set "
Job 36:21 for this hast thou c' rather than "
Ps 33:12 the people whom he hath c' for his "
78:31 smote down the c' men of Israel. *970
89: 3 I have made a covenant with my c', 972
19 exalted one c' out of the people. 970
105: 6 servant, ye children of Jacob his c'. 972
26 and Aaron whom he had c'. 977
43 with joy, and his c' with gladness: 972
106: 5 That I may see the good of thy c', "
23 had not Moses his c' stood before "
119:30 I have c' the way of truth: thy 977
173 help me; for I have c' thy precepts. "
132:13 the Lord hath c' Zion; he hath "
135: 4 the Lord hath c' Jacob unto himself, "
Pr 16:16 rather to be c' than silver! "
22: 1 A good name is rather to be c' "
Isa 1:29 for the gardens that ye have c'. "
41: 8 servant, Jacob whom I have c', "
9 I have c' thee, and not cast thee "
43:10 and my servant whom I have c': "
20 to give drink to my people, my c'. 972
44: 1 Israel, whom I have c': 977
2 and thou, Jesurun, whom I have c'. "
48:10 c' thee in the furnace of affliction. "
58: 5 Is it such a fast that I have c'? "
6 Is not this the fast that I have c'? "
65:15 your name for a curse unto my c': 972
66: 3 they have c' their own ways, and 977
Jer 8: 3 death shall be c' rather than life "
33:24 families which the Lord hath c', * 977
48:15 and his c' young men are gone 4005
49:19 and who is a c' man, that I may 977
50:44 from her: and who is a c' man, "
Eze 23: 7 with all them that were the c' *4005
Da 11:15 neither his c' people, neither "
Hag 2:23 for I have c' thee, saith the Lord 977
Zec 3: 2 the Lord that hath c' Jerusalem "
M't 12:18 my servant, whom I have c'; *140*
20:16 for many be called, but few c'. **1588*
22:14 many are called, but few are c'. "
M'r 13:20 the elect's sake, whom he hath c', **1586*
Lu 10:42 Mary hath c' that good part, which "
23:35 if he be Christ, the c' of God. *1588*
Joh 6:70 Have not I c' you twelve, and one **1586*
13:18 I know whom I have c': "
15:16 Ye have not c' me, * "
16 but I have c' you, and * "
19 I have c' you out of the world, * "
Ac 1: 2 the apostles whom he had c': "
24 whether of these two thou hast c', "
9:15 he is a c' vessel unto me, to bear *1589*
10:41 unto witnesses c' before of God, *4401*
15:22 to send c' men of their own **1586*
25 to send c' men unto you with our* "
22:14 hath c' thee, that thou shouldest **4400*
Ro 16:13 Salute Rufus c' in the Lord, and *1588*
1Co 1:27 God hath c' the foolish things of **1586*
27 God hath c' the weak things of * "
28 which are despised, hath God c', * "
2Co 8:19 who was also c' of the churches **5500*
Eph 1: 4 as he hath c' us in him before the **1586*
2Th 2:13 God hath from the beginning c' * *138*
2Ti 2: 4 he may please him who hath c' **4758*
Jas 2: 5 Hath not God c' the poor of this **1586*
1Pe 2: 4 but c' of God, and precious, **1588*
9 ye are a c' generation, a royal * "
Re 17:14 him are called, and c', and faithful. "

Chozeba (*ko-ze'-bah*) See also CHEZIB.
1Ch 4:22 and the men of C', and Joash, 3578

Christ (*krist*) see also ANTICHRIST; CHRISTIAN; CHRIST'S; CHRISTS; JESUS; MESSIAH.
M't 1: 1 book of the generation of Jesus C', *5547*
16 was born Jesus, who is called C'. "
17 unto C' are fourteen generations. "
18 the birth of Jesus C' was on this "
2: 4 of them where C' should be born. "
11: 2 heard in the prison the works of C', "
16:16 Thou art the C', the Son of the "
20 no man that he was Jesus the C'. "
22:42 What think ye of C'? whose son "
23: 8 one is your Master, even C'; and * "
10 for one is your Master, even C'. "
24: 5 my name, saying, I am C'; and "
23 Lo, here is C', or there; believe it "
26:63 whether thou be the C', the Son "
68 Prophesy unto us, thou C', Who is "
27:17 or Jesus which is called C'? "
22 with Jesus which is called C'? "
M'r 1: 1 of the gospel of Jesus C', "
8:29 saith unto him, Thou art the C'. "
9:41 because ye belong to C', verily I * "
12:35 How say the scribes that C' is the "
13: 6 saying, I am C'; and shall * "
21 Lo, here is C'; or, lo, he is there; *5547*
14:61 Art thou the C', the Son of the "
15:32 Let C' the King of Israel descend "
Lu 2:11 a Saviour, which is C' the Lord. "
26 before he had seen the Lord's C'. "
3:15 whether he were the C', or not; "
4:41 Thou art C' the Son of God. * "
41 for they knew that he was C'. "
9:20 answering said, The C' of God. "
20:41 say they that C' is David's son? "
21: 8 in my name, saying, I am C'; and* "
22:67 Art thou the C'? tell us. And he *5547*
23: 2 saying that he himself is C' a king. "
35 if he be C', the chosen of God. "
39 saying, If thou be C', save thyself "
24:26 Ought not C' to have suffered "
46 thus it behoved C' to suffer, and to "
Joh 1:17 grace and truth came by Jesus C'. "
20 but confessed, I am not the C'. "
25 if thou be not that C', nor Elias, "
41 which is, being interpreted, the C'. "
3:28 said, I am not the C', but that I am "
4:25 Messias cometh, which is called C': "
29 that even I did: is not this the C'? "
42 this is indeed the C', the Saviour of "
6:69 are sure that thou art that C', * "
7:26 indeed that this is the very C'? "
27 when C' cometh, no man knoweth "
31 When C' cometh, will he do more "
41 Others said, This is the C'. But "
41 Shall C' come out of Galilee? "
42 C' cometh of the seed of David, and "
9:22 man did confess that he was C', "
10:24 If thou be the C', tell us plainly. "
11:27 I believe that thou art the C', "
12:34 the law that C' abideth for ever: "
17: 3 Jesus C', whom thou hast sent. "
20:31 might believe that Jesus is the C', "
Ac 2:30 raise up C' to sit on his throne; * "
31 spake of the resurrection of C', "
36 ye have crucified, both Lord and C'. "
38 in the name of Jesus C' for the "
3: 6 In the name of Jesus C' of "
18 prophets, that C' should suffer, he "
20 And he shall send Jesus C', which "
4:10 that by the name of Jesus C' of "
26 the Lord, and against his C'. * "
5:42 to teach and preach Jesus C'. "
8: 5 Samaria, and preached C' unto "
12 and the name of Jesus C', they were "

Ac 8:37 that Jesus C· is the Son of God. *5547
9:20 preached C· in the synagogues, * "
22 proving that this is very C·. "
34 Jesus C· maketh thee whole: "
10:36 peace by Jesus C·: (he is Lord of "
11:17 believed on the Lord Jesus C·; "
15:11 the grace of the Lord Jesus C· "
26 for the name of our Lord Jesus C·. "
16:18 thee in the name of Jesus C· to "
31 Believe on the Lord Jesus C·, and* "
17: 3 C· must needs have suffered, and "
3 whom I preach unto you, is C·. "
18: 5 to the Jews that Jesus was C·. "
28 the scriptures that Jesus was C·. "
19: 4 after him, that is, on C· Jesus. * "
20:21 faith toward our Lord Jesus C·. "
24:24 him concerning the faith in C·. "
26:23 That C· should suffer, and that "
28:31 which concern the Lord Jesus C·, "
Ro 1: 1 Paul, a servant of Jesus C·, called "
3 Concerning his Son Jesus C· our * "
6 ye also the called of Jesus C·: * "
7 our Father, and the Lord Jesus C·. "
8 I thank my God through Jesus C· "
16 not ashamed of the gospel of C·: * "
2:16 judge the secrets of men by Jesus C· "
3:22 is by faith of Jesus C· unto all "
24 redemption that is in C· Jesus: "
5: 1 God through our Lord Jesus C·: "
6 in due time C· died for the ungodly. "
8 were yet sinners, C· died for us. "
11 through our Lord Jesus C·, by "
15 which is by one man, Jesus C·, "
17 shall reign in life by one, Jesus C·.) "
21 eternal life by Jesus C· our Lord. "
6: 3 were baptized into Jesus C· were "
4 as C· was raised up from the dead "
8 if we be dead with C·, we believe "
9 Knowing that C· being raised from "
11 God, through Jesus C· our Lord. "
23 eternal life through Jesus C· our "
7: 4 dead to the law by the body of C·; "
25 God through Jesus C· our Lord. "
8: 1 to them which are in C· Jesus, "
2 Spirit of life in C· Jesus hath "
9 any man have not the Spirit of C·, "
10 if C· be in you, the body is dead "
11 that raised up C· from the dead "
17 of God, and joint-heirs with C·; "
34 It is C· that died, yea rather, that "
35 separate us from the love of C·? "
39 love of God, which is in C· Jesus "
9: 1 I say the truth in C·, I lie not, my "
3 accursed from C· for my brethren, "
5 C· came, who is over all, God "
10: 4 C· is the end of the law for "
6 (that is, to bring C· down from "
7 (that is, to bring up C· again from "
12: 5 being many, are one body in C·, "
13:14 But put ye on the Lord Jesus C·, "
14: 9 C· both died, and rose, and revived, "
10 before the judgment seat of C·. * "
15 with thy meat, for whom C· died. "
18 that in these things serveth C· is "
15: 3 For even C· pleased not himself; "
5 another according to C· Jesus: "
6 the Father of our Lord Jesus C·. "
7 as C· also received us to the glory "
8 Jesus C· was a minister of the "
16 minister of Jesus C· to the Gentiles, "
17 I may glory through Jesus C· in "
18 things which C· hath not wrought "
19 fully preached the gospel of C·. "
20 not where C· was named, lest I "
29 the blessing of the gospel of C·. "
16: 3 Aquila my helpers in C· Jesus: "
5 the firstfruits of Achaia unto C·. "
7 who also were in C· before me. "
9 Urbane, our helper in C·, and "
10 Salute Apelles approved in C·. "
16 The churches of C· salute you. "
18 such serve not our Lord Jesus C·, "
20 of our Lord Jesus C· be with you. "
24 our Lord Jesus C· be with you all.* "
25 and the preaching of Jesus C·, "
27 wise, be glory through Jesus C· "
1Co 1: 1 apostle of Jesus C· through the will "
2 them that are sanctified in C· Jesus, "
2 call upon the name of Jesus C· "
3 and from the Lord Jesus C·. "
4 which is given you by Jesus C·; "
6 of C· was confirmed in you: "
7 the coming of our Lord Jesus C·: "
8 in the day of our Lord Jesus C·. "
9 of his Son Jesus C· our Lord. "
10 by the name of our Lord Jesus C·, "
12 and I of Cephas; and I of C·. "
13 Is C· divided? was Paul crucified "
17 C· sent me not to baptize, but to "
17 C· should be made of none effect. "
23 But we preach C· crucified, "
24 C· the power of God, and the "
30 But of him are ye in C· Jesus, "
2: 2 save Jesus C·, and him crucified. "
16 But we have the mind of C·. "
3: 1 even as unto babes in C·. "
11 that is laid, which is Jesus C·. "
23 ye are Christ's; and C· is God's. "
4: 1 ministers of C·, and stewards of "
10 sake, but ye are wise in C·; "
15 ten thousand instructors in C·, yet "
15 for in C· Jesus I have begotten "
17 of my ways which be in C·, "
5: 4 the name of our Lord Jesus C·, * "
4 the power of our Lord Jesus C·, * "

1Co 5: 7 C· our passover is sacrificed for 5547
6:15 bodies are the members of C·? "
15 I then take the members of C·, "
8: 6 Jesus C·, by whom are all things, "
11 brother perish, for whom C· died? "
12 conscience, ye sin against C·. "
9: 1 have I not seen Jesus C· our Lord?* "
12 we should hinder the gospel of C·. "
18 the gospel of C· without charge, * "
21 under the law to C·,) that I might "
10: 4 and that rock was C·. "
9 neither let us tempt C·, as some * "
16 communion of the blood of C·? "
16 communion of the body of C·? "
11: 1 of me, even as I also am of C·. "
3 that the head of every man is C·; "
3 man; and the head of C· is God. "
12:12 are one body: so also is C·. "
27 are the body of C·, and members "
15: 3 C· died for our sins according to "
12 if C· be preached that he rose "
13 of the dead, then is C· not risen: "
14 if C· be not risen, then is our "
15 of God that he raised up C·: "
16 rise not, then is not C· raised: "
17 C· be not raised, your faith is vain; "
18 also which are fallen asleep in C· "
19 this life only we have hope in C·, "
20 now is C· risen from the dead, "
22 in C· shall all be made alive. "
23 C· the firstfruits; afterward they "
31 which I have in C· Jesus our Lord, "
57 victory through our Lord Jesus C·. "
16:22 man love not the Lord Jesus C·, "
23 of our Lord Jesus C· be with you. "
24 love be with you all in C· Jesus. "
2Co 1: 1 of Jesus C· by the will of God, "
2 and from the Lord Jesus C·. "
3 the Father of our Lord Jesus C·, "
5 sufferings of C· abound in us, "
5 consolation also aboundeth by C·. "
19 C·, who was preached among you "
21 stablisheth us with you in C·, "
2:10 forgave I it in the person of C·; "
14 always causeth us to triumph in C·, "
15 unto God a sweet savour of C·, "
17 in the sight of God speak we in C·. "
3: 3 the epistle of C· ministered by us, "
4 have we through C· to God-ward: "
14 which vail is done away in C·. "
4: 4 light of the glorious gospel of C·, "
5 ourselves, but C· Jesus the Lord; "
6 glory of God in the face of Jesus C·. "
5:10 judgment seat of C·; that every "
14 For the love of C· constraineth us; "
16 we have known C· after the flesh, "
17 if any man be in C·, he is a new "
18 us to himself by Jesus C·, and hath "
19 God was in C·, reconciling the "
20 we are ambassadors for C·, as "
6:15 what concord hath C· with Belial? "
8: 9 the grace of our Lord Jesus C·, "
23 the churches, and the glory of C·. "
9:13 subjection unto the gospel of C·, "
10: 1 meekness and gentleness of C·, "
5 thought to the obedience of C·; "
14 in preaching the gospel of C·: "
11: 2 you as a chaste virgin to C·. "
3 from the simplicity that is in C·. "
10 truth of C· is in me, no man shall "
13 themselves into the apostles of C·. "
23 Are they ministers of C·? (I speak "
31 the Father of our Lord Jesus C·,* "
12: 2 a man in C· above fourteen years "
9 power of C· may rest upon me. "
19 we speak before God in C·: but "
13: 3 seek a proof of C· speaking in me, "
5 Jesus C· is in you, except ye be "
14 grace of the Lord Jesus C·, and "
Ga 1: 1 neither by man, but by Jesus C·, "
3 and from our Lord Jesus C·, "
6 grace of C· unto another gospel: "
7 would pervert the gospel of C·. "
10 should not be the servant of C·. "
12 but by the revelation of Jesus C·. "
22 of Judæa which were in C·: "
2: 4 in C· Jesus, that they might bring "
16 law, but by the faith of Jesus C·, "
16 we have believed in Jesus C·, "
16 be justified by the faith of C·, "
17 we seek to be justified by C·, "
17 is therefore C· the minister of sin? "
20 I am crucified with C·: "
20 yet not I, but C· liveth in me: "
21 by the law, then C· is dead in vain. "
3: 1 C· hath been evidently set forth, "
13 C· hath redeemed us from the "
14 on the Gentiles through Jesus C·; "
16 one, And to thy seed, which is C·. "
17 confirmed before of God in C·, * "
22 promise by faith of Jesus C· "
24 schoolmaster to bring us unto C·, "
26 of God by faith in C· Jesus. "
27 baptized into C· have put on C·. "
28 for ye are all one in C· Jesus. "
4: 7 then an heir of God through C·. * "
14 angel of God, even as C· Jesus. "
19 in birth again until C· be formed "
5: 1 wherewith C· hath made us free, "
2 C· shall profit you nothing. "
4 C· is become of no effect unto you, "
6 in Jesus C· neither circumcision "
6: 2 burdens, and so fulfil the law of C·. "
12 persecution for the cross of C·. "
14 cross of our Lord Jesus C·, by "

Ga 6:15 in C· Jesus neither circumcision *5547
18 Lord Jesus C· be with your spirit. "
Eph 1: 1 Paul, an apostle of Jesus C· by the "
1 and to the faithful in C· Jesus: "
2 and from the Lord Jesus C·. "
3 Father of our Lord Jesus C·, who "
3 in heavenly places in C·: "
5 children by Jesus C· to himself, "
10 all things in C·, both which are in "
12 his glory, who first trusted in C·. "
17 God of our Lord Jesus C·, the "
20 Which he wrought in C·, when he "
2: 5 quickened us together with C·, "
6 in heavenly places in C· Jesus: "
7 toward us through C· Jesus. "
10 in C· Jesus unto good works, "
12 without C·, being aliens from the "
13 now in C· Jesus, ye who sometimes "
13 are made nigh by the blood of C·. "
20 C· himself being the chief corner "
3: 1 prisoner of Jesus C· for you "
4 knowledge in the mystery of C·) "
6 his promise in C· by the gospel: "
8 the unsearchable riches of C·; "
9 created all things by Jesus C·: * "
11 which he purposed in C· Jesus "
14 Father of our Lord Jesus C·, * "
17 C· may dwell in your hearts by "
19 the love of C·, which passeth "
21 by C· Jesus throughout all ages, "
4: 7 to the measure of the gift of C·. "
12 for the edifying of the body of C·: "
13 of the stature of the fulness of C·: "
15 which is the head, even C·: "
20 ye have not so learned C·; "
5: 2 as C· also hath loved us, and hath "
5 in the kingdom of C· and of God. "
14 dead, and C· shall give thee light. "
20 in the name of our Lord Jesus C·; "
23 C· is the head of the church: "
24 as the church is subject unto C·, "
25 even as C· also loved the church, "
32 concerning C· and the church. "
6: 5 of your heart, as unto C·; "
6 the servants of C·, doing the will "
23 Father and the Lord Jesus C·. "
24 our Lord Jesus C· in sincerity. "
Ph'p 1: 1 the servants of Jesus C·, to all "
1 to all the saints in C· Jesus "
2 Father, and from the Lord Jesus C·. "
6 perform it until the day of Jesus C·: "
8 you all in the bowels of Jesus C·. "
10 without offence till the day of C·; "
11 are by Jesus C·, unto the glory "
13 my bonds in C· are manifest in all "
15 indeed preach C· even of envy and "
16 The one preach C· of contention, "
18 or in truth, C· is preached; "
19 supply of the Spirit of Jesus C·, "
20 C· shall be magnified in my body, "
21 For me to live is C·, and to die is "
23 to depart, and to be with C·; "
26 may be more abundant in Jesus C· "
27 as it becometh the gospel of C·: "
29 it is given in the behalf of C·, not "
2: 1 be therefore any consolation in C·, "
5 you, which was also in C· Jesus: "
11 Jesus C· is Lord, to the glory of God "
16 I may rejoice in the day of C·, "
30 for the work of C· he was nigh "
3: 3 rejoice in C· Jesus, and have no "
7 those I counted loss for C·. "
8 knowledge of C· Jesus my Lord: "
8 but dung, that I may win C·, "
9 which is through the faith of C·, "
12 I am apprehended of C· Jesus. "
14 the high calling of God in C· Jesus. "
18 are the enemies of the cross of C·: "
20 for the Saviour, the Lord Jesus C·: "
4: 7 hearts and minds through C· Jesus. "
13 C· which strengtheneth me. * "
19 to his riches in glory by C· Jesus. "
21 Salute every saint in C· Jesus. "
23 The grace of our Lord Jesus C· be "
Col 1: 1 an apostle of Jesus C· by the will "
2 saints and faithful brethren in C· "
2 Father and the Lord Jesus C·. * "
3 the Father of our Lord Jesus C·, "
4 we heard of your faith in C· Jesus, "
7 for you a faithful minister of C·; "
24 the afflictions of C· in my flesh for "
27 is C· in you, the hope of glory: "
28 every man perfect in C· Jesus: "
2: 2 and of the Father, and of C·; "
5 stedfastness of your faith in C·. "
6 therefore received C· Jesus the "
8 of the world, and not after C·. "
11 flesh by the circumcision of C·: "
17 but the body is of C·. * "
20 dead with C· from the rudiments "
3: 1 If ye then be risen with C·, "
1 where C· sitteth on the right hand "
3 your life is hid with C· in God. "
4 C·, who is our life, shall appear, "
11 but C· is all, and in all. "
13 as C· forgave you, so also do ye. * "
16 the word of C· dwell in you richly "
24 for ye serve the Lord C·. "
4: 3 speak the mystery of C·, for which "
12 a servant of C·, saluteth you, * "
1Th 1: 1 Father and in the Lord Jesus C·: "
1 Father, and the Lord Jesus C·. * "
3 hope in our Lord Jesus C·, in "
2: 6 burdensome, as the apostles of C·. "
14 which in Judæa are in C· Jesus: "

1Th 2:19 our Lord Jesus C· at his coming? *5547
3: 2 fellowlabourer in the gospel of C·, "
11 Lord Jesus C·, direct our way * "
13 the coming of our Lord Jesus C· * "
4:16 the dead in C· shall rise first: "
5: 9 salvation by our Lord Jesus C·, "
18 this is the will of God in C· Jesus "
23 the coming of our Lord Jesus C·. "
28 The grace of our Lord Jesus C· be "
2Th 1: 1 our Father and the Lord Jesus C·: "
2 our Father and the Lord Jesus C·. "
8 the gospel of our Lord Jesus C·: * "
12 the name of our Lord Jesus C· * "
12 of our God and the Lord Jesus C·. "
2: 1 the coming of our Lord Jesus C·, "
2 as that the day of C· is at hand. * "
14 the glory of our Lord Jesus C·. "
16 Now our Lord Jesus C· himself, "
3: 5 into the patient waiting for C·. "
6 in the name of our Lord Jesus C·, "
12 and exhort by our Lord Jesus C·, "
18 The grace of our Lord Jesus C· be "
1Ti 1: 1 Paul, an apostle of Jesus C· by the "
1 our Saviour, and Lord Jesus C·, "
2 our Father and Jesus C· our Lord. "
12 thank C· Jesus our Lord, who hath "
14 and love which is in C· Jesus. "
15 that C· Jesus came into the world "
16 first Jesus C· might shew forth "
2: 5 and men, the man C· Jesus; "
7 speak the truth in C·, and lie not;)* "
3:13 in the faith which is in C· Jesus. "
4: 6 be a good minister of Jesus C·, "
5:11 begun to wax wanton against C·, "
21 before God, and the Lord Jesus C·, "
6: 3 the words of our Lord Jesus C·, "
13 C· Jesus, who before Pontius Pilate "
14 appearing of our Lord Jesus C·: "
2Ti 1: 1 an apostle of Jesus C· by the will "
1 promise of life which is in C· Jesus, "
2 the Father and C· Jesus our Lord. "
9 in C· Jesus before the world began, "
10 appearing of our Saviour Jesus C·, "
13 and love which is in C· Jesus. "
2: 1 in the grace that is in C· Jesus. "
3 as a good soldier of Jesus C·. "
8 Remember that Jesus C· of the "
10 is in C· Jesus with eternal glory. "
19 that nameth the name of C· * "
3:12 live godly in C· Jesus shall suffer "
15 through faith which is in C· Jesus. "
4: 1 Lord Jesus C·, who shall judge "
22 Lord Jesus C· be with thy spirit. "
Tit 1: 1 an apostle of Jesus C·, according to "
4 and the Lord Jesus C· our Saviour. "
2:13 great God and our Saviour Jesus C·; "
3: 6 through Jesus C· our Saviour; "
Ph'm 1 Paul, a prisoner of Jesus C·, "
3 our Father and the Lord Jesus C·. "
6 thing which is in you in C· Jesus. "
8 be much bold in C· to enjoin thee "
9 now also a prisoner of Jesus C·. "
23 my fellowprisoner in C· Jesus; "
25 grace of our Lord Jesus C· be with "
Heb 3: 1 Priest of our profession, C· Jesus * "
6 C· as a son over his own house; "
14 For we are made partakers of C·, "
5: 5 also C· glorified not himself to be "
6: 1 the principles of the doctrine of C·, "
9:11 But C· being come an high priest "
14 much more shall the blood of C·, "
24 C· is not entered in to the holy places "
28 C· was once offered to bear the sins "
10:10 of the body of Jesus C· once for all. "
11:26 the reproach of C· greater riches "
13: 8 Jesus C· the same yesterday, and "
21 in his sight, through Jesus C·; "
Jas 1: 1 Lord Jesus C·, to the twelve tribes "
2: 1 faith of our Lord Jesus C·, the Lord "
1Pe 1: 1 Peter, an apostle of Jesus C·, to "
2 sprinkling of the blood of Jesus C·: "
3 and Father of our Lord Jesus C·, "
3 resurrection of Jesus C· from the "
7 glory at the appearing of Jesus C·: "
11 the spirit of C· which was in them "
11 beforehand the sufferings of C·, "
13 you at the revelation of Jesus C·; "
19 precious blood of C·, as of a lamb "
2: 5 acceptable to God by Jesus C·. "
21 because C· also suffered for us, "
3:16 your good conversation in C·. "
18 C· also hath once suffered for sins, "
21 by the resurrection of Jesus C·: "
4: 1 Forasmuch then as C· hath suffered "
11 may be glorified through Jesus C·, "
14 be reproached for the name of C·, "
5: 1 a witness of the sufferings of C·, "
10 his eternal glory by C· Jesus, "
14 with you all that are in C· Jesus. "
2Pe 1: 1 Peter, an apostle of Jesus C·, to "
1 of God and our Saviour Jesus C·: "
8 knowledge of our Lord Jesus C·. "
11 of our Lord and Saviour Jesus C·. "
14 as our Lord Jesus C· hath shewed "
16 and coming of our Lord Jesus C·, "
2:20 of the Lord and Saviour Jesus C·, "
3:18 of our Lord and Saviour Jesus C·. "
1Jo 1: 3 Father, and with his Son Jesus C·. "
7 and the blood of Jesus C· his Son * "
2: 1 the Father, Jesus C· the righteous: "
22 that denieth that Jesus is the C·? "
3:23 on the name of his son Jesus C·, "
4: 2 that Jesus C· is come in the flesh "
3 confesseth not that Jesus C· is * "
5: 1 believeth that Jesus is the C· is "

1Jo 5: 6 water and blood, even Jesus C·: 5547
20 is true, even in his Son Jesus C·. "
2Jo 3 Lord Jesus C·, the son of the Father, "
7 that Jesus C· is come in the flesh. "
9 abideth not in the doctrine of C·, "
9 that abideth in the doctrine of C·,* "
Jude 1 the servant of Jesus C·, and brother "
1 preserved in Jesus C·, and called: "
4 Lord God, and our Lord Jesus C·. "
17 the apostles of our Lord Jesus C·; "
21 the mercy of our Lord Jesus C· "
Re 1: 1 Revelation of Jesus C·, which God "
2 testimony of Jesus C·, and of all "
5 from Jesus C·, who is the faithful "
9 kingdom and patience of Jesus C·, "
9 and for the testimony of Jesus C·. "
11:15 of our Lord, and of his C·; "
12:10 our God, and the power of his C·: "
17 have the testimony of Jesus C·. * "
20: 4 reigned with C· a thousand years. "
6 shall be priests of God and of C·, "
22:21 Lord Jesus C· be with you all. * "

Christ Jesus See CHRIST and JESUS.

Christ's (*krists*)
Ro 15:30 for the Lord Jesus C· sake, and *5547
1Co 3:23 ye are C·; and Christ is God's. "
4:10 for C· sake, but ye are wise in "
7:22 is called, being free, is C· servant. "
15:23 fruits; afterward they that are C· "
2Co 2:12 C· gospel, and a door was opened* "
5:20 in C· stead, be ye reconciled to * "
10: 7 man trust to himself that he is C·,* "
7 think this again, that, as he is C·, "
7 even so are we C·. * "
12:10 in distresses for C· sake: "
Ga 3:29 if ye be C·, then are ye Abraham's "
5:24 are C· have crucified the flesh * "
Eph 4:32 God for C· sake hath forgiven * "
Ph'p 2:21 not the things which are Jesus C·.* "
1Pe 4:13 as ye are partakers of C· "

Christs (*krists*)
M't 24:24 For there shall arise false C·, and 5580
M'r 13:22 For false C· and false prophets "

Christian (*kris'-tyan*) See also CHRISTIANS.
Ac 26:28 thou persuadest me to be a C·. 5546
1Pe 4:16 if any man suffer as a C·, let him "

Christians (*kris'-tyans*)
Ac 11:26 disciples were called C· first in 5546

chronicles
1Ki 14:19 c· of the kings of Israel? 1697, 3117
29 c· of the kings of Judah? " "
15: 7, 23 c· of the kings of Judah? " "
31 c· of the kings of Israel? " "
16: 5, 14, 20, 27 c· of . . . Israel? " "
22:39 c· of the kings of Israel? " "
45 c· of the kings of Judah? " "
2Ki 1:18 c· of the kings of Israel? " "
8:23 c· of the kings of Judah? " "
10:34 c· of the kings of Israel? " "
12:19 c· of the kings of Judah? " "
13: 8, 12 c· of the kings of Israel? " "
14:15 c· of the kings of Israel? " "
18 c· of the kings of Judah? " "
28 c· of the kings of Israel? " "
15: 6 c· of the kings of Judah? " "
11, 15, 21, 26, 31 c· of . . . Israel? " "
36 c· of the kings of Judah? " "
20:20 c· of the kings of Judah? " "
21:17, 25 c· of the kings of Judah? " "
23:28 c· of the kings of Judah? " "
24: 5 c· of the kings of Judah? " "
1Ch 27:24 c· of King David. " "
Neh 12:23 book of the c· even until " "
Es 2:23 book of the c· before the king " "
6: 1 records of the c·; and they " "
10: 2 c· of the kings of Media and " "

chrysolite (*cris'-o-lite*)
Re 21:20 the seventh, c·; the eighth, beryl: 5555

chrysoprasus (*cris'-o-pra-sus*)
Re 21:20 the tenth, a c·; the eleventh, a 5556

Chub (*cub*)
Eze 30: 5 all the mingled people, and C·. 3552

Chun (*kun*)
1Ch 18: 8 from Tibhath, and from C·, cities 3560

church See also CHURCHES.
M't 16:18 upon this rock I will build my c·; 1577
18:17 tell it unto the c·: "
17 but if he neglect to hear the c·, "
Ac 2:47 the Lord added to the c· daily * "
5:11 fear came upon all the c·, and "
7:38 he, that was in the c· in the "
8: 1 against the c· which was at "
3 he made havock of the c·, "
11:22 the c· which was in Jerusalem: "
26 assembled themselves with the c·, "
12: 1 his hands to vex certain of the c·. "
5 without ceasing of the c· unto God "
13: 1 Now there were in the c· that was "
14:23 ordained them elders in every c·, "
27 and had gathered the c· together, "
15: 3 brought on their way by the c·, "
4 they were received of the c·, and of "
22 and elders, with the whole c·, "
18:22 gone up, and saluted the c·, he "
20:17 and called the elders of the c·. "
28 overseers, to feed the c· of God, "
Ro 16: 1 is a servant of the c· which is at "

Ro 16: 5 greet the c· that is in their house. 1577
23 mine host, and of the whole c·. "
subscr. by Phebe servant of the c· * "
1Co 1: 2 Unto the c· of God which is at "
4:17 I teach everywhere in every c·. "
6: 4 who are least esteemed in the c·. "
10:32 Gentiles; nor to the c· of God: "
11:18 when ye come together in the c·, "
22 or despise ye the c· of God, and "
12:28 God hath set some in the c·, "
14: 4 that prophesieth edifieth the c·. "
5 interpret, that the c· may receive "
12 excel to the edifying of the c·. "
19 in the c· I had rather speak five "
23 therefore the whole c· be come "
28 let him keep silence in the c·; "
35 for women to speak in the c·. "
15: 9 I persecuted the c· of God. "
16:19 with the c· that is in their house. "
2Co 1: 1 unto the c· of God which is "
Ga 1:13 I persecuted the c· of God, and "
Eph 1:22 the head over all things to the c·, "
3:10 might be known by the c· the "
21 glory in the c· by Christ Jesus "
5:23 Christ is the head of the c·: "
24 Therefore as the c· is subject unto "
25 as Christ also loved the c·, and "
27 present it to himself a glorious c·, "
29 even as the Lord the c·: "
32 concerning Christ and the c·. "
Ph'p 3: 6 Concerning zeal, persecuting the c·; "
4:15 no c· communicated with me "
Col 1:18 the head of the body, the c·: "
24 for his body's sake, which is the c·: "
4:15 and the c· which is in his house. "
16 it be read also in the c· of the "
1Th 1: 1 unto the c· of the Thessalonians "
2Th 1: 1 unto the c· of the Thessalonians "
1Ti 3: 5 take care of the c· of God?) "
15 the c· of the living God, the pillar "
5:16 let not the c· be charged; "
2Ti *subscr.* first bishop of the c· of the * "
Ti *subscr.* first bishop of the c· of the * "
Ph'm 2 to the c· in thy house: "
Heb 2:12 in the midst of the c· will I sing * "
12:23 general assembly and c· of the "
Jas 5:14 call for the elders of the c·; "
1Pe 5:13 The c· that is at Babylon, elected* "
3Jo 6 of thy charity before the c·: "
9 I wrote unto the c·: but "
10 and casteth them out of the c·. "
Rev 2: 1 the angel of the c· of Ephesus "
8 the angel of the c· in Smyrna "
12 to the angel of the c· in Pergamos "
18 the angel of the c· in Thyatira. "
3: 1 the angel of the c· in Sardis write; "
7 the angel of the c· in Philadelphia "
14 the angel of the c· of the Laodiceans "

churches
Ac 9:31 Then had the c· rest throughout *1577
15:41 and Cilicia, confirming the c·. "
16: 5 so were the c· established in the "
19:37 which are neither robbers of c·, *2417
Ro 16:4 but also all the c· of the Gentiles. 1577
16 The c· of Christ salute you. "
1Co 7:17 And so ordain I in all c·. "
11:16 custom, neither the c· of God. "
14:33 of peace, as in all c· of the saints. "
34 your women keep silence in the c·: "
16: 1 I have given order to the c· of "
19 The c· of Asia salute you. "
2Co 8: 1 bestowed on the c· of Macedonia; "
18 gospel throughout all the c·; "
19 was also chosen of the c· to travel "
23 they are the messengers of the c·, "
24 ye to them, and before the c·, "
11: 8 I robbed other c·, taking wages of "
28 me daily, the care of all the c·. "
12:13 ye were inferior to other c·, "
Ga 1: 2 unto the c· of Galatia: "
22 unto the c· of Judæa which were "
1Th 2:14 became followers of the c· of God "
2Th 1: 4 glory in you in the c· of God "
Re 1: 4 John to the seven c· which are in "
11 and send it unto the seven c· "
20 are the angels of the seven c·: "
20 which thou sawest are the seven c·. "
2: 7 what the Spirit saith unto the c·; "
11 the Spirit saith unto the c·; He "
17 the Spirit saith unto the c·; To "
23 all the c· shall know that I am he "
29 what the Spirit saith unto the c·. "
3: 6, 13, 22 the Spirit saith unto the c·. "
22:16 unto you these things in the c·. "

churl
Isa 32: 5 nor the c· said to be bountiful. 3596
7 The instruments also of the c· "

churlish
1Sa 25: 3 the man was c· and evil in his 7186

churning
Pr 30:33 c· of milk bringeth forth butter, 4330

Chushan-rishathaim (*cu"-shan-rish-a-tha'-im*)
J'g 3: 8 he sold them into the hand of C· 3573
8 of Israel served C· eight years. "
10 Lord delivered C· into his hand; "
10 and his hand prevailed against C·. "

Chuza (*cu'-zah*)
Lu 8: 3 the wife of C· Herod's steward, ‡5529

cieled
2Ch 3: 5 greater house he c· with fir tree, 2645
Jer 22:14 it is c· with cedar, and painted 5603

Eze 41:16 door, c' with wood round about, 7824
Hag 1: 4 to dwell in your c' houses, 5603

cieling
1Ki 6:15 the house, and the walls of the c': 5604

Cilicia (*sil-ish'-yah*)
Ac 6: 9 and of them of C' and of Asia, 2791
15:23 in Antioch and Syria and C': "
41 And he went through Syria and C'. "
21:39 am a Jew of Tarsus, a city in C', "
22: 3 born in Tarsus, a city in C', "
23:34 he understood that he was of C'; "
27: 5 we had sailed over the sea of C' "
Gal 1:21 into the regions of Syria and C'; "

cinnamon
Ex 30:23 and of sweet c' half so much, 7076
Pr 7:17 my bed with myrrh, aloes, and c'. "
Ca 4:14 calamus and c', with all trees of "
Re 18:13 c', and odours, and ointments, 2792

Cinneroth (*sin'-ne-roth*) See also CHINNEROTH.
1Ki 15:20 and all C', with all the land of 3672

circle
Isa 40:22 sitteth upon the c' of the earth, 2329

circuit See also CIRCUITS.
1Sa 7:16 he went from year to year in c' 5437
Job 22:14 he walketh in the c' of heaven. †2329
Ps 19: 6 and his c' unto the ends of it: 8622

circuits
Ec 1: 6 again according to his c'. 5439

circumcise See also CIRCUMCISED; CIRCUMCISING.
Ge 17:11 shall c' the flesh of your foreskin; *5243
De 10:16 C' therefore the foreskin of your 4135
30: 6 And the Lord thy God will c' thine "
Jos 5: 2 c' again the children of Israel the "
4 is the cause why Joshua did c': "
Jer 4: 4 C' yourselves to the Lord, and take "
Lu 1:59 day they came to c' the child; 4059
Joh 7:22 ye on the sabbath day c' a man. "
Ac 15: 5 That it was needful to c' them, "
21:21 saying that they ought not to c' "

circumcised See also UNCIRCUMCISED.
Ge 17:10 man child among you shall be c'. 4135
12 that is eight days old shall be c' "
13 must needs be circumcised: "
14 whose flesh of his foreskin is not c', "
23 and c' the flesh of their foreskin "
24 was c' in the flesh of his foreskin. "
25 when he was c' in the flesh of his "
26 the selfsame day was Abraham c', "
27 the stranger, were c' with him. "
21: 4 And Abraham c' his son Isaac "
34:15 that every male of you be c'; "
17 will not hearken unto us, to be c'; "
22 if every male among us be c', "
22 as they are c'. "
24 and every male was c', all that "
Ex 12:44 when thou hast c' him, then shall "
48 let all his males be c', and then let "
Le 12: 3 flesh of his foreskin shall be c'. "
Jos 5: 3 c' the children of Israel at the hill "
5 the people that came out were c'. "
5 of Egypt, them they had not c'. "
7 them Joshua c': for they were * "
7 they had not c' them by the way. "
Jer 9:25 all them which are c' with the "
Ac 7: 8 Isaac, and c' him the eighth day; 4059
15: 1 be c' after the manner of Moses, "
24 Ye must be c', and keep the law: "
16: 3 and took and c' him because of "
Ro 4:11 believe, though they be not c'; * 203
1Co 7:18 Is any man called being c'? 4059
18 let him not be c'. "
Ga 2: 3 a Greek, was compelled to be c': "
5: 2 if ye be c', Christ shall profit you * "
3 again to every man that is c', "
6:12 they constrain you to be c'; only "
13 they themselves who are c' keep "
13 desire to have you c', that they may "
Ph'p 3: 5 C' the eighth day, of the stock of 4061
Col 2:11 In whom also ye are c' with the 4059

circumcising
Jos 5: 8 they had done c' all the people, 4135
Lu 2:21 accomplished for the c' of the 4059

circumcision See also UNCIRCUMCISION.
Ex 4:26 husband thou art, because of the c'. 4139
Joh 7:22 Moses therefore gave unto you c'; 4061
23 man on the sabbath day receive c', "
Ac 7: 8 he gave him the covenant of c': "
10:45 they of the c' which believed "
11: 2 they that were of the c' contended "
Ro 2:25 For c' verily profiteth, if thou keep "
25 thy c' is made uncircumcision. "
26 uncircumcision be counted for c'? "
27 the letter and c' dost transgress "
28 is that c', which is outward in the "
29 c' is that of the heart, in the spirit, "
3: 1 what profit is there of c'? "
30 shall justify the c' by faith, and "
4: 9 blessedness then upon the c' only, "
10 when he was in c', or in "
10 Not in c', but in uncircumcision. "
11 And he received the sign of c', "
12 the father of c' to them who are not "
12 them who are not of the c' only, "
15: 8 a minister of the c' for the truth "
1Co 7:19 C' is nothing, and uncircumcision "
Ga 2: 7 gospel of the c' was unto Peter; "
8 Peter to the apostleship of the c', "
9 heathen, and they unto the c'. "
12 fearing them which were of the c'. "
5: 6 neither c' availeth any thing, "
11 if I yet preach c', why do I yet "
Ga 6:15 neither c' availeth any thing, 4061
Eph 2:11 C' in the flesh made by hands; "
Ph'p 3: 3 For we are the c', which worship "
Col 2:11 with the c' made without hands, "
11 sins of the flesh by the c' of Christ: "
3:11 c' nor uncircumcision, Barbarian, "
4:11 called Justus, who are of the c'. "
Tit 1:10 deceivers, specially they of the c': "

circumspect
Ex 23:13 that I have said unto you be c': *8104

circumspectly
Eph 5:15 that ye walk c', not as fools, * 199

Cis (*sis*) See also KISH.
Ac 13:21 Saul the son of C', a man of the 2797

cistern See also CISTERNS.
2Ki 18:31 every one the waters of his c': 953
Pr 5:15 Drink waters out of thine own c', "
Ec 12: 6 or the wheel broken at the c'. "
Isa 36:16 every one the waters of his own c'; "

cisterns
Jer 2:13 hewed them out c', broken c', 877

cities
Ge 13:12 Lot dwelled in the c' of the plain, 5892
19:25 overthrew those c', and all the plain, "
25 and all the inhabitants of the c', "
29 God destroyed the c' of the plain, "
29 overthrew the c' in which Lot dwelt. "
35: 5 the terror of God was upon the c' "
41:35 let them keep food in the c'. "
48 and laid up the food in the c': "
47:21 removed them to c' from one end "
Ex 1:11 built for Pharaoh treasure c', "
Lev 25:32 Notwithstanding the c' of the "
32 and the houses of the c' of their "
33 houses of the c' of the Levites "
34 the field of the suburbs of their c' "
26:25 gathered together within your c', "
31 I will make your c' waste, and "
33 shall be desolate, and your c' waste. "
Nu 13:19 what c' they be that they dwell in, "
28 and the c' are walled, and very "
21: 2 then I will utterly destroy their c'. "
3 utterly destroyed them and their c': "
25 Israel took all these c': and Israel "
25 dwelt in all the c' of the Amorites, "
31:10 burnt all their c' wherein they "
32:16 cattle, and c' for our little ones: "
17 ones shall dwell in the fenced c' "
24 Build you c' for your little ones, "
26 shall be there in the c' of Gilead: "
33 with the c' thereof in the coasts, "
33 the c' of the country round about. "
36 and Beth-haran, fenced c': "
38 unto the c' which they builded. "
35: 2 of their possession c' to dwell in; "
2 unto the Levites suburbs for the c' "
3 the c' shall they have to dwell in; "
4 And the suburbs of the c', which "
5 be to them the suburbs of the c'. "
6 among the c' which ye shall give "
6 there shall be six c' for refuge, "
6 them ye shall add forty and two c'. "
7 all the c' which ye shall give to "
7 Levites shall be forty and eight c': "
8 And the c' which ye shall give "
8 give of his c' unto the Levites "
11 ye shall appoint you c' to be "
11 to be c' of refuge for you; "
12 they shall be unto you c' for refuge "
13 And of these c' which ye shall give "
13 six c' shall ye have for refuge. "
14 give three c' on this side Jordan, "
14 three c' shall ye give in the land "
14 which shall be c' of refuge. "
15 These six c' shall be a refuge, "
De 1:22 and into what c' we shall come. "
28 the c' are great and walled up "
2:34 took all his c' at that time, "
35 the spoil of the c' which we took. "
37 nor unto the c' in the mountains, "
3: 4 we took all his c' at that time, "
4 took not from them, threescore c', "
5 All these c' were fenced with high "
7 spoil of the c', we took for a prey "
10 the c' of the plain, and all Gilead, "
10 c' of the kingdom of Og in Bashan. "
12 half mount Gilead, and the c' "
19 abide in your c' which I have given "
4:41 Then Moses severed three c' on "
42 that fleeing unto one of these c' he "
6:10 to give thee great and goodly c', "
9: 1 c' great and fenced up to heaven, "
13:12 thou shalt hear say in one of thy c', "
19: 1 and dwellest in their c', and in "
2 three c' for thee in the midst of "
5 he shall flee unto one of those c', "
7 Thou shalt separate three c' for "
9 then shalt thou add three c' more "
11 and fleeth into one of these c': "
20:15 Thus shalt thou do unto all the c' "
15 are not of the c' of these nations. "
16 But of the c' of these people, which "
21: 2 they shall measure unto the c' "
Jos 9:17 and came unto their c' on the third "
17 c' were Gibeon, and Chephirah, "
10: 2 a great city, as one of the royal c', "
19 them not to enter into their c': "
20 of them entered into fenced c'. "
37 all the c' thereof, and all the souls "
39 king thereof, and all the c' thereof; "
11:12 all the c' of those kings, and all the "
13 c' that stood still in their strength, "
14 all the spoil of these c', and the "
Jos 11:21 them utterly with their c'. 5892
13:10 c' of Sihon king of the Amorites, "
17 Heshbon, and all her c' that are in "
21 all the c' of the plain, and all the "
23 families, the c' and the villages "
25 all the c' of Gilead, and half the "
28 families, the c', and their villages. "
30 which are in Bashan, threescore c': "
31 c' of the kingdom of Og in Bashan, "
14: 4 c' to dwell in, with their suburbs "
12 that the c' were great and fenced: "
15: 9 out to the c' of mount Ephron; "
21 uttermost c' of the tribe of the "
32 all the c' are twenty and nine, "
36 fourteen c' with their villages. "
41 sixteen c' with their villages. "
44 nine c' with their villages. "
51 eleven c' with their villages. "
54 nine c' with their villages; "
57 ten c' with their villages. "
59 six c' with their villages. "
60 two c' with their villages. "
62 six c' with their villages. "
16: 9 separate c' for the children "
9 all the c' with their villages. "
17: 9 these c' of Ephraim are among "
9 are among the c' of Manasseh; "
12 out the inhabitants of those c'; "
18: 9 the land, and described it by c' "
21 c' of the tribe of the children of "
24 twelve c' with their villages: "
28 fourteen c' with their villages. "
19: 6 thirteen c' with their villages: "
7 four c' and their villages: "
8 that were round about these c' "
15 twelve c' with their villages. "
16 these c' with their villages. "
22 sixteen c' with their villages. "
23 the c' and their villages. "
30 twenty and two c' with their "
31 these c' with their villages. "
35 And the fenced c' are Ziddim, Zer, "
38 nineteen c' with their villages. "
39 the c' and their villages. "
48 these c' with their villages. "
20: 2 Appoint out for you c' of refuge, "
4 flee unto one of those c' shall stand "
9 c' appointed for all the children of "
21: 2 to give us c' to dwell in, with the "
3 Lord, these c' and their suburbs. "
4 the tribe of Benjamin, thirteen c'. "
5 the half tribe of Manasseh, ten c'. "
6 of Manasseh in Bashan, thirteen c'. "
7 of the tribe of Zebulun, twelve c'. "
8 by lot unto the Levites these c' "
9 these c' which are here mentioned "
16 nine c' out of those two tribes. "
18 Almon with her suburbs; four c'. "
19 All the c' of the children of Aaron, "
19 were thirteen c' with their suburbs. "
20 they had the c' of their lot out of "
22, 24 with her suburbs; four c'. "
25 with her suburbs; two c'. "
26 All the c' were ten with their "
27 with her suburbs; two c'. "
29 with her suburbs; four c'. "
31 Rehob with her suburbs; four c'. "
32 Kartan with her suburbs; three c'. "
33 All the c' of the Gershonites were "
33 were thirteen c' with their suburbs. "
35 Nahalal with her suburbs; four c'. "
37 Mephaath with her suburbs; four c'. "
39 Jazer with her suburbs; four c' in "
40 the c' for the children of Merari by "
40 Levites, were by their lot twelve c. "
41 All the c' of the Levites within the "
41 forty and eight c' with their "
42 These c' were every one with their "
42 about them: thus were all these c'. "
24:13 c' which ye built not, and ye dwell "
J'g 10: 4 they had thirty c', which are called "
11:26 the c' that be along by the coasts "
33 come to Minnith, even twenty c', "
12: 7 buried in one of the c' of Gilead. "
20:14 themselves together out of the c' "
15 numbered at that time out of the c' "
42 them which came out of the c' "
48 they set on fire all the c' that they "
21:23 repaired the c', and dwelt in them. "
1Sa 6:18 the number of all the c' of the "
18 of fenced c', and of country villages, "
7:14 the c' which the Philistines had "
18: 6 women came out of all c' of Israel, "
30:29 in the c' of the Jerahmeelites, and "
29 which were in the c' of the Kenites, "
31: 7 dead, they forsook the c', and fled; "
2Sa 2: 1 go up into any of the c' of Judah? "
3 and they dwelt in the c' of Hebron. "
8: 8 and from Berothai, c' of Hadadezer, "
10:12 people, and for the c' of our God: "
12:31 the c' of the children of Ammon. "
20: 6 he get him fenced c', and escape "
24: 7 all the c' of the Hivites, and of the "
1Ki 4:13 threescore great c' with walls and "
8:37 besiege them in the land of their c'; 8179
9:11 Solomon gave Hiram twenty c' in 5892
12 came out from Tyre to see the c' "
13 What c' are these which thou hast "
19 the c' of store that Solomon had, "
19 and c' for his chariots, "
19 and c' for his horsemen, "
10:26 he bestowed in the c' for chariots, "
12:17 Israel which dwelt in the c' of "
13:32 high places which are in the c' of "
15:20 he had against the c' of Israel, "
23 he did, and the c' which he built, "

1Ki 20:34 The c' which my father took from 5892
22:39 all the c' that he built, are they "
2Ki 3:25 And they beat down the c', and on "
13:25 son of Hazael the c', which he had "
25 and recovered the c' of Israel. "
17: 6 Gozan, and in the c' of the Medes. "
9 them high places in all their c', "
24 placed them in the c' of Samaria "
24 Samaria, and dwelt in the c' "
26 and placed in the c' of Samaria, "
29 every nation in their c' wherein "
18:11 and in the c' of the Medes: "
13 come up against all the fenced c' "
19:25 shouldest be to lay waste fenced c' "
23: 5 the high places in the c' of Judah, "
8 all the priests out of the c' of Judah, "
19 the high places that were in the c' "
1Ch 2:22 Jair, who had three and twenty c' "
23 towns thereof, even threescore c'. "
4:31 These were their c' unto the reign "
32 and Tochen, and Ashan, five c': "
33 that were round about the same c', "
6:57 the sons of Aaron they gave the c' "
60 All their c' throughout their "
60 their families were thirteen c'. "
61 of the family of that tribe, were c' *
61 tribe of Manasseh, by lot, ten c'. 5892
62 Manasseh in Bashan, thirteen c'. "
63 of the tribe of Zebulun, twelve c'. "
64 Israel gave to the Levites these c' "
65 these c', which are called by their "
66 the sons of Kohath had c' of their "
67 unto them, of the c' of refuge, "
9: 2 dwelt in their possessions in their c' "
10: 7 they forsook their c', and fled: "
13: 2 Levites which are in their c' and "
18: 8 and from Chun, c' of Hadarezer, "
19: 7 themselves together from their c', "
13 people, and for the c' of our God: "
20: 3 so dealt David with all the c' of "
27:25 the fields, in the c', and in the "
2Ch 1:14 which he placed in the chariot c', "
6:28 besiege them in the c' of their 8179
8: 2 c' which Huram had restored 5892
4 wilderness, and all the store c', "
5 fenced c', with walls, gates, and "
6 all the store c' that Solomon had, "
6 and all the chariot c', "
6 and the c' of the horsemen, "
9:25 he bestowed in the chariot c', and "
10:17 Israel that dwelt in the c' of Judah, "
11: 5 in Jerusalem, and built c' for "
10 Judah and in Benjamin fenced c'. "
12: 4 he took the fenced c' which "
13:19 and took c' from him, Bethel with "
14: 5 out of all the c' of Judah the high "
6 he built fenced c' in Judah: for "
7 unto Judah, Let us build these c', "
14 they smote all the c' round about "
14 them: and they spoiled all the c'; "
15: 8 c' which he had taken from mount "
16: 4 captains of his armies against the c' "
4 and all the store c' of Naphtali. "
17: 2 placed forces in all the fenced c' of "
2 and in the c' of Ephraim, which "
7 to teach in the c' of Judah. "
9 throughout all the c' of Judah, "
12 in Judah castles, and c' of store. "
13 much business in the c' of Judah: "
19 fenced c' throughout all Judah. "
19: 5 fenced c' of Judah, city by city, "
10 brethren that dwell in their c', "
20: 4 out of all the c' of Judah they "
21: 3 things, with fenced c' in Judah: "
23: 2 the Levites out of all the c' of "
24: 5 Go out unto the c' of Judah and "
25:13 fell upon the c' of Judah, from "
26: 6 and built c' about Ashdod, "
27: 4 he built c' in the mountains "
28:18 invaded the c' of the low country, "
31: 1 went out to the c' of Judah, "
1 his possession, into their own c'. "
6 Judah, that dwelt in the c' of "
15 in the c' of the priests, in their "
19 fields of the suburbs of their c', "
32: 1 encamped against the fenced c', "
29 Moreover he provided him c', and "
33:14 war in all the fenced c' of Judah. "
34: 6 so did he in the c' of Manasseh, "
Ezr 2:70 the Nethinims, dwelt in their c', "
70 and all Israel in their c'. "
3: 1 children of Israel were in the c', "
4:10 and set in the c' of Samaria, *7141
10:14 taken strange wives in our c' 5892
Ne 7:73 and all Israel, dwelt in their c'; "
73 children of Israel were in their c'. "
8:15 and proclaim in all their c', "
9:25 took strong c', and a fat land, "
10:37 tithes in all the c' of our tillage. "
11: 1 nine parts to dwell in other c'. "
3 in the c' of Judah dwelt every one "
3 in his possesion in their c', "
20 the c' of Judah, every one in his "
12:44 of the fields of the c' the portions "
Es 9: 2 themselves together in their c' "
Job 15:28 he dwelleth in desolate c', and in "
Ps 9: 6 and thou hast destroyed c'; their "
69:35 and will build the c' of Judah: "
Isa 1: 7 c' are burned with fire: your land, "
6:11 c' be wasted without inhabitant, "
14:17 and destroyed the c' thereof; "
21 fill the face of the world with c'. "
17: 2 The c' of Aroer are forsaken: "
9 strong c' be as a forsaken bough, "
19:18 five c' in the land of Egypt speak "
33: 8 hath despised the c', he regardeth "

Isa 36: 1 all the defenced c' of Judah, 5892
37:26 be to lay waste defenced c' "
40: 9 say unto the c' of Judah, Behold "
42:11 the wilderness and the c' thereof "
44:26 and to the c' of Judah, Ye shall be "
54: 3 the desolate c' to be inhabited. "
61: 4 they shall repair the waste c', the "
64:10 Thy holy c' are a wilderness, "
Jer 1:15 and against all the c' of Judah. "
2:15 c' are burned without inhabitant. "
28 the number of thy c' are thy gods, "
4: 5 and let us go into the defenced c'. "
7 thy c' shall be laid waste, without "
16 their voice against the c' of Judah. "
26 the c' thereof were broken down "
5: 6 leopard shall watch over their c': "
17 shall impoverish thy fenced c', "
7:17 what they do in the c' of Judah "
34 to cease from the c' of Judah, "
8:14 let us enter into the defenced c', "
9:11 will make the c' of Judah desolate, "
10:22 to make the c' of Judah desolate, "
11: 6 all these words in the c' of Judah, "
12 Then shall the c' of Judah and "
13 number of thy c' were thy gods, "
13:19 c' of the south shall be shut up, "
17:26 shall come from the c' of Judah "
20:16 the c' which the Lord overthrew, "
22: 6 and c' which are not inhabited. "
25:18 Jerusalem, and the c' of Judah, "
26: 2 speak unto all the c' of Judah, "
31:21 turn again to these thy c'. "
23 of Judah and in the c' thereof, "
24 in Judah itself, and in all the c' "
32:44 Jerusalem, and in the c' of Judah, "
44 and in the c' of the mountains, "
44 and in the c' of the valley, "
44 and in the c' of the south: "
33:10 c' of Judah, and in the streets of "
12 c' thereof, shall be an habitation "
13 In the c' of the mountains, in the "
13 c' of the vale, and in the c' of the "
13 Jerusalem, and in the c' of Judah, "
34: 1 and against all the c' thereof, "
7 and against all the c' of Judah "
7 Azekah: for these defenced c' "
7 remained of the c' of Judah. "
22 make the c' of Judah a desolation "
36: 6 all Judah that come out of their c'. "
9 the c' of Judah unto Jerusalem. "
40: 5 governor over the c' of Judah, "
10 in your c' that ye have taken. "
44: 2 upon all the c' of Judah; and, "
6 and was kindled in the c' of Judah "
17 and our princes, in the c' of Judah, "
21 that ye burned in the c' of Judah, "
48: 9 for the c' thereof shall be desolate, "
15 spoiled, and gone up out of her c', "
24 all the c' of the land of Moab, far "
28 ye that dwell in Moab, leave the c', "
49: 1 and his people dwell in his c'? "
13 the c' thereof shall be perpetual "
18 and the neighbour c' thereof,
50:32 I will kindle a fire in his c', and it 5892
40 Gomorrah and the neighbour c' "
51:43 c' are a desolation, a dry land, 5892
La 5:11 and the maids in the c' of Judah. "
Eze 6: 6 the c' shall be laid waste, "
12:20 And the c' that are inhabited shall "
19: 7 palaces, and he laid waste their c'; "
25: 9 open the side of Moab from the c', "
9 his c' which are on his frontiers, "
26:19 like the c' that are not inhabited; "
29:12 that are desolate, and her c' "
12 among the c' that are laid waste "
30: 7 and her c' shall be in the midst "
7 of the c' that are wasted. "
17 and these c' shall go into captivity. "
35: 4 I will lay thy c' waste, and thou 5892
9 and thy c' shall not return: and "
36: 4 and to the c' that are forsaken, "
10 the c' shall be inhabited, and the "
33 also cause you to dwell in the c', "
35 ruined c' are become fenced, "
38 waste c' be filled with flocks of "
39: 9 in the c' of Israel shall go forth, "
Da 11:15 and take the most fenced c': *
Ho 8:14 Judah hath multiplied fenced c': "
14 but I will send a fire upon his c', "
11: 6 the sword shall abide on his c', "
13:10 that may save thee in all thy c'? "
Am 4: 6 cleanness of teeth in all your c', "
8 three c' wandered unto one city, "
9:14 they shall build the waste c', and "
Ob 20 shall possess the c' of the south. "
Mic 5:11 I will cut off the c' of thy land, "
14 so will I destroy thy c'. "
7:12 Assyria, and from the fortified c', "
Zep 1:16 and alarm against the fenced c', "
3: 6 their c' are destroyed, so that "
Zec 1:12 Jerusalem and on the c' of Judah, "
17 My c' through prosperity shall yet "
7: 7 in prosperity, and the c' thereof "
8:20 and the inhabitants of many c': "
M't 9:35 Jesus went about all the c' and 4172
10:23 over the c' of Israel, till the Son "
11: 1 to teach and to preach in their c'. "
20 Then began he to upbraid the c' "
14:13 followed him on foot out of the c'. "
M'r 6:33 and ran afoot thither out of all c', "
56 into villages, or c', or country, "
Lu 4:43 kingdom of God to other c' also: "
13:22 went through the c' and villages, "
19:17 have thou authority over ten c'. "
19 to him, Be thou also over five c'. "
Ac 5:16 out of the c' round about "

Ac 8:40 he preached in all the c', till he 4172
14: 6 Lystra and Derbe, c' of Lycaonia, "
16: 4 through the c', they delivered "
26:11 them even unto strange c'. "
2Pe 2: 6 c' of Sodom and Gomorrha into "
Jude 7 Gomorrha, and the c' about them "
Re 16:19 parts, and the c' of the nations "

citizen See also CITIZENS.
Lu 15:15 himself to a c' of that country; *4177
Ac 21:39 in Cilicia, a c' of no mean city: "

citizens See also FELLOWCITIZENS.
Lu 19:14 But his c' hated him, and sent a 4177

city See also CITIES.
Ge 4:17 and he builded a c', and called 5892
17 called the name of the c', after "
10:11 and the c' Rehoboth, and Calah, "
12 and Calah: the same is a great c'. "
11: 4 let us build us a c' and a tower, "
5 the Lord came down to see the c' "
8 and they left off to build the c'. "
18:24 be fifty righteous within the c': "
26 Sodom fifty righteous within the c', "
28 destroy all the c' for lack of five? "
19: 4 of the c', even the men of Sodom, "
12 whatsoever thou hast in the c', "
14 for the Lord will destroy this c'. "
15 consumed in the iniquity of the c'. "
16 forth, and set him without the c'. "
20 this c' is near to flee unto, and it "
21 I will not overthrow this c', for the "
22 the name of the c' was called Zoar. "
23:10 in at the gate of his c', saying, "
18 that went in at the gate of his c'. "
24:10 Mesopotamia, unto the c' of Nahor. "
11 to kneel down without the c' "
13 of the men of the c' come out "
26:33 the name the c' is Beer-sheba "
28:19 name of that c' was called Luz "
33:18 Jacob came to Shalem, a c' of "
18 and pitched his tent before the c'. "
34:20 came unto the gate of their c', "
20 with the men of their c', saying, "
24 that went out of the gate of his c'; "
24 that went out of the gate of his c'. "
25 c' boldly, and slew all the males. "
27 upon the slain, and spoiled the c', "
28 and that which was in the c', "
35:27 c' of Arbah, which is Hebron. *7151
36:32 name of his c' was Dinhabah. 5892
35 the name of his c' was Avith. "
39 the name of his c' was Pau; and "
41:48 which was round about every c', "
44: 4 when they were gone out of the c', "
13 his ass, and returned to the c'. "
Ex 9:29 As soon as I am gone out of the c', "
33 Moses went out of the c' from "
Le 14:40 an unclean place without the c': "
41 that they scrape off without the c' "
45 carry them forth out of the c' "
53 let go the living bird out of the c' "
25:29 a dwelling house in a walled c', "
30 the house that is in the walled c' "
33 sold, and the c' of his possession, "
Nu 20:16 Kadesh, a c' in the uttermost of "
21:26 Heshbon was the c' of Sihon the "
27 c' of Sihon be built and prepared: "
28 a flame from the c' of Sihon: 7151
22:36 meet him unto a c' of Moab, 5892
24:19 him that remaineth of the c'. "
35: 4 the wall of the c' and outward a "
5 shall measure from without the c' "
5 the c' shall be in the midst: "
25 shall restore him to the c' "
26 the border of the c' of his refuge, "
27 him without the borders of the c' "
28 remained in the c' of his refuge "
32 that is fled to the c' of his refuge, "
De 2:34 and the little ones, of every c', "
36 and from the c' that is by the "
36 there was not one c' too strong 7151
3: 4 not a c' which we took not from "
6 women, and children, of every c'. 5892
13:13 the inhabitants of their c', saying, "
15 smite the inhabitants of that c' "
16 and shalt burn with fire the c', "
19:12 elders of his c' shall send and fetch "
20:10 When thou comest nigh unto a c' "
14 and all that is in the c', even all the "
19 When thou shalt besiege a c' a long "
20 shalt build bulwarks against the c' "
21: 3 the c' which is next unto the slain "
3 even the elders of that c' shall take "
4 elders of that c' shall bring down "
6 all the elders of that c', that are "
19 him out unto the elders of his c', "
20 shall say unto the elders of his c', "
21 all the men of his c' shall stone "
22:15 the elders of the c' in the gate: "
17 the cloth before the elders of the c'. "
18 elders of that c' shall take that "
21 the men of her c' shall stone her "
23 and a man find her in the c', "
24 both out unto the gate of that c', "
24 she cried not, being in the c'; "
25: 8 the elders of his c' shall call him, "
28: 3 Blessed shalt thou be in the c', "
16 Cursed shalt thou be in the c', and "
34: 3 of Jericho, the c' of palm "
Jos 3:16 far from the c' Adam, that is "
6: 3 And ye shall compass the c', all ye "
3 go round about the c' once. Thus "
4 seventh day ye shall compass the c' "
5 wall of the c' shall fall down flat, "
7 Pass on, and compass the c', and "
11 ark of the Lord compassed the c'. "

Jos 6:14 second day they compassed the c' 5892
15 compassed the c' after the same "
15 day they compassed the c' seven "
16 for the Lord hath given you the c'. "
17 the c' shall be accursed, even it, "
20 people went up into the c', every "
20 before him, and they took the c'. "
21 destroyed all that was in the c', "
24 And they burnt the c' with fire, "
26 that riseth up and buildeth this c' "
8: 1 king of Ai, and his people, and his c', "
2 lay thee an ambush for the c' behind "
4 lie in wait against the c', "
4 even behind the c': "
4 go not very far from the c', "
5 with me, will approach unto the c': "
6 we have drawn them from the c'; "
7 the ambush, and seize upon the c': "
8 when ye have taken the c', "
8 that ye shall set the c' on fire: "
11 drew nigh, and came before the c', "
12 and Ai, on the west side of the c'. "
13 host that was on the north of the c', "
13 liers in wait on the west of the c', "
14 the men of the c' went out against "
14 ambush against him behind the c'. "
16 and were drawn away from the c'. "
17 and they left the c' open, and "
18 he had in his hand toward the c'. "
19 they entered into the c', and took it, "
19 and hasted and set the c' on fire. "
20 the smoke of the c' ascended up to "
21 the ambush had taken the c', and "
21 that the smoke of the c' ascended "
22 And the other issued out of the c' "
27 the spoil of that c' Israel took for "
29 the entering of the gate of the c', "
10: 2 Gibeon was a great c', as one of "
11:19 not a c' that made peace with the "
13: 9, 16 c'... in the midst of the river, "
15:13 the c' of Arba the father of Anak, *7151
13 which c' is Hebron. *
62 Nibshan, and the c' of Salt, 5892
18:14 Kirjath-jearim, a c' of the "
19:29 the strong c' Tyre; and the coast "
50 gave him the c' which he asked, "
50 he built the c', and dwelt therein. "
20: 4 at the entering of the gate of the c', "
4 in the ears of the elders of that c', "
4 shall take him into the c' unto them, "
6 shall dwell in that c', until he stand "
6 return, and come unto his own c', "
6 unto the c' from whence he fled. "
21:11 they gave them the c' of Arba *7151
11 which c' is Hebron, in the hill *
12 fields of the c', and the villages 5892
13, 21, 27, 32, 38 c' of refuge ... slayer; "
J'g 1: 8 the sword, and set the c' on fire. "
16 out of the c' of palm trees with "
17 name of the c' was called Hormah. "
23 the name of the c' before was Luz.) "
24 saw a man come forth out of the c', "
24 the entrance into the c', and we will "
25 them the entrance into the c', "
25 they smote the c' with the edge of "
26 land of the Hittites and built a c', "
3:13 and possessed the c' of palm trees. "
6:27 household, and the men of the c', "
28 when the men of the c' arose early "
30 the men of the c' said unto Joash, "
8:16 And he took the elders of the c', "
17 and slew the men of the c'. "
27 ephod thereof, and put it in his c', "
9:30 Zebul the ruler of the c' heard "
31 they fortify the c' against thee. "
33 rise early, and set upon the c': "
35 the entering of the gate of the c': "
43 were come forth out of the c'; "
44 in the entering of the gate of the c': "
45 Abimelech fought against the c' all "
45 that day; and he took the c', "
45 and beat down the c' and sowed it "
51 was a strong tower within the c', "
51 and women, and all they of the c', "
14:18 the men of the c' said unto him on "
16: 2 him all night in the gate of the c', "
3 took the doors of the gate of the c', "
17: 8 the man departed out of the c' "
18:27 and burnt the c' with fire. "
28 they built a c' and dwelt therein. "
29 they called the name of the c' Dan, "
29 name of the c' was Laish at the first. "
19:11 turn in into this c' of the Jebusites, "
12 hither into the c' of a stranger, "
15 sat him down in a street of the c': "
17 man in the street of the c': "
22 men of the c', certain sons of Belial, "
20:11 Israel were gathered against the c', "
31 were drawn away from the c'; "
32 them from the c' unto the highways. "
37 smote all the c' with the edge of "
38 with smoke rise up out of the c'. "
40 began to arise up out of the c' "
40 the flame of the c' ascended up to "
48 as well the men of every c', as the "
Ru 1:19 all the c' was moved about them, "
2:18 took it up, and went into the c': "
3:11 the c' of my people doth know 8179
15 on her: and she went into the c'. 5892
4: 2 took ten men of the elders of the c', "
1Sa 1: 3 this man went up out of his c' "
4:13 when the man came into the c', "
13 told it, all the c' cried out. "
5: 9 hand of the Lord was against the c' "
9 he smote the men of the c', "

1Sa 5:11 destruction throughout all the c'; 5892
12 cry of the c' went up to heaven, "
8:22 Go ye every man unto his c'. "
9: 6 there is in this c' a man of God, "
10 the c' where the man of God was. "
11 as they went up the hill to the c', "
12 for he came to day to the c'; for "
13 As soon as ye be come into the c', "
14 they went up into the c': and "
14 when they were come into the c', "
25 from the high place into the c', "
27 going down to the end of the c', "
10: 5 thou art come thither to the c', "
15: 5 Saul came to a c' of Amalek, and "
20: 6 he might run to Beth-lehem his c': "
29 family hath a sacrifice in the c'; "
40 him, Go, carry them to the c'. "
42 and Jonathan went into the c'. "
22:19 Nob, the c' of the priests, smote he "
23:10 to destroy the c' for my sake. "
27: 5 thy servant dwell in the royal c' "
28: 3 him in Ramah, even in his own c'. "
30: 3 David and his men came to the c', "
2Sa 5: 7 Zion: the same is the c' of David. "
9 fort, and called it the c' of David. "
6:10 unto him into the c' of David: but "
12 the house of Obed-edom into the c' "
16 ark of the Lord came into the c' "
10: 3 to search the c', and to spy it out, "
14 and entered into the c'. So Joab "
11:16 to pass, when Joab observed the c', "
17 the men of the c' went out, and "
20 approached ye so nigh unto the c' "
25 battle more strong against the c', "
12: 1 There were two men in one c'; "
26 of Ammon, and took the royal c'. "
27 and have taken the c' of waters. "
28 encamp against the c', and take it: "
28 lest I take the c', and it be called "
30 he brought forth the spoil of the c' "
15: 2 Of what c' art thou? And he said, "
12 David's counseller, from his c', "
14 smite the c' with the edge of the "
24 had done passing out of the c'. "
25 back the ark of God into the c': "
27 return into the c' in peace, and "
34 But if thou return to the c', and say "
37 David's friend came into the c', "
17:13 if he be gotten into a c', then shall "
13 all Israel bring ropes to that c', "
17 not be seen to come into the c': "
23 him home to his house, to his c', "
18: 3 that thou succour us out of the c'. "
19: 3 by stealth that day into the c', "
37 die in mine own c', and be buried "
20:15 they cast up a bank against the c', "
16 cried a wise woman out of the c', "
19 to destroy a c' and a mother in "
21 and I will depart from the c'. "
22 they retired from the c', every man "
24: 5 on the right side of the c' that lieth "
1Ki 1:41 of the c' being in an uproar? 7151
45 c' rang again. This is the noise "
2:10 and was buried in the c' of David. 5892
3: 1 brought her into the c' of David, "
8: 1 of the Lord out of the c' of David, "
16 I chose no c' out of all the tribes "
44 pray unto the Lord toward the c' "
48 the c' which thou hast chosen, "
9:16 the Canaanites that dwelt in the c', "
24 came up out of the c' of David "
11:27 the breaches of the c' of David "
32 sake, the c' which I have chosen "
36 Jerusalem, the c' which I have "
43 was buried in the c' of David his "
13:25 they came and told it in the c' "
29 the old prophet came to the c', to "
14:11 that dieth of Jeroboam in the c' "
12 when thy feet enter into the c', the "
21 the c' which the Lord did choose "
31 buried with his fathers in the c' of "
15: 8 they buried him in the c' of David: "
24 buried with his fathers in the c' of "
16: 4 Him that dieth of Baasha in the c' "
18 when Zimri saw that the c' was "
24 called the name of the c' which he "
17:10 when he came to the gate of the c', "
20: 2 to Ahab king of Israel into the c', "
12 themselves in array against the c'. "
19 the provinces came out of the c', "
30 the rest fled to Aphek, into the c'; "
30 Ben-hadad fled and came into the c', "
21: 8 to the nobles that were in his c', "
11 the men of his c', even the elders "
11 who were the inhabitants in his c', "
13 they carried him forth out of the c', "
24 Him that dieth of Ahab in the c' "
22:26 Amon the governor of the c', and "
36 saying, Every man to his c', and "
50 buried with his fathers in the c' of "
2Ki 2:19 the men of the c' said unto Elisha, "
19 the situation of this c' is pleasant, "
23 forth little children out of the c', "
3:19 ye shall smite every fenced c', "
19 and every choice c', "
6:14 by night, and compassed the c' "
15 an host compassed the c' both "
19 not the way, neither is this the c': "
7: 4 If we say, We will enter into the c', "
4 then the famine is in the c', "
10 and called unto the porter of the c': "
12 When they come out of the c', we "
7:12 them alive, and get into the c'. "
13 remain, which are left in the c', "
8:24 with his fathers in the c' of David: 5892

2Ki 9:15 go forth nor escape out of the c' 5892
28 with his fathers in the c' of David. "
10: 2 chariots and horses, a fenced c', "
5 he that was over the c', the elders "
6 the great men of the c', which "
25 went to the c' of the house of Baal. "
11:20 the land rejoiced, and the c' was in "
12:21 with his fathers in the c' of David: "
14:20 with his fathers in the c' of David, "
15: 7 with his fathers in the c' of David: "
38 in the c' of David his father: and "
16:20 with his fathers in the c' of David: "
17: 9 of the watchman to the fenced c'. "
18: 8 of the watchman to the fenced c'. "
30 this c' shall not be delivered into "
19:13 the king of the c' of Sepharvaim, "
32 He shall not come into this c', "
33 and shall not come into this c', "
34 I will defend this c', to save it, "
20: 6 I will deliver thee and this c' out "
6 I will defend this c' for mine own "
20 and brought water into the c', are "
23: 8 of Joshua the governor of the c', "
8 left hand at the gate of the c'. "
17 And the men of the c' told him, "
27 and will cast off this c' Jerusalem "
24:10 and the c' was besieged. "
11 of Babylon came against the c', "
25: 2 the c' was besieged unto the "
3 the famine prevailed in the c', "
4 And the c' was broken up, and all "
4 the Chaldees were against the c' "
11 the people that were left in the c', "
19 out of the c' he took an officer that "
19 which were found in the c', and "
19 the land that were found in the c': "
1Ch 1:43 the name of his c' was Dinhabah. "
46 the name of his c' was Avith. "
50 name of his c' was Pai; and his "
6:56 the fields of the c', and the villages "
57 namely, Hebron, the c' of refuge, *
11: 5 castle of Zion, which is the c' of 5892
7 they called it the c' of David. "
8 he built the c' round about, even "
8 and Joab repaired the rest of the c'. "
13:13 home to himself to the c' of David, "
15: 1 David made him houses in the c' of "
29 came to the c' of David, that "
19: 9 in array before the gate of the c': "
15 his brother, and entered into the c'. "
20: 2 exceeding much spoil out of the c'. "
2Ch 5: 2 of the Lord out of the c' of David, "
6: 5 I chose no c' among all the tribes "
34 they pray unto thee toward this c' "
38 and toward the c' which thou hast "
8:11 of Pharaoh out of the c' of David "
9:31 he was buried in the c' of David "
11:12 in every several c' he put shields "
23 Benjamin, unto every fenced c': "
12:13 the c' which the Lord had chosen "
16 and was buried in the c' of David: "
14: 1 they buried him in the c' of David: "
15: 6 was destroyed of nation, and c' of c': "
16:14 made for himself in the c' of David, "
18:25 to Amon the governor of the c', "
19: 5 the fenced cities of Judah, c' by c', "
21: 1 with his fathers in the c' of David, "
20 they buried him in the c' of David, "
23:21 and the c' was quiet, after that "
24:16 in the c' of David among the kings, "
25 they buried him in the c' of David, "
25:28 with his fathers in the c' of Judah. "
27: 9 they buried him in the c' of David: "
28:15 Jericho, the c' of palm trees, "
25 in every several c' of Judah he "
27 they buried him in the c', even in "
29:20 and gathered the rulers of the c', "
30:10 the posts passed from c' to c' "
31:19 in every several c', the men that "
32: 3 which were without the c': "
5 repaired Millo in the c' of David, "
6 in the street of the gate of the c', "
18 them; that they might take the c'. "
30 to the west side of the c' of David. "
33:14 built a wall without the c' of David, "
15 and cast them out of the c'. "
34: 8 Maaseiah the governor of the c', "
Ezr 2: 1 Judah, every one unto his c'; "
4:12 the rebellious and the bad c', 7149
13 if this c' be builded, and the walls "
15 know that this c' is a rebellious c', "
15 which cause was this c' destroyed. "
16 if this c' be builded again, and the "
19 and it is found that this c' of old "
21 and that this c' be not builded, "
10:14 the elders of every c', and the 5892
Neh 2: 3 when the c', the place of my father's "
5 the c' of my father's sepulchres, "
8 house, and for the wall of the c', "
3:15 the stairs that go down from the c' "
7: 4 the c' was large and great: but the "
6 to Judah, every one unto his c'; "
11: 1 to dwell in Jerusalem the holy c', "
9 of Senuah was second over the c'. "
18 the Levites in the holy c' were "
12:37 by the stairs of the c' of David, "
13:18 this evil upon us, and upon this c'? "
Es 3:15 but the c' Shushan was perplexed. "
4: 1 went out into the midst of the c', "
6 unto the street of the c', which "
6: 9, 11 through the street of the c', "
8:11 the Jews which were in every c' "
15 and the c' of Shushan rejoiced "
17 in every province, and in every c', "
9:28 every province, and every c'; "

Job 24:12 Men groan from out of the c', 5892
29: 7 out to the gate through the c', 7176
39: 7 scorneth the multitude of the c', 7151
Ps 31:21 kindness in a strong c'. 5892
46: 4 shall make glad the c' of God, "
48: 1 the c' of our God, in the mountain "
2 north, the c' of the great King. 7151
8 in the c' of the Lord of hosts, 5892
8 in the c' of our God: "
55: 9 seen violence and strife in the c'. "
59: 6, 14 dog, and go round about the c'. "
60: 9 will bring me into the strong c'? "
72:16 they of the c' shall flourish like "
87: 3 are spoken of thee, O c' of God. "
101: 8 doers from the c' of the Lord. "
107: 4 they found no c' to dwell in. "
7 they might go to a c' of habitation. "
36 may prepare a c' for habitation; "
108:10 will bring me into the strong c'? "
122: 3 is builded as a c' that is compact "
127: 1 except the Lord keep the c', "
Pr 1:21 in the c' she uttereth her words, "
8: 3 the gates, at the entry of the c', 7176
9: 3 upon the highest places of the c', "
14 in the high places of the c', "
10:15 rich man's wealth is his strong c': 7151
11:10 the righteous, the c' rejoiceth: "
11 of the upright the c' is exalted: 7176
16:32 spirit than he that taketh a c'. 5892
18:11 rich man's wealth is his strong c', 7151
19 harder to be won than a strong c': "
21:22 man scaleth the c' of the mighty, 5892
25:28 like a c' that is broken down, "
29: 8 men bring a c' into a snare: 7151
Ec 7:19 mighty men which are in the c'. 5892
8:10 they were forgotten in the c' "
9:14 There was a little c', and few men "
15 he by his wisdom delivered the c'; "
10:15 knoweth not how to go to the c'. "
Ca 3: 2 will rise now, and go about the c' "
3 that go about the c' found me: "
5: 7 that went about the c' found me, "
Isa 1: 8 of cucumbers, as a besieged c'. "
21 is the faithful c' become an harlot! 7151
26 be called, The c' of righteousness, 5892
26 of righteousness, the faithful c' 7151
14: 4 the golden c' ceased! 4062
31 Howl, O gate; cry, O c'; 5892
17: 1 is taken away from being a c', "
19: 2 against his neighbour; c' against c', "
18 The c' of destruction. "
22: 2 of stirs, a tumultuous c', "
2 a joyous c': thy slain men 7151
9 the breaches of the c' of David, 5892
23: 7 this your joyous c', whose "
8 against Tyre, the crowning c', ‡
11 against the merchant c', *
16 Take an harp, go about the c', 5892
24:10 c' of confusion is broken down: 7151
12 In the c' is left desolation, 5892
25: 2 thou hast made of a c' an heap; "
2 of a defenced c' a ruin: 7151
2 a palace of strangers to be no c'; 5892
3 the c' of the terrible nations shall 7151
26: 1 We have a strong c'; salvation 5892
5 the lofty c', he layeth it low; 7151
27:10 the defenced c' shall be desolate, 5892
29: 1 Ariel, the c' where David dwelt! 7151
32:13 houses of joy in the joyous c': "
14 multitude of the c' shall be left; 5892
19 the c' shall be low in a low place. "
33:20 Zion, the c' of our solemnities: 7151
36:15 this c' shall not be delivered into 5892
37:13 the king of the c' of Sepharvaim, "
33 He shall not come into this c', nor "
34 and shall not come into this c', saith "
35 I will defend this c' to save it "
38: 6 I will deliver thee and this c' out "
6 and I will defend this c'. "
45:13 he shall build my city, and he "
48: 2 they call themselves of the holy c', "
52: 1 O Jerusalem, the holy c': "
60:14 call thee, The c' of the Lord, "
62:12 Sought out, A c' not forsaken. "
66: 6 A voice of noise from the c', "
Jer 1:18 made thee this day a defenced c', "
3:14 I will take you one of a c', "
4:29 whole c' shall flee for the noise "
29 every c' shall be forsaken, and not "
6: 6 this is the c' to be visited; "
8:16 the c', and those that dwell therein. "
14:18 if I enter into the c', then behold "
15: 8 suddenly, and terrors upon the c'.* "
17:24 burden through the gates of this c' "
25 there enter into the gates of this c' "
25 and this c' shall remain for ever. "
19: 8 I will make this c' desolate, and an "
11 will I break this people and this c', "
12 and even make this c' as Tophet: "
15 upon this c' and upon all her towns "
20: 5 deliver all the strength of this c', "
21: 4 them into the midst of this c'. "
6 will smite the inhabitants of this c', "
7 left in this c' from the pestilence, "
9 He that abideth in this c' shall "
10 have set my face against this c' "
22: 8 many nations shall pass by this c', "
8 Lord done thus unto this great c'? "
23:39 you, and the c' that I gave you "
25:29 I begin to bring evil on the c' "
26: 6 and will make this c' a curse to all "
9 this c' shall be desolate without "
11 he hath prophesied against this c', "
12 this house and against this c' "
15 upon yourselves, and upon this c', "
26:20 who prophesied against this c' "

Jer 27:17 should this c' be laid waste? 5892
19 the vessels that remain in this c', "
29: 7 And seek the peace of the c' "
16 the people that dwelleth in this c', "
30:18 c' shall be builded upon her own "
31:38 the c' shall be built to the Lord "
32: 3 this c' into the hand of the king "
24 mounts, they are come unto the c' "
24 and the c' is given into the hand of "
25 for the c' is given into the hand of "
28 I will give this c' into the hand of "
29 that fight against this c', "
29 shall come and set fire on this c', "
31 For this c' hath been to me as a "
36 concerning this c', whereof ye say "
33: 4 concerning the houses of this c', "
5 I have hid my face from this c'. "
34: 2 I will give this c' into the hand of "
22 cause them to return to this c'; "
37: 8 and fight against this c', and take "
10 tent; and burn this c' with fire. "
21 all the bread in the c' were spent. "
38: 2 that remaineth in this c' shall die "
3 This c' shall surely be given into "
4 men of war that remain in this c', "
9 there is no more bread in the c'. "
17 and this c' shall not be burned "
18 shall this c' be given into the hand "
23 shalt cause this c' to be burned "
39: 2 of the month, the c' was broken up. "
4 went forth out of the c' by night, "
9 the people that remained in the c', "
16 will bring my words upon this c' "
41: 7 they came into the midst of the c', "
46: 8 the c' and the inhabitants thereof. "
47: 2 c', and them that dwell therein: "
48: 8 spoiler shall come upon every c', "
8 and no c' shall escape: "
49:25 is the c' of praise not left, "
25 the c' of my joy! 7151
51:31 king of Babylon that his c' is taken 5892
52: 5 the c' was besieged unto the "
6 the famine was sore in the c', so "
7 the c' was broken up, and all the "
7 went forth out of the c' by night "
7 were by the c' round about:) "
15 the people that remained in the c', "
25 took also out of the c' an eunuch, "
25 which were found in the c'; "
25 were found in the midst of the c'. "
La 1: 1 How doth the c' sit solitary, "
19 elders gave up the ghost in the c', "
2:11 swoon in the streets of the c'. 7151
12 wounded in the streets of the c', 5892
15 c' that men call The perfection "
3:51 of all the daughters of my c'. "
Eze 4: 1 thee, and pourtray upon it the c', "
3 of iron between thee and the c': "
5: 2 a third part in the midst of the c', "
7:15 and he that is in the c', famine and "
23 and the c' is full of violence. "
9: 1 that have charge over the c' "
4 Go through the midst of the c', "
5 Go ye after him through the c', "
7 went forth, and slew in the c'. "
9 and the c' full of perverseness: "
10: 2 and scatter them over the c'. "
11: 2 and give wicked counsel in this c': "
3 this c' is the caldron, and we be the "
6 multiplied your slain in this c', 5892
7 and this c' is the caldron: but I will "
11 This c' shall not be your caldron, "
23 up from the midst of the c', 5892
23 which is on the east side of the c'. "
17: 4 he set it in a c' of merchants. "
21:19 at the head of the way to the c'. "
22: 2 wilt thou judge the bloody c'? "
3 The c' sheddeth blood in the midst "
24: 6 Woe to the bloody c', to the pot "
9 Woe to the bloody c'! I will even "
26:10 enter into a c' wherein is made "
17 the renowned c', which wast "
19 I shall make thee a desolate c', "
27:32 saying, What c' is like Tyrus, *
33:21 me, saying, The c' is smitten. 5892
39:16 name of the c' shall be Hamonah. "
40: 1 year after that the c' was smitten, "
2 the frame of a c' on the south. "
43: 3 when I came to destroy the c': "
45: 6 possession of the c' five thousand "
7 possession of the c', before the "
7 before the possession of the c', "
48:15 place for the c', for dwelling, "
15 c' shall be in the midst thereof. "
17 suburbs of the c' shall be toward "
18 food unto them that serve the c'. "
19 that serve the c' shall serve it "
20 with the possession of the c'. "
21 and of the possession of the c', "
22 from the possession of the c', "
30 out of the c' on the north side, "
31 the gates of the c' shall be after "
35 name of the c' from that day shall "
Da 9:16 away from thy c' Jerusalem, "
18 c' which is called by thy name: "
19 thy c' and thy people are called by "
24 thy people and upon thy holy c', "
26 destroy the c' and the sanctuary; "
Ho 6: 8 is a c' of them that work iniquity, 7151
11: 9 and I will not enter into the c'. 5892
Joe 2: 9 shall run to and fro in the c'; "
Am 3: 6 a trumpet be blown in the c', "
6 there be evil in a c', and the Lord "
4: 7 I caused it to rain upon one c', "
7 it not to rain upon another c': "
8 cities wandered unto one c' "

Am 5: 3 c' that went out by a thousand 5892
6: 8 deliver up the c' with all that is "
7:17 wife shall be an harlot in the c', "
Jon 1: 2 go to Nineveh, that great c', and "
3: 2 go unto Nineveh, that great c', "
3 Nineveh was an exceeding great c' "
4 Jonah began to enter into the c' "
4: 5 Jonah went out of the c', and sat "
5 on the east side of the c', "
5 see what would become of the c'. "
11 not I spare Nineveh, that great c', "
Mic 4:10 shalt thou go forth out of the c', 7151
6: 9 Lord's voice crieth unto the c', 5892
Na 3: 1 Woe to the bloody c'! it is all full "
Hab 2: 8 the violence of the land, of the c', 7151
12 and stablisheth a c' by iniquity! "
17 of the c', and of all that dwell "
Zep 2:15 rejoicing c' that dwelt carelessly, 5892
3: 1 and polluted, to the oppressing c'! "
Zec 8: 3 shall be called a c' of truth; "
5 c' shall be full of boys and girls "
21 the inhabitants of one c' shall go to "
14: 2 c' shall be taken, and the houses 5892
2 the c' shall go forth into captivity, "
2 shall not be cut off from the c'. "
M't 2:23 and dwelt in a c' called Nazareth: 4172
4: 5 taketh him up into the holy c', "
5:14 A c' that is set on an hill cannot be "
35 for it is the c' of the great King. "
8:33 and went their ways into the c', "
34 whole c' came out to meet Jesus: "
9: 1 over, and came into his own c'. "
10: 5 c' of the Samaritans enter ye not: "
11 c' or town ye shall enter, "
14 ye depart out of that house or c', "
15 day of judgment, than for that c'. "
23 when they persecute you in this c', "
12:25 c' or house divided against itself "
21:10 all the c' was moved, saying, Who "
17 went out of the c' into Bethany; "
18 returned into the c', he hungered. "
22: 7 and burned up their c'. "
23:34 and persecute them from c' to c': "
26:18 Go into the c' to such a man, and "
27:53 went into the holy c', and appeared "
28:11 of the watch came into the c', "
M'r 1:33 all the c' was gathered together "
45 no more openly enter into the c', "
5:14 told it in the c', and in the country. "
6:11 day of judgment, than for that c'. * "
11:19 was come, he went out of the c'. "
14:13 Go ye into the c', and there shall "
16 went forth, and came into the c', "
Lu 1:26 a c' of Galilee, named Nazareth, "
39 with haste, into a c' of Juda; "
2: 3 taxed, every one into his own c'. "
4 out of the c' of Nazareth, into "
4 Judæa, unto the c' of David, "
11 day in the c' of David a Saviour, "
39 Galilee, to their own c' Nazareth. "
4:26 save unto Sarepta, a c' of Sidon, *
29 up, and thrust him out of the c', 4172
29 hill whereon their c' was built, "
31 to Capernaum, a c' of Galilee, "
5:12 was in a certain c', behold a man * "
7:11 he went into a c' called Nain; "
12 he came nigh to the gate of the c', "
12 much people of the c' was with her. "
37 And, behold, a woman in the c', "
8: 1 throughout every c' and village, * "
4 were come to him out of every c', "
27 him out of the c' a certain man, "
34 and went and told it in the c' "
39 published throughout the whole c' "
9: 5 when ye go out of that c', shake "
10 to the c' called Bethsaida. "
10: 1 into every c' and place, whither "
8, 10 whatsoever c' ye enter, and "
11 Even the very dust of your c', "
12 day for Sodom, than for that c'. "
14:21 into the streets and lanes of the c', "
18: 2 There was in a c' a judge, which "
3 And there was a widow in that c'; "
19:41 beheld the c', and wept over it, "
22:10 when ye are entered into the c', "
23:19 a certain sedition made in the c', "
51 of Arimathæa, a c' of the Jews: "
24:49 tarry ye in the c' of Jerusalem, "
Joh 1:44 the c' of Andrew and Peter. "
4: 5 Then cometh he to a c' of Samaria, "
8 gone away unto the c' to buy meat. "
28 went her way into the c', and saith "
30 Then they went out of the c', and "
39 the Samaritans of that c' believed "
11:54 into a c' called Ephraim, and "
19:20 was crucified was nigh to the c': "
Ac 7:58 And cast him out of the c', and "
8: 5 went down to the c' of Samaria, "
8 And there was great joy in that c'. "
9 in the same c' used sorcery, and "
9: 6 Arise, and go into the c', and it "
10: 9 and drew nigh unto the c', "
11: 5 I was in the c' of Joppa praying: "
12:10 iron gate that leadeth unto the c'; "
13:44 came almost the whole c' together "
50 and the chief men of the c', "
14: 4 multitude of the c' was divided: "
13 Jupiter, which was before their c', "
19 drew him out of the c', supposing "
20 he rose up, and came into the c': "
21 preached the gospel to that c', "
15:21 in every c' them that preach him, "
36 and visit our brethren in every c' "
16:12 chief c' of that part of Macedonia, "
12 in that c' abiding certain days. "
13 went out of the c' by a river side, * "

Ac 16:14 of purple, of the c' of Thyatira, 4172
20 do exceedingly trouble our c', "
39 them to depart out of the c'. "
17: 5 set all the c' on an uproar, "
6 unto the rulers of the c', crying, 4173
8 rulers of the c', when they heard "
16 the c' wholly given to idolatry. 4172
18:10 for I have much people in this c'. "
19:29 whole c' was filled with confusion: "
19:35 how that the c' of the Ephesians "
20:23 Holy Ghost witnesseth in every c', "
21: 5 till we were out of the c': and we "
29 in the c' Trophimus an Ephesian, "
30 the c' was moved, and the people "
39 which am a Jew of Tarsus, a c' *
39 in Cilicia, a citizen of no mean c': 4172
22: 3 am a Jew, born in Tarsus, a c' *
3 Cilicia, yet brought up in this c' 4172
24:12 in the synagogues, nor in the c': "
25:23 principal men of the c', at Festus' "
27: 5 we came to Myra, a c' of Lycia. "
8 whereunto was the c' of Lasea. 4172
Ro 16:23 Erastus the chamberlain of the c' "
2Co 11:26 in perils in the c', in perils in "
32 king kept the c' of the Damascenes "
subscr. written from Philippi, a c' *
1Ti *subscr.* is the chiefest c' of Phrygia *3390
Tit 1: 5 ordain elders in every c', as I had 4172
Heb 11:10 For he looked for a c' which hath "
16 he hath prepared for them a c'. "
12:22 c' of the living God, the heavenly "
13:14 have we no continuing c', but we "
Jas 4:13 go into such a c', and continue "
Re 3:12 the name of the c' of my God, "
11: 2 holy c' shall they tread under foot "
8 lie in the street of the great c', "
13 and the tenth part of the c' fell, "
14: 8 is fallen, is fallen, that great c', * "
20 was trodden without the c', "
16:19 the great c' was divided into three "
17:18 is that great c', which reigneth "
18:10 great c' Babylon, that mighty c'! "
16 that great c', that was clothed "
18 What c' is like unto this great c'! "
19 alas that great c', wherein were "
21 great c' Babylon be thrown down, "
20: 9 saints about, and the beloved c': "
21: 2 saw the holy c', new Jerusalem, "
10 and shewed me that great c', the "
14 of the c' had twelve foundations, "
15 a golden reed to measure the c', "
16 And the c' lieth foursquare, and "
16 he measured the c' with the reed, "
18 the c' was pure gold, like unto "
19 the foundations of the wall of the c' "
21 the street of the c' was pure gold, "
23 the c' had no need of the sun, "
22:14 in through the gates into the c'. "
19 out of the holy c', and from the "

clad See also CLOTHED.
1Ki 11:29 c' himself with a new garment; 3680
Isa 59:17 and was c' with zeal as a cloke. 5844

clamorous
Pr 9:13 foolish woman is c': she is simple, 1993

clamour
Eph 4:31 anger, and c', and evil speaking, 2906

clap See also CLAPPED; CLAPPETH.
Job 27:23 Men shall c' their hands at him, 5606
Ps 47: 1 O c' your hands, all ye people; 8628
98: 8 Let the floods c' their hands: let 4222
Isa 55:12 of the field shall c' their hands. "
La 2:15 pass by c' their hands at thee; 5606
Na 3:19 shall c' the hands over thee: 8628

clapped
2Ki 11:12 and they c' their hands, and said, 5221
Eze 25: 6 thou hast c' thine hands, and 4222

clappeth
Job 34:37 he c' his hands among us, and 5606

Clauda (*claw'-dah*)
Ac 27:16 certain island which is called C'. *2802

Claudia (*claw'-de-ah*)
2Ti 4:21 and C', and all the brethren. 2803

Claudius (*claw'-de-us*)
Ac 11:28 to pass in the days of C' Cæsar. 2804
18: 2 C' had commanded all Jews to "
23:26 C' Lysias unto the most excellent "

clave
Ge 22: 3 and c' the wood for the burnt 1234
34: 3 And his soul c' unto Dinah the 1692
Nu 16:31 ground c' asunder that was under 1234
J'g 15:19 But God c' an hollow place that "
Ru 1:14 but Ruth c' unto her. 1692
1Sa 6:14 and they c' the wood of the cart, 1234
2Sa 20: 2 men of Judah c' unto their king, 1692
23:10 and his hand c' unto the sword: "
1Ki 11: 2 Solomon c' unto these in love. "
2Ki 18: 6 he c' to the Lord, and departed not "
Ne 10:29 They c' to their brethren, their 2388
Ps 78:15 He c' the rocks in the wilderness, 1234
Isa 48:21 he c' the rock also, and the "
Ac 17:34 men c' unto him, and believed: 2853

claws
De 14: 6 cleaveth the cleft into two c', and *6541
Da 4:33 feathers, and his nails like birds' c'.
Zec 11:16 fat, and tear their c' in pieces. *6541

clay
1Ki 7:46 king cast them, in the c' ground 4568
2Ch 4:17 in the c' ground between Succoth "
Job 4:19 them that dwell in houses of c', 2563
10: 9 thou hast made me as the c'; and "
13:12 ashes, your bodies to bodies of c'. "
Job 27:16 and prepare raiment as the c'; 2563
33: 6 I also am formed out of the c'. "
38:14 It is turned as c' to the seal; and "
Ps 40: 2 out of the miry c', and set my feet 2916
Isa 29:16 be esteemed as the potter's c': 2563
41:25 and as the potter treadeth c'. 2916
45: 9 c' say to him that fashioneth it, 2563
64: 8 thou art our father; we are the c', "
Jer 18: 4 that he made of c' was marred "
6 as the c' is in the potter's hand, so "
43: 9 them in the c' in the brickkiln, *4423
Da 2:33 feet part of iron and part of c'. 2635
34 were of iron and c', and brake them "
35 iron, the c', the brass, the silver, "
41 part of potter's c', and part of iron, "
41 sawest the iron mixed with miry c'. "
42 were part of iron, and part of c', "
43 sawest iron mixed with miry c', "
43 even as iron is not mixed with c'. "
45 in pieces the iron, the brass, the c', "
Na 3:14 go into c', and tread the morter, 2916
Hab 2: 6 that ladeth himself with thick c! *5671
Joh 9: 6 and made c' of the spittle, and he 4081
6 eyes of the blind man with the c', "
11 man that is called Jesus made c', "
14 when Jesus made the c', and "
15 He put c' upon mine eyes, and "
Ro 9:21 not the potter power over the c', "

clean See also UNCLEAN.
Ge 7: 2 Of every c' beast thou shalt take 2889
2 of beasts that are not c' by two, "
8 Of c' beasts, and of "
8 beasts that are not c', "
8:20 every c' beast, and of every c' fowl, "
35: 2 bo c', and change your garments: *2891
Le 4:12 a c' place where the ashes are 2889
6:11 without the camp unto a c' place. "
7:19 all that be c' shall eat thereof. "
10:10 and between unclean and c'; "
14 shoulder shall ye eat in a c' place; "
11:36 is plenty of water, shall be c': "
37 which is to be sown, it shall be c'. "
47 between the unclean and the c', "
12: 8 for her, and she shall be c'. 2891
13: 6 the priest shall pronounce him c': "
6 he shall wash his clothes, and be c'. "
13 he shall pronounce him c' that "
13 it is all turned white: he is c'. 2889
17 the priest shall pronounce him c' 2891
17 that hath the plague: he is c'. 2889
23 the priest shall pronounce him c'. 2891
28 the priest shall pronounce him c': "
34 pronounce him c': and he shall "
34 wash his clothes, and be c'. 2891
37 the scall is healed, he is c': 2889
37 the priest shall pronounce him c'. 2891
39 groweth in the skin; he is c'. 2889
40 he is bald; yet is he c'. "
41 he is forehead bald: yet is he c'. "
58 the second time, and shall be c'. 2891
59 to pronounce it c', or to pronounce "
14: 4 be cleansed two birds alive and c', 2889
7 and shall pronounce him c', and 2891
8 himself in water, that he may be c': "
9 flesh in water, and he shall be c'. "
11 the priest that maketh him c' "
11 the man that is to be made c', and "
20 for him, and he shall be c'. "
48 priest shall pronounce the house c', "
53 for the house: and it shall be c'. "
57 unclean, and when it is c': this is 2889
15: 8 spit upon him that is c'; then he "
13 in running water, and shall be c'. 2891
28 days, and after that she shall be c'. "
16:30 ye may be c' from all your sins "
17:15 until the even: then shall he be c'. "
20:25 between c' beasts and unclean, 2889
25 and between unclean fowls and c': "
22: 4 of the holy things, until he be c'. 2891
7 the sun is down, he shall be c', "
23:22 thou shalt not make c' riddance *
Nu 5:28 woman be not defiled, but be c'; 2889
8: 7 and so make themselves c'. *2891
9:13 But the man that is c', and is not 2889
18:11 every one that is c' in thy house "
13 every one that is c' in thine house "
19: 9 a man that is c' shall gather up "
9 up without the camp in a c' place, "
12 on the seventh day he shall be c': 2891
12 the seventh day he shall not be c'. "
18 a c' person shall take hyssop, and 2889
19 and the c' person shall sprinkle "
19 himself in water, and shall be c' 2891
31:23 through the fire, and it shall be c': "
24 and ye shall be c', and afterward "
De 12:15 the unclean and the c' may eat 2889
22 the unclean and the c' shall eat of "
14:11 Of all c' birds ye shall eat. "
20 But of all c' fowls ye may eat. "
15:22 unclean and the c' person shall "
23:10 not c' by reason of uncleanness "
Jos 3:17 all the people were passed c' over 8552
4: 1 people were c' passed over Jordan, "
11 people were c' passed over, that "
1Sa 20:26 he is not c'; surely he is not c'. 2889
2Ki 5:10 again to thee, and thou shalt be c'. 2891
12 may I not wash in them, and be c'? "
13 he saith to thee, Wash, and be c'? "
14 of a little child, and he was c'. "
2Ch 30:17 for every one that was not c', to 2889
Job 9:30 and make my hands never so c'; 2141
11: 4 doctrine is pure, and I am c' in 1249
14: 4 Who can bring a c' thing out of an 2889
15:14 What is man, that he should be c'? 2135
15 the heavens are not c' in his sight. 2141
Job 17: 9 and he that hath c' hands shall 2891
25: 4 or how can he be c' that is born 2135
33: 9 I am c' without transgression, I 2134
Ps 19: 9 The fear of the Lord is c', 2889
24: 4 He that hath c' hands, and a pure 5355
51: 7 me with hyssop, and I shall be c': 2891
10 Create in me a c' heart, O God; 2889
73: 1 even to such as are of a c' heart. *1249
77: 8 Is his mercy c' gone for ever? 656
Pr 14: 4 Where no oxen are, the crib is c': 1249
16: 2 ways of a man are c' in his own 2134
20: 9 can say, I have made my heart c', 2135
Ec 9: 2 to the good and to the c', and to 2889
Isa 1:16 Wash you, make you c'; put away 2135
24:19 broken down, the earth is c' 6565
28: 8 so that there is no place c'.
30:24 that ear the ground shall eat c' *2548
52:11 be ye c', that bear the vessels of 1305
66:20 bring an offering in a c' vessel 2889
Jer 13:27 wilt thou not be made c'? 2891
Eze 22:26 between the unclean and the c', 2889
36:25 Then will I sprinkle c' water "
25 and ye shall be c': from all your 2891
44:23 between the unclean and the c'. 2889
Joe 1: 7 he hath made it c' bare, and cast
Zec 11:17 his arm shall be c' dried up, and
M't 8: 2 thou wilt, thou canst make me c'. "
3 him, saying, I will; be thou c'. "
23:25 for ye make c' the outside of the * "
26 the outside of them may be c'. 2513
27:59 the body, he wrapped it in a c' "
M'k 1:40 wilt, thou canst make me c'. 2511
41 saith unto him, I will; be thou c'. "
Lu 5:12 thou wilt, thou canst make me c'. 2511
13 him, saying, I will: be thou c'. "
11:39 Now do ye Pharisees make c' * "
41 behold, all things are c' unto you. 2513
Joh 13:10 but is c' every whit: "
10 and ye are c', but not all. "
11 therefore said he, Ye are not all c'. "
15: 3 Now ye are c' through the word "
Ac 18: 6 upon your own heads; I am c': "
2Pe 2:18 those that were c' escaped from *3689
Re 19: 8 arrayed in fine linen, c' and white: *2513
14 clothed in fine linen, white and c'. * "

cleanness See also UNCLEANNESS.
2Sa 22:21 to the c' of my hands hath he 1252
25 according to my c' in his eye sight. "
Ps 18:20 to the c' of my hands hath he "
24 the c' of my hands in his eyesight. "
Am 4: 6 I also have given you c' of teeth 5356

cleanse See also CLEANSED; CLEANSETH; CLEANSING.
Ex 29:36 and thou shalt c' the altar, when 2398
Lev 14:49 he shall take to c' the house two "
52 And he shall c' the house with the "
16:19 seven times, and c' it, and hallow 2891
30 an atonement for you, to c' you, "
Nu 8: 6 children of Israel, and c' them. "
7 shalt thou do unto them, to c' "
15 and thou shalt c' them, and offer "
21 an atonement for them to c' them. "
2Ch 29:15 of the Lord, to c' the house of the "
16 house of the Lord, to c' it, "
Neh 13:22 the Levites that they should c' * "
Ps 19:12 c' thou me from secret faults. *5352
51: 2 mine iniquity, and c' me from my "
119: 9 Wherewithal shall a young man c' 2135
Jer 4:11 people, not to fan, nor to c', 1305
33: 8 And I will c' them from all their 2891
Eze 36:25 from all your idols, will I c' you. "
37:23 they have sinned, and will c' them: "
39:12 of them, that they may c' the land. "
14 upon the face of the earth, to c' it: "
16 Thus shall they c' the land. "
43:20 thus shalt thou c' and purge it. 2398
22 and they shall c' the altar, "
22 as they did c' it with the bullock. "
45:18 blemish, and c' the sanctuary: "
Joe 3:21 For I will c' their blood that I 5352
M't 10: 8 c' the lepers, raise the dead, cast 2511
23:26 c' first that which is within the "
2Co 7: 1 let us c' ourselves from all "
Eph 5:26 That he might sanctify and c' it * "
Jas 4: 8 C' your hands, ye sinners; and "
1Jo 1: 9 to c' us from all unrighteousness. "

cleansed
Lev 11:32 until the even; so it shall be c' *2891
12: 7 and she shall be c' from "
14: 4 take for him that is to be c' two "
7 upon him that is to be c' from the "
8 he that is to be c' shall wash his "
14, 17 right ear of him that is to be c', "
18 the head of him that is to be c': "
19 for him that is to be c' from his "
25, 28 right ear of him that is to be c', "
29 the head of him that is to be c', to "
31 atonement for him that is to be c' "
15:13 when he that hath an issue is c' "
28 if she be c' of her issue, then she "
Nu 35:33 the land cannot be c' of the blood *3722
Jos 22:17 which we are not c' until this day, 2891
2Ch 29:18 have c' all the house of the Lord, "
30:18 not c' themselves, yet did they eat "
19 though he be not c' according to "
34: 5 their altars, and c' Judah and *2891
Ne 13: 9 and they c' the chambers: "
30 Thus c' I them from all strangers, "
Job 35: 3 I have, if I be c' from my sin? "
Ps 73:13 Verily I have c' my heart in vain, 2135
Eze 22:24 Thou art the land that is not c', 2891
36:33 In the day that I shall have c' you * "
44:26 after he is c', they shall reckon 2893
Da 8:14 then shall the sanctuary be c'. 6663
Joe 3:21 their blood that I have not c': 5352

M't 8: 3 immediately his leprosy was c'. 2511
11: 5 lepers are c', and the deaf hear, "
M'r 1:42 departed from him and he was c'. * "
Lu 4:27 and none of them was c', saving "
7:22 the lepers are c', the deaf hear, "
17:14 to pass, as they went, they were c'. "
17 Were there not ten c'? but where "
Ac 10:15 What God hath c', that call not thou "
11: 9 What God hath c', that call not thou "

cleanseth
Job 37:21 the wind passeth, and c' them. ‡2891
Pr 20:30 blueness of a wound c' away evil: *8562
1Jo 1: 7 blood of Jesus Christ his Son c' us 2511

cleansing
Le 13: 7 been seen of the priest for his c', 2893
35 much in the skin after his c'; "
14: 2 law of the leper in the day of his c': "
23 them on the eighth day for his c' "
32 get that which pertaineth to his c'. "
15:13 to himself seven days for his c', "
Nu 6: 9 shave his head in the day of his c', "
Eze 43:23 When thou hast made an end of c' "
M'r 1:44 and offer for thy c' those things 2512
Lu 5:14 and offer for thy c', according as "

clear See also CLEARER; CLEARING.
Ge 24: 8 shalt be c' from this my oath: 5352
41 shalt thou be c' from this my oath, "
41 thou shalt be c' from my oath. 5355
44:16 or how shall we c' ourselves? 6663
Ex 34: 7 will by no means c' the guilty; 5352
2Sa 23: 4 the earth by c' shining after rain.
Ps 51: 4 speakest, and be c' when thou 2135
Ca 6:10 fair as the moon, c' as the sun, 1249
Isa 18: 4 like a c' heat upon herbs, and like 6703
Am 8: 9 will darken the earth in the c' day: 216
Zec 14: 6 the light shall not be c', nor dark: *3368
2Co 7:11 approved yourselves to be c' in * 53
Re 21:11 like a jasper stone, c' as crystal; 2929
18 was pure gold, like unto c' glass. *2513
22: 1 river of water of life, c' as crystal, *2986

clearer
Job 11:17 age shall be c' than the noonday; 6965

clearing
Nu 14:18 no means c' the guilty, visiting *5352
2Co 7:11 in you, yea, what c' of yourselves, 627

clearly
Job 33: 3 my lips shall utter knowledge c'. *1305
M't 7: 5 then shalt thou see c' to cast out 1227
M'r 8:25 restored, and saw every man c'. 5081
Lu 6:42 then shalt thou see c' to pull out 1227
Ro 1:20 are c' seen, being understood by 2529

clearness
Ex 24:10 were the body of heaven in his c'. 2892

cleave See also CLAVE; CLEAVED; CLEAVETH; CLEFT; CLOVEN.
Ge 2:24 shall c' unto his wife: and they 1692
Le 1:17 shall c' it with the wings thereof, *8156
De 4: 4 But ye that did c' unto the Lord 1695
10:20 to him shalt thou c', and swear by 1692
11:22 in all his ways, and to c' unto him; "
13: 4 shall serve him, and c' unto him. "
17 shall c' nought of the cursed thing "
28:21 make the pestilence c' unto thee, "
60 they shall c' unto thee. "
30:20 and that thou mayest c' unto him: "
Jos 22: 5 to c' unto him and to serve him, "
23: 8 But c' unto the Lord your God, as "
12 and c' unto the remnant of these "
2Ki 5:27 of Naaman shall c' unto thee, "
Job 38:38 and the clods c' fast together? "
Ps 74:15 c' the fountain and the flood: 1234
101: 3 it shall not c' to me. 1692
102: 5 groaning my bones c' to my skin. "
137: 6 tongue c' to the roof of my mouth; "
Isa 14: 1 they shall c' to the house of Jacob. 5596
Jer 13:11 so have I caused to c' unto me the 1692
Eze 3:26 tongue c' to the roof of thy mouth, "
Da 2:43 they shall not c' one to another, 1693
11:34 shall c' to them with flatteries. *3867
Hab 3: 9 didst c' the earth with rivers. 1234
Zec 14: 4 of Olives shall c' in the midst "
M't 19: 5 c' to his wife: and they twain 4347
M'r 10: 7 and mother, and c' to his wife; "
Ac 11:23 they would c' unto the Lord. "
Ro 12: 9 c' to that which is good. 2853

cleaved
2Ki 3: 3 Nevertheless he c' unto the sins 1692
Job 29:10 tongue c' to the roof of their "
31: 7 if any blot hath c' to mine hands; "

cleaveth
De 14: 6 and c' the cleft into two claws, *8157
Job 16:13 he c' my reins asunder, and doth 6398
19:20 My bone c' to my skin and to my 1692
Ps 22:15 and my tongue c' to my jaws; "
41: 8 disease, say they, c' fast unto him: 3332
44:25 our belly c' unto the earth. 1692
119:25 My soul c' unto the dust: quicken "
141: 7 when one cutteth and c' wood 1234
Ec 10: 9 that c' wood shall be endangered "
Jer 13:11 the girdle c' to the loins of a man, 1692
La 4: 4 The tongue of the sucking child c' "
8 their skin c' to their bones; it is 6821
Lu 10:11 dust of your city, which c' on us, 2853

cleft See also CLEFTS; CLIFT.
De 14: 6 cleaveth the c' into two claws. *8156
Mic 1: 4 the valleys shall be c', as wax 1234

clefts See also CLIFTS.
Ca 2:14 in the c' of the rock, in the secret 2288
Isa 2:21 To go into the c' of the rocks, *5366
Jer 49:16 thou that dwellest in the c' of the 2288
Am 6:11 and the little house with c'. 1233
Ob 3 that dwellest in the c' of the rock, 2288

clemency
Ac 24: 4 hear us of thy c' a few words. 1932

Clement (*clem'-ent*)
Ph'p 4: 3 in the gospel, with C' also, and 2815

Cleopas (*cle'-o-pas*) See also ALPHÆUS; CLEOPHAS.
Lu 24:18 one of them, whose name was C', 2810

Cleophas (*cle'-o-fas*) See also CLEOPAS.
Joh 19:25 Mary the wife of C', and Mary *2832

clerk See TOWNCLERK.

cliff See also CLIFFS.
2Ch 20:16 they come up by the c' of Ziz; *4608

cliffs
Job 30: 6 in the c' of the valleys, in caves *6178

clift See also CLEFT.
Ex 33:22 put thee in a c' of the rock, *5366

clifts See also CLEFTS.
Isa 57: 5 under the c' of the rocks? *5585

climb See also CLIMBED; CLIMBETH.
Jer 4:29 and c' up upon the rocks: 5927
Joe 2: 7 shall c' the wall like men of war; "
9 they shall c' up upon the houses; "
Am 9: 2 though they c' up to heaven, "

climbed
1Sa 14:13 Jonathan c' up upon his hands 5927
Lu 19: 4 c' up into a sycomore tree to see 305

climbeth
Joh 10: 1 c' up some other way, the same 305

clipped
Jer 48:37 shall be bald, and every beard c': 1639

cloak See CLOKE.

clods
Job 7: 5 with worms and c' of dust; 1487
21:33 The c' of the valley shall be sweet 7263
38:38 and the c' cleave fast together? "
Isa 28:24 and break the c' of his ground? ‡7702
Ho 10:11 and Jacob shall break his c'. "
Joe 1:17 seed is rotten under their c', 4053

cloke
Isa 59:17 was clad with zeal as a c'. ‡4598
M't 5:40 thy coat, let him have thy c' also. 2440
Lu 6:29 him that taketh away thy c' "
Joh 15:22 they have no c' for their sin *4392
1Th 2: 5 nor a c' of covetousness; God is "
2Ti 4:13 The c' that I left at Troas with 5341
1Pe 2:16 liberty for a c' of maliciousness, 1942

close See also CLOSED; CLOSER; CLOSEST; DISCLOSE; INCLOSE.
Nu 5:13 of her husband, and be kept c', 5956
2Sa 22:46 be afraid out of their c' places. 4526
1Ch 12: 1 he yet kept himself c' because of 6113
Job 28:21 kept c' from the fowls of the air. 5641
41:15 shut up together as with a c' seal. 6862
Ps 18:45 be afraid out of their c' places. 4526
Jer 42:16 c' after you there in Egypt; *1692
Da 8: 7 saw him come c' unto the ram, 681
Am 9:11 and c' up the breaches thereof; 1443
Lu 9:36 And they kept it c', and told no *4601
Ac 27:13 thence, they sailed c' by Crete. 788

closed See also INCLOSED.
Ge 2:21 c' up the flesh instead thereof; 5462
20:18 the Lord had fast c' up all the 6113
Nu 16:33 and the earth c' upon them: 3680
J'g 3:22 and the fat c' upon the blade, 5462
Isa 1: 6 they have not been c', neither 2115
29:10 sleep, and hath c' your eyes: 6105
Da 12: 9 the words are c' up and sealed *5640
Jon 2: 5 the depth c' me round about, *5437
M't 13:15 their eyes they have c'; lest at 2576
Lu 4:20 c' the book, and he gave it again 4428
Ac 28:27 their eyes have they c'; lest they 2576

closer
Pr 18:24 that sticketh c' than a brother.

closest
Jer 22:15 because thou c' thyself in cedar? *8474

closet See also CLOSETS.
Joe 2:16 and the bride out of her c'. 2646
M't 6: 6 thou prayest, enter into thy c', *5009

closets
Lu 12: 3 ye have spoken in the ear in c' *5009

cloth See CLOTHS; SACKCLOTH.
Nu 4: 6 spread over it a c' wholly of blue, 899
7 they shall spread a c' of blue, "
8 spread upon them a c' of scarlet, "
9 they shall take a c' of blue, "
11 they shall spread a c' of blue, "
12 put them in a c' of blue, and cover "
13 and spread a purple c' thereon: "
De 22:17 spread the c' before the elders *8071
1Sa 19:13 bolster, and covered it with a c'. * 899
21: 9 wrapped in a c' behind the ephod: 8071
2Sa 20:12 cast a c' upon him, when he saw * 899
2Ki 8:15 he took a thick c', and dipped it *4346
Isa 30:22 them away as a menstruous c'; *
M't 9:16 of new c' unto an old garment, 4470
27:59 wrapped it in a clean linen c', 4616
M'r 2:21 of new c' on an old garment: 4470
14:51 linen c' cast about his naked body; 4616
52 And he left the linen c', and fled "

clothe See also CLOTHED; CLOTHES; CLOTHEST; CLOTHING.
Ex 40:14 his sons, and c' them with coats: *3847
Est 4: 4 she sent raiment to c' Mordecai, "
Ps 132:16 also c' her priests with salvation: "
18 His enemies will I c' with shame: "
Pr 23:21 shall c' a man with rags. "
Isa 22:21 And I will c' him with thy robe, 3847
49:18 shalt surely c' thee with them all, "
50: 3 I c' the heavens with blackness, "
Eze 26:16 c' themselves with trembling; "
34: 3 ye c' you with the wool, ye kill them "
Hag 1: 6 ye c' you, but there is none warm; "
Zec 3: 4 c' thee with change of raiment. "
M't 6:30 if God so c' the grass of the field, 294
30 shall he not much more c' you, "
Lu 12:28 If then God so c' the grass, which 294
28 how much more will he c' you, "

clothed See also CLAD; UNCLOTHED.
Ge 3:21 make coats of skins, and c' them. 3847
Le 8: 7 and c' him with the robe, and put "
2Sa 1:24 over Saul, who c' you in scarlet, "
1Ch 15:27 was c' with a robe of fine linen, 3736
21:16 the elders of Israel, who were c' 3680
2Ch 6:41 thy priests... be c' with salvation, 3847
18: 9 c' in their robes, and they sat * "
28:15 c' all that were naked among them, "
Es 4: 2 the king's gate c' with sackcloth. 3830
Job 7: 5 My flesh is c' with worms and 3847
8:22 hate thee shall be c' with shame; "
10:11 hast c' me with skin and flesh, "
29:14 on righteousness, and it c' me: "
39:19 thou c' his neck with thunder? "
Ps 35:26 let them be c' with shame and "
65:13 The pastures are c' with flocks; "
93: 1 he is c' with majesty; † "
1 the Lord is c' with strength, † "
104: 1 art c' with honour and majesty. "
109:18 As he c' himself with cursing "
29 mine adversaries be c' with shame, "
132: 9 priests be c' with righteousness; "
Pr 31:21 her household are c' with scarlet. "
Isa 61:10 he hath c' me with the garments of "
Eze 7:27 prince shall be c' with desolation, "
9: 2 among them was c' with linen, "
3 called to the man c' with linen, "
11 And, behold, the man c' with linen, "
10: 2 spake unto the man c' with linen, "
6 commanded the man c' with linen, "
7 of him that was c' with linen: "
16:10 c' thee also with broidered work, "
23: 6 c' with blue, captains and rulers, "
12 and rulers c' most gorgeously, "
38: 4 c' with all sorts of armour, "
44:17 shall be c' with linen garments; "
Da 5: 7 shall be c' with scarlet, and have 3848
16 thou shalt be c' with scarlet, "
29 and they c' Daniel with scarlet, "
10: 5 behold a certain man c' in linen, 3847
12: 6 one said to the man c' in linen, "
7 I heard the man c' in linen, "
Zep 1: 8 as are c' with strange apparel. "
Zec 3: 3 Joshua was c' with filthy garments, "
5 head, and c' him with garments. "
M't 6:31 or, Wherewithal shall we be c'? 4016
11: 8 A man c' in soft raiment? 294
25:36 Naked, and ye c' me: I was sick, 4016
38 thee in? or naked, and c' thee? "
43 naked and ye c' me not: sick, "
M'r 1: 6 And John was c' with camel's hair, 1746
5:15 and c', and in his right mind: 2439
15:17 c' him with purple, and platted *1746
16: 5 c' in a long white garment; *4016
Lu 7:25 see? A man c' in soft raiment? 294
8:35 at the feet of Jesus, c', and in his 2439
16:19 was c' in purple and fine linen, 1737
2Co 5: 2 earnestly desiring to be c' upon 1902
3 being c' we shall not be found 1746
4 would be unclothed, but c' upon, 1902
1Pe 5: 5 be c' with humility: for God *1463
Re 1:13 c' with a garment down to the 1746
3: 5 shall be c' in white raiment; *4016
18 raiment, that thou mayest be c', * "
4: 4 sitting, c' in white raiment; * "
7: 9 c' with white robes, and palms in * "
10: 1 from heaven, c' with a cloud: * "
11: 3 threescore days, c' in sackcloth. "
12: 1 a woman c' with the sun, and the * "
15: 6 c' in pure and white linen, and *1746
18:16 city, that was c' in fine linen, *4016
19:13 c' with a vesture dipped in blood: * "
14 c' in fine linen, white and clean. 1746

clothes See also SACKCLOTHES.
Ge 37:29 in the pit; and he rent his c'. 899
34 And Jacob rent his c', and put *8071
44:13 Then they rent their c', and "
49:11 in wine, and his c' in the blood *5497
Ex 12:34 being bound up in their c' upon 8071
19:10 let them wash their c', "
14 people, and they washed their c'. * "
Le 10: 6 your heads, neither rend your c'; 899
11:25 shall wash his c', and be unclean "
28 carcase of them shall wash his c', "
40 carcase of it shall wash his c', "
40 shall wash his c', and be unclean "
13: 6, 34 shall wash his c', and be clean. "
45 c' shall be rent, and his head bare, "
14: 8 wash his c', and shave off all his hair, "
9 he shall wash his c', also he shall "
47 lieth in the house shall wash his c'; "
47 eateth in the house shall wash his c'. "
15: 5, 6, 7, 8, 10, 11, 13, 21, 22, 27 wash his c', "
16:26, 28 shall wash his c', and bathe "
32 shall put on the linen c', even * "
17:15 he shall both wash his c', and "
21:10 uncover his head, nor rend his c'; "
Nu 8: 7 let them wash their c', and so make "
21 purified, and they washed their c'; "
14: 6 that searched the land, rent their c': "
19: 7 Then the priest shall wash his c', "
8 that burneth her shall wash his c' "

Nu 19:10 of the heifer shall wash his *c*, 899
19 purify himself, and wash his *c*, "
21 of separation shall wash his *c*; "
31:24 wash your *c* on the seventh day, "
De 29: 5 *c* are not waxen old upon you, 8008
Jos 7: 6 Joshua rent his *c*, and fell to the 8071
J'g 11:35 that he rent his *c*, and said, Alas, 899
1Sa 4:12 with his *c* rent, and with earth 4055
19:24 he stripped off his *c* also, and 899
2Sa 1: 2 camp from Saul with his *c* rent, "
11 David took hold on his *c*, and rent "
3:31 Rend your *c*, and gird you with "
13:31 servants stood by with their *c* rent. "
19:24 nor washed his *c*, from the day the "
1Ki 1: 1 they covered him with *c*, but he gat "
21:27 that he rent his *c*, and put "
2Ki 2:12 he took hold of his own *c*, and "
5: 7 that he rent his *c*, and said, Am I "
8 the king of Israel had rent his *c*, "
8 hast thou rent thy *c*? let him come "
6:30 the woman, that he rent his *c*; "
11:14 Athaliah rent her *c*, and cried, "
18:37 to Hezekiah with their *c* rent, "
19: 1 rent his *c*, and covered himself "
22:11 book of the law, that he rent his *c*. "
19 hast rent thy *c*, and wept before "
2Ch 23:13 Then Athaliah rent her *c*, and said, "
34:19 words of the law, that he rent his *c*. "
27 before me, and didst rend thy *c*, "
Ne 4:23 none of us put off our *c*, saving "
9:21 their *c* waxed not old, and their 8008
Es 4: 1 Mordecai rent his *c*, and put on 899
Job 9:31 and mine own *c* shall abhor me. 8008
Pr 6:27 bosom, and his *c* not be burned? 899
Isa 36:22 to Hezekiah with their *c* rent, "
37: 1 heard it, that he rent his *c*, "
Jer 41: 5 and their *c* rent, and having cut "
Eze 16:39 shall strip thee also of thy *c*, "
23:26 strip thee out of thy *c*, and take "
27:20 in precious *c* for chariots. * "
24 in blue *c*, and broidered work, *1545
Am 2: 8 lay themselves down upon *c* laid 899
M't 21: 7 put on them their *c*, and they **2440*
24:18 field return back to take his *c*. * "
26:65 Then the high priest rent his *c*, * "
M'r 5:28 If I may but touch his *c*, I shall * "
30 and said, Who touched my *c*? * "
14:63 Then the high priest rent his *c*, *5509*
15:20 and put his own *c* on him, **2440*
Lu 2: 7 and wrapped him in swaddling *c*, *4683*
12 the babe wrapped in swaddling *c*, "
8:27 and ware no *c*, neither abode in *2440*
19:36 they spread their *c* in the way. "
24:12 the linen *c* laid by themselves, **3608*
Joh 19:40 and wound it in linen *c* with the * "
20: 5 looking in, saw the linen *c* lying; * "
6 and seeth the linen *c* lie, "
7 not lying with the linen *c*, but * "
Ac 7:58 the witnesses laid down their *c* **2440*
14:14 rent their *c*, and ran in among * "
16:22 the magistrates rent off their *c*, * "
22:23 cast off their *c*, and threw dust * "

clothest
Jer 4:30 thou *c* thyself with crimson, 3847

clothing
Job 22: 6 and stripped the naked of their *c*. 899
24: 7 the naked to lodge without *c*, 3830
10 cause him to go naked without *c*, "
31:19 seen any perish for want of *c*, "
Ps 35:13 were sick, my *c* was sackcloth: "
45:13 within: her *c* is of wrought gold. "
Pr 27:26 lambs are for thy *c*, and the goats "
31:22 her *c* is silk and purple. "
25 Strength and honour are her *c*; "
Isa 3: 6 Thou hast *c*, be thou our ruler, 8071
7 my house is neither bread nor *c*: "
23:18 sufficiently, and for durable *c*. 4374
59:17 the garments of vengeance for *c*, 8516
Jer 10: 9 blue and purple is their *c*: they 3830
M't 7:15 come to you in sheep's *c*, but *1742*
11: 8 wear soft *c* are in kings' houses. *
M'r 12:38 which love to go in long *c*, and **4749*
Ac 10:30 stood before me in bright *c*, **2066*
Jas 2: 3 to him that weareth the gay *c*,

cloths
Ex 31:10 the *c* of service, and the holy * 899
35:19 The *c* of service, to do service in * "
39: 1 they made *c* of service, to do * "
41 The *c* of service to do service in * "

cloud See also CLOUDS.
Ge 9:13 I do set my bow in the *c*, and it 6051
14 when I bring a *c* over the earth, "
14 the bow shall be seen in the *c*: "
16 And the bow shall be in the *c*; "
Ex 13:21 them by day in a pillar of a *c*, "
22 took not away the pillar of the *c* "
14:19 the *c* went from before their face, "
20 it was a *c* and darkness to them, "
24 the pillar of fire and of the *c*, "
16:10 of the Lord appeared in the *c*. "
19: 9 I come unto thee in a thick *c*, "
16 and a thick *c* upon the mount, "
24:15 a *c* covered the mount. "
16 the *c* covered it six days: and "
16 Moses out of the midst of the *c*. "
18 went into the midst of the *c*, "
34: 5 And the Lord descended in the *c*, "
40:34 a *c* covered the tent of the "
35 *c* abode thereon, and the glory "
36 when the *c* was taken up from "
37 But if the *c* were not taken up, "
38 the *c* of the Lord was upon the "
Le 16: 2 in the *c* upon the mercy seat. "
13 that the *c* of the incense may "
Nu 9:15 the *c* covered the tabernacle. "

Nu 9:16 the *c* covered it by day, and the 6051
17 And when the *c* was taken up "
17 in the place where the *c* abode, "
18 as long as the *c* abode upon the "
19 *c* tarried long upon the tabernacle "
20 when the *c* was a few days upon "
21 when the *c* abode from even unto "
21 *c* was taken up in the morning, "
21 by night that the *c* was taken up, "
22 the *c* tarried upon the tabernacle, "
10:11 that the *c* was taken up "
12 the *c* rested in the wilderness of "
34 the *c* of the Lord was upon them "
11:25 And the Lord came down in a *c*, "
12: 5 came down in the pillar of the *c*, "
10 And the *c* departed from off the "
14:14 that thy *c* standeth over them, "
14 by day time in a pillar of a *c*, "
16:42 behold, the *c* covered it, and the "
De 1:33 ye should go, and in a *c* by day. "
5:22 the *c*, and of the thick darkness, "
31:15 the tabernacle in a pillar of a *c*: "
15 and the pillar of the *c* stood over "
1Ki 8:10 the *c* filled the house of the Lord, "
11 stand to minister because of the *c*: "
18:44 ariseth a little *c* out of the sea, 5645
2Ch 5:13 the house was filled with a *c*, 6051
14 to minister by reason of the *c*: "
Ne 9:19 the pillar of the *c* departed not "
Job 3: 5 let a *c* dwell upon it; let the 6053
7: 9 *c* is consumed and vanisheth away: 6051
22:13 he judge through the dark *c*? *6205
26: 8 the *c* is not rent under them. 6051
9 and spreadeth his *c* upon it. "
30:15 my welfare passeth away as a *c*. 5645
36:32 by the *c* that cometh betwixt. *
37:11 he wearieth the thick *c*: 5645
11 he scattereth his bright *c*: 6051
15 caused the light of his *c* to shine? "
38: 9 made the *c* the garment thereof, "
Ps 78:14 daytime also he led them with a *c*, "
105:39 He spread a *c* for a covering; and "
Pr 16:15 favour is as a *c* of the latter rain. 5645
Isa 4: 5 a *c* and smoke by day, and the 6051
18: 4 a *c* of dew in the heat of harvest. 5645
19: 1 the Lord rideth upon a swift *c*, "
25: 5 the heat with the shadow of a *c*: "
44:22 I have blotted out, as a thick *c*, "
22 as a *c*, thy sins: return unto me; 6051
60: 8 Who are these that fly as a *c*, 5645
La 2: 1 the daughter of Zion with a *c* 5743
3:44 hast covered thyself with a *c*, 6051
Eze 1: 4 a great *c*, and a fire infolding itself, "
28 that is in the *c* in the day of rain, "
8:11 and a thick *c* of incense went up. "
10: 3 and the *c* filled the inner court. "
4 the house was filled with the *c*, "
30:18 as for her, a *c* shall cover her, "
32: 7 I will cover the sun with a *c*, and "
38: 9 shalt be like a *c* to cover the land, "
16 as a *c* to cover the land; it shall "
Ho 6: 4 your goodness is as a morning *c*, "
13: 3 they shall be as the morning *c*, "
M't 17: 5 a bright *c* overshadowed them: *3507*
5 and behold a voice out of the *c*, "
M'r 9: 7 a *c* that overshadowed them: "
7 and a voice came out of the *c*, "
Lu 9:34 a *c*, and overshadowed them: "
34 as they entered into the *c*. "
35 there came a voice out of the *c*, "
12:54 ye see a *c* rise out of the west, "
21:27 in a *c* with power and great glory. "
Ac 1: 9 a *c* received him out of their sight. "
1Co 10: 1 all our fathers were under the *c*, "
2 Moses in the *c* and in the sea; "
Heb 12: 1 with so great a *c* of witnesses, *3509*
Re 10: 1 from heaven, clothed with a *c*: *3507*
11:12 ascended up to heaven in a *c*; "
14:14 and behold a white *c*, and upon the "
14 upon the *c* one sat like unto the Son "
15 to him that sat on the *c*, Thrust "
16 sat on the *c* thrust in his sickle "

clouds
De 4:11 darkness, *c*, and thick darkness. *6051
J'g 5: 4 the *c* also dropped water. 5645
2Sa 22:12 waters, and thick *c* of the skies. "
23: 4 even a morning without *c*; "
1Ki 18:45 was black with *c* and wind, "
Job 20: 6 and his head reach unto the *c*; "
22:14 Thick *c* are a covering to him, "
26: 8 up the waters in his thick *c*; "
35: 5 *c* which are higher than thou. *7834
36:28 *c* do drop and distil upon man * "
29 the spreadings of the *c*, 5645
32 With *c* he covereth the light; *3709
37:16 know the balancings of the *c*, 5645
21 bright light which is in the *c*: *7834
38:34 thou lift up thy voice to the *c*, 5645
37 can number the *c* in wisdom? 7834
Ps 18:11 waters and thick *c* of the skies. 5645
12 before him his thick *c* passed, "
36: 5 faithfulness reacheth unto the *c*. *7834
57:10 and thy truth unto the *c*. * "
68:34 and his strength is in the *c*. "
77:17 The *c* poured out water: the 5645
78:23 commanded the *c* from above, *7834
97: 2 *C* and darkness are round about 6051
104: 3 who maketh the *c* his chariot: 5645
108: 4 thy truth reacheth unto the *c*. *7834
147: 8 Who covereth the heaven with *c*, 5645
Pr 3:20 and the *c* drop down the dew. *7834
8:28 When he established the *c* above: * "
25:14 is like *c* and wind without rain. 5387
Ec 11: 3 If the *c* be full of rain, they empty 5645
4 regardeth the *c* shall not reap. "
12: 2 nor the *c* return after the rain: "

Isa 5: 6 I will also command the *c* that 5645
14:14 ascend above the heights of the *c*; "
Jer 4:13 he shall come up as *c*, and his 6053
Da 7:13 of man came with the *c* of heaven 6050
Joe 2: 2 a day of *c* and of thick darkness, 6051
Na 1: 3 and the *c* are the dust of his feet. "
Zep 1:15 a day of *c* and thick darkness, "
Zec 10: 1 the Lord shall make bright *c*, *2385
M't 24:30 in the *c* of heaven with power *3507*
26:64 and coming in the *c* of heaven. "
M'r 13:26 the Son of man coming in the *c* "
14:62 and coming in the *c* of heaven. "
1Th 4:17 up together with them in the *c*, "
2Pe 2:17 *c* that are carried with a * "
Jude 12 *c* they are without water, carried "
Re 1: 7 Behold he cometh with *c*; and "

cloudy
Ex 33: 9 *c* pillar descended, and stood *6051
10 the people saw the *c* pillar stand * "
Ne 9:12 them in the day by a *c* pillar; * "
Ps 99: 7 spake unto them in the *c* pillar: * "
Eze 30: 3 day of the Lord is near, a *c* day; * "
34:12 scattered in the *c* and dark day. "

clouted
Jos 9: 5 old shoes and *c* upon their feet, ‡2921

clouts
Jer 38:11 old cast *c* and old rotten rags, 5499
12 Put now these old cast *c* and "

clove See CLAVE.

cloven See also CLOVENFOOTED.
De 14: 7 or of them that divide the *c* hoof; 8156
Ac 2: 3 appeared unto them *c* tongues **1266*

clovenfooted
Le 11: 3 the hoof, and is *c*, 8156, 8157, 6541
7 the hoof, and be *c*, " "
26 the hoof, and is not *c*, " "

cluster See also CLUSTERS.
Nu 13:23 a branch with one *c* of grapes, 811
24 the *c* of grapes which the children "
Ca 1:14 My beloved is unto me as a *c* of "
Isa 65: 8 As the new wine is found in the *c*, "
Mic 7: 1 there is no *c* to eat: my soul "

clusters
Ge 40:10 the *c* thereof brought forth ripe 811
De 32:32 grapes of gall, their *c* are bitter: "
1Sa 25:18 and an hundred *c* of raisins, 6778
30:12 cake of figs, and two *c* of raisins: "
Ca 7: 7 and thy breasts to *c* of grapes. 811
8 breasts shall be as *c* of the vine, "
Re 14:18 the *c* of the vine of the earth; *1009*

Cnidus (*ni'-dus*)
Ac 27: 7 scarce were come over against *C*, *2834*

coal See also COALS.
2Sa 14: 7 so they shall quench my *c* which 1513
Isa 6: 6 having a live *c* in his hand, 7531
47:14 there shall not be a *c* to warm at, 1513
La 4: 8 Their visage is blacker than a *c*; 7815

coals
Le 16:12 take a censer full of burning *c* 1513
2Sa 22: 9 devoured: *c* were kindled by it. "
13 before him were *c* of fire "
1Ki 19: 6 there was a cake baken on the *c*, 7529
Job 41:21 His breath kindleth *c*, and a 1513
Ps 18: 8 devoured: *c* were kindled by it. "
12 passed, hail stones and *c* of fire. "
13 his voice; hail stones and *c* of fire. "
120: 4 of the mighty, with *c* of juniper. "
140:10 let burning *c* fall upon them: let "
Pr 6:28 Can one go upon hot *c*, and his "
25:22 thou shalt heap *c* of fire upon his "
26:21 As *c* are to burning 6352
21 are to burning *c*, and wood to *1513
Ca 8: 6 the *c* thereof are *c* of fire, which *7565
Isa 44:12 the tongs both worketh in the *c*, 6352
19 baked bread upon the *c* thereof; 1513
54:16 the smith that bloweth the *c* 6352
Eze 1:13 was like burning *c* of fire, 1513
10: 2 and fill thine hand with *c* of fire "
24:11 Then set it empty upon the *c* "
Hab 3: 5 and burning *c* went forth at his *7565
Joh 18:18 who had made a fire of *c*; for it *439*
21: 9 they saw a fire of *c* there, and fish "
Ro 12:20 thou shalt heap *c* of fire on his *440*

coast See also COASTS.
Ex 10: 4 I bring the locusts into thy *c*: *1366
Nu 13:29 the sea, and by the *c* of Jordan. *3027
20:23 by the *c* of the land of Edom, *1366
22:36 Arnon, which is in the utmost *c*.* "
24:24 shall come from the *c* of Chittim, 3027
34: 3 of Zin along by the *c* of Edom, * "
3 the outmost *c* of the salt sea *7097
11 *c* shall go down from Shepham *1366
De 2: 4 through the *c* of your brethren * "
18 over through Ar, the *c* of Moab, * "
3:17 Jordan, and the *c* thereof, * "
11:24 uttermost sea shall your *c* be, * "
16: 4 seen with thee in all thy *c* seven * "
19: 8 the Lord thy God enlarge thy *c*, * "
Jos 1: 4 down of the sun, shall be your *c*. * "
12: 4 And the *c* of Og king of Bashan, * "
23 The king of Dor in the *c* of Dor, *5299
13:16 their *c* was from Aroer, that is *1366
25 their *c* was Jazer, and all the * "
30 And their *c* was from Mahanaim, * "
15: 1 uttermost part of the south *c*. * "
4 out of that *c* were at the sea: * "
4 this shall be your south *c*. * "
12 the great sea, and the *c* thereof. * "
12 is the *c* of the children of Judah, * "
21 toward the *c* of Edom southward * "
16: 3 to the *c* of Japhleti, unto the *c* * "

Jos 17: 7 the c' of Manasseh was from *1366
9 And the c' descended unto the * "
9 the c' of Manasseh also was on * "
18: 5 Judah shall abide in their c' on * "
11 and the c' of their lot came forth * "
19 of Jordan: this was the south c'. * "
19:22 the c' reacheth to Tabor, and * "
29 the c' turneth to Ramah, and to * "
29 and the c' turneth to Hosah; * "
29 at the sea from the c' to Achzib: *2256
33 their c' was from Heleph, from *1366
34 then the c' turneth westward to * "
41 the c' of the inheritance was * "
47 the c' of the children of Dan went* "
J'g 1:18 Gaza with the c' thereof, * "
18 and Askelon with the c' thereof. * "
18 and Ekron with the c' thereof. * "
36 And the c' of the Amorites was * "
11:20 not Israel to pass through his c': * "
1Sa 6: 9 by the way of his own c' to * "
7:13 no more into the c' of Israel: * "
27: 1 any more in any c' of Israel: * "
30:14 the c' which belongeth to Judah, * "
2Ki 14:25 He restored the c' of Israel from *1366
1Ch 4:10 me indeed, and enlarge my c', * "
Eze 25:16 destroy the remnant of the sea c'. 2348
47:16 which is by the c' of Hauran. *1366
48: 1 the c' of the way of Hethlon, as *3027
1 northward, to the c' of Hamath; *3027
Zep 2: 5 unto the inhabitants of the sea c', 2256
6 the sea c' shall be dwellings and "
7 the c' shall be for the remnant of "
M't 4:13 which is upon the sea c'. *3864
Lu 6:17 from the sea c' of Tyre and Sidon, 3882

coasts
Ex 10:14 and rested in all the c' of Egypt: *1366
19 one locust in all the c' of Egypt. * "
Nu 21:13 out of the c' of the Amorites: * "
32:33 with the cities thereof in the c', *1367
34: 2 the land of Canaan with the c' * "
12 your land with the c' thereof * "
De 3:14 of Argob unto the c' of Geshuri *1366
19: 3 divide the c' of thy land, which * "
28:40 olive trees throughout all thy c', * "
Jos 9: 1 in all the c' of the great sea over *2348
18: 5 Joseph shall abide in their c' on *1366
20 Benjamin by the c' thereof *1367
19:49 land for inheritance by their c', * "
J'g 11:22 all the c' of the Amorites, *1366
26 that be along by the c' of Arnon, *3027
18: 2 five men from their c', men of *7098
19:29 sent her into all the c' of Israel. *1366
1Sa 5: 6 even Ashdod and the c' thereof. * "
7:14 and the c' thereof did Israel * "
11: 3 unto all the c' of Israel: * "
7 throughout all the c' of Israel * "
2Sa 21: 5 in any of the c' of Israel, * "
1Ki 1: 3 throughout all the c' of Israel, * "
2Ki 10:32 smote them in all the c' of Israel; * "
15:16 therein, and the c' thereof from * "
1Ch 6:54 their castles in their c', * "
66 had cities of their c' out of the * "
21:12 throughout all the c' of Israel. ‡ "
2Ch 11:13 resorted to him out of all their c'.* "
Ps 105:31 flies, and lice in all their c'. * "
33 brake the trees of their c'. * "
Jer 25:32 up from the c' of the earth. *3411
31: 8 them from the c' of the earth, * "
50:41 up from the c' of the earth. * "
Eze 33: 2 take a man of their c', and set *7097
Joel 3: 4 Zidon, and all the c' of Palestine? *1552
M't 2:16 and in all the c' thereof, from *3725
8:34 he would depart out of their c'. * "
15:21 departed into the c' of Tyre and *3313
22 out of the same c', and cried *3725
39 came into the c' of Magdala. * "
16:13 Jesus came into the c' of Caesarea *3313
19: 1 and came into the c' of Judæa *3725
M'k 5:17 pray him to depart out of their c'.* "
7:31 departing from the c' of Tyre * "
31 the midst of the c' of Decapolis. * "
10: 1 and cometh into the c' of Judæa * "
Ac 13:50 and expelled them out of their c'.* "
19: 1 passed through the upper c' *3313
26:20 throughout all the c' of Judæa, *5561
27: 2 meaning to sail by the c' of Asia; *5117

coat See also COATS.
Ge 37: 3 made him a c' of many colours. 3801
23 out of his c', his c' of many colours "
31 they took Joseph's c', and killed "
31 and dipped the c' in the blood; "
32 they sent the c' of many colours, "
32 whether it be thy son's c' or no. "
33 it, and said, It is my son's c'; "
Ex 28: 4 and a broidered c', a mitre, and "
39 embroider the c' of fine linen, "
29: 5 put upon Aaron the c', and the "
Lev 8: 7 he put upon him the c', and "
16: 4 He shall put on the holy linen c', "
1Sa 2:19 his mother made him a little c', *4598
17: 5 he was armed with a c' of mail; 8302
5 and the weight of the c' was "
38 he armed him with a c' of mail. "
2 Sa 15:32 came to meet him with his c' rent,3801
Job 30:18 me about as the collar of my c'. "
Ca 5: 3 I have put off my c'; how shall I ‡ "
M't 5:40 at the law, and take away thy c', 5509
Lu 6:29 forbid not to take thy c' also. "
Joh 19:23 and also his c': now the c' was "
21: 7 he girt his fisher's c' unto him, 1903

coat of mail See COAT and MAIL.

coats
Gen 3:21 did the Lord God make c' of skins, 3801
Ex 28:40 Aaron's sons thou shalt make c', 3801
29: 8 his sons, and put c' upon them. "
39:27 they made c' of fine linen of "
40:14 sons, and clothe them with c': "
Le 8:13 put c' upon them, and girded them "
10: 5 carried them in their c' out of the "
Da 3:21 bound in their c', their hosen *5622
27 neither were their c' changed, * "
M't 10:10 neither two c', neither shoes, 5509
M'r 6: 9 sandals; and not put on two c'. "
Lu 3:11 He that hath two c', let him "
9: 3 money; neither have two c' apiece. "
Ac 9:39 shewing the c' and garments which "

cock See also COCKCROWING; PEACOCKS.
M't 26:34 this night, before the c' crow, thou 220
74 And immediately the c' crew. "
75 Before the c' crow, thou shalt deny "
M'r 14:30 before the c' crow twice, thou shalt "
68 into the porch; and the c' crew. "
72 the second time the c' crew. "
72 said unto him, Before the c' crow "
Lu 22:34 the c' shall not crow this day, "
60 while he yet spake, the c' crew. "
61 Before the c' crow, thou shalt deny "
Joh 13:38 The c' shall not crow, till thou hast "
18:27 and immediately the c' crew. "

cockatrice See also COCKATRICE'; COCKATRICES.
Isa 14:29 shall come forth a c', and his †‡6848

cockatrice'
Isa 11: 8 shall put his hand on the c' den. †‡6848
59: 5 They hatch c' eggs, and weave the†‡ "

cockatrices
Jer 8:17 I will send serpents, c', among, †‡6848

cockcrowing
M'r 13:35 at midnight, or at the c', or in the 219

cockle
Job 31:40 instead of wheat, and c' instead of 890

coffer
1Sa 6: 8 a trespass offering, in a c' by the 712
11 the c' with the mice of gold and "
15 and the c' that was with it, wherein "

coffin
Ge 50:26 and he was put in a c' in Egypt. 727

cogitations
Dan 7:28 my c' much troubled me, and *7476

Col See COL-HOZEH.

cold
Ge 8:22 and c' and heat, and summer 7120
Job 24: 7 they have no covering in the c'. 7135
37: 9 whirlwind: and c' out of the north. "
Ps 147:17 who can stand before his c'? "
Pr 20: 4 will not plow by reason of the c'; *2779
25:13 As the c' of snow in the time of 6793
20 away a garment in c' weather, 7135
25 c' waters to a thirsty soul, so is 7119
Jer 18:14 shall the c' flowing waters that "
Na 3:17 camp in the hedges in the c' day, 7135
M't 10:42 these little ones a cup of c' water 5593
24:12 the love of many shall wax c'. 5594
Joh 18:18 made a fire of coals; for it was c': 5592
Ac 28: 2 present rain, and because of the c'. "
2Co 11:27 in fastings often, in c' and "
Re 3:15 that thou art neither c' nor hot: 5593
15 I would thou wert c' or hot. "
16 and neither c' nor hot, I will spue "

Col-hozeh (*col-ho'-zeh*)
Ne 3:15 repaired Shallum the son of C', 3626
11: 5 the son of Baruch, the son of C', "

collar See also COLLARS.
Job 30:18 me about as the c' of my coat. 6310

collars
J'g 8:26 and c', and purple raiment *5188

collection
2Ch 24: 6 out of Jerusalem the c', according *4864
9 to the Lord the c' that Moses * "
1Co 16: 1 concerning the c' for the saints, 3048

college
2Ki 22:14 she dwelt in Jerusalem in the c';) *4932
2Ch 34:22 she dwelt in Jerusalem in the c':) * "

collops
Job 15:27 maketh c' of fat on his flanks. ‡6371

colony
Ac 16:12 part of Macedonia, and a c': *2862

color See COLOUR.

Colossæ See COLOSSE.

Colosse (*co-los'-see*) See also COLOSSIANS.
Col 1: 2 in Christ which are at C': 2857

Colossians (*co-los'-yans*)
Col *subscr.* Written from Rome to the C' *2858

colour See also COLOURED; COLOURS.
Le 13:55 plague have not changed his c', 5869
Nu 11: 7 c' thereof as the c' of bdellium. * "
Pr 23:31 when it giveth his c' in the cup, "
Eze 1: 4 midst thereof as the c' of amber, ‡ "
7 like the c' of burnished brass. ‡ "
16 was like unto the c' of a beryl: ‡ "
22 as the c' of the terrible crystal, ‡ "
27 And I saw as c' of amber, as ‡ "
8: 2 of brightness, as the c' of amber. ‡ "
10: 9 wheels was as the c' of a beryl ‡ "
Da 10: 6 feet like in c' to polished brass, "
Ac 27:30 under c' as though they would 4392
Re 17: 4 arrayed in purple and scarlet c', *

coloured
Re 17: 3 sit upon a scarlet c' beast,

colours
Ge 37: 3 he made him a coat of many c'. 6446
23 coat of many c' that was on him; "
32 And they sent the coat of many c', "
J'g 5:30 to Sisera a prey of divers c', 6648
30 a prey of divers c' of needlework, "
30 of divers c' of needlework on both "
2Sa 13:18 a garment of divers c' upon her: 6446
19 rent her garment of divers c' "
1Ch 29: 2 glistering stones, and of divers c', 7553
Isa 54:11 I will lay thy stones with fair c', 6320
Eze 16:16 thy high places with divers c', 2921
17: 3 of feathers, which had divers c', 7553

colt See also COLTS
Ge 49:11 ass's c' unto the choice vine; 1121
Job 11:12 man be born like a wild ass's c'. 5895
Zec 9: 9 and upon a c' the foal of an ass. "
M't 21: 2 find an ass tied, and a c' with her: 4454
5 an ass, and a c' the foal of an ass. "
7 brought the ass, and the c', and put "
M'r 11: 2 ye shall find a c' tied, whereon "
4 and found the c' tied by the door "
5 them, What do ye, loosing the c'? "
7 brought the c' to Jesus, and cast "
Lu 19:30 entering ye shall find a c' tied, "
33 as they were loosing the c', the "
33 unto them, Why loose ye the c'? "
35 cast their garments upon the c', "
Joh 12:15 king cometh, sitting on an ass's c'. "

colts
Ge 32:15 milch camels with their c', forty 1121
J'g 10: 4 sons that rode on thirty ass c', 5895
12:14 rode on threescore and ten ass c': "

combs See HONEYCOMBS.

come See also CAME; COMEST; COMETH; COMING; BECOME; OVERCOME.
Ge 4:14 it shall c' to pass, that every one 1961
6:13 end of all flesh is c' before me; 935
18 and thou shalt c' into the ark, thou, "
20 two of every sort shall c' unto thee, "
7: 1 C' thou and all thy house into the "
12:11 was c' near to enter into Egypt, 7126
14 when Abram was c' into Egypt, 935
15: 4 shall c' forth out of thine own 3318
14 they c' out with great substance. "
16 they shall c' hither again: for the 7725
17: 6 thee, and kings shall c' out of thee. 3318
18: 5 therefore are ye c' to your servant.5674
21 the cry of it, which is c' unto me; 935
19:22 cannot do any thing till thou be c' "
31 to c' in unto us after the manner "
32 C', let us make our father drink 3212
20: 4 Abimelech had not c' near her: 7126
13 whither we shall c', say of me, 935
22: 5 and worship, and c' again to you. 7725
24:13 of the city c' out to draw water: 3318
31 C' in, thou blessed of the Lord; 935
43 c' to pass, that when the virgin 1961
26:27 Wherefore c' ye to me, seeing ye 935
27:21 C' near, I pray thee, that I may 5066
26 C' near now, and kiss me, my son. "
40 it shall c' to pass when thou shalt 1961
28:21 I c' again to my father's house 7725
30:16 Thou must c' in unto me; for 935
33 answer for me in time to c', *4279
33 c' for my hire before thy face: 935
31:44 c' thou, let us make a covenant, 3212
32: 8 If Esau c' to the one company, 935
11 him, lest he will c' and smite me, "
33:14 until I c' unto my Lord unto Seir. "
34: 5 his peace until they were c'. * "
35:11 kings shall c' out of thy loins; 3318
16 but a little way to c' to Ephrath: 935
37:10 mother and thy brethren indeed c' "
13 c', and I will send thee unto them. 3212
20 C' now therefore, and let us slay "
23 Joseph was c' unto his brethren, 935
27 C', and let us sell him to the 3212
38:16 pray thee, let me c' in unto thee; 935
16 that thou mayest c' in unto me? "
41:29 there c' seven years of great plenty "
35 the food of those good years that c', "
54 seven years of dearth began to c', "
42: 7 Whence c' ye? And they said, "
9 the nakedness of the land ye are c'. "
10 but to buy food are thy servants c'. "
12 the nakedness of the land ye are c'. "
15 your youngest brother c' hither. "
21 therefore is this distress c' upon us. "
44:23 Except your youngest brother c' 3381
30 when I c' to thy servant my father, 935
31 It shall c' to pass, when he seeth 1961
34 the evil that shall c' on my father. 4672
45: 4 C' near to me, I pray you. And 5066
9 c' down unto me, tarry not: 3381
11 all that thou hast, c' to poverty.
16 Joseph's brethren are c': and it 935
18 and c' unto me: and I will give you "
19 wives, and bring your father, and c'. "
46:31 My brethren, ... are c' unto me; "
33 it shall c' to pass, when Pharaoh 1961
47: 1 they have, are c' out of the land 935
4 to sojourn in the land are we c'; "
5 and thy brethren are c' unto thee: "
24 it shall c' to pass in the increase 1961
48: 7 a little way to c' unto Ephrath: 935
49: 6 soul, c' not thou into their secret; "
10 until Shiloh c'; and unto him shall "
50: 5 my father, and I will c' again. 7725
Ex 1:10 C' on, let us deal wisely with 3051
10 and it c' to pass, that, when there 1961
19 ere the midwives c' in unto them, 935
2:18 is it that ye are c' so soon to day? "

Ex 3: 8 And I am c' down to deliver them 3381
9 children of Israel is c' unto me: 935
10 C' now therefore, and I will send 3212
13 I c' unto the children of Israel, 935
18 c', thou and the elders of Israel, "
21 and it shall c' to pass, that, when 1961
4: 8, 9 c' to pass, if they will not believe "
7:15 by the river's brink against he c';*7125
8: 3 c' into thine house, and into thy 935
4 the frogs shall c' up both on thee, 5927
5 cause frogs to c' up upon the land "
9:19 the hail shall c' down upon them, 3381
10:12 they may c' up upon the land 5927
26 serve the Lord, until we c' thither. 935
11: 8 these thy servants shall c' down 3381
12:23 not suffer the destroyer to c' in 935
25 And it shall c' to pass, when ye 1961
25 be c' to the land which the Lord 935
26 it shall c' to pass, when your 1961
48 then let him c' near and keep it; 7126
13:14 thy son asketh thee in time to c', 4279
14:26 may c' again upon the Egyptians, 7725
16: 5 And it shall c' to pass, that on 1961
9 C' near before the Lord: for he 7126
17: 6 and there shall c' water out of it, 3318
18: 6 father in law Jethro am c' unto 935
8 the travail that had c' upon them 4672
15 the people c' unto me to enquire 935
16 have a matter, they c' unto me; "
19: 2 and were c' to the desert of Sinai, "
9 c' unto thee in a thick cloud, "
11 third day the Lord will c' down 3381
13 they shall c' up to the mount. 5927
15 third day: c' not at your wives. 5066
22 also, which c' near to the Lord, "
23 cannot c' up to mount Sinai: 5927
24 thou shalt c' up, thou, and Aaron "
24 through to c' up unto the Lord, "
20:20 for God is c' to prove you, and 935
24 I will c' unto thee, and I will bless "
21:14 if a man c' presumptuously upon "
22: 9 parties shall c' before the judges; 935
27 and it shall c' to pass, when 1961
23:27 to whom thou shalt c', and I will 935
24: 1 C' up unto the Lord, thou, and 5927
2 Moses alone shall c' near the Lord:5066
2 they shall not c' nigh; neither "
12 Lord said unto Moses, C' up to me 5927
14 until we c' again unto you: and, 7725
14 to do, let him c' unto them. 5066
25:32 shall c' out of the sides of it; *3318
33 the six branches that c' out of * "
28:43 when they c' in unto the tabernacle* 935
43 when they c' near unto the altar 5066
30:20 c' near to the altar to minister, "
32: 1 to c' down out of the mount, 3381
26 Lord's side? let him c' unto me. 935
33: 5 I will c' up into the midst of thee *5927
22 it shall c' to pass, while my glory 1961
34: 2 and c' up in the morning unto 5927
3 And no man shall c' up with thee, "
30 they were afraid to c' nigh him. 5066
35:10 wise hearted among you shall c', 935
36: 2 him up to c' unto the work 7126
Le 4:23 hath sinned, c' to his knowledge;*3045
28 hath sinned, c' to his knowledge: * "
10: 3 sanctified in them that c' nigh 7138
4 C' near, carry your brethren *7126
6 wrath c' upon all the people: *
12: 4 nor c' into the sanctuary, until 935
13:16 he shall c' unto the priest; "
14: 8 that he shall c' into the camp, "
34 ye be c' into the land of Canaan, "
35 he that owneth the house shall c' "
39 shall c' again the seventh day, 7725
43 if the plague c' again, and break "
44 Then the priest shall c' and look, 935
48 priest shall c' in, and look upon it, "
15:14 and c' before the Lord unto the door "
16: 2 that he c' not at all times into the "
3 shall Aaron c' into the holy place: "
17 until he c' out, and have made an 3318
23 Aaron shall c' into the tabernacle 935
24 put on his garments, and c' forth, 3318
26 and afterward c' into the camp. 935
28 afterward he shall c' into the camp. "
19:19 of linen and woollen c' upon thee. 5927
23 when ye shall c' into the land, 935
21:21 shall c' nigh to offer the offering 5066
21 shall not c' nigh to offer the bread "
23 nor c' nigh unto the altar, because "
23:10 When ye be c' into the land which 935
25: 2 c' into the land which I give you, "
22 c' in ye shall eat of the old store. "
25 if any of his kin c' to redeem it, "
Nu 1: 1 were c' out of the land of Egypt, 3318
4: 5 setteth forward, Aaron shall c', * 935
15 sons of Kohath shall c' to bear it; "
5:14 spirit of jealousy c' upon him, 5674
14 the spirit of jealousy c' upon him, "
27 it shall c' to pass, that if she 1961
6: 5 shall no rasor c' upon his head: 5674
6 he shall c' at no dead body. 935
8:19 when the children of Israel c' nigh 5066
9: 1 after they were c' out of the land 3318
10:29 c' thou with us, and we will do 3212
11:17 I will c' down and talk with thee 3381
20 until it c' out at your nostrils, 3318
23 shall c' to pass unto thee or not. 7136
12: 4 C' out ye three unto the 3318
13:21 Rehob, as men c' to Hamath. * 935
33 sons of Anak, which c' of the giants: "
14:30 ye shall not c' into the land, 935
15: 2 When ye be c' into the land of "
18 When ye c' into the land whither I "

Nu 16: 5 cause him to c' near unto him: 7126
5 will he cause to c' near unto him. "
12 which said, We will not c' up: 5927
14 of these men? we will not c' up. "
40 c' near to offer incense before 7126
17: 5 c' to pass, that the man's rod, 1961
18: 3 they shall not c' nigh the vessels 7126
4 stranger shall not c' nigh unto you. "
22 c' nigh the tabernacle of the "
19: 7 he shall c' into the camp, 935
14 all that c' into the tent, and all * "
20: 5 have ye made us to c' up 5927
18 lest I c' out against thee with the 3318
21: 8 it shall c' to pass, that every one 1961
27 C' into Heshbon, let the city of 935
22: 5 is a people c' out from Egypt: 3318
6 C' now therefore, I pray thee, 3212
11 there is a people c' out of Egypt, 3318
11 c' now, curse me them; 3212
14 Balaam refuseth to c' with us. 1980
17 c' therefore, I pray thee, curse 3212
20 If the men c' to call thee, rise up, 935
36 Balak he d that Balaam was c', "
38 Lo, I am c' unto thee: have I now "
23: 3 the Lord will c' to meet me: and 7136
7 C', curse me Jacob, and c', defy 3212
13 C', I pray thee, with me unto "
27 C', I pray thee, I will bring thee "
24:14 c' therefore, and I will advertise "
17 there shall c' a Star out of Jacob, 1869
19 Out of Jacob shall c' he that *3381
24 shall c' from the coast of Chittim, "
26:29 c' the family of the Gileadites. *
27:21 at his word they shall c' in, both 935
31:24 ye shall c' into the camp. "
33:38 the children of Israel were c' 3318
55 then it shall c' to pass, that those *1961
56 Moreover it shall c' to pass, "
34: 2 ye c' into the land of Canaan; 935
35:10 When ye be c' over Jordan into *5674
26 if the slayer shall at any time c' *3318
32 c' again to dwell in the land, 7725
De 1:20 Ye are c' unto the mountain of the 935
22 into what cities we shall c'. "
2:14 we were c' over the brook Zered, 5674
4:30 all these things are c' upon thee, 4672
46 they were c' forth out of Egypt: *3318
6:20 thy son asketh thee in time to c', 4279
7:12 Wherefore it shall c' to pass, if ye 1961
10: 1 c' up unto me into the mount, 5927
11:13 And it shall c' to pass, if ye shall 1961
29 it shall c' to pass, when the Lord "
12: 5 seek, and thither thou shalt c': 935
9 For ye are not as yet c' to the rest "
13: 2 the sign or the wonder c' to pass, "
14:29 shall c', and shall eat and be "
15:19 firstling males that c' of thy herd*3205
17: 9 And thou shalt c' unto the priests 935
14 thou art c' unto the land which "
18: 6 if a Levite c' from any of thy gates "
6 c' with all the desire of his mind "
9 When thou art c' into the land "
19 it shall c' to pass, that whosoever 1961
22 thing follow not, nor c' to pass, 935
20: 2 ye are c' nigh unto the battle, *7126
21: 2 and thy judges shall c' forth, 3318
5 the sons of Levi shall c' near; 5066
23:10 he shall not c' within the camp: 935
11 he shall c' into the camp again. "
24: 1 and it c' to pass that she find no *1961
9 ye were c' forth out of Egypt. *3318
25: 1 and they c' unto judgment, 5066
9 Then shall his brother's wife c' "
17 ye were c' forth out of Egypt; *3318
26: 1 when thou art c' in unto the land 935
3 c' unto the country which the Lord "
27:12 when ye are c' over Jordan; 5674
28: 1 c' to pass, if thou shalt hearken 1961
2 these blessings shall c' on thee, 935
7 shall c' out against thee one way, 3318
15 it shall c' to pass, if thou wilt not 1961
15 all these curses shall c' upon thee, 935
24 shall it c' down upon thee, 3381
43 and thou shalt c' down very low. "
45 all these curses shall c' upon thee, 935
52 high and fenced walls c' down, 3381
63 shall c' to pass, that as the Lord 1961
29:19 And it c' to pass, when he heareth "
22 So that the generation to c' of 314
22 that shall c' from a far land, 935
30: 1 And it shall c' to pass, when 1961
1 all these things are c' upon thee, 935
31: 2 can no more go out and c' in: "
11 When all Israel is c' to appear "
17 Are not these evils c' upon us, 4672
21 shall c' to pass, when many evil 1961
32:35 shall c' upon them make haste. 6264
33:16 c' upon the head of Joseph, 935
Jos 2: 3 forth the men that are c' to thee, "
3 c' to search out all the country. "
18 Behold, when we c' into the land, "
3: 4 c' not near unto it, that ye may 7126
8 ye are c' to the brink of the water 935
9 C' hither, and hear the words of 5066
13 And it shall c' to pass, as soon as 1961
13 waters that c' down from above; 3381
15 as they that bare the ark were c' 935
4: 6 ask their fathers in time to c', 4279
16 that they c' up out of Jordan. 5927
17 saying, C' ye up out of Jordan. "
18 c' up out of the midst of Jordan, "
21 in time to c', saying, What men 4279
5:14 the host of the Lord am I now c'. 935
6: 5 c' to pass, that when they make *1961
19 c' into the treasury of the Lord. 935

Jos 7:14 which the Lord taketh shall c' 7126
14 which the Lord shall take shall c' "
8: 5 and it shall c' to pass, when they 1961
5 c' out against us, as at the first, 3318
6 (For they will c' out after us) till "
9: 6 We be c' from a far country: now 935
8 are ye? and from whence c' ye? "
9 thy servants are c' because of the "
10: 4 C' up unto me, and help me, that 5927
6 c' up to us quickly, and save us, "
24 C' near, put your feet upon the 7126
11:20 should c' against Israel in battle, 7122
14:11 war, both to go out, and to c' in. 935
18: 4 and they shall c' again to me, "
8 and describe it, and c' again to me, 7725
20: 6 and c' unto his own city, and unto 935
22:24 In time to c' your children might 4279
27 say to our children in time to c', "
28 to our generations in time to c', "
23: 7 ye c' not among these nations, 935
14 all are c' to pass unto you, and not "
15 Therefore it shall c' to pass, that 1961
15 as all good things are c' upon you, 935
J'g 1: 3 C' up with me into my lot, that 5927
24 the spies saw a man c' forth out 3318
34 would not suffer them to c' down 3381
3:27 when he was c', that he blew a 935
4:20 man doth c' and enquire of thee, "
22 C', and I will shew thee the 3212
6: 4 till thou c' unto Gaza, and left no 935
18 pray thee, until I c' unto thee, "
18 I will tarry until thou c' again. 7725
7:13 And when Gideon was c', behold, 935
17 I c' to the outside of the camp, "
24 C' down against the Midianites, 3381
8: 9 When I c' again in peace, I will 7725
9:10 tree, C' thou, and reign over us. 3212
12 vine, C' thou, and reign over us. "
14 bramble, C' thou, and reign over us. "
15 c' and put your trust in my 935
15 let fire c' out of the bramble, and 3318
20 let fire c' out from Abimelech, "
20 fire c' out from the men of Shechem, "
24 and ten sons of Jerubbaal might c', 935
29 Increase thine army, and c' out. 3318
31 his brethren be c' to Shechem; 935
33 is with him c' out against thee, 3318
36 there c' people down from the top 3381
37 c' people down by the middle * "
37 another company c' along by the 935
43 were c' forth out of the city; *3318
11: 6 C', and be our captain, that we 3212
7 why are ye c' unto me now when 935
12 thou art c' against me to fight in "
33 Aroer, even till thou c' to Minnith, "
12: 3 are ye c' up unto me this day, 5927
13: 5 and no rasor shall c' on his head: "
8 which thou didst send c' again 935
12 said, Now let thy words c' to pass. "
17 that when thy sayings c' to pass we "
15:10 Why are ye c' up against us? And 5927
10 To bind Samson are we c' "
12 We are c' down to bind thee, that 3381
16: 2 saying, Samson is c' hither. 935
17 There hath not c' a rasor upon 5927
18 C' up this once, for he hath "
18:10 ye shall c' unto a people secure, 935
19:11 C', I pray thee, and let us turn in 3212
13 C', and let us draw near to one of "
23 that this man is c' into mine house, 935
29 And when he was c' into his house, "
20:10 they c' to Gibeah of Benjamin, "
41 saw that evil was c' upon them. 5060
21: 3 why is this c' to pass in Israel, 1961
21 daughters of Shiloh c' out to dance 3318
21 then c' ye out of the vineyards, and "
22 brethren c' unto us to complain, 935
Ru 1:19 when they were c' to Beth-lehem, "
2:11 art c' unto a people which thou 1980
12 whose wings thou art c' to trust. 935
14 At mealtime c' thou hither, and 5066
4: 3 Naomi, that is c' again out of the 7725
11 woman that is c' into thine house 935
1Sa 1:11 shall no rasor c' upon his head. 5927
20 when the time was c' about after 8622
2: 3 arrogancy c' out of your mouth: 3318
31 Behold, the days c', that I will cut 935
34 that shall c' upon thy two sons, on "
36 shall c' to pass, that every one 1961
36 c' and crouch to him for a piece 935
4: 3 the people were c' into the camp, "
6 of the Lord was c' into the camp. "
7 they said, God is c' into the camp. "
5: 5 nor any that c' into Dagon's house, "
6: 7 on which there hath c' no yoke, 5927
21 c' ye down, and fetch it up to you. 3381
9: 5 when they were c' to the land of 935
5 C', and let us return; lest my 3212
9 spake C', and let us go to the seer: "
10 Well said; c', let us go. So they "
13 As soon as ye be c' into the city, 935
13 the people will not eat until he c', "
14 and when they were c' into the city,* "
16 because their cry is c' unto me. "
25 they were c' down from the high 3381
10: 3 thou shalt c' to the plain of Tabor, 935
5 that thou shalt c' to the hill of God, "
5 it shall c' to pass, when thou art 1961
5 thou art c' thither to the city, 935
6 of the Lord will c' upon thee, 6743
7 when these signs are c' unto thee, 935
8 c' down unto thee, to offer burnt 3381
8 till I c' to thee, and shew thee what 935
11 that is c' unto the son of Kish? 1961
20 to c' near, the tribe of Benjamin *7126

1Sa 10:21 to c' near by their families, the *7126
22 if the man should yet c' thither. 935
11: 3 to save us, we will c' out to thee. 3318
10 To morrow we will c' out unto you, "
14 C', and let us go to Gilgal, and 3212
12: 8 When Jacob was c' into Egypt, 935
13:12 The Philistines will c' down now 3381
14: 1 C', and let us go over to the 3212
6 C', and let us go over unto the "
9 Tarry until we c' to you; then we 5060
10 if they say thus, C' up unto us; 5927
11 Hebrews c' forth out of the holes 3318
12 C' up to us, and we will shew you 5927
12 C' up after me: for the Lord hath "
26 when the people were c' into the 935
16: 2 say, I am c' to sacrifice to the Lord. "
5 I am c' to sacrifice unto the Lord: "
5 and c' with me to the sacrifice. "
6 when they were c', that he looked "
11 will not sit down till he c' hither. "
16 c' to pass, when the evil spirit 1961
17: 8 Why are ye c' out to set your 3318
8 you, and let him c' down to me. 3381
25 ye seen this man that is c' up? 5927
25 surely to defy Israel is he c' up: "
28 art c' down that thou mightest 3381
44 C' to me, and I will give thy flesh 3212
45 but I c' to thee in the name of the 935
52 until thou c' to the valley, and to * "
19:16 And when the messengers were c' * "
20: 9 were determined by my father to c' "
11 C', and let us go out into the 3212
19 c' to the place where thou didst 935
21 then c' thou: for there is peace to "
24 when the new moon was c', the 1961
37 when the lad was c' to the place 935
21:15 shall this fellow c' into my house? "
22: 3 my mother, I pray thee, c' forth, 3318
23: 3 much more then if we c' to Keilah 3212
7 told Saul that David was c' to 935
10 that Saul seeketh to c' to Keilah, "
11 will Saul c' down, as thy servant 3381
11 And the Lord said, He will c' down. "
15 David saw that Saul was c' out to 3318
20 Now therefore, O king, c' down 3381
20 the desire of thy soul to c' down; "
23 and c' ye again to me with the 7725
23 c' to pass, if he be in the land, 1961
27 Haste thee, and c'; for the 3212
24:14 After whom is the king of Israel c' 3318
25: 8 we c' in a good day: give, I pray 935
19 before me; behold, I c' after you. "
30 c' to pass, when the Lord shall 1961
34 hadst hasted and c' to meet me, 935
40 when the servants of David were c' "
26: 4 and understood that Saul was c' in "
10 him; or his day shall c' to die; "
20 king of Israel is c' out to seek a 3318
22 let one of the young men c' over 5674
29:10 servants that are c' with thee: 935
30: 1 when David and his men were c' to "
31: 4 lest these uncircumcised c' and "
2Sa 1: 9 me: for anguish is c' upon me, *270
2:24 went down when they were c' to 935
3:23 the host that was with him were c', "
26 when Joab was c' out from David, 3318
5: 6 thou shalt not c' in hither: 935
6 David cannot c' in hither. "
8 the lame shall not c' into the house. "
13 of Jerusalem, after he was c' from "
23 and c' upon them over against the "
25 from Geba until thou c' to Gazer. "
6: 9 How shall the ark of the Lord c' to "
7:19 house for a great while to c'. "
9: 6 the son of Saul, was c' unto David, *935
10:11 thee, then I will c' and help thee. 1980
11: 7 And when Uriah was c' unto him, 935
12: 4 the wayfaring man that was c' unto "
4 it for the man that was c' to him. "
13: 5 let my sister Tamar c', and give me "
6 when the king was c' to see him, "
6 I pray thee, let Tamar my sister c', "
11 unto her, C' lie with me, my sister. "
35 Behold, the king's sons c': as thy "
14: 3 And c' to the king, and speak on * "
15 Now therefore that I am c' to speak "
29 but he would not c' to him: and "
29 the second time, he would not c'. "
32 C' hither, that I may send thee to "
32 Wherefore am I c' from Geshur? it "
15: 4 any suit or cause might c' unto me, "
28 until there c' word from you to "
32 that when David was c' to the top of "
16: 7 C' out, c' out, thou bloody man, *3318
16 David's friend, was c' unto 935
17: 2 And I will c' upon him while he is "
6 when Hushai was c' to Absalom, "
9 and it will c' to pass, when some 1961
12 So shall we c' upon him in some 935
17 they might not be seen to c' into "
27 it came to pass, when David was c' "
19:11 all Israel is c' to the king, even to "
18 before the king, as he was c' over 5674
20 I am c' the first this day of all the 935
25 when he was c' to Jerusalem to "
30 as my lord the king is c' again in "
33 C' thou over with me, and I will 5674
39 when the king was c' over, the * "
20:16 C' near hither, that I may speak *7126
17 when he was c' near unto her, * "
24:13 Shall seven years of famine c' unto 935
21 my lord the king c' to his servant? "
1Ki 1:12 therefore c', let me, I pray thee, 3212
14 I also will c' in after thee, and 935
21 c' to pass, when my lord the king 1961
23 And when he was c' in before the 935

1Ki 1: 35 Then ye shall c' up after him, 5927
35 that he may c' and sit upon my 935
42 C' in; for thou art a valiant man, "
45 are c' up from thence rejoicing, 5927
2:30 Thus saith the king, C' forth. 3318
41 Jerusalem to Gath, and was c' 7725
3: 7 I know not how to go out or c' in. 935
6: 1 the children of Israel were c' out 3318
8:10 when the priests were c' out of the "
19 thy son that shall c' forth out of "
31 and the oath c' before thine altar *935
42 when he shall c' and pray toward "
10: 2 and when she was c' to Solomon, "
11: 2 neither shall they c' in unto you: "
12: 1 all Israel were c' to Shechem to "
5 yet for three days, then c' again 7725
12 saying, C' to me again the third "
20 heard that Jeroboam was c' again, "
21 And when Rehoboam was c' to 935
13: 7 C' home with me, and refresh "
15 said unto him, C' home with me, 3212
22 thy carcase shall not c' unto the 935
32 Samaria, shall surely c' to pass. 1961
14: 6 C' in, thou wife of Jeroboam; 935
13 of Jeroboam shall c' to the grave, "
15:17 to go out or c' in to Asa king of "
19 c' and break thy league with *3212
17:18 art thou c' unto me to call my sin 935
21 let this child's soul c' into him 7725
18:12 c' to pass, as soon as I am gone 1961
12 and so when I c' and tell Ahab, 935
30 said unto all the people, C' near 5066
19:17 c' to pass, that him that escapeth 1961
20:17 There are men c' out of Samaria. 3318
18 Whether they be c' out for peace, "
18 alive; or whether they be c' out "
22 king of Syria will c' up against 5927
33 whether anything would c' from * "
33 he caused him to c' up into the 5927
22:27 of affliction, until I c' in peace. 935
2Ki 1: 4 c' down from that bed on which 3381
6 thou shalt not c' down from that "
9 God, the king hath said, C' down. "
10 then let fire c' down from heaven, "
11 the king said, C' down quickly. "
12 let fire c' down from heaven, and "
16 shalt not c' down off that bed "
3:21 heard that the kings were c' up 5927
4: 1 c' to take unto him my two sons 935
4 And when thou art c' in, thou * "
22 to the man of God, and c' again. 7725
32 when Elisha was c' into the house, 935
36 And when she was c' in unto him, "
5: 6 when this letter is c' unto thee, "
8 let him c' now to me, and "
10 and thy flesh shall c' again to thee, 7725
11 He will surely c' out to me, 3318
22 be c' to me from mount Ephraim 935
6: 9 thither the Syrians are c' down. *5185
20 when they were c' into Samaria, 935
7: 4 Now therefore c', and let us fall 3212
5 they were c' to the uttermost part 935
6 of the Egyptians, to c' upon us. "
9 some mischief will c' upon us: *4672
9 c', that we may go and tell the 3212
12 When they c' out of the city, we 3318
8: 1 c' upon the land seven years. 935
7 saying, The man of God is c' hither. "
9:16 Ahaziah king of Judah was c' 3381
30 when Jehu was c' to Jezreel, 935
34 And when he was c' in, he did eat "
10: 6 c' to me to Jezreel by to morrow "
16 C' with me, and see my zeal 3212
25 and slay them; let none c' forth. 3381
11: 9 that were to c' in on the sabbath, 935
14: 8 C', let us look one another in the 3212
16: 7 c' up, and save me out of the hand 5927
12 the king was c' from Damascus, 935
18:13 did Sennacherib king of Assyria c' 5927
17 And when they were c' up, they "
25 Am I now c' up without the Lord "
31 and c' out to me, and then eat ye 3318
32 Until I c' and take you away to a 935
19: 3 the children are c' to the birth, "
9 he is c' out to fight against thee. 3318
23 multitude of my chariots I am c' 5927
28 thy tumult is c' up into mine ears, "
32 He shall not c' into this city, 935
32 nor c' before it with shield, 6923
33 not c' into this city, saith the Lord. 935
20:14 They are c' from a far country, "
17 Behold, the days c', that all that "
1Ch 9:25 to c' after seven days from time "
10: 4 lest these uncircumcised c' "
11: 5 David, Thou shalt not c' hither. "
12:17 c' peaceably unto me to help me, "
17 c' to betray me to mine enemies, "
31 name, to c' and make David king. 935
14:14 and c' upon them over against "
16:29 c' before him: worship the Lord "
17:11 And it shall c' to pass, when thy 1961
17 house for a great while to c', "
19: 3 are not his servants c' unto thee 935
9 the kings that were c' were by "
24:19 to c' into the house of the Lord, "
29:12 Both riches and honour c' of thee, "
14 for all things c' of thee, and of "
2Ch 1:10 out and c' in before this people: 935
5:11 were c' out of the holy place: 3318
6: 9 but thy son which shall c' forth "
22 and the oath c' before thine altar 935
32 but is c' from a far country for "
32 if they c' and pray in this house; "
8:11 the ark of the Lord hath c'. "
9: 1 and when she was c' to Solomon, "
10: 1 to Shechem were all Israel c' "

2Ch 10: 5 C' again unto me after three days.7725
12 C' again to me on the third day. "
11: 1 Rehoboam was c' to Jerusalem, 935
13:13 caused an ambushment to c' "
16: 1 let none go out or c' in to Asa "
18:14 And when he was c' to the king, "
19:10 what cause soever shall c' to you "
10 Lord, and so wrath c' upon you, 1961
20:11 c' to cast us out of thy possession, 935
16 they c' up by the cliff of Ziz; 5927
22 which were c' against Judah; 935
22: 7 for when he was c', he went out "
23: 6 But let none c' into the house of "
8 his men that were to c' in on the "
15 when she was c' to the entering * "
25:10 the army that was c' to him out "
14 Amaziah was c' from the slaughter "
17 C', let us see one another in the 3212
28:17 Edomites had c' and smitten Judah,935
29:31 c' near and bring sacrifices and 5066
30: 1 that they should c' to the house 935
5 should c' to keep the passover "
9 they shall c' again into this land: 7725
32: 2 saw that Sennacherib was c', 935
4 should the kings of Assyria c', "
21 when he was c' into the house "
35:21 I c' not against thee this day, "
Ezr 3: 1 when the seventh month was c', 5060
8 that were c' out of the captivity 935
4:12 are c' unto Jerusalem, building 858
6:21 of Israel, which were c' again out 7725
8:35 which were c' out of the captivity 935
9:13 after all that is c' upon us for "
10: 8 would not c' within three days, * "
14 c' at appointed times, and with "
Ne 2: 7 convey me over till I c' to Judah; "
10 that there was c' a man to seek "
17 c', and let us build up the wall 3212
4: 8 together to c' and to fight against 935
11 we c' in the midst among them, "
6: 2 C', let us meet together in some 3212
3 work, so that I cannot c' down: 3381
3 whilst I leave it, and c' down to "
7 C' now therefore, and let us take 3212
10 for they will c' to slay thee; 935
10 yea, in the night will they c' "
8:17 were c' again out of the captivity 7725
9:32 hath c' upon us, on our kings, 4672
13: 1 not c' into the congregation * 935
22 and that they should c' and keep "
Es 1:12 Vashti refused to c' at the kings "
17 shall c' abroad unto all women, 3318
19 Vashti c' no more before king 935
2:12 when every maid's turn was c' 5060
15 was c' to go in unto the king, "
4:11 shall c' unto the king into the 935
11 to c' in unto the king these thirty "
14 thou art c' to the kingdom *5060
5: 4 c' this day unto the banquet 935
8 let the king and Haman c' to the "
12 the queen did let no man c' in "
6: 4 Haman was c' into the outward "
5 And the king said, Let him c' in. "
8: 6 evil that shall c' unto my people? 4672
9:26 and which had c' unto them, 5060
Job 2:11 heard of all this evil that was c' 935
11 to c' to mourn with him and "
3: 6 let it not c' into the number "
7 let no joyful voice c' therein. "
25 which I greatly feared is c' upon * 857
25 which I was afraid of is c' unto me.*935
4: 5 But now it is c' upon thee, and "
5:26 Thou shalt c' to thy grave in a "
7: 9 down to the grave shall c' up no 5927
8:22 of the wicked shall c' to nought. * "
9:32 should c' together in judgment. 935
13:13 speak, and let c' on me what will. 5674
16 hypocrite shall not c' before him. 935
14:14 time will I wait, till my change c'. "
21 His sons c' to honour, and he "
15:21 the destroyer shall c' upon him. 935
16:22 When a few years are c', 857
17:10 you all, do ye return, and c' now: 935
18:20 They that c' after him shall be "
19:12 His troops c' together, and raise 935
20:22 hand of the wicked shall c' upon "
22:21 thereby good shall c' unto thee. "
23: 3 that I might c' even to his seat! "
10 tried me, I shall c' forth as gold. 3318
26:10 the day and night c' to an end. *
34:28 cry of the poor to c' unto him, 935
37:13 He causeth it to c', whether for 4672
38:11 Hitherto shalt thou c', but no 935
41:13 who can c' to him with his double "
16 that no air can c' between them. "
Ps 5: 7 c' into thy house in the multitude "
7: 9 of the wicked c' to an end; "
16 his violent dealing shall c' down 3381
9: 6 destructions are c' to a perpetual "
14: 7 salvation of Israel were c' out "
17: 2 c' forth from thy presence; 3318
22:31 They shall c', and shall declare 935
24: 7, 9 and the King of glory shall c' in. "
32: 6 they shall not c' nigh unto him. *5060
9 bridle, lest they c' near unto thee.*7126
34:11 C', ye children, hearken unto me: 3212
35: 8 Let destruction c' upon him 935
36:11 not the foot of pride c' against me, "
40: 7 Then said I, Lo, I c': in the "
41: 6 if he c' to see me, he speaketh "
42: 2 shall I c' and appear before God? "
44:17 All this is c' upon us; yet have we "
46: 8 C', behold the works of the Lord, 3212
50: 3 Our God shall c', and shall not 935
52:title David is c' to the house of "
53: 6 salvation of Israel were c' out of Zion

Ps 55: 5 and trembling are c' upon me, 935
65: 2 prayer, unto thee shall all flesh c'.
66: 5 C' and see the works of God: 3212
16 C' and hear, all ye that fear God, "
68:31 Princes shall c' out of Egypt; 857
69: 1 waters are c' in unto my soul. 935
2 I am c' into deep waters, where "
27 them not c' into thy righteousness. "
71:18 power to every one that is to c'. "
72: 6 He shall c' down like rain upon 3381
78: 4 shewing to the generation to c' 314
6 That the generation to c' might "
79: 1 O God, the heathen are c' into 935
11 Let the sighing of the prisoner c' "
80: 2 strength, and c' and save us. 3212
83: 4 C', and let us cut them off from "
86: 9 whom thou hast made shall c' 935
88: 2 Let my prayer c' before thee: * "
8 shut up, and I cannot c' forth. 3318
91: 7 but it shall not c' nigh thee. 5066
10 neither shall any plague c' nigh 7126
95: 1 O c', let us sing unto the Lord: 3212
2 Let us c' before his presence 6923
6 O c', let us worship and bow down: 935
96: 8 offering, and c' into his courts. "
100: 2 c' before his presence with singing. "
101: 2 O when wilt thou c' unto me? "
102: 1 O Lord, and let my cry c' unto thee. "
13 favour her, yea, the set time, is c'. "
18 be written for the generation to c': 314
109:17 cursing, so let it c' unto him: * 935
18 it c' into his bowels like water, "
119:41 Let thy mercies c' also unto me, "
77 Let thy tender mercies c' unto me, "
169 Let my cry c' near before thee. 7126
170 my supplication c' before thee: 935
126: 6 doubtless c' again with rejoicing, "
132: 3 I will not c' into the tabernacle "
144: 5 thy heavens, O Lord, and c' down: 3381
Pr 1:11 C' with us, let us lay wait for 3212
3:28 thy neighbour, Go, and c' again, 7725
5: 8 c' not nigh the door of her house: 7126
6: 3 c' into the hand of thy friend; 935
11 So shall thy poverty c' as one that "
15 Therefore shall his calamity c' "
7:18 C', let us take our fill of love until 3212
20 will c' home at the day appointed. 935
9: 5 C', eat of my bread, and drink 3212
10:24 the wicked, it shall c' upon him: 935
11:27 mischief, it shall c' unto him. "
12:13 the just shall c' out of trouble. 3318
20:13 not sleep, lest thou c' to poverty; "
22:16 the rich, shall surely c' to want. * "
23:21 the glutton shall c' to poverty: "
24:25 good blessing shall c' upon them. 935
34 So shall thy poverty c' as one that "
25: 4 shall c' forth a vessel for the finer. *3318
7 said unto thee, C' up hither; than 5927
26: 2 the curse causeless shall not c'. *935
28:22 that poverty shall c' upon him. "
31:25 she shall rejoice in time to c'. 314
Ec 1: 7 place from whence the rivers c' *1980
11 remembrance of things that are to c' 314
11 with those that shall c' after. 1961
16 Lo, I am c' to great estate, * "
2:16 the days to c' shall all be forgotten. 935
3:16 also that c' after shall not rejoice 314
7:18 he that feareth God shall c' forth 3318
8:10 had c' and gone from the place * 935
9: 2 All things c' alike to all: there is "
12: 1 while the evil days c' not, nor 935
Ca 2:10 love, my fair one, and c' away. 3212
12 of the singing of birds is c', 5060
13 love, my fair one, and c' away. 3212
4: 8 C' with me from Lebanon, 935
16 O north wind; and c', thou south; "
16 Let my beloved c' into his garden, "
5: 1 I am c' into my garden, my sister, "
7:11 C', my beloved, let us go forth 3212
Isa 1:12 When ye c' to appear before me, 935
18 C' now, and let us reason 3212
23 doth the cause of the widow c' 935
2: 2 And it shall c' to pass in the last 1961
3 C' ye, and let us go up to the 3212
5 O house of Jacob, c' ye, and let us "
3:24 it shall c' to pass, that instead of 1961
4: 3 c' to pass, that he that is left in "
5: 6 shall c' up briers and thorns: 5927
19 One of Israel draw nigh and c', 935
26 behold, they shall c' with speed "
7: 7 stand, neither shall it c' to pass. 1961
17 house, days that have not c', 935
18 shall c' to pass in that day, that 1961
19 And they shall c', and shall rest 935
21 c' to pass in that day, that a man 1961
22 c' to pass, for the abundance of "
23 c' to pass in that day, that every "
24 and with bows shall men c' 935
25 not c' thither the fear of briers "
8: 7 shall c' up over all his channels, 5927
10 and it shall c' to nought; * "
21 shall c' to pass, that when they 1961
10: 3 desolation which shall c' from far? 935
12 c' to pass, that when the Lord 1961
20 c' to pass in that day, that the "
27 c' to pass in that day, that his "
28 c' to Aiath, he is passed to Migron; 935
11: 1 And there shall c' forth a rod out 3318
11 c' to pass in that day, that the 1961
13: 5 They c' from a far country, from 935
6 it shall c' as a destruction from "
22 her time is near to c', and her days "
14: 3 c' to pass in the day that the Lord 1961
8 no feller is c' up against us. 5927
24 thought, so shall it c' to pass; 1961
29 of the serpent's root shall c' forth 3318

Isa 14:31 shall c' from the north a smoke, 935
16: 8 they are c' even unto Jazer, *5060
12 c' to pass, when it is seen that 1961
12 shall c' to his sanctuary to pray; 935
17: 4 And in that day it shall c' to pass, 1961
19: 1 cloud, and shall c' into Egypt: 935
23 the Assyrian shall c' into Egypt, "
21:12 enquire, enquire ye: return, c'. 857
22: 7 shall c' to pass, that thy choicest 1961
20 And it shall c' to pass in that day, "
23:15 c' to pass in that day, that Tyre "
17 c' to pass after the end of seventy "
24:10 is shut up, that no man may c' in. 935
18 shall c' to pass that he who fleeth 1961
21 And it shall c' to pass in that day, "
26:20 C', my people, enter thou into thy 3212
27: 6 shall cause them that c' of Jacob 935
11 women c', and set them on fire: "
12 c' to pass in that day, that the 1961
13 And it shall c' to pass in that day, "
13 shall c' which were ready to perish 935
28:15 it shall not c' unto us: for we have "
29:24 shall c' to understanding, 3045
30: 6 whence c' the young and old lion, "
8 the time to c' for ever and ever: 314
29 c' into the mountain of the Lord, 935
31: 4 so shall the Lord of hosts c' down 3381
32:10 fail, the gathering shall not c'. 935
13 of my people shall c' up thorns 5927
34: 1 C' near, ye nations, to hear; and 7126
1 and all things that c' forth of it. 6631
3 shall c' up out of their carcases, 5927
5 it shall c' down upon Idumea, 3381
7 unicorns shall c' down with them, "
13 thorns shall c' up in her palaces, 5927
35: 4 God will c' with vengeance, 935
4 he will c' and save you. "
10 and c' to Zion with songs and "
36:10 am I now c' up without the Lord 5927
16 c' out to me: and eat ye every one 3318
17 Until I c' and take you away to a 935
37: 3 the children are c' to the birth, "
9 is c' forth to make war with thee. 3318
24 multitude of my chariots am I c' 5927
29 tumult, is c' up into mine ears, "
33 He shall not c' into this city, nor 935
33 nor c' before it with shields, 6923
34 not c' into this city, saith the Lord. 935
39: 3 are c' from a far country unto me, "
6 Behold, the days c', that all that is "
40:10 Lord God will c' with strong hand, "
41: 1 c' near; then let them speak: 5066
1 us c' near together to judgment. 7126
22 declare us things for to c'. 935
23 things that are to c' hereafter, 857
25 the north, and he shall c': "
25 c' upon princes as upon morter. 935
42: 9 the former things are c' to pass, "
23 hearken and hear for the time to c'? "
44: 7 are coming, and shall c', 935
45:11 things to c' concerning my sons, 857
14 stature, shall c' over unto thee, 5674
14 be thine: they shall c' after thee; *3212
14 in chains they shall c' over, and 5674
20 Assemble yourselves and c'; 935
24 even to him shall men c'; "
47: 1 C' down, and sit in the dust, O 3381
9 these two things shall c' to thee 935
9 they shall c' upon thee in their "
11 Therefore shall evil c' upon thee; "
11 shall c' upon thee suddenly, "
13 things that shall c' upon thee. "
48: 1 are c' forth out of the waters of 3318
16 C' ye near unto me, hear ye this; 7126
49:12 these shall c' from far: and, lo, 935
18 themselves together, and c' to thee. "
50: 8 let him c' near to me. 5066
51:11 and c' with singing unto Zion; 935
19 two things are c' unto thee; *7122
52: 1 there shall no more c' into thee 935
54:14 for it shall not c' near thee. 7126
55: 1 c' ye to the waters, and he that 3212
1 hath no money; c' ye, buy, and eat; "
1 yea, c', buy wine and milk "
3 Incline your ear, and c' unto me: "
13 the thorn shall c' up the fir tree, 5927
13 and instead of the brier shall c' up "
56: 1 for my salvation is near to c', 935
9 ye beasts of the field, c' to devour, 857
12 C' ye, say they, I will fetch wine, "
57: 1 is taken away from the evil to c'. "
59:19 the enemy shall c' in like a flood, 935
20 And the Redeemer shall c' to Zion, "
60: 1 Arise, shine; for thy light is c', "
3 the Gentiles shall c' to thy light, 1980
4 together, they c' to thee: 935
4 thy sons shall c' from far, and thy "
5 forces of the Gentiles shall c' unto "
6 all they from Sheba shall c': they "
7 they shall c' up with acceptance 5927
13 of Lebanon shall c' unto thee, 935
14 of them that afflicted thee shall c' 1980
63: 4 and the year of my redeemed is c'. 935
64: 1 that thou wouldest c' down, that 3381
65: 5 c' not near to me; for I am holier 5066
17 shall not be remembered, nor c' 5927
24 c' to pass, that before they call, 1961
66:15 behold, the Lord will c' with fire, 935
18 and their thoughts: it shall c', * "
18 they shall c', and see my glory. "
23 And it shall c' to pass, that from 1961
23 all flesh c' to worship before me, 935
Jer 1:15 and they shall c', and they shall "
2: 3 shall c' upon them, saith the Lord. "
31 we will c' no more unto thee? "
3:16 c' to pass, when ye be multiplied 1961

Jer 3:16 neither shall it c' to mind: 5927
18 shall c' together out of the land 935
22 we c' unto thee; for thou art the 857
4: 4 lest my fury c' forth like fire, *3318
7 lion is c' up from his thicket, *5927
9 it shall c' to pass at that day, 1961
12 from those places shall c' unto me: 935
13 he shall c' up as clouds, 5927
16 watchers c' from a far country, 935
5:12 neither shall evil c' upon us; "
19 it shall c' to pass, when ye shall 1961
6: 3 their flocks shall come unto her; 935
26 spoiler shall suddenly c' upon us. "
7:10 And c' and stand before me in this "
32 behold, the days c', saith the Lord, "
8:16 for they are c', and have devoured "
9:17 mourning women, that they may c'; "
17 cunning women, that they may c': "
21 death is c' up into our windows, 5927
25 Behold, the days c', saith the Lord, 935
10:22 Behold, the noise of the bruit is c', "
12: 9 c' ye, assemble all the beasts *3212
9 beasts of the field, c' to devour, *857
12 The spoilers are c' upon all high 935
13:18 your principalities shall c' down, 3381
20 them that c' from the north: 935
22 Wherefore c' these things upon 7122
15: 2 c' to pass, if they say unto thee, 1961
16:10 And it shall c' to pass, when thou "
14 behold, the days c', saith the Lord, 935
19 the Gentiles shall c' unto thee "
17:15 word of the Lord? let it c' now. "
19 whereby the kings of Judah c' in, "
24 it shall c' to pass, if ye diligently 1961
26 And they shall c' from the cities 935
18:14 waters that c' from another place *
18 C', and let us devise devices 3212
18 C', and let us smite him with the "
19: 6 the days c', saith the Lord, that 935
20: 6 thou shalt c' to Babylon, and "
21:13 Who shall c' down against us? 5181
22:23 thou be when pangs c' upon thee, 935
23: 5 days c', saith the Lord, that I will "
7 days c', saith the Lord, that they "
17 No evil shall c' upon you. "
25: 3 word of the Lord hath c' unto me, 1961
12 c' to pass, when seventy years "
31 c' even to the ends of the earth; 935
26: 2 c' to worship in the Lord's house, "
27: 3 c' to Jerusalem unto Zedekiah king "
7 until the very time of his land c': "
8 c' to pass, that the nation and 1961
28: 9 of the prophet shall c' to pass, 935
30: 3 For, lo, the days c', saith the Lord, "
8 For it shall c' to pass in that day, 1961
31: 9 They shall c' with weeping, 935
12 Therefore they shall c' and sing "
16 and they shall c' again from the 7725
17 shall c' again to their own border; "
27, 31, 38 Behold, the days c', saith 935
28 And it shall c' to pass, that like 1961
32: 7 thine uncle shall c' unto thee, 935
23 hast caused all this evil to c' 7122
24 they are c' unto the city to take 935
24 thou hast spoken is c' to pass; 1961
29 shall c' and set fire on this city, 935
33: 5 They c' to fight with the Chaldeans, "
14 days c', saith the Lord, that I will "
35:11 C', and let us go to Jerusalem for "
36: 6 all Judah that c' out of their cities. "
14 in the ears of the people, and c'. 3212
29 king of Babylon shall certainly c' 935
37: 5 Pharaoh's army was c' forth out 3318
7 Pharaoh's army, which is c' forth "
8 And the Chaldeans shall c' again, 7725
19 The king of Babylon shall not c' 935
38:25 and they c' unto thee, and say "
40: 3 therefore this thing is c' upon 1961
4 to c' with me into Babylon, 935
4 c'; and I will look well unto thee: "
4 but if it seem ill unto thee to c' "
10 the Chaldeans, which will c' unto us: "
41: 6 unto them, C' to Gedaliah the son "
42: 4 c' to pass, that whatsoever thing 1961
16 it shall c' to pass, that the sword, "
46: 9 C' up, ye horses; and rage, ye *5927
9 let the mighty men c' forth; *3318
13 king of Babylon should c' and 935
18 as Carmel by the sea, so shall he c'. "
21 the day of their calamity was c' "
22 c' against her with axes, as hewers "
47: 5 Baldness is c' upon Gaza; "
48: 2 c', and let us cut it off from being 3212
8 And the spoiler shall c' upon 935
12 days c', saith the Lord, that I will "
16 The calamity of Moab is near to c', "
18 Dibon, c' down from thy glory, 3381
18 the spoiler of Moab shall c' upon 5927
21 judgment is c' upon the plain 935
45 fire shall c' forth out of Heshbon, *3318
49: 2 behold, the days c', saith the Lord, 935
4 her treasures, saying, Who shall c' "
9 If grapegatherers c' to thee, * "
14 and c' against her, and rise up to "
19 he shall c' up like a lion from the 5927
22 he shall c' up and fly as the eagle, "
36 the outcasts of Elam shall not c'. 935
39 it shall c' to pass in the latter days, 1961
50: 4 the children of Israel shall c', they 935
5 C', and let us join ourselves to the "
9 I will raise and cause to c' up 5927
26 C' against her from the utmost 935
27 for their day is c', the time of their "
31 for thy day is c', the time that I will "
41 Behold, a people shall c' from the* "
44 he shall c' up like a lion from the 5927

Jer 51:10 c', and let us declare in Zion the 935
13 thine end is c', and the measure "
27 cause the horses to c' up as the 5927
33 and the time of her harvest shall c'.935
42 The sea is c' up upon Babylon: 5927
46 a rumour shall both c' one year, 935
46 in another year shall c' a rumour,
47 behold, the days c', that I will do 935
48 for the spoilers shall c' unto her "
50 and let Jerusalem c' into your 5927
51 for strangers are c' into the 935
52 behold, the days c', saith the Lord, "
53 from me shall spoilers c' unto her, "
56 Because the spoiler is c' upon her, "
60 all the evil that should c' upon "
La 1: 4 none c' to the solemn feasts: "
14 they are wreathed, and c' up upon 5927
22 Let all their wickedness c' before 935
3:47 Fear and a snare is c' upon us, 1961
4:18 days are fulfilled; for our end is c'.935
5: 1 what is c' upon us: consider, and 1961
Eze 5: 4 thereof shall a fire c' forth into 3318
7: 2 the end is c' upon the four corners 935
3 Now is the end c' upon thee, and *
5 evil, an only evil, behold, is c'. *935
6 An end is c', the end is c': it "
6 for thee; behold, it is c'. * "
7 c' unto thee, O thou that dwellest "
7 the time is c', the day of trouble is "
10 Behold the day, behold, it is c': * "
12 The time is c', the day draweth "
26 Mischief shall c' upon mischief, "
9: 6 c' not near any man upon whom 5066
11: 5 for I know the things that c' into 4609
16 the countries where they shall c'. 935
18 And they shall c' thither, and they "
12:16 among the heathen whither they c';"
25 that I shall speak shall c' to pass*6213
27 he seeth is for many days to c', "
13:18 the souls alive that c' unto you? "
14:22 they shall c' forth unto you, and 3318
16: 7 art c' to excellent ornaments; * 935
16 the like things shall not c', "
33 that they may c' unto thee on "
17:12 the king of Babylon is c' to * "
18: 6 neither hath c' near to a 7126
20: 3 Are ye c' to enquire of me? As I 935
21:19 of the king of Babylon may c': "
19 both twain shall c' forth out of 3318
20 that the sword may c' to Rabbath 935
24 I say, that ye are c' to remembrance,
25 whose day is c', when iniquity 935
27 until he c' whose right it is; and I "
29 wicked, whose day is c', when "
22: 3 that her time may c', and maketh "
4 to draw near, and art c' even unto "
23:24 And they shall c' against thee "
40 ye have sent for men to c' from far, "
24: 8 That it might cause fury to c' up 5927
14 it shall c' to pass, and I will do it; 835
26 escapeth in that day shall c' unto "
26: 3 will cause many nations to c' up 5927
3 the sea causeth his waves to c' up. "
16 princes of the sea shall c' down 3381
27:29 pilots of the sea, shall c' down from "
30: 4 And the sword shall c' upon Egypt, 935
6 pride of her power shall c' down: 3381
9 great pain shall c' upon them, *1961
32:11 of the king of Babylon shall c' 935
33: 3 If when he seeth the sword c' upon "
4 if the sword c', and take him away, "
6 if the watchman see the sword c', "
6 if the sword c', and take any "
30 C', I pray you, and hear what is "
31 And they c' unto thee as the people "
33 this cometh to pass, (lo, it will c',) "
34:26 I will cause the shower to c' down 3381
36: 8 Israel; for they are at hand to c'. 935
37: 9 C' from the four winds, O breath, "
12 graves, and cause you to c' up 5927
38: 8 thou shalt c' into the land that is 935
9 Thou shalt ascend and c' like "
10 It shall also c' to pass, that at the 1961
10 same time shall things c' into thy 5927
13 Art thou c' to take a spoil? hast 935
15 And thou shalt c' from thy place "
16 And thou shalt c' up against my 5927
18 And it shall c' to pass at the same 1961
18 time when Gog shall c' against the 935
18 that my fury shall c' up in my 5927
39: 2 will cause thee to c' up from the "
8 Behold, it is c', and it is done, * 935
11 And it shall c' to pass in that 1961
17 Assemble yourselves, and c'; 935
40:46 the sons of Levi, which c' near to 7131
44:13 they shall not c' near unto me, 5066
13 nor to c' near to any of my holy "
15 they shall c' near to me to 7126
16 they shall c' near to my table, to "
17 it shall c' to pass, that when they 1961
17 no wool shall c' upon them, 5927
25 they shall c' at no dead person 935
45: 4 which shall c' near to minister 7131
46: 9 the people of the land shall c' 935
47: 9 And it shall c' to pass, that every 1961
9 whithersoever the rivers shall c'. 935
9 because these waters shall c' "
10 And it shall c' to pass, that the 1961
20 the border, till a man c' over * 935
22 And it shall c' to pass, that ye 1961
23 shall c' to pass, that in what tribe "
Da 2:29 what should c' to pass hereafter: 1934
29 to thee what shall c' to pass. "
45 to the king what shall c' to pass "
3: 2 to c' to the dedication of the 858

Da 3:26 of the most high God, c' forth, 5312
26 forth, and c' hither. Then 858
4:24 which is c' upon my lord the 4291
8: 7 I saw him c' close unto the ram, 5060
23 when the transgressors are c' to the full,
9:13 all this evil is c' upon us: yet 935
22 I am now c' forth to give thee 3318
23 I am c' to shew thee; for thou art 935
26 people of the prince that shall c' "
10:12 words were heard, and I am c' for "
14 Now I am c' to make thee "
20 knowest thou wherefore I c' unto "
20 lo, the prince of Grecia shall c'. "
11: 6 shall c' to the king of the north to "
7 which shall c' with an army, "
9 So the king of the south shall c' "
10 and one shall certainly c', and "
11 and shall c' forth and fight with 3318
13 and shall certainly c' after certain 935
15 So the king of the north shall c', "
21 but he shall c' in peaceably, and "
23 for he shall c' up, and shall 5927
29 he shall return, and c' toward the 935
30 For the ships of Chittim shall c' "
11:40 king of the north shall c' against 8175
45 yet he shall c' to his end, and 935
Ho 1: 5 it shall c' to pass at that day, 1961
10 c' to pass, that in the place where "
11 they shall c' up out of the land: *5927
2:21 c' to pass in that day, I will hear, 1961
4:15 c' not ye unto Gilgal, neither go 935
6: 1 C', and let us return unto the 3212
3 and he shall c' unto us as the rain, 935
8: 1 He shall c' as an eagle against the *
9: 4 not c' into the house of the Lord. 935
7 The days of visitation are c', "
7 the days of recompence are c'; "
10: 8 thistle shall c' up on their altars; 5927
12 till he c' and rain righteousness 935
13:13 c' upon him: he is an unwise son; "
15 an east wind shall c', the wind of 935
15 the wind of the Lord shall c' up 5927
Joe 1: 6 a nation is c' up upon my land, "
13 c', lie all night in sackcloth, ye 935
15 from the Almighty shall it c'. "
2:20 and his stink shall c' up, 5927
20 and his ill savour shall c' up, "
23 cause to c' down for you the rain, 3381
28 And it shall c' to pass afterward, 1961
31 and the terrible day of the Lord c'. 635
32 c' to pass, that whosoever shall 1961
3: 9 of war draw near; let them c' up: 5927
11 Assemble yourselves, and c', all ye 935
11 cause thy mighty ones to c' down, 5181
12 c' up to the valley of Jehoshaphat: 5927
13 c', get you down; for the press is 935
18 And it shall c' to pass in that day, 1961
18 a fountain shall c' forth out of the 3318
Am 4: 2 the days shall c' upon you, that he 935
4 C' to Beth-el, and transgress; at "
10 the stink of your camps to c' up 5927
5: 5 and Beth-el shall c' to nought. 1961
9 shall c' against the fortress. 935
6: 3 the seat of violence to c' near; 5066
9 shall c' to pass, if there remain ten 1961
8: 2 is c' upon my people of Israel; 935
9 And it shall c' to pass in that day, 1961
11 days c', saith the Lord God, that 935
9:13 the days c', saith the Lord, that the "
Ob 21 saviours shall c' up on mount 5927
Jon 1: 2 wickedness is c' up before me. "
7 C', and let us cast lots, that we 3212
4: 6 and made it to c' up over Jonah, 5927
Mic 1: 3 will c' down, and tread upon the 3381
9 for it is c' unto Judah; he is 935
9 is c' unto the gate of my people * 5060
15 c' unto Adullam, the glory of 935
2:13 The breaker is c' up before them:*5927
3:11 none evil can c' upon us. 935
4: 1 c' to pass, that the mountain of 1961
2 many nations shall c', and say, 1980
2 C', and let us go up to the 3212
8 unto thee shall it c', even the first 857
8 kingdom shall c' to the daughter 935
5: 2 out of thee shall he c' forth unto 3318
5 Assyrian shall c' into our land: 935
10 shall c' to pass in that day, saith 1961
6: 6 Wherewith shall I c' before the 6923
6 c' before him with burnt offerings, "
7:12 c' even to thee from Assyria, 935
Na 1:11 There is one c' out of thee, *3318
2: 1 that dasheth in pieces is c' up 5927
3: 7 c' to pass, that all they that look 1961
Hab 1: 8 their horsemen shall c' from far; 935
9 They shall c' all for violence: "
2: 3 it will surely c', it will not tarry. "
Zep 1: 8 c' to pass in the day of the Lord's 1961
10 it shall c' to pass in that day, * "
12 And it shall c' to pass at that time "
2: 2 of the Lord c' upon you, before 935
2 the day of the Lord's anger c' "
Hag 1: 2 The time is not c', the time that "
2: 7 the desire of all nations shall c': "
22 and their riders shall c' down, 3381
Zec 1:21 Then said I, What c' these to do? 935
21 but these are c' to fray them, to "
2: 6 Ho, ho, c' forth, and flee from the *
10 I c', and I will dwell in the midst 935
6:10 c' from Babylon, and c' thou the "
15 that are far off shall c' and build "
15 And this shall c' to pass, if ye will 1961
7:13 it is c' to pass, that as he cried, * "
8:13 c' to pass, that as ye were a curse "
20 shall yet c' to pass, that there shall "
20 c' people, and the inhabitants 935

Zec 8:22 people and strong nations shall c' 935
23 In those days it shall c' to pass, "
11: 2 forest of the vintage is c' down. 3381
12: 9 it shall c' to pass in that day, that 1961
9 nations that c' against Jerusalem. 935
13: 2 And it shall c' to pass in that day, 1961
3 And it shall c' to pass, that when "
4 And it shall c' to pass in that day, "
8 And it shall c' to pass, that in all "
14: 5 my God shall c', and all the saints 935
6, 13 it shall c' to pass in that day, 1961
16 And it shall c' to pass, that every "
17 will not c' up of all the families, *5927
18 of Egypt go not up, and c' not, * 935
18, 19 that c' not up to keep the feast *5927
21 they that sacrifice shall c' and take 935
Mal 3: 1 shall suddenly c' to his temple, "
1 behold, he shall c', saith the Lord * "
5 I will c' near to you to judgment; 7126
4: 6 lest I c' and smite the earth 935
M't 2: 2 east, and are c' to worship him, *2064*
6 out of thee shall c' a Governor, *1831*
8 I may c' and worship him also. *2064*
11 when they were c' into the house,* "
3: 7 and Sadducees c' to his baptism, * "
7 to flee from the wrath to c'? *3195*
5:17 that I am c' to destroy the law, *2064*
17 I am not c' to destroy, but to fulfil. "
24 and then c' and offer thy gift. *"
26 shalt by no means c' out thence, *1831*
6:10 Thy kingdom c'. Thy will be done *2064*
7:15 which c' to you in sheep's clothing, "
8: 1 was c' down from the mountain, *2597*
7 unto him, I will c' and heal him. *2064*
8 thou shouldest c' under my roof: *1525*
9 to another, C', and he cometh; *2064*
11 shall c' from the east and west, *2240*
14 Jesus was c' into Peter's house, *2064*
16 When the even was c', they *1096*
28 when he was c' to the other side *2064*
29 art thou c' hither to torment us "
32 when they were c' out, they went *1831*
9:13 I am not c' to call the righteous, *2064*
15 days will c', when the bridegroom "
18 c' and lay thy hand upon her, and "
28 And when he was c' into the house, "
10:12 ye c' into an house, salute it. *1525*
13 worthy, let your peace c' upon it; *2064*
23 of Israel, till the Son of man be c'. "
34 I am c' to send peace on earth: * "
35 I am c' to set a man at variance * "
11: 3 Art thou he that should c', or do * "
14 is Elias, which was for to c'. "
28 C' unto me, all ye that labour *1205*
12:28 kingdom of God is c' unto you. *5348*
32 neither in the world to c'. *3195*
44 when he is c', he findeth it empty, *2064*
13:32 so that the birds of the air c' "
49 the angels shall c' forth, and *1831*
54 he was c' into his own country, *2064*
14:23 when the evening was c', he was *1096*
28 bid me c' unto thee on the water. *2064*
29 And he said, C'. And when "
29 Peter was c' down out of the ship,*2597*
32 when they were c' into the ship, *1684*
15:18 c' forth from the heart; and they *1831*
16: 5 when his disciples were c' to the *2064*
24 If any man will c' after me, "
27 Son of man shall c' in the glory "
17:10 scribes that Elias must first c'? "
11 Elias truly shall first c', and * "
12 unto you, That Elias is c' already, "
14 when they were c' to the multitude, "
24 when they were c' to Capernaum, "
25 when he was c' into the house, *1525*
18: 7 must needs be that offences c'; *2064*
11 For the Son of man is c' to save * "
19:14 forbid them not, to c' unto me: "
21 in heaven: and c' and follow me. *1204*
20: 8 So when even was c', the lord of *1096*
21: 1 and were c' to Bethphage, unto *2064*
10 when he was c' into Jerusalem, *1525*
23 when he was c' into the temple, *2064*
38 c', let us kill him, and let us seize *1205*
22: 3 wedding: and they would not c'. *2064*
4 ready: c' unto the marriage. *1205*
23:35 That upon you may c' all the *2064*
36 shall c' upon this generation. *2240*
24: 5 For many shall c' in my name, *2064*
6 all these things must c' to pass, *1096*
14 and then shall the end c'. *2240*
17 is on the housetop not c' down *2597*
42 not what hour your Lord doth c'. *2064*
43 what watch the thief would c', * "
50 The lord of that servant shall c' *2240*
25:31 When the Son of man shall c' in *2064*
34 C', ye blessed of my Father, *1205*
26:20 Now when the even was c', he sat *1096*
50 Friend, wherefore art thou c'? *3918*
55 Are ye c' out as against a thief *1831*
27: 1 When the morning was c', all the *1096*
33 when they were c' unto a place *2064*
40 of God, c' down from the cross. *2597*
42 let him now c' down from the cross, "
49 whether Elias will c' to save him.*2064*
57 When the even was c', there *1096*
64 lest his disciples c' by night, *2064*
28: 6 C', see the place where the Lord *1205*
14 if this c' to the governor's ears, *191*
M'r 1:17 C' ye after me, and I will make *1205*
24 art thou c' to destroy us? I know *2064*
25 thy peace, and c' out of him. *1831*
29 when they were c' out of the "
2: 3 And they c' unto him, bringing *2064*
4 And when they could not c' nigh *4331*

M'r 2:18 they c' and say unto him, Why do 2064
20 But the days will c', when the "
4:22 but that it should c' abroad. "
29 sickle, because the harvest is c'. 3936
35 same day, when the even was c'. 1096
5: 2 when he was c' out of the ship, 1831
8 C' out of the man, thou unclean "
15 And they c' to Jesus, and see him 2064
18 when he was c' into the ship, *1684
23 c' and lay thy hands on her, 2064
39 when he was c' in, he saith unto *1525
6: 2 when the sabbath day was c', 1096
21 when a convenient day was c', "
31 C' ye yourselves apart into a 1205
47 when even was c', the ship was in 1096
54 when they were c' out of the ship, 1831
7: 4 And when they c' from the market, "
15 the things which c' out of him, *1607
23 these evil things c' from within, * "
30 when she was c' to her house, * 565
8:34 Whosoever will c' after me, let 2064
9: 1 kingdom of God c' with power. "
11 scribes that Elias must first c'? "
13 That Elias is indeed c', and they "
25 I charge thee, c' out of him, 1831
28 when he was c' into the house, 1525
29 This kind can c' forth by nothing, 1831
10:14 Suffer the little children to c' 2064
21 c', take up the cross, and follow 1204
30 in the world to c' eternal life. 2064
35 c' unto him, saying, Master, we 4365
11:11 and now the eventide was c', *1511
12 when they were c' from Bethany, *1831
15 And they c' to Jerusalem: and 2064
19 when even was c', he went out *1096
23 which he saith shall c' to pass; * "
27 And they c' again to Jerusalem: 2064
27 there c' to him the chief priests, "
12: 7 is the heir; c', let us kill him, 1205
9 c' and destroy the husbandmen, 2064
14 And when they were c', they say "
18 Then c' unto him the Sadducees, "
13: 6 For many shall c' in my name, "
29 shall see these things c' to pass, *1096
14: 8 she is c' aforehand to anoint *4301
41 it is enough, the hour is c'; 2064
45 And as soon as he was c', he goeth "
48 Are ye c' out, as against a thief, 1831
15:30 Save thyself, and c' down from 2597
33 when the sixth hour was c', there 1096
36 Elias will c' to take him down. *2064
42 now when the even was c', 1096
16: 1 they might c' and anoint him. 2064
Lu 1:35 Holy Ghost shall c' upon thee, 1904
43 the mother of my Lord should c' 2064
2:15 this thing which is c' to pass, 1096
3: 7 to flee from the wrath to c'? 3195
4:34 art thou c' to destroy us? I know 2064
35 Hold thy peace, and c' out of him. 1831
36 unclean spirits, and they c' out. "
5: 7 that they should c' and help them. 2064
17 which were c' out of every town "
35 But the days will c', when the "
7: 3 he would c' and heal his servant. "
7 I myself worthy to c' unto thee: "
8 and to another, C', and he cometh; "
19 Art thou he that should c'? * "
20 When the men were c' unto him, 3854
20 Art thou he that should c'? *2064
34 The Son of man is c' eating and "
8: 4 were c' to him out of every city, *1975
17 not be known and c' abroad. 2064
19 could not c' at him for the press. 4940
29 spirit to c' out of the man. 1831
41 that he would c' into his house: 1525
9:23 If any man will c' after me, 2064
26 when he shall c' in his own glory,* "
37 they were c' down from the hill, 2718
51 when the time was c' that he 4845
54 that we command fire to c' down 2597
56 is not c' to destroy men's lives, *2064
10: 1 whither he himself would c'. "
9 The kingdom of God is c' nigh 1448
11 that the kingdom of God is c' nigh "
35 when I c' again, I will repay thee. 1880
11: 2 Thy kingdom c'. Thy will be 2064
6 mine in his journey is c' to me, 3854
20 kingdom of God is c' upon you. 5348
22 he shall c' upon him, and 1904
33 which c' in may see the light. *1531
12:37 and will c' forth and serve them. 3928
38 if he shall c' in the second watch, 2064
38 or c' in the third watch, * "
39 what hour the thief would c', * "
46 The lord of that servant will c' 2240
49 I am c' to send fire on the earth; *2064
51 Suppose ye that I am c' to give 3854
13: 7 I c' seeking fruit on this fig tree, 2064
14 them therefore c' and be healed, "
29 they shall c' from the east, and 2240
35 the time c' when we shall say, * "
14: 9 that bade thee and him c' and 2064
17 C'; for all things are now ready. "
20 a wife, and therefore I cannot c'. "
23 compel them to c' in, that my 1525
26 If any man c' to me, and hate not*2064
27 bear his cross, and c' after me, "
15:27 Thy brother is c'; and thy father 2240
30 as soon as this thy son was c', *2064
16:26 that would c' from thence. "
28 lest they also c' into this place 2064
17: 1 but that offences will c': but woe "
1 unto him, through whom they c'! "
7 when he is c' from the field, 1525
20 the kingdom of God should c', 2064
22 The days will c', when ye shall "

Lu 17:31 let him not c' down to take it *2597
18:16 little children to c' unto me, 2064
22 in heaven: and c', follow me. 1204
30 in the world to c' life everlasting. 2064
35 as he was c' nigh unto Jericho, *1448
40 when he was c' near, he asked "
19: 5 make haste, and c' down; for 2597
9 day is salvation c' to this house, 1096
10 For the Son of man is c' to seek *2064
13 said unto them, Occupy till I c'. "
29 he was c' nigh to Bethphage and *1448
37 when he was c' nigh, even now * "
41 when he was c' near, he beheld * "
43 the days shall c' upon thee, that 2240
20:14 is the heir: c', let us kill him, *1205
16 c' and destroy these husbandmen, 2064
21: 6 the days will c', in the which "
7 these things shall c' to pass? 1096
8 for many shall c' in my name, 2064
9 these things must first c' to pass; 1096
28 these things begin to c' to pass, "
31 ye see these things c' to pass, * "
34 that day c' upon you unawares. 2186
35 as a snare shall it c' on all them 1904
36 these things that shall c' to pass, 1096
22:14 when the hour was c', he sat down, "
18 the kingdom of God shall c'. 2064
45 and was c' to his disciples, he * "
52 the elders, which were c' to him, 3854
52 Be ye c' out, as against a thief, 1831
23:33 when they were c' to the place, *565
24:12 at that which was c' to pass. 1096
18 things which are c' to pass there "
Joh 1:31 am I c' baptizing with water. *2064
39 He saith unto them, C' and see. "
46 good thing c' out of Nazareth? 1511
46 Philip saith unto him, C' and see. 2064
2: 4 with thee? mine hour is not yet c'. 2240
3: 2 thou art a teacher c' from God: 2064
19 light is c' into the world, and men "
26 baptizeth, and all men c' to him. "
4:15 not, neither c' hither to draw. "
16 call thy husband, and c' hither. "
25 is called Christ: when he is c', "
29 C', see a man, which told me all 1205
40 the Samaritans were c' unto him,*2064
45 Then when he was c' into Galilee,* "
47 that Jesus was c' out of Judæa 2240
47 would c' down, and heal his son: 2597
49 Sir, c' down ere my child die. "
54 was c' out of Judæa into Galilee. 2064
5:14 lest a worse thing c' unto thee. *1096
24 shall not c' into condemnation; *2064
29 And shall c' forth; they that have 1607
40 ye will not c' to me, that ye might 2064
43 I am c' in my Father's name, and "
43 another shall c' in his own name, "
6: 5 saw a great company c' unto him,* "
14 a truth that prophet that should c'* "
15 would c' and take him by force, "
16 And when even was now c', his *1096
17 And Jesus was not c' to them. 2064
37 Father giveth me shall c' to me; 2240
44 No man can c' to me, except the 2064
65 c' unto me, except it were given "
7: 6 My time is not yet c': but your 3918
8 for my time is not yet full c'. *4137
28 I am not c' of myself, but he that 2064
30 because his hour was not yet c'. "
34 where I am, thither ye cannot c'. "
36 where I am, thither ye cannot c'? "
37 let him c' unto me, and drink. "
41 Shall Christ c' out of Galilee? "
8:14 ye cannot tell whence I c', and "
20 him; for his hour was not yet c'. "
21 sins: whither I go, ye cannot c'. "
22 saith, Whither I go, ye cannot c'. * "
9:39 I am c' into this world, that they * "
10:10 I am c' that they might have life, * "
11:27 Son of God, which should c' into * "
28 Master is c', and calleth for thee. *3918
30 Jesus was not yet c' into the town, 2064
32 Mary was c' where Jesus was, * "
34 said unto him, Lord, c' and see. "
43 a loud voice, Lazarus, c' forth. 1204
48 the Romans shall c' and take 2064
56 that he will not c' to the feast? "
12:12 people that were c' to the feast, "
23 the hour is c', that the Son of man "
35 lest darkness c' upon you: *2638
46 I am c' a light into the world, 2064
13: 1 Jesus knew that his hour was c' "
3 was c' from God, and went to God;*1831
19 Now I tell you before it c', that, 1096
19 when it is c' to pass, ye may "
33 Whither I go, ye cannot c'; so 2064
14: 3 I will c' again, and receive you "
18 you comfortless: I will c' to you. "
23 we will c' unto him, and make our "
28 I go away, and c' again unto you.* "
29 c' to pass, that, when it is c' to 1096
15:22 not c' and spoken unto them, 2064
26 But when the Comforter is c', "
16: 4 that when the time shall c', ye "
7 Comforter will not c' unto you; "
8 And when he is c', he will reprove "
13 when he, the Spirit of truth, is c', "
13 he will shew you things to c'. "
21 because her hour is c': but as "
28 Father, and am c' into the world: "
32 cometh, yea, is now c', that ye shall "
17: 1 Father, the hour is c'; glorify thy "
11 are in the world, and I c' to thee. "
13 And now c' I to thee; and these "
18: 4 all things that should c' upon him,*"
21: 4 when the morning was now c', *1096

Joh 21: 9 then as they were c' to land, * 576
12 Jesus saith unto them, C' and dine. 1205
22, 23 he tarry till I c', what is that to 2064
Ac 1: 6 they therefore were c' together, 4905
8 the Holy Ghost is c' upon you: 1904
11 shall so c' in like manner as ye 2064
13 when they were c' in, they went 1525
2: 1 the day of Pentecost was fully c', 4845
17 And it shall c' to pass in the last *1511
20 and notable day of the Lord c': 2064
21 it shall c' to pass, that whosoever *1511
3:19 the times of refreshing shall c' 2064
23 shall c' to pass, that every soul, *1511
5:38 be of men, it will c' to nought: *2647
7: 3 c' into the land which I shall 1204
7 after that shall they c' forth, and 1834
34 and am c' down to deliver them. 2597
34 c', I will send thee into Egypt. 1204
8:15 were c' down, prayed for them, 2597
24 which ye have spoken c' upon me. 1904
27 c' to Jerusalem for to worship, 2064
31 he would c' up and sit with him. 305
39 they were c' up out of the water, "
9:26 when Saul was c' to Jerusalem, 3854
38 he would not delay to c' to them. 1330
39 When he was c', they brought 3854
10: 4 c' up for a memorial before God. * 305
21 is the cause wherefore ye are c'? 3918
27 many that were c' together. 4905
28 or c' unto one of another nation; 4334
33 hast well done that thou art c'. 3854
11: 2 Peter was c' up to Jerusalem, 305
11 were three men already c' unto the*2186
20 when they were c' to Antioch, 1525
12:11 Peter was c' to himself, he said, 1096
13:40 lest that c' upon you, which is 1904
14:11 The gods are c' down to us in the 2597
27 And when they were c', and had 3854
15: 4 when they were c' to Jerusalem, "
16: 7 After they were c' to Mysia, they 2064
9 saying, C' over into Macedonia, 1224
15 c' into my house, and abide there. 1525
18 of Jesus Christ to c' out of her. 1831
37 c' themselves and fetch us out. 2064
17: 6 upside down are c' hither also; 3918
15 for to c' to him with all speed, 2064
18: 2 lately c' from Italy, with his wife "
5 Silas and Timotheus were c' from*2718
27 who, when he was c', helped them 3854
19: 4 him which should c' after him, 2064
32 wherefore they were c' together. 4905
20:11 therefore was c' up again, and * 305
18 And when they were c' to him, he 3854
21:11 when he was c' unto us, he took *2064
17 when we were c' to Jerusalem, 1096
22 multitude must needs c' together; 4905
22 for they will hear that thou art c'.*2064
22: 6 my journey, and was c' nigh *1448
17 I was c' again to Jerusalem, even *5290
23:15 he c' near, are ready to kill him. 1448
35 when thine accusers are also c'. 3854
24: 8 his accusers to c' unto thee: *2064
22 the chief captain shall c' down, 2597
23 to minister or c' unto him. *4334
25 judgment to c', Felix. 3195, 1511
25: 1 Festus was c' into the province, 1910
7 And when he was c', the Jews 3854
17 when they were c' hither, without 4905
23 when Agrippa was c', and Bernice, 2064
26: 7 God day and night, hope to c'. *2658
22 and Moses did say should c': 1096
27: 7 were c' over against Cnidus, "
16 much work to c' by the boat: *4031 "
27 when the fourteenth night was c', "
28: 6 no harm c' to him, they changed "
17 they were c' together, he said 4905
Ro 1:10 by the will of God to c' unto you. 2064
13 oftentimes I purposed to c' unto "
3: 8 Let us do evil, that good may c'? "
23 For all have sinned, and c' short *5302
5:14 the figure of him that was to c'. 3195
8:38 things present, nor things to c', "
9: 9 At this time will I c', and Sarah 2064
26 shall c' to pass, that in the place *1511
11:11 salvation is c' unto the Gentiles,
25 fulness of the Gentiles be c' in. 1525
26 shall c' out of Sion the Deliverer, 2240
15:23 these many years to c' unto you; 2064
24 journey into Spain, I will c' to: * "
28 I will c' by you into Spain. * 565
29 when I c' unto you, I shall c' in 2064
32 That I may c' unto you with joy "
16:19 obedience is c' abroad unto all men. 864
1Co 1: 7 So that ye c' behind in no gift; 5302
2: 6 of this world, that c' to nought: *2673
3:22 or things to c'; all are yours; 3195
4: 5 the Lord c', who both will bring 2064
18 as though I would not c' to you * "
19 c' to you shortly, if the Lord will, "
21 shall I c' unto you with a rod, or "
7: 5 c' together again, that Satan *4905
10:11 whom the ends of the world are c'.2658
11:17 ye c' together not for the better, 4905
18 when ye c' together in the church, "
20 When ye c' together therefore * "
26 shew the Lord's death till he c'. 2064
33 when ye c' together to eat, tarry 4905
34 c' not together unto condemnation.*"
34 rest will I set in order when I c'. 2064
13:10 when that which is perfect is c', "
14: 6 if I c' unto you speaking with "
23 the whole church be c' together *4905
23 c' in those that are unlearned, 1525
24 there c' in one that believeth not, "
26 when ye c' together, every one of 4905
15:35 and with what body do they c'? 2064

1Co 16: 2 there be no gatherings when I c'. 2064
3 And when I c', whomsoever ye *3854
5 Now I will c' unto you, when I 2064
10 Now if Timotheus c', see that he "
11 in peace, that he may c' unto me: "
12 I greatly desired him to c' unto "
12 but his will was not at all to c' at "
12 this time; but he will c' when he "
2Co 1:15 I was minded to c' unto you before, "
16 to c' again out of Macedonia unto "
2: 1 that I would not c' again to you in "
6:17 c' out from among them, and be 1831
7: 5 For when we were c' into 2064
9: 4 haply if they of Macedonia c' with "
10:14 for we are c' as far as to you also *5348
12: 1 I will c' to visions and revelations 2064
14 third time I am ready to c' to you: "
20 lest, when I c', I shall not find you "
21 lest, when I c' again, my God will "
13: 2 other, that, if I c' again, I will not "
Ga 2:11 But when Peter was c' to Antioch,* "
12 but when they were c', he * "
21 for if righteousness c' by the law * "
3:14 blessing of Abraham might c' on 1096
19 till the seed should c' to whom 2064
25 But after that faith is c', we are "
4: 4 the fulness of the time was c', * "
Eph 1:21 but also in that which is to c': 3195
2: 7 that in the ages to c' he might 1904
4:13 Till we all c' in the unity of the *2658
Ph'p 1:27 that whether I c' and see you, or 2064
2:24 Lord that I also myself shall c' "
Col 1: 6 Which is c' unto you as it is in all 3918
2:17 are a shadow of things to c'; 3195
4:10 if he c' unto you, receive him;) 2064
1Th 1:10 delivered us from the wrath to c'. "
2:16 for the wrath is c' upon them to 5348
18 we would have c' unto you, even 2064
2Th 1:10 When he shall c' to be glorified in "
2: 3 for that day shall not c', except * "
3 except there c' a falling away *2064
1Ti 2: 4 c' unto the knowledge of the truth. "
3:14 hoping to c' unto thee shortly: "
4: 8 now is, and of that which is to c'. 3195
13 Till I c', give attendance to 2064
6:19 foundation against the time to c', 3195
2Ti 3: 1 last days perilous times shall c'. 1764
7 never able to c' to the knowledge 2064
4: 3 the time will c' when they will not 1511
9 Do thy diligence to c' shortly 2064
21 Do thy diligence to c' before winter. "
Tit 3:12 be diligent to c' unto me to "
Heb 2: 5 put in subjection the world to c', 3195
4: 1 any of you should seem to c' short 5302
16 Let us therefore c' boldly unto *4334
6: 5 and the powers of the world to c', 3195
7: 5 c' out of the loins of Abraham: 1831
25 that c' unto God by him, seeing *4334
8: 8 Behold, the days c', saith the 2064
9:11 But Christ being c' an high priest 3854
11 high priest of good things to c', 3195
10: 1 a shadow of good things to c', 3195
7 Then said I, Lo, I c' (in the 2240
9 Then said he, Lo, I c' to do thy "
37 and he that shall c' will 2064
37 will c', and will not tarry. *2240
11:20 Esau concerning things to c'. 3195
24 Moses, when he was c' to years, *1096
12:18 For ye are not c' unto the mount 4334
22 But ye are c' unto mount Sion, "
13:14 city, but we seek one to c'. 3195
23 with whom, if he c' shortly, I will 2064
Jas 2: 2 if there c' unto your assembly a 1525
2 there c' in also a poor man in vile "
4: 1 From whence c' wars and fightings
1 c' they not hence, even of your lusts
5: 1 miseries that shall c' upon you. *1904
1Pe 1:10 the grace that should c' unto you:
4:17 For the time is c' that judgment
2Pe 3: 3 there shall c' in the last days 2064
9 that all should c' to repentance. 5562
10 But the day of the Lord will c' as 2240
1Jo 2:18 heard that antichrist shall c', *2064
4: 2 that Jesus Christ is c' in the flesh "
3 Christ is c' in the flesh is not of * "
3 ye have heard that it should c'; * "
5:20 know that the Son of God is c', 2240
2Jo 7 confess not that Jesus Christ is c'*2064
10 If there c' any unto you, and bring* "
12 I trust to c' unto you, and speak "
3Jo 10 Wherefore, if I c', I will remember "
Re 1: 1 which must shortly c' to pass; 1096
4 and which was, and which is to c'; 2064
8 and which was, and which is to c'. "
2: 5 or else I will c' unto thee quickly, "
16 I will c' unto thee quickly, and will "
25 ye have already, hold fast till I c'. 2240
3: 3 I will c' on thee as a thief, and thou "
3 shalt not know what hour I will c' "
9 behold, I will make them to c' and "
10 of temptation, which shall c' upon 2064
11 Behold, I c' quickly: hold that fast "
20 open the door, I will c' in to him, 1525
4: 1 which said, C' up hither, and I 305
8 which was, and is, and is to c'. 2064
6: 1 one of the four beasts saying, C' "
3 I heard the second beast say, C' "
5 the third beast say, C' and see. "
7 the fourth beast say, C' and see. "
17 the great day of his wrath is c'; "
9:12 and, behold, there c' two woes "
10: 1 I saw another mighty angel c' *2597
11:12 saying unto them, C' up hither. 305
17 which art, and wast, and art to c';*2064
18 thy wrath is c', and the time of * "
12:10 Now is c' salvation, and strength, 1096
Re 12:12 the devil is c' down unto you, *2597
13:13 so that he maketh fire c' down "
14: 7 for the hour of his judgment is c': 2064
15 the time is c' for thee to reap; for "
15: 4 all nations shall c' and worship 2240
16:13 unclean spirits like frogs c' out *
15 I c' as a thief. Blessed is he that 2064
17: 1 C' hither; I will shew unto thee 1204
10 the other is not yet c'; and when 2064
18: 1 I saw another angel c' down from 2597
4 C' out of her, my people, that ye *1831
8 Therefore shall her plagues c' in 2240
10 in one hour is thy judgment c'. 2064
17 so great riches is c' to nought. *2049
19: 7 the marriage of the Lamb is c', 2064
17 C' and gather yourselves together 1205
20: 1 I saw an angel c' down from *2597
21: 9 C' hither, I will shew thee the 1204
22: 7 Behold, I c' quickly: blessed is he 2064
12 behold, I c' quickly; and my "
17 the Spirit and the bride say, C'. "
17 And let him that heareth say, C'. "
17 And let him that is athirst c'. "
20 Surely I c' quickly. Amen. "
20 Even so, c', Lord Jesus. "

comeliness
Isa 53: 2 he hath no form nor c'; and when 1926
Eze 16:14 for it was perfect through my c', * "
27:10 they set forth thy c'. "
Da 10: 8 for my c' was turned in me into 1935
1Co 12:23 parts have more abundant c'. 2157

comely See also UNCOMELY.
1Sa 16:18 in matters, and a c' person, 8389
Job 41:12 his power, nor his c' proportion. ‡2433
Ps 33: 1 for praise is c' for the upright. 5000
147: 1 for it is pleasant; and praise is c'. "
Pr 30:29 go well, yea, four are c' in going: *3190
Ec 5:18 it is good and c' for one to eat and 3303
Ca 1: 5 I am black, but c', O ye daughters 5000
10 Thy cheeks are c' with rows of 4998
2:14 voice, and thy countenance is c'. 5000
4: 3 thy speech is c': thy temples are "
6: 4 love, as Tirzah, c' as Jerusalem, "
Isa 4: 2 earth shall be excellent and c' for 8597
Jer 6: 2 daughter of Zion to a c' and 5000
1Co 7:35 you, but for that which is c', *2158
11:13 is it c' that a woman pray unto *4241
12:24 For our c' parts have no need: but 2158

comers
Heb 10: 1 continually make the c' thereunto*4334

comest
Ge 10:19 Sidon, as thou c' to Gerar, unto *935
13:10 of Egypt, as thou c' unto Zoar. "
24:41 this my oath, when thou c' to my "
De 2:19 And when thou c' nigh over 7126
20:10 When thou c' nigh unto a city to * "
23:24 When thou c' into thy neighbour's 935
25 When thou c' into the standing corn "
28: 6 when thou c' in, and blessed shalt "
19 when thou c' in, and cursed shalt "
J'g 17: 9 said unto him, Whence c' thou? "
18:23 that thou c' with such a company? 2199
19:17 goest thou? and whence c' thou? 935
1Sa 15: 7 thou c' to Shur, that is over against* "
16: 4 C' thou peaceably? "
17:43 Am I a dog, that thou c' to me "
45 Thou c' to me with a sword, and "
2Sa 1: 3 unto him, From whence c' thou? "
3:13 when thou c' to see my face. "
1Ki 2:13 she said, C' thou peaceably? And "
19:15 and when thou c', anoint Hazael to "
2Ki 5:25 Elisha said unto him, Whence c' "
9: 2 And when thou c' thither, look out 935
Job 1: 7 said unto Satan, Whence c' thou? "
2: 2 From whence c' thou? And Satan "
Jer 51:61 When thou c' to Babylon, and shalt "
Jon 1: 8 and whence c' thou? What is thy "
M't 3:14 and c' thou to me? 2064
Lu 23:42 remember me when thou c' into "
2Ti 4:13 when thou c', bring with thee, and "

cometh See also BECOMETH; OVERCOMETH.
Ge 24:43 when the virgin c' forth to draw 3318
29: 6 his daughter c' with the sheep. 935
30:11 And Leah said, A troop c': and * "
32: 6 he c' to meet thee, and four 1980
37:19 Behold, this dreamer c'. 935
48: 2 thy son Joseph c' unto thee: "
Ex 4:14 he c' forth to meet thee: and when 3318
8:20 he c' forth to the water; and say "
13:12 every firstling that c' of a beast 7698
28:35 when he c' out, that he die not. 3318
29:30 when he c' into the tabernacle of 935
Le 11:34 on which such water c' shall be "
Nu 1:51 the stranger that c' nigh shall be 7131
3:10, 38 stranger that c' nigh shall be "
5:30 the spirit of jealousy c' upon him, 5674
12:12 he c' out of his mother's womb. 3318
17:13 Whosoever c' any thing near unto 7131
18: 7 the stranger that c' nigh shall be "
21:13 that c' out of the coasts of the 3318
26: 5 Hanoch, of whom c' the family of *
De 18: 8 that which c' of the sale of his
23:11 when evening c' on, he shall wash 6437
13 and cover that which c' from thee: 6627
28:57 that c' out from between her feet, 3318
J'g 11:31 whatsoever c' forth of the doors "
13:14 eat of any thing that c' of the vine, "
1Sa 4: 3 when it c' among us, it may save *935
9: 6 all that he saith c' surely to pass: "
11: 7 Whosoever c' not forth after Saul 3318
20:27 Wherefore c' not the son of Jesse 935
29 he c' not unto the king's table. * "
25: 8 whatsoever c' to thine hand unto 4672
28:14 An old man c' up; and he is 5927
2Sa 13: 5 and when thy father c' to see thee, 935
18:27 good man, and c' with good tidings. "
1Ki 8:41 but c' out of a far country for thy * "
14: 5 wife of Jeroboam c' to ask a thing "
5 when she c' in, that she shall feign "
2Ki 4:10 when he c' to us, that he shall turn "
6:32 when the messenger c', shut the "
9:18 came to them, but he c' not again. 7725
20 even unto them, and c' not again: "
10: 2 Now as soon as this letter c' to you, 935
11: 8 and he that c' within the ranges, let "
8 king as he goeth out and as he c' in. "
12: 4 all the money that c' into any 5927
9 on the right side as one c' into the 935
1Ch 16:33 because he c' to judge the earth. "
29:16 thine holy name c' of thine hand,
2Ch 13: 9 so that whosoever c' to consecrate 935
20: 2 There c' a great multitude against "
9 If, when evil c' upon us, as the * "
12 this great company that c' against "
23: 7 whosoever else c' into the house, "
7 be ye with the king when he c' in, "
Job 3:21 long for death, but it c' not; and
24 For my sighing c' before I eat, and 935
5: 6 affliction c' not forth of the dust, 3318
21 be afraid of destruction when it c'. 935
26 a shock of corn c' in in his season. 5927
14: 2 He c' forth like a flower, and is 3318
18 the mountain falling c' to nought, 5034
20:25 is drawn, and c' out of the body; 3318
25 glittering sword c' out of his gall:1980
21:17 oft c' their destruction upon them! 935
27: 9 his cry when trouble c' upon him? "
28: 5 for the earth, out of it c' bread: 3318
20 Whence then c' wisdom? and 935
36:32 by the cloud that c' betwixt. *6293
37: 9 Out of the south c' the whirlwind: 935
22 Fair weather c' out of the north: 857
Ps 30: 5 a night, but joy c' in the morning.
62: 1 God: from him c' my salvation.
75: 6 For promotion c' neither from the
78:39 passeth away, and c' not again. 7725
96:13 Lord: for he c', for he c' to judge 935
98: 9 Lord; for he c' to judge the earth: "
118:26 Blessed be he that c' in the name "
121: 1 the hills, from whence c' my help. * "
2 My help c' from the Lord, which
Pr 1:26 I will mock when your fear c'; 935
27 When your fear c' as desolation, "
27 and your destruction c' as a 857
27 distress and anguish c' upon * 935
2: 6 out of his mouth c' knowledge and
3:25 desolation of the wicked, when it c'. 935
11: 2 When pride c', then c' shame: "
8 and the wicked c' in his stead. "
13: 5 man is loathsome, and c' to shame.
10 by pride c' contention: but with 5414
12 but when the desire c', it is a tree 935
18: 3 When the wicked c', then c' also "
17 but his neighbour c' and searcheth "
29:26 every man's judgment c' from the Lord.
Ec 1: 4 another generation c': but the earth "
2:12 the man do that c' after the king? "
4:14 For out of prison he c' to reign; *3318
5: 3 a dream c' through the multitude 935
6: 4 For he c' in with vanity, and "
11: 8 All that c' is vanity.
Ca 2: 8 he c' leaping upon the mountains, "
3: 6 Who is this that c' out of the 5927
8: 5 Who is this that c' up from the "
Isa 13: 9 Behold, the day of the Lord c', 935
21: 1 it c' from the desert, from a terrible "
9 here c' a chariot of men, a couple "
12 The morning c', and also the night: 857
24:18 and he that c' up out of the midst 5927
26:21 Lord c' out of his place to punish 3318
28:29 This also c' forth from the Lord
30:13 whose breaking c' suddenly at an 935
27 the name of the Lord c' from far, "
42: 5 earth, and that which c' out of it; 6631
55:10 as the rain c' down, and the snow 3381
62:11 salvation c'; behold, his reward is 935
63: 1 Who is this that c' from Edom, "
Jer 6:20 To what purpose c' there to me "
22 a people c' from the north country, "
17: 6 shall not see when good c'; but "
8 shall not see when heat c', but her "
18:14 Lebanon which c' from the rock *
43:11 when he c', he shall smite the * 935
46: 7 Who is this that c' up as a flood, *5927
20 c'; it c' out of the north. * 935
47: 4 Because of the day that c' to spoil "
50: 3 there c' up a nation against her, 5927
La 3:37 he that saith, and it c' to pass, 1961
Eze 4:12 with dung that c' out of man, 6627
7:25 destruction c'; and they shall seek 935
14: 4 and c' to the prophet; I the Lord "
4 will answer him that c' according * "
7 and c' to a prophet to enquire of "
20:32 And that which c' into your mind 5927
21: 7 For the tidings; because it c': and 935
7 be weak as water: behold, it c', "
24:24 and when this c', ye shall know "
30: 9 in the day of Egypt: for, lo, it c'. "
33:30 the word that c' forth from the 3318
31 as the people c', and they sit 935
33 And when this c' to pass, (lo, it will "
47: 9 shall live whither the river c'. "
Da 11:16 But he that c', against him shall do "
12:12 waiteth, and c' to the thousand 5060
Ho 7: 1 and the thief c' in, and the troop *935
Joe 2: 1 for the day of the Lord c', for it is "
Mic 1: 3 the Lord c' forth out of his place, 3318
5: 6 when he c' into our land, and when 935
7: 4 watchmen and thy visitation c'; * "
Hab 3:16 when he c' up unto the people, he 5927

Zec 9: 9 thy King c' unto thee: he is just, 935
14: 1 day of the Lord c', and thy spoil "
Mal 4: 1 the day c', that shall burn as an "
1 the day that c' shall burn them up, "
M't 3:11 but he that c' after me is mightier 2064
13 Then c' Jesus from Galilee to 3854
5:37 is more than these c' of evil. *1511
8: 9 and to another, Come, and he c'; 2064
13:19 then c' the wicked one, and "
15:11 that which c' out of the mouth, *1607
17:27 and take up the fish that first c' up; 305
18: 7 that man by whom the offence c'! 2064
21: 5 c' unto thee, meek, and sitting "
9 Blessed is he that c' in the name of "
40 lord therefore of the vineyard c', * "
23:39 Blessed is he that c' in the name of "
24:27 as the lightning c' out of the east, 1831
44 as ye think not the Son of man c'. 2064
46 whom his lord when he c' shall "
25: 6 made, Behold, the bridegroom c'; * "
13 hour wherein the Son of man c'. * "
19 the lord of those servants c', and "
26:36 Then c' Jesus with them unto a "
40 And he c' unto the disciples, and "
45 Then c' he to his disciples, and 2064
M'r 1: 7 There c' one mightier than I "
3:20 the multitude c' together again, 4905
4:15 Satan c' immediately, and taketh 2064
5:22 there c' one of the rulers of the "
38 he c' to the house of the ruler "
6:48 he c' unto them, walking upon the "
7:20 That which c' out of the man, *1607
8:22 c' to Bethsaida; and they bring *2064
38 he c' in the glory of his Father "
9:12 Elias verily c' first, and restoreth "
10: 1 thence, and c' into the coasts "
11: 9 he that c' in the name of the Lord: "
10 of our father David, that c' in the "
13:35 master of the house c', at even, "
14:17 the evening he c' with the twelve. "
37 he c', and findeth them sleeping, "
41 And he c' the third time, and saith "
43 while he yet spake, c' Judas, one 3854
66 there c' one of the maids of the 2064
Lu 3:16 but one mightier than I c', "
6:47 c' to me, and heareth my sayings, "
7: 8 and to another, Come, and he c'; "
8:12 then c' the devil, and taketh away "
49 spake, there c' one from the ruler "
11:25 And when he c', he findeth it swept "
12:36 When he c' and knocketh, they "
37 the lord when he c' shall find "
40 the Son of man c' at an hour when "
43 when he c' shall find so doing. "
54 There c' a shower; and so it is. "
55 will be heat; and it c' to pass. 1096
13:35 Blessed is he that c' in the name 2064
14:10 he that bade thee c', he may say "
31 meet him that c' against him with "
15: 6 he c' home, he calleth together "
17:20 of God c' not with observation: "
18: 8 Son of man c', shall he find faith "
19:38 that c' in the name of the Lord: "
Joh 1: 9 every man that c' into the world. * "
15 c' after me is preferred before me: "
30 me c' a man which is preferred "
3: 8 canst not tell whence it c', and "
20 c' to the light, lest his deeds "
21 he that doeth truth c' to the light, "
31 He that c' from above is above all: "
31 that c' from heaven is above all. "
4: 5 Then c' he to a city of Samaria, "
7 There c' a woman of Samaria to "
21 the hour c', when ye shall neither "
23 But the hour c', and now is, when "
25 Messias c', which is called Christ: "
35 four months, and then c' harvest? "
5:44 not the honour that c' from God "
6:33 bread of God is he which c' down 2597
35 that c' to me shall never hunger; 2064
37 c' to me I will in no wise cast out. "
45 learned of the Father, c' unto me. "
50 bread which c' down from heaven, 2597
7:27 when Christ c', no man knoweth 2064
31 Christ c', will he do more miracles* "
42 Christ c' of the seed of David, "
9: 4 night c', when no man can work. "
10:10 The thief c' not, but for to steal, "
11:38 in himself c' to the grave. 2064
12:13 that c' in the name of the Lord. "
15 King c', sitting on an ass's colt. "
22 Philip c' and telleth Andrew: and "
13: 6 c' he to Simon Peter: and Peter "
14: 6 man c' unto the Father, but by me. "
30 the prince of this world c', and hath "
15:25 But this c' to pass, that the word "
16: 2 the time c', that whosoever killeth 2064
25 time c', when I shall no more speak "
32 the hour c', yea, is now come, "
18: 3 c' thither with lanterns and "
20: 1 c' Mary Magdalene early, when it "
2 she runneth, and c' to Simon Peter, "
6 Then c' Simon Peter following "
21:13 Jesus then c', and taketh bread, "
Ac 10:32 when he c', shall speak unto thee. *3854
13:25 there c' one after me, whose shoes 2064
18:21 this feast that c' in Jerusalem: * "
Ro 4: 9 C' this blessedness then upon *
10:17 So then faith c' by hearing, and
1Co 15:24 Then c' the end, when he shall
2Co 11: 4 For if he that c' preacheth another 2064
28 that which c' upon me daily, *1999
Ga 5: 8 This persuasion c' not of him *
Eph 5: 6 of these things c' the wrath of God 2064
Col 3: 6 the wrath of God c' on the children "
1Th 5: 2 the day of the Lord so c' as a thief "
1Th 5: 3 sudden destruction c' upon them, 2186
1Ti 6: 4 strifes of words, whereof c' envy, 1096
Heb 6: 7 in the rain that c' oft upon it, 2064
10: 5 when he c' into the world, he
11: 6 for he that c' to God must believe 4334
Jas 1:17 c' down from the Father of lights,*2591
Jude 14 the Lord c' with ten thousands of *2064
Re 1: 7 Behold, he c' with clouds; and "
3:12 new Jerusalem, which c' down 2597
11:14 behold, the third woe c' quickly. 2064
17:10 when he c', he must continue a "

come to pass See COME and PASS.

comfort See also COMFORTABLE; COMFORTED; COMFORTETH; COMFORTLESS; COMFORTS.
Ge 5:29 shall c' us concerning our work 5162
18: 5 and c' ye your hearts; after that 5582
27:42 c' himself, purposing to kill thee. 5162
37:35 all his daughters rose up to c' him; "
J'g 19: 5 C' thine heart with a morsel of 5582
8 said, C' thine heart, I pray thee.
2Sa 10: 2 David sent to c' him by the hand 5162
1Ch 7:22 and his brethren came to c' him. "
19: 2 David sent messengers to c' him "
2 of Ammon to Hanun, to c' him. "
Job 2:11 to mourn with him and to c' him. "
6:10 should I yet have c'; yea, I would ‡5165
7:13 My bed shall c' me, my couch 5162
9:27 my heaviness, and c' myself: *1082
10:20 alone, that I may take c' a little, "
21:34 How then c' ye me in vain, seeing 5162
Ps 23: 4 thy rod and thy staff they c' me. "
71:21 and c' me on every side. "
119:50 This is my c' in my affliction: for "
76 merciful kindness be for my c', "
82 saying, When wilt thou c' me? "
Ca 2: 5 with flagons, c' me with apples: 7502
Isa 22: 4 to c' me, because of the spoiling 5162
40: 1 C' ye, c' ye my people, saith your "
51: 3 the Lord shall c' Zion: * "
3 he will c' all her waste places; * "
19 by whom shall I c' thee? "
57: 6 Should I receive c' in these? * "
61: 2 to c' all that mourn; "
66:13 comforteth, so will I c' you; "
Jer 8:18 I would c' myself against sorrow, 4010
16: 7 to c' them for the dead; neither 5162
31:13 into joy, and will c' them, "
La 1: 2 none to c' her: all her friends "
17 is none to c' her: the Lord hath "
21 I sigh: there is none to c' me: "
2:13 I may c' thee, O virgin daughter "
Eze 14:23 And they shall c' you, when ye see "
16:54 in that thou art a c' unto them. "
Zec 1:17 and the Lord shall yet c' Zion, "
10: 2 they c' in vain: therefore they "
M't 9:22 Daughter, be of good c'; thy faith*2293
M'r 10:49 of good c', rise; he calleth thee. * "
Lu 8:48 Daughter, be of good c': thy faith* "
Joh 11:19 to Martha and Mary, to c' them *3888
Ac 9:31 and in the c' of the Holy Ghost, 3874
Ro 15: 4 patience and c' of the scriptures "
1Co 14: 3 and exhortation, and c'. 3889
2Co 1: 3 of mercies, and the God of all c'; 3874
4 that we may be able to c' them 3870
4 by the c' wherewith we ourselves 3874
2: 7 to forgive him, and c' him, lest 3870
7: 4 I am filled with c', I am exceeding 3874
13 we were comforted in your c': "
13:11 Be perfect, be of good c', be of *3870
Eph 6:22 and that he might c' your hearts. "
Ph'p 2: 1 if any c' of love, if any fellowship *3890
19 that I also may be of good c', 2174
Col 4: 8 your estate, and c' your hearts; 3870
11 which have been a c' unto me. 3931
1Th 3: 2 to c' you concerning your faith: 3870
4:18 c' one another with these words. "
5:11 c' yourselves together, and edify * "
14 c' the feebleminded, support the *3888
2Th 2:17 C' your hearts, and stablish you 3870

comfortable
2Sa 14:17 my lord the king shall now be c': 4496
Zec 1:13 with good words and c' words. 5150

comfortably
2Sa 19: 7 speak c' unto thy servants: 5921, 3820
2Ch 30:22 spake c' unto all the Levites "
32: 6 spake c' to them, saying, " 3824
Isa 40: 2 Speak ye c' to Jerusalem, " 3820
Ho 2:14 speak c' unto her. "

comforted See also COMFORTEDST.
Ge 24:67 Isaac was c' after his mother's 5162
37:35 he refused to be c'; and he said, "
38:12 wife died; and Judah was c', "
50:21 And he c' them, and spake kindly "
Ru 2:13 for that thou hast c' me, and for "
2Sa 12:24 And David c' Bath-sheba his wife, "
13:39 he was c' concerning Amnon, "
Job 42:11 they bemoaned him, and c' him "
Ps 77: 2 not: my soul refused to be c'. "
86:17 Lord, hast holpen me, and c' me. "
119:52 of old, O Lord; and have c' myself. "
Isa 49:13 the Lord hath c' his people, and "
52: 9 the Lord hath c' his people, he "
54:11 tossed with tempest, and not c', "
66:13 ye shall be c' in Jerusalem. "
Jer 31:15 children refused to be c' for her "
Eze 5:13 rest upon them, and I will be c': "
14:22 and ye shall be c' concerning "
31:16 shall be c' in the nether parts "
32:31 shall be c' over all his multitude, "
M't 2:18 would not be c', because they 3870
5: 4 that mourn: for they shall be c'. "
Lu 16:25 but now he is c', and thou art "
Joh 11:31 in the house, and c' her, when *3888
Ac 16:40 the brethren, they c' them, and 3870
20:12 alive, and were not a little c'. "
Ro 1:12 that I may be c' together with you. 4837
1Co 14:31 may learn, and all may be c'. 3870
2Co 1: 4 wherewith we ourselves are c' "
6 or whether we be c', it is for your "
7: 6 down, c' us by the coming of Titus; "
7 wherewith he was c' in you, "
13 we were c' in your comfort: yea, "
Col 2: 2 That their hearts might be c', "
1Th 2:11 ye know how we exhorted and c' *3888
3: 7 we were c' over you in all our 3870

comfortedst
Isa 12: 1 is turned away, and thou c' me. *5162

comforter See also COMFORTERS.
Ec 4: 1 oppressed, and they had no c'; 5162
1 was power; but they had no c'.
La 1: 9 down wonderfully: she had no c'. 5162
16 the c' that should relieve my soul "
Joh 14:16 and he shall give you another C', 3875
26 the C', which is the Holy Ghost, "
15:26 But when the C' is come, whom I "
16: 7 the C' will not come unto you; but "

comforters
2Sa 10: 3 that he hath sent c' unto thee? 5162
1Ch 19: 3 he hath sent c' unto thee? are not "
Job 16: 2 miserable c' are ye all. "
Ps 69:20 none; and for c', but I found none. "
Na 3: 7 whence shall I seek c' for thee? "

comforteth
Job 29:25 as one that c' the mourners. 5162
Isa 51:12 I, even I, am he that c' you: "
66:13 As one whom his mother c', so will "
2Co 1: 4 Who c' us in all our tribulation, 3870
7: 6 that c' those that are cast down, "

comfortless
Joh 14:18 I will not leave you c': I will *3737

comforts
Ps 94:19 within me thy c' delight my soul. 8575
Isa 57:18 and restore c' unto him and to 5150

coming See also COMINGS.
Ge 24:63 and, behold, the camels were c'. 935
30:30 hath blessed thee since my c': *7272
Nu 22:16 hinder them from c' unto me: 1980
33:40 of the c' of the children of Israel. 935
J'g 5:28 Why is his chariot so long in c'? "
1Sa 10: 5 a company of prophets c' down 3381
16: 4 of the town trembled at his c', *7122
22: 9 saw the son of Jesse c' to Nob, 935
25:26 withholden thee from c' to shed * "
33 me this day from c' to shed blood, * "
29: 6 thy going out and thy c' in with me "
6 of thy c' unto me unto this day: "
2Sa 3:25 know thy going out and thy c' in, 4126
24:20 saw the king and his servants c' 5674
2Ki 10:15 son of Rechab c' to meet him: "
13:20 invaded the land at the c' in of the 935
19:27 and thy going out, and thy c' in, "
2Ch 22: 7 was of God by c' to Joram: for * "
Ezr 3: 8 in the second year of their c' unto "
Ps 19: 5 bridegroom c' out of his chamber, 3318
37:13 for he seeth that his day is c'. 935
121: 8 and thy c' in from this time forth, "
Pr 8: 3 city, at the c' in at the doors. 3996
Isa 14: 9 to meet thee at thy c': it stirreth 935
32:19 When it shall hail, c' down on *3381
37:28 and thy c' in, and thy rage against 935
44: 7 and the things that are c', and 857
Jer 8: 7 swallow observe the time of their c'; 935
Da 4:23 watcher and an holy one c' down 5182
Mic 7:15 According to the days of thy c' *3318
Hab 3: 4 he had horns c' out of his hand:
Mal 3: 2 who may abide the day of his c'? 935
4: 5 before the c' of the great and * "
M't 8:28 devils, c' out of the tombs, *1831
16:28 the Son of man c' in his kingdom. 2064
24: 3 what shall be the sign of thy c', 3952
27 also the c' of the Son of man be. "
30 they shall see the Son of man c' 2064
37, 39 also the c' of the Son of man 3952
48 heart, My lord delayeth his c'; *2064
25:27 at my c' I should have received "
26:64 and c' in the clouds of heaven. "
M'r 1:10 straightway c' up out of the water, 305
6:31 for there were many c' and going, 2064
13:26 see the Son of man c' in the clouds "
36 c' suddenly he find you sleeping. "
14:62 and c' in the clouds of heaven. "
15:21 passed by, c' out of the country, "
Lu 2:38 she c' in that instant gave thanks 2186
9:42 And as he was yet a c', the devil 4334
12:45 My lord delayeth his c'; and 2064
18: 5 by her continual c' she weary me. "
19:23 at my c' I might have required "
21:26 things which are c' on the earth: 1904
27 shall they see the Son of man c' 2064
23:26 a Cyrenian, c' out of the country, "
29 behold, the days are c', in the which "
36 c' to him, and offering him 4334
Joh 1:27 c' after me is preferred before me, 2064
29 John seeth Jesus c' unto him, "
47 Jesus saw Nathanael c' to him, "
5: 7 but while I am c', another steppeth "
25 The hour is c', and now is, when "
28 for the hour is c', in the which all "
10:12 seeth the wolf c', and leaveth the "
11:20 as she heard that Jesus was c', "
12:12 that Jesus was c' to Jerusalem, "
Ac 7:52 before of the c' of the Just One; 1660
9:12 a man named Ananias c' in, 1525
28 with them c' in and going out *1531
10: 3 an angel of God c' in to him, 1525
25 as Peter was c' in, Cornelius met *1525

Ac 13:24 had first preached before his c' 1529
17:10 Berea: who c' thither went into *3854
27:33 while the day was c' on, 3195, 1096
Ro 15:22 much hindered from c' to you. 2064
1Co 1: 7 waiting for the c' of our Lord * 602
15:23 they that are Christ's at his c'. 3952
16:17 glad of the c' of Stephanus and "
2Co 7: 6 comforted us by the c' of Titus; "
7 And not by his c' only, but by the "
13: 1 This is the third time I am c' 2064
Ph'p 1:26 for me by my c' to you again. *3952
1Th 2:19 our Lord Jesus Christ at his c'? "
3:13 at the c' of our Lord Jesus Christ "
4:15 remain unto the c' of the Lord "
5:23 the c' of our Lord Jesus Christ. "
2Th 2: 1 by the c' of our Lord Jesus "
8 with the brightness of his c': "
9 him, whose c' is after the working "
Jas 5: 7 brethren, unto the c' of the Lord. "
8 the c' of the Lord draweth nigh. "
1Pe 2: 4 To whom c', as unto a living stone, 4334
2Pe 1:16 power and c' of our Lord Jesus 3952
3: 4 Where is the promise of his c'? "
12 unto the c' of the day of God, "
1Jo 2:28 be ashamed before him at his c'. "
Re 13:11 beast c' up out of the earth; 305
21: 2 new Jerusalem, c' down from God 2597

comings
Eze 43:11 and the c' in thereof, and all 4126

command See also COMMANDED; COMMANDEST; COMMANDETH; COMMANDING; COMMANDMENT.
Ge 18:19 c' his children and his household 6680
27: 8 according to that which I c' thee. "
50:16 Thy father did c' before he died, "
Ex 7: 2 shalt speak all that I c' thee: "
8:27 Lord our God, as he shall c' us. 559
18:23 do this thing, and God c' thee 6680
27:20 And thou shalt c' the children of "
34:11 thou that which I c' thee this day: "
Le 6: 9 C' Aaron and his sons, saying, "
13:54 the priest shall c' that they wash "
14: 4 Then shall the priest c' to take "
5 priest shall c' that one of the birds "
36 the priest shall c' that they empty "
40 priest shall c' that they take away "
24: 2 C' the children of Israel that they "
25:21 I will c' my blessing upon you "
Nu 5: 2 C' the children of Israel, that they "
9: 8 the Lord will c' concerning you. "
28: 2 C' the children of Israel, and say "
34: 2 C' the children of Israel, and say "
35: 2 C' the c' of Israel, that they give "
36: 6 which the Lord doth c' concerning "
De 2: 4 c' thou the people, saying, Ye are "
4: 2 add unto the word which I c' you, "
2 of the Lord your God which I c' "
40 I c' thee this day, that it may go "
6: 2 commandments, which I c' thee, "
6 words, which I c' thee this day, "
7:11 judgments, which I c' thee this "
8: 1 the commandments which I c' thee "
11 statutes, which I c' thee this day: "
10:13 and his statutes, which I c' thee "
11: 8 the commandments which I c' you "
13 my commandments which I c' "
22 these commandments which I c' "
27 your God, which I c' you this day: "
28 the way which I c' you this day, "
12:11 shall ye bring all that I c' you; "
14 thou shalt do all that I c' thee. "
28 all these words which I c' thee, "
32 What thing soever I c' you, "
13:18 his commandments which I c' thee "
15: 5 these commandments which I c' "
11 therefore I c' thee, saying, Thou "
15 therefore I c' thee this thing to day. "
18:18 unto them all that I shall c' him. "
19: 7 Wherefore I c' thee, saying, Thou "
9 which I c' thee this day, to love the "
24:18, 22 I c' thee to do this thing. "
27: 1 which I c' you this day. "
4 set up these stones, which I c' you "
10 statutes, which I c' thee this day. "
28: 1 I c' thee this day, that the Lord "
8 Lord shall c' the blessing upon thee "
13 which I c' thee this day, to observe "
14 the words which I c' thee this day, "
15 statutes which I c' thee this day; "
30: 2 all that I c' thee this day, thou and "
8 his commandments which I c' thee "
11 which I c' thee this day, it is not "
16 In that I c' thee this day to love "
32:46 shall c' your children to observe to "
Jos 1:11 c' the people, saying, Prepare you "
3: 8 c' the priests that bear the ark "
4: 3 c' ye them, saying, Take you hence "
16 C' the priests that bear the ark "
11:15 so did Moses c' Joshua, and so did "
1Sa 16:16 Let our lord now c' thy servants, 559
1Ki 5: 6 c' thou that they hew me cedar 6680
11:38 hearken unto all that I c' thee, "
2Ch 7:13 I c' the locusts to devour the land, "
Job 39:27 the eagle mount up at thy c', 6310
Ps 42: 8 Lord will c' his lovingkindness 6680
44: 4 God: c' deliverances for Jacob. "
Isa 5: 6 also c' the clouds that they rain "
45:11 the work of my hands c' ye me. "
Jer 1: 7 I c' thee thou shalt speak. "
17 speak unto them all that I c' thee: "
11: 4 according to all which I c' you; "
26: 2 the words that I c' thee to speak "
27: 4 And c' them to say unto their * "
34:22 I will c', saith the Lord, and cause "
La 1:10 whom thou didst c' that they "
Am 9: 3 thence will I c' the serpent, and 6680
4 thence will I c' the sword, and it "
9 For, lo, I will c', and I will sift "
M't 4: 3 c' that these stones be made bread. 2036
19: 7 Why did Moses then c' to give a 1781
27:64 C' therefore that the sepulchre be 2753
M'r 10: 3 unto them, What did Moses c' you? 1781
Lu 4: 3 c' this stone that it be made bread. 2036
8:31 he would not c' them to go out 2004
9:54 wilt thou that we c' fire to come *2036
Joh 15:14 if ye do whatsoever I c' you. 1781
17 These things I c' you, that ye love "
Ac 5:28 Did not we straitly c' you that ye *3853
15: 5 c' them to keep the law of Moses. * "
16:18 I c' thee in the name of Jesus "
1Co 7:10 unto the married I c', yet not I, * "
2Th 3: 4 and will do the things which we c' "
6 we c' you, brethren, in the name "
12 that are such we c' and exhort "
1Ti 4:11 These things c' and teach. "

commanded See also COMMANDEDST.
Ge 2:16 And the Lord God c' the man, 6680
3:11 the tree, whereof I c' thee that "
17 the tree, of which I c' thee, saying, "
6:22 all that God c' him, so did he. "
7: 5 unto all that the Lord c' him. "
9 the female, as God had c' Noah. "
16 of all flesh, as God had c' him: "
12:20 Pharaoh c' his men concerning * "
21: 4 eight days old, as God had c' him. "
32: 4 And he c' them, saying, Thus shall "
17 And he c' the foremost, saying, "
19 so c' he the second, and the third, "
42:25 Then Joseph c' to fill their sacks, "
44: 1 And he c' the steward of his house, "
45:19 Now thou art c', this do ye; "
47:11 of Rameses, as Pharaoh had c'. "
50: 2 And Joseph c' his servants the "
12 unto him according as he c' them: "
Ex 1:17 not as the king of Egypt c' them, 1696
4:28 all the signs which he had c' him. *6680
5: 6 And Pharaoh c' the same day the "
7: 6 as the Lord c' them, so did they. "
10 Aaron did so as the Lord had c': "
20 and Aaron did so, as the Lord c'; "
12:28 and did as the Lord had c' Moses "
50 as the Lord c' Moses and Aaron, "
16:16 the Lord hath c', Gather of it every "
34 As the Lord c' Moses, so Aaron laid "
19: 7 these words which the Lord c' him. "
23:15 as I c' thee, in the time appointed "
29:35 which I have c' thee: seven days "
31: 6 all that I have c' thee; "
11 that I have c' thee shall they do. "
32: 8 out of the way which I c' them: "
34: 4 as the Lord had c' him, and took "
18 as I c' thee, in the time of the month "
34 that which he was c'. "
35: 1 words which the Lord hath c', "
4 the thing which the Lord c', "
10 make all that the Lord hath c'; "
29 which the Lord had c' to be made "
36: 1 all that the Lord had c'. "
5 work, which the Lord c' to make. "
38:22 made all that the Lord c' Moses. "
39: 1 for Aaron; as the Lord c' Moses. "
5 twined linen; as the Lord c' Moses. "
7 of Israel; as the Lord c' Moses. "
21 ephod; as the Lord c' Moses. "
26 to minister in; as the Lord c' Moses. "
29 needlework; as the Lord c' Moses. "
31 the mitre; as the Lord c' Moses. "
32 that the Lord c' Moses, so did they. "
42 all that the Lord c' Moses, so "
43 the Lord had c', even so had they "
40:16 that the Lord c' him, so did he. "
19 upon it; as the Lord c' Moses. "
21 testimony; as the Lord c' Moses. "
23 Lord; as the Lord had c' Moses. "
25 the Lord; as the Lord c' Moses. "
27 thereon; as the Lord c' Moses. "
29 meat offering; as the Lord c' "
32 they washed; as the Lord c' Moses. "
Le 7:36 Which the Lord c' to be given them "
38 the Lord c' Moses in mount Sinai, "
38 in the day that he c' the children of "
8: 4 And Moses did as the Lord c' him; "
5 thing which the Lord c' to be done. "
9 holy crown; as the Lord c' Moses. "
13 bonnets upon them; as the Lord c' "
17 without the camp; as the Lord c' "
21 unto the Lord; as the Lord c' "
29 it was Moses' part; as the Lord c' "
31 as I c', saying, Aaron and his sons "
34 the Lord hath c' to do, to make an "
35 that ye die not: for so I am c'. "
36 which the Lord c' by the hand "
9: 5 Moses c' before the tabernacle "
6 the Lord c' that ye should do: "
7 for them; as the Lord c'. "
10 upon the altar; as the Lord c' Moses. "
21 before the Lord; as Moses c'. "
10: 1 the Lord, which he c' them not. "
13 made by fire: for so I am c'. "
15 for ever; as the Lord hath c'. "
18 eaten it in the holy place, as I c'. "
16:34 And he did as the Lord c' Moses. "
17: 2 the Lord hath c', saying, "
24:23 Israel did as the Lord c' Moses. "
27:34 the Lord c' Moses for the children "
Nu 1:19 the Lord c' Moses, so he numbered "
54 according to all that the Lord c' "
2:33 of Israel; as the Lord c' Moses. "
34 all that the Lord c' Moses: so they "
3:16 of the Lord, as he was c'. "
Nu 3:42 the Lord c' him, all the firstborn 6680
51 of the Lord, as the Lord c' Moses. "
4:49 of him, as the Lord c' Moses. "
8: 3 candlestick, as the Lord c' Moses. "
20 that the Lord c' Moses concerning "
22 the Lord had c' Moses concerning "
9: 5 Lord c' Moses, so did the children "
15:23 the Lord hath c' you by the hand "
23 the day that the Lord c' Moses, * "
36 and he died; as the Lord c' Moses. "
16:47 Aaron took as Moses c', and ran *1696
17:11 did so: as the Lord c' him, so did 6680
19: 2 the Lord hath c', saying, Speak "
20: 9 before the Lord, as he c' him. "
27 Moses did as the Lord c': and they "
26: 4 the Lord c' Moses and the children "
27:11 of judgment, as the Lord c' Moses. "
22 And Moses did as the Lord c' him: "
23 gave him a charge, as the Lord c' *1696
29:40 according to all that the Lord c' 6680
30: 1 the thing which the Lord hath c'. "
16 the Lord c' Moses, between a man "
31: 7 the Lord c' Moses; and they slew "
21 the law which the Lord c' Moses; "
31 the priest did as the Lord c' Moses. "
41 the priest, as the Lord c' Moses. "
47 of the Lord; as the Lord c' Moses. "
32:28 So concerning them Moses c' * "
34:13 c' the children of Israel, saying, "
13 Lord c' to give unto the nine tribes, "
29 Lord c' to divide the inheritance "
36: 2 Lord c' my lord to give the land "
2 my lord was c' by the Lord to give "
5 And Moses c' the children of "
10 as the Lord c' Moses, so did the "
13 the Lord c' by the hand of Moses "
De 1:18 I c' you at that time all the things "
19 as the Lord our God c' us; and we "
41 all that the Lord our God c' us. "
3:18 And I c' you at that time, "
21 And I c' Joshua at that time, "
4: 5 even as the Lord my God c' me, "
13 which he c' you to perform, "
14 the Lord c' me at that time to "
5:12 it, as the Lord thy God hath c' "
15 the Lord thy God c' thee to keep "
16 the Lord thy God hath c' thee; "
32 the Lord your God hath c' you: "
33 which the Lord your God hath c' "
6: 1 the Lord your God c' to teach "
17 statutes, which he hath c' thee. "
20 the Lord our God hath c' you? "
24 And the Lord c' us to do all these "
25 the Lord our God, as he hath c' us. "
9:12 out of the way which I c' them; "
16 the way which the Lord had c' you. "
10: 5 they be, as the Lord c' me. "
12:21 as I have c' thee, and thou shalt "
13: 5 the Lord thy God c' thee to walk "
17: 3 of heaven, which I have not c' "
18:20 I have not c' him to speak, or that "
20:17 as the Lord thy God hath c' thee: "
24: 8 as I c' them, so ye shall observe "
26:13 which thou hast c' me: I have not "
14 to all that thou hast c' me. "
16 the Lord thy God hath c' thee to * "
27: 1 c' the people, saying, Keep all the "
28:45 and his statutes which he c' thee: "
29: 1 the Lord c' Moses to make with "
31: 5 commandments which I have c' you. "
10 And Moses c' them, saying, At the "
25 That Moses c' the Levites, "
29 the way which I have c' you; and "
33: 4 Moses c' us a law, even the "
34: 9 and did as the Lord c' Moses. "
Jos 1: 7 which Moses my servant c' thee: "
9 Have not I c' thee? Be strong "
10 Then Joshua c' the officers of the "
13 the servant of the Lord c' you, "
3: 3 And they c' the people, saying, "
4: 8 as Joshua c', and took up twelve "
10 the Lord c' Joshua to speak unto "
10 according to all that Moses c' "
17 Joshua therefore c' the priests, "
6:10 Joshua had c' the people, saying, "
7:11 my covenant which I c' them: for "
8: 4 And he c' them, saying, Behold, ye "
8 See, I have c' you. "
27 word of the Lord, which he c' "
29 Joshua c' that they should take "
31 the servant of the Lord c' the "
33 the servant of the Lord had c' "
35 all that Moses c', which Joshua "
9:24 the Lord thy God c' his servant "
10:27 Joshua c', and they took them "
40 as the Lord God of Israel c'. "
11:12 Moses the servant of the Lord c'. "
15 As the Lord c' Moses his servant, "
15 undone of all that the Lord c' "
20 destroy them, as the Lord c' Moses. "
13: 6 for an inheritance, as I have c' "
14: 2 as the Lord c' by the hand of Moses, "
5 As the Lord c' Moses, so the "
17: 4 The Lord c' Moses to give us an "
21: 2 The Lord c' by the hand of Moses "
8 with their suburbs, as the Lord c' "
22: 2 the servant of the Lord c' you, "
2 obeyed my voice in all that I c' you: "
23:16 which he c' you, and have gone "
J'g 2:20 my covenant which I c' their "
3: 4 which he c' their fathers by the "
4: 6 the Lord God of Israel c', saying, "
13:14 all that I c' her let her observe. "
21:10 and c' them, saying, Go and smite "
20 Therefore they c' the children of "

Ru 2:15 Boaz c' his young men, saying, 6680
1Sa 2:29 I have c' in my habitation; and "
13:13 which he c' thee: for now would "
14 and the Lord hath c' him to be * "
14 not kept that which the Lord c' "
17:20 and went, as Jesse had c' him; "
18:22 And Saul c' his servants, saying, "
20:29 he hath c' me to be there: and "
21: 2 The king hath c' me a business, "
2 I send thee, and what I have c' "
2Sa 4:12 And David c' his young men, and "
5:25 David did so, as the Lord had c' "
7: 7 whom I c' to feed my people "
11 the time that I c' judges to be over "
9:11 my lord the king hath c' his * "
13:28 Now Absalom had c' his servants, "
28 have not I c' you? be courageous. "
29 unto Amnon as Absalom had c'. "
18: 5 And the king c' Joab and Abishai "
21:14 they performed all that the king c'. "
24:19 of Gad, went up as the Lord c'. "
1Ki 2:46 So the king c' Benaiah the son of "
5:17 And the king c', and they brought "
8:58 his judgments, which he c' our "
9: 4 all that I have c' thee, and wilt "
11:10 And had c' him concerning this "
10 kept not that which the Lord c'. "
11 which I have c' thee, I will surely "
13:21 which the Lord thy God c' thee, "
15: 5 any thing that he c' him all the "
17: 4 I have c' the ravens to feed thee "
9 I have c' a widow woman there to "
22:31 the king of Syria c' his thirty and "
2Ki 11: 5 And he c' them, saying, This is the "
9 Jehoiada the priest c': and they "
15 But Jehoiada the priest c' the "
14: 6 wherein the Lord c', saying, The "
16:15 And king Ahaz c' Urijah the priest, "
16 according to all that king Ahaz c'. "
17:13 the law which I c' your fathers, "
27 Then the king of Assyria c', saying, "
34 which the Lord c' the children of "
18: 6 which the Lord c' Moses. "
12 Moses the servant of the Lord c', "
21: 8 all that I have c' them, and "
8 the law that my servant Moses c' "
22:12 And the king c' Hilkiah the priest, "
23: 4 And the king c' Hilkiah the high "
21 And the king c' all the people, "
1Ch 6:49 Moses the servant of God had c'. "
14:16 David therefore did as God c' him: "
15:15 thereon, as Moses c' according to "
16:15 which he c' to a thousand "
40 of the Lord, which he c' Israel; "
17: 6 whom I c' to feed my people. "
10 I c' judges to be over my people "
21:17 Is it not I that c' the people to be 559
18 Then the angel of the Lord c' Gad "
27 And the Lord c' the angel; and he "
22: 2 And David c' to gather together "
17 David also c' all the princes of 6680
23:31 according to the order c' unto *
24:19 as the Lord God of Israel had c' 6680
2Ch 7:17 I have c' thee, and shalt observe "
8:14 so had David the man of God c'. 4687
14: 4 And c' Judah to seek the Lord God 559
18:30 king of Syria had c' the captains 6680
23: 8 that Jehoiada the priest had c', "
25: 4 Lord c', saying, The fathers shall "
29:21 And he c' the priests the sons of 559
24 the king c' that the burnt offering "
27 And Hezekiah c' to offer the burnt "
30 king and the princes c' the Levites "
31: 4 Moreover he c' the people that "
11 Hezekiah c' to prepare chambers "
32:12 c' Judah and Jerusalem, saying, "
33: 8 to do all that I have c' them, 6680
16 c' Judah to serve the Lord God of 559
34:20 the king c' Hilkiah, and Ahikam 6680
35:21 God c' me to make haste: forbear 559
Ezr 4: 3 the king of Persia hath c' us. 6680
19 And I c', and search hath *7761, 2942
5: 3 Who hath c' you to build * "
9 Who c' you to build this * "
7:23 Whatsoever is c' by the God 4480, 2941
9:11 Which thou hast c' by thy servants 6680
Ne 8: 1 which the Lord had c' to Israel. "
14 the Lord had c' by Moses, that the "
13: 5 which was c' to be given to the *4687
9 Then I c', and they cleansed the 559
19 I c' that the gates should be shut, "
22 And I c' the Levites that they should "
Es 1:10 he c' Mehuman, Biztha, Harbona, "
17 king Ahasuerus c' Vashti the queen "
3: 2 king had so c' concerning him. 6680
12 Haman had c' unto the king's "
4:13 Mordecai c' to answer Esther, *559
17 according to all that Esther had c' 6680
6: 1 he c' to bring the book of records 559
8: 9 that Mordecai c' unto the Jews, 6680
9:14 And the king c' it so to be done: 559
25 he c' by letters that his wicked "
Job 38:12 Hast thou c' the morning since 6680
42: 9 and did according as the Lord c' 1696
Ps 7: 6 to the judgment that thou hast c'. 6680
33: 9 was done; he c', and it stood fast. "
68:28 Thy God hath c' thy strength: "
78: 5 he c' our fathers, that they should "
23 Though he had c' the clouds from "
105: 8 forever, the word which he c' to a "
106:34 concerning whom the Lord c' 559
111: 9 he hath c' his covenant for ever: 6680
119: 4 hast c' us to keep thy precepts "
138 testimonies that thou hast c' are "
133: 3 the Lord c' the blessing, even life "
Ps 148: 5 for he c', and they were created. 6680
Isa 13: 3 I have c' my sanctified ones, I have "
34:16 my mouth it hath c', and his spirit "
45:12 and all their host have I c'. "
48: 5 my molten image, hath c' them. "
Jer 7:22 c' them in the day that I brought "
23 But this thing c' I them, saying, "
23 the ways that I have c' you, that it "
31 I c' them not, neither came it into "
11: 4 I c' your fathers in the day that I "
8 I c' them to do; but they did them "
13: 5 it by Euphrates, as the Lord c' me. "
6 from thence, which I c' thee to hide "
14:14 neither have I c' them, neither "
17:22 sabbath day, as I c' your fathers. "
19: 5 offerings unto Baal, which I c' not, "
23:32 nor c' them: therefore they shall "
26: 8 Lord had c' him to speak unto all "
29:23 I have not c' them; even I know, "
32:35 I c' them not, neither came it into "
35: 6 of Rechab our father c' us, saying, "
10 all that Jonadab our father c' us. "
14 he c' his sons not to drink wine, "
16 of their father, which he c' them. "
18 all that he hath c' you: "
36: 5 And Jeremiah c' Baruch, saying, "
8 Jeremiah the prophet c' him, "
26 the king c' Jerahmeel the son of "
37:21 Then Zedekiah the king c' that "
38:10 Then the king c' Ebed-melech the "
27 all these words that the king had c'. "
50:21 to all that I have c' thee. "
51:59 Jeremiah the prophet c' Seraiah "
La 1:17 the Lord hath c' concerning Jacob, "
2:17 his word that he had c' in the days "
Eze 9:11 saying, I have done as thou hast c' "
10: 6 when he had c' the man clothed "
12: 7 And I did so as I was c': I brought "
24:18 I did in the morning as I was c'. "
37: 7 I prophesied as I was c': and as I "
10 I prophesied as he c' me, and the "
Da 2: 2 the king c' to call the magicians, 559
12 and c' to destroy all the wise men 560
46 c' that they should offer an oblation "
3: 4 To you it is c', O people, nations, "
13 in his rage and fury c' "
19 he spake, and c' that they should "
20 And he c' the most mighty men "
4:26 whereas they c' to leave the stump "
5: 2 c' to bring the golden and silver "
29 c' Belshazzar, and they clothed "
6:16 Then the king c', and they brought "
23 and c' that they should take Daniel "
24 And the king c', and they brought "
Am 2:12 c' the prophets, saying, Prophesy 6680
Zec 1: 6 I c' my servants the prophets, "
Mal 4: 4 which I c' unto him in Horeb for "
M't 8: 4 offer the gift that Moses c', for a 4367
10: 5 and c' them, saying, Go not into *3853
14: 9 he c' it to be given her. 2753
19 he c' the multitude to sit down on "
15: 4 For God c', saying, Honour thy *1781
35 he c' the multitude to sit down 2753
18:25 his lord c' him to be sold, and his "
21: 6 went, and did as Jesus c' them, *4367
27:58 Pilate c' the body to be delivered. 2753
28:20 whatsoever I have c' you: and, lo, 1781
M'r 1:44 those things which Moses c', for 4367
5:43 c' that something should be given 2036
6: 8 And c' them that they should *3853
27 and c' his head to be brought 2004
39 he c' them to make all sit down 3853
8: 6 And he c' the people to sit down 3853
7 c' to set them also before them. 2036
10:49 stood still, and c' him to be called.* "
11: 6 even as Jesus had c': and they let *1781
13:34 and c' the porter to watch. "
Lu 5:14 according as Moses c', for a 4367
8:29 (For he had c' the unclean spirit ‡3853
55 and he c' to give her meat. 1299
9:21 and c' them to tell no man 3853
14:22 it is done as thou hast c', and yet *2004
17: 9 he did the things that were c' him? 1299
10 those things which are c' you, say, "
18:40 c' him to be brought unto him: 2753
19:15 c' these servants to be called unto 2036
Joh 8: 5 Now Moses in the law c' us, 1781
Ac 1: 4 c' them that they should not *3853
4:15 when they had c' them to go aside 2753
18 and c' them not to speak at all nor *3853
5:34 c' to put the apostles forth a little 2753
40 they c' that they should not speak *3853
8:38 he c' the chariot to stand still: 2753
10:33 all things that are c' thee of God. 4367
42 he c' us to preach unto the people, *3853
48 he c' them to be baptized in the 4367
12:19 c' that they should be put to 2753
13:47 the Lord c' us, saying, I have set 1781
16:22 their clothes, and c' to beat them. 2753
18: 2 Claudius had c' all Jews to depart 1299
21:33 and c' him to be bound with two 2753
34 he c' him to be carried into the "
22:24 chief captain c' him to be brought "
30 c' the chief priests and all their "
23: 2 Ananias c' them that stood by him 2004
10 c' the soldiers to go down, and to 2753
31 the soldiers, as it was c' them, 1299
35 he c' him to be kept in Herod's 2753
24:23 he c' a centurion to keep Paul, *1299
25: 6 seat c' Paul to be brought. 2753
17 and c' the man to be brought forth. "
21 c' him to be kept till I might send "
27:43 c' that they which could swim "
1Co 14:34 c' to be under obedience, as *
2Co 4: 6 For God, who c' the light to shine *2036
1Th 4:11 with your own hands, as we c' *3853
2Th 3:10 this we c' you, that if any would "
Heb 12:20 not endure that which was c', *1291
Re 9: 4 was c' them that they should not *4483

commandedst
Ne 1: 7 thou c' thy servant Moses. 6680
8 the word that thou c' thy servant "
9:14 c' them precepts, statutes, and laws, "
Jer 32:23 of all that thou c' them to do: "

commander
Isa 55: 4 a leader and c' to the people. 6680

commandest
Jos 1:16 All that thou c' us we will do, *6680
18 thy word in all that thou c' him, "
Ac 23: 3 and c' me to be smitten contrary 2753

commandeth
Ex 16:32 is the thing which the Lord c', *6680
Nu 32:25 Thy servants will do as my lord c'. "
Job 9: 7 Which c' the sun, and it riseth not; 559
36:10 c' that they return from iniquity. "
32 and c' it not to shine by the cloud *6680
37:12 they may do whatsoever he c' "
Ps 107:25 For he c', and raiseth the stormy 559
La 3:37 to pass, when the Lord c' it not? 6680
Am 6:11 the Lord c', and he will smite "
M'r 1:27 c' he even the unclean spirits, 2004
Lu 4:36 power he c' the unclean spirits "
8:25 he c' even the winds and water, "
Ac 17:30 but now c' all men every where to 3853

commanding
Ge 49:33 Jacob had made an end of c' his *6680
M't 11: 1 an end of c' his twelve disciples, 1299
Ac 24: 8 C' his accusers to come unto *2753
1Ti 4: 3 c' to abstain from meats, which

commandment See also COMMANDMENTS.
Ge 45:21 according to the c' of Pharaoh, 6310
Ex 17: 1 journeys, according to the c' of "
25:22 give thee in c' unto the children 6680
34:32 gave them in c' all that the Lord "
36: 6 Moses gave c', and they caused "
38:21 was counted according to the c' 6310
Nu 3:39 numbered at the c' of the Lord, "
4:37 did number according to the c' of "
41 according to the c' of the Lord. "
49 According to the c' of the Lord they "
9:18 At the c' of the Lord the children "
18 Israel journeyed, and at the c' of "
20 the tabernacle; according to the c' "
20 the c' of the Lord they journeyed. "
23 At the c' of the Lord they rested "
23 the c' of the Lord they journeyed: "
23 c' of the Lord by the hand of Moses. "
10:13 their journey according to the c' of "
13: 3 by the c' of the Lord sent them "
14:41 do ye transgress the c' of the Lord? "
15:31 hath broken his c', that soul shall 4687
23:20 Behold, I have received c' to bless:
24:13 c' of the Lord to do either good *6310
27:14 ye rebelled against my c' in the * "
33: 2 their journeys by the c' of the Lord: "
38 the c' of the Lord, and died there, "
De 1: 3 the Lord had given him in c' unto 6680
26 rebelled against the c' of the Lord 6310
43 against the c' of the Lord, and "
9:23 against the c' of the Lord your God, "
17:20 that he turn not aside from the c', 4687
30:11 For this c' which I command thee "
Jos 1:18 that doth rebel against thy c', 6310
8: 8 city on fire: according to the c' *1697
15:13 the c' of the Lord to Joshua, even 6310
17: 4 according to the c' of the Lord, he "
21: 3 at the c' of the Lord, these cities "
22: 3 of the c' of the Lord your God. 4687
5 But take diligent heed to do the c' "
1Sa 12:14 and not rebel against the c' of the 6310
15 but rebel against the c' of the Lord, "
13:13 hast not kept the c' of the Lord 4687
15:13 have performed the c' of the Lord. 1697
24 transgressed the c' of the Lord, 6310
2Sa 12: 9 despised the c' of the Lord, to do *1697
1Ki 2:43 c' that I have charged thee with? 4687
13:21 not kept the c' which the Lord "
2Ki 17:34 after the law and c' which the Lord "
37 the law, and the c', which he wrote "
18:36 king's c' was, saying, Answer him "
23:35 according to the c' of Pharaoh: 6310
24: 3 c' of the Lord came this upon Judah, "
1Ch 12:32 all their brethren were at their c'. "
14:12 David gave a c', and they were 559
28:21 people will be wholly at thy c'. 1697
2Ch 8:13 according to the c' of Moses, 4687
15 not from the c' of the king "
14: 4 and to do the law and the c'. "
19:10 between law and c', statutes and "
24: 6 according to the c' of Moses the *
8 at the king's c' they made a chest,* 559
21 at the c' of the king in the court 4687
29:15 according to the c' of the king, by "
25 to the c' of David, and of Gad the "
25 the c' of the Lord by his prophets. "
30: 6 and Judah, and according to the c' "
12 c' of the king and of the princes, "
31: 5 as soon as the c' came abroad, 1697
13 at the c' of Hezekiah the king, *4662
35:10 courses according to the king's c'. 4687
15 to the c' of David, and Asaph, "
16 according to the c' of king Josiah. "
Ezr 4:21 Give ye now c' to cause these men 2942
21 until another c' shall be given *2941
6:14 according to the c' of the God of * "
14 and according to the c' of Cyrus, 2942
8:17 And I sent them with c' unto Iddo 3318
10: 3 that tremble at the c' of our God; 4687

Ne 11:23 the king's c' concerning them, 4687
12:24 the c' of David the man of God, "
45 the c' of David, and of Solomon "
Es 1:12 refused to come at the king's c' 1697
15 she hath not performed the c' of *3982
19 let there go a royal c' from him, 1697
2: 8 when the king's c' and his decree "
20 for Esther did the c' of Mordecai, 3982
3: 3 transgressest thou the king's c'? 4687
14 a c' to be given in every province *1881
15 being hastened by the king's c', 1697
4: 3 the king's c' and his decree came, "
5 and gave him a c' to Mordecai, *6680
10 and gave him c' unto Mordecai; * "
8:13 the writing for a c' to be given *1881
14 and pressed on by the king's c'. 1697
17 the king's c' and his decree came,* "
9: 1 when the king's c' and his decree "
Job 23:12 gone back from the c' of his lips; 4687
Ps 19: 8 c' of the Lord is pure, enlightening "
71: 3 thou hast given c' to save me; 6680
119:96 but thy c' is exceeding broad. 4687
147:15 sendeth forth his c' upon earth: 565
Pr 6:20 keep thy father's c', and forsake 4687
23 c' is a lamp; and the law is light; "
8:29 the waters should not pass his c': 6310
13:13 feareth the c' shall be rewarded. 4687
19:16 keepeth the c' keepeth his own "
Ec 8: 2 counsel thee to keep the king's c',*6310
5 keepeth the c' shall feel no evil 4687
Isa 23:11 the Lord hath given a c' against 6680
36:21 not a word: for the king's c' was, 4687
Jer 35:14 none, but obey their father's c': "
16 performed the c' of their father, "
18 the c' of Jonadab your father, "
La 1:18 for I have rebelled against his c': 6310
Da 3:22 because the king's c' was urgent, 4406
9:23 the c' came forth, and I am come 1697
25 the going forth of the c' to restore "
Ho 5:11 he willingly walked after the c'. *6673
Na 1:14 Lord hath given a c' concerning 6680
Mal 2: 1 O ye priests, this c' is for you. 4687
4 that I have sent this c' unto you, "
M't 8:18 he gave c' to depart unto the *2753*
15: 3 Why do ye also transgress the c' *1785*
6 made the c' of God of none effect * "
22:36 which is the great c' in the law? "
38 This is the first and great c'. "
M'r 7: 8 laying aside the c' of God, ye hold "
9 Full well ye reject the c' of God, "
12:28 Which is the first c' of all? "
30 strength: this is the first c'. * "
31 there is none other c' greater than "
Lu 15:29 transgressed I at any time thy c':* "
23:56 the sabbath day according to the c'. "
Joh 10:18 This c' have I received of my "
11:57 the Pharisees had given a c', "
12:49 he gave me a c', what I should "
50 And I know that his c' is life "
13:34 A new c' I give unto you, That ye "
14:31 as the Father gave me c', even so *1781*
15:12 This is my c', That ye love *1785*
Ac 15:24 to whom we gave no such c': *1291*
17:15 and receiving a c' unto Silas and *1785*
23:30 gave c' to his accusers also to say **3853*
25:23 at Festus' c' Paul was brought **2753*
Ro 7: 8 taking occasion by the c', wrought *1785*
9 but when the c' came, sin revived "
10 And the c', which was ordained "
11 taking occasion by the c', deceived "
12 the c' holy, and just, and good. "
13 that sin by the c' might appear "
13: 9 and if there be any other c', "
16:26 the c' of the everlasting God, *2003*
1Co 7: 6 this by permission, and not of c'. "
25 I have no c' of the Lord: yet I give "
2Co 8: 8 I speak not by c', but by occasion "
Eph 6: 2 which is the first c' with promise; *1785*
1Ti 1: 1 by the c' of God our Saviour, *2003*
5 Now the end of the c' is charity **3852*
6:14 That thou keep this c' without *1785*
Tit 1: 3 according to the c' of God our *2003*
Heb 7: 5 priesthood, have a c' to take tithes *1785*
16 not after the law of a carnal c', "
18 disannulling of the c' going before "
11:22 and gave c' concerning his bones. *1781*
23 were not afraid of the king's c'. *1297*
2Pe 2:21 to turn from the holy c' delivered *1785*
3: 2 and of the c' of us the apostles of "
1Jo 2: 7 I write no new c' unto you, "
7 but an old c' which ye had from the "
7 The old c' is the word which ye "
8 Again, a new c' I write unto you, "
3:23 And this is his c', That we should "
23 love one another, as he gave us c'. "
4:21 And this c' have we from him, That "
2Jo 4 have received a c' from the Father. "
5 though I wrote a new c' unto thee, "
6 This is the c', That, as ye have "

commandments
Ge 26: 5 my c', my statutes, and my laws. 4687
Ex 15:26 and wilt give ear to his c', and keep "
16:28 refuse ye to keep my c' and my "
20: 6 them that love me, and keep my c'. "
24:12 a law, and c' which I have written;* "
34:28 words of the covenant, the ten c'. 1697
Le 4: 2 against any of the c' of the Lord *4687
13 any the c' of the Lord concerning* "
22 ignorance against any of the c' * "
27 against any of the c' of the Lord * "
5:17 to be done by the c' of the Lord; * "
22:31 Therefore shall ye keep my c', "
26: 3 and keep my c', and do them; "
14 and will not do all these c'; "
15 that ye will not do all my c', but "
27:34 These are the c', which the Lord "
Nu 15:22 all these c', which the Lord hath 4687
39 remember all the c' of the Lord, "
40 do all my c', and be holy unto your "
36:13 These are the c' and the judgments, "
De 4: 2 ye may keep the c' of the Lord "
13 to perform, even ten c'; and he 1697
40 his statutes, and his c', which I 4687
5:10 them that love me and keep my c'. "
29 keep all my c' always, that it might "
31 all the c', and the statutes, and * "
6: 1 Now these are the c', the statutes,* "
2 his statutes and his c', which I "
17 keep the c' of the Lord your God, "
25 to do all these c' before the Lord * "
7: 9 and keep his c' to a thousand "
11 keep the c', and the statutes, and* "
8: 1 All the c' which I command thee * "
2 whether thou wouldest keep his c', "
6 the c' of the Lord thy God, to walk "
11 keeping his c', and his judgments, "
10: 4 the ten c', which the Lord spake 1697
13 To keep the c' of the Lord, and 4687
11: 1 his judgments, and his c', alway. "
8 keep all the c' which I command * "
13 my c' which I command you this "
22 shall diligently keep all these c' * "
27 A blessing, if ye obey the c' of the "
28 if ye will not obey the c' of the Lord "
13: 4 keep his c', and obey his voice, and "
18 Lord thy God, to keep all his c' "
15: 5 observe to do all these c' which I * "
19: 9 shalt keep all these c' to do them, * "
26:13 to all thy c' which thou hast * "
13 I have not transgressed thy c', "
17 and his c', and his judgments, and "
18 thou shouldest keep all his c'; "
27: 1 Keep all the c' which I command * "
10 and do his c', and his statutes, "
28: 1 to do all his c' which I command "
9 keep the c' of the Lord thy God, "
13 if that thou hearken unto the c' of "
15 to observe to do all his c' and his "
45 thy God, to keep his c' and his "
30: 8 do all his c' which I command thee "
10 thy God, to keep his c' and his "
16 walk in his ways, and to keep his c' "
31: 5 unto all the c' which I have * "
Jos 22: 5 and to keep his c', and to cleave "
J'g 2:17 walked in, obeying the c' of the "
3: 4 they would hearken unto the c' of "
1Sa 15:11 and hath not performed my c'. 1697
1Ki 2: 3 his statutes, and his c', and his 4687
3:14 to keep my statutes and my c', as "
6:12 and keep all my c' to walk in them; "
8:58 to keep his c', and his statutes, "
61 and to keep his c', as at this day. "
9: 6 keep my c' and my statutes which "
11:34 he kept my c' and my statutes: "
38 my statutes and my c', as David my "
14: 8 David, who kept my c', and who "
18:18 ye have forsaken the c' of the Lord, "
2Ki 17:13 your evil ways, and keep my c' and "
16 they left all the c' of the Lord "
19 Judah kept not the c' of the Lord "
18: 6 but kept his c', which the Lord "
23: 3 to keep his c' and his testimonies "
1Ch 28: 7 if he be constant to do my c' "
8 seek for all the c' of the Lord "
29:19 son a perfect heart, to keep thy c', "
2Ch 7:19 my statutes and my c', which I "
17: 4 and walked in his c', and not after "
24:20 Why transgress ye the c' of the "
31:21 and in the c', to seek his God, he "
34:31 after the Lord, and to keep his c', "
Ezr 7:11 of the words of the c' of the Lord, "
9:10 for we have forsaken thy c', "
14 break thy c', and join in affinity "
Ne 1: 5 that love him, and observe his c': "
7 and have not kept the c', nor the "
9 and keep my c', and do them; "
9:13 and true laws, good statutes and c': "
16 necks, and hearkened not to thy c', "
29 and hearkened not unto thy c', but "
34 nor hearkened unto thy c' and "
10:29 do all the c' of the Lord our God, "
Ps 78: 7 works of God, but keep his c': "
89:31 my statutes, and keep not my c'; "
103:18 those that remember his c' to do *6490
20 do his c', hearkening unto the *1697
111: 7 judgment; all his c' are sure. *6490
10 have all they that do his c': †
112: 1 that delighteth greatly in his c'. 4687
119: 6 when I have respect unto all thy c'. "
10 O let me not wander from thy c'. "
19 hide not thy c' from me. "
21 cursed, which do err from thy c'. "
32 I will run the way of thy c', when "
35 Make me to go in the path of thy c'; "
47 I will delight myself in thy c', "
48 hands also will I lift up unto thy c', "
60 and delayed not to keep thy c'. "
66 for I have believed thy c'. "
73 that I may learn thy c'. "
86 All thy c' are faithful: they "
98 Thou through thy c' hast made me "
115 For I will keep the c' of my God. "
127 I love thy c' above gold; yea, "
131 and panted: for I longed for thy c'. "
143 yet thy c' are my delights. "
151 O Lord; and all thy c' are truth. "
166 for thy salvation, and done thy c'. "
172 for all thy c' are righteousness. "
176 servant; for I do not forget thy c'. "
Pr 2: 1 words, and hide my c' with thee; "
3: 1 but let thine heart keep my c': "
4: 4 my words: keep my c', and live. "
7: 1 and lay up my c' with thee. 4687
2 Keep my c', and live; and my law "
10: 8 The wise in heart will receive c': "
Ec 12:13 Fear God, and keep his c': for this "
Isa 48:18 thou hadst hearkened to my c'! "
Da 9: 4 and to them that keep his c'; "
Am 2: 4 and have not kept his c', and *2706
M't 5:19 shall break one of these least c', *1785*
15: 9 teaching for doctrines the c' of **1778*
19:17 wilt enter into life, keep the c'. *1785*
22:40 On these two c' hang all the law "
M'r 7: 7 teaching for doctrines the c' of **1778*
10:19 Thou knowest the c', Do not kill, *1785*
12:29 of all the c' is, Hear, O Israel; "
Lu 1: 6 in all the c' and ordinances of the "
18:20 Thou knowest the c', Do not commit "
Joh 14:15 If ye love me, keep my c'. "
21 He that hath my c', and keepeth "
15:10 If ye keep my c', ye shall abide in "
10 kept my Father's c', and abide in "
Ac 1: 2 had given c' unto the apostles **1781*
1Co 7:19 but the keeping of the c' of God. *1785*
14:37 I write unto you are the c' of the "
Eph 2:15 law of c' contained in ordinances; "
Col 2:22 after the c' and doctrines of men?**1778*
4:10 touching whom ye received c': *1785*
1Th 4: 2 ye know what c' we gave you **3852*
Tit 1:14 Jewish fables, and c' of men, *1785*
1Jo 2: 3 that we know him, if we keep his c'. "
4 and keepeth not his c', is a liar, "
3:22 because we keep his c', and do those "
24 he that keepeth his c' dwelleth in "
5: 2 when we love God, and keep his c'. "
3 love of God, that we keep his c': "
3 and his c' are not grievous. "
2Jo 6 this is love, that we walk after his c'. "
Re 12:17 her seed, which keep the c' of God, "
14:12 here are they that keep the c' of God, "
22:14 Blessed are they that do his c', * "

commend See also COMMENDED; COMMENDETH; COMMENDING.
Lu 23:46 into thy hands I c' my spirit: *3908*
Ac 20:32 brethren, I c' you to God, and to "
Ro 3: 5 But if our unrighteousness c' the *4921*
16: 1 I c' unto you Phebe our sister, "
2Co 3: 1 Do we begin again to c' ourselves? "
5:12 c' not ourselves again unto you, * "
10:12 with some that c' themselves: "

commendation
2Co 3: 1 some others, epistles of c' to you, *4956*
1 or letters of c' from you? * "

commended
Ge 12:15 her, and c' her before Pharaoh: *1984
Pr 12: 8 be c' according to his wisdom: "
Ec 8:15 Then I c' mirth, because a man 7623
Lu 16: 8 the lord c' the unjust steward, *1867*
Ac 14:23 they c' them to the Lord, on whom *3908*
2Co 12:11 I ought to have been c' of you: *4921*

commendeth
Ro 5: 8 But God c' his love toward us, *4921*
1Co 8: 8 But meat c' us not to God: **3936*
2Co 10:18 not he that c' himself is approved, *4921*
18 but whom the Lord c'. "

commending
2Co 4: 2 truth c' ourselves to every man's *4921*

commission See also COMMISSIONS.
Ac 26:12 with authority and c' from the *2011*

commissions
Ezr 8:36 And they delivered the king's c' 1881

commit See also COMMITTED; COMMITTEST; COMMITTETH; COMMITTING.
Ex 20:14 Thou shalt not c' adultery. 5003
Le 5:15 If a soul c' a trespass, and sin *4600
17 and c' any of these things which *6213
6: 2 If a soul sin, and c' a trespass 4600
18:26 and shall not c' any of these *6213
29 whosoever shall c' any of these * "
29 the souls that c' them shall be * "
30 that ye c' not any one of these * "
20: 5 to c' whoredom with Molech, ‡2181
Nu 5: 6 When a man or woman shall c' 6213
6 any sin that men c', to do a "
12 and c' a trespass against him, 4600
25: 1 the people began to c' whoredom 2181
31:16 to c' trespass against the Lord 4560
De 5:18 Neither shalt thou c' adultery. 5003
19:20 c' no more any such evil among 6213
Jos 22:20 the son of Zerah c' a trespass 4600
2Sa 7:14 If he c' iniquity, I will chasten 5753
2Ch 21:11 of Jerusalem to c' fornication, *2181
Job 5: 8 unto God would I c' my cause: 7760
34:10 from the Almighty, that he should c' "
Ps 31: 5 Into thine hand I c' my spirit: *6485
37: 5 C' thy way unto the Lord; trust 1556
Pr 16: 3 C' thy works unto the Lord, "
12 to kings to c' wickedness: for the 6213
Isa 22:21 c' thy government into his hand: 5414
23:17 and shall c' fornication with *2181
Jer 7: 9 ye steal, murder, and c' adultery, 5003
9: 5 weary themselves to c' iniquity. 5753
23:14 they c' adultery, and walk in lies: 5003
37:21 should c' Jeremiah into the court*6485
44: 7 Wherefore c' ye this great evil 6213
Eze 3:20 his righteousness, and c' iniquity, "
8:17 that they c' the abominations "
17 which they c' here? "
16:17 didst c' whoredom with them, *2181
34 followeth thee to c' whoredoms: ‡2181
43 thou shalt not c' this lewdness 6213
20:30 and c' ye whoredom after their *2181
22: 9 midst of thee they c' lewdness. *6213
23:43 Will they now c' whoredoms with ‡2181
33:13 and c' iniquity, all his 6213

Ho 4:10 they shall c' whoredom, and ‡2181
13 daughters shall c' whoredom, ‡ "
13 your spouses shall c' adultery. 5003
14 when they c' whoredom, nor your ‡2181
14 spouses when they c' adultery: 5003
6: 9 consent: for they c' lewdness. *6313
7: 1 they c' falsehood; and the thief 6466
M't 5:27 Thou shalt not c' adultery: 3431
32 causeth her to c' adultery: *3429
19: 9 which is put away doth c' adultery.* "
18 Thou shalt not c' adultery, 3431
M'r 10:19 Do not c' adultery,
Lu 12:48 did c' things worthy of stripes, *4160
16:11 c' to your trust the true riches? 4100
18:20 Do not c' adultery, 3431
Joh 2:24 Jesus did not c' himself unto *4100
Ro 1:32 which c' such things are worthy *4238
2: 2 them which c' such things. * "
22 a man should not c' adultery, 3431
22 dost thou c' adultery?
22 idols, dost thou c' sacrilege? *2416
13: 9 Thou shalt not c' adultery, 3431
1Co 10: 8 Neither let us c' fornication, 4203
1Ti 1:18 This charge I c' unto thee, 3908
2Ti 2: 2 the same c' thou to faithful men,
Jas 2: 9 ye c' sin, and are convinced of the 2038
11 that said, Do not c' adultery, 3431
11 Now if thou c' no adultery,
1Pe 4:19 c' the keeping of their souls to 3908
1Jo 3: 9 is born of God doth not c' sin; *4160
Re 2:14 unto idols, and to c' fornication. 4203
20 to c' fornication, and to eat things "
22 them that c' adultery with her 3431

committed
Ge 39: 8 he hath c' all that he hath to my *5414
22 of the prison c' to Joseph's hand "
Le 4:35 for his sin that he hath c', it *2398
5: 7 his trespass, which he hath c', * "
18:30 which were c' before you, *6213
20:13 of them have c' an abomination: "
23 for they c' all these things, and * "
Nu 15:24 be c' by ignorance without the * "
De 17: 5 or that woman, which have c' * "
21:22 man have c' a sin worthy of death, 1961
Jos 7: 1 children of Israel c' a trespass 4600
22:16 that ye have c' against the God "
31 c' this trespass against the Lord: "
J'g 20: 6 c' lewdness and folly in Israel. 6213
1Ki 8:47 we have c' wickedness; *7561
14:22 with their sins which they had c', 2398
27 and c' them unto the hands of the 6485
1Ch 10:13 for his transgression which he c' 4600
2Ch 12:10 shields of brass, and c' them 6485
34:16 All that was c' to thy servants, 5414
Ps 106: 6 we have c' iniquity, we have done 5753
Jer 2:13 For my people have c' two evils; 6213
3: 8 backsliding Israel c' adultery 5003
9 and c' adultery with stones and "
5: 7 then c' adultery, and assembled "
30 horrible thing is c' in the land; *1961
6:15 when they had c' abomination? 6213
8:12 they had c' abomination? nay, "
16:10 that we have c' against the Lord 2398
29:23 they have c' villany in Israel, and *6213
39:14 and c' him unto Gedaliah the son 5414
40: 7 c' unto him men, and women, 6485
41:10 of the guard had c' to Gedaliah "
44: 3 wickedness which they have c' to 6213
9 which they have c' in the land "
22 abominations which ye have c'; "
Eze 6: 9 the evils which they have c' in all "
15: 8 have c' a trespass, saith the Lord 4600
16:26 c' fornication with the Egyptians 2181
50 and c' abomination before me: 6213
51 hath Samaria c' half of thy sins; 2398
52 c' more abominable than they: 8581
18:12 to the idols, hath c' abomination, 6213
21 from all his sins that he hath c', "
22 his trangressions that he hath c', "
27 his wickedness that he hath c', "
28 his transgressions that he hath c', "
20:27 have c' a trespass against me. 4600
43 for all your evils that ye have c'. 6213
22:11 And one hath c' abomination with "
23: 3 they c' whoredoms in Egypt; ‡2181
3 c' whoredoms in their youth: ‡ "
7 she c' her whoredoms with them,‡5414
37 they have c' adultery, and blood 5003
37 their idols have they c' adultery, "
33:13 for his iniquity that he hath c', 6213
16 None of his sins that he hath c' 2398
29 abominations which they have c'. 6213
43: 8 abominations that they have c': "
44:13 abominations which they have c'. "
Da 9: 5 sinned, and have c' iniquity, *5753
Ho 1: 2 land hath c' great whoredom, ‡2181
4:18 have c' whoredom continually: ‡ "
Mal 2:11 an abomination is c' in Israel 6213
M't 5:28 hath c' adultery with her already 3431
M'r 15: 7 c' murder in the insurrection. 4160
Lu 12:48 to whom men have c' much, of *3908
Joh 5:22 c' all judgment unto the Son: *1325
Ac 8: 3 men and women c' them to prison. 3860
25:11 or have c' any thing worthy of 4238
26 he had c' nothing worthy of death, "
27:40 they c' themselves unto the sea, *1439
28:17 c' nothing against the people, *4160
Ro 3: 2 them were c' the oracles of God. *4100
1Co 9:17 a dispensation of the gospel is c' * "
10: 8 fornication, as some of them c', 4203
2Co 5:19 and hath c' unto us the word of 5087
11: 7 I c' an offence in abasing myself *4160
12:21 lasciviousness which they have c'. 4238
Ga 2: 7 uncircumcision was c' unto me, *4100
1Ti 1:11 which was c' to my trust.
6:20 keep that which is c' to thy trust, 3872
2Ti 1:12 able to keep that which I have c' 3866
14 That good thing which was c' unto 3872
Tit 1: 3 preaching, which is c' unto me *4100
Jas 5:15 if he have c' sins, they shall be 4160
1Pe 2:23 but c' himself to him that judgeth 3860
Jude 15 deeds which they have ungodly c',* 764
Re 17: 2 of the earth have c' fornication, 4203
18: 3 have c' fornication with her, and "
9 who have c' fornication and lived "

committest
Ho 5: 3 O Ephraim, thou c' whoredom, ‡2181

committeth
Le 20:10 man that c' adultery with another 5003
10 c' adultery with his neighbour's "
Ps 10:14 the poor c' himself unto thee; 5800
Pr 6:32 whoso c' adultery with a woman 5003
Eze 8: 6 that the house of Israel c' here, 6213
16:32 But as a wife that c' adultery, 5003
18:24 c' iniquity, and doeth according 6213
26 and c' iniquity, and dieth in them; "
33:18 and c' iniquity, he shall even die "
M't 5:32 her that is divorced c' adultery. 3429
19: 9 marry another, c' adultery: and "
M'r 10:11 another, c' adultery against her. "
12 married to another, she c' adultery. "
Lu 16:18 marrieth another c' adultery: 3431
18 away from her husband c' adultery. "
Joh 8:34 c' sin is the servant of sin. 4160
1Co 6:18 but he that c' fornication sinneth 4203
1Jo 3: 4 Whosoever c' sin transgresseth *4160
8 He that c' sin is of the devil; for * "

committing
Eze 33:15 without c' iniquity; he shall 6213
Ho 4: 2 stealing, and c' adultery, they 5003

commodious
Ac 27:12 the haven was not c' to winter in, 428

common See also COMMONWEALTH.
Le 4:27 c' people sin through ignorance, 776
Nu 16:29 If these men die the c' death of
1Sa 21: 4 is no c' bread under mine hand, 2455
5 and the bread is in a manner c', "
Ec 6: 1 and it is c' among men: *7227
Jer 26:23 into the graves of the c' people. 1121
31: 5 and shall eat them as c' things. *2490
Eze 23:42 men of the c' sort were brought 7230
M't 27:27 took Jesus into the c' hall, and †‡4232
M'r 12:37 the c' people heard him gladly. 4183
Ac 2:44 and had all things c'; 2839
4:32 but they had all things c'. "
5:18 put them in the c' prison. *1219
10:14 any thing that is c' or unclean. 2839
15 cleansed, that call not thou c'. 2840
28 not call any man c' or unclean. 2839
11: 8 for nothing c' or unclean hath at "
9 cleansed, that call not thou c'. "
1Co 10:13 you but such as is c' to man: * 442
Tit 1: 4 mine own son after the c' faith: 2839
Jude 3 write unto you of the c' salvation, "

common hall See COMMON and HALL.

commonly
M't 28:15 is c' reported among the Jews *1310
1Co 5: 1 It is reported c' that there is *3654

common people See COMMON, and PEOPLE.

commonwealth
Eph 2:12 being aliens from the c' of Israel, 4174

commotion See also COMMOTIONS.
Jer 10:22 great c' out of the north country, 7494

commotions
Lu 21: 9 ye shall hear of wars and c', * 181

commune See also COMMUNED; COMMUNING.
Ge 34: 6 out unto Jacob to c' with him. 1696
Ex 25:22 and I will c' with thee from above "
1Sa 18:22 C' with David secretly, and say, "
19: 3 I will c' with my father of thee; "
Job 4: 2 we assay to c' with thee, wilt thou 1697
Ps 4: 4 c' with your own heart upon your 559
64: 5 they c' of laying snares privily; 5608
77: 6 I c' with mine own heart: and my 7878

communed
Ge 23: 8 And he c' with them, saying, If it 1696
34: 8 And Hamor c' with them, saying, "
20 and c' with the men of their city, "
42:24 and c' with them, and took from * "
43:19 and they c' with him at the door * "
J'g 9: 1 and c' with them, and with all "
1Sa 9:25 Samuel c' with Saul upon the top "
25:39 David sent and c' with Abigail, * "
1Ki 10: 2 she was come to Solomon, she c' "
2Ki 22:14 and they c' with her. "
2Ch 9: 1 she was come to Solomon, she c' "
Ec 1:16 I c' with mine own heart, saying, "
Da 1:19 And the king c' with them; and "
Zec 1:14 that c' with me said unto me, * "
Lu 6:11 c' one with another what they 1255
22: 4 and c' with the chief priests and 4814
24:15 they c' together and reasoned, 3656
Ac 24:26 him the oftener, and c' with him. "

communicate See also COMMUNICATED.
Ga 6: 6 c' unto him that teacheth in all 2841
Ph'p 4:14 that ye did c' with my affliction. *4790
1Ti 6:18 ready to distribute, willing to c'; 2843
Heb 13:16 to do good and to c' forget not: 2842

communicated
Ga 2: 2 c' unto them that gospel which I * 394
Ph'p 4:15 church c' with me as concerning *2841

communication See also COMMUNICATIONS.
2Sa 3:17 And Abner had c' with the elders 1697
2Ki 9:11 Ye know the man, and his c'. *7879
M't 5:37 your c' be, Yea, yea; Nay, nay: *3056
Eph 4:29 Let no corrupt c' proceed out of * "
Col 3: 8 filthy c' out of your mouth. * 148
Ph'm 6 The c' of thy faith may become *2842

communications
Lu 24:17 What manner of c' are these that 3056
1Co 15:33 evil c' corrupt good manners. †‡3657

communion
1Co 10:16 not the c' of the blood of Christ? 2842
16 it not the c' of the body of Christ? "
2Co 6:14 what c' hath light with darkness? "
13:14 the c' of the Holy Ghost, be with "

communing
Ge 18:33 as he had left c' with Abraham: 1696
Ex 31:18 he had made an end of c' with him "

compact See also COMPACTED.
Ps 122: 3 as a city that is c' together: 2266

compacted
Eph 4:16 and c' by that which every joint *4822

companied See also ACCOMPANIED.
Ac 1:21 these men which have c' with us 4905

companies
J'g 7:16 three hundred men into three c', 7218
20 the three c' blew the trumpets, "
9:34 wait against Shechem in four c'. "
43 divided them into three c', and "
44 other c' ran upon all the people "
1Sa 11:11 Saul put the people in three c'; "
13:17 camp of the Philistines in three c': "
2Ki 5: 2 the Syrians had gone out by c', *1416
1Ch 9:18 they were porters in the c' of the *4264
28: 1 c' that ministered to the king by 4256
Ne 12:31 two great c' of them that gave thanks,
40 So stood the two c' of them that gave
Job 6:19 the c' of Sheba waited for them. 1979
Isa 21:13 O ye travelling c' of Dedanim. ‡ 736
57:13 criest, let thy c' deliver thee; *
Eze 26: 7 with horsemen, and c', and much 6951
M'r 6:39 sat down by c' upon the green 4849

companion See COMPANIONS.
Ex 32:27 brother, and every man his c', 7453
J'g 14:20 Samson's wife was given to his c', 4828
15: 2 I gave her to thy c': is not her "
6 his wife, and given her to his c'. "
1Ch 27:33 the Archite was the king's c': *7453
Job 30:29 brother to dragons, and a c' to owls."
Ps 119:63 am a c' of all them that fear thee, 2270
Pr 13:20 but a c' of fools shall be destroyed? 7462
28: 7 but he that is a c' of riotous men "
24 the same is the c' of a destroyer. 2270
Mal 2:14 yet is she thy c', and the wife of 2278
Ph'p 2:25 my brother, and c' in labour, *4904
Re 1: 9 and c' in tribulation, and in the *4791

companions See also COMPANIONS'.
J'g 11:38 she went with her c', and bewailed 7464
14:11 they brought thirty c' to be with 4828
Ezr 4: 7 Tabeel, and the rest of their c', 3675
9 the rest of their c'; the Dinaites, "
17 the rest of their c' that dwell in "
23 Shimshai the scribe, and their c', "
5: 3 Shethar-boznai, and their c', and "
6 Shethar-boznai, and his c' the "
6: 6 Shethar-boznai, and your c' the "
13 Shethar-boznai, and their c', "
Job 35: 4 will answer thee, and thy c' with 7453
41: 6 Shall the c' make a banquet of *2271
Ps 45:14 the virgins her c' that follow her 7464
Ca 1: 7 aside by the flocks of thy c'? 2270
8:13 the c' hearken to thy voice: "
Isa 1:23 are rebellious, and c' of thieves: "
Eze 37:16 and for the children of Israel his c': "
16 for all the house of Israel his c': "
Da 2:17 Mishael, and Azariah, his c': 2269
Ac 19:29 of Macedonia, Paul's c' in travel, 4898
Heb 10:33 ye became c' of them that were so *2844

companions'
Ps 122: 8 For my brethren and c' sakes, 7453

company See also ACCOMPANY; COMPANIED; COMPANIES.
Ge 32: 8 If Esau come to the one c', 4264
8 then the other c' which is left "
21 himself lodged that night in the c'. "
35:11 a c' of nations shall be of thee, 6951
37:25 a c' of Ishmeelites came from 736
50: 9 and it was a very great c'. 4264
Nu 14: 7 they spake unto all the c' of the *5712
16: 5 unto all his c', saying, Even "
6 you censers, Korah, and all his c'; "
11 thou and all thy c' are gathered "
16 and all thy c' before the Lord, * "
40 he be not as Korah, and as his c'. "
22: 4 Now shall this c' lick up all that *6951
26: 9 in the c' of Korah, when they 5712
10 when that c' died, what time the "
27: 3 in the c' of them that gathered "
3 against the Lord in the c' of Korah; "
J'g 9:37 and another c' come along by the 7218
44 Abimelech, and the c' that was * "
18:23 that thou comest with such a c'? 2199
1Sa 10: 5 thou shalt meet a c' of prophets *2256
10 behold, a c' of prophets met him; * "
13:17 one c' turned unto the way that 7218
18 And another c' turned the way to "
18 Beth-horon: and another c' turned "
19:20 they saw the c' of the prophets 3862
30:15 thou bring me down to this c'? *1416
15 I will bring thee down to this c'. "
23 the c' that came against us into * "
2Ki 5:15 he and all his c', and came, 4264
9:17 he spied the c' of Jehu as he came, 8229
17 and said, I see a c'. And Joram "
2Ch 9: 1 with a very great c', and camels *2428
20:12 have no might against this great c' 1995
24:24 Syrians came with a small c' of

Ne 12:38 And the other c' of them that
Job 16: 7 thou hast made desolate all my c'. 5712
34: 8 Which goeth in c' with the 2274
Ps 55:14 unto the house of God in c'. *7285
68:11 great was the c' of those that *6635
30 Rebuke the c' of spearmen, the *2416
106:17 and covered the c' of Abiram. 5712
18 And a fire was kindled in their c'; "
Pr 29: 3 he that keepeth c' with harlots 7462
Ca 1: 9 c' of horses in Pharaoh's chariots.*
6:13 As it were the c' of two armies. *4246
Jer 31: 8 a great c' shall return thither. 6951
Eze 16:40 They shall also bring up a c' * "
17:17 with his mighty army and great c' "
23:46 I will bring up a c' upon them, * "
47 And the c' shall stone them with * "
27: 6 the c' of the Ashurites have made *1323
27 in all thy c' which is in the midst 6951
34 all thy c' in the midst of thee shall "
32: 3 my net over thee with a c' of many "
22 Asshur is there and all her c': his "
23 and her c' is round about her "
38: 4 great c' with bucklers and shields, "
7 all thy c' that are assembled unto* "
13 hast thou gathered thy c' to take a "
15 horses, a great c', and a mighty "
Ho 6: 9 c' of priests murder in the way 2267
Lu 2:44 him to have been in the c', went *4923*
5:29 c' of publicans and of others that *3793*
6:17 and the c' of his disciples, and a * "
22 shall separate you from their c', "
9:14 them sit down by fifties in a c'. *2828*
38 a man of the c' cried out, saying, *3793*
11:27 certain woman of the c' lifted up * "
12:13 And one of the c' said unto him, * "
23:27 great c' of people, and of women, *4128*
24:22 certain women also of our c' made us
Joh 6: 5 saw a great c' come unto him, *3793*
Ac 4:23 go, they went to their own c', *2398*
6: 7 and a great c' of the priests were *3793*
10:28 is a Jew to keep c', or come unto *2853*
13:13 when Paul and his c' loosed *3588, 4012*
15:22 chosen men of their own c'
17: 5 gathered a c', and set all the city *3792*
21: 8 day we that were of Paul's c' *4012*
Ro 15:24 somewhat filled with your c'.
1Co 5: 9 epistle not to c' with fornicators: *4874*
11 written unto you not to keep c', "
2Th 3:14 that man, and have no c' with him. "
Heb 12:22 to an innumerable c' of angels, *3461*
Re 18:17 all the c' in ships, and sailors, *3658*

comparable
La 4: 2 The precious sons of Zion, c' to 5537

compare See also COMPARABLE; COMPARED; COMPARING.
Isa 40:18 what likeness will ye c' unto him? 6186
46: 5 and c' me, that we may be like? 4911
M'r 4:30 what comparison shall we c' it? *3846*
2Co 10:12 or c' ourselves with some that *4793*

compared
Ps 89: 6 who in the heaven can be c' unto 6186
Pr 3:15 thou canst desire are not to be c' 7737
8:11 may be desired are not to be c' to "
Ca 1: 9 I have c' thee, O my love, to a 1819
Ro 8:18 not worthy to be c' with the glory

comparing
1Co 2:13 c' spiritual things with spiritual. ‡*4793*
2Co 10:12 c' themselves among themselves, "

comparison
J'g 8: 2 have I done now in c' of you?
3 what was I able to do in c' of you?
Hag 2: 3 is it not in your eyes in c' of it as *3644
M'r 4:30 or with what c' shall we compare *3850*

compass See also COMPASSED; COMPASSEST; COMPASSETH; COMPASSING.
Ex 27: 5 put it under the c' of the altar *3749
38: 4 under the c' thereof beneath unto * "
Nu 21: 4 way of the Red sea, to c' the land 5437
34: 5 And the border shall fetch a c' * "
Jos 6: 3 And ye shall c' the city, all ye men "
4 ye shall c' the city seven times, "
7 Pass on, and c' the city, and let him "
15: 3 and fetched a c' to Karkaa: * "
2Sa 5:23 fetch a c' behind them, and come * "
1Ki 7:15 line of twelve cubits did c' either * "
23 of thirty cubits did c' it round * "
35 was there a round c' of half a cubit 5439
2Ki 3: 9 they fetched a c' of seven days' *5437
11: 8 And ye shall c' the king round 5362
2Ch 4: 2 from brim to brim, round in c', *5439
2 a line of thirty cubits did c' it 5437
3 oven, which did c' it round about: "
23: 7 And the Levites shall c' the king 5362
Job 16:13 His archers c' me round about, 5437
40:22 willows of the brook c' him about. "
Ps 5:12 with favour wilt thou c' him as 5849
7: 7 congregation of the people c' thee 5437
17: 9 from my deadly enemies, who c' 5362
26: 6 so will I c' thine altar, O Lord: 5437
32: 7 thou shalt c' me about with songs "
10 Lord, mercy shall c' him about. "
49: 5 the iniquity of my heels shall c' me "
140: 9 for the head of those that c' me 4524
142: 7 the righteous shall c' me about; 3803
Pr 8:27 he set a c' upon the face of the *2329
Isa 44:13 and he marketh it out with the c', *4230
50:11 c' yourselves about with sparks: * 247
Jer 31:22 earth, A woman shall c' a man. *5437
39 hill Gareb, and shall c' about to * "
52:21 a fillet of twelve cubits did c' it; "
Hab 1: 4 for the wicked doth c' about the 3803
M't 23:15 for ye c' sea and land to make one *4013*
Lu 19:43 a trench about thee, and c' thee *4033*
Ac 28:13 thence we fetched a c', and came **4022*

compassed
Ge 19: 4 c' the house round, both old and 5437
De 2: 1 and we c' mount Seir many days. "
3 Ye have c' this mountain long "
Jos 6:11 So the ark of the Lord c' the city, * "
14 the second day they c' the city once, "
15 c' the city after the same manner "
15 on that day they c' the city seven * "
15:10 And the border c' from Baalah "
18:14 and c' the corner of the sea * "
J'g 11:18 and c' the land of Edom, and the "
16: 2 And they c' him in, and laid wait "
1Sa 23:26 Saul and his men c' David and his 5849
2Sa 18:15 c' about and smote Absalom, 5437
22: 5 waves of death c' me, the floods 661
6 The sorrows of hell c' me about; *5437
2Ki 6:14 they came by night, and c' the city 5362
15 host c' the city both with horses *5437
8:21 smote the Edomites which c' him "
2Ch 18:31 Therefore they c' about him to * "
21: 9 smote the Edomites which c' him "
33:14 and c' about Ophel, and raised it "
Job 19: 6 and hath c' me with his net. 5362
26:10 hath c' the waters with bounds, *2328
Ps 17:11 They have now c' us in our steps: 5437
18: 4 The sorrows of death c' me, and 661
5 The sorrows of hell c' me about: *5437
22:12 Many bulls have c' me: strong "
16 For dogs have c' me: the assembly "
40:12 innumerable evils have c' me 661
88:17 water; they c' me about together. 5362
109: 3 They c' me about also with words 5437
116: 3 The sorrows of death c' me, and 661
118:10 All nations c' me about: but in 5437
11 c' me about; yea, they c' me about: "
12 They c' me about like bees; they "
La 3: 5 me, and c' me with gall and travel. 5362
Jon 2: 3 the floods c' me about: all thy *5437
5 The waters c' me about, even to 661
Lu 21:20 shall see Jerusalem c' with armies, *2944*
Heb 5: 2 himself also is c' with infirmity. *4029*
11:30 they were c' about seven days. *2944*
12: 1 are c' about with so great a cloud *4029*
Re 20: 9 and c' the camp of the saints about, *2944*

compassest
Ps 139: 3 Thou c' my path and my lying *2219

compasseth
Ge 2:11 c' the whole land of Havilah, 5437
13 that c' the whole land of Ethiopia. "
Jos 19:14 the border c' it on the north side * "
Ps 73: 6 pride c' them about as a chain; *6059
Ho 11:12 Ephraim c' me about with lies, 5437

compassing
1Ki 7:24 were knops c' it, ten in a cubit, *5437
24 c' the sea round about: the knops 5362
2Ch 4: 3 c' the sea round about. Two rows "

compassion See also COMPASSIONS.
Ex 2: 6 And she had c' on him, and said, 2550
De 13:17 thee mercy, and have c' upon thee, 7355
30: 3 captivity, and have c' upon thee, "
1Sa 23:21 of the Lord: for ye have c' on me. 2550
1Ki 8:50 c' before them who carried them 7356
50 that they may have c' on them: 7355
2Ki 13:23 had c' on them, and had respect "
2Ch 30: 9 children shall find c' before them 7356
36:15 because he had c' on his people, 2550
17 had no c' on young man or maiden, "
Ps 78:38 he, being full of c', forgave their ‡7349
86:15 a God full of c', and gracious, ‡ "
111: 4 Lord is gracious and full of c'. ‡ "
112: 4 and full of c', and righteous, ‡ "
145: 8 Lord is gracious, and full of c'; ‡ "
Isa 49:15 she should not have c' on the son 7355
Jer 12:15 I will return, and have c' on them, "
La 3:32 will he have c' according to the "
Eze 16: 5 to have c' upon thee; but thou 2550
Mic 7:19 he will have c' upon us; he will 7355
M't 9:36 he was moved with c' on them, *4697*
14:14 was moved with c' toward them, "
15:32 I have c' on the multitude, because "
18:27 was moved with c', and loosed him, "
33 have had c' on thy fellow servant, **1653*
20:34 Jesus had c' on them, and touched *4697*
M'r 1:41 Jesus, moved with c', put forth "
5:19 for thee, and hath had c' on thee. **1653*
6:34 was moved with c' toward them, *4697*
8: 2 I have c' on the multitude, because "
9:22 have c' on us, and help us. "
Lu 7:13 he had c' on her, and said unto her, "
10:33 when he saw him, he had c' on him, "
15:20 his father saw him, and had c', "
Ro 9:15 will have c' on whom I will have c'. *3627*
Heb 5: 2 Who can have c' on the ignorant, **3356*
10:34 For ye had c' of me in my bonds, *4834*
1Pe 3: 8 having c' one of another, love **4835*
1Jo 3:17 shutteth up his bowels of c' from him,
Jude 22 have c', making a difference: **1653*

compassions
La 3:22 consumed, because his c' fail not. 7355
Zec 7: 9 shew mercy and c' every man to *7356

compel See also COMPELLED.
Le 25:39 thou shalt not c' him to serve as *5647
Es 1: 8 none did c': for so the king had 597
M't 5:41 shall c' thee to go a mile, go with *29*
M'r 15:21 they c' one Simon a Cyrenian, who "
Lu 14:23 c' them to come in, that my house **315*

compelled
1Sa 28:23 together with the woman, c' him; *6555
2Ch 21:11 fornication, and c' Judah thereto. *5080
M't 27:32 him they c' to bear his cross. * *29*
Ac 26:11 and c' them to blaspheme; and * *315*
2Co 12:11 a fool in glorying; ye have c' me: "
Ga 2: 3 a Greek, was c' to be circumcised: "

compellest
Ga 2:14 why c' thou the Gentiles to live *315*

complain See also COMPLAINED; COMPLAINING.
J'g 21:22 come unto us to c', that we will say 7378
Job 7:11 c' in the bitterness of my soul. 7878
31:38 the furrows likewise thereof c'; *1058
La 3:39 Wherefore doth a living man c', 596

complained
Nu 11: 1 when the people c', it displeased* 596
Ps 77: 3 I c', and my spirit was *7878

complainers
Jude 16 are murmurers, c', walking after *3202*

complaining
Ps 144:14 that there be no c' in our streets. *6682

complaint See also COMPLAINTS.
1Sa 1:16 abundance of my c' and grief have 7879
Job 7:13 my couch shall ease my c'; "
9:27 I will forget my c', I will leave off "
10: 1 I will leave my c' upon myself; "
21: 4 is my c' to man? And if it were so, "
23: 2 to day is my c' bitter: my stroke is "
Ps 55: 2 I mourn in my c', and make a "
102 *title* poureth out his c' before the Lord. "
142: 2 I poured out my c' before him; "

complaints
Ac 25: 7 and grievous c' against Paul, * *157*

complete
Le 23:15 seven sabbaths shall be c': 8549
Col 2:10 are c' in him, which is the head **4137*
4:12 perfect and c' in all the will of God.* "

composition
Ex 30:32 any other like it, after the c' of it: 4971
37 according to the c' thereof: it shall "

compound See also COMPOUNDETH.
Ex 30:25 an ointment c' after the art of the *4842

compoundeth
Ex 30:33 Whosoever c' any like it, or 7543

comprehend See also COMPREHENDED.
Job 37: 5 doeth he, which we cannot c'. 3045
Eph 3:18 able to c' with all saints what is **2638*

comprehended
Isa 40:12 and c' the dust of the earth in a 3557
Joh 1: 5 and the darkness c' it not. **2638*
Ro 13: 9 it is briefly c' in this saying, * *346*

Conaniah (*co-na-ni'-ah*) See also CONONIAH.
2Ch 35: 9 C' also, and Shemaiah, and 3562

conceal See also CONCEALED; CONCEALETH.
Ge 37:26 slay our brother, and c' his blood? 3680
De 13: 8 neither shalt thou c' him: "
Job 27:11 is with the Almighty will I not c'. 3582
41:12 I will not c' his parts, nor his *2790
Pr 25: 2 It is the glory of God to c' a thing: 5641
Jer 50: 2 publish and c' not: say, 3582

concealed
Job 6:10 not c' the words of the Holy One. *3582
Ps 40:10 I have not c' thy lovingkindness "

concealeth
Pr 11:13 is of a faithful spirit c' the matter. 3680
12:23 A prudent man c' knowledge: but "

conceit See also CONCEITS.
Pr 18:11 and as an high wall in his own c'. *4906
26: 5 lest he be wise in his own c'. 5869
12 thou a man wise in his own c'? "
16 The sluggard is wiser in his own c' "
28:11 The rich man is wise in his own c'; "

conceits
Ro 11:25 be wise in your own c'; *3844, 1438*
12:16 Be not wise in your own c'. "

conceive See also CONCEIVED; CONCEIVING.
Ge 30:38 should c' when they came to drink. *3179
41 cattle did c', that Jacob laid "
41 that they might c' among the rods. "
Nu 5:28 shall be free, and shall c' seed. 2232
J'g 13: 3 but thou shalt c', and bear a son. 2029
5 lo, thou shalt c', and bear a son; 2030
7 thou shalt c', and bear a son; "
Job 15:35 They c' mischief, and bring forth 2029
Ps 51: 5 and in sin did my mother c' me. 3179
Isa 7:14 a virgin shall c', and bear a son, 2030
33:11 shall c' chaff, ye shall bring forth 2029
59: 4 c' mischief, and bring forth iniquity. "
Lu 1:31 thou shalt c' in thy womb, and *4815*
Heb 11:11 received strength to c' seed, *2602*

conceived
Ge 4: 1 and she c', and bare Cain, and 2029
17 and she c', and bare Enoch: and "
16: 4 went in unto Hagar, and she c': "
4 when she saw that she had c', her "
5 when she saw that she had c', I "
21: 2 Sarah c', and bare Abraham a son "
25:21 and Rebekah his wife c'. "
29:32 And Leah c', and bare a son, "
33, 34 she c' again, and bare a son; "
35 And she c' again, and bare a son: "
30: 5 Bilhah c', and bare Jacob a son. "
7 And Bilhah Rachel's maid c' again, "
17 she c', and bare Jacob the fifth son. "
19 And Leah c' again, and bare Jacob "
23 And she c', and bare a son; "
39 And the flocks c' before the rods. 3179
31:10 pass at the time that the cattle c'. "
38: 3 And she c', and bare a son; 2029
4 and she c' again, and bare a son; "
5 And she yet again c', and bare *3254
18 in unto her, and she c' by him. 2029
Ex 2: 2 the woman c', and bare a son: "
Le 12: 2 If a woman have c' seed, and *2232
Nu 11:12 Have I c' all this people? have I 2029
1Sa 1:20 after Hannah had c', that she bare "

1Sa 2:21 that she c', and bare three sons 2029
2Sa 11: 5 And the woman c', and sent and "
2Ki 4:17 And the woman c', and bare a son "
1Ch 7:23 she c', and bare a son, and he "
Job 3: 3 was said, There is a man child c'. "
Ps 7:14 and hath c' mischief, and brought "
Ca 3: 4 into the chamber of her that c' me. "
Isa 8: 3 and she c', and bare a son. "
Jer 49:30 hath c' a purpose against you. 2803
Ho 1: 3 which c', and bare him a son. 2029
6 she c' again, and bare a daughter. "
8 Loruhamah, she c', and bare a son. "
2: 5 harlot: she that c' them hath done "
M't 1:20 that which is c' in her is of the 1080
Lu 1:24 his wife Elisabeth c', and hid 4815
36 hath also c' a son in her old age: "
2:21 before he was c' in the womb. "
Ac 5: 4 why hast thou c' this thing in 5087
Ro 9:10 when Rebecca also had c' 2845, 2192
Jas 1:15 Then when lust hath c', it bringeth 4815

conceiving
Isa 59:13 c' and uttering from the heart 2029

conception
Ge 3:16 multiply thy sorrow and thy c'; 2032
Ru 4:13 the Lord gave her c', and she bare "
Ho 9:11 from the womb, and from the c'. "

concern See also CONCERNETH; CONCERNING.
Ac 28:31 things which c' the Lord Jesus *4012
2Co 11:30 glory of the things which c' mine "

concerneth
Ps 138: 8 that which c' me: thy mercy, 1157
Eze 12:10 This burden c' the prince in

concerning
Ge 5:29 comfort us c' our work and toil
19:21 accepted thee c' this thing also,
24: 9 and sware to him c' that matter. 5921
26:32 c' the well which they had 5921, 182
42:21 are verily guilty c' our brother, 5921
Ex 6: 8 the land, c' the which I did swear
24: 8 made with you c' all these words. 5921
Le 4: 2 the Lord c' things which ought *
13, 22 c' things which should not be *
26 atonement for him as c' his sin,
27 c' things which ought not to be *
5: 6 atonement for him c' his sin.
18 for him c' his ignorance 5921
6: 3 which was lost, and lieth c' it, *
18 c' the offerings of the Lord *
23: 2 C' the feasts of the Lord, *
27:32 And c' the tithe of the herd, *
Nu 8:20 Lord commanded Moses c' the *
22 commanded Moses c' the Levites, 5921
9: 8 the Lord will command c' you.
10:29 Lord hath spoken good c' Israel. 5921
14:30 the land, c' which I sware to
30: 1 tribes c' the children of Israel, *
12 out of her lips c' her vows,
12 or c' the bond of her soul,
32:28 So c' them Moses commanded
36: 6 c' the daughters of Zelophehad
Jos 14: 6 man of God c' me and thee in 5921, 182
23:14 Lord your God spake c' you; 5921
J'g 15: 3 Samson said c' them, Now shall *
21: 5 a great oath c' him that came not
Ru 4: 7 c' redeeming and c' changing, 5921
1Sa 3:12 which I have spoken c' his house: 413
25:30 good that he hath spoken c' thee, 5921
2Sa 3: 8 to day with a fault c' this woman?
7:25 c' thy servant, and c' his house, 5921
11:18 David all the things c' the war;
13:39 for he was comforted c' Amnon, 5921
14: 8 and I will give charge c' thee.
18: 5 captains charge c' Absalom. 5921, 1697
1Ki 2: 4 his word which he spake c' me, 5921
27 which he spake c' the house of Eli "
5: 8 will do all thy desire c' timber
8 of cedar, and c' timber of fir.
6:12 C' this house which thou art
8:41 Moreover c' a stranger, that is 413
10: 1 c' the name of the Lord, she
11: 2 nations c' which the Lord said
10 had commanded him c' this thing, 5921
22: 8 doth not prophesy good c' me, "
18 would prophesy no good c' me, "
23 Lord hath spoken evil c' thee. "
2Ki 10:10 Lord spake c' the house of Ahab: "
17:15 c' whom the Lord had charged
19:21 that the Lord hath spoken c' him; 5921
32 the Lord c' the king of Assyria, 413
22:13 c' the words of this book that is 5921
13 unto all that which is written c' us. "
1Ch 11:10 to the word of the Lord c' Israel. "
17:23 that thou hast spoken c' thy servant "
23 and c' his house be established for "
19: 2 to comfort him c' his father. "
22:12 and give thee charge c' Israel,
23:14 Now c' Moses the man of God, *
24:21 C' Rehabiah: of the sons of *
29 C' Kish: the son of Kish was *
26: 1 C' the divisions of the porters: *
21 As c' the sons of Laadan; the *
2Ch 6:32 Moreover c' the stranger, which 413
8:15 c' any matter, or c' the treasures.
12:15 of Iddo the seer c' genealogies? *
15:16 c' Maachah the mother of Asa
24:27 Now c' his sons, and the greatness
31: 6 And c' the children of Israel *
9 and the Levites c' the heaps. 5921
34:21 c' the words of the book that
26 God of Israel c' the words which *
Ezr 5: 5 answer by letter c' this matter. 5922
17 pleasure to us c' this matter.
6: 3 a decree c' the house of God
7:14 enquire c' Judah and Jerusalem. 5922
Ezr 10: 2 hope in Israel c' this thing. 5921
Ne 1: 2 and I asked them c' the Jews "
2 of the captivity, and c' Jerusalem. "
9:23 them into the land, c' which thou
11:23 king's commandment c' them, 5921
24 in all matters c' the people.
13:14 Remember me, O my God, c' this, 5921
22 Remember me, O my God, c' this also,
Es 3: 2 king had so commanded c' him.
9:26 of that which they had seen c' this 5921
Job 36:33 noise thereof sheweth c' it, "
33 the cattle also c' the vapour. "
Ps 7 *title* the Lord, c' the words of Cush
17: 4 C' the works of men, by the *
73: 8 speak wickedly c' oppression: *
90:13 let it repent thee c' thy servants. 5921
106:34 not destroy the nations, c' whom *
119:128 I esteem all thy precepts c' all things
152 C' thy testimonies, I have *
135:14 repent himself c' his servants. 5921
Ec 1:13 search out by wisdom c' all things "
3:18 I said in mine heart c' the estate* "
7:10 dost not enquire wisely c' this. "
Isa 1: 1 of Amoz, which he saw c' Judah "
2: 1 Amoz saw c' Judah and Jerusalem. "
8: 1 write in it with a man's pen c' *
16:13 Lord hath spoken c' Moab since 413
23: 5 As at the report c' Egypt, so *
29:22 Abraham, c' the house of Jacob, 413
30: 7 therefore have I cried c' this,
37: 9 he heard say c' Tirhakah king 5921
22 Lord hath spoken c' him; The
33 Lord c' the king of Assyria, He 413
45:11 c' my sons, and c' the work of my 5921
Jer 7:22 c' burnt offerings or 5921, 1697
14: 1 to Jeremiah c' the dearth.
15 saith the Lord c' the prophets 5921
16: 3 c' the sons, and c' the daughters "
3 and c' their mothers that bare "
3 and c' their fathers that begat "
18: 7, 9 c' a nation, and c' a kingdom, "
22:18 thus saith the Lord c' Jehoiakim 413
23:15 the Lord of hosts c' the prophets; 5921
25: 1 came to Jeremiah c' all the people "
27:19 c' [413] the pillars, and c' the sea, "
19 c' the bases, and c' the residue "
21 c' the vessels that remain in the "
29:31 Thus saith the Lord c' Shemaiah 413
30: 4 Lord spake c' Israel and c' Judah. "
32:36 c' the city, whereof ye say, "
33: 4 of Israel, c' the houses of this city, 5921
4 and c' the houses of the kings "
39:11 gave charge c' Jeremiah to "
42:19 The Lord hath said c' you, "
44: 1 c' all the Jews which dwell in 413
49: 1 C' the Ammonites, thus saith *
7 C' Edom, thus saith the Lord *
23 C' Damascus. Hamath is *
28 C' Kedar, and c' the kingdoms *
52:21 And c' the pillars, the height *
La 1:17 Lord hath commanded c' Jacob
Eze 13:16 which prophesy c' Jerusalem, 413
14: 7 to enquire of him c' me; *
22 c' the evil that I have brought 5921
22 c' all that I have brought upon 854
18: 2 proverb c' the land of Israel, 5921
21:28 the Lord God c' the Ammonites, 413
28 and c' their reproach;
36: 6 Prophesy therefore c' the land 5921
44: 5 I say unto thee c' all the ordinances
45:14 C' the ordinance of oil, *
47:14 c' the which I lifted up mine hand
Da 2:18 God of heaven c' this secret; 5922
5:29 made a proclamation c' him,
6: 4 against Daniel c' the kingdom; *6655
5 against him c' the law of his God.
12 the king c' the king's decree; 5922
17 might not be changed c' Daniel.
7:12 As c' the rest of the beasts, *
8:13 the vision c' the daily sacrifice,
Am 1: 1 which he saw c' Israel in the 5921
Ob 1 saith the Lord God c' Edom; "
Mic 1: 1 c' Samaria and Jerusalem. 5921
3: 5 saith the Lord c' the prophets "
Na 1:14 given a commandment c' thee,
Hag 2:11 Ask now the priests c' the law,
M't 4: 6 give his angels charge c' thee: 4012
11: 7 to say unto the multitudes c' John, "
16:11 I spake it not to you c' bread, "
M'r 5:16 and also c' the swine.
7:17 disciples asked him c' the parable* "
Lu 2:17 which was told them c' this child.* "
7:24 to speak unto the people c' John, "
18:31 by the prophets c' the Son of man* "
22:37 for the things c' me have an end. *4012
24:19 C' Jesus of Nazareth, which was "
27 scriptures the things c' himself. "
44 and in the psalms, c' me. "
Joh 7:12 among the people c' him: "
32 murmured such things c' him; "
9:18 believe c' him, that he had been "
11:19 to comfort them c' their brother. "
Ac 1:16 c' Judas, which was guide to them "
2:25 David speaketh c' him, I foresaw 1519
8:12 the things c' the kingdom of God, 4012
13:34 And as c' that he raised him up 3754
19: 8 the things c' the kingdom of God. 4012
39 any thing c' other matters, * "
21:24 whereof they were informed c' thee. "
22:18 will not receive thy testimony c' me. "
23:15 something more perfectly c' him:* "
24:24 and heard him c' the faith in Christ. "
25:16 for himself c' the crime laid against "
28:21 received letters out of Judæa c' thee, "
22 as c' this sect, we know that every "
23 persuading them c' Jesus, both "
Ro 1: 3 C' his son Jesus Christ our Lord, 4012
9: 5 as c' the flesh Christ came, who 2596
27 Esaias also crieth c' Israel, 5228
11:28 As c' the gospel, they are enemies*2596
16:19 which is good, and simple c' evil. *1519
1Co 5: 3 present, c' him that hath so done *
7: 1 Now c' the things whereof ye 4012
25 Now c' virgins I have no "
8: 4 As c' therefore the eating of those "
12: 1 Now c' spiritual gifts, brethren, I "
16: 1 C' the collection for the saints, as I "
2Co 8:23 and fellowhelper c' you: *1519
11:21 I speak as c' reproach, as though *2596
Eph 4:22 c' the former conversation the old *
5:32 I speak c' Christ and the church. *1519
Ph'p 3: 6 C' zeal, persecuting the church: *2596
4:15 with me as c' giving and *1519, 3056
1Th 3: 2 and to comfort you c' your faith: 4012
4:13 c' them which are asleep, that ye "
5:18 will of God in Christ Jesus c' you,*1519
1Ti 1:19 c' faith have made shipwreck: 4012
6:21 professing have erred c' the faith. "
2Ti 2:18 Who c' the truth have erred, "
3: 8 minds, reprobate c' the faith. "
Heb 7:14 Moses spake nothing c' priesthood. "
11:20 blessed Jacob and Esau c' things "
22 gave commandment c' his bones "
1Pe 4:12 c' the fiery trial which is to try you, "
2Pe 3: 9 Lord is not slack c' his promise, 4814
1Jo 2:26 have I written unto you c' them 4012

concision
Ph'p 3: 2 of evil workers, beware of the c'. 2699

conclude See also CONCLUDED.
Ro 3:28 Therefore we c' that a man is *3049

concluded
Ac 21:25 we have written and c' that they *2919
Ro 11:32 For God hath c' them all in *4788
Ga 3:22 the scripture hath c' all under * "

conclusion
Ec 12:13 Let us hear the c' of the whole *5490

concord
2Co 6:15 And what c' hath Christ with 4857

concourse
Pr 1:21 She crieth in the chief place of c', 1993
Ac 19:40 we may give an account of this c'. 4963

concubine See also CONCUBINES.
Ge 22:24 And his c', whose name was 6370
35:22 Bilhah his father's c': and Israel "
36:12 Timna was c' to Eliphaz Esau's son; "
J'g 8:31 And his c' that was in Shechem, "
19: 1 who took to him a c' out of "
2 his c' played the whore against "
9 and his c', and his servant, his "
10 his c' also was with him. "
24 my daughter a maiden, and his c'; "
25 so the man took his c', and brought "
27 the woman his c' was fallen down "
29 laid hold on his c', and divided her "
20: 4 I and my c', to lodge. "
5 my c' have they forced, that she is "
6 And I took my c', and cut her in "
2Sa 3: 7 And Saul had a c', whose name was "
7 thou gone in unto my father's c'? "
21:11 the daughter of Aiah, the c' of Saul, "
1Ch 1:32 the sons of Keturah, Abraham's c': "
2:46 And Ephah, Caleb's c', bare Haran, "
48 Maachah, Caleb's c', bare Sheber. "
7:14 his c' the Aramitess bare Machir "

concubines
Ge 25: 6 the sons of the c', which Abraham 6370
2Sa 5:13 David took him more c' and wives "
15:16 ten women, which were c', to keep "
16:21 Go in unto thy father's c', which "
22 Absalom went in unto his father's c' "
19: 5 of thy wives, and the lives of thy c'; "
20: 3 the ten women his c', whom he had "
1Ki 11: 3 and three hundred c': and his "
1Ch 3: 9 beside the sons of the c', and "
2Ch 11:21 above all his wives and his c': "
21 and threescore c'; and begat "
Es 2:14 chamberlain, which kept the c': "
Ca 6: 8 and fourscore c', and virgins "
9 the queens and the c', and they "
Da 5: 2 his wives, and his c', might drink 3904
3 his wives, and his c', drank in them. "
23 and thy c', have drunk wine in "

concupiscence
Ro 7: 8 wrought in me all manner of c'. *1939
Col 3: 5 evil c', and covetousness, which * "
1Th 4: 5 Not in the lust of c', even as the * "

condemn See also CONDEMNED; CONDEMNEST; CONDEMNETH; CONDEMNING.
Ex 22: 9 whom the judges shall c', he shall 7561
De 25: 1 the righteous, and c' the wicked. "
Job 9:20 mine own mouth shall c' me: "
10: 2 Do not c' me; shew me wherefore "
34:17 wilt thou c' him that is most just? "
40: 8 wilt thou c' me, that thou mayest "
Ps 37:33 in his hand, nor c' him when he is "
94:21 the righteous, and c' the innocent "
109:31 him from those that c' his soul. *8199
Pr 12: 2 a man of wicked devices will he c'. 7561
Isa 50: 9 who is he that shall c' me? lo, they "
54:17 in judgment thou shalt c'. This is "
M't 12:41 and shall c' it: because they 2632
42 and shall c' it: for she came from "
20:18 they shall c' him to death, "
M'r 10:33 they shall c' him to death, and shall "
Lu 6:37 c' not, and ye shall not be 2613
11:31 of this generation, and c' them: 2632
32 with this generation, and shall c' it "
Joh 3:17 Son into the world to c' the world; *2919

Joh 8:11 Neither do I c' thee: go, and sin 2632
2Co 7: 3 I speak not this to c' you: for I 2633
1Jo 3:20 For if our heart c' us, God is 2607
21 if our heart c' us not, then have "

condemnation
Lu 23:40 seeing thou art in the same c'? 2917
Joh 3:19 And this is the c', that light is *2920
5:24 shall not come into c'; but is * "
Ro 5:16 for the judgment was by one to c', 2631
18 judgment came upon all men to c'; "
8: 1 now no c' to them which are in "
1Co 11:34 ye come not together unto c'. *2917
2Co 3: 9 For if the administration of c' be 2633
1Ti 3: 6 he fall into the c' of the devil. 2917
Jas 3: 1 we shall receive the greater c'. * "
5:12 your way, nay; lest ye fall into c'.*5272
Jude 4 before of old ordained to this c', 2917

condemned
2Ch 36:3 and c' the land in an hundred †‡6064
Job 32: 3 no answer, and yet had c' Job. 7561
Ps 109: 7 be judged, let him be c': *3318, 7563
Am 2: 8 drink the wine of the c' in the *6064
M't 12: 7 ye would not have c' the guiltless. 2613
37 and by thy words thou shalt be c'. * "
27: 3 when he saw that he was c', 2632
M'r 14:64 they all c' him to be guilty of death."
Lu 6:37 and ye shall not be c': forgive, 2613
24:20 delivered him to be c' to 1519, 2917
Joh 3:18 believeth on him is not c': but he *2919
18 that believeth not is c' already, * "
8:10 hath no man c' thee? *2632
Ro 8: 3 c' sin in the flesh: "
1Co 11:32 that we should not be c' with "
Tit 2: 8 Sound speech, that cannot be c'; 176
3:11 and sinneth, being c' of himself. * 843
Heb 11: 7 by the which he c' the world, and 2632
Jas 5: 6 Ye have c' and killed the just; 2613
9 lest ye be c': behold, the judge *2632
2Pe 2: 6 c' them with an overthrow, "

condemnest
Ro 2: 1 judgest another, thou c' thyself; 2632

condemneth
Job 15: 6 Thine own mouth c' thee, and 7561
Pr 17:15 and he that c' the just, even they "
Ro 8:34 Who is he that c'? It is Christ †2632
14:22 Happy is he that c' not himself *2919

condemning
1Ki 8:32 c' the wicked, to bring his way 7561
Ac 13:27 they have fulfilled them in c' him. 2919

condescend
Ro 12:16 but c' to men of low estate. 4879

condition See also CONDITIONS.
1Sa 11: 2 On this c' will I make a covenant

conditions
Lu 14:32 and desireth c' of peace. 4314

conduct See also CONDUCTED.
2Sa 19:15 king, to c' the king over Jordan. *5674
31 the king, to c' him over Jordan. 7971
1Co 16:11 but c' him forth in peace, that he *4311

conducted
2Sa 19:40 the people of Judah c' the king, *5674
Ac 17:15 c' Paul brought him unto Athens: 2525

conduit *(con'-dit)*
2Ki 18:17 stood by the c' of the upper pool, 8585
20:20 he made a pool, and a c', and "
Isa 7: 3 the end of the c' of the upper pool "
36: 2 he stood by the c' of the upper pool "

coney See also CONIES.
Le 11: 5 c', because he cheweth the cud, 8227
De 14: 7 camel, and the hare, and the c': "

confection
Ex 30:35 c' after the art of the apothecary, *7545

confectionaries
1Sa 8:13 take your daughters to be c', ‡7543

confederacy
Isa 8:12 Say ye not, A c', to all them to *7195
12 this people shall say, A c'; neither* "
Ob 7 All the men of thy c' have brought 1285

confederate
Ge 14:13 these were c' with Abram. 1167, 1285
Ps 83: 5 they are c' against thee: *1285, 3772
Isa 7: 2 Syria is c' with Ephraim. And 5117

conference
Ga 2: 6 in c' added nothing to me: *4323

conferred
1Ki 1: 7 And he c' with Joab the son 1961, 1697
Ac 4:15 they c' among themselves, 4820
25:12 Then Festus, when he had c' with 4814
Ga 1:16 I c' not with flesh and blood: 4323

confess See also CONFESSED; CONFESSETH; CONFESSING.
Le 5: 5 he shall c' that he hath sinned 3034
16:21 and c' over him all the iniquities "
26:40 If they shall c' their iniquity, and "
Nu 5: 7 c' their sin which they have done: "
1Ki 8:33 and c' thy name, and pray, and "
35 and c' thy name, and turn from 3034
2Ch 6:24 c' thy name, and pray and make "
26 toward this place, and c' thy name, "
Ne 1: 6 c' the sins of the children of Israel, "
Job 40:14 Then will I also c' unto thee that "
Ps 32: 5 I will c' my transgressions unto "
M't 10:32 shall c' me before men, him will I 3670
32 will I c' also before my Father "
Lu 12: 8 shall c' me before men, him "
8 shall the Son of man also c' before "
Joh 9:22 any man did c' that he was Christ, "
12:42 the Pharisees they did not c' him, "
Ac 23: 8 but the Pharisees c' both. "
Ac 24:14 But this I c' unto thee, that after 3670
Ro 10: 9 c' with thy mouth the Lord Jesus, "
14:11 and every tongue shall c' to God. 1843
15: 9 c' to thee among the Gentiles, * "
Ph'p 2:11 should c' that Jesus Christ is Lord, "
Jas 5:16 C' your faults one to another, and "
1Jo 1: 9 If we c' our sins, he is faithful and 3670
4:15 c' that Jesus is the Son of God, "
2Jo 7 who c' not that Jesus Christ is "
Re 3: 5 will c' his name before my Father, 1843

confessed
Ezr 10: 1 when he had c', weeping and *3034
Ne 9: 2 stood and c' their sins, and the "
3 another fourth part they c', and "
Joh 1:20 he c', and denied not; but 3670
20 c', I am not the Christ. "
Ac 19:18 and c', and showed their deeds. *1843
Heb 11:13 and c' that they were strangers 3670

confesseth
Pr 28:13 c' and forsaketh them shall have 3034
1Jo 4: 2 Every spirit that c' that Jesus 3670
3 every spirit that c' not that Jesus "

confessing
Da 9:20 praying, and c' my sin and the 3034
M't 3: 6 of him in Jordan, c' their sins. 1843
M'r 1: 5 in the river of Jordan, c' their sins. "

confession
Jos 7:19 make c' unto him; and tell me 8426
2Ch 30:22 and making c' to the Lord God of 3034
Ezr 10:11 make c' unto the Lord God of 8426
Da 9: 4 Lord my God, and made my c', 3034
Ro 10:10 mouth c' is made unto salvation; 3670
1Ti 6:13 Pontius Pilate witnessed a good c': 3671

confidence See also CONFIDENCES.
J'g 9:26 men of Shechem put their c' in * 982
2Ki 18:19 c' is this wherein thou trustest? 986
Job 4: 6 not this thy fear, thy c', thy hope, 3690
18:14 His c' shall be rooted out of his *4009
31:24 to the fine gold, Thou art my c'; "
Ps 65: 5 the c' of all the ends of the earth, "
118: 8 in the Lord than to put c' in man. 982
9 the Lord than to put c' in princes. "
Pr 3:26 the Lord shall be thy c', and 3689
14:26 the fear of the Lord is strong c': 4009
21:22 the strength of the c' thereof. "
25:19 C' in an unfaithful man in time of "
Isa 30:15 and in c' shall be your strength: 985
36: 4 c' is this wherein thou trustest? 986
Jer 48:13 was ashamed of Beth-el their c'. 4009
Eze 28:26 they shall dwell with c', when I * 983
29:16 be no more the c' of the house 4009
Mic 7: 5 a friend, put ye not c' in a guide: 982
Ac 28:31 with all c', no man forbidding *3954
2Co 1:15 in this c' I was minded to come 4006
2: 3 having c' in you all, that my joy 3982
7:16 I have c' in you in all things. *2292
8:22 the great c' which I have in you. 4006
10: 2 c', wherewith I think to be bold "
11:17 foolishly, in this c' of boasting. 5287
Ga 5:10 have c' in you through the Lord, 3982
Eph 3:12 and access with c' by the faith 4006
Ph'p 1:25 And having this c', I know that I 3982
3: 3 and have no c' in the flesh. "
3: 4 might also have c' in the flesh. 4006
2Th 3: 4 have c' in the Lord touching you, 3982
Ph'm 21 Having c' in thy obedience I wrote "
Heb 3: 6 if we hold fast the c' and the *3954
14 if we hold the beginning of our c' 5287
10:35 therefore your c', which hath *3954
1Jo 2:28 we may have c', and not be * "
3:21 then have we c' toward God. * "
5:14 is the c' that we have in him, * "

confidences
Jer 2:37 the Lord hath rejected thy c', and 4009

confident
Ps 27: 3 against me, in this will I be c'. 982
Pr 14:16 but the fool rageth, and is c'. "
Ro 2:19 c' that thou thyself art a guide 3982
2Co 5: 6 Therefore we are always c', *2292
8 are c', I say, and willing rather * "
9: 4 in this same c' boasting. *5287
Ph'p 1: 6 Being c' of this very thing, that 3982
14 waxing c' by my bonds, are much "

confidently
Lu 22:59 another c' affirmed, saying, Of a 1340

confirm See also CONFIRMED; CONFIRMETH; CONFIRMING.
Ru 4: 7 changing, for to c' all things; 6965
1Ki 1:14 in after thee, and c' thy words. 4390
2Ki 15:19 be with him to c' the kingdom 2388
Es 9:29 to c' this second letter of Purim. 6965
31 To c' these days of Purim in their "
Ps 68: 9 thou didst c' thine inheritance, 3559
Isa 35: 3 and c' the feeble knees. 553
Eze 13: 6 hope that they would c' the word.*6965
Da 9:27 And he shall c' the covenant *1396
11: 1 stood to c' and to strengthen him. 2388
Ro 15: 8 to c' the promises made unto the 950
1Co 1: 8 Who shall also c' you unto the end, "
2Co 2: 8 would c' your love toward him. 2964

confirmation
Ph'p 1: 7 in the defence and c' of the gospel, 951
Heb 6:16 an oath for c' is to them an end of "

confirmed
2Sa 7:24 thou hast c' to thyself thy people *3559
2Ki 14: 5 the kingdom was c' in his hand, *2388
1Ch 14: 2 Lord had c' him king over Israel, *3559
16:17 And hath c' the same to Jacob 5975
Es 9:32 Esther c' these matters of Purim; 6965
Ps 105:10 c' the same unto Jacob for a law, 5975
Da 9:12 And he hath c' his words, which 6965
Ac 15:32 with many words, and c' them. 1991
1Co 1: 6 testimony of Christ was c' in you: 950
Ga 3:15 a man's covenant, yet if it be c', 2964
17 that was c' before of God in Christ, 4300
Heb 2: 3 c' unto us by them that heard him; 950
6:17 of his counsel, c' it by an oath: *3315

confirmeth
Nu 30:14 he c' them, because he held his *6965
De 27:26 Cursed be he that c' not all the "
Isa 44:26 That c' the word of his servant, "

confirming
M'r 16:20 c' the word with signs following. 950
Ac 14:22 C' the souls of the disciples, and 1991
15:41 Syria and Cilicia, c' the churches. "

confiscation
Ezr 7:26 c' of goods, or to imprisonment. 6065

conflict
Ph'p 1:30 the same c' which ye saw in me, 73
Col 2: 1 knew what great c' I have for you,* "

conformable
Ph'p 3:10 being made c' unto his death; *4832

conformed
Ro 8:29 to be c' to the image of his Son, 4832
12: 2 And be not c' to this world: but *4964

confound See also CONFOUNDED.
Ge 11: 7 and there c' their language, 1101
9 the Lord did there c' the language "
Jer 1:17 faces, lest I c' thee before them. *2865
1Co 1:27 things of the world to c' the wise;*2617
27 c' the things which are mighty; * "

confounded
2Ki 19:26 they were dismayed and c'; 954
Job 6:20 were c' because they had hoped; "
Ps 22: 5 trusted in thee, and were not c'. ‡‡ "
35: 4 Let them be c' and put to shame‡‡ "
40:14 Let them be ashamed and c' 2659
69: 6 let not those that seek thee be c' *3637
70: 2 Let them be ashamed and c' 2659
71:13 Let them be c' and consumed ‡‡ 954
24 for they are c', for they are brought "
83:17 Let them be c' and troubled for * "
97: 7 C' be all they that serve graven ‡‡ "
129: 5 Let them all be c' and turned ‡‡ "
Isa 1:29 ye shall be c' for the gardens 2659
19: 9 that weave net works, shall be c'.‡‡ 954
24:23 Then the moon shall be c', 2659
37:27 they were dismayed and c': 954
41:11 shall be ashamed and c': they 3637
45:16 They shall be ashamed, and also c'."
17 ye shall not be ashamed nor c' "
50: 7 me; therefore shall I not be c': "
54: 4 neither be thou c'; for thou shalt "
Jer 9:19 we are greatly c', because we have 954
10:14 founder is c' by the graven image:*3001
14: 3 they were ashamed and c', 3637
15: 9 she hath been ashamed and c': 2659
17:18 them be c' that persecute me, ‡‡ 954
18 let not me be c': let them be "
22:22 then shalt thou be ashamed and c' 3637
31:19 I was ashamed, yea, even c', "
46:24 daughter of Egypt shall be c'; *3001
48: 1 Kiriathaim is c' and taken: * "
1 Misgab is c' and dismayed. * "
20 Moab is c'; for it is broken down:* "
49:23 Hamath is c', and Arpad: for ‡‡ 954
50: 2 Bel is c', Merodach is broken *3001
2 her idols are c', her images are * "
12 Your mother shall be sore c'; ‡‡ 954
51:17 founder is c' by the graven image:*3001
47 her whole land shall be c', ‡‡ 954
51 We are c', because we have "
Eze 16:52 be thou c' also, and bear thy shame,"
54 and mayest be c' in all that thou *3637
63 thou mayest remember, and be c', 954
36:32 be ashamed and c' for your own 3637
Mic 3: 7 ashamed, and the diviners c': 2659
7:16 The nations shall see and be c'. * 954
Zec 10: 5 the riders on horses shall be c'. 3001
Ac 2: 6 came together, and were c', 4797
9:22 and c' the Jews which dwelt at "
1Pe 2: 6 believeth on him shall not be c'. *2617

confused
Isa 9: 5 of the warrior is with c' noise, *7494
Ac 19:32 for the assembly was c'; *4797

confusion
Le 18:23 to lie down thereto: it is c'. 8397
20:12 they have wrought c'; their blood "
1Sa 20:30 to thine own c', and unto the c' of *1322
Ezr 9: 7 and to c' of face, as it is this day. "
Job 10:15 I am full of c'; therefore see *7036
Ps 35: 4 be turned back and brought to c' *2659
26 be ashamed and brought to c' * "
44:15 My c' is continually before me, *3639
70: 2 and put to c', that desire my hurt.*3637
71: 1 let me never be put to c'. ‡‡ 954
109:29 themselves with their own c', *1322
Isa 24:10 The city of c' is broken down: 8414
30: 3 in the shadow of Egypt your c'. 3639
34:11 stretch out upon it the line of c', 8414
41:29 molten images are wind and c'. "
45:16 they shall go to c' together that 3639
61: 7 and for c' they shall rejoice ‡ "
Jer 3:25 our c' covereth us: for we have "
7:19 to the c' of their own faces? 1322
20:11 their everlasting c' shall never *3639
Da 9: 7 but unto us c' of faces, as at this 1322
8 Lord, to us belongeth c' of face, "
Ac 19:29 the whole city was filled with c': 4799
1Co 14:33 For God is not the author of c', 181
Jas 3:16 there is c' and every evil work. "

congealed
Ex 15: 8 the depths were c' in the heart of 7087

congratulate
1Ch 18:10 and to c' him, because he had *1288

congregation See also CONGREGATIONS.
Ex 12: 3 Speak ye unto all the c' of Israel, 5712
6 whole assembly of the c' of Israel "
19 be cut off from the c' of Israel, "
47 All the c' of Israel shall keep it. "
16: 1 the c' of the children of Israel came "
2 And the whole c' of the children of "
9 Say unto all the c' of the children "
10 Aaron spake unto the whole c' of "
22 all the rulers of the c' came and "
17: 1 all the c' of the children of Israel "
27:21 the tabernacle of the c' without *4150
28:43 in unto the tabernacle of the c', * "
29: 4 door of the tabernacle of the c', * "
10 before the tabernacle of the c': * "
11 door of the tabernacle of the c'. * "
30 into the tabernacle of the c' of * "
32 door of the tabernacle of the c'. * "
42 door of the tabernacle of the c' of * "
44 sanctify the tabernacle of the c', * "
30:16 service of the tabernacle of the c';* "
18 between the tabernacle of the c' * "
20 go into the tabernacle of the c', * "
26 anoint the tabernacle of the c' * "
36 in the tabernacle of the c', where * "
31: 7 tabernacle of the c', and the ark * "
33: 7 called it the Tabernacle of the c'.* "
7 out unto the tabernacle of the c',* "
34:31 all the rulers of the c' returned 5712
35: 1 And Moses gathered all the c' of the "
4 spake unto all the c' of the children "
20 c' of the children of Israel departed "
21 work of the tabernacle of the c', *4150
38: 8 door of the tabernacle of the c'. * "
25 that were numbered of the c' 5712
30 door of the tabernacle of the c', *4150
39:32 tabernacle of the tent of the c' * "
40 for the tent of the c', * "
40: 2, 6 tabernacle of the tent of the c'.* "
7 the tent of the c' and the altar, * "
12 door of the tabernacle of the c', * "
22 the table in the tent of the c', * "
24 candlestick in the tent of the c', * "
26 the tent of the c' before the vail: * "
29 tabernacle of the tent of the c', * "
30 the tent of the c' and the altar, * "
32 they went into the tent of the c', * "
34 cloud covered the tent of the c', * "
35 to enter into the tent of the c', * "
Le 1: 1 out of the tabernacle of the c', * "
3 the tabernacle of the c' before * "
5 door of the tabernacle of the c'. * "
3: 2 door of the tabernacle of the c': * "
8, 13 before the tabernacle of the c':* "
4: 4 tabernacle of the c' before the * "
5 it to the tabernacle of the c': * "
7 is in the tabernacle of the c'; * "
7 door of the tabernacle of the c'. * "
13 And if the whole c' of Israel sin 5712
14 the c' shall offer a young bullock,*6951
14 before the tabernacle of the c'. *4150
15 And the elders of the c' shall lay 5712
16 blood to the tabernacle of the c': *4150
18 that is in the tabernacle of the c',* "
18 door of the tabernacle of the c'. * "
21 it is a sin offering for the c'. *6951
6:16 tabernacle of the c' they shall eat*4150
26 court of the tabernacle of the c'. * "
30 into the tabernacle of the c' to * "
8: 3 gather thou all the c' together 5712
3, 4 door of the tabernacle of the c'.*4150
5 And Moses said unto the c', 5712
31 door of the tabernacle of the c': *4150
33 tabernacle of the c' in seven days,* "
35 door of the tabernacle of the c' * "
9: 5 before the tabernacle of the c'; * "
5 the c' drew near and stood before 5712
23 went into the tabernacle of the c',*4150
10: 7 door of the tabernacle of the c', * "
9 go into the tabernacle of the c', * "
17 the iniquity of the c', to make 5712
12: 6 door of the tabernacle of the c', *4150
14:11 door of the tabernacle of the c': * "
23 door of the tabernacle of the c', * "
15:14 door of the tabernacle of the c', * "
29 door of the tabernacle of the c'. * "
16: 5 shall take of the c' of the children 5712
7 door of the tabernacle of the c'. *4150
16 he do for the tabernacle of the c',* "
17 man in the tabernacle of the c' * "
17 and for all the c' of Israel. *6951
20 and the tabernacle of the c', *4150
23 come into the tabernacle of the c',* "
33 for the tabernacle of the c', * "
33 and for all the people of the c'. *6951
17: 4, 5, 6, 9 of the tabernacle of the c'. *4150
19: 2 Speak unto all the c' of the 5712
21 door of the tabernacle of the c', *4150
24: 3 in the tabernacle of the c', shall * "
14 and let all the c' stone him. 5712
16 the c' shall certainly stone him: "
Nu 1: 1 Sinai, in the tabernacle of the c'. *4150
2 Take ye the sum of all the c' 5712
16 were the renowned of the c', "
18 they assembled all the c' together "
53 there be no wrath upon the c' "
2: 2 about the tabernacle of the c' *4150
17 the tabernacle of the c' shall set * "
3: 7 and the charge of the whole c' 5712
7 before the tabernacle of the c', *4150
8 of the tabernacle of the c', * "
25 in the tabernacle of the c' * "
25 door of the tabernacle of the c', * "
38 before the tabernacle of the c', * "

Nu 4: 3 work in the tabernacle of the c'. *4150
4 Kohath in the tabernacle of the c',* "
15 Kohath in the tabernacle of the c'.* "
23 work in the tabernacle of the c'. * "
25 and the tabernacle of the c', * "
25 door of the tabernacle of the c', * "
28 in the tabernacle of the c': * "
30 work of the tabernacle of the c'. * "
31 service in the tabernacle of the c';* "
33 service in the tabernacle of the c',* "
34 the chief of the c' numbered the 5712
35 work in the tabernacle of the c': *4150
37 service in the tabernacle of the c',* "
39 work in the tabernacle of the c', * "
41 service in the tabernacle of the c', * "
43 work in the tabernacle of the c', * "
47 burden in the tabernacle of the c',* "
6:10, 13 door of the tabernacle of the c':* "
18 door of the tabernacle of the c', * "
7: 5 service of the tabernacle of the c';* "
89 gone into the tabernacle of the c'* "
8: 9 before the tabernacle of the c': * "
15 service of the tabernacle of the c': * "
19 Israel in the tabernacle of the c', * "
20 all the c' of the children of Israel, 5712
22 service in the tabernacle of the c' *4150
24 service of the tabernacle of the c': * "
26 brethren in .. tabernacle of the c',* "
10: 3 door of the tabernacle of the c'. * "
7 But when the c' is to be gathered *6951
11:16 them unto the tabernacle of the c',*4150
12: 4 three unto the tabernacle of the c'.* "
13:26 all the c' of the children of Israel, 5712
26 and unto all the c', and shewed "
14: 1 And all the c' lifted up their voice, "
2 And the whole c' said unto them, "
5 assembly of the c' of the children "
10 all the c' bade stone them with "
10 the tabernacle of the c' before all*4150
27 shall I bear with this evil c', 5712
35 surely do it unto all this evil c', "
36 made all the c' to murmur against "
15:15 shall be both for you of the c', *6951
24 without the knowledge of the c', 5712
24 that all the c' shall offer one young "
25 for the c' of the children of Israel, "
26 forgiven all the c' of the children "
33 and Aaron, and unto all the c'. "
35 the c' shall stone him with stones "
36 c' brought him without the camp, 5712
16: 2 the assembly, famous in the c', 4150
3 seeing all the c' are holy, every 5712
3 lift ye up yourselves above the c'*6951
9 separated you from the c' of Israel,5712
9 to stand before the c' to minister "
18 door of the tabernacle of the c' *4150
19 Korah gathered all the c' against 5712
19 door of the tabernacle of the c': *4150
19 the Lord appeared unto all the c'. 5712
21 yourselves from among this c', "
22 thou be wroth with all the c'? "
24 Speak unto the c', saying, Get you "
26 he spake unto the c', saying, "
33 they perished from among the c'. *6951
41 morrow all the c' of the children 5712
42 where the c' was gathered against "
42 toward the tabernacle of the c': *4150
43 before the tabernacle of the c'. * "
45 Get you up from among this c', 5712
46 go quickly unto the c', and make "
47 and ran into the midst of the c'; *6951
50 door of the tabernacle of the c': *4150
17: 4 them up in the tabernacle of the c'* "
18: 4 charge of the tabernacle of the c',* "
6 service of the tabernacle of the c'. * "
21 service of the tabernacle of the c'.* "
22 come nigh the tabernacle of the c',* "
23 service of the tabernacle of the c',* "
31 service in the tabernacle of the c'.* "
19: 4 tabernacle of the c' seven times: * "
9 for the c' of the children of Israel 5712
20 shall be cut off from among the c',*6951
20: 1 even the whole c', into the desert 5712
2 And there was no water for the c': "
4 have ye brought up the c' of the *6951
6 door of the tabernacle of the c', *4150
8 thou shalt give the c' and their 5712
10 Moses and Aaron gathered the c' *6951
11 the c' drank, and their beasts 5712
12 ye shall not bring this c' into the *6951
22 even the whole c', journeyed from 5712
27 mount Hor in the sight of all the c'. "
29 when all the c' saw that Aaron "
25: 6 in the sight of all the c' of the "
6 door of the tabernacle of the c'. *4150
7 he rose up from among the c', 5712
26: 2 Take the sum of all the c' of the "
9 which were famous in the c', who "
27: 2 the princes and all the c', "
2 door of the tabernacle of the c', *4150
14 in the strife of the c', to sanctify 5712
16 set a man over the c', "
17 the c' of the Lord be not as sheep "
19 and before all the c'; and give him "
20 the c' of the children of Israel may "
21 Israel with him, even all the c'. "
22 and before all the c': "
31:12 unto the c' of the children of Israel, "
13 all the princes of the c', went forth "
16 was a plague among the c' of the "
26 and the chief fathers of the c': "
27 to battle, and between all the c': "
43 half that pertained unto the c' "
54 unto the tabernacle of the c', for a *4150
32: 2 and unto the princes of the c', 5712
4 before the c' of Israel, is a land for "

Nu 35:12 until he stand before the c' in 5712
24 c' shall judge between the slayer "
25 c' shall deliver the slayer out of "
25 the c' shall restore him to the city "
De 23: 1, 2 shall not enter into the c' of the *6951
2 shall he not enter into the c' of the* "
3 Moabite shall not enter into the c' * "
3 shall they not enter into the c' of * "
8 of them shall enter into the c' * "
31:14 in the tabernacle of the c', *4150
14 in the tabernacle of the c'. * "
30 spake in the ears of all the c' of * "
33: 4 even the inheritance of the c' of *6952
Jos 8:35 Joshua read not before all the c' *6951
9:15 the princes of the c' sware unto 5712
18 because the princes of the c' had "
18 all the c' murmured against the "
19 all the princes said unto all the c', "
21 drawers of water unto all the c'; "
27 drawers of water for the c', and for "
18: 1 whole c' of the children of Israel "
1 set up the tabernacle of the c' *4150
19:51 door of the tabernacle of the c'. * "
20: 6 until he stand before the c' for 5712
9 until he stood before the c'. "
22:12 c' of the children of Israel gathered "
16 Thus saith the whole c' of the Lord, "
17 was a plague in the c' of the Lord, "
18 will be wroth with the whole c' of "
20 wrath fell on all the c' of Israel? "
30 the princes of the c' and heads of "
J'g 20: 1 c' was gathered together as one "
21: 5 came not up with the c' unto the *6951
10 c' sent thither twelve thousand 5712
13 the whole c' sent some to speak "
16 elders of the c' said, How shall we "
1Sa 2:22 door of the tabernacle of the c'. *4150
1Ki 8: 4 the tabernacle of the c', and all * "
5 c' of Israel, that were assembled 5712
14 blessed all the c' of Israel: 6951
14 (and all the c' of Israel stood;) "
22 in the presence of all the c' of "
55 blessed all the c' of Israel with a "
65 all Israel with him, a great c', "
12: 3 Jeroboam and all the c' of Israel "
20 sent and called him unto the c', 5712
1Ch 6:32 place of the tabernacle of the c' *4150
9:21 door of the tabernacle of the c'. * "
13: 2 David said unto all the c' of *6951
4 the c' said that they would do so: * "
23:32 charge of the tabernacle of the c',*4150
28: 8 of all Israel the c' of the Lord, 6951
29: 1 the king said unto all the c', "
10 blessed the Lord before all the c': "
20 David said to all the c', Now bless "
20 all the c' blessed the Lord God "
2Ch 1: 3 Solomon, and all the c' with him, "
3 there was the tabernacle of the c'*4150
5 Solomon and the c' sought unto it. 6951
6 was at the tabernacle at the c', *4150
13 before the tabernacle of the c', * "
5: 5 ark, and the tabernacle of the c', * "
6 c' of Israel that were assembled 5712
6: 3 blessed the whole c' of Israel: 6951
3 and all the c' of Israel stood. "
12 the presence of all the c' of Israel, "
13 upon his knees before all the c' of "
7: 8 Israel with him, a very great c', "
20: 5 stood in the c' of Judah and "
14 of the Lord in the midst of the c'; "
23: 3 all the c' made a covenant with "
24: 6 and of the c' of Israel, for the "
28:14 before the princes and all the c'. "
29:23 offering before the king and the c'; "
28 all the c' worshipped, and the "
31 the c' brought in sacrifices and "
32 burnt offerings, which the c' brought, "
30: 2 all the c' in Jerusalem, to keep "
4 pleased the king and all the c'. "
13 the second month, a very great c'. "
17 there were many in the c' that "
24 give to the c' a thousand bullocks "
24 princes gave to the c' a thousand "
25 all the c' of Judah, with the priests "
25 all the c' that came out of Israel, "
31:18 their daughters, through all the c': "
Ezr 2:64 whole c' together was forty and two "
10: 1 a very great c' of men and women "
8 himself separated from the c' of "
12 Then all the c' answered and said "
14 now our rulers of all the c' stand, "
Ne 5:13 all the c' said, Amen, and praised "
7:66 whole c' together was forty and two "
8: 2 brought the law before the c' both "
17 all the c' of them that were come "
13: 1 not come into the c' of God * "
Job 15:34 c' of hypocrites shall be desolate,*5712
30:28 I stood up, and I cried in the c'. *6951
Ps 1: 5 sinners in the c' of the righteous. 5712
7: 7 shall the c' of the people compass "
22:22 midst of the c' will I praise thee. 6951
25 shall be of thee in the great c': "
26: 5 have hated the c' of evil doers; "
35:18 give thee thanks in the great c': "
40: 9 righteousness in the great c': "
10 and thy truth from the great c'. "
58: 1 speak righteousness, O c'? * 482
68:10 Thy c' hath dwelt therein: thou, 2416
74: 2 Remember thy c', which thou hast 5712
19 forget not the c' of thy poor *2416
75: 2 When I shall receive the c' I will *4150
82: 1 God standeth in the c' of the 5712
89: 5 faithfulness also in the c' of the *6951
107:32 him also in the c' of the people, * "
111: 1 of the upright, and in the c'. 5712
149: 1 and his praise in the c' of saints. *6951

Pr 5:14 in all evil in the midst of the c' 6951
21:16 shall remain in the c' of the dead. "
26:26 be shewed before the whole c'.
Isa 14:13 sit also upon the mount of the c'. 4150
Jer 6:18 know, O c', what is among them. 5712
30:20 and their c' shall be established
La 1:10 they should not enter into thy c'. 6951
Ho 7:12 chastise them, as their c' hath 5712
Joe 2:16 Gather the people, sanctify the c', 6951
Mic 2: 5 a cord by lot in the c' of the Lord. "
Ac 13:43 Now when the c' was broken up, *4864

congregations
Ps 26:12 in the c' will I bless the Lord. 4721
68:26 Bless ye God in the c', even the "
74: 4 roar in the midst of thy c'; *4150

Coniah (*co-ni'-ah*) See also JEHOIACHIN.
Jer 22:24 though C' the son of Jehoiakim 3659
28 this man C' a despised broken idol? "
37: 1 son of Josiah reigned instead of C' "

conies
Ps 104:18 goats; and the rocks for the c'. 8227
Pr 30:26 The c' are but a feeble folk, yet "

Cononiah (*co-no-ni'-ah*) See also CONANIAH.
2Ch 31:12 over which C' the Levite was ruler, 3562
13 overseers under the hand of C' "

conquer See also CONQUERING.
Re 6: 2 went forth conquering, and to c'. 3528

conquering
Re 6: 2 he went forth c', and to conquer. 3528

conquerors
Ro 8:37 we are more than c' through him 5245

conscience See also CONSCIENCES.
Joh 8: 9 being convicted by their own c', *4893
Ac 23: 1 have lived in all good c' before God "
24:16 to have always a c' void of offence "
Ro 2:15 their c' also bearing witness, and "
9: 1 my c' also bearing me witness. "
13: 5 for wrath, but also for c' sake. "
1Co 8: 7 for some with c' of the idol unto * "
7 and their c' being weak is defiled. "
10 shall not the c' of him which is weak "
12 and wound their weak c', ye sin "
10:25 eat, asking no question for c' sake: "
27 eat, asking no question for c' sake. "
28 sake that showed it, and for c' sake: "
29 C', I say, not thine own, but of the "
29 liberty judged of another man's c'? "
2Co 1:12 is this, the testimony of our c', "
4: 2 ourselves to every man's c' in the "
1Ti 1: 5 a good c', and of faith unfeigned: "
19 Holding faith, and a good c'; "
3: 9 mystery of the faith in a pure c'. "
4: 2 their c' seared with a hot iron; "
2Ti 1: 3 from my forefathers with pure c', "
Tit 1:15 even their mind and c' is defiled. "
Heb 9: 9 perfect, as pertaining to the c'; "
14 purge your c' from dead works "
10: 2 should have had no more c' of sins. "
22 hearts sprinkled from an evil c', "
13:18 we trust we have a good c', "
1Pe 2:19 if a man for c' toward God endure "
3:16 Having a good c'; that whereas "
21 answer of a good c' toward God,) "

consciences
2Co 5:11 also are made manifest in your c'. 4893

consecrate See also CONSECRATED.
Ex 28: 3 make Aaron's garments to c' him, *6942
41 anoint them, and c' them, 4390, 3027
29: 9 shalt c' Aaron and his sons. " "
33 to c' and to sanctify them: " "
35 seven days shalt thou c' them. " "
30:30 Aaron and his sons, and c' them, *6942
32:29 C' yourselves to day to the 4390, 3027
Le 8:33 for seven days shall he c' you. " "
16:32 he shall c' to minister in " "
Nu 6:12 And he shall c' unto the Lord the *5144
1Ch 29: 5 c' his service this day unto 4390, 3027
2Ch 13: 9 to c' himself with a young " "
Eze 43:26 and they shall c' themselves. " "
Mic 4:13 and I will c' their gain unto the *2763

consecrated
Ex 29:29 anointed therein, and to be c' 4390, 3027
Le 21:10 and that is c' to put on the " "
Nu 3: 3 whom he c' to minister in the " "
Jos 6:19 of brass and iron, are c' unto the *6944
J'g 17: 5 and c' one of his sons, 4390, 3027
12 And Micah c' the Levite; " "
1Ki 13:33 he c' him, and he became one " "
2Ch 26:18 Aaron, that are c' to burn incense: 6942
29:31 have c' yourselves unto the 4390, 3027
33 the c' things were six hundred 6942
31: 6 which were c' unto the Lord their "
Ezr 3: 5 set feasts of the Lord that were c', "
Heb 7:28 the Son, who is c' for evermore. *5048
10:20 way, which he hath c' for us, *1457

consecration See also CONSECRATIONS.
Ex 29:22 for it is a ram of c': 4394
26 breast of the ram of Aaron's c', "
27 of the ram of the c', even of that "
31 thou shalt take the ram of the c'. "
Le 8:22 the other ram, the ram of c': "
29 of the ram of c' it was Moses' part; "
33 until the days of your c' be at an "
Nu 6: 7 because the c' of his God is upon *5145
9 he hath defiled the head of his c'; * "

consecrations
Ex 29:34 And if ought of the flesh of the c', *4394
Le 7:37 and of the c', and of the sacrifice * "
8:28 they were c' for a sweet savour: * "
31 bread that is in the basket of c'. * "

consent See also CONSENTED; CONSENTING.
Ge 34:15 But in this will we c' unto you: 225
22 Only herein will the men c' unto us "
23 only let us c' unto them, and they "
De 13: 8 Thou shalt not c' unto him, 14
J'g 11:17 but he would not c': * "
1Sa 11: 7 and they came out with one c'. * 376
1Ki 20: 8 him, Hearken not unto him, nor c'. 14
Ps 83: 5 consulted together with one c': 3820
Pr 1:10 if sinners entice thee, c' thou not. 14
Ho 6: 9 priests murder in the way by c': *7926
Zep 3: 9 the Lord, to serve him with one c'. "
Lu 14:18 with one c' began to make excuse.
Ro 7:16 I c' unto the law that it is good. 4852
1Co 7: 5 except it be with c' for a time, 4859
1Ti 6: 3 and c' not to wholesome words, 4334

consented See also CONSENTEDST.
2Ki 12: 8 the priests c' to receive no more 225
Da 1:14 So he c' to them in this matter, *8085
Lu 23:51 same had not c' to the counsel and 4784
Ac 18:20 longer time with them, he c' not; 1962

consentedst
Ps 50:18 then thou c' with him, and hast 7521

consenting
Ac 8: 1 And Saul was c' unto his death. 4909
22:20 standing by, and c' unto his death, "

consider See also CONSIDERED; CONSIDEREST; CONSIDERETH; CONSIDERING.
Ex 33:13 and c' that this nation is thy 7200
Le 13:13 Then the priest shall c': and, * "
De 4:39 Know therefore this day, and c' *7725
8: 5 Thou shalt also c' in thine heart, 3045
32: 7 c' the years of many generations: 995
29 that they would c' their latter end! "
J'g 18:14 now therefore c' what ye have to 3045
19:30 c' of it, take advice, and speak 7760
1Sa 12:24 for c' how great things he hath 7200
25:17 therefore know and c' what thou "
2Ki 5: 7 wherefore c', I pray you, and see 3045
Job 11:11 wickedness also; will he not then c' 995
23:15 when I c', I am afraid of him. "
34:27 and would not c' any of his ways: *7919
37:14 and c' the wondrous works of God. 995
Ps 5: 1 O Lord, c' my meditation. "
8: 3 When I c' thy heavens, the work 7200
9:13 c' my trouble which I suffer of * "
13: 3 C' and hear me, O Lord my God: 5027
25:19 C' mine enemies; for they are 7200
37:10 thou shalt diligently c' his place, 995
45:10 Hearken, O daughter, and c', 7200
48:13 well her bulwarks, c' her palaces; 6448
50:22 Now c' this, ye that forget God, 995
64: 9 they shall wisely c' of his doing. 7919
119:95 I will c' thy testimonies. 995
153 C' mine affliction, and deliver me: 7200
159 C' how I love thy precepts: "
Pr 6: 6 the ant, thou sluggard; c' her ways, "
23: 1 c' diligently what is before thee: 995
24:12 he that pondereth the heart c' it? "
Ec 5: 1 for they c' not that they do evil. *3045
7:13 C' the work of God: for who 7200
14 in the day of adversity c': God also "
Isa 1: 3 not know, my people doth not c'. 995
5:12 neither c' the operation of his 7200
14:16 narrowly look upon thee, and c' thee 995
18: 4 I will c' in my dwelling place *5027
41:20 they may see, and know, and c', 7760
22 that we may c' them, and 7760, 3820
43:18 neither c' the things of old. 995
52:15 they had not heard shall they c'. * "
Jer 2:10 and c' diligently, and see if there "
9:17 C' ye, and call for the mourning "
23:20 in the latter days ye shall c' it * "
30:24 in the latter days ye shall c' it. * "
La 1:11 see, O Lord, and c'; for I am *5027
2:20 Behold, O Lord, and c' to whom * "
5: 1 c', and behold our reproach. * "
Eze 12: 3 may be they will c', though they 7200
Da 9:23 the matter, and c' the vision. 995
Ho 7: 2 they c' not in their hearts that I 559
Hag 1: 5, 7 hosts; C' your ways. 7760, 3820, 5921
2:15 c' from this day and upward, 7760, 3820
18 C' now from this day and " "
18 Lord's temple was laid, c' it. " "
M't 6:28 C' the lilies of the field, how they 2648
Lu 12:24 C' the ravens: for they neither 2657
27 C' the lilies how they grow: they "
Joh 11:50 Nor c' that it is expedient for us, *1260
Ac 15: 6 came together for to c' of this 1492
2Ti 2: 7 C' what I say; and the Lord give 3539
Heb 3: 1 c' the Apostle and High Priest 2657
7: 4 Now c' how great this man was, 2334
10:24 let us c' one another to provoke 2657
12: 3 For c' him that endured such 357

considered
1Ki 3:21 but when I had c' it in the morning, 995
5: 8 I have c' the things which thou *8085
Job 1: 8 Hast thou c' my servant Job, 7760, 3820
2: 3 Hast thou c' my servant Job, " "
Ps 31: 7 thou hast c' my trouble; thou *7200
77: 5 have c' the days of old, the years 2803
Pr 24:32 I saw, and c' it well: I looked 7896, 3820
Ec 4: 1 and c' all the oppressions that *7200
4 Again, I c' all travail, and every * "
15 I c' all the living which walk * "
9: 1 I c' in my heart even to declare *5414
Da 7: 8 I c' the horns, and, behold, there 7920
M'r 6:52 For they c' not the miracle of the *4920
Ac 11: 6 I c', and saw fourfooted beasts 2657
12:12 And when he had c' the thing, 4894
Ro 4:19 he c' not his own body now dead, 2657

considerest
Jer 33:24 C' thou not what this people have 7200
M't 7: 3 but c' not the beam that is in 2657

considereth
Ps 33:15 hearts alike; he c' all their works. 995
41: 1 Blessed is he that c' the poor: 7919
Pr 21:12 wisely c' the house of the wicked: "
28:22 c' not that poverty shall come *3045
29: 7 The righteous c' the cause of the * "
31:16 She c' a field, and buyeth it: 2161
Isa 44:19 none c' in his heart, neither is *7725
Eze 18:14 and c', and doeth not such like, *7200
28 Because he c', and turneth away "

considering
Isa 57: 1 none c' that the righteous is taken 995
Da 8: 5 I was c', behold, an he goat came "
Ga 6: 1 c' thyself, lest thou also be *4648
Heb 13: 7 c' the end of their conversation. 333

consist See also CONSISTETH.
Col 1:17 things, and by him all things c'. 4921

consisteth
Lu 12:15 man's life c' not in the abundance 2076

consolation See also CONSOLATIONS.
Jer 16: 7 give them the cup of c' to drink 8575
Lu 2:25 waiting for the c' of Israel: 3874
6:24 for ye have received your c'. "
Ac 4:36 being interpreted, The son of c',) * "
15:31 had read, they rejoiced for the c'. "
Ro 15: 5 the God of patience and c' grant * "
2Co 1: 5 in us, so our c' also aboundeth * "
6 it is for your c' and salvation, "
6 we be comforted, it is for your c' * "
7 so shall ye be also of the c'. * "
7: 7 but by the c' wherewith he was * "
Ph'p 2: 1 any c' in Christ, if any comfort * "
2Th 2:16 given us everlasting c' and good * "
Ph'm 7 we have great joy and c' in thy * "
Heb 6:18 we might have a strong c', who * "

consolations
Job 15:11 Are the c' of God small with thee? 8575
21: 2 my speech, and let this be your c'. "
Isa 66:11 satisfied with the breasts of her c'; "

consorted
Ac 17: 4 believed, and c' with Paul and 4345

conspiracy
2Sa 15:12 the c' was strong; for the people 7195
2Ki 12:20 servants arose, and made a c', and "
14:19 Now they made a c' against "
15:15 acts of Shallum, and his c' "
30 the son of Elah made a c' "
17: 4 the king of Assyria found c' in "
2Ch 25:27 they made a c' against him "
Jer 11: 9 the Lord said unto me, A c' is "
Eze 22:25 There is a c' of her prophets in the "
Ac 23:13 than forty which had made this c'. 4945

conspirators
2Sa 15:31 Ahithophel is among the c' with 7194

conspired
Ge 37:18 they c' against him to slay him. 5230
1Sa 22: 8 all of you have c' against me, and 7194
13 Why have ye c' against me, thou "
1Ki 15:27 c' against him; and Baasha smote "
16: 9 c' against him, as he was in Tirzah "
16 Zimri hath c', and hath also slain "
2Ki 9:14 Jehoshaphat the son of Nimshi c' "
10: 9 I c' against my master, and slew "
15:10 And Shallum the son of Jabesh c' "
25 c' against him, and smote him in "
21:23 And the servants of Amon c' "
24 that had c' against king Amon; "
2Ch 24:21 And they c' against him, and "
25 his own servants c' against him for "
26 And these are they that c' against "
33:24 And his servants c' against him, "
25 slew all them that had c' against "
Ne 4: 8 c' all of them together to come "
Am 7:10 Amos hath c' against thee in the "

constant
1Ch 28: 7 he be c' to do my commandments 2388

constantly
Pr 21:28 man that heareth speaketh c'. ††5331
Ac 12:15 she c' affirmed that it was even *1340
Tit 3: 8 things I will that thou affirm c'. *1226

constellations
Isa 13:10 stars of heaven and the c' thereof 3685

constrain See also CONSTRAINED; CONSTRAINETH.
Ga 6:12 they c' you to be circumcised; * 315

constrained
2Ki 4: 8 she c' him to eat bread. And so 2388
M't 14:22 Jesus c' his disciples to get into a 315
M'r 6:45 straightway he c' his disciples to "
Lu 24:29 But they c' him, saying, Abide 3849
Ac 16:15 And she c' us. "
28:19 I was c' to appeal unto Cæsar; 315

constraineth
Job 32:18 the spirit within me c' me. 6693
2Co 5:14 the love of Christ c' us; because 4912

constraint
1Pe 5: 2 thereof, not by c', but willingly; 317

consult See also CONSULTED; CONSULTETH.
Ps 62: 4 They only c' to cast him down 3289

consultation
M'r 15: 1 priests held a c' with the elders 4824

consulted
1Ki 12: 6 Rehoboam c' with the old men, *3289
8 and c' with the young men that * "
1Ch 13: 1 And David c' with the captains of "
2Ch 20:21 when he had c' with the people, * "
Ne 5: 7 Then I c' with myself, and I 4427
Ps 83: 3 and c' against thy hidden ones. *3289
5 have c' together with one consent: "
Eze 21:21 he c' with images, he looked in 7592

Da 6: 7 have c' together to establish a 3272
Mic 6: 5 now what Balak, king of Moab c', 3289
Hab 2:10 Thou hast c' shame to thy house "
M't 26: 4 c' that they might take Jesus by *4823
Joh 12:10 the chief priests c' that they *1011

consulter
De 18:11 or a c' with familiar spirits, or a 7592

consulteth
Lu 14:31 c' whether he be able with ten *1011

consume See also CONSUMED; CONSUMETH; CONSUMING.
Ge 41:30 and the famine shall c' the land; 3615
Ex 32:10 that I may c' them: and I will "
12 c' them from the face of the earth? "
33: 3 people: lest I c' thee in the way. "
5 in a moment, and c' thee: therefore "
Le 26:16 that shall c' the eyes, and cause "
Nu 16:21 that I may c' them in a moment. "
45 that I may c' them as in a moment. "
De 5:25 this great fire will c' us: if we 398
7:16 And thou shalt c' all the people "
22 thou mayest not c' them at once, 3615
28:38 for the locust shall c' it. 2628
42 of thy land shall the locust c'. *3423
32:22 and shall c' the earth with her * 398
Jos 24:20 turn and do you hurt, and c' you, 3615
1Sa 2:33 to c' thine eyes, and to grieve thine "
2Ki 1:10, 12 heaven, and c' thee and thy fifty. 398
Ne 9:31 thou didst not utterly c' them, *3615
Es 9:24 to c' them, and to destroy them; 2000
Job 15:34 shall c' the tabernacles of bribery. 398
20:26 a fire not blown shall c' him; it * "
24:19 and heat c' the snow waters: 1497
Ps 37:20 c'; into smoke shall they c' away. 3615
39:11 thou makest his beauty to c' away 4529
49:14 their beauty shall c' in the grave 1086
59:13 C' them in wrath, c' them, that 3615
78:33 their days did he c' in vanity, "
Isa 7:20 and it shall also c' the beard. 5595
10:18 shall c' the glory of his forest, 3615
27:10 down, and c' the branches thereof. "
Jer 8:13 surely c' them, saith the Lord: 5486
14:12 I will c' them by the sword, and 3615
49:27 shall c' the palaces of Ben-hadad.* 398
Eze 4:17 and c' away for their iniquity. *4743
13:13 hailstones in my fury to c' it. 3615
20:13 them in the wilderness, to c' them. "
21:28 to c' because of the glittering: * 398
22:15 will c' thy filthiness out of thee. 8552
24:10 kindle the fire, c' the flesh, and * "
35:12 desolate, they are given us to c'. * 402
Da 2:44 and c' all these kingdoms, and it 5487
7:26 c' and to destroy it unto the end. 8046
Ho 11: 6 and shall c' his branches, and 3615
Zep 1: 2 c' all things from off the land, 5486
3 I will c' man and beast; "
3 I will c' the fowls of heaven, "
Zec 5: 4 and shall c' it with the timber 3615
14:12 Their flesh shall c' away 4743
12 eyes shall c' away in their holes, "
12 and their tongue shall c' away in "
Lu 9:54 down from heaven, and c' them, 355
2Th 2: 8 the Lord shall c' with the spirit * "
Jas 4: 3 that ye may c' it upon your lusts. *1159

consumed
Ge 19:15 lest thou be c' in the iniquity of 5595
17 to the mountain, lest thou be c'. "
31:40 in the day the drought c' me, and 398
Ex 3: 2 with fire, and the bush was not c'. "
15: 7 wrath, which c' them as stubble. * "
22: 6 standing corn, or the field, be c' "
Le 6:10 which the fire hath c' with the "
9:24 and c' upon the altar the burnt "
Nu 11: 1 and c' them that were in the * "
12:12 the flesh is half c' when he cometh "
14:35 in this wilderness they shall be c'. 8552
16:26 lest ye be c' in all their sins. 5595
35 c' the two hundred and fifty men * 398
17:13 shall we be c' with dying? *8552
21:28 hath c' Ar of Moab, and the lords * 398
25:11 I c' not the children of Israel in 3615
32:13 in the sight of the Lord, was c'. 8552
De 2:15 among the host, until they were c'. "
16 when all the men of war were c' "
28:21 he have c' thee from off the land, 3615
Jos 5: 6 which came out of Egypt, were c'. 8552
8:24 of the sword, until they were c', "
10:20 great slaughter, till they were c', "
J'g 6:21 and c' the flesh and the unleavened 398
1Sa 12:25 ye shall be c', both ye and your 5595
15:18 fight against them until they be c'. 3615
2Sa 21: 5 The man that c' us, and that "
22:38 not again until I had c' them. "
39 I have c' them, and wounded them, "
1Ki 18:38 and c' the burnt sacrifice, and the 398
22:11 Syrians, until thou have c' them. 3615
2Ki 1:10 heaven, and c' him and his fifty. 398
12 God came down from heaven, and c' "
7:13 of the Israelites that are c':) 8552
13:17 Syrians in Aphek, till thou have c' 3615
19 smitten Syria till thou hadst c' it: "
2Ch 7: 1 and c' the burnt offering and the 398
8: 8 whom the children of Israel c' not, 3615
18:10 shalt push Syria until they be c'. "
Ezr 9:14 till thou hadst c' us, so that "
Ne 2: 3 the gates thereof are c' with fire? 398
13 the gates thereof were c' with fire. "
Job 1:16 sheep, and the servants, and c' them; "
4: 9 breath of his nostrils are they c'. 3615
6:17 hot, they are c' out of their place. 1846
7: 9 cloud is c' and vanisheth away: 3615
19:27 though my reins be c' within me. "
33:21 His flesh is c' away, that it cannot "
Ps 6: 7 Mine eye is c' because of grief; *6244
Ps 18:37 did I turn again till they were c'. 3615
31: 9 mine eye is c' with grief, yea, *6244
10 iniquity, and my bones are c'. "
39:10 I am c' by the blow of thine hand. 3615
71:13 Let them be confounded and c' "
73:19 they are utterly c' with terrors. 8552
78:63 The fire c' their young men; and * 398
90: 7 we are c' by thine anger, and 3615
102: 3 For my days are c' like smoke, * "
104:35 Let the sinners be c' out of the 8552
119:87 They had almost c' me upon 3615
139 My zeal hath c' me, because mine 6789
Pr 5:11 thy flesh and thy body are c', 3615
Isa 1:28 that forsake the Lord shall be c'. "
16: 4 the oppressors are c' out of the 8552
29:20 scorner is c', and all that watch *3615
64: 7 c' us, because of our iniquities. 4127
66:17 shall be c' together, saith the *5486
Jer 5: 3 thou hast c' them, but they have 3615
6:29 the lead is c' of the fire; the 8552
9:16 after them, till I have c' them. 3615
10:25 devoured him, and c' him, and "
12: 4 the beasts are c', and the birds; 5595
14:15 famine shall those prophets be c'. 8552
16: 4 they shall be c' by the sword, and 3615
20:18 my days should be c' with shame? "
24:10 till they be c' from off the land 8552
27: 8 until I have c' them by his hand. "
36:23 until all the roll was c' in the fire "
44:12 and they shall all be c', and fall "
12 they shall even be c' by the sword "
18 have been c' by the sword and by "
27 are in the land of Egypt shall be c' "
49:37 after them, till I have c' them: 3615
La 2:22 brought up hath mine enemy c'. "
3:22 Lord's mercies that we are not c', 8552
Eze 5:12 with famine shall they be c' in the 3615
13:14 ye shall be c' in the midst thereof: "
19:12 and withered; the fire c' them. 398
22:31 I have c' them with the fire of my 3615
24:11 that the scum of it may be c'. 8552
34:29 be no more c' with hunger in the 622
43: 8 wherefore I have c' them in mine 398
47:12 shall the fruit thereof be c': *8552
Da 11:16 which by his hand shall be c'. *3615
Mal 3: 6 ye sons of Jacob are not c'. "
Ga 5:15 take heed that ye be not c' one of 355

consumeth
Job 13:28 he, as a rotten thing, c', as a 1086
22:20 the remnant of them the fire c'. * 398
31:12 it is a fire that c' to destruction, "
Isa 5:24 flame c' the chaff, so their root *7503

consuming
De 4:24 the Lord thy God is a c' fire, * 398
9: 3 as a c' fire he shall destroy them, * "
Heb 12:29 For our God is a c' fire. 2654

consummation
Da 9:27 until the c', and that determined 3617

consumption
Le 26:16 terror, c', and the burning ague, 7829
De 28:22 The Lord shall smite thee with a c', "
Isa 10:22 the c' decreed shall overflow with 3631
23 God of hosts shall make a c', *3617
28:22 a c', even determined upon the * "

contain See also CONTAINED; CONTAINETH; CONTAINING.
1Ki 8:27 heaven of heavens cannot c' thee; 3557
18:32 great as would c' two measures of 1004
2Ch 2: 6 heaven of heavens cannot c' him? 3557
6:18 heaven of heavens cannot c' thee; "
Eze 45:11 that the bath may c' the tenth 5375
Joh 21:25 even the world itself could not c' 5562
1Co 7: 9 if they cannot c', let them marry: *1467

contained
1Ki 7:26 of lilies: it c' two thousand baths. *3557
38 of brass: one laver c' forty baths: "
Ro 2:14 by nature the things c' in the law,*
Eph 2:15 of commandments c' in ordinances;
1Pe 2: 6 also it is c' in the scripture, 4023

containeth
Eze 23:32 and had in derision; it c' much. 3557

containing
Joh 2: 6 of the Jews, c' two or three firkins 5562

contemn See also CONTEMNED; CONTEMNETH.
Ps 10:13 Wherefore doth the wicked c' God? 5006
Eze 21:13 what if the sword c' even the rod? *3988

contemned
Ps 15: 4 In whose eyes a vile person is c'; * 959
107:11 c' the counsel of the most High: 5006
Ca 8: 7 for love, it would utterly be c'. 936
Isa 16:14 and the glory of Moab shall be c'. *7034

contemneth
Eze 21:10 it c' the rod of my son, as every 3988

contempt See also CONTEMPTIBLE.
Es 1:18 shall there arise too much c' and 963
Job 12:21 He poureth c' upon princes, and 937
31:34 or did the c' of families terrify me, "
Ps 107:40 He poureth c' upon princes, and "
119:22 Remove from me reproach and c'; "
123: 3 for we are exceedingly filled with c'. "
4 at ease, and with the c' of the proud. "
Pr 18: 3 wicked cometh, then cometh also c'. "
Isa 23: 9 to bring into c' all the honourable 7043
Da 12: 2 some to shame and everlasting c'. 1860

contemptible
Mal 1: 7 ye say, The table of the Lord is c'. 959
12 the fruit thereof, even his meat, is c'. "
2: 9 have I also made you c' and base "
2Co 10:10 is weak, and his speech c'. *1848

contemptuously
Ps 31:18 and c' against the righteous. * 937

contend See also CONTENDED; CONTENDEST; CONTENDETH; CONTENDING.
De 2: 9 neither c' with them in battle: 1624
24 possess it, and c' with him in battle. "
Job 9: 3 If he will c' with him, he cannot 7378
13: 8 his person? will ye c' for God? "
Pr 28: 4 such as keep the law c' with them. 1624
Ec 6:10 neither may he c' with him that 1777
Isa 49:25 I will c' with him that contendeth 7378
50: 8 who will c' with me? let us stand "
57:16 I will not c' for ever, neither will I "
Jer 12: 5 how canst thou c' with horses? 8474
18:19 the voice of them that c' with me. 3401
Am 7: 4 the Lord God called to c' by fire, 7378
Mic 6: 1 c' thou before the mountains, and "
Jude 3 ye should earnestly c' for the faith 1864

contended
Ne 13:11 Then c' I with the rulers, and 7378
17 Then I c' with the nobles of Judah, "
25 I c' with them, and cursed them, "
Job 31:13 when they c' with me; "
Isa 41:12 them, even them that c' with thee: 4695
Ac 11: 2 of the circumcision c' with him, 1252

contendest
Job 10: 2 me wherefore thou c' with me. 7378

contendeth
Job 40: 2 Shall he that c' with the Almighty *7378
Pr 29: 9 If a wise man c' with a foolish *8199
Isa 49:25 with him that c' with thee, and 3401

contending
Jude 9 when c' with the devil he disputed 1252

content
Ge 37:27 flesh. And his brethren were c'. *8085
Ex 2:21 And Moses was c' to dwell with 2974
Le 10:20 Moses heard that, he was c'. *3190, 5869
Jos 7: 7 would to God we had been c', and 2974
J'g 17:11 And the Levite was c' to dwell "
19: 6 Be c', I pray thee, and tarry all "
2Ki 5:23 Naaman said, Be c', take two "
6: 3 one said, Be c', I pray thee, and go * "
Job 6:28 Now therefore be c', look upon * "
Pr 6:35 neither will he rest c', though thou 14
M'r 15:15 Pilate, willing to c' the 2425, 3588, 4160
Lu 3:14 and be c' with your wages. 714
Ph'p 4:11 state I am, therewith to be c'. 842
1Ti 6: 8 raiment let us be therewith c'. 714
Heb 13: 5 be c' with such things as ye have: "
3Jo 10 with malicious words: and not c' "

contention See CONTENTIONS.
Pr 13:10 by pride cometh c': but with the 4683
17:14 leave off c', before it be meddled 7379
18: 6 A fool's lips enter into c', and his "
22:10 out the scorner, and c' shall go out; 4066
Jer 15:10 a man of c' to the whole earth! "
Hab 1: 3 there are that raise up strife and c'. "
Ac 15:39 And the c' was so sharp between 3948
Ph'p 1:16 The one preach Christ of c', not *2052
1Th 2: 2 the gospel of God with much c'. * 73

contentions
Pr 18:18 The lot causeth c' to cease, and 4079
19 and their c' are like the bars of a "
19:13 the c' of a wife are a continual "
23:29 who hath c'? who hath babbling? "
1Co 1:11 that there are c' among you. 2054
Tit 3: 9 genealogies, and c', and strivings* "

contentious
Pr 21:19 with a c' and an angry woman. 4066
26:21 so is a c' man to kindle strife. "
27:15 rainy day and a c' woman are alike. "
Ro 2: 8 But unto them that are c', *1537, 2052
1Co 11:16 But if any man seem to be c', 5380

contentment
1Ti 6: 6 godliness with c' is great gain. 841

continence See INCONTINENCY.

continual
Ex 29:42 a c' burnt offering throughout 8548
Nu 4: 7 the c' bread shall be thereon: "
28: 3 day by day, for a c' burnt offering. "
6 It is a c' burnt offering, which was "
10 the c' burnt offering, and his drink "
15 offered, beside the c' burnt offering, "
23 which is for a c' burnt offering. "
24 offered beside the c' burnt offering, "
31 them beside the c' burnt offering, "
29:11 and the c' burnt offering, and the "
16 beside the c' burnt offering, his "
19, 22 beside the c' burnt offering, and "
25 beside the c' burnt offering, his "
28 beside the c' burnt offering, and "
31, 34 beside the c' burnt offering, his "
38 beside the c' burnt offering, and "
2Ki 25:30 his allowance was a c' allowance "
2Ch 2: 4 for the c' shewbread, and for the "
Ezr 3: 5 the c' burnt offering, both of the "
Ne 10:33 for the c' meat offering, "
33 and for the c' burnt offering, "
Pr 15:15 of a merry heart hath a c' feast. "
19:13 of a wife are a c' dropping. 2956
27:15 A c' dropping in a very rainy day "
Isa 14: 6 wrath with a c' stroke, 1115, 5627
Jer 48: 5 c' weeping shall go up; for in "
52:34 a c' diet given him of the king 8548
Eze 39:14 sever out men of c' employment, "
46:15 morning for a c' burnt offering. "
Lu 18: 5 lest by her c' coming 1519, 5056
Ro 9: 2 great heaviness and c' sorrow * 88

continually
Ge 6: 5 of his heart was only evil c'. 3605, 3117
8: 3 returned from off the earth c': 1980, 7725
5 decreased c' until the tenth month: 1980
Ex 28:29 a memorial before the Lord c'. 8548
30 upon his heart before the Lord c'. "

Ex 29:38 of the first year day by day c'. 8548
Le 24: 2 to cause the lamps to burn c'. "
3 the morning before the Lord c': "
4 pure candlestick before the Lord c'. "
8 set it in order before the Lord c', "
Jos 6:13 went on c', and blew with the 1980
1Sa 18:29 became David's enemy c'. 3605, 3117
2Sa 9: 7 shalt eat bread at my table c'. 8548
13 he did eat c' at the king's table; "
15:12 people increased c' with Absalom. 1980
19:13 of the host before me c' 3605, 3117
1Ki 10: 8 which stand c' before thee, 8548
2Ki 4: 9 of God, which passeth by us c'. "
25:29 he did eat bread c' before him "
1Ch 16: 6 with trumpets c' before the ark "
11 his strength, seek his face c'. * "
37 to minister before the ark c', "
40 the altar of the burnt offering c' "
23:31 unto them, c' before the Lord: "
2Ch 9: 7 which stand c' before thee, "
12:15 Rehoboam and Jeroboam c'. 3605, 3117
24:14 house of the Lord c' all the days 8548
Job 1: 5 Thus did Job c'. 3605, 3117
Ps 34: 1 praise shall c' be in my mouth. 8548
35:27 let them say c', Let the Lord be "
38:17 and my sorrow is c' before me. "
40:11 and thy truth c' preserve me. "
16 salvation say c', The Lord be "
42: 3 and night, while they c' say 3605, 3117
44:15 My confusion is c' before * "
50: 8 to have been c' before me. 8548
52: 1 goodness of God endureth c'. 3605, 3117
58: 7 away as waters which run c': *
69:23 and make their loins c' to shake. 8548
70: 4 say c', Let God be magnified. "
71: 3 whereunto I may c' resort: "
6 my praise shall be c' of thee. "
14 I will hope c', and will yet praise "
72:15 also shall be made for him c'; "
73:23 Nevertheless I am c' with thee: "
74:23 rise up against thee increaseth c'. "
109:10 his children be c' vagabonds, *
15 Let them be before the Lord c', 8548
19 girdle wherewith he is girded c'. "
119:44 So shall I keep thy law c' for ever "
109 My soul is c' in my hand: "
117 have respect unto thy statutes c'. "
140: 2 c' are they gathered together 3605, 3117
Pr 6:14 he deviseth mischief c'; 6256
21 Bind them c' upon thine heart, 8548
Ec 1: 6 it whirleth about c', and the wind
Isa 21: 8 I stand c' upon the watchtower 8548
49:16 thy walls are c' before me. "
51:13 hast feared c' every day because "
52: 5 name c' every day is blasphemed. "
58:11 And the Lord shall guide thee c', "
60:11 thy gates shall be open c'; "
65: 3 that provoketh me to anger c' "
Jer 6: 7 before me is grief and wounds. "
33:18 and to do sacrifice c'. 3605, 3117
52:33 he did c' eat bread before him 8548
Eze 46:14 offering c' by a perpetual ordinance "
Da 6:16 Thy God whom thou servest c', 8411
20 is thy God, whom thou servest c', "
Ho 4:18 they have committed whoredom c': "
12: 6 and wait on thy God c'. 8548
Ob 16 so shall all the heathen drink c', "
Na 3:19 hath not thy wickedness passed c'? "
Hab 1:17 not spare c' to slay the nations? "
Lu 24:53 And were c' in the temple, 1725
Ac 6: 4 will give ourselves c' to prayer, *4342
10: 7 of them that waited on him c'; "
Ro 13: 6 attending c' upon this very thing. "
Heb 7: 3 of God; abideth a priest c'. 1519, 1336
10: 1 offered year by year c' make "
13:15 the sacrifice of praise to God c'. 1275

continuance
De 28:59 great plagues, and of long c', 539
59 and sore sicknesses, and of long c'. "
Ps 139:16 which in c' were fashioned, *3117
Isa 64: 5 in those is c', and we shall be *5769
Ro 2: 7 by patient c' in well doing seek *5281

continue See also CONTINUED; CONTINUETH; CONTINUING.
Ex 21:21 if he c' a day or two, he shall not 5975
Le 12: 4 she shall then c' in the blood of 3427
5 she shall c' in the blood of her "
1Sa 12:14 c' following the Lord your God: *1961
13:14 now thy kingdom shall not c': 6965
2Sa 7:29 it may c' for ever before thee: 1961
1Ki 2: 4 That the Lord may c' his word *6965
Job 15:29 neither shall his substance c', "
17: 2 doth not mine eye c' in their †‡3885
Ps 36:10 c' thy lovingkindness unto them 4900
49:11 is, that their houses shall c' for ever,
102:28 children of thy servants shall c'. 7931
119:91 They c' this day according to *5975
Isa 5:11 that c' until night, till wine * 309
Jer 32:14 that they may c' many days. 5975
Da 11: 8 shall c' more years than the king* "
M't 15:32 they c' with me now three days, 4357
Joh 8:31 If ye c' in my word, then are ye *3306
15: 9 I loved you: c' ye in my love. * "
Ac 13:43 them to c' in the grace of God. 1961
14:22 exhorting them to c' in the faith, 1696
26:22 I c' unto this day, witnessing *2476
Ro 6: 1 Shall we c' in sin, that grace 1961
11:22 if thou c' in his goodness: "
Gal 2: 5 of the gospel might c' with you. 1265
Ph'p 1:25 I shall abide and c' with you all *4839
Col 1:23 If ye c' in the faith grounded 1961
4: 2 C' in prayer, and watch in the 4342
1Ti 2:15 if they c' in faith and charity 3306
4:16 c' in them: for in doing this thou 1961
2Ti 3:14 c' thou in the things which thou *3306
Heb 7:23 suffered to c' by reason of death: *3887
13: 1 Let brotherly love c'. 3306
Jas 4:13 and c' there a year, and buy, *4160
2Pe 3: 4 all things c' as they were from 1265
1Jo 2:24 remain in you, ye also shall c' *3306
Re 13: 5 him to c' forty and two months. 4160
17:10 cometh, he must c' a short space. 3306

continued
Ge 40: 4 and they c' a season in ward. 1961
J'g 5:17 Asher c' on the seashore, *3427
Ru 1: 2 country of Moab, and c' there. 1961
2: 7 hath c' even from the morning 5975
1Sa 1:12 she c' praying before the Lord, 7235
2Sa 6:11 ark of the Lord c' in the house *3427
1Ki 22: 1 they c' three years without war "
2Ch 29:28 this c' until the burnt offering
Ne 5:16 also I c' in the work of this wall, 2388
Job 27: 1 Moreover Job c' his parable, and *3254
29: 1 Moreover Job c' his parable, and * "
Ps 72:17 shall be c' as long as the sun: 5125
Da 1:21 And Daniel c' even unto the 1961
Lu 6:12 and c' all night in prayer to God. 1273
22:28 c' with me in my temptations 1265
Joh 2:12 they c' there not many days. *3306
8: 7 So when they c' asking him, 1961
11:54 and there c' with his disciples. *1304
Ac 1:14 all c' with one accord in prayer 4342
2:42 they c' steadfastly in the apostles' "
8:13 he c' with Philip, and wondered, "
12:16 But Peter c' knocking, and when 1961
15:35 Paul also and Barnabas c' in *1304
18:11 c' there a year and six months, *2523
19:10 c' by the space of two years; 1096
20: 7 and c' his speech until midnight. *3905
27:33 c' fasting, having taken nothing. *1300
Heb 8: 9 they c' not in my covenant, 1696
1Jo 2:19 would no doubt have c' with us: 3306

continueth
Job 14: 2 fleeth also as a shadow, and c' not. 5975
Gal 3:10 every one that c' not in all things 1696
1Ti 5: 5 c' in supplications and prayers 4357
Heb 7:24 this man, because he c' ever, *3306
Jas 1:25 law of liberty, and c' therein, 3887

continuing
Jer 30:23 a c' whirlwind: it shall fall with *1641
Ac 2:46 And they, c' daily with one accord *4342
Ro 12:12 tribulations; c' instant in prayer; "
Heb 13:14 here have we no c' city, but we *3306

contradicting
Ac 13:45 were spoken by Paul, c' and * 483

contradiction
Heb 7: 7 without all c' the less is blessed * 485
12: 3 c' of sinners against himself, * "

contrariwise
2Co 2: 7 that c' ye ought rather to forgive 5121
Ga 2: 7 But c', when they saw that the "
1Pe 3: 9 railing for railing: but c' blessing; "

contrary See also CONTRARIWISE.
Le 26:21 if ye walk c' unto me, and will 7147
23 but will walk c' unto me; "
24 Then will I also walk c' unto you, "
27 but walk c' unto me; "
28 I will walk c' unto you also in fury; "
40 and that also they have walked c' "
41 I also have walked c' unto them, "
Es 9: 1 (though it was turned to the c',
Eze 16:34 the c' is in thee from other women 2016
34 unto thee, therefore thou art c'. "
M't 14:24 for the wind was c'. 1727
M'r 6:48 for the wind was c' unto them: "
Ac 17: 7 these all do c' to the decrees of 561
18:13 men to worship God c' to the law. 3844
23: 3 commandest me to be smitten c' to 3891
26: 9 many things c' to the name of 1727
27: 4 Cyprus, because the winds were c'. "
Ro 11:24 graffed c' to nature into a good 3844
16:17 c' to the doctrine which ye have "
Ga 5:17 these are c' the one to the other: 480
Col 2:14 which was c' to us, and took it out 5227
1Th 2:15 not God, and are c' to all men: 1727
1Ti 1:10 thing that is c' to sound doctrine; 480
Tit 2: 8 is of the c' part may be ashamed, 1727

contribution
Ro 15:26 to make a certain c' for the poor 2842

contrite
Ps 34:18 saveth such as be of a c' spirit. 1793
51:17 a broken and a c' heart, O God, 1794
Isa 57:15 also that is of a c' and humble 1793
15 to revive the heart of the c' ones. 1792
66: 2 him that is poor and of a c' spirit, 5223

controversies
2Ch 19: 8 judgment of the Lord, and for c', 7379

controversy See also CONTROVERSIES.
De 17: 8 being matters of c' within thy 7379
19:17 the men, between whom the c' is, "
21: 5 by their word shall every c' and "
25: 1 If there be a c' between men, "
2Sa 15: 2 any man that had a c' came to * "
Isa 34: 8 year of recompences for the c' of ‡ "
Jer 25:31 Lord hath a c' with the nations, "
Eze 44:24 in c' they shall stand in judgment; "
Ho 4: 1 the Lord hath a c' with the "
12: 2 Lord hath also a c' with Judah, "
Mic 6: 2 Hear ye, O mountains, the Lord's c', "
2 the Lord hath a c' with his people, "
1Ti 3:16 without c' great is the mystery 3672

convenient
Pr 30: 8 feed me with food c' for me: *2706
Jer 40: 4 whither it seemeth good and c' 3477
5 go wheresoever it seemeth c' unto "
M'r 6:21 And when a c' day was come, 2121
Ac 24:25 when I have a c' season, I will call 2540
Ro 1:28 do those things which are not c'; *2520
1Co 16:12 come when he shall have c' time. *2119
Eph 5: 4 nor jesting, which are not c': * 433
Ph'm 8 to enjoin thee that which is c', * "

conveniently
M'r 14:11 he sought how he might c' betray 2122

conversant
Jos 8:35 the strangers that were c' among 1980
1Sa 25:15 as long as we were c' with them, "

conversation
Ps 37:14 to slay such as be of upright c'. *1870
50:23 him that ordereth his c' aright ‡ "
2Co 1:12 we have had our c' in the world, * 390
Ga 1:13 ye have heard of my c' in time * 391
Eph 2: 3 we all had our c' in times past * 390
4:22 put off concerning the former c' * 391
Ph'p 1:27 let your c' be as it becometh the *4176
3:20 our c' is in heaven; from whence *4175
1Ti 4:12 in word, in c', in charity, in spirit, * 391
Heb 13: 5 your c' be without covetousness; *5158
7 considering the end of their c'. * 391
Jas 3:13 shew out of a good c' his works * "
1Pe 1:15 so be ye holy in all manner of c'; * "
18 from your vain c' received by * "
2:12 Having your c' honest among * "
3: 1 be won by the c' of the wives; * "
2 While they behold your chaste c' * "
16 falsely accuse your good c' in * "
2Pe 2: 7 with the filthy c' of the wicked: * "
3:11 be in all holy c' and godliness, * "

conversion
Ac 15: 3 declaring the c' of the Gentiles: 1995

convert See also CONVERTED; CONVERTETH; CONVERTING; CONVERTS.
Isa 6:10 with their heart, and c', and be *7725
Jas 5:19 from the truth, and one c' him; 1994

converted
Ps 51:13 and sinners shall be c' unto thee. 7725
Isa 60: 5 of the sea shall be c' unto thee, *2015
M't 13:15 and should be c', and I should *1994
18: 3 Except ye be c', and become as *4762
M'r 4:12 they should be c', and their sins *1994
Lu 22:32 and when thou art c', strengthen * "
Joh 12:40 and be c', and I should heal them. * "
Ac 3:19 Repent ye therefore, and be c', * "
28:27 should be c', and I should heal * "

converteth
Jas 5:20 he which c' the sinner from the 1994

converting
Ps 19: 7 of the Lord is perfect, c' the soul: *7725

converts
Isa 1:27 with judgment, and her c' with 7725

convey See also CONVEYED.
1Ki 5: 9 will c' them by sea in floats unto *7760
Ne 2: 7 river, that they may c' me over *5674

conveyed
Joh 5:13 for Jesus had c' himself away, 1593

convicted
Joh 8: 9 being c' by their own conscience, *1651

convince See also CONVINCED; CONVINCETH.
Tit 1: 9 exhort and to c' the gainsayers. *1651
Jude 15 to c' all that are ungodly among *1827

convinced
Job 32:12 there was none of you that c' Job, 3198
Ac 18:28 For he mightily c' the Jews, *1246
1Co 14:24 unlearned, he is c' of all, he is *1651
Jas 2: 9 c' of the law as transgressors. "

convinceth
Joh 8:46 Which of you c' me of sin? *1651

convocation See also CONVOCATIONS.
Ex 12:16 first day there shall be an holy c', 4744
16 seventh day there shall be an holy c' "
Le 23: 3 is the sabbath of rest, an holy c'; "
7 first day ye shall have an holy c': "
8 in the seventh day is an holy c': "
21 that it may be an holy c' unto you: "
24 of blowing of trumpets, an holy c'. "
27 of atonement: it shall be an holy c' "
35 On the first day shall be an holy c': "
36 the eighth day shall be an holy c' "
Nu 28:18 In the first day shall be an holy c'; "
25 seventh day ye shall have an holy c'; "
26 be out, ye shall have an holy c'; "
29: 1 the month, ye shall have an holy c'; "
7 of this seventh month an holy c'; "
12 month ye shall have an holy c'; "

convocations
Le 23: 2 ye shall proclaim to be holy c', 4744
4 the feasts of the Lord, even holy c', "
37 ye shall proclaim to be holy c', to "

cook See also COOKS.
1Sa 9:23 Samuel said unto the c', Bring the 2876
24 And the c' took up the shoulder, "

cooks
1Sa 8:13 to be confectionaries, and to be c', 2876

cool
Ge 3: 8 in the garden in the c' of the day; 7307
Lu 16:24 finger in water, and c' my tongue; 2711

Coos (*co'-os*)
Ac 21: 1 with a straight course unto C', 2972

copied
Pr 25: 1 Hezekiah king of Judah c' out. 6275

coping
1Ki 7: 9 from the foundation unto the c', 2947

copper See also COPPERSMITH.
Ezr 8:27 two vessels of fine c', precious as *5178

coppersmith
2Ti 4:14 Alexander the c' did me much *5471*

copulation
Le 15:16 if any man's seed of c' go out 7902
17 whereon is the seed of c', shall be "
18 whom man shall lie with seed of c', "

copy See also COPIED.
De 17:18 he shall write him a c' of this law 4932
Jos 8:32 a c' of the law of Moses, which he "
Ezr 4:11 This is the c' of the letter that 6573
23 when the c' of king Artaxerxes' "
5: 6 The c' of the letter that Tatnai, "
7:11 Now this is the c' of the letter that "
Es 3:14 The c' of the writing for a 6572
4: 8 the c' of the writing of the decree "
8:13 The c' of the writing for a "

cor
Eze 45:14 tenth part of a bath out of the c'. 3734

coral
Job 28:18 No mention shall be made of c', 7215
Eze 27:16 and fine linen, and c', and agate. "

Corban (*cor'-ban*)
M'r 7:11 It is C', that is to say, a gift, *2878*

cord See also ACCORD; CORDS; DISCORD; RECORD.
Jos 2:15 down by a c' through the window: 2256
Job 30:11 hath loosed my c', and afflicted 3499
41: 1 or his tongue with a c' which 2256
Ec 4:12 threefold c' is not quickly broken. 2339
12: 6 Or ever the silver c' be loosed, or 2256
Mic 2: 5 cast a c' by lot in the congregation* "

cords
Ex 35:18 the pins of the court, and their c', 4340
39:40 his c', and his pins, and all the "
Nu 3:26 c' of it for all the service thereof. "
37 sockets, their pins, and their c'. "
4:26 their c', and all the instruments of "
32 their pins, and their c', with all "
J'g 15:13 they bound him with two new c',*5688
14 the c' that were upon his arms * "
Es 1: 6 fastened with c' of fine linen and 2256
Job 36: 8 and be holden in c' of affliction; "
Ps 2: 3 and cast away their c' from us. 5688
118:27 with c', even unto the horns "
129: 4 cut asunder the c' of the wicked. "
140: 5 have hid a snare for me, and c'; 2256
Pr 5:22 be holden with the c' of his sins. "
Isa 5:18 that draw iniquity with c' of vanity, "
33:20 any of the c' thereof be broken. "
54: 2 lengthen thy c', and strengthen 4340
Jer 10:20 is spoiled, all my c' are broken: "
38: 6 they let down Jeremiah with c'. 2256
11 them down by c' into the dungeon "
12 under thine armholes under the c'. "
13 they drew up Jeremiah with c', "
Eze 27:24 of rich apparel, bound with c', "
Ho 11: 4 I drew them with c' of a man, with "
Joh 2:15 he had made a scourge of small c',*4979*

Core (*co'-ree*) See also KORAH.
Jude 11 perished in the gainsaying of C'. *2879*

coriander
Ex 16:31 and it was like c' seed, white; 1407
Nu 11: 7 And the manna was as c' seed, and "

Corinth (*cor'-inth*) See also CORINTHIANS; CORINTHUS.
Ac 18: 1 from Athens, and came to C'; *2882*
19: 1 while Apollos was at C', Paul "
1Co 1: 2 the church of God which is at C', to "
2Co 1: 1 church of God which is at C', with "
23 spare you I came not as yet unto C'. "
2Ti 4:20 Erastus abode at C': but "

Corinthians (*co-rin'-the-uns*)
Ac 18: 8 many of the C' hearing believed, *2881*
1Co *subscr.* The first epistle to the C' was * "
2Co 6:11 O ye C', our mouth is open unto "
subscr. The second epistle to the C' was* "

Corinthus (*co-rin'-thus*) See also CORINTH.
Ro *subscr.* Written to the Romans from C', *2882*

cormorant
Le 11:17 the little owl, and the c', and the 7994
De 14:17 and the gier eagle, and the c', "
Isa 34:11 c' and the bittern shall possess *6893
Zep 2:14 the c' and the bittern shall lodge * "

corn See also CORNFLOOR.
Ge 27:28 earth, and plenty of c' and wine: ‡1715
37 c' and wine have I sustained him: ‡ "
41: 5 seven ears of c' came up upon ‡
35 and lay up c' under the hand of ‡1250
49 Joseph gathered c' as the sand ‡
57 into Egypt to Joseph for to buy c';‡
42: 1 saw that there was c' in Egypt, ‡7668
2 heard that there is c' in Egypt: ‡
3 went down to buy c' in Egypt. ‡1250
5 the sons of Israel came to buy c' ‡
19 c' for the famine of your houses: ‡7668
25 to fill their sacks with c', and to ‡1250
26 laded their asses with the c', ‡7668
43: 2 the c' which they had brought ‡ "
44: 2 and his c' money. And he did ‡ "
45:23 ten she asses laden with c' and ‡1250
47:14 the c' which they had bought: ‡7668
Ex 22: 6 so that the stacks of c', ‡
6 or the standing c, or the field, ‡7054
Le 2:14 of the firstfruits green ears of c' ‡
14 even c' beaten out of full ears. ‡1643
16 part of the beaten c' thereof, and ‡ "
23:14 eat neither bread, nor parched c',‡ "
Nu 18:27 the c' of the threshingfloor, ‡1715
De 7:13 of thy land, thy c', and thy wine, ‡ "
11:14 gather in thy c', and thy wine, ‡ "
12:17 the tithe of thy c', or of thy wine, ‡ "
14:23 the tithe of thy c', of thy wine. ‡ "
De 16: 9 to put the sickle to the c'. ‡7054
13 that thou hast gathered in thy c', *1637
18: 4 also of thy c', of thy wine ‡1715
23:25 the standing c' of thy neighbour, ‡7054
25 unto thy neighbour's standing c'. ‡ "
25: 4 ox when he treadeth out the c'. ‡
28:51 leave thee either c', wine, or oil, ‡1715
33:28 be upon a land of c' and wine; ‡ "
Jos 5:11 did eat of the old c' of the land ‡5669
11 parched c' in the selfsame day. ‡
12 eaten of the old c' of the land; ‡5669
J'g 15: 5 the standing c' of the Philistines, ‡7054
5 shocks, and also the standing c', ‡ "
Ru 2: 2 glean ears of c' after him in ‡
14 he reached her parched c', and ‡
3: 7 down at the end of the heap of c':‡6194
1Sa 17:17 an ephah of this parched c', and ‡
25:18 five measures of parched c', and ‡
2Sa 17:19 and spread ground c' thereon; ‡7383
28 and parched c', and beans, and ‡
2Ki 4:42 and full ears of c' in the husk ‡3759
18:32 a land of c' and wine, a land of ‡1715
2Ch 31: 5 in abundance the firstfruits of c', ‡ "
32:28 for the increase of c', and wine, ‡ "
Ne 5: 2 therefore we take up c' for them, ‡ "
3 buy c', because of the dearth. ‡ "
10 exact of them money and c': * "
11 of the c', the wine, and the oil, ‡ "
10:39 offering of the c', of the new wine,‡ "
13: 5 vessels, and the tithes of the c', ‡ "
12 all Judah the tithe of the c' and ‡ "
Job 5:26 age, like as a shock of c' cometh ‡
24: 6 reap every one his c' in the field: *1098
24 off as the tops of the ears of c'. ‡
39: 4 grow up with c'; they go forth, *1250
Ps 4: 7 than in the time that their c' and ‡1715
65: 9 thou preparest them c', when "
13 also are covered over with c'; ‡1250
72:16 be an handful of c' in the earth ‡
78:24 given them of the c' of heaven. ‡1715
Pr 11:26 He that withholdeth c', the ‡1250
Isa 17: 5 the harvestman gathereth the c', ‡7054
21:10 threshing, and the c' of my floor: ‡1121
28:28 Bread c' is bruised; because he ‡
36:17 own land, a land of c' and wine, ‡1715
37:27 as c' blasted before it be grown up.‡
62: 8 no more give thy c' to be meat ‡1715
La 2:12 mothers, Where is c' and wine? ‡ "
Eze 36:29 call for the c', and will increase it,‡ "
Ho 2: 8 I gave her c', and wine, and oil, ‡ "
9 and take away my c' in the time ‡ "
22 the earth shall hear the c', and ‡ "
7:14 assemble themselves for c' and ‡ "
10:11 and loveth to tread out the c'; ‡
14: 7 they shall revive as the c', and ‡1715
Joe 1:10 the c' is wasted: the new wine is ‡ "
17 down; for the c' is withered. ‡ "
2:19 I will send you c', and wine, and ‡ "
Am 8: 5 be gone, that we may sell c'? ‡7668
9: 9 like as c' is sifted in a sieve, "
Hag 1:11 the mountains, and upon the c', ‡1715
Zec 9:17 c' shall make the young men ‡ "
M't 12: 1 the sabbath day through the c'; *4702*
1 and began to pluck the ears of c', *4719*
M'r 2:23 that he went through the c' fields*4702*
23 they went to pluck the ears of c'. *4719*
4:28 ear, after that the full c' in the ear. *4621*
Lu 6: 1 that he went through the c' fields;*4702*
1 disciples plucked the ears of c', *4719*
Joh 12:24 Except a c' of wheat fall into the *2848*
Ac 7:12 heard that there was c' in Egypt, *4621*
1Co 9: 9 of the ox that treadeth out the c'.
1Ti 5:18 muzzle the ox that treadeth out the c'.

Cornelius (*cor-ne'-le-us*)
Ac 10: 1 C', a centurion of the band *2883*
3 to him, and saying unto him, C'. "
7 which spake unto C' was departed,* "
17 the men which were sent from C' "
21 which were sent unto him from C':* "
22 said, C' the centurion, a just man, "
24 C' waited for them, and had called "
25 C' met him, and fell down at his "
30 C' said, Four days ago I was fasting "
31 C', thy prayer is heard, and thine "

corner See also CORNERS.
Ex 36:25 north c', he made twenty boards, *6285
Le 21: 5 shave off the c' of their beard, "
Jos 18:14 the c' of the sea southward, from * "
2Ki 11:11 from the right c' of the temple *3802
11 to the left c' of the temple, "
14:13 gate of Ephraim unto the c' gate, 6438
2Ch 25:23 gate of Ephraim to the c' gate, 6437
26: 9 towers in Jerusalem at the c' gate,6438
28:24 altars in every c' of Jerusalem. "
Ne 3:24 of the wall, even unto the c'. "
31 and to the going up of the c'. "
32 between the going up of the c' "
Job 38: 6 or who laid the c' stone thereof; "
Ps 118:22 become the head stone of the c'. "
144:12 daughters may be as c' stones, 2106
Pr 7: 8 through the street near her c'; 6438
12 and lieth in wait at every c'.) "
21: 9 to dwell in a c' of the housetop, "
25:24 to dwell in the c' of the housetop, "
Isa 28:16 precious c' stone, a sure foundation:"
30:20 thy teachers be removed into a c' *3671
Jer 31:38 Hananeel unto the gate of the c'. 6438
40 unto the c' of the horse gate "
48:45 shall devour the c' of Moab, and 6285
51:26 not take of thee a stone for a c', 6438
Eze 46:21 behold, in every c' of the court 4742
Am 3:12 in Samaria in the c' of a bed, 6285
Zec 10: 4 Out of him came forth the c', 6438
14:10 the c' gate, and from the tower 6434
M't 21:42 same is become the head of the c':*1137*
M'r 12:10 is become the head of the c': *1137*
Lu 20:17 same is become the head of the c'? "
Ac 4:11 which is become the head of the c'. "
26:26 for this thing was not done in a c'. "
Eph 2:20 Christ himself being the chief c' *204*
1Pe 2: 6 I lay in Sion a chief c' stone, elect, "
7 same is made the head of the c', *1137*

corner-gate See CORNER and GATE.

corners
Ex 25:12 put them in the four c' thereof; *6471
26 the rings in the four c' that are 6285
26:23 make for the c' of the tabernacle 4742
24 both; they shall be for the two c'. "
27: 2 horns of it upon the four c' thereof:6438
4 brasen rings in the four c' thereof.7098
30: 4 by the two c' thereof, upon the *6763
36:28 made he for the c' of the tabernacle4742
29 did to both of them in both the c'. "
37: 3 gold, to be set by the four c' of it; *6471
13 put the rings upon the four c' that 6285
27 by the two c' of it, upon the two *6763
38: 2 horns thereof on the four c' of it; 6438
Le 19: 9 not wholly reap the c' of thy field, 6285
27 shall not round the c' of your heads,"
27 shalt thou mar the c' of thy beard. "
23:22 riddance of the c' of thy field 6285
Nu 24:17 and shall smite the c' of Moab, "
De 32:26 said, I would scatter them into c', *6284
1Ki 7:30 four c' thereof had undersetters: *6471
34 to the four c' of one base: and the 6438
Ne 9:22 and didst divide them into c': *6285
Job 1:19 smote the four c' of the house, 6438
Isa 11:12 from the four c' of the earth. 3671
Jer 9:26 are in the utmost c', that dwell 6285
25:23 all that are in the utmost c', "
49:32 them that are in the utmost c'; "
Eze 7: 2 come upon the four c' of the land. 3671
41:22 and the c' thereof, and the length 4740
43:20 and on the four c' of the settle, 6438
45:19 upon the four c' of the settle of the "
46:21 to pass by the four c' of the court; 4742
22 In the four c' of the court there "
22 these four c' were of one measure.7106
Zec 9:15 bowls, and as the c' of the altar. 2106
M't 6: 5 in the c' of the streets, that they *1137*
Ac 10:11 knit at the four c', and let down *746*
11: 5 let down from heaven by four c'; "
Re 7: 1 standing on the four c' of the earth,*1137*

corner-stone See CORNER and STONE.

cornet See also CORNETS.
1Ch 15:28 with sound of the c', and with 7782
Ps 98: 6 With trumpets and sound of c' "
Da 3: 5 ye hear the sound of the c', flute, 7162
7 people heard the sound of the c', "
10 that shall hear the sound of the c', "
15 ye hear the sound of the c', flute, "
Ho 5: 8 Blow ye the c' in Gibeah, and the 7782

cornets
2Sa 6: 5 on timbrels, and on c', and on *4517
2Ch 15:14 and with trumpets, and with c'. 7782

cornfloor
Ho 9: 1 loved a reward upon every c'. 1637, 1715

corpse See also CORPSES.
M'r 6:29 they came and took up his c', *4430*

corpses
2Ki 19:35 behold, they were all dead c'. ‡6297
Isa 37:36 behold, they were all dead c'. ‡ "
Na 3: 3 c'; they stumble upon their c': 1472

correct See also CORRECTED; CORRECTETH.
Ps 39:11 thou with rebukes dost c' man 3256
94:10 the heathen, shall not he c'? 3198
Pr 29:17 C' thy son, and he shall give thee 3256
Jer 2:19 thine own wickedness shall c' thee, "
10:24 O Lord, c' me, but with judgment; "
30:11 I will c' thee in measure, and will "
46:28 but c' thee in measure; yet will I "

corrected
Pr 29:19 A servant will not be c' by words: 3256
Heb 12: 9 fathers of our flesh which c' us, *3810*

correcteth
Job 5:17 happy is the man whom God c': 3198
Pr 3:12 For whom the Lord loveth he c'; * "

correction
Job 37:13 whether for c', or for his land, 7626
Pr 3:11 neither be weary of his c': *8433
7:22 as a fool to the c' of the stocks; 4148
15:10 C' is grievous unto him that "
22:15 rod of c' shall drive it far from him. "
23:13 Withhold not c' from the child: "
Jer 2:30 they received no c': your own "
5: 3 they have refused to receive c': "
7:28 nor receiveth c': truth is perished,* "
Hab 1:12 thou hast established them for c'. 3198
Zep 3: 2 she received not c'; she trusted 4148
2Ti 3:16 for reproof, for c', for instruction *1882*

corrupt See also CORRUPTED; CORRUPTETH; CORRUPTIBLE; CORRUPTING.
Ge 6:11 The earth also was c' before God, 7843
12 it was c'; for all flesh had corrupted "
De 4:16 Lest ye c' yourselves, and make you "
25 and shall c' yourselves, and make a "
31:29 ye will utterly c' yourselves, "
Job 17: 1 breath is c', my days are extinct, *2254
Ps 14: 1 They are c', they have done 7843
38: 5 My wounds stink and are c' 4743
53: 1 C' are they, and have done 7843
73: 8 They are c', and speak wickedly *4167
Pr 25:26 troubled fountain, and a c' spring.*7843
Eze 20:44 according to your c' doings, O ye "
23:11 was more c' in her inordinate love "
Da 2: 9 have prepared lying and c' words 7844

Da 11:32 shall he c' by flatteries: but the *2610
Mal 1:14 sacrificeth unto the Lord a c' *7843
2: 3 I will c' your seed, and spread *1605
M't 6:19 where moth and rust doth c', and* 853
20 neither moth nor dust doth c', * "
7:17 a c' tree bringeth forth evil fruit. 4550
18 neither can a c' tree bring forth "
12:33 make the tree c', and his fruit c': "
Lu 6:43 tree bringeth not forth c' fruit; "
43 neither doth a c' tree bring forth "
1Co 15:33 evil communications c' good 5351
2Co 2:17 many, which c' the word of God: *2585
Eph 4:22 old man, which is c' according to 5351
29 Let no c' communication proceed 4550
1Ti 6: 5 disputings of men of c' minds, *1311
2Ti 3: 8 men of c' minds, reprobate *2704
Jude 10 those things they c' themselves. *5351
Re 19: 2 which did c' the earth with her "

corrupted
Ge 6:12 flesh had c' his way upon the earth.7843
Ex 8:24 land was c' by reason of the swarm "
32: 7 out of Egypt, have c' themselves: "
De 9:12 out of Egypt have c' themselves; "
32: 5 They have c' themselves, their * "
J'g 2:19 c' themselves more than their * "
Eze 16:47 wast c' more than they in all thy* "
28:17 thou hast c' thy wisdom by reason "
Ho 9: 9 They have deeply c' themselves, "
Zep 3: 7 rose early, and c' all their doings. "
Mal 2: 8 ye have c' the covenant of Levi, "
2Co 7: 2 we have c' no man, we have 5351
11: 3 your minds should be c' from the "
Jas 5: 2 Your riches are c', and your 4595

corrupters
Isa 1: 4 children that are c': they have *7843
Jer 6:28 brass and iron; they are all c'. * "

corrupteth
Lu 12:33 approacheth, neither moth c'. * 1311

corruptible See also INCORRUPTIBLE.
Ro 1:23 into an image made like to c' man, 5349
1Co 9:25 they do it to obtain a c' crown; "
15:53 this c' must put on incorruption, "
54 So when this c' shall have put on "
1Pe 1:18 were not redeemed with c' things, "
23 not of c' seed, but of incorruptible, "
3: 4 in that which is not c', even the * 862

corrupting
Da 11:17 the daughter of women, c' her: 7843

corruption See also INCORRUPTION.
Le 22:25 their c' is in them, and blemishes 4893
2Ki 23:13 the right hand of the mount of c', 4889
Job 17:14 said to c', Thou art my father: 7845
Ps 16:10 suffer thine Holy One to see c'. "
49: 9 still live for ever, and not see c'. "
Isa 38:17 delivered it from the pit of c': 1097
Da 10: 8 was turned in me into c', and I 4889
Jon 2: 6 thou brought up my life from c', *7845
Ac 2:27 suffer thine Holy One to see c'. 1312
31 in hell, neither his flesh did see c'. "
13:34 to return to c', he said on this wise, "
35 not suffer thine Holy One to see c'. "
36 laid unto his fathers, and saw c': "
37 whom God raised again, saw no c'. "
Ro 8:21 delivered from the bondage of c' 5356
1Co 15:42 It is sown in c'; it is raised in "
50 neither doth c' inherit incorruption. "
Ga 6: 8 shall of the flesh reap c'; but he "
2Pe 1: 4 escaped the c' that is in the world "
2:12 utterly perish in their own c'; * "
19 themselves are the servants of c': "

corruptly
2Ch 27: 2 And the people did yet c'. 7843
Ne 1: 7 We have dealt very c' against thee.2254

Cosam (*co'-sam*)
Lu 3:28 Addi, which was the son of C'. 2973

cost See COSTLY.
2Sa 19:42 have we eaten at all of the king's c'?
24:24 of that which doth c' me nothing. 2600
1Ch 21:24 nor offer burnt offerings without c'. "
Lu 14:28 not down first, and counteth the c'.1160

costliness
Re 18:19 ships in the sea by reason of her c'! 5094

costly
1Ki 5:17 c' stones, and hewed stones, 3368
7: 9 All these were of c' stones, "
10 the foundation was of c' stones, "
11 And above were c' stones, after the "
Joh 12: 3 of ointment of spikenard, very c', *4186
1Ti 2: 9 or gold, or pearls, or c' array: 4185

cotes See also SHEEPCOTES.
2Ch 32:28 of beasts, and c' for flocks. * 220

cottage See also COTTAGES.
Isa 1: 8 daughter of Zion is left as a c' in *5521
24:20 and shall be removed like a c'; *4412

cottages
Zep 2: 6 c' for shepherds, and folds for 3741

couch See also COUCHED; COUCHES; COUCHETH; COUCHING.
Ge 49: 4 thou it: he went up to my c'. 3326
Job 7:13 my c' shall ease my complaint; 4904
38:40 When they c' in their dens, and 7742
Ps 6: 6 I water my c' with my tears. 6210
Am 3:12 of a bed, and in Damascus in a c'. "
Lu 5:19 through the tiling with his c' into 2826
24 take up thy c', and go unto thine "

couched
Ge 49: 9 he c' as a lion, and as an old lion; 7257
Nu 24: 9 He c', he lay down as a lion, and 3766

couches
Am 6: 4 stretch themselves upon their c', 6210
Ac 5:15 and laid them on beds and c', 2895

coucheth
De 33:13 and for the deep that c' beneath, 7257

couching See also COUCHINGPLACE.
Ge 49:14 Issachar is a strong ass c' down 7257

couchingplace
Eze 25: 5 and the Ammonites a c' for flocks:*4769

could See also COULDEST.
Ge 13: 6 so that they c' not dwell together. 3201
27: 1 his eyes were dim, so that he c' not see, "
36: 7 were strangers c' not bear them 3201
37: 4 they hated him, and c' not speak "
41: 8 there was none that c' interpret them "
21 it c' not be known that they had "
24 there was none that c' declare it to me. "
43: 7 c' we certainly know that he "
45: 1 Then Joseph c' not refrain himself 3201
3 his brethren c' not answer him; "
48:10 dim for age, so that he c' not see. "
Ex 2: 3 when she c' not longer hide him, "
7:21 and the Egyptians c' not drink of "
24 for they c' not drink of the water of "
8:18 bring forth lice, but they c' not. "
9:11 magicians c' not stand before Moses "
12:39 out of Egypt, and c' not tarry, "
15:23 c' not drink of the waters of Marah, "
Nu 9: 6 c' not keep the passover on that "
Jos 7:12 the children of Israel c' not stand * "
15:63 of Judah c' not drive them out: "
17:12 children of Manasseh c' not drive "
J'g 1:19 c' not drive out the inhabitants of the
2:14 that they c' not any longer stand 3201
3:22 that he c' not draw the dagger out*
6:27 of the city, that he c' not do it by day,
12: 6 he c' not frame to pronounce it right.
14:14 they c' not in three days expound 3201
17: 8 to sojourn where he c' find a place:
20:16 one c' sling stones at an hair breadth,
Ru 3:14 rose up before one c' know another.
1Sa 3: 2 to wax dim, that he c' not see; 3201
4:15 eyes were dim, that he c' not see. "
10:21 they sought him, he c' not be found.
23:13 and went whithersoever they c' go.
30:10 they c' not go over the brook Besor.
21 so faint that they c' not follow David,
2Sa 1:10 I was sure that he c' not live after that
3:11 he c' not answer Abner a word 3201
17:20 had sought and c' not find them, "
22:39 wounded them, that they c' not *
1Ki 5: 3 David my father c' not build an 3201
8: 5 oxen, that c' not be told nor numbered
11 priests c' not stand to minister 3201
13: 4 he c' not pull it in again to him. "
14: 4 But Ahijah c' not see; for his eyes "
2Ki 3:26 the king of Edom; but they c' not. "
4:40 And they c' not eat thereof. "
16: 5 besieged Ahaz, but c' not overcome "
1Ch 12: 2 and c' use both the right hand and the
8 for the battle, that c' handle shield and
33 which c' keep rank; they were not of
38 All these men of war, that c' keep rank,
21:30 But David c' not go before it to 3201
2Ch 4:18 weight of the brass c' not be found out.
5: 6 which c' not be told nor numbered for
14 priests c' not stand to minister by 3201
7: 2 priests c' not enter into the house "
13: 7 tenderhearted, and c' not withstand
14:13 that they c' not recover themselves;
20:25 more than they c' carry away: and
25: 5 war, that c' handle spear and shield.
15 c' not deliver their own people *
29:34 c' not flay all the burnt offerings: 3201
30: 3 For they c' not keep it at that time, "
32:14 c' deliver his people out of mine "
34:12 all that c' skill of instruments
Ezr 2:59 c' not shew their father's house, 3201
3:13 the people c' not discern the noise of
5: 5 they c' not cause them to cease, *
Ne 7:61 c' not shew their father's house, 3201
8: 2 all that c' hear with understanding,
3 and those that c' understand; and
13:24 c' not speak in the Jews' language, 5234
Es 6: 1 that night c' not the king sleep, 5074
7: 4 the enemy c' not countervail the king's
9: 2 no man c' withstand them; for the fear
Job 4:16 It stood still, but I c' not discern the
16: 4 I also c' speak as ye do; if your souls
4 c' heap up words against you,
31:23 his highness I c' not endure. 3201
Ps 37:36 I sought him, but he c' not be found.
55:12 then I c' have borne it: neither was
73: 7 they have more than heart c' wish.
78:44 their floods, that they c' not drink.
Ca 5: 6 I sought him, but I c' not find him;
Isa 5: 4 c' have been done more to my vineyard,
7: 1 but c' not prevail against it. 3201
30: 5 of a people that c' not profit
33:23 c' not well strengthen their mast,
23 they c' not spread the sail:
41:28 asked of them, c' answer a word. *
46: 2 they c' not deliver the burden, 3201
Jer 6:15 ashamed, neither c' they blush: 3045
8:12 ashamed, neither c' they blush: "
15: 1 my mind c' not be toward this people:
20: 9 with forbearing, and I c' not stay. *3201
24: 2 c' not be eaten, they were so bad.
44:22 So that the Lord c' no longer bear,3201
La 4:14 men c' not touch their garments. * "
17 for a nation that c' not save us.
Eze 31: 8 in the garden of God c' not hide him:
47: 5 a river that I c' not pass over: 3201
5 a river that c' not be passed over.
Da 5: 8 but they c' not read the writing, 3546
15 they c' not shew the interpretation "
6: 4 but they c' find none occasion, nor 3202
8: 4 any that c' deliver out of his hand;
7 none that c' deliver the ram out of his
Ho 5:13 c' he not heal you, nor cure you *3201
Jon 1:13 they c' not: for the sea wrought,
M't 17:16 and they c' not cure him. 1410
19 Why c' not we cast him out? "
26:40 What, c' ye not watch with me 2480
27:24 When Pilate saw that he c' prevail *
M'r 1:45 insomuch that Jesus c' no more 1410
2: 4 And when they c' not come nigh "
3:20 that c' not so much as eat bread. "
5: 3 and no man c' bind him, no, not "
4 neither c' any man tame him. *2480
6: 5 he c' there do no mighty work, 1410
19 have killed him; but she c' not: "
7:24 man know it: but he c' not be hid. "
9:18 cast him out; and they c' not. *2489
28 privately, Why c' not we cast him 1410
14: 8 She hath done what she c': she is 2192
Lu 1:22 he came out, he c' not speak unto 1410
5:19 And when they c' not find by what*
6:48 that house, and c' not shake it: 2480
8:19 and c' not come to him for the 1410
43 physicians, neither c' be healed 2480
9:40 cast him out; and they c' not. 1410
13:11 and c' in no wise lift up herself. "
14: 6 And they c' not answer him again 2480
19: 3 who he was; and c' not for the 1410
48 And c' not find what they might do:
20: 7 that they c' not tell whence it *5342
26 And they c' not take hold of his *2480
Joh 9:33 were not of God, he c' do nothing. 1410
11:37 C' not this man, which opened the "
12:39 Therefore they c' not believe, "
21:25 even the world itself c' not contain*
Ac 4:14 they c' say nothing against it. 2192
11:17 what was I, that I c' withstand 1415
13:39 from which ye c' not be justified 1410
21:34 and when he c' not know the "
22:11 And when I c' not see for the
25: 7 Paul, which they c' not prove. 2480
27:15 and c' not bear up into the wind, 1410
43 that they which c' swim should "
Ro 8: 3 For what the law c' not do, 102
9: 3 For I c' wish that myself were
1Co 3: 1 And I, brethren, c' not speak unto 1410
13: 2 all faith, so that I c' remove *
2Co 3: 7 Israel c' not stedfastly behold 1410
13 Israel c' not stedfastly look to *
11: 1 Would to God ye c' bear with me
Ga 3:21 a law given which c' have given 1410
1Th 3: 1 when we c' no longer forbear,
5 cause, when I c' no longer forbear,
Heb 3:19 So we see that they c' not enter *1410
6:13 because he c' swear by no greater, 2192
9: 9 and sacrifices, that c' not make *1410
12:20 (For they c' not endure that which
Re 7: 9 great multitude, which no man c' 1410
14: 3 and no man c' learn that song but "

couldest
Jer 3: 5 and done evil things as thou c'. *3201
Eze 16:28 and yet c' not be satisfied. *
Da 2:47 seeing thou c' reveal this secret. *3202
M'r 14:37 c' not thou watch one hour? *2480
Joh 19:11 Thou c' have no power at all

coulter See also COULTERS.
1Sa 13:20 every man his share, and his c'. 855

coulters
1Sa 13:21 and for the c', and for the forks, 855

council See also COUNCILS.
Ps 68:27 princes of Judah and their c', 7277
M't 5:22 Raca, shall be in danger of the c': 4892
12:14 Pharisees went out, and held a c' *4824
26:59 and elders, and all the c', sought 4892
M'r 14:55 chief priests and all the c' sought "
15: 1 and scribes and the whole c', and "
Lu 22:66 and led him into their c', saying, "
Joh 11:47 chief priests and the Pharisees a c'. "
Ac 4:15 to go aside out of the c', they "
5:21 and called the c' together, and all "
27 they set them before the c': "
34 Then stood there up one in the c', "
41 from the presence of the c', "
6:12 him, and brought him to the c', "
15 And all that sat in the c', looking "
22:30 and all their c' to appear, and "
23: 1 Paul, earnestly beholding the c', "
6 he cried out in the c', Men and "
15 Now therefore ye with the c' signify "
20 down Paul to morrow into the c', "
28 I brought him forth into their c': "
24:20 while I stood before the c', "
25:12 he had conferred with the c', 4824

councils
M't 10:17 they will deliver you up to the c', 4892
M'r 13: 9 they shall deliver you up to c'; "

counsel See also COUNSELLED; COUNSELS.
Ex 18:19 I will give thee c', and God shall 3289
Nu 27:21 the priest, who shall ask c', for *
31:16 through the c' of Balaam, to 1697
De 32:28 For they are a nation void of c', 6098
Jos 9:14 and asked not c' at the mouth of
J'g 18: 5 Ask c', we pray thee, of God,
20: 7 give here your advice and c', 6098
18 and asked c' of God, and said,
23 and asked c' of the Lord, saying, *
1Sa 14:37 And Saul asked c' of God, Shall I
2Sa 15:31 turn the c' of Ahithophel into 6098
34 for me defeat the c' of Ahithophel. "
16:20 Give c' among you what we shall "
23 And the c' of Ahithophel, which he "

2Sa 16:23 so was all the c' of Ahithophel both 6098
17: 7 The c' that Ahithophel hath given "
11 I c' that all Israel be generally 3289
14 The c' of Hushai the Archite 6098
14 is better than the c' of Ahithophel. "
14 to defeat the good c' of Ahithophel, "
15 Thus and thus did Ahithophel c' 3289
23 saw that his c' was not followed, 6098
20:18 They shall surely ask c' at Abel: "
1Ki 1:12 let me, I pray thee, give thee c', 6098
12: 8 he forsook the c' of the old men, "
9 What c' give ye that we may 3289
13 forsook the old men's c' that they 6098
14 to them after the c' of the young "
28 Whereupon the king took c', and 3289
2Ki 6: 8 and took c' with his servants, "
18:20 I have c' and strength for the war.6098
1Ch 10:13 asking c' of one that had a familiar "
2Ch 10: 6 Rehoboam took c' with the old 3289
6 What c' give ye me to return "
8 forsook the c' which the old men 6098
8 and took c' with the young men 3289
13 forsook the c' of the old men, 6098
22: 5 He walked also after their c', and "
25:16 Art thou made of the king's c'? 3289
16 hast not hearkened unto my c'. 6098
30: 2 For the king had taken c', and 3289
23 whole assembly took c' to keep "
32: 3 He took c' with his princes and "
Ezr 10: 3 according to the c' of my lord, 6098
8 according to the c' of the princes "
Ne 4:15 God had brought their c' to nought, "
6: 7 and let us take c' together. 3289
Job 5:13 the c' of the froward is carried 6098
10: 3 shine upon the c' of the wicked? "
12:13 strength, he hath c' and "
18: 7 and his own c' shall cast him down. "
21:16 the c' of the wicked is far from me. "
22:18 but the c' of the wicked is far from "
29:21 waited, and kept silence at my c'. "
38: 2 Who is this that darkeneth c' by "
42: 3 Who is he that hideth c' without "
Ps 1: 1 walketh not in the c' of the ungodly, "
2: 2 the rulers take c' together, 3245
13: 2 How long shall I take c' in my 6098
14: 6 Ye have shamed the c' of the poor, "
16: 7 the Lord, who hath given me c': 3289
20: 4 own heart, and fulfil all thy c'. 6098
31:13 while they took c' together 3245
33:10 The Lord bringeth the c' of the 6098
11 The c' of the Lord standeth for "
55:14 We took sweet c' together, and 5475
64: 2 Hide me from the secret c' of the "
71:10 that lay wait for my soul take c' 3289
73:24 Thou shalt guide me with thy c', 6098
83: 3 They have taken crafty c' against 5475
106:13 works; they waited not for his c': 6098
43 they provoked him with their c', "
107:11 contemned the c' of the most High, "
Pr 1:25 ye have set at nought all my c', "
30 They would none of my c': "
8:14 C' is mine, and sound wisdom: "
11:14 Where no c' is, the people fall: *8458
12:15 that hearkeneth unto c' is wise. 6098
15:22 Without c' purposes are 5475
19:20 Hear c', and receive instruction, 6098
21 nevertheless the c' of the Lord, "
20: 5 C' in the heart of man is like deep "
18 Every purpose is established by c': "
21:30 nor c' against the Lord. "
24: 6 wise c' thou shalt make thy war: *8458
27: 9 of a man's friend by hearty c'. 6098
Ec 8: 2 I c' thee to keep the king's
Isa 5:19 the c' of the Holy One of Israel 6098
7: 5 have taken evil c' against thee, *3289
8:10 Take c' together, and it shall 6098
11: 2 the spirit of c' and might, "
16: 3 Take c', execute judgment; make "
19: 3 and I will destroy the c' thereof: "
11 the c' of the wise counsellers "
17 because of the c' of the Lord of * "
23: 8 hath taken this c' against Tyre, *3289
28:29 which is wonderful in c', 6098
29:15 hide their c' from the Lord, "
30: 1 Lord, that take c', but not of me; "
36: 5 I have c' and strength for war: "
40:14 With whom took he c', and who 3289
44:26 the c' of his messengers; 6098
45:21 let them take c' together: 3289
46:10 My c' shall stand, and I will do 6098
11 the man that executeth my c' "
Jer 18:18 nor c' from the wise, nor the word "
23 thou knowest all their c' against "
19: 7 I will make void the c' of Judah "
23:18 hath stood in the c' of the Lord, *5475
22 if they had stood in my c', * "
32:19 Great in c', and mighty in work: 6098
38:15 if I give thee c', wilt thou not 3289
49: 7 is c' perished from the prudent? 6098
20 hear the c' of the Lord, that he "
30 hath taken c' against you, "
50:45 hear ye the c' of the Lord, "
Eze 7:26 priest, and c' from the ancients. "
11: 2 and give wicked c' in this city: "
Da 2:14 answered with c' and wisdom 5843
4:27 let my c' be acceptable unto thee, 4431
Ho 4:12 My people ask c' at their stocks, "
10: 6 shall be ashamed of his own c'. 6098
Mic 4:12 neither understand they his c': "
Zec 6:13 c' of peace shall be between them "
M't 22:15 took c' how they might entangle 4824
27: 1 and elders of the people took c' "
7 And they took c', and bought "
28:12 and had taken c', they gave large "
M'r 3: 6 took c' with the Herodians "
Lu 7:30 lawyers rejected the c' of God 1012
23:51 consented to the c' and deed of 1012
Joh 11:53 they took c' together for to put 4823
18:14 was he which gave c' to the Jews, "
Ac 2:23 determinate c' and foreknowledge 1012
4:28 thy hand and thy c' determined "
5:33 heart, and took c' to slay them. *1011
38 this c' or this work be of men, 1012
9:23 the Jews took c' to kill him: *4823
20:27 declare unto you all the c' of God. 1012
27:42 soldiers' c' was to kill the prisoners, "
Eph 1:11 after the c' of his own will: "
Heb 6:17 the immutability of his c', "
Re 3:18 I c' thee to buy of me gold 4823

counselled
2Sa 16:23 which he c' in those days, was as if 3289
17:15 and thus and thus have I c'. "
21 hath Ahithophel c' against you. "
Job 26: 3 How hast thou c' him that hath "

counseller See also COUNSELLERS; COUNSELLOR.
[*Most editions have uniformly* COUNSELLOR *and* COUNSELLORS.]
2Sa 15:12 David's c', from his city, even 3289
1Ch 26:14 for Zechariah his son, a wise c', "
27:32 Jonathan David's uncle was a c', "
33 Ahithophel was the king's c': "
2Ch 22: 3 mother was his c' to do wickedly. "
Isa 3: 3 the c', and the cunning artificer, "
9: 6 shall be called Wonderful, C', "
40:13 Who being his c' hath taught him? 6098
41:28 there was no c', that, when I asked 3289
Mic 4: 9 is thy c' perished? for pangs have "
Na 1:11 against the Lord, a wicked c'. * "

counsellers
2Ch 22: 4 they were his c' after the death 3289
Ezr 4: 5 hired c' against them, to frustrate "
7:14 of the king, and of his seven c', 3272
15 king and his c' have freely offered "
28 me before the king, and his c', 3289
8:25 which the king, and his c', "
Job 3:14 With kings and c' of the earth, "
12:17 He leadeth c' away spoiled, "
Ps 119:24 also are my delight and my c'. 6098
Pr 11:14 multitude of c' there is safety. 3289
12:20 but to the c' of peace is joy. "
15:22 in the multitude of c' they are "
24: 6 multitude of c' there is safety. "
Isa 1:26 and thy c' as at the beginning: "
19:11 counsel of the wise c' of Pharaoh "
Da 3: 2, 3 treasurers, the c', the sheriffs, 1884
24 said unto his c', Did not we cast 1907
27 king's c', being gathered together, "
4:36 c' and my lords sought unto me; "
6: 7 c', and the captains, have consulted "

counsellor See also COUNSELLER.
M'r 15:43 of Arimathæa, an honourable c', 1010
Lu 23:50 was a man named Joseph, a c'; "
Ro 11:34 or who hath been his c'? 4825

counsels
Job 37:12 turned round about by his c': *8458
Ps 5:10 let them fall by their own c'; 4156
81:12 and they walked in their own c'. "
Pr 1: 5 shall attain unto wise c': 8458
12: 5 the c' of the wicked are deceit. "
22:20 things in c' and knowledge, 4156
Isa 25: 1 thy c' of old are faithfulness 6098
47:13 in the multitude of thy c'. "
Jer 7:24 in the c' and in the imagination 4156
Ho 11: 6 them, because of their own c'. "
Mic 6:16 ye walk in their c'; that I should "
1Co 4: 5 manifest the c' of the hearts: 1012

count See also ACCOUNT; COUNTED; COUNTETH; COUNTING; RECOUNT.
Ex 12: 4 shall make your c' for the lamb. 3699
Le 19:23 c' the fruit thereof as uncircumcised: "
23:15 c' unto you from the morrow 5608
25:27 c' the years of the sale thereof, 2803
52 then he shall c' with him, * "
Nu 23:10 Who can c' the dust of Jacob, 4487
1Sa 1:16 C' not thine handmaid for a 5414
Job 19:15 my maids, c' me for a stranger: 2803
31: 4 see my ways, and c' all my steps? *5608
Ps 87: 6 The Lord shall c', when he writeth "
139:18 If I should c' them, they are "
22 I c' them mine enemies. 1961
Mic 6:11 Shall I c' them pure with the *
Ac 20:24 neither c' I my life dear unto *2192
Ph'p 3: 8 I c' all things but loss for the 2233
8 do c' them but dung, that I may "
13 Brethren, I c' not myself to have 3049
2Th 1:11 God would c' you worthy of this 515
3:15 c' him not as an enemy, but 2233
1Ti 6: 1 c' their own masters worthy of "
Ph'm 17 If thou c' me therefore a partner, 2192
Jas 1: 2 c' it all joy when ye fall into 2233
5:11 we c' them happy which endure. *3106
2Pe 2:13 as they that c' it pleasure to riot 2233
3: 9 as some men c' slackness; but is "
Re 13:18 hath understanding c' the number 5585

counted
Ge 15: 6 he c' it to him for righteousness. 2803
30:33 that shall be c' stolen with me. "
31:15 Are we not c' of him strangers? 2803
Ex 38:21 as it was c', according to the 6485
Le 25:31 shall be c' as the fields of the *2803
Nu 18:30 it shall be c' unto the Levites "
Jos 13: 3 is c' to the Canaanite: five lords "
1Ki 1:21 son Solomon shall be c' offenders. "
3: 8 be numbered nor c' for multitude. 5608
1Ch 21: 6 But Levi and Benjamin c' he not 6485
23:24 they were c' by number of names "
Ne 13:13 they were c' faithful, and their 2803
Job 18: 3 Wherefore are we c' as beasts, "
41:29 Darts are c' as stubble: he "
Ps 44:22 we are c' as sheep for the slaughter. "
88: 4 I am c' with them that go down 2803
106:31 was c' unto him for righteousness "
Pr 17:28 he holdeth his peace, is c' wise: "
27:14 it shall be c' a curse to him. "
Isa 5:28 horses' hoofs shall be c' like flint, "
32:15 the fruitful field be c' for a forest. "
33:18 where is he that c' the towers? 5608
40:15 are c' as the small dust of the 2803
17 are c' to him less than nothing, "
Ho 8:12 they were c' as a strange thing. "
M't 14: 5 because they c' him as a prophet 2192
M'r 11:32 men c' John, that he was a prophet.* "
Ac 5:41 that they were c' worthy to suffer 2661
19:19 they c' the price of them, and found 4860
Ro 2:26 shall not his uncircumcision be c' *3049
4: 3 c' unto him for righteousness. * "
5 his faith is c' for righteousness * "
9: 8 of the promise are c' for the seed. * "
Ph'p 3: 7 gain to me, those I c' loss for 2233
2Th 1: 5 may be c' worthy of the kingdom 2661
1Ti 1:12 that he c' me faithful, putting me 2233
5:17 well be c' worthy of double honour, 515
Heb 3: 3 was c' worthy of more glory than "
7: 6 whose descent is not c' from them 1075
10:29 hath c' the blood of the covenant, 2233

countenance See also COUNTENANCES.
Ge 4: 5 Cain was very wroth, and his c' fell. 6440
6 why is thy c' fallen? "
31: 2 Jacob beheld the c' of Laban, "
5 I see your father's c', that it is "
Ex 23: 3 Neither shalt thou c' a poor man *1921
Nu 6:26 The Lord lift up his c' upon thee, 6440
De 28:50 nation of fierce c', which shall not "
J'g 13: 6 his c' was like the c' of an angel 4758
1Sa 1:18 eat, and her c' was no more sad. 6440
16: 7 Look not on his c', or on the 4758
12 of a beautiful c', and goodly 5869
17:42 youth, and ruddy, and of a fair c'. 4758
25: 3 and of a beautiful c': 8389
2Sa 14:27 she was a woman of a fair c'. 4758
2Ki 8:11 And he settled his c' stedfastly, 6440
Ne 2: 2 Why is thy c' sad, seeing thou art "
3 why should not my c' be sad, "
Job 14:20 thou changest his c', and sendest "
29:24 light of my c' they cast not down. "
Ps 4: 6 lift thou up the light of thy c' "
10: 4 through the pride of his c', 639
11: 7 his c' doth behold the upright. *6440
21: 6 him exceeding glad with thy c'. * "
42: 5 praise him for the help of his c'. "
11 health of my c', and my God. "
43: 5 health of my c', and my God. "
44: 3 light of thy c', because thou hadst "
80:16 they perish at the rebuke of thy c'. "
89:15 walk, O Lord, in the light of c': "
90: 8 secret sins in the light of thy c'. "
Pr 15:13 merry heart maketh a cheerful c': "
16:15 the light of the king's c' is life; "
25:23 an angry c' a backbiting tongue. "
27:17 sharpeneth the c' of his friend. "
Ec 7: 3 by the sadness of the c' the heart "
Ca 2:14 let me see thy c', let me hear 4758
14 is thy voice, and thy c' is comely. "
5:15 his c' is as Lebanon, excellent as * "
Isa 3: 9 The shew of their c' doth witness 6440
Eze 27:35 they shall be troubled in their c'. "
Da 1:13 and the c' of the children that 4758
5: 6 the king's c' was changed, and 2122
9 his c' was changed in him, and "
10 nor let thy c' be changed: "
7:28 and my c' changed in me: but I "
8:23 a king of fierce c', and 6440
M't 6:16 the hypocrites, of a sad c': 4659
28: 3 His c' was like lightning, and his *2397
Lu 9:29 his c' was altered, and 4383
Ac 2:28 make me full of joy with thy c'. "
2Co 3: 7 of Moses for the glory of his c'; * "
Re 1:16 and his c' was as the sun shineth 3799

countenances
Da 1:13 Then let our c' be looked upon 4758
15 their c' appeared fairer and "

countervail
Es 7: 4 the enemy could not c' the king's *7737

counteth
Job 19:11 he c' me unto him as one of his 2803
33:10 he c' me for his enemy, "
Lu 14:28 and c' the cost, whether he hath 5585

counting
Ec 7:27 saith the preacher, c' one by one, *

countries
Ge 10:20 after their tongues, in their c', * 776
26: 3 give all these c', and I will * "
4 give unto thy seed all these c'; * "
41:57 all c' came into Egypt to Joseph "
Jos 13:32 These are the c' which Moses did*
14: 1 And these are the c' which the *
17:11 and her towns, even three c'. *5316
2Ki 18:35 gods of the c', that have delivered 776
1Ch 22: 5 and of glory throughout all c': "
29:30 over all the kingdoms of the c'. "
2Ch 11:23 all the c' of Judah and Benjamin,* "
12: 8 service of the kingdoms of the c'. "
15: 5 upon all the inhabitants of the c'.* "
20:29 on all the kingdoms of those c', "
34:33 out of all the c' that pertained "
Ezr 3: 3 because of the people of those c': "
4:20 over all c' beyond the river; *
Ps 110: 6 wound the heads over many c'. 776
Isa 8: 9 and give ear, all ye of far c': "
37:18 waste all the nations, and their c', "
Jer 23: 3 my flock out of all c' whither I have "
8 from all c' whither I had driven "
28: 8 prophesied both against many c', "
32:37 will gather them out of all c', "

Jer 40:11 that were in all the c', heard that 776
Eze 5: 5 the nations and c' that are round "
6 more than the c' that are round "
6: 8 be scattered throughout the c'. "
11:16 have scattered them among the c', "
16 them as a little sanctuary in the c' "
17 assemble you out of the c' where "
12:15 and disperse them in the c'. "
20:23 and disperse them through the c'; "
32 heathen, as the families of the c', "
34 gather you out of the c' wherein "
41 c' wherein ye have been scattered; "
22: 4 and a mocking to all c'. "
15 disperse thee in the c', and will "
25: 7 cause thee to perish out of the c': "
29:12 midst of the c' that are desolate, "
12 will disperse them through the c'. "
30: 7 midst of the c' that are desolate, "
23 disperse them through the c'. "
26 and disperse them among the c'; "
32: 9 the c' which thou hast not known. "
34:13 and gather them from the c', "
35:10 and these two c' shall be mine, "
36:19 were dispersed through the c': "
24 gather you out of all c', and will "
Da 9: 7 all the c' whither thou hast driven "
11:40 he shall enter in the c', and shall "
41 many c' shall be overthrown: "
42 forth his hand also upon the c': 776
Zec 10: 9 they shall remember me in far c'; "
Lu 21:21 that are in the c' enter thereinto. *5561*

country See also COUNTRIES; COUNTRYMEN.
Ge 12: 1 Get thee out of thy c', and from thy 776
14: 7 smote all the c' of the Amalekites, 7704
19:28 the smoke of the c' went up as * 776
20: 1 toward the south c', and dwelled * "
24: 4 thou shalt go unto my c', and to "
62 for he dwelt in the south c'. * "
25: 6 lived, eastward, unto the east c'. * "
29:26 It must not be so done in our c', *4725
30:25 mine own place, and to my c'. 776
32: 3 the land of Seir, the c' of Edom. *7704
9 Return unto thy c', and to thy 776
34: 2 Hivite, prince of the c', saw her, * "
36: 6 went into the c' from the face of * "
42:30 and took us for spies of the c'. "
33 man, the lord of the c', said unto * "
47:27 of Egypt, in the c' of Goshen; * "
Le 16:29 whether it be one of your own c', * 249
17:15 whether it be one of your own c', * "
24:22 stranger, as for one of your own c': * "
25:31 be counted as the fields of the c': 776
Nu 15:13 All that are born of the c' shall do * 249
20:17 pass, I pray thee, through thy c': * 776
21:20 c' of Moab, to the top of Pisgah, *7704
32: 4 the c' which the Lord smote * 776
33 the cities of the c' round about. * "
De 3:14 Manasseh took all the c' of Argob *2256
4:43 in the plain c', of the Reubenites; 776
26: 3 come unto the c' which the Lord * "
Jos 2: 2 of Israel to search out the c'. * "
3 be come to search out all the c'. * "
24 the inhabitants of the c' do faint * "
6:22 men that had spied out the c', * "
27 was noised throughout all the c'. * "
7: 2 Go up and view the c'. And the * "
9: 6 We be come from a far c': now "
9 From a very far c' thy servants are "
11 inhabitants of our c' spake to us, "
10:40 Joshua smote all the c' of the hills, "
41 and all the c' of Goshen, even unto "
11:16 all the south c', and all the land "
12: 7 the kings of the c' which Joshua * 776
8 and in the south c'; the Hittites, * "
13: 6 of the hill c' from Lebanon "
21 of Sihon, dwelling in the c'. * 776
17:15 then get thee up to the wood c', * "
19:51 made an end of dividing the c'. * 776
21:11 Hebron, in the hill c' of Judah, "
22: 9 to go unto the c' of Gilead, to the * 776
J'g 8:28 c' was in quietness forty years * "
11:21 Amorites, the inhabitants of that c'. "
12:12 in Aijalon in the c' of Zebulun. * "
16:24 the destroyer of our c', which slew "
18:14 that went to spy out the c' of Laish, "
20: 6 c' of the inheritance of Israel: 7704
Ru 1: 1 to sojourn in the c' of Moab, he, "
2 And they came into the c' of Moab, "
6 might return from the c' of Moab: "
6 for she had heard in the c' of Moab "
22 returned out of the c' of Moab: "
2: 6 with Naomi out of the c' of Moab: "
4: 3 come again out of the c' of Moab, "
1Sa 6: 1 c' of the Philistines seven months "
18 of fenced cities, and of c' villages, 6521
14:21 the camp from the c' round about, "
27: 5 me a place in some town in the c', 7704
7 the time that David dwelt in the c' "
11 dwelleth in the c' of the Philistines. "
2Sa 15:23 all the c' wept with a loud voice, 776
18: 8 scattered over the face of all the c': "
21:14 in the c' of Benjamin in Zelah, "
1Ki 4:19 the son of Uri was in the c' of * "
19 Gilead, in the c' of Sihon king * "
30 the children of the east c', and all * "
8:41 out of a far c' for thy name's sake; 776
10:13 turned and went to her own c', * "
15 and of the governors of the c'. "
11:21 that I may go to mine own c', "
22 thou seekest to go to thine own c'? "
20:27 but the Syrians filled the c'. "
22:36 and every man to his own c'. "
2Ki 3:20 and the c' was filled with water. * "
24 the Moabites, even in their c'. * "
18:35 delivered their c' out of mine hand, 776
20:14 They are come from a far c', even "

1Ch 8: 8 begat children in the c' of Moab, *7704
20: 1 the c' of the children of Ammon, 776
2Ch 6:32 a far c' for thy great name's sake, "
9:14 governors of the c' brought gold "
26:10 in the low c', and in the plains: * "
28:18 invaded the cities of the low c', * "
30:10 the c' of Ephraim and Manasseh 776
Ne 12:28 plain c' round about Jerusalem, * "
Pr 25:25 soul, so is good news from a far c'. 776
Isa 1: 7 Your c' is desolate, your cities are "
13: 5 They come from a far c', from the "
22:18 toss thee like a ball into a large c': "
39: 3 are come from a far c' unto me, "
46:11 executeth my counsel from a far c': "
Jer 2: 7 I brought you into a plentiful c', * "
4:16 watchers come from a far c', and "
6:20 and the sweet cane from a far c'? "
22 a people cometh from the north c', "
8:19 them that dwell in a far c': * "
10:22 great commotion out of the north c', "
22:10 no more, nor see his native c'. "
26 another c', where ye were not born; "
23: 8 out of the north c', and from all "
31: 8 I will bring them from the north c', "
32: 8 which is in the c' of Benjamin: * "
44: 1 Noph, and in the c' of Pathros, "
46:10 hath a sacrifice in the north c' by "
47: 4 the remnant of the c' of Caphtor. * 339
48:21 upon the plain c'; upon Holon, 776
50: 9 great nations from the north c': "
51: 9 let us go every one into his own c': "
Eze 20:38 out of the c' where they sojourn, * "
42 into the c' for the which I lifted up "
25: 9 the glory of the c', Beth-jeshimoth, "
32:15 and the c' shall be destitute of * "
34:13 in all the inhabited places of the c'. "
47: 8 issue out toward the east c', *1552
22 be unto you as born in the c' * 249
Ho 12:12 Jacob fled into the c' of Syria, *7704
Jon 1: 8 what is thy c'? and of what people 776
4: 2 saying, when I was yet in my c'? 127
Zec 6: 6 go forth into the north c'; and the 776
6 go forth toward the south c'. "
8 that go toward the north c' have "
8 quieted my spirit in the north c'. "
8: 7 save my people from the east c', "
7 and from the west c'; "
M't 2:12 into their own c' another way. *5561*
8:28 side into the c' of the Gergesenes, "
9:31 abroad his fame in all that c'. *1093*
13:54 he was come into his own c', he *3968*
57 without honour, save in his own c', "
14:35 all that c' round about, and *4066*
21:33 and went into a far c': *589*
25:14 a man travelling into a far c', who "
M'r 5: 1 into the c' of the Gadarenes. *5561*
10 not send them away out of the c'. "
14 told it in the city, and in the c'. *68*
6: 1 and came into his own c'; and *3968*
4 without honour, but in his own c', "
36 go into the c' round about, and into *68*
56 into villages, or cities, or c', "
12: 1 husbandmen, and went into a far c'. *589*
15:21 coming out of the c', the father of *68*
16:12 they walked, and went into the c'. "
Lu 1:39 and went into the hill c' with haste, "
65 throughout all the hill c' of Judæa, "
2: 8 were in the same c' shepherds *5561*
3: 3 into all the c' about Jordan, *4066*
4:23 Capernaum, do also here in thy c'. *3968*
24 prophet is accepted in his own c'. "
37 every place of the c' round about. *4066*
8:26 at the c' of the Gadarenes, which *5561*
34 and told it in the city and in the c'. *68*
37 c' of the Gadarenes round about *4066*
9:12 may go into the towns and c' round *68*
15:13 took his journey into a far c', and *5561*
15 joined himself to a citizen of that c'; "
19:12 went into a far c' to receive for "
20: 9 went into a far c' for a long time. *589*
23:26 a Cyrenian, coming out of the c', *68*
Joh 4:44 hath no honour in his own c'. *3968*
11:54 unto a c' near to the wilderness, *5561*
55 went out of the c' up to Jerusalem "
Ac 4:36 a Levite, and of the c' of Cyprus, *1085*
7: 3 Get the out of thy c', and from *1093*
12:20 c' was nourished by the king's c'. *5561*
13: 7 deputy of the c', Sergius Paulus, * "
18:23 all the c' of Galatia and Phrygia *5561*
27:27 that they drew near to some c'; "
Heb 11: 9 of promise, as in a strange c', "
14 declare plainly that they seek a c'. *3968*
15 mindful of that c' from whence "
16 But now they desire a better c', "

countrymen
2Co 11:26 in perils by mine own c', in perils *1085*
1Th 2:14 suffered like things of your own c', *4853*

couple See also COUPLED; COUPLETH; COUPLING.
Ex 26: 6 and c' the curtains together with 2266
9 c' five curtains by themselves, "
11 and c' the tent together, that it "
36:18 of brass to c' the tent together, "
39: 4 shoulderpieces for it, to c' it * "
J'g 19: 3 servant with him, and a c' of asses: 6776
2Sa 13: 6 make me a c' of cakes in my sight, 8147
16: 1 him, with a c' of asses saddled, 6776
Isa 21: 7 a chariot with a c' of horsemen, * "
9 of men, with a c' of horsemen. * "

coupled
Ex 26: 3 five curtains shall be c' together 2266
3 c' one to another. "
24 they shall be c' together beneath, *8382
24 they shall be c' together above *8535
36:10 And he c' the five curtains one 2266
10 five curtains he c' one unto another. "

Ex 36:13 and c' the curtains one unto 2266
16 And he c' five curtains by "
29 And they were c' beneath, *8382
29 c' together at the head thereof, *8535
39: 4 by the two edges was it c'. *2266
1Pe 3: 2 chaste conversation c' with fear.

coupleth
Ex 26:10 the edge of the curtain which c' *2279
36:17 of the curtain which c' the second. * "

coupling See also COUPLINGS.
Ex 26: 4 from the selvedge in the c'; 2279
4 curtain, in the c' of the second. 4225
5 that is in the c' of the second; "
10 curtain that is outmost in the c', 2279
28:27 over against the other c' thereof, 4225
36:11 from the selvedge in the c': "
11 side of another curtain, in the c' "
12 which was in the c' of the second: "
17 edge of the curtain in the c', "
39:20 over against the other c' thereof, "

couplings
2Ch 34:11 buy hewn stone, and timber for c', 4226

courage See also DISCOURAGE; ENCOURAGE.
Nu 13:20 And be ye of good c', and bring 2388
De 31: 6 Be strong and of a good c', fear not 553
7, 23 Be strong and of a good c': for "
Jos 1: 6 Be strong and of a good c': for unto "
9 Be strong and of a good c'; be not "
18 only be strong and of a good c'. "
2:11 did there remain any more c' *7307
10:25 be strong and of good c': for thus 553
2Sa 10:12 Be of good c', and let us play the 2388
1Ch 19:13 Be of good c', and let us behave "
22:13 be strong, and of good c'; dread not, 553
28:20 Be strong and of good c', and do it: "
2Ch 15: 8 Oded the prophet, he took c', and 2388
Ezr 10: 4 with thee: be of good c', and do it. "
Ps 27:14 Wait on the Lord: be of good c', "
31:24 Be of good c', and he shall "
Isa 41: 6 said to his brother, Be of good c'. "
Da 11:25 shall stir up his power and his c' 3824
Ac 28:15 saw, he thanked God, and took c'. *2294*

courageous
Jos 1: 7 Only be thou strong and very c', 553
23: 6 Be ye therefore very c' to keep 2388
2Sa 13:28 I commanded you? be c', and be "
2Ch 32: 7 Be strong and c', be not afraid * 553
Am 2:16 And he that is c' among the 533, 3820

courageously
2Ch 19:11 Deal c', and the Lord shall be 2388

course See also CONCOURSE; COURSES; WATER-COURSE.
1Ch 27: 1 of every c' were twenty and four 4256
2 Over the first c' for the first month "
2 in his c' were twenty and four "
4 over the c' of the second month "
4 and of his c' was Mikloth also the "
4 in his c' likewise were twenty and "
5 and in his c' were twenty and four "
6 and in his c' was Ammizabad his "
7, 8, 9, 10, 11, 12, 13, 14, 15 and in his
c' were twenty and four thousand. 4256
28: 1 that ministered to the king by c', "
2Ch 5:11 and did not then wait by c': * "
Ezr 3:11 And they sang together by c' in * "
Ps 82: 5 of the earth are out of c'. *4131
Jer 8: 6 every one turned to his c', as the 4794
23:10 their c' is evil, and their force is "
Lu 1: 5 Zacharias, of the c' of Abia: *2183*
8 before God in the order of his c', "
Ac 13:25 as John fulfilled his c', he said, *1408*
16:11 we came with a straight c' to *2113*
20:24 that I might finish my c' with joy, *1408*
21: 1 we came with a straight c' unto *4144*
7 when we had finished our c' from * "
1Co 14:27 three, and that by c'; and let one *3313*
Eph 2: 2 according to the c' of this world, *165*
2Th 3: 1 word of the Lord may have free c', *5143*
2Ti 4: 7 I have finished my c', I have kept *1408*
Jas 3: 6 setteth on fire the c' of nature; *5164*

courses
J'g 5:20 stars in their c' fought against 4546
1Ki 5:14 ten thousand a month by c': a 2487
1Ch 23: 6 divided them into c' among the 4256
27: 1 the king in any matter of the c', "
28:13 Also for the c' of the priests and "
21 behold, the c' of the priests and the "
2Ch 8:14 the c' of the priests to their service, "
14 the porters also by their c' at every "
23: 8 the priest dismissed not the c'. "
31: 2 appointed the c' of the priests and "
2 and the Levites after their c', "
15 to give to their brethren by c', as "
16 their charges according to their c'; "
17 in their charges by their c'; "
35: 4 fathers, after your c', according to "
10 the Levites in their c', according to "
Ezr 6:18 and the Levites in their c', for the 4255
Isa 44: 4 as willows by the water c'. *2988

court See also COURTS.
Ex 27: 9 thou shalt make the c' of the 2691
9 hangings for the c' of fine twined "
12 the breadth of the c' on the west "
13 the breadth of the c' on the east "
16 for the gate of the c' shall be an "
17 the pillars round about the c' shall "
18 The length of the c' shall be an "
19 all the pins of the c', shall be of "
35:17 The hangings of the c', his pillars, "
17 the hanging for the door of the c', "
18 the pins of the c', and their cords, "
38: 9 he made the c': on the south side "
9 the hangings of the c' were of fine "

Ex 38:15 And for the other side of the c' 2691
16 All the hangings of the c' round "
17 and all the pillars of the c' were "
18 the hanging for the gate of the c' "
18 answerable to the hangings of the c'. "
20 and of the c' round about, were of "
31 the sockets of the c' round about, "
31 and the sockets of the c' gate, "
31 all the pins of the c' round about. "
39:40 The hangings of the c', his pillars, "
40 the hanging for the c' gate, his "
40: 8 thou shalt set up the c' round "
8 hang up the hanging at the c' gate. "
33 he reared up the c' round about "
33 set up the hanging of the c' gate. "
Le 6:16 place; in the c' of the tabernacle "
26 be eaten, in the c' of the tabernacle "
Nu 3:26 the hangings of the c', and the "
26 curtain for the door of the c', "
37 And the pillars of the c' round "
4:26 And the hangings of the c', and the "
26 the door of the gate of the c', "
32 the pillars of the c' round about, "
2Sa 17:18 which had a well in his c'; whither "
1Ki 6:36 he built the inner c' with three "
7: 8 another c' within the porch, which "
9 on the outside toward the great c'. "
12 And the great c' round about was "
12 both for the inner c' of the house "
8:64 hallow the middle of the c' that "
2Ki 20: 4 was gone out into the middle c', *5892
2Ch 4: 9 he made the c' of the priests, 2691
9 and the great c', 5835
9 and doors for the c', "
6:13 and had set it in the midst of the c': "
7: 7 hallowed the middle of the c' that 2691
20: 5 house of the Lord, before the new c', "
24:21 in the c' of the house of the Lord. "
29:16 into the c' of the house of the Lord. "
Ne 3:25 that was by the c' of the prison. "
Es 1: 5 in the c' of the garden of the king's "
2:11 before the c' of the women's house, "
4:11 unto the king into the inner c', "
5: 1 stood in the inner c' of the king's "
2 Esther the queen standing in the c', "
6: 4 the king said, Who is in the c'? "
4 into the outward c' of the king's "
5 Behold, Haman standeth in the c'. "
Isa 34:13 of dragons, and a c' for owls. 2681
Jer 19:14 he stood in the c' of the Lord's 2691
26: 2 Stand in the c' of the Lord's house, "
32: 2 was shut up in the c' of the prison, "
8 came to me in the c' of the prison "
12 Jews that sat in the c' of the prison. "
33: 1 yet shut up in the c' of the prison, "
36:10 in the higher c', at the entry of the "
20 they went in to the king into the c', "
37:21 Jeremiah into the c' of the prison, "
21 remained in the c' of the prison. "
38: 6 that was in the c' of the prison: "
13 remained in the c' of the prison. "
28 abode in the c' of the prison until "
39:14 Jeremiah out of the c' of the prison, "
15 shut up in the c' of the prison, "
Eze 8: 7 brought me to the door of the c'; "
16 brought me into the inner c' of the "
10: 3 and the cloud filled the inner c'. "
4 the c' was full of the brightness "
5 was heard even to the outer c', "
40:14 unto the post of the c' round about "
17 brought he me into the outer c', "
17 a pavement made for the c' round "
19 forefront of the inner c' without, "
20 gate of the outward c' that looked "
23 the gate of the inner c' was over "
27 a gate in the inner c' toward "
28 he brought me to the inner c' "
31 thereof were toward the utter c'; "
32 he brought me into the inner c' "
34 were toward the outward c'; "
37 thereof were toward the utter c'; "
44 the singers in the inner c', which "
47 measured the c', an hundred cubits "
41:15 temple, and the porches of the c'; "
42: 1 brought me forth into the utter c', "
3 cubits which were for the inner c', "
3 which was for the utter c', "
7 toward the utter c' on the forepart "
8 chambers that were in the utter c' "
9 goeth into them from the utter c'. "
10 the thickness of the wall of the c' "
14 the holy place into the utter c', "
43: 5 and brought me into the inner c'; "
44:17 enter in at the gates of the inner c', "
17 minister in the gates of the inner c', "
19 they go forth into the utter c', "
19 even into the utter c' to the people, "
21 when they enter into the inner c'. "
27 unto the inner c', to minister "
45:19 posts of the gate of the inner c'. "
46: 1 gate of the inner c' that looketh "
20 bear them not out into the utter c', "
21 brought me forth into the utter c', "
21 me to pass by the corners of the c'; "
21 corner of the c' there was a c'. "
22 corners of the c' there were courts "
Am 7:13 chapel, and it is the king's c'. *1004
Re 11: 2 the c' which is without the temple *833*

courteous
1Pe 3: 8 as brethren, be pitiful, be c': *5391*

courteously
Ac 27: 3 Julius c' entreated Paul, *5364*
28: 7 us, and lodged us three days c'. *5390*

courts
2Ki 21: 5 two c' of the house of the Lord. 2691
23:12 Manasseh had made in the two c' 2691
1Ch 23:28 in the c', and in the chambers, "
28: 6 he shall build my house and my c': "
12 of the c' of the house of the Lord, "
2Ch 23: 5 all the people shall be in the c' of "
33: 5 two c' of the house of the Lord. "
Ne 8:16 roof of his house, and in their c', "
16 and in the c' of the house of God, "
13: 7 preparing him a chamber in the c' "
Ps 65: 4 thee, that he may dwell in thy c': "
84: 2 even fainteth for the c' of the Lord: "
10 For a day in thy c' is better than "
92:13 shall flourish in the c' of our God. "
96: 8 an offering, and come into his c'. "
100: 4 into his c' with praise: be thankful "
116:19 In the c' of the Lord's house, "
135: 2 in the c' of the house of our God, "
Isa 1:12 this at your hand, to tread my c'? "
62: 9 drink it in the c' of my holiness. "
Eze 9: 7 and fill the c' with the slain: "
42: 6 not pillars as the pillars of the c': "
46:22 were c' joined of forty cubits long "
Zec 3: 7 and shalt also keep my c', and I will "
Lu 7:25 live delicately, are in the king's c'.

cousin See also COUSINS.
Lu 1:36 And, behold, thy c' Elizabeth, *4773*

cousins
Lu 1:58 her neighbours and her c' heard *4773*

covenant See also COVENANTBREAKERS; COVENANTED; COVENANTS.
Ge 6:18 with thee will I establish my c'; 1285
9: 9 behold, I establish my c' with you, "
11 I will establish my c' with you; "
12 This is the token of the c' which "
13 shall be for a token of a c' between "
15 I will remember my c', which is "
16 the everlasting c' between God "
17 This is the token of the c', which "
15:18 the Lord made a c' with Abram, "
17: 2 I will make my c' between me and "
4 for me, behold, my c' is with thee, "
7 I will establish my c' between me "
7 for an everlasting c', to be a God "
9 Thou shalt keep my c' therefore, "
10 This is my c', which ye shall keep, "
11 a token of the c' betwixt me and "
13 and my c' shall be in your flesh "
13 in your flesh for an everlasting c'. "
14 his people; he hath broken my c'. "
19 I will establish my c' with him "
19 with him for an everlasting c', "
21 my c' will I establish with Isaac, "
21:27 and both of them made a c'. "
32 Thus they made a c' at Beer-sheba: "
26:28 and let us make a c' with thee; "
31:44 let us make a c', I and thou; "
Ex 2:24 God remembered his c' with "
6: 4 I have also established my c' with "
5 and I have remembered my c'. "
19: 5 and keep my c', then ye shall be "
23:32 Thou shalt make no c' with them, "
24: 7 And he took the book of the c', "
8 Behold, the blood of the c', which "
31:16 generations, for a perpetual c'. "
34:10 Behold, I make a c': before all "
12 lest thou make a c' with the "
15 Lest thou make a c' with the "
27 of these words I have made a c' "
28 upon the tables the words of the c', "
Le 2:13 the salt of the c' of thy God to be "
24: 8 of Israel by an everlasting c'. "
26: 9 and establish my c' with you. "
15 but that ye break my c': "
25 shall avenge the quarrel of my c': "
42 will I remember my c' with Jacob, "
42 and also my c' with Isaac, "
42 and also my c' with Abraham "
44 and to break my c' with them: for "
45 remember the c' of their ancestors, "
Nu 10:33 the ark of the c' of the Lord went "
14:44 the ark of the c' of the Lord, and "
18:19 it is a c' of salt for ever before the "
25:12 I give unto him my c' of peace: "
13 the c' of an everlasting priesthood; "
De 4:13 And he declared unto you his c', "
23 lest ye forget the c' of the Lord "
31 nor forget the c' of thy fathers "
5: 2 Lord our God made a c' with us in "
3 The Lord made not this c' with our "
7: 2 thou shalt make no c' with them, "
9 keepeth c' and mercy with them "
12 God shall keep unto thee the c' and "
8:18 that he may establish his c' which "
9: 9 the tables of the c' which the Lord "
11 stone, even the tables of the c'. "
15 the two tables of the c' were in my "
10: 8 to bear the ark of the c' of the Lord, "
17: 2 in transgressing his c', "
29: 1 These are the words of the c', "
1 the c' which he made with them "
9 Keep therefore the words of this c', "
12 That thou shouldest enter into c' "
14 with you only do I make this c' "
21 curses of the c' that are written "
25 have forsaken the c' of the Lord "
31: 9 which bare the ark of the c' of the "
16 break my c' which I have made "
20 and provoke me, and break my c'. "
25 which bare the ark of the c' of the "
26 in the side of the ark of the c' of "
33: 9 thy word, and kept thy c'. "
Jos 3: 3 When ye see the ark of the c' of "
6 Take up the ark of the c', and pass "
6 they took up the ark of the c', "
8 that bear the ark of the c', saying, "
Jos 3:11 the ark of the c' of the Lord of the 1285
14 bearing the ark of the c' before the "
17 priests that bare the ark of the c' "
4: 7 cut off before the ark of the c' of "
9 which bare the ark of the c' stood: "
18 bare the ark of the c' of the Lord "
6: 6 Take up the ark of the c', "
8 and the ark of the c' of the Lord "
7:11 also transgressed my c' which I "
15 he hath transgressed the c' of the "
8:33 which bare the ark of the c' of "
23:16 When ye have transgressed the c' "
24:25 Joshua made a c' with the people "
J'g 2: 1 I will never break my c' with you. "
20 people hath transgressed my c' "
20:27 the ark of the c' of God was there "
1Sa 4: 3 Let us fetch the ark of the c' of the "
4 from thence the ark of the c' of the "
4 there with the ark of the c' of God. "
5 the ark of the c' of the Lord came "
11: 1 Make a c' with us, and we will "
2 condition will I make a c' with you,* "
18: 3 Jonathan and David made a c', 1285
20: 8 brought thy servant into a c' of the "
16 Jonathan made a c' with the house "
23:18 two made a c' before the Lord: 1285
2Sa 15:24 bearing the ark of the c' of God: "
23: 5 made with me an everlasting c', "
1Ki 3:15 and stood before the ark of the c' "
6:19 there the ark of the c' of the Lord. "
8: 1 might bring up the ark of the c' of "
6 brought in the ark of the c' of the "
9 when the Lord made a c' with the "
21 wherein is the c' of the Lord, 1285
23 who keepest c' and mercy with "
11:11 thou hast not kept my c' and my "
19:10, 14 of Israel have forsaken thy c', "
20:34 send thee away with this c'. "
34 So he made a c' with him, "
2Ki 11: 4 and made a c' with them, and took "
17 Jehoiada made a c' between the "
13:23 because of his c' with Abraham, "
17:15 c' that he made with their fathers, "
35 With whom the Lord had made a c'. "
38 the c' that I have made with you "
18:12 but transgressed his c', and all "
23: 2 words of the book of the c' which "
3 made a c' before the Lord, to walk "
3 words of this c' that were written "
3 And all the people stood to the c'. "
21 it is written in the book of this c'. "
1Ch 11: 3 David made a c' with them in "
15:25 went to bring up the ark of the c' "
26 Levites that bare the ark of the c' "
28 Israel brought up the ark of the c' "
29 the ark of the c' of the Lord came "
16: 6 before the ark of the c' of God. "
15 Be ye mindful always of his c'; "
16 Even of the c' which he made "
17 to Israel for an everlasting c', "
37 before the ark of the c' of the Lord "
17: 1 but the ark of the c' of the Lord "
22:19 bring the ark of the c' of the Lord, "
28: 2 house of rest for the ark of the c' "
18 and covered the ark of the c' of "
2Ch 5: 2 the ark of the c' of the Lord out 1285
7 brought in the ark of the c' of "
10 when the Lord made a c' with "
6:11 wherein is the c' of the Lord, 1285
14 which keepest c', and shewest "
13: 5 and to his sons by a c' of salt? "
15:12 into a c' to seek the Lord "
21: 7 because of the c' that he had made "
23: 1 son of Zichri, into c' with him. "
3 congregation made a c' with the "
16 Jehoiada made a c' between him, "
29:10 a c' with the Lord God of Israel, "
34:30 the book of the c' that was found "
31 made a c' before the Lord, "
31 to perform the words of the c' "
32 did according to the c' of God, "
Ezr 10: 3 let us make a c' with our God "
Ne 1: 5 that keepeth c' and mercy for them "
9: 8 madest a c' with him to give the land "
32 God, who keepest c' and mercy, "
38 we make a sure c', and write "
13:29 and the c' of the priesthood, and 1285
Job 31: 1 I made a c' with mine eyes; why "
41: 4 Will he make a c' with thee? "
Ps 25:10 as keep his c' and his testimonies. "
14 and he will shew them his c'. "
44:17 have we dealt falsely in thy c'. "
50: 5 made a c' with me by sacrifice. "
16 shouldest take my c' in thy mouth? "
55:20 with him: he hath broken his c'. "
74:20 have respect unto the c': for "
78:10 They kept not the c' of God, and "
37 neither were they stedfast in his c'. "
89: 3 I have made a c' with my chosen, "
28 my c' shall stand fast with him. "
34 My c' will I not break, nor alter "
39 made void the c' of thy servant: "
103:18 To such as keep his c', and to those "
105: 8 hath remembered his c' for ever, "
9 Which c' he made with Abraham, "
10 and to Israel for an everlasting c': 1285
106:45 he remembered for them his c', "
111: 5 he will ever be mindful of his c'. "
9 he hath commanded his c' for ever: "
132:12 If thy children will keep my c' and "
Pr 2:17 and forgetteth the c' of her God. "
Isa 24: 5 ordinance, broken the everlasting c'. "
28:15 We have made a c' with death, and "
18 c' with death shall be disannulled, "
33: 8 he hath broken the c', he hath "
42: 6 give thee for a c' of the people, for "

Isa 49: 8 give thee for a c' of the people, to 1285
54:10 neither shall the c' of my peace be "
55: 3 make an everlasting c' with you, "
56: 4 please me, and take hold of my c'; "
6 and taketh hold of my c'; "
57: 8 and made thee a c' with them; "
59:21 As for me, this is my c' with them, 1285
61: 8 make an everlasting c' with them. "
Jer 3:16 The ark of the c' of the Lord: "
11: 2 Hear ye the words of this c', and "
3 obeyeth not the words of this c', "
6 Hear ye the words of this c', and do "
8 upon them all the words of this c', "
10 of Judah having broken my c' "
14:21 remember, break not thy c' with us. "
22: 9 Because they have forsaken the c' "
31:31 will make a new c' with the house "
32 Not according to the c' that I made "
32 which my c' they brake, although I "
33 shall be the c' that I will make "
32:40 I will make an everlasting c' with "
33:20 If ye can break my c' of the day, "
20 and my c' of the night, "
21 also my c' be broken with David "
25 If my c' be not with day and night, "
34: 8 had made a c' with all the people "
10 which had entered into the c', "
13 a c' with your fathers in the day "
15 made a c' before me in the house "
18 men that have transgressed my c', "
18 not performed the words of the c' "
50: 5 to the Lord in a perpetual c' that "
Eze 16: 8 and entered into a c' with thee, saith "
59 despised the oath in breaking the c'. "
60 I will remember my c' with thee in "
60 establish unto thee an everlasting c'. "
61 for daughters, but not by thy c'. "
62 I will establish my c' with thee; "
17:13 and made a c' with him, and hath "
14 by keeping of his c' it might stand. "
15 he break the c', and be delivered? "
16 whose c' he brake, even with him "
18 despised the oath by breaking the c', "
19 and my c' that he hath broken, "
20:37 bring you into the bond of the c': "
34:25 will make with them a c' of peace, "
37:26 will make a c' of peace with them; "
26 shall be an everlasting c' with them: "
44: 7 they have broken my c' because "
Da 9: 4 keeping the c' and mercy to them "
27 he shall confirm the c' with many "
11:22 yea, also the prince of the c'. "
28 heart shall be against the holy c'; "
30 indignation against the holy c': "
30 with them that forsake the holy c'. "
32 such as do wickedly against the c' "
Ho 2:18 in that day will I make a c' for them "
6: 7 like men have transgressed the c': "
8: 1 they have transgressed my c', "
10: 4 swearing falsely in making a c': "
12: 1 do make a c' with the Assyrians, "
Am 1: 9 remembered not the brotherly c': "
Zec 9:11 by the blood of thy c' I have sent "
11:10 that I might break my c' which I "
Mal 2: 4 that my c' might be with Levi, "
5 My c' was with him of life and "
8 ye have corrupted the c' of Levi, "
10 by profaning the c' of our fathers? "
14 companion, and the wife of thy c'. "
3: 1 the messenger of the c', whom ye "
Lu 1:72 to remember his holy c'; *1242*
Ac 3:25 c' which God made with our fathers, "
7: 8 And he gave him the c' of "
Ro 11:27 this is my c' unto them, when I shall "
Ga 3:15 Though it be but a man's c', "
17 the c', that was confirmed before "
Heb 8: 6 he is the mediator of a better c', "
7 if that first c' had been faultless, "
8 will make a new c' with the house *1242*
9 Not according to the c' that I made "
9 they continued not in my c', and "
10 this is the c' that I will make with "
13 In that he saith, A new c', he "
9: 1 Then verily the first c' had also "
4 the ark of the c' overlaid round *1242*
4 and the tables of the c'; "
10:16 This is the c' that I will make with "
29 the blood of the c', wherewith he "
12:24 Jesus the mediator of the new c', "
13:20 the blood of the everlasting c', "

covenantbreakers
Ro 1:31 c', without natural affection. *802*

covenanted
2Ch 7:18 as I have c' with David thy father 3772
Hag 2: 5 I c' with you when ye came out of "
M't 26:15 they c' with him for thirty pieces **2476*
Lu 22: 5 glad, and c' to give him money. *4934*

covenants
Ro 9: 4 glory, and the c', and the giving *1242*
Ga 4:24 for these are the two c'; the one "
Eph 2:12 strangers from the c' of promise, "

cover See also COVERED; COVERETH; COVERING; DISCOVER; RECOVER; UNCOVER.
Ex 10: 5 they shall c' the face of the earth, 3680
21:33 a man shall dig a pit, and not c' it, "
25:29 and bowls thereof, to c' withal: of *5258
26:13 side and on that side, to c' it. 3680
28:42 breeches to c' their nakedness; "
33:22 and will c' thee with my hand while 5526
37:16 bowls, and his covers to c' withal, *5258
40: 3 and c' the ark with the vail. *5526
Le 13:12 the leprosy c' all the skin of him 3680
16:13 the incense may c' the mercy seat "
17:13 blood thereof, and c' it with dust. "
Nu 4: 5 c' the ark of testimony with it: 3680
7 the bowls, and covers to c' withal: *5258
8 and c' the same with a covering 3680
9 and c' the candlestick of the light, "
11 and c' it with a covering of badgers' "
12 c' them with a covering of badgers' "
22: 5 they c' the face of the earth, and "
De 23:13 and c' that which cometh from thee: "
33:12 Lord shall c' him all the day *2645
1Sa 24: 3 Saul went in to c' his feet: and 5526
1Ki 7:18 to c' the chapiters that were upon 3680
41 two networks, to c' the two bowls of "
42 to c' the two bowls of the chapiters "
2Ch 4:12 two wreaths to c' the two pommels "
13 each wreath, to c' the two pommels "
Ne 4: 5 And c' not their iniquity, and let "
Job 16:18 c' not thou my blood, and let my "
21:26 and the worms shall c' them. * "
22:11 and abundance of waters c' thee. "
38:34 abundance of waters may c' thee? "
40:22 trees c' him with their shadow; 5526
Ps 91: 4 He shall c' thee with his feathers, "
104: 9 they turn not again to c' the earth 3680
109:29 them c' themselves with their own 5844
139:11 Surely the darkness shall c' me; *7779
140: 9 mischief of their own lips c' them. 3680
Isa 11: 9 the Lord, as the waters c' the sea. "
14:11 under thee, and the worms c' thee. 4374
22:17 captivity, and will surely c' thee. *5844
26:21 and shall no more c' her slain. 3680
30: 1 that c' with a covering, but not ‡5258
58: 7 seest the naked, that thou c' him; 3680
59: 6 neither shall they c' themselves "
60: 2 darkness shall c' the earth, and "
6 multitude of camels shall c' thee. "
Jer 46: 8 I will go up, and will c' the earth; "
Eze 7:18 and horror shall c' them; "
12: 6 thou shalt c' thy face, that thou "
12 he shall c' his face, that he see not "
24: 7 the ground, to c' it with dust; "
17 and c' not thy lips, and eat not the 5844
22 ye shall not c' your lips, nor eat "
26:10 his horses their dust shall c' thee: 3680
19 and great waters shall c' thee; "
30:18 a cloud shall c' her, and her "
32: 7 I will c' the heaven, and make the "
7 I will c' the sun with a cloud, "
37: 6 and c' you with skin, and put 7159
38: 9 like a cloud to c' the land, thou, 3680
16 as a cloud to c' the land; it shall "
Ho 2: 9 flax given to c' her nakedness. * "
10: 8 shall say to the mountains, C' us; "
Ob 10 shame shall c' thee, and thou shalt "
Mic 3: 7 yea, they shall all c' their lips; 5844
7:10 and shame shall c' her which said 3680
Hab 2:14 glory of the Lord, as the waters c' "
17 violence of Lebanon shall c' thee, "
M'r 14:65 to spit on him, and to c' his face, *4028*
Lu 23:30 Fall on us; and to the hills, C' us. *2572*
1Co 11: 7 For a man indeed ought not to c' **2619*
1Pe 4: 8 charity shall c' the multitude of **2572*

covered See also COVEREDST; DISCOVERED; RECOVERED; UNCOVERED.
Ge 7:19 under the whole heaven, were c'. 3680
20 and the mountains were c'. "
9:23 c' the nakedness of their father; "
24:65 she took a vail, and c' herself. "
38:14 and c' her with a vail, and wrapped "
15 because she had c' her face. "
Ex 8: 6 the frogs came up, and c' the land "
10:15 For they c' the face of the whole "
14:28 waters returned, and c' the chariots "
15: 5 depths have c' them: they sank * "
10 the sea c' them: they sank as lead "
16:13 quails came up, and c' the camp: "
24:15 and a cloud c' the mount. "
16 and the cloud c' it six days: "
37: 9 and c' with their wings over the *5526
40:21 and c' the ark of the testimony; * "
34 Then a cloud c' the tent of the 3680
Le 13:13 if the leprosy have c' all his flesh, "
Nu 4:20 when the holy things are c', *1104
7: 3 six c' wagons, and twelve oxen; 6632
9:15 cloud c' the tabernacle, namely, 3680
16 the cloud c' it by day, and the "
16:42 the cloud c' it, and the glory of "
De 32:15 thick, thou art c' with fatness; *3780
Jos 24: 7 the sea upon them, and c' them; 3680
J'g 4:18 she c' him with a mantle. "
19 and gave him drink, and c' him. "
1Sa 19:13 for his bolster, and c' it with a "
28:14 and he is c' with a mantle. 5844
2Sa 15:30 had his head c', and he went 2645
30 c' every man his head, and they "
19: 4 the king c' his face, and the king 3813
1Ki 1: 1 and they c' him with clothes, 3680
6: 9 and c' the house with beams and 5603
15 he c' them on the inside with 6823
15 and c' the floor of the house with "
20 and so c' the altar which was of "
35 and c' them with gold fitted upon * "
7: 3 And it was c' with cedar above 5603
7 and it was c' with cedar from one "
8: 7 and the cherubims c' the ark and 5526
2Ki 19: 1 and c' himself with sackcloth, 3680
2 of the priests, c' with sackcloth, "
1Ch 28:18 and c' the ark of the covenant 5526
2Ch 5: 8 and the cherubims c' the ark and 3680
Ne 3:15 he built it, and c' it, and set up 2926
Es 6:12 mourning, and having his head c'. 2645
7: 8 mouth, they c' Haman's face. "
Job 23:17 neither hath he c' the darkness *3680
31:33 If I c' my transgressions as Adam, "
Ps 32: 1 is forgiven, whose sin is c'. "
44:15 the shame of my face hath c' me, "
19 and c' us with the shadow of death. "
Ps 65:13 valleys also are c' over with corn; 5848
68:13 the wings of a dove c' with silver, 2645
69: 7 reproach; shame hath c' my face. 3680
71:13 let them be c' with reproach and 5844
80:10 The hills were c' with the shadow 3680
85: 2 people, thou hast c' all their sin. "
89:45 thou hast c' him with shame. 5844
106:11 And the waters c' their enemies: 3680
17 and c' the company of Abiram. "
139:13 thou hast c' me in my mother's ‡5526
140: 7 thou hast c' my head in the day "
Pr 24:31 nettles had c' the face thereof, 3680
26:23 a potsherd c' with silver dross. *6823
26 Whose hatred is c' by deceit, 3680
Ec 6: 4 his name shall be c' with darkness. "
Isa 6: 2 with twain he c' his face, "
2 and with twain he c' his feet, "
29:10 your rulers, the seers hath he c'. "
37: 1 and c' himself with sackcloth, "
2 of the priests c' with sackcloth, "
51:16 I have c' thee in the shadow of mine "
61:10 he hath c' me with the robe of 3271
Jer 14: 3 confounded, and c' their heads. *2645
4 ashamed, they c' their heads. * "
51:42 she is c' with the multitude of the 3680
51 shame hath c' our faces: for "
La 2: 1 Lord c' the daughter of Zion with 5743
3:16 stones, he hath c' me with ashes. 3728
43 Thou hast c' with anger, and 5526
44 Thou hast c' thyself with a cloud, "
Eze 1:11 and two c' their bodies. 3680
23 had two, which c' on this side, and "
23 had two, which c' on that side, their "
16: 8 over thee, and c' thy nakedness: "
10 fine linen, and I c' thee with silk. "
18: 7 hath c' the naked with a garment; "
16 hath c' the naked with a garment, "
24: 8 of a rock, that it should not be c'. "
27: 7 Elishah was that which c' thee. *4374
31:15 I c' the deep for him, and I 3680
37: 8 them, and the skin c' them above: 7159
41:16 and the windows were c'; 3680
Jon 3: 6 and c' him with sackcloth, and sat "
8 man and beast be c' with sackcloth, "
Hab 3: 3 His glory c' the heavens, and the "
M't 8:24 the ship was c' with the waves: *2572*
10:26 there is nothing c', that shall not "
Lu 12: 2 there is nothing c', that shall not *4780*
Ro 4: 7 forgiven, and whose sins are c'. *1943*
1Co 11: 4 having his head c', dishonoureth *2596*
6 the woman be not c', let her also **2619*
6 shorn or shaven, let her be c'.* "

coveredst
Ps 104: 6 Thou c' it with the deep as with a 3680
Eze 16:18 broidered garments, and c' them: "

coverest
De 22:12 vesture, wherewith thou c' thyself. 3680
Ps 104: 2 Who c' thyself with light as with 5844

covereth See also UNCOVERETH.
Ex 29:13 all the fat that c' the inwards, 3680
22 and the fat that c' the inwards, "
Le 3: 3, 9, 14 the fat that c' the inwards, "
4: 8 the fat that c' the inwards, "
7: 3 and the fat that c' the inwards, "
9:19 and that which c' the inwards, 4374
Nu 22:11 which c' the face of the earth: 3680
J'g 3:24 he c' his feet in his summer 5526
Job 9:24 he c' the faces of the judges 4374
15:27 Because he c' his face with his *3680
36:30 it, and c' the bottom of the sea. "
32 With clouds he c' the light; "
Ps 73: 6 violence c' them as a garment. 5848
109:19 him as the garment which c' him, 5844
147: 8 Who c' the heaven with clouds, 3680
Pr 10: 6, 11 but violence c' the mouth of the "
12 up strifes: but love c' all sins. "
12:16 but a prudent man c' shame. * "
17: 9 He that c' a transgression seeketh "
28:13 that c' his sins shall not prosper: "
Jer 3:25 and our confusion c' us: for we * "
Eze 28:14 art the anointed cherub that c'; 5526
Mal 2:16 one c' violence with his garment, 3680
Lu 8:16 a candle, c' it with a vessel, *2572*

covering See also COVERINGS; DISCOVERING; RECOVERING.
Ge 8:13 Noah removed the c' of the ark, 4372
20:16 he is to thee a c' of the eyes, unto 3682
Ex 22:27 For that is his c' only, it is his "
25:20 c' the mercy seat with their wings, 5526
26: 7 to be a c' upon the tabernacle: * 168
14 a c' for the tent of rams' skins, 4372
14 and a c' above of badgers' skins. "
35:11 tabernacle, his tent, and his c', "
12 mercy seat, and the vail of the c', *4539
36:19 a c' for the tent of rams' skins 4372
19 a c' of badgers' skins above that. "
39:34 the c' of rams' skins dyed red, * "
34 and the c' of badgers' skins, * "
34 and the vail of the c', 4539
40:19 the c' of the tent above upon it; 4372
21 set up the vail of the c', and *4539
Le 13:45 shall put a c' upon his upper lip, *5844
Nu 3:25 the tent, the c' thereof, and the 4372
4: 5 they shall take down the c' vail, *4539
6 the c' of badgers' skins, and 3681
8 same with a c' of badgers' skins, 4372
10 within a c' of badgers' skins, "
11 cover it with a c' of badgers' skins, "
12 them with a c' of badgers' skins, "
14 upon it a c' of badgers' skins, and 3681
15 made an end of c' the sanctuary, 3680
25 his c', and the c' of the badgers' 4372
16:38, 39 plates for a c' of the altar: 6826
19:15 no c' bound upon it, is unclean. 6781

2Sa 17:19 spread a c' over the well's mouth, 4539
Job 22:14 Thick clouds are a c' to him, that 5643
24: 7 that they have no c' in the cold. 3682
26: 6 him, and destruction hath no c'. "
31:19 clothing, or any poor without c'; "
Ps 105:39 He spread a cloud for a c'; and 4539
Ca 3:10 the c' of it of purple, the midst *4817
Isa 22: 8 he discovered the c' of Judah, 4539
25: 7 face of the c' cast over all people, 3875
28:20 and the c' narrower than that he 4541
30: 1 that cover with a c', but not of ‡ "
22 c' of thy graven images of silver, *6826
50: 3 and I make sackcloth their c'. 3682
Eze 28:13 every precious stone was thy c', 4540
16 I will destroy thee, O c' cherub, 5526
Mal 2:13 c' the altar of the Lord with tears, 3680
1Co 11:15 for her hair is given her for a c'. 4018

coverings
Pr 7:16 decked my bed with c' of tapestry, *4765
31:22 She maketh herself c' of tapestry;* "

covers
Ex 25:29 and c' thereof, and bowls thereof, *7184
37:16 and his c' to cover withal, of pure* "
Nu 4: 7 the bowls, and c' to cover withal:* "

covert
1Sa 25:20 came down by the c' of the hill, 5643
2Ki 16:18 c' for the sabbath that they had *4329
Job 38:40 and abide in the c' to lie in wait? 5521
40:21 in the c' of the reed, and fens. 5643
Ps 61: 4 I will trust in the c' of thy wings. "
Isa 4: 6 a c' from storm and from rain. 4563
16: 4 be thou a c' to them from the face 5643
32: 2 wind, and a c' from the tempest; "
Jer 25:38 hath forsaken his c', as the lion: 5520

covet See also COVETED; COVETETH.
Ex 20:17 shalt not c' thy neighbour's house, 2530
17 shalt not c' thy neighbour's wife, "
De 5:21 shalt thou c' thy neighbour's house, 183
Mic 2: 2 And they c' fields, and take them 2530
Ro 7: 7 law had said, Thou shalt not c'. 1937
13: 9 Thou shalt not c'; and if there be "
1Co 12:31 But c' earnestly the best gifts: *2206
14:39 c' to prophesy, and forbid not to "

coveted
Jos 7:21 then I c' them, and took them; 2530
Ac 20:33 I have c' no man's silver, or gold, 1937
1Ti 6:10 while some c' after, they have *3713

coveteth
Pr 21:26 He c' greedily all the day long: 183
Hab 2: 9 him that c' an evil covetousness *1214

covetous See COVETOUSNESS.
Ps 10: 3 blesseth the c', whom the Lord 1214
Lu 16:14 the Pharisees also, who were c', *5366
1Co 5:10 or with the c', or extortioners, or 4123
11 or c', or an idolator, or a railer, or "
6:10 nor c', nor drunkards, nor revilers, "
Eph 5: 5 nor c' man, who is an idolater, "
1Ti 3: 3 patient, not a brawler, not c'; * 866
2Ti 3: 2 lovers of their own selves, c', *5366
2Pe 2:14 have exercised with c' practices; *4124

covetousness
Ex 18:21 fear God, men of truth, hating c'; *1215
Ps 119:36 thy testimonies, and not to c'. "
Pr 28:16 hateth c' shall prolong his days. "
Isa 57:17 the iniquity of his c' was I wroth, "
Jer 6:13 them every one is given to c'; and "
8:10 the greatest is given to c', from "
22:17 are not but for c', and for to shed "
51:13 is come, and the measure of thy c'. "
Eze 33:31 their heart goeth after their c'. * "
Hab 2: 9 coveteth an evil c' to his house, * "
M'r 7:22 Thefts, c', wickedness, deceit, *4124
Lu 12:15 Take heed, and beware of c': "
Ro 1:29 wickedness, c', maliciousness; * "
2Co 9: 5 of bounty, and not as of c'. * "
Eph 5: 3 all uncleanness, or c', let it not be "
Col 3: 5 and c', which is idolatry: "
1Th 2: 5 as ye know, nor a cloke of c'; "
Heb 13: 5 your conversation be without c'; * 866
2Pe 2: 3 through c' shall they with feigned 4124

cow See also COW'S; KINE.
Le 22:28 And whether it be c' or ewe, ye 7794
Nu 18:17 But the firstling of a c', or the "
Job 21:10 their c' calveth, and casteth not 6510
Isa 7:21 man shall nourish a young c', 5697
11: 7 And the c' and the bear shall feed; 6510
Am 4: 3 every c' at that which is before her; "

cow's
Eze 4:15 me, Lo, I have given thee c' dung 1241

Coz *(coz)*
1Ch 4: 8 And C' begat Anub, and Zobebah, 6976

Cozbi *(coz'-bi)*
Nu 25:15 woman that was slain was C', 3579
18 of Peor, and in the matter of C', "

crackling
Ec 7: 6 as the c' of thorns under a pot, 6963

cracknels
1Ki 14: 3 take with thee ten loaves and c', ‡5350

craft See also CRAFTSMAN; WITCHCRAFT.
Da 8:25 cause c' to prosper in his hand; 4820
M'r 14: 1 how they might take him by c', *1388
Ac 18: 3 because he was of the same c', *3673
19:25 by this c' we have our wealth. *2039
27 not only this our c' is in danger *3313
Re 18:22 craftsman, of whatsoever c' he be, 5078

craftiness
Job 5:13 taketh the wise in their own c': 6193
Lu 20:23 But he perceived their c', and 3834
1Co 3:19 He taketh the wise in their own c'. "
2Co 4: 2 not walking in c', nor handling the "
Eph 4:14 the sleight of men, and cunning c', "

craftsman See also CRAFTSMEN.
De 27:15 the work of the hands of the c', 2796
Re 18:22 no c', of whatsoever craft he be, 5079

craftsmen
2Ki 24:14 and all the c' and smiths: none 2796
16 and c' and smiths a thousand, all "
1Ch 4:14 of Charashim; for they were c'. "
Ne 11:35 Lod, and Ono, the valley of c'. "
Ho 13: 2 all of it the work of the c': 2796
Ac 19:24 brought no small gain unto the c'; 5079
38 and the c' which are with him, "

crafty
Job 5:12 disappointeth the devices of the c', 6175
15: 5 thou choosest the tongue of the c'. "
Ps 83: 3 They have taken c' counsel against 6191
2Co 12:16 being c', I caught you with guile. 3835

crag
Job 39:28 upon the c' of the rock, and the ‡8127

Crane
Isa 38:14 a c' or a swallow, so did I chatter: 5483
Jer 8: 7 the c' and the swallow observe "

crashing
Zep 1:10 and a great c' from the hills. 7667

craved
M'r 15:43 Pilate, and c' the body of Jesus. * 154

craveth
Pr 16:26 for his mouth c' it of him, 404

create See also CREATED; CREATETH.
Ps 51:10 C' in me a clean heart, O God; 1254
Isa 4: 5 Lord will c' upon every dwelling "
45: 7 I form the light, and c' darkness: "
7 I make peace, and c' evil: "
57:19 I c' the fruit of the lips; Peace, "
65:17 I c' new heavens and a new earth: "
18 rejoice for ever in that which I c': "
18 behold, I c' Jerusalem a rejoicing, "

created
Ge 1: 1 God c' the heaven and the earth. 1254
21 And God c' great whales, and every "
27 So God c' man in his own image, "
27 in the image of God c' he him; "
27 male and female c' he them. "
2: 3 his work which God c' and made. "
4 and of the earth, when they were c', "
5: 1 In the day that God c' man, in the "
2 Male and female c' he them; and "
2 in the day when they were c'. "
6: 7 I will destroy man whom I have c' "
De 4:32 that God c' man upon the earth, "
Ps 89:12 and the south thou hast c' them: "
102:18 the people which shall be c' shall "
104:30 sendest forth thy spirit, they are c': "
148: 5 he commanded, and they were c'. "
Isa 40:26 behold who hath c' these things, "
41:20 the Holy One of Israel hath c' it. "
42: 5 he that c' the heavens, and "
43: 1 thus saith the Lord that c' thee, "
7 I have c' him for my glory, I have "
45: 8 I the Lord have c' it. "
12 made the earth, and c' man upon it: "
18 the Lord that c' the heavens; God "
18 he c' it not in vain, he formed it to "
48: 7 They are c' now, and not from the "
54:16 c' the smith that bloweth the coals "
16 I have c' the waster to destroy. "
Jer 31:22 hath c' a new thing in the earth, "
Eze 21:30 in the place where thou wast c', "
28:13 thee in the day that thou wast c'. "
15 from the day that thou wast c', till "
Mal 2:10 hath not one God c' us? why do we "
M'r 13:19 which God c' unto this time, neither 2936
1Co 11: 9 was the man c' for the woman; but "
Eph 2:10 c' in Christ Jesus unto good works, "
3: 9 in God, who c' all things by Jesus "
4:24 after God is c' in righteousness "
Col 1:16 by him were things c', that are in "
16 all things were c' by him, and for "
3:10 after the image of him that c' him: "
1Ti 4: 3 which God hath c' to be received "
Re 4:11 for thou hast c' all things, and for* "
11 thy pleasure they are and were c'. "
10: 6 who c' heaven, and the things that "

createth
Am 4:13 and c' the wind, and declareth 1254

creation
M'r 10: 6 But from the beginning of the c' 2937
13:19 not from the beginning of the c' "
Ro 1:20 from the c' of the world are clearly "
8:22 that the whole c' groaneth and "
2Pe 3: 4 were from the beginning of the c' "
Re 3:14 the beginning of the c' of God; "

Creator
Ec 12: 1 Remember now thy C' in the days 1254
Isa 40:28 the C' of the ends of the earth, "
43:15 your Holy One, the c' of Israel, * "
Ro 1:25 more than the C', who is blessed 2936
1Pe 4:19 well doing, as unto a faithful C'. 2939

creature See also CREATURES.
Ge 1:20 the moving c' that hath life, and 8318
21 every living c' that moveth, which 5315
24 the earth bring forth the living c' "
2:19 called every living c', that was the "
9:10 every living c' that is with you, of "
12 me and you and every living c' "
15 and every living c' of all flesh; "
16 between God and every living c' "
Le 11:46 every living c' that moveth in the "
46 every c' that creepeth upon the "
Eze 1:20, 21 spirit of the living c' was in the 2416
22 upon the heads of the living c' "
10:15 This is the living c' that I saw by "
10:17 spirit of the living c' was in them. 2416
20 This is the living c' that I saw by "
M'r 16:15 and preach the gospel to every c'. *2937
Ro 1:25 and served the c' more than the "
8:19 the earnest expectation of the c' * "
20 For the c' was made subject to * "
21 Because the c' itself also shall be* "
39 nor any other c', shall be able to "
2Co 5:17 he is a new c': old things are "
Ga 6:15 uncircumcision, but a new c'. "
Col 1:15 God, the firstborn of every c': * "
23 which was preached to every c' "
1Ti 4: 4 For every c' of God is good and 2938
Heb 4:13 Neither is there any c' that is not 2937
Re 5:13 And every c' which is in heaven, *2938

creatures
Isa 13:21 houses shall be full of doleful c'; 255
Eze 1: 5 came the likeness of four living c'. 2416
13 the likeness of the living c', their "
13 up and down among the living c'; "
14 And the living c' ran and returned "
15 Now as I beheld the living c', "
15 upon the earth by the living c', "
19 when the living c' went, the wheels "
19 and when the living c' were lifted "
3:13 noise of the wings of the living c' "
Jas 1:18 be a kind of firstfruits of his c'. 2938
Re 8: 9 third part of the c' which were in "

credible See INCREDIBLE.

creditor See CREDITORS.
De 15: 2 Every c' that lendeth 1167, 4874, 3027
2Ki 4: 1 and the c' is come to take unto 5383
Lu 7:41 There was a certain c' which had *1157

creditors
Isa 50: 1 which of my c' is it to whom I 5383

creek
Ac 27:39 they discovered a certain c' with *2859

creep See also CREEPETH; CREEPING; CREPT.
Le 11:20 All fowls that c', going upon all *8318
29 the creeping things that c' upon 8317
31 unclean to you among all that c': 8318
42 all creeping things that c' upon 8317
Ps 104:20 the beasts of the forest do c' forth 7430
Eze 38:20 and all creeping things that c' "
2Ti 3: 6 are they which c' into houses, 1744, 1519

creepeth
Ge 1:25 and every thing that c' upon the 7431
26 every creeping thing that c' upon 7430
30 to every thing that c' upon the "
7: 8 and of every thing that c' upon the "
14 and every creeping thing that c' "
21 and of every creeping thing that c' 8317
8:17 and of every creeping thing that c' 7430
19 fowl, and whatsoever c' upon the * "
Le 11:41 every creeping thing that c' upon 8317
43 with any creeping thing that c', "
44 manner of creeping thing that c' *7430
46 of every creature that c' upon the 8317
20:25 manner of living thing that c' on *7430
De 4:18 The likeness of any thing that c' "

creeping
Ge 1:24 cattle, and c' thing, and beast of 7431
26 over every c' thing that creepeth "
6: 7 the c' thing, and the fowls of the "
20 every c' thing of the earth after "
7:14 and every c' thing that creepeth "
21 and of beast, and of every c' thing 8318
23 the c' things, and the fowl of the 7431
8:17 of every c' thing that creepeth "
19 Every beast, every c' thing, and "
Le 5: 2 carcase of unclean c' things, and 8318
11:21 every flying c' thing that goeth "
23 all other flying c' things, which "
29 among the c' things that creep "
41 every c' thing that creepeth upon "
42 hath more feet among all c' things "
43 abominable with any c' thing that "
44 with any manner of c' thing that "
22: 5 whosoever toucheth any c' thing, "
De 14:19 every c' thing that flieth is unclean "
1Ki 4:33 of fowl, and of c' things, and of 7431
Ps 104:25 things c' innumerable, both small "
148:10 c' things, and flying fowl: "
Eze 8:10 and behold every form of c' things, "
38:20 field, and all c' things that creep "
Hos 2:18 with the c' things of the ground: "
Hab 1:14 as the c' things, that have no ruler "
Ac 10:12 and wild beasts, and c' things, and 2062
11: 6 wild beasts, and c' things, and "
Ro 1:23 fourfooted beasts, and c' things. "

crept
Jude 4 For there are certain men c' in 3921

Crescens *(cres'-sens)*
2Ti 4:10 C' to Galatia, Titus unto 2913

Cretans See CRETES; CRETIANS.

Crete *(creet)* See also CRETES.
Ac 27: 7 suffering us, we sailed under C', 2914
12 which is an haven of C', and lieth "
13 thence, they sailed close by C'. "
21 me, and not have loosed from C', "
Tit 1: 5 For this cause left I thee in C', "

Cretes *(creets)* See also CRETIANS.
Ac 2:11 C' and Arabians, we do hear *2912

Cretians *((cre'-shuns)* See also CRETES.
Tit 1:12 The C' are always liars, evil 2912
subscr bishop of the church of the C' * "

crew
M't 26:74 And immediately the cock c'. 5455
M'r 14:68 out into the porch; and the cock c'. "
72 And the second time the cock c'. "

Lu 22:60 while he yet spake, the cock c'. 5455
Joh 18:27 again: and immediately the cock c'. "

crib
Job 39: 9 to serve thee, or abide by thy c'? 18
Pr 14: 4 Where no oxen are, the c' is clean: "
Isa 1: 3 owner, and the ass his master's c': "

cried
Ge 27:34 he c' with a great and exceeding 6817
39:14 me, and I c' with a loud voice: 7121
15 that I lifted up my voice and c', "
18 as I lifted up my voice and c', that "
41:43 they c' before him, Bow the knee: "
55 people c' to Pharaoh for bread: 6817
45: 1 and he c', Cause every man to go 7121
Ex 2:23 and they c', and their cry came up 2199
5:15 the children of Israel came and c' 6817
8:12 Moses c' unto the Lord because of "
14:10 and the children of Israel c' out "
15:25 And he c' unto the Lord; and the "
17: 4 And Moses c' unto the Lord, saying, "
Nu 11: 2 And the people c' unto Moses; "
12:13 And Moses c' unto the Lord, saying, "
14: 1 lifted up their voice, and c'; 5414
20:16 And when we c' unto the Lord, 6817
De 22:24 the damsel, because she c' not, "
27 the betrothed damsel c', and there "
26: 7 And when we c' unto the Lord God "
Jos 24: 7 And when they c' unto the Lord, * "
J'g 3: 9 And when the children of Israel c' 2199
15 But when the children of Israel c' "
4: 3 And the children of Israel c' unto 6817
5:28 and c' through the lattice, 2980
6: 6 and the children of Israel c' unto 2199
7 when the children of Israel c' unto "
7:20 they c', The sword of the Lord, 7121
21 all the host ran, and c', and fled. *7321
9: 7 and lifted up his voice, and c', 7121
10:10 and the children of Israel c' unto 2199
12 and ye c' to me, and I delivered 6817
18:23 they c' unto the children of Dan. 7121
1Sa 4:13 and told it, all the city c' out. 2199
5:10 that the Ekronites c' out, saying, "
7: 9 and Samuel c' unto the Lord for "
12: 8 and your fathers c' unto the Lord, "
10 they c' unto the Lord, and said, "
15:11 and he c' unto the Lord all night. "
17: 8 and c' unto the armies of Israel, 7121
20:37 Jonathan c' after the lad, and said, "
38 Jonathan c' after the lad, make "
24: 8 out of the cave, and c' after Saul, "
26:14 And David c' to the people, and to "
28:12 woman saw Samuel, she c' with a 2199
2Sa 18:25 watchman c', and told the king. 7121
19: 4 and the king c' with a loud voice, 2199
20:16 Then c' a wise woman out of the 7121
22: 7 and c' to my God: and he did hear "
1Ki 13: 2 he c' against the altar in the word "
4 had c' against the altar in Beth-el, "
21 And he c' unto the man of God "
32 which he c' by the word of the Lord "
17:20 he c' unto the Lord, and said, "
21 the child three times, and c' unto "
18:28 they c' aloud, and cut themselves "
20:39 he c' unto the king: and he said, 6817
22:32 against him: and Jehoshaphat c' 2199
2Ki 2:12 and he c', My father, my father, 6817
4: 1 Now there c' a certain woman of "
40 they c' out, and said, O thou man "
6: 5 and he c', and said, Alas, master! "
26 there c' a woman unto him, saying, "
8: 5 c' to the king for her house and "
11:14 Athaliah rent her clothes, and c', 7121
18:28 Then Rab-shakeh stood and c' with "
20:11 And Isaiah the prophet c' unto the "
1Ch 5:20 they c' to God in the battle, and he 2199
2Ch 13:14 and they c' unto the Lord, and the 6817
14:11 And Asa c' unto the Lord his God, 7121
18:31 Jehoshaphat c' out, and the Lord 2199
32:18 Then they c' with a loud voice in 7121
20 the son of Amoz, prayed and c' to 2199
Ne 9: 4 and c' with a loud voice unto the "
27 they c' unto thee, thou heardest 6817
28 when they returned, and c' unto 2199
Es 4: 1 and c' with a loud and a bitter cry; "
Job 29:12 I delivered the poor that c', 7768
30: 5 c' after them as after a thief;) *7321
28 up, and I c' in the congregation. *7768
Ps 3: 4 I c' unto the Lord with my voice, *7121
18: 6 and c' unto my God: he heard 7768
41 They c', but there was none to "
22: 5 They c' unto thee, and were 2199
24 when he c' unto him, he heard. 7768
30: 2 O Lord my God, I c' unto thee, "
8 I c' to thee, O Lord; and unto the 7121
31:22 supplications when I c' unto thee. 7768
34: 6 This poor man c', and the Lord 7121
66:17 I c' unto him with my mouth, "
77: 1 I c' unto God with my voice, *6817
88: 1 I have c' day and night before thee: "
13 unto thee have I c', O Lord; and 7768
107: 6 Then they c' unto the Lord in 6817
13 Then they c' unto the Lord in 2199
119:145 I c' with my whole heart; *7121
146 I c' unto thee; save me, and I * "
147 dawning of the morning, and c': 7768
120: 1 In my distress I c' unto the Lord, 7121
130: 1 Out of the depths have I c' unto "
138: 3 day when I c' thou answeredst * "
142: 1 I c' unto the Lord with my voice; *2199
5 I c' unto thee, O Lord: I said, "
Isa 6: 3 And one c' unto another, and said, 7121
4 moved at the voice of him that c', "
21: 8 And he c', A lion: My lord, "
30: 7 therefore have I c' concerning * "
36:13 Then Rabshakeh stood, and c' with "
Jer 4:20 Destruction upon destruction is c'; 7121
20: 8 For since I spake, I c' out, *2199
8 I c' violence and spoil; *7121
La 2:18 Their heart c' unto the Lord, 6817
4:15 they c' unto them, Depart ye; 7121
Eze 9: 1 He c' also in mine ears with a loud "
8 I fell upon my face, and c', 2199
10:13 As for the wheels, it was c' unto *7121
11:13 fell I down upon my face, and c' 2199
Da 3: 4 Then an herald c' aloud, To you 7123
4:14 He c' aloud, and said thus, "
5: 7 The king c' aloud to bring in the "
6:20 he c' with a lamentable voice unto 2200
Ho 7:14 And they have not c' unto me 2199
Jon 1: 5 and c' every man unto his god, "
14 they c' unto the Lord, and said, 7121
2: 2 And said, I c' by reason of mine * "
2 out of the belly of hell c' I, and 7768
3: 4 he c', and said, Yet forty days, and 7121
Zec 1: 4 former prophets have c', saying, "
6: 8 Then c' he unto me, and spake 2199
7: 7 the Lord hath c' by the former 7121
13 as he c', and they would not hear; "
13 so they c', and I would not hear, * "
M't 8:29 behold, they c' out, saying, 2896
14:26 is a spirit; and they c' out for fear. "
30 beginning to sink, he c', saying, "
15:22 c' unto him, saying, Have mercy 2905
20:30 c' out, saying, Have mercy on us, 2896
31 but they c' the more, saying, "
21: 9 c', saying, Hosanna to the son of "
27:23 But they c' out the more, saying, "
46 Jesus c' with a loud voice, saying, 310
50 Jesus, when he had c' again with 2896
M'r 1:23 with an unclean spirit; and he c' 349
26 torn him, and c' with a loud voice, *2896
3:11 c', saying, Thou art the Son of God. "
5: 7 c' with a loud voice, and said, * "
6:49 it had been a spirit, and c' out: 349
9:24 c' out, and said with tears, Lord, 2896
26 the spirit c', and rent him sore, "
10:48 but he c' the more a great deal, "
11: 9 and they that followed, c', saying, "
15:13 they c' out again, Crucify him. "
14 they c' out the more exceedingly, "
34 hour Jesus c' with a loud voice, 994
37 And Jesus c' with a loud voice, * 863
39 saw that he so c' out, and gave *2896
Lu 4:33 unclean devil, and c' out with a 349
8: 8 he had said these things, he c', 5455
28 When he saw Jesus, he c' out, and 349
9:38 a man of the company c' out, 310
16:24 he c' and said, Father Abraham, 5455
18:38 he c', saying, Jesus, thou son of 994
39 he c' so much the more, Thou son 2896
23:18 they c' out all at once, saying, 349
21 But they c', saying, Crucify him, *2019
46 when Jesus had c' with a loud ‡5455
Joh 1:15 and c', saying, This was he of 2896
7:28 Then c' Jesus in the temple as he "
37 Jesus stood and c', saying, If any "
11:43 he c' with a loud voice, Lazarus, 2905
12:13 to meet him, and c', Hosanna: 2896
44 Jesus c' and said, He that "
18:40 Then c' they all again, saying, 2905
19: 6 saw him, they c' out, saying, "
12 the Jews c' out, saying, If thou 2896
15 they c' out, Away with him, 2905
Ac 7:57 they c' out with a loud voice, 2896
60 and c' with a loud voice, Lord, "
16:17 and c', saying, These men are the "
28 Paul c' with a loud voice, saying, 5455
19:28 and c' out, saying, Great is Diana 2896
32 Some therefore c' one thing, and "
34 c' out, Great is Diana of the "
21:34 some c' one thing, some another, * 994
22:23 And as they c' out, and cast off 2905
24 he might know wherefore they c' *2019
23: 6 he c' out in the council, Men and 2896
24:21 I c' standing among them, "
Re 6:10 they c' with a loud voice, saying, "
7: 2 and he c' with a loud voice to the "
10 And c' with a loud voice, saying, * "
10: 3 And c' with a loud voice, as when "
3 when he had c', seven thunders "
12: 2 And she being with child c, * "
14:18 c' with a loud cry to him that had *5455
18: 2 And he c' mightily with a strong 2896
18 And c' when they saw the smoke "
19 and c', weeping and wailing, "
19:17 and he c' with a loud voice, "

cries
Jas 5: 4 the c' of them which have reaped 995

criest
Ex 14:15 Wherefore c' thou unto me? 6817
1Sa 26:14 Who art thou that c' to the king? 7121
Pr 2: 3 Yea, if thou c' after knowledge, * "
Isa 57:13 When thou c', let thy companies 2199
Jer 30:15 Why c' thou for thine affliction? "

crieth
Ge 4:10 the voice of thy brother's blood c' 6817
Ex 22:27 he c' unto me, that I will hear; "
Job 24:12 the soul of the wounded c' out: 7768
Ps 72:12 shall deliver the needy when he c'; "
84: 2 my heart and my flesh c' out for *7442
Pr 1:20 Wisdom c' without; she uttereth "
21 c' in the chief place of concourse, 7121
8: 3 She c' at the gates, at the entry 7442
9: 3 she c' upon the highest places of 7121
Isa 26:17 in pain, and c' out in her pangs; 2199
40: 3 of him that c' in the wilderness, 7121
Jer 12: 8 it c' out against me: *5414, 6963
Mic 6: 9 The Lord's voice c' unto the city, 7121
M't 15:23 for she c' after us. 2896
Lu 9:39 him, and he suddenly c' out; "
Ro 9:27 Esaias also c' concerning Israel, 2896
Jas 5: 4 is of you kept back by fraud, c': "

crime See also CRIMES.
Job 31:11 For this is an heinous c'; yea, 2154
Ac 25:16 concerning the c' laid against him. *1462

crimes
Eze 7:23 for the land is full of bloody c', 4941
Ac 25:27 signify the c' laid against him. * 156

crimson
2Ch 2: 7 in purple, and c', and blue, 3758
14 blue, and in fine linen, and in c'; "
3:14 purple, and c', and fine linen, "
Isa 1:18 though they be red like c', 8438
Jer 4:30 thou clothest thyself with c', *8144

cripple
Ac 14: 8 a c' from his mother's womb, 5560

crisping
Isa 3:22 the wimples, and the c' pins, *2754

crisping-pins See CRISPING and PINS.

Crispus (*cris'-pus*)
Ac 18: 8 And C', the chief ruler of the 2921
1Co 1:14 I baptized none of you, but C' and "

crookbackt
Le 21:20 Or c', or a dwarf, or that hath a ‡1384

crooked
De 32: 5 are a perverse and c' generation. 6618
Job 26:13 hand hath formed the c' serpent. *1281
Ps 125: 5 turn aside unto their c' ways, 6128
Pr 2:15 Whose ways are c', and they 6141
Ec 1:15 is c' cannot be made straight: 5791
7:13 straight, which he hath made c'? "
Isa 27: 1 even leviathan that c' serpent; 6129
40: 4 and the c' shall be made straight, 6121
42:16 them, and c' things straight. 4625
45: 2 and make the c' places straight: *1921
59: 8 they have made them c' paths: 6140
La 3: 9 he hath made my paths c'. 5753
Lu 3: 5 the c' shall be made straight, 4646
Ph'p 2:15 midst of a c' and perverse nation, "

crop See also CROPPED.
Le 1:16 pluck away his c' with his feathers, 4760
Eze 17:22 I will c' off from the top of his 6998

cropped
Eze 17: 4 c' off the top of his young twigs, 6998

cross See also CROSSWAY.
M't 10:38 And he that taketh not his c', 4716
16:24 deny himself, and take up his c', "
27:32 him they compelled to bear his c'. "
40 Son of God, come down from the c'. "
42 let him now come down from the c', "
M'r 8:34 deny himself, and take up his c', "
10:21 take up the c', and follow me. * "
15:21 and Rufus, to bear his c'. "
30 and come down from the c'. "
32 descend now from the c', that we "
Lu 9:23 himself, and take up his c' daily, "
14:27 whosoever doth not bear his c', "
23:26 and on him they laid the c', that "
Joh 19:17 And he bearing his c' went forth "
19 wrote a title, and put it on the c'. "
25 stood by the c' of Jesus his mother, "
31 should not remain upon the c' on "
1Co 1:17 lest the c' of Christ should be made "
18 the preaching of the c' is to them "
Ga 5:11 then is the offence of the c' ceased. "
6:12 should suffer persecution for the c' "
14 save in the c' of our Lord Jesus "
Eph 2:16 unto God in one body by the c', "
Ph'p 2: 8 death, even the death of the c'. "
3:18 are the enemies of the c' of Christ: "
Col 1:20 peace through the blood of his c', "
2:14 out of the way, nailing it to his c'; "
Heb 12: 2 endured the c', despising the shame, "

crossway
Ob 14 shouldest thou have stood in the c', 6563

crouch See also CROUCHETH.
1Sa 2:36 c' to him for a piece of silver *7812

croucheth
Ps 10:10 He c', and humbleth himself, 1794

crow See also COCKCROWING; CREW.
M't 26:34 this night, before the cock c', thou 5455
75 Before the cock c', thou shalt deny "
M'r 14:30 before the cock c' twice, thou shalt "
72 him, Before the c' crow twice, thou "
Lu 22:34 the cock shall not c' this day, before "
61 him, Before the cock c', thou shalt "
Joh 13:38 The cock shall not c', till thou hast "

crown See also CROWNED; CROWNEST; CROWNETH; CROWNING; CROWNS.
Ge 49:26 and on the c' of the head of him 6936
Ex 25:11 make upon it a c' of gold round 2213
24 and make thereto a c' of gold "
25 make a golden c' to the border. "
29: 6 put the holy c' upon the mitre. 5145
30: 3 shalt make unto it a c' of gold 2213
4 thou make to it under the c' of it, "
37: 2 and made a c' of gold to it round "
11 and made thereunto a c' of gold "
12 made a c' of gold for the border "
26 also he made unto it a c' of gold "
27 of gold for it under the c' thereof, "
39:30 they made the plate of the holy c' 5145
Le 8: 9 put the golden plate, the holy c'; "
21:12 c' of the anointing oil of his God "
De 33:20 the arm with the c' of the head. 6936
2Sa 1:10 took the c' that was upon his head, 5145
12:30 And he took their king's c' from 5850
14:25 his foot even to the c' of his head 6936
2Ki 11:12 and put the c' upon him, 5145
1Ch 20: 2 David took the c' of their king 5850

2Ch 23:11 son, and put upon him the c', 5145
Es 1:11 queen before the king with the c' 3804
2:17 he set the royal c' upon her head, "
6: 8 c' royal which is set upon his head. "
8:15 and with a great c' of gold, 5850
Job 2: 7 the sole of his foot unto his c'. 6936
19: 9 and taken the c' from my head. 5850
31:36 and bind it as a c' to me. "
Ps 21: 3 a c' of pure gold on his head. "
89:39 hast profaned his c' by casting it 5145
132:18 upon himself shall his c' flourish. "
Pr 4: 9 a c' of glory shall she deliver to 5850
12: 4 woman is a c' to her husband: "
14:24 The c' of the wise is their riches: "
16:31 The hoary head is a c' of glory, "
17: 6 Children's children are the c' of "
27:24 the c' endure to every generation? 5145
Ca 3:11 behold king Solomon with the c' 5850
Isa 3:17 Lord will smite with a scab the c' 6936
28: 1 the c' of pride, to the drunkards 5850
3 The c' of pride, the drunkards of "
5 Lord of hosts be for a c' of glory, "
62: 3 Thou shalt also be a c' of glory "
Jer 2:16 have broken the c' of thy head. 6936
13:18 down, even the c' of your glory. 5850
48:45 c' of the head of the tumultuous 6936
La 5:16 The c' is fallen from our head: 5850
Eze 16:12 and a beautiful c' upon thine head. "
21:26 the diadem, and take off the c': "
Zec 9:16 shall be as the stones of a c', 5145
M't 27:29 they had platted a c' of thorns, 4735
M'r 15:17 and platted a c' of thorns, "
Joh 19: 2 the soldiers platted a c' of thorns, "
5 wearing the c' of thorns, and the "
1Co 9:25 to obtain a corruptible c'; but we "
Ph'p 4: 1 and longed for, my joy and c', "
1Th 2:19 hope, or joy, or c' of rejoicing? "
2Ti 4: 8 up for me a c' of righteousness, "
Jas 1:12 he shall receive the c' of life, "
1Pe 5: 4 a c' of glory that fadeth not away. "
Re 2:10 and I will give thee a c' of life. "
3:11 thou hast, that no man take thy c'. "
6: 2 and a c' was given unto him: "
12: 1 upon her head a c' of twelve stars: "
14:14 having on his head a golden c', "

crowned See also CROWNEDST.
Ps 8: 5 c' him with glory and honour. *5849
Pr 14:18 prudent are c' with knowledge. 3803
Ca 3:11 wherewith his mother c' him in 5849
Na 3:17 Thy c' are as the locusts, and thy 4502
2Ti 2: 5 yet is he not c', except he strive 4737
Heb 2: 9 death, c' with glory and honour; "

crownedst
Heb 2: 7 thou c' him with glory and honour, 4737

crownest
Ps 65:11 c' the year with thy goodness; 5849

crowneth
Ps 103: 4 who c' thee with lovingkindness 5849

crowning
Isa 23: 8 counsel against Tyre, the c' city, ‡5849

crowns
Eze 23:42 and beautiful c' upon their heads. 5850
Zec 6:11 take silver and gold, and make c', "
14 And the c' shall be to Helem, "
Re 4: 4 they had on their heads c' of gold. 4735
10 and cast their c' before the throne, "
9: 7 heads were as it were c' like gold, "
12: 3 and seven c' upon his heads. *1238
13: 1 and upon his horns ten c', and * "
19:12 and on his head were many c'; * "

crucified
M't 26: 2 Son of man is betrayed to be c'. 4717
27:22 all say unto him, Let him be c'. "
23 out the more, saying, Let him be c'. "
26 he delivered him to be c'. "
35 And they c' him, and parted his "
38 were there two thieves c' with him, "
44 also, which were c' with him, 4957
28: 5 that ye seek Jesus, which was c'. 4717
M'r 15:15 when he had scourged him, to be c'. "
24 when they had c' him, they parted* "
25 was the third hour, and they c' him. "
32 that were c' with him reviled him. 4957
16: 6 Jesus of Nazareth, which was c': 4717
Lu 23:23 requiring that he might be c'. "
33 called Calvary, there they c' him, "
24: 7 and be c', and the third day rise "
20 to death, and have c' him. "
Joh 19:16 him therefore unto them to be c'. "
18 Where they c' him, and two others "
20 place where Jesus was c' was nigh "
23 soldiers, when they had c' Jesus, "
32 the other which was c' with him. 4957
41 Now in the place where he was c' 4717
Ac 2:23 wicked hands have c' and slain: *4362
36 same Jesus, whom ye have c', 4717
4:10 Christ of Nazareth, whom ye c', "
Ro 6: 6 that our old man is c' with him, 4957
1Co 1:13 was Paul c' for you? or were ye 4717
23 we preach Christ c', unto the Jews "
2: 2 you, save Jesus Christ, and him c'. "
8 would not have c' the Lord of glory. "
2Co 13: 4 he was c' through weakness, "
Ga 2:20 I am c' with Christ: nevertheless 4957
3: 1 evidently set forth, c' among you? 4717
5:24 have c' the flesh with the affections "
6:14 by whom the world is c' unto me, "
Re 11: 8 Egypt, where also our Lord was c'. "

crucify See also CRUCIFIED.
M't 20:19 and to scourge, and to c' him: 4717
23:34 some of them ye shall kill and c'; "
27:31 and led him away to c' him. "
M'r 15:13 they c' out again, C' him. "
15:14 out the more exceedingly, C' him. 4717
20 and led him out to c' him. "
27 And with him they c' two thieves; "
Lu 23:21 they cried, saying, C' him, c' him. "
Joh 19: 6 cried out, saying, C' him, c' him. "
6 Take ye him, and c' him: for I find "
10 not that I have power to c' thee, "
15 away with him, c' him. Pilate saith "
15 Shall I c' your King? The chief "
Heb 6: 6 they c' to themselves the Son of God 388

cruel
Ge 49: 7 and their wrath, for it was c': 7185
Ex 6: 9 of spirit, and for c' bondage. "
De 32:33 dragons, and the c' venom of asps. 393
Job 30:21 Thou art become c' to me: with thy "
Ps 25:19 and they hate me with c' hatred. 2555
71: 4 of the unrighteous and c' man. 2556
Pr 5: 9 others, and thy years unto the c': 394
11:17 he that is c' troubleth his own flesh. "
12:10 tender mercies of the wicked are c'. "
17:11 a c' messenger shall be sent against "
27: 4 is c', and anger is outrageous; 395
Ca 8: 6 jealousy is c' as the grave: the coals
Isa 13: 9 Lord cometh, c' both with wrath 394
19: 4 over into the hand of a c' lord; 7186
Jer 6:23 they are c', and have no mercy; 394
30.14 the chastisement of a c' one, for "
50:42 they are c', and will not shew mercy: "
La 4: 3 daughter of my people is become c', 393
Heb 11:36 others had trial of c' mockings *

cruelly
Eze 18:18 father, because he c' oppressed, 6233

cruelty
Ge 49: 5 instruments of c' are in their *2555
J'g 9:24 the c' done to the threescore and * "
Ps 27:12 against me, and breathe out c'. "
74:20 are full of the habitations of c'. * "
Eze 34: 4 and with c' have ye ruled them. *6531

crumbs
M't 15:27 dogs eat of the c' which fall from 5589
M'r 7:28 the table eat of the children's c'. "
Lu 16:21 to be fed with the c' which fell "

cruse
1Sa 26:11 and the c' of water, and let us go. 6835
12 the c' of water from Saul's bolster; "
16 and the c' of water that was at his "
1Ki 14: 3 and a c' of honey, and go to him: 1228
17:12 in a barrel, and a little oil in a c': 6835
14 waste, neither shall the c' of oil fail, "
16 not, neither did the c' of oil fail, "
19: 6 and a c' of water at his head. "
2Ki 2:20 Bring me a new c', and put salt 6746

crush See also CRUSHED.
Job 39:15 that the foot may c' them, or that 2115
La 1:15 against me to c' my young men: 7665
3:34 c' under his feet all the prisoners 1792
Am 4: 1 which c' the needy, which say to 7533

crushed
Le 22:24 bruised, or c', or broken, or cut; 3807
Nu 22:25 c' Balaam's foot against the wall: 3905
De 28:33 be only oppressed and c' alway: 7533
Job 4:19 which are c' before the moth? 1792
5: 4 they are c' in the gate, neither is "
Isa 59: 5 is c' breaketh out into a viper. 2116
Jer 51:34 he hath c' me, he hath made me 2000

cry See also CRIED; CRIES; CRIEST; CRIETH; CRYING.
Ge 18:20 c' of Sodom and Gomorrah is 2201
21 altogether according to the c' of it, 6818
19:13 the c' of them is waxen great "
27:34 a great and exceeding bitter c', "
Ex 2:23 their c' came up unto God by 7775
3: 7 and have heard their c' by reason 6818
9 c' of the children of Israel is come "
5: 8 they c', saying, Let us go and 6817
11: 6 shall be great c' throughout all 6818
12:30 there was a great c' in Egypt; "
22:23 and they c' at all unto me, 6817
23 I will surely hear their c'; 6818
32:18 is it the voice of them that c' 6030
Le 13:45 and shall c', Unclean, unclean. 7121
Nu 16:34 about them fled at the c' of them: 6963
De 15: 9 he c' unto the Lord against thee, 7121
24:15 he c' against thee unto the Lord, "
J'g 10:14 Go and c' unto the gods which ye 2199
1Sa 5:12 c' of the city went up to heaven. 7775
7: 8 Cease not to c' unto the Lord our 2199
8:18 And ye shall c' out in that day "
9:16 because their c' is come unto me. 6818
2Sa 19:28 have I yet to c' any more unto the 2199
22: 7 and my c' did enter into his ears. 7775
1Ki 8:28 unto the c' and to the prayer, 7440
18:27 C' aloud: for he is a god; either 7121
2Ki 8: 3 she went forth to c' unto the king 6817
2Ch 6:19 to hearken unto the c' and the 7440
13:12 sounding trumpets to c' alarm *7321
20: 9 and c' unto thee in our affliction, 2199
Ne 5: 1 there was a great c' of the people 6818
6 I heard their c' and these words. 2201
9: 9 heardest their c' by the Red sea; "
Es 4: 1 cried with a loud and a bitter c'; "
9:31 matters of the fastings and their c'. "
Job 16:18 and let my c' have no place. "
19: 7 I c' out of wrong, but I am not 6817
7 I c' aloud, but there is no 7768
27: 9 Will God hear his c' when trouble 6818
30:20 I c' unto thee, and thou dost not 7768
24 though they c' in his destruction. 7769
31:38 If my land c' against me, or 2199
34:28 c' of the poor to come unto him, 6818
28 and he heareth the c' of the "
35: 9 they make the oppressed to c': 2199
9 they c' out by reason of the arm 7768
12 they c', but none giveth answer, 6817
36:13 they c' not when he bindeth them. 7768
38:41 when his young ones c' unto God, "
Ps 5: 2 unto the voice of my c', my King, 7773
9:12 forgetteth not the c' of the humble. 6818
17: 1 attend unto my c', give ear unto 7440
18: 6 and my c' came before him, even 7775
22: 2 O my God, I c' in the daytime, 7121
27: 7 Hear, O Lord, when I c' with my "
28: 1 Unto thee will I c', O Lord my * "
2 when I c' unto thee, when I lift 7768
34:15 his ears are open unto their c'. 7775
17 The righteous c', and the Lord *6817
39:12 and give ear unto my c'; hold not 7775
40: 1 inclined unto me, and heard my c'. "
55:17 at noon; will I pray, and c' aloud: *1993
56: 9 I c' unto thee, then shall mine *7121
57: 2 I will c' unto God most high; unto "
61: 1 Hear my c', O God; attend unto 7440
2 of the earth will I c' unto thee, *7121
86: 3 O Lord: for I c' unto thee daily. "
88: 2 incline thine ear unto my c'; 7440
89:26 He shall c' unto me, Thou art my 7121
102: 1 and let my c' come unto thee. 7775
106:44 affliction, when he heard their c': 7440
107:19 c' unto the Lord in their trouble, 2199
28 c' unto the Lord in their trouble, 6817
119:169 Let my c' come near before thee, 7440
141: 1 Lord, I c' unto thee: make haste *7121
1 my voice, when I c' unto thee. * "
142: 6 Attend unto my c'; for I am 7440
145:19 hear their c', and will save them. 7775
147: 9 and to the young ravens which c'. 7121
Pr 8: 1 Doth not wisdom c'? and 7121
21:13 his ears at the c' of the poor, 2201
13 he also shall c' himself, 7121
Ec 9:17 c' of him that ruleth among fools. 2201
Isa 5: 7 for righteousness, but behold a c'. 6818
8: 4 child shall have knowledge to c', 7121
12: 6 C' out and shout, thou inhabitant 6670
13:22 wild beasts of the islands shall c' 6030
14:31 Howl, O gate; c', O city; thou, 2199
15: 4 Heshbon shall c', and Elealeh; * "
4 soldiers of Moab shall c' out; 7321
5 My heart shall c' out for Moab; *2199
5 shall raise up a c' of destruction. 2201
8 For the c' is gone round about the "
19:20 shall c' unto the Lord because of 6817
24:14 they shall c' aloud from the sea. 6670
29: 9 and wonder; c' ye out, and c': *8173
30:19 unto thee at the voice of thy c'; 2201
33: 7 their valiant ones shall c' without: 6817
34:14 the satyr shall c' to his fellow; 7121
40: 2 and c' unto her, that her warfare is "
6 The voice said, C'. "
6 And he said, what shall I c'? "
42: 2 He shall not c', nor lift up, nor 6817
13 he shall c', yea, roar; he shall 7321
14 will I c' like a travailing woman; 6463
43:14 the Chaldeans, whose c' is in the *7440
46: 7 yea, one shall c' unto him, yet 6817
54: 1 forth into singing, and c' aloud, 6670
58: 1 C' aloud, spare not, lift up thy 7121
9 thou shalt c', and he shall say, 7768
65:14 ye shall c' for sorrow of heart, 6817
Jer 2: 2 and c' in the ears of Jerusalem, 7121
3: 4 thou not from this time c' unto me, "
4: 5 in the land: c', gather together, "
7:16 lift up c' nor prayer for them, 7440
8:19 c' of the daughter of my people 7775
11:11 though they shall c' unto me, 2199
12 go, and c' unto the gods unto "
14 lift up a c' or prayer for them: 7440
14 the time that they c' unto me for 7121
14: 2 the c' of Jerusalem is gone up. 6682
12 they fast, I will not hear their c'; 7440
18:22 a c' be heard from their houses, 2201
20:16 let him hear the c' in the morning, "
22:20 Go up to Lebanon, and c'; and lift 6817
20 up thy voice in Bashan, and c' from "
25:34 Howl, ye shepherds, and c'; and 2199
36 A voice of the c' of the shepherds, 6818
31: 6 shall c', Arise ye, and let us go 7121
46:12 and thy c' hath filled the land: 6682
17 They did c' there, Pharaoh king *7121
47: 2 then the men shall c', and all the 2199
48: 4 her little ones have caused a c' 2201
5 have heard a c' of destruction. 6818
20 it is broken down: howl and c'; 2199
31 I will c' out for all Moab; mine "
34 c' of Heshbon even unto Elealeh, 2201
49: 3 c', ye daughters of Rabbah, gird 6817
21 at the c' the noise thereof was 6818
29 they shall c' unto them, Fear is 7121
50:46 c' is heard among the nations. 2201
51:54 sound of a c' cometh from Babylon, "
La 2:19 Arise, c' out in the night: in the 7442
3: 8 Also when I c' and shout, he 2199
56 ear at my breathing, at my c'. 7775
Eze 8:18 though they c' in mine ears with 7121
9: 4 that c' for all the abominations 602
21:12 C' and howl, son of man: for it 2199
24:17 Forbear to c', make no mourning * 602
26:15 wounded c', when the slaughter "
27:28 the sound of the c' of thy pilots 2201
30 and shall c' bitterly, and shall cast 2199
Ho 5: 8 Ramah: c' aloud at Beth-aven, *7321
8: 2 Israel shall c' unto me, My God, 2199
Joe 1:14 and c' unto the Lord, * "
19 O Lord, to thee will I c': for the 7121
20 beasts of the field c' also unto *6165
Am 3: 4 young lion c' out of his den, 5414, 6963
Jon 1: 2 that great city, and c' against it; 7121
3: 8 and c' mightily unto God: "
Mic 3: 4 Then shall they c' unto the Lord, 2199
5 with their teeth, and c', Peace: 7121

Mic 4: 9 why dost thou c' out aloud: is 7321
Na 2: 8 Stand, stand, shall they c'; but none
Hab 1: 2 O Lord, how long shall I c', and 7768
2 c' out unto thee of violence, and 2199
2:11 the stone shall c' out of the wall, "
Zep 1:10 noise of a c' from the fish gate, 6818
14 mighty man shall c' there bitterly.*6873
Zec 1:14 C' thou, saying, Thus saith the 7121
17 C' yet, saying, Thus saith the Lord "
M't 12:19 He shall not strive, nor c'; *2905
25: 6 at midnight there was a c' made, 2906
M'r 10:47 he began to c' out, and say, Jesus, 2896
Lu 18: 7 own elect, which c' day and night 994
19:40 stones would immediately c' out. 2896
Ac 23: 9 And there arose a great c': and *2906
Ro 8:15 whereby we c', Abba, Father. 2896
Ga 4:27 and c' thou that travailest not: 994
Re 14:18 and cried with a loud c' to him *2906

crying
1Sa 4:14 Eli heard the noise of the c', 6818
2Sa 13:19 hand on her head, and went on c'. 2201
Job 39: 7 regardeth he the c' of the driver. *8663
Ps 69: 3 I am weary of my c': my throat 7121
Pr 19:18 let not thy soul spare for his c'. *4191
30:15 hath two daughters, c', Give, give.
Isa 22: 5 walls, and of c' to the mountains. 7771
24:11 is a c' for wine in the streets; 6682
65:19 heard in her, nor the voice of c'. 2201
Jer 48: 3 of c' shall be from Horonaim, *6818
Zec 4: 7 thereof with shoutings, c', Grace,*
Mal 2:13 with weeping, and with c' out, * 603
M't 3: 3 voice of one c' in the wilderness, 994
9:27 c', and saying, Thou son of David, 2896
21:15 and the children c' in the temple, "
M'r 1: 3 voice of one c' in the wilderness, 994
5: 5 and in the tombs, c', and cutting *2896
15: 8 the multitude c' aloud began to * 310
Lu 3: 4 voice of one c' in the wilderness, 994
4:41 out of many, c' out, and saying, 2896
Joh 1:23 the voice of one c' in the wilderness,994
Ac 8: 7 unclean spirits, c' with loud voice, "
14:14 ran in among the people, c' out, 2896
17: 6 unto the rulers of the city, c', 994
21:28 C' out, Men of Israel, help: This 2896
36 followed after, c', Away with him. "
25:24 c' that he ought not to live any 1916
Ga 4: 6 into your hearts, c', Abba, Father. 2896
Heb 5: 7 with strong c' and tears unto him 2906
Re 14:15 c' with a loud voice to him that 2896
21: 4 neither sorrow, nor c', neither 2906

crystal
Job 28:17 The gold and the c' cannot equal *2137
Eze 1:22 as the colour of the terrible c', 7140
Re 4: 6 was a sea of glass like unto c': 2930
21:11 like a jasper stone, clear as c'; 2929
22: 1 river of water of life, clear as c'. 2930

cubit See also CUBITS.
Ge 6:16 a c' shalt thou finish it above; 520
Ex 25:10 a c' and a half the breadth thereof, "
10 a c' and a half the height thereof. "
17 a c' and a half the breadth thereof. "
23 and a c' the breadth thereof, and "
23 a c' and a half the height thereof. "
26:13 And a c' on the one side, "
13 and a c' on the other side of that "
16 a c' and a half shall be the breadth "
30: 2 A c' shall be the length thereof, and "
2 a c' the breadth thereof; foursquare "
36:21 and the breadth of a board one c' "
37: 1 and a c' and a half the breadth of it, "
1 and a c' and a half the height of it: "
6 one c' and a half the breadth thereof, "
10 and a c' the breadth thereof, "
10 a c' and a half the height thereof. "
25 the length of it was a c', "
25 and the breadth of it a c'; "
De 3:11 breadth of it, after the c' of a man. "
J'g 3:16 had two edges, of a c' length; 1574
1Ki 7:24 knops compassing it, ten in a c', *520
31 the chapiter and above was a c': "
31 work of the base, a c' and an half: "
32 a wheel was a c' and half a c'. "
35 a round compass of half a c' high: "
2Ch 4: 3 ten in a c', compassing the sea * "
Eze 40: 5 six cubits long by the c' and an hand "
12 one c' on this side, "
12 the space was one c' on that side: "
42 of a c' and an half long, "
42 and a c' and an half broad, "
42 and one c' high: "
42: 4 breadth inward, a way of one c'; "
43:13 The c' is a c' and an hand breadth; "
13 even the bottom shall be a c', "
13 and the breadth a c', "
14 two cubits, and the breadth one c'; "
14 four cubits, and the breadth one c'. "
17 border about it shall be half a c'; "
17 bottom thereof shall be a c' about; "
M't 6:27 can add one c' unto his stature? 4083
Lu 12:25 can add to his stature one c'?

cubits
Ge 6:15 the ark shall be three hundred c', 520
15 the breadth of it fifty c', "
15 and the height of it thirty c'. "
7:20 Fifteen c' upward did the waters "
Ex 25:10, 17 two c' and a half shall be the "
23 two c' shall be the length thereof, "
26: 2 curtain shall be eight and twenty c', "
2 the breadth of one curtain four c': "
8 of one curtain shall be thirty c', and "
8 the breadth of one curtain four c': "
16 Ten c' shall be the length of a "
27: 1 wood, five c' long, and five c' broad; "
1 the height thereof shall be three c'. "
9 fine twined linen of an hundred c' "
Ex 27:11 be hangings of an hundred c' long, "
12 side shall be hangings of fifty c': 520
13 east side eastward shall be fifty c'. "
14 side of the gate shall be fifteen c': "
15 side shall be hangings fifteen c': "
16 shall be an hanging of twenty c', 520
18 of the court shall be an hundred c', "
18 and the height five c' of fine twined "
30: 2 two c' shall be the height thereof; "
36: 9 one curtain was twenty and eight c', "
9 the breadth of one curtain four c': "
15 length of one curtain was thirty c', "
15 and four c' was the breadth of one "
21 The length of a board was ten c', "
37: 1 two c' and a half was the length of "
6 c' and a half was the length thereof, "
10 two c' was the length thereof, and "
25 and two c' was the height of it; the "
38: 1 five c' was the length thereof, "
1 and five c' the breadth thereof; "
1 and three c' the height thereof. "
9 of fine twined linen, an hundred c': "
11 the hangings were an hundred c', "
12 side were hangings of fifty c', "
13 for the east side eastward fifty c'. "
14 one side of the gate were fifteen c'; "
15 hand, were hangings of fifteen c'; "
18 twenty c' was the length, and the "
18 the breadth was five c', answerable "
Nu 11:31 and as it were two c' high upon the "
35: 4 and outward a thousand c' round "
5 east side two thousand c', "
5 the south side two thousand c', "
5 the west side two thousand c', "
5 on the north side two thousand c'; "
De 3:11 nine c' was the length thereof, "
11 and four c' the breadth of it, "
Jos 3: 4 about two thousand c' by measure: "
1Sa 17: 4 whose height was six c' and a span. "
1Ki 6: 2 the length thereof was threescore c', "
2 the breadth thereof twenty c', "
2 and the height thereof thirty c'. 520
3 twenty c' was the length thereof, "
3 and ten c' was the breadth thereof "
6 nethermost chamber was five c', "
6 and the middle was six c' broad, "
6 and the third was seven c' broad: "
10 against all the house, five c' high: "
16 he built twenty c' on the sides of "
17 temple before it, was forty c' long. "
20 forepart was twenty c' in length, "
20 and twenty c' in breadth, "
20 and twenty c' in the height thereof. "
23 cherubims of olive tree, each ten c' "
24 c' was the one wing of the cherub, "
24 five c' the other wing of the cherub: "
24 part of the other were ten c'. "
25 And the other cherub was ten c': "
26 height of the one cherub was ten c', "
7: 2 the length thereof was an hundred c', "
2 and the breadth thereof fifty c', "
2 and the height thereof thirty c', "
6 the length thereof was fifty c', "
6 and the breadth thereof thirty c': "
10 stones of ten c', and stones of eight c'. "
15 of brass, of eighteen c' high apiece: "
15 line of twelve c' did compass either "
16 one chapiter was five c', and the "
16 of the other chapiter was five c': "
19 of lily work in the porch, four c'. "
23 a molten sea, ten c' from the one "
23 and his height was five c': and "
23 a line of thirty c' did compass it "
27 four c' was the length of one base, "
27 and four c' the breadth thereof, "
27 and three c' the height of it. "
38 every laver was four c': and upon "
2Ki 14:13 the corner gate, four hundred c'. "
25:17 one pillar was eighteen c', and the "
17 the height of the chapiter three c'; "
1Ch 11:23 a man of great stature, five c' high; "
2Ch 3: 3 The length, by c' after the first "
3 measure was threescore c', "
3 and the breadth twenty c'. "
4 the breadth of the house, twenty c', "
8 length whereof was twenty c', "
8 and the breadth thereof twenty c': "
11 the cherubims were twenty c' long: "
11 wing of the one cherub was five c', "
11 the other wing was likewise five c', "
12 wing of the other cherub was five c', "
12 the other wing was five c' also, "
13 spread themselves forth twenty c': "
15 house two pillars of thirty and five c'" "
15 the top of each of them was five c'. "
4: 1 twenty c' the length thereof, "
1 and twenty c' the breadth thereof, "
1 and ten c' the height thereof. "
2 a molten sea of ten c' from brim to "
2 brim, round in compass, and five c' "
2 a line of thirty c' did compass "
6:13 a brasen scaffold, of five c' long, "
13 and five c' broad, and three c' high, "
25:23 to the corner gate, four hundred c'. "
Ezr 6: 3 the height thereof threescore c', 521
3 the breadth thereof threescore c'; "
Neh 3:13 and a thousand c' on the wall unto 520
Es 5:14 Let a gallows be made of fifty c' "
7: 9 Behold also, the gallows fifty c' high, "
Jer 52:21 height of one pillar was eighteen c'; "
21 and a fillet of twelve c' did compass "
22 height of one chapiter was five c', "
Eze 40: 5 a measuring reed of six c' long by "
7 the little chambers were five c'; "
9 the porch of the gate, eight c'; "
9 and the posts thereof, two c'; "
Eze 40:11 the entry of the gate, ten c'; and 520
11 the length of the gate, thirteen c'. "
12 chambers were six c' on this side, "
12 and six c' on that side. "
13 breadth was five and twenty c', door "
14 He made also posts of threescore c', "
15 porch of the inner gate were fifty c'. "
19 without, an hundred c' eastward and "
21 the length thereof was fifty c', "
21 and the breadth five and twenty c'. "
23 from gate to gate an hundred c'. "
25 the length was fifty c', and the "
25 breadth five and twenty c'. "
27 gate toward the south an hundred c'. "
29 it was fifty c' long, and "
29 and five and twenty c' broad. "
30 about were five and twenty c' long, "
30 and five c' broad. "
33 it was fifty c' long, "
33 and five and twenty c' broad. "
36 the length was fifty c', and the "
36 breadth five and twenty c'. "
47 an hundred c' long, and "
47 an hundred c' broad, four square; "
48 post of the porch, five c' on this side, "
48 and five c' on that side: "
48 of the gate was three c' on this side, "
48 and three c' on that side. "
49 length of the porch was twenty c', "
49 and the breadth eleven c'; "
41: 1 posts, six c' broad on the one side, "
1 and six c' broad on the other side, "
2 breadth of the door was ten c'; "
2 sides of the door were five c' on the "
2 side, and five c' on the other side: "
2 the length thereof, forty c': "
2 and the breadth, twenty c'. "
3 door two c'; and the door, six c'; "
3 the breadth of the door, seven c'. "
4 the length thereof, twenty c'; "
4 and the breadth, twenty c'. "
5 the wall of the house, six c'; "
5 of every side chamber, four c'. "
8 were a full reed of six great c'. "
9 side chamber without, was five c': "
10 was the wideness of twenty c' round "
11 place that was left was five c' round "
12 the west was seventy c' broad; "
12 was five c' thick round about, "
12 and the length thereof ninety c'. "
13 the house an hundred c' long; and "
13 walls thereof, an hundred c' long; "
14 place toward the east, an hundred c'. "
15 the other side, an hundred c', with "
22 altar of wood was three c' high, "
22 and the length thereof two c'; "
42: 2 Before the length of an hundred c' "
2 door, and the breadth was fifty c'. "
3 Over against the twenty c' which
4 a walk of ten c' breadth inward, 520
7 the length thereof was fifty c'. "
8 were in the utter court was fifty c': "
8 the temple were an hundred c'. "
43:13 measures of the altar after the c': "
14 to the lower settle shall be two c', "
14 the greater settle shall be four c', "
15 the altar shall be four c'; and from "
16 the altar shall be twelve c' long, "
17 the settle shall be fourteen c' long "
45: 2 fifty c' round about for the suburbs 520
46:22 were courts joined of forty c' long "
47: 3 he measured a thousand c', and 520
Da 3: 1 whose height was threescore c', 521
1 and the breadth thereof six c': "
Zec 5: 2 the length thereof is twenty c', 520
2 and the breadth thereof ten c'. "
Joh 21: 8 but as it were two hundred c',) 4083
Re 21:17 an hundred and forty and four c', "

cuckow
Le 11:16 the night hawk, and the c', and *7828
De 14:15 the night hawk, and the c', and * "

cucumbers
Nu 11: 5 freely; the c', and the melons, 7180
Isa 1: 8 as a lodge in a garden of c', 4750

cud
Le 11: 3 cheweth the c', among the beasts, 1625
4 of them that chew the c', or of "
4, 5, 6 because he cheweth the c', but "
7 yet he cheweth not the c'; he is "
26 nor cheweth the c', are unclean "
De 14: 6 cheweth the c' among the beasts, "
7 of them that chew the c', or of "
7 for they chew the c', but divide "
8 yet cheweth not the c', it is "

cumbered
Lu 10:40 But Martha was c' about much 4049

cumbereth
Lu 13: 7 cut it down; why c' it the ground? *2673

cumbrance
De 1:12 can I myself alone bear your c', 2960

cumi *(coo'-mi)*
M'r 5:41 unto her, Talitha c'; which is, 2891

cummin
Isa 28:25 and scatter the c', and cast in the 3646
27 wheel turned about upon the c'; "
27 with a staff, and the c' with a rod. "
M't 23:23 pay tithe of mint and anise and c', 2951

cunning
Ge 25:27 Esau was a c' hunter, a man of 3045
Ex 26: 1 cherubims of c' work shalt thou ‡2803
31 and fine twined linen of c' work: ‡ "
28: 6 fine twined linen, with c' work. ‡ "
15 breastplate of judgment with c' ‡ "

Ex 31: 4 devise c' works, to work in gold, ‡4284
35:33 to make any manner of c' work. ‡ "
35 and of the c' workman, and of the ‡2803
35 and of those that devise c' work. ‡4284
36: 8 cherubims of c' work made he ‡2803
35 cherubims made he it of c' work. ‡ "
38:23 an engraver and a c' workman, ‡ "
39: 3 in the fine linen, with c' work. ‡ "
8 the breastplate of c' work, like ‡ "
1Sa 16:16 seek out a man, who is a c' player 3045
18 that is c' in playing, and a mighty "
1Ki 7:14 c' to work all works in brass. ‡1847
1Ch 22:15 c' men for every manner of work. ‡2450
25: 7 all that were c', was two hundred* 995
2Ch 2: 7 c' to work in gold, and in silver, ‡2450
7 skill to grave with c' the men that "
13 now I have sent a c' man, endued "
14 be put to him, with thy c' men, "
14 and with the c' men of my lord "
26:15 engines, invented by c' men, to be 2803
Ps 137: 5 let my right hand forget her c'
Ca 7: 1 of the hands of a c' workman. ‡ 542
Isa 3: 3 counseller, and the c' artificer, ‡2450
40:20 seeketh unto a him c' workman ‡ "
Jer 9:17 may come; and send for c' women, "
10: 9 they are all the work of c' men. ‡ "
Da 1: 4 and c' in knowledge, and 3045
Eph 4:14 sleight of men, and c' craftiness. *

cunningly
2Pe 1:16 have not followed c' devised fables,

cup See also CUPBEARER; CUPS.
Ge 40:11 and Pharaoh's c' was in my hand: 3563
11 pressed them into Pharaoh's c', "
11 I gave the c' into Pharaoh's hand. "
13 deliver Pharaoh's c' into his hand, "
21 he gave the c' into Pharaoh's hand: "
44: 2 And put my c', the silver c', in the 1375
12 c' was found in Benjamin's sack. "
16 he also with whom the c' is found. "
17 man in whose hand the c' is found, "
2Sa 12: 3 and drank of his own c', and lay 3563
1Ki 7:26 was wrought like the brim of a c', "
2Ch 4: 5 like the work of the brim of a c', "
Ps 11: 6 this shall be the portion of their c'. "
16: 5 of mine inheritance and of my c': "
23: 5 head with oil; my c' runneth over. "
73:10 and waters of a full c' are wrung out "
75: 8 hand of the Lord there is a c', 3563
116:13 I will take the c' of salvation, and "
Pr 23:31 when it giveth his colour in the c',3599
Isa 51:17 of the Lord the c' of his fury; 3563
17 the dregs of the c' of trembling, "
22 of thine hand the c' of trembling, "
22 even the dregs of the c' of my fury; "
Jer 16: 7 the c' of consolation to drink for "
25:15 the wine c' of this fury at my hand, "
17 took I the c' at the Lord's hand, "
28 take the c' at thine hand to drink, "
49:12 judgment was not to drink of the c' "
51: 7 Babylon hath been a golden c' in "
La 4:21 the c' also shall pass through unto "
Eze 23:31 will I give her c' into thine hand. "
32 of thy sister's c' deep and large: "
33 c' of astonishment and desolation, "
33 with the c' of thy sister Samaria. "
Hab 2:16 c' of the Lord's right hand shall be "
Zec 12: 2 make Jerusalem a c' of trembling 5592
M't 10:42 c' of cold water only in the name 4221
20:22 drink of the c' that I shall drink of, "
23 Ye shall drink indeed of my c', and "
23:25 outside of the c' and of the platter, "
26 first that which is within the c' "
26:27 he took the c', and gave thanks, "
39 possible, let this c' pass from me: "
42 this c' may not pass away from me, "
M'r 9:41 give you a c' of water to drink "
10:38 ye drink of the c' that I drink of? "
39 indeed drink of the c' that I drink "
14:23 And he took the c', and when he "
36 take away this c' from me: "
Lu 11:39 make clean the outside of the c' "
22:17 he took the c', and gave thanks, "
20 Likewise also the c' after supper, "
20 This c' is the new testament in my "
42 if thou be willing, remove this c' "
Joh 18:11 c' which my Father hath given me, "
1Co 10:16 The c' of blessing which we bless, "
21 Ye cannot drink the c' of the Lord, "
21 and the c' of devils: "
11:25 same manner also he took the c', "
25 This c' is the new testament in my "
26 and drink this c', ye do shew "
27 drink this c' of the Lord, unworthily, "
28 of that bread, and drink of that c'. "
Re 14:10 into the c' of his indignation; "
16:19 the c' of the wine of the fierceness "
17: 4 having a golden c' in her hand full "
18: 6 in the c' which she hath filled, fill "

cupbearer See also CUPBEARERS.
Ne 1:11 For I was the king's c'. 4945

cupbearers
1Ki 10: 5 their apparel, and his c', and his 4945
2Ch 9: 4 their apparel; his c' also, and their "

cups
1Ch 28:17 and the bowls, and the c': 7184
Isa 22:24 from the vessels of c', even to all 101
Jer 35: 5 pots full of wine, and c', and I 3563
52:19 and the spoons, and the c'; that 4518
M'r 7: 4 as the washing of c', and pots, 4221
8 as the washing of pots and c':

curdled
Job 10:10 as milk, and c' me like cheese? 7087

cure See also CURED; CURES; INCURABLE; PROCURE.
Jer 33: 6 I will bring it health and c', 4832
6 and I will c' them, and will reveal 7495
Ho 5:13 you, nor c' you of your wound. 1455
M't 17:16 and they could not c' him. 2323
Lu 9: 1 over all devils, and to c' diseases. "

cured
Jer 46:11 for thou shalt not be c'. *8585
M't 17:18 child was c' from that very hour. 2323
Lu 7:21 he c' many of their infirmities and "
Joh 5:10 said unto him that was c', It is the "

cures
Lu 13:32 and I do c' to day and to morrow, 2392

curious
Ex 28: 8 And the c' girdle of the ephod, †‡
27, 28 above the c' girdle of the †‡
29: 5 with the c' girdle of the ephod: †‡
35:32 devise c' works, to work in gold, †‡4284
39: 5 And the c' girdle of his ephod, †‡
20, 21 above the c' girdle of the †‡
Le 8: 7 with the c' girdle of the ephod, †‡
Ac 19:19 used c' arts brought their books 4021

curiously
Ps 139:15 c' wrought in the lowest parts 7551

current
Ge 23:16 c' money with the merchant. 5674

curse See also CURSED; CURSES; CURSEST; CURSETH; CURSING.
Ge 8:21 I will not again c' the ground any 7043
12: 3 and c' him that curseth thee: and in 779
27:12 I shall bring a c' upon me, and not 7045
13 Upon me be thy c', my son: "
Ex 22:28 gods, nor c' the ruler of thy people. 779
Le 19:14 Thou shalt not c' the deaf, nor 7043
Nu 5:18, 19 bitter water that causeth the c': 779
21 Lord make thee a c' and an oath 423
22 water that causeth the c' shall go 779
24 bitter water that causeth the c'. "
24, 27 water that causeth the c' shall "
27 woman shall be a c' among her 423
22: 6 I pray thee, c' me this people; 779
11 come now, c' me them; 6895
12 shalt not c' the people: for they 779
17 I pray thee, c' me this people. 6895
23: 7 Come, c' me Jacob, and come, 779
8 How shall I c', whom God hath not 5344
11 I took thee to c' mine enemies, 6895
13 all: and c' me them from thence. "
25 c' them at all, nor bless them at all. "
27 mayest c' me them from thence. "
24:10 I called thee to c' mine enemies, "
De 11:26 you this day a blessing and a c'; 7045
28 a c', if ye will not obey the "
29 and the c' upon mount Ebal. "
23: 4 Pethor of Mesopotamia, to c' thee. 7043
5 God turned the c' into a blessing 7045
27:13 shall stand upon mount Ebal to c'; "
29:19 he heareth the words of this c', 423
30: 1 the blessing and the c', which I 7045
Jos 6:18 and make the camp of Israel a c', *2764
24: 9 Balaam the son of Beor to c' you: 7043
J'g 5:23 C' ye Meroz, said the angel 779
23 c' ye bitterly the inhabitants "
9:57 upon them came the c' of Jotham 7045
2Sa 16: 9 should this dead dog c' my lord 7043
10 let him c', because the Lord hath * "
10 Lord hath said unto him, C' David. "
11 let him alone, and let him c': for "
1Ki 2: 8 a grievous c' in the day when I 7045
2Ki 22:19 should become a desolation and a c', "
Ne 10:29 entered into a c', and into an oath, 423
13: 2 against them, that he should c' 7043
2 God turned the c' into a blessing. 7045
Job 1:11 and he will c' thee to thy face. *1288
2: 5 and he will c' thee to thy face. * "
9 c' God, and die. * "
3: 8 Let them c' it that 5344
8 that c' the day, who are 779
31:30 to sin by wishing a c' to his soul. 423
Ps 62: 4 their mouth, but they c' inwardly. 7043
109:28 Let them c', but bless thou: "
Pr 3:33 The c' of the Lord is in the house 3994
11:26 corn, the people shall c' him: but 5344
24:24 him shall the people c', nations "
26: 2 the c' causeless shall not come. 7045
27:14 morning, it shall be counted a c' "
28:27 his eyes shall have many a c'. 3994
30:10 lest he c' thee, and thou be found 7043
Ec 7:21 lest thou hear thy servant c' thee: "
10:20 C' not the king, no not in thy "
20 c' not the rich in thy bedchamber: "
Isa 8:21 and c' their king and their God, "
24: 6 hath the c' devoured the earth, 423
34: 5 and upon the people of my c', to 2764
43:28 given Jacob to the c', and Israel "
65:15 ye shall leave your name for a c' 7621
Jer 15:10 every one of them doth c' me. 7043
24: 9 and a proverb, a taunt and a c', 7045
25:18 astonishment, an hissing, and a c'; "
26: 6 will make this city a c' to all the "
29:18 to be a c', and an astonishment, * 423
22 them shall be taken up a c' by all 7045
42:18 an astonishment, and a c', and a "
44: 8 ye might be a c' and a reproach "
12 an astonishment, and a c', and a "
22 astonishment, and a c', without an "
49:13 a reproach, a waste, and a c'; and "
La 3:65 sorrow of heart, thy c' unto them. 8381
Da 9:11 the c' is poured upon us, and the 423
Zec 5: 3 is the c' that goeth forth over the "
8:13 ye were a c' among the heathen. 7045
Mal 2: 2 I will even send a c' upon you, 3994
2 and I will c' your blessings: 779
Mal 3: 9 are cursed with a c': for ye have 3994
4: 6 come and smite the earth with a c'.2764
M't 5:44 bless them that c' you, do good to *2672
26:74 Then began he to c' and to swear, 2653
M'r 14:71 But he began to c', and to swear, 332
Lu 6:28 Bless them that c' you, and pray 2672
Ac 23:12 and bound themselves under a c', 332
14 bound ourselves under a great c', "
Ro 12:14 persecute you: bless, and c' not. 2672
Ga 3:10 works of the law are under the c': 2671
13 redeemed us from the c' of the "
13 law, being made a c' for us: "
Jas 3: 9 therewith c' we men, which are 2672
Re 22: 3 there shall be no more c': but the 2652

cursed See also ACCURSED; CURSEDST.
Ge 3:14 thou art c' above all cattle, and 779
17 c' is the ground for thy sake; in "
4:11 now art thou c' from the earth, "
5:29 ground which the Lord hath c'. "
9:25 he said, C' be Canaan; a servant of "
27:29 c' be every one that curseth thee, "
49: 7 C' be their anger, for it was fierce; "
Le 20: 9 hath c' his father or his mother; 7043
24:11 the name of the Lord, and c'. "
14 forth him that hath c' without the "
23 forth him that had c' out of the "
Nu 22: 6 and he whom thou cursest is c'. 779
23: 8 I curse, whom God hath not c'? 6895
24: 9 and c' is he that curseth thee. 779
De 7:26 lest thou be a c' thing like it: *2764
26 abhor it; for it is a c' thing. * "
13:17 cleave nought of the c' thing to * "
27:15 C' be the man that maketh any 779
16 C' be he that setteth light by his "
17 C' be he that removeth his "
18 C' be he that maketh the blind to "
19 C' be he that perverteth the "
20 C' be he that lieth with his father's "
21 C' be he that lieth with any manner "
22 C' be he that lieth with his sister, "
23 C' be he that lieth with his mother "
24 C' be he that smiteth his neighbour "
25 C' be he that taketh reward to slay "
26 C' be he that confirmeth not all the "
28:16 C' shalt thou be in the city, "
16 and c' shalt thou be in the field. "
17 C' shall be thy basket and thy store. "
18 C' shall be the fruit of thy body, "
19 C' shalt thou be when thou comest "
19 c' shalt thou be when thou goest "
Jos 6:26 C' be the man before the Lord, that "
9:23 therefore ye are c', and there shall "
J'g 9:27 eat and drink, and c' Abimelech. 7043
21:18 C' be he that giveth a wife to 779
1Sa 14:24, 28 C' be the man that eateth any "
17:43 Philistine c' David by his gods: 7043
26:19 of men, c' be they before the Lord; 779
2Sa 16: 5 came forth, and c' still as he came. 7043
7 said Shimei when he c', Come out, "
13 and c' as he went, and threw stones "
19:21 because he c' the Lord's anointed? "
1Ki 2: 8 which c' me with a grievous curse "
2Ki 2:24 c' them in the name of the Lord. "
9:34 now this c' woman, and bury her: 779
Ne 13:25 contended with them, and c' them, 7043
Job 1: 5 sinned, and c' God in their hearts.*1288
3: 1 Job his mouth, and c' his day. 7043
5: 3 but suddenly I c' his habitation. 5344
24:18 their portion is c' in the earth: he 7043
Ps 37:22 they that be c' of him shall be cut "
119:21 hast rebuked the proud that are c'. 779
Ec 7:22 thyself likewise hast c' others. 7043
Jer 11: 3 C' be the man that obeyeth not the 779
17: 5 C' be the man that trusteth in man, "
20:14 C' be the day wherein I was born: "
15 C' be the man who brought tidings "
48:10 C' be he that doeth the work "
10 c' be he that keepeth back his "
Mal 1:14 c' be the deceiver, which hath in "
2: 2 yea, I have c' them already, because "
3: 9 Ye are c' with a curse: for ye have "
M't 25:41 Depart from me, ye c', into 2672
Joh 7:49 who knoweth not the law are c'. *1944
Ga 3:10 C' is every one that continueth "
13 C' is every one that hangeth on a "
2Pe 2:14 covetous practices; c' children: *2671

cursedst
J'g 17: 2 about which thou c', and spakest * 422
M'r 11:21 behold, the fig tree which thou c' 2672

curses
Nu 5:23 the priest shall write these c' in 423
De 28:15, 45 these c' shall come upon thee, 7045
29:20 all the c' that are written in this * 423
21 according to all the c' of the "
27 to bring upon it all the c' that are *7045
30: 7 put all these c' upon thine enemies, 423
2Ch 34:24 all the c' that are written in the "

cursest
Nu 22: 6 and he whom thou c' is cursed. 779

curseth
Ge 12: 3 and curse him that c' thee: and in 7043
27:29 cursed be every one that c' thee, 779
Ex 21:17 And he that c' his father, or his 7043
Le 20: 9 every one that c' his father or his "
24:15 Whosoever c' his God shall bear "
Nu 24: 9 thee, and cursed is he that c' thee. 779
Pr 20:20 Whoso c' his father or his mother, 7043
30:11 There is a generation that c' their "
M't 15: 4 He that c' father or mother, let *2551
M'r 7:10 Whoso c' father or mother, let him* "

cursing See also CURSINGS.
Nu 5:21 the woman with an oath of c', 423
De 28:20 The Lord shall send upon thee c', 3994
30:19 life and death, blessing and c': *7045

2Sa 16:12 will requite me good for his c' 7045
Ps 10: 7 His mouth is full of c' and deceit 423
59:12 for c' and lying which they speak. "
109:17 As he loved c', so let it come unto 7045
18 he clothed himself with c' like as "
Pr 29:24 he heareth c', and bewrayeth it * 423
Ro 3:14 Whose mouth is full of c' and 685
Heb 6: 8 nigh unto c'; whose end is to be *2671
Jas 3:10 mouth proceedeth blessing and c'. "

cursings
Jos 8:34 of the law, the blessings and c', *7045

curtain See also CURTAINS.
Ex 26:2 The length of one c' shall be eight 3407
2 the breadth of one c' four cubits: "
4 upon the edge of the one c' from "
4 in the uttermost edge of another c', "
5 loops shalt thou make in the one c', "
5 the edge of the c' that is in the "
8 length of one c' shall be thirty "
8 breadth of one c' four cubits; and "
9 double the sixth c' in the forefront "
10 edge of the one c' that is outmost "
10 fifty loops in the edge of the c' "
12 the half c' that remaineth, shall "
36: 9 The length of one c' was twenty "
9 the breadth of one c' four cubits: "
11 loops of blue on the edge of one c' "
11 the uttermost side of another c', "
12 Fifty loops made he in one c', and "
12 the edge of the c' which was "
12 the loops held one c' to another. * "
15 length of one c' was thirty cubits, 3407
15 cubits was the breadth of one c': "
17 upon the uttermost edge of the c' "
17 made he upon the edge of the c', "
Nu 3:26 the c' for the door of the court, *4539
Ps 104: 2 out the heavens like a c': 3407
Isa 40:22 stretcheth out the heavens as a c', 1852

curtains
Ex 26: 1 ten c' of fine twined linen, and 3407
2 every one of the c' shall have one "
3 five c' shall be coupled together "
3 other five c' shall be coupled one to "
6 couple the c' together with the "
7 thou shalt make c' of goats' hair "
7 eleven c' shalt thou make. "
8 the eleven c' shall be all of one "
9 thou shalt couple five c' by "
9 and six c' by themselves, and shalt "
12 remaineth of the c' of the tent, "
13 in the length of the c' of the tent, "
36: 8 ten c' of fine twined linen, and blue "
9 the c' were all of one size. "
10 he coupled the five c' one unto "
10 the other five c' he coupled one "
13 coupled the c' one unto another "
14 made c' of goats' hair for the tent "
14 eleven c' he made them. "
15 the eleven c' were of one size. "
16 five c' by themselves, and six c' by "
Nu 4:25 shall bear the c' of the tabernacle, "
2Sa 7: 2 the ark of God dwelleth within c'. "
1Ch 17: 1 of the Lord remaineth under c'. "
Ca 1: 5 of Kedar, as the c' of Solomon. "
Isa 54: 2 and let them stretch forth the c' of "
Jer 4:20 spoiled, and my c' in a moment. "
10:20 and to set up my c'. "
49:29 shall take to themselves their c', "
Hab 3: 7 the c' of the land of Midian did "

Cush (*cush*) See also ETHIOPIA.
Ge 10: 6 the sons of Ham; C', and Mizraim, 3568
7 the sons of C'; Seba, and Havilah, "
8 C' begat Nimrod: he began to be "
1Ch 1: 8 sons of Ham; C', and Mizraim, "
9 the sons of C'; Seba, and Havilah, "
10 C' begat Nimrod: he began to be "
Ps 7 *title* the words of C' the Benjamite. "
Isa 11:11 from Pathros, and from C', and "

Cushan (*cu'-shan*) See also CHUSHAN-RISHATHAIM.
Hab 3: 7 I saw the tents of C' in affliction: 3572

Cushi (*cu'-shi*)
2Sa 18:21 said Joab to C', Go tell the king *3569
21 And C' bowed himself unto Joab, * "
22 I pray thee, also run after C'. * "
23 way of the plain, and overran C'. * "
31 And, behold, C' came; and C' said,* "
32 said unto C', Is the young man * "
32 C' answered, The enemies of my * "
Jer 36:14 the son of C', unto Baruch, saying, "
Zep 1: 1 unto Zephaniah the son of C', "

custody
Nu 3:36 under the c' and charge of the *6486
Es 2: 3 the women, unto the c' of Hege the 3027
8 the palace, to the c' of Hegai, that "
8 the king's house, to the c' of Hegai, "
14 the women, to the c' of Shaashgaz, "

custom See also ACCUSTOM; CUSTOMS.
Ge 31:35 for the c' of women is upon me. *1870
J'g 11:39 And it was a c' in Israel, 2706
1Sa 2:13 priest's c' with the people was, 4941
Ezr 3: 4 according to the c', as the duty * "
4:13 they not pay toll, tribute, and c', 1983
20 and toll, tribute, and c', was paid "
7:24 toll, tribute, or c', upon them. "
Jer 32:11 sealed according to the law and c 2706
M't 9: 9 sitting at the receipt of c': 5058
17:25 of the earth take c' or tribute? 5056
M'r 2:14 sitting at the receipt of c', *5058
Lu 1: 9 to the c' of the priest's office, his 1485
2:27 do for him after the c' of the law, 1480
42 Jerusalem after the c' of the feast. 1485
4:16 as his c' was, he went into 3588, 1486
5:27 Levi, sitting at the receipt of c': *5058
Joh 18:39 ye have a c', that I should release 4914
Ro 13: 7 is due; c' to whom c'; fear to whom 5056
1Co 11:16 we have no such c', neither the 4914

customs
Le 18:30 any one of these abominable c', 2708
Jer 10: 3 the c' of the people are vain: "
Ac 6:14 the c' which Moses delivered us. 1485
16:21 teach c' which are not lawful for us "
21:21 neither to walk after the c'. "
26: 3 to be expert in all c' and questions "
28:17 the people, or c' of our fathers, "

cut See also CUTTEST; CUTTETH; CUTTING.
Ge 9:11 neither shall all flesh be c' off any 3772
17:14 shall be c' off from his people; "
Ex 4:25 and c' off the foreskin of her son, "
9:15 shalt be c' off from the earth. 3582
12:15 soul shall be c' off from Israel. 3772
19 be c' off from the congregation "
23:23 Jebusites; and I will c' them off. 3582
29:17 thou shalt c' the ram in pieces, 5408
30:33, 38 even be c' off from his people. 3772
31:14 that soul shall be c' off from among "
34:13 images, and c' down their groves: "
39: 3 and c' it into wires, to work it in 7112
Le 1: 6 offering, and c' it into his pieces. 5408
12 And he shall c' it into his pieces, "
7:20, 21 even that soul shall be c' off 3772
25 the soul that eateth it shall be c' off "
27 even that soul shall be c' off from "
8:20 And he c' the ram into pieces; 5408
17: 4 and that man shall be c' off from 3772
9 even that man shall be c' off from "
10 c' him off from among his people. "
14 whosoever eateth it shall be c' off. "
18:29 that commit them shall be c' off "
19: 8 and that soul shall be c' off from "
20: 3 c' him off from among his people; "
5 and will c' him off, and all that go "
6 and will c' him off from among "
17 c' off in the sight of their people: "
18 and both of them shall be c' off "
22: 3 shall be c' off from my presence: "
24 or crushed, or broken, or c'; "
23:29 day, he shall be c' off from among "
26:30 places, and c' down your images, "
Nu 4:18 C' ye not off the tribe of the families "
9:13 even the same soul shall be c' off "
13:23 and c' down from thence a branch "
24 the children of Israel c' down from "
15:30 that soul shall be c' off from among "
31 that soul shall utterly be c' off; "
19:13 that soul shall be c' off from Israel: "
20 that soul shall be c' off from among "
De 7: 5 c' down their groves, and burn *1438
12:29 thy God shall c' off the nations 3772
14: 1 ye shall not c' yourselves, nor 1413
19: 1 thy God hath c' off the nations, 3772
5 with the axe to c' down the tree, "
20:19 and thou shalt not c' them down "
20 shalt destroy and c' them down; "
23: 1 or hath his privy member c' off, "
25:12 Then thou shalt c' off her hand, 7112
Jos 3:13 the waters of Jordan shall be c' off 3772
16 salt sea, failed, and were c' off: "
4: 7 of Jordan were c' off before the ark "
7 the waters of Jordan were c' off: "
7: 9 and c' off our name from the earth: "
11:21 and c' off the Anakims from the "
17:15 and c' down for thyself there in 1254
18 a wood, and thou shalt c' it down: "
23: 4 all the nations that I have c' off. 3772
J'g 1: 6 c' off his thumbs and his great toes, 7112
7 thumbs and their great toes c' off, "
6:25 c' down the grove that is by it: 3772
26 the grove which thou shalt c' down. "
28 grove was c' down that was by it, "
30 because he hath c' down the grove "
9:48 c' down a bough from the trees, "
49 c' down every man his bough, "
20: 6 and c' her in pieces, and sent her 5408
21: 6 There is one tribe c' off from Israel 1438
Ru 4:10 the name of the dead be not c' off 3772
1Sa 2:31 that I will c' off thine arm, and 1438
33 I shall not c' off from mine altar, 3772
5: 4 the palms of his hands were c' off "
17:51 him, and c' off his head therewith. "
20:15 thou shalt not c' off thy kindness "
15 the Lord hath c' off the enemies "
24: 4 and c' off the skirt of Saul's robe "
5 because he had c' off Saul's skirt. "
11 that I c' off the skirt of thy robe, "
21 thou wilt not c' off my seed after "
28: 9 he hath c' off those that have "
31: 9 they c' off his head, and stripped 3772
2Sa 4:12 c' off their hands and their feet, 7112
7: 9 and have c' off all thine enemies 3772
10: 4 and c' off their garments in the "
20:22 And they c' off the head of Sheba "
1Ki 9: 7 will I c' off Israel out of the land "
11:16 until he had c' off every male "
13:34 even to c' it off, and to destroy it 3582
14:10 will c' off from Jeroboam him 3772
14 shall c' off the house of Jeroboam "
18: 4 when Jezebel c' off the prophets of "
23 c' it in pieces, and lay it on wood, 5408
28 cried aloud, and c' themselves 1413
33 c' the bullock in pieces, and laid 5408
21:21 and will c' off from Ahab him that 3772
2Ki 6: 4 they came to Jordan, they c' down 1504
6 he c' down a stick, and cast it in 7094
9: 8 and I will c' off from Ahab him 3772
10:32 the Lord began to c' Israel short: 7096
16:17 And king Ahaz c' off the borders 7112
18: 4 c' down the groves, and brake 3772
16 Hezekiah c' off the gold from the 7112
2Ki 19:23 will c' down the tall cedar trees 3772
23:14 and c' down the groves, and filled "
24:13 c' in pieces all the vessels of gold 7112
1Ch 17: 8 and have c' off all thine enemies 3772
19: 4 and c' off their garments in the "
20: 3 and c' them with saws, and with 7787
2Ch 2: 8 skill to c' timber in Lebanon; 3772
10 servants, the hewers that c' timber, "
16 we will c' wood out of Lebanon, "
14: 3 images, and c' down the groves: *1438
15:16 Asa c' down her idol, and stamped 3772
22: 7 anointed to c' off the house of Ahab. "
26:21 c' off from the house of the Lord: 1504
28:24 and c' in pieces the vessels of 7112
31: 1 and c' down the groves, and *1438
32:21 Lord sent an angel, which c' off all 3582
34: 4 on high above them, he c' down; *1438
7 c' down all the idols throughout * "
Job 4: 7 where were the righteous c' off? 3582
6: 9 loose his hand, and c' me off! 1214
8:12 in his greenness, and not c' down, 6998
14 Whose hope shall be c' off, and *6990
11:10 If he c' off, and shut up, or *2498
14: 2 flower, and is c' down: he fleeth 5243
7 is hope of a tree, if it be c' down, 3772
18:16 above shall his branch be c' off. 5243
21:21 his months is c' off in the midst? 2686
22:16 Which were c' down out of time, *7059
20 our substance is not c' down, but 3582
23:17 was not c' off before the darkness, 6789
24:24 and c' off as the tops of the ears 5243
30: 4 Who c' up mallows by the bushes, *6998
36:20 people are c' off in their place. 5927
Ps 12: 3 Lord shall c' off all flattering lips, 3772
31:22 I am c' off from before thine eyes: 1629
34:16 to c' off the remembrance of them 3772
37: 2 they shall soon be c' down like 5243
9 evildoers shall be c' off: but those 3772
22 be cursed of him shall be c' off. "
28 seed of the wicked shall be c' off. "
34 when the wicked are c' off, thou "
38 the end of the wicked shall be c' off. "
54: 5 enemies: c' them off in thy truth. *6789
58: 7 let them be as c' in pieces. 4135
75:10 of the wicked also will I c' off; 1438
76:12 He shall c' off the spirit of princes: 1219
80:16 It is burned with fire, it is c' down: 3683
83: 4 Come, and let us c' them off from 3582
88: 5 and they are c' off from thy hand. 1504
16 thy terrors have c' me off. 6789
90: 6 it is c' down, and withereth. 4135
10 it is soon c' off, and we fly away. *1504
94:23 c' them off in their own wickedness *6789
23 the Lord our God shall c' them off. "
101: 5 his neighbour, him will I c' off: * "
8 that I may c' off all wicked doers 3772
107:16 and c' the bars of iron in sunder. 1438
109:13 Let his posterity be c' off; and in 3772
15 he may c' off the memory of them "
129: 4 c' asunder the cords of the wicked. 7112
143:12 of thy mercy c' off mine enemies, 6789
Pr 2:22 shall be c' off from the earth, 3772
10:31 the froward tongue shall be c' out. "
23:18 thine expectation shall not be c' off. "
24:14 thy expectation shall not be c' off. "
Isa 9:10 the sycomores are c' down, but we 1438
14 Lord will c' off from Israel head 3772
10: 7 destroy and c' off nations not a few. "
34 And he shall c' down the thickets 5362
11:13 adversaries of Judah shall be c' off: 3772
14:12 art thou c' down to the ground, 1438
22 and c' off from Babylon the name, 3772
15: 2 be baldness, and every beard c' off. 1438
18: 5 both c' off the sprigs with pruning 3772
5 away and c' down the branches. 8456
22:25 removed, and be c' down, and fall; *1438
25 that was upon it shall be c' off: 3772
29:20 that watch for iniquity are c' off: "
33:12 thorns c' up shall they be burned 3683
37:24 c' down the tall cedars thereof, 3772
38:12 have c' off like a weaver my life: *7088
12 c' me off with pining sickness: 1214
45: 2 and c' in sunder the bars of iron: 1438
48: 9 for thee, that I c' thee not off. 3772
19 name should not have been c' off "
51: 9 Art thou not it that hath c' Rahab, 2672
53: 8 c' off out of the land of the living: 1504
55:13 sign that shall not be c' off. 3772
56: 5 name, that shall not be c' off. "
66: 3 lamb, as if he c' off a dog's neck; * "
Jer 7:28 and is c' off from their mouth. 3772
29 C' off thine hair, O Jerusalem, 1494
9:21 to c' off the children from without, 3772
11:19 and let us c' him off from the land "
16: 6 nor c' themselves, nor make 1413
22: 7 shall c' down thy choice cedars, 3772
25:37 peaceable habitations are c' down *1826
34:18 c' the calf in twain, and passed 3772
36:23 he c' it with the penknife, and 7167
41: 5 and having c' themselves, with 1413
44: 7 c' off from you man and woman, 3772
8 that ye might c' yourselves off, "
11 you for evil, and to c' off all Judah. "
46:23 They shall c' down her forest, "
47: 4 c' off from Tyrus and Zidon every "
5 Ashkelon is c' off with the *1820
5 how long wilt thou c' thyself? 1413
48: 2 let us c' it off from being a nation. 3772
2 thou shalt be c' down, O Madmen; *1826
25 The horn of Moab is c' off, and 1438
49:26 men of war shall be c' off in that *1826
50:16 C' off the sower from Babylon, 3772
23 the hammer of the whole earth c' 1438
30 of war shall be c' off in that day, *1826
51: 6 soul: be not c' off in her iniquity; "
62 against this place, to c' it off, 3772

La 2: 3 He hath c' off in his fierce anger 1438
3:53 have c' off my life in the dungeon, 6789
54 then I said, I am c' off. 1504
Eze 6: 6 and your images may be c' down, *1438
14: 8 c' him off from the midst of my 3772
13 will c' off man and beast from it: "
17 that I c' off man and beast from it: "
19 to c' off from it man and beast: 3772
21 to c' off from it man and beast? "
16: 4 thy navel was not c', neither wast "
17: 9 and c' off the fruit thereof, that it 7082
17 forts, to c' off many persons: 3772
21: 3 will c' off from thee the righteous "
4 I will c' off from thee the righteous "
25: 7 I will c' thee off from the people, "
13 will c' off man and beast from it; "
16 and I will c' off the Cherethims, "
29: 8 and c' off man and beast out of thee. "
30:15 I will c' off the multitude of No. "
31:12 of the nations, have c' him off, "
35: 7 c' off from it him that passeth out "
37:11 is lost: we are c' off for our parts. 1504
39:10 out of the field, neither c' down 2404
Da 2: 5 ye shall be c' in pieces, and your 5648
34 a stone was c' out without hands, 1505
45 stone was c' out of the mountain "
3:29 shall be c' in pieces, and their 5648
4:14 and c' off his branches, shake off 7113
9:26 shall Messiah be c' off, but not for 3772
Ho 8: 4 them idols, that they may be c' off. "
10: 7 her king is c' off as the foam upon 1820
15 the king of Israel utterly be c' off. "
Joe 1: 5 for it is c' off from your mouth. 3772
9 the drink offering is c' off from the "
16 not the meat c' off before our eyes, "
Am 1: 5 and c' off the inhabitants from the "
8 c' off the inhabitant from Ashdod, "
2: 3 c' off the judge from the midst "
3: 14 horns of the altar shall be c' off, 1438
9: 1 c' them in the head, all of them; *1214
Ob 5 (how art thou c' off!) would 1820
9 Esau may be c' off by slaughter. 3772
10 and thou shalt be c' off for ever. "
14 c' off those of his that did escape; "
Mic 5: 9 all thine enemies shall be c' off. "
10 I will c' off thy horses out of the "
11 I will c' off the cities of thy land, "
12 c' off witchcrafts out of thine hand; "
13 Thy graven images also will I c' off, "
Na 1:12 shall they be c' down, when he 1494
14 will I c' off the graven image and 3772
15 through thee; he is utterly c' off. "
2:13 I will c' off thy prey from the earth, "
3:15 the sword shall c' thee off, it shall "
Hab 3:17 flock shall be c' off from the fold, 1504
Zep 1: 3 I will c' off man from off the land, 3772
4 c' off the remnant of Baal from "
11 the merchant people are c' down; *1820
11 all they that bear silver are c' off. 3772
3: 6 I have c' off the nations: their "
7 their dwelling should not be c' off, "
Zec 5: 3 every one that stealeth shall be c' †5352
3 every one that sweareth shall be c' † "
9: 6 c' off the pride of the Philistines. 3772
10 c' off the chariot from Ephraim, "
Zec 9:10 and the battle bow shall be c' off: 3772
11: 8 Three shepherds also I c' off in 3582
9 and that that is to be c' off, "
9 let it be c' off; "
10 even Beauty, and c' it asunder, 1438
14 Then I c' asunder mine other staff, "
16 those that be c' off, neither shall 3582
12: 3 with it shall be c' in pieces, *8295
13: 2 will c' off the names of the idols 3772
8 therein shall be c' off and die; "
14: 2 of the people shall not be c' off "
Mal 2:12 The Lord will c' off the man that "
M't 5:30 c' it off, and cast it from thee: *1581*
18: 8 c' them off, and cast them from "
21: 8 c' down branches from the trees, *2875*
24:51 shall c' him asunder, and appoint *1371*
M'r 9:43 if thy hand offend thee, c' it off: *609*
45 if thy foot offend thee, c' it off: "
11: 8 c' down branches off the trees, *2875*
14:47 the high priest, and c' off his ear. * *851*
Lu 12:46 will c' him in sunder, and will *1371*
13: 7 c' it down; why cumbereth it the *1581*
9 after that thou shalt c' it down. "
22:50 priest, and c' off his right ear. * *851*
Joh 18:10 servant, and c' off his right ear. *609*
26 kinsman whose ear Peter c' off, "
Ac 5:33 that, they were c' to the heart, *1282*
7:54 they were c' to the heart, and they "
27:32 soldiers c' off the ropes of the boat, *609*
Ro 9:28 and c' it short in righteousness: *4932*
11:22 otherwise thou also shalt be c. off. *1581*
24 thou wert c' out of the olive tree "
2Co 11:12 I may c' off occasion from them "
Gal 5:12 were even c' off which trouble you. ‡ *609*

Cuth (*cuth*) See also CUTHAH.
2Ki 17:30 and the men of C' made Nergal, 3575

Cuthah (*cu'-thah*) See also CUTH.
2Ki 17:24 men from Babylon, and from C' 3575

cuttest
De 24:19 thou c' down thine harvest in *7114

cutteth
Job 28:10 c' out rivers among the rocks; 1234
Ps 46: 9 bow, and c' the spear in sunder; 7112
141: 7 when one c' and cleaveth wood *6398
Pr 26: 6 hand of the fool c' off the feet, 7096
Jer 10: 3 for one c' a tree out of the forest, 3772
22:14 and c' him out windows; 7167

cutting See also CUTTINGS.
Ex 31: 5 And in c' of stones, to set them, 2799
35:33 And in the c' of stones, to set them, "
Isa 38:10 I said in the c' off of my days, *1824
Hab 2:10 thy house by c' off many people, 7096
M'r 5: 5 crying, and c' himself with stones. *2629*

cuttings
Le 19:28 not make any c' in your flesh for 8296
21: 5 nor make any c' in their flesh. "
Jer 48:37 upon all the hands shall be c', 1417

cymbal See also CYMBALS.
1Co 13: 1 sounding brass, or a tinkling c'. *2950*

cymbals
2Sa 6: 5 and on cornets, and on c'. 6767
1Ch 13: 8 with timbrels, and with c'. 4700
15:16 psalteries and harps and c'. "
19 to sound with c' of brass; "
28 with trumpets, and with c', "
16: 5 but Asaph made a sound with c'; "
42 with trumpets and c' for those "
25: 1 harps, with psalteries, and with c': "
6 with c', psalteries, and harps, "
2Ch 5:12 having c' and psalteries and harps, "
13 trumpets and c' and instruments "
29:25 the Lord with c', with psalteries, "
Ezr 3:10 the sons of Asaph with c', to praise "
Ne 12:27 with singing, with c', psalteries, "
Ps 150: 5 Praise him upon the loud c': 6767
5 him upon the high sounding c'. "

cypress
Isa 44:14 and taketh the c' and the oak. *8645

Cyprus (*si'-prus*)
Ac 4:36 Levite, and of the country of C', *2954*
11:19 and C', and Antioch, preaching "
20 them were men of C' and Cyrene, "
13: 4 and from thence they sailed to C'. "
15:39 took Mark, and sailed unto C'; "
21: 3 when we had discovered C', we left "
16 with them one Mnason of C', "
27: 4 we sailed under C', because the "

Cyrene (*si-re'-ne*) See also CYRENIAN.
M't 27:32 a man of C', Simon by name: *2957*
Ac 2:10 of Libya about C', and strangers "
11:20 were men of Cyprus and C', which "
13: 1 and Lucius of C', and Manaen, "

Cyrenian (*si-re'-ne-an*) See also CYRENIANS.
M'r 15:21 compel one Simon a C', who *2956
Lu 23:26 laid hold upon one Simon, a C', "

Cyrenians (*si-re'-ne-ans*)
Ac 6: 9 of the Libertines, and C', and *2956*

Cyrenius (*si-re'-ne-us*)
Lu 2: 2 when C' was governor of Syria.) *2958*

Cyrus (*si'-rus*)
2Ch 36:22 the first year of C' king of Persia, 3566
22 the Lord stirred up the spirit of C' "
23 Thus saith C' king of Persia, "
Ezr 1: 1 the first year of C' king of Persia, "
1 the Lord stirred up the spirit of C' "
2 Thus saith C' king of Persia, "
7 C' the king brought forth the "
8 those did C' king of Persia bring "
3: 7 to the grant that they had of C' "
4: 3 as king C' the king of Persia hath "
5 all the days of C' king of Persia, "
5:13 first year of C' the king of Babylon 3567
13 the same king C' made a decree "
14 those did C' the king take out of "
17 was made of C' the king to build "
6: 3 year of C' the king the same C' "
14 to the commandment of C', "
Isa 44:28 saith of C', He is my shepherd, 3566
45: 1 the Lord to his anointed, to C', "
Da 1:21 even unto the first year of king C'. "
6:28 and in the reign of C' the Persian. 3567
10: 1 the third year of C' king of Persia 3566

D.

Dabareh (*dab'-a-reh*) See also DABARETH.
Jos 21:28 D' with her suburbs, 1705

Dabbasheth (*dab'-ba-sheth*)
Jos 19:11 and reached to D', and reached 1708

Daberath (*dab'-e-rath*) See also DABASEH.
Jos 19:12 and then goeth out to D', 1705
1Ch 6:72 D' with her suburbs, "

dagger
J'g 3:16 Ehud made him a d' which had two *2719
21 took the d' from his right thigh, * "
22 he could not draw the d' out * "

Dagon See also BETH-DAGON; DAGON'S.
J'g 16:23 great sacrifice unto D' their god, 1712
1Sa 5: 2 brought it into the house of D', "
2 and set it by D'. "
3 behold, D' was fallen upon his face "
3 took D', and set him in his place "
4 behold, D' was fallen upon his face "
4 the head of D' and both the palms "
4 the stump of D' was left to him. "
5 neither the priests of D', nor any "
5 house, tread on the threshold of D' "
7 is sore upon us, and upon D' "
1Ch 10:10 his head in the temple of D'. "

Dagon's
1Sa 5: 5 any that come into D' house, 1712

daily
Ex 5:13 Fulfil your works, your d' tasks, 3117
19 your bricks of your d' tasks. "
16: 5 twice as much as they gather d'. "
Nu 4:16 the d' meat offering and the *8548
28:24 this manner ye shall offer d', 3117
29: 6 d' burnt offering, and his meat *8548
J'g 16:16 pressed him d' with her words, 3117
2Ki 25:30 a d' rate for every day, * "
2Ch 31:16 his d' portion for their service * "
Ezr 3: 4 the d' burnt offerings by number, "
Ne 5:18 prepared for me d' was one *3117, 259
Es 3: 4 when they spake d' unto him, 3117
Ps 13: 2 having sorrow in my heart d'? *3119
42:10 while they say d' unto me, *3605,3117
56: 1 he fighting d' oppresseth me. "
Ps 56: 2 enemies would d' swallow me *3605,3117
61: 8 I may d' perform my vows. "
68:19 who d' loadeth us with benefits, "
72:15 and d' shall he be praised. *3605, "
74:22 foolish...reproacheth thee d'* "
86: 3 O Lord for I cry unto thee d'* "
88: 9 Lord, I...called d' upon thee, "
17 They came round about me d'* "
Pr 8:30 and I was d' his delight, "
34 watching d' at my gates, "
Isa 58: 2 Yet they seek me d', and delight "
Jer 7:25 d' rising up early and sending "
20: 7 I am in derision d', every one *3605, "
8 unto me and a derision, d'. * "
37:21 d' a piece of bread out of the "
Eze 30:16 Noph shall have distresses d'. *3119
45:23 without blemish d' the seven days ;3117
23 and a kid of the goats d' "
46:13 shalt d' prepare a burnt offering "
Da 1: 5 appointed them a d' provision "
8:11 the d' sacrifice was taken away, *8548
12 given him against the d' sacrifice* "
13 vision concerning the d' sacrifice,* "
11:31 shall take away the d' sacrifice, * "
12:11 d' sacrifice shall be taken away, * "
Ho 12: 1 d' increaseth lies and *3605, 3117
M't 6:11 Give us this day our d' bread. *1967*
26:55 I sat d' with you teaching *2596, 2250*
M'r 14:49 was d' with you in the temple " "
Lu 9:23 and take up his cross d', " "
11: 3 us day by day our d' bread. *1967*
19:47 he taught d' in the temple. *2596, 2250*
22:53 d' with you in the temple, " "
Ac 2:46 continuing d' with one accord* " "
47 Lord added to the church d' * " "
3: 2 whom they laid d' at the gate " "
5:42 And d' in the temple, and in * *3956*, "
6: 1 neglected in the d' ministration. *2522*
16: 5 increased in number d'. *2596, 2250*
17:11 searched the scriptures d', " "
17 the market d' with them *2596, 3956*, "
19: 9 disputing d' in the school *2596* "
1Co 15:31 Jesus our Lord, I die d'. " "
2Co 11:28 which cometh upon me d', " "
Heb 3:13 exhort one another d,' *2596, 1538, 2250*
7:27 Who needeth not d', as *2596*, "
10:11 priest standeth d' ministering* " "
Jas 2:15 naked, and destitute of d' food, *2184*

dainties
Ge 49:20 fat, and he shall yield royal d'. 4574
Ps 141: 4 and let me not eat of their d'. 4516
Pr 23: 3 not desirous of his d': for they 4303

dainty See also DAINTIES.
Job 33:20 abhorreth bread, and his soul d' 8378
Pr 23: 6 neither desire thou his d' meats: *4303
Re 18:14 things which were d' and goodly *3045*

Dalaiah (*dal-a-i'-ah*) See also DELAIAH.
1Ch 3:24 Johanan, and D', and Anani, 1806

dale
Ge 14:17 of Shaveh, which is the king's d'. *6010
2Sa 18:18 a pillar, which is in the king's d': "

Dalmanutha (*dal-ma-nu'-thah*)
M'r 8:10 and came into the parts of D'. *1148*

Dalmatia (*dal-ma'-she-ah*)
2Ti 4:10 Crescens to Galatia, Titus unto D'. *1149*

Dalphon (*dal'-fon*)
Es 9: 7 Parshandatha, and D', and 1813

dam
Ex 22:30 seven days it shall be with his d'; 517
Le 22:27 shall be seven days under the d'; "
De 22: 6 and the d' sitting upon the young, "
6 shalt not take the d' with the "
7 thou shalt in any wise let the d' go, "

damage See also ENDAMAGE.
Ezr 4:22 why should d' grow to the hurt 2257
Es 7: 4 not countervail the king's d'. 5143
Pr 26: 6 off the feet, and drinketh d'. 2555
Da 6: 2 and the king should have no d'. 5142
Ac 27:10 will be with hurt and much d', *2209*
2Co 7: 9 that ye might receive d' by us in *2210*

Damaris (*dam'-a-ris*)
Ac 17:34 and a woman named D', and *1152*

Damascenes (*dam-as-senes'*)
2Co 11:32 the king kept the city of the D' *1153*

Damascus (*da-mas'-cus*) See also DAMASCENES; SYRIA-DAMASCUS.
Ge 14:15 which is on the left hand of D'. 1834
15: 2 of my house is this Eliezer of D'?† "
2Sa 8: 5 when the Syrians of D' came to "
6 David put garrisons in Syria of D': "
1Ki 11:24 they went to D', and dwelt therein. "
24 and reigned in D'. "
15:18 king of Syria, that dwelt at D', "
19:15 on thy way to the wilderness of D': "
20:34 shalt make streets for thee in D'. "
2Ki 5:12 Abana and Pharpar, rivers of D', "
8: 7 Elisha came to D'; and Ben-hadad "
9 even of every good thing of D', "
14:28 how he recovered D', and Hamath, "
16: 9 king of Assyria went up against D', "
10 king Ahaz went to D' to meet "
10 and saw an altar that was at D': "
11 that king Ahaz had sent from D': "
11 against king Ahaz came from D'. "
12 when the king was come from D', "
1Ch 18: 5 when the Syrians of D' came to "
2Ch 16: 2 king of Syria, that dwelt at D', "
24:23 spoil of them unto the king of D'. "
28: 5 captives, and brought them to D'. "
23 he sacrificed unto the gods of D', "
Ca 7: 4 Lebanon which looketh toward D'. "
Isa 7: 8 the head of Syria is D', "
8 and the head of D' is Rezin; "
8: 4 the riches of D' and the spoil of "
10: 9 is not Samaria as D'? "
17: 1 The burden of D'. Behold, "
1 D' is taken away from being a city, "
3 and the kingdom from D', and the "
Jer 49:23 Concerning D'. Hamath is "
24 D' is waxed feeble, and turneth "
27 I will kindle a fire in the wall of D', "
Eze 27:18 D' was thy merchant in the "
47:16 which is between the border of D' "
17 the border of D', and the north "
18 and from D', and from Gilead, "
48: 1 the border of D' northward, to the "
Am 1: 3 For three transgressions of D', "
5 I will break also the bar of D', "
3:12 and in D' in a couch. *1833
5:27 to go into captivity beyond D', 1834
Zec 9: 1 and D' shall be the rest thereof: "
Ac 9: 2 And desired of him letters to D' 1154
3 as he journeyed, he came near D': "
8 the hand, and brought him into D'. "
10 there was a certain disciple at D', "
19 with the disciples which were at D'. "
22 the Jews which dwelt at D', "
27 how he had preached boldly at D' "
22: 5 and went to D', to bring them "
6 and was come nigh unto D' "
10 Arise, and go into D'; and there it "
11 that were with me, I came into D'. "
26:12 Whereupon as I went to D' with "
20 But shewed first unto them of D', "
2Co 11:32 In D' the governor under Aretas "
Ga 1:17 Arabia, and returned again unto D'. "

Dammim (*dam'-mim*) See EPHES-DAMMIM; PAS-DAMMIM.

damnable
2Pe 2: 1 privily shall bring in d' heresies, * 684

damnation
M't 23:14 ye shall receive the greater d'. *2917
33 how can ye escape the d' of hell? *2920
M'r 3:29 but is in danger of eternal d': * "
12:40 these shall receive greater d'. *2917
Lu 20:47 the same shall receive greater d'. * "
Joh 5:29 unto the resurrection of d'. *2920
Ro 3: 8 good may come? whose d' is just.*2917
13: 2 shall receive to themselves d'. * "
1Co 11:29 eateth and drinketh d' to himself,* "
1Ti 5:12 Having d', because they have cast* "
2Pe 2: 3 not, and their d' slumbereth not. * 684

damned
M'r 16:16 he that believeth not shall be d'. *2632
Ro 14:23 he that doubteth is d' if he eat, * "
2Th 2:12 That they all might be d' who *2919

damsel See also DAMSEL'S; DAMSELS.
Ge 24:14 the d' to whom I shall say, 5291
16 And the d' was very fair to look "
28 And the d' ran, and told them of "
55 Let the d' abide with us a few "
57 We will call the d', and enquire "
34: 3 and he loved the d', and "
3 spake kindly unto the d'. "
4 saying, Get me this d' to wife. 3207
12 unto me: but give me the d' to 5291
De 22:15 father of the d', and her mother, "
19 unto the father of the d', because "
20 of virginity be not found for the d': "
21 they shall bring out the d' to the "
23 a d' that is a virgin be betrothed "
24 the d', because she cried not, "
25 if a man find a betrothed d' in the "
26 unto the d' thou shalt do nothing; "
26 there is in the d' no sin "
27 the betrothed d' cried, and there "
28 If a man find a d' that is a virgin, "
J'g 5:30 to every man a d' or two; 7356
19: 3 the father of the d' saw him, 5291
Ru 2: 5 over the reapers, Whose d' is this? "
6 It is the Moabitish d' that came "
1Ki 1: 3 So they sought for a fair d' "
4 And the d' was very fair, "
M't 14:11 in a charger, and given to the d': 2877
26:69 and a d' came unto him, saying, *3814
M'r 5:39 the d' is not dead, but sleepeth. *3813
40 father and the mother of the d', "
40 and entereth in where the d' was * "
5:41 he took the d' by the hand, *3813
41 interpreted, D', I say unto thee, 2877
42 the d' arose, and walked; for she "
6:22 the king said unto the d', Ask of "
28 and gave it to the d': and "
28 the d' gave it to her mother. "
Joh 18:17 Then saith the d' that kept the *3814
Ac 12:13 a d' came to hearken, named * "
16:16 a certain d' possessed with a * "

damsel's
De 22:15 bring forth the tokens of the d' 5291
16 And the d' father shall say unto "
29 shall give unto the d' father fifty "
J'g 19: 4 the d' father, retained him; and "
5 d' father said unto his son in law, "
6 the d' father had said unto the "
8 and the d' father said, Comfort "
9 his father in law, the d' father, "

damsels
Ge 24:61 Rebekah arose, and her d', and 5291
1Sa 25:42 with five d' of hers that went "
Ps 68:25 were the d' playing with timbrels. 5959

Dan (*dan*) See also DANITES; DAN-JAAN; LAISH; MAHANEH-DAN.
Ge 14:14 and pursued them unto D'. 1835
30: 6 therefore called she his name D'. "
35:25 of Bilhah, Rachel's handmaid; D', "
46:23 And the sons of D'; Hushim. "
49:16 D' shall judge his people, as one of "
17 D' shall be a serpent by the way, "
Ex 1: 4 D', and Naphtali, Gad, and Asher. "
31: 6 of Ahisamach, of the tribe of D': "
35:34 Ahisamach, of the tribe of D'. "
38:23 of the tribe of D', an engraver, "
Le 24:11 of Dibri, of the tribe of D':) "
Nu 1:12 Of D'; Ahiezer the son of "
38 children of D', by their generations, "
39 of them, even of the tribe of D', "
2:25 The standard of the camp of D' "
25 the captain of the children of D' "
31 were numbered in the camp of D' "
7:66 prince of the children of D', * "
10:25 of the camp of the children of D' "
13:12 the tribe of D', Ammiel the son of "
26:42 the sons of D' after their families: "
42 families of D' after their families "
34:22 of the tribe of the children of D', "
De 27:13 Gad, and Asher, and Zebulun, D', "
33:22 of D' he said, D' is a lion's whelp: "
34: 1 all the land of Gilead, unto D', "
Jos 19:40 for the tribe of the children of D' "
47 of the children of D' went out "
47 the children of D' went up to fight "
47 and called Leshem, D', after "
47 the name of D' their father. "
48 of the tribe of the children of D' "
21: 5 and out of the tribe of D', and out "
23 of the tribe of D', Elteketh with her "
J'g 1:34 Amorites forced the children of D' "
5:17 and why did D' remain in ships? "
13:25 him at times in the camp of D' * "
18: 2 children of D' sent of their family "
16 which were of the children of D', "
22 and overtook the children of D'. "
23 they cried unto the children of D'. "
25 the children of D' said unto him, "
26 the children of D' went their way: "
29 they called the name of the city D', "
29 after the name of D' their father, "
30 children of D' set up the graven "
30 sons were priests to the tribe of D'* "
20: 1 man, from D' even to Beer-sheba, "
1Sa 3:20 Israel from D' even to Beer-sheba "
2Sa 3:10 Judah, from D' even to Beer-sheba "
17:11 thee, from D' even to Beer-sheba, "
24: 2 Israel, from D' even to Beer-sheba, "
15 people from D' even to Beer-sheba "
1Ki 4:25 fig tree, from D' even to Beer-sheba, "
12:29 Beth-el, and the other put he in D'. "
30 before the one, even unto D'. "
15:20 and D', and Abel-beth-maachah, "
2Ki 10:29 in Beth-el, and that were in D'. "
1Ch 2: 2 D', Joseph, and Benjamin, "
21: 2 Israel from Beer-sheba even to D'; "
27:22 Of D', Azareel the son of Jeroham. "
2Ch 2:14 a woman of the daughters of D', "
16: 4 smote Ijon, and D', and Abel-maim, "
30: 5 Israel, from Beer-sheba even to D', "
Jer 4:15 For a voice declareth from D', and "
8:16 of his horses was heard from D': "
Eze 27:19 D' also and Javan going to and * "
48: 1 east and west; a portion for D'. "
2 the border of D', from the east side "
32 gate of Benjamin, one gate of D'. "
Am 8:14 and say, Thy god, O D', liveth; "

dance See also DANCED; DANCES; DANCING.
J'g 21:21 of Shiloh come out to d' in dances, 2342
Job 21:11 like a flock, and their children d'. 7540
Ps 149: 3 praise his name in the d': let 4234
150: 4 Praise him with the timbrel and d': "
Ec 3: 4 a time to mourn, and a time to d'; 7540
Isa 13:21 there, and satyrs shall d' there. "
Jer 31:13 shall the virgin rejoice in the d', 4234
La 5:15 our d' is turned into mourning. "

danced
J'g 21:23 to their number, of them that d', 2342
2Sa 6:14 David d' before the Lord with all 3769
M't 11:17 unto you, and ye have not d'; 3738
14: 6 the daughter of Herodias d' before "
M'r 6:22 the said Herodias came in, and d', "
Lu 7:32 unto you, and ye have not d'; "

dances
Ex 15:20 her with timbrels and with d'. 4246
J'g 11:34 him with timbrels and with d': "
21:21 of Shiloh come out to dance in d', 4246
1Sa 21:11 sing one to another of him in d', "
29: 5 they sang one to another in d', "
Jer 31: 4 shalt go forth in the d' of them "

dancing
Ex 32:19 that he saw the calf, and the d': 4246
1Sa 18: 6 singing and d', to meet king Saul, "
30:16 eating and drinking, and d', *2287
2Sa 6:16 saw king David leaping and d' 3769
1Ch 15:29 saw king David d' and playing: 7540
Ps 30:11 for me my mourning into d': 4234
Lu 15:25 the house, he heard musick and d'. 5525

dandled
Isa 66:12 and be d' upon her knees. 8173

danger See also ENDANGER.
M't 5:21, 22 shall be in d' of the judgment: 1777
22 shall be in d' of the council: but "
22 thou fool, shall be in d' of hell fire. "
M'r 3:29 is in d' of eternal damnation: * "
Ac 19:27 not only this our craft is in d' 2793
40 we are in d' to be called in question "

dangerous
Ac 27: 9 when sailing was now d', 2000

Daniel See also BELTESHAZZAR.
1Ch 3: 1 D', of Abigail the Carmelitess: 1840
Ezr 8: 2 of the sons of Ithamar; D': of the "
Ne 10: 6 D', Ginnethon, Baruch, "
Eze 14:14 three men, Noah, D', and Job, "
20 Noah, D', and Job, were in it, "
28: 3 Behold, thou art wiser than D'; "
Da 1: 6 children of Judah, D', Hananiah, "
7 for he gave unto D' the name of "
8 But D' purposed in his heart that "
9 God had brought D' into favour "
10 prince of the eunuchs said unto D', "
11 said D' to Melzar, whom the prince "
11 of the eunuchs had set over D', "
17 D' had understanding in all visions "
19 them all was found none like D', "
21 D' continued even unto the first "
2:13 they sought D' and his fellows 1841
14 Then D' answered with counsel "
15 made the thing known to D'. "
16 Then D' went in, and desired of the "
17 Then D' went to his house, and "
18 that D' and his fellows should not "
19 was the secret revealed unto D' "
19 Then D' blessed the God of heaven, "
20 D' answered and said, Blessed be "
24 Therefore D' went in unto Arioch, "
25 Then Arioch brought in D' before "
26 The king answered and said to D', "
27 D' answered in the presence of the "
46 upon his face, and worshipped D', "
47 king answered unto D', and said, "
48 the king made D' a great man, "
49 Then D' requested of the king, and "
49 but D' sat in the gate of the king. "
4: 8 at the last D' came in before me, "
19 D', whose name was Belteshazzar, "
5:12 in the same D', whom the king "
12 now let D' be called, and he will "
13 was D' brought in before the king. "
13 the king spake and said unto D', "
13 Art thou that D', which art of "
17 Then D' answered and said before "
29 and they clothed D' with scarlet, "
6: 2 presidents; of whom D' was first: "
3 Then this D' was preferred above "
4 sought to find occasion against D' "
5 find any occasion against this D', "
10 when D' knew that the writing was "
11 and found D' praying and making "
13 D', which is of the children of the "
14 set his heart on D' to deliver him: "
16 and they brought D', and cast him "
16 the king spake and said unto D', "
17 not be changed concerning D'. "
20 with a lamentable voice unto D': "
20 and the king spake and said to D', "
20 O D', servant of the living God, "
21 Then said D' unto the king, O king, "
23 that they should take D' up out of "
23 the den. So D' was taken up "
24 those men which had accused D', "
26 and fear before the God of D': "
27 hath delivered D' from the power "
28 D' prospered in the reign of Darius, "
7: 1 D' had a dream and visions of "
2 D' spake and said, I saw in my "
15 I D' was grieved in my spirit "
28 As for me D', my cogitations much "
8: 1 unto me, even unto me D', 1840
15 it came to pass, when I, even I D', "
27 And I D' fainted, and was sick "
9: 2 In the first year of his reign I D' "
22 and said, O D', I am now come forth "
10: 1 a thing was revealed unto D', "
2 In those days I D' was mourning "
7 And I D' alone saw the vision: "
11 he said unto me, O D', a man "
12 Then said he unto me, Fear not, D': "
12: 4 But thou, O D', shut up the words, "
5 D' looked, and behold, there stood "
9 And he said, Go thy way, D': "
M't 24:15 spoken of by D' the prophet, 1158
M'r 13:14 spoken of by D' the prophet, * "

Danites (*dan'-ites*)
J'g 13: 2 of Zorah, of the family of the D', 1839
18: 1 the tribe of the D' sought them "
11 from thence of the family of the D', "
1Ch 12:35 And of the D' expert in war "

Dan-jaan (*dan-ja'-an*)
2Sa 24: 6 they came to D', and about to 1842

Dannah (*dan'-nah*)
Jos 15:49 D', and Kirjath-sannah, which is 1837
Dara (*da'-rah*) See also DARDA.
1Ch 2: 6 and Heman, and Calcol, and D': 1873
Darda (*dar'-dah*) See also DARA.
1Ki 4:31 Chalcol, and D', the son of Mahol: 1862
dare See also DURST.
Job 41:10 None is so fierce that d' stir him
Ro 5: 7 man some would even d' to die. 5111
15:18 For I will not d' to speak of "
1Co 6: 1 D' any of you, having a matter "
2Co 10:12 For we d' not make ourselves * "
Darius (*da-ri'-us*)
Ezr 4: 5 until the the reign of D' king of 1867
24 the second year of the reign of D' 1868
5: 5 till the matter came to D': and then "
6 this side of the river, sent unto D' "
7 thus; Unto D' the king, all peace. "
6: 1 Then D' the king made a decree, "
12 I D' have made a decree; let it be "
13 to that which D' the king had sent, "
14 the commandment of Cyrus, and D', "
15 the sixth year of the reign of D' "
Ne 12:22 also the priests, to the reign of D' 1867
Da 5:31 D' the Median took the kingdom, 1868
6: 1 It pleased D' to set over the "
6 thus unto him, King D', live forever. "
9 Wherefore king D' signed the "
25 Then king D' wrote unto all people, "
28 Daniel prospered in the reign of D', "
9: 1 year of D' the son of Ahasuerus, 1867
11: 1 I in the first year of D' the Mede, "
Hag 1: 1 In the second year of D' the king, "
15 in the second year of D' the king. "
2:10 month, in the second year of D', "
Zec 1: 1 month, in the second year of D', "
7 Sebat, in the second year of D', "
7: 1 in the fourth year of king D', "
dark See also DARKISH.
Ge 15:17 the sun went down, and it was d', 5939
Le 13: 6 if the plague be somewhat d', *3544
21 the skin, but be somewhat d'; * "
26 other skin, but be somewhat d'; * "
28 the skin, but it be somewhat d'; * "
56 the plague be somewhat d' after * "
Nu 12: 8 apparently, and not in d' speeches; 2420
Jos 2: 5 when it was d', that the men went 2822
2Sa 22:12 round about him, d' waters, *2841
Ne 13:19 gates of Jerusalem began to be d' 6751
Job 3: 9 stars of the twilight thereof be d'; 2821
12:25 grope in the d' without light, 2822
18: 6 light shall be d' in his tabernacle, 2821
22:13 he judge through the d' cloud? *6205
24:16 In the d' they dig through houses, 2822
Ps 18:11 round about him were d' waters *2824
35: 6 Let their way be d' and slippery: 2822
49: 4 open my d' saying upon the harp. 2420
74:20 the d' places of the earth are full 4285
78: 2 I will utter d' sayings of old: 2420
88:12 thy wonders be known in the d'? 2822
105:28 He sent darkness, and made it d'; 2821
Pr 1: 6 of the wise, and their d' sayings. 2420
7: 9 evening, in the black and d' night:* 653
Isa 29:15 their works are in the d', and they 4285
45:19 secret, in a d' place of the earth: *2822
Jer 13:16 stumble upon the d' mountains, 5399
La 3: 6 He hath sent me in d' places, 4285
Eze 8:12 the house of Israel do in the d', 2822
32: 7 and make the stars thereof d'; 6937
8 of heaven will I make d' over thee, "
34:12 scattered in the cloudy and d' day. 6205
Da 8:23 and understanding d' sentences, 2420
Joe 2:10 the sun and the moon shall be d',*6937
Am 5: 8 maketh the day d' with night: 2821
20 very d', and no brightness in it? 651
Mic 3: 6 and it shall be d' unto you, that 2821
6 and the day shall be d' over them. *6937
Zec 14: 6 light shall not be clear, nor d': *7087
Lu 11:36 full of light, having no part d', 4652
Joh 6:17 And it was now d', and Jesus was 4653
20: 1 Magdalene early, when it was yet d', "
2Pe 1:19 light that shineth in a d' place, 850
darken See also DARKENED; DARKENETH.
Am 8: 9 will d' the earth in the clear day: 2821
darkened
Ex 10:15 earth, so that the land was d'; 2821
Ps 69:23 Let their eyes be d', that they see "
Ec 12: 2 stars, be not d', nor the clouds "
3 that look out of the windows be d', "
Isa 5:30 light is d' in the heavens thereof. "
9:19 the Lord of hosts is the land d', *6272
13:10 sun shall be d' in his going forth, 2821
24:11 all joy is d', the mirth of the 6150
Eze 30:18 shall be d', when I shall break *2821
Joe 3:15 sun and the moon shall be d', 6937
Zec 11:17 his right eye shall be utterly d', 3543
M't 24:29 of those days shall the sun be d', 4654
M'r 13:24 the sun shall be d', and the moon "
Lu 23:45 And the sun was d', and the veil * "
Ro 1:21 and their foolish heart was d'. "
11:10 Let their eyes be d', that they may "
Eph 4:18 Having the understanding d', "
Re 8:12 so as the third part of them was d', "
9: 2 and the sun and the air were d' "
darkeneth
Job 38: 2 Who is this that d' counsel by 2821
darkish
Le 13:39 skin of their flesh be d' white: *3544
darkly
1Co 13:12 we see through a glass, d'; 1722, 135
darkness
Ge 1: 2 d' was upon the face of the deep. 2822
4 God divided the light from the d'. 2822
5 Day, and the d' he called Night. "
18 and to divide the light from the d': "
15:12 horror of great d' fell upon him. 2825
Ex 10:21 may be d' over the land of Egypt, 2822
21 even d' which may be felt. "
22 there was a thick d' in all the land "
14:20 it was a cloud and d' to them, "
20:21 drew near unto the thick d' 6205
De 4:11 unto the midst of heaven, with d', 2822
11 clouds, and thick d'. 6205
5:22 the cloud, and of the thick d', with "
23 voice out of the midst of the d', 2822
28:29 as the blind gropeth in d', 653
Jos 24: 7 d' between you and the Egyptians, 3990
1Sa 2: 9 the wicked shall be silent in d'; 2822
2Sa 22:10 and d' was under his feet. 6205
12 he made d' pavilions round about 2822
29 and the Lord will lighten my d'. "
1Ki 8:12 he would dwell in the thick d'. 6205
2Ch 6: 1 he would dwell in the thick d'. "
Job 3: 4 Let that day be d'; let not God 2822
5 Let d' and the shadow of death "
6 for that night, let d' seize upon it; 652
5:14 meet with d' in the day time, 2822
10:21 Even to the land of d', and the "
22 A land of d', as 5890
22 as d' itself; and of the shadow ‡652
22 and where the light is as d'. "
12:22 discovereth deep things out of d', 2822
15:22 that he shall return out of d', "
23 knoweth that the day of d' is ready "
30 He shall not depart out of d'; "
17:12 the light is short because of d'. "
13 I have made my bed in the d'. "
18:18 be driven from light into d', and "
19: 8 he hath set d' in my paths. "
20:26 d' shall be hid in his secret places: "
22:11 Or d', that thou canst not see; "
23:17 I was not cut off before the d', "
17 neither hath he covered the d' * 652
28: 3 He setteth an end to d', and 2822
3 the stones of d', and the * 652
29: 3 by his light I walked through d'; 2822
30:26 I waited for light, there came d'. 652
34:22 There is no d', nor shadow of 2822
37:19 order our speech by reason of d' "
38: 9 thick d' a swaddlingband for it, 6205
19 and as for d', where is the place 2822
Ps 18: 9 and d' was under his feet. 6205
11 He made d' his secret place; 2822
28 my God will enlighten my d'. "
82: 5 understand; they walk on in d': 2825
88: 6 lowest pit, in d', in the deeps. *4285
18 me, and mine acquaintance into d'. "
91: 6 the pestilence that walketh in d'; 652
97: 2 and d' are round about him: 6205
104:20 Thou makest d', and it is night: 2822
105:28 He sent d', and made it dark; "
107:10 Such as sit in d' and in the shadow "
14 He brought them out of d' and the "
112: 4 upright there ariseth light in the d': "
139:11 I say, Surely the d' shall cover me; "
12 Yea, the d' hideth not from thee; "
12 d' and the light are both alike to 2825
143: 3 he hath made me to dwell in d', *4285
Pr 2:13 to walk in the ways of d'; 2822
4:19 The way of the wicked is as d: 653
20:20 shall be put out in obscure d'. 2822
Ec 2:13 folly, as far as light excelleth d'. "
14 head; but the fool walketh in d': "
5:17 All his days also he eateth in d', "
6: 4 vanity, and departeth in d', and "
4 his name shall be covered with d'. "
11: 8 let him remember the days of d'; "
Isa 5:20 put d' for light, and light for d'; "
30 behold d' and sorrow, and the light "
8:22 behold trouble and d', dimness of 2825
22 and they shall be driven to d'. 653
9: 2 The people that walked in d' have 2822
29:18 out of obscurity, and out of d'. "
42: 7 them that sit in d' out of the prison "
16 I will make d' light before them. 4285
45: 3 I will give thee the treasures of d', 2822
7 I form the light, and create d': "
47: 5 Sit thou silent, and get thee into d', "
49: 9 to them that are in d', Shew "
50:10 walketh in d', and hath no light? 2825
58:10 and thy d' be as the noon day: 653
59: 9 for brightness, but we walk in d'. "
60: 2 the d' shall cover the earth, 2822
2 and gross d' the people: 6205
Jer 2:31 unto Israel? a land of d'? 3991
13:16 before he cause d', and before 2821
16 of death, and make it gross d'. 6205
Jer 23:12 as slippery ways in the d': 653
La 3: 2 led me, and brought me into d', 2822
Eze 32: 8 over thee, and set d' upon thy land." "
Da 2:22 he knoweth what is in the d', 2816
Joe 2: 2 A day of d' and of gloominess, 2822
2 a day of clouds and of thick d', 6205
31 The sun shall be turned into d', 2822
Am 4:13 that maketh the morning d', and 5890
5:18 the day of the Lord is d', and not 2822
20 shall not the day of the Lord be d', "
Mic 7: 8 I sit in d', the Lord shall be a light "
Na 1: 8 and d' shall pursue his enemies. "
Zep 1:15 a day of d' and gloominess, "
15 a day of clouds and thick d'. 6205
M't 4:16 The people which sat in d' saw 4655
6:23 thy whole body shall be full of d'. 4652
23 in thee be d', how great is that d'! 4655
8:12 shall be cast out into outer d': "
10:27 What I tell you in d', that speak 4653
22:13 away, and cast him into outer d'; 4655
25:30 unprofitable servant into outer d': "
27:45 there was d' over all the land 4655
M'r 15:33 there was d' over the whole land "
Lu 1:79 To give light to them that sit in d' "
11:34 is evil, thy body also is full of d'. 4652
35 light which is in thee be not d'. 4655
12: 3 whatsoever ye have spoken in d' 4653
22:53 is your hour, and the power of d'. 4655
23:44 there was a d' over all the earth "
Joh 1: 5 And the light shineth in d'; and 4653
5 and the d' comprehended it not. "
3:19 men loved d' rather than light, 4655
8:12 followeth me shall not walk in d', 4653
12:35 the light, lest d' come upon you: "
35 for he that walketh in d' knoweth "
46 on me should not abide in d'. "
Ac 2:20 The sun shall be turned into d', 4655
13:11 there fell on him a mist and a d'; "
26:18 to turn them from d' to light, "
Ro 2:19 a light of them which are in d', "
13:12 cast off the works of d', and let us "
1Co 4: 5 to light the hidden things of d', "
2Co 4: 6 the light to shine out of d', hath "
6:14 communion hath light with d'? "
Eph 5: 8 ye were sometimes d', but now are "
11 with the unfruitful works of d', "
6:12 the rulers of the d' of this world, "
Col 1:13 delivered us from the power of d', "
1Th 5: 4 But ye, brethren, are not in d', "
5 we are not of the night, nor of d'. "
Heb 12:18 nor unto blackness, and d', and "
1Pe 2: 9 hath called you out of d' into his "
2Pe 2: 4 delivered them into chains of d', 2217
17 the mist of d' is reserved for ever. 4655
1Jo 1: 5 light, and in him is no d' at all. 4653
6 and walk in d', we lie, and do not 4655
2: 8 because the d' is past, and the 4653
9 brother, is in d' even until now. "
11 is in d', and walketh in d', "
11 goeth, because that d' hath blinded "
Jude 6 in everlasting chains under d' 2217
13 the blackness of d' for ever. 4655
Re 16:10 and his kingdom was full of d'; *4656
Darkon (*dar'-kon*)
Ezr 2:56 of Jaalah, the children of D', the 1874
Ne 7:58 of Jaala, the children of D', the "
darling
Ps 22:20 my d' from the power of the dog. 3173
35:17 my d' from the lions. "
dart See also DARTS.
Job 41:26 spear, the d', nor the habergeon. 4551
Pr 7:23 Till a d' strike through his liver; *2671
Heb 12:20 or thrust through with a d': *1002
darts
2Sa 18:14 he took three d' in his hand, 7626
2Ch 32: 5 d' and shields in abundance. *7973
Job 41:29 D' are counted as stubble: he *8455
Eph 6:16 all the fiery d' of the wicked. 956
dash See also DASHED; DASHETH.
2Ki 8:12 wilt d' their children, and rip up 7376
Ps 2: 9 thou shalt d' them in pieces like 5310
91:12 thou d' thy foot against a stone. 5062
Isa 13:18 shall d' the young men to pieces; 7376
Jer 13:14 d' them one against another, 5310
M't 4: 6 thou d' thy foot against a stone. 4350
Lu 4:11 thou d' thy foot against a stone. "
dashed
Ex 15: 6 hand, O Lord, hath d' in pieces *7492
Isa 13:16 children also shall be d' to pieces 7376
Ho 10:14 the mother was d' in pieces upon "
13:16 their infants shall be d' in pieces, "
Na 3:10 children also were d' in pieces "
dasheth
Ps 137: 9 that taketh and d' thy little ones 5310
Na 2: 1 He that d' in pieces is come 6327
Dathan (*da'-than*)
Nu 16: 1 D' and Abiram, the sons of Eliab, 1885
12 Moses sent to call D' and Abiram, "
24 of Korah, D', and Abiram. "
25 Moses rose up and went unto D' "
27 from the tabernacle of Korah, D', "
27 side: and D' and Abiram came out, "
26: 9 Nemuel, and D', and Abiram. "
9 This is that D' and Abiram, which "
De 11: 6 what he did unto D' and Abiram, "
Ps 106:17 earth opened and swallowed up D', "
daub See also DAUBED; DAUBING.
Eze 13:11 d' it with untempered morter, 2902
daubed
Ex 2: 3 d' it with slime and with pitch, 2560
Eze 13:10 d' it with untempered morter: *2902
12 daubing wherewith ye have d' it? "
14 down the wall that ye have d' "
15 have d' it with untempered morter, "
15 no more, neither they that d' it; "
22:28 And her prophets have d' them "
daubing
Eze 13:12 Where is the d' wherewith ye 2915
daughter See also DAUGHTER'S; DAUGHTERS.
Ge 11:29 Milcah, the d' of Haran, the 1323
31 and Sarai his d' in law, his son 3618
20:12 she is the d' of my father, 1323
12 but not the d' of my mother; "
24:23 Whose d' art thou? tell me, I pray "
24 d' of Bethuel the son of Milcah, "
47 Whose d' art thou? And she said, "
47 The d' of Bethuel, Nahor's son, "
48 master's brother's d' unto his son. "
25:20 the d' of Bethuel the Syrian of "
26:34 Judith the d' of Beeri the Hittite, "
34 and Bashemath the d' of Elon the "
28: 9 Mahalath the d' of Ishmael "
29: 6 his d' cometh with the sheep. "

Ge 29:10 Jacob saw Rachel the d' of Laban 1323
18 years for Rachel thy younger d'. "
23 took Leah his d', and brought her "
24 gave unto his d' Leah Zilpah his "
28 gave him Rachel his d' to wife also. "
29 Laban gave to Rachel his d' "
30:21 afterwards she bare a d', and "
34: 1 And Dinah the d' of Leah, "
3 clave unto Dinah the d' of Jacob, "
5 that he had defiled Dinah his d': "
7 Israel in lying with Jacob's d'; "
8 son Shechem longeth for your d': "
17 then will we take our d', and we "
19 he had delight in Jacob's d': "
36: 2 the d' of Elon the Hittite, "
2 d' of Anah the d' of Zibeon the "
3 Bashemath Ishmael's d', sister of "
14 Aholibamah the d' of Anah "
14 the d' of Zibeon, Esau's wife "
18 the d' of Anah, Esau's wife. "
25 and Aholibamah the d' of Anah. "
39 the d' of Matred, the d' of Mezahab. "
38: 2 there a d' of a certain Canaanite, "
11 said Judah to Tamar his d' in law, 3618
12 the d' of Shuah Judah's wife died; 1323
16 not that she was his d' in law.) 3618
24 Tamar thy d' in law hath played "
41:45 gave him to wife Asenath the d' of 1323
50 Asenath the d' of Poti-pherah "
46:15 with his d' Dinah: all the souls of "
18 whom Laban gave to Leah his d', "
20 Asenath the d' of Poti-pherah "
25 Laban gave unto Rachel his d', "
Ex 1:16 but if it be a d', then she shall live. "
22 every d' ye shall save alive. "
2: 1 took to wife a d' of Levi. "
5 And the d' of Pharaoh came down "
7 said his sister to Pharaoh's d', "
8 And Pharaoh's d' said to her, Go. "
9 Pharaoh's d' said unto her, Take "
10 she brought him unto Pharaoh's d', "
21 he gave Moses Zipporah his d'. "
6:23 Elisheba, d' of Amminadab, sister "
20:10 thou, nor thy son, nor thy d', "
21: 7 man sell his d' to be a maidservant, "
31 a son, or have gored a d', "
Le 12: 6 or for a d', she shall bring "
18: 9 d' of thy father, or d' of thy mother, "
10 The nakedness of thy son's d', "
10 or of thy daughter's d', "
11 nakedness of thy father's wife's d', "
15 the nakedness of thy d' in law: 3618
17 nakedness of a woman and her d', 1323
17 shalt thou take her son's d', "
17 or her daughter's d', "
19:29 Do not prostitute thy d', to cause "
20:12 if a man lie with his d' in law, 3618
17 take his sister, his father's d', 1323
17 or his mother's d', "
21: 2 for his son, and for his d', and for "
9 d' of any priest, if she profane "
22:12 if the priest's d' also be married "
13 But if the priest's d' be a widow, "
24:11 was Shelomith, the d' of Dibri, "
Nu 25:15 slain was Cozbi, the d' of Zur; "
18 Cozbi, the d' of a prince of Midian, "
26:46 of the d' of Asher was Sarah. "
59 wife was Jochebed, the d' of Levi, "
27: 8 his inheritance to pass unto his d'. "
9 if he have no d', then he shall give "
30:16 between the father and his d', "
36: 8 every d', that possesseth an "
De 5:14 work, thou, nor thy son, nor thy d', "
7: 3 d' thou shalt not give unto his son, "
3 d' shalt thou take unto thy son. "
12:18 thou, and thy son, and thy d', "
13: 6 thy mother, or thy son, or thy d', "
16:11 thy d', and thy manservant, and "
14 thou, and thy son, and thy d', "
18:10 his son or his d' to pass through "
22:16 I gave my d' unto this man to wife, "
17 I found not thy d' a maid; and yet "
27:22 the d' of his father, or the d' of his "
28:56 toward her son, and toward her d', "
Jos 15:16 will I give Achsah my d' to wife. "
17 he gave him Achsah his d' to wife. "
J'g 1:12 will I give Achsah my d' to wife. "
13 he gave him Achsah his d' to wife. "
11:34 his d' came out to meet him "
34 her he had neither son nor d'. "
35 Alas, my d'! thou hast brought me "
40 yearly to lament the d' of Jephthah "
19:24 Behold, here is my d' a maiden, "
21: 1 any of us give his d' unto Benjamin "
Ru 1:22 the Moabitess, her d' in law, with 3618
2: 2 she said unto her, Go, my d'. 1323
8 unto Ruth, Hearest thou not, my d'? "
20 Naomi said unto her d' in law, 3618
22 Naomi said unto Ruth her d' in law, "
22 It is good, my d', that thou go 1323
3: 1 My d', shall I not seek rest for thee, "
10 Blessed be thou of the Lord, my d': "
11 And now, my d', fear not; I will do "
16 Who art thou, my d'? And she told "
18 Then said she, Sit still, my d', "
4:15 thy d' in law, which loveth thee, 3618
1Sa 1:16 thine handmaid for a d' of Belial: ‡1323
4:19 And his d' in law, Phinehas' wife. 3618
14:50 was Ahinoam, the d' of Ahimaaz: 1323
17:25 riches, and will give him his d', "
18:17 Behold my elder d' Merab, her will "
19 Saul's d' should have been given "
20 And Michal Saul's d' loved David: "
27 gave him Michal his d' to wife. "
28 that Michal Saul's d' loved him. "
25:44 But Saul had given Michal his d'. "
2Sa 3: 3 Maacah the d' of Talmai king of 1323
7 name was Rizpah, the d' of Aiah: "
13 thou first bring Michal Saul's d', "
6:16 Michal Saul's d' looked through a "
20 And Michal the d' of Saul come out "
23 Michal the d' of Saul had no child "
11: 3 this Bath-sheba, the d' of Eliam, "
12: 3 bosom, and was unto him as a d'. "
14:27 three sons, and one d', whose name "
17:25 went in to Abigail the d' of Nahash, "
21: 8 the d' of Aiah, whom she bare unto "
8 five sons of Michal the d' of Saul, "
10 the d' of Aiah took sackcloth, and "
11 David what Rizpah the d' of Aiah, "
1Ki 3: 1 took Pharaoh's d', and brought her "
4:11 Taphath the d' of Solomon to wife: "
15 took Basmath the d' of Solomon to "
7: 8 also an house for Pharaoh's d', "
9:16 given it for a present unto his d', "
24 Pharaoh's d' came up out of the "
11: 1 together with the d' of Pharaoh, "
15: 2, 10 Maachah, the d' of Abishalom. "
16:31 to wife Jezebel the d' of Ethbaal "
22:42 name was Azubah the d' of Shilhi. "
2Ki 8:18 for the d' of Ahab was his wife: "
26 the d' of Omri king of Israel. "
9:34 bury her for she is a king's d'. "
11: 2 Jehosheba the d' of king Joram, "
14: 9 Give thy d' to my son to wife: "
15:33 name was Jerusha the, d' of Zadok. "
18: 2 also was Abi, the d' of Zachariah. "
19:21 virgin the d' of Zion hath despised "
21 the d' of Jerusalem hath shaken "
21:19 Meshullemeth, the d' of Haruz of "
22: 1 Jedidah, the d' of Adaiah of "
23:10 or his d' to pass through the fire "
31 Hamutal, the d' of Jeremiah of "
36 Zebudah, the d' of Pedaiah of "
24: 8 Nehushta, the d' of Elnathan of "
18 Hamutal, the d' of Jeremiah of "
1Ch 1:50 the d' of Matred, the d' of Mezahab. "
2: 3 of the d' of Shua the Canaanitess.* "
4 Tamar his d' in law bare him 3618
21 Hezron went in to the d' of Machir 1323
35 Sheshan gave his d' to Jarha his "
49 and the d' of Caleb was Achsa. "
3: 2 son of Maachah the d' of Talmai "
5 of Bath-shua the d' of Ammiel: "
4:18 the d' of Pharaoh, which Mered "
7:24 (And his d' was Sherah, who built "
15:29 Michal the d' of Saul looking out at "
2Ch 8:11 Solomon brought up the d' of "
11:18 Mahalath the d' of Jerimoth the 1121
18 Abihail the d' of Eliab 1323
20 took Maachah the d' of Absalom; "
21 the d' of Absalom above all his "
13: 2 Michaiah the d' of Uriel of Gibeah. "
20:31 was Azubah the d' of Shilhi. "
21: 6 he had the d' of Ahab to wife: "
22: 2 also was Athaliah the d' of Omri. "
11 Jehoshabeath, the d' of the king, "
11 So Jehoshabeath, the d' of king 1323
25:18 Give thy d' to my son to wife: "
27: 1 also was Jerushah, the d' of Zadok. "
29: 1 was Abijah, the d' of Zechariah. "
Ne 6:18 had taken the d' of Meshullam "
Es 2: 7 that is, Esther, his uncle's d': "
7 were dead, took for his own d'. "
15 Esther, the d' of Abihail the uncle "
15 who had taken her for his d', "
9:29 Esther the queen, the d' of Abihail, "
Ps 9:14 in the gates of the d' of Zion: "
45:10 Hearken, O d', and consider, and "
12 And the d' of Tyre shall be there "
13 The king's d' is all glorious within: "
137: 8 O d' of Babylon, who art to be "
Ca 7: 1 O prince's d'! the joints of thy "
Isa 1: 8 the d' of Zion is left as a cottage "
10:30 Lift up thy voice, O d' of Gallim: "
32 against the mount of the d' of Zion. 1004
16: 1 unto the mount of the d' of Zion. 1323
22: 4 the spoiling of the d' of my people. "
23:10 d' of Tarshish: there is no more "
12 thou oppressed virgin, d' of Zidon: "
37:22 virgin, the d' of Zion, hath despised "
22 the d' of Jerusalem hath shaken "
47: 1 O virgin d' of Babylon, sit on the "
1 no throne, O d' of the Chaldeans: "
5 darkness, O d' of the Chaldeans: "
52: 2 of thy neck, O captive d' of Zion. "
62:11 Say ye to the d' of Zion, "
Jer 4:11 wilderness toward the d' of my "
31 the voice of the d' of Zion, "
6: 2 I have likened the d' of Zion "
14 the hurt of the d' of my people *
23 war against thee, O d' of Zion. 1323
26 O d' of my people, gird thee "
8:11 hurt of the d' of my people slightly. "
19 the cry of the d' of my people "
21 the hurt of the d' of my people "
22 the health of the d' of my people "
9: 1 the slain of the d' of my people! "
7 I do for the d' of my people? "
14:17 for the virgin d' of my people is "
31:22 go about, O thou backsliding d'? "
46:11 balm, O virgin, the d' of Egypt: "
19 O thou d' dwelling in Egypt, "
24 d' of Egypt shall be confounded; "
48:18 Thou d' that dost inhabit Dibon, "
49: 4 O backsliding d'? that trusted "
50:42 against thee, O d' of Babylon. "
51:33 The d' of Babylon is like a "
52: 1 the d' of Jeremiah of Libnah. "
La 1: 6 from the d' of Zion all her beauty "
15 the virgin, the d' of Judah, "
2: 1 the Lord covered the d' of Zion "
La 2: 2 strongholds of the d' of Judah; 1323
4 the tabernacle of the d' of Zion: "
5 hath increased in the d' of Judah "
8 destroy the wall of the d' of Zion: "
10 The elders of the d' of Zion sit "
11 destruction of the d' of my people; "
13 liken to thee, O d' of Jerusalem? "
13 comfort thee, O virgin d' of Zion? "
15 their head at the d' of Jerusalem, "
18 O wall of the d' of Zion, let tears "
3:48 destruction of the d' of my people. "
4: 3 the d' of my people is become cruel, "
6 the iniquity of the d' of my people "
10 destruction of the d' of my people. "
21 and be glad, O d' of Edom, "
22 is accomplished, O d' of Zion; "
22 O d' of Edom; he will discover thy "
Eze 14:20 shall deliver neither son nor d'; "
16:44 As is the mother, so is her d'. "
45 Thou art thy mother's d', that "
22:11 hath lewdly defiled his d' in law; 3618
11 humbled his sister, his father's d'. 1323
44:25 for son, or for d', for brother, "
Da 11: 6 for the king's d' of the south "
17 shall give him the d' of women, "
Ho 1: 3 took Gomer the d' of Diblaim; "
6 conceived again, and bare a d'. "
Mic 1:13 of the sin to the d' of Zion: "
4: 8 the strong hold of the d' of Zion, "
8 shall come to the d' of Jerusalem. "
10 O d' of Zion, like a woman in travail: "
13 Arise and thresh, O d' of Zion: "
5: 1 thyself in troops, O d' of troops: "
7: 6 d' riseth up against her mother, "
6 d' in law against her mother in 3618
Zep 3:10 even the d' of my dispersed, shall 1323
14 Sing, O d' of Zion; shout, O Israel; "
14 all the heart, O d' of Jerusalem. "
Zec 2: 7 dwellest with the d' of Babylon. "
10 Sing and rejoice, O d' of Zion: "
9: 9 Rejoice greatly, O d' of Zion; "
9 shout, O d' of Jerusalem: "
Mal 2:11 hath married the d' of a strange god. "
M't 9:18 My d' is even now dead: but 2364
22 D', be of good comfort; thy faith "
10:35 and the d' against her mother, "
35 and the d' in law against her 3565
37 loveth son or d' more than me 2364
14: 6 the d' of Herodias danced before "
15:22 my d' is grievously vexed with a "
28 And her d' was made whole from "
21: 5 Tell ye the d' of Sion, Behold, "
M'r 5:23 little d' lieth at the point of death: 2365
34 D', thy faith hath made thee whole; 2364
35 Thy d' is dead: why troublest thou "
6:22 the d' of the said Herodias came "
7:25 young d' had an unclean spirit, 2365
26 cast forth the devil out of her d'. 2364
29 the devil is gone out of thy d'. "
30 and her d' laid upon the bed. * "
Lu 2:36 the d' of Phanuel, of the tribe of "
8:42 he had one only d', about twelve "
48 D', be of good comfort: thy faith "
49 Thy d' is dead; trouble not the "
12:53 against the d', and the d' against "
53 d' in law, and the d' in law against 3565
13:16 a d' of Abraham, whom Satan 2364
Joh 12:15 Fear not, d' of Sion: behold, thy "
Ac 7:21 Pharaoh's d' took him up and "
Heb 11:24 be called the son of Pharaoh's d'; "

daughter-in-law See DAUGHTER and LAW.

daughter's
Le 18:10 daughter, or thy d' daughter, 1323
17 or her d' daughter, to uncover her "
De 22:17 are the tokens of my d' virginity. "

daughters
Ge 5: 4 years: and he begat sons and d': 1121
7, 10, 13, 16, 19, 22, 26, 30 and begat sons and d':
6: 1 earth, and d' were born unto them. "
2 the sons of God saw the d' of men "
4 came in unto the d' of men, and they "
11:11, 13, 15, 17, 19, 21, 23, 25, and begat sons and d'.
19: 8 have two d' which have not known "
12 in law, and thy sons, and thy d', "
14 sons in law, which married his d', "
15 and thy two d', which are here; "
16 and upon the hand of his two d'; "
30 in the mountain, and his two d'; "
30 dwelt in a cave, he and his two d'. "
36 Thus were both the d' of Lot with "
24: 3 my son of the d' of the Canaanites, "
13 and the d' of the men of the city "
37 d' of the Canaanites, in whose land "
27:46 my life because of the d' of Heth: "
46 Jacob take a wife of the d' of Heth, "
46 these which are of the d' of the land, "
28: 1 not take a wife of the d' of Canaan. "
2 d' of Laban thy mother's brother. "
6 not take a wife of the d' of Canaan; "
8 Esau seeing that the d' of Canaan "
29:16 Laban had two d': the name of the "
30:13 for the d' will call me blessed: "
31:26 carried away my d', as captives "
28 me to kiss my sons and my d'? "
31 take by force thy d' from me. "
41 thee fourteen years for thy two d', "
43 These d' are my d', and these "
43 can I do this day unto these my d', "
50 If thou shalt afflict my d', or if thou "
50 shalt take other wives beside my d', "
55 and kissed his sons and his d', "
34: 1 went out to see the d' of the land. "
9 and give your d' unto us, and take "

Ge 34: 9 and take our d' unto you. 1121
16 Then we will give our d' unto you, "
16 and we will take your d' unto us, "
21 let us take their d' to us for wives, "
21 and let us give them our d'. "
36: 2 wives of the d' of Canaan; Adah "
6 his wives, and his sons, and his d', "
37:35 and his d' rose up to comfort "
46: 7 his d', and his sons' d', and all "
15 and his d' were thirty and three. "
Ex 2:16 the priest of Midian had seven d': "
20 And he said unto his d', And where "
3:22 upon your sons, and upon your d'; "
6:25 took him one of the d' of Putiel to "
10: 9 with our sons and with our d', "
21: 4 she have born him sons or d'; "
9 with her after the manner of d'. "
32: 2 wives, of your sons, and of your d', "
34:16 take of their d' unto thy sons, "
16 and their d' go a whoring after "
Le 10:14 and thy sons, and thy d' with thee: "
26:29 the flesh of your d' shall ye eat. "
Nu 18:11 to thy sons and to thy d' with thee, "
19 and thy sons and thy d' with thee, "
21:29 and his d', into captivity unto Sihon "
25: 1 whoredom with the d' of Moab. "
26:33 Hepner had no sons, but d': and "
33 names of the d' of Zelophehad were "
27: 1 Then came the d' of Zelophehad, "
1 these are the names of his d'; "
7 The d' of Zelophehad speak right: "
36: 2 Zelophehad our brother unto his d'. "
6 concerning the d' of Zelophehad, "
10 so did the d' of Zelophehad: "
11 the d' of Zelophehad, were married "
De 12:12 ye, and your sons, and your d', "
31 sons and their d' they have burnt "
23:17 be no whore of the d' of Israel, "
28:32 Thy sons and thy d' shall be given "
41 Thou shalt beget sons and d', but "
53 the flesh of thy sons and of thy d', "
32:19 provoking of his sons, and of his d'. "
Jos 7:24 of gold, and his sons, and his d', "
17: 3 had no sons, but d': and these "
3 and these are the names of his d', "
6 Because the d' of Manasseh had an "
J'g 3: 6 they took their d' to be their wives, "
6 and gave their d' to their sons, "
11:40 d' of Israel went yearly to lament "
12: 9 he had thirty sons, and thirty d', "
9 thirty d' from abroad for his sons. "
14: 1, 2 of the d' of the Philistines: "
3 among the d' of thy brethren, or "
21: 7 give them of our d' to wives? "
18 may not give them wives of our d': "
21 the d' of Shiloh come out to dance "
21 man his wife of the d' of Shiloh, "
Ru 1: 6 she arose with her d' in law, 3618
7 her two d' in law with her; "
8 Naomi said unto her two d' in law, "
11 my d': why will ye go with me? 1121
12 Turn again, my d', go your way; "
13 nay, my d'; for it grieveth me "
1Sa 1: 4 to all her sons and her d', portions: "
2:21 and bare three sons and two d'. "
8:13 And he will take your d' to be "
14:49 names of his two d' were these; "
30: 3 their sons, and their d', were taken "
6 man for his sons and for his d': "
19 neither sons nor d', neither spoil, "
2Sa 1:20 lest the d' of the Philistines rejoice, "
20 d' of the uncircumcised triumph. "
24 Ye d' of Israel, weep over Saul, "
5:13 were yet sons and d' born to David. "
13:18 with such robes were the king's d' "
19: 5 the lives of thy sons and of thy d', "
2Ki 17:17 their d' to pass through the fire, "
1Ch 2:34 Sheshon had no sons, but d'. "
4:27 Shimei had sixteen sons and six d'; "
7:15 and Zelophehad had d'. "
14: 3 and David begat more sons and d'. "
23:22 died, and had no sons, but d': "
25: 5 Heman fourteen sons and three d'. "
2Ch 2:14 son of a woman of the d' of Dan, "
11:21 and eight sons, and threescore d'.) "
13:21 twenty and two sons, and sixteen d'. "
24: 3 wives; and he begat sons and d'. "
28: 8 women, sons, and d', and took also "
29: 9 our sons and our d' and our wives "
31:18 their sons, and their d', through all "
Ezr 2:61 of the d' of Barzillai the Gileadite, "
9: 2 taken of their d' for themselves, "
12 give not your d' unto their sons, "
12 neither take their d' unto your sons, "
Ne 3:12 part of Jerusalem, he and his d'. "
4:14 your sons, and your d', your wives, "
5: 2 our sons, and our d', are many: "
5 our sons and our d' to be servants, "
5 our d' are brought unto bondage "
7:63 which took one of the d' of Barzillai, "
10:28 their sons, and their d', every one "
30 our d' unto the people of the land, "
30 nor take their d' for our sons: "
13:25 not give your d' unto their sons, "
25 nor take their d' unto your sons, "
Job 1: 2 unto him seven sons and three d'. "
13 his sons and his d' were eating and "
18 Thy sons and thy d' were eating "
42:13 had also seven sons and three d'. "
15 found so fair as the d' of Job: "
Ps 45: 9 Kings' d' were among thy "
48:11 let the d' of Judah be glad, "
97: 8 the d' of Judah rejoiced because of "
106:37 sacrificed their sons and their d' "
38 blood of their sons and of their d', "
144:12 that our d' may be as corner stones, "
Pr 30:15 horseleach hath two d', crying, 1121
31:29 Many d' have done virtuously, but "
Ec 12: 4 d' of musick shall be brought low; "
Ca 1: 5 O ye d' of Jerusalem, as the tents "
2: 2 so is my love among the d'. "
7 I charge you, O ye d' of Jerusalem, "
3: 5 I charge you, O ye d' of Jerusalem, "
10 with love, for the d' of Jerusalem. "
11 Go forth, O ye d' of Zion, and "
5: 8 I charge you, O d' of Jerusalem, "
16 is my friend, O d' of Jerusalem. "
6: 9 The d' saw her, and blessed her; "
8: 4 I charge you, O d' of Jerusalem, "
Isa 3:16 Because the d' of Zion are haughty, "
17 crown of the head of the d' of Zion, "
4: 4 away the filth of the d' of Zion, "
16: 2 the d' of Moab shall be at the fords "
32: 9 hear my voice, ye careless d'; "
43: 6 and my d' from the ends of the earth; "
49:22 thy d' shall be carried upon their "
56: 5 name better than of sons and of d': "
60: 4 thy d' shall be nursed at thy side. "
Jer 3:24 their herds, their sons and their d'. "
5:17 which thy sons and thy d' should eat: "
7:31 their sons and their d' in the fire; "
9:20 teach your d' wailing, and every "
11:22 and their d' shall die by famine: "
14:16 wives, nor their sons, nor their d': "
16: 2 neither shalt thou have sons or d' "
3 concerning the d' that are born in "
19: 9 flesh of their d', and they shall eat "
29: 6 beget sons and d'; and take wives "
6 and give your d' to husbands, "
6 that they may bear sons and d'; "
32:35 their d' to pass through the fire "
35: 8 our wives, our sons, nor our d'; "
41:10 the king's d', and all the people "
43: 6 and the king's d', and every person "
48:46 taken captives, and thy d' captives. "
49: 2 her d' shall be burned with fire: "
3 cry, ye d' of Rabbah, gird you with "
La 3:51 because of all the d' of my city. "
Eze 13:17 against the d' of thy people, which "
14:16 deliver neither sons nor d'; they "
18 deliver neither sons nor d', but they "
22 both sons and d': behold, they shall "
16:20 thou hast taken thy sons and thy d', "
27 the d' of the Philistines, which are "
46 Samaria, she and her d' that dwell "
46 thy right hand, is Sodom and her d'. "
48 hast not done, she nor her d', as "
48 thou hast done, thou and thy d'. "
49 idleness was in her and in her d', "
53 the captivity of Sodom and her d', "
53 the captivity of Samaria and her d', "
55 When thy sisters, Sodom and her d', "
55 Samaria and her d', shall return "
55 then thou and thy d' shall return "
57 of thy reproach of the d' of Syria, "
57 about her, the d' of the Philistines, "
61 I will give them unto thee for d', "
23: 2 two women, the d' of one mother: "
4 mine, and they bare sons and d'. "
10 they took her sons and her d', and "
25 they shall take thy sons and thy d'; "
47 shall slay their sons and their d', "
24:21 your sons and your d' whom ye "
25 their minds, their sons and their d', "
26: 6 And her d' which are in the field "
8 He shall slay with the sword thy d' "
30:18 and her d' shall go into captivity. "
32:16 the d' of the nations shall lament "
18 and the d' of the famous nations, "
Hos 4:13 your d' shall commit whoredom, "
14 I will not punish your d' when they "
Joe 2:28 sons and your d' shall prophesy, "
3: 8 I will sell your sons and your d' into the "
Am 7:17 and thy d' shall fall by the sword, "
Lu 1: 5 his wife was of the d' of Aaron, 2364
23:28 D' of Jerusalem, weep not for me, "
Ac 2:17 sons and your d' shall prophesy, "
21: 9 four d', virgins, which did prophesy. "
2Co 6:18 ye shall be my sons and d', saith "
1Pe 3: 6 whose d' ye are, as long as ye do* 2364

David See also David's.
Ru 4:17 father of Jesse, the father of D'. 1732
22 begat Jesse, and Jesse begat D'. "
1Sa 16:13 the Spirit of the Lord came upon D' "
19 Send me D' thy son, which is with "
20 sent them by D' his son unto Saul. "
21 D' came to Saul, and stood before "
22 Let D', I pray thee, stand before "
23 D' took a harp, and played with his "
17:12 Now D' was the son of that "
14 D' was the youngest: and the three "
15 D' went and returned from Saul "
17 Jesse said unto D' his son, Take "
20 D' rose up early in the morning, "
22 D' left his carriage in the hand of "
23 same words: and D' heard them. "
26 D' spake to the men that stood by "
28 anger was kindled against D', "
29 D' said, What have I now done? "
31 words were heard which D' spake, "
32 D' said to Saul, Let no man's heart "
33 Saul said to D', Thou art not able "
34 D' said unto Saul, Thy servant "
37 D' said moreover, The Lord that "
37 Saul said unto D', Go, and the "
38 Saul armed D' with his armour, "
39 D' girded his sword upon his "
39 D' said unto Saul, I cannot go "
39 And D' put them off him. "
41 came on and drew near unto D'; "
42 looked about, and saw D', "
43 the Philistine said unto D', Am I a "
1Sa 17:43 Philistine cursed D' by his gods. 1732
44 the Philistine said to D', Come to "
45 Then said D' to the Philistine, "
48 and came and drew nigh to meet D', "
48 that D' hasted and ran toward the "
49 D' put his hand in his bag, and "
50 So D' prevailed over the Philistine "
50 was no sword in the hand of D'. "
51 Therefore D' ran, and stood upon "
54 D' took the head of the Philistine, "
55 when Saul saw D' go forth against "
57 as D' returned from the slaughter "
58 D' answered, I am the son of thy "
18: 1 was knit with the soul of D', and "
3 Jonathan and D' made a covenant, "
4 and gave it to D', and his garments, "
5 D' went out whithersoever Saul "
6 when D' was returned from the "
7 slain his thousands, and D' his ten "
8 They have ascribed unto D' ten "
9 Saul eyed D' from that day and "
10 and D' played with his hand, as at "
11 I will smite D' even to the wall "
11 And D' avoided out of his presence "
12 Saul was afraid of D', because the "
14 D' behaved himself wisely in all "
16 But all Israel and Judah loved D', "
17 Saul said to D', Behold my elder "
18 D' said unto Saul, Who am I? and "
19 should have been given to D', that "
20 Michal Saul's daughter loved D': "
21 Wherefore Saul said to D', Thou "
22 Commune with D' secretly, and say, "
23 spake these words in the ears of D'. "
23 And D' said, Seemeth it to you a "
24 On this manner spake D'. "
25 Thus shall ye say to D', The king "
25 Saul thought to make D' fall by the "
26 when his servants told D' these "
26 it pleased D' well to be the king's "
27 Wherefore D' arose and went, he "
27 D' brought their foreskins, and "
28 knew that the Lord was with D', "
29 Saul was yet the more afraid of D'; "
30 D' behaved himself more wisely "
19: 1 servants, that they should kill D'. "
2 Saul's son delighted much in D': "
2 Jonathan told D', saying, Saul my "
4 Jonathan spake good of D' unto "
4 sin against his servant, against D'; "
5 against innocent blood, to slay D' "
7 Jonathan called D', and Jonathan "
7 Jonathan brought D' to Saul, and "
8 and D' went out, and fought with "
9 hand: and D' played with his hand. "
10 Saul sought to smite D' even to the "
10 and D' fled, and escaped that night. "
12 So Michal let D' down through a "
14 Saul sent messengers to take D', "
15 the messengers again to see D', "
18 So D' fled, and escaped, and came "
19 Behold, D' is at Naioth in Ramah. "
20 Saul sent messengers to take D': "
22 said, Where are Samuel and D'? "
20: 1 D' fled from Naioth in Ramah, and "
3 D' sware moreover, and said, Thy "
4 Then said Jonathan unto D', "
5 D' said unto Jonathan, Behold, "
6 D' earnestly asked leave of me that "
10 Then said D' to Jonathan, Who "
11 Jonathan said unto D', Come, and "
12 Jonathan said unto D', O Lord God "
12 if there be good toward D', and I "
15 Lord hath cut off the enemies of D' "
16 a covenant with the house of D', "
17 Jonathan caused D' to swear again, "
18 Jonathan said to D', To morrow * "
24 So D' hid himself in the field: and "
28 And Jonathan answered Saul, D' "
33 determined of his father to slay D'. "
34 for he was grieved for D', because "
35 at the time appointed with D', and "
39 only Jonathan and D' knew the "
41 D' arose out of a place toward the "
41 with another, until D' exceeded. "
42 Jonathan said to D', Go in peace, "
21: 1 Then came D' to Nob to Ahimelech "
1 was afraid at the meeting of D', "
2 D' said unto Ahimelech the priest, "
4 the priest answered D', and said, "
5 D' answered the priest, and said "
8 D' said unto Ahimelech, And is "
9 D' said, There is none like that; "
10 D' arose, and fled that day for fear "
11 Is not this D' the king of the land? "
11 slain his thousands, and D' his ten "
12 D' laid up these words in his heart, "
22: 1 D' therefore departed thence, and "
3 D' went thence to Mizpeh of Moab: "
4 the while that D' was in the hold. "
5 the prophet Gad said unto D', "
5 Then D' departed, and came into "
6 Saul heard that D' was discovered, "
14 among all thy servants as D', "
17 because their hand also is with D', "
20 Abiathar, escaped, and fled after D'. "
21 Abiathar shewed D' that Saul had "
22 D' said unto Abiathar, I knew it "
23: 1 Then they told D', saying, Behold, "
2 Therefore D' enquired of the Lord, "
2 the Lord said unto D', Go, and "
4 D' enquired of the Lord yet again. "
5 So D' and his men went to Keilah, "
5 D' saved the inhabitants of Keilah. "
6 the son of Ahimelech fled to D' "
7 it was told Saul that D' was come "

1Sa 23: 8 to Keilah, to besiege D· and his 1732
9 D· knew that Saul secretly practised "
10 Then said D·, O Lord God of Israel, "
12 Then said D·, Will the men of "
13 Then D· and his men, which were "
13 was told Saul that D· was escaped "
14 D· abode in the wilderness in "
15 D· saw that Saul was come out to "
15 D· was in the wilderness of Ziph "
16 arose, and went to D· into the wood, "
18 and D· abode in the wood, and "
19 Doth not D· hide himself with us "
24 but D· and his men were in the "
25 they told D·: wherefore he came "
25 pursued after D· in the wilderness "
26 and D· and his men on that side of "
26 and D· made haste to get away "
26 Saul and his men compassed D· "
28 returned from pursuing after D·, "
29 D· went up from thence, and dwelt "
24: 1 D· is in the wilderness of En-gedi. "
2 and went to seek D· and his men "
3 D· and his men remained in the "
4 the men of D· said unto him, "
4 D· arose, and cut off the skirt of "
7 So D· stayed his servants with "
8 D· also arose afterward, and went "
8 D· stooped with his face to the "
9 D· said to Saul, Wherefore hearest "
9 saying, Behold, D· seeketh thy "
16 when D· had made an end of "
16 said, Is this thy voice, my son D·? "
17 he said to D·, Thou art more "
22 And D· sware unto Saul. And Saul "
22 but D· and his men gat them up "
25: 1 D· arose, and went down to the "
4 D· heard in the wilderness that "
5 And D· sent out ten young men, "
5 and D· said unto the ten young "
8 unto thy servants, and to thy son D·. "
9 words in the name of D·, and ceased. "
10 Who is D·? and who is the son of "
13 D· said unto his men, Gird ye on "
13 and D· also girded on his sword: "
13 went up after D· about four hundred "
14 D· sent messengers out of the "
20 D· and his men came down against "
21 D· had said, Surely in vain have I "
22 also do God unto the enemies of D·, "
23 when Abigail saw D·, she hasted, "
23 lighted off the ass, and fell before D· "
32 D· said to Abigail, Blessed be the "
35 So D· received of her hand that "
39 when D· heard that Nabal was dead, "
39 And D· sent and communed with "
40 when the servants of D· were come "
40 D· sent us unto thee, to take thee "
42 went after the messengers of D·, "
43 D· also took Ahinoam of Jezreel; "
26: 1 Doth not D· hide himself in the "
2 to seek D· in the wilderness of Ziph. "
3 But D· abode in the wilderness, and "
4 D· therefore sent out spies, and "
5 D· arose, and came to the place "
5 D· beheld the place where Saul lay, "
6 Then answered D· and said to "
7 D· and Abishai came to the people "
8 Then said Abishai to D·, God hath "
9 D· said to Abishai, Destroy him not: "
10 D· said furthermore, As the Lord "
12 So D· took the spear and the cruse "
13 Then D· went over to the other side, "
14 D· cried to the people, and to Abner "
15 D· said to Abner, Art not thou a "
17 Is this thy voice, my son D·? "
17 And D· said, It is my voice, my lord, "
21 I have sinned: return, my son D·; "
22 D· answered and said, Behold the "
25 Then Saul said to D·, "
25 Blessed be thou, my son D·: "
25 So D· went on his way, and Saul "
27: 1 D· said in his heart, I shall now "
2 D· arose, and he passed over with "
3 D· dwelt with Achish at Gath, "
3 even D· with his two wives, "
4 it was told Saul that D· was fled to "
5 D· said unto Achish, If I have now "
7 And the time that D· dwelt in the "
8 And his men went up, and "
9 D· smote the land, and left neither "
10 D· said, Against the south of Judah, "
11 D· saved neither man nor woman "
11 So did D·, and so will be his "
12 Achish believed D·, saying, He hath "
28: 1 Achish said unto D·, Know thou "
2 D· said to Achish, Surely thou "
2 Achish said to D·, Therefore will I "
17 given it to thy neighbor, even to D·: "
29: 2 D· and his men passed on in the "
3 Is not this D·, the servant of Saul "
5 Is not this D·, of whom they sang "
5 slew his thousands, and D· his ten "
6 Then Achish called D·, and said "
8 D· said unto Achish, But what "
9 Achish answered and said to D·, I "
11 So D· and his men rose up early "
30: 1 when D· and his men were come to "
3 So D· and his men came to the "
4 Then D· and the people that were "
6 D· was greatly distressed; for the "
6 D· encouraged himself in the Lord "
7 D· said to Abiathar the priest, "
7 brought thither the ephod to D·. "
8 D· enquired at the Lord, saying, "
9 So D· went, he and the six hundred "
10 D· pursued, he and four hundred "

1Sa 30:11 and brought him to D·, and gave 1732
13 And D· said unto him, To whom "
15 D· said to him, Canst thou bring "
17 D· smote them from the twilight "
18 D· recovered all that the "
18 and D· rescued his two wives. "
19 taken to them: D· recovered all. "
20 D· took all the flocks and the herds "
21 D· came to the two hundred men, "
21 faint that they could not follow D·, "
21 and they went forth to meet D·, "
21 when D· came near to the people, "
22 Belial, of those that went with D·, "
23 Then said D·, Ye shall not do so, "
26 when D· came to Ziklag, he sent of "
31 where D· himself and his men were "
2Sa 1: 1 D· was returned from the slaughter "
1 D· had abode two days in Ziklag; "
2 And so it was, when he came to D·, "
3 D· said unto him, From whence "
4 D· said unto him, How went the "
5 D· said unto the young man that "
11 Then D· took hold on his clothes, "
13 D· said unto the young man that "
14 D· said unto him, How wast thou "
15 D· called one of the young men, "
16 D· said unto him, Thy blood be "
17 D· lamented with this lamentation "
2: 1 D· enquired of the Lord, saying, "
1 D· said, Whither shall I go up? "
2 D· went up thither, and his two "
3 were with him did D· bring up, "
4 And there they anointed D· king "
4 they told D·, saying, That the men "
5 D· sent messengers unto the men "
10 the house of Judah followed D·. "
11 time that D· was king in Hebron "
13 of Zeruiah, and the servants of D·, "
15 and twelve of the servants of D·, "
17 Israel, before the servants of D·, "
31 the servants of D· had smitten of "
3: 1 house of Saul and the house of D·: "
1 D· waxed stronger and stronger, "
2 unto D· were sons born in Hebron: "
5 These were born to D· in Hebron. "
6 house of Saul and the house of D·, "
8 delivered thee into the hand of D·, "
9 as the Lord hath sworn to D·, even "
10 set up the throne of D· over Israel "
12 sent messengers to D· on his behalf, "
14 D· sent messengers to Ish-bosheth "
17 Ye sought for D· in times past to "
18 for the Lord hath spoken of D·, "
18 By the hand of my servant D· I will "
19 went also to speak in the ears of D· "
20 So Abner came to D· to Hebron, "
20 D· made Abner and the men that "
21 Abner said unto D·, I will arise and "
21 D· sent Abner away; and he went "
22 the servants of D· and Joab came "
22 Abner was not with D· in Hebron; "
26 when Joab was come out from D·, "
26 well of Sirah: but D· knew it not. "
28 afterward when D· heard it, he said, "
31 And D· said to Joab, and to all the "
31 king D· himself followed the bier. "
35 people came to cause D· to eat "
35 while it was yet day, D· sware, "
4: 8 the head of Ish-bosheth unto D· "
9 And D· answered Rechab and "
12 D· commanded his young men, and "
5: 1 came all the tribes of Israel to D· "
3 king D· made a league with them "
3 they anointed D· king over Israel. "
4 D· was thirty years old when he "
6 spake unto D·, saying, Except thou "
6 thinking, D· cannot come in hither. "
7 D· took the strong hold of Zion: "
7 the same is the city of D·. "
8 D· said on that day, Whosoever "
9 So D· dwelt in the fort, "
9 and called it the city of D·. "
9 D· built round about from Millo "
10 D· went on, and grew great, "
11 king of Tyre sent messengers to D·, "
11 and they built D· an house. "
12 D· perceived that the Lord had "
13 D· took him more concubines and "
13 yet sons and daughters born to D·. "
17 had anointed D· king over Israel, "
17 Philistines came up to seek D·; "
17 and D· heard of it, and went "
19 D· enquired of the Lord, saying, "
19 the Lord said unto D·, Go up: "
20 And D· came to Baal-perazim, "
20 and D· smote them there, "
21 and D· and his men burned them. "
23 when D· enquired of the Lord, he "
25 And D· did so, as the Lord had "
6: 1 D· gathered together all the chosen "
2 D· arose, and went with all the "
5 And D· and all the house of Israel "
8 D· was displeased, because the "
9 D· was afraid of the Lord that day, "
10 D· would not remove the ark of the "
10 Lord unto him in the city of D·: "
10 but D· carried it aside into the "
12 was told king D·, saying, The Lord "
12 So D· went and brought up the ark "
12 into the city of D· with gladness. "
14 D· danced before the Lord with all "
14 and D· was girded with a linen "
15 So D· and all the house of Israel "
16 the Lord came into the city of D·, "
16 saw king D· leaping and dancing "
17 tabernacle that D· had pitched for "

2Sa 6:17 and D· offered burnt offerings 1732
18 as D· had made an end of offering "
20 D· returned to bless his household. "
20 daughter of Saul came to meet D·, "
21 D· said unto Michal, It was before "
7: 5 Go and tell my servant D·, Thus "
8 shalt thou say unto my servant D·, "
17 so did Nathan speak unto D·. "
18 Then went king D· in, and sat "
20 what can D· say more unto thee? "
26 of thy servant D· be established "
8: 1 D· smote the Philistines, and "
1 D· took Metheg-ammah out of the "
3 D· smote also Hadadezer, the son "
4 D· took from him a thousand "
4 D· houghed all the chariot horses, "
5 D· slew of the Syrians two and "
6 D· put garrisons in Syria of "
6 the Syrians became servants to D·, "
6 preserved D· whithersoever he "
7 D· took the shields of gold that "
8 king D· took exceeding much brass. "
9 Toi king of Hamath heard that D· "
10 sent Joram his son unto king D·, "
11 Which also king D· did dedicate "
13 D· gat him a name when he "
14 And the Lord preserved D· "
15 And D· reigned over all Israel; "
15 D· executed judgment and justice "
9: 1 D· said, Is there yet any that is left "
2 when they had called him unto D·, "
5 Then king D· sent, and fetched "
6 come unto D·, he fell on his face, "
6 And D· said, Mephibosheth. "
7 D· said unto him, Fear not: for I "
10: 2 Then said D·, I will shew kindness "
2 D· sent to comfort him by the hand "
3 that D· doth honour thy father, "
3 hath not D· rather sent his servants "
5 When they told it unto D·, he sent "
6 saw that they stank before D·, "
7 when D· heard of it, he sent Joab, "
17 was told D·, he gathered all Israel "
17 set themselves in array against D·, "
18 D· slew the men of seven hundred "
11: 1 D· sent Joab, and all his servants "
1 But D· tarried still at Jerusalem. "
2 that D· arose from off his bed, and "
3 D· sent and enquired after the "
4 D· sent messengers, and took her; "
5 conceived, and sent and told D·, "
6 D· sent to Joab, saying, Send me "
6 And Joab sent Uriah to D·. "
7 D· demanded of him how Joab did, "
8 D· said to Uriah, Go down to thy "
10 had told D·, saying, Uriah went "
10 D· said unto Uriah, camest thou "
11 Uriah said unto D·, The ark, and "
12 And D· said to Uriah, Tarry here "
13 when D· had called him, he did eat "
14 D· wrote a letter to Joab, and sent "
17 of the people of the servants of D·; "
18 Joab sent and told D· all the things "
22 come and shewed D· all that Joab "
23 messenger said unto D·, Surely the "
25 Then D· said unto the messenger, "
27 the mourning was passed, D· sent "
27 thing that D· had done displeased "
12: 1 the Lord sent Nathan unto D·. "
7 Nathan said to D·, Thou art the "
13 D· said unto Nathan, I have sinned "
13 Nathan said unto D·, The Lord "
15 that Uriah's wife bare unto D·, "
16 D· therefore besought God for the "
16 and D· fasted, and went in, "
18 servants of D· feared to tell him "
19 D· saw that his servants whispered, "
19 D· perceived that the child was "
19 D· said unto his servants, Is the "
20 Then D· arose from the earth, and "
24 D· comforted Bath-sheba his wife, "
27 Joab sent messengers to D·, and "
29 D· gathered all the people together, "
31 So D· and all the people returned "
13: 1 Absalom the son of D· had a fair "
1 Amnon the son of D· loved her. "
7 Then D· sent home to Tamar, "
21 king D· heard of all these things, "
30 came to D·, saying, Absalom hath "
37 D· mourned for his son every day. "
39 the soul of king D· longed to go 1732
15:13 came a messenger to D·, saying, "
14 D· said unto all his servants that "
22 D· said to Ittai, Go and pass over. "
30 D· went up by the ascent of mount "
31 told D·, saying, Ahithophel is among "
31 D· said, O Lord, I pray thee, turn "
32 when D· was come up to the top of "
33 Unto whom D· said, If thou passest "
16: 1 when D· was a little past the top of "
5 when king D· came to Bahurim, "
6 And he cast stones at D·, and "
6 at all the servants of king D·: "
10 Lord hath said unto him, Curse D·. "
11 D· said to Abishai, and to all his "
13 as D· and his men went by the way, "
23 of Ahithophel both with D· and "
17: 1 I will arise and pursue after D· "
16 and tell D·, saying, Lodge not this "
17 and they went and told king D·. "
21 and told king D·, and said unto "
21 said unto D·, Arise, and pass quickly "
22 Then D· arose, and all the people "
24 D· came to Mahanaim. And Absalom "
27 when D· was come to Mahanaim, "
29 sheep, and cheese of kine, for D·, "

2Sa 18: 1 D' numbered the people that were 1732
2 D' sent forth a third part of the "
7 slain before the servants of D'. "
9 Absalom met the servants of D'. "
24 D' sat between the two gates: and "
19:11 D' sent to Zadok and to Abiathar "
16 the men of Judah to meet king D'. "
22 D' said, What have I to do with "
43 have also more right in D' than ye: "
20: 1 We have no part in D', neither "
2 man of Israel went up from after D', "
3 D' came to his house at Jerusalem; "
6 D' said to Abishai, Now shall Sheba "
11 favoureth Joab, and he that is for D', "
21 against the king, even against D': "
26 Jairite was a chief ruler about D'. "
21: 1 was a famine in the days of D', "
1 and D' enquired of the Lord. And "
3 D' said unto the Gibeonites, What "
7 D' and Jonathan the son of Saul. "
11 it was told D' what Rizpah the "
12 D' went and took the bones of Saul "
15 D' went down, and his servants "
15 Philistines: and D' waxed faint. "
16 new sword, thought to have slain D'. "
17 the men of D' sware unto him, "
21 the brother of D' slew him. * "
22 and fell by the hand of D', and by "
22: 1 D' spake unto the Lord the words "
51 mercy to his anointed, unto D', "
23: 1 these be the last words of D'. "
1 D' the son of Jesse said, and the "
8 of the mighty men whom D' had: "
9 of the three mighty men with D', "
13 came to D' in the harvest time "
14 D' was then in an hold, and the "
15 D' longed, and said, Oh that one "
16 and took it, and brought it to D', "
23 And D' set him over his guard. "
24: 1 he moved D' against them to say, "
10 D' said unto the Lord, I have "
11 when D' was up in the morning, "
12 Go and say unto D', Thus saith the "
13 So Gad came to D', and told him, "
14 D' said unto Gad, I am in a great "
17 D' spake unto the Lord when he "
18 Gad came that day to D', and said "
19 D', according to the saying of Gad, "
21 D' said, To buy the threshingfloor "
22 Araunah said unto D', Let my lord "
24 So D' bought the threshingfloor "
25 D' built there an altar unto the "
1Ki 1: 1 Now king D' was old and stricken "
8 mighty men which belonged to D', "
11 and D' our lord knoweth it not? "
13 Go and get thee in unto king D', "
28 Then king D' answered and said, "
31 Let my lord king D' live for ever. "
32 D' said, Call me Zadok the priest, "
37 than the throne of my lord king D'. "
43 king D' hath made Solomon king. "
47 came to bless our lord king D', "
2: 1 of D' drew nigh that he should die; "
10 So D' slept with his fathers, "
10 and was buried in the city of D'. "
11 the days that D' reigned over Israel "
12 sat Solomon upon the throne of D' "
24 and set me on the throne of D' "
26 the ark of the Lord God before D' "
32 my father D' not knowing thereof, "
33 but upon D', and upon his seed, "
44 that thou didst to D' my father: "
45 throne of D' shall be established "
3: 1 and brought her into the city of D', "
3 in the statutes of D' his father: "
6 hast shewed unto thy servant D' "
7 made thy servant king instead of D' "
14 as thy father D' did walk, then I "
5: 1 for Hiram was ever a lover of D'. "
3 Thou knowest how that D' my "
5 the Lord spake unto D' my father, "
7 hath given unto D' a wise son "
6:12 which I spake unto D' thy father: "
7:51 which D' his father had dedicated; "
8: 1 out of the city of D', which is Zion. "
15 which spake with his mouth unto D' "
16 but I chose D' to be over my people "
17 it was in the heart of D' my father "
18 the Lord said unto D' my father, "
20 I am risen up in the room of D' "
24 Who hast kept with thy servant D' "
25 keep with thy servant D' my father "
26 thou spakest unto thy servant D' "
66 that the Lord had done for D' his "
9: 4 D' thy father walked, in integrity "
5 I promised to D' thy father, saying, "
24 came up out of the city of D' unto "
11: 4 as was the heart of D' his father. "
6 not fully after the Lord, as did D' "
12 not do it for D' thy father's sake: "
13 to thy son for D' my servant's sake, "
15 to pass, when D' was in Edom, "
21 Hadad heard in Egypt that D' slept "
24 when D' slew them of Zobah: "
27 the breaches of the city of D' "
33 my judgments, as did D' his father "
34 D' my servant's sake, whom I chose, "
36 D' my servant may have a light 1732
38 commandments, as D' my servant "
38 thee a sure house, as I built for D', "
39 I will for this afflict the seed of D', "
43 buried in the city of D' his father: "
12:16 What portion have we in D'? "
16 now see to thine own house, D'. "
19 rebelled against the house of D' "
20 none that followed the house of D', "

1Ki 12:26 kingdom return to the house of D': 1732
13: 2 shall be born unto the house of D', "
14: 8 kingdom away from the house of D', "
8 hast not been as my servant D', "
31 with his fathers in the city of D'. "
15: 3 Lord his God, as the heart of D' "
5 D' did that which was right in the "
8 they buried him in the city of D' "
11 in the eyes of the Lord, as did D' "
24 of D' his father: and Jehoshaphat "
22:50 fathers in the city of D' his father: "
2Ki 8:19 Judah for D' his servant's sake. "
24 with his fathers in the city of D': "
9:28 with his fathers in the city of D'. "
12:21 with his fathers in the city of D': "
14: 3 yet not like D' his father: he did "
20 with his fathers in the city of D'. "
15: 7 with his fathers in the city of D': "
38 fathers in the city of D' his father "
16: 2 Lord his God, like D' his father. "
20 with his fathers in the city of D': "
17:21 rent Israel from the house of D'; "
18: 3 according to all that D' his father "
20: 5 Thus saith the Lord, the God of D' "
21: 7 house, of which the Lord said to D', "
22: 2 and walked in all the way of D' "
1Ch 2:15 Ozem the sixth, D' the seventh "
3: 1 these were the sons of D', which "
9 These were all the sons of D', "
4:31 their cities unto the reign of D'. "
6:31 D' set over the service of song "
7: 2 whose number was in the days of D' "
9:22 D' and Samuel the seer did ordain "
10:14 and turned the kingdom unto D' "
11: 1 Israel gathered themselves to D' "
3 and D' made a covenant with them "
3 they anointed D' king over Israel, "
4 D' and all Israel went to Jerusalem, "
5 the inhabitants of Jebus said to D', "
5 Nevertheless D' took the castle "
5 of Zion, which is the city of D'. "
6 D' said, Whosoever smiteth the "
7 D' dwelt in the castle; therefore "
7 they called it the city of D'. "
9 So D' waxed greater and greater: "
10 chief of the mighty men whom D' "
11 number of the mighty men whom D' "
13 He was with D' at Pas-dammim, 1732
15 went down to the rock to D', "
16 D' was then in the hold, and the "
17 D' longed, and said, Oh that one "
18 and took it, and brought it to D': "
18 but D' would not drink of it, "
25 and D' set him over his guard. "
12: 1 they that came to D' to Ziklag, "
8 there separated themselves unto D' "
16 and Judah to the hold unto D'. "
17 D' went out to meet them, and "
18 Thine are we, D', and on thy side, "
18 D' received them, and made them "
19 there fell some of Manasseh to D', "
21 D' against the band of the rovers: "
22 day there came to D' to help him, "
23 came to D' to Hebron, to turn the "
31 name, to come and make D' king. "
38 to make D' king over all Israel: "
38 were of one heart to make D' king. "
39 there they were with D' three days, "
13: 1 D' consulted with the captains of "
2 D' said unto all the congregation "
5 So D' gathered all Israel together, "
6 D' went up, and all Israel, to "
8 D' and all Israel played before God "
11 D' was displeased, because the "
12 D' was afraid of God that day, "
13 So D' brought not the ark home "
13 to himself to the city of D', "
14: 1 king of Tyre sent messengers to D', "
2 D' perceived that the Lord had "
3 D' took more wives at Jerusalem: "
3 D' begat more sons and daughters. "
8 when the Philistines heard that D' "
8 the Philistines went up to seek D'. "
8 And D' heard of it, and went out "
10 D' enquired of God, saying, Shall I "
11 and D' smote them there. Then "
11 D' said, God hath broken in upon "
12 D' gave a commandment, and they "
14 Therefore D' enquired again of God; "
16 D' therefore did as God commanded "
17 fame of D' went out into all lands; "
15: 1 D' made him houses in the city "
1 houses in the city of D', 1732
2 Then D' said, None ought to carry "
3 D' gathered all Israel together to "
4 D' assembled the children of Aaron, "
11 D' called for Zadok and Abiathar "
16 D' spake to the chief of the Levites "
25 So D', and the elders of Israel, and "
27 D' was clothed with a robe of fine "
27 D' also had upon him an ephod of "
29 came to the city of D', that Michal "
29 at a window saw king D' dancing "
16: 1 the tent that D' had pitched for it: "
2 D' had made an end of offering "
7 day D' delivered first this psalm "
43 D' returned to bless his house. "
17: 1 to pass, as D' sat in his house, "
1 that D' said to Nathan the prophet, "
2 Nathan said unto D', Do all that is "
4 Go and tell D' my servant, Thus "
7 shalt thou say unto my servant D', "
15 so did Nathan speak unto D'. "
16 D' the king came and sat before "
18 What can D' speak more to thee "
24 let the house of D' thy servant be "

1Ch 18: 1 pass, that D' smote the Philistines, 1732
3 D' smote Hadarezer king of Zobah "
4 D' took from him a thousand "
4 D' also houghed all the chariot "
5 D' slew of the Syrians two and "
6 D' put garrisons in "
6 Thus the Lord preserved D' "
7 D' took the shields of gold that "
8 brought D' very much brass, "
9 Tou king of Hamath heard how D' "
10 sent Hadoram his son to king D', "
11 king D' dedicated unto the Lord, "
13 Thus the Lord preserved D' "
14 So D' reigned over all Israel, and "
17 of D' were chief about the king. "
19: 2 D' said, I will shew kindness unto "
2 D' sent messengers to comfort "
2 servants of D' came into the land * "
3 Thinkest thou that D' doth honour "
5 told D' how the men were served. "
6 had made themselves odious to D', "
8 when D' heard of it, he sent Joab, "
17 And it was told D'; and he gathered "
17 D' had put the battle in array "
18 D' slew of the Syrians seven "
19 they made peace with D', and "
20: 1 But D' tarried at Jerusalem. And "
2 D' took the crown of their king "
3 Even so dealt D' with all the cities "
3 D' and all the people returned to "
8 and they fell by the hand of D', and "
21: 1 and provoked D' to number Israel. "
2 D' said to Joab, and to the rulers of "
5 of the number of people unto D'. "
8 D' said unto God, I have sinned "
10 Go and tell D', saying, Thus saith "
11 Gad came to D', and said unto him, "
13 D' said unto Gad, I am in a great "
16 D' lifted up his eyes, and saw the "
16 Then D' and the elders of Israel, "
17 D' said unto God, Is it not I that "
18 Lord commanded Gad to say to D', "
18 that D' should go up, and set up "
19 D' went up at the saying of Gad, "
21 as D' came to Ornan, Ornan looked "
21 and saw D', and went out of the "
21 bowed himself to D' with his face "
22 Then D' said to Ornan, Grant me "
23 Ornan said unto D', Take it to thee, "
24 king D' said to Ornan, Nay; but I "
25 So D' gave to Ornan for the place "
26 D' built there an altar unto the "
28 time when D' saw that the Lord "
30 D' could not go before it to enquire "
22: 1 Then D' said, This is the house of "
2 D' commanded to gather together "
3 D' prepared iron in abundance for "
4 brought much cedar wood to D' "
5 D' said, Solomon my son is young "
5 So D' prepared abundantly before "
7 D' said to Solomon, My son, as for "
17 D' also commanded all the princes "
23: 1 when D' was old and full of days, "
6 D' divided them into courses "
25 For D' said, The Lord God of Israel "
27 last words of D' the Levites were "
24: 3 D' distributed them, both Zadok of "
31 sons of Aaron in the presence of D' "
25: 1 Moreover D' and the captains of "
26:26 D' the king, and the chief fathers, "
31 the fortieth year of the reign of D' "
32 D' made rulers over the Reubenites, "
27:18 Elihu, one of the brethren of D': "
23 D' took not the number of them "
24 of the chronicles of king D'. "
28: 1 D' assembled all the princes of "
2 D' the king stood up upon his feet, "
11 Then D' gave to Solomon his son "
19 All this, said D', the Lord made me "
20 D' said to Solomon his son, Be 1732
29: 1 Furthermore D' the king said unto "
9 D' the king also rejoiced with great "
10 D' blessed the Lord before all the "
10 D' said, Blessed be thou, Lord God "
20 D' said to all the congregation, "
22 the son of D' king the second time, "
23 as king instead of D' his father, and "
24 all the sons likewise of king D', "
26 Thus D' the son of Jesse reigned "
29 acts of D' the king, first and last, "
2Ch 1: 1 And Solomon the son of D' was "
4 ark of God had D' brought up from "
4 the place which D' had prepared "
8 hast shewed great mercy unto D' "
9 let thy promise unto D' my father "
2: 3 thou didst deal with D' my father, "
7 whom D' my father did provide. "
12 hath given to D' the king a wise son, "
14 with the cunning men of my lord D' "
17 D' his father had numbered them; "
3: 1 Lord appeared unto D' his father, "
1 the place that D' had prepared "
5: 1 brought in all the things that D' his "
2 out of the city of D', which is Zion. "
6: 4 with his mouth to my father D', "
6 and have chosen D' to be over my "
7 it was in the heart of D' my father "
8 But the Lord said to D' my father, "
10 I am risen up in the room of D' "
15 which hast kept with thy servant D' "
16 keep with thy servant D' my father "
17 hast spoken unto thy servant D'. "
42 remember the mercies of D' thy "
7: 6 which D' the king had made to "
6 when D' praised by their ministry; "
10 that the Lord had shewed unto D', "

2Ch 7:17 as *D* thy father walked, and do 1732
18 as I have covenanted with *D* thy "
8:11 out of the city of *D* unto the house "
11 shall not dwell in the house of *D* "
14 according to the order of *D* his "
14 had *D* the man of God commanded. "
9:31 he was buried in the city of *D* his "
10:16 What portion have we in *D*? and "
16 now, *D*, see to thine own house. "
19 rebelled against the house of *D* "
11:17 years they walked in the way of *D* "
18 daughter of Jerimoth the son of *D* "
12:16 and was buried in the city of *D*: "
13: 5 kingdom over Israel to *D* forever, "
6 servant of Solomon the son of *D*, "
8 in the hand of the sons of *D*; "
14: 1 they buried him in the city of *D*: "
16:14 made for himself in the city of *D*, "
17: 3 in the first ways of his father *D*, "
21: 1 with his fathers in the city of *D*. "
7 would not destroy the house of *D*, "
7 covenant that he had made with *D*, "
12 saith the Lord God of *D* thy father, "
20 they buried him in the city of *D*, "
23: 3 Lord hath said of the sons of *D*. "
18 whom *D* had distributed in the "
18 singing, as it was ordained by *D*. "
24:16 in the city of *D* among the kings, "
25 in the city of *D*, but they buried "
27: 9 they buried him in the city of *D*: "
28: 1 of the Lord, like *D* his father: "
29: 2 according to all that *D* his father "
25 to the commandment of *D*, and of "
26 stood with the instruments of *D*, "
27 the instruments ordained by *D* "
30 with the words of *D*, and of Asaph "
30:26 the time of Solomon the son of *D* "
32: 5 repaired Millo in the city of *D*, "
30 to the west side of the city of *D*. "
33 of the sepulchres of the sons of *D*: "
33: 7 God had said to *D* and to Solomon "
14 built a wall without the city of *D*, "
34: 2 walked in the ways of *D* his father, "
3 began to seek after the God of *D* "
35: 3 house which Solomon the son of *D* "
4 according to the writing of *D* "
15 to the commandment of *D*, and of "
Ezr 3:10 after the ordinance of *D* king of "
8: 2 of the sons of *D*; Hattush. "
20 of the Nethinims, whom *D* and "
Ne 3:15 that go down from the city of *D*. "
16 over against the sepulchres of *D*, "
12:24 to the commandment of *D* the man "
36 with the musical instruments of *D* "
37 up by the stairs of the city of *D*, "
37 above the house of *D*, even unto "
45 to the commandment of *D*, and of "
46 For in the days of *D* and Asaph of "
Ps 3:*title* A Psalm of *D*, when he fled from "
4:*title* on Neginoth, A Psalm of *D*. "
5:*title* upon Nehiloth, A Psalm of *D*. "
6:*title* upon Sheminith, A Psalm of *D*. "
7:*title* Shiggaion of *D*, which he sang "
8:*title* upon Gittith, A Psalm of *D*. "
9:*title* upon Muth-labben, A Psalm of *D*. "
11:*title* chief Musician, A Psalm of *D*. "
12:*title* upon Sheminith, A Psalm of *D*. "
13:*title* chief Musician, A Psalm of *D*. "
14:*title* chief Musician, A Psalm of *D*. "
15:*title* A Psalm of *D*. "
16:*title* Michtam of *D*. "
17:*title* A Prayer of *D*. "
18:*title* A Psalm of *D*, the servant of the "
50 to *D*, and to his seed for evermore. "
19:*title* chief Musician, A Psalm of *D*. "
20:*title* chief Musician, A Psalm of *D*. "
21:*title* chief Musician, A Psalm of *D*. "
22:*title* Aijeleth Shahar, A Psalm of *D*. "
23:*title* A Psalm of *D*. "
24:*title* A Psalm of *D*. "
25:*title* A Psalm of *D*. "
26:*title* A Psalm of *D*. "
27:*title* A Psalm of *D*. "
28:*title* A Psalm of *D*. "
29:*title* A Psalm of *D*. "
30:*title* the dedication of the house of *D*. "
31:*title* chief Musician, A Psalm of *D*. "
32:*title* A Psalm of *D*, Maschil. "
34:*title* A Psalm of *D*, when he changed "
35:*title* A Psalm of *D*. "
36:*title* A Psalm of *D* the servant of the "
37:*title* A Psalm of *D*. "
38:*title* A Psalm of *D*, to bring to "
39:*title* even to Jeduthun, A Psalm of *D*. "
40:*title* chief Musician, A Psalm of *D*. "
41:*title* chief Musician, A Psalm of *D*. "
51:*title* A Psalm of *D*, when Nathan, the "
52:*title* A Psalm of *D*, when Doeg the "
title *D* is come to the house of "
53:*title* Mahalath, Maschil, A Psalm of *D*. "
54:*title* A Psalm of *D*, when the Ziphims "
title said to Saul, Doth not *D* hide "
55:*title* Neginoth, Maschil, A Psalm of *D*. "
56:*title* Michtam of *D*, when the "
57:*title* Michtam of *D*, when he fled from "
58:*title* Al-taschith, Michtam of *D*. "
59:*title* Michtam of *D*; when Saul sent, "
60:*title* Michtam of *D*, to teach; when he "
61:*title* upon Neginah, A Psalm of *D*. "
62:*title* to Jeduthun, A Psalm of *D*. "
63:*title* A Psalm of *D*, when he was in the "
64:*title* chief Musician, A Psalm of *D*. "
65:*title* Musician, A Psalm and Song of *D*. "
68:*title* Musician, A Psalm or Song of *D*. "
69:*title* upon Shoshannim, A Psalm of *D*. "
70:*title* A Psalm of *D*, to bring to "

Ps 72:20 The prayers of *D* the son of Jesse 1732
78:70 He chose *D* also his servant, and "
86:*title* A Prayer of *D*. "
89: 3 I have sworn unto *D* my servant, "
20 I have found *D* my servant; with "
35 that I will not lie unto *D*. "
49 which thou swearest unto *D* in "
101:*title* A Psalm of *D*. "
103:*title* A Psalm of *D*. "
108:*title* A Song or Psalm of *D*. "
109:*title* chief Musician, A Psalm of *D*. "
110:*title* A Psalm of *D*. "
122:*title* A Song of degrees of *D*. "
5 the thrones of the house of *D*. "
124:*title* A Song of degrees of *D*. "
131:*title* A Song of degrees of *D*. "
132: 1 Lord, remember *D*, and all his "
11 Lord hath sworn in truth unto *D*; "
17 There will I make the horn of *D* "
133:*title* A Song of degrees of *D*. "
138:*title* A Psalm of *D*. "
139:*title* chief Musician, A Psalm of *D*. "
140:*title* chief Musician, A Psalm of *D*. "
141:*title* A Psalm of *D*. "
142:*title* Maschil of *D*; A Prayer when he "
143:*title* A Psalm of *D*. "
144:*title* A Psalm of *D*. "
10 who delivereth *D* his servant from "
Pr 1: 1 Proverbs of Solomon, the son of *D*, "
Ec 1: 1 words of the Preacher, the son of *D*, "
Ca 4: 4 Thy neck is like the tower of *D* "
Isa 7: 2 it was told the house of *D*, saying, "
13 said, Hear ye now, O house of *D*; "
9: 7 upon the throne of *D*, and upon "
16: 5 in truth in the tabernacle of *D*, "
22: 9 the breaches of the city of *D*, "
22 key of the house of *D* will I lay "
29: 1 to Ariel, the city where *D* dwelt! "
38: 5 the Lord, the God of *D* thy father, "
55: 3 even the sure mercies of *D*. "
Jer 17:25 sitting upon the throne of *D*, "
21:12 O house of *D*, thus saith the Lord; "
22: 2 that sittest upon the throne of *D*, "
4 kings sitting upon the throne of *D*, "
30 sitting upon the throne of *D*, and "
23: 5 raise unto *D* a righteous Branch, "
29:16 that sitteth upon the throne of *D*, "
30: 9 *D* their king, whom I will raise up "
33:15 righteousness to grow up unto *D*; "
17 *D* shall never want a man to sit "
21 my covenant be broken with *D* "
22 so will I multiply the seed of *D* "
26 seed of Jacob, and *D* my servant, "
36:30 none to sit upon the throne of *D*: "
Eze 34:23 feed them, even my servant *D*; "
24 servant *D* a prince among them; "
37:24 *D* my servant shall be king over "
25 my servant *D* shall be their prince "
Ho 3: 5 Lord their God, and *D* their king; "
Am 6: 5 instruments of musick, like *D*; "
9:11 will I raise up the tabernacle of *D* "
Zec 12: 7 that the glory of the house of *D* "
8 them at that day shall be as *D*; "
8 the house of *D* shall be as God, "
10 I will pour upon the house of *D*, "
12 the family of the house of *D* apart, "
13: 1 fountain opened to the house of *D* "
M't 1: 1 son of *D*, the son of Abraham. 1138
6 Jesse begat *D* the king; and *D* "
17 generations from Abraham to *D* "
17 *D* until the carrying away into "
20 Joseph, thou son of *D*, fear not to "
9:27 Thou son of *D*, have mercy on us. "
12: 3 have ye not read what *D* did, "
23 said, Is not this the son of *D*? "
15:22 Lord, thou son of *D*; my daughter "
20:30, 31 on us, O Lord, thou son of *D*. "
21: 9 Hosanna to the son of *D*: Blessed "
15 Hosanna to the son of *D*; they "
22:42 They say unto him, The son of *D*. "
43 How then doth *D* in spirit call him "
45 If *D* then call him Lord, how is "
M'r 2:25 Have ye never read what *D* did, "
10:47 Jesus, thou son of *D*, have mercy "
48 Thou son of *D*, have mercy on me. "
11:10 of our father *D*, that cometh in "
12:35 that Christ is the son of *D*? "
36 *D* himself said by the Holy Ghost, "
37 *D* therefore himself calleth him "
Lu 1:27 was Joseph, of the house of *D*; "
32 him the throne of his father *D*: "
69 in the house of his servant *D*; "
2: 4 unto the city of *D*, which is called "
4 was of the house and lineage of *D*:) "
11 is born this day in the city of *D* "
3:31 Nathan, which was the son of *D*, "
6: 3 what *D* did, when himself was an "
18:38 Jesus, thou son of *D*, have mercy "
39 Thou son of *D*, have mercy on me. "
20:42 And *D* himself saith in the book "
44 *D* therefore calleth him Lord, how "
Joh 7:42 Christ cometh of the seed of *D*, "
42 town of Bethlehem, where *D* was? "
Ac 1:16 the Holy Ghost by the mouth of *D* "
2:25 For *D* speaketh concerning him, "
29 speak unto you of the patriarch *D*, "
34 *D* is not ascended into the heavens: "
4:25 Who by the mouth of thy servant *D* "
7:45 of our fathers, unto the days of *D*; "
13:22 up unto them *D* to be their king; "
22 I have found *D* the son of Jesse, "
34 give you the sure mercies of *D*. "
36 For *D*, after he had served his own "
15:16 build again the tabernacle of *D*, "
Ro 1: 3 which was made of the seed of *D* "
4: 6 *D* also describeth the blessedness "

Ro 11: 9 *D* saith, Let their table be made 1138
2Ti 2: 8 Jesus Christ of the seed of *D* "
Heb 4: 7 limiteth a certain day, saying in *D*, "
11:32 *D* also, and Samuel, and of the "
Re 3: 7 he that hath the key of *D*, he that "
5: 5 Root of *D*, hath prevailed to open "
22:16 am the root and the offspring of *D*. "

David's

1Sa 18:29 became *D* enemy continually. 1732
19:11 sent messengers unto *D* house, "
11 Michal *D* wife told him, saying, "
20:16 require it at the hand of *D* enemies. "
25 side, and *D* place was empty: "
27 month, that *D* place was empty: "
23: 3 And *D* men said unto him, Behold, "
24: 5 afterward, that *D* heart smote him, "
25: 9 when *D* young men came, they "
12 So *D* young men turned their way, "
44 *D* wife, to Phalti the son of Laish, "
26:17 Saul knew *D* voice, and said, Is "
30: 5 *D* two wives were taken captives, "
20 cattle, and said, this is *D* spoil. "
2Sa 2:30 lacked of *D* servants, nineteen "
3: 5 sixth, Ithream, by Eglah *D* wife. "
5: 8 the blind that are hated of *D* soul, "
8: 2 the Moabites became *D* servants,* "
14 they of Edom became *D* servants.* "
18 and *D* sons were chief rulers. "
10: 2 *D* servants came into the land of "
4 *D* servants, and shaved off the one "
12: 5 *D* anger was greatly kindled "
30 stones: and it was set on *D* head. "
13: 3 son of Shimeah *D* brother: and "
32 of Shimeah *D* brother, answered "
15:12 the Gilonite, *D* counseller, from "
37 So Hushai *D* friend came into the "
16:16 Hushai the Archite, *D* friend, "
19:41 all *D* men with him, over Jordan? "
24:10 *D* heart smote him after that he "
11 unto the prophet Gad, *D* seer, "
1Ki 1:38 Solomon to ride upon king *D* mule, "
11:32 one tribe for my servant *D* sake, "
15: 4 for *D* sake did the Lord his God "
2Ki 11:10 give king *D* spears and shields, "
19:34 sake, and for my servant *D* sake. "
20: 6 sake, and for my servant *D* sake. "
1Ch 18: 2 the Moabites became *D* servants,* "
6 the Syrians became *D* servants,* "
13 the Edomites became *D* servants.* "
19: 4 Wherefore Hanun took *D* servants, "
20: 2 in it: and it was set upon *D* head: "
7 of Shimea *D* brother slew him. "
21: 9 the Lord spake unto Gad, *D* seer, "
27:31 the substance which was king *D*. "
32 *D* uncle was a counseller, "
2Ch 23: 9 and shields, that had been king *D*, "
Ps 132:10 For thy servant *D* sake turn not "
145:*title* *D* Psalm of praise. * "
Isa 37:35 sake, and for my servant *D* sake. "
Jer 13:13 kings that sit upon *D* throne, "
Lu 20:41 say they that Christ is *D* son? 1138

dawn See also DAWNING.

M't 28: 1 began to *d* toward the first day 2020
2Pe 1:19 until the day *d*, and the day star 1306

dawning

Jos 6:15 rose early about the *d* of the day, 5927
J'g 19:26 the woman in the *d* of the day, 6437
Job 3: 9 neither let it see the *d* of the day:*6079
7: 4 to and fro unto the *d* of the day. 5399
Ps 119:147 prevented the *d* of the morning, "

day See also DAY'S; DAYS; DAYSMAN; DAYSPRING; DAYTIME; HOLYDAY; MIDDAY; NOONDAY; YESTERDAY.

Ge 1: 5 God called the light *D*, and the 3117
5 and the morning were the first *d*. "
8 and the morning were the second *d*. "
13 and the morning were the third *d*. "
14 to divide the *d* from the night; "
16 the greater light to rule the *d*, "
18 rule over the *d* and over the night, "
19 and the morning were the fourth *d*. "
23 and the morning were the fifth *d*. "
31 and the morning were the sixth *d*. "
2: 2 the seventh *d* God ended his work "
2 and he rested on the seventh *d* "
3 God blessed the seventh *d*, and "
4 in the *d* that the Lord God made "
17 in the *d* that thou eatest thereof "
3: 5 in the *d* ye eat thereof, then your "
8 the garden in the cool of the *d*: "
4:14 thou hast driven me out this *d* "
5: 1 In the *d* that God created man, "
2 in the *d* when they were created. "
7:11 the seventeenth *d* of the month, "
11 the same *d* were all the fountains "
13 In the selfsame *d* entered Noah, "
8: 4 on the seventeenth *d* of the month, "
14 seven and twentieth *d* of the month, "
22 and *d* and night shall not cease. "
15:18 same *d* the Lord made a covenant "
17:23 the selfsame *d*, as God had said "
26 *d* was Abraham circumcised, "
18: 1 the tent door in the heat of the *d*; "
19:37 father of the Moabites unto this *d*. "
38 children of Ammon unto this *d*. "
21: 8 made a great feast the same *d* "
26 neither yet heard I of it, but to *d*. "
22: 4 third *d* Abraham lifted up his eyes, "
14 as it is said to this *d*, In the mount "
24:12 send me good speed this *d*, and "
42 I came this *d* unto the well, and "
25:31 said, Sell me this *d* thy birthright. "
33 Swear to me this *d*; and he sware "
26:32 it came to pass the same *d*, that "

Ge 26:33 the city is Beer-sheba unto this d'. 3117
27: 2 I know not the d' of my death: "
45 deprived also of you both in one d'? "
29: 7 it is yet high d', neither is it time "
30:32 will pass through all thy flock to d', "
35 he removed that d' the he goats "
31:22 it was told Laban on the third d' "
39 whether stolen by d', or stolen by "
40 the d' the drought consumed me, "
43 this d' unto these my daughters, "
48 between me and thee this d'. "
32:24 him until the breaking of the d'. 7837
26 Let me go, for the d' breaketh. "
32 hollow of the thigh, unto this d': 3117
33:13 men should overdrive them one d', "
16 Esau returned that d' on his way "
34:25 it came to pass on the third d', "
35: 3 answered me in the d' of my distress, "
20 pillar of Rachel's grave unto this d'. "
39:10 as she spake to Joseph d' by d', "
40: 7 Wherefore look ye so sadly to d'? "
20 it came to pass the third d', which "
41: 9 I do remember my faults this d': "
42:13 youngest is this d' with our father, "
18 Joseph said unto them the third d', "
32 youngest is this d' with our father "
47:23 bought you this d' and your land "
26 over the land of Egypt unto this d', "
48:15 fed me all my life long unto this d', "
20 he blessed them that d', saying, "
50:20 as it is this d', to save much people "
Ex 2:13 he went out the second d', behold, "
18 it that ye are come so soon to d'? "
5: 6 Pharaoh commanded the same d' * "
14 yesterday and to d', as heretofore? "
6:28 the d' when the Lord spake unto "
8:22 I will sever in that d' the land of "
10: 6 have seen, since the d' that they "
6 were upon the earth unto this d'. "
13 east wind upon the land all that d', "
28 in that d' thou seest my face thou "
12: 3 In the tenth d' of this month "
6 fourteenth d' of the same month: 3117
14 d' shall be unto you for a memorial; "
15 first d' ye shall put away leaven "
15 the first d' until the seventh d', "
16 in the first d' there shall be an holy "
16 the seventh d' there shall be an "
17 in this selfsame d' have I brought "
17 observe this d' in your generations "
18 fourteenth d' of the month at even, "
18 one and twentieth d' of the month "
41 the selfsame d' it came to pass, "
51 it came to pass the selfsame d', "
13: 3 Remember this d', in which ye "
4 This d' came ye out in the month "
6 and in the seventh d' shall be a "
8 thou shalt shew thy son in that d', "
21 the Lord went before them by d' 3119
21 them light; to go by d' and night: "
22 the pillar of the cloud by d', nor "
14:13 which he will shew to you to d': 3117
13 Egyptians whom ye have seen to d', "
30 the Lord saved Israel that d' out of "
16: 1 the fifteenth d' of the second month "
4 gather a certain rate every d', that "
5 on the sixth d' they shall prepare "
22 on the sixth d' they gathered twice "
23 bake that which ye will bake to d',* "
25 that to d'; for to d' is a sabbath 3117
25 to d' ye shall not find it in the "
26 but on the seventh d', which is the "
27 on the seventh d' for to gather, "
29 he giveth you on the sixth d' the "
29 out of his place on the seventh d'. "
30 the people rested on the seventh d'. "
19: 1 the same d' came they into the "
10 sanctify them to d' and to morrow, "
11 be ready against the third d': for "
11 the third d' the Lord will come "
15 Be ready against the third d': come "
16 it came to pass on the third d' in "
20: 8 Remember the sabbath d', to keep "
10 But the seventh d' is the sabbath "
11 rested the seventh d': wherefore "
11 the Lord blessed the sabbath d', "
21:21 if he continue a d' or two he shall "
22:30 on the eighth d' thou shalt give it "
23:12 the seventh d' thou shalt rest: that "
24:16 and the seventh d' he called unto "
29:36 thou shalt offer every d' a bullock "
38 two lambs of the first year d' by d' "
31:15 doeth any work in the sabbath d'. "
17 and on the seventh d' he rested, "
32:28 there fell of the people that d' "
29 Consecrate yourselves to d' to the "
29 bestow upon you a blessing this d'. "
34 nevertheless in the d' when I visit "
34:11 that which I command thee this d': "
21 but on the seventh d' thou shalt "
35: 2 but on the seventh d' there shall be "
2 to you an holy d', a sabbath of "
3 habitations upon the sabbath d'. 3117
40: 2 On the first d' of the first month "
17 second year, on the first d' of the "
37 they journeyed not till the d' that 3117
38 was upon the tabernacle by d', 3119
Le 6: 5 in the d' of his trespass offering. 3117
20 Lord in the d' when he is anointed; "
7:15 eaten the same d' that it is offered; "
16 the same d' that he offereth his "
17 the sacrifice on the third d' shall be "
18 be eaten at all on the third d', "
35 in the d' when he presented them "
36 in the d' that he anointed them, "
38 in the d' that he commanded the "

Le 8:34 As he hath done this d', so the 3117
35 d' and night seven days, and keep 3119
9: 1 it came to pass on the eighth d', 3117
4 to d' the Lord will appear unto you. "
10:19 this d' have they offered their sin "
19 I had eaten the sin offering to d', "
12: 3 And in the eighth d' the flesh of "
13: 5 shall look on him the seventh d': "
6 look on him again the seventh d': "
27 shall look upon him the seventh d': "
32, 34 in the seventh d' the priest shall "
51 on the plague on the seventh d': "
14: 2 the leper in the d' of his cleansing: "
9 it shall be on the seventh d', that "
10 And on the eighth d' he shall take "
23 shall bring them on the eighth d' "
39 shall come again the seventh d', "
15:14 And on the eighth d' he shall take "
29 And on the eighth d' she shall take "
16:29 on the tenth d' of the month, ye "
30 in that d' shall the priest make an 3117
19: 6 it shall be eaten the same d' ye "
6 if ought remain until the third d', "
7 if it be eaten at all on the third d', "
22:27 from the eighth d' and thenceforth "
28 it and her young both in one d'. "
30 On the same d' it shall be eaten up; "
23: 3 but the seventh d' is the sabbath of "
5 In the fourteenth d' of the first "
6 the fifteenth d' of the same month 3117
7 In the first d' ye shall have an holy "
8 seventh d' is an holy convocation "
12 ye shall offer that d' when ye wave "
14 until the selfsame d' that ye have "
15 from the d' that ye brought the "
21 shall proclaim on the selfsame d', "
24 seventh month in the first d' of the "
27 Also on the tenth d' of this seventh "
27 there shall be a d' of atonement: 3117
28 ye shall do no work in that same d': "
28 for it is a d' of atonement, "
29 not be afflicted in that same d', "
30 doeth any work in that same d', "
32 in the ninth d' of the month at even, "
34 The fifteenth d' of this seventh 3117
35 On the first d' shall be an holy "
36 on the eighth d' shall be an holy "
37 every thing upon his d': "
39 in the fifteenth d' of the seventh "
39 on the first d' shall be a sabbath, "
39 on the eighth d' shall be a sabbath. "
40 ye shall take you on the first d' "
25: 9 the jubile to sound on the tenth d' "
9 in the d' of atonement shall ye 3117
27:23 give thine estimation in that d', "
Nu 1: 1, 18 on the first d' of the second month, "
3: 1 in the d' that the Lord spake with 3117
13 the d' that I smote all the firstborn "
6: 9 his head in the d' of his cleansing, "
9 on the seventh d' shall he shave it. "
10 And on the eighth d' he shall bring "
11 shall hallow his head that same d'. "
7: 1 to pass on the d' that Moses "
10 in the d' that it was anointed, even "
11 each prince on his d', for the "
12 offered his offering the first d' "
18 On the second d' Nethaneel the son "
24 On the third d' Eliab the son of "
30 On the fourth d' Elizur the son of "
36 On the fifth d' Shelumiel the son of "
42 On the sixth d' Eliasaph the son of "
48 On the seventh d' Elishama the son "
54 On the eighth d' offered Gamaliel "
60 On the ninth d' Abidan the son of "
66 On the tenth d' Ahiezer the son of "
72 On the eleventh d' Pagiel the son of "
78 On the twelfth d' Ahira the son of "
84 in the d' when it was anointed, "
8:17 on the d' that I smote every "
9: 3 In the fourteenth d' of this month, "
5 the fourteenth d' of the first month "
6 not keep the passover on that d': "
6 Moses and before Aaron on that d': "
11 The fourteenth d' of the second "
15 And on the d' that the tabernacle "
16 alway: the cloud covered it by d',* "
21 whether it was by d' or by night 3119
10:10 Also in the d' of your gladness, 3117
11 the twentieth d' of the second "
34 of the Lord was upon them by d', 3119
11:19 Ye shall not eat one d', nor two 3117
32 the people stood up all that d', and "
32 all that night, and all the next d', "
14:14 by d' time in a pillar of a cloud, 3119
34 each d' for a year, shall ye bear 3117
15:23 the d' that the Lord commanded "
32 gathered sticks upon the sabbath d'. "
19:12 himself with it on the third d', "
12 and on the seventh d' he shall be "
12 he purify not himself the third d', "
12 then the seventh d' he shall not be "
19 upon the unclean on the third d', "
19 and on the seventh d': and on the "
19 seventh d' he shall purify himself, "
22:30 since I was thine unto this d'? "
25:18 the d' of the plague for Peor's sake. "
28: 3 without spot d' by d', for a "
9 And on the sabbath d' two lambs of "
16 in the fourteenth d' of the first "
17 in the fifteenth d' of this month "
18 In the first d' shall be an holy "
25 And on the seventh d' ye shall "
26 Also in the d' of the first fruits, "
29: 1 On the first d' of the month, "
1 it is a d' of blowing the trumpets 3117
7 on the tenth d' of this seventh "

Nu 29:12 the fifteenth d' of the seventh 3117
17 And on the second d' ye shall offer "
20 And on the third d' eleven bullocks, "
23 And on the fourth d' ten bullocks, "
26 And on the fifth d' nine bullocks, "
29 And on the sixth d' eight bullocks, "
32 And on the seventh d' seven "
35 On the eighth d' ye shall have a "
30: 5 her in the d' that he heareth; "
7 at her in the d' that he heard it: "
8 her on the d' that he heard it; "
12 void on the d' he heard them; "
14 hold his peace at her from d' to d'; "
14 at her in the d' that he heard them. "
31:19 and your captives on the third d', "
19 and on the seventh d'. "
24 wash your clothes on the seventh d', "
33: 3 the fifteenth d' of the first month; "
38 Egypt, in the first d' of the fifth "
De 1: 3 on the first d' of the month, that "
10 are this d' as the stars of heaven 3117
33 should go, and in a cloud by d'. 3119
39 which in that d' had no knowledge 3117
2:18 Ar, the coast of Moab, this d': "
22 in their stead even unto this d': "
25 This d' will I begin to put the dread "
30 thy hand, as appeareth this d'. "
3:14 Bashan-havoth-jair, unto this d'. "
4: 4 are alive every one of you this d'. "
8 which I set before you this d'? "
10 the d' that thou stoodest before "
15 on the d' that the Lord spake unto "
20 of inheritance, as ye are this d'. "
26 earth to witness against you this d', "
32 since the d' that God created man "
38 for an inheritance, as it is this d'. "
39 Know therefore this d', and "
40 which I command thee this d', that "
5: 1 which I speak in your ears this d', "
3 who are all of us here alive this d'. "
12 Keep the sabbath d' to sanctify it, "
14 But the seventh d' is the sabbath "
15 thee to keep the sabbath d'. "
24 we have seen this d' that God doth "
6: 6 which I command thee this d', "
24 preserve us alive, as it is at this d'. "
7:11 command thee this d', to do them. "
8: 1 this d' shall ye observe to do, that "
11 which I command thee this d': "
18 unto thy fathers, as, it is this d'. "
19 testify against you this d' that ye "
9: 1 art to pass over Jordan this d', "
3 Understand therefore this d', that "
7 the d' that thou didst depart out "
10 the fire in the d' of the assembly. "
24 Lord from the d' that I knew you. "
10: 4 of the fire in the d' of the assembly: "
8 to bless in his name, unto this d'. "
13 command thee this d' for thy good? "
15 above all people, as it is this d'. "
11: 2 And know ye this d': for I speak not "
4 hath destroyed them unto this d'; "
8 command you this d', that ye may "
13 command you this d', to love the "
26 I set before you this d' a blessing "
27 God, which I command you this d': "
28 I command you this d', to go after "
32 which I set before you this d'. "
12: 8 the things that we do here this d', "
13:18 command thee this d', to do that "
15: 5 which I command thee this d'. "
15 I command thee this thing to d'. "
16: 3 mayest remember the d' when "
4 sacrificedst the first d' at even, "
8 the seventh d' shall be a solemn "
18:16 in the d' of the assembly, saying, "
19: 9 command thee this d', to love the "
20: 3 ye approach this d' unto battle "
21:23 shalt in any wise bury him that d'; "
24:15 his d' thou shalt give him his hire, "
26: 3 I profess this d' unto the Lord "
16 This d' the Lord thy God hath "
17 the Lord this d' to be thy God, "
18 Lord hath avouched thee this d' to "
27: 1 which I command you this d'. "
2 on the d' when ye shall pass over "
4 which I command you this d', in "
9 d' thou art become the people of "
10 which I command thee this d'. "
11 charged his people the same d', "
28: 1 thee this d', that the Lord thy God, "
13 I command thee this d', to observe "
14 I command thee this d', to the "
15 which I command thee this d'; "
32 longing for them all the d' long: "
66 thou shalt fear d' and night, and 3119
29: 4 and ears to hear, unto this d'. 3117
10 Ye stand this d' all of you before "
12 thy God maketh with thee this d': "
13 That he may establish thee to d' "
15 that standeth here with us this d' "
15 that is not here with us this d': "
18 whose heart turneth away this d' "
28 into another land, as it is this d'. "
30: 2 I command thee this d', thou and "
8 which I command thee this d'. "
11 I command thee this d', it is not "
15 I have set before thee this d' life "
16 this d' to love the Lord thy God, "
18 I denounce unto you this d', that ye "
19 heaven and earth to record this d' "
31: 2 and twenty years old this d'; "
17 kindled against them in that d', "
17 so that they will say in that d', "
18 I will surely hide my face in that d' "
22 wrote this song the same d',

De 31:27 I am yet alive with you this d'. 3117
32:35 the d' of their calamity is at hand, "
46 I testify among you this d', which "
48 spake unto Moses that selfsame d', "
33:12 shall cover him all the d' long, "
34: 6 of his sepulchre unto this d'. "
Jos 1: 8 meditate therein d' and night, 3119
3: 7 d' will I begin to magnify thee 3117
4: 9 and they are there unto this d'. "
14 that d' the Lord magnified Joshua "
19 on the tenth d' of the first month, "
5: 9 This d' have I rolled away the 3117
9 place is called Gilgal unto this d'. "
10 on the fourteenth d' of the month "
11 parched corn in the selfsame d'. "
6: 4 and the seventh d' ye shall compass "
10 mouth, until the d' I bid you shout; "
14 the second d' they compassed the "
15 it came to pass on the seventh d', "
15 about the dawning of the d', 7837
15 that d' they compassed the city 3117
25 even unto this d'; because she hid "
7:25 the Lord shall trouble thee this d'. "
26 a great heap of stones unto this d'. "
26 The valley of Achor, unto this d'. "
8:25 all that fell that d', both of men "
28 ever, even a desolation unto this d'. "
29 stones, that remaineth unto this d'. "
9:12 on the d' we came forth to go unto "
17 unto their cities on the third d'. "
27 Joshua made them that d' hewers "
27 of the Lord, even unto this d', "
10:12 in the d' when the Lord delivered "
13 not to go down about a whole d'. "
14 no d' like that before it or after it, "
27 which remain until this very d'. "
28 that d' Joshua took Makkedah, "
32 it on the second d', and smote it "
35 they took it on that d', and smote it "
35 therein he utterly destroyed that d', "
13:13 among the Israelites until this d'. "
14: 9 Moses sware on that d', saying, "
10 this d' fourscore and five years old. "
11 d' as I was in the d' that Moses sent "
12 the Lord spake in that d'; "
12 for thou heardest in that d' "
14 unto this d', because that he wholly "
15:63 of Judah at Jerusalem unto this d'. "
16:10 this d', and serve under tribute. "
22: 3 these many days unto this d', "
16 to turn away this d' from following "
16 rebel this d' against the Lord. "
17 we are not cleansed until this d', "
18 ye must turn away this d' from "
18 and it will be, seeing ye rebel to d' "
22 the Lord, (save us not this d',) "
29 this d' from following the Lord, "
31 This d' we perceive that the Lord "
23: 8 as ye have done unto this d'. "
9 stand before you unto this d'. "
14 this d' I am going the way of all "
24:15 choose you this d' whom ye will "
25 a covenant with the people that d', "
J'g 1:21 in Jerusalem unto this d'. "
26 is the name thereof unto this d'. "
3:30 So Moab was subdued that d' "
4:14 this is the d' in which the Lord "
23 God subdued on that d' Jabin the "
5: 1 son of Abinoam on that d', saying, "
6:24 unto this d' it is yet in Ophrah "
27 could not do it by d', that he did 3119
32 that d' he called him Jerubbaal, 3117
9:18 against my father's house this d', "
19 his house this d', then rejoice ye "
45 fought against the city all that d'; "
10: 4 are called Havoth-jair unto this d', "
15 us only, we pray thee, this d'. "
11:27 the Judge be judge this d' between "
12: 3 are ye come up unto me this d', "
13: 7 the womb to the d' of his death. "
10 that came unto me the other d'. "
14:15 the seventh d', that they said unto "
17 it came to pass on the seventh d', "
18 said unto him on the seventh d' "
15:19 which is in Lehi unto this d'. "
16: 2 when it is d', we shall kill him. *1242
18: 1 that d' all their inheritance had 3117
12 Mahaneh-dan unto this d': behold, "
30 the d' of the captivity of the land. "
19: 5 it came to pass on the fourth d', "
8 morning on the fifth d' to depart: "
9 the d' draweth toward evening, I "
9 behold, the d' groweth to an end, "
11 d' was far spent; and the servant "
25 when the d' began to spring, they 7837
26 dawning of the d', and fell down 1242
30 the d' that the children of Israel 3117
30 of the land of Egypt unto this d': "
20:21 d' twenty and two thousand men. "
22 put themselves in array the first d'. "
24 children of Benjamin the second d'. "
25 them out of Gibeah the second d', "
26 fasted that d' until even, and "
30 of Benjamin on the third d', "
35 that d' twenty and five thousand "
46 all which fell that d' of Benjamin "
21: 3 should be to d' one tribe lacking "
6 one tribe cut off from Israel this d'. "
Ru 2:19 Where hast thou gleaned to d'? "
19 name with whom I wrought to d' is "
3:18 he hath finished the thing this d'. "
4: 5 What d' thou buyest the field of "
9 witnesses this d', that I have "
10 this place; ye are witnesses this d'. "
14 which hath not left thee this d' "
1Sa 2:34 one d' they shall die both of them. "

1Sa 3:12 In that d' I will perform against Eli 3117
4: 3 the Lord smitten us to d' before the "
12 came to Shiloh the same d' with his "
16 I fled to d' out of the army. "
5: 5 of Dagon in Ashdod unto this d'. "
6:15 sacrifices the same d' unto the Lord. "
16 they returned to Ekron the same d'. "
18 unto this d' in the field of Joshua, "
7: 6 and fasted on that d', "
10 a great thunder on that d' "
8: 8 since the d' that I brought them up "
8 out of Egypt even unto this d', "
18 ye shall cry out in that d' because "
18 Lord will not hear you in that d'. "
9:12 he came to d' to the city; for there "
12 a sacrifice of the people to d' "
15 in his ear a d' before Saul came, "
19 ye shall eat with me to d', "
24 Saul did eat with Samuel that d'. "
26 about the spring of the d', that 7837
10: 2 art departed from me to d', then 3117
9 those signs came to pass that d'. "
19 ye have this d' rejected your God, "
11:11 Ammonites until the heat of the d': "
13 not a man be put to death this d': "
13 for to d' the Lord hath wrought "
12: 2 you from my childhood unto this d'. "
5 his anointed is witness this d', that "
17 Is it not wheat harvest to d'? "
18 Lord sent thunder and rain that d': "
13:22 it came to pass in the d' of battle, "
14: 1 it came to pass upon a d', "
23 the Lord saved Israel that d': "
24 of Israel were distressed that d': "
28 man that eateth any food this d'. "
30 the people had eaten freely to d' "
31 they smote the Philistines that d' "
33 roll a great stone unto me this d'. "
37 he answered him not that d'. "
38 wherein this sin hath been this d'. "
45 he hath wrought with God this d'. "
15:28 kingdom of Israel from thee this d', "
35 to see Saul until the d' of his death: "
16:13 upon David from that d' forward. "
17:10 I defy the armies of Israel this d'; "
46 This d' will the Lord deliver thee "
46 this d' unto the fowls of the air, "
18: 2 Saul took him that d', and would "
9 Saul eyed David from that d' and "
21 Thou shalt this d' be my son in law "
19:24 lay down naked all that d' and all "
20: 5 in the field unto the third d' at even. "
12 to morrow any time, or the third d', "
26 Saul spake not any thing that d': 3117
27 was the second d' of the month, "
27 neither yesterday, nor to d'? 3117
34 meat the second d' of the month: "
21: 5 though it were sanctified this d' "
6 in the d' when it was taken away. "
7 servants of Saul was there that d', "
10 fled that d' for fear of Saul, "
22: 8, 13 me, to lie in wait, as at this d'? "
18 slew on that d' fourscore and five "
22 I knew it that d', when Doeg the "
23:14 Saul sought him every d', but God "
24: 4 Behold the d' of which the Lord "
10 this d' thine eyes have seen how "
10 the Lord had delivered thee to d' "
18 thou hast shewed this d' how that "
19 that thou hast done unto me this d'. "
25: 8 we come in a good d': give, I pray "
16 both by night and d', all the while 3119
32 sent thee this d' to meet me: 3117
33 which hast kept me this d' from "
26: 8 enemy into thine hand this d': "
10 his d' shall come to die; "
19 they have driven me out this d' "
21 was precious in thine eyes this d': "
23 delivered thee into my hand to d', "
24 thy life was much set by this d' "
27: 1 I shall now perish one d' by the "
6 Achish gave him Ziklag that d': "
6 the kings of Judah unto this d'. "
10 Whither have ye made a road to d'? "
28:18 done this thing unto thee this d'. "
20 he had eaten no bread all the d', "
29: 3 since he fell unto me unto this d'? "
6 d' of thy coming ... unto this d': "
8 I have been with thee unto this d', "
30: 1 were come to Ziklag on the third d', "
17 unto the evening of the next d': 4283
25 it was so from that d' forward, 3117
25 an ordinance for Israel unto this d'. "
31: 6 all his men, that same d' together. "
2Sa 1: 2 came even to pass on the third d', "
2:17 was a very sore battle that d'; "
32 they came to Hebron at break of d'. 215
3: 8 shew kindness this d' unto the 3117
8 thou chargest me to d' with a fault "
35 eat meat while it was yet d', "
37 all Israel understood that d' that it "
38 great man fallen this d' in Israel? "
39 I am this d' weak, though anointed "
4: 3 were sojourners there until this d'.) "
5 about the heat of the d' to the "
8 avenged my lord the king this d' "
5: 8 David said on that d', Whosoever "
6: 8 of the place Perez-uzzah to this d'. "
9 was afraid of the Lord that d', "
20 glorious was the king of Israel to d', "
20 who uncovered himself to d' "
23 no child unto the d' of her death. "
7: 6 even to this d', but have walked in "
11:12 Tarry here to d' also, and to "
12 Uriah abode in Jerusalem that d', "
12:18 it came to pass on the seventh d', "

2Sa 13: 4 the king's son, lean from d' to d'? 1242
32 from the d' that he forced his sister 3117
37 David mourned for his son every d'. "
14:22 d' thy servant knoweth that I have "
15:20 should I this d' make thee go up "
16: 3 To d' shall the house of Israel "
12 me good for his cursing this d'. "
18: 7 was there a great slaughter that d' "
8 wood devoured more people that d' "
18 unto this d', Absalom's place. "
20 Thou shalt not bear tidings this d', "
20 thou shalt bear tidings another d': "
20 this d' thou shalt bear no tidings, "
31 the Lord hath avenged thee this d' "
19: 2 the victory that d' was turned into "
2 for the people heard say that d' "
3 people gat them by stealth that d' "
5 shamed this d' the faces of all thy "
5 which this d' have saved thy life, "
6 thou hast declared this d', that "
6 this d' I perceive, that if Absalom "
6 lived, and all we had died this d', "
19 the d' that my lord the king went "
20 I am come the first this d' "
22 ye should this d' be adversaries "
22 put to death this d' in Israel? for do "
22 not I know that I am this d' king "
24 from the d' the king departed until "
24 the d' he came again in peace. "
35 I am this d' fourscore years old: "
20: 3 shut up unto the d' of their death, "
21:10 of the air to rest on them by d'. 3119
22: 1 the d' that the Lord had delivered 3117
19 me in the d' of my calamity: "
23:10 wrought a great victory that d'; "
24:18 Gad came that d' to David, and "
1Ki 1:25 gone down this d', and hath slain "
30 so will I certainly do this d'. "
48 one to sit on my throne this d', "
51 king Solomon swear unto me to d' "
2: 8 the d' when I went to Mahanaim: "
24 shall be put to death this d'. "
37 the d' thou goest out, and passest "
42 the d' thou goest out, and walkest "
3: 6 to sit on his throne, as it is this d'. "
18 came to pass the third d' after that "
4:22 Solomon's provision for one d' was "
5: 7 Blessed be the Lord this d', which "
8: 8 and there they are unto this d'. "
16 Since the d' that I brought forth "
24 with thine hand, as it is this d'. "
28 servant prayeth before thee to d': "
29 toward this house night and d', "
59 the Lord our God d' and night, 3119
61 his commandments, as at this d'. 3117
64 The same d' did the king hallow "
66 eighth d' he sent the people away: "
9:13 the land of Cabul unto this d'. "
21 tribute of bondservice unto this d'. "
10:12 trees, nor were seen unto this d'. "
12: 7 servant unto this people this d', "
12 came to Rehoboam the third d', "
12 Come to me again the third d'. "
19 the house of David unto this d'. "
32 the fifteenth d' of the month, like "
33 fifteenth d' of the eighth month, *
13: 3 he gave a sign the same d', "
11 the man of God had done that d' "
14:14 off the house of Jeroboam that d': "
16:16 over Israel that d' in the camp. "
17:14 d' that the Lord sendeth rain "
18:15 surely shew thyself unto him to d'. "
36 known this d' that thou art God "
20:13 deliver it into thine hand this d'; "
29 seventh d' the battle was joined: "
29 thousand footmen in one d'. "
22: 5 at the word of the Lord to d'. "
25 thou shalt see in that d', when thou "
35 the battle increased that d': and "
2Ki 2: 3, 5 thy master from thy head to d'? "
22 the waters were healed unto this d', "
4: 8 it fell on a d', that Elisha passed to "
11 it fell on a d', that he came thither, "
18 it fell on a d', that he went out "
23 Wherefore wilt thou go to him to d'? "
6:28 thy son, that we may eat him to d', "
29 I said unto her on the next d', "
31 Shaphat shall stand on him this d'. "
7: 9 this d' is a d' of good tidings, "
8: 6 since the d' that she left the land, "
22 the hand of Judah unto this d'. "
10:27 it a draught house unto this d'. "
14: 7 name of it Joktheel unto this d'. "
15: 5 was a leper unto the d' of his death, "
16: 6 Elath, and dwelt there unto this d'. "
17:23 own land to Assyria unto this d'. "
34 this d' they do after the former "
41 fathers, so do they unto this d'. "
19: 3 This d' is a d' of trouble, "
20: 5 on the third d' thou shalt go up "
8 the house of the Lord the third d'? "
17 laid up in store unto this d', "
21:15 the d' their fathers came forth out "
15 of Egypt, even unto this d'. "
25: 3 d' of the fourth month of the famine "
8 on the seventh d' of the month "
27 seven and twentieth d' of the month, "
30 daily rate for every d', all the days 3117
1Ch 4:41 destroyed them utterly unto this d'. "
43 and dwelt there unto this d'. "
5:26 to the river Gozan, unto this d'. "
9:33 in that work d' and night. 3119
11:22 slew a lion in a pit in a snowy d'. *3117
12:22 d' by d' there came to David to "
13:11 place is called Perez-uzza to this d'. "
12 David was afraid of God that d', "

1Ch 16: 7 *d* David delivered first this psalm 3117
23 forth from *d* to *d* his salvation. "
17: 5 dwelt in an house since the *d* that "
5 I brought up Israel unto this *d*; "
26:17 Levites northward four a *d*, "
17 southward four a *d*, and toward "
28: 7 and my judgments, as at this *d*. "
29: 5 his service this *d* unto the Lord? "
21 on the morrow after that *d*, even a "
22 drink before the Lord on that *d* "
2Ch 3: 2 began to build in the second *d* of "
5: 9 And there it is unto this *d*. 3117
6: 5 since the *d* that I brought forth "
15 with thine hand, as it is this *d*. "
20 open upon this house *d* and night, 3119
7: 9 *d* they made a solemn assembly: 3117
10 And on the three and twentieth *d* "
8: 8 make to pay tribute until this *d*. "
13 Even after a certain rate every *d*, "
14 as the duty of every *d* required: "
16 *d* of the foundation of the house of "
10:12 came to Rehoboam on the third *d*, "
12 Come again to me on the third *d*. "
19 the house of David unto this *d*. "
18: 4 at the word of the Lord to *d*. "
24 thou shalt see on that *d* when "
34 battle increased that *d*: howbeit "
20:26 on the fourth *d* they assembled "
26 valley of Berachah, unto this *d*. "
21:10 the hand of Judah unto this *d*. "
15 by reason of the sickness *d* by *d*. "
24:11 they did *d* by *d*, and gathered "
26:21 the *d* of his death, and dwelt in a "
28: 6 twenty thousand in one *d*, which "
29:17 on the first *d* of the first month "
17 and on the eighth *d* of the month "
17 in the sixteenth *d* of the first month "
30:15 fourteenth *d* of the second month: "
21 priests praised the Lord *d* by *d*, 3117
35: 1 the fourteenth *d* of the first month. "
16 Lord was prepared the same *d*, 3117
21 I come not against thee this *d*, "
25 their lamentations to this *d*, and "
Ezr 3: 4 as the duty of every *d* required; "
6 the first *d* of the seventh month "
6: 9 let it be given them *d* by *d* 3118
15 finished on the third *d* of the month "
19 the fourteenth *d* of the first month. "
7: 9 upon the first *d* of the first month "
9 on the first *d* of the fifth month "
8:31 river of Ahava on the twelfth *d* of "
33 fourth *d* was the silver and the 3117
9: 7 a great trespass unto this *d*; and "
7 to confusion of face, as it is this *d*. "
15 remain yet escaped, as it is this *d*: "
10: 9 on the twentieth *d* of the month; "
13 work of one *d* or two: for we are 3117
16 in the first *d* of the tenth month "
17 by the first *d* of the first month. "
Ne 1: 6 pray before thee now, *d* and night, 3119
11 I pray thee, thy servant this *d*, 3117
4: 2 will they make an end in a *d*? "
9 watch against them *d* and night, 3119
22 guard to us, and labour on the *d*. 3117
5:11 I pray you, to them, even this *d*, "
6:15 twenty and fifth *d* of the month "
8: 2 the first *d* of the seventh month. 3117
9 *d* is holy unto the Lord your God; "
10 this *d* is holy unto our Lord: "
11 Hold your peace, for the *d* is holy; "
13 And on the second *d* were gathered "
17 *d* had not the children of Israel "
18 Also *d* by *d*, from the first "
18 *d* unto the last *d*, "
18 and on the eighth *d* was a solemn "
9: 1 Now in the twenty and fourth *d* "
3 one fourth part of the *d*; "
10 get thee a name, as it is this *d*. "
12 them in the *d* by a cloudy pillar; 3119
19 departed not from them by *d*, "
32 the kings of Assyria unto this *d*. 3117
36 Behold, we are servants this *d*, "
10:31 victuals on the sabbath *d* to sell, "
31 on the sabbath, or on the holy *d*: "
11:23 for the singers, due for every *d*. "
12:43 that *d* they offered great sacrifices, "
47 the porters, every *d* his portion: "
13: 1 On that *d* they read in the book "
15 into Jerusalem on the sabbath *d*: "
15 in the *d* wherein they sold victuals. "
17 ye do, and profane the sabbath *d*? "
19 be brought in on the sabbath *d*. "
22 gates, to sanctify the sabbath *d*. "
Es 1:10 *d*, when the heart of the king "
18 of Persia and Media say this *d* "
2:11 Mordecai walked every *d* before "
3: 7 *d* to *d*, and from month to month, "
12 thirteenth *d* of the first month, "
13 one *d*, even upon the thirteenth *d* "
14 should be ready against that *d*. "
4:16 nor drink three days, night or *d*: "
5: 1 it came to pass on the third *d*, "
4 the king and Haman come this *d* "
9 Then went Haman forth that *d* "
7: 2 again unto Esther on the second *d* "
8: 1 On that *d* did the king Ahasuerus "
9 the three and twentieth *d* thereof; "
12 Upon one *d* in all the provinces 3117
12 upon the thirteenth *d* of the twelfth "
13 should be ready against that *d* 3117
17 gladness, a feast and a good *d*. "
9: 1 on the thirteenth *d* of the same, "
1 the *d* that the enemies of the Jews "
11 On that *d* the number of those that "
15 together on the fourteenth *d* "
17 On the thirteenth *d* of the month "

Es 9:17 on the fourteenth *d* of the same
17 and made it a *d* of feasting and 3117
18 on the thirteenth *d* thereof,
18 the fifteenth *d* of the same they
18 made it a *d* of feasting and 3117
19 the fourteenth *d* of the month Adar "
19 month Adar a *d* of gladness and
19 and feasting, and a good *d*, 3117
21 the fourteenth *d* of the month Adar, "
21 and the fifteenth *d* of the same, "
22 from mourning into a good *d*: that "
Job 1: 4 in their houses, every one his *d*; "
6 Now there was a *d* when the sons of "
13 there was a *d* when his sons and "
2: 1 Again there was a *d* when the sons "
3: 1 Job his mouth, and cursed his *d*. "
3 Let the *d* perish wherein I was "
4 Let that *d* be darkness; let not "
5 let the blackness of the *d* terrify it. "
8 Let them curse it that curse the *d*, "
9 let it see the dawning of the *d*: *7837
7: 4 and fro unto the dawning of the *d*. 5399
14: 6 accomplish, as an hireling, his *d*. 3117
15:23 the *d* of darkness is ready at his "
17:12 They change the night into *d*: the "
18:20 shall be astonied at his *d*, as they "
19:25 stand at the latter *d* upon the *
20:28 flow away in the *d* of his wrath. 3117
21:30 to the *d* of destruction? they shall "
30 brought forth to the *d* of wrath. "
23: 2 Even to *d* is my complaint bitter: "
26:10 until the *d* and night come to an* 216
38:23 against the *d* of battle and war? 3117
Ps 1: 2 in his law doth he meditate *d* and 3119
2: 7 Son; this *d* have I begotten thee. 3117
7:11 angry with the wicked every *d*. "
18:*title* in the *d* that the Lord delivered "
18 in the *d* of my calamity: but the "
19: 2 *D* unto *d* uttereth speech, and "
20: 1 Lord hear thee in the *d* of trouble; "
25: 5 on thee do I wait all the *d*. "
32: 3 through my roaring all the *d* long. "
4 *d* and night thy hand was heavy 3119
35:28 of thy praise all the *d* long. 3117
37:13 for he seeth that his *d* is coming. "
38: 6 I go mourning all the *d* long. "
12 and imagine deceits all the *d* long. "
42: 3 My tears have been my meat *d* 3119
44: 8 In God we boast all the *d* long, 3117
22 For thy sake are we killed all the *d* "
50:15 call upon me in the *d* of trouble: "
55:10 *D* and night they go about it upon 3119
56: 5 Every *d* they wrest my words: 3117
59:16 and refuge in the *d* of my trouble. "
71: 8 and with thy honour all the *d*. "
15 and thy salvation all the *d*; "
24 thy righteousness all the *d* long: "
73:14 all the *d* long have I been plagued, "
74:16 The *d* is thine, the night also is "
77: 2 in the *d* of my trouble I sought the "
78: 9 turned back in the *d* of battle. "
42 the *d* when he delivered them from "
81: 3 appointed, on our solemn feast *d*. "
84:10 a *d* in thy courts is better than a "
86: 7 the *d* of my trouble I will call upon "
88: 1 I have cried *d* and night before thee: "
89:16 name shall they rejoice all the *d*: "
91: 5 for the arrow that flieth by *d*; 3119
92:*title* Psalm or Song for the sabbath *d*. 3117
95: 7 To *d* if ye will hear his voice, "
8 in the *d* of temptation in the "
96: 2 forth his salvation from *d* to *d*. "
102: 2 in the *d* when I am in trouble; "
2 in the *d* when I call answer me "
8 enemies reproach me all the *d*; "
110: 3 be willing in the *d* of thy power, "
5 through kings in the *d* of his wrath. "
118:24 This is the *d* which the Lord hath "
119:91 They continue this *d* according to "
97 it is my meditation all the *d*. "
164 Seven times a *d* do I praise thee "
121: 6 The sun shall not smite thee by *d*, 3119
136: 8 The sun to rule by *d*: for his 3117
137: 7 of Edom in the *d* of Jerusalem; "
138: 3 In the *d* when I cried thou "
139:12 the night shineth as the *d*: the "
140: 7 hast covered my head in the *d* of "
145: 2 Every *d* will I bless thee; "
146: 4 in that very *d* his thoughts perish. "
Pr 4:18 more and more unto the perfect *d*. "
6:34 not spare in the *d* of vengeance. "
7:14 this *d* have I payed my vows. "
20 come home at the *d* appointed. *
11: 4 Riches profit not in the *d* of wrath: "
16: 4 the wicked for the *d* of evil. "
21:26 He coveteth greedily all the *d* long: "
31 horse is prepared against the *d* "
22:19 I have made known to thee this *d*, "
23:17 the fear of the Lord all the *d* long. "
24:10 If thou faint in the *d* of adversity, "
27: 1 for thou knowest not what a *d* may "
10 house in the *d* of thy calamity: "
15 dropping in a very rainy *d* and a "
Ec 7: 1 the *d* of death than the *d* of one's "
14 In the *d* of prosperity be joyful, "
14 but in the *d* of adversity consider: "
8: 8 hath he power in the *d* of death: "
16 there is that neither *d* nor night "
12: 3 In the *d* when the keepers of the "
Ca 2:17 Until the *d* break, and the shadows "
3:11 in the *d* of his espousals, and in "
11 the *d* of the gladness of his heart. "
4: 6 Until the *d* break, and the shadows "
8: 8 in the *d* when she shall be spoken "
Isa 2:11 alone shall be exalted in that *d*. "
12 the *d* of the Lord of hosts shall be "

Isa 2:17 alone shall be exalted in that *d*. 3117
20 In that *d* a man shall cast his idols "
3: 7 In that *d* shall he swear, saying, I "
18 In that *d* the Lord will take away "
4: 1 In that *d* seven women shall take "
2 In that *d* shall the branch of the "
5 a cloud and smoke by *d*, and the 3119
5:30 in that *d* they shall roar against 3117
7:17 from the *d* that Ephraim departed "
18 to pass in that *d*, that the Lord "
20 In the same *d* shall the Lord shave "
21 to pass in that *d*, that a man shall "
23 to pass in that *d*, that every place "
9: 4 oppressor, as in the *d* of Midian. "
14 tail, branch and rush, in one *d*. "
10: 3 will ye do in the *d* of visitation, "
17 his thorns and his briers in one *d*; "
20 to pass in that *d*, that the remnant "
27 to pass in that *d*, that his burden "
32 yet shall he remain at Nob that *d*: "
11:10 in that *d* there shall be a root of "
11 to pass in that *d*, that the Lord "
16 in the *d* that he came up out of the "
12: 1 in that *d* thou shalt say, O Lord, I "
4 And in that *d* shall ye say, Praise "
13: 6 the *d* of the Lord is at hand; "
9 the *d* of the Lord cometh, cruel "
13 and in the *d* of his fierce anger. "
14: 3 to pass in the *d* that the Lord "
17: 4 in that *d* it shall come to pass, that "
7 At that *d* shall a man look to his "
9 In that *d* shall his strong cities be "
11 In the *d* shalt thou make thy plant "
11 in the *d* of grief and of desperate "
19:16 In that *d* shall Egypt be like unto "
18 In that *d* shall five cities in the "
19 In that *d* shall there be an altar to "
21 shall know the Lord in that *d*, "
23 In that *d* shall there be a highway "
24 In that *d* shall Israel be the third "
20: 6 isle shall say in that *d*, Behold, "
22: 5 it is a *d* of trouble, and of treading "
8 thou didst look in that *d* to the "
12 in that *d* did the Lord God of "
20 to pass in that *d*, that I will call "
25 In that *d*, saith the Lord of hosts, "
23:15 to pass in that *d*, that Tyre shall "
24:21 to pass in that *d*, that the Lord "
25: 9 it shall be said in that *d*, Lo, this "
26: 1 In that *d* shall this song be sung "
27: 1 In that *d* the Lord with his sore "
2 In that *d* sing ye unto her, A "
3 it, I will keep it night and *d*. "
8 wind in the *d* of the east wind. "
12 to pass in that *d*, that the Lord "
13 to pass in that *d*, that the great "
28: 5 In that *d* shall the Lord of hosts "
19 shall it pass over, by *d* and by "
24 Doth the plowman plow all *d* to *
29:18 in that *d* shall the deaf hear the "
30:23 in that *d* shall thy cattle feed in "
25 in the *d* of the great slaughter, "
26 in the *d* that the Lord bindeth up "
31: 7 in that *d* every man shall cast "
34: 8 is the *d* of the Lord's vengeance, "
10 not be quenched night nor *d*; 3119
37: 3 This *d* is a *d* of trouble, 3117
38:12, 13 from *d* even to night wilt thou "
19 he shall praise thee, as I do this *d*: "
39: 6 have laid up in store until this *d*, "
43:13 before the *d* was I am he; "
47: 9 come to thee in a moment in one *d*, "
48: 7 before the *d* when thou heardest "
49: 8 and in a *d* of salvation have I "
51:13 hast feared continually every *d* "
52: 5 continually every *d* is blasphemed. "
6 they shall know in that *d* that I "
56:12 to morrow shall be as this *d*, "
58: 3 in the *d* of your fast ye find "
4 ye shall not fast as ye do this *d*, "
5 a *d* for a man to afflict his soul? "
5 and an acceptable *d* to the Lord? "
10 thy darkness be as the noon *d*: *
13 doing thy pleasure on my holy *d*; 3117
59:10 We stumble at noon *d* as in the *
60:11 they shall not be shut *d* nor night; 3119
19 shall be no more thy light by *d*; "
61: 2 the *d* of vengeance of our God; 3117
62: 6 never hold their peace *d* nor night; "
63: 4 the *d* of vengeance is in mine "
65: 2 have spread out my hands all the *d* "
5 a fire that burneth all the *d*. "
66: 8 be made to bring forth in one *d*? "
Jer 1:10 I have this *d* set thee over the "
18 I have made thee this *d* a defenced "
3:25 from our youth even unto this *d*, "
4: 9 it shall come to pass at that *d*, "
6: 4 the *d* goeth away, for the shadows "
7:22 in the *d* that I brought them out "
25 Since the *d* that your fathers came "
25 of the land of Egypt unto this *d* "
9: 1 that I might weep *d* and night for 3119
11: 4 in the *d* that I brought them 3117
5 milk and honey, as it is this *d*. "
7 in the *d* that I brought them up "
7 the land of Egypt even unto this *d*, "
12: 3 prepare them for the *d* of slaughter. "
14:17 run down with tears night and *d*, 3119
15: 9 is gone down while it was yet *d*: "
16:13 there shall ye serve other gods *d* "
19 my refuge in the *d* of affliction, 3117
17:16 have I desired the woeful *d*; "
17 thou art my hope in the *d* of evil. "
18 bring upon them the *d* of evil, "
21 bear no burden on the sabbath *d*, "
22 of your houses on the sabbath *d*, "

Jer 17:22 work, but hallow ye the sabbath d'. 3117
24 gates of this city on the sabbath d', "
24 hallow the sabbath d', to do no "
27 hallow the sabbath d', and not to "
27 of Jerusalem on the sabbath d'; "
18:17 the face, in the d' of their calamity."
20:14 Cursed be the d' wherein I was "
14 let not the d' wherein my mother "
25: 3 even unto this d', that is the three "
18 and a curse; as it is this d'; "
33 slain of the Lord shall be at that d' "
27:22 until the d' that I visit them, "
30: 7 Alas! for that d' is great, so that "
8 come to pass in that d', saith the "
31: 6 For there shall be a d', that the "
32 in the d' that I took them by the "
35 giveth the sun for a light by d', 3119
32:20 even unto this d', and in Israel, "
20 made thee a name, as at this d'; "
31 d' that they built it even unto this d';"
33:20 break my covenant of the d', 3117
20 there should not be d' and night 3119
25 covenant be not with d' and night, "
34:13 the d' that I brought them forth 3117
35:14 unto this d' they drink none, but "
36: 2 from the d' I spake unto thee, "
2 days of Josiah, even unto this d'. "
6 Lord's house upon the fasting d': "
30 body shall be cast out in the d' "
38:28 the d' that Jerusalem was taken: "
39:16 accomplished in that d' before thee."
17 I will deliver thee in that d', "
40: 4 I loose thee this d' from the chains "
41: 4 d' after he had slain Gedaliah, "
42:19 that I have admonished you this d'."
21 I have this d' declared it to you; "
44: 2 this d' they are a desolation, "
6 wasted and desolate, as at this d'. "
10 not humbled even unto this d', "
22 without an inhabitant, as at this d'."
23 happened unto you, as at this d'. "
46:10 For this is the d' of the Lord God "
10 of hosts, a d' of vengeance, "
21 d' of their calamity was come upon "
47: 4 the d' that cometh to spoil all the "
48:41 men's hearts in Moab at that d' "
49:22 at that d' shall the heart of the "
26 shall be cut off in that d', "
50:27 their d' is come, the time of their "
30 of war shall be cut off in that d', "
31 thy d' is come, the time that I will "
51: 2 in the d' of trouble they shall be "
52: 4 month, in the tenth d' of the month, "
6 ninth day of the month, the famine "
11 in prison till the d' of his death. 3117
12 in the tenth d' of the month, which "
31 in the five and twentieth d of the "
34 every d' a portion until the d of 3117
La 1:12 me in the d' of his fierce anger. "
13 me desolate and faint all the d'. "
21 bring the d' that thou hast called, "
2: 1 his footstool in the d' of his anger! "
7 as in the d' of a solemn feast. "
16 this is the d' that we looked for; "
18 down like a river d' and night: 3119
21 thou hast slain them in the d' of 3117
22 solemn d' my terrors round about, "
22 so that in the d' of the Lord's anger "
3: 3 his hand against me all the d'. "
14 people; and their song all the d'. "
57 Thou drewest near in the d' that I "
62 their device against me all the d'. "
Eze 1: 1 in the fifth d' of the month, as I was "
2 In the fifth d' of the month, which "
28 is in the cloud in the d' of rain, 3117
2: 3 against me, even unto this very d'. "
4: 6 appointed thee each d' for a year. "
10 be by weight, twenty shekels a d': "
7: 7 the d' of trouble is near, and not "
10 Behold the d', behold, it is come: "
12 is come, the d' draweth near: "
19 in the d' of the wrath of the Lord: "
8: 1 in the fifth d' of the month, as I "
12: 3 and remove by d' in their sight; 3119
4 forth thy stuff by d' in their sight, "
7 I brought forth my stuff by d', "
13: 5 the battle in the d' of the Lord. 3117
16: 4 in the d' thou wast born thy navel "
5 in the d' that thou wast born. "
56 by thy mouth in the d' of thy pride, "
20: 1 the tenth d' of the month, that "
5 In the d' when I chose Israel, 3117
6 In the d' that I lifted up mine hand "
29 is called Bamah unto this d'. "
31 all your idols, even unto this d': "
21:25 prince of Israel, whose d' is come, "
29 of the wicked, whose d' is come, "
22:24 rained upon in the d' of indignation."
23:38 defiled my sanctuary in the same d',"
39 came the same d' into my sanctuary "
24: 1 month, in the tenth d' of the month, "
2 write thee the name of the d', 3117
2 even of this same d': "
2 against Jerusalem this same d'. "
25 in the d' when I take from them "
26 in that d' shall come unto thee, "
27 that d' shall thy mouth be opened "
26: 1 year, in the first d' of the month, "
18 isles tremble in the d' of thy fall; 3117
27:27 of the seas in the d' of thy ruin. "
28:13 in the d' that thou wast created. "
15 from the d' that thou wast created, "
29: 1 in the twelfth d' of the month, the "
17 the first d' of the month, the word "
21 In that d' will I cause the horn of 3117
30: 2 Howl ye, Woe worth the d'! "

Eze 30: 3 For the d' is near, even the d' of 3117
3 the Lord is near, a cloudy d'; "
9 In that d' shall messengers go forth "
9 upon them, as in the d' of Egypt: "
18 the d' shall be darkened, when I "
20 in the seventh d' of the month, that
31: 1 the first d' of the month, that the
15 In the d' when he went down to 3117
32: 1 first d' of the month, that the word
10 his own life, in the d' of thy fall. 3117
17 in the fifteenth day of the month,
33:12 in the d' of his transgression: 3117
12 in the d' that he turneth from his "
12 in the d' that he sinneth. "
21 in the fifth d' of the month, that one
34:12 the d' that he is among his sheep 3117
12 scattered in the cloudy and dark d'."
36:33 In the d' that I shall have cleansed "
38:14 In that d' when my people of Israel "
19 in that d' there shall be a great "
39: 8 this is the d' whereof I have spoken."
11 to pass in that d', that I will "
13 the d' that I shall be glorified, "
22 their God from that d' and forward."
40: 1 in the tenth d' of the month,
1 in the selfsame d' the hand of the 3117
43:18 in the d' when they shall make it, "
22 the second d' thou shalt offer a kid "
25 every d' a goat for a sin offering: "
27 upon the eighth d', and so forward, "
44:27 d' that he goeth into the sanctuary,"
45:18 the first month, in the first d' of the
20 And so shalt thou do the seventh d'
21 the fourteenth d' of the month, 3117
22 upon that d' shall the prince "
25 the fifteenth d' of the month, "
46: 1 in the d' of the new moon it shall "
4 in the sabbath d' shall be six lambs"
6 the day of the new moon it shall be "
12 as he did on the sabbath d': then "
48:35 of the city from that d' shall be, "
Da 6:10 upon his knees three times a d', 3118
13 maketh his petition three times a d'."
9: 7 confusion of faces, as at this d'; 3117
15 gotten thee renown, as at this d'; "
10: 4 And in the four and twentieth d' "
12 from the first d' that thou didst set "
Ho 1: 5 it shall come to pass at that d', "
11 great shall be the d' of Jezreel. "
2: 3 as in the d' that she was born, "
15 as in the d' when she came up out "
16 shall be at that d', saith the Lord, "
18 in that d' will I make a covenant "
21 it shall come to pass in that d', "
4: 5 Therefore shalt thou fall in the d', "
5: 9 Ephraim shall be desolate in the d' "
6: 2 in the third d' he will raise us up, "
7: 5 in the d' of our king the princes "
9: 5 What will ye do in the solemn d', "
5 in the d' of the feast of the Lord? "
10:14 Beth-arbel in the d' of battle: "
Joe 1:15 for the d'! for the d' of the Lord "
2: 1 the d' of the Lord cometh, for it is "
2 A d' of darkness and of gloominess,"
2 d' of clouds and of thick darkness, "
11 the d' of the Lord is great and very "
31 and the terrible d' of the Lord come."
3:14 d' of the Lord is near in the valley "
18 it shall come to pass in that d', "
Am 1:14 in the d' of battle, with a tempest "
14 in the d' of the whirlwind: "
2:16 shall flee away naked in that d'. "
3:14 in the d' that I shall visit the "
5: 8 and maketh the d' dark with night: "
18 you that desire the d' of the Lord! "
18 the d' of the Lord is darkness, "
20 not the d' of the Lord be darkness, "
6: 3 Ye that put far away the evil d', "
8: 3 temple shall be howlings in that d', "
9 it shall come to pass in that d', "
9 darken the earth in the clear d': "
10 the end thereof as a bitter d'. "
13 In that d' shall the fair virgins "
9:11 In that d' will I raise up the "
Ob 8 shall I not in that d', saith the Lord,"
11 in the d' that thou stoodest on the "
11 in the d' that the strangers "
12 d' of thy brother in the d' that he "
12 in the d' of their destruction; "
12 spoken proudly in the d' of distress."
13 people in the d' of their calamity; "
13 affliction in the d' of their calamity,"
13 in the d' of their calamity; "
14 did remain in the d' of distress. "
15 the d' of the Lord is near upon all "
Jon 4: 7 the morning rose the next d', 4283
Mic 2: 4 In that d' shall one take up 3117
3: 6 the d' shall be dark over them. "
4: 6 In that d', saith the Lord, will I "
5:10 it shall come to pass in that d', "
7: 4 the d' of thy watchmen and thy "
11 d' that thy walls are to be built, "
11 d' shall the decree be far removed. "
12 In that d' also he shall come "
Na 1: 7 a strong hold in the d' of trouble; "
2: 3 in the d' of his preparation, and "
3:17 camp in the hedges in the cold d', "
Hab 3:16 I might rest in the d' of trouble: "
Zep 1: 7 the d' of the Lord is at hand: "
8 come to pass in the d' of the Lord's "
9 In the same d' also will I punish "
10 it shall come to pass in that d', "
14 The great d' of the Lord is near, "
14 the voice of the d' of the Lord: "
15 That d' is a d' of wrath, "
15 a d' of trouble and distress, "

Zep 1:15 a d' of wasteness and desolation, 3117
15 a d' of darkness and gloominess, "
15 a d' of clouds and thick darkness, "
16 A d' of the trumpet and alarm "
18 in the d' of the Lord's wrath; "
2: 2 before the d' pass as the chaff, "
2 before the d' of the Lord's anger "
3 hid in the d' of the Lord's anger. "
4 drive out Ashdod at the noon d', *
3: 8 the d' that I rise up to the prey: 3117
11 that d' shalt thou not be ashamed "
16 that d' it shall be said to Jerusalem,"
Hag 1: 1 in the first d' of the month, came "
15 In the four and twentieth d' of the "
2: 1 one and twentieth d' of the month,
10 In the four and twentieth d' of the
15 consider from this d' and upward, 3117
18 now from this d' and upward, "
18 four and twentieth d' of the ninth "
18 from the d' that the foundation of "
19 from this d' will I bless you. "
20 four and twentieth d' of the month,
23 In that d', saith the Lord of hosts,3117
Zec 1: 7 the four and twentieth d' of the "
2:11 be joined to the Lord in that d', "
3: 9 the iniquity of that land in one d'. "
10 In that d', saith the Lord of hosts, "
4:10 despised the d' of small things? "
6:10 come thou the same d', and go "
7: 1 the fourth d' of the ninth month,
8: 9 in the d' that the foundation of 3117
9:12 even to d' do I declare that I will "
16 their God shall save them in that d' "
11:11 And it was broken in that d': and "
12: 3 in that d' will I make Jerusalem "
4 that d', saith the Lord, I will smite "
6 that d' will I make the governors "
8 that d' shall the Lord defend the "
8 he that is feeble ... at that d' "
9 it shall come to pass in that d', "
11 in that d' shall there be a great "
13: 1 In that d' there shall be a fountain "
2 it shall come to pass in that d', "
4 in that d', that the prophets shall "
14: 1 d' of the Lord cometh, and thy "
3 when he fought in the d' of battle. "
4 his feet shall stand in that d' "
6 it shall come to pass in that d', "
7 be one d' which shall be known "
7 to the Lord, not d', nor night: "
8 be in that d', that living waters "
9 in that d' shall there be one Lord, "
13 it shall come to pass in that d', "
20 In that d' shall there be upon the "
21 in that d' there shall be no more "
Mal 3: 2 who may abide the d' of his coming?"
17 that d' when I make up my jewels; "
4: 1 the d' cometh, that shall burn as an "
1 and the d' that cometh shall burn "
3 in the d' that I shall do this, "
5 great and dreadful d' of the Lord: "
M't 6:11 Give us this d' our daily bread. 4594
30 the grass of the field, which to d' is,"
34 Sufficient unto the d' is the evil 2250
7:22 Many will say to me in that d', "
10:15 in the d' of judgment, than for that "
11:22 for Tyre and Sidon at the d' of "
23 would have remained until this d'.4594
24 of Sodom in the d' of judgment, 2250
12: 1 Jesus went on the sabbath d' "
2 lawful to do upon the sabbath d'.*
8 is Lord even of the sabbath d'. *
11 fall into a pit on the sabbath d'.
36 thereof in the d' of judgment. 2250
13: 1 The same d' went Jesus out of "
16: 3 It will be foul weather to d': for 4594
21 and be raised again the third d'. 2250
17:23 third d' he shall be raised again. "
20: 2 with the laborers for a penny a d', "
6 Why stand ye here all the d' idle? "
12 the burden and heat of the d'. "
19 the third d' he shall rise again. "
21:28 Son, go work to d' in my vineyard. 4594
22:23 d' came to him the Sadducees, 2250
46 any man from that d' forth ask "
24:20 winter, neither on the sabbath d':*
36 d' and hour knoweth no man, 2250
38 until the d' that Noe entered into "
50 a d' when he looketh not for him, "
25:13 know neither the d' nor the hour "
26: 5 But they said, not on the feast d',*
17 the first d' of the feast of unleavened
29 d' when I drink it new with you 2250
27: 8 The field of blood, unto this d'. 4594
19 suffered many things this d' in a "
62 Now the next d', that followed *1887
62 the d' of the preparation,
64 be made sure until the third d', 2250
28: 1 began to dawn toward the first d'
15 among the Jews until this d'. 4594
M'r 1:21 on the sabbath d' he entered into
35 rising up a great while before d', 1773
2:23 the corn fields on the sabbath d';
24 why do they on the sabbath d'
3: 2 would heal him on the sabbath d';
4:27 sleep, and rise night and d', and 2250
35 same d', when the even was come, "
5: 5 And always, night and d', he was "
6: 2 when the sabbath d' was come, *
11 Gomorrha in the d' of judgment, *2250
21 when a convenient d' was come, "
35 And when the d' was now far spent,5610
9:31 killed, he shall rise the third d'. *2250
10:34 the third d' he shall rise again. * "
13:32 of that d' and that hour knoweth "
14: 2 But they said, Not on the feast d',*

M'r 14:12 the first d' of unleavened bread, 2250
25 until that I drink it new "
30 That this d', even in this night, 4594
15:42 that is, the d' before the sabbath, "
16: 2 first d' of the week, they came unto "
9 risen early the first d' of the week, "
Lu 1:20 not able to speak, until the d' that 2250
59 eighth d' they came to circumcise "
80 deserts till the d' of his shewing "
2:11 unto you is born this d' in the city 4594
37 fastings and prayers night and d'. 2250
4:16 the synagogue on the sabbath d', "
21 This d' is this scripture fulfilled 4594
42 And when it was d', he departed 2250
5:17 a certain d', as he was teaching, * "
26 We have seen strange things to d'. 4594
6: 7 he would heal on the sabbath d'; "
13 when it was d', he called 2250
23 Rejoice ye in that d', and leap for "
7:11 the d' after, that he went into a * "
8:22 it came to pass on a certain d', * "
9:12 when the d' began to wear away, "
22 slain, and be raised the third d'. "
37 that on the next d', when they "
10:12 more tolerable in that d' for Sodom, "
11: 3 d' by d' our daily bread. 3588, 2596, "
12:28 grass, which is to d' in the field 4594
46 d' when he looketh not for him, 2250
13:14 healed on the sabbath d', and *
14 healed, and not on the sabbath d'. 2250
16 from this bond on the sabbath d'? "
31 The same d' there came certain * "
32 I do cures to d' and to morrow, 4594
32 the third d' I shall be perfected *
33 Nevertheless I must walk to d', 4594
33 and the d' following: for it cannot
14: 1 to eat bread on the sabbath d', *
3 lawful to heal on the sabbath d'? *
5 pull him out on the sabbath d'? 2250
16:19 fared sumptuously every d': "
17: 4 seven times in a d', and seven "
4 times in a d' turn again to thee, * "
24 also the Son of man be in his d'. "
27 d' that Noe entered into the ark, "
29 same d' that Lot went out of Sodom "
30 d' when the Son of man is revealed. "
31 In that d', he which shall be upon "
18: 7 which cry d' and night unto him, "
33 the third d' he shall rise again. "
19: 5 to d' I must abide at thy house. 4594
9 d' is salvation come to this house, "
42 at least in this thy d', the things 2250
21:34 that d' come upon you unawares. "
37 And in the d' time he was teaching "
22: 7 came the d' of unleavened bread, "
34 the cock shall not crow this d', 4594
66 as soon as it was d', the elders 2250
23:12 the same d' Pilate and Herod were "
43 I say unto thee, To d' shalt thou 4594
54 that d' was the preparation, and 2250
56 rested the sabbath d' according to*
24: 1 Now upon the first d' of the week,
7 and the third d' rise again. 2250
13 them went that same d' to a village "
21 and beside all this, to d' is *4594
21 is the third d' since these things 2250
29 evening, and the d' is far spent. "
46 rise from the dead the third d': "
Joh 1:29 next d' John seeth Jesus coming *1887
35 the next d' after John stood, and * "
39 abode with him that d': for it 2250
43 d' following Jesus would go forth *1887
2: 1 the third d' there was a marriage 2250
23 at the passover, in the feast d', *
5: 9 on the same d' was the sabbath. 2250
10 is the sabbath d': it is not lawful *
16 these things on the sabbath d'. *
6:22 The d' following, when the people *1887
39 raise it up again at the last d'. 2250
40, 44, 54 raise him up at the last d'. "
7:22 ye on the sabbath d' circumcise a *
23 If a man on the sabbath d' receive *
23 whit whole on the sabbath d'? *
37 In the last d', that great 2250
37 that great d' of the feast, Jesus
8:56 Abraham rejoiced to see my d': 2250
9: 4 him that sent me, while it is d': "
14 And it was the sabbath d' when *
16 he keepeth not the sabbath d'. *
11: 9 there not twelve hours in the d'? 2250
9 If any man walk in the d', "
24 in the resurrection at the last d'. "
53 Then from that d' forth they took "
12: 7 against the d' of my burying hath "
12 On the next d' much people that *1887
48 same shall judge him in the last d'. 2250
14:20 At that d' ye shall know that I "
16:23 in that d' ye shall ask me nothing. "
26 At that d' ye shall ask in my name: "
19:31 upon the cross on the sabbath d', *
31 (for that sabbath d' was an high
31 was an high d',) besought
42 of the Jews' preparation d'; *
20: 1 The first d' of the week cometh
19 the same d' at evening, being the 2250
19 first d' of the week, when the doors "
Ac 1: 2 Until the d' in which he was taken "
22 John, unto that same d' that he was "
2: 1 the d' of Pentecost was fully come, "
15 it is but the third hour of the d'. "
20 before that great and notable d' of "
29 sepulchre is with us unto this d'. "
41 the same d' there were added unto "
4: 3 put them in hold unto the next d': * 839
9 If we this d' be examined of the 4594
7: 8 and circumcised him the eighth d'; 2250
Ac 7:26 And the next d' he shewed himself 2250
9:24 watched the gates d' and night to "
10: 3 the ninth hour of the d' an angel of "
40 Him God raised up the third d', "
12:18 Now as soon as it was d', there was "
21 And upon a set d' Herod, arrayed in "
13:14 the synagogue on the sabbath d', "
27 which are read every sabbath d', *
33 Son, this d' have I begotten thee. 4594
44 And the next sabbath d' came *
14:20 the next d' he departed with *1887
15:21 the synagogues every sabbath d'. *
16:11 Samothracia, and the next d' to "
35 when it was d', the magistrates 2250
17:31 Because he hath appointed a d', in "
20: 7 And upon the first d' of the week, "
11 a long while, even till break of d', 827
15 next d' over against Chios; and "
15 the next d' we arrived at Samos, "
15 and the next d' we came to Miletus. "
16 at Jerusalem the d' of Pentecost. 2250
18 from the first d' that I came into "
26 I take you to record this d', 4594
31 warn every one night and d' with 2250
21: 1 and the d' following unto Rhodes, "
7 and abode with them one d'. 2250
8 the next d' we that were of Paul's *
18 And the d' following Paul went "
26 and the next d' purifying himself 2250
22: 3 toward God, as ye all are this d'. 4594
23: 1 conscience before God until this d'. 2250
12 And when it was d', certain of the "
24:21 called in question by you this d'. 4594
25: 6 and the next d' sitting on the *1887
26: 2 I shall answer for myself this d' 4594
7 serving God d' and night, hope to 2250
22 I continue unto this d', witnessing "
29 but also all that hear me this d', 4594
27: 3 And the next d' we touched at Sidon.
18 the next d' they lightened the ship;
19 And the third d' we cast out with
29 stern, and wished for the d'. 2250
33 while the d' was coming on, "
33 to take meat, saying, This d' is 4594
33 is the fourteenth d' that ye have 2250
39 And when it was d', they knew not "
28:13 after one d' the south wind blew, "
16 we came the next d' to Puteoli: "
23 when they had appointed him a d', 2250
Ro 2: 5 the d' of wrath and revelation "
16 In the d' when God shall judge "
8:36 we are killed all the d' long; "
10:21 All d' long I have stretched forth "
11: 8 not hear;) unto this d'. *4594
13:12 the d' is at hand: let us therefore "
13 Let us walk honestly, as in the d'; "
14: 5 esteemeth one d' above another: "
5 another esteemeth every d' alike. "
6 that regardeth the d', regardeth * "
6 and he that regardeth not the d', * "
1Co 1: 8 in the d' of our Lord Jesus Christ. "
3:13 for the d' shall declare it, because "
4:13 of all things unto this d'. * 737
5: 5 saved in the d' of the Lord Jesus. 2250
10: 8 one d' three and twenty thousand. "
15: 4 he rose again the third d' according "
16: 2 Upon the first d' of the week let "
2Co 1:14 ours in the d' of the Lord Jesus. 2250
3:14 for until this d' remaineth 4594
15 unto this d', when Moses is read, "
4:16 inward man is renewed d' by d'. 2250
6: 2 d' of salvation have I succoured "
2 behold, now is the d' of salvation.) "
11:25 a night and a d' I have been in the 3574
Eph 4:30 sealed unto the d' of redemption. 2250
6:13 to withstand in the evil d', "
Ph'p 1: 5 gospel from the first d' until now; "
6 it until the d' of Jesus Christ: "
10 without offence till the d' of Christ; "
2:16 I may rejoice in the d' of Christ, "
3: 5 Circumcised the eighth d', of the "
Col 1: 6 since the d' ye heard of it, and "
9 we also, since the d' we heard it, "
1Th 2: 9 for labouring night and d', because "
3:10 Night and d' praying exceedingly "
5: 2 d' of the Lord so cometh as a thief "
4 that that d' should overtake you "
5 of light, and the children of the d': "
8 But let us, who are of the d', "
2Th 1:10 among you was believed) in that d'. "
2: 2 as that the d' of Christ is at hand. "
3 for that d' shall not come, except *
3: 8 labour and travail night and d', 2250
1Ti 5: 5 and prayers night and d'. "
2Ti 1: 3 thee in my prayers night and d'; "
12 committed unto him against that d'. "
18 find mercy of the Lord in that d': "
4: 8 judge, shall give me at that d': "
Heb 1: 5 this d' have I begotten thee? 4594
3: 7 saith, To d' if ye will hear his voice, "
8 d' of temptation in the wilderness: 2250
13 while it is called To d'; lest any of 4594
15 While it is said, To d' if ye will hear "
4: 4 in a certain place of the seventh d' "
4 And God did rest the seventh d' 2250
7 Again, he limiteth a certain d', "
7 To d', after so long a time, 4594
7 To d' if ye will hear his voice, "
8 have spoken of another d'. 2250
5: 5 my Son, to d' have I begotten thee. 4594
8: 9 d' when I took them by the hand 2250
10:25 as ye see the d' approaching. "
13: 8 yesterday, and to d', and for ever. 4594
Jas 4:13 ye that say, To d' or to morrow we "
5: 5 hearts, as in a d' of slaughter. 2250
1Pe 2:12 glorify God in the d' of visitation. "
2Pe 1:19 in a dark place, until the d' dawn, 2250
19 the d' star arise in your hearts: 5459
2: 8 his righteous soul from d' to d' 2250
9 the d' of judgment to be punished: "
13 in pleasure to riot in the d' time. "
3: 7 against the d' of judgment and "
8 d' is with the Lord as a thousand "
8 and a thousand years as one d'. "
10 But the d' of the Lord will come "
12 unto the coming of the d' of God, "
1Jo 4:17 boldness in the d' of judgment: "
Jude 6 unto the judgment of the great d'. "
Re 1:10 I was in the Spirit on the Lord's d', "
4: 8 and they rest not d' and night, "
6:17 the great d' of his wrath is come; "
7:15 him d' and night in his temple: "
8:12 d' shone not for a third part of it, "
9:15 for an hour, and a d', and a month, "
12:10 them before our God d' and night. "
14:11 and they have no rest d' nor night, "
16:14 of that great d' of God Almighty. "
18: 8 shall her plagues come in one d', "
20:10 d' and night for ever and ever. "
21:25 shall not be shut at all by d': "

day's
Nu 11:31 it were a d' journey on this side, 3117
31 were a d' journey on the other side, "
1Ki 19: 4 he himself went a d' journey "
1Ch 16:37 continually, as every d' work "
Es 9:13 according unto this d' decree, and "
Jon 3: 4 a d' journey, and he cried, and said, "
Lu 2:44 a d' journey; and they sought 2250
Ac 1:12 Jerusalem a sabbath d' journey. "
19:40 in question for this d' uproar, 4594

days
Ge 1:14 for seasons, and for d', and years: 3117
3:14 shalt thou eat all the d' of thy life: "
17 eat of it all the d' of thy life; "
5: 4 d' of Adam after he had begotten "
5 the d' that Adam lived were nine "
8 the d' of Seth were nine hundred "
11 the d' of Enos were nine hundred "
14 d' of Cainan were nine hundred "
17 d' of Mahalaleel were eight hundred "
20 the d' of Jared were nine hundred "
23 the d' of Enoch were three hundred "
27 d' of Methuselah were nine hundred "
31 d' of Lamech were seven hundred "
6: 3 d' shall be an hundred and twenty "
4 giants in the earth in those d'; "
7: 4 For yet seven d', and I will cause it "
4 to rain upon the earth forty d' "
10 it came to pass after seven d', "
12 the rain was upon the earth forty d' "
17 flood was forty d' upon the earth; "
24 the earth an hundred and fifty d'. "
8: 3 the end of the hundred and fifty d' "
6 at the end of forty d', that Noah "
10, 12 he stayed yet other seven d'; "
9:29 the d' of Noah were nine hundred "
10:25 in his d' was the earth divided; "
11:32 d' of Terah were two hundred and "
14: 1 to pass in the d' of Amraphel "
17:12 he that is eight d' old shall be "
21: 4 being eight d' old, as God had "
34 in the Philistines' land many d'. "
24:55 the damsel abide with us a few d', "
25: 7 the d' of the years of Abraham's "
24 her d' to be delivered were fulfilled, "
26: 1 that was in the d' of Abraham. "
15 servants had digged in the d' "
18 in the d' of Abraham his father; "
27:41 The d' of mourning for my father "
44 him a few d', until thy brother's "
29:20 they seemed unto him but a few d', "
21 my d' are fulfilled, that I may go "
30:14 in the d' of wheat harvest, and "
35:28 the d' of Isaac were an hundred "
29 his people, being old and full of d': "
37:34 and mourned for his son many d'. "
40:12 The three branches are three d': "
13 Yet within three d' shall Pharaoh "
18 The three baskets are three d': "
19 within three d' shall Pharaoh lift "
42:17 all together into ward three d'. "
47: 9 d' of the years of my pilgrimage "
9 and evil have the d' of the years of "
9 and have not attained unto the d' "
9 in the d' of their pilgrimage. "
49: 1 which shall befall you in the last d'. "
50: 3 forty d' were fulfilled for him; for "
3 d' of those which are embalmed: "
3 for him threescore and ten d'. "
4 the d' of his mourning were past, "
10 a mourning for his father seven d'. "
Ex 2:11 And it came to pass in those d', "
7:25 seven d' were fulfilled, after that "
10:22 in all the land of Egypt three d': "
23 any from his place for three d': "
12:15 d' shall ye eat unleavened bread; "
19 Seven d' shall there be no leaven "
13: 6 d' thou shalt eat unleavened bread, "
7 bread shall be eaten seven d'; "
15:22 went three d' in the wilderness, "
16:26 Six d' ye shall gather it; "
29 the sixth day the bread of two d'; "
20: 9 Six d' shalt thou labour, and do all "
11 d' the Lord made heaven and earth, "
12 thy d' may be long upon the land "
22:30 seven d' it shall be with his dam; "
23:12 Six d' thou shalt do thy work, "
15 eat unleavened bread seven d', "
26 the number of thy d' I will fulfil. "
24:16 the cloud covered it six d': and the "
18 Moses was in the mount forty d' "

Ex 29:30 shall put them on seven *d'*, when 3117
35 *d'* shalt thou consecrate them. “
37 Seven *d'* thou shalt make an “
31:15 Six *d'* may work be done; but in “
17 in six *d'* the Lord made heaven and “
34:18 Seven *d'* thou shalt eat unleavened “
21 Six *d'* thou shalt work, but on the “
28 he was there with the Lord forty *d'* “
35: 2 Six *d'* shall work be done, but on “
Le 8:33 in seven *d'*, until the *d'* of your “
33 seven *d'* shall he consecrate you. “
35 congregation day and night seven *d'*, “
12: 2 she shall be unclean seven *d'*; “
2 according to the *d'* of the separation “
4 her purifying three and thirty *d'*; “
4 the *d'* of her purifying be fulfilled. “
5 her purifying threescore and six *d'*. “
6 the *d'* of her purifying are fulfilled, “
13: 4 him that hath the plague seven *d'*: “
5 shall shut him up seven *d'* more: “
21, 26 shall shut him up seven *d'*: “
31 the plague of the scall seven *d'*: “
33 up him that hath the scall seven *d'* “
46 All the *d'* wherein the plague shall “
50 up it that hath the plague seven *d'*: “
54 he shall shut it up seven *d'* more: “
14: 8 abroad out of his tent seven *d'*. “
38 and shut up the house seven *d'*: “
15:13 he shall number to himself seven *d'* “
19 she shall be put apart seven *d'*: “
24 he shall be unclean seven *d'*; and “
25 many *d'* out of the time of her “
25 *d'* of the issue of her uncleanness “
25 shall be as the *d'* of her separation: “
26 she lieth all the *d'* of her issue “
28 shall number to herself seven *d'*, “
22:27 it shall be seven *d'* under the dam; “
23: 3 Six *d'* shall work be done: but the “
6 seven *d'* ye must eat unleavened “
8 made by fire unto the Lord seven *d'*: “
16 sabbath shall ye number fifty *d'*; “
34 tabernacles for seven *d'* unto the “
36 Seven *d'* ye shall offer an offering “
39 a feast unto the Lord seven *d'*: “
40 before the Lord your God seven *d'*. “
41 unto the Lord seven *d'* in the year. “
42 Ye shall dwell in booths seven *d'*; “
Nu 6: 4 All the *d'* of his separation shall he “
5 the *d'* of the vow of his separation “
5 his head: until the *d'* be fulfilled, “
6 the *d'* that he separateth himself “
8 All the *d'* of his separation he is “
12 the *d'* of his separation, and shall “
12 the *d'* that were before shall be lost, “
13 *d'* of his separation are fulfilled: “
9:19 upon the tabernacle many *d'*, then “
20 when the cloud was a few *d'* “
22 whether it were two *d'*, or a month, “
10:10 and in your solemn *d'*, and in the *
11:19 shall not eat one day nor two *d'*, 3117
19 five *d'*, neither ten *d'*, nor twenty *d'*; “
12:14 she not be ashamed seven *d'*? “
14 shut out from the camp seven *d'*, “
15 shut out from the camp seven *d'*: “
13:25 searching of the land after forty *d'*. “
14:34 After the number of the *d'* in “
34 even forty *d'*, each day for a year, “
19:11 any man shall be unclean seven *d'*. “
14 the tent, shall be unclean seven *d'*. “
16 a grave, shall be unclean seven *d'*. “
20:29 they mourned for Aaron thirty *d'*, “
24:14 do to thy people in the latter *d'*. “
28:17 seven *d'* shall unleavened bread be “
24 daily, throughout the seven *d'*, “
29:12 a feast unto the Lord seven *d'*: “
31:19 abide without the camp seven *d'*: “
De 1:46 ye abode in Kadesh many *d'*, “
46 according unto the *d'* that ye abode “
2: 1 we compassed mount Seir many *d'*. “
4: 9 from thy heart all the *d'* of thy life: “
10 fear me all the *d'* that they shall live “
26 shall not prolong your *d'* upon it, “
30 even in the latter *d'*, if thou turn “
32 ask now of the *d'* that are past, “
40 prolong thy *d'* upon the earth, “
5:13 Six *d'* thou shalt labour, and do all “
16 that thy *d'* may be prolonged, and “
33 that ye may prolong your *d'* in the “
6: 2 all the *d'* of thy life; and that thy *d'* “
9: 9 I abode in the mount forty *d'* “
11 at the end of forty *d'* and forty “
18 the Lord, as at the first, forty *d'* “
25 I fell down before the Lord forty *d'* “
10:10 according to the first time, forty *d'* “
11: 9 that ye may prolong your *d'* in the “
21 That your *d'* may be multiplied, “
21 and the *d'* of your children, “
21 give them, as the *d'* of heaven “
12: 1 all the *d'* that ye live upon the “
16: 3 seven *d'* shalt thou eat unleavened “
3 of Egypt all the *d'* of thy life. “
4 with thee in all thy coast seven *d'*; “
8 Six *d'* thou shalt eat unleavened “
13 the feast of tabernacles seven *d'*, “
15 Seven *d'* shalt thou keep a solemn “
17: 9 the judge that shall be in those *d'*, “
19 read therein all the *d'* of his life: “
20 that he may prolong his *d'* in his “
19:17 judges, which shall be in those *d'*; “
22: 7 that thou mayest prolong thy *d'*. “
19, 29 may not put her away all his *d'*. “
23: 6 their prosperity all thy *d'* for ever. “
25:15 that thy *d'* may be lengthened in “
26: 3 the priest that shall be in those *d'*, “
30:18 ye shall not prolong your *d'* upon “
20 is thy life, and the length of thy *d'*: “

De 31:14 thy *d'* approach that thou must die: 3117
29 evil will befall you in the latter *d'*; “
32: 7 Remember the *d'* of old, consider “
47 ye shall prolong your *d'* in the land, “
33:25 and as thy *d'*, so shall thy strength “
34: 8 in the plains of Moab thirty *d'*: “
8 so the *d'* of weeping and mourning “
Jos 1: 5 before thee all the *d'* of thy life: “
11 within three *d'* ye shall pass over “
2:16 hide yourselves there three *d'*, “
22 mountain and abode there three *d'*, “
3: 2 it came to pass after three *d'*, “
4:14 feared Moses, all the *d'* of his life. “
6: 3 once. Thus shalt thou do six *d'*. “
14 the camp: so they did six *d'*. “
9:16 the end of three *d'* after they had “
20: 6 priest that shall be in those *d'*: “
22: 3 left your brethren these many *d'* “
24:31 Israel served the Lord all the *d'* of “
31 Joshua, and all the *d'* of the elders “
J'g 2: 7 people served the Lord all the *d'* of “
7 Joshua, and all the *d'* of the elders “
18 their enemies all the *d'* of the judge: “
5: 6 In the *d'* of Shamgar the son of “
6 Anath, in the *d'* of Jael, “
8:28 forty years in the *d'* of Gideon. “
11:40 of Jephthah the Gileadite four *d'* “
14:12 the seven *d'* of the feast, and find it “
14 they could not in three *d'* expound “
17 she wept before him the seven *d'*, “
15:20 *d'* of the Philistines twenty years. “
17: 6 In those *d'* there was no king in “
18: 1 those *d'* there was no king in Israel: “
1 in those *d'* the tribe of the Danites “
19: 1 it came to pass in those *d'*, when “
4 he abode with him three *d'*: so “
20:27 of God was there in those *d'*, “
28 stood before it in those *d'*), saying, “
21:25 those *d'* there was no king in Israel: “
Ru 1: 1 in the *d'* when the judges ruled, “
1Sa 1:11 unto the Lord all the *d'* of his life, “
2:31 *d'* come, that I will cut off thine “
3: 1 the Lord was precious in those *d'*; “
7:13 against the Philistines all the *d'* of “
15 Samuel judged Israel all the *d'* of “
9:20 thine asses that were lost three *d'* “
10: 8 *d'* shalt thou tarry, till I come “
13: 8 he tarried seven *d'*, according to “
11 thou camest not within the *d'* “
14:52 against the Philistines all the *d'* of “
17:12 an old man in the *d'* of Saul. “
16 and presented himself forty *d'*. “
18:26 law: and the *d'* were not expired. “
20:19 when thou hast staid three *d'*, “
21: 5 kept from us about these three *d'*, 8543
25:10 there be many servants now a *d'* 3117
28 not been found in thee all thy *d'*. “
38 it came to pass about ten *d'* after, “
28: 1 it came to pass in those *d'*, that the “
29: 3 which hath been with me these *d'*, “
30:12 nor drunk any water, three *d'* and “
13 because three *d'* agone I fell sick. “
31:13 at Jabesh, and fasted seven *d'*. 3117
2Sa 1: 1 David had abode two *d'* in Ziklag; “
7:12 when thy *d'* be fulfilled, and thou “
16:23 which he counselled in those *d'*, “
20: 4 the men of Judah within three *d'*, “
21: 1 was a famine in the *d'* of David “
9 the *d'* [3117] of harvest, in the first *d'*, “
24: 8 end of nine months and twenty *d'*. 3117
1Ki 2: 1 the *d'* of David drew nigh that he “
11 And the *d'* that David reigned over “
38 Shimei dwelt in Jerusalem many *d'*. “
3: 2 the name of the Lord, until those *d'*. “
13 the kings like unto thee all thy *d'*. “
14 walk, then I will lengthen thy *d'*. “
4:21 served Solomon all the *d'* of his life. “
25 Beer-sheba, all the *d'* of Solomon. “
8:40 fear thee all the *d'* that they live “
65 *d'* and seven *d'*, even fourteen *d'*. “
10:21 nothing accounted of in the *d'* of “
11:12 in thy *d'* I will not do it for David “
25 to Israel all the *d'* of Solomon, “
34 him prince all the *d'* of his life “
12: 5 Depart yet for three *d'*, then come “
14:20 the *d'* which Jeroboam reigned “
30 and Jeroboam all their *d'*. * “
15: 5 commanded him all the *d'* of his “
6 and Jeroboam all the *d'* of his life. “
14 perfect with the Lord all his *d'*. “
16, 32 Baasha king of Israel all their *d'*. “
16:15 did Zimri reign seven *d'* in Tirzah. “
34 In his *d'* did Hiel the Beth-elite “
17:15 and her house, did eat many *d'*. “
18: 1 it came to pass after many *d'*, “
19: 8 the strength of that meat forty *d'* “
20:29 one over against the other seven *d'*. “
21:29 evil in his *d'*: but in his son's *d'* “
22:46 which remained in the *d'* of his “
2Ki 2:17 sought three *d'*, but found him not. “
8:20 In his *d'* Edom revolted from “
10:32 In those *d'* the Lord began to cut “
12: 2 *d'* wherein Jehoiada the priest “
13: 3 the son of Hazael, all their *d'*. * “
22 oppressed Israel all the *d'* of “
15:18 he departed not all his *d'* from the “
29 In the *d'* of Pekah king of Israel “
37 In those *d'* the Lord began to send “
18: 4 unto those *d'* the children of Israel “
20: 1 In those *d'* was Hezekiah sick “
6 I will add unto thy *d'* fifteen years; “
17 Behold, the *d'* come, that all that is “
19 if peace and truth be in my *d'*? “
23:22 from the *d'* of the judges that “
22 Israel, nor in all the *d'* of the kings “
29 In his *d'* Pharaoh-nechoh king of “

2Ki 24: 1 In his *d'* Nebuchadnezzar king of 3117
25:29 continually before him all the *d'* of “
30 for every day, all the *d'* of his life. “
1Ch 1:19 because in his *d'* the earth was “
4:41 the *d'* of Hezekiah king of Judah, “
5:10 in the *d'* of Saul they made war “
17 In the *d'* of Jotham king of Judah, “
17 in the *d'* of Jeroboam king of Israel. “
7: 2 number was in the *d'* of David “
22 their father mourned many *d'*, and “
9:25 and were to come after seven *d'* “
10:12 oak in Jabesh, and fasted seven *d'*. “
12:39 they were with David three *d'*, “
13: 3 enquired not at it in the *d'* of Saul. “
17:11 when thy *d'* be expired that thou “
21:12 else three *d'* the sword of the Lord, “
22: 9 and quietness unto Israel in his *d'*. “
23: 1 when David was old and full of *d'*, “
29:15 our *d'* on the earth are as a shadow, “
28 age, full of *d'*, riches, and honour: “
2Ch 7: 8 Solomon kept the feast seven *d'*, “
9 seven *d'*, and the feast seven *d'*. “
9:20 accounted of in the *d'* of Solomon. “
10: 5 Come again unto me after three *d'*. “
13:20 recover strength again in the *d'* of “
14: 1 In his *d'* the land was quiet “
15:17 heart of Asa was perfect all his *d'*. “
20:25 three *d'* in gathering of the spoil, “
21: 8 In his *d'* the Edomites revolted “
24: 2 in the sight of the Lord all the *d'* “
14 continually all the *d'* of Jehoiada. “
15 was full of *d'* when he died; “
26: 5 sought God in the *d'* of Zechariah, “
29:17 the house of the Lord in eight *d'*; “
30:21 feast of unleavened bread seven *d'* “
22 eat throughout the feast seven *d'*, “
23 took counsel to keep other seven *d'*: “
23 and they kept other seven *d'* “
32:24 In those *d'* Hezekiah was sick to “
26 upon them in the *d'* of Hezekiah. “
34:33 all his *d'* they departed not from “
35:17 feast of unleavened bread seven *d'*. “
18 from the *d'* of Samuel the prophet; “
36: 9 reigned three months and ten *d'* “
Ezr 4: 2 him since the *d'* of Esar-haddon “
5 their purpose, all the *d'* of Cyrus “
7 *d'* of Artaxerxes wrote Bishlam, “
6:22 feast of unleavened bread seven *d'* “
8:15 there abode we in tents three *d'*: “
32 and abode there three *d'*. “
9: 7 *d'* of our fathers have we been “
10: 8 would not come within three *d'*, “
9 unto Jerusalem within three *d'*. “
Ne 1: 4 wept, and mourned certain *d'*, “
2:11 Jerusalem, and was there three *d'*. “
5:18 in ten *d'* store of all sorts of wine: “
6:15 month Elul, in fifty and two *d'*. “
17 in those *d'* the nobles of Judah “
8:17 since the *d'* of Jeshua the son of “
18 they kept the feast seven days; “
12: 7 their brethren in the *d'* of Jeshua. “
12 in the *d'* of Joiakim were priests, “
22 The Levites in the *d'* of Eliashib, “
23 until the *d'* of Johanan the son of “
26 These were in the *d'* of Joiakim “
26 the *d'* of Nehemiah the governor, “
46 in the *d'* of David and Asaph of old “
47 in the *d'* of Zerubbabel, “
47 and in the *d'* of Nehemiah, “
13: 6 after certain *d'* obtained I leave of “
15 In those *d'* saw I in Judah some “
23 In those *d'* also saw I Jews that “
Est 1: 1 to pass in the *d'* of Ahasuerus, “
2 That in those *d'*, when the king “
4 excellent majesty many *d'*, even “
4 an hundred and fourscore *d'*. “
5 when these *d'* were expired, the “
5 both unto great and small, seven *d'*, “
2:12 so were the *d'* of their purifications “
21 In those *d'*, while Mordecai sat in “
4:11 in unto the king these thirty *d'*. “
16 neither eat nor drink three *d'*, “
9:22 As the *d'* wherein the Jews rested “
22 should make them *d'* of feasting “
26 they called these *d'* Purim after “
27 that they would keep these two *d'* “
28 these *d'* should be remembered “
28 these *d'* of Purim should not fail “
31 confirm these *d'* of Purim in their “
Job 1: 5 the *d'* of their feasting were gone “
2:13 with him upon the ground seven *d'* “
3: 6 be joined unto the *d'* of the year, “
7: 1 *d'* also like the *d'* of an hireling? “
6 My *d'* are swifter than a weaver's “
16 me alone; for my *d'* are vanity. “
8: 9 our *d'* upon earth are a shadow:) “
9:25 Now my *d'* are swifter than a post: “
10: 5 Are thy *d'* as the *d'* of man? “
5 are thy years as man's *d'*, “
20 Are not my *d'* few? cease then, “
12:12 in length of *d'* understanding. “
14: 1 born of a woman is of few *d'*, “
5 Seeing his *d'* are determined, the “
14 all the *d'* of my appointed time “
15:20 man travaileth with pain all his *d'*, “
17: 1 my *d'* are extinct, the graves are “
11 My *d'* are past, my purposes are “
21:13 They spend their *d'* in wealth, and “
24: 1 they that know him not see his *d'*? “
29: 2 in the *d'* when God preserved me; “
4 As I was in the *d'* of my youth, “
18 I shall multiply my *d'* as the sand. “
30:16 the *d'* of affliction have taken hold “
27 the *d'* of affliction prevented me. “
32: 7 *D'* should speak, and multitude “
33:25 shall return to the *d'* of his youth: “

Job 36:11 shall spend their *d*· in prosperity, 3117
38:12 the morning since thy *d*·; "
21 the number of thy *d*· is great? "
42:17 Job died, being old and full of *d*·. "
Ps 21: 4 length of *d*· for ever and ever. "
23: 6 shall follow me all the *d*· of my life: "
27: 4 of the Lord all the *d*· of my life, "
34:12 loveth many *d*·, that he may see "
37:18 The Lord knoweth the *d*· of the "
19 *d*· of famine they shall be satisfied. "
39: 4 the measure of my *d*·, what it is; "
5 made my *d*· as an hand breadth; "
44: 1 what work thou didst in their *d*·, "
49: 5 should I fear in the *d*· of evil, "
55:23 shall not live out half their *d*·; "
72: 7 his *d*· shall the righteous flourish; "
77: 5 I have considered the *d*· of old, "
78:33 their *d*· did he consume in vanity, "
89:29 his throne as the *d*· of heaven. "
45 *d*· of his youth hast thou shortened: "
90: 9 *d*· are passed away in thy wrath: "
10 The *d*· of our years are threescore "
12 So teach us to number our *d*·, "
14 may rejoice and be glad all our *d*·. "
15 *d*· wherein thou hast afflicted us, "
94:13 him rest from the *d*· of adversity, "
102: 3 my *d*· are consumed like smoke, "
11 *d*· are like a shadow that declineth; "
23 in the way, he shortened my *d*·. "
24 me not away in the midst of my *d*·: "
103:15 As for man, his *d*· are as grass: "
109: 8 Let his *d*· be few; and let another "
119:84 many are the *d*· of thy servant? "
128: 5 of Jerusalem all the *d*· of thy life. "
143: 5 I remember the *d*· of old; "
144: 4 his *d*· are as a shadow that passeth "
Pr 3: 2 For length of *d*·, and long life, "
16 Length of *d*· is in her right hand; "
9:11 by me thy *d*· shall be multiplied, "
10:27 The fear of the Lord prolongeth *d*·: "
15:15 All the *d*· of the afflicted are evil: "
28:16 covetousness shall prolong his *d*·. "
31:12 and not evil all the *d*· of her life. "
Ec 2: 3 heaven all the *d*· of their life. "
16 *d*· to come shall all be forgotten. "
23 all his *d*· are sorrows, and his "
5:17 his *d*· also he eateth in darkness, "
18 all the *d*· of his life, which God "
20 much remember the *d*· of his life; "
6: 3 the *d*· of his years be many, "
12 all the *d*· of his vain life which he "
7:10 former *d*· were better than these? "
15 In the *d*· of my vanity: there is a "
8:12 times, and his *d*· be prolonged, yet "
13 neither shall he prolong his *d*·, 3117
15 *d*· of his life, which God giveth * "
9: 9 the *d*· of the life of thy vanity, "
9 sun, all the *d*· of thy vanity: "
11: 1 thou shalt find it after many *d*·. "
8 him remember the *d*· of darkness; "
9 cheer thee in the *d*· of thy youth, "
12: 1 now thy Creator in the *d*· of thy "
1 youth, while the evil *d*· come not, "
Isa 1: 1 in the *d*· of Uzziah, Jotham, Ahaz, "
2: 2 it shall come to pass in the last *d*·, "
7: 1 it came to pass in the *d*· of Ahaz "
17 *d*· that have not come, from the day "
13:22 and her *d*· shall not be prolonged. "
23: 7 whose antiquity is of ancient *d*·? "
15 according to the *d*· of one king: "
24:22 after many *d*· shall they be visited. "
30:26 sevenfold, as the light of seven *d*·, "
32:10 Many *d*· and years shall ye be "
38: 1 In those *d*· was Hezekiah sick unto "
5 I will add unto thy *d*· fifteen years. "
10 I said in the cutting off of my *d*·, "
20 all the *d*· of our life in the house of "
39: 6 Behold, the *d*· come, that all that "
8 shall be peace and truth in my *d*·. "
51: 9 awake, as in the ancient *d*·, in the "
53:10 he shall also prolong his *d*·, and "
60:20 *d*· of thy mourning shall be ended. "
63: 9 and carried them all the *d*· of old. "
11 he remembered the *d*· of old, "
65:20 thence an infant of *d*·, nor an old "
20 man that hath not filled his *d*·: "
22 as the *d*· of a tree are the *d*· of my "
Jer 1: 2 in the *d*· of Josiah the son of "
3 in the *d*· of Jehoiakim the son of "
2:32 forgotten me *d*· without number. "
3: 6 me in the *d*· of Josiah the king, "
16 in those *d*·, saith the Lord, they "
18 In those *d*· the house of Judah "
5:18 in those *d*·, saith the Lord, I will "
6:11 the aged with him that is full of *d*·. "
7:32 behold, the *d*· come, saith the Lord, "
9:25 *d*· come, saith the Lord, that I will "
13: 6 it came to pass after many *d*·, "
16: 9 and in your *d*·, the voice of mirth, "
14 the *d*· come, saith the Lord, that it "
17:11 leave them in the midst of his *d*·, "
19: 6 the *d*· come, saith the Lord, that "
20:18 *d*· should be consumed with shame? "
22:30 that shall not prosper in his *d*·: "
23: 5 Behold, the *d*· come, saith the Lord, "
6 In his *d*· Judah shall be saved, "
7 the *d*· come, saith the Lord, that "
20 in the latter *d*· ye shall consider it "
25:34 the *d*· of your slaughter and of your "
26:18 the *d*· of Hezekiah king of Judah, "
30: 3 the *d*· come, saith the Lord, that I "
24 in the latter *d*· ye shall consider it. "
31:27 Behold, the *d*· come, saith the Lord, "
29 In those *d*· they shall say no more, "
31 the *d*· come, saith the Lord, that I "
33 After those *d*·, saith the Lord, I will "

Jer 31:38 the *d*· come, saith the Lord, that 3117
32:14 that they may continue many *d*·. "
33:14 the *d*· come, saith the Lord, that I "
15 In those *d*·, and at that time, "
16 In those *d*· shall Judah be saved, "
35: 1 *d*· of Jehoiakim the son of Josiah "
7 all your *d*· ye shall dwell in tents; "
7 that ye may live many *d*· in the "
8 us, to drink no wine all our *d*·, "
36: 2 from the *d*· of Josiah, even unto "
37:16 had remained there many *d*·; "
42: 7 it came to pass after ten *d*·, "
46:26 as in the *d*· of old, saith the Lord. "
48:12 the *d*· come, saith the Lord, that I "
47 in the latter *d*·, saith the Lord. "
49: 2 the *d*· come, saith the Lord, that I "
39 shall come to pass in the latter *d*·. "
50: 4, 20 In those *d*·, and in that time, "
51:47 Therefore, behold, the *d*· come, that "
52 Wherefore, behold, the *d*· come, "
52:33 before him all the *d*· of his life. "
34 his death, all the *d*· of his life. "
La 1: 7 in the *d*· of her affliction and of her "
7 that she had in the *d*· of old, "
2:17 he had commanded in the *d*· of old: "
4:18 end is near, our *d*· are fulfilled; "
5:21 be turned; renew our *d*· as of old. "
Eze 3:15 astonished among them seven *d*·. "
16 came to pass at the end of seven *d*·, "
4: 4 according to the number of the *d*· "
5 according to the number of the *d*·, "
5 three hundred and ninety *d*·: so "
6 of the house of Judah forty *d*·: "
8 thou hast ended the *d*· of thy siege. "
9 the *d*· that thou shalt lie upon thy "
9 side, three hundred and ninety *d*· "
5: 2 when the *d*· of the siege are fulfilled: "
12:22 The *d*· are prolonged, and every "
23 The *d*· are at hand, and the effect "
25 in your *d*·, O rebellious house, will "
27 *d*· to come, and he prophesieth "
16:22 the *d*· of thy youth, when thou wast "
43 the *d*· of thy youth, but hast fretted "
60 with thee in the *d*· of thy youth, "
22: 4 hast caused thy *d*· to draw near, "
14 in the *d*· that I shall deal with thee? "
23:19 to remembrance the *d*· of her youth, "
38: 8 After many *d*· thou shalt be visited: "
16 it shall be in the latter *d*·, and I "
17 which prophesied in those *d*· "
43:25 Seven *d*· shalt thou prepare every "
26 Seven *d*· shall they purge the altar "
27 when these *d*· are expired, it shall "
44:26 shall reckon unto him seven *d*·. "
45:21 a feast of seven *d*·; unleavened "
23 seven *d*· of the feast he shall "
23 without blemish daily the seven *d*·; "
25 the feast of the seven *d*·, according "
46: 1 six working *d*·; but on the sabbath "
Da 1:12 thy servants, I beseech thee, ten *d*·; "
14 matter, and proved them ten *d*·. "
15 end of ten *d*· their countenances "
18 at the end of the *d*· that the king "
2:28 what shall be in the latter *d*·. 3118
44 And in the *d*· of these kings "
4:34 the end of the *d*· I Nebuchadnezzar "
5:11 and in the *d*· of thy father "
6: 7 of any God or man for thirty *d*·, "
12 of any God or man within thirty *d*·, "
7: 9 and the Ancient of *d*· did sit, "
13 and came to the Ancient of *d*·, "
22 Until the Ancient of *d*· came, and "
8:14 and three hundred *d*·; *6153, 1242
26 for it shall be for many *d*·. *3117
27 fainted, and was sick certain *d*·; "
10: 2 In those *d*· I Daniel was mourning "
13 withstood me one and twenty *d*·: "
14 befall thy people in the latter *d*·: "
14 for yet the vision is for many *d*·. "
11:20 within few *d*· he shall be destroyed, "
33 by captivity, and by spoil, many *d*·. "
12:11 thousand two hundred and ninety *d*·. "
12 hundred and five and thirty *d*·. "
13 stand in thy lot at the end of the *d*·. "
Ho 1: 1 in the *d*· of Uzziah, Jotham, Ahaz, "
1 Judah, and in the *d*· of Jeroboam "
2:11 her feast *d*·, her new moons, *
13 I will visit upon her the *d*· of 3117
15 as in the *d*· of her youth, and as in "
3: 3 Thou shalt abide for me many *d*·; "
4 of Israel shall abide many *d*· "
5 and his goodness in the latter *d*·. "
6: 2 After two *d*· will he revive us: "
9: 7 The *d*· of visitation are come, "
7 the *d*· of recompence are come; "
9 as in the *d*· of Gibeah: therefore he "
10: 9 hast sinned from the *d*· of Gibeah: "
12: 9 as in the *d*· of the solemn feast. "
Joe 1: 2 in your *d*·, or even in the *d*· of your "
2: 29 those *d*· will I pour out my spirit. "
3: 1 behold, in those *d*·, and in that "
Am 1: 1 in the *d*· of Uzziah king of Judah, "
1 in the *d*· of Jeroboam the son of "
4: 2 the *d*· shall come upon you, that he "
5:21 I hate, I despise your feast *d*·, *
8:11 the *d*· come, saith the Lord God, 3117
9:11 I will build it as in the *d*· of old: "
13 the *d*· come, saith the Lord, that "
Jon 1:17 was in the belly of the fish three *d*· "
3: 4 Yet forty *d*·, and Nineveh shall be "
Mic 1: 1 in the *d*· of Jotham, Ahaz, and "
4: 1 in the last *d*· it shall come to pass, "
7:14 and Gilead, as in the *d*· of old. "
15 According to the *d*· of thy coming "
20 unto our fathers from the *d*· of old. "
Hab 1: 5 I will work a work in your *d*·. "

Zep 1: 1 in the *d*· of Josiah the son of 3117
Hag 2:16 Since those *d*· were, when one *
Zec 8: 6 remnant of this people in these *d*·, 3117
9 ye that hear in these *d*· these words "
10 before these *d*· there was no hire "
11 this people as in the former *d*·, "
15 have I thought in these *d*· to do "
23 In those *d*· it shall come to pass, "
14: 5 in the *d*· of Uzziah king of Judah: "
Mal 3: 4 unto the Lord, as in the *d*· of old, "
7 from the *d*· of your fathers ye are "
M't 2: 1 in the *d*· of Herod the king, 2250
3: 1 In those *d*· came John the Baptist, "
4: 2 when he had fasted forty *d*·, "
9:15 but the *d*· will come, when the "
11:12 from the *d*· of John the Baptist "
12: 5 on the sabbath *d*· the priests in "
10 it lawful to heal on the sabbath *d*·? *
12 lawful to do well on the sabbath *d*·. *
40 Jonas was three *d*· and three 2250
40 three *d*· and three nights in the "
15:32 continue with me now three *d*·, "
17: 1 And after six *d*· Jesus taketh Peter, "
23:30 If we had been in the *d*· of our "
24:19 to them that give suck in those *d*·! "
22 except those *d*· should be shortened, "
22 sake those *d*· shall be shortened. "
29 After the tribulation of those *d*· "
37 But as the *d*· of Noe were, "
38 For as in the *d*· that were before "
26: 2 after two *d*· is the feast of the "
61 and to build it in three *d*·. "
27:40 and buildest it in three *d*·, save "
63 After three *d*· I will rise again. "
M'r 1: 9 in those *d*·, that Jesus came from "
13 there in the wilderness forty *d*·, "
2: 1 into Capernaum after some *d*·; "
20 But the *d*· will come, when the "
20 then shall they fast in those *d*·. * "
26 of God in the *d*· of Abiathar *1909
3: 4 to do good on the sabbath *d*·, or *
8: 1 In those *d*· the multitude being 2250
2 have now been with me three *d*·, "
31 killed, and after three *d*· rise again. "
9: 2 after six *d*· Jesus taketh with him "
13:17 to them that give suck in those *d*·! "
19 For in those *d*· shall be affliction, "
20 had shortened those *d*·, no flesh "
20 chosen, he hath shortened the *d*·. "
24 in those *d*·, after that tribulation, "
14: 1 After two *d*· was the feast of the "
58 within three *d*· I will build another "
15:29 temple, and buildest it in three *d*·, "
Lu 1: 5 There was in the *d*· of Herod, "
23 soon as the *d*· of his ministration "
24 after those *d*· his wife Elisabeth "
25 in the *d*· wherein he looked on me, "
39 Mary arose in those *d*·, and went "
75 before him, all the *d*· of our life. "
2: 1 in those *d*·, that there went out a "
6 the *d*· were accomplished that she "
21 eight *d*· were accomplished for the "
22 when the *d*· of her purification "
43 when they had fulfilled the *d*·, "
46 that after three *d*· they found him "
4: 2 forty *d*· tempted of the devil. And "
2 in those *d*· he did eat nothing: "
25 were in Israel in the *d*· of Elias, "
31 taught them on the sabbath *d*·. *
5:35 But the *d*· will come, when the 2250
35 then shall they fast in those *d*·. "
6: 2 not lawful to do on the sabbath *d*·? *
9 lawful on the sabbath *d*· to do good, "
12 it came to pass in those *d*·, that he 2250
9:28 about an eight *d*· after these "
36 told no man in those *d*· any of those "
13:14 There are six *d*· in which men "
15:13 not many *d*· after the younger son "
17:22 The *d*· will come, when ye shall "
22 to see one of the *d*· of the Son of "
26 as it was in the *d*· of Noe, so shall "
26 be also in the *d*· of the Son of man. "
28 as it was in the *d*· of Lot; "
19:43 For the *d*· shall come upon thee, "
20: 1 on one of those *d*·, as he taught "
21: 6 the *d*· will come, in the which there "
22 For these be the *d*· of vengeance, "
23 that give suck, in these *d*·! "
23:29 behold, the *d*· are coming, in the "
24:18 come to pass there in these *d*·? "
Joh 2:12 they continued there not many *d*·. "
19 in three *d*· I will raise it up. "
20 wilt thou rear it up in three *d*·? "
4:40 and he abode there two *d*·. "
43 after two *d*· he departed thence, "
11: 6 abode two *d*· still in the same place "
17 he had lain in the grave four *d*· "
39 for he hath been dead four *d*·. 5066
12: 1 Jesus six *d*· before the passover 2250
20:26 after eight *d*· again his disciples "
Ac 1: 3 being seen of them forty *d*·, and "
5 the Holy Ghost not many *d*· hence. "
15 And in those *d*· Peter stood up "
2:17 it shall come to pass in the last *d*·, "
18 pour out in those *d*· of my Spirit; "
3:24 have likewise foretold of these *d*·. "
5:36 before these *d*· rose up Theudas, "
37 in the *d*· of the taxing, and drew "
6: 1 And in those *d*·, when the number "
7:41 they made a calf in those *d*·, "
45 our fathers, unto the *d*· of David; "
9: 9 And he was three *d*· without sight, "
19 Saul certain *d*· with the disciples "
23 *d*· were fulfilled, the Jews took "
37 came to pass in those *d*·, that she "
43 tarried many *d*· in Joppa with one "

Ac 10:30 Four d' ago I was fasting until this 2250
48 prayed they him to tarry certain d'. "
11:27 And in these d' came prophets "
28 pass in the d' of Claudius Cæsar. 1909
12: 3 were the d' of unleavened bread. 2250
13:31 he was seen many d' of them "
41 for I work a work in your d', "
15:36 some d' after Paul said unto "
16:12 in that city abiding certain d'. "
18 this did she many d'. But Paul, "
17: 2 three sabbath d' reasoned with them "
20: 6 Philippi after the d' of unleavened 2250
6 five d'; where we abode seven d'. "
21: 4 we tarried there seven d': who said "
5 we had accomplished those d', "
10 And as we tarried there many d', "
15 And after those d' we took up our "
26 the accomplishment of the d' of "
27 the seven d' were almost ended, "
38 Egyptian, which before these d' "
24: 1 And after five d' Ananias the high "
11 there are yet but twelve d' since I "
24 after certain d', when Felix came "
25: 1 three d' he ascended from Cæsarea "
6 among them more than ten d', "
13 And after certain d' king Agrippa "
14 when they had been there many d', "
27: 7 when we had sailed slowly many d', "
20 sun nor stars in many d' appeared, "
28: 7 and lodged us three d' courteously. "
12 Syracuse, we tarried there three d'. "
14 desired to tarry with them seven d': "
17 after three d' Paul called the chief "
Ga 1:18 and abode with him fifteen d'. "
4:10 Ye observe d', and months, "
Eph 5:16 the time, because the d' are evil. "
Col 2:16 the new moon, or of the sabbath d'.* "
2Ti 3: 1 last d' perilous times shall come. 2250
Heb 1: 2 in these last d' spoken unto us "
5: 7 Who in the d' of his flesh, when "
7: 3 beginning of d', nor end of life; "
8: 8 Behold, the d' come, saith the Lord, "
10 the house of Israel after those d', "
10:16 will make with them after those d', "
32 call to remembrance the former d', "
11:30 were compassed about seven d'. "
12:10 they verily for a few d' chastened "
Jas 5: 3 treasure together for the last d'. "
1Pe 3:10 that will love life, and see good d', "
20 of God waited in the d' of Noah, "
2Pe 3: 3 shall come in the last d' scoffers, "
Re 2:10 ye shall have tribulation ten d': "
13 in those d' wherein Antipas was "
9: 6 in those d' shall men seek death, "
10: 7 But in the d' of the voice of the "
11: 3 two hundred and threescore d', "
6 rain not in the d' of their prophecy: "
9 dead bodies three d' and a half, "
11 three d' and a half the Spirit of life "
12: 6 two hundred and threescore d'. "

days'
Ge 30:36 three d' journey betwixt himself 3117
31:23 pursued after him seven d' journey; "
Ex 3:18 we beseech thee, three d' journey "
5: 3 we pray thee, three d' journey into "
8:27 d' journey into the wilderness, "
Nu 10:33 of the Lord three d' journey: "
33 them in the three d' journey: "
33: 8 three d' journey in the wilderness "
De 1: 2 are eleven d' journey from Horeb "
1Sa 11: 3 Give us seven d' respite, that we "
2Sa 24:13 three d' pestilence in thy land? "
2Ki 3: 9 a compass of seven d' journey: "
Jon 3: 3 great city of three d' journey. "

daysman
Job 9:33 Neither is there any d' betwixt us, 3198

dayspring
Job 38:12 caused the d' to know his place; 7837
Lu 1:78 d' from on high hath visited us, 395

daystar See DAY and STAR.

daytime See also DAY and TIME.
Job 5:14 They meet with darkness in the d', 3119
24:16 marked for themselves in the d': "
Ps 22: 2 O my God, I cry in the d', but thou "
42: 8 his lovingkindness in the d', and in "
78:14 d' also he led them with a cloud, "
Isa 4: 6 a shadow in the d' from the heat, "
21: 8 upon the watchtower in the d', "

deacon See also DEACONS.
1Ti 3:10 let them use the office of a d', *1247
13 that have used the office of a d', * "

deacons
Ph'p 1: 1 Philippi, with the bishops and d': 1249
1Ti 3: 8 Likewise must the d' be grave, "
12 the d' be the husbands of one wife, "

dead
Ge 20: 3 art but a d' man, for the woman 4191
23: 3 stood up from before his d', "
4 that I may bury my d' out of my "
6 of our sepulchres bury thy d'; "
6 but that thou mayest bury thy d'. "
8 that I should bury my d' out of my "
11 people give I it thee: bury thy d'. "
13 and I will bury my d' there. "
15 me and thee? bury therefore thy d'. "
42:38 for his brother is d', and he is "
44:20 and his brother is d', and he alone "
50:15 that their father was d', they said, "
Ex 4:19 men are d' which sought thy life. "
9: 7 one of the cattle of the Israelites d'. "
12:30 a house where there was not one d'. "
33 for they said, We be all d' men. "
14:30 Israel saw the Egyptians d' upon "
21:34 and the d' beast shall be his. 4191
35 the d' ox also they shall divide. "
36 and the d' shall be his own. "
Le 11:31 when they be d', shall be unclean 4194
32 when they are d', doth fall, it shall "
19:28 cuttings in your flesh for the d', 5315
21: 1 shall none be defiled for the d' "
11 shall he go in to any d' body, 4191
22: 4 thing that is unclean by the d', 5315
Nu 5: 2 whosoever is defiled by the d': "
6: 6 he shall come at no d' body. 4191
11 him, for that he sinned by the d', 5315
9: 6, 7 defiled by the d' body of a man, "
10 unclean by the reason of a d' body, "
12:12 Let her not be as one d', 4191
16:48 stood between the d' and the living; "
19:11 He that toucheth the d' body of any "
13 Whosoever toucheth the d' body "
13 of any man that is d', and "
16 or a d' body, or a bone of a man, "
18 or one slain, or one d', or a grave: "
20:29 that Aaron was d', they mourned 1478
De 2:16 men of war were consumed and d' 4191
14: 1 between your eyes for the d'. "
8 flesh, nor touch their d' carcass.* 5038
25: 5 the wife of the d' shall not marry 4191
6 the name of his brother which is d', "
26:14 nor given ought thereof for the d': "
Jos 1: 2 Moses my servant is d'; now "
J'g 2:19 the judge was d', that they returned, "
3:25 their lord was fallen down d' "
4: 1 of the Lord, when Ehud was d'. "
22 into her tent, behold, Sisera lay d', "
5:27 he bowed, there he fell down d'. 7703
8:33 as soon as Gideon was d', that the 4191
9:55 Israel saw that Abimelech was d', "
16:30 the d' which he slew at his death "
20: 5 have they forced, that she is d'. "
Ru 1: 8 as ye have dealt with the d', "
2:20 to the living and to the d'. "
4: 5 the d', to raise up the name of the d' "
10 name of the d' upon his inheritance, "
10 the name of the d' be not cut off "
1Sa 4:17 Hophni and Phinehas, are d', and "
19 in law and her husband were d', "
17:51 saw their champion was d', they "
24:14 after a d' dog, after a flea. "
25:39 David heard that Nabal was d', "
28: 3 Now Samuel was d', and all Israel "
31: 5 armourbearer saw that Saul was d', "
7 Saul and his sons were d', they "
2Sa 1: 4 the people also are fallen and d'; "
4 Saul and Jonathan his son are d' "
5 Saul and Jonathan his son be d'? "
2: 7 your master Saul is d', and also the "
4: 1 Abner was d' in Hebron, his hands "
10 Saul is d', thinking to have brought "
9: 8 such a d' dog as I am? "
11:21 Thy servant Uriah the Hittite is d' "
24 some of the king's servants be d', "
24 Uriah the Hittite is d' also. "
26 Uriah her husband was d', she "
12:18 to tell him that the child was d': "
18 if we tell him that the child is d'? "
19 perceived that the child was d': "
19 unto his servants, Is the child d'? "
19 And they said, He is d'. "
21 the child was d', thou didst rise "
23 he is d', wherefore should I fast? "
13:32 Amnon only is d': for by the "
33 that all the king's sons are d': "
33 for Amnon only is d'. "
39 Amnon, seeing he was d'. "
14: 2 a long time mourned for the d': "
5 woman, and mine husband is d'. "
16: 9 this d' dog curse my lord the king? "
18:20 because the king's son is d'. "
19:10 we anointed over us, is d' in battle. "
28 my father's house were but d' men 4194
1Ki 3:20 laid her d' child in my bosom. 4191
21 my child suck, behold, it was d': "
22 the d' is thy son. And this said, "
22 No; but the d' is thy son, and "
23 and thy son is the d': and the other "
23 saith, Nay; but thy son is the d', "
11:21 Joab the captain of the host was d', "
13:31 When I am d', then bury me in the "
21:14 saying, Naboth is stoned, and is d'. "
15 that Naboth was stoned, and was d', "
15 for Naboth is not alive, but d'. "
16 Ahab heard that Naboth was d', "
2Ki 3: 5 when Ahab was d', that the king 4194
4: 1 Thy servant my husband is d'; and 4191
32 child was d', and laid upon his bed. "
8: 5 he had restored a d' body to life, "
11: 1 of Ahaziah saw that her son was d', "
19:35 morning, behold, they were all d' ‡ "
23:30 servants carried him in a chariot d' "
1Ch 1:44 when Bela was d', Jobab the son * "
45 And when Jobab was d', Husham * "
46 when Husham was d', Hadad * "
47 And when Hadad was d', Samlah * "
48 And when Samlah was d', Shaul * "
49 when Shaul was d', Baal-hanan * "
50 And when Baal-hanan was d', * "
2:19 And when Azubah was d', Caleb * "
24 after that Hezron was d' in 4194
10: 5 saw that Saul was d', he fell 4191
7 Saul and his sons were d', then "
2Ch 20:24 they were d' bodies fallen to the 6297
25 riches with the d' bodies, and "
22:10 Ahaziah saw that her son was d'. 4191
Es 2: 7 her father and mother were d', 4194
Job 1:19 the young men, and they are d'; 4191
26: 5 D' things are formed from under *7496
Ps 31:12 I am forgotten as a d' man 4191
76: 6 and horse are cast into a d' sleep. "
79: 2 The d' bodies of thy servants 5038
88: 5 Free among the d', like the slain 4191
10 Wilt thou shew wonders to the d'? "
10 shall the d' arise and praise thee? *7496
106:28 and ate the sacrifices of the d'. 4191
110: 6 fill the places with the d' bodies; 1472
115:17 The d' praise not the Lord, 4191
143: 3 as those that have been long d'. "
Pr 2:18 death, and her paths unto the d'. 7496
9:18 knoweth not that the d' are there; "
21:16 in the congregation of the d'. "
Ec 4: 2 praised the d' which are already d' 4191
9: 3 and after that they go to the d'. "
4 a living dog is better than a d' lion. "
5 but the d' know not any thing, "
10: 1 D' flies cause the ointment of the 4194
Isa 8:19 their God? for the living to the d'? 4191
14: 9 it stirreth up the d' for thee, 7496
22: 2 slain with the sword, nor d' in 4191
26:14 They are d', they shall not live; "
19 Thy d' men shall live, together "
19 with my d' body shall they arise. 5038
19 the earth shall cast out the d'. 7496
37:36 behold, they were all d' corpses. ‡4191
59:10 are in desolate places as d' men "
Jer 16: 7 to comfort them for the d'; "
22:10 Weep ye not for the d', neither "
26:23 cast his d' body into the graves 5038
31:40 the whole valley of the d' bodies, 6297
33: 5 fill them with the d' bodies of men, "
34:20 their d' bodies shall be for meat 5038
36:30 and his d' body shall be cast out "
41: 9 cast all the d' bodies of the men, 6297
La 3: 6 as they that be d' of old. 4191
Eze 6: 5 And I will lay the d' carcasses *
24:17 make no mourning for the d', 4191
44:25 they shall come at no d' person "
31 any thing that is d' of itself, or 5038
Am 8: 3 there shall be many d' bodies 6297
Hag 2:13 unclean by a d' body touch any of
M't 2:19 But when Herod was d', behold, 5053
20 for they are d' which sought the 2348
8:22 me; and let the d' bury their d'. 3498
9:18 My daughter is even now d': but 5053
24 for the maid is not d', but sleepeth. 599
10: 8 lepers, raise the d', cast out 3498
11: 5 the d' are raised up, and the poor "
14: 2 Baptist; he is risen from the d'; "
17: 9 of man be risen again from the d'. "
22:31 touching the resurrection of the d', "
32 God is not the God of the d', but "
23:27 within full of d' men's bones, and "
27:64 He is risen from the d': so the last "
28: 4 did shake, and became as d' men. "
7 that he is risen from the d'; "
M'r 5:35 which said, Thy daughter is d': 599
39 the damsel is not d', but sleepeth. "
6:14 the Baptist was risen from the d', 3498
16 beheaded: he is risen from the d'.* "
9: 9 Son of man were risen from the d'. "
10 what the rising from the d' should "
26 out of him: and he was as one d'; "
26 insomuch that many said, He is d'. 599
12:25 when they shall rise from the d', 3498
26 as touching the d', that they rise: "
27 He is not the God of the d', "
15:44 marvelled if he were already d': 2348
44 whether he had been any while d'. 599
Lu 7:12 there was a d' man carried out, 2348
15 And he that was d' sat up, 3498
22 the deaf hear, the d' are raised. "
8:49 Thy daughter is d'; trouble not 2348
52 not; she is not d', but sleepeth. 599
53 to scorn, knowing that she was d'. "
9: 7 that John was risen from the d'; 3498
60 unto him, Let the d' bury their d': * "
10:30 and departed, leaving him half d'. 2253
15:24 For this my son was d', and is 3498
32 for this thy brother was d', and is "
16:30 if one went unto them from the d', "
31 though one rose from the d'. "
20:35 and the resurrection from the d', "
37 Now that the d' are raised, even "
38 For he is not a God of the d', "
24: 5 seek ye the living among the d'? "
46 to rise from the d' the third day: "
Joh 2:22 therefore he was risen from the d', "
5:21 as the Father raiseth up the d', "
25 when the d' shall hear the voice "
6:49 in the wilderness, and are d'. * 599
58 fathers did eat manna, and are d': * "
8:52 Abraham is d', and the prophets; ‡ "
53 Abraham, which is d'? ‡ "
53 and the prophets are d': ‡ "
11:14 unto them plainly, Lazarus is d'. "
25 though he were d', yet shall he live: * "
39 the sister of him that was d', 2348
39 for he hath been d' four days. "
41 the place where the d' was laid. *2348
44 And he that was d' came forth, "
12: 1 Lazarus was which had been d'. * "
1 d' whom he raised from the d', 3498
9 whom he had raised from the d'. "
17 him from the d', bare record. "
19:33 that he was d' already, they brake 2348
20: 9 he must rise again from the d'. 3498
21:14 after that he was risen from the d'. "
Ac 2:29 that he is both d' and buried, *5053
3:15 God hath raised from the d'; 3498
4: 2 Jesus the resurrection from the d'. "
10 whom God raised from the d', even "
5:10 men came in and found her d', "
7: 4 thence, when his father was d', he 599
10:41 with him after he rose from the d'. 3498
42 to be the Judge of quick and d'.

Ac 13:30 But God raised him from the d': 3498
34 that he raised him up from the d', "
14:19 city, supposing he had been d'. 2348
17: 3 and risen again from the d'; 3498
31 he hath raised him from the d'. "
32 heard of the resurrection of the d', "
20: 9 the third loft, and was taken up d'. "
23: 6 the hope and resurrection of the d' "
24:15 shall be a resurrection of the d', * "
21 Touching the resurrection of the d' "
25:19 of one Jesus, which was d', whom 2348
26: 8 you, that God should raise the d'? 3498
23 first that should rise from the d', "
28: 6 or fallen down d' suddenly: but "
Ro 1: 4 by the resurrection from the d': "
4:17 God, who quickeneth the d', "
19 not his own body now d', *3499
24 Jesus our Lord from the d'; Who 3498
5:15 the offence of one many be d', * 599
6: 2 How shall we, that are d' to sin, * "
4 Christ was raised up from the d' 3498
7 For he that is d' is freed from sin.* 599
8 if we be d' with Christ, we believe* "
9 raised from the d' dieth no more: 3498
11 to be d' indeed unto sin, but alive "
13 as those that are alive from the d', "
7: 2 if the husband be d', she is loosed* 599
3 if her husband be d', she is free * "
4 ye also are become d' to the law 2289
4 to him who is raised from the d', 3498
6 being d' wherein we were held; * 599
8 For without the law sin was d'. 3498
8:10 the body is d' because of sin; "
11 up Jesus from the d' dwell in you, "
11 that raised up Christ from the d' "
10: 7 bring up Christ again from the d'. "
9 hath raised him from the d', thou "
11:15 of them be, but life from the d'? "
14: 9 be Lord both of the d' and living. "
1Co 7:39 but if her husband be d', she is at 2837
15:12 preached that he rose from the d', 3498
12 there is no resurrection of the d'? "
13 if there be no resurrection of the d', "
15 if so be that the d' rise not. "
16 For if the d' rise not, then is not "
20 now is Christ risen from the d', "
21 came also the resurrection of the d'. "
29 which are baptized for the d', * "
29 if the d' rise not at all? why are * "
29 they then baptized for the d'? * "
32 it me, if the d' rise not? "
35 How are the d' raised up? and with "
42 also is the resurrection of the d'. "
52 the d' shall be raised incorruptible, "
2Co 1: 9 but in God which raiseth the d': "
5:14 one died for all, then were all d': * 599
Ga 1: 1 who raised him from the d'; *3498
2:19 I through the law am d' to the * 599
21 the law, then Christ is d' in vain. * "
Eph 1:20 when he raised him from the d', 3498
2: 1 were d' in trespasses and sins; "
5 when we were d' in sins, hath "
5:14 and arise from the d', and Christ "
Ph'p 3:11 unto the resurrection of the d'. "
Col 1:18 the firstborn from the d'; "
2:12 who hath raised him from the d'. "
13 And you, being d' in your sins "
20 if ye be d' with Christ from the * 599
3: 3 For ye are d', and your life is hid * "
1Th 1:10 whom he raised from the d', even 3498
4:16 the d' in Christ shall rise first: "
1Ti 5: 6 in pleasure is d' while she liveth. 2348
2Ti 2: 8 of David was raised from the d' 3498
11 For if we be d' with him, we shall*4880
4: 1 shall judge the quick and the d' 3498
Heb 6: 1 repentance from d' works, and of "
2 and of resurrection of the d', and "
9:14 your conscience from d' works to "
17 of force after men are d': * "
11: 4 by it he being d' yet speaketh. 599
12 even of one, and him as good as d',3499
19 to raise him up, even from the d'; 3498
35 received their d' raised to life "
13:20 brought again from the d' our Lord "
Jas 2:17 hath not works, is d', being alone. "
20 that faith without works is d'? * "
26 the body without the spirit is d', "
26 so faith without works is d' also. "
1Pe 1: 3 of Jesus Christ from the d', "
21 that raised him up from the d', and "
2:24 that we, being d' to sins, should * 581
4: 5 to judge the quick and the d'. 3498
6 preached also to them that are d', "
Jude 12 without fruit, twice d', plucked 599
Re 1: 5 the first begotten of the d', and 3498
17 saw him, I fell at his feet as d'. "
18 I am he that liveth, and was d'; "
2: 8 last, which was d', and is alive; "
3: 1 a name that thou livest, and art d'. "
11: 8 d' bodies shall lie in the streets 4430
9 shall see their d' bodies three days "
9 shall not suffer their d' bodies to "
18 time of the d', that they should 3498
14:13 Blessed are the d' which die in the "
16: 3 became as the blood of a d' man: "
20: 5 the rest of the d' lived not again "
12 And I saw the d', small and great, "
12 and the d' were judged out of "
13 gave up the d' which were in it, "
13 death and hell delivered up the d' "

deadly
1Sa 5:11 was a d' destruction throughout 4194
Ps 17: 9 my d' enemies, who compass me 5315
Eze 30:24 groanings of a d' wounded man.
M'r 16:18 and if they drink any d' thing, 2286
Jas 3: 8 an unruly evil, full of d' poison. 2287
Re 13: 3 d' wound was healed: and all *2288
12 whose d' wound was healed. * "

deadness
Ro 4:19 yet the d' of Sarah's womb: 3500

deaf
Ex 4:11 who maketh the dumb, or d', or 2795
Le 19:14 Thou shalt not curse the d', nor "
Ps 38:13 But I, as a d' man, heard not; "
58: 4 the d' adder that stoppeth her ear; "
Isa 29:18 in that day shall the d' hear "
35: 5 ears of the d' shall be unstopped. "
42:18 Hear, ye d'; and look, ye blind, "
19 d', as my messenger that I sent? "
43: 8 eyes, and the d' that have ears. "
Mic 7:16 their mouth, their ears shall be d'.2790
M't 11: 5 and the d' hear, the dead are 2974
M'r 7:32 was d', and had an impediment "
37 he maketh both the d' to hear, and "
9:25 Thou dumb and d' spirit, I charge "
Lu 7:22 the d' hear, the dead are raised, "

deal See also DEALEST; DEALETH; DEALING; DEALS; DEALT.
Ge 19: 9 now will we d' worse with thee,
21:23 thou wilt not d' falsely with me,
24:49 if ye will d' kindly and truly with 6213
32: 9 and I will d' well with thee: *
34:31 Should he d' with our sister as 6213
47:29 and d' kindly and truly with me; "
Ex 1:10 let us d' wisely with them; lest
8:29 let not Pharaoh d' deceitfully any
21: 9 d' with her after the manner 6213
23:11 thou shalt d' with thy vineyard, "
Ex 29:40 the one lamb a tenth d' of flour *
Le 14:21 and one tenth d' of fine flour *
19:11 shall not steal, neither d' falsely,*
Nu 11:15 if thou d' thus with me, kill me, 6213
15: 4 a tenth d' of flour mingled with *
28:13 And a several tenth d' of flour *
21 several tenth d' shalt thou offer *
29 several tenth d' unto one lamb *
29: 4 And one tenth d' for one lamb, *
10 A several tenth d' for one lamb, *
15 a several tenth d' to each lamb *
De 7: 5 shall ye d' with them; ye shall 6213
Jos 2:14 will d' kindly and truly with thee. "
Ru 1: 8 the Lord d' kindly with you, as ye "
1Sa 20: 8 shalt d' kindly with thy servant; "
2Sa 18: 5 D' gently for my sake with the
2Ch 2: 3 didst d' with David my father, 6213
3 dwell therein, even so d' with me
19:11 D' courageously, and the Lord 6213
Job 42: 8 lest I d' with you after your folly, "
Ps 75: 4 D' not foolishly: and to the
105:25 to d' subtilly with his servants.
119:17 D' bountifully with thy servant, 1580
124 D' with thy servant according 6213
142: 7 thou shalt d' bountifully with me. 1580
Pr 12:22 they that d' truly are his delight. 6213
Isa 26:10 of uprightness will he d' unjustly,
33: 1 an end to d' treacherously,
1 shall d' treacherously with thee.
48: 8 wouldst d' very treacherously,
52:13 my servant shall d' prudently,
58: 7 to d' thy bread to the hungry, 6536
Jer 12: 1 happy that d' very treacherously?
18:23 d' thus with them in the time of 6213
21: 2 Lord will d' with us according to "
Eze 8:18 Therefore will I also d' in fury: "
16:59 d' with thee as thou hast done "
18: 9 kept my judgments, to d' truly; "
22:14 the days that I shall d' with thee? "
23:25 they shall d' furiously with thee: "
29 they shall d' with thee hatefully, "
31:11 he shall surely d' with him: "
Da 1:13 thou seest, d' with thy servants. "
11: 7 and shall d' against them, and "
Hab 1:13 upon them that d' treacherously,
Mal 2:10 why do we d' treacherously every
15 let none d' treacherously against
16 spirit, that ye d' not treacherously.
M'r 7:36 so much the more a great d' 4054
10:48 he cried the more a great d'.

dealer See also DEALERS.
Isa 21: 2 the treacherous d' dealeth

dealers
Isa 24:16 the treacherous d' have dealt
16 yea, the treacherous d' have dealt very

dealest
Ex 5:15 d' thou thus with thy servants? 6213
Isa 33: 1 d' treacherously, and they dealt

dealeth
J'g 18: 4 d' Micah with me, and hath *6213
1Sa 23:22 told me that he d' very subtilly.
Pr 10: 4 He becometh poor that d' with 6213
13:16 prudent man d' with knowledge: * "
14:17 He that is soon angry d' foolishly: "
21:24 his name, who d' in proud wrath.* "
Isa 21: 2 treacherous dealer d' treacherously;
Jer 6:13 the priest every one d' falsely. 6213
8:10 unto the priest every one d' falsely. "
Heb 12: 7 God d' with you as with sons; 4374

dealing See also DEALINGS.
Ps 7:16 his violent d' shall come down *

dealings
1Sa 2:23 of your evil d' by all this people 1697
Joh 4: 9 had no d' with the Samaritans. 4798

deals
Le 14:10 three tenth d' of fine flour for *
23:13 two tenth d' of fine flour mingled *
17 two wave loaves of two tenth d': *
24: 5 two tenth d' shall be in one cake. *
Nu 15: 6 two tenth d' of flour mingled *
15: 9 three tenth d' of flour mingled *
28: 9 and two tenth d' of flour for a *
12 three tenth d' of flour for a meat *
12 two tenth d' of flour for a meat *
20 three tenth d' shall ye offer for a *
20 and two tenth d' for a ram; *
28 three tenth d' unto one bullock, *
28 two tenth d' unto one ram, *
29: 3 three tenth d' for a bullock, *
3 and two tenth d' for a ram, *
9 three tenth d' to a bullock, *
9 and two tenth d' to one ram, *
14 three tenth d' unto every bullock *
14 two tenth d' to each ram *

dealt
Ge 16: 6 when Sarai d' hardly with her
33:11 God hath d' graciously with me,
43: 6 Wherefore d' ye so ill with me,
Ex 1:20 God d' well with the midwives:
14:11 wherefore hast thou d' thus with 6213
18:11 the thing wherein they d' proudly
21: 8 seeing he hath d' deceitfully with
J'g 9:16 if ye have d' well with Jerubbaal 6213
19 ye then have d' truly and sincerely "
23 men of Shechem d' treacherously
Ru 1: 8 as ye have d' with the dead, 6213
20 the Almighty hath d' very bitterly
1Sa 24:18 thou hast d' well with me: for as 6213
25:31 when the Lord shall have d' well
2Sa 6:19 And he d' among all the people, 2505
2Ki 12:15 workmen: for they d' faithfully. 6213
21: 6 and d' with familiar spirits and "
22: 7 hand, because they d' faithfully.
1Ch 16: 3 And he d' to every one of Israel, 2505
20: 3 so d' David with all the cities *6213
2Ch 6:37 done amiss, and have d' wickedly;
11:23 And he d' wisely, and dispersed of
33: 6 d' with a familiar spirit, and with 6213
Ne 1: 7 d' very corruptly against thee,
9:10 that they d' proudly against them.
16 they and our fathers d' proudly
29 yet they d' proudly and hearkened
Job 6:15 My brethren have d' deceitfully as
Ps 13: 6 he hath d' bountifully with me. 1580
44:17 have we d' falsely in thy covenant.
78:57 d' unfaithfully like their fathers:
103:10 hath not d' with us after our sins; 6213
116: 7 hath d' bountifully with thee. 1580
119:65 hast d' well with thy servant, 6213
78 for they d' perversely with me *
147:20 He hath not d' so with any nation: 6213
Isa 24:16 dealers have d' treacherously; yea,
16 have d' very treacherously.
33: 1 d' not treacherously with thee!
Jer 3:20 have ye d' treacherously with me,
5:11 d' very treacherously against me,
12: 6 have d' treacherously with thee;
La 1: 2 have d' treacherously with her,
Eze 22: 7 of thee have they d' by oppression 6213
25:12 d' against the house of Judah "
15 the Philistines have d' by revenge, "
Ho 5: 7 d' treacherously against the Lord:
6: 7 have d' treacherously against me.
Joe 2:26 your God that hath d' wondrously 6213
Zec 1: 6 our doings, so hath he d' with us. "
Mal 2:11 Judah hath d' treacherously, and
14 hast d' treacherously: yet is she
Lu 1:25 Thus hath the Lord d' with me *4160
2:48 why hast thou thus d' with us? "
Ac 7:19 The same d' subtilly with our 2686
25:24 the Jews have d' with me, both *1793
Ro 12: 3 as God hath d' to every man 3307

dear
Jer 31:20 Is Ephraim my d' son? is he a 3357
Lu 7: 2 who was d' unto him, was sick, 1784
Ac 20:24 count I my life d' unto myself, 5093
Eph 5: 1 followers of God, as d' children; * 27
Col 1: 7 our d' fellowservant, who is * "
13 into the kingdom of his d' Son: * 26
1Th 2: 8 souls, because ye were d' unto us. 27

dearly
Jer 12: 7 the d' beloved of my soul
Ro 12:19 D' beloved, avenge not *
1Co 10:14 Wherefore, my d' beloved, flee *
2Co 7: 1 these promises d' beloved, let us *
12:19 do all things d' beloved for *
Ph'p 4: 1 my brethren d' beloved and longed*
1 fast in the Lord, my d' beloved *
2Ti 1: 2 To Timothy my d' beloved son: *
Ph'm 1 unto Philemon our d' beloved *
1Pe 2:11 D' beloved, I beseech you as *

dearth
Ge 41:54 seven years of d' began to come, *7458
54 said, and the d' was in all lands; * "
2Ki 4:38 and there was a d' in the land; "
2Ch 6:28 If there be d' in the land, "
Ne 5: 3 might buy corn, because of the d'. "
Jer 14: 1 to Jeremiah concerning the d'. *1226
Ac 7:11 there came a d' over all the land *3042
11:28 be great d' throughout all the "

death See also DEATHS.
Ge 21:16 Let me not see the d' of the child. 4194
24:67 was comforted after his mother's d'
25:11 after the d' of Abraham, that God 4194
26:11 his wife shall surely be put to d'. 4191
18 after the d' of Abraham: and he 4194
27: 2 I know not the day of my d': "
7 before the Lord before my d'. "
10 he may bless thee before his d'. "
Ex 10:17 take away from me this d' only. "
19:12 mount shall be surely put to d': 4191
21:12 he die shall be surely put to d'. "
15 his mother, shall be surely put to d'. "
16 hand, he shall surely be put to d'. "

Ex 21:17 his mother shall surely be put to d'.4191
29 his owner also shall be put to d'. "
22:19 a beast shall surely be put to d'. "
31:14 defileth it shall surely be put to d': "
15 day, he shall surely be put to d'. "
35: 2 work therein shall be put to d'. "
Le 16: 1 after the d' of the two sons of 4194
19:20 they shall not be put to d', because 4191
20: 2 he shall surely be put to d': the "
9 shall be surely put to d': he hath "
10 adulteress shall surely be put to d'. "
11, 12 them shall surely be put to d'; "
13 they shall surely be put to d'; their "
15 he shall surely be put to d': and ye "
16 they shall surely be put to d'; their "
27 a wizard, shall surely be put to d': "
24:16 he shall surely be put to d', and all "
16 of the Lord, shall be put to d'. "
17 any man shall surely be put to d'. "
21 a man, he shall be put to d'. "
27:29 but shall surely be put to d'. "
Nu 1:51 that cometh nigh shall be put to d'. "
3:10, 38 cometh nigh shall be put to d'. "
15:35 The man shall be surely put to d': "
16:29 these men die the common d' of all 4194
18: 7 that cometh nigh shall be put to d'. 4191
23:10 Let me die the d' of the righteous, 4194
35:16, 17, 18 murderer... be put to d'. 4191
21 smote him shall surely be put to d': "
25 unto the d' of the high priest, 4194
28 until the d' of the high priest: "
28 but after the d' of the high priest "
35:30 the murderer shall be put to d' by*7523
31 a murderer, which is guilty of d' 4191
31 but he shall surely be put to d'. "
32 land, until the d' of the priest. 4194
De 13: 5 of dreams, shall be put to d'; 4191
9 be first upon him to put him to d', "
17: 6 shall he that is worthy of d' be * "
6 be put to d'; but at the mouth of "
6 witness he shall not be put to d'. "
7 upon him to put him to d', and "
19: 6 whereas he was not worthy of d', 4194
21:22 committed a sin worthy of d', "
22 and he be to be put to d', 4191
22:26 in the damsel no sin worthy of d': 4194
24:16 The fathers shall not be put to d' 4191
16 the children be put to d' for the "
16 shall be put to d' for his own sin. "
30:15 life and good, and d' and evil; 4194
19 I have set before you life and d', "
31:27 how much more after my d'? "
29 I know that after my d' ye will "
33: 1 the children of Israel before his d'. "
Jos 1: 1 after the d' of Moses the servant of "
18 he shall be put to d': only be 4191
2:13 have, and deliver our lives from d'. 4194
20: 6 until the d' of the high priest "
J'g 1: 1 after the d' of Joshua it came to "
5:18 jeoparded their lives unto the d' 4191
6:31 let him be put to d' whilst it is yet "
13: 7 the womb to the day of his d'. 4194
16:16 his soul was vexed unto d'; 4191
30 the dead which he slew at his d' 4194
20:13 that we may put them to d', and 4191
21: 5 saying, He shall surely be put to d'. "
Ru 1:17 if ought but d' part thee and me. 4194
2:11 since the d' of thine husband: "
1Sa 4:20 about the time of her d' the women 4191
11:12 men, that we may put them to d'. "
13 There shall not a man be put to d' "
15:32 Surely the bitterness of d' is past. 4194
35 to see Saul until the day of his d': "
20: 3 but a step between me and d'. "
22:22 I have occasioned the d' of all the "
2Sa 1: 1 came to pass after the d' of Saul, 4194
23 in their d' they were not divided: "
6:23 had no child unto the day of her d'. "
8: 2 two lines measured he to put to d', 4191
15:21 whether in d' or life, even there 4194
19:21 shall not Shimei be put to d' for 4191
22 shall there any man be put to d' "
20: 3 shut up unto the day of their d', "
21: 9 and were put to d' in the days of "
22: 5 When the waves of d' compassed 4194
6 the snares of d' prevented me; "
1Ki 2: 8 I will not put thee to d' with the 4191
24 Adonijah shall be put to d' this day. "
26 thou art worthy of d': but 4194
26 not at this time put thee to d', 4191
11:40 in Egypt until the d' of Solomon. 4194
2Ki 1: 1 against Israel after the d' of Ahab. "
2:21 thence any more d' or barren land. "
4:40 man of God, there is d' in the pot. "
14: 6 fathers shall not be put to d' for 4191
6 nor the children be put to d' * "
6 but every man shall be put to d' * "
17 after the d' of Jehoash son of 4194
15: 5 a leper unto the day of his d'. "
20: 1 days was Hezekiah sick unto d'. *4191
1Ch 22: 5 prepared abundantly before his d'. 4194
2Ch 15:13 God of Israel should be put to d', 4191
22: 4 after the d' of his father to his 4194
23: 7 the house, he shall be put to d': *4191
24:17 after the d' of Jehoiada came the 4194
25:25 after the d' of Joash son of "
26:21 a leper unto the day of his d', "
32:24 Hezekiah was sick to the d', and 4191
33 did him honour at his d'. 4194
Ezr 7:26 whether it be unto d', or to 4193
Es 4:11 one law of his to put him to d', 4191
Job 3: 5 Let darkness and the shadow of d' 6757
21 long for d', but it cometh not; 4194
5:20 he shall redeem thee from d': "
7:15 and d' rather than my life. "
10:21 of darkness and the shadow of d'; 6757

Job 10:22 itself; and of the shadow of d', 6757
12:22 out to light the shadow of d'. "
16:16 on my eyelids is the shadow of d'; "
18:13 firstborn of d' shall devour his ‡4194
24:17 to them even as the shadow of d': 6757
17 the terrors of the shadow of d'. "
27:15 of him shall be buried in d': 4194
28: 3 of darkness, and the shadow of d'. 6757
22 Destruction and d' say, We have 4194
30:23 thou wilt bring me to d', and to the "
34:22 is no darkness, nor shadow of d', 6757
38:17 Have the gates of d' been opened 4194
17 the doors of the shadow of d'? 6757
Ps 6: 5 in d' there is no remembrance of 4194
7:13 for him the instruments of d'; he "
9:13 liftest me up from the gates of d': "
13: 3 lest I sleep the sleep of d'; "
18: 4 The sorrows of d' compassed me, "
5 the snares of d' prevented me. "
22:15 brought me into the dust of d'. "
23: 4 the valley of the shadow of d', 6757
33:19 To deliver their soul from d', and 4194
44:19 covered us with the shadow of d'. 6757
48:14 he will be our guide even unto d'. 4192
49:14 d' shall feed on them; and the 4194
55: 4 the terrors of d' are fallen upon me. "
15 Let d' seize upon them, and "
56:13 hast delivered my soul from d': "
68:20 the Lord belong the issues from d'. "
73: 4 there are no bands in their d': "
78:50 spared not their soul from d', "
89:48 he that liveth, and shall not see d'? "
102:20 those that are appointed to d'; 8546
107:10 darkness and in the shadow of d', 6757
14 of darkness and the shadow of d', "
18 they draw near unto the gates of d'. 4194
116: 3 The sorrows of d' compassed me, "
8 delivered my soul from d', mine "
15 of the Lord is the d' of his saints. "
118:18 he hath not given me over unto d'. "
Pr 2:18 her house inclineth unto d', and "
5: 5 Her feet go down to d'; her steps "
7:27 going down to the chambers of d'. "
8:36 all they that hate me love d'. "
10: 2 righteousness delivereth from d'. "
11: 4 righteousness delivereth from d'. "
19 evil pursueth it to his own d'. "
12:28 the pathway thereof there is no d'. "
13:14 to depart from the snares of d'. "
14:12 the end thereof are the ways of d'. "
27 to depart from the snares of d'. "
32 the righteous hath hope in his d'. "
16:14 of a king is as messengers of d': "
25 the end thereof are the ways of d'. "
18:21 D' and life are in the power of the "
21: 6 to and fro of them that seek d'. "
24:11 them that are drawn unto d', and "
26:18 casteth firebrands, arrows, and d', "
Ec 7: 1 day of d' than the day of one's birth. "
26 more bitter than d' the woman, "
8: 8 power in the day of d': and there is "
Ca 8: 6 love is strong as d'; jealousy is "
Isa 9: 2 the land of the shadow of d', upon 6757
25: 8 He will swallow up d' in victory; 4194
28:15 We have made a covenant with d', "
18 your covenant with d' shall be "
38: 1 days was Hezekiah sick unto d'. 4191
18 d' can not celebrate thee: they 4194
53: 9 wicked, and with the rich in his d'; "
12 hath poured out his soul unto d': "
Jer 2: 6 drought, and of the shadow of d', 6757
8: 3 d' shall be chosen rather than 4194
9:21 d' is come up into our windows, "
13:16 he turn it into the shadow of d', 6757
15: 2 Such as are for d', to d'; and such 4194
18:21 let their men be put to d'; let "
21: 8 the way of life, and the way of d'. "
26:15 if ye put me to d', ye shall surely 4191
19 and all Judah put him at all to d'? "
21 the king sought to put him to d': "
24 hand of the people to put him to d'. "
38: 4 let this man be put to d': for thus "
15 wilt thou not surely put me to d'? "
16 I will not put thee to d', neither "
25 we will not put thee to d'; also "
43: 3 that they might put us to d', and "
11 such as are for d' to d'; and such 4194
52:11 in prison till the day of his d'. "
27 smote them, and put them to d' 4191
34 a portion until the day of his d', 4194
La 1:20 bereaveth, at home there is as d'. "
Eze 18:32 pleasure in the d' of him that dieth, "
31:14 they are all delivered unto d', to the "
33:11 no pleasure in the d' of the wicked; "
Ho 13:14 I will redeem them from d': O d', "
Am 5: 8 turneth the shadow of d' into the 6757
Jon 4: 9 well to be angry, even unto d'. 4194
Hab 2: 5 his desire as hell, and is as d', "
M't 2:15 was there until the d' of Herod: 5054
4:16 in the region and shadow of d' 2288
10:21 deliver up the brother to d', 2288
21 and cause them to be put to d'. 2289
14: 5 he would have put him to d', 615
15: 4 or mother, let him die the d'. 2288
16:28 shall not taste of d', till they see "
20:18 and they shall condemn him to d', "
26:38 exceeding sorrowful, even unto d': "
59 against Jesus, to put him to d'; 2289
66 and said, He is guilty of d'. 2288
27: 1 against Jesus, to put him to d': 2289
M'r 5:23 daughter lieth at the point of d': 2079
7:10 let him die the d': But ye say, 2288
9: 1 shall not taste of d', till they have "
10:33 shall condemn him to d', and shall "
13:12 shall betray the brother to d', "
12 shall cause them to be put to d'. 2289

M'r 14: 1 him by craft, and put him to d'. * 615
34 is exceeding sorrowful unto d': and 2288
55 against Jesus to put him to d'; and 2289
64 condemned him to be guilty of d'. 2288
Lu 1:79 and in the shadow of d', to guide "
2:26 that he should not see d', before "
9:27 which shall not taste of d', till they "
18:33 scourge him, and put him to d': * 615
21:16 shall they cause to be put to d'. 2289
22:33 thee; both into prison, and to d'. 2288
23:15 nothing worthy of d' is done unto "
22 found no cause of d' in him: I will "
32 led with him to be put to d'. 337
24:20 to be condemned to d', and have 2288
Joh 4:47 for he was at the point of d'. 599
5:24 but is passed from d' unto life. 2288
8:51 my saying, he shall never see d'. "
52 saying, he shall never taste of d'. "
11: 4 This sickness is not unto d', but "
13 Jesus spake of his d': but they "
53 together for to put him to d'. 615
12:10 they might put Lazarus also to d'; "
33 signifying what d' he should die. 2288
18:31 lawful for us to put any man to d'; 615
32 signifying what d' he should die. 2288
21:19 by what d' he should glorify God. "
Ac 2:24 up, having loosed the pains of d': "
8: 1 Saul was consenting unto his d'. 336
12:19 that they should be put to d'. 520
13:28 they found no cause of d' in him, 2288
22: 4 I persecuted this way unto the d', "
20 by, and consenting unto his d', * 336
23:29 charge worthy of d' or of bonds. 2288
25:11 committed any thing worthy of d', "
25 committed nothing worthy of d', "
26:10 when they were put to d', I gave 337
31 nothing worthy of d' or of bonds. 2288
28:18 there was no cause of d' in me. "
Ro 1:32 such things are worthy of d', "
5:10 by the d' of his Son, much more, "
12 and d' by sin; and so d' passed "
14 d' reigned from Adam to Moses, "
17 man's offence d' reigned by one; "
21 That as sin hath reigned unto d', "
6: 3 Christ were baptized into his d'? "
4 with him by baptism into d': "
5 in the likeness of his d', we shall be "
9 d' hath no more dominion over him. "
16 of sin unto d', or of obedience "
21 the end of those things is d'. "
23 For the wages of sin is d'; but the "
7: 5 to bring forth fruit unto d'. "
10 life, I found to be unto d'. "
13 which is good made d' unto me? "
13 might appear sin, working d' in me "
24 me from the body of this d'? "
8: 2 free from the law of sin and d'. "
6 to be carnally minded is d'; "
38 neither d', nor life, nor angels, nor "
1Co 3:22 or life, or d', or things present, "
4: 9 last, as it were appointed to d': 1935
11:26 ye do shew the Lord's d' till he 2288
15:21 by man came d', by man came "
26 that shall be destroyed is d'. "
54 D' is swallowed up in victory. "
55 O d', where is thy sting? O grave "
56 sting of d' is sin; and the strength "
2Co 1: 9 had the sentence of d' in ourselves, "
10 delivered us from so great a d', "
2:16 one we are the savour of d' unto d'; "
3: 7 the ministration of d', written and "
4:11 delivered unto d' for Jesus' sake, "
12 then d' worketh in us, but life in "
7:10 the sorrow of the world worketh d'. "
Ph'p 1:20 whether it be by life, or by d'. "
2: 8 and became obedient unto d', "
8 even the d' of the cross. "
27 he was sick nigh unto d': but God "
30 he was nigh unto d', not regarding "
3:10 made conformable unto his d'; "
Col 1:22 In the body of his flesh through d', "
2Ti 1:10 who hath abolished d', and "
Heb 2: 9 for the suffering of d', crowned "
9 God should taste of d' for every man. "
14 through d' he might destroy him "
14 that had the power of d', "
15 fear of d' were all their lifetime "
5: 7 to save him from d', and was heard "
7:23 to continue by reason of d': "
9:15 by means of d', for the redemption "
16 must also of necessity be the d' "
11: 5 that he should not see d'; "
Jas 1:15 it is finished, bringeth forth d'. "
5:20 save a soul from d', and shall hide "
1Pe 3:18 being put to d' in the flesh, 2289
1Jo 3:14 we have passed from d' unto life, 2288
14 not his brother abideth in d'. "
5:16 a sin which is not unto d', he shall "
16 life for them that sin not unto d'. "
16 There is a sin unto d': I do not "
17 and there is a sin not unto d'. "
Re 1:18 the keys of hell and of d'. "
2:10 be thou faithful unto d', and I will "
11 shall not be hurt of the second d'. "
23 I will kill her children with d'; "
6: 8 his name that sat on him was D', "
8 and with hunger, and with d', "
9: 6 men seek d', and shall not find it; "
6 and d' shall flee from them. "
12:11 loved not their lives unto the d'. "
13: 3 as it were wounded to d'; and his "
18: 8 day, d', and mourning, and famine; "
20: 6 the second d' hath no power, but "
13 d' and hell delivered up the dead "
14 d' and hell were cast into the * "
14 lake of fire. This is the second d'. * "

Re 21: 4 be no more *d'*, neither sorrow, *2288*
8 brimstone: which is the second *d'*. "

deaths
Jer 16: 4 They shall die of grievous *d'*; 4463
Eze 28: 8 the *d'* of them that are slain
10 die the *d'* of the uncircumcised 4194
2Co 11:23 prisons more frequent in *d'* oft. *2288*

Debar See Lo-debar.

debase
Isa 57: 9 didst *d'* thyself even unto hell. 8213

debate See also debates.
Pr 25: 9 *D'* thy cause with thy neighbour 7378
Isa 27: 8 forth, thou wilt *d'* with it: * "
58: 4 fast for strife and *d'*, and to smite *4683
Ro 1:29 murder, *d'*, deceit, malignity; **2054*

debates
2Co 12:20 there be *d'*, envyings, wraths, **2054*

Debir (*de'-bur*) See also Kirjath-sannah; Kirjath-sepher.
Jos 10: 3 unto *D'* king of Eglon, saying, 1688
38 and all Israel with him, to *D'*; "
39 did to *D'*, and to the king thereof; "
11:21 from Hebron, from *D'*, from Anab, "
12:13 king of *D'*, one; the king of Geder, "
13:26 Mahanaim unto the border of *D'*; "
15: 7 the border went up toward *D'* "
15 up thence to the inhabitants of *D'*: "
15 of *D'* before was Kirjath-sepher. "
49 and Kirjath-sannah, which is *D'*, "
21:15 Holon with her suburbs, and *D'* "
J'g 1:11 up against the inhabitants of *D'*: "
11 of *D'* before was Kirjath-sepher. "
1Ch 6:58 Hilen with her suburbs, *D'* with "

Deborah (*deb'-o-rah*)
Ge 35: 8 But *D'* Rebekah's nurse died, 1683
J'g 4: 4 *D'*, a prophetess, the wife of "
5 dwelt under the palm tree of *D'*, "
9 *D'* arose, and went with Barak "
10 and *D'* went up with him. "
14 *D'* said unto Barak, Up; for this "
5: 1 Then sang *D'* and Barak the son of "
7 until that I *D'* arose, that I arose "
12 Awake, awake, *D'*: awake, awake, "
15 princes of Issachar were with *D'*; "

debt See also debts; indebted.
1Sa 22: 2 every one that was in *d'*, and 5378
2Ki 4: 7 sell the oil, and pay thy *d'*, 5386
Ne 10:31 and the exaction of every *d'*. 3027
M't 18:27 him, and forgave him the *d'*. *1156*
30 prison, till he should pay the *d'*. **3784*
32 I forgave thee all that *d'*, because *3782*
Ro 4: 4 not reckoned of grace, but of *d'*. *3783*

debtor See also debtors.
Eze 18: 7 hath restored to the *d'* his pledge, 2326
M't 23:16 the gold of the temple, he is a *d'*! *3784*
Ro 1:14 I am *d'* both to the Greeks, and *3781*
Ga 5: 3 he is a *d'* to do the whole law. "

debtors
M't 6:12 our debts, as we forgive our *d'*. *3781*
Lu 7:41 certain creditor which had two *d'*: *5533*
16: 5 called every one of his lord's *d'* "
Ro 8:12 we are *d'*, not to the flesh, *3781*
15:27 them verily; and their *d'* they are. "

debts
Pr 22:26 of them that are sureties for *d'*. 4859
M't 6:12 forgive us our *d'*, as we forgive *3783*

Decapolis (*de-cap'-o-lis*)
M't 4:25 and from *D'*, and from Jerusalem, *1179*
M'r 5:20 and began to publish in *D'* how "
7:31 the midst of the coasts of *D'*. "

decay See also decayed; decayeth.
Le 25:35 and fallen in *d'* with thee; *4131

decayed
Ne 4:10 of the bearers of burdens is *d'*, 3782
Isa 44:26 and I will raise up the *d'* places *2723

decayeth
Job 14:11 the flood *d'* and drieth up: ‡ 2717
Ec 10:18 slothfulness the building *d'*; *4355
Heb 8:13 that which *d'* and waxeth old **3822*

decease See also deceased.
Lu 9:31 spake of his *d'* which he should *1841*
2Pe 1:15 may be able after my *d'* to have "

deceased
Isa 26:14 they are *d'*, they shall not rise: 7496
M't 22:25 when he had married a wife, *d'*, *5053*

deceit See also deceitful; deceits.
Job 15:35 and their belly prepareth *d'*. 4820
27: 4 nor my tongue utter *d'*. 7423
31: 5 if my foot hath hasted to *d'*; 4820
Ps 10: 7 His mouth is full of cursing and *d'* "
36: 3 of his mouth are iniquity and *d'*: "
50:19 to evil, and thy tongue frameth *d'*. "
55:11 *d'* and guile depart not from her *8496
72:14 shall redeem their soul from *d'* * "
101: 7 *d'* shall not dwell within my 7423
119:118 statutes: for their *d'* is falsehood. 8649
Pr 12: 5 the counsels of the wicked are *d'*. 4820
17 but a false witness *d'*. "
20 *D'* is in the heart of them that "
14: 8 but the folly of fools is *d'*. "
20:17 Bread of *d'* is sweet to a man; *8267
26:24 and layeth up *d'* within him; 4820
26 Whose hatred is covered by *d'*, *4860
Isa 53: 9 neither was any *d'* in his mouth. 4820
Jer 5:27 their houses full of *d'*: therefore "
8: 5 hold fast *d'*, they refuse to return. 8649
9: 6 habitation is in the midst of *d'*; 4820
6 through *d'* they refuse to know me, "
8 it speaketh *d'*: one speaketh "
14:14 nought, and the *d'* of their heart. 8649
Jer 23:26 of the *d'* of their own heart; 8649
Ho 11:12 and the house of Israel with *d'*: 4820
12: 7 the balances of *d'* are in his hand: "
Am 8: 5 and falsifying the balances by *d'*? "
Zep 1: 9 houses with violence and *d'*. "
M'r 7:22 wickedness, *d'*, lasciviousness, an *1388*
Ro 1:29 full of envy, murder, debate, *d'*, "
3:13 their tongues they have used *d'*; *1387*
Col 2: 8 through philosophy and vain *d'*, *539*
1Th 2: 3 our exhortation was not of *d'*, **4106*

deceitful
Ps 5: 6 will abhor the bloody and *d'* man. 4820
35:20 devise *d'* matters against them "
43: 1 me from the *d'* and unjust man. "
52: 4 words, O thou *d'* tongue. "
55:23 bloody and *d'* men shall not live "
78:57 were turned aside like a *d'* bow. 7423
109: 2 of the *d'* are opened against me: *4820
120: 2 from lying lips, and from a *d'* 7423
Pr 11:18 The wicked worketh a *d'* work: 8267
14:25 but a *d'* witness speaketh lies. *4820
23: 3 his dainties: for they are *d'* meat. 3577
27: 6 but the kisses of an enemy are *d'*. *6280
29:13 and the *d'* man meet together: *8501
31:30 Favour is *d'*, and beauty is vain: 8267
Jer 17: 9 The heart is *d'* above all things, 6121
Ho 7:16 High: they are like a *d'* bow: 7423
Mic 6:11 and with the bag of *d'* weights? 4820
12 their tongue is *d'* in their mouth. 7423
Zep 3:13 *d'* tongue be found in their mouth: 8649
2Co 11:13 false apostles, *d'* workers, *1386*
Eph 4:22 corrupt according to the *d'* lusts; * *539*

deceitfully
Ge 34:13 Shechem and Hamor his father *d'*, *4820
Ex 8:29 let not Pharaoh deal *d'* any more 2048
21: 8 seeing he hath dealt *d'* with her. 898
Le 6: 4 thing which he hath *d'* gotten. *6231
Job 6:15 brethren have dealt *d'* as a brook, 898
13: 7 for God? and talk *d'* for him? 7423
Ps 24: 4 his soul unto vanity, nor sworn *d'*. 4820
52: 2 like a sharp razor, working *d'*. 7423
Jer 48:10 doeth the work of the Lord *d'*, * "
Da 11:23 he shall work *d'*: for he shall 4820
2Co 4: 2 nor handling the word of God *d'*, *1389*

deceitfulness
M't 13:22 the *d'* of riches, choke the word, *539*
M'r 4:19 the *d'* of riches, and the lusts of "
Heb 3:13 be hardened through the *d'* of sin. "

deceits
Ps 38:12 and imagine *d'* all the day long. 4820
Isa 30:10 us smooth things, prophesy *d'*: 4123

deceivableness
2Th 2:10 with all *d'* of unrighteousness in * *539*

deceive See also deceived; deceiveth; deceiving.
2Sa 3:25 that he came to *d'* thee, and to 6601
2Ki 4:28 did I not say, Do not *d'* me? 7952
18:29 Let not Hezekiah *d'* you: for he 5377
19:10 God in whom thou trustest *d'* thee, "
2Ch 32:15 let not Hezekiah *d'* you, nor "
Pr 24:28 cause; and *d'* not with thy lips. 6601
Isa 36:14 Let not Hezekiah *d'* you: for he 5377
37:10 God, in whom thou trustest, *d'* thee, "
Jer 9: 5 will *d'* every one his neighbour, 2048
29: 8 that be in the midst of you *d'* you, 5377
37: 9 *D'* not yourselves, saying, The "
Zec 13: 4 they wear a rough garment to *d'*: 3584
M't 24: 4 Take heed that no man *d'* you. **4105*
5 I am Christ; and shall *d'* many. * "
11 shall rise and shall *d'* many. * "
24 they shall *d'* the very elect. * "
M'r 13: 5 Take heed lest any man *d'* you: * "
6 I am Christ; and shall *d'* many. * "
Ro 16:18 speeches *d'* the hearts of the **1818*
1Co 3:18 Let no man *d'* himself. If any **4105*
Eph 4:14 whereby they lie in wait to *d'*; **4106*
5: 6 Let no man *d'* you with vain words: *538*
2Th 2: 3 Let no man *d'* you by any means: **1818*
1Jo 1: 8 we *d'* ourselves, and the truth *4105*
3: 7 let no man *d'* you: he that doeth * "
Re 20: 3 that he should *d'* the nations no "
8 go out to *d'* the nations which are "

deceived
Ge 31: 7 your father hath *d'* me, and 2048
Le 6: 2 violence, or hath *d'* his neighbour; 6231
De 11:16 that your heart be not *d'*, 6601
1Sa 19:17 Why hast thou *d'* me so, and sent 7411
28:12 Why hast thou *d'* me? for thou art "
2Sa 19:26 my servant *d'* me: for thy servant "
Job 12:16 the *d'* and the deceiver are his. 7683
15:31 not him that is *d'* trust in vanity: *8582
31: 9 If mine heart have been *d'* by a *6601
Pr 20: 1 whosoever is *d'* thereby is not *7686
Isa 19:13 the princes of Noph are *d'*; 5377
44:20 a *d'* heart had turned him aside, 2048
Jer 4:10 thou hast greatly *d'* this people 5377
20: 7 thou hast *d'* me, and I was *d'*: ‡6601
49:16 Thy terribleness hath *d'* thee, 5377
La 1:19 I called for my lovers, but they *d'* 7411
Eze 14: 9 if the prophet be *d'* when he hath 6601
9 I the Lord have *d'* that prophet, "
Ob 3 pride of thine heart hath *d'* thee, 5377
7 at peace with thee hath *d'* thee, "
Lu 21: 8 Take heed that ye be not *d'*: **4105*
Joh 7:47 the Pharisees, Are ye also *d'*? * "
Ro 7:11 *d'* me, and by it slew me. *1818*
1Co 6: 9 Be not *d'*: neither fornicators, nor *4105*
15:33 Be not *d'*: evil communications "
Ga 6: 7 Be not *d'*; God is not mocked: "
1Ti 2:14 Adam was not *d'*, but the woman * *538*
14 being *d'* was in the transgression. * "
2Ti 3:13 worse, deceiving, and being *d'*. *4105*
Tit 3: 3 *d'*, serving divers lusts and "
Re 18:23 thy sorceries were all nations *d'*. *4105*
19:20 with which he *d'* them that had "
20:10 the devil that *d'* them was cast "

deceiver See also deceivers.
Ge 27:12 I shall seem to him as a *d'*; 8591
Job 12:16 the deceived and the *d'* are his. 7686
Mal 1:14 cursed be the *d'*, which hath in 5230
M't 27:63 we remember that that *d'* said, *4108*
2Jo 7 This is a *d'* and an antichrist. "

deceivers
2Co 6: 8 good report: as *d'*, and yet true; *4108*
Tit 1:10 unruly and vain talkers and *d'*, *5423*
2Joh 7 For many *d'* are entered into the *4108*

deceiveth
Pr 26:19 the man that *d'* his neighbour, 7411
Joh 7:12 said, Nay; but he *d'* the people. **4105*
Ga 6: 3 when he is nothing, he *d'* himself. *5422*
Jas 1:26 his tongue, but *d'* his own heart, *538*
Re 12: 9 Satan, which *d'* the whole world: **4105*
13:14 *d'* them that dwell on the earth "

deceiving See also deceivings.
2Ti 3:13 worse and worse, *d'*, and being *4105*
Jas 1:22 hearers only, *d'* your own selves. **3884*

deceivings
2Pe 2:13 their own *d'* while they feast, † *539*

decently
1Co 14:40 all things be done *d'* and in order. *2156*

decided
1Ki 20:40 judgment be; thyself hast *d'* it. 2782

decision
Joe 3:14 multitudes in the valley of *d'*: for 2742
14 the Lord is near in the valley of *d'*. "

deck See also decked; deckest; decketh.
Job 40:10 *D'* thyself now with majesty 5710
Jer 10: 4 *d'* it with silver and with gold; 3302

decked See also deckedst.
Pr 7:16 I have *d'* my bed with coverings *7234
Eze 16:11 I *d'* thee also with ornaments, 5710
13 wast thou *d'* with gold and silver; "
Ho 2:13 she *d'* herself with her earrings "
Re 17: 4 *d'* with gold and precious stones *5558*
18:16 *d'* with gold, and precious stones, "

deckedst
Eze 16:16 and *d'* thy high places with divers *6213
23:40 and *d'* thyself with ornaments, 5710

deckest
Jer 4:30 thou *d'* thee with ornaments of 5710

decketh
Isa 61:10 as a bridegroom *d'* himself with 3547

declaration
Es 10: 2 *d'* of the greatness of Mordecai *6575
Job 13:17 and my *d'* with your ears. 262
Lu 1: 1 to set forth in order a *d'* of those **1335*
2Co 8:19 and *d'* of your ready mind: *

declare See also declared; declareth; declaring.
Ge 41:24 was none that could *d'* it to me. 5046
De 1: 5 began Moses to *d'* this law, saying, 874
Jo 20: 4 and shall *d'* his cause in the ears 1696
J'g 14:12 *d'* it me within the seven days of 5046
13 if ye cannot *d'* it me, then shall ye "
15 that he may *d'* unto us the riddle, "
1Ki 22:13 prophets *d'* good unto the king "
1Ch 16:24 *D'* his glory among the heathen; 5608
2Ch 18:12 the words of the prophets *d'* good "
Es 4: 8 and to *d'* unto her, and to charge 5046
Job 12: 8 the fishes of the sea shall *d'* unto 5608
15:17 that which I have seen I will *d'*; "
21:31 Who shall *d'* his way to his face? 5046
28:27 Then did he see it, and *d'* it; 5608
31:37 I would *d'* unto him the number 5046
38: 4 *d'*, if thou hast understanding. "
18 earth? *d'* if thou knowest it all. "
40: 7 of thee, and *d'* thou unto me. 3045
42: 4 of thee, and *d'* thou unto me. "
Ps 2: 7 I will *d'* the decree: the Lord *5608
9:11 *d'* among the people his doings. 5046
19: 1 The heavens *d'* the glory of God: 5608
22:22 *d'* thy name unto my brethren: "
31 *d'* his righteousness unto a people 5046
30: 9 praise thee? shall it *d'* thy truth? "
38:18 For I will *d'* mine iniquity; "
40: 5 if I would *d'* and speak of them, "
50: 6 heavens shall *d'* his righteousness: "
16 hast thou to do to *d'* my statutes, 5608
64: 9 and shall *d'* the work of God; 5046
66:16 and I will *d'* what he hath done 5608
73:28 that I may *d'* all thy works. * "
75: 1 is near thy wondrous works *d'*. * "
9 But I will *d'* for ever; I will 5046
78: 6 and *d'* them to their children: *5608
96: 3 *D'* his glory among the heathen, "
97: 6 The heavens *d'* his righteousness, 5046
102:21 To *d'* the name of the Lord in 5608
107:22 and *d'* his works with rejoicing. "
118:17 but live, and *d'* the works of the "
145: 4 and shall *d'* thy mighty acts. 5046
3 acts: and I will *d'* thy greatness. 5608
Ec 9: 1 to *d'* all this, that the righteous, * 952
Isa 3: 9 they *d'* their sin as Sodom, they 5046
12: 4 *d'* his doings among the people, 3045
21: 6 let him *d'* what he seeth. 5046
41:22 or *d'* us things for to come. 8085
42: 9 new things do I *d'*: before they 5046
12 unto the Lord, and *d'* his praise "
43: 9 who among them can *d'* this, "
26 *d'* thou, that thou mayest be *5608
44: 7 as I, shall call, and shall *d'* it, 5046
45:19 I *d'* things that are right. "
48: 6 all this; and will not ye *d'* it? "
20 with a voice of singing *d'* ye, "

Isa 53: 8 and who shall d' his generation? *7878
57:12 I will d' thy righteousness, and 5046
66:19 and they shall d' my glory among "
Jer 4: 5 D' ye in Judah, and publish in "
5:20 D' this in the house of Jacob, "
9:12 d' it, for what the land perisheth "
31:10 and d' it in the isles afar off, "
38:15 If I d' it unto thee, wilt thou not "
25 D' unto us now what thou hast "
42: 4 I will d' it unto you; I will keep "
20 d' unto us, and we will do it. "
46:14 D' ye in Egypt, and publish in "
50: 2 D' ye among the nations, and "
28 to d' in Zion the vengeance of the "
51:10 and let us d' in Zion the work of 5608
Eze 12:16 they may d' all their abominations "
23:36 d' unto them their abominations; 5046
40: 4 d' all that thou seest to the house "
Da 4:18 d' the interpretation thereof, 560
Mic 1:10 D' ye it not at Gath, weep ye not *5046
3: 8 to d' unto Jacob his transgression, "
Zec 9:12 even to day do I d' that I will "
M't 13:36 D' unto us the parable of the *5419
15:15 unto him, D' unto us this parable. "
Joh 17:26 them thy name, and will d' it: *1107
Ac 8:33 and who shall d' his generation? 1334
13:32 we d' unto you glad tidings, how *2097
41 though a man d' it unto you. 1555
17:23 worship, him d' I unto you. *2605
20:27 to d' unto you the counsel of God. 312
Ro 3:25 to d' his righteousness for the *1732
26 To d', I say, at this time his * "
1Co 3:13 for the day shall d' it, because 1213
11:17 Now in this that I d' unto you *3853
15: 1 brethren I d' unto you the gospel *1107
Col 4: 7 state shall Tychicus d' unto you, * "
Heb 2:12 will d' thy name unto my brethren, 518
11:14 d' plainly that they seek a *1718
1Jo 1: 3 seen and heard d' we unto you, 518
5 d' unto you, that God is light, * 312

declared
Ex 9:16 my name may be d' throughout 5608
Le 23:44 And Moses d' unto the children 1696
Nu 1:18 and they d' their pedigrees after
15:34 was not d' what should be done 6567
De 4:13 And he d' unto you his covenant 5046
2Sa 19: 6 thou hast d' this day, that thou "
Ne 8:12 the words that were d' unto them. 3045
Job 26: 3 hast thou plentifully d' the thing "
Ps 40:10 I have d' thy faithfulness and thy 559
71:17 have I d' thy wondrous works. 5046
77:14 d' thy strength among the people. *3045
88:11 Shall thy lovingkindness be d' 5608
119:13 With my lips have I d' all the "
26 I have d' my ways, and thou "
Isa 21: 2 A grievous vision is d' unto me; 5046
10 of Israel, have I d' unto you. "
41:26 Who hath d' from the beginning, "
43:12 I have d', and have saved, and I "
44: 8 from that time, and have d' it? "
45:21 who hath d' this from ancient *5085
48: 3 I have d' the former things from 5046
5 from the beginning d' it to thee; "
14 among them hath d' these things? "
Jer 36:13 Then Michaiah d' unto them all "
42:21 And now I have this day d' it "
Lu 8:47 d' unto him before all the people 518
Joh 1:18 the Father, he hath d' him: 1834
17:26 I have d' unto them thy name, *1107
Ac 9:27 d' unto them how he had seen the 1334
10: 8 when he had d' all these things *1834
12:17 d' unto them how the Lord had 1334
15: 4 d' all things that God had done * 312
14 Simeon hath d' how God at the 1834
21:19 d' particularly what things God * "
25:14 d' Paul's cause unto the king, * 394
Ro 1: 4 d' to be the Son of God with power, 3724
9:17 my name might be d' throughout *1229
1Co 1:11 it hath been d' unto me of you, *1213
2Co 3: 3 manifestly d' to be the epistle of *5319
Col 1: 8 Who also d' unto us your love 1213
Re 10: 7 d' to his servants the prophets. 2097

declareth
Isa 41:26 there is none that d', yea, there is 5046
Jer 4:15 For a voice d' from Dan, and "
Ho 4:12 and their staff d' unto them: for "
Am 4:13 d' unto man what is his thought, "

declaring
Isa 46:10 D' the end from the beginning, 5046
Ac 15: 3 d' the conversion of the Gentiles: 1555
12 d' what miracles and wonders *1834
1Co 2: 1 d' unto you the testimony of God. 2605

decline See also DECLINED; DECLINETH.
Ex 23: 2 d' after many to wrest judgment: *5186
De 17:11 shalt not d' from the sentence *5493
Ps 119:157 do I not d' from thy testimonies. *5186
Pr 4: 5 neither d' from the words of my "
7:25 Let not thine heart d' to her ways, 7847

declined
2Ch 34: 2 d' neither to the right hand, nor *5493
Job 23:11 his way have I kept, and not d'. *5186
Ps 44:18 have our steps d' from thy way; * "
119:51 yet have I not d' from thy law. * "

declineth
Ps 102:11 days are like a shadow that d'; 5186
109:23 gone like the shadow when it d': "

decrease See also DECREASED.
Ps 107:38 and suffereth not their cattle to d'. 4591
Joh 3:30 He must increase, but I must d'. 1642

decreased
Ge 8: 5 the waters d' continually until 2637

decree See also DECREED; DECREES.
2Ch 30: 5 So they established a d' to make 1697
Ezr 5:13 Cyrus made a d' to build this 2942
17 that a d' was made of Cyrus the "
6: 1 Darius the king made a d', and "
3 same Cyrus the king made a d' "
8 I make a d' what ye shall do to "
11 I have made a d', that whosoever "
12 I Darius have made a d'; let it "
7:13 I make a d', that all they of the "
21 I Artaxerxes the king, do make a d' "
Es 1:20 the king's d' which he shall make 6599
2: 8 and his d' was heard, and when 1881
3:15 and the d' was given in Shushan "
4: 3 commandment and his d' came, "
8 the copy of the writing of the d' "
8:14 And the d' was given at Shushan "
17 commandment and his d' came, "
9: 1 and his d' drew near to be put in "
13 according unto this day's d', and let "
14 the d' was given at Shushan; and "
32 And the d' of Esther confirmed *3982
Job 22:28 Thou shalt also d' a thing, and it 1504
28:26 When he made a d' for the rain, 2706
Ps 2: 7 I will declare the d': the Lord hath "
148: 6 made a d' which shall not pass. "
Pr 8:15 reign, and princes d' justice. 2710
29 When he gave to the sea his d', *2706
Isa 10: 1 unto them that d' unrighteous 2710
Jer 5:22 of the sea by a perpetual d', 2706
Da 2: 9 there is but one d' for you: *1882
13 And the d' went forth that wise men "
15 is the d' so hasty from the king? "
3:10 Thou, O king, hast made a d', 2942
29 I make a d', That every people, "
4: 6 Therefore made I a d' to bring in "
17 by the d' of the watchers, and the 1510
24 and this is the d' of the most High, "
6: 7 to make a firm d', that whosoever * 633
8 O king, establish the d', and sign * "
9 signed the writing and the d'. * "
12 king concerning the king's d'; * "
12 Hast thou not signed a d', that * "
13 nor the d' that thou hast signed, * "
15 no d' nor statute which the king * "
26 I make a d', That in every 2942
Jon 3: 7 the d' of the king and his nobles, 2940
Mic 7:11 day shall the d' be far removed. 2706
Zep 2: 2 Before the d' bring forth, before "
Lu 2: 1 there went out a d' from Cæsar 1378

decreed
Es 2: 1 and what was d' against her. 1504
9:31 and as they had d' for themselves *6965
Job 38:10 brake up for it my d' place †‡2706
Isa 10:22 the consumption d' shall overflow *2782
1Co 7:37 hath so d' in his heart that he *2919

decrees
Isa 10: 1 that decree unrighteous d', and 2711
Ac 16: 4 delivered them the d' for to keep, 1378
17: 7 all do contrary to the d' of Cæsar "

Dedan (*de'-dan*) See also DEDANIM.
Ge 10: 7 sons of Raamah; Sheba, and D'. 1719
25: 3 Jokshan begat Sheba and D'. "
3 the sons of D' were Asshurim, and "
1Ch 1: 9 sons of Raamah; Sheba, and D'. "
32 sons of Jokshan; Sheba, and D'. "
Jer 25:23 D', and Tema, and Buz, and all "
49: 8 dwell deep, O inhabitants of D'; "
Eze 25:13 they of D' shall fall by the sword. "
27:15 The men of D' were thy merchants; "
20 D' was thy merchant in precious "
38:13 Sheba, and D', and the merchants "

Dedanim (*ded'-a-nim*) See also DODANIM.
Isa 21:13 O ye travelling companies of D'. *1720

dedicate See also DEDICATED; DEDICATING.
De 20: 5 battle, and another man d' it. 2596
2Sa 8:11 Which also king David did d' 6942
1Ch 26:27 did they d' to maintain the house "
2Ch 2: 4 to d' it to him, and to burn "

dedicated
De 20: 5 new house, and hath not d' it? 2596
J'g 17: 3 wholly d' the silver unto the Lord *6942
2Sa 8:11 silver and gold that he had d' "
1Ki 7:51 which David his father had d'; 6944
8:63 and all the children of Israel d' 2596
15:15 things which his father had d', 6944
15 the things which himself had d', "
2Ki 12: 4 money of the d' things that is * "
18 kings of Judah, had d', and his 6942
1Ch 18:11 king David d' unto the Lord, * "
26:20 over the treasures of the d' things 6944
26 all the treasures of the d' things, "
26 the captains of the host, had d'. 6942
28 Joab the son of Zeruiah, had d'; "
28 and whosoever had d' any thing, "
28:12 of the treasuries of the d' things: 6944
2Ch 5: 1 things that David his father had d'; "
7: 5 and all the people d' the house 2596
15:18 the things that his father had d', 6944
18 and that he himself had d', "
24: 7 d' things of the house of the Lord "
31:12 and the d' things faithfully: over "
Eze 44:29 every d' thing in Israel shall be *2764
Heb 9:18 testament was d' without blood. 1457

dedicating
Nu 7:10 princes offered for d' of the altar *2598
11 on his day, for the d' of the altar. * "

dedication
Nu 7:84 the d' of the altar, in the day 2598
88 This was the d' of the altar, "
2Ch 7: 9 they kept the d' of the altar "
Ezr 6:16 kept the d' of this house of God 2597
17 And offered at the d' of this house "
Ne 12:27 at the d' of the wall of Jerusalem 2598
27 to keep the d' with gladness, "
Ps 30:*title* at the d' of the house of David. 2598
Da 3: 2 come to the d' of the image 2597
3 together unto the d' of the image "
Joh 10:22 at Jerusalem the feast of the d'. 1456

deed See also DEEDS; INDEED.
Ge 44:15 What d' is this that ye have done? 4639
Ex 9:16 And in very d' for this cause 199
J'g 19:30 There was no such d' done nor
1Sa 25:34 For in very d', as the Lord God of 199
26: 4 that Saul was come in very d'. *3559
2Sa 12:14 by this d' thou hast given great 1697
2Ch 6:18 But will God in very d' dwell with men
Es 1:17 For this d' of the queen shall 1697
18 have heard of the d' of the queen. "
Lu 23:51 to the counsel and d' of them; 4234
24:19 mighty in d' and word before God 2041
Ac 4: 9 good d' done to the impotent man, 2108
Ro 15:18 Gentiles obedient, by word and d', 2041
1Co 5: 2 hath done this d' might be taken "
3 him that hath so done this d', *
2Co 10:11 also in d' when we are present. 2041
Col 3:17 ye do in word or d', do all in the "
Jas 1:25 man shall be blessed in his d'. *4162
1Jo 3:18 tongue; but in d' and in truth. 2041

deeds See also ALMSDEEDS.
Ge 20: 9 thou hast done d' unto me that 4639
1Ch 16: 8 make known his d' among the *5949
2Ch 35:27 And his d', first and last, behold, *1697
Ezr 9:13 for our evil d', and for our 4639
Ne 6:19 reported his good d' before him,
13:14 wipe not out my good d' that I
Ps 28: 4 Give them according to their d'. *6467
105: 1 make known his d' among the *5949
Isa 59:18 According to their d', 1578
Jer 5:28 overpass the d' of the wicked: 1697
25:14 them according to their d', and 6467
Lu 11:48 ye allow the d' of your fathers: *2041
23:41 the due reward of our d': 3739, 4238
Joh 3:19 because their d' were evil. *2041
20 lest his d' should be reproved. * "
21 his d' may be made manifest, * "
8:41 Ye do the d' of your father. * "
Ac 7:22 was mighty in words and in d'. * "
19:18 confessed, and shewed their d'. 4234
24: 2 and that very worthy d' are done *2735
Ro 2: 6 to every man according to his d': *2041
3:20 by the d' of the law there shall no * "
28 faith without the d' of the law. * "
8:13 do mortify the d' of the body, 4234
2Co 12:12 and wonders, and mighty d'. *1411
Col 3: 9 put off the old man with his d'; *4234
2Pe 2: 8 to day with their unlawful d'; 2041
2Jo 11 speed is partaker of his evil d'. * "
3Jo 10 his d' which he doeth, prating * "
Jude 15 of all their ungodly d' which * "
Re 2: 6 hatest the d' of the Nicolaitanes * "
22 except they repent of their d'. * "
16:11 and repented not of their d'. * "

deemed
Ac 27:27 shipmen d' that they drew near *5282

deep See also DEEPER; DEEPS.
Ge 1: 2 was upon the face of the d'. 8415
2:21 God caused a d' sleep to fall upon 8639
7:11 fountains of the great d' broken 8415
8: 2 The fountains also of the d' and "
15:12 down, a d' sleep fell upon Abram; 8639
49:25 blessings of the d' that lieth under, 8415
De 33:13 for the d' that coucheth beneath, "
1Sa 26:12 d' sleep from the Lord was fallen 8639
Job 4:13 when d' sleep falleth on men, "
12:22 He discovereth d' things out of 6013
33:15 when d' sleep falleth upon men, 8639
38:30 and the face of the d' is frozen. 8415
41:31 maketh the d' to boil like a pot: 4688
32 would think the d' to be hoary. 8415
Ps 36: 6 thy judgments are a great d': "
42: 7 D' calleth unto d' at the noise of "
64: 6 one of them, and the heart, is d'. 6013
69: 2 I sink in d' mire, where there is no 4688
2 I am come into d' waters, where 4615
14 hate me, and out of the d' waters. "
15 neither let the d' swallow me up, 4688
80: 9 and didst cause it to take d' root, 8328
92: 5 and thy thoughts are very d'. 6009
95: 4 In his hand are the d' places of the 4278
104: 6 Thou coveredst it with the d' as 8415
107:24 Lord, and his wonders in the d'. 4688
135: 6 in the seas, and all d' places. *8415
140:10 into the fire; into d' pits, that 4113
Pr 8:28 the fountains of the d': 8415
18: 4 of a man's mouth are as d' waters, 6013
19:15 casteth into a d' sleep: and an 8639
20: 5 in the heart of man is like d' water; 6013
22:14 mouth of strange women is a d' pit; "
23:27 whore is a d' ditch; and a strange "
Ec 7:24 far off, and exceeding d', who can "
Isa 29:10 the spirit of d' sleep, and hath 8639
15 Woe unto them that seek d' to 6009
30:33 he hath made it d' and large: "
44:27 That saith to the d', Be dry, 6683
51:10 sea, the waters of the great d'; * 8415
63:13 That led them through the d', as * "
Jer 49: 8 dwell d', O inhabitants of Dedan; 6009
30 dwell d' O ye inhabitants of Hazor, "
Eze 23:32 shalt drink of thy sister's cup d' 6013
26:19 when I shall bring up the d' upon 8415
31: 4 the d' set him up on high with her "
15 I covered the d' for him, and I "
32:14 Then will I make their waters d', *8257
34:18 to have drunk of the d' waters, *4950
Da 2:22 revealeth the d' and secret things: 5994
8:18 I was in a d' sleep on my face 7290
10: 9 then was I in a d' sleep on my face. "
Am 7: 4 it devoured the great d', and did 8415

Jon 2: 3 thou hadst cast me into the d', *4688
Hab 3:10 the d' uttered his voice, and lifted 8415
Lu 5: 4 Launch out into the d', and let 899
6:48 built an house, and digged d', 2532, 900
8:31 them to go out into the d'. * 12
Joh 4:11 to draw with, and the well is d': 901
Ac 20: 9 being fallen into a d' sleep:
Ro 10: 7 Who shall descend into the d'? * 12
1Co 2:10 things, yea, the d' things of God. 899
2Co 8: 2 their d' poverty abounded unto the "
11:25 and a day I have been in the d'; 1037

deeper
Le 13: 3 plague in sight be d' than the skin, 6013
4 and in sight be not d' than the skin, "
25 and it be in sight d' than the skin; "
30 if it be in sight d' than the skin; "
31 it be not in sight d' than the skin 6013
32 in sight d' than the skin; "
34 nor be in sight d' than the skin; * "
Job 11: 8 d' than hell; what canst thou know? "
Isa 33:19 a people of d' speech than thou *6012

deeply
Isa 31: 6 children of Israel have d' revolted 6009
Ho 9: 9 They have d' corrupted themselves, "
M'r 8:12 he sighed d' in his spirit, and saith, 389

deepness
M't 13: 5 because they had no d' of earth: 899

deeps
Ne 9:11 thou threwest into the d', as a *4688
Ps 88: 6 lowest pit, in darkness, in the d'. "
148: 7 the earth, ye dragons, and all d': 8415
Zec 10:11 the d' of the river shall dry up: *4688

deer See also FALLOWDEER.
De 14: 5 the roebuck, and the fallow d', *3180

defamed
1Co 4:13 Being d', we intreat: we are made 987

defaming
Jer 20:10 For I heard the d' of many, fear 1681

defeat
2Sa 15:34 me d' the counsel of Ahithophel. 6565
17:14 d' the good counsel of Ahithophel, "

defence See also DEFENCED.
Nu 14: 9 their d' is departed from them, 6738
2Ch 11: 5 Jerusalem, and built cities for d' 4692
Job 22:25 the Almighty shall be thy d', and *1220
Ps 7:10 My d' is of God, which saveth *4043
31: 2 for an house of d' to save me. 4686
59: 9 wait upon thee: for God is my d'. *4869
16 thou hast been my d' and refuge * "
17 God is my d', and the God of my * "
62: 2 and my salvation; he is my d'; * "
6 he is my d'; I shall not be moved. * "
89:18 For the Lord is our d'; and the *4043
94:22 the Lord is my d'; and my God *4869
Ec 7:12 wisdom is a d', and money is a d': 6738
Isa 4: 5 upon all the glory shall be a d'. *2646
19: 6 the brooks of d' shall be emptied *4692
33:16 place of d' shall be the munition 4869
Na 2: 5 and the d' shall be prepared. *5526
Ac 19:33 have made his d' unto the people. 626
22: 1 hear ye my d', which I make 627
Ph'p 1: 7 d' and confirmation of the gospel, "
17 I am set for the d' of the gospel. * "

defenced
Isa 25: 2 of a d' city a ruin: a palace of ‡1219
27:10 Yet the d' city shall be desolate ‡ "
36: 1 against all the d' cities of Judah, †‡ "
37:26 to lay waste d' cities into ruinous †‡ "
Jer 1:18 have made thee this day a d' city, ‡4013
4: 5 and let us go into the d' cities. ‡ "
8:14 and let us enter into the d' cities, ‡ "
34: 7 for these d' cities remained of ‡ "
Eze 21:20 and to Judah in Jerusalem the d'. ‡1219

defend See also DEFENDED; DEFENDEST; DEFENDING.
J'g 10: 1 arose to d' Israel Tola the son of *3467
2Ki 19:34 For I will d' this city, to save it, 1598
20: 6 will d' this city for mine own sake, "
Ps 20: 1 name of the God of Jacob d' thee; *7682
59: 1 d' me from them that rise up * "
82: 3 D' the poor and fatherless: do *8199
Isa 31: 5 the Lord of hosts d' Jerusalem; *1598
37:35 For I will d' this city to save it "
38: 6 of Assyria: and I will d' this city. "
Zec 9:15 The Lord of hosts shall d' them; "
12: 8 In that day shall the Lord d' the "

defended
2Sa 23:12 and d' it, and slew the Philistines: 5337
Ac 7:24 suffer wrong, he d' him; and smote 292

defendest
Ps 5:11 because thou d' them: let them 5526

defending
Isa 31: 5 d' also he will deliver it; and *1598

defer See also DEFERRED; DEFERRETH.
Ec 5: 4 d' not to pay it; for he hath no 309
Isa 48: 9 will I d' mine anger, and for my 748
Da 9:19 d' not, for thine own sake, O my 309

deferred
Ge 34:19 young man d' not to do the thing, 309
Pr 13:12 Hope d' maketh the heart sick: 4900
Ac 24:22 of that way, he d' them, and said, 306

deferreth
Pr 19:11 discretion of a man d' his anger; * 748

defied
Nu 23: 8 defy, whom the Lord hath not d'? 2194
1Sa 17:36 seeing he hath d' the armies of 2778
45 armies of Israel, whom thou hast d'. "
2Sa 21:21 And when he d' Israel, Jonathan "
23: 9 when they d' the Philistines that "
1Ch 20: 7 But when he d' Israel, Jonathan "

defile See also DEFILED; DEFILETH.
Le 11:44 neither shall ye d' yourselves 2930
15:31 when they d' my tabernacle that is "
18:20 neighbour's wife, to d' thyself with "
23 thou lie with any beast to d' thyself "
24 D' not ye yourselves in any of these "
28 spue not you out also, when ye d' it, "
30 that ye d' not yourselves therein: "
20: 3 to d' my sanctuary, and to profane "
21: 4 shall not d' himself, being a chief "
11 nor d' himself for his father, or for "
22: 8 not eat to d' himself therewith: "
Nu 5: 3 that they d' not their camps, in the "
35:34 D' not therefore the land which ye "
2Ki 23:13 children of Ammon, did the king d'. "
Ca 5: 3 my feet; how shall I d' them? 2936
Isa 30:22 Ye shall d' also the covering of thy 2930
Jer 32:34 called by my name, to d' it. "
Eze 7:22 robbers shall enter into it, and d' *2490
9: 7 he said unto them, D' the house, 2930
20: 7 d' not yourselves with the idols of "
18 nor d' yourselves with their idols: "
22: 3 maketh idols against herself to d' "
28: 7 and they shall d' thy brightness. 2490
33:26 ye d' every one his neighbour's 2930
37:23 Neither shall they d' themselves "
43: 7 shall the house of Israel no more d', "
44:25 no dead person to d' themselves: "
25 husband, they may d' themselves. "
Da 1: 8 he would not d' himself with the 1351
8 that he might not d' himself. "
M't 15:18 the heart; and they d' the man. 2840
20 are the things which d' a man: "
M'k 7:15 entering into him can d' him: but "
15 him, those are they that d' the man. "
18 into the man, it cannot d' him; "
23 come from within, and d' the man. "
1Co 3:17 If any man d' the temple of God, *5351
1Ti 1:10 that d' themselves with mankind, * 733
Jude 8 these filthy dreamers d' the flesh, 3392

defiled See also DEFILEDST.
Ge 34: 2 and lay with her, and d' her. *6031
5 Jacob heard that he had d' Dinah 2930
13 he had d' Dinah their sister: "
27 because they had d' their sister. "
Le 5: 3 that a man shall be d' withal, and * "
11:43 them, that ye should be d' thereby. 2933
13:46 shall be in him he shall be d'; *2930
15:32 from him, and is d' therewith; "
18:24 all these the nations are d' which "
25 the land is d': therefore I do visit "
27 before you, and the land is d'; "
19:31 wizards, to be d' by them: I am the "
21: 1 There shall none be d' for the * "
3 no husband; for her may he be d'. * "
Nu 5: 2 and whosoever is d' by the dead: *2931
13 kept close, and she be d', and 2930
14 jealous of his wife, and she be d': "
14 of his wife, and she be not d': "
20 if thou be d', and some man have "
27 if she be d', and have done trespass "
28 if the woman be not d', but be "
29 instead of her husband, and is d'; "
6: 9 and he hath d' the head of his * "
12 lost, because his separation was d'. "
9: 6 men, who were d' by the dead *2931
7 We are d' by the dead body of a * "
19:20 hath d' the sanctuary of the Lord: 2930
De 21:23 that thy land be not d', which the * "
22: 9 the fruit of thy vineyard, be d'. *6942
24: 4 after that she is d'; for that is 2930
2Ki 23: 8 and d' the high places where the "
10 And he d' Topheth, which is in "
1Ch 5: 1 forasmuch as he d' his father's 2490
Neh 13:29 they have d' the priesthood, 1351
Job 16:15 and d' my horn in the dust. *5953
Ps 74: 7 they have d' by casting down the *2490
79: 1 thy holy temple have they d'; 2930
106:39 Thus were they d' with their own "
Isa 24: 5 The earth also is d' under the *2610
59: 3 your hands are d' with blood, and 1351
Jer 2: 7 when ye entered, ye d' my land, 2930
3: 9 she d' the land, and committed *2610
16:18 because they have d' my land, *2490
19:13 be d' as the place of Tophet, *2931
Eze 4:13 Israel eat their d' bread among "
5:11 thou hast d' my sanctuary with 2930
7:24 and their holy places shall be d'. *2490
18: 6 hath d' his neighbour's wife, 2930
11 and d' his neighbour's wife, "
15 hath not d' his neighbour's wife, "
20:43 wherein ye have been d': and ye * "
22: 4 and hast d' thyself in thine idols "
11 hath lewdly d' his daughter in law; "
23: 7 with all their idols she d' herself. "
13 Then I saw that she was d', that "
17 they d' her with their whoredom, "
38 they have d' my sanctuary in the "
28:18 Thou hast d' thy sanctuaries by *2490
36:17 dwelt in their own land, they d' it 2930
43: 8 they have even d' my holy name "
Hos 5: 3 whoredom, and Israel is d'. "
6:10 whoredom of Ephraim, Israel is d'. "
Mic 4:11 that say, Let her be d', and let our 2610
M'k 7: 2 eat bread with d', that is to say, 2839
Joh 18:28 lest they should be d'; but that 3392
1Co 8: 7 their conscience being weak is d'. 3435
Tit 1:15 but unto them that are d' and 3392
15 their mind and conscience is d'. "
Heb 12:15 you, and thereby many be d'; "
Rev 3: 4 which have not d' their garments; 3435
14: 4 which were not d' with women; "

defiledst
Ge 49: 4 then d' thou it: he went up to 2490

defileth
Ex 31:14 every one that d' it shall surely *2490
Nu 19:13 d' the tabernacle of the Lord; 2930
35:33 for blood it d' the land: and the *2610
M't 15:11 into the mouth d' a man; but that 2840
11 out of the mouth, this d' a man. "
20 with unwashen hands d' not a man. "
M'k 7:20 of the man, that d' the man. "
Jas 3: 6 members, that it d' the whole body, 4695
Re 21:27 enter into it any thing that d', *2840

defraud See also DEFRAUDED.
Le 19:13 Thou shalt not d' thy neighbour, *6231
M'r 10:19 D' not, Honour thy father and 650
1Co 6: 8 Nay, ye do wrong, and d', and that "
7: 5 D' ye not one the other, except it "
1Th 4: 6 and d' his brother in any matter: *4122

defrauded
1Sa 12: 3 I taken? or whom have I d'? 6231
4 Thou hast not d' us, nor oppressed "
1Co 6: 7 rather suffer yourselves to be d'? 650
2Co 7: 2 no man, we have d' no man. *4122

defy See also DEFIED.
Nu 23: 7 me Jacob, and come, d' Israel. 2194
8 hath not cursed? or how shall I d', "
1Sa 17:10 I d' the armies of Israel this day; 2778
25 surely to d' Israel is he come up: "
26 that he should d' the armies of the 2778

degenerate
Jer 2:21 art thou turned into the d' plant 5494

degree See also DEGREES.
1Ch 15:18 of the second d', Zechariah, Ben, "
17:17 to the estate of a man of high d', "
Ps 62: 9 d' are vanity, and men of high d' "
Lu 1:52 seats, and exalted them of low d'. 5011
1Ti 3:13 purchase to themselves a good d', * 898
Jas 1: 9 Let the brother of low d' rejoice 5011

degrees
2Ki 20: 9 the shadow go forward ten d', *4609
9 or go back ten d'? "
10 for the shadow to go down ten d': * "
10 shadow return backward ten d'. * "
11 the shadow ten d' backward, by * "
Ps 120 *title* A Song of d'. "
121 *title* A Song of d'. "
122 *title* A Song of d' of David. "
123 *title* A Song of d'. "
124 *title* A Song of d' of David. "
125 *title* A Song of d'. "
126 *title* A Song of d'. "
127 *title* A Song of d' for Solomon. "
128 *title* A Song of d'. "
129 *title* A Song of d'. "
130 *title* A Song of d'. "
131 *title* A Song of d' of David. "
132 *title* A Song of d'. "
133 *title* A Song of d' of David. "
134 *title* A Song of d'. "
Isa 38: 8 bring again the shadow of the d', * "
8 Ahaz, ten d' backward. So the sun * "
8 ten d', by which d' it was gone * "

Dehavites (*de-ha'-vites*)
Ezr 4: 9 the D', and the Elamites, 1723

Dekar (*de'-kar*)
1Ki 4: 9 The son of D', in Makaz, and in *1857

Delaiah (*del-a-i'-ah*) See also DALAIAH.
1Ch 24:18 The three and twentieth to D', 1806
Ezr 2:60 The children of D', the children of "
Ne 6:10 house of Shemaiah the son of D' "
7:62 The children of D', the children of "
Jer 36:12 and D' the son of Shemaiah, "
25 Nevertheless Elnathan and D' and "

delay See also DELAYED; DELAYETH.
Ex 22:29 Thou shalt not d' to offer the 309
Ac 9:38 that he would not d' to come 3635
25:17 without any d' on the morrow 311

delayed
Ex 32: 1 Moses d' to come down out of the 954
Ps 119:60 I made haste, and d' not to keep 4102

delayeth
M't 24:48 My lord d' his coming; and shall *5549
Lu 12:45 My lord d' his coming; and shall "

delectable
Isa 44: 9 their d' things shall not profit; 2530

delicacies
Rev 18: 3 through the abundance of her d'. *4764

delicate See also DELICATES.
De 28:54 is tender among you, and very d', 6028
56 The tender and d' woman among "
Isa 47: 1 no more be called tender and d'. "
Jer 6: 2 to a comely and d' woman. 6026
Mic 1:16 and poll thee for thy d' children; *8588

delicately
1Sa 15:32 And Agag came unto him d'. ‡4574
Pr 29:21 He that d' bringeth up his servant 6445
La 4: 5 They that did feed d' are desolate 4574
Lu 7:25 and live d', are in kings' courts. 5172

delicateness
De 28:56 of her foot upon the ground for d' 6026

delicates
Jer 51:34 he hath filled his belly with my d', ‡5730

deliciously
Re 18: 7 glorified herself, and lived d', *4763
9 and lived d' with her, shall * "

delight See also DELIGHTED; DELIGHTEST; DELIGHTETH; DELIGHTS; DELIGHTSOME.
Ge 34:19 he had d' in Jacob's daughter: 2654
Nu 14: 8 If the Lord d' in us, then he will "
De 10:15 the Lord had a d' in thy fathers 2836
21:14 if thou have no d' in her, then 2654

1Sa 15:22 Hath the Lord as great d' in burnt 2656
18:22 the king hath d' in thee, and all 2654
2Sa 15:26 I have no d' in thee; behold, here "
24: 3 doth my lord the king d' in this "
Es 6: 6 To whom would the king d' to do "
Job 22:26 then shalt thou have thy d' in the 6026
27:10 Will he d' himself in the Almighty? "
34: 9 that he should d' himself with God.7521
Ps 1: 2 But his d' is in the law of the Lord; 2656
16: 3 excellent, in whom is all my d'. "
37: 4 D' thyself also in the Lord; and 6026
11 d' themselves in the abundance "
40: 8 I d' to do thy will, O my God: 2654
62: 4 they d' in lies: they bless with 7521
68:30 thou the people that d' in war. 2654
94:19 me thy comforts d' my soul. 8173
119:16 I will d' myself in thy statutes: "
24 Thy testimonies also are my d' 8191
35 for therein do I d'. 2654
47 d' myself in thy commandments, 8173
70 fat as grease; but I d' in thy law. "
77 I may live: for thy law is my d'. 8191
174 O Lord; and thy law is my d'. "
Pr 1:22 the scorners d' in their scorning, 2531
2:14 and d', in the frowardness of the 1523
8:30 I was daily his d', rejoicing always 8191
11: 1 but a just weight is his d'. 7522
20 but such as are upright are his d'. "
12:22 but they that deal truly are his d'. "
15: 8 the prayer of the upright is his d'. "
16:13 Righteous lips are the d' of kings; "
18: 2 fool hath no d' in understanding. 2654
19:10 D' is not seemly for a fool; *8588
24:25 them that rebuke him shall be d', 5276
29:17 he shall give d' unto thy soul. 4574
Ca 2: 3 under his shadow with great d', 2530
Isa 1:11 I d' not in the blood of bullocks, 2654
13:17 as for gold, they shall not d' in it. "
55: 2 let your soul d' itself in fatness, 6026
58: 2 me daily, and d' to know my ways, 2654
Isa 58: 2 take d' in approaching to God. 2654
13 call the sabbath a d', the holy of 6027
14 shalt thou d' thyself in the Lord; 6026
Jer 6:10 reproach; they have no d' in it. 2654
9:24 these things I d', saith the Lord. "
Mal 3: 1 of the covenant, whom ye d' in: 2655
Ro 7:22 For I d' in the law of God after 4913

delighted
1Sa 19: 2 Saul's son d' much in David: 2654
2Sa 22:20 delivered me, because he d' in me. "
1Ki 10: 9 which d' in thee, to set thee on the "
2Ch 9: 8 which d' in thee to set thee on his "
Ne 9:25 and d' themselves in thy great 5727
Es 2:14 no more, except the king d' in her, 2654
Ps 18:19 delivered me, because he d' in me. "
22: 8 deliver him, seeing he d' in him. * "
109:17 as he d' not in blessing, so let it be "
Isa 65:12 did choose that wherein I d' not. "
66: 4 and chose that in which I d' not. "
11 and be d' with the abundance 6026

delightest
Ps 51:16 thou d' not in burnt offering. *7521

delighteth
Es 6: 6 man whom the king d' to honour? 2654
7 man whom the king d' to honour, "
9 withal whom the king d' to honour "
9, 11 whom the king d' to honour. "
Ps 37:23 Lord: and he d' in his way. "
112: 1 d' greatly in his commandments. "
147:10 d' not in the strength of the horse: "
Pr 3:12 a father the son in whom he d'. 7521
Isa 42: 1 mine elect, in whom my soul d'; "
62: 4 the Lord d' in thee, and thy land 2654
66: 3 their soul d' in their abominations. "
Mic 7:18 for ever, because he d' in mercy. "
Mal 2:17 and he d' in them; or, Where is the "

delights
2Sa 1:24 you in scarlet, with other d', *5730
Ps 119:92 Unless thy law had been my d', *8191
143 thy commandments are my d'. * "
Pr 8:31 my d' were with the sons of men. * "
Ec 2: 8 and the d' of the sons of men, 8588
Ca 7: 6 pleasant art thou, O love, for d'!

delightsome
Mal 3:12 for ye shall be a d' land, 2656

Delilah (*de-li'-lah*)
J'g 16: 4 of Sorek, whose name was D'. 1807
6 D' said to Samson, Tell me, I pray "
10 D' said unto Samson, Behold, thou "
12 D' therefore took new ropes, and "
13 D' said unto Samson, Hitherto thou "
18 D' saw that he had told her all "

deliver See also DELIVERED; DELIVEREST; DELIVERETH; DELIVERING.
Ge 32:11 D' me, I pray thee, from the hand 5337
37:22 to d' him to his father again. *7725
40:13 d' Pharaoh's cup into his hand, *5414
42:34 will I d' you your brother, and ye "
37 d' him into my hand, and I will "
Ex 3: 8 I am come down to d' them 5337
5:18 yet shall ye d' the tale of bricks. 5414
21:13 but God d' him into his hand; 579
22: 7 a man shall d' unto his neighbour 5414
10 If a man d' unto his neighbour "
26 thou shalt d' it unto him by that *7725
23:31 d' the inhabitants of the land into 5414
Le 26:26 shall d' you your bread again 7725
Nu 21: 2 If thou wilt indeed d' this people 5414
35:25 congregation shall d' the slayer 5337
De 1:27 to d' us into the hand of the 5414
2:30 that he might d' him into thy hand, "
3: 2 d' him, and all his people, into * "
De 7: 2 Lord thy God shall d' them before 5414
16 the Lord thy God shall d' thee; "
23 the Lord thy God shall d' them unto "
24 shall d' their kings into thine hand, "
19:12 d' him into the hand of the avenger "
23:14 the midst of thy camp, to d' thee, 5337
15 not d' unto his master the servant 5462
24:13 shalt d' him the pledge again *7725
25:11 to d' her husband out of the hand 5337
32:39 any that can d' out of my hand. "
Jos 2:13 have, and d' our lives from death.* "
7: 7 to d' us into the hand of the 5414
8: 7 the Lord your God will d' it into "
11: 6 about this time will I d' them up "
20: 5 d' the slayer up into his hand; 5462
J'g 4: 7 and I will d' him into thine hand. 5414
7: 7 I save you, and d' the Midianites "
10:11 not I d' you from the Egyptians * "
13 wherefore I will d' you no more. *3467
14 let them d' you in the time of * "
15 d' us only, we pray thee, this day. 5337
11: 9 and the Lord d' them before me, 5414
30 d' the children of Ammon into mine "
13: 5 he shall begin to d' Israel out of *3467
15:12 that we may d' thee into the hand 5414
13 fast, and d' thee into their hand: "
20:13 Now therefore d' us the men, the "
28 I will d' them into thine hand. "
1Sa 4: 8 who shall d' us out of the hand of 5337
7: 3 he will d' you out of the hand of the "
14 the coasts thereof did Israel d' out "
12:10 but now d' us out of the hand of our "
21 things, which cannot profit nor d'; "
14:37 d' them into the hand of Israel? 5414
17:37 he will d' me out of the hand of 5337
46 the Lord d' thee into mine hand; 5462
23: 4 d' the Philistines into thine hand. 5414
11 Will the men of Keilah d' me up 5462
12 Will the men of Keilah d' me and "
12 Lord said, They will d' thee up. "
20 to d' him into the king's hand. "
24: 4 I will d' thine enemy into thine 5414
15 and d' me out of thine hand. 8199
26:24 him d' me out of all tribulation. 5337
28:19 Lord will also d' Israel with thee 5414
19 the Lord also shall d' the host into "
30:15 nor d' me into the hands of my 5462
2Sa 3:14 D' me my wife Michal, which I 5414
5:19 wilt thou d' them into mine hand? "
19 will doubtless d' the Philistines into "
14: 7 D' him that smote his brother that "
16 d' his handmaid out of the hand 5337
20:21 d' him only, and I will depart 5414
1Ki 8:46 d' them to the enemy, so that they "
18: 9 thou wouldst d' thy servant into "
20: 5 Thou shalt d' me thy silver, and "
13 I will d' it into thine hand "
28 I d' all this great multitude into "
22: 6 shall d' it into the hand of the king. "
12 Lord shall d' it into the king's hand "
15 shall d' into the hand of the king. "
2Ki 3:10, 13 d' them into the hand of Moab! "
18 he will d' the Moabites also into "
12: 7 d' it for the breaches of the house. "
17:39 he shall d' you out of the hand of 5337
18:23 will d' thee two thousand horses. *5414
29 he shall not be able to d' you 5337
30 The Lord will surely d' us, and this "
32 you, saying, The Lord will d' us, "
35 the Lord should d' Jerusalem out "
20: 6 I will d' thee and this city out of the "
21:14 and d' them into the hand of their 5414
22: 5 And let them d' it into the hand of "
1Ch 14:10 thou d' them into mine hand? "
10 for I will d' them into thine hand. "
16:35 and d' us from the heathen, that 5337
2Ch 6:36 angry with them, and d' them over 5414
18: 5 God will d' it into the king's hand. "
11 shall d' it into the hand of the king. "
25:15 could not d' their own people *5337
20 that he might d' them into the 5414
28:11 and d' the captives again, which *7725
32:11 The Lord our God shall d' us out 5337
13 d' their lands out of mine hand? "
14 d' his people out of mine hand, "
14 God should be able to d' you out "
15 able to d' his people out of mine "
15 your God d' you out of mine hand? "
17 God of Hezekiah d' his people out "
Ezr 7:19 those d' thou before the God of 8000
Ne 9:28 many times didst thou d' them 5337
Job 5: 4 neither is there any to d' them. "
19 He shall d' thee in six troubles: "
6:23 D' me from the enemy's hand? 4422
10: 7 there is none that can d' out of 5337
22:30 d' the island of the innocent: 4422
33:24 D' him from going down to the 6308
28 He will d' his soul from going *6299
36:18 a great ransom cannot d' thee, *5186
Ps 6: 4 Return, O Lord, d' my soul: oh 2502
7: 1 that persecute me, and d' me: 5337
2 in pieces, while there is none to d'. "
17:13 d' my soul from the wicked, 6403
22: 4 trusted, and thou didst d' them. "
8 on the Lord that he would d' him: "
8 d' him, seeing he delighted in †5337
20 D' my soul from the sword; my "
25:20 O keep my soul, and d' me: "
27:12 D' me not over unto the will of 5414
31: 1 d' me in thy righteousness. 6403
2 d' me speedily: be thou my strong 5337
15 d' me from the hand of mine "
33:17 he d' any by his great strength. 4422
19 To d' their soul from death, and 5337
37:40 d' them: he shall d' them from *6403
Ps 39: 8 D' me from all my transgressions: 5337
40:13 Be pleased, O Lord, to d' me: "
41: 1 Lord will d' him in time of trouble. 4422
2 thou wilt not d' him unto the will 5414
43: 1 O d' me from the deceitful and 6403
50:15 the day of trouble: I will d' thee, 2502
22 in pieces, and there be none to d'. 5337
51:14 D' me from bloodguiltiness, O God, "
56:13 not thou d' my foot from falling, "
59: 1 D' me from mine enemies, O my 5337
2 D' me from the workers of iniquity, "
69:14 D' me out of the mire, and let me "
18 d' me because of mine enemies. *6299
70: 1 Make haste, O God, to d' me; 5337
71: 2 D' me in thy righteousness, and "
4 D' me, O my God, out of the *6403
11 for there is none to d' him. 5337
72:12 shall d' the needy when he crieth; "
74:19 O d' not the soul of thy turtledove 5414
79: 9 d' us, and purge away our sins, 5337
82: 4 D' the poor and needy: rid them 6403
89:48 shall he d' his soul from the hand 4422
91: 3 he shall d' thee from the snare 5337
14 will I d' him: I will set him on 6403
15 I will d' him, and honour him 2502
106:43 Many times did he d' them; but 5337
109:21 thy mercy is good, d' thou me. "
116: 4 Lord, I beseech thee, d' my soul. 4422
119:134 D' me from the oppression of *6299
119:153 mine affliction and d' me: for I 2502
154 Plead my cause, and d' me: *1350
170 d' me according to thy word. 5337
120: 2 D' my soul, O Lord, from lying "
140: 1 D' me, O Lord, from the evil man: 2502
142: 6 d' me from my persecutors; for 5337
143: 9 D' me, O Lord, from mine enemies: "
144: 7 and d' me out of great waters, "
11 and d' me from the hand of strange "
Pr 2:12 To d' thee from the way of the evil "
16 To d' thee from the strange woman, "
4: 9 a crown of glory shall she d' to 4042
6: 3 this now, my son, and d' thyself, 5337
5 D' thyself as a roe from the hand "
11: 6 of the upright shall d' them: "
12: 6 mouth of the upright shall d' them. "
19:19 if thou d' him, yet thou must "
23:14 and shall d' his soul from hell. "
24:11 If thou forbear to d' them that are "
Ec 8: 8 neither shall wickedness d' those 4422
Isa 5:29 away safe, and none shall d' it. 5337
19:20 a great one, and he shall d' them. "
29:11 men d' to one that is learned, 5414
31: 5 defending also he will d' it, 5337
36:14 he shall not be able to d' you. "
15 The Lord will surely d' us: this city "
18 you, saying, The Lord will d' us. "
20 that the Lord should d' Jerusalem "
38: 6 And I will d' thee and this city "
43:13 there is none that can d' out of my "
44:17 D' me; for thou art my god. "
20 he cannot d' his soul, nor say, "
46: 2 they could not d' the burden, but 4422
4 I will carry, and will d' you. "
47:14 they shall not d' themselves from 5337
50: 2 or have I no power to d'? "
57:13 let thy companies d' thee; but the "
Jer 1: 8 I am with thee to d' thee, saith "
19 with thee, saith the Lord, to d' thee. "
15: 9 the residue of them will I d' to the 5414
20 to save thee and to d' thee, 5337
21 And I will d' thee out of the hand "
18:21 d' up their children to the famine, 5414
20: 5 will d' all the strength of the city,* "
21: 7 I will d' Zedekiah king of Judah, "
12 and d' him that is spoiled out of 5337
22: 3 and d' the spoiled out of the hand "
24: 9 And I will d' them to be removed *5414
29:18 and will d' them to be removed "
21 I will d' them into the hand of "
38:19 lest they d' me into their hand, "
20 They shall not d' thee. Obey, I "
39:17 But I will d' thee in that day, 5337
18 I will surely d' thee, and thou *4422
42:11 and to d' you from his hand. 5337
43: 3 to d' us into the hand of the 5414
11 and d' such as are for death to *
46:26 and I will d' them into the hand 5414
51: 6 and d' every man his soul: be *4422
45 and d' ye every man his soul * "
La 5: 8 there is none that doth d' us out 6561
Eze 7:19 gold shall not be able to d' them 5337
11: 9 and d' you into the hands of 5414
13:21 and d' my people out of your 5337
23 for I will d' my people out of your "
14:14 they should d' but their own souls "
16 d' neither sons nor daughters; they "
18 d' neither sons nor daughters, but "
20 shall d' neither son nor daughter; "
20 they shall but d' their own souls "
21:31 and d' thee into the hand of 5414
23:28 I will d' thee into the hand of them "
25: 4 I will d' thee to the men of the "
7 and will d' thee for a spoil to the "
33: 5 taketh warning shall d' his soul. *4422
12 of the righteous shall not d' him 5337
34:10 I will d' my flock from their mouth, "
12 and will d' them out of all places "
Da 3:15 who is that God that shall d' you 7804
17 is able to d' us from the burning "
17 he will d' us out of thine hand, "
29 God that can d' after this sort. 5338
6:14 set his heart on Daniel to d' him: 7804
14 going down of the sun to d' him. *5338
16 servest continually, he will d' thee. 7804
20 able to d' thee from the lions? "

Da 8: 4 was there any that could *d'* out of 5337
7 was none that could *d'* the ram "
Hos 2:10 shall *d'* her out of mine hand. "
11: 8 how shall I *d'* thee, Israel? 4042
Am 1: 6 captivity, to *d'* them up to Edom: 5462
2:14 shall the mighty *d'* himself: 4422
15 swift of foot shall not *d'* himself: "
15 he that rideth the horse *d'* himself. "
6: 8 therefore will I *d'* up the city 5462
Jon 4: 6 head, to *d'* him from his grief. 5337
Mic 5: 6 shall he *d'* us from the Assyrian, "
8 teareth in pieces, and none can *d'*. "
6:14 shalt take hold, but shalt not *d'*; *6403
Zep 1:18 shall be able to *d'* them in the day 5337
Zec 2: 7 *D'* thyself, O Zion, that dwellest *4422
11: 6 I will *d'* the men every one 4672
6 out of their hand I will not *d'* them. 5337
M't 5:25 adversary *d'* thee to the judge, 3860
25 and the judge *d'* thee to the officer, "
6:13 temptation, but *d'* us from evil: 4506
10:17 will *d'* you up to the councils, 3860
19 But when they *d'* you up, take "
21 the brother shall *d'* up the brother "
20:19 And shall *d'* him to the Gentiles "
24: 9 Then shall they *d'* you up to the "
26:15 and I will *d'* him unto you? "
27:43 let him *d'* him now, if he will have 4506
M'r 10:33 and shall *d'* him to the Gentiles: 3860
13: 9 they shall *d'* you up to councils; "
11 and *d'* you up, take no thought "
Lu 11: 4 temptation; but *d'* us from evil. *4506
12:58 the judge *d'* thee to the officer, 3860
20:20 that so they might *d'* him unto the "
Ac 7:25 God by his hand would *d'* them: *1325
34 and am come down to *d'* them. 1807
21:11 and shall *d'* him into the hands of 3860
25:11 no man may *d'* me unto them. *5483
16 to *d'* any man to die, before that * "
Ro 7:24 who shall *d'* me from the body of 4506
1Co 5: 5 To *d'* such an one unto Satan 3860
2Co 1:10 a death, and doth *d'*: in whom 4506
10 we trust that he will yet *d'* us; "
Ga 1: 4 that he might *d'* us from this 1807
2Ti 4:18 the Lord shall *d'* me from every 4506
Heb 2:15 and *d'* them who through fear of 525
2Pe 2: 9 The Lord knoweth how to *d'* the 4506

deliverance See also DELIVERANCES.
Ge 45: 7 save your lives by a great *d'*. 6413
J'g 15:18 Thou hast given this great *d'* 8668
2Ki 5: 1 Lord had given *d'* unto Syria: * "
13:17 The arrow of the Lord's *d'*, * "
17 the arrow of *d'* from Syria * "
1Ch 11:14 Lord saved them by a great *d'*. * "
2Ch 12: 7 but I will grant them some *d'*; 6413
Ez 9:13 hast given us such *d'* as this; * "
Es 4:14 enlargement and *d'* arise to the 2020
Ps 18:50 Great *d'* giveth he to his king; 3444
32: 7 me about with the songs of *d'*. 6405
Isa 26:18 we have not wrought any *d'* in 3444
Joel 2:32 and in Jerusalem shall be *d'* *6413
Ob 17 upon Mount Zion shall be *d'* * "
Lu 4:18 to preach *d'* to the captives, and * 859
Heb 11:35 were tortured, not accepting *d'*; 629

deliverances
Ps 44: 4 O God: command *d'* for Jacob. *3444

delivered See also DELIVEREDST.
Ge 9: 2 sea; into your hand are they *d'*. 5414
14:20 hath *d'* thine enemies into thy 4042
25:24 her days to be *d'* were fulfilled, 3205
32:16 And he *d'* them into the hand of 5414
37:21 and he *d'* him out of their hands; 5337
Ex 1:19 and are *d'* ere the midwives come 3205
2:19 An Egyptian *d'* us out of the hand 5337
5:23 neither hast thou *d'* thy people at "
12:27 the Egyptians, and *d'* our houses. "
18: 4 *d'* me from the sword of Pharaoh: "
8 way, and how the Lord *d'* them. "
9 whom he had *d'* out of the hand "
10 who hath *d'* you out of the hand of "
10 of Pharaoh, who hath *d'* the people "
Le 6: 2 which was *d'* him to keep, or in *6487
4 which was *d'* him to keep, or the * "
26:25 and ye shall be *d'* into the 5414
Nu 21: 3 and *d'* up the Canaanites; and they "
34 I have *d'* him into thy hand, "
31: 5 they were *d'* out of the thousands 4560
De 2:33 And the Lord our God *d'* him 5414
36 the Lord our God *d'* all unto us: "
3: 3 So the Lord our God *d'* into our "
5:22 of stone, and *d'* them unto me. * "
9:10 And the Lord *d'* unto me two tables "
20:13 God hath *d'* it into thine hands, * "
21:10 the Lord thy God hath *d'* them "
31: 9 and *d'* it unto the priests the sons "
Jos 2:24 the Lord hath *d'* into our hands "
9:26 and *d'* them out of the hand of the 5337
10: 8 I have *d'* them into thine hand; 5414
12 the Lord *d'* up the Amorites before "
19 the Lord your God hath *d'* them "
30 And the Lord *d'* it also, and the "
32 And the Lord *d'* Lachish into the "
11: 8 *d'* them into the hand of Israel, "
21:44 the Lord *d'* all their enemies into "
22:31 ye have *d'* the children of Israel 5337
24:10 so I *d'* you out of his hand. "
11 and I *d'* them into your hand. 5414
J'g 1: 2 I have *d'* the land into his hand. "
4 and the Lord *d'* the Canaanites "
2:14 and he *d'* them into the hands of "
16 which *d'* them out of the hand of *3467
18 and *d'* them out of the hand of * "
23 neither *d'* he them into the hand 5414
3: 9 children of Israel who *d'* them, *3467
10 the Lord *d'* Chushan-rishathaim 5414
28 hath *d'* your enemies the Moabites "

J'g 3:31 ox-goad: and he also *d'* Israel. *3467
4:14 hath *d'* Sisera into thine hand: 5414
5:11 are *d'* from the noise of archers *
6: 1 *d'* them into the hand of Midian 5414
9 And I *d'* you out of the hand of 5337
13 and *d'* us into the hands of the 5414
7: 9 I have *d'* it into thine hand. "
14 into his hand hath God *d'* Midian, "
15 the Lord hath *d'* into your hand "
8: 3 God hath *d'* into your hands the "
7 when the Lord hath *d'* Zebah and "
22 *d'* us from the hand of Midian. *3467
34 Lord their God, who had *d'* them 5337
9:17 *d'* you out of the hand of Midian: "
10:12 and I *d'* you out of their hand. *3467
11:21 the Lord God of Israel *d'* Sihon 5414
32 the Lord *d'* them into his hands. "
12: 2 ye *d'* me not out of their hands. *3467
3 And when I saw that ye *d'* me not, "
3 the Lord *d'* them into my hand: 5414
13: 1 and the Lord *d'* them into the hand "
16:23 hath *d'* Samson our enemy into our "
24 hath *d'* into our hands our enemy, "
1Sa 4:19 was with child, near to be *d'*: 3205
10:18 and *d'* you out of the hand of the 5337
12:11 and *d'* you out of the hand of your "
14:10 hath *d'* them into our hand: 5414
12 *d'* them into the hand of Israel. "
48 *d'* Israel out of the hands of them 5337
17:35 and *d'* it out of his mouth: "
37 *d'* me out of the paw of the lion, "
23: 7 God hath *d'* him into mine hand; 5234
14 God *d'* him not into his hand. 5414
24:10 the Lord had *d'* thee to day "
18 Lord had *d'* me into thine hand, 5462
26: 8 *d'* thine enemy into thine hand "
23 the Lord *d'* thee into my hand 5414
30:23 and *d'* the company that came "
2Sa 3: 8 not *d'* thee into the hand of David, 4672
10:10 the rest of the people he *d'* *5414
12: 7 I *d'* thee out of the hand of Saul; 5337
16: 8 and the Lord hath *d'* the kingdom 5414
18:28 hath *d'* up the men that lifted 5462
19: 9 and he *d'* us out of the hand of *4422
21: 6 Let seven men of his sons be *d'* 5414
9 And he *d'* them into the hands of "
22: 1 the Lord had *d'* him out of the 5337
18 He *d'* me from my strong enemy, "
20 he *d'* me, because he delighted in 2502
44 *d'* me from the strivings of my 6403
49 hast *d'* me from the violent man. *5337
1Ki 3:17 *d'* of a child with her in the house 3205
18 the third day after that I was *d'*, "
18 that this woman was *d'* also: "
13:26 Lord hath *d'* him unto the lion, 5414
15:18 and *d'* them into the hand of his "
17:23 and *d'* him unto his mother: and "
2Ki 12:15 they *d'* the money to be bestowed "
13: 3 *d'* them into the hand of Hazael "
17:20 *d'* them into the hand of spoilers, "
18:30 shall not be *d'* into the hand * "
33 any of the gods of the nations, *d'* 5337
34 *d'* Samaria out of mine hand? "
35 *d'* their country out of mine hand, "
19:10 Jerusalem shall not be *d'* into *5414
11 utterly: and shalt thou be *d'*? 5337
12 the gods of the nation *d'* them "
22: 7 the money that was *d'* into their 5414
9 and have *d'* it into the hand of "
10 Hilkiah the priest hath *d'* me a "
1Ch 5:20 Hagarites were *d'* into their hand, "
11:14 *d'* it, and slew the Philistines; *5337
16: 7 David *d'* first this psalm to thank *5414
19:11 the rest of the people he *d'* unto * "
2Ch 13:16 and God *d'* them into thine hand. "
16: 8 Lord, he *d'* them into thine hand. "
18:14 and they shall be *d'* into your hand "
23: 9 Moreover Jehoiada the priest *d'* to "
24:24 *d'* a very great host into their hand. "
28: 5 Lord his God *d'* him into the hand "
5 he was also *d'* into the hand of "
9 he hath *d'* them into your hand, "
29: 8 and he hath *d'* them to trouble, "
32:17 not *d'* their people out of mine 5337
34: 9 the high priest, they *d'* the money 5414
15 Hilkiah *d'* the book to Shaphan "
17 *d'* it into the hand of the overseers, "
Ezr 5:14 and they were *d'* unto one, 3052
8:31 *d'* us from the hand of the enemy, 5337
36 they *d'* the king's commissions 5414
9: 7 our priests, been *d'* into the hand "
Es 6: 9 let this apparel and horse be *d'* 5414
Job 16:11 God hath *d'* me to the ungodly, *5462
22:30 *d'* by the pureness of thine hands. 4422
23: 7 I be *d'* for ever from my judge 6403
29:12 I *d'* the poor that cried, and the 4422
Ps 7: 4 have *d'* him that without cause 2502
18:*title* the Lord *d'* him from the hand 5337
17 He *d'* me from my strong enemy, "
19 he *d'* me, because he delighted in 2502
43 hast *d'* me from the strivings 6403
48 *d'* me from the violent man. *5337
22: 5 They cried unto thee and were *d'*: 4422
33:16 a mighty man is not *d'* by much 5337
34: 4 and *d'* me from all my fears. "
54: 7 he hath *d'* me out of all trouble: "
55:18 He hath *d'* my soul in peace *6299
56:13 thou hast *d'* my soul from death: 5337
60: 5 That thy beloved may be *d'*; save 2502
69:14 me be *d'* from them that hate me, 5337
78:42 he *d'* them from the enemy. *6299
61 And *d'* his strength into captivity, 5414
81: 6 his hands were *d'* from the pots. *5674
7 calledst in trouble, and I *d'* thee; 2502
86:13 and thou hast *d'* my soul from the 5337
107: 6 he *d'* them out of their distresses. "

Ps 107:20 *d'* them from their destructions. 4422
108: 6 That thy beloved may be *d'*: save 2502
116: 8 thou hast *d'* my soul from death, "
Pr 11: 8 The righteous is *d'* out of trouble, "
9 knowledge shall the just be *d'*. "
21 seed of the righteous shall be *d'*. 4422
28:26 walketh wisely, he shall be *d'*. "
Ec 9:15 and he by his wisdom *d'* the city; "
Isa 20: 6 to be *d'* from the king of Assyria: 5337
29:12 And the book is *d'* to him that is 5414
34: 2 he hath *d'* them to the slaughter. "
36:15 this city shall not be *d'* into the * "
18 the gods of the nations *d'* his land 5337
19 have they *d'* Samaria out of my "
20 that have *d'* their land out of my "
37:11 them utterly; and shalt thou be *d'*? "
12 Have the gods of the nations *d'* them "
38:17 hast in love to my soul *d'* it from the "
49:24 mighty, or the lawful captive *d'*? 4422
25 the prey of the terrible shall be *d'*: "
66: 7 came, she was *d'* of a man child. "
Jer 7:10 are *d'* to do all these abominations? 5337
20:13 he hath *d'* the soul of the poor "
32: 4 surely be *d'* into the hand of the 5414
16 when I had *d'* the evidence of the "
36 It shall be *d'* into the hand of the * "
34: 3 shalt surely be taken, and *d'* into * "
37:17 thou shalt be *d'* into the hand of the "
46:24 she shall be *d'* into the hand of the "
La 1:14 Lord hath *d'* me into their hands, "
Eze 3:19 iniquity; but thou hast *d'* thy soul. 5337
21 warned; also thou hast *d'* thy soul. "
14:16 they only shall be *d'*, but the land "
18 they only shall be *d'* themselves. "
16:21 and *d'* them to cause them to pass 5414
27 and *d'* thee unto the will of them "
17:15 he break the covenant, and be *d'*? *4422
23: 9 I have *d'* her into the hand of her 5414
31:11 I have therefore *d'* him into the * "
14 they are all *d'* unto death, to the "
32:20 she is *d'* to the sword: draw her "
33: 9 iniquity; but thou hast *d'* thy soul. 5337
34:27 and *d'* them out of the hand of those "
Da 3:28 hath sent his angel, and *d'* his 7804
6:27 who hath *d'* Daniel from the power "
12: 1 thy people shall be *d'*, every one 4422
Joel 2:32 the name of the Lord shall be *d'*: "
Am 1: 9 they *d'* up the whole captivity to 5462
9: 1 escapeth of them I shall not be *d'* *4422
Ob 14 neither shouldest thou have *d'* up *5462
Mic 4:10 there shalt thou be *d'*; there the *5337
Hab 2: 9 that he may be *d'* from the power "
Mal 3:15 they that tempt God are even *d'*. ‡4422
M't 11:27 All things are *d'* unto me of my 3860
18:34 and *d'* him to the tormentors, till "
25:14 and *d'* unto them his goods. "
27: 2 and *d'* him to Pontius Pilate the "
18 that for envy they had *d'* him. "
26 Jesus, he *d'* him to be crucified. "
58 commanded the body to be *d'*. *591
M'r 7:13 your tradition, which ye have *d'*: 3860
9:31 is *d'* into the hands of men, and * "
10:33 the Son of man shall be *d'* unto the "
15: 1 him away, and *d'* him to Pilate. *3860
10 chief priests had *d'* him for envy.* "
15 and *d'* Jesus, when he had scourged "
Lu 1: 2 Even as they *d'* them unto us, "
57 time came that she should be *d'*; 5088
74 that we being *d'* out of the hand 4506
2: 6 accomplished that she should be *d'*. 5088
4: 6 of them; for that is *d'* unto me; 3860
17 was *d'* unto him the book of the 1929
7:15 And he *d'* him to his mother *1325
9:42 and *d'* him again to his father. *591
44 Son of man shall be *d'* into the 3860
10:22 things are *d'* to me of my Father. "
12:58 that thou mayest be *d'* from him; *525
18:32 For he shall be *d'* unto the Gentiles, 3860
19:13 *d'* them ten pounds, and said unto *1325
23:25 but he *d'* Jesus to their will. 3860
24: 7 must be *d'* into the hands of sinful "
20 and our rulers *d'* him to be "
Joh 16:21 as soon as she is *d'* of the child, 1080
18:30 we would not have *d'* him up unto 3860
35 chief priests have *d'* thee unto me: "
36 that I should not be *d'* to the Jews: "
19:11 therefore he that *d'* me unto thee "
16 Then *d'* he him therefore unto "
Ac 2:23 Him being *d'* by the determinate 1560
3:13 whom ye *d'* up, and denied him 3860
6:14 the customs which Moses *d'* us. "
7:10 And *d'* him out of all his afflictions, 1807
12: 4 and *d'* him to four quaternions of 3860
11 and hath *d'* me out of the hand of 1807
15:30 together, they *d'* the epistle: 1929
16: 4 *d'* them the decrees for to keep 3860
23:33 *d'* the epistle to the governor, 325
27: 1 they *d'* Paul and certain other 3860
28:16 the centurion *d'* the prisoners to * "
17 yet was I *d'* prisoner from "
Ro 4:25 Who was *d'* for our offences, and "
6:17 form of doctrine which was *d'* you. "
7: 6 now we are *d'* from the law, *2673
8:21 shall be *d'* from the bondage of 1659
32 own Son, but *d'* him up for us all, 3860
15:31 That I may be *d'* from them that 4506
1Co 11: 2 ordinances, as I *d'* them to you. 3860
23 which also I *d'* unto you, that the "
15: 3 For I *d'* unto you first of all that "
24 when he shall have *d'* up the "
2Co 1:10 Who *d'* us from so great a death, 4506
4:11 are alway *d'* unto death for Jesus' 3860
Col 1:13 *d'* us from the power of darkness, 4506
1Th 1:10 Jesus which *d'* us from the wrath* "
2Th 3: 2 we may be *d'* from unreasonable "
1Ti 1:20 whom I have *d'* unto Satan, that 3860

2Ti 3:11 out of them all the Lord d· me. 4506
4:17 was d· out of the mouth of the lion. "
Heb 11:11 and was d· of a child when she *5088
2Pe 2: 4 d· them into chains of darkness, *3860
7 And d· just Lot, vexed with the 4506
21 holy commandment d· unto them. 3860
Jude 3 faith which was once d· unto the "
Re 12: 2 in birth, and pained to be d·. 5088
4 woman which was ready to be d·, "
20:13 death and hell d· up the dead *1325

deliveredst
Ne 9:27 Therefore thou d· them into the 5414
M't 25:20 Lord, thou d· unto me five talents: 3860
22 Lord, thou d· unto me two talents: "

deliverer
J'g 3: 9 the Lord raised up a d· to the *3467
15 the Lord raised them up a d·, * "
18:28 there was no d·, because it was 5337
2Sa 22: 2 rock, and my fortress, and my d·; 6403
Ps 18: 2 my fortress, and my d·; my God, "
40:17 thou art my help and my d·; make "
70: 5 thou art my help and my d·; O Lord, "
144: 2 my high tower, and my d·; my "
Ac 7:35 God send to be a ruler and a d· by 3086
Ro 11:26 shall come out of Sion the D·, 4506

deliverest
Ps 35:10 which d· the poor from him that 5337
Mic 6:14 which thou d· will I give up to *6403

delivereth
Job 36:15 He d· the poor in his affliction, 2502
Ps 18:48 He d· me from mine enemies: *6403
34: 7 them that fear him, and d· them. 2502
17 d· them out of all their troubles. *5337
19 the Lord d· him out of them all. "
97:10 he d· them out of the hand of the "
144:10 who d· David his servant from *6475
Pr 10: 2 but righteousness d· from death. 5337
11: 4 but righteousness d· from death. "
14:25 A true witness d· souls: but a "
31:24 and d· girdles unto the merchant. 5414
Isa 42:22 for a prey, and none d·; for a spoil, 5337
Da 6:27 He d· and rescueth, and he 7804

delivering
Lu 21:12 d· you up to the synagogues, and 3860
Ac 22: 4 and d· into prisons both men and "
26:17 D· thee from the people, and from 1807

delivery
Isa 26:17 draweth near the time of her d·, 3205

delusion See also DELUSIONS.
2Th 2:11 God shall send them strong d·. *4106

delusions
Isa 66: 4 I also will choose their d·, 8586

demand See also DEMANDED.
Job 38: 3 for I will d· of thee, and answer 7592
40: 7 like a man: I will d· of thee, and "
42: 4 will speak: I will d· of thee, and "
Da 4:17 the d· by the word of the holy ones: 7595

demanded
Ex 5:14 were beaten, and d·, Wherefore 559
2Sa 11: 7 David d· of him how Joab did, *7592
Da 2:27 The secret which the king hath d· 7593
M't 2: 4 he d· of them where Christ should *4441
Lu 3:14 soldiers likewise d· of him, saying, *1905
17:20 when he was d· of the Pharisees, * "
Ac 21:33 and d· who he was, and what *4441

Demas (*de'-mas*)
Col 4:14 the beloved physician, and D·, 1214
2Ti 4:10 For D· hath forsaken me, having "
Ph'm 24 Marcus, Aristarchus, D·, Lucas, "

Demetrius (*de-me'-tre-us*)
Ac 19:24 For a certain man named D·, a 1216
38 Wherefore if D·, and the craftsmen "
3Jo 12 D· hath good report of all men, "

demonstration
1Co 2: 4 in d· of the Spirit and of power: 585

den See also DENS.
Ps 10: 9 in wait secretly as a lion in his d·: 5520
Isa 11: 8 his hand on the cockatrice' d·. 3975
Jer 7:11 a d· of robbers in your eyes? 4631
9:11 heaps, and a d· of dragons; and I *4583
10:22 desolate, and a d· of dragons. * "
Da 6: 7 shall be cast into the d· of lions. 1358
12 d· of lions? The king answered "
16 and cast him into the d· of lions. "
17 and laid upon the mouth of the d·; "
19 went in haste unto the d· of lions. "
20 when he came to the d· he cried "
23 should take Daniel up out of the d·. "
23 Daniel was taken up out of the d·, "
24 they cast them into the d· of lions, "
24 they came at the bottom of the d·. "
Am 3: 4 will a young lion cry out of his d·, 4585
M't 21:13 but ye have made it a d· of thieves. 4693
M'r 11:17 but ye have made it a d· of thieves. "
Lu 19:46 but ye have made it a d· of thieves. "

denied
Ge 18:15 Sarah d·, saying, I laughed not; 3584
1Ki 20: 7 my gold; and I d· him not. 4513
Job 31:28 have d· the God that is above. *3584
M't 26:70 he d· before them all, saying, 720
72 again he d· with an oath, I do not "
M'r 14:68 But he d·, saying, I know not, "
70 And he d· it again. And a little after, "
Lu 8:45 When all d·, Peter and they that "
12: 9 be d· before the angels of God. 533
22:57 he d· him, saying, Woman, I know 720
Joh 1:20 he confessed, and d· not; but "
13:38 crow, till thou hast d· me thrice. 533
18:25 He d· it, and said, I am not. 720
27 Peter then d· again: and "

Ac 3:13 d· him in the presence of Pilate, 720
14 ye d· the Holy One and the Just, "
1Ti 5: 8 he hath d· the faith, and is worse "
Re 2:13 hast not d· my faith, even in those* "
3: 8 word, and hast not d· my name. * "

denieth
Lu 12: 9 he that d· me before men shall be 720
1Jo 2:22 he that d· that Jesus is the Christ? "
22 that d· the Father and the Son. "
23 Whosoever d· the Son, the same "

denounce
De 30:18 I d· unto you this day, that ye 5046

dens
J'g 6: 2 of Israel made them the d· which 4492
Job 37: 8 Then the beasts go into d·, and * 695
38:40 When they couch in their d·, and 4585
Ps 104:22 and lay them down in their d·. "
Ca 4: 8 from the lions' d·, from the "
Isa 32:14 forts and towers shall be for d· 4631
Na 2:12 with prey, and his d· with ravin. 4585
Heb 11:38 and in d· and caves of the earth *4693
Rev 6:15 hid themselves in the d· and in * "

deny See also DENIED; DENIETH; DENYING.
Jos 24:27 unto you, lest ye d· your God. 3584
1Ki 2:16 one petition of thee, d· me not. 7725
Job 8:18 then it shall d· him, saying, I have 3584
Pr 30: 7 d· me them not before I die: 4513
9 be full, and d· thee, and say, Who 3584
M't 10:33 whosoever shall d· me before men, 720
33 him will I also d· before my Father "
16:24 come after me, let him d· himself, 533
26:34 cock crow, thou shalt d· me thrice. "
35 die with thee, yet will I not d· thee. "
75 cock crow, thou shalt d· me thrice. "
M'r 8:34 let him d· himself, and take up "
14:30 crow twice, thou shalt d· me thrice. "
31 I will not d· thee in any wise. "
72 twice, thou shalt d· me thrice. "
Lu 9:23 come after me, let him d· himself, "
20:27 d· that there is any resurrection; * 483
22:34 thrice d· that thou knowest me. 533
61 cock crow, thou shalt d· me thrice. "
Ac 4:16 Jerusalem; and we cannot d· it. 720
2Ti 2:12 if we d· him, he also will d· us: "
13 faithful: he cannot d· himself. "
Tit 1:16 but in works they d· him, being "

denying
2Ti 3: 5 of godliness, but d· the power * 720
Tit 2:12 d· ungodliness and worldly lusts, "
2Pe 2: 1 d· the Lord that bought them, "
Jude 4 d· the only Lord God, and our Lord "

depart See also DEPARTED; DEPARTETH; DEPARTING.
Ge 13: 9 or if thou d· to the right hand, *
49:10 sceptre shall not d· from Judah, 5493
Ex 8:11 And the frogs shall d· from thee, "
29 that the swarms of flies may d· "
18:27 And Moses let his father in law d·; 7971
21:22 so that her fruit d· from her, 3318
33: 1 D·, and go up hence, thou and 3212
Le 25:41 And then shall he d· from thee, *3318
Nu 10:30 but I will d· to mine own land, 3212
16:26 D·, I pray you, from the tents of 5493
De 4: 9 lest they d· from thy heart all the "
9: 7 from the day that thou didst d· *3318
Jos 1: 8 This book of the law shall not d· 4185
24:28 So Joshua let the people d·, *7971
J'g 6:18 D· not hence, I pray thee, 4185
7: 3 let him return and d· early from 6852
19: 5 he rose up to d·: and the damsel's 3212
7 the man rose up to d·, his father "
8 the morning on the fifth day to d·: "
9 the man rose up to d·, he, and his "
1Sa 15: 6 d·, get you down from among 5493
22: 5 d·, and get thee into the land of 3212
29:10 in the morning, and have light, d·. "
11 and his men rose up early to d· "
30:22 they may lead them away, and d·. "
2Sa 7:15 mercy shall not d· away from him, 5493
11:12 and to morrow I will let thee d·. 7971
12:10 shall never d· from thine house; 5493
15:14 make speed to d·, lest he overtake 3212
20:21 and I will d· from the city. "
22:23 statutes, I did not d· from them. 5493
1Ki 11:21 Let me d·, that I may go to mine 7971
12: 5 unto them, D· yet for three days, 3212
24 returned to d·, according to the * "
15:19 king of Israel, that he may d· from 5927
2Ch 16: 3 king of Israel, that he may d· from "
18:31 God moved them to d· from him. "
35:15 might not d· from their service; 5493
Job 7:19 long wilt thou not d· from me, *8159
15:30 He shall not d· out of darkness; 5493
20:28 The increase of his house shall d·, 1540
21:14 they say unto God, D· from us; 5493
22:17 Which said unto God, D· from us: "
28:28 to d· from evil is understanding. "
Ps 6: 8 D· from me, all ye workers of "
34:14 D· from evil, and do good; seek "
37:27 D· from evil, and do good; and "
55:11 and guile d· not from her streets. 4185
101: 4 froward heart shall d· from me: 5493
119:115 D· from me, ye evildoers: for I "
139:19 d· from me therefore, ye bloody "
Pr 3: 7 fear the Lord, and d· from evil. "
21 let not them d· from thine eyes: 3868
4:21 Let them not d· from thine eyes; "
5: 7 d· not from the words of my 5493
13:14 to d· from the snares of death. "
19 abomination to fools to d· from "
14:27 to d· from the snares of death. "
15:24 that he may d· from hell beneath. "
16: 6 fear of the Lord men d· from evil. "

Pr 16:17 of the upright is to d· from evil: 5493
17:13 evil shall not d· from his house. 4185
22: 6 he is old, he will not d· from it. 5493
27:22 not his foolishness d· from him. "
Isa 11:13 The envy also of Ephraim shall d·, "
14:25 shall his yoke d· from off them, "
25 burden d· from off their shoulders. "
52:11 D· ye, d· ye, go ye out from thence, "
54:10 the mountains shall d·, and the 4185
10 but my kindness shall not d· from "
59:21 have put in thy mouth, shall not d· "
Jer 6: 8 lest my soul d· from thee; lest *3363
17:13 and they that d· from me shall be 3249
31:36 ordinances d· from before me, 4185
32:40 that they shall not d· from me. 5493
37: 9 The Chaldeans shall surely d· 1980
9 from us: for they shall not d·. "
50: 3 they shall d·, both man and beast.* "
La 4:15 They cried unto them, D· ye; it 5493
15 it is unclean; d·, d·, touch not: "
Eze 16:42 my jealously shall d· from thee, "
Hos 9:12 woe also to them when I d· from "
Mic 2:10 Arise ye, and d·; for this is not 3212
Zec 10:11 sceptre of Egypt shall d· away. 5493
M't 7:23 d· from me, ye that work iniquity. 672
8:18 gave the commandment to d· unto 565
34 he would d· out of their coasts. 3327
10:14 ye d· out of that house or city, *1831
14:16 unto them, They need not d·; * 565
25:41 D· from me, ye cursed, into 4198
M'r 5:17 pray him to d· out of their coasts. 565
6:10 abide till ye d· from that place. 1831
11 ye d· thence, shake off the dust *1607
Lu 2:29 lettest thou thy servant d· in peace, 630
4:42 that he should not d· from them. *4198
5: 8 saying, D· from me; for I am a 1831
8:37 besought him to d· from them; 565
9: 4 into, there abide, and thence d·. 1831
12:59 thou shalt not d· thence, till thou * "
13:27 d· from me, all ye workers of 868
31 Get thee out, and d· hence: for *4198
21:21 which are in the midst of it d· out 1633
Joh 7: 3 D· hence, and go into Judæa, 3327
13: 1 that he should d· out of this world "
16: 7 but if I d·, I will send him unto *4198
Ac 1: 4 they should not d· from Jerusalem 5562
16:36 therefore d·, and go in peace. *1831
39 desired them to d· out of the city. * "
18: 2 all Jews to d· from Rome: 5562
20: 7 them, ready to d· on the morrow; 1826
22:21 D·: for I will send thee far hence 4198
23:22 then let the young man d·, and * 630
25: 4 himself would d· shortly thither. 1607
27:12 part advised to d· thence also, * 321
1Co 7:10 not the wife d· from her husband 5562
11 she d·, let her remain unmarried, "
15 if the unbelieving d·, let him d·. * "
2Co 12: 8 thrice, that it might d· from me. 868
Ph'p 1:23 having a desire to d·, and to be 360
1Ti 4: 1 some shall d· from the faith, * 868
2Ti 2:19 name of Christ d· from iniquity. "
Jas 2:16 say unto them, D· in peace, be ye *5217

departed
Ge 12: 4 Abram d·, as the Lord had spoken *3212
4 old when he d· out of Haran. *3318
14:12 and his goods, and d·. 3212
21:14 and she d·, and wandered in the "
24:10 the camels of his master, and d·: "
26:17 And Isaac d· thence, and pitched "
31 and they d· from him in peace. "
31:40 and my sleep d· from mine eyes. *5074
55 and Laban d·, and returned unto 3212
37:17 They are d· hence; for I heard 5265
42:26 asses with the corn, and d· thence. 3212
45:24 his brethren away, and they d·: "
Ex 19: 2 For they were d· from Rephidim, 5265
33:11 d· not out of the tabernacle. 4185
35:20 of the children of Israel d· 3318
Le 13:58 if the plague be d· from them, 5493
Nu 10:33 d· from the mount of the Lord *5265
12: 9 kindled against them; and he d·. 3212
10 cloud d· from off the tabernacle; *5493
14: 9 their defence is d· from them, * "
44 Moses, d· not out of the camp. 4185
22: 7 the elders of Midian d· with the 3212
33: 3 they d· from Rameses in the first *5265
6 And they d· from Succoth, and * "
8 they d· from before Pi-hahiroth, * "
13 And they d· from Dophkah, and * "
15 And they d· from Rephidim, and * "
17 they d· from Kibroth-hattaavah, * "
18 And they d· from Hazeroth, and * "
19 And they d· from Rithmah, and * "
20 And they d· from Rimmon-parez, * "
27 And they d· from Tahath, and * "
30 And they d· from Hashmonah, * "
31 And they d· from Moseroth, and * "
35 And they d· from Ebronah, and * "
41 And they d· from mount Hor, and * "
42 And they d· from Zalmonah, and * "
43 And they d· from Punon, and * "
44 And they d· from Oboth, and * "
45 And they d· from Iim, and pitched * "
48 d· from the mountains of Abarim, * "
De 1:19 when we d· from Horeb, we went * "
24: 2 when she is d· out of his house, 3318
Jos 2:21 she sent them away, and they d·: 3212
22: 9 and d· from the children of Israel "
J'g 6:21 angel of the Lord d· out of his 1980
9:55 that Abimelech was dead they d· 3212
16:20 he wist not that the Lord was d· 5493
17: 8 And the man d· out of the city 3212
18: 7 Then the five men d·, and came to "
21 So they turned and d·, and put "
19:10 he rose up and d·, and came over "

J'g 21:24 And the children of Israel d' 1980
1Sa 4:21 saying, The glory is d' from Israel: 1540
22 is d' from Israel: for the ark of God "
6: 6 let the people go, and they d'? 3212
10: 2 When thou art d' from me to day, "
15: 6 So the Kenites d' from among the 5493
16:14 the Spirit of the Lord d' from Saul, "
23 and the evil spirit d' from him. "
18:12 with him, and was d' from Saul. "
20:42 he arose and d': and Jonathan 3212
22: 1 David therefore d' thence, and "
5 David d', and came into the forest "
23:13 six hundred, d' out of Keilah, 3318
28:15 God is d' from me, and answereth 5493
16 seeing the Lord is d' from thee, "
2Sa 6:19 So all the people d' every one 3212
11: 8 Uriah d' out of the king's house, 3318
12:15 And Nathan d' unto his house. 3212
17:21 after they were d', that they came "
19:24 the day the king d' until the day "
22:22 have not wickedly d' from my God. 7561
1Ki 12: 5 again to me. And the people d'. 3212
16 So Israel d' unto their tents. "
14:17 Jeroboam's wife arose, and d', and "
19:19 So he d' thence, and found Elisha "
20: 9 the messengers d', and brought "
36 as thou art d' from me a lion shall 1980
36 as soon as he was d' from him, 3212
38 So the prophet d', and waited "
2Ki 1: 4 shalt surely die. And Elijah d'. "
3: 3 to sin; he d' not therefrom. 5493
27 they d' from him, and returned 5265
5: 5 d', and took with him ten talents 3212
19 So he d' from him a little way. "
24 he let the men go, and they d'. "
8:14 So he d' from Elisha, and came to "
10:12 he arose and d', and came to 935
15 when he was d' thence, he lighted 3212
29 Jehu d' not from after them, 5493
31 d' not from the sins of Jeroboam, "
13: 2 Israel to sin; he d' not therefrom. "
6 They d' not from the sins of the "
11 d' not from all the sins of Jeroboam "
14:24 d' not from all the sins of Jeroboam "
15: 9 he d' not from the sins of Jeroboam "
18 he d' not all his days from the sins "
24, 28 d' not from the sins of Jeroboam "
17:22 he did; they d' not from them; "
18: 6 and d' not from following him, "
19: 8 that he was d' from Lachish. 5265
36 So Sennacherib king of Assyria d', "
1Ch 16:43 And all the people d' every man 3212
21: 4 Joab d', and went throughout all 3318
2Ch 8:15 d' not from the commandment 5493
10: 5 three days. And the people d'. 3212
20:32 d' not from it, doing that which *5493
21:20 and d' without being desired. 3212
24:25 And when they were d' from him, "
34:33 d' not from following the Lord, 5493
Ezr 8:31 we d' from the river of Ahava 5265
Ne 9:19 cloud d' not from them by day, 5493
Ps 18:21 have not wickedly d' from my God. 7561
34:title who drove him away, and he d'. 3212
105:38 Egypt was glad when they d': 3318
119:102 have not d' from thy judgments:*5493
Isa 7:17 from the day that Ephraim d' "
37: 8 that he was d' from Lachish. 5265
37 So Sennacherib king of Assyria d', "
38:12 Mine age is d', and is removed * "
Jer 29: 2 smiths were d' from Jerusalem: 3318
37: 5 of them, they d' from Jerusalem. *5927
41:10 d' to go over to the Ammonites. 3212
17 they d', and dwelt in the habitation "
La 1: 6 of Zion all her beauty is d': 3318
Eze 6: 9 their whorish heart, which hath d' 5493
10:18 the glory of the Lord d' from off *3318
Da 4:31 The kingdom is d' from thee. 5709
Ho 10: 5 thereof, because it is d' from it. 1540
Mal 2: 8 ye are d' out of the way; *5493
M't 2: 9 they d'; and, lo, the star, which *4198
12 d' into their own country another 402
13 when they were d', behold, the angel "
14 mother by night, and d' into Egypt: "
4:12 into prison, he d' into Galilee; * "
9: 7 And he arose and d' to his house 565
27 And when Jesus d' thence, two *3855
31 when they were d', spread abroad *1831
11: 1 he d' thence to teach and to preach 3327
7 as they d', Jesus began to say *4198
12: 9 And when he was d' thence, he 3327
13:53 these parables, he d' thence. 3332
14:13 he d' thence by ship into a desert * 402
15:21 and d' into the coasts of Tyre and * "
29 Jesus d' from thence, and came 3327
16: 4 Jonas. And he left them, and d'. 565
17:18 he d' out of him: and the child *1831
19: 1 he d' from Galilee, and came unto 3332
15 his hands on them, and d' thence. 4198
20:29 d' from Jericho, a great multitude*1607
24: 1 and d' from the temple: and his *4198
27: 5 in the temple, and d', and went 402
60 the door of the sepulchre, and d'. 565
28: 8 they d' quickly from the sepulchre 1831
M'r 1:35 he went out, and d' into a solitary 565
42 the leprosy d' from him, and he was * "
5:20 he d', and began to publish in * "
6:32 they d' into a desert place by ship * "
46 he d' into a mountain to pray. "
8:13 the ship again d' to the other side. "
9:30 And they d' thence, and passed *1831
Lu 1:23 he d' to his own house. 565
38 word. And the angel d' from her. "
2:37 which d' not from the temple, 868
4:13 he d' from him for a season. "
42 was day, he d' and went into *1831

Lu 5:13 the leprosy d' from him. 565
25 d' to his own house, glorifying God. "
7:24 the messengers of John were d', "
8:35, 38 out of whom the devils were d' *1831
9: 6 d', and went through the towns, "
33 as they d' from him, Peter said *1316
10:30 him, d', leaving him half dead. 565
35 morrow when he d', he took out *1831
24:12 clothes laid by themselves, and d',* 565
Joh 4: 3 Judæa, and d' again into Galilee. "
43 after two days he d' thence, and * "
5:15 The man d', and told the Jews * "
6:15 d' again into a mountain himself * 402
12:36 These things spake Jesus, and d', 565
Ac 5:41 And they d' from the presence of 4198
10: 7 spake unto Cornelius was d', he 565
11:25 Then d' Barnabas to Tarsus, for *1831
12:10 forthwith the angel d' from him. 868
17 And he d', and went into another 1831
13: 4 d' unto Seleucia; and from thence *2718
14 when they d' from Perga, they *1330
14:20 he d' with Barnabas to Derbe. *1831
15:38 d' from them from Pamphylia, * 868
39 they d' asunder one from the 673
40 Paul chose Silas, and d', being *1831
16:40 they comforted them, and d', "
17:15 come to him with all speed, they d'. 1826
33 So Paul d' from among them. *1831
18: 1 Paul d' from Athens, and came to 5562
7 he d' thence, and entered into a 1831
23 he d', and went over all the country "
19: 9 he d' from them, and separated 868
12 and the diseases d' from them, 525
20: 1 and d' for to go into Macedonia. 1831
11 even till break of day, so he d'. "
21: 5 we d' and went our way; and they "
8 that were of Paul's company d', and "
22:29 Then straightway they d' from him 868
28:10 when we d', they laded us with * 321
11 we d' in a ship of Alexandria, * "
25 not among themselves, they d', 630
29 Jews d', and had great reasoning* 565
Phil 4:15 when I d' from Macedonia, no 1831
Ph'm 15 For perhaps he therefore d' for a *5563
2Ti 4:10 and is d' unto Thessalonica; *4198
Re 6:14 the heaven d' as a scroll when it is* 673
18:14 lusted after are d' from thee, and* 565
14 and goodly are d' from thee, and * "

departeth
Job 27:21 carrieth him away, and he d': 3212
Pr 14:16 A wise man feareth, and d' from 5493
Ec 6: 4 and d' in darkness, and his name 3212
Isa 59:15 and he that d' from evil maketh 5493
Jer 3:20 a wife treacherously d' from her
17: 5 and whose heart d' from the Lord. 5493
Na 3: 1 lies and robbery; the prey d' not; 4185
Lu 9:39 bruising him hardly d' from him, 672

departing
Ge 35:18 her soul was in d' (for she died), 3318
Ex 16: 1 after their d' out of the land of "
Isa 59:13 d' away from our God, speaking *5253
Da 9: 5 even by d' from thy precepts and *5493
11 transgressed thy law, even by d', "
Hos 1: 2 great whoredom, d' from the Lord.
M'r 6:33 And the people saw them d', and *5217
7:31 again, d' from the coast of Tyre *1831
Ac 13:13 John d' from them returned to * 672
20:29 I know this, that after my d' 867
He 3:12 unbelief, in d' from the living God.* 868
11:22 the d' of the children of Israel *1841

departure
Eze 26:18 the sea shall be troubled at thy d'. 3318
2Ti 4: 6 and the time of my d' is at hand. 359

deposed
Da 5:20 he was d' from his kingly throne, 5182

deprived
Ge 27:45 why should I be d' also of you *7921
Job 39:17 God hath d' her of wisdom, 5382
Isa 38:10 I am d' of the residue of my years. 6485

depth See also DEPTHS.
Job 28:14 The d' saith, It is not in me: *8415
38:16 walked in the search of the d'? * "
Ps 33: 7 layeth up the d' in storehouses. * "
Pr 8:27 compass upon the face of the d': * "
25: 3 for height, and the earth for d', 6012
Isa 7:11 ask it either in the d' or in the 6009
Jon 2: 5 the d' closed me round about, the *8415
M't 18: 6 were drowned in the d' of the sea. 3989
M'r 4: 5 because it had no d' of earth: *899
Ro 8:39 Nor height, nor d', nor any other "
11:33 O the d' of the riches both of the "
Eph 3:18 the breadth, and length, and d', and "

depths
Ex 15: 5 The d' have covered them; they *8415
8 d' were congealed in the heart * "
De 8: 7 of fountains and d' that spring out * "
Ps 68:22 again from the d' of the sea: 4688
71:20 up again from the d' of the earth. 8415
77:16 afraid: the d' also were troubled. "
78:15 them drink as out of the great d'. "
106: 9 so he led them through the d', "
107:26 they go down again to the d': "
130: 1 Out of the d' have I cried unto thee, 4615
Pr 3:20 By his knowledge the d' are 8415
8:24 When there were no d', I was "
9:18 her guests are in the d' of hell. 6010
Isa 51:10 that hath made the d' of the sea 4615
Eze 27:34 by the seas in the d' of the waters "
Mic 7:19 their sins into the d' of the sea. 4688
Re 2:24 have not known the d' of Satan, * 899

deputed
2Sa 15: 3 there is no man d' of the king to hear

deputies
Est 8: 9 the d' and rulers of the provinces *6346
9: 3 the d' and officers of the king, * "
Ac 19:38 the law is open, and there are d': * 446

deputy See also DEPUTIES.
1Ki 22:47 no king in Edom: a d' was king. 5324
Ac 13: 7 was with the d' of the country, * 446
8 turn away the d' from the faith. * "
12 Then the d', when he saw what * "
18:12 when Gallio was d' of Achaia, * "

Derbe (*der'-by*)
Ac 14: 6 and fled unto Lystra and D', 1191
20 he departed with Barnabas to D'. "
16: 1 Then came he to D' and Lystra: "
20: 4 and Secundus; and Gaius of D', and "

deride See also DERIDED.
Hab 1:10 they shall d' every strong hold; *7832

derided
Lu 16:14 all these things: and they d' him.*1592
23:35 the rulers also with them d' him. * "

derision
Job 30: 1 are younger than I have me in d', 7832
Ps 2: 4 the Lord shall have them in d'. 3932
44:13 a scorn and a d' to them that are 7047
59: 8 shalt have all the heathen in d'. 3932
79: 4 a scorn and d' to them that are 7047
119:51 proud have had me greatly in d': 3887
Jer 20: 7 am in d' daily, every one mocketh*7814
8 a reproach unto me, and a d', 7047
48:26 and he also shall be in d'. 7814
27 was not Israel a d' unto thee? "
39 so shall Moab be a d' and a "
La 3:14 I was a d' to all my people; "
Eze 23:32 laughed to scorn and had in d'; 3932
36: 4 which became a prey and d' to the "
Hos 7:16 shall be their d' in the land of Egypt."

descend See also DESCENDED; DESCENDETH; DESCENDING.
Nu 34:11 and the border shall d', and shall*3381
1Sa 26:10 he shall d' into battle, and perish.* "
Ps 49:17 his glory shall not d' after him. "
Isa 5:14 he that rejoiceth, shall d' into it. "
Eze 26:20 them that d' into the pit, with the "
31:16 them that d' into the pit: and all "
M'r 15:32 Let Christ the king of Israel d' *2597
Ac 11: 5 A certain vessel d', as it had been* "
Ro 10: 7 Or, Who shall d' into the deep? "
1Th 4:16 Lord himself shall d' from heaven "

descended
Ex 19:18 the Lord d' upon it in fire: and 3381
33: 9 the cloudy pillar d', and stood at "
34: 5 And the Lord d' in the cloud, "
De 9:21 the brook that d' out of the mount. "
Jos 2:23 returned, and d' from the mountain, "
17: 9 And the coast d' unto the river * "
18:13 the border d' to Ataroth-adar, * "
16 and d' to the valley of Hinnom, * "
16 south, and d' to En-rogel, * "
17 and d' to the stone of Bohan the * "
Ps 133: 3 d' upon the mountains of Zion: * "
Pr 30: 4 ascended up into heaven, or d'? "
M't 7:25, 27 And the rain d', and the floods 2597
28: 2 for the angel of the Lord d' from "
Lu 3:22 the Holy Ghost d' in a bodily shape "
Ac 24: 1 the high priest d' with the elders,* "
Eph 4: 9 but that he also d' first into the "
10 He that d' is the same also that "

descendeth
Jas 3:15 This wisdom d' not from above, *2718

descending
Ge 28:12 angels of God ascending and d' 3381
M't 3:16 Spirit of God d' like a dove, 2597
M'r 1:10 the Spirit like a dove d' upon him "
Joh 1:32 I saw the Spirit d' from heaven "
33 whom thou shalt see the Spirit d', "
51 angels of God ascending and d' "
Ac 10:11 a certain vessel d' unto him, "
Re 21:10 Jerusalem, d' out of heaven from "

descent
Lu 19:37 at the d' of the mount of Olives, 2600
Heb 7: 3 without mother, without d', * 35
6 whose d' is not counted from *1075

describe See also DESCRIBED; DESCRIBETH.
Jos 18: 4 and go through the land, and d' it 3789
6 Ye shall therefore d' the land into "
8 them that went to d' the land, "
8 walk through the land, and d' it, "

described
Jos 18: 9 and d' it by cities into seven parts 3789
J'g 8:14 and he d' unto him the princes of "

describeth
Ro 4: 6 as David also d' the blessedness *3004
10: 5 Moses d' the righteousness which*1125

description
Jos 18: 6 and bring the d' hither to me

descry
J'g 1:23 the house of Joseph sent to d' *8446

desert See also DESERTS.
Ex 3: 1 to the backside of the d', and *4057
5: 3 three days' journey into the d', * "
19: 2 were come to the d' of Sinai, and * "
23:31 and from the d' unto the river: * "
Nu 20: 1 into the d' of Zin in the first * "
27:14 in the d' of Zin, in the strife of * "
33:16 removed from the d' of Sinai, and* "
De 32:10 He found him in a d' land, and "
2Ch 26:10 he built towers in the d', and * "
Job 24: 5 wild asses in the d', go they forth * "

Ps 28: 4 hands; render to them their d·. 1576
78:40 and grieve him in the d·! 3452
102: 6 I am like an owl of the d·. *2723
106:14 and tempted God in the d·. 3452
Isa 13:21 beasts of the d· shall lie there; 6728
21: 1 burden of the d· of the sea. *4057
1 through; so it cometh from the d·,* "
34:14 The wild beasts of the d· shall 6728
35: 1 the d· shall rejoice, and blossom 6160
6 break out, and streams in the d·. "
40: 3 make straight in the d· a highway "
41:19 I will set in the d· the fir tree, "
43:19 wilderness, and rivers in the d·. 3452
20 rivers in the d·, to give drink to my "
51: 3 her d· like the garden of the Lord; 6160
Jer 17: 6 like the heath in the d·, and shall "
25:24 people that dwell in the d·, *4057
50:12 wilderness, a dry land, and a d·. 6160
39 Therefore the wild beasts of the d· 6728
Eze 47: 8 go down into the d·, and go into *6160
M't 14:13 by ship into a d· place apart: 2048
15 This is a d· place, and the time is "
24:26 Behold, he is in the d·; go not * "
M'r 1:45 was without in d· places: and they "
6:31 yourselves apart into a d· place, "
32 they departed into a d· place by "
35 This is a d· place, and now the "
Lu 4:42 departed and went into a d· place: "
9:10 into a d· place belonging to the * "
12 for we are here in a d· place. "
Joh 6:31 fathers did eat manna in the d·; * "
Ac 8:26 Jerusalem unto Gaza, which is d·. "

deserts
Isa 48:21 he led them through the d·: he 2723
Jer 2: 6 a land of d· and of pits, 6160
Eze 7:27 and according to their d· will I 4941
13: 4 are like the foxes in the d·. *2723
Lu 1:80 and was in the d· till the day of 2048
Heb 11:38 wandered in d·, and in mountains,*2047

deserve See also DESERVETH; DESERVING.
Ezr 9:13 us less than our iniquities d·, and

deserveth
Job 11: 6 of thee less than thine iniquity d·.

deserving
J'd 9:16 according to the d· of his hands; 1576

desirable
Eze 23: 6 rulers, all of them d· young men, 2531
12 riding upon horses, all of them d· "
23 d· young men, captains and rulers, "

desire See also DESIRABLE; DESIRED; DESIRES; DESIREST; DESIRETH; DESIRING.
Ge 3:16 thy d· shall be to thy husband, 8669
4: 7 unto thee shall be his d·, and thou "
Ex 10:11 serve the Lord; for that ye did d·. 1245
34:24 neither shall any man d· thy land 2530
De 5:21 shalt thou d· thy neighbour's wife "
7:25 shalt not d· the silver or gold * "
18: 6 come with all the d· of his mind 183
21:11 and hast a d· unto her, that thou 2836
J'g 8:24 I would d· a request of you, 7592
1Sa 9:20 on whom is all the d· of Israel? *2532
23:20 according to all the d· of thy soul 183
2Sa 23: 5 all my salvation, and all my d·, 2656
1Ki 2:20 I d· one small petition of thee; *7592
5: 8 I will do all thy d· concerning 2656
9 thou shalt accomplish my d·, in "
10 fir trees according to all his d·. "
9: 1 all Solomon's d· which he was 2837
11 according to all his d·,) that then 2656
10:13 unto the queen of Sheba all her d·, "
2Ki 4:28 Did I d· a son of my lord? 7592
2Ch 9:12 to the queen of Sheba all her d·, 2656
15:15 sought him with their whole d·; 7522
Ne 1:11 who d· to fear thy name: and *2655
Job 13: 3 and I d· to reason with God. 2654
14:15 thou wilt have a d· to the work of 3700
21:14 we d· not the knowledge of thy 2654
31:16 withheld the poor from their d·, 2656
35 my d· is, that the Almighty would *8420
33:32 speak, for I d· to justify thee. 2654
34:36 My d· is that Job may be tried * 15
36:20 D· not the night, when people are 7602
Ps 10: 3 wicked boasteth of his heart's d·, 8378
17 hast heard the d· of the humble: "
21: 2 Thou hast given him his heart's d·, "
38: 9 Lord, all my d· is before thee; "
40: 6 and offering thou didst not d·; *2654
45:11 shall the king greatly d· thy beauty:183
54: 7 mine eye hath seen his d· upon mine
59:10 let me see my d· upon mine enemies.
70: 2 put to confusion, that d· my hurt.*2655
73:25 upon earth that I d· beside thee. 2654
78:29 for he gave them their own d·; *8378
92:11 shall see my d· upon mine enemies,
11 ears shall hear my d· of the wicked
112: 8 he see his d· upon his enemies.
10 the d· of the wicked shall perish. 8378
118: 7 therefore shall I see my d· upon them
145:16 satisfiest the d· of every living 7522
19 He will fulfil the d· of them that "
Pr 3:15 all the things thou canst d· are 2656
10:24 but the d· of the righteous shall 8378
11:23 The d· of the righteous is only good: "
13:12 when the d· cometh, it is a tree of "
19 The d· accomplished is sweet to "
18: 1 Through d· a man, having separated "
19:22 The d· of a man is his kindness: ‡ "
21:25 The d· of the slothful killeth him; "
23: 6 neither d· thou his dainty meats: 183
24: 1 men, neither d· to be with them. "
Ec 6: 9 than the wandering of the d·: 5315
12: 5 be a burden, and d· shall fail: † 35
Ca 7:10 beloved's, and his d· is toward me. 8669
Isa 26: 8 the d· of our soul is to thy name, 8378
53: 2 no beauty that we should d· him. 2530
Jer 22:27 whereunto they d· to return, *5375, 5315
42:22 the place whither ye d· to go 2654
44:14 which they have a d· to return 5375, 5315
Eze 24:16 away from thee the d· of thine 4261
21 strength, the d· of your eyes, "
25 of their glory, the d· of their eyes, "
Da 2:18 That they would d· mercies of the 1156
11:37 nor the d· of women, nor regard 2532
Ho 10:10 It is in my d· that I should chastise 183
Am 5:18 Woe unto you that d· the day of "
Mic 7: 3 he uttereth his mischievous d·: *5315
Hab 2: 5 who enlargeth his d· as hell, and "
Hag 2: 7 the d· of all nations shall come: *2532
M'r 9:35 If any man d· to be first, *2309
10:35 do for us whatsoever we shall d·.* 154
11:24 What things soever ye d·, when * "
15: 8 began to d· him to do as he had * "
Lu 17:22 ye shall d· to see one of the days 1937
20:46 the scribes, which d· to walk in 2309
22:15 With d· I have desired to eat this 1939
Ac 23:20 The Jews have agreed to d· thee *2065
28:22 we d· to hear of thee what thou 515
Ro 10: 1 Brethren, my heart's d· and prayer 2107
15:23 having a great d· these many * 1974
1Co 14: 1 and d· spiritual gifts, but rather 2206
2Co 7: 7 he told us your earnest d·, your * 1972
11 yea, what vehement d·, yea, what * "
11:12 from them which d· occasion; 2309
12: 6 For though I would d· to glory, "
Ga 4: 9 ye d· again to be in bondage? "
20 I d· to be present with you now, * "
21 Tell me, ye that d· to be under the "
6:12 As many as d· to make a fair shew "
13 but d· to have you circumcised, "
Eph 3:13 I d· that ye faint not at my * 154
Ph'p 1:23 having a d· to depart, and to be 1939
4:17 Not because I d· a gift: * 1934
17 but I d· fruit that may abound * "
Col 1: 9 and to d· that ye might be filled * 154
1Th 2:17 to see your face with great d·. 1939
1Ti 3: 1 If a man d· the office of a bishop, *3713
Heb 6:11 And we d· that every one of you 1937
11:16 But now they d· a better country, 3713
Jas 4: 2 kill, and d· to have, and cannot *2206
1Pe 1:12 which things the angels d· to look 1937
2: 2 d· the sincere milk of the word, *1971
Re 9: 6 and shall d· to die, and death shall 1937

desired See also DESIREDST.
Ge 3: 6 and a tree to be d· to make one 2530
1Sa 12:13 chosen, and whom ye have d·! *7592
1Ki 9:19 that which Solomon d· to build in 2836
2Ch 8: 6 all that Solomon d· to build in "
11:23 And he d· many wives. *7592
21:20 and departed without being d·. 2532
Es 2:13 whatsoever she d· was given her 559
Job 20:20 shall not save of that which he d·.*2530
Ps 19:10 More to be d· are they than gold, "
27: 4 One thing have I d· of the Lord, *7592
107:30 bringeth them unto their d· haven.†2656
132:13 he hath d· it for his habitation. 183
14 here will I dwell; for I have d· it. "
Pr 8:11 all the things that may be d· are 2656
21:20 There is treasure to be d· and oil *2530
Ec 2:10 whatsoever mine eyes d· I kept 7592
Isa 1:29 the oaks which ye have d·, and ye 2530
26: 9 With my soul have I d· thee 183
Jer 17:16 neither have I d· the woeful day; "
Da 2:16 Daniel went in, and d· of the king 1156
23 known unto me now what we d· "
Ho 6: 6 For I d· mercy, and not sacrifice *2654
Mic 7: 1 my soul d· the first ripe fruit * 183
Zep 2: 1 gather together, O nation not d·; *3700
M't 13:17 righteous men have d· to see those 1939
16: 1 d· him that he would shew them *1905
M'r 15: 6 one prisoner, whomsoever they d·.* 154
Lu 7:36 And one of the Pharisees d· him 2065
9: 9 things? And he d· to see him. *2212
10:24 prophets and kings have d· to see 2309
22:15 With desire I have d· to eat this 1937
31 Satan hath d· to have you, that *1809
23:25 into prison, whom they had d·; * 154
Jo 12:21 d· him, saying, Sir, we would see *2065
Ac 3:14 the Just, and d· a murderer to * 154
7:46 d· to find a tabernacle for the God * "
8:31 And he d· Philip that he would *3870
9: 2 d· of him letters to Damascus to * 154
12:20 their friend, d· peace; because * "
13: 7 and d· to hear the word of God. *1934
21 afterward they d· a king: and * 154
28 yet d· they Pilate that he should * "
16:39 them out, and d· them to depart *2065
18:20 When they d· him to tarry longer * "
25: 3 d· favour against him, that he * 154
28:14 and were d· to tarry with them *3870
1Co 16:12 Apollos, I greatly d· him to come * "
2Co 8: 6 Insomuch that we d· Titus, that * "
12:18 I d· Titus, and with him I sent * "
1Jo 5:15 the petitions that we d· of him. * 154

desiredst
De 18:16 According to all that thou d· of the 7592
M't 18:32 all that debt, because thou d· me: *3870

desires
Ps 37: 4 give thee the d· of thine heart. 4862
140: 8 Grant not, O Lord, the d· of the 3970
Eph 2: 3 fulfilling the d· of the flesh and of 2307

desirest
Ps 51: 6 thou d· truth in the inward parts: 2654
16 For thou d· not sacrifice; else * "

desireth
De 14:26 or for whatsoever thy soul d·: *7592
1Sa 2:16 take as much as thy soul d·; 8378
18:25 The king d· not any dowry, 2656
1Sa 20: 4 Whatsoever thy soul d·, 559
2Sa 3:21 reign over all that thine heart d·. 8378
1Ki 11:37 according to all that thy soul d·, "
Job 7: 2 As a servant earnestly d· the 7602
23:13 what his soul d·, even that he 183
Ps 34:12 What man is he that d· life, 2655
68:16 the hill which God d· to dwell in; *2530
Pr 12:12 The wicked d· the net of evil men: "
13: 4 The soul of the sluggard d·, and 183
21:10 The soul of the wicked d· evil: "
Ec 6: 2 for his soul of all that he d·, "
Lu 5:39 drunk old wine straightway d· new: 2309
14:32 and d· conditions of peace. *2065
1Ti 3: 1 of a bishop, he d· a good work. 1937

desiring
M't 12:46 without, d· to speak with him. *2212
47 without, d· to speak with thee. * "
20:20 and d· a certain thing of him. * 154
Lu 8:20 stand without, d· to see thee. 2309
16:21 d· to be fed with the crumbs 1937
Ac 9:38 d· him that he would not delay *3870
19:31 d· him that he would not * "
25:15 d· to have judgment against him. * 154
2Co 5: 2 earnestly d· to be clothed upon *1971
1Th 3: 6 d· greatly to see us, as we also * "
1Ti 1: 7 D· to be teachers of the law; 2309
2Ti 1: 4 Greatly d· to see thee, being 1971

desirous
Pr 23: 3 Be not d· of his dainties: for they 183
Lu 23: 8 for he was d· to see him a long 2309
Joh 16:19 they were d· to ask him, and said "
2Co 11:32 garrison, d· to apprehend me: * "
Gal 5:26 Let us not be d· of vain glory, *2755
1Th 2: 8 So being affectionately d· of you, 2442

desolate
Ge 47:19 not die, that the land be not d·. 3456
Ex 23:29 lest the land become d·, and the 8077
Le 26:22 and your high ways shall be d·. 8074
33 your land shall be d·, and your *8077
34 as long as it lieth d·, and ye be in 8074
35 As long as it lieth d·, it shall rest; "
43 while she lieth d· without them: "
2Sa 13:20 Tamar remained d· in her brother 8076
2Ch 36:21 as long as she lay d·, she kept 8074
Job 3:14 built d· places for themselves; *2723
15:28 he dwelleth in d· cities, and in 3582
34 of hypocrites shall be d·, and fire *1565
16: 7 hast made d· all my company. 8074
30: 3 in former time d· and waste. *7722
38:27 satisfy the d· and waste ground, "
Ps 25:16 upon me; for I am d· and afflicted. 3173
34:21 hate the righteous shall be d·. * 816
22 them that trust in him shall be d·.* "
40:15 Let them be d· for a reward of 8074
69:25 Let their habitation be d·; and "
109:10 bread also out of their d· places. 2723
143: 4 me; my heart within me is d·. 8074
Isa 1: 7 Your country is d·, your cities are 8077
7 in your presence, and it is d·, "
3:26 being d· shall sit upon the ground. 5352
5: 9 many houses shall be d·, even 8047
6:11 and the land be utterly d·, *8077
7:19 all of them in the d· valleys, 1327
13: 9 fierce anger, to lay the land d·: *8047
22 shall cry in their d· houses, 490
15: 6 the waters of Nimrim shall be d·: 4923
24: 6 they that dwell therein are d·: * 816
27:10 the defenced city shall be d·, * 910
49: 8 cause to inherit the d· heritages; 8076
19 thy waste and thy d· places, and 8074
21 children, and am d·, a captive, *1565
54: 1 the children of the d· than the 8074
3 make the d· cities to be inhabited. 8077
59:10 we are in d· places as dead men. * 820
62: 4 thy land any more be termed D·: 8077
Jer 2:12 be ye very d·, saith the Lord, 2717
4: 7 his place to make thy land d·; 8047
27 The whole land shall be d·; yet *8077
6: 8 lest I make thee d·, a land not * "
7:34 bride: for the land shall be d·. *2723
9:11 will make the cities of Judah d·, *8077
10:22 to make the cities of Judah d·, * "
25 and have made his habitation d·. *8074
12:10 pleasant portion a d· wilderness. 8077
11 They have made it d·, and *8074
11 being d· it mourneth unto me; *8077
11 the whole land is made d·, because 8074
18:16 To make their land d·, and a *8047
19: 8 I will make this city d·, and an * "
25:38 for their land is d· because of * "
26: 9 this city shall be d· without an 2717
32:43 It is d· without man or beast; 8077
33:10 which ye say shall be d· without *2717
10 streets of Jerusalem, that are d·, 8074
12 Again in this place, which is d· *2717
44: 6 they are wasted and d·, as at 8077
46:19 for Noph shall be waste and d· *3341
48: 9 for the cities thereof shall be d·, *8047
34 waters also of Nimrim shall be d·. 4923
49: 2 it shall be a d· heap, and her 8077
20 shall make their habitations d· 8074
50: 3 shall make her land d·, and none 8047
13 but it shall be wholly d·: 8077
45 he shall make their habitation d· 8074
51:26 but thou shalt be d· for ever, 8077
62 but that it shall be d· for ever. "
La 1: 4 feasts: all her gates are d·: and 8076
13 made me d· and faint all the day. "
16 my children are d·, because the "
3:11 in pieces: he hath made me d·. "
4: 5 They that did feed delicately are d· 8074
5:18 the mountain of Zion, which is d·, "
Eze 6: 4 And your altars shall be d·, and "
6 the high places shall be d·; that 3456
6 may be laid waste and made d·, 816

Eze 6:14 and make the land d·, yea, *8077
14 more d· than the wilderness *8047
12:19 that her land may be d· from all 3456
20 waste, and the land shall be d·; *8077
14:15 spoil it, so that it be d·, "
16 delivered, but the land shall be d·. "
15: 8 I will make the land d·, because "
19: 7 he knew their d· places, and he * 490
7 their cities; and the land was d·, 3456
20:26 that I might make them d·, to the 8074
25: 3 land of Israel, when it was d·; * "
13 I will make it d· from Teman; 2723
26:19 I shall make thee a d· city, 2717
20 of the earth, in places d· of old, 2723
29: 9 the land of Egypt shall be d· *8077
10 of Egypt utterly waste and d·, * "
12 I will make the land of Egypt d· * "
12 midst of the countries that are d·, 8074
12 laid waste shall be d· forty years: 8077
30: 7 they shall be d· in the midst of 8074
7 midst of the countries that are d·, "
14 And I will make Pathros d·, and "
32:15 I shall make the land of Egypt d·, 8077
33:28 For I will lay the land most d·, *8077
28 mountains of Israel shall be d·, 8074
29 when I have laid the land most d· *8077
35: 3 I will make thee most d·. * "
4 cities waste, and thou shalt be d·, "
7 will I make mount Seir most d·, * "
12 They are laid d·, they are given 8074
14 rejoiceth, I will make thee d·. 8077
15 house of Israel, because it was d·, 8074
15 I do unto thee: thou shalt be d·, 8077
36: 3 Because they have made you d·, 8074
4 to the valleys, to the d· wastes, 8076
34 And the d· land shall be tilled, 8074
34 whereas it lay d· in the sight *8077
35 This land that was d· is become 8074
35 waste and d· and ruined cities "
36 places, and plant that that was d·: "
38:12 thine hand upon the d· places *2723
Da 9:17 upon thy sanctuary that is d·, 8074
27 he shall make it d·, even until the "
27 shall be poured upon the d·. †8076
11:31 the abomination that maketh d·. 8074
12:11 abomination that maketh d· set up, "
Ho 5: 9 Ephraim shall be d· in the day *8047
13:16 Samaria shall become d·; for she* 816
Joe 1:17 the garners are laid d·, the barns 8074
18 the flocks of sheep are made d·. 816
2: 3 behind them a d· wilderness; 8077
20 him into a land barren and d·, "
3:19 and Edom shall be a d· wilderness, "
Am 7: 9 high places of Isaac shall be d·, 8074
Mic 1: 7 the idols thereof will I lay d·: 8077
6:13 making thee d· because of thy sins. 8074
7:13 land shall be d· because of them 8077
Zep 3: 6 their towers are d·; I made their 8074
Zec 7:14 the land was d· after them, that "
14 for they laid the pleasant land d·. 8047
Mal 1: 4 return and build the d· places; *2723
M't 23:38 your house is left unto you d·. 2048
Lu 13:35 your house is left unto you d·: "
Ac 1:20 Let his habitation be d·, and let "
Gal 4:27 the d· hath many more children "
1Ti 5: 5 that is a widow indeed, and d·, 3443
Re 17:16 shall make her d· and naked, 2049
18:19 for in one hour is she made d·. "

desolation See also DESOLATIONS.
Le 26:31 bring your sanctuaries unto d·, 8074
32 And I will bring the land into d·: "
Jos 8:28 for ever, even a d· unto this day. 8077
2Ki 22:19 should become a d· and a curse, 8047
2Ch 30: 7 gave them up to d·, as ye see. "
Job 30:14 in the d· they rolled themselves *7722
Ps 73:19 How are they brought into d·, 8047
Pr 1:27 When your fear cometh as d·, *7584
3:25 neither of the d· of the wicked, 7722
Isa 10: 3 and in the d· which shall come "
17: 9 of Israel: and there shall be d·. 8077
24:12 In the city is left d·, and the gate 8047
47:11 d· shall come upon thee suddenly, 7722
51:19 d·, and destruction, and the 7701
64:10 is a wilderness, Jerusalem a d·. 8077
Jer 22: 5 that this house shall become a d·. 2723
25:11 this whole land shall be a d·, "
18 make them a d·, an astonishment, "
34:22 Judah a d· without an inhabitant. 8077
44: 2 this day they are a d·, and no man 2723
22 therefore is your land a d·, and an "
49:13 Bozrah shall become a d·, *8047
17 Edom shall be a d·: every one * "
33 for dragons, and a d· for ever: 8077
50:23 Babylon become a d· among the 8047
51:29 Babylon a d· without an inhabitant. "
43 Her cities are a d·, a dry land, * "
La 3:47 come upon us, d· and destruction. *7612
Eze 7:27 prince shall be clothed with d·, 8077
23:33 the cup of astonishment and d·, "
Da 8:13 transgression of d·, to give both *8074
Ho 12: 1 he daily increaseth lies and d·; 7701
Joe 3:19 Egypt shall be a d·, and Edom 8077
Mic 6:16 that I should make thee a d·, 8047
Zep 1:13 a booty, and their houses a d·: "
15 a day of wasteness, and d·, a day 4875
2: 4 be forsaken, and Ashkelon a d·: 8077
9 and salt pits, and a perpetual d·: "
13 will make Nineveh a d·, and dry "
14 d· shall be in the thresholds: 2721
15 how is she become a d·, a place 8047
M't 12:25 against itself is brought to d·; 2049
24:15 the abomination of d·, spoken of 2050
M'r 13:14 ye shall see the abomination of d·, 2050
Lu 11:17 against itself is brought to d·; 2049
21:20 know that the d· thereof is nigh. 2050

desolations
Ezr 9: 9 to repair the d· thereof, and to *2723
Ps 46: 8 what d· he hath made in the 8047
74: 3 thy feet unto the perpetual d·; *4876
Isa 61: 4 they shall raise up the former d·, 8074
4 cities, the d· of many generations. "
Jer 25: 9 and an hissing, and perpetual d·. 2723
12 and will make it perpetual d·. *8077
Eze 35: 9 I will make thee perpetual d·, and "
Da 9: 2 years in the d· of Jerusalem. 2723
18 thine eyes, and behold our d·, 8074
26 end of the war d· are determined. "

despair See also DESPAIRED.
1Sa 27: 1 and Saul shall d· of me, to seek 2976
Ec 2:20 my heart to d· of all the labour "
2Co 4: 8 we are perplexed, but not in d·; 1820

despaired
2Co 1: 8 insomuch that we d· even of life: 1820

desperate
Job 6:26 and speeches of one that is d·, 2976
Isa 17:11 the day of grief and of d· sorrow. 605

desperately
Jer 17: 9 above all things, and d· wicked: 605

despise See also DESPISED; DESPISEST; DESPISETH; DESPISING.
Le 26:15 if ye shall d· my statutes, or if *3988
1Sa 2:30 and they that d· me shall be lightly 959
2Sa 19:43 why then did ye d· us, that our 7043
Es 1:17 that they shall d· their husbands * 959
Job 5:17 d· not thou the chastening of the 3988
9:21 my soul: I would d· my life. "
10: 3 shouldst d· the work of thine hands, "
31:13 did d· the cause of my manservant "
Ps 51:17 heart, O God, thou wilt not d·. 959
73:20 awakest, thou shalt d· their image. "
102:17 destitute, and not d· their prayer. "
Pr 1: 7 fools d· wisdom and instruction. 936
3:11 d· not the chastening of the Lord; 3988
6:30 Men do not d· a thief, if he steal 936
23: 9 he will d· the wisdom of thy words. "
22 d· not thy mother when she is old. "
Isa 30:12 Because ye d· this word, and trust 3988
Jer 4:30 thy lovers will d· thee, they "
23:17 They say still unto them that d· 5006
La 1: 8 all that honoured her d· her, 2107
Eze 16:57 of the Philistines, which d· thee *7590
28:26 upon all those that d· them "
Am 5:21 I hate, I d· your feast days, and I 3988
Mal 1: 6 you, O priests, that d· my name. 959
M't 6:24 hold to the one, and d· the other. 2706
18:10 ye d· not one of these little ones; "
Lu 16:13 hold to the one, and d· the other. "
Ro 14: 3 Let not him that eateth d· him *1848
1Co 11:22 or d· ye the church of God, 2706
16:11 Let no man therefore d· him: 1848
1Th 5:20 D· not prophesyings. Prove all "
1Ti 4:12 Let no man d· thy youth; but be 2706
6: 2 masters, let them not d· them, "
Tit 2:15 authority. Let no man d· thee. 4065
Heb 12: 5 d· not thou the chastening of *3643
2Pe 2:10 uncleanness, and d· government. 2706
Jude 8 d· dominion, and speak evil of * 114

despised
Ge 16: 4 her mistress was d· in her eyes. 7043
5 conceived, I was d· in her eyes: "
25:34 way: thus Esau d· his birthright. 959
Le 26:43 because they d· my judgments, *3988
Nu 11:20 ye have d· the Lord which is * "
14:31 know the land which ye have d·. * "
15:31 he hath d· the word of the Lord, 959
J'g 9:38 this the people that thou hast d·? 3988
1Sa 10:27 And they d· him, and brought him 959
2Sa 6:16 and she d· him in her heart. "
12: 9 d· the commandment of the Lord, "
10 because thou hast d· me, and hast "
2Ki 19:21 the daughter of Zion hath d· thee, "
1Ch 15:29 and she d· him in her heart. "
2Ch 36:16 and d· his words, and misused his "
Ne 2:19 and d· us, and said, What is this "
4: 4 Hear, O our God; for we are d·: 939
Job 12: 5 a lamp d· in the thought of him * 937
19:18 young children d· me; I arose, *3988
Ps 22: 6 of men, and d· of the people. 959
24 not d· nor abhorred the afflictions "
53: 5 because God hath d· them. *3988
106:24 Yea, they d· the pleasant land, "
119:141 I am small and d·: yet do not I 959
Pr 1:30 counsel: they d· all my reproof. 5006
5:12 and my heart d· reproof; "
12: 8 is of a perverse heart shall be d·. 937
9 He that is d·, and hath a servant, *7034
Ec 9:16 the poor man's wisdom is d·, 959
Ca 8: 1 kiss thee; yea, I should not be d·. 937
Isa 5:24 d· the word of the Holy One of 5006
33: 8 he hath d· the cities, he regardeth 3988
37:22 d· thee, and laughed thee to scorn; 959
53: 3 He is d· and rejected of men; a "
3 he was d·, and we esteemed him not. "
60:14 all they that d· thee shall bow 5006
Jer 33:24 they have d· my people, that they* "
49:15 the heathen, and d· among men. 959
La 2: 6 d· in the indignation of his anger 5006
Eze 16:59 hast d· the oath in breaking the 959
17:16 oath he d·, and whose covenant "
18 Seeing he d· the oath by breaking "
19 surely mine oath that he hath d·, "
20:13 they d· my judgments, which if *3988
16 they d· my judgments, and walked* "
24 d· my statutes, and had polluted * "
22: 8 Thou hast d· mine holy things, 959
28:24 round about them, that d· them; *7590
Am 2: 4 they have d· the law of the Lord, *3988
Ob 2 the heathen: thou art greatly d·. 959
Zec 4:10 hath d· the day of small things? 937
Mal 1: 6 Wherein have we d· thy name? 959
Lu 18: 9 were righteous, and d· others: *1848
Ac 19:27 Diana should be d·, *1519, 3762, 3049
1Co 1:28 things which are d·, hath God 1848
4:10 ye are honourable, but we are d·. * 820
Ga 4:14 in my flesh ye d· not, nor rejected; 1848
Heb 10:28 He that d· Moses' law died without* 114
Jas 2: 6 But ye have d· the poor. Do not * 818

despisers
Ac 13:41 Behold, ye d·, and wonder, and 2707
2Ti 3: 3 fierce, d· of those that are good, * 865

despisest
Ro 2: 4 d· thou the riches of his goodness 2706

despiseth
Job 36: 5 God is mighty, and d· not any: 3988
Ps 69:33 the poor, and d· not his prisoners. 959
Pr 11:12 void of wisdom d· his neighbour: 936
13:13 Whoso d· the word shall be "
14: 2 that is perverse in his ways d· him. 959
21 He that d· his neighbour sinneth: 936
15: 5 A fool d· his father's instruction: 5006
20 but a foolish man d· his mother. 959
32 refuseth instruction d· his own 3988
19:16 but he that d· his ways shall die. * 959
30:17 father, and d· to obey his mother, 936
Isa 33:15 he that d· the gain of oppressions, 3988
49: 7 to him whom man d·, to him whom 960
Lu 10:16 he that d· you d· me; * 114
16 and he that d· me d· him that sent* "
1Th 4: 8 He therefore that d·, d· not man, * "

despising
Heb 12: 2 the cross, d· the shame, and is 2706

despite See also DESPITEFUL.
Eze 25: 6 rejoiced in heart with all thy d· 7589
Heb 10:29 and hath done d· unto the Spirit 1796

despiteful
Eze 25:15 taken vengeance with a d· heart, *7589
36: 5 with d· minds, to cast it out for * "
Ro 1:30 Backbiters, haters of God, d·, * 5197

despitefully
M't 5:44 pray for them which d· use you, * 1908
Lu 6:28 pray for them which d· use you. "
Ac 14: 5 to use them d·, and to stone them,* 5195

destitute
Ge 24:27 not left d· my master of his mercy *5800
Ps 102:17 will regard the prayer of the d·, 6199
141: 8 is my trust; leave not my soul d·. 6168
Pr 15:21 joy to him that is d· of wisdom: *2638
Eze 32:15 and the country shall be d· of that 8047
1Ti 6: 5 corrupt minds and d· of the truth,* 650
Heb 11:37 being d·, afflicted, tormented; 5302
Jas 2:15 be naked, and d· of daily food, *3007

destroy See also DESTROYED; DESTROYEST; DESTROYETH; DESTROYING.
Ge 6: 7 And the Lord said, I will d· man 4229
13 I will d· them with the earth. 7843
17 to d· all flesh, wherein is the breath "
7: 4 that I have made will I d· from off 4229
9:11 more be a flood to d· the earth. 7843
15 more become a flood to d· all flesh. "
18:23 d· the righteous with the wicked? *5595
24 wilt thou also d· and not spare * "
28 thou d· all the city for lack of five? 7843
28 there forty and five, I will not d· it. "
31 I will not d· it for twenty's sake. "
32 I will not d· it for ten's sake. "
19:13 we will d· this place, because the "
13 the Lord hath sent us to d· it. "
14 place; for the Lord will d· this city. "
Ex 8: 9 to d· the frogs from thee and thy *3772
12:13 be upon you to d· you, when I 4889
15: 9 my sword, my hand shall d· them. 3423
23:27 d· all the people to whom thou *2000
34:13 But ye shall d· their altars, *5422
Le 23:30 same soul will I d· from among his 6
26:22 d· your cattle, and make you few 3772
30 And I will d· your high places, 8045
44 to d· them utterly, and to break 3615
Nu 21: 2 then I will utterly d· their cities. 2763
24:17 and d· all the children of Sheth. *6979
19 and shall d· him that remaineth 6
32:15 and ye shall d· all this people. 7843
33:52 before you, and d· all their pictures, 6
52 and d· all their molten images, "
De 1:27 hand of the Amorites, to d· us. 8045
2:15 to d· them from among the host, 2000
4:31 d· thee, nor forget the covenant of 7843
6:15 and d· thee from off the face of 8045
7: 2 smite them, and utterly d· them; 2763
4 against you, and d· thee suddenly. 8045
5 ye shall d· their altars, and break *5422
10 hate him to their face, to d· them: 6
23 and shall d· them with a mighty *2000
24 thou shalt d· their name from * 6
9: 3 a consuming fire he shall d· them, 8045
3 thou drive them out, and d· them* 6
14 Let me alone, that I may d· them, 8045
19 was wroth against you to d· you. "
25 the Lord had said he would d· you. "
26 God, d· not thy people and thine 7843
10:10 and the Lord would not d· thee. "
12: 2 Ye shall utterly d· all the places, 6
3 and d· the names of them out of * "
20:17 But thou shalt utterly d· them; 2763
19 shalt not d· the trees thereof by 7843
20 thou shalt d· and cut them down; "
28:63 Lord will rejoice over you to d· you, 6
31: 3 d· these nations from before thee, 8045
32:25 shall d· both the young man and 7921
33:27 thee; and shall say, D· them. 8045

Jos 7: 7 hand of the Amorites, to d' us? * 6
12 d' the accursed from among you. 8045
9:24 to d' all the inhabitants of the land "
11:20 that he might d' them utterly, 2763
20 favour, but that he might d' them, 8045
22:33 d' the land wherein the children 7843
J'g 6: 5 they entered into the land to d' it. "
21:11 Ye shall utterly d' every male, 2763
1Sa 15: 3 smite Amalek, and utterly d' all "
6 the Amalekites, lest I d' you with 622
9 and would not utterly d' them: 2763
18 d' the sinners the Amalekites, "
23:10 to d' the city for my sake. 7843
24:21 that thou wilt not d' my name 8045
26: 9 D' him not: for who can stretch 7843
15 came one of the people in to d' the "
2Sa 1:14 hand to d' the Lord's anointed? "
14: 7 and we will d' the heir also: 8045
11 revengers of blood to d' any more, 7843
11 lest they d' my son. And he said, 8045
16 the man that would d' me and my "
20:19 seekest to d' a city and a mother 4191
20 that I should swallow up or d'. 7843
22:41 I might d' them that hate me. *6789
24:16 his hand upon Jerusalem to d' it, 7843
1Ki 9:21 also were not able utterly to d', 2763
13:34 and to d' it from off the face of the 8045
16:12 did Zimri d' all the house Baasha, "
2Ki 8:19 Yet the Lord would not d' Judah 7843
10:19 he might d' the worshippers of Baal 6
13:23 would not d' them, neither cast 7843
18:25 Lord against this place to d' it? "
25 Go up against this land, and d' it. "
24: 2 sent them against Judah to d' it, 6
1Ch 21:15 an angel unto Jerusalem to d' it: 7843
2Ch 12: 7 I will not d' them, but I will grant "
12 he would not d' him altogether: "
20:23 Seir, utterly to slay and d' them: 8045
23 every one helped to d' another, 4889
21: 7 would not d' the house of David, 7843
25:16 God hath determined to d' thee, "
35:21 who is with me, that he d' thee not. "
Ezr 6:12 d' all kings and people, that shall*4049
12 to alter and to d' this house of God2255
Es 3: 6 Haman sought to d' all the Jews 8045
13 to d', to kill, and to cause to perish, "
4: 7 treasuries for the Jews, to d' them. 6
8 was given at Shushan to d' them, 8045
8: 5 which he wrote to d' the Jews which 6
11 d', to slay, and to cause to perish, 8045
9:24 devised against the Jews to d' them, 6
24 to consume them, and to d' them; "
Job 2: 3 him, to d' him without cause. 1104
6: 9 it would please God to d' me; *1792
8:18 If he d' him from his place, *1104
10: 8 round about; yet thou dost d' me. "
19:26 my skin worms d' this body, †5362
Ps 5: 6 shalt d' them that speak leasing: 6
10 D' thou them, O God; let them * 816
18:40 I might d' them that hate me. *6789
21:10 fruit shalt thou d' from the earth, 6
28: 5 d' them, and not build them up. *2040
40:14 that seek after my soul to d' it; 5595
52: 5 God shall likewise d' thee for ever, 5422
55: 9 D', O Lord, and divide their 1104
63: 9 those that seek my soul, to d' it, 7722
69: 4 they that would d' me, being *6789
74: 8 Let us d' them together: they *3238
101: 8 early d' all the wicked of the land; 6789
106:23 he would d' them, had not Moses 8045
23 his wrath, lest he should d' them. 7843
34 They did not d' the nations, 8045
118:10, 11, 12 of the Lord will I d' them. *4135
119:95 wicked have waited for me to d' me: 6
143:12 and d' all them that afflict my soul: "
144: 6 out thine arrows, and d' them. *1949
145:20 but all the wicked will he d'. 8045
Pr 1:32 the prosperity of fools shall d' them. 6
11: 3 of transgressors shall d' them. 7703
15:25 will d' the house of the proud: *5255
21: 7 of the wicked shall d' them; *1641
Ec 5: 6 and d' the work of thine hands? 2254
7:16 why shouldest thou d' thyself? 8074
Isa 3:12 and d' the way of thy paths. 1104
10: 7 d' and cut off nations not a few. 8045
11: 9 shall not hurt nor d' in all my 7843
15 Lord shall utterly d' the tongue of 2763
13: 5 indignation, to d' the whole land. 2254
9 d' the sinners thereof out of it. 8045
19: 3 and I will d' the counsel thereof: 1104
23:11 city, to d' the strong holds thereof. 8045
25: 7 And he will d' in this mountain 1104
32: 7 wicked devices to d' the poor with 2254
36:10 Lord against this land to d' it? 7843
10 Go up against this land, and d' it. "
42:14 I will d' and devour at once. *5395
51:13 as if he were ready to d'? 7843
54:16 I have created the waster to d'. 2254
65: 8 D' it not; for a blessing is in it: 7843
8 sakes, that I may not d' them all. "
25 They shall not hurt nor d' in all my "
Jer 1:10 to pull down, and to d', and to 6
5:10 Go ye up upon her walls, and d'; 7843
6: 5 by night, and let us d' her palaces. "
11:19 Let us d' the tree with the fruit "
12:17 pluck up and d' that nation, * 6
13:14 nor have mercy, but d' them. 7843
15: 3 of the earth, to devour and d'. "
6 my hand against thee, and d' thee; "
7 I will d' my people, since they return 6
17:18 d' them with double destruction. 7665
18: 7 to pull down, and to d' it; 6
23: 1 Woe be unto the pastors that d' and "
25: 9 utterly d' them, and make them 2763
31:28 break down, and to d', and to afflict: 6
36:29 certainly come and d' this land, 7843

Jer 46: 8 I will d' the city and the inhabitants 6
48:18 and he shall d' thy strong holds. *7843
49: 9 they will d' till they have enough. "
38 and will d' from thence the king 6
50:21 waste and utterly d' after them, 2763
26 her up as heaps, and d' her utterly: "
51: 3 men, d' ye utterly all her host. "
11 device is against Babylon, to d' it; 7843
20 and with thee will I d' kingdoms; "
La 2: 8 Lord hath purposed to d' the wall "
3:66 Persecute and d' them in anger 8045
Eze 5:16 and which I will send to d' you: 7843
6: 3 and I will d' your high places. 6
9: 8 wilt thou d' all the residue of Israel 7843
14: 9 and will d' him from the midst 8045
21:31 of brutish men, and skilful to d'. 4889
22:27 to shed blood, and to d' souls, 6
30 the land, that I should not d' it; 7843
25: 7 I will d' thee; and thou shalt know 8045
15 heart, to d' it for the old hatred; 4889
16 and d' the remnant of the sea coast. 6
26: 4 they shall d' the walls of Tyrus, 7843
12 walls, and d' thy pleasant houses: 5422
28:16 I will d' thee, O covering cherub, 6
30:11 shall be brought to d' the land: 7843
13 I will also d' the idols, and I will 6
32:13 I will d' also all the beasts thereof "
34:16 I will d' the fat and the strong; 8045
43: 3 saw when I came to d' the city: 7843
Da 2:12 to d' all the wise men of Babylon. 7
24 to d' the wise men of Babylon. "
24 D' not the wise men of Babylon: "
4:23 Hew the tree down, and d' it; 2255
7:26 consume and to d' it unto the end. 7
8:24 d' wonderfully, and shall prosper, 7843
24 d' the mighty and the holy people. "
25 heart, and by peace shall d' many: "
9:26 shall d' the city and the sanctuary; "
11:26 portion of his meat shall d' him, 7665
44 shall go forth with great fury to d', 8045
Ho 2:12 will d' her vines and her fig trees, *8074
4: 5 the night, and I will d' thy mother 1820
11: 9 I will not return to d' Ephraim: 7843
Am 9: 8 and I will d' it from off the face of 8045
8 I will not utterly d' the house of "
Ob 8 even d' the wise men out of Edom, 6
Mic 2:10 it is polluted, it shall d' you, *2254
5:10 of thee, and I will d' thy chariots: 6
14 of thee: so will I d' thy cities. 8045
Zep 2: 5 the Philistines, I will even d' thee, 6
13 against the north, and d' Assyria; "
Hag 2:22 d' the strength of the kingdoms 8045
Zec 12: 9 seek to d' all the nations that come "
Mal 3:11 he shall not d' the fruits of your 7843
M't 2:13 seek the young child to d' him. 622
5:17 not that I am come to d' the law, 2647
17 I am not come to d', but to fulfil. "
10:28 able to d' both soul and body in 622
12:14 against him, how they might d' him. "
21:41 He will miserably d' those wicked "
26:61 said, I am able to d' the temple 2647
27:20 should ask Barabbas, and d' Jesus. 622
M'r 1:24 art thou come to d' us? I know thee "
3: 6 against him, how they might d' him. "
9:22 and into the waters, to d' him: "
11:18 sought how they might d' him: "
12: 9 will come and d' the husbandmen, "
14:58 I will d' this temple that is made 2647
Lu 4:34 Nazareth? art thou come to d' us? 622
6: 9 or to do evil? to save life, or to d' it? "
9:56 is not come to d' men's lives, but * "
19:47 chief of the people sought to d' him, "
20:16 come and d' these husbandmen, "
Joh 2:19 D' this temple, and in three days 3089
10:10 for to steal, and to kill, and to d': 622
Ac 6:14 Jesus of Nazareth shall d' this 2647
Ro 14:15 D' not him with thy meat, for whom 622
14:20 For meat d' not the work of God. *2647
1Co 1:19 I will d' the wisdom of the wise, 622
3:17 temple of God, him shall God d'; 5351
6:13 God shall d' both it and them. *2673
2Th 2: 8 and shall d' with the brightness * "
Heb 2:14 through death he might d' him * "
Jas 4:12 who is able to save and to d': 622
1Jo 3: 8 that he might d' the works of the 3089
Re 11:18 d' them which d' the earth. 1311

destroyed

Ge 7:23 And every living substance was d' 4229
23 and they were d' from the earth: "
13:10 before the Lord d' Sodom and 7843
19:29 when God d' the cities of the plain, "
34:30 and I shall be d', I and my house. 8045
Ex 10: 7 knowest thou not yet that Egypt is d'? 6
22:20 Lord only, he shall be utterly d'. 2763
Nu 21: 3 and they utterly d' them and their "
De 1:44 and d' you in Seir, even unto *3807
2:12 them, when they had d' them from 8045
21 but the Lord d' them before them; "
22 in Seir, when he d' the Horims "
23 out of Caphtor, d' them, and dwelt "
34 and utterly d' the men, and the 2763
3: 6 And we utterly d' them, as we did "
4: 3 thy God hath d' them from among 8045
26 days upon it, but shall utterly be d'. "
7:20 hide themselves from thee, be d'.* 6
23 destruction, until they be d'. 8045
24 before thee, until thou have d' them. "
9: 8 was angry with you to have d' you. "
20 angry with Aaron to have d' him: "
11: 4 how the Lord hath d' them unto this 6
12:30 after that they be d' from before 8045
28:20 until thou be d', and until thou "
24 down upon thee, until thou be d'. "
45 and overtake thee, till thou be d'; "
48 thy neck, until he have d' thee. "

De 28:51 fruit of thy land, until thou be d'. 8045
51 thy sheep, until he have d' thee. * 6
61 bring upon thee, until thou be d'. 8045
31: 4 the land of them, whom he d'. "
Jos 2:10 Sihon and Og, whom ye utterly d'. 2763
6:21 And they utterly d' all that was in "
8:26 until he had utterly d' all the "
10: 1 taken Ai, and had utterly d' it, "
28 and the king thereof he utterly d'. "
35 were therein he utterly d' that day. "
37 but d' it utterly, and all the souls "
39 and utterly d' all the souls that "
40 but utterly d' all that breathed, "
11:12 he utterly d' them, as Moses the "
14 until they had d' them, neither left 8045
21 Joshua d' them utterly with their 2763
23:15 until he have d' you from off this 8045
24: 8 and d' them from before you. "
J'g 1:17 Zephath, and utterly d' it. 2763
4:24 until they had d' Jabin king of 3772
6: 4 and d' the increase of the earth, 7843
20:21 Gibeah, and d' down to the ground "
25 second day, and d' down to the "
35 and the children of Israel d' of the "
42 the cities they d' in the midst of "
21:16 remain, seeing the women are d' 8045
17 Benjamin, that a tribe be not d' *4229
1Sa 5: 6 Ashdod, and he d' them, and smote 8074
15: 8 and utterly d' all the people with 2763
9 and refuse, that they d' utterly. "
15 and the rest we have utterly d'. "
20 and have utterly d' the Amalekites. "
21 which should have been utterly d'. *2764
2Sa 11: 1 they d' the children of Ammon, 7843
21: 5 we should be d' from remaining 8045
22:38 pursued mine enemies, and d' them; "
24:16 the angel that d' the people, 7843
1Ki 15:13 and Asa d' her idol, and burnt it *3772
29 that breathed, until he had d' him, 8045
2Ki 10:17 in Samaria, till he had d' him, "
28 Thus Jehu d' Baal out of Israel. "
11: 1 she arose and d' all the seed royal. 6
13: 7 the king of Syria had d' them, "
19:12 them which my fathers have d'; 843
17 of Assyria have d' the nations *2717
18 stone, therefore they have d' them. 6
21: 3 which Hezekiah his father had d'; "
9 nations whom the Lord d' before 8045
1Ch 4:41 and d' them utterly unto this day, 2763
5:25 land, whom God d' before them. 8045
20: 1 Joab smote Rabbah, and d' it. *2040
21:12 three months to be d' before thy *5595
15 and said to the angel that d', *7843
2Ch 14:13 for they were d' before the Lord, 7665
15: 6 And nation was d' of nation, *3807
20:10 turned from them, and d' them not; 8045
22:10 she arose and d' all the seed royal 1696
24:23 and d' all the princes of the people 7843
31: 1 until they had utterly d' them all. 3615
32:14 nations that my fathers utterly d', 2763
33: 9 whom the Lord had d' before the 8045
34:11 which the kings of Judah had d'. 7843
36:19 d' all the goodly vessels thereof. "
Ezr 4:15 for which cause was this city d'. *2718
5:12 who d' this house, and carried the 5642
Es 3: 9 it be written that they may be d': 6
4:14 and thy father's house shall be d': "
7: 4 to be d', to be slain, and to perish. 8045
9: 6 Jews slew and d' five hundred men. 6
12 Jews have slain and d' five hundred "
Job 4:20 They are d' from morning to 3807
19:10 He hath d' me on every side, *5422
34:25 in the night, so that they are d'. 1792
Ps 9: 5 thou hast d' the wicked, thou hast 6
6 hast d' cities; their memorial *5428
11: 3 If the foundations be d', what can 2040
37:38 transgressors shall be d' together: 8045
73:27 thou hast d' all them that go a 6789
78:38 their iniquity, and d' them not: 7843
45 them; and frogs, which d' them. "
47 he d' their vines with hail, and 2026
92: 7 it is that they shall be d' for ever: 8045
137: 8 of Babylon, who art to be d'; 7703
Pr 13:13 despiseth the word shall be d': *2254
13:20 a companion of fools shall be d'. *7321
23 there is that is d' for want of 5595
29: 1 shall suddenly be d', and that *7665
Isa 9:16 they that are led of them are d'. 1104
10:27 and the yoke shall be d' because 2254
14:17 and d' the cities thereof; *2040
20 because thou hast d' thy land, 7843
26:14 therefore hast thou visited and d' 8045
34: 2 he hath utterly d' them, he hath 2763
37:12 them which my fathers have d', 7843
19 stone: therefore they have d' them. 6
48:19 not have been cut off nor d' from 8045
Jer 12:10 Many pastors have d' my vineyard, 7843
22:20 passages: for all thy lovers are d'. 7665
48: 4 Moab is d'; her little ones have "
8 and the plain shall be d', as the 8045
42 And Moab shall be d' from being a "
51: 8 Babylon is suddenly fallen and d': 7665
51:55 Babylon, and d' out of her the great 6
La 2: 5 he hath d' his strong holds, and 7843
6 hath d' his places of the assembly: "
9 he hath d' and broken her bars: 6
Eze 26:17 How art thou d', that wast inhabited "
27:32 the d' in the midst of the sea? *1822
30: 8 when all her helpers shall be d'. 7665
32:12 the multitude thereof shall be d'. 8045
Da 2:44 kingdom, which shall never be d': 2255
6:26 kingdom that which shall not be d', "
7:11 the beast was slain, and his body d', 7
14 kingdom that which shall not be d' 2255
11:20 but within few days he shall be d', 7665
Ho 4: 6 My people are d' for lack of 1820

Ho 10: 8 Aven, the sin of Israel, shall be d': 8045
13: 9 O Israel, thou hast d' thyself, but*7843
Am 2: 9 Yet d' I the Amorite before them. 8045
9 yet I d' his fruit from above, "
Zep 3: 6 passeth by: their cities are d', 6658
M't 22: 7 and d' those murderers, and burned 622
Lu 17:27 the flood came, and d' them all. "
29 from heaven, and d' them all. "
Ac 3:23 shall be d' from among the people. 1842
9:21 Is not this he that d' them which *4199
13:19 And when he had d' seven nations 2507
19:27 her magnificence should be d', * "
Ro 6: 6 that the body of sin might be d', *2673
1Co 10: 9 tempted and were d' of serpents. * 622
10 and were d' of the destroyer. * "
15:26 The last enemy that shall be d' *2673
2Co 4: 9 forsaken; cast down, but not d'; 622
Ga 1:23 the faith which once he d'. 4199
2:18 build again the things which I d', 2647
Heb 11:28 lest he that d' the first born *3645
2Pe 2:12 beasts, made to be taken and d', 5356
Jude 5 afterward d' them that believed not. 622
Re 8: 9 the third part of the ships were d'. 1311

destroyer See also DESTROYERS.
Ex 12:23 will not suffer the d' to come in 7843
J'g 16:24 the d' of our country, which slew 2717
Job 15:21 the d' shall come upon him. *7703
Ps 17: 4 kept me from the paths of the d'. *6530
Pr 28:24 the same is the companion of a d'. 7843
Jer 4: 7 and the d' of the Gentiles is on his "
1Co 10:10 and were destroyed of the d'. 3644

destroyers
Job 33:22 the grave, and his life to the d'. 4191
Isa 49:17 thy d' and they that made thee 2040
Jer 22: 7 And I will prepare d' against thee, 7843
50:11 O ye d' of mine heritage, because*8154

destroyest
Job 14:19 earth; and thou d' the hope of man. 6
Jer 51:25 the Lord, which d' all the earth: 7843
M't 27:40 Thou that d' the temple, and 2647
M'r 15:29 Ah, thou that d' the temple, and "

destroyeth
De 8:20 As the nations which the Lord d'* 6
Job 9:22 He d' the perfect and the wicked. 3615
12:23 increaseth the nations, and d' them: 6
Pr 6:32 he that doeth it d' his own soul. *7843
11: 9 with his mouth d' his neighbour: "
31: 3 thy ways to that which d' kings. 4229
Ec 7: 7 man mad; and a gift d' the heart. 6
9:18 war: but one sinner d' much good. "

destroying
De 3: 6 of Heshbon, utterly d' the men, 2763
13:15 d' it utterly, and all that is therein, "
Jos 11:11 edge of the sword, utterly d' them: "
2Ki 19:11 to all lands, by d' them utterly: "
1Ch 21:12 angel of the Lord d' throughout 7843
15 and as he was d', the Lord beheld* "
Isa 28: 2 a tempest of hail and a d' storm, 6986
37:11 by d' them utterly; and shalt thou2763
Jer 2:30 your prophets, like a d' lion 7843
51: 1 that rise up against me, a d' wind; "
25 I am against thee, O d' mountain, 4889
La 2: 8 not withdrawn his hand from d': 1104
Eze 9: 1 every man with his d' weapon in 4892
20:17 eye spared them from d' them, 7843

destruction See also DESTRUCTIONS.
De 7:23 destroy them with a mighty d', *4103
32:24 burning heat, and with bitter d': 6986
1Sa 5: 9 the city with a very great d': *4103
11 there was a deadly d' throughout* "
1Ki 20:42 whom I appointed to utter d', 2764
2Ch 22: 4 the death of his father to his d'. 4889
7 the d' of Ahaziah was of God by 8395
26:16 his heart was lifted up to his d': *7843
Es 8: 6 how can I endure to see the d' of my 13
9: 5 slaughter, and d', and did what 12
Job 5:21 neither shalt thou be afraid of d' 7701
22 At d' and famine thou shalt laugh: "
18:12 and d' shall be ready at his side. * 343
21:17 oft cometh their d' upon them! * "
20 His eyes shall see his d', and he 3589
30 is reserved to the day of d'? * 343
26: 6 him, and d' hath no covering. * 11
28:22 D' and death say, We have heard "
30:12 against me the ways of their d'. 343
24 grave, though they cry in his d'. 6365
31: 3 Is not d' to the wicked? * 343
12 it is a fire that consumeth to d', 11
23 d' from God was a terror to me, * 343
29 If I rejoiced at the d' of him that 6365
Ps 35: 8 d' come upon him at unawares; 7722
8 into that very d' let him fall. "
55:23 bring them down into the pit of d': 7845
73:18 thou castedst them down into d'. 4876
88:11 grave? or thy faithfulness in d'? 11
90: 3 turnest man to d'; and sayest, 1793
91: 6 the d' that wasteth at noonday. 6986
103: 4 Who redeemeth thy life from d'; 7845
Pr 1:27 your d' cometh as a whirlwind; * 343
10:14 the mouth of the foolish is near d'. 4288
15 the d' of the poor is their poverty. "
29 but d' shall be to the workers of "
13: 3 openeth wide his lips shall have d'. "
14:28 want of people is the d' of the prince. "
15:11 Hell and d' are before the Lord: * 11
16:18 Pride goeth before d', and an 7667
17:19 that exalteth his gate seeketh d'. "
18: 7 A fool's mouth is his d', and his 4288
12 Before d' the heart of man is 7667
21:15 but d' shall be to the workers of 4288
24: 2 their heart studieth d', and their *7701
27:20 Hell and d' are never full; * 10
31: 8 all such as are appointed to d'. *2475
Isa 1:28 And the d' of the transgressors 7667
10:25 cease, and mine anger in their d'. 8399
13: 6 come as a d' from the Almighty. 7701
14:23 will sweep it with the besom of d', 8045
15: 5 they shall raise up a cry of d'. 7667
19:18 one shall be called, The city of d'. 2041
24:12 and the gate is smitten with d'. 7591
49:19 the land of thy d', shall even now*2035
51:19 desolation, and d', and the famine, 7667
59: 7 wasting and d' are in their paths. "
60:18 wasting nor d' within thy borders; "
Jer 4: 6 evil from the north and a great d'. "
20 D' upon d' is cried; for the whole "
6: 1 out of the north, and great d'. "
17:18 and destroy them with double d'. 7670
46:20 but d' cometh; it cometh out of 7171
48: 3 Horonaim, spoiling and great d'. 7667
5 the enemies have heard a cry of d'. "
50:22 battle is in the land and of great d'. "
51:54 and great d' from the land of the "
La 2:11 d' of the daughter of my people; "
3:47 come upon us, desolation and d'. "
48 d' of the daughter of my people. "
4:10 d' of the daughter of my people. "
Eze 5:16 which shall be for their d', 4889
7:25 D' cometh; and they shall seek 7089
32: 9 bring thy d' among the nations, 7667
Ho 7:13 d' unto them! because they have 7701
9: 6 lo, they are gone because of d': "
13:14 O grave, I will be thy d': 6987
Joe 1:15 and as a d' from the Almighty 7701
Ob 12 of Judah in the day of their d'; 6
Mic 2:10 destroy you, even with a sore d'. 2256
Zec 14:11 there shall be no more utter d'; *2764
M't 7:13 broad is the way that leadeth to d', 684
Ro 3:16 D' and misery are in their ways: 4938
9:22 vessels of wrath fitted to d'. 684
1Co 5: 5 unto Satan for the d' of the flesh, 3639
2Co 10: 8 edification, and not for your d', *2506
13:10 me to edification, and not to d'. * "
Ph'p 3:19 Whose end is d', whose God is * 684
1Th 5: 3 sudden d' cometh upon them, 3639
2Th 1: 9 be punished with everlasting d' "
1Ti 6: 9 drown men in d' and perdition. "
2Pe 2: 1 bring upon themselves swift d'. 684
3:16 other scriptures, unto their own d'. "

destructions
Ps 9: 6 d' are come to a perpetual end: *2723
35:17 rescue my soul from their d', 7722
107:20 and delivered them from their d'. 7825

detain See also DETAINED.
J'g 13:15 I pray thee, let us d' thee, 6113
16 Though thou d' me, I will not eat "

detained
1Sa 21: 7 there that day, d' before the Lord; 6113

determinate
Ac 2:23 delivered by the d' counsel and 3724

determination
Zep 3: 8 for my d' is to gather the nations, 4941

determine See DETERMINED.
Ex 21:22 and he shall pay as the judges d'

determined
1Sa 20: 7 be sure that evil is d' by him. 3615
9 evil were d' by my father to come "
1Sa 20:33 Jonathan knew that it was d' of his "
25:17 evil is d' against our master. "
2Sa 13:32 this hath been d' from the day 7760
2Ch 2: 1 Solomon d' to build an house for * 559
25:16 know that God hath d' to destroy 3289
Es 7: 7 there was evil d' against him by 3615
Job 14: 5 Seeing his days are d', the number 2782
Isa 10:23 consumption, even d', in the midst "
19:17 hosts, which he hath d' against it.*3289
28:22 a consumption, even d' upon 2782
Da 9:24 Seventy weeks are d' upon thy *2852
26 end of the war desolations are d'. 2782
27 that d' shall be poured upon the "
11:36 for that that is d' shall be done. "
Lu 22:22 Son of man goeth, as it was d': 3724
Ac 3:13 Pilate, when he was d' to let him 2919
4:28 counsel d' before to be done. *4309
11:29 d' to send relief unto the brethren 3724
15: 2 they d' that Paul and Barnabas, *5021
37 Barnabas d' to take with them *1011
17:26 hath d' the times before appointed, 3724
19:39 shall be d' in a lawful assembly. *1956
20:16 Paul had d' to sail by Ephesus, 2919
25:25 Augustus, I have d' to send him. "
27: 1 when it was d' that we should sail "
1Co 2: 2 For I d' not to know any thing "
2Co 2: 1 But I d' this with myself, that I "
Tit 3:12 for I have d' there to winter. "

detest See also DETESTABLE.
De 7:26 thou shalt utterly d' it, and thou 8262

detestable
Jer 16:18 their d' and abominable things. 8251
Eze 5:11 sanctuary with all thy d' things. "
7:20 and of their d' things therein: "
11:18 all the d' things thereof from 8251
21 d' things and their abominations, "
37:23 idols, nor with their d' things, "

Deuel (*de-oo'-el*) See also REUEL.
Nu 1:14 of Gad; Eliasaph the son of D'. 1845
7:42 sixth day Eliasaph the son of D', "
47 offering of Eliasaph the son of D'. "
10:20 Gad was Eliasaph the son of D'. "

device See also DEVICES.
2Ch 2:14 to find out every d' which shall 4284
Es 8: 3 his d' that he had devised against "
9:25 by letters that his wicked d', which 4284
Ps 21:11 they imagined a mischievous d', "
140: 8 further not his wicked d'; lest "
Ec 9:10 for there is no work, nor d', nor 2808
Jer 18:11 and devise a d' against you: 4284
51:11 for his d' is against Babylon, 4209
La 3:62 their d' against me all the day. *1902
Ac 17:29 stone, graven by art and man's d'. 1761

devices
Job 5:12 He disappointeth the d' of the 4284
21:27 d' which ye wrongfully imagine 4209
Ps 10: 2 let them be taken in the d' that "
33:10 he maketh the d' of the people *4284
37: 7 who bringeth wicked d' to pass. 4209
Pr 1:31 and be filled with their own d'. 4156
12: 2 man of wicked d' will he condemn. 4209
14:17 a man of wicked d' is hated. "
19:21 are many d' in a man's heart; 4284
Isa 32: 7 he deviseth wicked d' to destroy 2154
Jer 11:19 they had devised d' against me, 4284
18:12 we will walk after our own d', "
18 let us devise d' against Jeremiah; "
Da 11:24 forecast his d' against the strong "
25 they shall forecast d' against him. "
2Co 2:11 we are not ignorant of his d'. 3540

devil See also DEVILS.
M't 4: 1 wilderness to be tempted of the d'. 1228
5 d' taketh him up into the holy city, "
8 Again the d' taketh him up into "
11 Then the d' leaveth him, and, "
9:32 a dumb man possessed with a d'. ‡1139
33 when the d' was cast out, the ‡1140
11:18 and they say, He hath a d'. ‡ "
12:22 one possessed with a d', blind, 1139
13:39 enemy that sowed them is the d'; 1228
15:22 is grievously vexed with a d' ‡1139
17:18 Jesus rebuked the d'; and he ‡1140
25:41 prepared for the d' and his angels: 1228
M'r 5:15, 16 was possessed with the d'. ‡1139
18 that had been possessed with a d',‡ "
7:26 that he would cast forth the d' ‡1140
29 d' is gone out of thy daughter. ‡ "
30 she found the d' gone out, and her‡ "
Lu 4: 2 Being forty days tempted of the d'. 1228
3 the d' said unto him, If thou be "
5 d', taking him up into an high "
6 the d' said unto him, All this will "
13 d' had ended all the temptation, "
33 had a spirit of an unclean d', ‡1140
35 when the d' had thrown him in ‡ "
7:33 wine; and ye say, He hath a d'. ‡ "
8:12 cometh the d', and taketh away 1228
29 of the d' into the wilderness ‡1142
9:42 d' threw him down, and tare him. ‡1140
11:14 casting out a d', and it was dumb. ‡ "
14 to pass when the d' was gone out, ‡ "
Joh 6:70 twelve, and one of you is a d'? 1228
7:20 and said, Thou hast a d': ‡1140
8:44 Ye are of your father the d', 1228
8:48 art a Samaritan, and hast a d'? ‡1140
49 Jesus answered, I have not a d'; ‡ "
52 Now we know that thou hast a d'. ‡ "
10:20 many of them said, He hath a d', ‡ "
21 the words of him that hath a d'. ‡1139
21 a d' open the eyes of the blind? ‡1140
13: 2 d' having now put into the heart 1228
Ac 10:38 all that were oppressed of the d'; "
13:10 thou child of the d', thou enemy "
Eph 4:27 Neither give place to the d'. "
6:11 stand against the wiles of the d'. "
1Ti 3: 6 into the condemnation of the d'. "
7 reproach and the snare of the d'. "
2Ti 2:26 out of the snare of the d', who "
Heb 2:14 power of death, that is, the d'; "
Jas 4: 7 Resist the d', and he will flee from "
1Pe 5: 8 because your adversary the d', "
1Jo 3: 8 that committeth sin is of the d'; "
8 d' sinneth from the beginning. "
8 might destroy the works of the d'. "
10 manifest, and the children of the d': "
Jude 9 when contending with the d' he "
Re 2:10 the d' shall cast some of you into "
12: 9 that old serpent, called the D', and "
12 the d' is come down unto you, "
20: 2 that old serpent, which is the D', "
10 the d' that deceived them was cast "

devilish
Jas 3:15 above, but is earthly, sensual, d'. 1141

devils
Le 17: 7 offer their sacrifices unto d', after*8163
De 32:17 sacrificed unto d', not to God; *7700
2Ch 11:15 and for the d', and for the calves *8163
Ps 106:37 sons and their daughters unto d',*7700
M't 4:24 which were possessed with d', ‡1139
7:22 in thy name have cast out d'? ‡1140
8:16 that were possessed with d': ‡1139
28 met him two possessed with d', ‡ "
31 So the d' besought him, saying, If ‡1142
33 befallen to the possessed of the d'. ‡1139
9:34 Pharisees said, He casteth out d' ‡1140
34 through the prince of the d'. ‡ "
10: 8 lepers, raise the dead, cast out d': ‡ "
12:24 This fellow doth not cast out d', ‡ "
24 by Beelzebub the prince of the d'. ‡ "
27 if I by Beelzebub cast out d', ‡ "
28 if I cast out d' by the Spirit of ‡ "
M'r 1:32 them that were possessed with d'. ‡1139
34 diseases, and cast out many d'; ‡1140
34 and suffered not the d' to speak, ‡ "
39 all Galilee, and cast out d'. ‡ "
3:15 sicknesses, and to cast out d': ‡ "
22 and by the prince of the d' ‡ "
22 casteth he out d'. ‡ "

M'r 5:12 all the d' besought him, saying, ‡1142
6:13 they cast out many d', and ‡1140
9:38 one casting out d' in thy name, ‡ "
16: 9 out of whom he had cast seven d'. ‡ "
17 my name shall they cast out d'; ‡ "
Lu 4:41 d' also came out of many, crying ‡ "
8: 2 out of whom went seven d', ‡ "
27 a certain man, which had d' long ‡ "
30 because many d' were entered ‡ "
33 Then went the d' out of the man, ‡ "
35 of whom the d' were departed, ‡ "
36 possessed of the d' was healed. ‡*1139
38 the man out of whom the d' were ‡1140
9: 1 power and authority over all d', ‡ "
49 Master, we saw one casting out d' ‡ "
10:17 even the d' are subject unto us ‡ "
11:15 casteth out d' through Beelzebub ‡ "
15 the chief of the d'. ‡ "
18 I cast out d' through Beelzebub. ‡ "
19 if I by Beelzebub cast out d', ‡ "
20 with the finger of God cast out d', ‡ "
13:32 I cast out d', and I do cures ‡ "
1Co 10:20 sacrifice to d', and not to God: ‡ "
20 ye should have fellowship with d'. ‡ "
21 cup of the Lord, and the cup of d': ‡ "
21 Lord's table, and of the table of d'. ‡ "
1Ti 4: 1 spirits, and doctrines of d'; ‡ "
Jas 2:19 the d' also believe, and tremble. ‡ "
Re 9:20 that they should not worship d', ‡ "
16:14 For they are the spirits of d', ‡1142
18: 2 is become the habitation of d', ‡ "

devise See also DEVISED; DEVISETH.
Ex 31: 4 To d' cunning works, to work in 2803
35:32 And to d' curious works, to work in "
35 and of those that d' cunning work. "
2Sa 14:14 yet doth he d' means, that his * "
Ps 35: 4 to confusion that d' my hurt. "
20 d' deceitful matters against them "
41: 7 against me do they d' my hurt. "
Pr 3:29 D' not evil against thy neighbour, 2790
14:22 Do they not err that d' evil? but "
22 shall be to them that d' good. "
16:30 shutteth his eyes to d' froward 2803
Jer 18:11 and d' a device against you: return "
18 let us d' devices against Jeremiah; "
Eze 11: 2 the men that d' mischief, and give "
Mic 2: 1 Woe to them that d' iniquity, and "
3 against this family do I d' an evil, "

devised
2Sa 21: 5 that d' against us that we should 1819
1Ki 12:33 in the month which he had d' 908
Es 8: 3 that he had d' against the Jews. 2803
5 reverse the letters d' by Haman 4284
9:24 had d' against the Jews to destroy 2803
25 which he d' against the Jews, "
Ps 31:13 they d' to take away my life. 2161
Jer 11:19 they had d' devices against me, 2803
48: 2 in Heshbon they had d' evil "
51:12 the Lord hath both d' and done 2161
La 2:17 hath done that which he had d'; "
2Pe 1:16 not followed cunningly d' fables, 4679

deviseth
Ps 36: 4 He d' mischief upon his bed; he 2803
52: 2 tongue d' mischiefs; like a sharp "
Pr 6:14 heart, he d' mischief continually; 2790
18 heart that d' wicked imaginations, "
16: 9 A man's heart d' his ways; but the 2803
24: 8 He that d' to do evil shall be "
Isa 32: 7 he d' wicked devices to destroy 3289
8 But the liberal d' liberal things; "

devote See also DEVOTED.
Le 27:28 that a man shall d' unto the Lord 2763

devoted
Le 27:21 unto the Lord, as a field d'; 2764
28 no d' thing, that a man shall devote "
28 every d' thing is most holy unto "
29 None d', which shall be "
29 which shall be d' of men, 2763
Nu 18:14 Every thing d' in Israel shall be 2764
Ps 119:38 servant, who is d' to thy fear. †‡

devotions
Ac 17:23 I passed by, and beheld your d', *4574

devour See also DEVOURED; DEVOUREST; DEVOURETH; DEVOURING.
Ge 49:27 the morning he shall d' the prey, 398
De 32:42 blood, and my sword shall d' flesh; "
J'g 9:15 and d' the cedars of Lebanon. "
20 and d' the men of Shechem, and the "
20 house of Millo, and d' Abimelech. "
2Sa 2:26 Shall the sword d' for ever? "
2Ch 7:13 command the locusts to d' the land, "
Job 18:13 It shall d' the strength of his skin: "
13 born of death shall d' his strength. "
Ps 21: 9 wrath, and the fire shall d' them. "
50: 3 silence: a fire shall d' before him, "
80:13 wild beasts of the field doth d' it. *7462
Pr 30:14 to d' the poor from off the earth, 398
Isa 1: 7 strangers d' it in your presence, "
9:12 shall d' Israel with open mouth. "
18 it shall d' the briers and thorns, "
10:17 and it shall burn and d' his thorns "
26:11 of thine enemies shall d' them. "
31: 8 not of a mean man, shall d' him: "
33:11 your breath, as fire, shall d' you. "
42:14 I will destroy and d' at once. *7602
56: 9 beasts of the field, come to d', 398
Jer 2: 3 all that d' him shall offend: "
5:14 people wood, and it shall d' them. "
12: 9 the beasts of the field, come to d'. 402
12 the sword of the Lord shall d' 398
15: 3 of the earth, to d' and destroy. "
17:27 shall d' the palaces of Jerusalem, "
21:14 and it shall d' all things round "
30:16 Therefore all they that d' shall be "
Jer 46:10 and the sword shall d', and it shall 398
14 sword shall d' round about thee. "
48:45 and shall d' the corner of Moab, * "
50:32 and it shall d' all round about him. "
Eze 7:15 famine and pestilence shall d' him. "
15: 7 fire, and another fire shall d' them; "
20:47 it shall d' every green tree in thee, "
23:37 them through the fire to d' them. * 402
28:18 it shall d' thee, and I will bring 398
34:28 the beast of the land d' them; * "
36:14 thou shalt d' men no more, neither "
Da 7: 5 thus unto it, Arise, d' much flesh. 399
23 and shall d' the whole earth, "
Ho 5: 7 now shall a month d' them with 398
8:14 and it shall d' the palaces thereof. "
11: 6 and d' them, because of their own "
13: 8 and there will I d' them like a lion: "
Am 1: 4 shall d' the palaces of Ben-hadad. "
7 which shall d' the palaces thereof: "
10 of Tyrus, which shall d' the palaces "
12 shall d' the palaces of Bozrah. "
14 and it shall d' the palaces thereof, "
2: 2 Moab, and it shall d' the palaces "
5 shall d' the palaces of Jerusalem. "
5: 6 in the house of Joseph, and d' it, "
Ob 18 shall kindle in them, and d' them; "
Na 2:13 the sword shall d' thy young lions: "
3:13 enemies: the fire shall d' thy bars. "
15 There shall the fire d' thee: the "
Hab 3:14 was as to d' the poor secretly. "
Zec 9:15 and they shall d', and subdue with "
11: 1 that the fire may d' thy cedars. "
12: 6 and they shall d' all the people "
M't 23:14 ye d' widows' houses, and for *2719
M'r 12:40 which d' widows' houses, and for "
Lu 20:47 Which d' widows' houses, and for * "
2Co 11:20 if a man d' you, if a man take * "
Ga 5:15 if ye bite and d' one another, "
Heb 10:27 which shall d' the adversaries. 2068
1Pe 5: 8 about, seeking whom he may d': 2666
Re 12: 4 for to d' her child as soon as 2719

devoured
Ge 31:15 and hath quite d' also our money. 398
37:20 Some evil beast hath d' him: and "
33 an evil beast hath d' him: Joseph "
41: 7 And the seven thin ears d' the *1104
24 And the thin ears d' the seven * "
Le 10: 2 and d' them, and they died before 398
Nu 26:10 the fire d' two hundred and fifty "
De 31:17 and they shall be d', and many evils "
32:24 and d' with burning heat, and 3898
2Sa 18: 8 the wood d' more people 398
8 that day than the sword d'. "
22: 9 and fire out of his mouth d': "
Ps 18: 8 and fire out of his mouth d': "
78:45 flies among them, which d' them; "
79: 7 For they have d' Jacob, and laid "
105:35 and d' the fruit of their ground. * "
Isa 1:20 ye shall be d' with the sword: "
24: 6 hath the curse d' the earth, "
Jer 2:30 own sword hath d' your prophets, "
3:24 shame hath d' the labour of our "
8:16 they are come, and have d' the land, "
10:25 have eaten up Jacob, and d' him, "
30:16 they that devour thee shall be d'; "
50: 7 All that found them have d' them: "
17 the king of Assyria hath d' him; "
51:34 the king of Babylon hath d' me, "
La 4:11 it hath d' the foundations thereof. "
Eze 15: 5 when the fire hath d' it, and it is "
16:20 thou sacrificed unto them to be d'. "
19: 3 learned to catch the prey; it d' men. "
6 to catch the prey, and d' men. "
14 branches, which hath d' her fruit, "
22:25 they have d' souls; they have taken "
23:25 thy residue shall be d' by the fire. "
33:27 will I give to the beasts to be d', "
39: 4 to the beasts of the field to be d'. 402
Da 7: 7 teeth: it d' and brake in pieces, 399
19 which d', brake in pieces, and "
Ho 7: 7 an oven, and have d' their judges; 398
9 Strangers have d' his strength, and "
Joe 1:19 to thee will I cry for the fire hath d' "
20 the fire hath d' the pastures of the "
Am 4: 9 increased, the palmerworm d' them: "
7: 4 and it d' the great deep, and did eat "
Na 1:10 they shall be d' as stubble fully ‡ "
Zep 1:18 shall be d' by the fire of his jealousy: "
3: 8 be d' with the fire of my jealousy. "
Zec 9: 4 and she shall be d' with fire. "
M't 13: 4 the fowls came and d' them up: 2719
M'r 4: 4 fowls of the air came and d' it up. "
Lu 8: 5 and the fowls of the air d' it. "
15:30 hath d' thy living with harlots, "
Re 20: 9 out of heaven, and d' them. "

devourer
Mal 3:11 I will rebuke the d' for your sakes, 398

devourest
Eze 36:13 Thou land d' up men, and hast * 398

devoureth
2Sa 11:25 sword d' one as well as another: 398
Pr 19:28 mouth of the wicked d' iniquity. *1104
20:25 man who d' that which is holy, *3216
Isa 5:24 Therefore as the fire d' the stubble, 398
La 2: 3 a flaming fire, which d' round about. "
Eze 15: 4 the fire d' both the ends of it, "
Joe 2: 3 A fire d' before them; and behind "
5 a flame of fire that d' the stubble, "
Hab 1:13 when the wicked d' the man that *1104
Re 11: 5 their mouth, and d' their enemies: 2719

devouring
Ex 24:17 like d' fire on the top of the mount 398
Ps 52: 4 Thou lovest all d' words, O thou 1105
Isa 29: 6 tempest, and the flame of d' fire. 398
30:27 and his tongue as a d' fire: "
30 and with the flame of a d' fire, "
33:14 us shall dwell with the d' fire? "

devout
Lu 2:25 the same man was just and d', 2126
Ac 2: 5 Jews, d' men, out of every nation "
8: 2 And d' men carried Stephen to his "
10: 2 A d' man, and one that feared God 2152
7 a d' soldier of them that waited on "
13:50 stirred up the d' and honourable 4576
17: 4 of the d' Greeks a great multitude, "
17 the Jews, and with the d' persons, "
22:12 a d' man according to the law, 2152

dew
Ge 27:28 God give thee of the d' of heaven, 2919
39 and of the d' of heaven from above; "
Ex 16:13 the d' lay round about the host. "
14 when the d' that lay was gone "
Nu 11: 9 when the d' fell upon the camp "
De 32: 2 my speech shall distil as the d', "
33:13 for the d', and for the deep "
28 also his heavens shall drop down d'. "
J'g 6:37 if the d' be on the fleece only, "
38 wringed the d' out of the fleece, "
39 upon all the ground let there be d'. "
40 there was d' on all the ground. "
2Sa 1:21 Gilboa, let there be no d', neither "
17:12 light upon him as the d' falleth "
1Ki 17: 1 there shall not be d' nor rain "
Job 29:19 the d' lay all night upon my branch. "
38:28 who hath begotten the drops of d'? "
Ps 110: 3 thou hast the d' of thy youth. "
133: 3 the d' [2919] of Hermon, and as the d' *
Pr 3:20 and the clouds drop down the d'. 2919
19:12 his favour is as d' upon the grass. "
Ca 5: 2 for my head is filled with d', "
Isa 18: 4 like a cloud of d' in the heat of "
26:19 for thy d' is as the d' of herbs, "
Da 4:15 let it be wet with the d' of heaven, 2920
23 d' of heaven, and let his portion be "
25 they shall wet thee with the d' of "
33 and his body was wet with the d' of "
5:21 body was wet with the d' of heaven; "
Ho 6: 4 and as the early d' it goeth away. 2919
13: 3 and as the early d' that passeth "
14: 5 I will be as the d' unto Israel: "
Mic 5: 7 many people as a d' from the Lord, "
Hag 1:10 heaven over you is stayed from d', "
Zec 8:12 the heavens shall give their d'; "

diadem
Job 29:14 judgment was as a robe and a d'. 6797
Isa 28: 5 and for a d' of beauty, unto the 6843
62: 3 a royal d' in the hand of thy God. 6797
Eze 21:26 Remove the d', and take off the *4701

dial
2Ki 20:11 which it had gone down in the d' 4609
Isa 38: 8 which is gone down in the sun d' "

diamond
Ex 28:18 an emerald, a sapphire, and a d'. 3095
39:11 an emerald, a sapphire, and a d'. "
Jer 17: 1 and with the point of a d': 8068
Eze 28:13 the sardius, topaz, and the d', 3095

Diana (*di-an'-ah*)
Ac 19:24 which made silver shrines for D' 735
27 the temple of the great goddess D' "
28 Great is D' of the Ephesians. "
34 out, Great is D' of the Ephesians. "
35 worshipper of the great goddess D', "

Diblaim (*dib'-la-im*)
Ho 1: 3 took Gomer the daughter of D'; 1691

Diblath (*dib'-lath*)
Eze 6:14 than the wilderness toward D', 1689

Diblathaim See ALMON-DIBLATHAIM; BETH-DIBLATHAIM.

Dibon (*di'-bon*) See also DIBON-GAD; DIMON.
Nu 21:30 Heshbon is perished even unto D', 1769
32: 3 Ataroth, and D', and Jazer, and "
34 And the children of Gad built D', "
Jos 13: 9 all the plain of Medeba unto D'; "
17 D', and Bamoth-baal, and "
Ne 11:25 at D', and in the villages thereof, "
Isa 15: 2 He is gone up to Bajith, and to D', "
Jer 48:18 daughter that dost inhabit D', "
22 And upon D', and upon Nebo, and "

Dibon-gad (*di'-bon-gad'*)
Nu 33:45 from Iim, and pitched in D'. 1769
46 removed from D', and encamped "

Dibri (*dib'-ri*)
Le 24:11 Shelomith, the daughter of D', 1704

did See also DIDDEST; DIDST.
Ge 3: 6 and d' eat, and gave also unto her
6 husband with her; and he d' eat.
12 she gave me of the tree, and I d' eat.
13 serpent beguiled me, and I d' eat.
21 unto his wife d' the Lord God make
6:22 Thus d' Noah; according to all 6213
22 God commanded him, so d' he.
7: 5 Noah d' according unto all that the
20 cubits upward d' the waters prevail;
11: 9 because the Lord d' there confound
9 thence d' the Lord scatter them
18: 8 under the tree, and they d' eat.
13 Wherefore d' Sarah laugh,
19: 3 and d' bake unleavened bread,
21: 1 d' unto Sarah as he had spoken. 6213
22: 1 that God d' tempt Abraham and
23 these eight Milcah d' bear to Nahor,
24:54 and they d' eat and drink,
25:28 because he d' eat of his venison:
34 and he d' eat and drink, and rose up

Ge 26:20 the herdmen of Gerar d' strive *
30 and they d' eat and drink,
27:25 brought it near to him, and he d' eat:
29:25 d' not I serve with thee for
28 Jacob d' so, and fulfilled her week: 6213
30:40 And Jacob d' separate the lambs,
41 the stronger cattle d' conceive,
31:46 and they d' eat thereupon the heap.
54 and they d' eat bread,
35: 5 and they d' not pursue after the
38:10 which he d' displeased the Lord: 6213
11 he die also, as his brethren d'. *
39: 3 Lord made all that he d' to prosper 6213
6 save the bread which he d' eat.
19 this manner d' thy servant to me; 6213
22 they d' there, he was the doer of it. "
23 that which he d', the Lord made "
40:17 birds d' eat them out of the basket
23 Yet d' not the chief butler remember
41: 4 and the lean fleshed kine d' eat up
12 to his dream he d' interpret.
20 illfavored kine d' eat up the first
42:20 ye shall not die. And they d' so. 6213
25 way: and thus d' he unto them. * "
43: 3 man d' solemnly protest unto us,
17 And the man d' as Joseph bade; 6213
30 bowels d' yearn upon his brother:
32 which d' eat with him,
44: 2 And he d' according to the word 6213
45: 5 for God d' send me before you to
21 And the children of Israel d' so: 6213
47:22 d' eat their portion which Pharaoh
48:15 fathers Abraham and Isaac d' walk,
50:12 his sons d' unto him according as 6213
15 all the evil which we d' unto him. 1580
16 father d' command before he died,
17 they d' unto thee evil: and now, 1580
Ex 1:11 d' set over them taskmasters
17 and d' not as the king of Egypt 6213
2:13 he said to him that d' the wrong,
4:30 and d' the signs in the sight of the 6213
5: 8 which they d' make heretofore,
19 the children of Israel d' see that
6: 8 the which I d' swear to give it to *
7: 6 Aaron d' as the Lord commanded 6213
6 Lord commanded them, so d' they. "
10 d' so as the Lord had commanded: "
11 magicians of Egypt, they also d' in "
20 And Moses and Aaron d' so, as the "
22 magicians of Egypt d' so with their "
23 d' he set his heart to this also.
8: 7 d' so with their enchantments, 6213
13 d' according to the word of Moses; "
17 they d' so; for Aaron stretched "
18 d' so with their enchantments "
24 the Lord d' so; and there came "
31 the Lord d' according to the word "
9: 6 Lord d' that thing on the morrow, "
7 and he d' not let the people go.
10:11 for that ye d' desire. *
15 they d' eat every herb of the land,
11:10 And Moses and Aaron d' all these 6213
12:28 children of Israel went away, and d' "
28 Moses and Aaron, so d' they. "
35 the children of Israel d' according "
50 Thus d' all the children of Israel; "
50 Moses and Aaron, so d' they. "
51 Lord d' bring the children of Israel
13: 8 that which the Lord d' unto me 6213
14: 4 I am the Lord. And they d' so. "
12 the word that we d' tell thee in *
31 the Lord d' upon the Egyptians: 6313
16: 3 and when we d' eat bread to the full;
17 And the children of Israel d' so, 6213
18 and when they d' mete it with an
24 and it d' not stink, neither was
35 the children of Israel d' eat manna
35 they d' eat manna, until they
17: 2 the people d' chide with Moses
6 And Moses d' so in the sight of 6213
10 Joshua d' as Moses had said to him, "
18: 7 his father in law, and d' obeisance,
14 father in law saw all that he d' to 6213
24 in law, and d' all that he had said. "
19: 4 seen what I d' unto the Egyptians, "
24:11 nobles of the children of....and d' eat
32:12 For mischief d' he bring them out,
21 What d' this people unto thee, 6213
28 the children of Levi d' according "
33: 4 and no man d' put on him his
34:28 d' neither eat bread, nor drink water.
35:24 that d' offer an offering of silver
25 that were wise hearted d' spin
36:22 thus d' he make for all the boards
29 d' both of them in both the corners. 6213
39: 3 And they d' beat the gold into
21 d' bind the breastplate by his rings
32 children of Israel d' according to 6213
32 Lord commanded Moses, so d' they. "
43 And Moses d' look upon all the *
40:16 Thus d' Moses: according to all 6213
16 command him, so d' he. And it "
Le 4:20 bullock as he d' with the bullock "
8: 4 Moses d' as the Lord commanded "
9 d' he put the golden plate
36 Aaron and his sons d' all the 6213
9:14 d' wash the inwards and the legs, *
10: 7 d' according to the word of Moses. 6213
16:15 he d' with the blood of the bullock, "
34 d' as the Lord commanded Moses. "
24:23 Israel d' as the Lord commanded "
26:35 it d' not rest in your sabbaths, *
27:24 possession of the land d' belong. *
Nu 1:54 commanded Moses, so d' they. 6213
54 the children of Israel d' according "

Nu 2:34 the children of Israel d' according 6213
4:37 Moses and Aaron d' number *
41 Moses and Aaron d' number *
5: 4 so d' the children of Israel. 6213
4 And the children of Israel d' so, "
7:18 prince of Issachar, d' offer:
24 children of Zebulun, d' offer: *
30 the children of Reuben, d' offer: *
36 the children of Simeon, d' offer: *
8: 3 Aaron d' so; he lighted the lamps 6213
20 d' the children of Israel unto them. "
20 d' to the Levites according unto all "
22 the Levites, so d' they unto them. "
9: 5 Moses, so d' the children of Israel. "
10:21 the other d' set up the tabernacle
11: 5 which we d' eat in Egypt freely;
25 they prophesied, and d' not cease.
14:22 my miracles, which I d' in Egypt,*6213
37 those men that d' bring up the evil
17:11 d' so: as the Lord commanded 6213
11 commanded him, so d' he. "
20:27 Moses d' as the Lord commanded: "
21:14 What he d' in the Red sea, and *2052
23: 2 Balak d' as Balaam had spoken; 6213
30 And Balak d' as Balaam had said, "
25: 2 and the people d' eat,
27:22 Moses d' as the Lord commanded 6213
31:31 d' as the Lord commanded Moses. "
32: 8 d' your fathers, when I sent them "
36:10 so d' the daughters of Zelophehad: "
De 1:30 to all that he d' for you in Egypt "
32 ye d' not believe the Lord your God,
2:12 as Israel d' unto the land of his 6213
22 As he d' to the children of Esau, "
29 Moabites which dwell in Ar, d' unto "
3: 6 we d' unto Sihon king of Heshbon, "
4: 3 eyes have seen what the Lord d' "
4 d' cleave unto the Lord your God
33 D' ever people hear the voice of God
34 to all that the Lord your God d' 6213
5:23 for the mountain d' burn with fire,
7:18 Lord thy God d' unto Pharaoh, 6213
8: 3 neither d' thy fathers know;
4 neither d' thy foot swell,
9: 9 I neither d' eat nor drink water:
18 I d' neither eat bread nor drink
11: 3 which he d' in the midst of Egypt 6213
4 what he d' unto the army of Egypt, "
5 he d' unto you in the wilderness, "
6 he d' unto Dathan and Abiram, "
7 great acts of the Lord which he d' "
12:30 How d' these nations serve their *
24: 9 what the Lord thy God d' unto 6213
25:17 Remember what Amalek d' unto "
29: 2 Ye have seen all that the Lord d' "
31: 4 do unto them as he d' to Sihon and "
32:12 the Lord alone d' lead him,
38 which d' eat the fat of their sacrifices
33: 9 neither d' he acknowledge his
34: 9 and d' as the Lord commanded 6213
Jos 2:10 what ye d' unto the two kings of "
11 hearts d' melt, neither d' there remain
4: 8 children of Israel d' so as Joshua 6213
18 over all his banks, as they d' before.
20 d' Joshua pitch in Gilgal.
23 as the Lord your God d' to the Red 6213
5: 4 cause why Joshua d' circumcise
11 and they d' eat of the old corn
12 but they d' eat of the fruit of the
14 and d' worship, and said unto him,
15 is holy. And Joshua d' so. 6213
6:14 into the camp: so they d' six days. "
9: 4 They d' work wilily, and went
9 fame of him, and all that he d' in "
10 d' to the two kings of the Amorites, "
26 And so d' he unto them, and "
10:23 And they d' so, and brought forth "
28 d' to the king of Makkedah as he d'* "
30 d' unto the king thereof as he d' * "
39 he had done to Hebron, so he d' to "
42 kings and their land d' Joshua take
11: 9 Joshua d' unto them as the Lord 6213
12 all the kings of them, d' Joshua take
13 Hazor only; that d' Joshua burn.
15 Moses command Joshua, and so d' 6213
12: 6 Them d' Moses the...smite: *
13:12 for these d' Moses smite,
22 d' the children of Israel slay with the
32 which Moses d' distribute for
14: 5 Moses, so the children of Israel d', 6213
17:13 but d' not utterly drive them out.
22:20 D' not Achan the son of Zerah commit
33 and d' not intend to go up against *
24: 5 according to that which I d' among 6213
13 a land for which ye d' not labour, *
17 and which d' those great signs in 6213
J'g 1:21 children of Benjamin d' not drive out
27 Neither d' Manasseh drive out the
28 and d' not utterly drive them out.
29 Neither d' Ephraim drive out the *
30 Neither d' Zebulun drive out the *
31 Neither d' Asher drive out the *
32 for they d' not drive them out.
33 Neither d' Naphtali drive out the *
2: 7 works of the Lord, that he d' for *6213
11 And the children of Israel d' evil in "
17 of the Lord; but they d' not so. "
22 As their fathers d' keep it, or not.
3: 7 And the children of Israel d' evil 6213
12 the children of Israel d' evil again "
16 he d' gird it under his raiment *
4: 1 the children of Israel again d' evil 6213
5:17 and why d' Dan remain in ships?
6: 1 the children of Israel d' evil in the 6213
20 pour out the broth. And he d' so. "

J'g 6:27 and d' as the Lord had said unto 6213
27 do it by day, that he d' it by night. "
40 And God d' so that night: for it was "
8: 1 And they d' chide with him sharply.
15 with whom ye d' upbraid me,
25 and d' cast therein every man the
9:27 and d' eat and drink,
56 of Abimelech, which he d' unto 6213
57 the men of Shechem d' God render
10: 6 And the children of Israel d' evil 6213
11 D' not I deliver you from the
12 and the Maonites, d' oppress you;
11: 7 D' not ye hate me, and expel me,
25 d' he ever strive against Israel,
26 Why therefore d' ye not recover them
39 father, who d' with her, according 6213
13: 1 Israel d' evil again in the sight of "
19 and the angel d' wondrously; "
21 angel of the Lord d' no more appear
14: 9 and they d' eat: but he told not
15:11 As they d' unto me, so have I done 6213
16:21 and he d' grind in the prison house
17: 6 every man d' that which was right 6213
19: 4 so they d' eat and drink,
6 and d' eat and drink both of them
8 and they d' eat both of them.
21 and d' eat and drink.
21:22 for ye d' not give unto them at this
23 the children of Benjamin d' so, 6213
25 every man d' that which was right "
Ru 2:14 and she d' eat, and was sufficed,
19 blessed be he that d' take knowledge
3: 6 unto the floor, and d' according 6213
4:11 which two d' build the house of Israel:
1Sa 1: 7 And as he d' so year by year, when 6213
18 went her way, and d' eat,
2:11 And the child d' minister unto the 1961
14 So they d' in Shiloh unto all the 6213
22 heard all that his sons d' unto all "
27 D' I plainly appear unto the house
28 and d' I choose him out of all the
28 and d' I give unto the house of thy
3: 7 Now Samuel d' not yet know the Lord.
19 and d' let none of his words fall to the
4:20 neither d' she regard it.
6: 6 d' they not let the people go,
10 And the men d' so; and took two 6213
7: 4 children of Israel d' put away Baalim
14 and the coasts thereof d' Israel deliver
9:24 So Saul d' eat with Samuel that day.
12: 7 Lord, which he d' to you and to 6213
13: 6 then the people d' hide themselves in
14:32 and the people d' eat them with the
43 I d' but taste a little honey with the
15: 2 remember that which Amalek d' to 6213
16: 4 Samuel d' that which the Lord 6213
19: 5 for he d' put his life in his hand,
20:34 and d' eat no meat the second day
21:11 d' they not sing one to another of
22:15 D' I then begin to enquire of God*
17 and d' not shew it to me.
18 and five persons that d' wear
25: 4 David heard...that Nabal d' shear
27:11 saying, So d' David, and so will be 6213
28:24 and d' bake unleavened bread thereof:
25 and they d' eat. Then they rose up,
30:11 and he d' eat; and they made
2Sa 1: 2 he fell to the earth, and d' obeisance.
2: 3 were with him d' David bring up,
3:36 whatsoever the king d' pleased 6213
5:25 And David d' so, as the Lord had "
7:17 so d' Nathan speak unto David.
8:11 king David d' dedicate unto the
9: 6 fell on his face, and d' reverence.
13 he d' eat continually at the king's
11: 7 Joab d', and how the people d', *7965
13 he d' eat and drink before him;
20 ye so nigh...when ye d' fight? *
21 d' not a woman cast a piece of
12: 3 it d' eat of his own meat,
6 because he d' this thing, and 6213
17 neither d' he eat bread with them.
20 bread before him, and he d' eat.
31 and thus d' he unto all the cities 6213
13: 8 and d' bake the cakes.
29 the servants of Absalom d' unto 6213
14: 4 face to the ground, and d' obeisance,
15: 6 this manner d' Absalom to all 6213
17:15 Thus and thus d' Ahithophel counsel
19:19 that which thy servant d' perversely
28 among them that d' eat at thine own
43 why then d' ye despise us,
20: 6 more harm than d' Absalom: take
21: 6 whom the Lord d' choose. *
22: 7 and he d' hear my voice out of his*
7 my cry d' enter into his ears. *
11 he rode upon a cherub, and d' fly:
23 I d' not depart from them. *
37 so that my feet d' not slip.
43 then d' I beat them as small as the
43 I d' stamp them as the mire of the
43 and d' spread them abroad.
23:17 These things d' these three 6213
22 These things d' Benaiah the son of "
24:23 things d' Araunah, as a king, *
1Ki 1:16 Bath-sheba bowed, and d' obeisance
31 and d' reverence to the king,
2: 5 the son of Zeruiah d' to me, and 6213
5 what he d' to the two captains
35 and Zadok the priest d' the king put
42 D' I not make thee to swear by the
3: 4 burnt offerings d' Solomon offer upon
14 as thy father David d' walk,
21 it was not my son, which I d' bear.
5:18 builders and Hiram's d' hew them.

1Ki 7:15 a line of twelve cubits *d'* compass
18 and so *d'* he for the other chapiter 6213
23 a line of thirty cubits *d'* compass it
46 the plain of Jordan *d'* the king cast
51 the gold, and the vessels, *d'* he put *
8: 5 even those *d'* the priests...bring up.
64 the same day *d'* the king hallow
9:21 upon those *d'* Solomon levy a tribute
22 the children of Israel *d'* Solomon
24 then *d'* he build Millo.
25 And three times in a year *d'* Solomon
10:29 kings of Syria, *d'* they bring them out
11: 6 And Solomon *d'* evil in the sight 6213
6 after the Lord, as *d'* David his
7 Then *d'* Solomon build an high place
8 likewise *d'* he for all his strange 6213
16 For six months *d'* Joab remain *
25 beside the mischief that Hadad *d'*:
33 and my judgments as *d'* David his
38 as David my servant *d'*; 6213
41 and all that he *d'*, and his wisdom, "
12: 9 which thy father *d'* put upon us
11 now whereas my father *d'* lade
32 So *d'* he in Beth-el, sacrificing 6213
13:19 and *d'* eat bread in his house,
22 which the Lord *d'* say to thee, *
14: 4 And Jeroboam's wife *d'* so, and 6213
16 who *d'* sin, and who made Israel *
21 the city which the Lord *d'* choose*
22 And Judah *d'* evil in the sight of 6213
24 and they *d'* according to all the "
29 and all that he *d'*, are they not "
15: 4 for David's sake *d'* the Lord...give him
5 Because David *d'* that which was 6213
7 and all that he *d'*, are they not "
11 And Asa *d'* that which was right in "
11 of the Lord, as *d'* David his father.
23 and all that he *d'*, and the cities 6213
26 he *d'* evil in the sight of the Lord, "
28 king of Judah *d'* Baasha slay him
31 and all that he *d'*, are they not 6213
34 he *d'* evil in the sight of the Lord, "
16: 5 and what he *d'*, and his might, are "
7 the evil that he *d'* in the sight of "
12 Thus *d'* Zimri destroy all the house
14 Elah, and all that he *d'*, are they 6213
15 of Asa king of Judah *d'* Zimri reign
19 in his sin which he *d'*, to make 6213
25 and *d'* worse than all that were *
27 the acts of Omri which he *d'*, and 6213
30 And Ahab the son of Omri *d'* evil "
33 Ahab *d'* more to provoke the Lord
34 In his days *d'* Hiel the Bethelite build
17: 5 So he went and *d'* according unto 6213
15 And she went and *d'* according to "
16 neither *d'* the cruse of oil fail,
18:13 told my lord what I *d'* when 6213
34 And they *d'* it the second time.
34 And they *d'* it the third time.
19: 6 And he *d'* eat and drink,
8 And he arose, and *d'* eat and drink,
21 gave unto the people, and they *d'* eat.
20:25 unto their voice, and *d'* so. 6213
33 Now the men *d'* diligently observe *
33 and *d'* hastily catch it: *
21:11 in his city, *d'* as Jezebel had 6213
13 Naboth *d'* blaspheme God and the
25 which *d'* sell himself to work wicked
26 he *d'* very abominably in following
26 to all things as *d'* the Amorites, 6213
22:18 *D'* I not tell thee that he would
39 acts of Ahab, and all that he *d'*, 6213
52 he *d'* evil in the sight of the Lord, "
2Ki 1:18 the acts of Ahaziah which he *d'*. 6213
2:18 *D'* I not say unto you, Go not?
4: 1 thy servant *d'* fear the Lord:
28 *D'* I desire a son of my Lord?
28 *D'* I not say, do not deceive me?
44 he set it before them, and they *d'* eat,
6: 6 and the iron *d'* swim. *
29 we boiled my son, and *d'* eat him:
7: 8 into one tent, and *d'* eat and drink,
8: 2 *d'* after the saying of the man 6213
18 as *d'* the house of Ahab: for the
18 was his wife: and he *d'* evil in the
23 of Joram, and all that he *d'*, are
25 Ahab king of Israel *d'* Ahaziah...begin
27 *d'* evil in the sight of the Lord, 6213
27 as *d'* the house of Ahab: for he
9:27 they *d'* so at the going up to Gur.*
34 was come in, he *d'* eat and drink.
10:19 But Jehu *d'* it in subtilty, to the 6213
34 and all that he *d'*, and all his might,"
11: 3 Athaliah *d'* reign over the land. *
9 captains over the hundreds *d'* 6213
10 over hundreds *d'* the priest give *
12: 2 And Jehoash *d'* that which was 6213
11 the hands of them that *d'* the work,"
19 and all that he *d'*, are they not "
13: 2 And he *d'* that which was evil in the"
7 neither *d'* he leave of the people *
8 and all that he *d'*, and his might, "
11 And he *d'* that which was evil in "
12 acts of Joash, and all that he *d'*. "
25 three times *d'* Joash beat him,
14: 3 And he *d'* that which was right 6213
3 he *d'* according to all things "
3 as Joash his father *d'*. * "
4 as yet the people *d'* sacrifice and *
15 acts of Jehoash which he *d'*, and 6213
24 and he *d'* that which was evil in "
28 of Jeroboam, and all that he *d'*, "
15: 3 And he *d'* that which was right "
6 and all that he *d'*, are they not "
8 king of Judah *d'* Zachariah...reign

2Ki 15: 9 And he *d'* that which was evil in 6213
18 *d'* that which was evil in the sight "
21 and all that he *d'*, are they not "
24 And he *d'* that which was evil in "
26 and all that he *d'*, behold, they are "
28 And he *d'* that which was evil in "
31 the acts of Pekah, and all that he *d'*,"
34 And he *d'* that which was right in "
34 he *d'* according to all that his "
36 acts of Jotham, and all that he *d'*, "
16: 2 and *d'* not that which was right "
16 *d'* Urijah the priest, according to all"
19 the acts of Ahaz which he *d'*, are "
17: 2 And he *d'* that which was evil in "
9 children of Israel *d'* secretly those
11 the high places, as *d'* the heathen
14 that *d'* not believe in the Lord *
22 the sins of Jeroboam which he *d'*;6213
40 Howbeit they *d'* not hearken,
40 *d'* after their former manner. *6213
41 as *d'* their fathers, so do they unto "
18: 3 And he *d'* that which was right in "
3 to all that David his father *d'*. * "
4 children of Israel *d'* burn incense
11 of Assyria *d'* carry away Israel *
13 king Hezekiah *d'* Sennacherib...come
16 time *d'* Hezekiah cut off the gold
21: 2 And he *d'* that which was evil in 6213
3 grove, as *d'* Ahab king of Israel "
9 do more evil than *d'* the nations
11 above all that the Amorites *d'*, 6213
17 and all that he *d'*, and his sin that "
20 And he *d'* that which was evil in "
20 Lord, as his father Manasseh *d'*. "
25 the acts of Amon which he *d'*, "
22: 2 And he *d'* that which was right in "
23: 9 *d'* eat of the unleavened bread
13 of Ammon, *d'* the king defile.
19 and *d'* to them according to all 6213
24 *d'* Josiah put away, that he might
28 and all that he *d'*, are they not 6213
32 And he *d'* that which was evil in "
37 he *d'* that which was evil in the "
24: 3 according to all that he *d'*; "
5 all that he *d'*, are they not written "
9 And he *d'* that which was evil in "
11 and his servants *d'* besiege it. *
19 And he *d'* that which was evil in 6213
25:11 *d'* Nebuzar-adan...carry away.
13 *d'* the Chaldees break in pieces,
27 *d'* lift up the head of Jehoiachin
29 and he *d'* eat bread continually
1Ch 4:27 *d'* all their family multiply,
9:22 David and Samuel the Seer *d'* ordain
11:19 things *d'* these three mightiest. 6213
24 *d'* Benaiah the son of Jehoiada "
14:16 therefore *d'* as God commanded "
15:13 because ye *d'* it not at the first, *
24 *d'* blow with the trumpets before
17:15 so *d'* Nathan speak unto David
23:24 that *d'* the work for the service 6213
26:27 *d'* they dedicate to maintain
27:26 And over them that *d'* the work 6213
29:22 And *d'* eat and drink before the Lord
2Ch 1: 7 In that night *d'* God appear unto
2: 7 whom David my father *d'* provide
4: 2 line of thirty cubits *d'* compass *
3 which *d'* compass it round about:
16 *d'* Huram his father make to
17 of the Jordan *d'* the king cost them
5: 5 *d'* the priests and the Levites bring
11 and *d'* not then wait by course:
8: 8 *d'* Solomon make to pay tribute
9 of Israel *d'* Solomon make no
10: 9 that thy father *d'* put upon us?
12:14 *d'* evil, because he prepared not 6213
13:20 Neither *d'* Jeroboam recover
14: 2 And Asa *d'* that which was good 6213
15: 4 when they in their trouble *d'* turn*
6 *d'* vex them with all adversity.
18:16 I *d'* see all Israel scattered upon *
17 *D'* I not tell thee that he would
19: 8 in Jerusalem *d'* Jehoshaphat set
20:35 after this *d'* Jehoshaphat join
35 of Israel, who *d'* very wickedly: 6213
21: 6 like as *d'* the house of Ahab: for "
10 same time also *d'* Libnah revolt
22: 4 Wherefore he *d'* evil in the sight 6213
23: 8 Levites and all Judah *d'* according "
24: 2 Joash *d'* that which was right "
7 *d'* they bestow on Baalim.
11 Thus they *d'* day by day, and 6213
12 gave it to such as *d'* the work of "
25: 2 And he *d'* that which was right in "
4 but *d'* as it is written in the law
12 alive *d'* the children of Judah carry
27 the time that Amaziah *d'* turn
26: 4 And he *d'* that which was right in 6213
4 to all that his father Amaziah *d'* * "
22 *d'* Isaiah the prophet,...write.
27: 2 And he *d'* that which was right 6213
2 to all that his father Uzziah *d'*: * "
2 And the people *d'* yet corruptly.
5 So much *d'* the children of Ammon pay
28: 1 he *d'* not that which was right 6213
16 *d'* king Ahaz send unto the kings
22 of his distress *d'* he trespass yet
29: 2 And he *d'* that which was right 6213
19 Ahaz in his reign *d'* cast away
34 the Levites *d'* help them,
30:18 yet *d'* they eat the passover
22 they *d'* eat throughout the feast
24 Hezekiah king of Judah *d'* give
31:20 *d'* Hezekiah throughout all Judah 6213
21 he *d'* it with all his heart, and "

2Ch 32: 3 and they *d'* help him. *
9 After this *d'* Sennacherib...send
33 Jerusalem *d'* him honour at his 6213
33: 2 *d'* that which was evil in the sight "
17 *d'* sacrifice still in the high places,
22 But he *d'* that which was evil 6213
22 Lord, as *d'* Manasseh his father: "
34: 2 And he *d'* that which was right in "
6 *d'* he in the cities of Manasseh,
12 the men *d'* the work faithfully: 6213
32 the inhabitants of Jerusalem *d'* "
35: 3 David king of Israel *d'* build
12 And so *d'* they with the oxen.
36: 5 and he *d'* that which was evil in 6213
8 and his abominations which he *d'*, "
9 and he *d'* that which was evil in "
12 he *d'* that which was evil in the "
Ezr 1: 8 *d'* Cyrus king of Persia bring forth
11 All these *d'* Sheshbazzar bring up with
5:14 those *d'* Cyrus the king take out
6:13 the king had sent, so they *d'* speedily.
21 had separated themselves....*d'* eat,
10: 6 he *d'* eat no bread, nor drink
16 the children of the captivity *d'* so. 6213
Ne 2:16 not whither I went, or what I *d'*; "
16 nor to the rest that *d'* the work. "
3: 3 gate *d'* the sons of Hassenaah build,
5:13 *d'* according to this promise. 6213
15 but so *d'* not I, because of the fear "
9:25 so they *d'* eat, and were filled,
28 they *d'* evil again before thee: 6213
11:12 their brethren that *d'* the work "
13: 7 evil that Eliashib *d'* for Tobiah, * "
10 and the singers, that *d'* the work "
18 *D'* [6213] not your fathers thus, and *d'*
26 *D'* not Solomon king of Israel sin
26 *d'* outlandish women cause to sin.
Es 1: 8 none *d'* compel: for so the king *
21 king *d'* according to the word of 6213
2: 4 pleased the king; and he *d'* so. "
11 to know how Esther *d'*, and what 7965
20 for Esther *d'* the commandment 6213
3: 1 things *d'* king Ahasuerus promote
2, 5 bowed not, nor *d'* him reverence,
4:17 *d'* according to all that Esther 6213
5:12 Esther the Queen *d'* let no man
8: 1 that day *d'* the king Ahasuerus give
9: 5 and *d'* what they would unto those 6213
Job 1: 5 Thus *d'* Job continually. "
2:10 In all this *d'* not Job sin with his lips.
3:11 why *d'* I not give up the ghost
12 Why *d'* the knees prevent me?
6:22 *D'* I say, Bring unto me?
28:27 Then *d'* he see it, and declare it;
30:25 *D'* not I weep for him that was in
31:13 If I *d'* despise the cause of my
15 *D'* not he that made me in the
15 *d'* not one fashion us in the womb?
32 The stranger *d'* not lodge in the
34 *D'* I fear a great multitude, *
34 or *d'* the contempt of families *
42: 9 and *d'* according as the Lord 6213
11 and *d'* eat bread with him in his
Ps 14: 2 if there were any that *d'* understand,
18:10 upon a cherub, and *d'* fly: yea,
10 he *d'* fly upon the wings of the *
22 I *d'* not put away his statutes *
36 that my feet *d'* not slip. *
37 neither *d'* I turn again till they *
42 Then *d'* I beat them small as the dust
42 I *d'* cast them out as the dirt in the
31:11 they that *d'* see me without fled
35:11 False witnesses *d'* rise up; *
15 they *d'* tear me, and ceased not:
41: 9 which *d'* eat of my bread,
44: 3 neither *d'* their own arm save them:
45: 9 upon the right hand *d'* stand the *
51: 5 and in sin *d'* my mother conceive me.
53: 2 there were any that *d'* understand,
2 that *d'* seek God.
55:12 that *d'* magnify himself against me;
66: 6 there *d'* we rejoice in him.
68:12 Kings of armies *d'* flee apace: *
78:12 Marvellous things *d'* he in the 6213
25 Man *d'* eat angel's food:
29 so they *d'* eat, and were well filled:
33 their days *d'* he consume in vanity,
36 Nevertheless they *d'* flatter him *
38 and *d'* not stir up all his wrath.
40 How oft *d'* they provoke him
102:19 from heaven *d'* the Lord behold the
105:35 And *d'* eat up all the herbs in
106:34 They *d'* not destroy the nations,
43 Many times *d'* he deliver them;
119:23 also *d'* sit and speak against *
23 but thy servant *d'* meditate in thy*
135: 6 pleased, that *d'* he in heaven, and 6213
139:16 Thine eyes *d'* see my substance, yet
142: 1 unto the Lord *d'* I make my *
Pr 1:29 and *d'* not choose the fear of the
Isa 5:25 and the hills *d'* tremble,
6: 2 and with twain he *d'* fly.
9: 1 afterward *d'* more grievously *
10:10 and whose graven images *d'* excel
13: 1 which Isaiah the son of Amoz *d'* see.
14:16 that *d'* shake kingdoms;
20: 2 And he *d'* so, walking naked and 6213
22:12 that day *d'* the Lord God of hosts call
38:14 or a swallow, so *d'* I chatter:
14 I *d'* mourn as a dove:
42:24 *d'* not the Lord, he against whom
48: 3 I *d'* them suddenly, and they came 6213
53: 4 yet we *d'* esteem him stricken
58: 2 as a nation that *d'* righteousness, 6213
65:12 when I called, ye *d'* not answer;

Isa 65:12 when I spake, ye d' not hear:
12 d' evil before mine eyes, and d' *6213
66: 4 when I called, none d' answer:
4 when I spake, they d' not hear:
4 but they d' evil before mine eyes, 6213
Jer 7:12 and see what I d' to it for the "
26 they d' worse than their fathers.
11: 8 but they d' them not. 6213
14: 6 the wild asses d' stand in the high *
6 their eyes d' fail, *
15: 4 for that which he d' in Jerusalem. 6213
16 and I d' eat them;
22:15 d' not thy father eat and drink,
26:19 D' Hezekiah king of Judah...put him
19 d' he not fear the Lord,
31:19 I d' bear the reproach of my youth.
36: 8 the son of Neriah d' according to 6213
37: 2 d' hearken unto the words of the
38:12 the cords. And Jeremiah d' so, 6213
44:19 d' we make her cakes to worship
21 d' not the Lord remember them,
46:15 because the Lord d' drive them.
17 They d' cry there, Pharaoh king *
21 they d' not stand, because the day
52: 2 And he d' that which was evil in 6213
21 fillet of twelve cubits d' compass it;
33 and he d' continually eat bread
La 1: 7 and none d' help her:
7 and d' mock at her sabbaths.
4: 5 They that d' feed delicately are
Eze 3: 3 Then d' I eat it; and it was in
6:13 the place where they d' offer sweet
11 22 Then d' the cherubims lift up their
12: 7 And I d' so as I was commanded: 6213
16:49 neither d' she strengthen the hand
17: 7 this vine d' bend her roots toward
18:18 and d' that which is not good 6213
20: 8 they d' not every man cast away
8 neither d' they forsake the idols of
17 neither d' I make an end of them
24:18 I d' in the morning as I was 6213
27:25 ships of Tarshish d' sing of thee, *
31: 6 branches d' all the beasts...bring
34: 6 and none d' search or seek after
8 neither d' my shepherds search for
43:22 as they d' cleanse it with the
46:12 as he d' on the sabbath day: *6213
Da 1:15 children which d' eat the portion of
3:24 D' not we cast three men bound
4: 7 but they d' not make known unto
33 and d' eat grass as oxen,
6:10 as he d' aforetime. 5648
7: 9 and the Ancient of days d' sit,
8: 4 but he d' according to his will, 6213
27 I rose up, and d' the king's "
10: 3 neither d' I anoint myself at all,
Ho 2: 8 For she d' not know that I gave her
9:17 because they d' not hearken unto
10: 9 of iniquity d' not overtake them. *
13: 5 I d' know thee in the wilderness,
Am 1:11 because he d' pursue his brother
11 and d' cast off all pity,
11 and his anger d' tear perpetually,
5:19 As if a man d' flee from a lion. *
7: 4 and d' eat up a part.
Ob 14 to cut off those of his that d' escape;
14 those of his that d' remain in the
Jon 3:10 do unto them: and he d' it not. 6213
4: 8 when the sun d' arise, *
Na 2:12 The lion d' tear in pieces enough
Hab 1: 1 which Habakkuk the prophet d' see.
3: 6 the perpetual hills d' bow:
7 of the land of Midian d' tremble.
Hag 1: 9 I d' blow upon it.
12 the people d' fear before the Lord.
14 they came and d' work in the 6213
Zec 1: 4 but they d' not hear,
6 d' they not take hold of your
21 so that no man d' lift up his head:
7: 5 seventy years d' ye at all fast *
6 when ye d' eat, and when ye d' drink,
6 d' not ye eat for yourselves,
9: 3 Tyrus d' build herself a stronghold,
Mal 2: 6 and d' turn many away from
15 And d' not he make one?
M't 1:24 being raised from sleep d' as 4160
2:22 that Archelaus d' reign in Judæa *
9:19 and so d' his disciples.
12: 3 Have ye not read what David d' 4160
4 and d' eat the shewbread,
13:58 And he d' not many mighty works 4160
14:20 And they d' all eat, and were filled:
15: 7 well d' Esaias prophesy of you,
37 And they d' all eat, and were filled:
38 they that d' eat were four thousand
17: 2 and his face d' shine as the sun,
19: 7 Why d' Moses then command to give
20: 5 and ninth hour, and d' likewise. 4160
21: 6 went and d' as Jesus commanded "
15 the wonderful things that he d', "
25 Why d' ye not them believe him?
31 twain d' the will of his father? 4160
36 and they d' unto them likewise.
42 D' ye never read in the scriptures,
25:44 and d' not minister unto thee?
45 as ye d' it not to one of the least 4160
45 of these, ye d' it not to me. "
26:12 on my body, she d' it for my burial. "
19 disciples d' as Jesus had appointed "
21 And as they d' eat, he said,
67 Then d' they spit in his face,
27: 9 of the children of Israel d' value;
35 upon my vesture d' they cast lots. *
51 and the earth d' quake,
28: 4 for fear of him the keepers d' shake,
8 d' run to bring his disciples word. *

M't 28:15 money and d' as they were taught. 4160
M'r 1: 4 John d' baptize in the wilderness, *
6 he d' eat locusts and wild honey;
32 And at even, when the sun d' set,
2:25 read what David d', when he had 4160
26 and d' eat the shewbread,
3: 8 great things he d', came unto him. 4160
4: 8 and d' yield fruit that sprang up *
5:20 and all men d' marvel.
6:20 he d' many things, and heard *4160
42 And they d' all eat, and were filled.
44 they that d' eat of the loaves were
8: 6 d' set them before the people. *
8 So they d' eat, and were filled:
10: 3 What d' Moses command you?
11:31 Why then d' ye not believe him?
12:44 they d' cast in of their abundance;
44 of her want d' cast in all that she had,
14:18 and as they sat and d' eat; *
22 as they d' eat, Jesus took bread, *
59 neither so d' their witness agree
65 the servants d' strike him with *
15:19 and d' spit upon him,
Lu 4: 2 and in those days he d' eat nothing:
6: 1 and d' eat, rubbing them in their
3 what David d', when himself was 4160
4 and d' take and eat the shewbread,
10 and he d' so: and his hand was 4160
23 the like manner d' their fathers "
26 for so d' their fathers to the false "
49 the stream d' beat vehemently, *
7:38 and d' wipe them with the hairs of *
9:15 And they d' so, and made them all 4160
17 And they d' eat, and were all filled:
43 at all things which Jesus d', he 4160
53 And they d' not receive him,
54 consume them, even as Elias did? *4160
11:40 d' not he that made that which is
12:47 neither d' according to his will, 4160
48 d' commit things worthy of stripes,
15:16 with the husks that the swine d' eat:
17: 9 because he d' things that were 4160
27, 28 They d' eat, they drank, *
19:22 and reaping that I d' not sow:
24:32 D' not our heart burn within us, *
43 and d' eat before them.
Joh 1:45 the law, and the prophets, d' write,
2:11 of miracles d' Jesus, in Cana of 4160
23 they saw the miracles which he d'. "
24 But Jesus d' not commit himself
4:29 all things that ever I d': is not 4160
39 He told me all that ever I d'. "
45 the things that he d' at Jerusalem "
54 miracle that Jesus d', when he was "
5:16 therefore d' the Jews persecute Jesus,
6: 2 which he d' on them that were 4160
14 miracle that Jesus d', said, This "
23 where they d' eat bread,
26 but because ye d' eat of the loaves, *
31 fathers d' eat manna in the desert; *
49 your fathers d' eat manna in the
58 not as your fathers d' eat manna,
7: 5 For neither d' his brethren believe
19 D' not Moses give you the law,
8:40 of God: this d' not Abraham, 4160
9: 2 Master, who d' sin, this man, or his
18 But the Jews d' not believe
22 man d' confess that he was Christ, *
26 What d' he to thee? how opened 4160
27 and ye d' not hear:
10: 8 but the sheep d' not hear them.
41 John d' no miracle: but all things 4160
11:45 seen the things which Jesus d', *
12:36 and d' hide himself from them. *
42 the Pharisees they d' not confess him,
15:24 which none other man d'. they 4160
18:15 followed Jesus, and so d' another
26 D' not I see thee in the garden with
34 or d' others tell it thee of me?
19:24 for my vesture they d' cast lots.
24 things therefore the soldiers d'. 4160
20: 4 other disciples d' outrun Peter *
30 other signs truly d' Jesus in 4160
21: 7 and d' cast himself into the sea. *
25 many other things which Jesus d', 4160
Ac 2:22 which God d' by him in the midst *
26 Therefore d' my heart rejoice, *
31 neither his flesh d' see corruption.
40 many other words d' he testify *
46 d' eat their meat with gladness and
3:17 through ignorance ye d' it, 4238
17 as d' also your rulers.
4:25 Why d' the heathen rage, and the
5:28 D' not we straitly command you *
6: 8 faith and power, d' great wonders *4160
7:27 that d' his neighbour wrong thrust 91
35 the same d' God send to be a ruler *
51 as your fathers d', so do ye.
8: 6 seeing the miracles which he d'. 4160
9: 9 and neither d' eat nor drink.
36 works and almsdeeds which she d'. 4160
10:39 of all things which he d' both in
41 who d' eat and drink with him after
11:17 God gave them the like gift as he d'
30 Which also they d', and sent it to 4160
12: 8 bind on thy sandals, so he d'.
14:17 in that he d' good, and gave us rain 15
15: 8 Holy Ghost, even as he d' unto us;
14 God at the first d' visit the Gentiles
16:18 And this d' she many days. But 4160
19:14 and chief of the priests which d' so. "
21: 9 virgins, which d' prophesy.
26:10 thing I also d' in Jerusalem: 4160
22 and Moses d' say should come:
Ro 1:26 even their women d' change the *
28 even as they d' not like to retain *

Ro 3: 3 For what if some d' not believe? *
5:20 grace d' much more abound:
7: 5 d' work in our members to bring *
8:29 For whom he d' foreknow, *
29 d' predestinate to be conformed *
30 whom he d' predestinate, *
10:19 D' not Israel know?
1Co 4: 8 and I would to God ye d' reign,
10: 3 d' all eat the same spiritual meat;
4 d' all drink the same spiritual drink:
15:27 which d' put all things under him.
2Co 1:17 d' I use lightness?
2: 9 For to this end also d' I write,
5:20 as though God d' beseech you *
7: 8 though I d' repent:
12 I d' it not for his cause that had *
8: 5 this they d', not as we hoped, *
12:16 But be it so, I d' not burden you:
17 D' I make a gain of you by any of
18 D' Titus make a gain of you?
Ga 2:12 he d' eat with the Gentiles:
4: 8 ye d' service unto them which *
5: 7 Ye d' run well: who *
7 who d' hinder you that ye should not
Ph'p 4:14 d' communicate with my affliction.
2Th 3: 8 Neither d' we eat any man's bread
1Ti 1:13 because I d' it ignorantly in
2Ti 4:14 Alexander the coppersmith d' me 1731
Heb 3:16 when they had heard, d' provoke:
4: 2 word preached d' not profit them:
4 God d' rest the seventh day from
10 his own works, as God d' from his.
7:19 bringing in of a better hope d'.
27 for this he d' once, when he offered 4160
9: 9 him that d' the service perfect, *3000
1Pe 1:11 Christ which was in them d' signify.
12 unto us they d' minister the things,
2:22 Who d' no sin, neither was guile 4160
Re 12: 4 and d' cast them to the earth:
13:14 the wound by a sword, and d' live. *
19: 2 which d' corrupt the earth with her
21:23 for the glory of God d' lighten it,

diddest See also DIDST.
Ac 7:28 thou d' the Egyptian yesterday? * 337

didst See also DIDDEST.
Ge 12:18 Why d' thou not tell me that
18:15 Nay; but thou d' laugh.
20: 6 I know that thou d' this in the *6213
21:26 neither d' thou tell me,
31:27 Wherefore d' thou flee away
27 and d' not tell me,
39 of my hand d' thou require it,
Ex 15:10 Thou d' blow with thy wind,
40:15 as thou d' anoint their father,
De 3: 2 as thou d' unto Sihon king of 6213
9: 7 from the day that thou d' depart *
32:14 and thou d' drink the pure *
33: 8 whom thou d' prove at Massah,
8 and with whom thou d' strive
Jos 2:18 window which thou d' let us down by:
8: 2 thou d' unto Jericho and her king: 6213
1Sa 3: 6, 8 Here am I; for thou d' call me. *
15:19 Wherefore d' thou not obey the
19 but d' fly upon the spoil,
19 and d' evil in the sight of the 6213
19: 5 thou sawest it, and d' rejoice:
20:19 the place where thou d' hide thyself
25:25 of my lord, whom thou d' send.
2Sa 11:10 Why then d' thou not go down
12:12 For thou d' it secretly: but I will 6213
21 thou d' fast and weep for the child,
21 thou d' rise and eat bread.
13:16 the other that thou d' unto me. 6213
18:11 and why d' thou not smite him
19:28 yet d' thou set thy servant among
1Ki 1:13 D' not thou, my lord, O king, swear
2:44 that thou d' to David my father: 6213
8:18 thou d' well that it was in thine
20: 9 All that thou d' send for to thy
21:10 Thou d' blaspheme God and the king.
1Ch 17:22 For thy people Israel d' thou make
2Ch 2: 3 As thou d' deal with David my father,
3 and d' send him cedars to build him
6: 8 d' well in that it was in thine heart:
16: 8 because thou d' rely on the Lord,
20: 7 who d' drive out the inhabitants
34:27 thou d' humble thyself before God,
27 and d' rend thy clothes, and weep *
Ne 9: 7 the God, who d' choose Abram,
9 and d' see the affliction of our *
10 So d' thou get thee a name, as it is
11 And thou d' divide the sea before them,
17 wonders that thou d' among them; 6213
21 forty years d' thou sustain them in the
22 and d' divide them into corners:
28 and many times d' thou deliver them
30 Yet many years d' thou forbear them,
31 thou d' not utterly consume them,
34 wherewith thou d' testify against
Ps 22: 4 they trusted, and thou d' deliver them.
9 thou d' make me hope when I was upon
30: 7 thou d' hide thy face, and I was
39: 9 not my mouth; because thou d' it. 6213
40: 6 and offering thou d' not desire; *
44: 1 what work thou d' in their days, 6466
2 how thou d' drive out the heathen
2 how thou d' afflict the people,
60:10 d' not go out with our armies? *
68: 7 thou d' march through the wilderness;
9 Thou, O God, d' send a plentiful rain,
9 thou d' confirm thine inheritance,
73:18 d' set them in slippery places: *
74:13 Thou d' divide the sea by thy strength:
15 Thou d' cleave the fountain and the
76: 8 Thou d' cause judgment to be heard

Ps 80: 9 and *d'* cause it to take deep root,*
Isa 14:12 which *d'* weaken the nations!
22: 8 and thou *d'* look in that day to the
47: 6 thou *d'* shew them no mercy;
7 so that thou *d'* not lay these things to
7 *d'* remember the latter end of it.
48: 6 and thou *d'* not know them. *
54: 1 barren, thou that *d'* not bear;
1 thou that *d'* not travail with child:
57: 9 and *d'* increase thy perfumes,
9 and *d'* send thy messengers far off,
9 and *d'* debase thyself even unto hell.
63:14 so *d'* thou lead thy people,
64: 3 When thou *d'* terrible things 6213
Jer 32:22 which thou *d'* swear to their fathers
36:17 How *d'* thou write all these words
45: 3 Thou *d'* say, Woe is me now!
La 1:10 thou *d'* command that they should
Eze 16:13 thou *d'* eat fine flour, and honey,
13 and thou *d'* prosper into a kingdom,
15 But thou *d'* trust in thine own beauty,
16 And of thy garments thou *d'* take, and
17 and *d'* commit whoredom with them,
36 which thou *d'* give unto them;
23:40 for whom thou *d'* wash thyself,
27:33 *d'* enrich the kings of the earth with
29: 7 thou *d'* break, and rend all their
35:15 As thou *d'* rejoice at the inheritance
Da 10:12 *d'* set thine heart to understand,
Ho 10:13 because thou *d'* trust in thy way,
Hab 3: 8 that thou *d'* ride upon thine horses
9 Thou *d'* cleave the earth with rivers.
12 Thou *d'* march through the land in
12 thou *d'* thresh the heathen in anger
14 Thou *d'* strike through with his slaves
15 Thou *d'* walk through the sea with
M't 14:31 wherefore *d'* thou doubt?
20:13 *d'* not thou agree with me for a penny?
Lu 7:46 My head with oil thou *d'* not anoint.
19:21 and reapest that thou *d'* not sow.
Joh 17: 8 believed that thou *d'* send me.
Ac 11: 3 uncircumcised, and *d'* eat with them.
1Co 4: 7 hast thou that thou *d'* not receive?
7 now if thou *d'* receive it, why dost thou
Heb 2: 7 and *d'* set him over the works of thy
Re 17: 7 Wherefore *d'* thou marvel?

Didymus (*did'-i-mus*) See also THOMAS.
Joh 11:16 said Thomas, which is called *D'*, *1324*
20:24 one of the twelve, called *D'*, "
21: 2 Simon Peter, and Thomas called *D'*."

die See also DEAD; DIED; DIETH; DYING.
Ge 2:17 eatest thereof thou shalt surely *d'*. 4191
3: 3 neither shall ye touch it, lest ye *d'*. "
4 the woman, Ye shall not surely *d'*: "
6:17 thing that is in the earth shall *d'*. 1478
19:19 lest some evil take me, and I *d'*: 4191
20: 7 thou shalt surely *d'*, thou, and all "
25:32 Behold, I am at the point to *d'*: "
26: 9 Because I said, Lest I *d'* for her. "
27: 4 my soul may bless thee before I *d'*. "
30: 1 Give me children, or else I *d'*. "
33:13 them one day, all the flock will *d'*. "
38:11 Lest peradventure he *d'* also, as "
42: 2 thence; that we may live, and not *d'*. "
20 be verified, and ye shall not *d'*. "
43: 8 go; that we may live, and not *d'*, "
44: 9 it be found, both let him *d'*, and we "
22 leave his father, his father would *d'*. "
31 lad is not with us, that he will *d'*: "
45:28 I will go and see him before I *d'*. "
46:30 Now let me *d'*, since I have seen "
47:15 why should we *d'* in thy presence? "
19 Wherefore shall we *d'* before thine "
19 seed, that we may live, and not *d'*, "
29 time drew nigh that Israel must *d'*: "
48:21 said unto Joseph, Behold, I *d'*: "
50: 5 made me swear, saying, Lo, I *d'*: "
24 Joseph said unto his brethren, I *d'*: "
Ex 7:18 the fish that is in the river shall *d'*, "
9: 4 there shall nothing *d'* of all that is "
19 down upon them, and they shall *d'*. "
10:28 thou seest my face thou shalt *d'*. "
11: 5 in the land of Egypt shall *d'*, "
14:11 us away to *d'* in the wilderness? "
12 that we should *d'* in the wilderness. "
20:19 not God speak with us, lest we *d'*. "
21:12 that smiteth a man, so that he *d'*, "
14 from mine altar, that he may *d'*. "
18 or with his fist, and he *d'* not, "
20 a rod, and he *d'* under his hand; "
28 a man or a woman, that they *d'*: "
35 man's ox hurt another's, that he *d'*; "
22: 2 up, and be smitten that he *d'*, "
10 it *d'*, or be hurt, or driven away, "
14 and it be hurt, or *d'*, the owner "
28:35 he cometh out, that he *d'* not. "
43 that they bear not iniquity, and *d'*: "
30:20 wash with water that they *d'* not;4191
21 and their feet, that they *d'* not: "
Le 8:35 charge of the Lord, that ye *d'* not; "
10: 6 rend your clothes, lest ye *d'*, "
7 of the congregation, lest ye *d'*: "
9 of the congregation, lest ye *d'*: "
11:39 any beast of which ye may eat, *d'*; "
15:31 they *d'* not in their uncleanness, "
16: 2 is upon the ark; that he *d'* not: "
13 the testimony, that he *d'* not: "
20:20 their sin: they shall *d'* childless. "
22: 9 lest they bear sin for it, and *d'* "
Nu 4:15 touch any holy thing, lest they *d'*. "
19 that they may live, and not *d'*, "
20 holy things are covered, lest they *d'*. "
6: 7 or for his sister, when they *d'*: 4194
9 any man *d'* very suddenly by him, 4191

Nu 14:35 consumed, and there they shall *d'*. 4191
16:29 If these men *d'* the common death "
17:10 from me, that they *d'* not. "
12 saying, Behold we *d'*, we perish, *1478
13 tabernacle of the Lord shall *d'*: *4191
18: 3 that neither they, nor ye also, *d'*. "
22 lest they bear sin, and *d'*. "
32 the children of Israel, lest ye *d'*. "
20: 4 that we and our cattle should *d'* "
26 unto his people, and shall *d'* there, "
21: 5 of Egypt to *d'* in the wilderness? "
23:10 me *d'* the death of the righteous, "
26:65 They shall surely *d'* in the "
27: 8 If a man *d'*, and have no son, "
35:12 that the manslayer *d'* not, until he "
16 instrument of iron, so that he *d'*, * "
17,18 wherewith he may *d'*, and he *d'*,* "
20 him by laying of wait, that he *d'*;* "
21 him with his hand, that he *d'*: * "
23 wherewith a man may *d'*, seeing "
23 cast it upon him, that he *d'*, * "
30 any person to cause him to *d'*. "
De 4:22 I must *d'* in this land, I must not "
5:25 Now therefore why should we *d'*? "
25 our God any more, then we shall *d'*. "
13:10 stone him with stones, that he *d'*; "
17: 5 stone them with stones, till they *d'*. "
12 the judge, even that man shall *d'*: "
18:16 great fire any more that I *d'* not. "
20 gods, even that prophet shall *d'*. "
19: 5 upon his neighbour, that he *d'*; "
11 smite him mortally that he *d'*, "
12 avenger of blood, that he may *d'*. "
20: 5, 6, 7 lest he *d'* in the battle, and "
21:21 stone him with stones, that he *d'*: "
22:21 stone her with stones that she *d'*: "
22 then they shall both of them *d'*, "
24 stone them with stones that they *d'*; "
25 man only that lay with her shall *d'*: "
24: 3 if the latter husband *d'*, which took "
7 that thief shall *d'*; and thou shalt "
25: 5 dwell together, and one of them *d'*, "
31:14 days approach that thou must *d'*: "
32:50 And *d'* in the mount whither thou "
33: 6 Let Reuben live, and not *d'*; and let "
Jos 20: 9 not *d'* by the hand of the avenger "
J'g 6:23 thee; fear not: thou shalt not *d'*. "
30 Bring out thy son, that he may *d'*: "
13:22 We shall surely *d'*, because we have "
15:18 and now shall I *d'* for thirst, and "
16:30 Let me *d'* with the Philistines. "
Ru 1:17 Where thou diest, will I *d'*, and "
1Sa 2:33 the increase of thine house shall *d'* "
34 in one day they shall *d'* both of "
12:19 the Lord thy God, that we *d'* not: "
14:39 my son, he shall surely *d'*. "
43 in mine hand, and, lo, I must *d'*. "
44 for thou shalt surely *d'*, Jonathan. "
45 Shall Jonathan *d'*, who hath "
20: 2 God forbid; thou shalt not *d'*: "
14 kindness of the Lord, that I *d'* not: "
31 unto me, for he shall surely *d'*. "
22:16 Thou shalt surely *d'*, Ahimelech, "
26:10 his day shall come to *d'*; or he "
16 ye are worthy to *d'*, because ye 4194
28: 9 for my life, to cause me to *d'*? 4191
2Sa 11:15 that he may be smitten, and *d'*. "
12: 5 done this thing shall surely *d'*: 4194
13 away thy sin; thou shalt not *d'*. 4191
14 is born unto thee shall surely *d'*. "
14:14 For we must needs *d'*, and are as "
18: 3 neither if half of us *d'*, will they "
19:23 said unto Shimei, Thou shalt not *d'*. "
37 that I may *d'* in mine own city, "
1Ki 1:52 shall be found in him, he shall *d'*. "
2: 1 David drew nigh that he should *d'*; "
30 he said, Nay; but I will *d'* here. "
37 certain that thou shalt surely *d'*: "
42 whither, that thou shalt surely *d'*? "
14:12 into the city, the child shall *d'*. "
17:12 that we may eat it, and *d'*. "
19: 4 for himself that he might *d'*; "
21:10 out, and stone him, that he may *d'*. "
2Ki 1: 4, 6, 16 gone up, but shalt surely *d'*. "
7: 3 Why sit we here until we *d'*? "
4 is in the city and we shall *d'* there: "
4 and if we sit still here, we *d'* also. "
4 and if they kill us, we shall but *d'*. "
8:10 showed me that he shall surely *d'*. "
18:32 that ye may live, and not *d'*: "
20: 1 for thou shalt *d'*, and not live. "
2Ch 25: 4 The fathers shall not *d'* for the "
4 neither shall the children *d'* for the "
4 but every man shall *d'* for his own "
32:11 to *d'* by famine and by thirst, "
Job 2: 9 thine integrity? curse God, and *d'*. "
4:21 they *d'*, even without wisdom. "
12: 2 and wisdom shall *d'* with you. "
14: 8 the stock thereof *d'* in the ground; "
14 If a man *d'*, shall he live again? "
27: 5 that I should justify you: till I *d'* 1478
29:18 Then I said, I shall *d'* in my nest, "
34:20 In a moment shall they *d'*, and the 4191
36:12 they shall *d'* without knowledge. 1478
14 They *d'* in youth, and their life is 4191
Ps 41: 5 When shall he *d'*, and his name "
49:10 For he seeth that wise men *d'*, "
79:11 those that are appointed to *d'*; *8546
82: 7 But ye shall *d'* like men, and fall 4191
88:15 I am afflicted and ready to *d'* from 1478
104:29 they *d'*, and return to their dust. "
118:17 I shall not *d'*, but live, and declare 4191
Pr 5:23 He shall *d'* without instruction; "
10:21 but fools *d'* for want of wisdom. "
15:10 he that hateth reproof shall *d'*. "

Pr 19:16 he that despiseth his ways shall *d'*.4191
23:13 him with the rod, he shall not *d'*. "
30: 7 deny me them not before I *d'*: "
Ec 3: 2 A time to be born, and a time to *d'*; "
7:17 why shouldest thou *d'* before thy "
9: 5 the living know that they shall *d'*: "
Isa 22:13 drink; for to-morrow we shall *d'*. "
14 not be purged from you till ye *d'*, "
18 there shalt thou *d'*, and there the "
38: 1 for thou shalt *d'*, and not live. "
51: 6 they that dwell therein shall *d'* in "
12 be afraid of a man that shall *d'*, "
14 that he should not *d'* in the pit, "
65:20 the child shall *d'* an hundred years "
66:24 their worm shall not *d'*, neither "
Jer 11:21 Lord, that thou *d'* not by our hand: "
22 young men shall *d'* by the sword; "
22 sons and their daughters shall *d'* "
16: 4 They shall *d'* of grievous deaths; "
6 the great and the small shall *d'* in "
20: 6 Babylon, and there thou shalt *d'*, "
21: 6 they shall *d'* of a great pestilence. "
9 He that abideth in this city shall *d'* "
22:12 he shall *d'* in the place whither they "
26 not born; and there shall ye *d'*. "
26: 8 him, saying, Thou shalt surely *d'*. "
11 This man is worthy to *d'*; for he *4194
16 This man is not worthy to *d'*: * "
27:13 will ye *d'*, thou and thy people, 4191
28:16 this year thou shalt *d'*, because "
31:30 But every one shall *d'* for his own "
34: 4 Thou shalt not *d'* by the sword: "
5 Thou shalt *d'* in peace: and with "
37:20 Jonathan the scribe, lest I *d'* there. "
38: 2 that remaineth in this city shall *d'* "
9 and he is like to *d'* for hunger "
10 out of the dungeon, before he *d'*. "
24 these words, and thou shalt not *d'*. "
26 to Jonathan's house, to *d'* there. "
42:16 in Egypt; and there ye shall *d'*. "
17 they shall *d'* by the sword, by the "
22 know certainly that ye shall *d'* by "
44:12 they shall *d'*, from the least even "
Eze 3:18 Thou shalt surely *d'*; and thou "
18 the same wicked man shall *d'* in "
19 way, he shall *d'* in his iniquity; "
20 he shall *d'*: because thou hast not "
20 him warning, he shall *d'* in his sin, "
5:12 of thee shall *d'* with the pestilence, "
6:12 He that is far off shall *d'* of the "
12 remaineth and is besieged shall *d'* "
7:15 he that is in the field shall *d'* with "
12:13 not see it, though he shall *d'* there. "
13:19 to slay the souls that should not *d'*, "
17:16 in the midst of Babylon he shall *d'*. "
18: 4 the soul that sinneth, it shall *d'*. "
13 he shall surely *d'*; his blood shall "
17 he shall not *d'* for the iniquity of "
18 even he shall *d'* in his iniquity. "
20 The soul that sinneth, it shall *d'*. "
21 he shall surely live, he shall not *d'*. "
23 at all that the wicked should *d'*? *4194
24 hath sinned, in them shall he *d'*. 4191
26 that he hath done shall he *d'*. "
28 he shall surely live, he shall not *d'*. "
31 why will ye *d'*, O house of Israel? "
28: 8 and thou shalt *d'* the deaths of them "
10 Thou shalt *d'* the deaths of the "
33: 8 thou shalt surely *d'*; if thou dost "
8 his way, that wicked man shall *d'* "
9 his way he shall *d'* in his iniquity; "
11 why will ye *d'*, O house of Israel? "
13 hath committed, he shall *d'* for it. "
14 Thou shalt surely *d'*; if he turn "
15 he shall surely live, he shall not *d'*. "
18 iniquity, he shall even *d'* thereby. "
27 the caves shall *d'* of the pestilence. "
Am 2: 2 and Moab shall *d'* with tumult, "
6: 9 in one house, that they shall *d'*, "
7:11 Jeroboam shall *d'* by the sword, "
17 thou shalt *d'* in a polluted land: "
9:10 the sinners of my people shall *d'* "
Jon 4: 3 is better for me to *d'* than to live. 4194
8 wished in himself to *d'*, and said, 4191
8 It is better for me to *d'* than to live."
Hab 1:12 mine Holy One? we shall not *d'*. "
Zec 11: 9 feed you: that that dieth, let it *d'*; "
13: 8 therein shall be cut off and *d'*; 1478
M't 15: 4 or mother, let him *d'* the death. *5053*
22:24 Master, Moses said, If a man *d'*, *599*
26:35 Though I should *d'* with thee, yet "
M'r 7:10 let him *d'* the death: But ye say, *5053*
12:19 If a man's brother *d'*, and leave *599*
14:31 If I should *d'* with thee, I will not *4880*
Lu 7: 2 him, was sick, and ready to *d'*. **5053*
20:28 If any man's brother *d'*, having a *599*
28 wife, and he *d'* without children, * "
36 Neither can they *d'* any more: for "
Joh 4:49 Sir, come down ere my child *d'*. "
6:50 a man may eat thereof, and not *d'*. "
8:21 seek me, and shall *d'* in your sins: "
24 that ye shall *d'* in your sins: for if "
24 unto you ye shall *d'* in your sins. "
11:16 also go, that we may *d'* with him. "
26 and believeth in me shall never *d'*. "
50 one man should *d'* for the people, "
51 that Jesus should *d'* for that nation; "
12:24 wheat fall into the ground and *d'*, "
24 it abideth alone: but if it *d'*, it "
33 signifying what death he should *d'*. "
18:14 one man should *d'* for the people. *622*
32 signifying what death he should *d'*.*599*
19: 7 and by our law he ought to *d'*, "
21:23 that disciple should not *d'*: yet "
23 said not unto him, He shall not *d'*; "

Ac 21:13 also to d' at Jerusalem for the 599
25:11 worthy of death, I refuse not to d': "
16 Romans to deliver any man to d',* 684
Ro 5: 7 for a righteous man will one d': 599
7 man some would even dare to d'. "
8:13 ye live after the flesh, ye shall d': "
14: 8 whether we d', we d' unto the Lord: "
8 therefore, or d', we are the Lord's. "
1Co 9:15 better for me to d', than that any "
15:22 For as in Adam all d', even so "
31 in Christ Jesus our Lord, I d' daily. "
32 eat and drink; for to morrow we d'. "
36 is not quickened, except it d': "
2Co 7: 3 our hearts to d' and live with you. 4880
Ph'p 1:21 to live is Christ, and to d' is gain. 599
Heb 7: 8 here men that d' receive tithes; "
9:27 it is appointed unto men once to d', "
Re 3: 2 which remain, that are ready to d': "
9: 6 not find it; and shall desire to d', "
14:13 are the dead which d' in the Lord "

died
Ge 5: 5 and thirty years: and he d'. 4191
8 and twelve years: and he d'. "
11 hundred and five years: and he d'. "
14 hundred and ten years: and he d'. "
17 ninety and five years: and he d'. "
20 sixty and two years: and he d'. "
27 sixty and nine years: and he d'. "
31 seventy and seven years: and he d'. "
7:21 And all flesh d' that moved upon 1478
22 all that was in the dry land, d'. 4191
9:29 hundred and fifty years: and he d'. "
11:28 Haran d' before his father Terah "
32 five years: and Terah d' in Haran. "
23: 2 And Sarah d' in Kirjath-arba; the "
25: 8 d' in a good old age, an old man, "
17 and he gave up the ghost and d'; "
18 he d' in the presence of all his *5307
35: 8 But Deborah Rebekah's nurse d', 4191
18 soul was in departing, (for she d') "
19 And Rachel d', and was buried in "
29 Isaac gave up the ghost, and d', "
36:33 And Bela d', and Jobab the son of "
34 And Jobab d', and Husham of the "
35 And Husham d', and Hadad the son "
36 And Hadad d', and Samlah of "
37 Samlah d', and Saul of Rehoboth "
38 Saul d', and Baal-hanan the son of "
39 Baal-hanan the son of Achbor d', "
38:12 daughter of Shuah Judah's wife d'; "
46:12 and Onan d' in the land of Canaan. "
48: 7 Rachel d' by me in the land of "
50:16 father did command before he d', 4194
26 Joseph d', being an hundred and 4191
Ex 1: 6 Joseph d', and all his brethren, "
2:23 of time that the king of Egypt d': "
7:21 the fish that was in the river d'; "
8:13 and the frogs d' out of the houses, "
9: 6 and all the cattle of Egypt d': "
6 of the children of Israel d' not one. "
16: 3 Would to God we had d' by the "
Lev 10: 2 them, and they d' before the Lord. "
16: 1 offered before the Lord, and d'; "
17:15 soul that eateth that which d' of *5038
Nu 3: 4 and Abihu d' before the Lord, 4191
14: 2 we had d' in the land of Egypt! "
2 God we had d' in this wilderness! "
37 up the evil report upon the land, d' "
15:36 stoned him with stones, and he d'; "
16:49 they that d' in the plague were "
49 that d' about the matter of Korah. "
20: 1 Miriam d' there, and was buried "
3 Would God that we had d' when 1478
3 our brethren d' before the Lord! "
28 Aaron d' there in the top of the 4191
21: 6 and much people of Israel d'. "
25: 9 those that d' in the plague were "
26:10 when that company d', what time 4194
11 the children of Korah d' not. 4191
19 and Onan d' in the land of Canaan. "
61 And Nadab and Abihu d', when "
27: 3 Our father d' in the wilderness, and "
3 d' in his own sin, and had no sons. "
33:38 of the Lord, and d' there, "
39 old when he d' in mount Hor. 4194
De 10: 6 Aaron d', and there he was buried ;4191
32:50 Aaron thy brother d' in mount Hor, "
34: 5 Moses the servant of the Lord d' "
7 and twenty years old when he d': 4194
Jos 5: 4 d' in the wilderness by the way, 4191
10:11 them unto Azekah, and they d': "
11 more which d' with hailstones than "
24:29 of Nun, the servant of the Lord, d'. "
33 Eleazar the son of Aaron d'; and "
J'g 1: 7 him to Jerusalem, and there he d'. "
2: 8 of Nun, the servant of the Lord, d', "
21 which Joshua left when he d': "
3:11 And Othniel the son of Kenaz d'. "
4:21 fast asleep and weary. So he d'. "
8:32 And Gideon the son of Joash d' "
9:49 the men of the tower of Shechem d' "
54 man thrust him through, and he d'. "
10: 2 twenty and three years, and d', "
5 And Jair d', and was buried in "
12: 7 Then d' Jephthah the Gileadite, and "
10 Then d' Ibzan, and was buried at "
12 And Elon the Zebulonite d', and was "
15 son of Hillel the Pirathonite d', "
Ru 1: 3 Elimelech Naomi's husband d'; "
5 and Chilion d' also both of them; "
1Sa 4:18 and his neck brake, and he d': "
5:12 the men that d' not were smitten "
14:45 rescued Jonathan, that he d' not. "
25: 1 Samuel d'; and all the Israelites "
37 that his heart d' within him, and he "
1Sa 25:38 the Lord smote Nabal, that he d'. 4191
31: 5 upon his sword, and d' with him. "
6 So Saul d', and his three sons, "
2Sa 1:15 And he smote him that he d'. "
2:23 and d' in the same place: and it "
23 Asahel fell down and d' stood still. "
31 hundred and threescore men d'. "
3:27 under the fifth rib, that he d', "
33 said, D' Abner as a fool dieth? * "
6: 7 and there he d' by the ark of God. "
10: 1 king of the children of Ammon d', "
18 captain of their host, who d' there. "
11:17 and Uriah the Hittite d' also. "
21 the wall, that he d' in Thebez? "
12:18 the seventh day, that the child d'. "
17:23 and hanged himself, and d', and "
18:33 would God I had d' for thee, "
19: 6 all we had d' this day, then it had "
20:10 struck him not again; and he d'. "
24:15 there d' of the people from Dan "
1Ki 2:25 and he fell upon him that he d'. "
46 and fell upon him, that he d'. "
3:19 woman's child d' in the night; "
12:18 stoned him with stones, that he d'. "
14:17 threshold of the door, the child d': "
16:18 house over him with fire, and d', "
22 so Tibni d', and Omri reigned. "
21:13 stoned him with stones, that he d'. "
22:35 against the Syrians, and d' at even: "
37 So the king d', and was brought to "
2Ki 1:17 So he d' according to the word of "
4:20 on her knees till noon, and then d'. "
7:17 upon him in the gate, and he d', as "
20 upon him in the gate, and he d'. "
8:15 spread it on his face, so that he d': "
9:27 he fled to Megiddo, and d' there. "
12:21 his servants, smote him, and he d'; "
13:14 sick of his sickness whereof he d'. "
20 And Elisha d', and they buried him. "
24 So Hazael king of Syria d'; and "
23:34 he came to Egypt, and d' there. "
25:25 and smote Gedaliah, that he d', "
1Ch 1:51 Hadad d' also. And the dukes of "
2:30 but Seled d' without children. "
32 and Jether d' without children. "
10: 5 fell likewise on the sword, and d'. "
6 So Saul d', and his three sons, "
6 and all his house d' together. "
13 So Saul d' for his transgression "
13:10 and there he d' before God. "
19: 1 king of the children of Ammon d', "
23:22 And Eleazar d', and had no sons, "
24: 2 Nadab and Abihu d' before their "
29:28 And he d' in a good old age, "
2Ch 10:18 stoned him with stones, that he d'. "
13:20 the Lord struck him, and he d'. "
16:13 and d' in the one and fortieth year "
18:34 time of the sun going down he d'. "
21:19 sickness: so he d' of sore diseases. "
24:15 and was full of days when he d'; "
15 years old was he when he d'. 4194
22 And when he d', he said, The Lord 4191
25 slew him on his bed, and he d': "
35:24 him to Jerusalem, and he d', "
Job 3:11 Why d' I not from the womb? "
42:17 Job d', being old and full of days. "
Isa 6: 1 In the year that king Uzziah d' 4194
14:28 In the year that king Ahaz d' "
Jer 28:17 So Hananiah the prophet d' the 4191
Eze 11:13 Pelatiah the son of Benaiah d'. "
24:18 and at even my wife d'; and I did "
Ho 13: 1 when he offended in Baal, he d'. "
M't 22:27 And last of all the woman d' also. 599
M'r 12:21 the second took her, and d', neither "
22 seed: last of all the woman d' also. "
Lu 16:22 it came to pass, that the beggar d', "
22 rich man also d', and was buried; "
20:29 a wife, and d' without children. * "
30 her to wife, and he d' childless. "
31 and they left no children, and d'. "
32 Last of all the woman d' also. "
Joh 11:21, 32 here, my brother had not d'. 599
37 even this man should not have d'? "
Ac 7:15 Egypt, and d', he, and our fathers, 5053
9:37 days, that she was sick, and d': 599
Ro 5: 6 time Christ d' for the ungodly. "
8 were yet sinners, Christ d' for us. "
6:10 in that he d', he d' unto sin once: "
7: 9 came, sin revived, and I d'. "
8:34 It is Christ that d', yea rather, "
14: 9 To this end Christ both d', and rose, "
15 with thy meat, for whom Christ d'. "
1Co 8:11 brother perish, for whom Christ d'? "
15: 3 how that Christ d' for our sins "
2Co 5:14 one d' for all, then were all dead: "
15 that he d' for all, that they which "
15 but unto him which d' for them, "
1Th 4:14 that Jesus d' and rose again, even "
5:10 Who d' for us, that, whether we "
Heb 10:28 Moses' law d' without mercy under* "
11:13 These all d' in faith, not having "
22 By faith Joseph when he d', made 5053
Re 8: 9 were in the sea, and had life, d'; * 599
11 many men d' of the waters, "
16: 3 every living soul d' in the sea. "

diest
Ru 1:17 Where thou d', will I die, and 4191

diet
Jer 52:34 And for his d', there was a * 737
34 there was a continual d' given * "

dieth
Le 7:24 fat of the beast that d' of itself, 5038
22: 8 That which d' of itself, or is torn "
Nu 19:14 when a man d' in a tent: 4191
De 14:21 eat of any thing that d' of itself: 5038
2Sa 3:33 said, Died Abner as a fool d'? 4194
1Ki 14:11 Him that d' of Jeroboam in the 4191
11 eat; and him that d' in the field "
16: 4 Him that d' of Baasha in the city "
4 and him that d' of his in the fields "
21:24 Him that d' of Ahab in the city "
24 eat; and him that d' in the field "
Job 14:10 But man d', and wasteth away: "
21:23 One d' in his full strength, being "
25 d' in the bitterness of his soul, "
Ps 49:17 when he d' he shall carry nothing 4194
Pr 11: 7 a wicked man d', his expectation "
Ec 2:16 And how d' the wise man? as the*4191
3:19 as the one d', so d' the other; 4194
Isa 50: 2 is no water, and d' for thirst. 4191
59: 5 he that eateth of their eggs d', "
Eze 4:14 eaten of that which d' of itself, 5038
18:26 iniquity, and d' in them; 4191
32 pleasure in the death of him that d', "
Zec 11: 9 feed you: that that d', let it die; "
M'r 9:44, 46 Where their worm d' not, and *5053
48 Where their worm d' not, and "
Ro 6: 9 raised from the dead, d' no more; 599
14: 7 himself, and no man d' to himself. "

differ See also DIFFERETH; DIFFERING.
1Co 4: 7 maketh thee to d' from another? 1252

difference See also DIFFERENCES.
Ex 11: 7 the Lord doth put a d' between 6395
Le 10:10 And that ye may put d' between holy 914
11:47 d' between the unclean and the "
20:25 shall therefore put d' between * "
Eze 22:26 they have put no d' between the "
26 have they showed d' between "
44:23 the d' between the holy and "
Ac 15: 9 no d' between us and them, *1252
Ro 3:22 that believe: for there is no d': *1293
10:12 no d' between the Jew and the * "
1Co 7:34 There is d' also between a wife 3307
Jude 22 have compassion, making a d': *1252

differences
1Co 12: 5 there are d' of administrations, *1243

differeth
1Co 15:41 for one star d' from another star 1308
Ga 4: 1 a child, d' nothing from a servant, 1308

differing
Ro 12: 6 gifts d' according to the grace 1313

dig See also DIGGED; DIGGETH.
Ex 21:33 if a man shall d' a pit, and not 3738
De 8: 9 whose hills thou mayest d' brass. 2672
23:13 thou shalt d' therewith, and shalt 2658
Job 3:21 d' for it more than for hid treasures: "
6:27 and ye d' a pit for your friend. *3738
11:18 yea, thou shalt d' about thee, *2658
24:16 the dark they d' through houses, 2864
Eze 8: 8 Son of man, d' now in the wall: "
12: 5 D' thou through the wall in their "
12 d' through the wall to carry out, "
Am 9: 2 Though they d' into hell, thence "
Lu 13: 8 till I shall d' about it, and dung it: 4626
16: 3 I cannot d'; to beg I am ashamed. "

digged See also DIGGEDST.
Ge 21:30 unto me, that I have d' this well. 2658
26:15 had d' in the days of Abraham "
18 Isaac d' again the wells of water; "
18 which they had d' in the days of "
19 Isaac's servants d' in the valley, "
21 And they d' another well, and "
22 from thence, and d' another well; "
25 there Isaac's servants d' a well. 3738
32 the well which they had d', and 2658
49: 6 their selfwill they d' down a wall.*6131
50: 5 in my grave which I have d' for 3738
Ex 7:24 the Egyptians d' round about the 2658
Nu 21:18 The princes d' the well, "
18 the nobles of the people d' it, *3738
De 6:11 wells d', which thou diggedst not,*2672
2Ki 19:24 d' and drunk strange waters, 5365
2Ch 26:10 in the desert, and d' many wells: *2672
Ne 9:25 houses full of all goods, wells d', * "
Ps 7:15 He made a pit, and d' it, and is 2658
35: 7 cause they have d' for my soul. "
57: 6 they have d' a pit before me, into 3738
94:13 until the pit be d' for the wicked. "
119:85 The proud have d' pits for me, "
Isa 5: 6 it shall not be pruned, nor d'; *5737
7:25 on all hills that shall be d' with "
37:25 I have d', and drunk water; and 5365
51: 1 hole of the pit whence ye are d'. "
Jer 13: 7 Then I went to Euphrates, and d', 2658
18:20 they have d' a pit for my soul. 3738
22 they have d' a pit to take me, "
Eze 8: 8 and when I had d' in the wall, 2864
12: 7 in the even I d' through the wall "
M't 21:33 and d' a winepress in it, and built 3736
25:18 and d' in the earth, and hid his "
M'r 12: 1 and d' a place for the winefat, "
Lu 6:48 d' deep, and laid the foundation 4626
Ro 11: 3 and d' down thine altars; 2679

diggedst
De 6:11 wells digged, which thou d' not, *2672

diggeth
Pr 16:27 An ungodly man d' up evil: and *3738
26:27 Whoso d' a pit shall fall therein: "
Ec 10: 8 He that d' a pit shall fall into it; 2658

dignities
2Pe 2:10 are not afraid to speak evil of d'. 1391
Jude 8 dominion, and speak evil of d'.

dignity See also DIGNITIES.
Ge 49: 3 the excellency of d', and the 7613
Es 6: 3 What honour and d' has been done 1420

Ec 10: 6 Folly is set in great *d*, and the 4791
Hab 1: 7 *d* shall proceed of themselves. 7613

Diklah (*dik'-lah*)
Ge 10:27 And Hadoram, and Uzal, and *D*, 1853
1Ch 1:21 Hadoram also, and Uzal, and *D*, "

Dilean (*dil'-e-an*)
Jos 15:38 and *D*, and Mizpeh, and Joktheel,1810

diligence
Pr 4:23 Keep thy heart with all *d*; for out 4929
Lu 12:58 way, give *d* that thou mayest be *2039*
Ro 12: 8 he that ruleth, with *d*; he that *4710*
2Co 8: 7 and knowledge, and in all *d*, and * "
2Ti 4: 9 thy *d* to come shortly unto me: *4704*
21 Do thy *d* to come before winter. "
Heb 6:11 the same *d* to the full assurance *4710*
2Pe 1: 5 giving all *d*, add to your faith "
10 give *d* to make your calling and "
Jude 3 when I gave all *d* to write unto "

diligent
De 19:18 judges shall make *d* inquisition: 3190
Jos 22: 5 *d* heed to do the commandment 3966
Ps 64: 6 they accomplish a *d* search:
77: 6 heart: and my spirit made *d* search.
Pr 10: 4 the hand of the *d* maketh rich. 2742
12:24 The hand of the *d* shall bear rule: "
27 substance of a *d* man is precious. "
13: 4 the soul of the *d* shall be made fat. "
21: 5 The thoughts of the *d* tend only to "
22:29 thou a man *d* in his business? 4106
27:23 Be thou *d* to know the state of
2Co 8:22 often proved *d* in many things, *4705
22 but now much more *d*, upon 4707
Tit 3:12 *d* to come unto me to Nicopolis: *4704
2Pe 3:14 *d* that ye may be found of him in* "

diligently
Ex 15:26 If thou wilt *d* hearken to the voice
Le 10:16 And Moses *d* sought the goat of
De 4: 9 keep thy soul *d*, lest thou forget 3966
6: 7 teach them *d* unto thy children, 8150
17 Ye shall *d* keep the commandments
11:13 hearken *d* unto my commandments
22 For if ye shall *d* keep all these
13:14 make search, and ask *d*; and, 3190
17: 4 hast heard of it, and enquired *d*, "
24: 8 of leprosy, that thou observe *d*, 3966
28: 1 if thou shalt hearken *d* unto the
1Ki 20:33 did *d* observe whether any thing 5172
Ezr 7:23 let it be *d* done for the house of * 149
Job 13:17 Hear *d* my speech, and my
21: 2 Hear *d* my speech, and let this be
Ps 37:10 thou shalt *d* consider his place, 995
119: 4 us to keep thy precepts *d*. 3966
Pr 7:15 *d* to seek thy face, and I have 7836
11:27 He that *d* seeketh good procureth "
23: 1 ruler, consider *d* what is before thee:
Isa 21: 7 he hearkened *d* with much heed 7182
55: 2 hearken *d* unto me, and eat ye that
Jer 2:10 and consider *d*, and see if there 3966
12:16 if they will *d* learn the ways
17:24 if ye *d* hearken unto me, saith the
Zec 6:15 will *d* obey the voice of the Lord
M't 2: 7 of them *d* what time the star *
8 search *d* for the young child; * *199*
16 had *d* enquired of the wise men, *
Lu 15: 8 house, and seek *d* till she find it? *1960*
Ac 18:25 he spake and taught *d* the things* *199*
1Ti 5:10 *d* followed every good work.
2Ti 1:17 Rome, he sought me out very *d*, *4706*
Tit 3:13 and Apollos on their journey *d*, *4709*
Heb 11: 6 reward of them that *d* seek him. **1567*
12:15 Looking *d* lest any man fail of *
1Pe 1:10 have enquired and searched *d*,

dim
Ge 27: 1 was old, and his eyes were *d*, 3543
48:10 the eyes of Israel were *d* for age, 3513
De 34: 7 his eye was not dim, nor his 3543
1Sa 3: 2 his eyes began to wax *d*, that he 3544
4:15 his eyes were *d*, that he could *6965
Job 17: 7 eye also is *d* by reason of sorrow,3543
Isa 32: 3 of them that see shall not be *d*, 8159
La 4: 1 How is the gold become *d*! how 6004
5:17 for these things our eyes are *d*. 2821

diminish See also DIMINISHED; DIMINISHING; MINISH.
Ex 5: 8 ye shall not *d* ought thereof: for 1639
21:10 duty of marriage, shall he not *d*. "
Le 25:16 thou shalt *d* the price of it: 4591
De 4: 2 neither shall ye *d* ought from it, 1639
12:32 not add thereto, nor *d* from it. "
Jer 26: 2 speak unto them; *d* not a word: † "
Eze 5:11 therefore will I also *d* thee; "
29:15 for I will *d* them, that they shall 4591

diminished See also MINISHED.
Ex 5:11 ought of your work shall be *d*. 1639
Pr 13:11 gotten by vanity shall be *d*: 4591
Isa 21:17 children of Kedar, shall be *d*: * "
Jer 29: 6 may be increased there, and not *d*. "
Eze 16:27 and have *d* thine ordinary food, 1639

diminishing
Ro 11:12 and the *d* of them the riches of **2275*

Dimnah (*dim'-nah*)
Jos 21:35 *D* with her suburbs, Nahalal 1829

dimness
Isa 8:22 and darkness, *d* of anguish; *4588
9: 1 the *d* shall not be such as was *4155

Dimon (*di'-mon*) See also DIBON; DIMONAH.
Isa 15: 9 waters of *D* shall be full of blood: 1775
9 I will bring more upon *D*, "

Dimonah (*di-mo'-nah*) See also DIMON.
Jos 15:22 Kinah, and *D*, and Adadah. 1776

Dinah See also DINAH'S.
Ge 30:21 daughter, and called her name *D*. 1783
34: 1 *D* the daughter of Leah, which "
3 soul clave unto *D* the daughter of "
5 Jacob heard that he had defiled *D* "
13 he had defiled *D* their sister: "
26 took *D* out of Shechem's house, "
46:15 Padan-aram, with his daughter *D*:"

Dinah's
Ge 34:25 Simeon, and Levi, *D* brethren, 1783

Dinaites (*di'-na-ites*)
Ezr 4: 9 the *D*, the Apharsathchites, 1784

dine See also DINED.
Ge 43:16 these men shall *d* with me at noon. 398
Lu 11:37 besought him to *d* with him: *709*
Joh 21:12 saith unto them, Come and *d*. * "

dined
Joh 21:15 So when they had *d*, Jesus saith * *709*

Dinhabah (*din'-ha-bah*)
Ge 36:32 and the name of his city was *D*. 1838
1Ch 1:43 and the name of his city was *D*. "

dinner
Pr 15:17 is a *d* of herbs where love is, 737
M't 22: 4 Behold, I have prepared my *d*: *712*
Lu 11:38 had not first washed before *d*. "
14:12 When thou makest a *d* or a supper, "

Dionysius (*di-on-ish'-yus*)
Ac 17:34 the which was *D* the Areopagite, *1354*

Diotrephes (*di-ot'-re-feez*)
3Jo 9 I wrote unto the church: but *D*, *1361*

dip See also DIPPED; DIPPETH.
Ex 12:22 *d* it in the blood that is in the 2881
Le 4: 6 shall *d* his finger in the blood, "
17 *d* his finger in some of the blood, "
14: 6 shall *d* them and the living bird "
16 the priest shall *d* his right finger "
51 *d* them in the blood of the slain "
Nu 19:18 and *d* it in the water, and sprinkle "
De 33:24 and let him *d* his foot in oil. "
Ru 2:14 and *d* thy morsel in the vinegar. "
Lu 16:24 that he may *d* the tip of his finger *911*

dipped
Ge 37:31 and *d* the coat in the blood; 2881
Le 9: 9 and he *d* his finger in the blood, "
Jos 3:15 were *d* in the brim of the water, "
1Sa 14:27 and *d* it in an honeycomb, and put "
2Ki 5:14 *d* himself seven times in Jordan, "
8:15 and *d* it in water, and spread it on "
Ps 68:23 thy foot may be *d* in the blood ††4272
Joh 13:26 give a sop when I have *d* it. * *911*
26 had *d* the sop, he gave it to Judas *1686*
Re 19:13 with a vesture *d* in blood: * *911*

dippeth
M't 26:23 He that *d* his hand with me in **1686*
M'r 14:20 that *d* with me in the dish. "

direct See also DIRECTED; DIRECTETH.
Ge 46:28 to *d* his face unto Goshen; *3384
Ps 5: 3 will I *d* my prayer unto thee, *6186
Pr 3: 6 him, and he shall *d* thy paths. 3474
11: 5 of the perfect shall *d* his way: "
Ec 10:10 but wisdom is profitable to *d*. 3787
Isa 45:13 and I will *d* all his ways: *3474
61: 8 and I will *d* their work in truth, *5414
Jer 10:23 man that walketh to *d* his steps. 3559
1Th 3:11 Christ, *d* our way unto you. *2720*
2Th 3: 5 *d* your hearts into the love of God, "

directed
Job 32:14 hath not *d* his words against me: 6186
Ps 119: 5 ways were *d* to keep thy statutes!*3559
Isa 40:13 Who hath *d* the spirit of the Lord, 8505

directeth
Job 37: 3 He *d* it under the whole heaven, *3474
Pr 16: 9 way: but the Lord *d* his steps. 3559
21:29 as for the upright, he *d* his way. * "

direction
Nu 21:18 it, by the *d* of the lawgiver, *

directly
Nu 19: 4 blood *d* before the tabernacle*413,5227
Eze 42:12 even the way *d* before the wall 1903

dirt
J'g 3:22 his belly; and the *d* came out. *6574
Ps 18:42 them out as the *d* in the streets. *2916
Isa 57:20 whose waters cast up mire and *d*. "

disallow See also DISALLOWED.
Nu 30: 5 if her father *d* her in the day that 5106

disallowed
Nu 30: 5 her, because her father *d* her. 5106
8 her husband *d* her on the day that "
11 his peace at her, and *d* her not: "
1Pe 2: 4 *d* indeed of men, but chosen of * *593*
7 the stone which the builders *d*, * "

disannul See also DISANNULLED; DISANNULLETH; DISANNULLING.
Job 40: 8 Wilt thou also *d* my judgment? ‡6565
Isa 14:27 purposed, and who shall *d* it? ‡ "
Ga 3:17 years after, cannot *d*, that it *208*

disannulled
Isa 28:18 covenant with death shall be *d*, ‡3722

disannulleth
Ga 3:15 no man *d*, or addeth thereto. * *114*

disannulling
Heb 7:18 verily a *d* of the commandment *115*

disappoint See also DISAPPOINTED; DISAPPOINTETH.
Ps 17:13 Arise, O Lord, *d* him, cast him *6923

disappointed
Pr 15:22 Without counsel purposes are *d*: 6565

disappointeth
Job 5:12 He *d* the devices of the crafty, *6565

discern See also DISCERNED; DISCERNETH; DISCERNING.
Ge 31:32 *d* thou what is thine with me, 5234
38:25 *D*, I pray thee, whose are these, "
2Sa 14:17 lord the king to *d* good and bad: 8085
19:35 can I *d* between good and evil? 3045
1Ki 3: 9 I may *d* between good and bad: 995
11 understanding to *d* judgment; 8085
Ezr 3:13 the people could not *d* the noise 5234
Job 4:16 I could not *d* the form thereof: "
6:30 cannot my taste *d* perverse things ?995
Eze 44:23 them to *d* between the unclean 3045
Jon 4:11 that cannot *d* between their right "
Mal 3:18 and *d* between the righteous and 7200
M't 16: 3 ye can *d* the face of the sky; *1252*
3 but can ye not *d* the signs of the
Lu 12:56 ye can *d* the face of the sky and **1381*
56 is it that ye do not *d* this time? *
Heb 5:14 exercised to *d* both good and evil. *1253*

discerned
Ge 27:23 he *d* him not, because his hands 5234
1Ki 20:41 and the king of Israel *d* him that "
Pr 7: 7 I *d* among the youths, a young 995
1Co 2:14 because they are spiritually *d*. * *350*

discerner
Heb 4:12 and is a *d* of the thoughts and **2924*

discerneth
Ec 8: 5 and a wise man's heart *d* both 3045

discerning
1Co 11:29 himself, not *d* the Lord's body. **1252*
12:10 to another *d* of spirits; to another *1253*

discharge See also DISCHARGED.
Ec 8: 8 and there is no *d* in that war; 4917

discharged
1Ki 5: 9 and will cause them to be *d* there,*5310

disciple See also DISCIPLES.
M't 10:24 The *d* is not above his master, *3101*
25 It is enough for the *d* that he be as "
42 water only in the name of a *d*, "
27:57 who also himself was Jesus' *d*: *3100*
Lu 6:40 The *d* is not above his master: *3101*
14:26 own life also, he cannot be my *d*. "
27 come after me, cannot be my *d*. "
33 that he hath, he cannot be my *d*. "
Joh 9:28 Thou art his *d*; but we are Moses' "
18:15 another *d*: that *d* was known "
16 Then went out that other *d*, which "
19:26 and the *d* standing by, whom he "
27 Then saith he to the *d*, Behold thy "
27 from that hour that *d* took her "
38 of Arimathæa, being a *d* of Jesus, "
20: 2 to the other *d*, whom Jesus loved, "
3 went forth, and that other *d*, "
4 and the other *d* did outrun Peter, "
8 Then went in also that other *d*, "
21: 7 Therefore that *d* whom Jesus loved "
20 seeth the *d* whom Jesus loved "
23 that that *d* should not die; "
24 This is the *d* which testifieth of "
Ac 9:10 *d* at Damascus, named Ananias; "
26 believed not that he was a *d*. "
36 Joppa a certain *d* named Tabitha,*3102*
16: 1 *d* was there, named Timotheus, *3101*
21:16 *d*, with whom we should lodge. "

disciples See also DISCIPLES'; FELLOWDISCIPLES.
Isa 8:16 seal the law among my *d*. 3928
M't 5: 1 he was set, his *d* came unto him: *3101*
8:21 another of his *d* said unto him, "
23 into a ship, his *d* followed him. "
25 his *d* came to him, and awoke * "
9:10 and sat down with him and his *d*. "
11 they said unto his *d*, Why eateth "
14 came to him the *d* of John, saying, "
14 fast oft, but thy *d* fast not? "
19 and followed him, and so did his *d*. "
37 saith he unto his *d*, The harvest "
10: 1 had called unto him his twelve *d*, "
11: 1 end of commanding his twelve *d*, "
2 of Christ, he sent two of his *d*, "
12: 1 *d* were an hungred, and began to "
2 thy *d* do that which is not lawful "
49 forth his hand toward his *d*, "
13:10 And the *d* came, and said unto him, "
36 into the house: and his *d* came "
14:12 his *d* came, and took up the body, "
15 his *d* came to him, saying, This is "
19 loaves to his *d*, and the *d* to the "
22 constrained his *d* to get into a ship, "
26 the *d* saw him walking on the sea, "
15: 2 Why do thy d transgress the "
12 Then came his *d*, and said unto him, "
23 And his *d* came and besought him, "
32 Jesus called his *d* unto him, and "
33 his *d* say unto him, Whence "
36 and brake them, and gave to his *d*, "
36 and the *d* to the multitude. "
16: 5 his *d* were come to the other side, "
13 he asked his *d*, saying, Whom do "
20 Then charged he his *d* that they "
21 to shew unto his *d*, how that he "
24 said Jesus unto his *d*, If any man "
17: 6 when the *d* heard it, they fell "
10 his *d* asked him, saying, Why then "
13 Then the *d* understood that he "
16 I brought him to thy *d*, and they "
19 Then came the *d* to Jesus apart, "
18: 1 came the *d* unto Jesus, saying, "
19:10 His *d* say unto him, If the case "
13 and pray: and the *d* rebuked them. "
23 Then said Jesus unto his *d*, Verily "
25 When his *d* heard it, they were "

M't 20:17 took the twelve d' apart in the way, 3101
21: 1 of Olives, then sent Jesus two d', "
6 And the d' went, and did as Jesus "
20 when the d' saw it, they marvelled, "
22:16 sent out unto him their d' with the "
23: 1 to the multitude, and to his d', "
24: 1 his d' came to him for to shew him "
3 the d' came unto him privately, "
26: 1 he said unto his d', Ye know that "
8 his d' saw it, they had indignation, "
17 the d' came to Jesus, saying unto "
18 passover at thy house with my d'. "
19 the d' did as Jesus had appointed "
26 gave it to the d', and said, Take, "
35 thee. Likewise also said all the d'. "
36 and saith unto the d', Sit ye here "
40 he cometh unto the d', and findeth "
45 Then cometh he to his d', and saith "
56 Then all the d' forsook him, and "
27:64 lest his d' come by night, and steal "
28: 7 d' that he is risen from the dead; "
8 and did run to bring his d' word. "
9 And as they went to tell his d', "
13 Say ye, His d' came by night, "
16 eleven d' went away into Galilee, "
M'r 2:15 together with Jesus and his d': "
16 they said unto his d', How is it "
18 And the d' of John and of the "
18 Why do the d' of John and of the "
18 Pharisees fast, but thy d' fast not? "
23 his d' began, as they went, to pluck "
3: 7 himself with his d' to the sea: "
9 spake to his d', that a small ship "
4:34 he expounded all things to his d'. "
5:31 his d' said unto him, Thou seest "
6: 1 own country; and his d' follow him. "
29 when his d' heard of it, they came "
35 his d' came unto him, and said, "
41 them to his d' to set before them: "
45 constrained his d' to get into the "
7: 2 they saw some of his d' eat bread "
5 Why walk not thy d' according to "
17 his d' asked him concerning the "
8: 1 Jesus called his d' unto him, and "
4 his d' answered him, From whence "
6 gave to his d' to set before them; "
10 entered into a ship with his d', "
14 Now the d' had forgotten to take *
27 went out, and his d', into the towns 3101
27 and by the way he asked his d', "
33 looked on his d', he rebuked Peter, "
34 people unto him with his d' also, "
9:14 when he came to his d', he saw a "
18 I spake to thy d' that they should "
28 his d' asked him privately, Why "
31 taught his d', and said unto them, "
10:10 in the house his d' asked him "
13 his d' rebuked those that brought "
23 and saith unto his d', How hardly "
24 the d' were astonished at his words. "
46 went out of Jericho with his d' "
11: 1 he sendeth forth two of his d', "
14 for ever. And his d' heard it. "
12:43 he called unto him his d', and saith "
13: 1 one of his d' saith unto him, "
14:12 d' said unto him, Where wilt thou "
13 he sendeth forth two of his d', "
14 shall eat the passover with my d'? "
16 his d' went forth, and came into "
32 and he saith to his d', Sit ye here, "
16: 7 tell his d' and Peter that he goeth "
Lu 5:30 murmured against his d', saying, "
33 Why do the d' of John fast often, "
33 likewise the d' of the Pharisees "
6: 1 his d' plucked the ears of corn, 3101
13 was day, he called unto him his d': "
17 company of his d', and a great "
20 And he lifted up his eyes on his d', "
7:11 and many of his d' went with him, "
18 the d' of John shewed him of all "
19 John calling unto him two of his d' "
8: 9 his d' asked him, saying, What "
22 he went into a ship with his d': "
9: 1 he called his twelve d' together, * "
14 he said to his d', Make them sit "
16 and gave to the d' to set before "
18 praying, his d' were with him: "
40 I besought thy d' to cast him out; "
43 said unto his d', Let these sayings "
54 And when his d' James and John "
10:23 he turned him unto his d', and said "
11: 1 one of his d' said unto him, Lord, "
1 as John also taught his d'. "
12: 1 he began to say unto his d' first of "
22 he said unto his d', Therefore I say "
16: 1 he said also unto his d', There was "
17: 1 Then said he unto the d', It is "
22 said unto the d', The days will come, "
18:15 his d' saw it, they rebuked them. "
19:29 of Olives, he sent two of his d', "
37 d' began to rejoice and praise God "
39 unto him, Master, rebuke thy d'. "
20:45 unto his d', Beware of the scribes, "
22:11 eat the passover with my d'? "
39 Olives; and his d' also followed him. "
45 was come to his d', he found them "
Joh 1:35 John stood, and two of his d'; "
37 And the two d' heard him speak, "
2: 2 called, and his d', to the marriage. "
11 glory; and his d' believed on him. "
12 and his brethren, and his d': "
17 his d' remembered that it was "
22 his d' remembered that he had said "
3:22 came Jesus and his d' into the land "
25 between some of John's d' and the "
4: 1 and baptized more d' than John, "

Joh 4: 2 himself baptized not, but his d',) 3101
8 (For his d' were gone away unto "
27 upon this came his d', and marvelled "
31 the meanwhile his d' prayed him, "
33 Therefore said the d' one to "
6: 3 and there he sat with his d'. "
8 One of his d', Andrew, Simon "
11 distributed to the d', and the d' to * "
12 he said unto his d', Gather up the "
16 his d' went down unto the sea, "
22 whereinto his d' were entered, * "
22 Jesus went not with his d' into the "
22 that his d' were gone away alone; "
24 was not there, neither his d', they "
60 Many therefore of his d', when they "
61 himself that his d' murmured at it, "
66 many of his d' went back, and "
7: 3 that thy d' also may see the works "
8:31 word, then are ye my d' indeed; "
9: 2 his d' asked him, saying, Master, "
27 it again? will ye also be his d'? "
28 his disciple; but we are Moses' d'. "
11: 7 saith he to his d', Let us go into "
8 His d' say unto him, Master, the "
12 Then said his d', Lord, if he sleep, "
54 and there continued with his d'. "
12: 4 Then saith one of his d', Judas "
16 understood not his d' at the first: "
13:22 Then the d' looked one on another, "
23 one of his d', whom Jesus loved. "
35 know that ye are my d', if ye have "
15: 8 much fruit; so shall ye be my d'. "
16:17 Then said some of his d' among "
29 His d' said unto him, Lo, now "
18: 1 he went forth with his d' over the "
1 the which he entered, and his d'. "
2 resorted thither with his d'. "
17 not thou also one of this man's d'? "
19 priest then asked Jesus of his d', "
25 Art not thou also one of his d'? "
20:10 Then the d' went away unto their "
18 Magdalene came and told the d' "
19 shut where the d' were assembled "
20 Then were the d' glad, when they "
25 The other d' therefore said unto "
26 his d' were within, and Thomas "
30 did Jesus in the presence of his d', "
21: 1 himself again to the d' at the sea "
2 of Zebedee, and two other of his d'. "
4 the d' knew not that it was Jesus. "
8 And the other d' came in a little "
12 And none of the d' durst ask him, "
14 Jesus shewed himself to his d', "
Ac 1:15 stood up in the midst of the d', * "
6: 1 number of the d' was multiplied, "
2 called the multitude of the d' unto "
7 the number of the d' multiplied in "
9: 1 against the d' of the Lord, went "
19 certain days with the d' which "
25 Then the d' took him by night, "
26 assayed to join himself to the d': "
38 and the d' had heard that Peter "
11:26 And the d' were called Christians "
29 Then the d', every man according "
13:52 And the d' were filled with joy, "
14:20 Howbeit, as the d' stood round "
22 Confirming the souls of the d', and "
28 they abode long time with the d'. "
15:10 a yoke upon the neck of the d', "
18:23 in order, strengthening all the d' "
27 exhorting the d' to receive him: "
19: 1 Ephesus; and finding certain d', "
9 and separated the d', disputing "
30 people, the d' suffered him not. "
20: 1 Paul called unto him the d', and "
7 the d' came together to break * "
30 things, to draw away d' after them. "
21: 4 And finding d', we tarried there "
16 also certain of the d' of Cæsarea, "

disciples'
Joh 13: 5 to wash the d' feet, and to wipe 3101

discipline
Job 36:10 He openeth also their ear to d', *4148

disclose
Isa 26:21 the earth also shall d' her blood, 1540

discomfited
Ex 17:13 And Joshua d' Amalek and his 2522
Nu 14:45 smote them, and d' them, even *3807
Jos 10:10 And the Lord d' them before 1949
J'g 4:15 And the Lord d' Sisera, and all his 2000
8:12 and Zalmunna, and d' all the host. 2729
1Sa 7:10 the Philistines, and d' them; and 1949
2Sa 22:15 them; lightning, and d' them. 2000
Ps 18:14 shot out lightnings, and d' them. 1949
Isa 31: 8 and his young men shall be d'. *4522

discomfiture
1Sa 14:20 and there was a very great d'. 4103

discontented
1Sa 22: 2 every one that was d', 4751, 5315

discontinue
Jer 17: 4 And thou, even thyself, shalt d' 8058

discord
Pr 6:14 continually; he soweth d'. 4066
19 that soweth d' among brethren. 4090

discourage See also DISCOURAGED.
Nu 32: 7 d' ye the heart of the children of 5106

discouraged
Nu 21: 4 the soul of the people was much d' 7114
32: 9 they d' the heart of the children 5106
De 1:21 thee: fear not, neither be d'. *2865
28 our brethren have d' our heart, *4549

Isa 42: 4 He shall not fail nor be d', till 7533
Col 3:21 children to anger, lest they be d'. 120

discover See also DISCOVERED; DISCOVERETH; DISCOVERING.
De 22:30 wife, nor d' his father's skirt. *1540
1Sa 14: 8 and we will d' ourselves unto them. "
Job 41:13 can d' the face of his garment? * "
Pr 18: 2 but that his heart may d' itself. * "
25: 9 and d' not a secret to another: * "
Isa 3:17 Lord will d' their secret parts. *6168
Jer 13:26 Therefore will I d' thy skirts *2834
La 4:22 of Edom; he will d' thy sins. ‡1540
Eze 16:37 will d' thy nakedness unto them, ‡ "
Ho 2:10 now will I d' her lewdness in the ‡ "
Mic 1: 6 I will d' the foundations thereof. ‡ "
Na 3: 5 will d' thy skirts upon thy face, ‡ "

discovered
Ex 20:26 that thy nakedness be not d' ‡1540
Le 20:18 he hath d' her fountain, and she *6168
1Sa 14:11 And both of them d' themselves 1540
22: 6 Saul heard that David was d', 3045
2Sa 22:16 foundations of the world were d', *1540
Ps 18:15 foundations of the world were d' * "
Isa 22: 8 And he d' the covering of Judah, ‡ "
57: 8 thou hast d' thyself to another ‡ "
Jer 13:22 thine iniquity are thy skirts d', ‡ "
La 2:14 they have not d' thine iniquity, ‡ "
Eze 13:14 foundation thereof shall be d', ‡ "
16:36 thy nakedness d' through thy ‡ "
57 thy wickedness was d', as at the ‡ "
21:24 that your transgressions are d', ‡ "
22:10 In thee have they d' their fathers' ‡ "
23:10 These d' her nakedness: they ‡ "
18 she d' her whoredoms, and d' her ‡ "
29 thy whoredoms shall be d', both ‡ "
Ho 7: 1 the iniquity of Ephraim was d', ‡ "
Ac 21: 3 when we had d' Cyprus, we left * 398
27:39 they d' a certain creek with a *2657

discovereth
Job 12:22 He d' deep things out of darkness, ‡1540
Ps 29: 9 and d' the forests: and in his *2834

discovering
Hab 3:13 d' the foundation unto the neck. *6168

discreet
Ge 41:33 look out a man d' and wise, 995
39 none so d' and wise as thou art: "
Tit 2: 5 To be d', chaste, keepers at home, *4998

discreetly
M'r 12:34 saw that he answered d', he said 3562

discretion
Ps 112: 5 he will guide his affairs with d'. *4941
Pr 1: 4 the young man knowledge and d'. 4209
2:11 D' shall preserve thee, "
3:21 eyes: keep sound wisdom and d': "
5: 2 That thou mayest regard d', and "
11:22 a fair woman which is without d'. 2940
19:11 d' of a man deferreth his anger; 7922
Isa 28:26 his God doth instruct him to d', *4941
Jer 10:12 out the heavens by his d'. *8394

disdained
1Sa 17:42 and saw David, he d' him: for he 959
Job 30: 1 whose fathers I would have d' to 3988

disease See also DISEASED; DISEASES.
2Ki 1: 2 whether I shall recover of this d'. *2483
8: 8, 9 Shall I recover of this d'? * "
2Ch 16:12 until his d' was exceeding great: "
12 yet in his d' he sought not to the "
21:15 sickness by d' of thy bowels, until 4245
18 his bowels with an incurable d'. 2483
Job 30:18 By the great force of my d' is my
Ps 38: 7 are filled with a loathsome d': "
41: 8 An evil d', say they, cleaveth fast 1697
Ec 6: 2 this is vanity, and it is an evil d'. 2483
M't 4:23 all manner of d' among the people. 3119
9:35 and every d' among the people. "
10: 1 of sickness and all manner of d'. "
Joh 5: 4 whole of whatsoever d' he had. *3553

diseased
1Ki 15:23 his old age he was d' in his feet. 2470
2Ch 16:12 year of his reign was d' in his feet, "
Eze 34: 4 The d' have ye not strengthened, 2456
21 pushed all the d' with your horns, "
M't 9:20 was d' with an issue of blood *
14:35 unto him all that were d'; *2560, 2192
M'r 1:32 unto him all that were d', * "
Joh 6: 2 which he did on them that were d'.* 770

diseases
Ex 15:26 put none of these d' upon thee, 4245
De 7:15 put none of the evil d' of Egypt, 4064
28:60 bring upon thee all the d' of Egypt, "
2Ch 21:19 his sickness: so he died of sore d'. 8463
24:25 (for they left him in great d',) his 4251
Ps 103: 3 iniquities; who healeth all thy d'; 8463
M't 4:24 that were taken with divers d' 3554
M'r 1:34 many that were sick of divers d', "
Lu 4:40 any sick with divers d' brought "
6:17 him; and to be healed of their d': "
9: 1 over all devils, and to cure d'. "
Ac 19:12 and the d' departed from them, "
28: 9 which had d' in the island, came, 769

disfigure
M't 6:16 for they d' their faces, that they 853

disgrace
Jer 14:21 do not d' the throne of thy glory: 5034

disguise See also DISGUISED; DISGUISETH.
1Ki 14: 2 Arise, I pray thee, and d' thyself, 8138
22:30 I will d' myself and enter into the 2664
2Ch 18:29 I will d' myself and will go to the "

disguised
1Sa 28: 8 And Saul d' himself, and put on 2664

1Ki 20:38 and *d*· himself with ashes upon 2664
22:30 And the king of Israel *d*· himself, "
2Ch 18:29 So the king of Israel *d*· himself; "
35:22 but *d*· himself, that he might fight "

disguiseth
Job 24:15 shall see me: and *d*· his face. 5643

dish See DISHES; SNUFFDISH.
J'y 5:25 brought forth butter in a lordly *d*·.5602
2Ki 21:13 as a man wipeth a *d*·, wiping it, 6747
M't 26:23 dippeth his hand with me in the *d*·,*5165*
M'r 14:20 that dippeth with me in the *d*·, "

Dishan (*di'-shan*) See also DISHON.
Ge 36:21 And Dishon, and Ezer, and *D*·: 1789
28 The children of *D*· are these; Uz "
30 Duke Dishon, duke Ezer, duke *D*·: "
1Ch 1:38 and Dishon, and Ezar, and *D*·. "
42 The sons of *D*·; Uz, and Aran. "

dishes
Ex 25:29 thou shalt make the *d*· thereof, 7086
37:16 the table, his *d*·, and his spoons, "
Nu 4: 7 put thereon the *d*·, and the spoons, "

Dishon (*di'-shon*) See also DISHAN.
Ge 36:21 And *D*·, and Ezer, and Dishan: 1788
25 *D*·, and Aholibamah the daughter "
26 are the children of *D*·; Hemdan, "
30 Duke *D*·, duke Ezer, duke Dishan: "
1Ch 1:38 and *D*·, and Ezar, and Dishan. "
41 The sons of Anah; *D*·. And the "
41 sons of *D*·; Amram, and Eshban, "

dishonest
Eze 22:13 smitten mine hand at thy *d*· gain 1215
27 to destroy souls, to get *d*· gain. "

dishonesty
2Co 4: 2 renounced the hidden things of *d*·,* *152*

dishonour See also DISHONOUREST; DISHONOURETH.
Ezr 4:14 meet for us to see the king's *d*·, 6173
Ps 35:26 be clothed with shame and *d*· that 3639
69:19 and my shame, and my *d*·; mine "
71:13 be covered with reproach and *d*· "
Pr 6:33 A wound and *d*· shall he get; 7036
Joh 8:49 honour my Father, and ye do *d*· me.*818*
Ro 1:24 to *d*· their own bodies between * "
9:21 unto honour, and another unto *d*? *819*
1Co 15:43 It is sown in *d*·; it is raised in "
2Co 6: 8 By honour and *d*·, by evil report "
2Ti 2:20 some to honour, and some to *d*·. "

dishonourest
Ro 2:23 breaking the law *d*· thou God? *818*

dishonoureth
Mic 7: 6 son *d*· the father, the daughter 5034
1Co 11: 4 his head covered, *d*· his head. *2617*
5 her head uncovered *d*· her head: "

disinherit
Nu 14:12 with the pestilence, and *d*· them, 3423

dismayed
De 31: 8 thee: fear not, neither be *d*·. 2865
Jos 1: 9 neither be thou *d*·: for the Lord "
8: 1 neither be thou *d*·: take all the "
10:25 Fear not, nor be *d*·, be strong and "
1Sa 17:11 Philistine, they were *d*·, and greatly "
2Ki 19:26 they were *d*· and confounded; "
1Ch 22:13 courage; dread not, nor be *d*·. "
28:20 fear not, nor be *d*·: for the Lord "
2Ch 20:15 Be not afraid nor *d*· by reason of "
17 fear not, nor be *d*·; to morrow go "
32: 7 be not afraid nor *d*· for the king of "
Isa 21: 3 of it; I was *d*· at the seeing of it. 926
37:27 they were *d*· and confounded: 2865
41:10 be not *d*·; for I am thy God: 8159
23 that we may be *d*·, and behold it "
Jer 1:17 be not *d*· at their faces, lest I 2865
8: 9 ashamed, they are *d*· and taken: "
10: 2 be not *d*· at the signs of heaven; "
2 for the heathen are *d*· at them. "
17:18 be confounded: let them be *d*·, "
18 but let not me be *d*·: bring upon "
23: 4 they shall fear no more, nor be *d*·, "
30:10 neither be *d*·, O Israel: for, lo, "
46: 5 Wherefore have I seen them *d*· 2844
27 be not *d*·, O Israel: for, behold, 2865
48: 1 Misgab is confounded and *d*·. * "
49:37 For I will cause Elam to be *d*· "
50:36 mighty men; and they shall be *d*·. "
Eze 2: 6 of their words, nor be *d*· at their "
3: 9 neither be *d*· at their looks, though "
Ob 9 mighty men, O Teman, shall be *d*·, "

dismaying
Jer 48:39 a derision and a *d*· to all them ‡4288

dismissed
2Ch 23: 8 Jehoiada the priest *d*· not the 6362
Ac 15:30 So when they were *d*·, they came *630*
19:41 thus spoken, he *d*· the assembly. "

disobedience
Ro 5:19 by one man's *d*· many were made *3876*
2Co 10: 6 to revenge all *d*·, when your "
Eph 2: 2 now worketh in the children of *d*·: *543*
5: 6 of God upon the children of *d*·. "
Col 3: 6 of God cometh on the children of *d*·: "
Heb 2: 2 transgression and *d*· received a *3876*

disobedient
1Ki 13:26 the man of God, who was *d*· unto 4784
Ne 9:26 Nevertheless they were *d*·, and "
Lu 1:17 the *d*· to the wisdom of the just; *545*
Ac 26:19 was not *d*· unto the heavenly vision: "
Ro 1:30 of evil things, *d*· to parents, "
10:21 unto a *d*· and gainsaying people. *544*
1Ti 1: 9 but for the lawless and *d*·, for the * *506*
2Ti 3: 2 blasphemers, *d*· to parents, *545*
Tit 1:16 being abominable, and *d*·, and unto "
3: 3 sometimes foolish, *d*·, deceived, "

1Pe 2: 7 but unto them which be *d*·, * *544*
8 stumble at the word, being *d*·: "
3:20 Which sometime were *d*·, when "

disobeyed
1Ki 13:21 hast *d*· the mouth of the Lord, *4784

disorderly
2Th 3: 6 every brother that walketh *d*·, *814*
7 behaved not ourselves *d*· among *812*
11 some which walk among you *d*·, *814*

dispatch
Eze 23:47 and *d*· them with their swords; 1254

dispensation
1Co 9:17 a *d*· of the gospel is committed **3622*
Eph 1:10 That in the *d*· of the fulness of "
3: 2 heard of the *d*· of the grace of God "
Col 1:25 according to the *d*· of God which "

disperse See also DISPERSED.
1Sa 14:34 *D*· yourselves among the people, 6327
Pr 15: 7 The lips of the wise *d*· knowledge: 2219
Eze 12:15 and *d*· them in the countries. "
20:23 and *d*· them through the countries; "
22:15 and *d*· thee in the countries, and "
29:12 and *d*· them through the countries. "
30:23 will *d*· them through the countries. "
26 and *d*· them among the countries; "

dispersed
2Ch 11:23 *d*· of all his children throughout 6555
Es 3: 8 and *d*· among the people in all 6504
Ps 112: 9 He hath *d*·, he hath given to the 6340
Pr 5:16 Let thy fountains be *d*· abroad, 6327
Isa 11:12 gather together the *d*· of Judah 5310
Eze 36:19 were *d*· through the countries: 2219
Zep 3:10 the daughter of my *d*·, shall bring6327
Joh 7:35 unto the *d*· among the Gentiles? **1290*
Ac 5:37 as many as obeyed him, were *d*·. **1287*
2Co 9: 9 He hath *d*· abroad; he hath given**4650*

dispersions
Jer 25:34 of your slaughter and of your *d*· *8600

displayed
Ps 60: 4 may be *d*· because of the truth. 5127

displease See also DISPLEASED.
Ge 31:35 Let it not *d*· my lord that I cannot 2734
Nu 22:34 *d*· thee, I will get me back 7489, 5869
1Sa 29: 7 thou *d*· not the lords of 6213, 7451, "
2Sa 11:25 Let not this thing *d*· thee, for 7489, "
Pr 24:18 the Lord see it, and it *d*· him, " "

displeased
Ge 38:10 which he did *d*· the Lord: *7489, 5869
48:17 And when Joseph...it *d*· him: " "
Nu 11: 1 complained, it *d*· the Lord: *7451, 241
1Sa 8: 6 But the thing *d*· Samuel, 7489, 5869
18: 8 and the saying *d*· him; and he " "
2Sa 6: 8 And David was *d*·, because the 2734
11:27 thing that David had done *d*·7489, 5869
1Ki 1: 6 his father had not *d*· him at any 6087
20:43 went to his house heavy and *d*·, 2198
21: 4 came into his house heavy and *d*· "
1Ch 13:11 And David was *d*·, because the 2734
21: 7 God was *d*· with this thing; 3415, 5869
Ps 60: 1 thou hast been *d*·; O turn thyself* 599
Isa 59:15 it *d*· him that there was no 7489, 5869
Da 6:14 was sore *d*· with himself, and set 888
Jon 4: 1 But it *d*· Jonah exceedingly, 7489, 5869
Hab 3: 8 the Lord *d*· against the rivers? 2734
Zec 1: 2 The Lord hath been sore *d*· with 7107
15 I am very sore *d*· with the heathen "
15 at ease: for I was but a little *d*·, "
M't 21:15 son of David; they were sore *d*·, * *23*
M'r 10:14 Jesus saw it, he was much *d*·, * "
41 began to be much *d*· with James * "
Ac 12:20 Herod was highly *d*· with them of *2371*

displeasure
De 9:19 was afraid of the anger and hot *d*·, 2534
J'g 15: 3 though I do them a *d*·. *7451
Ps 2: 5 and vex them in his sore *d*·. 2740
6: 1 neither chasten me in thy hot *d*·. 2534
38: 1 neither chasten me in thy hot *d*·. "

disposed
Job 34:13 who hath *d*· the whole world? 7760
37:15 thou know when God *d*· them, * "
Ac 18:27 he was *d*· to pass into Achaia, * *1014*
1Co 10:27 you to a feast, and ye be *d*· to go; *2309*

disposing
Pr 16:33 the whole *d*· thereof is of the Lord. 4941

disposition
Ac 7:53 the law by the *d*· of angels, **1296*

dispossess See also DISPOSSESSED.
Nu 33:53 And ye shall *d*· the inhabitants *3423
De 7:17 more than I; how can I *d*· them? "

dispossessed
Nu 32:39 and *d*· the Amorite which was 3423
J'g 11:23 God of Israel hath *d*· the Amorites "

disputation See also DISPUTATIONS.
Ac 15: 2 no small dissension and *d*· with **4803*

disputations
Ro 14: 1 receive ye, but not to doubtful *d*·. *1253*

dispute See also DISPUTED; DISPUTING.
Job 23: 7 the righteous might *d*· with him;*3198

disputed
M'r 9:33 that ye *d*· among yourselves by **1260*
34 they had *d*· among themselves, *1256*
Ac 9:29 and *d*· against the Grecians: *4802*
17:17 *d*· he in the synagogue with the **1256*
Jude 9 he *d*· about the body of Moses, "

disputer
1Co 1:20 where is the *d*· of this world? *4804*

disputing See also DISPUTINGS.
Ac 6: 9 and of Asia, *d*· with Stephen. *4802*

Ac 15: 7 when there had been much *d*·, *4803*
19: 8 three months, *d*· and persuading **1256*
9 *d*· daily in the school of one * "
24:12 me in the temple *d*· with any man, "

disputings
Ph'p 2:14 without murmurings and *d*·: ‡*1261*
1Ti 6: 5 Perverse *d*· of men of corrupt **3859*

disquiet See also DISQUIETED.
Jer 50:34 and *d*· the inhabitants of Babylon. 7264

disquieted
1Sa 28:15 Why hast thou *d*· me, to bring me 7264
Ps 39: 6 shew: surely they are *d*· in vain: 1993
42: 5 and why art thou *d*· in me? hope "
11 why art thou *d*· within me? hope "
43: 5 why art thou *d*· within me? hope "
Pr 30:21 For three things the earth is *d*·, *7264

disquietness
Ps 38: 8 I have roared by reason of the *d*· 5100

dissembled See also DISSEMBLETH.
Jos 7:11 and have also stolen, and *d*· also, 3584
Jer 42:20 For ye *d*· in your hearts, when ye*8582
Ga 2:13 other Jews *d*· likewise with him; *4942*

dissemblers
Ps 26: 4 neither will I go in with *d*·. 5956

dissembleth
Pr 26:24 he that hateth *d*· with his lips, 5234

dissension
Ac 15: 2 had no small *d*· and disputation *4714*
23: 7 a *d*· between the Pharisees and the "
10 And when there arose a great *d*·, "

dissimulation
Ro 12: 9 Let love be without *d*·. Abhor * *505*
Ga 2:13 was carried away with their *d*·. *5272*

dissolve See also DISSOLVED; DISSOLVEST; DISSOLVING.
Da 5:16 interpretations, and *d*· doubts: 8271

dissolved
Ps 75: 3 the inhabitants therefore are *d*·: 4127
Isa 14:31 thou, whole Palestina, art *d*·: * "
24:19 the earth is clean *d*·, the earth 6565
34: 4 all the host of heaven shall be *d*·, 4743
Na 2: 6 and the palace shall be *d*·. 4127
2Co 5: 1 house of this tabernacle were *d*·, *2647*
2Pe 3:11 that all these things shall be *d*·, *3089*
12 heavens being on fire shall be *d*·, "

dissolvest
Job 30:22 upon it, and *d*· my substance. 4127

dissolving
Da 5:12 hard sentences, and *d*· of doubts, 8271

distaff
Pr 31:19 and her hands hold the *d*·. 6418

distant
Ex 36:22 equally *d*· one from another: *7947

distil
De 32: 2 my speech shall *d*· as the dew, 5140
Job 36:28 clouds do drop and *d*· upon man 7491

distinction
1Co 14: 7 they give a *d*· in the sounds, *1293*

distinctly
Ne 8: 8 in the book in the law of God *d*·, 6567

distracted
Ps 88:15 while I suffer thy terrors I am *d*·. 6323

distraction
1Co 7:35 attend upon the Lord without *d*·. *563*

distress See also DISTRESSED; DISTRESSES.
Ge 35: 3 answered me in the day of my *d*·, 6869
42:21 therefore is this *d*· come upon us. "
De 2: 9 *D*· not the Moabites, neither *6696
19 Ammon, *d*· them not, nor meddle* "
28:53 thine enemies shall *d*· thee: †6693
55 thine enemies shall *d*· thee in all † "
57 enemy shall *d*· thee in thy gates. † "
J'g 11: 7 unto me now when ye are in *d*? 6887
1Sa 22: 2 And every one that was in *d*·, 4689
2Sa 22: 7 In my *d*· I called upon the Lord, 6862
1Ki 1:29 redeemed my soul out of all *d*·, *6869
2Ch 28:22 And in the time of his *d*· did he 6887
Ne 2:17 Ye see the *d*· that we are in, *7451
9:37 pleasure, and we are in great *d*·. 6869
Ps 4: 1 enlarged me when I was in *d*·; 6862
18: 6 In my *d*· I called upon the Lord, "
118: 5 I called upon the Lord in *d*·: 4712
120: 1 In my *d*· I cried unto the Lord, 6869
Pr 1:27 *d*· and anguish cometh upon you. "
Isa 25: 4 a strength to the needy in his *d*·, 6862
29: 2 Yet I will *d*· Ariel, and there shall 6693
7 and her munition, and that *d*· her, "
Jer 10:18 and will *d*· them, that they may 6887
La 1:20 O Lord; for I am in *d*·: my bowels "
Ob 12 spoken proudly in the day of *d*·. 6869
14 that did remain in the day of *d*·. "
Zep 1:15 a day of trouble and *d*·, a day of 4691
17 And I will bring *d*· upon men, 6887
Lu 21:23 there shall be great *d*· in the land, *318*
25 and upon the earth *d*· of nations, *4928*
Ro 8:35 tribulation, or *d*·, or persecution, **4730*
1Co 7:26 this is good for the present *d*·, *318*
1Th 3: 7 our affliction and *d*· by your faith: "

distressed
Ge 32: 7 Jacob was greatly afraid and *d*·: 3334
Nu 22: 3 and Moab was *d*· because of the 6973
J'g 2:15 them: and they were greatly *d*·. 3334
10: 9 so that Israel was sore *d*·. "
1Sa 13: 6 (for the people were *d*·,) then the 5065
14:24 the men of Israel were *d*· that day: "
28:15 And Saul answered, I am sore *d*·; 6887
30: 6 And David was greatly *d*·; for the 3334
2Sa 1:26 I am *d*· for thee, my brother 6887

2Ch 28:20 d' him, but strengthened him not. 6696
2Co 4: 8 troubled on every side, yet not d'; *4729

distresses
Ps 25:17 O bring thou me out of my d'. 4691
107: 6 he delivered them out of their d'. "
13 he saved them out of their d'. "
19 he saveth them out of their d'. "
28 he bringeth them out of their d'. "
Eze 30:16 and Noph shall have d' daily. *6862
2Co 6: 4 in afflictions, in necessities, in d', 4730
12:10 persecutions, in d' for Christ's sake: "

distribute See also DISTRIBUTED; DISTRIBUTETH; DISTRIBUTING.
Jos 13:32 Moses did d' for inheritance in *5157
2Ch 31:14 to d' the oblations of the Lord, 5414
Ne 13:13 was to d' unto their brethren. 2505
Lu 18:22 d' unto the poor, and thou shalt 1239
1Ti 6:18 works, ready to d', willing to 2130

distributed
Jos 14: 1 Israel, d' for inheritance to them. 5157
1Ch 24: 3 David d' them, both Zadok of *2505
2Ch 23:18 whom David had d' in the house of "
Joh 6:11 he d' to the disciples, and the 1239
1Co 7:17 as God hath d' to every man, 3307
2Co 10:13 rule which God hath d' to us, * "

distributeth
Job 21:17 God d' sorrows in his anger. 2505

distributing
Ro 12:13 D' to the necessity of saints; *2841

distribution
Ac 4:35 feet: and d' was made unto every 1239
2Co 9:13 and for your liberal d' unto them, *2842

ditch See also DITCHES.
Job 9:31 Yet shalt thou plunge me in the d',7845
Ps 7:15 is fallen into the d' which he "
Pr 23:27 For a whore is a deep d'; and a 7745
Isa 22:11 Ye made also a d' between the *4724
M't 15:14 blind, both shall fall into the d' * 999
Lu 6:39 they not both fall into the d'? * "

ditches
2Ki 3:16 Make this valley full of d': *1356

divers See also DIVERSE.
De 22: 9 sow thy vineyard with d' seeds: *3610
11 a garment of d' sorts, as of *8162
25:13 shalt not have in thy bag d' weights,
14 not have in thine house d' measures,
J'g 5:30 to Sisera a prey of d' colours, 6648
30 a prey of d' colours of needlework, "
30 of d' colours of needlework "
2Sa 13:18 she had a garment of d' colours 6446
19 rent her garment of d' colours "
1Ch 29: 2 glistering stones, and of d' colours.7553
2Ch 16:14 filled with sweet odours and d' kinds
21: 4 and d' also of the princes of Israel.
30:11 d' of Asher and Manasseh and 582
Ps 78:45 sent d' sorts of flies among them,*
105:31 came d' sorts of flies, and lice *
Pr 20:10 D' weights, and d' measures,
23 D' weights are an abomination
Ec 5: 7 words there are also d' vanities:†‡
Eze 16:16 thy high places with d' colours, 2921
17: 3 of feathers, which had d' colours, 7553
M't 4:24 with d' diseases and torments, 4164
24: 7 and earthquakes, in d' places.
M'r 1:34 many that were sick of d' diseases, 4164
8: 3 for d' of them came from far. *5100
13: 8 shall be earthquakes in d' places,
Lu 4:40 sick with d' diseases brought 4164
21:11 great earthquakes shall be in d'
Ac 19: 9 But when d' were hardened, and *5100
1Co 12:10 to another d' kind of tongues;
2Ti 3: 6 with sins, led away with d' lusts, 4164
Tit 3: 3 serving d' lusts and pleasures,
Heb 1: 1 times and in d' manners spake in 4187
2: 4 and with d' miracles, and gifts of *4164
9:10 meats and drinks, and d' washings, 1313
13: 9 with d' and strange doctrines. 4164
Jas 1: 2 when ye fall into d' temptations; * "

diverse See also DIVERS.
Le 19:19 cattle gender with a d' kind: 3610
Es 1: 7 vessels being d' one from another,)8138
3: 8 their laws are d' from all people; "
Da 7: 3 the sea, d' one from another. 8133
7 and it was d' from all the beasts "
19 which was d' from all the others, "
23 which shall be d' from all kingdoms,"
24 and he shall be d' from the first, "

diversities
1Co 12: 4 Now there are d' of gifts, but the 1243
6 there are d' of operations, but it "
28 helps, governments, d' of tongues *1085

divide See also DIVIDED; DIVIDETH; DIVIDING.
Ge 1: 6 let it d' the waters from the waters. 914
14 to d' the day from the night; "
18 to d' the light from the darkness: "
49: 7 will d' them in Jacob, and scatter 2505
27 at night he shall d' the spoil. "
Ex 14:16 thine hand over the sea, and d' it: 1234
15: 9 I will overtake, I will d' the spoil; 2505
21:35 the live ox, and d' the money of it; 2673
35 the dead ox also they shall d'. "
26:33 the vail shall d' unto you between 914
Le 1:17 thereof, but shall not d' it asunder: "
5: 8 neck, but shall not d' it asunder: "
11: 4 cud, or of them that d' the hoof: *6536
7 the swine, though he d' the hoof, "
Nu 31:27 And d' the prey into two parts; 2673
33:54 And ye shall d' the land by lot for *5157
34:17 which shall d' the land unto you: "
18 tribe, to d' the land by inheritance. "
29 Lord commanded to d' the inheritance
De 14: 7 or of them that d' the cloven hoof; *6536
7 chew the cud, but d' not the hoof;* "
19: 3 d' the coasts ... into three parts,
Jos 1: 6 shalt thou d' for an inheritance *
13: 6 d' thou it by lot unto the Israelites*5307
7 d' this land for an inheritance 2505
18: 5 And they shall d' it into seven "
22: 8 d' the spoil of your enemies with "
2Sa 19:29 said, Thou and Ziba d' the land. "
1Ki 3:25 D' the living child in two, and 1504
26 be neither mine nor thine, but d' it."
Ne 9:11 thou didst d' the sea before them, 1234
22 and didst d' them into corners: *2505
Job 27:17 and the innocent shall d' the silver. "
Ps 55: 9 Destroy, O Lord, and d' their 6385
60: 6 I will d' Shechem, and mete out 2505
74:13 Thou didst d' the sea by thy 6565
108: 7 will rejoice, I will d' Shechem, and 2505
Pr 16:19 than to d' the spoil with the proud. "
Isa 9: 3 rejoice when they d' the spoil. "
53:12 Therefore will I d' him a portion 5312
12 he shall d' the spoil with the strong; "
Eze 5: 1 balances to weigh, and d' the hair. 2505
45: 1 Moreover, when ye shall d' by lot 5307
47:21 So shall ye d' this land unto you 2505
22 shall d' it by lot for an inheritance 5307
48:29 ye shall d' by lot unto the tribes "
Da 11:39 and shall d' the land for gain. 2505
Lu 12:13 that he d' the inheritance with me. 3307
22:17 Take this, and d' it among 1266

divided
Ge 1: 4 God d' the light from the darkness. 914
7 and d' the waters which were under "
10: 5 were the isles of the Gentiles d' 6504
25 in his days was the earth d'; 6385
32 by these were the nations d' in the 6504
14:15 And he d' himself against them, 2505
15:10 and d' them in the midst, and laid 1334
10 another: but the birds d' he not. "
32: 7 and he d' the people that was with 2673
33: 1 And he d' the children unto Leah, "
Ex 14:21 dry land, and the waters were d'. 1234
Nu 26:53 Unto these the land shall be d' 2505
55 the land shall be d' by lot: "
56 shall the possession thereof be d' "
31:42 which Moses d' from the men that 2673
De 4:19 which the Lord thy God hath d' 2505
32: 8 d' to the nations their inheritance,*
Jos 14: 5 Israel did, and they d' the land. 2505
18:10 there Joshua d' the land unto the "
19:51 d' for an inheritance by lot in *
23: 4 I have d' unto you by lot *5307
J'g 5:30 have they not d' the prey; to 2505
7:16 And he d' the three hundred men 2673
9:43 and d' them into three companies, "
19:29 and d' her, together with her 5408
2Sa 1:23 in their death they were not d': 6504
1Ki 16:21 Then were the people of Israel d' 2505
18: 6 So they d' the land between them "
2Ki 2: 8 they were d' hither and thither, 2673
1Ch 1:19 in his days the earth was d': 6385
23: 6 And David d' them into courses 2505
24: 4 of Ithamar; and thus were they d'. "
5 Thus were they d' by lot, one sort "
2Ch 35:13 and d' them speedily among all *7323
Job 38:25 Who hath d' a watercourse for the*6385
Ps 68:12 that tarried at home d' the spoil. 2505
78:13 He d' the sea, and caused them *1234
55 and d' them an inheritance by *5307
136:13 To him which d' the Red sea into 1504
Isa 33:23 is the prey of a great spoil d'; 2505
34:17 his hand hath d' it unto them by "
51:15 the Lord thy God, that d' the sea,*7280
La 4:16 anger of the Lord hath d' them; 2505
Eze 37:22 neither shall they be d' into two 2673
Da 2:41 of iron, the kingdom shall be d'; 6386
5:28 Thy kingdom is d', and given 6537
11: 4 and shall be d' toward the four 2673
Ho 10: 2 Their heart is d'; now shall they 2505
Am 7:17 and thy land shall be d' by line; "
Mic 2: 4 away he hath d' our fields. * "
Zec 14: 1 and thy spoil shall be d' in the "
M't 12:25 Every kingdom d' against itself is 3307
25 city or house d' against itself "
26 Satan, he is d' against himself; "
M'r 3:24 if a kingdom be d' against itself, "
25 if a house be d' against itself, "
26 and be d', he cannot stand, but hath "
6:41 the two fishes d' he among them all."
Lu 11:17 Every kingdom d' against itself is 1266
17 house d' against a house falleth "
18 If Satan also be d' against himself, 1266
12:52 there shall be five in one house d', "
53 father shall be d' against the son, "
15:12 And he d' unto them his living. 1244
Ac 13:19 he d' their land to them by lot. *2624
14: 4 the multitude of the city was d': 4977
23: 7 and the multitude was d'. "
1Co 1:13 Is Christ d'? was Paul crucified 3307
Re 16:19 the great city was d' into three 1096

divider
Lu 12:14 made me a judge or a d' over you? 3312

divideth
Le 11: 4, 5 the cud; but d' not the hoof; *6536
6 the cud, but d' not the hoof; * "
26 every beast which d' the hoof, * "
De 14: 8 the swine, because it d' the hoof,* "
Job 26:12 He d' the sea with his power, *7280
Ps 29: 7 The Lord d' the flames of fire. *2672
Jer 31:35 which d' the sea when the waves *7280
M't 25:32 as a shepherd d' his sheep from * 873
Lu 11:22 he trusted, and d' his spoils. 1239

dividing
Jos 19:49 end of d' the land for inheritance*
51 made an end of d' the country. 2505
Isa 63:12 d' the water before them, to *1234
Da 7:25 a time and times and the d' of *6387
1Co 12:11 d' to every man severally as he 1244
2Ti 2:15 rightly d' the word of truth. *3718
Heb 4:12 even to the d' asunder of soul and 3311

divination See also DIVINATIONS.
Nu 22: 7 with the rewards of d' in their 7081
23:23 is there any d' against Israel: "
De 18:10 or that useth d', or an observer "
2Ki 17:17 used d' and enchantments, and "
Jer 14:14 a false vision and d', and a thing "
Eze 12:24 vain vision nor flattering d' within 4738
13: 6 vanity and lying d', saying, The 7081
7 have ye not spoken a lying d', 4738
21:21 head of the two ways, to use d': 7081
22 hand was the d' for Jerusalem, "
23 be unto them as a false d' in their 7080
Ac 16:16 possessed with a spirit of d' met us, 4436

divinations
Eze 13:23 see no more vanity, nor divine d': 7081

divine See also DIVINETH; DIVINING.
Ge 44:15 such a man as I can certainly d'? 5172
1Sa 28: 8 d' unto me by the familiar spirit, 7080
Pr 16:10 A d' sentence is in the lips of the 7081
Eze 13: 9 that see vanity, and that d' lies: 7080
23 no more vanity, nor d' divinations 7081
21:29 whiles they d' a lie unto thee, 7080
Mic 3: 6 unto you, that ye shall not d'; "
11 the prophets thereof d' for money: "
Heb 9: 1 had also ordinances of d' service, 2999
2Pe 1: 3 According as his d' power hath 2304
4 might be partakers of the d' nature."

diviners
De 18:14 observers of times, and unto d': 7080
1Sa 6: 2 called for the priests and the d', "
Isa 44:25 of the liars, and maketh d' mad; "
Jer 27: 9 to your d', nor to your dreamers, "
29: 8 Let not your prophets and your d'. "
Mic 3: 7 ashamed, and the d' confounded: "
Zec 10: 2 and the d' have seen a lie, "

divineth
Ge 44: 5 and whereby indeed he d'? 5172

divining
Eze 22:28 seeing vanity, and d' lies unto 7080

division See also DIVISIONS.
Ex 8:23 I will put a d' between my people 6304
2Ch 35: 5 and after the d' of the families *2515
Lu 12:51 I tell you, Nay; but rather d': 1267
Joh 7:43 there was a d' among the people 4978
9:16 there was a d' among them. "
10:19 There was a d' therefore again "

divisions
Jos 11:23 to their d' by their tribes. 4256
12: 7 a possession according to their d'; "
18:10 of Israel according to their d'. "
J'g 5:15 For the d' of Reuben ... thoughts *6391
16 the d' of Reuben ... searchings * "
1Ch 24: 1 are the d' of the sons of Aaron. *4256
26: 1 Concerning the d' of the porters:* "
12 these were the d' of the porters, * "
19 These are the d' of the porters * "
2Ch 35: 5 according to the d' of the families 6391
12 according to the d' of the families 4653
Ezr 6:18 they set the priests in their d', 6392
Ne 11:36 of the Levites were d' in Judah, 4256
Ro 16:17 them which cause d' and offences 1370
1Co 1:10 that there be no d' among you; 4978
3: 3 you envying, and strife, and d', 1370
11:18 hear that there be d' among you; 4978

divorce See also DIVORCED; DIVORCEMENT.
Jer 3: 8 away, and given her a bill of d'; *3748

divorced
Le 21:14 widow, or a d' woman, or profane, 1644
22:13 priest's daughter be a widow, or d', "
Nu 30: 9 of a widow, and of her that is d', "
M't 5:32 her that is d' committeth adultery.* 630

divorcement
De 24: 1 then let him write her a bill of d', 3748
3 hate her, and write her a bill of d' "
Isa 50: 1 Where is the bill of your mother's d',"
M't 5:31 let him give her a writing of d': 647
19: 7 command to give a writing of d', "
M'r 10: 4 Moses suffered to write a bill of d', "

Dizahab (*diz'-a-hab*)
De 1: 1 and Laban, and Hazeroth, and D'. 1774

do See also ADO; DID; DOEST; DOETH; DOING; DONE; UNDO.
Ge 6:17 I, even I, d' bring a flood of waters
9:13 I d' set my bow in the cloud, and it
11: 6 and this they begin to d': and now 6213
6 which they have imagined to d'. "
16: 6 hand; d' to her as it pleaseth thee. "
18: 5 they said, So d', as thou hast said. "
17 Abraham that thing which I d'; "
19 Lord, to d' justice and judgment; "
25 from thee to d' after this manner, "
25 the Judge of all the earth d' right? "
29 said, I will not d' it for forty's sake. "
30 I will not d' it, if I find thirty there. "
19: 7 you, brethren, d' not so wickedly. "
8 you, and d' ye to them as is good 6213
8 only unto these men d' nothing; "
22 for I cannot d' any thing till thou "
21:23 thou shalt d' unto me, and to the "
22:12 the lad, neither d' thou any thing "
24:42 thou d' prosper my way which I go: "
25:32 profit shall this birthright d' to me? "
26:29 That thou wilt d' us no hurt, as 6213
27:37 and what shall I d' now unto thee, "
46 what good shall my life d' me? "
30:31 if thou wilt d' this thing for me, I 6213

Ge 31:16 God hath said unto thee, d'. 6213
29 power of my hand to d' you hurt: "
43 and what can I d' this day unto "
32:12 saidst, I will surely d' thee good,
34:14 We cannot d' this thing, to give 6213
19 man deferred not to d' the thing, "
37:13 D' not thy brethren feed the flock in
39: 9 can I d' this great wickedness, 6213
11 into the house to d' his business; "
40: 8 D' not interpretations belong to God?
41: 9 I d' remember my faults this day:
25 Pharaoh what he is about to d'. 6213
28 to d' he sheweth unto Pharaoh. "
34 Let Pharaoh d' this, and let him "
55 Joseph; what he saith to you, d'. "
42: 1 Why d' ye look one upon another?
18 This d', and live; for I fear God: 6213
22 D' not sin against the child;
43:11 so now, d' this; take of the best 6213
44: 7 thy servants should d' according "
17 said, God forbid that I should d' so: "
45:17 Say unto your brethren, This d' ye; "
19 thou art commanded, this d' ye; "
47:30 he said, I will d' as thou hast said. "
Ex 1:16 When ye d' the office of a midwife to
3:20 I will d' in the midst thereof: 6213
4:15 will teach you what ye shall d'. "
17 wherewith thou shalt d' signs. "
21 d' all those wonders before Pharaoh, "
5: 4 Wherefore d' ye, Moses and Aaron, "
17 Let us go and d' sacrifice to the *
6: 1 see what I will d' to Pharaoh: 6213
8: 8 may d' sacrifice unto the Lord. *
26 Moses said, It is not meet so to d'; 6213
9: 5 To morrow the Lord shall d' this "
15:26 d' that which is right in his sight, "
17: 2 wherefore d' ye tempt the Lord?
4 What shall I d' unto this people? 6213
18:16 d' make them know the statutes *
20 and the work that they must d'. 6213
23 If thou shalt d' this thing, and God "
19: 8 the Lord hath spoken we will d'. "
20: 9 thou labour, and d' all thy work: "
10 in it thou shalt not d' any work, "
21: 7 not go out as the menservants d'. 3318
11 if he d' not these three unto her, 6213
22:30 shalt thou d' with thine oxen, and "
23: 2 shalt not follow a multitude to d' evil;
12 Six days thou shalt d' thy work, 6213
22 his voice, and d' all that I speak; "
24 them, nor d' after their works: "
24: 3 which the Lord hath said will we d'. "
7 that the Lord hath said will we d', "
14 any man have any matters to d', *1167
29: 1 is the thing that thou shalt d' unto 6213
35 And thus shalt thou d' unto Aaron, "
41 shalt d' according to the meat "
31:11 commanded thee shall they d'. "
32:14 he thought to d' unto his people. "
18 the noise of them that sing d' I hear.
33: 5 may know what to d' unto thee. 6213
17 I will d' this thing also that thou "
34:10 all thy people I will d' marvels, "
10 thing that I will d' with thee. "
15 gods, and d' sacrifice unto their gods,
35: 1 commanded, that ye should d' 6213
19 to d' service in the holy place. *
35 weaver, even of them that d' any 6213
36: 2 up to come unto the work to d' it: "
39: 1, 41 to d' service in the holy place, *
Le 4: 2 and shall d' against any of them: 6213
3 that is anointed d' sin according *
20 And he shall d' with the bullock 6213
20 offering, so shall he d' with this: "
5: 1 if he d' not utter it, then he shall
4 his lips to d' evil, or to d' good,
8:34 the Lord hath commanded to d', 6213
9: 6 commanded that ye should d': "
10: 9 D' not drink wine nor strong *
16:15 and d' with that blood as he did 6213
16 so shall he d' for the tabernacle "
29 souls, and d' no work at all, "
18: 3 wherein ye dwelt, shall ye not d': "
3 whither I bring you, shall ye not d': "
4 Ye shall d' my judgments, and "
5 if a man d', he shall live in them: "
25 therefore I d' visit the iniquity
19:15 Ye shall d' no unrighteousness in 6213
29 D' not prostitute thy daughter, *
35 Ye shall d' no unrighteousness in 6213
37 judgments, and d' them: I am the "
20: 4 d' any ways hide their eyes from *
8 keep my statutes, and d' them: 6213
22 all my judgments, and d' them: "
21: 6 the bread of their God, they d' offer:
15 for I the Lord d' sanctify him. *
23 for I the Lord d' sanctify them. *
22: 9 it: I the Lord d' sanctify them. *
16 for I the Lord d' sanctify them. *
31 my commandments, and d' them: 6213
23: 3 ye shall d' no work therein: "
7 ye shall d' no servile work therein. "
8 ye shall d' no servile work "
21 ye shall d' no servile work therein: "
25 Ye shall d' no servile work therein: "
28 shall d' no work in that same day: "
31 Ye shall d' no manner of work: it "
35 ye shall d' no servile work therein. "
36 and ye shall d' no servile work "
25:18 Wherefore ye shall d' my statutes, "
18 keep my judgments, and d' them; "
45 strangers that d' sojourn among you,
26: 3 my commandments, and d' them; 6213
14 not d' all these commandments; "
15 will not d' all my commandments, "
16 I also will d' this unto you; I will "

Le 27:11 of which they d' not offer a sacrifice
Nu 2: 5 those that d' pitch next unto him
3: 7 congregation, to d' the service of 5647
8 of Israel, to d' the service of the "
4: 3 to d' the work in the tabernacle of 6213
19 d' unto them, that they may live, "
23 the service, to d' the work in the 5647
30 the service, to d' the work of the "
37, 41 d' service in the tabernacle * "
47 to d' the service of the ministry, "
5: 6 to d' a trespass against the Lord, 6213
6:21 d' after the law of his separation. "
7: 5 to d' the service of the tabernacle 5647
8: 7 And thus shalt thou d' unto them, 6213
15 the Levites go in to d' the service 5647
19 to d' the service of the children of "
22 Levites in to d' their service "
26 the charge, and shall d' no service. "
26 Thus shalt thou d' unto the 6213
9:14 the manner thereof, so shall ye d': "
10:29 with us, and we will d' thee good: "
32 goodness the Lord shall d' unto us, 3190
32 the same will we d' unto thee. "
11:27 and Medad d' prophesy in the camp.
14:28 in mine ears, so will I d' to you: 6213
35 will surely d' it unto all this evil "
41 Wherefore d' ye now transgress
15:12 shall ye d' to every one according 6213
13 of the country shall d' these things "
14 as ye d', so he shall d'. "
20 ye d' the heave offering of the
39 of the Lord, and d' them; 6213
40 and d' all my commandments, "
16: 6 This d'; Take you censers, Korah, "
9 near to himself to d' the service 5647
28 sent me to d' all these works; 6213
18: 6 gift for the Lord, to d' the service 5647
23 But the Levites shall d' the service "
21:34 d' to him as thou didst unto Sihon 6213
22:17 d' whatsoever thou sayest unto me: "
18 Lord my God, to d' less or more. "
20 say unto thee, that shalt thou d'. "
30 was I ever wont to d' so unto thee? "
23:19 he said, and shall he not d' it? "
26 the Lord speaketh, that I must d'? "
24:13 d' either good or bad of mine own "
14 thee what this people shall d' "
18 and Israel shall d' valiantly. * "
28:18 shall d' no manner of servile work "
25 ye shall d' no servile work. "
26 ye shall d' no servile work: "
29: 1 ye shall d' no servile work: it is a "
7 ye shall not d' any work therein: "
12 ye shall d' no servile work, and ye "
35 ye shall d' no servile work therein: "
39 things ye shall d' unto the Lord * "
30: 2 he shall d' according to all that "
32:20 If ye will d' this thing, if ye will "
23 But if ye will not d' so, behold, ye "
24 and d' that which hath proceeded "
25 Thy servants will d' as my lord "
31 unto thy servants, so will we d'. "
33:56 shall d' unto you, as I thought to d' "
De 1:14 hast spoken is good for us to d'. "
18 all the things which ye should d'. "
44 you, and chased you, as bees d', "
3: 2 thou shalt d' unto him as thou "
21 so shall the Lord d' unto all the "
24 or in earth, that can d' according "
4: 1 which I teach you, for to d' them, "
5 that ye should d' so in the land "
6 Keep therefore and d' them; for "
14 that ye might d' them in the land "
25 shall d' evil in the sight of the Lord "
5: 1 learn them, and keep, and d' them. "
13 Six days thou shall labour, and d' "
14 in it thou shalt not d' any work, "
27 and we will hear it, and d' it. "
31 teach them, that they may d' them "
32 Ye shall observe to d' therefore as "
6: 1 to teach you, that ye might d' them "
3 O Israel, and observe to d' it; "
18 And thou shalt d' that which is "
24 Lord commanded us to d' all these "
25 if we observe to d' all these "
7:11 I command thee this day, to d' them. "
12 and keep, and d' them, that the "
19 shall the Lord thy God d' unto all "
8: 1 shall ye observe to d', that ye may "
16 prove thee, to d' thee good at thy "
19 if thou d' at all forget the Lord *
11:22 to d' them, to love the Lord your 6213
32 And ye shall observe to d' all the "
12: 1 which ye shall observe to d' in the "
4 Ye shall not d' so unto the Lord "
8 not d' after all the things that we d' "
14 and there thou shalt d' all that I "
25 d' that which is right in the sight "
30 serve their gods? even so will I d' "
31 Thou shalt not d' so unto the Lord "
32 I command you, observe to d' it: "
13:11 and shall d' no more any such "
18 d' that which is right in the sight "
15: 5 to observe to d' all these "
17 maidservant thou shalt d' likewise. "
19 shalt d' no work with the firstling
16: 8 Lord thy God: thou shalt d' no 6213
12 and thou shalt observe and d' "
17:10 And thou shalt d' according to the "
10 to d' according to all that they "
11 they shall tell thee, thou shalt d': "
12 man that will d' presumptuously, "
13 and d' no more presumptuously. "
18: 7 as all his brethren the Levites d', "
9 shalt not learn to d' after the 6213
12 all that d' these things are an * "

De 18:14 God hath not suffered thee so to d'.
19: 9 to d' them, which I command 6213
19 Then shall ye d' unto him, as he "
20: 3 fear not, and d' not tremble, *
15 Thus shalt thou d' unto all the 6213
18 That they teach you not to d' after "
21: 9 when thou shalt d' that which is "
22: 3 d' with his ass; and so shalt thou d' "
3 hast found, shalt thou d' likewise: "
5 all that d' so are an abomination * "
24: 8 and d' according to all that the "
8 them, so ye shall observe to d'. "
18, 22 therefore I command thee to d' "
25:16 For all that d' such things, and all "
16 all that d' unrighteously, are an "
26:16 hath commanded thee to d' these "
16 thou shalt therefore keep and d' "
27:10 and d' his commandments and his "
26 not all the words of this law to d' "
28: 1 thy God, to observe and to d' all his "
13 thee this day, to observe and to d' "
15 thy God, to observe to d' all his "
20 settest thine hand unto for to d', "
58 If thou wilt not observe to d' all the "
63 rejoiced over you to d' you good,
29: 9 this covenant, and d' them, that 6213
9 ye may prosper in all that ye d'. "
14 Neither with you only d' I make this
29 that we may d' all the words of 6213
30: 5 and he will d' thee good, and
8 and d' all his commandments 6213
12, 13 that we may hear it, and d' it? "
14 thy heart, that thou mayest d' it. "
31: 4 And the Lord shall d' unto them as "
5 that ye may d' unto them according "
12 and observe to d' all the words of "
29 ye will d' evil in the sight of the "
32: 6 D' ye thus requite the Lord,
46 your children to observe to d', 6213
34:11 the Lord sent him to d' in the land "
Jos 1: 2 the land which I d' give to them,
7 to d' according to all the law, 6213
8 to d' according to all that is written "
16 thou commandest us we will d', "
2:24 the country d' faint because of us.
3: 5 morrow the Lord will d' wonders 6213
6: 3 Thus shalt thou d' six days. "
7: 9 what wilt thou d' unto thy great "
8: 2 And thou shalt d' to Ai and her king "
8 of the Lord shall ye d'. "
9:20 This we will d' to them: we will "
25 right unto thee to d' unto us, d'. "
10:25 thus shall the Lord d' to all your "
22: 5 take diligent heed to d' the "
24 What have ye to d' with the Lord
27 that we might d' the service of the 5647
23: 6 courageous to keep and to d' all 6213
12 Else if ye d' in any wise go back,
24:13 which ye planted not d' ye eat.
20 will turn and d' you hurt, and consume
J'g 6:27 of the city, that he could not d' 6213
7:17 unto them, Look on me, and d' "
17 it shall be that, as I d', so shall ye d'. "
8: 3 was I able to d' in comparison of "
9:33 thou d' to them as thou shalt find "
48 What ye have seen me d', make "
48 make haste, and d' as I have done. "
10:15 d' thou unto us whatsoever seemeth "
11:10 if we d' not so according to thy "
12 What hast thou to d' with me, that
36 unto the Lord, d' to me according 6213
13: 8 teach us what we shall d' unto the "
12 child, and how shall we d' unto †4640
17 come to pass we may d' thee honour?
14:10 for so used the young men to d'. 6213
15: 3 Philistines, though I d' them a "
10 come up, to d' to him as he hath "
17:13 know I that the Lord will d' me good.
18:14 D' ye know that there is in these
14 consider what ye have to d' 6213
18 the priest unto them, What d' ye? "
19:23 nay, I pray you, d' not so wickedly:
23 into mine house, d' not this folly. 6213
24 d' with them what seemeth good "
24 but unto this man d' not so vile a "
20: 9 the thing which we will d' to "
10 that they may d', when they come "
21: 7 How shall we d' for wives for them "
11 this is the thing that ye shall d', "
16 How shall we d' for wives for them "
Ru 1:17 the Lord d' so to me, and more also, "
2: 9 eyes be on the field that they d' reap,
3: 4 he will tell thee what thou shalt d'. 6213
5 All thou sayest unto me I will d'. "
11 I will d' for thee all that thou "
13 well; let him d' the kinsman's part:
13 but if he will not d' the part of a
13 will I d' the part of a kinsman to
4:11 and d' thou worthily in Ephratah, 6213
1Sa 1:23 said unto her, D' what seemeth "
2:23 he said unto them, Why d' ye such "
35 priest, that shall d' according to "
3:11 Behold, I will d' a thing in Israel, "
17 God d' so to thee, and more also, if "
18 let him d' what seemeth him good. "
5: 8 What shall we d' with the ark of the "
6: 2 What shall we d' to the ark of the "
6 Wherefore then d' ye harden your
7: 3 If ye d' return unto the Lord with
8: 8 served other gods, so d' they also 6213
10: 2 you, saying, What shall I d' for my "
7 that thou d' as occasion serve thee; "
8 and shew thee what thou shalt d'. "
11:10 ye shall d' with us all that seemeth "
12:16 which the Lord will d' before your "
25 But if ye shall still d' wickedly, ye

1Sa 14: 7 said unto him, D' all that is in 6213
36 D' whatsoever seemeth good unto "
40 unto Saul, D' what seemeth good "
44 And Saul answered, God d' so and "
16: 3 will shew thee what thou shalt d': "
20: 2 my father will d' nothing either * "
4 thy soul desireth, I will even d' it "
13 The Lord d' so and much more to "
13 if it please my father to d' thee evil,
30 d' not I know that thou hast
22: 3 till I know what God will d' for me. 6213
24: 4 that thou mayest d' to him as it "
6 Lord forbid that I should d' this "
25:17 and consider what thou wilt d'; "
22 So and more also d' God unto the "
26:21 I will no more d' thee harm, because
25 David: thou shalt both d' great 6213
28: 2 shalt know what thy servant can d'. "
15 known unto me what I shall d'. "
29: 3 the Philistines, What d' these Hebrews
30:23 Ye shall not d' so, my brethren, 6213
2Sa 3: 8 which against Judah d' shew "
9 So d' God to Abner, and more "
9 sworn to David, even so I d' to him; "
18 Now then d' it: for the Lord hath "
35 So d' God to me, and more also, if "
7: 3 Nathan said to the king, Go, d' all "
23 to make him a name, and to d' for "
25 establish it for ever, and d' as thou "
9:11 his servant, so shall thy servant d'. "
10:12 Lord d' that which seemeth him "
11:11 soul liveth, I will not d' this thing. "
12: 9 commandment of the Lord, to d' "
12 but I will d' this thing before all "
13: 2 thought it hard for him to d' any "
12 in Israel: d' not thou this folly. "
15: 4 unto me, and I would d' him justice! "
5 nigh to him to d' him obeisance, "
15 thy servants are ready to d' "
26 let him d' to me as seemeth good 6213
16:10 What have I to d' with you, ye sons of
11 more now may this Benjamite d' it?
20 among you what we shall d'. 6213
17: 6 shall we d' after his saying? if not, "
18: 4 What seemeth you best I will d'. "
32 rise against thee to d' thee hurt, be as
19:13 God d' so to me, and more also, if 6213
18 and to d' what he thought good. "
19 neither d' thou remember that which
22 What have I to d' with you, ye sons of
22 for d' not I know that I am this day
27 d' therefore what is good in thine 6213
37 and d' to him what shall seem "
38 will d' to him that which shall seem "
38 shalt require of me, that will I d' "
20: 6 the son of Bichri d' us more harm "
17 And he answered, I d' hear.
21: 3 What shall I d' for you? and 6213
4 ye shall say, that will I d' for you. "
23:17 that I should d' this: is not this the "
24:12 of them, that I may d' it unto thee. "
1Ki 1:30 even so will I certainly d' this day. 6213
2: 6 D' therefore according to thy "
9 knowest what thou oughtest to d' "
23 God d' so to me, and more also, if "
31 the king said unto him, D' as he "
38 hath said, so will thy servant d'. "
3:28 wisdom of God was in him, to d' "
5: 8 and I will d' all thy desire "
8:32 Then hear thou in heaven, and d', "
39 and forgive, and d', and give to "
43 and d' according to all that the "
43 fear thee, as d' thy people Israel; * "
9: 1 which he was pleased to d', That 6213
4 to d' according to all that I have "
10: 9 made he thee king, to d' judgment "
11:12 I will not d' it for David thy "
33 have not walked in my ways, to d' "
38 and d' that is right in my sight, to "
12: 6 d' ye advise that I may answer *
27 If this people go up to d' sacrifice *6213
14: 8 to d' that only which was right in "
17:13 go and d' as thou hast said: but "
18 What have I to d' with thee, O thou
18:34 And he said, D' it the second time.
34 And he said, D' it the third time.
19: 2 So let the gods d' to me, and more 6213
20: 9 I will d': but this thing I may not d'. "
10 The gods d' so unto me, and more "
24 And d' this thing, Take the kings "
22:22 prevail also: go forth, and d' so. "
2Ki 2: 9 Ask what I shall d' for thee, before "
3:13 What have I to d' with thee? get
4: 2 What shall I d' for thee? tell me, 6213
16 thou man of God, d' not lie unto thine
28 did I not say, D' not deceive me?
5:13 the prophet had bid thee d' some 6213
6:15 Alas, my master! how shall we d'? 6213
27 And he said, If the Lord d' not help
31 God d' so and more also to me, if 6213
7: 9 We d' not well: this day is a day of "
8:12 the evil that thou wilt d' unto the "
13 servant a dog, that he should d' "
9:18, 19 What hast thou to d' with peace?
10: 5 and will d' all that thou shalt bid 6213
5 d' thou that which is good in thine "
19 I have a great sacrifice to d' to Baal:
11: 5 This is the thing that ye shall d'; 6213
17:12 said unto them, Ye shall not d' this "
15 that they should not d' like them. "
17 sold themselves to d' evil in the "
34 Unto this day they d' after the "
34 they fear not the Lord, neither d' "
36 and to him shall ye d' sacrifice, *
37 shall observe to d' for evermore; 6213
41 so d' they unto this day

2Ki 18:12 would not hear them, nor d' them. 6213
19:31 of the Lord of hosts shall d' this. * "
20: 9 that the Lord will d' the thing that "
21: 8 observe to d' according to all that "
9 seduced them to d' more evil than "
22: 9 hand of them that d' the work, * "
13 this book, to d' according unto all "
1Ch 11:19 that I should d' this thing: shall I "
12:32 to know what Israel ought to d'; "
13: 4 said that they would d' so: for "
16:21 He suffered no man to d' them wrong:
22 anointed, and d' my prophets no harm.
40 d' according to all that is written*
17: 2 D' all that is in thine heart; for 6213
23 for ever, and d' as thou hast said. "
19:13 the Lord d' that which is good in "
21: 8 thee, d' away the iniquity of thy *5674
10 them, that I may d' it unto thee. 6213
23 let my lord the king d' that which "
28: 7 constant to d' my commandments "
10 sanctuary: be strong, and d' it. "
20 and of good courage, and d' it: "
29:19 and to d' all these things, and to "
2Ch 6:23 hear thou from heaven, and d', "
33 and d' according to all that the "
7:17 d' according to all that I have "
9: 8 king over them, to d' judgment "
14: 4 d' the law and the commandment. "
18:21 also prevail: go out, and d' even so. "
19: 6 Take heed what ye d': for ye judge "
7 be upon you; take heed and d' it: "
9 shall ye d' in the fear of the Lord, "
10 this d', and ye shall not trespass. "
20:12 neither know we what to d': "
22: 3 was his counseller to d' wickedly.
23: 4 This is the thing that ye shall d'; 6213
25: 8 But if thou wilt go, d' it, be strong "
9 shall we d' for the hundred talents "
30:12 one heart to d' the commandment "
32:10 Whereon d' ye trust, that ye abide
33: 8 will take heed to d' all that I have 6213
9 and to d' worse than the heathen.* "
34:16 to thy servants, they d' it. "
21 d' after all that is written in this "
35: 6 they may d' according to the word "
21 What have I to d' with thee, thou king
Ezr 4: 2 for we seek your God, as ye d'; "
2 we d' sacrifice unto him since the
3 Ye have nothing to d' with us
22 now that ye fail not to d' this: *5648
6: 8 what ye shall d' to the elders of
7:10 and to d' it, and to teach in Israel 6213
18 to d' with the rest of the silver 5648
18 that d' after the will of your God.
21 I Artaxerxes the king, d' make
26 whosoever will not d' the law of 5648
10: 4 be of good courage, and d' it. 6213
5 should d' according to this word. "
11 your fathers, and d' his pleasure: "
12 As thou hast said, so must we d'. "
Ne 1: 9 my commandments, and d' them; "
2:12 in my heart to d' at Jerusalem: "
19 What is this thing that ye d'? "
4: 2 What d' these feeble Jews? "
5: 9 I said, It is not good that ye d': "
12 them; so will we d' as thou sayest. "
12 should d' according to this promise. "
6: 2 they thought to d' me mischief. "
13 should be afraid, and d' so, and sin, "
9:24 might d' with them as they would. "
29 which if a man d', he shall live in "
10:29 and d' all the commandments of "
13:17 What evil thing is this that ye d', "
21 d' so again, I will lay hands on you.
27 hearken unto you to d' all this 6213
Es 1: 8 should d' according to every man's "
15 shall we d' unto the queen Vashti "
3:11 to d' with them as it seemeth good "
4:11 of the king's provinces, d' know, that
5: 5 he may d' as Esther hath said. *6213
8 d' to morrow as the king hath said. "
6: 6 the king delight to d' honour more "
10 said, and d' even so to Mordecai "
7: 5 presume in his heart to d' so? "
9:13 in Shushan to d' to morrow also "
23 undertook to d' as they had begun, "
Job 6: 4 terrors of God d' set themselves in
26 D' ye imagine to reprove words,
7:20 what shall I d' unto thee, O thou 6466
9:13 proud helpers d' stoop under him.
10: 2 D' not condemn me; shew me
11: 8 as heaven; what canst thou d'? 6466
13: 2 ye know, the same d' I know also:
9 another, d' ye so mock him? *
10 if ye d' secretly accept persons.
14 Wherefore d' I take my flesh in *
20 Only d' not two things unto me: 6213
15: 3 wherewith he can d' no good? 5953
12 and what d' thy eyes wink at,
16: 4 I also could speak as ye d':
17:10 all, d' ye return, and come now: *
19:22 Why d' ye persecute me as God,
20: 2 Therefore d' my thoughts cause me
21: 7 Wherefore d' the wicked live, become
29 and d' ye not know their tokens,
22:17 can the Almighty d' for them? 6466
24: 1 d' they that know him not see
31:14 shall I d' when God riseth up?
32: 9 d' the aged understand judgment.*
34:10 God, that he should d' wickedness;
12 God will not d' wickedly, neither
32 done iniquity, I will d' no more. 6466
36:28 Which the clouds d' drop and *
37:12 d' whatsoever he commandeth 6467
39: 1 thou mark when the hinds d' calve?
41: 8 him, remember the battle, d' no more.

Job 42: 2 know that thou canst d' every thing,
Ps 2: 1 Why d' the heathen rage, and the
7: 1 my God, in thee d' I put my trust:
11: 3 what can the righteous d'? 6466
12: 2 with a double heart d' they speak.
16: 1 for in thee d' I put my trust.
25: 1 thee, O Lord, d' I lift up my soul.
5 on thee d' I wait all the day.
34:14 Depart from evil, and d' good; 6213
16 Lord is against them that d' evil, "
36: 3 off to be wise, and to d' good.
37: 3 Trust in the Lord and d' good; 6213
8 not thyself in any wise to d' evil. *
27 Depart from evil, and d' good; 6213
38:15 For in thee, O Lord, d' I hope:
40: 8 I delight to d' thy will, O my God: 6213
41: 7 against me d' they devise my hurt.
50:16 hast thou to d' to declare my statutes,
51:18 D' good in thy good pleasure
56: 4 fear what flesh can d' unto me. 6213
11 afraid what man can d' unto me. "
58: 1 D' ye indeed speak righteousness,
1 d' ye judge uprightly, O ye sons of
60:12 God we shall d' valiantly: for he 6213
64: 4 suddenly d' they shoot at him, and fear
71: 1 In thee, O Lord, d' I put my trust:
82: 3 d' justice to the afflicted and needy.
83: 9 D' unto them as unto the 6213
86: 4 unto thee, O Lord, d' I lift up my soul.
89:50 how d' I bear in my bosom the
92: 7 all the workers of iniquity d' flourish;
95:10 a people that d' err in their heart,
103:18 his commandments to d' them. 6213
20 that d' his commandments, * "
21 of his, that d' his pleasure. "
104:20 beasts of the forest d' creep forth.
105:14 suffered no man to d' them wrong:
15 anointed, and d' my prophets no harm.
107:23 that d' business in great waters; 6213
108:13 Through God we shall d' valiantly: "
109:21 But d' thou for me, O God the * "
111:10 they that d' his commandments: "
118: 6 fear: what can man d' unto me? "
119: 3 They also d' no iniquity: they 6466
21 which d' err from thy commandments.
35 commandments; for therein d' I
83 yet d' I not forget thy statutes.
109 yet d' I not forget thy law.
113 vain thoughts: but thy law d' I love.
132 as thou usest to d' unto those that
141 yet d' not I forget thy precepts.
153 for I d' not forget thy law.
157 yet d' I not decline from thy *
163 lying: but thy law d' I love.
164 seven times a day d' I praise thee
176 I d' not forget thy commandments.
125: 4 D' good, O Lord, unto those that
129: 8 Neither d' they which go by say,
130: 5 and in his word d' I hope.
131: 1 neither d' I exercise myself in
137: 6 If I d' not remember thee, let my *
139:21 D' not I hate them, O Lord, that hate
143: 8 morning: for in thee d' I trust:
10 Teach me to d' thy will; for thou 6213
Pr 2:14 Who rejoice to d' evil, and delight "
3:27 in the power of thine hand to d' it. "
6: 3 D' this now, my son, and deliver "
30 Men d' not despise a thief, if he
8:13 and the froward mouth, d' I hate.
10:23 as sport to a fool to d' mischief: 6213
14:22 D' they not err that devise evil?
17: 7 much less d' lying lips a prince.
19: 7 brethren of the poor d' hate him:
7 how much more d' his friends go
19 deliver him, yet thou must d' it again.
20:30 so d' stripes the inward parts of *
21: 3 To d' justice and judgment is 6213
7 because they refuse to d' judgment. "
15 It is joy to the just to d' judgment: "
24: 8 He that deviseth to d' evil shall be
29 I will d' so to him as he hath done 6213
25: 8 lest thou know not what to d' in "
28:12 When righteous men d' rejoice, *
31:12 She will d' him good and not evil 1580
Ec 2: 3 which they should d' under the 6213
11 labour that I had laboured to d': "
12 what can the man d' that cometh
3:12 rejoice, and to d' good in his life. 6213
4: 8 For whom d' I labour, and bereave
5: 1 they consider not that they d' evil. 6213
6: 6 no good: d' not all go to one place?
8:11 men is fully set in them to d' evil. 6213
12 Though a sinner d' evil an hundred "
9:10 hand findeth to d', d' it with thy "
10:10 iron be blunt, and he d' not whet the
11: 5 how the bones d' grow in the womb
Ca 1: 3 therefore d' the virgins love thee.
8: 8 what shall we d' for our sister in 6213
Isa 1:16 before mine eyes; cease to d' evil; "
17 Learn to d' well; seek judgment,
5: 5 you what I will d' to my vineyard, 6213
9:13 neither d' they seek the Lord of *
10: 3 will ye d' in the day of visitation, 6213
11 so d' to Jerusalem and her idols? "
14:21 that they d' not rise, nor possess *
19:15 or tail, branch or rush, may d'. 6213
21 shall d' sacrifice and oblation; *5647
23: 4 neither d' I nourish up young men,*
24: 4 people of the earth d' languish.
7 all the merryhearted d' sigh.
18 the foundations of the earth d' shake.
27: 3 I the Lord d' keep it; I will water
28:21 that he may d' his work, his 6213
29:13 and with their lips d' honour me,
14 I will proceed to d' a marvellous work
37:32 of the Lord of hosts shall d' this. *6213

Isa 38: 7 that the Lord will d' this thing that 6213
19 he shall praise thee, as I d' this day:
41:23 yea, d' good, or d' evil, that we
42: 9 and new things d' I declare:
16 These things will I d' unto them, 6213
43:19 Behold, I will d' a new thing; "
45: 7 I the Lord d' all these things. * "
46:10 and I will d' all my pleasure: "
11 I have purposed it, I will also d' it. "
48:11 even for mine own sake, will I d' it: "
14 will d' his pleasure on Babylon, * "
55: 2 Wherefore d' ye spend money for that
56: 1 Keep ye judgment, and d' justice: 6213
57: 4 Against whom d' ye sport yourselves?
58: 4 ye shall not fast as ye d' this day,*
64: 6 and we all d' fade as a leaf;
65: 8 so will I d' for my servants' sakes,6213
Jer 2: 8 walked after things that d' not profit.
18 hast thou to d' in the way of Egypt,
18 hast thou to d' in the way of Assyria,
4:22 they are wise to d' evil, but to
22 to d' good they have no knowledge.
30 thou art spoiled,what wilt thou d'? 6213
5:28 right of the needy d' they not judge.
31 what will ye d' in the end thereof ?6213
7:10 We are delivered to d' all these "
14 Therefore will I d' unto this house, "
17 Seest thou not what they d' in the "
19 D' they provoke me to anger?
19 d' they not provoke themselves to
8: 8 How d' ye say, We are wise,
14 Why d' we sit still? assemble
9: 7 for how shall I d' for the daughter 6213
10: 5 for they cannot d' evil, neither
5 also is it in them to d' good.
11: 4 Obey my voice, and d' them, 6213
6 words of this covenant, and d' them. "
8 which I commanded them to d': "
15 hath my beloved to d' in mine house,
12: 5 then how wilt thou d' in the 6213
13:12 D' we not certainly know that every
23 then may ye also d' good, that are
23 that are accustomed to d' evil.
14: 7 d' thou it for thy name's sake: *6213
21 D' not abhor us, for thy name's sake,
21 d' not disgrace the throne of thy glory:
17:22 neither d' ye any work, but hallow 6213
24 sabbath day, to d' no work therein; "
18: 6 cannot I d' with you as this potter? "
8 evil that I thought to d' unto them "
10 If it d' evil in my sight, that it obey "
12 we will every one d' the imagination "
19:12 Thus will I d' unto this place, saith "
22: 3 and d' no wrong, d' no violence to
4 For if ye d' this thing indeed, 6213
15 and d' judgment and justice, and "
17 oppression, and for violence, to d' it. "
23:24 D' not I fill heaven and earth?
25: 6 hands; and I will d' you no hurt.
26: 3 which I purpose to d' unto them 6213
14 d' with me as seemeth good and "
28: 6 the Lord d' so: the Lord perform "
29:32 good that I will d' for my people, "
30: 6 wherefore d' I see every man with
31:20 I d' earnestly remember him still:
32:23 that thou commandest them to d': 6213
35 they should d' this abomination, "
40 away from them, to d' them good; "
41 rejoice over them to d' them good, "
33: 9 shall hear all the good that I d' 6213
18 meat offerings, and to d' sacrifice "
36: 3 which I purpose to d' unto them; "
38: 5 for he is not he that can d' any thing
39:12 d' him no harm; but d' unto him 6213
40:16 Thou shalt not d' this thing: for "
42: 2 as thine eyes d' behold us:)
3 and the thing that we may d'. 6213
5 if we d' not even according to all "
20 declare unto us, and we will d' it. "
44: 4 Oh, d' not this abominable thing "
17 we will certainly d' whatsoever * "
50:15 as she hath done, d' unto her. "
21 saith the Lord, and d' according to "
29 that she hath done, d' unto her: "
51:47 that I will d' judgment upon the "
52 that I will d' judgment upon her "
55 when her waves d' roar like great
La 1: 4 The ways of Zion d' mourn,
22 and d' unto them, as thou hast 5953
2:11 Mine eyes d' fail with tears,
Eze 2 4 I d' send thee unto them;
5 9 And I will d' in thee that which I 6213
9 and whereunto I will not d' any "
6:10 I would d' this evil unto them. "
7:27 I will d' unto them after their way, "
8: 6 seest thou what they d'? even the "
9 abominations that they d' here. "
12 of the house of Israel d' in the dark, "
13 greater abominations that they d'. "
11:20 and d' them: and they shall be my "
15: 3 be taken thereof to d' any work? * "
16: 5 pitied thee, to d' any of these unto "
18: 5 but if a man be just and d' that "
21 d' that which is lawful and right, "
20:11 man d', he shall even live in them. "
13 man d', he shall even live in them; "
19 keep my judgments, and d' them; "
21 to d' them, which if a man d', he "
21:24 all your doings your sins d' appear;
22:14 Lord have spoken it, and will d' it.6213
23:48 taught not to d' after your lewdness. "
24:14 and I will d' it; I will not go back, "
22 And ye shall d' as I have done: ye "
24 to all that he hath done shall ye d': "
25: 8 Because that Moab and Seir d' say,
14 they shall d' in Edom according 6213

Eze 33: 9 if he d' not turn from his way, *
14, 19 and d' that which is lawful and6213
31 but they will not d' them: for with "
32 thy words, but they d' them not. "
34: 2 to the shepherds of Israel that d' feed
35:11 even d' according to thine anger, 6213
15 so will I d' unto thee: thou shalt "
36:11 and will d' better unto you than at
22 I d' not this for your sakes, O 6213
27 keep my judgments and d' them. "
32 Not for your sakes d' I this, saith "
36 Lord have spoken it, and I will d' it. "
37 house of Israel, to d' it for them; "
37:24 observe my statues, and d' them. "
28 I the Lord d' sanctify Israel, *
39:17 my sacrifice that I d' sacrifice for
43:11 ordinances thereof, and d' them. 6213
44:13 near unto me, to d' the office of a*
45:20 And so shalt thou d' the seventh 6213
25 shall he d' the like in the feast of "
Da 3:14 d' not ye serve my gods, nor *
4:26 have known that the heavens d' rule.
9:18 for we d' not present our supplications
19 O Lord, hearken and d'; defer not 6213
11: 3 dominion, and d' according to his "
16 shall d' according to his own will, "
17 thus shall he d': and he shall give "
24 he shall d' that which his fathers "
27 shall be to d' mischief, and they
28 he shall d' exploits, and return to 6213
30 so shall he d'; he shall even return "
32 and such as d' wickedly against
32 the people that d' know their God*
32 shall be strong, and d' exploits, 6213
36 king shall d' according to his will; "
39 he d' in the most strong holds * "
12:10 but the wicked shall d' wickedly:
Ho 4:18 her rulers with shame d' love,
6: 4 Ephraim,what shall I d' unto thee?6213
4 Judah, what shall I d' unto thee? "
7:10 d' not return to the Lord their God,*
15 yet d' they imagine mischief against
9: 5 What will ye d' in the solemn day,6213
10: 3 what then should a king d' to us? "
15 So shall Beth-el d' unto you "
12: 1 and they d' make a covenant with
14: 8 What have I to d' any more with idols?
Joe 1:18 How d' the beasts groan?
2:21 for the Lord will d' great things, *6213
22 pastures of the wilderness d' spring
3: 4 what have ye to d' with me, O Tyre,
Am 3: 7 the Lord God will d' nothing, but 6213
10 know not to d' right, saith the Lord, "
4:12 thus will I d' unto thee, O Israel: "
12 because I will d' this unto thee, "
Jon 1:11 What shall we d' unto thee, that "
3:10 that he would d' unto them: and "
4: 9 he said, I d' well to be angry,
Mic 2: 3 against this family d' I devise an evil,
7 d' not my words d' good to him
11 in the spirit and falsehood d' lie,
6: 8 to d' justly, and to love mercy, 6213
7: 3 that they may d' evil with both hands
Na 1: 9 What d' ye imagine against the Lord?
Zep 1:12 will not d' good,
12 neither will he d' evil.
3: 5 not d' iniquity: every morning 6213
13 Israel shall not d' iniquity, nor "
Hag 2: 3 and how d' ye see it now?
12 and with his skirt d' touch bread,
Zec 1: 5 and the prophets, d' they live for ever?
6 Lord of hosts thought to d' unto us,6213
21 What come these to d'? And he "
5:10 Whither d' these bear the ephah?
8:15 days to d' well unto Jerusalem
16 things that ye shall d'; Speak ye 6213
9:12 even to day d' I declare that I will
12: 7 of Jerusalem d' not magnify *
Mal 1:10 d' ye kindle fire on mine altar *
2: 2 because ye d' not lay it to heart.
10 why d' we deal treacherously every
4: 1 and all that d' wickedly shall be *6213
3 day that I d' this, saith the Lord "
M't 5: 6 Blessed are they which d' hunger*
15 neither d' men light a candle, and
19 whosoever shall d' and teach them,4160
44 d' good to them that hate you, * "
46 d' not even the publicans the same? "
47 what d' ye more than others? "
47 d' not even the publicans so? "
6: 1 Take heed that ye d' not your alms "
2 d' not sound a trumpet before thee,
2 as the hypocrites d' in the 4160
7 repetitions, as the heathen d':
20 where thieves d' not break through
26 they sow not, neither d' they reap,
28 they toil not, neither d' they spin:
32 all these things d' the Gentiles seek:
7:12 ye would that men should d' to you,4160
12 d' ye even so to them: for this is "
16 D' men gather grapes of thorns,
8: 9 D' this, and he doeth it. 4160
9:14 Why d' we and the Pharisees fast oft,
17 Neither d' men put new wine into old
28 ye that I am able to d' this? 4160
11: 3 or d' we look for another?
4 again these things which ye d' hear
12: 2 thy disciples d' that which is not 4160
2 not lawful to d' upon the sabbath "
12 Wherefore it is lawful to d' well "
27 whom d' your children cast them out?
50 For whosoever shall d' the will 4160
13:13 neither d' they understand.
41 and them which d' iniquity; 4160
14: 2 mighty works d' shew forth
15: 2 Why d' thy disciples transgress the

M't 15: 3 Why d' ye also transgress the
16: 9 D' ye not yet understand,
11 How is it that ye d' not understand
13 Whom d' men say that I the Son of
17:25 of whom d' the kings of the earth take
18:10 in heaven their angels d' always behold
35 heavenly Father d' also unto you, 4160
19:16 what good thing shall I d', that I "
18 Thou shalt d' no murder. Thou *
20:13 I d' thee no wrong: didst not thou 91
15 for me to d' what I will with mine 4160
32 will ye that I shall d' unto you? "
21:21 ye shall not only d' this which is "
24, 27 by what authority I d' these "
40 will he d' unto those husbandmen? "
22:29 Ye d' err, not knowing the Scriptures,
23: 3 you observe, that observe and d'; 4160
3 but d' not ye after their works: "
3 for they say and d' not. "
5 But all their works they d' for to "
26:72 I d' not know the man. *
27:19 thou nothing to d' with that just man:
22 What shall I d' then with Jesus 4160
M'r 1:24 have we to d' with thee, thou Jesus
27 spirits, and they d' obey him. *
2:18 Why d' the disciples of John and of
24 why d' they on the sabbath day 4160
3: 4 to d' good on the sabbath days, 15
4 to d' evil? to save life, or to kill? 2554
35 whosoever shall d' the will of God,
5: 7 What have I to d' with thee, Jesus
6: 5 he could there d' no mighty work, 4160
14 d' shew forth themselves in him.
7: 7 Howbeit in vain d' they worship me,
8 many other such like things ye d'.*4160
12 ye suffer him no more to d' ought "
13 and many such like things d' ye. "
18 D' ye not perceive, that whatsoever
8:18 and d' ye not remember?
21 How is it that ye d' not understand?
27 Whom d' men say that I am?
9:22 canst d' any thing, have compassion
39 no man which shall d' a miracle 4160
10:17 what shall I d' that I may inherit
19 D' not commit adultery, D' not kill,
19 D' not steal, D' not bear false witness,
35 that thou shouldest d' for us 4160
36 What would ye that I should d' "
51 What wilt thou that I should d' "
11: 3 Why d' ye this? say ye that the "
5 them, What d' ye, loosing the colt? "
26 But if ye d' not forgive, neither *
28 this authority to d' these things? 4160
29, 33 by what authority I d' these "
12: 9 the lord of the vineyard d'? he "
24 D' ye not therefore err, because *
27 living: ye therefore d' greatly err.
13:11 neither d' ye premeditate: *
14: 7 ye will ye may d' them good: but 4160
15: 8 desire him to d' as he had ever done
12 I shall d' unto him whom ye call 4160
Lu 2:27 to d' for him after the custom of
3:10 saying, What shall we d' then? "
11 that hath meat, let him d' likewise. "
12 him, Master, what shall we d'? "
14 And what shall we d'? And he ‡ "
14 D' violence to no man, neither 1286
4:23 d' also here in thy country. 4160
34 have we to d' with thee, thou Jesus
5:30 Why d' ye eat and drink with publicans
33 Why d' the disciples of John fast
6: 2 Why d' ye that which is not lawful 4160
2 to d' on the sabbath days? "
9 on the sabbath days to d' good, 15
9 or to d' evil? 2554
11 what they might d' to Jesus. 4160
27 Love your enemies, d' good to them "
31 would that men should d' to you, "
31 d' ye also to them likewise. "
33 And if ye d' good to them which
33 d' good to you, what thank have ye? 15
33 for sinners also d' even the same. 4160
35 love your enemies, and d' good, 15
44 For of thorns men d' not gather figs,
46 and d' not the things which I say? 4160
7: 4 worthy for whom he should d' this: 3930
8 servant, D' this, and he doeth it. 4160
8:21 hear the word of God, and d' it. "
28 What have I to d' with thee, Jesus,
10:11 dust...we d' wipe off against you:
25 shall I d' to inherit eternal life? 4160
28 answered right: this d', and thou "
37 unto him, Go, and d' thou likewise. "
11:19 by whom d' your sons cast them out?
39 Now d' ye Pharisees make clean the
12: 4 have no more that they can d'. 4160
17 What shall I d', because I have no "
18 will I d': I will pull down my barns, "
26 not able to d' that thing which is least
30 all these things d' the nations of the
56 that ye d' not discern this time? *
13:32 I d' cures to day and to morrow, *2005
15:29 these many years d' I serve thee,
16: 3 What shall I d'? for my lord 4160
4 I am resolved what to d', that, "
17:10 that which was our duty to d'. "
18:18 shall I d' to inherit eternal life? "
20 D' not commit adultery, D' not kill,
20 D' not steal, D' not bear false witness
41 thou that I shall d' unto thee? 4160
19:31 Why d' ye loose him?
48 could not find what they might d': 4160
20: 8 by what authority I d' these things. "
13 What shall I d'? I will send my "
15 lord of the vineyard d' unto them? "
22:19 you: this d' in remembrance of me. "

Lu 22:23 it was that should d' this thing. 4238
23:31 d' these things in a green tree 4160
34 for they know not what they d'.
24:38 why d' thoughts arise in your hearts?
Joh 2: 4 what have I to d' with thee? mine
5 Whatsoever he saith unto you, d' 4160
3: 2 for no man can d' these miracles "
11 We speak that we d' know,
4:34 My meat is to d' the will of him 4160
5:19 The Son can d' nothing of himself, "
19 what he seeth the Father d': for "
30 I can of mine own self d' nothing; "
36 same works that I d', bear witness "
45 D' not think that I will accuse you to
6: 6 himself knew what he would d'. 4160
28 What shall we d', that we might "
38 not to d' mine own will, but the "
7: 4 thou d' these things, shew thyself "
17 If any man will d' his will, he shall "
26 D' the rulers know indeed that *
31 will he d' more miracles than 4160
8:11 neither d' I condemn thee: go and
28 and that I d' nothing of myself; 4160
29 for I d' always those things that "
38 and ye d' that which ye have seen "
39 ye would d' the works of Abraham. "
41 Ye d' the deeds of your father. "
43 d' ye not understand my speech?
44 the lusts of your father ye will d'. 4160
46 the truth, why d' ye not believe me?
49 and ye d' dishonour me.
9:15 and I washed, and d' see.
16 that is a sinner d' such miracles? 4160
33 not of God, he could d' nothing. "
10:25 that I d' in my Father's name, "
32 for which of these works d' ye stone me?
37 If I d' not the work of my Father, 4160
38 if I d', though ye believe not me, "
11:12 Lord, if he sleep, he shall d' well.*4982
47 What d' we? for this man doeth 4160
13: 7 What I d' thou knowest not now; "
15 ye should d' as I have done to you. "
17 things, happy are ye if ye d' them, "
27 That thou doest, d' quickly. "
14:12 the works that I d' shall he d' also; "
12 works than these shall he d'; "
13 that will I d', that the Father may "
14 any thing in my name, I will d' it. "
31 commandment, even so I d'. Arise, "
15: 5 for without me ye can d' nothing. "
14 ye d' whatsoever I command you,* "
21 But all these things will they d' "
16: 3 these things will they d' unto you, "
19 D' ye enquire among yourselves of
31 D' ye now believe?
17: 4 work which thou gavest me to d'. 4160
21:21 Lord, and what shall this man d?
Ac 1: 1 Jesus began both to d' and teach, 4160
2:11 we d' hear them speak in our tongues
37 and brethren, what shall we d'? 4160
4:16 What shall we d' to these men? "
28 For to d' whatsoever thy hand and "
5:35 to d' as touching these men. 4238
7:26 why d' ye wrong one to another? 91
51 as your fathers did, so d' ye.
9: 6 have me to d'? And the Lord *4160
6 be told thee what thou must d'. "
10: 6 thee what thou oughtest to d' * "
14:15 Sirs, why d' ye these things? "
15:29 ye shall d' well. Fare ye well. *4238
36 of the Lord, and see how they d'. *2192
16:20 Jews, d' exceedingly trouble our city,
28 D' thyself no harm: for we are 4238
30 Sirs, what must I d' to be saved? 4160
37 now d' they thrust us out privily?
17: 7 all d' contrary to the decrees *4160
19:36 be quiet, and to d' nothing rashly. "
21:23 D' therefore this that we say to "
22:10 I said, What shall I d', Lord? "
10 which are appointed for thee to d'. "
23:21 But d' not thou yield unto them:
24:10 I d' the more cheerfully answer for
16 and herein d' I exercise myself,
25: 9 willing to d' the Jews a pleasure, *2698
26: 9 ought to d' many things contrary 4238
20 d' works meet for repentance, * "
Ro 1:28 to d' those things which are not 4160
32 not only d' the same, but have
32 pleasure in them that d' them. *4238
2: 3 them which d' such things, and * "
8 and d' not obey the truth, *
14 have not the law, d' by nature 4160
3: 8 Let us d' evil, that good may come? "
31 D' we then make void the law
7:15 For that which I d' I allow not: 2716
15 for what I would, that d' I not; *4238
15 but what I hate, that d' I. 4160
16 If then I d' that which I would not "
17 it is no more I that d' it, but sin 2716
19 the good that I would I d' not: but 4160
19 evil which I would not, that I d'. *4238
20 Now if I d' that I would not, 4160
20 no more I that d' it, but sin that 2716
21 I would d' good, evil is present 4160
8: 3 law could not d', in that it was weak
5 flesh d' mind the things of the flesh;
13 d' mortify the deeds of the body,
25 then d' we with patience wait for it.
12: 8 giveth, let him d' it with simplicity;
15 Rejoice with them that d' rejoice,*
13: 3 d' that which is good, and thou 4160
4 But if thou d' that which is evil, "
15:31 that d' not believe in Judæa; *
1Co 5:12 I to d' to judge them also that are
12 d' not ye judge them that are
6: 2 D' ye not know that the saints shall

1Co 6: 7 Why d' ye not rather take wrong?*
7 d' ye not rather suffer yourselves*
8 Nay, ye d' wrong, and defraud,
7:36 let him d' what he will, 4160
9: 3 answer to them that d' examine me
13 D' ye not know that they which
17 For if I d' this thing willingly, I 4238
23 And this I d' for the gospel's sake, 4160
25 d' it to obtain a corruptible crown;
10:22 D' we provoke the Lord to jealousy?
31 ye d', d' all to the glory of God. 4160
11:24 this d' in remembrance of me. "
25 this d' ye, as oft as ye drink it in "
26 ye d' show the Lord's death till *
12:30 d' all speak with tongues?
30 d' all interpret?
15:29 Else what shall they d' which are 4160
35 and with what body d' they come?
16: 1 even so d' ye. Upon the first day 4160
5 for I d' pass through Macedonia.
10 the work of the Lord, as I also d'.
2Co 1:17 d' I purpose according to the flesh,
3: 1 D' we begin again to commend
5: 4 that are in this tabernacle d' groan,
7: 8 I d' not repent, though I did repent:
8: 1 d' you to wit of the grace of God *1107
10 only to d', but also to be forward 4160
23 Whether any d' enquire of Titus,
10: 3 we d' not war after the flesh: *
7 D' ye look on things after the *
11: 8 wages of them to d' you service. *
12 But what I d', that I will d', that 4160
12:19 but we d' all things, dearly
13: 7 d' no evil; d' that which is honest, 4160
8 we can d' nothing against the truth,
Ga 1:10 d' I now persuade men, or God? *
10 or d' I seek to please men? *
2:10 which I also was forward to d'. 4160
14 and not as d' the Jews,
14 to live as d' the Jews? We who
21 d' not frustrate the grace of God:*
3:10 in the book of the law to d' them. 4160
4:21 d' ye not hear the law?
5: 3 he is a debtor to d' the whole law. 4160
11 why d' I yet suffer persecution? *
17 d' the things that ye would. 4160
21 that they which d' such things *4238
6:10 let us d' good unto all men, *2038
Eph 3:20 is able to d' exceeding abundantly 4160
6: 9 d' the same things unto them, "
21 know my affairs, and how I d', 4238
Ph'p 1:18 and I therefore d' rejoice,
2:13 and to d' of his good pleasure. *1754
14 D' all things without murmurings 4160
18 For the same cause also d' ye joy,
3: 8 loss of all things, and d' count them
13 but this one thing I d', forgetting
4: 9 heard, and seen in me, d': and *4238
13 can d' all things through Christ 2480
Col 1: 9 d' not cease to pray for you,
3:13 as Christ forgave you, so also d' ye.
17 ye d' in word or deed, d' all in 4160
23 And whatsoever ye d', "
23 d' it heartily, as to the Lord, *2038
1Th 3:12 even as we d' toward you:
4:10 And indeed ye d' it toward all the 4160
11 be quiet, and to d' your business 4238
5: 6 let us not sleep, as d' others; but
11 one another, even as also ye d'. 4160
24 calleth you, who also will d' it. "
2Th 3: 4 that ye both d', and will d' the "
1Ti 1: 4 edifying which is in faith: so d'.
6: 2 rather d' them service, because *1398
18 That they d' good, that they be rich 14
2Ti 2:23 knowing that they d' gender strifes.
3: 8 so d' these also resist the truth: men
4: 5 d' the work of an evangelist, make 4160
9 D' thy diligence to come shortly 4704
21 D' thy diligence to come before "
Ph'm 14 thy mind would I d' nothing; 4160
21 thou wilt also d' more than I say. "
Heb 3:10 They d' always err in their heart;
4: 3 For we which have believed d' enter
13 him with whom we have to d'. 3588, 3056
6: 3 And this will we d' if God permit. 4160
10 have ministered to the saints and d'
11 every one of you d' shew the same*
10: 7 written of me,) to d' thy will, O God 4160
9 Lo, I come to d' thy will, O God. "
11: 3 not made of things which d' appear.
29 assaying to d' were drowned.
13: 6 not fear what man shall d' unto me.
16 to d' good and to communicate 2140
17 that they may d' it with joy, 4160
19 beseech you the rather to d' this, "
21 in every good work to d' his will, "
Jas 1:16 D' not err, my beloved brethren.
2: 6 D' not rich men oppress you,
7 D' they not blaspheme that worthy
8 neighbour as thyself, ye d' well: 4160
11 that said, D' not commit adultery,
11 said also, D' not kill.
12 So speak ye, and so d', as they 4160
4: 5 D' ye think that the scripture saith
15 we shall live, and d' this, or that. 4160
17 to him that knoweth to d' good, "
5:19 any of you d' err from the truth,
1Pe 1:21 Who by him d' believe in God, *
2:14 for the praise of them that d' well. 17
20 if, when ye d' well, and suffer for it, 15
3: 6 daughters ye are, as long as ye d' "
11 him eschew evil, and d' good; 4160
12 Lord is against them that d' evil. "
4:11 let him d' it as of the ability *
2Pe 1:10 for if ye d' these things, ye shall 4160
19 ye d' well that ye take heed, as

2Pe 3:16 they d' also the other Scriptures,
1Jo 1: 6 we lie, and d' not the truth: 4160
2: 3 hereby we d' know that we know*
3:22 d' those things that are pleasing 4160
4:14 and d' testify that the Father *
5:16 I d' not say that he shall pray for it.
3Jo 1: 6 a godly sort, thou shalt d' well: 4160
Re 2: 5 and repent, and d' the first works; "
3: 9 they are Jews, and are not, but d' lie; "
18 thy nakedness d' not appear; *
9:19 and with them they d' hurt.
13:14 which he had the power to d' in 4160
14:13 and their works d' follow them. *
19:10 See thou d' it not: I am thy fellow
21:24 the kings of the earth d' bring their
22: 9 saith he unto me, See thou d' it not;
14 they that d' his commandments, 4160

doctor See also DOCTORS.
Ac 5:34 named Gamaliel, a d' of the law, 3547

doctors
Lu 2:46 sitting in the midst of the d', 1320
5:17 and d' of the law sitting by, 3547

doctrine See also DOCTRINES.
De 32: 2 My d' shall drop as the rain, 3948
Job 11: 4 My d' is pure, and I am clean in "
Pr 4: 2 I give you good d', forsake ye not "
Isa 28: 9 shall he make to understand d'? *8052
29:24 that murmured shall learn d'. ‡3948
Jer 10: 8 the stock is a d' of vanities. *4148
M't 7:28 people were astonished at his d': *1322
16:12 of the d' of the Pharisees and of * "
22:33 they were astonished at his d'. * "
M'r 1:22 they were astonished at his d': * "
27 what new d' is this? for with * "
4: 2 and said unto them in his d', * "
11:18 people was astonished at his d'. * "
12:38 he said unto them in his d', * "
Lu 4:32 they were astonished at his d': * "
Joh 7:16 My d' is not mine, but his that * "
17 he shall know of the d', whether * "
18:19 of his disciples, and of his d'. * "
Ac 2:42 in the apostles' d' and fellowship,* "
5:28 filled Jerusalem with your d', * "
13:12 astonished at the d' of the Lord, * "
17:19 what this new d', whereof thou * "
Ro 6:17 form of d' which was delivered * "
16:17 offences contrary to the d' which * "
1Co 14: 6 or by prophesying, or by d'? * "
26 of you hath a psalm, hath a d', * "
Eph 4:14 about with every wind of d', 1319
1Ti 1: 3 some that they teach no other d', "
10 that is contrary to sound d'; 1319
4: 6 up in words of faith and of good d', "
13 to reading, to exhortation, to d'. * "
16 unto thyself, and unto the d'; * "
5:17 who labour in the word and d'. * "
6: 1 God and his d' be not blasphemed. "
3 to the d' which is according to "
2Ti 3:10 thou hast fully known my d', * "
16 is profitable for d', for reproof, * "
4: 2 with all longsuffering and d'. *1322
3 they will not endure sound d'; 1319
Tit 1: 9 able by sound d' both to exhort "
2: 1 things which become sound d': "
7 in d' shewing uncorruptness, "
10 adorn the d' of God our Saviour "
Heb 6: 1 leaving the principles of the d' ‡3056
2 Of the d' of baptisms, and of *1322
2Jo 9 abideth not in the d' of Christ, * "
9 that abideth in the d' of Christ, * "
10 bring not this d', receive him not * "
Re 2:14 that hold the d' of Balaam, who * "
15 hold the d' of the Nicolaitanes, * "
24 as many as have not this d', * "

doctrines
M't 15: 9 for d' the commandments of men. 1319
M'r 7: 7 for d' the commandments of men. "
Col 2:22 the commandments and d' of men? "
1Ti 4: 1 seducing spirits, and d' of devils; "
Heb 13: 9 about with divers and strange d'. *1322

Dodai (*do'-dahee*) See also DODO.
1Ch 27: 4 second month was D' an Ahohite, 1739

Dodanim (*do'-da-nim*) See also RODANIM.
Ge 10: 4 and Tarshish, Kittim, and D'. 1721
1Ch 1: 7 and Tarshish, Kittim, and D'.

Dodavah (*do'da-vah*)
2Ch 20:37 Then Eliezer the son of D' of *1735

Dodo (*do'-do*) See also DODAI.
J'g 10: 1 the son of D', a man of Issachar; 1734
2Sa 23: 9 Eleazar the son of D' the Ahohite, "
24 Elhanan the son of D' of Beth-lehem. "
1Ch 11:12 him was Eleazar the son of D', "
26 Elhanan the son of D' of Beth-lehem, "

Doeg (*do'-eg*)
1Sa 21: 7 his name was D', an Edomite, 1673
22: 9 Then answered D' the Edomite, "
18 the king said to D', Turn thou, "
18 D' the Edomite turned, and he fell "
22 when D' the Edomite was there, "
Ps 52 *title* when D' the Edomite came and "

doer See also DOERS.
Ge 39:22 did there, he was the d' of it. 6213
2Sa 3:39 Lord shall reward the d' of evil "
Ps 31:23 plentifully rewardeth the proud d'. "
Pr 17: 4 wicked d' giveth heed to false lips;*
2Ti 2: 9 as an evil d', even unto bonds; *2557
Jas 1:23 hearer of the word, and not a d', 4163
25 hearer, but a d' of the work, "
4:11 not a d' of the law, but a judge. "

doers
2Ki 22: 5 the hand of the d' of the work, *6213
5 them give it to the d' of the work, * "

Job 8:20 neither will he help the evil d·:*
Ps 26: 5 hated the congregation of evil d·;*
101: 8 that I may cut off all wicked d· *6466
Ro 2:13 d· of the law shall be justified. 4163
Jas 1:22 be ye d· of the word, and not "

doest See also DOST.
Ge 4: 7 If thou d· well, shalt thou not be
7 and if thou d· not well, sin lieth at
31:22 is with thee in all that thou d·: 6213
Ex 18:14 What is this thing that thou d· to "
17 unto him, The thing that thou d· is "
De 12:28 when thou d· that which is good "
14:29 work of thine hand which thou d·. "
15:18 shall bless thee in all that thou d·. "
J'g 11:27 thou d· me wrong to war against "
1Ki 2: 3 mayest prosper in all that thou d·, "
19: 9 he said unto him, What d· thou here, "
13 and said, What d· thou here, Elijah? "
20:22 mark, and see what thou d·: for 6213
Job 9:12 will say unto him, What d· thou? "
35: 6 what d· thou against him? or if *6466
6 be multiplied, what d· thou unto 6213
Ps 49:18 men will praise thee, when thou d· well "
77:14 Thou art the God that d· wonders: 6213
86:10 thou art great, and d· wondrous "
119:68 Thou art good, and d· good; teach me "
Ec 8: 4 may say unto him, What d· thou? 6213
Jer 11:15 when thou d· evil, then thou rejoicest. "
15: 5 go aside to ask how thou d·? *7965
Eze 12: 9 said unto thee, What d· thou? 6213
16:30 seeing thou d· all these things, the "
24:19 these things are to us, that thou d· "
Da 4:35 or say unto him, What d· thou? 5648
Jon 4: 4 the Lord, D· thou well to be angry? "
9 D· thou well to be angry for the gourd? "
M't 6: 2 when thou d· thine alms, do not 4160
3 But when thou d· alms, let not "
21:23 By what authority d· thou these "
M'r 11:28 By what authority d· thou these "
Lu 20: 2 by what authority d· thou these "
Joh 2:18 seeing that thou d· these things? "
3: 2 that thou d·, except God be with "
7: 3 may see the works that thou d·. "
13:27 That thou d·, do quickly. "
Ac 22:26 Take heed what thou d·: for this * "
Ro 2: 1 thou that judgest d· the same *4238
3 and d· the same, that thou shalt 4160
Jas 2:19 that there is one God; thou d· well: "
3Jo 5 d· faithfully whatsoever thou d· to "

doeth See also DOTH.
Ge 31:12 seen all that Laban d· unto thee. 6213
Ex 31:14 whosoever d· any work therein, "
15 whosoever d· any work in the "
35: 2 whosoever d· work therein shall be "
Le 4:27 while he d· somewhat against * "
6: 3 of all these that a man d·, sinning "
23:30 whatsoever soul it be that d· any "
Nu 15:30 soul that d· ought presumptuously, "
24:23 who shall live when God d· this! 7760
Job 5: 9 d· great things and unsearchable; 6213
9:10 Which d· great things past finding "
23:13 his soul desireth, even that he d·. "
24:21 and d· not good to the widow. "
37: 5 great things d· he, which we 6213
Ps 1: 3 and whatsoever he d· shall prosper. "
14: 1 works, there is none that d· good. "
3 there is none that d· good, no, not "
15: 3 nor d· evil to his neighbour, nor "
5 He that d· these things shall never "
53: 1 iniquity: there is none that d· good. "
3 there is none that d· good, no, not "
72:18 of Israel, who only d· wondrous "
106: 3 and he that d· righteousness at all "
118:15, 16 hand of the Lord d· valiantly. "
136: 4 him who alone d· great wonders: "
Pr 6:32 he that d· it destroyeth his own soul. "
11:17 The merciful man d· good to his 1580
15: 7 but the heart of the foolish d· not so.
17:21 He that begetteth a fool d· it to his
22 A merry heart d· good like a *
28:17 A man that d· violence to the *
Ec 2: 2 is mad: and of mirth, What d· it? 6213
3:14 I know that, whatsoever God d·, it "
14 and God d· it, that men should fear "
7:20 just man upon earth, that d· good, "
8: 3 for he d· whatsoever pleaseth him. "
Isa 49:18 bind them on thee, as a bride d·. *
56: 2 Blessed is the man that d· this, 6213
Jer 5:19 Wherefore d· the Lord our God all "
48:10 Cursed be he that d· the work of the "
Eze 17:15 shall he escape that d· such things? "
18:10 and that d· the like to any one of "
11 And that d· not any of those duties, "
14 and considereth, and d· not such "
24 iniquity, and d· according to all the "
24 that the wicked man d·, shall he "
27 and d· that which is lawful and "
Da 4:35 and he d· according to his will 5648
9:14 in all his work which he d·: 6213
Am 9:12 saith the Lord that d· this. "
Mal 2:12 the man that d· this, the master "
17 Every one that d· evil is good in "
M't 6: 3 what thy right hand d·: 4160
7:21 but he that d· the will of my Father "
24 and d· them, I will liken him unto "
26 and d· them not, shall be likened "
8: 9 my servant, Do this, and he d· it. "
Lu 6:47 my sayings, and d· them, I will "
49 heareth, and d· not, is like a man "
7: 8 my servant, Do this, and he d· it. 4238
Joh 3:20 For every one that d· evil hateth 4160
21 But he that d· truth cometh to the "
5:19 for what things soever he d·, "
19 these also d· the Son likewise. "
20 him all things that himself d·: and "
Joh 7: 4 there is no man that d· any thing 4160
51 hear him, and know what he d·? "
9:31 and d· his will, him he heareth. "
11:47 What do we? for this man d· many "
14:10 dwelleth in me, he d· the works. "
15:15 knoweth not what his lord d·: but "
16: 2 will think that he d· God service. *4374
Ac 15:17 the Lord who d· all these things. *4160
26:31 This man d· nothing worthy of 4238
Ro 2: 9 soul of man that d· evil, of the *
3:12 there is none that d· good, no, not 4160
10: 5 the man which d· those things "
13: 4 wrath upon him that d· evil. 4238
1Co 6:18 that a man d· is without the body; 4160
7:37 he will keep his virgin, d· well. * "
38 giveth her in marriage, d· well; "
38 her not in marriage d· better. * "
Ga 3: 5 d· he it by the works of the law, or "
12 The man that d· them shall live 4160
Eph 6: 8 whatsoever good thing any man d·, "
Col 3:25 But he that d· wrong shall receive 91
Ja 4:17 knoweth to do good, and d· it not, 4160
1Jo 2:17 but he that d· the will of God "
29 that d· righteousness is born of him. "
3: 7 that d· righteousness is righteous, "
10 Whosoever d· not righteousness is "
3Jo 10 remember his deeds which he d·, "
11 He that d· good is of God: but he 15
11 he that d· evil hath not seen God. 2554
Re 13:13 And he d· great wonders, so that 4160

dog See also DOG'S; DOGS.
Ex 11: 7 shall not a d· move his tongue, 3611
De 23:18 the price of a d·, into the house "
J'g 7: 5 with his tongue, as a d· lappeth, "
1Sa 17:43 Am I a d·, that thou comest to me "
24:14 after a dead d·, after a flea. "
2Sa 9: 8 look upon such a dead d· as I am? "
16: 9 Why should this dead d· curse my "
2Ki 8:13 is thy servant a d·, that he should "
Ps 22:20 darling from the power of the d·. "
59: 6 they make a noise like a d·, and go "
14 let them make a noise like a d·, "
Pr 26:11 As a d· returneth to his vomit, "
17 one that taketh a d· by the ears. "
Ec 9: 4 living d· is better than a dead lion. "
2Pe 2:22 The d· is turned to his own vomit 2965

dog's
2Sa 3: 8 Am I a d· head, which against 3611
Isa 66: 3 a lamb, as if he cut off a d· neck; "

dogs
Ex 22:31 the field; ye shall cast it to the d·. 3611
1Ki 14:11 in the city shall the d· eat; and him "
16: 4 Baasha in the city shall the d· eat; "
21:19 place where d· licked the blood of "
19 Naboth shall d· lick thy blood, "
23 The d· shall eat Jezebel by the wall "
24 Ahab in the city, the d· shall eat: "
22:38 and the d· licked up his blood; "
2Ki 9:10 the d· shall eat Jezebel in the "
36 shall d· eat the flesh of Jezebel: "
Job 30: 1 to have set with the d· of my flock. "
Ps 22:16 For d· have compassed me: the "
68:23 and the tongue of thy d· in the "
Isa 56:10 all ignorant, they are all dumb d·, "
11 Yea, they are greedy d· which can "
Jer 15: 3 and the d· to tear, and the fowls "
M't 7: 6 not that which is holy unto the d·, 2965
15:26 bread, and to cast it to d·. 2952
27 yet the d· eat of the crumbs which "
M'k 7:27 bread, and to cast it unto the d·. "
28 yet the d· under the table eat of the "
Lu 16:21 the d· came and licked his sores. 2965
Phil 3: 2 Beware of d·, beware of evil "
Re 22:15 For without are d·, and sorcerers, "

doing See also DOINGS.
Ge 31:28 hast now done foolishly in so d· *6213
44: 5 ye have done evil in so d·. "
Ex 15:11 fearful in praises, d· wonders? "
Nu 20:19 I will only, without d· any thing "
De 9:18 in d· wickedly in the sight of the 6213
1Ki 7:40 Hiram made an end of d· all the "
16:19 he sinned in d· evil in the sight of "
22:43 d· that which was right in the eyes "
2Ki 21:16 in d· that which was evil in the "
1Ch 22:16 Arise therefore and be d·, and the "
2Ch 20:32 and departed not from it, d· that "
Ez 9: 1 d· according to their abominations, "
Ne 6: 3 I am doing a great work, so that 6213
Job 32:22 in so d· my Maker would soon *
Ps 64: 9 shall wisely consider of his d·. 4640
66: 5 is terrible in his d· toward the 5949
118:23 This is the Lord's d·; it is 854
Isa 56: 2 keepeth his hand from d· any evil. 6213
58:13 d· thy pleasure on my holy day; "
13 honour him, not d· thine own ways, "
M't 21:42 this is the Lord's d·, and it is *1096
24:46 when he cometh shall find so d·. 4160
M'k 12:11 This was the Lord's d·, and it is *1096
Lu 12:43 when he cometh shall find so d·. 4160
Ac 10:38 who went about d· good, and 2109
24:20 found any evil d· in me, while I 92
Ro 2: 7 by patient continuance in well d· 2041
12:20 for in so d· thou shalt heap coals 4160
2Co 8:11 Now therefore perform the d· of it; "
Ga 6: 9 be weary in well d·: for in due "
Eph 6: 6 servants of Christ, d· the will of "
7 With good will d· service, as to 1398
2Th 3:13 brethren, be not weary in well d·. 2569
1Ti 4:16 for in d· this thou shalt both save 4160
5:21 one before another, d· nothing by "
1Pe 2:15 that with well d· ye may put to 15
3:17 be so, that ye suffer for well d· "
17 than for evil d·. 2554
4:19 of their souls to him in well d·, as 16

doings
Le 18: 3 after the d· of the land of Egypt 4640
3 and after the d· of the land of "
De 28:20 of the wickedness of thy d·, 4611
J'g 2:19 they ceased not from their own d. "
1Sa 25: 3 was churlish and evil in his d·: "
2Ch 17: 4 and not after the d· of Israel. 4640
Ps 9:11 declare among the people his d·. 5949
77:12 all thy work, and talk of thy d·. "
Pr 20:11 Even a child is known by his d·, 4611
Isa 1:16 put away the evil of your d· from "
3: 8 and their d· are against the Lord, "
10 they shall eat the fruit of their d·. "
12: 4 declare his d· among the people, 5949
Jer 4: 4 it, because of the evil of your d·. 4611
18 Thy way and thy d· have procured "
7: 3 Amend your ways and your d·, "
5 amend your ways and your d·; "
11:18 then thou shewedst me their d·. "
17:10 and according to the fruit of his d·. "
18:11 make your ways and your d· good. "
21:12 because of the evil of your d·. "
14 according to the fruit of your d·. "
23: 2 visit upon you the evil of your d·, "
22 way, and from the evil of their d·. "
25: 5 and from the evil of your d·, and "
26: 3 because of the evil of their d·. "
13 amend your ways and your d·, "
32:19 according to the fruit of his d·: "
35:15 his evil way, and amend your d·, "
44:22 because of the evil of your d·, and "
Eze 14:22 shall see their way and their d·: 5949
23 ye see their ways and their d·: "
20:44 nor according to your corrupt d·, "
21:24 in all your d·, your sins do appear; "
24:14 and according to thy d·, shall they "
36:17 by their own way and by their d·: "
19 according to their d· I judged them, "
31 own evil ways, and your d· that 4611
Hos 4: 9 ways, and reward them their d·. "
5: 4 They will not frame their d· to turn "
7: 2 now their own d· have beset them "
9:15 for the wickedness of their d· I "
12: 2 to his d· will he recompense him. "
Mic 2: 7 are these his d·? do not my words "
3: 4 behaved themselves ill in their d·. "
7:13 therein, for the fruit of their d·. "
Zep 3: 7 early, and corrupted all their d·. 5949
11 thou not be ashamed for all thy d·, "
Zec 1: 4 and from your evil d·: but they did 4611
6 according to our d·, so hath he "

doleful
Isa 13:21 houses shall be full of d· creatures; 255
Mic 2: 4 and lament with a d· lamentation, 5093

dominion See also DOMINIONS.
Ge 1:26 and let them have d· over the fish 7287
28 and have d· over the fish of the sea, "
27:40 pass when thou shalt have the d·, *7300
37: 8 shalt thou indeed have d· over us? 4910
Nu 24:19 shall come he that shall have d·, 7287
J'g 5:13 made him that remaineth have d·* "
13 made me have d· over the mighty.* "
14: 4 the Philistines had d· over Israel. *4910
1Ki 4:24 he had d· over all the region on 7287
9:19 and in all the land of his d·. 4475
2Ki 20:13 in his house, nor in all his d·, "
1Ch 4:22 Saraph, who had the d· in Moab, 1166
18: 3 his d· by the river Euphrates. 3027
2Ch 8: 6 throughout all the land of his d·. 4475
21: 8 from under the d· of Judah, and *3027
Ne 9:28 so that they had the d· over them: 7287
37 also they have d· over our bodies, *4910
Job 25: 2 D· and fear are with him, he
38:33 canst thou set the d· thereof in 4896
Ps 8: 6 Thou madest him to have d· over 4910
19:13 let them not have d· over me: "
49:14 and the upright shall have d· over 7287
72: 8 He shall have d· also from sea to "
103:22 his works in all places of his d·: 4475
114: 2 was his sanctuary, and Israel his d·. "
119:133 let not iniquity have d· over me. 7980
145:13 and thy d· endureth throughout 4475
Isa 26:13 beside thee have had d· over us: 1166
39: 2 nor in all his d·, that Hezekiah 4475
Jer 34: 1 the kingdoms of the earth of his d·. "
51:28 thereof, and all the land of his d·. "
Da 4: 3 and his d· is from generation to 7985
22 and thy d· to the end of the earth. "
34 whose d· is an everlasting d·, "
6:26 That in every d· of my kingdom "
26 his d· shall be even unto the end. "
7: 6 four heads; and d· was given to it. "
12 they had their d· taken away: "
14 there was given him d·, and glory, "
14 his d· is an everlasting d·, "
26 and they shall take away his d·, "
27 And the kingdom and d·, and the "
11: 3 up, that shall rule with great d·, 4474
4 according to his d· which he ruled: 4915
5 be strong above him, and have d·: 4910
5 his d· shall be a great 4474
5 shall be a great d·. 4475
Mic 4: 8 shall it come, even the first d·;
Zec 9:10 and his d· shall be from sea to 4915
M't 20:25 princes of the Gentiles exercise d· *2634
Ro 6: 9 death hath no more d· over him. 2961
14 sin shall not have d· over you: "
7: 1 the law hath d· over a man as long "
2Co 1:24 that we have d· over your faith, * "
Eph 1:21 might, and d·, and every name that 2963
1Pe 4:11 be praise and d· for ever and ever. 2904
5:11 To him be glory and d· for ever "
Jude 8 despise d·, and speak evil of 2963
25 d· and power, both now and ever. 2904
Re 1: 6 to him be glory and d· for ever "

dominions
Da 7:27 all d' shall serve and obey him. 7985
Col 1:16 or d', or principalities, or powers: 2963

done See also UNDONE.
Ge 3:13 What is this that thou hast d'? 6213
14 Because thou hast d' this, thou art "
4:10 What hast thou d'? the voice of "
8:21 every living thing, as I have d'. "
9:24 knew what his younger son had d' "
12:18 is this that thou hast d' unto me? "
18:21 whether they have d' altogether "
20: 5 of my hands have I d' this. "
9 What hast thou d' unto us? "
9 thou hast d' deeds unto me that "
9 unto me that ought not to be d'. "
10 thou, that thou hast d' this thing? "
21:23 kindness that I have d' unto thee, "
26 I wot not who hath d' this thing: "
22:16 because thou hast d' this thing, "
24:15 pass, before he had d' speaking, 3615
19 when she had d' giving him drink, "
19 also, until they have d' drinking. "
22 pass, as the camels had d' drinking, "
45 I had d' speaking in mine heart, "
66 Isaac all things that he had d'. 6213
26:10 What is this thou hast d' unto us? "
29 have d' unto thee nothing but good, "
27:19 d' according as thou badest me: "
45 that which thou hast d' to him: "
28:15 I have d' that which I have spoken "
29:25 What is this thou hast d' unto me? "
26 It must not be so d' in our country, "
30:26 my service which I have d' thee. *5647
31:26 What hast thou d', that thou hast 6213
28 hast now d' foolishly in so doing. "
34: 7 which thing ought not to be d'. 6213
40:15 and here also have I d' nothing "
42:28 is this that God hath d' unto us? "
44: 5 divineth? ye have d' evil in so doing. "
15 What deed is this that ye have d'? 6213
Ex 1:18 Why have ye d' this thing, and "
2: 4 to wit what would be d' to him. "
3:16 that which is d' to you in Egypt: "
5:23 he hath d' evil to this people; †‡
10: 2 which I have d' among them; 7760
12:16 no manner of work shall be d' in 6213
16 eat, that only may be d' of you. "
13: 8 This is d' because of that which *
14: 5 Why have we d' this, that we have 6213
18: 1 of all that God had d' for Moses, "
8 that the Lord had d' unto Pharaoh "
9 which the Lord had d' to Israel, "
21:31 judgment shall it be d' unto him. "
31:15 Six days may work be d'; but in "
34:10 have not been d' in all the earth, *1254
33 Moses had d' speaking with them, 3615
35: 2 Six days shall work be d', but on 6213
39:43 d' it as the Lord had commanded, "
43 even so had they d' it: and Moses "
Le 4: 2 things which ought not to be d', "
13 and they have d' somewhat against "
13 should not be d', and are guilty; "
22 When a ruler hath sinned, and d' * "
22 things which should not be d', "
27 things which ought not to be d', "
5:16 for the harm that he hath d' in "
17 to be d' by the commandments 6213
6: 7 he hath d' in trespassing therein.* "
8: 5 the Lord commanded to be d'. "
34 As he hath d' this day, so the Lord "
11:32 vessel it be, wherein any work is d', "
18:27 have the men of the land d', which "
19:22 for his sin which he hath d': "
22 he hath d' shall be forgiven him.* "
23: 3 six days shall work be d': but 6213
24:19 he hath d', so shall it be d' to him; "
20 so shall it be d' to him again. *5414
Nu 5: 7 their sin which they have d': 6213
27 d' trespass against her husband,* "
12:11 wherein we have d' foolishly, and "
15:11 Thus shall it be d' for one bullock, 6213
34 declared what should be d' to him. "
16:28 have not d' them of mine own mind. "
22: 2 that Israel had d' to the Amorites. 6213
28 What have I d' unto thee, that "
23:11 What hast thou d' unto me? "
27: 4 name of our father be d' away *1639
32:13 d' evil in the sight of the Lord, 6213
De 3:21 God hath d' unto these two kings: "
10:21 d' for thee these great and terrible "
12:31 Lord, which he hateth, have they d' "
19:19 to have d' unto his brother: * "
25: 9 So shall it be d' unto that man "
26:14 d' according to all that thou hast "
29:24 Wherefore hath the Lord d' thus "
32:27 and the Lord hath not d' all this. 6466
Jos 5: 8 d' circumcising all the people, 8552
7:19 tell me now what thou hast d'; 6213
20 and thus and thus have I d': "
9: 3 what Joshua had d' unto Jericho "
24 of you, and have d' this thing. "
10: 1 d' to Jericho and her king, "
1 so he had d' to Ai and her "
32 to all that he had d' to Libnah. "
35 to all that he had d' to Lachish. "
37 to all that he had d' to Eglon; "
39 as he had d' to Hebron, so he did "
39 as he had d' also to Libnah, and to "
22:24 rather d' it for fear of this thing, "
23: 3 all that the Lord your God hath d' "
8 God, as ye have d' unto this day. * "
24: 7 seen what I have d' in Egypt: "
20 you, after that he hath d' you good. "
31 Lord, that he had d' for Israel. *6213
J'g 1: 7 have d', so God hath requited me. "
2: 2 my voice: why have ye d' this? "
J'g 2:10 yet the works which he had d' *6213
3:12 Israel, because they had d' evil "
6:29 another, Who hath d' this thing? "
29 the son of Joash hath d' this thing. "
8: 2 What have I d' now, in comparison "
9:16 Now therefore, if ye have d' truly* "
16 d' unto him according to the "
24 That the cruelty d' to the three "
48 do, make haste, and do as I have d'. "
11:37 Let this thing be d' for me: 6213
14: 6 or his mother what he had d'. "
15: 6 Philistines said, Who hath d' this? "
7 Though ye have d' this, yet will * "
10 up, to do to him as he hath d' to us. "
11 is this that thou hast d' unto us? "
11 unto me, so have I d' unto them. "
19:30 There was no such deed d' nor 1961
20:12 wickedness is this that is d' * "
Ru 2:11 hast d' unto thy mother in law 6213
3: 3 shall have d' eating and drinking. 3615
16 told her all that the man had d' 6213
1Sa 4:16 What is there d', my son? *1697
6: 9 to Beth-shemesh, then he hath d' 6213
8: 8 works which they have d' since the "
11: 7 Samuel, so shall it be d' unto his "
12:17 ye have d' in the sight of the Lord, "
20 not: ye have d' all this wickedness: "
24 consider how great things he hath d' "
13:11 Samuel said, What hast thou d'? 6213
13 said to Saul, Thou hast d' foolishly: "
14:43 Tell me what thou hast d'. 6213
17:26 shall be d' to the man that killeth "
27 it be d' to the man that killeth him. "
29 David said, What have I now d'? "
19:18 told him all that Saul had d' to him. "
20: 1 before Jonathan, What have I d'? "
32 shall he be slain? what hath he d'? "
34 because his father had d' him shame. "
24:19 that thou hast d' unto me this day. 6213
25:30 the Lord shall have d' to my lord "
26:16 thing is not good that thou hast d'. "
18 for what have I d'? or what evil is "
28: 9 thou knowest what Saul hath d', "
17 the Lord hath d' to him, as he * "
18 therefore hath the Lord d' this "
29: 8 unto Achish, But what have I d'? "
31:11 the Philistines had d' to Saul; "
2Sa 2: 6 because ye have d' this thing. "
3:24 and said, What hast thou d'? "
7:21 thou d' all these great things, * "
11:27 But the thing that David had d' "
12: 5 the man that hath d' this thing "
21 thing is this that thou hast d'? "
13:12 such thing ought to be d' in Israel: "
14:20 hath thy servant Joab d' this thing: "
21 Behold now, I have d' this thing: "
15:24 all the people had d' passing out 8552
16:10 Wherefore hast thou d' so? 6213
21:11 Aiah, the concubine of Saul, had d'. "
23:20 who had d' many acts, he slew "
24:10 sinned greatly in that I have d': "
10 for I have d' very foolishly. For "
17 sinned, and I have d' wickedly: "
17 but these sheep what have they d'? 6213
1Ki 1: 6 Why hast thou d' so? "
27 thing d' by my lord the king, "
3:12 Behold, I have d' according to thy 6213
8:47 have sinned, and have d' perversely, "
66 that the Lord had d' for David *6213
9: 8 Why hath the Lord d' thus unto "
11:11 Forasmuch as this is d' of thee, "
13:11 the man of God had d' that day 6213
14: 9 But hast d' evil above all that were "
22 above all that their fathers had d'. "
15: 3 which he had d' before him: and "
18:36 d' all these things at thy word. "
19: 1 all that Elijah had d', and withal "
20 for what have I d' to thee? "
22:53 to all that his father had d'. "
2Ki 4:13 what is to be d' for thee? wouldest "
14 what is then to be d' for her? "
5:13 wouldest thou not have d' it? "
7:12 what the Syrians have d' to us. "
8: 4 great things that Elisha hath d'. "
10:10 Lord hath d' that which he spake "
30 thou hast d' well in executing that "
30 hast d' unto the house of Ahab 6213
15: 3 all that his father Amaziah had d'; "
9 as his fathers had d': he departed "
34 to all that his father Uzziah had d'. "
17: 4 he had d' year by year: therefore "
19:11 what the kings of Assyria have d' 6213
25 long ago how I have d' it, and of "
20: 3 have d' that which is good in thy "
21:11 Judah hath d' these abominations, "
11 and hath d' wickedly above all "
15 they have d' that which was evil "
23:17 that thou hast d' against the altar "
19 the acts that he hath d' in Beth-el. "
32, 37 to all that his fathers had d'. "
24: 9 to all that his father had d'. "
19 to all that Jehoiakim had d'. "
1Ch 10:11 that the Philistines had d' to Saul, "
11:22 who had d' many acts; he slew two "
16:12 marvellous works that he hath d', 6213
17:19 hast thou d' all this greatness, * "
21: 8 because I have d' this thing; "
8 for I have d' very foolishly. "
17 have sinned and d' evil indeed; "
17 for these sheep, what have they d'? 6213
2Ch 6:37 We have sinned, we have d' amiss, "
7:21 Why hath the Lord d' thus unto 6213
11: 4 for this thing is d' of me. * "
16: 9 Herein thou hast d' foolishly: "
24:16 because he had d' good in Israel, 6213
22 Jehoiada his father had d' to "
2Ch 25:16 because thou hast d' this, and hast 6213
29: 2 to all that David his father had d'. "
6 d' that which was evil in the sight "
36 for the thing was d' suddenly. "
30: 5 they had not d' it of a long time *6213
32:13 what I and my fathers have d' "
25 according to the benefit d' unto him; "
31 wonder that was d' in the land, "
Ezr 6:12 made a decree; let it be d' with 5648
7:21 require of you, it be d' speedily, "
23 let it be diligently d' for the house "
9: 1 Now when these things were d', 3615
10: 3 let it be d' according to the law. 6213
Ne 5:19 all that I have d' for this people. "
6: 8 There are no such things d' as "
9 from the work, that it be not d'. 6213
8:17 not the children of Israel d' so. "
9:33 for thou hast d' right, * "
33 but we have d' wickedly: "
13:14 deeds that I have d' for the house 6213
Es 1:16 hath not d' wrong unto the king "
2: 1 and what she had d', and what 6213
4: 1 Mordecai perceived all that was d', "
6: 3 hath been d' to Mordecai for this? "
3 him, There is nothing d' for him. "
6 What shall be d' unto the man 6213
9 Thus shall it be d' to the man "
11 Thus shall it be d' unto the man "
9:12 they d' in the rest of the king's "
12 request further? and it shall be d'. "
14 the king commanded it so to be d': "
Job 21:31 shall repay him what he hath d'? "
34:29 whether it be d' against a nation, "
32 if I have d' iniquity, I will do no 6466
Ps 7: 3 O Lord my God, if I have d' this; 6213
14: 1 they have d' abominable works, "
22:31 be born, that he hath d' this. 6213
33: 4 and all his works are d' in truth. "
9 For he spake, and it was d'; he "
40: 5 works which thou hast d', and thy 6213
50:21 These things hast thou d', and I "
51: 4 sinned, and d' this evil in thy sight: "
52: 9 because thou hast d' it: and I will "
53: 1 and have d' abominable iniquity: "
66:16 what he hath d' for my soul. 6213
71:19 who hast d' great things: O God, "
74: 3 hath d' wickedly in the sanctuary. "
78: 4 wonderful works that he hath d'. 6213
98: 1 for he hath d' marvellous things: "
105: 5 marvellous works that he hath d'; "
106: 6 iniquity, we have d' wickedly. "
21 saviour, which had d' great things "
109:27 hand; that thou, Lord, hast d' it. 6213
111: 8 are d' in truth and uprightness. "
115: 3 d' whatsoever he hath pleased. "
119:121 I have d' judgment and justice: "
166 and d' thy commandments. "
120: 3 what shall be d' unto thee, thou 3254
126: 2 hath d' great things for them. 6213
3 Lord hath d' great things for us; "
Pr 3:30 if he have d' thee no harm. 1580
4:16 sleep not, except they have d' mischief; "
24:29 do so to him as he hath d' to me: 6213
30:20 saith, I have d' no wickedness. 466
32 hast d' foolishly in lifting up thyself, "
31:29 daughters have d' virtuously, 6466
Ec 1: 9 which is d' is that which shall be d': "
13 things that are d' under heaven: "
14 works that are d' under the sun; "
2:12 that which hath been already d'. "
4: 1 that are d' under the sun: "
3 the evil work that is d' under the "
8: 9 my heart unto every work that is d' "
10 in the city where they had so d': "
14 a vanity which is d' upon the earth; "
16 business that is d' upon the earth: "
17 cannot find out the work that is d' "
9: 3 things that are d' under the sun, "
6 any thing that is d' under the sun. "
Isa 5: 4 have been d' more to my vineyard, "
4 that I have not d' in it? "
10:11 d' unto Samaria and her idols, so "
13 strength of my hand I have d' it, "
12: 5 for he hath d' excellent things: "
24:13 grapes when the vintage is d'. 3615
25: 1 thou hast d' wonderful things; 6213
33:13 that are far off, what I have d'; "
37:11 the kings of Assyria have d' to all "
26 heard long ago, how I have d' it: "
38: 3 and have d' that which is good in "
15 unto me, and himself hath d' it: "
41: 4 Who hath wrought and d' it, "
20 the hand of the Lord hath d' this, "
44:23 ye heavens; for the Lord hath d' it: "
46:10 the things that are not yet d', "
48: 5 say, Mine idol hath d' them, "
53: 9 because he had d' no violence, "
Jer 2:23 the valley, know what thou hast d': "
3: 5 thou hast spoken and d' evil things "
6 which backsliding Israel hath d'? "
7 after she had d' all these things, "
16 neither shall that be d' any more. "
5:13 thus shall it be d' unto them. "
7:13 because ye have d' all these works, "
14 your fathers, as I have d' to Shiloh. "
30 children of Judah have d' evil in "
8: 6 saying, What have I d'? "
11:17 d' against themselves to provoke * "
16:12 have d' worse than your fathers; "
18:13 the virgin of Israel hath d' a very "
22: 8 hath the Lord d' thus unto this "
30:15 I have d' these things unto thee. "
24 until he have d' it, and until he * "
31:37 that they have d', saith the Lord. "
32:23 they have d' nothing of all that "
30 children of Judah have only d' evil "

Jer 32:32 have d' to provoke me to anger, 6213
34:15 d' right in my sight, in proclaiming "
35:10 obeyed, and d' according to all "
18 d' according unto all that he hath "
38: 9 these men have d' evil in all that "
9 have d' to Jeremiah the prophet, 6213
40: 3 brought it, and d' according as he "
41:11 the son of Nethaniah had d', "
42:10 the evil that I have d' unto you. "
44:17 as we have d', we, and our fathers, "
48:19 that escapeth, and say, What is d'? "
50:15 as she hath d', do unto her. 6213
29 according to all that she hath d', "
51:12 both devised and d' that which "
24 they have d' in Zion in your sight "
35 The violence d' to me and to my flesh
52: 2 all that Jehoiakim had d'. 6213
La 1:12 which is d' unto me, wherewith ‡5953
21 they are glad that thou hast d' it: 6213
22 unto them, as thou hast d' unto 5953
2:17 The Lord hath d' that which he 6213
20 to whom thou hast d' this. 5953
Eze 3:20 his righteousness which he hath d' 6213
5: 7 d' according to the judgments "
9 which I have not d', and whereunto "
9: 4 that be d' in the midst thereof. "
11 d' as thou hast commanded me. "
11:12 d' after the manners of the heathen "
12:11 have d', so shall it be d' unto them "
28 shall be d', saith the Lord God, * "
14:23 I have not d' without cause all that "
23 I have d' in it, saith the Lord God. "
16:47 nor d' after their abominations: "
48 hath not d', she nor her daughters, "
48 hast d', thou and thy daughters. "
51 abominations which thou hast d'. "
54 confounded in all that thou hast d', "
59 deal with thee as thou hast d', "
63 toward thee for all that thou hast d', "
17:18 and hath d' all these things, he "
24 Lord have spoken and have d' it. "
18:13 he hath d' all these abominations; "
14 his father's sins which he hath d', "
19 d' that which is lawful and right, "
19 hath d' them, he shall surely live. "
22 that he hath d' he shall live. "
24 he hath d' shall not be mentioned: "
26 that he hath d' shall he die. "
23:38 Moreover this they have d' unto me: "
39 they d' in the midst of mine house. "
24:22 And ye shall do as I have d': ye "
24 according to all that he hath d' "
33:16 d' that which is lawful and right; "
39: 8 Behold, it is come, and it is d', "
24 have I d' unto them, and hid my *6213
43:11 of all that they have d', shew them "
44:14 and for all that shall be d' therein. "
Da 6:22 thee, O King, have I d' no hurt. 5648
9: 5 have d' wickedly, and have rebelled, "
12 hath not been d' as hath been d' 6213
15 we have sinned, we have d' wickedly. "
11:24 which his fathers have not d', nor 6213
36 that that is determined shall be d'. "
Hos 2: 5 conceived them hath d' shamefully: "
Joel 2:20 because he hath d' great things. 6213
Am 3: 6 and the Lord hath not d' it? "
Ob 1:15 as thou hast d', it shall be d' unto "
Jo 1:10 Why hast thou d' this? For the "
14 O Lord, hast d' as it pleased thee. "
Mic 6: 3 what have I d' unto thee? and "
Zep 3: 4 they have d' violence to the law, "
Zec 7: 3 as I have d' these so many years? 6213
Mal 2:13 And this have ye d' again, "
M't 1:22 Now all this was d', that it might *1096
6:10 Thy will be d' in earth "
7:22 in thy name d' many wonderful *4160
8:13 so be it d' unto thee. 1096
11:20 most of his mighty works were d', "
21 which were d' in you, "
21 had been d' in Tyre and Sidon, "
23 which have been d' in thee, "
23 had been d' in Sodom, it would "
13:28 An enemy hath d' this. 4160
17:12 but have d' unto him whatsoever "
18:19 it shall be d' for them of my Father 1096
31 saw what was d', they were very "
31 told unto their lord all that was d'. "
21: 4 All this was d', that it might be * "
21 this which is d' to the fig tree, but "
21 cast into the sea; and it shall be d'. 1096
23:23 these ought ye to have d', and not 4160
25:21 Well d', thou good and faithful "
23 Well d', good and faithful servant; "
40 as ye have d' it unto one of the *4160
40 brethren, ye have d' it unto me. "
26:13 that this woman hath d', be told for "
42 except I drink it, thy will be d'. 1096
56 But all this was d' that the * "
27:23 Why, what evil hath he d'? But 4160
54 and those things that were d', 1096
28:11 priests all the things that were d'.* "
M'r 4:11 all these things are d' in parables: "
5:14 to see what it was that was d'. * "
19 the Lord hath d' for thee, and 4160
20 great things Jesus had d' for him: "
20 to see her that had d' this thing. "
33 knowing what was d' in her, came 1096
6:30 both what they had d', and what 4160
7:37 He hath d' all things well; "
9:13 they have d' unto him whatsoever "
13:30 pass, till all these things be d'. *1096
14: 8 She hath d' what she could: she 4160
9 this also that she hath d' shall be "
15: 8 do as he had ever d' unto them. * "
14 what evil hath he d'? And they "
Lu 1:49 he that is mighty hath d' to me "

Lu 3:19 all the evils which Herod had d'. 4160
4:23 whatsoever we have heard d' in 1096
5: 6 when they had this d', they inclosed 4160
8:34 that fed them saw what was d', *1096
35 they went out to see what was d'; * "
39 great things God hath d' unto 4160
39 how great things Jesus had d' unto "
56 should tell no man what was d'. 1096
9: 7 heard all that was d' by him: and "
10 told him all that they had d'. 4160
10:13 works had been d' in Tyre and 1096
13 which have been d' in you, they "
11: 2 Thy will be d', as in heaven, so in * "
42 these ought ye to have d', and not 4160
13:17 glorious things that were d' by 1096
14:22 it is d' as thou hast commanded "
16: 8 because he had d' wisely; for the 4160
17:10 when ye shall have d' all those "
10 unprofitable servants: we have d' "
22:42 not my will, but thine, be d'. 1096
23: 8 have seen some miracle d' by him. "
15 worthy of death is d' unto him 4238
22 time, Why, what evil hath he d'? 4160
31 what shall be d' in the dry? 1096
41 this man hath d' nothing amiss. 4238
47 saw what was d', he glorified God, 1096
48 the things which were d', smote "
24:21 day since these things were d'. * "
35 what things were d' in the way, * "
Joh 1:28 These things were d' in Bethabara 1096
5:16 because he had d' these things on *4160
29 they that have d' good, unto the "
29 of life; and they that have d' evil 4238
7:21 I have d' one work, and ye all 4160
31 than these which this man hath d'? "
11:46 them what things Jesus had d'. "
12:16 and that they had d' these things "
18 they heard that he had d' this "
37 But though he had d' so many "
13:12 Know ye what I have d' to you? "
15 ye should do as I have d' to you. "
15: 7 what ye will, and it shall be d' 1096
24 If I had not d' among them the 4160
18:35 thee unto me: what hast thou d'? "
19:36 For these things were d', that the *1096
Ac 2:43 wonders and were d' by the "
4: 7 by what name, have ye d' this? 4160
9 the good deed d' to the impotent
16 notable miracle hath been d' by *1096
21 glorified God for that which was d'. "
28 determined before to be d'. * "
30 may be d' by the name of thy holy "
5: 7 not knowing what was d', came in, "
8:13 miracles and signs which were d', * "
9:13 much evil he hath d' to thy saints *4160
10:16 This was d' thrice: and the vessel 1096
33 and thou hast d' well that thou 4160
11:10 And this was d' three times: and 1096
12: 9 true which was d' by the angel; "
13:12 when he saw what was d', "
14: 3 signs and wonders to be d' by their "
11 saw what Paul had d', they lifted 4160
13 and would have d' sacrifice with the
18 that they had not d' sacrifice unto *
27 all that God had d' with them, and 4160
15: 4 all things that God had d' with "
21:14 The will of the Lord be d'. 1096
33 who he was, and what he had d'. 4160
24: 2 worthy deeds are d' unto this *1096
25:10 have I d' no wrong, as thou very 91
26:26 this thing was not d' in a corner. 4238
28: 9 So when this was d', others also, 1096
Ro 9:11 neither having d' any good or evil, 4238
1Co 5: 2 that he that hath d' this deed 4160
3 him that hath so d' this deed, *2716
9:15 that it should be so d' unto me: 1096
13:10 which is in part shall be d' away. 2673
14:26 Let all things be d' unto edifying. 1096
40 Let all things be d' decently and in "
16:14 all your things be d' with charity. "
2Co 3: 7 which glory was to be d' away: *2673
11 For if that which is d' away was * "
14 which vail is d' away in Christ. "
5:10 may receive the things d' in his body,
10 according to that he hath d', 4238
7:12 that had d' the wrong, nor for his * 91
Eph 5:12 those things which are d' of them 1096
6:13 in the evil day, and having d' all, 2716
Ph'p 2: 3 Let nothing be d' through strife or
4:14 Notwithstanding ye have well d', *4160
Col 3:25 for the wrong which he hath d': 91
4: 9 unto you all things which are d' here.
Tit 3: 5 righteousness which we have d', *4160
Heb 10:29 hath d' despite unto the Spirit of 1796
36 after ye have d' the will of God, 4160
Re 16:17 from the throne, saying, It is d'. 1096
21: 6 And he said unto me, It is d'. * "
22: 6 things which must shortly be d'. * "
door See also DOORKEEPER; DOORS.
Ge 4: 7 doest not well, sin lieth at the d'. 6607
6:16 and the d' of the ark shalt thou set "
18: 1 he sat in the tent d' in the heat of "
2 ran to meet them from the tent d', "
10 Sarah heard it in the tent d', "
19: 6 Lot went out at the d' unto them, "
6 and shut the d' after him, 1817
9 and came near to break the d'. "
10 house to them, and shut to the d'. "
11 the men that were at the d' 6607
11 wearied themselves to find the d'. "
43:19 with him at the d' of the house, "
Ex 12: 7 on the d' post of the houses, *4947
22 go out at the d' of his house 6607
23 the Lord will pass over the d', "
21: 6 he shall also bring him to the d', 1817
6 unto the d' post; and his master 4201

Ex 26:36 shalt make an hanging for the d' 6607
29: 4 bring unto the d' of the tabernacle "
11 Lord, by the d' of the tabernacle "
32 in the basket, by the d' of the "
42 at the d' of the tabernacle of the "
33: 8 and stood every man at his tent d', "
9 stood at the d' of the tabernacle, "
10 pillar stand at the tabernacle d': "
10 worshipped, every man in his tent d'. "
35:15 and the hanging for the d' at the "
17 hanging for the d' of the court, *8179
36:37 for the tabernacle d' of blue, 6607
38: 8 which assembled at the d' of the "
30 the sockets to the d' of the "
39:38 the hanging for the tabernacle d', "
40: 5 and put the hanging of the d' to the "
6 before the d' of the tabernacle of "
12 and his sons unto the d' of the "
28 he set up the hanging at the d' "
29 by the d' of the tabernacle of the "
Le 1: 3 voluntary will at the d' of the "
5 the altar that is by the d' of the "
3: 2 kill it at the d' of the tabernacle "
4: 4 unto the d' of the tabernacle "
7 which is at the d' of the tabernacle "
18 burnt offering, which is at the d' of "
8: 3 congregation together unto the d' "
4 was gathered together unto the d' "
31 the flesh at the d' of the tabernacle "
33 And ye shall not go out of the d' "
35 Therefore shall ye abide at the d' "
10: 7 And ye shall not go out from the d' "
12: 6 sin offering, unto the d' of the "
14:11 Lord, at the d' of the tabernacle "
23 the priest, unto the d' of the "
38 the house to the d' of the house, "
15:14 Lord unto the d' of the tabernacle "
29 the priest, to the d' of the "
16: 7 at the d' of the tabernacle of the "
17: 4 And bringeth it not unto the d' of "
5 unto the Lord, unto the d' of the "
6 altar of the Lord at the d' of "
9 bringeth it not unto the d' of the "
19:21 offering unto the Lord, unto the d' "
Nu 3:25 for the d' of the tabernacle "
26 the curtain for the d' of the court, "
4:25 for the d' of the tabernacle "
26 the hanging for the d' of the gate "
6:10 priest, to the d' of the tabernacle "
13 unto the d' of the tabernacle "
18 his separation at the d' of the "
10: 3 at the d' of the tabernacle "
11:10 every man in the d' of his tent: "
12: 5 stood in the d' of the tabernacle, "
16:18 stood in the d' of the tabernacle "
19 them unto the d' of the tabernacle "
27 and stood in the d' of their tents, "
50 returned unto Moses unto the d' of "
20: 6 unto the d' of the tabernacle of the "
25: 6 before the d' of the tabernacle "
27: 2 the congregation, by the d' of the "
De 11:20 upon the d' posts of thine house, 4201
15:17 it through his ear unto the d', 1817
22:21 to the d' of her father's house, 6607
31:15 stood over the d' of the tabernacle. "
Jos 19:51 Lord, at the d' of the tabernacle "
J'g 4:20 Stand in the d' of the tent, and it "
9:52 went hard unto the d' of the tower "
19:22 beat at the d', and spake to the 1817
26 down at the d' of the man's house 6607
27 fallen down at the d' of the house, "
1Sa 2:22 that assembled at the d' of the "
2Sa 11: 9 Uriah slept at the d' of the king's "
13:17 from me, and bolt the d' after her. 1817
18 her out, and bolted the d' after her. "
1Ki 6: 8 The d' for the middle chamber 6907
33 made he for the d' of the temple "
34 leaves of the one d' were folding, 1817
34 and the two leaves of the other d' "
14: 6 her feet, as she came in at the d', 6607
17 threshold of the d', the child died; *1004
27 kept the d' of the king's house. 6607
2Ki 4: 4 thou shalt shut the d' upon thee 1817
5 shut the d' upon her and upon her "
15 had called her, she stood in the d'. 6607
21 shut the d' upon him, and went out.
33 and shut the d' upon them twain, 1817
5: 9 at the d' of the house of Elisha. 6607
6:32 the d', and hold him fast at the d': 1817
9: 3 Then open the d', and flee, and "
10 And he opened the d', and fled. "
12: 9 that kept the d' put therein ‡5592
22: 4 keepers of the d' have gathered ‡ "
23: 4 keepers of the d', to bring forth ‡ "
25:18 and the three keepers of the d': ‡ "
1Ch 9:21 porter of the d' of the tabernacle 6607
Ne 3:20 unto the d' of the house of Eliashib "
21 from the d' of the house of Eliashib "
Es 2:21 which kept the d', were wroth, ‡5592
6: 2 the keepers of the d', who sought ‡ "
Job 31: 9 laid wait at my neighbour's d'; 6607
34 silence, and went not out of the d'? "
Ps 141: 3 my mouth; keep the d' of my lips. 1817
Pr 5: 8 come not nigh the d' of her house: 6607
9:14 she sitteth at the d' of her house, "
26:14 As the d' turneth upon his hinges, 1817
Ca 5: 4 the hole of the d', and my bowels
8: 9 if she be a d', we will enclose 1817
Isa 6: 4 posts of the d' moved at the voice *5592
Jer 35: 4 of Shallum, the keeper of the d': ‡ "
52:24 and the three keepers of the d': ‡ "
Eze 8: 3 to the d' of the inner gate that 6607
7 brought me to the d' of the court; "
8 had digged in the wall, behold a d'. "
14 he brought me to the d' of the gate "
16 at the d' of the temple of the Lord, "

Eze 10:19 one stood at the d' of the east gate 6607
11: 1 and behold at the d' of the gate five "
40:13 and twenty cubits, d' against d'. "
41: 2 breadth of the d' was ten cubits; * "
2 the sides of the d' were five cubits * "
3 and measured the post of the d', * "
3 two cubits; and the d', six cubits. * "
3 the breadth of the d', seven cubits* "
11 one d' toward the north, and "
11 another d' toward the south: "
16 The d' posts, and the narrow *5592
16 against the d', cieled with wood * "
17 To that above the d', even unto 6607
20 From the ground unto above the d' "
24 leaves for the one d', and...other d'.1817
42: 2 hundred cubits was the north d', 6607
12 was a d' in the head of the way, "
46: 3 shall worship at the d' of this gate "
47: 1 me again unto the d' of the house; "
Hos 2:15 the valley of Achor for a d' of hope: "
Am 9: 1 he said, Smite the lintel of the d', "
M't 6: 6 when thou hast shut thy d', 2374
25:10 marriage: and the d' was shut. "
27:60 stone to the d' of the sepulchre, "
28: 2 rolled back the stone from the d',* "
M'r 1:33 was gathered together at the d'. "
2: 2 no, not so much as about the d': "
11: 4 colt tied by the d' without in a place "
15:46 stone unto the d' of the sepulchre. "
16: 3 stone from the d' of the sepulchre? "
Lu 11: 7 the d' is now shut, and my children "
13:25 is risen up, and hath shut to the d', "
25 to knock at the d', saying, Lord, "
Joh 10: 1 by the d' into the sheepfold, but "
2 the d' is the shepherd of the sheep. "
7 unto you, I am the d' of the sheep. "
9 I am the d': by me if any man "
18:16 Peter stood at the d' without. "
16 spake unto her that kept the d', 2377
17 the damsel that kept the d' "
Ac 5: 9 at the d', and shall carry thee out. 2374
12: 6 before the d' kept the prison. "
13 Peter knocked at the d' of the gate, "
16 and when they had opened the d',* "
14:27 opened the d' of faith unto the 2374
1Co 16: 9 a great d' and effectual is opened "
2Co 2:12 and a d' was opened unto me "
Col 4: 3 open unto us a d' of utterance, "
Jas 5: 9 the judge standeth before the d'. * "
Re 3: 8 set before thee an open d', "
20 I stand at the d', and knock: if any "
20 man hear my voice, and open the d', "
4: 1 a d' was opened in heaven: "

doorkeeper See also DOORKEEPERS.
Ps 84:10 I had rather be a d' in the house 5605

doorkeepers
1Ch 15:23 and Elkanah were d' for the ark. 7778
24 and Jehiah were d' for the ark. "

door-post See DOOR and POST.

doors
Jos 2:19 shall go out of the d' of thy house 1817
J'g 3:23 the d' of the parlour upon him, "
24 the d' of the parlour were locked, "
25 he opened not the d' of the parlour; "
11:31 cometh forth of the d' of my house "
16: 3 took the d' of the gate of the city, "
19:27 and opened the d' of the house, and "
1Sa 3:15 the d' of the house of the Lord. "
21:13 scrabbled on the d' of the gate, and "
1Ki 6:31 the oracle he made d' of olive tree: "
32 The two d' also were of olive tree; "
34 the two d' were of fir tree: the two "
7: 5 all the d' and posts were square, 6607
50 of the d' of the inner house, the 1817
50 place, and for the d' of the house, "
2Ki 18:16 the d' of the temple of the Lord, "
1Ch 22: 3 the nails of the d' of the gates, "
2Ch 3: 7 and the d' thereof, with gold; "
4: 9 great court and d' for the court, "
9 and overlaid the d' of them with "
22 the inner d' thereof for the most "
22 and the d' of the house of the "
23: 4 Levites, shall be porters of the d'; 5592
28:24 up the d' of the house of the Lord. 1817
29: 3 the d' of the house of the Lord, "
7 have shut up the d' of the porch, "
34: 9 the Levites that kept the d' had ††5592
Ne 3: 1 set up the d' of it; even unto the 1817
3,6,13,14,15 and set up the d' thereof, "
6: 1 that time I had not set up the d' "
10 let us shut the d' of the temple: "
7: 1 I had set up the d', and the porters, "
3 let them shut the d' and bar them: "
Job 3:10 up the d' of my mother's womb, "
31:32 but I opened my d' to the traveller. "
38: 8 Or who shut up the sea with d', "
10 decreed place, and set bars and d', "
17 thou seen the d' of the shadow *8179
41:14 Who can open the d' of his face? 1817
Ps 24: 7 be ye lift up, ye everlasting d'; 6607
9 lift them up, ye everlasting d'; "
78:23 and opened the d' of heaven, 1817
Pr 8: 3 city, at the coming in at the d'. 6607
34 waiting at the posts of my d'. "
Ec 12: 4 the d' shall be shut in the streets, 1817
Isa 26:20 shut thy d' about thee: hide "
57: 8 Behind the d' also and the posts "
Eze 33:30 and in the d' of the houses, 6607
41:11 And the d' of the side chambers "
23 and the sanctuary had two d'. 1817
24 the d' had two leaves apiece, "
25 on the d' of the temple, cherubims "
42: 4 and their d' toward the north. 6607
11 fashions, and according to their d'. "
Eze 42:12 according to the d' of the chambers 6607
Mic 7: 5 keep the d' of my mouth from her "
Zec 11: 1 Open thy d', O Lebanon, that the 1817
Mal 1:10 that would shut the d' for nought? "
M't 24:33 it is near, even at the d'. 2374
M'r 13:29 it is nigh, even at the d'. "
Joh 20:19 when the d' were shut where the "
26 the d' being shut, and stood in the "
Ac 5:19 opened the prison d', and brought "
23 standing without before the d': "
16:26 immediately all the d' were opened, "
27 seeing the prison d' open, he drew "
21:30 and forthwith the d' were shut. "

Dophkah (*dof'-kah*)
Nu 33:12 of Sin, and encamped in D'. 1850
13 And they departed from D', and "

Dor (*dor*) See also EN-DOR.
Jos 11: 2 the borders of D' on the west, 1756
12:23 The king of D' in the coast of D', "
17:11 the inhabitants of D' and her towns, "
J'g 1:27 the inhabitants of D' and her towns, "
1Ki 4:11 of Abinadab, in all the region of D'; "
1Ch 7:29 and her towns, D' and her towns. "

Dorcas (*dor'-cas*) See also TABITHA.
Ac 9:36 by interpretation is called D': 1393
39 D' made, while she was with them. "

dost See also LOEST.
Ge 32:29 is it that thou d' ask after my name?
44: 4 thou d' overtake them, say unto them,
De 9: 5 d' thou go to possess their land:
24:10 thou d' lend thy brother any thing,
11 the man to whom thou d' lend shall
J'g 14:16 Thou d' but hate me, and lovest me
1Sa 24:14 after whom d' thou pursue? after
28:16 Wherefore then d' thou ask of me,
1Ki 2:22 d thou ask Abishag the Shunammite
21: 7 D' thou now govern the kingdom of
2Ki 18:20 Now on whom d' thou trust, that
2Ch 6:26 their sin, when thou d' afflict them;
Ne 2: 4 For what d' thou make request?
Job 2: 9 D' thou still retain thine integrity?
7:21 d' thou not pardon my transgression
10: 8 round about; yet thou d' destroy
14: 3 And d' thou open thine eyes upon
16 d' thou not watch over my sin?
15: 8 d' thou not restrain wisdom for thyself?
30:20 unto thee, and thou d' not hear me:
33:13 Why d' thou strive against him?
37:15 D' thou know when God disposed
16 D' thou know the balancings of the
Ps 39:11 thou with rebukes d' correct man for
43: 2 why d' thou cast me off? why go *
44:12 and d' not increase thy wealth *
99: 4 thou d' establish equity, thou executest
Pr 4: 8 to honour, when thou d' embrace her.
Ec 7:10 d' not enquire wisely concerning this.
Ca 5: 9 that thou d' so charge us?
Isa 26: 7 most upright, d' weigh the path of the
36: 5 now on whom d' thou trust, that thou
Jer 32: 3 Wherefore d' thou prophesy, and say,
40:14 D' thou certainly know that Baalis
48:18 daughter that d' inhabit Dibon, *
La 5:20 Wherefore d' thou forget us for ever,
Eze 2: 6 and thou d' dwell among scorpions:
32:19 Whom d' thou pass in beauty?
33: 8 if thou d' not speak to warn the
Mic 4: 9 why d' thou cry out aloud? is there
Hab 1: 3 Why d' thou shew me iniquity, and
Lu 10:40 Lord, d' thou not care that my sister
23:40 D' not thou fear God, seeing thou art
Joh 6:30 believe thee? what d' thou work?
9:34 and d' thou teach us? And they cast
35 D' thou believe on the Son of God?
10:24 How long d' thou make us to doubt?
13: 6 Lord, d' thou wash my feet?
Ro 2:21 man should not steal, d' thou steal?
22 d' thou commit adultery? thou that
22 idols, d' thou commit sacrilege?
27 and circumcision d' transgress *
14:10 But why d' thou judge thy brother?
10 or why d' thou set at nought thy
1Co 4: 7 why d' thou glory, as if thou hadst
Re 6:10 Lord, holy and true, d' thou not judge

dote See also DOTED; DOTING.
Jer 50:36 and they shall d': a sword is upon 2973

doted
Eze 23: 5 and she d' on her lovers, on the 5689
7 with all on whom she d': with all "
9 of the Assyrians, upon whom she d'. "
12 She d' upon the Assyrians her "
16 she saw them with her eyes, she d' "
20 For she d' upon their paramours, "

doth See also DOETH.
Ge 3: 5 God d' know that in the day ye eat
27:42 Esau, as touching thee, d' comfort
45: 3 d' my father yet live?
Ex 7:17 how that the Lord d' put a difference
31:13 am the Lord that d' sanctify you.*
32:11 why d' thy wrath wax hot against thy
31 when they are dead, d' fall, it shall be
Le 11:32 d' touch them, when they be dead,
25:16 years of the fruits d' he sell unto thee.
Nu 5:21 the Lord d' make thy thigh to rot,
16: 7 the man whom the Lord d' choose,
36: 6 thing which the Lord d' command
De 1:20 Lord our God d' give unto us. *
25 the Lord our God d' give us. *
31 God bare thee, as a man d' bear his
5:24 this day that God d' talk with man,
8: 3 that man d' not live by bread only,
3 of the mouth of the Lord d' man live.
9: 4 the Lord d' drive them out from before
5 thy God d' drive them out from before
De 11:10 d' the Lord thy God require of thee,
18 He d' execute the judgment of the
16:19 a gift d' blind the eyes of the wise,
18:12 the Lord thy God d' drive them out
20:16 the Lord thy God d' give thee for *
31: 6 thy God, he it is that d' go with thee;
8 Lord, he it is that d' go before thee;
Jos 1:18 Whosoever he be that d' rebel *
20: 4 when he that d' flee unto one of *
J'g 4:20 any man d' come and enquire of thee,
Ru 3:11 for all the city of my people d' know
1Sa 9:13 because he d' bless the sacrifice; and
23:19 D' not David hide himself with us
26: 1 D' not David hide himself in the hill
18 Wherefore d' my lord thus pursue
20 flea, as when one d' hunt a partridge
2Sa 10: 3 Thinkest thou that David d' honour
14:13 for the king d' speak this thing *
13 in that the king d' not fetch home
14 d' God respect any person: yet d'
19: 8 Behold, the king d' sit in the gate.
20 servant d' know that I have sinned:
24: 3 but why d' my lord the king delight
24 that which d' cost me nothing. *
1Ki 1:11 Adonijah the son of Haggith d' reign,
13 throne? why then d' Adonijah reign?
22: 8 d' not prophesy good concerning me,
2Ki 2:15 The spirit of Elijah d' rest on Elisha.
5: 7 this man d' send unto me to recover
1Ch 19: 3 thou that David d' honour thy father,
21: 3 then d' my lord require this thing?
2Ch 6:33 and fear thee, as d' thy people Israel,
32:11 D' not Hezekiah persuade you to give
Job 1: 9 said, D' Job fear God for nought?
4:21 D' not their excellency which is *
5: 6 d' trouble spring out of the ground;
6: 5 D' the wild ass bray when he hath
25 but what d' your arguing reprove?
8: 3 D' God pervert judgment? or d' the
12:11 D' not the ear try words? and the
15:12 Why d' thine heart carry thee away?
16:13 my reins asunder, and d' not spare;
17: 2 d' not mine eye continue in their*
22:13 How d' God know? can he judge
23: 9 On the left hand, where he d' work,
24:19 d' the grave those which have sinned.
25: 3 upon whom d' not his light arise?
31: 4 D' not he see my ways, and count all
35:16 d' Job open his mouth in vain;
36: 7 he d' establish them for ever, and
39:26 D' the hawk fly by thy wisdom, and
27 D' the eagle mount up at thy
41:18 By his neesings a light d' shine, *
Ps 1: 2 and in his law d' he meditate day and
10: 2 his pride d' persecute the poor: *
8 in the secret places d' he murder the
9 d' catch the poor, when he draweth
13 Wherefore d' the wicked contemn
11: 7 his countenance d' behold the *
29: 9 in his temple d' every one speak *
41:11 because mine enemy d' not triumph
54:*title* D' not David hide himself with us?
59: 7 their lips: for who, say they, d' hear?
68:33 lo, he d' send out his voice, and *
73:11 How d' God know? and is there
74: 1 why d' thine anger smoke against
77: 8 d' his promise fail for evermore?
80:13 boar out of the wood d' waste it,
13 wild beast of the field d' devour it.*
92: 6 neither d' a fool understand this.
119:129 therefore d' my soul keep them.
130: 5 d' wait, and in his word do I hope.
147: 2 The Lord d' build up Jerusalem:
Pr 6:16 These six things d' the Lord hate:*
8: 1 D' not wisdom cry? and understanding
14:10 stranger d' not intermeddle with his
22: 5 d' keep his soul shall be far from *
24:12 d' not he that pondereth the heart
12 keepeth thy soul, d' not he know it?
25:23 so d' an angry countenance a
26:14 upon his hinges, so d' the slothful
27: 9 so d' the sweetness of a man's friend
24 and d' the crown endure to every
29: 6 but the righteous d' sing and rejoice.
30:11 and d' not bless their mother.
31:11 husband d' safely trust in her, *
Ec 10: 1 so d' a little folly him that is in
Ca 2: 6 and his right hand d' embrace me.
Isa 1: 3 but Israel d' not know,
3 my people d' not consider.
23 d' the cause of the widow come unto
3: 1 the Lord of hosts, d' take away from
9 shew of their countenance d' witness
10: 7 neither d' his heart think so;
28:24 D' the plowman plow all day to sow?
24 d' he open and break the clods of his
25 d' he not cast abroad the fitches,
26 d' instruct him to discretion, and d'
30:33 a stream of brimstone, d' kindle it.
42:11 the villages that Kedar d' inhabit:
44:14 an ash, and the rain d' nourish it.
52: 6 that day that I am he that d' speak:
59: 9 us, neither d' judgment overtake us:
Jer 2:11 glory for that which d' not profit.
10: 7 for to thee d' it appertain:
12: 1 d' the way of the wicked prosper?
14:10 therefore the Lord d' not accept them:
15:10 yet every one of them d' curse me.
23:14 none d' return from his wickedness:
30: 6 whether a man d' travail with child?
31:10 keep him, as a shepherd d' his flock.
49: 1 why then d' their king inherit Gad,
51:43 d' any son of man pass thereby.
La 1: 1 How d' the city sit solitary, that was
3:33 For he d' not afflict willingly nor
39 Wherefore d' a living man complain.

La 5: 8 *d'* deliver us out of their hand. *
Eze 3:20 When a righteous man *d'* turn from
21 and he *d'* not sin, he shall surely live
18:19 Why? *d'* not the son bear the iniquity
20:49 me, *D'* he not speak in parables? *
Ho 4:14 the people that *d'* not understand
5: 5 pride of Israel *d'* testify to his face:
Mic 6: 8 and what *d'* the Lord require of thee,
Hab 1: 4 and judgment *d'* never go forth: for
4 *d'* compass about the righteous;
Zep 3: 5 morning *d'* he bring his judgment
M't 6:19 where moth and rust *d'* corrupt,
20 neither moth nor rust *d'* corrupt,
12:24 This fellow *d'* not cast out devils,
17:24 *D'* not your master pay tribute?
18:12 *d'* he not leave the ninety and nine,
19: 9 is put away *d'* commit adultery.
22:43 then *d'* David in spirit call him Lord,
24:42 not what hour your Lord *d'* come.*
26:46 he is at hand that *d'* betray me.
M'r 2: 7 *d'* this man thus speak blasphemies?
22 new wine *d'* burst the bottles,
8:12 *d'* this generation seek after a sign?
Lu 1:46 My soul *d'* magnify the Lord,
6:43 neither *d'* a corrupt tree bring *
11:36 a candle *d'* give thee light.
13:15 Thou hypocrite, *d'* not each one of
34 a hen *d'* gather her brood under *
14:27 And whosoever *d'* not bear his cross,
15: 4 if he lose one of them, *d'* not leave the
8 lose one piece, *d'* not light a candle,
17: 9 *D'* he thank that servant because he
22:26 that is chief, as he that *d'* serve.
Joh 2:10 beginning *d'* set forth good wine; *
6:61 said unto them, *D'* this offend you?
7:51 *D'* our law judge any man, before
9:19 born blind? how then *d'* he now see?
10:17 Therefore *d'* my Father love me,
Ac 4:10 even by him *d'* this man stand here
8:36 what *d'* hinder me to be baptized?
22: 5 the high priest *d'* bear me witness,
26:24 much learning *d'* make thee mad.
Ro 8:24 seeth, why *d'* he yet hope for? *
9:19 Why *d'* he yet find fault? For who
14: 6 to the Lord he *d'* not regard it. *
1Co 9: 9 *D'* God take care for oxen? *
11:14 *D'* not even nature itself teach you,
13: 5 *D'* not behave itself unseemly,
15:50 *d'* corruption inherit incorruption.
2Co 1:10 so great a death, and *d'* deliver: *
3: 9 *d'* the ministration of righteousness
Eph 5:13 *d'* make manifest is light. *
Col 1: 6 *d'* also in you, since the day ye heard
1Th 2:11 you, as a father *d'* his children. *
2Th 2: 7 mystery of iniquity *d'* already work:
2Ti 2:17 their word will eat as *d'* a canker:
Heb 1:11 all shall wax old as *d'* a garment;
12: 1 the sin which *d'* so easily beset us,
Jas 2:14 What *d'* it profit, my brethren, though
16 to the body; what *d'* it profit?
3:11 *D'* a fountain send forth at the same
5: 6 killed the just; and he *d'* not resist
1Pe 3:21 even baptism *d'* also now save us,
5:13 you; and so *d'* Marcus my son.
1Jo 3: 2 and it *d'* not yet appear what we *
9 is born of God *d'* not commit sin;*
3Jo 1:10 *d'* he himself receive the brethren,
Re 19:11 righteousness he *d'* judge and make

Dothan (*do'-than*)
Ge 37:17 I heard them say, Let us go to *D'*. 1886
17 his brethren, and found them in *D'*. "
2Ki 6:13 him, saying, Behold, he is in *D'*. "

doting
1Ti 6: 4 but *d'* about questions and strifes *3552*

double See also DOUBLED; DOUBLETONGUED.
Ge 43:12 take *d'* money in your hand; 4932
15 they took *d'* money in their hand, "
Ex 22: 4 or sheep; and he shall restore *d'*. 8147
7 the thief be found, let him pay *d'*. "
9 shall pay *d'* unto his neighbour. "
26: 9 and shalt *d'* the sixth curtain in 3717
39: 9 they made the breastplate *d'*: a "
De 15:18 worth a *d'* hired servant to thee, 4932
21:17 by giving him a *d'* portion of all 8147
2Ki 2: 9 *d'* portion of thy spirit be upon me. "
1Ch 12:33 they were not of *d'* heart.
Job 11: 6 of wisdom, that they are *d'* *3718
41:13 who can come to him with his *d'* "
Ps 12: 2 and with a *d'* heart do they speak.
Isa 40: 2 received of the Lord's hand *d'* for 3718
61: 7 shall have *d'*; and for confusion 4932
7 they shall possess the *d'*: "
Jer 16:18 their iniquity and their sin *d'*; "
17:18 destroy them with *d'* destruction. "
Zec 9:12 that I will render *d'* unto thee; "
1Ti 5:17 be counted worthy of *d'* honour, *1362*
Jas 1: 8 A *d'* minded man is unstable in all *1374*
4: 8 purify your hearts, ye *d'* minded. "
Re 18: 6 rewarded you, and *d'* unto her *1363*
6 *d'* according to her works: *3588, 1362*
6 which she hath filled fill to her *d'*. "

doubled
Ge 41:32 for that the dream was *d'* unto 8138
Ex 28:16 Foursquare it shall be being *d'*: *3717
39: 9 the breadth thereof, being *d'*. "
Eze 21:14 and let the sword be *d'* the third "

double-minded See DOUBLE and MINDED.

doubletongued
1Ti 3: 8 not *d'*, not given to much wine, *1351*

doubt See also DOUBTED; DOUBTETH; DOUBTFUL; DOUBTING; DOUBTLESS; DOUBTS.
Ge 37:33 Joseph is without *d'* rent in pieces.
De 28:66 life shall hang in *d'* before thee:
Job 12: 2 No *d'* but ye are the people, 551
M't 14:31 faith, wherefore didst thou *d'*? *1365*
21:21 If ye have faith, and *d'* not, ye *1252*
M'r 11:23 shall not *d'* in his heart, but shall "
Lu 11:20 no *d'* the kingdom of God is come* *686*
Jo 10:24 dost thou make us to *d'*? **142, 5590*
Ac 2:12 were all amazed, and were in *d'*, **1280*
28: 4 No *d'* this man is a murderer, *3843*
1Co 9:10 our sakes, no *d'*, this is written: **1063*
Gal 4:20 voice; for I stand in *d'* of you. * *639*
1Jo 2:19 they would no *d'* have continued *

doubted
M't 28:17 worshipped him: but some *d'*. *1365*
Ac 5:24 they *d'* of them whereunto this **1280*
10:17 while Peter *d'* in himself what * "
25:20 *d'* of such manner of questions, * *639*

doubteth
Ro 14:23 he that *d'* is damned if he eat, *1252*

doubtful
Lu 12:29 drink, neither be ye of *d'* mind. *3349*
Ro 14: 1 ye, but not to *d'* disputations. *1261*

doubting
Joh 13:22 on another, *d'* of whom we spake. *639*
Ac 10:20 and go with them, *d'* nothing: *1252*
11:12 bade me go with them, nothing *d'*.* "
1Ti 2: 8 holy hands, without wrath and *d'*. **1261*

doubtless
Nu 14:30 *D'* ye shall not come into the * 518
2Sa 5:19 I will *d'* deliver the Philistines *
Ps 126: 6 *d'* come again with rejoicing, *
Isa 63:16 *D'* thou art our Father, though *3588
1Co 9: 2 unto others, yet *d'* I am to you: **1065*
2Co 12: 1 not expedient for me *d'* to glory. **1211*
Ph'p 3: 8 Yea *d'*, and I count all things **3304*

doubts
Da 5:12 and dissolving of *d'*, were found 7001
16 interpretations, and dissolve *d'*: "

dough
Ex 12:34 the people took their *d'* before it 1217
39 baked unleavened cakes of the *d'* "
Nu 15:20 a cake of the first of your *d'* for an 6182
21 the first of your *d'* ye shall give "
Ne 10:37 the firstfruits of your *d'*, and our "
Jer 7:18 the women knead their *d'*, to 1217
Eze 44:30 the first of your *d'*, that he may 6182
Ho 7: 4 after he hath kneaded the *d'*, 1217

dove See also DOVE'S; DOVES; TURTLEDOVE.
Ge 8: 8 he sent forth a *d'* from him, to 3123
9 the *d'* found no rest for the sole of "
10 again he sent forth the *d'* out of "
11 *d'* came in to him in the evening; "
12 seven days; and sent forth the *d'*; "
Ps 55: 6 O that I had wings like a *d'*! for "
68:13 ye be as the wings of a *d'* covered "
Ca 2:14 O my *d'*, that art in the clefts of "
5: 2 to me, my sister, my love, my *d'*, "
6: 9 My *d'*, my undefiled is but one; "
Isa 38:14 I did mourn as a *d'*: mine eyes fail "
Jer 48:28 be like the *d'* that maketh her nest "
Ho 7:11 Ephraim also is like a silly *d'* "
11:11 as a *d'* out of the land of Assyria: "
M't 3:16 Spirit of God descending like a *d'*, *4058*
M'r 1:10 and the Spirit like a *d'* descending "
Lu 3:22 in a bodily shape like a *d'* upon "
Joh 1:32 descending from heaven like a *d'*, "

dove's
2Ki 6:25 fourth part of a cab of *d'* dung 1686

doves See also DOVES'; TURTLEDOVES.
Ca 5:12 His eyes are as the eyes of *d'* 3123
Isa 59:11 like bears, and mourn sore like *d'*: "
60: 8 and as the *d'* to their windows? "
Eze 7:16 shall be on the mountains like *d'* "
Na 2: 7 lead her as with the voice of *d'*, "
M't 10:16 as serpents, and harmless as *d'*. *4058*
21:12 the seats of them that sold *d'*, "
M'r 11:15 the seats of them that sold *d'*; "
Jo 2:14 that sold oxen and sheep and *d'*, "
16 said unto them that sold *d'*, Take "

doves'
Ca 1:15 thou art fair; thou hast *d'* eyes. *3123
4: 1 thou hast *d'* eyes within thy locks:* "

down See also DOWNSITTING; DOWNWARD.
Ge 11: 5 the Lord came *d'* to see the city 3381
7 Go to, let us go *d'*, and there "
12:10 Abram went *d'* into Egypt to "
15:11 fowls came *d'* upon the carcasses, "
12 And when the sun was going *d'*, 935
17 to pass, that, when the sun went *d'*, "
18:21 I will go *d'* now, and see whether 3381
19: 4 But before they lay *d'*, the men
33, 35 perceived not when she lay *d'*.
21:16 and sat her *d'* over against him
23:12 And Abraham bowed *d'* himself 7812
24:11 he made his camels to kneel *d'* 1288
14 Let *d'* thy pitcher, I pray thee, 5186
16 and she went *d'* to the well, and 3381
18 let *d'* her pitcher upon her hand, "
26 And the man bowed *d'* his head, *6915
45 and she went *d'* unto the well, and 3381
46 she let *d'* her pitcher from her "
48 And I bowed *d'* my head, and *6915
26: 2 Go not *d'* into Egypt; dwell in 3381
27:29 thee, and nations bow *d'* to thee: 7812
29 thy mother's sons bow *d'* to thee: "
28:11 and lay *d'* in that place to sleep.
37:10 come to bow *d'* ourselves to thee 7812
25 And they sat *d'* to eat bread: and
25 going to carry it *d'* to Egypt. 3381
35 I will go *d'* into the grave unto my "
38: 1 Judah went *d'* from his brethren, "
39: 1 Joseph was brought *d'* to Egypt; "
1 which had brought him *d'* thither. "
Ge 42: 2 get you *d'* thither, and buy for us 3381
3 Joseph's ten brethren went *d'* to "
6 came, and bowed *d'* themselves 7812
38 shall ye bring *d'* my gray hairs 3381
43: 4 we will go *d'* and buy thee food: "
5 not send him, we will not go *d'*: "
7 would say, Bring your brother *d'*? "
11 and carry *d'* the man a present, "
15 and rose up, and went *d'* to Egypt, "
20 came indeed *d'* at the first time "
22 other money have we brought *d'* "
28 And they bowed *d'* their heads, *6915
44:11 they speedily took *d'* every man 3381
21 Bring him *d'* unto me, that I may "
23 your youngest brother come *d'* with "
26 And we said, We cannot go *d'*: if "
26 be with us, then will we go *d'*: "
29 ye shall bring *d'* my gray hairs "
31 shall bring *d'* the gray hairs of thy "
45: 9 come *d'* unto me, tarry not: "
13 and bring *d'* my father hither. "
46: 3 fear not to go *d'* into Egypt; for I "
4 I will go *d'* with thee into Egypt; "
49: 6 selfwill they digged *d'* a wall. *6131
8 children shall bow *d'* before thee. 7812
9 stooped *d'*, he couched as a lion,
14 a strong ass couching *d'* between
50:18 went and fell *d'* before his face;
Ex 2: 5 daughter of Pharaoh came *d'* to 3381
15 of Midian: and he sat *d'* by a well.
3: 8 I am come *d'* to deliver them out 3381
7:10 cast *d'* his rod before Pharaoh,
12 they cast *d'* every man his rod,
9:19 the hail shall come *d'* upon them, 3381
11: 8 servants shall come *d'* unto me, "
8 and bow *d'* themselves unto me, 7812
17:11 and when he let *d'* his hand, 5117
12 steady until the going *d'* of the sun. 935
19:11 third day the Lord will come *d'* in 3381
14 Moses went *d'* from the mount "
20 Lord came *d'* upon mount Sinai, "
21 Go *d'*, charge the people, lest they "
24 Away, get thee *d'*, and thou shalt "
25 So Moses went *d'* unto the people, "
20: 5 shalt not bow *d'* thyself to them, 7812
22:26 unto him by that the sun goeth *d'*: 935
23:24 shalt not bow *d'* to their gods, 7812
24 and quite break *d'* their images. *7665
32: 1 to come *d'* out of the mount, 3381
6 people sat *d'* to eat and to drink,
7 said unto Moses, Go, get thee *d'*; 3381
15 and went *d'* from the mount, "
34:13 images, and cut *d'* their groves:
29 Moses came *d'* from mount Sinai 3381
29 when he came *d'* from the mount, "
Le 9:22 came *d'* from offering of the sin "
11:35 for pots, they shall be broken *d'*: *5422
14:45 And he shall break *d'* the house, "
18:23 before a beast to lie *d'* thereto: 7250
19:16 Thou shalt not go up and *d'* as a
20:16 unto any beast, and lie *d'* thereto, 7250
22: 7 when the sun is *d'*, he shall be 935
26: 1 in your land, to bow *d'* unto it: 7812
6 in the land, and ye shall lie *d'*,
30 places, and cut *d'* your images,
Nu 1:51 the Levites shall take it *d'*: 3381
4: 5 shall take *d'* the covering vail, "
10:17 And the tabernacle was taken *d'*; "
11:17 I will come *d'* and talk with thee "
25 And the Lord came *d'* in a cloud, "
12: 5 came *d'* in the pillar of the cloud, "
13:23 and cut *d'* from thence a branch
24 which the children of Israel cut *d'*
14:45 Amalekites came *d'*, and the 3381
16:30 and they go *d'* quick into the pit; "
33 went *d'* alive into the pit, and the "
20:15 How our fathers went *d'* into Egypt, "
28 And Moses and Eleazar came *d'* "
21:15 brooks that goeth *d'* to the *5186
22:27 of the Lord, she fell *d'* under 7257
31 bowed *d'* his head, and fell flat *6915
23:24 he shall not lie *d'* until he eat of 7901
24: 9 He couched, he lay *d'* as a lion, and "
25: 2 people did eat, and bowed *d'* to 7812
33:52 and quite pluck *d'* all their high *8045
34:11 And the coast shall go *d'* from 3381
De 1:25 brought it *d'* unto us, and brought "
5: 9 Thou shalt not bow *d'* thyself unto 7812
6: 7 when thou liest *d'*, and when thou 7901
7: 5 and break *d'* their images and
5 cut *d'* their groves, and
9: 3 he shall bring them *d'* before thy 3665
12 Arise, get thee *d'* quickly from 3381
15 I turned and came *d'* from the "
18 I fell *d'* before the Lord, as at the
25 Thus I fell *d'* before the Lord forty
25 and forty nights, as I fell *d'* at the
10: 5 and came *d'* from the mount, and 3381
22 Thy fathers went *d'* into Egypt "
11:19 when thou liest *d'*, and when thou
30 way where the sun goeth *d'*, 3996
12: 3 and ye shall hew *d'* the graven 1438
16: 6 at the going *d'* of the sun, at the 935
19: 5 a stroke with the ax to cut *d'* the
20:19 and thou shalt not cut them *d'*
20 thou shalt destroy and cut them *d'*;
21: 4 elders of that city shall bring *d'* 3381
22: 4 brother's ass or his ox fall *d'* by
23:11 when the sun is *d'*, he shall come 935
24:13 pledge again when the sun goeth *d'*. "
15 neither shall the sun go *d'* upon it; "
19 thou cuttest *d'* thine harvest *
25: 2 shall cause him to lie *d'*, and to be
26: 4 and set it *d'* before the altar of the
5 and he went *d'* into Egypt, and 3381
15 Look *d'* from thy holy habitation.

De 28:24 from heaven shall it come d· upon 3381
43 and thou shalt come d· very low. "
52 thy high and fenced walls come d·. "
33: 3 and they sat d· at thy feet; 8497
28 his heavens shall drop d· dew. 6201
Jos 1: 4 great sea toward the going d· of 3996
2: 8 And before they were laid d·, 7901
15 Then she let them d· by a cord 3381
18 window which thou didst let us d· "
3:13 from the waters that come d· from "
16 the waters which came d· from "
16 and those that came d· toward the "
4: 8 they lodged, and laid them d·
6: 5 walls of the city shall fall d· flat,
20 shout, that the wall fell d· flat,
7: 5 and smote them in the going d·: 4174
8:29 and as soon as the sun was d·, 935
29 should take his carcase d· from 3381
10:11 in the going d· to Beth-horon, 4174
11 the Lord cast d· great stones from
13 hasted not to go d· about a whole day.
27 at the time of the going d· of the
27 and they took them d· off the trees,3381
15:10 and went d· to Beth-shemesh, and "
16: 3 goeth d· westward to the coast of "
7 And it went d· from Janohah to "
17:15 and cut d· for thyself there in the
18 is a wood, and thou shalt cut it d·:
18:16 border came d· to the end of the 3381
18 northward, and went d· unto "
24: 4 Jacob and his children went d· "
J'g 1: 9 Judah went d· to fight against the "
34 not suffer them to come d· to the "
2: 2 ye shall throw d· their altars: 5422
19 to serve them, and to bow d· unto 7812
3:25 their lord was fallen d· dead on the
27 the children of Israel went d· with 3381
28 And they went d· after him, and "
4:14 Barak went d· from mount Tabor, "
15 so that Sisera lighted d· off his "
5:11 people of the Lord go d· to the "
14 out of Machi came d· governors, "
21 thou hast trodden d· strength. *
27 feet he bowed, he fell, he lay d·: *7901
27 where he bowed, there he fell d·
6:25 and throw d· the altar of Baal that 2040
25 hath, and cut d· the grove that is
26 the grove which thou shalt cut d·.
28 the altar of Baal was cast d·, 5422
28 and the grove was cut d· that was
30 because he hath cast d· the altar
30 and because he hath cut d· the
31 because one hath cast d· his altar. 5422
32 because he hath thrown d· his altar. "
7: 4 bring them d· unto the water, and 3381
5 So he brought d· the people unto the "
5 that boweth d· upon his knees to
6 all the rest of the people bowed d·
9 Arise, get thee d· unto the host; 3381
10 But if thou fear to go d·, go thou "
10 with Phurah thy servant d· to the "
11 hands be strengthened to go d· "
11 Then went he d· with Phurah his "
24 Come d· against the Midianites, and "
8: 9 again in peace, I will break d· this 5242
17 And he beat d· the tower of Penuel, "
9:36 Behold, there come people d· from 3381
37 See there come people d· by the "
45 that was therein, and beat d· the 5422
48 and cut d· a bough from the trees,
49 all the people likewise cut d· every
11:37 go up and d· upon the mountains, 3381
14: 1 And Samson went d· to Timnath, "
5 Then went Samson d·, and his "
7 And he went d·, and talked with the "
10 So his father went d· unto the "
18 seventh day before the sun went d·,
19 and he went d· to Ashkelon, and 3381
15: 8 and he went d· and dwelt in the "
12 We are come d· to bind thee, that "
16:21 his eyes, and brought him d· to "
31 the house of his fathers came d·, "
19: 6 And they sat d·, and did eat and drink
14 and the sun went d· upon them when
15 he sat him d· in a street of the city:
26 and fell d· at the door of the man's
27 his concubine was fallen d· at the
20:21 of Gibeah, and destroyed d· to the
25 destroyed d· to the ground of the
32 They are smitten d· before us, as at
39 Surely they are smitten d· before us,
43 and trode them d· with ease over
Ru 3: 3 upon thee, and get thee d· to the 3381
4 And it shall be, when he lieth d·, 7901
4 uncover his feet, and lay thee d·; "
6 And she went d· unto the floor, 3381
7 he went to lie d· at the end of the 7901
7 uncovered his feet, and laid her d·. "
13 liveth: lie d· until the morning. "
4: 1 up to the gate, and sat him d· there:
1 such a one! turn aside, sit d· here.
1 And he turned aside, and sat d·.
2 said, Sit ye d· here. And they sat d·.
1Sa 2: 6 he bringeth d· to the grave, and 3381
3: 2 when Eli was laid d· in his place, 7901
3 and Samuel was laid d· to sleep; "
5 lie d· again. And he ... lay d·. "
6 I called not, my son; lie d· again. "
9 Eli said unto Samuel, Go, lie d·: "
9 went and lay d· in his place. "
6:15 And the Levites took d· the ark of 3381
18 Abel, whereon they set d· the ark
21 the ark of the Lord; come ye d·, 3381
9:25 come d· from the high place into "
27 were going d· to the end of the city, "
10: 5 coming d· from the high place "

1Sa 10: 8 shalt go d· before me to Gilgal; 3381
8 behold, I will come d· unto thee, "
13:12 The Philistines will come d· now "
20 Israelites went d· to the Philistines, "
14:16 went on beating d· one another. *
36 Let us go d· after the Philistines 3381
37 Shall I go d· after the Philistines? "
15: 6 get you d· from among the "
12 passed on, and gone d· to Gilgal. "
16:11 we will not sit d· till he come hither.
17: 8 you, and let him come d· to me. 3381
28 said, Why comest thou d· hither? "
28 thou art come d· that thou mightest "
52 Philistines fell d· by the way to
19:12 let David d· through a window: 3381
24 lay d· naked all that day and all
20:19 then thou shalt go d· quickly, 3381
24 the king sat him d· to eat meat.
21:13 his spittle fall d· upon his beard. 3381
22: 1 it, they went d· thither to him. "
23: 4 and said, Arise, go d· to Keilah; "
6 came d· with an ephod in his hand. "
8 to go d· to Keilah, to besiege David "
11 And the Lord said, He will come d· "
11 come d· as thy servant hath heard? "
20 O king, come d· according to all "
20 the desire of thy soul to come d·; "
25 wherefore he came d· into a rock, "
25: 1 went d· to the wilderness of Paran. "
20 that she came d· by the covert of "
20 and his men came d· against her; "
26: 2 Saul arose, and went d· to the "
6 Who will go d· with me to Saul to "
6 Abishai said, I will go d· with thee. "
29: 4 let him not go d· with us to battle, "
30:15 Canst thou bring me d· to this "
15 will bring thee d· to this company. "
16 And when he had brought him d·, "
24 part is that goeth d· to the battle, "
31: 1 and fell d· slain in mount Gilboa.
2Sa 2:16 so they fell d· together: wherefore
13 the pool of Gibeon: and they sat d·
23 and he fell d· there, and died in
23 where Asahel fell d· and died stood
24 and the sun went d· when they were
3:35 or ought else, till the sun be d·. 935
5:17 of it, and went d· to the hold. 3381
8: 2 with a line, casting them d· to the 7901
11: 8 Go d· to thy house, and wash thy 3381
9 lord, and went not d· to his house. "
10 Uriah went not d· unto his house, "
10 why then didst thou not go d· unto "
13 servants of his lord, but went not d· "
13: 5 Lay thee d· on thy bed, and make 7901
6 So Amnon lay d· and made himself "
8 Amnon's house; and he was laid d·. "
15:20 make thee go up and d· with us? 5128
24 and they set d· the ark of God; 3332
17:18 court; whither they went d·. 3381
18:28 he fell d· to the earth upon his *7812
19:16 hasted and came d· with the men 3381
18 Shimei the son of Gera fell d· before
20 of all the house of Joseph to go d· 3381
24 Mephibosheth the son of Saul came d· "
31 Gileadite came d· from Rogelim, "
20:15 battered the wall, to throw it d·. 5307
21:15 and David went d·, and his 3381
22:10 the heavens also, and came d·; "
28 that thou mayest bring them d·. "
48 and that bringeth d· the people 8213
23:13 of the thirty chief went d·, 3381
20 he went d· also and slew a lion in "
21 but he went d· to him with a staff "
1Ki 1:25 he is gone d· this day, and hath slain "
33 mule, and bring him d· to Gihon; "
38 and the Pelethites, went d·, and "
53 and they brought him d· from the "
2: 6 let not his hoar head go d· to the "
8 he came d· to meet me at Jordan, "
9 his hoar head bring thou d· to the "
19 and sat d· on his throne, and caused a
5: 9 shall bring them d· from Lebanon 3381
8:33 When thy people Israel be smitten d·
17:23 and brought him d· out of the 3381
18:30 altar of the lord that was broken d·.
40 Elijah brought them d· to the 3281
42 he cast himself d· upon the earth, 1457
44 and get thee d·, that the rain stop 3381
19: 4 and came and sat down under a
6 and drink, and laid him d· again 7901
10 covenant, thrown d· thine altars, 2040
14 thrown d· thine altars, and slain "
21: 4 And he laid him d· upon his bed, 7901
16 Ahab rose up to go d· to the 3381
18 Arise, go d· to meet Ahab king of "
18 whither he is gone d· to possess it. "
22: 2 the king of Judah came d· to the "
36 about the going d· of the sun,
2Ki 1: 2 And Ahaziah fell d· through a
4 Thou shalt not come d· from that 3381
6 therefore thou shalt not come d· "
9 God, the king hath said, Come d·. "
10 let fire come d· from heaven, and "
10 thy fifty. And there came d· fire "
11 the king said, Come d· quickly. "
12 let fire come d· from heaven, and "
12 fifty. And the fire of God came d· "
14 Behold, there came d· fire from "
15 Go d· with him: be not afraid of "
15 he arose, and went d· with him unto "
16 thou shalt not come d· off that bed "
2: 2 thee. So they went d· to Beth-el. "
3:12 the king of Edom went d· to him. "
25 And they beat d· the cities, and 2040
5:14 went he d·, and dipped himself 3381
18 I bow d· myself in the house of *7812

2Ki 5:21 he lighted d· from his chariot to
6: 4 to the Jordan they cut d· wood,
6 And he cut d· a stick, and cast it
9 thither the Syrians are come d·. 5181
18 And when they came d· to him, 3381
33 the messenger came d· unto him: "
7:17 when the king came d· to him. "
8:29 king of Judah went d· to see Joram "
9:16 Judah was come d· to see Joram. "
24 and he sunk d· in his chariot.
33 Throw her d·. So...threw her d·: 8058
10:13 we go d· to salute the children of 3381
27 they brake d· the image of Baal, 5422
27 and brake d· the house of Baal. "
11: 6 house, that it be not broken d·. *4535
18 the house of Baal, and break it d·; 5422
19 they brought d· the king from the 3381
12:20 of Millo, which goeth d· to Silla. "
13:14 king of Israel came d· unto him, "
21 and when the man was let d·, and *3212
14: 9 in Lebanon, and trode d· the thistle.
13 brake d· the wall of Jerusalem
16:17 and took d· the sea from off the 3381
18: 4 and cut d· the groves, and brake
19:16 Lord, bow d· thine ear, and hear: *5186
23 and will cut d· the tall cedars
20:10 the shadow to go d· ten degrees: *5186
11 by which it had gone d· in the 3381
21:13 wiping it, and turning it upside d·.
23: 5 he put d· the idolatrous priests, 7673
7 And he brake d· the houses of the 5422
8 and brake d· the high places of
12 did the king beat d·, and "
12 and brake them d· from thence, 7323
14 and cut d· the groves, and filled
15 and the high places he brake d·, 5422
25:10 brake d· the walls of Jerusalem
1Ch 5:22 For there fell d· many slain, *
7:21 because they came d· to take 3381
10: 1 and fell d· slain in mount Gilboa.
11:15 went d· to the rock to David, into 3381
22 he went d· and slew a lion in a pit "
23 and he went d· to him with a staff. "
29:20 and bowed d· their heads, and 6915
2Ch 6:13 kneeled d· upon his knees before
7: 1 the fire came d· from heaven, 3381
3 of Israel saw how the fire came d·, "
13:17 so there fell d· slain of Israel five
14: 3 and brake d· the images,
3 and cut d· the groves:
15:16 Asa cut d· her idol, and stamped
18: 2 certain years he went d· to Ahab 3381
34 time of the sun going d· he died.
20:16 To morrow go ye d· against them: 3381
22: 6 Jehoram king of Judah went d· to "
23:17 the house of Baal, and brake it d·, 5422
20 and brought d· the king from the 3381
25: 8 power to help, and to cast d·. 3782
12 cast them d· from the top of the rock,
14 and bowed d· himself before them, 7812
18 Lebanon, and trode d· the thistle.
23 brake d· the wall of Jerusalem
26: 6 and brake d· the wall of Gath, and
31: 1 in pieces, and cut d· the groves, and 1438
1 and threw d· the high places and 5422
32:30 brought it straight d· to the west 4295
33: 3 Hezekiah his father had broken d·, 5422
34: 4 brake d· the altars of Baalim in
4 on high above them, he cut d·; 1438
7 when he had broken d· the altars 5422
7 powder, and cut d· all the idols 1438
36: 3 the king of Egypt put him d· at *5493
19 brake d· the wall of Jerusalem, 5422
Ezr 6:11 be pulled d· from his house, *
9: 3 of my beard, and sat d· astonied.
10: 1 weeping and casting himself d· 5307
16 sat d· in the first day of the tenth
Ne 1: 3 of Jerusalem also is broken d·,
4 I sat d· and wept, and mourned
2:13 Jerusalem, which were broken d·,
3:15 the stairs that go d· from the city 3381
4: 3 even break d· their stone wall.
6: 3 I cannot come d·: why should the 3381
3 I leave it, and come d· to you? "
16 much cast d· in their own eyes: 5307
9:13 camest d· also upon mount Sinai, 3381
Es 3:15 the king and Haman sat d· to drink;
8: 3 fell d· at his feet, and besought
Job 1: 7 and from walking up and d· in it.
20 and fell d· upon the ground, and
2: 2 and from walking up and d· in it.
8 and he sat d· among the ashes. *
13 they sat d· with him upon the ground
6:21 see my casting d· and are afraid *
7: 4 When I lie d·, I say, When shall I 7901
9 so he that goeth d· to the grave 3381
19 me alone till I swallow d· my spittle?
8:12 and not cut d·, it withereth before
11:19 Also thou shalt lie d·, and none 7257
12:14 breaketh d·, and it cannot be built 2040
14: 2 forth as a flower, and is cut d·:
7 is hope of a tree, if it be cut d·,
12 So man lieth d·, and riseth not: 7901
17: 3 Lay d· now, put me in a surety *
16 shall go d· to the bars of the pit, 3381
18: 7 and his counsel shall cast him d·.
20:11 shall lie d· with him in the dust. 7901
15 He hath swallowed d· riches, and he
18 shall not swallow it d·: according
21:13 in a moment go d· to the grave. 5181
26 They shall lie d· alike in the dust, 7901
22:16 Which were cut d· out of time, *
20 our substance is not cut d·, but *
29 When men are cast d·, then thou 8213
27:19 The rich man shall lie d·, but he 7901
29:24 my countenance they cast not d·. 5307

Job 31:10 and let others bow *d*· upon her. 3766
32:13 God thrusteth him *d*·, not man. *
33:24 him from going *d*· to the pit: 3381
36:27 they pour *d*· rain according to the*
40:12 and tread *d*· the wicked in their place.
41: 1 with a cord which thou lettest *d*·?*8257
9 one be cast *d*· even at the sight 2904
Ps 3: 5 I laid me *d*· and slept; I awaked; 7901
4: 8 both lay me *d*· in peace, and sleep; "
7: 5 yea, let him tread *d*· my life upon the
16 dealing shall come *d*· upon his 3381
9:15 The heathen are sunk *d*· in the pit
14: 2 Lord looked *d*· from heaven upon
17:11 have set their eyes bowing *d*· to 5186
13 disappoint him, cast him *d*·: 3766
18: 9 the heavens also, and came *d*·: 3381
27 but wilt bring *d*· high looks. 8213
20: 8 They are brought *d*· and fallen: 3766
22:29 that go *d*· to the dust shall bow 3381
23: 2 me to lie *d*· in green pastures, 7257
28: 1 like them that go *d*· into the pit. 3381
30: 3 that I should not go *d*· to the pit.
9 in my blood, when I go *d*· to the pit?"
31: 2 Bow *d*· thine ear to me; deliver 5186
35:14 I bowed *d*· heavily, as one that 7817
36:12 they are cast *d*·, and shall not be 1760
37: 2 For they shall soon be cut *d*· like 5243
14 to cast *d*· the poor and needy, and 5307
24 he shall not be utterly cast *d*·: for 2904
38: 6 I am bowed *d*· greatly; I go 7817
42: 5 Why art thou cast *d*·, O my soul? "
6 God, my soul is cast *d*· within me: "
11 Why art thou cast *d*·, O my soul? "
43: 5 Why art thou cast *d*·, O my soul? "
44: 5 thee will we push *d*· our enemies:
25 our soul is bowed *d*· to the dust: 7743
50: 1 the sun unto the going *d*· thereof.
53: 2 God looked *d*· from heaven upon
55:15 let them go *d*· quick into hell: 3381
23 shalt bring them *d*· into the pit of "
56: 7 thine anger cast *d*· the people, O God.
57: 6 my soul is bowed *d*·: they have
59:11 bring them *d*·, O Lord our shield. 3381
15 Let them wander up and *d*· for meat,
60:12 it is that shall tread *d*· our enemies,
62: 4 They only consult to cast him *d*·
72: 6 He shall come *d*· like rain upon 3381
11 all kings shall fall *d*· before him: 7812
73:18 castedst them *d*· into destruction. 5307
74: 6 they break *d*· the carved work
7 by casting *d*· the dwellingplace *
75: 7 he putteth *d*· one, and setteth up 8213
78:16 caused waters to run *d*· like rivers.
24 And had rained *d*· manna upon them
31 smote *d*· the chosen men of Israel. 3766
80:12 thou then broken *d*· her hedges,
14 look *d*· from heaven, and behold,
16 It is burned with fire, it is cut *d*·:
85:11 shall look *d*· from heaven.
86: 1 Bow *d*· thine ear, O Lord, hear 5186
88: 4 am counted with them that go *d*· 3381
89:23 I will beat *d*· his foes before his
40 hast broken *d*· all his hedges;
44 cast his throne *d*· to the ground.
90: 6 in the evening it is cut *d*·, and
95: 6 come, let us worship and bow *d*·: 3766
102:10 hast lifted me up, and cast me *d*·.*
19 he hath looked *d*· from the height
104: 8 they go *d*· by the valleys unto ‡3381
19 the sun knoweth his going *d*·.
22 and lay them *d*· in their dens. 7257
107:12 brought *d*· their heart with labour; 3665
12 they fell *d*·, and there was none 3782
23 that go *d*· to the sea in ships, 3381
26 they go *d*· again to the depths:
108:13 he that shall tread *d*· our enemies.
109:23 am tossed up and *d*· as the locust.
113: 3 sun unto the going *d*· of the same
115:17 any that go *d*· into silence. 3381
119:118 hast trodden *d*· all them that err*
136 Rivers of waters run *d*· mine eyes,
133: 2 head, that ran *d*· upon the beard, 3381
2 that went *d*· to the skirts of his
137: 1 rivers of Babylon, there we sat *d*·,
139: 3 my path and my lying *d*· 7252
143: 3 smitten my life *d*· to the ground;
7 unto them that go *d*· into the pit. 3381
144: 5 thy heavens, O Lord, and come *d*·: "
145:14 up all those that be bowed *d*·.
146: 8 raiseth them that are bowed *d*·:
9 the wicked he turneth upside *d*·.
147: 6 casteth the wicked *d*· to the 8213
Pr 1:12 as those that go *d*· into the pit: 3381
3:20 and the clouds drop *d*· the dew. 7491
24 When thou liest *d*·, thou shalt not 7901
24 thou shalt lie *d*·, and thy sleep
5: 5 Her feet go *d*· to death; 3381
7:26 she hath cast *d*· many wounded:
27 to hell, going *d*· to the chambers 3381
14: 1 plucketh it *d*· with her hands. 8045
18: 8 go *d*· into the innermost parts of 3381
21:22 and casteth *d*· the strength of the "
22:17 Bow *d*· thine ear, and hear the *5186
23:34 lieth *d*· in the midst of the sea, 7901
24:31 stone wall thereof was broken *d*·. 2040
25:26 A righteous man falling *d*· before*
28 is like a city that is broken *d*·,
26:22 go *d*· into the innermost parts of 3381
Ec 1: 5 also ariseth, and the sun goeth *d*·,
3: 3 a time to break *d*·, and a time to
Ca 2: 3 I sat *d*· under his shadow with great
6: 2 beloved is gone *d*· into his garden, 3381
11 I went *d*· into the garden of nuts "
7: 9 that goeth *d*· sweetly, causing the
Isa 2: 9 And the mean man boweth *d*·, 7817
11 . . . shall be bowed *d*·, "

Isa 2:17 loftiness of man shall be bowed *d*·, 7817
5: 5 and break *d*· the wall thereof,
5 and it shall be trodden *d*·:
15 mean man shall be brought *d*·, 7817
9:10 The bricks are fallen *d*·, but we *
10 the sycamores are cut *d*·, but we 1438
10: 4 Without me they shall bow *d*· 3766
6 and to tread them *d*· like the mire
13 I have put *d*· the inhabitants like 3381
33 ones of stature shall be hewn *d*·, 1438
34 And he shall cut *d*· the thickets
11: 6 leopard shall lie *d*· with the kid; 7257
7 young ones shall lie *d*· together: "
14: 8 Since thou art laid *d*·, no feller is 7901
11 pomp is brought *d*· to the grave, 3381
12 art thou cut *d*· to the ground, 1438
15 thou shalt be brought *d*· to hell, 3381
19 that go *d*· to the stones of the pit; "
30 the needy shall lie *d*· in safety: 7257
16: 8 of the heathen have broken *d*·
17: 2 be for flocks, which shall lie *d*·, 7257
18: 2 a nation meted out and trodden *d*·,
5 away and cut *d*· the branches.
21: 3 was bowed *d*· at the hearing of it;*
22: 5 day of trouble, and of treading *d*·,
5 breaking *d*· the walls, and of
10 and the houses have ye broken *d*· 5422
19 from thy state shall he pull thee *d*·.
25 and be cut *d*·, and fall; 1438
24: 1 it waste, and turneth it upside *d*·,
10 The city of confusion is broken *d*·:
19 The earth is utterly broken *d*·, *
25: 5 bring *d*· the noise of strangers, 3665
10 Moab shall be trodden *d*· under
10 straw is trodden *d*· for the dunghill.
11 and he shall bring *d*· their pride *8213
12 fort of thy walls shall he bring *d*·, 7817
26: 5 bringeth *d*· them that dwell on "
6 The foot shall tread it *d*·,
27:10 and there shall he lie *d*·, 7257
28: 2 cast *d*· to the earth with the hand.
18 then ye shall be trodden *d*· by it.
29: 4 And thou shalt be brought *d*·, 8213
16 your turning of things upside *d*·
30: 2 That walk to go *d*· into Egypt, 3381
30 show the lighting *d*· of his arm, 5183
31 shall the Assyrian be beaten *d*·, *
31: 1 that go *d*· to Egypt for help; 3381
3 he that is holpen shall fall *d*·, *
4 so shall the Lord of hosts come *d*· 3381
32:19 hail, coming *d*· on the forest; * "
33: 9 Lebanon is ashamed and hewn *d*·:*
20 that shall not be taken *d*·; *
34: 4 and all their host shall fall *d*·, *
5 it shall come *d*· upon Idumea, 3381
7 unicorn shall come *d*· with them, "
37:24 will cut *d*· the tall cedars thereof,
38: 8 is gone *d*· in the sun dial of Ahaz,
8 by which degrees it was gone *d*·.
18 they that go *d*· into the pit cannot 3381
42:10 ye that go *d*· to the sea, and all "
43:14 have brought *d*· all their nobles, "
17 they shall lie *d*· together, they shall"
44:14 He heweth him *d*· cedars,
15 it a graven image, and falleth *d*· 5456
17 falleth *d*· unto it, and worshippeth "
19 fall *d*· to the stock of a tree? "
45: 8 Drop *d*·, ye heavens, from above,
8 the skies pour *d*· righteousness:
14 and they shall fall *d*· unto thee, 7812
46: 1 Bel boweth *d*·, Nebo stoopeth, 3766
2 They stoop, they bow *d*· together; "
6 they fall *d*·, yea, they worship. 5456
47: 1 Come *d*·, and sit in the dust, 3381
49:23 shall bow *d*· to thee with their 7812
50:11 ye shall lie *d*· in sorrow. 7901
51:23 Bow *d*·, that we may go over: 7812
52: 2 arise, and sit *d*·, O Jerusalem: ‡
4 went *d*· aforetime into Egypt 3381
55:10 For as the rain cometh *d*·, and the "
56:10 sleeping, lying *d*·, loving to 7901
58: 5 to bow *d*· his head as a bulrush,
60:14 *d*· at the soles of thy feet; 7812
20 Thy sun shall no more go *d*·;
63: 6 And I will tread *d*· the people in
6 and I will bring *d*· their strength*
14 a beast goeth *d*· into the valley, 3381
15 Look *d*· from heaven,
18 our adversaries have trodden *d*· thy
64: 1 that thou wouldest come *d*·, 3381
1 the mountains might flow *d*· at
3 looked not for, thou camest *d*·, 3381
3 mountains flowed *d*· at thy
65:10 place for the herds to lie *d*· in, 7257
12 shall all bow *d*· to the slaughter: 3766
Jer 1:10 to root out, and to pull *d*·, and to
10 throw *d*·, to build, and to plant. *2040
3:25 We lie *d*· in our shame, 7901
4:26 the cities thereof were broken *d*· 5422
6: 6 Hew ye *d*· trees, and cast a mount
15 they shall be cast *d*·, saith the 3782
8:12 they shall be cast *d*·, saith the Lord."
9:18 our eyes may run *d*· with tears,
13:17 and run *d*· with tears, because
18 Humble yourselves, sit *d*·: for
18 your principalities shall come *d*·, 3381
14:17 Let mine eyes run *d*· with tears
15: 9 sun is gone *d*· while it was yet day:
18: 2 and go *d*· to the potter's house, 3381
3 Then I went *d*· to the potter's "
7 and to pull *d*·, and to destroy it;
21:13 Who shall come *d*· against us? 5181
22: 1 Go *d*· to the house of the king 3381
7 shall cut *d*· thy choice cedars,
24: 6 build them, and not pull them *d*·;
25:37 cut *d*· because of the fierce anger*

Jer 26:10 sat *d*· in the entry of the new gate*
31:28 pluck up, and to break *d*·, and 5422
28 and to throw *d*·, and to destroy *2040
40 nor thrown *d*· any more for ever.
33: 4 are thrown *d*· by the mounts, 5422
12 causing their flock to lie *d*·. 7901
36:12 went *d*· into the king's house, 3381
15 Sit *d*· now, and read it in our ears.
38: 6 they let *d*· Jeremiah with cords. 7971
11 and let them *d*· by cords into the "
39: 8 brake *d*· the walls of Jerusalem. 5422
42:10 and not pull you *d*·, and I will
45: 4 which I have built will I break *d*·, 2040
46: 5 their mighty ones are beaten *d*·,
23 They shall cut *d*· her forest,
48: 2 thou shalt be cut *d*·, O Madmen; *
5 for in the going *d*· of Horonaim 4174
15 men are gone *d*· to the slaughter, 3381
18 come *d*· from thy glory, and sit in "
20 it is broken *d*·: howl and cry;
39 How is it broken *d*·! how hath
49:16 I will bring thee *d*· from thence, 3381
50:15 her walls are thrown *d*·: for it is 2040
27 bullocks; let them go *d*· to the 3381
51:25 and roll thee *d*· from the rocks, and
40 I will bring them *d*· like lambs to 3381
52:14 brake *d*· all the walls of Jerusalem 5422
La 1: 9 she came *d*· wonderfully: 3381
16 mine eye runneth *d*· with water,
2: 1 and cast *d*· from heaven unto
2 he hath thrown *d*· in his wrath 2040
2 brought them *d*· to the ground:
10 hang *d*· their heads to the ground. 3381
17 thrown *d*·, and hath not pitied: 2040
18 tears run *d*· like a river day and night:
3:48 eye runneth *d*· with rivers of water
49 eye trickleth *d*·, and ceaseth not,
50 Till the Lord look *d*·, and behold
63 their sitting *d*·, and their rising up;
Eze 1:13 it went up and *d*· among the living
24 they stood, they let *d*· their wings. 7503
25 stood, and had let *d*· their wings. "
6: 4 and I will cast *d*· your slain men 5307
6 and your images may be cut *d*·, 1438
11:13 Then fell I *d*· upon my face, and
13:14 I break *d*· the wall that ye have 2040
14 and bring it *d*· to the ground,
16:39 throw *d*· thine eminent place, 2040
39 shall break *d*· thy high places: 5422
17:24 have brought *d*· the high tree, 8213
19: 2 thy mother? A lioness: she lay *d*· *7257
6 went up and *d*· among the lions,
12 she was cast *d*· to the ground,
24:16 neither shall thy tears run *d*·.
26: 4 and break *d*· her towers: I will 2040
9 axes he shall break *d*· thy towers. 5422
11 shall he tread *d*· all thy streets: he
11 shall go *d*· to the ground. 3381
12 and they shall break *d*· thy walls, 2040
16 shall come *d*· from their thrones, 3381
20 I shall bring thee *d*· with them "
20 with them that go *d*· to the pit, "
27:29 shall come *d*· from their ships, "
28: 8 They shall bring thee *d*· to the pit, "
14 thou hast walked up and *d*· in the
30: 4 her foundations shall be broken *d*·. 2040
6 pride of her power shall come *d*·: 3381
25 the arms of Pharaoh shall fall *d*·;
31:12 are gone *d*· from his shadow, and
14 with them that go *d*· to the pit. 3381
15 day when he went *d*· to the grave "
16 when I cast him *d*· to hell with "
17 They also went *d*· into hell with "
18 thou be brought *d*· with the trees "
32:18 and cast them *d*·, even her, and the "
18 with them that go *d*· into the pit. "
19 go *d*·, and be thou laid with the "
21 gone *d*·, they lie uncircumcised, "
24 are gone *d*· uncircumcised into "
24 with them that go *d*· to the pit. "
25 that go *d*· to the pit: he is put in "
27 gone *d*· to hell with their weapons "
29 with them that go *d*· to the pit. "
30 which are gone *d*· with the slain; "
30 with them that go *d*· to the pit. "
34:15 them to lie *d*·, saith the Lord God. 7901
18 ye must tread *d*· with your feet the
26 I will cause the shower to come *d* 3381
37: 1 and set me *d*· in the midst of a valley
38:20 the mountains shall be thrown *d*·, 2040
39:10 cut *d*· any out of the forests; for
47: 1 came *d*· from under from the right 3381
8 and go *d*· into the desert, and go "
Da 3: 5 ye fall *d*· and worship the golden
6 falleth not *d*· and worshippeth
7 fell *d*· and worshipped the golden
10 shall fall *d*· and worship the golden
11 falleth not *d*· and worshippeth,
15 ye fall *d*· and worship the image
23 fell *d*· bound into the midst of the
4:13 an holy one came *d*· from heaven; 5182
14 Hew *d*· the tree, and cut off his
23 one coming *d*· from heaven, and 5182
23 Hew the tree *d*·, and destroy it;
5:19 and whom he would he put *d*·. 8214
6:14 till the going *d*· of the sun 4606
7: 9 till the thrones were cast *d*·, and *
23 and shall tread it *d*· and break it
8: 7 but he cast him *d*· to the ground,
10 and it cast *d*· some of the host 5307
11 place of his sanctuary was cast *d*·.
12 and it cast *d*· the truth to the
11:12 shall cast *d*· many ten thousands: 5307
26 and many shall fall *d*· slain.
Ho 2:18 will make them to lie *d*· safely. 7901
7:12 I will bring them *d*· as the fowls 3381

Ho 10: 2 he shall break d' their altars, he *
Joe 1:17 the barns are broken d'; for the 2040
2:23 cause to come d' for you the rain, 3381
3: 2 will bring them d' into the valley "
11 mighty ones to come d', O Lord. 5181
13 come, get you d'; for the press is *3381
18 mountains shall drop d' new wine,
Am 2: 8 lay themselves d' upon clothes
3:11 and he shall bring d' thy strength 3381
5:24 let judgment run d' as waters, and
6: 2 go d' to Gath of the Philistines: 3381
8: 9 the sun to go d' at noon, and I will
9: 2 thence will I bring them d': 3381
Ob 1: 3 shall bring me d' to the ground? "
4 I bring thee d', saith the Lord. "
16 and they shall swallow d', and they
Jon 1: 3 went d' to Joppa; and he found 3381
3 fare thereof, and went d' into it, "
5 Jonah was gone d' into the sides "
2: 6 I went d' to the bottoms of the "
Mic 1: 3 and will come d', and tread upon "
4 that are poured d' a steep place.
6 I will pour d' the stones thereof
12 but evil came d' from the Lord 3381
3: 6 the sun shall go d' over the prophets,
5: 8 both treadeth d', and teareth in pieces,
11 and throw d' all thy strong holds: 2040
6:14 and thy casting d' shall be in the
7:10 shall she be trodden d' as the mire
Na 1: 6 the rocks are thrown d' by him *5422
12 thus shall they be cut d', when he
Zep 1:11 the merchant people are cut d'; *
2: 7 Ashkelon shall they lie d' in the 7257
14 And flocks shall lie d' in the midst "
15 a place for beasts to lie d' in! 4769
3:13 they shall feed and lie d', and none "
Hag 2:22 riders shall come d', every one 3381
Zec 10: 5 which tread d' their enemies in the
11 Assyria shall be brought d', and 3381
12 shall walk up and d' in his name,
11: 2 forest of the vintage is come d'. 3381
Mal 1: 4 I will throw d'; and they shall 2040
11 even unto the going d' of the same
4: 3 ye shall tread d' the wicked;
M't 2:11 and fell d', and worshipped him: 4098
3:10 not forth good fruit is hewn d', 1581
4: 6 the Son of God, cast thyself d': 2736
9 if thou wilt fall d' and worship me.4098
7:19 is hewn d', and cast into the fire. 1581
8: 1 When he was come d' from the 2597
11 shall sit d' with Abraham, and 347
32 swine ran violently d' a steep place 2596
9:10 and sinners came and sat d' 347
11:23 shall be brought d' to hell: 2601
13:48 and sat d', and gathered the good 2523
14:29 when Peter was come d' out of the 2597
15:29 into a mountain, and sat d' there.*2521
30 and cast them d' at Jesus' feet; 4496
35 multitudes to sit d' on the ground. 377
17: 9 And as they came d' from the 2597
14 kneeling d' to him, and saying, *
18:26 The servant therefore fell d', and
29 And his fellow servant fell d' at his
21: 8 others cut d' branches from the *2875
24: 2 that shall not be thrown d'. 2647
17 housetop not come d' to take any 2597
26:20 even was come, he sat d' with the * 345
27: 5 And he cast d' the pieces of silver 4496
19 he was set d' on the judgment *2521
36 And sitting d' they watched him * "
40 If thou be the Son of God, come d' 2597
42 let him now come d' from the cross. "
M'r 1: 7 not worthy to stoop d' and unloose.
40 and kneeling d' to him, and saying
2: 4 they let d' the bed wherein the sick 5465
3:11 fell d' before him, and cried,
22 the scribes which came d' from 2597
5:13 the herd ran violently d' a steep 2596
33 came and fell d' before him, and
6:39 to make all sit d' by companies 347
40 they sat d' in ranks, by hundreds, 377
8: 6 the people to sit d' on the ground: "
9: 9 And as they came d' from the 2597
35 he sat d', and called the twelve, 2523
11: 8 and others cut d' branches off the *2875
13: 2 that shall not be thrown d'. 2647
15 on the housetop not go d' into 2597
15:30 and come d' from the cross.
36 Elias will come to take him d'. 2507
46 and took him d', and wrapped him "
Lu 1:52 He hath put d' the mighty from
2:51 And he went d' with them, and 2597
3: 9 good fruit is hewn d', and cast 1581
4: 9 of God, cast thyself d' from hence: 2736
20 again to the minister, and sat d'. 2523
29 they might cast him d' headlong. 2630
31 And came d' to Capernaum, a city 2718
5: 3 he sat d', and taught the people 2523
4 and let d' your nets for a draught. 5465
5 at thy word will I let d' the net.
8 he fell d' at Jesus' knees, saying,
19 and let him d' through the tiling 2524
29 of others that sat d' with them. *2621
6:17 he came d' with them, and stood 2597
38 good measure, pressed d', and shaken
7:36 the Pharisee's house, and sat d' to 347
8: 5 it was trodden d', and the fowls *2662
23 and there came d' a storm of wind 2597
28 he cried out, and fell d' before him,
33 herd ran violently d' a steep place 2596
41 fell d' at Jesus' feet, and besought
47 and falling d' before him, she
9:14 Make them sit d' by fifties in a 2625
15 and made them all sit d'. 347
37 when they were come d' from the 2778
42 the devil threw him d', and tare him.

Lu 9:44 Let these sayings sink d' into *
54 fire to come d' from heaven, and 2597
10:15 to heaven, shall be thrust d' to 2601
30 A certain man went d' from 2597
31 chance there came d' a certain
11:37 and he went in, and sat d' to meat. 377
12:18 I will pull d' my barns, and 2507
37 them to sit d' to meat, and will 347
13: 7 cut it d'; why cumbereth it the 1581
9 after that thou shalt cut it d'. "
29 and shall sit d' in the kingdom 347
14: 8 sit not d' in the highest room; 2625
10 go and sit d' in the lowest room, 377
28 sitteth not d' first, and counteth 2523
31 sitteth not d' first, and consulteth "
16: 6 thy bill, and sit d' quickly, and
17: 7 the field, Go and sit d' to meat? 377
16 And fell d' on his face at his feet,*
31 him not come d' to take it away: 2597
18:14 this man went d' to his house "
19: 5 make haste, and come d'; for "
6 And he made haste, and came d', "
21 takest up that thou layedst not d',
22 taking up that I laid not d', and
21: 6 that shall not be thrown d'. 2647
24 Jerusalem shall be trodden d' of the
22:14 he sat d', and the twelve apostles 377
41 a stone's cast, and kneeled d', and
44 drops of blood falling d' to the 2597
55 and were set d' together, 4776
55 Peter sat d' among them. *2521
23:53 And he took it d', and wrapped it 2507
24: 5 bowed d' their faces to the earth,
12 and stooping d', he beheld the *3879
Joh 2:12 this he went d' to Capernaum, 2597
3:13 but he that came d' from heaven,* "
4:47 he would come d', and heal his son:"
49 Sir, come d' ere my child die, "
51 as he was now going d', his servants "
5: 4 angel went d' at a certain season * "
7 another steppeth d' before me, 2597
6:10 Make the men sit d'. Now there 377
10 So the men sat d', in number
11 disciples to them that were set d'; 345
16 his disciples went d' unto the sea, 2597
33 which cometh d' from heaven, "
38 For I came d' from heaven, not "
41 bread which came d' from heaven. "
42 he saith, I came d' from heaven? "
50 which cometh d' from heaven, that "
51 living bread which came d' from "
58 bread which came d' from heaven: "
8: 2 and he sat d', and taught them. 2523
6 Jesus stooped d', and with his 2736
8 And again he stooped d', and wrote "
10:15 and I lay d' my life for the sheep.
17 because I lay d' my life, that I
18 I lay it d' of myself. I have power
18 to lay it d', and I have power to
11:32 she fell d' at his feet, saying unto
13:12 and was set d' again, he said unto 377
37 I will lay d' my life for thy sake.
38 Wilt thou lay d' thy life for my
15:13 that a man lay d' his life for his
19:13 and sat d' in the judgment seat in 2523
20: 5 And he stooping d', and looking *3879
11 she stooped d', and looked into * "
Ac 4:35 laid them d' at the apostles' feet:
5: 5 hearing these words fell d', and
10 Then fell she d' straightway at his
7:15 So Jacob went d' into Egypt, and 2597
34 and am come d' to deliver them. "
58 laid d' their clothes at a young
60 And he kneeled d', and cried with a
8: 5 Philip went d' to the city of 2718
15 when they were come d', prayed 2597
26 way that goeth d' from Jerusalem "
38 and they went d' both into the water "
9:25 and let him d' by the wall in a 2524
30 they brought him d' to Cesarea, 2609
32 he came d' also to the saints 2718
40 and kneeled d', and prayed; and
10:11 corners, and let d' to the earth: 2524
20 and get thee d', and go with them, 2597
21 Then Peter went d' to the men "
25 fell d' at his feet, and worshipped
11: 5 great sheet, let d' from heaven by 2524
12:19 he went d' from Judæa to Cæsarea, 2718
13:14 on the sabbath day, and sat d'. 2523
29 they took him d' from the tree, 2507
14:11 The gods are come d' to us in the 2597
25 Perga, they went d' into Attalia: "
15: 1 men which came d' from Judæa 2718
16 of David, which is fallen d'; and
16: 8 passing by Mysia came d' to 2597
13 and we sat d', and spake unto the 2523
29 and fell d' before Paul and Silas,
17: 6 turned the world upside d' are 387
18:22 the church, he went d' to Antioch. 2597
19:35 image which fell d' from Jupiter?
20: 9 he sunk d' with sleep, and 2736
9 and fell d' from the third loft,
10 And Paul went d', and fell on him, 2597
36 he kneeled d', and prayed with them
21: 5 and we kneeled d' on the shore, and
10 there came d' from Judæa a 2718
32 and ran d' unto them: and when 2701
22:30 and brought Paul d', and set him 2609
23:10 commanded the soldiers to go d', 2597
15 that he bring him d' unto you 2609
20 thou wouldest bring d' Paul "
24:22 chief captain shall come d', I 2597
25: 5 you are able, go d' with me, 4782
6 he went d' unto Cæsarea; and 2597
7 which came d' from Jerusalem "
27:27 as we were driven up and d' in *1308

Ac 27:30 when they had let d' the boat into*5465
28: 6 or fallen d' dead suddenly: but 2667
Ro 10: 6 to bring Christ d' from above:) 2609
11: 3 and digged d' thine altars; and 2679
10 and bow d' their back alway. 4781
16: 4 Who have for my life laid d' their 5294
1Co 10: 7 The people sat d' to eat and drink, 2523
14:25 and so falling d' on his face he
15:24 when he shall have put d' all rule *2673
2Co 4: 9 cast d', but not destroyed; 2598
7: 6 those that are cast d', comforted *5011
10: 4 to the pulling d' of strong holds:) 2506
5 Casting d' imaginations, and 2507
11:33 a basket was I let d' by the wall, 5465
Eph 2:14 and hath broken d' the middle wall of
4:26 let not the sun go d' upon your 1931
Heb 1: 3 himself purged our sins, sat d' on 2523
11:30 the walls of Jericho fell d',
12:12 which hang d', and the feeble 3935
Jas 1:17 cometh d' from the Father of lights, 2597
5: 4 labourers who have reaped d' *
1Pe 1:12 Holy Ghost sent d' from heaven; *
2Pe 2: 4 but cast them d' to hell,
1Joh 3:16 because he laid d' his life
16 we ought to lay d' our lives "
Re 1:13 clothed with a garment d' to the foot,
3:12 Jerusalem, which cometh d' out 2597
21 d' with my Father in his throne. 2523
4:10 The four and twenty elders fall d'
5: 8 elders fell d' before the Lamb,
14 the four and twenty elders fell d'
10: 1 angel come d' from heaven, 2597
12:10 accuser of our brethren is cast d', 2598
12 for the devil is come d' unto you, 2597
13:13 maketh fire come d' from heaven "
18: 1 I saw another angel come d' from "
21 great city Babylon be thrown d',
19: 4 and the four beasts fell d' and
20: 1 an angel come d' from heaven, 2597
9 and fire came d' from God out of "
21: 2 Jerusalem, coming d' from God out"
22: 8 I fell d' to worship before the feet

downsitting
Ps 139: 2 Thou knowest my d' and mine 3427

downward
2Ki 19:30 shall yet again take root d', and 4295
Ec 3:21 the spirit of the beast that goeth d' "
Isa 37:31 shall again take root d', and bear "
Eze 1:27 appearance of his loins even d', I saw"
8: 2 appearance of his loins even d', fire;"

dowry
Ge 30:20 hath endued me with a good d'; 2065
34:12 Ask me never so much d' and gift, 4119
Ex 22:17 pay money according to the d' of "
1Sa 18:25 The king desireth not any d', but "

drag See also DRAGGING.
Hab 1:15 net, and gather them in their d': 4365
16 burn incense unto their d'; because"

dragging
Joh 21: 8 cubits,) d' the net with fishes. 4951

dragon See also DRAGONS.
Neh 2:13 even before the d' well, and *8577
Ps 91:13 the young lion and the d' shalt "
Isa 27: 1 he shall slay the d' that is in the ‡ "
51: 9 cut Rahab, and wounded the d'? ‡ "
Jer 51:34 hath swallowed me up like a d', ‡ "
Eze 29: 3 the great d' that lieth in the midst "
Rev 12: 3 behold a great red d', having 1404
4 the d' stood before the woman "
7 his angels fought against the d'; "
7 and the d' fought and his angels, "
9 the great d' was cast out, that "
13 when the d' saw that he was cast "
16 the flood which the d' cast out "
17 the d' was wroth with the woman, "
13: 2 and the d' gave him his power, "
4 they worshipped the d' which gave "
11 like a lamb, and he spake as a d'. "
16:13 out of the mouth of the d', "
20: 2 he laid hold on the d', that old "

dragons
De 32:33 Their wine is the poison of d', 8577
Job 30:29 I am a brother to d', and a * "
Ps 44:19 sore broken us in the place of d',* "
74:13 thou breakest the heads of the d' "
148: 7 the earth, ye d', and all deeps: "
Isa 13:22 and d' in their pleasant palaces: * "
34:13 it shall be an habitation of d', * "
35: 7 in the habitation of d', where * "
43:20 honour me, the d' and the owls: * "
Jer 9:11 Jerusalem heaps, and a den of d';* "
10:22 Judah desolate, and a den of d', * "
14: 6 they snuffed up the wind like d';* "
49:33 Hazor shall be a dwelling for d', * "
51:37 a dwellingplace for d', an * "
Mic 1: 8 make a wailing like the d', and * "
Mal 1: 3 waste for the d' of the wilderness.*8568

dragon-well See DRAGON and WELL.

drams
1Ch 29: 7 talents and ten thousand d', * 150
Ezr 2:69 and one thousand d' of gold, *1871
8:27 of gold, of a thousand d'; and * 150
Ne 7:70 thousand d' of gold, fifty basons, *1871
71 twenty thousand d' of gold, and * "
72 gave was twenty thousand d' *1871

drank
Ge 9:21 And he d' of the wine, and was 8354
24:46 I d', and she made the camels drink "
27:25 he brought him wine, and he d'. "
43:34 they d', and were merry with him. "
Nu 20:11 and the congregation d', and their "
De 32:38 d' the wine of their drink offerings? "

2Sa 12: 3 and d' of his own cup, and lay in 8354
1Ki 13:19 bread in his house, and d' water. "
17: 6 evening; and he d' of the brook.
Da 1: 5 and of the wine which he d': 4960
8 nor with the wine which he d':
5: 1 and d' wine before the thousand. 8355
3 his wives, and his concubines, d' "
4 They d' wine, and praised the gods "
M'r 14:23 it to them: and they all d' of it. *4095*
Lu 17:27 They did eat, they d', they married "
28 they did eat, they d', they bought, "
Joh 4:12 us the well, and d' thereof himself, "
1Co 10: 4 for they d' of that spiritual Rock "

draught
2Ki 10:27 made it d' house unto this day. 4280
M't 15:17 and is cast out into the d'? *856*
M'r 7:19 goeth out into the d', purging * "
Lu 5: 4 and let down your nets for a d'. *61*
9 at the d' of the fishes which they "

draught-house See DRAUGHT and HOUSE.

drave See also DROVE.
Ex 14:25 that they d' them heavily: so that 5090
Jos 16:10 they d' not out the Canaanites 3423
24:12 d' them out from before you, 1644
18 the Lord d' out from before us "
J'g 1:19 he d' out the inhabitants of the 3423
6: 9 and d' them out from before you, 1644
1Sa 30:20 and the herds, which they d' 5090
2Sa 6: 3 sons of Abinadab, d' the new cart. "
2Ki 16: 6 and d' the Jews from Elath: 5394
17:21 d' Israel from following the Lord, 5071
1Ch 13: 7 and Uzza and Ahio d' the cart. 5090
Ac 7:45 whom God d' out before the face *1856
18:16 d' them from the judgment seat. *556*

draw See also DRAWETH; DRAWING; DRAWN; DREW; WITHDRAW.
Ge 24:11 that women go out to d' water. 7579
13 of the city come out to d' water: "
19 I will d' water for thy camels also, "
20 ran unto the well to d' water, "
43 virgin cometh forth to d' water, "
44 I will also d' for thy camels: "
Ex 3: 5 D' not nigh hither: put off thy
12:21 D' out and take you a lamb 4900
15: 9 I will d' my sword, mine hand 7324
Le 26:33 and will d' out a sword after you: "
J'g 3:22 he could not d' the dagger out 8025
4: 6 and d' toward mount Tabor, and 4900
7 And I will d' unto thee to the river "
9:54 D' thy sword, and slay me, that 8025
19:13 us d' near to one of these places
20:32 and d' them from the city unto 5423
1Sa 9:11 maidens going out to d' water, 7579
14:36 Let us d' near hither unto God.
38 D' ye near hither, all the chief of
31: 4 his armourbearer, D' thy sword, 8025
2Sa 17:13 and we will d' it into the river, 5498
1Ch 10: 4 D' thy sword, and thrust me 8025
Job 21:33 and every man shall d' after him. 4900
40:23 that he can d' up Jordan *1518
41: 1 Canst thou d' out leviathan with 4900
Ps 28: 3 D' me not away with the wicked, "
35: 3 D' out also the spear, and stop 7324
69:18 D' nigh unto my soul, and redeem
73:28 is good for me to d' near to God:
85: 5 wilt thou d' out thine anger to all 4900
107:18 d' near unto the gates of death.
119:150 d' nigh that follow after mischief:
Pr 20: 5 of understanding will d' it out. 1802
Ec 12: 1 d' nigh, when thou shalt say,
Ca 1: 4 D' me, we will run after thee: 4900
Isa 5:18 d' iniquity with cords of vanity, "
19 of the Holy One of Israel d' nigh
12: 3 Therefore with joy shall ye d' 7579
29:13 people d' near me with their mouth,
45:20 d' near together, ye that are escaped
57: 3 But d' near hither, ye sons of the
4 mouth, and d' out the tongue? ‡ 748
58:10 d' out thy soul to the hungry, 6329
66:19 d' the bow, to Tubal, and Javan, 4900
Jer 30:21 and I will cause him to d' near,
46: 3 and shield, and d' near to battle.
49:20 shall d' them out; surely he shall *5498
50:45 of the flock shall d' them out: * "
La 4: 3 sea monsters d' out the breast, 2502
Eze 5: 2 in the wind; and I will d' out a 7324
12 I will d' out a sword after them. "
9: 1 charge over the city to d' near,
12:14 will d' out the sword after them. 7324
21: 3 and will d' forth my sword out of 3318
22: 4 thy days to d' near, and art
28: 7 d' their swords against the beauty 7324
30:11 d' their swords against Egypt, "
32:20 d' her and all her multitudes. 4900
Joe 3: 9 let all the men of war d' near;
Na 3:14 D' thee waters for the siege, 7579
Hag 2:16 press at for to d' out fifty vessels 2834
Joh 2: 8 saith unto them, D' out now, and *501*
4: 7 a woman of Samaria to d' water: "
11 Sir, thou hast nothing to d' with, *502*
15 not, neither come hither to d'. *501*
6:44 Father which hath sent me d' him: *1670*
12:32 the earth, will d' all men unto me. "
21: 6 now they were not able to d' it for "
Ac 20:30 to d' away disciples after them. *645*
Heb 7:19 by the which we d' nigh unto God.
10:22 Let us d' near with a true heart *4334*
38 but if any man d' back, my soul *5288
39 we are not of them who d' back *5289
Jas 2: 6 rich men oppress you, and d' you *1670
4: 8 D' nigh to God, and he will d' nigh

drawer See also DRAWERS.
De 29:11 the hewer of thy wood unto the d' 7579

drawers
Jos 9:21 hewers of wood and d' of water 7579
23 d' of water for the house of my God. "
27 d' of water for the congregation, "

drawest See WITHDRAWEST.

draweth See also WITHDRAWETH.
De 25:11 and the wife of the one d' near
J'g 19: 9 the day d' toward evening, 7503
Job 24:22 He d' also the mighty with his 4900
33:22 his soul d' near unto the grave,
Ps 10: 9 when he d' him into his net. 4900
88: 3 my life d' nigh unto the grave.
Isa 26:17 d' near the time of her delivery,
Eze 7:12 the day d' near: let not the
M't 15: 8 This people d' nigh unto me with*
Lu 21: 8 the time d' near: go ye not *
28 for your redemption d' nigh.
Jas 5: 8 the coming of the Lord d' nigh. *

drawing
J'g 5:11 archers in the places of d' water, 4857
Joh 6:19 the sea, and d' nigh unto the ship: *1096*

drawn See also WITHDRAWN.
Nu 22:23, 31 and his sword d' in his hand: 8025
De 21: 3 which hath not d' in the yoke; 4900
30:17 but shall be d' away, and worship 5080
Jos 5:13 against him with his sword d' 8025
8: 6 till we have d' them from the city; 5423
16 and were d' away from the city. "
15: 9 And the border was d' from the 8388
9 and the border was d' to Baalah, "
11 and the border was d' to Shicron, "
18:14 And the border was d' thence, "
17 And was d' from the north, and "
J'g 20:31 were d' away from the city; and 5423
Ru 2: 9 that which the young men have d'. 7579
1Ch 21:16 having a d' sword in his hand 8025
Job 20:25 It is d', and cometh out of the * "
Ps 37:14 The wicked have d' out the sword, 6605
55:21 than oil, yet were they d' swords. 6609
Pr 24:11 them that are d' unto death, *3947
Isa 21:15 the swords, from the d' sword, 5203
28: 9 the milk, and d' from the breasts. 6267
Jer 22:19 burial of an ass, d' and cast forth 5498
31: 3 lovingkindness have I d' thee. 4900
La 2: 3 he hath d' back his right hand 7725
Eze 21: 5 I the Lord have d' forth my sword 3318
28 The sword, the sword is d': for 6605
Ac 11:10 all were d' up again into heaven. *385*
Jas 1:14 when he is d' away of his own lust, *1828*

dread See also DREADFUL.
Ge 9: 2 the fear of you and the d' of you 2844
Ex 15:16 Fear and d' shall fall upon them; 6343
De 1:29 D' not, neither be afraid of them. 6206
2:25 the d' of thee and the fear of thee 6343
11:25 and the d' of you upon all the land 4172
1Ch 22:13 courage; d' not, nor be dismayed. *3372
Job 13:11 afraid? and his d' fall upon you? 6343
21 and let not thy d' make me afraid. * 367
Isa 8:13 fear, and let him be your d'. 6206

dreadful
Ge 28:17 How d' is this place! this is none 3372
Job 15:21 A d' sound is in his ears: *6343
Eze 1:18 were so high that they were d'; 3374
Da 7: 7 a fourth beast, d' and terrible, *1763
19 from all the others, exceeding d', * "
9: 4 O Lord, the great and d' God, 3372
Hab 1: 7 They are terrible and d': their "
Mal 1:14 name is d' among the heathen. * "
4: 5 the great and d' day of the Lord: * "

dream See also DREAMED; DREAMETH; DREAMS.
Ge 20: 3 to Abimelech in a d' by night, 2472
6 And God said unto him in a d', "
31:10 and saw in a d', and, behold, the "
11 spake unto me in a d', saying, "
24 came to Laban the Syrian in a d' "
37: 5 Joseph dreamed a d', and he told "
6 you, this d' which I have dreamed: "
9 he dreamed yet another d', and "
9 Behold, I have dreamed a d' "
10 What is this d' that thou hast "
40: 5 they dreamed a d' both of them, "
5 each man his d' in one night, "
5 to the interpretation of his d', "
8 We have dreamed a d', and there "
9 chief butler told his d' to Joseph, "
9 In my d', behold, a vine was "
16 I also was in my d', and, behold, I "
41: 7 awoke, and, behold, it was a d'. "
8 Pharaoh told them his d'; but there "
11 we dreamed a d' in one night, I and "
11 to the interpretation of his d'. "
12 to each man according to his d' "
15 I have dreamed a d', and there is "
15 that thou canst understand a d' "
17 In my d', behold, I stood upon the "
22 I saw in my d', and, behold, seven "
25 The d' of Pharaoh is one: God "
26 ears are seven years: the d' is one. "
32 for that the d' was doubled unto "
Nu 12: 6 and will speak unto him in a d'. "
J'g 7:13 a man that told a d' unto his fellow, "
13 and said, Behold, I dreamed a d', "
15 Gideon heard the telling of the d', "
1Ki 3: 5 Lord appeared to Solomon in a d' "
15 awoke; and, behold, it was a d'. "
Job 20: 8 He shall fly away as a d', and shall "
33:15 In a d', in a vision of the night, "
Ps 73:20 As a d' when one awaketh; "
126: 1 Zion, we were like them that d'. "
Ec 5: 3 a d' cometh through the multitude "
Isa 29: 7 shall be as a d' of a night vision. "
Jer 23:28 The prophet that hath a d', let him "
28 let him tell a d': and he that hath "

Da 2: 3 I have dreamed a d', and my spirit 2472
3 was troubled to know the d'. "
4 tell thy servants the d', and we 2493
5 not make known unto me the d', "
6 But if ye shew the d', and the "
6 honour: therefore shew me the d', "
7 the king tell his servants the d', "
9 not make known unto me the d', "
9 therefore tell me the d', and I shall "
26 able to make known unto me the d' "
28 Thy d', and the visions of thy head "
36 This is the d'; and we will tell the "
45 and the d' is certain, and the "
4: 5 I saw a d' which made me afraid, 2493
6 unto me the interpretation of the d'. "
7 and I told the d' before them; "
8 and before him I told the d', "
9 tell me the visions of my d' that I "
18 This d' I king Nebuchadnezzar "
19 let not the d', or the interpretation "
19 the d' be to them that hate thee, "
7: 1 Daniel had a d' and visions of his "
1 then he wrote the d', and told the "
Joe 2:28 your old men shall d' dreams, your 2492
M't 1:20 Lord appeared unto him in a d', *3677*
2:12 being warned of God in a d' that "
13 Lord appeareth to Joseph in a d', "
19 Lord appeareth in a d' to Joseph "
22 being warned of God in a d', he "
27:19 this day in a d' because of him. "
Ac 2:17 and your old men shall d' dreams: *1798*

dreamed
Ge 28:12 And he d', and behold a ladder set 2492
37: 5 And Joseph d' a dream, and he told "
6 you, this dream which I have d': "
9 And he d' yet another dream, and "
9 Behold, I have d' a dream more; "
10 is this dream that thou hast d'? "
40: 5 And they d' a dream both of them, "
8 We have d' a dream, and there is no "
41: 1 of two full years, that Pharaoh d': "
5 he slept and d' the second time: "
11 And we d' a dream in one night, I "
11 we d' each man according to the "
15 unto Joseph, I have d' a dream, "
42: 9 the dreams which he d' of them, "
J'g 7:13 said, Behold, I d' a dream, and, "
Jer 23:25 name, saying, I have d', I have d'. "
29: 8 dreams, which ye cause to be d'. "
Da 2: 1 Nebuchadnezzar d' dreams, "
3 I have d' a dream, and my spirit "

dreamer See also DREAMERS.
Ge 37:19 Behold, this d' cometh. 1167, 2472
De 13: 1 you a prophet, or a d' of dreams, 2492
3 that prophet, or that d' of dreams: "
5 that prophet, or that d' of dreams, "

dreamers
Jer 27: 9 nor to your d', nor to your *2492
Jude 8 Likewise also these filthy d' defile *1797*

dreameth
Isa 29: 8 as when an hungry man d', and, 2492
8 as when a thirsty man d', "

dreams
Ge 37: 8 hated him yet the more for his d', 2472
20 see what will become of his d'. "
41:12 he interpreted to us our d'; to each "
42: 9 Joseph remembered the d' which "
De 13: 1 or a dreamer of d', and giveth thee "
3 that prophet, or that dreamer of d': "
5 that prophet, or that dreamer of d'. "
1Sa 28: 6 neither by d', nor by Urim, nor by "
15 neither by prophets, nor by d': "
Job 7:14 Then thou scarest me with d', and "
Ec 5: 7 in the multitude of d' and many "
Jer 23:27 to forget my name by their d' "
32 against them that prophesy false d', "
29: 8 neither hearken to your d' which "
Da 1:17 understanding in all visions and d'. "
2: 1 Nebuchadnezzar dreamed d', "
2 for to shew the king his d'. "
5:12 interpreting of d', and shewing of 2493
Joe 2:28 your old men shall dream d', your 2472
Zec 10: 2 seen a lie, and have told false d'; "
Ac 2:17 and your old men shall dream d': *1797*

dregs
Ps 75: 8 but the d' thereof, all the wicked 8105
Isa 51:17 thou hast drunken the d' of the *6907
22 even the d' of the cup of my fury; * "

dress See also DRESSED; DRESSETH.
Ge 2:15 of Eden to d' it and to keep it. 5647
18: 7 young man; and he hasted to d' it. 6213
De 28:39 shalt plant vineyards, and d' them, 5647
2Sa 12: 4 to d' for the wayfaring man that 6213
13: 5 meat, and d' the meat in my sight, "
7 Amnon's house, and d' him meat. "
1Ki 17:12 that I may go in and d' it for me "
18:23 I will d' the other bullock, and lay "
25 one bullock for yourselves, and d' it "

dressed See also UNDRESSED.
Ge 18: 8 milk, and the calf which he had d', 6213
Le 7: 9 all that is d' in the fryingpan, "
1Sa 25:18 and five sheep ready d', and five "
2Sa 12: 4 and d' it for the man that was come "
19:24 had neither d' his feet, nor trimmed "
1Ki 18:26 which was given them, and they d' "
Heb 6: 7 for them by whom it is d'. *1090*

dresser See also DRESSERS.
Lu 13: 7 said he unto the d' of his vineyard. *289*

dressers See also VINEDRESSERS.
2Ch 26:10 and vine d' in the mountains, and 3755

dresseth
Ex 30: 7 when he d' the lamps, he shall 3190

drew See also DREWEST; WITHDREW.
Ge 18:23 And Abraham *d'* near, and said,
24:45 down unto the well, and *d'* water: 7579
37:28 and they *d'* and lifted up Joseph 4900
38:29 to pass, as he *d'* back his hand, 7725
47:29 time *d'* nigh that Israel must die: "
Ex 2:10 Because I *d'* him out of the water.4871
16 they came and *d'* water, and filled1802
19 and also *d'* water enough for us, "
14:10 when Pharaoh *d'* nigh, the
20:21 *d'* near unto the thick darkness
Le 9: 5 and all the congregation *d'* near
Jos 8:11 went up, and *d'* nigh, and came
26 Joshua *d'* not his hand back, 7725
J'g 8:10 thousand men that *d'* sword. 8025
20 But the youth *d'* not his sword: "
20: 2 thousand footmen that *d'* sword. "
15 six thousand men that *d'* sword, "
17 thousand men that *d'* sword: "
25, 35 men; all these *d'* the sword. "
37 liers in wait *d'* themselves along, 4900
46 thousand men that *d'* the sword; 8025
Ru 4: 8 for thee. So he *d'* off his shoe. "
1Sa 7: 6 together to Mizpeh, and *d'* water, 7579
10 the Philistines *d'* near to battle
9:18 Saul *d'* near to Samuel in the gate,
17:16 the Philistine *d'* near morning
40 and he *d'* near to the Philistine.
41 Philistine came on and *d'* near
48 arose, and came and *d'* nigh
51 *d'* it out of the sheath thereof, 8025
2Sa 10:13 And Joab *d'* nigh, and the people
18:25 And he came apace, and *d'* near.
22:17 he *d'* me out of many waters; 4871
23:16 and *d'* water out of the well of 7579
24: 9 valiant men that *d'* the sword; 8025
1Ki 2: 1 Now the days of David *d'* nigh
8: 8 And they *d'* out the staves, * 748
22:34 certain man *d'* a bow at a venture,4900
2Ki 3:26 hundred men that *d'* swords, 8025
9:24 *d'* a bow with his full strength,
1Ch 11:18 of the Philistines, and *d'* water 7579
19:14 people that were with him *d'* nigh
16 and *d'* forth the Syrians that were3318
21: 5 thousand men that *d'* swords: 8025
5 ten thousand men that *d'* sword. "
2Ch 5: 9 they *d'* out the staves of the ark, * 748
14: 8 that bare shields and *d'* bows, 1869
18:33 certain man *d'* a bow at a venture 4900
Es 5: 2 So Esther *d'* near, and touched
9: 1 and his decree *d'* near to be put
Ps 18:16 he *d'* me out of many waters. 4871
Isa 41: 5 the earth were afraid, *d'* near,
Jer 38:13 they *d'* up Jeremiah with cords, 4900
Ho 11: 4 I *d'* them with cords of a man, "
Zep 3: 2 Lord; she *d'* not near to her God.
M't 13:48 they *d'* to shore, and sat down, *307*
21: 1 they *d'* nigh unto Jerusalem,
34 when the time of the fruit *d'* near,
26:51 and *d'* his sword, and struck a *645*
M'r 6:53 Gennesaret, and *d'* to the shore. **4358*
14:47 them that stood by *d'* a sword, *4685*
Lu 15: 1 Then *d'* near unto him all the *
25 he came and *d'* nigh to the house,
22: 1 feast of unleavened bread *d'* nigh,
47 *d'* near unto Jesus to kiss him.
23:54 preparation, and the sabbath *d'* on.*2020*
24:15 Jesus himself *d'* near, and went
28 And they *d'* nigh unto the village,
Joh 2: 9 servants which *d'* the water knew;) *501*
18:10 Peter having a sword *d'* it, and *1670*
21:11 Peter went up, and *d'* the net to "
Ac 5:37 *d'* away much people after him: *868*
7:17 the time of the promise *d'* nigh,
31 and as he *d'* near to behold it, *4334*
10: 9 and *d'* nigh unto the city, Peter
14:19 Paul, *d'* him out of the city, **4951*
16:19 Paul and Silas, and *d'* them into **1670*
27 he *d'* out his sword, and would *4685*
17: 6 *d'* Jason and certain brethren **4951*
19:33 *d'* Alexander out of the multitude,**4264*
21:30 and *d'* him out of the temple: **1670*
27:27 they *d'* near to some country; **4317*
Re 12: 4 *d'* the third part of the stars **4951*

drewest
La 3:57 Thou *d'* near in the day that I

dried See also DRIEDST.
Ge 8: 7 until the waters were *d'* up from 3001
13 were *d'* up from off the earth: 2717
14 of the month, was the earth *d'*. *3001
Le 2:14 green ears of corn *d'* by the fire, *7033
Nu 6: 3 nor eat moist grapes, or *d'*. 3002
11: 6 now our soul is *d'* away; there 3001
Jos 2:10 *d'* up the water of the Red sea "
4:23 God *d'* up the waters of Jordan "
23 which he *d'* up from before us, "
5: 1 the Lord had *d'* up the waters of "
J'g 16: 7 green withs that were never *d'*, 2717
8 green withs which had not been *d'*,"
1Ki 13: 4 he put forth against him, *d'* up, 3001
17: 7 that the brook *d'* up, because "
2Ki 19:24 with the sole of my feet have I *d'* *2717
Job 18:16 His roots shall be *d'* up beneath, 3001
28: 4 they are *d'* up, they are gone *1809
Ps 22:15 strength is *d'* up like a potsherd; 3001
69: 3 my throat is *d'*: mine eyes fail 2787
106: 9 Red sea also, and it was *d'* up: 2717
Isa 5:13 their multitude *d'* up with thirst.*6704
19: 5 river shall be wasted and *d'* up. *3001
6 shall be emptied and *d'* up: 2717
37:25 the sole of my feet have I *d'* * "
51:10 thou not it which hath *d'* the sea, "
Jer 23:10 of the wilderness are *d'* up. 3001
50:38 waters; and they shall be *d'* up: "
Eze 17:24 have *d'* up the green tree, and have"
19:12 the east wind *d'* up her fruit: 3001
37:11 they say, Our bones are *d'*, and "
Ho 9:16 their root is *d'* up, they shall bear "
13:15 and his fountain shall be *d'* up: 2717
Joe 1:10 the new wine is *d'* up, the oil 3001
12 The vine is *d'* up, and the fig tree* "
20 the rivers of waters are *d'* up, and "
Zec 11:17 his arm shall be clean *d'* up, and "
M'r 5:29 fountain of her blood was *d'* up; *3583*
11:20 the fig tree *d'* up from the roots. * "
Re 16:12 and the water thereof was *d'* up,

driedst
Ps 74:15 flood: thou *d'* up mighty rivers. 3001

drieth
Job 14:11 the flood decayeth and *d'* up: 3001
Pr 17:22 but a broken spirit *d'* the bones. "
Na 1: 4 it dry, and *d'* up all the rivers: 2717

drink See also DRANK; DRINKETH; DRINKING; DRINKS; DRUNK.
Ge 19:32 let us make our father *d'* wine, 8248
33 And they made their father *d'* wine "
34 make him *d'* wine this night also; "
35 And they made their father *d'* wine"
21:19 with water, and gave the lad *d'*. "
24:14 pitcher, I pray thee, that I may *d'*; 8354
14 and she shall say, *D'*, and I will "
14 I will give thy camels *d'* also: 8248
17 Let me, I pray thee, *d'* a little 1572
18 And she said, *D'*, my lord: and 8354
18 upon her hand, and gave him *d'*. 8248
19 when she had done giving him *d'*, "
43 a little water of thy pitcher to *d'*; "
44 And she say to me, Both *d'* thou, 8354
45 unto her, Let me *d'*, I pray thee. 8248
46 from her shoulder, and said, *D'*, 8354
46 I will give thy camels *d'* also: 8248
46 and she made the camels *d'* also. 8354
54 they did eat and *d'*, he and the "
25:34 he did eat and *d'*, and rose up, and "
26:30 a feast, and they did eat and *d'*. "
30:38 when the flocks came to *d'*, that "
38 conceive when they came to *d'*. "
35:14 poured a *d'* offering thereon, 5262
Ex 7:18 Egyptians shall lothe to *d'* of the 8354
21 the Egyptians could not *d'* of the "
24 about the river for water to *d'*; "
24 for they could not *d'* of the water "
15:23 they could not *d'* of the waters of "
24 Moses, saying, What shall we *d'*? "
17: 1 was no water for the people to *d'*. "
2 Give us water that we may *d'*. "
6 out of it, that the people may *d'*. "
24:11 they saw God, and did eat and *d'*. "
29:40 hin of wine for a *d'* offering. 5262
41 according to the *d'* offering thereof,"
30: 9 shall ye pour *d'* offering thereon. "
32: 6 people sat down to eat and to *d'*, 8354
20 and made the children of Israel *d'* 8248
34:28 neither eat bread, nor *d'* water. 8354
Le 10: 9 Do not *d'* wine nor strong 8354
9 wine nor strong *d'*, thou, nor thy 7941
11:34 all *d'* that may be drunk in 4945
23:13 and the *d'* offering thereof 5262
18 and their *d'* offerings, even an "
37 a sacrifice, and *d'* offerings, every "
Nu 5:24 cause the woman to *d'* the bitter 8248
26 cause the woman to *d'* the water. "
27 he hath made her to *d'* the water, "
6: 3 himself from wine and strong *d'*, 7941
3 and shall *d'* no vinegar of wine, 8354
3 of wine, or vinegar of strong *d'*, 7941
3 shall he *d'* any liquor of grapes 8354
15 offering, and their *d'* offerings. 5262
17 meat offering, and his *d'* offering. "
20 that the Nazarite may *d'* wine. 8354
15: 5 of an hin of wine for a *d'* offering 5262
7 for a *d'* offering thou shalt offer "
10 for a *d'* offering half an hin of wine, "
24 and his *d'* offering, according to "
20: 5 neither is there any water to *d'*. 8354
8 congregation and their beasts *d'*. 8248
17 neither will we *d'* of the water 8354
19 if I and my cattle *d'* of thy water, "
21:22 we will not *d'* of the waters "
23:24 prey, and *d'* the blood of the slain. "
28: 7 And the *d'* offering thereof shall 5262
7 unto the Lord for a *d'* offering. "
8 and as the *d'* offering thereof, thou "
9 oil, and the *d'* offering thereof: "
10 burnt offering, and his *d'* offering. "
14 their *d'* offerings shall be half an "
15, 24 offering, and his *d'* offering. "
31 blemish) and their *d'* offerings. "
29: 6 *d'* offerings, according unto their "
11 offering of it, and their *d'* offerings. "
16 meat offering, and his *d'* offering. "
18 their *d'* offerings for the bullocks, "
19 thereof, and their *d'* offerings. "
21 meat offering and their *d'* offerings "
22 meat offering, and his *d'* offering. "
24 their *d'* offerings for the bullocks, "
25 meat offering, and his *d'* offering. "
27 meat offering and their *d'* offerings "
28 meat offering, and his *d'* offering. "
30 offering and their *d'* offerings "
31 meat offering, and his *d'* offering. "
33 their *d'* offerings for the bullocks, "
34 meat offering, and his *d'* offering. "
37 meat offering and their *d'* offerings "
38 meat offering, and his *d'* offering. "
39 and for your *d'* offerings, and for "
33:14 was no water for the people to *d'*. 8354
De 2: 6 them for money, that ye may *d'*. "
28 water for money, that I may *d'*: "
9: 9 neither did eat bread, nor *d'* water, "
9:18 neither eat bread nor *d'* water, 8354
14:26 for wine, or for strong *d'*, or for 7941
28:39 but shalt neither *d'* of the wine, 8354
29: 6 have ye drunk wine or strong *d'*: 7941
32:14 *d'* the pure blood of the grape. *8354
38 the wine of their *d'* offerings? 5257
J'g 4:19 I pray thee, a little water to *d'*; 8248
19 and gave him *d'*, and covered him. "
7: 5 boweth down upon his knees to *d'*.8354
6 bowed down upon their knees to *d'* "
9:27 eat and *d'*, and cursed Abimelech. "
13: 4 and *d'* not wine nor strong "
4 not wine nor strong *d'*, and eat 7941
7 no wine nor strong *d'*, neither "
7 and now *d'* no wine nor strong 8354
14 neither let her *d'* wine or strong "
14 wine or strong *d'*, nor eat any 7941
19: 4 did eat and *d'*, and lodged there. 8354
6 did eat and *d'* both of them "
21 washed their feet, and did eat and *d'*."
Ru 2: 9 and *d'* of that which the young men"
1Sa 1:15 drunk neither wine nor strong *d'*,7941
30:11 eat; and they made him *d'* water: 8248
2Sa 11:11 to eat and to *d'*, and to lie with my 8354
13 he did eat and *d'* before him; "
16: 2 be faint in the wilderness may *d'*. "
19:35 taste what I eat or what I *d'*? "
23:15 one would give me *d'* of the water 8248
16 he would not *d'* thereof, but 8354
17 lives? therefore he would not *d'* it. "
1Ki 1:25 they eat and *d'* before him, and say,"
13: 8 neither will I eat bread nor *d'* water"
9 Eat no bread, nor *d'* water,nor turn"
16 will I eat bread nor *d'* water with "
17 shalt eat no bread nor *d'* water "
18 he may eat bread and *d'* water. "
22 Eat no bread, and *d'* no water; "
17: 4 be, that thou shalt *d'* of the brook; "
10 water into a vessel, that I may *d'*. "
18:41 unto Ahab, Get thee up, eat and *d'*; "
42 Ahab went up to eat and to *d'*. "
19: 6 he did eat and *d'*, and laid him "
8 eat and *d'*, and went in the strength"
2Ki 3:17 water, that ye may *d'*, both ye, and "
6:22 that they may eat and *d'*, and go to "
7: 8 into one tent, and did eat and *d'*, "
9:34 was come in, he did eat and *d'*, "
16:13 and poured his *d'* offering, and 5262
15 offering, and their *d'* offerings; "
18:27 and *d'* their own piss with you? 8354
31 and *d'* ye every one the waters "
1Ch 11:17 would give me *d'* of the water 8248
18 David would not *d'* of it, but poured8354
19 shall I *d'* the blood of these men "
19 it. Therefore he would not *d'* it. "
29:21 lambs, with their *d'* offerings, 5262
22 did eat and *d'* before the Lord 8353
2Ch 28:15 and gave them to eat and to *d'*, 8248
29:35 and the *d'* offerings for every 5262
Ezr 3: 7 meat, and *d'*, and oil, unto them 4960
7:17 their *d'* offerings, and offer them 5261
10: 6 he did eat no bread, nor *d'* water: 8354
Ne 8:10 eat the fat, and *d'* the sweet, "
12 went their way to eat, and to *d'*, "
Es 1: 7 gave them *d'* in vessels of gold, 8248
3:15 king and Haman sat down to *d'*; 8354
4:16 neither eat nor *d'* three days, night "
Job 1: 4 sisters to eat and to *d'* with them. "
21:20 *d'* of the wrath of the Almighty. "
22: 7 not given water to the weary to *d'*, 8248
Ps 16: 4 *d'* offerings of blood will I not 5262
36: 8 thou shalt make them *d'* of the 8248
50:13 of bulls, or *d'* the blood of goats? 8354
60: 3 to *d'* the wine of astonishment. 8248
69:21 thirst they gave me vinegar to *d'*. "
75: 8 wring them out, and *d'* them. 8354
78:15 gave them *d'* as out of the great 8248
44 floods, that they could not *d'*. 8354
80: 5 tears to *d'* in great measure. 8248
102: 9 and mingled my *d'* with weeping, 8249
104:11 give *d'* to every beast of the field: 8248
110: 7 shall *d'* of the brook in the way: 8354
Pr 4:17 and *d'* the wine of violence. "
5:15 *D'* waters out of thine own cistern, "
9: 5 eat of my bread, and *d'* of the wine "
20: 1 is a mocker, strong *d'* is raging: 7941
23: 7 Eat and *d'*, saith he to thee; 8354
25:21 be thirsty, give him water to *d'*: 8248
31: 4 it is not for kings to *d'* wine; 8354
4 wine; nor for princes strong *d'*: 7941
5 Lest they *d'*, and forget the law, 8354
6 Give strong *d'* unto him that is 7941
7 Let him *d'*, and forget his 8354
Ec 2:24 that he should eat and *d'*, and "
3:13 every man should eat and *d'*, and "
5:18 comely for one to eat and to *d'* "
8:15 to eat, and to *d'*, and to be merry: "
9: 7 *d'* thy wine with a merry heart; "
Ca 5: 1 eat, O friends; *d'*, yea, 8354
5 yea, *d'* abundantly, O beloved. 7937
8: 2 I would cause thee to *d'* of spiced 8248
Isa 5:11 that they may follow strong *d'*; 7941
22 them that are mighty to *d'* wine, 8354
22 of strength to mingle strong *d'*: 7941
21: 5 watch in the watchtower, eat, *d'*: 8354
22:13 drinking wine: let us eat and *d'*; "
24: 9 They shall not *d'* wine with a song; "
9 strong *d'* shall be bitter to them 7941
9 shall be bitter to them that *d'* it. 8354
28: 7 strong *d'* are out of the way; 7941
7 have erred through strong *d'*, "
7 out of the way through strong *d'*; "
29: 9 stagger, but not with strong *d'*. "
32: 6 he will cause the *d'* of the thirsty 4945
36:12 and *d'* their own piss with you? 8354
16 *d'* ye every one the waters of his "

Isa 43:20 desert, to give d' to my people, 8248
51:22 thou shalt no more d' it again: 8354
56:12 will fill ourselves with strong d'; 7941
57: 6 hast thou poured a d' offering, 5262
62: 8 the stranger shall not d' thy wine, 8354
9 d' it in the courts of my holiness. "
65:11 d' offering unto that number. *4469
13 shall d', but ye shall be thirsty: 8354
Jer 2:18 to d' the waters of Sihor? or what "
18 to d' the waters of the river? "
7:18 d' offerings unto other gods, that 5262
8:14 and given us water of gall to d'. 8248
9:15 and give them water of gall to d'. "
16: 7 them the cup of consolation to d' "
8 to sit with them to eat and to d'. 8354
19:13 have poured out d' offerings unto 5262
22:15 did not thy father eat and d'. 8354
23:15 make them d' the water of gall: 8248
25:15 to whom I send thee, to d' it. "
16 And they shall d', and be moved, 8354
17 and made all the nations to d'. 8248
26 of Sheshach shall d' after them. 8354
27 D' ye, and be drunken, and spue, "
28 take the cup at thine hand to d', "
28 Lord of hosts; Ye shall certainly d'. "
32:29 out d' offerings unto other gods, 5262
35: 2 and give them wine to d'. 8248
5 I said unto them, D' ye wine. 8354
6 We will d' no wine: for Jonadab "
6 Ye shall d' no wine, neither ye, "
8 to d' no wine all our days, "
14 commanded his sons not to d' wine, "
14 for unto this day they d' none, "
44:17, 18 pour out d' offerings unto her, 5262
19 poured out d' offerings unto her, "
19 and pour out d' offerings unto her, "
25 to pour out d' offerings unto her: "
49:12 whose judgment was not to d' of 8354
12 but thou shalt surely d' of it. "
Eze 4:11 shalt d' also water by measure, "
11 from time to time shalt thou d'. "
16 they shall d' water by measure, "
12:18 and d' thy water with trembling "
19 d' their water with astonishment, "
20:28 poured out there their d' offerings. 5262
23:32 Thou shalt d' of thy sister's cup 8354
34 shalt even d' it and suck it out, "
25: 4 fruit, and they shall d' thy milk. "
31:14 in their height, all that d' water: "
16 all that d' water, shall be comforted "
34:19 they d' that which ye have fouled "
39:17 that ye may eat flesh, and d' blood. "
18 d' the blood of the princes of the "
19 and d' blood till ye be drunken, "
44:21 Neither shall any priest d' wine, "
45:17 meat offerings, and d' offerings, 5262
Da 1:10 appointed your meat and your d': 4960
12 pulse to eat, and water to d'. 8354
16 and the wine that they should d'; 4960
5: 2 his concubines, might d' therein. 8355
Ho 2: 5 and my flax, mine oil and my d'. 8250
4:18 Their d' is sour: they have 5435
Joe 1: 9 the d' offering is cut off from the 5262
13 and the d' offering is withholden "
2:14 a d' offering unto the Lord your "
3: 3 girl for wine, that they might d'. 8354
Am 2: 8 they d' the wine of the condemned "
12 ye gave the Nazarites wine to d'; 8248
4: 1 masters, Bring, and let us d'. 8354
8 unto one city, to d' water; "
5:11 but ye shall not d' wine of them. "
6: 6 That d' wine in bowls, and anoint "
9:14 vineyards, and d' the wine thereof; "
Ob 16 all the heathen d' continually, "
16 yea, they shall d', and they "
Jon 3: 7 let them not feed, nor d' water: "
Mic 2:11 thee of wine and of strong d'; 7941
6:15 and sweet wine, but shalt not d' 8354
Hab 2:15 him that giveth his neighbour d', 8248
16 d' thou also, and let thy foreskin 8354
Zep 1:13 but not d' the wine thereof. "
Hag 1: 6 ye d', but ye are not filled 8354
6 but ye are not filled with d'; 7937
Zec 7: 6 did eat, and when ye did d', 8354
6 yourselves, and d' for yourselves? "
9:15 they shall d', and make a noise "
M't 6:25 ye shall eat, or what ye shall d'; 4095
31 What shall we d'? or, Wherewithal "
10:42 whosoever shall give to d' unto 4222
20:22 to d' of the cup that I shall d' of, 4095
23 Ye shall d' indeed of my cup, "
24:49 to eat and d' with the drunken; "
25:35 I was thirsty, and ye gave me d': 4222
37 or thirsty, and gave thee d'? "
42 I was thirsty and ye gave me no d': "
26:27 to them, saying, D' ye all of it; 4095
29 I will not d' henceforth of this fruit "
29 day when I d' it new with you "
42 except I d' it, thy will be done. "
27:34 vinegar to d' mingled with gall: "
34 tasted thereof, he would not d'. "
48 on a reed, and gave him to d'. "
M'r 9:41 shall give you a cup of water to d' 4222
10:38 can ye d' of the cup that I d' of? 4095
39 indeed d' of the cup that I d' of; "
14:25 I will d' no more of the fruit of the "
25 vine, until that day that I d' it new "
15:23 And they gave him to d' wine * "
36 gave him to d', saying, Let alone; 4222
16:18 and if they d' any deadly thing, 4095
Lu 1:15 shall d' neither wine nor strong 4095
15 neither wine nor strong d'; 4608
5:30 do ye eat and d' with publicans 4095
33 Pharisees; but thine eat and d'? "
12:19 thine ease, eat, d', and be merry. "
29 ye shall eat, or what ye shall d'. "

Lu 12:45 to eat and d', and to be drunken; 4095
17: 8 afterward thou shalt eat and d'? "
22:18 will not d' of the fruit of the vine, "
30 That ye may eat and d' at my table "
Joh 4: 7 Jesus saith unto her, Give me to d'. "
9 askest d' of me, which am a woman "
10 Give me to d'; thou wouldest "
6:53 and d' his blood, ye have no life "
55 and my blood is d' indeed. 4213
7:37 let him come unto me, and d'. 4095
18:11 hath given me, shall I not d' it? "
Ac 9: 9 sight, and neither did eat nor d'. "
10:41 who did eat and d' with him 4844
23:12 they would neither eat nor d' till 4095
21 they will neither eat nor d' till "
Ro 12:20 if he thirst, give him d': for in so 4222
14:17 of God is not meat and d'; *4213
21 nor to d' wine, nor any thing 4095
1Co 9: 4 we not power to eat and to d'? "
10: 4 And did all d' the same spiritual 4095
4 same spiritual d': for they drank 4188
7 The people sat down to eat and d', 4095
21 Ye cannot d' the cup of the Lord, "
31 Whether therefore ye eat, or d', or "
11:22 ye not houses to eat and to d' in? "
25 this do ye, as oft as ye d' it, "
26 ye eat this bread, and d' this cup, "
27 d' this cup of the Lord, unworthily, "
28 of that bread, and d' of that cup. "
12:13 all made to d' into one Spirit. 4222
15:32 let us eat and d'; for to morrow 4095
Col 2:16 judge you in meat, or in d', 4213
1Ti 5:23 D' no longer water, but use a *5202
Re 14: 8 because she made all nations d' 4222
10 The same shall d' of the wine 4095
16: 6 thou hast given them blood to d'; "

drinkers
Joe 1: 5 howl, all ye d' of wine, because of 8354

drinketh
Ge 44: 5 Is not this it in which my lord d', 8354
De 11:11 d' water of the rain of heaven: "
Job 6: 4 poison whereof d' up my spirit: "
15:16 man, which d' iniquity like water? "
34: 7 Job, who d' up scorning like water? "
40:23 Behold, he d' up a river, and *6231
Pr 26: 6 cutteth off the feet, and d' damage. 8354
Isa 29: 8 behold, he d'; but he awaketh, "
44:12 he d' no water, and is faint. "
M'r 2:16 d' with publicans and sinners? 4095
Joh 4:13 d' of this water shall thirst again: "
14 But whosoever d' of the water that "
6:54 and d' my blood, hath eternal life; "
56 eateth my flesh, and d' my blood, "
1Co 11:29 For he that eateth and d' "
29 unworthily, eateth and d' damnation "
Heb 6: 7 the earth which d' in the rain "

drinking
Ge 24:19 also, until they have done d'. 8354
22 to pass, as the camels had done d', "
Ru 3: 3 he shall have done eating and d'. "
1Sa 30:16 earth, eating and d', and dancing, "
1Ki 4:20 eating and d', and making merry. "
10:21 all king Solomon's d' vessels were 4945
16: 9 in Tirzah, d' himself drunk in the 8354
20:12 message, as he was d', he and the "
16 Ben-hadad was d' himself drunk in "
1Ch 12:39 David three days, eating and d': "
2Ch 9:20 all the d' vessels of king Solomon 4945
Es 1: 8 And the d' was according to the 8360
Job 1:13 his daughters were eating and d' 8354
18 thy daughters were eating and d' "
Isa 22:13 sheep, eating flesh, and d' wine: "
M't 11:18 John came neither eating nor d', 4095
19 Son of man came eating and d', "
24:38 they were eating and d', marrying "
Lu 7:33 neither eating bread nor d' wine; "
34 Son of man is come eating and d'; "
10: 7 eating and d' such things as they "

drink-offering See DRINK and OFFERING.

drinks
Heb 9:10 Which stood only in meats and d', 4188

drive See also DRAVE; DROVE; DRIVEN; DRIVETH; DRIVING; OVERDRIVE.
Ex 6: 1 with a strong hand shall he d' them 1644
23:28 which shall d' out the Hivite, the "
29 I will not d' them out from before "
30 By little and little I will d' them "
31 and thou shalt d' them out before "
33: 2 and I will d' out the Canaanite, the "
34:11 I d' out before thee the Amorite, the "
Nu 22: 6 and that I may d' them out of the * "
11 to overcome them, and d' them out. "
33:52 ye shall d' out all the inhabitants 3423
55 if ye will not d' out the inhabitants "
De 4:38 To d' out nations from before thee "
9: 3 so shalt thou d' them out, and "
4 the Lord doth d' them out from "
5 the Lord thy God doth d' them out "
11:23 Then will the Lord d' out all these "
18:12 the Lord thy God doth d' them out "
Jos 3:10 and that he will without fail d' out "
13: 6 them will I d' out from before the "
14:12 then I shall be able to d' them out, "
15:63 children of Judah could not d' them "
17:12 children of Mannasseh could not d' "
13 but did not utterly d' them out. "
18 thou shalt d' out the Canaanites, "
23: 5 and d' them from out of your sight; "
13 your God will no more d' out any "
J'g 1:19 could not d' out the inhabitants of "
21 the children of Benjamin did not d' "
27 Manasseh d' out the inhabitants of "
28 and did not utterly d' them out. "
29 did Ephraim d' out the Canaanites* "

J'g 1:30 did Zebulun d' out the inhabitants *3423
31 did Asher d' out the inhabitants * "
32 land: for they did not d' them out. "
33 did Naphtali d' out the inhabitants* "
2: 3 I will not d' them out from before 1644
21 I also will not henceforth d' out 3423
11:24 the Lord our God shall d' out * "
2Ki 4:24 D', and go forward; slack not thy 5090
2Ch 20: 7 didst d' out the inhabitants of this 3423
Job 18:11 side, and shall d' him to his feet. *6327
24: 3 d' away the ass of the fatherless, 5090
Ps 44: 2 thou didst d' out the heathen with 3423
68: 2 is driven away, so d' them away: 5086
Pr 22:15 the rod of correction shall d' it far
Isa 22:19 I will d' thee from thy station, *1920
Jer 24: 9 all places whither I shall d' them. 5080
27:10 that I should d' you out, and ye "
15 that I might d' you out, and that "
46:15 not, because the Lord did d' them. 1920
Eze 4:13 Gentiles, whither I will d' them. 5080
Da 4:25 they shall d' thee from men, and *2957
32 And they shall d' thee from men, * "
Hos 9:15 I will d' them out of mine house, 1644
Joe 2:20 and will d' him into a land barren 5080
Zep 2: 4 they shall d' out Ashdod at the 1644
Ac 27:15 up into the wind, we let her d'. *1929

driven
Ge 4:14 thou hast d' me out this day from 1644
Ex 10:11 they were d' out from Pharaoh's "
22:10 die, or be hurt, or d' away, no man 7617
Nu 32:21 until he hath d' out his enemies 3423
De 4:19 shouldest be d' to worship them, *5080
30: 1 whither the Lord thy God hath d' "
4 If any of thine be d' out unto the * "
Jos 23: 9 the Lord hath d' out from before 3423
1Sa 26:19 for they have d' me out this day 1644
Job 6:13 and is wisdom d' quite from me? 5080
13:25 thou break a leaf d' to and fro? 5086
18:18 He shall be d' from light into 1920
30: 5 They were d' forth from among 1644
Ps 40:14 let them be d' backward and put *5472
68: 2 As smoke is d' away, so drive 5086
114: 3 it, and fled: Jordan was d' back. 5437
5 thou Jordan, that thou wast d' * "
Pro 14:32 The wicked is d' away in his *1760
Isa 8:22 they shall be d' to darkness. 5080
19: 7 by the brooks, shall wither, be d' 5086
41: 2 sword, and as d' stubble to his bow. "
Jer 8: 3 the places whither I have d' them. 5080
16:15 the lands whither he had d' them: "
23: 2 scattered my flock, and d' them "
3 all countries whither I have d' them. "
8 all countries whither I had d' them; "
23:12 they shall be d' on, and fall 1760
29:14 all the places whither I have d' 5080
18 the nations whither I have d' them: "
32:37 all countries, whither I have d' "
40:12 all places whither they were d', "
43: 5 nations, whither they had been d', "
46:28 the nations whither I have d' thee: "
49: 5 and ye shall be d' out every man "
50:17 the lions have d' him away: "
Eze 31:11 have d' him out for his wickedness. 1644
34: 4 brought again that which was d' 5080
16 bring again that which was d' away, "
Da 4:33 he was d' from men, and did eat 2957
5:21 he was d' from the sons of men; "
9: 7 countries whither thou hast d' 5080
Ho 13: 3 chaff that is d' with the whirlwind 5590
Mic 4: 6 I will gather her that is d' out, 5080
Zep 3:19 and gather her that was d' out; "
Lu 8:29 d' of the devil into the wilderness.) 1643
Ac 27:17 strake sail, and so were d'. 5342
27 we were d' up and down in Adria, 1308
Jas 1: 6 the sea d' with the wind and tossed. 416
3: 4 are d' of fierce winds, yet are they 1643

driver
1Ki 22:34 he said unto the d' of his chariot, 7395
Job 39: 7 regardeth he the crying of the d'. 5065

driveth
2Ki 9:20 son of Nimshi; for he d' furiously. 5090
Ps 1: 4 the chaff which the wind d' away. 5086
Pr 25:23 The north wind d' away rain: so *2342
M'r 1:12 spirit d' him into the wilderness. 1544

driving
J'g 2:23 without d' them out hastily; 3423
2Ki 9:20 and the d' is like the d' of Jehu 4491
1Ch 17:21 by d' out nations from before thy 1644

dromedaries
1Ki 4:28 and d' brought they unto the *7409
Es 8:10 mules, camels, and young d': *7424
Isa 60: 6 the d' of Midian and Ephah; 1070

dromedary See also DROMEDARIES.
Jer 2:23 a swift d' traversing her ways; 1072

drop See also DROPPED; DROPPETH; DROPPING; DROPS.
De 32: 2 My doctrine shall d' as the rain, 6201
33:28 also his heaven shall d' down dew. "
Job 36:28 the clouds do d' and distil upon *5140
Ps 65:11 goodness; and thy paths d' fatness. 7491
12 They d' upon the pastures of the "
Pr 3:20 and the clouds d' down the dew. "
5: 3 woman d' as an honeycomb, 5197
Ca 4:11 my spouse, d' as the honeycomb: "
Isa 40:15 a d' of a bucket, and are counted 4752
45: 8 D' down, ye heavens, from above, 7491
Eze 20:46 and d' thy word toward the south, 5197
21: 2 and d' thy word toward the holy "
Joel 3:18 the mountains shall d' down new "
Am 7:16 d' not thy word against the house "
9:13 and the mountains shall d' sweet "

dropped
J'g 5: 4 the heavens d', the clouds also d' 5197

1Sa 14:26 behold, the honey d'; but no man 1982
2Sa 21:10 until water d' upon them out of *5413
Job 29:22 and my speech d' upon them. 5197
Ps 68: 8 heavens also d' at the presence of "
Ca 5: 5 my hands d' with myrrh, and my "

droppeth
Ec 10:18 the hands the house d' through. *1811

dropping
Pr 19:13 of a wife are a continual d'. 1812
27:15 A continual d' in a very rainy day "
Ca 5:13 lilies, d' sweet smelling myrrh. 5197

drops
Job 36:27 he maketh small the d' of water: 5197
38:28 who hath begotten the d' of dew? 96
Ca 5: 2 my locks with the d' of the night. 7447
Lu 22:44 as it were great d' of blood falling 2361

dropsy
Lu 14: 2 man before him which had the d'. 5203

dross
Ps 119:119 all the wicked of the earth like d':5509
Pr 25: 4 Take away the d' from the silver, "
26:23 a potsherd covered with silver d'. "
Isa 1:22 Thy silver is become d', thy wine "
25 purely purge away thy d', and take "
Eze 22:18 house of Israel is to me become d'; "
18 they are even the d' of silver. "
19 all become d', behold, therefore "

drought
Ge 31:40 in the day the d' consumed me, 2721
De 8:15 serpents, and scorpions, and d', *6774
Job 24:19 D' and heat consume the snow 6723
Ps 32: 4 is turned into the d' of summer. 2725
Isa 58:11 and satisfy thy soul in d', and *6710
Jer 2: 6 through a land of d', and of the 6723
17: 8 not be careful in the year of d', 1226
50:38 A d' is upon her waters; and they 2721
Hos 13: 5 wilderness, in the land of great d'. 8514
Hag 1:11 I called for a d' upon the land, 2721

drove See also DRAVE; DROVES.
Ge 3:24 So he d' out the man; and he 1644
15:11 carcases, Abram d' them away. 5380
32:16 every d' by themselves; and said 5739
16 put a space betwixt d' and d'. "
33: 8 What meanest thou by all this d' *4264
Ex 2:17 came and d' them away: but 1644
Nu 21:32 and d' out the Amorites that were 3423
Jos 15:14 Caleb d' thence the three sons of "
1Ch 8:13 who d' away the inhabitants of *1272
Ps 34:*title* who d' him away, and he 1644
Hab 3: 6 and d' asunder the nations; and 5425
Joh 2:15 he d' them all out of the temple, *1544

droves
Ge 32:19 all that followed the d', saying, 5739

drown See also DROWNED.
Ca 8: 7 neither can the floods d' it: if a 7857
1Ti 6: 9 which d' men in destruction and 1036

drowned
Ex 15: 4 his chosen captains also are d' *2883
Am 8: 8 and it shall be cast out and d', as *8248
9: 5 and shall be d', as by the flood of * "
M't 18: 6 he were d' in the depth of the sea.*2670
Heb 11:29 Egyptians assaying to do were d'.*2666

drowsiness
Pr 23:21 d' shall clothe a man with rags. 5124

drunk See also DRUNKEN.
Le 11:34 all drink that may be d' in every 8354
De 29: 6 neither have ye d' wine or strong "
32:42 make mine arrows d' with blood, 7937
J'g 15:19 and when he had d', his spirit 8354
Ru 3: 7 when Boaz had eaten and d', and "
1Sa 1: 9 in Shiloh, and after they had d'. "
15 I have d' neither wine nor strong "
30:12 eaten no bread, nor d' any water, "
2Sa 11:13 and he made him d': and at even 7937
1Ki 13:22 and d' water in the place, of the 8354
23 after he had d', that he saddled "
16: 9 drinking himself d' in the house of 7910
20:16 drinking himself d' in the pavilions,"
2Ki 6:23 when they had eaten and d', he 8354
19:24 digged and d' strange waters, and "
Ca 5: 1 I have d' my wine with my milk: "
Isa 37:25 I have digged, and d' water; and "
51:17 which hast d' at the hand of the "
63: 6 and make them d' in my fury, 7937
Jer 46:10 and made d' with their blood: *7301
51:57 And I will make d' her princes, 7937
Eze 34:18 to have d' of the deep waters, 8354
Da 5:23 have d' wine in them; and thou 8355
Ob 16 have d' upon my holy mountain, 8354
Lu 5:39 No man also having d' old wine 4095
13:26 have eaten and d' in thy presence, "
Joh 2:10 when men have well d', then 3184
Eph 5:18 And be not d' with wine, wherein*3182
Re 17: 2 have been made d' with the wine* "
18: 3 all nations have d' of the wine *

drunkard See also DRUNKARDS.
De 21:20 voice; he is a glutton, and a d'. 5435
Pr 23:21 the d' and the glutton shall come "
26: 9 goeth up into the hand of a d', 7910
Isa 24:20 shall reel to and fro like a d', * "
1Co 5:11 railer, or a d', or an extortioner; 3183

drunkards
Ps 69:12 and I was the song of the d'. 8354, 7941
Isa 28: 1 of pride, to the d' of Ephraim, 7910
3 crown of pride, the d' of Ephraim, "
Joe 1: 5 Awake, ye d', and weep; and howl, "
Na 1:10 while they are drunken as d', †‡5435
1Co 6:10 nor d', nor revilers, nor 3183

drunken
Ge 9:21 he drank of the wine, and was d'; 7943
1Sa 1:13 Eli thought she had been d'. 7910
1Sa 1:14 How long wilt thou be d'? put 7937
25:36 within him, for he was very d': 7910
Job 12:25 them to stagger like a d' man. "
Ps 107:27 and stagger like a d' man, "
Isa 19:14 a d' man staggereth in his vomit. "
29: 9 they are d', but not with wine; 7937
49:26 shall be d' with their own blood, "
51:17 thou hast d' the dregs of the cup 8354
21 and d', but not with wine: 7937
Jer 23: 9 I am like a d' man, and like a 7910
25:27 Drink ye, and be d', and spue, 7937
48:26 Make ye him d': for he magnified "
49:12 of the cup have assuredly d'; * "
51: 7 that made all the earth d': "
7 the nations have d' of her wine; *8354
39 feasts, and I will make them d', 7937
La 3:15 hath made me d' with wormwood.*7301
4:21 thou shalt be d', and shalt make 7937
5: 4 We have d' our water for money; 8354
Eze 39:19 and drink blood till ye be d', 7943
Na 1:10 while they are d' as drunkards, †5435
3:11 Thou also shalt be d': thou shalt 7937
Hab 2:15 to him, and makest him d' also, "
M't 24:49 and to eat and drink with the d'; 3184
Lu 12:45 eat and drink, and to be d'; 3182
17: 8 till I have eaten and d'; and 4095
Ac 2:15 these are not d', as ye suppose, 3184
1Co 11:21 one is hungry, and another is d'. "
1Th 5: 7 they that be d' are d' in the night. "
Re 17: 6 d' with the blood of the saints, "

drunkenness
De 29:19 mine heart, to add d' to thirst: *7302
Ec 10:17 for strength, and not for d'! 8358
Jer 13:13 inhabitants of Jerusalem, with d'.7943
Eze 23:33 shalt be filled with d' and sorrow, "
Lu 21:34 and d', and cares of this life, 3178
Ro 13:13 rioting and d', not in chambering "
Ga 5:21 Envyings, murders, d', revellings, "

Drusilla (*dru-sil'-lah*)
Ac 24:24 when Felix came with his wife D', 1409

dry See also DRIED; DRIETH; DRYSHOD.
Ge 1: 9 let the d' land appear: and it was 3004
10 And God called the d' land Earth; "
7:22 of all that was in the d' land, died. 2724
8:13 the face of the ground was d'. *2720
Ex 4: 9 pour it upon the d' land: and the 3004
9 become blood upon the d' land. 3006
14:16 of Israel shall go on d' ground 3004
21 the sea d' land, and the waters 2724
22 of the sea upon the d' ground: 3004
29 of Israel walked upon d' land "
15:19 children of Israel went on d' land "
Le 7:10 offering mingled with oil, and d', 2720
13:30 it is a d' scall, even a leprosy upon*5424
Jos 3:17 stood firm on d' ground in the 2724
17 Israelites passed over on d' ground,"
4:18 were lifted up unto the d' land, "
22 came over this Jordan on d' land. 3004
9: 5 their provision was d' and mouldy. 3001
12 behold, it is d', and it is mouldy: "
J'g 6:37 be d' upon all the earth beside, 2721
39 it now be d' only upon the fleece, "
40 for it was d' upon the fleece only, "
2Ki 2: 8 they two went over on d' ground. 2724
Ne 9:11 midst of the sea on the d' land; 3004
Job 12:15 the waters, and they d' up: also 3001
13:25 wilt thou pursue the d' stubble? 3002
15:30 the flame shall d' up his branches.3001
Ps 63: 1 for thee in a d' and thirsty land, 6723
66: 6 He turned the sea into d' land: 3004
68: 6 the rebellious dwell in a d' land. *6707
95: 5 and his hands formed the d' land. 3006
105:41 ran in the d' places like a river. 6723
107:33 the watersprings into d' ground; *6774
35 and d' ground into watersprings. 6723
Pr 17: 1 is a d' morsel, and quietness 2720
Isa 25: 5 strangers, as the heat in a d' place;*6724
32: 2 as rivers of water in a d' place, "
41:18 and the d' land springs of water. 6723
42:15 and d' up all their herbs; and I 3001
15 islands, and I will d' up the pools. "
44: 3 and floods upon the d' ground: 3004
27 saith to the deep, Be d', 2717
27 and I will d' up thy rivers. 3001
50: 2 at my rebuke I d' up the sea, 2717
53: 2 as a root out of a d' ground: 6723
56: 3 say, Behold, I am a d' tree. 3002
Jer 4:11 A d' wind of the high places *6703
50:12 a d' land, and a desert. 6723
51:36 I will d' up her sea, and make 2717
36 and make her springs d'. 3001
43 a d' land, and a wilderness, 6723
Eze 17:24 have made the d' tree to flourish: 3002
19:13 in a d' and thirsty ground. 6723
20:47 tree in thee, and every d' tree: 3002
30:12 I will make the rivers d', and sell 2724
37: 2 valley; and, lo, they were very d'. 3002
4 O ye d' bones, hear the word of "
Ho 2: 3 set her like a d' land, and slay 6723
9:14 miscarrying womb and d' breasts.6784
13:15 and his spring shall become d', 954
Jon 1: 9 hath made the sea and the d' land.3004
2:10 vomited out Jonah upon the d' land. "
Na 1: 4 rebuketh the sea, and maketh it d',3001
10 be devoured as stubble fully d'. †3002
Zep 2:13 desolation, and d' like a wilderness.6723
Hag 2: 6 and the sea, and the d' land; 2724
Zec 10:11 the deeps of the river shall d' up:3001
M't 12:43 he walketh through d' places, * 504
Lu 11:24 he walketh through d' places, * "
23:31 what shall be done in the d'? 3584
Heb 11:29 through the Red sea as by d' land: "

dry-ground See DRY and GROUND.

dry-land See DRY and LAND.

dryshod
Isa 11:15 streams, and make men go over d'.5275

due See also DUES.
Le 10:13 it is thy d', and thy sons' d', 2706
14 they be thy d', and thy sons d', "
26: 4 I will give thee rain in d' season, *
Nu 28: 2 offer unto me in their d' season. "
De 11:14 rain of your land in his d' season,*
18: 3 be the priest's d' from the people, 4941
32:35 their foot shall slide in d' time: *
1Ch 15:13 sought him not after the d' order.*
16:29 Give unto the Lord the glory d'
Ne 11:23 for the singers, d' for every day. *1697
Ps 29: 2 Lord the glory d' unto his name;
96: 8 the Lord the glory d' unto his name:
104:27 give them their meat in d' season.
145:15 them their meat in d' season.
Pr 3:27 good from them to whom it is d', 1167
15:23 a word spoken in d' season, how
Ec 10:17 princes eat in d' season, for strength,
M't 18:34 pay all that was d' unto him. 3784
24:45 to give them meat in d' season?
Lu 12:42 their portion of meat in d' season?
23:41 receive the d' reward of our deeds: 514
Ro 5: 6 in d' time Christ died for the ungodly.
13: 7 dues: tribute to whom tribute is d';
1Co 7: 3 unto the wife d' benevolence: 3784
15: 8 as of one born out of d' time. ‡
Ga 6: 9 for in d' season we shall reap, 2398
1Ti 2: 6 for all, to be testified in d' time. * "
Tit 1: 3 in d' time manifested his word * "
1Pe 5: 6 that he may exalt you in d' time:

dues
Ro 13: 7 Render therefore to all their d': 3782

dug See DIGGED.

duke See also DUKES.
Ge 36:15 d' Teman, d' Omar, 441
15 d' Zepho, d' Kenaz, "
16 D' Korah, d' Gatam, and d' Amalek: "
17 d' Nahath, d' Zerah, "
17 d' Shammah, d' Mizzah: "
18 d' Jeush, d' Jaalam, d' Korah: "
29 d' Lotan, d' Shobal, "
29 d' Zibeon, d' Anah, "
30 D' Dishon, d' Ezer, d' Dishan: "
40 d' Timnah, d' Alvah, d' Jetheth, "
41 D' Aholibamah, d' Elah, d' Pinon, "
42 D' Kenaz, d' Teman, d' Mibzar, "
43 D' Magdiel, d' Iram: "
1Ch 1:51 d' Timnah, d' Aliah, d' Jetheth, "
52 D' Aholibamah, d' Elah, d' Pinon, "
53 D' Kenaz, d' Teman, d' Mibzar, "
54 D' Magdiel, d' Iram. "

dukes
Ge 36:15 These were d' of the sons ‡ 441
16 are the d' that came of Eliphaz ‡ "
17 are the d' that came of Reuel ‡ "
18 the d' that came of Aholibamah ‡ "
19 is Edom, and these are their d'. ‡ "
21 these are the d' of the Horites, ‡ "
29 the d' that came of the Horites; ‡ "
30 are the d' that came of Hori, ‡ "
30 among their d' in the land of Seir.‡ "
40 of the d' that came of Esau, ‡ "
43 these be the d' of Edom, ‡ "
Ex 15:15 the d' of Edom shall be amazed; ‡ *5257
Jos 13:21 were d' of Sihon, dwelling in the *5257
1Ch 1:51 And the d' of Edom were; ‡ 441
54 These are the d' of Edom. ‡

dulcimer
Da 3: 5, 10, 15 d', and all kinds of musick, 5481

dull
M't 13:15 their ears are d' of hearing, and 917
Ac 28:27 their ears are d' of hearing, and "
Heb 5:11 seeing ye are d' of hearing. 3576

Dumah (*doo'-mah*)
Ge 25:14 Mishma, and D', and Massa, 1746
Jos 15:52 Arab, and D', and Eshean, "
1Ch 1:30 and D', Massa, Hadad, and Tema, "
Isa 21:11 The burden of D'. He calleth to "

dumb
Ex 4:11 or who maketh the d', or deaf, 483
Ps 38:13 and I was as a d' man that openeth "
39: 2 I was d' with silence, I held my 481
9 I was d', I opened not my mouth; "
Pr 31: 8 Open thy mouth for the d' in the 483
Isa 35: 6 and the tongue of the d' sing: "
53: 7 a sheep before her shearers is d', 481
56:10 they are all d' dogs, they cannot 483
Eze 3:26 thou shalt be d', and shalt not be 481
24:27 shalt speak, and be no more d': "
33:22 was opened, and I was no more d'. "
Da 10:15 toward the ground, and I became d'. "
Hab 2:18 trusteth therein, to make d' idols? 483
19 Awake; to the d' stone, Arise, 1748
M't 9:32 brought to him a d' man possessed 2974
33 devil was cast out, the d' spake: "
12:22 with a devil, blind, and d': and he "
22 that the blind and d' both spake "
15:30 blind, d', maimed, and many others,"
31 when they saw the d' to speak, "
M'r 7:37 deaf to hear, and the d' to speak. 216
9:17 my son, which hath a d' spirit; "
25 Thou d' and deaf spirit, I charge "
Lu 1:20 shalt be d', and not able to speak, *4623
11:14 casting out a devil, and it was d'. 2974
14 devil was gone out, the d' spake. "
Ac 8:32 like a lamb d' before his shearer, 880
1Co 12: 2 carried away unto these d' idols, "
2Pe 2:16 d' ass speaking with man's voice "

dung See also DUNGHILL.
Ex 29:14 bullock, and his skin, and his d', 6569

Le 4:11 his legs, and his inwards, and his d', 6569
8:17 and his hide, his flesh, and his d', "
16:27 skins, their flesh, and their d'. "
Nu 19: 5 flesh, and her blood, with her d', "
1Ki 14:10 as a man taketh away d', till it be 1557
2Ki 6:25 fourth part of a cab of dove's d' 2755
9:37 Jezebel shall be as d' upon the face 1828
18:27 they may eat their own d', 2716 (6675)
Ne 2:13 and to the d' port, and viewed the 830
3:13 cubits on the wall unto the d' gate. "
14 But the d' gate repaired Malchiah "
12:31 upon the wall toward the d' gate: "
Job 20: 7 shall perish for ever like his own d':1561
Ps 83:10 they became as d' for the earth. 1828
Isa 36:12 may eat their own d', 2716 (6675)
Jer 8: 2 they shall be for d' upon the face 1828
9:22 shall fall as d' upon the open field, "
16: 4 they shall be as d' upon the face of "
25:33 they shall be d' upon the ground. "
Eze 4:12 and thou shalt bake it with d' that 1561
15 Lo I have given thee cow's d' 6832
15 fo man's d', and thou shalt 1561
Zep 1:17 as dust, and their flesh as the d'. "
Mal 2: 3 spread d' upon your faces, even 6569
3 even the d' of your solemn feasts; "
Lu 13: 8 I shall dig about it, and d' it: 906, 2874
Ph'p 3: 8 and do count them but d', that I *4657

dungeon
Ge 40:15 that they should put me into the d'.953
41:14 brought him hastily out of the d': "
Ex 12:29 the captive that was in the d':1004, "
Jer 37:16 was entered into the d', "
38: 6 cast him into the d' of Malchiah the "
6 And in the d' there was no water, but "
7 they had put Jeremiah into the d'; "
9 whom they have cast into the d'; and "
10 Jeremiah the prophet out of the d', "
11 let them down by cords into the d' to "
13 cords, and took him up out of the d': "
La 3:53 They have cut off my life in the d', "
55 thy name, O Lord, out of the low d'. "

dung-gate See DUNG and GATE.

dunghill See also DUNGHILLS.
1Sa 2: 8 lifted up the beggar from the d', 830
Ezr 6:11 his house be made a d' for this. 5122
Ps 113: 7 and lifteth the needy out of the d'; 830
Isa 25:10 as straw is trodden down for the d'. 4087
Da 2: 5 your houses shall be made a d'. 5122
3:29 their houses shall be made a d': "
Lu 14:35 for the land, nor yet for the d'; 2874

dunghills
La 4: 5 brought up in scarlet embrace d'. 830

Dura (*doo'-rah*)
Da 3: 1 he set it up in the plain of D', in the 1757

durable
Pr 8:18 yea, d' riches and righteousness. 6276
Isa 23:18 sufficiently, and for d' clothing. 6266

dureth See also ENDURETH.
M't 13:21 root in himself, but d' for a while:*2076

durst
Es 7: 5 that d' presume in his heart to do so?
Job 32: 6 d' not shew you mine opinion. 3372
M't 22:46 neither d' any man from that day 5111
M'r 12:34 no man after that d' ask him any "
Lu 20:40 they d' not ask him any question "
Joh 21:12 none of the disciples d' ask him, "
Ac 5:13 And of the rest d' no man join "
7:32 Moses trembled, and d' not behold. "
Jude 9 d' not bring against him a railing "

dust
Ge 2: 7 Lord God formed man of the d' of 6083
3:14 and d' shalt thou eat all the days of "
19 wast thou taken; for d' thou art, "
19 and unto d' shalt thou return. "
13:16 as the d' of the earth: so that if a "
16 man can number the d' of the earth, "
18:27 Lord, which am but d' and ashes: "
28:14 shall be as the d' of the earth, "
Ex 8:16 smite the d' of the land, that it "
17 and smote the d' of the earth, "
17 in beast; all the d' of the land "
9: 9 And it shall become small d' in all 80
Le 14:41 they shall pour out the d' that *6083
17:13 blood thereof, and cover it with d'. "
Nu 5:17 and of the d' that is in the floor of "
23:10 Who can count the d' of Jacob, "
De 9:21 until it was as small as d': and "
21 I cast the d' thereof into the brook "
28:24 the rain of thy land powder and d': "
32:24 the poison of serpents of the d'. "
Jos 7: 6 and put d' upon their heads. "
1Sa 2: 8 raiseth up the poor out of the d', "
2Sa 16:13 threw stones at him, and cast d'. "
22:43 I beat them as small as the d' of "
1Ki 16: 2 I exalted thee out of the d', "
18:38 the wood, and the stones, and the d', "
20:10 if the d' of Samaria shall suffice "
2Ki 13: 7 and had made them like the d' by "
23:12 cast the d' of them into the brook "
2Ch 1: 9 people like the d' of the earth "
34: 4 and made d' of them, and strowed 1854
Job 2:12 sprinkled d' upon their heads 6083
4:19 whose foundation is in the d', "
5: 6 affliction cometh not forth of the d', "
7: 5 with worms and with clods of d'; "
21 now shall I sleep in the d'; and "
10: 9 wilt thou bring me into d' again? "
14:19 grow out of the d' of the earth; "
16:15 and defiled my horn in the d'. "
17:16 our rest together is in the d'. "
20:11 shall lie down with him in the d' "
21:26 They shall lie down alike in the d', "
22:24 Then shalt thou lay up gold as d', "
Job 27:16 Though he heap up silver as the d',6083
28: 6 sapphires: and it hath d' of gold. "
30:19 I am become like d' and ashes. "
34:15 man shall turn again unto d'. "
38:38 When the d' groweth into hardness, "
39:14 earth, and warmeth them in d', "
40:13 Hide them in the d' together; "
42: 6 and repent in d' and ashes. "
Ps 7: 5 and lay mine honour in the d'. "
18:42 I beat them small as the d' before "
22:15 brought me into the d' of death. "
29 they that go down to the d' shall "
30: 9 Shall the d' praise thee? shall it "
44:25 our soul is bowed down to the d': "
72: 9 and his enemies shall lick the d'. "
78:27 rained flesh also upon them as d', "
102:14 stones, and favour the d' thereof. "
103:14 he remembereth that we are d'. "
104:29 they die, and return to their d'. "
113: 7 raiseth up the poor out of the d', "
119:25 My soul cleaveth unto the d': "
Pr 8:26 highest part of the d' of the world. "
Ec 3:20 all are of the d', and all turn to d' "
12: 7 shall the d' return to the earth "
Isa 2:10 and hide thee in the d', for fear of "
5:24 their blossom shall go up as d': 80
25:12 to the ground, even to the d'. 6083
26: 5 he bringeth it even to the d'. "
19 and sing, ye that dwell in d': "
29: 4 speech shall be low out of the d', "
4 speech shall whisper out of the d'. "
5 strangers shall be like small d', 80
34: 7 their d' made fat with fatness. 6083
9 and the d' thereof into brimstone, "
40:12 comprehended the d' of the earth "
15 as the small d' of the balance: 7834
41: 2 gave them as the d' to his sword, 6083
47: 1 Come down, and sit in the d', "
49:23 and lick up the d' of thy feet; "
52: 2 Shake thyself from the d'; arise, "
65:25 and d' shall be the serpent's meat. "
La 2:10 have cast up d' upon their heads; "
3:29 He putteth his mouth in the d'; "
Eze 24: 7 the ground, to cover it with d'; "
26: 4 I will also scrape her d' from her, "
10 his horses their d' shall cover thee: 80
12 timber and thy d' in the midst of 6083
27:30 shall cast up d' upon their heads, "
Da 12: 2 many of them that sleep in the d' "
Am 2: 7 that pant after the d' of the earth "
Mic 1:10 of Aphrah roll thyself in the d'. "
7:17 shall lick the d' like a serpent, "
Na 1: 3 the clouds are the d' of his feet. 80
3:18 thy nobles shall dwell in the d': *
Hab 1:10 they shall heap d', and take it. 6083
Zep 1:17 blood shall be poured out as d', "
Zec 9: 3 heaped up silver as the d', and fine "
M't 10:14 city, shake off the d' of your feet. 2868
M'r 6:11 shake off the d' under your feet 5522
Lu 9: 5 shake off the very d' from your feet 2868
10:11 Even the very d' of your city, which "
Ac 13:51 they shook off the d' of their feet "
22:23 clothes, and threw d' into the air, "
Re 18:19 And they cast d' on their heads, 5522

duty
Ex 21:10 and her d' of marriage, shall he not
De 25: 5 d' of an husband's brother unto her.
7 the d' of my husband's brother.
2Ch 8:14 as the d' of every day required: 1697
Ezr 3: 4 as the d' of every day required; "
Ec 12:13 for this is the whole d' of man.
Lu 17:10 done that which was our d' to do. 3784
Ro 15:27 their d' is also to minister unto * "

dwarf
Le 21:20 crookbackt, or a d', or that hath 1851

dwell See also DWELLED; DWELLEST; DWELLETH; DWELLING; DWELT.
Ge 4:20 the father of such as d' in tents, 3427
9:27 he shall d' in the tents of Shem; 7931
13: 6 that they might d' together: for 3427
6 so that they could not d' together. "
16:12 he shall d' in the presence of all 7931
19:30 he feared to d' in Zoar: and he 3427
20:15 thee: d' where it pleaseth thee. "
24: 3 the Canaanites, among whom I d': "
37 the Canaanites, in whose land I d': "
26: 2 d' in the land which I shall tell 7931
30:20 now will my husband d' with me, 2082
34:10 And ye shall d' with us: and the 3427
10 d' and trade ye therein, and get you "
16 and we will d' with you, and we "
21 therefore let them d' in the land, "
22 consent unto us for to d' with us, "
23 unto them, and they will d' with us. "
35: 1 go up to Beth-el, and d' there: and "
36: 7 than that they might d' together; "
45:10 thou shalt d' in the land of Goshen, "
46:34 ye may d' in the land of Goshen; "
47: 4 servants d' in the land of Goshen. "
6 make thy father and brethren to d'; "
6 in the land of Goshen let them d': "
49:13 Zebulun shall d' at the haven of 7931
Ex 2:21 Moses was content to d' with the 3427
8:22 Goshen, in which my people d', 5975
15:17 thou hast made for thee to d' in, 3427
23:33 They shall not d' in thy land, lest "
25: 8 that I may d' among them. 7931
29:45 d' among the children of Israel, "
46 that I may d' among them: I am "
Le 13:46 he shall d' alone; without the camp3427
20:22 whither I bring you to d' therein, "
23:42 Ye shall d' in booths seven days; "
42 Israelites born shall d' in booths: "
43 children of Israel to d' in booths, "
25:18 ye shall d' in the land in safety. "
Le 25:19 your fill, and d' therein in safety. 3427
26: 5 the full, and d' in your land safely. "
32 your enemies which d' therein "
Nu 5: 3 camps, in the midst whereof I d'. 7931
13:19 what the land is that they d' in, 3427
19 that they d' in, whether in tents, "
28 people be strong that d' in the land, "
29 The Amalekites d' in the land of * "
29 the Amorites, d' in the mountains: "
29 and the Canaanites d' by the sea, * "
14:30 make you d' therein, save Caleb 7931
23: 9 the people shall d' alone, and shall "
32:17 ones shall d' in the fenced cities 3427
33:53 of the land, and d' therein: for I "
55 vex you in the land wherein ye d'. "
35: 2 of their possession cities to d' in; "
3 the cities shall they have to d' in; "
32 should come again to d' in the land, "
34 ye shall inhabit, wherein I d': for 7931
34 d' among the children of Israel. "
De 2: 4 children of Esau, which d' in Seir; 3427
29 children of Esau which d' in Seir, "
29 and the Moabites which d' in Ar, "
11:30 which d' in the champaign over "
31 ye shall possess it, and d' therein. "
12:10 and d' in the land which the Lord "
10 round about, so that ye d' in safety; "
11 to cause his name to d' there; 7931
13:12 God hath given thee to d' there, 3427
17:14 possess it, and shalt d' therein, "
23:16 He shall d' with thee, even among "
25: 5 If brethren d' together, and one of "
28:30 and thou shalt not d' therein: "
30:20 that thou mayest d' in the land "
33:12 Lord shall d' in safety by him; 7931
12 he shall d' between his shoulders.* "
28 Israel then shall d' in safety * "
Jos 9: 7 Peradventure ye d' among us; 3427
22 from you; when ye d' among us? "
10: 6 d' in the mountains are gathered "
13:13 the Maachathites d' among the * "
14: 4 cities to d' in, with their suburbs "
15:63 Jebusites d' with the children * "
16:10 but the Canaanites d' among the* "
17:12 Canaanites would d' in that land. "
16 that d' in the land of the valley "
20: 4 place, that he may d' among them. "
6 And he shall d' in that city, "
21: 2 of Moses to give us cities to d' in, "
24:13 ye built not, and ye d' in them; "
15 the Amorites, in whose land ye d': "
J'g 1:21 Jebusites d' with the children * "
27 Canaanites would d' in that land. "
35 Amorites would d' in mount Heres "
6:10 in whose land ye d': but ye have "
9:41 they should not d' in Shechem. "
17:10 Micah said unto him, D' with me, "
11 the Levite was content to d' with "
18: 1 sought them an inheritance to d' in; "
1Sa 12: 8 and made them d' in this place. "
27: 5 country, that I may d' there: for "
5 why should thy servant d' in the "
2Sa 7: 2 I d' in an house of cedar, but the ark "
5 build me an house for me to d' in? "
10 that they may d' in a place of their 7931
1Ki 2:36 house in Jerusalem, and d' there, 3427
3:17 I and this woman d' in one house; "
6:13 And I will d' among the children 7931
8:12 The Lord said that he would d' in "
13 built thee an house to d' in, a *2073
27 will God indeed d' on the earth? 3427
17: 9 belongeth to Zidon, and d' there: "
2Ki 4:13 I d' among mine own people. "
6: 1 the place where we d' with thee "
2 a place there, where we may d'. "
17:27 let them go and d' there, "
25:24 d' in the land, and serve the king "
1Ch 17: 1 I d' in an house of cedars, "
4 not build me an house to d' in: "
9 and they shall d' in their place, 7931
23:25 may d' in Jerusalem for ever: "
2Ch 2: 3 build him an house to d' therein, 3427
6: 1 he would d' in the thick darkness. 7931
18 will God in very deed d' with men 3427
8: 2 the children of Israel to d' there. "
11 shall not d' in the house of David "
19:10 brethren that d' in their cities, "
Ezr 4:17 companions that d' in Samaria, 3488
6:12 hath caused his name to d' there 7932
Ne 8:14 the children of Israel should d' in 3427
11: 1 to d' in Jerusalem the holy city, "
2 themselves to d' at Jerusalem. "
Job 3: 5 stain it; let a cloud d' upon it; 7931
4:19 in them that d' in houses of clay, "
11:14 wickedness d' in thy tabernacles. "
18:15 It shall d' in his tabernacle, "
19:15 They that d' in mine house, and 1481
30: 6 To d' in the cliffs of the valleys, 7931
Ps 4: 8 Lord, only makest me d' in safety. 3427
5: 4 neither shall evil d' with thee. *1481
15: 1 who shall d' in thy holy hill? 7931
23: 6 I will d' in the house of the Lord 3427
24: 1 world, and they that d' therein. "
25:13 His soul shall d' at ease; and his 3885
27: 4 I may d' in the house of the Lord 3427
37: 3 So shalt thou d' in the land, and 7931
27 and do good; and d' for evermore. "
29 inherit the land, and d' therein for "
65: 4 that he may d' in thy courts: "
8 They also that d' in the uttermost 3427
68: 6 but the rebellious d' in a dry land. 7931
16 hill which God desireth to d' in; *3427
16 yea, the Lord will d' in it for ever. 7931
18 Lord God might d' among them "
69:25 and let none d' in their tents. 3427
35 that they may d' there, and have * "

Ps 69:36 they that love his name shall d' 7931
72: 9 that d' in the wilderness shall bow
78:55 made the tribes of Israel to d' 7931
84: 4 Blessed are they that d' in thy 3427
10 to d' in the tents of wickedness. 1752
85: 9 that glory may d' in our land. 7931
98: 7 world, and they that d' therein. 3427
101: 6 the land, that they may d' with me: "
7 shall not d' within my house: "
107: 4 way; they found no city to d' in. *4186
34 of them that d' therein. 3427
36 there he maketh the hungry to d'. "
120: 5 I d' in the tents of Kedar! 7931
132:14 here will I d'; for I have desired it. 3427
133: 1 brethren to d' together in unity! "
139: 9 and d' in the uttermost parts of the 7931
140:13 upright shall d' in thy presence. 3427
143: 3 he hath made me to d' in darkness, "
Pr 1:33 hearkeneth unto me shall d' 7931
2:21 the upright shall d' in the land, "
8:12 I wisdom d' with prudence, and * "
21: 9 to d' in the corner of the housetop, 3427
19 It is better to d' in the wilderness, "
25:24 to d' in the corner of the housetop, "
Isa 6: 5 I d' in the midst of a people of "
9: 2 that d' in the land of the shadow * "
11: 6 wolf also shall d' with the lamb, 1481
13:21 owls shall d' there, and satyrs 7931
16: 4 Let mine outcasts d' with thee, 1481
23:13 them that d' in the wilderness: †
18 them that d' before the Lord, to 3427
24: 6 they that d' therein are desolate: "
26: 5 down them that d' on high; the "
19 and sing, ye that d' in dust: for 7931
30:19 For the people shall d' in Zion at 3427
32:16 shall d' in the wilderness, and 7931
18 d' in a peaceable habitation, *3427
33:14 shall d' with the devouring fire? 1481
14 shall d' with everlasting "
16 He shall d' on high: his place of 7931
24 the people that d' therein shall 3427
34:11 the raven shall d' in it: and he 7931
17 generation shall they d' therein. "
40:22 them out as a tent to d' in: 3427
49:20 give place to me that I may d'. "
51: 6 d' therein shall die in like manner: "
57:15 I d' in the high and holy place, 7931
58:12 The restorer of paths to d' in. 3427
65: 9 and my servants shall d' there. 7931
Jer 4:29 forsaken, and not a man d' therein. 3427
7: 3 I will cause you to d' in this place. 7931
7 will I cause you to d' in this place, "
8:16 city, and those that d' therein. 3427
19 of them that d' in a far country: * "
9:26 corners, that d' in the wilderness: 3427
12: 4 wickedness of them that d' therein? "
20: 6 all that d' in thine house shall go "
23: 6 Israel shall d' safely: and this 7931
8 they shall d' in their own land. 3427
24: 8 them that d' in the land of Egypt: "
25: 5 and d' in the land that the Lord "
24 people that d' in the desert, 7931
27:11 they shall till it, and d' therein. 3427
29: 5 Build ye houses, and d' in them; "
28 build ye houses, and d' in them; "
32 a man to d' among his people; "
31:24 And there shall d' in Judah itself, "
32:37 and I will cause them to d' safely: "
33:16 and Jerusalem shall d' safely: 7931
35: 7 all your days ye shall d' in tents; 3427
9 Nor to build houses for us to d' in: "
11 Syrians: so we d' at Jerusalem. "
15 and ye shall d' in the land which "
40: 5 and d' with him among the people: "
9 d' in the land, and serve the king "
10 for me, behold, I will d' at Mizpah, "
10 and d' in your cities that ye have "
42:13 We will not d' in this land, neither "
14 of bread: and there will we d': "
43: 4 Lord, to d' in the land of Judah. "
5 driven, to d' in the land of Judah; *1481
44: 1 which d' in the land of Egypt, *3427
1 which d' at Migdol, and at * "
8 whither ye be gone to d', that *1481
13 I will punish them that d' in the 3427
14 have a desire to return to d' there: "
26 Judah that d' in the land of Egypt; "
47: 2 the city, and them that d' therein: "
48: 9 desolate, without any to d' therein. "
28 O ye that d' in Moab, leave the * "
28 cities, and d' in the rock, and be 7931
49: 1 and his people d' in his cities? 3427
8 Flee ye, turn back, d' deep, O "
18 neither shall a son of man d' in it. *1481
30 Flee, get you far off, d' deep, O ye 3427
31 gates nor bars which d' alone. 7931
33 nor any son of man d' in it. *1481
50: 3 none shall d' therein: they shall 3427
39 beasts of the islands shall d' there, "
39 and the owls shall d' therein: and "
40 shall any son of man d' therein. *1481
51: 1 against them that d' in the midst 3427
Eze 2: 6 thou dost d' among scorpions: "
12:19 violence of all them that d' therein. "
16:46 daughters that d' at thy left hand: * "
17:23 and under it shall d' all fowl 7931
23 the branches thereof shall they d'. "
28:25 then shall they d' in their land 3427
26 And they shall d' safely therein, "
26 yea, they shall d' with confidence, "
32:15 shall smite all them that d' therein, "
34:25 and they shall d' safely in the "
28 but they shall d' safely, and none "
36:28 And ye shall d' in the land that "
33 also cause you to d' in the cities, * "
37:25 And they shall d' in the land that "

Eze 37:25 and they shall d' therein, even they, 3427
38: 8 and they shall d' safely all of them. "
11 that are at rest, that d' safely, "
12 that d' in the midst of the land. "
39: 6 among them that d' carelessly "
9 they that d' in the cities of Israel "
43: 7 where I will d' in the midst of the 7931
9 and I will d' in the midst of them "
Da 2:38 wheresoever the children of men d', 1753
4: 1 that d' in all the earth; Peace be "
6:25 that d' in all the earth; Peace be "
Ho 9: 3 shall not d' in the Lord's land; 3427
12: 9 make thee to d' in tabernacles, "
14: 7 They that d' under his shadow "
Joe 3:20 Judah shall d' for ever, and * "
Am 3:12 be taken out that d' in Samaria * "
5:11 but ye shall not d' in them; "
9: 5 all that d' therein shall mourn: "
Mic 4:10 and thou shalt d' in the field, 7931
7:13 because of them that d' therein, 3427
14 which d' solitarily in the wood, 7931
Na 1: 5 the world, and all that d' therein. 3427
3:18 thy nobles shall d' in the dust: *7931
Hab 2: 8 the city, and of all that d' therein. 3427
17 city, and of all that d' therein. "
Zep 1:18 of all them that d' in the land. "
Hag 1: 4 to d' in your cieled houses, and "
Zec 2:10 I come, and I will d' in the midst 7931
11 people: and I will d' in the midst "
8: 3 will d' in the midst of Jerusalem: "
4 and old women d' in the streets 3427
8 shall d' in the midst of Jerusalem: 7931
9: 6 And a bastard shall d' in Ashdod, 3427
14:11 And men shall d' in it, and there "
M't 12:45 and they enter in and d' there: 2730
Lu 11:26 and they enter in, and d' there: "
21:35 all them that d' on the face of the 2521
Ac 1:20 and let no man d' therein: 2730
2:14 and all ye that d' at Jerusalem, "
4:16 to all them that d' in Jerusalem; "
7: 4 into this land, wherein ye now d'. "
13:27 For they that d' at Jerusalem, and "
17:26 to d' on all the face of the earth, "
28:16 Paul was suffered to d' by himself *3306
Ro 8: 9 that the Spirit of God d' in you. *3611
11 raised up Jesus from the dead d' * "
1Co 7:12 and she be pleased to d' with him, "
13 if he be pleased to d' with her, "
2Co 6:16 God hath said, I will d' in them, 1774
Eph 3:17 That Christ may d' in your hearts 2730
Col 1:19 that in him should all fulness d'; "
3:16 Let the word of Christ d' in you 1774
1Pe 3: 7 husbands d' with them according 4924
1Jo 4:13 know we that we d' in him, *3306
Re 3:10 try them that d' upon the earth. 2730
6:10 blood on them that d' on the earth? "
7:15 the throne shall d' among them. *4637
11:10 they that d' upon the earth shall 2730
10 tormented them that d' on the earth. "
12:12 heavens, and ye that d' in them. 4637
13: 6 and them that d' in heaven. "
8 all that d' upon the earth shall 2730
12 which d' therein to worship the "
14 And deceiveth them that d' on the "
14 saying to them that d' on the earth, "
14: 6 to preach unto them that d' on "
17: 8 and they that d' on the earth shall "
21: 3 and he will d' with them, and they 4637

dwelled See also DWELT.
Ge 13: 7 the Perizzite d' then in the land. 3427
12 Abram d' in the land of Canaan, "
12 and Lot d' in the cities of the plain, "
20: 1 and d' between Kadesh and Shur, * "
Ru 1: 4 and they d' there about ten years. "
1Sa 12:11 on every side, and ye d' safe. "

dwellers
Isa 18: 3 of the world, and d' on the earth, 7931
Ac 1:19 known unto all the d' at Jerusalem; 2730
2: 9 and the d' in Mesopotamia, and in "

dwellest
De 12:29 them, and d' in their land; 3427
19: 1 them, and d' in their cities, "
26: 1 and possessest it, and d' therein; "
2Ki 19:15 which d' between the cherubims, * "
Ps 80: 1 that d' between the cherubims, * "
123: 1 O thou that d' in the heavens. "
Ca 8:13 Thou that d' in the gardens, the "
Isa 10:24 O my people that d' in Zion, "
37:16 that d' between the cherubims, * "
47: 8 to pleasures, that d' carelessly, "
Jer 49:16 O thou that d' in the clefts of the 7931
51:13 O thou that d' upon many waters, "
La 4:21 Edom, that d' in the land of Uz; 3427
Eze 7: 7 O thou that d' in the land: "
12: 2 thou d' in the midst of a rebellious "
Ob 3 that d' in the clefts of the rock, 7931
Zec 2: 7 d' with the daughter of Babylon. 3427
Joh 1:38 Master,) where d' thou? *3306
Re 2:13 and where thou d', even where 2730

dwelleth
Le 19:34 the stranger that d' with you *1481
25:39 And if thy brother that d' by thee *
47 and thy brother that d' by him *
Nu 13:18 people that d' therein, whether 3427
De 33:20 he d' as a lion, and teareth the arm 7931
Jos 6:25 and she d' in Israel even unto *3427
22:19 wherein the Lord's tabernacle d', 7931
1Sa 4: 4 which d' between the cherubims: *3427
27:11 while he d' in the country of the * "
2Sa 6: 2 that d' between the cherubims. * "
7: 2 the ark of God d' within curtains. "
1Ch 13: 6 that d' between the cherubims, * "
Job 15:28 And he d' in desolate cities, and *7931
38:19 Where is the way where light d'? * "

Job 39:28 She d' and abideth on the rock, 7931
Ps 9:11 to the Lord, which d' in Zion: 3427
26: 8 the place where thine honour d'. 4908
91: 1 He that d' in the secret place of the 3427
113: 5 the Lord our God, who d' on high, * "
135:21 of Zion, which d' at Jerusalem. 7931
Pr 3:29 seeing he d' securely by thee. 3427
Isa 8:18 of hosts, which d' in mount Zion. 7931
33: 5 for he d' on high: he hath filled "
Jer 29:16 of all the people that d' in this *3427
44: 2 desolation, and no man d' therein, "
49:31 nation that d' without care, "
51:43 a land wherein no man d', neither "
La 1: 3 she d' among the heathen, she "
Eze 16:46 that d' at thy right hand, is Sodom "
17:16 the place where the king d' that "
38:14 when my people of Israel d' safely, 3427
Da 2:22 darkness, and the light d' with 8271
Ho 4: 3 every one that d' therein shall 3427
Joe 3:21 cleansed: for the Lord d' in Zion. 7931
Am 8: 8 every one mourn that d' therein? 3427
M't 23:21 by it, and by him that d' therein. 2730
Joh 6:56 my blood, d' in me, and I in him. *3306
14:10 the Father that d' in me, he doeth * "
17 for he d' with you, and shall be * "
Ac 7:48 the most High d' not in temples 2730
17:24 of heaven and earth, d' not in temples "
Ro 7:17 that do it, but sin that d' in me. 3611
18 is, in my flesh,) d' no good thing: "
20 I that do it, but sin that d' in me. "
8:11 bodies by his Spirit that d' in you. 1774
1Co 3:16 and that the Spirit of God d' in you? 3611
Col 2: 9 in him d' all the fulness of the 2730
2Ti 1:14 the Holy Ghost which d' in us. 1774
Jas 4: 5 The spirit that d' in us lusteth *2730
2Pe 3:13 earth, wherein d' righteousness. "
1Jo 3:17 how d' the love of God in him? *3306
24 his commandments d' in him, * "
4:12 God d' in us, and his love is * "
15 God d' in him, and he in God. * "
16 he that d' in love d' in God, and * "
2Jo 2 the truth's sake, which d' in us, * "
Re 2:13 slain among you, where Satan d'. 2730

dwelling See also DWELLINGPLACE; DWELLINGS.
Ge 10:30 their d' was from Mesha, as thou 4186
25:27 Jacob was a plain man, d' in tents. 3427
27:39 thy d' shall be the fatness of the 4186
Le 25:29 if a man sell a d' house in a walled "
Nu 21:15 that goeth down to the d' of Ar, 3427
Jos 13:21 dukes of Sihon, d' in the country. * "
1Ki 8:30 and hear thou in heaven thy d' "
39 Then hear thou in heaven thy d' "
43 Hear thou in heaven thy d' place, "
49 supplication in heaven thy d' place, "
21: 8 were in his city, d' with Naboth. "
2Ki 17:25 the beginning of their d' there, that "
1Ch 6:32 they ministered before the d' *4908
54 are their d' places throughout 4186
2Ch 6: 2 a place for thy d' for ever. *3427
21 hear thou from thy d' place, even "
30 hear thou from heaven thy d' place, "
33 even from thy d' place, and do "
39 even from thy d' place, their prayer, "
30:27 came up to his holy d' place, *4583
36:15 his people, and on his d' place: "
Job 8:22 and the d' place of the wicked * 168
21:28 are the d' places of the wicked? *4908
Ps 49:11 their d' places to all generations; "
14 consume in the grave from their d'. *2073
52: 5 pluck thee out of thy d' place, * 168
74: 7 down the d' place of thy name 4908
76: 2 and his d' place in Zion. 4585
79: 7 Jacob, and laid waste his d' place. *5116
90: 1 Lord, thou hast been our d' place 4583
91:10 shall any plague come nigh thy d'. * 168
Pr 21:20 and oil in the d' of the wise; 5116
24:15 against the d' of the righteous; * "
Isa 4: 5 every d' place of mount Zion, *4349
18: 4 I will consider in my d' place "
Jer 46:19 O thou daughter d' in Egypt, *3427
49:33 Hazor shall be a d' for dragons, 4583
Eze 38:11 all of them d' without walls, and 3427
48:15 the city, for d', and for suburbs: 4186
Da 2:11 gods, whose d' is not with flesh. 4070
4:25, 32 thy d' shall be with the beasts "
5:21 and his d' was with the wild asses: "
Joe 3:17 the Lord your God d' in Zion, 7931
Na 2:11 Where is the d' of the lions, *4583
Zep 3: 7 so their d' should not be cut off, "
M'r 5: 3 Who had his d' among the tombs; 2731
Ac 2: 5 And there were d' at Jerusalem 2730
19:17 Greeks also d' at Ephesus; and * "
1Ti 6:16 d' in the light which no man can 3611
Heb 11: 9 d' in tabernacles with Isaac and 2730
2Pe 2: 8 righteous man d' among them, 1460

dwelling-house See DWELLING and HOUSE.

dwellingplace See also DWELLING and PLACE; DWELLINGPLACES.
Nu 24:21 Strong is thy d', and thou puttest 4186
Jer 51:37 Babylon shall become heaps, a d' 4583
1Co 4:11 are buffeted, have no certain d'; 790

dwellingplaces
Jer 30:18 tents, and have mercy on his d'; 4908
51:30 women: they have burned her d'; "
Eze 6: 6 In all your d' the cities shall be 4186
37:23 I will save them out of all their d', "
Hab 1: 6 possess the d' that are not theirs. 4908

dwellings
Ex 10:23 of Israel had light in their d'. 4186
Le 3:17 throughout all your d', that ye eat "
7:26 fowl or of beast, in any of your d'. "
23: 3 sabbath of the Lord in all your d'. "
14 your generations in all your d'. "
21 for ever in all your d' throughout "

Le 23:31 your generations in all your d'. 4186
Nu 35:29 your generations in all your d'. "
Job 18:19 nor any remaining in his d'. *4033
21 such are the d' of the wicked, 4908
39: 6 and the barren land his d'. * "
Ps 55:15 wickedness is in their d', and *4033
87: 2 Zion more than all the d' of Jacob.4908
Isa 32:18 and in sure d', and in quiet resting "
Jer 9:19 because our d' have cast us out. "
Eze 25: 4 thee, and to make their d' in thee: "
Zep 2: 6 And the sea coast shall be d' and *5116

dwelt See also DWELLED.
Ge 4:16 the Lord, and d' in the land of Nod, 3427
11: 2 land of Shinar; and they d' there. "
31 came unto Haran, and d' there. "
13:18 and d' in the plain of Mamre, "
14: 7 Amorites, that d' in Hazezon-tamar."
12 who d' in Sodom, and his goods, "
13 for he d' in the plain of Mamre 7931
16: 3 after Abram had d' ten years in 3427
19:29 the cities in the which Lot d'. "
30 and d' in the mountain, and his two"
30 and he d' in a cave, he and his two "
21:20 grew, and d' in the wilderness, "
21 he d' in the wilderness of Paran: "
22:19 and Abraham d' at Beer-sheba. "
23:10 Ephron d' among the children of* "
24:62 for he d' in the south country. "
25:11 Isaac d' by the well Lahai-roi. "
18 they d' from Havilah unto Shur, 7931
26: 6 And Isaac d' in Gerar: 3427
17 the valley of Gerar, and d' there. "
35:22 when Israel d' in that land, that 7931
36: 8 Thus d' Esau in mount Seir: 3427
37: 1 And Jacob d' in the land wherein "
38:11 Tamar went and d' in her father's "
47:27 And Israel d' in the land of Egypt, "
50:22 And Joseph d' in Egypt, he, and his"
Ex 2:15 and d' in the land of Midian: "
12:40 of Israel, who d' in Egypt, * "
Le 18: 3 the land of Egypt, wherein ye d', "
26:35 sabbaths, when ye d' upon it. "
Nu 14:25 the Canaanites d' in the valley.) * "
45 Canaanites which d' in that hill, "
20:15 we have d' in Egypt a long time; "
21: 1 which d' in the south, heard tell "
25 and Israel d' in all the cities of the "
31 Israel d' in the land of the Amorites."
34 Amorites, which d' at Heshbon. "
31:10 all their cities wherein they d', 4186
32:40 Manasseh; and he d' therein. 3427
33:40 which d' in the south in the land of"
De 1: 4 which d' in Heshbon, and Og the "
4 which d' at Astaroth in Edrei: "
6 have d' long enough in this mount:"
44 which d' in that mountain, came "
2: 8 Esau, which d' in Seir, through * "
10 Emims d' therein in times past, "
12 Horims also d' in Seir beforetime; "
12 before them, and d' in their stead; "
20 giants d' therein in old time; "
21 them, and d' in their stead: "
22 children of Esau, which d' in Seir,* "
22 and d' in their stead even unto "
23 the Avims which d' in Hazerim, "
23 them, and d' in their stead.) "
3: 2 the Amorites, which d' at Heshbon."
4:46 who d' at Heshbon, whom Moses "
8:12 built goodly houses, and d' therein;"
29:16 we have d' in the land of Egypt; "
33:16 will of him that d' in the bush: 7931
Jos 2:15 and she d' upon the wall. 3427
7: 7 and d' on the other side Jordan! "
9:16 and that they d' among them. "
12: 2 who d' in Heshbon, and ruled "
4 that d' at Ashtaroth and at Edrei, "
16:10 the Canaanites that d' in Gezer: "
19:47 possessed it, and d' therein, and "
50 he built the city, and d' therein. "
21:43 they possessed it, and d' therein. "
22:33 the children of Reuben and Gad d'. "
24: 2 d' on the other side of the flood "
7 d' in the wilderness a long season. "
8 d' on the other side Jordan; "

Jos 24:18 the Amorites which d' in the land:3427
J'g 1: 9 Canaanites, that d' in the mountain,"
10 Canaanites that d' in Hebron: "
16 they went and d' among the people."
29 the Canaanites that d' in Gezer; "
29 but the Canaanites d' in Gezer "
30 but the Canaanites d' among them,"
32 Asherites d' among the Canaanites,"
33 but he d' among the Canaanites, "
3: 3 Hivites that d' in mount Lebanon, "
5 of Israel d' among the Canaanites, "
4: 2 d' in Harosheth of the Gentiles. "
5 d' under the palm tree of Deborah "
8:11 the way of them that d' in tents 7931
29 Joash went and d' in his own 3427
9:21 went to Beer, and d' there, for fear "
41 And Abimelech d' at Arumah: and "
10: 1 he d' in Shamir in mount Ephraim. "
11: 3 and d' in the land of Tob: "
26 Israel d' in Heshbon and her towns,"
15: 8 and d' in the top of the rock Etam. "
18: 7 they d' careless, after the manner "
28 they built a city, and d' therein. "
21:23 repaired the cities, and d' in them. "
Ru 2:23 and d' with her mother in law. "
1Sa 19:18 and Samuel went and d' in Naioth. "
22: 4 and they d' with him all the while "
23:29 and d' in strong holds at En-gedi. "
27: 3 And David d' with Achish at Gath, "
7 d' in the country of the Philistines "
31: 7 Philistines came and d' in them. "
2Sa 2: 3 and they d' in the cities of Hebron. "
5: 9 David d' in the fort, and called it "
7: 6 I have not d' in any house since "
9:12 all that d' in the house of Ziba 4186
13 Mephibosheth d' in Jerusalem: 3427
14:28 So Absalom d' two full years in "
1Ki 2:38 Shimei d' in Jerusalem many days."
4:25 And Judah and Israel d' safely, "
7: 8 his house where he d' had another* "
9:16 the Canaanites that d' in the city, "
11:24 went to Damascus, and d' therein, "
12: 2 and Jeroboam d' in Egypt; "
17 which d' in the cities of Judah, "
25 in mount Ephraim, and d' therein; "
13:11 there d' an old prophet in Beth-el; "
25 the city where the old prophet d'. "
15:18 of Syria, that d' at Damascus. "
21 of Ramah, and d' in Tirzah. "
17: 5 went and d' by the brook Cherith, "
2Ki 13: 5 children of Israel d' in their tents, "
15: 5 his death, and d' in a several house."
16: 6 Elath, and d' there unto this day. "
17:24 Samaria, and d' in the cities thereof."
28 came and d' in Beth-el, and taught "
29 in their cities wherein they d'. "
19:36 and returned, and d' at Nineveh. "
22:14 she d' in Jerusalem in the college;) "
1Ch 2:55 of the scribes which d' at Jabez; "
4:23 d' among plants and hedges: * "
23 there they d' with the king "
28 d' at Beer-sheba, and Moladah, "
40 they of Ham had d' there of old. "
41 this day, and d' in their rooms: "
43 escaped, and d' there unto this day."
5: 8 who d' in Aroer, even unto Nebo "
10 they d' in their tents throughout "
11 the children of Gad d' over against "
16 And they d' in Gilead in Bashan, "
22 d' in their steads until the captivity."
23 tribe of Manasseh d' in the land: "
7:29 In these d' the children of Joseph "
8:28 chief men. These d' in Jerusalem. "
29 Gibeon d' the father of Gibeon; * "
32 d' with their brethren in Jerusalem,"
9: 2 Now the first inhabitants that d' "
3 in Jerusalem d' of the children of 3427
16 that d' in the villages of the "
34 generations; these d' at Jerusalem."
35 in Gibeon d' the father of Gibeon; "
38 d' with their brethren at Jerusalem,"
10: 7 Philistines came and d' in them. "
11: 7 And David d' in the castle; "
17: 5 I have not d' in an house since the "

2Ch 10:17 that d' in the cities of Judah, 3427
11: 5 And Rehoboam d' in Jerusalem, "
16: 2 king of Syria, that d' at Damascus, "
19: 4 And Jehoshaphat d' at Jerusalem: "
20: 8 And they d' therein, and have built "
26: 7 the Arabians that d' in Gur-baal, "
21 d' in a several house, being a leper; "
28:18 villages thereof: and they d' there. "
30:25 of Israel, and that d' in Judah, "
31: 4 the people that d' in Jerusalem to "
6 that d' in the cities of Judah, they "
34:22 she d' in Jerusalem in the college:)"
Ezr 2:70 the Nethinims, d' in their cities, "
Ne 3:26 the Nethinims d' in Ophel, unto the "
4:12 the Jews which d' by them came, "
7:73 all Israel, d' in their cities; and "
11: 1 of the people d' at Jerusalem: "
3 the province that d' in Jerusalem: "
3 but in the cities of Judah d' every "
4 at Jerusalem d' certain of the "
6 sons of Perez that d' at Jerusalem "
21 the Nethinims d' in Ophel: and "
25 of Judah d' at Kirjath-arba, "
30 they d' from Beer-sheba unto the *2583
31 also of Benjamin from Geba d' at "
13:16 There d' men of Tyre also therein, 3427
Es 9:19 that d' in the unwalled towns, * "
Job 22: 8 and the honourable man d' in it. "
29:25 and d' as a king in the army, 7931
Ps 68:10 congregation hath d' therein: 3427
74: 2 mount Zion, wherein thou hast d'. 7931
94:17 my soul had almost d' in silence. "
120: 6 My soul hath long d' with him * "
Isa 13:20 neither shall it be d' in from "
29: 1 to Ariel, the city where David d'! *2583
37:37 and returned, and d' at Nineveh. 3427
Jer 35:10 But we have d' in tents, and have "
39:14 home: so he d' among the people. "
40: 6 and d' with him among the people "
41:17 And they departed, and d' in the "
44:15 all the people that d' in the land of "
50:39 neither shall it be d' in from 7931
Eze 3:15 that d' by the river of Chebar, and 3427
31: 6 and under his shadow d' all great "
17 that d' under his shadow in the "
36:17 the house of Israel d' in their own "
37:25 wherein your fathers have d'; "
39:26 when they d' safely in their land, "
Da 4:12 the fowls of the heaven d' in the 1753
21 which the beasts of the field d', "
Zep 2:15 rejoicing city that d' carelessly, 3427
M't 2:23 and d' in a city called Nazareth: *2730*
4:13 he came and d' in Capernaum, "
Lu 1:65 on all that d' round about them: *4039*
13: 4 all men that d' in Jerusalem? **2730*
Joh 1:14 and d' among us, (and we beheld *4637*
39 They came and saw where he d', **3306*
Ac 7: 2 Mesopotamia, before he d' in *2730*
4 Chaldeans, and d' in Charran: "
9:22 the Jews which d' at Damascus, "
32 to the saints which d' at Lydda. "
35 all that d' at Lydda and Saron saw "
11:29 the brethren which d' in Judæa: "
13:17 when they d' as strangers in the **3940*
19:10 all they which d' in Asia heard *2730*
17 of all the Jews which d' there, "
28:30 Paul d' two whole years in his **3306*
2Ti 1: 5 which d' first in thy grandmother *1774*

dyed
Ex 25: 5 rams' skins d' red, and badgers'
26:14 rams' skins d' red, and a covering
35: 7 rams' skins d' red, and badgers'
36:19 rams' skins d' red, and a covering
39:34 rams' skins d' red, and the covering
Isa 63: 1 with d' garments from Bozrah? 2556
Eze 23:15 exceeding in d' attire upon their 2871

dying
Nu 17:13 shall we be consumed with d'? *1478
M'r 12:20 and the first took a wife, and d' *599*
Lu 8:42 years of age, and she lay a d'. "
2Co 4:10 bearing about in the body the d' *3500*
6: 9 known; as d', and, behold, we live; *599*
Heb 11:21 Jacob, when he was a d', blessed "

E.

each
Ge 15:10 laid e' piece one against another; 376
35:25 took e' man his sword, and came "
40: 5 them, e' man his dream in one night, "
5 one night, e' man according to the "
41:11 dreamed e' man according to the "
12 to e' man according to his dream he "
45:22 he gave e' man changes of raiment; "
Ex 18: 7 asked e' other of their welfare; "
30:34 of e' shall there be a like weight. 905
Nu 1:44 e' one was for the house of his 376
7: 3 of the princes, and for e' one an ox: "
11 offer their offering, e' prince on his 259
85 E' charger of silver weighing an "
85 thirty shekels, e' bowl seventy: "
14:34 even forty days, e' day for a year,* "
16:17 and Aaron, e' of you his censer. 376
17: 6 him a rod apiece, for e' prince one, "
29:14 two tenth deals to e' ram of the 259
15 a several tenth deal to e' lamb * "
Jos 18: 4 from among you three men for e' "
22:14 with him ten princes, of e' chief 259
14 e' one was an head of the house * "
J'g 8:18 e' one resembled the children of a "
21:22 not to e' man his wife in the war: "

Ru 1: 8 return e' to her mother's house: 802
9 e' of you in the house of her husband."
1Ki 4: 7 e' man his month in a year made 259
6:23 two cherubims of olive tree, e' ten "
22:10 sat e' on his throne, having put on 376
2Ki 9:21 e' in his chariot, and they went out "
15:20 of e' man fifty shekels of silver, 259
1Ch 20: 6 six on e' hand, and six on e' foot: "
2Ch 3:15 the top of e' of them was five cubits. "
4:13 two rows of pomegranates on e' 259
9:18 stays on e' side of the sitting "
Ne 13:24 according to the language of e' people. "
Ps 85:10 and peace have kissed e' other. "
Isa 2:20 they made e' one for himself to * "
6: 2 seraphims: e' one had six wings; 259
35: 7 of dragons, where e' lay, shall be * "
57: 2 e' one walking in his uprightness "
Eze 4: 6 have appointed thee e' day for a year, "
40:16 and upon e' post were palm trees. "
48 and measured e' post of the porch, "
Lu 13:15 doth not e' one of you on the *1538*
Ac 2: 3 fire, and it sat upon e' of them. "
Ph'p 2: 3 let e' esteem other better than *240*
2Th 1: 3 all toward e' other aboundeth; * "
Re 4: 8 And the four beasts had e' of them *303*

eagle See also EAGLE'S; EAGLES.
Le 11:13 the e', and the ossifrage, and the 5404
18 and the pelican and the gier e', *7360
De 14:12 not eat: the e', and the ossifrage, 5404
17 the gier e', and the cormorant, *7360
28:49 the earth, as swift as the e' flieth; 5404
32:11 As an e' stirreth up her nest, "
Job 9:26 as the e' that hasteth to the prey. "
39:27 Doth the e' mount up at thy "
Pr 23: 5 fly away as an e' toward heaven. "
30:19 The way of an e' in the air; "
Jer 48:40 Behold, he shall fly as an e', "
49:16 make thy nest as high as the e', "
22 and fly as the e', and spread his "
Eze 1:10 they four also had the face of an e'. "
10:14 and the fourth the face of an e'. "
17: 3 A great e' with great wings, long "
7 There was also another great e' "
Ho 8: 1 He shall come as an e' against the "
Ob 4 Though thou exalt thyself as the e'. "
Mic 1:16 enlarge thy baldness as the e'; "
Hab 1: 8 they shall fly as the e' that hasteth "
Re 4: 7 the fourth beast was like a flying e'. *105*
12:14 were given two wings of a great e', "

eagle's
Ps 103: 5 thy youth is renewed like the e'. *5404
Da 7: 4 was like a lion, and had e' wings; 5403
eagles See also EAGLES'.
2Sa 1:23 they were swifter than e', they 5404
Pr 30:17 and the young e' shall eat it. "
Isa 40:31 shall mount up with wings as e'; "
Jer 4:13 his horses are swifter than e'. "
La 4:19 swifter than the e' of the heaven: "
M't 24:28 is, there will the e' be gathered 105
Lu 17:37 is, thither will the e' be gathered "
eagles'
Ex 19: 4 and how I bare you on e' wings, 5404
Da 4:33 his hairs were grown like e' 5403
ear See also EARED; EARING; EARRINGS; EARS; PLOW.
Ex 9:31 for the barley was in the e', 24
15:26 wilt give e' to his commandments, 238
21: 6 his master shall bore his e' through 241
29:20 upon the tip of the right e' of Aaron, "
20 upon the tip of the right e' of his "
Le 8:23 upon the tip of Aaron's right e', "
24 upon the tip of their right e', and "
14:14, 17, 25, 28 tip of the right e' of him "
De 1:45 to your voice, nor give e' unto you. 238
15:17 it through his e' unto the door, 241
32: 1 Give e', O ye heavens, and I will 238
J'g 5: 3 give e', O ye princes; I, even I, will "
1Sa 8:12 and will set them to e' his ground,*2790
9:15 had told Samuel in his e' a day * 241
2Ki 19:16 Lord, bow down thine e', and hear: "
2Ch 24:19 them: but they would not give e'. 238
Ne 1: 6 Let thine e' now be attentive, and 241
11 thine e' be attentive to the prayer "
9:30 yet would they not give e': 238
Job 4:12 mine e' received a little thereof. 241
12:11 Doth not the e' try words? and the "
13: 1 mine e' hath heard and understood "
29:11 the e' heard me, then it blessed me; "
21 Unto me men gave e', and waited, 8085
32:11 I gave e' to your reasons, whilst * 238
34: 2 give e' unto me, ye that have "
3 the e' trieth words, as the mouth 241
36:10 openeth also their e' to discipline, "
42: 5 of thee by the hearing of the e': "
Ps 5: 1 Give e' to my words, O Lord, 238
10:17 thou wilt cause thine e' to hear: 241
17: 1 my cry, give e' unto my prayer, 238
6 incline thine e' unto me, and hear 241
31: 2 Bow down thine e' to me; deliver "
39:12 give e' unto my cry; hold not thy 238
45:10 and consider, and incline thine e'; 241
49: 1 give e', all ye inhabitants of the 238
4 I will incline mine e' to a parable: 241
54: 2 give e' to the words of my mouth. 238
55: 1 Give e' to my prayer, O God; "
58: 4 deaf adder that stoppeth her e'; 241
71: 2 incline thine e' unto me, and save "
77: 1 my voice; and he gave e' unto me. 238
78: 1 Give e', O my people, to my law: "
80: 1 Give e', O Shepherd of Israel, "
84: 8 give e', O God of Jacob. "
86: 1 down thine e', O Lord, hear me: 241
6 Give e', O Lord, unto my prayer; 238
88: 2 incline thine e' unto my cry; 241
94: 9 planted the e', shall he not hear? "
102: 2 trouble; incline thine e' unto me: "
116: 2 he hath inclined his e' unto me, "
141: 1 give e' unto my voice, when I cry 238
143: 1 O Lord, give e' to my supplications: "
Pr 2: 2 thou incline thine e' unto wisdom, 241
4:20 incline thine e' unto my sayings. "
5: 1 bow thine e' to my understanding: "
13 mine e' to them that instructed me! "
15:31 The e' that heareth the reproof of "
17: 4 liar giveth e' to a naughty tongue. 238
18:15 e' of the wise seeketh knowledge. 241
20:12 The hearing e', and the seeing eye, "
22:17 Bow down thine e', and hear the "
25:12 a wise reprover upon an obedient e'. "
28: 9 away his e' from hearing the law, "
Ec 1: 8 nor the e' filled with hearing. "
Isa 1: 2 O heavens, and give e', O earth: 238
10 give e' unto the law of our God, "
8: 9 and give e', all ye of far countries: "
28:23 Give ye e', and hear my voice; "
30:24 young asses that e' the ground *5647
32: 9 daughters; give e' unto my speech. 238
37:17 Incline thine e', O Lord, and hear; 241
42:23 among you will give e' to this? 238
48: 8 time that thine e' was not opened: 241
50: 4 wakeneth mine e' to hear as the "
5 The Lord God hath opened mine e', "
51: 4 give e' unto me, O my nation: 238
55: 3 Incline your e', and come unto me: 241
59: 1 his e' heavy, that it cannot hear: "
64: 4 not heard, nor perceived by the e', 238
Jer 6:10 behold, their e' is uncircumcised, 241
7:24 nor inclined their e', but walked in "
26 nor inclined their e', but hardened "
9:20 e' receive the word of his mouth, "
11: 8 nor inclined their e', but walked "
13:15 ye, and give e'; be not proud: 238
17:23 neither inclined their e', but made 241
25: 4 nor inclined your e' to hear. "
34:14 unto me, neither inclined their e'. "
35:15 but ye have not inclined your e', "
44: 5 nor inclined their e' to turn from "
La 3:56 hide not thine e' at my breathing, "
Da 9:18 O my God, incline thine e', and hear; "
Ho 5: 1 give ye e', O house of the king; 238
Joe 1: 2 Hear this, ye old men, and give e', "
Am 3:12 two legs, or a piece of an e'; 241
M't 10:27 what ye hear in the e', that preach 3775
26:51 high priest's, and smote off his e'. 5621
M'r 4:28 first the blade, then the e', after 4719
28 after that the full corn in the e'. "
14:47 high priest, and cut off his e'. 5621
Lu 12: 3 which ye have spoken in the e' 3775
22:50 high priest, and cut off his right e'. "
51 he touched his e', and healed him. 5621
Joh 18:10 servant, and cut off his right e'. "
26 his kinsman whose e' Peter cut off, "
1Co 2: 9 nor e' heard, neither have entered 3775
12:16 And if the e' shall say, Because I "
Re 2: 7, 11, 17, 29 He that hath an e', let him "
3: 6, 13, 22 He that hath an e', let him "
13: 9 If any man have an e', let him hear. "
eared See also PLOWED.
De 21: 4 which is neither e' nor sown, *5647
earing See also PLOWING.
Ge 45: 6 there neither be e' nor harvest. *2758
Ex 34:21 in e' time and in harvest thou * "
early
Ge 19: 2 rise up e', and go on your ways. 7925
27 Abraham gat up e' in the morning "
20: 8 Abimelech rose e' in the morning, "
21:14 Abraham rose up e' in the morning, "
22: 3 Abraham rose up e' in the morning, "
28:18 Jacob rose up e' in the morning, "
31:55 e' in the morning Laban rose up, "
Ex 8:20 Rise up e' in the morning, and "
9:13 Moses, Rise up e' in the morning, "
24: 4 and rose up e' in the morning, "
32: 6 And they rose up e' on the morrow, "
34: 4 Moses rose up e' in the morning, "
Nu 14:40 And they rose up e' in the morning, "
Jos 3: 1 And Joshua rose e' in the morning; "
6:12 And Joshua rose e' in the morning, "
15 e' about the dawning of the day, "
7:16 Joshua rose up e' in the morning, "
8:10 Joshua rose up e' in the morning, "
14 they hasted and rose up e', and the "
J'g 6:28 when the men of the city arose e' "
38 for he rose up e' on the morrow, "
7: 1 Then Jerubbaal, . . . rose up e', "
3 and depart e' from mount Gilead. *6852
9:33 rise e', and set upon the city: 7925
19: 5 when they arose e' in the morning, "
8 And he arose e' in the morning "
9 to morrow get you e' on your way, "
21: 4 the morrow, that the people rose e', "
1Sa 1:19 And they rose up in the morning e', "
5: 3 they of Ashdod arose e' on the "
4 when they arose e' on the morrow "
9:26 they arose e': and it came to pass "
15:12 when Samuel rose e' to meet Saul "
17:20 David rose up e' in the morning, "
29:10 now rise up e' in the morning "
10 and as soon as ye be up e' in the "
11 So David and his men rose up e' to "
2Sa 15: 2 And Absalom rose up e', and stood "
2Ki 3:22 And they rose up e' in the morning, "
6:15 of the man of God was risen e', "
19:35 when they arose e' in the morning, "
2Ch 20:20 And they rose e' in the morning, "
29:20 Then Hezekiah the king rose e', "
Job 1: 5 and rose up e' in the morning, "
Ps 46: 5 shall help her, and that right e'. 1242
57: 8 I myself will awake e'. 7837
63: 1 art my God; e' will I seek thee: ‡7836
78:34 and enquired e' after God. "
90:14 satisfy us e' with thy mercy; *1242
101: 8 I will e' destroy all the wicked of * "
108: 2 and harp: I myself will awake e'. 7837
127: 2 It is vain for you to rise up e', 7925
Pr 1:28 they shall seek me e', but they *7836
8:17 that seek me e' shall find me. * "
27:14 voice, rising e' in the morning, 7925
Ca 7:12 Let us get up e' to the vineyards; "
Isa 5:11 Woe unto them that rise up e' "
26: 9 within me will I seek thee e': ‡7836
37:36 they arose e' in the morning, 7925
Jer 7:13 you, rising up e' and speaking, "
25 rising up e' and sending them: "
11: 7 rising e' and protesting, saying, "
25: 3 unto you, rising e' and speaking; "
4 rising e' and sending them; "
26: 5 rising up e', and sending them, "
29:19 rising up e' and sending them; "
32:33 rising up e' and teaching them, "
35:14 rising e' and speaking; but ye "
15 rising up e' and sending them, "
44: 4 rising e' and sending them, "
Da 6:19 king arose very e' in the morning, 8238
Ho 5:15 affliction they will seek me e'. *7836
6: 4 as the e' dew it goeth away. 7925
13: 3 as the e' dew that passeth away, "
Zep 3: 7 but they rose e', and corrupted all "
M't 20: 1 went out e' in the morning to 260, 4404
M'r 16: 2 And very e' in the morning the "
9 risen e' the first day of the week, "
Lu 21:38 the people came e' in the morning 3719
24: 1 very e' in the morning, they came 3722
22 which were e' at the sepulchre; 3721
Joh 8: 2 And e' in the morning he came 3722
18:28 it was e'; and they themselves 4405
20: 1 cometh Mary Magdalene e', when 4404
Ac 5:21 e' in the morning, and taught. *3722
Jas 5: 7 he receive the e' and latter rain. 4406
earnest
Ro 8:19 the e' expectation of the creature 603
2Co 1:22 the e' of the Spirit in our hearts. 728
5: 5 given unto us the e' of the Spirit. "
7: 7 he told us your e' desire, your *1972
8:16 put the same e' care into the heart 4710
Eph 1:14 Which is the e' of our inheritance 728
Ph'p 1:20 to my e' expectation and my hope, 603
Heb 2: 1 we ought to give the more e' heed 4056
earnestly
Nu 22:37 Did I not e' send unto thee to call thee?
1Sa 20: 6 say, David e' asked leave of me that
28 David e' asked leave of me to go to
Ne 3:20 the son of Zabbai e' repaired 2734
Job 7: 2 As a servant e' desireth the shadow,
Jer 11: 7 For I e' protested unto your fathers
31:20 him, I do e' remember him still:
Mic 7: 3 may do evil with both hands e', *3190
Lu 22:44 in an agony he prayed more e': 1617
56 and e' looked upon him, and said,* 816
Ac 3:12 why look ye so e' on us, * "
23: 1 Paul, e' beholding the council, * "
1Co 12:31 But covet e' the best gifts: *2206
2Co 5: 2 e' desiring to be clothed upon *1971
Jas 5:17 prayed e' that it might not rain: *4335
Jude 3 ye should e' contend for the faith 1864
earneth
Hag 1: 6 he that e' wages, e' wages to put it 7936
earring See also EARRINGS.
Ge 24:22 golden e' of half a shekel weight, *5141
30 came to pass, when he saw the e' * "
47 I put the e' upon her face, * "
Job 42:11 and every one an e' of gold. * "
Pr 25:12 an e' of gold, and an ornament of "
earrings
Ge 35: 4 their e' which were in their ears;*5141
Ex 32: 2 Break off the golden e', which * "
3 people brake off the golden e' * "
35:22 e', and rings, and tablets, all jewels "
Nu 31:50 chains, and bracelets, rings, e', 5694
J'g 8:24 me every man the e' of his prey. 5141
24 (For they had golden e', because they "
25 every man the e' of his prey. "
26 And the weight of the golden e' "
Isa 3:20 and the tablets, and the e', *3908
Eze 16:12 e' in thine ears, and a beautiful 5694
Ho 2:13 herself with her e' and her jewels, 5141
ears
Ge 20: 8 and told all these things in their e': 241
35: 4 earrings which were in their e'; "
41: 5 seven e' of corn came up upon 7641
6 seven thin e' and blasted with the "
7 And the seven thin e' devoured the "
7 devoured the seven rank and full e'. "
22 seven e' came up in one stalk, "
23 seven e', withered, thin, and "
24 thin e' devoured the seven good e': "
26 the seven good e' are seven years: "
27 the seven empty e' blasted with "
44:18 speak a word in my lord's e', 241
50: 4 I pray you, in the e' of Pharaoh, "
Ex 10: 2 mayest tell in the e' of thy son, "
11: 2 Speak now in the e' of the people, "
17:14 rehearse it in the e' of Joshua: "
32: 2 which are in the e' of your wives, "
3 earrings which were in their e', "
Le 2:14 of thy firstfruits green e' of corn * 24
14 even corn beaten out of full e'. *3759
23:14 nor parched corn, nor green e', "
Nu 11:18 ye have wept in the e' of the Lord, 241
14:28 as ye have spoken in mine e', so "
De 5: 1 which I speak in your e' this day, "
23:25 pluck the e' with thine hand; 4425
29: 4 eyes to see, and e' to hear, unto this 241
31:28 I may speak these words in their e', "
30 Moses spake in the e' of all the "
32:44 this song in the e' of the people, "
Jos 20: 4 his cause in the e' of the elders "
J'g 7: 3 proclaim in the e' of the people, "
9: 2 Speak, I pray you, in the e' of all "
3 in the e' of all the men of Shechem "
17: 2 and spakest of also in mine e', "
Ru 2: 2 and glean e' of corn after him 7641
1Sa 3:11 the e' of every one that heareth 241
8:21 rehearse them in the e' of the Lord. "
11: 4 the tidings in the e' of the people: "
15:14 bleating of the sheep in mine e', "
18:23 those words in the e' of David. "
2Sa 3:19 also spake in the e' of Benjamin: "
19 also to speak in the e' of David "
7:22 all that we have heard with our e'. "
22: 7 my cry did enter into his e'. "
2Ki 4:42 e' of corn in the husk thereof. 3759
18:26 in the e' of the people that are on 241
19:28 tumult is come up into mine e', "
21:12 of it, both his e' shall tingle. "
23: 2 read in their e' all the words of the "
1Ch 17:20 all that we have heard with our e'. "
2Ch 6:40 and let thine e' be attent unto the "
7:15 and mine e' attent unto the prayer "
34:30 read in their e' all the words of the "
Ne 8: 3 and the e' of all the people were "
Job 13:17 and my declaration with your e'. "
15:21 A dreadful sound is in his e': "
24:24 off as the tops of the e' of corn. 7641
28:22 heard the fame thereof with our e'. 241
33:16 Then he openeth the e' of men, "
36:15 openeth their e' in oppression. * "
Ps 18: 6 came before him, even into his e'. "
34:15 and his e' are open unto their cry. "
40: 6 mine e' hast thou opened: "
44: 1 We have heard with our e', O God, "
78: 1 incline your e' to the words of my "
92:11 mine e' shall hear my desire of "
115: 6 They have e', but they hear not: "
130: 2 let thine e' be attentive to the voice "
135:17 They have e', but they hear not; "
Pr 21:13 Whoso stoppeth his e' at the cry "
23: 9 Speak not in the e' of a fool: * "
12 thine e' to the words of knowledge. "
26:17 one that taketh a dog by the e'. "
Isa 5: 9 In mine e' said the Lord of hosts, "
6:10 and make their e' heavy, and shut

Isa 6:10 their eyes, and hear with their e'. 241
11: 3 reprove after the hearing of his e': "
17: 5 and reapeth the e' with his arm; 7641
5 it shall be as he that gathereth e' "
22:14 revealed in mine e' by the Lord 241
30:21 And thine e' shall hear a word "
32: 3 e' of them that hear shall hearken. "
33:15 stoppeth his e' from hearing of "
35: 5 e' of the deaf shall be unstopped. "
36:11 in the e' of the people that are on "
37:29 tumult, is come up into mine e', "
42:20 opening the e', but he heareth not. "
43: 8 have eyes, and the deaf that have e'. "
49:20 other, shall say again in thine e', "
Jer 2: 2 Go and cry in the e' of Jerusalem, "
5:21 which have e', and hear not: "
19: 3 whosoever heareth, his e' shall "
26:11 as ye have heard with your e'. "
15 speak all these words in your e'. "
28: 7 this word that I speak in thine e', "
7 and in the e' of all the people; "
29:29 this letter in the e' of Jeremiah "
36: 6 in the e' of the people in the Lord's "
6 in the e' of all Judah that come out "
10 house, in the e' of all the people. "
13 read the book in the e' of the people. "
14 hast read in the e' of the people, "
15 down now, and read it in our e'. "
15 So Baruch read it in their e'. "
20 all the words in the e' of the king. "
21 Jehudi read it in the e' of the king, "
21 and in the e' of all the princes "
Eze 3:10 thine heart, and hear with thine e'. "
8:18 cry in mine e' with a loud voice, "
9: 1 cried also in mine e' with a loud "
12: 2 they have e' to hear, and hear not: "
16:12 and earrings in thine e', and a "
23:25 take away thy nose and thine e'; "
24:26 cause thee to hear it with thine e'? "
40: 4 thine eyes, and hear with thine e', "
44: 5 and hear with thine e' all that I say "
Mic 7:16 their mouth, their e' shall be deaf. "
Zec 7:11 and stopped their e', that they "
M't 11:15 He that hath e' to hear, let him 3775
12: 1 and began to pluck the e' of corn, 4719
13: 9 Who hath e' to hear, let him hear. 3775
15 and their e' are dull of hearing, "
15 their eyes, and hear with their e', "
16 and your e', for they hear. "
43 Who hath e' to hear, let him hear. "
28:14 if this come to the governor's e', 191
M'r 2:23 went, to pluck the e' of corn. 4719
4: 9 He that hath e' to hear, let him 3775
23 If any man have e' to hear, "
7:16 If any man have e' to hear, let * "
33 and put his fingers into his e', "
35 straightway his e' were opened, 189
8:18 and having e', hear ye not? 3775
Lu 1:44 thy salutation sounded in mine e', "
4:21 this scripture fulfilled in your e'. "
6: 1 disciples plucked the e' of corn, 4719
8: 8 He that hath e' to hear, let him 3775
9:44 sayings sink down into your e': "
14:35 He that hath e' to hear, let him "
Ac 7:51 and uncircumcised in heart and e', "
57 and stopped their e', and ran upon "
11:22 came unto the e' of the church "
17:20 certain strange things to our e': 189
28:27 and their e' are dull of hearing, 3775
27 their eyes, and hear with their e', "
Ro 11: 8 and e' that they should not hear;) "
2Ti 4: 3 teachers, having itching e'; 189
4 turn away their e' from the truth, "
Jas 5: 4 entered into the e' of the Lord 3775
1Pe 3:12 his e' are open unto their prayers: "

earth See also EARTHQUAKE.
Ge 1: 1 God created the heaven and the e'. 776
2 And the e' was without form, and "
10 And God called the dry land E'; "
11 said, Let the e' bring forth grass, "
11 whose seed is in itself, upon the e': "
12 And the e' brought forth grass, "
15 to give light upon the e': and it was "
17 to give light upon the e', "
20 and fowl that may fly above the e' in "
22 and let fowl multiply in the e'. "
24 Let the e' bring forth the living "
24 and beast of the e' after his kind: "
25 God made the beast of the e' after "
25 thing that creepeth upon the e' * 127
26 and over all the e', and over every 776
26 thing that creepeth upon the e'. "
28 multiply, and replenish the e', and "
28 living thing that moveth upon the e'. "
29 which is upon the face of all the e', "
30 to every beast of the e', and to "
30 thing that creepeth upon the e', "
2: 1 the heavens and the e' were finished "
4 of the heavens and of the e' when "
4 day that the Lord God made the e' "
5 of the field before it was in the e', "
5 had not caused it to rain upon the e', "
6 there went up a mist from the e', "
4:11 now art thou cursed from the e', * 127
12 vagabond shalt thou be in the e'. 776
14 this day from the face of the e'; * 127
14 fugitive and a vagabond in the e'; 776
6: 1 multiply upon the face of the e', * 127
4 were giants in the e' in those days; 776
5 of man was great in the e', and that "
6 that he had made man on the e', "
7 created from the face of the e'; * 127
11 e' also was corrupt before God, 776
11 the e' was filled with violence. "
12 God looked upon the e', and, behold, "
12 had corrupted his way upon the e', "
Ge 6:13 for the e' is filled with violence 776
13 I will destroy them with the e'. "
17 bring a flood of waters upon the e', "
17 every thing that is in the e' shall die. "
20 of every creeping thing of the e' * 127
7: 3 seed alive upon the face of all the e'. 776
4 I will cause it to rain upon the e' "
4 destroy from off the face of the e'.* 127
6 the flood of waters was upon the e'. 776
8 thing that creepeth upon the e', * 127
10 waters of the flood were upon the e'. 776
12 the rain was upon the e' forty days "
14 creepeth upon the e' after his kind, "
17 flood was forty days upon the e'; "
17 and it was lift up above the e'. "
18 increased greatly upon the e'; "
19 prevailed exceedingly upon the e'; "
21 flesh died that moved upon the e', "
21 thing that creepeth upon the e', "
23 they were destroyed from the e': "
24 the waters prevailed upon the e' "
8: 1 God made a wind to pass over the e', "
3 the waters returned from off the e' "
7 were dried up from off the e'. "
9 were on the face of the whole e': "
11 waters were abated from off the e'. "
13 were dried up from off the e': "
14 day of the month, was the e' dried. "
17 thing that creepeth upon the e'; "
17 may breed abundantly in the e', "
17 be fruitful, and multiply upon the e'. "
19 whatsoever creepeth upon the e', "
22 While the e' remaineth, seed time "
9: 1 and multiply, and replenish the e'. "
2 shall be upon every beast of the e', "
2 upon all that moveth upon the e',* 127
7 bring forth abundantly in the e', 776
10 of every beast of the e' with you; "
10 of the ark, to every beast of the e'. "
11 more be a flood to destroy the e'. "
13 a covenant between me and the e'. "
14 when I bring a cloud over the e', "
16 of all flesh that is upon the e'. "
17 and all flesh that is upon the e'. "
19 then was the whole e' overspread. "
10: 8 began to be a mighty one in the e'. "
25 in his days was the e' divided; "
32 were the nations divided in the e' "
11: 1 the whole e' was of one language, "
4 abroad upon the face of the whole e'. "
8 thence upon the face of all the e': "
9 confound the language of all the e': "
9 abroad upon the face of all the e'. "
12: 3 shall all families of the e' be blessed. 127
13:16 make thy seed as the dust of the e': 776
16 a man can number the dust of the e', "
14:19 God, possessor of heaven and e': "
22 God, the possessor of heaven and e', "
18:18 the nations of the e' shall be blessed "
25 not the Judge of all the e' do right? "
19:23 The sun was risen upon the e' when "
31 there is not a man in the e' to come "
31 us after the manner of all the e': "
22:18 all the nations of the e' be blessed; "
24: 3 of heaven, and the God of the e', "
52 the Lord, bowing himself to the e'. "
26: 4 all the nations of the e' be blessed; "
15 them, and filled them with e'. 6083
27:28 the fatness of the e', and plenty of 776
39 shall be the fatness of the e', and of "
28:12 behold a ladder set up on the e', "
14 shall be as the dust of the e', "
14 all the families of the e' be blessed. 127
37:10 down ourselves to thee to the e'? 776
41:47 the e' brought forth by handfuls. "
56 was over all the face of the e': "
42: 6 before him with their faces to the e'. "
43:26 bowed themselves to him to the e'. "
45: 7 to preserve you a posterity in the e', "
48:12 himself with his face to the e', "
16 a multitude in the midst of the e'. "
Ex 8:17 and smote the dust of the e', "
22 I am the Lord in the midst of the e'. "
9:14 there is none like me in all the e'. "
15 thou shalt be cut off from the e'. "
16 be declared throughout all the e'. "
29 know how that the e' is the Lord's. "
33 the rain was not poured upon the e'. "
10: 5 they shall cover the face of the e', "
5 that one cannot be able to see the e': "
6 the day that they were upon the e' 127
15 they covered the face of the whole e', 776
15:12 right hand, the e' swallowed them. "
19: 5 all people: for all the e' is mine: "
20: 4 or that is in the e' beneath, or "
4 that is in the water under the e': "
11 days the Lord made heaven and e', "
24 An altar of e' thou shalt make unto 127
31:17 days the Lord made heaven and e', 776
32:12 them from the face of the e'? 127
33:16 that are upon the face of the e'. "
34: 8 and bowed his head toward the e', 776
10 as have not been done in all the e', "
Le 11: 2 all the beasts that are on the e'. "
21 feet, to leap withal upon the e'; "
29 things that creep upon the e'; "
41 thing that creepeth upon the e' "
42 things that creep upon the e', "
44 thing that creepeth upon the e'. "
46 creature that creepeth upon the e': "
15:12 the vessel of e', that he toucheth *2789
26:19 as iron, and your e' as brass: 776
Nu 11:31 cubits high upon the face of the e'. "
12: 3 which were upon the face of the e'.) 127
14:21 the e' shall be filled with the glory 776
16:30 and the e' open her mouth, and * 127
Nu 16:32 And the e' opened her mouth, and 776
33 and the e' closed upon them: and "
34 Lest the e' swallow us up also. "
22: 5 they cover the face of the e', and they "
11 which covereth the face of the e': "
26:10 And the e' opened her mouth, and "
De 3:24 what God is there in heaven or in e', "
4:10 that they shall live upon the e', 127
17 of any beast that is on the e', the 776
18 that is in the waters beneath the e': "
26 I call heaven and e' to witness "
32 that God created man upon the e', "
36 upon e' he shewed thee his great fire; "
39 above, and upon the e' beneath: "
40 mayest prolong thy days upon the e' 127
5: 8 or that is in the e' beneath, or that 776
8 is in the waters beneath the e': "
6:15 thee from off the face of the e'. 127
7: 6 that are upon the face of the e'. "
10:14 the e' also, with all that therein is. 776
11: 6 now the e' opened her mouth, and "
21 as the days of heaven upon the e'. "
12: 1 all the days that ye live upon the e'. 127
16 ye shall pour it upon the e' as water, 776
19 as long as thou livest upon the e'.* 127
24 thou shalt pour it upon the e' as 776
13: 7 from the one end of the e' even unto "
7 even unto the other end of the e'; "
14: 2 all the nations that are upon the e'. 127
26: 2 the first of all the fruit of the e', * "
28: 1 on high above all nations of the e': 776
10 all people of the e' shall see that thou "
23 and the e' that is under thee shall be "
25 into all the kingdoms of the e'. "
26 the air, and unto the beasts of the e', "
49 from afar, from the end of the e', "
64 end of the e' even unto the other; "
30:19 call heaven and e' to record this day "
31:28 and e' to record against them. "
32: 1 hear, O e', the words of my mouth. "
13 ride on the high places of the e', "
22 consume the e' with her increase, "
33:16 And for the precious things of the e' "
17 people together to the ends of the e': "
Jos 2:11 in heaven above, and in e' beneath. "
3:11 the Lord of all the e' passeth over "
13 Lord of all the e', shall rest in the "
4:24 That all the people of the e' might "
5:14 Joshua fell on his face to the e', and "
7: 6 and fell to the e' upon his face before "
9 cut off our name from the e': "
21 they are hid in the e' in the midst "
23:14 I am going the way of all the e': "
J'g 3:25 lord was fallen down dead on the e'. "
5: 4 the e' trembled, and the heavens "
6: 4 destroyed the increase of the e', "
37 it be dry upon all the e' beside, * "
18:10 no want of anything that is in the e'. "
1Sa 2: 8 the pillars of the e' are the Lord's, "
10 Lord shall judge the ends of the e'; "
4: 5 a great shout, so that the e' rang "
12 rent, and with e' upon his head. 127
5: 3 was fallen upon his face to the e' * 776
14:15 also trembled, and the e' quaked: "
17:46 air, and to the wild beasts of the e'; "
46 that all the e' may know that there "
49 and he fell upon his face to the e'. "
20:15 every one from the face of the e'. 127
24: 8 stooped with his face to the e', and 776
25:41 bowed herself on her face to the e', "
26: 8 the spear even to the e' at once, "
20 let not my blood fall to the e' before "
28:13 I saw gods ascending out of the e'. "
20 fell straightway all along on the e', "
23 So he rose from the e', and sat upon "
30:16 were spread abroad upon all the e',* "
2Sa 1: 2 clothes rent, and e' upon his head: 127
2 he fell to the e', and did obeisance. 776
4:11 and take you away from the e'? "
7: 9 of the great men that are in the e'. "
23 nation in the e' is like thy people, "
12:16 in, and lay all night upon the e'. "
17 to him, to raise him up from the e': "
20 Then David arose from the e', and "
13:31 tare his garments, and lay on the e'; "
14: 7 name nor remainder upon the e'. 127
11 not one hair of thy son fall to the e'. 776
20 know all things that are in the e'. "
15:32 his coat rent, and e' upon his head: 127
18: 9 up between the heaven and the e'; 776
28 he fell down to the e' upon his face "
22: 8 Then the e' shook and trembled; "
43 them as small as the dust of the e', "
23: 4 tender grass springing out of the e' "
1Ki 1:31 bowed with her face to the e', and "
40 the e' rent with the sound of them. "
52 not an hair of him fall to the e': "
2: 2 I go the way of all the e': be thou "
4:34 from all kings of the e', which had "
8:23 in heaven above, or on e' beneath, "
27 will God indeed dwell on the e'? "
43 that all people of the e' may know "
53 from among all the people of the e', "
60 all the people of the e' may know "
10:23 exceeded all the kings of the e' for "
24 And all the e' sought to Solomon, "
13:34 destroy it from off the face of the e'. 127
17:14 the Lord sendeth rain upon the e'. "
18: 1 and I will send rain upon the e'. "
42 he cast himself down upon the e', 776
2Ki 5:15 that there is no God in all the e', "
17 servant two mules' burden of e'? 127
10:10 there shall fall unto the e' nothing 776
19:15 alone, of all the kingdoms of the e'; "
15 thou hast made heaven and e'. "
19 the kingdoms of the e' may know "

1Ch 1:10 he began to be mighty upon the e·. 776
19 in his days the e· was divided: "
16:14 God; his judgments are in all the e·. "
23 Sing unto the Lord, all the e·; "
30 Fear before him, all the e·: the "
31 let the e· rejoice: and let men say "
33 because he cometh to judge the e·. "
17: 8 of the great men that are in the e·. "
21 what one nation in the e· is like thy "
21:16 stand between the e· and the heaven, "
22: 8 hast shed much blood upon the e· "
29:11 in the heaven and in the e· is thine; "
15 our days on the e· are as a shadow, "
2Ch 1: 9 like the dust of the e· in multitude. "
2:12 that made heaven and e·, who hath "
6:14 thee in the heaven, nor in the e·; "
18 very deed dwell with men on the e·? "
33 people of the e· may know thy name, "
9:22 passed all the kings of the e· in "
23 kings of the e· sought the presence "
16: 9 and fro throughout the whole e·, "
20:24 were dead bodies fallen to the e·, "
32:19 the gods of the people of the e·, "
36:23 All the kingdoms of the e· hath the "
Ezr 1: 2 given me all the kingdoms of the e·; "
5:11 of the God of heaven and e·, and 772
Ne 9: 1 with sackclothes, and e· upon them. 127
6 e·, and all things that are therein, 776
Job 1: 7 From going to and fro in the e·, "
8 that there is none like him in the e·, "
2: 2 From going to and fro in the e·, "
3 that there is none like him in the e·, "
3:14 With kings and counsellors of the e·, "
5:10 Who giveth rain upon the e·, and "
22 thou be afraid of the beasts of the e·. "
25 offspring as the grass of the e·. "
7: 1 an appointed time to man upon e·? "
8: 9 our days upon e· are a shadow:) "
19 and out of the e· shall others grow. 6083
9: 6 shaketh the e· out of her place, and 776
24 The e· is given into the hand of the "
11: 9 thereof is longer than the e·, and "
12: 8 Or speak to the e·, and it shall "
15 them out, and they overturn the e·. "
24 of the chief of the people of the e·, "
14: 8 the root thereof wax old in the e·, "
19 which grow out of the dust of the e·; "
15:19 whom alone the e· was given, * "
29 the perfection thereof upon the e·. "
16:18 O e·, cover not thou my blood, "
18: 4 shall the e· be forsaken for thee? "
17 shall perish from the e·, and he "
19:25 stand at the latter day upon the e·: 6083
20: 4 since man was placed upon e·, 776
27 and the e· shall rise up against him. "
22: 8 for the mighty man, he had the e·; "
24: 4 the poor of the e· hide themselves "
18 their portion is cursed in the e·: "
26: 7 and hangeth the e· upon nothing. "
28: 2 Iron is taken out of the e·, 6083
5 for the e·, out of it cometh bread: 776
24 For he looketh to the ends of the e·, "
30: 6 caves of the e·, and in the rocks. 6083
8 men: they were viler than the e·.* 776
34:13 given him a charge over the e·? "
35:11 us more than the beasts of the e·, "
37: 3 his lightning unto the ends of the e·. "
6 saith to the snow, Be thou on the e·; "
12 upon the face of the world in the e·.* "
17 quieteth the e· by the south wind? "
38: 4 when I laid the foundations of the e·? "
13 might take hold of the ends of the e·, "
18 perceived the breadth of the e·? "
24 scattereth the east wind upon the e·? "
26 To cause it to rain on the e·, * "
33 set the dominion thereof in the e·? "
39:14 Which leaveth her eggs in the e·, "
41:33 Upon e· there is not his like, 6083
Ps 2: 2 The kings of the e· set themselves, 776
8 parts of the e· for thy possession. "
10 be instructed, ye judges of the e·. "
7: 5 him tread down my life upon the e·, "
8: 1, 9 excellent is thy name in all the e·! "
10:18 man of the e· may no more oppress. "
12: 6 as silver tried in a furnace of e·, "
16: 3 But to the saints that are in the e·, "
17:11 their eyes bowing down to the e·; "
18: 7 Then the e· shook and trembled; "
19: 4 line is gone out through all the e·, "
21:10 fruit shalt thou destroy from the e·, "
22:29 All they that be fat upon e· shall eat "
24: 1 The e· is the Lord's, and the "
25:13 and his seed shall inherit the e·. * "
33: 5 e· is full of the goodness of the Lord. "
8 Let all the e· fear the Lord: "
14 upon all the inhabitants of the e·. "
34:16 remembrance of them from the e·. "
37: 9 Lord, they shall inherit the e·. * "
11 But the meek shall inherit the e·;* "
22 blessed of him shall inherit the e·;* "
41: 2 he shall be blessed upon the e·: "
44:25 our belly cleaveth unto the e·. "
45:16 mayest make princes in all the e·. "
46: 2 we fear, though the e· be removed, "
6 he uttered his voice, the e· melted. "
8 desolations he hath made in the e·. "
9 was to cease unto the end of the e·; "
10 am God: I will be exalted in the e·. "
47: 2 he is a great King over all the e·. "
7 For God is the King of all the e·: "
9 shields of the e· belong unto God: "
48: 2 joy of the whole e·, is mount Zion, "
10 thy praise unto the ends of the e·: "
50: 1 the e· from the rising of the sun "
4 heavens from above, and to the e·, "
57: 5, 11 let thy glory be above all the e·. "

Ps 58: 2 violence of your hands in the e·. 776
11 he is a God that judgeth in the e·. "
59:13 in Jacob unto the ends of the e·. "
60: 2 hast made the e· to tremble; * "
61: 2 From the end of the e· will I cry "
63: 9 go into the lower parts of the e·. "
65: 5 confidence of all the ends of the e·, "
9 Thou visitest the e·, and waterest it: "
66: 4 All the e· shall worship thee, and "
67: 2 That thy way may be known upon e·, "
4 and govern the nations upon e·. "
6 Then shall the e· yield her increase; "
7 all the ends of the e· shall fear him. "
68: 8 The e· shook, the heavens also "
32 unto God, ye kingdoms of the e·; "
69:34 Let the heaven and e· praise him, "
71:20 up again from the depths of the e·. "
72: 6 grass: as showers that water the e·. "
8 the rivers unto the ends of the e·. "
16 shall be an handful of corn in the e· "
16 shall flourish like grass of the e·. "
19 the whole e· be filled with his glory; "
73: 9 their tongue walketh through the e·. "
25 there is none upon e· that I desire "
74:12 salvation in the midst of the e·. "
17 hast set all the borders of the e·: "
20 the dark places of the e· are full of "
75: 3 e· and all the inhabitants thereof "
8 wicked of the e· shall wring them out, "
76: 8 heaven; the e· feared, and was still. "
9 to save all the meek of the e·. "
12 he is terrible to the kings of the e·. "
77:18 the world: the e· trembled and shook. "
78:69 e· which he hath established forever. "
79: 2 thy saints unto the beasts of the e·. "
82: 5 all the foundations of the e· are out "
8 Arise, O God, judge the e·: for thou "
83:10 they became as dung for the e·. 127
18 art the most high over all the e·. 776
85:11 Truth shall spring out of the e·; "
89:11 The heavens are thine, the e· also is "
27 higher than the kings of the e·. "
90: 2 or ever thou hadst formed the e· "
94: 2 Lift up thyself, thou judge of the e·: "
95: 4 hand are the deep places of the e·: "
96: 1 sing unto the Lord, all the e·. "
9 holiness: fear before him, all the e·. "
11 rejoice, and let the e· be glad; "
13 for he cometh to judge the e·: "
97: 1 let the e· rejoice; let the multitude "
4 world: the e· saw, and trembled. "
5 presence of the Lord of the whole e·. "
9 thou, Lord, art high above all the e·: "
98: 3 all the ends of the e· have seen the "
4 noise unto the Lord, all the e·: "
9 for he cometh to judge the e·: "
99: 1 the cherubims; let the e· be moved. "
102:15 and all the kings of the e· thy glory. "
19 heaven did the Lord behold the e·; "
25 thou laid the foundation of the e·: "
103:11 the heaven is high above the e·, "
104: 5 Who laid the foundations of the e·, "
9 they turn not again to cover the e·. "
13 the e· is satisfied with the fruit of "
14 may bring forth food out of the e·; "
24 the e· is full of thy riches. "
30 thou renewest the face of the e·. * 127
32 looketh on the e·, and it trembleth: 776
35 sinners be cousumed out of the e·, "
105: 7 his judgments are in all the e·. "
106:17 e· opened and swallowed up Dathan, "
108: 5 and thy glory above all the e·; "
109:15 the memory of them from the e·. "
112: 2 His seed shall be mighty upon e·: "
113: 6 that are in heaven, and in the e·! "
114: 7 Tremble, thou e·, at the presence "
115:15 the Lord which made heaven and e·. "
16 but the e· hath he given to the "
119:19 I am a stranger in the e·: "
64 The e·, O Lord, is full of thy mercy: "
87 had almost consumed me upon e·; "
90 thou hast established the e·, and it "
119 puttest away all the wicked of the e· "
121: 2 the Lord, which made heaven and e·. "
124: 8 the Lord, who made heaven and e·. "
134: 3 The Lord that made heaven and e· "
135: 6 that did he in heaven, and in e·, "
7 to ascend from the ends of the e·; "
136: 6 To him that stretched out the e· "
138: 4 All the kings of the e· shall praise "
139:15 in the lowest parts of the e·. "
140:11 speaker be established in the e·: "
141: 7 and cleaveth wood upon the e·. "
146: 4 goeth forth, he returneth to his e·; 127
6 Which made heaven, and e·, the 776
147: 8 who prepareth rain for the e·, who "
15 forth his commandment upon e·: "
148: 7 Praise the Lord from the e·, "
11 Kings of the e·, and all people; "
11 princes, and all judges of the e·: "
13 his glory is above the e· and heaven. "
Pr 2:22 wicked shall be cut off from the e·,* "
3:19 by wisdom hath founded the e·; "
8:16 even all the judges of the e·. "
23 the beginning, or ever the e· was. "
26 as yet he had not made the e·, "
29 appointed the foundations of the e·: "
31 in the habitable part of his e·; "
10:30 the wicked shall not inhabit the e·. * "
11:31 shall be recompensed in the e·: "
17:24 of a fool are in the ends of the e·. "
25: 3 for height, and the e· for depth, "
30: 4 established all the ends of the e·? "
14 to devour the poor from off the e·, "
16 the e· that is not filled with water; "
21 For three things the e· is disquieted, "

Pr 30:24 things which are little upon the e·, 776
Ec 1: 4 but the e· abideth for ever. "
3:21 that goeth downward to the e·? "
5: 2 God is in heaven, and thou upon e·: "
9 the profit of the e· is for all: "
7:20 there is not a just man upon e·, that "
8:14 a vanity which is done upon the e·; "
16 business that is done upon the e·: "
10: 7 walking as servants upon the e·. "
11: 2 what evil shall be upon the e·. "
3 they empty themselves upon the e·: "
12: 7 Then shall the dust return to the e· "
Ca 2:12 The flowers appear on the e·; "
Isa 1: 2 Hear, O heavens, and give ear, O e·: "
2:19 rocks, and into the caves of the e·. 6083
19, 21 ariseth to shake terribly the e·. 776
4: 2 fruit of the e· shall be excellent * "
5: 8 placed alone in the midst of the e·!* "
26 unto them from the end of the e·: "
6: 3 the whole e· is full of his glory. "
8:22 And they shall look unto the e·; "
10:14 are left, have I gathered all the e·; "
11: 4 with equity for the meek of the e·: "
4 and he shall smite the e· with the rod "
9 the e· shall be full of the knowledge "
12 from the four corners of the e·. "
12: 5 things: this is known in all the e·. "
13:13 and the e· shall remove out of her "
14: 7 The whole e· is at rest, and is quiet: "
9 even all the chief ones of the e·; "
16 the man that made the e· to tremble, "
26 that is purposed upon the whole e·: "
18: 3 of the world, and dwellers on the e·, "
6 and to the beasts of the e·: and the "
6 all the beasts of the e· shall winter "
23: 8 are the honourable of the e·? "
9 contempt all the honourable of the e·. "
17 the world upon the face of the e·. 127
24: 1 the Lord maketh the e· empty, 776
4 The e· mourneth and fadeth away, "
4 haughty people of the e· do languish. "
5 The e· also is defiled under the "
6 hath the curse devoured the e·, "
6 the inhabitants of the e· are burned, "
16 From the uttermost part of the e· "
17 upon thee, O inhabitant of the e·. "
18 the foundations of the e· do shake. "
19 The e· is utterly broken down, the "
19 e· is clean dissolved, the e· is moved "
20 The e· shall reel to and fro like a "
21 the kings of the e· upon the e·. 127
25: 8 he take away from off all the e·: 776
26: 9 when thy judgments are in the e·, "
15 it far unto all the ends of the e·. * "
18 wrought any deliverance in the e·; "
19 and the e· shall cast out the dead. "
21 to punish the inhabitants of the e· "
21 the e· also shall disclose her blood, "
28: 2 shall cast down to the e· with the "
22 even determined upon the whole e·. "
30:23 bread of the increase of the e·. * 127
33: 9 The e· mourneth and languisheth:* 776
34: 1 let the e· hear, and all that is "
37:16 alone, of all the kingdoms of the e·: "
16 thou hast made heaven and e·. "
20 all the kingdoms of the e· may know "
40:12 and comprehended the dust of the e· "
21 from the foundations of the e·? "
22 that sitteth upon the circle of the e·, "
23 he maketh the judges of the e· as "
24 stock shall not take root in the e·: "
28 the Creator of the ends of the e·, "
41: 5 the ends of the e· were afraid, "
9 have taken from the ends of the e·, "
42: 4 till he have set judgment in the e·: "
5 he that spread forth the e·, and that "
10 his praise from the end of the e·, "
43: 6 daughters from the ends of the e·; "
44:23 shout, ye lower parts of the e·: "
24 that spreadeth abroad the e· by "
45: 8 let the e· open, and let them bring "
9 strive with the potsherds of the e·. 127
12 I have made the e·, and created 776
18 God himself that formed the e· and "
19 secret, in a dark place of the e·: * "
22 be ye saved, all the ends of the e·: "
48:13 hath laid the foundation of the e·, "
20 utter it even to the end of the e·; "
49: 6 my salvation unto the end of the e·. "
8 to establish the e·, to cause to * "
13 Sing, O heavens; and be joyful, O e·; "
23 with their face toward the e·, and "
51: 6 and look upon the e· beneath: for "
6 the e· shall wax old like a garment, "
13 and laid the foundations of the e·; "
16 and lay the foundations of the e·, "
52:10 all the ends of the e· shall see the "
54: 5 The God of the whole e· shall he be "
9 Noah should no more go over the e·; "
55: 9 the heavens are higher than the e·, "
10 but watereth the e·, and maketh it "
58:14 ride upon the high places of the e·, "
60: 2 the darkness shall cover the e·, "
61:11 as the e· bringeth forth her bud, "
62: 7 make Jerusalem a praise in the e·. "
63: 6 bring down their strength to the e·. "
65:16 he who blesseth himself in the e· "
16 and he that sweareth in the e· shall "
17 I create new heavens and a new e·: "
66: 1 throne, and the e· is my footstool: "
8 Shall the e· be made to bring forth* "
22 as the new heavens and the new e·, "
Jer 4:23 I beheld the e·, and, lo, it was "
28 For this shall the e· mourn, and the "
6:19 Hear, O e·: behold, I will bring evil "
22 be raised from the sides of the e·, "

Jer 7:33 heaven, and for the beasts of the e'; 776
8: 2 be for dung upon the face of the e'. 127
9: 3 valiant for the truth upon the e': * 776
24 and righteousness, in the e': "
10:10 at his wrath the e' shall tremble, "
11 not made the heavens and the e', 778
11 even they shall perish from the e'. 772
12 He hath made the e' by his power, 776
13 to ascend from the ends of the e'; "
14: 4 for there was no rain in the e', * "
15: 3 and the beasts of the e', to devour "
4 removed into all kingdoms of the e', "
10 a man of contention to the whole e'! "
16: 4 as dung upon the face of the e': * 127
4 heaven, and for the beasts of the e'. 776
19 unto thee from the ends of the e', "
17:13 from me shall be written in the e', "
19: 7 heaven, and for the beasts of the e'. "
22:29 O e', e', e', hear the word of the Lord. "
23: 5 judgment and justice in the e'. * "
24 Do not I fill heaven and e'? saith the "
24: 9 into all the kingdoms of the e' for "
25:26 which are upon the face of the e': 127
29 upon all the inhabitants of the e', 776
30 against all the inhabitants of the e'. "
31 shall come even to the ends of the e'; "
32 be raised from the coasts of the e'. "
33 at that day from one end of the e' "
33 even unto the other end of the e': "
26: 6 a curse to all the nations of the e'. "
27: 5 I have made the e', the man and the "
28:16 cast thee from off the face of the e': 127
29:18 to all the kingdoms of the e', to be a 776
31: 8 them from the coasts of the e', "
22 hath created a new thing in the e', "
37 foundations of the e' searched out "
32:17 made the heaven and the e' by thy "
33: 9 before all the nations of the e', which "
25 the ordinances of heaven and e'; "
34: 1 army, and all the kingdoms of the e' "
17 into all the kingdoms of the e'. "
20 heaven, and to the beasts of the e'. "
44: 8 among all the nations of the e'? "
46: 8 will go up, and will cover the e'; "
49:21 The e' is moved at the noise of their "
50:23 whole e' cut asunder and broken! "
41 raised up from the coasts of the e'. "
46 taking of Babylon the e' is moved, "
51: 7 hand, that made all the e' drunken: "
15 He hath made the e' by his power, "
16 to ascend from the ends of the e': "
25 Lord, which destroyest all the e': "
41 the praise of the whole e' surprised! "
48 Then the heaven and the e', and all "
49 shall fall the slain of all the e'. * "
La 2: 1 cast down from heaven unto the e' "
11 my liver is poured upon the e', "
15 of beauty, The joy of the whole e'? "
3:34 his feet all the prisoners of the e', "
4:12 The kings of the e', and all the "
Eze 1:15 behold one wheel upon the e' by the "
19 creatures were lifted up from the e', "
21 those were lifted up from the e', "
7:21 to the wicked of the e' for a spoil; "
8: 3 up between the e' and the heaven, "
12 not; the Lord hath forsaken the e'. "
9: 9 The Lord hath forsaken the e', and "
10:16 their wings to mount up from the e', "
19 mounted up from the e' in my sight: "
26:20 set thee in the low parts of the e', "
27:33 thou didst enrich the kings of the e' "
28:18 will bring thee to ashes upon the e' "
31:12 all the people of the e' are gone "
14 death, to the nether parts of the e', "
16 in the nether parts of the e'. "
18 Eden unto the nether parts of the e': "
32: 4 the beasts of the whole e' with thee. "
18 unto the nether parts of the e', with "
24 into the nether parts of the e', which "
34: 6 scattered upon all the face of the e', "
27 and the e' shall yield her increase, "
35:14 When the whole e' rejoiceth, I will "
38:20 things that creep upon the e', 127
20 men that are upon the face of the e', "
39:14 remain upon the face of the e', *776
18 the blood of the princes of the e', "
43: 2 and the e' shined with his glory. "
Da 2:10 There is not a man upon the e' 3007
35 mountain, and filled the whole e'. 772
39 which shall bear rule over all the e'. "
4: 1 languages, that dwell in all the e'; "
10 behold a tree in the midst of the e', "
11 sight thereof to the end of all the e': "
15 the stump of his roots in the e', "
15 the beasts in the grass of the e': "
20 and the sight thereof to all the e'; "
22 thy dominion to the end of the e'. "
23 stump of the roots thereof in the e', "
35 And all the inhabitants of the e' "
35 among the inhabitants of the e': "
6:25 languages, that dwell in all the e'; "
27 and wonders in heaven and in e', "
7: 4 and it was lifted up from the e', "
17 which shall arise out of the e'. "
23 shall be the fourth kingdom upon e', "
23 and shall devour the whole e', and "
8: 5 west on the face of the whole e', 776
12: 2 them that sleep in the dust of the e' 127
Ho 2:18 sword and the battle out of the e', *776
21 heavens, and they shall hear the e'; "
22 And the e' shall hear the corn, "
23 I will sow her unto me in the e'; "
6: 3 latter and former rain unto the e'. "
Joe 2:10 The e' shall quake before them; "
30 in the heavens and in the e', "
3:16 the heavens and the e' shall shake: "

Am 2: 7 That pant after the dust of the e' 776
3: 2 known of all the families of the e': 127
5 a bird fall in a snare upon the e', 776
5 one take up a snare from the e', * 127
4:13 upon the high places of the e', 776
5: 7 leave off righteousness in the e', "
8 them out upon the face of the e': "
8: 9 will darken the e' in the clear day: "
9: 6 hath founded his troop in the e'; "
6 them out upon the face of the e': "
8 destroy it from off the face of the e'; 127
9 not the least grain fall upon the e'. 776
Jon 2: 6 the e' with her bars was about me "
Mic 1: 2 Hear, all ye people; hearken, O e', "
3 tread upon the high places of the e'. "
4:13 unto the Lord of the whole e'. "
5: 4 he be great unto the ends of the e'. "
6: 2 ye strong foundations of the e': "
7: 2 good man is perished out of the e': "
17 of their holes like worms of the e': "
Na 1: 5 and the e' is burned at his presence, "
2:13 I will cut off thy prey from the e', "
Hab 2:14 e' shall be filled with the knowledge "
20 let all the e' keep silence before him. "
3: 3 and the e' was full of his praise. "
6 He stood, and measured the e': "
9 Thou didst cleave the e' with rivers. "
Zep 2: 3 ye the Lord, all ye meek of the e', "
11 he will famish all the gods of the e'; "
3: 8 the e' shall be devoured with the fire "
20 praise among all people of the e', "
Hag 1:10 and the e' is stayed from her fruit. "
2: 6 the heavens, and the e', and the sea, "
21 I will shake the heavens and the e'; "
Zec 1:10 to walk to and fro through the e'. "
11 walked to and fro through the e', "
11 all the e' sitteth still, and is at rest. "
4:10 run to and fro through the whole e'. "
14 stand by the Lord of the whole e'. "
5: 3 forth over the face of the whole e':* "
6 resemblance through all the e'. * "
9 ephah between the e' and the heaven. "
6: 5 standing before the Lord of all the e'. "
7 and fro through the e': and he said, "
7 hence, walk to and fro through the e'. "
7 walked to and fro through the e'. "
9:10 the river even to the ends of the e'. "
12: 1 and layeth the foundation of the e', "
3 though all the people of the e' be "
14: 9 Lord shall be king over all the e': "
17 families of the e' unto Jerusalem "
Mal 4: 6 come and smite the e' with a curse. "
M't 5: 5 meek: for they shall inherit the e'. 1093
13 Ye are the salt of the e': but if the "
18 Till heaven and e' pass, one jot or "
35 Nor by the e'; for it is his footstool: "
6:10 will be done in e', as it is in heaven. "
19 for yourselves treasures upon e', "
9: 6 hath power on e' to forgive sins, "
10:34 I am come to send peace on e': "
11:25 O Father, Lord of heaven and e', "
12:40 three nights in the heart of the e'. "
42 uttermost parts of the e' to hear "
13: 5 where they had not much e': "
5 because they had no deepness of e': "
16:19 whatsoever thou shalt bind on e' "
19 whatsoever thou shalt loose on e' "
17:25 whom doth the kings of the e' take "
18:18 Whatsoever ye shall bind on e' "
18 and whatsoever ye shall loose on e' "
19 if two of you shall agree on e' as "
23: 9 no man your father upon the e': "
35 righteous blood shed upon the e', "
24:30 shall the tribes of the e' mourn, "
35 Heaven and e' shall pass away, but "
25:18 one went and digged in the e', "
25 went and hid thy talent in the e': "
27:51 e' did quake, and the rocks rent; "
28:18 given unto me in heaven and in e'. "
M'r 2:10 Son of man hath power on e' to "
4: 5 ground; where it had not much e'; "
5 because it had no depth of e': "
28 e' bringeth forth fruit of herself; "
31 it is sown in the e', is less than "
31 all the seeds that be in the e': "
9: 3 as no fuller on e' can white them. "
13:27 from the uttermost part of the e' "
31 Heaven and e' shall pass away: "
Lu 2:14 on e' peace, good will toward men. "
5:24 the Son of man hath power upon e' "
6:49 built an house upon the e'; "
10:21 O Father, Lord of heaven and e', "
11: 2 be done, as in heaven, so in e'. * "
31 from the utmost parts of the e' to "
12:49 I am come to send fire on the e'; "
51 that I am come to give peace on e'? "
56 the face of the sky and of the e'; "
16:17 is easier for heaven and e' to pass, "
18: 8 shall he find faith on the e'? "
21:25 and upon the e' distress of nations, "
26 which are coming on the e'; *3625
33 Heaven and e' shall pass away: 1093
35 dwell on the face of the whole e'. "
23:44 was a darkness over all the e' * "
24: 5 bowed down their faces to the e', "
Joh 3:31 he that is of the e' is earthly, "
31 and speaketh of the e': "
12:32 if I be lifted up from the e', "
17: 4 I have glorified thee on the e': "
Ac 1: 8 unto the uttermost part of the e'. "
2:19 and signs in the e' beneath; blood, "
3:25 the kindreds of the e' be blessed. "
4:24 which hast made heaven, and e', "
26 The kings of the e' stood up, "
7:49 my throne, and e' is my footstool: "
8:33 for his life is taken from the e'. "

Ac 9: 4 he fell to the e', and heard a voice 1093
8 Saul arose from the e'; and when "
10:11 corners, and let down to the e': "
12 of fourfooted beasts of the e', and "
11: 6 and saw fourfooted beasts of the e', "
13:47 salvation unto the ends of the e'. "
14:15 God, which made heaven, and e', "
17:24 is Lord of heaven and e', dwelleth "
26 to dwell on all the face of the e', "
22:22 with such a fellow from the e': "
26:14 when we were all fallen to the e', "
Ro 9:17 be declared throughout all the e'. "
28 will the Lord make upon the e'. "
10:18 their sound went into all the e', "
1Co 8: 5 gods, whether in heaven or in e', "
10:26 For the e' is the Lord's, and the "
28 for the e' is the Lord's, and the * "
15:47 The first man is of the e', earthy: "
Eph 1:10 are in heaven, and which are on e'; "
3:15 family in heaven and e' is named, "
4: 9 into the lower parts of the e'? "
6: 3 thou mayest live long on the e'. "
Ph'p 2:10 things in heaven, and things in e', 1919
10 and things under the e'; 2709
Col 1:16 are in heaven, and that are in e', 1093
20 whether they be things in e', or "
3: 2 above, not on things on the e'. "
5 members which are upon the e'; "
2Ti 2:20 but also of wood and of e'; and 3749
Heb 1:10 hast laid the foundation of the e'; 1093
6: 7 the e' which drinketh in the rain * "
8: 4 For if he were on e', he should not "
11:13 strangers and pilgrims on the e': "
38 and in dens and caves of the e'. "
12:25 who refused him that spake on e', "
26 Whose voice then shook the e': "
26 once more I shake not the e' only, "
Jas 5: 5 Ye have lived in pleasure on the e', "
7 for the precious fruit of the e', "
12 neither by heaven, neither by the e', "
17 it rained not on the e' by the space "
18 and the e' brought forth her fruit. "
2Pe 3: 5 the e' standing out of the water "
7 heavens and the e', which are now, "
10 the e' also and the works that are "
13 look for new heavens and a new e', "
1Jo 5: 8 are three that bear witness in e', * "
Re 1: 5 the prince of the kings of the e'. "
7 all kindreds of the e' shall wail "
3:10 to try them that dwell upon the e'. "
5: 3 nor in e', neither under the e', "
6 of God sent forth into all the e'. "
10 and we shall reign on the e'. "
13 and on the e', and under the e', "
6: 4 thereon to take peace from the e', "
8 them over the fourth part of the e', "
8 death, and with the beasts of the e'. "
10 blood on them that dwell on the e'? "
13 the stars of heaven fell unto the e', "
15 kings of the e', and the great men, "
7: 1 on the four corners of the e', "
1 holding the four winds of the e', "
1 the wind should not blow on the e', "
2 to whom it was given to hurt the e' "
3 Saying, Hurt not the e', neither the "
8: 5 altar, and cast it into the e': "
7 and they were cast upon the e': "
13 woe, to the inhabiters of the e' by "
9: 1 a star fall from heaven unto the e': "
3 of the smoke locusts upon the e': "
3 the scorpions of the e' have power. "
4 should not hurt the grass of the e', "
10: 2 the sea, and his left foot on the e', "
5 stand upon the sea and upon the e' "
6 e', and the things that therein are, "
8 upon the sea and upon the e'. "
11: 4 standing before the God of the e'. "
6 to smite the e' with all plagues, "
10 that dwell upon the e' shall rejoice "
10 tormented them that dwelt on the e'. "
18 destroy them which destroy the e'. "
12: 4 and did cast them to the e': "
9 he was cast out into the e', "
12 Woe to the inhabiters of the e' and "
13 saw that he was cast unto the e', "
16 And the e' helped the woman, "
16 and the e' opened her mouth, "
13: 8 dwell upon the e' shall worship "
11 beast coming up out of the e'; "
12 causeth the e' and them which "
13 heaven on the e' in the sight of men, "
14 deceiveth them that dwell on the e' "
14 saying to them that dwell on the e', "
14: 3 which were redeemed from the e'. "
6 unto them that dwell on the e', "
7 him that made heaven, and e', "
15 for the harvest of the e' is ripe. "
16 thrust in his sickle on the e'; "
16 and the e' was reaped. "
18 the clusters of the vine of the e'; "
19 angel thrust his sickle into the e', "
19 and gathered the vine of the e', "
16: 1 the wrath of God upon the e'. "
2 poured out his vial upon the e'; "
14 of the e' and of the whole world, * "
18 not since men were upon the e', "
17: 2 With whom the kings of the e' have "
2 of the e' have been made drunk "
5 harlots and abominations of the e' "
8 dwell upon the e' shall wonder, "
18 reigneth over the kings of the e'. "
18: 1 the e' was lightened with his glory. "
3 the e' have committed fornication "
3 merchants of the e' are waxed rich "
9 kings of the e', who have committed "
11 the merchants of the e' shall weep "

Re 18:23 were the great men of the e·; 1098
24 all that were slain upon the e·. "
19: 2 corrupt the e· with her fornication, "
19 the beast, and the kings of the e·, "
20: 8 in the four quarters of the e·, "
9 went up on the breadth of the e·, "
11 the e· and the heaven fled away; "
21: 1 I saw a new heaven and a new e·: "
1 and first e· were passed away; "
24 the kings of the e· do bring their "

earthen See also EARTHY.
Le 6:28 the e· vessel wherein it is sodden 2789
11:33 every e· vessel, whereinto any of "
14: 5 birds be killed in an e· vessel "
50 the one of the birds in an e· vessel "
Nu 5:17 take holy water in an e· vessel; "
2Sa 17:28 beds, and basons, and e· vessels, 3335
Jer 19: 1 Go and get a potter's e· bottle, 2789
32:14 and put them in an e· vessel, "
La 4: 2 are they esteemed as e· pitchers, "
2Co 4: 7 have this treasure in e· vessels, 3749

earthly See also EARTHY.
Joh 3:12 If I have told you e· things, 1919
31 that is of the earth is e·, *1537, 3588, 1093
2Co 5: 1 if our e· house of this tabernacle 1919
Ph'p 3:19 their shame, who mind e· things.) "
Jas 3:15 above, but is e·, sensual, devilish. "

earthquake See also EARTHQUAKES.
1Ki 19:11 and after the wind an e·; 7494
11 but the Lord was not in the e·: "
12 after the e· a fire; but the Lord "
Isa 29: 6 and with e·, and great noise, "
Am 1: 1 two years before the e·. "
Zec 14: 5 the e· in the days of Uzziah "
M't 27:54 saw the e·, and those things that 4578
28: 2 behold, there was a great e·: "
Ac 16:26 And suddenly there was a great e·, "
Re 6:12 lo, there was a great e·; "
8: 5 and lightnings, and an e·. "
11:13 same hour was there a great e·, "
13 and in the e· were slain of men "
19 and an e·, and great hail. "
16:18 and there was a great e·, "
18 so mighty an e·, and so great. "

earthquakes
M't 24: 7 and e·, in divers places. 4578
M'r 13: 8 there shall be e· in divers places, "
Lu 21:11 great e· shall be in divers places "

earthy See also EARTHEN; EARTHLY.
1Co 15:47 The first man is of the earth, e·: 5517
48 As is the e·, such are they also "
48 such are they also that are e·: "
49 we have born the image of the e·, "

ease See also EASED; DISEASE.
De 23:13 when thou wilt e· thyself abroad,*3427
28:65 these nations shalt thou find no e·,7280
J'g 20:43 and trode them down with e· *4496
2Ch 10: 4 e· thou somewhat the grievous *7043
9 E· somewhat the yoke that thy * "
Job 7:13 my couch shall e· my complaint; 5375
12: 5 the thought of him that is at e·. 7600
16:12 I was at e·, but he hath broken 7961
21:23 being wholly at e· and quiet. 7946
Ps 25:13 His soul shall dwell at e·; and 2896
123: 4 scorning of those that are at e·, 7600
Isa 1:24 will e· me of mine adversaries, 5162
32: 9 Rise up, ye women that are at e·; 7600
11 Tremble, ye women that are at e·; "
Jer 46:27 and be in rest and at e·, 7599
48:11 Moab hath been at e· from his "
Eze 23:42 a voice of a multitude being at e· 7961
Am 6: 1 Woe to them that are at e· in Zion,7600
Zec 1:15 with the heathen that are at e·: "
Lu 12:19 take thine e·, eat, drink, and be 373

eased
Job 16: 6 though I forbear, what am I e·? 1980
2Co 8:13 I mean not that other men be e·, 425

easier
Ex 18:22 so shall it be e· for thyself, 7043
M't 9: 5 whether is e·, to say, Thy sins be 2123
19:24 It is e· for a camel to go through "
M'r 2: 9 Whether it is e· to say to the sick "
10:25 It is e· for a camel to go through "
Lu 5:23 Whether is e·, to say, Thy sins be "
16:17 it is e· for heaven and earth to pass, "
18:25 For it is e· for a camel to go through "

easily
1Co 13: 5 not e· provoked, thinketh no evil;*
Heb 12: 1 the sin which doth so e· beset us,

east See also EASTWARD.
Ge 2:14 goeth toward the e· of Assyria *6926
3:24 at the e· of the garden of Eden 6924
4:16 the land of Nod, on the e· of Eden.6926
10:30 was...Sephar a mount of the e·. 6924
11: 2 pass, as they journeyed from the e·, "
12: 8 a mountain on the e· of Beth-el, "
8 his tent, having...Hai on the e·: "
13:11 and Lot journeyed e·: and they "
25: 6 eastward, unto the e· country. "
28:14 abroad to the west, and to the e·, "
29: 1 into the land of the people of the e·. "
41: 6 ears and blasted with the e· wind 6921
23 ears...blasted with the e· wind, "
27 empty ears blasted with the e· wind "
Ex 10:13 brought an e· wind upon the land "
13 the e· wind brought the locusts. "
14:21 to go back by a strong e· wind "
27:13 breadth of the court on the e· side6924
38:13 for the e· side eastward fifty cubits. "
Le 1:16 it beside the altar on the e· part, "
Nu 2: 3 on the e· side toward the rising of "
3:38 the tabernacle toward the e·, * "
10: 5 the camps that lie on the e· parts 6924
23: 7 out of the mountains of the e·, "
34:10 your e· border from Hazar-enan "
11 to Riblah, on the e· side of Ain; "
35: 5 from without the city on the e· side "
Jos 4:19 Gilgal, in the e· border of Jericho.4217
7: 2 to Ai,....on the e· side of Beth-el, 6924
11: 3 And to the Canaanite on the e· 4217
12: 1 and all the plain on the e·: * "
3 the sea of Chinneroth on the e·, * "
3 even the salt sea on the e·, * "
15: 5 the e· border was the salt sea, 6924
16: 1 the water of Jericho on the e·, 4217
5 of their inheritance on the e· side* "
6 passed by it on the e· to Janohah; "
17:10 north, and in Issachar on the e·. "
18: 7 beyond Jordan on the e·, * "
20 the border of it on the e· side. 6924
19:13 passeth on along on the e· * "
J'g 6: 3 the children of the e·,....came up "
33 children of the e· were gathered "
7:12 all the children of the e· lay along "
8:10 the hosts of the children of the e·: "
11 them that dwelt in tents on the e· "
11:18 came by the e· side of the land 4217,8121
21:19 on the e· side of the highway "
1Ki 4:30 all the children of the e· country, 6924
7:25 and three looking toward the e·: 4217
1Ch 4:39 unto the e· side of the valley, "
5:10 tents throughout all the e· land "
6:78 on the e· side of Jordan, were "
9:24 the e·, west, north, and south. "
12:15 toward the e·, and toward the west. "
2Ch 4: 4 three looking toward the e·: and "
10 on the right side of the e· end, *6924
5:12 stood at the e· end of the altar, 4217
29: 4 them together into the e· street, "
31:14 the porter toward the e·, was "
Ne 3:26 the water gate toward the e·, "
29 the keeper of the e· gate. "
Job 1: 3 greatest of all the men of the e·. 6924
15: 2 and fill his belly with the e· wind?6921
27:21 The e· wind carrieth him away, "
38:24 which scattereth the e· wind upon "
Ps 48: 7 ships of Tarshish with an e· wind. "
75: 6 cometh neither from the e·, 4161
78:26 He caused an e· wind to blow in 6921
103:12 far as the e· is from the west, 4217
107: 3 from the e·, and from the west, "
Isa 2: 6 they be replenished from the e·, 6924
11:14 shall spoil them of the e· together: "
27: 8 wind in the day of the e· wind. 6921
41: 2 up the righteous man from the e·, 4217
43: 5 I will bring thy seed from the e·, "
46:11 Calling a ravenous bird from the e·, "
Jer 18:17 scatter them as with an e· wind 6921
19: 2 is by the entry of the e· gate, *2777
31:40 of the horse gate toward the e·, 4217
49:28 and spoil the men of the e·. 6924
Eze 8:16 their faces toward the e·; and they "
16 worshipped the sun toward the e·. "
10:19 stood at the door of the e· gate 6931
11: 1 brought me unto the e· gate "
23 mountain which is on the e· side 6924
17:10 when the e· wind toucheth it? 6921
19:12 the e· wind dried up her fruit: "
25: 4 deliver thee to the men of the e· 6924
10 Unto the men of the e· with the "
27:26 the e· wind hath broken thee in 6921
39:11 passengers on the e· of the sea; 6926
40: 6 gate which looketh toward the e·, 6921
22 the gate that looketh toward the e·; "
23 toward the north, and toward the e·; "
32 into the inner court toward the e·: "
44 at the side of the e· gate "
41:14 the separate place toward the e·, "
42: 9 was the entry on the e· side, "
10 the wall of the court toward the e·, "
12 before the wall toward the e·, "
15 whose prospect is toward the e·, "
16 He measured the e· side with the "
43: 1 the gate that looketh toward the e·: "
2 came from the way of the e·: "
4 whose prospect is toward the e·. "
17 his stairs shall look toward the e·. "
44: 1 which looketh toward the e·; "
45: 7 and from the e· side eastward: 6924
7 west border unto the e· border. 6921
46: 1 court that looketh toward the e· "
12 gate that looketh toward the e·, "
47: 1 of the house stood toward the e·, "
8 waters issue out toward the e· *6930
18 the e· side ye shall measure from 6921
18 from the border unto the e· sea. 6931
18 And this is the e· side. 6921
48: 1 these are his sides e· and west; "
2 border of Dan, from the e· side "
3 border of Asher, from the e· side "
4 border of Naphtali, from the e· side "
5 border of Manasseh, from the e· "
6 border of Ephraim, from the e· side "
7 border of Reuben, from the e· side "
8 border of Judah, from the e· side "
8 the e· side unto the west side: "
10 and toward the e· ten thousand in "
16 the e· side four thousand and five "
17 the e· two hundred and fifty, "
21 the oblation toward the e· border, "
23 from the e· side unto the west side, "
24 from the e· side unto the west "
25 border of Simeon, from the e· side "
26 border of Issachar, from the e· side "
27 border of Zebulun, from the e· side "
32 at the e· side four thousand and "
Da 8: 9 the south ,and toward the e·, 4217
11:44 But tidings out of the e· and out "
Ho 12: 1 and followeth after the e· wind: 6921
13:15 an e· wind shall come, the wind "
Joe 2:20 with his face toward the e· sea, *6931
Am 8:12 from the north even to the e·, 4217
Jon 4: 5 and sat on the e· side of the city, 6924
8 God prepared a vehement e· wind;6921
Hab 1: 9 faces shall sup up as the e· wind, "
Zec 8: 7 save my people from the e· 4217
14: 4 is before Jerusalem on the e·, 6924
4 the midst thereof toward the e· 4217
M't 2: 1 men from the e· to Jerusalem, 395
2 we have seen his star in the e·, "
9 the star, which they saw in the e·, "
8:11 shall come from the e· and west, "
24:27 the lightning cometh out of the e·, "
Lu 13:29 they shall come from the e·, and "
Rev 7: 2 angel ascending from the e·, * "
16:12 the way of the kings of the e· * "
21:13 On the e· three gates; on the north "

Easter
Ac 12: 4 intending after E· to bring him *3957

east-side See EAST and SIDE.

eastward
Ge 2: 8 God planted a garden e· of Eden; 6924
13:14 southward, and e·, and westward: "
25: 6 yet lived, e·, unto the east country. "
Ex 27:13 east side e· shall be fifty cubits. 4217
38:13 the east side e· fifty cubits. "
Le 16:14 his finger upon the mercy seat e·;6924
Nu 3:38 e·, shall be Moses, and Aaron *4217
32:19 fallen to us on this side Jordan e·. "
34: 3 outmost coast of the salt sea e·: 6924
11 side of the sea of Chinnereth e·: "
15 Jericho e·, toward the sunrising. "
De 3:17 sea, under Ashdoth-pisgah e·. 4217
27 northward, and southward, and e·, "
4:49 the plain on this side Jordan e·, "
Jos 11: 8 and unto the valley of Mizpeh e·; "
13: 8 gave them, beyond Jordan e·, "
27 on the other side Jordan e·, "
32 other side Jordan, by Jericho, e·. "
16: 6 about e· unto Taanath-shiloh, "
19:12 from Sarid e· toward the sunrising 6924
20: 8 other side Jordan by Jericho e·, 4217
1Sa 13: 5 in Michmash, e· from Beth-aven. 6926
1Ki 7:39 on the right side of the house e·, 6924
17: 3 Get thee hence, and turn thee e·, "
2Ki 10:33 Jordan e·, all...land of Gilead, 4217,8121
13:17 And he said, Open the window e·. 6924
1Ch 5: 9 And e· he inhabited unto the 4217
7:28 e· Naaran, and westward Gezer, "
9:18 waited in the king's gate e·: "
26:14 the lot e· fell to Shelemiah. "
17 E· were six Levites, northward four "
Ne 12:37 even unto the water gate e·. "
Eze 11: 1 Lord's house, which looketh e·: 6921
40:10 little chambers of the gate e· 1870, "
19 hundred cubits e· and northward.* "
45: 7 and from the east side e·: "
47: 1 the threshold of the house e·: "
2 gate by the way that looketh e·; "
3 the line in his hand went forth e·, "
48:18 residue...shall be ten thousand e·, "

east wind See EAST and WIND.

easy See also EASIER.
Pr 14: 6 knowledge is e· unto him that 7043
M't 11:30 For my yoke is e·, and my burden 5543
1Co 14: 9 tongue words e· to be understood, 2154
Jas 3:17 e· to be intreated, full of mercy 2138

eat See also ATE; EATEN; EATEST; EATETH; EATING.
Ge 2:16 garden thou mayest freely e·: 398
17 thou shalt not e· of it: for in the "
3: 1 not e· of every tree of the garden? "
2 We may e· of the fruit of the trees "
3 God hath said, Ye shall not e· of it, "
5 know that in the day ye e· thereof, "
6 and did e·, and gave also unto her "
6 husband with her; and he did e·. "
11 thee that thou shouldest not e·? "
12 she gave me of the tree, and I did e·. "
13 serpent beguiled me, and I did e·. "
14 dust shalt thou e· all the days of thy "
17 saying, Thou shalt not e· of it: "
17 thou e· of it all the days of thy life; "
18 thou shalt e· the herb of the field; "
19 the sweat of thy face shalt thou e· "
22 take also of the tree of life, and e·, "
9: 4 the blood thereof, shall ye not e·. "
18: 8 under the tree, and they did e·. "
19: 3 unleavened bread, and they did e·. "
24:33 was set meat before him to e·: "
33 but he said, I will not e·, "
54 And they did e· and drink, he and "
25:28 he did e· of his venison: 6310
34 he did e· and drink, and rose up, 398
26:30 made them a feast, and they did e· "
27: 4 bring it to me, that I may e·; "
7 me savoury meat, that I may e·, "
10 may e·, and that he may bless thee "
19 sit and e· of my venison, that thy "
25 and I will e· of my son's venison, "
25 it near to him, and he did e·: "
31 arise, and e· of his son's venison, "
28:20 I go, and will give me bread to e·, "
31:46 and they did e· there upon the heap. "
54 and called his brethren to e· bread, "
54 did e· bread, and tarried all night "
32:32 children of Israel e· not of the sinew "
37:25 and they sat down to e· bread: "
39: 6 save the bread which he did e·. "
40:17 birds did e· them out of the basket "
19 and the birds shall e· thy flesh "

Ge 41: 4 did e' up the seven well favoured 398
20 the...kine did e' up the first seven "
43:25 that they should e' bread there. "
32 Egyptians, which did e' with him, "
32 not e' bread with the Hebrews; "
45:18 and ye shall e' the fat of the land. "
47:22 and did e' their portion which "
Ex 2:20 call him, that he may e' bread. "
10: 5 and they shall e' the residue of "
5 shall e' every tree which groweth "
12 and e' every herb of the land, "
15 they did e' every herb of the land, "
12: 7 houses, wherein they shall e' it. "
8 shall e' the flesh in that night "
8 with bitter herbs they shall e' it. "
9 E' not of it raw, nor sodden at all "
11 And thus shall ye e' it; with your "
11 and ye shall e' it in haste: "
15 days shall ye e' unleavened bread; "
16 save that which every man must e', "
18 ye shall e' unleavened bread, until "
20 Ye shall e' nothing leavened; in all "
20 shall ye e' unleavened bread. "
43 There shall no stranger e' thereof: "
44 him, then shall he e' thereof. "
45 an hired servant shall not e' thereof. "
48 no uncircumcised person shall e' "
13: 6 thou shalt e' unleavened bread, "
16: 3 when we did e' bread to the full; "
8 give you in the evening flesh to e', "
12 At even ye shall e' flesh, and in the "
15 which the Lord hath given you to e'. 402
25 And Moses said, E' that to day; 398
35 the children of Israel did e' manna "
35 they did e' manna, until they came "
18:12 e' bread with Moses' father in law "
22:31 shall ye e' any flesh that is torn "
23:11 that the poor of thy people may e': "
11 the beasts of the field shall e'. "
15 e' unleavened bread seven days, "
24:11 they saw God, and did e' and drink. "
29:32 And Aaron and his sons shall e' "
33 And they shall e' those things "
33 but a stranger shall not e' thereof, "
32: 6 people sat down to e' and to drink, "
34:15 and thou e' of his sacrifice; "
18 thou shalt e' unleavened bread, "
28 neither e' bread, nor drink water. "
Le 3:17 that ye e' neither fat nor blood. "
6:16 thereof shall Aaron and his sons e': "
16 the congregation they shall e' it. "
18 the children of Aaron shall e' of it. "
26 that offereth it for sin shall e' it: "
29 among the priests shall e' thereof: "
7: 6 among the priests shall e' thereof: "
19 all that be clean shall e' thereof. "
21 and e' of the flesh of the sacrifice "
23 Ye shall e' no manner of fat, "
24 but ye shall in no wise e' of it. "
26 ye shall e' no manner of blood, "
8:31 and there e' it with the bread that is "
31 Aaron and his sons shall e' it. "
10:12 and e' it without leaven beside the "
13 And ye shall e' it in the holy place, "
14 and heave shoulder shall ye e' "
11: 2 ye shall e' among all the beasts "
3 among the beasts, that shall ye e'. "
4 Nevertheless these shall ye not e' "
8 Of their flesh shall ye not e', "
9 ye e' of all that are in the waters: "
9 and in the rivers, them shall ye e'. "
11 ye shall not e' of their flesh, "
21 Yet these may ye e' of every flying "
22 even these of them ye may e'; "
39 any beast, of which ye may e', 402
42 them ye shall not e'; for they are 398
17:12 No soul of you shall e' blood, "
12 any stranger...among you e' blood. "
14 Ye shall e' the blood of no manner "
19:25 fifth year shall ye e' of the fruit "
26 not e' anything with the blood. "
21:22 He shall e' the bread of his God, "
22: 4 he shall not e' of the holy things, "
6 and shall not e' of the holy things, "
7 shall afterward e' the holy things; "
8 he shall not e' to defile himself "
10 no stranger e' of the holy thing: "
10 shall not e' of the holy thing. "
11 he shall e' of it, and he that is born "
11 they shall e' of his meat. "
12 she may not e' of an offering "
13 she shall e' of her father's meat: "
13 there shall no stranger e' thereof. "
14 if a man e' of the holy thing "
16 when they e' their holy things: "
23: 6 days ye must e' unleavened bread. "
14 And ye shall e' neither bread, nor "
24: 9 they shall e' it in the holy place: "
25:12 ye shall e' the increase thereof out "
19 shall e' your fill, and dwell therein "
20 What shall we e' the seventh year? "
22 and e' yet of old fruit until the ninth "
22 ye shall e' of the old store. "
26: 5 ye shall e' your bread to the full, "
10 ye shall e' old store, and bring forth "
16 for your enemies shall e' it. "
26 ye shall e', and not be satisfied. "
29 ye shall e' the flesh of your sons, "
29 flesh of your daughters shall ye e'. "
38 land of your enemies shall e' you "
Nu 6: 3 nor e' moist grapes, or dried. "
4 shall he e' nothing that is made "
9:11 and e' it with unleavened bread "
11: 4 Who shall give us flesh to e'? "
5 remember the fish, which we did e' "
13 Give us flesh, that we may e'. "

Nu 11:18 and ye shall e' flesh: for ye have 398
18 Who shall give us flesh to e'? "
18 will give you flesh, and ye shall e'. "
19 shall not e' one day, nor two days, "
21 that they may e' a whole month. "
15:19 when ye e' of the bread of the land, "
18:10 most holy place shalt thou e' it; "
10 every male shall e' it: "
11 is clean in thy house shall e' of it. "
13 is clean in thine house shall e' of it. "
31 And ye shall e' it in every place, "
23:24 not lie down until he e' of the prey, "
24: 8 he shall e' up the nations "
25: 2 the people did e', and bowed down "
De 2: 6 of them for money, that ye may e'; "
28 me meat for money, that I may e'; "
4:28 see, nor hear, nor e', nor smell. "
8: 9 A land wherein thou shalt e' bread "
9: 9 did e' bread nor drink water: "
18 neither e' bread, nor drink water, "
11:15 that thou mayest e' and be full. "
12: 7 there ye shall e' before the Lord "
15 kill and e' flesh in all thy gates, "
15 and the clean may e' thereof, "
16 Only ye shall not e' the blood; "
17 mayest not e' within thy gates "
18 thou must e' them before the Lord "
20 and thou shalt say, I will e' flesh, "
20 because thy soul longeth to e' flesh; "
20 thou mayest e' flesh, whatsoever "
21 and thou shalt e' in thy gates "
22 so thou shalt e' them: the unclean "
22 and the clean shall e' of them alike. "
23 be sure that thou e' not the blood: "
23 mayest not e' the life with the flesh. "
24 Thou shalt not e' it; thou shalt pour "
25 Thou shalt not e' it; that it may go "
27 and thou shalt e' the flesh. "
14: 3 shalt not e' any abominable thing. "
4 are the beasts which ye shall e': "
6 among the beasts, that ye shall e'. "
7 Nevertheless these ye shall not e' "
8 ye shall not e' of their flesh, "
9 shall e' of all that are in the waters: "
9 that have fins and scales shall ye e': "
10 not fins and scales ye may not e'; "
11 Of all clean birds ye shall e'. "
12 are they of which ye shall not e': "
20 But of all clean fowls ye may e'. "
21 Ye shall not e' of anything that "
21 is in thy gates, that he may e' it; "
23 And thou shalt e' before the Lord "
26 thou shalt e' there before the Lord "
29 come, and shall e' and be satisfied; "
15:20 Thou shalt e' it before the Lord "
22 Thou shalt e' it within thy gates: "
23 thou shalt not e' the blood thereof; "
16: 3 shalt e' no leavened bread with it; "
3 seven days shalt thou e' unleavened "
7 And thou shalt roast and e' it "
8 Six days shalt thou e' unleavened "
18: 1 shall e' the offerings of the Lord "
8 They shall have like portions to e', "
20: 6 battle, and another man e' of it. *2490
14 shalt e' the spoil of thine enemies, 398
19 for thou mayest e' of them, and "
23:24 then thou mayest e' grapes thy fill "
26:12 that they may e' within thy gates, "
27: 7 e' there, and rejoice before the Lord "
28:31 and thou shalt not e' thereof: "
33 which thou knowest not e' up: "
39 grapes; for the worms shall e' them. "
51 he shall e' the fruit of thy cattle, "
53 shalt e' the fruit of thine own body, "
55 his children whom he shall e': "
57 shall e' them for want of all things "
32:13 might e' the increase of the fields; "
38 did e' the fat of their sacrifices, "
Jos 5:11 And they did e' of the old corn "
12 but they did e' of the fruit of the "
24:13 which ye planted not do ye e'. "
J'g 9:27 e' and drink, and cursed Abimelech. "
13: 4 and e' not any unclean thing: "
7 drink, neither e' any unclean thing: "
14 She may not e' of any thing that "
14 nor e' any unclean thing: all that I "
16 I will not e' of thy bread: "
14: 9 he gave them, and they did e': "
19: 4 did e' and drink, and lodged there. "
6 they sat down, and did e' and drink "
8 and they did e' both of them. "
21 their feet, and did e' and drink. "
Ru 2:14 e' of the bread, and dip thy morsel "
14 and she did e', and was sufficed, "
1Sa 1: 7 therefore she wept, and did not e'. "
18 the woman went her way, and did e', "
2:36 that I may e' a piece of bread. "
9:13 he go up to the high place to e': "
13 the people will not e' until he come, "
13 afterwards they e' that be bidden. "
19 for ye shall e' with me to day, "
24 set it before thee, and e': for unto "
24 So Saul did e' with Samuel that day. "
14:32 people did e' them with the blood. "
33 in that they e' with the blood. "
34 slay them here, and e'; and sin not "
20:24 the king sat him down to e' meat. "
34 and did e' no meat the second day "
28:22 e', that thou mayest have strength, "
23 he refused, and said, I will not e'. "
25 before his servants; and they did e'. "
30:11 and gave him bread, and he did e'; "
2Sa 3:35 to cause David to e' meat while it 1262
9: 7 thou shalt not e' bread at my table 398
10 master's son may have food to e': "
10 thy master's son shall e' bread "

2Sa 9:11 e' at my table, as one of the king's 398
13 he did e' continually at the king's "
11:11 into mine house, to e' and to drink, "
13 And...he did e' and drink before him; "
12: 3 it did e' of his own meat, "
17 neither did he e' bread with them. 1262
20 set bread before him, and he did e'. 398
21 thou didst rise and e' bread. "
13: 5 that I may see it, and e' it at her hand. "
6 that I may e' at her hand. 1262
9 before him; but he refused to e'. 398
10 that I may e' of thine hand. 1262
11 had brought them unto him to e', 398
16: 2 fruit for the young men to e'; "
17:29 the people that were with him, to e': "
19:28 them that did e' at thine own table. "
35 taste what I e' or what I drink? "
1Ki 1:25 they e' and drink before him, "
2: 7 be of those that e' at thy table: "
13: 8 neither will I e' bread nor drink "
9 E' no bread, nor drink water, nor "
15 Come home with me, and e' bread. "
16 neither will I e' bread nor drink "
17 Thou shalt e' no bread nor drink "
18 he may e' bread and drink water. "
19 and did e' bread in his house, "
22 E' no bread, and drink no water; "
14:11 in the city shall the dogs e'; and "
11 the field shall the fowls of the air e': "
16: 4 Baasha in the city shall the dogs e'; "
4 fields shall the fowls of the air e'. "
17:12 that we may e' it, and die. "
15 she, and he, and her house, did e' "
18:19 hundred, which e' at Jezebel's table. "
41 Get thee up, e' and drink; for there "
42 Ahab went up to e' and to drink. "
19: 5 and said unto him, Arise and e'. "
6 did e' and drink, and laid him down "
7 Arise and e'; because the journey is "
8 he arose, and did e' and drink, "
21 unto the people, and they did e'. "
21: 4 his face, and would e' no bread. "
7 arise, and e' bread, and let thine "
23 dogs shall e' Jezebel by the wall "
24 Ahab in the city the dogs shall e'; "
24 field shall the fowls of the air e'. "
2Ki 4: 8 she constrained him to e' bread. "
8 he turned in thither to e' bread. "
40 they poured out for the men to e'. "
40 And they could not e' thereof. "
41 for the people, that they may e'. "
42 unto the people, that they may e'. "
43 Give the people, that they may e'; "
43 shall e', and shall leave thereof. "
44 set it before them, and they did e', "
6:22 e' and drink, and go to their master. "
28 thy son, that we may e' him to day, "
28 and we will e' my son to-morrow. "
29 we boiled my son, and did e' him: "
29 Give thy son, that we may e' him: "
7: 2 thine eyes, but shalt not e' thereof. "
8 into one tent, and did e' and drink, "
19 thine eyes, but shalt not e' thereof. "
9:10 dogs shall e' Jezebel in the portion "
34 he did e' and drink, and said, Go, "
36 the portion of Jezreel shall dogs e' "
18:27 that they may e' their own dung, "
31 e' ye every man of his own vine, "
19:29 e' this year such things as grow "
29 vineyards, and e' the fruits thereof. "
23: 9 they did e' of the unleavened bread "
25:29 did e' bread continually before him "
1Ch 29:22 did e' and drink before the Lord "
2Ch 28:15 and gave them to e' and to drink, "
30:18 did they e' the passover otherwise "
22 and they did e' throughout the feast "
31:10 we have had enough to e', and * "
Ezr 2:63 should not e' of the most holy things, "
6:21 seek the Lord God of Israel, did e', "
9:12 and e' the good of the land, "
10: 6 he did e' no bread, nor drink water: "
Ne 5: 2 for them, that we may e', and live. "
7:65 should not e' of the most holy things. "
8:10 e' the fat, and drink the sweet, "
12 the people went their way to e', "
9:25 so they did e', and were filled, "
36 our fathers to e' the fruit thereof "
Es 4:16 neither e' nor drink three days, "
Job 1: 4 to e' and to drink with them. "
3:24 For my sighing cometh before I e'. 3899
31: 8 let me sow, and let another e'; 398
42:11 did e' bread with him in his house: "
Ps 14: 4 e' up my people as they e' bread, "
22:26 The meek shall e' and be satisfied: "
29 fat upon earth shall e' and worship: "
27: 2 came upon me to e' up my flesh, "
41: 9 I trusted, which did e' of my bread, "
50:13 Will I e' the flesh of bulls, or drink "
53: 4 e' up my people as they e' bread: "
78:24 down manna upon them to e', "
25 Man did e' angels' food: he sent "
29 So they did e', and were well filled: "
102: 4 so that I forget to e' my bread. "
105:35 did e' up all the herbs in their land, "
127: 2 up late, to e' the bread of sorrows: "
128: 2 shalt e' the labour of thine hands: "
141: 4 let me not e' of their dainties. 3898
Pr 1:31 e' of the fruit of their own way, 398
4:17 they e' the bread of wickedness, 3898
9: 5 Come, e' of my bread, and drink of "
13: 2 e' good by the fruit of his mouth: 398
2 of the transgressors shall e' violence. "
18:21 they that love it shall e' the fruit 398
23: 1 thou sittest to e' with a ruler, 3898
6 E' thou not the bread of him that "
7 E' and drink, said he to thee; 398

Pr 24:13 e' thou honey, because it is good; 398
25:16 e' so much as is sufficient for thee, "
21 give him bread to e'; and if he be "
27 It is not good to e' much honey: "
27:18 fig tree shall e' the fruit thereof: "
30:17 and the young eagles shall e' it. "
Ec 2:24 than that he should e' and drink, "
25 For who can e', or who else can "
3:13 that every man should e' and drink, "
5:11 they are increased that e' them: "
12 sweet, whether he e' little or much: "
18 comely for one to e' and to drink, "
19 hath given him power to e' thereof, "
6: 2 God giveth him not power to e' "
8:15 than to e', and to drink, "
9: 7 e' thy bread with joy, and drink "
10:16 and thy princes e' in the morning! "
17 and thy princes e' in due season, "
Ca 4:16 garden, and e' his pleasant fruits. "
5: 1 e', O friends; drink, yea, drink "
Isa 1:19 ye shall e' the good of the land: "
3:10 shall e' the fruit of their doings. "
4: 1 We will e' our own bread, and "
5:17 of the fat ones shall strangers e'. "
7:15 Butter and honey shall he e', that "
22 he shall e' butter: for butter "
22 and honey shall every one e' "
9:20 and he shall e' on the left hand, "
20 they shall e' every man the flesh of "
11: 7 the lion shall e' straw like the ox. "
21: 5 watch in the watchtower, e', drink: "
22:13 drinking wine: let us e' and drink; "
23:18 to e' sufficiently, and for durable "
30:24 shall e' clean provender, which "
36:12 that they may e' their own dung, "
16 and e' ye every one of his vine, "
37:30 shall e' this year such as groweth "
30 vineyards, and e' the fruit thereof. "
50: 9 the moth shall e' them up. "
51: 8 For the moth shall e' them up like "
8 the worm shall e' them like wool: "
55: 1 come ye, buy, and e'; yea, come, "
2 and e' ye that which is good, "
61: 6 shall e' the riches of the Gentiles, "
62: 9 that have gathered it shall e' it, "
65: 4 which e' swine's flesh, and broth "
13 Behold, my servants shall e', but "
21 vineyards, and e' the fruit of them. "
22 they shall not plant, and another e': "
25 lion shall e' straw like the bullock: "
Jer 2: 7 to e' the fruit thereof and the "
5:17 And they shall e' up thine harvest "
17 sons and thy daughters should e': "
17 e' up thy flocks and thine herds: "
17 they shall e' up thy vines "
7:21 unto your sacrifices, and e' flesh. "
15:16 were found, and I did e' them; "
16: 8 to sit with them to e' and to drink. "
19: 9 I will cause them to e' the flesh of "
9 they shall e' every one the flesh of "
22:15 did not thy father e' and drink, "
22 wind shall e' up all thy pastors, *7462
29: 5 gardens, and e' the fruit of them; 398
28 and plant gardens, and e' the fruit "
31: 5 shall e' them as common things. *
41: 1 there they did e' bread together 398
52:33 and he did continually e' bread "
La 2:20 Shall the women e' their fruit, and "
Eze 2: 8 open thy mouth, and e' that I give "
3: 1 Son of man, e' that thou findest; "
1 e' this roll, and go speak "
2 and he caused me to e' that roll. "
3 Son of man, cause thy belly to e', "
3 did I e' it; and it was in my mouth "
4: 9 days shalt thou e' thereof. "
10 thy meat which thou shalt e' shall "
10 from time to time shalt thou e' it. "
12 thou shalt e' it as barley cakes, "
13 thus shall the children of Israel e' "
16 and they shall e' bread by weight, "
5:10 the fathers shall e' the sons "
10 and the sons shall e' their fathers; "
12:18 man, e' thy bread with quaking, "
19 e' their bread with carefulness, "
16:13 thou didst e' fine flour, and honey, "
22: 9 thee they e' upon the mountains: * "
24:17 and e' not the bread of men. "
22 your lips, nor e' the bread of men. "
25: 4 they shall e' thy fruit, and they "
33:25 Ye e' with the blood, and lift up "
34: 3 Ye e' the fat, and ye clothe you with "
19 e' that which ye have trodden 7462
39:17 ye may e' flesh, and drink blood. 398
18 shall e' the flesh of the mighty, "
19 And ye shall e' fat till ye be full, "
42:13 Lord shall e' the most holy things: "
44: 3 he shall sit in it to e' bread "
29 They shall e' the meat offering, and "
31 The priests shall not e' of any thing "
Da 1:12 let them give us pulse to e', "
13 e' of the portion of the king's meat: "
15 did e' the portion of the king's meat. "
4:25 they shall make thee to e' grass 2939
32 make thee to e' grass as oxen, "
33 and did e' grass as oxen, and his 399
Ho 2:12 the beasts of the field shall e' them. 398
4: 8 They e' up the sin of my people, * "
10 they shall e', and not have enough: "
8:13 of mine offerings, and e' it; "
9: 3 shall e' unclean things in Assyria. "
4 that e' thereof shall be polluted: "
Joe 2:26 And ye shall e' in plenty, and be "
Am 6: 4 and e' the lambs out of the flock, "
7: 4 the great deep, and did e' up a part.* "
12 there e' bread, and prophesy there: "
9:14 gardens, and e' the fruit of them. "

Ob 1: 7 they that e' thy bread have laid a "
Mic 3: 3 Who also e' the flesh of my people, 398
6:14 Thou shalt e', but not be satisfied; "
7: 1 vintage: there is no cluster to e': "
Na 3:15 e' thee up like the cankerworm: * "
Hab 1: 8 as the eagle that hasteth to e'. * "
Hag 1: 6 ye e', but ye have not enough; "
Zec 7: 6 when ye did e', and when ye did "
6 did not ye e' for yourselves, and "
11: 9 e' every one the flesh of another. "
16 he shall e' the flesh of the fat, "
M't 6:25 what ye shall e', or what ye shall 5315
31 saying, What shall we e'? or, What "
12: 1 pluck the ears of corn, and to e'. 2068
4 and did e' the shewbread, 5315
4 which was not lawful for him to e', "
14:16 not depart; give ye them to e'. "
20 And they did all e', and were filled: "
15: 2 wash not their hands when they e' 2068
20 but to e' with unwashen hands 5315
27 the dogs e' of the crumbs which 2068
32 three days, and have nothing to e': 5315
37 they did all e', and were filled: "
38 did e' were four thousand men, 2068
24:49 to e' and drink with the drunken; "
26:17 prepare for thee to e' the passover? 5315
21 as they did e', he said, Verily I say 2068
26 said, Take, e'; this is my body. 5315
M'r 1: 6 he did e' locusts and wild honey; 2068
2:16 e' with publicans and sinners, * "
26 and did e' the shewbread, which is 5315
26 not lawful to e' but for the priests, "
3:20 could not so much as e' bread. "
5:43 should be given her to e'. "
6:31 had no leisure so much as to e'. "
36 bread: for they have nothing to e'. "
37 said unto them, Give ye them to e'. "
37 of bread, and give them to e'? "
42 And they did all e', and were filled. "
44 And they that did e' of the loaves* "
7: 2 saw some of his disciples e' bread*2068
3 e' not, holding the tradition of "
4 except they wash, they e' not. "
5 but e' bread with unwashen hands? "
28 yet the dogs under the table e' of "
8: 1 having nothing to e', Jesus called 5315
2 days, and have nothing to e': "
8 So they did e', and were filled: "
11:14 No man e' fruit of thee hereafter "
14:12 and prepare that thou mayest e' "
14 where I shall e' the passover with "
18 as they sat and did e', Jesus said, 2068
22 as they did e', Jesus took bread, * "
22 said, Take, e'; this is my body. 5315
Lu 4: 2 in those days he did e' nothing: "
5:30 ye e' and drink with publicans 2068
33 Pharisees; but thine e' and drink? "
6: 1 and did e', rubbing them in their "
4 did take and e' the shewbread, 5315
4 not lawful to e' but for the priests "
7:36 him that he would e' with him. "
9:13 unto them, Give ye them to e'. "
17 And they did e', and were all filled: "
10: 8 e' such things as are set before 2068
12:19 take thine ease, e', drink, and be 5315
22 for your life, what ye shall e'; "
29 seek not ye what ye shall e', "
45 to e' and drink, and to be drunken; 2068
14: 1 to e' bread on the sabbath day, 5315
15 Blessed is he that shall e' bread in "
15:16 the husks that the swine did e': 2068
23 and let us e', and be merry: 5315
17: 8 afterward thou shalt e' and drink? "
27 They did e', they drank, they *2068
28 they did e', they drank, they * "
22: 8 us the passover, that we may e'. 5315
11 where I shall e' the passover with "
15 I have desired to e' this passover "
16 I will not any more e' thereof, "
30 That ye may e' and drink at my 2068
24:43 he took it, and did e' before them. 5315
Joh 4:31 prayed him, saying, Master, e'. "
32 I have meat to e' that ye know not "
33 any man brought him ought to e'? "
6: 5 we buy bread, that these may e'? "
23 the place where they did e' bread,* "
26 but because ye did e' of the loaves,* "
31 Our fathers did e' manna in the * "
31 gave them bread from heaven to e'. "
49 Your fathers did e' manna in the "
50 that a man may e' thereof, and not "
51 if any man e' of this bread, "
52 can this man give us his flesh to e'? "
53 Except ye e' the flesh of the Son of "
58 not as your fathers did e' manna, "
18:28 but that they might e' the passover. "
Ac 2:46 did e' their meat with gladness *3335
9: 9 sight, and neither did e' nor drink. 5315
10:13 Rise, Peter; kill, and e'. "
41 who did e' and drink with him 4906
11: 3 uncircumcised, and didst e' with "
7 Arise, Peter; slay and e'. 5315
23:12 they would neither e' nor drink "
14 we will e' nothing until we have *1089
21 an oath, that they will neither e' 5315
27:35 he had broken it, he began to e'. 2068
Ro 14: 2 believeth that he may e' all things: 5315
21 It is good neither to e' flesh, nor to "
23 that doubteth is damned if he e', "
1Co 5:11 with such a one no not to e'. 4906
8: 7 e' it as a thing offered unto an 2068
8 neither, if we e', are we the better; 5315
8 if we e' not, are we the worse. "
10 e' those things which are offered 2068
13 I will e' no flesh while the world 5315
9: 4 Have we not power to e' and to "

1Co 10: 3 did all e' the same spiritual meat; 5315
7 people sat down to e' and drink, "
18 are they which e' of the sacrifices 2068
25 is sold in the shambles, that e', "
27 whatsoever is set before you, e', "
28 e' not for his sake that shewed it, "
31 Whether therefore ye e', or drink, "
11:20 this is not to e' the Lord's supper. 5315
22 have ye not houses to e' and to 2068
24 Take, e'; this is my body, which *5315
26 as often as ye e' this bread, 2068
27 whosoever shall e' this bread, and "
28 and so let him e' of that bread, "
33 when ye come together to e', tarry 5315
34 man hunger, let him e' at home; 2068
15:32 let us e' and drink; for to-morrow 5315
Ga 2:12 James, he did e' with the Gentiles: 4906
2Th 3: 8 Neither did we e' any man's 5315
10 not work, neither should he e'. 2068
12 with quietness they work, and e' "
2Ti 2:17 word will e' as doth a canker: 3542, 2192
Heb 13:10 they have no right to e' which 5315
Jas 5: 3 and shall e' your flesh as it were "
Rev 2: 7 will I give to e' of the tree of life, "
14 to e' things sacrificed unto idols, "
17 will I give to e' of the hidden * "
20 to e' things sacrificed unto idols. "
10: 9 Take it, and e' it up; and it shall 2719
17:16 and shall e' her flesh, and burn her 5315
19:18 That ye may e' the flesh of kings, "

eaten

Ge 3:11 Hast thou e' of the tree, whereof I 398
17 hast e' of the tree, of which I "
6:21 unto thee of all food that is e', "
14:24 that which the young men have e', "
27:33 I have e' of all before thou camest, "
31:38 the rams of thy flock have I not e'. "
41:21 when they had e' them 935, 413, 7130
21 that they had e' them; " " "
43: 2 when they had e' up the corn 398
Ex 12:46 In one house shall it be e'; "
13: 3 there shall no leavened bread be e'. "
7 Unleavened bread shall be e' seven "
21:28 and his flesh shall not be e'; "
22: 5 cause a field or vineyard to be e', 1197
29:34 it shall not be e', because it is holy. 398
Le 6:16 with unleavened bread shall it be e' "
23 be wholly burnt: it shall not be e'. "
26 in the holy place shall it be e', "
30 no sin offering....shall be e': "
7: 6 it shall be e' in the holy place: "
15 shall be e' the same day that it is "
16 it shall be e' the same day that he "
16 the remainder of it shall be e': "
18 his peace offerings be e' at all "
19 any unclean thing shall not be e'; "
10:17 Wherefore have ye not e' the sin "
18 ye should indeed have e' it in the "
19 and if I had e' the sin offering "
11:13 they shall not be e', they are an "
34 Of all meat which may be e', "
41 an abomination; it shall not be e'. "
47 between the beast that may be e' "
47 and the beast that may not be e'. "
17:13 any beast or fowl that may be e'; "
19: 6 It shall be e' the same day ye offer "
7 if it be e' at all on the third day, "
23 it shall not be e' of. "
22:30 On the same day it shall be e' "
Nu 28:17 days shall unleavened bread be e'. "
De 6:11 when thou shalt have e' and be * "
8:10 when thou hast e' and art full, * "
12 Lest when thou hast e' and art full, "
12:22 the roebuck and the hart is e', "
14:19 unto you: they shall not be e'. "
20: 6 vineyard, and hath not yet e' of it?*2490
26:14 I have not e' thereof in my 398
29: 6 Ye have not e' bread, neither have "
31:20 and they shall have e' and filled "
Jos 5:12 after they had e' of the old corn "
Ru 3: 7 when Boaz had e' and drunk, and "
1 Sa 1: 9 Hannah rose up after they had e' in "
14:30 if haply the people had e' freely "
28:20 he had e' no bread all the day, "
30:12 and when he had e', his spirit came "
12 for he had e' no bread, nor drunk "
2 Sa 19:42 have we e' at all of the king's cost? "
1Ki 13:22 and hast e' bread and drunk water "
23 it came to pass, after he had e' "
28 the lion had not e' the carcase, "
2Ki 6:23 and when they had e' and drunk, "
Ne 5:14 my brethren have not e' the bread "
Job 6: 6 Can that which is unsavoury be e' "
13:28 as a garment that is moth e'. "
31:17 Or have e' my morsel myself alone, "
17 the fatherless hath not e' thereof; "
39 If I have e' the fruits thereof "
Ps 69: 9 the zeal of thine house hath e' me "
102: 9 For I have e' ashes like bread, "
Pr 9:17 and bread e' in secret is pleasant. "
23: 8 The morsel which thou hast e' 398
Ca 5: 1 I have e' my honeycomb with my "
Isa 3:14 for ye have e' up the vineyard; "
5: 5 hedge thereof, and it shall be e' up; "
6:13 it shall return, and shall be e': 1197
44:19 I have roasted flesh, and e' it: 398
Jer 10:25 for they have e' up Jacob, and * "
24: 2 naughty figs, which could not be e', "
3 evil, very evil, that cannot be e', "
8 as the evil figs, which cannot be e', "
29:17 like vile figs, that cannot be e', "
31:29 The fathers have e' a sour grape, "
Eze 4:14 have I not e' of that which dieth "
18: 2 The fathers have e' sour grapes, "
6 and hath not e' upon the mountains, "
11 even hath e' upon the mountains. "

Eze 18:15 hath not e· upon the mountains, 398
34:18 to have e· up the good pasture, *7462
45:21 days; unleavened bread shall be e·. 398
Ho 10:13 ye have e· the fruit of lies: "
Joe 1: 4 worm hath left hath the locust e·; "
4 hath left hath the cankerworm e·; "
4 hath left hath the caterpiller e·. "
2:25 the years that the locust hath e·. "
M't 14:21 And they that had e· were about 2068
M'r 8: 9 And they that had e· were about *5315
Lu 13:26 We have e· and drunk in thy "
17: 8 till I have e· and drunken; and "
Joh 2:17 zeal of thine house hath e· me up. 2719
6:13 and above unto them that had e·. 977
Ac 10:10 very hungry, and would have e·: *1089
14 for I have never e· anything that 5315
12:23 and he was e· of worms, 4662
20:11 had broken bread, and e·, and 1089
27:38 when they had e· enough, they 2880
Rev 10:10 as soon as I had e· it, 5315

eater See also EATERS.
J'g 14:14 Out of the e· came forth meat, 398
Isa 55:10 to the sower, and bread to the e·: "
Nah 3:12 even fall into the mouth of the e·. "

eaters
Pro 23:20 among riotous e· of flesh: 2151

eatest
Ge 2:17 the day that thou e· thereof thou 398
1Sa 1: 8 weepest thou? and why e· thou not? "
1Ki 21: 5 spirit so sad, that thou e· no bread? "

eateth
Ex 12:15 whosoever e· leavened bread from 398
19 whosoever e· that which is leavened, "
Lev 7:18 the soul that e· of it shall bear his "
20 But the soul that e· of the flesh "
25 For whosoever e· the fat of the "
25 even the soul that e· it shall be cut "
27 Whatsoever soul it be that e· any "
11:40 And he that e· of the carcase "
14:47 and he that e· in the house shall "
17:10 that e· any manner of blood; I will "
10 against that soul that e· blood, "
14 whosoever e· it shall be cut off. "
15 every soul that e· that which died "
19: 8 Therefore every one that e· it shall "
Nu 13:32 e· up the inhabitants thereof; and "
1Sa 14:24 the man that e· any food until "
28 Cursed be the man that e· any food "
Job 5: 5 the hungry e· up, and taketh it "
21:25 soul, and never e· with pleasure. * "
40:15 he e· grass as an ox. "
Ps 106:20 the similitude of an ox that e· grass. "
Pr 13:25 The righteous e· to the satisfying of "
30:20 she e·, and wipeth her mouth, "
31:27 and e· not the bread of idleness. "
Ec 4: 5 together, and e· his own flesh. "
5:17 All his days also he e· in darkness, "
6: 2 but a stranger e· it: this is vanity, "
Isa 28: 4 it is yet in his hand he e· it up. 1104
29: 8 man dreameth, and, behold, he e·; 398
44:16 with part thereof he e· flesh; "
59: 5 he that e· of their eggs dieth, "
Jer 31:30 every man that e· the sour grape, "
M't 9:11 e· your Master with publicans 2068
M'r 2:16 How is it that he e· and drinketh "
14:18 you, One of you which e· with me "
Lu 15: 2 receiveth sinners, and e· with them. 4906
Joh 6:54 Whoso e· my flesh, and drinketh 5176
56 He that e· my flesh, and drinketh "
57 so he that e· me, even he shall live "
58 he that e· of this bread shall live "
13:18 He that e· bread with me hath lifted "
Ro 14: 2 another, who is weak, e· herbs. 2068
3 Let not him that e· despise him that "
3 e· not; and let not him which e· not "
3 not judge him that e·: "
6 He that e·, e· to the Lord, for he "
6 God thanks; and he that e· not, "
6 not, to the Lord he e· not, "
20 it is evil for that man who e· with "
23 because he e· not of faith: "
1Co 9: 7 and e· not of the fruit thereof? "
7 and e· not of the milk of the flock? "
11:29 he that e· and drinketh unworthily, "
29 e· and drinketh damnation to "

eating
Ex 12: 4 every man according to his e· shall 400
16:16 of it every man according to his e·. "
18 every man according to his e·. "
21 every man according to his e·: and "
J'g 14: 9 went on e·, and came to his father 398
Ru 3: 3 until he shall have done e· and "
1Sa 14:34 sin not against the Lord in e· "
30:16 e· and drinking, and dancing, "
1Ki 1:41 as they had made an end of e·. "
4:20 e· and drinking, and making merry. "
2Ki 4:40 as they were e· of the pottage, "
1Ch 12:39 David three days, e· and drinking: "
Job 1:13 his sons and his daughters were e· "
18 thy sons and thy daughters were e· "
20:23 rain it upon him while he is e·. 3894
Isa 22:13 killing sheep, e· flesh, and drinking 398
66:17 e· swine's flesh, and the abomination, "
Am 7: 2 when they had made an end of e· "
M't 11:18 John came neither e· nor drinking, 2068
19 Son of man came e· and drinking, "
24:38 were e· and drinking, marrying 5176
26:26 And as they were e·, Jesus took 2068
Lu 7:33 the Baptist came neither e· bread "
34 The Son of man is come e· and "
10: 7 remain, e· and drinking such "
1Co 8: 4 the e· of those things that are 1035
11:21 For in e· every one taketh before 5315

Ebal (e'-bal)
Ge 36:23 Alvan, and Manaheth, and E·, 5858
De 11:29 and the curse upon mount E·. "
27: 4 command you this day, in mount E·, "
13 shall stand upon mount E· to curse; "
Jos 8:30 Lord God of Israel in mount E·, "
33 half of them over against mount E·; "
1Ch 1:22 And E·, and Abimael, and Sheba, "
40 Alian, and Manahath, and E·, "

Ebed (e'-bed) See also EBED-MELECH.
J'g 9:26 Gaal the son of E· came with his 5651
28 Gaal the son of E· said, Who is "
30 the words of Gaal the son of E·, his "
31 Behold, Gaal the son of E· and his "
35 Gaal the son of E· went out, and "
Ezr 8: 6 E· the son of Jonathan, and with "

Ebed-melech (e''-bed-me'-lek)
Jer 38: 7 Now when E· the Ethiopian, 5663
8 E· went forth out of the king's "
10 Then the king commanded E· the "
11 So E· took the men with him, "
12 E· the Ethiopian said unto "
39:16 Go and speak to E· the Ethiopian, "

Ebenezer (eb-en-e'-zur)
1Sa 4: 1 to battle, and pitched beside E·: 72
5: 1 and brought it from E· unto Ashdod. "
7:12 and called the name of it E·. "

Eber (e'-bur) See also HEBER.
Ge 10:21 the father of all the children of E·, 5677
24 begat Salah; and Salah begat E·. "
25 And unto E· were born two sons: "
11:14 lived thirty years, and begat E·: "
15 Salah lived after he begat E· "
16 And E· lived four and thirty years, "
17 And E· lived after he begat Peleg "
Nu 24:24 shall afflict E·, and he also shall "
1Ch 1:18 begat Shelah, and Shelah begat E·. "
19 And unto E· were born two sons; "
25 E·, Peleg, Reu, "
8:12 E·, and Misham, and Shamed, who "
Ne 12:20 of Sallai, Kallai; of Amok, E·; "

Ebiasaph (e-bi'-a-saf) See also ABIASAPH.
1Ch 6:23 Elkanah his son, and E· his son, 43
37 the son of Assir, the son of E·, "
9:19 the son of Kore, the son of E·, "

ebony
Eze 27:15 a present horns of ivory and e·. 1894

Ebronah (eb-ro'-nah)
Nu 33:34 Jotbathah, and encamped at E·. *5684
35 And they departed from E·, and * "

Ed (ed)
Jos 22:34 children of Gad called the altar E·:

Edar (e'-dar) See also EDER.
Ge 35:21 his tent beyond the tower of E·. *5740

Eden (e'-dun)
Ge 2: 8 planted a garden eastward in E·; 5731
10 went out of E· to water the garden; "
15 him into the garden of E· to dress it "
3:23 him forth from the garden of E·, "
24 east of the garden of E· Cherubims, "
4:16 the land of Nod, on the east of E·. "
2Ki 19:12 of E· which were in Thelasar? "
2Ch 29:12 of Zimnah, and E· the son of Joah: "
31:15 next him were E·, and Miniamin, "
Isa 37:12 of E· which were in Telassar? "
51: 3 will make her wilderness like E·, "
Eze 27:23 Haran, and Canneh, and E·, the "
28:13 hast been in E· the garden of God; "
31: 9 trees of E·, that were in the garden "
16 the trees of E·, the choice and best "
18 greatness among the trees of E·? "
18 brought down with the trees of E· "
36:35 is become like the garden of E·; "
Joe 2: 3 is as the garden of E· before them, "
Am 1: 5 the sceptre from the house of E·: "

Eder (e'-dur) See also EDAR.
Jos 15:21 were Kabzeel, and E·, and Jagur, 5740
1Ch 23:23 Mahli, and E·, and Jeremoth, three. "
24:30 Mahli, and E·, and Jerimoth. "

edge See also EDGES; SELVEDGE; TWOEDGED.
Ge 34:26 with the e· of the sword, 6310
Ex 13:20 Etham, in the e· of the wilderness. 7097
17:13 people with the e· of the sword. 6310
26: 4 upon the e· of the one curtain 8193
4 uttermost e· of another curtain, "
5 thou make in the e· of the curtain 7097
10 make fifty loops on the e· of the 8193
10 fifty loops in the e· of the curtain "
36:11 of blue on the e· of one curtain "
12 made he in the e· of the curtain 7097
17 the uttermost e· of the curtain "
17 made he upon the e· of the curtain "
Nu 21:24 smote him with the e· of the sword, 6310
33: 6 Etham, which is in the e· of the 7097
37 Hor, in the e· of the land of Edom. "
De 13:15 that city with the e· of the sword, 6310
15 thereof, with the e· of the sword. "
20:13 thereof with the e· of the sword: "
Jos 6:21 and ass, with the e· of the sword. "
8:24 all fallen on the e· of the sword, "
24 smote it with the e· of the sword. "
10:28 smote it with the e· of the sword, "
30 he smote it with the e· of the sword, "
32, 35, 37 and smote it with the e· of "
39 smote them with the e· of the sword, "
11:11 therein with the e· of the sword, "
12 smote them with the e· of the sword, "
14 they smote with the e· of the sword, "
13:27 the e· of the sea of Chinnereth *7097
19:47 smote it with the e· of the sword, 6310
J'g 1: 8 smitten it with the e· of the sword, "
25 the city with the e· of the sword; "
4:15 all his host, with the e· of the sword 6310
16 Sisera fell upon the e· of the sword; "
18:27 smote them with the e· of the sword, "
20:37 the city with the e· of the sword. "
48 smote them with the e· of the sword, "
21:10 with the e· of the sword, with the "
1Sa 15: 8 the people with the e· of the sword. "
22:19 smote he with the e· of the sword, "
19 and sheep, with the e· of the sword. "
2Sa 15:14 the city with the e· of the sword. "
2Ki 10:25 them with the e· of the sword; "
Job 1:15 servants with the e· of the sword; "
17 servants with the e· of the sword; "
Ps 89:43 also turned the e· of his sword, 6697
Ec 10:10 and he do not whet the e·, 6440
Jer 21: 7 them with the e· of the sword; 6310
31:29 the children's teeth are set on e·. 6949
30 his teeth shall be set on e·. "
Eze 18: 2 the children's teeth are set on e·? "
Lu 21:24 shall fall by the e· of the sword, 4750
Heb 11:34 escaped the e· of the sword, out of "

edges
Ex 28: 7 joined at the two e· thereof; *7098
39: 4 two e· was it coupled together. *7099
J'g 3:16 a dagger which had two e·, 6366
Re 2:12 hath the sharp sword with two e·; 1366

edification
Ro 15: 2 his neighbour for his good to e·. *3619
1Co 14: 3 speaketh unto men to e·, * "
2Co 10: 8 the Lord hath given us for e·, * "
13:10 the Lord hath given me to e·, * "

edified
Ac 9:31 the churches rest...and were e·; 3618
1Co 14:17 thanks well, but the other is not e·. "

edifieth
1Co 8: 1 puffeth up, but charity e·. 3618
14: 4 an unknown tongue e· himself; "
4 he that propesieth e· the church. "

edify See also EDIFIED; EDIFIETH; EDIFYING.
Ro 14:19 wherewith one may e· another. 3619
1Co 10:23 lawful for me, but all things e· not. 3618
1Th 5:11 together, and e· one another, "

edifying
1Co 14: 5 that the church may receive e·. 3619
12 may excel to the e· of the church. "
26 Let all things be done unto e·. "
2Co 12:19 things, dearly beloved, for your e·. "
Eph 4:12 for the e· of the body of Christ: * "
16 unto the e· of itself in love. * "
29 which is good to the use of e·, * "
1Ti 1: 4 than godly e· which is in faith: *3618

Edom (e'-dum) See also EDOMITES; ESAU; IDUMEA; OBED-EDOM.
Ge 25:30 therefore was his name called E·. 123
32: 3 the land of Seir, the country of E·. "
36: 1 the generations of Esau, who is E·. "
8 Esau in mount Seir; Esau is E·. "
16 came of Eliphaz in the land of E·; "
17 came of Reuel in the land of E·; "
19 are the sons of Esau, who is E·, "
21 children of Seir in the land of E·. "
31 kings that reigned in the land of E·, "
32 Bela the son of Beor reigned in E·: "
43 these be the dukes of E·, "
Ex 15:15 the dukes of E· shall be amazed; "
Nu 20:14 from Kadesh unto the king of E·, "
18 E· said unto him, Thou shalt not "
20 E· came out against him with much "
21 E· refused to give Israel passage "
23 by the coast of the land of E·, "
21: 4 to compass the land of E·: "
24:18 And E· shall be a possession, "
33:37 in the edge of the land of E·. "
34: 3 of Zin along by the coast of E· "
Jos 15: 1 border of E· the wilderness of Zin "
21 of Judah toward the coast of E· "
J'g 5: 4 marchedst out of the field of E·, "
11:17 sent messengers unto the king of E·, "
17 but the king of E· would not hearken "
18 and compassed the land of E·, "
1Sa 14:47 against E·, and against the kings of "
2Sa 8:14 And he put garrisons in E·; "
14 throughout all E· put he garrisons. "
14 they of E· became David's servants.* "
1Ki 9:26 of the Red sea, in the land of E·. "
11:14 he was of the king's seed in E·. "
15 came to pass, when David was in E·, "
15 he had smitten every male in E·; "
16 he had cut off every male in E·: "
22:47 There was then no king in E·: "
2Ki 3: 8 way through the wilderness of E·. "
9 king of Judah, and the king of E·: "
12 the king of E· went down to him. "
20 there came water by the way of E·, "
26 through even unto the king of E·: "
8:20 E· revolted from under the hand of "
22 Yet E· revolted from under the hand "
14: 7 He slew of E· in the valley of salt "
10 Thou hast indeed smitten E·, "
1Ch 1:43 kings that reigned in the land of E· "
51 the dukes of E· were; duke Timnah, "
54 Iram. These are the dukes of E·. "
18:11 from E·, and from Moab, and from "
13 And he put garrisons in E·; and all "
2Ch 8:17 at the sea side in the land of E·. "
25:20 they sought after the gods of E·. "
Ps 60:*title* smote in E· in the valley of salt "
8 over E· will I cast out my shoe: "
9 Who will lead me into E·? "
83: 6 of E·, and the Ishmaelites; "
108: 9 over E· will I cast out my shoe; "
10 who will lead me into E·? "
137: 7 the children of E· in the day of "

Isa 11:14 lay their hand upon E· and Moab; 123
63: 1 Who is this that cometh from E·, "
Jer 9:26 Egypt, and Judah, and E·, and the "
25:21 E·, and Moab, and the children of "
27: 3 And send them to the king of E·, "
40:11 among the Ammonites, and in E·, "
49: 7 concerning E·, thus saith the Lord "
17 Also E· shall be a desolation: "
20 that he hath taken against E·; "
22 the heart of the mighty men of E· "
La 4:21 and be glad, O daughter of E·, "
22 thine iniquity, O daughter of E·; "
Eze 25:12 E· hath dwelt against the house of "
13 also stretch out mine hand upon E·, "
14 I will lay my vengeance upon E· "
14 do in E· according to mine anger "
32:29 There is E·, her kings, and all her "
Da 11:41 out of his hand, even E·, and Moab, "
Joe 3:19 E· shall be a desolate wilderness, "
Am 1: 6 captivity to deliver them up to E·: "
9 up the whole captivity to E·, and "
11 For three transgressions of E·, and "
2: 1 burned the bones of the king of E· "
9:12 they may possess the remnant of E·, "
Ob 1 saith the Lord God concerning E·; "
8 even destroy the wise men out of E·, "
Mal 1: 4 E· saith, We are impoverished, "

Edomite (*e'-dum-ite*) See also EDOMITES.
De 23: 7 Thou shalt not abhor an E·: 130
1Sa 21: 7 and his name was Doeg, an E·, "
22: 9 Then answered Doeg the E·, "
18 And Doeg the E· turned, and he fell "
22 day, when Doeg the E· was there, "
1Ki 11:14 unto Solomon, Hadad the E·: 130
Ps 52:*title* Doeg the E· came and told Saul, "

Edomites (*e'-dum-ites*)
Ge 36: 9 Esau the father of the E· in mount 130
43 he is Esau the father of the E·. "
1Ki 11: 1 E·, Zidonians, and Hittites; "
17 Hadad fled, he and certain E· "
2Ki 8:21 smote the E· which compassed him 130
1Ch 18:12 the son Zeruiah slew of the E· "
13 all the E· became David's servants. "
2Ch 21: 8 In his days the E· revolted from "
9 smote the E· which compassed him "
10 So the E· revolted from under the "
25:14 come from the slaughter of the E·, "
19 sayest, Lo, thou hast smitten the E·; "
28:17 E· had come and smitten Judah, "

Edrei (*ed'-re-i*)
Nu 21:33 all his people, to the battle at E·. 154
De 1: 4 which dwelt at Astaroth in E·: "
3: 1 and all his people, to battle at E·. "
10 all Bashan, unto Salchah and E·, "
Jos 12: 4 that dwelt at Ashtaroth and at E·, "
13:12 reigned in Ashtaroth and in E·, "
31 half Gilead, and Ashtaroth, and E·, "
19:37 And Kedesh, and E·, and En-hazor, "

effect See also EFFECTED.
Nu 30: 8 shall make her vow...of none e·: *6565
2Ch 34:22 and they spake to her to that e·. "
Ps 33:10 devices of the people of none e·. 5106
Isa 32:17 the e· of righteousness quietness 5656
Jer 48:30 his lies shall not so e· it. *6213
Eze 12:23 hand, and the e· of every vision. 1697
M't 15: 6 commandment of God of none e· * *208*
M'r 7:13 the word of God of none e· * "
Ro 3: 3 make the faith of God without e·? *2673*
4:14 and the promise made of none e·: "
9: 6 word of God hath taken none e·. **1601*
1Co 1:17 Christ should be made of none e·.**2758*
Gal 3:17 make the promise of none e·. *2673*
5: 4 Christ is become of no e· unto * "

effected
2Ch 7:11 own house, he prosperously e·. 6743

effectual
1Co 16: 9 a great door and e· is opened *1756*
2Co 1: 6 which is e· in the enduring of the **1754*
Eph 3: 7 by the e· working of his power. **1753*
4:16 the e· working in the measure of * "
Ph'm 6 become e· by the acknowledging *1756*
Jas 5:16 e· fervent prayer of a righteous **1754*

effectually
Gal 2: 8 (For he that wrought e· in Peter **1754*
1Th 2:13 which e· worketh also in you * "

effeminate
1Co 6: 9 adulterers, nor e·, nor abusers of *3120*

egg See also EGGS.
Job 6: 6 any taste in the white of an e·? 2495
Lu 11:12 Or if he shall ask an e·, will he *5609*

eggs
De 22: 6 whether they be young ones, or e·, 1000
6 upon the young, or upon the e·, "
Job 39:14 Which leaveth her e· in the earth, "
Isa 10:14 as one gathereth e· that are left, "
59: 5 They hatch cockatrice' e·, and "
5 he that eateth of their e· dieth, "
Jer 17:11 As the partridge sitteth on e·, "

Eglah (*eg'-lah*) See also MICHAL.
2Sa 3: 5 Ithream, by E· David's wife. 5698
1Ch 3: 3 the sixth, Ithream by E· his wife. "

Eglaim (*eg'-la-im*) See also EN-EGLAIM.
Isa 15: 8 the howling thereof unto E·. 97

Eglon (*eg'-lon*)
Jos 10: 3 and unto Debir king of E·, saying, 5700
5 the king of Lachish, the king of E·, "
23 the king of Lachish, the king of E·. "
34 Lachish Joshua passed unto E·, "
36 And Joshua went up from E·, "
37 to all that he had done to E·; "
12:12 The king of E·, one; the king of "
15:39 Lachish, Bozkath, and E·, 5700
J'g 3:12 Lord strengthened E· the king of "
14 children of Israel served E· the "
15 Israel sent a present unto E· the "
17 brought the present unto E· the "
17 And E· was a very fat man. "

Egypt (*e'-jipt*) See also EGYPTIAN; MIZRAIM.
Ge 12:10 and Abram went down into E· 4714
11 was come near to enter into E·, "
14 when Abram was come into E·, "
13: 1 Abram went up out of E·, he, "
10 of the Lord, like the land of E·, "
15:18 given this land, from the river of E· "
21:21 him a wife out of the land of E·. "
25:18 E·, as thou goest toward Assyria: "
26: 2 and said, Go not down into E·; "
37:25 going to carry it down to E·. "
28 and they brought Joseph into E·. "
36 sold him into E· unto Potiphar, "
39: 1 Joseph was brought down to E·; "
40: 1 that the butler of the king of E· "
1 offended their lord the king of E·. "
5 the baker of the king of E·, which "
41: 8 the magicians of E·, and all the "
19 in all the land of E· for badness: "
29 throughout all the land of E·: "
30 be forgotten in the land of E·; "
33 and set him over the land of E·. "
34 up the fifth part of the land of E· "
36 which shall be in the land of E·; "
41 have set thee over all the land of E·. "
43 him ruler over all the land of E·. "
44 hand or foot in all the land of E·. "
45 went out over all the land of E·. "
46 he stood before Pharaoh king of E·. "
46 went throughout all the land of E·. "
48 which were in the land of E·, and "
53 that was in the land of E·, "
54 all the land of E· there was bread. "
55 all the land of E· was famished, "
56 famine waxed sore in the land of E·. "
57 And all the countries came into E· "
42: 1 saw that there was corn in E·, "
2 heard that there is corn in E·: "
3 went down to buy corn in E·. "
43: 2 which they had brought out of E·, "
15 and went down to E·, and stood "
45: 4 your brother, whom ye sold into E·. "
8 throughout all the land of E·. "
9 God hath made me lord of all E·: "
13 tell my father of all my glory in E·, "
18 give you the good of the land of E·, "
19 you wagons out of the land of E· "
20 good of all the land of E· is yours. "
23 laden with the good things of E·, "
25 they went up out of E·, and came "
26 governor over all the land of E·. "
46: 3 fear not to go down into E·; for "
4 I will go down with thee into E·; "
6 and came into E·, Jacob, and all "
7 seed brought he with him into E·. "
8 of Israel, which came into E·, "
20 unto Joseph in the land of E· were "
26 that came with Jacob into E·, "
27 Joseph, which were born him in E·, "
27 which came into E·, were "
47: 6 The land of E· is before thee; in "
11 them a possession in the land of E·, "
13 the land of E· and all the land of "
14 that was found in the land of E·, "
15 money failed in the land of E·, "
20 all the land of E· for Pharaoh; "
21 from one end of the borders of E· "
26 made it a law over the land of E· "
27 Israel dwelt in the land of E·, "
28 And Jacob lived in the land of E· "
29 bury me not, I pray thee, in E·: "
30 thou shalt carry me out of E·, "
48: 5 born unto thee in the land of E· "
5 I came unto thee into E·, are mine; "
50: 7 and all the elders of the land of E·, "
14 Joseph returned into E·, he, and "
22 Joseph dwelt in E·, he, and his "
26 and he was put in a coffin in E·. "
Ex 1: 1 of Israel, which came into E·; "
5 for Joseph was in E· already. "
8 there arose up a new king over E·, "
15 And the king of E· spake to the "
17 and did not as the king of E· "
18 And the king of E· called for the "
2:23 of time, that the king of E· died: "
3: 7 of my people which are in E·, and "
10 the children of Israel out of E·. "
11 the children of Israel out of E·? "
12 brought forth the people out of E·, "
16 that which is done to you in E·: "
17 you up out of the affliction of E· "
18 unto the king of E·, and ye shall "
19 the king of E· will not let you go, "
20 stretch out my hand, and smite E· "
4:18 unto my brethren which are in E·, "
19 in Midian, Go, return into E·: "
20 and he returned to the land of E·: "
21 return into E·, see that thou do all "
5: 4 the king of E· said unto them, "
12 throughout all the land of E· to "
6:11 speak unto Pharaoh king of E·, "
13 and unto Pharaoh king of E·, "
13 of Israel out of the land of E·. "
26 from the land of E· according to "
27 spake to Pharaoh king of E·, "
27 out the children of Israel from E·: "
28 spake unto Moses in the land of E·. "
29 thou unto Pharaoh king of E· all "
7: 3 and my wonders in the land of E·. "
4 lay my hand upon E·, and bring "
Ex 7: 4 land of E· by great judgments. 4714
5 stretch forth mine hand upon E·, "
11 magicians of E·, they also did in "
19 thine hand upon the waters of E·, "
19 blood throughout all the land of E·, "
21 blood throughout all the land of E·. "
22 the magicians of E· did so with "
8: 5 to come up upon the land of E·. "
6 his hand over the waters of E·; "
6 came up,and covered the land of E·. "
7 up frogs upon the land of E·. "
16 become lice throughout all...of E·. "
17 became lice throughout all...of E·. "
24 houses, and into all the land of E·: "
9: 4 of Israel and the cattle of E·: "
6 and all the cattle of E· died: "
9 small dust in all the land of E·, "
9 beast, throughout all the land of E·. "
18 hail, such as hath not been in E· "
22 may be hail in all the land of E·, "
22 field, throughout the land of E·. "
23 rained hail upon the land of E·. "
24 none like it in all the land of E· "
25 smote throughout all the land of E· "
10: 2 what things I have wrought in E·, "
7 thou not yet that E· is destroyed? "
12 over the land of E· for the locusts, "
12 may come up upon the land of E·, "
13 forth his rod over the land of E·, "
14 went up over all the land of E·, "
14 and rested in all the coasts of E·: "
15 field, through all the land of E·. "
19 one locust in all the coasts of E·. "
21 be darkness over the land of E·, "
22 in all the land of E· three days: "
11: 1 more upon Pharaoh, and upon E·; "
3 was very great in the land of E·, "
4 will I go out into the midst of E·: "
5 firstborn in the land of E· shall die, "
6 cry throughout all the land of E·, "
9 be multiplied in the land of E·. "
12: 1 Moses and Aaron in the land of E·, "
12 through the land of E· this night, "
12 all the firstborn in the land of E·, "
12 gods of E· I will execute judgment: "
13 you, when I smite the land of E·. "
17 your armies out of the land of E·: "
27 of the children of Israel in E·, "
29 all the firstborn in the land of E·, "
30 and there was a great cry in E·; "
39 which they brought forth out of E·, "
39 because they were thrust out of E·, "
40 who dwelt in E·, was four hundred "
41 Lord went out from the land of E·. "
42 them out from the land of E·: "
51 of Israel out of the land of E· "
13: 3 day, in which ye came out from E·, "
8 me when I came forth out of E·. "
9 the Lord brought thee out of E·. "
14 the Lord brought us out from E·, "
15 in the land of E·, both the firstborn "
16 the Lord brought us forth out of E·. "
17 see war, and they return to E·: "
18 harnessed out of the land of E·. "
14: 5 the king of E· that the people fled: "
7 the chariots of E·, and captains "
8 the heart of Pharaoh king of E·, "
11 Because there were no graves in E·, "
11 us, to carry us forth out of E·? "
12 that we did tell thee in E·, saying, "
16: 1 departing out of the land of E·. "
3 hand of the Lord in the land of E·, "
6 you out from the land of E·: "
32 you forth from the land of E·. "
17: 3 thou hast brought us up out of E·, "
18: 1 hath brought Israel out of E·; "
19: 1 gone forth out of the land of E·, "
20: 2 brought thee out of the land of E·, "
22:21 ye were strangers in the land of E·. "
23: 9 ye were strangers in the land of E·. "
15 in it thou camest out from E·: "
29:46 out of the land of E·, that I may "
32: 1 us up out of the land of E·, "
4 thee up out of the land of E·. "
7 broughtest out of the land of E·, "
8 thee up out of the land of E·. "
11 brought forth out of the land of E· "
23 brought us up out of the land of E·, "
33: 1 brought up out of the land of E·, "
34:18 Abib thou camest out from E·. "
Le 11:45 of the land of E·, to be your God: "
18: 3 the land of E·, wherein ye dwelt, "
19:34 strangers in the land of E·: I am "
36 brought you out of the land of E·. "
22:33 brought you out of the land of E·, "
23:43 brought them out of the land of E·: "
25:38 forth out of the land of E·, to give "
42 forth out of the land of E·: they "
55 forth out of the land of E·: I am "
26:13 forth out of the land of E·, that ye "
45 forth out of the land of E· in the "
Nu 1: 1 come out of the land of E·, saying, "
3:13 all the firstborn in the land of E· "
8:17 of E· I sanctified them for myself. "
9: 1 come out of the land E·, saying, "
11: 5 fish, which we did eat in E· freely; "
18 eat? for it was well with us in E·: "
20 Why came we forth out of E·? "
13:22 built seven years before Zoan in E·.) "
14: 2 we had died in the land of E·! "
3 not better for us to return into E·? "
4 captain, and let us return into E·. "
19 people, from E· even until now. "
22 I did in E· and in the wilderness, "
15:41 brought you out of the land of E·, "
20: 5 up out of E·, to bring us in unto "

Nu 20:15 E', and we have dwelt in E' a long 4714
16 hath brought us forth out of E': "
21: 5 out of E' to die in the wilderness? "
22: 5 is a people come out from E': "
11 out of E', which covereth the face "
23:22 God brought them out of E'; he "
24: 8 God brought him forth out of E'; "
26: 4 went forth out of the land of E'. "
59 her mother bare to Levi in E': "
32:11 of the men that came up out of E', "
33: 1 went forth out of the land of E' "
38 the land of E', in the first day of "
34: 5 from Azmon unto the river of E', "
De 1:27 the land of E', to deliver us into "
30 did for you in E' before your eyes; "
4:20 of the iron furnace, even out of E'; "
34 Lord your God did for you in E' "
37 with his mighty power out of E'; "
45 after they came forth out of E', "
46 they were come forth out of E': "
5: 6 brought thee out of the land of E', "
15 wast a servant in the land of E', "
6:12 thee forth out of the land of E', "
21 We were Pharaoh's bondmen in E'; "
21 the Lord brought us out of E' with "
22 wonders, great and sore, upon E', "
7: 8 the hand of Pharaoh king of E'. "
15 none of the evil diseases of E', "
18 did unto Pharaoh, and unto all E'; "
8:14 thee forth out of the land of E', "
9: 7 didst depart out of the land of E', "
12 thou hast brought forth out of E' "
26 out of E' with a mighty hand. "
10:19 were strangers in the land of E'. "
22 Thy fathers went down into E' with "
11: 3 acts, which he did in the midst of E' "
3 unto Pharaoh the king of E', and "
4 what he did unto the army of E', "
10 it, is not as the land of E', from "
13: 5 brought you out of the land of E', "
10 brought thee out of the land of E', "
15:15 wast a bondman in the land of E', "
16: 1 God brought thee forth out of E' by "
3 forth out of the land of E' in haste: "
3 out of the land of E' all the days of "
6 that thou camest forth out of E'. "
12 that thou wast a bondman in E': "
17:16 cause the people to return to E', "
20: 1 brought thee up out of the land of E'. "
23: 4 way, when ye came forth out of E'; "
24: 9 that ye were come forth out of E'. "
18 that thou wast a bondman in E', "
22 wast a bondman in the land of E': "
25:17 when ye were come forth out of E'; "
26: 5 and he went down into E', and "
8 the Lord brought us forth out of E' "
28:27 will smite thee with the botch of E', "
60 upon thee all the diseases of E', "
68 Lord shall bring thee into E' again "
29: 2 before your eyes in the land of E' "
16 we have dwelt in the land of E'; "
25 them forth out of the land of E': "
34:11 sent him to do in the land of E' "
Jos 2:10 for you, when ye came out of E'; "
5: 4 All the people that came out of E', "
4 the way, after they came out of E'. "
5 way as they came forth out of E', "
6 men of war, which came out of E', "
9 I rolled away the reproach of E' "
9: 9 of him, and all that he did in E', "
13: 3 From Sihor, which is before E', "
15: 4 and went out unto the river of E'; "
47 her villages, unto the river of E', "
24: 4 his children went down into E'. "
5 and I plagued E', according to that "
6 I brought your fathers out of E': "
7 have seen what I have done in E': "
14 other side of the flood, and in E'; "
17 our fathers out of the land of E', "
32 of Israel brought up out of E', "
J'g 2: 1 said, I made you to go up out of E', "
12 brought them out of the land of E', "
6: 8 Israel, I brought you up from E', "
13 not the Lord bring us up from E'? "
11:13 land, when they came up out of E', "
16 When Israel came up from E', "
19:30 came up out of the land of E' unto "
1Sa 2:27 thy father, when they were in E' "
8: 8 day that I brought them up out of E' "
10:18 I brought up Israel out of E', and "
12: 6 fathers up out of the land of E'. "
8 When Jacob was come into E', and "
8 brought forth your fathers out of E', "
15: 2 the way, when he came up from E'. "
6 when they came up out of E'. "
7 to Shur, that is over against E'. "
27: 8 to Shur, even unto the land of E'. "
30:13 I am a young man of E', servant 4713
2Sa 7: 6 up the children of Israel out of E', 4714
23 thou redeemedst to thee from E', "
1Ki 3: 1 affinity with Pharaoh king of E', "
4:21 and unto the border of E': they "
30 country, and all the wisdom of E'. "
6: 1 were come out of the land of E', "
8: 9 they came out of the land of E'. "
16 my people Israel out of E', I chose "
21 brought them out of the land of E'. "
51 thou broughtest forth out of E', "
53 broughtest our fathers out of E', "
65 in of Hamath unto the river of E', "
9: 9 their fathers out of the land of E', "
16 For Pharaoh king of E' had gone "
10:28 had horses brought out of E', and "
29 and went out of E' for six hundred "
11:17 servants with him, to go into E'; "
18 came to E', unto Pharaoh king of E': "

1Ki 11:21 And when Hadad heard in E' that 4714
40 fled into E', unto Shishak king of E', "
40 and was in E' until the death of "
12: 2 son of Nebat, who was yet in E', "
2 Solomon, and Jeroboam dwelt in E'; "
28 brought thee up out of the land of E'. "
14:25 that Shishak king of E' came up "
2Ki 17: 4 sent messengers to So king of E', "
7 them up out of the land of E', "
7 the hand of Pharaoh king of E', "
36 you up out of the land of E' with "
18:21 of this bruised reed, even upon E', "
21 is Pharaoh king of E' unto all that "
24 put thy trust on E' for chariots and "
21:15 their fathers came forth out of E', "
23:29 Pharaoh-nechoh king of E' went up "
34 and he came to E', and died there. "
24: 7 And the king of E' came not again "
7 had taken from the river of E' unto "
7 all that pertained to the king of E'. "
25:26 arose, and came to E': for they "
1Ch 13: 5 Israel together, from Shihor of E' "
17:21 whom thou hast redeemed out of E'? "
2Ch 1:16 had horses brought out of E', and "
17 and brought forth out of E' a "
5:10 Israel, when they came out of E'. "
6: 5 forth my people out of the land of E' "
7: 8 in of Hamath unto the river of E'. "
22 them forth out of the land of E', "
9:26 Philistines, and to the border of E'. "
28 unto Solomon horses out of E', "
10: 2 the son of Nebat, who was in E', "
2 that Jeroboam returned out of E'. "
12: 2 king Rehoboam, Shishak king of E' "
3 that came with him out of E'; "
9 Shishak king of E' came up against "
20:10 they came out of the land of E', "
26: 8 abroad even to the entering in of E'; "
35:20 Necho king of E' came up to fight "
36: 3 And the king of E' put him down at "
4 the king of E' made Eliakim his "
4 his brother, and carried him to E'. "
Ne 9: 9 the affliction of our fathers in E', "
18 that brought thee up out of E', "
Ps 68:31 Princes shall come out of E'; "
78:12 of their fathers, in the land of E', "
43 he had wrought his signs in E', and "
51 And smote all the firstborn in E'; "
80: 8 Thou hast brought a vine out of E': "
81: 5 he went out through the land of E': "
10 brought thee out of the land of E': "
105:23 Israel also came into E'; and Jacob "
38 E' was glad when they departed: "
106: 7 understood not thy wonders in E'; "
21 which had done great things in E'; "
114: 1 When Israel went out of E', the "
135: 8 Who smote the firstborn of E', both "
9 into the midst of thee, O E', "
136:10 that smote E' in their firstborn: "
Pr 7:16 carved works, with fine linen of E'. "
Isa 7:18 uttermost part of the rivers of E', "
10:24 against thee, after the manner of E'. "
26 he lift it up after the manner of E'. "
11:11 and from E', and from Pathros, and "
16 he came up out of the land of E'. "
19: 1 The burden of E'. Behold, the Lord "
1 swift cloud, and shall come into E': "
1 and the idols of E' shall be moved "
1 and the heart of E' shall melt in "
3 And the spirit of E' shall fail in the "
12 of hosts hath purposed upon E'. "
13 they have also seduced E', even "
14 and they have caused E' to err in "
15 shall there be any work for E', "
16 day shall E' be like unto women: "
17 of Judah shall be a terror unto E', "
18 five cities in the land of E' speak "
19 Lord in the midst of the land of E', "
20 the Lord of hosts in the land of E': "
21 the Lord shall be known to E', and "
22 And the Lord shall smite E': he "
23 shall there be a highway out of E' "
23 the Assyrian shall come into E', and "
24 shall Israel be the third with E' "
25 Blessed be E' my people, and "
20: 3 for a sign and wonder upon E' and "
4 uncovered, to the shame of E'. "
5 expectation, and of E' their glory. "
23: 5 As at the report concerning E', so "
27:12 of the river unto the stream of E', "
13 and the outcasts in the land of E', "
30: 2 That walk to go down into E', and "
2 and to trust in the shadow of E'! "
3 the trust in the shadow of E' your "
31: 1 that go down to E' for help; and "
36: 6 the staff of this broken reed, on E'; "
6 so is Pharaoh king of E' to all that "
9 servants, and put thy trust on E' "
43: 3 I gave E' for thy ransom, Ethiopia "
45:14 The labour of E', and merchandise "
52: 4 people went down aforetime into E' "
Jer 2: 6 brought us up out of the land of E', "
18 hast thou to do in the way of E', "
36 thou also shalt be ashamed of E', "
7:22 brought them out of the land of E', "
25 came forth out of the land of E' "
9:26 E', and Judah, and Edom, and the "
11: 4 them forth out of the land of E', "
7 them up out of the land of E', "
16:14 of Israel out of the land of E'; "
23: 7 of Israel out of the land of E'; "
24: 8 them that dwell in the land of E': "
25:19 Pharaoh king of E', and his "
26:21 afraid, and fled, and went into E'; "
22 the king sent men into E', namely, "
22 and certain men with him into E'. "

Jer 26:23 they fetched forth Urijah out of E', 4714
31:32 bring them out of the land of E'; "
32:20 signs and wonders in the land of E', "
21 people Israel out of the land of E' "
34:13 them forth out of the land of E', out "
37: 5 army was come forth out of E': "
7 to help you, shall return to E' into "
41:17 Bethlehem, to go to enter into E', "
42:14 but we will go into the land of E', "
15 set your faces to enter into E', "
16 overtake you there in the land of E', "
16 follow close after you there in E'; "
17 that set their faces to go into E' "
18 you, when ye shall enter into E': "
19 of Judah; Go ye not into E': "
43: 2 sent thee to say, Go not into E' to "
7 they came into the land of E': for "
11 he shall smite the land of E', "
12 fire in the houses of the gods of E'; "
12 array himself with the land of E', "
13 that is in the land of E'; and the "
44: 1 Jews which dwell in the land of E', "
8 unto other gods in the land of E', "
12 their faces to go into the land of E' "
12 consumed, and fall in the land of E'; "
13 them that dwell in the land of E', "
14 which are gone into the land of E' "
15 people that dwelt in the land of E', "
24 all Judah that are in the land of E': "
26 Judah that dwell in the land of E'; "
26 man of Judah in all the land of E', "
27 the land of E' shall be consumed by "
28 shall return out of the land of E' "
28 into the land of E' to sojourn there, "
30 give Pharaoh-hophra king of E' "
46: 2 Against E', against the army of "
2 Pharaoh-necho king of E', which "
8 E' riseth up like a flood, and his "
11 balm, O virgin, the daughter of E': "
13 come and smite the land of E'. "
14 Declare ye in E', and publish in "
17 Pharaoh king of E' is but a noise; "
19 O thou daughter dwelling in E', "
20 E' is like a very fair heifer, but "
24 The daughter of E' shall be "
25 of No, and Pharaoh, and E', with "
Eze 17:15 sending his ambassadors into E', "
19: 4 him with chains into the land of E'. "
20: 5 known unto them in the land of E', "
6 to bring them forth of the land of E' "
7 not yourselves with the idols of E': "
8 did they forsake the idols of E': "
8 them in the midst of the land of E'. "
9 them forth out of the land of E'. "
10 to go forth out of the land of E', "
36 in the wilderness of the land of E', "
23: 3 they committed whoredoms in E'; "
8 her whoredoms brought from E': "
19 played the harlot in the land of E'. "
27 brought from the land of E': "
27 them, nor remember E' any more. "
27: 7 linen with broidered work from E' "
29: 2 face against Pharaoh king of E', "
2 against him, and against all E': "
3 Pharaoh king of E', the great "
6 E' shall know that I am the Lord, "
9 the land of E' shall be desolate "
10 make the land of E' utterly waste "
12 I will make the land of E' desolate "
14 will bring again the captivity of E', "
19 I will give the land of E' unto "
20 given him the land of E' for his "
30: 4 And the sword shall come upon E', "
4 when the slain shall fall in E', "
6 They also that uphold E' shall fall; "
8 when I have set a fire in E', and "
9 upon them, as in the day of E': "
10 make the multitude of E' to cease "
11 shall draw their swords against E', "
13 no more a prince of the land of E': "
13 I will put a fear in the land of E'. "
15 fury upon Sin, the strength of E'; "
16 And I will set fire in E': Sin shall "
18 I shall break there the yokes of E': "
19 will I execute judgments in E': "
21 the arm of Pharaoh king of E'; "
22 I am against Pharaoh king of E', "
25 stretch it out upon the land of E'. "
31: 2 speak unto Pharaoh king of E', "
32: 2 lamentation for Pharaoh king of E', "
12 they shall spoil the pomp of E', "
15 shall make the land of E' desolate, "
16 shall lament for her, even for E', "
18 man, wail for the multitude of E', "
Da 9:15 people forth out of the land of E' "
11: 8 carry captives into E' their gods, "
42 and the land of E' shall not escape. "
43 over all the precious things of E': "
Ho 2:15 she came up out of the land of E'. "
7:11 without heart: they call to E', "
16 be their derision in the land of E'. "
8:13 their sins: they shall return to E'. "
9: 3 Ephraim shall return to E', and "
6 E' shall gather them up, Memphis "
11: 1 him, and called my son out of E'. "
5 shall not return into the land of E', "
11 shall tremble as a bird out of E', "
12: 1 and oil is carried into E'. "
9 thy God from the land of E' will yet "
13 the Lord brought Israel out of E', "
13: 4 Lord thy God from the land of E', "
Joe 3:19 E' shall be a desolation, and Edom "
Am 2:10 up from the land of E', and led you "
3: 1 up from the land of E', saying, "
9 and in the palaces in the land of E', "
4:10 pestilence after the manner of E': "

Am 8: 8 and drowned, as by the flood of E·. 4714
9: 5 be drowned, as by the flood of E·. "
7 up Israel out of the land of E·? "
Mic 6: 4 thee up out of the land of E·, "
7:15 of thy coming out of the land of E· "
Na 3: 9 Ethiopa and E· were her strength, "
Hag 2: 5 with you when ye came out of E·, "
Zec 10:10 them again also out of the land of E·, "
11 and the sceptre of E· shall depart "
14:18 if the family of E· go not up, and "
19 This shall be the punishment of E·, "
M't 2:13 flee into E·, and be thou there 125
14 by night, and departed into E·: "
15 Out of E· have I called my son. "
19 in a dream to Joseph in E·, "
Ac 2:10 in E·, and in the parts of Libya "
7: 9 with envy, sold Joseph into E·: "
10 the sight of Pharaoh king of E·; "
10 he made him governor over E· "
11 came a dearth over all the land of E· "
12 Jacob heard that there was corn in E·, "
15 Jacob went down into E·, and died, "
17 people grew and multiplied in E·, "
34 of my people which is in E·, "
34 now come, I will send thee into E·. "
36 wonders and signs in the land of E·, "
39 hearts turned back again into E·, "
40 brought us out of the land of E·, "
13:17 as strangers in the land of E·, "
Heb 3:16 that came out of E· by Moses. "
8: 9 to lead them out of the land of E·; "
11:26 riches than the treasures in E·: "
27 By faith he forsook E·, not fearing "
Jude 5 the people out of the land of E·, "
Re 11: 8 spiritually is called Sodom and E·, "

Egyptian (*e-jip'-shun*) See also EGYPTIAN'S; EGYPTIANS.
Ge 16: 1 an E·, whose name was Hagar. 4713
3 wife, took Hagar her maid the E·, "
21: 9 Sarah saw the son of Hagar the E·, "
25:12 Hagar the E·, Sarah's handmaid, "
39: 1 an E·, bought him of the hands of "
2 in the house of his master the E·. "
Ex 1:19 women are not as the E· women; "
2:11 he spied an E· smiting an Hebrew, "
12 slew the E·, and hid him in the sand. "
14 to kill me, as thou killedst the E·? "
19 An E· delivered us out of the hand "
Le 24:10 woman, whose father was an E·, "
De 23: 7 thou shalt not abhor an E·; because "
1Sa 30:11 And they found an E· in the field, "
2Sa 23:21 And he slew an E·, a goodly man: "
21 the E· had a spear in his hand; "
1Ch 2:34 And Sheshan had a servant, an E·, "
11:23 slew an E·, a man of great stature, "
Isa 11:15 destroy the tongue of the E· sea; 4714
19:23 and the E· into Assyria, and "
Ac 7:24 was oppressed, and smote the E·: 124
28 as thou didst the E· yesterday? "
21:38 Art not thou that E·, which before "

Egyptian's (*e-jip'-shuns*)
Ge 39: 5 the Lord blessed the E· house for 4713
2Sa 23:21 plucked the spear out of the E· "
1Ch 11:23 E· hand was a spear like a weaver's "
23 out of the E· hand, and slew him "

Egyptians (*e-jip'-shuns*)
Ge 12:12 when the E· shall see thee, that 4713
14 Abram was come into Egypt, the E· "
41:55 Pharaoh said unto all the E·, Go 4714
56 storehouses, and sold unto the E·; "
43:32 by themselves, and for the E·, 4713
32 the E· might not eat bread with the "
32 is an abomination unto the E·. 4714
45: 2 the E· and the house of Pharaoh "
46:34 is an abomination unto the E·. "
47:15 the E· came unto Joseph, and said, "
20 for the E· sold every man his field, "
50: 3 the E· mourned for him threescore "
11 is a grievous mourning to the E·: "
Ex 1:13 the E· made the children of Israel "
3: 8 them out of the hand of the E·, "
9 wherewith the E· oppress them. "
21 people favour in the sight of the E·: "
22 and ye shall spoil the E·. "
6: 5 whom the E· kept in bondage; "
6 from under the burdens of the E·, "
7 from under the burdens of the E·. "
7: 5 E· shall know that I am the Lord, "
18 the E· shall lothe to drink of the "
21 and the E· could not drink of "
24 E· digged round about the river "
8:21 the houses of the E· shall be full "
26 abomination of the E· to the Lord "
26 abomination of the E· before their "
9:11 the magicians, and upon all the E·. "
10: 6 and the houses of all the E·; "
11: 3 people favour in the sight of the E·. "
7 a difference between the E· and "
12:23 will pass through to smite the E·; "
27 when he smote the E·, and "
30 and all his servants, and all the E·; "
33 E· were urgent upon the people, "
35 borrowed of the E· jewels of silver, "
36 people favour in the sight of the E·, "
36 required. And they spoiled the E·. "
14: 4 E· may know that I am the Lord. "
9 But the E· pursued after them, all "
10 the E· marched after them; and "
12 alone, that we may serve the E·? "
12 been better for us to serve the E·, "
13 the E· whom ye have seen to day, "
17 I will harden the hearts of the E·, "
18 E· shall know that I am the Lord, "
20 between the camp of the E· and *

Ex 14:23 E· pursued, and went in after them 4714
24 looked unto the host of the E· "
24 and troubled the host of the E·, "
25 the E· said, Let us flee from the "
25 fighteth for them against the E·. "
26 waters may come again upon the E·, "
27 the E· fled against it; and the Lord "
27 the E· in the midst of the sea. "
30 day out of the hand of the E·; "
30 saw the E· dead upon the sea shore. "
31 which the Lord did upon the E·: "
15:26 which I have brought upon the E·: "
18: 8 and to the E· for Israel's sake, "
9 delivered out of the hand of the E·. "
10 you out of the hand of the E·, "
10 from under the hand of the E·. "
19: 4 have seen what I did unto the E·. "
32:12 Wherefore should the E· speak, "
Nu 14:13 the Lord, Then the E· shall hear it, "
20:15 the E· vexed us, and our fathers: "
33: 3 high hand in the sight of all the E·. "
4 the E· buried all their firstborn, "
De 26: 6 E· evil entreated us, and afflicted 4713
Jos 24: 6 E· pursued after your fathers 4714
7 and the E·, and brought the sea 4713
J'g 6: 9 you out of the hand of the E·, 4714
10:11 Did not I deliver you from the E·, "
1Sa 4: 8 are the Gods that smote the E· "
6: 6 do ye harden your hearts, as the E· "
10:18 the E·, and out of the hand of all "
2Ki 7: 6 the Hittites, and the kings of the E·, "
Ezr 9: 1 Ammonites, the Moabites, the E·, 4713
Isa 19: 2 I will set the E· against the E·: 4714
4 And the E· will I give over into the "
21 E· shall know the Lord in that day, "
24 E· shall serve with the Assyrians. "
20: 4 Assyria lead away...E· prisoners, *
30: 7 the E· shall help in vain, and to *
31: 3 the E· are men, and not God; and "
Jer 43:13 the gods of the E· shall he burn *
La 5: 6 to the E·, and to the Assyrians, "
Eze 16:26 committed fornication with the E· "
23:21 in bruising thy teats by the E· for "
29:12 scatter the E· among the nations, "
13 of forty years will I gather the E· "
30:23, 26 scatter the E· among the "
Ac 7:22 in all the wisdom of the E·, 124
Heb 11:29 E· assaying to do were drowned. "

Ehi (*e'-hi*) See also AHARAH.
Ge 46:21 Gera, and Naaman, E·, and Rosh, 278

Ehud (*e'-hud*)
J'g 3:15 raised them up a deliverer, E· 261
16 E· made him a dagger which had "
20 And E· came unto him; and he was "
20 E· said, I have a message from God "
21 E· put forth his left hand, and took "
23 E· went forth through the porch, "
26 And E· escaped while they tarried, "
4: 1 of the Lord, when E· was dead. "
1Ch 7:10 Benjamin, and E·, and Chenaanah, "
8: 6 And these are the sons of E·: these "

eight See also EIGHTEEN.
Ge 5: 4 Seth were e· hundred years: 8083
7 e· hundred and seven years, and "
10 e· hundred and fifteen years, "
13 e· hundred and forty years, "
16 Jared e· hundred and thirty years, "
17 e· hundred ninety and five years: "
19 begat Enoch e· hundred years, and "
17:12 is e· days old shall be circumcised "
21: 4 his son Isaac being e· days old, as "
22:23 these e· Milcah did bear to Nahor, "
Ex 26: 2 shall be e· and twenty cubits, "
25 And they shall be e· boards, and "
36: 9 curtain was twenty and e· cubits, "
30 And there were e· boards; and "
Nu 2:24 and e· thousand and an hundred, "
3:28 e· thousand and six hundred, "
4:48 were e· thousand and five hundred "
7: 8 four wagons and e· oxen he gave "
29:29 on the sixth day e· bullocks, "
35: 7 Levites shall be forty and e· cities: "
De 2:14 Zered, was thirty and e· years; "
Jos 21:41 forty and e· cities with their "
J'g 3: 8 Chushan-rishathaim e· years. "
12:14 and he judged Israel e· years. "
1Sa 4:15 Eli was ninety and e· years old; "
17:12 was Jesse; and he had e· sons: "
2Sa 23: 8 against e· hundred, whom he slew "
24: 9 e· hundred thousand valiant men "
1Ki 7:10 of ten cubits, stones of e· cubits. "
2Ki 8:17 he reigned e· years in Jerusalem. "
10:36 Samaria was twenty and e· years. "
22: 1 Josiah was e· years old when he "
1Ch 12:24 six thousand and e· hundred, "
30 twenty thousand and e· hundred, "
35 and e· thousand and six hundred. "
16:38 their brethren, three score and e·; "
23: 3 man, was thirty and e· thousand. "
24: 4 and e· among the sons of Ithamar "
25: 7 was two hundred fourscore and e·. "
2Ch 11:21 begat twenty and e· sons, and "
13: 3 e· hundred thousand chosen men, "
21: 5 he reigned e· years in Jerusalem. "
20 he reigned in Jerusalem e· years, "
29:17 the house of the Lord in e· days; "
34: 1 Josiah was e· years old when he "
36: 9 Jehoiachin was e· years old when "
Ezr 2: 6 thousand and e· hundred and twelve. "
16 Ater of Hezekiah, ninety and e·. "
23 Anathoth, an hundred twenty and e·. "
41 Asaph, an hundred twenty and e·. "
8:11 and with him twenty and e· males. "
Ne 7:11 and e· hundred and eighteen. "
13 Zattu, e· hundred forty and five. "

Ne 7:15 Binnui, six hundred forty and e·. 8083
16 Bebai, six hundred twenty and e·. "
21 Ater of Hezekiah, ninety and e·. "
22 three hundred twenty and e·. "
26 an hundred fourscore and e·. "
27 an hundred twenty and e·. "
44 of Asaph, an hundred forty and e·. "
45 of Shobai, an hundred thirty and e·. "
11: 6 threescore and e· valiant men. "
8 Sallai, nine hundred twenty and e·. "
12 were e· hundred twenty and two: "
14 of valour an hundred twenty and e·: "
Ec 11: 2 a portion to seven, and also to e·; "
Jer 41:15 escaped from Johanan with e· men, "
52:29 from Jerusalem e· hundred thirty "
Eze 40: 9 he the porch of the gate, e· cubits; "
31, 34, 37 going up to it had e· steps. "
41 e· tables, whereupon they slew "
Mic 5: 5 shepherds, and e· principal men. "
Lu 2:21 when e· days were accomplished 3638
9:28 an e· days after these sayings, "
Joh 5: 5 an infirmity thirty and e· years. "
20:26 after e· days again his disciples "
Ac 9:33 which had kept his bed e· years, "
1Pe 3:20 is, e· souls were saved by water. "

eighteen
Ge 14:14 house, three hundred and e·, 8083, 6240
J'g 3:14 the king of Moab e· years. " "
10: 8 children of Israel: e· years, " "
20:25 Israel again e· thousand men; " "
44 Benjamin e· thousand men; " "
2Sa 8:13 salt, being e· thousand men. " "
1Ki 7:15 brass, e· cubits high apiece: " "
2Ki 24: 8 Jehoiachin was e· years old " "
25:17 of one pillar was e· cubits, " "
1Ch 12:31 tribe of Manasseh e· thousand, " "
18:12 the valley of salt e· thousand. " "
26: 9 and brethren, strong men, e·. " "
29: 7 of brass e· thousand talents, 7239, 8083
2Ch 11:21 for he took e· wives, and 8083, 6240
Ezr 8: 9 him two hundred and e· males. " "
18 his sons and his brethren, e·; " "
Ne 7:11 eight hundred and e·. " "
Jer 52:21 of one pillar was e· cubits; " "
Eze 48:35 about e· thousand measures; " "
Lu 13: 4 Or those e·, upon whom 1176, 2532, 3638
11 spirit of infirmity e· years, " " "
16 lo, these e· years, be " " "

eighteenth
1Ki 15: 1 the e· year of king Jeroboam 8083, 6240
2Ki 3: 1 Israel in Samaria the e· year " "
22: 3 in the e· year of king Josiah, " "
23:23 in the e· year of king Josiah, " "
1Ch 24:15 to Hezer, the e· to Aphses, " "
25:25 The e· to Hanani, he, his sons, " "
2Ch 13: 1 the e· year of king Jeroboam " "
34: 8 in the e· year of his reign, " "
35:19 e· year of the reign of Josiah " "
Jer 32: 1 the e· year of Nebuchadrezzar. " "
52:29 the e· year of Nebuchadrezzar " "

eighteen thousand See EIGHTEEN and THOUSAND.

eighth
Ex 22:30 the e· day thou shalt give it me. 8066
Le 9: 1 it came to pass on the e· day, "
12: 3 the e· day the flesh of his foreskin "
14:10 e· day he shall take two he lambs "
23 he shall bring them on the e· day "
15:14 e· day he shall take to him two "
29 e· day she shall take unto her two "
22:27 from the e· day and thenceforth "
23:36 e· day shall be a holy convocation "
39 on the e· day shall be a sabbath. "
25:22 ye shall sow the e· year, and eat "
Nu 6:10 e· day he shall bring two turtles, "
7:54 the e· day offered Gamaliel the son "
29:35 On the e· day ye shall have a "
1Ki 6:38 month Bul, which is the e· month, "
8:66 the e· day he sent the people away: "
12:32 ordained a feast in the e· month, "
33 the fifteenth day of the e· month, "
16:29 in the thirty and e· year of Asa 8083
2Ki 15: 8 the thirty and e· year of Azariah "
24:12 took him in the e· year of his reign. "
1Ch 12:12 Johanan the e·, Elzabad the e· 8066
24:10 to Hakkoz, the e· to Abijah, "
25:15 The e· to Jeshaiah, he, his sons "
26: 5 Peulthai the e·: for God blessed "
27:11 The e· captain for the e· month "
2Ch 7: 9 e· day they made a solemn assembly: "
29:17 and on the e· day of the month "
34: 3 For in the e· year of his reign, 8083
Ne 8:18 the e· day was a solemn assembly, 8066
Eze 43:27 upon the e· day, and so forward, "
Zec 1: 1 In the e· month, in the second year "
Lu 1:59 e· day they came to circumcise 3590
Ac 7: 8 and circumcised him the e· day; "
Ph'p 3: 5 Circumcised the e· day, of the 3637
2Pe 2: 5 but saved Noah the e· person, *3590
Re 17:11 was, and is not, even he is the e·, "
21:20 the e·, beryl; the ninth, a topaz; "

eight hundred See EIGHT and HUNDRED.

eightieth
1Ki 6: 1 in the four hundred and e· year 8084

eight thousand See EIGHT and THOUSAND.

eighty
Ge 5:25 an hundred e· and seven years, 8084
26 seven hundred e· and two years, "
28 lived an hundred e· and two years, "

either See also NEITHER.
Ge 31:24 speak not to Jacob e· good or bad.
29 thou speak not to Jacob e· good or bad.
Le 10: 1 took e· of them his censer, and * 376

Le 13:49 or in the skin, e' in the warp, or * 176
51, 53 in the garment, e' in the warp, "
57 still in the garment, e' in the warp, "
58 And the garment, e' warp, or woof, "
59 or linen, e' in the warp, or woof, "
22:23 E' a bullock or a lamb that hath "
25:49 E' his uncle, or his uncle's son, * 176
Nu 6: 2 e' man or woman shall separate 376
22:26 no way to turn e' to the right hand
24:13 e' good or bad of mine own mind;
De 17: 3 e' the sun, or moon, or any of *
28:51 also shall not leave thee e' corn, *
J'g 9: 2 e' that all the sons of Jerubbaal, *
1Sa 20: 2 will do nothing e' great or small,
25:31 e' that thou hast shed blood causeless,
30: 2 slew not any, e' great or small, *
1Ki 7:15 did compass e' of them about. 8145
10:19 and there were stays on e' side
18:27 e' he is talking, or he is pursuing,3588
1Ch 21:12 E' three years' famine; or three 518
2Ch 18: 9 king of Judah sat e' of them on * 376
Ec 9: 1 man knoweth e' love or hatred *1571
11: 6 not whether shall prosper, e' this*
Isa 7:11 ask it e' in the depth, or in the
17: 8 e' the groves, or the images.
Eze 21:16 one way or other, e' on the right *
M't 6:24 for e' he will hate the one, and 2228
12:33 E' make the tree good, and his "
Lu 6:42 E' how canst thou say to thy * "
15: 8 E' what woman having ten pieces* "
16:13 two masters: for e' he will hate "
Joh 19:18 on e' side one, and Jesus in 1782, 2532
Ac 17:21 but e' to tell, or to hear some 2228
1Co 14: 6 shall speak to you e' by revelation, "
Ph'p 3:12 attained, e' were already perfect:* "
Jas 3:12 bear olive berries? e' a vine, figs?* "
Re 22: 2 and on e' side of the river, *1782, 2532

Eker (*e'-ker*)
1Ch 2:27 were, Maaz, and Jamin, and E'. 6134

Ekron (*ec'-ron*) See also Ekronites.
Jos 13: 3 Egypt, even unto the borders of E'6138
15:11 unto the side of E' northward: "
45 E', with her towns and her villages: "
46 From E' even unto the sea, all "
19:43 Elon, and Thimnathah, and E', "
J'g 1:18 with the coast thereof, and E' "
1Sa 5:10 they sent the ark of God to E'. "
10 pass, as the ark of God came to E', "
6:16 had seen it, they returned to E' "
17 one, for Gath one, for E' one; "
7:14 to Israel, from E' even unto Gath; "
17:52 the valley, and to the gates of E'. "
52 even unto Gath, and unto E'. "
2Ki 1: 2 enquire of Baal-zebub the god of E' "
3, 6 of Baal-zebub the god of E'? "
16 enquire of Baal-zebub the god of E', "
Jer 25:20 and E', and the remnant of Ashdod, "
Am 1: 8 I will turn mine hand against E': "
Zep 2: 4 and E' shall be rooted up. "
Zec 9: 5 and E'; for her expectation shall "
7 in Judah, and E' as a Jebusite. "

Ekronites (*ek'-ron-ites*)
Jos 13: 3 the Gittites, and the E'; also the 6139
1Sa 5:10 that the E' cried out, saying, They "

El See Beth-el; El-beth-el; El-elohe-israel; El-haran; Jiphthah-el; Migdal-el.

Eladah (*el'-a-dah*)
1Ch 7:20 E' his son, and Tahath his son, * 497

Elah (*e'-lah*)
Ge 36:41 Duke Aholibamah, duke E', duke 425
1Sa 17: 2 and pitched by the valley of E', "
19 were in the valley of E', fighting "
21: 9 thou slewest in the valley of E', "
1Ki 4:18 Shimei the son of E', in Benjamin. "
16: 6 E' his son reigned in his stead. "
8 E' the son of Baasha to reign "
13 sins of Baasha, and the sins of E' "
14 the rest of the acts of E', and all "
2Ki 15:30 the son of E' made a conspiracy "
17: 1 began Hoshea the son of E' to reign "
18: 1 the third year of Hoshea son of E' "
9 seventh year of Hoshea son of E' "
1Ch 1:52 Duke Aholibamah, duke E', duke "
4:15 Jephunneh; Iru, E', and Naam: "
15 and the sons of E', even Kenaz. "
9: 8 the son of Jeroham, and E' "

Elam (*e'-lam*) See also Elamites; Persia.
Ge 10:22 children of Shem; E', and Ashur, 5867
14: 1 Chedorlaomer king of E', and "
9 With Chedorlaomer the king of E', "
1Ch 1:17 The sons of Shem; E', and Asshur, "
8:24 Hananiah, and E', and Antothijah, "
26: 3 E' the fifth, Jehohanan the sixth, "
Ezr 2: 7 The children of E', a thousand two "
31 The children of the other E', "
8: 7 And of the sons of E'; Jeshaiah "
10: 2 son of Jehiel, one of the sons of E', "
26 sons of E'; Mattaniah, Zechariah, "
Ne 7:12 children of E', a thousand two "
34 The children of the other E', "
10:14 people; Parosh, Pahath-moab, E', "
12:42 and Malchijah, and E', and Ezer. "
Isa 11:11 and from Cush, and from E', and "
21: 2 Go up, O E': besiege, O Media; "
22: 6 E' bare the quiver with chariots "
Jer 25:25 and all the kings of E', and all the "
49:34 Jeremiah the prophet against E', "
35 Behold, I will break the bow of E', "
36 upon E' will I bring the four winds "
36 the outcasts of E' shall not come. "
37 For I will cause E' to be dismayed "
38 And I will set my throne in E', and "
39 bring again the captivity of E', "
Eze 32:24 is E and all her multitude round 5867
Da 8: 2 which is in the province of E'; "

Elamites (*e'-lam-ites*) See also Persians.
Ezr 4: 9 the Dehavites, and the E', 5962
Ac 2: 9 Parthians, and Medes, and E', 1639

Elasah (*el'-a-sah*) See also Eleasa.
Ezr 10:22 Nethaneel, Jozabad, E'. 501
Jer 29: 3 hand of E' the son of Shaphan, "

Elath (*e'-lath*) See also Eloth.
De 2: 8 the way of the plain from E', 359
2Ki 14:22 built E', and restored it to Judah, "
16: 6 king of Syria recovered E' to Syria, "
6 and drave the Jews from E': "
6 Syrians came to E', and dwelt there "

El-beth-el (*el-beth'-el*)
Ge 35: 7 an altar, and called the place E'; 416

Eldaah (*el'-da-ah*)
Ge 25: 4 and Hanoch, and Abidah, and E'. 420
1Ch 1:33 and Henoch, and Abida, and E'. "

Eldad (*el'-dad*)
Nu 11:26 the name of the one was E', 419
27 E' and Medad do prophesy in the "

elder See also elders.
Ge 10:21 the brother of Japheth the e', *1419
25:23 and the e' shall serve the younger.7227
27:42 these words of Esau her e' son 1419
29:16 the name of the e' was Leah, "
1Sa 18:17 Behold my e' daughter Merab, "
1Ki 2:22 for he is mine e' brother; "
Job 15:10 men, much e' than thy father. "
32: 4 because they were e' than he.2205,3117
Eze 16:46 thine e' sister is Samaria, she and1419
61 sisters, thine e' and thy younger: "
23: 4 names of them were Aholah the e', "
Lu 15:25 Now his e' son was in the field: 4245
Ro 9:12 The e' shall serve the younger. 3187
1Ti 5: 1 Rebuke not an e', but entreat him 4245
2 e' women as mothers; the younger "
19 an e' receive not an accusation, "
1Pe 5: 1 I exhort, who am also an e', 4850
5 submit yourselves unto the e'. 4245
2Jo 1 The e' unto the elect lady and her "
3Jo 1 The e' unto the well beloved Gaius, "

elders
Ge 50: 7 of Pharaoh, the e' of his house, 2205
7 all the e' of the land of Egypt, "
Ex 3:16 Go, and gather the e' of Israel "
18 come, thou and the e' of Israel, "
4:29 gathered together all the e' of the "
12:21 Moses called for all the e' of Israel, "
17: 5 take with thee of the e' of Israel; "
6 did so in the sight of the e' of "
18:12 Aaron came, all the e' of Israel, "
19: 7 called for the e' of the people, "
24: 1 seventy of the e' of Israel; and "
9 and seventy of the e' of Israel: "
14 he said unto the e', Tarry ye here "
Le 4:15 the e' of the congregation shall "
9: 1 and his sons, and the e' of Israel; "
Nu 11:16 seventy men of the e' of Israel, "
16 knowest to be the e' of the people, "
24 seventy men of the e' of the people, "
25 and gave it unto the seventy e': "
30 the camp, he and the e' of Israel. "
16:25 and the e' of Israel followed him. "
22: 4 Moab said unto the e' of Midian, "
7 And the e' of Moab and the "
7 and the e' of Midian departed "
De 5:23 heads of your tribes, and your e'; "
19:12 Then the e' of his city shall send "
21: 2 thy e' and thy judges shall come "
3 e' of that city shall take an heifer, "
4 And the e' of that city shall bring "
6 And all the e' of that city, "
19 him out unto the e' of his city, "
20 shall say unto the e' of his city, "
22:15 virginity unto the e' of the city "
16 damsel's father shall say unto the e', "
17 the cloth before the e' of the city. "
18 And the e' of that city shall take "
25: 7 go up to the gate unto the e', "
8 the e' of his city shall call him, "
9 unto him in the presence of the e', "
27: 1 with the e' of Israel commanded "
29:10 your e', and your officers, with all "
31: 9 and unto all the e' of Israel. "
28 Gather unto me all the e' of your "
32: 7 thy e', and they will tell thee. "
Jos 7: 6 eventide, he and the e' of Israel, "
8:10 he and the e' of Israel, before the "
33 all Israel, and their e', and officers, "
9:11 our e' and all the inhabitants "
20: 4 his cause in the ears of the e' of "
23: 2 for their e', and for their heads, "
24: 1 and called for the e' of Israel, "
31 days of the e' that overlived Joshua, "
J'g 2: 7 days of the e' that outlived Joshua, "
8:14 and the e' thereof, even three score "
16 And he took the e' of the city, "
11: 5 the e' of Gilead went to fetch "
7 Jephthah said unto the e' of Gilead, "
8 e' of Gilead said unto Jephthah, "
9 Jephthah said unto the e' of Gilead, "
10 the e' of Gilead said unto Jephthah, "
11 Jephthah went with the e' of Gilead, "
21:16 the e' of the congregation said, "
Ru 4: 2 took ten men of the e' of the city. "
4 and before the e' of my people. "
9 And Boaz said unto the e', "
11 and the e', said, We are witnesses. "
1Sa 4: 3 the e' of Israel said, Wherefore "
8: 4 Then all the e' of Israel gathered "
11: 3 the e' of Jabesh said unto him, "
15:30 thee, before the e' of my people, 2205
16: 4 the e' of the town trembled at his "
30:26 he sent of the spoil unto the e' of "
2Sa 3:17 communication with the e' of "
5: 3 the e' of Israel came to the king "
12:17 the e' of his house arose, and went "
17: 4 Absalom well, and all the e' of "
15 Absalom and the e' of Israel; "
19:11 Speak unto the e' of Judah, saying, "
1Ki 8: 1 Solomon assembled the e' of Israel, "
3 And all the e' of Israel came, "
20: 7 king of Israel called all the e' of "
8 And all the e' and all the people "
21: 8 and sent the letters unto the e' and "
11 even the e' and the nobles who were "
2Ki 6:32 and the e' sat with him; "
32 came to him, he said to the e', "
10: 1 unto the rulers of Jezreel, to the e', "
5 the e' also, and the bringers up "
19: 2 and the e' of the priests, covered "
23: 1 gathered unto him all the e' of "
1Ch 11: 3 Therefore came all the e' of Israel, "
15:25 So David, and the e' of Israel, "
21:16 Then David and the e' of Israel, "
2Ch 5: 2 Then Solomon assembled the e' of "
4 And all the e' of Israel came; "
34:29 gathered together all the e' of "
Ezr 5: 5 of their God was upon the e' of 7868
9 Then asked we those e', and said "
6: 7 and the e' of the Jews build this "
8 what ye shall do to the e' of these "
14 And the e' of the Jews builded, "
10: 8 counsel of the princes and the e', 2205
14 with them the e' of every city, "
Ps 107:32 praise him in the assembly of the e'. "
Pr 31:23 when he sitteth among the e' of the "
Isa 37: 2 and the e' of the priests covered "
Jer 26:17 Then rose up certain of the e' of "
29: 1 Jerusalem unto the residue of the e' "
La 1:19 my priests and mine e' gave up the "
2:10 The e' of the daughter of Zion "
4:16 priests, they favoured not the e'. "
5:12 the faces of e' were not honoured. "
14 The e' have ceased from the gate, "
Eze 8: 1 and the e' of Judah sat before me, "
14: 1 Then came certain of the e' of "
20: 1 certain of the e' of Israel came to "
3 of man speak unto the e' of Israel, "
Joe 1:14 assembly, gather the e' and all the* "
2:16 congregation, assemble the e', * "
M't 15: 2 transgress the tradition of the e'? 4245
16:21 suffer many things of the e' and "
21:23 and the e' of the people came unto "
26: 3 scribes, and the e' of the people, "
47 chief priests and e' of the people. "
57 scribes and the e' were assembled. "
59 the chief priests, and e', and all * "
27: 1 chief priests and e' of the people "
3 silver to the chief priests and e', "
12 accused of the chief priests and e', "
20 the chief priests and e' persuaded "
41 with the scribes and e', said, "
28:12 they were assembled with the e', "
M'r 7: 3 holding the tradition of the e'. "
5 according to the tradition of the e', "
8:31 and be rejected of the e', and of the "
11:27 priests, and the scribes, and the e', "
14:43 priests and the scribes and the e'. "
53 priests and the e' and the scribes. "
15: 1 with the e' and scribes and the "
Lu 7: 3 he sent unto him the e' of the Jews, "
9:22 and be rejected of the e' and chief "
20: 1 scribes came upon him with the e', "
22:52 captains of the temple, and the e', "
66 the e' of the people and the chief 4244
Ac 4: 5 that their rulers, and e', and 4245
8 of the people, and e' of Israel, "
23 chief priests and e' had said unto "
6:12 the people, and the e', and the "
11:30 and sent it to the e' by the hands "
14:23 ordained them e' in every church, "
15: 2 unto the apostles and e' about this "
4 and of the apostles and e', and they "
6 And the apostles and e' came "
22 Then pleased it the apostles and e', "
23 The apostles and e' and brethren † "
16: 4 were ordained of the apostles and e' "
20:17 and called the e' of the church. "
21:18 and all the e' were present. "
22: 5 and all the estate of the e': 4244
23:14 came to the chief priests and e', 4245
24: 1 high priest descended with the e', "
25:15 the chief priests and the e' of the "
1Ti 5:17 Let the e' that rule well be counted "
Tit 1: 5 ordain e' in every city, as I had "
Heb 11: 2 For by it the e' obtained a good "
Jas 5:14 let him call for the e' of the church; "
1Pe 5: 1 The e' which are among you I "
Re 4: 4 I saw four and twenty e' sitting, "
10 The four and twenty e' fall down "
5: 5 And one of the e' saith unto me, "
6 and in the midst of the e', "
8 and four and twenty e' fell down "
11 and the beasts and the e': "
14 the four and twenty e' fell down "
7:11 and about the e' and the four beasts, "
13 And one of the e' answered, saying "
11:16 the four and twenty e', which sat "
14: 3 before the four beasts, and the e': "
19: 4 the four and twenty e' and the four "

eldest
Ge 24: 2 Abraham said unto his e' servant *2205
27: 1 he called Esau his e' son, and *1419
15 took goodly raiment of her e' son* "
44:12 began at the e', and left at the "
Nu 1:20 children of Reuben, Israel's e' son.*1060

Nu 26: 5 Reuben, the e· son of Israel: the *1060
1Sa 17:13 And the three e· sons of Jesse 1419
14 and the three e· followed Saul. "
28 Eliab his e· brother heard when he "
2Ki 3:27 Then he took his e· son that 1060
2Ch 22: 1 of men . . . had slain all the e·. 7223
Job 1:13, 18 wine in their e· brother's 1060
Joh 8: 9 beginning at the e·, even unto the 4245

Elead (e'-le-ad)
1Ch 7:21 and Ezer, and E·, whom the men 496

Elealeh (el-e-a'-leh)
Nu 32: 3 Heshbon, and E·, and Shebam, 500
37 of Reuben built Heshbon, and E·, "
Isa 15: 4 And Heshbon shall cry, and E·: "
16: 9 with my tears, O Heshbon, and E·: "
Jer 48:34 the cry of Heshbon even unto E·, "

Eleasah (el-e'-a-sah) See also ELASAH.
1Ch 2:39 begat Helez, and Helez begat E·, 501
40 E· begat Sisamai, and Sisamai "
8:37 Rapha was his son, E· his son, "
9:43 Rephaiah his son, E· his son, "

Eleazar (el-e-a'-zar)
Ex 6:23 bare him Nadab, and Abihu, E·, 499
25 E· Aaron's son took him one of the "
28: 1 even Aaron, Nadab and Abihu, E· "
Le 10: 6 Moses said unto Aaron, and unto E· "
12 spake unto Aaron, and unto E· "
16 and he was angry with E· and "
Nu 3: 2 Nadab the firstborn, and Abihu, E·, "
4 E· and Ithamar ministered in the "
32 E· the son of Aaron the priest shall "
4:16 to the office of E· the son of Aaron "
16:37 Speak unto E· the son of Aaron the "
39 E· the priest took the brazen "
19: 3 ye shall give her unto E· the priest, "
4 E· the priest shall take of her blood "
20:25 Take Aaron and E· his son, and "
26, 28 garments, and put them upon E· "
28 Moses and E· came down from the "
25: 7 when Phinehas, the son of E·, the "
11 Phinehas, the son of E·, the son of "
26: 1 Lord spake unto Moses and unto E· "
3 E· the priest spake with them in "
60 was born Nadab, and Abihu, E· "
63 Moses and E· the priest, who "
27: 2 stood before Moses, and before E· "
19 And set him before E· the priest, "
21 he shall stand before E· the priest, "
22 took Joshua, and set him before E· "
31: 6 them and Phinehas the son of E· "
12 and the spoil, unto Moses, and E· "
13 Moses, and E· the priest, and all "
21 E· the priest said unto the men of "
26 thou, and E· the priest, and the "
29 it of their half, and give it unto E· "
31 Moses and E· the priest did as the "
41 the Lord's heave offering, unto E· "
51, 54 Moses and E· the priest took the "
32: 2 E· the priest, and unto the princes "
28 Moses commanded E· the priest, "
34:17 E· the priest, and Joshua the son "
De 10: 6 E· his son ministered in the priest's "
Jos 14: 1 in the land of Canaan, which E· the "
17: 4 they came near before E· the priest, "
19:51 are the inheritances, which E· the "
21: 1 the fathers of the Levites unto E· "
22:13 of Gilead, Phinehas the son of E· "
31 the son of E· the priest said unto "
32 the son of E· the priest, and the "
24:33 E· the son of Aaron died; and they "
J'g 20:28 son of E·, the son of Aaron, stood "
1Sa 7: 1 sanctified E· his son to keep the ark "
2Sa 23: 9 after him was E· the son of Dodo "
1Ch 6: 3 of Aaron; Nadab, and Abihu, E·, "
4 E· begat Phinehas, Phinehas begat "
50 these are the sons of Aaron, E· his "
9:20 Phinehas the son of E· was the "
11:12 after him was E· the son of Dodo, "
23:21 The sons of Mahli; E·, and Kish. "
22 E· died, and had no sons, "
24: 1 of Aaron; Nadab, and Abihu, E·, "
2 therefore E and Ithamar executed "
3 both Zadok of the sons of E·, and "
4 chief men found of the sons of E· "
4 Among the sons of E· there were "
5 were of the sons of E·, and of the "
6 household being taken for E·, "
28 Of Mahli came E·, who had no sons. "
Ezr 7: 5 the son of E·, the son of Aaron the "
8:33 and with him was E· the son of "
10:25 Miamin, and E·, and Malchijah, "
Ne 12:42 Shemaiah, and E·, and Uzzi, 499
M't 1:15 And Eliud begat E·; and E· begat 1648

elect See also ELECTED; ELECT'S.
Isa 42: 1 e·, in whom my soul delighteth; * 972
45: 4 sake, and Israel mine e·, * "
65: 9 mine e· shall inherit it, and my * "
22 mine e· shall long enjoy the work * "
M't 24:24 they shall deceive the very e·. 1588
31 and shall gather together his e· "
M'r 13:22 if it were possible, even the e·. "
27 and shall gather together his e· "
Lu 18: 7 shall not God avenge his own e·, "
Ro 8:33 any thing to the charge of God's e'? "
Col 3:12 Put on therefore, as the e· of God, "
1Ti 5:21 Lord Jesus Christ, and the e· angels, "
Tit 1: 1 according to the faith of God's e·, "
1Pe 1: 2 E· according to the foreknowledge* "
2: 6 a chief corner stone, e·, precious: "
2Joh 1 The elder unto the e· lady and her "
13 The children of thy e· sister greet "

elected
1Pe 5:13 e· together with you, saluteth you;*4899

election
Ro 9:11 the purpose of God according to e· 1589
11: 5 according to the e· of grace. "
7 the e· hath obtained it, and the rest "
28 as touching the e·, they are beloved "
1Th 1: 4 brethren beloved, your e· of God. "
2Pe 1:10 make your calling and e· sure: "

elect's
M't 24:22 for the e· sake those days shall be 1588
M'r 13:20 for the e· sake, whom he hath "
2Ti 2:10 endure all things for the e· sakes, "

El-elohe-Israel (el-el-o''-he-iz'-rah-el)
Ge 33:20 there an altar, and called it E· 415

elements
Ga 4: 3 in bondage under the e· of the *4747
9 to the weak and beggarly e·, * "
2Pe 3:10 the e· shall melt with fervent heat, "
12 the e· shall melt with fervent heat? "

Eleph (e'-lef)
Jos 18:28 And Zelah, E·, and Jebusi which is 507

eleven
Ge 32:22 took....his e· sons, and passed 259, 6240
37: 9 and the moon and the e· stars " "
Ex 26: 7 e· curtains shalt thou make. 6249, "
8 e· curtains shall be all of one " "
36:14 e· curtains he made them. " "
15 the e· curtains were of one " "
Nu 29:20 on the third day e· bullocks, " "
De 1: 2 e· days' journey from Horeb 259 "
Jos 15:51 e· cities with their villages. " "
J'g 16: 5 one of us e· hundred pieces of 505, 3967
17: 2 e· hundred shekels of silver " "
3 restored the e· hundred shekels" "
2Ki 23:36 reign; and he reigned e· years 259, 6240
24:18 reign, and he reigned e· years " "
2Ch 36: 5, 11 and he reigned e· years in " "
Jer 52: 1 reigned e· years in Jerusalem. " "
Eze 40:49 and the breadth e· cubits; 6249, "
M't 28:16 Then the e· disciples went away 1733
M'r 16:14 he appeared unto the e· as they "
Lu 24: 9 told all these things unto the e·, "
33 found the e· gathered together, "
Ac 1:26 was numbered with the e· apostles. "
2:14 Peter, standing up with the e·, "

eleven hundred See also ELEVEN and HUNDRED.

eleventh
Nu 7:72 the e· day Pagiel...offered: 6249, 6240
De 1: 3 in the fortieth year, in the e· " "
1Ki 6:38 in the e· year, in the month 259 "
2Ki 9:29 in the e· year of Joram the " "
25: 2 the e· year of king Zedekiah. 6249 "
1Ch 12:13 the tenth, Machbanai the e·. " "
24:12 The e· to Eliashib, the twelfth" "
25:18 The e· to Azareel, he, his sons, " "
27:14 The e· captain for the e· month" "
Jer 1: 3 of the e· year of Zedekiah the " "
39: 2 in the e· year of Zedekiah, in " "
52: 5 was besieged unto the e· year " "
Eze 26: 1 in the e· year, in the first day " "
30:20 came to pass in the e· year, 259, "
31: 1 the e· year, in the third month, " "
Zec 1: 7 twentieth day of...e· month, 6249, "
M't 20: 6 about the e· hour he went out, 1734
9 that were hired about the e· hour, "
Re 21:20 the e·, a jacinth; the twelfth, an "

Elhanan (el-ha'-nan)
2Sa 21:19 where E· the son of Jaare-oregim, 445
23:24 E· the son of Dodo of Bethlehem, "
1Ch 11:26 brother of Joab, E· the son of Dodo "
20: 5 E· the son of Jair slew Lahmi "

Eli (e'-li) See also ELI'S; ELOI.
1Sa 1: 3 sons of E·, Hophni and Phinehas, 5941
9 now E· the priest sat upon a seat "
12 Lord, that E· marked her mouth. "
13 E· thought she had been drunken. "
14 And E· said unto her, How long "
17 Then E· answered and said, Go in "
25 and brought the child to E·. "
2:11 minister unto the Lord before E· "
12 sons of E· were sons of Belial; "
20 And E· blessed Elkanah and his "
22 Now E· was very old, and heard "
27 a man of God unto E·, and said "
3: 1 ministered unto the Lord before E·. "
2 when E· was laid down in his place, "
5 And he ran unto E·, and said, Here "
6 And Samuel arose and went to E·, "
8 he arose and went to E·, and said, "
8 And E· perceived that the Lord had "
9 E· said unto Samuel, Go, lie down: "
12 I will perform against E· all things "
14 I have sworn unto the house of E·, "
15 Samuel feared to shew E· the vision. "
16 Then E· called Samuel, and said, "
4: 4 sons of E·, Hophni and Phinehas, "
11 E·, Hophni and Phinehas, were slain. "
13 E· sat upon a seat by the wayside "
14 E· heard the noise of the crying, "
14 man came in hastily, and told E·. "
15 Now E· was ninety and eight "
16 And the man said unto E·, I am he "
14: 3 son of Phinehas, the son of E·, "
1Ki 2:27 spake concerning the house of E· "
M't 27:46 E·, E·, lama sabachthani? that is 2241

Eliab (e'-le-ab) See also ELIAB'S; ELIEL.
Nu 1: 9 Of Zebulun; E· the son of Helon. 446
2: 7 E· the son of Helon shall be captain "
7:24 the third day E· the son of Helon, "
29 the offering of E· the son of Helon. "
10:16 of the children of Zebulun was E· "
16: 1 Dathan and Abiram, the sons of E·, "
12 Dathan and Abiram, the sons of E·: "
26: 8 And the sons of Pallu; E·. 446
9 the sons of E·; Nemuel, and Dathan, "
De 11: 6 the sons of E·, the son of Reuben: "
1Sa 16: 6 he looked on E·, and said, Surely "
17:13 were E· the firstborn, and next unto "
28 E· his eldest brother heard when "
1Ch 2:13 And Jesse begat his firstborn E·, "
6:27 E· his son, Jeroham his son, "
12: 9 Obadiah the second, E· the third, "
15:18 Jehiel, and Unni, E·, and Benaiah, "
20 Unni, and E·, and Maaseiah, "
16: 5 Mattithiah, and E·, and Benaiah, "
2Ch 11:18 Abihail the daughter of E· the son "

Eliab's (e'-le-abs)
1Sa 17:28 E· anger was kindled against 446

Eliada (e'-li'-a-dah) See also ELIADAH.
2Sa 5:16 Elishama, and E·, and Eliphalet. 450
1Ch 3: 8 E·, and Eliphelet, nine. "
2Ch 17:17 E· a mighty man of valour, "

Eliadah (e-li'-a-dah) See also ELIADA.
1Ki 11:23 Rezon the son of E·, which fled * 450

Eliah (e-li'-ah) See also ELIJAH.
1Ch 8:27 Jaresiah, and E·, and Zichri, 452
Ezr 10:26 and Abdi, and Jeremoth, and E·. "

Eliahba (e-li'-ah-bah)
2Sa 23:32 E· the Shaalbonite, of the sons of 455
1Ch 11:33 the Baharumite, E· the Shaalbonite, "

Eliakim (e-li'-a-kim) See also JEHOIAKIM.
2Ki 18:18 there came out to them E· the son 471
26 Then said E· the son of Hilkiah, "
37 Then came E· the son of Hilkiah, "
19: 2 And he sent E·, which was over the "
23:34 Pharaoh-nechoh made E· the son of "
2Ch 36: 4 of Egypt made E· his brother king "
Ne 12:41 the priests; E·, Maaseiah, Miniamin, "
Isa 22:20 I will call my servant E· the son of "
36: 3 Then came forth unto him E·, "
11 Then said E·, and Shebna and Joah "
22 Then came E·, the son of Hilkiah, "
37: 2 And he sent E·, who was over the "
M't 1:13 Abiud begat E·; and E· begat Azor;1662
Lu 3:30 Jonan, which was the son of E·, "

Eliam (e'-le-am)
2Sa 11: 3 Bath-sheba, the daughter of E·, 463
23:34 E· the son of Ahithophel the "

Elias (e-li'-as) See also ELIJAH.
M't 11:14 is Elias, which was for to come. *2243
16:14 some, E·; and others, Jeremias, * "
17: 3 Moses and E· talking with him. * "
4 and one for Moses, and one for E·.* "
10 scribes that E· must first come? * "
11 E· truly shall first come, and * "
12 unto you, That E· is come already,* "
27:47 This man calleth for E·. * "
49 whether E· will come to save him.* "
M'r 6:15 Others said, That it is E·. * "
8:28 but some say, E·; and others, * "
9: 4 unto them E· with Moses: * "
5 and one for Moses, and one for E·.* "
11 that E· must first come? * "
12 E· verily cometh first, and * "
13 unto you, That E· is indeed come,* "
15:35 Behold, he calleth E·. * "
36 whether E· will come to take him* "
Lu 1:17 in the spirit and power of E·, * "
4:25 were in Israel in the days of E·, * "
26 But unto none of them was E· * "
9: 8 of some, that E· had appeared; * "
19 but some say, E·; and others say,* "
30 men, which were Moses and E·: * "
33 and one for Moses, and one for E·:* "
54 consume them, even as E· did? * "
Joh 1:21 What then? Art thou E·? And he* "
25 nor E·, neither that prophet? * "
Ro 11: 2 what the scripture saith of E·? * "
Jas 5:17 E· was a man subject to like * "

Eliasaph (e-li'-a-saf)
Nu 1:14 Of Gad; E· the son of Deuel. 460
2:14 of the sons of Gad shall be E· "
3:24 Gershonites shall be E· the son of "
7:42 the sixth day E· the son of Deuel, "
47 the offering of E· the son of Deuel. "
10:20 tribe of the children of Gad was E· "

Eliashib (e-li'-a-shib)
1Ch 3:24 Hodaiah, and E·, and Pelaiah, 475
24:12 eleventh to E·, the twelfth to Jakim, "
Ezr 10: 6 chamber of Johanan the son of E·: "
24 Of the singers also; E·: "
27 Elioenai, E·, Mattaniah, "
36 Vaniah, Meremoth, E·, "
Ne 3: 1 Then E· the high priest rose up "
20 unto the door of the house of E· "
21 from the door of the house of E· "
21 even to the end of the house of E·. "
12:10 Joiakim also begat E·, "
10 and E· begat Joiada, "
22 Levites in the days of E·, Joiada, "
23 the days of Johanan the son of E·. "
13: 4 E· the priest, having the oversight "
7 the evil that E· did for Tobiah, "
28 the son of E· the high priest, was "

Eliathah (e-li'-a-thah)
1Ch 25: 4 Hanani, E·, Giddalti, 448
27 The twentieth to E·, he, his sons, "

Elidad (e-li'-dad)
Nu 34:21 of Benjamin, E· the son of Chislon. 449

Eliel (e'-le-el) See also ELIAH.
1Ch 5:24 Epher, and Ishi, and E·, and Azriel, 447
6:34 the son of Jeroham, the son of E·, "
8:20 And Elienai, and Zilthai, and E·, "
22 And Ishpan, and Heber, and E·, "

1Ch 11:46 E· the Mahavite, and Jeribai 447
47 E·, and Obed, and Jasiel the "
12:11 Attai the sixth, E· the seventh, "
15: 9 E· the chief, and his brethren "
11 Shemaiah, and E·, and Amminadab, "
2Ch 31:13 Jozabad, and E·, and Ismachiah, "

Elienai (*e-li-e'-nahee*)
1Ch 8:20 E·, and Zilthai, and Eliel, 462

Eliezer (*e-li-e'-zur*)
Ge 15: 2 the steward of my house is this E· 461
Ex 18: 4 the name of the other was E·; "
1Ch 7: 8 Zemira, and Joash, and E·, "
15:24 Benaiah, and E·, the priests, did "
23:15 of Moses were, Gershom, and E·. "
17 sons of E· were, Rehabiah the chief. "
17 And E· had none other sons; "
26:25 brethren by E·; Rehabiah his son, "
27:16 the ruler of the Reubenites was E· "
2Ch 20:37 Then E· the son of Dodavah of "
Ezr 8:16 Then sent I for E·, for Ariel, "
10:18 Maaseiah, and E·, and Jarib, "
23 Pethahiah, Judah, and E·. "
31 of the sons of Harim, E·, Ishijah, "
Lu 3:29 which was the son of E·, *1663*

Elihoenai (*e-li-ho-e'-nahee*) See also ELIOENAI.
Ezr 8: 4 E· the son of Zerahiah, and with * 454

Elihoreph (*e-li-ho'-ref*)
1Ki 4: 3 E· and Ahiah, the sons of Shisha, 456

Elihu (*e-li'-hew*)
1Sa 1: 1 the son of E·, the son of Tohu, 453
1Ch 12:20 Jozabad, and E·, and Zilthai, "
26: 7 strong men, E·, and Semachiah, "
27:18 E·, one of the brethren of David: "
Job 32: 2 Then was kindled the wrath of E· "
4 E· had waited till Job had spoken, "
5 E· saw that there was no answer "
6 E· the son of Barachel the Buzite "
34: 1 E· answered and said, "
35: 1 E· spake moreover, and said, "
36: 1 E· also proceeded, and said, "

Elijah (*e-li'-jah*) See also ELIAH; ELIAS.
1Ki 17: 1 E· the Tishbite, who was of the 452
13 E· said unto her, Fear not; go and "
15 did according to the saying of E·: "
16 of the Lord, which he spake by E·. "
18 she said unto E·, What have I to do "
22 the Lord heard the voice of E·; and "
23 E· took the child, and brought him "
23 and E· said, See, thy son liveth. "
24 the woman said to E·, Now by this "
18: 1 Lord came to E· in the third year, "
2 E· went to shew himself unto Ahab. "
7 was in the way, behold, E· met him: "
7 Art thou that my lord E·? "
8 go, tell thy lord, Behold, E· is here. "
11 Go, tell thy lord, Behold, E· is here. "
14 Go, tell thy lord, Behold, E· is here: "
15 E· said, As the Lord of hosts liveth, "
16 and Ahab went to meet E·. "
17 it came to pass, when Ahab saw E·, "
21 E· came unto all the people, and "
22 Then said E· unto the people, I, "
25 E· said unto the prophets of Baal, "
27 E· mocked them, and said, Cry "
30 E· said unto all the people, Come "
31 E· took twelve stones, according to "
36 E· the prophet came near, and said, "
40 And E· said unto them, Take the "
40 E· brought them down to the brook "
41 E· said unto Ahab, Get thee up, eat "
42 E· went up to the top of Carmel; "
46 the hand of the Lord was on E·; "
19: 1 told Jezebel all that E· had done, "
2 Jezebel sent a messenger unto E·, "
9 unto him, What doest thou here, E·? "
13 it was so, when E· heard it, that he "
13 and said, What doest thou here, E·? "
19 and E· passed by him, and cast his "
20 he left the oxen, and ran after E·, "
21 Then he arose, and went after E·, "
21:17 the Lord came to E· the Tishbite, "
20 Ahab said to E·, Hast thou found "
28 word of the Lord came to E· the "
2Ki 1: 3 said to E· the Tishbite, Arise, go up "
4 shalt surely die. And E· departed. "
8 And he said, It is E· the Tishbite. "
10 E· answered and said to the captain "
12 E· answered and said unto them, "
13 came and fell on his knees before E·, "
15 the angel of the Lord said unto E·, "
17 of the Lord which E· had spoken. "
2: 1 Lord would take up E· into heaven "
1 E· went with Elisha from Gilgal. "
2 E· said unto Elisha, Tarry here, I "
4 E· said unto him, Elisha, tarry here, "
6 E· said unto him, Tarry, I pray thee, "
8 E· took his mantle, and wrapped it "
9 E· said unto Elisha, Ask what I "
11 E· went up by a whirlwind into "
13 He took up also the mantle of E· "
14 And he took the mantle of E· that "
14 Where is the Lord God of E·? "
15 The spirit of E· doth rest on Elisha. "
3:11 poured water on the hand of E·. "
9:36 which he spake by his servant E· the "
10:10 which he spake by his servant E·. "
17 of the Lord, which he spake to E·. "
2Ch 21:12 there came a writing to him from E· "
Ezr 10:21 Maaseiah, and E·, and Shemaiah, "
Mal 4: 5 I will send you E· the prophet "

Elika (*e-li'-kah*)
2Sa 23:25 the Harodite, E· the Harodite, 470

Elim (*e'-lim*) See also BEER-ELIM.
Ex 15:27 they came to E·, where were twelve 362
16: 1 they took their journey from E·, "
1 Sin, which is between E· and Sinai, "
Nu 33: 9 from Marah, and came unto E·: "
9 in E· were twelve fountains of water, "
10 And they removed from E·, and "

Elimelech (*e-lim'-e-lek*) See also ELIMELECH'S.
Ru 1: 2 And the name of the man was E·, 458
3 And E· Naomi's husband died; "
2: 1 man of wealth, of the family of E·; "
3 Boaz, who was of the kindred of E·. "

Elimelech's (*e-lim'-e-leks*)
Ru 4: 3 of land, which was our brother E·: 458
9 that I have bought all that was E·, "

Elioenai (*e-li-o-e'-nahee*) See also ELIHOENAI.
1Ch 3:23 sons of Neariah: E·, and Hezekiah, 454
24 the sons of E· were, Hodaiah, and "
4:36 E·, and Jaakobah, and Jeshohaiah, "
7: 8 Eliezer, and E·, and Omri, "
26: 3 Jehohanan the sixth, E· the * "
Ezr 10:22 the sons of Pashur; E·, Maaseiah, "
27 of the sons of Zattu; E·, Eliashib, "
Ne 12:41 Michaiah, E·, Zechariah, and "

Eliphal (*el'-i-fal*)
1Ch 11:35 Sacar the Hararite, E· the son of Ur, 465

Eliphalet (*e-lif'-a-let*) See also ELIPHELET; ELPALET.
2Sa 5:16 Elishama, and Eliada, and E·. * 467
1Ch 14: 7 Elishama, and Beeliada, and E·. * "

Eliphaz (*el'-if-az*)
Ge 36: 4 And Adah bare to Esau E·; 464
10 E· the son of Adah the wife of Esau, "
11 the sons of E· were Teman, Omar, "
12 Timna was concubine to E· Esau's "
12 and she bare to E· Amalek: "
15 sons of E· the firstborn son of Esau; "
16 these are the dukes that came of E· "
1Ch 1:35 The sons of Esau; E·, Reuel. "
36 The sons of E·; Teman, and Omar, "
Job 2:11 E· the Temanite, and Bildad the "
4: 1 E· the Temanite answered and said, "
15: 1 Then answered E· the Temanite, "
22: 1 E· the Temanite answered and said, "
42: 7 the Lord said to E· the Temanite, "
9 So E· the Temanite and Bildad the "

Elipheleh (*e-lif'-e-leh*)
1Ch 15:18 Mattithiah, and E·, and Mikneiah, 465
21 E·, and Mikneiah, and Obed-edom, "

Eliphelet (*e-lif'-e-let*) See also ELIPHALET.
2Sa 23:34 E· the son of Ahasbai, the son of 467
1Ch 3: 6 Ibhar also, and Elishama, and E·, "
8 Elishama, and Eliada, and E·, nine. "
8:39 Jehush the second, and E· the third. "
Ezr 8:13 whose names are these, E·, Jeiel, "
10:33 Zabad, E·, Jeremai, Manasseh, "

Eli's (*e'-lize*)
1Sa 3:14 the iniquity of E· house shall not 5941

Elisabeth (*e-liz'-a-beth*) See also ELISABETH'S.
Lu 1: 5 of Aaron, and her name was E·. *1665*
7 child, because that E· was barren, "
13 thy wife E· shall bear thee a son, "
24 those days his wife E· conceived, "
36 behold, thy cousin E·, she hath also "
40 house of Zacharias, and saluted E·. "
41 E· heard the salutation of Mary, "
41 E· was filled with the Holy Ghost: "

Elisabeth's (*e-liz'-a-beths*)
Lu 1:57 Now E· full time came that she *1665*

Elisæus See ELISEUS.

Eliseus (*el-i-se'-us*) See also ELISHA.
Lu 4:27 in the time of E· the prophet; *1666*

Elisha (*e-li'-shah*) See also ELISEUS.
1Ki 19:16 E· the son Shaphat of Abel-meholah 477
17 from the sword of Jehu shall E· slay. "
19 he departed thence, and found E· "
2Ki 2: 1 Elijah went with E· from Gilgal. "
2 Elijah said unto E·, Tarry here, "
2 E· said unto him, As the Lord "
3 were at Beth-el came forth to E·, "
4 Elijah said unto him, E·, tarry here, "
5 that were at Jericho came to E·, "
9 Elijah said unto E·, Ask what I "
9 E· said, I pray thee, let a double "
12 E· saw it, and he cried, My father, "
14 and thither: and E· went over. "
15 The spirit of Elijah doth rest on E·. "
19 the men of the city said unto E·, "
22 to the saying of E· which he spake. "
3:11 Here is E· the son of Shaphat, "
13 E· said unto the king of Israel, What "
14 E· said, As the Lord of hosts liveth, "
4: 1 of the sons of the prophets unto E·, "
2 E· said unto her, What shall I do "
8 on a day, that E· passed to Shunem, "
17 season that E· had said unto her, "
32 when E· was come into the house, "
38 E· came again to Gilgal: and there "
5: 8 when E· the man of God had heard "
9 stood at the door of the house of E·. "
10 E· sent a messenger unto him, "
20 Gehazi, the servant of E· the man "
25 E· said unto him, Whence comest "
6: 1 sons of the prophets said unto E·, "
12 but E·, the prophet that is in Israel, "
17 E· prayed, and said, Lord, I pray "
17 and chariots of fire round about E·. "
18 E· prayed unto the Lord, and said, "
18 according to the word of E·. "
19 E· said unto them, This is not the "
20 E· said, Lord, open the eyes of these "
2Ki 6:21 the king of Israel said unto E·, 477
31 the head of E· the son of Shaphat "
32 E· sat in his house, and the elders "
7: 1 E· said, Hear ye the word of the Lord; "
8: 1 Then spake E· unto the woman, "
4 the great things that E· hath done. "
5 is her son, whom E· restored to life. "
7 And E· came to Damascus; and "
10 E· said unto him, Go, say unto him, "
13 E· answered, The Lord hath shewed "
14 So he departed from E·, and came "
14 said to him, What said E· to thee? "
9: 1 E· the prophet called one of the "
13:14 E· was fallen sick of his sickness "
15 E· said unto him, Take bow and "
16 E· put his hands upon the king's "
17 Then E· said, Shoot. And he shot. "
20 And E· died, and they buried him. "
21 the man into the sepulchre of E·: "
21 down, and touched the bones of E·, "

Elishah (*e-li'-shah*)
Ge 10: 4 the sons of Javan; E·, and Tarshish, 473
1Ch 1: 7 the sons of Javan; E·, and Tarshish, "
Eze 27: 7 blue and purple from the isles of E· "

Elishama (*e-lish'-a-mah*) See also ELISHUA.
Nu 1:10 Ephraim; E· the son of Ammihud: 476
2:18 of the sons of Ephraim shall be E· "
7:48 seventh day E· the son of Ammihud, "
53 this was the offering of E· the son of "
10:22 over his host was E· the son of "
2Sa 5:16 E·, and Eliada, and Eliphalet. "
2Ki 25:25 the son of E·, of the seed royal, "
1Ch 2:41 Jekamiah, and Jekamiah begat E·. "
3: 6 Ibhar also, and E·, and Eliphalet, "
8 E·, and Eliada, and Eliphelet, nine. "
7:26 Ammihud his son, E· his son, "
14: 7 E·, and Beeliada, and Eliphalet. "
2Ch 17: 8 and with them E· and Jehoram, "
Jer 36:12 even E· the scribe, and Delaiah "
20 in the chamber of E· the scribe, "
21 out of E· the scribe's chamber. "
41: 1 the son of Nethaniah the son of E·, "

Elishaphat (*e-lish'-a-fat*)
2Ch 23: 1 and E· the son of Zichri, into 478

Elisheba (*e-lish'-e-bah*)
Ex 6:23 Aaron took him E·, daughter of 472

Elishua (*e-lish'-oo-ah*) See also ELISHAMA.
2Sa 5:15 Ibhar also, and E·, and Nepheg, 474
1Ch 14: 5 And Ibhar, and E·, and Elpalet, "

Elite See BETH-ELITE.

Eliud (*e-li'-ud*)
M't 1:14 begat Achim; and Achim begat E·; *1664*
15 And E· begat Eleazar; and "

Elizabeth See ELISABETH.

Elizaphan (*e-liz'-a-fan*) See also ELZAPHAN.
Nu 3:30 of the Kohathites shall be E· 469
34:25 of Zebulun, E· the son of Parnach. "
1Ch 15: 8 the sons of E·; Shemaiah the chief, "
2Ch 29:13 of the sons of E·; Shimri, and Jeiel: "

Elizur (*e-li'-zur*)
Nu 1: 5 of Reuben; E· the son of Shedeur. 468
2:10 the children of Reuben shall be E· "
7:30 fourth day E· the son of Shedeur, "
35 this was the offering of E· the son "
10:18 host was E· the son of Shedeur. "

Elkanah (*el-ka'-nah*)
Ex 6:24 the sons of Korah; Assir, and E·, 511
1Sa 1: 1 and his name was E·, the son of "
4 when the time was that E· offered, "
8 Then said E· her husband to her, "
19 and E· knew Hannah his wife; "
21 the man E·, and all his house, went "
23 E· her husband said unto her, Do "
2:11 And E· went to Ramah to his house. "
20 And Eli blessed E· and his wife, "
1Ch 6:23 E· his son, and Ebiasaph his son, "
25 sons of E·; Amasai, and Ahimoth. "
26 As for E·: the sons of E·; Zophai "
27 Jeroham his son, E· his son. "
34 The son of E·, the son of Jeroham, "
35 The son of Zuph, the son of E·, "
36 The son of E·, the son of Joel, "
9:16 the son of E·, that dwelt in the "
12: 6 E·, and Jesiah, and Azareel, "
15:23 Berechiah and E· were door keepers "
2Ch 28: 7 and E· that was next to the king "

Elkohshite (*el'-ko-shite*)
Na 1: 1 book of the vision of Nahum the E·. 512

Ellasar (*el'-la-sar*)
Ge 14: 1 Arioch king of E·, Chedorlaomer 495
9 and Arioch king of E·; four kings "

Elmodam (*el-mo'-dam*)
Lu 3:28 which was the son of E·, which *1678*

elms
Ho 4:13 under oaks and poplars and E·, * 424

Elnaam (*el-na'-am*)
1Ch 11:46 and Joshaviah, the sons of E·, 493

Elnathan (*el-na'-than*)
2Ki 24: 8 the daughter of E· of Jerusalem. 494
Ezr 8:16 for E·, and for Jarib, and for E·, "
16 and for E·, men of understanding. "
Jer 26:22 E· the son of Achbor, and certain "
36:12 E· the son of Achbor, and Gemariah "
25 Nevertheless E· and Delaiah and "

Elohe See EL-ELOHE-ISRAEL.

Eloi (*e-lo'-ee*) See also ELI.
M'r 15:34 E·, E·, lama sabachthani? *1682*

Elon (*e'-lon*) See also ELON-BETH-HANAN; ELONITES.
Ge 26:34 Bashemath the daughter of *E'* the 356
36: 2 Adah the daughter of *E'* the "
46:14 sons of Zebulun; Sered, and *E'*, "
Nu 26:26 of *E'* the family of the Elonites: "
Jos 19:43 *E'*, and Thimnathah, and Ekron, "
J'g 12:11 And after him *E'*, a Zebulonite, "
12 And *E'* the Zebulonite died, and was "

Elon-beth-hanan (*e''-lon-beth-ha'-nan*)
1Ki 4: 9 and Beth-shemesh, and *E'*: 358

Elonites (*e'-lon-ites*)
Nu 26:26 of Elon, the family of the *E'*: 440

eloquent
Ex 4:10 O my Lord, I am not *e'*, 376, 1697
Isa 3: 3 artificer, and the *e'* orator. * 995
Ac 18:24 an *e'* man, and mighty in the *3052

Eloth (*e'-loth*) See also ELATH.
1Ki 9:26 Ezion-geber, which is beside *E'*, 359
2Ch 8:17 *E'*, at the sea side in the land of "
26: 2 He built *E'*, and restored it to Judah, "

Elpaal (*el-pa'-al*)
1Ch 8:11 Hushim he begat Abitub, and *E'*. 508
12 The sons of *E'*; Eber, and Misham, "
18 Jezliah, and Jobab, the sons of *E'*; "

Elpalet (*el-pa'-let*) See also ELIPHALET.
1Ch 1:15 Ibhar, and Elishua, and *E'*, 467

El-paran (*el-pa'-ran*)
Ge 14: 6 unto *E'*, which is by the wilderness. 364

else
Ge 30: 1 Give me children, or *e'* I die. 369
42:16 or *e'* by the life of Pharaoh 518, 3808
Ex 8:21 *E'*, if thou wilt not let my people 3588
10: 4 *E'*, if thou refuse to let my people "
Nu 20:19 without doing anything *e'*, go though
De 4:35 he is God; there is none *e'* beside 5750
39 the earth beneath: there is none *e'*. "
Jos 23:12 *E'* if ye do in any wise go back, 3588
J'g 7:14 This is nothing *e'* save the sword
2Sa 3:35 if I taste bread, or ought *e'*, till the
15:14 for we shall not *e'* escape from
1Ki 8:60 is God, and that there is none *e'*. 5750
1Ch 21:12 or *e'* three days the sword of the 518
2Ch 23: 7 and whosoever *e'* cometh into the*
Ne 2: 2 this is nothing *e'* but sorrow of
Ps 51:16 thou desirest not sacrifice; *e'* would I
Ec 2:25 or who *e'* can hasten hereunto, *
Isa 45: 5 am the Lord, and there is none *e'*, 5750
6 I am the Lord, and there is none *e'*. "
14 and there is none *e'*, there is no God. "
18 I am the Lord; and there is none *e'*. "
21 and there is no God *e'* beside me; a "
22 for I am God, and there is none *e'*. "
46: 9 I am God, and there is none *e'*; I "
47: 8 I am, and none *e'* beside me; I shall "
10 I am, and none *e'* beside me.
Jo 2:27 am the Lord your God, and none *e'*: "
M't 6:24 either he will hate the one, . . . or *e'* he
9:17 *e'* the bottles break, and the wine *1490*
12:29 Or *e'* how can one enter into the *
33 or *e'* make the tree corrupt, and *
M'r 2:21 *e'* the new piece that filled it up *1490*
22 *e'* the new wine doth burst the bottles, "
Lu 5:37 *e'* the new wine will burst the bottles, "
14:32 Or *e'*, while the other is yet a great "
16:13 or *e'* he will hold to the one,
Joh 14:11 or *e'* believe me for the very works' *1490*
Ac 17:21 spent their time in nothing *e'*, but *2087*
24:20 Or *e'* let these same here say,
Ro 2:15 accusing or *e'* excusing one *2532*
1Co 7:14 *e'* were your children unclean; *1893, 686*
14:16 *E'* when thou shalt bless with the *1893*
15:29 *E'* what shall they do which are "
Ph'p 1:27 come and see you, or *e'* be absent,*
Re 2: 5 or *e'* I will come unto thee quickly, *1490*
16 Repent; or *e'* I will come unto thee "

Eltekeh (*el'-te-keh*)
Jos 19:44 And *E'*, and Gibbethon, and Baalath, 514
21:23 out of the tribe of Dan, *E'* with her "

Eltekon (*el'-te-kon*)
Jos 15:59 Maarath, and Beth-anoth, and *E'*; 515

Eltolad (*el-to'-lad*)
Jos 15:30 And *E'*, and Chesil, and Hormah, 513
19: 4 And *E'*, and Bethul, and Hormah, "

Elul (*e'-lul*)
Ne 6:15 and fifth day of the month *E'*, 435

Eluzai (*e-loo'-zahee*)
1Ch 12: 5 *E'*, and Jerimoth, and Bealiah, 498

Elymas (*el'-i-mas*) See also BAR-JESUS.
Ac 13: 8 But *E'* the sorcerer (for so is his *1681*

Elzabad (*el'-za-bad*)
1Ch 12:12 Johanan the eighth, *E'* the ninth, 443
26: 7 *E'*, whose brethren were strong "

Elzaphan (*el'-za-fan*) See also ELIZAPHAN.
Ex 6:22 the sons of Uzziel; Mishael, and *E'*, 469
Lev 10: 4 Moses called Mishael and *E'*, "

embalm See also EMBALMED.
Ge 50: 2 the physicians to *e'* his father: 2590

embalmed
Ge 50: 2 and the physicians *e'* Israel. 2590
3 the days of those which are *e'*: "
26 and they *e'* him, and he was put in "

embassy See AMBASSAGE.

emboldened
1Co 8:10 of him which is weak be *e'* to eat *3618*

emboldeneth
Job 16: 3 what *e'* thee that thou answerest? *4834

embrace See also EMBRACED; EMBRACING.
2Ki 4:16 time of life, thou shalt *e'* a son. 2263
Job 24: 8 *e'* the rock for want of a shelter. "
Pr 4: 8 to honour when thou dost *e'* her. "
5:20 and *e'* the bosom of a stranger? "
Ec 3: 5 a time to *e'*, and a time to refrain "
Ca 2: 6 and his right hand doth *e'* me. "
8: 3 and his right hand should *e'* me. "
La 4: 5 that were brought up in scarlet *e'* "

embraced
Ge 29:13 he ran to meet him, and *e'* him, 2263
33: 4 Esau ran to meet him, and *e'* him, "
48:10 he kissed them, and *e'* them. "
Ac 20: 1 unto him the disciples, and *e'* * *782*
He 11:13 *e'* them, and confessed that they *

embracing
Ec 3: 5 a time to refrain from *e'*; 2263
Ac 20:10 and fell on him, and *e'* him said, *4843*

embroider
Ex 28:39 And thou shalt *e'* the coat of fine *7660

embroiderer
Ex 35:35 manner of work, . . . and of the *e'*, 7551
38:23 and an *e'* in blue, and in purple, "

Emek See BETH-EMEK.

emerald See also EMERALDS.
Ex 28:18 And the second row shall be an *e'*, 5306
39:11 an *e'*, a sapphire, and a diamond. "
Eze 28:13 sapphire, the *e'*, and the carbuncle, "
Re 4: 3 in sight like unto an *e'*. *4664*
21:19 a chalcedony; the fourth, an *e'*; *4665*

emeralds
Eze 27:16 they occupied in thy fairs with *e'*, 5306

emerods (*em'-e-rods*)
De 28:27 and with the *e'*, and with the scab, 6076
1Sa 5: 6 smote them with *e'*, even Ashdod * "
9 they had *e'* in their secret parts. * "
12 died not were smitten with the *e'*: * "
6: 4 Five golden *e'*, and five golden * "
5 ye shall make images of your *e'*, * "
11 and the images of their *e'*. *2914
17 these are the golden *e'* which the * "

Emims (*e'-mims*)
Ge 14: 5 and the *E'* in Shaveh Kiriathaim, * 368
De 2:10 *E'* dwelt therein in times past, * "
11 but the Moabites call them *E'*. * "

eminence See PRE-EMINENCE.

eminent
Eze 16:24 also built unto thee an *e'* place, 1354
31 thou buildest thine *e'* place in the "
39 shall throw down thine *e'* place, "
17:22 upon an high mountain and *e'*: 8524

Emmanuel (*em-man'-uel*) See also IMMANUEL.
M't 1:23 they shall call his name *E'*, *1694*

Emmaus (*em'-ma-us*)
Lu 24:13 to a village called *E'*, which was *1695*

Emmor (*em'-mor*) See also HAMOR.
Ac 7:16 of the sons of *E'* the father of *1697*

empire
Es 1:20 published throughout all his *e'*, *4438

employ See also EMPLOYED; EMPLOYMENT.
De 20:19 to *e'* them in the siege: *935, 6440

employed
1Ch 9:33 for they were *e'* in that work day 5921
Ezr 10:15 Tikvah were *e'* about this matter: *5975

employment
Eze 39:14 shall sever out men of continual *e'*,

emptied
Ge 24:20 she hasted, and *e'* her pitcher 6168
42:35 to pass as they *e'* their sacks, 7324
2Ch 24:11 officer came and *e'* the chest, 6168
Ne 5:13 thus be he shaken out, and *e'*. 7386
Isa 19: 6 defence shall be *e'* and dried up; *1809
24: 3 The land shall be utterly *e'*, and 1238
Jer 48:11 hath not been *e'* from vessel to 7324
Na 2: 2 for the emptiers have *e'* them out, 1238

emptiers
Na 2: 2 for the *e'* have emptied them out, 1238

emptiness
Isa 34:11 of confusion, and the stones of *e'*. 922

empty See also EMPTIED.
Ge 31:42 thou hadst sent me away now *e'*. 7387
37:24 the pit was *e'*; there was no water 7386
41:27 the seven *e'* ears blasted with the "
Ex 3:21 when ye go, ye shall not go *e'*: 7387
23:15 and none shall appear before me *e'*:) "
34:20 And none shall appear before me *e'*. "
Le 14:36 command that they *e'* the house, 6437
De 15:13 thou shalt not let him go away *e'*: 7387
16:16 shall not appear before the Lord *e'*: "
J'g 7:16 *e'* pitchers, and lamps within the 7385
Ru 1:21 hath brought me home again *e'*: 7387
3:17 Go not *e'* unto thy mother in law. "
1Sa 6: 3 send it not *e'*; but in any wise "
20:18 missed because thy seat will be *e'*. 6485
25 side, and David's place was *e'*. "
27 that David's place was *e'*: and Saul "
2Sa 1:22 the sword of Saul returned not *e'*. 7387
2Ki 4: 3 borrow thee vessels...*e'* vessels; 7385
Job 22: 9 Thou hast sent widows away *e'*, 7387
26: 7 out the north over the *e'* place, 8414
Ec 11: 3 they *e'* themselves upon the earth: 7324
Isa 24: 1 the Lord maketh the earth *e'*, 1238
29: 8 he awaketh, and his soul is *e'*: 7385
32: 6 to make *e'* the soul of the hungry, 7324
Jer 14: 3 returned with their vessels *e'*; 7387
48:12 shall *e'* his vessels, and break 7324
51: 2 shall fan her, and shall *e'* her land: 1238
34 he hath made me an *e'* vessel, 7385

Eze 24:11 set it *e'* upon the coals thereof, 7385
Hos 10: 1 Israel is an *e'* vine, he bringeth *1238
Na 2:10 She is *e'*, and void, and waste: 950
Hab 1:17 Shall they therefore *e'* their net, 7324
Zec 4:12 through the two golden pipes *e'* "
M't 12:44 he findeth it *e'*, swept, and *4980*
M'r 12: 3 beat him, and sent him away *e'*. *2756*
Lu 1:53 the rich he hath sent *e'* away. "
20:10 beat him, and sent him away *e'*. "
11 shamefully, and sent him away *e'*. "

emulation See also EMULATIONS.
Ro 11:14 I may provoke to *e'* them which *3863*

emulations
Ga 5:20 hatred, variance, *e'*, wrath, strife, *2205*

En See EN-DOR; EN-EGLAIM; EN-GANNIM; EN-GEDI; EN-HADDAH; EN-HAKKORE; EN-HAZOR; EN-MISHPAT; EN-RIMMON; EN-ROGEL; EN-SHEMESH; EN-TAPPUAH.

enabled
1Ti 1:12 Jesus our Lord, who hath *e'* me, *1743*

Enam (*e'-nam*)
Jos 15:34 and En-gannim, Tappuah, and *E'*, 5879

Enan (*e'-nan*) See also HAZAR-ENAN.
Nu 1:15 Of Naphtali; Ahira the son of *E'*. 5881
2:29 shall be Ahirah the son of *E'*. "
7:78 the twelfth day Ahira the son of *E'*, "
83 the offering of Ahira the son of *E'*. "
10:27 Naphtali was Ahira the son of *E'*. "

encamp See also ENCAMPED; ENCAMPETH; ENCAMPING.
Ex 14: 2 turn and *e'* before Pi-hahiroth, 2583
2 before it shall ye *e'* by the sea. "
Nu 1:50 shall minister unto it, and shall *e'* "
2:17 as they *e'*, so shall they set forward, "
27 And those that *e'* by him shall be † "
3:38 But those that *e'* before the † "
10:31 how we are to *e'* in the wilderness, "
2Sa 12:28 and *e'* against the city, and take it: "
Job 19:12 and *e'* round about my tabernacle. "
Ps 27: 3 Though an host should *e'* against "
Zec 9: 8 And I will *e'* about mine house "

encamped
Ex 13:20 and *e'* in Etham, in the edge of the 2583
15:27 and they *e'* there by the waters. "
18: 5 where he *e'* at the mount of God: "
Nu 33:10 and *e'* by the Red Sea. † "
11 and *e'* in the wilderness of Sin. † "
12 and *e'* in Dophkah. † "
13 and *e'* in Alush. † "
14 and *e'* at Rephidim, where was no † "
17 and *e'* at Hazeroth. † "
24 and *e'* in Haradah. † "
26 and *e'* at Tahath. † "
30 and *e'* at Moseroth. † "
32 and *e'* at Hor-hagidgad. † "
34 and *e'* at Ebronah. † "
35 and *e'* at Ezion-gaber. † "
46 and *e'* in Almon-diblathaim. † "
Jos 4:19 and *e'* in Gilgal, in the east border "
5:10 And the children of Israel *e'* in "
10: 5 and *e'* before Gibeon, and made war "
31 and *e'* against it, and fought "
34 and they *e'* against it, and fought "
J'g 6: 4 And they *e'* against them, and "
9:50 and *e'* against Thebez, and took it. "
10:17 gathered together, and *e'* in Gilead. "
17 together, and *e'* in Mizpeh. "
20:19 morning, and *e'* against Gibeah. "
1Sa 11: 1 and *e'* against Jabesh-gilead: "
13:16 but the Philistines *e'* in Michmash. "
2Sa 11:11 my lord, are *e'* in the open fields; "
1Ki 16:15 And the people were *e'* against "
16 the people that were *e'* heard say, "
1Ch 11:15 the Philistines *e'* in the valley of "
2Ch 32: 1 and *e'* against the fenced cities, "

encampeth
Ps 34: 7 The angel of the Lord *e'* round 2583
53: 5 the bones of him that *e'* against "

encamping
Ex 14: 9 and overtook them *e'* by the sea, 2583

enchanter See also ENCHANTERS.
De 18:10 spirits, or an *e'*, or a witch, 5172

enchanters
Jer 27: 9 your *e'*, nor to your sorcerers, *6049

enchantment See also ENCHANTMENTS.
Le 19:26 neither shall ye use *e'*, *5172
Nu 23:23 there is no *e'* against Jacob, "
Ec 10:11 the serpent will bite without *e'*; *3908

enchantments
Ex 7:11 did in like manner with their *e'*. 3858
22 of Egypt did so with their *e'*: 3909
8: 7 the magicians did so with their *e'*, "
18 did so with their *e'* to bring forth "
Nu 24: 1 to seek for *e'*, but he set his face 5172
2Ki 17:17 and used divination and *e'*, and "
21: 6 and observed times, and used *e'*, "
2Ch 33: 6 also he observed times, and used *e'*, "
Isa 47: 9 the great abundance of thine *e'*. 2267
12 Stand now with thine *e'*, and with "

encountered
Ac 17:18 and of the Stoicks, *e'* him. *4820*

encourage See also ENCOURAGED.
De 1:38 he shall go in thither: *e'* him: 2388
3:28 charge Joshua, and *e'* him, and "
2Sa 11:25 and overthrow it: and *e'* thou him. "
Ps 64: 5 They *e'* themselves in an evil "

encouraged
J'g 20:22 the men of Israel *e'* themselves, 2388
1Sa 30: 6 but David *e'* himself in the Lord "
2Ch 31: 4 that they might be *e'* in the law of * "

2Ch 35: 2 and e' them to the service of the 2388
Isa 41: 7 So the carpenter e' the goldsmith, "
end See ENDEST; ENDETH; ENDING; ENDLESS; ENDS.
Ge 6:13 The e' of all flesh is come before 7093
8: 3 after the e' of the hundred and 7097
6 came to pass at the e' of forty days,7093
23: 9 which is in the e' of his field; 7097
27:30 as Isaac had made an e' of blessing3615
41: 1 it came to pass at the e' of two full 7093
47:21 from one e' of the borders of Egypt7097
21 even to the other e' thereof. "
49:33 And when Jacob had made an e' of 3615
Ex 8:22 to the e' thou mayest know that I 4616
12:41 at the e' of the four hundred and 7093
23:16 in the e' of the year, when thou 3318
25:19 one cherub on the one e', and the 7098
19 the other cherub on the other e': "
26:28 the boards shall reach from e' to e'.7097
31:18 choses, when he had made an e' of 3615
34:22 of ingathering at the year's e'. 8622
36:33 the boards from the one e' to the 7097
37: 8 One cherub on the e' on this side, 7098
8 and another cherub on the other e' "
Le 8:33 of your consecration be at an e': *4390
16:20 hath made an e' of reconciling 3615
17: 5 To the e' that the children of 4616
Nu 4:15 have made an e' of covering 3615
16:31 as he had made an e' of speaking "
23:10 and let my last e' be like his!
24:20 but his latter e' shall be that he perish
De 8:16 to do thee good at thy latter e';
9:11 at the e' of forty days and forty 7093
11:12 even unto the e' of the year. 319
13: 7 from the one e' of the earth even 7097
7 even unto the other e' of the earth;"
14:28 At the e' of three years thou shalt "
15: 1 At the e' of every seven years thou7093
17:16 to the e' that he should multiply 4616
20 to the e' that he may prolong his "
20: 9 officers have made an e' speaking 3615
26:12 thou hast made an e' of tithing all "
28:49 from the e' of the earth, as swift 7097
64 from the one e' of the earth even "
31:10 At the e' of every seven years, 7093
24 Moses had made an e' of writing 3615
32:20 I will see what their e' shall be: 319
29 they would consider their latter e'!
45 And Moses made an e' of speaking 3615
Jos 8:24 Israel had made an e' of slaying "
9:16 to pass at the e' of three days 7097
10:20 Israel had made an e' of slaying 3615
15: 5 sea, even unto the e' of Jordan. 7097
8 at the e' of the valley of the giants* "
18:15 from the e' of Kirjath-jearim, * "
16 down to the e' of the mountain * "
19 salt sea at the south e' of Jordan: "
19:49 they had made an e' of dividing 3615
51 So they made an e' of dividing the "
J'g 3:18 when he had made an e' to offer "
6:21 Lord put forth the e' of the staff 7097
11:39 to pass at the e' of two months, 7093
15:17 he had made an e' of speaking, 3615
19: 9 behold, the day groweth to an e', 2583
Ru 2:23 unto the e' of barley harvest and 3615
3: 7 at the e' of the heap of corn: 7097
10 more kindness at the latter e' than
1Sa 3:12 I begin, I will also make an e'. 3615
9:27 going down to the e' of the city, 7097
10:13 he had made an e' of prophesying,3615
13:10 as he had made an e' of offering "
14:27 he put forth the e' of the rod 7097
43 a little honey with the e' of the rod "
18: 1 he had made an e' of speaking 3615
24:16 David had made an e' of speaking "
2Sa 2:23 Abner with the hinder e' of the spear
26 it will be bitterness in the latter e'?
6:18 David had made an e' of offering 3615
11:19 thou hast made an e' of telling "
13:36 as he had made an e' of speaking, "
14:26 every year's e' that he polled it: 7093
24: 8 at the e' of nine months and twenty7097
1Ki 1:41 as they had made an e' of eating. 3615
2:39 to pass at the e' of three years, 7093
3: 1 he had made an e' of building 3615
7:40 So Hiram made an e' of doing all "
8:54 Solomon had made an e' of praying"
9:10 to pass at the e' of twenty years, 7097
2Ki 8: 3 came to pass at the seven years' e'."
10:21 of Baal was full from one e' to 6310
25 as he had made an e' of offering 3615
18:10 at the e' of three years they took it:7097
21:16 Jerusalem from one e' to another;6310
1Ch 16: 2 David had made an e' of offering 3615
2Ch 4:10 sea on the right side of the east e',*
5:12 stood at the east e' of the altar,
7: 1 Solomon had made an e' of praying,3615
8: 1 to pass at the e' of twenty years, 7093
20:16 find them at the e' of the brook, 5490
23 had made an e' of the inhabitants 3615
21:19 of time, after the e' of two years, 7093
24:10 chest, until they had made an e'. 3615
23 came to pass at the e' of the year, 8622
29:17 sixteenth day...they made an e'. 3615
29 they had made an e' of offering, "
Ezr 9:11 filled it from one e' to another 6310
10:17 they made an e' with all the men 3615
Ne 3:21 to the e' of the house of Eliashib. 8503
4: 2 will they make an e' in a day? 3615
Job 6:11 and what is mine e', that I should 7093
8: 7 thy latter e' should greatly increase.
16: 3 Shall vain words have an e'? 7093
18: 2 ere ye make an e' of words? *7078
26:10 the day and night come to an e'. *8503
28: 3 He setteth an e' to darkness, 7093
34:36 that Job may be tried unto the e' 5331
Job 42:12 the Lord blessed the latter e' of Job
Ps 7: 9 of the wicked come to an e'; 1584
9: 6 are come to a perpetual e': 8552
19: 4 their words to the e' of the world. 7097
6 forth is from the e' of the heaven, "
30:12 To the e' that my glory may sing 4616
37:37 for the e' of that man is peace. 319
38 e' of the wicked shall be cut off. "
39: 4 Lord, make me to know mine e', 7093
46: 9 to cease unto the e' of the earth; 7097
61: 2 From the e' of the earth will I cry "
73:17 God; then understood I their e'. 319
102:27 and thy years shall have no e'. 8552
107:27 man, and are at their wit's e'. 1104
119:33 I shall keep it unto the e'. 6118
96 have seen an e' of all perfection: 7093
112 statutes alway, even unto the e'. 6118
Pr 5: 4 But her e' is bitter as wormwood, 319
14:12 e' thereof are the ways of death. "
13 the e' of that mirth is heaviness. "
16:25 the e' thereof are the ways of death."
19:20 thou mayest be wise in thy latter e'.
20:21 the e' thereof shall not be blessed. 319
23:18 For surely there is an e'; and * "
25: 8 what to do in the e' thereof, "
Ec 3:11 from the beginning to the e'. 5490
4: 8 yet is there no e' of all his labour;7093
16 There is no e' of all the people, "
7: 2 for that is the e' of all men; 5490
8 Better is the e' of a thing than the 319
14 e' that man should find nothing 1700
10:13 the e' of his talk is mischievous 319
12:12 making many books there is no e';7093
Isa 2: 7 is there any e' of their treasures; 7097
7 is there any e' of their chariots; "
5:26 unto them from the e' of the earth: "
7: 3 at the e' of the conduit of the upper "
9: 7 and peace there shall be no e', 7093
13: 5 far country, from the e' of heaven,* "
16: 4 for the extortioner is at an e', * 657
23:15 the e' of seventy years shall Tyre 7093
17 pass after the e' of seventy years, "
33: 1 make an e' to deal treacherously, 5239
38:12, 13 wilt thou make an e' of me. 7999
41:22 and know the latter e' of them;
42:10 his praise from the e' of the earth,7097
45:17 world without e'. 5704, 5769, 5703
46:10 the e' from the beginning, 319
47: 7 didst remember the latter e' of it.
48:20 it even to the e' of the earth; 7097
49: 6 salvation unto the e' of the earth. "
62:11 proclaimed unto the e' of the world,"
Jer 1: 3 unto the e' of the eleventh year 8537
3: 5 will he keep it to the e'? 5331
4:27 yet will I not make a full e'. 3615
5:10 but make not a full e': take away "
18 I will not make a full e' with you. "
31 what will ye do in the e' thereof? 319
12: 4 He shall not see our last e'.
12 from the one e' of the land 7097
12 even to the other e' of the land: "
17:11 and at his e' shall be a fool. 319
25:33 from one e' of the earth even 7097
33 unto the other e' of the earth: "
26: 8 had made an e' of speaking all 3615
29:11 of evil, to give you an expected e'. 319
30:11 I make a full e' of all nations 3615
11 yet will I not make a full e' of thee:"
31:17 And there is hope in thine e', 319
34:14 At the e' of seven years let ye go 7093
43: 1 had made an e' of speaking unto 3615
44:27 until there be an e' of them. "
46:28 will make a full e' of all the nations "
28 I will not make a full e' of thee, "
51:13 thine e' is come, and the measure 7093
31 that his city is taken at one e', *7097
63 made an e' of reading this book, 3615
La 1: 9 she remembereth not her last e';
4:18 our e' is near, our days are fulfilled;7093
18 for our e' is come. "
Eze 3:16 to pass at the e' of seven days, 7097
7: 2 An e', the e' is come upon the four 7093
3 Now is the e' come upon thee, "
6 An e' is come, the e' is come: "
11:13 God! wilt thou make a full e' of 3615
20:17 neither did I make an e' of them "
26 to the e' that they might know 4616
21:25 when iniquity shall have an e', 7093
29 their iniquity shall have an e'. "
29:13 At the e' of forty years will I gather "
31:14 To the e' that none of all the trees 4616
35: 5 that their iniquity had an e': 7093
39:14 after the e' of seven months shall 7097
41:12 at the e' toward the west was *6285
42:15 he had made an e' of measuring 3615
43:23 hast made an e' of cleansing it, "
48: 1 From the north e' to the coast of 7097
Da 1: 5 at the e' thereof they might stand 7117
15 And at the e' of ten days their "
18 at the e' of the days that the king "
4:11 thereof to the e' of all the earth: 5491
22 thy dominion to the e' of the earth."
29 the e' of twelve months he walked 7118
34 the e' of the days I Nebuchadnezzar"
6:26 dominion shall be even unto the e'.5491
7:26 and to destroy it unto the e'. "
28 Hitherto is the e' of the matter. "
8:17 time of the e' shall be the vision. 7093
19 in the last e' of the indignation: *
19 the time appointed the e' shall be.7093
9:24 and to make an e' of sins, 2856
26 the e' thereof shall be with a flood,7093
26 and unto the e' of the war "
11: 6 in the e' of years they shall join "
27 the e' shall be at the time appointed."
35 even to the time of the e': "
Da 11:40 at the time of the e' shall the king 7093
45 yet he shall come to his e', "
12: 4 book, even to the time of the e': "
6 it be to the e' of these wonders? "
8 shall be the e' of these things? * 319
9 and sealed till the time of the e'. 7093
13 go thou thy way till the e' be: "
13 stand in thy lot at the e' of the days."
Am 3:15 the great houses shall have an e', 5486
5:18 to what e' is it for you? *
7: 2 they had made an e' of eating 3615
8: 2 The e' is come upon my people 7093
10 and the e' thereof as a bitter day. 319
Ob 9 to the e' that every one of the 4616
Na 1: 8 will make an utter e' of the place 3615
9 the Lord? he will make an utter e': "
2: 9 for there is none e' of the store 7097
3: 3 there is none e' of their corpses; "
Hab 2: 3 but at the e' it shall speak, 7093
M't 10:22 endureth to the e' shall be saved. 5056
11: 1 when Jesus had made an e' of 5055
13:39 the harvest is the e' of the world; 4930
40 so shall it be in the e' of this world."
49 So shall it be at the e' of the world:"
24: 3 and of the e' of the world? "
6 come to pass, but the e' is not yet. 5056
13 he that shall endure unto the e', "
14 and then shall the e' come. "
31 from one e' of heaven to the other. 206
26:58 with the servants, to see the e'. 5056
28: 1 the e' of the sabbath, as it began *3796
20 even unto the e' of the world. 4930
M'r 3:26 he cannot stand, but hath an e'. 5056
13: 7 the e' shall not be yet. "
13 but he that shall endure unto the e'."
Lu 1:33 of his kingdom there shall be no e'."
18: 1 a parable unto them to this e', that men
21: 9 but the e' is not by and by. 5056
22:37 things concerning me have an e'. * "
Joh 13: 1 world, he loved them unto the e'. "
18:37 To this e' was I born, and for this
Ac 7:19 to the e' they might not live. 1519
Ro 1:11 to the e' ye may be established; "
4:16 the e' the promise might be sure "
6:21 for the e' of those things is death. 5056
22 and the e' everlasting life. "
10: 4 For Christ is the e' of the law "
14: 9 to this e' Christ both died, and rose
1Co 1: 8 shall also confirm you unto the e',5056
15:24 Then cometh the e', when he shall "
2Co 1:13 shall acknowledge even to the e'; "
2: 9 to this e' also did I write, that I might
3:13 the e' of that which is abolished: 5056
11:15 e' shall be according to their works."
Eph 3:21 ages, world without e'. 165, 3588, 165
Ph'p 3:19 Whose e' is destruction, whose God 5056
1Th 3:13 To the e' he may stablish your 1519
1Ti 1: 5 Now the e' of the commandment 5056
Heb 3: 6 of the hope firm unto the e'. "
14 our confidence stedfast unto the e';"
6: 8 cursing; whose e' is to be burned. "
11 full assurance of hope unto the e': "
16 is to them an e' of all strife. *4009
7: 3 beginning of days, nor e' of life; 5056
9:26 e' of the world hath he appeared 4930
13: 7 the e' of their conversation. *1545
Jas 5:11 and have seen the e' of the Lord; 5056
1Pe 1: 9 Receiving the e' of your faith, "
13 and hope to the e' for the grace *5049
4: 7 But the e' of all things is at hand:5056
17 what shall the e' be of them that "
2Pe 2:20 the latter e' is worse with them *2078
Re 2:26 and keepeth my works unto the e',5056
21: 6 the beginning and the e', I will give "
22:13 Omega, the beginning and the e', "
endamage
Ezr 4:13 so thou shalt e' the revenue of ‡5142
endanger See also ENDANGERED.
Da 1:10 then shall ye make me e' my head 2325
endangered
Ec 10: 9 he that cleaveth wood shall be e' 5533
endeavour See also ENDEAVOURED; ENDEAVOURING; ENDEAVOURS.
2Pe 1:15 I will e' that ye may be able after *4704
endeavoured
Ac 16:10 we e' to go into Macedonia, *2212
1Th 2:17 e' the more abundantly to see 4704
endeavouring
Eph 4: 4 E' to keep the unity of the Spirit *4704
endeavours
Ps 28: 4 to the wickedness of their e': *4611
ended
Ge 2: 2 And on the seventh day God e' *3615
41:53 years of plenteousness,...were e'.* "
47:18 When that year was e', they came 8552
De 31:30 of this song, until they were e'. "
34: 8 and mourning for Moses were e'. "
Ru 2:21 until they have e' all my harvest. 3615
2Sa 20:18 so they e' the matter. 8552
1Ki 7:51 So was e' all the work that king *7999
2Ch 29:34 till the work was e', and until the 3615
Job 31:40 The words of Job are e'. 8552
Ps 72:20 of David the son of Jesse are e'. 3615
Isa 60:20 days of thy mourning shall be e'. 7999
Jer 8:20 the summer is e', and we are not 3615
Eze 4: 8 till thou hast e' the days of thy *
M't 7:28 when Jesus had e' these sayings, 4931
Lu 4: 2 and when they were e', he *4931
13 And when the devil had e' all the * "
7: 1 when he had e' all his sayings 4137
Joh 13: 2 supper being e', the devil having *1096
Ac 19:21 After these things were e', Paul 4137
21:27 the seven days were almost e', *4931

endeth
Isa 24: 8 the noise of them that rejoice *e'*. 2308
ending
Re 1: 8 Omega, the beginning and the *e'*.*5056
endless
1Ti 1: 4 to fables and *e'* genealogies, which 562
Heb 7:16 but after the power of an *e'* life. 179
En-dor (*en'-dor*)
Jos 17:11 and the inhabitants of *E'* and her 5874
1Sa 28: 7 that hath a familiar spirit at *E'*. "
Ps 83:10 Which perished at *E'*: they became "
endow See also ENDUED.
Ex 22:16 he shall surely *e'* her to be his *4117
ends
Ex 25:18 in the two *e'* of the mercy seat. 7098
19 the cherubims on the two *e'* thereof. "
28:14 two chains of pure gold at the *e'*;*4020
22 the *e'* of wreathen work of pure *1383
23 on the two *e'* of the breastplate. 7098
24 are on the *e'* of the breastplate "
25 And the other two *e'* of the two "
26 upon the two *e'* of the breastplate "
37: 7 on the two *e'* of the mercy seat; "
8 cherubims on the two *e'* thereof. 7099
38: 5 four rings for the four *e'* of the "
39:15 the breastplate chains at the *e'*, *1383
16 in the two *e'* of the breastplate. 7098
17 rings on the *e'* of the breastplate. "
18 two *e'* of the two wreathen chains "
19 on the two *e'* of the breastplate, "
De 33:17 together to the *e'* of the earth: 657
1Sa 2:10 Lord shall judge the *e'* of the earth;"
1Ki 8: 8 the *e'* of the staves were seen out 7218
2Ch 5: 9 the *e'* of the staves were seen from "
Job 28:24 he looketh to the *e'* of the earth, 7098
37: 3 lightning unto the *e'* of the earth. 3671
38:13 take hold of the *e'* of the earth, "
Ps 19: 6 and his circuit unto the *e'* of it: 7098
22:27 All the *e'* of the world shall 657
48:10 thy praise unto the *e'* of the earth:7099
59:13 in Jacob unto the *e'* of the earth. 657
65: 5 confidence of all the *e'* of the earth,7099
67: 7 all the *e'* of the earth shall fear 657
72: 8 the river unto the *e'* of the earth. "
98: 3 all the *e'* of the earth have seen the "
135: 7 to ascend from the *e'* of the earth;7097
Pr 17:24 of a fool are in the *e'* of the earth. "
30: 4 established all the *e'* of the earth? 657
Isa 26:15 far unto all the *e'* of the earth. *7097
40:28 the Creator of the *e'* of the earth, 7098
41: 5 the *e'* of the earth were afraid, "
9 have taken from the *e'* of the earth, "
43: 6 my daughters from the *e'* of the *7097
45:22 saved, all the *e'* of the earth: 657
52:10 all the *e'* of the earth shall see the "
Jer 10:13 vapours to ascend from the *e'* of 7097
16:19 shall come unto thee from the *e'* of 657
25:31 come even to the *e'* of the earth; *7097
51:16 vapours to ascend from the *e'* of the "
Eze 15: 4 the fire devoureth both the *e'* of it,7098
Mic 5: 4 be great unto the *e'* of the earth. 657
Zec 9:10 the river even to the *e'* of the earth. "
Ac 13:47 salvation unto the *e'* of the earth. *2078
Ro 10:18 their words unto the *e'* of the world.4009
1Co 10:11 upon whom the *e'* of the world are5056
endued See also ENDOW.
Ge 30:20 God hath *e'* me with a good *2064
2Ch 2:12 a wise son, *e'* with prudence and 3045
13 man, *e'* with understanding, "
Lu 24:49 until ye be *e'* with power from on *1746
Jas 3:13 *e'* with knowledge among you? *1990
endure See also ENDURED; ENDURETH; ENDURING.
Ge 33:14 me and the children be able to *e'*,*7272
Ex 18:23 then thou shalt be able to *e'*. 5975
Es 8: 6 how can I *e'* to see the evil that 3201
6 how can I *e'* to see the destruction "
Job 8:15 hold it fast, but it shall not *e'*. 6965
31:23 of his highness I could not *e'*. *
Ps 9: 7 But the Lord shall *e'* for ever: *3427
30: 5 weeping may *e'* for a night, but *3885
72: 5 as long as the sun and moon *e'*, *6440
17 His name shall *e'* for ever: 1961
89:29 His seed also will I make to *e'* forever, "
36 His seed shall *e'* for ever, and his 1961
102:12 thou, O Lord, shalt *e'* for ever; *3427
26 shall perish, but thou shalt *e'*: 5975
104:31 glory of the Lord shall *e'* for ever:1961
Pr 27:24 ever: and doth the crown *e'* to every
Eze 22:14 Can thine heart *e'*, or can thine 5975
M't 24:13 But he that shall *e'* unto the end, *5278
M'r 4:17 and so *e'* but for a time: 2076
13:13 but he that shall *e'* unto the end, *5278
2Th 1: 4 and tribulations that ye *e'*: 430
2Ti 2: 3 therefore *e'* hardness, as a good *2553
10 Therefore I *e'* all things for the 5278
4: 3 they will not *e'* sound doctrine; 430
5 *e'* afflictions, do the work of an *2553
Heb 12: 7 If ye *e'* chastening, God dealeth 5278
20 (For they could not *e'* that which 5342
Jas 5:11 we count them happy which *e'*. *5278
1Pe 2:19 conscience toward God *e'* grief, *5297
endured
Ps 81:15 their time should have *e'* for ever.*1961
Ro 9:22 *e'* with much longsuffering the 5342
2Ti 3:11 what persecutions I *e'*: but out of 5297
Heb 6:15 And so, after he had patiently *e'*, 3114
10:32 ye *e'* a great fight of afflictions; 5278
11:27 for he *e'*, as seeing him who is 2594
12: 2 *e'* the cross, despising the shame, 5278
3 him that *e'* such contradiction "
endureth See also DURETH.
1Ch 16:34 he is good; for his mercy *e'* for ever.
41 Lord because his mercy *e'* for ever;
2Ch 5:13 he is good; for his mercy *e'* for ever:
7: 3 he is good; for his mercy *e'* for ever:
6 Lord, because his mercy *e'* for ever,
20:21 the Lord; for his mercy *e'* for ever.
Ezr 3:11 his mercy *e'* for ever toward Israel.
Ps 30: 5 For his anger *e'* but a moment; *
52: 1 the goodness of God *e'* continually.
72: 7 peace so long as the moon *e'*. *1097
100: 5 and his truth *e'* to all generations.*
106: 1 he is good: for his mercy *e'* for ever.
107: 1 he is good: for his mercy *e'* for ever.
111: 3 and his righteousness *e'* for ever. 5975
10 commandments: his praise *e'* for "
112: 3 and his righteousness *e'* for ever. "
9 poor; his righteousness *e'* for ever; "
117: 2 and the truth of the Lord *e'* for ever.
118: 1 is good: because his mercy *e'* for ever.
2 Israel now say, that his mercy *e'* for
3 Aaron now say, that his mercy *e'* for
4 Lord say, that his mercy *e'* for ever.
29 he is good: for his mercy *e'* for ever.
119:160 thy righteous judgments *e'* for ever.
135:13 Thy name, O Lord, *e'* for ever;
136: 1 he is good: for his mercy *e'* for ever.
2 of gods: for his mercy *e'* for ever.
3 of lords: for his mercy *e'* for ever.
4 wonders: for his mercy *e'* for ever.
5 heavens: for his mercy *e'* for ever.
6 the waters: for his mercy *e'* for ever.
7 lights: for his mercy *e'* for ever:
8 by day: for his mercy *e'* for ever:
9 by night: for his mercy *e'* for ever.
10 firstborn: for his mercy *e'* for ever,
11 among them: for his mercy *e'*
12 out arm: for his mercy *e'* for ever.
13 into parts: for his mercy *e'* for ever.
14 the midst of it: for his mercy *e'* for ever.
15 the Red sea: for his mercy *e'* for ever.
16 wilderness: for his mercy *e'* for ever.
17 great kings: for his mercy *e'* for ever.
18 famous kings: for his mercy *e'* for ever.
19 the Amorites: for his mercy *e'* for ever.
20 of Bashan: for his mercy *e'* for ever.
21 an heritage: for his mercy *e'* for ever.
22 his servant: for his mercy *e'* for ever.
23 low estate: for his mercy *e'* for ever:
24 our enemies: for his mercy *e'* for ever.
25 to all flesh: for his mercy *e'* for ever.
26 of heaven: for his mercy *e'* for ever.
138: 8 thy mercy, O Lord, *e'* for ever: forsake
145:13 and thy dominion *e'* throughout all
Jer 33:11 for his mercy *e'* for ever: and of them
M't 10:22 that *e'* to the end shall be saved. 5278
Joh 6:27 which *e'* unto everlasting life, *3306
1Co 13: 7 hopeth all things, *e'* all things. 5278
Jas 1:12 is the man that *e'* temptation: "
1Pe 1:25 the word of the Lord *e'* for ever. *3306
enduring
Ps 19: 9 of the Lord is clean, *e'* for ever: 5975
2Co 1: 6 is effectual in the *e'* of the same 5281
Heb 10:34 a better and an *e'* substance. *3306
Eneas See ÆNEAS.
En-eglaim (*en-eg'-la-im*)
Eze 47:10 from Engedi even unto *E'*; 5882
enemies See also ENEMIES'.
Ge 14:20 delivered thine *e'* into thy hand. 6862
22:17 seed shall possess the gate of his *e'*;341
49: 8 hand shall be in the neck of thine *e'*; "
Ex 1:10 they join also unto our *e'*, and 8130
23:22 I will be an enemy unto thine *e'*, 341
27 make all thine *e'* turn their backs "
32:25 unto their shame among their *e'*:) 6965
Le 26: 7 And ye shall chase your *e'*, 341
8 and your *e'* shall fall before you "
16 seed in vain, for your *e'* shall eat it. "
17 ye shall be slain before your *e'*: "
32 your *e'* which dwell therein shall be "
36 their hearts in the lands of their *e'*; "
37 no power to stand before your *e'*. "
38 the land of your *e'* shall eat you up. "
41 them into the land of their *e'*; "
44 when they be in the land of their *e'*, "
Nu 10: 9 ye shall be saved from your *e'*. "
35 Lord, and let thine *e'* be scattered; "
14:42 ye be not smitten before your *e'*. "
23:11 I took thee to curse mine *e'*, "
24: 8 he shall eat up the nations his *e'*,*6862
10 I called thee to curse mine *e'*, 341
18 also shall be a possession for his *e'*; "
32:21 driven out his *e'* from before him, "
De 1:42 lest ye be smitten before your *e'*. "
6:19 out all thine *e'* from before thee, "
12:10 he giveth you rest from all your *e'* "
20: 1 goest out to battle against thine *e'*, "
3 this day unto battle against your *e'*: "
4 to fight for you against your *e'*, "
14 thou shalt eat the spoil of thine *e'*, "
21:10 goest forth to war against thine *e'*, "
23: 9 host goeth forth against thine *e'*, "
14 to give up thine *e'* before thee; "
25:19 given thee rest from all thine *e'* "
28: 7 Lord shall cause thine *e'* that rise "
25 thee to be smitten before thine *e'*: "
31 sheep shall be given unto thine *e'*, "
48 Therefore shalt thou serve thine *e'* "
53 wherewith thine *e'* shall distress "
55 thine *e'* shall distress thee in all *
68 ye shall be sold unto your *e'* for "
30: 7 put all these curses upon thine *e'*, "
32:31 our *e'* themselves being judges. "
41 will render vengeance to mine *e'*,*6862
33: 7 be thou an help to him from his *e'*.* "
29 thine *e'* shall be found liars unto 341
Jos 7: 8 turneth their backs before their *e'*! 341
12 Israel could not stand before their *e'*, "
12 turned their backs before their *e'*, "
13 thou canst not stand before thine *e'*, "
10:13 avenged themselves upon their *e'*. "
19 but pursue after your *e'*, and smite "
25 thus shall the Lord do to all your *e'* "
21:44 stood not a man of all their *e'* before "
44 delivered all their *e'* into their hand. "
22: 8 divide the spoil of your *e'* with your "
23: 1 rest unto Israel from all their *e'* "
J'g 2:14 sold them into the hands of their *e'* "
14 any longer stand before their *e'*. "
18 out of the hand of their *e'* all the "
3:28 for the Lord hath delivered your *e'* "
5:31 So let all thine *e'* perish, "
8:34 out of the hands of all their *e'* on "
11:36 taken vengeance for thee of thine *e'*, "
1Sa 2: 1 my mouth is enlarged over mine *e'*; "
4: 3 save us out of the hand of our *e'*. "
12:10 deliver us out of the hand of our *e'*, "
11 out of the hand of your *e'* on every "
14:24 that I may be avenged on mine *e'*. "
30 spoil of their *e'* which they found? "
47 against all his *e'* on every side, "
18:25 to be avenged of the king's *e'*. "
20:15 Lord hath cut off the *e'* of David "
16 require it at the hand of David's *e'*. "
25:22 also do God unto the *e'* of David, "
26 let thine *e'*, and they that seek evil "
29 souls of thine *e'*, them shall he sling "
29: 8 go fight against the *e'* of my lord "
30:26 the spoil of the *e'* of the Lord; "
2Sa 3:18 out of the hand of all their *e'*. "
5:20 hath broken forth upon mine *e'* "
7: 1 rest round about from all his *e'*; "
9 cut off all thine *e'* out of thy sight, "
11 caused thee to rest from all thine *e'*. "
12:14 great occasion to the *e'* of the Lord "
18:19 the Lord hath avenged him of his *e'*. "
32 The *e'* of my lord the king, and all "
19: 6 thine *e'*, and hatest thy friends. *8130
9 saved us out of the hand of our *e'*, 341
22: 1 him out of the hand of all his *e'*, and "
4 so shall I be saved from mine *e'*. "
38 I have pursued mine *e'*, and "
41 also given me the necks of mine *e'*. "
49 bringeth me forth from mine *e'*: "
24:13 flee three months before thine *e'*,*6862
1Ki 3:11 nor hast asked the life of thine *e'*; 341
8:48 their soul, in the land of their *e'*, "
2Ki 17:39 you out of the hand of all your *e'*. "
21:14 them into the hand of their *e'*; "
14 a prey and a spoil to all their *e'*; "
1Ch 12:17 be come to betray me to mine *e'*, *6862
14:11 God hath broken in upon mine *e'* 341
17: 8 and have cut off all thine *e'* from "
10 Moreover I will subdue all thine *e'*. "
21:12 while that the sword of thine *e'* "
22: 9 I will give him rest from all his *e'* "
2Ch 1:11 or honour, nor the life of thine *e'*,*8130
6:28 their *e'* besiege them in the cities 341
34 go out to war against their *e'* by the "
36 deliver them over before their *e'*,* "
20:27 made them to rejoice over their *e'*. "
29 fought against the *e'* of Israel, "
25:20 deliver them into the hands of their *e'*, "
Ne 4:15 our *e'* heard that it was known 341
5: 9 the reproach of the heathen our *e'*? "
6: 1 the Arabian, and the rest of our *e'*, "
16 that when all our *e'* heard thereof, "
9:27 them into the hand of their *e'*, *6862
27 saved out of the hand of their *e'*. * "
28 thou them in the hand of their *e'*, 341
Es 8:13 to avenge themselves on their *e'*. "
9: 1 the day that the *e'* of the Jews hoped "
5 Thus the Jews smote all their *e'* "
16 and had rest from their *e'*, and slew "
22 the Jews rested from their *e'*, "
Job 19:11 me unto him as one of his *e'*. *6862
Ps 3: 7 thou hast smitten all mine *e'* 341
5: 8 because of mine *e'*; make thy way 8324
6: 7 waxeth old because of all mine *e'*.*6887
10 Let all mine *e'* be ashamed and 341
7: 6 because of the rage of mine *e'*: *6887
8: 2 strength because of thine *e'*, that* "
9: 3 When mine *e'* are turned back, 341
10: 5 for all his *e'*, he puffeth at them. *6887
17: 9 from my deadly *e'*, who compass me341
18:*title* him from the hand of all his *e'*, "
3 so shall I be saved from mine *e'*. "
37 I have pursued mine *e'*, and "
40 also given me the necks of mine *e'*; "
48 He delivereth me from mine *e'*: "
21: 8 Thine hand shall find out all thine *e'*: "
23: 5 me in the presence of mine *e'*: 6887
25: 2 let not mine *e'* triumph over me. 341
19 consider mine *e'*; for they are many; "
27: 2 even mine *e'* and my foes, came *6862
6 head be lfted up above mine *e'* 341
11 a plain path, because of mine *e'*. 8324
12 not over unto the will of mine *e'*: *6862
31:11 was a reproach among all mine *e'*,*6887
15 me from the hand of mine *e'*, 341
35:19 Let not them that are mine *e'* "
37:20 and the *e'* of the Lord shall be as "
38:19 But mine *e'* are lively, and they "
41: 2 deliver him unto the will of his *e'*. "
5 Mine *e'* speak evil of me, When "
42:10 mine *e'* reproach me; while they *6887
44: 5 thee will we push down our *e'*: *6862
7 thou hast saved us from our *e'*, * "
45: 5 in the heart of the king's *e'*: 341
54: 5 He shall reward evil unto mine *e'*:8324
7 hath seen his desire upon mine *e'*. 341
56: 2 Mine *e'* would daily swallow me 8324

Ps 56: 9 then shall mine e· turn back: 341
59: 1 Deliver me from mine e·, O my God:"
10 me see my desire upon mine e·. 8324
60:12 it is that shall tread down our e·.*6862
66: 3 shall thine e· submit themselves 341
68: 1 God arise, let his e· be scattered: "
21 God shall wound the head of his e·, "
23 be dipped in the blood of thine e·, "
69: 4 being mine e· wrongfully, are mighty:"
18 deliver me because of mine e·. "
71:10 For mine e· speak against me; "
72: 9 and his e· shall lick the dust. "
74: 4 Thine e· roar in the midst of thy *6887
23 Forget not the voice of thine e·: * "
78:53 but the sea overwhelmed their e·. 341
66 smote his e· in the hinder parts: *6862
80: 6 our e· laugh among themselves. 341
81:14 I should soon have subdued their e·,"
83: 2 For, lo, thine e· make a tumult: "
89:10 scattered thine e· with thy strong "
42 thou hast made all his e· to rejoice. "
51 Wherewith thine e· have reproached,"
92: 9 For, lo, thine e·, O Lord, "
9 for, lo, thine e· shall perish; "
11 shall see my desire on mine e·. 7790
97: 3 burneth up his e· round about. *6862
102: 8 Mine e· reproach me all the day; 341
105:24 made them stronger than their e·.*6862
106:11 And the waters covered their e·: * "
42 Their e· also oppressed them, and 341
108:13 it is that shall tread down our e·.*6862
110: 1 until I make thine e· thy footstool. 341
2 rule thou in the midst of thine e·. "
112: 8 he see his desire upon his e·. *6862
119:98 hast made me wiser than mine e·: 341
139 mine e· have forgotten thy words.*6862
157 are my persecutors and mine e·;* "
127: 5 but they shall speak with the e· 341
132:18 His e· will I clothe with shame: "
136:24 hath redeemed us from our e·: *6862
138: 7 hand against the wrath of mine e·. 341
139:20 thine e· take thy name in vain. 6145
22 hatred: I count them mine e·. 341
143: 9 Deliver me, O Lord, from mine e·: "
12 And of thy mercy cut off mine e·, "
Pr 16: 7 maketh even his e· to be at peace "
Isa 1:24 and avenge me of mine e·: "
9:11 and join his e· together; "
26:11 of thine e· shall devour them. *6862
42:13 he shall prevail against his e·. 341
59:18 adversaries, recompence to his e·; "
62: 8 thy corn to be meat for thine e·; "
66: 6 rendereth recompence to his e·. "
14 and his indignation toward his e·. "
Jer 12: 7 my soul into the hand of her e·. "
15: 9 deliver to the sword before their e·, "
14 make thee to pass with thine e· "
17: 4 I will cause thee to serve thine e· "
19: 7 to fall by the sword before their e·, "
9 and straitness, wherewith their e·, "
20: 4 shall fall by the sword of their e·, "
5 I give into the hand of their e·, "
21: 7 and into the hand of their e·, "
34:20 give them into the hand of their e·, "
21 I give into the hand of their e·, "
44:30 king of Egypt into the hand of his e·,"
48: 5 e· have heard a cry of destruction.*6862
49:37 Elam to be dismayed before their e·,341
La 1: 2 with her, they are become her e·. "
5 are the chief, her e· prosper; "
21 mine e· have heard of my trouble; "
2:16 thine e· have opened their mouth "
3:46 All our e· have opened their mouths"
52 Mine e· chased me sore, like a bird, "
Eze 39:23 them into the hand of their e·: *6862
Da 4:19 interpretation thereof to thine e·.*6146
Am 9: 4 go into captivity before their e·, 341
Mic 4:10 thee from the hand of thine e·. "
5: 9 all thine e· shall be cut off. "
7: 6 a man's e· are the men of his own "
Na 1: 2 he reserveth wrath for his e·. "
8 and darkness shall pursue his e·. "
3:13 be set wide open unto thine e·: "
Zec 10: 5 which tread down their e· in the "
M't 5:44 Love your e·, bless them that curse 2190
22:44 till I make thine e· thy footstool? "
M'r 12:36 till I make thine e· thy footstool. "
Lu 1:71 That we should be saved from our e·,"
74 delivered out of the hand of our e· "
6:27 Love your e·, do good to them that "
35 love ye your e·, and do good, "
19:27 But those mine e·, which would not"
43 thine e· shall cast a trench about "
20:43 Till I make thine e· thy footstool. "
Ro 5:10 when we were e·, we were reconciled"
11:28 they are e· for your sakes: "
1Co 15:25 till he hath put all e· under his feet."
Ph'p 3:18 that they are the e· of the cross of "
Col 1:21 e· in your mind by wicked works, "
Heb 1:13 until I make thine e· thy footstool? "
10:13 till his e· be made his footstool. "
Re 11: 5 their mouth and devoureth their e·:"
12 and their e· beheld them. "

enemies'
Le 26:34 and ye be in your e· land; 341
39 their iniquity in your e· lands; "
Eze 39:27 gathered them out of their e· lands, "

enemy See also ENEMIES; ENEMY'S.
Ex 15: 6 Lord hath dashed in pieces the e·. 341
9 The e· said, I will pursue, I will "
23:22 I will be an e· unto thine enemies, 340
Le 26:25 delivered into the hand of the e·. 341
Nu 10: 9 the e· that oppresseth you, then * "
35:23 that he die, and was not his e·, "
De 28:57 wherewith thine e· shall distress "
32:27 not that I feared the wrath of the e·,341
42 beginning of revenges upon the e·. "
33:27 he shall thrust out the e· from "
J'g 16:23 hath delivered Samson our e· into "
24 hath delivered into our hands our e·,"
1Sa 2:32 shalt see an e· in my habitation, *6862
18:29 Saul became David's e· continually. 341
19:17 and sent away mine e·, that he is "
24: 4 will deliver thine e· into thine hand, "
19 For if a man find his e·, will he let "
26: 8 hath delivered thine e· into thine "
28:16 thee, and is become thine e·? *6145
2Sa 4: 8 the son of Saul thine e·, which 341
22:18 He delivered me from my strong e·, "
1Ki 8:33 Israel be smitten down before the e·, "
37 if their e· besiege them in the land "
44 go out to battle against their e·, "
46 them, and deliver them to the e·, "
46 captives unto the land of the e·, "
21:20 Hast thou found me, O mine e·? "
2Ch 6:24 be put to the worse before the e·, "
25: 8 shall make thee fall before the e·: "
26:13 to help the king against the e·. "
Ezr 8:22 help us against the e· in the way: "
31 delivered us from the hand of the e·, "
Es 3:10 the Agagite, the Jews' e·. 6887
7: 4 the e· could not countervail the *6862
6 and e· is this wicked Haman. 341
8: 1 Haman the Jews' e· unto Esther 6887
9:10 Hammedatha, the e· of the Jews, "
24 the Agagite, the e· of all the Jews, "
Job 13:24 and holdest me for thine e·? 341
16: 9 mine e· sharpeneth his eyes upon *6862
27: 7 Let mine e· be as the wicked, 341
33:10 he counteth me for his e·, "
Ps 7: 4 that without cause is mine e·:) *6887
5 Let the e· persecute my soul, 341
8: 2 that thou mightest still the e· and "
9: 6 O thou e·, destructions are come "
13: 2 how long shall mine e· be exalted "
4 Lest mine e· say, I have prevailed "
18:17 He delivered me from my strong e·, "
31: 8 shut me up into the hand of the e·: "
41:11 mine e· doth not triumph over me. "
42: 9 because of the oppression of the e·? "
43: 2 because of the oppression of the e·? "
44:10 us to turn back from the e·: *6862
16 by reason of the e· and avenger. 341
55: 3 Because of the voice of the e·, "
12 For it was not an e· that reproached "
61: 3 and a strong tower from the e·. "
64: 1 preserve my life from fear of the e·. "
74: 3 all that the e· hath done wickedly "
10 shall the e· blaspheme thy name "
18 this, that the e· hath reproached, "
78:42 he delivered them from the e·. *6862
89:22 The e· shall not exact upon him; 341
106:10 them from the hand of the e·. "
107: 2 redeemed from the hand of the e·;*6862
143: 3 the e· hath persecuted my soul; 341
Pr 24:17 Rejoice not when thine e· falleth, "
25:21 If thine e· be hungry, give him 8130
27: 6 the kisses of an e· are deceitful. "
Isa 59:19 the e· shall come in like a flood, *6862
63:10 he was turned to be their e·, 341
Jer 6:25 for the sword of the e· and fear is on "
15:11 I will cause the e· to entreat thee "
18:17 as with an east wind before the e·; "
30:14 thee with the wound of an e·, "
31:16 come again from the land of the e·. "
44:30 king of Babylon, his e·, and that "
La 1: 5 gone into captivity before the e·. *6862
7 people fell into the hand of the e·,* "
9 for the e· hath magnified himself. 341
16 desolate, because the e· prevailed. "
2: 3 his right hand from before the e·, "
4 He hath bent his bow like an e·: "
5 The Lord was as an e·: he hath "
7 hath given up into the hand of the e· "
17 he hath caused thine e· to rejoice "
22 brought up hath mine e· consumed. "
4:12 and the e· should have entered into "
Eze 36: 2 Because the e· hath said against you,"
Ho 8: 3 is good: the e· shall pursue him. "
Mic 2: 8 my people is risen up as an e·: "
7: 8 Rejoice not against me, O mine e·: "
10 Then she that is mine e· shall see it,"
Na 3:11 seek strength because of the e·. "
Zep 3:15 he hath cast out thine e·: "
M't 5:43 thy neighbour, and hate thine e·. 2190
13:25 his e· came and sowed tares among"
28 unto them, An e· hath done this. "
39 The e· that sowed them is the devil;"
Lu 10:19 and over all the power of the e·: "
Ac 13:10 devil, thou e· of all righteousness, "
Ro 12:20 Therefore if thine e· hunger, feed "
1Co 15:26 The last e· that shall be destroyed "
Gal 4:16 Am I therefore become your e·, "
2Th 3:15 Yet count him not as an e·, "
Jas 4: 4 friend of the world is the e· of God. "

enemy's
Ex 23: 4 If thou meet thine e· ox or his ass 341
Job 6:23 Deliver me from the e· hand? *6862
Ps 78:61 and his glory into the e· hand. * "

enflaming See also INFLAME.
Isa 57: 5 E· yourselves with idols under *2552

engaged
Jer 30:21 for who is this that e· his heart to *6148

En-gannim (en-gan'-nim)
Jos 15:34 And Zanoah, and E·, Tappuah, 5873
19:21 Remeth, and E·, and En-haddah, "
21:29 Jarmuth with her suburbs, E· with"

En-gedi (en-ghe'-di) See also HAZAZON-TAMAR.
Jos 15:62 and the city of Salt, and E·; 5872
1Sa 23:29 and dwelt in strong holds at E·. 5872
24: 1 David is in the wilderness of E·. "
2Ch 20: 2 be in Hazazon-tamar, which is E·. "
Ca 1:14 camphire in the vineyards of E·. "
Eze 47:10 fishers shall stand upon it from E· "

engines
2Ch 26:15 And he made in Jerusalem e·, 2810
Eze 26: 9 he shall set e· of war against thy 4239

engrafted See also GRAFFED.
Jas 1:21 with meekness the e· word, which *1721

engrave See also ENGRAVEN; ENGRAVINGS.
Ex 28:11 shalt thou e· the two stones with 6605
Zec 3: 9 behold, I will e· the graving thereof. "

engraven
2Co 3: 7 written and e· in stones, was 1795

engraver
Ex 28:11 With the work of an e· in stone, 2796
35:35 all manner of work, of the e·, "
38:23 an e·, and a cunning workman, "

engravings
Ex 28:11 in stone, like the e· of a signet, 6603
21 names, like the e· of a signet; "
36 upon it, like the e· of a signet, "
39:14 names, like the e· of a signet, "
30 writing, like to the e· of a signet, "

En-haddah (en-had'-dah)
Jos 19:21 and E·, and Beth-pazzez; 5876

En-hakkore (en-hak'-ko-re)
J'g 15:19 he called the name thereof E·. 5875

En-hazor (en-ha'-zor)
Jos 19:37 And Kedesh, and Edrei, and E·, 5877

enjoin See also ENJOINED.
Ph'm 8 much bold in Christ to e· thee 2004

enjoined
Es 9:31 and Esther the queen had e· them, 6965
Job 36:23 Who hath e· him his way? who 6485
Heb 9:20 which God hath e· unto you. *1781

enjoy See also ENJOYED.
Le 26:34 shall the land e· her sabbaths, 7521
34 the land rest, and e· her sabbaths. "
43 shall e· her sabbaths, while she "
Nu 36: 8 children of Israel may e· every *3423
De 28:41 daughters, but thou shalt not e· *1961
Jos 1:15 land of your possession, and e· it,*3423
Ec 2: 1 with mirth, therefore e· pleasure: 7200
24 he should make his soul e· good in "
3:13 and e· the good of all his labour, "
5:18 eat and to drink, and to e· the good "
Isa 65:22 long e· the work of their hands. 1086
Ac 24: 2 Seeing that by thee we e· great 5177
1Ti 6:17 giveth us richly all things to e·; 619
Heb 11:25 than to e· the pleasures of sin 2192. "

enjoyed
2Ch 36:21 until the land had e· her sabbaths: 7521

enlarge See also ENLARGED; ENLARGETH; ENLARGING.
Ge 9:27 God shall e· Japheth, and he shall 6601
Ex 34:24 before thee, and e· thy borders: 7337
De 12:20 When the Lord thy God shall e· thy "
19: 8 if the Lord thy God e· thy coast, "
1Ch 4:10 wouldest bless....and e· my coast, 7235
Ps 119:32 when thou shalt e· my heart. 7337
Isa 54: 2 E· the place of thy tent, and let "
Am 1:13 that they might e· their border: "
Mic 1:16 e· thy baldness as the eagle for; "
M't 23: 5 e· the borders of their garments, 3170

enlarged
1Sa 2: 1 my mouth is e· over mine enemies; 7337
2Sa 22:37 Thou hast e· my steps under me; "
Ps 4: 1 thou hast e· me when I was in * "
18:36 Thou hast e· my steps under me, "
25:17 The troubles of my heart are e·: "
Isa 5:14 Therefore hell hath e· herself, "
57: 8 gone up; thou hast e· thy bed, "
60: 5 thine heart shall fear, and be e·; "
2Co 6:11 is open unto you, our heart is e·. 4115
13 unto my children,) be ye also e·. "
10:15 that we shall be e· by you *3170

enlargement
Es 4:14 shall there e· and deliverance *7305

enlargeth
De 33:20 Blessed be he that e· Gad: 7337
Job 12:23 he e· the nations, and straiteneth †7849
Hab 2: 5 who e· his desire as hell, and is 7337

enlarging
Eze 41: 7 there was an e·, and a winding *7337

enlighten See also ENLIGHTENED; ENLIGHTENING.
Ps 18:28 Lord my God will e· my darkness. *5050

enlightened
1Sa 14:27 his mouth; and his eyes were e·. 215
29 mine eyes have been e·, because "
Job 33:30 to be e· with the light of the living. "
Ps 97: 4 His lightnings e· the world: * "
Eph 1:18 of your understanding being e·; 5461
Heb 6: 4 those who were once e·, and have "

enlightening
Ps 19: 8 of the Lord is pure, e· the eyes. 215

En-mishpat (en-mish'-pat) See also KADESH.
Ge 14: 7 they returned, and came to E·, 5880

enmity
Ge 3:15 put e· between thee and the woman, 342
Nu 35:21 Or in e· smite him with his hand, "
22 thrust him suddenly without e·, "
Lu 23:12 were at e· between themselves. 2189
Ro 8: 7 the carnal mind is e· against God: "

Eph 2:15 abolished in his flesh the e', 2189
16 having slain the e' thereby: "
Jas 4: 4 friendship of the world is e' with "
Enoch (e'-nok) See also HENOCH.
Ge 4:17 and she conceived, and bare E': 2585
17 after the name of his son, E'. "
18 unto E' was born Irad: and Irad "
5:18 and two years, and he begat E': "
19 Jared lived after he begat E' eight "
21 And E' lived sixty and five years, "
22 E' walked with God after he begat "
23 the days of E' were three hundred "
24 E' walked with God: and he was not; "
Lu 3:37 which was the son of E', which 1802
Heb 11: 5 By faith E' was translated that he "
Jude 14 E' also, the seventh from Adam, "
Enon See ÆNON.
Enos (e'-nos) See also ENOSH.
Ge 4:26 called his name E': then began * 583
5: 6 and five years, and begat E': * "
7 And Seth lived after he begat E' * "
9 E' lived ninety years, and begat * "
10 E' lived after he begat Cainan * "
11 the days of E' were nine hundred* "
Lu 3:38 Which was the son of E', which 1800
Enosh (e'-nosh) See also ENOS.
1Ch 1: 1 Adam, Sheth, E', 583
enough
Ge 24:25 have both straw and provender e', 7227
33: 9 Esau said, I have e', my brother; "
11 with me, and because I have e'. 3605
34:21 behold, it is large e' for them; 3027
45:28 Israel said, It is e'; Joseph my 7227
Ex 2:19 and also drew water e' for us, *
9:28 Intreat the Lord (for it is e') that 7227
36: 5 much more than e' for the service 1767
De 1: 6 Ye have dwelt long e' in this mount; "
2: 3 compassed this mountain long e': "
Jos 17:16 The hill is not e' for us: 4672
2Sa 24:16 It is e': stay now thine hand. And 7227
1Ki 19: 4 It is e'; now, O Lord, take away "
1Ch 21:15 It is e', stay now thine hand. And "
2Ch 31:10 we have had e' to eat, and have 7644
Pr 27:27 have goats' milk e' for thy food, 1767
28:19 persons shall have poverty e'. 7644
30:15 yea, four things say not, It is e': 1952
16 and the fire that saith not, It is e'. "
Isa 56:11 dogs which can never have e', 7654
Jer 49: 9 they will destroy till they have e'. 1767
Ho 4:10 they shall eat, and not have e': 7644
Ob 5 not have stolen till they had e'? 1767
Na 2:12 did tear in pieces e' for his whelps, "
Hag 1: 6 little; ye eat, but ye have not e'; 7654
Mal 3:10 that there shall not be room e' 1767
M't 10:25 It is e' for the disciple that he be 713
25: 9 lest there be not e' for us and you: 714
M'r 14:41 your rest: it is e', the hour is come 566
Lu 15:17 have bread e' and to spare, and I 4052
22:38 he said unto them, It is e'. 2425
Ac 27:38 they had eaten e', they lightened 2880
enquire See also ENQUIRED; ENQUIREST; ENQUIRY.
Ge 24:57 We will call the damsel, and e' at *7592
25:22 And she went to e' of the Lord. *1875
Ex 18:15 people come unto me to e' of God:* "
De 12:30 that thou e' not after their gods, * "
13:14 shalt thou e', and make search, * "
17: 9 and e'; and they shall shew thee * "
J'g 4:20 man doth come and e' of thee, *7592
1Sa 9: 9 when a man went to e' of God, *1875
17:56 E' thou whose son the stripling is.*7592
22:15 Did I then begin to e' of God for * "
28: 7 that I may go to her, and e' of her.*1875
1Ki 22: 5 E', I pray thee, at the word of the* "
7 besides, that we might e' of him?* "
8 by whom we may e' of the Lord: * "
2Ki 1: 2 e' of Baal-zebub the god of Ekron* "
3 that ye go to e' of Baal-zebub * "
6 thou sendest to e' of Baal-zebub * "
16 e' of Baal-zebub the god of Ekron,* "
16 no God in Israel to e' of his word?* "
3:11 that we may e' of the Lord by him?* "
8: 8 and e' of the Lord by him, * "
16:15 altar shall be for me to e' by. *1239
22:13 Go ye, e' of the Lord for me, *1875
18 which sent you to e' of the Lord, * "
1Ch 10:13 had a familiar spirit, to e' of it; * "
18:10 his son to king David, to e' of his *7592
21:30 could not go before it to e' of God:*1875
2Ch 18: 4 E', I pray thee, at the word of the* "
6 besides, that we might e' of him?* "
7 by whom we may e' of the Lord: * "
32:31 sent unto him to e' of the wonder* "
34:21 Go, e' of the Lord for me, and for* "
26 who sent you to e' of the Lord, * "
Ezr 7:14 to ' concerning Judah and *1240
Job 8: 8 e', I pray thee, of the former age, *7592
Ps 27: 4 the Lord, and to e' in his temple. *1239
Ec 7:10 dost not e' wisely concerning this.*7592
Isa 21:12 if ye will e', e' ye: return, come, *1158
Jer 21: 2 E', I pray thee, of the Lord for us;*1875
37: 7 that sent you unto me to e' of me;* "
Eze 14: 7 prophet to e' of him concerning * "
20: 1 of Israel came to e' of the Lord, * "
3 Are ye come to e' of me? * "
M't 10:11 e' who in it is worthy; and there *1833
Lu 22:23 began to e' among themselves, *4802
Joh 16:19 Do ye e' among yourselves of that*2212
Ac 9:11 e' in the house of Judas for one * "
19:39 But if ye e' any thing concerning *1934
23:15 as though ye would e' something *1231
20 as though they would e' somewhat*4441
2Co 8:23 Whether any do e' of Titus, he is *

enquired
De 17: 4 e diligently, and, behold, it be *1875
J'g 6:29 And when they e' and asked, * "
8:14 a young man..., and e' of him: *7592
20:27 children of Israel e' of the Lord. * "
1Sa 10:22 they e' of the Lord further, if the * "
22:10 And he e' of the Lord for him, * "
13 and hast e' of God for him, * "
23: 2 Therefore David e' of the Lord, * "
4 David e' of the Lord yet again. * "
28: 6 And when Saul e' of the Lord, * "
30: 8 And David e' at the Lord, saying, * "
2Sa 2: 1 that David e' of the Lord, saying, * "
5:19 And David e' of the Lord, saying, * "
23 when David e' of the Lord, he said,* "
11: 3 David sent and e' after the woman.*1875
16:23 as if a man had e' at the oracle *7592
21: 1 year; and David e' of the Lord. *1245
1Ch 10:14 And e' not of the Lord: therefore *1875
13: 3 we e' not at it in the days of Saul.* "
14:10 And David e' of God, saying, *7592
14 Therefore David e' again of God;* "
Ps 78:34 returned and e' early after God. *7836
Eze 14: 3 should I be e' of at all by them? *1875
20: 3 Lord God, I will not be e' of by you.* "
31 and shall I be e' of by you, O house* "
31 Lord God, I will not be e' of by you.*
36:37 I will yet for this be e' of by the *1875
Da 1:20 king e' of them, he found them *1245
Zep 1: 6 sought the Lord, nor e' for him. *1875
M't 2: 7 e' of them diligently what time the* 198
16 had diligently e' of the wise men.* "
Joh 4:52 Then e' he of them the hour *4441
2Co 8:23 or our brethren be e' of, they *
1Pe 1:10 have e' and searched diligently, *1567
enquirest
Job 10: 6 That thou e' after mine iniquity, *1245
enquiry
Pr 20:25 and after vows to make e'. *1239
Ac 10:17 had made e' for Simon's house, *1331
enrich See also ENRICHED; ENRICHEST.
1Sa 17:25 king will e' him with great riches, 6238
Eze 27:33 thou didst e' the kings of the earth "
enriched
1Co 1: 5 in every thing ye are e' by him, 4148
2Co 9:11 e' in every thing to all bountifulness, "
enrichest
Ps 65: 9 greatly e' it with the river of God, 6238
En-rimmon (en-rim'-mon) See also AIN and RIMMON.
Ne 11:29 And at E', and at Zareah, and at 5884
En-rogel (en-ro'-ghel)
Jos 15: 7 the goings out thereof were at E': 5883
18:16 on the south, and descended to E', "
2Sa 17:17 and Ahimaaz stayed by E'; "
1Ki 1: 9 stone of Zoheleth, which is by E', "
ensample See also ENSAMPLES; EXAMPLE.
Ph'p 3:17 walk as ye have us for an e'. 5179
2Th 3: 9 to make ourselves an e' unto you "
2Pe 2: 6 making them an e' unto those *5262
ensamples
1Co 10:11 things happened unto them for e':*5179
1Th 1: 7 that ye were e' to all that believe* "
1Pe 5: 3 but being e' to the flock. "
En-shemesh (en-she'-mesh)
Jos 15: 7 passed toward the waters of E', 5885
18:17 and went forth to E', and went "
ensign See also ENSIGNS.
Nu 2: 2 the e' of their father's house: * 226
Isa 5:26 he will lift up an e' to the nations 5251
11:10 shall stand for an e' of the people; "
12 he shall set up an e' for the nations, "
18: 3 lifteth up an e' on the mountains; "
30:17 and as an e' on an hill. "
31: 9 his princes shall be afraid of the e', "
Zec 9:16 lifted up as an e' upon his land. *5264
ensigns
Ps 74: 4 they set up their e' for signs. 226
ensnared
Job 34:30 reign not, lest the people be e'. *4170
ensue See also PURSUE.
1Pe 3:11 let him seek peace, and e' it. *1377
entangle See also ENTANGLED; ENTANGLETH.
M't 22:15 how they might e' him in his talk.*3802
entangled
Ex 14: 3 of Israel, They are e' in the land, 943
Ga 5: 1 e' again with the yoke of bondage, 1758
2Pe 2:20 they are again e' therein, and 1707
entangleth
2Ti 2: 4 e' himself with the affairs of this 1707
En-tappuah (en-tap'-poo-ah)
Jos 17: 7 hand, unto the inhabitants of E'. 5887
enter See also ENTERED; ENTERETH; ENTERING.
Ge 12:11 he was come near to e' into Egypt, 935
Ex 40:35 Moses was not able to e' into the "
Nu 4: 3 that e' into the host, to do the work "
23 all that e' in to perform service, "
5:24, 27 causeth the curse shall e' into "
20:24 for he shall not e' into the land "
De 23: 1 member cut off, shall not e' into the "
2 A bastard shall not e' into the "
2 generation shall he not e' into the "
3 or Moabite shall not e' into the "
3 generation shall they not e' into the "
8 begotten of them shall not e' into the "
29:12 thou shouldest e' into covenant 5674

Jos 10:19 them not to e' into their cities: 935
J'g 18: 9 and to e' to possess the land. "
2Sa 22: 7 and my cry did e' into his ears. *
1Ki 14:12 when thy feet e' into the city, 935
22:30 myself, and e' into the battle; * "
2Ki 7: 4 If we say, We will e' into the city, "
11: 5 that e' in on the sabbath shall * "
19:23 e' into the lodgings of his borders, "
2Ch 7: 2 priests could not e' into the house "
23:19 unclean in any thing should e' in. "
30: 8 and e' into his sanctuary, which he "
Ne 2: 8 for the house that I shall e' into. "
Es 4: 2 none might e' into the king's gate "
Job 22: 4 he e' with thee into judgment? * "
34:23 that he should e' into judgment *1980
Ps 37:15 sword shall e' into their own heart, 935
45:15 they shall e' into the king's palace. "
95:11 that they should not e' into my rest. "
100: 4 E' into his gates with thanksgiving, "
118:20 into which the righteous shall e'. "
143: 2 And e' not into judgment with thy "
Pr 4:14 E' not into the path of the wicked, "
18: 6 A fool's lips e' into contention, "
23:10 and e' not into the fields of the "
Isa 2:10 E' into the rock, and hide thee in "
3:14 The Lord will e' into judgment with "
26: 2 which keepeth the truth may e' in. "
20 people, e' thou into thy chambers, "
37:24 will e' into the height of his border, "
57: 2 shall e' into peace: they shall rest* "
59:14 in the street, and equity cannot e'. "
Jer 7: 2 that e' in at these gates to worship "
8:14 and let us e' into the defenced cities, "
14:18 if I e' into the city, then behold "
16: 5 E' not into the house of mourning, "
17:20 Jerusalem, that e' in by these gates: "
25 Then shall there e' into the gates "
21:13 who shall e' into our habitations? "
22: 2 thy people that e' in by these gates: "
4 then shall there e' in by the gates "
41:17 Bethlehem, to go to e' into Egypt, "
42:15 set your faces to e' into Egypt, "
18 when ye shall e' into Egypt: "
La 1:10 should not e' into thy congregation. "
3:13 caused the arrows of his quiver to e' "
Eze 7:22 for the robbers shall e' into it. "
13: 9 they e' into the land of Israel; "
20:38 shall not e' into the land of Israel: "
26:10 when he shall e' into thy gates, "
10 as men e' into a city wherein is "
37: 5 I will cause breath to e' into you, "
42:14 When the priests e' therein, then "
44: 2 and no man shall e' in by it; "
3 he shall e' by the way of the porch "
9 in flesh, shall e' into my sanctuary, "
16 They shall e' into my sanctuary, "
17 when they e' in at the gates of the "
21 when they e' into the inner court. "
46: 2 And the prince shall e' by the way "
8 And when the prince shall e', he "
Da 11: 7 army, and shall e' into the fortress "
17 He shall also set his face to e' *
24 He shall e' peaceably even upon *
40 and he shall e' into the countries, "
41 shall e' also into the glorious land, "
Ho 11: 9 and I will not e' into the city. "
Joe 2: 9 they shall e' in at the windows "
Am 5: 5 seek not Bethel, nor e' into Gilgal, "
Jon 3: 4 And Jonah began to e' into the city "
Zec 5: 4 and it shall e' into the house of the "
M't 5:20 e' into the kingdom of heaven. 1525
6: 6 thou prayest, e' into thy closet, "
7:13 E' ye in at the strait gate: "
21 Lord, shall e' into the kingdom of "
10: 5 city of the Samaritans e' ye not: "
11 whatsoever city or town ye shall e', "
12:29 one e' into a strong man's house, "
45 and they e' in and dwell there: "
18: 3 not e' into the kingdom of heaven. "
8 thee to e' into life halt or maimed, "
9 for thee to e' into life with one eye, "
19:17 if thou wilt e' into life, keep the "
23 shall hardly e' into the kingdom of "
24 to e' into the kingdom of God. "
25:21, 23 e' thou into the joy of thy lord. "
26:41 that ye e' not into temptation: "
M'r 1:45 no more openly e' into the city, "
3:27 can e' into a strong man's house, "
5:12 swine, that we may e' into them. "
6:10 place soever ye e' into an house, "
9:25 of him, and e' no more into him. "
43 for thee to e' into life maimed, "
45 better for thee to e' halt into life, "
47 thee to e' into the kingdom of God "
10:15 little child, he shall not e' therein. "
23 shall...e' into the kingdom of God! "
24 riches to e' into the kingdom of God! "
25 man to e' into the kingdom of God. "
13:15 neither e' therein, to take any "
14:38 pray, lest ye e' into temptation. "
Lu 7: 6 thou shouldest e' under my roof: * "
8:16 they which e' in may see the light. 1531
32 would suffer them to e' into them. 1525
9: 4 house ye e' into, there abide, "
10: 5 whatsoever house ye e', first say, "
8 into whatsoever city ye e', "
10 But into whatsoever city ye e', "
11:26 and they e' in, and dwell there: "
13:24 Strive to e' in at the strait gate: "
24 seek to e' in, and shall not be able. "
18:17 child shall in no wise e' therein. "
24 riches e' into the kingdom of God! "
25 man to e' into the kingdom of God. "
21:21 are in the countries e' thereinto. "
22:40 that ye e' not into temptation. "

Lu 22:46 pray, lest ye e' into temptation. 1525
24:26 things, and to e' into his glory? "
Joh 3: 4 can he e' the second time into his "
5 cannot e' into the kingdom of God. "
10: 9 if any man e' in, he shall be saved, "
Ac 14:22 e' into the kingdom of God. "
20:29 grievous wolves e' in among you, "
Heb 3:11 They shall not e' into my rest.) "
18 that they should not e' into his rest, "
19 that they could not e' in because "
4: 3 which have believed do e' into rest, "
3 wrath, if they shall e' into my rest: "
5 again, If they shall e' into my rest. "
6 that some must e' therein, and they "
11 therefore to e' into that rest, lest "
10:19 boldness to e' into the holiest by 1529
Re 15: 8 was able to e' into the temple, 1525
21:27 there shall in no wise e' into it "
22:14 e' in through the gates into the city. "

entered
Ge 7:13 In the selfsame day e' Noah, and 935
19: 3 unto him, and e' into his house; "
23 the earth when Lot e' into Zoar. * "
31:33 Leah's tent, and e' into Rachel's "
43:30 and he e' into his chamber, and "
Ex 33: 9 as Moses e' into the tabernacle, "
Jos 2: 3 which are e' into thine house: for "
8:19 and they e' into the city, and took it, "
10:20 of them e' into fenced cities. "
J'g 6: 5 they e' into the land to destroy it. "
9:46 they e' into an hold of the house "
2Sa 10:14 Abishai, and e' into the city. "
2Ki 7: 8 again, and e' into another tent, "
9:31 as Jehu e' in at the gate, "
1Ch 19:15 and e' into the city. Then Joab "
2Ch 12:11 king e' into the house of the Lord, "
15:12 e' into a covenant to seek the Lord "
27: 2 howbeit he e' not into the temple "
32: 1 and e' into Judah, and encamped "
Ne 2:15 and e' by the gate of the valley, "
10:29 e' into a curse, and into an oath, "
Job 38:16 Hast thou e' into the springs of the "
22 Hast thou e' into the treasures of "
Jer 2: 7 but when ye e', ye defiled my land, "
9:21 and is e' into our palaces, to cut off "
34:10 which had e' into the covenant, "
37:16 was e' into the dungeon, and into * "
La 1:10 the heathen e' into her sanctuary, "
4:12 should have e' into the gates * "
Eze 2: 2 the spirit e' into me when he spake "
3:24 Then the spirit e' into me, and set "
16: 8 and e' into a covenant with thee, "
36:20 when they e' unto the heathen, * "
41: 6 and they entered into the wall "
44: 2 the God of Israel, hath e' in by it, "
Ob 11 and foreigners e' into his gates, * "
13 shouldest not have e' into the gate "
Hab 3:16 rottenness e' into my bones, and I "
M't 8: 5 when Jesus was e' into Capernaum, 1525
23 when he was e' into a ship, 1684
9: 1 he e' into a ship, and passed over, "
12: 4 How he e' into the house of God, 1525
24:38 the day that Noe e' into the ark, "
M'r 1:21 he e' into the synagogue, and "
29 they e' into the house of Simon *2064
2: 1 again he e' into Capernaum after 1525
3: 1 he e' again into the synagogue; "
4: 1 he e' into a ship, and sat in the sea; 1684
5:13 went out, and e' into the swine: 1525
6:56 whithersoever he e', into villages, 1531
7:17 when he was e' into the house 1525
24 e' into an house, and would have "
8:10 he e' into a ship with his disciples, 1684
11: 2 as soon as ye be e' into it, *1531
11 Jesus e' into Jerusalem, and into 1525
Lu 1:40 And e' into the house of Zacharias, "
4:38 synagogue, and e' into Simon's "
5: 3 he e' into one of the ships, which 1684
6: 6 e' into the synagogue and taught: 1525
7: 1 people, he e' into Capernaum. "
44 I e' into thine house, thou gavest "
8:30 many devils were e' into him. "
33 e' into the swine: and the herd ran "
9:34 feared as they e' into the cloud. 1525
52 they went, and e' into a village "
10:38 that he e' into a certain village: "
11:52 ye e' not in yourselves, and them "
17:12 as he e' into a certain village, "
27 day that Noe e' into the ark, "
19: 1 Jesus e' and passed through "
22: 3 Then e' Satan into Judas surnamed "
10 when ye are e' into the city, there "
24: 3 they e' in, and found not the body "
Joh 4:38 and ye are e' into their labours. "
6:17 e' into a ship, and went over the 1684
22 whereinto his disciples were e', * "
13:27 after the sop Satan e' into him. 1525
18: 1 was a garden, into the which he e', "
33 Then Pilate e' into the judgment "
21: 3 They went forth, and e' into a ship 305
Ac 3: 2 ask alms of them that e' into the 1531
8 and e' with them into the temple, 1525
5:21 they e' into the temple early in the "
9:17 went his way, and e' into the house; "
10:24 And the morrow after they e' into "
11: 8 hath at any time e' into my mouth. "
12 and we e' into the man's house: "
16:40 and e' into the house of Lydia: "
18: 7 and e' into a certain man's house, *2064
19 e' the synagogue, and reasoned 1525
19:30 Paul would have e' in unto the * "
21: 8 we e' into the house of Philip "
26 with them e' into the temple, to *1524
23:16 e' into the castle, and told Paul. 1525
25:23 and was e' into the place of hearing, "
Ac 28: 8 to whom Paul e' in, and prayed, 1525
Ro 5:12 sin e' into the world, and death by "
20 Moreover the law e', that the *3922
1Co 2: 9 neither have e' into the heart of 305
He 4: 6 e' not in because of unbelief: *1525
10 For he that is e' into his rest, he "
6:20 Whither the forerunner is for us e', "
9:12 he e' in once into the holy place, "
24 For Christ is not e' into the holy "
Jas 5: 4 are e' into the ears of the Lord "
2Jo 7 deceivers are e' into the world, * "
Re 11:11 spirit of life from God e' into them, "

entereth
Nu 4:30 that e' into the service, to do the 935
35, 39, 43 that e' into the service, for * "
2Ch 31:16 every one that e' into the house of * "
Pr 2:10 When wisdom e' into thine heart, * "
17:10 A reproof e' more into a wise man 5181
Eze 21:14 which e' into their privy chambers. "
42:12 toward the east, as one e' into them. 935
46: 9 he that e' in by the way of the north "
9 he that e' by the way of the south "
M't 15:17 whatsoever e' in at the mouth *1531
M'r 5:40 e' in where the damsel was lying.* "
7:18 from without e' into the man, "
19 Because it e' not into his heart, * "
Lu 22:10 him into the house where he e' in. *1531
Joh 10: 1 He that e' not by the door into the 1525
2 But he that e' in by the door is "
He 6:19 which e' into that within the veil;* "
9:25 as the high priest e' into the holy "

entering See also ENTRANCE.
Ex 35:15 at the e' in of the tabernacle, *6607
Jos 8:29 at the e' of the gate of the city, "
13: 5 unto the e' into Hamath. 935
20: 4 at the e' of the gate of the city, 6607
J'g 3: 3 unto the e' in of Hamath. 935
9:35 in the e' of the gate of the city: 6607
40 even unto the e' of the gate. "
44 in the e' of the gate of the city: "
18:16 Dan, stood by the e' of the gate. "
17 priest stood in the e' of the gate "
2Sa 10: 8 in array at the e' in of the gate: "
11:23 them even unto the e' of the gate. "
1Ki 6:31 And for the e' of the oracle he made "
8:65 from the e' in of Hamath unto the 935
19:13 and stood in the e' in of the cave. 6607
2Ki 7: 3 leprous men at the e' in of the gate: "
10: 8 two heaps at the e' in of the gate "
23: 8 in the e' in of the gate of Joshua "
11 at the e' in of the house of the 935
1Ch 5: 9 unto the e' in of the wilderness "
13: 5 Egypt even unto the e' of Hemath, "
2Ch 7: 8 from the e' in of Hamath unto the "
18: 9 void place at the e' in of the gate *6607
23: 4 part of you e' on the sabbath * 935
13 king stood at his pillar at the e' *3996
15 when she was come to the e' of "
26: 8 abroad even to the e' in of Egypt; 935
33:14 even to the e' in at the fish gate, "
Isa 23: 1 so that there is no house, no e' in: "
Jer 1:15 at the e' of the gates of Jerusalem, 6607
17:27 e' in at the gates of Jerusalem *935
Eze 44: 5 mark well the e' in of the house, 3996
Am 6:14 afflict you from the e' in of Hemath 935
M't 23:13 suffer ye them that are e' to go in. 1525
M'r 4:19 the lusts of other things e' in, 1531
7:15 that e' into him can defile him; * "
8:13 e' into the ship again departed 1684
16: 5 e' into the sepulchre, they saw a 1525
Lu 11:52 them that were e' in ye hindered. "
19:30 in the which at your e' ye shall *1531
Ac 8: 3 As for Saul, ... e' into every house, "
27: 2 e' into a ship of Adramyttium, *1910
1Th 1: 9 what manner of e' in we had unto 1529
He 4: 1 being left us of e' into his rest, 1525

enterprise
Job 5:12 hands cannot perform their e'. 8454

entertain See also ENTERTAINED.
He 13: 2 Be not forgetful to e' strangers: *5381

entertained
He 13: 2 some have e' angels unawares. 3579

entice See also ENTICED; ENTICETH.
Ex 22:16 if a man e' a maid that is not 6601
De 13: 6 e' thee secretly, saying, Let us go 5496
J'g 14:15 E' thy husband, that he may 6601
16: 5 E' him, and see wherein his great "
2Ch 18:19 Who shall e' Ahab king of Israel, "
20 before the Lord, and said, I will e' "
21 Thou shalt e' him, and thou shalt "
Pr 1:10 My son, if sinners e' thee, consent "

enticed
Job 31:27 my heart hath been secretly e', 6601
Jer 20:10 Peradventure he will be e', and ‡ "
Jas 1:14 drawn away of his own lust, and e'. 1185

enticeth
Pr 16:29 A violent man e' his neighbour, 6601

enticing
1Co 2: 4 with e' words of man's wisdom, *3981
Col 2: 4 should beguile you with e' words, *4086

entire
Jas 1: 4 that ye may be perfect and e', 3648

entrance See also ENTERING; ENTRANCES; ENTRY.
Nu 34: 8 border unto the e' of Hamath; *935
J'g 1:24 Shew us... the e' into the city, 3996
25 when he shewed them the e' into "
1Ki 18:46 ran before Ahab to the e' of Jezreel. 935
22:10 in the e' of the gate of Samaria; 6607
1Ch 4:39 they went to the e' of Gedor, *3996
2Ch 12:10 that kept the e' of the king's *6607
Ps 119:130 The e' of thy words giveth light; *6608
Eze 40:15 the face of the gate of the e' 2978
1Th 2: 1 know our e' in unto you, that it *1529
2Pe 1:11 an e' shall be ministered unto you "

entrances
Mi 5: 6 land of Nimrod in the e' thereof: 6607

entreat See also ENTREATED; ENTREATETH; INTREAT.
Jer 15:11 cause the enemy to e' thee well *6293
Ac 7: 6 and e' them evil four hundred 2559

entreated See also INTREATED.
Ge 12:16 he e' Abram well for her sake: ‡
Ex 5:22 hast thou so evil e' this people? ‡
De 26: 6 And the Egyptians evil e' us, ‡
M't 22: 6 e' them spitefully, and slew them. 5195
Lu 18:32 shall be mocked, and spitefully e', "
20:11 e' him shamefully, and sent him * 818
Ac 7:19 evil e' our fathers, so that they 2559
27: 3 Julius courteously e' Paul, and *5530
1Th 2: 2 before, and were shamefully e', 5195

entreateth
Job 24:21 He evil e' the barren that beareth*

entreaty See INTREATY.

entries
Eze 40:38 the chambers and the e' thereof *6607

entry See also ENTERING; ENTRANCE; ENTRIES.
2Ki 16:18 king's e' without, turned he from 3996
1Ch 9:19 of the Lord, were keepers of the e'. "
2Ch 4:22 e' of the house, the inner doors 6607
Pr 8: 3 at the e' of the city, at the coming 6310
Jer 19: 2 which is by the e' of the east gate, 6607
26:10 sat down in the e' of the new gate "
36:10 court, at the e' of the new gate "
38:14 prophet unto him into the third e' 3996
43: 9 is at the e' of Pharaoh's house 6607
Eze 8: 5 this image of jealousy in the e'. 872
27: 3 art situate at the e' of the sea, 3996
40:11 the breadth of the e' of the gate, *6607
40 goeth up to the e' of the north gate, "
42: 9 was the e' on the east side, 3996
46:19 he brought me through the e', "

envied
Ge 26:14 and the Philistines e' him. 7065
30: 1 no children, Rachel e' her sister; "
37:11 his brethren e' him; but his father "
Ps 106:16 They e' Moses also in the camp, "
Ec 4: 4 this a man is e' of his neighbour. 7068
Eze 31: 9 that all the trees of Eden,... e' him. 7065

envies
1Pe 2: 1 guile, and hypocrisies, and e', and 5355

enviest
Nu 11:29 unto him, E' thou for my sake? *7065

envieth
1Co 13: 4 charity e' not; charity vaunteth 2206

envious
Ps 37: 1 neither be thou e' against the 7065
73: 3 For I was e' at the foolish, when "
Pr 24: 1 Be not thou e' against evil men, "
19 neither be thou e' at the wicked; "

environ
Jos 7: 9 shall e' us round, and cut off our *5437

envy See also ENVIABLE; ENVIED; ENVIES; ENVIEST; ENVYING.
Job 5: 2 and e' slayeth the silly one. *7068
Pr 3:31 E' thou not the oppressor, and 7065
14:30 but e' the rottenness of the bones. 7068
23:17 Let not thine heart e' sinners: but 7065
27: 4 who is able to stand before e'? *7068
Ec 9: 6 their hatred, and their e', is now "
Isa 11:13 The e' also of Ephraim shall depart, "
13 Ephraim shall not e' Judah, and 7065
26:11 for their e' at the people; yea, *7068
Eze 35:11 according to thine e' which thou "
M't 27:18 that for e' they had delivered him. 5355
M'r 15:10 priests had delivered him for e'. "
Ac 7: 9 patriarchs, moved with e', sold *2206
13:45 were filled with e', and spake *2205
17: 5 which believed not, moved with e' *2206
Ro 1:29 full of e', murder, debate, deceit, 5355
Ph'p 1:15 preach Christ even of e' and strife; "
1Ti 6: 4 whereof cometh e', strife, railings, "
Tit 3: 3 living in malice and e', hateful, "
Jas 4: 5 that dwelleth in us lusteth to e'? * "

envying See also ENVYINGS.
Ro 13:13 wantonness, not in strife and e'. *2205
1Co 3: 3 e', and strife, and divisions, are * "
Ga 5:26 one another, e' one another. 5354
Jas 3:14 But if ye have bitter e' and strife *2205
16 For where e' and strife is, there * "

envyings
2Co 12:20 e', wraths, strifes, backbitings, *2205
Ga 5:21 E', murders, drunkenness, 5355

Epænetus (*ep-en'-e-tus*)
Ro 16: 5 Salute my well beloved E', who 1866

Epaphras (*ep'-a-fras*)
Col 1: 7 As ye also learned of E' our dear 1889
4:12 E', who is one of you, a servant of "
Ph'm 23 salute thee E', my fellowprisoner "

Epaphroditus (*e-paf-ro-di'-tus*)
Ph'p 2:25 it necessary to send to you E', 1891
4:18 having received of E' the things "
subscr. the Philippians from Rome by E'. "

Epenetus See EPAENETUS.

ephah (*e'-fah*)
Ex 16:36 an omer is the tenth part of an e'. 374
Le 5:11 the tenth part of an e' of fine flour "
6:20 the tenth part of an e' of fine flour "
19:36 just weights, a just e', and a just "
Nu 5:15 tenth part of an e' of barley meal; "

Nu 28: 5 And a tenth part of an e· of flour 374
J'g 6:19 unleavened cakes of an e· of flour: "
Ru 2:17 and it was about an e· of barley. "
1Sa 1:24 one e· of flour, and a bottle of wine, "
17:17 brethren an e· of this parched corn, "
Isa 5:10 seed of an homer shall yield an e·. "
Eze 45:10 and a just e·, and a just bath. "
11 The e· and the bath shall be of one "
11 the e· the tenth part of an homer "
13 part of an e· of an homer of wheat. "
13 part of an e· of an homer of barley: "
24 an e· for a bullock, and an e· for a "
24 a ram, and an hin of oil for an e·. "
46: 5 offering shall be an e· for a ram, "
5 to give, and an hin of oil to an e·. "
7 an e· for a bullock, and an e· for a "
7 unto, and an hin of oil to an e·. "
11 an e· to a bullock, and an e· to a ram, "
11 to give, and an hin of oil to an e·. "
14 morning, the sixth part of an e·, "
Am 8: 5 making the e· small, and the shekel "
Zec 5: 6 This is an e· that goeth forth. "
7 sitteth in the midst of the e·. "
8 he cast it into the midst of the e·; "
9 they lifted up the e· between the "
10 Whither do these bear the e·? "

Ephah (e'-fah)
Ge 25: 4 And the sons of Midian; E·, and 5891
1Ch 1:33 E·, and Epher, and Henoch, and "
2:46 E·, Caleb's concubine, bare Haran, "
47 And Pelet, and E·, and Shaaph. "
Isa 60: 6 the dromedaries of Midian and E·; "

Ephai (e'-fahee)
Jer 40: 8 the sons of E· the Netophathite, 5778

Epher (e'-fur)
Ge 25: 4 sons of Midian; Ephah, and E·, 6081
1Ch 1:33 Ephah, and E·, and Henoch, and "
4:17 were, Jether, and Mered, and E·, "
5:24 the house of their fathers, even E·, "

Ephes-dammin (e''-fes-dam'-min) See also PAS-DAMMIN.
1Sa 17: 1 Shochoh and Azekah, in E·. 658

Ephesian (e-fe'-zheun) See also EPHESIANS.
Ac 21:29 him in the city Trophimus an E·. *2180*

Ephesians (e-fe'-zheuns)
Ac 19:28 saying, Great is Diana of the E·. *2180*
34 cried out, Great is Diana of the E·. "
35 the city of the E· is a worshipper "
Eph *subs.* Written from Rome unto the E· "
2Ti *subs.* first bishop of the church of the E·. "

Ephesus (ef'-e-sus) See also EPHESIAN.
Ac 18:19 And he came to E·, and left them *2181*
21 God will. And he sailed from E·. "
24 mighty in the scriptures, came to E·. "
19: 1 through the upper coasts came to E·: "
17 and Greeks also dwelling at E·; "
26 that not alone at E·, but almost "
35 Ye men of E·, what man is there "
20:16 Paul had determined to sail by E·. "
17 And from Miletus he sent to E·, "
1Co 15:32 I have fought with beasts at E·, "
16: 8 I will tarry at E· until Pentecost. "
Eph 1: 1 to the saints which are at E·, "
1Ti 1: 3 besought thee to abide still at E·, "
2Ti 1:18 he ministered unto me at E·, "
4:12 And Tychicus have I sent to E·. "
Re 1:11 unto E·, and unto Smyrna, and "
2: 1 angel of the church of E· write; "

Ephlal (ef'-lal)
1Ch 2:37 Zabad begat E·, and E· begat 654

ephod (e'-fod)
Ex 25: 7 and stones to be set in the e·. 646
28: 4 a breastplate, and an e·, and a robe, "
6 they shall make the e· of gold, "
8 And the curious girdle of the e·, * 642
12 upon the shoulders of the e· for 646
15 after the work of the e· thou shalt "
25 shoulderpieces of the e· before it. "
26 is in the side of the e· inward. "
27 the two sides of the e· underneath, "
27 above the curious girdle of the e·. "
28 rings thereof unto the rings of the e· "
28 above the curious girdle of the e·, "
28 breastplate be not loosed from the e·. "
31 make the robe of the e· all of blue. "
29: 5 and the robe of the e·, and the e·, "
5 with the curious girdle of the e·: "
35: 9, 27 and stones to be set for the e·; "
39: 2 he made the e· of gold, blue, "
5 And the curious girdle of his e·, * 642
7 them on the shoulders of the e·, 646
8 like the work of the e·; of gold, "
18 shoulderpieces of the e·, before it. "
19 was on the side of the e· inward. "
20 the two sides of the e· underneath, "
20 above the curious girdle of the e·. "
21 his rings unto the rings of the e· with "
21 above the curious girdle of the e·, "
21 it might not be loosed from the e·; "
22 And he made the robe of the e· of "
Le 8: 7 put the e· upon him, and he girded "
7 with the curious girdle of the e·, "
J'g 8:27 And Gideon made an e· thereof, "
17: 5 made an e·, and teraphim, and "
18:14 there is in these houses an e·, "
17 took the graven image, and the e·, "
18 fetched the carved image, the e·, "
20 he took the e·, and the teraphim, "
1Sa 2:18 being a child, girded with a linen e·. "
28 to wear an e· before me? and did "
14: 3 priest in Shiloh, wearing an e·. "
21: 9 wrapped in a cloth behind the e·: "
22:18 persons that did wear a linen e·. 646
23: 6 came down with an e· in his hand. "
9 the priest, Bring hither the e·. "
30: 7 I pray thee, bring me hither the e·. "
7 And Abiathar brought thither the e· "
2Sa 6:14 David was girded with a linen e·. "
1Ch 15:27 David also had upon him an e· of "
Ho 3: 4 without an e·, and without teraphim: "

Ephod (e'-fod)
Nu 34:23 Manasseh, Hanniel the son of E·. 641

ephphatha (ef'-fath-ah)
M'r 7:34 unto him, E·, that is, Be opened. *2188*

Ephraim (e'-fra-im) See also EPHRAIMITE; EPHRAIM'S; EPHRAIN.
Ge 41:52 name of the second called he E·: 669
46:20 were born Manasseh and E·, which "
48: 1 him his two sons, Manasseh and E·. "
5 now thy two sons, E· and Manasseh, "
13 E· in his right hand toward Israel's "
17 his right hand upon the head of E·, "
20 God make thee as E· and as "
20 and he set E· before Manasseh. "
Nu 1:10 of E·; Elishama the son of Ammihud: "
32 namely, of the children of E·, "
33 even of the tribe of E·, were forty "
2:18 be the standard of the camp of E· "
18 the captain of the sons of E· shall "
24 were numbered of the camp of E· "
7:48 prince of the children of E·, offered: "
10:22 of the camp of the children of E· "
13: 8 Of the tribe of E·, Oshea the son "
26:28 families were Manasseh and E·. "
35 the sons of E· after their families: "
37 are the families of the sons of E· "
34:24 of the tribe of the children of E·, "
De 33:17 they are the ten thousands of E·, "
34: 2 all Naphtali, and the land of E·, "
Jos 14: 4 were two tribes, Manasseh and E·: "
16: 4 Manasseh and E·, took their "
5 the border of the children of E· "
8 of the tribe of the children of E· "
9 separate cities for the children of E· "
17: 8 belonged to the children of E·; "
9 these cities of E· are among the cities "
15 if mount E· be too narrow for thee. "
17 the house of Joseph, even to E· "
19:50 Even Timnath-serah in mount E·: "
20: 7 and Shechem in mount E·, "
21: 5 of the families of the tribe of E·, "
20 of their lot out of the tribe of E·. "
21 with her suburbs in mount E·, "
24:30 Timnath-serah, ... is in mount E·, "
33 which was given him in mount E·. "
J'g 1:29 did E· drive out the Canaanites "
2: 9 in the mount of E·, on the north side "
3:27 a trumpet in the mountain of E·, "
4: 5 Ramah and Bethel in mount E·: "
5:14 Out of E· was there a root of them "
7:24 throughout all mount E·, saying, "
24 the men of E· gathered themselves "
8: 1 the men of E· said unto him, Why "
2 the gleaning of the grapes of E· "
10: 1 he dwelt in Shamir in mount E·. "
9 and against the house of E·; "
12: 1 men of E· gathered themselves "
4 of Gilead, and fought with E·: "
4 and the men of Gilead smote E·, "
4 Ye Gileadites are fugitives of E· "
15 in Pirathon in the land of E·, "
17: 1 there was a man of mount E·, "
8 to mount E· to the house of Micah, "
18: 2 who when they came to mount E·, "
13 they passed thence unto mount E·, "
19: 1 sojourning on the side of mount E·, "
16 which was also of mount E·; and "
18 toward the side of mount E·; "
1Sa 1: 1 Ramathaim-zophim, of mount E·, "
9: 4 he passed through mount E·, and "
14:22 had hid themselves in mount E·, "
2Sa 2: 9 and over E·, and over Benjamin, "
13:23 in Baal-hazor, which is beside E·: "
18: 6 and the battle was in the wood of E·; "
20:21 but a man of mount E·, Sheba the "
1Ki 4: 8 The son of Hur, in mount E·: "
12:25 built Shechem in mount E·, "
2Ki 5:22 there be come to me from mount E· "
14:13 from the gate of E· unto the corner "
1Ch 6:66 of their coasts out of the tribe of E·. "
67 Shechem in mount E· with her "
7:20 sons of E·; Shuthelah, and Bered "
22 E· their father mourned many days, "
9: 3 of the children of E·, and Manasseh; "
12:30 the children of E· twenty thousand "
27:10 the Pelonite, of the children of E·: "
14 Pirathonite, of the children of E·: "
20 Of the children of E·, Hoshea the "
2Ch 13: 4 Zemaraim, which is in mount E·, "
15: 8 which he had taken from mount E·, "
9 the strangers with them out of E· "
17: 2 and in the cities of E·, which Asa "
19: 4 people from Beer-sheba to mount E·, "
25: 7 to wit, with all the children of E·. "
10 that was come to him out of E·, "
23 from the gate of E· to the corner "
28: 7 Zichri, a mighty man of E·, slew "
12 of the heads of the children of E·, "
30: 1 and wrote letters also to E· and "
10 to city through the country of E· "
18 of people, even many of E·, "
31: 1 in E· also and Manasseh, until they "
34: 6 and E·, and Simeon, even unto "
9 and E·, and of all the remnant of "
Ne 8:16 in the street of the gate of E· "
12:39 And from above the gate of E·, "
Ps 60: 7 E· also is the strength of mine head; 669
78: 9 The children of E·, being armed, "
67 and chose not the tribe of E·: "
80: 2 E· and Benjamin and Manasseh "
108: 8 E· also is the strength of mine head; "
Isa 7: 2 saying, Syria is confederate with E·. "
5 Syria, E·, and the son of Remaliah, "
8 and five years shall E· be broken, "
9 And the head of E· is Samaria, "
17 day that E· departed from Judah; "
9: 9 all the people shall know, even E· "
21 Manasseh, E·; and E·, Manasseh: "
11:13 The envy also of E· shall depart, "
13 E· shall not envy Judah, "
13 and Judah shall not vex E·. "
17: 3 fortress also shall cease from E·, "
28: 1 to the drunkards of E·, whose "
3 the drunkards of E·, shall be trodden "
Jer 4:15 publisheth affliction from mount E·. "
7:15 brethren, even the whole seed of E·. "
31: 6 the watchmen upon the mount E· "
9 to Israel, and E· is my firstborn. "
18 surely heard E· bemoaning himself "
20 Is E· my dear son? is he a pleasant "
50:19 shall be satisfied upon mount E· "
Eze 37:16 For Joseph, the stick of E·, "
19 which is in the hand of E·, and the "
48: 5 unto the west side, a portion for E·. "
6 by the border of E·, from the east "
Ho 4:17 E· is joined to idols: let him alone. "
5: 3 I know E·, and Israel is not hid "
3 for now, O E·, thou committest "
5 therefore shall Israel and E· fall "
9 E· shall be desolate in the day of "
11 E· is oppressed and broken in "
12 will I be unto E· as a moth, "
13 E· saw his sickness, and Judah "
13 then went E· to the Assyrian, and "
14 I will be unto E· as a lion, "
6: 4 O E·, what shall I do unto thee? "
10 there is the whoredom of E·, "
7: 1 the iniquity of E· was discovered, "
8 E·, he hath mixed himself among "
8 E· is a cake not turned. "
11 E· also is like a silly dove without "
8: 9 E· hath hired lovers. "
11 E· hath made many altars to sin, "
9: 3 but E· shall return to Egypt, "
8 watchman of E· was with my God: "
11 As for E·, their glory shall fly away "
13 E·, as I saw Tyrus, is planted in "
13 E· shall bring forth his children "
16 E· is smitten, their root is dried up, "
10: 6 E· shall receive shame, and Israel "
11 E· is as an heifer that is taught, "
11 I will make E· to ride; Judah shall "
11: 3 I taught E· also to go, taking them "
8 How shall I give thee up, E·? "
9 I will not return to destroy E·: "
12 E· compasseth me about with lies, "
12: 1 E· feedeth on wind, and followeth "
8 E· said, Yet I am become rich, "
14 E· provoked him to anger most "
13: 1 When E· spake trembling, he "
12 The iniquity of E· is bound up; "
14: 8 E· shall say, What have I to do any "
Ob 1:19 they shall possess the fields of E·, "
Zec 9:10 I will cut off the chariot from E·, "
13 filled the bow with E·, and raised "
10: 7 And they of E· shall be like a mighty "
Joh 11:54 into a city called E·, and there *2187*

Ephraimite (e'-fra-im-ite) See also EPHRAIMITES.
J'g 12: 5 said unto him, Art thou an E·? 673

Ephraimites (e'-fra-im-ites)
Jos 16:10 Canaanites dwell among the E· *669
J'g 12: 4 fugitives of Ephraim among the E·,* "
5 passages of Jordan before the E·:* "
5 those E· which were escaped said,* "
6 there fell at that time of the E· * "

Ephraim's (e'-fra-ims)
Ge 48:14 and laid it upon E· head, who was 669
17 to remove it from E· head unto "
50:23 Joseph saw E· children of the third "
Jos 17:10 Southward it was E·, and northward "

Ephrain (e'-fra-in) See also EPHRAIM; EPHRON.
2Ch 13:19 and E· with the towns thereof. *6085

Ephratah (ef'-rat-ah) See also BETHLEHEM; CALEB-EPHRATAH; EPHRATH; EPHRATHITE.
Ru 4:11 and do thou worthily in E·, * 672
1Ch 2:50 the son of Hur, the firstborn of E·;* "
4: 4 E·, the father of Beth-lehem. * "
Ps 132: 6 Lo, we heard of it at E·: we found* "
Mic 5: 2 But thou Beth-lehem E·, though "

Ephrath (e'-frath) See also EPHRATAH.
Ge 35:16 was but a little way to come to E·: 672
19 and was buried in the way to E·, "
48: 7 but a little way to come unto E·: "
7 I buried her there in the way of E·; "
1Ch 2:19 Caleb took unto him E·, which bare "

Ephrathite (ef'-rath-ite) See also EPHRATHITES.
1Sa 1: 1 of John, the son of Zuph, an E·: * 673
17:12 Now David was the son of that E· "
1Ki 11:26 Jeroboam the son of Nebat, an E·* "

Ephrathites (ef'-rath-ites)
Ru 1: 2 E· of Beth-lehem-judah. 673

Ephron (e'-fron) See also EPHRAIM; EPHRAIN.
Ge 23: 8 for me to E· the son of Zohar, 6085
10 And E· dwelt among the children "
10 E· the Hittite answered Abraham "
13 he spake unto E· in the audience "
14 And E· answered Abraham, saying "

Ge 23:16 And Abraham hearkened unto E';6085
16 Abraham weighed to E' the silver, "
17 of E', which was in Machpelah, "
25: 9 of E' the son of Zohar the Hittite, "
49:29 that is in the field of E' the Hittite, "
30 with the field of E' the Hittite for a "
50:13 of a burying place of E' the Hittite, "
Jos 15: 9 went out to the cities of mount E'; "

Epicureans (*ep-i-cu-re'-ans*)
Ac 17:18 certain philosophers of the E', *1946

epistle See also EPISTLES.
Ac 15:30 together, they delivered the e': 1992
23:33 delivered the e' to the governor, * "
Ro 16:22 I Tertius, who wrote this e', "
1Co 5: 9 I wrote unto you in an e' "
subscr. The first e' to the Corinthians was
2Co 3: 2 are our e' written in our hearts, 1992
3 the e' of Christ ministered by us, "
7: 8 I perceive that the same e' hath "
subscr. The second e' to the Corinthians
Col 4:16 when this e' is read among you, 1992
16 that ye likewise read the e' from
1Th 5:27 this e' be read unto all the holy 1992
subscr. The first e' unto the Thessalonians
2Th 2:15 whether my word, or our e'. 1992
3:14 our word by this e', note that man, "
17 which is the token in every e': "
subscr. The second e' to the Thessalonians
2Ti *subscr.* The second e' unto Timotheus,
2Pe 3: 1 second e', beloved, I now write 1992

epistles
2Co 3: 1 e' of commendation to you, or 1992
2Pe 3:16 As also in all his e', speaking in "

equal See also EQUALS; UNEQUAL.
Job 28:17 gold and the crystal cannot e' it: 6186
19 topaz of Ethiopia shall not e' it, "
Ps 17: 2 behold the things that are e'. *4339
55:13 it was thou, a man mine e', 6187
Pr 26: 7 The legs of the lame are not e': *1809
Isa 40:25 will ye liken me, or shall I be e'? 7737
46: 5 will ye liken me, and make me e', "
La 2:13 what shall I e' to thee, that I may "
Eze 18:25 The way of the Lord is not e'. 8505
25 house of Israel; Is not my way e'? "
29 The way of the Lord is not e'. O "
29 of Israel, are not my ways e'? "
33:17 The way of the Lord is not e': but "
17 as for them, their way is not e'. "
20 The way of the Lord is not e'. "
M't 20:12 thou hast made them e' unto us, 2470
Lu 20:36 for they are e' unto the angels; 2465
Joh 5:18 making himself e' with God. 2470
Ph'p 2: 6 it not robbery to be e' with God: * "
Col 4: 1 servants that which is just and e':2471
Re 21:16 breadth and the height of it are e'.2470

equality
2Co 8:14 But by an e', that now at this time 2471
14 your want: that there may be e': "

equally See also UNEQUALLY.
Ex 36:22 e' distant one from another: *7947

equals
Ga 1:14 many my e' in mine own nation, *4915

equity See also INIQUITY.
Ps 98: 9 the world, and the people with e'. 4339
99: 4 dost establish e', thou executest "
Pr 1: 3 justice, and judgment, and e'; "
2: 9 and judgment, and e'; yea, every "
17:26 good, nor to strike princes for e'. *3476
Ec 2:21 and in knowledge, and in e'; *3788
Isa 11: 4 with e' for the meek of the earth: 4334
59:14 in the street, and e' cannot enter.*5229
Mic 3: 9 abhor judgment, pervert all e'. 3477
Mal 2: 6 walked with me in peace and e', *4334

Er (*ur*)
Ge 38: 3 a son; and he called his name E'. 6147
6 And Judah took a wife for E' his "
7 E', Judah's firstborn, was wicked "
46:12 the sons of Judah; E', and Onan, "
12 but E' and Onan died in the land "
Nu 26:19 sons of Judah were E', and Onan: "
19 and E' and Onan died in the land "
1Ch 2: 3 The sons of Judah; E', and Onan, "
3 And E', the firstborn of Judah, "
4:21 son of Judah were, E' the father "
Lu 3:28 Elmodam, which was the son of E',2262

Eran (*e'-ran*) See also ERANITES.
Nu 26:36 of E', the family of the Eranites. 6197

Eranites (*e'-ran-ites*)
Nu 26:36 of Eran, the family of the E'. 6198

Erastus (*e-ras'-tus*)
Ac 19:22 Timotheus and E'; but he himself 2037
Ro 16:23 E' the chamberlain of the city "
2Ti 4:20 E' abode at Corinth: but Trophimus "

ere
Ex 1:19 delivered e' the midwives come 2962
Nu 11:33 their teeth, e' it was chewed, "
14:11 how long will it be e' they believe *3808
1Sa 3: 3 And e' the lamp of God went out *2962
2Sa 2:26 it be then, e' thou bid the people 3808
2Ki 6:32 but e' the messenger came to him,2962
Job 18: 2 How long will it be e' ye make an *
Jer 47: 6 how long will it be e' thou be quiet?3808
Ho 8: 5 how long will it be e' they attain "
Joh 4:49 Sir, come down e' my child die. 4250

Erech (*e'-rek*) See also ARCHEVITES.
Ge 10:10 Babel, and E', and Accad, and 751

erected
Ge 33:20 And he e' there an altar, 5324

Eri (*e'-ri*) See also ERITES.
Ge 46:16 Ezbon, E', and Arodi, and Areli. 6179
Nu 26:16 of E', the family of the Erites: "

Erites (*e'-rites*)
Nu 26:16 of Eri, the family of the E': 6180

err See also ERRED; ERRETH.
2Ch 33: 9 So Manasseh made Judah....to e', 8582
Ps 95:10 is a people that do e' in their heart, "
119:21 rebuked the proud... which do e' *7686
118 hast trodden down all them that e' "
Pr 14:22 Do they not e' that devise evil? 8582
19:27 the instruction that causeth to e' 7686
Isa 3:12 which lead thee cause thee to e', 8582
9:16 of this people cause them to e'; "
19:14 they have caused Egypt to e' in * "
28: 7 they e' in vision, they stumble in 7686
30:28 of the people, causing them to e'. 8582
35: 8 men, though fools, shall not e' "
63:17 why hast thou made us to e' from "
Jer 23:13 and caused my people Israel to e'. "
32 cause my people to e' by their lies, "
Ho 4:12 whoredoms hath caused them to e', "
Am 2: 4 and their lies caused them to e', "
Mic 3: 5 prophets that make my people e', "
M't 22:29 Ye do e', not knowing the 4105
M'r 12:24 Do ye not therefore e', because ye "
27 ye therefore do greatly e'. "
Heb 3:10 They do alway e' in their heart; "
Jas 1:16 Do not e', my beloved brethren. * "
5:19 Brethren, if any of you do e' from "

errand
Ge 24:33 not eat, until I have told mine e'. 1697
J'g 3:19 I have a secret e' unto thee, "
2Ki 9: 5 I have an e' to thee, O captain. "

erred
Le 5:18 his ignorance wherein he e' and 7683
Nu 15:22 if ye have e', and not observed all* "
1Sa 26:21 the fool, and have e' exceedingly. "
Job 6:24 me to understand wherein I have e'. "
19: 4 And be it indeed that I have e', "
Ps 119:110 I have e' not from thy precepts. *8582
Isa 28: 7 they also have e' through wine, *7686
7 priest and the prophet have e' * "
29:24 They also that e' in spirit shall *8582
1Ti 6:10 they have e' from the faith, and * 635
21 have e' concerning the faith. 795
2Ti 2:18 Who concerning the truth have e', "

erreth
Pr 10:17 but he that refuseth reproof e'. 8582
Eze 45:20 every one that e', and for him that 7686

error See also ERRORS.
2Sa 6: 7 God smote him there for his e'; 7944
Job 19: 4 mine e' remaineth with myself. 4879
Ec 5: 6 neither say thou...it was an e': 7684
10: 5 as an e' which proceedeth from the "
Isa 32: 6 and to utter e' against the Lord, 8432
Da 6: 4 neither was there any e' or fault 7960
M't 27:64 so the last e' shall be worse than 4106
Ro 1:27 that recompence of their e' which "
Jas 5:20 the sinner from the e' of his way "
2Pe 2:18 escape from them who live in e'. "
3:17 being led away with the e' of the "
1Jo 4: 6 spirit of truth, and the spirit of e'. "
Jude 11 ran greedily after the e' of Balaam "

errors
Ps 19:12 Who can understand his e'? 7691
Jer 10:15 are vanity, and the work of e': *8595
51:18 They are vanity, the work of e': * "
Heb 9: 7 himself, and for the e' of the people: 51

Esaias (*e-sah'-yas*) See also ISAIAH.
M't 3: 3 spoken of by the prophet E', *2268
4:14 was spoken by E' the prophet, * "
8:17 fulfilled which was spoken by E' * "
12:17 fulfilled which was spoken by E' * "
13:14 fulfilled the prophecy of E', * "
15: 7 hypocrites, well did E' prophesy * "
M'r 7: 6 Well hath E' prophesied of you * "
Lu 3: 4 in the book of the words of E' * "
4:17 him the book of the prophet E'. * "
Joh 1:23 the Lord, as said the prophet E'. * "
12:38 That the saying of E' the prophet* "
39 could not believe, because that E'* "
41 These things said E', when he * "
Ac 8:28 sitting in his chariot read E' the * "
30 heard him read the prophet E', * "
28:25 Well spake the Holy Ghost by E' * "
Ro 9:27 E' also crieth concerning Israel, * "
29 and as E' said before, Except the* "
10:16 E' saith, Lord, who hath believed* "
20 But E' is very bold, and saith, I * "
15:12 And again, E' saith, There shall * "

Esar-haddon (*e''-zar-had'-dun*)
2Ki 19:37 E' his son reigned in his stead. 634
Ezr 4: 2 since the days of E' king of Assur, "
Isa 37:38 E' his son reigned in his stead. "

Esau (*e'-saw*) See also EDOM; ESAU'S.
Ge 25:25 they called his name E'. 6215
27 E' was a cunning hunter, a man of "
28 Isaac loved E', because he did eat "
29 E' came from the field, and he was "
30 E' said to Jacob, Feed me, I pray "
32 E' said, Behold, I am at the point "
34 Then Jacob gave E' bread and "
34 Thus E' despised his birthright. "
26:34 And E' was forty years old when he "
27: 1 he called E' his eldest son, and said "
5 heard when Isaac spake to E' "
5 And E' went to the field to hunt for "
6 I heard thy father speak unto E' "
11 Behold, E' my brother is a hairy "
15 goodly raiment of her eldest son E', "
19 Jacob said unto his father, I am E' "
Ge 27:21 whether thou be my very son E' or 6215
22 but the hands are the hands of E'. "
24 he said, Art thou my very son E'? "
30 that E' his brother came in from "
32 said, I am thy son, thy firstborn E'. "
34 when E' heard the words of his "
37 Isaac answered and said unto E', "
38 E' said unto his father, Hast thou "
38 E' lifted up his voice, and wept. "
41 And E' hated Jacob because of the "
41 E' said in his heart, The days of "
42 these words of E' her elder son "
42 Behold, thy brother E', as touching "
28: 6 When E' saw that Isaac had blessed "
8 And E' seeing that the daughters of "
9 Then went E' unto Ishmael, and "
32: 3 sent messengers before him to E' "
4 shall ye speak unto my lord E'; "
6 We came to thy brother E', and "
8 If E' come to the one company, "
11 of my brother, from the hand of E': "
13 hand a present for E' his brother; "
17 When E' my brother meeteth thee, "
18 sent unto my lord E': and, behold, "
19 this manner shall ye speak unto E', "
33: 1 and, behold, E' came, and with him "
4 And E' ran to meet him, and "
9 E' said, I have enough, my brother; "
15 And E' said, Let me now leave "
16 So E' returned that day on his way "
35: 1 from the face of E' thy brother. "
29 his sons E' and Jacob buried him. "
36: 1 generations of E', who is Edom. "
2 E' took his wives of the daughters "
4 And Adah bare to E' Eliphaz; "
5 these are the sons of E', which "
6 And E' took his wives, and his sons, "
8 dwelt E' in Mount Seir: E' is Edom. "
9 of E' the father of the Edomites in "
10 the son of Adah the wife of E', "
10 son of Bashemath the wife of E'. "
14 she bare to E' Jeush, and Jaalam, "
15 were dukes of the sons of E': "
15 of Eliphaz, the firstborn son of E'; "
19 are the sons of E', who is Edom, "
40 of the dukes that came of E', "
43 he is E' the father of the Edomites. "
De 2: 4 children of E', which dwell in Seir; "
5 Seir unto E' for a possession. "
8 children of E', which dwelt in Seir, "
12 the children of E' succeeded them, "
22 As he did to the children of E', "
29 children of E' which dwelt in Seir, "
Jos 24: 4 I gave unto Isaac Jacob and E': "
4 and I gave unto E' mount Seir, "
1Ch 1:34 The sons of Isaac; E' and Israel. "
35 The sons of E'; Eliphaz, Reuel, "
Jer 49: 8 bring the calamity of E' upon him, "
10 But I have made E' bare, I have "
Ob 6 are the things of E' searched out! "
8 the wise men out of the mount of E'? "
9 every one of the mount of E' may "
18 and the house of E' for stubble, "
18 any remaining of the house of E'; "
19 shall possess the mount of E'; "
21 Zion to judge the mount of E'; "
Mal 1: 2 Was not E' Jacob's brother? saith "
3 I hated E', and laid his mountains "
Ro 9:13 I loved, but E' have I hated. 2269
Heb 11:20 By faith Isaac blessed Jacob and E' "
12:16 fornicator, or profane person, as E', "

Esau's (*e'-saws*)
Ge 25:26 his hand took hold on E' heel; 6215
27:23 hairy, as his brother E' hands: "
28: 5 Rebekah, Jacob's and E' mother. "
36:10 are the names of E' sons; Eliphaz "
12 was concubine to Eliphaz E' son; "
12 were the sons of Adah E' wife. "
13 the sons of Bashemath E' wife. "
14 of Zibeon, E' wife: and she bare "
17 these are the sons of Reuel E' son; "
17 are the sons of Bashemath E' wife. "
18 the sons of Aholibamah E' wife; "
18 the daughter of Anah, E' wife. "

escape See also ESCAPED; ESCAPETH; ESCAPING.
Ge 19:17 E' for thy life; look not behind 4422
17 e' to the mountain, lest thou be "
19 I cannot e' to the mountain, lest "
20 Oh, let me e' thither, (is it not "
22 Haste thee, e' thither; for I can not "
32: 8 company which is left shall e'. 6413
Jos 8:22 let none of them remain or e'. 6412
1Sa 27: 1 I should speedily e' into the land 4422
1 so shall I e' out of his hand. "
2Sa 15:14 we shall not else e' from Absalom:6413
20: 6 lest he get him fenced cities, and e'5337
1Ki 18:40 let not one of them e'. And they 4422
2Ki 9:15 then let none go forth nor e' 6412
10:24 If any of the men...e', 4422
19:31 and they that e' out of mount Zion:6413
Ezr 9: 8 to leave us a remnant to e', "
Es 4:13 thou shalt e' in the king's house, 4422
Job 11:20 they shall not e', and their hope*4498, 6
Ps 55: 8 my e' from the windy storm and *4655
56: 7 Shall they e' by iniquity? in thine 6405
71: 2 cause me to e': incline thine ear *6403
141:10 own nets, whilst that I withal e'. 5674
Pr 19: 5 he that speaketh lies shall not e'. 4422
Ec 7:26 pleaseth God shall e' from her; "
Isa 20: 6 of Assyria: and how shall we e'? "
37:32 and they that e' out of mount Zion:6413
66:19 I will send those that e' of them 6412
Jer 11:11 they shall not be able to e'; 3318
25:35 nor the principal of the flock to e'.6413
32: 4 shall not e' out of the hand of the 4422

Jer 34: 3 thou shalt not *e·* out of his hand, 4422
38:18, 23 shalt not *e·* out of their hand. "
42:17 none of them shall remain or *e·* 6412
44:14 of Egypt to sojourn there, shall *e·* "
14 shall return but such as shall *e·*. "
28 a small number that *e·* the sword "
46: 6 flee away, nor the mighty man *e·*; 4422
48: 8 no city shall *e·*: the valley also "
50:28 The voice of them that flee and *e·* 6412
29 let none thereof *e·*: recompense 6413
Eze 6: 8 ye may have some that shall *e·* 6412
9 they that *e·* of you shall remember "
7:16 But they that *e·* of them shall 6403
16 But they that...of them shall *e·*, 6412
17:15 shall he *e·* that doeth such things?4422
18 all these things, he shall not *e·*. "
Da 11:41 But these shall *e·* out of his hand,* "
42 and the land of Egypt shall not *e·*. 6413
Joe 2: 3 yea, and nothing shall *e·* them. "
Ob 14 to cut off those of his that did *e·*; 6412
M't 23:33 ye *e·* the damnation of hell? *5343, 575*
Lu 21:36 worthy to *e·* all these things *1628*
Ac 27:42 of them should swim out, and *e·*. *1309*
Ro 2: 3 thou shalt *e·* the judgment of God? *1628*
1Co 10:13 temptation also make a way to *e·*, *1545*
1Th 5: 3 with child; and they shall not *e·*. *1628*
Heb 2: 3 How shall we *e·*, if we neglect so "
12:25 earth, much more shall not we *e·*, *5343*

escaped
Ge 14:13 And there came one that had *e·*, 6412
Ex 10: 5 the residue of that which is *e·*, 6413
Nu 21:29 he hath given his sons that *e·*, *6412
De 23:15 servant which is *e·* from his master5337
J'g 3:26 Ehud *e·* while they tarried, and 4422
26 quarries, and *e·* unto Seirath. "
29 of valour; and there *e·* not a man. "
12: 5 those Ephraimites which were *e·* *6412
21:17 for them that be *e·* of Benjamin, 6413
1Sa 14:41 were taken: but the people *e·*. 3318
19:10 and David fled, and *e·* that night. 4422
12 and he went, and fled, and *e·*. "
17 away mine enemy, that he is *e*? "
18 David fled, and *e·*, and came to "
22: 1 thence, and *e·* to the cave Adullam: "
20 sons of Ahimelech...*e·*, and fled "
23:13 that David was *e·* from Keilah; "
30:17 and there *e·* not a man of them, "
2Sa 1: 3 Out of the camp of Israel am I *e·*. "
4: 6 Rechab and Baanah his brother *e·*. "
1Ki 20:20 Ben-hadad the king of Syria *e·* "
2Ki 19:30 that is *e·* of the house of Judah 6413
37 they *e·* into the land of Armenia. 4422
1Ch 4:43 of the Amalekites that were *e·*. 6413
2Ch 16: 7 the host of the king of Syria *e·* 4422
20:24 fallen to the earth, and none *e·*. 6413
30: 6 the remnant of you, that are *e·* "
36:20 them that had *e·* from the sword 7611
Ezr 9:15 we remain yet *e·*, as it is this day: 6413
Ne 1: 2 concerning the Jews that had *e·*, "
Job 1:15, 16, 17, 19 I only am *e·* alone to tell 4422
19:20 I am *e·* with the skin of my teeth. "
Ps 124: 7 Our soul is *e·* as a bird out of the "
7 the snare is broken, and we are *e·*. "
Isa 4: 2 for them that are *e·* of Israel. 6413
10:20 such as are *e·* of the house of Jacob. "
37:31 that is *e·* of the house of Judah "
38 and they *e·* into the land of 4422
45:20 ye that are *e·* of the nations: 6412
Jer 41:15 Ishmael the son of Nethaniah *e·* 4422
51:50 Ye that have *e·* the sword, 6412
La 2:22 the day of the Lord's anger none *e·* "
Eze 24:27 mouth be opened to him which is *e·*, "
33:21 one that had *e·* out of Jerusalem "
22 evening, afore he that was *e·* came; "
Joh 10:39 him: but he *e·* out of their hand, **1831*
Ac 27:44 pass, that they *e·* all safe to land, *1295*
28: 1 when they were *e·*, then they knew "
4 whom, though he hath *e·* the sea, "
2Co 11:33 was I let down by the wall, and *e·* *1628*
Heb 11:34 of fire, *e·* the edge of the sword, *5343*
12:25 For if they *e·* not who refused him "
2Pe 1: 4 having *e·* the corruption that is in *668*
2:18 those that were clean *e·* from them* "
20 For if after they have *e·* the "

escapeth
1Ki 19:17 him that *e·* the sword of Hazael 4422
17 him that *e·* from the sword of Jehu "
Isa 15: 9 lions upon him that *e·* of Moab, 6413
Jer 48:19 him that fleeth, and her that *e·*, 4422
Eze 24:26 he that *e·* in that day shall come 6412
Am 9: 1 he that *e·* of them shall not be "

escaping
Ezr 9:14 should be no remnant nor *e·*? *6413

eschew See also ESCHEWED; ESCHEWETH.
1Pe 3:11 Let him *e·* evil, and do good; **1578*

eschewed
Job 1: 1 one that feared God, and *e·* evil. ‡5493

escheweth
Job 1: 8 one that feareth God and *e·* evil? ‡5493
2: 3 one that feareth God, and *e·* evil? ‡ "

Esek (*e'-sek*)
Ge 26:20 he called the name of the well *E·*; 6320

Esh-baal (*esh'-ba-al*) See also ISH-BOSHETH.
1Ch 8:33 Malchi-shua, and Abinadab, and *E·*.792
9:39 Malchi-shua, and Abinadab, and *E·*. "

Esh-ban (*esh'-ban*)
Ge 36:26 Hemdan, and *E·*, and Ithran, 790
1Ch 1:41 Amram, and *E·*, and Ithran. "

Eshcol (*esh'-col*)
Ge 14:13 brother of *E·*, and brother of Aner: 812
24 men which went with me, Aner, *E·*, "
Nu 13:23 they came unto the brook of *E·*, 812
24 The place was called the brook *E·*, "
32: 9 they went up unto the valley of *E·*, "
De 1:24 came unto the valley of *E·*, and "

Eshean (*esh'-e-an*)
Jos 15:52 Arab, and Dumah, and *E·*, 824

Eshek (*e'-shek*)
1Ch 8:39 And the sons of *E·* his brother 6232

Eshkalonites (*esh'-ka-lon-ites*)
Jos 13: 3 Ashdothites, the *E·*, the Gittites, * 832

Eshtaol (*esh'-ta-ol*) See also ESHTAULITES.
Jos 15:33 in the valley, *E·*, and Zoreah, 847
19:41 Zorah, and *E·*, and Ir-shemesh, "
J'g 13:25 camp of Dan between Zorah and *E·*. "
16:31 buried him between Zorah and *E·* "
18: 2 of valour, from Zorah, and from *E·*, "
8 unto their brethren to Zorah and *E·*: "
11 out of Zorah and out of *E·*, "

Eshtaulites (*esh'-ta-u-lites*)
1Ch 2:53 the Zareathites, and the *E·*. * 848

Eshtemoa (*esh-te-mo'-ah*) See also ESHTEMOH.
Jos 21:14 and *E·* with her suburbs, 851
1Sa 30:28 and to them which were in *E·*, "
1Ch 4:17 and Ishbah the father of *E·*. "
19 Garmite, and *E·* the Maachathite. "
6:57 Jattir, and *E·*, with their suburbs, "

Eshtemoh (*esh'-te-moh*) See also ESHTEMOA.
Jos 15:50 Anab, and *E·*, and Anim, 851

Eshton (*esh'-ton*)
1Ch 4:11 Mehir, which was the father of *E·*. 850
12 *E·* begat Beth-rapha, and Paseah, "

Esli (*es'-li*)
Lu 3:25 which was the son of *E·*, which *2069*

especially
Ps 31:11 but *e·* among my neighbours, *3966
Ac 26: 3 *E·* because I know thee to be *3122*
Ga 6:10 men, *e·* unto them who are of the "
1Ti 5:17 *e·* they who labour in the word and "
2Ti 4:13 the books, but *e·* the parchments. "

espied
Ge 42:27 of them opened his sack ... he *e·* 7200
Eze 20: 6 into a land that I had *e·* for them, 8446

espousals
Ca 3:11 crowned him in the day of his *e·*, 2861
Jer 2: 2 of thy youth, the love of thine *e·*, 3623

espoused
2Sa 3:14 my wife Michal, which I *e·* to me * 781
M't 1:18 When as his mother Mary was *e·* **3423*
Lu 1:27 To a virgin *e·* to a man whose * "
2: 5 To be taxed with Mary his *e·* wife,* "
2Co 11: 2 For I have *e·* you to one husband, *718*

espy See also ESPIED; SPY.
Jos 14: 7 sent...from Kadesh-barnea to *e·* *7270
Jer 48:19 stand by the way, and *e·*; ask him 6822

Esrom (*es'-rom*) See also HEZRON.
M't 1: 3 Phares begat *E·*; and *E·* begat **2074*
Lu 3:33 which was the son of *E·*, which * "

essay See ASSAY.

establish See also ESTABLISHED; ESTABLISHETH; STABLISH.
Ge 6:18 with thee will I *e·* my covenant; 6965
9: 9 behold, I *e·* my covenant with you, "
11 And I will *e·* my covenant with you; "
17: 7 And I will *e·* my covenant between "
19 and I will *e·* my covenant with him "
21 my covenant will I *e·* with Isaac, "
Le 26: 9 you, and *e·* my covenant with you. "
Nu 30:13 her husband may *e·* it, or her "
De 8:18 that he may *e·* his covenant which "
28: 9 The Lord shall *e·* thee an holy people "
29:13 That he may *e·* thee to day "
1Sa 1:23 only the Lord *e·* his word. So the "
2Sa 7:12 and I will *e·* his kingdom. 3559
25 concerning his house, *e·* it for *6965
1Ki 9: 5 Then I will *e·* the throne of thy "
15: 4 after him, and to *e·* Jerusalem. 5975
1Ch 17:11 and I will *e·* his kingdom. 3559
22:10 and I will *e·* the throne of his "
28: 7 Moreover I will *e·* his kingdom "
2Ch 9: 8 loved Israel, to *e·* them for ever, 5975
Job 36: 7 yea, he doth *e·* them for ever, *3427
Ps 7: 9 but *e·* the just: for the righteous *3559
48: 8 God will *e·* it for ever. Selah. "
87: 5 and the highest himself shall *e·* her. "
89: 2 thy faithfulness shalt thou *e·* in the "
4 Thy seed will I *e·* for ever, "
90:17 and *e·* thou the work of our hands "
17 the work of our hands *e·* thou it. "
99: 4 thou dost *e·* equity, thou executest "
Pr 15:25 he will *e·* the border of the widow.5324
Isa 9: 7 and to *e·* it with judgment and 5582
49: 8 of the people, to *e·* the earth, to *6965
62: 7 And give him no rest, till he *e·*, 3559
Jer 33: 2 the Lord that formed it, to *e·* it; "
Eze 16:60 I will *e·* unto thee an everlasting 6965
62 And I will *e·* my covenant with thee; "
Da 6: 7 together to *e·* a royal statute, 6966
8 Now, O king, *e·* the decree, "
11:14 exalt themselves to *e·* the vision. 5975
Am 5:15 and *e·* judgment in the gate: 3322
Ro 3:31 God forbid: yea, we *e·* the law. *2476*
10: 3 about to *e·* their own righteousness, "
1Th 3: 2 to *e·* you, and to comfort you *4741*
Heb 10: 9 the first, that he may *e·* the second.*2476*

established See also STABLISHED.
Ge 9:17 the covenant, which I have *e·* 6965
41:32 because the thing is *e·* by God, 3559
Ex 6: 4 I have also *e·* my covenant with 6965
15:17 O Lord, which thy hands have *e·*. 3559
Lev 25:30 then the house ... shall be *e·* *6965
De 19:15 witnesses, shall the matter be *e·*. "
32: 6 hath he not made thee, and *e·* thee?3559
1Sa 3:20 knew that Samuel was *e·* to be a 539
13:13 the Lord have *e·* thy kingdom *3559
20:31 shalt not be *e·*, nor thy kingdom. "
24:20 the kingdom of Israel shall be *e·* 6965
2Sa 5:12 Lord had *e·* him king over Israel, 3559
7:16 thy kingdom shall be *e·* for ever. * 539
16 thy throne shall be *e·* for ever. 3559
26 house of thy servant David be *e·* "
1Ki 2:12 and his kingdom was *e·* greatly. "
24 the Lord liveth, which hath *e·* me, "
45 throne of David shall be *e·* before "
46 the kingdom was *e·* in the hand of "
1Ch 17:14 his throne shall be *e·* for evermore. "
23 let the thing ... be *e·* for ever, 539
24 Let it even be *e·*, that thy name be "
24 let the house of David ... be *e·* 3559
2Ch 1: 9 unto David my father be *e·*: 539
12: 1 when Rehoboam had *e·* the 3559
20:20 so shall ye be *e·*; believe his 539
25: 3 when the kingdom was *e·* to him, 2388
30: 5 So they *e·* a decree to make 5975
Job 21: 8 Their seed is *e·* in their sight 3559
22:28 and it shall be *e·* unto thee: 6965
Ps 24: 2 and *e·* it upon the floods. 3559
40: 2 feet upon a rock, and *e·* my goings. "
78: 5 For he *e·* a testimony in Jacob, 6965
69 earth which he hath *e·* for ever 3245
89:21 with whom my hand shall be *e·*: 3559
37 It shall be *e·* for ever as the moon, "
93: 2 Thy throne is *e·* of old: thou art "
96:10 the world also shall be *e·* that it * "
102:28 their seed shall be *e·* before thee. "
112: 8 His heart is *e·*, he shall not be 5564
119:90 thou hast *e·* the earth, and it 3559
140:11 Let not an evil speaker be *e·* "
Pr 3:19 by understanding hath he *e·* the "
4:26 and let all thy ways be *e·*. "
8:28 when he *e·* the clouds above: * 553
12: 3 man shall not be *e·* by wickedness:3559
19 The lip of truth shall be *e·* for ever: "
15:22 of counsellors they are *e·*. 6965
16: 3 and thy thoughts shall be *e·*. 3559
12 the throne is *e·* by righteousness. "
20:18 Every purpose is *e·* by counsel: "
24: 3 and by understanding it is *e·*: "
25: 5 and his throne shall be *e·* in "
29:14 his throne shall be *e·* for ever. "
30: 4 hath *e·* all the ends of the earth? 6965
Isa 2: 2 of the Lord's house shall be *e·* 3559
7: 9 believe, surely ye shall not be *e·*. 539
16: 5 in mercy shall the throne be *e·*: 3559
45:18 he hath *e·* it, he created it "
54:14 In righteousness shalt thou be *e·*: "
Jer 10:12 hath *e·* the world by his wisdom, "
30:20 their congregation shall be *e·* "
51:15 by his power, he hath *e·* the world "
Da 4:36 I was *e·* in my kingdom, 8627
Mic 4: 1 be *e·* in the top of the mountains, 3559
Hab 1:12 thou hast *e·* them for correction. 3245
Zec 5:11 and it shall be *e·*, and set there *3559
M't 18:16 witnesses every word may be *e·*. *2476*
Ac 16: 5 were the churches *e·* in the faith,**4732*
Ro 1:11 to the end ye may be *e·*; *4741*
2Co 13: 1 witnesses shall every word be *e·*. *2476*
Heb 8: 6 was *e·* upon better promises. **3549*
13: 9 that the heart be *e·* with grace; *950*
2Pe 1:12 and be *e·* in the present truth. *4741*

establisheth
Nu 30:14 then he *e·* all her vows, or all her 6965
Pr 29: 4 The king by judgment *e·* the land: 5975
Da 6:15 nor statute which the king *e·* 6966

establishment
2Ch 32: 1 After these things, and the *e·* * 571

estate See also ESTATES; STATE.
1Ch 17:17 regarded me according to the *e·* 8448
Es 1:19 give her royal *e·* unto another
Ps 136:23 Who remembered us in our low *e·*:
Ec 1:16 Lo, I am come to great *e·*, *
3:18 concerning the *e·* of the sons of *1700
Eze 16:55, 55 shall return to their former *e·*,
55 shall return to your former *e·*.
Da 11: 7 shall one stand up in his *e·*, *3653
20 Then shall stand up in his *e·* * "
21 And in his *e·* shall stand up a vile * "
38 in his *e·* shall he honour the God * "
Ac 22: 5 and all the *e·* of the elders:
Lu 1:48 the low *e·* of his handmaiden:
Ro 12:16 condescend to men of low *e·*. *
Col 4: 8 he might know your *e·*, and *3588, 4012*
Jude 6 which kept not their first *e·*, *

estates
Eze 36:11 I will settle you after your old *e·*,
M'r 6:21 captains, and chief *e·* of Galilee; *

esteem See also ESTEEMED; ESTEEMETH; ESTEEMING.
Job 36:19 Will he *e·* thy riches? no, not *6186
Ps 119:128 I *e·* all thy precepts...to be right;
Isa 53: 4 yet we did *e·* him stricken, 2803
Ph'p 2: 3 *e·* other better than themselves. **2233*
1Th 5:13 And to *e·* them very highly in love *

esteemed
De 32:15 lightly *e·* the Rock of his salvation.5034
1Sa 2:30 despise me shall be lightly *e·*. 7043
18:23 I am a poor man, and lightly *e·*? "
Job 23:12 I have *e·* the words of his mouth *6845
Pr 17:28 shutteth his lips is *e·* a man of
Isa 29:16 shall be *e·* as the potter's clay *2803
17 fruitful field shall be *e·* as a forest?* "
53: 3 was despised, and we *e·* him not. "

La 4: 2 are they e' as earthern pitchers, 2803
Lu 16:15 which is highly e' among men *
1Co 6: 4 them to judge who are least e' *1848

esteemeth
Job 41:27 He e' iron as straw, and brass *2803
Ro 14: 5 One man e' one day above another:2919
5 another e' every day alike.
14 but to him that e' any thing to be *3049

esteeming
He 11:26 E' the reproach of Christ greater *2233

Esther (*est'-thur*) See also ESTHER'S; HADASSAH.
Es 2: 7 brought up Hadassah, that is, E', 635
8 E' was brought also unto the king's "
10 E' had not shewed her people nor "
11 to know how E' did, and what "
15 Now when the turn of E', the "
15 E' obtained favour in the sight of "
16 E' was taken unto king Ahasuerus "
17 king loved E' above all the women, "
20 E' had not yet shewed her kindred "
20 E' did the commandment of "
22 who told it unto E' the queen; "
22 and E' certified the king thereof "
4: 5 Then called E' for Hatach, one of "
8 to shew it unto E', and to declare "
9 Hatach came and told E' the words "
10 Again E' spake unto Hatach, and "
13 Mordecai commanded to answer E', "
15 E' bade them return Mordecai this "
17 to all that E' had commanded "
5: 1 that E' put on her royal apparel, "
2 when the king saw E' the queen "
2 held out to E' the golden sceptre "
2 E' drew near, and touched the top "
3 What wilt thou queen E'? "
4 E' answered, If it seem good unto "
5 that he may do as E' had said. "
5 the banquet that E' had prepared. "
6 said unto E' at the banquet of wine, "
7 Then answered E', and said, My "
12 E' the queen did let no man come "
6:14 the banquet that E' had prepared. "
7: 1 came to banquet with E' the queen. "
2 the king said again unto E' on the "
2 What is thy petition, queen E'? "
3 E' the queen answered and said, "
5 answered and said unto E' the "
6 E' said, The adversary and enemy "
7 to make request for his life to E' "
8 upon the bed whereon E' was. "
8: 1 the Jews' enemy unto E' the queen. "
1 E' had told what he was unto her. "
2 E' set Mordecai over the house of "
3 E' spake yet again before the king, "
4 out the golden sceptre toward E'. "
4 E' arose, and stood before the king. "
7 Ahasuerus said unto E' the queen "
7 have given E' the house of Haman, "
9:12 the king said unto E' the queen, "
13 Then said E', If it please the king, "
25 when E' came before the king, *
29 Then E' the queen, the daughter of 635
31 E' the queen had enjoined them, "
32 the decree of E' confirmed these "

Esther's (*es'-thurs*)
Es 2:18 and his servants, even E' feast; 635
4: 4 E' maids and her chamberlains "
12 they told to Mordecai E' words. "

estimate
Le 27:14 then the priest shall e' it, whether 6186
14 as the priest shall e' it, so shall "

estimation See also ESTIMATIONS.
Le 5:15 with thy e' by shekels of silver, 6187
18 with thy e', for a trespass offering, "
6: 6 with thy e', for a trespass offering, "
27: 2 shall be for the Lord by thy e'. "
3 And thy e' shall be of the male "
3 thy e' shall be fifty shekels of silver, "
4 thy e' shall be thirty shekels. "
5 then thy e' shall be of the male "
6 e' shall be of the male five shekels "
6 for the female thy e' shall be three "
7 thy e' shall be fifteen shekels. "
8 But if he be poorer than thy e', "
13 add a fifth part thereof unto thy e'. "
15 part of the money of thy e' unto it, "
16 e' shall be according to the seed "
17 year of jubile, according to thy e' "
18 and it shall be abated from thy e'. "
19 part of the money of thy e' unto it, "
23 unto him the worth of thy e', even "
23 he shall give thine e' in that day, "
27 redeem it according to thine e', "
27 it shall be sold according to thy e'. "
Nu 18:16 according to thine e', for the money "

estimations
Le 27:25 thy e' shall be according to the 6187

estranged
Job 19:13 mine acquaintance are verily e' 2114
Ps 58: 3 The wicked are e' from the womb: "
78:30 They were not e' from their lust. "
Jer 19: 4 and have e' this place, and have 5234
Eze 14: 5 they are all e' from me through 2114

Etam (*e'-tam*)
J'g 15: 8 dwelt in the top of the rock E'. 5862
11 went to the top of the rock E', and "
1Ch 4: 3 And these were of the father of E'; "
32 their villages were, E' and Ain, "
2Ch 11: 6 He built even Bethlehem, and E', "

eternal
De 33:27 The e' God is thy refuge, and 6924
Isa 60:15 I will make thee an e' excellency, 5769
M't 19:16 shall I do, that I may have e' life? 166
25:46 but the righteous into life e'. "
M'r 3:29 in danger of e' damnation: "
10:17 I do that I may inherit e' life? "
30 and in the world to come e' life. "
Lu 10:25 what shall I do to inherit e' life? "
18:18 what shall I do to inherit e' life? "
Joh 3:15 should not perish, but have e' life. "
4:36 and gathereth fruit unto life e': "
5:39 for in them ye think ye have e' life: "
6:54 and drinketh my blood, hath e' life; "
68 thou hast the words of e' life. "
10:28 And I give unto them e' life; "
12:25 this world shall keep it unto life e'. "
17: 2 he should give e' life to as many as "
3 this is life e', that they might know "
Ac 13:48 many as were ordained to e' life. "
Ro 1:20 even his e' power and Godhead; 126
2: 7 honour and immortality, e' life: 166
5:21 through righteousness unto e' life "
6:23 but the gift of God is e' life through "
2Co 4:17 exceeding and e' weight of glory; "
18 the things which are not seen are e'. "
5: 1 made with hands, e' in the heavens. "
Eph 3:11 According the e' purpose which 165
1Ti 1:17 Now unto the King e', immortal, "
6:12 lay hold on e' life, whereunto thou 166
19 that they may lay hold on e' life. * "
2Ti 2:10 is in Christ Jesus with e' glory. "
Tit 1: 2 In hope of e' life, which God, that "
3: 7 according to the hope of e' life. "
Heb 5: 9 became the author of e' salvation "
6: 2 of the dead, and of e' judgment. "
9:12 having obtained e' redemption "
14 who through the e' Spirit offered "
15 the promise of e' inheritance. "
1Pe 5:10 who hath called us unto his e' glory "
1Jo 1: 2 shew unto you that e' life, which "
2:25 he hath promised us, even e' life. "
3:15 no murderer hath e' life abiding in "
5:11 that God hath given to us e' life, "
13 ye may know that ye have e' life, "
20 This is the true God, and e' life. "
Jude 7 suffering the vengeance of e' fire. "
21 of our Lord Jesus Christ unto e' life. "

eternity
Isa 57:15 and lofty One that inhabiteth e', 5703

Etham (*e'-tham*)
Ex 13:20 and encamped in E', in the edge of 864
Nu 33: 6 and pitched in E', which is in the "
7 they removed from E', and turned "
8 journey in the wilderness of E', "

Ethan (*e'-than*)
1Ki 4:31 than E' the Ezrahite, and Heman, 387
1Ch 2: 6 And the sons of Zera; Zimri, and E', "
8 And the sons of E'; Azariah. "
6:42 The son of E', the son of Zimmah, "
44 E' the son of Kishi, the son of Abdi, "
15:17 of Merari their brethren, E' the son "
19 the singers, Heman, Asaph, and E', "
Ps 89:*title* Maschil of E' the Ezrahite. "

Ethanim (*eth'-a-nim*)
1Ki 8: 2 at the feast in the month E', 388

Ethbaal (*eth'-ba-al*)
1Ki 16:31 to wife Jezebel the daughter of E' 856

Ether (*e'-ther*)
Jos 15:42 Libnah, and E', and Ashan, 6281
19: 7 Ain, Remmon, and E', and Ashan; "

Ethiopia (*e-the-o'-pe-ah*) See also CUSH; ETHIOPIAN.
Ge 2:13 compasseth the whole land of E' *3568
2Ki 19: 9 heard say of Tirhakah king of E', "
Es 1: 1 reigned from India even unto E', "
8: 9 which are from India unto E', "
Job 28:19 The topaz of E' shall not equal it, "
Ps 68:31 E' shall soon stretch out her hands "
87: 4 behold Philistia, and Tyre, with E'; "
Isa 18: 1 which is beyond the rivers of E': "
20: 3 wonder upon Egypt and upon E'; "
5 afraid and ashamed of E' their "
37: 9 concerning Tirhakah king of E', "
43: 3 thy ransom, E' and Seba for thee. "
45:14 of Egypt, and merchandise of E' "
Eze 29:10 even unto the borders of E'. "
30: 4 and great pain shall be in E', "
5 E', and Libya, and Lydia, and all "
38: 5 Persia, E', and Libya with them; * "
Na 3: 9 E' and Egypt were her strength, "
Zep 3:10 From beyond the rivers of E' my "
Ac 8:27 and, behold, a man of E', 128

Ethiopian See also ETHIOPIANS.
Nu 12: 1 against Moses because of the E' *3569
1 for he had married an E' woman. * "
2Ch 14: 9 out against them Zerah the E' "
Jer 13:23 Can the E' change his skin, or the "
38: 7 Now when Ebed-melech the E', "
10 commanded Ebed-melech the E', "
12 Ebed-melech the E' said unto "
39:16 and speak to Ebed-melech the E', "

Ethiopians
2Ch 12: 3 Lubims, the Sukkiims, and the E'. 3569
14:12 the Lord smote the E' before Asa, "
12 before Judah; and the E' fled. "
13 and the E' were overthrown, "
16: 8 Were not the E' and the Lubims "
21:16 Arabians, that were near the E': "
Isa 20: 4 Egyptians prisoners, and the E' * "
Jer 46: 9 E' and the Libyans, that handle * "
Eze 30: 9 to make the careless E' afraid, "
Da 11:43 and the E' shall be at his steps. "
Am 9: 7 not as children of the E' unto me, "
Zep 2:12 Ye E' also, ye shall be slain 3569
Ac 8:27 under Candace queen of the E', 128

Ethnan (*eth'-nan*)
1Ch 4: 7 Zereth, and Jezoar, and E'. 869

Ethni (*eth'-ni*) See also JEATERAI.
1Ch 6:41 The son of E', the son of Zerah, 867

Eubulus (*yu-bu'-lus*)
2Ti 4:21 E' greeteth thee, and Pudens, and 2103

Eunice (*yu-ni'-see*)
2Ti 1: 5 Lois, and thy mother E'; and I am 2131

eunuch See also EUNUCHS.
Isa 56: 3 neither let the e' say, Behold, I 5631
Jer 52:25 e', which had the charge of the * "
Ac 8:27 an e' of great authority under 2135
34 the e' answered Philip, and said, "
36 the e' said, See, here is water; "
38 the water, both Philip and the e'; "
39 that the e' saw him no more: "

eunuchs
2Ki 9:32 looked out to him two or three e'. 5631
20:18 and they shall be e' in the palace of "
Isa 39: 7 and they shall be e' in the palace of "
56: 4 thus saith the Lord unto the e' "
Jer 29: 2 and the queen, and the e', the "
34:19 the princes of Jerusalem, the e', "
Jer 38: 7 Ethiopian, one of the e' which * "
41:16 the children, and the e', whom "
Da 1: 3 Ashpenaz the master of his e', "
7 the prince of the e' gave names: "
8 he requested of the prince of the e' "
9 tender love with the prince of the e'. "
10 prince of the e' said unto Daniel, "
11 prince of the e' had set over Daniel, "
18 prince of the e' brought them in "
M't 19:12 For there are some e', which were 2135
12 and there are some e', which 2134
12 which were made e' of men: "
12 and there be e', which have made 2135
12 have made themselves e' for the 2134

Euodias (*yu-o'-de-as*)
Ph'p 4: 2 beseech E', and beseech Syntyche,*2136

Euphrates (*yu-fra'-teze*)
Ge 2:14 Assyria. And the fourth river is E'. 6578
15:18 unto the great river, the river E': "
De 1: 7 unto the great river, the river E'. "
11:24 from the river, the river E', even "
Jos 1: 4 unto the great river, the river E', "
2Sa 8: 3 recover his border at the river E'.* "
2Ki 23:29 the king of Assyria to the river E': "
24: 7 river of Egypt unto the river E' "
1Ch 5: 9 the wilderness from the river E': "
18: 3 his dominion by the river E'. "
2Ch 35:20 to fight against Carchemish by E': "
Jer 13: 4 upon thy loins, and arise, go to E', "
5 went, and hid it by E', as the Lord "
6 Arise, go to E', and take the girdle "
7 Then I went to E', and digged, and "
46: 2 of Egypt, which was by the river E' "
6 towards the north by the river E'. "
10 the north country by the river E'. "
51:63 it, and cast it into the midst of E': "
Re 9:14 are bound in the great river E'. 2166
16:12 his vial upon the great river E'; "

Euroclydon (*yu-roc'-lid-on*)
Ac 27:14 a tempestuous wind, called E'. 2148

Eutychus (*yu'-tik-us*)
Ac 20: 9 a certain young man named E', 2161

evangelist See also EVANGELISTS.
Ac 21: 8 entered the house of Philip the e', 2099
2Ti 4: 5 afflictions, do the work of an e', "

evangelists
Eph 4:11 and some, e'; and some, pastors 2099

Eve (*eev*)
Ge 3:20 Adam called his wife's name E'; 2332
4: 1 And Adam knew E' his wife; and "
2Co 11: 3 the serpent beguiled E' through 2096
1Ti 2:13 Adam was first formed, then E'.

even See also EVENING; EVENTIDE.
Ge 6:17 behold, I e' I, do bring a flood *
9: 3 e' as the green herb have I given *
10: 9 E' as Nimrod the mighty hunter *
19 and Zeboim, e' unto Lasha. *
21 e' to him were children born. *1571
13: 3 from the south e' to Bethel, *
10 e' as the garden of the Lord, *
14:23 from a thread e' to a shoelatchet, *5704
19: 1 came two angels to Sodom at e'; 6153
4 men of the city, e' the men of Sodom,
9 pressed sore upon the man, e' Lot,
20: 5 she, e' she herself said, He is my 1571
21:10 be heir with my son, e' with Isaac.
24:11 e' the time that women go to draw*
26:28 e' betwixt us and thee, and let us
27:34 Bless me, e' me also, O my father. 1571
38 bless me, e' me also, O my father.
34:29 spoiled e' all that was in the house.
35:14 with him, e' a pillar of stone; *
37:18 e' before he came unto them, *
44:18 servant: for thou art e' as Pharaoh.
46:18 she bare unto Jacob, e' sixteen souls.
34 our youth e' until now, both we,
47: 2 some of his brethren, e' five men,*
21 of the borders of Egypt e' to the other
49:22 Joseph is..., e' a fruitful bough *
25 E' by the God of thy father, who
Ex 3: 1 mountain of God, e' to Horeb. *
4:16 e' he shall be to thee instead of *
22 Israel is my son, e' my firstborn: *
23 will slay thy son, e' thy firstborn.*
9:18 foundation thereof e' until now.
10:12 eat every herb of the land, e' all 853

Ex 10:21 e' darkness that may be felt.
11: 5 e' unto the firstborn of the
12:15 e' the first day ye shall put away 389
18 fourteenth day of the month at e', 6153
18 twentieth day of the month at e'. "
19 e' that soul shall be cut off from *
38 flocks, and herds, e' very much cattle.
41 e' the selfsame day it came to pass,
14:23 the sea, e' all Pharaoh's horses, *
16: 6 At e', then ye shall know that the 6153
12 At e' ye shall eat flesh, and in the "
13 that at e' the quails came up, and "
18:14 by thee from morning unto e'? "
23:31 e' unto the sea of the Philistines,
25: 9 instruments thereof, e' so shall ye
19 e' of the mercy seat shall ye make *
27: 5 be e' to the midst of the altar. *
28: 1 e' Aaron, Nadab and Abihu, Eleazar
8 e' of gold, of blue, and purple, *
17 of stones, e' four rows of stones: *
42 from the loins e' unto the thighs
29:27 e' of that which is for Aaron, and of
28 e' their heave offering unto the Lord.
39 other lamb thou shalt offer at e': 6153
41 other lamb thou shalt offer at e', "
30: 8 Aaron lighteth the lamps at e',
21 e' to him and to his seed throughout
23 so much, e' two hundred shekels,
33 upon a stranger, shall e' be cut off*
38 to smell thereto, shall e' be cut off*
32:29 e' every man upon his son, and *3588
35:35 e' of them that do any work, and of
36: 2 e' every one whose heart stirred
37: 3 e' two rings upon the one side of it,
9 e' to the mercy seatward were *
38:21 of the tabernacle, e' of the tabernacle
24 e' the gold of the offering, was twenty
39:37 e' with the lamps to be set in order,
43 Lord had commanded, e' so had they
Le 1: 2 offering of the cattle, e' of the herd,
2:14 corn dried by the fire, e' corn *
3:14 his offering, e' an offering made by
4:12 E' the whole bullock shall he carry
17 before the Lord e' before the vail.*
5:12 of it, e' a memorial thereof, and * 853
6: 5 shall e' restore it in the principal,
15 e' the memorial of it, unto the *
7: 8 e' the priest shall have to himself
20 upon him, e' that soul shall be cut*
21 the Lord, e' that soul shall be cut*
25 e' the soul that eateth it shall be
27 of blood, e' that soul shall be cut *
8: 9 mitre, e' upon his forefront, did *
11:11 They shall be e' an abomination *
22 E' these of them ye may eat; the
24 shall be unclean until the e'. 6153
25 clothes, and be unclean until the e'."
27 carcase shall be unclean until the e'."
28 clothes, and be unclean until the e':"
31 dead, shall be unclean until the e'. "
32 and it shall be unclean until the e';"
39 thereof shall be unclean until the e'."
40 clothes, and be unclean until the e': "
40 and be unclean until the e'. "
13:12 from his head e' to his foot,
18 e' in the skin thereof, was a boil, *
30 it is a dry scall, e' a leprosy upon*
38 bright spots, e' white bright spots,
14: 9 e' all his hair he shall shave off: and
31 E' such as he is able to get, the one
46 up shall be unclean until the e'. 6153
15: 5, 6, 7, 8 and be unclean until the e'. "
10 him shall be unclean until the e'. "
10, 11, 16, 17, 18 unclean until the e'. "
19 her shall be unclean until the e'. "
21, 22 and be unclean until the e'. "
23 he shall be unclean until the e'. "
27 water, and be unclean until the e'. "
16:32 linen clothes, e' the holy garments:
17: 5 e' that they may bring them unto
9 e' that man shall be cut off from
10 I will e' set my face against that *
13 e' pour out the blood thereof, *
15 and be unclean until the e': 6153
18: 9, 10 e' their nakedness thou shalt not
29 e' the souls that commit them shall
19:21 e' a ram for a trespass offering.
20:10 e' he that committeth adultery with
22: 6 such shall be unclean until e', 6153
23: 2 convocations, e' these are my feasts.
4 of the Lord, e' holy convocations,
5 day of the first month at e' 6153
16 E' unto the morrow after the
18 e' an offering made by fire, of sweet
32 the ninth day of the month at e', 6153
32 from e' unto e', shall ye celebrate "
24: 7 e' an offering made by fire unto the
26:16 I will e' appoint over you terror, *
28 I, e' I, will chastise you seven * 637
34 e' then shall the land rest, and enjoy
43 because, e' because they despised
27: 3 twenty years old e' unto sixty
3 e' thy estimation shall be fifty
5 years old e' unto twenty years old,
6 a month old e' unto five years old,
18 the years that remain, e' unto *
23 e' unto the year of the jubilee: *
24 e' to him to whom the possession of
32 e' of whatsoever passeth under *
Nu 1:21 e' of the tribe of Reuben, were *
23 e' of the tribe of Simeon, were *
25 e' of the tribe of Gad, were forty *
27 e' of the tribe of Judah, were *
29 e' of the tribe of Issachar, were *
31 e' of the tribe of Zebulun, were *
33 e' of the tribe of Ephraim, were *

Nu 1:35 e' of the tribe of Manasseh, were *
37 e' of the tribe of Benjamin, were *
39 e' of the tribe of Dan, were *
41 e' of the tribe of Asher, were *
43 e' of the tribe of Naphtali, were *
46 E' all they that were numbered were
3:22 e' those that were numbered of them
38 e' before the tabernacle of the *
47 shalt e' take five shekels apiece *
4: 3 e' until fifty years old, all that
14 e' the censers, the fleshhooks, *
30 e' unto fifty years old shalt thou
35 years old and upward e' unto fifty
39 and upward e' unto fifty years old,
40 E' those that were numbered of them,
43 e' unto fifty years old, every one
44 E' those that were numbered of them
47 e' unto fifty years old, every one
48 E' those that were numbered of them,
5: 8 unto the Lord, e' to the priest; *
26 e' the memorial thereof, and burn*
6: 4 from the kernels e' to the husk.
7:10 e' the princes offered their offering
8: 8 e' fine flour mingled with oil, *
16 e' instead of the firstborn of all the
9: 3 fourteenth day of this month, at e',6153
5 day of the first month at e' in the "
11 day of the second month at e' they "
13 e' the same soul shall be cut off *
15 and at e' there was upon the 6153
21 abode from e' unto the morning,* "
11:20 But e' a whole month, until it *5704
12: 8 mouth to mouth, e' apparently,
14:19 from Egypt e' until now.
34 e' forty days, each day for a year,
34 e' forty years, and ye shall know
37 E' those men that did bring up the
45 discomfited them, e' unto Hormah.
15:23 E' all that the Lord hath commanded
16: 5 E' to morrow the Lord will shew*
5 e' him whom he hath chosen will
17: 6 fathers' houses, e' twelve rods:
18:21 e' the service of the tabernacle of
26 e' a tenth part of the tithe. *
29 e' the hallowed part thereof out of it.853
19: 7 shall be unclean until the e'. 6153
8 and shall be unclean until the e'. "
10 and be unclean until the e': "
19 in water, shall be clean at e'. "
21 shall be unclean until e'. "
22 it shall be unclean until e'. "
20: 1 e' the whole congregation, into the
22 e' the whole congregation, journeyed
29 e' all the house of Israel.
21:24 e' unto the children of Ammon:
26 out of his hand, e' unto Arnon.
30 is perished e' unto Dibon, and
30 laid them waste e' unto Nophah,
25:13 e' the covenant of an everlasting*
14 e' that was slain with the *
27:21 with him, e' all the congregation.
28: 4 other lamb shalt thou offer at e'; 6153
8 other lamb shalt thou offer at e': "
31:47 E' of the children of Israel's half,
51 them, e' all wrought jewels.
32: 4 E' the country which the Lord *
33 them, e' to the children of Gad,
33 e' the cities of the country round
33:49 from Beth-jesimoth e' unto
34: 2 e' the land of Canaan with the
6 e' have the great sea for a border:*
36:10 E' as the Lord commanded Moses,
De 1:44 you in Seir, e' unto Hormah.
2:22 in their stead e' unto this day:
23 e' unto Azzah, the Caphtorims, *
36 e' unto Gilead, there was not one
3:16 from Gilead e' unto the river Jabbok,
16 the border e' unto the river Jabbok,
17 from Chinnereth e' unto the sea
17 the sea, e' the salt sea, under *
4: 5 e' as the Lord my God commanded
13 to perform, e' ten commandments;
19 stars, e' all the host of heaven,
20 e' out of Egypt, to be unto him a *
24 consuming fire, e' a jealous God. *
30 e' in the latter days, if thou turn *
48 e' unto mount Sion, which is Hermon,
49 e' unto the sea of the plain,
5: 3 but with us, e' us, who are all of
23 e' all the heads of your tribes,
9: 9 e' the tables of the covenant which
11 e' the tables of the covenant.
21 e' until it was as small as dust: *
10:15 e' you above all people, as it is this
11:12 the year e' unto the end of the
24 e' unto the uttermost sea shall
12: 5 e' unto his habitation shall you
22 E' as the roebuck and the hart 389
30 e' so will I do likewise. 1571
31 for e' their sons and their "
13: 7 the earth, e' unto the other end
16: 3 bread therewith, e' the bread of
4 first day at e', remain all night 6153
6 sacrifice the passover at e', "
17: 5 e' that man or that woman, and
18:20 e' that prophet shall die. *
20:14 e' all the spoil thereof, shalt thou
21: 3 e' the elders of that city shall take
22:26 e' so is this matter:
23: 2 e' to his tenth generation shall 1571
3 e' to their tenth generation shall "
16 e' among you, in that place *
18 for e' both these are abomination 1571
23 e' a freewill offering, according *
25:18 e' all that were feeble behind *
26: 9 e' a land that floweth with *

De 28:59 e' great plagues, and of long
64 of the earth e' unto the other;
64 have known, e' wood and stone.
67 Would God it were e'! and at e' 6153
29:24 E' all nations shall say,
31:21 e' now, before I have brought ‡
32:31 e' our enemies themselves being
39 that I, e' I, am he, and there is
33: 4 e' the inheritance of the *
Jos 1: 2 e' to the children of Israel.
4 e' unto the great river, the river
2: 1 Go view the land, e' Jericho. *
24 for e' all the inhabitants of the *1571
3:16 of the plain, e' the salt sea, failed,
5: 4 e' all the men of war, died in the
10 fourteenth day of the month at e' 6153
6:17 e' it, and all that are therein, to the
25 in Israel e' unto this day; *
7: 5 before the gate e' unto Shebarim,
11 e' taken of the accursed thing, 1571
11 put it e' among their own stuff. "
8: 4 the city, e' behind the city: *
11 e' the people of war that were with
13 e' all the host that was on the north
25 e' all the men of Ai.
28 e' a desolation unto this day.
9:20 we will e' let them live, lest *
27 e' unto this day, in the place *
10:41 Kadesh-barnea e' unto Gaza,
41 country of Goshen, e' unto Gibeon.
11: 4 e' as the sand that is upon the sea
17 E' from the mount Halak, *
17 e' unto Baal-gad in the valley of
12: 2 Gilead, e' unto the river Jabbok,
3 e' the salt sea on the east,
7 e' unto the mount Halak,
13: 3 e' unto the borders of Ekron
8 e' as Moses the servant of the Lord
24 e' unto the children of Gad *
27 e' unto the edge of the sea of *
31 e' to the one half of the children
14:10 e' since the Lord spake this word*
11 e' so is my strength now, for
15: 1 e' to the border of Edom the *
5 e' unto the end of Jordan.
13 e' the city of Arba the father of
46 From Ekron e' unto the sea,
16: 5 e' the border of their inheritance
17:11 and her towns, e' three countries.
17 e' to Ephraim and to Manasseh,
19: 1 e' for the tribe of the children of
28 and Kanah, e' unto great Zidon;
32 e' for the children of Naphtali
50 e' Timnath-serah in mount
21:20 e' they had the cities of their lot *
23: 4 e' unto the great sea westward.
12 e' these that remain among you,
24: 2 e' Terah, the father of Abraham,
12 e' the two kings of the Amorites;
18 e' the Amorites which dwelt in the
J'g 3: 1 e' as many of Israel as had not
9 e' Othniel the son of Kenaz, 853
4:13 e' nine hundred chariots of iron,
5: 3 I, e' I, will sing unto the Lord;
5 e' that Sinai from before the Lord
11 e' the righteous acts toward the
15 e' Issachar, and also Barak: *
6: 3 the east, e' they came up against*
25 e' the second bullock of seven years
7:22 fellow, e' throughout all the host:*
8:14 e' threescore and seventeen men.*
19 e' the sons of my mother: *
27 put it in his city, e' in Ophrah:
9:40 e' unto the entering of the gate.
11:13 of Egypt, from Arnon e' unto Jabbok,
22 Amorites, from Arnon e' unto Jabbok.
22 the wilderness e' unto Jordan.
33 e' till thou come to Minnith, *
33 e' twenty cities, and unto the plain
36 e' of the children of Ammon.
18:15 e' unto the house of Micah, and
19:16 there came an old man . . . at e', 6153
20: 1 from Dan e' to Beer-sheba,
2 e' of all the tribes of Israel,
23 wept before the Lord until e', 6153
26 and fasted that day until e', "
33 e' out of the meadows of Gibeah.
21: 2 abode there till e' before God, 6153
Ru 2: 7 continued e' from the morning 227
15 her glean e' among the sheaves, 1571
17 she gleaned in the field until e', 6153
1Sa 3:20 from Dan e' to Beer-sheba knew
5: 6 e' Ashdod and the coasts thereof. 853
6:18 e' unto the great stone of Abel,
19 e' he smote of the people fifty
7:14 from Ekron e' unto Gath;
8: 8 e' unto this day, wherewith they
14 e' the best of them, and give them
14:21 e' they also turned to be with
22 e' they also followed hard after
17:40 in a shepherd's bag...e' in a scrip;
52 e' unto Gath, and unto Ekron.
18: 4 e' to his sword, and to his bow,
11 smite David e' to the wall with it.
19:10 David e' to the wall with the javelin:
20: 4 I will e' do it for thee.
5 the field unto the third day at e'. 6153
16 Lord e' require it at the hand of *
25 set...e' upon a seat by the wall:
25:25 regard this man of Belial, e' Nabal:
27 it e' be given unto the young men*
26: 8 him...e' to the earth at once, *
27: 3 e' David with his two wives,
8 e' unto the land of Egypt.
28: 3 him in Ramah, e' in his own city.
17 it to thy neighbour, e' to David:

1Sa 30:17 the twilight e' unto the evening
26 the elders of Judah, e' to his friends,
2Sa 1: 2 It came e' to pass on the third day,
12 and fasted until e', for Saul, and 6153
2: 5 unto your Lord, e' unto Saul,
3: 9 to David, e' so I do to him; 3588
10 from Dan e' to Beer-sheba.
15 e' from Phaltiel the son of Laish.
6: 5 e' on harps, and on psalteries, *
19 e' among the whole multitude of
7: 6 out of Egypt, e' to this day,
23 like thy people, e' like Israel,
8: 2 e' with two lines measured he to *
10: 4 their garments...e' to their buttocks,
11:13 at e' he went out to lie on his bed 6153
23 were upon them e' unto the entering
14:25 his foot e' to the crown of his head
15:12 from his city, e' from Giloh,
21 e' there also will thy servant be. 3588
17:11 from Dan e' to Beer-sheba,
18: 5 with the young man, e' with Absalom.
19:11 come to the king, e' to his house. *
14 e' as the heart of one man;
32 very aged man, e' fourscore years
20: 2 from Jordan e' to Jerusalem.
21 against the king, e' against David:
22:42 e' unto the Lord, but he answered
23: 4 e' a morning without clouds; *
24: 2 from Dan e' to Beer-sheba,
7 south of Judah e' to Beer-sheba.*
15 e' to the time appointed:
15 Dan e' to Beer-sheba seventy
1Ki 1:26 But me, e' me thy servant,
30 E' as I sware unto thee by the *3588
30 e' so will I certainly do this day, * "
37 e' so be he with Solomon, and
48 mine eyes e' seeing it.
2:22 e' for him, and for Abiathar the priest,
4:12 e' unto the place that is beyond *
24 from Tiphsah e' to Azzah,
25 from Dan e' to Beer-sheba,
29 e' as the sand that is on the sea shore.
33 e' unto the hyssop that springeth
6:16 he e' built them for it within, *
16 e' for the oracle, e' for the most holy
7: 7 e' the porch of judgment:
9 e' from the foundation unto the coping.
10 costly stones, e' great stones,
42 e' two rows of pomegranates for *
51 e' the silver, and the gold, 853
8: 4 e' those did the priests and the Levites
6 e' under the wings of the cherubims.
29 e' toward the place of which thou
39 for thou, e' thou only, knowest the
65 and seven days, e' fourteen days.
11:26 Jeroboam...e' he lifted up his *
35 will give it unto thee, e' ten tribes.
12:27 e' unto Rehoboam king of Judah,
30 went to worship... e' unto Dan.
33 e' in the month which he had devised
13:34 e' to cut it off, and to destroy it
14:14 that day: but what? e' now. 1571
15:13 Maachah...e' her he removed *
28 E' in the third year of Asa king of
16: 7 e' for all the evil that he did in *
18:22 I, e' I only, remain a prophet of the
26 from morning e' until noon,
19:10, 14 and I, e' I only, am left; and they
20: 3 children, e' the goodliest, are mine.
14 E' by the young men of the *
15 people, e' all the children of Israel,
21:11 e' the elders and the nobles who were
13 against him, e' against Naboth, in the
19 shall dogs lick thy blood, e' thine.1571
22:35 was stayed up...and died at e': 6153
2Ki 3:24 Moabites, e' in their own country.*
26 e' unto the king of Edom:
4: 3 of thy neighbours, e' empty vessels;
5:22 Behold, e' now there be come...two
7: 6 of horses, e' the noise of a great host:
7 e' the camp as it was, and fled for
13 they are e' as all the multitude of*
8: 6 she left the land, e' until now.
9 a present...e' of every good thing
9: 4 e' the young man the prophet, went
6 anointed thee king...e' over Israel.
20 saying, He came e' unto them, and
10: 3 Look e' out the best and meetest *
14 e' two and forty men;
33 e' Gilead and Bashan.
11: 2 they hid him, e' him and his nurse,
5 shall e' be keepers of the watch *
7 e' they shall keep the watch of the
12: 4 e' the money of every one that *
14:10 e' thou, and Judah with thee?
29 e' with the kings of Israel;
15:20 e' of all the mighty men of wealth,
17:16 molten images, e' two calves,
18: 8 e' unto Gaza, and the borders *
10 e' in the sixth year of Hezekiah,
21 e' upon Egypt, on which if a man
19:15 thou art the God, e' thou alone,
19 thou art the Lord God, e' thou only.
22 e' against the Holy One of Israel.
20:14 from a far country, e' from Babylon.
21:15 out of Egypt, e' unto this day.
22:16 e' all the words of the book which
24:14 e' ten thousand captives, and all the
16 the men of might, e' seven thousand,
16 e' them the king of Babylon brought
25:22 e' over them he made Gedaliah . . .
23 e' Ishmael the son of Nethaniah, and
1Ch 2:23 the towns thereof, e' threescore cities.
4:15 and the sons of Elah, e' Kenaz. *
39 e' unto the east side of the valley,
42 e' of the sons of Simeon, five hundred

1Ch 5: 8 e' unto Nebo and Baal-meon
24 e' Epher, and Ishi, and Eliel, and
26 e' the Reubenites, and the Gadites,
6:39 e' Asaph the son of Berachiah,
10:13 e' against the word of the Lord, *
11: 2 time past, e' when Saul was king, 1571
12: 2 e' of Saul's brethren of Benjamin.*
40 e' unto Issachar and Zebulun and
13: 5 from Shihor of Egypt e' unto the
14:16 smote the host . . . from Gibeon e'
16:16 E' of the covenant which he made*
19 When ye were but few, e' a few, *
17: 7 from the sheepcote, e' from *
24 Let it e' be established, *
24 Lord of hosts is . . . e' a God to Israel:
20: 3 E' so dealt David with all the *
21: 2 Israel from Beer-sheba e' unto Dan;
12 e' the pestilence, in the land, and the
17 e' I it is that have sinned and done evil
23:24 e' the chief of the fathers, as they were
30 morning . . . and likewise at e'; 6153
24:31 e' the principal fathers over against
25: 7 e' all that were cunning, was two
26:12 divisions of the porters, e' among
21 e' of Laadan the Gershonite, *
31 e' among the Hebronites, according to
28:15 E' the weight for the candlesticks*
19 e' all the works of this pattern.
20 the Lord God, e' my God, will be with
21 e' they shall be with thee for all *
29: 4 E' three thousand talents of gold,
21 e' a thousand bullocks, a thousand
2Ch 2: 3 As thou didst deal with David . . . e' so
9 E' to prepare me timber in abundance:
5: 7 e' under the wings of the cherubims:
13 It came e' to pass, as the trumpeters
13 was filled with a cloud, e' the house of
6:21 dwelling place, e' from heaven; and
33 e' from thy dwelling place, and do
39 e' from thy dwelling place, their prayer
8:10 chief of king Solomon's officers, e' two
13 E' after a certain rate every day,
13 e' in the feast of unleavened bread,
9:26 from the river e' unto the land of
11: 6 He built e' Beth-lehem, and Etam, and
13: 3 e' four hundred thousand chosen men:
5 e' to him and to his sons by a covenant
17: 7 to his princes, e' to Ben-hail, and to
8 he sent Levites, e' Shemaiah, and
18:13 e' what my God saith, that will *3588
21 prevail: go out, and do e' so.
34 against the Syrians until the e': 6153
19:10 ye shall e' warn them that they *
20: 4 e' out of all the cities of Judah 1571
24:14 e' vessels to minister, and to offer
25:13 from Samaria e' unto Beth-horon,
19 thou shouldest fall, e' thou, and Judah
26: 8 spread abroad e' to the entering in
19 leprosy e' rose up in his forehead*
28:10 are there not with you,e' with you,7535
27 buried him in the city, e' in
30: 5 from Beer-sheba e' to Dan,
10 and Manasseh e' unto Zebulun:
18 e' many of Ephraim, and Manasseh,
27 to his holy dwelling place, e' unto
31:16 e' unto every one that entereth into
33:14 e' to the entering in at the fish gate,
34: 6 and Simeon, e' unto Naphtali,
11 E' to the artificers and builders gave
24 e' all the curses that are written in the
27 I have e' heard thee also, saith *
33 e' to serve the Lord their God.
Ezr 1: 8 E' those did Cyrus king of Persia
3: 3 e' burnt offerings morning and evening.
4: 5 e' until the reign of Darius king
11 sent unto him,e' unto Artaxerxes*
5: 1 unto the Jews . . . e' unto them, *
16 since that time e' until now
6: 8 of the king's goods, e' of the tribute
7:11 e' a scribe of the words of the
21 And I, e' I Artaxerxes the king,
8:25 e' the offering of the house of our God,
26 I e' weighed unto their hand six
9: 1 e' of the Canaanites, the Hittites,
Ne 2:13 e' before the dragon well,
3: 1 e' unto the tower of Meah they
10 e' over against his house.
21 e' to the end of the house of
24 of the wall, e' unto the corner, *
27 e' unto the wall of Ophel. *
4: 3 E' that which they build, 1571
3 he shall e' break down their stone*
13 e' set the people after their families
5: 8 and will ye e' sell your brethren? 1571
11 Restore...e' this day, their lands, their
13 e' thus be he shaken out, and 3602
14 twentieth year e' unto the two and
15 yea, e' their servants bare rule
8:13 e' to understand the words of the law.
9: 6 Thou, e' thou, art Lord alone;
12:23 e' until the days of Johanan the son
37 e' unto the water gate eastward.
38 tower of the furnaces e' unto the broad
39 e' unto the sheep gate:
43 Jerusalem was heard e' afar off.
13:26 e' him did outlandish women
Es 1: 1 from India e' unto Ethiopia,
4 e' an hundred and fourscore days.
2:18 made a great feast...e' Esther's 853
3: 6 e' the people of Mordecai.
13 e' upon the thirteenth day of the
4: 2 came e' before the king's gate: 5704
5: 3 it shall be e' given thee to the half
6 e' to the half of the kingdom it
6:10 and do e' so to Mordecai the Jew,
7: 2 e' to the half of the kingdom.

Job 4: 8 E' as I have seen, they that plow*
21 they die, e' without wisdom. *
5: 5 and taketh it e' out of the thorns,
6: 9 E' that it would please God to destroy
10:21 e' to the land of darkness and the
15:26 runneth upon him, e' on his neck,*
17: 5 e' the eyes of his children shall fail.
11 e' the thoughts of my heart.
18:13 e' the firstborn of death shall *
21: 6 E' when I remember I am afraid,
23: 2 E' to day is my complaint bitter: 1571
3 that I might come e' to his seat!
13 his soul desireth, e' that he doeth.
24:17 them e' as the shadow of death: *
25: 5 Behold e' to the moon, and it
28: 4 e' the waters forgotten of the *
31: 6 me be weighed in an e' balance, 6664
34:17 Shall e' he that hateth right govern? 637
36:16 E' so would he have removed *
41: 9 cast down e' at the sight of him? 1571
42:16 his son's sons, e' four generations.
Ps 18: 6 before him, e' into his ears. *
41 e' unto the Lord, but he answered
21: 4 e' length of days for ever and ever.
24: 9 e' lift them up, ye everlasting *
26:12 My foot standeth in an e' place: 4334
27: 2 wicked, e' mine enemies and my foes,
35:23 to my judgment, e' unto my cause,
39:*title* the chief Musician, e' to Jeduthun,
2 I held my peace, e' from good;
40: 3 in my mouth, e' praise unto our God:
45:12 e' the rich among the people shall
47: 9 e' the people of the God of *
48:14 he will be our guide e' unto death.
50: 1 The mighty God, e' the Lord, ‡
7 I am God, e' thy God.
55:19 e' he that abideth of old.
57: 4 I lie e' among them that are set *
4 e the sons of men, whose teeth are
59:12 let them e' be taken in their pride:
64: 3 to shoot their arrows, e' bitter words:
65: 4 thy house, e' thy holy temple. *
67: 6 God, e' our own God, shall bless us.
68: 8 e' Sinai itself was moved at the ‡
17 thousand, e' thousands of angels:
19 loadeth...with benefits, e' the God of
24 e' the goings of my God, my King,
26 e' the Lord, from the fountain of
71:16 thy righteousness, e' of thine only.
22 e' thy truth, O my God:
73: 1 e' to such as are of a clean heart.
74: 3 e' all that the enemy hath done *
11 thy hand, e' thy right hand?
76: 7 Thou, e' thou, art to be feared:
77: 1 e' unto God with my voice;
78: 6 know them, e' the children which *
54 e' to this mountain, which his right
84: 2 yea, e' fainteth for the courts of 1571
3 e' thine altars, O Lord of hosts, my 853
90: 2 e' from everlasting to everlasting,
11 e' according to thy fear, so is thy*
91: 9 e' the most High, thy habitation:*
105:17 e' Joseph, who was sold for a *
20 e' the ruler of the people, and let
106: 7 him at the sea, e' at the Red sea.
38 blood, e' the blood of their sons
107:43 e' they shall understand the *
108: 1 and give praise, e' with my glory. 637
109:16 might e' slay the broken in heart.*
113: 8 e' with the princes of his people.
115:16 e' the heavens, are the Lord's: *
118:27 e' unto the horns of the altar.
119:41 e' thy salvation, according to thy
112 thy statutes alway, e' unto the end.
121: 8 time forth, and e' for evermore. *
125: 2 from henceforth e' for ever. *
131: 2 my soul is e' as a weaned child. *
133: 2 down upon the beard, e' Aaron's beard:
3 the blessing, e' life for evermore.
136:22 E' an heritage unto Israel his servant:
137: 7 it, e' to the foundation thereof.
139:10 E' there shall thy hand lead me, 1571
11 e' the night shall be light about *
146:10 e' thy God, O Zion, unto all *
148:14 e' of the children of Israel, a people
Pr 2:16 e' from the stranger which flattereth
3:12 e' as a father the son in whom he
8:16 e' all the judges of the earth.
14:13 E' in laughter the heart is 1571
20 is hated e' of his own neighbour: "
16: 4 e' the wicked for the day of evil. "
7 he maketh e' his enemies to be at "
17:15 e' they both are abomination to * "
28 E' a fool, when he holdeth his "
20:11 E' a child is known by his doings, "
12 Lord hath made e' both of them. "
22:19 known to thee this day, e' to thee. 637
23:15 my heart shall rejoice, e' mine. 1571
28: 9 e' his prayer shall be abomination. "
30: 1 of Jakeh, e' the prophecy: *
1 spake unto Ithiel, e' unto Ithiel *
Ec 2:12 e' that which hath been already 853
15 so it happeneth e' to me; 1571
3:19 e' one thing befalleth them:
4:16 e' of all that have been before them:
7:25 of folly, e' of foolishness and *
9: 1 in my heart e' to declare all this,
11: 5 e' so thou knowest not the works 3602
12:10 was upright, e' words of truth.
Ca 4: 2 flock of sheep that are e' shorn,
Isa 1: 6 soul of the foot e' unto the head
13 iniquity, e' the solemn meeting. *
4: 3 be called holy, e' every one that is
5: 9 shall be desolate, e' great and fair,
7: 6 in the midst...e' the son of Tabeal:
17 e' the king of Assyria. 853

Isa 7:23 it shall e' be for briers and thorns.
8: 7 and many, e' the king of Assyria, 853
8 he shall reach e' to the neck;
9: 7 justice from henceforth e' for ever.
9 all the people...e' Ephraim and the
10:21 shall return, e' the remnant of Jacob,
23 e' determined, in the midst of all *
13: 3 e' them that rejoice in my highness.
5 e' the Lord, and the weapons of his
12 precious than fine gold; e' a man
14: 9 e' all the chief ones of the earth;
18 kings...e' all of them, lie in glory, *
15: 4 shall be heard e' unto Jahaz:
16: 6 e' of his haughtiness, and his pride,
8 they are come e' unto Jazer they
18: 2 e' in vessels of bulrushes upon the
19:13 e' they that are the stay of the *
22 they shall return e' to the Lord, *
24 e' a blessing in the midst of the *
20: 4 e' with their buttocks uncovered,*
22:15 unto this treasurer, e' unto Shebna,
24 e' to all the vessels of flagons.
23: 4 spoken, e' the strength of the sea,*
24:15 e' the name of the Lord God of
16 songs, e' glory to the righteous. *
25: 5 e' the heat with the shadow of a *
10 e' as straw is trodden down for the
12 to the ground, e' to the dust.
26: 5 he layeth it low, e' to the ground;
5 he bringeth it e' to the dust.
6 tread it down, e' the feet of the poor,
27: 1 e' leviathan that crooked *
28:22 e' determined upon the whole *
29: 7 fight against Ariel, e' all that fight
8 It shall e' be as when an hungry *
14 e' a marvellous work and a wonder:
32: 7 e' when the needy speaketh right.
35: 2 rejoice e' with joy and singing: 637
4 e' God with a recompence; *
37:16 thou art the God, e' thou alone,
20 thou art the Lord, e' thou only.
23 e' against the Holy One of Israel.
38:11 I shall not see the Lord, e' the Lord,
12 sickness: from day e' to night wilt
13 my bones: from day e' to night wilt
39: 3 country unto me, e' from Babylon.
40:30 E' the youths shall faint and be weary,
41: 3 e' by the way that he had not gone
12 e' them that contended with thee:
28 e' among them, and there was no
43: 7 E' every one that is called by my*
11 I, e' I, am the Lord;
19 e' make a way in the wilderness, 637
25 I, e' I, am he that blotteth out
44: 8 ye are e' my witnesses. *
17 maketh a god, e' his graven image:
28 e' saying to Jerusalem, Thou shalt be
45: 4 have e' called thee by thy name: *
12 I, e' my hands, have stretched out
24 e' to him shall men come;
46: 4 And e' to your old age I am he;
4 e' to hoar hairs will I carry you:
4 e' I will carry, and will deliver *
47:15 e' thy merchants, from thy youth:*
48: 5 I have e' from the beginning *
6 have showed you new...e' hidden
7 e' before the day when thou *
11 For mine own sake, e' for mine *
15 I, e' I, have spoken;
20 utter it e' to the end of the earth;*
49:10 e' by the springs of water shall he
19 of thy destruction shall e' now be *3588
25 E' the captives of the mighty 1571
51:12 I, e' I, am he that comforteth you:
22 e' the dregs of the cup of my fury;
55: 3 e' the sure mercies of David.
56: 5 E' unto them will I give in mine *
7 E' them will I bring to my holy
57: 6 e' to them hast thou poured a 1571
7 e' thither wentest thou up to offer* "
9 didst debase thyself e' unto hell.
11 have not I held my peace e' of old,
65: 6 e' recompense into their bosom, *
66: 2 e' to him that is poor and of a contrite
Jer 3:25 from your youth e' unto this day,
4:12 E' a full wind from those places *
6:11 e' the husband with the wife 1571
13 the least of them e' unto the greatest
13 from the prophet e' unto the priest
19 e' the fruit of their thoughts,
7:11 Behold, e' I have seen it, 1571
15 e' the whole seed of Ephraim. 853
25 unto this day I have e' sent *
8:10 from the least e' unto the greatest
10 from the prophet e' unto the priest
9:15 will feed them, e' this people, with
22 E' the carcases of men shall fall *
10:11 e' they shall perish from the
11: 7 e' unto this day, rising early and
13 e' altars to burn incense unto Baal.
23 e' the year of their visitation.
12: 6 For e' thy brethren, and the house 1571
6 of thy father, e' they have dealt
12 from the one end of the land e' to
13:10 to worship them, shall e' be as this
13 inhabitants of this land, e' the kings
14 one against another, e' the fathers
18 shall come down, e' the crown of your
15:13 for all thy sins, e' in all thy borders.
16: 5 e' lovingkindness and mercies. 853
17: 4 And thou, e' thyself, shalt discontinue
10 I try the reins, e' to give every man
27 not to bear a burden, e' entering *
19:11 E' so will I break this people, 3602
12 and e' make this city as Tophet:
21: 5 with a strong arm, e' in anger,
Jer 22:25 whose face thou fearest, e' into the
23:12 e' the year of their visitation.
19 in fury, e' a grievous whirlwind: *
33 I will e' forsake you, *
34 I will e' punish that man
39 behold, I, e' I, will utterly forget *
24: 2 very good figs, e' like the figs
25: 3 Amon king of Judah, e' unto this day,
13 e' all that is written in this book.
31 noise shall come e' to the ends of
33 one end of the earth e' unto the other
28: 6 E' the prophet Jeremiah said,
11 E' so will I break the yoke 3602
29:23 I have not commanded them; e' I*
30: 7 none is like it: it is e' the time
31: 2 grace in the wilderness; e' Israel,
19 I was ashamed, yea, e' confounded,1571
21 heart toward the highway, e' the way
32: 9 weighed him the money, e' seventeen
20 land of Egypt, e' unto this day,
31 they built it e' unto this day,
33:10 beast, e' in the cities of Judah,
24 he hath e' cast them off? *
34:20 I will e' give them into the hand
36: 2 the days of Josiah, e' unto this day.
12 all the princes sat there e' Elishama
39: 3 in the middle gate, e' Nergal-sharezer,
12 do unto him e' as he shall say 3651
14 E' they sent and took Jeremiah, *
40: 7 in the fields, e' they and their men,
8 to Mizpah, e' Ishmael the son
12 E' all the Jews returned out *
41: 1 the princes of the king, e' ten men*
3 that were with him, e' with Gedaliah,
5 and from Samaria, e' fourscore men,
10 that were in Mizpah, e' the king's 853
16 son of Ahikam, e' mighty men
42: 1 from the least e' unto the greatest,
2 Lord thy God, e' for all this remnant;
5 if we do not e' according to all 3651
8 from the least e' to the greatest,
43: 1 him to them, e' all these words, 853
6 E' men, and women, and children,* "
7 thus came they e' to Tahpanhes.
44:10 are not humbled e' unto this day,
12 they shall e' be consumed. *
12 from the least e' unto the greatest,
15 a great multitude, e' all the people
45: 4 I will pluck up, e' this whole land.*
46:25 and their kings; e' Pharaoh,
48:32 they reach e' to the sea of Jazer:
34 the cry of Heshbon e' unto Elealeh,
34 Elealeh, and e' unto Jahaz,
34 from Zoar e' unto Horonaim,
44 I will bring upon it, e' upon Moab,
49:37 evil upon them, e' my fierce anger, 853
50: 7 the habitation of justice, e' the Lord,
21 land of Merathaim, e' against it,
51: 9 and is lifted up e' to the skies.
56 is come upon her, e' upon Babylon,
60 come upon Babylon, e' all these 853
La 4: 3 E' the sea monsters draw out 1571
Eze 1:27 of his loins e' upward, *
27 of his loins e' downward, *
2: 3 against me, e' unto this very day.
4: 1 upon it the city, e' Jerusalem: 853
13 said, E' thus shall the children 3602
14 from my youth up e' till now
5: 8 Behold, I, e' I, am against thee, 1571
6: 3 Behold, I, e' I, will bring a sword
7:14 the trumpet, e' to make all ready; *
8: 2 of his loins e' downward, *
2 from his loins e' upward, *
9: 1 to draw near, e' every man *
10: 2 the wheels, e' under the cherub, *
5 was heard e' to the outer court,
12 full of eyes round about, e' the wheels
11:15 thy brethren, e' thy brethren,
17 e' gather you from the people, *
12: 4 thou shalt go forth at e' in their 6153
7 in the e' I digged through the wall "
13:10 Because, e' because they have seduced
13 I will e' rend it with a stormy wind
20 will let the souls go, e' the souls that
14:10 prophet shall be e' as the punishment
22 e' concerning all that I have brought
16:19 thou hast e' set it before them
37 e' gather them round about against
59 I will e' deal with thee as thou hast
17: 9 e' without great power or many ‡
16 whose covenant he brake, e' with him
19 hath broken, e' it will I recompense
18:11 but e' hath eaten upon the 1571
18 lo, e' he shall die in his iniquity. *
20:11 13, 21 he shall e' live in them. *
31 all your idols, e' unto this day: *
21:13 if the sword contemn e' the rod? 1571
28 concerning their reproach; e' say*
22: 4 art come e' unto thy years: *
18 they are e' the dross of silver. *
23:34 Thou shalt e' drink it and suck it out,
24: 2 the name of the day, e' this same
4 pieces thereof into it, e' every good
9 will e' make the pile for fire great. *
18 and at e' my wife died; 6153
29:10 tower of Syene e' unto the border
30: 3 the day is near, e' the day of the Lord
32: 6 thou swimmest, e' to the mountains;
16 shall lament for her, e' for Egypt, *
18 cast them down, e' her,
31 all his multitude, e' Pharaoh
32 are slain with the sword, e' Pharaoh
33:18 he shall e' die thereby.
34:11 Behold, I, e' I, will both search
20 Behold, I, e' I, will judge between the
23 shall feed them, e' my servant 853
Eze 34:30 and they, e' the house of Israel,
35: 6 e' blood shall pursue thee. *
11 I will e' do according to thine *
15 and all Idumea, e' all of it:
36: 2 Aha, e' the ancient high places *
10 the house of Israel, e' all of it:
12 to walk upon you, e' my people 853
37:19 put them with him, e' with the stick "
25 they shall dwell therein, e' they,
38: 4 of armour, e' a great company *
39:17 sacrifice for you, e' a great sacrifice
40:14 e' unto the post of the court *
41:17 the door, e' unto the inner house,
42:12 the head of the way, e' the way
43: 1 e' the gate that looketh toward the
3 I saw, e' according to the vision
8 have e' defiled my holy name *
13 e' the bottom shall be a cubit, *
14 upon the ground e' to the lower *
14 settle e' to the greater settle *
44: 6 rebellious, e' to the house of Israel,
7 to pollute it, e' my house, 853
10 they shall e' bear their iniquity. *
19 into the utter court, e' into the utter
47:10 from En-gedi e' unto En-eglaim;
19 from Tamar e' to the waters of *
48: 3, 6 from the east side e' unto the west
10 for them, e' for the priests,
28 the border shall be e' from Tamar
Da 1:21 Daniel continued e' unto the first
2:43 e' as iron is not mixed with clay. 1887
4:15 roots in the earth, e' with a band
23 e' with a band of iron and brass, *
5:14 I have e' heard of thee,
6:26 dominion shall be e' unto the end
7:11 I beheld e' till the beast was slain, 5705
18 the kingdom for ever, e' for ever "
20 before whom three fell; e' of that horn
8: 1 appeared unto me, e' unto me Daniel,
10 it waxed great, e' to the host of heaven;
11 magnified himself e' to the prince of
15 when I, e' I Daniel, had seen
9: 5 have rebelled, e' by departing
11 transgressed thy law, e' by departing
21 I was speaking in prayer, e' the man*
25 the wall, e' in troublous times
27 e' until the consummation,
11: 1 Darius the Mede, e' I, stood to *
4 shall be plucked up, e' for others
10 be stirred up, e' to his fortress,
11 fight with him, e' with the king
24 enter peaceably e' upon the fattest
24 the strong holds, e' for a time.
30 he shall e' return, and have
35 make them white, e' to the time
41 escape out of his hand, e' Edom, *
12: 1 was a nation e' to that same time:
4 the book e' to the time of the end:
Ho 2:20 I will e' betroth thee unto me
5:14 I, e' I, will tear and go away;
9:16 will I slay e' the beloved fruit of *
12: 5 E' the Lord God of hosts;
Joe 1: 2 in your days, or e' in the days * 518
12 and the apple tree, e' all the trees
2: 2 after it, e' to the years of many
12 ye e' to me with all your heart,
14 e' a meat offering and a drink offering
Am 2:11 Is it not e' thus, O ye children 637
3:11 then shall be e' round about the land;
5: 1 up against you, e' a lamentation,*
20 not light? e' very dark, and no
8: 4 e' to make the poor of the land to*
12 from the north e' to the east,
14 e' they shall fall and never rise
Ob 7 brought thee e' to the border:
8 e' destroy the wise men out of *
11 cast lots upon Jerusalem, e' thou 1571
20 Canaanites; e' unto Zarephath;
Jon 2: 5 compassed me about, e' to the soul:
3: 5 greatest of them e' to the least
4: 9 do well to be angry, e' unto death.
Mic 1: 9 gate of my people, e' to Jerusalem.
2: 2 oppress a man in his house, e' a man
8 E' of late my people is risen *
10 you e' with a sore destruction.
11 shall e' be the prophet of this people.
3: 4 he will e' hide his face from them*
5 they e' prepare war against him.
4: 7 from henceforth, e' for ever.
8 it come, e' the first dominion; *
10 thou shalt go e' to Babylon; *
7:12 he shall come e' to thee *
12 from the fortress e' to the river,
Na 2:11 where the lion, e' the old lion, *
3:12 they shall e' fall into the mouth *
Hab 1: 2 e' cry out unto thee of violence, *
3: 9 oaths of the tribes, e' thy word. *
13 e' for the salvation with thine
Zep 1:14 e' the voice of the day of the Lord:
18 shall make e' a speedy riddance *
2: 5 I will e' destroy thee, *
9 e' the breeding of nettles, *
11 from his place, e' all the isles
3: 8 mine indignation, e' all my fierce
10 my suppliants, e' the daughter
15 the king of Israel, e' the Lord,
20 bring you again, e' in the time *
Hag 2:18 the ninth month, e' from the day*
Zec 3: 2 O Satan; e' the Lord that hath *
6:10 of the captivity, e' of Heldai,
13 E' he shall build the temple
7: 1 the ninth month, e' in Chisleu; *
5 and seventh month, e' those seventy
5 did ye at all fast unto me, e' to me?
8:23 e' shall take hold of the skirt of him
9: 7 he that remaineth, e' he, shall be *1571

Zec 9:10 dominion shall be from sea e· to *
10 and from the river e· to the ends *
12 e· to day do I declare that I will 1571
11: 7 flock of slaughter, e· you, O poor *3651
10 I took my staff, e· Beauty, * 853
14 asunder mine other staff, e· Bands, "
12: 6 in her own place, e· in Jerusalem.
14:16 shall e· go up from year to year *
17 the Lord of hosts, e· upon them *
Mal 1:10 Who is there e· among you *1571
11 rising of the sun e· unto the going
12 the fruit thereof, e· his meat,
2: 2 I will e· send a curse upon you, *
3 your faces, e· the dung of your
3: 1 to his temple, e· the messenger *
7 E· from the days of your fathers
9 ye have robbed me, e· this whole
15 that tempt God are e· delivered. *
M't 5:46 do not e· the publicans the same? 2532
47 do not e· publicans so? "
48 perfect, e· as your Father *5618
6:29 That e· Solomon in his glory was 3761
7:12 do ye e· so to them: for this is 2532
17 E· so every good tree bringeth
8:16 When the e· was come, they 3798
27 that e· the winds and the sea 2532
9:18 My daughter is e· now dead: but 737
11:26 E· so, Father: for so it seemed *
12: 8 Son of man is Lord e· of the *2532
45 E· so shall it be also unto this
13:12 taken away e· that he hath. 2532
15:28 be it unto thee e· as thou wilt.
18:14 E· so it is not the will of your
33 on thy fellowservant, e· as I had 2532
20: 8 So when e· was come, the lord of 3798
14 unto this last, e· as unto thee. 2532
28 E· as the Son of man came not 5618
23: 8 one is your Master, e· Christ; *
10 one is your Master, e· Christ.
28 E· so ye also outwardly appear
37 e· as a hen gathereth her 3739, 5158
24:27 and shineth e· unto the west;
33 that it is near, e· at the doors.
25:29 taken away e· that which he hath. 2532
26:20 Now when the e· was come, he sat 3798
38 is exceedingly sorrowful, e· unto
27:57 e· was come, there came a rich 3798
28:20 e· unto the end of the world.
M'r 1:27 commandeth he e· the unclean 2532
32 at e·, when the sun did set, 3798, 1096
4:25 shall be taken e· that which he 2532
35 when the e· was come, he saith 3798
36 took him e· as he was in the ship.
41 of man is this, that e· the wind 2532
6: 2 e· such mighty works are wrought* "
47 And when e· was come, the ship 3798
10:45 For e· the son of man came not *2532
11: 6 them e· as Jesus had commanded: 2531
19 when e· was come, he went out *3796
12:44 all that she had, e· all her living.
13:22 if it were possible, e· the elect. *2532
29 know that it is nigh, e· at the doors.
35 at e·, or at midnight, or at the 3796
14:30 thee, That this day, e· in this night,
54 e· into the palace of the high priest: 2193
15:42 And now when the e· was come, 3798
Lu 1: 2 E· as they delivered them unto us, 2531
15 Ghost, e· from his mother's womb. 2089
2:15 Let us now go e· unto Bethlehem,
6:33 for sinners also do e· the same. 2532
8:18 be taken e· that which he seemeth "
25 he commandeth e· the winds and "
9:54 consume them, e· as Elias did? * "
10:11 E· the very dust of your city, "
17 saying, Lord, e· the devils are "
21 e· so, Father: for so it seemed *3483
12: 7 But e· the very hairs of your head *2532
41 this parable unto us, or e· to all? "
57 and why e· of yourselves judge "
17:30 E· thus shall it be in the days *
18:11 or e· as this publican. 2532
19:26 him that hath not, e· that he hath "
32 e· as he had said unto them. 2531
37 when he was come nigh, e· now 2536
42 If thou hadst known, e· thou, 2532
44 shall lay thee e· with the ground, *
20:37 are raised, e· Moses shewed at 2532
24:24 found it e· as the woman had said: 3779
Joh 1:12 to become the sons of God, e· to them
3:13 came down from heaven, e· the Son
14 e· so must the Son of man be lifted
5:21 e· so the Son quickeneth whom he 2532
23 honour the Son, e· as they honour 2531
45 that accuseth you, e· Moses,
6:16 And when e· was now come, *3798
57 he that eateth me, e· he shall live *2548
8: 9 beginning at the eldest, e· unto the
25 E· the same that I said unto you 2532
41 we have one Father, e· God.
43 e· because ye can not hear my word.
10:15 e· so know I the Father: and I lay 2504
11:22 But I know, that e· now, 2532
37 have caused that e· this man * "
12:50 e· as the Father said unto me, 2531
14:17 E· the Spirit of truth;
31 gave me commandment, e· so I do.
15:10 e· as I have kept my Father's 2531
26 from the Father, e· the Spirit of truth,
17:14 e· as I am not of the world. 2531
16 They are not of the world, e· as I "
18 e· so have I also sent them 2504
22 they may be one e· as we are one: 2531
20:21 hath sent me, e· so send I you. 2504
21:25 e· the world itself could not 3761
Ac 2:39 are afar off, e· as many as
4:10 e· by him doth this man stand *
Ac 5:37 and all, e· as many as obeyed him,
39 be found e· to fight against God. 2532
9:17 the Lord, e· Jesus, hath appeared
10:41 chosen before of God, e· to us,
11: 5 by four corners; and it came e· to 891
12:15 constantly affirmed that it was e· so.
15: 8 Holy Ghost, e· as he did unto us. 2532
11 we shall be saved, e· as they. *2548
20:11 talked a long while, e· till break
22:17 e· while I prayed in the temple *
26:11 I persecuted them e· unto strange 2532
27:25 it shall be e· as it was told me. 3779
Ro 1:13 fruit among you also, e· as among 2532
20 e· his eternal power and Godhead;
26 for e· their women did change the *5037
28 e· as they did not like to retain God 2531
3:22 E· the righteousness of God 1161
4: 6 E· as David also describeth the 2509
17 whom he believed, e· God,
5: 7 peradventure some would e· dare to die.
14 from Adam to Moses, e· over them 2532
18 e· so by the righteousness of one "
21 e· so might grace reign through "
6: 4 e· so we also should walk in *
19 e· so now yield your members 3779
7: 4 married to another, e· to him who
8:23 e· we ourselves groan within 2532
34 who is e· at the right hand of God, "
9:10 conceived by one, e· by our father
17 unto Pharaoh, E· for this same *
24 E· us, whom he hath called, 2532
30 e· the righteousness which is of 1161
10: 8 word is nigh thee, e· in thy mouth*
11: 5 E· so then at this present time 2532
31 E· so have these also now not
15: 3 For e· Christ pleased not himself; *2532
6 glorify God, e· the Father of our * "
1Co 1: 6 E· as the testimony of Christ was 2531
2: 7 in a mystery, e· the hidden wisdom,
11 e· so the things of God knoweth no 2532
3: 1 as unto carnal, e· as unto babes *
5 e· as the Lord gave to every man? *2532
4:11 E· unto this present hour we both
5: 7 For e· Christ our passover is 2532
7: 7 I would that all men were e· as I "
8 good for them if they abide e· as I. 2504
9:14 E· so hath the Lord ordained 2532
10:33 E· as I please all men in all things, 2504
11: 1 e· as I also am of Christ. 2531
5 that is e· all one as she were *2532
12 e· so is the man also by the woman;
14 Doth not e· nature itself teach you, 3761
12: 2 these dumb idols, e· as ye were *5613
13:12 shall I know e· as also I am known 2531
14: 7 And e· things without life giveth 3676
12 E· so ye, forasmuch as ye are *2532
15:22 e· so in Christ shall all be made * "
24 the kingdom of God, e· the Father; "
16: 1 churches of Galatia e· so do ye. * "
2Co 1: 3 Blessed be God, e· the Father of * "
8 that we despaired e· of life: * "
13 shall acknowledge e· to the end; * "
14 e· as ye also are ours in the day 2509
19 preached among you by us, e· by me
3:10 For e· that which was made *2532
15 But e· unto this day, when Moses *2193
18 from glory to glory, e· as by the Spirit
7:14 e· so our boasting, which I made *2532
10: 7 is Christ's, e· so are we Christ's. * "
13 a measure to reach e· unto you. "
11:12 they may be found e· as we. "
13: 9 this also we wish e· your perfection.
Ga 2:16 e· we have believed in Jesus 2532
3: 6 E· as Abraham believed God, and 2531
4: 3 E· so we, when we were children, *2532
14 as an angel of God, e· as Christ Jesus.
29 after the Spirit, e· so it is now. 2532
5:12 I would they were e· cut off
14 law is fulfilled in one word, e· in this:
Eph 2: 3 children of wrath, e· as others. 2532
5 E· when we were dead in sins, "
15 in his flesh the enmity, e· the law of
4: 4 one Spirit, e· as ye are called 2532
15 which is the head, e· Christ;
32 forgiving one another, e· as God 2532
5:12 it is a shame e· to speak of those "
23 the wife, e· as Christ is the head * "
25 love your wives, e· as Christ also 2531
29 cherisheth it, e· as the Lord the 2532
33 so love his wife e· as himself. 5613
Ph'p 1: 7 E· as it is meet for me to think this 2531
15 preach Christ e· of envy 2532
2: 8 obedient unto death, e· the death *1161
3:15 God shall reveal e· this unto you. 2532
18 now tell you e· weeping, "
21 he is able e· to subdue all things "
4:16 For e· Thessalonica ye sent once "
Col 1:14 e· the forgiveness of sins: *
26 E· the mystery which hath
3:13 e· as Christ forgave you, so also do 2532
1Th 1:10 whom he raised from the dead, e· Jesus,
2: 2 But e· after that we had suffered *2532
4 e· so we speak; not as pleasing
7 gentle among you; e· as a nurse *
14 e· as they have of the Jews: 2532
18 e· I Paul, once and again; but *3303
19 Are not e· ye in the presence 2532
3: 4 suffer tribulation; e· as it came to "
12 toward all men, e· as we do toward "
13 holiness before God, e· our Father.* "
4: 3 will of God, e· your sanctification *
5 concupiscence, e· as the Gentiles 2532
13 that ye sorrow not, e· as others "
14 e· so them also which sleep in "
5:11 e· as also ye do. 2531
2Th 2: 9 E· him, whose coming is after
2Th 2:16 and God, e· our Father, 2532
3: 1 be glorified, e· as it is with you: "
10 For e· when we were with you,
1Ti 3:11 E· so must their wives be grave, *5615
6: 3 wholesome words, e· the words
2Ti 2: 9 as an evil doer, e· unto bonds; *
Tit 1:12 One of themselves, e· a prophet *
15 e· their mind and conscience is *2532
Ph'm 19 thou owest unto me e· thine own *
Heb 1: 9 God, e· thy God, hath anointed *
4:12 e· to the dividing asunder of soul
5:14 of full age, e· those who by reason
6:20 for us entered, e· Jesus made *
7: 4 whom e· the patriarch Abraham *2532
11:12 sprang there e· of one, * "
19 to raise him up, e· from the dead; "
Jas 2:17 E· so faith, if it hath not works, "
3: 5 E· so the tongue is a little member* "
9 bless we God, e· the Father; "
4: 1 come they not hence, e· of your lusts
14 It is e· a vapour, that appeareth *1063
1Pe 1: 9 end of your faith, e· the salvation
2: 8 rock of offence, e· to them which *
21 e· hereunto were ye called: *
3: 4 not corruptible, e· the ornament *
6 E· as Sara obeyed Abraham, *5613
21 whereunto e· baptism doth also
4:10 received the gift, e· so minister *
2Pe 1:14 e· as our Lord Jesus Christ 2532
2: 1 among the people, e· as there shall* "
1 damnable heresies, e· denying the "
3:15 e· as our beloved brother Paul also 2531
1Jo 2: 6 so to walk, e· as he walked.
9 is in darkness e· until now.
18 antichrist shall come, e· now are 2532
25 he hath promised us, e· eternal life.
27 e· as it hath taught you, ye shall 2531
3: 3 purifieth himself, e· as he is pure. "
7 is righteous, e· as he is righteous. "
4: 3 it should come; and e· now *2532
5: 4 overcometh the world, e· our faith.
6 by water and blood, e· Jesus Christ;
3Jo 2 health, e· as thy soul prospereth. 2531
3 e· as thou walkest in the truth. "
Jude 7 E· as Sodom and Gomorrha, and 5613
23 hating e· the garment spotted 2532
Re 1: 7 because of him. E· so, Amen. 3483
2:13 thou dwellest, e· where Satan's
13 denied my faith, e· in those days 2532
27 e· as I received of my father. *2504
3: 4 hast a few names e· in Sardis *2532
21 e· as I also overcame, and am set *2504
6:13 fell unto the earth, e· as a fig tree*
14:20 e· unto the horse bridles,
16: 7 E· so, Lord God Almighty, true *3483
17:11 e· he is the eighth, *2532
18: 6 Reward her e· as she rewarded you, "
21:11 e· like a jasper stone, clear as *5613
22:20 E· so, come, Lord Jesus. *3483

evening See also EVEN; EVENINGS; EVENTIDE.
Ge 1: 5 e· and the morning were the first 6153
8 e· and the morning were the second "
13 e· and the morning were the third "
19 e· and the morning were the fourth "
23 e· and the morning were the fifth "
31 e· and the morning were the sixth "
8:11 the dove came in to him in the e·; * "
24:11 at the time of the e·, even the time "
29:23 it came to pass in the e·, "
30:16 Jacob came out of the field in the e·, "
Ex 12: 6 Israel shall kill it in the e·. * "
16: 8 shall give you in the e· flesh to eat, "
18:13 Moses from the morning unto the e·. "
27:21 shall order it from e· to morning "
Le 24: 3 e· unto the morning before the Lord "
De 23:11 when e· cometh on, he shall wash "
Jos 10:26 hanging upon the trees until the e·. "
J'g 19: 9 now the day draweth toward e·, 6150
1Sa 14:24 man that eateth any food until e·, 6153
17:16 drew near morning and e·, 6150
30:17 unto the e· of the next day: 6153
1Ki 17: 6 and bread and flesh in the e·; "
18:29, 36 the offering of the e· sacrifice, "
2Ki 16:15 e· meat offering, and the king's 6153
1Ch 16:40 continually morning and e·, "
2Ch 2: 4 burnt offerings morning and e·, "
13:11 Lord every morning and every e· "
11 the lamps thereof, to burn every e·: "
31: 3 the morning and e· burnt offerings, "
Ezr 3: 3 burnt offerings morning and e·. "
9: 4 I sat astonied until the e· sacrifice. "
5 at the e· sacrifice I arose up from "
Es 2:14 e· she went, and on the morrow "
Job 4:20 are destroyed from morning to e·: "
Ps 55:17 E·, and morning, and at noon, "
59: 6 They return at e·: they make a "
14 at e· let them return; and let them "
65: 8 the morning and e· to rejoice. "
90: 6 the e· it is cut down, and withereth. "
104:23 forth unto his work...until the e·. "
141: 2 up of my hands as the e· sacrifice. "
Pr 7: 9 in the e·, in the black and dark "
Ec 11: 6 in the e· withhold not thine hand: "
Jer 6: 4 shadows of the e· are stretched out. "
Eze 33:22 of the Lord was upon me in the e·, "
46: 2 gate shall not be shut until the e·. "
Da 8:26 vision of the e· and the morning * "
9:21 about the time of the e· oblation. "
Hab 1: 8 are more fierce than the e· wolves: "
Zep 2: 7 shall they lie down in the e·: "
3: 3 judges are e· wolves; they gnaw "
Zec 14: 7 at e· time it shall be light. "
M't 14:15 when it was e·, his disciples came *3798
23 e· was come, he was there alone. * "
16: 2 When it is e·, ye say, it will be fair "
M'r 14:17 in the e· he cometh with the twelve, 3798

Lu 24:29 toward e', and the day is far spent, 2073
Joh 20:19 same day at e', being the first 3798
Ac 28:23 the prophets, from morning till e'. 2073

evenings
Jer 5: 6 a wolf of the e' shall spoil them, 6160

eveningtide See also EVENTIDE.
2Sa 11: 2 it came to pass in an e', *6256, 6153
Isa 17:14 And behold at e' trouble; * "

event
Ec 2:14 one e' happeneth to them all. 4745
9: 2 one e' to the righteous, and to the "
3 that there is one e' unto all: "

eventide See also EVENINGTIDE.
Ge 24:63 Isaac went out...at the e': 6256, 6153
Jos 7: 6 the ark of the Lord until the e', * "
8:29 he hanged on a tree until e': 6256, "
M'r 11:11 and now the e' was come, 3798, 5610
Ac 4: 3 the next day: for it was now e'. 2073

ever See also EVERLASTING; EVERMORE; NEVER; SOEVER.
Ge 3:22 life, and eat, and live for e': 5769
13:15 I give it, and to thy seed for e'. "
43: 9 let me bear the blame for e': 3605, 3117
44:32 the blame to my father for e'. "
Ex 3:15 this is my name for e', and 5769
12:14 a feast by an ordinance for e'. "
17 by an ordinance for e'. "
24 to thee and to thy sons for e'. "
14:13 them again no more for e'. "
15:18 Lord shall reign for e' [5769] and e' 5703
19: 9 thee, and believe thee for e'. 5769
21: 6 and he shall serve him for e'. "
27:21 it shall be a statute for e' unto "
28:43 it shall be a statute for e' unto him "
29:28 for e' from the children of Israel; "
30:21 it shall be a statute for e' to them, "
31:17 the children of Israel for e': "
32:13 and they shall inherit it for e'. "
Le 6:13 e' be burning upon the altar; *8548
18 statute for e' in your generations 5769
22 a statute for e' unto the Lord; "
7:34 for e' from among the children "
36 for e' throughout their generations. "
10: 9 for e' throughout your generations: "
15 a statute for e'; as the Lord hath "
16:29 shall be a statute for e' unto you: "
31 afflict your souls, by a statute for e'. "
17: 7 shall be a statute for e' unto them "
23:14 for e' throughout your generations "
21 statute for e' in all your dwellings "
31 for e' throughout your generations "
41 statute for e' in your generations: "
24: 3 statute for e' in your generations. "
25:23 The land shall not be sold for e': *6783
30 shall be established for e' to him * "
46 shall be your bondmen for e': 5769
Nu 10: 8 for e' throughout your generations. "
15:15 for e' in your generations: "
18: 8 to thy sons, by an ordinance for e'. "
11, 19 with thee, by a statute for e': "
19 of salt for e' before the Lord "
23 for e' throughout your generations, "
19:10 among them, for a statute for e'. "
22:30 which thou hast ridden e' since *5750
30 was I e' wont to do so unto thee? "
24:20 end shall be that he perish for e'. *5703
24 and he also shall perish for e'. * "
De 4:33 Did e' people hear the voice of God
40 thy God giveth thee, for e'. 3605, 3117
5:29 and with their children for e'! 5769
12:28 with thy children after thee for e', "
13:16 it shall be a heap for e'; "
15:17 and he shall be thy servant for e'. "
18: 5 Lord, him and his sons for e'. 3605, 3117
19: 9 and to walk e' in his ways; "
23: 3 congregation of the Lord for e': 5769
6 prosperity all thy days for e'. "
28:46 wonder, and upon thy seed for e'. "
29:29 unto us and to our children for e', "
32:40 and say, I live for e'. "
Jos 4: 7 unto the children of Israel for e'. "
24 fear the Lord your God for e'. 3605, 3117
8:28 Ai, and made it an heap for e'. 5769
14: 9 and thy children's for e', "
J'g 11:25 did he e' strive against Israel,
25 or did he e' fight against them,
1Sa 1:22 the Lord, and there abide for e'. 5769
2:30 should walk before me for e': "
32 old man in thine house for e'. 3605, 3117
35 before mine anointed for e'. "
3:13 I will judge his house for e' 5769
14 with sacrifice nor offering for e'. "
13:13 thy kingdom upon Israel for e'. "
20:15 thy kindness from my house for e': "
23 Lord between thee and me for e'. "
42 my seed and thy seed for e'. "
27:12 he shall be my servant for e'. "
28: 2 keeper of mine head for e'. 3605, 3117
2Sa 2:26 Shall the sword devour for e'? 5331
3:28 guiltless before the Lord for e' 5769
7:13 the throne of his kingdom for e'. "
16 established for e' before thee: "
16 throne shall be established for e'. "
24 to be a people unto thee for e': "
25 his house, establish it for e', "
26 let thy name be magnified for e', "
29 continue for e' before thee: "
29 thy servant be blessed for e'. "
1Ki 1:31 lord king David live for e'. "
2:33 the head of his seed for e': "
33 be peace for e' from the Lord. "
45 established before the Lord for e'. "
5: 1 Hiram was e' a lover of David. 3605, 3117
8:13 place for thee to abide in for e'. 5769
1Ki 9: 3 to put my name there for e'; 5769
5 kingdom upon Israel for e', "
10: 9 the Lord loved Israel for e', "
11:39 seed of David, but not for e'. 3605, 3117
12: 7 they will be thy servants for e'. "
2Ki 5:27 thee, and unto thy seed for e'. 5769
21: 7 will I put my name for e': "
1Ch 15: 2 and to minister unto him for e'. "
16:34 for his mercy endureth for e'. "
36 the Lord God of Israel for e' "
36 Lord God of Israel...and e', *5704, "
41 for his mercy endureth for e'; "
17:12 I will stablish his throne for e'. "
14 house and in my kingdom for e': "
22 thou make thine own people for e'; "
23 his house be established for e', "
24 thy name may be magnified for e', "
27 it may be before thee for e': "
27 and it shall be blessed for e'. "
22:10 of his kingdom over Israel for e'. "
23:13 he and his sons for e', to burn "
13 to bless in his name for e'. "
25 dwell in Jerusalem for e': "
28: 4 to be king over Israel for e': "
7 establish his kingdom for e', "
8 for your children after you for e'. "
9 he will cast thee off for e'. 5703
29:10 Lord God of Israel our father, for e' 5769
10 of Israel our father,...and e'. 5704, "
18 for e' in the imagination of "
2Ch 2: 4 an ordinance for e' to Israel. "
5:13 for his mercy endureth for e': "
6: 2 a place for thy dwelling for e'. "
7: 3 for his mercy endureth for e'. "
6 because his mercy endureth for e', "
16 that my name may be there for e': "
9: 8 to establish them for e', "
10: 7 will be thy servants for e'. 3605, 3117
13: 5 over Israel to David for e', 5769
20: 7 of Abraham thy friend for e'? "
21 for his mercy endureth for e'. "
21: 7 to him and to his sons for e'. *3605, 3117
30: 8 he hath sanctified for e': 5769
33: 4 shall my name be for e'. "
7 will I put my name for e': 5865
Ezr 3:11 for his mercy endureth for e' 5769
9:12 their peace or their wealth for e': "
12 inheritance to your children for e'. "
Ne 2: 3 king, Let the king live for e': "
9: 5 the Lord your God for e' and e': "
13: 1 the congregation of God for e'; "
Job 4: 7 who e' perished, being innocent? or
20 they perish for e' without any 5331
14:20 Thou prevailest for e' against him, "
19:24 pen and lead in the rock for e'! 5703
20: 7 he shall perish for e' like his own 5331
23: 7 so should I be delivered for e' from "
36: 7 yea, he doth establish them for e', "
41: 4 take him for a servant for e'? 5769
Ps 5:11 let them e' shout for joy, because "
9: 5 thou hast put out their name for e'. "
5 hast put out their name...and e'. 5703
7 the Lord shall endure for e': 5769
18 of the poor shall not perish for e'. 5703
10:16 The Lord is King for e' 5769
16 The Lord is King...and e'. 5703
12: 7 from this generation for e', 5769
13: 1 thou forget me, O Lord? for e'? 5331
19: 9 the Lord is clean, enduring for e': 5703
21: 4 even length of days for e' 5769
4 even length of days...and e'. 5703
6 made him most blessed for e': "
22:26 him: your heart shall live for e'. "
23: 6 the house of the Lord for e'. 753, 3117
25: 6 for they have been e' of old.
15 Mine eyes are e' toward the Lord; 8548
28: 9 them also, and lift them up for e'. 5769
29:10 the Lord sitteth King for e'. "
30:12 give thanks unto thee for e'. "
33:11 counsel of the Lord standeth for e', "
37:18 and their inheritance shall be for e'. "
26 is e' merciful, and lendeth; *3605, 3117
28 they are preserved for e': 5769
29 the land, and dwell therein for e'. 5703
41:12 settest me before thy face for e'. 5769
44: 8 and praise thy name for e'. "
23 Lord? arise, cast us not off for e'. 5331
45: 2 God hath blessed thee for e'. 5769
6 Thy throne, O God, is for e' "
6 Thy throne, O God, is...and e'; 5703
17 shall the people praise thee for e' 5769
17 the people praise thee...and e'. 5703
48: 8 God will establish it for e'. 5769
14 God is our God for e' [5769] and e': 5703
49: 8 precious, and it ceaseth for e':) 5769
9 That he should still live for e' *5331
11 their houses shall continue for e', 5769
51: 3 and my sin is e' before me. 8548
52: 5 shall likewise destroy thee for e', 5331
8 trust in the mercy of God for e' 5769
8 trust in the mercy of God...and e'. 5703
9 will praise thee for e', because 5769
61: 4 will abide in thy tabernacle for e': "
7 He shall abide before God for e': "
8 I sing praise unto thy name for e', 5703
66: 7 He ruleth by his power for e'; 5769
68:16 the Lord will dwell in it for e'. 5331
72:17 name shall endure for e': 5769
19 be his glorious name for e': "
73:26 heart, and my portion for e'. "
74: 1 why hast thou cast us off for e'? 5331
10 enemy blaspheme thy name for e'? "
19 the congregation of thy poor for e'. "
75: 9 I will declare for e'; I will 5769
77: 7 Will the Lord cast off for e'?
8 Is his mercy clean gone for e'? 5331
Ps 78:69 he hath established for e'. 5769
79: 5 Lord? wilt thou be angry for e'? 5331
13 will give thee thanks for e': 5769
81:15 should have endured for e'. "
83:17 be confounded and troubled for e'; 5703
85: 5 thou be angry with us for e'? 5769
89: 1 of the mercies of the Lord for e': "
2 Mercy shall be built up for e': "
4 Thy seed will I establish for e', "
29 also will I make to endure for e', 5703
36 His seed shall endure for e', 5769
37 It shall be established for e' as "
46 Lord? wilt thou hide thyself for e'? 5331
90: 2 or e' thou hadst formed the earth
92: 7 that they shall be destroyed for e': 5703
93: 5 thine house, O Lord, for e'. * 753, 3117
102:12 thou O Lord, shalt endure for e'; 5769
103: 9 neither will he keep his anger for e'. "
104: 5 should not be removed for e'. 5769, 5703
31 glory of the Lord...endure for e': 5769
105: 8 remembered his covenant for e', "
106: 1 for his mercy endureth for e'. "
107: 1 for his mercy endureth for e'. "
110: 4 Thou art a priest for e' after the "
111: 3 his righteousness endureth for e'. 5703
5 will e' be mindful of his covenant. 5769
8 They stand fast for e' 5703
8 They stand fast...and e', 5769
9 remembered his covenant for e': "
10 his praise endureth for e'. "
112: 3 his righteousness endureth for e'. 5703
6 he shall not be moved for e': 5769
9 his righteousness endureth for e'; 5703
117: 2 truth of the Lord endureth for e'. 5769
118: 1 because his mercy endureth for e'. "
2, 3, 4 that his mercy endureth for e'. "
29 for his mercy endureth for e'. "
119:44 I keep thy law continually for e' "
44 I keep thy law continually...and e'. 5703
89 For e', O Lord, thy word is settled 5769
98 enemies: for they are e' with me. "
111 have I taken as a heritage for e': "
152 thou hast founded them for e'. "
160 judgments endureth for e'. "
125: 1 be removed, but abideth for e'. "
2 people from henceforth even for e'.* "
131: 3 Lord from henceforth and for e'. * "
132:14 This is my rest for e': here will I 5703
135:13 Thy name, O Lord, endureth for e'; 5769
136: 1, 2, 3, 4, 5, 6 his mercy endureth for e' "
7, 8, 10, 11 his mercy endureth for e' "
9, 12, 15, 16 his mercy endureth for e'. "
13, 14, 17, 18, 19, 20, 21, 23 for his mercy endureth for e.: "
22, 24, 25, 26 his mercy endureth for e'. "
138: 8 thy mercy, O Lord, endureth for e': "
145: 1 and I will bless thy name for e' "
1 and I will bless thy name...and e'. 5703
2 and I will praise thy name for e' 5769
2 and I will praise thy name...and e'. 5703
21 all flesh bless his holy name for e' 5769
21 flesh bless his holy name...and e'. 5703
146: 6 which keepeth truth for e': 5769
10 The Lord shall reign for e', "
148: 6 hath also stablished them for e' 5703
6 hath also stablished them...and e'. 5769
Pr 8:23 the beginning, or e' the earth ‡6924
12:19 truth shall be established for e': 5703
27:24 for riches are not for e': 5769
29:14 throne shall be established for e'. 5703
Ec 1: 4 but the earth abideth for e'. 5769
2:16 more than of the fool for e'; "
3:14 God doeth, it shall be for e': "
9: 6 they any more a portion for e' "
12: 6 Or e' the silver cord be loosed, ‡
Ca 6:12 Or e' I was aware, my soul made ‡3808
Isa 9: 7 from henceforth even for e'. 5769
26: 4 Trust ye in the Lord for e': 5703
28:28 because he will not e' be threshing 5331
30: 8 may be for the time to come for e' 5703
8 be for the time to come... and e': 5769
32:14 and towers shall be for dens for e', "
17 quietness and assurance for e'. "
33:20 thereof shall e' be removed, *5331
34:10 smoke thereof shall go up for e': 5769
10 none shall pass through it for e' 5331
17 they shall possess it for e', from 5769
40: 8 word of our God shall stand for e' "
47: 7 saidst, I shall be a lady for e': "
51: 6 but my salvation shall be for e', "
8 but my righteousness shall be for e', "
57:16 For I will not contend for e', "
59:21 Lord, from henceforth and for e'. "
60:21 they shall inherit the land for e', "
64: 9 neither remember iniquity for e': 5703
65:18 But be ye glad and rejoice for e' "
Jer 3: 5 Will he reserve his anger for e'?
12 and I will not keep anger for e'. 5769
7: 7 gave to your fathers, for e' and e'.* "
17: 4 anger, which shall burn for e'. "
25 and this city shall remain for e'. "
25: 5 and to your fathers for e' and e': * "
31:36 a nation before me for e'. 3605, 3117
40 nor thrown down any more for e'. 5769
32:39 that they may fear me for e', 3605, 3117
33:11 for his mercy endureth for e': 5769
35: 6 neither ye, nor your sons for e': "
19 man to stand before me for e'. 3605, 3117
49:33 dragons, and a desolation for e': 5769
50:39 shall be no more inhabited for e'; 5331
51:26 but thou shalt be desolate for e', 5769
62 but that it shall be desolate for e'. "
La 3:31 For the Lord will not cast off for e': "
5:19 Thou O Lord, remainest for e'; "
20 dost thou forget us for e', 5331
Eze 37:25 and their children's children for e': 5769

Eze 37:25 David shall be their prince for e'. 5769
43: 7 midst of the children of Israel for e'. "
9 will dwell in the midst of them for e'. "
Da 2: 4 O king, live for e': tell thy servants 5957
20 Blessed be...of God for e' and e': "
44 kingdoms, and it shall stand for e'. "
3: 9 Nebuchadnezzar, O king, live for e'. "
4:34 and honoured him that liveth for e', "
5:10 O king, live for e': let not thy "
6: 6 unto him, King Darius, live for e'. "
21 unto the king, O king, live for e'. "
24 all their bones in pieces or e' they‡3809
26 the living God, and stedfast for e', 5957
7:18 kingdom for e', even for e' and e'. "
12: 3 righteousness as the stars for e' 5769
3 righteousness as the stars...and e'. 5703
7 and sware by him that liveth for e' 5769
Ho 2:19 I will betroth thee unto me for e'; "
Joe 2: 2 there hath not been e' the like, "
3:20 But Judah shall dwell for e', "
Am 1:11 and he kept his wrath for e': 5331
Ob 10 thou shalt be cut off for e'. 5769
Jon 2: 6 with her bars was about me for e': "
Mic 2: 9 have ye taken away my glory for e'. "
4: 5 name of the Lord our God for e' "
5 name of the Lord our God...and e'. 5703
7 Zion from henceforth, even for e'. 5769
7:18 he retaineth not his anger for e', 5703
Zec 1: 5 prophets, do they live for e'? 5769
Mal 1: 4 the Lord hath indignation for e'. "
M't 6:13 power, and the glory, for e'. * 165
21:19 on thee henceforward for e'. "
24:21 world to this time, no, nor e' shall 3364
M'r 11:14 fruit of thee hereafter for e'. 165
15: 8 as he had e' done unto them. * 104
Lu 1:33 over the house of Jacob for e'; 165
55 Abraham, and to his seed for e'. "
15:31 Son, thou art e' with me, and all 3842
Joh 4:29 told me all things that e' I did: 3745
39 testified, He told me all that e' I did. "
6:51 this bread, he shall live for e': 165
58 of this bread shall live for e'. "
8:35 abideth not in the house for e': "
35 but the Son abideth for e'. "
10: 8 All that e' came before me are *3745
12:34 law that Christ abideth for e': 165
14:16 he may abide with you for e'; "
18:20 I e' taught in the synagogue, and 3842
Ac 23:15 and we, or e' he come near, are 4253
Ro 1:25 Creator, who is blessed for e'. 165
9: 5 is over all, God blessed for e'. "
11:36 To whom be glory for e'. Amen. "
16:27 through Jesus Christ for e'. "
2Co 9: 9 his righteousness remaineth for e'. "
Ga 1: 5 To whom be glory for e' and e'. "
Eph 5:29 For no man e' yet hated his own 4218
Ph'p 4:20 Father be glory for e' and e'. 165
1Th 4:17 and so shall we e' be with the 3842
5:15 but e' follow that which is good, * "
1Ti 1:17 honour and glory for e' and e'. 165
2Ti 3: 7 E' learning, and never able to 3842
4:18 to whom be glory for e' and e'. 165
Ph'm 15 thou shouldest receive him for e'; 166
Heb 1: 8 thy throne, O God, is for e' and e'; 165
5: 6 Thou art a priest for e' after the "
6:20 made an high priest for e' after the "
7:17, 21 Thou art a priest for e' after the "
24 this man, because he continueth e', "
25 he e' liveth to make intercession 3842
10:12 for e' sat down on the right 1336
14 he hath perfected for e' them "
13: 8 yesterday, and to day, and for e'. 165
21 whom be glory for e' and e'. "
1Pe 1:23 which liveth and abideth for e'. * "
25 the word of the Lord endureth for e'. "
4:11 praise and dominion for e' and e'. "
5:11 glory and dominion for e' and e'. "
2Pe 2:17 of darkness is reserved for e' * "
3:18 be glory both now and for e'. 2250, "
1Jo 2:17 doeth the will of God abideth for e'. "
2Jo 2 and shall be with us for e'. "
Jude 13 the blackness of darkness for e'. "
25 and power, both now and for e'. *3956, "
Re 1: 6 be glory and dominion for e' and e'. "
4: 9 throne, who liveth for e' and e', "
10 worship him that liveth for e' and e', "
5:13 and unto the Lamb for e' and e'. "
14 him that liveth for e' and e'. * "
7:12 be unto our God for e' and e'. "
10: 6 by him that liveth for e' and e', "
11:15 and he shall reign for e' and e'. "
14:11 torment ascendeth up for e' and e': "
15: 7 God, who liveth for e' and e'. "
19: 3 her smoke rose up for e' and e'. "
20:10 tormented day and night for e' and e'. "
22: 5 and they shall reign for e' and e'. "

everlasting

Ge 9:16 I may remember the e' covenant 5769
17: 7 an e' covenant, to be a God unto "
8 for an e' possession; and I will be "
13 be in your flesh for an e' covenant. "
19 with him for an e' covenant, "
21:33 name of the Lord, the e' God. "
48: 4 after thee for an e' possession. "
49:26 the utmost bound of the e' hills: "
Ex 40:15 an e' priesthood throughout their "
Le 16:34 this shall be an e' statute unto you, "
24: 8 of Israel by an e' covenant. "
Nu 25:13 the covenant of an e' priesthood; "
De 33:27 and underneath are the e' arms: "
2Sa 23: 5 hath made with me an e' covenant, "
1Ch 16:17 and to Israel for an e' covenant, "
Ps 24: 7 be ye lift up, ye e' doors; "
9 even lift them up, ye e' doors; "
41:13 Lord God of Israel from e', and to e'. "
90: 2 even from e' to e', thou art God. "
Ps 93: 2 established of old; thou art from e'. 5769
100: 5 the Lord is good; his mercy is e'; * "
103:17 mercy of the Lord is from e' to e' "
105:10 and to Israel for an e' covenant: "
106:48 the Lord God of Israel from e' to e': "
112: 6 shall be in e' remembrance. "
119:142 Thy righteousness is an e' "
144 of thy testimonies is e': * "
139:24 and lead me in the way e'. "
145:13 Thy kingdom is an e' kingdom, "
Pr 8:23 I was set up from e', from the "
10:25 the righteous is an e' foundation. "
Isa 9: 6 The e' Father, The Prince of Peace. 5703
24: 5 ordinance, broken the e' covenant. 5769
26: 4 in the Lord Jehovah is e' strength: "
33:14 us shall dwell with e' burnings? "
35:10 and e' joy upon their heads: "
40:28 not heard, that the e' God, the Lord, "
45:17 in the Lord with an e' salvation: "
51:11 e' joy shall be upon their head: "
54: 8 with e' kindness will I have mercy "
55: 3 I will make an e' covenant with you, "
13 an e' sign that shall not be cut off. "
56: 5 I will give them an e' name, "
60:19 Lord shall be unto thee an e' light, "
20 the Lord shall be thine e' light, "
61: 7 e' joy shall be unto them. "
8 I will make an e' covenant with "
63:12 to make himself an e' name? "
16 redeemer; thy name is from e'. "
Jer 10:10 the living God, and an e' king: "
20:11 their e' confusion shall never be "
23:40 I will bring an e' reproach upon "
31: 3 I have loved thee with an e' love: "
32:40 I will make an e' covenant with "
Eze 16:60 establish unto thee an e' covenant. "
37:26 shall be an e' covenant with them: "
Da 4: 3 his kingdom is an e' kingdom, 5957
34 whose dominion is an e' dominion, "
7:14 his dominion is an e' dominion, "
27 whose kingdom is an e' kingdom, "
9:24 and to bring in e' righteousness, 5769
12: 2 some to e' life, and some to shame "
2 to shame and e' contempt. "
Mic 5: 2 forth have been from of old, from e'. "
Hab 1:12 Art thou not from e', O Lord 6924
3: 6 the e' mountains were scattered. *5703
6 hills did bow: his ways are e'. 5769
M't 18: 8 or two feet to be cast into e' fire. * 166
19:29 and shall inherit e' life. "
25:41 from me, ye cursed, into e' fire, * "
46 shall go away into e' punishment: * "
Lu 16: 9 receive you into e' habitations. * "
18:30 and in the world to come life e'. * "
Joh 3:16 should not perish, but have e' life. * "
36 believeth on the Son hath e' life; * "
4:14 of water springing up into e' life. * "
5:24 on him that sent me, hath e' life, * "
6:27 meat which endureth unto e' life, * "
40 on him, may have e' life: * "
47 believeth on me hath e' life. * "
12:50 that his commandment is life e': * "
Ac 13:46 yourselves unworthy of e' life, lo, * "
Ro 6:22 unto holiness, and the end e' life. * "
16:26 the commandment of the e' God, "
Ga 6: 8 shall of the spirit reap life e'. * "
2Th 1: 9 be punished with e' destruction * "
2:16 and hath given us e' consolation * "
1Ti 1:16 believe on him to life e'. * "
6:16 to whom be honour and power e'. * "
Heb 13:20 the blood of the e' covenant, * "
2Pe 1:11 to the e' kingdom of our Lord and * "
Jude 6 he hath reserved in e' chains 126
Re 14: 6 having the e' gospel to preach * 166

evermore

De 28:29 oppressed and spoiled e', *3605, 3117
2Sa 22:51 unto David, and to his seed for e'. 5769
2Ki 17:37 ye shall observe to do for e'; 3605, 3117
1Ch 17:14 throne shall be established for e'. *5769
Ps 16:11 hand there are pleasures for e'. 5331
18:50 David, and to his seed for e'. 5769
37:27 and do good; and dwell for e'. "
77: 8 doth his promise fail for e'? 1755
86:12 I will glorify thy name for e'. 5769
89:28 My mercy will I keep for him for e'. "
52 Blessed be the Lord for e'. Amen. "
92: 8 thou, Lord, art most high for e'. "
105: 4 and his strength: seek his face e'. 8548
106:31 unto all generations for e'. 5769
113: 2 from this time forth and for e'. "
115:18 from this time forth and for e'. "
121: 8 from this time forth, and even for e'. "
132:12 shall also sit upon thy throne for e'. 5703
133: 3 the blessing, even life for e'. 5769
Eze 37:26 in the midst of them for e'. "
28 shall be in the midst of them for e'. "
Joh 6:34 Lord, e' give us this bread. 3842
2Co 11:31 Christ, which is blessed for e', 3588, 165
1Th 5:16 Rejoice e'. *3842
Heb 7:28 Son, who is consecrated for e'. 3588, 165
Re 1:18 I am alive for e', "

every

Ge 1:21 and e' living creature that 3605
21 and e' winged fowl after his kind: "
25 e' thing that creepeth upon the "
26 over e' creeping thing that creepeth "
28 e' living thing that moveth upon "
29 given you e' herb bearing seed, "
29 and e' tree, in the which is the "
30 e' beast of the earth, and to e' fowl "
30 and to e' thing that creepeth "
30 I have given e' green herb for meat: "
31 God saw e' thing that he had made, "
2: 5 And e' plant of the field before * "
5 and e' herb of the field before * "
Ge 2: 9 to grow e' tree that is pleasant 3605
16 e' tree of the garden thou mayest "
19 God formed e' beast of the field, "
19 and e' fowl of the air; "
20 and to e' beast of the field; "
3: 1 not eat of e' tree of the garden? * "
14 cattle, and above e' beast of the field; "
24 flaming sword which turned e' way, "
4:14 e' one that findeth me shall slay *3605
22 instructor of e' artificer in brass "
6: 5 e' imagination of the thoughts "
17 e' thing that is in the earth shall "
19 And of e' living thing of all flesh, "
19 two of e' sort shalt thou bring "
20 of e' creeping thing of the earth "
20 two of e' sort shall come unto thee, "
7: 2 Of e' clean beast thou shalt take "
4 e' living substance that I have "
8 and of e' thing that creepeth "
14 They, and e' beast after his kind, "
14 and e' creeping thing that creepeth "
14 and e' fowl after his kind "
14 e' bird of e' sort. "
21 and of e' creeping thing that "
21 upon the earth, and e' man. "
23 And e' living substance was "
8: 1 Noah, and e' living thing, and all "
17 Bring forth with thee e' living thing "
17 and of e' creeping thing that "
19 E' beast, e' creeping thing, and e' "
20 and took of e' clean beast, "
20 and of e' clean fowl, "
21 smite any more e' thing living, "
9: 2 upon e' beast of the earth, "
3 E' moving thing that liveth "
5 at the hand of e' man's brother "
10 And with e' living creature that 3605
10 and of e' beast of the earth "
12 e' living creature that is with you, "
15 e' living creature of all flesh; "
16 e' living creature of all flesh that "
10: 5 e' one after his tongue, after their 376
13:10 it was well watered e' where, 3605
16:12 his hand will be against e' man, "
12 and e' man's hand against him; "
17:10 E' man child among you shall be "
12 e' man child in your generations, "
23 e' male among the men of "
20:13 at e' place whither we shall come, "
27:29 cursed be e' one that curseth thee, "
30:33 e' one that is not speckled and 3605
35 e' one that had some white in it, "
32:16 e' drove by themselves; "
34:15 e' male of you be circumcised; 3605
22 e' male among us be circumcised, "
23 and e' beast of theirs be ours? * "
24 e' male was circumcised, "
41:48 which was round about e' city, "
42:25 e' man's money into his sack, "
35 e' man's bundle of money was "
43:21 behold, e' man's money was in "
44: 1 and put e' man's money in his "
11 took down e' man his sack "
11 opened e' man his sack. "
13 laded e' man his ass, "
45: 1 Cause e' man to go out from me. 3605
46:34 for e' shepherd is an abomination "
47:20 Egyptians sold e' man his field, "
49:28 e' one according to his blessing "
Ex 1: 1 e' man and his household came "
22 E' son that is born ye shall cast 3605
22 e' daughter ye shall save alive. "
3:22 But e' woman shall borrow of her "
7:12 they cast down e' man his rod, 376
9:19 upon e' man and beast which 3605
22 and upon e' herb of the field, "
25 hail smote e' herb of the field, "
25 break e' tree of the field. "
10: 5 shall eat e' tree which groweth "
12 eat e' herb of the land, "
15 did eat e' herb of the land, "
11: 2 let e' man borrow of his neighbour, "
2 e' woman of her neighbour, "
12: 3 shall take to them e' man a lamb, "
4 e' man according to his eating "
16 save that which e' man must eat, 3605
13:12 e' firstling that cometh of a "
13 And e' firstling of an ass "
14: 7 captains over e' one of them. * "
16: 4 gather a certain rate e' day, "
16 Gather of it e' man according to "
16 an omer for e' man, according to * "
16 take ye e' man for them which are "
18 gathered e' man according to his "
21 And they gathered it e' morning, "
21 morning, e' man according to his "
29 e' man in his place, let no man go "
18:22 e' great matter they shall bring 3605
22 e' small matter they shall judge: "
26 e' small matter they judged "
25: 2 of e' man that giveth it willingly 3605
26: 2 e' one of the curtains shall have * "
28:21 e' one with his name shall they be 376
29:36 And thou shalt offer e' day "
30: 7 thereon sweet incense e' morning: "
12 give e' man a ransom for his soul "
13 e' one that passeth among them 3605
14 E' one that passeth among them "
31:14 e' one that defileth it shall surely "
32:27 Put e' man his sword by his side, "
27 slay e' man his brother, "
27 and e' man his companion, "
27 and e' man his neighbour. "
29 e' man upon his son, and upon his "
33: 7 e' one which sought the Lord 3605
8 e' man at his tent door, and looked 376

Ex 33:10 worshipped, e' man in his tent door.
34:19 e' firstling among thy cattle, *3605
35:10 And e' wise hearted among you "
21 they came, e' one whose heart "
21 e' one whom his spirit made "
22 and e' man that offered offered "
23 And e' man, with whom was "
24 E' one that did offer an offering "
24 e' man, with whom was found "
29 unto the Lord, e' man and woman, "
36: 1 and e' wise hearted man, in whom "
2 and e' wise hearted man, in whose "
2 e' one whose heart stirred him "
3 free offerings e' morning.
4 came e' man from his work
8 And e' wise hearted man among 3605
30 silver, under e' board two sockets. 259
38:26 for e' man, that is, half a shekel, *
26 e' one that went to be numbered. 3605
39:14 e' one with his name, according to 376
Le 2:13 And e' oblation of thy meat 3605
6:12 burn wood on it e' morning,
18 e' one that toucheth them shall *3605
23 For e' meat offering for the priest "
7: 6 E' male among the priests shall "
10 And e' meat offering, mingled "
11:21 ye eat of e' flying creeping thing * "
26 The carcases of e' beast which "
26 e' one that toucheth them shall be "
33 And e' earthen vessel, whereinto "
34 may be drunk in e' such vessel "
35 And e' thing whereupon any part "
41 e' creeping thing that creepeth "
46 of e' living creature that moveth "
46 and of e' creature that creepeth "
15: 4 E' bed, whereon he lieth that hath "
12 e' vessel of wood shall be rinsed "
17 And e' garment, and e' skin, "
20 And e' thing that she lieth upon "
20 e' thing also that she sitteth upon "
26 E' bed whereon she lieth "
17:15 e' soul that eateth that which died "
19: 3 Ye shall fear e' man his mother,
8 Therefore e' one that eateth it
10 gather e' grape of thy vineyard; *
20: 9 e' one that curseth his father or 376
23:37 e' thing upon his day: *
24: 8 E' sabbath he shall set it in order
25:10 return e' man unto his possession,
10 shall return e' man unto his family.
13 return e' man unto his possession.
27:28 e' devoted thing is most holy 3605
Nu 1: 2 e' male by their polls;
4 a man of e' tribe 376
4 e' one head of the house of his "
20, 22 e' male from twenty years old 3605
52 e' man by his own camp,
52 and e' man by his own standard,
2: 2 E' man of the children of Israel
17 e' man in his place by their
34 e' one after their families, according 376
3:15 e' male from a month old 3605
4:19 appoint them e' one to his service 376
30, 35, 39, 43 e' one that entereth into 3605
47 e' one that came to do the service "
49 e' one according to his service, and 376
5: 2 e' leper, and e' one that hath an 3605
9 e' offering of all the holy things "
10 And e' man's hallowed things
7: 5 to e' man according to his service.
8:16 instead of such as open e' womb, *3605
17 I smote e' firstborn in the land * "
11:10 e' man in the door of his tent:
13: 2 e' tribe of their fathers shall ye 376
2 a man, e' one a ruler among them. 3605
15:12 so shall ye do to e' one according
16: 3 congregation are holy, e' one of 3605
17 take e' man his censer, and put
17 before the Lord e' man his censer,
18 And they took e' man his censer,
27 the tabernacle of Korah,...on e' side: 376
17: 2 and take of e' one of them a rod *
2 write thou e' man's name upon
6 e' one of their princes gave him *3605
9 looked, and took e' man his rod.
18: 7 office for e' thing of the altar, 3605
9 e' oblation of theirs, "
9 e' meat offering "
9 e' sin offering of theirs, e' trespass "
10 e' male shall eat it: "
11 e' one that is clean in thy house "
13 e' one that is clean in thine house "
14 E' thing devoted in Israel shall be "
15 E' thing that openeth the matrix "
29 ye shall offer e' heave offering "
31 ye shall eat it in e' place, "
19:15 And e' open vessel, which hath no "
21: 8 E' one that is bitten,
23: 2 Balaam offered on e' altar a bullock
4 I have offered upon e' altar a bullock
14, 30 a bullock and a ram on e' altar.
25: 5 Slay ye e' one his men that 376
26:54 to e' one shall his inheritance be
28:10 is the burnt offering of e' sabbath,
14 burnt offering for e' month
21 deal shalt thou offer for e' lamb,
29:14 three tenth deals unto e' bullock 259
30: 4 and e' bond wherewith she hath 3605
9 But e' vow of a widow, and of her*
11 e' bond wherewith she bound 3605
13 E' vow, and e' binding oath
31: 4 Of e' tribe a thousand, throughout
5 of Israel, a thousand of e' tribe,
6 to the war, a thousand of e' tribe,
17 Now therefore kill e' male among 3605
17 and kill e' woman that hath known "

Nu 31:23 E' thing that may abide the fire, 3605
50 what e' man hath gotten, of jewels
53 had taken spoil, e' man for himself.)
32:18 inherited e' man his inheritance.
27 pass over, e' man armed for war, 3605
29 Jordan, e' man armed to battle, "
33:54 e' man's inheritance shall be in *
34:18 take one prince of e' tribe,
35: 8 e' one shall give of his cities 376
15 e' one that killeth any person 3605
36: 7 e' one of the children of Israel 376
8 may enjoy e' man the inheritance
9 but e' one of the tribes of the 376
De 1:16 between e' man and his brother, *
22 came near unto me e' one of you, 3605
41 on e' man his weapons of war, 376
2:34 of e' city, we left none to remain: 3605
3: 6 and children, of e' city. "
20 return e' man, unto his possession,
4: 4 are alive e' one of you this day. 3605
8: 3 but by e' word that proceedeth "
11:24 E' place whereon the soles of your "
12: 2 and under e' green tree:
8 e' man whatsoever is right in his
13 offerings in e' place that thou 3605
31 for e' abomination to the Lord, "
13:16 and all the spoil thereof e' whit, 3632
14: 6 And e' beast that parteth the hoof, 3605
14 And e' raven after his kind, "
19 And e' creeping thing that flieth * "
15: 1 end of e' seven years thou shalt
2 E' creditor that lendeth ought 3605
16:17 E' man shall give as he is able,
19: 3 that e' slayer may flee thither. 3605
20:13 thou shalt smite e' male thereof "
21: 5 shall e' controversy and e' stroke "
23: 9 keep thee from e' wicked thing. "
24:16 e' man shall be put to death
26:11 shalt rejoice in e' good thing *3605
28:61 Also e' sickness, and e' plague "
30: 9 plenteous in e' work * "
31:10 At the end of e' seven years,
33: 3 e' one shall receive of thy words.
Jos 1: 3 E' place that the sole of your foot 3605
3:12 of Israel, out of e' tribe a man.
4: 2 the people, out of e' tribe a man,
4 of Israel, out of e' tribe a man:
5 take you up e' man of you a stone
10 until e' thing was finished that 3605
6: 5 shall ascend up e' man straight
20 e' man straight before him, and
11:14 e' man they smote with the edge 3605
21:42 were e' one with their suburbs round
24:28 e' man unto his inheritance.
J'g 2: 6 e' man unto his inheritance to
5:30 to e' man a damsel or two; 7218
7: 5 E' one that lappeth of the water 3605
5 e' one that boweth down upon his "
7 people go e' man unto his place.
8 of Israel e' man unto his tent,
16 a trumpet in e' man's hand, *3605
18 on e' side of all the camp,
21 and they stood e' man in his place
22 e' man's sword against his fellow,
8:24 me e' man the earrings of his prey.
25 cast therein e' man the earrings of
34 of all their enemies on e' side: 5437
9:49 cut down e' man his bough,
55 they departed e' man unto his place.
16: 5 e' one of us eleven hundred pieces 376
17: 6 e' man did that which was right
20:16 e' one could sling stones at an 3605
48 as well the men of e' city, *
21:11 destroy e' male, and e' woman 3605
21 and catch you e' man his wife
24 e' man to his tribe and to his family,
24 thence e' man to his inheritance.
25 e' man did that which was right in
1Sa 2:36 e' one that is left in thine house 3605
3:11 ears of e' one that heareth it shall "
18 Samuel told him e' whit, "
4:10 fled e' man into his tent:
8:22 Go ye e' man unto his city.
10:25 people away, e' man to his house.
12:11 your enemies on e' side, and ye 5437
13: 2 he sent e' man to his tent.
20 to sharpen e' man his share, and
14:20 e' man's sword was against his
34 Bring me hither e' man his ox,
34 and e' man his sheep,
34 e' man his ox with him that night,
47 against all his enemies on e' side, 5437
15: 9 but e' thing that was vile 3605
20:15 And e' one from the face of the earth. 376
22: 2 and e' one that was in distress, 3605
2 and e' one that was in debt, "
2 and e' one that was discontented, "
7 son of Jesse give e' one of you "
23:14 And Saul sought him e' day,
25:10 away e' man from his master.
13 Gird ye on e' man his sword.
13 they girded on e' man his sword;
26:23 The Lord render to e' man his
27: 3 e' man with his household, even
30: 6 e' man for his sons and for his
22 e' man his wife and his children,
2Sa 2: 3 e' man with his household: and
16 e' one his fellow by the head, 376
27 e' one from following his brother. "
6:19 to e' one a cake of bread, and a "
19 people departed e' one to his house. "
13: 9 And they went out e' man from him.
29 e' man gat him up upon his mule,
37 David mourned for his son e' day. 3605
14:26 was at e' year's end that he polled it: "
15: 4 e' man which hath any suit or 3605

2Sa 15:30 covered e' man his head, and they
36 send unto me e' thing that ye can 3605
18:17 all Israel fled e' one to his tent. 376
19: 8 Israel had fled e' man to his tent.
20: 1 e' man to his tents, O Israel. 376
2 e' man of Israel went up from * "
12 saw that e' one that came by him 3605
22 from the city, e' man to his tent.
21:20 had on e' hand six fingers,
20 on e' foot six toes,
1Ki 1:49 rose up, and went e' man his way.
4:25 e' man under his vine and under
27 e' man in his month: they lacked
28 e' man according to his charge.
5: 3 which were about him on e' side, 5437
4 God hath given me rest on e' side, "
7:30 e' base had four brasen wheels, 259
30 at the side of e' addition. * 376
36 the proportion of e' one, and * "
38 and e' laver was four cubits: 259
38 and upon e' one of the ten bases
8:38 which shall know e' man the plague
39 to e' man according to his ways,
9: 8 e' one that passeth by it shall be 3605
10:25 they brought e' man his present,
11:15 had smitten e' male in Edom; 3605
16 until he cut off e' male in Edom: "
12:24 return e' man to his house; for
14:23 groves, on e' high hill, 3605
23 and under e' green tree. "
19:18 and e' mouth which hath not
20:20 And they slew e' one his man: 376
24 e' man out of his place, and put "
22:17 let them return e' man to his house
28 Hearken, O people, e' one of you. *3605
36 E' man to his city, and
36 e' man to his own country.
2Ki 3:19 smite e' fenced city, and e' choice 3605
19 and shall fell e' good tree, "
19 mar e' good piece of land "
25 on e' good piece of land
25 cast e' man his stone,
6: 2 and take thence e' man a beam,
8: 9 of e' good thing of Damascus, 3605
9:13 took e' man his garment, and put
11: 8 e' man with his weapons in his
9 they took e' man his men that were
11 guard stood, e' man with weapons
12: 4 the money of e' one that passeth 3605
4 the money that e' man is set at, *
5 them, e' man of his acquaintance:
14: 6 but e' man shall be put to death
12 and they fled e' man to their tents.
16: 4 the hills, and under e' green tree. 3605
17:10 in e' high hill, and under e' green "
29 Howbeit e' nation made gods
29 e' nation in their cities wherein
18:31 eat ye e' man of his own vine, and
31 e' one of his fig...and drink ye e' one 376
23:35 e' one according to his taxation, "
25: 9 e' great man's house burnt he 3605
30 a daily rate for e' day, all the days
1Ch 9:27 the opening thereof e' morning *
32 shewbread, to prepare it e' sabbath.
13: 1 hundreds, and with e' leader. 3605
2 send abroad our brethren e' where,
16: 3 dealt to e' one of Israel, both man 376
3 man and woman, to e' one a loaf
37 before the ark continually, as e' day's
43 departed e' man to his house:
22:15 men for e' manner of work. *3605
18 he not given you rest on e' side? 5437
23:30 And to stand e' morning to thank
26:13 cast lots...for e' gate.
32 for e' matter pertaining to God, 3605
27: 1 of e' course were twenty and four 259
28:14 instruments of e' kind of service: 3605
15 by weight for e' candlestick,
15 according to the use of e' candlestick.
28:16 tables of shewbread, for e' table;
17 he gave gold by weight for e' bason;
21 workmanship e' willing skilful 3605
2Ch 2:14 to find out e' device which * "
6:29 e' one shall know his own sore 376
30 e' man according unto all his ways,
7:21 an astonishment to e' one that 3605
8:13 Even after a certain rate e' day,
14 as the duty of e' day required:
9:21 e' three years once came the ships
24 they brought e' man his present,
10:16 e' man to your tents, O Israel:
11: 4 return e' man to his house; for this
12 And in e' special city he put 3605
23 Benjamin, unto e' fenced city:
13:11 e' morning and e' evening burnt
11 lamps thereof, to burn e' evening:
14: 7 he hath given us rest on e' side. 5437
18:16 therefore e' man to his house
20:23 e' one helped to destroy another. 376
27 they returned, e' man of Judah 3605
23: 7 e' man with his weapons in his
8 e' man his men that were to come
10 e' man having his weapon in his
25: 4 but e' man shall die for his own sin.
22 and they fled e' man to his tent.
28: 4 the hills, and under e' green tree. 3605
24 altars in e' corner of Jerusalem. "
25 And in e' several city of Judah "
29:35 drink offerings for e' burnt offering.
30:17 for e' one that was not clean, 3605
18 The good Lord pardon e' one
31: 1 e' man to his possession, into their
2 e' man according to his service,
16 even unto e' one that entereth 3605
19 in e' several city, the men that "
21 And in e' work that he began "

2Ch 32:22 and guided them on e' side. 5437
35:15 and the porters waited at e' gate;
Ezr 2: 1 and Judah, e' one unto his city; 376
3: 4 as the duty of e' day required;
5 of e' one that willingly offered 3605
6: 5 at Jerusalem, e' one to his place,
8:34 and by weight of e' one: *3605
9: 4 assembled unto me e' one that
10:14 with them the elders of e' city,
Ne 3:28 e' one over against his house. 376
4:15 to the wall, e' one unto his work. "
17 e' one with one of his hands "
18 e' one had his sword girded by his "
22 Let e' one with his servant lodge "
23 e' one put them off for washing. "
5: 7 exact usury, e' one of his brother. "
13 shake out e' man from his house,
7: 3 e' one in his watch, and e' one to be376
6 and to Judah, e' one unto his city; "
8:16 e' one upon the roof of his house,
10:28 e' one having knowledge, and 3605
31 and the exaction of e' debt.
11: 3 e' one in his possession in their 376
20 of Judah, e' one in his inheritance. "
23 be for the singers, due for e' day.
12:47 the singers and the porters, e' day
13:10 were fled e' one to his field. 376
30 the Levites, e' one in his business; "
Es 1: 8 do according to e' man's pleasure.
22 king's provinces, into e' province
22 to e' people after their language, 376
22 that e' man should bear rule in *
22 to the language of e' people.
2:11 Mordecai walked e' day before the
12 Now when e' maid's turn was come
13 came e' maiden unto the king; *
3:12 governors that were over e' province,
12 rulers of e' people of e' province
12 to e' people after their language;
14 to be given in e' province 3605
4: 3 And in e' province, whithersoever "
6:13 e' thing that had befallen him. "
8: 9 unto e' province according to
9 and unto e' people after their
11 Jews which were in e' city to 3605
13 to be given in e' province was "
17 And in e' province, and in e' city. "
9:27 their appointed time e' year; "
28 e' [3605] generation, e' family,
28 e' province, and e' city;
Job 1: 4 their houses, e' one his day; * 376
10 about all that he hath on e' side? 5437
2:11 came e' one from his own place; 376
12 and they rent e' one his mantle,
7:18 visit him e' morning, and try him e'
12:10 the soul of e' living thing, 3605
18:11 shall make him afraid on e' side, 5437
19:10 He hath destroyed me on e' side,
20:22 e' hand of the wicked shall come 3605
21:33 and e' man shall draw after him, * "
24: 6 They reap e' one his corn *
28:10 his eye seeth e' precious thing. 3605
34:11 and cause e' man to find according
36:25 E' man may see it; *3605
37: 7 sealeth up the hand of e' man; "
39: 8 he searcheth after e' green thing. "
40:11 behold e' one that is proud, "
12 Look on e' one that is proud, "
42: 2 thou canst do e' thing, * "
11 e' man also gave him a piece of
11 and e' one an earring 376
Ps 7:11 angry with the wicked e' day. 3605
12: 2 vanity e' one with his neighbour: 376
8 The wicked walk on e' side, 5437
29: 9 doth e' one speak of his glory. 3605
31:13 fear was on e' side: 5437
32: 6 For this shall e' one that is godly 3605
39: 5 e' man at his best state is altogether"
6 e' man walketh in a vain shew:
11 surely e' man is vanity. Selah. 3605
50:10 For e' beast of the forest is mine, "
53: 3 E' one of them is gone back: "
56: 5 E' day they wrest my words: * "
58: 8 let e' one of them pass away: *
62:12 to e' man according to his work.
63:11 e' one that sweareth by him shall 3605
64: 6 inward thought of e' one of them, 376
65:12 the little hills rejoice on e' side. *
68:30 till e' one submit himself with *
69:34 the seas, and e' thing that moveth 3605
71:18 thy power to e' one that is to come. "
21 and comfort me on e' side. *5437
73:14 plagued, and chastened e' morning.
84: 7 e' one of them in Zion appeareth
92: 2 and thy faithfulness e' night,
104:11 drink to e' beast of the field: 3605
115: 8 so is e' one that trusteth in them. "
119:101 my feet from e' evil way, "
104 therefore I hate e' false way. "
128 and I hate e' false way. "
160 e' one of thy righteous judgments "
128: 1 Blessed is e' one that feareth "
135:18 so is e' one that trusteth in them. "
145: 2 E' day I will bless thee; "
16 the desire of e' living thing. "
150: 6 Let e' thing that hath breath "
Pr 1:19 the ways of e' one that is greedy "
2: 9 yea, e' good path.
3:18 happy is e' one that retaineth her.
7:12 and lieth in wait at e' corner.) 3605
13:16 E' prudent man dealeth with "
14: 1 E' wise woman buildeth her house:
15 The simple believeth e' word: 3605
15: 3 The eyes of the Lord are in e' place, "
16: 5 E' one that is proud in heart "
19: 6 e' man that is a friend to him "

Pr 20: 3 but e' fool will be meddling. 3605
6 e' one his own goodness: but a 376
18 E' purpose is established by counsel:
21: 2 E' way of a man is right in his 3605
5 of e' one that is hasty only to want. "
24:12 to e' man according to his works?
26 E' man shall kiss his lips *
27: 7 soul e' bitter thing is sweet. 3605
24 crown endure to e' generation? *
29:26 e' man's judgment cometh from *
30: 5 E' word of God is pure: 3605
Ec 3: 1 To e' thing there is a season, "
1 to e' purpose under the heaven: "
11 e' thing beautiful in his time: "
13 that e' man should eat and drink, "
17 for e' purpose and for e' work. "
4: 4 all travail, and e' right work, "
5:19 E' man also to whom God hath "
8: 6 Because to e' purpose there is "
9 unto e' work that is done under "
10: 3 he saith to e' one that he is a fool. "
15 wearieth e' one of them,
12:14 God shall bring e' work into 3605
14 with e' secret thing, whether it be "
Ca 3: 8 e' man hath his sword upon his
4: 2 whereof e' one bear twins, 3605
6: 6 whereof e' one beareth twins,
8: 11 e' one for the fruit thereof was to 376
Isa 1:23 e' one loveth gifts, and followeth 3605
2:12 be upon e' one that is proud * "
12 and upon e' one that is lifted up;* "
15 e' high tower, and upon e' fenced "
3: 5 be oppressed, e' one by another, 376
5 and e' one by his neighbour: "
4: 3 even e' one that is written among 3605
5 create upon e' dwelling place * "
7:22 honey shall e' one eat that is "
23 that e' place shall be, where "
9: 5 For e' battle of the warrior is * "
17 e' one is an hypocrite and an "
17 and e' mouth speaketh folly, "
20 eat e' man the flesh of his own
13: 7 e' man's heart shall melt: 3605
14 e' man turn to his own people, and
14 flee e' one into his own land. 376
15 E' one that is found shall be 3605
15 and e' one that is joined unto "
14:18 in glory, e one in his own house. 376
15: 2 and e' beard cut off. 3605
3 in their streets, e' one shall howl, "
16: 7 for Moab, e' one shall howl: "
19: 2 e' one against his brother, 376
2 and e' one against his neighbour; "
7 and e' thing sown by the brooks *3605
14 Egypt to err in e' work thereof, "
17 e' one that maketh mention "
24:10 e' house is shut up, "
27: 3 I will water it e' moment:
25 and upon e' high mountain 3605
30:25 and upon e' high hill, "
32 And in e' place where the grounded"
31: 7 e' man shall cast away his idols
33: 2 be thou their arm e' morning,
34:15 be gathered, e' one with her mate. 802
36:16 eat ye e' one of his vine, and e' one 376
16 drink ye e' one the waters of his "
40: 4 E' valley shall be exalted 3605
4 e' mountain and hill shall be made "
41: 6 helped e' one his neighbour; 376
6 and e' one said to his brother, "
43: 7 e' one that is called by my name: 3605
44:23 O forest, and e' tree therein: "
45:23 unto me e' knee shall bow, "
23 e' tongue shall swear. "
47:15 they shall wander e' one to his 376
51:13 feared continually e' day because*3605
52: 5 continually e' day is blasphemed.* "
53: 6 we have turned e' one to his own 376
54:17 e' tongue that shall rise against 3605
55: 1 Ho, e' one that thirsteth, "
56: 6 e' one that keepeth the sabbath "
11 e' one for his gain, from his quarter.*376
57: 5 with idols under e' green tree, 3605
58: 6 that ye break e' yoke? "
Jer 1:15 shall set e' one his throne at the 376
2:20 when upon e' high hill and under 3605
20 under e' green tree thou wanderest, "
3: 6 gone up upon e' high mountain and "
6 and under e' green tree, and there "
13 to the strangers under e' green tree, "
4:29 e' city shall be forsaken, "
5: 8 e' one neighed after his neighbour's 376
6: 3 they shall feed e' one in his place. "
13 e' one is given to covetousness; 3605
13 unto the priest e' one dealeth "
25 the enemy and fear is on e' side. 5437
8: 6 e' one turned to his course, 3605
10 for e' one from the least even unto "
10 the priest e' one dealeth falsely. "
9: 4 ye heed e' one of his neighbour, 376
4 for e' brother will utterly supplant 3605
4 e' neighbour will walk with slanders. "
5 deceive e' one his neighbour, 376
20 e' one her neighbour lamentation. 802
10:14 E' man is brutish in his 3605
14 e' founder is confounded by the "
11: 8 walked e' one in the imagination 376
12: 4 and the herbs of e' field wither, *3605
15 e' man to his heritage, and e' man
13:12 E' bottle shall be filled with wine: 3605
12 know that e' bottle shall be filled "
15:10 e' one of them doth curse me. "
16:12 e' one after the imagination of his 376
16 from e' mountain, and from e' hill, 3605
17:10 give e' man according to his ways,
18:11 return ye now e' one from his evil 376

Jer 18:12 we will e' one do the imagination 376
16 e' one that passeth thereby shall 3605
19: 8 e' one that passeth thereby shall be"
9 and they shall eat e' one the flesh 376
20: 7 daily, e' one mocketh me. 3605
10 defaming of many, fear on e' side. 5437
22: 7 thee, e' one with his weapons; 376
8 shall say e' man to his neighbour,
23:17 they say unto e' one that walketh 3605
27 they tell e' man to his neighbour,
30 my words e' one from his neighbour.376
35 ye say e' one to his neighbour, and "
35 and e' one to his brother, "
36 e' man's word shall be his burden;
25: 5 Turn ye again now e' one from his 376
26: 3 and turn e' man from his evil way,
29:26 for e' man that is mad, and maketh
30: 6 I see e' man with his hands on his 3605
16 e' one of them, shall go into
31:25 replenished e' sorrowful soul.
30 e' one shall die for his own iniquity:376
34 teach no more e' man his neighbour,
34 and e' man his brother,
32:19 to give e' one according to his ways376
34: 9 e' man should let his manservant,
9 and e' man his maidservant,
10 e' one should let his manservant, 376
10 and e' one his maidservant, go free, "
14 let ye go e' man his brother
15 proclaiming liberty e' man to his
16 e' man his servant, and e' man his
17 e' one to his brother, and e' man to
35:15 Return ye now e' man from his evil
36: 3 return e' man from his evil way;
7 return e' one from his evil way: 376
37:10 rise up e' man in his tent,
43: 6 and e' person that Nebuzar-adan 3605
47: 4 from Tyrus and Zidon e' helper "
48: 8 spoiler shall come upon e' city, "
37 For e' head shall be bald, "
37 and e' beard clipped: "
49: 5 ye shall be driven out e' man
17 e' one that goeth by it shall be 3605
29 cry unto them, Fear is on e' side. 5437
50:13 e' one that goeth by Babylon shall 3605
16 shall turn e' one to his people, and 376
16 and they shall flee e' one "
42 e' one put in array, like a man to the
51: 6 and deliver e' man his soul:
9 go e' one into his own country: 376
17 E' man is brutish by his 3605
17 e' founder is confounded by the "
29 for e' purpose of the Lord shall be*
45 and deliver ye e' man his soul
56 men are taken, e' one of their *
52:34 e' day a portion until the day of his
La 2:19 for hunger in the top of e' street. 3605
3:23 They are new e' morning: great is
4: 1 poured out in the top of e' street. 3605
Eze 1: 6 e' one had four faces, and e' one
9 went e' one straight forward. 376
11 two wings of e' one were joined "
12 they went e' one straight forward: "
23 e' one had two, which covered on "
23 this side, and e' one had two, "
6:13 upon e' high hill,...under e' green 3605
13 and under e' thick oak, the place "
7:16 all of them mourning, e' one for his 376
8:10 and behold e' form of creeping 3605
11 with e' man his censer in his hand;
12 e' man in the chambers of his
9: 1 even e' man with his destroying
2 and e' man a slaughter weapon
10:14 And e' one had four faces:
19 and e' one stood at the door *
21 E' one had four faces apiece, and
21 and e' one four wings;
22 they went e' one straight forward. 376
11: 5 into your mind, e' one of them, *
12:14 And I will scatter toward e' wind 3605
22 The days are prolonged, and e' "
23 at hand, and the effect of e' vision. "
13:18 kerchiefs upon the head of e' stature"
14: 4 E' man of the house of Israel
7 e' one of the house of Israel, 376
16:15 thy fornications on e' one that 3605
24 made thee an high place in e' street. "
25 built thy high place at e' head of "
25 opened thy feet to e' one that "
31 eminent place in the head of e' way, "
31 makest thine high place in e' street; "
33 may come unto thee on e' side 5437
44 Behold, e' one that useth proverbs 3605
17:23 under it shall dwell all fowl of e' "
18:30 e' one according to his ways, saith 376
19: 8 the nations set against him on e' 5437
20: 7 Cast ye away e' man the
8 they did not e' man cast away
28 then they saw e' high hill, and all 3605
39 Go ye, serve ye e' one his idols, 376
47 e' green tree in thee, and e' dry 3605
21: 7 and e' heart shall melt, and all "
7 and e' spirit shall faint, "
10 the rod of my son, as e' tree. "
22: 6 e' one were in thee to their power 376
23:22 bring them against thee on e' side; 5437
24: 4 even e' good piece, the thigh, and 3605
26:16 and shall tremble at e' moment, and
28:13 e' precious stone was thy covering, 3605
23 by the sword upon her on e' side; 5437
29:18 e' head was made bald, and 3605
18 and e' shoulder was peeled; "
32:10 and they shall tremble at e' moment,
10 e' man for his own life, in the day
33:20 I will judge you e' one after his ways376
26 and ye defile e' one his neighbour's "

Eze 33:30 e· one to his brother, saying, 376
34: 6 the mountains, and upon e· high 3605
8 my flock became meat to e· beast* "
36: 3 and swallowed you up on e· side, 5437
37:21 and will gather them on e· side, "
38:20 and e· wall shall fall to the ground3605
21 e· man's sword shall be against "
39: 4 unto the ravenous birds of e· sort,3605
17 Speak unto e· feathered fowl, and "
17 and to e· beast of the field, "
17 gather yourselves on e· side to 5437
40: 7 e· little chamber was one reed long, "
41: 5 and the breadth of e· side chamber, "
5 round about the house on e· side. 5437
10 round about the house on e· side. "
18 and e· cherub had two faces; "
43:25 shalt thou prepare e· day a goat for a "
44: 5 e· going forth of the sanctuary, 3605
29 and e· dedicated thing in Israel "
30 fruits of all things, and e· oblation "
30 of e· sort of your oblations, * "
45:20 for e· one that erreth, and for him 376
46:13 thou shalt prepare it e· morning. * "
14 a meat offering for it e· morning, * "
15 e· offering, and the oil, e· morning* "
18 e· man from his possession. "
21 in e· corner of the court there was a "
47: 9 come to pass, that e· thing that 3605
9 and e· thing shall live whither the "
Da 3:10 that e· man that shall hear the 3606
29 e· people, nation, and language, "
6:12 that e· man that shall ask a petition "
26 in e· dominion of my kingdom * "
11:36 and magnify himself above e· god, 3605
12: 1 e· one shall be found written in "
Ho 4: 3 e· one that dwelleth therein shall "
9: 1 thou hast loved a reward upon e· "
Joe 2: 7 and they shall march e· one on his 376
8 they shall walk e· one in his path: 1397
Am 2: 8 clothes laid to pledge by e· altar, 3605
4: 3 e· cow at that which is before her; 802
4 bring your sacrifices e· morning, "
8: 3 be many dead bodies in e· place; 3605
8 e· one mourn that dwelleth therein? "
10 all loins, and baldness upon e· head; "
Ob 9 e· one of the mount of Esau 376
Jon 1: 5 and cried e· man unto his god, "
7 and they said e· one to his fellow, 376
3: 8 them turn e· one from his evil way, "
Mic 4: 4 sit e· man under his vine and under "
5 walk e· one in the name of his god, 376
7: 2 hunt e· man his brother with a net. "
Hab 1:10 they shall divide e· stronghold; for3605
Zep 2:11 e· one from his place, even all the 376
15 e· one that passeth by her shall 3605
3: 5 e· morning doth he bring his judgment "
19 fame in e· land where they have *3605
Hag 1: 9 ye run e· man unto his own house. "
2:14 and so is e· work of their hands; 3605
22 e· one by the sword of his brother. 376
Zec 3:10 call e· man his neighbour under "
5: 3 e· one that stealeth shall be cut 3605
3 e· one that sweareth shall be cut "
7: 9 compassions e· man to his brother: "
8: 4 e· man with his staff in his hand "
10 men e· one against his neighbour. "
16 e· man the truth to his neighbour; "
10: 1 to e· one grass in the field. 376
4 out of him e· oppressor together. 3605
11: 6 e· one into his neighbour's hand, 376
9 rest eat e· one the flesh of another.802
12: 4 smite e· horse with astonishment,3605
4 e· horse of the people with blindness. "
12 the land shall mourn, e· family apart; "
14 families that remain, e· family apart, "
13: 4 be ashamed e· one of his vision. 376
14:13 e· one on the hand of his neighbour, "
16 e· one that is left of all the nations 3605
21 e· pot in Jerusalem and in Judah "
Mal 1:11 in e· place incense shall be offered "
2:10 do we deal treacherously e· man "
17 E· one that doeth evil is good in 3605
M't 3:10 e· tree which bringeth not forth 3956
4: 4 but by e· word that proceedeth out "
7: 8 For e· one that asketh receiveth; "
17 so e· good tree bringeth forth good "
19 E· tree that bringeth not forth good "
21 Not e· one that saith unto me, "
26 e· one that heareth these sayings "
8:33 e· thing, and what was befallen "
9:35 healing e· sickness and e· disease* "
12:25 E· kingdom divided against "
25 e· city or house divided against "
36 e· idle word that men shall speak "
13:47 the sea, and gathered of e· kind: "
52 e· scribe which is instructed "
15:13 E· plant, which my heavenly Father "
16:27 e· man according to his works. 1538
18:16 e· word may be established. 3956
35 e· one his brother their trespasses.1538
19: 3 put away his wife for e· cause? 3956
29 e· one that hath forsaken houses, "
20: 9 they received e· man a penny. 303
10 likewise received e· man a penny. "
25:15 e· man according to his several *1538
29 e· one that hath shall be given, 3956
26:22 e· one of them to say unto him, 1538
M'r 1:45 they came to him from e· quarter. 3836
7:14 Hearken unto me e· one of you, *3956
8:25 restored, and saw e· man clearly. * 537
9:49 e· one shall be salted with fire, 3956
49 and e· sacrifice shall be salted * "
13:34 and to e· man his work, and *1538
15:24 them, what e· man should take. *5100
16:15 preach the gospel to e· creature. *3956
20 went forth, and preached e· where 3837

Lu 2: 3 to be taxed, e· one into his own city.1538
23 E· male that openeth the womb 3956
41 e· year at the feast of the passover.2596
3: 5 E· valley shall be filled, 3956
5 and e· mountain and hill shall be "
9 e· tree therefore which bringeth not "
4: 4 but by e· word of God. * "
37 fame of him went out into e· place "
40 laid his hands on e· one of them, 1538
5:17 come out of e· town of Galilee, 3956
6:30 Give to e· man that asketh of thee; "
40 but e· one that is perfect shall be as "
44 e· tree is known by his own fruit. *1538
8: 1 that he went throughout e· city *2596
4 were come to him out of e· city, "
9: 6 the gospel, and healing e· where. 3837
43 they wondered e· one at all things*3956
10: 1 into e· city and place, whither he "
11: 4 forgive e· one that is indebted to "
10 For e· one that asketh receiveth; "
17 E· kingdom divided against itself "
16: 5 called e· one of his lord's debtors *1538
16 and e· man presseth into it. 3956
19 and fared sumptuously e· day: 2596
18:14 e· one that exalteth himself shall 3956
19:15 how much e· man had gained *5101
26 e· one which hath shall be given; 3956
43 and keep thee in on e· side, 3840
Joh 1: 9 lighteth e· man that cometh into 3956
2:10 E· man at the beginning doth set "
3: 8 e· one that is born of the Spirit. "
20 e· one that doeth evil hateth the "
6: 7 e· one of them may take a little. 1538
40 e· one which seeth the Son, and 3956
45 E· man therefore that hath heard, "
7:23 I have made a man e· whit whole 3650
53 e· man went unto his own house. 1538
13:10 but is clean e· whit: and ye are 3650
15: 2 E· branch in me that beareth not 3956
2 and e· branch that beareth fruit, "
16:32 be scattered, e· man to his own, 1538
18:37 E· one that is of the truth heareth 3956
19:23 four parts, to e· soldier a part; 1538
21:25 if they should be written e· one, 2596
Ac 2: 5 out of e· nation under heaven. 3956
6 e· man heard them speak in his 1538
8 hear we e· man in our own tongue, "
38 and be baptized e· one of you "
43 fear came upon e· soul: and many 3956
45 all men, as e· man had need. *5100
3:23 shall come to pass, that e· soul, 3956
26 in turning away e· one of you 1538
4:35 e· man according as he had need.* "
5:16 and they were healed e· one. 537
42 and in e· house, they ceased not *2596
8: 3 entering into e· house, and haling "
4 e· where preaching the word. *1330
10:35 in e· nation he that feareth him, 3956
11:29 e· man according to his ability, 1538
13:27 which are read e· sabbath day, 3956
14:23 ordained them elders in e· church,2596
15:21 in e· city them that preach him, "
21 in the synagogues e· sabbath day. 3956
36 and visit our brethren in e· city "
16:26 and e· one's bands were loosed. "
17:27 he be not far from e· one of us: *1538
30 commandeth all men e· where to 3837
18: 4 in the synagogue e· sabbath, 3956
20:23 Holy Ghost witnesseth in e· city, 2596
31 to warn e· one night and day 1538
21:26 be offered for e· one of them. "
28 that teacheth all men e· where 3837
22:19 beat in e· synagogue them that 2596
26:11 them oft in e· synagogue, *3956
28: 2 and received us e· one, because * "
22 e· where it is spoken against. 3837
Ro 1:16 salvation to e· one that believeth; 3956
2: 6 to e· man according to his deeds: 1538
9 e· soul of man that doeth evil, 3956
10 to e· man that worketh good, to the "
3: 2 Much e· way: chiefly, because that "
4 but e· man a liar; as it is written, "
19 that e· mouth may be stopped, and "
10: 4 to e· one that believeth. "
12: 3 to e· man that is among you, not "
3 as God hath dealt to e· man 1538
5 and e· one members one of *2596
13: 1 e· soul be subject unto the higher 3956
14: 5 another esteemeth e· day alike. "
5 Let e· man be fully persuaded *1538
11 e· knee shall bow to me, 3956
11 and e· tongue shall confess to God. "
12 e· one of us shall give account *1538
15: 2 e· one of us please his neighbour * "
1Co 1: 2 with all that in e· place call upon 3956
5 That in e· thing ye are enriched "
12 e· one of you saith, I am of Paul; *1538
3: 5 as the Lord gave to e· man? * "
8 e· man shall receive his own * "
10 let e· man take heed how he * "
13 E· man's work shall be made * "
13 the fire shall try e· man's work * "
4: 5 shall e· man have praise of God. * "
17 as I teach e· where in 3837
17 as I teach...in e· church. 3956
6:18 E· sin that a man doeth is without "
7: 2 let e· man have his own wife, *1538
2 and let e· woman have her own * "
7 e· man hath his proper gift of * "
17 distributed to e· man, as the Lord* "
17 as the Lord hath called e· one, so* "
20 e· man abide in the same calling * "
24 let e· man, wherein he is called, "
8: 7 Howbeit there is not in e· man *3956
9:25 And e· man that striveth for the "
10:24 but e· man another's wealth. *1538

1Co 11: 3 the head of e· man is Christ; 3956
4 E· man praying or prophesying, "
5 But e· woman that prayeth or "
21 in eating e· one taketh before *1538
12: 7 given to e· man to profit withal. * "
11 to e· man severally as he will. "
18 e· one of them in the body, * "
14:26 e· one of you hath a psalm, * "
15:23 But e· man in his own order: * "
30 stand we in jeopardy e· hour? 3956
38 and to e· seed his own body. *1538
16: 2 e· one of you lay by him in store, * "
16 and to e· one that helpeth with us, 3956
2Co 2:14 his knowledge by us in e· place. "
4: 2 to e· man's conscience in the sight "
8 We are troubled on e· side, 1722,
5:10 e· one may receive the things *1538
7: 5 but we were troubled on e· side; 3956
8: 7 as ye abound in e· thing, 376
9: 7 E· man according as he *1538
8 may abound to e· good work: 3956
11 in e· thing to all bountifulness, "
10: 5 e· high thing that exalteth itself "
5 e· thought to the obedience of "
13: 1 shall e· word be established. "
Ga 3:10 e· one that continueth not in all "
13 is e· one that hangeth on a tree: "
5: 3 For I testify again to e· man that "
6: 4 let e· man prove his own work, *1538
5 e· man shall bear his own burden.* "
Eph 1:21 and e· name that is named, not 3956
4: 7 unto e· one of us is given grace *1538
14 about with e· wind of doctrine, 3596
16 by that which e· joint supplieth, "
16 in the measure of e· part, *1520, 1538
25 e· man truth with his neighbour: * "
5:24 to their own husbands in e· thing. 3956
33 let e· one of you in particular *2596, 1520
Ph'p 1: 3 upon e· remembrance of you, *3956
4 in e· prayer of mine for you all "
18 notwithstanding, e· way, whether "
2: 4 not e· man on his own things, *1538
4 but e· man also on the things of "
9 a name which is above e· name: 3596
10 name of Jesus e· knee should bow, "
11 And that e· tongue should confess "
4: 6 e· thing by prayer and supplication "
12 e· where and in all things I am * "
21 Salute e· saint in Christ Jesus. "
Col 1:10 being fruitful in e· good work, "
15 God, the firstborn of e· creature: * "
23 to e· creature which is under "
28 warning e· man, and teaching e· man "
28 that we may present e· man "
4: 6 ye ought to answer e· man. *1519, 1538
1Th 1: 8 in e· place your faith to God-ward 3956
2:11 and charged e· one of you, *1538
4: 4 That e· one of you should know * "
5:18 In e· thing give thanks: for this 3956
2Th 1: 3 the charity of e· one of you all *1538
2:17 stablish you in e· good word and 3956
3: 6 e· brother that walketh disorderly, "
17 which is the token in e· epistle: "
1Ti 2: 8 that men pray e· where, 1722, "
4: 4 For e· creature of God is good, "
5:10 diligently followed e· good work. "
2Ti 2:19 Let e· one that nameth the name "
21 and prepared unto e· good work. "
4:18 shall deliver me from e· evil work, "
Tit 1: 5 and ordain elders in e· city, as I 2596
16 and unto e· good work reprobate. 3956
3: 1 to be ready to e· good work, "
Ph'm 6 the acknowledging of e· good thing "
Heb 2: 2 e· transgression and disobedience "
9 God should taste death for e· man. "
3: 4 For e· house is builded by some "
5: 1 For e· high priest taken from among "
13 For e· one that useth milk is "
6:11 desire that e· one of you do shew *1538
8: 3 For e· high priest is ordained to 3956
11 e· man his neighbour, and e· man 1538
9: 7 high priest alone once e· year, "
19 spoken e· precept to all the people 3956
25 the high priest entereth...e· year *2596
10: 3 again made of sins e· year. "
11 And e· priest standeth daily 3956
12: 1 let us lay aside e· weight, and the "
6 and scourgeth e· son whom he "
13:21 in e· good work to do his will, "
Jas 1:14 e· man is tempted, when he is *1538
17 E· good gift and e· perfect gift 3956
19 let e· man be swift to hear, slow to "
3: 7 For e· kind of beasts, and of birds, "
16 there is confusion and e· evil work. "
1Pe 1:17 according to e· man's work, *1538
2:13 yourself to e· ordinance of man 3956
3:15 answer to e· man that asketh you "
4:10 As e· man hath received the gift, *1538
1Jo 2:29 e· one that doeth righteousness is 3956
3: 3 And e· man that hath this hope "
4: 1 believe not e· spirit, but try the "
2 E· spirit that confesseth that Jesus "
3 And e· spirit that confesseth not "
7 e· one that loveth is born of God, "
5: 1 e· one that loveth him that begat, * "
Re 1: 7 e· eye shall see him, and they also "
2:23 I will give unto e· one of you *1538
5: 8 having e· one of them harps, and * "
9 out of e· kindred, and tongue, 3956
13 And e· creature which is in heaven, "
6:11 were given unto e· one of them; *1538
14 e· mountain and island were 3956
15 e· bondman, and e· free man, hid "
14: 6 e· nation, and kindred, and tongue, "
16: 3 and e· living soul died in the sea. "
20 And e· island fled away, and the

Re 16:21 *e'* stone about the weight of a
18: 2 the hold of *e'* foul spirit, and a cage *3956*
2 of *e'* unclean and hateful bird. "
17 *e'* shipmaster, and all the company "
20:13 were judged *e'* man according to *1538*
21:21 *e'* several gate was of one pearl: * "
22: 2 yielded her fruit *e'* month: *2596,1520,* "
12 to give *e'* man according as his * "
18 I testify unto *e'* man that heareth *3956*

everyone See EVERY and ONE.

everything See EVERY and THING.

everywhere See EVERY and WHERE.

Evi (*e'-vi*)
Nu 31: 8 namely, *E'*, and Rekem, and Zur, 189
Jos 13:21 with the princes of Midian, *E'*, and "

evidence See also EVIDENCES.
Jer 32:10 I subscribed the *e'*, and sealed it, *5612
11 So I took the *e'* of the purchase, * "
12 And I gave the *e'* of the purchase * "
14 this *e'* of the purchase, * "
14 and this *e'* which is open; * "
16 delivered the *e'* of the purchase * "
Heb 11: 1 the *e'* of things not seen. †‡*1650*

evidences
Jer 32:14 Take these *e'*, this evidence of the *5612
44 and subscribe *e'*, and seal them, * "

evident
Job 6:28 for it is *e'* unto you if I lie. *5921, 6440
Ga 3:11 in the sight of God, it is *e'*: for, *1212*
Ph'p 1:28 is to them an *e'* token of perdition, *1732*
Heb 7:14 For it is *e'* that our Lord sprang *4271*
15 And it is yet far more *e'*: for that *2612*

evidently
Ac 10: 3 He saw in a vision *e'*, about the **5320*
Ga 3: 1 Jesus Christ hath been *e'* set forth, *4270*

evil See also EVILDOER; EVILFAVOUREDNESS; EVILS.
Ge 2: 9 tree of knowledge of good and *e'*. 7451
17 of the knowledge of good and *e'*. "
3: 5 be as gods, knowing good and *e'*. "
22 as one of us, to know good and *e'*: "
6: 5 of his heart was only *e'* continually. "
8:21 imagination of man's heart is *e'* "
19:19 lest some *e'* take me, and I die: "
37: 2 unto his father their *e'* report. "
20 Some *e'* beast hath devoured him: "
33 an *e'* beast hath devoured him; "
44: 4 have ye rewarded *e'* for good? "
5 ye have done *e'* in so doing. 7489
34 lest...I see the *e'* that shall come 7451
47: 9 few and *e'* have the days of the "
48:16 which redeemed me from all *e'*, "
50:15 the *e'* which we did unto him. "
17 their sin; for they did unto thee *e'*: "
20 for you, ye thought *e'* against me; "
Ex 5:19 Israel did see they were in *e'* case, "
22 hast thou so *e'* entreated this ‡7489
23 he hath done *e'* to this people; "
10:10 look to it; for *e'* is before you. 7451
23: 2 not follow a multitude to do *e'*; "
32:12 repent of this *e'* against thy people. "
14 *e'* which he thought to do unto his "
33: 4 the people heard these *e'* tidings, "
Le 5: 4 pronouncing with his lips to do *e'*, 7489
26: 6 I will rid *e'* beasts out of the land, 7451
Nu 13:32 they brought up an *e'* report of 1681
14:27 I bear with this *e'* congregation, 7451
35 do it unto all this *e'* congregation, "
37 that did bring up the *e'* report "
20: 5 to bring us in unto this *e'* place? "
32:13 the generation, that had done *e'* in "
De 1:35 these men of this *e'* generation see "
39 knowledge between good and *e'*, "
4:25 do *e'* in the sight of the Lord "
7:15 none of the *e'* diseases of Egypt, "
13: 5 So shalt thou put the *e'* away "
15: 9 thine eye be *e'* against thy poor 7489
17: 7 put the *e'* away from among you. 7451
12 shalt put away the *e'* from Israel. "
19:19 put the *e'* away from among you. "
20 commit no more any such *e'* among "
21:21 so shalt thou put *e'* away from "
22:14 and bring up an *e'* name upon her, "
19 brought up an *e'* name upon a "
21 thou put *e'* away from among you. "
22 shalt thou put away *e'* from Israel. "
24 thou shalt put away *e'* from among "
24: 7 shalt put *e'* away from among you. "
26: 6 the Egyptians *e'* entreated us, ‡7489
28:54 eye shall be *e'* toward his brother, "
56 her eye shall be *e'* toward the "
29:21 Lord shall separate him unto *e'* 7451
30:15 life and good, and death and *e'*; "
31:29 *e'* will befall you in the latter days; "
29 will do *e'* in the sight of the Lord, "
Jos 23:15 Lord bring upon you all *e'* things, "
24:15 if it seem *e'* unto you to serve the 7489
J'g 2:11 children of Israel did *e'* in the 7451
15 the Lord was against them for *e'*, "
3: 7 did *e'* in the sight of the Lord, "
12 did *e'* again in the sight of the Lord: "
12 they had done *e'* in the sight of the "
4: 1 the children of Israel again did *e'* "
6: 1 children of Israel did *e'* in the sight "
9:23 God sent an *e'* spirit between "
57 all the *e'* of the men of Shechem * "
10: 6 did *e'* again in the sight of the Lord, "
13: 1 did *e'* again in the sight of the Lord; "
20:13 death, and put away *e'* from Israel. "
34 but they knew not that *e'* was near "
41 saw that *e'* was come upon them. "
1Sa 2:23 I hear of your *e'* dealings by all this "
6: 9 he hath done us this great *e'*: "
12:19 have added unto all our sins this *e'*, 7451
15:19 didst *e'* in the sight of the Lord? "
16:14 an *e'* spirit from the Lord troubled "
15 *e'* spirit from God troubleth thee. "
16 the *e'* spirit from God is upon thee, "
23 it came to pass, when the *e'* spirit "
23 the *e'* spirit departed from him. "
18:10 *e'* spirit from God came upon Saul, "
19: 9 *e'* spirit from the Lord was upon "
20: 7 sure that *e'* is determined by him. "
9 certainly that *e'* were determined "
13 if it please my father to do thee *e'*, "
24:11 *e'* nor transgression in mine hand, "
17 whereas I have rewarded thee *e'*. "
25: 3 was churlish and *e'* in his doings: "
17 *e'* is determined against our master, "
21 he hath requited me *e'* for good. "
26 they that seek *e'* to my lord, "
28 and *e'* hath not been found in thee "
39 and hath kept his servant from *e'*: "
26:18 or what *e'* is in mine hand? "
29: 6 I have not found *e'* in thee "
2Sa 3:39 reward the doer of *e'* according * "
12: 9 the Lord to do *e'* in his sight? * "
11 I will raise up *e'* against thee "
13:16 *e'* in sending me away is greater* "
15:14 us suddenly, and bring *e'* upon us, "
17:14 Lord might bring *e'* upon Absalom. "
19: 7 than all the *e'* that befell thee "
35 I discern between good and *e'*? * "
24:16 the Lord repented him of the *e'*, "
1Ki 5: 4 neither adversary nor *e'* occurrent. "
9: 9 Lord brought upon them all this *e'*. "
11: 6 Solomon did *e'* in the sight of the "
13:33 Jeroboam returned not from his *e'* "
14: 9 done *e'* above all that were before 7489
10 *e'* upon the house of Jeroboam, 7451
22 Judah did *e'* in the sight of the Lord, "
15:26, 34 did *e'* in the sight of the Lord, "
16: 7 *e'* that he did in the sight of the Lord, "
19 in doing *e'* in the sight of the Lord, "
25 Omri wrought *e'* in the eyes of the "
30 Ahab the son of Omri did *e'* in the "
17:20 also brought *e'* upon the widow 7489
21:20 thou hast sold thyself to work *e'* 7451
21 Behold, I will bring *e'* upon thee, "
29 I will not bring the *e'* in his days: "
29 in his son's days will I bring the *e'* "
22: 8 doth not prophesy good...but *e'*. "
18 he would prophesy no good...but *e'*? "
23 Lord hath spoken *e'* concerning "
52 he did *e'* in the sight of the Lord, "
2Ki 3: 2 wrought *e'* in the sight of the Lord; "
6:33 Behold, this *e'* is of the Lord; "
8:12 I know the *e'* that thou wilt do "
18 he did *e'* in the sight of the Lord. "
27 and did *e'* in the sight of the Lord, "
13: 2 was *e'* in the sight of the Lord, "
11 did that which was *e'* in the sight "
14:24 And he did that which was *e'* in the "
15: 9, 18, 24, 28 was *e'* in the sight of the "
17: 2 was *e'* in the sight of the Lord, "
13 Turn ye from your *e'* ways, and "
17 to do *e'* in the sight of the Lord, "
21: 2 was *e'* in the sight of the Lord, "
9 seduced them to do more *e'* than "
12 bringing such *e'* upon Jerusalem "
15 done that which was *e'* in my sight, "
16 doing that which was *e'* in the sight "
20 did that which was *e'* in the sight "
22:16 I will bring *e'* upon this place, "
20 all the *e'* which I will bring upon "
23:32, 37 he did that which was *e'* in the "
24: 9, 19 that which was *e'* in the sight "
1Ch 2: 3 Er, the firstborn of Judah, was *e'** "
4:10 thou wouldest keep me from *e'*, "
7:23 because it went *e'* with his house. "
21:15 and he repented him of the *e'*, "
17 is that have sinned and done *e'* *7489
2Ch 7:22 he brought all this *e'* upon them. 7451
12:14 he did *e'*, because he prepared "
18: 7 good unto me, but always *e'*: "
17 prophesy good unto me, but *e'*? "
22 Lord hath spoken *e'* against thee. "
20: 9 *e'* cometh upon us, as the sword, "
21: 6 was *e'* in the eyes of the Lord, "
22: 4 he did *e'* in the sight of the Lord "
29: 6 done that which was *e'* in the eyes "
33: 2 was *e'* in the sight of the Lord, "
6 much *e'* in the sight of the Lord, "
22 did that which was *e'* in the sight "
34:24 I will bring *e'* upon this place, "
28 *e'* that I will bring upon this place, "
36: 5 *e'* in the sight of the Lord his God. "
9 was *e'* in the sight of the Lord. "
12 he did that which was *e'* in the "
Ezr 9:13 is come upon us for our *e'* deeds, "
Ne 6:13 might have matter for an *e'* report, "
9:28 they did *e'* again before thee: "
13: 7 understood of the *e'* that Eliashib "
17 What *e'* thing is this that ye do, "
18 our God bring all this *e'* upon us, "
27 to do all this great *e'*, to transgress "
Es 7: 7 there was *e'* determined against "
8: 6 *e'* that shall come unto my people? "
Job 1: 1 that feared God, and eschewed *e'*. "
8 that feareth God, and escheweth *e'*? "
2: 3 that feareth God, and escheweth *e'*? "
10 God, and shall we not receive *e'*? "
11 this *e'* that was come upon him, "
5:19 seven there shall no *e'* touch thee. "
8:20 neither will he help the *e'* doers: 7489
24:21 He *e'* entreateth the barren that *7462
28:28 depart from *e'* is understanding. 7451
30:26 for good, then *e'* came upon me: "
31:29 lifted up myself when *e'* found him: "
Job 35:12 because of the pride of *e'* men. 7451
42:11 the *e'* that the Lord had brought "
Ps 5: 4 neither shall *e'* dwell with thee. "
7: 4 If I have rewarded *e'* unto him "
10:15 arm of the wicked and the *e'* man: "
15: 3 nor doeth *e'* to his neighbour, nor "
21:11 For they intended *e'* against thee: "
23: 4 I will fear no *e'*: for thou art "
34:13 Keep thy tongue from *e'*, and thy "
14 Depart from *e'*, and do good; seek "
16 the Lord is against them that do *e'*, "
21 *E'* shall slay the wicked: and they "
35:12 They rewarded me *e'* for good to "
36: 4 is not good; he abhorreth not *e'*. "
37: 8 not thyself in any wise to do *e'*. *7489
19 not be ashamed in the *e'* time: 7451
27 Depart from *e'*, and do good; and "
38:20 They also that render *e'* for good "
40:14 backward...that wish me *e'*. * "
41: 5 Mine enemies speak *e'* of me, "
8 An *e'* disease, say they, cleaveth 1100
49: 5 should I fear in the days of *e'*, 7451
50:19 Thou givest thy mouth to *e'*, and "
51: 4 and done this *e'* in thy sight: "
52: 3 Thou lovest *e'* more than good; "
54: 5 shall reward *e'* unto mine enemies: "
56: 5 their thoughts are against me for *e'*. "
64: 5 encourage themselves in an *e'* "
78:49 by sending *e'* angels among them. "
90:15 the years wherein we have seen *e'*. "
91:10 There shall no *e'* befall thee, "
97:10 Ye that love the Lord, hate *e'*: "
109: 5 have rewarded me *e'* for good, "
20 that speak *e'* against my soul. "
112: 7 He shall not be afraid of *e'* tidings: "
119:101 refrained my feet from every *e'* "
121: 7 Lord shall preserve thee from all *e'*: "
140: 1 Deliver me, O Lord, from the *e'* "
11 an *e'* speaker be established "
11 *e'* shall hunt the violent man to 7451
141: 4 not my heart to any *e'* thing, "
Pr 1:16 their feet run to *e'*, and make haste "
33 and shall be quiet from fear of *e'*. "
2:12 me from the way of the *e'* man, "
14 Who rejoice to do *e'*, and delight "
3: 7 fear the Lord, and depart from *e'*. "
29 not *e'* against thy neighbour, "
4:14 go not in the way of *e'* men. "
27 to the left: remove thy foot from *e'*. "
5:14 I was almost in all *e'* in the midst "
6:24 To keep thee from the *e'* woman, "
8:13 The fear of the Lord is to hate *e'*: "
13 pride, and arrogancy, and the *e'* "
11:19 *e'* pursueth it to his own death. "
12:12 wicked desireth the net of *e'* men: "
20 the heart of them that imagine *e'*: "
21 shall no *e'* happen to the just: 205
13:19 to fools to depart from *e'*. 7451
21 *E'* pursueth sinners: but to the "
14:16 man feareth, and departeth from *e'*: "
19 The *e'* bow before the good; "
22 Do they not err that devise *e'*? "
15: 3 eyes of the Lord...beholding the *e'* "
15 All the days of the afflicted are *e'*: "
28 the wicked poureth out *e'* things. "
16: 4 even the wicked for the day of *e'*. "
6 of the Lord men depart from *e'*. "
17 of the upright is to depart from *e'*: "
27 An ungodly man diggeth up *e'*: * "
30 his lips he bringeth *e'* to pass. "
17:11 An *e'* man seeketh only rebellion: "
13 Whoso rewardeth *e'* for good, "
13 *e'* shall not depart from his house. "
19:23 he shall not be visited with *e'*. "
20: 8 A king...scattereth away all *e'* with "
22 Say not thou I will recompense *e'*; "
30 of a wound cleanseth away *e'*: "
21:10 The soul of the wicked desireth *e'*: "
22: 3 A prudent man foreseeth the *e'*, "
23: 6 bread of him that hath an *e'* eye, "
24: 1 Be not thou envious against *e'* men, "
8 He that deviseth to do *e'* shall be 7489
19 Fret not thyself because of *e'* men, "
20 shall be no reward to the *e'* man; 7451
27:12 A prudent man foreseeth the *e'*, "
28: 5 *E'* men understand not judgment: "
10 righteous to go astray in an *e'* way, "
22 hasteth to be rich hath an *e'* eye, "
29: 6 the transgression of an *e'* man "
30:32 or if thou hast thought *e'*, lay thine "
31:12 She will do him good and not *e'* 7451
Ec 2:21 This also is vanity and a great *e'*. "
4: 3 *e'* work that is done under the sun. "
5: 1 they consider not that they do *e'*. "
13 a sore *e'* which I have seen "
14 riches perish by *e'* travail: and he "
16 this also is a sore *e'*, that in all "
6: 1 *e'* which I have seen under the sun, "
2 and it is an *e'* disease. "
8: 3 stand not in an *e'* thing; for he "
5 the commandment shall feel no *e'* "
11 sentence against an *e'* work is not "
11 men is fully set in them to do *e'*. "
12 a sinner do *e'* an hundred times, "
9: 3 *e'* among all things that are done "
3 heart of the sons of men is full of *e'*, "
12 fishes that are taken in an *e'* net, "
12 sons of men snared in an *e'* time, "
10: 5 *e'* which I have seen under the sun, "
11: 2 not what *e'* shall be upon the earth. "
10 put away *e'* from thy flesh: "
12: 1 while the *e'* days come not, nor the "
14 it be good, or whether it be *e'*. "
Isa 1:16 put away the *e'* of your doings 7455
16 before mine eyes, cease to do *e'*; 7489
3: 9 rewarded *e'* unto themselves. 7451

Isa 5:20 them that call e' good, and good e'; 7451
7: 5 taken e' counsel against thee, "
15 that he may know to refuse the e', "
16 child shall know to refuse the e', "
13:11 will punish the world for their e', "
31: 2 he also is wise, and will bring e', "
32: 7 instruments also of the churl are e': "
33:15 shutteth his eyes from seeing e'; "
41:23 do good, or do e', that we may be 7489
45: 7 I make peace, and create e': I 7451
47:11 Therefore shall e' come upon thee; "
56: 2 his hand from doing any e'. "
57: 1 righteous is taken away from the e' "
59: 7 Their feet run to e', and they "
15 he that departeth from e' maketh "
65:12 hear; but did e' before mine eyes, "
66: 4 but they did e' before mine eyes, "
Jer 1:14 an e' shall break forth upon all the "
2: 3 e' shall come upon them, saith the "
19 it is an e' thing and bitter, "
3: 5 hast spoken and done e' things "
17 the imagination of their e' heart. "
4: 4 because of the e' of your doings. 7455
6 I will bring e' from the north, 7451
22 they are wise to do e', but to 7489
5:12 neither shall e' come upon us; 7451
6: 1 for e' appeareth out of the north, "
19 I will bring e' upon this people, "
7:24 in the imagination of their e' heart, "
30 Judah have done e' in my sight, "
8: 3 them that remain of this e' family, "
9: 3 they proceed from e' to e', and "
10: 5 they cannot do e', neither also 7489
11: 8 the imagination of their e' heart: 7451
11 Behold, I will bring e' upon them, "
15 thou doest e', then thou rejoicest. "
17 hath pronounced e' against thee, "
17 for the e' of the house of Israel, "
23 e' upon the men of Anathoth, "
12:14 all mine e' neighbours, that touch "
13:10 e' people, which refuse to hear "
23 ye...that are accustomed to do e'. 7489
15:11 entreat thee well in the time of e' 7451
16:10 all this great e' against us? "
12 the imagination of his e' heart, "
17:17 thou art my hope in the day of e'. "
18 bring upon them the day of e', "
18: 8 If that nation,...turn from their e', "
8 I will repent of the e' that I thought "
10 If it do e' in my sight, that it "
11 I frame e' against you, and devise "
11 ye now every one from his e' way, "
12 do the imagination of his e' heart. "
20 Shall e' be recompensed for good? "
19: 3 I will bring e' upon this place, "
15 will bring upon this city...all the e' "
21:10 set my face against the city for e', "
12 because of the e' of your doings. 7455
23: 2 visit upon you the e' of your doings, "
10 their course is e', and their force 7451
12 I will bring e' upon them, even "
17 No e' shall come upon you. "
22 turned them from their e' way, 7451
22 and from the e' of their doings. 7455
24: 3 the e',very e',that cannot be eaten,*7451
3 cannot be eaten, they are so e'. *7455
8 the e' figs, which cannot be eaten,*7451
8 cannot be eaten, they are so e'; *7455
25: 5 ye now every one from his e' way. 7451
5 and from the e' of your doings, 7455
29 I begin to bring e' on the city 7489
32 e' shall go forth from nation to 7451
26: 3 turn every man from his e' way, "
3 that I may repent me of the e', "
3 because of the e' of their doings. 7455
13 the Lord will repent him of the e' 7451
19 the Lord repented him of the e' "
19 procure great e' against our souls. "
28: 8 war, and of e', and of pestilence. "
29:11 thoughts of peace, and not of e', "
17 cannot be eaten, they are so e'. *7455
32:23 all this e' to come upon them: 7451
30 have only done e' before me from "
32 the e' of the children of Israel "
42 all this great e' upon this people, "
35:15 now every man from his e' way, "
17 all the e' that I have pronounced "
36: 3 all the e' which I purpose to do "
3 return every man from his e' way; "
7 return every one from his e' way: "
31 all the e' that I have pronounced "
38: 9 these men have done e' in all 7489
39:16 my words upon this city for e', 7451
40: 2 pronounced this e' upon this place. "
41:11 the e' that Ishmael...had done, "
42: 6 it be good, or whether it be e', "
10 I repent me of the e' that I have "
17 escape from the e' that I will bring "
44: 2 seen all the e' that I have brought "
7 Wherefore commit ye this great e' "
11 will set my face against you for e', "
17 and were well, and saw no e'. "
22 because of the e' of your doings, 7455
23 this e' is happened unto you, 7451
27 I will watch over them for e', "
29 words shall surely stand...for e': "
45: 5 I will bring e' upon all flesh, "
48: 2 they have devised e' against it: "
49:23 for they have heard e' tidings: "
37 and I will bring e' upon them, "
51:24 their e' that they have done in Zion "
60 e' that should come upon Babylon, "
64 the e' that I will bring upon her: "
52: 2 which was e' in the eyes of the Lord, "
La 3:38 High proceedeth not e' and good? "
Eze 5:16 upon them the e' arrows of famine. "

Eze 5:17 upon you famine and e' beasts, 7451
6:10 said in vain that I would do this e' "
11 all the e' abominations of the house "
7: 5 An e', an only e', behold, is come. "
14:22 the e' that I have brought upon "
33:11 turn ye from your e' ways; for "
34:25 will cause the e' beasts to cease "
36:31 ye remember your own e' ways, "
38:10 thou shalt think an e' thought: "
Da 9:12 by bringing upon us a great e': "
13 all this e' is come upon us: "
14 hath the Lord watched upon the e', "
Joel 2:13 and repenteth him of the e'. "
Am 3: 6 shall there be e' in a city, "
5:13 that time; for it is an e' time. "
14 Seek good, and not e', that ye may "
15 Hate the e', and love the good, "
6: 3 Ye that put far away the e' day, "
9: 4 will set mine eyes upon them for e', "
10 The e' shall not overtake...us. "
Jo 1: 7, 8 for whose cause that e' is upon us. "
3: 8 turn every one from his e' way, "
10 that they turned from their e' way; "
10 God repented of the e', that he had "
4: 2 and repentest thee of the e'. "
Mic 1:12 e' came down from the Lord unto "
2: 1 and work e' upon their beds! "
3 against this family do I devise an e', "
3 go haughtily: for this time is e'. "
3: 2 Who hate the good, and love the e'; "
11 none e' can come upon us. "
7: 3 they may do e' with both hands "
Na 1:11 that imagineth e' against the Lord, "
Hab 1:13 art of purer eyes than to behold e', "
2: 9 that coveteth an e' covetousness "
9 delivered from the powers of e'! "
Zep 1:12 not do good, neither will he do e'. 7489
3:15 thou shalt not see e' any more. 7451
Zec 1: 4 Turn ye now from your e' ways, "
4 and from your e' doings: "
7:10 none of you imagine e' against his "
8:17 let none of you imagine e' in your "
Mal 1: 8 blind for the sacrifice, is it not e'? "
8 offer the lame and sick, is it not e'? "
2:17 Every one that doeth e' is good "
M't 5:11 and shall say all manner of e' 4190, 4487
37 is more than these cometh of e'. 4190
39 unto you, That ye resist not e': "
45 maketh his sun to rise on the e' "
6:13 but deliver us from e': "
23 in thine eye be e', thy whole body "
34 Sufficient unto the day is the e' 2549
7:11 If ye then, being e', know how to 4190
17 corrupt tree bringeth forth e' fruit. "
18 good tree cannot bring forth e' fruit, "
9: 4 Wherefore think ye e' in your "
12:34 how can ye, being e', speak good "
35 an e' man out of the e' treasure "
35 bringeth forth e' things. "
39 An e' and adulterous generation "
15:19 of the heart proceed e' thoughts, "
20:15 Is thine eye e', because I am good? "
24:48 and if that e' servant shall say 2556
27:23 Why, what e' hath he done? "
M'r 3: 4 on the sabbath day, or to do e'? *2554
7:21 e' thoughts, adulteries, *2556
22 lasciviousness, an e' eye, 4190
23 these e' things come from within, "
9:39 that can lightly speak e' of me. 2551
15:14 Why, what e' hath he done? 2556
Lu 6: 9 to do good, or to do e'? *2554
22 and cast out your name as e', 4190
35 unto the unthankful and to the e'. "
45 and an e' man out of the e' treasure "
45 bringeth forth that which is e': "
7:21 and plagues, and of e' spirits; "
8: 2 healed of e' spirits and infirmities, "
11: 4 but deliver us from e'. * "
13 If ye then, being e', know how to "
29 This is an e' generation: they seek "
34 when thine eye is e', thy body also "
16:25 likewise Lazarus e' things: but 2556
23:22 Why, what e' hath he done? "
Joh 3:19 light, because their deeds were e'. 4190
20 every one that doeth e' hateth the † 5337
5:29 they that have done e', unto the † "
7: 7 of it, that the works thereof are e'. 4190
17:15 should keep them from the e'. "
18:23 answered him, If I have spoken e', 2560
23 bear witness of the e': but if well, 2556
Ac 7: 6 entreat them e' four hundred 2559
19 e' entreated our fathers, so that "
9:13 of this man, how much e' he hath 2556
14: 2 made their minds e' affected 2559
19: 9 but spake e' of that way before the "
12 the e' spirits went out of them. 4190
13 call over them which had e' spirits "
15 the e' spirit answered and said, "
16 the man in whom the e' spirit was "
23: 5 Thou shalt not speak e' of the ruler 2560
9 We find no e' in this man: 2556
24:20 have found any e' doing in me, * 92
Ro 1:30 inventors of e' things, disobedient 2556
2: 9 every soul of man that doeth e', "
3: 8 that we say,) Let us do e', that good "
7:19 but the e' which I would not, "
21 do good, e' is present with me. "
9:11 having done any good or e', * "
12: 9 Abhor that which is e'; cleave to 4190
17 Recompense to no man e' for e'. 2556
21 Be not overcome of e', but "
21 but overcome e' with good. "
13: 3 terror to good works, but to the e'. "
4 But if thou do that which is e', "
4 wrath upon him that doeth e'. "
14:16 Let not then your good be e' spoken of:

Ro 14:20 but it is e' for that man who eateth 2556
16:19 is good, and simple concerning e'. "
1Co 10: 6 we should not lust after e' things, "
30 why am I e' spoken of for that for 987
13: 5 easily provoked, thinketh no e'; 2556
15:33 e' communications corrupt good "
2Co 6: 8 by e' report and good report: 1426
13: 7 I pray to God that ye do no e'; 2556
Ga 1: 4 deliver us from this present e' 4190
Eph 4:31 clamour, and e' speaking, be put * 988
5:16 the time, because the days are e'. 4190
6:13 be able to withstand in the e' day, "
Ph'p 3: 2 of dogs, beware of e' workers, 2556
Co 3: 5 e' concupiscence, and covetousness," "
1Th 5:15 See that none render e' for e' "
22 Abstain from all appearance of e'. 4190
2Th 3: 3 stablish you, and keep you from e'. "
1Ti 6: 4 envy, strife, railings, e' surmisings, "
10 love of money is the root of all e': 2556
2Ti 2: 9 as an e' doer, even unto bonds: *2557
3:13 But e' men and seducers shall wax 4190
4:14 the coppersmith did me much e': 2556
18 deliver me from every e' work, 4190
Tit 1:12 e' beasts, slow bellies. 2556
2: 8 having no e' thing to say of you. 5337
3: 2 speak e' of no man, to be no 987
Heb 3:12 any of you an e' heart of unbelief, 4190
5:14 to discern both good and e'. 2556
10:22 sprinkled from an e' conscience, 4190
Jas 1:13 God cannot be tempted with e', 2556
2: 4 are become judges of e' thoughts? 4190
3: 8 an unruly e', full of deadly poison. 2556
16 is confusion and every e' work. *5337
4:11 Speak not e' one of another, *2635
11 that speaketh e' of his brother, * "
11 speaketh e' of the law, and * "
16 boastings: all such rejoicing is e'. 4190
1Pe 2: 1 and envies, and all e' speakings, 2636
3: 9 Not rendering e' for e', or railing 2556
10 refrain his tongue from e', "
11 Let him eschew e', and do good; "
12 Lord is against them that do e'. "
16 speak e' of you, as of evildoers, *2635
17 for well doing, than for e' doing. 2554
4: 4 excess of riot, speaking e' of you: 987
14 on their part he is e' spoken of, * "
2Pe 2: 2 of truth shall be e' spoken of. "
10 not afraid to speak e' of dignities * "
12 speak e' of the things that they * "
1Jo 3:12 Because his own works were e', 4190
2Jo 11 is partaker of his e' deeds. "
3Jo 11 follow not that which is e', but 2556
11 that doeth e' hath not seen God. 2554
Jude 8 despise dominion, and speak e' of* 987
10 these speak e' of those things * "
Re 2: 2 canst not bear them which are e': 2556

evil-affected See EVIL and AFFECTED.

evildoer See also EVIL and DOER; EVILDOERS.
Isa 9:17 every one is a hypocrite and an e' 7489
1Pe 4:15 or as an e', or as a busybody 2555

evildoers
Ps 37: 1 Fret not thyself because of e', 7489
9 e' shall be cut off: but those that "
94:16 will rise up for me against the e'? "
119:115 Depart from me, ye e': for I will "
Isa 1: 4 a seed of e', children that are "
14:20 seed of e' shall never be renowned. "
31: 2 arise against the house of the e', "
Jer 20:13 soul of the poor from the hand of e'. "
23:14 strengthen also the hands of e', "
1Pe 2:12 they speak against you as e', 2555
14 by him for the punishment of e', "
3:16 speak evil of you, as of e', * "

evil-doing See EVIL and DOING.

evilfavouredness
De 17: 1 wherein is blemish, or any e': 1697, 7451

Evil-merodach (*e'-vil-mer'-o-dak*)
2Ki 25:27 that *E'* king of Babylon in the year 192
Jer 52:31 *E'* king of Babylon in the first year "

evils
De 31:17 e' and troubles shall befall them; 7451
17 Are not these e' come upon us, "
18 e' which they shall have wrought,* "
21 e' and troubles are befallen them, "
Ps 40:12 innumerable e' have compassed me "
Jer 2:13 my people have committed two e'; "
Eze 6: 9 the e' which they have committed "
20:43 all your e' that ye have committed. "
Lu 3:19 all the e' which Herod had done, 4190

evil-speaking See EVIL and SPEAKING.

ewe See also EWES.
Ge 21:28 Abraham set seven e' lambs of 3535
29 What mean these seven e' lambs "
30 seven e' lambs shalt thou take "
Le 14:10 and one e' lamb of the first year "
22:28 cow or e', ye shall not kill it and 7716
Nu 6:14 and one e' lamb of the first year 3535
2Sa 12: 3 one little e' lamb, which he had "

ewe-lamb See EWE and LAMB.

ewes
Ge 31:38 thy e' and thy she goats have not 7353
32:14 two hundred e', and twenty rams, "
Ps 78:71 following the e' great with young 5763

exact See also EXACTED; EXACTETH.
De 15: 2 shall not e' it of his neighbour, 5065
3 foreigner thou mayest e' it again: "
Ne 5: 7 Ye e' usury, every one of his 5378
10 and my brethren, . . . might e' *5383
11 the corn, . . . that ye e' of them. "
Ps 89:22 The enemy shall not e' upon him; 5378
Isa 58: 3 pleasure, and e' all your labours. 5065
Lu 3:13 *E'* no more than that which is *4238

exacted
2Ki 15:20 Menahem e· the money of Israel, 3318
23:35 he e· the silver and the gold of 5065
exacteth
Job 11: 6 God e· of thee less than thine 5382
exaction See also EXACTIONS.
Ne 10:31 year, and the e· of every debt. 4855
exactions
Eze 45: 9 take away your e· from my people, 1646
exactors
Isa 60:17 peace, and thine e· righteousness. 5065
exalt See also EXALTED; EXALTEST; EXALTETH.
Ex 15: 2 my father's God, and I will e· him. 7311
1Sa 2:10 and e· the horn of his anointed. "
Job 17: 4 therefore shalt thou not e· them. "
Ps 34: 3 and let us e· his name together. "
37:34 shall e· thee to inherit the land: "
66: 7 let not the rebellious e· themselves. "
92:10 But my horn shalt thou e· like the* "
99: 5 E· ye the Lord our God, and "
9 E· the Lord our God, and worship "
107:32 e· him also in the congregation "
118:28 thou art my God, I will e· thee. "
140: 8 device; lest they e· themselves. "
Pr 4: 8 E· her, and she shall promote thee: 5549
Isa 13: 2 e· the voice unto them, shake *7311
14:13 I will e· my throne above the stars "
25: 1 thou art my God; I will e· thee, "
Eze 21:26 e· him that is low, and abase him 1361
29:15 neither shall it e· itself any more *5375
31:14 e· themselves for their height, 1361
Da 11:14 the robbers of thy people shall e· *5375
36 shall e· himself, and magnify 7311
Ho 11: 7 most High, none at all would e· him. "
Ob 4 Though thou e· thyself as the *1361
M't 23:12 And whosoever shall e· himself 5312
2Co 11:20 a man e· himself, if a man smite *1869
1Pe 5: 6 that he may e· you in due time: 5312
exalted
Nu 24: 7 and his kingdom shall be e·. 5375
1Sa 2: 1 mine horn is e· in the Lord: 7311
2Sa 5:12 had e· his kingdom for his people 5375
22:47 and e· be the God of the rock of 7311
1Ki 1: 5 the son of Haggith e· himself, 5375
14: 7 I e· thee from among the people, 7311
16: 2 Forasmuch as I e· thee out of the "
2Ki 19:22 against whom hast thou e· thy "
1Ch 29:11 thou art e· as head above all. 5375
Ne 9: 5 name, which is e· above all 7311
Job 5:11 which mourn may be e· to safety. 7682
24:24 They are e· for a little while, 7426
36: 7 them forever, and they are e·. 1361
Ps 12: 8 when the vilest men are e·. 7311
13: 2 how long shall mine enemy be e· "
18:46 let the God of my salvation be e·. "
21:13 Be thou e·, Lord, in thine own "
46:10 I will be e· among the heathen, "
10 I will be e· in the earth. "
47: 9 belong unto God: he is greatly e·. 5927
57: 5 thou e·, O God, above the heavens: 7311
11 thou e·, O God, above the heavens: "
75:10 horns of the righteous shall be e·.* "
89:16 thy righteousness shall they be e·. "
17 in thy favour our horn shall be e· "
19 e· one chosen out of the people. "
24 in my name shall his horn be e·. "
97: 9 thou art e· far above all gods. 5927
108: 5 thou e·, O God, above the heavens: 7311
112: 9 his horn shall be e· with honour. "
118:16 The right hand of the Lord is e·: 7426
Pr 11:11 of the upright the city is e·: 7311
Isa 2: 2 and shall be e· above the hills; 5375
11, 17 Lord alone shall be e· in that 7682
5:16 But the Lord of hosts shall be e· 1361
12: 4 make mention that his name is e·. 7682
30:18 and therefore he will be e·, 7311
33: 5 The Lord is e·, for he dwelleth on 7682
10 now will I be e·; now will I lift up 7311
37:23 against whom hast thou e· thy voice, "
40: 4 Every valley shall be e·, and every 5375
49:11 and my highways shall be e·. 7311
52:13 he shall be e· and extolled, and be "
Eze 17:24 have e· the low tree, have dried 1361
19:11 was e· among the thick branches, "
31: 5 Therefore his height was e· above "
Ho 13: 1 Ephraim e· himself in Israel; 5375
6 filled, and their heart was e·; 7311
Mic 4: 1 and it shall be e· above the hills; 5375
M't 11:23 which art e· unto heaven, shalt be 5312
23:12 shall humble himself, shalt be e·. "
Lu 1:52 seats, and e· them of low degree. "
10:15 which art e· to heaven, shalt be "
14:11 that humbleth himself shall be e·. "
18:14 that humbleth himself shall be e·. "
Ac 2:33 being by the right hand of God e·, "
5:31 Him hath God e· with his right * "
13:17 e· the people when they dwelt as "
2Co 11: 7 abasing myself that ye might be e·. "
12: 7 lest I should be e· above measure 5229
7 lest I should be e· above measure. "
Ph'p 2: 9 God also hath highly e· him, 5251
Jas 1: 9 low degree rejoice in that he is e·: *5311
exaltest
Ex 9:17 e· thou thyself against my people, 5549
exalteth
Job 36:22 Behold, God e· by his power: *7682
Ps 148:14 also e· the horn of his people, *7311
Pr 14:29 he that is hasty of spirit e· folly. "
34 Righteousness e· a nation: but sin "
17:19 e· his gate seeketh destruction. *1361
Lu 14:11 e· himself shall be abased; 5312
18:14 one that e· himself shall be abased; "

2Co 10: 5 every high thing that e· itself *1869
2Th 2: 4 Who opposeth and e· himself 5229
examination
Ac 25:26 that, after e· had, I might have 351
examine See also EXAMINED; EXAMINING.
Ezr 10:16 the tenth month to e· the matter. 1875
Ps 26: 2 E· me, O Lord, and prove me; 974
1Co 9: 3 to them that do e· me in this, 350
11:28 let a man e· himself, and so let *1381
2Co 13: 5 E· yourselves, whether ye be in *3985
examined
Lu 23:14 I, having e· him before you, 350
Ac 4: 9 If we this day be e· of the good deed "
12:19 found him not, he e· the keepers, "
22:24 he should be e· by scourging; 426
29 him which should have e· him: * "
28:18 Who, when they had e· me, 350
examining
Ac 24: 8 e· of whom thyself mayest take 350
example See also ENSAMPLE; EXAMPLES.
M't 1:19 make her a public e·, was minded 3856
Joh 13:15 For I have given you an e·, that 5262
1Ti 4:12 be thou an e· of the believers, *5179
Heb 4:11 after the same e· of unbelief. 5262
8: 5 serve unto the e· and shadow * "
Jas 5:10 for an e· of suffering affliction, "
1Pe 2:21 leaving us an e·, that ye should 5261
Jude 7 for an e·, suffering the vengeance 1164
examples
1Co 10: 6 Now these things were our e·, 5179
exceed See also EXCEEDED; EXCEEDEST; EXCEEDETH; EXCEEDING.
De 25: 3 he may give him, and not e·: 3254
3 lest, if he should e·, and beat him "
M't 5:20 your righteousness shall e· the 4052
2Co 3: 9 of righteousness e· in glory. "
exceeded
1Sa 20:41 one with another, until David e·. 1431
1Ki 10:23 So king Solomon e· all the kings "
Job 36: 9 transgressions that they have e·. *1396
exceedest
2Ch 9: 6 thou e· the fame that I heard. 3254
exceedeth
1Ki 10: 7 thy wisdom and prosperity e· the 3254
exceeding See also EXCEEDINGLY.
Ge 15: 1 shield, and thy e· great reward. 3966
17: 6 And I will make thee e· fruitful, "
27:34 with a great and e· bitter cry, "
Ex 1: 7 multiplied, and waxed e· mighty; "
19:16 the voice of the trumpet e· loud; "
Nu 14: 7 to search it, is an e· good land. "
1Sa 2: 3 Talk no more so e· proudly; "
2Sa 8: 8 king David took e· much brass. 3966
12: 2 The rich man had e· many flocks "
1Ki 4:29 wisdom and understanding e· much, "
7:47 because they were e· many: "
1Ch 20: 2 also e· much spoil out of the city. "
22: 5 the Lord must be e· magnifical, 4605
2Ch 11:12 and made them e· strong. 7235, 3966
14:14 for there was e· much spoil in *7235
16:12 until his disease was e· great: 4605
32:27 Hezekiah had e· much riches and 3966
Ps 21: 6 him e· glad with thy countenance. *2302
43: 4 altar of God, unto God my e· joy: 8057
119:96 thy commandment is e· broad. 3966
Pr 30:24 the earth, but they are e· wise: "
Ec 7:24 That which is far off, and e· deep, "
Jer 48:29 pride of Moab, (he is e· proud) *3966
Eze 9: 9 Israel and Judah is e· great, "
16:13 and thou wast e· beautiful, and "
23:15 e· in dyed attire upon their heads, 5628
37:10 upon their feet, an e· great army. 3966
47:10 fish of the great sea, e· many. "
Da 3:22 and the furnace e· hot, the flame 3493
6:23 was the king e· glad for him, 7689
7:19 e· dreadful, whose teeth were of 3493
8: 9 waxed e· great, toward the south, 3499
Jon 3: 3 Nineveh was an e· great city 430
4: 6 Jonah was e· glad of the gourd. 1419
M't 2:10 they rejoiced with e· great joy. 4970
16 of the wise men, was e· wroth, 3029
4: 8 him up into an e· high mountain, "
5:12 Rejoice, and be e· glad: for great "
8:28 coming out of the tombs, e· fierce, 3029
17:23 And they were e· sorry. 4970
26:22 And they were e· sorrowful, and "
38 soul is e· sorrowful, even unto 4036
M'r 6:26 And the king was e· sorry; yet for "
9: 3 became shining, e· white as snow; 3029
14:34 soul is e· sorrowful unto death: 4036
Lu 23: 8 Herod saw Jesus he was e· glad: 3029
Ac 7:20 and was e· fair, and nourished 3588, 2316
Ro 7:13 sin...might become e· sinful. 2596, 5236
2Co 4:17 a far more e· and eternal *1519, "
7: 4 am e· joyful in all our tribulation. *5248
9:14 for the e· grace of God in you. 5235
Eph 1:19 And what is the e· greatness of "
2: 7 shew the e· riches of his grace "
3:20 e· abundantly above all that we 5228
1Ti 1:14 Lord was e· abundant with faith *5250
1Pe 4:13 ye may be glad also with e· joy.
2Pe 1: 4 us e· great and precious promises:
Jude 24 the presence of his glory with e· joy,
Re 16:21 the plague thereof was e· great. 4970
exceedingly See also EXCEEDING.
Ge 7:19 prevailed e· upon the earth; 3966
13:13 and sinners before the Lord e·. "
16:10 I will multiply thy seed e·, *7235
17: 2 and thee, and will multiply thee e·. 3966
20 multiply him e·; twelve princes "
27:33 And Isaac trembled very e·. 1419

Ge 30:43 And the man increased e·, and 3966
47:27 and grew, and multiplied e·. "
1Sa 26:21 the fool, and have erred e·. 7235, "
2Sa 13:15 Then Amnon hated her e·; *1419, "
2Ki 10: 4 But they were e· afraid, and said, "
1Ch 29:25 the Lord magnified Solomon e· 4605
2Ch 1: 1 was with him, and magnified him e·. "
17:12 great e·; and he built in Judah "
26: 8 for he strengthened himself e·. * "
Ne 2:10 it grieved them e· that there was 1419
Es 4: 4 Then was the queen e· grieved; 3966
Job 3:22 Which rejoice e·, and are glad, 413, 1524
Ps 68: 3 yea, let them e· rejoice. *8057
106:14 But lusted e· in the wilderness,
119:167 testimonies; and I love them e·. 3966
123: 3 for we are e· filled with contempt. 7227
4 soul is e· filled with the scorning "
Isa 24:19 dissolved, the earth is moved e·. "
Da 7: 7 strong e·; and it had great iron 3493
Jon 1:10 Then were the men e· afraid, and 1419
16 Then the men feared the Lord e·, "
4: 1 it displeased Jonah e·, and he was "
M't 19:25 they were e· amazed, saying, Who 4970
M'r 4:41 they feared e·, and said one 5401, 3173
15:14 they cried out the more e·, Crucify 4056
Ac 16:20 being Jews, do e· trouble our city, 1613
26:11 and being e· mad against them, 4057
27:18 we being e· tossed with a tempest, 4971
2Co 7:13 e· the more joyed we for the joy of 4056
Ga 1:14 more e· zealous of the traditions "
1Th 3:10 Night and day praying e· 5228, 1537, 4053
2Th 1: 3 your faith groweth e·, and the charity "
Heb 12:21 Moses said, I e· fear and quake:) 1630
excel See also EXCELLED; EXCELLEST; EXCELLETH.
Ge 49: 4 as water, thou shalt not e·; ††3498
1Ch 15:21 with harps on the Sheminith to e·. *5329
Ps 103:20 that e· in strength, that do his *1368
Isa 10:10 whose graven images did e· them of
1Co 14:12 that ye may e· to the edifying of *4052
excelled
1Ki 4:30 Solomon's wisdom e· the wisdom 7227
excellency
Ge 49: 3 e· of dignity, and the e· of power: ‡3499
Ex 15: 7 the greatness of thine e· thou hast 1347
De 33:26 and in his e· on the sky. 1346
29 and who is the sword of thy e·! "
Job 4:21 Doth not their e· which is in them *3499
13:11 Shall not his e· make you afraid? ‡7613
20: 6 Though his e· mount up to the 7863
37: 4 with the voice of his e·; and he will *1347
40:10 thyself now with majesty and e·; 1363
Ps 47: 4 the e· of Jacob whom he loved. ‡1347
62: 4 to cast him down from his e·: ‡7613
68:34 his e· is over Israel, and his 1346
Ec 7:12 but the e· of knowledge is, that 3504
Isa 13:19 the beauty of the Chaldees' e·, *1347
35: 2 the e· of Carmel and Sharon, 1926
2 of the Lord, and the e· of our God. "
60:15 I will make thee an eternal e·, 1347
Eze 24:21 the e· of your strength, the desire* "
Am 6: 8 I abhor the e· of Jacob, and hate "
8: 7 hath sworn by the e· of Jacob, "
Na 2: 2 turned away the e· of Jacob, "
2 as the e· of Israel: "
1Co 2: 1 you, came not with e· of speech 5247
2Co 4: 7 the e· of the power may be of God, *5236
Ph'p 3: 8 the e· of the knowledge of Christ 5242
excellent
Es 1: 4 and the honour of his e· majesty 1420
Job 37:23 he is e· in power, and in judgment, 7689
Ps 8: 1, 9 e· is thy name in all the earth! 117
16: 3 to the e·, in whom is all my delight. "
36: 7 e· is thy loving kindness, O God! *3368
76: 4 Thou art more glorious and e· than 117
141: 5 it shall be an e· oil, which shall *7218
148:13 his name alone is e·; his glory is *7682
150: 2 him according to his e· greatness. 7230
Pr 8: 6 for I will speak of e· things; 5057
12:26 The righteous is more e· than his *8446
17: 7 E· speech becometh not a fool; 3499
27 of understanding is of an e· spirit. *7119
22:20 not I written to thee e· things in 7991
Ca 5:15 Lebanon, e· as the cedars. 977
Isa 4: 2 the fruit of the earth shall be e· 1347
12: 5 for he hath done e· things: 1348
28:29 in counsel, and e· in working. 1431
Eze 16: 7 thou art come to e· ornaments: 5716
Da 2:31 image, whose brightness was e·, 3493
4:36 and e· majesty was added unto me, "
5:12 Forasmuch as an e· spirit, and "
14 and e· wisdom is found in thee. "
6: 3 because an e· spirit was in him; "
Lu 1: 3 in order, most e· Theophilus, 2903
Ac 23:26 unto the most e· governor Felix "
Ro 2:18 the things that are more e·, being 1308
1Co 12:31 shew I unto you a more e· way. 2596, 5236
Ph'p 1:10 ye may approve things that are e·; 1308
Heb 1: 4 obtained a more e· name than they. 1313
8: 6 hath he obtained a more e· ministry, "
11: 4 a more e· sacrifice than Cain, 4119
2Pe 1:17 a voice to him from the e· glory. ‡3169
excellest
Pr 31:29 virtuously, but thou e· them all. 5927
excelleth
Ec 2:13 Then I saw that wisdom e· folly, 3504
13 as far as light e· darkness. "
2Co 3:10 by reason of the glory that e·. *5235
except See also EXCEPTED.
Ge 31:42 E· the God of my father, the God 3884
32:26 let thee go, e· thou bless me. 3588, 518
42:15 e· your youngest brother come "
43: 3 e· your brother be with you. 1115

Ge 43: 5 not see my face, e' your brother 1115
10 e' we had lingered, surely now we 3884
44:23 E' your youngest brother 518, 3808
26 e' our youngest brother be with 369
47:26 e' the land of the priests only, *7535
Nu 16:13 e' thou make thyself altogether *3588
De 32:30 e' their Rock had sold 518, 3808, 3588
Jos 7:12 e' ye destroy the accursed 518, 3808
1Sa 25:34 e' thou hadst hasted and 3588, 3884
2Sa 3: 9 God to Abner, and more also, e', *3588
13 not see my face, e' thou first 3588, 518
5: 6 E' thou take away the blind " "
2Ki 4:24 not thy riding for me, e' I bid " "
Es 2:14 e' the king delighted in her, " "
4:11 e' such to whom the king shall 905
Ps 127: 1 E' the Lord build the house, 518, 3808
1 e' the Lord keep the city, the " "
Pr 4:16 sleep not, e' they have done " "
Isa 1: 9 E' the Lord of hosts had left unto 3884
Da 2:11 e' the gods, whose dwelling is not 3861
3:28 nor any god, e' their own God. "
6: 5 Daniel, e' we find it against him "
Am 3: 3 walk together, e' they be agreed? 1115
M't 5:20 e' your righteousness shall exceed 3362
12:29 e' he first bind the strong man? "
18: 3 E' ye be converted, and become as "
19: 9 e' it be for fornication, and shall 1508
24:22 e' those days should be shortened, "
26:42 e' I drink it, thy will be done. 3362
M'r 3:27 e' he will first bind the strong man; "
7: 3 e' they wash their hands oft, "
4 e' they wash, they eat not. "
13:20 e' that the Lord had shortened 1508
Lu 9:13 e' we should go and buy meat for 1509
13: 3, 5 e' ye repent, ye shall all likewise 3362
Joh 3: 2 that thou doest, e' God be with him. "
3 E' a man be born again, he cannot "
5 E' a man be born of water and of "
27 e' it be given him from heaven. "
4:48 E' ye see signs and wonders, ye "
6:44 e' the Father which hath sent me "
53 E' ye eat the flesh of the Son of "
65 e' it were given unto him of my "
12:24 E' a corn of wheat fall into the "
15: 4 e' it abide in the vine; no more can "
4 no more can ye, e' ye abide in me. "
19:11 e' it were given thee from above: 1508
20:25 E' I shall see in his hands the print 3362
Ac 8: 1 were all scattered...e' the apostles. 4133
31 How can I, e' some man should 3362
15: 1 E' ye be circumcised after the "
24:21 E' it be for this one voice, that I 2228
26:29 such as I am, e' these bonds. 3923
27:31 E' these abide in the ship, ye 3362
Ro 7: 7 e' the law had said, Thou shalt not 1508
9:29 E' the Lord of Sabaoth had left us "
10:15 e' they be sent, as it is written, 3362
1Co 7: 5 e' it be with consent for a time, 1509
14: 5 tongues, e' he interpret, that 1622, 1508
6 e' I shall speak to you either by *3362
7 e' they give a distinction in the * "
9 e' ye utter by the tongue words * "
15:36 sowest is not quickened, e' it die: "
2Co 12:13 e' it be that I myself was not 1508
13: 5 is in you, e' ye be reprobates? * 1509
2Th 2: 3 e' there come a falling away first, 3362
2Ti 2: 5 not crowned, e' he strive lawfully. "
Re 2: 5 out of his place, e' thou repent. "
22 e' they repent of their deeds. "

excepted
1Co 15:27 that he is e', which did put 1622

excess
M't 23:25 they are full of extortion and e'. 192
Eph 5:18 drunk with wine, wherein is e'; * 810
1Pe 4: 3 e' of wine, revellings, *3632
4 e' of riot, speaking evil of you: 401

exchange
Ge 47:17 them bread in e' for horses, and
Le 27:10 and the e' thereof shall be holy. *8545
Job 28:17 and the e' of it shall not be ‡ "
Eze 48:14 e', nor alienate the first fruits 4171
M't 16:26 shall a man give in e' for his soul? 465
M'r 8:37 shall a man give in e' for his soul? "

exchangers
M't 25:27 to have put my money to the e', *5133

exclude See also EXCLUDED.
Ga 4:17 yea, they would e' you, that ye *1576

excluded
Ro 3:27 Where is boasting then? It is e'. 1576

excusable See INEXCUSABLE.

excuse See also EXCUSED; EXCUSING.
Lu 14:18 with one consent began to make e'. 3868
Ro 1:20 so that they are without e': 379
2Co 12:19 that we e' ourselves unto you? * 626

excused
Lu 14:18 and see it: I pray thee have me e'. 3868
19 prove them: I pray thee have me e'.

excusing
Ro 2:15 accusing or else e' one another;) 626

execration
Jer 42:18 be an e', and an astonishment, 423
44:12 shall be an e', and an astonishment,

execute See also EXECUTED; EXECUTEST; EXECUTETH; EXECUTING.
Ex 12:12 will e' judgment: I am the Lord. 6213
Nu 5:30 priest shall e' upon her all this law. "
8:11 may e' the service of the Lord. *5647
De 10:18 e' the judgment of the fatherless 6213
1Ki 6:12 and e' my judgments, and keep all "
Ps 119:84 when wilt thou e' judgment on "
149: 7 To e' vengeance upon the heathen, "
9 To e' upon them the judgment "
Isa 16: 3 Take counsel, e' judgment; make 6213
Jer 7: 5 thoroughly e' judgment between "
21:12 E' judgment in the morning, and 1777
22: 3 saith the Lord; E' ye judgment 6213
23: 5 and prosper, and shall e' judgment "
33:15 and he shall e' judgment and "
Eze 5: 8 and will e' judgments in the midst "
10 and I will e' judgments in thee, "
15 when I shall e' judgment in thee "
11: 9 and will e' judgments among you. "
16:41 and e' judgments upon thee in the "
25:11 I will e' judgments upon Moab; "
17 will e' great vengeance upon them "
30:14 and will e' judgments in No. "
19 Thus will I e' judgments in Egypt: "
45: 9 e' judgment and justice, take away "
Ho 11: 9 not e' the fierceness of mine anger, "
Mic 5:15 And I will e' vengeance in anger "
7: 9 my cause, and e' judgment for me: "
Zec 7: 9 E' true judgment, and shew 8199
8:16 e' the judgment of truth and peace "
Joh 5:27 authority to e' judgment also, 4160
Ro 13: 4 a revenger to e' wrath upon him *
Jude 15 To e' judgment upon all, and to 4160

executed See also EXECUTEDST.
Nu 33: 4 gods also the Lord e' judgments 6213
De 33:21 he e' the justice of the Lord, "
2Sa 8:15 David e' judgment and justice "
1Ch 6:10 (he it is that e' the priest's office in the
18:14 e' judgment and justice among 6213
24: 2 and Ithamar e' the priest's office,
2Ch 24:24 they e' judgment against Joash. 6213
Ezr 7:26 judgment be e' speedily upon him, 5648
Ps 106:30 stood up Phinehas, and e' judgment:
Ec 8:11 an evil work is not e' speedily, 6213
Jer 23:20 until he have e', and till he have "
Eze 11:12 neither e' my judgments, but have "
18: 8 hath e' true judgment between "
17 hath e' my judgments, hath walked "
20:24 they had not e' my judgments, "
23:10 for they had e' judgment upon her. "
28:22 I shall have e' judgments in her, "
26 when I have e' judgments upon all "
39:21 see my judgment that I have e', "
Lu 1: 8 that while he e' the priest's office 2407

executedst
1Sa 28:18 e' his fierce wrath upon Amalek, *6213

executest
Ps 99: 4 e' judgment and righteousness in 6213

executeth
Ps 9:16 by the judgment which he e': *6213
103: 6 The Lord e' righteousness and "
146: 7 e' judgment for the oppressed: "
Isa 46:11 the man that e' my counsel from *
Jer 5: 1 if there be any that e' judgment, *6213
Joe 2:11 for he is strong that e' his word: "

executing
2Ki 10:30 thou hast done well in e' that 6213
2Ch 11:14 them off from e' the priest's office *
22: 8 when Jehu was e' judgment upon

execution
Es 9: 1 decree drew near to be put in e'. 6213

executioner
M'r 6:27 king sent an e', and commanded *4688

exempted
1Ki 15:22 none was e': and they took away 5355

exercise See also EXERCISED; EXERCISETH.
Ps 131: 1 do I e' myself in great matters, 1980
Jer 9:24 the Lord which e' lovingkindness, 6213
M't 20:25 Gentiles e' dominion over them, *2634
25 are great e' authority upon them. 2715
M'r 10:42 the Gentiles e' lordship over them; *2634
42 great ones e' authority upon them. 2715
Lu 22:25 kings of the earth e' lordship *2961
25 they that e' authority upon them *1850
Ac 24:16 herein do I e' myself, to have alway 778
1Ti 4: 7 e' thyself rather unto godliness. 1128
8 For bodily e' profiteth little: but 1129

exercised
Ec 1:13 sons of man to be e' therewith. 6031
3:10 to the sons of men to be e' in it. "
Eze 22:29 and e' robbery, and have vexed
Heb 5:14 e' to discern both good and evil. 1128
12:11 unto them which are e' thereby. "
2Pe 2:14 have e' with covetous practices; "

exerciseth
Re 13:12 e' all the power of the first beast 4160

exhort See also EXHORTED; EXHORTETH; EXHORTING.
Ac 2:40 did he testify and e', saying, Save 3870
27:22 now I e' you to be of good cheer: 3867
2Co 9: 5 it necessary to e' the brethren, *3870
1Th 4: 1 and e' you by the Lord Jesus, "
5:14 we e' you, brethren, warn them "
2Th 3:12 and e' by our Lord Jesus Christ, "
1Ti 2: 1 I e' therefore, that, first of all, "
6: 2 These things teach and e'. "
2Ti 4: 2 rebuke, e' with all long suffering "
Tit 1: 9 to e' and to convince the gainsayers. "
2: 6 likewise e' to be sober minded. "
9 E' servants to be obedient unto their
15 speak, and e', and rebuke with all 3870
Heb 3:13 But e' one another daily, while it "
1Pe 5: 1 I e', who am also an elder, "
Jude 3 me to write unto you, and e' you* "

exhortation
Lu 3:18 e' preached he unto the people. *3870
Ac 13:15 any word of e' for the people, 3874
20: 2 and had given them much e'. 3870
Ro 12: 8 Or he that exhorteth, on e': *3874
1Co 14: 3 edification, and e', and comfort. † "
2Co 8:17 For indeed he accepted the e'; "
1Th 2: 3 For our e' was not of deceit, "
1Ti 4:13 to reading, to e', to doctrine. "
Heb 12: 5 forgotten the e' which speaketh "
13:22 brethren, suffer the word of e': "

exhorted
Ac 11:23 and e' them all, that with purpose 3870
15:32 e' the brethren with many words, "
1Th 2:11 As ye know how we e' and *

exhorteth
Ro 12: 8 Or he that e', on exhortation: 3870

exhorting
Ac 14:22 e' them to continue in the faith, 3870
18:27 e' the disciples to receive him: *4389
Heb 10:25 but e' one another: and so much 3870
1Pe 5:12 written briefly, e', and testifying "

exile
2Sa 15:19 art a stranger, and also an e'. 1540
Isa 51:14 The captive e' hasteneth that he 6808

exorcists
Ac 19:13 vagabond Jews, e', took upon them 1845

expectation
Ps 9:18 the e' of the poor shall not perish 8615
62: 5 my e' is from him. "
Pr 10:28 the e' of the wicked shall perish. "
11: 7 man dieth, his e' shall perish: "
23 the e' of the wicked is wrath. "
23:18 and thine e' shall not be cut off. * "
24:14 and thy e' shall not be cut off. * "
Isa 20: 5 Ethiopia their e', and of Egypt 4007
6 such is our e', whither we flee "
Zec 9: 5 Ekron; for her e' shall be ashamed; "
Lu 3:15 as the people were in e', 4328
Ac 12:11 all the e' of the people of the Jews. 4329
Ro 8:19 the earnest e' of the creature 603
Ph'p 1:20 to my earnest e' and my hope, "

expected
Jer 29:11 not of evil, to give you an e' end. *8615

expecting
Ac 3: 5 e' to receive something of them. 4328
Heb 10:13 e' till his enemies be made his 1551

expedient
Joh 11:50 Nor consider that it is e' for us, 4851
16: 7 It is e' for you that I go away: "
18:14 it was e' that one man should die "
1Co 6:12 unto me, but all things are not e': "
10:23 but all things are not e': "
2Co 8:10 this is e' of you, who have begun "
12: 1 not e' for me doubtless to glory. "

expel See also EXPELLED.
Jos 23: 5 shall e' them from before you, *1920
J'g 11: 7 Did not ye hate me, and e' me *1644

expelled
Jos 13:13 of Israel e' not the Geshurites, *3423
J'g 1:20 e' thence the three sons of Anak. †‡ "
2Sa 14:14 his banished be not e' from him. *5080
Ac 13:50 and e' them out of their coasts. *1544

expences
Ezr 6: 4 and let the e' be given out of the *5313
8 forthwith e' be given unto these * "

expense See EXPENCES.

experience
Ge 30:27 by e' that the Lord hath blessed *5172
Ec 1:16 my heart had great e' of wisdom 7200
Ro 5: 4 And patience, e'; and e', hope: *1382

experiment
2Co 9:13 by the e' of this ministration *1382

expert
1Ch 12:33 e' in war, with all instruments of *6186
35 of the Danites e' in war twenty * "
36 battle, e' in war, forty thousand. * "
Ca 3: 8 being e' in war: every man hath 3925
Jer 50: 9 shall be as of a mighty e' man; 7919
Ac 26: 3 be e' in all customs and questions 1109

expired
1Sa 18:26 and the days were not e'. 4390
2Sa 11: 1 after the year was e', at the time *8666
1Ch 17:11 when thy days be e' that thou *4390
20: 1 after the year was e', at the time *8666
2Ch 36:10 was e', king Nebuchadnezzar * "
Es 1: 5 And when these days were e', *4390
Eze 43:27 these days are e', it shall be, *3615
Ac 7:30 And when forty years were e', †4137
Re 20: 7 when the thousand years are e', *5055

exploits
Da 11:28 and he shall do e', and return to *
32 God shall be strong, and do e'.

expound See also EXPOUNDED.
J'g 14:14 they could not in three days e' *5046

expounded
J'g 14:19 unto them which e' the riddle. *5046
M'r 4:34 he e' all things to his disciples. 1956
Lu 24:27 he e' unto them in all the *1329
Ac 11: 4 e' it by order unto them, saying, 1620
18:26 and e' unto him the way of God "
28:23 to whom he e' and testified the "

express See also EXPRESSED.
Heb 1: 3 and the e' image of his person, *5481

expressed
Nu 1:17 men which are e' by their names: 5344
1Ch 12:31 which were e' by name, to come "
16:41 were e' by name, to give thanks "
2Ch 28:15 which were e' by name rose up, "
31:19 the men that were e' by name, to "
Ezr 8:20 all of them were e' by name.

expressly
1Sa 20:21 If I e' say unto the lad, Behold, * 559
Eze 1: 3 word of the Lord came e' unto Ezekiel
1Ti 4: 1 Now the Spirit speaketh e'. 4490

extend See also EXTENDED; EXTENDETH.
Ps 109:12 Let there be none to e' mercy 4900
Isa 66:12 I will e' peace to her like a river, 5186

extended
Ezr 7:28 e' mercy unto me before the king, 5186
9: 9 hath e' mercy unto us in the sight "

extendeth
Ps 16: 2 my goodness e' not to thee; *

extinct
Job 17: 1 breath is corrupt, my days are e', 2193
Isa 43:17 they are e', they are quenched as 1846

extol See also EXTOLLED.
Ps 30: 1 I will e' thee, O Lord; for thou 7311
68: 4 e' him that rideth upon the *5549
145: 1 I will e' thee, my God, O king; 7311
Da 4:37 I Nebuchadnezzar praise and e' 7313

extolled
Ps 66:17 and he was e' with my tongue. 7318
Isa 52:13 he shall be exalted and e', and be *5375

extortion
Eze 22:12 gained of thy neighbours by e', *6233
M't 23:25 they are full of e' and excess. 724

extortioner See also EXTORTIONERS.
Ps 109:11 Let the e' catch all that he hath; 5383
Isa 16: 4 the e' is at an end, the spoiler 4160
1Co 5:11 a railer, or a drunkard, or an e'; 727

extortioners
Lu 18:11 not as other men are, e', unjust, 727
1Co 5:10 covetous, or e', or with idolaters; "
6:10 revilers, nor e', shall inherit the "

extreme
De 28:22 an e' burning, and with the sword,*2746

extremity
Job 35:15 he knoweth it not in great e': *6580

eye See also EYEBROWS; EYED; EYELIDS; EYE'S EYES; EYESALVE; EYESERVICE; EYESIGHT; EYE-WITNESSES.
Ex 21:24 E' for e', tooth for tooth, hand for 5869
26 if a man smite the e' of his servant, "
26 or the e' of his maid, that it perish; "
Le 21:20 or that hath a blemish in his e', "
24:20 e' for e', tooth for tooth: as he "
De 7:16 e' shall have no pity upon them: "
13: 8 neither shall thine e' pity him, "
15: 9 thine e' be evil against thy poor "
19:13 Thine e' shall not pity him, but "
21 And thine e' shall not pity; "
21 but life shall go for life, e' for e', "
25:12 hand, thine e' shall not pity her. "
28:54 e' shall be evil toward his brother, "
56 e' shall be evil toward the husband "
32:10 he kept him as the apple of his e'. "
34: 7 his e' was not dim, nor his natural "
1Sa 24:10 but mine e' spared thee; and I "
2Sa 22:25 to my cleanness in his e' sight. 5869
Ezr 5: 5 e' of their God was upon the elders 5870
Job 7: 7 mine e' shall no more see good. 5869
8 The e' of him that hath seen me "
10:18 the ghost, and no e' had seen me! "
13: 1 Lo, mine e' hath seen all this, "
16:20 mine e' poureth out tears unto God. "
17: 2 e' continue in their provocation? "
7 e' also is dim by reason of sorrow, "
20: 9 The e' also which saw him shall see "
24:15 The e' also of the adulterer "
15 twilight, saying, No e' shall see me: "
28: 7 the vulture's e' hath not seen: "
10 his e' seeth every precious thing. "
29:11 and when the e' saw me, it gave "
42: 5 but now mine e' seeth thee. "
Ps 6: 7 e' is consumed because of grief; "
17: 8 Keep me as the apple of the e', "
31: 9 mine e' is consumed with grief, "
32: 8 I will guide thee with mine e'. "
33:18 the e' of the Lord is upon them "
35:19 neither let them wink with the e' "
21 Aha, aha, our e' hath seen it. "
54: 7 and mine e' hath seen his desire "
88: 9 e' mourneth by reason of affliction: "
92:11 Mine e' also shall see my desire "
94: 9 he that formed the e', shall he not "
Pr 7: 2 my law as the apple of thine e'. "
10:10 that winketh with the e' causeth "
20:12 The hearing ear, and the seeing e', "
22: 9 He that hath a bountiful e' shall "
23: 6 bread of him that hath an evil e', "
28:22 hasteth to be rich hath an evil e', "
30:17 The e' that mocketh at his father, "
Ec 1: 8 the e' is not satisfied with seeing, "
4: 8 is his e' satisfied with riches; * "
Isa 13:18 their e' shall not spare children. "
52: 8 they shall see e' to e', when the "
64: 4 neither hath the e' seen, O God, "
Jer 13:17 mine e' shall weep sore, and run "
La 1:16 mine e', mine e' runneth down with "
2: 4 slew all that were pleasant to the e' "
18 let not the apple of thine e' cease. "
3:48 Mine e' runneth down with rivers of "
49 Mine e' trickleth down, and ceaseth "
51 Mine e' affecteth mine heart "
Eze 5:11 neither shall mine e' spare, neither "
7: 4 And mine e' shall not spare thee, "
9 And mine e' shall not spare, neither "
8:18 mine e' shall not spare, neither "
9: 5 let not your e' spare, neither have "
10 for me also, mine e' shall not spare, "
16: 5 None e' pitied thee, to do any of "
Eze 20:17 e' spared them from destroying 5869
Mic 4:11 and let our e' look upon Zion. "
Zec 2: 8 you toucheth the apple of his e'. "
11:17 his arm, and upon his right e': "
17 right e' shall be utterly darkened. "
M't 5:29 if thy right e' offend thee, pluck it 3788
38 e' for an e', and a tooth for a tooth: "
6:22 The light of the body is the e': "
22 if therefore thine e' be single, "
23 But if thine e' be evil, thy whole "
7: 3 mote that is in thy brother's e', "
3 the beam that is in thine own e'? "
4 me pull out the mote out of thine e'; "
4 behold, a beam is in thine own e'? "
5 out the beam out of thine own e'; "
5 out the mote out of thy brother's e'. "
18: 9 if thine e' offend thee, pluck it out, "
9 thee to enter into life with one e', 3442
19:24 to go through the e' of a needle, 5169
20:15 Is thine e' evil, because I am good? 3788
M'r 7:22 an evil e', blasphemy, pride, "
9:47 if thine e' offend thee, pluck it out, "
47 the kingdom of God with one e', 3442
10:25 to go through the e' of a needle, 5168
Lu 6:41 the mote that is in thy brother's e', 3788
41 the beam that is in thine own e'? "
42 out the mote that is in thine e', "
42 the beam that is in thine own e'? "
42 first the beam out of thine own e', "
42 the mote that is in thy brother's e'. "
11:34 The light of the body is the e': "
34 therefore when thine e' is single, "
34 but when thine e' is evil, thy * "
18:25 camel to go through a needle's e', 5168
1Co 2: 9 E' hath not seen, nor ear heard, 3788
12:16 Because I am not the e', I am not "
17 If the whole body were an e', where "
21 the e' cannot say unto the hand, "
15:52 in the twinkling of an e', at the "
Re 1: 7 every e' shall see him, and they "

eyebrows
Le 14: 9 and his e', even all his hair 1354, 5869

eyed
Ge 29:17 Leah was tender e'; but Rachel *5869
1Sa 18: 9 Saul e' David from that day 5770

eyelids
Job 16:16 on my e' is the shadow of death; 6079
41:18 eyes are like the e' of the morning. "
Ps 11: 4 his e' try, the children of men. "
132: 4 mine eyes, or slumber to mine e', "
Pr 4:25 thine e' look straight before thee. "
6: 4 thine eyes, nor slumber to thine e'. "
25 neither let her take thee with her e'. "
30:13 and their e' are lifted up. "
Jer 9:18 and our e' gush out with waters. "

eye's
Ex 21:26 let him go free for his e' sake. 5869

eyes
Ge 3: 5 then your e' shall be opened, and 5869
6 and that it was pleasant to the e', "
7 the e' of them both were opened, "
6: 8 found grace in the e' of the Lord. "
13:10 Lot lifted up his e', and beheld "
14 Lift up now thine e', and look "
16: 4 her mistress was despised in her e'. "
5 I was despised in her e': the Lord "
18: 2 And he lifted up his e' and looked, "
19: 8 do ye to them as is good in your e': "
20:16 he is to thee a covering of the e', "
21:19 God opened her e', and she saw a "
22: 4 Abraham lifted up his e', and saw "
13 Abraham lifted up his e', and looked "
24:63 and he lifted up his e', and saw, "
64 Rebekah lifted up her e', and when "
27: 1 Isaac was old, and his e' were dim, "
30:27 if I have found favour in thine e', "
41 the rods before the e' of the cattle "
31:10 I lifted up mine e', and saw in a "
12 Lift up now thine e', and see, "
40 my sleep departed from mine e'. "
33: 1 Jacob lifted up his e', and looked, "
5 lifted up his e', and saw the women "
34:11 Let me find grace in your e', "
37:25 they lifted up their e' and looked, "
39: 7 his master's wife cast her e' upon "
41:37 was good in the e' of Pharaoh, "
37 and in the e' of all his servants. "
42:24 and bound him before their e'. "
43:29 lifted up his e', and saw his brother "
44:21 that I may set mine e' upon him. "
45:12 your e' see, and the e' of my brother "
46: 4 shall put his hand upon thine e'. "
47:19 shall we die before thine e', both "
48:10 the e' of Israel were dim for age, "
49:12 His e' shall be red with wine, "
50: 4 now I have found grace in your e', "
Ex 5:21 be abhorred in the e' of Pharaoh, "
21 and in the e' of his servants, "
8:26 of the Egyptians before their e', "
13: 9 for a memorial between thine e', "
16 and for frontlets between thine e': "
14:10 children of Israel lifted up their e', "
24:17 in the e' of the children of Israel. "
Le 4:13 be hid from the e' of the assembly, "
20: 4 the land do any ways hide their e' "
26:16 ague, that shall consume the e', "
Nu 5:13 be hid from the e' of her husband, "
10:31 thou mayest be to us instead of e', "
11: 6 beside this manna, before our e'. * "
15:39 your own heart and your own e', "
16:14 thou put out the e' of these men? "
20: 8 ye unto the rock before their e': "
12 sanctify me in the e' of the children "
Nu 22:31 the Lord opened the e' of Balaam, 5869
24: 2 Balaam lifted up his e', and he saw "
3 man whose e' are open hath said: * "
4 a trance, but having his e' open: "
15 man whose e' are open hath said: * "
16 a trance, but having his e' open: "
27:14 me at the water before their e': "
33:55 of them shall be pricks in your e', "
De 1:30 did for you in Egypt before your e'; "
3:21 Thine e' have seen all that the Lord "
27 and lift up thine e' westward, and "
27 and behold it with thine e': "
4: 3 Your e' have seen what the Lord "
9 things which thine e' have seen, "
19 And lest thou lift up thine e' unto "
34 did for you in Egypt before your e'? "
6: 8 be as frontlets between thine e'. "
22 all his household, before our e': "
7:19 temptations which thine e' saw, "
9:17 and brake them before your e'. "
10:21 things, which thine e' have seen. "
11: 7 your e' have seen all the great acts "
12 the e' of the Lord thy God are "
18 be as frontlets between your e'. "
12: 8 whatsoever is right in his own e'. "
13:18 which is right in the e' of the Lord "
14: 1 make any baldness between your e' "
16:19 a gift doth blind the e' of the wise, "
21: 7 neither have our e' seen it. "
24: 1 that she find no favour in his e', "
28:31 ox shall be slain before thine e', "
32 and thine e' shall look, and fail with "
34 be mad for the sight of thine e' "
65 a trembling heart, and failing of e', "
67 of thine e' which thou shalt see. "
29: 2 all that the Lord did before your e' "
3 temptations which thine e' have "
4 a heart to perceive, and e' to see, "
34: 4 caused thee to see it with thine e', "
Jos 5:13 he lifted up his e' and looked, "
23:13 thorns in your e', until ye perish "
24: 7 your e' have seen what I have done "
J'g 16:21 took him, and put out his e', "
28 of the Philistines for my two e'. "
17: 6 that which was right in his own e'. "
19:17 when he had lifted up his e', he saw "
21:25 that which was right in his own e'. "
Ru 2: 9 Let thine e' be on the field that "
10 have I found grace in thine e', * "
1Sa 2:33 shall be to consume thine e', and "
3: 2 and his e' began to wax dim, "
4:15 his e' were dim, that he could not "
6:13 lifted up their e', and saw the ark, "
11: 2 I may thrust out all your right e', "
12: 3 bribe to blind mine e' therewith? "
16 the Lord will do before your e'. "
14:27 and his e' were enlightened. "
29 how mine e' have been enlightened, "
20: 3 I have found grace in thine e'; "
29 if I have found favour in thine e', "
24:10 thine e' have seen how that the Lord "
25: 8 young men find favour in thine e': "
26:21 my soul was precious in thine e' "
24 much set by this day in mine e', "
24 much set by in the e' of the Lord, "
27: 5 I have now found grace in thine e', "
2Sa 6:20 to day in the e' of the handmaids "
12:11 I will take thy wives before thine e', "
13:34 that kept the watch lifted up his e', "
15:25 find favour in the e' of the Lord, "
18:24 and lifted up his e', and looked, "
19:27 therefore what is good in thine e'. "
22:28 thine e' are upon the haughty, "
24: 3 the e' of my lord the king may see "
1Ki 1:20 O king, the e' of all Israel are upon "
48 this day, mine e' even seeing it. "
8:29 e' may be open toward this house "
52 That thine e' may be open unto the "
9: 3 e' and mine heart shall be there "
10: 7 mine e' had seen it: and, behold, "
11:33 do that which is right in mine e', "
14: 4 Ahijah could not see; for his e' "
8 only which was right in mine e'; "
15: 5 was right in the e' of the Lord, "
11 that which was right in the e' of "
16:25 Omri wrought evil in the e' of * "
20: 6 whatsoever is pleasant in thine e', "
22:43 was right in the e' of the Lord: "
2Ki 4:34 and his e' upon his e', and his hands "
35 times, and the child opened his e'. "
6:17 Lord, I pray thee, open his e', "
17 opened the e' of the young man; "
20 Lord, open the e' of these men, "
20 And the Lord opened their e', "
7: 2, 19 thou shalt see it with thine e', "
10: 5 thou that which is good in thine e'. "
30 that which is right in mine e', "
19:16 open, Lord, thine e', and see: "
22 and lifted up thine e' on high? "
22:20 thine e' shall not see all the evil "
25: 7 the sons of Zedekiah before his e', "
7 and put out the e' of Zedekiah, "
1Ch 13: 4 was right in the e' of all the people. "
17:17 this was a small thing in thine e', "
21:16 And David lifted up his e', and saw "
23 do that which is good in his e': "
2Ch 6:20 e' may be open upon this house "
40 let, I beseech thee, thine e' be open, "
7:15 Now mine e' shall be open, and "
16 mine e' and mine heart shall be "
9: 6 mine e' had seen it: and, behold, "
14: 2 good and right in the e' of the Lord "
16: 9 the e' of the Lord run to and fro "
20:12 but our e' are upon thee. "
21: 6 was evil in the e' of the Lord. * "

2Ch 29: 6 evil in the e· of the Lord our God,*5869
8 to hissing, as ye see with your e·. “
34:28 neither shall thine e· see all the evil “
Ezr 3:12 house was laid before their e·. 5870
9: 8 that our God may lighten our e·. 5869
Ne 1: 6 e· open, that thou mayest hear “
6:16 much cast down in their own e·: “
Es 1:17 despise their husbands in their e·, “
8: 5 the king, and I be pleasing in his e·, “
Job 2:12 they lifted up their e· afar off, “
3:10 nor hid sorrow from mine e·. “
4:16 an image was before mine e·, “
7: 8 thine e· are upon me, and I am not. “
10: 4 Hast thou e· of flesh? or seest the “
11: 4 and I am clean in thine e·. “
20 But the e· of the wicked shall fail, “
14: 3 open thine e· upon such an one, “
15:12 and what do thy e· wink at, “
16: 9 enemy sharpeneth his e· upon me. “
17: 5 even the e· of his children shall fail. “
19:27 and mine e· shall behold, and not “
21: 8 and their offspring before their e·. “
20 His e· shall see his destruction, “
24:23 yet his e· are upon their ways. “
27:19 he openeth his e·, and he is not. “
28:21 it is hid from the e· of all living, “
29:15 I was e· to the blind, and feet was I “
31: 1 I made a covenant with mine e·; “
7 mine heart walked after mine e·, “
16 caused the e· of the widow to fail; “
32: 1 he was righteous in his own e·. “
34:21 his e· are upon the ways of man, “
36: 7 not his e· from the righteous: “
39:29 prey, and her e· behold afar off. “
40:24 He taketh it with his e·: his nose* “
41:18 and his e· are like the eyelids of the “
Ps 10: 8 e· are privily set against the poor. “
11: 4 his e· behold, his eyelids try, “
13: 3 lighten mine e·, lest I sleep “
15: 4 whose e· a vile person is contemned; “
17: 2 e· behold the things that are equal. “
11 they have set their e· bowing down “
19: 8 Lord is pure, enlightening the e·. “
25:15 Mine e· are ever toward the Lord; “
26: 3 lovingkindness is before mine e·: “
31:22 I am cut off from before thine e·: “
34:15 The e· of the Lord are upon the “
36: 1 there is no fear of God before his e·. “
2 he flattereth himself in his own e·, “
38:10 the light of mine e·, it also is gone “
50:21 set them in order before thine e·. “
66: 7 his e· behold the nations: let not “
69: 3 mine e· fail while I wait for my God. “
23 e· be darkened, that they see not; “
73: 7 Their e· stand out with fatness: “
77: 4 Thou holdest mine e· waking: I “
91: 8 Only with thine e· shalt thou behold “
101: 3 set no wicked thing before mine e·: “
6 Mine e· shall be upon the faithful “
115: 5 e· have they, but they see not: “
116: 8 soul from death, mine e· from tears, “
118:23 doing; it is marvellous in our e·. “
119:18 Open thou mine e·, that I may “
37 mine e· from beholding vanity; “
82 Mine e· fail for thy word, saying, “
123 Mine e· fail for thy salvation, and “
136 Rivers of waters run down mine e·, “
148 Mine e· prevent the night watches, “
121: 1 I will lift up mine e· unto the hills, “
123: 1 Unto thee lift I up mine e·, O thou “
2 as the e· of servants look unto the “
2 as the e· of a maiden unto the hand “
2 our e· wait upon the Lord our God, “
131: 1 is not haughty, nor mine e· lofty: “
132: 4 I will not give sleep to mine e·, “
135:16 e· have they, but they see not; “
139:16 Thine e· did see my substance, yet “
141: 8 But mine e· are unto thee, O God “
145:15 The e· of all wait upon thee; “
146: 8 The Lord openeth the e· of the blind: “
Pr 3: 7 Be not wise in thine own e·: 5869
21 let not them depart from thine e·: “
4:21 Let them not depart from thine e·; “
25 Let thine e· look right on, and let “
5:21 man are before the e· of the Lord, “
6: 4 Give not sleep to thine e·, nor “
13 winketh with his e·, he speaketh “
10:26 smoke to the e·, so is the sluggard “
12:15 way of a fool is right in his own e·: “
15: 3 e· of the Lord are in every place, “
30 light of the e· rejoiceth the heart: “
16: 2 of a man are clean in his own e·: “
30 shutteth his e· to devise froward “
17: 8 as a precious stone in the e· of him “
24 but the e· of a fool are in the ends “
20: 8 scattereth away all evil with his e·. “
13 open thine e·, and thou shalt be “
21: 2 way of a man is right in his own e·: “
10 findeth no favour in his e·. “
22:12 The e· of the Lord preserve “
23: 5 thine e· upon that which is not? “
26 and let thine e· observe my ways. “
29 cause? who hath redness of e·? “
33 Thine e· shall behold strange “
25: 7 prince whom thine e· have seen. “
27:20 so the e· of man are never satisfied. “
28:27 his e· shall have many a curse. “
29:13 the Lord lighteneth both their e·. “
30:12 that are pure in their own e·, “
13 O how lofty are their e·! “
Ec 2:10 e· desired I kept not from them, “
14 The wise man's e· are in his head; “
5:11 beholding of them with their e·? “
6: 9 Better is the sight of the e· than “
8:16 nor night seeth sleep with his e·:) “
11: 7 thing it is for the e· to behold the “
Ec 11: 9 heart, and in the sight of thine e·: 5869
Ca 1:15 thou art fair; thou hast doves' e·. “
4: 1 thou art fair; thou hast doves' e·. “
9 my heart with one of thine e·, “
5:12 His e· are as the e· of doves * “
6: 5 Turn away thine e· from me, for “
7: 4 e· like the fishpools in Heshbon: “
8:10 in his e· as one that found favour. “
Isa 1:15 I will hide mine e· from you: yea, “
16 of your doings from before mine e·; “
3: 8 Lord, to provoke the e· of his glory. “
16 stretched forth necks and wanton e·, “
5:15 the e· of the lofty shall be humbled: “
21 them that are wise in their own e·, “
6: 5 for mine e· have seen the King, “
10 their ears heavy, and shut their e·; “
10 lest they see with their e·, “
11: 3 not judge after the sight of his e·, “
13:16 be dashed to pieces before their e·; “
17: 7 and his e· shall have respect to the “
29:10 sleep, and hath closed your e·: “
18 the e· of the blind shall see out of “
30:20 but thine e· shall see thy teachers: “
32: 3 e· of them that see shall not be dim, “
33:15 and shutteth his e· from seeing evil; “
17 e· shall see the King in his beauty: “
20 thine e· shall see Jerusalem a quiet “
35: 5 the e· of the blind shall be opened, “
37:17 open thine e·, O Lord, and see: “
23 and lifted up thine e· on high? “
38:14 mine e· fail with looking upward: “
40:26 Lift up your e· on high, and behold “
42: 7 To open the blind e·, to bring out “
43: 8 forth the blind people that have e·, “
44:18 he hath shut their e·, that they “
49: 5 I be glorious in the e· of the Lord, “
18 Lift up thine e· round about, and “
51: 6 Lift up your e· to the heavens, “
52:10 made bare his holy arm in the e· “
59:10 we grope as if we had no e·: “
60: 4 Lift up thine e· round about, and “
65:12 but did evil before mine e·, and did “
16 because they are hid from mine e·. “
66: 4 but they did evil before mine e·, “
Jer 3: 2 up thine e· unto the high places, “
5: 3 are not thine e· upon the truth? “
21 which have e·, and see not; “
7:11 become a den of robbers in your e·? “
9: 1 and mine e· a fountain of tears, “
18 that our e· may run down with tears. “
13:20 Lift up your e·, and behold them “
14: 6 their e· did fail, because there was “
17 Let mine e· run down with tears “
16: 9 cease out of this place in your e·, “
17 mine e· are upon all their ways: “
17 is their iniquity hid from mine e·. “
20: 4 and thine e· shall behold it: and “
22:17 thine e· and thine heart are not “
24: 6 set mine e· upon them for good, “
29:21 he shall slay them before your e·; “
31:16 weeping, and thine e· from tears: “
32: 4 and his e· shall behold his e·; “
19 thine e· are open upon all the ways “
34: 3 thine e· shall behold the e· of the “
39: 6 Zedekiah in Riblah before his e·: “
7 Moreover he put out Zedekiah's e·, “
42: 2 few of many, as thine e· do behold “
52: 2 was evil in the e· of the Lord, *
10 the sons of Zedekiah before his e·: “
11 Then he put out the e· of Zedekiah; “
La 2:11 Mine e· do fail with tears, “
4:17 e· as yet failed for our vain help: “
5:17 for these things our e· are dim. “
Eze 1:18 rings were full of e· round about “
6: 9 their e·, which go a whoring after “
8: 5 Son of man, lift up thine e· now “
5 So I lifted up mine e·...the north, “
10:12 wheels, were full of e· round about, “
12: 2 a rebellious house, which have e· “
12 he see not the ground with his e·. “
18: 6 neither hath lifted up his e· to the “
12 and hath lifted up his e· to the idols “
15 neither hath lifted up his e· to the “
20: 7 man the abominations of his e·, “
8 away the abominations of their e·, “
24 e· were after their fathers' idols. “
21: 6 with bitterness sigh before their e·. “
22:26 hid their e· from my sabbaths, “
23:16 soon as she saw them with her e·,* “
27 thou shalt not lift up thine e· unto “
40 didst wash thyself, paintedst thy e·, “
24:16 from thee the desire of thine e· “
21 the desire of your e·, and that which “
25 their glory, the desire of their e·, “
33:25 lift up your e· toward your idols, “
36:23 be sanctified in you before their e·. “
37:20 be in thine hand before their e·. “
38:16 in thee, O Gog, before their e·. “
23 known in the e· of many nations, “
40: 4 Son of man, behold with thine e·, “
44: 5 mark well, and behold with thine e·, “
Da 4:34 Nebuchadnezzar lifted up mine e· 5870
7: 8 this horn were e· like the e· of man, “
20 even of that horn that had e·, “
8: 3 Then I lifted up mine e·, and saw, 5869
5 had a notable horn between his e·. “
21 great horn that is between his e· “
9:18 thine e·, and behold our desolations, “
10: 5 I lifted up mine e·, and looked, “
6 his e· as lamps of fire, and his arms “
Ho 13:14 shall be hid from mine e·. “
Joe 1:16 not the meat cut off before our e·, “
Am 9: 4 will set mine e· upon them for evil, “
8 the e· of the Lord God are upon “
Mic 7:10 mine e· shall behold her: now shall “
Hab 1:13 Thou art of purer e· than to behold “
Zep 3:20 back your captivity before your e·, 5869
Hag 2: 3 not in your e· in comparison of it “
Zec 1:18 Then lifted I up mine e·, and saw, “
2: 1 I lifted up mine e· again, and looked, “
3: 9 upon one stone shall be seven e·: “
4:10 they are the e· of the Lord, which “
5: 1 I turned, and lifted up mine e·, “
5 Lift up now thine e·, and see “
9 lifted I up mine e·, and looked, “
6: 1 Then I turned, and lifted up mine e·, “
8: 6 marvellous in the e· of the remnant “
6 it also be marvellous in mine e·? “
9: 1 the e· of man, as of all the tribes * “
8 for now have I seen with mine e·. “
12: 4 mine e· upon the house of Judah, “
14:12 their e· shall consume away in “
Mal 1: 5 your e· shall see, and ye shall say, “
M't 9:29 Then touched he their e·, saying, 3788
30 their e· were opened; and Jesus “
13:15 and their e· they have closed; “
15 time they should see with their e·, “
16 blessed are your e·, for they see: “
17: 8 when they had lifted up their e·, “
18: 9 rather than having two e· to be “
20:33 Lord, that our e· may be opened. “
34 on them, and touched their e·: “
34 their e· received sight, and they *3788
21:42 and it is marvellous in our e·? “
26:43 for their e· were heavy. “
M'r 8:18 Having e·, see ye not? having ears, “
23 and when he had spit on his e·, 3659
25 put his hands again upon his e·, 3788
9:47 having two e· to be cast into hell “
12:11 and it is marvellous in our e·? “
14:40 (for their e· were heavy,) neither “
Lu 2:30 For mine e· have seen thy salvation, “
4:20 And the e· of all them that were “
6:20 he lifted up his e· on his disciples, “
10:23 Blessed are the e· which see the “
16:23 And in hell he lifted up his e·, “
18:13 up so much as his e· unto heaven, “
19:42 but now they are hid from thine e·. “
24:16 e· were holden that they should “
31 And their e· were opened, and they “
Joh 4:35 Lift up your e·, and look on the “
6: 5 Jesus then lifted up his e·, and saw “
9: 6 he anointed the e· of the blind man “
10 him, How were thine e· opened? “
11 and anointed mine e·, and said “
14 made the clay, and opened his e·. “
15 He put clay upon mine e·, and I “
17 him, that he hath opened thine e·? “
21 who hath opened his e·, we know “
26 thee? how opened he thine e·? “
30 and yet he hath opened mine e·. “
32 that any man opened the e· of one “
10:21 Can a devil open the e· of the blind? “
11:37 which opened the e· of the blind, “
41 Jesus lifted up his e·, and said, “
12:40 He hath blinded their e·, and “
40 they should not see with their e·, “
17: 1 and lifted up his e· to heaven, and “
Ac 3: 4 Peter, fastening his e· upon him with “
9: 8 his e· were opened, he saw no man: 3788
18 from his e· as it had been scales: “
40 And she opened her e·: and when “
11: 6 when I had fastened mine e·, I “
13: 9 the Holy Ghost, set his e· on him, “
26:18 To open their e·, and to turn them 3788
28:27 and their e· have they closed; “
27 lest they should see with their e·, “
Ro 3:18 is no fear of God before their e·. “
11: 8 e· that they should not see, and “
10 Let their e· be darkened, that they “
Ga 3: 1 before whose e· Jesus Christ hath “
4:15 have plucked out your own e·, “
Eph 1:18 The e· of your understanding being “
Heb 4:13 and opened unto the e· of him with “
1Pe 3:12 For the e· of the Lord are over the “
2Pe 2:14 Having e· full of adultery, and that “
1Jo 1: 1 which we have seen with our e·, “
2:11 that darkness hath blinded his e·. “
16 lust of the e·, and the pride of life, “
Re 1:14 and his e· were as a flame of fire; “
2:18 hath his e· like unto a flame of fire, “
3:18 and anoint thine e· with eyesalve, “
4: 6 there four beasts full of e· before “
8 and they were full of e· within: “
5: 6 seven e·, which are the seven spirits “
7:17 wipe away all tears from their e·. “
19:12 His e· were as a flame of fire, “
21: 4 wipe away all tears from their e·; “

eyesalve
Re 3:18 and anoint thine eyes with e·, that 2854

eyeservice
Eph 6: 6 Not with e·, as menpleasers; but as 3787
Col 3:22 not with e·, as menpleasers; but in “

eyesight See also EYE and SIGHT.
Ps 18:24 cleanness of my hands in his e·. 5869

eyewitnesses
Lu 1: 2 which from the beginning were e·, 845
2Pe 1:16 but were e· of his majesty. 2030

Ezar (*e'-zar*) See also EZER.
1Ch 1:38 and Dishon, and E·, and Dishan. 687

Ezbai (*ez'-bahee*)
1Ch 11:37 Carmelite, Naarai the son of E·, 229

Ezbon (*ez'-bon*)
Ge 46:16 Haggi, Shuni, and E·, Eri, 675
1Ch 7: 7 the sons of Bela; E·, and Uzzi. “

Ezekias (*ez-e-ki'-as*) See also HEZEKIAH.
M't 1: 9 Achaz; and Achaz begat E·; 1478
10 And E· begat Manasses; and “

Ezekiel (*e-zeke'-yel*)
Eze 1: 3 the Lord came expressly unto *E*· 3168
24:24 Thus *E*· is unto you a sign: "
Ezel (*e'-zel*) See also BETH-EZEL.
1Sa 20:19 and shalt remain by the stone *E*·. 237
Ezem (*e'-zem*) See also AZEM.
1Ch 4:29 Bilhah, and at *E*·, and at Tolad, 6107
Ezer (*e'-zur*) See also ABI-EZER; EBEN-EZER; EZAR; ROMAMTI-EZER.
Ge 36:21 And Dishon, and *E*·, and Dishan: 687
27 The children of *E*· are these; Bilhan, "
30 Dishon, duke *E*·, duke Dishan: "
1Ch 1:42 The sons of *E*·; Bilhan, and Zavan, "
4: 4 and *E*· the father of Hushah. 5829
7:21 and *E*·, and Elead, whom the men 5827
12: 9 *E*· the first, Obadiah the second, 5829
Ne 3:19 next to him repaired *E*· the son of "
12:42 and Malchijah, and Elam, and *E*·. "
Ezion-gaber (*e''-ze-on-ga'-bur*) See also EZION-GEBER.
Nu 33:35 Ebronah, and encamped at *E*·. *6100
36 And they removed from *E*·, and * "
De 2: 8 from *E*·, we turned and passed *6100
2Ch 20:36 and they made the ships in *E*·. * "
Ezion-geber (*e''-ze-on-ghe'-bur*) See also EZION-GABER.
1Ki 9:26 made a navy of ships in *E*·, 6100
22:48 for the ships were broken at *E*·. "
2Ch 8:17 went Solomon to *E*·, and to Eloth, "
Eznite (*ez'-nite*)
2Sa 23: 8 the same was Adino the *E*·: he 6112
Ezra (*ez'-rah*) See also AZARIAH; EZRAHITE.
1Ch 4:17 of *E*· were, Jether, and Mered, 5830
Ezr 7: 1 *E*· the son of Seraiah, the son of "
6 This *E*· went up from Babylon; "
10 *E*· had prepared his heart to seek "
11 Artaxerxes gave unto *E*· the priest, "
12 king of kings, Unto *E*· the priest, "
21 whatsoever *E*· the priest, the scribe "
25 *E*·, after the wisdom of thy God, "
10: 1 Now when *E*· had prayed, and "
2 said unto *E*·, We have trespassed "
5 Then arose *E*·, and made the chief "
Ezr 10: 6 *E*· rose up from before the house 5830
10 *E*· the priest stood up, and said "
16 And *E*· the priest, with certain chief "
Ne 8: 1 and they spake unto *E*· the scribe "
2 And *E*· the priest brought the law "
4 *E*· the scribe stood upon a pulpit "
5 *E*· opened the book in the sight of "
6 *E*· blessed the Lord, the great God. "
9 and *E*· the priest the scribe, and the "
13 Levites, unto *E*· the scribe, even to "
12: 1 Seraiah, Jeremiah, *E*·, "
13 Of *E*·, Meshullam; of Amariah, "
26 and of *E*· the priest, the scribe. "
33 And Azariah, *E*·, Meshullam, "
36 of God, and *E*· the scribe before "
Ezrahite (*ez'-rah-hite*)
1Ki 4:31 than Ethan the *E*·, and Heman, 250
Ps 88:*title* Maschil of Heman the *E*·. "
89:*title* Maschil of Ethan the *E*·. "
Ezri (*ez'-ri*)
1Ch 27:26 ground was *E*· the son of Chelub: 5836
Ezrite See ABI-EZRITE.

F

fables
1Ti 1: 4 Neither give heed to *f* and endless 3454
4: 7 refuse profane and old wives' *f*, "
2Ti 4: 4 and shall be turned unto *f*. "
Tit 1:14 Not giving heed to Jewish *f*, and "
2Pe 1:16 not followed cunningly devised *f*, "
face See also FACES.
Ge 1: 2 darkness was upon the *f* of the 6440
2 Spirit of God moved upon the *f* of the "
29 which is upon the *f* of all the earth, "
2: 6 watered the whole *f* of the ground. "
3:19 In the sweat of thy *f* shalt thou eat 639
4:14 driven me out this day from the *f* 6440
14 of the earth; and from thy *f* shall I "
6: 1 to multiply on the *f* of the earth, "
7 destroy...from the *f* of the earth; "
7: 3 seed alive upon the *f* of all the earth. "
4 destroy from off the *f* of the earth. "
18 ark went upon the *f* of the waters. "
23 was upon the *f* of the ground, "
8: 8 abated from off the *f* of the ground; "
9 were on the *f* of the whole earth: "
13 behold, the *f* of the ground was dry. "
11: 4 upon the *f* of the whole earth. "
8 thence upon the *f* of all the earth: "
9 abroad upon the *f* of all the earth. "
16: 6 hardly with her, she fled from her *f*. "
8 I flee from the *f* of my mistress "
17: 3 And Abram fell on his *f*: "
17 Then Abraham fell upon his *f*, 639
19: 1 with his *f* toward the ground; "
13 great before the *f* of the Lord; *6440
24:47 and I put the earring upon her *f*,* 639
30:33 come for my hire before thy *f*: *6440
31:21 set his *f* toward the mount Gilead. "
32:20 and afterward I will see his *f*; "
30 for I have seen God *f* to *f*, "
33:10 I have seen thy *f*, as though I had "
10 though I had seen the *f* of God, "
35: 1 thou fleddest from the *f* of Esau "
7 he fled from the *f* of his brother. "
36: 6 from the *f* of his brother Jacob. * "
38:15 because she had covered her *f*. "
41:56 was over all the *f* of the earth: "
43: 3 Ye shall not see my *f*, except your "
5 unto us, Ye shall not see my *f*, "
31 he washed his *f*, and went out, "
44:23 with you, ye shall see my *f* no more. "
26 for we may not see the man's *f*, "
46:28 him unto Joseph, to direct his *f* * "
30 let me die, since I have seen thy *f*, "
48:11 I had not thought to see thy *f*: "
12 bowed himself with his *f* to the 639
50: 1 Joseph fell upon his father's *f*, 6440
18 went and fell down before his *f*; "
Ex 2:15 Moses fled from the *f* of Pharaoh, "
3: 6 Moses hid his *f*; for he was afraid "
10: 5 they shall cover the *f* of the earth, 5869
15 covered the *f* of the whole earth, "
28 see my *f* no more; for in that day 6440
28 thou seest my *f* thou shalt die. "
29 I will see thy *f* again no more. "
14:19 cloud went from before their *f*, *
25 Let us flee from the *f* of Israel; 6440
16:14 upon the *f* of the wilderness there "
32:12 to consume them from the *f* of the "
33:11 the Lord spake unto Moses *f* to *f*, "
16 that are upon the *f* of the earth. "
20 he said, Thou canst not see my *f*: "
23 but my *f* shall not be seen. "
34:29 wist not that the skin of his *f* shone "
30 behold, the skin of his *f* shone; "
33 he put a vail on his *f*. "
35 saw the *f* of Moses, that the skin of "
35 the skin of Moses' *f* shone: "
35 and Moses put the vail upon his *f* "
Le 13:41 the part of his head toward his *f*,* "
17:10 I will even set my *f* against that "
19:32 and honour the *f* of the old man, "
20: 3, 5 I will set my *f* against that man, "
6 I will even set my *f* against that "
26:17 And I will set my *f* against you, "
Nu 6:25 Lord make his *f* shine upon thee, "
11:31 cubits high upon the *f* of the earth. "
12: 3 which were upon the *f* of the earth.) "
14 If her father had but spit in her *f*, "
Nu 14:14 that thou Lord art seen *f* to *f*, 5869
16: 4 Moses heard it, he fell upon his *f*: 6440
19: 3 and one shall slay her before his *f*: "
22: 5 they cover the *f* of the earth, 5869
11 which covereth the *f* of the earth: "
31 and fell flat on his *f*. 639
24: 1 set his *f* toward the wilderness. 6440
De 1:17 shall not be afraid of the *f* of man; "
5: 4 Lord talked with you *f* to *f* in the "
6:15 thee from off the *f* of the earth. "
7: 6 that are upon the *f* of the earth. "
10 them that hate him to their *f*, "
10 he will repay him to his *f*. "
8:20 Lord destroyeth before your *f*, *
9: 3 bring them down before thy *f*: *
25: 2 and to be beaten before his *f*, "
9 and spit in his *f*, and shall answer 6440
28: 7 to be smitten before thy *f*: *
31 taken away from before thy *f*, "
31: 5 shall give them up before your *f*,*
17 and I will hide my *f* from them, 6440
18 I will surely hide my *f* in that day "
32:20 said, I will hide my *f* from them, "
34:10 whom the Lord knew *f* to *f*, "
Jos 5:14 Joshua fell on his *f* to the earth, "
7: 6 fell to the earth upon his *f* before "
10 liest thou thus upon thy *f*? "
J'g 6:22 seen an angel of the Lord *f* to *f*. "
Ru 2:10 Then she fell on her *f*, and bowed "
1Sa 5: 3 was fallen upon his *f* to the earth "
4 was fallen upon his *f* to the ground "
17:49 he fell upon his *f* to the earth. "
20:15 every one from the *f* of the earth. "
41 and fell on his *f* to the ground, 639
24: 8 David stooped with his *f* to the "
25:23 and fell before David on her *f*, 6440
41 bowed herself on her *f* to the earth, 639
26:20 earth before the *f* of the Lord: *6440
28:14 stooped with his *f* to the ground, 639
2Sa 2:22 how then should I hold up my *f* 6440
3:13 Thou shalt not see my *f*, except "
13 when thou comest to see my *f*. "
9: 6 he fell on his *f*, and did reverence. "
14: 4 she fell on her *f* to the ground, 639
22 Joab fell to the ground on his *f*, 6440
24 and let him not see my *f*. "
24 house, and saw not the king's *f*. "
28 and saw not the king's *f*. "
32 therefore let me see the king's *f*; "
33 himself on his *f* to the ground 639
18: 8 over the *f* of all the country: 6440
28 his *f* before the king, and said, 639
19: 4 But the king covered his *f*, 6440
24:20 king on his *f* upon the ground. 639
1Ki 1:23 the king with his *f* to the ground. "
31 bowed with her *f* to the earth, "
8:14 And the king turned his *f* about, 6440
13: 6 Intreat now the *f* of the Lord * "
34 destroy it from off the *f* of the earth. "
18: 7 he knew him, and fell on his *f*, "
42 and put his *f* between his knees. "
19:13 he wrapped his *f* in his mantle, "
20:38 himself with ashes upon his *f*. *5869
41 took the ashes away from his *f*; * "
21: 4 turned away his *f*, and would eat 6440
2Ki 4:29 lay my staff upon the *f* of the child. "
31 the staff upon the *f* of the child; "
8:15 spread it on his *f*, so that he died: "
9:30 she painted her *f*, and tired her *5869
32 he lifted up his *f* to the window, 6440
37 as dung upon the *f* of the field "
12:17 set his *f* to go up to Jerusalem. "
13:14 and wept over his *f*, and said, * "
14: 8 let us look one another in the *f*. "
11 Judah looked one another in the *f* "
18:24 thou turn away the *f* of one captain "
20: 2 he turned his *f* to the wall, "
1Ch 16:11 strength, seek his *f* continually. "
21:21 to David with his *f* to the ground. 639
2Ch 6: 3 And the king turned his *f*, and 6440
42 not away the *f* of thine anointed: "
7:14 and pray, and seek my *f*, "
20:18 head with his *f* to the ground: 639
25:17 let us see one another in the *f*. 6440
21 they saw one another in the *f*, "
30: 9 will not turn away his *f* from you, "
2Ch 32:21 with shame of *f* to his own land. 6440
35:22 Josiah would not turn his *f* from "
Ezr 9: 6 and blush to lift up my *f* to thee, "
7 to a spoil, and to confusion of *f*, "
Es 1:14 and Media, which saw the king's *f*, "
7: 8 mouth, they covered Haman's *f*. "
Job 1:11 and he will curse thee to thy *f*. "
2: 5 and he will curse thee to thy *f*. "
4:15 Then a spirit passed before my *f*; "
11:15 For then shalt thou lift up thy *f* "
13:24 Wherefore hidest thou thy *f*, and "
15:27 he covereth his *f* with his fatness, "
16: 8 in me beareth witness to my *f*. "
16 My *f* is foul with weeping, "
21:31 Who shall declare his way to his *f*? "
22:26 shalt lift up thy *f* unto God. "
23:17 covered the darkness from my *f*. "
24:15 see me: and disguiseth his *f*. "
26: 9 holdeth back the *f* of his throne, "
30:10 and spare not to spit in my *f*. "
33:26 he shall see his *f* with joy: "
34:29 and when he hideth his *f*, who "
37:12 the *f* of the world in the earth. "
38:30 and the *f* of the deep is frozen. "
41:13 discover the *f* of his garment? * "
14 Who can open the doors of his *f*? "
Ps 5: 8 thy way straight before my *f*. "
10:11 hideth his *f*; he will never see it. "
13: 1 how long wilt thou hide thy *f* "
17:15 will behold thy *f* in righteousness: "
21:12 thy strings against the *f* of them. "
22:24 hath he hid his *f* from him; "
24: 6 that seek thy *f*, O Jacob. Selah. "
27: 8 Seek ye my *f*; my heart said unto "
8 Thy *f*, Lord, will I seek. "
9 Hide not thy *f* far from me; "
30: 7 hide thy *f*, and I was troubled. "
31:16 thy *f* to shine upon thy servant: "
34:16 The *f* of the Lord is against them "
41:12 settest me before thy *f* for ever. "
44:15 shame of my *f* hath covered me, "
24 Wherefore hidest thou thy *f*, and "
51: 9 Hide thy *f* from my sins, "
67: 1 and cause his *f* to shine upon us; "
69: 7 shame hath covered my *f*. "
17 hide not thy *f* from thy servant; "
80: 3 O God, and cause thy *f* to shine; "
7 of hosts, and cause thy *f* to shine; "
19 of hosts, cause thy *f* to shine; "
84: 9 look upon the *f* of thine anointed. "
88:14 why hidest thou thy *f* from me? "
89:14 and truth shall go before thy *f*. "
23 beat down his foes before his *f*, * "
102: 2 Hide not thy *f* from me in the day "
104:15 and oil to make his *f* to shine, "
29 hidest thy *f*, they are troubled: "
30 thou renewest the *f* of the earth. "
105: 4 strength: seek his *f* evermore. "
119:135 Make thy *f* to shine upon thy "
132:10 not away the *f* of thine anointed. "
143: 7 faileth: hide not thy *f* from me, "
Pr 7:13 with an impudent *f* said unto him, "
15 thee, diligently to seek thy *f*, "
8:27 compass upon the *f* of the depth: "
21:29 A wicked man hardeneth his *f*: "
24:31 nettles had covered the *f* thereof, "
27:19 As in water *f* answereth to *f*, so "
Ec 8: 1 wisdom maketh his *f* to shine, "
1 boldness of his *f* shall be changed. "
Isa 6: 2 with twain he covered his *f*, "
8:17 his *f* from the house of Jacob, "
14:21 fill the *f* of the world with cities. "
16: 4 to them from the *f* of the spoiler: "
23:17 the world upon the *f* of the earth. "
25: 7 the *f* of the covering cast over all "
27: 6 fill the *f* of the world with fruit. "
28:25 he hath made plain the *f* thereof, "
29:22 neither shall his *f* now wax pale. "
36: 9 turn away the *f* of one captain "
38: 2 Hezekiah turned his *f* toward the "
49:23 with their *f* toward the earth, * 639
50: 6 my *f* from shame and spitting. 6440
7 have I set my *f* like a flint, "
54: 8 hid my *f* from thee for a moment; "
59: 2 your sins have hid his *f* from you, "
64: 7 thou hast hid thy *f* from us, "

Isa 65: 3 me to anger continually to my f: 6440
Jer 1:13 the f thereof is toward the north. "
2:27 their back unto me, and not their f: "
4:30 thou rentest thy f with painting,*5869
8: 2 for dung upon the f of the earth. 6440
13:26 I discover thy skirts upon thy f. "
16: 4 as dung upon the f of the earth: "
17 ways: they are not hid from my f, "
18:17 shew them the back, and not the f, "
21:10 I have set my f against this city "
22:25 of them whose f thou fearest, * "
25:26 which are upon the f of the earth: "
28:16 thee from off the f of the earth: "
32:31 should remove it from before my f, "
33 unto me the back, and not the f: "
33: 5 I have hid my f from this city. "
44:11 I will set my f against you "
La 2:19 like water before the f of the Lord: "
3:35 before the f of the most High, "
Eze 1:10 the f of a man, and the f of a lion, "
10 had the f of an ox on the left side; "
10 four also had the f of an eagle. "
28 fell upon my f, and I heard a voice "
3: 8 thy f strong against their faces, "
23 of Chebar: and I fell on my f. "
4: 3 and set thy f against it, and it shall "
7 shalt set thy f toward the siege "
6: 2 set thy f toward the mountains "
7:22 My f will I turn also from them, "
9: 8 I fell upon my f, and cried, "
10:14 the first f was the f of a cherub, "
14 the second f was the f of a man, "
14 and the third the f of a lion, "
14 and the fourth the f of an eagle. "
11:13 Then fell I down upon my f, "
12: 6 shalt cover thy f, that thou see not "
12 shall cover his f, that he see not "
13:17 set thy f against the daughters of "
14: 3 of their iniquity before their f: "
4, 7 of his iniquity before his f, and "
8 I will set my f against that man, "
15: 7 I will set my f against them; "
7 when I set my f against them. "
20:35 there will I plead with you f to f. "
46 man, set thy f toward the south, "
21: 2 man, set thy f toward Jerusalem, "
16 left, whithersoever thy f is set. "
25: 2 set thy f against the Ammonites, "
28:21 of man, set thy f against Zidon, "
29: 2 of man, set thy f against Pharaoh "
34: 6 upon all the f of the earth, "
35: 2 man, set thy f against mount Seir, "
38: 2 Son of man, set thy f against Gog, "
18 my fury shall come up in my f. * 639
20 that are upon the f of the earth, 6440
39:14 remain upon the f of the earth, "
23 therefore hid I my f from them, "
24 and hid my f from them. "
29 Neither will I hide my f any more "
40:15 And from the f of the gate of the * "
15 entrance unto the f of the porch * "
41:14 the breadth of the f of the house, "
19 f of a man was toward the palm "
19 f of a young lion toward the palm "
21 and the f of the sanctuary; "
25 upon the f of the porch without. "
43: 3 of Chebar; and I fell upon my f. "
44: 4 the Lord: and I fell upon my f. "
Da 2:46 Nebuchadnezzar fell upon his f, 600
8: 5 on the f of the whole earth, 6440
17 I was afraid, and fell upon my f: "
18 I was in a deep sleep on my f "
9: 3 I set my f unto the Lord God, "
8 to us belongeth confusion of f, "
17 thy f to shine upon thy sanctuary "
10: 6 f as the appearance of lightning, "
9 then was I in a deep sleep on my f, "
9 and my f toward the ground. "
15 I set my f toward the ground, "
11:17 He shall also set his f to enter "
18 shall he turn his f unto the isles, "
19 he shall turn his f toward the fort "
Ho 5: 5 pride of Israel doth testify to his f: "
15 their offence, and seek my f: "
7: 2 about: they are before my f. "
10 pride of Israel testifieth to his f: "
Joe 2: 6 Before their f the people shall be * "
20 with his f toward the east sea, * "
Am 5: 8 them out upon the f of the earth: "
9: 6 them out upon the f of the earth: "
8 destroy it from off the f of the earth; "
Mic 3: 4 he will even hide his f from them "
Na 2: 1 in pieces is come up before thy f: "
3: 5 discover thy skirts upon thy f, "
Zec 5: 3 over the f of the whole earth: "
M't 6:17 anoint thine head, and wash thy f; 4383
11:10 I send my messenger before thy f, "
16: 3 ye can discern the f of the sky; "
17: 2 and his f did shine as the sun, "
6 on their f, and were sore afraid. "
18:10 always behold the f of my Father "
26:39 and fell on his f, and prayed, "
67 Then did they spit in his f, "
M'r 1: 2 I send my messenger before thy f, "
14:65 to cover his f, and to buffet him, "
Lu 1:76 shalt go before the f of the Lord "
2:31 prepared before the f of all people; "
5:12 who seeing Jesus fell on his f, "
7:27 I send my messenger before thy f, "
9:51 set his f to go to Jerusalem, "
52 And sent messengers before his f: "
53 because his f was as though he "
10: 1 sent them two and two before his f "
12:56 ye can discern the f of the sky "
17:16 And fell down on his f at his feet, "
Lu 21:35 dwell on the f of the whole earth. 4383
22:64 struck him on the f, and asked * "
Joh 11:44 f was bound about with a napkin. 4799
Ac 2:25 the Lord always before my f, for 1799
6:15 saw his f as it had been the f of 4383
7:45 out before the f of our fathers, "
17:26 to dwell on all the f of the earth, "
20:25 shall see my f no more. "
38 that they should see his f no more. "
25:16 have the accusers f to f. "
1Co 13:12 a glass, darkly; but then f to f: "
14:25 and so falling down on his f "
2Co 3: 7 stedfastly behold the f of Moses "
13 which put a vail over his f, "
18 with open f beholding as in a glass "
4: 6 of God in the f of Jesus Christ. "
11:20 if a man smite you on the f. "
Ga 1:22 unknown by f unto the churches "
2:11 I withstood him to the f, "
Col 2: 1 as have not seen my f in the flesh; "
1Th 2:17 to see your f with great desire. "
3:10 that we might see your f, "
Jas 1:23 beholding his natural f in a glass: "
1Pe 3:12 the f of the Lord is against them "
2Jo 12 and speak f to f, that our joy may 4750
3Jo 14 see thee, and we shall speak f to f. "
Re 4: 7 the third beast had a f as a man, 4383
6:16 hide us from the f of him that "
10: 1 and his f was as it were the sun, "
12:14 a time, from the f of the serpent. "
20:11 from whose f the earth and the "
22: 4 And they shall see his f; "

faced See SHAMEFACEDNESS.

faces
Ge 9:23 and their f were backward, and 6440
18:22 their f from thence, and went *
30:40 and set the f of the flocks 6440
42: 6 with their f to the earth. 639
Ex 19: 7 before their f all these words *6440
20:20 his fear may be before your f, "
25:20 their f shall look one to another; "
20 shall the f of the cherubims be. "
37: 9 with their f one to another; even "
9 were the f of the cherubims. "
Le 9:24 they shouted, and fell on their f. "
Nu 14: 5 Moses and Aaron fell on their f "
16:22 they fell upon their f, and said, "
45 And they fell upon their f. "
20: 6 they fell upon their f: and the "
J'g 13:20 and fell on their f to the ground. "
18:23 turned their f, and said unto Micah, "
2Sa 19: 5 this day the f of all thy servants, "
1Ki 2:15 all Israel set their f on me, "
18:39 they fell on their f: and they said, "
1Ch 12: 8 whose f were like the f of lions, "
21:16 in sackcloth, fell upon their f. "
2Ch 3:13 feet, and their f were inward. "
7: 3 with their f to the ground upon the 639
29: 6 have turned away their f from 6440
Ne 8: 6 Lord with their f to the ground. 639
Job 9:24 he covereth the f of the judges 6440
40:13 and bind their f in secret. "
Ps 34: 5 and their f were not ashamed. "
83:16 Fill their f with shame; that they "
Isa 3:15 and grind the f of the poor? * "
13: 8 their f shall be as flames. "
25: 8 wipe away tears from off all f; "
53: 3 we hid as it were our f from him;* "
Jer 1: 8 Be not afraid of their f: for I am * "
17 be not dismayed at their f, "
5: 3 made their f harder than a rock; "
7:19 to the confusion of their own f? "
30: 6 all f are turned into paleness? "
42:15 If ye wholly set your f to enter "
17 all the men that set their f to "
44:12 that have set their f to go into "
50: 5 to Zion with their f thitherward, "
51:51 shame hath covered our f: for "
La 5:12 f of elders were not honoured. "
Eze 1: 6 And every one had four f, "
8 four had their f and their wings. "
10 As for the likeness of their f, "
11 Thus were their f: and their wings "
15 living creatures, with his four f. "
3: 8 thy face strong against their f, "
7:18 and shame shall be upon all f, "
8:16 and their f toward the east; "
10:14 And every one had four f: "
21 Every one had four f apiece, "
22 And the likeness of their f was "
22 was the same f which I saw "
14: 6 f from all your abominations. "
20:47 all f from the south to the north "
41:18 and every cherub had two f; "
Da 1:10 why should he see your f worse "
9: 7 us confusion of f, as at this day;* "
Joe 2: 6 all f shall gather blackness. "
Na 2:10 f of them shall gather blackness. "
Hab 1: 9 f shall sup up as the east wind, "
Mal 2: 3 and spread dung upon your f, "
M't 6:16 for they disfigure their f, that 4383
Lu 24: 5 bowed down their f to the earth, "
Re 7:11 fell before the throne on their f, "
9: 7 and their f were as the f of men. "
11:16 upon their f, and worshipped God, "

fade See also FADETH; FADING.
2Sa 22:46 Strangers shall f away, and they 5034
Ps 18:45 strangers shall f away, and be "
Isa 64: 6 and we all do f as a leaf; "
Jer 8:13 the fig tree, and the leaf shall f; 5034
Eze 47:12 whose leaf shall not f, neither * "
Jas 1:11 so also shall the rich man f away 3133

fadeth
Isa 1:30 shall be as an oak whose leaf f. 5034
Isa 24: 4 The earth mourneth and f away, 5034
4 the world languisheth and f away, "
40: 7 the flower f: because the spirit "
8 the flower f: but the word of "
1Pe 1: 4 undefiled, and that f not away, 263
5: 4 a crown of glory that f not away. 262

fading
Isa 28: 1 glorious beauty is a f flower, 5034
4 shall be a f flower, and as the "

fail See also FAILED; FAILETH; FAILING.
Ge 47:16 you for your cattle, if money f. 656
De 28:32 thine eyes shall look, and f with 3615
31: 6 he will not f thee, nor forsake 7503
8 he will not f thee, neither forsake "
Jos 1: 5 I will not f thee, nor forsake thee. "
3:10 that he will without f drive out from
J'g 11:30 without f deliver the children *
1Sa 2:16 Let them not f to burn the fat *
17:32 no man's heart f because of him ;5307
20: 5 f to sit with the king at meat:
30: 8 overtake them, and without f recover
2Sa 3:29 not f from the house of Joab 3772
1Ki 2: 4 there shall not f thee (said he)
8:25 There shall not f thee a man in "
9: 5 There shall not f thee a man upon "
17:14 neither shall the cruse of oil f, 2637
16 neither did the cruse of oil f, 2638
1Ch 28:20 will not f thee, nor forsake thee, 7503
2Ch 6:16 There shall not f thee a man in 3772
7:18 There shall not f thee a man to be "
Ezr 4:22 now that ye f not to do this: *7960
6: 9 given them day by day without f: "
Es 6:10 let nothing f of all that thou 5307
9:27 so as it should not f, that they 5674
28 should not f from among the Jews, "
Job 11:20 the eyes of the wicked shall f, 3615
14:11 As the waters f from the sea, 235
17: 5 the eyes of his children shall f. 3615
31:16 caused the eyes of the widow to f; "
Ps 12: 1 f from among the children of men. 6461
69: 3 eyes f while I wait for my God. 3615
77: 8 doth his promise f for evermore ?1584
89:33 nor suffer my faithfulness to f. 8266
119:82 Mine eyes f for thy word, 3615
123 Mine eyes f for thy salvation, "
Pr 22: 8 and the rod of his anger shall f. "
Ec 12: 5 and desire shall f: because man 6565
Isa 19: 3 And the spirit of Egypt shall f *1238
5 the waters shall f from the sea, 5405
21:16 and all the glory of Kedar shall f :3615
31: 3 and they shall f together. "
32: 6 cause the drink of the thirsty to f. 2637
10 the vintage shall f, the gathering 3615
34:16 no one of these shall f, none *5737
38:14 mine eyes f with looking upward: 1809
42: 4 shall not f nor be discouraged, 3543
51:14 nor that his bread should f. 2637
57:16 the spirit should f before me, 5848
58:11 spring of water, whose waters f 3576
Jer 14: 6 their eyes did f, because there 3615
15:18 and as waters that f? 3808, 539
48:33 and I have caused wine to f from *7673
La 2:11 Mine eyes do f with tears, my 3615
3:22 because his compassions f not. "
Ho 9: 2 and the new wine shall f in her. 3584
Am 8: 4 to make the poor of the land to f, 7673
Hab 3:17 the labour of the olive shall f, 3584
Lu 16: 9 when ye f, they may receive you 1587
17 than one tittle of the law to f. *4098
22:32 for thee, that thy faith f not: 1587
1Co 13: 8 there be prophecies, they shall f;*2673
Heb 1:12 same, and thy years shall not f. 1587
11:32 time would f me to tell of Gedeon, 1952
12:15 any man f of the grace of God; *5302

failed
Ge 42:28 and their heart f them, and they 3318
47:15 And when money f in the land *8552
Jos 3:16 the plain, even the salt sea, f, * "
21:45 f not ought of any good thing 5307
23:14 thing hath f of all the good things "
14 and not one thing hath f thereof. "
1Ki 8:56 there hath not f one word of all his "
Job 19:14 My kinsfolk have f, and my 2308
Ps 142: 4 refuge f me; no man cared for my 6
Ca 5: 6 my soul f when he spake: 3318
Jer 51:30 their might hath f; they became 5405
La 4:17 eyes as yet f for our vain help: *3615

faileth
Ge 47:15 thy presence? for the money f. 656
Job 21:10 Their bull gendereth, and f not; 1602
Ps 31:10 my strength f because of mine 3782
38:10 heart panteth, my strength f me: 5800
40:12 therefore my heart f me. * "
71: 9 me not when my strength f. 3615
73:26 My flesh and my heart f: "
109:24 and my flesh f of fatness. 3584
143: 7 O Lord; my spirit f: hide not 3615
Ec 10: 3 his wisdom f him, and he saith 2638
Isa 15: 6 grass f, there is no green thing. 3615
40:26 he is strong in power; not one f. *5737
41:17 and their tongue f for thirst, I the 5405
44:12 he is hungry, and his strength f: 369
59:15 truth f; and he that departeth *5737
Eze 12:22 prolonged, and every vision f? 6
Zep 3: 5 his judgment to light, he f not; 5737
Lu 12:33 treasure in the heavens that f not, 413
1Co 13: 8 Charity never f: but whether 1601

failing
De 28:65 a trembling heart, and f of eyes, 3631
Lu 21:26 Men's hearts f them for fear, * 674

fain
Job 27:22 he would f flee out of his hand. 1272
Lu 15:16 he would f have filled his belly 1937

faint See also FAINTED; FAINTEST; FAINTETH; FAINTHEARTED.
Ge 25:29 came from the field, and he was f: 5889
30 that same red pottage; for I am f: "
De 20: 3 let not your hearts f, fear not, 7401
8 lest his brethren's heart f as well*4549
25:18 when thou wast f and weary; 5889
Jos 2: 9 inhabitants of the land f because*4127
24 inhabitants of the country do f * "
J'g 8: 4 men that were with him, f, yet 5889
5 that follow me; for they be f, "
1Sa 14:28 And the people were f. 5774
31 and the people were very f. "
30:10 were so f that they could not go 6296
21 two hundred men, which were so f " "
2Sa 16: 2 such as be f in the wilderness 3287
21:15 Philistines: and David waxed f. 5774
Pr 24:10 If thou f in the day of adversity, 7503
Isa 1: 5 is sick, and the whole heart f. 1742
13: 7 Therefore shall all hands be f, *7503
29: 8 he awaketh, and, behold, he is f, 5889
40:29 He giveth power to the f; 3287
30 Even the youths shall f and be 3286
31 and they shall walk, and not f. "
44:12 he drinketh no water, and is f. "
Jer 8:18 sorrow, my heart is f in me. 1742
51:46 lest your heart f, and ye fear 7401
La 1:13 me desolate and f all the day. 1738
22 sighs are many, and my heart is f. 1742
2:19 young children, that f for hunger 5848
5:17 For this our heart is f; for these 1739
Eze 21: 7 and every spirit shall f, and all 3543
15 that their heart may f, and their*4127
Am 8:13 the fair virgins and young men f 5968
M't 15:32 lest they f in the way. 1590
M'r 8: 3 they will f by the way: "
Lu 18: 1 always to pray, and not to f; 1573
2Co 4: 1 we have received mercy, we f not; "
16 For which cause we f not; but "
Gal 6: 9 we shall reap, if we f not. 1590
Eph 3:13 Wherefore I desire that ye f not 1573
Heb 12: 3 be wearied and f in your minds. *1590
5 f when thou art rebuked of him: "

fainted
Ge 45:26 Jacob's heart f, for he believed 6313
47:13 all the land of Canaan f by reason 3856
Ps 27:13 I had f, unless I had believed
107: 5 thirsty, their soul f in them. 5848
Isa 51:20 Thy sons have f, they lie at the 5968
Jer 45: 3 I f in my sighing, and I find no *3021
Eze 31:15 the trees of the field f for him. 5969
Da 8:27 And I Daniel f, and was sick 1961
Jon 2: 7 When my soul f within me I 5848
4: 8 upon the head of Jonah, that he f, 5968
M't 9:36 they f, and were scattered *1590
Re 2: 3 hast laboured, and hast not f. *2577

faintest
Job 4: 5 it is come upon thee, and thou f; 3811

fainteth
Ps 84: 2 My soul longeth, yea, even f for 3615
119:81 My soul f for thy salvation: "
Isa 10:18 be as when a standardbearer f. 4549
40:28 of the ends of the earth, f not, 3286

fainthearted
De 20: 8 there that is fearful and f? 7390, 3824
Isa 7: 4 quiet; fear not, neither be f3824,*7401
Jer 49:23 they are f: there is sorrow on the*4127

faintness
Le 26:36 I will send a f into their hearts 4816

fair See also FAIRER; FAIREST; FAIRS.
Ge 6: 2 daughters of men that they were f; 2896
12:11 I know that thou art a f woman 3303
14 the woman that she was very f. "
24:16 damsel was very f to look upon, 2896
26: 7 because she was f to look upon. "
1Sa 17:42 ruddy, and of a f countenance. 3303
2Sa 13: 1 the son of David had a f sister, "
14:27 was a woman of a f countenance. "
1Ki 1: 3 So they sought for a f damsel "
4 damsel was very f, and cherished "
Es 1:11 for she was f to look on. 2896
2: 2 f young virgins sought for 2896, 4758
3 together all the f young virgins" "
7 maid was f and beautiful; 3303, 8389
Job 37:22 F weather cometh out of the *2091
42:15 so f as the daughters of Job: 3303
Pr 7:21 With her much f speech she 3948
11:22 so is a f woman which is without 3303
26:25 When he speaketh f, believe him 2603
Ca 1:15 Behold, thou art f, my love; 3302
15 behold, thou art f; thou hast dove's "
16 Behold, thou art f, my beloved, "
2:10 Rise up, my love, my f one, "
13 my love, my f one, and come "
4: 1 Behold, thou art f, my love; "
1 behold, thou art f; thou hast dove's "
7 Thou art all f, my love; "
10 How f is thy love, my sister, "
6:10 f as the moon, clear as the sun, 3303
7: 6 How f and how pleasant art thou, 3302
Isa 5: 9 be desolate, even great and f, 2896
54:11 will lay thy stones with f colours, 6320
Jer 4:30 in vain shalt thou make thyself f; 3302
11:16 olive tree, f, and of goodly fruit: 3303
12: 6 they speak f words unto thee. 2896
46:20 Egypt is like a very f heifer, 3304
Eze 16:17 Thou hast also taken thy f jewels 8597
39 and shall take thy f jewels, and "
23:26 and take away thy f jewels. "
31: 3 cedar in Lebanon with f branches, 3303
7 Thus was he f in his greatness, 3302
9 made him f by the multitude 3303
Da 4:12 The leaves thereof were f, and 8209
21 Whose leaves were f, and the fruit "
Ho 10:11 passed over upon her f neck: 2898
Am 8:13 In that day shall the f virgins 3303
Zec 3: 5 them set a f mitre upon his head.‡2889
5 they set a f mitre upon his head.‡ "
M't 16: 2 ye say, It will be f weather: 2105
Ac 7:20 was born, and was exceeding f, 791
27: 8 which is called The f havens; 2568
Ro 16:18 by good words and f speeches 2129
Gal 6:12 to make a f shew in the flesh, 2146

fairer
J'g 15: 2 her younger sister f than she? 2896
Ps 45: 2 art f than the children of men: 3302
Da 1:15 appeared f and fatter in flesh 2896

fairest
Ca 1: 8 O thou f among women, go thy 3303
5: 9 thou f among women? what is thy "
6: 1 O thou f among women? whither "

fair-havens See FAIR and HAVENS.

fairs
Eze 27:12 and lead, they traded in thy f. *5801
14 of Togarmah traded in thy f * "
16 occupied in thy f with emeralds,* "
19 going to an fro occupied in thy f:* "
22 in thy f with chief of all spices, * "
27 and thy f, thy merchandise, * "

faith See also FAITHFUL; FAITHLESS.
De 32:20 children in whom is no f. 529
Hab 2: 4 but the just shall live by his f. 530
M't 6:30 more clothe you, O ye of little f? 3640
8:10 I have not found so great f, no, not 4102
26 are ye fearful, O ye of little f? 3640
9: 2 Jesus seeing their f said unto the 4102
22 thy f hath made thee whole. "
29 According to your f be it unto you. "
14:31 O thou of little f, wherefore didst 3640
15:28 O woman, great is thy f: 4102
16: 8 O ye of little f, why reason ye 3640
17:20 If ye have f as a grain of mustard 4102
21:21 If ye have f, and doubt not, "
23:23 the law, judgment, mercy, and f: "
M'r 2: 5 When Jesus saw their f, he said "
4:40 how is it that ye have no f? "
5:34 Daughter, thy f hath made thee "
10:52 way; thy f hath made thee whole. "
11:22 saith unto them, Have f in God. "
Lu 5:20 when he saw their f, he said unto "
7: 9 I have not found so great f, no, not "
50 Thy f hath saved thee; go in peace. "
8:25 Where is your f? And they being "
48 thy f hath made thee whole; go in "
12:28 will he clothe you, O ye of little f? 3640
17: 5 unto the Lord, Increase our f. 4102
6 If ye had f as a grain of mustard "
19 way: thy f hath made thee whole. "
18: 8 shall he find f on the earth? "
42 thy sight: thy f hath saved thee. "
22:32 prayed for thee, that thy f fail not: "
Ac 3:16 his name through f in his name "
16 yea, the f which is by him "
6: 5 a man full of f and of the Holy "
7 the priests were obedient to the f. "
8 Stephen, full of f and power, * "
11:24 full of the Holy Ghost and of f: "
13: 8 to turn away the deputy from the f. "
14: 9 that he had f to be healed, "
22 exhorting them to continue in the f, "
27 how he had opened the door of f "
15: 9 purifying their hearts by f. "
16: 5 the churches established in the f, "
20:21 and f toward our Lord Jesus Christ. "
24:24 him concerning the f in Christ. "
26:18 are sanctified by f that is in me. "
Ro 1: 5 for obedience to the f among all "
8 that your f is spoken of throughout "
12 by the mutual f both of you and me. "
17 God revealed from f to f: as it is "
17 written, The just shall live by f. "
3: 3 make the f of God without effect?* "
22 which is by f of Jesus Christ unto "
25 propitiation through f in his blood, "
27 of works? Nay: but by the law of f. "
28 a man is justified by f without the "
30 justify the circumcision by f, and "
30 and uncircumcision through f. "
31 make void the law through f? "
4: 5 his f is counted for righteousness. "
9 for we say that f was reckoned to "
11 seal of the righteousness of the f "
12 walk in the steps of that f of our "
13 through the righteousness of f. "
14 f is made void, and the promise "
16 Therefore it is of f, that it might "
16 which is of the f of Abraham; "
19 being not weak in f, he considered "
20 but was strong in f, giving glory "
5: 1 being justified by f, we have peace "
2 we have access by f into this grace "
9:30 the righteousness which is of f. "
32 Because they sought it not by f, "
10: 6 But the righteousness which is of f "
8 is, the word of f, which we preach; "
17 So then f cometh by hearing, * "
11:20 broken off, and thou standest by f. "
12: 3 to every man the measure of f. "
6 according to the proportion of f; "
14: 1 Him that is weak in the f receive "
22 Hast thou f? have it to thyself "
23 because he eateth not of f: for "
23 whatsoever is not of f is sin. "
16:26 all nations for the obedience of f: "
1Co 2: 5 That your f should not stand in "
12: 9 To another f by the same Spirit; "
13: 2 though I have all f, so that I could "
13 And now abideth f, hope, charity, "
1Co 15:14 and your f is also vain. 4102
17 your f is vain; ye are yet in your "
16:13 Watch ye, stand fast in the f, "
2Co 1:24 that we have dominion over your f, "
24 of your joy: for by f ye stand. "
4:13 We having the same spirit of f, "
5: 7 (For we walk by f, not by sight:) "
8: 7 in f, and utterance, and knowledge, "
10:15 hope, when your f is increased, "
13: 5 yourselves, whether ye be in the f; "
Ga 1:23 now preacheth the f which once "
2:16 but by the f of Jesus Christ, "
16 be justified by the f of Christ, "
20 I live by the f of the Son of God, "
3: 2, 5 the law, or by the hearing of f? "
7 they which are of f, the same are "
8 justify the heathen through f, "
9 they which be of f are blessed "
11 for, The just shall live by f. "
12 And the law is not of f: "
14 promise of the Spirit through f. "
22 the promise by f of Jesus Christ "
23 But before f came, we were kept "
23 shut up unto the f, which should "
24 that we might be justified by f. "
25 But after that f is come, "
26 children of God by f in Christ "
5: 5 the hope of righteousness by f. "
6 but f which worketh by love. "
22 gentleness, goodness, f, * "
6:10 who are of the household of f. "
Eph 1:15 after I heard of your f in the Lord "
2: 8 by grace are ye saved through f; "
3:12 with confidence by the f of him. "
17 may dwell in your hearts by f; "
4: 5 One Lord, one f, one baptism, "
13 we all come in the unity of the f, "
6:16 Above all, taking the shield of f, "
23 and love with f, from God the "
Ph'p 1:25 for your furtherance and joy of f; "
27 together for the f of the gospel; "
2:17 the sacrifice and service of your f, "
3: 9 which is through the f of Christ, "
9 righteousness which is of God by f: "
Col 1: 4 Since we heard of your f in Christ "
23 If ye continue in the f grounded "
2: 5 the stedfastness of your f in Christ. "
7 stablished in the f, as ye have been "
12 through the f of the operation of "
1Th 1: 3 your work of f, and labour of love, "
8 f to God-ward is spread abroad; "
3: 2 to comfort you concerning your f: "
5 forbear, I sent to know your f, "
6 good tidings of your f and charity, "
7 affliction and distress by your f: "
10 that which is lacking in your f? "
5: 8 the breastplate of f and love; "
2Th 1: 3 your f groweth exceedingly, and "
4 for your patience and f in all your "
11 and the work of f with power: "
3: 2 for all men have not f. "
1Ti 1: 2 Timothy, my own son in the f: "
4 than godly edifying which is in f: "
5 conscience, and of f unfeigned: "
14 with f and love which is in Christ "
19 Holding f, and a good conscience; "
19 concerning f have made shipwreck: "
2: 7 of the Gentiles in f and verity. "
15 if they continue in f and charity "
3: 9 Holding the mystery of the f in a "
13 great boldness in the f which is in "
4: 1 some shall depart from the f, "
6 words of f and of good doctrine, "
12 in charity, in spirit, in f, in purity. "
5: 8 he hath denied the f, and is worse "
12 they have cast off their first f. ‡
6:10 they have erred from the f, "
11 godliness, f, love, patience, "
12 Fight the good fight of f, lay hold "
21 have erred concerning the f. "
2Ti 1: 5 the unfeigned f that is in thee, "
13 in f and love which is in Christ "
2:18 and overthrow the f of some. "
22 follow righteousness, f, charity, "
3: 8 minds, reprobate concerning the f. "
10 f, longsuffering, charity, patience, "
15 through f which is in Christ Jesus. "
4: 7 my course, I have kept the f: "
Tit 1: 1 according to the f of God's elect, "
4 mine own son after the common f: "
13 that they may be sound in the f; "
2: 2 sound in f, in charity, in patience. "
3:15 Greet them that love us in the f. "
Ph'm 5 Hearing of thy love and f, "
6 the communication of thy f may "
Heb 4: 2 not being mixed with f in them "
6: 1 dead works, and of f toward God, "
12 who through f and patience inherit "
10:22 a true heart in full assurance of f, "
23 hold fast the profession of our f *1680
38 Now the just shall live by f: 4102
11: 1 Now f is the substance of things "
3 Through f we understand that the "
4 By f Abel offered unto God a more "
5 By f Enoch was translated that he "
6 without f it is impossible to please "
7 By f Noah, being warned of God "
7 of the righteousness which is by f. "
8 By f Abraham, when he was called "
9 By f he sojourned in the land of "
11 Through f ... Sara herself received "
13 These all died in f, not having "
17 By f Abraham, when he was tried, "
20 By f Isaac blessed Jacob and Esau "
21 By f Jacob, when he was a dying, "
22 By f Joseph, when he died, made "

Heb 11:23 By *f* Moses, when he was born, 4102
24 By *f* Moses, when he was come to "
27 By *f* he forsook Egypt, not fearing "
28 Through *f* he kept the passover, "
29 By *f* he passed through the Red "
30 By *f* the walls of Jericho fell down, "
31 By *f* the harlot Rahab perished not "
33 Who through *f* subdued kingdoms, "
39 obtained a good report through *f*, "
12: 2 the author and finisher of our *f*; "
13: 7 whose *f* follow, considering the "
Jas 1: 3 trying of your *f* worketh patience. "
6 let him ask in *f*, nothing wavering. "
2: 1 My brethren, have not the *f* of our "
5 rich in *f*, and heirs of the kingdom "
14 though a man say he hath *f*, and "
14 have not works? can *f* save him? "
17 Even so *f*, if it hath not works, is "
18 Thou hast *f*, and I have works: "
18 shew me thy *f* without thy works, "
18 I will shew thee my *f* by my works. "
20 that *f* without works is dead? "
22 Seest thou how *f* wrought with his "
22 and by works was *f* made perfect? "
24 man is justified, and not by *f* only. "
26 so *f* without works is dead also. "
5:15 the prayer of *f* shall save the sick, "
1Pe 1: 5 through *f* unto salvation ready to "
7 That the trial of your *f*, being much "
9 Receiving the end of your *f*, "
21 your *f* and hope might be in God. "
5: 9 Whom resist stedfast in the *f*, "
2Pe 1: 1 obtained like precious *f* with us "
5 add to your *f* virtue: and to virtue "
1Jo 5: 4 overcometh the world, even our *f*. "
Jude 3 for the *f* which was once delivered "
20 up yourselves on your most holy *f*, "
Re 2:13 and hast not denied my *f*, "
19 and charity, and service, and *f*, "
13:10 the patience and the *f* of the saints. "
14:12 of God, and the *f* of Jesus. "

faithful See also UNFAITHFUL.
Nu 12: 7 who is *f* in all mine house. 539
De 7: 9 thy God, he is God, the *f* God, "
1Sa 2:35 I will raise me up a *f* priest, "
22:14 who is so *f* among all thy servants "
2Sa 20:19 that are peaceable and *f* in Israel: "
Ne 7: 2 he was a *f* man, and feared God 571
9: 8 foundest his heart *f* before thee, 539
13:13 for they were counted *f*, and their "
Ps 12: 1 the *f* fail from among the children "
31:23 for the Lord preserveth the *f*, "
89:37 and as a *f* witness in heaven. "
101: 6 sages shall be upon the *f* of the land, "
119:86 All thy commandments are *f*: 530
138 are righteous and very *f*. * "
Pr 11:13 he that is of a *f* spirit concealeth 539
13:17 but a *f* ambassador is health. 529
14: 5 A *f* witness will not lie: but a false "
20: 6 but a *f* man who can find? "
25:13 is a *f* messenger to them that send 539
27: 6 *F* are the wounds of a friend; "
28:20 A *f* man shall abound with 530
Isa 1:21 How is the *f* city become an harlot! 539
26 city of righteousness, the *f* city. "
8: 2 And I took unto me *f* witnesses to "
49: 7 because of the Lord that is *f*, "
Jer 42: 5 a true and *f* witness between us, "
Da 6: 4 forasmuch as he was *f*, neither 540
Ho 11:12 and is *f* with the saints. 539
M't 24:45 Who then is a *f* and wise servant, 4103
25:21 done, thou good and *f* servant: "
21 thou hast been *f* over a few things, "
23 Well done, good and *f* servant; "
23 thou hast been *f* over a few things, "
Lu 12:42 then is that *f* and wise steward, "
16:10 He that is *f* in that which is "
10 is least is *f* also in much: "
11 *f* in the unrighteous mammon, "
12 And if ye have not been *f* in that "
19:17 thou hast been *f* in a very little, "
Ac 16:15 have judged me to be *f* to the Lord, "
1Co 1: 9 God is *f*, by whom ye were called "
4: 2 stewards, that a man be found *f*. "
17 my beloved son, and *f* in the Lord, "
7:25 mercy of the Lord to be *f*. ‡ "
10:13 but God is *f*, who will not suffer "
Ga 3: 9 faith are blessed with *f* Abraham. "
Eph 1: 1 and to the *f* in Christ Jesus: "
6:21 and *f* minister in the Lord, "
Col 1: 2 saints and *f* brethren in Christ "
7 is for you a *f* minister in Christ; "
4: 7 a *f* minister and fellowservant in "
9 Onesimus, a *f* and beloved brother, "
1Th 5:24 *F* is he that calleth you, "
2Th 3: 3 Lord is *f*, who shall stablish you, "
1Ti 1:12 for that he counted me *f*, "
15 This is a *f* saying, and worthy of all "
3:11 slanderers, sober, *f* in all things. "
4: 9 This is a *f* saying and worthy of all "
6: 2 because they are *f* and beloved, * "
2Ti 2: 2 the same commit thou to *f* men, "
11 It is a *f* saying: For if we be dead "
13 yet he abideth *f*: he cannot deny "
Tit 1: 6 having *f* children not accused * "
9 the *f* word as he hath been taught, "
3: 8 This is a *f* saying, and these things "
Heb 2:17 be a merciful and *f* high priest in "
3: 2 was *f* to him that appointed him, "
2 also Moses was *f* in all his house. "
5 Moses verily was *f* in all his 4103
10:23 (for he is *f* that promised;) "
11:11 judged him *f* who had promised. "
1Pe 4:19 in well doing, as unto a *f* Creator. "
5:12 By Silvanus, a *f* brother unto you, "
1Jo 1: 9 he is *f* and just to forgive us our 4103
Re 1: 5 Jesus Christ who is the *f* witness, "
2:10 be thou *f* unto death, and I will "
13 Antipas was my *f* martyr, who was "
3:14 the Amen, the *f* and true witness, "
17:14 him are called, and chosen, and *f*. "
19:11 upon him was called *F* and True, "
21: 5 for these words are true and *f*. "
22: 6 These sayings are *f* and true: "

faithfully See also UNFAITHFULLY.
2Ki 12:15 on workmen: for they dealt *f*. 530
22: 7 their hand, because they dealt *f*. "
2Ch 19: 9 Lord, *f*, and with a perfect heart. "
31:12 tithes and the dedicated things *f*: "
34:12 And the men did the work *f*: "
Pr 29:14 The king that *f* judgeth the poor, 571
Jer 23:28 let him speak my word *f*. "
3Jo 5 doest *f* whatsoever thou doest *4103

faithfulness
1Sa 26:23 man his righteousness and his *f*: 530
Ps 5: 9 there is no *f* in their mouth; 3559
36: 5 thy *f* reacheth unto the clouds. 530
40:10 declared thy *f* and thy salvation: "
88:11 the grave? or thy *f* in destruction? "
89: 1 mouth will I make known thy *f* to all "
2 thy *f* shalt thou establish in the very "
5 thy *f* also in the congregation of the "
8 or to thy *f* round about thee? "
24 But my *f* and my mercy shall be with "
33 nor suffer my *f* to fail. "
92: 2 and thy *f* every night, "
119:75 that thou in *f* hast afflicted me. "
90 Thy *f* is unto all generations: "
143: 1 in thy *f* answer me, and in thy "
Isa 11: 5 and *f* the girdle of his reins. "
25: 1 counsels of old are *f* and truth. "
La 3:23 every morning: great is thy *f*. "
Ho 2:20 will even betroth thee unto me in *f*: "

faithless
M't 17:17 said, O *f* and perverse generation, 571
M'r 9:19 saith, O *f* generation, how long shall "
Lu 9:41 said, O *f* and perverse generation, "
Joh 20:27 and be not *f*, but believing. "

fall See also BEFALL; FALLEN; FALLEST; FALLETH; FALLING; FELL.
Ge 2:21 a deep sleep to *f* upon Adam, 5307
43:18 occasion against us, and *f* upon us, "
45:24 See that ye *f* not out by the way. 7264
49:17 that his rider shall *f* backward. *5307
Ex 5: 3 lest he *f* upon us with pestilence, 6293
15:16 and dread shall *f* upon them; *5307
21:33 and an ox or an ass *f* therein; "
Le 11:32 them, when they are dead, doth *f*, "
37 if any part of their carcase *f* upon "
38 any part of their carcase *f* thereon, "
19:29 lest the land *f* to whoredom, "
26: 7 and they shall *f* before you by the 5307
8 your enemies shall *f* before you by "
36 they shall *f* when none pursueth. "
37 they shall *f* one upon another, *3782
Nu 11:31 and let them *f* by the camp, 5203
14: 3 unto this land, to *f* by the sword, 5307
29 carcases shall *f* in this wilderness; "
32 they shall *f* in this wilderness. "
43 and ye shall *f* by the sword: "
34: 2 is the land that shall *f* unto you for "
De 22: 4 thy brother's ass or his ox *f* down * "
8 if any man *f* from thence. "
Jos 6: 5 the wall of the city shall *f* down "
J'g 8:21 Rise thou, and *f* upon us: 6293
15:12 unto me that ye will not *f* upon me "
18 thirst, and *f* into the hand of the 5307
Ru 2:16 let *f* also some of the handfuls *7997
3:18 thou know how the matter will *f*: 5307
1Sa 3:19 and did let none of his words *f* to "
14:45 shall not one hair of his head *f* to "
18:25 Saul thought to make David *f* by "
21:13 his spittle *f* down upon his beard. 3381
22:17 their hand to *f* upon the priests 6293
18 Turn thou, and *f* upon the priests. "
26:20 let not my blood *f* to the earth 5307
2Sa 1:15 said, Go near, and *f* upon him. 6293
14:11 shall not one hair of thy son *f* to 5307
24:14 us *f* now into the hand of the Lord; "
14 let me not *f* into the hand of man. "
1Ki 1:52 there shall not an hair of him *f* to "
2:29 Jehoiada, saying, Go, *f* upon him, 6293
31 as he hath said, and *f* upon him, "
22:20 go up and *f* at Ramoth-gilead? 5307
2Ki 7: 4 us *f* unto the host of the Syrians: "
10:10 shall *f* unto the earth nothing "
14:10 shouldest *f*, even thou, and Judah "
19: 7 will cause him to *f* by the sword "
1Ch 12:19 He will *f* to his master Saul "
21:13 *f* now into the hand of the Lord; "
13 let me not *f* into the hand of man. "
2Ch 18:19 that he may go up and *f* at "
21:15 until thy bowels *f* out by reason 3318
25: 8 God shall make thee *f* before *3782
19 shouldest *f*, even thou, and Judah "
Es 6:13 before whom thou hast began to *f*, "
13 but shalt surely *f* before him. "
Job 13:11 afraid? and his dread *f* upon you? "
31:22 arm *f* from my shoulder blade, "
Ps 5:10 let them *f* by their own counsels; "
9: 3 they shall *f* and perish at thy *3782
10:10 the poor may *f* by his strong ones. 5307
35: 8 into that very destruction let him *f*. "
37:24 Though he *f*, he shall not be "
45: 5 whereby the people *f* under thee. "
63:10 They shall *f* by the sword: they *5064
64: 8 make their own tongue to *f* upon *3782
72:11 kings shall *f* down before him: 7812
78:28 let it *f* in the midst of their camp, 5307
Ps 82: 7 and *f* like one of the princes. 5307
91: 7 A thousand shall *f* at thy side, "
118:13 thrust sore at me that I might *f*: "
140:10 Let burning coals *f* upon them: 4131
141:10 the wicked *f* into their own nets, 5307
145:14 The Lord upholdeth all that *f*, "
Pr 4:16 unless they cause some to *f*. 3782
10: 8 but a prating fool shall *f*. 3832
10 sorrow: but a prating fool shall *f*. "
11: 5 shall *f* by his own wickedness. 5307
14 Where no counsel is, the people *f*: "
28 that trusteth in his riches shall *f*: "
16:18 and an haughty spirit before a *f*. 3783
22:14 of the Lord shall *f* therein. 5307
24:16 the wicked shall *f* into mischief. *3782
26:27 diggeth a pit shall *f* therein: 5307
28:10 he shall *f* himself into his own pit: "
14 that hardeneth his heart shall *f* "
18 is perverse in his ways shall *f* at "
29:16 the righteous shall see their *f*. 4658
Ec 4:10 For if they *f*, the one will lift up 5307
10: 8 that diggeth a pit shall *f* into it; "
11: 3 if the tree *f* toward the south, "
Isa 3:25 Thy men shall *f* by the sword, "
8:15 among them shall stumble, and *f*, "
10: 4 and they shall *f* under the slain. "
34 Lebanon shall *f* by a mighty one. "
13:15 unto them shall *f* by the sword. "
22:25 removed, and be cut down, and *f*; "
24:18 noise of the fear shall *f* into the pit; "
20 and it shall *f*, and not rise again. "
28:13 they might go, and *f* backward, 3782
30:13 as a breach ready to *f*, swelling 5307
25 slaughter, when the towers *f*. "
31: 3 both he that helpeth shall *f*, and *3782
3 he that is holpen shall *f* down, 5307
8 the Assyrian *f* with the sword, "
34: 4 all their host shall *f* down, as *5034
37: 7 will cause him to *f* by the sword 5307
40:30 the young men shall utterly *f*: 3782
44:19 I *f* down to the stock of a tree? 5456
45:14 they shall *f* down unto thee, 7812
46: 6 they *f* down, yea, they worship. 5456
47:11 and mischief shall *f* upon thee; 5307
54:15 together against thee shall *f* for thy "
Jer 3:12 not cause mine anger to *f* upon * "
6:15 they shall *f* among them that *f*: "
21 the sons together shall *f* upon *3782
8: 4 Shall they *f*, and not arise? shall 5307
12 shall they *f* among them that *f*: "
9:22 Even the carcases of men shall *f* as "
15: 8 I have caused him to *f* upon it "
19: 7 and I will cause them to *f* by the "
20: 4 and they shall *f* by the sword "
23:12 shall be driven on, and *f* therein: "
19 shall *f* grievously upon the head *2342
25:27 be drunken, and spue, and *f*, 5307
34 ye shall *f* like a pleasant vessel, "
30:23 shall *f* with pain upon the head *2342
37:14 I *f* not away to the Chaldeans. 5307
39:18 thou shalt not *f* by the sword, "
44:12 and *f* in the land of Egypt, 5307
46: 6 and *f* toward the north by the * "
16 made many to *f*, yea, one fell *3782
48:44 fleeth from the fear shall *f* into 5307
49:21 is moved at the noise of their *f*, "
26 young men shall *f* in her streets, "
50:30 shall her young men *f* in the "
32 most proud shall stumble and *f*, "
51: 4 Thus the slain shall *f* in the land "
44 yea, the wall of Babylon shall *f*. "
47 all her slain shall *f* in the midst "
49 hath caused the slain of Israel to *f*, "
49 so at Babylon shall *f* the slain of "
La 1:14 he hath made my strength to *f*, *3782
Eze 5:12 a third part shall *f* by the sword 5307
6: 7 the slain shall *f* in the midst of you, "
11 for they shall *f* by the sword, "
12 that is near shall *f* by the sword; "
11:10 Ye shall *f* by the sword; I will "
13:11 morter, that it shall *f*: "
11 ye, O great hailstones, shall *f*; "
14 and it shall *f*, and ye shall be "
17:21 fugitives with all his bands shall *f* "
23:25 remnant shall fall by the sword: "
24: 6 piece by piece; let no lot *f* upon it. "
21 daughters whom ye have left shall *f* "
25:13 they of Dedan shall *f* by the sword. "
26:15 isles shake at the sound of thy *f*, 4658
18 isles tremble in the day of thy *f*; "
27:27 is in the midst of thee, shall *f* into 5307
34 in the midst of thee shall *f*. "
29: 5 thou shalt *f* upon the open fields; "
30: 4 when the slain shall *f* in Egypt, "
5 land that is in league, shall *f* with "
6 also that uphold Egypt shall *f*; "
6 shall they *f* in it by the sword, "
17 of Pi-beseth shall *f* by the sword. "
22 I will cause the sword to *f* out of "
25 the arms of Pharaoh shall *f* down; "
31:16 to shake at the sound of his *f*, 4658
32:10 his own life, in the day of thy *f*. "
12 will I cause thy multitude to *f*, "
20 They shall *f* in the midst of them "
33:12 he shall not *f* thereby in the day 3782
27 the wastes shall *f* by the sword. 5307
35: 8 rivers, shall they *f* that are slain "
36:15 shalt thou cause thy nations to *f*. *3782
38:20 and the steep places shall *f*, 5307
20 every wall shall *f* to the ground. "
39: 3 will cause thine arrows to *f* out of "
4 Thou shalt *f* upon the mountains "
5 Thou shalt *f* upon the open field: "
44:12 house of Israel to *f* into iniquity; *4383
47:14 and this land shall *f* unto you 5307

Da 3: 5 ye f down and worship the golden 5308
10 shall f down and worship the golden "
15 ye f down and worship the golden "
11:14 establish...vision; but they shall f. 3782
19 stumble and f, and not be found. 5307
26 overflow: and many shall f down "
33 yet they shall f by the sword, 3782
34 Now when they shall f, they shall "
35 of them of understanding shall f, "
Ho 4: 5 Therefore shalt thou f in the day,* "
5 and the prophet also shall f with* "
14 that doth not understand shall f.*3832
5: 5 shall Israel and Ephraim f in *3782
5 Judah also shall f with them. * "
7:16 their princes shall f by the sword 5307
10: 8 and to the hills, F on us. "
13:16 they shall f by the sword: their "
14: 9 the transgressors shall f therein. 3872
Joe 2: 8 when they f upon the sword, *5307
Am 3: 5 Can a bird f in a snare upon the "
14 be cut off, and f to the ground. "
7:17 sons and thy daughters shall f by "
8:14 they shall f, and never rise up "
9: 9 yet shall not the least grain f upon "
Mic 7: 8 enemy: when I f, I shall arise; "
Na 3:12 they shall even f into the mouth of "
M't 4: 9 wilt f down and worship me. 4098
7:27 and great was the f of it. 4431
10:29 them shall not f on the ground 4098
12:11 if it f into the pit on the sabbath 1706
15:14 blind, both shall f into the ditch. 4098
27 which f from their masters' table. "
21:44 whosoever shall f on this stone * "
44 on whomsoever it shall f, it will "
24:29 and the stars shall f from heaven, "
M'r 13:25 And the stars of heaven shall f. *1601
Lu 2:34 child is set for the f and rising *4431
6:39 shall they not both f into the ditch? 4098
8:13 and in time of temptation f away. 868
10:18 as lightning f from heaven. *4098
20:18 Whosoever shall f upon that * "
18 but on whomsoever it shall f, "
21:24 shall f by the edge of the sword, "
23:30 F on us; and to the hills, Cover us. "
Joh 12:24 wheat f into the ground and die, "
Ac 27:17 should f into the quicksands, *1601
32 ropes of the boat, and let her f off. "
34 shall not an hair f from the head*4098
Ro 11:11 they stumbled that they should f? "
11 through their f salvation is come 3900
12 Now if the f of them be the riches "
14:13 occasion to f in his brother's way.*4625
1Co 10:12 he standeth take heed lest he f. 4098
1Ti 3: 6 pride he f into the condemnation 1706
7 he f into reproach and the snare
6: 9 rich f into temptation and a snare,
Heb 4:11 lest any man f after the same 4098
6: 6 If they shall f away, to renew *3895
10:31 to f into the hands of the living 1706
Jas 1: 2 when ye f into divers temptations; 4045
5:12 nay; lest ye f into condemnation. 4098
2Pe 1:10 do these things, ye shall never f: *4417
3:17 f from your own stedfastness, 1601
Re 4:10 four and twenty elders f down 4098
6:16 mountains and rocks, F on us, "
9: 1 and I saw a star f from heaven "

fallen See also BEFALLEN.
Ge 4: 6 and why is thy countenance f? 5307
Le 13:40 the man whose hair is f off 4803
41 he that hath his hair f off "
25:35 and f in decay with thee; *4131, 3027
Nu 32:19 because our inheritance is f to us 935
Jos 2: 9 and that your terror is f upon us. 5307
8:24 were all f on the edge of the sword, "
J'g 3:25 their lord was f down dead on the "
18: 1 inheritance had not f unto them "
19:27 concubine was f down at the door "
1Sa 5: 3 was f upon his face to the earth "
4 was f upon his face to the ground "
26:12 from the Lord was f upon them. "
31: 8 found Saul and his three sons f in "
2Sa 1: 4 many of the people also are f and "
10 could not live after that he was f: "
12 because they were f by the sword. "
19 high places: how are the mighty f! "
25 How are the mighty f in the midst "
27 How are the mighty f, and the "
3:38 there is a prince and a great man f "
22:39 yea, they are f under my feet. "
2Ki 13:14 Now Elisha was f sick of his sickness "
1Ch 10: 8 they found Saul and his sons f in 5307
2Ch 20:24 were dead bodies f to the earth, "
29: 9 our fathers have f by the sword, "
Es 7: 8 Haman was f upon the bed where "
Job 1:16 The fire of God is f from heaven, "
Ps 7:15 is f into the ditch which he made. "
16: 6 are f unto me in pleasant places; "
18:38 they are f under my feet. * "
20: 8 They are brought down and f: "
36:12 There are the workers of iniquity f: "
55: 4 the terrors of death are f upon me. "
57: 6 whereof they are f themselves. "
69: 9 reproached thee are f upon me. "
Isa 3: 8 is ruined, and Judah is f: "
9:10 The bricks are f down, but we will "
14:12 How art thou f from heaven, "
16: 9 fruits and for thy harvest is f. "
21: 9 and said, Babylon is f, is f; "
26:18 have the inhabitants of the world f. "
59:14 truth is f in the street, and equity 3782
Jer 38:19 Jews that are f to the Chaldeans, 5307
46:12 mighty, they are f both together. "
48:32 the spoiler is f upon thy summer "
50:15 her foundations are f, her walls "
51: 8 Babylon is suddenly f and "
La 2:21 my young men are f by the sword; 5307
5:16 The crown is f from our head: "
Eze 13:12 the wall is f, shall it not be said "
31:12 all the valleys his branches are f, "
32:22 all of them slain, f by the sword: "
23, 24 all of them slain, f by the sword, "
27 that are f of the uncircumcised, "
Ho 7: 7 all their kings are f: there is none "
14: 1 for thou hast f by thine iniquity. 3782
Am 5: 2 The virgin of Israel is f; she 5307
9:11 the tabernacle of David that is f, "
Zec 11: 2 Howl, fir tree; for the cedar is f; "
Lu 14: 5 have an ass or an ox f into a pit, 1706
Ac 8:16 yet he was f upon none of them: 1968
15:16 of David, which is f down, 4098
20: 9 being f into a deep sleep: *2702
26:14 when we were all f to the earth, 2667
27:29 lest we should have f upon rocks,*1601
28: 6 should have swollen, or f down 2667
1Co 15: 6 but some are f asleep. 2837
18 also which are f asleep in Christ "
Ga 5: 4 by the law; ye are f from grace. 1601
Ph'p 1:12 happened unto me have f out 2064
Re 2: 5 from whence thou art f, 1601
14: 8 Babylon is f, is f, that great city. 4098
17:10 five are f, and one is, and the "
18: 2 Babylon the great is f, is f, "

fallest
Jer 37:13 Thou f away to the Chaldeans. 5307

falleth See also BEFALLETH.
Ex 1:10 when there f out any war, 7122
Le 11:33 vessel, whereinto any of them f, 5307
35 any part of their carcase f shall be "
Nu 33:54 in the place where his lot f; 3318
2Sa 3:29 or that f on the sword, or that 5307
34 as a man f before wicked men, "
17:12 as the dew f on the ground: "
Job 4:13 when deep sleep f on men, "
33:15 when deep sleep f upon men, "
Pr 13:17 wicked messenger f into mischief: "
17:20 that hath a perverse tongue f into "
24:16 For a just man f seven times, "
17 Rejoice not when thine enemy f, "
Ec 4:10 to him that is alone when he f; "
9:12 when it f suddenly upon them. "
11: 3 in the place where the tree f, "
Isa 34: 4 as the leaf f off from the vine, *5034
44:15 image, and f down thereto. 5456
17 he f down unto it, and worshippeth "
Jer 21: 9 f to the Chaldeans that besiege 5307
Da 3: 6 f not down and worshippeth shall 5308
11 whoso f not down and worshippeth. "
M't 17:15 for ofttimes he f into the fire, 4098
Lu 11:17 a house divided against a house f. "
15:12 the portion of goods that f to me. 1911
Ro 14: 4 his own master he standeth or f. 4098
Jas 1:11 the grass, and the flower thereof f, 1601
1Pe 1:24 and the flower thereof f away: "

fallible See INFALLIBLE.

falling
Nu 24: 4, 16 f into a trance, but having his 5307
Job 4: 4 have upholden him that was f, 3782
14:18 mountain f cometh to nought, 5307
Ps 56:13 not thou deliver my feet from f, 1762
116: 8 from tears, and my feet from f. "
Pr 25:26 A righteous man f down before *4131
Isa 34: 4 as a f fig from the fig tree. *5034
Lu 8:47 trembling, and f down before him, 4363
22:44 of blood f down to the ground. 2597
Ac 1:18 f headlong, he burst asunder 4248, 1096
27:41 And f into a place where two *4045
1Co 14:25 and so f down on his face he will 4098
2Th 2: 3 except there come a f away first, 646
Jude 24 that is able to keep you from f, * 679

fallow See also FALLOWDEER.
De 14: 5 and the roebuck and the f deer, *3180
Jer 4: 3 Break up your f ground, and sow 5215
Ho 10:12 break up your f ground: for it is "

fallowdeer See also FALLOW and DEER.
1Ki 4:23 harts, and roebucks, and f, *3180

fallow-ground See FALLOW and GROUND.

false See also FALSEHOOD; FALSIFYING.
Ex 20:16 Thou shalt not bear f witness 8267
23: 1 Thou shalt not raise a f report: 7723
7 Keep thee far from a f matter; 8267
De 5:20 Neither shalt thou bear f witness 7723
19:16 If a f witness rise up against any *2555
18 if the witness be a f witness, 8267
2Ki 9:12 they said, It is f; tell us now. "
Job 36: 4 truly my words shall not be f: "
Ps 27:12 f witnesses are risen up against "
35:11 F witnesses did rise up; they *2555
119:104 therefore I hate every f way. 8267
128 and I hate every f way. "
120: 3 done unto thee, thou f tongue? *7423
Pr 6:19 A f witness that speaketh lies, 8267
11: 1 A f balance is abomination to 4820
12:17 but a f witness deceit. 8267
14: 5 but a f witness will utter lies. "
17: 4 doer giveth heed to f lips; * 205
19: 5, 9 A f witness shall not be 8267
20:23 and a f balance is not good. 4820
21:28 A f witness shall perish: but the 3577
25:14 boasteth himself of a f gift is *8267
18 A man that beareth f witness "
Jer 14:14 you a f vision and divination, * "
23:32 them that prophesy f dreams, * "
37:14 Then said Jeremiah, It is f; "
La 2:14 have seen for thee f burdens and*7723
Eze 21:23 as a f divination in their sight, * "
Zec 8:17 and love no f oath: for all these 8267
10: 2 a lie, and have told f dreams; 7723
Mal 3: 5 and against f swearers, and 8267
M't 7:15 Beware of f prophets, which come 5578
15:19 thefts, f witness, blasphemies: 5577
19:18 Thou shalt not bear f witness, 5576
24:11 And many f prophets shall rise, 5578
24 For there shall arise f Christs, 5580
24 and f prophets, and shall shew 5578
26:59 sought f witness against Jesus, 5580
60 though many f witnesses came, 5575
60 At the last came two f witnesses, "
M'r 10:19 Do not bear f witness, Defraud 5576
13:22 For f Christs...shall rise, and shall 5580
22 and f prophets shall rise, and shall 5578
14:56 For many bare f witness against 5576
57 and bare f witness against him. "
Lu 6:26 their fathers to the f prophets. 5578
18:20 Do not bear f witness, Honour 5576
19: 8 from any man by f accusation, *4811
Ac 6:13 set up f witnesses, which said, 5571
13: 6 sorcerer, a f prophet, a Jew, 5578
Ro 13: 9 Thou shalt not bear f witness, *5576
1Co 15:15 we are found f witnesses of God; 5575
2Co 11:13 For such are f apostles, deceitful 5570
26 sea, in perils among f brethren; 5569
Ga 2: 4 because of f brethren unawares "
2Ti 3: 3 trucebreakers, f accusers, 1228
Tit 2: 3 not f accusers, not given to much* "
2Pe 2: 1 there were f prophets also among 5578
1 there shall be f teachers among 5572
1Jo 4: 1 because many f prophets are gone 5578
Re 16:13 out of the mouth of the f prophet. "
19:20 f prophet that wrought miracles "
20:10 the beast and the f prophet are, "

false-accusation See FALSE and ACCUSATION.

false-apostles See FALSE and APOSTLES.

false-brethren See FALSE and BRETHREN.

false-christs See FALSE and CHRISTS.

falsehood
2Sa 18:13 wrought f against mine own life: *8267
Job 21:34 your answers there remaineth f? 4604
Ps 7:14 mischief, and brought forth f. 8267
119:118 thy statutes: for their deceit is f. "
144: 8 their right hand is a right hand of f. "
11 their right hand is a right hand of f: "
Isa 28:15 under f have we hid ourselves: "
57: 4 of transgression, a seed of f, "
59:13 uttering from the heart words of f. "
Jer 10:14 for his molten image is f, and "
13:25 hast forgotten me, and trusted in f. "
51:17 for his molten image is f, and "
Ho 7: 1 for they commit f; and the thief "
Mic 2:11 walking in the spirit and f do lie, "

falsely
Ge 21:23 that thou wilt not deal f with me, 8266
Le 6: 3 it, and sweareth f; 5921, 8267
5 that about which he hath sworn f; "
19:11 Ye shall not steal, neither deal f, 3584
12 ye shall not swear by my name f, 8267
De 19:18 hath testified f against his brother; "
Ps 44:17 neither have we dealt f in thy 8266
Jer 5: 2 Lord liveth; surely they swear f. 8267
31 prophets prophesy f, and the "
6:13 unto the priest every one dealeth f. "
7: 9 and commit adultery, and swear f, "
8:10 unto the priest every one dealeth f. "
29: 9 prophesy f unto you in my name: "
40:16 for thou speakest f of Ishmael. "
43: 2 unto Jeremiah, Thou speakest f: "
Hos 10: 4 swearing f in making a covenant: 7723
Zec 5: 4 the house of him that sweareth f 8267
M't 5:11 all manner of evil against you f, 5574
Lu 3:14 neither accuse any f; and be *
1Ti 6:20 oppositions of science f so called: 5581
1Pe 3:16 ashamed that f accuse your *

false-prophet See FALSE and PROPHET.

false-teacher See FALSE and TEACHER.

false-witness See FALSE and WITNESS.

falsifying
Am 8: 5 and f the balances by deceit? *5791

fame See also DEFAME.
Ge 45:16 f thereof was heard in Pharaoh's 6963
Nu 14:15 which have heard the f of thee 8088
Jos 6:27 his f was noised throughout all 8089
9: 9 for we have heard the f of him, "
1Ki 4:31 his f was in all nations round 8034
10: 1 of Sheba heard of the f of Solomon 8088
7 exceedeth the f which I heard. 8052
1Ch 14:17 the f of David went out into all 8034
22: 5 magnifical, of f and of glory "
2Ch 9: 1 Sheba heard of the f of Solomon, 8088
6 thou exceedest the f that I heard. 8052
Es 9: 4 his f went out throughout all the 8089
Job 28:22 We have heard the f thereof with *8088
Isa 66:19 afar off, that have not heard my f, "
Jer 6:24 We have heard the f thereof: our 8089
Zep 3:19 I will get them praise and f in *8034
M't 4:24 his f went throughout all Syria: * 189
9:26 the f hereof went abroad into all 5345
31 spread abroad his f in all that 1310
14: 1 tetrarch heard of the f of Jesus. * 189
M'r 1:28 immediately his f spread abroad * "
Lu 4:14 and there went out a f of him 5345
37 the f of him went out into every *2279
5:15 went there a f abroad of him: *3056

familiar See also FAMILIARS.
Le 19:31 not them that have f spirits, "
20: 6 turneth after such as have f spirits, "
27 also or woman that hath a f spirit, "
De 18:11 or a consulter with f spirits, or a "
1Sa 28: 3 put away those that had f spirits, "

1Sa 28: 7 me a woman that hath a *f* spirit,
7 woman that hath a *f* spirit at En-dor.
8 divine unto me by the *f* spirit, and
9 hath cut off those that have *f* spirits,
2Ki 21: 6 and dealt with *f* spirits and wizards:
23:24 the workers with *f* spirits, and the
1Ch 10:13 counsel of one that had a *f* spirit,
2Ch 33: 6 and dealt with a *f* spirit, and with
Job 19:14 my *f* friends have forgotten me. 3045
Ps 41: 9 Yea, mine own *f* friend, in whom 7965
Isa 8:19 unto them that have *f* spirits, and
19: 3 and to them that have *f* spirits, and
29: 4 as of one that hath a *f* spirit,

familiars
Jer 20:10 all my *f* watched for my halting. *7965

familiar-spirit See FAMILIAR and SPIRIT.

families
Ge 10: 5 after their *f*, in their nations. 4940
18 were the *f* of the Canaanites "
20 are the sons of Ham, after their *f*, "
31 are the sons of Shem, after their *f*, "
32 These are the *f* of the sons of Noah, "
12: 3 shall all *f* of the earth be blessed. "
28:14 all the *f* of the earth be blessed. "
36:40 of Esau according to their *f*, "
47:12 with bread, according to their *f*. 2945
Ex 6:14 Carmi: these be the *f* of Reuben. 4940
15 women: these are the *f* of Simeon. "
17 and Shimi, according to their *f*. "
19 these are the *f* of Levi according "
24 these are the *f* of the Korhites. "
25 of the Levites according to their *f*. "
12:21 you a lamb according to your *f*, "
Le 25:45 and of their *f* that are with you, "
Nu 1: 2 the children of Israel, after their *f*, "
18 their pedigrees after their *f*, "
20, 22, 24, 26, 28, 30, 32, 34, 36, 38, 40 by their generations, after their *f*, "
42 their generations, after their *f*, by "
2:34 forward, every one after their *f*, "
3:15 children of Levi,...after their *f*: "
18 the sons of Gershon by their *f*; "
19 the sons of Kohath by their *f*; "
20 the sons of Merari by their *f*; "
20 These are the *f* of the Levites "
21 these are the *f* of the Gershonites. "
23 The *f* of the Gershonites shall "
27 these are the *f* of the Kohathites. "
29 The *f* of the sons of Kohath "
30 father of the *f* of the Kohathites "
33 these are the *f* of Merari. "
35 of the *f* of Merari was Zuriel "
39 throughout their *f*, all the males "
4: 2 the sons of Levi, after their *f*, "
18 tribe of the *f* of the Kohathites "
22 houses of their fathers, by their *f*; "
24 service of the *f* of the Gershonites, "
28 of the *f* of the sons of Gershon in "
29 shalt number them after their *f*, "
33 of the *f* of the sons of Merari, "
34 sons of the Kohathites after their *f*, "
36 were numbered of them by their *f* "
37 of the *f* of the Kohathites, all that "
38 of Gershon, throughout their *f*, "
40 throughout their *f*, by the house of "
41 of the *f* of the sons of Gershon, "
42 of the *f* of the sons of Merari, "
42 throughout their *f*, by the house of "
44 numbered of them after their *f*, "
45 of the *f* of the sons of Merari, "
46 of Israel, numbered after their *f*, "
11:10 people weep throughout their *f*, "
26: 7 These are the *f* of the Reubenites: "
12 The sons of Simeon after their *f*: "
14 These are the *f* of the Simeonites, "
15 The children of Gad after their *f*: "
18 These are the *f* of the children of "
20 sons of Judah after their *f* were; "
22 These are the *f* of Judah "
23 the sons of Issachar after their *f*: "
25 These are the *f* of Issachar "
26 the sons of Zebulun after their *f*: "
27 These are the *f* of the Zebulunites "
28 The sons of Joseph after their *f* "
34 These are the *f* of Manasseh, after "
35 the sons of Ephraim after their *f*: "
37 are the *f* of the sons of Ephraim "
37 are the sons of Joseph after their *f*. "
38 The sons of Benjamin after their *f*: "
41 the sons of Benjamin after their *f*: "
42 are the sons of Dan after their *f*; "
42 These are the *f* of Dan after their *f*. "
43 All the *f* of the Shuhamites, "
44 the children of Asher after their *f*: "
47 These are the *f* of the sons of Asher "
48 Of the sons of Naphtali after their *f*: "
50 *f* of Naphtali according to their *f*: "
57 of the Levites after their *f*: "
58 These are the *f* of the Levites: "
27: 1 of the *f* of Manasseh the son of "
33:54 for an inheritance among your *f*: "
36: 1 the *f* of the children of Gilead, * "
1 of the *f* of the sons of Joseph, "
12 married into the *f* of the sons of "
Jos 7:14 according to the *f* thereof; and "
13:15 inheritance according to their *f*. "
23 children of Reuben after their *f*, "
24 of Gad according to their *f*. "
28 the children of Gad after their *f*, "
29 children of Manasseh by their *f*, "
31 the children of Machir by their *f*. "
15: 1 the children of Judah by their *f*; "
12 round about according to their *f*. "
20 of Judah according to their *f*. "
Jos 16: 5 of Ephraim according to their *f* 4940
8 the children of Ephraim by their *f*. "
17: 2 children of Manasseh by their *f*; "
2 the son of Joseph by their *f*. "
18:11 came up according to their *f*: "
20 round about, according to their *f*. "
21 of Benjamin according to their *f* "
28 of Benjamin according to their *f*. "
19: 1 of Simeon according to their *f*: "
8 of Simeon according to their *f*. "
10 of Zebulun according to their *f*: "
16 of Zebulun according to their *f*, "
17 of Issachar according to their *f*. "
23 of Issachar according to their *f*, "
24 of Asher according to their *f*. "
31 of Asher according to their *f*, "
32 of Naphtali according to their *f*. "
39 of Naphtali according to their *f*, "
40 of Dan according to their *f*. "
48 of Dan according to their *f*, "
21: 4 for the *f* of the Kohathites: "
5 of the *f* of the tribe of Ephraim, "
6 of the *f* of the tribe of Issachar, "
7 The children of Merari by their *f* "
10 being of the *f* of the Kohathites, "
20 And the *f* of the children of Kohath, "
26 for the *f* of the children of Kohath "
27 of Gershon, of the *f* of the Levites, "
33 according to their *f* were thirteen "
34 unto the *f* of the children of Merari, "
40 the children of Merari by their *f* "
40 remaining of the *f* of the Levites, "
1Sa 9:21 and my family the least of all the *f* "
10:21 Benjamin to come near by their *f*, "
1Ch 2:53 And the *f* of Kirjath-jearim; the "
55 the *f* of the scribes which dwelt "
4: 2 These are the *f* of the Zorathites. "
8 the *f* of Aharhel the son of Harum. "
21 and the *f* of the house of them "
38 names were princes in their *f*: "
5: 7 And his brethren by their *f*, "
6:19 And these are the *f* of the Levites "
54 Aaron, of the *f* of the Kohathites: "
60 All their cities throughout their *f* "
62 of Gershom throughout their *f* "
63 given by lot, throughout their *f*, "
66 of the *f* of the sons of Kohath had "
7: 5 among all the *f* of Issachar were "
2Ch 35: 5 divisions of the *f* of the fathers *1004
5 division of the *f* of the Levites.*1004, 1
12 divisions of the *f* of the people,* " "
Ne 4:13 after their *f* with their swords, 4940
Job 31:34 did the contempt of *f* terrify me, "
Ps 68: 6 God setteth the solitary in *f*: 1004
107:41 and maketh him *f* like a flock. 4940
Jer 1:15 will call all the *f* of the kingdoms "
2: 4 all the *f* of the house of Israel: "
10:25 the *f* that call not on thy name: "
25: 9 and take all the *f* of the north, "
31: 1 the God of all the *f* of Israel, "
33:24 two *f* which the Lord hath chosen, "
Eze 20:32 as the *f* of the countries, to serve "
Am 3: 2 I known of all the *f* of the earth: "
Na 3: 4 and *f* through her witchcrafts. "
Zec 12:14 *f* that remain, every family apart, "
14:17 come up of all the *f* of the earth "

family See also FAMILIES.
Le 20: 5 that man, and against his *f*, 4940
25:10 shall return every man unto his *f*. "
41 and shall return unto his own *f*, "
47 or to the stock of the stranger's *f*: "
49 is nigh of kin unto him of his *f* "
Nu 3:21 Gershon was the *f* of the Libnites, "
21 and the *f* of the Shimites: "
27 Kohath was the *f* of the Amramites, "
27 and the *f* of the Izeharites, "
27 and the *f* of the Hebronites, "
27 and the *f* of the Uzzielites: "
33 Merari was the *f* of the Mahlites, "
33 and the *f* of the Mushites: "
26: 5 cometh the *f* of the Hanochites: "
5 of Pallu, the *f* of the Palluites: "
6 Of Hezron, the *f* of the Hezronites: "
6 of Carmi, the *f* of the Carmites. "
12 Nemuel, the *f* of the Nemuelites: "
12 of Jamin, the *f* of the Jaminites: "
12 of Jachin, the *f* of the Jachinites: "
13 Of Zerah, the *f* of the Zarhites: "
13 of Shaul, the *f* of the Shaulites. "
15 of Zephon, the *f* of the Zephonites: "
15 of Haggi, the *f* of the Haggites: "
15 of Shuni, the *f* of the Shunites: "
16 Of Ozni, the *f* of the Oznites: "
16 of Eri, the *f* of the Erites: "
17 Of Arod, the *f* of the Arodites: "
17 of Areli, the *f* of the Arelites. "
20 of Shelah, the *f* of the Shelanites: "
20 of Pharez, the *f* of the Pharzites: "
20 of Zerah, the *f* of the Zarhites. "
21 of Hezron, the *f* of the Hezronites: "
21 of Hamul, the *f* of the Hamulites. "
23 of Tola, the *f* of the Tolaites: "
23 of Pua, the *f* of the Punites: "
24 Of Jashub, the *f* of the Jashubites: "
24 Shimron, the *f* of the Shimronites. "
26 of Sered, the *f* of the Sardites: "
26 of Elon, the *f* of the Elonites: "
26 of Jahleel, the *f* of the Jahleelites. "
29 of Machir, the *f* of the Machirites: "
29 Gilead come the *f* of the Gileadites. "
30 of Jeezer, the *f* of the Jeezerites: "
30 of Helek, the *f* of the Helekites: "
31 of Asriel, the *f* of the Asrielites: "
31 Shechem, the *f* of the Shechemites: "
32 Shemida, the *f* of the Shemidaites: "
Nu 26:32 Hepher, the *f* of the Hepherites. 4940
35 Shuthelah, the *f* of the Shuthalhites: "
35 of Becher, the *f* of the Bachrites: "
35 of Tahan, the *f* of the Tahahamites, "
36 of Eran, the *f* of the Eranites. "
38 of Bela, the *f* of the Belaites: "
38 of Ashbel, the *f* of the Ashbelites: "
38 of Ahiram, the *f* of the Ahiramites: "
39 Shupham, the *f* of the Shuphamites: "
39 Hupham, the *f* of the Huphamites. "
40 of Ard, the *f* of the Ardites: "
40 of Naaman, the *f* of the Naamites. "
42 Shuham, the *f* of the Shuhamites. "
44 of Jimna, the *f* of the Jimnites: "
44 of Jesui, the *f* of the Jesuites: "
44 of Beriah, the *f* of the Beriites. "
45 of Heber, the *f* of the Heberites: "
45 Malchiel, the *f* of the Malchielites. "
48 Jahzeel, the *f* of the Jahzeelites: "
48 of Guni, the *f* of the Gunites: "
49 of Jezer, the *f* of the Jezerites: "
49 of Shillem, the *f* of the Shillemites. "
57 Gershon, the *f* of the Gershonites: "
57 Kohath, the *f* of the Kohathites: "
57 of Merari, the *f* of the Merarites. "
58 of the Levites: the *f* of the Libnites, "
58 the *f* of the Hebronites, "
58 the *f* of the Mahlites, "
58 the *f* of the Mushites, "
58 the *f* of the Korathites. "
27: 4 be done away from among his *f*, "
11 that is next to him of his *f*, "
36: 6 only to the *f* of the tribe of their "
8 wife unto one of the *f* of the tribe "
12 or the tribe of the *f* of their father. "
De 29:18 in *f*, or tribe, whose heart turneth "
Jos 7:14 the *f* which the Lord shall take "
17 And he brought the *f* of Judah; "
17 and he took the *f* of the Zarhites: "
17 he brought the *f* of the Zarhites "
J'g 1:25 they let go the man and all his *f*. "
6:15 behold, my *f* is poor in Manasseh, 504
9: 1 and with all the *f* of the house of 4940
13: 2 of Zorah, of the *f* of the Danites, "
17: 7 the *f* of Judah, who was a Levite, "
18: 2 of Dan sent of their *f* five men "
11 from thence of the *f* of the Danites, "
19 unto a tribe and a *f* in Israel? "
21:24 every man to his tribe and to his *f*, "
Ru 2: 1 of wealth, of the *f* of Elimelech; "
1Sa 9:21 my *f* the least of all the families "
10:21 the *f* of Matri was taken, "
18:18 my life, or my father's *f* in Israel, "
20: 6 yearly sacrifice there for all the *f*. "
29 for our *f* hath a sacrifice in the city. "
2Sa 14: 7 *f* is risen against thine handmaid, "
16: 5 a man of the *f* of the house of Saul, "
1Ch 4:27 neither did all their *f* multiply, like "
6:61 were left of the *f* of that tribe, "
70 the *f* of the remnant of the sons "
71 given out of the *f* of the half tribe "
13:14 ark of God remained with the *f* of 1004
Es 9:28 every *f*, every province, and every 4940
Jer 3:14 one of a city, and two of a *f*, "
8: 3 of them that remain of this evil *f*, "
Am 3: 1 the whole *f* which I brought up "
Mic 2: 3 against this *f* do I devise an evil, "
Zec 12:12 shall mourn, every *f* apart; "
12 the *f* of the house of David apart, "
12 the *f* of the house of Nathan apart, "
13 The *f* of the house of Levi apart, "
13 the *f* of Shimei apart, and their "
14 families that remain, every *f* apart, "
14:18 if the *f* of Egypt go not up, "
Eph 3:15 *f* in heaven and earth is named, 3965

famine See also FAMINES.
Ge 12:10 And there was a *f* in the land: 7458
10 for the *f* was grievous in the land. "
26: 1 And there was a *f* in the land, "
1 beside the first *f* that was in the "
41:27 east wind shall be seven years of *f*. "
30 arise after them seven years of *f*; "
30 and the *f* shall consume the land; "
31 in the land by reason of that *f* * "
36 against the seven years of *f*, which "
36 the land perish not through the *f*. "
50 before the years of *f* came, "
56 And the *f* was over all the face of "
56 and the *f* waxed sore in the land of "
57 that the *f* was so sore in all lands. "
42: 5 the *f* was in the land of Canaan. "
19 corn for the *f* of your houses: 7459
33 food for the *f* of your households, "
43: 1 And the *f* was sore in the land. 7458
45: 6 years hath the *f* been in the land: "
11 yet there are five years of *f*; "
47: 4 the *f* is sore in the land of Canaan: "
13 for the *f* was very sore, so that the "
13 Canaan fainted by reason of the *f*. "
20 because the *f* prevailed over them: "
Ru 1: 1 that there was a *f* in the land. "
2Sa 21: 1 there was a *f* in the days of David "
24:13 Shall seven years of *f* come unto "
1Ki 8:37 If there be in the land *f*, "
18: 2 And there was a sore *f* in Samaria. "
2Ki 6:25 there was a great *f* in Samaria: "
7: 4 then the *f* is in the city, "
8: 1 the Lord hath called for a *f*; "
25: 3 month the *f* prevailed in the city, "
1Ch 21:12 Either three years' *f*; or three "
2Ch 20: 9 judgment, or pestilence, or *f*, "
32:11 to die by *f* and by thirst, "
Job 5:20 In *f* he shall redeem thee from "
22 At destruction and *f* thou shalt *3720
30: 3 For want and *f* they were solitary; "

Ps 33:19 and to keep them alive in f. 7458
37:19 days of f they shall be satisfied. 7459
105:16 he called for a f upon the land: 7458
Isa 14:30 I will kill thy root with f, "
51:19 and the f, and the sword: "
Jer 5:12 neither shall we see sword nor f: "
11:22 and their daughters shall die by f: "
14:12 them by the sword, and by the f, "
13 the sword, neither shall ye have f; "
15 and f shall not be in this land; "
15 f shall those prophets be consumed. "
16 because of the f and the sword; "
18 behold them that are sick with f! "
15: 2 such as are for the f, to the f; "
16: 4 consumed by the sword, and by f; "
18:21 deliver up their children to the f, "
21: 7 from the sword, and from the f, "
9 die by the sword, and by the f, "
24:10 I will send the sword, the f, "
27: 8 with the sword, and with the f, "
13 thy people, by the sword, by the f, "
29:17 send upon them the sword, the f, "
18 them with the sword, with the f, "
32:24 because of the sword, and of the f, "
36 Babylon by the sword, and by the f, "
34:17 to the pestilence, and to the f; "
38: 2 shall die by the sword, by the f, "
42:16 and the f, whereof ye were afraid, "
17 shall die by the sword, by the f, "
22 ye shall die by the sword, by the f, "
44:12, 12 by the sword and by the f: "
13 Jerusalem, by the sword, by the f, "
18 by the sword and by the f. "
27 by the sword and by the f, until "
52: 6 month the f was sore in the city, "
La 5:10 an oven because of the terrible f. "
Eze 5:12 and with f shall they be consumed "
16 upon them the evil arrows of f, "
16 and I will increase the f upon you, "
17 So will I send upon you f and evil "
6:11 they shall fall by the sword, by the f, "
12 and is besieged shall die by the f: "
7:15 the pestilence and the f within: "
15 f and pestilence shall devour him. "
12:16 them from the sword, from the f, "
14:13 and will send f upon it, "
21 and the f, and the noisome beast, "
36:29 and lay no f upon you. "
30 shall receive no more reproach of f "
Am 8:11 that I will send a f in the land, "
11 not a f of bread, nor a thirst of "
Lu 4:25 when great f was throughout all 3042
15:14 there arose a mighty f in that land; "
Ro 8:35 or f, or nakedness, or peril, or "
Re 18: 8 day, death, and mourning, and f; "

famines
M't 24: 7 there shall be f, and pestilences, 3042
M'r 13: 8 and there shall be f and troubles: "
Lu 21:11 and f, and pestilences; and fearful "

famish See also FAMISHED.
Pr 10: 3 the soul of the righteous to f: 7456
Zep 2:11 will f all the gods of the earth; 7329

famished
Ge 41:55 when all the land of Egypt was f, 7456
Isa 5:13 and their honourable men are f, 7458

famous See also INFAMOUS.
Nu 16: 2 assembly, f in the congregation, *7148
26: 9 which were f in the congregation, *7121
Ru 4:11 Ephratah...f in Beth-lehem: 7121, 8034
14 that his name may be f in Israel. 7121
1Ch 5:24 mighty men of valour, f men, 8034
12:30 f throughout the house of their "
Ps 74: 5 A man was f according as he had *3045
136:18 And slew f kings: for his 117
Eze 23:10 she became f among women, *8034
32:18 the daughters of the f nations, 117

fan
Isa 30:24 with the shovel and with the f. 4214
41:16 Thou shalt f them, and the wind ‡2219
Jer 4:11 not to f, nor to cleanse, ‡ "
15: 7 And I will f them...in the gates †‡ "
7 And I will...with a f in the gates 4214
51: 2 Babylon fanners, that shall f her, ‡2219
M't 3:12 Whose f is in his hand, and he 4425
Lu 3:17 Whose f is in his hand, and he will "

fanners
Jer 51: 2 Babylon f, that shall fan her, *2114

far See also AFAR; FARTHER.
Ge 18:25 That be f from thee to do after 2486
25 as the wicked, that be f from thee: "
44: 4 and not yet f off, Joseph said 7368
Ex 8:28 ye shall not go very f away: "
23: 7 Keep thee f from a false matter; "
Nu 2: 2 f off about the tabernacle of the *5048
De 12:21 name there be too f from thee, 7368
13: 7 nigh unto thee, or f off from thee, 7350
14:24 if the place be too f from thee, 7368
20:15 the cities which are very f off 7350
28:49 bring a nation against thee from f, "
29:22 that shall come from a f land, "
30:11 from thee, neither is it f off. "
Jos 3:16 heap very f from the city Adam, *7368
8: 4 go not very f from the city, "
9: 6 We be come from a f country: 7350
9 f country thy servants are come "
22 We are very f from you; when ye "
J'g 9:17 and adventured his life f, and *5048
18: 7 they were f from the Zidonians, 7350
28 it was f from Zidon, and they had "
19:11 by Jebus, the day was f spent; 3966
1Sa 2:30 the Lord saith, Be it f from me; 2486
20: 9 Jonathan said, F be it from thee: "
22:15 be it f from me: let not the king "
2Sa 15:17 in a place that was f off. *4801
20:20 said, F be it, f be it from me, 2486
23:17 he said, Be it f from me, "
1Ki 8:41 cometh out of a f country for thy 7350
46 the land of the enemy, f or near; "
2Ki 20:14 They are come from a f country, "
2Ch 6:32 but is come from a f country "
36 unto a land f off or near; "
26:15 And his name spread f abroad; "
Ezr 6: 6 the river, be ye f from thence: 7352
Ne 4:19 the wall, one f from another. 7350
Es 9:20 king Ahasuerus, both nigh and f, "
Job 5: 4 His children are f from safety, "
11:14 be in thine hand, put it f away, "
13:21 Withdraw thine hand f from me: "
19:13 hath put my brethren f from me, "
21:16 counsel of the wicked is f from me. "
22:18 but the counsel of the wicked is f "
23 shalt put away iniquity f from thy "
30:10 abhor me, they flee f from me, * "
34:10 f be it from God, that he should 2486
Ps 10: 5 are f above out of his sight: 5048
22: 1 art thou so f from helping me, 7350
11 Be not f from me; for trouble is 7368
19 be not thou f from me, O Lord: "
27: 9 Hide not thy face f from me; *
35:22 O Lord, be not f from me. 7368
38:21 O my God, be not f from me. "
55: 7 Lo, then would I wander f off, "
71:12 O God, be not f from me: "
73:27 that are f from thee shall perish: 7369
88: 8 put away mine acquaintance f 7368
18 and friend hast thou put f from me, "
97: 9 thou art exalted f above all gods. 3966
103:12 As f as the east is from the west, 7350
12 so f hath he removed our "
109:17 so let it be f from him. 7368
119:150 they are f from thy law. "
155 Salvation is f from the wicked: 7350
Pr 4:24 and perverse lips put f from thee. 7368
5: 8 Remove thy way f from her, "
15:29 The Lord is f from the wicked: 7350
19: 7 do his friends go f from him? 7368
22: 5 keep his soul shall be f from them. "
15 rod of correction shall drive it f "
25:25 is good news from a f country. 4801
27:10 that is near than a brother f off. 7350
30: 8 Remove f from me vanity and 7369
31:10 for her price is f above rubies. 7350
Ec 7:23 be wise; but it was f from me. "
24 That which is f off, and exceeding "
Isa 5:26 an ensign to the nations from f, "
6:12 Lord have removed men f away, 7368
8: 9 give ear, all ye of f countries: 4801
10: 3 which shall come from f? "
13: 5 They come from a f country, from "
17:13 they shall flee f off, and shall "
19: 6 they shall turn the rivers f away;*
22: 3 together, which have fled from f.*7350
26:15 removed it f unto all the ends of*7368
29:13 removed their heart f from me "
30:27 name of the Lord cometh from f, 4801
33:13 Hear, ye that are f off, what I 7350
17 behold the land that is very f off. 4801
39: 3 They are come from a f country 7350
43: 6 not back; bring my sons from f, "
46:11 my counsel from a f country: 4801
12 that are f from righteousness: 7350
13 righteousness; it shall not be f off, 7368
49: 1 and hearken, ye people, from f; 7350
12 Behold, these shall come from f: "
19 swallowed thee up shall be f away. 7368
54:14 thou shalt be f from oppression; "
57: 9 didst send thy messengers f off, 7350
19 Peace, peace to him that is f off, "
59: 9 Therefore is judgment f from us, 7368
11 salvation, but it is f off from us. "
60: 4 thy sons shall come from f, and 7350
9 to bring thy sons from f, their "
Jer 2: 5 that they are gone f from me, 7368
4:16 watchers come from a f country, 4801
5:15 bring a nation upon you from f, "
6:20 the sweet cane from a f country? "
8:19 of them that dwell in a f country; "
12: 2 mouth, and f from their reins. 7350
25:26 the kings of the north, f and near, "
27:10 to remove you f from your land; 7368
48:24 of the land of Moab, f or near. 7350
47 Thus f is the judgment of Moab. 2008
49:30 Flee, get you f off, dwell deep, 3966
51:64 Thus f are the words of Jeremiah. 2008
La 1:16 relieve my soul is f from me: 7368
3:17 thou hast removed my soul f off 2186
Eze 6:12 He that is f off shall die 7350
7:20 therefore have I set it f from *5079
8: 6 go f off from my sanctuary? 7368
11:15 Get you f from the Lord: "
16 I have cast them f off among the "
12:27 of the times that are f off. 7350
22: 5 and those that be f from thee, "
23:40 sent for men to come from f, 4801
43: 9 carcases of their kings, f from me, 7350
44:10 Levites that are gone away f from "
Da 9: 7 that are near, and that are f off, "
11: 2 fourth shall be f richer than they 1419
Joe 2:20 I will remove f off from you the 7368
3: 6 remove them f from their border. "
8 the Sabeans, to a people f off: 7350
Am 6: 3 Ye that put f away the evil day, "
Mic 4: 7 her that was cast f off a strong nation: "
7:11 shall the decree be f removed. 7368
Hab 1: 8 their horsemen shall come from f; 7350
Zec 6:15 they that are f off shall come "
10: 9 shall remember me in f countries: 4801
M't 15: 8 but their heart is f from me. 4206
16:22 Be it f from thee, Lord: 2436
M't 21:33 and went into a f country: *
25:14 man travelling into a f country, *
M'r 6:35 when the day was now f spent, 4183
35 and now the time is f passed: "
7: 6 but their heart is f from me. 4206
8: 3 for divers of them came from f. 3113
12: 1 and went into a f country. *
34 not f from the kingdom of God. 3112
13:34 as a man taking a f journey, *
Lu 7: 6 was now not f from the house, 3112
15:13 his journey into a f country, 3117
19:12 went into a f country to receive "
20: 9 went into a f country for a long time.
22:51 and said, Suffer ye thus f. 2193
24:29 and the day is f spent. "
50 them out as f as to Bethany, *2193
Joh 21: 8 for they were not f from land, 3112
Ac 11:19 Stephen travelled as f as Phenice, 2193
22 that he should go as f as Antioch. "
17:27 he be not f from every one 3112
22:21 I will send thee f hence unto the "
28:15 to meet us as f as Appii forum, 891
Ro 13:12 night is f spent, the day is at hand:
2Co 4:17 for us a f more exceeding *1519, 5236
10:14 we are come as f as to you also in 891
Eph 1:21 F above all principality, and 5231
2:13 ye who sometimes were f off are 3112
4:10 ascended up f above all heavens, 5231
Ph'p 1:23 Christ; which is f better: 4183, 3123
Heb 7:15 And it is yet f more evident: *4054

fare See also FARED; FAREWELL; SEAFARING; WARFARE; WAYFARING; WELFARE.
1Sa 17:18 and look how thy brethren f, 7965
Jon 1: 3 he paid the f thereof, and went 7939
Ac 15:29 ye shall do well. F ye well. 4517

fared
Lu 16:19 and f sumptuously every day: *2165

farewell See also FARE and WELL.
Lu 9:61 but let me first go bid them f, 657
Ac 18:21 But bade them f, saying, I must * "
23:30 what they had against him. F. *4517
2Co 13:11 Finally, brethren, f. Be perfect, 5463

faring See SEAFARING; WAYFARING.

farm
M't 22: 5 and went their ways, one to his f, 68

far-off See FAR and OFF.

farther See also FURTHER.
Ec 8:17 yea f; though a wise man think *
M't 26:39 And he went a little f, and fell *4281
M'r 1:19 And when he had gone a little f *4260
10: 1 by the f side of Jordan: *4008

farthing See also FARTHINGS.
M't 5:26 thou hast paid the uttermost f. 2835
10:29 not two sparrows sold for a f? ‡ 787
M'r 12:42 in two mites, which make a f. 2835

farthings
Lu 12: 6 not five sparrows sold for two f, ‡ 787

fashion See also FASHIONED; FASHIONETH; FASHIONING; FASHIONS.
Ge 6:15 f which thou shalt make it of: *
Ex 26:30 according to the f thereof which 4941
37:19 made after the f of almonds *
1Ki 6:38 according to all the f of it. 4941
2Ki 16:10 the f of the altar, and the pattern 1823
Job 31:15 did not one f us in the womb? 3559
Eze 43:11 the house, and the f thereof, 8498
M'r 2:12 We never saw it on this f. 3779
Lu 9:29 the f of his countenance was 1491
Ac 7:44 to the f that he had seen. *5179
1Co 7:31 for the f of this world passeth 4976
Ph'p 2: 8 And being found in f as a man, "
Jas 1:11 the grace of the f of it perisheth: 4383

fashioned
Ex 32: 4 and f it with a graving tool, 3335
Job 10: 8 hands have made me and f me 6213
Ps 119:73 hands have made me and f me: 3559
139:16 which in continuance were f, 3335
Isa 22:11 had respect unto him that f it "
Eze 16: 7 thy breasts are f, and thine hair 3559
Ph'p 3:21 be f like unto his glorious body, *4832

fashioneth
Ps 33:15 He f their hearts alike; he 3335
Isa 44:12 the coals, and f it with hammers, "
45: 9 Shall the clay say to him that f it, "

fashioning
1Pe 1:14 not f yourselves according to the 4964

fashions
Eze 42:11 out were both according to their f, 4941

fast See also FASTED; FASTING; STEDFAST.
Ge 20:18 Lord had f closed up all the wombs
J'g 4:21 for he was f asleep and weary. *
15:13 No, but we will bind thee f, "
16:11 they bind me f with new ropes *
Ru 2: 8 but abide here f by my maidens:
21 Thou shalt keep f by my young men,
23 So she kept f by the maidens of Boaz
2Sa 12:21 didst f and weep for the child, 6684
23 he is dead, wherefore should I f? "
1Ki 21: 9 Proclaim a f, and set Naboth 6685
12 proclaimed a f, and set Naboth "
2Ki 6:32 and hold him f at the door:
2Ch 20: 3 proclaimed a f throughout all 6685
Ezr 5: 8 and this work goeth f on, * 629
8:21 Then I proclaimed a f there, 6685
Es 4:16 and f ye for me, and neither eat 6684
16 and my maidens will f likewise; "
Job 2: 3 and still he holdeth f his integrity,
8:15 he shall hold it f, but it shall not
27: 6 My righteousness I hold f, and will
38:38 and the clods cleave f together?

Ps 33: 9 he commanded, and it stood f.
38: 2 For thine arrows stick f in me,
41: 8 disease, say they, cleaveth f unto him:
65: 6 his strength setteth f the mountains:
89:28 my covenant shall stand f with him.
111: 8 They stand f for ever and ever, *
Pr 4:13 Take f hold of instruction; let her not
Isa 58: 3 Behold, in the day of your f ye 6685
4 ye f for strife and debate, 6684
4 ye shall not f as ye do this day, "
5 Is it such a f that I have chosen? 6685
5 wilt thou call this a f, and an "
6 not this the f that I have chosen? "
Jer 8: 5 they hold f deceit, they refuse to
14:12 When they f, I will not hear their 6684
36: 9 proclaimed a f before the Lord 6685
46:14 Stand f, and prepare thee; for *
48:16 and his affliction hasteth f. 3966
50:33 took them captives held them f:
Joe 1:14 Sanctify ye a f, call a solemn 6685
2:15 sanctify a f, call a solemn assembly: "
Jon 1: 5 and he lay, and was f asleep.
3: 5 and proclaimed a f, and put on 6685
Zec 7: 5 did ye all f unto me, even to me? 6684
8:19 The f of the fourth month, 6685
19 and the f of the fifth, "
19 and the f of the seventh, "
19 and the f of the tenth, "
M't 6:16 Moreover when ye f, be not, as 3522
16 they may appear unto men to f. "
18 thou appear not unto men to f, "
9:14 Why do we and the Pharisees f oft, "
14 but thy disciples f not? "
15 from them, and then shall they f. "
26:48 that same is he: hold him f. *
M'r 2:18 of the Pharisees used to f: *3522
18 of John and of the Pharisees f, "
18 but thy disciples f not? "
19 children of the bridechamber f, "
19 bridegroom with..., they cannot f. "
20 then shall they f in those days. "
Lu 5:33 do the disciples of John f often, "
34 children of the bridechamber f, "
35 then shall they f in those days. "
18:12 I f twice in the week, "
Ac 16:24 made their feet f in the stocks. 805
27: 9 because the f was now already 3521
41 forepart stuck f, and remained *
1Co 16:13 Watch ye, stand f in the faith, quit
Ga 5: 1 Stand f therefore in the liberty
Ph'p 1:27 that ye stand f in one spirit, with one
4: 1 so stand f in the Lord, my dearly
1Th 3: 8 now we live, if ye stand f in the Lord.
5:21 hold f that which is good. 2722
2Th 2:15 brethren, stand f, and hold the
2Ti 1:13 Hold f the form of sound words, *
Tit 1: 9 Holding f the faithful word as he * 472
Heb 3: 6 if we hold f the confidence and 2722
4:14 let us hold f our profession.
10:23 Let us hold f the profession of our 2722
Re 2:13 and thou holdest f my name,
25 ye have already, hold f till I come.
3: 3 and hold f, and repent. *
11 hold that f which thou hast, that no

fasted
J'g 20:26 f that day until even, and offered 6684
1Sa 7: 6 and f on that day, and said there, "
31:13 tree at Jabesh, and f seven days. "
2Sa 1:12 and f until even, for Saul, "
12:16 and David f, and went in, "
22 child was yet alive, I f and wept: "
1Ki 21:27 and f, and lay in sackcloth, "
1Ch 10:12 oak in Jabesh, and f seven days. "
Ezr 8:23 So we f and besought our God "
Ne 1: 4 and f, and prayed before the God of "
Isa 58: 3 Wherefore have we f, say they, "
Zec 7: 5 When ye f and mourned in the "
M't 4: 2 when he had f forty days 3522
Ac 13: 2 they ministered to the Lord, and f, "
3 when they had f and prayed, "

fasten See also FASTENED; FASTENING.
Ex 28:14 and f the wreathen chains to the *5414
25 thou shalt f in the two ouches, * "
39:31 to f it on high upon the mitre; "
Isa 22:23 And I will f him as a nail 8628
Jer 10: 4 they f it with nails and with 2388

fastened
Ex 39:18 chains they f in the two ouches, *5414
40:18 and f his sockets, and set up the * "
J'g 4:21 and f it into the ground: *6795
16:14 And she f it with the pin, 8628
1Sa 31:10 and they f his body to the wall of "
2Sa 20: 8 with a sword f upon his loins in 6775
1Ki 6: 6 beams should not be f in the * 270
1Ch 10:10 and f his head in the temple of 8628
2Ch 9:18 which were f to the throne, 270
Es 1: 6 f with cords of fine linen and purple "
Job 38: 6 are the foundations thereof f? 2883
Ec 12:11 f by the masters of assemblies, 5193
Isa 22:25 shall the nail that is f in the sure 8628
41: 7 f it with nails, that it should not 2388
Eze 40:43 a hand broad, f round about: 3559
Lu 4:20 in the synagogue were f on him. 816
Ac 11: 6 which when I had f mine eyes, I "
28: 3 out of the heat, and f on his hand. 2510

fastening
Ac 3: 4 Peter, f his eyes upon him with 816

fastest
M't 6:17 when thou f, anoint thine head, 3522

fasting See also FASTINGS.
Ne 9: 1 of Israel were assembled with f, 6685
Es 4: 3 and f, and weeping, and wailing; "
Ps 35:13 I humbled my soul with f; "
69:10 and chastened my soul with f, 6685
109:24 My knees are weak through f; "
Jer 36: 6 the Lord's house upon the f day: * "
Da 6:18 palace, and passed the night f: 2908
9: 3 with f, and sackcloth, and ashes: 6685
Joe 2:12 and with f, and with weeping, and "
M't 15:32 I will not send them away f, lest 3523
17:21 not out but by prayer and f. *3521
M'r 8: 3 And if I send them away f to their 3523
9:29 by nothing, but by prayer and f. *3521
Ac 10:30 Four days ago I was f until this *3522
14:23 prayed with f, they commended 3521
27:33 ye have tarried and continued f, 777
1Co 7: 5 give yourselves to f and prayer; *3521

fastings
Es 9:31 the matters of the f and their cry. 6685
Lu 2:37 with f and prayers night and day. 3521
2Co 6: 5 in labours, in watchings, in f; "
11:27 in f often, in cold and nakedness. "

fastness See STEDFASTNESS.

fat See also FATFLESHED; FATLING; FATS; FATTED; FATTER; FATTEST; PRESSFAT; WINEFAT.
Ge 4: 4 his flock and of the f thereof. 2459
41: 4 seven well favoured and f kine. 1277
20 did eat up the first seven f kine: "
45:18 ye shall eat the f of the land. 2459
49:20 Out of Asher his bread shall be f, 8082
Ex 23:18 shall the f of my sacrifice remain 2459
29:13 shalt take all the f that covereth "
13 kidneys, and the f that is upon "
22 thou shalt take of the ram the f "
22 the f that covereth the inwards, "
22 and the f that is upon them, "
Le 1: 8 the head, and the f, in order upon 6309
12 his pieces, with his head and his f: "
3: 3 the f that covereth the inwards, 2459
3 all the f that is upon the inwards, "
4 and the f that is on them, "
9 the f thereof, and the whole rump, "
9 the f that covereth the inwards, "
9 all the f that is upon the inwards, "
10 the f that is upon them, which is "
14 the f that covereth the inwards, "
14 all the f that is upon the inwards, "
15 and the f that is upon them, "
16 savour: all the f is the Lord's. "
17 that ye eat neither f nor blood. "
4: 8 shall take off from it all the f of the "
8 the f that covereth the inwards, "
8 and the f that is upon the inwards, "
9 and the f that is upon them, "
19 he shall take all his f from him, "
26 he shall burn all his f upon the "
26 as the f of the sacrifice of "
31 shall take away all the f thereof, "
31 as the f is taken away from off "
35 shall take away all the f thereof, "
35 as the f of the lamb is taken away "
6:12 he shall burn thereon the f of the "
Le 7: 3 offer of it all the f thereof; 2459
3 the f that covereth the inwards, "
4 and the f that is on them, "
23 Ye shall eat no manner of f, "
24 And the f of the beast that dieth "
24 and the f of that which is torn "
25 whosoever eateth the f of the beast, "
30 f with the breast, it shall he bring, "
31 And the priest shall burn the f "
33 the peace offerings, and the f, "
8:16 the f that was upon the inwards, "
16 the two kidneys, and their f, and "
20 head, and the pieces, and the f. 6309
25 he took the f, and the rump, and 2459
25 the f that was upon the inwards, "
25 the two kidneys, and their f, and "
26 and put them on the f, and upon "
9:10 But the f, and the kidneys, and "
19 And the f of the bullock and of the "
20 they put the f upon the breasts, "
20 and he burnt the f upon the altar: "
24 altar the burnt offering and the f: "
10:15 the offerings made by fire of the f, "
16:25 And the f of the sin offering shall "
17: 6 and burn the f for a sweet savour "
Nu 13:20 land is, whether it be f or lean, 8082
18:17 shalt burn their f for an offering 2459
De 31:20 filled themselves, and waxen f; 1878
32:14 with f of lambs, and rams of the 2459
14 with the f of kidneys of wheat; "
15 Jeshurun waxed f, and kicked: 8080
15 art waxen f, thou art grown thick, "
38 did eat the f of their sacrifices, 2459
J'g 3:17 and Eglon was a very f man. 1277
22 and the f closed upon the blade, 2459
1Sa 2:15 Also before they burnt the f, "
16 Let them not fail to burn the f "
29 yourselves f with the chiefest of 1254
15:22 and to hearken than the f of rams. 2459
28:24 And the woman had a f calf *4770
2Sa 1:22 from the f of the mighty, the bow 2459
1Ki 1: 9 slew sheep and oxen and f cattle *4806
19 he hath slain oxen and f cattle * "
25 slain oxen and f cattle and sheep * "
4:23 Ten f oxen, and twenty oxen out 1277
8:64 and the f of the peace offerings: 2459
64 and the f of the peace offerings. "
1Ch 4:40 they found f pasture and good, 8082
2Ch 7: 7 and the f of the peace offerings, 2459
7 the meat offerings, and the f. "
29:35 with the f of the peace offerings, "
35:14 offerings and the f until night; "
Ne 8:10 eat the f, and drink the sweet, 4924
9:25 took strong cities, and a f land, 8082
25 and were filled, and became f, and "
Ne 9:35 and in the large and f land which 8082
Job 15:27 maketh collops of f on his flanks. 6371
Ps 17:10 They are inclosed in their own f: 2459
22:29 All they that be f upon earth shall 1879
37:20 Lord shall be as the f of lambs: †3368
92:14 they shall be f and flourishing; *1879
119:70 Their heart is as f as grease; 2954
Pr 11:25 The liberal soul shall be made f: 1878
13: 4 soul of the diligent shall be made f. "
15:30 a good report maketh the bones f. "
28:25 trust in the Lord shall be made f. "
Isa 1:11 rams, and the f of fed beasts; 2459
5:17 the waste places of the f ones 4220
6:10 Make the heart of this people f, 8082
10:16 send among his f ones leanness; 4924
25: 6 unto all people a feast of f things, 8081
6 of f things full of marrow, "
28: 1 are on the head of the f valleys of "
4 which is on the head of the f valley, "
30:23 and it shall be f and plenteous: 1879
34: 6 it is made f with fatness, 1878
6 with the f of the kidneys of rams: 2459
7 their dust made f with fatness. 1878
43:24 hast thou filled me with the f of 2459
58:11 drought, and make f thy bones: *2502
Jer 5:28 They are waxen f, they shine: 8080
50:11 ye are grown f as the heifer *6335
Eze 34: 3 Ye eat the f, and ye clothe you 2459
14 in a f pasture shall they feed 8082
16 will destroy the f and the strong; "
20 I will judge between the f cattle 1277
39:19 And ye shall eat f till ye be full, 2459
44: 7 my bread, the f and the blood, "
15 offer unto me the f and the blood, "
45:15 out of the f pastures of Israel: ‡4945
Am 5:22 peace offerings of your f beasts. 4806
Hab 1:16 by them their portion is f, 8082
Zec 11:16 but he shall eat the flesh of the f, 1277

fatfleshed
Ge 41: 2 seven well favoured kine and f; 1277
18 seven kine, f and well favoured; "

father See also FATHERLESS; FATHER'S; FATHERS.
Ge 2:24 a man leave his f and his mother, 1
4:20 was the f of such as dwell in tents, "
21 the f of all such as handle the harp "
9:18 and Ham is the f of Canaan. "
22 And Ham, the f of Canaan, saw the "
22 saw the nakedness of his f, "
23 and covered the nakedness of their f; "
10:21 Shem also, the f of all the children "
11:28 And Haran died before his f Terah "
29 the f of Milcah, and the f of Iscah. "
17: 4 thou shalt be a f of many nations. "
5 f of many nations have I made thee. "
19:31 Our f is old, and there is not a man "
32 Come, let us make our f drink wine, "
32 that we may preserve seed of our f. "
33 made their f drink wine that night: "
33 firstborn went in, and lay with her f; "
34 Behold, I lay yesternight with my f: "
34 that we may preserve seed of our f. "
35 And they made their f drink wine "
36 of Lot with child by their f. "
37 the same is the f of the Moabites "
38 is the f of the children of Ammon "
20:12 she is the daughter of my f, but not "
22: 7 Abraham his f, and said, My f: "
21 and Kemuel the f of Aram, "
26: 3 which I swear unto Abraham thy f; "
15 digged in the days of Abraham his f, "
18 digged in the days of Abraham his f; "
18 by which his f had called them. "
24 I am the God of Abraham thy f; "
27: 6 I heard thy f speak unto Esau thy "
9 make them savoury meat for thy f, "
10 And thou shalt bring it to thy f, "
12 My f peradventure will feel me, "
14 savoury meat, such as his f loved. "
18 came unto his f, and said, My f: "
19 And Jacob said unto his f, I am Esau "
22 Jacob went near unto Isaac his f; "
26 And his f Isaac said unto him, Come "
30 out from the presence of Isaac his f, "
31 and brought it unto his f, and said "
31 and said unto his f, Let my f arise, "
32 And Isaac his f said unto him, Who "
34 when Esau heard the words of his f, "
34 and said unto his f, Bless me, even "
34 Bless me, even me also, O my f. "
38 Esau said unto his f, Hast thou but "
38 but one blessing, my f? bless me, "
38 bless me, even me also, O my f. "
39 And Isaac his f answered and said "
41 the blessing wherewith his f blessed "
41 the days of mourning for my f are at "
28: 2 the house of Bethuel thy mother's f; "
7 Jacob obeyed his f and his mother, "
8 of Canaan pleased not Isaac his f; "
13 am the Lord God of Abraham thy f, "
29:12 and she ran and told her f. "
31: 5 the God of my f hath been with me. "
6 all my power I have served your f. "
7 And your f hath deceived me, and "
9 hath taken away the cattle of your f, "
16 which God hath taken from our f, "
18 for to go to Isaac his f in the land "
29 but the God of your f spake unto me "
35 And she said to her f, Let it not "
42 Except the God of my f, the God of "
53 the God of their f, judge betwixt us. "
53 sware by the fear of his f Isaac. "
32: 9 Jacob said, O God of my f Abraham, "
9 and God of my f Isaac, the Lord

Ge 33:19 children of Hamor, Shechem's f, 1
34: 4 Shechem spake unto his f Hamor, "
6 Hamor the f of Shechem went out "
11 Shechem said unto her f and unto "
13 answered Shechem and Hamor his f "
19 than all the house of his f. "
35:18 but his f called him Benjamin. "
27 Jacob came unto Isaac his f unto "
36: 9 of Esau the f of the Edomites in "
24 as he fed the asses of Zibeon his f. "
43 he is Esau the f of the Edomites. "
37: 1 wherein his f was a stranger, * "
2 brought unto his f their evil report. "
4 saw that their f loved him more than "
10 And he told it to his f, and to his "
10 and his f rebuked him, and said "
11 but his f observed the saying. "
22 to deliver him to his f again. "
32 they brought it to their f; and said, "
35 Thus his f wept for him. "
38:13 thy f in law goeth up to Timnath 2524
25 she sent to her f in law, saying, "
42:13 the youngest is this day with our f. 1
29 And they came unto Jacob their f "
32 be twelve brethren, sons of our f; "
32 the youngest is this day with our f "
35 they and their f saw the bundles "
36 And Jacob their f said unto them, "
37 Reuben spake unto his f, saying, "
43: 2 their f said unto them, Go again, "
7 Is your f yet alive? have ye another "
8 And Judah said unto Israel his f, "
11 And their f Israel said unto them, "
23 the God of your f, hath given you "
27 and said, Is your f well, the old man "
28 Thy servant our f is in good health, "
44:17 get you up in peace unto your f. "
19 saying, Have ye a f, or a brother? "
20 my lord, We have a f, an old man, "
20 his mother, and his f loveth him. "
22 The lad cannot leave his f: "
22 for if he should leave his f, "
22 his f would die. "
24 we came up unto thy servant my f, 1
25 And our f said, Go again, and buy "
27 thy servant my f said unto us, "
30 when I come to thy servant my f, "
31 the gray hairs of thy servant our f "
32 became surety for the lad unto my f, "
32 then I shall bear the blame to my f "
34 For how shall I go up to my f, "
34 see the evil that shall come on my f. "
45: 3 I am Joseph; doth my f yet live? "
8 he hath made me a f to Pharaoh, "
9 Haste ye, and go up to my f, "
13 tell my f of all my glory in Egypt, "
13 haste and bring down my f hither. "
18 take your f and your households, 1
19 and bring your f, and come. "
23 to his f he sent after his manner; "
23 and meat for his f by the way. "
25 land of Canaan unto Jacob their f, "
27 the spirit of Jacob their f revived: "
46: 1 sacrifices unto the God of his f Isaac. "
3 I am God, the God of thy f: "
5 carried Jacob their f, and their "
29 and went up to meet Israel his f, "
47: 1 and said, My f and my brethren, and "
5 Thy f and thy brethren are come "
6 make thy f and brethren to dwell; "
7 And Joseph brought in Jacob his f, "
11 placed his f and his brethren, and "
12 nourished his f, and his brethren, "
48: 1 told Joseph, Behold, thy f is sick: "
9 Joseph said unto his f, They are "
17 Joseph saw that his f laid his right "
18 said unto his f, Not so, my f: for "
19 his f refused, and said, I know it, "
49: 2 and hearken unto Israel your f. "
25 Even by the God of thy f, who shall "
26 The blessings of thy f have prevailed "
28 is it that their f spake unto them, "
50: 2 the physicians to embalm his f: "
5 My f made me swear, saying, Lo, "
5 go up, I pray thee, and bury my f, "
6 Pharaoh said, Go up, and bury thy f, "
7 And Joseph went up to bury his f: "
10 a mourning for his f seven days. "
14 went up with him to bury his f, "
14 after he had buried his f. "
15 brethren saw that their f was dead, "
16 Thy f did command before he died, "
17 the servants of the God of thy f. "
Ex 2:18 when they came to Reuel their f, "
3: 1 the flock of Jethro his f in law, 2859
6 I am the God of thy f, 1
4:18 returned to Jethro his f in law, 2859
18: 1 priest of Midian, Moses' f in law, "
2 Then Jethro, Moses' f in law, took "
4 God of my f, said he, was mine help, 1
5 Jethro, Moses' f in law, came with 2859
6 I thy f in law Jethro am come unto "
7 went out to meet his f in law, "
8 And Moses told his f in law all that "
12 And Jethro, Moses' f in law, took a "
12 to eat bread with Moses' f in law "
14 when Moses' f in law saw that he "
15 And Moses said unto his f in law, "
17 And Moses' f in law said unto him, "
24 hearkened to the voice of his f in "
27 And Moses let his f in law depart; "
20:12 Honour thy f and thy mother: 1
21:15 he that smiteth his f, or his mother "
17 he that curseth his f, or his mother "
22:17 If her f utterly refuse to give her "
40:15 as thou didst anoint their f, "
Le 18: 7 The nakedness of thy f, or the 1
9 thy sister, the daughter of thy f, "
11 begotten of thy f, she is thy sister, "
19: 3 every man his mother, and his f, "
20: 9 For every man that curseth his f "
9 he hath cursed his f or his mother; "
21: 2 for his mother, and for his f, "
9 she profaneth her f: she shall be "
11 nor defile himself for his f, "
24:10 whose f was an Egyptian, 1121, 376
Nu 3: 4 office in the sight of Aaron their f. 1
24 chief of the house of the f of the * "
30 f of the families of the Kohathites* "
35 the f of the families of Merari * "
6: 7 not make himself unclean for his f, "
10:29 the Midianite, Moses' f in law, 2859
11:12 nursing f beareth the sucking child, "
12:14 If her f had but spit in her face, 1
18: 2 the tribe of Levi, the tribe of thy f, "
27: 3 Our f died in the wilderness, "
4 the name of our f be done away "
4 among the brethren of our f. "
7 inheritance of their f to pass unto "
11 And if his f have no brethren, "
30: 4 her f hear her vow, and her bond "
4 her f shall hold his peace at her: "
5 if her f disallow her in the day "
5 because her f disallowed her. "
16 between the f and his daughter, "
36: 6 the tribe of their f shall they marry. "
8 the family of the tribe of her f, "
12 the tribe of the family of their f. "
De 5:16 Honour thy f and thy mother, "
21:13 and bewail her f and her mother "
18 will not obey the voice of his f, "
19 shall his f and his mother lay hold "
22:15 Then shall the f of the damsel, "
16 And the damsel's f shall say "
19 give them unto the f of the damsel, "
29 shall give unto the damsel's f fifty "
26: 5 A Syrian ready to perish was my f, "
27:16 be he that setteth light by his f "
22 with his sister, the daughter of his f, "
32: 6 is not he thy f that hath bought thee? "
7 ask thy f, and he will shew thee; "
33: 9 Who said unto his f and to his mother, "
Jos 2:13 that ye will save alive my f, "
18 shalt bring thy f, and thy mother, "
6:23 brought out Rahab, and her f, and "
15:13 the city of Arba the f of Anak, "
18 she moved him to ask of her f a field: "
17: 1 of Manasseh, the f of Gilead: "
4 among the brethren of our f. "
19:47 after the name of Dan their f. "
21:11 the city of Arba the f of Anak, "
24: 2 Terah, the f of Abraham, and the f "
3 took your f Abraham from the other "
32 the sons of Hamor the f of Shechem "
J'g 1:14 she moved him to ask of her f a field: "
16 Moses' f in law, went up out of *2859
4:11 Hobab the f in law of Moses, * "
6:25 the altar of Baal that thy f hath, 1
8:32 Joash his f, in Ophrah of the "
9: 1 of the house of his mother's f, "
17 my f fought for you, and adventured "
28 the men of Hamor the f of Shechem: "
56 Abimelech, which he did unto his f, "
11:36 And she said unto him, My f, if thou "
37 she said unto her f, Let this thing "
39 she returned unto her f, who did "
14: 2 up, and told his f and his mother, "
3 his f and his mother said unto him, "
3 Samson said unto his f, Get her for "
4 But his f and his mother knew not "
5 went Samson down, and his f and "
6 he told not his f or his mother "
9 came to his f and mother, and he "
10 So his f went down unto the woman: "
16 have not told it my f nor my mother, "
15: 1 her f would not suffer him to go in. "
2 And her f said, I verily thought "
6 and burnt her and her f with fire. "
16:31 brethren and all the house of his f "
31 the burying-place of Manoah his f. "
17:10 and be unto me a f and a priest, "
18:19 and be to us a f and a priest: "
29 after the name of Dan their f, "
19: 3 when the f of the damsel saw him, "
4 And his f in law,...retained him; 2859
4 law, the damsel's f, retained him; 1
5 damsel's f said unto his son in law, "
6 damsel's f had said unto the man, "
7 his f in law urged him: therefore 2859
8 damsel's f said, Comfort thine heart, 1
9 his f in law,...said unto him, Behold 2859
9 law, the damsel's f, said unto him, 1
Ru 2:11 thou hast left thy f and thy mother, "
4:17 he is the f of Jesse, the f of David. "
1Sa 2:25 not unto the voice of their f, "
27 appear unto the house of thy f, "
28 did I give unto the house of thy f "
30 thy house, and the house of thy f, "
4:19 that her f in law and her husband 2524
21 of her f in law and her husband. "
9: 3 the asses of Kish Saul's f were lost. 1
5 lest my f leave caring for the asses, "
10: 2 thy f hath left the care of the asses, "
12 and said, But who is their f? "
14: 1 But he told not his f. "
27 But Jonathan heard not when his f "
28 Thy f straightly charged the people "
29 My f hath troubled the land: "
51 Kish was the f of Saul; and Ner the "
51 the f of Abner was the son of Abiel. "
19: 2 Saul my f seeketh to kill thee: "
3 stand beside my f in the field "
1Sa 19: 3 I will commune with my f of thee; 1
4 spake good of David unto Saul his f, "
20: 1 and what is my sin before thy f, "
2 behold, my f will do nothing either "
2 and why should my f hide this thing "
3 Thy f certainly knoweth that I have "
6 If thy f at all miss me, then say, "
8 shouldest thou bring me to thy f? "
9 determined by my f to come upon "
10 what if thy f answer thee roughly? "
12 when I have sounded my f about "
13 but if it please my f to do thee evil, "
13 as he hath been with my f. "
32 Jonathan answered Saul his f, and "
33 it was determined of his f to slay "
34 because his f had done him shame. "
22: 3 Let my f and my mother, I pray "
15 nor to all the house of my f: "
23:17 the hand of Saul my f shall not find "
17 and that also Saul my f knoweth. "
24:11 Moreover, my f, see, yea, see the "
2Sa 2:32 buried him in the sepulchre of his f, "
3: 8 this day unto the house of Saul thy f, "
6:21 Lord, which chose me before thy f, "
7:14 I will be his f, and he shall be my "
9: 7 thee all the land of Saul thy f; "
10: 2 as his f shewed kindness unto me. "
2 by the hand of his servants for his f. "
3 thou that David doth honour thy f, "
13: 5 and when thy f cometh to see thee, "
16: 3 restore me the kingdom of my f. "
21 that thou art abhorred of thy f: "
17: 8 thou knowest thy f and his men, "
8 and thy f is a man of war, and will "
10 knoweth that thy f is a mighty man, "
23 was buried in the sepulchre of his f. "
19:37 and be buried by the grave of my f "
21:14 in the sepulchre of Kish his f: "
1Ki 1: 6 his f had not displeased him at any "
2:12 upon the throne of David his f; "
24 set me on the throne of David my f, "
26 ark of the Lord before David my f, "
26 in all wherein my f was afflicted. "
31 me, and from the house of my f. * "
32 my f David not knowing thereof, "
44 that thou didst to David my f: "
3: 3 in the statutes of David his f: "
6 shewed unto thy servant David my f "
7 servant king instead of David my f: "
14 as thy f David did walk, then I will "
5: 1 him king in the room of his f: "
3 Thou knowest how that David my f "
5 the Lord spake unto David my f, "
6:12 which I spake unto David thy f: "
7:14 and his f was a man of Tyre, "
51 which David his f had dedicated; "
8:15 with his mouth unto David my f, "
17 And it was in the heart of David my f "
18 and the Lord said unto David my f, "
20 risen up in the room of David my f, "
24 kept with thy servant David my f "
25 keep with thy servant David my f "
26 thou unto thy servant David my f. "
9: 4 before me, as David thy f walked, "
5 as I promised to David thy f, "
11: 4 as was the heart of David his f. "
6 after the Lord, as did David his f. "
27 breaches of the city of David his f. "
33 my judgments, as did David his f. "
43 was buried in the city of David his f: "
12: 4 Thy f made our yoke grievous: "
4 thou the grievous service of thy f, "
6 that stood before Solomon his f "
9 yoke which thy f did put upon us "
10 saying, Thy f made our yoke heavy, "
11 whereas my f did lade you with "
11 my f hath chastised you with whips, "
14 My f made your yoke heavy, and "
14 my f also chastised you with whips, "
13:11 them they told also to their f. "
12 their f said unto them, What way "
15: 3 he walked in all the sins of his f, "
3 his God, as the heart of David his f. "
11 eyes of the Lord, as did David his f. "
15 things which his f had dedicated, "
19 thee, and between my f and thy f: "
24 fathers in the city of David his f; "
26 and walked in the way of his f, "
19:20 thee, kiss my f and my mother, "
20:34 cities, which my f took from thy f, "
34 Damascus, as my f made in Samaria. "
22:43 walked in the ways of Asa his f; "
46 which remained in the days of his f "
50 fathers in the city of David his f; "
52 and walked in the way of his f, "
53 according to all that his f had done. "
2Ki 2:12 My f, my f, the chariot of Israel, "
3: 2 not like his f, and like his mother: "
2 image of Baal that his f had made. "
13 get thee to the prophets of thy f, "
4:18 he went out to his f to the reapers. "
19 he said unto his f, My head, my head. "
5:13 My f, if the prophet had bid thee do "
6:21 My f, shall I smite them? shall I "
9:25 thou rode together after Ahab his f, "
13:14 and said, O my f, my f, the chariot "
25 the hand of Jehoahaz his f by war. "
14: 3 yet not like David his f: "
3 to all things as Joash his f did. "
5 which had slain the king his f. "
21 him king instead of his f Amaziah. "
15: 3 to all that his f Amaziah had done; "
34 to all that his f Uzziah had done. "
38 fathers in the city of David his f: "
16: 2 Lord his God, like David his f. "
18: 3 according to all that David his f did. "

2Ki 20: 5 the Lord, the God of David thy *f*, 1
21: 3 which Hezekiah his *f* had destroyed; "
20 of the Lord, as his *f* Manasseh did. "
21 all the way that his *f* walked in, "
21 served the idols that his *f* served, "
22: 2 walked in all the way of David his *f*, "
23:34 king in the room of Josiah his *f*, "
24: 9 according to all that his *f* had done. "
1Ch 2:17 and the *f* of Amasa was Jether "
21 daughter of Machir the *f* of Gilead, "
23 the sons of Machir the *f* of Gilead. "
24 bare him Ashur the *f* of Tekoa. "
42 which was the *f* of Ziph; and the "
42 sons of Mareshah the *f* of Hebron. "
44 begat Raham, the *f* of Jorkoam: "
45 and Maon was the *f* of Beth-zur. "
49 Shaaph the *f* of Madmannah, "
49 Sheva the *f* of Machbenah, "
49 and the *f* of Gibea: "
50 Shobal the *f* of Kirjath-jearim, "
51 Salma the *f* of Beth-lehem, "
51 Hareph the *f* of Beth-gader. "
52 Shobal the *f* of Kirjath-jearim had "
55 the *f* of the house of Rechab. "
4: 3 And these were of the *f* of Etam; "
4 Penuel the *f* of Gedor, "
4 and Ezer the *f* of Hushah. "
4 of Ephratah, the *f* of Beth-lehem. "
5 Ashur the *f* of Tekoa had two wives, "
11 Mehir, which was the *f* of Eshton. "
12 and Tehinnah the *f* of Ir-nahash. "
14 Joab the *f* of the valley of Charashim, "
17 and Ishbah the *f* of Eshtemoa. "
18 bare Jered the *f* of Gedor, "
18 and Heber the *f* of Socho, "
18 and Jekuthiel the *f* of Zanoah. "
19 of Naham, the *f* of Keilah the "
21 were, Er the *f* of Lecah, "
21 and Laadah the *f* of Mareshah, "
7:14 bare Machir the *f* of Gilead: "
22 Ephraim their *f* mourned many "
31 Malchiel, who is the *f* of Birzavith. "
8:29 at Gibeon dwelt the *f* of Gibeon 25
9:19 the house of his *f*, the Korahites,* 1
35 in Gibeon dwelt the *f* of Gibeon, 25
17:13 will be his *f*, and he shall be my son: 1
19: 2 because his *f* shewed kindness to me. "
2 to comfort him concerning his *f*. "
3 thou that David doth honour thy *f*, "
22:10 be my son, and I will be his *f*; "
24: 2 Nadab and Abihu died before their *f*, "
19 their manner, under Aaron their *f*, "
25: 3 under the hands of their *f* Jeduthun, "
6 were under the hands of their *f* "
26: 6 throughout the house of their *f*: "
10 yet his *f* made him the chief;) "
28: 4 me before all the house of my *f* "
4 house of Judah, the house of my *f*; "
4 among the sons of my *f* he liked me "
6 him to be my son, and I will be his *f*. "
9 my son, know thou the God of thy *f*, "
29:10 of Israel our *f*, for ever and ever. "
23 as king instead of David his *f*, "
2Ch 1: 8 great mercy unto David my *f*, "
9 unto David my *f* be established: "
2: 3 As thou didst deal with David my *f*, "
7 whom David my *f* did provide. "
14 and his *f* was a man of Tyre, "
14 cunning men of my lord David thy *f*. "
17 David his *f* had numbered them; "
3: 1 the Lord appeared unto David his *f*, "
4:16 instruments did Huram his *f* make "
5: 1 that David his *f* had dedicated; "
6: 4 with his mouth to my *f* David, "
7 Now it was in the heart of David my *f* "
8 But the Lord said to David my *f*, "
10 risen up in the room of David my *f*, "
15 kept with thy servant David my *f* "
16 keep with thy servant David my *f* "
7:17 before me as David thy *f* walked, "
18 I have covenanted with David thy *f*, "
8:14 to the order of David his *f*, "
9:31 was buried in the city of David his *f*: "
10: 4 Thy *f* made our yoke grievous: "
4 the grievous servitude of thy *f*, "
6 had stood before Solomon his *f* "
9 yoke that thy *f* did put upon us? "
10 Thy *f* made our yoke heavy, but "
11 my *f* put a heavy yoke upon you, "
11 my *f* chastised you with whips, but I "
14 My *f* made your yoke heavy, but I "
14 my *f* chastised you with whips, but I "
15:18 the things that his *f* had dedicated, "
16: 3 there was between my *f* and thy *f*: "
17: 2 Ephraim, which Asa his *f* had taken. "
3 in the first ways of his *f* David, "
4 sought to the Lord God of his *f*, "
20:32 he walked in the way of Asa his *f*, "
21: 3 And their *f* gave them great gifts of "
4 risen up to the kingdom of his *f*, "
12 the Lord God of David thy *f*, "
12 in the ways of Jehoshaphat thy *f*, "
22: 4 death of his *f* to his destruction, "
24:22 Jehoiada his *f* had done to him, "
25: 3 that had killed the king his *f*. "
26: 1 king in the room of his *f* Amaziah. "
4 according to all that his *f* Amaziah "
27: 2 according to all that his *f* Uzziah "
28: 1 sight of the Lord, like David his *f*: "
29: 2 to all that David his *f* had done. "
33: 3 Hezekiah his *f* had broken down, "
22 as did Manasseh his *f*; for Amon 1
22 which Manasseh his *f* had made, "
23 as Manasseh his *f* had humbled "
34: 2 walked in the ways of David his *f*, "
3 to seek after the God of David his *f*: "

Es 2: 7 for she had neither *f* nor mother, 1
7 when her *f* and mother were dead, "
Job 15:10 aged men, much elder than thy *f*. "
17:14 said to corruption, Thou art my *f*: "
29:16 I was a *f* to the poor: and the cause "
31:18 was brought up with me, as with a *f*, "
38:28 Hath the rain a *f*? or who hath "
42:15 and their *f* gave them inheritance "
Ps 27:10 my *f* and my mother forsake me, "
68: 5 A *f* of the fatherless, and a judge of "
89:26 He shall cry unto me, Thou art my *f*, "
103:13 Like as a *f* pitieth his children, so "
Pr 1: 8 My son, hear the instruction of thy *f*, "
3:12 as a *f* the son in whom he delighteth. "
4: 1 ye children, the instruction of a *f*, "
10: 1 A wise son maketh a glad *f*: but a "
15:20 A wise son maketh a glad *f*: but a "
17:21 and the *f* of a fool hath no joy. "
25 A foolish son is a grief to his *f*, and "
19:13 foolish son is the calamity of his *f*: "
26 that wasteth his *f*, and chaseth †‡ "
20:20 Whoso curseth his *f* or his mother, "
23:22 Hearken unto thy *f* that begat thee, "
24 The *f* of the righteous shall greatly "
25 Thy *f* and thy mother shall be glad, "
28: 7 of riotous men shameth his *f*. "
24 Whoso robbeth his *f* or his mother, "
29: 3 loveth wisdom rejoiceth his *f*: but he "
30:11 is a generation that curseth their *f*, "
17 The eye that mocketh at his *f*, and "
Isa 3: 6 of his brother of the house of his *f*, "
8: 4 to cry, My *f*, and my mother, "
9: 6 everlasting *F*, The Prince of Peace. "
22:21 and he shall be a *f* to the inhabitants "
38: 5 the Lord, the God of David thy *f*, "
19 *f* to the children shall make known "
43:27 Thy first *f* hath sinned, and thy "
45:10 Woe unto him that saith unto his *f*, "
51: 2 Look unto Abraham your *f*, and "
58:14 with the heritage of Jacob thy *f*: "
63:16 Doubtless thou art our *f*, though "
16 thou, O Lord, art our *f*, our "
64: 8 But now, O Lord, thou art our *f*; "
Jer 2:27 Saying to a stock, Thou art my *f*; "
3: 4 My *f*, thou art the guide of my youth? "
19 I said, Thou shalt call me, My *f*; "
12: 6 thy brethren, and the house of thy *f*, "
16: 7 drink for their *f* or for their mother. "
20:15 man who brought tidings to my *f*, "
22:11 which reigned instead of Josiah his *f*, "
15 did not thy *f* eat and drink, and do "
31: 9 for I am a *f* to Israel, and Ephraim "
35: 6 our *f* commanded us, saying, Ye shall "
8 for Jonadab the son of Rechab our *f* "
10 that Jonadab our *f* commanded us. "
16 the commandment of their *f*, "
18 commandment of Jonadab your *f*, "
Eze 16: 3 thy *f* was an Amorite, and thy mother "
45 an Hittite, and your *f* an Amorite. "
18: 4 souls are mine; as the soul of the *f*, "
17 shall not die for the iniquity of his *f*, "
18 As for his *f*, because he cruelly "
19 the son bear the iniquity of the *f*? "
20 shall not bear the iniquity of the *f*, "
20 neither shall the *f* bear the iniquity "
22: 7 have they set light by *f* and mother: "
44:25 but for *f*, or for mother, or for son, "
Da 5: 2 golden and silver vessels which his *f* 2
11 and in the days of thy *f* light and "
11 the king Nebuchadnezzar thy *f*, "
11 the king, I say, thy *f*, made master "
13 the king my *f* brought out of Jewry? "
18 God gave Nebuchadnezzar thy *f* a "
Am 2: 7 a man and his *f* will go in unto the "
Mic 7: 6 For the son dishonoureth the *f*, the "
Zec 13: 3 then his *f* and his mother that begat "
3 and his *f* and his mother that begat "
Mal 1: 6 A son honoureth his *f*, and a servant "
6 then I be a *f*, where is mine honour? "
2:10 Have we not all one *f*? hath not one "
M't 2:22 Judæa in the room of his *f* Herod, 3962
3: 9 We have Abraham to our *f*: for I "
4:21 in a ship with Zebedee their *f*, "
22 left the ship and their *f*, and "
5:16 glorify your *F* which is in heaven. "
45 ye may be the children of your *F* "
48 even as your *F* which is in heaven "
6: 1 of your *F* which is in heaven. "
4 and thy *F* which seeth in secret "
6 pray to thy *F* which is in secret; "
6 and thy *F* which seeth in secret "
8 your *F* knoweth what things ye "
9 *F* which art in heaven, Hallowed "
14 your heavenly *F* will also forgive "
15 neither will your *F* forgive your "
18 but unto thy *F* which is in secret: "
18 and thy *F*, which seeth in secret, "
26 yet your heavenly *F* feedeth them. "
32 for your heavenly *F* knoweth that "
7:11 how much more shall your *F* which "
21 he that doeth the will of my *F* "
8:21 suffer me first to go and bury my *f*. "
10:20 Spirit of your *F* which speaketh "
21 the *f* the child: and the children "
29 fall on the ground without your *F*. "
32 will I confess also before my *F* "
33 him will I also deny before my *F* "
35 set a man at variance against his *f*, "
37 He that loveth *f* or mother more "
11:25 I thank thee, O *F*, Lord of heaven "
26 Even so, *F*: for so it seemed good "
27 delivered unto me of my *F*: and no "
27 man knoweth the Son, but the *F*; "
27 neither knoweth any man the *F*, "
12:50 whosoever shall do the will of my *F* "
13:43 the sun in the kingdom of their *F*. "

M't 15: 4 Honour thy *f* and mother: and, 3962
4 He that curseth *f* or mother, let him "
5 Whosoever shall say to his *f* or his "
6 And honour not his *f* or his mother, "
13 my heavenly *F* hath not planted, "
16:17 but my *F* which is in heaven. "
27 shall come in the glory of his *F* "
18:10 do always behold the face of my *F* "
14 Even so it is not the will of your *F* "
19 it shall be done for them of my *F* "
35 shall my heavenly *F* do also unto "
19: 5 shall a man leave *f* and mother, "
19 Honour thy *f* and thy mother: "
29 or brethren, or sisters, or *f*, or "
20:23 for whom it is prepared of my *F*. "
21:31 them twain did the will of his *f*? "
23: 9 call no man your *f* upon the earth: "
9 one is your *F*, which is in heaven. "
24:36 angels in heaven, but my *F* only. "
25:34 Come, ye blessed of my *F*, inherit "
26:39 O my *F*, if it be possible, let this "
42 O my *F*, if this cup may not pass "
53 that I cannot now pray to my *F*, "
28:19 baptizing them in the name of the *F*, "
M'r 1:20 they left their *f* Zebedee in the ship "
5:40 he taketh the *f* and the mother of "
7:10 Honour thy *f* and thy mother; and "
10 Whoso curseth *f* or mother, let him "
11 If a man shall say to his *f* or mother, "
12 him no more to do ought for his *f* "
8:38 cometh in the glory of his *F* with the "
9:21 he asked his *f*, How long is it ago "
24 And straightway the *f* of the child "
10: 7 this cause shall a man leave his *f* "
19 not, Honour thy *f* and mother. "
29 brethren, or sisters, or *f*, or mother, "
11:10 be the kingdom of our *f* David, "
25 that your *F* also which is in heaven "
26 neither will your *F* which is in "
13:12 and the *f* the son; and the children "
32 neither the Son, but the *F*. "
14:36 he said, Abba, *F*, all things are "
15:21 *f* of Alexander and Rufus, to bear "
Lu 1:32 unto him the throne of his *f* David: "
59 Zacharias, after the name of his *f*. "
62 And they made signs to his *f*, how "
67 his *f* Zacharias was filled with the "
73 which he sware to our *f* Abraham, "
2:48 behold, thy *f* and I have sought thee "
3: 8 We have Abraham to our *f*: for I "
6:36 merciful, as your *F* also is merciful. "
8:51 *f* and the mother of the maiden. "
9:42 and delivered him again to his *f*. "
59 suffer me first to go and bury my *f*. "
10:21 I thank thee, O *F*, Lord of heaven "
21 even so, *F*; for so it seemed good "
22 things are delivered to me of my *F*: "
22 but the *F*; and who the *F* is, but "
11: 2 say, Our *F* which art in heaven, "
11 bread of any of you that is a *f*, "
13 much more shall your heavenly *F* "
12:30 your *F* knoweth that ye have need "
53 The *f* shall be divided against the "
53 son, and the son against the *f*; "
14:26 and hate not his *f*, and mother, "
15:12 of them said to his *f*, *F*, give me "
18 I will arise and go to my *f*, and "
18 say unto him, *F*, I have sinned "
20 And he arose, and came to his *f*. "
20 his *f* saw him, and had compassion, "
21 *F*, I have sinned against heaven, "
22 But the *f* said to his servants, "
27 and thy *f* hath killed the fatted calf, "
28 therefore came his *f* out, and "
29 said to his *f*, Lo, these many years "
16:24 And he cried and said, *F* Abraham, "
27 I pray thee therefore, *f*, that thou "
30 And he said, Nay, *f* Abraham, but "
18:20 Honour thy *f* and thy mother. "
22:29 as my *F* hath appointed unto me; "
42 Saying, *F*, if thou be willing, "
23:34 *F*, forgive them; for they know "
46 *F*, into thy hands I commend my "
24:49 I send the promise of my *F* upon "
Joh 1:14 as of the only begotten of the *F*,) "
18 in the bosom of the *F*, he hath "
3:35 The *F* loveth the Son, and hath "
4:12 Art thou greater than our *f* Jacob, "
21 nor yet at Jerusalem, worship the *F*. "
23 shall worship the *F* in spirit and "
23 in truth: for the *F* seeketh such to "
53 So the *f* knew that it was at the "
5:17 My *F* worketh hitherto, and I work. "
18 but said also that God was his *F*, "
19 but what he seeth the *F* do: for "
20 For the *F* loveth the Son, and "
21 For as the *F* raiseth up the dead, "
22 For the *F* judgeth no man, but "
23 Son, even as they honour the *F*. "
23 honoureth not the *F* which hath "
26 For as the *F* hath life in himself; "
30 but the will of the *F* which hath * "
36 the works which the *F* hath given "
36 bear witness of me, that the *F* hath "
37 And the *F* himself, which hath sent "
45 that I will accuse you to the *F*: "
6:27 for him hath God the *F* sealed. "
32 but my *F* giveth you the true bread "
37 All that the *F* giveth me shall come "
42 whose *f* and mother we know? "
44 except the *F* which hath sent me "
45 hath learned of the *F*, cometh unto "
46 Not that any man hath seen the *F*, "
46 which is of God, he hath seen the *F*. "
57 As the living *F* hath sent me, and "
57 and I live by the *F*: so he that "

Joh 6:65 it were given unto him of my F. 3962
8:16 but I and the F that sent me. "
18 and the F that sent me beareth "
19 they unto him, Where is thy F? "
19 ye neither know me, nor my F: "
19 ye should have known my F also. "
27 not that he spake to them of the F. "
28 as my F hath taught me, I speak "
29 the F hath not left me alone; * "
38 which I have seen with my F: "
38 which ye have seen with your f. "
39 said unto him, Abraham is our f. "
41 Ye do the deeds of your f. "
41 we have one F, even God. "
42 If God were your F, ye would love "
44 Ye are of your f the devil, and the "
44 and the lusts of your f ye will do: "
44 for he is a liar, and the f of it. "
49 but I honour my F, and ye do "
53 Art thou greater than our f "
54 it is my F that honoureth me; "
56 Your f Abraham rejoiced to see my "
10:15 As the F knoweth me, even so "
15 even so know I the F: "
17 Therefore doth my F love me, "
18 have I received of my F. "
29 My F which gave them me, is "
30 I and my F are one. "
32 have I shewed you from my F; "
36 him, whom the F hath sanctified, "
37 not the works of my F, believe me "
38 that the F is in me, and I in him. "
11:41 F, I thank thee that thou hast "
12:26 serve me, him will my F honour. "
27 F, save me from this hour; but "
28 F, glorify thy name. Then came "
49 but the F which sent me, he gave "
50 even as the F said unto me, so I "
13: 1 depart out of this world unto the F, "
3 that the F had given all things into "
14: 6 cometh unto the F, but by me. "
7 ye should have known my F also: "
8 Lord, shew us the F, and it "
9 hath seen the F; and how sayest "
9 thou then, Shew us the F? "
10 I am in the F, and the F in me? "
10 but the F that dwelleth in me, he "
11 Believe me that I am in the F, "
11 and the F in me: or else believe "
12 shall he do; because I go unto my F. "
13 that the F may be glorified in the "
16 And I will pray the F, and he shall "
20 that I am in my F, and ye in me, "
21 loveth me shall be loved of my F, "
23 and my F will love him, and we "
26 whom the F will send in my name, "
28 because I said, I go unto the F: "
28 for my F is greater than I. "
31 may know that I love the F; and as "
31 as the F gave me commandment, "
15: 1 and my F is the husbandman. "
8 Herein is my F glorified, that ye "
9 As the F hath loved me, so have I "
15 things that I have heard of my F "
16 ye shall ask of the F in my name, "
23 that hateth me hateth my F also. "
24 have they hated both me and my F. "
26 I will send unto you from the F, "
26 which proceedeth from the F, "
16: 3 they have not known the F, nor me. "
10 because I go to my F, and ye see "
15 things that the F hath are mine: "
16 shall see me, because I go to the F. "
17 and, Because I go to the F? "
23 ye shall ask the F in my name, "
25 shall shew you plainly of the F. "
26 that I will pray the F for you: "
27 For the F himself loveth you, "
28 I came forth from the F, and am "
28 leave the world, and go to the F. "
32 alone, because the F is with me. "
17: 1 F, the hour is come; glorify thy "
5 And now, O F, glorify thou me "
11 Holy F, keep through thine own "
21 as thou, F, art in me, and I in thee, "
24 F, I will that they also, whom thou "
25 O righteous F, the world hath not "
18:11 cup which my F hath given me, "
13 for he was f in law to Caiphas, 3995
20:17 I am not yet ascended to my F: 3962
17 I ascend unto my F, and your F, "
21 as my F hath sent me, even so "
Ac 1: 4 but wait for the promise of the F, "
7 the F hath put in his own power. "
2:33 received of the F the promise of "
7: 2 appeared unto our f Abraham, "
4 when his f was dead, he removed "
14 and called his f Jacob to him, "
16 sons of Emmor the f of Sychem. * "
16: 1 but his f was a Greek: 3962
3 knew all that his f was a Greek. "
28: 8 that the f of Publius lay sick of a "
Ro 1: 7 and peace from God our F, and the "
4: 1 our f, as pertaining to the flesh, * "
11 be the f of all them that believe, "
12 And the f of circumcision to them "
12 of that faith of our f Abraham, "
16 Abraham, who is the f of us all, "
17 I have made thee a f of many "
18 become the f of many nations, "
6: 4 the dead by the glory of the F, "
8:15 adoption, whereby we cry, Abba, F. "
9:10 by one, even by our f Isaac; "
15: 6 God, even the F of our Lord Jesus "
1Co 1: 3 and peace, from God our F, and "
8: 6 one God, the F, of whom are all "

1Co 15:24 the kingdom to God, even the F; 3962
2Co 1: 2 from God our F, and from the "
3 even the F of our Lord Jesus "
3 the F of mercies, and the God of "
6:18 And will be a F unto you, and ye "
11:31 The God and F of our Lord Jesus "
Gal 1: 1 and God the F, who raised him "
3 peace from God the F, and from "
4 to the will of God and our F: "
4: 2 until the time appointed of the f. "
6 unto your hearts, crying, Abba, F. "
Eph 1: 2 from God our F, and from "
3 be the God and F of our Lord "
17 the F of glory, may give unto you "
2:18 access by one Spirit unto the F. "
3:14 my knees unto the F of our Lord "
4: 6 One God and F of all, who is above "
5:20 unto God and the F in the name "
31 a man leave his f and mother, "
6: 2 Honour thy f and mother; which "
23 from God the F and the Lord Jesus "
Ph'p 1: 2 from God our F, and from the Lord "
2:11 to the glory of God the F. "
22 as a son with the f, he hath served "
4:20 Now unto God and our F be glory "
Col 1: 2 and peace, from God our F and "
3 God and the F of our Lord Jesus "
12 Giving thanks unto the F, which "
19 For it pleased the F that in him "
2: 2 and of the F, and of Christ; *3962
3:17 thanks to God and the F by him. "
1Th 1: 1 in God the F and in the Lord "
1 and peace, from God our F, and * "
3 in the sight of God and our F; "
2:11 of you, as a f doth his children, "
3:11 Now God himself and our F, and "
13 holiness before God, even our F, "
2Th 1: 1 in God our F and the Lord Jesus "
2 and peace, from God our F and the "
2:16 and God, even our F, which hath "
1Ti 1: 2 peace, from God our F and Jesus "
5: 1 an elder, but intreat him as a f; "
2Ti 1: 2 peace, from God the F and Christ "
Tit 1: 4 and peace, from God the F and the "
Ph'm 3 and peace, from God our F and the "
Heb 1: 5 And again, I will be to him a F, "
7: 3 Without f, without mother, 540
10 he was yet in the loins of his f, 3962
12: 7 for what son is he whom the f "
9 unto the F of spirits, and live? "
Jas 1:17 cometh down from the F of lights, "
27 undefiled before God and the F is "
2:21 Was not Abraham our f justified "
3: 9 bless we God, even the F; and "
1Pe 1: 2 the foreknowledge of God the F, "
3 Blessed be the God and F of our "
17 And if ye call on the F, who "
2Pe 1:17 For he received from God the F "
1Jo 1: 2 eternal life, which was with the F, "
3 our fellowship is with the F, and "
2: 1 we have an advocate with the F, "
13 because ye have known the F. "
15 the love of the F is not in him. "
16 is not of the F, but is of the world. "
22 that denieth the F and the Son. "
23 the Son, the same hath not the F: "
23 acknowledgeth the Son hath the F "
24 continue in the Son, and in the F. 3962
3: 1 of love the F hath bestowed upon "
4:14 F sent the Son to be the Saviour "
5: 7 F, the Word, and the Holy Ghost:* "
2Jo 3 and peace from God the F, and from "
3 the Son of the F, in truth and love. "
4 a commandment from the F. "
9 he hath both the F and the Son. "
Jude 1 that are sanctified by God the F, "
Re 1: 6 and priests unto God and his F; "
2:27 even as I received of my F. "
3: 5 confess his name before my F, "
21 set down with my F in his throne. "

father-in-law See FATHER and LAW.

fatherless
Ex 22:22 not afflict any widow, or f child. 3490
24 be widows, and your children f. "
De 10:18 the judgment of the f and widow, "
14:29 and the stranger, and the f, and "
16:11 and the stranger, and the f, and "
14 the stranger, and the f, and the "
24:17 of the stranger, nor of the f; "
19, 20, 21 for the stranger, for the f, "
26:12 Levite, the stranger, the f, and the "
13 and unto the stranger, to the f, and "
27:19 judgment of the stranger, f, and "
Job 6:27 overwhelm the f, and ye dig a pit "
22: 9 arms of the f have been broken. "
24: 3 They drive away the ass of the f, "
9 They pluck the f from the breast, "
29:12 the poor that cried, and the f, and "
31:17 and the f hath not eaten thereof; "
21 lifted up my hand against the f, "
Ps 10:14 thou art the helper of the f. "
18 to judge the f and the oppressed, "
68: 5 A father of the f, and a judge of "
82: 3 Defend the poor and f: do justice "
94: 6 the stranger, and murder the f. "
109: 9 Let his children be f, and his wife "
12 be any to favour his f children. "
146: 9 he relieveth the f and widow: but "
Pr 23:10 enter not into the fields of the f: "
Isa 1:17 judge the f, plead for the widow. "
23 they judge not the f, neither doth "
9:17 neither shall have mercy on their f "
10: 2 and that they may rob the f! "
Jer 5:28 not the cause, the cause of the f, "
7: 6 oppress not the stranger, the f, and "

Jer 22: 3 no violence to the stranger, the f, 3490
49:11 Leave thy f children, I will preserve "
La 5: 3 We are orphans and f, our 369, 1
Eze 22: 7 in thee have they vexed the f and 3490
Ho 14: 3 for in thee the f findeth mercy. "
Zec 7:10 oppress not the widow, nor the f, "
Mal 3: 5 in his wages, the widow, and the f, "
Jas 1:27 To visit the f and widows in their 3737

father's
Ge 9:23 and they saw not their f nakedness. 1
12: 1 thy kindred, and from thy f house, "
20:13 me to wander from my f house, "
24: 7 which took me from my f house, "
23 is there room in thy f house for us to "
38 But thou shalt go unto my f house, "
40 of my kindred, and of my f house: "
26:15 which his f servants had digged in "
28:21 So that I come again to my f house "
29: 9 Rachel came with her f sheep: for "
12 told Rachel that he was her f brother, "
31: 1 taken away all that was our f; and "
1 that which was our f hath he gotten "
5 I see your f countenance, that it is "
14 inheritance for us in our f house? "
19 stolen the images that were her f. "
30 thou sore longedst after thy f house, "
35:22 and lay with Bilhah his f concubine: "
37: 2 with the sons of Zilpah, his f wives: "
12 brethren went to feed their f flock "
38:11 Remain a widow at thy f house, "
11 Tamar went and dwelt in her f house. "
41:51 forget all my toil, and all my f house. "
46:31 his brethren, and unto his f house, "
31 My brethren, and my f house, "
47:12 brethren, and all his f household, "
48:17 and he held up his f hand, "
49: 4 thou wentest up to thy f bed; "
8 thy f children shall bow down before "
50: 1 And Joseph fell upon his f face, "
8 and his brethren, and his f house: "
22 dwelt in Egypt, he, and his f house: "
Ex 2:16 the troughs to water their f flock. "
6:20 him Jochebed his f sister to wife 1733
15: 2 my f God, and I will exalt him 1
Le 16:32 in the priest's office in his f stead. "
18: 8 The nakedness of thy f wife shalt "
8 not uncover: it is thy f nakedness. "
11 nakedness of thy f wife's daughter, "
12 uncover the nakedness of thy f sister: "
12 she is thy f near kinswoman. "
14 the nakedness of thy f brother, "
20:11 the man that lieth with his f wife "
11 hath uncovered his f nakedness: "
17 shall take his sister, his f daughter, "
19 mother's sister, nor of thy f sister: "
22:13 and is returned unto her f house, "
13 she shall eat of her f meat: "
Nu 2: 2 with the ensign of their f house: "
18: 1 and thy sons and thy f house * "
27: 7 inheritance among their f brethren; "
10 his inheritance unto his f brethren. "
30: 3 being in her f house in her youth; "
16 yet in her youth in her f house. "
36:11 unto their f brothers' sons: 1730
De 22:21 damsel to the door of her f house, 1
21 to play the whore in her f house: "
30 A man shall not take his f wife, "
30 nor discover his f skirt. "
27:20 be he that lieth with his f wife; "
20 because he uncovereth his f skirt. "
Jos 2:12 shew kindness unto my f house, "
18 all thy f household, home unto thee. "
6:25 the harlot alive, and her f household, "
J'g 6:15 and I am the least in my f house. "
25 Take thy f young bullock, even the "
27 because he feared his f household, "
9: 5 he went unto his f house at Ophrah, "
18 ye are risen up against my f house "
11: 2 Thou shalt not inherit our f house; "
7 and expel me out of my f house? "
14:15 lest we burn thee and thy f house "
19 and he went up to his f house. "
19: 2 away from him unto her f house "
3 she brought him into her f house: "
1Sa 2:31 thine arm, and the arm of thy f house, "
9:20 not on thee, and on all thy f house? "
17:15 to feed his f sheep at Beth-lehem. "
25 and make his f house free in Israel. "
34 Thy servant kept his f sheep, "
18: 2 him go no more home to his f house. "
18 is my life, or my f family in Israel, "
22: 1 when his brethren and all his f house "
11 son of Ahitub, and all his f house, "
16 Ahimelech, thou, and all thy f house. "
22 of all the persons of thy f house. "
24:21 destroy my name out of my f house. "
2Sa 3: 7 thou gone in unto my f concubine? "
29 head of Joab, and on all his f house; "
9: 7 kindness for Jonathan thy f sake, "
14: 9 be on me, and on my f house: "
15:34 as I have been thy f servant hitherto, "
16:19 as I have served in thy f presence, "
21 Go in unto thy f concubines, which "
22 went in unto his f concubines in the "
19:28 of my f house were but dead men "
24:17 against me, and against my f house. "
1Ki 11:12 will not do it for David thy f sake: "
17 certain Edomites of his f servants "
12:10 shall be thicker than my f loins. "
18:18 Israel; but thou and thy f house, "
2Ki 10: 3 and set him on his f throne, "
23:30 and made him king in his f stead. "
24:17 made Mattaniah his f brother 1730
1Ch 5: 1 forasmuch as he defiled his f bed, 1
7: 2 Shemuel, heads of their f house, * "

1Ch 7:40 heads of their *f* house, choice and* 1
12:28 his *f* house twenty and two captains."
21:17 be on me, and on my *f* house; "
23:11 according to their *f* house. "
2Ch 2:13 understanding, of Huram my *f*, "
10:10 shall be thicker than my *f* loins. "
21:13 slain thy brethren of thy *f* house, "
36: 1 made him king in his *f* stead in "
Ezr 2:59 they could not shew their *f* house,* "
Ne 1: 6 both I and my *f* house have sinned. "
Es 4:14 and thy *f* house shall be destroyed: "
Ps 45:10 thine own people, and thy *f* house; "
Pr 4: 3 I was my *f* son, tender and only * "
6:20 My son, keep thy *f* commandment,* "
13: 1 A wise son heareth his *f* instruction: "
15: 5 A fool despiseth his *f* instruction: "
27:10 and thy *f* friend forsake not: "
Isa 7:17 thy people, and upon thy *f* house, "
22:23 for a glorious throne to his *f* house. "
24 upon him all the glory of his *f* house, "
Jer 35:14 but obey their *f* commandment: "
Eze 18:14 a son, that seeth all his *f* sins which "
22:11 humbled his sister, his *f* daughter. "
M't 26:29 new with you in my *F* kingdom. 3962
Lu 2:49 I must be about my *F* business? "
9:26 in his *F*, and of the holy angels.* "
12:32 it is your *F* good pleasure to give "
15:17 hired servants of my *f* have bread "
16:27 wouldest send him to my *f* house: "
Joh 2:16 make not my *F* house an house of "
5:43 I am come in my *F* name, and ye "
6:39 And this is the *F* will which hath* "
10:25 that I do in my *F* name, they bear "
29 to pluck them out of my *F* hand. "
14: 2 In my *F* house are many mansions: "
24 not mine, but the *F* which sent me. "
15:10 I have kept my *F* commandments, "
Ac 7:20 was nourished up in his *f* house "
1Co 5: 1 that one should have his *f* wife. "
Re 14: 1 having his *F* name written in * "

fathers See also FATHERS'; FOREFATHERS.
Ge 15:15 And thou shalt go to thy *f* in peace; 1
31: 3 Return unto the land of thy *f*, "
46:34 until now, both we, and also our *f*: "
47: 3 shepherds, both we, and also our *f*. "
9 of the years of the life of my *f* in the "
30 But I will lie with my *f*, and thou "
48:15 my *f* Abraham and Isaac did walk, "
16 name of my *f* Abraham and Isaac; "
21 you again unto the land of your *f*. "
49:29 bury me with my *f* in the cave that is "
Ex 3:13 The God of your *f* hath sent me unto "
15 of Israel, the Lord God of your *f*, "
16 unto them, The Lord God of your *f*, "
4: 5 believe that the Lord God of their *f*, "
6:25 the heads of the *f* of the Levites * "
10: 6 thy *f*, nor thy fathers' *f* have seen, "
12: 3 according to the house of their *f*,* "
13: 5 he sware unto thy *f* to give thee, "
11 as he sware unto thee and to thy *f*, "
20: 5 visiting the iniquity of the *f* upon the "
34: 7 visiting the iniquity of the *f* upon the "
Le 25:41 possession of his *f* shall he return. "
26:39 iniquities of their *f* shall they pine "
40 and the iniquity of their *f*, with their "
Nu 1: 2 families, by the house of their *f*, * "
4 one head of the house of his *f*. "
16 princes of the tribes of their *f*, "
18, 20 house of their *f*, according * "
22 by the house of their *f*, those that * "
24, 26, 28, 30, 32, 34, 36, 38, 40 by the
house of their *f*, according to * "
44 eachone was for the house of his *f*.* "
45 the house of their *f*, from twenty* "
47 Levites after the tribe of their *f* were "
2:32 of Israel by the house of their *f*: * "
34 according to the house of their *f*. * "
3:15 of Levi after the house of their *f*,* "
20 according to the house of their *f*.* "
4: 2 families, by the house of their *f*,* "
22 throughout the houses of their *f*,* "
29 families by the house of their *f*; * "
34 and after the house of their *f*, * "
38 and by the house of their *f*, * "
40 by the house of their *f*, were two * "
42 families, by the house of their *f*, * "
46 and after the house of their *f*, * "
7: 2 heads of the house of their *f*, * "
11:12 which thou swarest unto their *f*? "
13: 2 every tribe of their *f* shall ye send "
14:18 visiting the iniquity of the *f* upon "
23 the land which I sware unto their *f*, "
17: 2 according to the house of their *f*,* "
2 according to the house of their *f* * "
3 the head of the house of their *f*. * "
20:15 How our *f* went down into Egypt, "
15 the Egyptians vexed us, and our *f*: "
26:55 the names of the tribes of their *f* "
31:26 the chief *f* of the congregation: * "
32: 8 Thus did your *f*, when I sent them "
28 and the chief *f* of the tribes of the * "
33:54 according to the tribes of your *f* "
34:14 Reuben according to...of their *f*, * "
14 Gad according to the...of their *f*, * "
36: 1 And the chief *f* of the families of * "
1 the chief *f* of the children of Israel: "
3 taken from the inheritance of our *f*, "
4 the inheritance of the tribe of our *f*. "
7 the inheritance of the tribe of his *f*. "
8 every man the inheritance of his *f*. "
De 1: 8 which the Lord sware unto your *f*, "
11 (The Lord God of your *f* make you "
21 the Lord God of thy *f* hath said "
35 which I sware to give unto your *f*, "
4: 1 which the Lord God of your *f* giveth "
31 nor forget the covenant of thy *f* which "
De 4:37 because he loved thy *f*, therefore he 1
5: 3 made not this covenant with our *f*, "
9 visiting the iniquity of the *f* upon the "
6: 3 the Lord God of thy *f* hath promised "
10 the land which he sware unto thy *f*, "
18 which the Lord sware unto thy *f*, "
23 the land which he sware unto our *f*. "
7: 8 oath, which he had sworn unto your *f*, "
12 the mercy which he sware unto thy *f*: "
13 the land which he sware unto thy *f* "
8: 1 which the Lord sware unto your *f*. "
3 knewest not, neither did thy *f* know; "
16 with manna, which thy *f* knew not, "
18 covenant which he sware unto thy *f*, "
9: 5 word which the Lord sware unto thy *f*, "
10:11 the land, which I sware unto their *f* "
15 the Lord had a delight in thy *f* "
22 Thy *f* went down into Egypt with "
11: 9 which the Lord sware unto your *f* "
21 which the Lord sware unto your *f* "
12: 1 the land, which the Lord God of thy *f* "
13: 6 thou hast not known, thou, nor thy *f*; "
17 as he hath sworn unto thy *f*; "
19: 8 coast, as he hath sworn unto thy *f*, "
8 which he promised to give unto thy *f*; "
24:16 The *f* shall not be put to death for "
16 children be put to death for the *f*: "
26: 3 which the Lord sware unto our *f* for "
7 we cried unto the Lord God of our *f*, "
15 given us, as thou swarest unto our *f*, "
27: 3 as the Lord God of thy *f* hath "
28:11 Lord sware unto thy *f* to give thee. "
36 neither thou nor thy *f* have known; "
64 neither thou nor thy *f* have known, "
29:13 as he hath sworn unto thy *f*, "
25 covenant of the Lord God of their *f*, "
30: 5 into the land which thy *f* possessed, "
5 and multiply thee above thy *f*. "
9 as he rejoiced over thy *f*: "
20 which the Lord sware unto thy *f*, "
31: 7 the Lord hath sworn unto their *f* "
16 Behold, thou shalt sleep with thy *f*; "
20 the land which I sware unto their *f*, "
32:17 newly up, whom your *f* feared not. "
Jos 1: 6 I sware unto their *f* to give them. "
4: 6 children ask their *f* in time to * "
21 children shall ask their *f* in time to 1
5: 6 which the Lord sware unto their *f* "
14: 1 the heads of the *f* of the tribes * "
18: 3 land which the Lord God of your *f* "
19:51 the heads of the *f* of the tribes * "
21: 1 the heads of the *f* of the Levites * "
1 unto the heads of the *f* of the tribes "
43 which he sware to give unto their *f*; "
44 all that he sware unto their *f*: "
22:14 an head of the house of their *f* * "
28 altar of the Lord, which our *f* made, "
24: 2 Your *f* dwelt on the other side of the "
6 And I brought your *f* out of Egypt: "
6 the Egyptians pursued after your *f* "
14 the gods which your *f* served on the "
15 gods which your *f* served that were "
17 brought us up and our *f* out of the "
J'g 2: 1 the land which I sware unto your *f*; "
10 were gathered unto their *f*: and there "
12 they forsook the Lord God of their *f*, "
17 the way which their *f* walked in, "
19 themselves more than their *f*, "
20 covenant which I commanded their *f*, "
22 as their *f* did keep it, or not. "
3: 4 which he commanded their *f* by the "
6:13 his miracles which our *f* told us of, "
21:22 when their *f* or their brethren come "
1Sa 12: 6 brought your *f* up out of the land "
7 which he did to you and to your *f*. "
8 and your *f* cried unto the Lord, "
8 brought forth your *f* out of Egypt, "
15 against you, as it was against your *f*. "
2Sa 7:12 and thou shalt sleep with thy *f*, "
1Ki 1:21 lord the king shall sleep with his *f*, "
2:10 David slept with his *f*, and was buried "
8: 1 the chief of the *f* of the children * "
21 the Lord, which he made with our *f* "
34 land which thou gavest unto their *f*. "
40 land which thou gavest unto our *f*. "
48 land, which thou gavest unto their *f*, "
53 thou broughtest our *f* out of Egypt, "
57 be with us, as he was with our *f*: "
58 which he commanded our *f*. "
9: 9 brought forth their *f* out of the land "
11:21 in Egypt that David slept with his *f*, "
43 Solomon slept with his *f*, and was "
13:22 come unto the sepulchre of thy *f*. "
14:15 good land, which he gave to their *f*, "
20 he slept with his *f*, and Nadab his "
22 above all that their *f* had done. "
31 And Rehoboam slept with his *f*, "
31 and was buried with his *f* in the city "
15: 8 Abijam slept with his *f*; and they "
12 all the idols that his *f* had made. "
24 Asa slept with his *f*, and was buried "
24 with his *f* in the city of David his "
16: 6 Baasha slept with his *f*, and was "
28 Omri slept with his *f*, and was buried "
19: 4 for I am not better than my *f*. "
21: 3 should give the inheritance of my *f* "
4 not give thee the inheritance of my *f*. "
22:40 Ahab slept with his *f*; and Ahaziah "
50 And Jehoshaphat slept with his *f*, "
50 and was buried with his *f* in the city "
2Ki 8:24 And Joram slept with his *f*, "
24 and was buried with his *f* in the city "
9:28 in his sepulchre with his *f* in the city "
10:35 And Jehu slept with his *f*: and they "
12:18 his *f*, kings of Judah, had dedicated, "
21 and they buried him with his *f* in the "
2Ki 13: 9 Jehoahaz slept with his *f*; and they 1
13 And Joash slept with his *f*; and "
14: 6 The *f* shall not be put to death for "
6 children be put to death for the *f*; "
16 Jehoash slept with his *f*, and was "
20 was buried at Jerusalem with his *f* "
22 after that the king slept with his *f*. "
29 Jeroboam slept with his *f*, even with "
15: 7 So Azariah slept with his *f*; and they "
7 buried him with his *f* in the city of "
9 as his *f* had done: he departed not "
22 And Menahem slept with his *f*; and "
38 And Jotham slept with his *f*, "
38 and was buried with his *f* in the city "
16:20 And Ahaz slept with his *f*, "
20 and was buried with his *f* in the city "
17:13 the law which I commanded your *f*, "
14 like to the neck of their *f*, "
15 covenant that he made with their *f*, "
41 as did their *f*, so do they unto this "
19:12 them which my *f* have destroyed; "
20:17 that which thy *f* have laid up in "
21 And Hezekiah slept with his *f*: and "
21: 8 the land which I gave their *f*; "
15 since the day their *f* came forth "
18 Manasseh slept with his *f*, and was "
22 he forsook the Lord God of his *f*, "
22:13 our *f* have not hearkened unto the "
20 I will gather thee unto thy *f*, "
23:32, 37 according to all that his *f* had "
24: 6 So Jehoiakim slept with his *f*: "
1Ch 4:38 house of their *f* increased greatly* "
5:13 brethren of the house of their *f* * "
15 chief of the house of their *f*. * "
24 the heads of the house of their *f*,* "
24 and heads of the house of their *f*.* "
25 trespassed against the God of their *f*, "
6:19 the Levites according to their *f*. * "
7: 4 after the house of their *f*, were * "
7, 9 heads of the house of their *f*, * "
11 by the heads of their *f*, mighty * "
8: 6 these are the heads of the *f* of * "
10 were his sons, heads of the *f*. * "
13 who were heads of the *f* of the * "
28 These were heads of the *f*, * "
9: 9 of the *f* in the house of their *f*. * "
13 heads of the house of their *f*, * "
19 and their *f*, being over the host "
33 chief of the *f* of the Levites, * "
34 These chief *f* of the Levites were * "
12:17 the God of our *f* look thereon, and "
30 throughout the house of their *f*. * "
15:12 chief of the *f* of the Levites: * "
17:11 that thou must go to be with thy *f*, "
23: 9 the chief of the *f* of Laadan. * "
24 Levi after the house of their *f*; * "
24 the chief of the *f*, as they were * "
24: 4 chief men of the house of their *f*,* "
4 according to the house of their *f*.* "
6 before the chief of the *f* of the * "
30 Levites after the house of their *f*.* "
31 the chief of the *f* of the priests * "
31 and Levites, even the principal *f* * "
26:13 according to the house of their *f*, * "
21 the Gershonite Laadan, chief *f*, * "
26 David the king, and the chief *f*, * "
31 to the generations of his *f*. * "
32 and seven hundred chief *f*, * "
27: 1 chief *f* and captains of thousands* "
29: 6 the chief of the *f* and princes * "
15 and sojourners, as were all our *f*: "
18 Abraham, Isaac, and of Israel, our *f*, "
20 blessed the Lord God of their *f*, "
2Ch 1: 2 in all Israel, the chief of the *f*. * "
5: 2 chief of the *f* of the children of * "
6:25 thou gavest to them and to their *f*. "
31 land which thou gavest unto our *f*. "
38 land, which thou gavest unto their *f*, "
7:22 they forsook the Lord God of their *f*, "
9:31 Solomon slept with his *f*, and he "
11:16 unto the Lord God of their *f*. "
12:16 Rehoboam slept with his *f*, and was "
13:12 not against the Lord God of your *f*; "
18 relied upon the Lord God of their *f*. "
14: 1 Abijah slept with his *f*, and they "
4 to seek the Lord God of their *f*, and "
15:12 to seek the Lord God of their *f* with "
16:13 And Asa slept with his *f*, and died "
17:14 according to the house of their *f*: * "
19: 4 back unto the Lord God of their *f*. "
8 and of the chief of the *f* of Israel, * "
20: 6 And said, O Lord God of our *f*, "
33 their hearts unto the God of their *f*. "
21: 1 Now Jehoshaphat slept with his *f*, "
1 and was buried with his *f* in the city "
10 had forsaken the Lord God of his *f*. "
19 for him, like the burning of his *f*. "
23: 2 and the chief of the *f* of Israel, * "
24:18 house of the Lord God of their *f*, "
24 forsaken the Lord God of their *f*. "
25: 4 The *f* shall not die for the children, "
4 shall the children die for the *f*, "
5 according to the houses of their *f*,* "
28 buried him with his *f* in the city "
26: 2 after that the king slept with his *f*. "
12 whole number of the chief of the *f* * "
23 So Uzziah slept with his *f*, and they "
23 buried him with his *f* in the field "
27: 9 Jotham slept with his *f*, and they "
28: 6 forsaken the Lord God of their *f*. "
9 because the Lord God of your *f* was "
25 to anger the Lord God of his *f*. "
27 And Ahaz slept with his *f*, and they "
29: 5 the house of the Lord God of your *f*, "
6 for our *f* have trespassed, and done "
9 lo, our *f* have fallen by the sword, "

2Ch 30: 7 And be not ye like your f, 1
7 against the Lord God of their f, "
8 be ye not stiffnecked, as your f were, "
19 to seek God, the Lord God of his f, "
22 confession to the Lord God of their f. "
31:17 priests by the house of their f, * "
32:13 what I and my f have done unto all "
14 nations that my f utterly destroyed, "
15 hand, and out of the hand of my f: "
33 Hezekiah slept with his f, and they "
33: 8 which I have appointed for your f; "
12 greatly before the God of his f, "
20 So Manasseh slept with his f, "
34:21 because our f have not kept the word "
28 Behold, I will gather thee to thy f, "
32 covenant of God, the God of their f. "
33 following the Lord, the God of their f. "
35: 4 by the houses of your f, after * "
5 of the f of your brethren * "
24 in one of the sepulchres of his f. "
36:15 the Lord God of their f sent to them "
Ezr 1: 5 Then rose up the chief of the f * "
2:68 And some of the chief of the f, * "
3:12 Levites and chief of the f, who * "
4: 2 and to the chief of the f, and said,* "
3 of the chiefs of the f of Israel, * "
15 in the book of the records of thy f: 2
5:12 f had provoked the God of heaven "
7:27 Blessed be the Lord God of our f, 1
8: 1 These are now the chief of their f,* "
28 offering unto the Lord God of your f. "
29 and chief of the f of Israel, * "
9: 7 Since the days of our f have we "
10:11 unto the Lord God of your f, and do "
16 the f, after the house of their f, * "
Ne 7:70 of the f gave unto the work. * "
71 of the f gave to the treasure * "
8:13 together the chief of the f * "
9: 2 sins, and the iniquities of their f. "
9 didst see the affliction of our f "
16 But they and our f dealt proudly, "
23 which thou hadst promised to their f, "
32 and on our f, and on all thy people, "
34 our priests, nor our f, kept thy law, "
36 the land that thou gavest unto our f "
10:34 after the houses of our f, at times* "
11:13 And his brethren, chief of the f, * "
12:12 were priests, the chief of the f: * "
22 were recorded chief of the f: * "
23 the chief of the f, were written * "
13:18 Did not your f thus, and did not "
Job 8: 8 thyself to the search of their f: "
15:18 wise men have told from their f, "
30: 1 whose f I would have disdained to "
Ps 22: 4 Our f trusted in thee: they trusted, "
39:12 and a sojourner, as all my f were. "
44: 1 O God, our f have told us, what "
45:16 Instead of thy f shall be thy children, "
49:19 shall go to the generation of his f; "
78: 3 and known, and our f have told us. "
5 Israel, which he commanded our f, "
8 And might not be as their f, "
12 things did he in the sight of their f, "
57 and dealt unfaithfully like their f: "
95: 9 When your f tempted me, proved "
106: 6 We have sinned with our f, we have "
7 Our f understood not thy wonders "
109:14 the iniquity of his f be remembered "
Pr 17: 6 and the glory of children are their f. "
19:14 and riches are the inheritance of f: "
22:28 landmark, which thy f have set. "
Isa 14:21 children for the iniquity of their f; "
37:12 which my f have destroyed, as Gozan, "
39: 6 that which thy f have laid up in "
49:23 And kings shall be thy nursing f, "
64:11 house, where our f praised thee, 1
65: 7 the iniquities of your f together, "
Jer 2: 5 iniquity have your f found in me, "
3:18 given for an inheritance unto your f. "
24 hath devoured the labour of our f "
25 the Lord our God, we and our f, "
6:21 the f and the sons together shall fall "
7: 7 the land that I gave to your f, "
14 which I gave to you and to your f, "
18 and the f kindle the fire, and the "
22 For I spake unto your f, "
25 Since the day that your f came forth "
26 they did worse than their f. "
9:14 Baalim, which their f taught them: "
16 neither they nor their f have known: "
11: 4 Which I commanded your f in the "
5 oath which I have sworn unto your f, "
7 I earnestly protested unto your f "
10 covenant which I made with their f. "
13:14 even the f and the sons together, "
14:20 wickedness, and the iniquity of our f: "
16: 3 concerning their f that begat them "
11 Because your f have forsaken me, "
12 ye have done worse than your f; "
13 ye know not, neither ye nor your f; "
15 their land that I gave unto their f. "
19 Surely our f have inherited lies, "
17:22 sabbath day, as I commanded your f. "
19: 4 neither they nor their f have known, "
23:27 as their f have forgotten my name "
39 the city that I gave you and your f, "
24:10 that I gave unto them and to their f. "
25: 5 hath given unto you and to your f "
30: 3 to the land that I gave to their f, "
31:29 The f have eaten a sour grape, "
32 covenant that I made with their f "
32:18 recompensest the iniquity of the f "
22 land, which thou didst swear to their f "
34: 5 and with the burnings of thy f, the "
13 I made a covenant with your f in the "
14 but your f hearkened not unto me, "

Jer 35:15 I have given to you and to your f: 1
44: 3 not, neither they, ye, nor your f. "
9 forgotten the wickedness of your f, "
10 I set before you, and before your f. "
17 as we have done, we, and our f, "
21 ye, and your f, your kings, and your "
47: 3 the f shall not look back to their "
50: 7 even the Lord, the hope of their f. "
La 5: 7 Our f have sinned, and are not; "
Eze 2: 3 their f have transgressed against "
5:10 Therefore the f shall eat the sons in "
10 and the sons shall eat their f; "
18: 2 saying, The f have eaten sour grapes, "
20: 4 to know the abominations of their f: "
18 Walk ye not in the statutes of your f, "
27 Yet in this your f have blasphemed "
30 polluted after the manner of your f? "
36 Like as I pleaded with your f in the "
42 up mine hand to give it to your f. "
36:28 the land that I gave to your f; "
37:25 wherein your f have dwelt; and they "
47:14 up mine hand to give it unto your f: "
Da 2:23 praise thee, O thou God of my f, 2
9: 6 our princes, and our f, and to all 1
8 to our princes, and to our f, because "
16 and for the iniquities of our f, "
11:24 f have not done, nor his fathers' f; "
37 shall he regard the God of his f, nor "
38 and a god whom his f knew not shall "
Ho 9:10 I saw your f as the firstripe in the fig "
Joe 1: 2 or even in the days of your f? "
Am 2: 4 after the which their f have walked: "
Mic 7:20 hast sworn unto our f from the days "
Zec 1: 2 been sore displeased with your f. "
4 Be ye not as your f, unto whom the "
5 Your f where are they? and the "
6 did they not take hold of your f? "
8:14 when your f provoked me to wrath. "
Mal 2:10 by profaning the covenant of our f? "
3: 7 Even from the days of your f ye are "
4: 6 the heart of the f to the children, "
6 the heart of the children to their f, "
M't 23:30 we had been in the days of our f, 3962
32 ye up then the measure of your f. "
Lu 1:17 to turn the hearts of the f to the "
55 As he spake to our f, to Abraham, "
72 the mercy promised to our f, "
6:23 did their f unto the prophets. "
26 so did their f to the false prophets. "
11:47 prophets, and your f killed them. "
48 that ye allow the deeds of your f: "
Joh 4:20 f worshipped in this mountain; "
6:31 Our f did eat manna in the desert; "
49 f did eat manna in the wilderness, "
58 not as your f did eat manna, "
7:22 because it is of Moses, but of the f;) "
Ac 3:13 God of our f, hath glorified his Son "
22 For Moses truly said unto the f, * "
25 which God made with our f, "
5:30 The God of our f raised up Jesus, "
7: 2 Men, brethren, and f, hearken; "
11 and our f found no sustenance. "
12 Egypt, he sent out our f first. "
15 Egypt, and died, he, and our f, "
19 evil entreated our f, so that they "
32 Saying, I am the God of thy f, "
38 the mount Sina, and with our f: "
39 To whom our f would not obey, "
44 f had the tabernacle of witness "
45 Which also our f that came after "
45 drave out before the face of our f, "
51 as your f did, so do ye. "
52 have not your f persecuted? "
13:17 chose our f, and exalted the people "
32 which was made unto the f, "
36 and was laid unto his f, and saw "
15:10 our f nor we were able to bear? "
22: 1 Men, brethren, and f, hear ye "
3 manner of the law of the f, 3971
14 God of our f hath chosen thee, 3962
24:14 so worship I the God of my f, 3971
26: 6 promise made of God unto our f: 3962
28:17 the people, or customs of our f, 3971
25 Esaias the prophet unto our f, 3962
Ro 9: 5 Whose are the f, and of whom "
15: 8 the promises made unto the f: "
1Co 4:15 yet have ye not many f: "
10: 1 all our f were under the cloud, "
Ga 1:14 zealous of the traditions of my f. 3967
Eph 6: 4 ye f, provoke not your children to 3962
Col 3:21 F, provoke not your children to "
1Ti 1: 9 for murderers of f and murderers 3964
Heb 1: 1 spake in time past unto the f by 3962
3: 9 When your f tempted me, proved "
8: 9 that I made with their f in the day "
12: 9 Furthermore we have had f of our "
1Pe 1:18 received by tradition from your f; 3970
2Pe 3: 4 since the f fell asleep, all things 3962
1Jo 2:13 I write unto you, f, because ye "
14 I have written unto you, f, because "

fathers'
Ex 6:14 These be the heads of their f houses: 1
10: 6 fathers, nor thy f fathers have seen, "
Nu 17: 6 according to their f houses, even "
26: 2 upward, throughout their f house, "
32:14 ye are risen up in your f stead, an "
Ne 2: 3 the place of my f sepulchres, lieth "
5 the city of my f sepulchres, that I "
Eze 20:24 their eyes were after their f idols. "
22:10 they discovered their f nakedness: "
Ro 11:28 they are beloved for the f sakes. 3962

fathoms
Ac 27:28 sounded, and found it twenty f: 3712
28 again, and found it fifteen f. "

fatling See also FATLINGS.
Isa 11: 6 young lion and the f together; 4806

fatlings
1Sa 15: 9 and of the f, and the lambs, 4932
2Sa 6:13 he sacrificed oxen and f. *4806
Ps 66:15 unto thee burnt sacrifices of f, 4220
Eze 39:18 bullocks, all of them f of Bashan. 4806
M't 22: 4 my oxen and my f are killed, 4619

fatness
Ge 27:28 of heaven, and the f of the earth, 4924
39 dwelling shall be the f of the earth, "
De 32:15 thick, thou art covered with f; *
J'g 9: 9 Should I leave my f, wherewith 1880
Job 15:27 he covereth his face with his f, 2459
36:16 thy table should be full of f. 1880
Ps 36: 8 satisfied with the f of thy house; "
63: 5 be satisfied as with marrow and f; "
65:11 goodness; and thy paths drop f. "
73: 7 Their eyes stand out with f: 2459
109:24 and my flesh faileth of f. 8081
Isa 17: 4 the f of his flesh shall wax lean. 4924
34: 6 it is made fat with f, and with the 2459
7 and their dust made fat with f. "
55: 2 let your soul delight itself in f. 1880
Jer 31:14 the soul of the priests with f, "
Ro 11:17 the root and f of the olive tree; 4096

fats
Joe 2:24 the f shall overflow with wine and 3342
3:13 the press is full, the f overflow; "

fatted
1Ki 4:23 and fallowdeer, and f fowl. 75
Jer 46:21 the midst of her like f bullocks; *4770
Lu 15:23 And bring hither the f calf, and 4618
27 thy father hath killed the f calf, "
30 thou hast killed for him the f calf. "

fatter
Da 1:15 appeared fairer and f in flesh 1277

fattest
Ps 78:31 upon them, and slew the f of them, 4924
Da 11:24 upon the f places of the province; "

fault See also FAULTS; FAULTLESS.
Ex 5:16 but the f is in thine own people. 2398
De 25: 2 before his face, according to his f.*7564
1Sa 29: 3 I have found no f in him since 3972
2Sa 3: 8 with a f concerning this woman? 5771
Ps 59: 4 prepare themselves without my f: "
Da 6: 4 could find none occasion nor f; 7844
4 there any error or f found in him. "
M't 18:15 and tell him his f between thee 1651
M'r 7: 2 unwashen, hands, they found f *3201
Lu 23: 4 I find no f in this man. 158
14 have found no f in this man "
Joh 18:38 I find in him no f at all. * 156
19: 4 know that I find no f in him. * "
6 for I find no f in him. * "
Ro 9:19 Why doth he yet find f? For who 3201
1Co 6: 7 there is utterly a f among you, *2275
Ga 6: 1 if a man be overtaken in a f, *3900
Heb 8: 8 For finding f with them, he saith, 3201
Re 14: 5 are without f before the throne * 299

faultless
Heb 8: 7 if that first covenant had been f, 273
Jude 24 and to present you f before the * 299

faults
Ge 41: 9 I do remember my f this day: 2399
Ps 19:12 cleanse thou me from secret f. "
Jas 5:16 Confess your f one to another, *3900
1Pe 2:20 if, when ye be buffeted for your f,* 264

faulty
2Sa 14:13 this thing as one which is f, * 818
Ho 10: 2 now shall they be found f: * 816

favour See also FAVOURABLE; FAVOURED; FAVOUREST; FAVOURETH.
Ge 18: 3 now I have found f in thy sight, 2580
30:27 if I have found f in thine eyes, "
39:21 him f in the sight of the keeper "
Ex 3:21 will give this people f in the sight "
11: 3 And the Lord gave the people f in "
12:36 Lord gave the people f in the sight "
Nu 11:11 have I not found f in thy sight, "
15 if I have found f in thy sight; "
De 24: 1 pass that she find no f in his eyes, "
28:50 the old, nor shew f to the young: 2603
33:23 O Naphtali, satisfied with f, and 7522
Jos 11:20 and that they might have no f, 8467
Ru 2:13 Let me find f in thy sight, *2580
1Sa 2:26 and was in f both with the Lord, 2896
16:22 for he hath found f in my sight. 2580
20:29 if I have found f in thine eyes, "
25: 8 young men find f in thine eyes: "
29: 6 the lords f thee not. 2896
2Sa 15:25 if I shall find f in the eyes of the 2580
1Ki 11:19 Hadad found great f in the sight "
Ne 2: 5 if thy servant have found f in thy 3190
Es 2:15 Esther obtained f in the sight of 2580
17 she obtained grace and f in his ‡2617
5: 2 that she obtained f in his sight: 2580
8 If I have found f in the sight of the "
7: 3 If I have found f in thy sight, O "
8: 5 and if I have found f in his sight, "
Job 10:12 Thou hast granted me life and f, ‡2617
Ps 5:12 with f wilt thou compass him as 7522
30: 5 his f is life: weeping may endure "
7 f thou hast made my mountain "
35:27 glad, that f my righteous cause: 2655
44: 3 because thou hadst a f unto them. 7520
45:12 the people shall intreat thy f. 6440
89:17 thy f our horn shall be exalted. 7522
102:13 for the time to f her, yea, the set *2603
14 stones, and f the dust thereof. * "
106: 4 with the f that thou bearest unto 7522
109:12 neither let there be any to f his *2603

Ps 112: 5 man sheweth *f*, and lendeth: *2603
119:58 I intreated thy *f* with my whole 6440
Pr 3: 4 So shalt thou find *f* and good 2580
8:35 and shall obtain *f* of the Lord. 7522
11:27 seeketh good procureth *f*: but "
12: 2 good man obtaineth *f* of the Lord: "
13:15 Good understanding giveth *f*: 2580
14: 9 among the righteous there is *f*. *7522
35 king's *f* is toward a wise servant: "
16:15 *f* is as a cloud of the latter rain. "
18:22 thing, and obtaineth *f* of the Lord. "
19: 6 will intreat the *f* of the prince: 6440
12 his *f* is as dew upon the grass. 7522
21:10 neighbour findeth no *f* in his eyes. 2603
22: 1 *f* rather than silver and gold. 2580
28:23 find more *f* than he that flattereth "
29:26 Many seek the ruler's *f*; 6440
31:30 *F* is deceitful, and beauty is vain: ‡2580
Ec 9:11 nor yet *f* to men of skill; "
Ca 8:10 I in his eyes as one that found *f*. *7965
Isa 26:10 Let *f* be shewed to the wicked, 2603
27:11 formed them will shew them no *f*. "
60:10 but in my *f* have I had mercy on 7522
Jer 16:13 where I will not shew you *f*. 2594
Da 1: 9 God had brought Daniel into *f* ‡2617
Lu 1:30 for thou hast found *f* with God. *5485*
2:52 and in *f* with God and man. "
Ac 2:47 and having *f* with all the people. "
7:10 him *f* and wisdom in the sight of "
46 Who found *f* before God, and "
25: 3 And desired *f* against him, that "

favourable
J'g 21:22 Be *f* unto them for our sakes: *2603
Job 33:26 and he will be *f* unto him: 7520
Ps 77: 7 and will he be *f* no more? "
85: 1 thou hast been *f* unto thy land: "

favoured See also EVILFAVOUREDNESS.
Ge 29:17 Rachel was beautiful and well *f*. 4758
39: 6 was a goodly person, and well *f*. "
41: 2 out of the river seven well *f* kine "
3 seven other kine...ill *f* and "
4 the ill *f*...kine did eat up the seven "
4 kine did eat up the seven well *f* "
18 kine, fatfleshed and well *f*; 8389
19 poor and very ill *f* and leanfleshed, "
20 the lean and the ill *f* kine did eat "
21 were still ill *f*, as at the beginning. "
27 And the seven thin and ill *f* kine "
La 4:16 priests, they *f* not the elders. 2603
Da 1: 4 was no blemish, but well *f*, 4758
Lu 1:28 Hail, thou that art highly *f*, *5487*

favourest
Ps 41:11 By this I know that thou *f* me, *2654

favoureth
2Sa 20:11 He that *f* Joab, and he that is for 2654

fear See also FEARED; FEAREST; FEARETH; FEARFUL; FEARING; FEARS.
Ge 9: 2 the *f* of you and the dread of you 4172
15: 1 *F* not, Abram: I am thy shield, 3372
20:11 the *f* of God is not in this place; 3374
21:17 What aileth thee, Hagar? *f* not; 3372
26:24 *f* not, for I am with thee, and will "
31:42 and the *f* of Isaac, had been with 6343
53 Jacob sware by the *f* of his father "
32:11 I *f* him, lest he will come and 3373
35:17 *F* not; thou shalt have this son 3372
42:18 This do, and live; for I *f* God: 3373
43:23 he said, Peace be to you, *f* not: 3372
46: 3 *f* not to go down into Egypt; "
50:19 Joseph said unto them, *F* not: "
21 Now therefore *f* ye not: I will "
Ex 9:30 I know that ye will not yet *f* the "
14:13 *F* ye not, stand still, and see the "
15:16 *F* and dread shall fall upon them;* 367
18:21 people able men, such as *f* God, 3373
20:20 Moses said unto the people, *F* not: 3372
20 that his *f* may be before your 3374
23:27 I will send my *f* before thee, * 367
Le 19: 3 Ye shall *f* every man his mother, 3372
14 but shalt *f* thy God: I am the "
32 face of the old man, and *f* thy God: "
25:17 but thou shalt *f* thy God: for I am "
36 but *f* thy God; that thy brother "
43 with rigour; but shalt *f* thy God. "
Nu 14: 9 neither *f* ye the people of the land; "
9 the Lord is with us; *f* them not. "
21:34 Lord said unto Moses, *F* him not: "
De 1:21 said unto thee; *f* not, neither be "
2:25 the dread of thee and the *f* of thee 3374
3: 2 Lord said unto me, *F* him not: 3372
22 Ye shall not *f* them: for the Lord "
4:10 that they may learn to *f* me "
5:29 that they would *f* me, and keep all "
6: 2 That thou mightest *f* the Lord thy "
13 Thou shalt *f* the Lord thy God, "
24 to *f* the Lord our God, for our "
8: 6 to walk in his ways, and to *f* him. "
10:12 but to *f* the Lord thy God, "
20 Thou shalt *f* the Lord thy God; "
11:25 the *f* of you and the dread of you 6343
13: 4 the Lord your God, and *f* him, 3372
11 And all Israel shall hear, and *f*, "
14:23 thou mayest learn to *f* the Lord "
17:13 all the people shall hear, and *f*, "
19 that he may learn to *f* the Lord "
19:20 which remain shall hear, and *f*, "
20: 3 *f* not, and do not tremble, neither "
21:21 and all Israel shall hear, and *f*. "
28:58 that thou mayest *f* this glorious "
66 and thou shalt *f* day and night, 6342
67 for the *f* of thine heart wherewith 6343
67 heart wherewith thou shalt *f*, 6342
31: 6 *f* not, nor be afraid of them: 3372
8 *f* not, neither be dismayed. "

De 31:12 they may learn, and *f* the Lord 3372
13 and learn to *f* the Lord your God, "
Jos 4:24 that ye might *f* the Lord your God "
8: 1 *F* not, neither be thou dismayed: "
10: 8 Lord said unto Joshua, *F* them not: "
25 Joshua said unto them, *F* not, nor "
22:24 rather done it for *f* of this thing, *1674
24:14 Now therefore *f* the Lord, and 3372
J'g 4:18 my lord, turn in to me; *f* not. "
6:10 *f* not the gods of the Amorites, "
23 Peace be unto thee; *f* not: thou "
7:10 if thou *f* to go down, go thou 3373
9:21 dwelt there, for *f* of Abimelech 6440
Ru 3:11 my daughter, *f* not; I will do to 3372
1Sa 4:20 *F* not; for thou hast born a son. "
11: 7 And the *f* of the Lord fell on the *6343
12:14 If ye will *f* the Lord, and serve 3372
20 Samuel said unto the people, *F* not: "
24 Only *f* the Lord, and serve him in "
21:10 and fled that day for *f* of Saul, 6440
22:23 Abide thou with me, *f* not: 3372
23:17 And he said unto him, *F* not: "
26 haste to get away for *f* of Saul; 6440
2Sa 9: 7 And David said unto him, *F* not: 3372
13:28 Amnon; then kill him, *f* not: "
23: 3 be just, ruling in the *f* of God. 3374
1Ki 8:40 That they may *f* thee all the days 3372
43 to *f* thee, as do thy people Israel; "
17:13 Elijah said unto her, *F* not; "
18:12 I thy servant *f* the Lord from my "
2Ki 4: 1 that thy servant did *f* the Lord: 3373
6:16 he answered, *F* not: for they 3372
17:28 taught them how they should *f* the "
34 manners: they *f* not the Lord, 3373
35 saying, Ye shall not *f* other gods, 3372
36 him shall ye *f*, and him shall ye "
37 and ye shall not *f* other gods. "
38 neither shall ye *f* other gods. "
39 the Lord your God ye shall *f*; "
25:24 *F* not to be the servants of the "
1Ch 14:17 the Lord brought the *f* of him 6343
16:30 *F* before him, all the earth: *2342
28:20 do it: *f* not, nor be dismayed: 3372
2Ch 6:31 That they may *f* thee, to walk in "
33 and *f* thee, as doth thy people "
14:14 the *f* of the Lord came upon them: 6343
17:10 the *f* of the Lord fell upon all the "
19: 7 let the *f* of the Lord be upon you; "
9 Thus shall ye do in the *f* of the 3374
20:17 *f* not, nor be dismayed; 3372
29 And the *f* of God was on all the 6343
Ezr 3: 3 *f* was upon them because of the 367
Ne 1:11 thy servants, who desire to *f* thy 3372
5: 9 ought ye not to walk in the *f* of 3374
15 so did not I, because of the *f* of "
6:14 that would have put me in *f*. 3372
19 Tobiah sent letters to put me in *f*. "
Es 8:17 the *f* of the Jews fell upon them. 6343
9: 2 the *f* of them fell upon all people. "
3 the *f* of Mordecai fell upon them. "
Job 1: 9 said, Doth Job *f* God for nought? 3372
4: 6 Is not this thy *f*, thy confidence, 3374
14 *F* came upon me, and trembling, 6343
6:14 but he forsaketh the *f* of the 3374
9:34 and let not his *f* terrify me: * 367
35 Then would I speak, and not *f* him; 3372
11:15 shalt be stedfast, and shalt not *f*: "
15: 4 thou castest off *f*, and restrainest 3374
21: 9 Their houses are safe from *f*, 6343
22: 4 Will he reprove thee for *f* of thee? 3374
10 and sudden *f* troubleth thee; 6343
25: 2 Dominion and *f* are with him, "
28:28 the *f* of the Lord, that is wisdom; 3374
31:34 Did I *f* a great multitude, or *6206
37:24 Men do therefore *f* him: he 3372
39:16 her labour is in vain without *f*; 6343
22 He mocketh at *f*, and is not "
41:33 his like, who is made without *f*. 2844
Ps 2:11 Serve the Lord with *f*, and rejoice 3374
5: 7 and in thy *f* will I worship toward "
9:20 Put them in *f*, O Lord: that the 4172
14: 5 There were they in great *f*: for 6342
15: 4 honoureth them that *f* the Lord. 3373
19: 9 The *f* of the Lord is clean, 3374
22:23 Ye that *f* the Lord, praise him: 3373
23 and *f* him, all ye the seed of *1481
25 my vows before them that *f* him. 3373
23: 4 I will *f* no evil: for thou art with 3372
25:14 the Lord is with them that *f* him; 3373
27: 1 whom shall I *f*? the Lord is the 3372
3 my heart shall not *f*: though war "
31:11 and a *f* to mine acquaintance: 6343
13 *f* was on every side: while they *4032
19 hast laid up for them that *f* thee; 3373
33: 8 Let all the earth *f* the Lord: 3372
18 the Lord is upon them that *f* him; 3373
34: 7 round about them that *f* him, "
9 O *f* the Lord, ye his saints: 3372
9 is no want to them that *f* him. 3373
11 I will teach you the *f* of the Lord. 3374
36: 1 is no *f* of God before his eyes. 6343
40: 3 many shall see it, and *f*, and shall 3372
46: 2 Therefore will not we *f*, though "
48: 6 *F* took hold upon them there, *7461
49: 5 should I *f* in the days of evil, 3372
52: 6 The righteous also shall see, and *f*, "
53: 5 There were they in great *f*, 6343
5 There were...where no *f* was: "
55:19 therefore they *f* not God. 3372
56: 4 I will not *f* what flesh can do unto "
60: 4 a banner to them that *f* thee, 3373
61: 5 heritage of those that *f* thy name. "
64: 1 preserve my life from *f* of the 6343
4 do they shoot at him, and *f* not. 3372
9 all men shall *f*, and shall declare "
66:16 Come and hear, all ye that *f* God, 3373

Ps 67: 7 the ends of the earth shall *f* him. 3372
72: 5 They shall *f* thee as long as the "
85: 9 salvation is nigh them that *f* him; 3373
86:11 unite my heart to *f* thy name. 3372
90:11 even according to thy *f*, so is thy 3374
96: 9 *f* before him, all the earth. *2342
102:15 shall *f* the name of the Lord, 3372
103:11 mercy toward them that *f* him. 3373
13 the Lord pitieth them that *f* him. "
17 everlasting upon them that *f* him, "
105:38 for the *f* of them fell upon them. 6343
111: 5 given meat unto them that *f* him: 3373
10 The *f* of the Lord is the beginning 3374
115:11 Ye that *f* the Lord, trust in the 3373
13 He will bless them that *f* the Lord, "
118: 4 Let them now that *f* the Lord say, "
6 Lord is on my side; I will not *f*: 3372
119:38 servant, who is devoted to thy *f*. 3374
39 away my reproach which I *f*: *3025
63 companion of all them that *f* thee, 3372
74 They that *f* thee will be glad 3373
79 those that *f* thee turn unto me, "
120 My flesh trembleth for *f* of thee; 6343
135:20 ye that *f* the Lord, bless the Lord. 3373
145:19 the desire of them that *f* him: "
147:11 taketh pleasure in them that *f* him, "
Pr 1: 7 The *f* of the Lord is the beginning 3374
26 will mock when your *f* cometh; 6343
27 When your *f* cometh as desolation, "
29 did not choose the *f* of the Lord: 3374
33 and shall be quiet from *f* of evil. 6343
2: 5 thou understand the *f* of the Lord, 3374
3: 7 *f* the Lord, and depart from evil. 3372
25 Be not afraid of sudden *f*, 6343
8:13 The *f* of the Lord is to hate evil: 3374
9:10 The *f* of the Lord is the beginning "
10:24 The *f* of the wicked, it shall come 4034
27 *f* of the Lord prolongeth days: 3374
14:26 In the *f* of the Lord is strong "
27 *f* of the Lord is a fountain of life, "
15:16 Better is little with the *f* of the "
33 The *f* of the Lord is the instruction "
16: 6 by the *f* of the Lord men depart "
19:23 The *f* of the Lord tendeth to life: "
20: 2 The *f* of the king is as the roaring* 367
22: 4 humility and the *f* of the Lord 3374
23:17 be thou in the *f* of the Lord "
24:21 *f* thou the Lord and the king: 3372
29:25 The *f* of man bringeth a snare: 2731
Ec 3:14 God doeth it, that men should *f* 3372
5: 7 divers vanities: but *f* thou God. "
8:12 shall be well with them that *f* God, 3373
12 with them...which *f* before him: 3372
12:13 matter: *F* God, and keep his "
Ca 3: 8 because of *f* in the night. 6343
Isa 2:10 in the dust, for *f* of the Lord, * "
19 of the earth, for *f* of the Lord, * "
21 ragged rocks, for *f* of the Lord, * "
7: 4 Take heed, and be quiet; *f* not, 3372
25 thither the *f* of briers and thorns: 3374
8:12 neither *f* ye...nor be afraid. 3372
12 neither...their *f*, nor be afraid. 4172
13 let him be your *f*, and let him be "
11: 2 knowledge and of the *f* of the 3374
3 understanding in the *f* of the "
14: 3 from thy sorrow and from thy *f*, *7267
19:16 and *f* because of the shaking of 6342
21: 4 pleasure hath he turned into *f* *2731
24:17 *F*, and the pit, and the snare, 6343
18 who fleeth from the noise of the *f* "
25: 3 the terrible nations shall *f* thee. 3372
29:13 their *f* toward me is taught by 3374
23 and shall *f* the God of Israel. *6206
31: 9 pass over to his strong hold for *f*, *4032
33: 6 the *f* of the Lord is his treasure. 3374
35: 4 Be strong, *f* not: behold, your 3372
41:10 *F* thou not; for I am with thee: "
13 thee, *F* not; I will help thee. "
14 *F* not, thou worm Jacob, and ye "
43: 1 *F* not: for I have redeemed thee, "
5 *F* not: for I am with thee: I will "
44: 2 *F* not, O Jacob, my servant; "
8 *F* ye not, neither be afraid: have 6342
11 yet they shall *f*, and they shall be "
51: 7 *f* ye not the reproach of men, 3372
54: 4 *F* not; for thou shalt not be "
14 oppression; for thou shalt not *f*: "
59:19 shall they *f* the name of the Lord "
60: 5 and thine heart shall *f*, and be *6342
63:17 hardened our heart from thy *f*? 3374
Jer 2:19 that my *f* is not in thee, 6345
5:22 *F* ye not me? saith the Lord: 3372
24 Let us now *f* the Lord our God, "
6:25 enemy, and *f* is on every side. *4032
10: 7 Who would not *f* thee, O King 3372
20:10 of many, *f* on every side. *4032
23: 4 and they shall *f* no more, nor be 3372
26:19 did he not *f* the Lord, and 3373
30: 5 a voice of trembling, of *f*, and 6343
10 *f* thou not, O my servant Jacob, 3372
32:39 that they may *f* me for ever, "
40 I will put my *f* in their hearts, 3374
33: 9 and they shall *f* and tremble 6342
35:11 for *f* of the army of the Chaldeans, 6440
11 for *f* of the army of the Syrians: "
37:11 for *f* of Pharaoh's army, "
40: 9 *F* not to serve the Chaldeans: 3372
41: 9 for *f* of Baasha king of Israel: 6440
46: 5 *f* was round about, saith the *4032
27 *f* not thou, O my servant Jacob, 3372
28 *F* thou not, O Jacob my servant, "
48:43 *F*, and the pit, and the snare, 6343
44 He that fleeth from the *f* shall fall "
49: 5 I will bring a *f* upon thee, saith "
24 to flee, and *f* hath seized on her: *7374
29 unto them, *F* is on every side. *4032

Jer 50:16 for f of the oppressing sword they 6440
51:46 lest your heart faint, and ye f for 3372
La 3:47 F and a snare is come upon us, 6343
57 upon thee: thou saidst, F not. 3372
Eze 3: 9 f them not, neither be dismayed 3372
30:13 will put a f in the land of Egypt. 3374
Da 1:10 I f my lord the king, who hath 3373
6:26 and f before the God of Daniel: 1763
10:12 Then said he unto me, F not, 3372
19 O man greatly beloved, f not: "
Ho 3: 5 shall f the Lord and his goodness 6342
10: 5 inhabitants of Samaria shall f *1481
Joe 2:21 F not, O land; be glad and 3372
Am 3: 8 lion hath roared, who will not f? "
Jon 1: 9 I f the Lord, the God of heaven, 3373
Mic 7:17 God, and shall f because of thee. *3372
Zep 3: 7 I said, Surely thou wilt f me, "
16 be said to Jerusalem, F thou not: "
Hag 1:12 the people did f before the Lord. "
2: 5 remaineth among you: f ye not. "
Zec 8:13 f not, but let your hands be strong. "
15 the house of Judah: f ye not. "
9: 5 Ashkelon shall see it, and f; Gaza "
Mal 1: 6 if I be a master, where is my f? 4172
2: 5 the f wherewith he feared me, "
3: 5 and f not me, saith the Lord 3372
4: 2 But unto you that f my name 3373
M't 1:20 f not to take unto thee Mary 5399
10:26 F them not therefore: for there is "
28 f not them which kill the body, * "
28 f him which is able to destroy both "
31 F ye not therefore, ye are of more "
14:26 a spirit; and they cried out for f. 5401
21:26 we f the people; for all hold John 5399
28: 4 for f of him the keepers did shake, 5401
5 F not ye: for I know that ye seek 5399
8 sepulchre with f and great joy; 5401
Lu 1:12 was troubled, and f fell upon him. "
13 F not, Zacharias: for thy prayer 5399
30 F not, Mary: for thou hast found "
50 his mercy is on them that f him "
65 f came on all that dwelt round 5401
74 enemies might serve him without f, 870
2:10 F not: for, behold, I bring you *5399
5:10 And Jesus said unto Simon, F not; "
26 were filled with f, saying, We have 5401
7:16 came a f on all: and they glorified "
8:37 for they were taken with great f: "
50 F not: believe only, and she shall 5399
12: 5 whom ye shall f: F him, which "
5 yea, I say unto you, F him. "
7 F not therefore: ye are of more "
32 F not, little flock; for it is your "
18: 4 I f not God, nor regard man; "
21:26 Men's hearts failing them for f, 5401
23:40 Dost not thou f God, seeing thou 5399
Joh 7:13 openly of him for f of the Jews. 5401
12:15 F not, daughter of Sion: behold, 5399
19:38 but secretly for f of the Jews, 5401
20:19 assembled for f of the Jews, came 5401
Ac 2:43 f came upon every soul: and many "
5: 5 great f came on all them that heard "
11 great f came upon all the church, "
9:31 and walking in the f of the Lord, "
13:16 and ye that f God, give audience. 5399
19:17 f fell on them all, and the name 5401
27:24 F not, Paul; thou must be brought 5399
Ro 3:18 There is no f of God before their 5401
8:15 the spirit of bondage again to f; "
11:20 faith. Be not highminded, but f: 5399
13: 7 f to whom f; honour to whom 5401
1Co 2: 3 and in f, and in much trembling. "
16:10 he may be with you without f: "
2Co 7: 1 perfecting holiness in the f of God. 5401
11 what indignation, yea, what f, yea, "
15 with f and trembling ye received "
11: 3 But I f, lest by any means, as the 5399
12:20 For I f, lest, when I come, I shall "
Eph 5:21 one to another in the f of God. 5401
6: 5 with f and trembling, in singleness "
Ph'p 1:14 bold to speak the word without f. 870
2:12 salvation with f and trembling. 5401
1Ti 5:20 all, that others also may f. 5401, 2192
2Ti 1: 7 hath not given us the spirit of f; * 1167
Heb 2:15 who through f of death were all 5401
4: 1 Let us therefore f, lest, a promise 5399
11: 7 moved with f, prepared an ark 2125
12:21 I exceedingly f and quake:) 1630, 1510
28 with reverence and godly f: *2124
13: 6 I will not f what man shall do unto 5399
1Pe 1:17 time of your sojourning here in f: 5401
2:17 F God. Honour the king. 5399
18 subject to your masters with all f; 5401
3: 2 chaste conversation coupled with f. "
15 is in you with meekness and f: "
1Jo 4:18 There is no f in love; but perfect "
18 love casteth out f: because f hath "
Jude 12 feeding themselves without f: 870
23 others save with f, pulling them 5401
Re 1:17 saying unto me, F not; I am the 5399
2:10 F none of those things which thou "
11:11 great f fell upon them which saw 5401
18 saints, and them that f thy name, 5399
14: 7 F God, and give glory to him; "
15: 4 Who shall not f thee, O Lord, "
18:10, 15 afar off for the f of her torment, 5401
19: 5 that f him, both small and great. 5399

feared
Ge 19:30 for he f to dwell in Zoar: 3372
26: 7 for he f to say, She is my wife; "
Ex 1:17 the midwives f God, and did not as "
21 the midwives f God, that he made "
2:14 And Moses f, and said, Surely this "
9:20 He that f the word of the Lord 3373
14:31 people f the Lord, and believed 3372
De 25:18 and he f not God. 3373
32:17 up, whom your fathers f not. *8175
27 that I f the wrath of the enemy, 1481
Jos 4:14 sight of all Israel; and they f him, 3372
14 they f Moses, all the days of his life. "
10: 2 they f greatly, because Gibeon was "
J'g 6:27 because he f his father's household, "
8:20 he f, because he was yet a youth. "
1Sa 3:15 Samuel f to shew Eli the vision. "
12:18 all the people greatly f the Lord "
14:26 mouth: for the people f the oath. "
15:24 because I f the people, and obeyed "
2Sa 3:11 a word again, because he f him. "
10:19 the Syrians f to help the children "
12:18 And the servants of David f to tell "
1Ki 1:50 Adonijah f because of Solomon, "
3:28 they f the king: for they saw that "
18: 3 Obadiah f the Lord greatly: 3373
2Ki 17: 7 and had f other gods, 3372
25 they f not the Lord: therefore the "
32 they f the Lord, and made unto 3373
33 f the Lord, and served their own "
41 nations f the Lord, and served "
1Ch 16:25 he also is to be f above all gods. 3372
2Ch 20: 3 Jehoshaphat f, and set himself to "
Ne 7: 2 man, and f God above many. "
Job 1: 1 and one that f God, and eschewed 3373
3:25 thing which I greatly f is come *6342
Ps 76: 7 Thou, even thou, art to be f: 3372
8 the earth f, and was still, "
11 unto him that ought to be f. 4172
78:53 them on safely so that they f not: 6342
89: 7 God is greatly to be f in the 6206
96: 4 he is to be f above all gods. 3372
130: 4 with thee, that thou mayest be f. "
Isa 41: 5 The isles saw it, and f; the ends of "
51:13 and hast f continually every day *6342
57:11 whom hast thou been afraid or f, *3372
Jer 3: 8 her treacherous sister Judah f not, "
42:16 sword, which ye f, shall overtake *3373
44:10 they f, nor walked in my law, 3372
Eze 11: 8 Ye have f the sword; and I will "
Da 5:19 languages, trembled and f before 1763
Ho 10: 3 because we f not the Lord: what *3372
Jon 1:16 the men f the Lord exceedingly, "
Mal 2: 5 fear wherewith he f me, and was "
3:16 they that f the Lord spake often "
16 before him for them that f the Lord, "
M't 14: 5 he f the multitude, because they 5399
21:46 they f the multitude, because they "
27:54 f greatly, saying, Truly this was "
M'r 4:41 they f exceedingly, and said 5399, 5401
6:20 For Herod f John, knowing that 5399
11:18 they f him, because all the people "
32 Of men; they f the people: "
12:12 lay hold on him, but f the people: "
Lu 9:34 f as they entered into the cloud. "
45 they f to ask him of that saying. * "
18: 2 judge, which f not God, neither "
19:21 For I f thee, because thou art an "
20:19 and they f the people: for they "
22: 2 kill him; for they f the people. "
Joh 9:22 because they f the Jews: for the "
Ac 5:26 for they f the people, lest they "
10: 2 one that f God with all his house, "
16:38 they f, when they heard that they "
Heb 5: 7 and was heard in that he f; *2124

fearest
Ge 22:12 now I know that thou f God, 3373
Isa 57:11 even of old, and thou f me not? 3372
Jer 22:25 hand of them whose face thou f, *1481

feareth
1Ki 1:51 Behold, Adonijah f king Solomon: 3372
Job 1: 8 an upright man, one that f God, 3373
2: 3 an upright man, one that f God, "
Ps 25:12 What man is he that f the Lord? "
112: 1 Blessed is the man that f the 3372
128: 1 is every one that f the Lord; 3373
4 shall the man be blessed that f the "
Pr 13:13 but he that f the commandment "
14: 2 in his uprightness f the Lord: "
16 A wise man f, and departeth from "
28:14 Happy is the man that f alway: 6342
31:30 but a woman that f the Lord, 3373
Ec 7:18 he that f God shall come forth "
8:13 because he f not before God. "
9: 2 as he that f an oath. "
Isa 50:10 Who is among you that f the Lord, "
Ac 10:22 a just man, and one that f God, 5399
35 But in every nation he that f him, "
13:26 whosoever among you f God, * "
1Jo 4:18 He that f is not made perfect in "

fearful
Ex 15:11 f in praises, doing wonders? 3372
De 20: 8 What man is there that is f and 3373
28:58 fear this glorious and f name, 3372
J'g 7: 3 Whosoever is f and afraid, let 3373
Isa 35: 4 Say to them that are of a f heart, 4116
M't 8:26 Why are ye f, O ye of little faith? 1169
M'r 4:40 said unto them, Why are ye so f? "
Lu 21:11 f sights and great signs shall *5400
Heb 10:27 certain f looking for of judgment 5398
31 It is a f thing to fall into the hands "
Re 21: 8 the f, and unbelieving, and the 1169

fearfully
Ps 139:14 I am f and wonderfully made: 3372

fearfulness
Ps 55: 5 F and trembling are come upon 3374
Isa 21: 4 heart panted, f affrighted me: *6427
33:14 f hath surprised the hypocrites. *7461

fearing
Jos 22:25 children cease from f the Lord. 3372
M'r 5:33 But the woman f and trembling, 5399
Ac 23:10 the chief captain, f lest Paul 2125
27:17 and, f lest they should fall into 5399
27:29 f lest we should have fallen upon 5399
Ga 2:12 himself, f them which were of the "
Col 3:22 but in singleness of heart, f God: "
Heb 11:27 not f the wrath of the king: "

fears
Ps 34: 4 and delivered me from all my f. 4035
Ec 12: 5 and f shall be in the way, *2849
Isa 66: 4 and will bring their f upon them: 4035
2Co 7: 5 were fightings, within were f. 5401

feast See also FEASTED; FEASTING; FEASTS.
Ge 19: 3 he made them a f, and did bake 4960
21: 8 Abraham made a great f the same "
26:30 he made them a f, and they did eat "
29:22 men of the place, and made a f. "
40:20 he made a f unto all his servants: "
Ex 5: 1 that they may hold a f unto me 2287
10: 9 we must hold a f unto the Lord. 2282
12:14 ye shall keep it a f to the Lord "
14 shall keep it a f by an ordinance 2287
17 observe the f of unleavened bread; "
13: 6 in the seventh day shall be a f to 2282
23:14 Three times thou shalt keep a f 2287
15 keep the f of unleavened bread: 2282
16 And the f of harvest, the firstfruits "
16 and the f of ingathering, which is "
32: 5 To morrow is a f to the Lord. "
34:18 The f of unleavened bread shalt "
22 thou shalt observe the f of weeks, "
22 f of ingathering at the year's end. "
25 sacrifice of the f of the passover "
Le 23: 6 the f of unleavened bread unto the "
34 the f of tabernacles for seven days "
39 ye shall keep a f unto the Lord "
41 ye shall keep it a f unto the Lord "
Nu 28:17 fifteenth day of this month is the f: "
29:12 ye shall keep a f unto the Lord "
De 16:10 thou shalt keep the f of weeks "
13 shalt observe the f of tabernacles "
14 And thou shalt rejoice in thy f, "
15 days shalt thou keep a solemn f 2287
16 in the f of unleavened bread, and 2282
16 in the f of weeks, and in the f of "
31:10 of release, in the f of tabernacles, "
J'g 14:10 Samson made there a f; for so 4960
12 within the seven days of the f, "
17 seven days, while their f lasted: "
21:19 Behold, there is a f of the Lord 2282
1Sa 25:36 behold he held a f in his house, 4960
36 like the f of a king; and Nabal's "
2Sa 3:20 the men that were with him a f. "
1Ki 3:15 and made a f to all his servants. "
8: 2 at the f in the month Ethanim, 2282
65 at that time Solomon held a f, "
12:32 Jeroboam ordained a f in the "
32 like unto the f that is in Judah, "
33 a f unto the children of Israel; "
2Ch 5: 3 themselves unto the king in the f "
7: 8 Solomon kept the f seven days, "
9 seven days, and the f seven days. "
8:13 even in the f of unleavened bread, "
13 and in the f of weeks, "
13 and in the f of tabernacles. "
30:13 to keep the f of unleavened bread "
21 kept the f of unleavened bread "
22 eat throughout the f seven days. 4150
35:17 kept...the f of unleavened bread 2282
Ezr 3: 4 They kept also the f of tabernacles, "
6:22 kept the f of unleavened bread "
Ne 8:14 should dwell in booths in the f of "
18 And they kept the f seven days; "
Es 1: 3 he made a f unto all his princes 4960
5 king made a f unto all the people "
9 Vashti the queen made a f for the "
2:18 Then the king made a great f unto "
18 and his servants, even Esther's f; "
8:17 and gladness, a f and a good day. "
Ps 81: 3 appointed, on our solemn f day. 2282
Pr 15:15 a merry heart hath a continual f. 4960
Ec 10:19 A f is made for laughter, and 3899
Isa 25: 6 unto all people a f of fat things, 4960
6 a f of wines on the lees, "
La 2: 7 as in the day of a solemn f. *4150
Eze 45:21 the passover, a f of seven days; 2282
23 seven days of the f he shall prepare "
25 shall he do the like in the f of the "
Da 5: 1 the king made a great f to a 3900
Ho 2:11 her f days, her new moons, and 2282
9: 5 in the day of the f of the Lord? "
12: 9 as in the days of the solemn f. 4150
Am 5:21 I hate, I despise your f days, *2282
Zec 14:16 and to keep the f of tabernacles. "
18, 19 that come not up to keep the f "
M't 26: 2 two days is the f of the passover, *
5 But they said, Not on the f day, 1859
17 day of the f of unleavened bread *
27:15 at that f the governor was wont 1859
M'r 14: 1 two days was the f of the passover, "
2 But they said, Not on the f day, 1859
15: 6 Now at that f he released unto "
Lu 2:41 every year at the f of the passover. "
42 Jerusalem after the custom of the f. "
5:29 Levi made him a great f in his 1408
14:13 when thou makest a f, call the "
22: 1 the f of unleavened bread drew 1859
23:17 release one unto them at the f. "
Joh 2: 8 bear unto the governor of the f. 755
9 When the ruler of the f had tasted "
9 the governor of the f called the "
23 at the passover, in the f day, 1859
4:45 that he did at Jerusalem at the f: "
45 for they also went unto the f. "
5: 1 After this there was a f of the Jews; "
6: 4 a f of the Jews, was nigh. "
7: 2 the Jews' f of tabernacles was at "
8 Go ye up unto this f: "

Joh 7: 8 I go not up yet unto this *f*; 1859
10 then went he also up unto the *f*, "
11 Then the Jews sought him at the *f*, "
14 Now about the midst of the *f* Jesus "
37 last day, that great day of the *f*, "
10:22 Jerusalem the *f* of the dedication, 1456
11:56 that he will not come to the *f*? 1859
12:12 people that were come to the *f*, "
20 that came up to worship at the *f*: "
13: 1 Now before the *f* of the passover, "
29 we have need of against the *f*; "
Ac 18:21 I must by all means keep this *f* * "
1Co 5: 8 Therefore let us keep the *f*, 1858
10:27 them that believe not bid you to a *f*,
2Pe 2:13 deceivings while they *f* with you; 4910
Jude 12 of charity, when they *f* with you,

feast-day See FEAST and DAY.

feasted
Job 1: 4 his sons went and *f* in their *6213, 4960

feasting
Es 9:17, 18 and made it a day of *f* and 4960
19 Adar a day of gladness and *f*, "
22 they should make them days of *f* "
Job 1: 5 when the days of their *f* were "
Ec 7: 2 than to go to the house of *f*: "
Jer 16: 8 not also go into the house of *f*, "

feasts
Le 23: 2 Concerning the *f* of the Lord, *4150
2 convocations, even these are my *f*. "
4 These are the *f* of the Lord, even "
37 These are the *f* of the Lord, which "
44 of Israel the *f* of the Lord. "
Nu 15: 3 in your solemn *f*, to make a sweet "
29:39 do unto the Lord in your set *f*, "
1Ch 23:31 and on the set *f*, by number, "
2Ch 2: 4 and on the solemn *f* of the Lord "
8:13 new moons, and on the solemn *f* "
31: 3 the new moons, and for the set *f*, "
Ezr 3: 5 and of all the set *f* of the Lord "
Ne 10:33 the set *f*, and for the holy things, "
Ps 35:16 With hypocritical mockers in *f*, 4580
Isa 1:14 your appointed *f* my soul hateth: "
5:12 and pipe and wine, are in their *f*: 4960
Jer 51:39 In their heat I will make their *f*, "
La 1: 4 none come to the solemn *f*: *4150
2: 6 caused the solemn *f* and sabbaths* "
Eze 36:38 of Jerusalem in her solemn *f*; "
45:17 to give drink...offerings, in the *f*. 2282
46: 9 before the Lord in the solemn *f*, 4150
11 And in the *f* and in the solemnities 2282
Ho 2:11 sabbaths, and all her solemn *f*. *4150
Am 8:10 I will turn your *f* into mourning, 2282
Na 1:15 keep thy solemn *f*, perform thy "
Zec 8:19 joy and gladness, and cheerful *f*; 4150
Mal 2: 3 even the dung of your solemn *f*; †2282
M't 23: 6 love the uppermost rooms at *f*, 1173
M'r 12:39 and the uppermost rooms at *f*: "
Lu 20:46 and the chief rooms at *f*; "
Jude 12 are spots in your *f* of charity, *

feathered
Ps 78:27 and *f* fowls like as the sand *3671
Eze 39:17 Speak unto every *f* fowl, and to* "

feathers
Le 1:16 pluck away his crop with his *f*, *5133
Job 39:13 wings and *f* unto the ostrich? ‡2624
Ps 68:13 and her *f* with yellow gold. * 84
91: 4 He shall cover thee with his *f*, * 84
Eze 17: 3 great wings, long winged, full of *f*, 5133
7 with great wings and many *f*: "
Da 4:33 hairs were grown like eagles' *f*, "

fed
Ge 30:36 Jacob *f* the rest of Laban's flocks 7462
36:24 as he *f* the asses of Zibeon his "
41: 2 fatfleshed; and they *f* in a meadow. "
18 favoured; and they *f* in a meadow: "
47:17 and he *f* them with bread for all 5095
48:15 the God which *f* me all my life 7462
Ex 16:32 I have *f* you in the wilderness, 398
De 8: 3 to hunger, and *f* thee with manna, "
16 Who *f* thee in the wilderness with "
2Sa 20: 3 put them in ward, and *f* them, *3557
1Ki 18: 4 and *f* them with bread and water.) "
13 and *f* them with bread and water? "
1Ch 27:29 over the herds that *f* in Sharon 7462
Ps 37: 3 and verily thou shalt be *f*. †‡ "
78:72 *f* them according to the integrity "
81:16 He should have *f* them also with* 398
Isa 1:11 of rams, and the fat of *f* beasts; 4806
Jer 5: 7 when I had *f* them to the full, "
8 They were as *f* horses in the 2109
Eze 16:19 and honey, wherewith I *f* thee, 398
34: 3 ye kill them that are *f*: but ye *1277
8 but the shepherds *f* themselves, 7462
8 and *f* not my flock; "
Da 4:12 and all flesh was *f* of it. 2110
5:21 they *f* him with grass like oxen, 2939
Zec 11: 7 called Bands; and I *f* the flock. 7462
M't 25:37 thee an hungered, and *f* thee? 5142
M'r 5:14 they that *f* the swine fled, and 1006
Lu 8:34 they that *f* them saw what was "
16:21 desiring to be *f* with the crumbs 5526
1Co 3: 2 I have *f* you with milk, and not 4222

feeble See also FEEBLEMINDED; FEEBLER.
Ge 30:42 But when the cattle were *f*, he 5848
De 25:18 even all that were *f* behind thee, 2826
1Sa 2: 5 hath many children is waxed *f*. * 535
2Sa 4: 1 his hands were *f*, and all the 7503
2Ch 28:15 and carried all the *f* of them upon 3782
Ne 4: 2 What do these *f* Jews? will they 537
Job 4: 4 hast strengthened the *f* knees, 3766
Ps 38: 8 I am *f* and sore broken: *6313
105:37 and there was not one *f* person 3782
Pr 30:26 The conies are but a *f* folk, 3808, 6099
Isa 16:14 the remnant shall be very *3808, 3524
35: 3 hands, and confirm the *f* knees. 3782
Jer 6:24 our hands wax *f*: anguish hath 7503
49:24 Damascus is waxed *f*, and turneth "
50:43 and his hands waxed *f*: anguish "
Eze 7:17 All hands shall be *f*, and all knees "
21: 7 and all hands shall be *f*, "
Zec 12: 8 and he that is *f* among them at 3782
1Co 12:22 which seem to be more *f*, are 772
Heb 12:12 hang down, and the *f* knees. *3886

feebleminded
1Th 5:14 comfort the *f*, support the weak, *3642

feebleness
Jer 47: 3 to their children for *f* of hands; 7510

feebler
Ge 30:42 so the *f* were Laban's, and the 5848

feed See also FED; FEEDEST; FEEDETH; FEEDING.
Ge 25:30 *F* me, I pray thee, with that same 3938
29: 7 ye the sheep, and go and *f* them. 7462
30:31 I will again *f* and keep thy flock: "
37:12 went to *f* their father's flock in "
13 Do not thy brethren *f* the flock in "
16 tell me, I pray thee, where they *f*.* "
46:32 their trade hath been to *f* cattle;* "
Ex 22: 5 shall *f* in another man's field; 1197
34: 3 neither let the flocks nor herds *f* 7462
1Sa 17:15 from Saul to *f* his father's sheep "
2Sa 5: 2 Thou shalt *f* my people Israel, ‡ "
7: 7 to *f* my people Israel, saying, ‡ "
19:33 and I will *f* thee with me in *3557
1Ki 17: 4 commanded the ravens to *f* thee "
22:27 and *f* him with bread of affliction 398
1Ch 11: 2 Thou shalt *f* my people Israel, ‡7462
17: 6 I commanded to *f* my people, ‡ "
2Ch 18:26 and *f* him with bread of affliction 398
Job 24: 2 take away flocks, and *f* thereof. 7462
20 the worm shall *f* sweetly on him; "
Ps 28: 9 *f* them also, and lift them up ‡7462
49:14 death shall *f* on them; and the * "
78:71 brought him to *f* Jacob his people, "
Pr 10:21 The lips of the righteous *f* many: "
30: 8 *f* me with food convenient for me: 2963
Ca 1: 8 *f* thy kids beside the shepherds' 7462
4: 5 twins, which *f* among the lilies. "
6: 2 bed of spices, to *f* in the gardens, "
Isa 5:17 the lambs *f* after their manner, "
11: 7 And the cow and the bear shall *f*; "
14:30 And the firstborn of the poor shall *f*, "
27:10 there shall the calf *f*, and there "
30:23 shall thy cattle *f* in large pastures. "
40:11 shall *f* his flock like a shepherd: "
49: 9 They shall *f* in the ways, and their "
26 I will *f* them that oppress thee 398
58:14 *f* thee with the heritage of Jacob "
61: 5 strangers shall stand and *f* your 7462
65:25 wolf and the lamb shall *f* together, "
Jer 3:15 which shall *f* you with knowledge "
6: 3 they shall *f* every one in his place. "
9:15 I will *f* them, even this people, 398
23: 2 the pastors that *f* my people; 7462
4 over them which shall *f* them: "
15 I will *f* them with wormwood, and 398
50:19 he shall *f* on Carmel and Bashan, 7462
La 4: 5 They that did *f* delicately are 398
Eze 34: 2 the shepherds of Israel that do *f* 7462
2 not the shepherds *f* the flocks? "
3 that are fed; but ye *f* not the flock. "
10 shall the shepherds *f* themselves "
13 and *f* them upon the mountains of "
14 I will *f* them in a good pasture, "
14 in a fat pasture they shall *f* upon "
15 I will *f* my flock, and I will cause "
16 I will *f* them with judgment. "
23 he shall *f* them, even my servant "
23 he shall *f* them, and he shall be "
Da 11:26 that *f* of the portion of his meat* 398
Ho 4:16 the Lord will *f* them as a lamb 7462
9: 2 and the winepress shall not *f* them, "
Jon 3: 7 let them not *f*, nor drink water: "
Mic 5: 4 and *f* in the strength of the Lord, "
7:14 *F* thy people with thy rod, the "
14 let them *f* in Bashan and Gilead, "
Zep 2: 7 they shall *f* thereupon: in the * "
3:13 for they shall *f* and lie down, "
Zec 11: 4 *F* the flock of the slaughter; "
7 And I will *f* the flock of slaughter, "
9 Then said I, I will not *f* you: "
16 nor *f* that that standeth still: 3557
Lu 15:15 him into his fields to *f* swine. 1006
Joh 21:15 He saith unto him, *F* my lambs. "
16 He saith unto him, *F* my sheep. *4165
17 Jesus saith unto him, *F* my sheep. 1006
Ac 20:28 overseers, to *f* the church of God, 4165
Ro 12:20 if thine enemy hunger, *f* him; if 5595
1Co 13: 3 bestow all my goods to *f* the poor, "
1Pe 5: 2 *F* the flock of God which is *4165
Re 7:17 midst of the throne shall *f* them, * "
12: 6 that they should *f* her there a *5142

feedest
Ps 80: 5 *f* them with the bread of tears; 398
Ca 1: 7 my soul loveth, where thou *f*, 7462

feedeth
Pr 15:14 mouth of fools *f* on foolishness. 7462
Ca 2:16 I am his: he *f* among the lilies. "
6: 3 is mine: he *f* among the lilies. "
Isa 44:20 He *f* on ashes: a deceived heart "
Ho 12: 1 Ephraim *f* on wind, and followeth "
M't 6:26 yet your heavenly Father *f* them. 5142
Lu 12:24 and God *f* them: how much more "
1Co 9: 7 who *f* a flock, and eateth not 4165

feeding See also FEEDINGPLACE.
Ge 37: 2 was *f* the flock with his brethren; 7462
Job 1:14 oxen were plowing, and the asses *f* "
Eze 34:10 them to cease from *f* the flock; 7462
M't 8:30 them an herd of many swine *f*. 1006
M'r 5:11 mountains a great herd of swine *f*. "
Lu 8:32 many swine *f* on the mountain: "
17: 7 a servant plowing or *f* cattle, *4165
Jude 12 you, *f* themselves without fear: * "

feedingplace
Na 2:11 and the *f* of the young lions, 4829

feel See also FEELING; FELT.
Ge 27:12 will *f* me, and I shall seem to him 4959
21 I pray thee, that I may *f* thee, 4184
J'g 16:26 Suffer me that I may *f* the pillars "
Job 20:20 shall not *f* quietness in his belly, *3045
Ps 58: 9 Before your pots can *f* the thorns, 995
Ec 8: 5 the commandment shall *f* no evil *3045
Ac 17:27 if haply they might *f* after him, 5584

feeling
Eph 4:19 Who being past *f* have given 524
Heb 4:15 cannot be touched with the *f* of our 4834

feet
Ge 18: 4 wash your *f*, and rest yourselves 7272
19: 2 tarry all night, and wash your *f*, "
24:32 and water to wash his *f*, and the "
32 and the men's *f* that were with him. "
43:24 water, and they washed their *f*; "
49:10 nor a lawgiver from between his *f*, "
33 he gathered up his *f* into the bed, "
Ex 3: 5 put off thy shoes from off thy *f*, "
4:25 of her son, and cast it at his *f*, "
12:11 your shoes on your *f*, and your "
24:10 under his *f* as it were a paved work "
25:26 that are on the four *f* thereof. "
30:19 shall wash their hands and their *f* "
21 shall wash their hands and their *f*, "
37:13 that were in the four *f* thereof. "
40:31 washed their hands and their *f* "
Le 8:24 the great toes of their right *f*: * "
11:21 which have legs above their *f*, to "
23 creeping things, which have four *f*, "
42 more *f* among all creeping things "
Nu 20:19 anything else, go through on my *f*. "
De 2:28 only I will pass through on my *f*; "
11:24 the soles of your *f* shall tread * "
28:57 cometh out from between her *f*, "
33: 3 and they sat down at thy *f*; "
Jos 3:13 of the *f* of the priests that bear "
15 and the *f* of the priests that bare "
4: 3 where the priests' *f* stood firm, "
9 where the *f* of the priests which "
18 soles of the priests' *f* were lifted "
9: 5 old shoes and clouted upon their *f*, "
10:24 put your *f* upon the necks of these "
24 put their *f* upon the necks of them. "
14: 9 land whereon thy *f* have trodden* "
J'g 3:24 he covereth his *f* in his summer "
4:10 with ten thousand men at his *f*: "
15 chariot, and fled away on his *f*. "
17 fled away on his *f* to the tent "
5:27 At her *f* he bowed, he fell, he lay "
27 at her *f* he bowed, he fell: where "
19:21 they washed their *f*, and did eat "
Ru 3: 4 uncover his *f*, and lay thee down; 4772
7 came softly, and uncovered his *f*, "
8 behold, a woman lay at his *f*. "
14 she lay at his *f* until the morning: "
1Sa 2: 9 He will keep the *f* of his saints, 7272
14:13 upon his hands and upon his *f*, "
24: 3 and Saul went in to cover his *f*: "
25:24 And fell at his *f*, and said, "
41 to wash the *f* of the servants of "
2Sa 3:34 nor thy *f* put into fetters: as a "
4: 4 had a son that was lame of his *f*. "
12 cut off their hands and their *f*, "
9: 3 yet a son, which is lame on his *f*. "
13 and was lame on both his *f*. "
11: 8 to thy house, and wash thy *f*. "
19:24 had neither dressed his *f*, nor "
22:10 and darkness was under his *f*. "
34 He maketh my *f* like hind's *f*: "
37 so that my *f* did not slip. 7166
39 yea, they are fallen under my *f*. 7272
1Ki 2: 5 in his shoes that were on his *f*. "
5: 3 put them under the soles of his *f*. "
14: 6 Ahijah heard the sound of her *f*, "
12 when thy *f* enter into the city, "
15:23 old age he was diseased in his *f*. "
2Ki 4:27 she caught him by the *f*: but "
37 she went in, and fell at his *f*, "
6:32 sound of his master's *f* behind "
9:35 the skull, and the *f*, and the palms "
13:21 he revived, and stood up on his *f*. "
19:24 the sole of my *f* have I dried up 6471
21: 8 Neither will I make the *f* of Israel 7272
1Ch 28: 2 David the king stood up upon his *f*, "
2Ch 3:13 they stood on their *f*, and their "
16:12 was diseased in his *f*, until his "
Neh 9:21 not old, and their *f* swelled not. "
Es 8: 3 fell down at his *f*, and besought "
Job 12: 5 He that is ready to slip with his *f** "
13:27 puttest my *f* also in the stocks, "
27 a print upon the heels of my *f*. "
18: 8 is cast into a net by his own *f*, "
11 and shall drive him to his *f*. * "
29:15 and *f* was I to the lame. "
30:12 they push away my *f*, and they "
33:11 He putteth my *f* in the stocks, "
Ps 8: 6 hast put all things under his *f*: "
18: 9 and darkness was under his *f*. "
33 He maketh my *f* like hinds' *f*, "
36 under me, that my *f* did not slip. 7166
38 they are fallen under my *f*. 7272
22:16 they pierced my hands and my *f*. "
25:15 he shall pluck my *f* out of the net. "
31: 8 thou hast set my *f* in a large room. "

Ps 40: 2 and set my f upon a rock, 7272
47: 3 and the nations under our f. "
56:13 not thou deliver my f from falling, "
58:10 he shall wash his f in the blood 6471
66: 9 suffereth not our f to be moved. 7272
73: 2 for me, my f were almost gone; "
74: 3 f unto the perpetual desolations; 6471
91:13 dragon shalt thou trample under f. "
105:18 Whose f they hurt with fetters: 7272
115: 7 f have they, but they walk not: "
116: 8 from tears, and my f from falling. "
119:59 turned my f unto thy testimonies. "
101 refrained my f from every evil way "
105 Thy word is a lamp unto my f, "
122: 2 Our f shall stand within thy gates, "
Pr 1:16 their f run to evil, and make haste "
4:26 Ponder the path of thy f, and let "
5: 5 Her f go down to death; her steps "
6:13 speaketh with his f, he teacheth "
18 f that be swift in running to "
28 coals, and his f not be burned? "
7:11 her f abide not in her house: "
19: 2 he that hasteth with his f sinneth. "
26: 6 the hand of a fool cutteth off the f, "
29: 5 spreadeth a net for his f. *6471
Ca 5: 3 I have washed my f; how shall 7272
7: 1 How beautiful are thy f with 6471
Isa 3:16 making a tinkling with their f: 7272
18 tinkling ornaments about their f *
6: 2 with twain he covered his f, and 7272
7:20 the head, and the hair of the f: "
14:19 as a carcase trodden under f. "
23: 7 her own f shall carry her afar off 7272
26: 6 it down, even the f of the poor, "
28: 3 Ephraim, shall be trodden under f: "
32:20 thither the f of the ox and the ass. "
37:25 the sole of my f have I dried up 6471
41: 3 that he had not gone with his f. 7272
49:23 and lick up the dust of thy f; "
52: 7 the f of him that bringeth good "
59: 7 Their f run to evil, and they make "
60:13 make the place of my f glorious. "
14 down at the soles of thy f; "
Jer 13:16 your f stumble upon the dark "
14:10 they have not refrained their f, "
18:22 and hid snares for my f. "
38:22 thy f are sunk in the mire, and they "
La 1:13 he hath spread a net for my f, "
3:34 under his f all the prisoners * "
Eze 1: 7 And their f were straight f; "
7 and the sole of their f was like "
2: 1 Son of man, stand upon thy f, "
2 unto me, and set me upon my f, "
3:24 into me, and set me upon my f, "
16:25 opened thy f to every one that "
24:17 and put on thy shoes upon thy f, "
23 and your shoes upon your f: ye "
25: 6 hands, and stamped with the f, "
32: 2 troubledst the waters with thy f, "
34:18 down with your f the residue of "
18 must foul the residue with your f? "
19 which ye have trodden with your f; "
19 which ye have fouled with your f. "
37:10 lived, and stood up upon their f, "
43: 7 and the place of the soles of my f, "
Da 2:33 his f part of iron and part of clay. 7271
34 smote the image upon his f "
41 f and toes, part of potters' clay, "
42 And as the toes of the f "
7: 4 made stand upon the f as a man, "
7 stamped the residue with the f of "
19 stamped the residue with his f; "
10: 6 his arms and his f like in colour 4772
Na 1: 3 the clouds are the dust of his f. 7272
15 the f of him that bringeth good "
Hab 3: 5 burning coals went forth at his f. "
19 he will make my f like hinds' f, "
Zec 14: 4 And his f shall stand in that day "
12 while they stand upon their f, "
Mal 4: 3 ashes under the soles of your f "
M't 7: 6 they trample them under their f, 4228
10:14 city, shake off the dust of your f. "
15:30 and cast them down at Jesus' f; "
18: 8 than having two hands or two f "
29 fellowservant fell down at his f, * "
28: 9 they came and held him by the f, "
M'r 5:22 when he saw him, he fell at his f, "
6:11 dust under your f for a testimony "
7:25 and came and fell at his f: "
9:45 having two f to be cast into hell, "
Lu 1:79 guide our f into the way of peace. "
7:38 stood at his f behind him weeping, "
38 and began to wash his f with tears, "
38 kissed his f, and anointed them "
44 thou gavest me no water for my f: "
44 she hath washed my f with tears, "
45 hath not ceased to kiss my f. "
46 hath anointed my f with ointment. "
8:35 sitting at the f of Jesus, clothed, "
41 fell down at Jesus' f, and besought "
9: 5 off the very dust from your f for a "
10:39 which also sat at Jesus' f, and "
15:22 on his hand, and shoes on his f: "
17:16 And fell down on his face at his f, "
24:39 Behold my hands and my f, "
40 shewed them his hands and his f. "
Joh 11: 2 and wiped his f with her hair, "
32 she fell down at his f, saying unto "
12: 3 and anointed the f of Jesus, "
3 and wiped his f with her hair: "
13: 5 and began to wash the disciples' f, "
6 Lord, dost thou wash my f? "
8 Thou shalt never wash my f. "
9 Lord, not my f only, but also my "
10 needeth not save to wash his f, "
12 So after he had washed their f, "
Joh 13:14 and Master, have washed your f; 4228
14 also ought to wash one another's f. "
20:12 at the head, and the other at the f, "
Ac 3: 7 his f and ancle bones received 939
4:35 laid them down at the apostles' f: 4228
37 money, and laid it at the apostles' f. "
5: 2 part, and laid it at the apostles' f. "
9 the f of them which have buried "
10 fell she down straightway at his f, "
7:33 Put off thy shoes from thy f: "
58 their clothes at a young man's f, "
10:25 met him, and fell down at his f, "
13:25 of his f I am not worthy to loose. "
51 they shook off the dust of their f "
14: 8 impotent in his f, being a cripple "
10 loud voice, Stand upright on thy f. "
16:24 and made their f fast in the stocks. "
21:11 and bound his own hands and f, "
22: 3 in this city at the f of Gamaliel, "
26:16 But rise, and stand upon thy f: "
Ro 3:15 Their f are swift to shed blood: "
10:15 How beautiful are the f of them "
16:20 bruise Satan under your f shortly. "
1Co 12:21 nor again the head to the f, "
15:25 hath put all enemies under his f. "
27 he hath put all things under his f. "
Eph 1:22 And hath put all things under his f, "
6:15 your f shod with the preparation "
1Ti 5:10 if she have washed the saints' f, "
Heb 2: 8 all things in subjection under his f. "
12:13 And make straight paths for your f, "
Re 1:15 And his f like unto fine brass, "
17 I saw him, I fell at his f as dead. "
2:18 and his f are like fine brass; "
3: 9 to come and worship before thy f, "
10: 1 and his f as pillars of fire: "
11:11 and they stood upon their f; and "
12: 1 the sun, and the moon under her f, "
13: 2 and his f were as the f of a bear, "
19:10 I fell at his f to worship him. "
22: 8 before the f of the angel which "

feign See also FEIGNED; FEIGNEST.
2Sa 14: 2 thee, f thyself to be a mourner,
1Ki 14: 5 f herself to be another woman. 5234
Lu 20:20 sent forth spies which would f *5271

feigned See also UNFEIGNED.
1Sa 21:13 and f himself mad in their hands,
Ps 17: 1 that goeth not out of f lips. 4820
2Pe 2: 3 with f words make merchandise 4112

feignedly
Jer 3:10 me with her whole heart, but f. 8267

feignest
1Ki 14: 6 why f thou thyself to be another ?5234
Ne 6: 8 thou f them out of thine own heart. 908

Felix (fe'-lix) See also FELIX'.
Ac 23:24 him safe unto F the governor. 5344
26 unto the most excellent governor F "
24: 3 and in all places, most noble F, "
22 And when F heard these things, "
24 F came with his wife Drusilla, "
25 F trembled, and answered, Go thy "
27 and F, willing to shew the Jews a "
25 14 a certain man left in bonds by F: "

Felix' (fe'-lix)
Ac 24:27 Porcius Festus came into F room: 5344

fell See also BEFELL; FELLED; FELLEST; FELLING.
Ge 4: 5 very wroth, and his countenance f. 5307
14:10 and Gomorrah fled, and f there; "
15:12 a deep sleep f upon Abram; and, "
12 an horror of great darkness f upon "
17: 3 And Abram f on his face: and God "
17 Then Abraham f upon his face, "
33: 4 and f on his neck, and kissed him: "
44:14 they f before him on the ground. "
45:14 he f upon his brother Benjamin's "
46:29 and he f on his neck, and wept "
50: 1 Joseph f upon his father's face, "
18 his brethren also went and f down "
Ex 32:28 and there f of the people that day "
Le 9:24 they shouted, and f on their faces. "
16: 9 goat upon which the Lord's lot f, 5927
10 the goat, on which the lot f to be the "
Nu 11: 4 that was among them f a lusting:
9 when the dew f upon the camp 3381
9 in the night, the manna f upon it. "
14: 5 Moses and Aaron f on their faces 5307
16: 4 Moses heard it, he f upon his face: "
22 they f upon their faces, and said, "
45 And they f upon their faces. "
20: 6 and they f upon their faces: and "
22:27 angel of the Lord, she f down *7257
31 bowed down his head, and f flat 7812
De 9:18 And I f down before the Lord, 5307
25 Thus I f down before the Lord "
25 forty nights, as I f down at the first; "
Jos 5:14 Joshua f on his face to the earth, "
6:20 shout, that the wall f down flat, "
7: 6 and f to the earth upon his face "
8:25 so it was, that all that f that day, "
11: 7 suddenly; and they f upon them. "
16: 1 of Joseph, f from Jordan by †‡3318
17: 5 there f ten portions to Manasseh, 5307
22:20 wrath f on all the congregation 1961
J'g 4:16 and all the host of Sisera f upon 5307
5:27 feet he bowed, he f, he lay down: "
27 her feet he bowed, he f: where he "
27 bowed, there he f down dead. "
7:13 unto a tent, and smote it that it f, "
8:10 f an hundred and twenty thousand "
12: 6 f at that time of the Ephraimites "
13:20 and f on their faces to the ground. "
16:30 and the house f upon the lords, "
19:26 f down at the door of the man's "
J'g 20:44 f of Benjamin eighteen thousand 5307
46 So that all which f that day of "
Ru 2:10 Then she f on her face, and bowed "
1Sa 4:10 there f of Israel thirty thousand "
18 he f from off the seat backward "
11: 7 fear of the Lord f on the people, "
14:13 and they f before Jonathan; and "
17:49 and he f upon his face to the earth. "
52 the wounded of the Philistines f "
20:41 and f on his face to the ground, "
22:18 he f upon the priests, and slew 6293
25:23 and f before David on her face, 5307
24 And f at his feet, and said, "
28:20 Then Saul f straightway all along "
29: 3 found no fault in him since he f "
30:13 because three days agone I f sick. "
31: 1 f down slain in mount Gilboa. 5307
4 Saul took a sword, and f upon it. "
5 he f likewise upon his sword, and "
2Sa 1: 2 f to the earth, and did obeisance. "
2:16 they f down together: wherefore "
23 and he f down there, and died "
23 Asahel f down and died stood still. "
4: 4 as she made haste to flee, that he f, "
9: 6 he f on his face, and did reverence. "
11:17 and there f some of the people "
13: 2 that he f sick for his sister Tamar; "
14: 4 to the king, she f on her face 5307
22 Joab f to the ground on his face, "
18:28 And he f down to the earth *7812
19:18 Shimei the son of Gera f down 5307
20: 8 and as he went forth it f out. "
21: 9 and they f all seven together, "
22 and f by the hand of David, "
1Ki 2:25 and he f upon him that he died. 6293
32 f upon two men more righteous "
34 and f upon him, and slew him: "
46 and f upon him, that he died. "
14: 1 Abijah the son of Jeroboam f sick. "
17:17 the mistress of the house, f sick; "
18: 7 he knew him, and f on his face, 5307
38 Then the fire of the Lord f, "
39 people saw it, they f on their faces: "
20:30 f upon twenty and seven thousand "
2Ki 1: 2 Ahaziah f down through a lattice "
13 and f on his knees before Elijah, 3766
2:13 mantle of Elijah that f from him, 5307
14 mantle of Elijah that f from him, "
3:19 and shall f every good tree, "
4: 8 And it f on a day, that Elisha 1961
11 it f on a day, that he came thither "
18 the child was grown, it f on a day, "
37 she went in, and f at his feet, 5307
6: 5 the axe head f into the water: "
6 Where f it? And he shewed him "
7:20 And so it f out unto him: for the *1961
25:11 fugitives that f away to the king 5307
1Ch 5:10 Hagarites, who f by their hand: "
22 there f down many slain, because "
10: 1 and f down slain in mount Gilboa. "
4 Saul took a sword, and f upon it. "
5 f likewise on the sword, and died. "
12:19 there f some of Manasseh to David, "
20 there f to him of Manasseh, Adnah, "
20: 8 and they f by the hand of David, "
21:14 there f of Israel seventy thousand "
16 in sackcloth, f upon their faces, "
26:14 the lot eastward f to Shelemiah. "
27:24 f wrath for it against Israel; *1961
2Ch 13:17 so there f down slain of Israel 5307
15: 9 they f to him out of Israel "
17:10 And the fear of the Lord f upon 1961
20:18 inhabitants of Jerusalem f before *5307
21:19 f out by reason of his sickness: 3318
25:13 f upon the cities of Judah, from 6584
Ezr 9: 5 I f upon my knees, and spread 3766
Es 8: 3 f down at his f, and besought 5307
17 the fear of the Jews f upon them.* "
9: 2 fear of them f upon all people. * "
3 the fear of Mordecai f upon them.* "
Job 1:15 And the Sabeans f upon them, "
17 bands, and f upon the camels, 6584
19 and it f upon the young men, 5307
20 and f down upon the ground, and "
Ps 27: 2 up my flesh, they stumbled and f. "
78:64 Their priests f by the sword; and "
105:38 the fear of them f upon them. * "
107:12 they f down, and there was none 3782
Jer 39: 9 those that f away, that f to him, *5307
46:16 one f upon another: and they said, "
52:15 that f away, that f to the king "
La 1: 7 people f into the hand of the enemy, "
5:13 the children f under the wood. *3782
Eze 1:28 when I saw it, I f upon my face. 5307
3:23 of Chebar: and I f on my face. "
8: 1 of the Lord God f there upon me. "
9: 8 that I f upon my face, and cried, "
11: 5 the Spirit of the Lord f upon me, "
13 Then f I down upon my face, "
39:23 so f they all by the sword. "
43: 3 river Chebar; and I f upon my face. "
44: 4 of the Lord: and I f upon my face, "
Da 2:46 Nebuchadnezzar f upon his face, 5308
3: 7 f down and worshipped the golden "
23 f down bound into the midst of the "
4:31 there f a voice from heaven, saying, "
7:20 came up, and before whom three f; "
8:17 I was afraid, and f upon my face: 5307
10: 7 but a great quaking f upon them, "
Jon 1: 7 lots, and the lot f upon Jonah. "
M't 2:11 and f down, and worshipped him: 4098
7:25 and it f not: for it was founded "
27 and it f: and great was the fall of it. "
13: 4 some seeds f by the way side, and "
5 Some f upon stony places, where "
7 And some f among thorns; and "

M't 13: 8 But other f into good ground, and 4098
17: 6 they f on their face, and were sore "
18:26 therefore f down, and worshipped "
29 fellowservant f down at his feet. "
26:39 and f on his face, and prayed, "
M'r 3:11 they saw him, f down before him, 4363
4: 4 some f by the way side, and the 4098
5 And some f on stony ground, where "
7 And some f among thorns, and the "
8 And other f on good ground, and "
5:22 when he saw him, he f at his feet, "
33 came and f down before him, and 4363
7:25 and came and f at his feet: "
9:20 he f on the ground, and wallowed 4098
14:35 and f on the ground, and prayed "
Lu 1:12 troubled, and fear f upon him. 1968
5: 8 he f down at Jesus' knees, saying, 4363
12 f on his face, and besought him, 4098
6:49 immediately it f; and the ruin "
8: 5 he sowed, some f by the way side; "
6 And some f upon a rock; and as "
7 And some f among thorns; and the "
8 And other f on good ground, and "
14 which f among thorns are they, "
23 as they sailed he f asleep: and there "
28 cried out, and f down before him, 4363
41 he f down at Jesus' feet, and 4098
10:30 f among thieves, which stripped 4045
36 him that f among the thieves? 1706
13: 4 upon whom the tower in Siloam f, 4098
15:20 and ran, and f on his neck, 1968
16:21 which f from the rich man's table: 4098
17:16 f down on his face at his feet, "
Joh 11:32 f down at his feet, saying unto him, "
18: 6 backward, and f to the ground. 4098
Ac 1:25 from which Judas by transgression f, "
26 and the lot f upon Matthias; 4098
5: 5 f down, and gave up the ghost: "
10 Then f she down straightway at "
7:60 when he had said this, he f asleep. "
9: 4 f to the earth, and heard a voice 4098
18 there f from his eyes as it had been 634
10:10 made ready, he f into a trance, 1968
25 and f down at his feet, and 4098
44 the Holy Ghost f on all them which 1968
11:15 the Holy Ghost f on them, as on us "
12: 7 his chains f off from his hands. 1601
13:11 f on him a mist and a darkness; 1968
36 f on sleep, and was laid unto his "
16:29 and f down before Paul and Silas, 4363
19:17 and fear f on them all, and the 1968
35 which f down from Jupiter? 1356
20: 9 and f down from the third loft, 4098
10 Paul went down, and f on him, 1968
37 f on Paul's neck, and kissed him, "
22: 7 I f unto the ground, and heard 4098
Ro 11:22 on them which f, severity; but "
15: 3 that reproached thee f on me. 1968
1Co 10: 8 and f in one day three and twenty 4098
Heb 3:17 carcasses f in the wilderness? "
11:30 faith the walls of Jericho f down, "
2Pe 3: 4 since the fathers f asleep, all things "
Re 1:17 I saw him, I f at his feet as dead. 4098
5: 8 elders f down before the Lamb, "
14 f down and worshipped him that "
6:13 stars of heaven f unto the earth, "
7:11 f before the throne on their faces, "
8:10 there f a great star from heaven, "
10 f upon the third part of the rivers, "
11:11 fear f upon them which saw them. "
13 and the tenth part of the city f, "
16 f upon their faces, and worshipped "
16: 2 f a noisome and grievous sore *1096
19 and the cities of the nations f: 4098
21 there f upon men a great hail *2597
19: 4 and the four beasts f down and 4098
10 And I f at his feet to worship "
22: 8 I f down to worship before the feet "

felled
2Ki 3:25 and f all the good trees: only in 5307

feller
Isa 14: 8 no f is come up against us. 3772

fellest
2Sa 3:34 before wicked men, so f thou. *5307

felling
2Ki 6: 5 But as one was f a beam, 5307

felloes
1Ki 7:33 and their f, and their spokes, 2839

fellow See also FELLOWCITIZENS; FELLOWDISCIPLES; FELLOWHEIRS; FELLOWHELPER; FELLOWLABOURER; FELLOWPRISONER; FELLOW'S; FELLOWS; FELLOWSERVANT; FELLOWSHIP; FELLOWSOLDIER; FELLOWWORKERS; WORKFELLOW; YOKEFELLOW.
Ex 2:13 Wherefore smitest thou thy f? 7453
J'g 7:13 man that told a dream unto his f, "
14 his f answered and said, This is "
22 every man's sword against his f, "
1Sa 14:20 man's sword was against his f, "
21:15 have brought this f to play the mad
15 shall this f come into my house?
25:21 in vain I have kept all that this f hath
29: 4 Make this f return, that he may * 376
2Sa 2:16 caught every one his f by the head, 7453
1Ki 22:27 Put this f in the prison, and feed him
2Ki 9:11 wherefore came this mad f to thee?
2Ch 18:26 Put this f in the prison, and feed him
Ec 4:10 the one will lift up his f: 2270
Isa 34:14 and the satyr shall cry to his f; 7453
Jon 1: 7 And they said every one to his f, "
Zec 13: 7 and against the man that is my f, 5997
M't 12:24 This f doth not cast out devils, *
26:61 This f said, I am able to destroy *
71 This f was also with Jesus of *
Lu 22:59 a truth this f also was with him: *
23: 2 We found this f perverting the *
Joh 9:29 as for this f, we know not from *
Ac 18:13 Saying, This f persuadeth men *
22:22 Away with such a f from the
24: 5 found this man a pestilent f, and

fellowcitizens
Eph 2:19 but f with the saints, and of the 4847

fellowdisciples
Joh 11:16 Didymus, unto his f, Let us also 4827

fellowheirs
Eph 3: 6 That the Gentiles should be f, 4789

fellowhelper See also FELLOWHELPERS.
2Co 8:23 partner and f concerning you: *4904

fellowhelpers
3Jo 8 that we might be f to the truth. *4904

fellowlabourer See also FELLOWLABOURERS.
1Th 3: 2 our f in the gospel of Christ, *4904
Ph'm 1 our dearly beloved, and f, * "

fellowlabourers
Ph'p 4: 3 also, and with other my f, *4904
Ph'm 24 Demas, Lucas, my f. * "

fellowprisoner See also FELLOWPRISONERS.
Col 4:10 Aristarchus my f saluteth you, 4869
Ph'm 23 Epaphras, my f in Christ Jesus; "

fellowprisoners
Ro 16: 7 and Junia, my kinsmen, and my f, 4869

fellow's
2Sa 2:16 thrust his sword in his f side; 7453

fellows
J'g 11:37 bewail my virginity, I and my f. *7464
18:25 lest angry f run upon thee, and 582
2Sa 6:20 as one of the vain f shamelessly
Ps 45: 7 the oil of gladness above thy f. 2270
Isa 44:11 Behold, all his f shall be ashamed: "
Eze 37:19 and the tribes of Israel his f, * "
Da 2:13 they sought Daniel and his f *2269
18 that Daniel and his f should not * "
7:20 look was more stout than his f. 2273
Zec 3: 8 the high priest, thou, and thy f 7453
M't 11:16 markets, and calling unto their f, 2083
Ac 17: 5 certain lewd f of the baser sort, 435
Heb 1: 9 the oil of gladness above thy f. 3353

fellowservant See also FELLOWSERVANTS.
M't 18:29 And his f fell down at his feet, 4889
33 also have had compassion on thy f, "
Col 1: 7 Epaphras our dear f, who is for "
4: 7 minister and f in the Lord: "
Re 19:10 do it not: I am thy f, and of thy "
22: 9 do it not: for I am thy f, and of thy "

fellowservants
M't 18:28 went out, and found one of his f, 4889
31 So when his f saw what was done, "
24:49 And shall begin to smite his f, "
Re 6:11 their f also and their brethren, "

fellowship
Le 6: 2 or in f, or in a thing taken *8667, 3027
Ps 94:20 of iniquity have f with thee, 2266
Ac 2:42 and f, and in breaking of bread, 2842
1Co 1: 9 were called unto the f of his Son "
10:20 that ye should have f with devils. *2844
2Co 6:14 what f hath righteousness with 3352
8: 4 upon us the f of the ministering 2842
Ga 2: 9 and Barnabas the right hand of f; "
Eph 3: 9 see what is the f of the mystery, * "
5:11 And have no f with the unfruitful 4790
Ph'p 1: 5 your f in the gospel from the first 2842
2: 1 of love, if any f of the Spirit, "
3:10 and the f of his sufferings, "
1Jo 1: 3 ye also may have f with us: and "
3 truly our f is with the Father, "
6 If we say that we have f with him, "
7 light, we have f one with another, "

fellowsoldier
Ph'p 2:25 and companion in labour, and f, 4961
Ph'm 2 and Archippus our f, and to the "

fellowworkers
Col 4:11 only are my f unto the kingdom 4904

felt
Ge 27:22 and he f him, and said, The voice 4959
Ex 10:21 even darkness which may be f. "
Pr 23:35 I f it not: when shall I awake? 3045
M'r 5:29 f in her body that she was healed 1097
Ac 28: 5 beast into the fire, and f no harm. *3958

female
Ge 1:27 him; male and f created he them. 5347
5: 2 Male and f created he them; and "
6:19 with thee; they shall be male and f. "
7: 2 thee by sevens, the male and his f: 802
2 clean by two, the male and his f. "
3 air by sevens, the male and the f; 5347
9 into the ark, the male and the f, "
16 went in male and f of all flesh, "
Le 3: 1 whether it be a male or f, he shall "
6 flock; male or f, he shall offer it "
4:28 of the goats, a f without blemish, "
32 shall bring it a f without blemish. "
5: 6 a f from the flock, a lamb or a kid "
12: 7 her that hath born a male or a f. "
27: 4 if it be a f, then thy estimation "
5 and for the f ten shekels. "
6 and for the f thy estimation shall "
7 and for the f ten shekels. "
Nu 5: 3 Both male and f shall ye put out, "
De 4:16 the likeness of male or f, "
M't 19: 4 beginning made them male and f, 2338
M'r 10: 6 God made them male and f. "
Gal 3:28 there is neither male nor f: for "

fence See also DEFENCE; FENCED; OFFENCE.
Ps 62: 3 shall ye be, and as a tottering f. 1447

fenced See also DEFENCED.
Nu 32:17 ones shall dwell in the f cities ‡4013
36 f cities: and folds for sheep. ‡ "
De 3: 5 cities were f with high walls, ‡1219
9: 1 cities great and f up to heaven, ‡ "
28:52 thy high and f walls come down, ‡ "
Jos 10:20 of them entered into f cities. ‡4013
14:12 that the cities were great and f: ‡1219
19:35 the f cities are Ziddim, Zer, and ‡4013
1Sa 6:18 f cities, and of country villages, ‡ "
2Sa 20: 6 he get him f cities, and escape ‡1211
23: 7 that shall touch them must be f *4390
2Ki 3:19 And ye shall smite every f city, ‡4013
10: 2 a f city also, and armour; ‡ "
17: 9 of the watchmen to the f city. ‡ "
18: 8 of the watchmen to the f city. ‡ "
13 come up against all the f cities ‡1219
19:25 shouldest be to lay waste f cities ‡ "
2Ch 8: 5 f cities, with walls, gates, and ‡4692
11:10 Judah and in Benjamin f cities. ‡4694
23 unto every f city: and he gave ‡ "
12: 4 f cities which pertained to Judah, ‡ "
14: 6 And he built f cities in Judah: ‡ "
17: 2 placed forces in all the f cities ‡1219
19 whom the king put in the f cities ‡4013
19: 5 all the f cities of Judah, city by ‡1219
21: 3 things, with f cities in Judah: ‡4694
32: 1 encamped against the f cities, ‡1219
33:14 war in all the f cities of Judah. ‡ "
Job 10:11 f me with bones and sinews. *7753
19: 8 f up my way that I cannot pass, 1443
Isa 2:15 tower, and upon every f wall, ‡1219
5: 2 And he f it, and gathered out *5823
Jer 5:17 shall impoverish thy f cities, ‡4013
15:20 unto this people a f brasen wall: ‡1219
Eze 36:35 and ruined cities are become f, ‡ "
Da 11:15 and take the most f cities: and ‡4013
Ho 8:14 Judah had multiplied f cities: ‡1219
Zep 1:16 and alarm against the f cities, ‡ "

fenced-city See FENCED and CITY.

fenced-wall See FENCED and WALL.

fens
Job 40:21 in the covert of the reed, and f. *1207

ferret
Le 11:30 And the f, and the chameleon, * 604

ferry
2Sa 19:18 And there went over a f boat to 5679

ferry-boat See FERRY and BOAT.

fervent
Ac 18:25 being f in the spirit, he spake 2204
Ro 12:11 f in spirit; serving the Lord; "
2Co 7: 7 your f mind toward me; so that *2205
Jas 5:16 f prayer of a righteous man *
1Pe 4: 8 have f charity among yourselves: 1618
2Pe 3:10 the elements shall melt with f heat,
12 the elements shall melt with f heat?

fervently
Col 4:12 labouring f for you in prayers, *
1Pe 1:22 one another with a pure heart f: 1619

Festus (*fes'-tus*) See also FESTUS'.
Ac 24:27 Porcius F came into Felix' room: 5347
25: 1 F was come into the province, "
4 But F answered, that Paul should "
9 But F, willing to do the Jews a "
12 Then F, when he had conferred "
13 came unto Cæsarea to salute F. "
14 F declared Paul's cause unto the "
22 Then Agrippa said unto F, I would "
24 and F said, King Agrippa, and all "
26:24 F said with a loud voice, Paul, "
25 I am not mad, most noble F; "
32 Then said Agrippa unto F, This "

Festus' (*fes'-tus*)
Ac 25:23 at F commandment Paul was 5347

fetch See FETCHED; FETCHETH; FETCHT.
Ge 18: 5 And I will f a morsel of bread, 3947
27: 9 f me from thence two good kids "
13 obey my voice, and go f me them. "
45 will send, and f thee from thence: "
42:16 and let him f your brother, and ye "
Ex 2: 5 she sent her maid to f it. "
Nu 20:10 we f you water out of this rock? *3318
34: 5 the border shall f a compass *
De 19:12 of his city shall send and f him 3947
24:10 into his house to f his pledge. 5670
19 thou shalt not go again to f it: 3947
30: 4 and from thence will he f thee: "
J'g 11: 5 elders of Gilead went to f Jephthah "
20:10 to f victual for the people, that "
1Sa 4: 3 Let us f the ark of the covenant "
6:21 come ye down, and f it up to you. 5927
16:11 Send and f him: for we will not 3947
20:31 now send and f him unto me, for "
26:22 the young men come over and f it. "
2Sa 5:23 but f a compass behind them, *
14:13 the king doth not f home again 7725
20 To f about this form of speech *5437
1Ki 17:10 F me, I pray thee, a little water 3947
11 And as she was going to f it, "
2Ki 6:13 that I may send and f him. "
2Ch 18: 8 F quickly Micaiah the son of Imla.
Ne 8:15 and f olive branches, and pine 935
Job 36: 3 I will f my knowledge from afar, 5375
Isa 56:12 I will f wine, and we will fill 3947
Jer 36:21 the king sent Jehudi to f the roll: "
Ac 16:37 come themselves and f us out. *1806

fetched See also FETCHT.
Ge 18: 4 Let a little water, I pray you, be f, 3947
27:14 he went, and f, and brought them "

Jos 15: 3 and *f* a compass to Karkaa *
J'g 18:18 *f* the carved image, the ephod, 3947
1Sa 7: 1 and *f* up the ark of the Lord, 5927
10:23 And they ran and *f* him thence: 3947
2Sa 4: 6 though they would have *f* wheat; "
9: 5 king David sent, and *f* him out of "
11:27 sent and *f* her to his house, * 622
14: 2 and *f* thence a wise woman, and 3947
1Ki 7:13 king Solomon sent and *f* Hiram "
9:28 to Ophir, and *f* from thence gold. "
2Ki 3: 9 they *f* a compass of seven days' *
11: 4 Jehoiada sent and *f* the rulers 3947
2Ch 1:17 And they *f* up, and brought forth 5927
12:11 the guard came and *f* them, and *5375
Jer 26:23 they *f* forth Urijah out of Egypt, 3318
Ac 28:13 from thence we *f* a compass, and *

fetcheth
De 19: 5 his hand *f* a stroke with the axe 5080

fetcht See also FETCHED.
Ge 18: 7 and *f* a calf tender and good, *3947

fetters
J'g 16:21 and bound him with *f* of brass; 5178
2Sa 3:34 not bound, nor thy feet put into *f*: "
2Ki 25: 7 and bound him with *f* of brass, "
2Ch 33:11 and bound him with *f*, and carried "
36: 6 and bound him in *f*, to carry him "
Job 36: 8 And if they be bound in *f*, 2131
Ps 105:18 Whose feet they hurt with *f*: he 3525
149: 8 and their nobles with *f* of iron; "
M'r 5: 4 often bound with *f* and chains, 3976
4 and the *f* broken in pieces: "
Lu 8:29 kept bound with chains and in *f*; "

fever
De 28:22 with a consumption, and with a *f*, 6920
M't 8:14 wife's mother laid, and sick of a *f*. 4445
15 and the *f* left her: and she arose, 4446
M'r 1:30 wife's mother lay sick of a *f*, 4445
31 and immediately the *f* left her, 4446
Lu 4:38 mother was taken with a great *f*; "
39 and rebuked the *f*; and it left her: "
Joh 4:52 at the seventh hour the *f* left him. "
Ac 28: 8 lay sick of a *f* and of a bloody flux: "

few See also FEWER; FEWEST.
Ge 24:55 the damsel abide with us a *f* days
27:44 And tarry with him a *f* days, 259
29:20 they seemed unto him but a *f* days, "
34:30 I being *f* in number, they shall 4962
47: 9 *f* and evil have the days of the 4592
Le 25:52 if there remain but *f* years unto "
26:22 and make you *f* in number; 4591
Nu 9:20 when the cloud was a *f* days upon 4557
13:18 be strong or weak, *f* or many; 4592
26:54 and to *f* thou shalt give the less * "
56 be divided between many and *f*. * "
35: 8 but from them that have *f* 4592
8 ye shall give *f*: every one 4591
De 4:27 and ye shall be left *f* in number 4962
26: 5 and sojourned there with a *f*, and 4592
28:62 And ye shall be left *f* in number, "
33: 6 and let not his men be *f*. 4557
Jos 7: 3 labour thither; for they are but *f*. 4592
1Sa 14: 6 to save by many or by *f*. "
17:28 with whom hast thou left those *f* "
2Ki 4: 3 empty vessels; borrow not a *f*. 4591
1Ch 16:19 When ye were but *f*, even 4962
19 even a *f*, and strangers in it. 4592
2Ch 29:34 But the priests were too *f*, so "
Ne 2:12 I and some *f* men with me; "
7: 4 but the people were *f* therein, and "
Job 10:20 Are not my days *f*? cease then, "
14: 1 that is born of woman is of *f* days, 7116
16:22 When a *f* years are come, then I 4557
Ps 105:12 When they were but a *f* men in 4962
12 yea, very *f*, and strangers in it. 4592
109: 8 Let his days be *f*: and let another "
Ec 5: 2 therefore let thy words be *f*. "
9:14 a little city and *f* men within it; "
12: 3 grinders cease because they are *f*, "
Isa 10: 7 and cut off nations not a *f*. "
19 the trees of his forest shall be *f*, 4557
24: 6 earth are burned, and *f* men left. 4213
Jer 30:19 them, and they shall not be *f*; 4591
42: 2 we are left but a *f* of many, 4592
Eze 5: 3 also take thereof a *f* in number, "
12:16 I will leave a *f* men of them 4557
Da 11:20 *f* days he shall be destroyed, 259
M't 7:14 and *f* there be that find it. 3641
9:37 but the labourers are *f*; "
15:34 Seven, and a *f* little fishes. "
20:16 for many be called, but *f* chosen. * "
22:14 many are called, but *f* are chosen. "
25:21, 23 thou hast been faithful over a *f* "
M'r 6: 5 he laid hands upon a *f* sick folk, "
8: 7 And they had a *f* small fishes: "
Lu 10: 2 is great, but the labourers are *f*: "
12:48 shall be beaten with *f* stripes. "
13:23 Lord, are there *f* that be saved? "
Ac 17: 4 and of the chief women not a *f*. "
12 were Greeks, and of men, not a *f*. "
24: 4 us of thy clemency a *f* words. 4935
Eph 3: 3 (as I wrote afore in *f* words, 3641
Heb 12:10 verily for a *f* days chastened us "
13:22 a letter unto you in *f* words. 1024
1Pe 3:20 wherein *f*, that is, eight souls 3641
Re 2:14 But I have a *f* things against thee, "
20 I have a *f* things against thee, * "
3: 4 Thou hast a *f* names even in Sardis "

fewer
Nu 33:54 and to the *f* ye shall give the less 4592

fewest
De 7: 7 ye were the *f* of all people: 4592

fewness
Le 25:16 according to the *f* of years thou 4591

fidelity
Tit 2:10 but shewing all good *f*; that they 4102

field See also FIELDS.
Ge 2: 5 every plant of the *f* before it was 7704
5 every herb of the *f* before it grew: "
19 God formed every beast of the *f*, "
20 and to every beast of the *f*; "
3: 1 than any beast of the *f* which the "
14 and above every beast of the *f*; "
18 and thou shalt eat the herb of the *f*; "
4: 8 to pass, when they were in the *f*, "
23: 9 which is in the end of his *f*; "
11 the *f* give I thee, and the cave "
13 I will give thee money for the *f*; "
17 And the *f* of Ephron, which was in "
17 the *f*, and the cave which was "
17 and all the trees that were in the *f*, "
19 the cave of the *f* of Machpelah "
20 the *f*, and the cave that is therein, "
24:63 went out to meditate in the *f* at the "
65 man is this that walketh in the *f* to "
25: 9 the *f* of Ephron the son of Zohar "
10 The *f* which Abraham purchased "
27 a cunning hunter, a man of the *f*; "
29 and Esau came from the *f*, and he "
27: 3 and go out to the *f* and take me "
5 And Esau went to the *f* to hunt "
27 my son is as the smell of a *f* which "
29: 2 and behold a well in the *f*, "
30:14 found mandrakes in the *f*, and "
16 Jacob came out of the *f* in the "
31: 4 called Rachel and Leah to the *f* "
33:19 he bought a parcel of a *f*, * "
34: 5 sons were with his cattle in the *f*: "
7 sons of Jacob came out of the *f* "
28 and that which was in the *f*, "
36:35 smote Midian in the *f* of Moab, "
37: 7 we were binding sheaves in the *f*, "
15 behold, he was wandering in the *f*: "
39: 5 he had in the house, and in the *f*. "
41:48 the food of the *f*, which was round "
47:20 Egyptians sold every man his *f*, "
24 seed of the *f*, and for your food, "
49:29 in the *f* of Ephron the Hittite, "
30 In the cave that is in the *f* of "
30 with the *f* of Ephron the Hittite "
32 purchase of the *f* and of the cave "
50:13 the cave of the *f* of Machpelah, "
13 which Abraham bought with the *f* "
Ex 1:14 in all manner of service in the *f*: "
9: 3 thy cattle which is in the *f*, "
19 all that thou hast in the *f*; "
19 which shall be found in the *f*, "
21 servants and his cattle in the *f*. "
22 and upon every herb of the *f*, "
25 all that was in the *f*, both man and "
25 the hail smote every herb of the *f*, "
25 and brake every tree of the *f*. "
10: 5 which groweth for you out of the *f*: "
15 or in the herbs of the *f*, "
16:25 ye shall not find it in the *f*. "
22: 5 If a man shall cause a *f* or "
5 shall feed in another man's *f*; "
5 of the best of his own *f*, "
6 corn, or the *f* be consumed "
31 flesh that is torn of beasts in the *f*; "
23:11 the beasts of the *f* shall eat. "
16 which thou hast sown in the *f*: "
16 in thy labours out of the *f*. "
29 the beast of the *f* multiply against "
Le 14: 7 living bird loose into the open *f*. "
17: 5 which they offer in the open *f*, "
19: 9 wholly reap the corners of thy *f*, "
19 not sow thy *f* with mingled seed: "
23:22 riddance of the corners of thy *f* "
25: 3 Six years thou shalt sow thy *f*, "
4 thou shalt neither sow thy *f*, nor "
12 the increase thereof out of the *f*. "
34 the *f* of the suburbs of their cities "
26: 4 and the trees of the *f* shall yield "
27:16 unto the Lord some part of a *f* of "
17 his *f* from the year of jubile, "
18 he sanctify his *f* after the jubile "
19 he that sanctified the *f* will in any "
20 And if he will not redeem the *f*, "
20 or if he have sold the *f* to another "
21 But the *f* when it goeth out in the "
21 unto the Lord, as a *f* devoted; "
22 a man sanctify unto the Lord a *f* "
24 the *f* shall return unto him of "
28 and of the *f* of his possession, "
Nu 22: 4 ox licketh up the grass of the *f*. "
23 of the way, and went into the *f*: "
23:14 brought him into the *f* of Zophim, "
De 5:21 house, his *f*, or his manservant, "
7:22 lest the beasts of the *f* increase "
14:22 the *f* bringeth forth year by year. "
20:19 the tree of the *f* is man's life) "
21: 1 lying in the *f*, and it be not known "
22:25 find a betrothed damsel in the *f*, "
27 For he found her in the *f*, "
24:19 cuttest down thine harvest in thy *f*, "
19 and hast forgot a sheaf in the *f*, "
28: 3 blessed shalt thou be in the *f*. "
16 cursed shalt thou be in the *f*. "
38 carry much seed out into the *f*, "
Jos 8:24 all the inhabitants of Ai in the *f*, "
15:18 moved him to ask of her father a *f*: "
J'g 1:14 moved him to ask of her father a *f*: "
5: 4 marchedst out of the *f* of Edom, "
18 in the high places of the *f*. "
9:32 and lie in wait in the *f*: "
42 the people went out into the *f*; "
43 laid wait in the *f*, and looked, "
13: 9 the woman as she sat in the *f*: "
J'g 19:16 old man from his work out of the *f* 7704
20:31 the other to Gibeah in the *f*, "
Ru 2: 2 Let me now go to the *f*, and glean "
3 gleaned in the *f* after the reapers: "
3 part of the *f* belonging unto Boaz, "
8 Go not to glean in another *f*, "
9 be on the *f* that they do reap, "
17 she gleaned in the *f* until even, "
22 they meet thee not in any other *f*. "
4: 5 buyest the *f* of the hand of Naomi, "
1Sa 4: 2 they slew of the army in the *f* "
6:14 the *f* of Joshua, a Beth-shemite, "
18 remaineth unto this day in the *f* "
11: 5 came after the herd out of the *f*; "
14:15 trembling in the host, in the *f*, "
17:44 the air, and to the beasts of the *f*. "
19: 3 stand beside my father in the *f* "
20: 5 that I may hide myself in the *f* "
11 Come, and let us go out into the *f*. "
11 went out both of them into the *f*. "
24 So David hid himself in the *f*: "
35 that Jonathan went out into the *f* "
30:11 they found an Egyptian in the *f*, "
2Sa 10: 8 were by themselves in the *f*. "
11:23 and came out unto us into the *f*, "
14: 6 they two strove together in the *f*, "
30 See, Joab's *f* is near mine, and he 2513
30 Absalom's servants set the *f* on fire." "
31 have thy servants set my *f* on fire? "
17: 8 bear robbed of her whelps in the *f*: 7704
18: 6 So the people went out into the *f* "
20:12 out of the highway into the *f*, "
21:10 nor the beasts of the *f* by night. "
1Ki 11:29 and they two were alone in the *f*: "
14:11 and him that dieth in the *f* shall the "
21:24 and him that dieth in the *f* shall the "
2Ki 4:39 went out into the *f* to gather herbs, "
7:12 to hide themselves in the *f*, saying, "
8: 6 and all the fruits of the *f* since the "
9:25 in the portion of the *f* of Naboth "
37 the *f* in the portion of Jezreel; "
18:17 in the highway of the fuller's *f*. "
19:26 they were as the grass of the *f*, "
1Ch 1:46 smote Midian in the *f* of Moab, "
19: 9 come were by themselves in the *f*. "
27:26 them that did the work of the *f* "
2Ch 26:23 the *f* of the burial which belonged "
31: 5 and of all the increase of the *f*; "
Ne 13:10 were fled every one to his *f*. "
Job 5:23 in league with the stones of the *f*: "
23 beasts of the *f* shall be at peace "
24: 6 reap every one his corn in the *f*: "
40:20 where all the beasts of the *f* play. "
Ps 8: 7 yea, and the beasts of the *f*; "
50:11 the wild beasts of the *f* are mine. "
78:12 the land of Egypt, in the *f* of Zoan. "
43 and his wonders in the *f* of Zoan: "
80:13 the wild beast of the *f* doth devour "
96:12 Let the *f* be joyful, and all that is "
103:15 flower of the *f*, so he flourisheth. "
104:11 drink to every beast of the *f*: "
Pr 24:27 and make it fit for thyself in the *f*; "
30 I went by the *f* of the slothful, "
27:26 and the goats are the price of the *f*. "
31:16 She considereth a *f*, and buyeth it: "
Ec 5: 9 the king himself is served by the *f*. "
Ca 2: 7 and by the hinds of the *f*, that ye "
3: 5 and by the hinds of the *f*, that ye "
7:11 beloved, let us go forth into the *f*; "
Isa 5: 8 join house to house, that lay *f* to *f*, "
7: 3 in the highway of the fuller's *f*; "
10:18 of his forest, and of his fruitful *f*, "
16:10 and joy out of the plentiful *f*; "
29:17 shall be turned into a fruitful *f*, "
17 and the fruitful *f* shall be esteemed "
32:15 and the wilderness be a fruitful *f*, "
15 the fruitful *f* be counted for a forest. "
16 righteousness remain in the fruitful *f*. "
36: 2 in the highway of the fuller's *f*. 7704
37:27 they were as the grass of the *f*, "
40: 6 thereof is as the flower of the *f*: "
43:20 The beast of the *f* shall honour me, "
55:12 and all the trees of the *f* shall clap "
56: 9 ye beasts of the *f*, come to devour, "
Jer 4:17 As keepers of a *f*, are they against "
6:25 Go not forth into the *f*, nor walk "
7:20 and upon the trees of the *f*, "
9:22 fall as dung upon the open *f*, "
12: 4 and the herbs of every *f* wither, * "
9 assemble all the beasts of the *f*, "
14: 5 the hind also calved in the *f*, "
18 If I go forth into the *f*, then behold "
17: 3 O my mountain in the *f*, I will give "
18:14 cometh from the rock of the *f*? "
26:18 Zion shall be plowed like a *f*, "
27: 6 the beasts of the *f* have I given "
28:14 have given him the beasts of the *f* "
32: 7 Buy thee my *f* that is in Anathoth: "
8 Buy my *f*, I pray thee, that is in "
9 And I bought the *f* of Hanameel "
25 Buy thee the *f* for money, and "
35: 9 have we vineyard, nor *f*, nor seed: "
41: 8 for we have treasures in the *f*, of "
48:33 gladness is taken from the plentiful *f*
La 4: 9 for want of the fruits of the *f*. 7704
Eze 7:15 he that is in the *f* shall die with the "
16: 5 but thou wast cast out in the open *f*, "
7 to multiply as the bud of the *f*, "
17: 5 and planted it in a fruitful *f*: * "
24 all the trees of the *f* shall know "
20:46 against the forest of the south *f*, "
26: 6 her daughters which are in the *f* "
8 the sword thy daughters in the *f*: "
29: 5 beasts of the *f* and to the fowls * 776
31: 4 rivers unto all the trees of the *f*. 7704
5 exalted above all the trees of the *f*, "

Eze 31: 6 beasts of the f bring forth their 7704
13 beasts of the f shall be upon his "
15 all the trees of the f fainted for him."
32: 4 cast thee forth upon the open f. "
33:27 him that is in the open f will I "
34: 5 meat to all the beasts of the f, when"
8 meat to every beast of the f, because"
27 tree of the f shall yield her fruit, "
36:30 the increase of the f, that ye shall "
38:20 heaven, and the beasts of the f, "
39: 4 beasts of the field to be devoured. "
5 Thou shalt fall upon the open f: "
10 shall take no wood out of the f, "
17 and to every beast of the f, "
Da 2:38 the beasts of the f and the fowls 1251
4:12 the beasts of the f had shadow "
15 in the tender grass of the f; and let"
21 which the beasts of the f dwelt, "
23 in the tender grass of the f, and let"
23 portion be with the beasts of the f, "
25 shall be with the beasts of the f, "
32 shall be with the beasts of the f: "
Ho 2:12 beasts of the f shall eat them. 7704
18 with the beasts of the f, and with "
4: 3 languish, with the beasts of the f, "
10: 4 hemlock in the furrows of the f. "
Joe 1:10 f is wasted, the land mourneth; "
11 the harvest of the f is perished. "
12 all the trees of the f, are withered: "
19 hath burned all the trees of the f. "
20 beasts of the f cry also unto thee: "
2:22 Be not afraid, ye beasts of the f: "
Mic 1: 6 make Samaria as an heap of the f, "
3:12 Zion for your sake be plowed as a f. "
4:10 and thou shalt dwell in the f, "
Zec 10: 1 of rain, to every one grass in the f. "
Mal 3:11 her fruit before the time in the f, "
M't 6:28 Consider the lilies of the f, how they 68
30 so clothe the grass of the f, which "
13:24 which sowed good seed in his f: "
27 not thou sow good seed in thy f? "
31 a man took, and sowed in his f: "
36 us the parable of the tares of the f. "
38 The f is the world; the good seed "
44 is like unto treasure hid in a f; "
44 all that he hath, and buyeth that f. "
24:18 Neither let him which is in the f "
40 Then shall two be in the f; "
27: 7 bought with them the potter's f, "
8 that f was called, The f of blood, "
10 And gave them for the potter's f, "
M'r 13:16 him that is in the f not turn back "
Lu 2: 8 shepherds abiding in the f, keeping "
12:28 is to day in the f, and to-morrow "
15:25 Now his elder son was in the f: "
17: 7 and by, when he is come from the f, "
31 he that is in the f, let him likewise "
36 Two men shall be in the f; * "
Ac 1:18 purchased a f with the reward of 5564
19 f is called in their proper tongue, "
19 that is to say, The f of blood. "

fields
Ex 8:13 of the villages, and out of the f. 7704
Le 14:53 out of the city into the open f, * "
25:31 counted as the f of the country: "
27:22 is not of the f of his possession; * "
Nu 16:14 us inheritance of f and vineyards: "
19:16 slain with a sword in the open f, * "
20:17 we will not pass through the f, * "
21:22 we will not turn into the f, or into* "
De 11:15 I will send grass in thy f, "
32:13 might eat the increase of the f; * "
32 Sodom, and of the f of Gomorrah: 7709
Jos 21:12 the f of the city, and the villages 7704
J'g 9:27 And they went out into the f, * "
44 the people that were in the f, * "
1Sa 8:14 take your f, and your vineyards, "
22: 7 Jesse give every one of you good f "
25:15 with them, when we were in the f: "
2Sa 1:21 rain, upon you, nor f of offerings: "
11:11 encamped in the open f; shall I * "
1Ki 2:26 to Anathoth, unto thine own f; "
16: 4 and him that dieth of his in the f* "
2Ki 23: 4 Jerusalem in the f of Kidron, 7709
1Ch 6:56 the f of the city, and the villages 7704
16:32 let the f rejoice, and all that is * "
27:25 storehouses in the f, in the cities, "
2Ch 31:19 which were in the f of the suburbs "
Ne 11:25 And for the villages, with their f, "
30 Lachish, and the f thereof, at "
12:29 of the f of Geba and Azmaveth: "
44 into them out of the f of the cities "
Job 5:10 and sendeth waters upon the f: 2351
Ps 107:37 sow the f, and plant vineyards, 7704
132: 6 we found it in the f of the wood. * "
Pr 8:26 had not made the earth, nor the f, 2351
23:10 not into the f of the fatherless: 7704
Isa 16: 8 For the f of Heshbon languish, 7709
32:12 for the teats, for the pleasant f, 7704
Jer 6:12 with their f and wives together: "
8:10 their f to them that shall inherit "
13:27 abominations on the hills in the f.* "
31:40 the f unto the brook of Kidron, 8309
32:15 Houses and f and vineyards shall 7704
43 And f shall be bought in this land, "
44 Men shall buy f for money, and "
39:10 vineyards and f at the same time. 3010
40: 7 of the forces which were in the f, 7704
13 of the forces that were in the f, "
Eze 29: 5 thou shalt fall upon the open f; * "
Ho 12:11 heaps in the furrows of the f. * "
Ob 19 f of Ephraim, and the f of Samaria: * "
Mic 2: 2 covet f, and take them by violence; "
4 turning away he hath divided our f."
Hab 3:17 and the f shall yield no meat; 7709
M'r 2:23 that he went through the corn f on
Lu 6: 1 that he went through the corn f; and
15:15 sent him into his f to feed swine. 68
Joh 4:35 look on the f; for they are white 5561
Jas 5: 4 who have reaped down your f, "

fierce See also FIERCER.
Ge 49: 7 Cursed be their anger, for it was f; 5794
Ex 32:12 Turn from thy f wrath, and repent 2740
Nu 25: 4 f anger of the Lord may be turned "
32:14 augment yet the f anger of the "
De 28:50 A nation of f countenance, which 5794
1Sa 20:34 arose from the table in f anger, 2750
28:18 nor executedst his f wrath upon 2740
2Ch 28:11 f wrath of the Lord is upon you. "
13 and there is f wrath against Israel. "
29:10 that his f wrath may turn away "
Ezr 10:14 until the f wrath of our God for this"
Job 4:10 voice of the f lion, and the teeth 7826
10:16 Thou huntest me as a f lion: * "
28: 8 nor the f lion passed by it. "
41:10 None is so f that dare stir him up: 393
Ps 88:16 Thy f wrath goeth over me; thy
Isa 7: 4 the f anger of Rezin with Syria, 2750
13: 9 with wrath and f anger, to lay 2740
13 and in the day of his f anger. "
19: 4 and a f king shall rule over them, 5794
33:19 Thou shalt not see a f people, 3267
Jer 4: 8 f anger of the Lord is not turned 2740
26 of the Lord, and by his f anger. "
12:13 revenues because of the f anger of "
25:37 cut down because of the f anger of "
38 and because of his f anger. "
30:24 The f anger of the Lord shall not "
49:37 evil upon them, even my f anger, "
51:45 man his soul from the f anger of "
La 1:12 me in the day of his f anger. "
2: 3 He hath cut off in his f anger all 2750
4:11 he hath poured out his f anger, 2740
Da 8:23 a king of f countenance, and 5794
Jon 3: 9 and turn away from his f anger, 2740
Hab 1: 8 more f than the evening wolves: 2300
Zep 2: 2 the f anger of the Lord come upon 2740
3: 8 indignation, even all my f anger: "
M't 8:28 exceeding f, so that no man might 5467
Lu 23: 5 they were the more f, saying, *2001
2Ti 3: 3 false accusers, incontinent, f, 434
Jas 3: 4 driven of f winds, yet are they *4642

fierceness
De 13:17 turn from the f of his anger, 2740
Jos 7:26 turned from the f of his anger. "
2Ki 23:26 not from the f of his great wrath, "
2Ch 30: 8 the f of his wrath may turn away* "
Job 39:24 He swalloweth the ground with f 7494
Ps 78:49 cast upon them the f of his anger, 2740
85: 3 thyself from the f of thine anger. "
Jer 25:38 because of the f of the oppressor. "
Ho 11: 9 not execute the f of mine anger, "
Na 1: 6 can abide in the f of his anger? "
Re 16:19 of the wine of the f of his wrath. 2372
19:15 the f and wrath of Almighty God. "

fiercer
2Sa 19:43 words of the men of Judah were f 7185

fiery
Nu 21: 6 the Lord sent f serpents among 8314
8 a f serpent, and set it upon a pole: "
De 8:15 were f serpents, and scorpions, "
33: 2 right hand went a f law for them. 799
Ps 21: 9 Thou shalt make them as a f oven 784
Isa 14:29 fruit shall be a f flying serpent. 8314
30: 6 the viper and f flying serpent, "
Da 3: 6, 11 midst of a burning f furnace. 5135
15 the midst of a burning f furnace; "
17 us from the burning f furnace, "
20 to cast them into the burning f "
21, 23 into the midst of the burning f "
26 the mouth of the burning f furnace. "
7: 9 his throne was like the f flame, "
10 A f stream issued and came forth "
Eph 6:16 all the f darts of the wicked. 4448
Heb 10:27 and f indignation, which shall *4442
1Pe 4:12 the f trial which is to try you, 4451

fifteen
Ge 5:10 eight hundred and f years, 2568, 6240
7:20 F cubits upward did the "
25: 7 an hundred threescore and f 7657, 2568
Ex 27:14 of the gate shall be f cubits: 2568, 6240
15 shall be hangings f cubits: " "
38:14 side of the gate were f cubits; " "
15 were hangings of f cubits; " "
25 threescore and f shekels, 7657, 2568
Le 27: 7 estimation shall be f shekels, 2568, 6240
Nu 31:37 and threescore and f, 7657, 2568
J'g 8:10 about f thousand men, all 2568, 6240
2Sa 9:10 Ziba had f sons and twenty " "
19:17 house of Saul, and his f sons " "
1Ki 7: 3 forty five pillars, f in a row. " "
2Ki 14:17 Jehoahaz king of Israel f years. " "
20: 6 will add unto thy days f years; " "
2Ch 25:25 Jehoahaz king of Israel f years. " "
Isa 38: 5 will add unto thy days f years. " "
Eze 45:12 f shekels, shall be your 6235, 2568
Ho 3: 2 to me for f pieces of silver. 2568, 6240
Joh 11:18 unto Jerusalem, about f furlongs 1178
Ac 7:14 threescore and f souls. 1440, 4002
27:28 again, and found it f fathoms. 1178
Ga 1:18 Peter, and abode with him f days. "

fifteenth
Ex 16: 1 f day of the second month 2568, 6240
Le 23: 6 the f day of the same month " "
34 f day of this seventh month " "
39 the f day of the seventh month. " "
Nu 28:17 in the f day of this month is " "
29:12 f day of the seventh month ye " "
33: 3 the f day of the first month; 2568, 6240
1Ki 12:32 the eighth month, on the f day " "
33 the f day of the eighth month. " "
2Ki 14:23 In the f year of Amaziah the " "
1Ch 24:14 The f to Bilgah, the sixteenth " "
25:22 f to Jeremoth, he, his sons, " "
2Ch 15:10 the f year of the reign of Asa. " "
Es 9:18 f day of the same they rested, " "
21 and the f day of the same, " "
Eze 32:17 in the f day of the month, " "
45:25 seventh month, in the f day " "
Lu 3: 1 Now in the f year of the reign 4003

fifth
Ge 1:23 and the morning were the f day. 2549
30:17 conceived, and bare Jacob the f "
41:34 and take up the f part of the land 2567
47:24 that ye shall give the f part unto 2549
26 that Pharaoh should have the f 2569
Le 5:16 and shall add the f part thereto, 2549
6: 5 add the f part more thereto, and "
19:25 And in the f year shall ye eat of the"
22:14 then he shall put the f part thereof"
27:13 then he shall add a f part thereof "
15, 19 shall add the f part of the money"
27 and shall add a f part of it thereto:"
31 shall add thereto the f part thereof."
Nu 5: 7 and add unto it the f part thereof, "
7:36 On the f day Shelumiel the son of "
29:26 And on the f day nine bullocks, "
33:38 in the first day of the f month. "
Jos 19:24 the f lot came out for the tribe "
J'g 19: 8 morning on the f day to depart: "
2Sa 2:23 spear smote him under the f rib, *2570
3: 4 and the f, Shephatiah the son of 2549
27 smote him there under the f rib, *2570
4: 6 they smote him under the f rib: * "
20:10 smote him therewith in the f rib.* "
1Ki 6:31 lintel and side posts were a f part 2549
14:25 in the f year of king Rehoboam, "
2Ki 8:16 in the f year of Joram the son of 2568
25: 8 the f month, on the seventh day 2549
1Ch 2:14 Nethaneel the fourth, Raddai the f, "
3: 3 The f, Shephatiah of Abital: the "
8: 2 Nohah the fourth, and Rapha the f. "
12:10 the fourth, Jeremiah the f, "
24: 9 The f to Malchijah, the sixth to "
25:12 The f to Nethaniah, he, his sons, "
26: 3 Elam the f, Jehohanan the sixth, "
4 Sacar the fourth, Nethaneel the f, "
27: 8 The f captain for the f month "
2Ch 12: 2 in the f year of king Rehoboam "
Ezr 7: 8 came to Jerusalem in the f month, "
9 on the first day of the f month "
Ne 6: 5 the f time with an open letter "
15 finished in the twenty and f day 2568
Jer 1: 3 Jerusalem captive in the f month. 2549
28: 1 fourth year, and in the f month, "
36: 9 to pass in the f year of Jehoiakim "
52:12 in the f month, in the tenth day "
Eze 1: 1 in the f day of the month, as I was 2568
2 In the f day of the month, which "
2 the f year of king Jehoiachin's 2549
8: 1 in the f day of the month, as I sat 2568
20: 1 the seventh year, in the f month, 2549
33:21 in the f day of the month, that one 2568
Zec 7: 3 Should I weep in the f month, 2549
5 mourned in the f and seventh "
8:19 of the f, and the fast of the seventh, "
Re 6: 9 when he had opened the f seal, 3991
9: 1 And the f angel sounded, and I saw "
16:10 And the f angel poured out his vial "
21:20 The f, sardonyx; the sixth, sardius; "

fifties
Ex 18:21 rulers of f, and rulers of tens: 2572
25 rulers of hundreds, rulers of f, "
De 1:15 captains over f, and captains over "
1Sa 8:12 captains over f; and will set them "
2Ki 1:14 captains of the former f with their "
M'r 6:40 in ranks, by hundreds, and by f. 4004
Lu 9:14 them sit down by f in a company.* "

fiftieth
Le 25:10 And ye shall hallow the f year, 2572
11 A jubile shall that f year be unto "
2Ki 15:23 In the f year of Azariah king of "
27 In the two and f year of Azariah "

fifty See also FIFTIES.
Ge 6:15 the breadth of it f cubits, and 2572
7:24 the earth an hundred and f days. "
8: 3 the end of the hundred and f days "
9:28 flood three hundred and f years. "
29 of Noah were nine hundred and f "
18:24 Peradventure there be f righteous "
24 spare the place for the f righteous "
26 said, If I find in Sodom f righteous "
28 there shall lack five of the f "
Ex 26: 5 F loops shalt thou make in the "
5 one curtain, and f loops shalt thou "
6 thou shalt make f taches of gold, "
10 shalt make f loops on the edge of "
10 and f loops in the edge of the "
11 thou shalt make f taches of brass, "
27:12 side shall be hangings of f cubits: "
13 side eastward shall be f cubits. "
18 and the breadth f every where, "
30:23 even two hundred and f shekels, "
23 two hundred and f shekels, "
36:12 F loops made he in one curtain, "
12 and f loops made he in the edge "
13 And he made f taches of gold, "
17 f loops upon the uttermost edge "
17 and f loops made he upon the edge "
18 And he made f taches of brass "
38:12 side were hangings of f cubits, "

Ex 38:13 the east side eastward *f* cubits. 2572
26 and five hundred and *f* men. "
Le 23:16 sabbath shall ye number *f* days; "
27: 3 thy estimation shall be *f* shekels "
16 be valued at *f* shekels of silver. "
Nu 1:23 *f* and nine thousand and three "
25 five thousand six hundred and *f*. "
29 were *f* and four thousand and four "
31 were *f* and seven thousand and four "
43 were *f* and three thousand and four "
46 thousand and five hundred and *f*. "
2: 6 were *f* and four thousand and four "
8 were *f* and seven thousand and four "
13 were *f* and nine thousand and three "
15 thousand and six hundred and *f*. "
16 an hundred thousand and *f* and "
16 thousand and four hundred and *f*. "
30 were *f* and three thousand and four "
31 an hundred thousand and *f* and "
32 thousand and five hundred and *f*. "
4: 3 even until *f* years old, all that "
23 until *f* years old shalt thou number "
30 even unto *f* years old shalt thou "
35 upward even unto *f* years old, "
36 two thousand seven hundred and *f*. "
39, 43, 47 upward even unto *f* years "
8:25 the age of *f* years they shall cease "
16: 2 two hundred and *f* princes of the "
17 censer, two hundred and *f* censers; "
35 consumed the two hundred and *f* "
26:10 devoured two hundred and *f* men: "
34 them, *f* and two thousand and seven "
47 were *f* and three thousand and four "
31:30 thou shalt take one portion of *f*, "
47 Moses took one portion of *f*, both "
52 thousand seven hundred and *f* "
De 22:29 unto the damsel's father *f* shekels "
Jos 7:21 and a wedge of gold of *f* shekels "
1Sa 6:19 he smote of the people *f* thousand "
2Sa 15: 1 and *f* men to run before him. "
24:24 and the oxen for *f* shekels of silver. "
1Ki 1: 5 and *f* men to run before him. "
7: 2 and the breadth thereof *f* cubits, "
6 the length thereof was *f* cubits, "
9:23 five hundred and *f*, which bare rule "
10:29 and an horse for an hundred and *f*: "
18: 4 and hid them by *f* in a cave, "
13 the Lord's prophets by *f* in a cave, "
19 prophets of Baal four hundred and *f*, "
22 prophets are four hundred and *f* "
2Ki 1: 9 unto him a captain of *f* with his *f*. "
10 and said to the captain of *f*, "
10 and consume thee and thy *f*. "
10 and consumed him and his *f*. "
11 him another captain of *f* with his *f*. "
12 and consume thee and thy *f*. "
12 and consumed him and his *f*. "
13 a captain of the third *f* with his *f*. "
13 And the third captain of *f* went "
13 the life of these *f* thy servants, "
2: 7 *f* men of the sons of the prophets "
16 be with thy servants *f* strong men; "
17 They sent therefore *f* men: and "
13: 7 people to Jehoahaz but *f* horsemen, "
15: 2 and he reigned two and *f* years in "
20 of each man *f* shekels of silver, "
25 with him *f* men of the Gileadites: "
21: 1 and reigned *f* and five years in "
1Ch 5:21 of their camels *f* thousand, and "
21 two hundred and *f* thousand, "
8:40 and sons' sons, an hundred and *f*. "
9: 9 nine hundred and *f* and six. "
12:33 instruments of war, *f* thousand, "
2Ch 1:17 an horse for an hundred and *f*: "
2:17 an hundred and *f* thousand and "
3: 9 of the nails was *f* shekels of gold. "
8:10 two hundred and *f*, that bare rule "
18 four hundred and *f* talents of gold, "
26: 3 and he reigned *f* and two years in "
33: 1 and he reigned *f* and five years in "
Ezr 2: 7 thousand two hundred *f* and four. "
14 of Bigvai, two thousand *f* and six. "
15 of Adin, four hundred *f* and four. "
22 The men of Netophah, *f* and six. "
29 The children of Nebo, *f* and two. "
30 of Magbish, an hundred *f* and six. "
31 thousand two hundred *f* and four. "
37 of Immer, a thousand *f* and two. "
60 of Nekoda, six hundred *f* and two. "
8: 3 of the males an hundred and *f*. "
6 Jonathan, and with him *f* males. "
26 six hundred and *f* talents of silver, "
Ne 5:17 an hundred and *f* of the Jews and "
6:15 the month Elul, in *f* and two days. "
7:10 of Arah, six hundred *f* and two. "
12 thousand two hundred *f* and four. "
20 of Adin, six hundred *f* and five. "
33 of the other Nebo, *f* and two. "
34 thousand two hundred *f* and four. "
40 of Immer, a thousand *f* and two. "
70 *f* basons, five hundred and thirty "
Es 5:14 gallows be made of *f* cubits high, "
7: 9 also, the gallows *f* cubits high, "
Isa 3: 3 captain of *f*, and the honourable "
Eze 40:15 of the inner gate were *f* cubits. "
21 the length thereof was *f* cubits, "
25 the length was *f* cubits, and the "
29, 33 it was *f* cubits long, and five "
36 the length was *f* cubits, and the "
42: 2 and the breadth was *f* cubits. "
7 the length thereof was *f* cubits. "
8 in the utter court was *f* cubits: "
45: 2 and *f* cubits round about for the "
48:17 the north two hundred and *f*, "
17 the south two hundred and *f*, "
17 toward the east two hundred and *f*. "
Eze 48:17 the west two hundred and *f*. 2572
Hag 2:16 draw out *f* vessels out of the press. "
Lu 7:41 hundred pence, and the other *f*. 4004
16: 6 and sit down quickly, and write *f*. "
Joh 8:57 Thou art not yet *f* years old, "
21:11 an hundred and *f* and three: "
Ac 13:20 of four hundred and *f* years, "
19:19 found it *f* thousand pieces of 4002, 3461

fig See also FIGS.
Ge 3: 7 and they sewed *f* leaves together, 8384
De 8: 8 barley, and vines, and *f* trees, "
J'g 9:10 the trees said to the *f* tree, "
11 But the *f* tree said unto them, "
1Ki 4:25 his vine and under his *f* tree, "
2Ki 18:31 and every one of his *f* tree, "
Ps 105:33 their vines also and their *f* trees; "
Pr 27:18 Whoso keepeth the *f* tree shall eat "
Ca 2:13 *f* tree putteth forth her green figs, "
Isa 34: 4 as a falling *f* [ ] from the *f* tree * "
36:16 vine, and every one of his *f* tree, "
Jer 5:17 eat up thy vines and thy *f* trees: "
8:13 nor figs on the *f* tree, and the leaf "
Ho 2:12 destroy her vines and her *f* trees, "
9:10 as the firstripe in the *f* tree "
Joe 1: 7 vine waste, and barked my *f* tree, "
12 and the *f* tree languisheth; the "
2:22 the *f* tree and the vine do yield "
Am 4: 9 your vineyards and your *f* trees "
Mic 4: 4 under his *f* tree; and none shall "
Na 3:12 strong holds shall be like *f* trees "
Hab 3:17 the *f* tree shall not blossom, "
Hag 2:19 as yet the vine, and the *f* tree, "
Zec 3:10 the vine and under the *f* tree. "
M't 21:19 when he saw a *f* tree in the way, 4808
19 presently the *f* tree withered away. "
20 soon is the *f* tree withered away! "
21 do this which is done to the *f* tree, "
24:32 learn a parable of the *f* tree; "
M'r 11:13 a *f* tree afar off having leaves, "
20 they saw the *f* tree dried up "
21 the *f* tree which thou cursedst "
13:28 learn a parable of the *f* tree; "
Lu 13: 6 A certain man had a *f* tree planted "
7 come seeking fruit on this *f* tree, "
21:29 Behold the *f* tree, and all the trees; "
Joh 1:48 when thou wast under the *f* tree, "
50 I saw thee under the *f* tree, "
Jas 3:12 Can the *f* tree, my brethren, bear "
Re 6:13 a *f* tree casteth her untimely figs, "

fight See also FIGHTETH; FIGHTING; FOUGHT.
Ex 1:10 also unto our enemies, and *f* 3898
14:14 The Lord shall *f* for you, and ye "
17: 9 go out, *f* with Amalek: tomorrow "
De 1:30 he shall *f* for you, according to all "
41 we will go up and *f*, according to "
42 Go not up, neither *f*; for I am "
2:32 out he and all his people, to *f* *4421
3:22 your God he shall *f* for you. *3898
20: 4 to *f* for you against your enemies, "
10 thou comest nigh unto a city to *f* "
Jos 9: 2 to *f* with Joshua and with Israel, "
10:25 your enemies against whom ye *f*. "
11: 5 of Merom, to *f* against Israel. "
19:47 children of Dan went up to *f* * "
J'g 1: 1 Canaanites first, to *f* against them? "
3 we may *f* against the Canaanites; "
9 down to *f* against the Canaanites, "
8: 1 us not, when thou wentest to *f* "
9:38 out, I pray now, and *f* with them. "
10: 9 to *f* also against Judah, and "
18 is he that will begin to *f* against "
11: 6 that we may *f* with the children "
8 *f* against the children of Ammon, "
9 to *f* against the children of Ammon, "
12 come against me to *f* in my land? "
25 or did he ever *f* against them, "
32 the children of Ammon to *f* against "
12: 1 Wherefore passedst thou over to *f* "
3 unto me this day, to *f* against me? "
20:20 put themselves in array to *f* *4421
1Sa 4: 9 quit yourselves like men, and *f*. 3898
8:20 go out before us, and *f* our battles. "
13: 5 gathered themselves together to *f* "
15:18 and *f* against them until they be "
17: 9 If he be able to *f* with me, "
10 man, that we may *f* together. "
20 the host was going forth to the *f*, 4634
32 go and *f* with this Philistine. 3898
33 to go against this Philistine to *f* "
18:17 for me, and *f* the Lord's battles. "
23: 1 the Philistines *f* against Keilah, * "
28: 1 for warfare to *f* with Israel. "
29: 8 may not go *f* against the enemies "
2Sa 11:20 nigh unto the city when ye did *f*? "
1Ki 12:21 to *f* against the house of Israel, "
24 nor *f* against your brethren the "
20:23 us *f* against them in the plain, "
25 will *f* against them in the plain, "
26 up to Aphek, to *f* against Israel. 4421
22:31 *F* neither with small nor great, 3898
32 turned aside to *f* against him: "
2Ki 3:21 the kings were come up to *f* "
10: 3 and *f* for your master's house. "
19: 9 he is come out to *f* against thee: "
2Ch 11: 1 to *f* against Israel, that he might "
4 nor *f* against your brethren: "
13:12 *f* ye not against the Lord God "
18:30 *F* ye not with small or great, "
31 they compassed about him to *f*: "
20:17 shall not need to *f* in this battle: "
32: 2 purposed to *f* against Jerusalem, 4421
8 to help us, and to *f* our battles. 3898
35:20 Necho king of Egypt came up to *f* "
22 might *f* with him, and hearkened "
22 came to *f* in the valley of Megiddo. "
Ne 4: 8 to *f* against Jerusalem, and to 3898
14 and *f* for your brethren, your "
20 our God shall *f* for us. "
Ps 35: 1 *f* against them that *f* against me. "
56: 2 they be many that *f* against me, "
144: 1 to war, and my fingers to *f*: 4421
Isa 19: 2 and they shall *f* every one against 3898
29: 7 the nations that *f* against Ariel, 6633
7 even all that *f* against her and her "
8 be, that *f* against mount Zion. "
30:32 in battles of shaking will he *f* 3898
31: 4 to *f* for mount Zion, and for the 6633
Jer 1:19 they shall *f* against thee; but 3898
15:20 and they shall *f* against thee: "
21: 4 ye *f* against the king of Babylon, "
5 And I myself will *f* against you "
32: 5 though ye *f* with the Chaldeans, "
24 of the Chaldeans, that *f* against it, "
29 Chaldeans, that *f* against this city, "
33: 5 They come to *f* with the Chaldeans, "
34:22 and they shall *f* against it, and "
37: 8 again, and *f* against this city, "
10 army of the Chaldeans that *f* "
41:12 to *f* with Ishmael the son of "
51:30 men of Babylon have forborn to *f*, "
Da 10:20 will I return to *f* with the prince "
11:11 shall come forth and *f* with him, "
Zec 10: 5 and they shall *f*, because the Lord "
14: 3 forth, and *f* against those nations, "
14 Judah also shall *f* at Jerusalem; "
Joh 18:36 then would my servants *f*, 75
Ac 5:39 be found even to *f* against God. *2314
23: 9 let us not *f* against God. *2313
1Co 9:26 so *f* I, not as one that beateth 4438
1Ti 6:12 *F* the good...of faith, lay hold on 75
12 the good *f* of faith, lay hold on 73
2Ti 4: 7 I have *f* a good..., I have finished 75
7 a good *f*, I have finished my course, 73
Heb 10:32 endured a great *f* of afflictions; * 119
11:34 waxed valiant in *f*, turned to *4171
Jas 4: 2 ye *f* and war, yet ye have not. 3164
Re 2:16 *f* against them with the sword *4170

fighteth
Ex 14:25 the Lord *f* for them against the 3898
Jos 23:10 he it is that *f* for you, as he hath "
1Sa 25:28 my lord *f* the battles of the Lord. "

fighting See also FIGHTINGS.
1Sa 17:19 of Elah, *f* with the Philistines. 3898
2Ch 26:11 host of *f* men, that went 6213, 4421
Ps 56: 1 me up; he *f* daily oppresseth me. 3898

fightings
2Co 7: 5 without were *f*, within were fears. 3163
Jas 4: 1 come wars and *f* among you?

fig-leaves See FIG and LEAVES.

figs
Nu 13:23 the pomegranates, and of the *f*. 8384
20: 5 it is no place of seed, or of *f*, "
1Sa 25:18 two hundred cakes of *f*, and laid "
30:12 they gave him a piece of a cake of *f*, "
2Ki 20: 7 Isaiah said, Take a lump of *f*. 8384
1Ch 12:40 oxen, and meat, meal, cakes of *f*, "
Ne 13:15 also wine, grapes, and *f*, 8384
Ca 2:13 fig tree putteth forth her green *f*, 6291
Isa 38:21 Let them take a lump of *f*, 8384
Jer 8:13 nor *f* on the fig tree, and the leaf "
24: 1 two baskets of *f* were set before "
2 One basket had very good *f*, "
2 even like the *f* that are first ripe: "
2 other basket had very naughty *f*, "
3 I said, *F*; the good *f*, very good; "
5 Like these good *f*, so will I "
8 the evil, *f* which cannot be eaten, "
29:17 I will make them like vile *f*, "
Na 3:12 like fig trees with the firstripe *f*: "
M't 7:16 grapes of thorns, or *f* of thistles? 4810
M'r 11:13 for the time of *f* was not yet. "
Lu 6:44 of thorns men do not gather *f*, "
Jas 3:12 either a vine, *f*? so can no fountain "
Re 6:13 a fig tree casteth her untimely *f*, 3653

fig-tree See FIG and TREE.

figure See also DISFIGURE; FIGURES; TRANSFIGURED.
De 4:16 image, the similitude of any *f*, 5566
Isa 44:13 maketh it after the *f* of a man, 8403
Ro 5:14 is the *f* of him that was to come. 5179
1Co 4: 6 I have in a *f* transferred to myself 3345
Heb 9: 9 was a *f* for the time then present, †3850
11:19 also he received him in a *f*. † "
1Pe 3:21 like *f* whereunto even baptism * 499

figures
1Ki 6:29 carved *f* of cherubims and palm 4734
Ac 7:43 *f* which ye made to worship 5179
Heb 9:24 which are the *f* of the true; * 499

file
1Sa 13:21 had a *f* for the mattocks, 6477, 6310

fill See also FILLED; FILLEST; FILLETH; FILLING; FULFIL.
Ge 1:22 and *f* the waters in the seas, 4390
42:25 Joseph commanded to *f* their sacks "
44: 1 *F* the men's sacks with food, as "
Ex 10: 6 And they shall *f* thy houses, * "
16:32 *F* an omer of it to be kept *4393
Le 25:19 eat your *f*, and dwell therein 7648
De 23:24 thou mayest eat grapes thy *f* at "
1Sa 16: 1 *f* thine horn with oil, and go, 4390
1Ki 18:33 *F* four barrels with water, and "
Job 8:21 Till he *f* thy mouth with laughing, "
15: 2 and *f* his belly with the east wind? "
20:23 When he is about to *f* his belly, "
23: 4 and *f* my mouth with arguments. "
38:39 *f* the appetite of the young lions, * "
41: 7 thou *f* his skin with barbed irons? "

Ps 81:10 thy mouth wide, and I will *f* it. 4390
83:16 *F* their faces with shame; that "
110: 6 he shall *f* the places with the dead "
Pr 1:13 we shall *f* our houses with spoil: "
7:18 Come, let us take our *f* of love 7301
8:21 and I will *f* their treasures. 4390
Isa 8: 8 shall *f* the breadth of thy land, 4393
14:21 *f* the face of the world with cities.4390
27: 6 *f* the face of the world with fruit. "
56:12 *f* ourselves with strong drink; 5433
Jer 13:13 I will *f* all the inhabitants of 4390
23:24 Do not I *f* heaven and earth? "
33: 5 is to *f* them with the dead bodies "
51:14 Surely I will *f* thee with men, "
Eze 3: 3 and *f* thy bowels with this roll "
7:19 their souls, neither *f* their bowels: "
9: 7 and *f* the courts with the slain: "
10: 2 *f* thine hand with coals of fire "
24: 4 *f* it with the choice bones. "
30:11 and *f* the land with the slain. "
32: 4 *f* the beasts of the whole earth *7646
5 and *f* the valleys with thy height. 4390
35: 8 and I will *f* his mountains with "
Zep 1: 9 which *f* their masters' houses "
Hag 2: 7 and I will *f* this house with glory, "
M't 9:16 which is put in to *f* it up taketh 4138
15:33 as to *f* so great a multitude? 5526
23:32 *F* ye up then the measure of 4137
Joh 2: 7 *F* the water pots with water. 1072
Ro 15:13 *f* you with all joy and peace in 4137
Eph 4:10 that he might *f* all things.) "
Col 1:24 *f* up that which is behind of the 466
1Th 2:16 to *f* up their sins alway: for the 378
Re 18: 6 she hath filled *f* to her double. *2767

filled See also FILLEDST; FULFILLED.
Ge 6:11 the earth was *f* with violence. 4390
13 for the earth is *f* with violence "
21:19 went, and *f* the bottle with water, "
24:16 and *f* her pitcher, and came up. "
26:15 them, and *f* them with earth. "
Ex 1: 7 and the land was *f* with them. "
2:16 and *f* the troughs to water their "
16:12 morning ye shall be *f* with bread; 7646
28: 3 whom I have *f* with the spirit 4390
31: 3 And I have *f* him with the spirit "
35:31 And he hath *f* him with the spirit "
35 hath he *f* with wisdom of heart, "
40:34, 35 and the glory of the Lord *f* the "
Nu 14:21 the earth shall be *f* with the glory "
De 26:12 eat within thy gates, and be *f*: 7646
31:20 shall have eaten and *f* themselves, "
Jos 9:13 these bottles of wine, which we *f*, 4390
1Ki 7:14 and he was *f* with wisdom, and "
8:10 the cloud *f* the house of the Lord, "
11 glory of the Lord had *f* the house "
18:35 he *f* the trench also with water. "
20:27 but the Syrians *f* the country. "
2Ki 3:17 that valley shall be *f* with water, "
20 and the country was *f* with water. "
25 cast every man his stone, and *f* it; "
21:16 till he had *f* Jerusalem from one "
23:14 and *f* their places with the bones "
24: 4 for he *f* Jerusalem with innocent "
2Ch 5:13 the house was *f* with a cloud, "
14 glory of the Lord had *f* the house "
7: 1 the glory of the Lord *f* the house. "
2 glory of the Lord had *f* the Lord's "
16:14 which was *f* with sweet odours "
Ezr 9:11 have *f* it from one end to another "
Ne 9:25 so they did eat, and were *f*, 7646
Job 3:15 who *f* their houses with silver: 4390
16: 8 thou hast *f* me with wrinkles, *7059
22:18 *f* their houses with good things: 4390
Ps 38: 7 are *f* with a loathsome disease: "
71: 8 Let my mouth be *f* with thy praise "
72:19 the whole earth be *f* with his glory; "
78:29 they did eat, and were well *f*: 7646
80: 9 take deep root, and it *f* the land. 4390
104:28 thy hand, they are *f* with good. *7646
123: 3 are exceedingly *f* with contempt. "
4 exceedingly *f* with the scorning "
126: 2 was our mouth *f* with laughter, 4390
Pr 1:31 fruit of their own way, and be *f* 7646
3:10 shall thy barns be *f* with plenty, 4390
5:10 strangers be *f* with thy wealth; 7646
12:21 wicked shall be *f* with mischief. "
14:14 backslider in heart shall be *f* 7646
18:20 increase of his lips shall he be *f*.* "
20:17 his mouth shall be *f* with gravel. 4390
24: 4 shall the chambers be *f* with all "
25:16 thou be *f* therewith, and vomit 7646
30:16 the earth that is not *f* with water;* "
22 a fool when he is *f* with meat; "
Ec 1: 8 nor the ear *f* with hearing. 4390
6: 3 his soul be not *f* with good, 7646
7 and yet the appetite is not *f*. 4390
Ca 5: 2 head is *f* with dew, and my locks "
Isa 6: 1 up, and his train *f* the temple. "
4 and the house was *f* with smoke. "
21: 3 Therefore are my loins *f* with "
33: 5 he hath *f* Zion with judgment "
34: 6 sword of the Lord is *f* with blood, "
43:24 neither hast thou *f* me with the 7301
65:20 old man that hath not *f* his days: 4390
Jer 13:12 Every bottle shall be *f* with wine: "
12 every bottle shall be *f* with wine? "
15:17 thou hast *f* me with indignation. "
16:18 they have *f* mine inheritance with "
19: 4 have *f* this place with the blood "
41: 9 Ishmael the son of Nethaniah *f* it "
46:12 and the cry hath *f* the land: * "
51: 5 though their land was *f* with sin * "
34 hath *f* his belly with my delicates, "
La 3:15 He hath *f* me with bitterness, 7646
30 he is *f* full with reproach. "
Eze 8:17 have *f* the land with violence, 4390
10: 3 and the cloud *f* the inner court. "
4 the house was *f* with the cloud, "
11: 6 and ye have *f* the streets thereof "
23:33 Thou shalt be *f* with drunkenness "
28:16 *f* the midst of thee with violence, "
36:38 the waste cities be *f* with flocks "
39:20 Thus ye shall be *f* at my table 7646
43: 5 the glory of the Lord *f* the house. 4390
44: 4 the Lord *f* the house of the Lord: "
Da 2:35 mountain, and *f* the whole earth. 4391
Ho 13: 6 to their pasture, so were they *f*; 7646
6 they were *f*, and their heart was "
Na 2:12 and *f* his holes with prey, and his 4390
Hab 2:14 shall be *f* with the knowledge "
16 Thou art *f* with shame for glory: 7646
Hag 1: 6 but ye are not *f* with drink; "
Zec 9:13 *f* the bow with Ephraim, and 4390
15 and they shall be *f* like bowls, "
M't 5: 6 righteousness: for they shall be *f*. 5526
14:20 And they did all eat, and were *f*: "
15:37 And they did all eat, and were *f*: "
27:48 a spunge, and *f* it with vinegar, 4130
M'r 2:21 the new piece that *f* it up *4138
6:42 And they did all eat, and were *f*. 5526
7:27 Let the children first be *f*: "
8: 8 So they did eat, and were *f*: "
15:36 and *f* a spunge full of vinegar, 1072
Lu 1:15 he shall be *f* with the Holy Ghost, 4130
41 Elisabeth was *f* with the Holy "
53 He hath *f* the hungry with good 1705
67 Zacharias was *f* with the Holy 4130
2:40 strong in spirit, *f* with wisdom: 4137
3: 5 Every valley shall be *f*, and every "
4:28 these things, were *f* with wrath, 4130
5: 7 they came and *f* both the ships, "
26 and were *f* with fear, saying, "
6:11 And they were *f* with madness; "
21 hunger now: for ye shall be *f*. 5526
8:23 and they were *f* with water, *4845
9:17 And they did eat, and were all *f*: 5526
14:23 come in, that my house may be *f*: 1072
15:16 And he would fain have *f* his * "
Joh 2: 7 And they *f* them up to the brim. "
6:12 When they were *f*, he said unto 1705
13 and *f* twelve baskets with the 1072
26 ye did eat the loaves, and were *f*. 5526
12: 3 the house was *f* with the odour 4137
16: 6 sorrow hath *f* your heart. "
19:29 and they *f* a spunge with vinegar, *4130
Ac 2: 2 *f* all the house where they were 4137
4 were all *f* with the Holy Ghost, 4130
3:10 and they were *f* with wonder and "
4: 8 Then Peter, *f* with the Holy Ghost, "
31 were all *f* with the Holy Ghost, "
5: 3 hath Satan *f* thine heart to lie 4137
17 and were *f* with indignation, "
28 and, behold, ye have *f* Jerusalem "
9:17 and be *f* with the Holy Ghost. 4130
13: 9 Paul,) *f* with the Holy Ghost, set "
45 they were *f* with envy, and spake "
52 And the disciples were *f* with joy, 4137
19:29 whole city was *f* with confusion: 4130
Ro 1:29 Being *f* with all unrighteousness, 4137
15:14 *f* with all knowledge, able also to "
24 somewhat *f* with your company. *1705
2Co 7: 4 *f* with comfort, I am exceeding 4137
Eph 3:19 might be *f* with all the fulness of "
5:18 but be *f* with the Spirit; "
Ph'p 1:11 *f* with the fruits of righteousness, "
Col 1: 9 might be *f* with the knowledge "
2Ti 1: 4 that I may be *f* with joy; "
Jas 2:16 in peace, be ye warmed and *f*; 5526
Re 8: 5 *f* it with fire of the altar, and cast 1072
15: 1 in them is *f* up the wrath of God.*5055
8 the temple was *f* with smoke 1072
18: 6 she hath *f* fill to her double. *2767
19:21 the fowls were *f* with their flesh. 5526

filledst
De 6:11 all good things, which thou *f* not, 4390
Eze 27:33 thou *f* many people: thou didst 7646

fillest
Ps 17:14 whose belly thou *f* with thy hid 4390

fillet See also FILLETED; FILLETS.
Jer 52:21 *f* of twelve cubits did compass it;*2339

filleted
Ex 27:17 round about the court shall be *f* 2836
38:17 all the pillars of the court were *f* "
28 overlaid their chapiters, and *f* * "

filleth
Job 9:18 but *f* me with bitterness. 7646
Ps 84: 6 the rain also *f* the pools. *5844
107: 9 *f* the hungry soul with goodness. 4390
129: 7 Wherewith the mower *f* not his "
147:14 *f* thee with the finest of the wheat. 7646
Eph 1:23 the fulness of him that *f* all in all. 4137

fillets
Ex 27:10 and their *f* shall be of silver. 2838
11 the pillars and their *f* of silver. "
36:38 chapiters and their *f* with gold. "
38:10 and their *f* were of silver. "
11 and their *f* were of silver. "
12 of the pillars and their *f* of silver. "
17 of the pillars and their *f* of silver: "
19 their chapiters and their *f* of silver. "

filling See also FULFILLING.
Ac 14:17 *f* our hearts with food and 1705

filth
Isa 4: 4 the *f* of the daughters of Zion, 6675
Na 3: 6 I will cast abominable *f* upon thee,
1Co 4:13 are made as the *f* of the world, 4027
1Pe 3:21 putting away of the *f* of the flesh. 4509

filthiness
2Ch 29: 5 forth the *f* out of the holy place. 5079
Ezr 6:21 them from the *f* of the heathen of 2932
9:11 an unclean land with the *f* of the*5079
Pr 30:12 yet is not washed from their *f*. 6675
Isa 28: 8 all tables are full of vomit and *f*, "
La 1: 9 Her *f* is in her skirts; she 2932
Eze 16:36 Because thy *f* was poured out, 5178
22:15 will consume thy *f* out of thee. 2932
24:11 that the *f* of it may be molten in it. "
13 In thy *f* is lewdness: because I "
13 shalt not be purged from thy *f* "
36:25 ye shall be clean: from all your *f*, "
2Cor 7: 1 from all *f* of the flesh and spirit, *3436
Eph 5: 4 Neither *f*, nor foolish talking, nor 151
Jas 1:21 lay apart all *f* and superfluity 4507
Re 17: 4 full of abominations and *f* of her * 168

filthy
Job 15:16 more abominable and *f* is man, * 444
Ps 14: 3 aside, they are altogether become *f*: "
53: 3 back: they are altogether become *f*: "
Isa 64: 6 righteousnesses are as *f* rags; *5708
Zep 3: 1 Woe to her that is *f* and polluted, *4754
Zec 3: 3 was clothed with *f* garments, 6674
4 Take away the *f* garments from "
Col 3: 8 *f* communication out of your * 148
1Ti 3: 3 no striker, not greedy of *f* lucre; *
8 much wine, not greedy of *f* lucre;
Tit 1: 7 no striker, not given to *f* lucre; 150
11 they ought not, for *f* lucre's sake. "
1Pe 5: 2 not for *f* lucre, but of a ready mind; 147
2Pe 2: 7 vexed with the *f* conversation of * 766
Jude 8 also these *f* dreamers defile *
Re 22:11 he which is *f*, let him be *f* still: 4510

finally
2Co 13:11 *F*, brethren, farewell. Be perfect, 3063
Eph 6:10 *F*, my brethren, be strong in the "
Ph'p 3: 1 *F*, my brethren, rejoice in the Lord. "
4: 8 *F*, brethren, whatsoever things are "
2Th 3: 1 *F*, brethren, pray for us, that the "
1Pe 3: 8 *F*, be ye all of one mind, having 5056

find See also FINDEST; FINDETH; FINDING; FOUND.
Ge 18:26 If I *f* in Sodom fifty righteous 4672
28 If I *f* there forty and five, "
30 I will not do it, if I *f* thirty there. "
19:11 wearied themselves to *f* the door. "
32: 5 that I may *f* grace in thy sight. "
19 speak unto Esau, when ye *f* him. "
33: 8 to *f* grace in the sight of my lord. "
15 me *f* grace in the sight of my lord. "
34:11 Let me *f* grace in your eyes, "
38:22 I cannot *f* her; and also the men * "
41:38 Can we *f* such a one as this is, "
47:25 us *f* grace in the sight of my lord. "
Ex 5:11 get you straw where ye can *f* it: "
16:25 ye shall not *f* it in the field. "
33:13 that I may *f* grace in thy sight: "
Nu 32:23 be sure your sin will *f* you out. "
35:27 And the revenger of blood *f* him "
De 4:29 thou shalt *f* him, if thou seek him "
22:23 and a man *f* her in the city, "
25 if a man *f* a betrothed damsel "
28 a man *f* a damsel that is a virgin, "
24: 1 that she *f* no favour in his eyes, "
28:65 these nations shalt thou *f* no ease, "
J'g 9:33 to them as thou shalt *f* occasion. 4672
14:12 and *f* it out, then I will give you "
17: 8 sojourn where he could *f* a place; "
9 to sojourn where I may *f* a place. "
Ru 1: 9 that ye may *f* rest, each of you "
2: 2 in whose sight I shall *f* grace. "
13 Let me *f* favour in thy sight, "
1Sa 1:18 handmaid *f* grace in thy sight. "
9:13 ye shall straightway *f* him, "
13 about this time ye shall *f* him. "
10: 2 *f* two men by Rachel's sepulchre "
20:21 saying, Go *f* out the arrows. "
36 *f* out now the arrows which I shoot. "
23:17 of Saul my father shall not *f* thee; "
24:19 a man *f* his enemy, will he let him "
25: 8 let the young men *f* favour in thine "
2Sa 15:25 if I shall *f* favour in the eyes "
16: 4 that I may *f* grace in thy sight "
17:20 had sought and could not *f* them, "
1Ki 18: 5 peradventure we may *f* grass to "
12 he cannot *f* thee, he shall slay me: "
2Ch 2:14 and to *f* out every device which *2803
20:16 and ye shall *f* them at the end 4672
30: 9 your children shall *f* compassion "
32: 4 Assyria come, and *f* much water? 4672
Ezr 4:15 thou *f* in the book of the records, 7912
7:16 thou canst *f* in all the province "
Job 3:22 glad, when they can *f* the grave? 4672
11: 7 Canst thou by searching *f* out God? "
7 canst thou *f* out the Almighty "
17:10 cannot *f* one wise man among you. "
23: 3 that I knew where I might *f* him! "
34:11 man to *f* according to his ways. "
37:23 Almighty we cannot *f* him out: "
Ps 10:15 out his wickedness till thou *f* none. "
17: 3 tried me, and shalt *f* nothing; * "
21: 8 Thine hand shall *f* out all thine "
8 thy right hand shall *f* out those "
132: 5 Until I *f* out a place for the Lord, "
Pr 1:13 We shall *f* all precious substance, "
28 me early, but they shall not *f* me: "
2: 5 Lord, and *f* the knowledge of God. "
3: 4 *f* favour and good understanding "
4:22 are life unto those that *f* them, "
8: 9 right to them that *f* knowledge. "
12 and *f* out knowledge of witty "
17 that seek me early shall *f* me. "
16:20 a matter wisely shall *f* good: "

Pr 19: 8 keepeth understanding shall f 4672
20: 6 but a faithful man who can f? "
28:23 shall f more favour than he that "
31:10 Who can f a virtuous woman? "
Ec 3:11 no man can f out the work that God "
7:14 man should f nothing after him. "
24 exceeding deep, who can f it out? "
26 I f more bitter than death the "
27 one by one, to f out the account: "
28 yet my soul seeketh, but I f not: "
8:17 that a man cannot f out the work "
17 yet he shall not f it: yea, farther; "
17 yet shall he not be able to f it. "
11: 1 for thou shalt f it after many days." "
12:10 sought to f out acceptable words: "
Ca 5: 6 but I could not f him; I called him," "
8 if ye f my beloved, that ye tell him," "
8: 1 I should f thee without, I would kiss" "
Isa 34:14 and f for herself a place of rest. "
41:12 seek them, and shalt not f them, "
58: 3 day of your fast ye f pleasure, "
Jer 2:24 in her month they shall f her. "
5: 1 if ye can f a man, if there be any "
6:16 and ye shall f rest for your souls. "
10:18 distress them, that they may f it* "
29:13 And ye shall seek me, and f me, "
45: 3 in my sighing, and I f no rest. "
La 1: 6 like harts that f no pasture, "
2: 9 also f no vision from the Lord. "
Da 6: 4 to f occasion against Daniel 7912
4 but they could f none occasion "
5 not f occasion against this Daniel," "
5 Daniel, except we f it against him "
Ho 2: 6 that she shall not f her paths. 4672
7 seek them, but shall not f them: "
5: 6 they shall not f him; he hath "
12: 8 they shall f none iniquity in me "
Am 8:12 of the Lord, and shall not f it. "
M't 7: 7 seek, and ye shall f; knock, and 2147
14 and few there be that f it. "
10:39 loseth his life for my sake shall f it." "
11:29 ye shall f rest unto your souls. "
16:25 lose his life for my sake shall f it. "
17:27 thou shalt f a piece of money: "
18:13 if so be that he f it, verily I say "
21: 2 ye shall f an ass tied, and a colt "
22: 9 as many as ye shall f, bid to the "
24:46 when he cometh shall f so doing. "
M'r 11: 2 ye shall f a colt tied, whereon "
13 he might f any thing thereon: "
13:36 coming suddenly he f you sleeping." "
Lu 2:12 Ye shall f the babe wrapped in "
5:19 they could not f by what way * "
6: 7 might f an accusation against him." "
11: 9 given you; seek, and ye shall f; "
12:37 when he cometh shall f watching: "
38 and f them so, blessed are those "
43 when he cometh shall f so doing. "
13: 7 fruit on this fig tree, and f none: "
15: 4 that which is lost, until he f it? "
8 and seek diligently till she f it? "
18: 8 shall he f faith on the earth? "
19:30 your entering ye shall f a colt tied," "
48 could not f what they might do: "
23: 4 I f no fault in this man. "
Joh 7:34 shall seek me, and shall not f me: "
35 we shall not f him? will he go "
36 and shall not f me: and where I "
10: 9 shall go in and out, and f pasture. "
18:38 I f in him no fault at all. "
19: 4 may know that I f no fault in him. "
6 for I f no fault in him. "
21: 6 side of the ship, and ye shall f. "
Ac 7:46 to f a tabernacle for the God of "
17:27 might feel after him, and f him, "
23: 9 We f no evil in this man: "
Ro 7:18 that which is good I f not. * "
21 I f then a law, that, when I would "
9:19 Why doth he yet f fault? For who "
2Co 9: 4 with me, and f you unprepared, 2147
12:20 I shall not f you such as I would, "
2Ti 1:18 that he may f mercy of the Lord "
Heb 4:16 we may obtain mercy, and f grace "
Re 9: 6 seek death, and shall not f it; "
18:14 thou shalt f them no more at all. "

findest
Ge 31:32 with whomsoever thou f thy gods, 4672
Eze 3: 1 Son of man, eat that thou f; "

findeth
Ge 4:14 every one that f me shall slay me. 4672
Job 33:10 Behold, he f occasions against me, "
Ps 119:162 thy word as one that f great spoil. "
Pr 3:13 Happy is the man that f wisdom, "
8:35 whoso f me, f life, and shall "
17:20 hath a froward heart f no good: "
18:22 Whoso f a wife f a good thing, "
21:10 neighbour f no favour in his eyes. "
21 righteousness and mercy f life, 4672
Ec 9:10 Whatsoever thy hand f to do, do it "
La 1: 3 she f no rest: all her persecutors "
Ho 14: 3 in thee the fatherless f mercy. "
M't 7: 8 he that seeketh f; and to him 2147
10:39 He that f his life shall lose it: "
12:43 places, seeking rest, and f none. "
44 is come he f it empty, swept, and "
26:40 f them asleep, and saith unto "
M'r 14:37 he cometh, and f them sleeping, "
Lu 11:10 receiveth; and he that seeketh f; "
25 he f it swept and garnished. "
Joh 1:41 He first f his own brother Simon, "
43 and f Philip, and saith unto him, "
45 Philip f Nathanael, and saith unto "
5:14 Jesus f him in the temple, and "

finding
Ge 4:15 lest any f him should kill him. 4672

Job 9:10 doeth great things past f out; 2714
Isa 58:13 nor f thine own pleasure, nor 4672
Lu 11:24 and f none, he saith, I will return 2147
Ac 4:21 f nothing how they might punish "
19: 1 and f certain disciples, "
21: 2 And f a ship sailing over unto * "
4 f disciples, we tarried there seven* 429
Ro 11:33 and his ways past f out! * 421
Heb 8: 8 For f fault with them, he saith

fine See also FINEST; FINING; REFINE.
Ge 41:42 and arrayed him in vestures of f linen,
Ex 25: 4 scarlet, and f linen, and goats' hair,
26: 1 with ten curtains of f twined linen,
31 and f twined linen of cunning work:
36 and f twined linen, wrought with
27: 9 for the court of f twined linen of an
16 purple and scarlet, and f twined linen,
18 the height five cubits of f twined linen,
28: 5 and purple, and scarlet, and f linen.
6 purple, of scarlet, and f twined linen,
8 purple, and scarlet, and f twined linen.
15 of f twined linen, shalt thou make it.
39 shalt embroider the coat of f linen,
39 thou shalt make the mitre of f linen,
35: 6, 23 scarlet, and f linen, and goats' hair,
25 purple, and of scarlet, and of f linen.
35 in purple, in scarlet, and in f linen,
36: 8 made ten curtains of f twined linen,
35 and purple, and scarlet, and f twined
37 and f twined linen, of needlework;
38: 9 of the court were of f twined linen, an
16 round about were of f twined linen.
18 purple, and scarlet, and f twined linen:
23 in purple, and in scarlet, and f linen.
39: 2 purple, and scarlet, and f twined linen,
3 and in the scarlet, and in the f linen,
5 purple, and scarlet, and f twined linen;
8 purple, and scarlet, and f twined linen.
27 made coats of f linen of woven work
28 And a mitre of f linen, and goodly
28 and goodly bonnets of f linen, and
28 and linen breeches of f twined linen,
29 And a girdle of f twined linen, and
Le 2: 1 his offering shall be of f flour; and
4 shall be unleavened cakes of f flour
5 it shall be of f flour unleavened,
7 it shall be made of f flour with oil,
5:11 the tenth part of an ephah of f flour
6:20 the tenth part of an ephah of f flour
7:12 and cakes mingled with oil, of f flour,
14:10 and three tenth deals of f flour for
21 and one tenth deal of f flour mingled
23:13 two tenth deals of f flour mingled
17 tenth deals: they shall be of f flour;
24: 5 And thou shalt take f flour, and bake
Nu 6:15 cakes of f flour mingled with oil
7:13, 19, 25, 31, 37, 43, 49, 55, 61, 67, 73 both of them were full of f flour
79 both of them full of f flour mingled
8: 8 even f flour mingled with oil
1Ki 4:22 was thirty measures of f flour,
2Ki 7: 1 measure of f flour be sold for a shekel,
16 So a measure of f flour was sold
18 a measure of f flour for a shekel,
1Ch 4:21 house of them that wrought f linen,
9:29 the f flour, and the wine, and the oil,
15:27 was clothed with a robe of f linen,
23:29 and for the f flour for meat offering,
2Ch 2:14 in blue, and in f linen, and in crimson;
3: 5 which he overlaid with f gold, 2896
8 and he overlaid it with f gold, "
14 purple, and crimson, and f linen,
Ezr 8:27 two vessels of f copper, precious 6668
Es 1: 6 fastened with cords of f linen and
8:15 and with a garment of f linen and
Job 28: 1 place for gold where they f it. *2212
17 of it shall not be for jewels of f gold.
31:24 or have said to the f gold, Thou art my
Ps 19:10 yea, than much f gold: sweeter also
119:127 above gold; yea, above f gold.
Pr 3:14 and the gain thereof than f gold.
7:16 works, with f linen of Egypt. *
8:19 is better than gold, yea, than f gold;
25:12 and an ornament of f gold, so is a wise
31:24 She maketh f linen, and selleth *
Ca 5:11 His head is as the most f gold,
15 marble, set upon sockets of f gold:
Isa 3:23 The glasses, and the f linen, and the
13:12 a man more precious than f gold;
19: 9 Moreover they that work in f flax, *8305
La 4: 1 how is the most f gold changed! *
2 sons of Zion, comparable to f gold,
Eze 16:10 and I girded thee about with f linen,
13 and thy raiment was of f linen,
13 thou didst eat f flour, and honey,
19 thee, f flour, and oil, and honey, and
27: 7 F linen with broidered work from
16 and f linen, and coral, and agate.
46:14 of oil, to temper with the f flour;
Da 2:32 This image's head was of f gold, 2869
10: 5 were girded with f gold of Uphaz: *
Zec 9: 3 and f gold as the mire of the streets.
M'r 15:46 And he bought f linen, and took *
Lu 16:19 was clothed in purple and f linen,
Re 1:15 And his feet like unto f brass, *
2:18 and his feet are like f brass; *
18:12 and of pearls, and f linen, and purple,
13 and f flour, and wheat, and 4585
16 great city, that was clothed in f linen,
19: 8 that she should be arrayed in f linen,
8 the f linen is the righteousness of
14 clothed in f linen, white and clean.

finer
Pr 25: 4 come forth a vessel for the f. ‡6884

finest
Ps 81:16 them also with the f of the wheat: 2459
147:14 filleth thee with the f of the wheat. "

finger See also FINGERS.
Ex 8:19 Pharaoh, This is the f of God: 676
29:12 the horns of the altar with thy f, "
31:18 stone, written with the f of God. "
Le 4: 6 priest shall dip his f in the blood, "
17 the priest shall dip his f in some "
25 blood of the sin offering with his f, "
30 take of the blood thereof with his f, "
34 blood of the sin offering with his f, "
8:15 of the altar round about with his f, "
9: 9 he dipped his f in the blood, "
14:16 the priest shall dip his right f in "
16 sprinkle of the oil with his f seven "
27 shall sprinkle with his right f some "
16:14 and sprinkle it with his f seven "
14 of the blood with his f seven times. "
19 blood upon it with his f seven times. "
Nu 19: 4 shall take of her blood with his f, "
De 9:10 them was written with the f of God; "
1Ki 12:10 My little f shall be thicker than "
2Ch 10:10 My little f shall be thicker than "
Isa 58: 9 the putting forth of the f, and 676
Lu 11:20 with the f of God cast out devils, 1147
16:24 may dip the tip of his f in water, "
Joh 8: 6 with his f wrote on the ground, "
20:25 put my f into the print of the nails," "
27 Reach hither thy f, and behold my "

fingers
2Sa 21:20 that had on every hand six f, 676
1Ch 20: 6 f and toes were four and twenty, "
Ps 8: 3 thy heavens, the work of thy f, "
144: 1 my hands to war, and my f to fight: "
Pr 6:13 his feet, he teacheth with his f; "
7: 3 Bind them upon thy f, write them "
Ca 5: 5 my f with sweet smelling myrrh, "
Isa 2: 8 that which their own f have made: "
17: 8 that which his f have made, "
59: 3 and your f with iniquity; your lips "
Jer 52:21 the thickness thereof was four f: "
Da 5: 5 In the same hour came forth f of a 677
M't 23: 4 move them with one of their f. 1147
M'r 7:33 put his f into his ears, and he spit, "
Lu 11:46 the burdens with one of your f. "

fining
Pr 17: 3 The f pot is for silver, and the ‡4715
27:21 As the f pot for silver, and the ‡ "

fining-pot See FINING and POT.

finish See also FINISHED.
Ge 6:16 in a cubit shalt thou f it above; 3615
Da 9:24 to f the transgresssion, and to 3607
Zec 4: 9 his hands shall also f it; 1214
Lu 14:28 whether he have sufficient to f it? *535
29 foundation, and is not able to f it, 1615
30 to build, and was not able to f. "
Joh 4:34 that sent me, and to f his work. *5048
5:36 the Father hath given me to f, * "
Ac 20:24 I might f my course with joy, * "
Ro 9:28 will f the work, and cut it short *4931
2Co 8: 6 he would also f in you the same *2005

finished
Ge 2: 1 the heavens and the earth were f, 3615
Ex 39:32 of the tent of the congregation f: "
40:33 So Moses f the work. "
De 31:24 law in a book, until they were f, 8552
Jos 4:10 until every thing was f that the "
Ru 3:18 until he have f the thing this day. 3615
1Ki 6: 9 he built the house, and f it; "
14 Solomon built the house, and f it. "
22 until he had f all the house: 8552
38 eighth month, was the house f 3615
7: 1 and he f all his house. "
22 so was the work of the pillars f. 8552
9: 1 when Solomon had f the building 3615
25 the Lord. So he f the house. 7999
1Ch 27:24 Zeruiah began to number, but he f 3615
28:20 until thou hast f all the work for "
2Ch 4:11 Huram f the work that he was * "
5: 1 for the house of the Lord was f: 7999
7:11 Solomon f the house of the Lord, 3615
8:16 of the Lord, and until it was f. "
24:14 when they had f it, they brought* "
29:28 until the burnt offering was f. "
31: 1 Now when all this was f, all Israel "
7 and f them in the seventh month. "
Ezr 5:16 building, and yet it is not f. *8000
6:14 And they builded, and f it, 3635
15 this house was f on the third day 3319
Ne 6:15 So the wall was f in the twenty 7999
Da 5:26 numbered thy kingdom, and f it. *8000
12: 7 all these things shall be f. 3615
M't 13:53 when Jesus had f these parables, 5055
19: 1 when Jesus had f these sayings, "
26: 1 when Jesus had f all these sayings," "
Joh 17: 4 I have f the work which thou *5048
19:30 he said, It is f: and he bowed 5055
Ac 21: 7 And when we had f our course 1274
2Ti 4: 7 I have f my course, I have kept 5055
Heb 4: 3 works were f from the foundation 1096
Jas 1:15 sin, when it is f, bringeth forth * 658
Re 10: 7 the mystery of God should be f, 5055
11: 7 they shall have f their testimony, "
20: 5 until the thousand years were f. "

finisher
Heb 12: 2 Jesus the author and f of our *5047

finite See INFINITE.

fins
Le 11: 9 hath f and scales in the waters, 5579
10 have not f and scales in the seas, "
12 Whatsoever hath no f nor scales "

De 14: 9 have f and scales shall ye eat: 5579
10 not f and scales ye may not eat; "

fir
2Sa 6: 5 of instruments made of f wood, 1265
1Ki 5: 8 and concerning timber of f. "
10 gave Solomon cedar trees and f "
6:15 of the house with planks of f. "
34 the two doors were of f tree: "
9:11 with cedar trees and f trees, and "
2Ki 19:23 and the choice f trees thereof: "
2Ch 2: 8 Send me also cedar trees, f trees, "
3: 5 greater house he cieled with f tree, "
Ps 104:17 stork, the f trees are her house. "
Ca 1:17 are cedar, and our rafters of f. *1266
Isa 14: 8 Yea, the f trees rejoice at thee, 1265
37:24 and the choice f trees thereof: "
41:19 I will set in the desert the f tree, "
55:13 the thorn shall come up the f tree, "
60:13 f tree, the pine tree, and the box "
Eze 27: 5 thy ship boards of f trees of Senir: "
31: 8 f trees were not like his boughs, "
Ho 14: 8 I am like a green f tree. "
Na 2: 3 f trees shall be terribly shaken. * "
Zec 11: 2 f tree; for the cedar is fallen; "

fire See also FIREBRAND; FIREPANS; FIRES.
Ge 19:24 brimstone and f from the Lord out 784
22: 6 and he took the f in his hand, and a "
7 Behold, the f and the wood: "
Ex 3: 2 appeared unto him in a flame of f "
2 behold, the bush burned with f, "
9:23 the f ran along upon the ground; "
24 and f mingled with the hail, very "
12: 8 roast with f, and unleavened bread; "
9 but with f; his head with his legs, "
10 the morning ye shall burn with f. "
13:21 and by night in a pillar of f, "
22 nor the pillar of f by night, "
14:24 the pillar of f and of the cloud, "
19:18 the Lord descended upon it in f: "
22: 6 If f break out, and catch in thorns, "
6 that kindled the f shall surely 1200
24:17 like devouring f on the top of the 784
29:14 his dung, shalt thou burn with f: "
18, 25 offering made by f unto the Lord. "
34 shalt burn the remainder with f: 784
41 an offering made by f unto the Lord. "
30:20 an offering made by f unto the Lord: "
32:20 burnt it in the f, and ground it 784
24 then I cast it into the f, "
35: 3 Ye shall kindle no f throughout "
40:38 and f was on it by night, "
Le 1: 7 the priest shall put f upon the altar, "
7 and lay the wood in order upon the f: "
8 upon the wood that is on the f, "
9 burnt sacrifice, an offering made by f, "
12 upon the wood that is on the f: 784
13 offering made by f, of a sweet savour "
17 upon the wood that is upon the f: 784
17 offering made by f, of a sweet savour "
2: 2 offering made by f, of sweet savour "
3 the offerings of the Lord made by f. "
9 offering made by f, of sweet savour "
10 the offerings of the Lord made by f. "
11 any offering of the Lord made by f. "
14 green ears of corn dried by the f, 784
16 an offering made by f unto the Lord. "
3: 3 an offering made by f unto the Lord; "
5 upon the wood that is on the f: 784
5 offering made by f, of a sweet savour "
9 an offering made by f unto the Lord; "
11 the offering made by f unto the Lord. "
14 an offering made by f unto the Lord. "
16 offering made by f of a sweet savour "
4:12 burn him on the wood with f: 784
35 the offerings made by f unto the Lord: "
5:12 offerings made by f unto the Lord: "
6: 9 the f of the altar shall be burning 784
10 ashes which the f hath consumed "
12 f upon the altar shall be burning in "
13 The f shall ever be burning upon "
17 portion of my offerings made by f; "
18 the offerings of the Lord made by f: "
30 it shall be burnt in the f. 784
7: 5 an offering made by f unto the Lord: "
17 third day shall be burnt with f. 784
19 be burnt with f: and as for the flesh, "
25 an offering made by f unto the Lord: "
30 the offerings of the Lord made by f, "
35 the offerings of the Lord made by f, "
8:17 be burnt with f without the camp; 784
21 an offering made by f unto the Lord; "
28 an offering made by f unto the Lord. "
32 the bread shall ye burn with f. 784
9:11 he burnt with f without the camp. "
24 came a f out from before the Lord, "
10: 1 them his censer, and put f therein, "
1 offered strange f before the Lord, "
2 there went out f from the Lord, "
12 the offerings of the Lord made by f, "
13 the sacrifices of the Lord made by f: "
15 the offerings made by f of the fat, "
13:52 it shall be burnt in the f. 784
55 thou shalt burn it in the f; "
57 that wherein the plague is with f. "
16:12 a censer full of burning coals of f "
13 he shall put the incense upon the f "
27 they shall burn in the f their skins, "
18:21 seed pass through the f to Molech, "
19: 6 it shall be burnt in the f. 784
20:14 be burnt with f, both he and they; "
21: 6 the offerings of the Lord made by f, "
9 she shall be burnt with f. 784
21 the offerings of the Lord made by f: "
22:22 nor make an offering by f of them "
27 an offering made by f unto the Lord. "
Le 23: 8 ye shall offer an offering made by f "
13 an offering made by f unto the Lord "
18 an offering made by f, of sweet savour "
25 ye shall offer an offering made by f "
27 and offer an offering made by f "
36 ye shall offer an offering made by f "
36 ye shall offer an offering made by f "
37 to offer an offering made by f "
24: 7 an offering made by f unto the Lord. "
9 the offerings of the Lord made by f "
Nu 3: 4 offered strange f before the Lord, 784
6:18 put it in the f which is under the "
9:15 as it were the appearance of f, "
16 and the appearance of f by night. "
11: 1 f of the Lord burnt among them, "
2 unto the Lord, the f was quenched. "
3 because the f of the Lord burnt "
14:14 and in a pillar of f by night. "
15: 3 And will make an offering by f "
10 of wine, for an offering made by f, "
13 in offering an offering made by f, "
14 offering made by f, of a sweet savour "
25 a sacrifice made by f unto the Lord, "
16: 7 put f therein, and put incense 784
18 and put f in them, and laid incense "
35 there came out a f from the Lord, "
37 scatter thou the f yonder; for they "
46 put f therein from off the altar, "
18: 9 holy things, reserved from the f: "
17 offering made by f, for a sweet savour "
21:28 there is a f gone out of Heshbon, 784
26:10 time the f devoured two hundred "
61 offered strange f before the Lord. "
28: 2 bread for my sacrifices made by f, "
3 This is the offering made by f "
6 a sacrifice made by f unto the Lord. "
8 a sacrifice made by f, of a sweet "
13 a sacrifice made by f unto the Lord. "
19 ye shall offer a sacrifice made by f "
24 the meat of the sacrifice made by f, "
29: 6 a sacrifice made by f unto the Lord. "
13, 36 a sacrifice made by f, of a sweet "
31:10 and all their goodly castles, with f. 784
23 Every thing that may abide the f, "
23 ye shall make it go through the f, "
23 abideth not the f ye shall make go "
De 1:33 in f by night, to shew you by what "
4:11 the mountain burned with f unto "
12 unto you out of the midst of the f: "
15 Horeb out of the midst of the f; "
24 the Lord thy God is a consuming f, "
33 speaking out of the midst of the f, "
36 earth he shewed thee his great f; "
36 his words out of the midst of the f. "
5: 4 mount out of the midst of the f, "
5 ye were afraid by reason of the f, "
22 the mount out of the midst of the f, "
23 (for the mountain did burn with f,) "
24 his voice out of the midst of the f: "
25 for this great f will consume us: "
26 speaking out of the midst of the f, "
7: 5 burn their graven images with f. "
25 of their gods shall ye burn with f: "
9: 3 as a consuming f he shall destroy "
10 the mount out of the midst of the f "
15 and the mount burned with f: "
21 burnt it with f, and stamped it, "
10: 4 the mount out of the midst of the f "
12: 3 and burn their groves with f; "
31 have burnt in the f to their gods. "
13:16 and shalt burn with f the city, "
18: 1 offerings of the Lord made by f, "
10 his daughter to pass through the f, 784
16 neither let me see this great f "
32:22 For a f is kindled in mine anger, "
22 set on f the foundations of the 3857
Jos 6:24 And they burnt the city with f, 784
7:15 accursed thing shall be burnt with f, "
25 and burned them with f, after they "
8: 8 that ye shall set the city on f: "
19 and hasted and set the city on f. "
11: 6 and burn their chariots with f. "
9 and burnt their chariots with f. "
11 and he burnt Hazor with f. "
13:14 sacrifices of the Lord...made by f "
J'g 1: 8 of the sword, and set the city on f. 784
6:21 there rose up f out of the rock, "
9:15 let f come out of the bramble, "
20 let f come out from Abimelech, "
20 and let f come out from the men of "
49 and set the hold on f upon them; "
52 of the tower to burn it with f. "
12: 1 burn thine house upon thee with f. "
14:15 thee and thy father's house with f: "
15: 5 when he had set the brands on f, "
6 burnt her and her father with f. "
14 as flax that was burnt with f, "
16: 9 tow is broken when it toucheth the f. "
18:27 and burnt the city with f. "
20:48 also they set on f all the cities "
1Sa 2:28 offerings made by f of the children "
30: 1 Ziklag, and burned it with f; 784
3 behold, it was burned with f; "
14 and we burned Ziklag with f. "
2Sa 14:30 hath barley there; go and set it on f. "
30 servants set the field on f. "
31 have thy servants set my field on f? "
22: 9 and f out of his mouth devoured: "
13 before him were coals of f kindled. "
23: 7 they shall be utterly burned with f "
1Ki 9:16 taken Gezer, and burned it with f, "
16:18 the king's house over him with f, "
18:23 lay it on wood, and put no f under: "
23 lay it on wood, and put no f under: "
24 and the God that answereth by f, "
25 of your gods, but put no f under. "
1Ki 18:38 Then the f of the Lord fell, 784
19:12 a f; but the Lord was not in the f: "
12 and after the f a still small voice. "
2Ki 1:10 then let f come down from heaven, "
10 there came down f from heaven, "
12 let f come down from heaven, "
12 f of God came down from heaven, "
14 there came f down from heaven, "
2:11 a chariot of f, and horses of f, and "
6:17 was full of horses and chariots of f "
8:12 their strong holds wilt thou set on f, "
16: 3 made his son to pass through the f, "
17:17 daughters to pass through the f, "
31 burnt their children in f to "
19:18 And have cast their gods into the f: "
21: 6 he made his son pass through the f, "
23:10 to pass through the f to Molech. "
11 the chariots of the sun with f. "
25: 9 great man's house burnt he with f. "
1Ch 14:12 and they were burned with f. "
21:26 he answered him from heaven by f "
2Ch 7: 1 the f came down from heaven, "
3 Israel saw how the f came down, "
28: 3 and burnt his children in the f, "
33: 6 his children to pass through the f "
35:13 they roasted the passover with f "
36:19 burnt all the palaces thereof with f, "
Ne 1: 3 the gates thereof are burned with f. "
2: 3 gates thereof are consumed with f? "
13 gates thereof were consumed with f. "
17 the gates thereof are burned with f: "
9:12 and in the night by a pillar of f, "
19 neither the pillar of f by night, "
Job 1:16 The f of God is fallen from heaven, "
15:34 f shall consume the tabernacles of "
18: 5 the spark of his f shall not shine. "
20:26 a f not blown shall consume him: "
22:20 remnant of them the f consumeth. "
28: 5 it is turned up as it were f. * "
31:12 For it is a f that consumeth to "
41:19 and sparks of f leap out. "
Ps 11: 6 f and brimstone, and an horrible "
18: 8 and f out of his mouth devoured: "
12 passed, hail stones and coals of f. "
13 his voice; hail stones and coals of f. "
21: 9 wrath, and the f shall devour them. "
29: 7 the Lord divideth the flames of f. "
39: 3 while I was musing the f burned: "
46: 9 he burneth the chariot in the f. "
50: 3 a f shall devour before him, "
57: 4 even among them that are set on f. 3857
66:12 through f and through water: 784
68: 2 as wax melteth before the f, so let "
74: 7 They have cast f into thy sanctuary, "
78:14 and all the night with a light of f. "
21 so a f was kindled against Jacob, "
63 The f consumed their young men; "
79: 5 shall thy jealousy burn like f? "
80:16 It is burned with f, it is cut down: "
83:14 As the f burneth a wood, and as "
14 flame setteth the mountains on f; 3857
89:46 shall thy wrath burn like f? 784
97: 3 A f goeth before him, and burneth "
104: 4 spirits; his ministers a flaming f: "
105:32 rain, and flaming f in their land. "
39 and f to give light in the night. "
106:18 a f was kindled in their company; "
118:12 are quenched as the f of thorns: "
140:10 let them be cast into the f; "
148: 8 F, and hail; snow, and vapours; "
Pr 6:27 Can a man take f in his bosom, "
16:27 in his lips there is as a burning f. "
25:22 shalt heap coals of f upon his head, "
26:20 no wood is, there the f goeth out: 784
21 to burning coals, and wood to f; "
30:16 and the f that saith not, It is "
Ca 8: 6 the coals thereof are coals of f, "
Isa 1: 7 your cities are burned with f: "
4: 5 the shining of a flaming f by night: "
5:24 as the f devoureth the stubble, "
9: 5 shall be with burning and fuel of f. "
18 For wickedness burneth as the f: "
19 people shall be as the fuel of the f: "
10:16 a burning like the burning of a f. "
17 the light of Israel shall be for a f, "
26:11 the f of thine enemies shall devour "
27:11 women come, and set them on f 215
29: 6 and the flame of devouring f. 784
30:14 a sherd to take f from the hearth, "
27 and his tongue as a devouring f: "
30 the flame of a devouring f, with "
33 pile thereof is f and much wood: "
31: 9 saith the Lord, whose f is in Zion, 217
33:11 your breath, as f, shall devour you. 784
12 cut up shall they be burned in the f. "
14 shall dwell with the devouring f? "
37:19 And have cast their gods into the f: "
42:25 it hath set him on f round about, 3857
43: 2 when thou walkest through the f, 784
44:16 He burneth part thereof in the f; "
16 I am warm, I have seen the f: 217
19 I have burned part of it in the f; 784
47:14 as stubble; the f shall burn them; "
14 to warm at, nor f to sit before it. 217
50:11 Behold, all ye that kindle a f, 784
11 walk in the light of your f, and in "
54:16 that bloweth the coals in the f, "
64: 2 As when the melting f burneth, "
2 the f causeth the waters to boil, "
11 praised thee, is burned up with f: "
65: 5 a f that burneth all the day. "
66:15 behold, the Lord will come with f, "
15 and his rebuke with flames of f. "
16 For by f and by his sword will the "
24 neither shall their f be quenched; "
Jer 4: 4 lest my fury come forth like f. "

Jer 5:14 make my words in thy mouth f, 784
6: 1 up a sign of f in Beth-haccerem: *
29 the lead is consumed of the f; 784
7:18 and the fathers kindle the f, "
31 sons and their daughters in the f; "
11:16 he hath kindled f upon it, and the "
15:14 for a f is kindled in mine anger, "
17: 4 ye have kindled a f in mine anger, "
27 then will I kindle a f in the gates "
19: 5 to burn their sons with f for burnt "
20: 9 as a burning f shut up in my bones, "
21:10 and he shall burn it with f. "
12 lest my fury go out like f, "
14 and I will kindle a f in the forest "
22: 7 cedars, and cast them into the f. "
23:29 Is not my word like as a f? "
29:22 king of Babylon roasted in the f; "
32:29 shall come and set f on this city, "
34: 2 and he shall burn it with f: "
22 and take it, and burn it with f: "
36:22 and there was a f on the hearth "
23 into the f that was on the hearth, 784
23 all the roll was consumed in the f "
32 king of Judah had burned in the f: "
37: 8 and take it, and burn it with f. "
10 tent, and burn this city with f. "
38:17 this city shall not be burnt with f; "
18 and they shall burn it with f, "
23 cause this city to be burned with f. "
39: 8 the houses of the people, with f, "
43:12 And I will kindle a f in the houses "
13 Egyptians shall he burn with f. "
48:45 f shall come forth out of Heshbon, "
49: 2 daughters shall be burned with f: "
27 And I will kindle a f in the wall of "
50:32 and I will kindle a f in his cities, "
51:32 the reeds they have burned with f, "
58 high gates shall be burned with f; "
58 and the folk in the f, and they shall "
52:13 of the great men, burned he with f: "
La 1:13 above hath he sent f into my bones, "
2: 3 against Jacob like a flaming f, "
4 he poured out his fury like f. "
4:11 and hath kindled a f in Zion, "
Eze 1: 4 f infolding itself, and a brightness "
4 amber, out of the midst of the f. "
13 was like burning coals of f, "
13 the f was bright, and out of the f "
27 as the appearance of f round about "
27 as it were the appearance of f, "
5: 2 Thou shalt burn with f a third part 217
4 cast them into the midst of the f, 784
4 and burn them in the f; "
4 for thereof shall a f come forth into "
8: 2 a likeness as the appearance of f: "
2 downward, f; and from his loins "
10: 2 fill thine hand with coals of f from "
6 Take f from between the wheels, "
7 f that was between the cherubims, "
15: 4 into the f for fuel; the f devoureth "
5 when the f hath devoured it, "
6 which I have given to the f for fuel, "
7 they shall go out from one f, "
7 and another f shall devour them; "
16:21 them to pass through the f for them? "
41 they shall burn thine houses with f, 784
19:12 withered; the f consumed them. "
14 And f is gone out of a rod of her "
20:26 through the f all that openeth the "
31 your sons to pass through the f, 784
47 Behold, I will kindle a f in thee, "
21:31 against thee in the f of my wrath, "
32 Thou shalt be for fuel to the f; "
22:20 to blow the f upon it, to melt it; "
21 blow upon you in the f of my wrath, "
31 them with the f of my wrath: "
23:25 residue shall be devoured by the f. "
37 to pass for them through the f, to "
47 and burn up their houses with f. 784
24: 9 even make the pile for f great. *
10 Heap on wood, kindle the f, 784
12 her scum shall be in the f. "
28:14 down in the midst of the stones of f. "
16 from the midst of the stones of f. "
18 therefore will I bring forth a f from "
30: 8 when I have set a f in Egypt, "
14 will set f in Zoan, and will execute "
16 And I will set f in Egypt: "
36: 5 Surely in the f of my jealousy have "
38:19 in the f of my wrath have I spoken, "
22 great hailstones, f, and brimstone. "
39: 6 And I will send a f on Magog, "
9 and shall set on f and burn the * "
9 burn them with f seven years: * "
10 shall burn the weapons with f: * "
Da 3:22 the flame of the f slew those men 5135
24 bound into the midst of the f? "
25 loose, walking in the midst of the f, "
26 came forth of the midst of the f. "
27 whose bodies the f had no power, "
27 the smell of f had passed on them. "
7: 9 and his wheels as burning f. "
10: 6 and his eyes as lamps of f, 784
Ho 7: 6 morning it burneth as a flaming f. "
8:14 but I will send a f upon his cities, "
Joe 1:19 for the f hath devoured the pastures "
20 the f hath devoured the pastures "
2: 3 A f devoureth before them; and "
5 like the noise of a flame of f that "
30 blood, and f, and pillars of smoke. "
Am 1: 4 I will send a f into the house of "
7 I will send a f on the wall of Gaza, "
10 I will send a f on the wall of Tyrus, "
12 I will send a f upon Teman, "
14 will kindle a f in the wall of Rabbah, "
2: 2 I will send a f upon Moab, "
Am 2: 5 I will send a f upon Judah, 784
5: 6 lest he break out like f in the house "
7: 4 Lord God called to contend by f, "
Ob 18 And the house of Jacob shall be a f, "
Mic 1: 4 wax before the f, and as the waters "
7 thereof shall be burned with the f. "
Na 1: 6 his fury is poured out like f. "
3:13 the f shall devour thy bars. "
15 There shall the f devour thee; "
Hab 2:13 people shall labour in the very f, "
Zep 1:18 land shall be devoured by the f of "
3: 8 earth shall be devoured with the f "
Zec 2: 5 will be unto her a wall of f round "
3: 2 this a brand plucked out of the f? "
9: 4 and she shall be devoured with f. "
11: 1 that the f may devour thy cedars. "
12: 6 like an hearth of f among the wood, "
6 and like a torch of f in a sheaf; "
13: 9 bring the third part through the f, "
Mal 1:10 neither do ye kindle f on mine altar "
3: 2 for he is like a refiner's f, 784
M't 3:10 is hewn down, and cast into the f. 4442
11 with the Holy Ghost, and with f: "
12 up the chaff with unquenchable f. "
5:22 fool, shall be in danger of hell f. "
7:19 is hewn down, and cast into the f. "
13:40 are gathered and burned in the f; "
42 shall cast them into a furnace of f: "
50 cast them into the furnace of f: "
17:15 for ofttimes he falleth into the f, "
18: 8 feet to be cast into everlasting f. "
9 two eyes to be cast into hell f. "
25:41 into everlasting f, prepared for the "
M'r 9:22 it hath cast him into the f, "
43 the f that never shall be quenched: "
44 not, and the f is not quenched. * "
45 the f that never shall be quenched: "
46 not, and the f is not quenched. * "
47 two eyes to be cast into hell f: * "
48 not, and the f is not quenched. "
49 every one shall be salted with f, "
14:54 and warmed himself at the f. *5457
Lu 3: 9 is hewn down, and cast into the f. 4442
16 with the Holy Ghost and with f: "
17 he will burn with f unquenchable. "
9:54 that we command f to come down "
12:49 I am come to send f on the earth; "
17:29 it rained f and brimstone from "
22:55 And when they had kindled a f "
56 beheld him as he sat by the f. 5457
Joh 15: 6 them, and cast them into the f, 4442
18:18 had made a f of coals; for it was cold: "
21: 9 they saw a f of coals there, and fish "
Ac 2: 3 them cloven tongues like as of f, 4442
19 blood, and f, and vapour of smoke: "
7:30 the Lord in a flame of f in a bush. "
28: 2 they kindled a f, and received us 4443
3 of sticks, and laid them on the f, "
5 he shook off the beast into the f, 4442
Ro 12:20 shalt heap coals of f on his head. "
1Co 3:13 shall be revealed by f; and the f "
15 shall be saved; yet so as by f. "
2Th 1: 8 In flaming f taking vengeance on "
Heb 1: 7 and his ministers a flame of f. "
11:34 Quenched the violence of f, "
12:18 and that burned with f, nor unto "
29 For our God is a consuming f. "
Jas 3: 5 great a matter a little f kindleth! "
6 tongue is a f, a world of iniquity: "
6 setteth on f the course of nature; 5394
6 and it is set on f of hell. "
5: 3 shall eat your flesh as it were f. 4442
1Pe 1: 7 though it be tried with f, might "
2Pe 3: 7 reserved unto f against the day of "
12 being on f shall be dissolved, 4448
Jude 7 the vengeance of eternal f. 4442
23 fear, pulling them out of the f; "
Re 1:14 and his eyes were as a flame of f; "
2:18 hath his eyes like unto a flame of f, "
3:18 to buy of me gold tried in the f, "
4: 5 seven lamps of f burning before "
8: 5 and filled it with f of the altar, "
7 hail and f mingled with blood, "
8 a great mountain burning with f "
9:17 having breastplates of f, and of 4447
17 out of their mouths issued f and 4442
18 killed, by the f, and by the smoke, "
10: 1 and his feet as pillars of f: "
11: 5 f proceedeth out of their mouth, "
13:13 maketh f come down from heaven "
14:10 tormented with f and brimstone "
18 which had power over f; and cried "
15: 2 were a sea of glass mingled with f: "
16: 8 unto him to scorch men with f. "
17:16 eat her flesh, and burn her with f. "
18: 8 she shall be utterly burned with f: "
19:12 His eyes were as a flame of f, "
20 lake of f burning with brimstone. "
20: 9 and f came down from God out of "
10 into the lake of f and brimstone, "
14 hell were cast into the lake of f. "
15 of life was cast into the lake of f. "
21: 8 burneth with f and brimstone: "

firebrand See also FIREBRANDS.
J'g 15: 4 turned tail to tail, and put a f 3940
Am 4:11 ye were as a f plucked out of the * 181

firebrands
J'g 15: 4 and took f and turned tail to tail, 3940
Pro 26:18 As a mad man who casteth f, 2131
Isa 7: 4 for the two tails of these smoking f, 181

firepans
Ex 27: 3 and his fleshhooks, and his f: 4289
38: 3 and the fleshhooks, and the f: "
2Ki 25:15 And the f, and the bowls, and such "
Jer 52:19 the basons, and the f, and the bowls, "

fires
Isa 24:15 glorify ye the Lord in the f, even * 217

firkins
Joh 2: 6 containing two or three f apiece. 3355

firm See also AFFIRM; CONFIRM.
Jos 3:17 the covenant of the Lord stood f 3559
4: 3 where the priests' feet stood f, "
Job 41:23 they are f in themselves; they 3332
24 His heart is as f as a stone; they "
Ps 73: 4 but their strength is f. 1277
Dan 6: 7 and to make a f decree, *8631
Heb 3: 6 rejoicing of the hope f unto the end. 949

firmament
Gen 1: 6 Let there be a f in the midst of 7549
7 God made the f, and divided the "
7 which were under the f from the "
7 the waters which were above the f: "
8 And God called the f Heaven. "
14 Let there be lights in the f of the "
15 for lights in the f of heaven to give "
17 God set them in the f of heaven to "
20 earth in the open f of heaven. "
Ps 19: 1 and the f sheweth his handywork. "
150: 1 praise him in the f of his power. "
Eze 1:22 the likeness of the f upon the heads "
23 And under the f were their wings "
25 And there was a voice from the f "
26 And above the f that was over their "
10: 1 in the f that was above the head "
Dan 12: 3 shine as the brightness of the f; "

first See also FIRSTBORN; FIRSTBEGOTTEN; FIRSTFRUIT; FIRSTLING; FIRSTRIPE.
Gen 1: 5 and the morning were the f day. * 259
2:11 The name of the f is Pison: "
8: 5 on the f day of the month, were "
13 in the six hundredth and f year, in "
13 the f [7223] month, the f day of the "
13: 4 which he had made there at the f: 7223
25:25 And the f came out red, all over "
26: 1 the f famine that was in the days "
28:19 that city was called Luz at the f. "
38:28 saying, This came out f. "
41:20 did eat up the f seven fat kine: "
43:18 in our sacks at the f time are we 8462
20 we came indeed down at the f time "
Ex 4: 8 hearken to the voice of the f sign, 7223
12: 2 be the f month of the year to you. "
5 blemish, a male of the f year; ‡1121
15 the f day ye shall put away leaven 7223
15 from the f day until the seventh "
16 in the f day there shall be an holy "
18 In the f month, on the fourteenth "
22:29 to offer the f of thy ripe fruits, *4395
23:19 The f of the firstfruits of thy land 7225
28:17 the f row shall be a sardius, a *
17 carbuncle: this shall be the f row. 259
29:38 two lambs of the f year day by ‡1121
34: 1 tables of stone like unto the f: 7223
1 the words that were in the f tables, "
4 two tables of stone like unto the f: "
26 The f of the firstfruits of thy land 7225
39:10 the f row was a sardius, a topaz, *
10 a carbuncle: this was the f row. 259
40: 2 On the f day of the...month shalt 7223
2 On the...day of the f month shalt 259
17 the f month in the second year, 7223
17 on the f day of the month, that the 259
Le 4:21 and burn him as he burned the f 7223
5: 8 that which is for the sin offering f, "
9: 3 and a lamb, both of the f year, ‡1121
15 and offered it for sin, as the f. 7223
12: 6 shall bring a lamb of the f year ‡1121
14:10 and one ewe lamb of the f year ‡1323
23: 5 the fourteenth day of the f month 7223
7 In the f day ye shall have an holy "
12 lamb without blemish of the f ‡1121
18 lambs without blemish of the f ‡ "
19 two lambs of the f year for a ‡ "
24 In the seventh month, in the f day 259
35 On the f day shall be an holy 7223
39 on the f day shall be a sabbath, "
40 take you on the f day the boughs "
Nu 1: 1, 18 the f day of the second month, 259
2: 9 armies. These shall f set forth. 7223
6:12 shall bring a lamb of the f year ‡1121
14 Lord, one he lamb of the f year ‡ "
14 and one ewe lamb of the f year ‡1323
7:12 he that offered his offering the f 7223
15 one ram, one lamb of the f year, ‡1121
17 goats, five lambs of the f year: ‡ "
21 one lamb of the f year, for a ‡ "
23 five lambs of the f year: this ‡ "
27 one lamb of the f year, for a ‡ "
29 goats, five lambs of the f year: ‡ "
33 one ram, one lamb of the f year, ‡ "
35 five lambs of the f year: this ‡ "
39 one lamb of the f year, for a ‡ "
41 five lambs of the f year: this ‡ "
45 one ram, one lamb of the f year, ‡ "
47 goats, five lambs of the f year: ‡ "
51 one ram, one lamb of the f year, ‡ "
53 goats, five lambs of the f year: ‡ "
57 one ram, one lamb of the f year, ‡ "
59 goats, five lambs of the f year: ‡ "
63 one ram, one lamb of the f year, ‡ "
65 goats, five lambs of the f year: ‡ "
69 one ram, one lamb of the f year, ‡ "
71 goats, five lambs of the f year: ‡ "
75 one ram, one lamb of the f year, ‡ "
77 goats, five lambs of the f year: ‡ "
81 one ram, one lamb of the f year, ‡ "
83 goats, five lambs of the f year: ‡ "
87 the lambs of the f year twelve, ‡ "

Nu 7:88 the lambs of the *f* year sixty. ‡1121
9: 1 in the *f* month of the second year 7223
5 *f* month at even in the wilderness "
10:13 they *f* took their journey according "
14 In the *f* place went the standard "
15:20 up a cake of the *f* of your dough 7225
21 Of the *f* of your dough ye shall give "
27 bring a she goat of the *f* year ‡1323
18:13 whatsoever is *f* ripe in the land. *1061
20: 1 the desert of Zin in the *f* month: 7223
24:20 Amalek was the *f* of the nations; 7225
28: 3, 9 lambs of the *f* year without ‡1121
11 seven lambs of the *f* year without ‡ "
16 fourteenth day of the *f* month 7223
18 *f* day shall be an holy convocation; "
19 and seven lambs of the *f* year: ‡1121
27 ram, seven lambs of the *f* year; ‡ "
29: 1 in the seventh month, on the *f* day 259
2 seven lambs of the *f* year without ‡1121
8 and seven lambs of the *f* year ‡ "
13 and fourteen lambs of the *f* year; ‡ "
17, 20 fourteen lambs of the *f* year ‡ "
23, 26, 29, 32 two rams, and fourteen lambs of the *f* year without ‡ "
36 ram, seven lambs of the *f* year ‡ "
33: 3 from Rameses in the *f* month, 7223
3 on the fifteenth day of the *f* month; "
38 in the *f* day of the fifth month. 259
De 1: 3 the *f* day of the month, that Moses "
9:18 down before the Lord, as at the *f*, 7223
25 as I fell down at the *f*; because *
10: 1 two tables of stone like unto the *f*, 7223
2 the words that were in the *f* tables "
3 two tables of stone like unto the *f*, "
4 according to the *f* writing, the ten "
10 mount, according to the *f* time, "
11:14 the *f* rain and the latter rain, *3138
13: 9 thine hand shall be *f* upon him 7223
16: 4 thou sacrificedst the *f* day at even, "
17: 7 hands of the witnesses shall be *f* "
18: 4 *f* fleece of the fleece of thy sheep, 7225
26: 2 thou shalt take of the *f* of all the "
21 he provided the *f* part for himself, "
Jos 4:19 on the tenth day of the *f* month, 7223
8: 5 come out against us, as at the *f*, "
6 They flee before us, as at the *f*: "
21:10 Levi, had: for their's was the *f* lot. "
J'g 1: 1 for us against the Canaanites *f*, 8462
18:29 name of the city was Laish at the *f*. 7223
20:18 Which of us shall go up *f* to the 8462
18 Lord said, Judah shall go up *f*. "
22 themselves in array the *f* day. 7223
32 smitten down before us, as at the *f*. "
39 down before us, as in the *f* battle. "
1Sa 14:14 that *f* slaughter, which Jonathan "
35 same was the *f* altar that he built 2490
2Sa 3:13 *f* bring Michael Saul's daughter, 6440
17: 9 of them be overthrown at the *f*, 8462
19:20 I am come the *f* this day of all the 7223
43 that our advice should not be *f* "
21: 9 the days of harvest, in the *f* days, "
23:19 he attained not unto the *f* three. "
23 but he attained not unto the *f* three. "
1Ki 16:23 In the thirty and *f* year of Asa 259
17:13 make me thereof a little cake *f*, 7223
18:25 for yourselves, and dress it *f*; "
20: 9 send for to thy servant at the *f* "
17 princes of the provinces went out *f*; "
1Ch 9: 2 *f* inhabitants that dwelt in their "
11: 6 Whosoever smiteth the Jebusites *f* "
6 Joab the son of Zeruiah went *f* up, "
21 howbeit he attained not to the *f* three. "
25 but attained not to the *f* three: "
12: 9 Ezer the *f*, Obadiah the second, *7218
15 went over Jordan in the *f* month. 7223
15:13 because ye did it not at the *f*, "
16: 7 David delivered *f* this psalm to 7218
23:19 Jeriah the *f*, Amariah the second, * "
20 Micah the *f*, and Jesiah the * "
24: 7 the *f* lot came forth to Jehoiarib, 7223
21 of Rehabiah, the *f* was Isshiah. *7218
23 Jeriah the *f*, Amariah the second, *
25: 9 the *f* lot came forth for Asaph 7223
27: 2 Over the *f* course for the *f* month "
3 captains of the host for the *f* month. "
29:29 acts of David the king, *f* and last, "
2Ch 3: 3 *f* measure was threescore cubits, "
9:29 the acts of Solomon, *f* and last, "
12:15 the acts of Rehoboam, *f* and last, "
16:11 the acts of Asa, *f* and last, "
17: 3 in the *f* ways of his father David, "
20:34 the acts of Jehoshaphat, *f* and last, "
25:26 the acts of Amaziah, *f* and last, "
26:22 the acts of Uzziah, *f* and last, "
28:26 acts and of all his ways, *f* and last, "
29: 3 He in the *f* year of his reign, "
3 in the *f* month, opened the doors of "
17 on the *f* [259] day of the *f* month to "
17 in the sixteenth day of the *f* month "
35: 1 the fourteenth day of the *f* month. "
27 And his deeds, *f* and last, behold. "
36:22 the *f* year of Cyrus king of Persia, 259
Ezr 1: 1 the *f* year of Cyrus king of Persia, "
3: 6 From the *f* day of the seventh month "
12 men, that had seen the *f* house, 7223
5:13 But in the *f* year of Cyrus the king 2298
6: 3 In the *f* year of Cyrus the king "
19 the fourteenth day of the *f* month. 7223
7: 9 For upon the *f* day of the...month 259
9 day of the *f* month began he to go 7223
9 and on the *f* day of the fifth month 259
8:31 on the twelfth day of the *f* month, 7223
10:16 in the *f* day of the tenth month to 259
17 wives by the *f* day of the...month. "
17 wives by the...day of the *f* month. 7223
Ne 7: 5 of them which came up at the *f*, "
Ne 8: 2 the *f* day of the seventh month. 259
18 from the *f* day unto the last day, 7223
Es 1:14 which sat the *f* in the kingdom;) "
3: 7 In the *f* month, that is, the month "
12 the thirteenth day of the *f* month, "
Job 15: 7 Art thou the *f* man that was born? "
42:14 And he called the name of the *f*, "
Pr 18:17 He that is *f* in his own cause "
Isa 1:26 will restore thy judges as at the *f*, "
9: 1 when at the *f* he lightly afflicted * "
41: 4 the Lord, the *f*, and with the last; "
27 The *f* shall say to Zion, Behold, "
43:27 Thy *f* father hath sinned, and thy "
44: 6 I am the *f*, and I am the last; and "
48:12 he; I am the *f*, I also am the last. "
60: 9 the ships of Tarshish *f*, to bring "
Jer 4:31 that bringeth forth her *f* child, 1069
7:12 where I set my name at the *f*, 7223
16:18 *f* I will recompense their iniquity "
24: 2 even like the figs that are *f* ripe: 1073
25: 1 was the *f* year of Nebuchadrezzar 7224
33: 7 and will build them, as at the *f*. 7223
11 the captivity of the land, as at the *f*, "
36:28 words that were in the *f* roll, "
50:17 away: *f* the king of Assyria hath "
52:31 *f* year of his reign lifted up the head "
Eze 10:14 the *f* face was the face of a cherub, 259
26: 1 in the *f* day of the month, that the "
29:17 in the *f* month, in the...day of the 7223
17 in the *f* day of the month, the word 259
30:20 the *f* month, in the seventh day 7223
31: 1 in the *f* day of the month, that the 259
32: 1 in the *f* day of the month, that the "
40:21 were the measure of the *f* gate: 7223
44:30 And the *f* of all the firstfruits 7225
30 unto the priest the *f* of your dough, "
45:18 In the *f* month, in the...day of the 7223
18 in the *f* day of the month, thou shalt 259
21 In the *f* month, in the fourteenth 7223
46:13 of a lamb of the *f* year without ‡1121
Da 1:21 even unto the *f* year of king Cyrus. 259
6: 2 presidents of whom Daniel was *f*: *2298
7: 1 In the *f* year of Belshazzar king "
4 The *f* was like a lion, and had 6933
8 three of the *f* horns plucked up "
24 he shall be diverse from the *f*, * "
8: 1 which appeared unto me at the *f*. 8462
21 between his eyes is the *f* king. 7223
9: 1 In the *f* year of Darius the son of 259
2 In the *f* year of his reign I Daniel "
10: 4 and twentieth day of the *f* month, 7223
12 from the *f* day that thou didst set "
11: 1 Also I in the *f* year of Darius the 259
Ho 2: 7 go and return to my *f* husband: 7223
9:10 in the fig tree at her *f* time: but 7225
Joe 2:23 and the latter rain in the *f* month. 7223
Am 6: 7 captive with the *f* that go captive, 7218
Mic 4: 8 the *f* dominion; the kingdom *7223
Hag 1: 1 in the *f* day of the month, came the 259
2: 3 saw this house in her *f* glory? *7223
Zec 6: 2 In the *f* chariot were red horses; "
12: 7 also shall save the tents of Judah *f*, "
14:10 gate unto the place of the *f* gate. "
M't 5:24 *f* be reconciled to thy brother, 4412
6:33 But seek ye *f* the kingdom of God, "
7: 5 *f* cast out the beam out of thine "
8:21 suffer me *f* to go and bury my "
10: 2 The *f*, Simon, who is called Peter, 4413
12:29 except he *f* bind the strong man? 4412
45 of that man is worse than the *f*. 4413
13:30 Gather ye together *f* the tares, 4412
17:10 scribes that Elias must *f* come? "
11 Elias truly shall *f* come, and * "
27 take up the fish that *f* cometh up; 4413
19:30 But many that are *f* shall be last; "
30 shall be last; and the last shall be *f*. "
20: 8 beginning from the last unto the *f*. "
10 when the *f* came, they supposed "
16 the last shall be *f*, and the *f* last: "
21:28 and he came to the *f*, and said, "
31 They say unto him, The *f*. "
36 other servants more than the *f*: "
22:25 and the *f*, when he had married a "
38 is the *f* and great commandment. "
23:26 cleanse *f* that which is within the 4412
26:17 Now the *f* day of the feast of 4413
27:64 last error shall be worse than the *f*. "
28: 1 toward the *f* day of the week, 3391
M'r 3:27 he will *f* bind the strong man; 4412
4:28 *f* the blade, then the ear, after that "
7:27 Let the children *f* be filled: for it "
9:11 the scribes that Elias must *f* come? "
12 Elias verily cometh *f*, and restoreth "
35 man desire to be *f*, the same shall 4413
10:31 But many that are *f* shall be last; "
31 shall be last; and the last *f*. "
12:20 *f* took a wife, and dying left no "
28 Which is the *f* commandment of "
29 The *f* of all the commandments is, "
30 this is the *f* commandment. "
13:10 the gospel must *f* be published 4412
14:12 the *f* day of unleavened bread, 4413
16: 2 morning the *f* day of the week, 3391
9 early the *f* day of the week, 4413
9 he appeared *f* to Mary Magdalene, 4412
Lu 1: 3 of all things from the very *f*, 509
2: 2 taxing was *f* made when Cyrenius 4413
6: 1 the second sabbath after the *f*, *1207
42 hypocrite, cast out *f* the beam 4412
9:59 suffer me *f* to go and bury my "
61 but let me *f* go bid them farewell, "
10: 5 *f* say, Peace be to this house. "
11:26 of that man is worse than the *f*. 4413
38 had not *f* washed before dinner. 4412
12: 1 to say unto his disciples *f* of all, "
13:30 shall be *f*, and there are *f* which 4413
Lu 14:18 *f* said unto him, I have bought 4413
28 sitteth not down *f*, and counteth 4412
31 sitteth not down *f*, and consulteth "
16: 5 and said unto the *f*, How much 4413
17:25 But *f* must he suffer many things, 4412
19:16 Then came the *f*, saying, Lord, 4413
20:29 and the *f* took a wife, and died "
21: 9 these things must *f* come to pass; 4412
24: 1 Now upon the *f* day of the week, 3391
Joh 1:41 *f* findeth his own brother Simon, 4413
5: 4 then *f* after the troubling of the * "
8: 7 let him *f* cast a stone at her. "
10:40 place where John at *f* baptized; 4412
12:16 not his disciples at the *f*: but when "
18:13 And led him away to Annas *f*; for "
19:32 and brake the legs of the *f*, and of 4413
39 at the *f* came to Jesus by night, 4412
20: 1 *f* day of the week cometh Mary 3391
4 Peter, and came *f* to the sepulchre. 4413
8 which came *f* to the sepulchre, and "
19 being the *f* day of the week, 3391
Ac 3:26 Unto you *f* God, having raised up 4412
7:12 Egypt, he sent out our fathers *f*. "
11:26 were called Christians *f* in Antioch. "
12:10 past the *f* and the second ward, 4413
13:24 When John had *f* preached before his "
46 should *f* have been spoken to you: 4412
15:14 how God at the *f* did visit the "
20: 7 And upon the *f* day of the week, 3391
18 know, from the *f* day that I came 4413
26: 4 at the *f* among mine own nation * 746
20 shewed *f* unto them of Damascus 4412
23 should be the *f* that should rise 4413
27:43 cast themselves *f* into the sea, "
Ro 1: 8 *F*, I thank my God through Jesus 4412
16 to the Jew *f*, and also to the Greek. "
2: 9 the Jew *f*, and also of the Gentile; "
10 the Jew *f*, and also to the Gentile: "
10:19 *F* Moses saith, I will provoke you 4413
11:35 Or who hath *f* given to him, 4272
15:24 if *f* I be somewhat filled with your 4412
1Co 11:18 For *f* of all, when ye come "
12:28 *f* apostles, secondarily prophets, "
14:30 sitteth by, let the *f* hold his peace. 4413
15: 3 I delivered unto you *f* of all 1722, "
45 *f* man Adam was made a living "
46 that was not *f* which is spiritual, 4412
47 The *f* man is of the earth, earthy: 4413
16: 2 Upon the *f* day of the week let 3391
subscr. The *f* epistle to the Corinthians 4413
2Co 8: 5 *f* gave their own selves to the "
12 if there be *f* a willing mind, *4295
Ga 4:13 the gospel unto you at the *f*. 4386
Eph 1:12 who *f* trusted in Christ. *4276
4: 9 also descended *f* into the lower *4412
6: 2 *f* commandment with promise; 4413
Ph'p 1: 5 gospel from the *f* day until now; "
1Th 4:16 the dead in Christ shall rise *f*: 4412
subscr. *f* epistle unto the Thessalonians 4413
2Th 2: 3 except there come a falling away *f*, 4412
1Ti 1:16 in me *f* Jesus Christ might shew *4413
2: 1 *f* of all, supplications, prayers, 4412
13 Adam was *f* formed, then Eve. *4413
3:10 And let these also *f* be proved; 4412
5: 4 let them learn *f* to shew piety "
12 they have cast off their *f* faith. 4413
subscr. The *f* to Timothy was written for "
2Ti 1: 5 which dwelt *f* in thy grandmother 4412
2: 6 must be *f* partaker of the fruits. 4412
4:16 At my *f* answer no man stood with "
subscr. Timotheus, ordained the *f* bishop "
Tit 3:10 after the *f* and second admonition 3391
subscr. Titus, ordained the *f* bishop of the 4413
Heb 2: 3 which at the *f* began to be spoken 746
4: 6 they to whom it was *f* preached *4386
5:12 *f* principles of the oracles of God; 746
7: 2 *f* being by interpretation King of 4412
27 *f* for his own sins, and then for 4386
8: 7 that *f* covenant had been faultless, 4413
13 covenant, he hath made the *f* old. "
9: 1 Then verily the *f* covenant had "
2 the *f*, wherein was the candlestick, "
6 went always into the *f* tabernacle, "
8 while as the *f* tabernacle was yet "
15 that were under the *f* testament, "
18 the *f* testament was dedicated "
10: 9 He taketh away the *f*, that he may "
Jas 3:17 is *f* pure, then peaceable, gentle, 4412
1Pe 4:17 and if it *f* begin at us, what shall "
2Pe 1:20 Knowing this *f*, that no prophecy "
3: 3 Knowing this *f*, that there shall "
1Jo 4:19 love him, because he *f* loved us. 4413
Jude 6 which kept not their *f* estate, * 746
Re 1: 5 the *f* begotten of the dead, *4416
11 Alpha and Omega, the *f* and the *4413
17 Fear not; I am the *f* and the last: "
2: 4 because thou hast left thy *f* love. "
5 and do the *f* works; or else I will "
8 saith the *f* and the last, which was "
19 and the last to be more than the *f*. "
4: 1 and the *f* voice which I heard was "
7 And the *f* beast was like a lion, "
8: 7 The *f* angel sounded, and there "
13:12 all the power of the *f* beast before "
12 therein to worship the *f* beast, "
16: 2 the *f* went, and poured out his vial "
20: 5 This is the *f* resurrection. "
6 hath part in the *f* resurrection: "
21: 1 the *f* heaven and the *f* earth were "
19 the *f* foundation was jasper; the "
22:13 and the end, the *f* and the last. "

firstbegotten See also FIRST and BEGOTTEN.
Heb 1: 6 bringeth in the *f* into the world, *4416

firstborn
Ge 10:15 Canaan begat Sidon his *f*, and 1060

Ge 19:31 And the *f* said unto the younger, 1067
33 *f* went in, and lay with her father, "
34 *f* said unto the younger, Behold, "
37 *f* bare a son, and called his name "
22:21 Huz his *f*, and Buz his brother, 1060
25:13 *f* of Ishmael, Nebajoth; and Kedar, "
27:19 I am Esau thy *f*; I have done "
32 he said, I am thy son, thy *f* Esau. "
29:26 to give the younger before the *f*. 1067
35:23 Reuben, Jacob's *f*, and Simeon, 1060
36:15 sons of Eliphaz the *f* son of Esau; "
38: 6 And Judah took a wife for Er his *f*, "
7 Er, Judah's *f*, was wicked in the "
41:51 called the name of the *f* Manasseh: "
43:33 the *f* according to his birthright, "
46: 8 and his sons; Reuben, Jacob's *f*. "
48:14 for Manasseh was the *f*. "
18 Not so, my father: for this is the *f*; "
49: 3 Reuben, thou art my *f*, my might, "
Ex 4:22 Israel is my son, even my *f*: "
23 I will slay thy son, even thy *f*. "
6:14 the *f* of Israel; Hanoch and Pallu, "
11: 5 all the *f* in the land of Egypt shall "
5 die, from the *f* of Pharaoh that "
5 unto the *f* of the maidservant that "
5 the mill; and all the *f* of beasts. "
12:12 and will smite all the *f* in the land "
29 Lord smote all the *f* in the land of "
29 from the *f* of Pharaoh that sat on "
29 unto the *f* of the captive that was "
29 dungeon; and all the *f* of cattle. "
13: 2 Sanctify unto me all the *f*, "
13 the *f* of man among thy children "
15 the Lord slew all the *f* in the land "
15 of Egypt, both the *f* of man, and "
15 of man, and the *f* of beast: "
15 all the *f* of my children I redeem. "
22:29 the *f* of thy sons shalt thou give "
34:20 the *f* of thy sons thou shalt redeem. "
Nu 3: 2 Nadab the *f*, and Abihu, Eleazar, "
12 all the *f* that openeth the matrix "
13 Because all the *f* are mine; for on "
13 on the day that I smote all the *f* of "
13 I hallowed unto me all the *f* in "
40 Number all the *f* of the males of the "
41 instead of all the *f* among the "
42 all the *f* among the children of "
43 And all the *f* males by the number "
45 Take the Levites instead of all the *f* "
46 of the *f* of the children of Israel, * "
50 Of the *f* of the children of Israel "
8:16 even instead the *f* of all the children "
17 For all the *f* of the children of Israel "
17 day that I smote every *f* in the land "
18 have taken the Levites for all the *f* "
18:15 *f* of man shalt thou surely redeem, "
33: 4 the Egyptians buried all their *f*; "
De 21:15 the *f* son be hers that was hated: "
16 not make the son of the beloved *f* 1069
16 of the hated, which is indeed the *f*: 1060
17 the son of the hated for the *f*, "
17 strength; the right of the *f* is his. 1062
25: 6 *f* which she beareth shall succeed 1060
Jos 6:26 lay the foundation thereof in his *f*, "
17: 1 for he was the *f* of Joseph; "
1 for Machir the *f* of Manasseh, "
J'g 8:20 And he said unto Jether his *f*, "
1Sa 8: 2 Now the name of his *f* was Joel; "
14:49 the name of the *f* Merab, 1067
17:13 Eliab the *f*, and next unto him 1060
2Sa 3: 2 and his *f* was Amnon, of Ahinoam "
1Ki 16:34 foundation thereof in Abiram his *f*, "
1Ch 1:13 And Canaan begat Zidon his *f*, and "
29 The *f* of Ishmael, Nebaioth; then "
2: 3 And Er, the *f* of Judah, was evil "
13 begat his *f* Eliab, and Abinadab "
25 the *f* of Hezron were, Ram the *f*, "
27 the sons of Ram the *f* of Jerahmeel "
42 of Jerahmeel were, Mesha his *f*, "
50 Hur, the *f* of Ephratah; Shobal the "
3: 1 the *f* Amnon, of Ahinoam the "
15 *f* Johanan, the second Jehoiakim, "
4: 4 the sons of Hur, the *f* of Ephratah, "
5: 1 the sons of Reuben the *f* of Israel, "
1 (for he was the *f*; but, forasmuch "
3 I say, of Reuben the *f* of Israel were, "
6:28 the sons of Samuel; the *f* Vashni, "
8: 1 Now Benjamin begat Bela his *f*, "
30 And his *f* son Abdon, and Zur, and "
39 Ulam his *f*, Jehush the second, "
9: 5 Asaiah the *f*, and his sons. "
31 who was the *f* of Shallum the "
36 And his *f* son Abdon, then Zur, and "
26: 2 Zechariah the *f*, Jediael the second, "
4 were, Shemiah the *f*, Jehozabad the "
10 not the *f*, yet his father made him "
2Ch 21: 3 to Jehoram; because he was the *f*. "
Ne 10:36 Also the *f* of our sons, and of our "
Job 18:13 the *f* of death shall devour his ‡
Ps 78:51 And smote all the *f* in Egypt; "
89:27 Also I will make him my *f*, "
105:36 smote also all the *f* in their land, "
135: 8 Who smote the *f* of Egypt, "
136:10 him that smote Egypt in their *f*: "
Isa 14:30 And the *f* of the poor shall feed, "
Jer 31: 9 to Israel, and Ephraim is my *f*. "
Mic 6: 7 I give my *f* for my transgression, "
Zec 12:10 as one that is in bitterness for his *f*. "
M't 1:25 she had brought forth her *f* son: *4416
Lu 2: 7 And she brought forth her *f* son, "
Ro 8:29 be the *f* among many brethren. "
Col 1:15 God, the *f* of every creature: "
18 the beginning, the *f* from the dead: "
Heb 11:28 destroyed the *f* shall touch them. "
12:23 assembly and church of the *f*, "

firstfruit See also FIRSTFRUITS.
De 18: 4 *f* also of thy corn, of thy wine, *7225
Ro 11:16 if the *f* be holy, the lump is also 536

firstfruits
Ex 23:16 the *f* of thy labours, which thou 1061
19 The first of the *f* of thy land thou "
34:22 *f* of wheat harvest, and the feast "
26 first of the *f* of thy land thou shalt "
Le 2:12 the oblation of the *f*, ye shall offer 7225
14 offer a meat offering of thy *f* 1061
14 offer for the meat offering of thy *f* "
23:10 ye shall bring a sheaf of the *f* of 7225
17 they are the *f* unto the Lord. 1061
20 wave them with the bread of the *f* "
Nu 18:12 *f* of them which they shall offer 7725
28:26 Also in the day of the *f*, when ye 1061
De 26:10 I have brought the *f* of the land,* 7725
2Ki 4:42 bread of the *f*, twenty loaves of 1061
2Ch 31: 5 the *f* of corn, wine, and oil, and 7225
Ne 10:35 And to bring the *f* of our ground, 1061
35 and the *f* of all fruit trees, yearly "
37 should bring the *f* of our dough, 7225
12:44 for the *f*, and for the tithes, to "
13:31 at times appointed, and for the *f*. 1061
Pr 3: 9 with the *f* of all thine increase: 7225
Jer 2: 3 the Lord, and the *f* of his increase: "
Eze 20:40 and the *f* of your oblations, "
44:30 the first of all the *f* of all things, 1061
48:14 nor alienate the *f* of the land: 7225
Ro 8:23 which have the *f* of the Spirit, 536
16: 5 who is the *f* of Achaia unto Christ. "
1Co 15:20 and become the *f* of them that slept. "
23 Christ the *f*; afterward they that "
16:15 Stephanas, that it is the *f* of Achaia, "
Jas 1:18 be a kind of *f* of his creatures, "
Re 14: 4 the *f* unto God and to the Lamb. "

firstling See also FIRSTLINGS.
Ex 13:12 every *f* that cometh of a beast 6363
13 every *f* of an ass thou shalt redeem "
34:19 and every *f* among thy cattle, "
20 the *f* of an ass thou shalt redeem "
Le 27:26 Only the *f* of the beasts, which 1060
26 which should be the Lord's *f*, no 1069
Nu 18:15 the *f* of unclean beasts shalt thou 1060
17 But the *f* of a cow, or the *f* of a "
17 a sheep, or the *f* of a goat, thou "
De 15:19 All the *f* males that come of thy "
19 no work with the *f* of thy bullock, "
19 nor shear the *f* of thy sheep. "
33:17 glory is like the *f* of his bullock, "

firstlings
Ge 4: 4 also brought of the *f* of his flock 1062
Nu 3:41 instead of all the *f* among the 1060
De 12: 6 and the *f* of your herds 1062
17 the *f* of thy herds or of thy flock, "
14:23 the *f* of your herds and of your "
Ne 10:36 *f* of our herds and of our flocks, 1062

firstripe See also FIRST and RIPE.
Nu 13:20 was the time of the *f* grapes. 1061
Ho 9:10 I saw your fathers as the *f* in the 1063
Mic 7: 1 eat: my soul desired the *f* fruit. "
Na 3:12 be like fig trees with the *f* figs: "

fir-tree See FIR and TREE.

fir-wood See FIR and WOOD.

fish See also FISHERMEN; FISHER'S; FISHERS; FISHES; FISHHOOKS; FISHING; FISHPOOLS; FISH'S.
Ge 1:26, 28, dominion over the *f* of the sea. 1710
Ex 7:18 And the *f* that is in the river shall "
21 And the *f* that was in the river died; "
Nu 11: 5 remember the *f*, which we did eat "
22 or shall all the *f* of the sea be 1709
De 4:18 of any *f* that is in the waters 1710
2Ch 33:14 the entering in at the *f* gate, 1709
Ne 3: 3 *f* gate did the sons of Hassenaah "
12:39 above the *f* gate, and the tower "
13:16 which brought *f*, and all manner "
Job 41: 7 irons? or his head with *f* spears? "
Ps 8: 8 the *f* of the sea, and whatsoever "
105:29 into blood, and slew their *f*. 1710
Isa 19:10 make sluices and ponds for *f*. *5315
50: 2 their *f* stinketh, because there is 1710
Jer 16:16 and they shall *f* them; and after 1770
Eze 29: 4 I will cause the *f* of thy rivers to 1710
4 all the *f* of thy rivers shall stick "
5 thee and all the *f* of thy rivers: "
47: 9 be a very great multitude of *f*, "
10 *f* shall be according to their kinds, "
10 as the *f* of the great sea, "
Jon 1:17 the Lord had prepared a great *f* 1709
17 Jonah was in the belly of the *f* "
2:10 And the Lord spake unto the *f*, "
Zep 1:10 the noise of a cry from the *f* gate, "
M't 7:10 Or if he ask a *f*, will he give him 2486
17:27 take up the *f* that first cometh up; "
Lu 11:11 or if he ask a *f*, will he for a *f* give "
24:42 gave him a piece of a broiled *f*, "
Joh 21: 9 and *f* laid thereon, and bread. 3795
10 the *f* which ye have now caught. "
13 and giveth them, and *f* likewise. "

fishermen
Lu 5: 2 but the *f* were gone out of them. 231

fisher's
Joh 21: 7 he girt his *f* coat unto him, (for *1903

fishers
Isa 19: 8 The *f* also shall mourn, and all 1771
Jer 16:16 Behold, I will send for many *f*, 1728
Eze 47:10 that the *f* shall stand upon it "
M't 4:18 a net into the sea: for they were *f*. 231
19 I will make you *f* of men. "
M'r 1:16 a net into the sea: for they were *f*. "
17 I will make you to become *f* of men. "

fishes
Ge 9: 2 shall be upon all the *f* of the sea; 1709
1Ki 4:33 and of creeping things, and of *f*. "
Job 12: 8 the *f* of the sea shall declare unto "
Ec 9:12 the *f* that are taken in an evil net, "
Eze 38:20 So that the *f* of the sea, and the "
Ho 4: 3 the *f* of the sea also shall be taken "
Hab 1:14 makest men as the *f* of the sea, "
Zep 1: 3 and the *f* of the sea, and the "
M't 14:17 here but five loaves, and two *f*. 2486
19 took the five loaves, and the two *f*, "
15:34 said, Seven, and a few little *f*. 2485
36 took the seven loaves and the *f*, 2486
M'r 6:38 they say, Five, and two *f*. "
41 taken the five loaves and the two *f*, "
41 the two *f* divided he among them "
43 full of the fragments, and of the *f*. "
8: 7 And they had a few small *f*: 2485
Lu 5: 6 inclosed a great multitude of *f* 2486
9 draught of the *f* which they had "
9:13 no more but five loaves and two *f*; "
16 took the five loaves and the two *f*, "
Joh 6: 9 barley loaves, and two small *f*: 3795
11 and likewise of the *f* as much as "
21: 6 to draw it for the multitude of *f*. 2486
8 dragging the net with *f*. "
11 drew the net to land full of great *f*, "
1Co 15:39 and another of *f*, and another of birds. "

fish-gate See FISH and GATE.

fishhooks
Am 4: 2 and your posterity with *f*. 5518, 1729

fishing
Joh 21: 3 Peter saith unto them, I go a *f*. 232

fishpools
Ca 7: 4 thine eyes like the *f* in Heshbon *1295

fish's
Jon 2: 1 Lord his God out of the *f* belly, 1710

fist See also FISTS.
Ex 21:18 or with his *f*, and he die not, 106
Isa 58: 4 to smite with the *f* of wickedness: "

fists
Pr 30: 4 hath gathered the wind in his *f*? 2651

fit See also FITTED; FITTETH.
Le 16:21 by the hand of a *f* man into the *6261
1Ch 7:11 soldiers, *f* to go out for war *
12: 8 and men of war *f* for the battle, *
Job 34:18 Is it *f* to say to a king, Thou art
Pr 24:27 make it *f* for thyself in the field: *6257
Lu 9:62 back, is *f* for the kingdom of God. 2111
14:35 It is neither *f* for the land, nor yet "
Ac 22:22 it is not *f* that he should live. 2520
Col 3:18 husbands, as it is *f* in the Lord. * 433

fitches
Isa 28:25 cast abroad the *f*, and scatter the 7100
27 For the *f* are not threshed with a "
27 the *f* are beaten out with a staff, "
Eze 4: 9 and lentiles, and millet, and *f*, *3698

fitly
Pr 25:11 word *f* spoken is like apples, 5921, 655
Ca 5:12 washed with milk, and *f* set. ", 4402
Eph 2:21 all the building *f* framed together 4883
4:16 the whole body *f* joined together "

fitted
1Ki 6:35 with gold *f* upon the carved work. 3474
Pr 22:18 they shall withal be *f* in thy lips. *3559
Ro 9:22 vessels of wrath *f* to destruction: 2675

fitteth
Isa 44:13 he *f* it with planes, and he *6213

five
Ge 5: 6 lived an hundred and *f* years, 2568
11 nine hundred and *f* years: and "
15 Mahalaleel lived sixty and *f* years, "
17 eight hundred ninety and *f* years: "
21 Enoch lived sixty and *f* years, "
23 three hundred sixty and *f* years: "
30 *f* hundred ninety and *f* years, "
32 Noah was *f* hundred years old: "
11:11 *f* hundred years, and begat sons "
12 Arphaxad lived *f* and thirty years, "
32 were two hundred and *f* years: "
12: 4 Abram was seventy and *f* years old "
14: 9 of Ellasar; four kings with *f*. "
18:28 Peradventure there shall lack *f* of "
28 destroy all the city for lack of *f*? "
28 If I find there forty and *f*, I will "
43:34 Benjamin's mess was *f* times so "
45: 6 and yet there are *f* years, in the "
11 yet there are *f* years of famine; "
22 silver, and *f* changes of raiment. "
47: 2 some of his brethren, even *f* men, "
Ex 22: 1 he shall restore *f* oxen for an ox, "
26: 3 The *f* curtains shall be coupled "
3 other *f* curtains shall be coupled "
9 couple *f* curtains by themselves, "
26 *f* for the boards of the one side "
27 *f* bars for the boards of the other "
27 *f* bars for the boards of the side of "
37 make for the hanging *f* pillars "
37 thou shalt cast *f* sockets of brass "
27: 1 *f* cubits long, and *f* cubits broad; "
18 the height *f* cubits of fine twined "
30:23 of pure myrrh *f* hundred shekels, "
24 And of cassia *f* hundred shekels, "
36:10 the *f* curtains one unto another: "
10 the other *f* curtains he coupled "
16 coupled *f* curtains by themselves, "
31 *f* for the boards of the one side of "
32 *f* bars for the boards of the other "
32 and *f* bars for the boards of the "
38 *f* pillars of it with their hooks; "

Ex 36:38 but their *f* sockets were of brass. 2568
38: 1 *f* cubits was the length thereof, "
1 and *f* cubits the breadth thereof; "
18 height in the breadth was *f* cubits, "
26 three thousand and *f* hundred "
28 hundred seventy and *f* shekels "
Le 26: 8 *f* of you shall chase an hundred, "
27: 5 from *f* years old even unto twenty "
6 a month old even unto *f* years old, "
6 of the male *f* shekels of silver, "
Nu 1:21 and six thousand and *f* hundred. "
25 forty and *f* thousand six hundred "
33 forty thousand and *f* hundred. "
37 and *f* thousand and four hundred. "
41 and one thousand and *f* hundred. "
46 thousand and *f* hundred and fifty. "
2:11 and six thousand and *f* hundred. "
15 *f* thousand and six hundred and "
19 forty thousand and *f* hundred. "
23 and *f* thousand and four hundred. "
28 and one thousand and *f* hundred. "
32 thousand and *f* hundred and fifty. "
3:22 seven thousand and *f* hundred. "
47 shalt even take *f* shekels apiece "
50 and threescore and *f* shekels, "
4:48 and *f* hundred and fourscore. "
7:17, 23, 29, 35, 41, 47, 53, 59, 65, 71, 77, 83 *f* "
rams, *f* he goats, *f* lambs of the "
8:24 from twenty and *f* years old and "
11:19 two days, nor *f* days, neither ten "
18:16 for the money of *f* shekels, after "
26:18 forty thousand and *f* hundred. "
22 sixteen thousand and *f* hundred. "
27 threescore thousand and *f* hundred. "
37 and two thousand and *f* hundred. "
41 and *f* thousand and six hundred. "
50 and *f* thousand and four hundred. "
31: 8 *f* kings of Midian: Balaam also "
28 one soul of *f* hundred, both of the "
32 thousand and *f* thousand sheep, "
36 thirty thousand and *f* hundred "
39 thirty thousand and *f* hundred; "
43 seven thousand and *f* hundred "
45 thousand asses and *f* hundred, "
Jos 8:12 he took about *f* thousand men, "
10: 5 the *f* kings of the Amorites, "
16 But these *f* kings fled, and hid "
17 *f* kings are found hid in a cave "
22 bring out those *f* kings unto me "
23 brought forth those *f* kings unto "
26 and hanged them on *f* trees: "
13: 3 *f* lords of the Philistines; the "
14:10 these forty and *f* years, even since "
10 day fourscore and *f* years old. "
J'g 3: 3 *f* lords of the Philistines, "
18: 2 Dan sent of their family *f* men "
7 Then the *f* men departed, and "
14 answered the *f* men that went "
17 the *f* men that went to spy "
20:35 twenty and *f* thousand and an "
45 in the highways *f* thousand men; "
46 twenty and *f* thousand men that "
1Sa 6: 4 *F* golden emerods, and *f* golden "
16 when the *f* lords of the Philistines "
18 Philistines belonging to the *f* "
17: 5 was *f* thousand shekels of brass. "
40 *f* smooth stones out of the brook, "
21: 3 give me *f* loaves of bread "
22:18 fourscore and *f* persons that did "
25:18 and *f* sheep ready dressed, "
18 and *f* measures of parched corn, "
42 with *f* damsels of hers that went "
2Sa 4: 4 He was *f* years old when the "
21: 8 *f* sons of Michal the daughter of "
24: 9 were *f* hundred thousand men. "
1Ki 4:32 his songs were a thousand and *f*. "
6: 6 chamber was *f* cubits broad, "
10 against all the house, *f* cubits "
24 And *f* cubits was the one wing "
24 and *f* cubits the other wing "
7: 3 on forty *f* pillars, *f* in a row. "
16 one chapiter was *f* cubits, and the "
16 height of the other chapiter was *f* "
23 and his height was *f* cubits: and "
39 put *f* bases on the right side of the "
39 *f* on the left side of the house: "
49 *f* on the right side, "
49 and *f* on the left, "
9:23 Solomon's work, *f* hundred and "
22:42 Jehoshaphat was thirty and *f* "
42 and he reigned twenty and *f* years "
2Ki 6:25 a cab of dove's dung for *f* pieces "
7:13 *f* of the horses that remain, "
13:19 have smitten *f* or six times; "
14: 2 twenty and *f* years old when he "
15:33 *F* and twenty years old was he "
18: 2 Twenty and *f* years old was he "
19:35 hundred fourscore and *f* thousand: "
21: 1 reigned fifty and *f* years in "
23:36 twenty and *f* years old when he "
25:19 and *f* men of them that were in "
1Ch 2: 4 All the sons of Judah were *f*. "
6 and Dara, *f* of them in all. "
3:20 Hasadiah, Jushab-hesed, *f*. "
4:32 and Tochen, and Ashan, *f* cities: "
42 sons of Simeon, *f* hundred men, "
7: 3 and Ishiah, *f*: all of them chief "
7 and Jerimoth, and Iri, *f*; heads of "
11:23 of great stature, *f* cubits high; "
29: 7 *f* thousand talents and ten "
2Ch 3:11 one wing of the one cherub was *f* "
11 other wing was likewise *f* cubits "
12 of the other cherub was *f* cubits, "
12 the other wing was *f* cubits also, "
15 two pillars of thirty and *f* cubits "
15 top of each of them was *f* cubits. "

2Ch 4: 2 and *f* cubits the height thereof; 2568
6 lavers, and put *f* on the right hand, "
6 and *f* on the left, to wash in them: "
7 in the temple, *f* on the right hand, "
7 right hand, and *f* on the left. "
8 in the temple, *f* on the right side, "
8 right side, and *f* on the left. "
6:13 brasen scaffold, of *f* cubits long, "
13 and *f* cubits broad, and three cubits "
13:17 slain of Israel *f* hundred thousand "
15:19 *f* and thirtieth year of the reign "
20:31 thirty and *f* years old when he "
31 and he reigned twenty and *f* years "
25: 1 Amaziah was twenty and *f* years "
26:13 and seven thousand and *f* hundred, "
27: 1 Jotham was twenty and *f* years old "
8 He was *f* and twenty years old "
29: 1 when he was *f* and twenty years old, "
33: 1 and he reigned fifty and *f* years in "
35: 9 *f* thousand small cattle, and "
9 small cattle, and *f* hundred oxen. "
36: 5 Jehoiakim was twenty and *f* years "
Ezr 1:11 were *f* thousand and four hundred. "
2: 5 Arah, seven hundred seventy and *f*. "
8 of Zattu, nine hundred forty and *f*. "
20 children of Gibbar, ninety and *f*. "
33 Ono, seven hundred twenty and *f*. "
34 Jericho, three hundred forty and *f*. "
66 mules, two hundred forty and *f*; "
67 camels, four hundred thirty and *f*; "
69 and *f* thousand pound of silver, "
Ne 7:13 of Zattu, eight hundred forty and *f*. "
20 of Adin, six hundred fifty and *f*. "
25 children of Gibeon, ninety and *f*. "
36 Jericho, three hundred forty and *f*. "
67 hundred forty and *f* singing men "
68 mules, two hundred forty and *f*: "
69 camels, four hundred thirty and *f*: "
70 *f* hundred and thirty priests' "
Es 9: 6 slew and destroyed *f* hundred men. "
12 and destroyed *f* hundred men in "
16 their foes seventy and *f* thousand, "
Job 1: 3 camels, and *f* hundred yoke of oxen, "
3 of oxen, and *f* hundred she asses, "
Isa 7: 8 and within threescore and *f* years "
17: 6 four or *f* in the outmost fruitful "
19:18 that day shall *f* cities in the land "
30:17 at the rebuke of *f* shall ye flee: "
37:36 and fourscore and *f* thousand: "
Jer 52:22 of one chapiter was *f* cubits, "
30 seven hundred forty and *f* persons: "
31 in the *f* and twentieth day of the "
Eze 8:16 were about *f* and twenty men, "
11: 1 door of the gate *f* and twenty men; "
40: 1 In the *f* and twentieth year of our "
7 the little chambers were *f* cubits; "
13 breadth was *f* and twenty cubits. "
21, 25 the breadth *f* and twenty cubits. "
29 and *f* and twenty cubits broad. "
30 were *f* and twenty cubits long, "
30 long, and *f* cubits broad. "
33 and *f* and twenty cubits broad. "
36 the breadth *f* and twenty cubits. "
48 the porch, *f* cubits on this side, "
48 this side, and *f* cubits on that side: "
41: 2 the sides of the door were *f* cubits "
2 and *f* cubits on that side: "
9 chamber without, was *f* cubits: "
11 was left was *f* cubits round about. "
12 was *f* cubits thick round about, "
42:16 reed, *f* hundred reeds, with the "
17 the north side, *f* hundred reeds, "
18 the south side, *f* hundred reeds, "
19 and measured *f* hundred reeds "
20 round about, *f* hundred reeds long, "
20 and *f* hundred broad, to make "
45: 1 length of *f* and twenty thousand "
2 sanctuary *f* hundred in length, "
2 with *f* hundred in breadth, square "
3 length of *f* and twenty thousand, "
5 *f* and twenty thousand of length, "
6 of the city *f* thousand broad, "
6 and *f* and twenty thousand long, "
12 *f* and twenty shekels, fifteen "
48: 8 offer of *f* and twenty thousand "
9 shall be of *f* and twenty thousand "
10 the north *f* and twenty thousand "
10 the south *f* and twenty thousand "
13 shall have *f* and twenty thousand "
13 shall be *f* and twenty thousand. "
15 And the *f* thousand, that are left "
15 against the *f* and twenty thousand, "
16 north side four...and *f* hundred, "
16 south side four...and *f* hundred, "
16 east side four...and *f* hundred, "
16 west side four...and *f* hundred. "
20 *f* and twenty thousand by *f* and "
21 city, over against the *f* and twenty "
21 westward over against the *f* and "
30 the north side, four thousand and *f* "
32 the east side four thousand and *f* "
33 the south side four thousand and *f* "
34 the west side four thousand and *f* "
Da 12:12 hundred and *f* and thirty days. "
M't 14:17 here but *f* loaves, and two fishes. 4002
19 the *f* loaves, and the two fishes, "
21 were about *f* thousand men, 4000
16: 9 neither remember the *f* loaves of 4002
9 of the *f* thousand, and how many 4000
25: 2 And *f* of them were wise, "
2 were wise, and *f* were foolish. "
15 And unto one he gave *f* talents, "
16 he that had received the *f* talents "
16 and made them other *f* talents. "
20 so he that had received *f* talents "
20 came and brought other *f* talents, "

M't 25:20 thou deliveredst unto me *f* talents: 4000
20 gained beside them *f* talents more. "
M'r 6:38 they say, *F*, and two fishes. "
41 when he had taken the *f* loaves "
44 loaves were about *f* thousand men. "
8:19 When I brake the *f* loaves among 4002
19 loaves among the *f* thousand, how 4000
Lu 1:24 hid herself *f* months, saying, 4002
7:41 one owed *f* hundred pence, and 4001
9:13 more but *f* loaves and two fishes; 4002
14 For they were about *f* thousand 4000
16 the *f* loaves and the two fishes, 4002
12: 6 *f* sparrows sold for two farthings, "
52 there shall be *f* in one house "
14:19 I have bought *f* yoke of oxen, "
16:28 For I have *f* brethren; that he "
19:18 thy pound hath gained *f* pounds. "
19 Be thou also over *f* cities. "
Joh 4:18 For thou hast had *f* husbands; and "
5: 2 tongue Bethesda, having *f* porches. "
6: 9 which hath *f* barley loaves, and two "
10 in number about *f* thousand. 4000
13 fragments of the *f* barley loaves, 4002
19 rowed about *f* and twenty or thirty "
Ac 4: 4 of the men was about *f* thousand. "
20: 6 came unto them to Troas in *f* days; "
24: 1 And after *f* days Ananias the "
1Co 14:19 church I had rather speak *f* words "
15: 6 seen of above *f* hundred brethren 4001
2Co 11:24 *f* times received I forty stripes 3999
Rev 9: 5 should be tormented *f* months: 4002
10 power was to hurt men *f* months. "
17:10 *f* are fallen, and one is, and the "

five hundred See FIVE and HUNDRED.

five thousand See FIVE and THOUSAND.

five times See FIVE and TIMES.

fixed
Ps 57: 7 My heart is *f*, O God, my heart 3559
7 O God, my heart is *f*: I will sing "
108: 1 O God, my heart is *f*; I will sing "
112: 7 his heart is *f*, trusting in the Lord. "
Lu 16:26 us and you there is a great gulf *f*: 4741

flag See also FLAGS.
Job 8:11 can the *f* grow without water? 260

flagon See also FLAGONS.
2Sa 6:19 piece of flesh, and a *f* of wine. *809
1Ch 16: 3 piece of flesh, and a *f* of wine. * "

flagons
Ca 2: 5 Stay me with *f*, comfort me with *809
Isa 22:24 even to all the vessels of *f*. 5035
Hos 3: 1 to other gods, and love *f* of wine. *809

flags
Ex 2: 3 laid it in the *f* by the river's brink. 5488
5 when she saw the ark among the *f*, "
Isa 19: 6 the reeds and *f* shall wither. "

flakes
Job 41:23 *f* of his flesh are joined together: 4651

flame See also FLAMES; FLAMING; INFLAME.
Ex 3: 2 the Lord appeared unto him in a *f* 3827
Nu 21:28 a *f* from the city of Sihon: 3852
J'g 13:20 when the *f* went up toward heaven 3851
20 of the Lord ascended in the *f* of "
20:38 make a great *f* with smoke rise *4864
40 But when the *f* began to rise * "
40 the *f* of the city ascended up *3632
Job 15:30 the *f* shall dry up his branches, 7957
41:21 and a *f* goeth out of his mouth. 3851
Ps 83:14 as the *f* setteth the mountains 3852
106:18 the *f* burned up the wicked. "
Ca 8: 6 which hath a most vehement *f*. 7957
Isa 5:24 and the *f* consumeth the chaff, so 3852
10:17 and his Holy One for a *f*: "
29: 6 and the *f* of devouring fire. 3851
30:30 and with the *f* of a devouring fire. "
Isa 43: 2 neither shall the *f* kindle upon 3852
47:14 themselves from the power of the *f*: "
Jer 48:45 a *f* from the midst of Sihon, "
Eze 20:47 flaming *f* shall not be quenched. 7957
Da 3:22 the *f* of the fire slew those men 7631
7: 9 his throne was like the fiery *f*, * "
11 and given to the burning *f*. * 785
11:33 shall fall by the sword, and by *f*. 3852
Joe 1:19 the *f* hath burned all the trees "
2: 3 and behind them a *f* burneth: "
5 like the noise of a *f* of fire 3851
Ob 18 and the house of Joseph a *f*, 3852
Lu 16:24 for I am tormented in this *f*. 5395
Ac 7:30 in a *f* of fire in a bush. "
Heb 1: 7 and his ministers a *f* of fire. "
Re 1:14 and his eyes were as a *f* of fire; "
2:18 hath his eyes like unto a *f* of fire, "
19:12 His eyes were as a *f* of fire, "

flames
Ps 29: 7 voice of the Lord divideth the *f* 3852
Isa 13: 8 their faces shall be as *f*. *3851
66:15 and his rebuke with *f* of fire. "

flaming See also ENFLAMING.
Ge 3:24 *f* sword which turned every way, *3858
Ps 104: 4 and his ministers a *f* fire: ‡3857
105:32 and *f* fire in their land. 3852
Isa 4: 5 the shining of a *f* fire by night: "
La 2: 3 burned against Jacob like a *f* fire, "
Eze 20:47 the *f* flame shall not be quenched, "
Ho 7: 6 the morning it burneth as a *f* fire, "
Na 2: 3 shall be with *f* torches in the day* 784
2Th 1: 8 In *f* fire taking vengeance on 5395

flanks
Le 3: 4 is on them, which is by the *f*, *3689
10, 15 upon them which is by the *f*, * "
4: 9 is upon them, which is by the *f*, * "

Le 7: 4 is on them, which is by the f. *3689
Job 15:27 maketh collops of fat on his f. ‡ "
flash
Eze 1:14 the appearance of a f of lightning. 965
flat
Le 21:18 or he that hath a f nose, 2763
Nu 22:31 bowed down his head, and fell f * "
Jos 6: 5 wall of the city shall fall down f, 8478
20 that the wall fell down f, so that "
flatter See also FLATTERETH; FLATTERING.
Ps 5: 9 they f with their tongue. 2505
78:36 Nevertheless they did f him with *6601
flattereth
Ps 36: 2 For he f himself in his own eyes, 2505
Pr 2:16 stranger which f with her words; "
7: 5 stranger which f with her words. "
20:19 meddle not with him that f *6601
28:23 than he that f with the tongue. 2505
29: 5 A man that f his neighbour "
flatteries
Da 11:21 and obtain the kingdom by f. 2519
32 covenant shall he corrupt by f: 2514
34 many shall cleave to them with f. 2519
flattering
Job 32:21 let me give f titles unto man. 3655
22 I know not to give f titles; "
Ps 12: 2 f lips and with a double heart 2513
3 The Lord shall cut off all f lips, "
Pr 7:21 the f of her lips she forced him. 2506
26:28 and a f mouth worketh ruin. 2509
Eze 12:24 any vain vision nor f divination "
1Th 2: 5 used we f words, as ye know, *2850
flattery See also FLATTERIES.
Job 17: 5 that speaketh f to his friends, *2506
Pr 6:24 from the f of the tongue of a 2513
flax
Ex 9:31 the f and the barley was smitten: 6594
31 in the ear, and the f was bolled "
Jos 2: 6 and hid them with the stalks of f 6593
J'g 15:14 were upon his arms became of f "
Pr 31:13 seeketh wool, and f, and worketh "
Isa 19: 9 Moreover they that work in fine f, "
42: 3 smoking f shall he not quench: 6594
Eze 40: 3 with a line of f in his hand, 6593
Ho 2: 5 my wool and my f, mine oil and "
9 wool and my f given to cover her "
M't 12:20 smoking f shall he not quench, 3043
flay See also FLAYED.
Le 1: 6 And he shall f the burnt offering, 6584
2Ch 29:34 could not f all the burnt offerings: "
Mic 3: 3 and f their skin from off them; "
flayed
2Ch 35:11 hands, and the Levites f them. 6584
flea
1Sa 24:14 after a dead dog, after a f. 6550
26:20 of Israel is come out to seek a f. "
fled See also FLEDDEST.
Ge 14:10 kings of Sodom and Gomorrah f, 5127
10 that remained f to the mountain. "
16: 6 Sarai dealt hardly with her, she f 1272
31:20 in that he told him not that he f. "
21 So he f with all that he had; "
22 on the third day that Jacob was f. "
35: 7 he f from the face of his brother. "
39:12 his garment in her hand, and f, 5127
13 his garment in her hand, and was f "
15 with me and f, and got him out. "
18 left his garment with me, and f. "
Ex 2:15 Moses f from the face of Pharaoh, 1272
4: 3 and Moses f from before it. 5127
14: 5 king of Egypt that the people f: 1272
27 appeared; and the Egyptians f 5127
Nu 16:34 that were round about them f "
35:25 of his refuge, whither he was f: "
26 of his refuge, whither he was f; * "
32 for him that is f to the city of his "
Jos 7: 4 and they f before the men of Ai. "
8:15 and f by the way of the wilderness. "
20 the people that f to the wilderness. "
10:11 pass, as they f from before Israel, "
16 But these five kings f, and hid "
20: 6 unto the city from whence he f. "
J'g 1: 6 Adoni-bezek f; and they pursued "
4:15 his chariot, and f away on his feet. "
17 Sisera f away on his feet to the "
7:21 the host ran, and cried, and f. * "
22 and the host f to Beth-shittah "
8:12 And when Zebah and Zalmunna f, "
9:21 Jotham ran away, and f, and went 1272
40 and he f before him, and many 5127
51 thither f all the men and women, "
11: 3 Jephthah f from his brethren, 1272
20:45 and f toward the wilderness 5127
47 But six hundred men turned and f "
1Sa 4:10 and they f every man into his tent: "
16 and I f to day out of the army. "
17 Israel is f before the Philistines, "
14:22 they heard that the Philistines f, "
17:24 f from him, and were sore afraid. "
51 their champion was dead, they f. "
19: 8 slaughter; and they f from him. "
10 David f, and escaped that night. "
12 and he went, and f, and escaped. 1272
18 So David f, and escaped, and came "
20: 1 David f from Naioth in Ramah, "
21:10 and f that day for fear of Saul, "
22:17 and because they knew when he f, "
20 escaped, and f after David. "
23: 6 Abiathar the son of Ahimelech f "
27: 4 it was told Saul that David was f "
30:17 which rode upon camels, and f. 5127
31: 1 the men of Israel f from before "
1Sa 31: 7 saw that the men of Israel f, and 5127
7 they forsook the cities, and f; "
2Sa 1: 4 the people are f from the battle, "
4: 3 And the Beerothites f to Gittaim, 1272
4 and his nurse took him up, and f: 5127
10:13 Syrians: and they f before him. "
14 saw that the Syrians were f, "
14 then f they also before Abishai, "
18 And the Syrians f before Israel; "
13:29 gat him up upon his mule, and f. "
34 Absalom f. And the young man 1272
37 Absalom f, and went to Talmai, "
38 So Absalom f, and went to Geshur, "
18:17 all Israel f every one to his tent. 5127
19: 8 Israel had f every man to his tent. "
9 and now he is f out of the land 1272
23:11 the people f from the Philistines. "
1Ki 2: 7 f because of Absalom thy brother. "
28 And Joab f unto the tabernacle 5127
29 told king Solomon that Joab was f "
11:17 That Hadad f, he and certain 1272
23 which f from his lord Hadadezer "
40 Jeroboam arose, and f into Egypt, "
12: 2 he was f from the presence of king "
20:20 the Syrians f; and Israel pursued 5127
30 the rest f to Aphek, into the city; "
30 Ben-hadad f, and came into the "
2Ki 3:24 so that they f before them: "
7: 7 they arose and f in the twilight, "
7 camp as it was, and f for their life. "
8:21 and the people f into their tents. "
9:10 And he opened the door, and f. "
23 Joram turned his hands, and f, "
27 f by the way of the garden house. "
27 he f to Megiddo, and died there. "
14:12 they f every man to their tents. "
19 and he f to Lachish; but they sent "
25: 4 and all the men of war f by night "
1Ch 10: 1 the men of Israel f from before 5127
7 were in the valley saw that they f, "
7 they forsook their cities, and f: "
11:13 f from before the Philistines. "
19:14 the battle; and they f before him. "
15 saw that the Syrians were f, they "
15 they likewise f before Abishai his "
18 But the Syrians f before Israel; "
2Ch 10: 2 f from the presence of Solomon 1272
13:16 children of Israel f before Judah: 5127
14:12 Judah; and the Ethiopians f. "
25:22 and they f every man to his tent. "
27 and he f to Lachish: but they sent "
Ne 13:10 singers, that did the work, were f 1272
Ps 3 *title* he f from Absalom his son. "
31:11 they that did see me without f 5074
57 *title* he f from Saul in the cave. 1272
104: 7 At thy rebuke they f; at the voice 5127
114: 3 the sea saw it, and f: Jordan was "
Isa 10:29 is afraid; Gibeah of Saul is f. "
21:14 with their bread him that f. *5074
15 For they f from the swords, from "
22: 3 All thy rulers are f together, "
3 together, which have f from far. 1272
33: 3 noise of the tumult the people f; 5074
Jer 4:25 all the birds of the heavens were f. "
9:10 the heavens and the beast are f; "
26:21 afraid and f, and went into Egypt; 1272
39: 4 then they f, and went forth out of "
46: 5 are beaten down, and are f apace, 5127
21 back, and are f away together: "
48:45 They that f stood under the shadow "
52: 7 all the men of war f, and went 1272
La 4:15 when they f away and wandered, 5132
Da 10: 7 so that they f to hide themselves. 1272
Ho 7:13 them! for they have f from me: *5074
12:12 Jacob f into the country of Syria, 1272
Jon 1:10 knew that he f from the presence "
4: 2 I f before unto Tarshish: *1272
Zec 14: 5 ye f from before the earthquake 5127
M't 8:33 And they that kept them f, and 5343
26:56 the disciples forsook him, and f. "
M'r 5:14 And they that fed the swine f, and "
14:50 And they all forsook him, and f. "
52 cloth, and f from them naked. "
16: 8 quickly, and f from the sepulchre; "
Lu 8:34 they f and went and told it in the 5343
Ac 7:29 Then f Moses at this saying, and "
14: 6 and f unto Lystra and Derbe, 2703
16:27 that the prisoners had been f. *1628
19:16 they f out of that house naked "
Heb 6:18 who have f for refuge to lay hold 2703
Re 12: 6 the woman f into the wilderness, 5343
16:20 And every island f away, and the "
20:11 the earth and the heaven f away; "
fleddest
Ge 35: 1 when thou f from the face of Esau 1272
Ps 114: 5 ailed thee, O thou sea, that thou f? 5127
flee See also FLED; FLEETH; FLEEING.
Ge 16: 8 f from the face of my mistress 1272
19:20 now this city is near to f unto, 5127
27:43 arise, f thou to Laban my brother 1272
31:27 Wherefore didst thou f away "
Ex 9:20 made his servants and his cattle f 5127
14:25 Let us f from the face of Israel; "
21:13 thee a place wither he shall f. "
Le 26:17 and ye shall f when none pursueth "
36 and they shall f, as fleeing from a "
Nu 10:35 and let them that hate thee f "
24:11 Therefore now f thou to thy place: 1272
35: 6 that he may f thither: and to 5127
11 that the slayer may f thither, "
15 killeth any person unawares may f "
De 4:42 That the slayer might f thither, "
19: 3 that every slayer may f thither "
4 the slayer, which shall f thither, "
5 he shall f unto one of those cities, "
De 28: 7 and f before thee seven ways. 5127
25 and f seven ways before them: "
Jos 8: 5 first, that we will f before them, "
6 They f before us, as at the first: "
6 therefore we will f before them. "
20 they had no power to f this way "
20: 3 unawares and unwittingly may f "
4 And when he that doth f unto one "
9 any person at unawares might f "
J'g 20:32 Let us f, and draw them from the "
2Sa 4: 4 as she made haste to f, that he fell, "
15:14 and let us f: for we shall not else 1227
17: 2 people that are with him shall f; 5127
18: 3 for if we f away, they will not "
19: 3 steal away when they f in battle. "
24:13 or wilt thou f three months before "
1Ki 12:18 up to his chariot, to f to Jerusalem. "
2Ki 9: 3 open the door, and f, and tarry not. "
2Ch 10:18 to his chariot, to f to Jerusalem. "
Ne 6:11 Should such a man as I f? 1272
Job 9:25 they f away, they see no good. "
20:24 He shall f from the iron weapon, "
27:22 he would fain f out of his hand. "
30:10 abhor me, they f far from me, *7368
41:28 The arrow cannot make him f: 1272
Ps 11: 1 F as a bird to your mountain? 5110
64: 8 all that see them shall f away. *5074
68: 1 them also that hate him f before 5127
12 Kings of armies did f apace: 5074
139: 7 shall I f from thy presence? 1272
143: 9 enemies: I f unto thee to hide me. 3680
Pr 28: 1 wicked f when no man pursueth: 5127
17 of any person shall f to the pit; "
Ca 2:17 and the shadows f away, turn, my "
4: 6 and the shadows f away, I will "
Isa 10: 3 whom will ye f for help? and where "
31 of Gebim gather themselves to f.
13:14 f every one into his own land. 5127
15: 5 his fugitives shall f unto Zoar, an
17:13 and they shall f far off, and shall 5127
20: 6 we f for help to be delivered * "
30:16 f upon horses; therefore shall ye f: "
17 thousand shall f at the rebuke of one;
17 at the rebuke of five shall ye f: 5127
31: 8 but he shall f from the sword, "
35:10 sorrow and sighing shall f away.
48:20 f ye from the Chaldeans, with a 1272
51:11 sorrow and mourning shall f 5127
Jer 4:29 whole city shall f for the noise *1272
6: 1 gather yourselves to f out of the 5756
25:35 shepherds shall have no way to f, 4498
46: 6 the swift f away, nor the mighty 5127
48: 6 F, save your lives, and be like the "
9 Moab, that it may f and get away: *5323
49: 8 F ye, turn back, dwell deep, 5127
24 feeble, and turneth herself to f, "
30 F, get you far off, dwell deep, "
50:16 they shall f every one to his own "
28 voice of them that f and escape "
51: 6 F out of the midst of Babylon, "
Am 2:16 the mighty shall f away naked "
5:19 As if a man did f from a lion, "
7:12 go, f thee away into the land of 1272
9: 1 fleeth of them shall not f away, 5127
Jon 1: 3 Jonah rose up to f unto Tarshish 1272
Na 2: 8 yet they shall f away. Stand, 5127
3: 7 they that look upon thee shall f 5074
17 when the sun ariseth they f away, "
Zec 2: 6 and f from the land of the north, 5127
14: 5 And ye shall f to the valley of the "
5 yea, ye shall f, like as ye fled from "
M't 2:13 f into Egypt, and be thou there 5343
3: 7 you to f from the wrath to come? "
10:23 f ye into another: for verily I say "
24:16 them which be in Judæa f into the "
M'r 13:14 them that be in Judæa f to the "
Lu 3: 7 you to f from the wrath to come? "
21:21 them which are in Judæa f to the "
Joh 10: 5 will f from him: for they know not "
Ac 27:30 were about to f out of the ship, "
1Co 6:18 F fornication. Every sin that a "
10:14 my dearly beloved, f from idolatry. "
1Ti 6:11 O man of God, f these things; "
2Ti 2:22 F also youthful lusts: but follow "
Jas 4: 7 the devil, and he will f from you. "
Re 9: 6 and death shall f from them. * "
fleece
De 18: 4 the first of the f of thy sheep, 1488
J'g 6:37 I will put a f of wool in the floor; 1492
37 and if the dew be on the f only, "
38 thrust the f together, and wringed "
38 and wringed the dew out of the f, "
39 I pray thee, but this once with the f; "
39 let it now be dry only upon the f, "
40 for it was dry upon the f only. "
Job 31:20 if he were not warmed with the f 1488
fleeing
Le 26:36 they shall flee, as f from a sword; *4499
De 4:42 and that f unto one of these cities 5127
Job 30: 3 f into the wilderness in former *6207
fleeth
De 19:11 and f into one of these cities: *5127
Job 14: 2 he f also as a shadow, and 1272
Isa 24:18 who f from the noise of the fear 5127
Jer 48:19 ask him that f, and her that "
44 he that f from the fear shall fall 5211
Am 9: 1 he that f of them shall not flee *5127
Na 3:16 cankerworm spoileth, and f away. *5775
Joh 10:12 leaveth the sheep, and f: and the 5343
13 The hireling f, because he is an "
flesh See also FATFLESHED; FLESHHOOK; LEAN FLESHED.
Ge 2:21 closed up the f instead thereof; 1320
23 bone of my bones, and f of my f: "

Ge 2:24 and they shall be one *f*. 1320
6: 3 with man, for that he also is *f*: "
12 for all *f* had corrupted his way "
13 The end of all *f* is come before me; "
17 destroy all *f*, wherein is the breath "
19 And of every living thing of all *f*, "
7:15 two of all *f*, wherein is the breath "
16 went in male and female of all *f*, "
21 all *f* died that moved upon the "
8:17 of all *f*, both of fowl, and of cattle, "
9: 4 But *f* with the life thereof, which is "
11 neither shall all *f* be cut off any "
15 and every living creature of all *f*; "
15 become a flood to destroy all *f*. "
16 every living creature of all *f* that is "
17 established between me and all *f* "
17:11 circumcise the *f* of your foreskin; "
13 my covenant shall be in your *f* for "
14 whose *f* of his foreskin is not "
23 circumcised the *f* of their foreskin "
24, 25 circumcised in the *f* of his "
29:14 Surely thou art my bone and my *f*. "
37:27 for he is our brother and our *f*. "
40:19 and the birds shall eat thy *f* from "
Ex 4: 7 it was turned again as his other *f*. "
12: 8 they shall eat the *f* in that night, "
46 carry forth ought of the *f* abroad "
16: 3 when we sat by the *f* pots, "
8 give you in the evening *f* to eat, "
12 At even ye shall eat *f*, and in the "
21:28 and his *f* shall not be eaten; "
22:31 shall ye eat any *f* that is torn of "
29:14 the *f* of the bullock, and his skin, "
31 and seethe his *f* in the holy place. "
32 his sons shall eat the *f* of the ram, "
34 ought of the *f* of the consecrations, "
30:32 Upon man's *f* shall it not be poured, "
Le 4:11 all his *f*, with his head, and with "
6:10 breeches shall he put upon his *f*, "
27 Whatsoever shall touch the *f* "
7:15 And the *f* of the sacrifice of his "
17 remainder of the *f* of the sacrifice "
18 And if any of the *f* of the sacrifice "
19 *f* that toucheth any unclean thing "
19 as for the *f*, all that be clean shall "
20 But the soul that eateth of the *f* "
21 and eat of the *f* of the sacrifice of "
8:17 the bullock, and his hide, his *f*, "
31 Boil the *f* at the door of the "
32 And that which remaineth of the *f* "
9:11 And the *f* and the hide he burnt "
11: 8 Of their *f* shall ye not eat, and their "
11 ye shall not eat of their *f*, but ye "
12: 3 the eighth day the *f* of his foreskin "
13: 2 man shall have in the skin of his *f* "
2 and it be in the skin of his *f* like "
3 on the plague in the skin of his *f*: "
3 be deeper than the skin of his *f*, "
4 spot be white in the skin of his *f*, "
10 there be quick raw *f* in the rising; "
11 an old leprosy in the skin of his *f*, "
13 the leprosy have covered all his *f*, "
14 But when raw *f* appeareth in him, "
15 And the priest shall see the raw *f*, "
15 the raw *f* is unclean: it is a leprosy. "
16 Or if the raw *f* turn again, "
18 The *f* also, in which, even in the "
24 there be any *f*, in the skin whereof "
24 and the quick *f* that burneth have a "
38 in the skin of their *f* bright spots, 1320
39 bright spots in the skin of their *f* "
43 appeareth in the skin of the *f*: "
14: 9 also he shall wash his *f* in water, "
15: 2 hath a running issue out of his *f*, "
3 whether his *f* run with his issue, "
3 or his *f* be stopped from his issue, "
7 And he that toucheth the *f* of him "
13 and bathe his *f* in running water, "
16 then he shall wash all his *f* in "
19 and her issue in her *f* be blood, "
16: 4 have the linen breeches upon his *f*, "
4 shall he wash his *f* in water, and so "
24 And he shall wash his *f* with water "
26 bathe his *f* in water, and afterward "
27 their skins, and their *f*, and their "
28 clothes, and bathe his *f* in water, "
17:11 For the life of the *f* is in the blood: "
14 For it is the life of all *f*; "
14 eat the blood of no manner of *f*: "
14 for the life of all *f* is the blood "
16 nor bathe his *f*; then he shall bear "
19:28 not make any cuttings in your *f*, "
21: 5 nor make any cuttings in their *f*. "
22: 6 unless he wash his *f* with water. "
26:29 And ye shall eat the *f* of your sons, "
29 and the *f* of your daughters shall "
Nu 8: 7 and let them shave all their *f*, "
11: 4 said, Who shall give us *f* to eat? "
13 Whence should I have *f* to give unto "
13 saying, Give us *f*, that we may eat. "
18 to-morrow, and ye shall eat *f*: for "
18 saying, Who shall give us *f* to eat? "
18 therefore the Lord will give you *f*, "
21 thou hast said, I will give them *f*, "
33 And while the *f* was yet between "
12:12 of whom the *f* is half consumed "
16:22 the God of the spirits of all *f*, "
18:15 that openeth the matrix in all *f*, "
18 And the *f* of them shall be thine, "
19: 5 her skin, and her *f*, and her blood, "
7 and he shall bathe his *f* in water, "
8 and bathe his *f* in water, and shall "
27:16 the God of the spirits of all *f*, "
De 5:26 For who is there of all *f*, that hath "
12:15 kill and eat *f* in all thy gates, "
20 and thou shalt say, I will eat *f*, "
De 12:20 because thy soul longeth to eat *f*; 1320
20 thou mayest eat *f*, whatsoever "
23 mayest not eat the life with the *f*. "
27 the *f* and the blood, upon the altar "
27 thy God, and thou shalt eat the *f*. "
14: 8 ye shall not eat of their *f*, nor "
16: 4 shall there any thing of the *f*, "
28:53 *f* of thy sons and of thy daughters, "
55 *f* of his children whom he shall eat: "
32:42 and my sword shall devour *f*; "
J'g 6:19 the *f* he put in a basket, and he put "
20 Take the *f* and the unleavened "
21 touched the *f* and the unleavened "
21 consumed the *f* and the unleavened "
8: 7 I will tear your *f* with the thorns "
9: 2 that I am your bone and your *f*. "
1Sa 2:13 came, while the *f* was in seething, "
15 Give *f* to roast for the priest; for "
15 he will not have sodden *f* of thee; "
17:44 and I will give thy *f* unto the fowls "
25:11 and my *f* that I have killed for my 2878
2Sa 5: 1 Behold, we are thy bone and thy *f*. 1320
6:19 and a good piece of *f*, and a flagon 829
19:12 ye are my bones and my *f*: 1320
13 thou not of my bone, and of my *f*? "
1Ki 17: 6 him bread and *f* in the morning, "
6 and bread and *f* in the evening; "
19:21 boiled their *f* with the instruments "
21:27 sackcloth upon his *f*, and fasted, "
2Ki 4:34 and the *f* of the child waxed warm. "
5:10 and thy *f* shall come again to thee, "
14 his *f* came again like unto the *f* of "
6:30 had sackcloth within upon his *f*. "
9:36 shall dogs eat the *f* of Jezebel: "
1Ch 11: 1 Behold, we are thy bone and thy *f*. "
16: 3 a good piece of *f*, and a flagon of 829
2Ch 32: 8 With him is an arm of *f*; 1320
Ne 5: 5 Yet now our *f* is as the *f* of our "
Job 2: 5 now, and touch his bone and his *f*, "
4:15 my face; the hair of my *f* stood up: "
6:12 of stones? or is my *f* of brass? "
7: 5 My *f* is clothed with worms and "
10: 4 Hast thou eyes of *f*? or seest thou "
11 hast clothed me with skin and *f*, "
13:14 Wherefore do I take my *f* in my "
14:22 his *f* upon him shall have pain, "
19:20 cleaveth to my skin and to my *f*, "
22 and are not satisfied with my *f*? "
26 yet in my *f* shall I see God: "
21: 6 and trembling taketh hold on my *f*. "
31:31 said not, Oh that we had of his *f*! * "
33:21 His *f* is consumed away, that it "
25 His *f* shall be fresher than a "
34:15 All *f* shall perish together, and "
41:23 The flakes of his *f* are joined "
Ps 16: 9 my *f* also shall rest in hope. "
27: 2 came upon me to eat up my *f*, "
38: 3 There is no soundness in my *f* "
7 and there is no soundness in my *f*. "
50:13 Will I eat the *f* of bulls, or drink "
56: 4 I will not fear what *f* can do unto "
63: 1 my *f* longeth for thee in a dry and "
65: 2 unto thee shall all *f* come. "
73:26 My *f* and my heart faileth: but 7607
78:20 can he provide *f* for his people? "
27 rained *f* also upon them as dust, "
39 remembered that they were but *f*; 1320
79: 2 the *f* of thy saints unto the beasts "
84: 2 my heart and my *f* crieth out for "
109:24 fasting, and my *f* faileth of fatness. "
119:120 My *f* trembleth for fear of thee; "
136:25 Who giveth food to all *f*: for his "
145:21 and let all *f* bless his holy name "
Pr 4:22 find them, and health to all their *f*. "
5:11 thy *f* and thy body are consumed, "
11:17 that is cruel troubleth his own *f*. 7607
14:30 a sound heart is the life of the *f*: 1320
23:20 among riotous eaters of *f*: "
Ec 4: 5 together, and eateth his own *f*. "
5: 6 not thy mouth to cause thy *f* to sin; "
11:10 and put away evil from thy *f*: "
12:12 much study is a weariness of the *f*. "
Isa 9:20 every man the *f* of his own arm: "
17: 4 the fatness of his *f* shall wax lean. "
22:13 eating *f*, and drinking wine: "
31: 3 and their horses *f*, and not spirit. "
40: 5 and all *f* shall see it together: "
6 What shall I cry? All *f* is grass, "
44:16 with part thereof he eateth *f*; he "
19 I have roasted *f*, and eaten it: "
49:26 that oppress thee with their own *f*; "
26 and all *f* shall know that I the Lord "
58: 7 hide not thyself from thine own *f*? "
65: 4 which eat swine's *f*, and broth of "
66:16 will the Lord plead with all *f*: "
17 the midst, eating swine's *f*, and the "
23 all *f* come to worship before me, "
24 shall be an abhorring unto all *f*. "
Jer 7:21 unto your sacrifices, and eat *f*. "
11:15 and the holy *f* is passed from thee? "
12:12 the land: no *f* shall have peace. "
17: 5 in man, and maketh *f* his arm, "
19: 9 cause them to eat the *f* of their sons "
9 and the *f* of their daughters, "
9 eat every one the *f* of his friend in "
25:31 he will plead with all *f*; he will "
32:27 I am the Lord, the God of all *f*: "
45: 5 behold, I will bring evil upon all *f*, "
51:35 violence done to me and to my *f* 7607
La 3: 4 My *f* and my skin hath he made 1320
Eze 4:14 there abominable *f* into my mouth. "
11: 3 is the caldron, and we be the *f*. "
7 they are the *f*, and this city is the "
11 neither shall ye be the *f* in the midst "
19 take the stony heart out of their *f*, "
19 and will give them an heart of *f*: "
Eze 16:26 thy neighbours, great of *f*; and 1320
20:48 And all *f* shall see that I the Lord "
21: 4 forth out of his sheath against all *f* "
5 That all *f* may know that I the Lord "
23:20 whose *f* is as the *f* of asses, "
24:10 consume the *f*, and spice it well, "
32: 5 will lay thy *f* upon the mountains, "
36:26 away the stony heart out of your *f*, "
26 and I will give you an heart of *f*. "
37: 6 and will bring up *f* upon you, "
8 lo, the sinews and the *f* came up "
39:17 that ye may eat *f*, and drink blood. "
18 Ye shall eat the *f* of the mighty, "
40:43 and upon the tables was the *f* of the "
44: 7 and uncircumcised in *f*, to be in my "
9 nor uncircumcised in *f*, shall enter "
Da 1:15 appeared fairer and fatter in *f* "
2:11 gods, whose dwelling is not with *f*. 1321
4:12 and all *f* was fed of it. "
7: 5 thus unto it, Arise, devour much *f*. "
10: 3 came *f* nor wine in my mouth, 1320
Ho 8:13 They sacrifice *f* for the sacrifices "
Joe 2:28 will pour out my spirit upon all *f*; "
Mic 3: 2 and their *f* from off their bones; 7607
3 Who also eat the *f* of my people, "
3 and as *f* within the caldron. 1320
Zep 1:17 as dust, and their *f* as the dung. 3894
Hag 2:12 If one bear holy *f* in the skirt of 1320
Zec 2:13 Be silent, O all *f*, before the Lord: "
11: 9 rest eat every one the *f* of another. "
16 but he shall eat the *f* of the fat, "
14:12 Their *f* shall consume away while "
M't 16:17 *f* and blood hath not revealed it 4561
19: 5 and they twain shall be one *f*? "
6 they are no more twain, but one *f*. "
24:22 there should no *f* be saved: but "
26:41 indeed is willing, but the *f* is weak. "
M'r 10: 8 And they twain shall be one *f*: "
8 they are no more twain, but one *f*. "
13:20 no *f* should be saved: but for the "
14:38 truly is ready, but the *f* is weak. "
Lu 3: 6 And all *f* shall see the salvation of "
24:39 for a spirit hath not *f* and bones, "
Joh 1:13 nor of the will of the *f*, nor of the "
14 And the Word was made *f*, and "
3: 6 That which is born of the *f* is *f*; "
6:51 the bread that I will give is my *f*, "
52 can this man give us his *f* to eat? "
53 Except ye eat the *f* of the Son of "
54 Whoso eateth my *f*, and drinketh "
55 For my *f* is meat indeed, and my "
56 He that eateth my *f*, and drinketh "
63 quickeneth; the *f* profiteth nothing: "
8:15 judge after the *f*; I judge no man. "
17: 2 hast given him power over all *f*, "
Ac 2:17 pour out of my Spirit upon all *f*: "
26 also my *f* shall rest in hope: "
30 fruit of his loins, according to the *f*, "
31 neither his *f* did see corruption. "
Ro 1: 3 seed of David according to the *f*; "
2:28 which is outward in the *f*: "
3:20 shall no *f* be justified in his sight: "
4: 1 as pertaining to the *f*, hath found? "
6:19 because of the infirmity of your *f*: "
7: 5 For when we were in the *f*, "
18 in me, (that is, in my *f*,) "
25 but with the *f* the law of sin. "
8: 1 after the *f*, but after the Spirit. * "
3 in that it was weak through the *f*, "
3 Son in the likeness of sinful *f*, and "
3 for sin, condemned sin in the *f*: "
4 in us, who walk not after the *f*, "
5 For they that are after the *f* do "
5 do mind the things of the *f*; "
8 that are in the *f* cannot please God. "
9 But ye are not in the *f*, but in the "
12 we are debtors, not to the *f*, "
12 to live after the *f*. "
13 For if ye live after the *f*, ye shall "
9: 3 my kinsmen according to the *f*: "
5 as concerning the *f* Christ came, "
8 which are the children of the *f*, "
11:14 emulation them which are my *f*, "
13:14 and make not provision for the *f*, "
14:21 It is good neither to eat *f*, nor to 2907
1Co 1:26 not many wise men after the *f*, 4561
29 no *f* should glory in his presence. "
5: 5 Satan for the destruction of the *f*, "
6:16 for two, saith he, shall be one *f*. "
7:28 such shall have trouble in the *f*: "
8:13 eat no *f* while the world standeth, 2907
10:18 Behold Israel after the *f*: are not 4561
15:39 All *f* is not the same *f*: but there "
39 but there is one kind of *f* of men, "
39 another of *f* of beasts, another of "
50 that *f* and blood cannot inherit the "
2Co 1:17 do I purpose according to the *f*, "
4:11 be made manifest in our mortal *f*. "
5:16 know we no man after the *f*: yea, "
16 we have known Christ after the *f*, "
7: 1 all filthiness of the *f* and spirit, "
5 *f* had no rest, but we were troubled "
10: 2 as if we walked according to the *f*. "
3 in the *f*, we do not war after the *f*: "
11:18 Seeing that many glory after the *f*, "
12: 7 a thorn in the *f*, the messenger of "
Ga 1:16 I conferred not with *f* and blood: "
2:16 of the law shall no *f* be justified. "
20 the life which I now live in the *f* "
3: 3 are ye now made perfect by the *f*? "
4:13 infirmity of the *f* I preached "
14 my temptation which was in my *f* "
23 bondwoman was born after the *f* "
29 as then he that was born after the *f* "
5:13 not liberty for an occasion to the *f*, "
16 ye shall not fulfil the lust of the *f*. "

Ga 5:17 the *f* lusteth against the Spirit, 4561
17 and the Spirit against the *f*: "
19 the works of the *f* are manifest, "
24 crucified the *f* with the affections "
6: 8 soweth to his *f* shall of the *f* reap "
12 desire to make a fair show in the *f*, "
13 that they may glory in your *f*. "
Eph 2: 3 in the lusts of our *f*, fulfilling the "
3 desires of the *f* and of the mind; "
11 being in time past Gentiles in the *f*, "
11 is called the Circumcision in the *f* "
15 Having abolished in his *f* the "
5:29 no man ever yet hated his own *f*; "
30 his body, of his *f*, and of his bones. "
31 and they two shall be one *f*. "
6: 5 your masters according to the *f*, "
12 we wrestle not against *f* and blood, "
Ph'p 1:22 if I live in the *f*, this is the fruit of "
24 Nevertheless to abide in the *f* is "
3: 3 and have no confidence in the *f*. "
4 might also have confidence in the *f*. "
4 whereof he might trust in the *f*. "
Col 1:22 In the body of his *f* through death, "
24 in my *f* for his body's sake, which "
2: 1 as have not seen my face in the *f*; "
5 For though I be absent in the *f*, "
11 off the body of the sins of the *f* by "
13 and the uncircumcision of your *f*. "
23 honour to the satisfying of the *f*. "
3:22 your masters according to the *f*; "
1Ti 3:16 God was manifest in the *f*, justified "
Ph'm 16 both in the *f* and in the Lord? "
Heb 2:14 the children are partakers of *f* and "
5: 7 Who in the days of his *f*, when he "
9:13 sanctifieth to the purifying of the *f*: "
10:20 the veil, that is to say, his *f*; "
12: 9 we have had fathers of our *f* which "
Jas 5: 3 and shall eat your *f* as it were fire. "
1Pe 1:24 For all *f* is grass, and all the glory "
3:18 to death in the *f*, but quickened "
21 putting away of the filth of the *f*, "
4: 1 Christ hath suffered for us in the *f*, "
1 he that hath suffered in the *f* hath "
2 live the rest of his time in the *f* to "
6 be judged according to men in the *f*, "
2Pe 2:10 that walk after the *f* in the lust of "
18 allure through the lusts of the *f*. "
1Jo 2:16 the lust of the *f*, and the lust of the "
4: 2 that Jesus Christ is come in the *f* "
3 not that...Jesus Christ is come in the *f* * "
2Jo 7 that Jesus Christ is come in the *f*. "
Jude 7 going after strange *f*, are set forth "
8 these filthy dreamers defile the *f*, "
23 even the garment spotted by the *f*. "
Re 17:16 and shall eat her *f*, and burn her "
19:18 *f* of kings, and the *f* of captains, "
18 captains, and the *f* of mighty men, "
18 men, and the *f* of horses, and of "
18 and the *f* of all men, both free and "
21 the fowls were filled with their *f*. "

fleshhook See also FLESHHOOKS.
1Sa 2:13 with a *f* of three teeth in his hand; 4207
14 all that the *f* brought up the priest "

fleshhooks
Ex 27: 3 and his *f*, and his firepans: all the 4207
38: 3 and the *f*, and the firepans: all the "
Nu 4:14 the censers, the *f*, and the shovels, "
1Ch 28:17 pure gold for the *f*, and the bowls, "
2Ch 4:16 and the shovels, and the *f*, and all "

fleshly
2Co 1:12 not with *f* wisdom, but by the 4559
3: 3 but in *f* tables of the heart. *4560
Col 2:18 vainly puffed up by his *f* mind, "
1Pe 2:11 abstain from *f* lusts, which war 4559

flesh-pots See FLESH and POTS.

flew
1Sa 14:32 And the people *f* upon the spoil, 6213
Isa 6: 6 Then *f* one of the seraphims unto 5774

flies
Ex 8:21 I will send swarms of *f* upon thee, and
21 shall be full of swarms of *f*, and also
22 that no swarms of *f* shall be there;
24 there came a grievous swarm of *f* into
24 corrupted by reason of the swarm of *f*
29 that the swarms of *f* may depart from
31 and he removed the swarms of *f* from
Ps 78:45 He sent divers sorts of *f* among 6157
105:31 there came divers sorts of *f*, and "
Ec 10: 1 Dead *f* cause the ointment of the 2070

flieth
De 4:17 likeness of any winged fowl that *f* 5774
14:19 creeping thing that *f* is unclean *5775
28:49 the earth as swift as the eagle *f*; 1675
Ps 91: 5 nor for the arrow that *f* by day; 5774

flight
Le 26: 8 you shall put ten thousand to *f*: *7291
De 32:30 and two put ten thousand to *f*, 5127
1Ch 12:15 and they put to *f* all them of the 1272
Isa 52:12 not go out with haste, nor go by *f*: 4499
Am 2:14 the *f* shall perish from the swift, 4498
M't 24:20 But pray ye that your *f* be not in 5437
M'r 13:18 And pray ye that your *f* be not in* "
Heb 11:34 turned to *f* the armies of the aliens.

flint
De 8:15 forth water out of the rock of *f*; 2496
Ps 114: 8 the *f* into a fountain of waters. "
Isa 5:28 hoofs shall be counted like *f*, 6864
50: 7 have I set my face like a *f*, 2496
Eze 3: 9 As an adamant harder than *f* have 6864

flinty
De 32:13 and oil out of the *f* rock; 2496

floats See also FLOTES.
1Ki 5: 9 and I will convey them by sea in *f* *1702

flock See also FLOCKS.
Ge 4: 4 the firstlings of his *f* and the fat 6629
21:28 ewe lambs of the *f* by themselves. "
27: 9 Go now to the *f*, and fetch me two "
29:10 and watered the *f* of Laban his "
30:31 I will again feed and keep thy *f*. "
32 I will pass through all thy *f* to day, "
40 all the brown in the *f* of Laban; "
31: 4 and Leah to the field unto his *f*, "
38 rams of thy *f* have I not eaten. * "
33:13 them one day, all the *f* will die. * "
37: 2 years old was feeding the *f* with his "
12 went to feed their father's *f* in "
13 Do not thy brethren feed the *f* in "
38:17 I will send thee a kid from the *f*. 6629
Ex 2:16 troughs to water their father's *f*. "
17 helped them, and watered their *f*. "
19 enough for us, and watered the *f*. "
3: 1 kept the *f* of Jethro his father in "
1 the *f* to the backside of the desert, "
Le 1: 2 even of the herd, and of the *f*. "
3: 6 be of the *f*; male or female, he "
5: 6 female from the *f*, a lamb or a kid "
18 ram without blemish out of the *f*, "
6: 6 ram without blemish out of the *f*, "
27:32 the tithe of the herd, or of the *f*, "
Nu 15: 3 the Lord, of the herd, or of the *f*: "
De 12:17 firstlings of thy herds or of thy *f*, "
21 shalt kill of thy herd and of thy *f*, "
15:14 out of thy *f*, and out of thy floor, "
19 that come of thy herd and of thy *f* "
16: 2 of the *f* and the herd, in the place "
1Sa 17:34 and took a lamb out of the *f*: 5739
2Sa 12: 4 he spared to take of his own *f* and 6629
2Ch 35: 7 Josiah gave to the people, of the *f*, "
Ezr 10:19 they offered a ram of the *f* for their "
Job 21:11 send forth their little ones like a *f*, "
30: 1 to have set with the dogs of my *f*. "
Ps 77:20 Thou leddest thy people like a *f* by "
78:52 them in the wilderness like a *f*. 5739
80: 1 thou that leadest Joseph like a *f*; 6629
107:41 and maketh him families like a *f*. "
Ca 1: 7 thou makest thy *f* to rest at noon:
8 way forth by the footsteps of the *f*, 6629
4: 1 thy hair is as a *f* of goats, that 5739
2 Thy teeth are like a *f* of sheep "
6: 5 thy hair is as a *f* of goats that "
6 Thy teeth are as a *f* of sheep which "
Isa 40:11 He shall feed his *f* like a shepherd: "
63:11 sea with the shepherd of his *f*? 6629
Jer 13:17 Lord's *f* is carried away captive. 5739
20 where is the *f* that was given thee, "
20 was given thee, thy beautiful *f*? 6629
23: 2 have scattered my *f*, and driven "
3 I will gather the remnant of my *f* "
25:34 in the ashes, ye principal of the *f*: "
35 nor the principal of the *f* to escape. "
36 howling of the principal of the *f*, "
31:10 him, as a shepherd doth his *f*. 5739
12 young of the *f* and of the herd: 6629
49:20 the least of the *f* shall draw them "
50:45 the least of the *f* shall draw them "
51:23 with thee the shepherd and his *f*; 5739
Eze 24: 5 Take the choice of the *f*, and 6629
34: 3 are fed: but ye feed not the *f*. * "
6 my *f* was scattered upon all the * "
8 because my *f* became a prey, * "
8 and my *f* became meat to every * "
8 did my shepherds search for my *f*, * "
8 fed themselves, and fed not my *f*; * "
10 I will require my *f* at their hand, * "
10 them to cease from feeding the *f*; * "
10 I will deliver my *f* from their * "
12 As a shepherd seeketh out his *f* 5739
15 I will feed my *f*, and I will cause *6629
17 And as for you, O my *f*, thus saith "
19 And as for my *f*, they eat that * "
22 Therefore will I save my *f*, and "
31 And ye my *f*, the *f* of my pasture, * "
36:37 increase them with men like a *f*. "
38 the holy *f*, as the *f* of Jerusalem "
43:23, 25 a ram out of the *f* without "
45:15 And one lamb out of the *f*, out of "
Am 6: 4 and eat the lambs out of the *f*, and "
7:15 Lord took me as I followed the *f*, "
Jon 3: 7 beast, herd nor *f*, taste anything: "
Mic 2:12 as the *f* in the midst of their fold: 5739
4: 8 And thou, O tower of the *f*, the "
7:14 thy rod, the *f* of thine heritage, 6629
Hab 3:17 the *f* shall be cut off from the fold, "
Zec 9:16 in that day as the *f* of his people: "
10: 2 they went their way as a *f*, they * "
3 Lord of hosts hath visited his *f* 5739
11: 4 Feed the *f* of the slaughter; 6629
7 And I will feed the *f* of slaughter, "
7 even you, O poor of the *f*. "
7 I called Bands; and I fed the *f*. "
11 poor of the *f* that waited upon me "
17 idol shepherd that leaveth the *f*! "
Mal 1:14 which hath in his *f* a male, and 5739
M't 26:31 sheep of the *f* shall be scattered 4167
Lu 2: 8 watch over their *f* by night.
12:32 Fear not, little *f*; for it is your 4168
Ac 20:28 unto yourselves, and to all the *f*, "
29 in among you, not sparing the *f*. "
1Co 9: 7 who feedeth a *f*, and eateth not of 4167
7 eateth not of the milk of the *f*? "
1Pe 5: 2 the *f* of God which is among you, 4168
3 but being ensamples to the *f*. "

flocks
Ge 13: 5 with Abram, had *f*, and herds, 6629
24:35 he hath given him *f*, and herds, "
26:14 possession of *f*, and possession of "
29: 2 were three *f* of sheep lying by it; 5739
2 out of that well they watered the *f*: "
3 And thither were all the *f* gathered: "
8 until all the *f* be gathered together. "
30:36 Jacob fed the rest of Laban's *f*. 6629
38 which he had pilled before the *f* "
38 when the *f* came to drink, "
39 the *f* conceived before the rods, "
40 of the *f* toward the ringstraked, "
40 he put his own *f* by themselves, 5739
32: 5 and asses, *f*, and menservants, *6629
7 the *f*, and herds, and the camels, "
33:13 and the *f* and herds with young "
37:14 brethren, and well with the *f*: * "
16 thee, where they feed their *f*. *
45:10 and thy *f*, and thy herds, and all 6629
46:32 and they have brought their *f*, "
47: 1 my brethren, and their *f*, and their "
4 have no pasture for their *f*; for the "
17 exchange for horses, and for the *f*, "
50: 8 only their little ones, and their *f*, "
Ex 10: 9 with our *f* and with our herds will "
24 your *f* and your herds be stayed: "
12:32 Also take your *f* and your herds, "
38 and *f*, and herds, even very much "
34: 3 neither let the *f* nor herds feed "
Le 1:10 And if his offering be of the *f*, * "
5:15 ram without blemish out of the *f*, * "
Nu 11:22 Shall the *f* and the herds be slain "
31: 9 and all their *f*, and all their goods. 4735
30 of the asses, and of the *f*, of all 6629
32:26 Our little ones, our wives, our *f*, 4735
De 7:13 and the *f* of thy sheep, in the *6251
8:13 thy herds and thy *f* multiply, 6629
12: 6 of your herds and of your *f*: * "
14:23 of thy herds and of thy *f*; * "
28: 4, 18 kine and the *f* of thy sheep. *6251
51 of thy kine, or *f* of thy sheep, "
J'g 5:16 to hear the bleatings of the *f*? 5739
1Sa 30:20 David took all the *f* and the herds, 6629
2Sa 12: 2 had exceeding many *f* and herds: "
1Ki 20:27 them like two little *f* of kids; 2835
1Ch 4:39 valley, to seek pasture for their *f*. 6629
41 there was pasture there for their *f*. "
27:31 over the *f* was Jaziz the Hagerite. "
2Ch 17:11 the Arabians brought him *f*, seven "
32:28 manner of beasts, and cotes for *f*. 5739
29 and possessions of *f* and herds 6629
Ne 10:36 firstlings of our herds and of our *f*, "
Job 24: 2 they violently take away *f*, and 5739
Ps 65:13 The pastures are clothed with *f*; 6629
78:48 and their *f* to hot thunderbolts. 4735
Pr 27:23 to know the state of thy *f*, and 6629
Ca 1: 7 as one that turneth aside by the *f* 5739
Isa 17: 2 they shall be for *f*, which shall "
32:14 a joy of wild asses, a pasture of *f*; "
60: 7 the *f* of Kedar shall be gathered 6629
61: 5 shall stand and feed your *f*, and the "
65:10 And Sharon shall be a fold of *f*, "
Jer 3:24 their *f* and their herds, their sons "
5:17 shall eat up thy *f* and thine herds: "
6: 3 shepherds with their *f* shall come 5739
10:21 and all their *f* shall be scattered. 4830
31:24 and they that go forth with *f*. 5739
33:12 shepherds causing their *f* to lie 6629
13 the cities of Judah, shall the *f* pass "
49:29 tents and their *f* shall they take "
50: 8 as the he goats before the *f*. "
Eze 25: 5 Ammonites a couchingplace for *f*: "
34: 2 not the shepherds feed the *f*? * "
36:38 waste cities be filled with *f* of men; "
Hos 5: 6 with their *f* and with their herds "
Joe 1:18 the *f* of sheep are made desolate. 5739
Mic 5: 8 young lion among the *f* of sheep: "
Zep 2: 6 for shepherds, and folds for *f*. 6629
14 And *f* shall lie down in the midst 5739

flood See also FLOODS; WATERFLOOD.
Ge 6:17 I do bring a *f* of waters upon the 3999
7: 6 the *f* of waters was upon the earth. "
7 because of the waters of the *f*. "
10 waters of the *f* were upon the earth. "
17 *f* was forty days upon the earth; "
9:11 off any more by the waters of a *f*; "
11 neither shall there any more be a *f* "
15 waters shall no more become a *f* "
28 And Noah lived after the *f* three "
10: 1 them were sons born after the *f*. "
32 divided in the earth after the *f*. "
11:10 Arphaxad two years after the *f*: "
Jos 24: 2 dwelt on the other side of the *f* *5104
3 from the other side of the *f*, * "
14 served on the other side of the *f*, * "
15 were on the other side of the *f*, * "
Job 14:11 and the *f* decayeth and drieth up: * "
22:16 was overflown with a *f*: * "
28: 4 The *f* breaketh out from the *5158
Ps 29:10 The Lord sitteth upon the *f*; yea, 3999
66: 6 they went through the *f* on foot: *5104
74:15 cleave the fountain and the *f*: 5158
90: 5 carriest them away as with a *f*; 2229
Isa 28: 2 *f* of mighty waters overflowing, *2230
59:19 the enemy shall come in like a *f*, *5104
Jer 46: 7 Who is this that cometh up as a *f*, *2975
8 Egypt riseth up like a *f*, and his "
47: 2 and shall be an overflowing *f*, *5158
Dan 9:26 The end thereof shall be with a *f*, 7858
11:22 with the arms of a *f* shall they be "
Am 8: 8 and it shall rise up wholly as a *f*; *2975
8 drowned, as by the *f* of Egypt. * "
9: 5 it shall rise up wholly like a *f*; * "
5 be drowned, as by the *f* of Egypt. * "
Na 1: 8 But with an overrunning *f* he will 7858
M't 24:38 *f* they were eating and drinking, 2627
39 until the *f* came, and took them all "
Lu 6:48 when the *f* arose, the stream beat 4132

Lu 17:27 the *f* came, and destroyed them *2627*
2Pe 2: 5 bringing in the *f* upon the world "
Re 12:15 cast out of his mouth water as a *f* *4215
15 her to be carried away of the *f*. *4216
16 mouth, and swallowed up the *f* *4215

floods
Ex 15: 8 the *f* stood upright as an heap, 5140
2Sa 22: 5 *f* of ungodly men made me afraid ;5158
Job 20:17 He shall not see the rivers, the *f*. *5104
28:11 bindeth the *f* from overflowing; * "
Ps 18: 4 *f* of ungodly men made me afraid.5158
24: 2 and established it upon the *f*. 5104
32: 6 surely in the *f* of great waters *7858
69: 2 waters, where the *f* overflow me. 7641
78:44 rivers into blood; and their *f*, *5140
93: 3 The *f* have lifted up, O Lord, 5104
3 the *f* have lifted up their voice; "
3 the *f* lift up their waves. "
98: 8 the *f* clap their hands: let the hills "
Ca 8: 7 neither can the *f* drown it: if a "
Isa 44: 3 and *f* upon the dry ground: *5140
Eze 31:15 *f* thereof, and the great waters *5104
Jon 2: 3 and the *f* compassed me about: * "
M't 7:25, 27 and the *f* came, and the winds *4215*

floor See also BARNFLOOR; CORNFLOOR; FLOORS; THRESHINGFLOOR.
Ge 50:11 the mourning in the *f* of Atad, 1637
Nu 5:17 of the dust that is in the *f* of the 7172
De 15:14 out of thy flock, and out of thy *f*,*1637
J'g 6:37 will put a fleece of wool in the *f*;* "
Ru 3: 3 and get thee down to the *f*: "
6 And she went down unto the *f*, "
14 that a woman came unto the *f*. * "
1Ki 6:15 the *f* of the house, and the walls 7172
15 covered the *f* of the house with "
16 the *f* and the walls with boards "
30 And the *f* of the house he overlaid "
7: 7 from one side of the *f* to the other."
2Ch 34:11 to *f* the houses which the kings *7136
Isa 21:10 threshing, and the corn of my *f*: 1637
Ho 9: 2 The *f* and the winepress shall * "
13: 3 with the whirlwind out of the *f*, * "
Mic 4:12 them as the sheaves into the *f*. * "
M't 3:12 and he will throughly purge his *f*,* *257*
Lu 3:17 and he will throughly purge his *f*,* "

floors See also THRESHINGFLOORS.
Joe 2:24 And the *f* shall be full of wheat, 1637

flotes See also FLOATS.
2Ch 2:16 and we will bring it to thee in *f* by 7513

flour
Ex 29: 2 wheaten *f* shalt thou make them. 5560
40 tenth deal of *f* mingled with the "
Le 2: 1 his offering shall be of fine *f*; "
2 his handful of the *f* thereof, * "
4 shall be unleavened cakes of fine *f* "
5 it shall be of fine *f* unleavened, "
7 it shall be made of fine *f* with oil. "
5:11 the tenth part of an ephah of fine *f* "
6:15 take of it his handful, of the *f* * "
20 the tenth part of an ephah of fine *f* "
7:12 cakes mingled with oil, of fine *f*, "
14:10 and three tenth deals of fine *f* "
21 and one tenth deal of fine *f* "
23:13 shall be two tenth deals of fine *f* "
17 tenth deals: they shall be of fine *f*: "
24: 5 thou shalt take fine *f*, and bake "
Nu 6:15 cakes of fine *f* mingled with oil, "
7:13 both of them were full of fine *f* "
19, 25, 31, 37, 43, 49, 55, 61, 67, 73, 79 full of fine *f* mingled with oil for a "
8: 8 even fine *f* mingled with oil, "
15: 4 meat offering of a tenth deal of *f* "
6 offering two tenth deals of *f* "
9 offering of three tenth deals of *f* "
28: 5 an ephah of *f* for a meat offering, "
9 two tenth deals of fine *f* for a "
12 three tenth deals of fine *f* for a meat "
12 two tenth deals of *f* for a meat "
13 And a several tenth deal of *f* "
20 shall be of *f* mingled with oil: "
28 their meat offering of *f* mingled "
29: 3 shall be of *f* mingled with oil, "
9 shall be of *f* mingled with oil, "
14 shall be of *f* mingled with oil, "
J'g 6:19 cakes of an ephah of *f*: *7058
1Sa 1:24 bullocks, and one ephah of *f*, * "
28:24 and took *f*, and kneaded it, "
2Sa 13: 8 And she took *f*, and kneaded it, *1217
17:28 wheat, and barley, and *f*, and *7058
1Ki 4:22 was thirty measures of fine *f*, 5560
2Ki 7: 1 a measure of fine *f* be sold for a "
16 So a measure of fine *f* was sold for "
18 a measure of fine *f* for a shekel, "
1Ch 9:29 the fine *f*, and the wine, and the "
23:29 for the fine *f* for meat offering, "
Eze 16:13 thou didst eat fine *f*, and honey, "
19 gave thee fine *f*, and oil, and honey,"
46:14 to temper with the fine *f*; "
Re 18:13 fine *f*, and wheat, and beasts, *4585*

flourish See also FLOURISHED; FLOURISHETH; FLOURISHING.
Ps 72: 7 In his days shall the righteous *f*; 6524
16 and they of the city shall *f* like 6692
92: 7 all the workers of iniquity do *f*; "
12 The righteous shall *f* like the 6524
13 shall *f* in the courts of our God. "
132:18 upon himself shall his crown *f*. 6692
Pr 11:28 the righteous shall *f* as a branch. 6524
14:11 tabernacle of the upright shall *f*. "
Ec 12: 5 and the almond tree shall *f*, *5006
Ca 7:12 let us see if the vine *f*, *6524
Isa 17:11 shalt thou make thy seed to *f*: * "
66:14 your bones shall *f* like an herb: "
Eze 17:24 and have made the dry tree to *f*: "

flourished
Ca 6:11 and to see whether the vine *f*, *6524
Ph'p 4:10 your care of me hath *f* again; * *330*

flourisheth
Ps 90: 6 In the morning it *f*, and groweth 6692
103:15 as a flower of the field, so he *f*. "

flourishing
Ps 92:14 they shall be fat and *f*; *7488
Da 4: 4 mine house, and *f* in my palace: 7487

flow See also FLOWED; FLOWETH; FLOWING; OVERFLOW.
Job 20:28 his goods shall *f* away in the day 5064
Ps 147:18 wind to blow, and the waters *f*. 5140
Ca 4:16 that the spices thereof may *f* out. "
Isa 2: 2 and all nations shall *f* unto it. 5102
48:21 the waters to *f* out of the rock 5140
60: 5 thou shalt see, and *f* together, *5102
64: 1 might *f* down at thy presence, 2151
Jer 31:12 shall *f* together to the goodness 5102
51:44 the nations shall not *f* together "
Joe 3:18 the hills shall *f* with milk, and 3212
18 all the rivers of Judah shall *f* with "
Mic 4: 1 and people shall *f* unto it. 5102
Joh 7:38 belly shall *f* rivers of living water.*4482*

flowed See also OVERFLOWED.
Jos 4:18 and *f* over all his banks, as they *3212
Isa 64: 3 mountains *f* down at thy presence.2151
La 3:54 Waters *f* over mine head; then 6687

flower See also FLOWERS.
Ex 25:33 a knop and a *f* in one branch; 6525
33 other branch, with a knop and a *f*: "
37:19 in one branch, a knop and a *f*; "
19 another branch, a knop and a *f*: "
1Sa 2:33 shall die in the *f* of their age. 582
Job 14: 2 He cometh forth like a *f*, and is cut 6731
15:33 shall cast off his *f* as the olive. 5328
Ps 103:15 a *f* of the field, so he flourisheth. 6731
Isa 18: 5 sour grape is ripening in the *f*, 5328
28: 1 glorious beauty is a fading *f*, 6731
4 shall be a fading *f*, and as the 6733
40: 6 thereof is as the *f* of the field: 6731
7 the *f* fadeth: because the spirit "
8 *f* fadeth: but the word of our God "
Na 1: 4 the *f* of Lebanon languisheth. 6525
1Co 7:36 if she pass the *f* of her age, *5230*
Jas 1:10 because as the *f* of the grass *438*
11 the grass, and the *f* thereof falleth, "
1Pe 1:24 the glory of man as the *f* of grass. "
24 and the *f* thereof falleth away: "

flowers
Ex 25:31 his bowls, his knops, and his *f*, 6525
34 with their knops and their *f*. "
37:17 and his *f* were of the same: "
20 like almonds, his knops, and his *f*: "
Le 15:24 her *f* be upon him, he shall be *5079
33 And of her that is sick of her *f*, * "
Nu 8: 4 the *f* thereof, was beaten work: 6525
1Ki 6:18 knops and open *f*: all was cedar; 6731
29 palm trees and open *f*, within and "
32 palm trees and open *f*, and overlaid "
35 palm trees and open *f*: and covered "
7:26 the brim of a cup, with *f* of lilies: 6525
49 with the *f*, and the lamps, and the "
2Ch 4: 5 brim of a cup, with *f* of lilies; * "
21 And the *f*, and the lamps, and the "
Ca 2:12 The *f* appear on the earth; 5339
5:13 as a bed of spices, as sweet *f*: *4026

floweth See also OVERFLOWETH.
Le 20:24 land that *f* with milk and honey: *2100
Nu 13:27 surely it *f* with milk and honey; "
14: 8 land which *f* with milk and honey. "
16:13, 14 that *f* with milk and honey, * "
De 6: 3 land that *f* with milk and honey.* "
11: 9 land that *f* with milk and honey.* "
26: 9, 15 that *f* with milk and honey. "
27: 3 land that *f* with milk and honey;* "
31:20 land that *f* with milk and honey;* "
Jos 5: 6 land that *f* with milk and honey.* "

flowing See also OVERFLOWING.
Ex 3: 8 a land *f* with milk and honey; 2100
17 unto a land *f* with milk and honey."
13: 5 thee, a land *f* with milk and honey. "
33: 3 Unto a land *f* with milk and "
Pr 18: 4 wellspring of wisdom as a *f* brook.5042
Isa 66:12 the glory of the Gentiles like a *f* *7857
Jer 11: 5 to give them a land *f* with milk 2100
18:14 the cold *f* waters that come from *5140
32:22 a land *f* with milk and honey; 2100
49: 4 *f* valley, O backsliding daughter? "
Eze 20: 6 *f* with milk and honey, which is "
15 them, *f* with milk and honey, "

flown See OVERFLOWN.

flute
Da 3: 5 ye hear the sound of the cornet, *f*,4953
7 heard the sound of the cornet, *f*, "
10 hear the sound of the cornet, *f*, "
15 ye hear the sound of the cornet, *f*, "

fluttereth
De 32:11 up her nest, *f* over her young, 7363

flux
Ac 28: 8 sick of a fever and of a bloody *f*: *1420*

fly See also FLEW; FLIES; FLIETH; FLYING.
Ge 1:20 fowl that may *f* above the earth 5774
1Sa 15:19 but didst *f* upon the spoil, and 5860
2Sa 22:11 he rode upon a cherub, and did *f*: 5774
Job 5: 7 trouble, as the sparks *f* upward. "
20: 8 He shall *f* away as a dream, "
39:26 Doth the hawk *f* by thy wisdom, * 82
Ps 18:10 rode upon a cherub, and did *f*: 5774
10 yea, he did *f* upon the wings *1675
55: 6 would I *f* away, and be at rest. 5774
90:10 it is soon cut off, and we *f* away. "
Pr 23: 5 they *f* away as an eagle toward *5774
Isa 6: 2 his feet, and with twain he did *f*. "
7:18 shall hiss for the *f* that is in the 2070
11:14 they shall *f* upon the shoulders 5774
60: 8 Who are these that *f* as a cloud, "
Jer 48:40 Behold, he shall *f* as an eagle, 1675
49:22 shall come up and *f* as the eagle, "
Eze 13:20 hunt the souls to make them *f*, 6524
20 souls that ye hunt to make them *f*. "
Da 9:21 being caused to *f* swiftly, touched 3286
Ho 9:11 glory shall *f* away like a bird 5774
Hab 1: 8 shall *f* as the eagle that hasteth "
Re 12:14 she might *f* into the wilderness, *4072*
14: 6 saw another angel *f* in the midst* "
19:17 to all the fowls that *f* in the midst "

flying
Le 11:21 ye eat of every *f* creeping thing *5775
23 But all other *f* creeping things, * "
Ps 148:10 creeping things, and *f* fowl: 3671
Pr 26: 2 as the swallow by *f*, so the curse 5774
Isa 14:29 his fruit shall be a fiery *f* serpent. "
30: 6 the viper and fiery *f* serpent, "
31: 5 birds *f*, so will the Lord of hosts ‡ "
Zec 5: 1 and looked, and behold a *f* roll. "
2 And I answered, I see a *f* roll; "
Re 4: 7 fourth beast was like a *f* eagle. *4072*
8:13 *f* through the midst of heaven, "

foal See also FOALS.
Ge 49:11 Binding his *f* unto the vine, and 5895
Zec 9: 9 and upon a colt the *f* of an ass. 1121
M't 21: 5 and a colt the *f* of an ass. *5207*

foals
Ge 32:15 bulls, twenty she asses, and ten *f*.5895

foam See also FOAMETH; FOAMING.
Ho 10: 7 cut off as the *f* upon the water. 7110

foameth
M'r 9:18 he *f*, and gnasheth with his teeth, *875*
Lu 9:39 and it teareth him that he *f* again, *876*

foaming
M'r 9:20 on the ground, and wallowed *f*. *875*
Jude 13 of the sea, *f* out their own shame; *1890*

fodder
Job 6: 5 or loweth the ox over his *f*? 1098

foes
1Ch 21:12 to be destroyed before thy *f*, 6862
Es 9:16 their *f* seventy and five thousand,*8130
Ps 27: 2 even mine enemies and my *f*, 341
30: 1 and hast not made my *f* to rejoice "
89:23 beat down his *f* before his face, *6862
M't 10:36 And a man's *f* shall be they of his *2190*
Ac 2:35 Until I make thy *f* thy footstool. * "

fold See also BLINDFOLD; FOLDEN; FOLDETH; FOLDING; FOLDS; FOURFOLD; HUNDREDFOLD; INFOLDING; MANIFOLD; SEVENFOLD; SHEEPFOLD; SIXTYFOLD; TENFOLD; THIRTYFOLD; THREEFOLD; TWOFOLD.
Isa 13:20 shall the shepherds make their *f* *7257
65:10 And Sharon shall be a *f* of flocks, 5116
Eze 34:14 mountains of Israel shall their *f* "
14 there shall they lie in a good *f*, "
Mic 2:12 the flock in the midst of their *f*: *1699
Hab 3:17 flock shall be cut off from the *f*, 4356
Joh 10:16 I have, which are not of this *f*: *833*
16 shall be one *f*, and one shepherd.*4167*
Heb 1:12 as a vesture shalt thou *f* them up,*1667*

folden
Na 1:10 they be *f* together as thorns, ††5440

foldeth
Ec 4: 5 The fool *f* his hands together, 2263

folding See also INFOLDING.
1Ki 6:34 two leaves of the one door were *f*,1550
34 two leaves of the other door were *f*."
Pr 6:10 a little *f* of the hands to sleep: 2264
24:33 a little *f* of the hands to sleep: "

folds See also SHEEPFOLDS.
Nu 32:24 and *f* for your sheep; and do that1448
36 fenced cities: and *f* for sheep. "
Ps 50: 9 nor he goats out of thy *f*. 4356
Jer 23: 3 will bring them again to their *f*; 5116
Zep 2: 6 for shepherds, and *f* for flocks. 1448

folk See also FOLKS; KINSFOLK.
Ge 33:15 now leave with thee some of the *f* 5971
Pr 30:26 The conies are but a feeble *f*, "
Jer 51:58 and the *f* in the fire, and they *3816
M'r 6: 5 laid his hands upon a few sick *f* "
Joh 5: 3 a great multitude of impotent *f*, *

folks See also KINSFOLKS.
Ac 5:16 bringing sick *f*, and them which *

follow See also FOLLOWED; FOLLOWETH; FOLLOWING.
Ge 24: 5 will not be willing to *f* me unto 3212, 310
8 will not be willing to *f* thee, then" "
39 the woman will not *f* me. " "
44: 4 Up, *f* after the men; and when 7291
Ex 11: 8 and all the people that *f* thee: 7272
14: 4 that he shall *f* after them; 7291
17 and they shall *f* them: and * 310
21:22 and yet no mischief *f*: he shall 1961
23 And if any mischief *f*, then thou "
23: 2 not *f* a multitude to do evil; 1961, 310
De 16:20 is altogether just shalt thou *f*, 7291
18:22 if the thing *f* not, nor come to 1961
J'g 3:28 he said unto them, *F* after me: 7291
8: 5 bread unto the people that *f* me; 7272
9: 3 hearts inclined to *f* Abimelech ;935, 310
1Sa 25:27 young men that *f* my lord. 1980, 7272
30:21 so faint that they could not *f* 3212, 310
2Sa 17: 9 among the people that *f* Absalom. "
1Ki 18:21 God, *f* him: but if Baal, then *f* 3212, "
19:20 mother, and then I will *f* thee. " "
20:10 for all the people that *f* me. 7272

2Ki 6:19 f me, and I will bring you 3212, 310
Ps 23: 6 goodness and mercy shall f me 7291
38:20 I f the thing that good is. "
45:14 virgins her companions that f her 310
94:15 all the upright in heart shall f it. "
119:150 draw nigh that f after mischief: 7291
Isa 5:11 that they may f strong drink; "
51: 1 me, ye that f after righteousness, "
Jer 17:16 from being a pastor to f thee: * 310
42:16 f close after you there in Egypt; 1692
Eze 13: 3 foolish prophets, that f their 1980, 310
Ho 2: 7 And she shall f after her lovers, 7291
6: 3 if we f on to know the Lord: "
M't 4:19 he saith unto them, F me, *1205, 3694
8:19 I will f thee whithersoever thou 190
22 And Jesus said unto him, F me; "
9: 9 and he saith unto him, F me. "
16:24 and take up his cross, and f me. "
19:21 in heaven: and come and f me. "
M'r 2:14 and said unto him, F me. And he "
5:37 And he suffered no man to f him, 4870
6: 1 country; and his disciples f him. 190
8:34 and take up his cross, and f me. "
10:21 come, take up the cross, and f me. "
14:13 bearing a pitcher of water: f him. "
16:17 And these signs shall f them that 3877
Lu 5:27 and he said unto him, F me. 190
9:23 take up his cross daily, and f me. "
57 I will f thee whithersoever thou "
59 And he said unto another, F me. "
61 also said, Lord, I will f thee; "
17:23 go not after them, nor f them. 1377
18:22 treasure in heaven: and come, f me. 190
22:10 f him into the house where he "
49 were about him saw what would f, 2071
Joh 1:43 Philip, and saith unto him, F me. 190
10: 4 before them, and the sheep f him: "
5 And a stranger will they not f, "
27 and I know them, and they f me: "
12:26 If any man serve me, let him f me; "
13:36 not f me now; but thou shalt f me "
37 why cannot I f thee now? "
21:19 he saith unto him, F me. "
22 what is that to thee? f thou me. "
Ac 3:24 Samuel and those that f after, *2517
12: 8 thy garment about thee, and f me. 190
Ro 14:19 therefore f after the things which 1377
1Co 14: 1 F after charity, and desire "
Ph'p 3:12 I f after, if that I may apprehend* "
1Th 5:15 but ever f that which is good, "
2Th 3: 7 know how ye ought to f us: *3401
9 an ensample unto you to f us. * "
1Ti 5:24 and some men they f after. 1872
6:11 f after righteousness, godliness, 1377
2Ti 2:22 f righteousness, faith, charity, "
Heb 12:14 F peace with all men, and "
13: 7 whose faith f, considering the *3401
1Pe 1:11 and the glory that should f. 3326, 5023
2:21 example, that ye should f his steps: 1872
2Pe 2: 2 And many shall f their pernicious 1811
3Jo 11 Beloved, f not that which is evil, *3401
Re 14: 4 These are they which f the Lamb 190
13 and their works do f them. "

followed See also FOLLOWEDST.
Ge 24:61 f the man: and the servant 3212, 310
32:19 all that f the droves, saying, 1980, 310
Nu 14:24 hath f me fully, him will I bring "
16:25 and the elders of Israel f him. 3212, "
32:11 because they have not wholly f me: "
12 for they have wholly f the Lord. "
De 1:36 because he hath wholly f the Lord. "
4: 3 all the men that f Baal-peor, 1980, "
Jos 6: 8 the covenant of the Lord f them. "
14: 8 but I wholly f the Lord my God. "
9 because thou hast wholly f the Lord "
14 he wholly f the Lord God of Israel. "
J'g 2:12 and f other gods, of the gods 3212, "
9: 4 and light persons, which f him. "
49 his bough, and f Abimelech. "
1Sa 13: 7 and all the people f him trembling. "
14:22 even they also f hard after them 1692
17:13 and f Saul to the battle: *1980, 310
14 and the three eldest f Saul. "
31: 2 the Philistines f hard upon Saul 1692
2Sa 1: 6 chariots and horsemen f hard after "
2:10 the house of Judah f David. 1961, 310
3:31 And king David himself f the 1980, "
11: 8 and there f him a mess of meat 3318, "
17:23 saw that his counsel was not f, he 6213
20: 2 up from after David, and f Sheba 310
1Ki 12:20 none that f the house of David, "
14: 8 who f me with all his heart, 1980, "
16:21 half of the people f Tibni 1961, "
21 make him king; and half f Omri. "
22 the people that f Omri prevailed "
22 against the people that f Tibni "
18:18 Lord, and thou hast f Baalim. 3212, "
20:19 and the army which f them. "
2Ki 3: 9 and for the cattle that f them. 7272
4:30 And he arose, and f her. 3112, 310
5:21 So Gehazi f after Naaman. 7291
9:27 And Jehu f after him, and said, "
13: 2 and f the sins of Jeroboam the 3212, 310
17:15 they f vanity, and became vain " "
1Ch 10: 2 And the Philistines f hard after 1692
Ne 4:23 nor the men of the guard which f 310
Ps 68:25 the players on instruments f after; "
Eze 10:11 the head looked they f it; 3212, 310
Am 7:15 the Lord took me as I f the flock, * "
M't 4:20 straightway left their nets, and f 190
22 the ship and their father, and f him. "
25 f him great multitudes of people "
8: 1 mountain, great multitudes f him, "
10 and said to them that f, Verily I say "
23 into a ship, his disciples f him. "
M't 9: 9 Follow me. And he arose, and f 190
19 And Jesus arose, and f him, "
27 two blind men f him, crying, and "
12:15 great multitudes f him, and he "
14:13 they f him on foot out of the cities. "
19: 2 great multitudes f him; and he "
27 we have forsaken all, and f thee; "
28 That ye which have f me, in the "
20:29 Jericho, a great multitude f him. "
34 received sight, and they f him. "
21: 9 that went before, and that f, "
26:58 Peter f him afar off unto the high "
27:55 f Jesus from Galilee, ministering "
62 day, that f the day of the *2076, 3326
M'r 1:18 they forsook their nets, and f him. 190
36 they that were with him f after 2614
2:14 Follow me. And he arose and f him. 190
15 there were many, and they f him. "
3: 7 great multitude from Galilee f him, "
5:24 with him; and much people f him, "
10:28 have left all, and have f thee. "
32 and as they f, they were afraid. "
52 he received his sight, and f Jesus "
11: 9 that went before, and they that f, "
14:51 there f him a certain young man, "
54 Peter f him afar off, even into the "
15:41 when he was in Galilee, f him, and "
Lu 5:11 they forsook all, and f him. "
28 And he left all, rose up, and f him. "
7: 9 and said unto the people that f him, "
9:11 people, when they knew it, f him: "
18:28 we have left all, and f thee. "
43 he received his sight, and f him, "
22:39 and his disciples also f him. "
54 priest's house. And Peter f afar off. "
23:27 And there f him a great company of "
49 and the women that f him from 4870
55 f after, and beheld the sepulchre, 2628
Joh 1:37 heard him speak, and they f Jesus. 190
40 which heard John speak, and f him, "
6: 2 And a great multitude f him, "
11:31 rose up hastily and went out, f her, "
18:15 And Simon Peter f Jesus, and so did "
Ac 12: 9 And he went out, and f him; "
13:43 proselytes f Paul and Barnabas: "
16:17 same f Paul and us, and cried, 2628
21:36 the multitude of the people f after, 190
Ro 9:30 which f not after righteousness, 1377
31 Israel, which f after the law of "
1Co 10: 4 of that spiritual Rock that f them: 190
1Ti 5:10 have diligently f every good work. 1872
2Pe 1:16 we have not f cunningly devised 1811
Re 6: 8 was Death, and Hell f with him. 190
8: 7 there f hail and fire mingled with 1096
14: 8 and there f another angel, saying, 190
9 And the third angel f them, saying "
19:14 armies which were in heaven f him "

followedst
Ru 3:10 as thou f not young men, 3212, 310

followers
1Co 4:16 I beseech you, be ye f of me. *3402
11: 1 Be ye f of me, even as I also am * "
Eph 5: 1 Be ye therefore f of God, "
Ph'p 3:17 be f together of me, and mark *4831
1Th 1: 6 became f of us, and of the Lord, *3402
2:14 became f of the churches of God * "
Heb 6:12 but f of them who through faith * "
1Pe 3:13 if ye be f of that which is good? * "

followeth
2Ki 11:15 that f her kill with the sword. 935, 310
2Ch 23:14 whoso f her, let him be slain "
Ps 63: 8 My soul f hard after thee: 1692
Pr 12:11 but he that f vain persons is void 7291
15: 9 him that f after righteousness. "
21:21 He that f after righteousness and "
28:19 but he that f after vain persons "
Isa 1:23 loveth gifts, and f after rewards: "
Eze 16:34 none f thee to commit whoredoms: 310
Ho 12: 1 and f after the east wind: he 7291
M't 10:38 and f after me, is not worthy of * 190
M'r 9:38 in thy name, and he f not us: * "
38 we forbad him, because he f not * "
Lu 9:49 we forbad him, because he f not "
Joh 8:12 he that f me shall not walk in "

following
Ge 41:31 by reason of that famine f; *310, 3651
De 7: 4 will turn away thy son from f me, 310
12:30 thou be not snared by f them, * "
Jos 22:16 to turn away this day from f the "
18 must turn away this day from f the "
23 an altar to turn from f the Lord. "
29 to turn this day from f the Lord. "
J'g 2:19 in f other gods to serve them, 3212, 310
Ru 1:16 or to return from f after thee: "
1Sa 12:14 continue f the Lord your God: * 310
20 yet turn not aside from f the Lord. "
14:46 went up from f the Philistines: "
15:11 for he is turned back from f me, "
24: 1 returned from f the Philistines, "
2Sa 2:19 hand nor to the left from f Abner. "
21 would not turn aside from f of him. "
22 Asahel, Turn thee aside from f me: "
26 return from f their brethren? "
27 up every one from f his brother. * "
30 And Joab returned from f Abner: "
7: 8 from f the sheep, to be ruler over "
1Ki 1: 7 and they f Adonijah helped him. "
9: 6 if ye shall at all turn from f me, "
21:26 very abominably in f idols, 3212, "
2Ki 17:21 drave Israel from f the Lord, "
18: 6 departed not from f him, but kept "
1Ch 17: 7 sheepcote, even from f the sheep, "
2Ch 25:27 did turn away from f the Lord "
34:33 they departed not from f the Lord. "
Ps 48:13 ye may tell it to the generation f. 314
78:71 From f the ewes great with young 310
109:13 in the generation f let their name 312
M'r 16:20 confirming the word with signs f. *1872
Lu 13:33 and tomorrow, and the day f: 2192
Joh 1:38 Jesus turned, and saw them f, 190
43 The day f Jesus would go forth *1887
6:22 The day f, when the people * "
20: 6 Then cometh Simon Peter f him, 190
21:20 the disciple whom Jesus loved f; "
Ac 21: 1 and the day f unto Rhodes, and *1836
18 the day f Paul went in with us 1966
23:11 And the night f the Lord stood "
2Pe 2:15 f the way of Balaam the son of *1811

folly
Ge 34: 7 he had wrought f in Israel 5039
De 22:21 she hath wrought f in Israel, "
Jos 7:15 and because he hath wrought f "
J'g 19:23 come into mine house, do not this f. "
20: 6 committed lewdness and f in "
10 f that they have wrought in Israel. "
1Sa 25:25 Nabal is his name, and f is with "
2Sa 13:12 done in Israel: do not thou this f. "
Job 4:18 his angels he charged with f: 8417
24:12 yet God layeth not f to them. 8604
42: 8 lest I deal with you after your f, 5039
Ps 49:13 This their way is their f: 3689
85: 8 but let them not turn again to f. 3690
Pr 5:23 in the greatness of his f he shall 200
13:16 but a fool layeth open his f. "
14: 8 but the f of fools is deceit. "
18 The simple inherit f: but the "
24 but the foolishness of fools is f. "
29 he that is hasty of spirit exalteth f. "
15:21 F is joy to him that is destitute of "
16:22 but the instruction of fools is f. "
17:12 rather than a fool in his f. "
18:13 matter before he heareth it, it is f "
26: 4 Answer not a fool according to his f, "
5 Answer a fool according to his f, "
11 so a fool returneth to his f. "
Ec 1:17 and to know madness and f: 5531
2: 3 to lay hold on f, till I might see "
12 wisdom, and madness, and f: "
13 I saw that wisdom excelleth f, "
7:25 and to know the wickedness of f, 3689
10: 1 so doth a little f him that is in 5531
6 F is set in great dignity, and the 5529
Isa 9:17 and every mouth speaketh f. 5039
Jer 23:13 I have seen f in the prophets 8604
2Co 11: 1 bear with me a little in my f: * 877
2Ti 3: 9 their f shall be manifest unto all 454

food
Ge 2: 9 to the sight, and good for f; 3978
3: 6 saw that the tree was good for f, "
6:21 unto thee of all f that is eaten, "
21 and it shall be for f for thee, 402
41:35 And let them gather all the f 400
35 and let them keep f in the cities. "
36 And that f shall be for store to the "
48 And he gathered up all the f of the "
48 laid up the f in the cities: the f of "
42: 7 From the land of Canaan to buy f. "
10 but to buy f are thy servants come. "
33 and take f for the famine of your* "
43: 2 Go again, buy us a little f. 400
4 we will go down and buy thee f: "
20 down at the first time to buy f: "
22 down in our hands to buy f: "
44: 1 Fill the men's sacks with f, "
25 Go again, and buy us a little f. "
47:24 seed of the field, and for your f, "
24 and for f for your little ones. 398
Ex 21:10 her f, her raiment, and her duty 7607
Le 3:11, 16 it is the f of the offering made 3899
19:23 planted all manner of trees for f, 3978
22: 7 holy things; because it is his f. *3899
De 10:18 in giving him f and raiment. "
1Sa 14:24 be the man that eateth any f until "
24 So none of the people tasted any f. "
28 be the man that eateth any f this "
2Sa 9:10 master's son may have f to eat: * "
1Ki 5: 9 desire, in giving f for my household. "
11 thousand measures of wheat for f 4361
Job 23:12 mouth more than my necessary f. "
24: 5 wilderness yieldeth f for them ‡3899
38:41 provideth for the raven his f? ‡6718
40:20 the mountains bring him forth f. 944
Ps 78:25 Man did eat angels' f: he sent *3899
104:14 bring forth f out of the earth; "
136:25 Who giveth f to all flesh: for his "
146: 7 which giveth f to the hungry. "
147: 9 He giveth to the beast his f, "
Pr 6: 8 gathereth her f in the harvest. 3978
13:23 Much f is in the tillage of the poor: 400
27:27 have goats' milk enough for thy f, 3899
27 for the f of thy household, and for "
28: 3 sweeping rain which leaveth no f. "
30: 8 feed me with f convenient for me: "
31:14 she bringeth her f from afar. ‡ "
Eze 16:27 and have diminished thine ordinary f, "
48:18 f unto them that serve the city. 3899
Ac 14:17 our hearts with f and gladness. 5160
2Co 9:10 both minister bread for your f, 1035
1Ti 6: 8 having f and raiment let us be 1304
Jas 2:15 be naked, and destitute of daily f, 5160

fool See also FOOL'S; FOOLS.
1Sa 26:21 behold, I have played the f, and 5528
2Sa 3:33 said, Died Abner as a f dieth? 5036
Ps 14: 1 The f hath said in his heart, "
49:10 the f and the brutish person 3684
53: 1 The f hath said in his heart, 5036
92: 6 neither doth a f understand this. 3684

Pr 7:22 f to the correction of the stocks; * 191
10: 8 commandments: but a prating f "
10 sorrow: but a prating f shall fall. "
18 he that uttereth a slander, is a f. 3684
23 It is as sport to a f to do mischief: "
11:29 f shall be servant to the wise * 191
12:15 of a f is right in his own eyes: * "
13:16 but a f layeth open his folly. 3684
14:16 but the f rageth, and is confident. "
15: 5 f despiseth his father's instruction:191
17: 7 speech becometh not a f: 5036
10 than an hundred stripes into a f. 3684
12 rather than a f in his folly. "
16 in the hand of a f to get wisdom, "
21 He that begetteth a f doeth it to his "
21 and the father of a f hath no joy. 5036
24 the eyes of a f are in the ends of 3684
28 a f, when he holdeth his peace, 191
18: 2 A f hath no delight in 3684
19: 1 is perverse in his lips, and is a f. "
10 Delight is not seemly for a f; "
20: 3 but every f will be meddling. 191
23: 9 Speak not in the ears of a f: 3684
24: 7 Wisdom is too high for a f: 191
26: 1 So honour is not seemly for a f. 3684
4 Answer not a f according to his "
5 Answer a f according to his folly, "
6 a message by the hand of a f "
8 so is he that giveth honour to a f. "
10 rewardeth the f, and rewardeth "
11 so a f returneth to his folly. "
12 is more hope of a f than of him. "
27:22 Though thou shouldest bray a f in 191
28:26 trusteth in his own heart is a f: 3684
29:11 A f uttereth all his mind: "
20 is more hope of a f than of him. "
30:22 a f when he is filled with meat; 5036
Ec 2:14 but the f walketh in darkness: 3684
15 As it happeneth to the f, so it "
16 of the wise more than of the f "
16 how dieth the wise man? as the f. "
19 he shall be a wise man or a f? 5530
4: 5 The f foldeth his hands together,3684
6: 8 hath the wise more than the f? "
7: 6 so is the laughter of the f: "
10: 3 he that is a f walketh by the way,5530
3 he saith to every one that he is a f. "
12 but the lips of a f will swallow up 3684
14 A f also is full of words: 5536
Jer 17:11 and at his end shall be a f. 5036
Ho 9: 7 the prophet is a f, the spiritual 191
M't 5:22 but whosoever shall say, Thou f, 3474
Lu 12:20 Thou f, this night thy soul shall * 878
1Co 3:18 become a f, that he may be wise. 3474
15:36 Thou f, that which thou sowest * 878
2Co 11:16 Let no man think me a f; * "
16 yet as a f receive me, * "
23 (I speak as a f) I am more; *3912
12: 6 I shall not be a f; for I will say * 878
11 I am become a f in glorying; * "

foolish
De 32: 6 O f people and unwise? is not he 5036
21 them to anger with a f nation. "
Job 2:10 speakest as one of the f women 5039
5: 2 For wrath killeth the f man, 191
3 I have seen the f taking root: "
Ps 5: 5 The f shall not stand in thy *1984
39: 8 me not the reproach of the f. 5036
73: 3 For I was envious at the f, *1984
22 So f was I, and ignorant: I was *1198
74:18 the f people have blasphemed 5036
22 the f man reproacheth thee daily. "
Pr 9: 6 Forsake the f, and live; and go *6612
13 A f woman is clamorous: she is 3687
10: 1 a f son is the heaviness of his 3684
14 mouth of the f is near destruction. 191
14: 1 but the f plucketh it down with 200
3 In the mouth of the f is a rod of 191
7 Go from the presence of a f man, 3684
15: 7 but the heart of the f doeth not so. "
20 but a f man despiseth his mother. "
17:25 A f son is a grief to his father, "
19:13 A f son is the calamity of his "
21:20 but a f man spendeth it up. "
29: 9 wise man contendeth with a f man, 191
Ec 4:13 an old and f king, who will no 3684
7:17 neither be thou f: why shouldest 5530
10:15 The labour of the f wearieth *3684
Isa 44:25 and maketh their knowledge f; 5528
Jer 4:22 For my people is f, they have not 191
5: 4 they are f: for they know not 2973
21 Hear now this, O f people, 5530
10: 8 they are altogether brutish and f:3688
La 2:14 seen vain and f things for thee: *8602
Eze 13: 3 Woe unto the f prophets, that 5036
Zec 11:15 the instruments of a f shepherd. 196
M't 7:26 shall be likened unto a f man, 3474
25: 2 them were wise, and five were f. "
3 They that were f took their lamps, "
8 And the f said unto the wise, "
Ro 1:21 and their f heart was darkened. * 801
2:20 An instructor of the f, a teacher 878
10:19 by a f nation I will anger you. * 801
1Co 1:20 hath not God made f the wisdom 3471
27 God hath chosen the f things of 3474
Gal 3: 1 O f Galatians, who hath bewitched 453
3 Are ye so f? having begun in the "
Eph 5: 4 nor f talking, nor jesting, 3473
1Ti 6: 9 into many f and hurtful lusts, 453
2Ti 2:23 f and unlearned questions avoid, 3474
Tit 3: 3 ourselves also were sometimes f, 453
9 f questions, and genealogies, 3474
1Pe 2:15 to silence the ignorance of f men: 878

foolishly
Ge 31:28 thou hast now done f in so doing. 5528
Nu 12:11 wherein we have done f, and 2973
2Sa 24:10 servant; for I have done very f 5528
1Ch 21: 8 thy servant; for I have done very f." "
2Ch 16: 9 Herein thou hast done f: "
Job 1:22 sinned not, nor charged God f. †8604
Ps 75: 4 Deal not f: and to the wicked, *1984
Pr 14:17 He that is soon angry dealeth f: 200
30:32 If thou hast done f in lifting up 5034
2Co 11:17 but as it were f, in this *1722, 877
21 (I speak f,) I am bold also. * " "

foolishness
2Sa 15:31 the counsel of Ahithophel into f. 5528
Ps 38: 5 and are corrupt because of my f. 200
69: 5 O God, thou knowest my f; "
Pr 12:23 the heart of fools proclaimeth f. "
14:24 but the f of fools is folly. * "
15: 2 mouth of fools poureth out f. * "
14 the mouth of fools feedeth on f. * "
19: 3 The f of man perverteth his way: "
22:15 F is bound in the heart of a child; "
24: 9 The thought of f is sin: * "
27:22 yet will not his f depart from him. "
Ec 7:25 of folly, even of f and madness: 5531
10:13 of the words of his mouth is f: "
M'r 7:22 an evil eye, blasphemy, pride, f: 877
1Co 1:18 the cross is to them that perish, f;3472
21 the f of preaching to save them "
23 and unto the Greeks f; "
25 the f of God is wiser than men; 3474
2:14 for they are f unto him: 3472
3:19 wisdom of this world is f with God." "

fool's
Pr 12:16 A f wrath is presently known: but 191
18: 6 A f lips enter into contention, 3684
7 A f mouth is his destruction, "
26: 3 the ass, and a rod for the f back.* "
27: 3 a f wrath is heavier than them 191
Ec 5: 3 a f voice is known by multitude 3684
10: 2 but a f heart at his left. "

fools
2Sa 13:13 shalt be as one of the f in Israel. 5036
Job 12:17 and maketh the judges f. 1984
30: 8 They were children of f, yea, 5036
Ps 75: 4 I said unto the f, Deal not *1984
94: 8 and ye f, when will ye be wise? 3684
107:17 F, because of their transgression, 191
Pr 1: 7 f despise wisdom and instruction.* "
22 and f hate knowledge? 3684
32 prosperity of f shall destroy them. "
3:35 shame shall be the promotion of f. "
8: 5 ye f, be ye of an understanding "
10:21 but f die for want of wisdom. * 191
12:23 but the heart of f proclaimeth 3684
13:19 it is abomination to f to depart "
20 companion of f shall be destroyed." "
14: 8 but the folly of f is deceit. "
9 F make a mock at sin: but * 191
24 but the foolishness of f is folly. 3684
33 that which is in the midst of f "
15: 2 mouth of f poureth out foolishness "
14 mouth of f feedeth on foolishness. "
16:22 but the instruction of f is folly. 191
19:29 and stripes for the back of f. 3684
26: 7, 9 is a parable in the mouth of f. "
Ec 5: 1 than to give the sacrifice of f: "
4 for he hath no pleasure in f: "
7: 4 but the heart of f is in the house of "
5 for a man to hear the song of f. "
9 for anger resteth in the bosom of f." "
9:17 the cry of him that ruleth among f. "
Isa 19:11 Surely the princes of Zoan are f, * 191
13 The princes of Zoan are become f,2973
35: 8 wayfaring men, though f, shall not 191
M't 23:17 Ye f and blind: for whether is 3474
19 Ye f and blind: for whether is * "
Lu 11:40 Ye f, did not he that made that * 878
24:25 O f, and slow of heart to believe * 453
Ro 1:22 to be wise, they became f, 3471
1Co 4:10 We are f for Christ's sake, but ye 3474
2Co 11:19 For ye suffer f gladly, seeing ye * 878
Eph 5:15 circumspectly, not as f, but as * 781

foot See also AFOOT; BAREFOOT; BROKENFOOTED; CLOVENFOOTED; FEET; FOOTMEN; FOOTSTEPS; FOOTSTOOL; FOURFOOTED.
Ge 8: 9 found no rest for the sole of her f, 7272
41:44 shall no man lift up his hand or f "
Ex 12:37 about six hundred thousand on f 7273
21:24 for tooth, hand for hand, f for f, 7272
29:20 upon the great toe of their right f, "
30:18 a laver of brass, and his f also *3653
28 vessels, and the laver and his f. * "
31: 9 furniture, and the laver and his f,* "
35:16 his vessels, the laver and his f, * "
38: 8 the laver of brass, and the f of it * "
39:39 his vessels, the laver and his f, * "
40:11 laver and his f, and sanctify it. * "
Le 8:11 laver and his f, to sanctify them.* "
23 upon the great toe of his right f. 7272
13:12 from his head even to his f, * "
14:14 upon the great toe of his right f: "
17 upon the great toe of his right f, "
25 upon the great toe of his right f: "
28 upon the great toe of his right f, "
Nu 22:25 crushed Balaam's f against the "
De 2: 5 no, not so much as a f breadth; "
8: 4 did thy f swell, these forty years. "
11:10 wateredst it with thy f, as a garden "
19:21 for tooth, hand for hand, f for f, "
25: 9 and loose his shoe from off his f, "
28:35 from the sole of thy f unto the top "
56 the sole of her f upon the ground "
65 shall the sole of thy f have rest: "
29: 5 shoe is not waxen old upon thy f. "
32:35 their f shall slide in due time: "
33:24 and let him dip his f in oil. 7272
Jos 1: 3 the sole of your f shall tread upon, "
5:15 Loose thy shoe from off thy f; "
J'g 5:15 he was sent on f into the valley. * "
2Sa 2:18 was as light of f as a wild roe. "
14:25 the sole of his f even to the crown "
21:20 and on every f six toes, four and "
1Ch 20: 6 on each hand, and six on each f: "
2Ch 33: 8 any more remove the f of Israel 7272
Job 2: 7 the sole of his f unto his crown. "
23:11 My f hath held his steps, his way "
28: 4 the waters forgotten of the f: † "
31: 5 if my f hath hasted to deceit; "
39:15 forgetteth that the f may crush "
Ps 9:15 which they hid is their own f taken." "
26:12 My f standeth in an even place: "
36:11 Let not the f of pride come against "
38:16 when my f slippeth, they magnify "
66: 6 they went through the flood on f: "
68:23 thy f may be dipped in the blood of "
91:12 thou dash thy f against a stone. "
94:18 I said, My f slippeth; thy mercy, "
121: 3 will not suffer thy f to be moved: "
Pr 1:15 refrain thy f from their path: "
3:23 and thy f shall not stumble. "
26 shall keep thy f from being taken. "
4:27 to the left: remove thy f from evil. "
25:17 thy f from thy neighbour's house; "
19 broken tooth, and a f out of joint. "
Ec 5: 1 Keep thy f when thou goest to the "
Isa 1: 6 From the sole of the f even unto "
14:25 my mountains tread him under f: 947
18: 7 meted out and trodden under f, *4001
20: 2 and put off thy shoe from thy f. 7272
26: 6 The f shall tread it down, even the "
41: 2 from the east, called him to his f, "
58:13 turn away thy f from the sabbath, "
Jer 2:25 Withhold thy f from being unshod," "
12:10 have trodden my portion under f, 947
La 1:15 Lord hath trodden under f all *5541
Eze 1: 7 was like the sole of a calf's f: 7272
6:11 and stamp with thy f, and say, "
29:11 No f of man shall pass through it, "
11 nor f of beast shall pass through it, "
32:13 shall the f of man trouble them "
Da 8:13 the host to be trodden under f? 4823
Am 2:15 that is swift of f shall not deliver 7272
M't 4: 6 lest at any time thou dash thy f 4228
5:13 and to be trodden under f of men.2662
14:13 followed him on f out of the cities.3979
18: 8 if thy hand or thy f offend thee, 4228
22:13 Bind him hand and f, and take him "
M'r 9:45 And if thy f offend thee, cut it off: "
Lu 4:11 thou dash thy f against a stone. "
Joh 11:44 hand and f with graveclothes: "
Ac 7: 5 not so much as to set his f on: "
1Co 12:15 If the f shall say, Because I am not "
Heb 10:29 trodden under f the Son of God, 2662
Re 1:13 with a garment down to the f, 4158
10: 2 and he set his right f upon the 4228
2 sea, and his left f on the earth, * "
11: 2 the holy city shall they tread under f

foot-breadth See FOOT and BREADTH.

footmen
Nu 11:21 are six hundred thousand f; and 7273
J'g 20: 2 thousand f that drew sword. 376, "
1Sa 4:10 fell of Israel thirty thousand f. "
15: 4 two hundred thousand f, and ten "
22:17 king said unto the f that stood *7323
2Sa 8: 4 and twenty thousand f: and 376, 7273
10: 6 twenty thousand f, and of king "
1Ki 20:29 hundred thousand f in one day. "
2Ki 13: 7 and ten thousand f; for the king "
1Ch 18: 4 and twenty thousand f: 376, "
19:18 forty thousand f, and killed "
Jer 12: 5 If thou hast run with the f, "

footsteps
Ps 17: 5 in thy paths, that my f slip not. *6471
77:19 and thy f are not known. 6119
89:51 reproached the f of thine anointed. "
Ca 1: 8 thy way forth by the f of the flock, "

footstool
1Ch 28: 2 and for the f of our God, 1916, 7272
2Ch 9:18 to the throne, with a f of gold, 3534
Ps 99: 5 and worship at his f; for he 1916, 7272
110: 1 I make thine enemies thy f. " "
132: 7 we will worship at his f. " "
Isa 66: 1 and the earth is my f: where " "
La 2: 1 remembered not his f in the " "
M't 5:35 earth; for it is his f: 5286, *3588, 4228
22:44 thine enemies thy f? * " " "
M'r 12:36 thine enemies thy f. " * "
Lu 20:43 thine enemies thy f. " * "
Ac 2:35 make thy foes thy f. " * "
7:49 and earth is my f: " * "
Heb 1:13 thine enemies thy f? " * "
10:13 enemies be made his f. " * "
Jas 2: 3 or sit here under my f: 5286

for See in the APPENDIX; also FORASMUCH; FORBEAR; FORBID; FORGET; FORGIVE; FORSAKE; FORSOMUCH; FORSWEAR.

forasmuch See also FORSOMUCH.
Ge 41:39 F as God hath shewed thee all 310
Nu 10:31 f as thou knowest how 3588, 5921, 3651
De 12:12 f as he hath no part nor 3588
17:16 f as the Lord hath said unto you, Ye
Jos 17:14 f as the Lord hath blessed me 5704
J'g 11:36 f as the Lord hath taken 310, 834
1Sa 20:42 f as we have sworn both of us in the
24:18 f as when the Lord had 854, 834
2Sa 19:30 f as my lord the king is come 310, "
1Ki 11:11 unto Solomon, F as this is done3282, "
13:21 F as thou hast disobeyed the "
14: 7 F as I exalted thee from among "

1Ki 16: 2 *F* as I exalted thee out of the3282, 834
2Ki 1:16 *F* as thou hast sent messengers" "
1Ch 5: 1 *f* as he defiled his father's bed, "
2Ch 6: 8 *F* as it was in thine heart to *
Ezr 7:14 *F* as thou art sent of 3606, 6903, 1768
Isa 8: 6 *F* as this people refuseth the 3282, 365
29:13 *F* as this people draw near me " "
Jer 10: 6 *F* as there is none like unto thee,*
7 *f* as among all the wise men of the
Da 2:40 *f* as iron breaketh in 3606, 6903, 1768
41 *f* as thou sawest the iron " " "
45 *F* as thou sawest that " " "
4:18 *f* as all the wise men of " " "
5:12 *F* as an excellent spirit, " " "
6: 4 *f* as he was faithful, " " "
22 *f* as before him...was " " "
Am 5:11 *F* therefore as your treading is 3282
M't 18:25 But *f* as he had not to pay,
Lu 1: 1 *F* as many have taken in hand 1895
Ac 9:38 And *f* as Lydda was nigh to *5607
11:17 *F* then as God gave them the *1487
15:24 *F* as we have heard, that certain 1894
17:29 *F* then as we are the offspring of*
24:10 *F* as I know that thou hast been of
1Co 11: 7 *f* as he is the image and glory of God:
14:12 *f* as ye are zealous of spiritual *1893
15:58 *f* as ye know that your labour is not in
2Co 3: 3 *F* as ye are manifestly declared *
Heb 2:14 *F* then as the children are *1893
1Pe 1:18 *F* as ye know that ye were not *
4: 1 *F* then as Christ hath suffered for us

forbad
De 2:37 the Lord our God *f* us. 6680
M't 3:14 John *f* him, saying, I have need *1254
M'r 9:38 we *f* him, because he followeth 2967
Lu 9:49 we *f* him, because he followeth "
2Pe 2:16 *f* the madness of the prophet. * "

forbare
1Sa 23:13 and he *f* to go forth. 2308
2Ch 25:16 Then the prophet *f*, and said, I "
Jer 41: 8 So he *f*, and slew them not among "

forbear See also FORBARE; FORBEARETH; FORBEARING; FORBORN.
Ex 23: 5 and wouldest *f* to help him, 2308
De 23:22 But if thou shalt *f* to vow, "
1Ki 22: 6 battle, or shall I *f*? And they said, "
15 or shall we *f*? And he answered "
2Ch 18: 5 or shall I *f*? And they said, "
14 to battle, or shall I *f*? And he said, "
25:16 *f*; why shouldest thou be smitten? "
35:21 *f* thee from meddling with God, "
Ne 9:30 many years didst thou *f* them, *4900
Job 16: 6 and though I *f*, what am I eased? 2308
Pr 24:11 If thou *f* to deliver them that are *2820
Jer 40: 4 to come with me into Babylon, *f*: 2308
Eze 2: 5 will hear, or whether they will *f*, "
7 will hear, or whether they will *f*: "
3:11 will hear, or whether they will *f*. "
27 he that forbeareth, let him *f*: "
24:17 *F* to cry, make no mourning *1826
Zec 11:12 and if not, *f*. So they weighed 2308
1Co 9: 6 have not we power to *f* working? 2361
2Co 12: 6 I *f*, lest any man should think of 5339
1Th 3: 1 when we could no longer *f*, we 4722
5 when I could no longer *f*, I went "

forbearance
Ro 2: 4 the riches of his goodness and *f* 463
3:25 that are past, through the *f* of God; "

forbeareth
Nu 9:13 and *f* to keep the passover, even 2308
Eze 3:27 and he that *f*, let him forbear: 2310

forbearing
Pr 25:15 by long *f* is a prince persuaded, 639
Jer 20: 9 I was weary with *f*, and I could 3557
Eph 4: 2 *f* one another in love; 430
6: 9 things unto them, *f* threatening: 447
Col 3:13 *F* one another, and forgiving one 430

forbid See also FORBAD; FORBIDDEN; FORBIDDETH; FORBIDDING.
Ge 44: 7 God *f* that thy servants should ‡2486
17 God *f* that I should do so: ‡ "
Nu 11:28 said, My lord Moses, *f* them. 3607
Jos 22:29 God *f* that we should rebel ‡2486
24:16 God *f* that we should forsake the ‡ "
1Sa 12:23 God *f* that I should sin against ‡ "
14:45 God *f*: as the Lord liveth, ‡ "
20: 2 And he said unto him, God *f*; ‡ "
24: 6 he said unto his men, The Lord *f* "
26:11 The Lord *f* that I should stretch "
1Ki 21: 3 The Lord *f* it me, that I should "
1Ch 11:19 And said, My God *f* it me, "
Job 27: 5 God *f* that I should justify you: ‡ "
M't 19:14 and *f* them not, to come unto me: 2967
M'r 9:39 But Jesus said, *F* him not: "
10:14 to come unto me, and *f* them not: " "
Lu 6:29 *f* not to take thy coat also. * "
9:50 *F* him not: for he that is not "
18:16 and *f* them not: for of such is the "
20:16 heard it, they said, God *f*. 3361, 1096
Ac 10:47 Can any man *f* water, that these 2967
24:23 and that he should *f* none of his "
Ro 3: 4 God *f*: let God be true, but 3361, 1096
6 God *f*: for then how shall God " "
31 God *f*: yea, we establish the " "
6: 2 God *f*. How shall we, that are" "
15 law, but under grace? God *f*. " "
7: 7 Is the law sin? God *f*. Nay, I " "
13 made death unto me? God *f*. " "
9:14 unrighteousness...God? God *f*." "
11: 1 cast away his people? God *f*. " "
11 that they should fall? God *f*. " "
1Co 6:15 members of an harlot? God *f*. " "
14:39 and *f* not to speak with tongues. 2967

Ga 2:17 the ministers of sin? God *f*. 3361, 1096
3:21 the promises of God? God *f*: " "
6:14 God *f* that I should glory, * " "

forbidden
Le 5:17 things which are *f* to be done by *3808
De 4:23 the Lord thy God hath *f* thee. 6680
Ac 16: 6 *f* of the Holy Ghost to preach 2967

forbiddeth
3Jo 10 *f* them that would, and casteth 2967

forbidding
Lu 23: 2 *f* to give tribute to Cæsar, saying 2967
Ac 28:31 all confidence, no man *f* him. 209
1Th 2:16 *F* us to speak to the Gentiles 2967
1Ti 4: 3 *F* to marry, and commanding to "

forbore See FORBARE.

forborn
Jer 51:30 men of Babylon have *f* to fight, 2308

forborne See FORBORN.

force See also FORCED; FORCES; FORCIBLE; FORCING.
Ge 31:31 wouldest take by *f* thy daughters 1497
De 22:25 the man *f* her, and lie with her: 2388
34: 7 not dim, nor his natural *f* abated. 3893
1Sa 2:16 and if not, I will take it by *f*. 2394
2Sa 13:12 Nay, my brother, do not *f* me; 6031
Ezr 4:23 them to cease by *f* and power. 153
Es 7: 8 he *f* the queen also before me 3533
Job 30:18 By the great *f* of my disease 3581
40:16 and his *f* is in the navel of his 202
Jer 18:21 their blood by the *f* of the sword *3027
23:10 is evil, and their *f* is not right. 1369
48:45 of Heshbon because of the *f*: *3581
Eze 34: 4 but with *f* and with cruelty have 2394
35: 5 by the *f* of the sword in the time *3027
Am 2:14 strong shall not strengthen his *f*, 3581
M't 11:12 and the violent take it by *f*. 726
Joh 6:15 take him by *f*, to make him a king "
Ac 23:10 to take him by *f* from among them, "
Heb 9:17 a testament is of *f* after men are 949

forced
J'g 1:34 Amorites *f* the children of Dan 3905
20: 5 have they *f*, that she is dead. 6031
1Sa 13:12 I *f* myself therefore, and offered a 662
2Sa 13:14 than she, *f* her, and lay with her. 6031
22 because he had *f* his sister "
32 from the day that he *f* his sister "
Pr 7:21 the flattering of her lips she *f* him. 5080

forces
2Ch 17: 2 he placed *f* in all the fenced cities 2428
Job 36:19 nor all the *f* of strength. 3981
Isa 60: 5 the *f* of the Gentiles shall come *2428
11 unto thee the *f* of the Gentiles, * "
Jer 40: 7 when all the captains of the *f* which "
13 and all the captains of the *f* that "
41:11, 13, 16 the *f* that were with him, "
42: 1 Then all the captains of the *f*, and "
8 the *f* which were with him, and all "
43: 4 captains of the *f*, and all the people, "
5 all the captains of the *f*, took all "
Da 11:10 assemble a multitude of great *f*: "
38 shall he honour the God of *f*: *4581
Ob 11 carried away captive his *f*, and *2428

forcible
Job 6:25 How *f* are right words! but what 4834

forcing
De 20:19 destroy the trees thereof by *f* an *5080
Pr 30:33 *f* of wrath bringeth forth strife. 4330

ford See also FORDS.
Ge 32:22 and passed over the *f* Jabbok. 4569

fords
Jos 2: 7 the way to Jordan unto the *f*: 4569
J'g 3:28 the *f* of Jordan toward Moab, "
Isa 16: 2 Moab shall be at the *f* of Arnon. "

fore See AFORE; BEFORE; FORECAST; FOREFATHERS; FOREFRONT; FOREHEAD; FOREKNOW; FOREKNOWLEDGE; FOREMEN; FOREMOST; FOREPART; FOREORDAINED; FORERUNNER; FORESAW; FORESEETH; FORESEEING; FORESHIP; FORESKIN; FORETELL; FORWARD; FOREWARN; HERETOFORE; THERETOFORE; WHEREFORE.

forecast
Da 11:24 *f* his devices against the strong *2803
25 they shall *f* devices against him.* "

forefathers
Jer 11:10 back to the iniquities of their *f*, 1, 7223
2Ti 1: 3 whom I serve from my *f* with pure 4269

forefront
Ex 26: 9 in the *f* of the tabernacle. 4136, 6440
28:37 upon the *f* of the mitre it shall " "
Le 8: 9 upon his *f*, did he put the * " "
1Sa 14: 5 The *f* of the one was situate *8127
2Sa 11:15 in the *f* of the hottest battle, 4136, 6440
2Ki 16:14 the *f* of the house, from between "
2Ch 20:27 Jehoshaphat in the *f* of them, 7218
Eze 40:19 from the *f* of the lower gate unto 6440
19 the *f* of the inner court without "
47: 1 *f* of the house stood toward the "

forehead See also FOREHEADS.
Ex 28:38 And it shall be upon Aaron's *f*, 4696
38 and it shall be always upon his *f*, "
Le 13:41 he is *f* bald: yet is he clean. 1371
42 or bald *f*, a white reddish sore; 1372
42 in his bald head, or his bald *f*, "
43 or in his bald *f*, as the leprosy "
1Sa 17:49 and smote the Philistine in his *f*, 4696
49 that the stone sunk into his *f*; "
2Ch 26:19 the leprosy even rose up in his *f* "
20 behold, he was leprous in his *f*, "
Jer 3: 3 and thou hadst a whore's *f*, "

Eze 3: 8 *f* strong against their foreheads. 4696
9 harder than flint have I made thy *f*. "
16:12 And I put a jewel on thy *f*, * 639
Re 14: 9 and receive his mark in his *f*, 3359
17: 5 upon her *f* was a name written, "

foreheads
Eze 3: 8 forehead strong against their *f*. 4696
9: 4 set a mark upon the *f* of the men "
Re 7: 3 servants of our God in their *f*. 3359
9: 4 have not the seal of God in their *f*. "
13:16 in their right hand, or in their *f*: "
14: 1 Father's name written in their *f*. "
20: 4 received his mark upon their *f*, "
22: 4 and his name shall be in their *f*. "

foreigner See also FOREIGNERS.
Ex 12:45 A *f* and an hired servant shall *8453
De 15: 3 Of a *f* thou mayest exact it again: 5237

foreigners
Ob 11 and *f* entered into his gates, and 5237
Eph 2:19 ye are no more strangers and *f*, *3941

foreknew
Ro 11: 2 cast away his people which he *f*. 4267

foreknow See also FOREKNEW.
Ro 8:29 For whom he did *f*, he also did *4267

foreknowledge
Ac 2:23 and *f* of God, ye have taken, and 4268
1Pe 1: 2 Elect according to the *f* of God "

foremost
Ge 32:17 And he commanded the *f*, saying, 7223
33: 2 handmaids and their children *f*, "
2Sa 18:27 the running of the *f* is like the "

foreordained
1Pe 1:20 Who verily was *f* before the *4267

forepart
Ex 28:27 toward the *f* thereof, over against 6440
39:20 ephod underneath, toward the *f* "
1Ki 6:20 oracle in the *f* was twenty cubits * "
Eze 42: 7 court on the *f* of the chambers. * "
Ac 27:41 the *f* stuck fast, and remained *4408

forerunner
Heb 6:20 Whither the *f* is for us entered, 4274

foresaw
Ac 2:25 I *f* the Lord always before my *4308

foreseeing
Ga 3: 8 the scripture, *f* that God would 4275

foreseeth
Pr 22: 3 A prudent man *f* the evil, and *7200
27:12 A prudent man *f* the evil, and * "

foreship
Ac 27:30 have cast anchors out of the *f*. 4408

foreskin See also FORESKINS.
Ge 17:11 circumcise the flesh of your *f*; 6190
14 flesh of his *f* is not circumcised, "
23 circumcised the flesh of their *f*, "
24, 25 circumcised in the flesh of his *f*. "
Ex 4:25 stone, and cut off the *f* of her son, "
Le 12: 3 flesh of his *f* shall be circumcised, "
De 10:16 Circumcise therefore the *f* of your "
Hab 2:16 and let thy *f* be uncovered: *6188

foreskins
Jos 5: 3 of Israel at the hill of the *f*. 6190
1Sa 18:25 an hundred *f* of the Philistines, "
27 David brought their *f*, and they "
2Sa 3:14 an hundred *f* of the Philistines. "
Jer 4: 4 and take away the *f* of your heart, "

forest See also FORESTS.
1Sa 22: 5 and came into the *f* of Hareth. 3293
1Ki 7: 2 also the house of the *f* of Lebanon; "
10:17 in the house of the *f* of Lebanon. "
21 of the house of the *f* of Lebanon "
2Ki 19:23 and into the *f* of his Carmel. "
2Ch 9:16 in the house of the *f* of Lebanon "
20 of the house of the *f* of Lebanon "
Ne 2: 8 Asaph the keeper of the king's *f*, 6508
Ps 50:10 For every beast of the *f* is mine, 3293
104:20 all the beasts of the *f* do creep "
Isa 9:18 kindle in the thickets of the *f*, "
10:18 shall consume the glory of his *f*, "
19 And the trees of his *f* shall be few, "
34 shall cut down the thickets of the *f* "
21:13 In the *f* in Arabia shall ye lodge, "
22: 8 the armour of the house of the *f*. "
29:17 field shall be esteemed as a *f*? "
32:15 fruitful field be counted for a *f* "
19 shall hail, coming down on the *f*; "
37:24 border, and the *f* of his Carmel. "
44:14 himself among the trees of the *f*: "
23 O *f*, and every tree therein: "
56: 9 yea, all ye beasts in the *f*. "
Jer 5: 6 a lion out of the *f* shall slay them, "
10: 3 one cutteth a tree out of the *f*, "
12: 8 is unto me as a lion in the *f*; "
21:14 I will kindle a fire in the *f* thereof, "
26:18 the house as the high places of a *f*. "
46:23 They shall cut down her *f*, saith "
Eze 15: 2 which is among the trees of the *f*? "
6 vine tree among the trees of the *f*, "
20:46 prophesy against the *f* of the south "
47 And say to the *f* of the south, "
Ho 2:12 and I will make them a *f*, "
Am 3: 4 Will a lion roar in the *f*, when he "
Mic 3:12 the house as the high places of the *f*. "
5: 8 as a lion among the beasts of the *f*, "
Zec 11: 2 the *f* of the vintage is come down. "

forests
2Ch 27: 4 and in the *f* he built castles and 2793
Ps 29: 9 to calve, and discovereth the *f*: 3295
Eze 39:10 neither cut down any out of the *f*; 3293

foretell See also FORETOLD.
2Co 13: 2 and *f* you, as if I were present, *4302

foretold
M'r 13:23 behold, I have *f* you all things. *4280
Ac 3:24 have likewise *f* of these days. *4293

forever See EVER.

forewarn See also FORWARNED.
Lu 12: 5 I will *f* you whom ye shall fear: *5263

forewarned
1Th 4: 6 all such as we also have *f* you and 4277

forfeited
Ezr 10: 8 all his substance should be *f*, and 2763

forgat See also FORGOT.
Ge 40:23 remember Joseph, but *f* him. 7911
J'g 3: 7 and *f* the Lord their God, and "
1Sa 12: 9 when they *f* the Lord their God, "
Ps 78:11 And *f* his works, and his wonders "
106:13 They soon *f* his works; they "
21 They *f* God their saviour, which "
La 3:17 far off from peace: I *f* prosperity. 5382
Ho 2:13 went after her lovers, and *f* me, 7911

forgave See also FORGAVEST.
Ps 78:38 *f* their iniquity, and destroyed 3722
M't 18:27 loosed him, and *f* him the debt. 863
32 I *f* thee all that debt, because thou "
Lu 7:42 to pay, he frankly *f* them both. 5483
43 that he, to whom he *f* most. "
2Co 2:10 if I *f* any thing, to whom I *f* it, * "
10 for your sakes *f* I it in the person * "
Col 3:13 even as Christ *f* you, so also do ye. "

forgavest
Ps 32: 5 and thou *f* the iniquity of my sin. 5375
99: 8 thou wast a God that *f* them, "

forged
Ps 119:69 the proud have *f* a lie against me: 2950

forgers
Job 13: 4 But ye are *f* of lies, ye are all 2950

forget See also FORGAT; FORGETFUL; FORGETTEST; FORGETTETH; FORGETTING; FORGOT; FORGOTTEN.
Ge 27:45 and he *f* that which thou hast 7911
41:51 hath made me *f* all my toil, 5382
De 4: 9 lest thou *f* the things which thine 7911
23 lest ye *f* the covenant of the Lord "
31 nor *f* the covenant of thy fathers "
6:12 Then beware lest thou *f* the Lord, "
8:11 Beware that thou *f* not the Lord "
14 and thou *f* the Lord thy God, "
19 if thou do at all *f* the Lord thy God, "
9: 7 Remember, and *f* not, how thou "
25:19 under heaven; thou shalt not *f* it. "
1Sa 1:11 and not *f* thine handmaid, but "
2Ki 17:38 have made with you ye shall not *f*; "
Job 8:13 So are the paths of all that *f* God; "
9:27 If I say, I will *f* my complaint, "
11:16 Because thou shalt *f* thy misery, "
24:20 The womb shall *f* him; the worm "
Ps 9:17 and all the nations that *f* God. 7913
10:12 thine hand: *f* not the humble. 7911
13: 1 How long wilt thou *f* me, O Lord? "
45:10 *f* also thine own people, and thy "
50:22 ye that *f* God, lest I tear you in "
59:11 slay them not, lest my people *f*: "
74:19 *f* not the congregation of thy poor "
23 *F* not the voice of thine enemies: "
78: 7 and not *f* the works of God, "
102: 4 so that I *f* to eat my bread. "
103: 2 my soul, and *f* not all his benefits: "
119:16 thy statutes: I will not *f* thy word. "
83 yet do I not *f* thy statutes. "
93 I will never *f* thy precepts: for "
109 in my hand: yet do I not *f* thy law. "
141 yet do not I *f* thy precepts. "
153 deliver me: for I do not *f* thy law. "
176 I do not *f* thy commandments. "
137: 5 If I *f* thee, O Jerusalem, "
5 let my right hand *f* her cunning. "
Pr 3: 1 My son, *f* not my law; but let thine "
4: 5 get understanding: *f* it not; "
31: 5 Lest they drink, and *f* the law, "
7 Let him drink, and *f* his poverty, "
Isa 49:15 Can a woman *f* her sucking child, "
15 son of her womb? yea, they may *f*, "
15 yet will I not *f* thee. "
54: 4 shalt *f* the shame of thy youth, "
65:11 forsake the Lord, that *f* my holy 7913
Jer 2:32 Can a maid *f* her ornaments, 7911
23:27 to cause my people to *f* my name "
39 I, even I, will utterly *f* you, 5382
La 5:20 Wherefore dost thou *f* us for ever, 7911
Ho 4: 6 thy God, I will also *f* thy children. "
Am 8: 7 I will never *f* any of their works. "
Heb 6:10 to *f* your work and labour of love, 1950
13:16 do good and to communicate *f* not: "

forgetful
He 13: 2 Be not *f* to entertain strangers: *1950
Jas 1:25 being not a *f* hearer, but a doer *1953

forgetfulness
Ps 88:12 righteousness in the land of *f*? 5388

forgettest
Ps 44:24 and *f* our affliction and our 7911
Isa 51:13 And *f* the Lord thy maker, that * "

forgetteth
Job 39:15 And *f* that the foot may crush 7911
Ps 9:12 he *f* not the cry of the humble. "
Pr 2:17 and *f* the covenant of her God. 7913
Jas 1:24 *f* what manner of man he was. 1950

forgetting
Ph'p 3:13 *f* those things which are behind, 1950

forgive See also FORGAVE; FORGIVEN; FORGIVETH; FORGIVING.
Ge 50:17 *F*, I pray thee now the trespass, 5375
17 *f* the trespass of the servants of the "
Ex 10:17 Now therefore *f*, I pray thee, my "
32:32 Yet now, if thou wilt *f* their sin—; "
Nu 30: 5 the Lord shall *f* her, because her 5545
8 effect: and the Lord shall *f* her. "
12 void; and the Lord shall *f* her, "
Jos 24:19 he will not *f* your transgressions 5375
1Sa 25:28 I pray thee, *f* the trespass of thine "
1Ki 8:30 and when thou hearest, *f*. 5545
34 and *f* the sin of thy people Israel, "
36 and *f* the sin of thy servants, "
39 heaven thy dwelling place, and *f*, "
50 And *f* thy people that have sinned "
2Ch 6:21 heaven; and when thou hearest, *f*. "
25 hear thou from the heavens, and *f* "
27 hear thou from heaven, and *f* "
30 heaven, thy dwelling place, and *f*, "
39 and *f* thy people which have "
7:14 and will *f* their sin, and will heal "
Ps 25:18 my pain; and *f* all my sins. 5375
86: 5 Lord, art good and ready to *f*; 5546
Isa 2: 9 himself: therefore *f* them not. 5375
Jer 18:23 *f* not their iniquity, neither blot 3722
31:34 I will *f* their iniquity, and I will 5545
36: 3 that I may *f* their iniquity and "
Da 9:19 O Lord, hear; O Lord, *f*; "
Am 7: 2 O Lord God, *f*, I beseech thee: "
M't 6:12 *f* us our debts, as we *f* our * 863
14 For if ye *f* men their trespasses, "
14 your heavenly Father will also *f* "
15 if ye *f* not men their trespasses, "
15 will your Father *f* your trespasses. "
9: 6 hath power on earth to *f* sins, "
18:21 my brother sin against me and I *f* "
35 *f* not every one his brother their "
M'r 2: 7 who can *f* sins but God only? "
10 man hath power on earth to *f* sins, "
11:25 *f*, if ye have ought against any: "
25 may *f* you your trespasses. "
26 if ye do not *f*, neither will your * "
26 in heaven *f* your trespasses. * "
Lu 5:21 Who can *f* sins, but God alone? "
24 hath power upon earth to *f* sins, "
6:37 *f*, and ye shall be forgiven: * 630
11: 4 *f* us our sins; for we also *f* every 863
17: 3 and if he repent, *f* him. "
4 saying, I repent; thou shalt *f* him. "
23:34 Then said Jesus, Father, *f* them; "
2Co 2: 7 ought rather to *f* him, and comfort 5483
10 To whom ye *f* any thing, I *f* also: "
12:13 to you? *f* me this wrong. "
1Jo 1: 9 faithful and just to *f* us our sins, 863

forgiven
Le 4:20 for them, and it shall be *f* them. 5545
26 concerning his sin, and it shall be *f* "
31 for him, and it shall be *f* him. "
35 committed, and it shall be *f* him. "
5:10 hath sinned, and it shall be *f* him. "
13 of these, and it shall be *f* him: "
16 offering, and it shall be *f* him. "
18 it not, and it shall be forgiven him. "
6: 7 shall be *f* him for any thing of all "
19:22 which he hath done shall be *f* him. "
Nu 14:19 and as thou hast *f* this people, 5375
15:25 and it shall be *f* them; for it is 5545
26 it shall be *f* all the congregation "
28 for him; and it shall be *f* him. "
De 21: 8 And the blood shall be *f* them. 3722
Ps 32: 1 is he whose transgression is *f*, 5375
85: 2 Thou hast *f* the iniquity of thy "
Isa 33:24 that dwell therein shall be *f* their "
M't 9: 2 be of good cheer; thy sins be *f* 863
5 to say, Thy sins be *f* thee; "
12:31 and blasphemy shall be *f* unto "
31 the Holy Ghost shall not be *f* unto "
32 the Son of man, it shall be *f* him: "
32 Holy Ghost, it shall not be *f* him, "
M'r 2: 5 the palsy, Son, thy sins be *f* thee. "
9 Thy sins be *f* thee; or to say, Arise, "
3:28 All sins shall be *f* unto the sons of "
4:12 and their sins should be *f* them. "
Lu 5:20 unto him, Man, thy sins are *f* thee. "
23 Thy sins be *f* thee; or to say, Rise "
6:37 forgive, and ye shall be *f*: * 630
7:47 Her sins, which are many, are *f*; 863
47 to whom little is *f*, the same loveth "
48 he said unto her, Thy sins are *f*. "
12:10 the Son of man, it shall be *f* him; "
10 the Holy Ghost it shall not be *f*. "
Ac 8:22 thought of thine heart may be *f* thee. "
Ro 4: 7 are they whose iniquities are *f*, "
Eph 4:32 God for Christ's sake hath *f* you. *5483
Col 2:13 him, having *f* you all trespasses; "
Jas 5:15 sins, they shall be *f* him. 863
1Jo 2:12 because your sins are *f* you for "

forgiveness See also FORGIVENESSES.
Ps 130: 4 But there is *f* with thee, that thou 5547
M'r 3:29 the Holy Ghost hath never *f*, 859
Ac 5:31 repentance to Israel, and *f* of * "
13:38 preached unto you the *f* of sins: * "
26:18 that they may receive *f* of sins, "
Eph 1: 7 the *f* of sins, according to the "
Col 1:14 through his blood, even the *f* of sins: "

forgivenesses
Da 9: 9 to . . . God belong mercies and *f*, 5547

forgiveth
Ps 103: 3 Who *f* all thine iniquities; who 5545
Lu 7:49 Who is this that *f* sins also? 863

forgiving
Ex 34: 7 for thousands, *f* iniquity and 5375
Nu 14:18 of great mercy, *f* iniquity and "
Eph 4:32 *f* one another, even as God for 5483
Col 3:13 and *f* one another, if any man "

forgot See also FORGAT; FORGOTTEN.
De 24:19 and hast *f* a sheaf in the field, 7911

forgotten
Ge 41:30 and all the plenty shall be *f* in 7911
De 26:13 neither have I *f* them; "
31:21 for it shall not be *f* out of the "
32:18 and hast *f* God that formed thee. "
Job 19:14 and my familiar friends have *f* me. "
28: 4 even the waters *f* of the foot: "
Ps 9:18 the needy shall not always be *f*: "
10:11 hath said in his heart, God hath *f*: "
31:12 I am *f* as a dead man out of "
42: 9 Why hast thou *f* me? why go I "
44:17 yet have we not *f* thee, neither "
20 If we have *f* the name of our God, "
77: 9 Hath God *f* to be gracious? hath "
119:61 but I have not *f* thy law. "
139 because mine enemies have *f* thy "
Ec 2:16 in the days to come shall all be *f*. "
8:10 and they were *f* in the city where "
9: 5 for the memory of them is *f*. "
Isa 17:10 Because thou hast *f* the God of thy "
23:15 that Tyre shall be *f* seventy years, "
16 thou harlot that hast been *f*; "
44:21 Israel, thou shalt not be *f* of me. 5382
49:14 and my Lord hath *f* me. 7913
65:16 because the former troubles are *f*, 7911
Jer 2:32 yet my people have *f* me days "
3:21 they have *f* the Lord their God. "
13:25 because thou hast *f* me, and "
18:15 my people hath *f* me, they have "
20:11 their...confusion shall never be *f*. "
23:27 their fathers have *f* my name * "
40 shame, which shall not be *f*. "
30:14 All thy lovers have *f* thee; "
44: 9 *f* the wickedness of your fathers, "
50: 5 covenant that shall not be *f*. "
6 they have *f* their restingplace. "
La 2: 6 solemn feasts and sabbaths to be *f* "
Eze 22:12 and hast *f* me, saith the Lord God. "
23:35 Because thou hast *f* me, and cast "
Ho 4: 6 thou hast *f* the law of thy God, "
8:14 For Israel hath *f* his Maker, "
13: 6 therefore have they *f* me. "
M't 16: 5 side, they had *f* to take bread. *1950
M'r 8:14 disciples had *f* to take bread, * "
Lu 12: 6 not one of them is *f* before God? "
Heb 12: 5 And ye have *f* the exhortation 1585
2Pe 1: 9 hath *f* that he was purged 3024, 2983

forks
1Sa 13:21 the coulters, and for the *f*, 7969, 7053

form See also FORMED; FORMETH; FORMS; INFORM; PERFORM; REFORM; TRANSFORM.
Ge 1: 2 And the earth was without *f*, *8414
1Sa 28:14 said unto her, What *f* is he of? 8389
2Sa 14:20 To fetch about this *f* of speech *6440
2Ch 4: 7 of gold according to their *f*, and *4941
Job 4:16 I could not discern the *f* thereof: *4758
Isa 45: 7 I *f* the light, and create darkness: 3335
52:14 his *f* more than the sons of men: 8389
53: 2 he hath no *f* nor comeliness; "
Jer 4:23 earth, and, lo, it was without *f*, *8414
Eze 8: 3 he put forth the *f* of an hand, 8403
10 behold every *f* of creeping things, "
10: 8 the *f* of a man's hand under their "
43:11 shew them the *f* of the house, 6699
11 may keep the whole *f* thereof, "
Da 2:31 and the *f* thereof was terrible. *7299
3:19 the *f* of his visage was changed 6755
25 *f* of the fourth is like the Son of *7299
M'r 16:12 he appeared in another *f* unto 3444
Ro 2:20 which hast the *f* of knowledge 3446
6:17 that *f* of doctrine which was 5179
Ph'p 2: 6 Who, being in the *f* of God, 3444
7 took upon him the *f* of a servant, "
2Ti 1:13 Hold fast the *f* of sound words, *5296
3: 5 Having a *f* of godliness, but 3446

formed See also CONFORMED; DEFORMED; REFORMED; TRANSFORMED.
Ge 2: 7 And the Lord God *f* man of the 3335
8 he put the man whom he had *f*. "
19 the ground the Lord *f* every beast "
De 32:18 hast forgotten God that *f* thee. *2342
2Ki 19:25 of ancient times that I have *f* it? 3335
Job 26: 5 Dead things are *f* from under *2342
13 hand hath *f* the crooked serpent. * "
33: 6 I also am *f* out of the clay. 7169
Ps 90: 2 or ever thou hadst *f* the earth 2342
94: 9 that *f* the eye, shall he not see? 3335
95: 5 and his hands *f* the dry land. "
Pr 26:10 The great God that *f* all things *2342
Isa 27:11 he that *f* them will shew them 3335
37:26 of ancient times, that I have *f* it? "
43: 1 and he that *f* thee, O Israel, "
7 I have *f* him; yea, I have made "
10 before me there was no God *f*, "
21 This people have I *f* for myself; "
44: 2 and *f* thee from the womb, "
10 Who hath *f* a god, or molten a * "
21 have *f* thee; thou art my servant: "
24 and he that *f* thee from the womb, "
45:18 God himself that *f* the earth and "
18 he *f* it to be inhabited: I am the "
49: 5 the Lord that *f* me from the womb "
54:17 No weapon that is *f* against thee "
Jer 1: 5 Before I *f* thee in the belly "
33: 2 the Lord that *f* it, to establish it; "
Am 7: 1 *f* grasshoppers in the beginning "
Ro 9:20 the thing *f* say to him that *f* it, 4110
Gal 4:19 until Christ be *f* in you, 3445
1Ti 2:13 Adam was first *f*, then Eve. 4111

former
Ge 40:13 after the f manner when thou 7223
Nu 21:26 fought against the f king of Moab, "
De 24: 4 Her f husband, which sent her "
Ru 4: 7 this was the manner in f time 6440
1Sa 17:30 answered him again after the f 7223
2Ki 1:14 two captains of the f fifties with "
17:34 they do after the f manners: "
40 but they did after their f manner. "
Ne 5:15 the f governors that had been "
Job 8: 8 enquire, I pray thee, of the f age, "
30: 3 in f time desolate and waste. * 570
Ps 79: 8 not against us f iniquities: *7223
89:49 where are thy f lovingkindnesses, "
Ec 1:11 is no remembrance of f things; "
7:10 the f days were better than these? "
Isa 41:22 let them shew the f things, what "
42: 9 the f things are come to pass, "
43: 9 declare this, and shew us f things? "
18 Remember ye not the f things, "
46: 9 Remember the f things of old: "
48: 3 I have declared the f things from "
61: 4 shall raise up the f desolations, "
65: 7 will I measure their f work into * "
16 the f troubles are forgotten, "
17 and the f shall not be remembered, "
Jer 5:24 rain, both the f and the latter, 3138
10:16 for he is the f of all things: 3335
34: 5 f kings which were before thee, 7223
36:28 f words that were in the first roll, "
51:19 for he is the f of all things: 3335
Eze 16:55 shall return to their f estate, and 6927
55 shall return to their f estate, then "
55 shall return to your f estate. "
Da 11:13 a multitude greater than the f, 7223
29 but it shall not be as the f, "
Hos 6: 3 latter and f rain unto the earth. *3138
Joe 2:23 given you the f rain moderately, 4175
23 the f rain, and the latter rain "
Hag 2: 9 shall be greater than of the f, 7223
Zec 1: 4 unto whom the f prophets have "
7: 7 Lord hath cried by the f prophets, "
12 sent in his spirit by the f prophets: "
8:11 of this people as in the f days, "
14: 8 half of them toward the f sea, *6931
Mal 3: 4 the days of old, and as in f years. * "
Ac 1: 1 The f treatise have I made, O 4413
Eph 4:22 concerning the f conversation 4387
Heb 10:32 call to remembrance the f days, 4386
1Pe 1:14 according to the f lusts in your "
Re 21: 4 for the f things are passed away.*4413

formeth See also PERFORMETH.
Am 4:13 For, lo, he that f the mountains, 3335
Zec 12: 1 and f the spirit of man within him. "

forming See PERFORMING; TRANSFORMING.

forms
Eze 43:11 f thereof, and all the ordinances 6699
11 all the f thereof, and all the laws "

fornication See also FORNICATIONS.
2Ch 21:11 of Jerusalem to commit f, and *2181
Isa 23:17 and shall commit f with all the * "
Eze 16:26 Thou hast also committed f with "
29 hast moreover multiplied thy f *8457
M't 5:32 his wife, saving for the cause of f, 4202
19: 9 away his wife, except it be for f, "
Joh 8:41 We be not born of f; we have one "
Ac 15:20 from f, and from things strangled "
29 from things strangled, and from f: "
21:25 and from strangled, and from f. "
Ro 1:29 f, wickedness, covetousness, * "
1Co 5: 1 that there is f among you, and "
1 such f as is not so much as "
6:13 Now the body is not for f, "
18 Flee f. Every sin that a man doeth "
18 but he that committeth f sinneth 4203
7: 2 to avoid f, let every man have *4202
10: 8 Neither let us commit f, as some 4203
2Co 12:21 and f and lasciviousness which 4202
Ga 5:19 Adultery, f, uncleanness, "
Eph 5: 3 But f, and all uncleanness, or "
Col 3: 5 f, uncleanness, inordinate "
1Th 4: 3 that ye should abstain from f: "
Jude 7 giving themselves over to f, 1608
Re 2:14 unto idols, and to commit f. 4203
20 to commit f, and to eat things "
21 gave her space to repent of her f; 4202
9:21 nor of their f, nor of their thefts. "
14: 8 the wine of the wrath of her f. "
17: 2 of the earth have committed f 4203
2 drunk with the wine of her f. 4202
4 and filthiness of her f: "
18: 3 of the wine of the wrath of her f, "
3 have committed f with her, and 4203
9 who have committed f and lived "
19: 2 did corrupt the earth with her f, 4202

fornications
Eze 16:15 pouredst out thy f on every one *8457
M't 15:19 thoughts, murders, adulteries, f, 4202
M'r 7:21 evil thoughts, adulteries, f, "

fornicator See also FORNICATORS.
1Co 5:11 Man that is called a brother be a f, 4205
Heb 12:16 Lest there be any f, or profane "

fornicators
1Co 5: 9 an epistle not to company with f: 4205
10 altogether with the f of this world. "
6: 9 neither f, nor idolaters, nor "

forsake See FORSAKEN; FORSAKETH; FORSAKING; FORSOOK.
De 4:31 he will not f thee, neither destroy*7503
12:19 heed to thyself that thou f not 5800
14:27 thou shalt not f him; for he hath "
31: 6 he will not fail thee, nor f thee. "
8 will not fail thee, neither f thee: "
31:16 will f me, and break my covenant 5800
17 and I will f them, and I will hide "
Jos 1: 5 I will not fail thee, nor f thee. "
24:16 forbid that we should f the Lord, "
20 If ye f the Lord, and serve strange "
J'g 9:11 Should I f my sweetness, and my *2308
1Sa 12:22 the Lord will not f his people for 5203
1Ki 6:13 and will not f my people Israel. 5800
8:57 let him not leave us, nor f us: 5203
2Ki 21:14 And I will f the remnant of mine* "
1Ch 28: 9 if thou f him, he will cast thee off 5800
20 he will not fail thee, nor f thee. "
2Ch 7:19 if ye turn away, and f my statutes "
15: 2 but if ye f him, he will f you. "
Ezr 8:22 is against all them that f him. "
Ne 9:31 utterly consume them, nor f them; "
10:39 we will not f the house of our "
Job 20:13 Though he spare it, and f it not; * "
Ps 27: 9 leave me not, neither f me, O God "
10 my father and my mother f me, * "
37: 8 Cease from anger, and f wrath: "
38:21 F me not, O Lord: O my God, "
71: 9 f me not when my strength faileth. "
18 O God, f me not; until I have "
89:30 If his children f my law, and walk "
94:14 neither will he f his inheritance. "
119: 8 will keep thy statutes: O f me not "
53 of the wicked that f thy law. "
138: 8 f not the works of thine own 7503
Pr 1: 8 and f not the law of thy mother: 5203
3: 3 Let not mercy and truth f thee: 5800
4: 2 good doctrine, f ye not my law. "
6 F her not, and she shall preserve "
6:20 and f not the law of thy mother: 5203
9: 6 F the foolish, and live; and go *5800
27:10 and thy father's friend, f not; "
28: 4 that f the law praise the wicked: "
Isa 1:28 that f the Lord shall be consumed. "
41:17 the God of Israel will not f them. "
42:16 I do unto them, and not f them. "
55: 7 Let the wicked f his way, and the "
65:11 But ye are they that f the Lord, "
Jer 17:13 all that f thee shall be ashamed, "
23:33 I will even f you, saith the Lord.*5203
39 and I will f you, and the city * "
51: 9 but she is not healed: f her, 5800
La 5:20 thou forget us for ever, and f us "
Eze 20: 8 did they f the idols of Egypt: "
Da 11:30 them that f the holy covenant. "
Jon 2: 8 lying vanities f their own mercy. "
Ac 21:21 among the Gentiles to f Moses, 646, 575
Heb 13: 5 I will never leave thee, nor f thee. 1459

forsaken
De 28:20 doings, whereby thou hast f me. 5800
29:25 they have f the covenant of the * "
J'g 6:13 but now the Lord hath f us, *5203
10:10 have f our God, and also served 5800
13 have f me, and served other gods: "
1Sa 8: 8 have f me, and served other gods, "
12:10 have f the Lord, and have served "
1Ki 11:33 have f me, and have worshipped "
18:18 f the commandments of the Lord, "
19:10, 14 of Israel have f thy covenant, "
2Ki 22:17 Because they have f me, and have "
2Ch 12: 5 Thus saith the Lord, Ye have f me, "
13:10 our God, and we have not f him; "
11 Lord our God, but ye have f him. "
21:10 had f the Lord God of his fathers. "
24:20 have f the Lord, he hath also f you. "
24 hand, because they had f the Lord "
28: 6 men; because they had f the Lord "
29: 6 have f him, and have turned away "
34:25 f me, and have burned incense "
Ezr 9: 9 yet our God hath not f us "
10 for we have f thy commandments, "
Ne 13:11 Why is the house of God f? "
Job 18: 4 shall the earth be f for thee? "
20:19 oppressed and hath f the poor; "
Ps 9:10 hast not f them that seek thee. "
22: 1 my God, why hast thou f me? "
37:25 have I not seen the righteous f, "
71:11 God hath f him: persecute and "
Isa 1: 4 they have f the Lord, they have "
2: 6 thou hast f thy people the house 5203
7:16 that thou abhorrest shall be f of 5800
17: 2 The cities of Aroer are f: they "
9 his strong cities be as a f bough, "
27:10 the habitation f, and left like a 7971
32:14 palaces shall be f; the multitude 5203
49:14 Zion said, The Lord hath f me, 5800
54: 6 hath called thee as a woman f and "
7 For a small moment have I f thee; "
60:15 thou hast been f and hated, "
62: 4 Thou shalt no more be termed F; "
12 called, Sought out, A city not f. "
Jer 1:16 who have f me, and have burned "
2:13 have f me the fountain of living "
17 in that thou hast f the Lord thy "
19 that thou hast f the Lord thy God, "
4:29 every city shall be f, and not a man "
5: 7 thy children have f me, and sworn "
19 Like as ye have f me, and served "
7:29 and f the generation of his wrath.5203
9:13 they have f my law which I set 5800
19 we have f the land, because our "
12: 7 I have f mine house, I have left "
15: 6 Thou hast f me, saith the Lord, *5203
16:11 fathers have f me, saith the Lord, 5800
11 and have f me, and have not kept "
17:13 they have f the Lord, the fountain "
18:14 come from another place be f? *5428
19: 4 have f me, and have estranged 5800
22: 9 have f the covenant of the Lord * "
25:38 He hath f his covert, as the lion; "
51: 5 Israel hath not been f, nor Judah 488
Eze 8:12 not; the Lord hath f the earth. 5800
Eze 9: 9 say, The Lord hath f the earth. 5800
36: 4 the cities that are f, which became "
Am 5: 2 she is f upon her land; there is *5203
Zep 2: 4 Gaza shall be f, and Ashkelon 5800
M't 19:27 we have f all, and followed thee;* 863
29 every one that hath f houses, * "
27:46 my God, why hast thou f me? 1459
M'r 15:34 God, my God, why hast thou f me? "
2Co 4: 9 Persecuted, but not f; cast down, "
2Ti 4:10 Demas hath f me, having loved * "
2Pe 2:15 Which have f the right way, and *2641

forsaketh
Job 6:14 he f the fear of the Almighty. 5800
Ps 37:28 judgment, and f not his saints; "
Pr 2:17 Which f the guide of her youth, "
15:10 is grievous unto him that f the way; "
28:13 confesseth and f them shall have "
Lu 14:33 of you that f not all that he hath,* 657

forsaking
Isa 6:12 there be a great f in the midst *5805
Heb 10:25 Not f the assembling of ourselves 1459

forsomuch See also FORASMUCH; INASMUCH.
Lu 19: 9 f as he also is a son of Abraham. *2530

forsook See also FORSOOKEST.
De 32:15 then he f God which made him, 5203
J'g 2:12 f the Lord God of their fathers, 5800
13 they f the Lord, and served Baal "
10: 6 f the Lord, and served not him. "
1Sa 31: 7 they f the cities, and fled; and the "
1Ki 9: 9 Because they f the Lord their God, "
12: 8 he f the counsel of the old men, "
13 and f the old men's counsel that "
2Ki 21:22 he f the Lord God of his fathers, "
1Ch 10: 7 then they f their cities, and fled; "
2Ch 7:22 they f the Lord God of their fathers, "
10: 8 he f the counsel which the old men "
13 Rehoboam f the counsel of the old. "
12: 1 he f the law of the Lord, and all "
Ps 78:60 he f the tabernacle of Shiloh, 5203
119:87 earth; but I f not thy precepts. 5800
Isa 58: 2 f not the ordinance of their God; "
Jer 14: 5 also calved in the field, and f it, * "
M't 26:56 all the disciples f him, and fled. * 863
M'r 1:18 they f their nets, and followed "
14:50 And they all f him, and fled. "
Lu 5:11 land, they f all, and followed him.* "
2Ti 4:16 stood with me, but all men f me; 1459
Heb 11:27 By faith he f Egypt, not fearing 2641

forsookest
Ne 9:17 great kindness, and f them not. 5800
19 thy manifold mercies f them not. "

forswear
M't 5:33 Thou shalt not f thyself, but shalt 1964

fort See also FORTS.
2Sa 5: 9 David dwelt in the f, and called *4686
Isa 25:12 fortress of the high f of thy walls 4869
Eze 4: 2 and build a f against it, and cast *1785
21:22 to cast a mount, and to build a f.* "
26: 8 he shall make a f against thee, * "
Da 11:19 shall turn his face toward the f *4581

forth See also FORTHWITH; HENCEFORTH.
Ge 1:11 said, Let the earth bring f grass, 1876
12 And the earth brought f grass, 3318
20 God said, Let the waters bring f 8317
21 the waters brought f abundantly, "
24 earth bring f the living creature 3318
3:16 thou shalt bring f children; and 3205
18 thistles shall it bring f to thee; 6779
22 lest he put f his hand, and take 7971
23 God sent him f from the garden "
8: 7 and he sent f a raven, which went "
7 a raven, which went f to and fro, 3318
8 also he sent f a dove from him, to "
9 put f his hand, and took her, 7971
10 he sent f his dove out of the ark; "
12 sent f the dove; which returned not "
16 Go f of the ark, thou, and thy wife,3318
17 Bring f with thee every living "
18 And Noah went f, and his sons, "
19 their kinds, went f out of the ark. "
9: 7 bring f abundantly in the earth, 8317
18 of Noah, that went f of the ark, 3318
10:11 Out of that land went f Asshur, "
11:31 they went f with them from Ur of "
12: 5 and they went f to go into the land "
14:18 king of Salem brought f bread "
15: 4 come f out of thine own bowels, "
5 he brought him f abroad, and said, "
19:10 But the men put f their hand, 7971
16 they brought him f, and set him 3318
17 when they had brought f abroad, "
22:10 Abraham stretched f his hand, and "
24:43 virgin cometh f to draw water, 3318
45 Rebekah came f with her pitcher "
53 servant brought f jewels of silver, "
30:39 brought f cattle ringstraked, 3209
38:24 And Judah said, Bring her f, and 3318
25 When she was brought f, she sent "
29 said, How hast thou broken f? 6556
39:13 in her hand, and was fled f, 2351
40:10 budded, and her blossoms shot f; "
10 thereof brought f ripe grapes: 1310
41:47 the earth brought f by handfuls. 6213
42:15 Pharaoh ye shall not go f hence, 3318
Ex 3:10 that thou mayest bring f my people "
11 should bring f the children of Israel "
12 thou hast brought f the people "
4: 4 Put f thine hand and take it by 7971
4 he put f his hand and caught it "
14 behold, he cometh f to meet thee: 3318
5:20 as they came f from Pharaoh: "
7: 4 and bring f mine armies, and my "
5 stretch f mine hand upon Egypt, "

Ex 8: 3 shall bring f frogs abundantly, *8317
5 Stretch f thine hand with thy rod over
18 their enchantment to bring f lice, 3318
20 lo, he cometh f to the water; "
9: 9 be a boil breaking f with blains
10 a boil breaking f with blains
22 Stretch f thine hand toward heaven,
23 And Moses stretched f his rod toward
10:13 Moses stretched f his rod over the land
22 Moses stretched f his hand toward
12:31 get you f from among my people, 3318
39 which they brought f out of Egypt, "
46 shalt not carry f ought of the flesh "
13: 8 unto me when I came f out of Egypt. "
16 the Lord brought us f out of Egypt. "
14:11 with us, to carry us f out of Egypt? "
27 stretched f his hand over the sea,
15: 7 sentest f thy wrath, which consumed
13 in thy mercy hast led f the people *
16: 3 brought us f into this wilderness, 3318
32 when I brought you f from the land "
19: 1 Israel were gone f out of the land "
17 Moses brought f the people out of "
22 lest the Lord break f upon them.
24 unto the Lord lest he break f upon
25:20 cherubims shall stretch f their *
29:46 that brought them f out of the land 3318
32:11 which thou hast brought f out of "
Le 4:12 shall he carry f without the camp "
21 carry f the bullock without the "
6:11 carry f the ashes without the camp "
14: 3 priest shall go f out of the camp; "
45 shall carry them f out of the city "
16:24 come f, and offer his burnt offering, "
27 one carry f without the camp; "
22:27 or a sheep, or a goat, is brought f, 3205
24:14 Bring f him that hath cursed 3318
23 should bring f him that cursed "
25:21 shall bring f fruit for three years. 6213
38 brought you f out of the land of 3318
42 which I brought f out of the land "
55 whom I brought f out of the land "
26:10 bring f the old because of the new. "
13 which brought you f out of the land "
45 whom I brought f out of the land "
Nu 1: 3 are able to go f to war in Israel: "
20, 22, 24, 26, 28, 30, 32, 34, 36, 38, 40, 42,
all that were able to go f to war; "
45 were able to go f to war in Israel; "
2: 9 armies. These shall first set f. 5265
16 they shall set f in the second rank. "
11:20 Why came we f out of Egypt? 3318
31 there went f a wind from the Lord, 5265
17: 8 was budded, and brought f buds, 3318
19: 3 may bring her f without the camp, "
20: 8 rock, and it shall give f his water,
8 thou shalt bring f to them water 3318
16 hath brought us f out of Egypt; "
24: 6 As the valley are they spread f,
8 God brought him f out of Egypt; 4161
26: 4 went f out of the land of Egypt. 3318
31:13 went f to meet them without the "
33: 1 went f out of the land of Egypt "
34: 4 the going f thereof shall be from *8444
8 goings f of the border shall be to * "
De 1:27 hath brought us f out of the land 3318
2:23 which came f out of Caphtor, "
4:20 and brought you f out of the iron "
45 after they came f out of Egypt, "
46 they were come f out of Egypt: "
6:12 brought thee f out of the land of "
8:14 brought thee f out of the land of 4161
15 brought thee f out of the rock of "
9:12, 26 hast brought f out of the land 3318
14:22 the field bringeth f year by year. "
28 shalt bring f all the tithe of thine "
16: 1 brought thee f out of the land of "
3 for thou comest f out of the land "
3 when thou camest f out of the land "
6 that thou camest f out of Egypt. "
17: 5 then shalt thou bring f that man or "
21: 2 elders and thy judges shall come f, "
10 thou goest f to war against thine "
22:15 bring f the tokens of the damsel's "
23: 4 way, when ye came f out of Egypt; "
9 host goeth f against thine enemies, "
12 whither thou shalt go f abroad: "
24: 9 that we were come f out of Egypt. "
25:11 putteth f her hand, and taketh 7971
17 when ye were come f out of Egypt; 3318
26: 8 Lord brought us f out of Egypt "
29:25 he brought them f out of the land "
33: 2 he shined f from Mount Paran, and
14 fruits brought f by the sun, *
14 things put f by the moon. *1645
Jos 2: 3 Bring f the men that are come to 3318
5: 5 as they came f out of Egypt, them "
8: 9 Joshua therefore sent them f; and
9:12 day we came f to go unto you; 3318
10:23 so, and brought f those five kings "
18:11 coast of their lot came f between * "
17 went f to En-shemesh, and went f * "
19: 1 the second lot came f to Simeon, * "
J'g 1:24 spies saw a man come f out of the "
3:21 Ehud put f his left hand, and took 7971
23 Ehud went f through the porch, 3318
5:25 brought f water in a lordly dish. *7126
31 sun when he goeth f in his might. 3318
6: 8 brought you f out of the house of "
18 unto thee, and bring f my present, "
21 the Lord put f the end of the staff 7971
9: 8 went f on a time to anoint a king
43 were come f out of the city; 3318
11:31 whatsoever cometh f of the doors "
14:12 I will now put f a riddle unto you: 2330
13 Put f thy riddle, that we may hear "
J'g 14:14 Out of the eater came f meat, 3318
14 out of the strong came f sweetness. "
16 thou hast put f a riddle unto the 2330
15:15 of an ass, and put f his hand, 7971
19:22 Bring f the man that came into 3318
25 and brought her f unto them; "
20:21 children of Benjamin came f out "
25 And Benjamin went f against "
33 the liers in wait of Israel came f 1518
Ru 1: 7 Wherefore she went f out of the 3318
2:18 she brought f, and gave to her "
1Sa 11: 7 Whosoever cometh not f after "
12: 8 brought f your fathers up out "
14:11 Hebrews come f out of the holes "
27 wherefore he put f the end of the 7971
17:20 the host was going f to the fight, 3318
55 And when Saul saw David go f "
18:30 princes of the Philistines went f: "
30 came to pass, after they went f, "
22: 3 I pray thee, come f, and be with "
17 would not put f their hand to fall 7971
23:13 Keilah; and he forbare to go f. 3318
24: 6 to stretch f mine hand against him,
10 will not put f mine hand against 7971
26: 9 for who can stretch f his hand against
11 that I should stretch f mine hand
23 but I would not stretch f mine hand
30:21 and they went f to meet David, 3318
2Sa 1:14 thou not afraid to stretch f thine hand
5:20 The Lord hath broken f upon *
6: 6 Uzzah put f his hand to the ark 7971
11: 1 at the time when kings go f to *3318
12:30 And he brought f the spoil of the "
31 And he brought f the people that "
13:39 king David longed to go f unto "
15: 5 he put f his hand, and took him, 7971
16 And the king went f, and all his 3318
17 And the king went f, and all the "
16: 5 he came f, and cursed still as he * "
11 son, which came f of my bowels, "
18: 2 And David sent f a third part of the
2 I will surely go f with you myself 3318
3 Thou shalt not go f: for if we flee "
12 yet would I not put f mine hand 7971
19: 7 Now, therefore arise, go f, and 3318
7 swear by the Lord, if thou go not f, "
20: 8 and as he went f it fell out. "
22:20 He brought me f also into a large "
49 and that bringeth me f from mine 4161
1Ki 2:30 Thus saith the king, Come f. 3318
36 and go not f thence any whither. "
6:27 and they stretched f the wings of
8: 7 For the cherubims spread f their
19 thy son that shall come f out of 3318
22 spread f his hands toward heaven:
38 spread f his hands toward this house:
51 thou broughtest f out of Egypt, 3318
9: 9 who brought f their fathers out of "
13: 4 that he put f his hand from the 7971
4 And his hand which he put f
19:11 And he said, Go f, and stand upon 3318
20:33 Then Ben-hadad came f to him; "
21:13 They carried him f out of the city, "
22:21 there came f a spirit and stood "
22 I will go f and I will be a lying "
22 and prevail also; go f, and do so. "
2Ki 2: 3 were at Beth-el came f to Elisha, "
21 And he went f unto the spring of "
23 there came f little children out of "
24 And there came f two she bears "
6:15 was risen early, and gone f, "
8: 3 and she went f to cry unto the "
9:11 Then Jehu came f to the servants "
15 let none go f nor escape out of the "
10:22 Bring f vestments for all the "
22 And he brought them f vestments. "
25 and slay them; let none come f. "
26 And they brought f the images out "
11: 7 of all you that go f on the sabbath, "
12 And he brought f the king's son, * "
15 her f without the ranges; "
18: 7 whithersoever he went f: "
19: 3 there is no strength to bring f. 3205
31 Jerusalem shall go f a remnant, 3318
21:15 their fathers came f out of Egypt, "
23: 4 to bring f out of the temple of the "
1Ch 12:33, 36 such as went f to battle, * "
13: 9 Uzzah put f his hand to hold the 7971
14:11 like the breaking f of waters: *
15 for God is gone f before thee to *3318
16:23 shew f from day to day his 1319
19:16 and drew f the Syrians that were 3318
20: 1 Joab led f the power of the army,
24: 7 the first lot came f to Jehoiarib, 3318
25: 9 Now the first lot came f for Asaph "
26:16 and Hosah the lot came f *
2Ch 1:17 they fetched up, and brought f *3318
3:13 cherubims spread themselves f
5: 8 For the cherubims spread f their
6: 5 Since the day that I brought f my 3318
9 but thy son which shall come f out "
12 of Israel, and spread f his hands:
13 of Israel, and spread f his hands
29 shall spread f his hands in this
7:22 brought them f out of the land 3318
20:20 early in the morning, and went f "
20 and as they went f, Jehoshaphat
21: 9 Then Jehoram went f with his *5674
23:14 Have her f of the ranges; 3318
25: 5 able to go f to war, that could
11 and led f his people, and went to
26: 6 And he went f and warred against 3318
29: 5 and carry f the filthiness out of "
23 And they brought f the he goats *
32:21 that came f of his own bowels 3329
Ezr 1: 7 Also Cyrus the king brought f 3318
Ezr 1: 7 Nebuchadnezzer had brought f 3318
8 did Cyrus king of Persia bring f "
6: 5 took f out of the temple which is 5312
Ne 4:16 came to pass from that time f, that
8:15 Go f unto the mount, and fetch 3318
16 So the people went f, and brought "
9: 7 and broughtest him f out of Ur of "
15 broughtest f water for them out "
13: 8 I cast f all the household stuff
21 From that time f came they no more
Es 4: 6 So Hatach went f to Mordecai 3318
5: 9 went Haman f that day joyful and "
Job 1:11 But put f thine hand now, and 7971
12 upon himself put not f thine hand, "
12 went f from the presence of the 3318
2: 5 But put f thine hand now, and 7971
7 went Satan f from the presence 3318
5: 6 affliction cometh not f of the dust, "
8:16 and his branch shooteth f in his "
10:18 hast thou brought me f out of the "
11:17 thou shalt shine f, thou shalt be *
14: 2 He cometh f like a flower, and is 3318
9 it will bud, and bring f boughs 6213
15:35 and bring f vanity, and their belly 3205
21:11 They send f their little ones like a
30 they shall be brought f to the day
23:10 he hath tried me, I shall come f 3318
24: 5 wild asses in the desert, go they f "
28: 9 He putteth f his hand upon the 7971
11 that is hid bringeth he f to light. 3318
30: 5 They were driven f from among
38: 8 when it brake f, as if it had issued 1518
27 of the tender herb to spring f? 6779
32 Canst thou bring f Mazzaroth in 3318
39: 1 when the wild goats bring f? or 3205
2 thou the time when they bring f? "
3 they bring f their young ones, 6398
4 they go f, and return not unto 3318
40:20 the mountains bring him f food,
Ps 1: 3 that bringeth f his fruit in his 5414
7:14 mischief, and brought f falsehood. 3205
9: 1 I will shew f all thy marvellous
14 that I may shew f all thy praise
17: 2 Let my sentence come f from 3318
18:19 He brought me f also into a large "
19: 6 His going f is from the end of the 4161
37: 6 shall bring f thy righteousness 3318
44: 9 and goest not f with our armies. "
51:15 and my mouth shall shew f thy
55:20 He hath put f his hands against 7971
57: 3 God shall send f his mercy and his
66: 2 Sing f the honour of his name; make
68: 7 when thou wentest f before thy 3318
71:15 shall shew f thy righteousness *
78:52 But made his own people to go f 5265
79:13 we will show f thy praise to all 5608
80: 1 between the cherubims, shine f.
88: 8 am shut up, and I cannot come f. 3318
90: 2 the mountains were brought f, 3205
92: 2 To shew f thy lovingkindness
14 still bring f fruit in old age; 5107
96: 2 shew f his salvation from day to
104:14 that he may bring f food out of 3318
20 all the beasts of the forest do creep f,
23 Man goeth f unto his work and 3318
30 Thou sendest f thy spirit, they are
105:30 brought f frogs in abundance, *8317
37 brought them f also with silver 3318
43 he brought f his people with joy, "
106: 2 who can shew f all his praise?
107: 7 he led them f by the right way, *
108:11 thou, O God, go f with our hosts? 3318
113: 2 from this time f and for evermore.
115:18 from this time f and for evermore.
121: 8 thy coming in from this time f,
125: 3 the righteous put f their hands 7971
5 the Lord shall lead them f with
126: 6 He that goeth f and weepeth,
138: 7 thou shalt stretch f thine hand against
141: 2 be set f before thee as incense;
143: 6 I stretch f my hands unto thee:
144: 6 Cast f lightning, and scatter them:
13 our sheep may bring f thousands
146: 4 His breath goeth f, he returneth 3318
147:15 He sendeth f his commandment *
17 He casteth f his ice like morsels:
Pr 7:15 Therefore came I f to meet thee, 3318
8: 1 understanding put f her voice?
24 were no depths, I was brought f; 2342
25 before the hills was I brought f: "
9: 3 She hath sent f her maidens:
10:31 of the just bringeth f wisdom: 5107
12:17 truth sheweth f righteousness:
25: 4 shall come f a vessel for the finer. 3318
6 Put not f thyself in the presence *1921
8 Go not f hastily to strive, lest thou 3318
27: 1 not what a day may bring f. 3205
30:27 go they f all of them by bands; 3318
33 churning of milk bringeth f butter, "
33 of the nose bringeth f blood: "
33 forcing of wrath bringeth f strife. "
31:20 yea, she reacheth f her hands to 6566
Ec 2: 6 the wood that bringeth f trees: *6779
5:15 he came f of his mother's womb, 3318
7:18 God shall come f of them all. "
10: 1 apothecary to send f a stinking
Ca 1: 3 thy name is as ointment poured f,
8 go thy way f by the footsteps 3318
12 spikenard sendeth f the smell
2: 9 he looketh f at the windows, *
13 fig tree putteth f her green figs, *2590
3:11 Go f, O ye daughters of Zion, 3318
6:10 that looketh f as the morning,
7:11 let us go f into the field; 3318
12 and the pomegranates bud f: *5132
8: 5 there thy mother brought thee f: *2254

Ca 8: 5 she brought thee f that bare thee,2254
Isa 1:15 And when ye spread f your hands,
2: 3 for out of Zion shall go f the law, 3318
3:16 and walk with stretched f necks
5: 2 that it should bring f grapes, 6213
2 and it brought f wild grapes. "
4 that it should bring f grapes, "
4 brought it f wild grapes? "
25 and he hath stretched f his hand
7: 3 Go f now to meet Ahaz, thou, 3318
25 shall be for the sending f of oxen,
11: 1 And there shall come f a rod 3318
13:10 shall be darkened in his going f, "
14: 7 they break f into singing.
29 root shall come f a cockatrice,
23: 4 travail not, nor bring f children, 3205
25:11 And he shall spread f his hands in
11 as he that swimmeth spreadeth f his
26:18 have as it were brought f wind; 3205
27: 8 In measure, when it shooteth f, *
28:19 from the time that it goeth f *5674
29 cometh f from the Lord of hosts, 3318
31: 4 multitude of shepherds is called f
32:20 that send f thither the feet of the ox
33:11 chaff, ye shall bring f stubble: 3205
34: 1 and all things that come f of it. 6631
36: 3 Then came f unto him Eliakim, 3318
37: 3 there is not strength to bring f. 3205
9 come f to make war with thee. *3318
32 For out of Jerusalem shall go f "
36 Then the angel of the Lord went f, "
41:21 bring f your strong reasons, 5066
22 Let them bring them f, and shew "
42: 1 he shall bring f judgment to the 3318
3 bring f judgment unto truth. "
5 he that spread f the earth, *
9 before they spring f I tell you
13 Lord shall go f as a mighty man, 3318
43: 8 Bring f the blind people that have "
9 let them bring f their witnesses,*
17 bringeth f the chariot and horse, 4161
19 now it shall spring f; 6779
21 they shall shew f my praise.
44:23 break f into singing, ye
24 that stretcheth f the heavens alone;
45: 8 and let them bring f salvation, 6509
10 What hast thou brought f? *2342
48: 1 come f out of the waters of Judah,3318
3 and they went f out of my mouth, "
20 Go ye f of Babylon, flee ye from "
49: 9 mayest say to the prisoners, Go f; "
13 and break f into singing,
17 made thee waste shall go f of thee.3318
51: 5 my salvation is gone f, and mine "
13 that hath stretched f the heavens,
18 sons whom she hath brought f; 3205
52: 9 Break f into joy, sing together,
54: 1 break f into singing, and cry
2 and let them stretch f the curtains
3 shalt break f on the right hand *
16 that bringeth f an instrument 4161
55:10 and maketh it bring f and bud, 3205
11 So shall my word be that goeth f 3318
12 and be led f with peace: 2986
12 and the hills shall break f
58: 8 Then shall the light break f as
8 health shall spring f speedily:
9 the putting f of the finger, and 7971
59: 4 mischief, and bring f iniquity. 3205
60: 6 shew f the praises of the Lord. *
61:11 as the earth bringeth f her bud, 3318
11 that are sown in it to spring f;
11 and praise to spring f before all
62: 1 the righteousness thereof go f "
65: 9 I will bring f a seed out of Jacob, "
23 nor bring f for trouble: 3205
66: 7 she travailed, she brought f;
8 be made to bring f in one day? 2342
8 she brought f her children. 3205
9 and not cause to bring f? saith
9 shall I cause to bring f, and shut "
24 And they shall go f, and look 3318
Jer 1: 5 and before thou camest f out of "
9 Then the Lord put f his hand, 7971
14 the north an evil shall break f
2:27 stone, Thou hast brought me f: 3205
37 Yea, thou shalt go f from him, 3318
4: 4 lest my fury come f like fire, "
7 is gone f from his place to make "
31 anguish as of her that bringeth f
6:25 Go not f into the field, nor walk 3318
7:25 day that your fathers came f out "
10:13 and bringeth f the wind out of his "
20 my children are gone f of me,
20 there is none to stretch f my tent
11: 4 I brought them f out of the land 3318
12: 2 they grow, yea, they bring f fruit:6213
14:18 If I go f into the field, then
15: 1 out of my sight, and let them go f. "
2 Whither shall we go f? then thou "
19 and if thou take f the precious
17:22 carry f a burden out of your houses"
19: 2 And go f unto the valley of the son"
20: 3 Pashur brought f Jeremiah out of "
18 Wherefore came I f out of the "
22:11 which went f out of this place; "
19 cast f beyond the gates of Jerusalem,
23:15 profaneness gone f into all the 3318
19 the Lord is gone f in fury, even "
25:32 shall go f from nation to nation, "
26:23 they fetched f Urijah out of Egypt,"
29:16 not gone f with you into captivity;"
30:23 the Lord goeth f with fury, a "
31: 4 shalt go f in the dances of them "
24 and they that go f with flocks. *5265
39 shall yet go f over against it *3318

Jer 32:21 brought f thy people Israel out of 3318
34:13 I brought them f out of the land "
37: 5 Pharaoh's army was come f out of "
7 which is come f to help you, shall "
12 Jeremiah went f out of Jerusalem "
38: 2 he that goeth f to the Chaldeans "
8 Ebed-melech went f out of the "
17 wilt assuredly go f unto the king "
18 if thou wilt not go f to the king "
21 But if thou refuse to go f, this is "
22 Judah's house shall be brought f 4163
39: 4 and went f out of the city by night,3318
41: 6 went f from Mizpah to meet them, "
42:18 my fury hath been poured f upon
18 shall my fury be poured f upon you,
43:12 shall go f from thence in peace. 3318
44: 6 fury and mine anger was poured f,
17 every thing goeth f out of our 3318
46: 4 and stand f with your helmets;
9 and let the mighty men come f; 3318
48: 7 Chemosh shall go f into captivity "
45 fire shall come f out of Heshbon, "
49: 5 driven out every man right f; 6440
50: 8 and go f out of the land of the 3318
25 and hath brought f the weapons of"
51:10 The Lord hath brought f our "
16 and bringeth f the wind out of his "
44 and I will bring f out of his mouth "
52: 7 and went f out of the city by night "
31 and brought him f out of prison, "
La 1:17 Zion spreadeth f her hands, and
Eze 1:13 out of the fire went f lightning. 3318
22 the terrible crystal, stretched f over
3:22 Arise, go f into the plain, and I 3318
23 and went f into the plain: and, "
5: 4 come f into all the house of Israel. "
7:10 the morning is gone f; the rod hath "
8: 3 And he put f the form of an hand,7971
9: 7 go ye f. And they went f, and 3318
10: 7 cherub stretched f his hand from
11: 7 bring you f out of the midst of it. 3318
12: 4 Thou shalt bring f thy stuff by "
4 shalt go f at even in their sight, "
4 as they that go f into captivity. 4161
6 and carry it f in the twilight: 3318
7 I brought f my stuff by day, as "
7 I brought it f in the twilight, and "
12 in the twilight, and shall go f: "
14:22 shall be brought f, both sons and 4163
22 they shall come f unto you, and ye 3318
16:14 And thy renown went f among the "
17: 2 Son of man, put f a riddle, and 2330
6 a vine and brought f branches, 6213
6 branches, and shot f sprigs.
7 and shot f her branches toward him,
8 that it might bring f branches, 6213
23 and it shall bring f boughs, and 5375
18: 8 He that hath not given f upon usury,
13 Hath given f upon usury, and hath
20: 6 bring them f of the land of Egypt 3318
9 in bringing them f out of the land "
10 Wherefore I caused them to go f "
22 in whose sight I brought them f. "
38 bring them f out of the country "
21: 3 and will draw f my sword out of "
4 shall my sword go f out of his "
5 have drawn f my sword out of his "
19 twain shall come f out of one land:"
24:12 great scum went not f out of her: "
27: 7 which thou spreadest f to be thy *
10 they set f thy comeliness.
33 thy wares went f out of the seas, 3318
28:18 therefore will I bring f a fire from "
29:21 house of Israel bud f, and I will
30: 9 shall messengers go f from me 3318
31: 5 multitude of waters, when he shot f.
6 of the field bring f their young, 3205
32: 2 and thou camest f with thy rivers,1518
4 will cast thee f upon the open field,
33:30 that cometh f from the Lord. 3318
36: 8 ye shall shoot f your branches, and
20 and are gone f out of his land. 3318
38: 4 I will bring thee f, and all thine "
8 it is brought f out of the nations, "
39: 9 cities of Israel shall go f, and shall"
42: 1 he brought me f into the utter "
15 he brought me f toward the gate "
44: 5 every going f of the sanctuary. 4161
19 they go f into the utter court, 3318
46: 2 then he shall go f: but the gate "
8 he shall go f by the way thereof. "
9 go f by the way of the north gate: "
9 but shall go f over against it. "
10 and when they go f, shall go f. "
12 then he shall go f; and after his "
12 after his going f one shall shut the "
21 Then he brought me f into the "
47: 3 line in his hand went f eastward, "
8 which being brought f into the sea,"
10 shall be a place to spread f nets;*
12 it shall bring f new fruit according
Da 2:13 decree went f that the wise men 5312
14 which was gone f to slay the wise "
3:26 come f, and come hither. "
26 and Abed-nego, came f of the "
5: 5 In the same hour came f fingers "
7:10 stream issued and came f from "
8: 9 out of one of them came f a little 3318
9:15 brought thy people f out of the "
22 I am now come f to give thee skill "
23 the commandment came f, and I "
25 going f of the commandment 4161
10:20 and when I am gone f, lo, the 3318
11:11 shall come f and fight with him, "
11 shall set f a great multitude; 5975
13 and shall set f a multitude greater

Da 11:42 He shall stretch f his hand also upon
44 therefore he shall go f with great3318
Ho 6: 3 his going f is prepared as the 4161
5 are as the light that goeth f. 3318
9:13 shall bring f his children to the *3318
16 though they bring f, yet will I 3205
10: 1 he bringeth f fruit unto himself: 7737
13:13 of the breaking f of children. 4866
14: 5 and cast f his roots as Lebanon. 5221
Joe 2:16 bridegroom go f of his chamber 3318
3:18 fountain shall come f of the house "
Am 5: 3 which went f by an hundred shall "
7:17 go into captivity f of his land. *
8: 3 shall cast them f with silence.
5 that we may set f wheat, making 6605
Jon 1: 5 cast f the wares that were in the 2904
12 and cast me f into the sea: so "
15 cast him f into the sea: and the sea "
Mic 1: 3 Lord cometh f out of his place, 3318
11 Zaanan came not f in the morning "
4: 2 for the law shall go f of Zion, and "
10 labour to bring f, O daughter of 1518
10 go f out of the city, and thou 3318
5: 2 shall he come f unto me that is to "
2 be ruler in Israel; whose goings f 4163
3 which travaileth hath brought f: 3205
7: 9 he will bring me f to the light, 3318
Hab 1: 4 and judgment doth never go f: for "
3: 5 burning coals went f at his feet. "
13 Thou wentest f for the salvation "
Zep 2: 2 Before the decree bring f, before 3205
Hag 1:11 that which the ground bringeth f,3318
2:19 the olive tree, hath not brought f: 5375
Zec 1:16 shall be stretched f upon Jerusalem,
2: 3 angel that talked with me went f,3318
6 Ho, ho, come f, and flee from the *
3: 8 bring f my servant the Branch. 935
4: 7 and he shall bring f the headstone 3318
5: 3 curse that goeth f over the face of "
4 I will bring it f, saith the Lord of "
5 angel that talked with me went f, "
5 and see what is this that goeth f. "
6 This is an ephah that goeth f. "
6: 5 which go f from standing before "
6 therein go f into the north country;"
6 and the white go f after them; "
6 the grisled go f toward the south "
7 the bay went f, and sought to go "
9:11 I have sent f thy prisoners out of
14 arrow shall go f as the lightning: 3318
10: 4 Out of him came f the corner, "
12: 1 which stretcheth f the heavens,
14: 2 the city shall go f into captivity, 3318
3 Then shall the Lord go f, and fight "
Mal 4: 2 and ye shall go f, and grow up "
M't 1:21 And she shall bring f a son, and 5088
23 and shall bring f a son, and they "
25 till she had brought f her firstborn "
2:16 sent f, and slew all the children 649
3: 8 Bring f therefore fruits, meet for 4160
10 which bringeth not f good fruit "
7:17 good tree bringeth f good fruit; "
17 corrupt tree bringeth f evil fruit. "
18 good tree cannot bring f evil fruit, "
18 neither can a corrupt tree bring f "
19 tree that bringeth not f good fruit "
8: 3 And Jesus put f his hand, 1614
9: 9 as Jesus passed f from thence *3855
25 But when the people were put f, 1544
38 that he will send f labourers "
10: 5 These twelve Jesus sent f, and 649
16 Behold, I send you f as sheep "
12:13 Stretch f thine hand. 1614
13 And he stretched it f; "
20 till he send f judgment unto 1544
35 of the heart bringeth f good things:"
35 treasure bringeth f evil things. "
49 And he stretched f his hand 1614
13: 3 Behold a sower went f to sow; 1831
8 good ground, and brought f fruit, "
23 beareth fruit, and bringeth f, 4160
24 Another parable put he f unto *3908
26 sprung up, and brought f fruit, 4160
31 Another parable put he f unto 3908
41 The son of man shall send f his 649
43 Then shall the righteous shine f 1584
49 the angels shall come f, 1831
52 bringeth f out of his treasure 1544
14: 2 therefore mighty works do shew f*1754
14 And Jesus went f, and saw 1831
31 immediately Jesus stretched f 1614
15:18 mouth come f from the heart; 1831
16:21 From that time f began Jesus to *
21:43 to a nation bringing f the fruits 4160
22: 3 sent f his servants to call them 649
4 he sent f other servants, saying, "
7 sent f his armies, and destroyed *
46 from that day f ask him any more
24:26 go not f: behold, he is in the secret1831
32 and putteth f leaves, ye know that 1631
25: 1 went f to meet the bridegroom, 1831
M'r 1:38 there also: for therefore came I f. "
41 put f his hand, and touched him, 1614
2:12 and went f before them all: 1831
13 And he went f again by the sea side "
3: 3 he saith... Stand f. 1519, 3588, 3319
5 the man, Stretch f thine hand. 1614
6 And the Pharisees went f, and *1831
14 he might send them f to preach, 649
4: 8 brought f, some thirty, and some 5342
20 and bring f fruit, some thirtyfold, 2592
28 earth bringeth f fruit of herself; "
29 fruit is brought f, immediately he*3860
6: 7 to send them f by two and two; 649
14 mighty works do shew f *1754
17 Herod himself had sent f and laid 1614

M'r 6:24 And she went *f* and said unto her* 1831
7:26 he would cast *f* the devil out of 1544
8:11 the Pharisees came *f*, and began 1831
9:29 This kind can come *f* by nothing,* "
10:17 when he was gone *f* into the way, 1607
11: 1 sendeth *f* two of his disciples, *1614
13:28 and putteth *f* leaves, ye know that 1631
14:13 he sendeth *f* two of his disciples, 1614
16 his disciples went *f*, and came 1831
16:20 they went *f*, and preached every "
Lu 1: 1 to set *f* in order a declaration * 392
31 bring *f* a son, and shalt call his 5088
57 be delivered; and she brought *f* 1080
2: 7 she brought *f* her firstborn son, 5088
3: 7 that came *f* to be baptized of *1607
8 Bring *f* therefore fruits worthy of 4160
9 which bringeth not *f* good fruit "
5:13 he put *f* his hand, and touched 1614
27 after these things he went *f*, and 1831
6: 8 Rise up, and stand *f* in the midst.
8 And he arose and stood *f*.
10 unto the man, Stretch *f* thy hand. 1614
43 bringeth not *f* corrupt fruit; 4160
43 a corrupt tree bring *f* good fruit.
45 bringeth *f* that which is good; 4393
45 treasure of his heart bringeth *f*
7:17 of him went *f* throughout all 1831
8:14 when they have heard, go *f*, and *4198
15 and bring *f* fruit with patience.
22 of the lake. And they launched *f*. 321
27 And when he went *f* to land, 1831
10: 2 that he would send *f* labourers 1544
3 I send you *f* as lambs among 649
12:16 rich man brought *f* plentifully; 2164
37 and will come *f* and serve them. *3928
14: 7 put *f* a parable to those which *3004
15:22 Bring *f* the best robe, and put it 1627
20: 9 and let it *f* to husbandmen, and *1554
20 sent *f* spies, which should feign 649
21:30 When they now shoot *f*, ye see 4261
22:53 ye stretched *f* no hands against 1614
Joh 1:43 Jesus would go *f* into Galilee, 1831
2:10 doth set *f* good wine; and when *5087
11 and manifested *f* his glory; *5319
5:29 And shall come *f*; they that have 1607
8:42 I proceeded *f* and came from God; 1831
10: 4 when he putteth *f* his own sheep, 1544
11:43 a loud voice, Lazarus, come *f*. 1854
44 he that was dead came *f*, bound 1831
53 from that day *f* they took counsel
12:13 went *f* to meet him, and cried, 1831
15: 2 that it may bring *f* more fruit,*
24 if it die, it bringeth *f* much fruit.*
5 the same bringeth *f* much fruit: *
6 he is cast *f* as a branch, and is 1854
16 should go and bring *f* fruit, and *
16:28 I came *f* from the Father, and * 1831
30 that thou camest *f* from God. "
18: 1 *f* with his disciples over the brook "
4 went *f*, and said unto them, Whom "
19: 4 Pilate therefore went *f* again, *1854
4 unto them, Behold, I bring him *f* * "
5 came Jesus *f*, wearing the crown * "
13 he brought Jesus *f*, and sat down * "
17 went *f* into a place called the *1831
20: 3 Peter therefore went *f*, and that "
21: 3 went *f*, and entered into a ship "
18 thou shalt stretch *f* thy hands, 1614
Ac 1:26 And they gave *f* their lots; and *
2:33 he hath shed *f* this, which ye now 1632
4:30 By stretching *f* thine hand to heal; 1614
5:10 and, carrying her *f*, buried her by 1627
15 brought *f* the sick into the streets,* "
19 and brought them *f*, and said, *1806
34 put the apostles *f* a little space; 1854
7: 7 shall they come *f*, and serve me 1831
9:30 Cæsarea, and sent him *f* to Tarsus. 1821
40 Peter put them all *f*, and kneeled 1854
11:22 they sent *f* Barnabas, that he 1821
12: 1 the king stretched *f* his hands to 1911
4 Easter to bring him *f* to the people. 321
6 Herod would have brought him *f*. 4254
13: 4 being sent *f* by the Holy Ghost, 1599
16: 3 would Paul have to go *f* with him; 1831
17:18 to be a setter *f* of strange gods: 2604
21: 2 we went aboard, and set *f*. * 321
23:28 brought him *f* into their council:*2609
24: 2 he was called *f*, Tertullus began *2564
25:17 the man to be brought *f*. *
23 Paul was brought *f*. *
26 have brought him *f* before you, 4254
26: 1 Then Paul stretched *f* the hand, 1614
25 but speak *f* the words of truth and 669
27:21 Paul stood *f* in the midst of them,
Ro 3:25 Whom God hath set *f* to be a 4388
7: 4 that we should bring *f* fruit unto
5 our members to bring *f* fruit unto
10:21 I have stretched *f* my hands unto*1600
1Co 4: 9 God hath set *f* us the apostles 584
16:11 but conduct him *f* in peace, that *4311
Ga 3: 1 Christ hath been evidently set *f*, 4270
4: 4 God sent *f* his son, made of a 1821
6 God hath sent *f* the Spirit of his "
27 *f* and cry, thou that travailest 4486
Ph'p 2:16 Holding *f* the word of life; that I 1907
3:13 and reaching *f* unto those things*1901
Col 1: 6 and bringeth *f* fruit, as it doth *
1Ti 1:16 Jesus Christ might shew *f* all 1731
Heb 6: 7 bringeth *f* herbs meet for them 5088
13:13 Let us go *f* therefore unto him 1831
Jas 1:15 lust hath conceived, it bringeth *f** 616
15 it is finished, bringeth *f* death. 5088
3:11 Doth a fountain send *f* at the same 1032
5:18 and the earth brought *f* her fruit. 985
1Pe 2: 9 that ye should shew *f* the praises 1804
3Jo 7 for his name's sake they went *f*, 1831
Jude 7 are set *f* for an example, suffering 4295
Re 5: 6 seven spirits of God sent *f* into 649
6: 2 went *f* conquering, and to conquer. 1831
12: 5 And she brought *f* a man child, *5088
13 woman which brought *f* the man "
16:14 go *f* unto the kings of the earth 1607

forthwith
Ezr 6: 8 *f* expences be given unto these * 629
M't 13: 5 *f* they sprung up, because they *2112
26:49 *f* he came to Jesus, and said, * "
M'r 1:29 *f*, when they were come out of * "
43 charged him, and *f* sent him away;* "
5:13 And *f* Jesus gave them leave.
Joh 19:34 *f* came thereout blood and water.*2117
Ac 9:18 he received sight *f*, and arose, *3916
12:10 *f* the angel departed from him. *2112
21:30 and *f* the doors were shut. * "

fortieth
Nu 33:38 and died there, in the *f* year after 705
De 1: 3 and it came to pass in the *f* year, "
1Ch 26:31 In the *f* year of the reign of David "
2Ch 16:13 and died in the one and *f* year of "

fortified
2Ch 11:11 And he *f* the strong holds, and 2388
26: 9 turning of the wall, and *f* them.
Ne 3: 8 Jerusalem unto the broad wall. 5800
Mic 7:12 Assyria, and from the *f* cities, *4692

fortify See also FORTIFIED.
J'g 9:31 they *f* the city against thee. *6696
Ne 4: 2 Jews? will they *f* themselves? 5800
Isa 22:10 ye broken down to *f* the wall. 1219
Jer 51:53 should *f* the height of her strength,"
Na 2: 1 loins strong, *f* thy power mightily. 553
3:14 *f* thy strong holds: go into clay, *2388

fortress See also FORTRESSES.
2Sa 22: 2 The Lord is my rock, and my *f*, 4686
Ps 18: 2 rock, and my *f*, and my deliverer; "
31: 3 For thou art my rock and my *f*; "
71: 3 for thou art my rock and my *f*. "
91: 2 He is my refuge and my *f*: "
144: 2 My goodness, and my *f*; my high "
Isa 17: 3 *f* also shall cease from Ephraim, 4013
25:12 And the *f* of the high fort of thy "
Jer 6:27 a tower and a *f* among my people, "
10:17 the land, O inhabitant of the *f*. *4693
16:19 O Lord, my strength, and my *f*, *4581
Da 11: 7 shall enter into the *f* of the king "
10 and be stirred up, even to his *f*. "
Am 5: 9 spoiled shall come against the *f*. 4013
Mic 7:12 and from the *f* even to the river, *4693

fortresses
Isa 34:13 and brambles in the *f* thereof: 4013
Ho 10:14 and all thy *f* shall be spoiled, "

forts
2Ki 25: 1 they built *f* against it round about. 1785
Isa 29: 3 and I will raise *f* against thee. *4694
32:14 *f* and towers shall be for dens *6076
Jer 52: 4 and built *f* against it round about. 1785
Eze 17:17 casting up mounts, and building *f*, "
33:27 that be in the *f* and in the caves *4679

Fortunatus (*for-chu-na'-tus*)
1Co 16:17 the coming of Stephanas and *F* 5415
subscr. Philippi by Stephanas, and *F*. "

forty See also FORTY'S.
Ge 5:13 Mahalaleel eight hundred and *f* 705
7: 4 upon the earth *f* days and *f* nights; "
17 flood was *f* days upon the earth; "
8: 6 it came to pass at the end of *f* days, "
18:28 he said, If I find there *f* and five, "
29 there shall be *f* found there. "
25:20 Isaac was *f* years old when he took "
26:34 Esau was *f* years old when he took "
32:15 *f* kine, and ten bulls, twenty she "
47:28 Jacob was an hundred *f* and seven "
50: 3 And *f* days were fulfilled for him: "
Ex 16:35 of Israel did eat manna *f* years, "
24:18 in the mount *f* days and *f* nights. "
26:19 thou shalt make *f* sockets of silver "
21 And their *f* sockets of silver; two "
34:28 with the Lord *f* days and *f* nights; "
36:24 And *f* sockets of silver he made "
26 And their *f* sockets of silver; "
Le 25: 8 shall be unto thee *f* and nine years. "
Nu 1:21 *f* and six thousand and five hundred. "
25 *f* and five thousand six hundred "
33 were *f* thousand and five hundred. "
41 *f* and one thousand and five hundred. "
2:11 *f* and six thousand and five hundred. "
15 *f* and five thousand and six hundred "
19 were *f* thousand and five hundred. "
28 *f* and one thousand and five hundred. "
13:25 searching of the land after *f* days. "
14:33 wander in the wilderness *f* years, "
34 searched the land, even *f* days, "
34 bear your iniquities, even *f* years, "
26: 7 numbered of them were *f* and three "
18 them, *f* thousand and five hundred. "
41 *f* and five thousand and six hundred. "
50 were *f* and five thousand and four "
32:13 wander in the wilderness *f* years, "
35: 6 them ye shall add *f* and two cities. "
7 Levites shall be *f* and eight cities: "
De 2: 7 these *f* years the Lord thy God "
8: 2 these *f* years in the wilderness, "
4 did thy foot swell, these *f* years. "
9: 9 in the mount *f* days and *f* nights. "
11 at the end of *f* days and *f* nights, "
18 at the first, *f* days and *f* nights: "
25 before the Lord *f* days and *f* nights, "
10:10 the first time, *f* days and *f* nights; "
25: 3 *F* stripes he may give him, and "
29: 5 led you *f* years in the wilderness: "
Jos 4:13 About *f* thousand prepared for war 705
5: 6 walked *f* years in the wilderness, "
14: 7 *F* years old was I when Moses the "
10 as he said these *f* and five years, "
21:41 were *f* and eight cities with their "
J'g 3:11 And the land had rest *f* years. "
5: 8 seen among *f* thousand in Israel? "
31 And the land had rest *f* years. "
8:28 country was in quietness *f* years "
12: 6 Ephraimites *f* and two thousand. "
14 he had *f* sons and thirty nephews, "
13: 1 the hand of the Philistines *f* years. "
1Sa 4:18 And he had judged Israel *f* years. "
17:16 and presented himself *f* days. "
2Sa 2:10 Ish-bosheth Saul's son was *f* years "
5: 4 to reign, and he reigned *f* years. "
10:18 and *f* thousand horsemen, and "
15: 7 And it came to pass after *f* years, "
1Ki 2:11 reigned over Israel were *f* years: "
4:26 Solomon had *f* thousand stalls of "
6:17 temple before it, was *f* cubits long. "
7: 3 that lay on *f* five pillars, fifteen in "
38 one layer contained *f* baths: "
11:42 over all Israel was *f* years. "
14:21 Rehoboam was *f* and one years old "
15:10 And *f* and one years reigned he in "
19: 8 of that meat *f* days and *f* nights "
2Ki 2:24 tare *f* and two children of them. "
8: 9 of Damascus, *f* camels' burden, "
10:14 even two and *f* men; neither left he "
12: 1 *f* years reigned he in Jerusalem. "
14:23 and reigned *f* and one years. "
1Ch 5:18 were four and *f* thousand seven "
12:36 to battle, expert in war, *f* thousand. "
19:18 chariots, and *f* thousand footmen, "
29:27 he reigned over Israel was *f* years; "
2Ch 9:30 in Jerusalem over all Israel *f* years. "
12:13 Rehoboam was one and *f* years old "
22: 2 *F* and two years old was Ahaziah "
24: 1 he reigned *f* years in Jerusalem. "
Ezr 2: 8 of Zattu, nine hundred *f* and five. "
10 of Bani, six hundred *f* and two. "
24 children of Azmaveth, *f* and two. "
25 seven hundred and *f* and three. "
34 of Jericho, three hundred *f* and five. "
38 thousand two hundred *f* and seven. "
64 together was *f* and two 702, 7239
66 mules, two hundred *f* and five; 705
Ne 5:15 wine, beside *f* shekels of silver; "
7:13 of Zattu, eight hundred *f* and five. "
15 of Binnui, six hundred *f* and eight. "
28 men of Beth-azmaveth, *f* and two. "
29 and Beeroth, seven hundred *f* and "
36 Jericho, three hundred *f* and five. "
41 thousand two hundred *f* and seven. "
44 of Asaph, an hundred *f* and eight. "
62 of Nekoda, six hundred *f* and two. "
66 was *f* and two thousand three 702, 7239
67 two hundred *f* and five singing 705
68 mules, two hundred *f* and five: "
9:21 Yea, *f* years didst thou sustain them "
11:13 the fathers, two hundred *f* and two: "
Job 42:16 lived Job an hundred and *f* years, "
Ps 95:10 *F* years long was I grieved with "
Jer 52:30 seven hundred *f* and five persons: "
Eze 4: 6 of the house of Judah *f* days: "
29:11 neither shall it be inhabited *f* years. "
12 waste shall be desolate *f* years: "
13 At the end of *f* years will I gather "
41: 2 the length thereof, *f* cubits: and the "
46:22 were courts joined of *f* cubits long "
Am 2:10 you *f* years through the wilderness, "
5:25 offerings in the wilderness *f* years, "
Jon 3: 4 Yet *f* days, and Nineveh shall be "
M't 4: 2 he had fasted *f* days and *f* nights, 5062
M'r 1:13 was there in the wilderness *f* days, "
Lu 4: 2 Being *f* days tempted of the devil. "
Joh 2:20 *F* and six years was this temple "
Ac 1: 3 proofs, being seen of them *f* days, "
4:22 For the man was above *f* years old, "
7:23 And when he was full *f* years old, 5063
30 And when *f* years were expired, 5062
36 sea, and in the wilderness *f* years. "
42 space of *f* years in the wilderness? "
13:18 And about the time of *f* years 5063
21 Benjamin, by the space of *f* years. 5062
23:13 were more than *f* which had made "
21 for him of them more than *f* men, "
2Co 11:24 times received I *f* stripes save one. "
Heb 3: 9 me, and saw my works *f* years. "
17 with whom was he grieved *f* years? "
Re 7: 4 sealed an hundred and *f* and four "
11: 2 tread under foot *f* and two months. "
13: 5 him to continue *f* and two months. "
14: 1 with him an hundred *f* and four "
3 but the hundred and *f* and four "
21:17 an hundred and *f* and four cubits, "

forty's
Ge 18:29 he said, I will not do it for *f* sake. 705

forty-thousand See FORTY and THOUSAND.

forum
Ac 28:15 came to meet us as far as Appii *f*.* 675

forward See also HENCEFORWARD.
Ge 26:13 the man waxed great, and went *f*,*1980
Ex 14:15 children of Israel, that they go *f*: 5265
Nu 1:51 And when the tabernacle setteth *f*, "
2:17 of the congregation shall set *f*; "
17 so shall they set *f*, every man in "
24 they shall go *f* in the third rank.* "
34 and so they set *f*, every one after "
4: 5 And when the camp setteth *f*, "
15 as the camp is to set *f*; after that, "
10: 5 lie on the east parts shall go *f*. * "
17 and the sons of Merari set *f*,

Nu 10:18 of the camp of Reuben set f 5265
21 And the Kohathites set f, bearing "
22 of the children of Ephraim set f "
25 camp of the children of Dan set f. "
28 to their armies, when they set f. "
35 when the ark set f, that Moses "
21:10 And the children of Israel set f, * "
22: 1 And the children of Israel set f, * "
32:19 them on yonder side Jordan, or f;1973
J'g 9:44 that was with him, rushed f, and 6584
1Sa 10: 3 Then shalt thou go on f from 1973
16:13 upon David from that day f. 4605
18: 9 eyed David from that day and f. 1973
30:25 And it was so from that day f, 4605
2Ki 3:24 but they went f smiting the Moabites,
4:24 Drive, and go f; slack not thy riding
20: 9 shall the shadow go f ten degrees,
1Ch 23: 4 to set f the work of the house *5921
2Ch 34:12 to set it f; and other of the Levites,
Ezr 3: 8 to set f the work of the house *5921
9 set f the workmen in the house * "
Job 23: 8 I go f, but he is not there; 6924
30:13 they set f my calamity, they have3276
Jer 7:24 and went backward, and not f. 6440
Eze 1: 9 they went every one straight f. "
12 they went every one straight f: "
10:22 they went every one straight f: "
39:22 their God from that day and f. 1973
43:27 and so f, the priests shall make
Zec 1:15 and they helped f the affliction.
M'r 14:35 And he went f a little, and fell on 4281
Ac 19:33 the Jews putting him f. 4261
2Co 8:10 but also to be f a year ago. *2309
17 but being more f, of his own *4707
Gal 2:10 the same which I also was f to do.*4704
3Jo 6 if thou bring f on their journey 4311

forwardness
2Co 8: 8 by occasion of the f of others, *4710
9: 2 For I know the f of your mind, *4288

fought
Ex 17: 8 came Amalek, and f with Israel 3898
10 said to him, and f with Amalek: "
Nu 21: 1 then he f against Israel, and took "
23 to Jahaz, and f against Israel. "
26 who had f against the former king"
Jos 10:14 the Lord f for Israel. "
29 for f against Libnah: "
31, 34 against it, and f against it: "
36 unto Hebron; and they f against it:"
38 to Debir; and f against it: "
42 the Lord God of Israel f for Israel."
23: 3 your God is he that hath f for you. "
24: 8 and they f with you: and I gave "
11 the men of Jericho f against you, "
J'g 1: 5 they f against him, and they slew "
8 Now the children of Judah had f "
5:19 kings came and f, then f the kings"
20 They f from heaven; "
20 the stars in their courses f against"
9:17 (For my father f for you, and "
39 Shechem, and f with Abimelech. "
45 Abimelech f against the city all "
52 and f against it, and went hard "
11:20 in Jahaz, and f against Israel. "
12: 4 and f with Ephraim: and the men "
1Sa 4:10 And the Philistines f, and Israel "
12: 9 Moab, and they f against them. "
14:47 and f against all his enemies on "
19: 8 went out, and f with the Philistines,"
23: 5 Keilah, and f with the Philistines, "
31: 1 the Philistines f against Israel: "
2Sa 2:28 no more neither f they any more. "
8:10 he had f against Hadadezer, and "
10:17 in array against David, and f with "
11:17 the men of the city went out, and f "
12:26 And Joab f against Rabbah of the "
27 I have f against Rabbah, and have "
29 and f against it, and took it. "
21:15 and f against the Philistines. "
2Ki 8:29 he f against Hazael king of Syria. "
9:15 he f with Hazael king of Syria.) "
12:17 Syria went up, and f against Gath, "
13:12 f against Amaziah king of Judah, "
14:15 he f with Amaziah king of Judah, "
1Ch 10: 1 the Philistines f against Israel; "
18:10 he had f against Hadarezer, and "
19:17 the Syrians, they f with him. "
18 seven thousand men which f in * "
2Ch 20:29 the Lord f against the enemies 3898
22: 6 when he f with Hazeal king of Syria."
27: 5 He f also with the king of the "
Ps 109: 3 and f against me without a cause. "
Isa 20: 1 and f against Ashdod, and took it; "
63:10 enemy, and he f against them. "
Jer 34: 1 the people, f against Jerusalem, "
7 king of Babylon's army f against "
Zec 14: 3 as when he f in the day of battle. "
12 that have f against Jerusalem; *6633
1Co 15:32 I have f with beasts at Ephesus, 2341
2Ti 4: 7 I have f a good fight, I have 75
Re 12: 7 his angels f against the dragon; *4170
7 and the dragon f and his angels.* "

foul See also FOULED.
Job 16:16 My face is f with weeping, and 2560
Eze 34:18 ye must f the residue with your 7515
M't 16: 3 It will be f weather to day: for 5494
M'r 9:25 he rebuked the f spirit, saying * 169
Re 18: 2 hold of every f spirit, and a cage* "

fouled See also FOULEDST.
Eze 34:19 they drink that which ye have f 4833

fouledst
Eze 32: 2 with thy feet, and f their rivers. 7515

found See also CONFOUND; FOUNDED; FOUNDEST.
Ge 2:20 there was not f an help meet 4672
6: 8 Noah f grace in the eyes of the "
8: 9 f no rest for the sole of her foot, "
11: 2 that they f a plain in the land of "
16: 7 And the angel of the Lord f her "
18: 3 now I have f favour in thy sight, "
29 Peradventure there shall be forty f "
30 Peradventure there shall thirty be f "
31 there shall be twenty f there. "
32 Peradventure ten shall be f there. "
19:19 servant hath f grace in thy sight, "
26:19 f there a well of springing water. "
32 said unto him, We have f water. "
27:20 How is it that thou hast f it so "
30:14 and f mandrakes in the field, "
27 if I have f favour in thine eyes, "
31:33 tents, but he f them not "
34 all the tent, but f them not. "
35 he searched, but f not the images. "
37 hast thou f of all thy household "
33:10 if now I have f grace in thy sight, "
36:24 had f the mules in the wilderness, "
37:15 And a certain man f him, and, "
17 brethren, and f them in Dothan. "
32 This have we f: know now "
38:20 woman's hand: but he f her not. "
23 this kid, and thou hast not f her. "
39: 4 And Joseph f grace in his sight, "
44: 8 which we f in our sacks' mouths, "
9 of thy servants it be f, both let him "
10 he with whom it is f shall be my "
12 the cup was f in Benjamin's sack. "
16 God hath f out the iniquity of thy "
16 he also with whom the cup is f. "
17 man in whose hand the cup is f, "
47:14 the money that was f in the land "
29 If now I have f grace in thy sight, "
50: 4 If now I have f grace in your eyes, "
Ex 9:19 man and beast which shall be f in "
12:19 days shall there be no leaven f in "
15:22 in the wilderness, and f no water. "
16:27 for to gather, and they f none. "
21:16 or if he be f in his hand, he shall "
22: 2 If a thief be f breaking up, and be "
4 If the theft be certainly f in his "
7 if the thief be f, let him pay "
8 If the thief be not f, then the "
33:12 thou hast also f grace in my sight. "
13 if I have f grace in thy sight, "
16 people have f grace in thy sight? "
17 thou hast f grace in my sight, "
34: 9 now I have f grace in thy sight, "
35:23 with whom was f blue, and purple, "
24 was f shittim wood for any work "
Le 6: 3 Or have f that which was lost, "
4 or the lost thing which he f, "
Nu 11:11 have I not f favour in thy sight, "
15 if I have f favour in thy sight; "
15:32 they f a man that gathered sticks "
33 they that f him gathering sticks "
32: 5 if we have f grace in thy sight, "
De 17: 2 If there be f among you, within "
18:10 There shall not be f among you "
20:11 all the people that is f therein "
21: 1 If one be f slain in the land which "
22: 3 which he hath lost, and thou hast f, "
14 I came to her, I f her not a maid: "
17 I f not thy daughter a maid; "
20 virginity be not f for the damsel; "
22 If a man be f lying with a woman "
27 For he f her in the field, and the "
28 and lie with her, and they be f; "
24: 1 hath f some uncleanness in her: "
7 If a man be f stealing any of his "
32:10 He f him in a desert land, "
33:29 thine enemies shall be f liars * "
Jos 2:22 all the way, but f them not. 4672
10:17 The five kings are f hid in a cave "
J'g 1: 5 And they f Adoni-bezek in Bezek: "
6:17 If now I have f grace in thy sight, "
14:18 ye had not f out my riddle. "
15:15 he f a new jawbone of an ass, "
21:12 And they f among the inhabitants "
Ru 2:10 Why have I f grace in thine eyes, "
1Sa 9: 4 Shalisha, but they f them not: "
4 Benjamites, but they f them not. "
11 they f young maidens going out "
20 thy mind on them; for they are f. "
10: 2 which thou wentest to seek are f: "
16 us plainly that the asses were f. "
21 they sought him, he could not be f. "
12: 5 ye have not f ought in my hand. "
13:19 smith f throughout all the land "
22 was neither sword nor spear f in "
22 with Jonathan his son was there f. "
14:30 of their enemies which they f? "
16:22 for he hath f favour in my sight. "
20: 3 that I have f grace in thine eyes; "
29 if I have f favour in thine eyes, "
25:28 and evil hath not been f in thee all "
27: 5 If I have now f grace in thine eyes, "
29: 3 and I have f no fault in him since "
6 for I have not f evil in thee since "
8 what hast thou f in thy servant "
30:11 they f an Egyptian in the field, "
31: 8 that they f Saul and his three sons "
2Sa 7:27 hath thy servant f in his heart "
14:22 that I have f grace in thy sight, "
17:12 some place where he shall be f, "
13 be not one small stone f there. "
1Ki 1: 3 and f Abishag a Shunammite, and "
52 if wickedness shall be f in him, "
7:47 was the weight of the brass f out. 2713
11:19 Hadad f great favour in the sight4672
29 the Shilonite f him in the way; "

1Ki 13:14 and f him sitting under an oak: 4672
28 he went and f his carcase cast in "
14:13 in him there is f some good thing "
18:10 and nation, that they f thee not. "
19:19 and f Elisha the son of Shaphat, "
20:36 him, a lion f him, and slew him. "
37 Then he f another man, and said, "
21:20 Hast thou f me, O mine enemy? "
20 I have f thee: because thou hast "
2Ki 2:17 sought three days, but f him not. "
4:39 and f a wild vine, and gathered "
9:35 f no more of her than the skull, "
12: 5 wheresoever any breach shall be f. "
10 the money that was f in the house "
18 gold that was f in the treasures "
14:14 vessels that were f in the house "
16: 8 the silver and gold that was f in the "
17: 4 the king of Assyria f conspiracy "
18:15 the silver that was f in the house "
19: 8 and f the king of Assyria warring "
20:13 and all that was f in his treasures: "
22: 8 I have f the book of the law in the "
9 the money that was f in the house, "
13 the words of this book that is f: "
23: 2 book of the covenant which was f "
24 the book that Hilkiah the priest f "
25:19 which were f in the city, and the "
19 of the land that were f in the city: "
1Ch 4:40 And they f fat pasture and good, "
41 the habitations that were f there, "
10: 8 they f Saul and his sons fallen "
17:25 thy servant hath f in his heart to "
20: 2 and f it to weigh a talent of gold, "
24: 4 And there were more chief men f "
26:31 were f among them mighty men "
28: 9 thou seek him, he will be f of thee; "
29: 8 with whom precious stones were f "
2Ch 2:17 and they were f an hundred and "
4:18 the brass could not be f out. 2713
15: 2 ye seek him, he will be f of you; 4672
4 and sought him, he was f of them. "
15 desire; and he was f of them: "
19: 3 there are good things f in thee, "
20:25 they f among them in abundance "
21:17 that was f in the king's house, "
22: 8 and f the princes of Judah, and "
25: 5 and f them three hundred...men, "
24 vessels that were f in the house "
29:16 they f in the temple of the Lord "
34:14 Hilkiah the priest f a book of the "
15 I have f the book of the law in the "
17 the money that was f in the house "
21 the words of the book that is f: "
30 book of the covenant that was f in "
36: 8 and that which was f in him, "
Ezr 2:62 genealogy, but they were not f: "
4:19 and it is f that this city of old 7912
6: 2 And there was f at Achmetha, in "
8:15 f there none of the sons of Levi. 4672
10:18 priests there were f that had taken "
Ne 2: 5 and if thy servant have f favour in "
5: 8 peace, and f nothing to answer. 4672
7: 5 And I f a register of the genealogy "
5 at the first, and f written therein, "
64 by genealogy, but it was not f: "
8:14 And they f written in the law "
13: 1 and therein was f written, that the "
Es 2:23 made of the matter, it was f out; "
5: 8 If I have f favour in the sight of "
6: 2 it was f written, that Mordecai "
7: 3 If I have f favour in thy sight, "
8: 5 if I have f favour in his sight, "
Job 19:28 the root of the matter is f in me? "
20: 8 as a dream, and shall not be f: "
28:12 But where shall wisdom be f? and "
13 neither is it f in the land of the "
31:29 lifted up myself when evil f him: "
32: 3 because they had f no answer, and "
13 should say, We have f out wisdom: "
33:24 down to the pit: I have f a ransom. "
42:15 were no women f so fair as the "
Ps 32: 6 in a time when thou mayest be f: "
36: 2 his iniquity be f to be hateful. * "
37:36 sought him, but he could not be f. "
69:20 and for comforters, but I f none. "
76: 5 men of might have f their hands. "
84: 3 yea, the sparrow hath f an house, "
89:20 I have f David my servant; with "
107: 4 way; they f no city to dwell in. "
116: 3 upon me: I f trouble and sorrow. "
132: 6 we f it in the fields of the wood. "
Pr 6:31 But if he be f, he shall restore "
7:15 to seek thy face, and I have f thee. "
10:13 hath understanding wisdom is f: "
16:31 it be f in the way of righteousness. "
24:14 when thou hast f it, then there "
25:16 Hast thou f honey? eat so much "
30: 6 he reprove thee, and thou be f a liar. "
10 curse thee, and thou be f guilty. * "
Ec 7:27 this have I f, saith the preacher, 4672
28 man among a thousand have I f; "
28 among all those have I not f. "
29 this only have I f, that God hath "
9:15 Now there was f in it a poor wise "
Ca 3: 1, 2 I sought him, but I f him not. "
3 watchmen that go about the city f "
4 but I f him whom my soul loveth: "
5: 7 that went about the city f me, "
8:10 I in his eyes as one that f favour. "
Isa 10:10 As my hand hath f the kingdoms "
14 And my hand hath f as a nest the "
13:15 Every one that is f shall be thrust "
22: 3 all that are f in thee are bound "
30:14 there shall not be f in the bursting "
35: 9 it shall not be f there; but the "
37: 8 and f the king of Assyria warring "

Isa 39: 2 and all that was f in his treasures:4672
51: 3 joy and gladness shall be f therein, "
55: 6 ye the Lord while he may be f, "
57:10 thou hast f the life of thine hand;* "
65: 1 I am f of them that sought me not: "
8 As the new wine is f in the cluster, "
Jer 2: 5 What iniquity have your fathers f "
26 the thief is ashamed when he is f, "
34 in thy skirts is f the blood of the "
34 I have not f it by secret search, "
5:26 among my people are f wicked "
11: 9 A conspiracy is f among the men "
14: 3 came to the pits, and f no water; "
15:16 Thy words were f, and I did eat "
23:11 have I f their wickedness, saith "
29:14 And I will be f of you, saith the "
31: 2 were left of the sword f grace in "
41: 3 the Chaldeans that were f there, "
8 But ten men were f among them "
12 and f him by the great waters that "
48:27 was he f among thieves? for since "
50: 7 that f them have devoured them: "
20 shall not be f: for I will pardon "
24 art f, and also caught, because "
52:25 which were f in the city; and the "
25 that were f in the midst of the city. "
La 2:16 for; we have f, we have seen it. "
Eze 22:30 not destroy it: but I f none. "
26:21 yet shalt thou never be f again, "
28:15 created, till iniquity was f in thee. "
Da 1:19 them all was f none like Daniel, "
20 he f them ten times better than all "
2:25 I have f a man of the captives of "
35 that no place was f for them: 7912
5:11 wisdom of the gods, was f in him; "
12 doubts, were f in the same Daniel, "
14 and excellent wisdom is f in thee. "
27 in the balances, and art f wanting. "
6: 4 was there any error or fault f in "
11 and f Daniel praying and making "
22 before him innocency was f in me; "
23 no manner of hurt was f upon him, "
11:19 stumble and fall, and not be f. 4672
12: 1 every one that shall be f written "
Ho 9:10 I f Israel like grapes in the "
10: 2 now shall they be f faulty: "
12: 4 he f him in Beth-el, and there he 4672
8 I have f me out substance: in all "
14: 8 From me is thy fruit f. "
Jon 1: 3 and he f a ship going to Tarshish: "
Mic 1:13 the transgressions of Israel were f "
Zep 3:13 shall a deceitful tongue be f in "
Zec 10:10 and place shall not be f for them. "
Mal 2: 6 and iniquity was not f in his lips: "
M't 1:18 she was f with child of the Holy 2147
2: 8 child; and when ye have f him, "
8:10 I have not f so great faith, no, not "
13:44 when a man hath f, he hideth, "
46 he had f one pearl of great price, "
18:28 and f one of his fellowservants, "
20: 6 and f others standing idle, and "
21:19 f nothing thereon, but leaves only, "
22:10 all as many as they f, both bad "
26:43 he came and f them asleep again: "
60 But f none: yea, though many "
60 witnesses came, yet f they none.* "
27:32 they f a man of Cyrene, Simon by 2147
M'r 1:37 And when they had f him, they "
7: 2 unwashen, hands, they f fault. *
30 she f the devil gone out, and her 2147
11: 4 and f the colt tied by the door "
13 to it, he f nothing but leaves; "
14:16 and f as he had said unto them: "
40 returned, he f them asleep again, "
55 to put him to death; and f none. "
Lu 1:30 Mary: for thou hast f favour "
2:16 came with haste, and f Mary, and 429
45 And when they f him not, they 2147
46 they f him in the temple, sitting "
4:17 f the place where it was written, "
7: 9 I have not f so great faith, no, not "
10 f the servant whole that had been "
8:35 and f the man, out of whom the "
9:36 voice was past, Jesus was f alone. "
13: 6 sought fruit thereon, and f none. "
15: 5 when he hath f it, he layeth it on "
6 I have f my sheep which was lost. "
9 when she hath f it, she calleth "
9 for I have f the piece which I had "
24 alive again; he was lost, and is f. "
32 alive again; and was lost, and is f. "
17:18 There are not f that returned to "
19:32 and f even as he had said unto "
22:13 and f as he had said unto them: "
45 he f them sleeping for sorrow, "
23: 2 We f this fellow perverting the "
14 you, have f no fault in this man "
22 I have f no cause of death in him: "
24: 2 And they f the stone rolled away "
3 and f not the body of the Lord "
23 And when they f not his body, they "
24 and f it even so as the women had "
33 and f the eleven gathered together, "
Joh 1:41 We have f the Messias, which is, "
45 saith unto him, We have f him, "
2:14 And f in the temple those that sold "
6:25 And when they had f him on the "
9:35 and when he had f him, he said "
11:17 he f that he had lain in the grave "
12:14 he had f a young ass, sat thereon; "
Ac 5:10 young men came in, and f her dead, "
22 officers came, and f them not in "
23 prison truly f we shut in all safety, "
23 had opened, we f no man within. "
39 ye be f even to fight against God. "
7:11 and our fathers f no sustenance, "

Ac 7:46 Who f favour before God, and 2147
8:40 But Philip was f at Azotus: "
9: 2 that if he f any of this way, "
33 And there he f a certain man "
10:27 f many that were come together. "
11:26 when he had f him, he brought "
12:19 f him not, he examined the keepers, "
13: 6 f a certain sorcerer, a false prophet, "
22 I have f David the son of Jesse, "
28 though they f no cause of death "
17: 6 when they f them not, they drew "
23 I f an altar with this inscription, "
18: 2 And f a certain Jew named Aquila, "
19:19 f it fifty thousand pieces of silver. "
24: 5 we have f this man a pestilent "
12 they neither f me in the temple "
18 Jews from Asia f me purified in "
20 if they have f any evil doing in "
25:25 when I f that he had committed 2638
27: 6 And there the centurion f a ship 2147
28 sounded, and f it twenty fathoms: "
28 again, and f it fifteen fathoms. "
28:14 Where we f brethren, and were "
Ro 4: 1 as pertaining to the flesh, hath f? "
7:10 to life, I f to be unto death. "
10:20 was f of them that sought me not; "
1Co 4: 2 stewards, that a man be f faithful. "
15:15 Yea, and we are f false witnesses "
2Co 2:13 because I f not Titus my brother: "
5: 3 clothed we shall not be f naked. "
7:14 made before Titus, is f a truth. 1096
11:12 they may be f even as we. 2147
12:20 and that I shall be f unto you such "
Ga 2:17 we ourselves also are f sinners, "
Ph'p 2: 8 And being f in fashion as a man, "
3: 9 And be f in him, not having mine "
1Ti 3:10 of a deacon, being f blameless. *
2Ti 1:17 me out very diligently, and f me. 2147
Heb 11: 5 and was not f, because God had "
12:17 for he f no place of repentance, "
1Pe 1: 7 might be f unto praise and honour "
2:22 neither was guile f in his mouth: "
2Pe 3:14 that ye may be f of him in peace, "
2 Joh 4 f of thy children walking in truth, "
Re 2: 2 and are not, and hast f them liars: "
3: 2 for I have not f thy works perfect "
5: 4 no man was f worthy to open and "
12: 8 neither was their place f any more "
14: 5 And in their mouth was f no guile "
16:20 and the mountains were not f. "
18:21 and shall be f no more at all. "
22 he be, shall be f any more in thee; "
24 in her was f the blood of prophets, "
20:11 and there was f no place for them. "
15 And whosoever was not f written "

foundation See also FOUNDATIONS.
Ex 9:18 the f thereof even until now. *3245
Jos 6:26 he shall lay the f thereof in his "
1Ki 5:17 stones, to lay the f of the house. "
6:37 In the fourth year was the f of the "
7: 9 even from the f unto the coping, 4527
10 And the f was of costly stones, 3245
16:34 he laid the f thereof in Abiram his "
2Ch 8:16 unto the day of the f of the house 4143
23: 5 a third part at the gate of the f: 3247
31: 7 began to lay the f of the heaps, 3245
Ezr 3: 6 f of the temple of the Lord was not "
10 when the builders laid the f of the "
11 the f of the house of the Lord was "
12 when the f of the house was laid "
5:16 and laid the f of the house of God* 787
Job 4:19 whose f is in the dust, which are 3247
22:16 whose f was overflown with a flood: "
Ps 87: 1 His f is in the holy mountains. 3248
102:25 Of old hast thou laid the f of the 3245
137: 7 rase it, even to the f thereof. 3247
Pr 10:25 the righteous is an everlasting f. "
Isa 28:16 I lay in Zion for a f a stone, 3248
16 a precious corner stone, a sure f: 4143
44:28 to the temple, Thy f shall be laid. 3245
48:13 Mine hand also hath laid the f of "
Eze 13:14 the f thereof shall be discovered, 3247
Hab 3:13 discovering the f unto the neck. "
Hag 2:18 f of the Lord's temple was laid. 3245
Zec 4: 9 have laid the f of this house; 3248
8: 9 the day that the f of the house "
12: 1 and layeth the f of the earth. "
M't 13:35 secret from the f of the world. 2602
25:34 for you from the f of the world: "
Lu 6:48 deep, and laid the f on a rock: 2310
49 without a f built an house upon the "
11:50 shed from the f of the world, 2602
14:29 after he hath laid the f, and is not 2310
Joh 17:24 lovest me before the f of the world, 2602
Ro 15:20 build upon another man's f: 2310
1Co 3:10 I have laid the f, and another "
11 For other f can no man lay than "
12 upon this f gold, silver, precious "
Eph 1: 4 in him before the f of the world, 2602
2:20 built upon the f of the apostles 2310
1Ti 6:19 for themselves a good f against "
2Ti 2:19 the f of God standeth sure, having "
He 1:10 hast laid the f of the earth; 2311
4: 3 finished from the f of the world. 2602
6: 1 laying again the f of repentance 2310
9:26 suffered since the f of the world: 2602
1Pe 1:20 before the f of the world, but was "
Re 13: 8 Lamb slain from the f of the world. "
17: 8 of life from the f of the world, "
21:19 The first f was jasper; the second, 2310

foundations
De 32:22 on fire the f of the mountains. 4146
2Sa 22: 8 the f of heaven moved and shook, "
16 the f of the world were discovered, "
Ezr 4:12 the wall thereof, and joined the f. 787

Ezr 6: 3 let the f thereof be strongly laid; 787
Job 38: 4 thou when I laid the f of the earth? 3245
6 are the f thereof fastened? or who 134
Ps 11: 3 If the f be destroyed, what can the 8356
18: 7 the f also of the hills moved and 4146
15 the f of the world were discovered "
82: 5 all of the f of the earth are out of "
104: 5 Who laid the f of the earth, 4349
Pr 8:29 he appointed the f of the earth: 4146
Isa 16: 7 f of Kir-hareseth shall ye mourn;* 808
24:18 and the f of the earth do shake. 4146
40:21 understood from the f of the earth? "
51:13 and laid the f of the earth; 3245
16 and lay the f of the earth, "
54:11 and lay thy f with sapphires. "
58:12 up the f of many generations; 4146
Jer 31:37 and the f of the earth searched out "
50:15 her f are fallen, her walls are * 803
51:26 thee a corner, nor a stone for f; 4146
La 4:11 and it hath devoured the f thereof. 3247
Eze 30: 4 and her f shall be broken down. "
41: 8 f of the side chambers were a full 4328
Mic 1: 6 and I will discover the f thereof. 3247
6: 2 and ye strong f of the earth: 4146
Ac 16:26 the f of the prison were shaken: 2310
He 11:10 he looked for a city which hath f, "
Re 21:14 the wall of the city had twelve f, "
19 And the f of the wall of the city "

founded See also CONFOUNDED.
Ps 24: 2 For he hath f it upon the seas, 3245
89:11 fulness thereof, thou hast f them. "
104: 8 place which thou hast f for them. "
119:152 that thou hast f them for ever. "
Pro 3:19 Lord by wisdom hath f the earth; "
Isa 14:32 the Lord hath f Zion, and the poor "
23:13 Assyrian f it for them that dwell† "
Am 9: 6 and hath f his troop in the earth; "
M't 7:25 fell not: for it was f upon a rock. 2311
Lu 6:48 shake it: for it was f upon a rock.* "

founder
J'g 17: 4 and gave them to the f, who made 6884
Jer 6:29 f melteth in vain: for the wicked* "
10: 9 hands of the f: blue and purple * "
14 every f is confounded by the * "
51:17 every f is confounded by the * "

foundest
Ne 9: 8 f his heart faithful before thee. 4672

fountain See also FOUNTAINS.
Ge 16: 7 found her by a f of water in the 5869
7 by the f in the way to Shur. "
Le 11:36 Nevertheless a f or pit, wherein 4599
20:18 he hath discovered her f, and she 4726
18 she hath uncovered the f of her "
De 33:28 f of Jacob shall be upon a land 5869
Jos 15: 9 the f of the water of Nephtoah, 4599
1Sa 29: 1 Israelites pitched by a f which 5869
Ne 2:14 I went on to the gate of the f, "
3:15 the gate of the f repaired Shallun "
12:37 And at the f gate, which was over "
Ps 36: 9 For with thee is the f of life: 4726
68:26 the Lord, from the f of Israel. "
74:15 Thou didst cleave the f and the 4599
114: 8 water, the flint into a f of waters. "
Pr 5:18 Let thy f be blessed: and rejoice 4726
13:14 The law of the wise is a f of life, "
14:27 The fear of the Lord is a f of life, "
25:26 troubled f, and a corrupt spring. 4599
Ec 12: 6 or the pitcher be broken at the f, 4002
Ca 4:12 a spring shut up, a f sealed. 4599
15 a f of gardens, a well of living "
Jer 2:13 forsaken me the f of living waters, 4726
6: 7 As a f casteth out her waters, * 953
9: 1 waters, and mine eyes a f of tears, 4726
17:13 forsaken the Lord, the f of living "
Ho 13:15 and his f shall be dried up: 4599
Joel 3:18 a f shall come forth of the house "
Zec 13: 1 that day there shall be a f opened 4726
M'r 5:29 straightway the f of her blood 4077
Jas 3:11 Doth a f send forth at the same "
12 so can no f both yield salt water* "
Re 21: 6 that is athirst of the f of the water "

fountains
Ge 7:11 were all the f of the great deep 4599
8: 2 f also of the deep and the windows "
Nu 33: 9 in Elim were twelve f of water, *5869
De 8: 7 of f and depths that spring out of "
1Ki 18: 5 unto all f of water, and unto all 4599
2Ch 32: 3 to stop the waters of the f which 5869
4 stopped all the f, and the brook 4599
Pr 5:16 Let thy f be dispersed abroad, * "
8:24 when there were no f abounding "
28 he strengthened the f of the deep: 5869
Isa 41:18 and f in the midst of the valleys: 4599
Re 7:17 shall lead them unto living f of 4077
8:10 rivers, and upon the f of waters; "
14: 7 the sea, and the f of waters. "
16: 4 upon the rivers and f of waters: "

four See also FOURFOLD; FOURSCORE; FOURSQUARE; FOURTEEN.
Ge 2:10 parted, and became into f heads. 702
11:13 after he begat Salah f hundred and "
15 after he begat Eber f hundred and "
16 And Eber lived f and thirty years, "
17 after he begat Peleg f hundred "
14: 9 king of Ellasar; f kings with five. "
15:13 shall afflict them f hundred years; "
23:15 worth f hundred shekels of silver; "
16 Heth, f hundred shekels of silver, "
32: 6 and f hundred men with him. "
33: 1 and with him f hundred men. "
47:24 and f parts shall be your own, "
Ex 12:40 was f hundred and thirty years. "
41 the f hundred and thirty years, "
22: 1 an ox, and f sheep for a sheep. "

Ex 25:12 thou shalt cast *f* rings of gold for it, 702
12 and put them in the *f* corners "
26 shalt make for it *f* rings of gold, "
26 and put the rings in the *f* corners "
26 that are on the *f* feet thereof. "
34 *f* bowls made like unto almonds, "
26: 2, 8 breadth of one curtain *f* cubits, "
32 *f* pillars of shittim wood overlaid "
32 gold, upon the *f* sockets of silver. "
27: 2 horns of it upon the *f* corners "
4 net shalt thou make *f* brasen rings "
4 rings in the *f* corners thereof. "
16 and their pillars shall be *f*, "
16 and their sockets *f*. "
28:17 even *f* rows of stones: the first row "
36: 9 the breadth of one curtain *f* cubits: "
15 *f* cubits was the breadth of one "
36 *f* pillars of shittim wood, and "
36 he cast for them *f* sockets of silver. "
37: 3 And he cast for it *f* rings of gold, "
3 to be set by the *f* corners of it; "
13 And he cast for it *f* rings of gold, "
13 and put the rings upon the *f* corners "
13 that were in the *f* feet thereof. "
20 were *f* bowls made like almonds, "
38: 2 the horns thereof on the *f* corners "
5 And he cast *f* rings for the *f* ends "
19 And their pillars were *f*, "
19 and their sockets of brass *f*; "
29 thousand and *f* hundred shekels. "
39:10 they set in it *f* rows of stones: "
Le 11:20 fowls that creep, going upon all *f*, "
21 creeping thing that goeth upon all *f*, "
23 creeping things, which have *f* feet, "
27 manner of beasts that go on all *f*, "
42 and whatsoever goeth upon all *f*, "
Nu 1:29 fifty and *f* thousand and *f* hundred. "
31 and seven thousand and *f* hundred. "
37 and five thousand and *f* hundred. "
43 and three thousand and *f* hundred "
2: 6 fifty and *f* thousand and *f* hundred. "
8 and seven thousand and *f* hundred. "
9 and six thousand and *f* hundred, "
16 thousand and *f* hundred and fifty, "
23 and five thousand and *f* hundred. "
30 and three thousand and *f* hundred. "
7: 7 Two wagons and *f* oxen he gave "
8 *f* wagons and eight oxen he gave "
85 thousand and *f* hundred shekels, "
88 were twenty and *f* bullocks, the "
25: 9 plague were twenty and *f* thousand. "
26:25 threescore and *f* thousand and "
43 and *f* thousand and *f* hundred. "
47 and three thousand and *f* hundred. "
50 and five thousand and *f* hundred. "
De 3:11 and *f* cubits the breadth of it, "
22:12 upon the *f* quarters of thy vesture, "
Jos 19: 7 Ashan; *f* cities and their villages: "
21:18 Almon with her suburbs; *f* cities. "
22 Beth-horon with her suburbs; *f* "
24 Gath-rimmon with her suburbs; *f* "
29 En-gannim with her suburbs; *f* "
31 Rehob with her suburbs; *f* cities. "
35 Nahalal with her suburbs; *f* cities. "
37 Mephaath with her suburbs; *f* "
39 with her suburbs; *f* cities in all. "
J'g 9:34 against Shechem in *f* companies. "
11:40 of Jephthah the Gileadite *f* days "
19: 2 and was there *f* whole months. "
20: 2 *f* hundred thousand footmen that "
17 *f* hundred thousand men that drew "
47 in the rock Rimmon *f* months. "
21:12 *f* hundred young virgins, that had "
1Sa 4: 2 in the field about *f* thousand men. "
22: 2 with him about *f* hundred men. "
25:13 after David about *f* hundred men; "
27: 7 was a full year and *f* months. "
30:10 David pursued, he and *f* hundred "
17 save *f* hundred young men, which "
2Sa 21:20 six toes, *f* and twenty in number; "
22 These *f* were born to the giant in "
1Ki 6: 1 in the *f* hundred and eightieth year "
7: 2 upon *f* rows of cedar pillars, with "
19 lily work in the porch, *f* cubits. "
27 *f* cubits was the length of one base, "
27 and *f* cubits the breadth thereof, "
30 every base had *f* brasen wheels, "
30 *f* corners thereof had undersetters: "
32 under the borders were *f* wheels; "
34 *f* undersetters to the *f* corners of "
38 and every layer was *f* cubits: and "
42 *f* hundred pomegranates for the "
9:28 gold, *f* hundred and twenty talents, "
10:26 thousand and *f* hundred chariots, "
15:33 in Tirzah twenty and *f* years. "
18:19 the prophets of Baal *f* hundred and "
19 prophets of the groves *f* hundred, "
22 Baal's prophets are *f* hundred and "
33 Fill *f* barrels with water, and pour "
22: 6 together, about *f* hundred men, and "
2Ki 7: 3 And there were *f* leprous men at "
14:13 unto the corner gate, *f* hundred "
1Ch 3: 5 and Nathan, and Solomon, *f*, "
5:18 *f* and forty thousand seven hundred "
7: 1 and Pua, Jashub, and Shimrom, *f*, "
7 and two thousand and thirty and *f*. "
9:24 In *f* quarters were the porters, "
26 the *f* chief porters, were in their set "
12:26 Levi *f* thousand and six hundred. "
20: 6 whose fingers and toes were *f* and "
21: 5 *f* hundred threescore and ten "
20 his *f* sons with him hid themselves. "
23: 4 twenty and *f* thousand were to set "
5 Moreover *f* thousand were porters; "
5 and *f* thousand praised the Lord "
10 These *f* were the sons of Shimei. "

1Ch 23:12 Izhar, Hebron, and Uzziel, *f*. 702
24:18 the *f* and twentieth to Maaziah. "
25:31 *f* and twentieth to Romamti-ezer. "
26:17 northward *f* a day, southward *f* a "
18 *f* at the causeway, and two at "
27: 1 of every course were...*f* thousand "
2 in his course were... *f* thousand. "
4 likewise were...and *f* thousand. "
5, 7, 8, 9, 10, 11, 12, 13, 14, 15 and in
his course were twenty and *f* thousand.
2Ch 1:14 a thousand and *f* hundred chariots, "
4:13 *f* hundred pomegranates on the "
8:18 *f* hundred and fifty talents of gold, "
9:25 Solomon had *f* thousand stalls for "
13: 3 even *f* hundred thousand chosen "
18: 5 of prophets *f* hundred men, and "
25:23 the corner gate, *f* hundred cubits. "
Ezr 1:10 basons of a second sort *f* hundred. "
11 were five thousand and *f* hundred "
2: 7 a thousand two hundred fifty and *f*. "
15 of Adin, *f* hundred fifty and *f*. "
31 a thousand two hundred fifty and *f*. "
40 children of Hodaviah, seventy and *f*. "
67 Their camels, *f* hundred thirty and "
6:17 hundred rams, *f* hundred lambs; 703
Ne 6: 4 Yet they sent unto me *f* times 702
7:12 thousand two hundred fifty and *f*. "
23 Bezai, three hundred twenty and *f*. "
34 thousand two hundred fifty and *f*. "
43 children of Hodevah, seventy and *f*. "
69 Their camels, *f* hundred thirty "
11: 6 *f* hundred three score and eight "
18 were two hundred fourscore and *f*. "
Job 1:19 smote the *f* corners of the house, "
42:16 his sons' sons, even *f* generations. "
Pr 30:15 *f* things say not, It is enough: "
18 yea, *f* which I know not: "
21 and for *f* which it cannot bear: "
24 *f* things which are little upon the "
29 yea, *f* are comely in going: "
Isa 11:12 from the *f* corners of the earth. "
17: 6 *f* or five in the outmost fruitful "
Jer 15: 3 I will appoint over them *f* kinds, "
36:23 Jehudi had read three or *f* leaves, "
49:36 the *f* winds from the *f* quarters "
52:21 thickness thereof was *f* fingers: "
30 persons were *f* thousand and six "
Eze 1: 5 the likeness of *f* living creatures. "
6 And every one had *f* faces, "
6 and every one had *f* wings. "
8 *f* sides; and they *f* had their faces "
10 they *f* had the face of a man, "
10 and they *f* had the face of an ox on "
10 they *f* also had the face of an eagle. "
15 living creatures, with his *f* faces. "
16 they *f* had one likeness: and their "
17 went, they went upon their *f* sides: "
18 full of eyes round about them *f*. "
7: 2 upon the *f* corners of the land. "
10: 9 the *f* wheels by the cherubims, "
10 they *f* had one likeness, as if a "
11 went, they went upon their *f* sides; "
12 even the wheels that they *f* had. "
14 And every one had *f* faces: the "
21 Every one had *f* faces apiece, "
21 and every one *f* wings; "
14:21 when I send my *f* sore judgments "
37: 9 Come from the *f* winds, O breath, "
40:41 *F* tables were on this side, "
41 and *f* tables on that side, "
42 And the *f* tables were of hewn "
41: 5 of every side chamber, *f* cubits "
42:20 He measured it by the *f* sides: "
43:14 the greater settle shall be *f* cubits, "
15 So the altar shall be *f* cubits; "
15 altar and upward shall be *f* horns. "
16 square in the *f* squares thereof. "
17 fourteen broad in the *f* squares "
20 *f* horns of it, and on the *f* corners "
45:19 upon the *f* corners of the settle "
46:21 pass by the *f* corners of the court; "
22 In the *f* corners of the court were "
22 *f* corners were of one measure. "
23 in them round about them *f*, and "
48:16 the north side *f* thousand and five "
16 the south side *f* thousand and five "
16 the east side *f* thousand and five "
16 the west side *f* thousand and five "
30 on the north side, *f* thousand and "
32 at the east side, *f* thousand and "
33 at the side *f* thousand and "
34 At the west side *f* thousand and "
Da 1:17 these *f* children, God gave them "
3:25 Lo, I see *f* men loose, walking 703
7: 2 the *f* winds of the heaven strove "
3 And *f* great beasts came up from "
6 upon the back of it *f* wings of a "
6 the beast had also *f* heads; "
17 beasts, which are *f*, are *f* kings, "
8: 8 and for it came up *f* notable ones 702
8 toward the *f* winds of heaven. "
22 *f* stood up for it, *f* kingdoms shall "
10: 4 in the *f* and twentieth day of the "
11: 4 be divided toward the *f* winds of "
Am 1: 3 of Damascus, and for *f*, I will not "
6 of Gaza, and for *f*, I will not turn "
9 transgressions of Tyrus, and for *f*, "
11 of Edom, and for *f*, I will not turn "
13 Ammon, and for *f*, I will not turn "
2: 1 of Moab, and for *f*, I will not turn "
4 of Judah, and for *f*, I will not turn "
6 of Israel, and for *f*, I will not turn "
Hag 1:15 In the *f* and twentieth day of the "
2:10 In the *f* and twentieth day of the "
18 from the *f* and twentieth day of "

Hag 2:20 in the *f* and twentieth day of the 702
Zec 1: 7 Upon the *f* and twentieth day of "
18 and saw, and behold *f* horns. "
20 the Lord shewed me *f* carpenters. "
2: 6 as the *f* winds of the heaven, "
6: 1 there came *f* chariots out from "
5 are the *f* spirits of the heavens. "
M't 15:38 *f* thousand men, beside women 5070
16:10 the seven loaves of the *f* thousand, "
24:31 together his elect from the *f* 5064
M'r 2: 3 of the palsy, which was borne of *f*. "
8: 9 eaten were about *f* thousand: 5070
20 when the seven among *f* thousand, "
13:27 his elect from the *f* winds, 5064
Lu 2:37 of about fourscore and *f* years, "
Joh 4:35 not ye, There are yet *f* months, 5072
11:17 lain in the grave *f* days already. 5064
39 for he hath been dead *f* days. 5066
19:23 *f* parts, to every soldier a part; 5064
Ac 5:36 number of men, about *f* hundred, 5071
7: 6 entreat them evil *f* hundred years. "
10:11 great sheet knit at the *f* corners, 5064
30 *F* days ago I was fasting until 5067
11: 5 down from heaven by *f* corners; 5064
12: 4 and delivered him to *f* quaternions "
13:20 the space of *f* hundred and fifty *5071
21: 9 the same man had *f* daughters, 5064
23 We have *f* men which have a vow "
38 wilderness *f* thousand men that 5070
27:29 they cast *f* anchors out of the 5064
Ga 3:17 *f* hundred and thirty years after, 5071
Re 4: 4 throne were *f* and twenty seats: 5064
4 I saw *f* and twenty elders sitting, "
6 *f* beasts full of eyes before and "
8 And the *f* beasts had each of them "
10 The *f* and twenty elders fall down "
5: 6 of the throne and of the *f* beasts, "
8 *f* beasts and *f* and twenty elders "
14 And the *f* beasts said, Amen. "
14 *f* and twenty elders fell down * "
6: 1 one of the *f* beasts saying, Come "
6 in the midst of the *f* beasts say, "
7: 1 after these things I saw *f* angels "
1 on the *f* corners of the earth, "
1 holding the *f* winds of the earth, "
2 with a loud voice to the *f* angels, "
4 hundred and forty and *f* thousand "
11 about the elders and the *f* beasts, "
9:13 I heard a voice from the *f* horns* "
14 Loose the *f* angels which are "
15 And the *f* angels were loosed, "
11:16 the *f* and twenty elders, which sat "
14: 1 an hundred forty and *f* thousand, "
3 and before the *f* beasts, and the "
3 hundred and forty and *f* thousand "
15: 7 And one of the *f* beasts gave "
19: 4 the *f* and twenty elders and the *f* "
20: 8 are in the *f* quarters of the earth, "
21:17 an hundred and forty and *f* cubits, "

fourfold
2Sa 12: 6 And he shall restore the lamb *f*, 706
Lu 19: 8 false accusation, I restore him *f*. 5073

fourfooted
Ac 10:12 manner of *f* beasts of the earth, 5074
11: 6 and saw *f* beasts of the earth, "
Ro 1:23 *f* beasts, and creeping things. "

four hundred See FOUR and HUNDRED.

fourscore
Ge 16:16 Abram was *f* and six years old, 8084
35:28 of Isaac were an hundred and *f* "
Ex 7: 7 And Moses was *f* years old, "
7 and Aaron *f* and three years old, "
Nu 2: 9 hundred thousand and *f* thousand "
4:48 thousand and five hundred and *f*. "
Jos 14:10 I am this day *f* and five years old. "
J'g 3:30 And the land had rest *f* years. "
1Sa 22:18 slew on that day *f* and five persons "
2Sa 19:32 a very aged man, even *f* years old: "
35 I am this day *f* years old: and can "
1Ki 5:15 and *f* thousand hewers in the "
12:21 an hundred and *f* thousand chosen "
2Ki 6:25 an ass's head was sold for *f* pieces "
10:24 Jehu appointed *f* men without, "
19:35 an hundred *f* and five thousand: "
1Ch 7: 5 genealogies *f* and seven thousand. "
15: 9 Eliel the chief, and his brethren *f*: "
25: 7 was two hundred *f* and eight. "
2Ch 2: 2 and *f* thousand to hew in the "
18 and *f* thousand to be hewers in the "
11: 1 an hundred and *f* thousand chosen "
14: 8 two hundred and *f* thousand: all "
17:15 him two hundred and *f* thousand. "
18 an hundred and *f* thousand ready "
26:17 and with him *f* priests of the Lord, "
Ezr 8: 8 Michael, and with him *f* males. "
Ne 7:26 Netopha, an hundred *f* and eight. "
11:18 city were two hundred *f* and four. "
Es 1: 4 days, even an hundred and *f* days. "
Ps 90:10 if by reason of strength they be *f* "
Ca 6: 8 queens, and *f* concubines, and "
Isa 37:36 a hundred and *f* and five thousand: "
Jer 41: 5 and from Samaria, even *f* men, "
Lu 2:37 widow of about *f* and four years, 3589
16: 7 Take thy bill, and write *f*. "

fourscore thousand See FOURSCORE and THOUSAND.

foursquare
Ex 27: 1 the altar shall be *f*: and the height 7251
28:16 *F* it shall be being doubled; a span "
30: 2 *f* shall it be: and two cubits shall "
37:25 it was *f*; and two cubits was the "
38: 1 it was *f*; and three cubits the "
39: 9 It was *f*; they made the "

1Ki 7:31 with their borders, f, not round, 7251
Eze 40:47 an hundred cubits broad, f; "
48:20 ye shall offer the holy oblation f, 7243
Re 21:16 And the city lieth f, and the length 5068
fourteen
Ge 31:41 I served thee f years for thy 702, 6240
46:22 Jacob: all the souls were f. " "
Nu 1:27 f thousand and six hundred. " 7657
2: 4 f thousand and six hundred. " "
16:49 were f thousand and seven " "
29:13 and f lambs of the first year; " 6246
15 to each lamb of the f lambs: " "
17, 20 f lambs of the first year " "
23, 26, 29, 32 and f lambs of the " "
Jos 15:36 f cities with their villages. " "
18:28 f cities with their villages. " "
1Ki 8:65 and seven days, even f days. " "
1Ch 25: 5 And God gave to Heman f sons " "
2Ch 13:21 mighty, and married f wives. " "
Job 42:12 for he had f thousand sheep, " "
Eze 43:17 settle shall be f cubits long " "
17 f broad in the four squares " "
M't 1:17 Abraham to David are f generations 1180
17 into Babylon are f generations; "
17 unto Christ are f generations. "
2Co 12: 2 a man in Christ above f years ago, "
Ga 2: 1 f years after I went up again to "
fourteenth
Ge 14: 5 f year came Chedorlaomer, 702, 6240
Ex 12: 6 shall keep it up until the f day " "
18 on the f day of the month at " "
Le 23: 5 In the f day of the first month " "
Nu 9: 3 In the f day of this month, at " "
5 the passover on the f day of " "
11 f day of the second month at " "
28:16 in the f day of the first month " "
Jos 5:10 the passover on the f day of " "
2Ki 18:13 in the f year of king Hezekiah " "
1Ch 24:13 Huppah, the f to Jeshebeab, " "
25:21 f to Mattithiah, he, his sons, " "
2Ch 30:15 the passover on the f day of " "
35: 1 on the f day of the first month. " "
Ezr 6:19 the passover upon the f day " "
Es 9:15 on the f day also of the month " "
17 and on the f day of the same " "
18 and on the f thereof; " "
19 the f day of the month Adar " "
21 they should keep the f day of " "
Isa 36: 1 in the f year of king Hezekiah, " "
Eze 40: 1 in the f year after that the city " "
45:21 first month, in the f day of the " "
Ac 27:27 But when the f night was come, 5065
33 is the f day that ye have tarried "
fourteen thousand See FOURTEEN and THOUSAND.
fourth
Ge 1:19 and the morning were the f day. 7243
2:14 And the f river is Euphrates. "
15:16 the f generation they shall come "
Ex 20: 5 unto the third and f generation 7256
28:20 the f row a beryl, and an onyx, 7243
29:40 the f part of an hin of beaten oil; 7253
40 and the f part of an hin of wine "
34: 7 the third and to the f generation. 7256
39:13 the f row, a beryl, an onyx, 7243
Le 19:24 in the f year all the fruit thereof "
23:13 of wine, the f part of an hin. "
Nu 7:30 On the f day Elizur the son of "
14:18 unto the third and f generation. 7256
15: 4 with the f part of an hin of oil. 7243
5 And the f part of an hin of wine "
23:10 the number of the f part of Israel? 7255
28: 5 the f part of an hin of beaten oil. 7243
7 the f part of an hin for the one "
14 and a f part of an hin unto a lamb: "
29:23 And on the f day ten bullocks, "
De 5: 9 unto the third and f generation *7256
Jos 19:17 the f lot came out to Issachar, 7243
J'g 19: 5 And it came to pass on the f day, "
1Sa 9: 8 the f part of a shekel of silver: 7253
2Sa 3: 4 And the f, Adonijah the son of 7243
1Ki 6: 1 in the f year of Solomon's reign "
33 olive tree, a f part of the wall. "
37 In the f year was the foundation "
22:41 the f year of Ahab king of Israel. 702
2Ki 6:25 the f part of a cab of dove's dung 7255
10:30 children of the f generation shall 7243
15:12 of Israel unto the f generation. "
18: 9 in the f year of king Hezekiah, "
25: 3 of the f month the famine prevailed "
1Ch 2:14 Nethaneel the f, Raddai the fifth, 7243
3: 2 the f, Adonijah the son of Haggith: "
15 the third Zedekiah, the f Shallum. "
8: 2 Nohah the f, and Rapha the fifth. "
12:10 Mishmannah the f, Jeremiah the "
23:19 the third, Jekameam the f. "
24: 8 third to Harim, the f to Seorim, "
23 the third, Jekameam the f. "
25:11 The f to Izri, he, his sons, "
26: 2 the third, Jathniel the f, "
4 Joah the third, Sacar the f, and "
11 the third, Zechariah the f: "
27: 7 The f captain for the f month was "
2Ch 3: 2 month, in the f year of his reign. 702
20:26 And on the f day they assembled 7243
Ezr 8:33 Now on the f day was the silver "
Ne 9: 1 Now in the twenty and f day 702
3 their God one f part of the day; of 7243
3 and another f part they confessed, "
Jer 25: 1 Judah in the f year of Jehoiakim "
28: 1 the f year, and in the fifth month, "
36: 1 pass in the f year of Jehoiakim "
39: 2 the f month, the ninth day of the "
45: 1 the f year of Jehoiakim the son of "
Jer 46: 2 smote in the f year of Jehoiakim 7243
51:59 Babylon in the f year of his reign. "
52: 6 And in the f month, in the ninth day "
Eze 1: 1 in the f month, in the fifth day of "
10:14 and the f the face of an eagle. "
Da 2:40 And the f kingdom shall be strong 7244
3:25 the form of the f is like the Son of "
7: 7 and behold a f beast, dreadful and "
19 know the truth of the f beast, "
23 The f beast shall be the f kingdom "
11: 2 f shall be far richer than they all: 7243
Zec 6: 3 the f chariot grisled and bay horses. "
7: 1 pass in the f year of king Darius, 702
1 in the f day of the ninth month, "
8:19 The fast of the f month, and the 7243
M't 14:25 And in the f watch of the night 5067
M'r 6:48 and about the f watch of the night "
Re 4: 7 the f beast was like a flying eagle. "
6: 7 And when he had opened the f seal, "
7 I heard the voice of the f beast "
8 them over the f part of the earth, "
8:12 And the f angel sounded, and the "
16: 8 And the f angel poured out his vial "
21:19 a chalcedony; the f, an emerald; "
four thousand See FOUR and THOUSAND.
fowl See also FOWLS.
Ge 1:20 and f that may fly above the earth 5775
21 and every winged f after his kind: "
22 and let f multiply in the earth. "
26 of the sea, and over the f of the air, "
30 of the earth, and to every f of the air, "
2:19 and every f of the air; and brought "
20 and to the f of the air, and to every "
7:14 every f after his kind, every bird "
21 both of f, and of cattle, and of "
23 the f of the heaven; and they were "
8:17 both of f, and of cattle, and of "
19 every creeping thing, and every f, "
20 clean beast, and of every clean f, "
9: 2 and upon every f of the air, "
10 creature that is with you, of the f, "
Le 7:26 manner of blood, whether it be of f "
11:46 the law of the beasts, and of the f, "
17:13 hunteth and catcheth any beast or f "
20:25 souls abominable by beast, or by f, "
De 4:17 the likeness of any winged f that 6833
1Ki 4:23 and fallowdeer, and fatted f. 1257
33 he spake also of beasts, and of f, 5775
Job 28: 7 is a path which no f knoweth, *5861
Ps 8: 8 The f of the air, and the fish of the 6833
148:10 creeping things, and flying f: "
Jer 9:10 both the f of the heavens and the 5775
Eze 17:23 shall dwell all f of every wing; 6833
39:17 feathered f, and to every beast * "
44:31 or torn, whether it be f or beast. 5775
Da 7: 6 the back of it four wings of a f; 5776
fowler See also FOWLERS.
Ps 91: 3 thee from the snare of the f, and 3353
Pr 6: 5 as a bird from the hand of the f. "
Ho 9: 8 but the prophet is a snare of a f *3353
fowlers
Ps 124: 7 as a bird out of the snare of the f: 3369
fowls
Ge 6: 7 thing, and the f of the air; for it *5775
20 f after their kind, and of cattle * "
7: 3 Of f also of the air by sevens, * "
8 f, and of every thing that creepeth * "
15:11 f came down upon the carcases, *5861
Le 1:14 his offering to the Lord be of f, 5775
11:13 have in abomination among the f; "
20 All f that creep, going upon all * "
20:25 between unclean f and clean: * "
De 14:20 But of all clean f ye may eat. "
28:26 carcase shall be meat unto all f of * "
1Sa 17:44 and I will give thy flesh unto the f * "
46 the Philistines this day unto the f * "
1Ki 14:11 the field shall the f of the air eat: "
16: 4 the fields shall the f of the air eat. "
21:24 the field shall the f of the air eat. "
Ne 5:18 also f were prepared for me, and 6833
Job 12: 7 and the f of the air, and they shall 5775
28:21 kept close from the f of the air. "
35:11 us wiser than the f of heaven? "
Ps 50:11 I know all the f of the mountains: "
78:27 and feathered f like as the sand * "
79: 2 meat unto the f of the heaven, "
104:12 By them shall the f of the heaven * "
Isa 18: 6 unto the f of the mountains, *5861
6 the f shall summer upon them, * "
Jer 7:33 people shall be meat for the f of 5775
15: 3 the f of the heaven, and the beasts "
16: 4 shall be meat for the f of heaven, "
19: 7 to be meat for the f of the heaven, "
34:20 shall be for meat unto the f of the "
Eze 29: 5 field and to the f of the heaven. "
31: 6 the f of heaven made their nests "
13 all the f of the heaven remain, "
32: 4 all the f of the heaven to remain "
38:20 the sea and the f of the heaven, "
Da 2:38 and the f of the heaven hath he 5776
4:12 and the f of the heaven dwelt in 6853
14 it, and the f from his branches: "
21 the f of the heaven had their "
Ho 2:18 with the f of heaven, and with the 5775
4: 3 and with the f of heaven; yea, the "
7:12 them down as the f of heaven; I "
Zep 1: 3 I will consume the f of the heaven, "
M't 6:26 Behold, the f of the air: for they *4071
13: 4 the f came and devoured them * "
M'r 4: 4 and the f of the air came and * "
32 the f of the air may lodge under * "
Lu 8: 5 and the f of the air devoured it. * "
12:24 more are ye better than the f? * "
Lu 13:19 and the f of the air lodged in the *4071
Ac 10:12 creeping things, and f of the air. "
11: 6 creeping things, and f of the air. "
Re 19:17 saying to all the f that fly in the *3732
21 the f were filled with their flesh. * "
fox See also FOXES.
Ne 4: 3 if a f go up, he shall even break 7776
Lu 13:32 Go ye, and tell that f, Behold, I 258
foxes
J'g 15: 4 went and caught three hundred f, 7776
Ps 63:10 they shall be a portion for f. "
Ca 2:15 Take us the f, the little f, that "
La 5:18 is desolate, the f walk upon it. "
Eze 13: 4 are like the f in the deserts. "
M't 8:20 The f have holes, and the birds of 258
Lu 9:58 F have holes, and birds of the air "
fragments
M't 14:20 took up of the f that remained *2801
M'r 6:43 up twelve baskets full of the f, * "
8:19, 20 baskets full of f took ye up? * "
Lu 9:17 taken up of f that remained to * "
Joh 6:12 Gather up the f that remain, * "
13 filled twelve baskets with the f * "
frail
Ps 39: 4 that I may know how f I am. 2310
frame See also FRAMED; FRAMETH.
J'g 12: 6 could not f to pronounce it right. 3559
Ps 103:14 For he knoweth our f; he 3336
Jer 18:11 I f evil against you, and devise 3335
Eze 40: 2 by which was as the f of a city on 4011
Ho 5: 4 They will not f their doings to *5414
framed
Isa 29:16 or shall the thing f say of him ‡3336
16 say of him that f it, He had no ‡3335
Eph 2:21 In whom all the building fitly f 4883
Heb 11: 3 the worlds were f by the word of 2675
frameth
Ps 50:19 evil, and thy tongue f deceit. 6775
94:20 which f mischief by a law? 3335
frankincense
Ex 30:34 these sweet spices with pure f: 3828
Le 2: 1 oil upon it, and put f thereon: "
2 with all the f thereof; and the "
15 and lay f thereon: it is a meat "
16 with all the f thereof: it is an "
5:11 neither shall he put any f thereon: "
6:15 all the f which is upon the meat "
24: 7 shalt put pure f upon each row, "
Nu 5:15 put f thereon; for it is an offering "
1Ch 9:29 the oil, and the f, and the spices. "
Ne 13: 5 the f, and the vessels, and the "
9 with the meat offering and the f. "
Ca 3: 6 perfumed with myrrh and f, with "
4: 6 of myrrh, and to the hill of f. "
14 with all trees of f; myrrh and "
M't 2:11 gifts; gold, and f, and myrrh. 3030
Re 18:13 f, and wine, and oil, and fine flour, "
frankly
Lu 7:42 to pay, he f forgave them both. *5435
fraud See also DEFRAUD.
Ps 10: 7 full of cursing and deceit and f: *8496
Jas 5: 4 which is of you kept back by f, 650
fray
De 28:26 and no man shall f them away. ‡2729
Jer 7:33 and none shall f them away. ‡ "
Zec 1:21 but these are come to f them, ‡ "
freckled
Le 13:39 it is a f spot that groweth in the *933
free See also FREED; FREEMAN; FREEWILL; FREEWOMAN.
Ex 21: 2 in the seventh he shall go out f 2670
5 my children; I will not go out f: "
11 shall she go out f without money. *2600
26 let him go f for his eye's sake. 2670
27 let him go f for his tooth's sake. "
36: 3 brought yet unto him f offerings *5071
Le 19:20 to death, because she was not f. 2666
Nu 5:19 be thou f from this bitter water 5352
28 then she shall be f, and shall "
De 15:12 thou shalt let him go f from thee. 2670
13 thou sendest him out f from thee, "
18 sendest him away f from thee; "
24: 5 he shall be f at home one year, 5355
1Sa 17:25 his father's house f in Israel. 2670
1Ch 9:33 in the chambers were f: for they 6362
2Ch 29:31 and as many as were of a f heart *5081
Job 3:19 the servant is f from his master. 2670
39: 5 Who hath sent out the wild ass f? "
Ps 51:12 and uphold me with thy f spirit. ‡5082
88: 5 F among the dead, like the slain *2670
105:20 of the people, and let him go f. 6605
Isa 58: 6 and to let the oppressed go f, 2670
Jer 34: 9 an Hebrew or an Hebrewess, go f; "
10 every one his maidservant, go f, "
11 whom they had let go f, to return, "
14 thou shalt let him go f from thee: "
M't 15: 6 or his mother, he shall be f. *
17:26 unto him, Then are the children f 1658
M'r 7:11 be profited by me; he shall be f. *
Joh 8:32 and the truth shall make you f. 1659
33 sayest thou, Ye shall be made f? 1658
36 Son therefore shall make you f, 1659
36 ye shall be f indeed. 1658
Ac 22:28 And Paul said, But I was f born. *
Ro 5:15 the offence, so also is the f gift. 5486
16 but the f gift is of many offences "
18 the f gift came upon all men unto "
6:18 Being then made f from sin, ye 1659
20 ye were f from righteousness. 1658
22 But now being made f from sin. 1659

Ro 7: 3 she is f from that law; so that 1658
8: 2 hath made me f from the law of 1659
1Co 7:21 if thou mayest be made f, use it 1658
22 that is called, being f, is Christ's "
9: 1 Am I not an apostle? am I not f? "
19 For though I be f from all men, "
12:13 whether we be bond or f; and have "
Gal 3:28 Greek, there is neither bond nor f, "
4:26 But Jerusalem which is above is f, "
31 of the bondwoman, but of the f. * "
5: 1 wherewith Christ hath made us f, 1659
Eph 6: 8 whether he be bond or f. 1658
Col 3:11 Barbarian, Scythian, bond nor f: * "
2Th 3: 1 of the Lord may have f course, *
1Pe 2:16 As f, and not using your liberty 1658
Re 6:15 every bondman, and every f man, "
13:16 rich and poor, f and bond, to "
19:18 all men, both f and bond, both "

free-born See FREE and BORN.

freed
Jos 9:23 there shall none of you be f from *3772
Ro 6: 7 For he that is dead is f from sin. *1344

freedom
Le 19:20 at all redeemed, nor f given her; 2668
Ac 22:28 a great sum obtained I this f. *4174

freely
Ge 2:16 tree of the garden thou mayest f eat:
Nu 11: 5 which we did eat in Egypt f; *2600
1Sa 14:30 if haply the people had eaten f to day
Ezr 2:68 offered f for the house of God to *
7:15 and his counsellors have f offered unto
Ps 54: 6 I will f sacrifice unto thee: I *5071
Ho 14: 4 I will love them f: for mine anger "
M't 10: 8 f ye have received, f give. 1432
Ac 2:29 let me f speak unto you of 3326, 3954
26:26 before whom also I speak f: 3955
Ro 3:24 Being justified f by his grace 1432
8:32 shall he not with him also f give us
1Co 2:12 we might know the things that are f
2Co 11: 7 to you the gospel of God f? *1432
Re 21: 6 the fountain of the water of life f. "
22:17 let him take the water of life f.

freeman
1Co 7:22 being a servant, is the Lord's f: * 558

freewill See also FREE and WILL.
Le 22:18 all his f offerings, which they 5071
21 a f offering in beeves or sheep, "
23 mayest thou offer for a f offering; "
23:38 all your f offerings, which ye give "
Nu 15: 3 a vow, or in a f offering, or in your "
29:39 your vows, and your f offerings, for "
De 12: 6 your vows, and your f offerings, and "
17 thy f offerings, or heave offering of "
16:10 of a f offering of thine hand, which "
23:23 a f offering, according as thou hast "
2Ch 31:14 the f offerings of God, to distribute "
Ezr 1: 4 the f offering for the house of God "
3: 5 offered a f offering unto the Lord. "
7:13 which are minded of their own f 5069
16 with the f offering of the people, "
8:28 a f offering unto the Lord God of 5071
Ps 119:108 the f offerings of my mouth, O "

freewoman
Gal 4:22 by a bondmaid, the other by a f. 1658
23 but he of the f was by promise. "
30 not be heir with the son of the f. "

freeze See FROZEN.

frequent
2Co 11:23 in prisons more f, in deaths oft. *4056

fresh See also AFRESH; FRESHER; REFRESH.
Nu 11: 8 taste of it was as the taste of f oil. 3955
Job 29:20 My glory was f in me, and my 2319
Ps 92:10 I shall be anointed with f oil. 7488
Jas 3:12 both yield salt water and f. *1099

fresher
Job 33:25 His flesh shall be f than a child's: 7375

fret See also FRETTED; FRETTETH; FRETTING.
Le 13:55 burn it in the fire; it is f inward. 6356
1Sa 1: 6 sore, for to make her f, because 7481
Ps 37: 1 F not thyself because of 2734
7 f not thyself because of him who "
8 f not thyself in any wise to do evil. "
Pr 24:19 F not thyself because of evil men, "
Isa 8:21 hungry, they shall f themselves, 7107

fretted
Eze 16:43 hast f me in all these things; but ‡7264

fretteth
Pr 19: 3 and his heart f against the Lord. 2196

fretting
Le 13:51 the plague is a f leprosy; it is 3992
52 it is a f leprosy; it shall be burnt "
14:44 it is a f leprosy in the house: it is "

fried
Le 7:12 mingled with oil, of fine flour, f. *7246
1Ch 23:29 and for that which is f, and for * "

friend See also FRIENDS; FRIENDSHIP.
Ge 38:12 and his f Hirah the Adullamite. 7453
20 sent the kid by the hand of his f "
Ex 33:11 face, as a man speaketh unto his f. "
De 13: 6 or the wife of thy bosom, or thy f, "
J'g 14:20 whom he had used as his f. 7462
2Sa 13: 3 Amnon had a f, whose name was 7453
15:37 Hushai David's f came into 7463
16:16 Hushai the Archite, David's f "
17 Is this thy kindness to thy f? 7453
17 why wentest thou not with thy f? "
1Ki 4: 5 principal officer, and the king's f: 7463
2Ch 20: 7 seed of Abraham thy f for ever? 157
Job 6:14 pity should be shewed from his f; 7453
27 and ye dig a pit for your f. 7451
Ps 35:14 as though he had been my f or 7453
41: 9 mine own familiar f, in whom I trusted
88:18 Lover and f hast thou put far 7453
Pr 6: 1 son, if thou be surety for thy f, * "
3 art come into the hand of thy f; * "
3 thyself, and make sure thy f. * "
17:17 A f loveth at all times, and a "
18 surety in the presence of his f. * "
18:24 and there is f that sticketh closer 157
19: 6 man is a f to him that giveth gifts. 7453
22:11 of his lips the king shall be his f. "
27: 6 Faithful are the wounds of a f; 157
9 doth the sweetness of a man's f by 7453
10 Thine own f, and thy father's f, "
14 blesseth his f with a loud voice. "
17 a man... the countenance of his f. "
Ca 5:16 my f, O daughters of Jerusalem. "
Isa 41: 8 chosen, the seed of Abraham my f. 157
Jer 6:21 neighbour and his f shall perish. 7543
19: 9 eat every one the flesh of his f in "
Ho 3: 1 yet, love a woman beloved of her f, "
Mic 7: 5 Trust ye not in a f, put ye not "
M't 11:19 a f of publicans and sinners. 5384
20:13 F, I do thee no wrong: didst not 2083
22:12 F, how camest thou in hither not "
26:50 F, wherefore art thou come? "
Lu 7:34 a f of publicans and sinners! 5384
11: 5 Which of you shall have a f, and "
5 unto him, F, lend me three loaves; "
6 For a f of mine in his journey is "
8 and give him, because he is his f, "
14:10 F, go up higher: then shalt thou "
Joh 3:29 but the f of the bridegroom, which "
11:11 Our f Lazarus sleepeth; but I go, "
19:12 thou art not Cæsar's f: whosoever "
Ac 12:20 and having made Blastus their f, 3982
Jas 2:23 and he was called the F of God. 5384
4: 4 f of the world is the enemy of God. "

friendly
J'g 19: 3 to speak f unto her, and to bring *3820
Ru 2:13 spoken f unto thine handmaid, * "
Pr 18:24 friends must shew himself f: *7489

friends
Ge 26:26 and Ahuzzath one of his f, and 4828
1Sa 30:26 to his f, saying, Behold a present 7453
2Sa 3: 8 to his brethren, and to his f, and 4828
19: 6 thine enemies, and hatest thy f. *157
1Ki 16:11 of his kinsfolks, nor of his f. and 7453
Es 5:10 he sent and called for his f, 157
14 said Zeresh his wife and all his f "
6:13 told Zeresh his wife and all his f "
Job 2:11 when Job's three f heard of all 7453
16:20 My f scorn me: but mine eye "
17: 5 He that speaketh flattery to his f, "
19:14 and my familiar f have forgotten me.
19 All my inward f abhorred me: 4962
21 have pity upon me, O ye my f; 7453
32: 3 against his three f was his wrath "
42: 7 thee, and against thy two f: for ye "
10 when he prayed for his f: also the "
Ps 38:11 My lovers and my f stand aloof "
Pr 14:20 but the rich hath many f. 157
16:28 and a whisperer separateth chief f. 441
17: 9 he that...a matter separateth very f. "
18:24 A man that hath f must shew 7453
19: 4 Wealth maketh many f; but the "
7 more do his f go far from him? 4828
Ca 5: 1 eat, O f; drink, yea, drink 7453
Jer 20: 4 terror to thyself, and to all thy f: 157
6 be buried there, thou, and all thy f, "
38:22 say, Thy f have set thee on, 605, 7965
La 1: 2 her f have dealt treacherously 7453
Zec 13: 6 was wounded in the house of my f. 157
M'r 3:21 when his f heard of it, they 3588, 3844
5:19 Go home to thy f, and tell them 4674
Lu 7: 6 centurion sent f to him, saying, 5384
12: 4 And I say unto you my f, Be not "
14:12 call not thy f, nor thy brethren. "
15: 6 he calleth together his f and "
9 calleth her f and her neighbours "
29 I might make merry with my f: "
16: 9 to yourselves f of the mammon of "
21:16 brethren, and kinsfolks, and f; "
23:12 day Pilate and Herod were made f "
Joh 15:13 a man lay down his life for his f. "
14 Ye are my f, if ye do whatsoever "
15 I have called you f; for all things "
Ac 10:24 together his kinsmen and near f. "
19:31 the chief of Asia, which were his f, "
27: 3 to go unto his f to refresh himself. "
3Jo 14 Our f salute thee. "
14 Greet the f by name. "

friendship
Pr 22:24 Make no f with an angry man; 7462
Jas 4: 4 f of the world is enmity with God? 5373

fright See AFFRIGHT.

fringe See also FRINGES.
Nu 15:38 put upon the f of the borders a 6734
39 And it shall be unto you for a f, "

fringes
Nu 15:38 may make them f in the borders 6734
De 22:12 thee f upon the four quarters 1434

fro See also FROWARD.
Ge 8: 7 raven, which went forth to and f, 7725
2Ki 4:35 walked in the house to and f: 259, 2008
2Ch 16: 9 the eyes of the Lord run to and f 7751
Job 1: 7 From going to and f in the earth, "
2: 2 From going to and f in the earth, "
7: 4 I am full of tossings to and f "
13:25 break a leaf driven to and f? *
Ps 107:27 They reel to and f, and stagger
Pr 21: 6 a vanity tossed to and f of them
Isa 24:20 shall reel to and f like a drunkard.*
Isa 33: 4 as the running to and f of locusts*
49:21 a captive, and removing to and f?
Jer 5: 1 ye to and f through the streets 7751
49: 3 and run to and f by the hedges; "
Eze 27:19 Dan also and Javan going to and f*235
Da 12: 4 many shall run to and f, and 7751
Joe 2: 9 shall run to and f in the city; *8264
Am 8:12 they shall run to and f to seek the 7751
Zec 1:10 to walk to and f through the earth.
11 We have walked to and f through the
4:10 of the Lord, which run to and f 7751
6: 7 might walk to and f through the earth:
7 Get you hence, walk to and f through
7 So they walked to and f through the
Eph 4:14 tossed to and f, and carried about 2831

frogs
Ex 8: 2 will smite all thy borders with f: 6854
3 And the river shall bring forth f "
4 the f shall come up both on thee, "
5 and cause f to come upon the land "
6 the f came up, and covered the land "
7 and brought up f upon the land of "
8 that he may take away the f from "
9 the f from thee and thy houses, "
11 And the f shall depart from thee, "
12 of the f which he had brought "
13 and the f died out of the houses, "
Ps 78:45 and f, which destroyed them. "
105:30 land brought forth f in abundance, "
Re 16:13 I saw three unclean spirits like f 944

from See in the APPENDIX; also THEREFROM.

front See also FOREFRONT.
2Sa 10: 9 Joab saw that the f of the battle *6440
2Ch 3: 4 that was in the f of the house, * "

frontiers
Eze 25: 9 from his cities which are on his f, 7097

frontlets
Ex 13:16 and for f between thine eyes: 2903
De 6: 8 shall be as f between thine eyes. "
11:18 they may be as f between your eyes. "

frost See also HOARFROST.
Ge 31:40 consumed me, and the f by night; 7140
Ex 16:14 small as the hoar f on the ground. 3713
Job 37:10 By the breath of God f is given: *7140
38:29 and the hoary f of heaven, who 3713
Ps 78:47 and their sycamore trees with f. 2602
Jer 36:30 the heat, and in the night to the f. 7140

froward
De 32:20 for they are a very f generation, ‡8419
2Sa 22:27 with the f thou wilt shew thyself *6141
Job 5:13 counsel of the f is carried ‡6617
Ps 18:26 and with the f thou wilt shew *6141
26 with...thou wilt show thyself f. 6617
101: 4 A f heart shall depart from me: 6141
Pr 2:12 the man that speaketh f things; ‡8419
15 and they f in their paths: †‡3868
3:32 the f is abomination to the Lord:* "
4:24 Put away from thee a f mouth, ‡6143
6:12 man, walketh with a f mouth. "
8: 8 nothing f or perverse in them. *6617
13 and the f mouth, do I hate. ‡8419
10:31 but the f tongue shall be cut out. "
11:20 are of a f heart are abomination* 6141
16:28 A f man soweth strife: and a ‡8419
30 his eyes to devise f things: ‡ "
17:20 hath a f heart findeth no good: ‡6141
21: 8 way of man is f and strange: *2019
22: 5 snares are in the way of the f: ‡6141
1Pe 2:18 good and gentle, but also to the f. 4646

frowardly
Isa 57:17 he went on f in the way of his ‡7726

frowardness
Pro 2:14 delight in the f of the wicked; ‡8419
6:14 F is in his heart, he deviseth ‡ "
10:32 mouth of the wicked speaketh f. ‡ "

frozen
Job 38:30 and the face of the deep is f. 3920

fruit See also FIRSTFRUIT; FRUITFUL; FRUITS.
Ge 1:11 f tree yielding f after his kind, 6529
12 yielding f, whose seed was in itself, "
29 is the f of a tree yielding seed; "
3: 2 the f of the trees of the garden: "
3 f of the tree which is in the midst "
6 took of the f thereof, and did eat, "
4: 3 Cain brought of the f of the ground "
30: 2 from thee the f of the womb? "
Ex 10:15 f of the trees which the hail had "
21:22 so that her f depart from her, 3206
Le 19:23 the f thereof as uncircumcised: 6529
24 year all the f thereof shall be holy "
25 year shall ye eat of the f thereof, "
23:39 have gathered in the f of the land, *8393
25: 3 and gather in the f thereof; * "
19 And the land shall yield her f, 6529
21 and it shall bring forth f for three 8393
22 yet of old f until the ninth year; * "
26: 4 trees of the field shall yield their f. 6529
27:30 the f of the tree, is the Lord's: "
Nu 13:20 and bring of the f of the land. "
26 and shewed them the f of the land. "
27 and honey; and this is the f of it. "
De 1:25 And they took of the f of the land "
7:13 f of thy womb, and the f of thy "
11:17 that the land yield not her f; 2981
22: 9 lest the f of thy seed 4395
9 the f of thy vineyard, be defiled. *8393
26: 2 the first of all the f of the earth, 6529
28: 4 the f of thy body, and the f of thy "
4 ground, and the f of thy cattle, "
11 in the f of thy body, and in the f of "
11 cattle, and in the f of thy ground, "
18 f of thy body, and the f of thy land. "

De 28:33 f of thy land, and all thy labours, 6529
40 oil; for thine olive shall cast his f. "
42 All thy trees and f of thy land 6529
51 the f of thy cattle, and the f of thy "
53 shall eat the f of thine own body, "
30: 9 in the f of thy body, and in the f of "
9 thy cattle, and in the f of thy land, "
Jos 5:12 they did eat of the f of the land 8393
J'g 9:11 my sweetness, and my good f, 8270
2Sa 16: 2 bread and summer f for the young
2Ki 19:30 downward, and bear f upward. 6529
Ne 9:25 and f trees in abundance: 3978
36 to eat the f thereof and the good 6529
10:35 the firstfruits of all f of all trees, "
37 and the f of all manner of trees, "
Ps 1: 3 bringeth forth his f in his season; "
21:10 Their f shalt thou destroy from "
72:16 f thereof shall shake like Lebanon: "
92:14 shall still bring forth f in old age; 5107
104:13 satisfied with the f of thy works. 6529
105:35 devoured the f of their ground. "
127: 3 the f of the womb is his reward. "
132:11 Of the f of thy body will I set upon "
Pr 1:31 they eat of the f of their own way, "
8:19 My f is better than gold, yea, than "
10:16 the f of the wicked to sin. *8393
11:30 The f of the righteous is a tree 6529
12:12 the root of the righteous yieldeth f. "
14 with good by the f of his mouth: 6529
13: 2 shall eat good by the f of his mouth: "
18:20 satisfied with the f of his mouth; "
21 that love it shall eat the f thereof. "
27:18 the fig tree shall eat the f thereof: "
31:16 the f of her hands she planteth "
31 Give her of the f of her hands; "
Ca 2: 3 and his f was sweet to my taste. "
8:11 every one for the f thereof was to "
12 those that keep the f thereof two "
Isa 3:10 they shall eat the f of their doings. "
4: 2 the f of the earth shall be excellent "
10:12 the f of the stout heart of the king "
13:18 have no pity on the f of the womb; "
14:29 his f shall be a fiery flying serpent. "
27: 6 fill the face of the world with f. 8570
9 is all the f to take away his sin; 6529
28: 4 the hasty f before the summer; *1061
37:30 plant vineyards, and eat the f 6529
31 downward, and bear f upward: "
57:19 I create the f of the lips; 5108
65:21 plant vineyards, and eat the f of 6529
Jer 2: 7 eat the f thereof and the goodness "
6:19 f of their thoughts, because they "
7:20 and upon the f of the ground; "
11:16 olive tree, fair, and of goodly f: "
19 Let us destroy the tree with the f 3899
12: 2 they grow, yea, they bring forth f: 6529
17: 8 neither shall cease from yielding f. "
10 according to the f of his doings. "
21:14 according to the f of your doings, "
29: 5, 28 plant gardens, and eat the f of "
32:19 according to the f of his doings: "
La 2:20 Shall the women eat their f, and "
Eze 17: 8 that it might bear f, that it might "
9 cut off the f thereof, that it wither? "
23 bring forth boughs, and bear f: "
19:12 and the east wind dried up her f: "
14 which hath devoured her f, "
25: 4 they shall eat thy f, and they shall "
34:27 tree of the field shall yield her f, "
36: 8 and yield your f to my people "
11 they shall increase and bring f: *6509
30 I will multiply the f of the tree, 6529
47:12 the f thereof be consumed: "
12 it shall bring forth new f 1061
12 and the f thereof shall be for meat, 6529
Da 4:12 the f thereof much, and it was meat 4
14 off his leaves, and scatter his f: "
21 f thereof much, and in it was meat "
Ho 9:16 they shall bear no f: yea, though 6529
16 yet will I slay even the beloved f
10: 1 bringeth forth f unto himself: 6529
1 according to the multitude of his f "
13 ye have eaten the f of lies: "
14: 8 From me is thy f found. "
Joe 2:22 the tree beareth her f, the fig tree "
Am 2: 9 I destroyed his f from above, "
6:12 f of righteousness unto hemlock: "
7:14 and a gatherer of sycomore f: *
8: 1 and behold a basket of summer f.
2 And I said, A basket of summer f.
9:14 make gardens, and eat the f of 6529
Mic 6: 7 f of my body for the sin of my soul? "
7: 1 my soul desired the first ripe f. *
13 therein, for the f of their doings. 6529
Hab 3:17 neither shall f be in the vines; 2981
Hag 1:10 the earth is stayed from her f. "
Zec 8:12 vine shall give her f, and the 6529
Mal 1:12 and the f thereof, even his meat, 5108
3:11 your vine cast her f before the 7920
M't 3:10 which bringeth not forth good f 2590
7:17 good tree bringeth forth good f; "
17 corrupt tree bringeth forth evil f. "
18 good tree cannot bring forth evil f, "
18 a corrupt tree bring forth good f. "
19 tree that bringeth not forth good f "
12:33 the tree good, and his f good; "
33 the tree corrupt, and his f corrupt: "
33 for the tree is known by his f. "
13: 8 and brought forth f, some an "
23 also beareth f, and bringeth forth, 2592
26 sprung up, and brought forth f, 2590
21:19 no f grow on thee henceforward "
34 when the time of the f drew near, * "
26:29 henceforth of this f of the vine, 1081
M'r 4: 7 and choked it, and it yielded no f. 2590
8 and did yield f that sprang up "
M'r 4:20 and bring forth f, some thirtyfold, 2592
28 earth bringeth forth f of herself; "
29 But when the f is brought forth, 2590
11:14 No man eat f of thee hereafter "
12: 2 from the husbandmen of the f of * "
14:25 drink no more of the f of the vine, 1081
Lu 1:42 blessed is the f of thy womb. 2590
3: 9 bringeth forth not good f is hewn "
6:43 tree bringeth not forth corrupt f; "
43 a corrupt tree bring forth good f. "
44 every tree is known by his own f. "
8: 8 up, and bare f an hundredfold. "
14 and bring no f to perfection. 5062
15 and bring forth f with patience. 2592
13: 6 he came and sought f thereon, 2590
7 these three years I come seeking f "
9 And if it bear f, well: and if not, "
20:10 that they should give him of the f "
22:18 will not drink of the f of the vine, 1081
Joh 4:36 and gathereth f unto life eternal: 2590
12:24 if it die, it bringeth forth much f. "
15: 2 that beareth not f he taketh away: "
2 that beareth f, he purgeth it, "
2 that it may bring forth more f. "
4 the branch cannot bear f of itself, "
5 the same bringeth forth much f: "
8 glorified, that ye bear much f; "
16 ye should go and bring forth f, "
16 and that your f should remain: "
Ac 2:30 that of the f of his loins, he would "
Ro 1:13 I might have some f among you "
6:21 What f had ye then in those things "
22 ye have your f unto holiness, "
7: 4 we should bring forth f unto God. 2592
5 to bring forth f unto death. "
15:28 and have sealed to them this f, 2590
1Co 9: 7 and eateth not of the f thereof? "
Ga 5:22 But the f of the Spirit is love, "
Eph 5: 9 f of the Spirit is in all goodness "
Ph'p 1:22 this is the f of my labour: "
4:17 but I desire f that may abound "
Col 1: 6 bringeth forth f, as it doth also 2592
Heb 12:11 it yieldeth the peaceable f of 2590
13:15 the f of our lips giving thanks "
Jas 3:18 And the f of righteousness is sown "
5: 7 for the precious f of the earth, "
18 and the earth brought forth her f. "
Jude 12 tree whose f withereth, *5352
12 without f, twice dead, 175
Re 22: 2 and yielded her f every month: 2590

fruitful See also UNFRUITFUL.
Ge 1:22 Be f, and multiply, and fill the 6509
28 Be f, and multiply, and replenish "
8:17 be f, and multiply upon the earth. "
9: 1 Be f, and multiply, and replenish "
7 be ye f, and multiply; bring forth "
17: 6 And I will make thee exceeding f, "
20 will make him f, and will multiply "
26:22 and we shall be f in the land. "
28: 3 bless thee, and make thee f, "
35:11 be f and multiply; a nation "
41:52 God hath caused me to be f "
48: 4 Behold, I will make thee f, and "
49:22 Joseph is a f bough, even a f "
Ex 1: 7 the children of Israel were f, and "
Le 26: 9 respect unto you, and make you f, "
Ps 107:34 A f land into barrenness, for the 6529
128: 3 Thy wife shall be as a f vine 6509
148: 9 all hills; f trees, and all cedars; 6529
Isa 5: 1 a vineyard in a very f hill: 1121, 8081
10:18 of his forest, and of his f field, 3759
17: 6 the outmost f branches thereof, 6509
29:17 Lebanon shall be turned into a f 3759
17 field, and the f field shall be
32:12 the pleasant fields, for the f vine. 6509
15 wilderness be a f field, and the 3759
15 f field be counted for a forest. "
16 righteousness remain in the f field. "
Jer 4:26 lo, the f place was a wilderness, "
23: 3 and they shall be f and increase. 6509
Eze 17: 5 and planted it in a f field; 2233
19:10 she was f and full of branches 6509
Ho 13:15 he be f among his brethren, 6500
Ac 14:17 and f seasons, filling our hearts 2593
Col 1:10 being f in every good work, *2592

fruits
Ge 43:11 take of the best f in the land 2173
Ex 22:29 the first of thy ripe f, and of thy 4395
23:10 shalt gather in the f thereof: *8393
Le 25:15 the f he shall sell unto thee: * "
16 the f doth he sell unto thee. * "
22 until her f come in ye shall eat "
26:20 trees of the land yield their f. *6529
De 33:14 for the precious f brought forth 8393
2Sa 9:10 bring in the f, that thy master's son
16: 1 hundred of summer f, and a bottle
2Ki 8: 6 all the f of the field since the day 8393
19:29 vineyards, and eat the f thereof. *6529
Job 31:39 If I have eaten the f thereof 3581
Ps 107:37 which may yield f of increase. 6529
Ec 2: 5 trees in them of all kind of f: * "
Ca 4:13 with pleasant f; camphire, with "
16 his garden, and eat his pleasant f. "
6:11 to see the f of the valley, * 3
7:13 are all manner of pleasant f,
Isa 16: 9 for the shouting for thy summer f
33: 9 and Carmel shake off their f. *
Jer 40:10 gather ye wine, and summer f, and
12 gathered wine and summer f very
48:32 spoiler is fallen upon thy summer f
La 4: 9 for want of the f of the field. 8570
Mic 7: 1 they have gathered the summer f,
Mal 3:11 not destroy the f of your ground; 6529
M't 3: 8 therefore f meet for repentance: *2590
7:16 Ye shall know them by their f. "
M't 7:20 by their f ye shall know them. 2590
21:34 they might receive the f of it. "
41 render him the f in their seasons. "
43 bringeth forth the f thereof. "
Lu 3: 8 therefore f worthy of repentance; "
12:17 no room where to bestow my f? "
18 I bestow all my f and my goods, *1081
2Co 9:10 the f of your righteousness;
Ph'p 1:11 with the f of righteousness, 2590
2Ti 2: 6 must be first partaker of the f. "
Jas 3:17 full of mercy and good f, "
Re 18:14 the f that thy soul lusted after 3703
22: 2 which bare twelve manner of f, 2590

fruit-tree See FRUIT and TREE.

frustrate See also FRUSTRATETH.
Ezr 4: 5 to f their purpose, all the days 656
Ga 2:21 I do not f the grace of God: * 114

frustrateth
Isa 44:25 That f the tokens of the liars, 6565

fryingpan
Le 2: 7 a meat offering baken in the f. 4802
7: 9 all that is dressed in the f, "

fuel
Isa 9: 5 be with burning and f of fire. 3980
19 shall be as the f of the fire: "
Eze 15: 4 it is cast into the fire for f; 402
6 I have given to the fire for f, "
21:32 Thou shalt be for f to the fire; "

fugitive See also FUGITIVES.
Ge 4:12 a f and a vagabond shalt thou be 5128
14 I shall be a f and a vagabond "

fugitives
J'g 12: 4 Ye Gileadites are f of Ephraim 6412
2Ki 25:11 the f that fell away to the king *5307
Isa 15: 5 his f shall flee unto Zoar, an *1280
Eze 17:21 his f with all his bands shall fall 4015

fulfil See also FULFILLED; FULFILLING.
Ge 29:27 F her week, and we will give thee 4390
Ex 5:13 F your works, your daily tasks, 3615
23:26 the number of thy days I will f. 4390
1Ki 2:27 he might f the word of the Lord, "
1Ch 22:13 takest heed to f the statutes *6213
2Ch 36:21 To f the word of the Lord by the 4390
21 to f threescore and ten years. "
Job 39: 2 number the months that they f? "
Ps 20: 4 and f all thy counsel. "
5 the Lord f all thy petitions. "
145:19 He will f the desire of them that 6213
M't 3:15 us to f all righteousness. 4137
5:17 I am not come to destroy, but to f. "
Ac 13:22 heart, which shall f all my will. *4160
Ro 2:27 if it f the law, judge thee, 5055
13:14 provision for the flesh, to f the lusts
Ga 5:16 shall not f the lust of the flesh. 5055
6: 2 and so f the law of Christ. 378
Ph'p 2: 2 F ye my joy, that ye be 4137
Col 1:25 for you, to f the word of God; "
4:17 in the Lord, that thou f it. "
2Th 1:11 and f all the good pleasure of his "
Jas 2: 8 If ye f the royal law according to 5055
Re 17:17 to f his will, and to agree, and *4160

fulfilled
Ge 25:24 her days to be delivered were f, 4390
29:21 my days are f, that I may go "
28 Jacob did so, and f her week: "
50: 3 And forty days were f for him; "
3 for so are f the days of those "
Ex 5:14 Wherefore have ye not f your 3615
7:25 And seven days were f, after that 4390
Le 12: 4 until the days of her purifying be f. "
6 the days of her purifying are f, "
Nu 6: 5 until the days be f, in the which "
13 the days of his separation are f: "
2Sa 7:12 when thy days be f, and thou shalt "
14:22 hath f the request of his servant. *6213
1Ki 8:15 hath with his hand f it, saying, 4390
24 and hast f it with thine hand, "
2Ch 6: 4 who hath with his hands f "
15 and hast f it with thine hand, "
Ezr 1: 1 mouth of Jeremiah might be f, *3615
Job 36:17 f the judgment of the wicked: *4390
Jer 44:25 spoken with your mouths, and f "
La 2:17 he hath f his word that he had 1214
4:18 our end is near, our days are f; 4390
Eze 5: 2 when the days of the siege are f: "
Da 4:33 The same hour was the thing f 5487
10: 3 till three whole weeks were f. 4390
M't 1:22 this was done, that it might be f 4137
2:15 it might be f which was spoken "
17 Then was f that which was spoken "
23 that it might be f which was "
4:14 it might be f which was spoken "
5:18 from the law, till all be f. *1096
8:17 it might be f which was spoken 4137
12:17 be f which was spoken by Esaias "
13:14 And in them is f the prophecy 378
35 That it might be f which was 4137
21: 4 it might be f which was spoken by "
24:34 pass, till all these things be f. *1096
26:54 then shall the scriptures be f, 4137
56 of the prophets might be f. "
27: 9 was f that which was spoken "
35 it might be f which was spoken * "
M'r 1:15 The time is f, and the kingdom "
13: 4 when all these things shall be f? *4931
14:49 but the scriptures must be f. 4137
15:28 the scripture was f, which saith, * "
Lu 1:20 which shall be f in their season. "
2:43 And when they had f the days, 5048
4:21 day is this scripture f in your ears. 4137
21:22 things which are written may be f. "
24 until the times of the Gentiles be f. "
32 shall not pass away, till all be f. *1096

Lu 22:16 until it be f in the kingdom 4137
24:44 must be f, which were written "
Joh 3:29 this my joy therefore is f. ‡ "
12:38 might be f, which he spake, Lord, "
13:18 but that the scripture may be f. "
15:25 word might be f that is written "
17:12 that the scripture might be f. "
13 that they might have my joy f ‡ "
18: 9 saying might be f, which he spake, "
32 the saying of Jesus might be f, "
19:24 scripture might be f, which saith, "
28 that the scripture might be f, *5048
36 the scripture should be f, A bone 4137
Ac 1:16 scripture must needs have been f, "
3:18 should suffer, he hath so f. "
9:23 And after that many days were f, "
12:25 when they had f their ministry, 4137
13:25 as John f his course, he said, * "
27 have f them in condemning him. "
29 f all that was written of him, 5055
33 God hath f the same unto us 1603
14:26 for the work which they f. 4137
Ro 8: 4 of the law might be f in us, "
13: 8 loveth another hath f the law. "
2Co 10: 6 when your obedience is f. "
Ga 5:14 all the law is f in one word, "
Jas 2:23 the scripture was f which saith, "
Re 6:11 killed as they were, should be f. "
15: 8 of the seven angels were f. *5055
17:17 until the words of God shall be f.* "
20: 3 the thousand years should be f: * "

fulfilling
Ps 148: 8 vapours; stormy wind f his word: 6213
Ro 13:10 therefore love is the f of the law.*4138
Eph 2: 3 f the desires of the flesh and of *4160

full See also BEAUTIFUL; BOUNTIFUL; CHEERFUL; DECEITFUL; DESPITEFUL; DOUBTFUL; DREADFUL; FAITHFUL; FEARFUL; FORGETFUL; FRUITFUL; FULFIL; HANDFUL; HARMFUL; HATEFUL; HURTFUL; JOYFUL; LAWFUL; MERCIFUL; MINDFUL; MOURNFULLY; NEEDFUL; PAINFUL; PITIFUL; PLENTIFUL; POWERFUL; REPROACHFULLY; SCORNFUL; SHAMEFUL; SINFUL; SKILFUL; SLOTHFUL; SORROWFUL; THANKFUL; WATCHFUL; WILFULLY; WOEFUL; WONDERFUL; WRATHFUL; YOUTHFUL.
Ge 15:16 of the Amorites is not yet f. 8003
25: 8 an old man, and f of years; 7649
35:29 old and f of days: and his sons "
41: 1 at the end of two f years, 3117
7 the seven rank and f ears. 4392
22 came up in one stalk, f and good: "
43:21 money in f weight: and we have "
Ex 8:21 of the Egyptians shall be f 4390
16: 3 when we did eat bread to the f; 7648
8 in the morning bread to the f; 7646
33 put an omer f of manna therein, 4393
22: 3 he should make f restitution; *7999
Le 2:14 even corn beaten out of f ears. *3759
16:12 shall take a censer f of burning 4393
12 f of sweet incense beaten small, "
19:29 the land become f of wickedness. 4390
25:29 within a f year may he redeem it. 3117
30 within the space of a f year, 8549
26: 5 ye shall eat your bread to the f, 7648
Nu 7:13 both of them were f of fine flour. 4392
14 of ten shekels of gold, f of incense "
19 f of fine flour mingled with oil "
20 of gold of ten shekels, f of incense: "
25 f of fine flour mingled with oil "
26 spoon of ten shekels, f of incense "
31 both of them f of fine flour "
32 spoon of ten shekels, f of incense: "
37 f of fine flour mingled with oil "
38 spoon of ten shekels, f of incense "
43 both of them f of fine flour "
44 spoon of ten shekels, f of incense "
49 both of them f of fine flour "
50 spoon of ten shekels, f of incense: "
55 f of fine flour mingled with oil "
56 spoon of ten shekels, f of incense: "
61 f of fine flour mingled with oil "
62 spoon of ten shekels, f of incense: "
67 f of fine flour mingled with oil "
68 spoon of ten shekels, f of incense: "
73 f of fine flour mingled with oil "
74 spoon of ten shekels, f of incense: "
79 f of fine flour mingled with oil for "
80 spoon of ten shekels, f of incense: "
86 spoons were twelve, f of incense, "
22:18 give me his house f of silver 4393
24:13 give me his house f of silver "
De 6:11 houses f of all good things, 4392
11 thou shalt have eaten and be f; 7646
8:10 When thou hast eaten and art f, "
12 when thou hast eaten and art f, "
11:15 that thou mayest eat and be f. "
21:13 father and her mother a f month: 3117
33:23 f with the blessing of the Lord: 4392
34: 9 Nun was f of the spirit of wisdom; "
J'g 6:38 of the fleece, a bowl f of water. "
16:27 house was f of men and women; 4390
Ru 1:21 went out f, and the Lord hath "
2:12 and a f reward be given thee 8003
1Sa 2: 5 They that were f have hired out 7646
18:27 gave them in f tale to the king, 4390
27: 7 of the Philistines was a f year 3117
2Sa 8: 2 and with one f line to keep alive. 4393
13:23 it came to pass after two f years, 3117
14:28 Absalom dwelt two f years in "
23:11 a piece of ground f of lentiles: 4392
2Ki 3:16 Lord, Make this valley f of ditches. "
4: 4 shalt set aside that which is f. 4392
6 when the vessels were f, that she 4390
39 thereof wild gourds his lap f, 4393

2Ki 4:42 and f ears of corn in the husk *
6:17 the mountain was f of horses 4390
7:15 was f of garments and vessels, 4392
9:24 drew a bow with his f strength, 4390
10:21 of Baal was f from one end "
15:13 reigned a f month in Samaria. *3117
1Ch 11:13 a parcel of ground f of barley; 4392
21:22 grant it me for the f price: "
24 I will verily buy it for the f price: "
23: 1 David was old and f of days, 7646
29:28 f of days, riches, and honour: "
2Ch 24:15 and was f of days when he died; "
Ne 9:25 possessed houses f of all goods, 4392
Es 3: 5 then was Haman f of wrath. 4390
5: 9 he was f of indignation against * "
Job 5:26 shalt come to thy grave in a f age, 3624
7: 4 and I am f of tossings to and fro 7646
10:15 I am f of confusion; therefore see* "
11: 2 should a man f of talk be justified? "
14: 1 is of few days, and f of trouble. 7646
20:11 His bones are f of the sin of his 4390
21:23 One dieth in his f strength, being 8537
24 His breasts are f of milk, and 4390
32:18 I am f of matter, the spirit within "
36:16 thy table should be f of fatness. "
42:17 Job died, being old and f of days. 7646
Ps 10: 7 His mouth is f of cursing and 4390
17:14 they are f of children, and leave *7646
26:10 their right hand is f of bribes. 4390
29: 4 voice of the Lord is f of majesty. "
33: 5 the earth is f of the goodness of 4390
48:10 right hand is f of righteousness. "
65: 9 river of God, which is f of water: "
69:20 and I am f of heaviness: and I looked "
73:10 waters of a f cup are wrung out 4392
74:20 the earth are f of the habitations 4390
75: 8 it is f of mixture; and he poureth 4392
78:25 he sent them meat to the f. 7648
38 he, being f of compassion, forgave ‡
86:15 a God f of compassion, and gracious, ‡
88: 3 For my soul is f of troubles: 7654
104:16 trees of the Lord are f of sap; †‡ "
24 the earth is f of thy riches. 4390
111: 4 Lord is gracious and f of compassion. ‡
112: 4 he is gracious, and f of compassion, ‡
119:64 earth, O Lord, is f of thy mercy: 4390
127: 5 that hath his quiver f of them: "
144:13 That our garners may be f, 4392
145: 8 Lord is gracious, and f of compassion; ‡
Pr 17: 1 than an house f of sacrifices 4392
27: 7 f soul loatheth an honeycomb; 7646
20 Hell and destruction are never f; * "
30: 9 Lest I be f, and deny thee, and "
Ec 1: 7 yet the sea is not f; unto the 4392
8 All things are f of labour; man "
4: 6 both the hands f with travail *4393
9: 3 of the sons of men is f of evil, 4390
10:14 A fool also is f of words: *7235
11: 3 If the clouds be f of rain, they 4390
Isa 1:11 I am f of the burnt offerings of 7646
15 hear: your hands are f of blood. 4390
21 it was f of judgment; 4392
2: 7 land also is f of silver and gold, 4390
7 their land is also f of horses, "
8 Their land also is f of idols; "
6: 3 the whole earth is f of his glory. 4393
11: 9 earth shall be f of the knowledge 4390
13:21 shall be f of doleful creatures; "
15: 9 of Dimon shall be f of blood: "
22: 2 art f of stirs, a tumultuous city, 4392
7 valleys shall be f of chariots, 4390
25: 6 fat things f of marrow, of wines
28: 8 are f of vomit and filthiness, 4390
30:27 his lips are f of indignation, and "
51:20 they are f of the fury of the Lord, 4392
Jer 4:12 a f wind from those places shall "
27 yet will I not make a f end.
5: 7 when I had fed them to the f, 7646
10 but make not a f end: take away
18 I will not make a f end with you.
27 As a cage is f of birds, 4392
27 so are their houses f of deceit: "
6:11 I am f of the fury of the Lord; "
11 aged with him that is f of days. 4390
23:10 For the land is f of adulterers; "
28: 3 two f years will I bring again 3117
11 within the space of two f years.
30:11 though I make a f end of all nations
11 yet will I not make a f end of thee:
35: 5 pots f of wine, and cups, and I 4392
46:28 I will make a f end of all the nations
28 I will not make a f end of thee,
La 1: 1 solitary, that was f of people! 7227
3:30 he is filled f with reproach. 7646
Eze 1:18 their rings were f of eyes round 4392
7:23 the land is f of bloody crimes, 4390
23 and the city is f of violence. "
9: 9 and the land is f of blood, "
9 and the city f of perverseness: "
10: 4 the court was f of the brightness "
12 were f of eyes round about, 4392
11:13 Lord God! wilt thou make a f end
17: 3 longwinged, f of feathers, which 4392
19:10 she was fruitful and f of branches
28:12 f of wisdom, and perfect in 4392
32: 6 and the rivers shall be f of thee. 4390
15 destitute of that whereof it was f, 4393
37: 1 the valley which was f of bones, 4392
39:19 ye shall eat fat till ye be f, 7654
41: 8 the side chambers were a f reed 4393
Da 3:19 was Nebuchadnezzar f of fury, 4391
8:23 transgressors are come to the f, 8552
10: 2 was mourning three f weeks *3117
Joe 2:24 And the floors shall be f of wheat, 4390
3:13 the press is f, the fats overflow; "
Am 2:13 is pressed that is f of sheaves. 4392

Mic 3: 8 I am f of power by the spirit 4390
6:12 rich men thereof are f of violence, "
Na 3: 1 it is all f of lies and robbery; 4392
Hab 3: 3 the earth was f of his praise. 4390
Zec 8: 5 the city shall be f of boys and girls "
M't 6:22 the whole body shall be f of light. 5460
23 whole body shall be f of darkness.
13:48 Which, when it was f, they drew 4137
14:20 that remained twelve baskets f. 4134
15:37 that was left seven baskets f. "
23:25 within they are f of extortion 1073
27 are within f of dead men's bones, "
28 are f of hypocrisy and iniquity. 3324
M'r 4:28 after that the f corn in the ear. 4134
37 the ship, so that it was now f. *1072
6:43 baskets f of the fragments, *4134
7: 9 F well ye reject the commandment
8:19 many baskets f of fragments 4134
20 how many baskets f of fragments *4138
15:36 And one ran and filled a spunge f
Lu 1:57 Elisabeth's f time came that she *4130
4: 1 Jesus being f of the Holy Ghost 4134
5:12 behold a man f of leprosy: who "
6:25 Woe unto you that are f! for ye 1705
11:34 the whole body also is f of light; 5460
34 thy body also is f of darkness.
36 whole body therefore be f of light, 5460
36 the whole shall be f of light, as "
39 your inward part is f of ravening 1073
16:20 laid at his gate f of sores,
Joh 1:14 the Father,) f of grace and truth. 4134
7: 8 my time is not yet f come. *4137
15:11 and that your joy might be f. † "
16:24 receive, that your joy may be f. † "
19:29 was set a vessel f of vinegar: 3324
21:11 f of great fishes, an hundred and "
Ac 2:13 These men are f of new wine. *3325
28 thou shalt make me f of joy with 4137
6: 3 f of the Holy Ghost and wisdom, 4134
5 f of faith and of the Holy Ghost, "
8 Stephen, f of faith and power, "
7:23 when he was f forty years old, *4137
55 he, being f of the Holy Ghost, 4134
9:36 this woman was f of good works "
11:24 f of the Holy Ghost and of faith: "
13:10 f of all subtilty and all mischief, "
19:28 they were f of wrath, and cried * "
Ro 1:29 f of envy, murder, debate, deceit, 3324
3:14 is f of cursing and bitterness: 1073
15:14 that ye are also f of goodness, 3324
1Co 4: 8 Now ye are f, now ye are rich, *2880
Ph'p 2:26 you all, and was f of heaviness, *
4:12 both to be f and to be hungry, *5526
18 I am f, having received of 4137
Col 2: 2 the f assurance of understanding, 4136
2Ti 4: 5 of an evangelist, make f proof of †4135
Heb 5:14 belongeth to them that are of f *5046
6:11 f assurance of hope unto the end: *4136
10:22 in f assurance of faith, having * "
Jas 3: 8 an unruly evil, f of deadly poison. 3324
17 f of mercy and good fruits, without "
1Pe 1: 8 with joy unspeakable and f of glory:
2Pe 2:14 Having eyes f of adultery, and that 3324
1Jo 1: 4 you, that your joy may be f. †4137
2Jo 8 but that we receive a f reward. 4134
12 to face, that our joy may be f. †4137
Re 4: 6 f of eyes before and behind. 1073
8 they were f of eyes within: and "
5: 8 harps, and golden vials f of odours, "
15: 7 f of the wrath of God, who liveth "
16:10 his kingdom was f of darkness; * "
17: 3 f of names of blasphemy, having 1073
4 cup in her hand f of abominations "
21: 9 vials f of the seven last plagues, * "

fuller See also FULLER'S; FULLERS'.
M'r 9: 3 as no f on earth can white them. 1102

fuller's
2Ki 18:17 is in the highway of the f field. 3526
Isa 7: 3 pool in the highway of the f field; "
36: 2 pool in the highway of the f field. "

fullers'
Mal 3: 2 like a refiner's fire, and like f sope. 3526

fully See also MOURNFULLY; REPROACHFULLY; SHAMEFULLY; SKILFULLY; WILFULLY; WONDERFULLY.
Nu 7: 1 had f set up the tabernacle, *3615
14:24 and hath followed me f, him will 4392
Ru 2:11 It hath f been shewed me, all 5046
1Ki 11: 6 went not f after the Lord, as did 4390
Ec 8:11 heart of the sons of men is f set "
Na 1:10 be devoured as stubble f dry. * "
Ac 2: 1 the day of Pentecost was f come, *4845
Ro 4:21 And being f persuaded that, what 4135
14: 5 Let every man be f persuaded "
15:19 I have f preached the gospel of 4137
2Ti 3:10 thou hast f known my doctrine, *3877
4:17 the preaching might be f known, 4135
Re 14:18 for her grapes are f ripe.

fulness See also SKILFULNESS; SLOTHFULNESS; THANKFULNESS.
Nu 18:27 and as the f of the winepress. 4395
De 33:16 things of the earth and f thereof, 4393
1Ch 16:32 Let the sea roar, and the f thereof: "
Job 20:22 In the f of his sufficiency he shall 4390
Ps 16:11 in thy presence is f of joy; 7648
24: 1 is the Lord's, and the f thereof; 4393
50:12 world is mine, and the f thereof. "
89:11 the world and the f thereof, thou "
96:11 let the sea roar, and the f thereof. "
98: 7 Let the sea roar, and the f thereof; "
Eze 16:49 f of bread, and abundance of 7653
19: 7 was desolate, and the f thereof, 4393
Joh 1:16 of his f have all we received, 4138
Ro 11:12 Gentiles; how much more their f? "

Ro 11:25 the f of the Gentiles be come 4138
15:29 come in the f of the blessing "
1Co 10:26 is the Lord's, and the f thereof. "
28 is the Lord's, and the f thereof: * "
Gal 4: 4 when the f of the time was come "
Eph 1:10 dispensation of the f of times "
23 the f of him that filleth all in all. "
3:19 be filled with all the f of God. "
4:13 the stature of the f of Christ: "
Col 1:19 that in him should all f dwell; "
2: 9 all the f of the Godhead bodily. "

furbish See also FURBISHED.
Jer 46: 4 f the spears, and put on the 4838

furbished
Eze 21: 9 sword is sharpened, and also f: 4803
10 it is f that it may glitter: "
11 he hath given it to be f, "
11 and it is f, to give it into the hand "
28 the slaughter it is f, to consume "

furious
Pr 22:24 with a f man thou shalt not go: *2534
29:22 and a f man aboundeth in * "
Eze 5:15 and in fury, and in f rebukes. ‡ "
25:17 upon them with f rebukes; ‡ "
Da 2:12 the king was angry and very f, 7108
Na 1: 2 Lord revengeth, and is f; *1167, 2534

furiously
2Ki 9:20 son of Nimshi; for he driveth f. 7697
Eze 23:25 and they shall deal f with thee: *2534

furlongs
Lu 24:13 Jerusalem about threescore f. 4712
Joh 6:19 about five and twenty or thirty f, "
11:18 unto Jerusalem, about fifteen f off: "
Re 14:20 a thousand and six hundred f. "
21:16 the reed, twelve thousand f. "

furnace See also FURNACES.
Ge 15:17 behold a smoking f, and a 8574
19:28 went up as the smoke of a f. 3536
Ex 9: 8 to you handfuls of ashes of the f, "
10 And they took ashes of the f, "
19:18 ascended as the smoke of a f, "
De 4:20 you forth out of the iron f, 3564
1Ki 8:51 from the midst of the f of iron: "
Ps 12: 6 as silver tried in a f of earth, 5948
Pr 17: 3 and the f for gold: but the Lord 3564
27:21 and the f for gold; so is a man "
Isa 31: 9 and his f in Jerusalem. 8574
48:10 I have chosen thee in the f of 3564
Jer 11: 4 from the iron f, saying, Obey "
Eze 22:18 and lead, in the midst of the f; "
20 into the midst of the f, "
22 is melted in the midst of the f, "
Da 3: 6, 11 the midst of a burning fiery f. 861
15 into the midst of a burning fiery f; "
17 deliver us from the burning fiery f, "
19 heat the f one seven times more "
20 cast them into the burning fiery f. "
21 the midst of the burning fiery f. "
22 and the f exceeding hot, the flame "
23 the midst of the burning fiery f. "
26 to the mouth of the burning fiery f. "
M't 13:42 shall cast them into a f of fire: 2575
50 shall cast them into the f of fire: "
Re 1:15 as if they burned in a f; "
9: 2 as the smoke of a great f; "

furnaces
Ne 3:11 other piece, and the tower of the f. 8574
12:38 of the f even unto the broad wall; "

furnish See also FURNISHED.
De 15:14 f him liberally out of thy flock, 6059
Ps 78:19 God f a table in the wilderness? *6186
Isa 65:11 f the drink offering unto that *4390
Jer 46:19 f thyself to go into captivity: 6213, 3627

furnished
1Ki 9:11 Hiram the king of Tyre had f 5375
Pr 9: 2 she hath also f her table. 6186
M't 22:10 the wedding was f with guests. *4130
M'r 14:15 large upper room f and prepared: 4766
Lu 22:12 shew you a large upper room f: "
2Ti 3:17 throughly f unto all good works. 1822

furniture
Ge 31:34 the camel's f, and sat upon them. 3733
Ex 31: 7 and all the f of the tabernacle, 3627
8 the table and his f, and the * "
8 pure candlestick with all his f, * "
9 of burnt offering with all his f, * "
35:14 also for the light, and his f, * "
39:33 all his f, his taches, his boards, "
Na 2: 9 glory out of all the pleasant f. "

furrow See also FURROWS.
Job 39:10 unicorn with his band in the f? 8525

furrows
Job 31:38 the f likewise thereof complain; 8525
Ps 65:10 settlest the f thereof: thou makest 1417
129: 3 they made long their f. 4618
Eze 17: 7 it by the f of her plantation. *6170
10 wither in the f where it grew. * "
Ho 10: 4 as hemlock in the f of the field. 8525
10 bind themselves in their two f. *5869
12:11 are as heaps in the f of the fields. 8525

further: See also FARTHER; FURTHERED; FURTHERMORE.
Nu 22:26 the angel of the Lord went f, 3254
De 20: 8 shall speak f unto the people, "
1Sa 10:22 enquired of the Lord f, if the man 5750
Es 9:12 is thy request f? and it shall be
Job 38:11 shalt thou come, but no f: 3254
40: 5 yea, twice; but I will proceed no f. "
Ps 140: 8 f not his wicked device; lest they 6329
Ec 12:12 And f, by these, my son, be *3148
M't 26:65 what f need have we of witnesses? 2089
M'r 5:35 troublest thou the Master any f? "
14:63 What need we any f witnesses? "
Lu 22:71 What need we any f witness? "
24:28 as though he would have gone f. 4206
Ac 4:17 spread no f among the people, 1909, 4118
21 when they had f threatened them,
12: 3 he proceeded f to take Peter also.*
21:28 f brought Greeks also into the *2089
24: 4 I be not f tedious unto thee, 1909, 4118
27:28 when they had gone a little f, *1339
2Ti 3: 9 proceed no f: for their folly, 1909, 4118
He 7:11 f need was there that another 2089

furtherance
Ph'p 1:12 rather unto the f of the gospel; *4297
25 for your f and joy of faith; * "

furthered
Ezr 8:36 they f the people, and the house 5375

furthermore
Ex 4: 6 And the Lord said f unto him, 5750
De 4:21 F the Lord was angry with me *
9:13 F the Lord spake unto me, *
1Sa 26:10 David said f, As the Lord liveth, *
1Ch 17:10 F I tell thee that the Lord will *
27:16 F over the tribes of Israel: the *
29: 1 F David the king said unto *
2Ch 4: 9 F he made the court of the *
Job 34: 1 F Elihu answered and said, *
Eze 8: 6 He said f unto me, Son of man, *
23:40 And f, that ye have sent for men 637
2Co 2:12 F, when I came to Troas to *1161
1Th 4: 1 F then we beseech you, brethren, *3063
He 12: 9 F we have had fathers of our 1534

fury
Ge 27:44 until thy brother's f turn away; 2534
Le 26:28 walk contrary unto you also in f; ‡ "
Job 20:23 God shall cast the f of his wrath *2740
Isa 27: 4 F is not in me: who would set ‡2534
34: 2 and his f upon all their armies: ‡ "
42:25 upon him the f of his anger, ‡ "
51:13 because of the f of the oppressor, "
13 where is the f of the oppressor? "
17 of the Lord the cup of his f; ‡ "
20 they are full of the f of the Lord, ‡ "
22 the dregs of the cup of my f; ‡ "
59:18 f to his adversaries, recompence ‡ "
63: 3 anger, and trample them in my f; ‡ "
5 and my f, it upheld me. ‡ "
6 and make them drunk in my f, ‡ "
66:15 to render his anger with f, and ‡ "
Jer 4: 4 lest my f come forth like fire, ‡ "
6:11 I am full of the f of the Lord; ‡ "
7:20 mine anger and my f shall be ‡ "
10:25 Pour out thy f upon the heathen ‡ "
21: 5 and in f, and in great wrath. ‡ "
12 my f go out like fire, and burn ‡ "
23:19 the Lord is gone forth in f, ‡ "
25:15 Take the wine cup of this f at my ‡ "
30:23 of the Lord goeth forth with f, ‡ "
32:31 of mine anger and of my f ‡ "
37 and in my f, and in great wrath; ‡ "
33: 5 in mine anger and in my f, ‡ "
36: 7 f that the Lord hath pronounced ‡ "
42:18 and my f hath been poured forth ‡ "
18 my f be poured forth upon you, ‡ "
44: 6 f and mine anger was poured ‡ "
La 2: 4 he poured out his f like fire. ‡ "
4:11 Lord hath accomplished his f; ‡ "
Eze 5:13 cause my f to rest upon them, ‡ "
13 have accomplished my f in them. ‡ "
15 in f and in furious rebukes. ‡ "
6:12 I accomplish my f upon them. ‡ "
7: 8 Now will I shortly pour out my f ‡ "
8:18 Therefore will I also deal in f: ‡ "
9: 8 in thy pouring out of thy f ‡ "
13:13 with a stormy wind in my f; ‡ "
13 hailstones in my f to consume it. ‡ "
14:19 pour out my f upon it in blood, ‡ "
16:38 I will give thee blood in f ‡ "
42 I make my f toward thee to rest, ‡ "
19:12 plucked up in f, she was cast ‡ "
20: 8 I will pour out my f upon them, ‡ "
13 I would pour out my f upon them ‡ "
21 would pour out my f upon them, ‡ "
33 and with f poured out, will I rule ‡ "
34 stretched out arm, and with f ‡ "
21:17 and I will cause my f to rest: ‡ "
22:20 in mine anger and in my f, ‡ "
22 have poured out my f upon you, ‡ "
24: 8 That it might cause f to come up ‡ "
13 caused my f to rest upon thee. ‡ "
25:14 anger and according to my f; ‡ "
30:15 I will pour my f upon Sin, ‡ "
36: 6 in my jealousy and in my f, ‡ "
18 my f upon them for the blood ‡ "
38:18 my f shall come up in my face. ‡ "
Da 3:13 rage and f commanded to bring 2528
19 Then was Nebuchadnezzar full of f, "
8: 6 unto him in the f of his power. 2534
9:16 thine anger and thy f be turned ‡ "
11:44 go forth with great f to destroy, ‡ "
Mic 5:15 in anger and f upon the heathen, ‡ "
Na 1: 6 f is poured out like fire, and the ‡ "
Zec 8: 2 I was jealous for her with great f. ‡ "

G

Gaal (*gal'-al*)
J'g 9:26 And G the son of Ebed came with 1603
28 G the son of Ebed said, Who is "
30 words of G the son of Ebed, his "
31 Behold, G the son of Ebed and his "
35 G the son of Ebed went out, and "
36 G saw the people, he said to Zebul, "
37 G spake again and said, See, "
39 G went out before the men of "
41 thrust out G and his brethren, "

Gaash (*ga'-ash*)
Jos 24:30 on the north side of the hill of G. 1608
J'g 2: 9 on the north side of the hill G. "
2Sa 23:30 Hiddai of the brooks of G, "
1Ch 11:32 Hurai of the brooks of G, Abiel the "

Gaba (*ga'-bah*) See also GEBA.
Jos 18:24 and Ophni, and G; twelve cities *1387
Ezr 2:26 The children of Ramah and G, * "
Ne 7:30 The men of Ramah and G, * "

Gabbai (*gab'-bahee*)
Ne 11: 8 And after him G, Sallai, nine 1373

Gabbatha (*gab'-ba-thah*)
Joh 19:13 but in the Hebrew, G. 1042

Gaber See EZION-GABER.

Gabriel (*ga'-bre-el*)
Da 8:16 G, make this man to understand 1403
9:21 even the man G, whom I had seen "
Lu 1:19 I am G, that stand in the 1043
26 sixth month the angel G was sent "

gad See GADDEST.

Gad (*gad*) See also BAAL-GAD; DIBON-GAD; GADITE; MIGDAL-GAD.
Ge 30:11 and she called his name G. 1410
35:26 Leah's handmaid; G, and Asher: "
46:16 And the sons of G; Ziphion, and "
49:19 G, a troop shall overcome him: "
Ex 1: 4 Dan, and Naphtali, G, and Asher. "
Nu 1:14 Of G; Eliasaph the son of Deuel. "
24 Of the children of G, by their "
25 even of the tribe of G, were forty "
2:14 Then the tribe of G: and the "
14 captain of the sons of G shall be "
7:42 of the children of G, offered: "
10:20 of the children of G was Eliasaph "
13:15 Of the tribe of G, Geuel the son of "
26:15 The children of G after their "
18 families of the children of G "
32: 1 and the children of G had a very "
2 The children of G and the "
6 Moses said unto the children of G "
25 And the children of G and the "
29 If the children of G and the "
31 And the children of G and the "
33 even to the children of G, "
34 And the children of G built Dibon, "
34:14 tribe of the children of G according "
De 27:13 Reuben, G, and Asher, and "
33:20 And of G he said Blessed be he "
20 Blessed be he that enlargeth G: "
Jos 4:12 and the children of G, and half "
13:24 of G, even unto the children of G "
28 children of G after their families, "
18: 7 and G, and Reuben, and half the "
20: 8 out of the tribe of G, and Golan "
21: 7 out of the tribe of G, and out of 1410
38 And out of the tribe of G, Ramoth "
22: 9, 10, 11, 13, 15, 21 children of G and the "
25 of Reuben and children of G; "
30 children of G and the children of "
31 children of G, and to the children of "
32 children of G, out of the land of "
33 children of Reuben and G dwelt, "
34 children of G called the altar Ed: "
1Sa 13: 7 Jordan to the land of G and Gilead. "
22: 5 prophet G said unto David, Abide "
2Sa 24: 5 the river of G, and toward Jazer: "
11 unto the prophet G, David's seer, "
13 So G came to David, and told him, "
14 David said unto G, I am in a great "
18 And G came that day to David, "
19 according to the saying of G, went "
1Ch 2: 2 Benjamin, Naphtali, G, and Asher. "
5:11 And the children of G dwelt over "
6:63 out of the tribe of G, and out of the "
80 And out of the tribe of G; Ramoth "
12:14 sons of G, captains of the host: "
21: 9 And the Lord spake unto G, and "
11 So G came to David, and said unto "
13 David said unto G, I am in a great "
18 Lord commanded G to say to "
19 David went up at the saying of G, "
29:29 and in the book of G the seer, "
2Ch 29:25 of David, and of G the king's seer, "
Jer 49: 1 why then doth their king inherit G, "
Eze 48:27 unto the west side, G a portion. "
28 And by the border of G, at the "
34 one gate of G, one gate of Asher, "
Re 7: 5 Of the tribe of G were sealed 1045

Gadarenes (*gad-a-renes'*)
M'r 5: 1 sea, into the country of the *G*·. *1046
Lu 8:26 arrived at the country of the *G*·. * "
37 of the country of the *G*· round * "

Gaddah See HAZAR-GADDAH.

gaddest
Jer 2:36 Why *g*· thou about so much to 235

Gaddi (*gad'-di*)
Nu 13:11 tribe of Manasseh, *G*· the son of 1426

Gaddiel (*gad'-de-el*)
Nu 13:10 of Zebulun, *G*· the son of Sodi. 1427

Gader See BETH-GADER.

Gadi (*ga'-di*)
2Ki 15:14 Menahem the son of *G*· went up 1424
17 Menahem the son of *G*· to reign "

Gadite (*gad'-ite*) See also GADITES.
2Sa 23:36 of Zobah, Bani the *G*·. 1425

Gadites (*gad'-ites*)
De 3:12 the Reubenites and to the *G*·. 1425
16 unto the *G*· I gave from Gilead even "
4:43 Gilead, of the *G*·; and Golan in "
29: 8 and to the *G*·, and to the half tribe "
Jos 1:12 and to the *G*·, and to half the tribe "
12: 6 unto the Reubenites, and the *G*·, "
13: 8 the Reubenites and the *G*· have "
22: 1 and the *G*·, and the half tribe of "
2Ki 10:33 land of Gilead, the *G*·, and the "
1Ch 5:18 and the *G*·, and half the tribe of "
26 and the *G*·, and the half tribe of "
12: 8 And of the *G*· there separated "
37 and the *G*·, and of the half tribe of "
26:32 the *G*·, and the half tribe of "

Gaham (*ga'-ham*)
Ge 22:24 bare also Tebah, and *G*·, and 1514

Gahar (*ga'-har*)
Ezr 2:47 of Giddel, the children of *G*·, the 1515
Ne 7:49 of Giddel, the children of *G*·. "

gain See also AGAIN; GAINED; GAINS; GAINSAY.
J'g 5:19 they took no *g*· of money. 1214
Job 22: 3 or is it *g*· to him, that thou makest "
Pr 1:19 every one that is greedy of *g*·; "
3:14 and the *g*· thereof than fine gold. 8393
15:27 He that is greedy of *g*· troubleth 1214
28: 8 by usury and unjust *g*· increaseth*8636
Isa 33:15 despiseth the *g*· of oppressions, 1214
56:11 one for his *g*·, from his quarter. "
Eze 22:13 mine hand at thy dishonest *g*· "
27 destroy souls, to get dishonest *g*·. "
Da 2: 8 certainty that ye would *g*· the time, 2084
11:39 and shall divide the land for *g*·. *4242
Mic 4:13 consecrate their *g*· unto the Lord, 1214
M't 16:26 if he shall *g*· the whole world, and 2770
M'r 8:36 if he shall *g*· the whole world, and "
Lu 9:25 if he *g*· the whole world, and lose "
Ac 16:16 brought her masters much *g*· by 2039
19:24 brought no small *g*· unto the * "
1Co 9:19 unto all, that I might *g*· the more. 2770
20 that I might *g*· the Jews; "
20 that I might *g*· them that are under "
21 might *g*· them that are without law. "
22 that I might *g*· the weak: "
2Co 12:17 Did I make a *g*· of you by any *4122
18 Did Titus make a *g*· of you? * "
Ph'p 1:21 to live is Christ, and to die is *g*·. 2771
3: 7 But what things were *g*· to me, "
1Ti 6: 5 supposing that *g*· is godliness: *4200
6 with contentment is great *g*·. "
Jas 4:13 and buy and sell, and get *g*·: 2770

gained
Job 27: 8 though he hath *g*·, when God *1214
Eze 22:12 and thou hast greedily *g*· of thy "
M't 18:15 thee, thou hast *g*· thy brother. 2770
25:17 received two, he also *g*· other two. "
20 I have *g*· beside them five talents "
22 *g*· two other talents beside them. "
Lu 19:15 every man had *g*· by trading. 1281
16 thy pound hath *g*· ten pounds. *4333
18 thy pound hath *g*· five pounds. *4160
Ac 27:21 to have *g*· this harm and loss. *2770

gains
Ac 16:19 the hope of their *g*· was gone, *2039

gainsay See also GAINSAYING.
Lu 21:15 shall not be able to *g*· nor resist. 471

gainsayers
Tit 1: 9 to exhort and to convince the *g*·. 483

gainsaying
Ac 10:29 came I unto you without *g*·, 369
Ro 10:21 a disobedient and *g*· people. 483
Jude 11 and perished in the *g*· of Core. 485

Gaius (*gah'-yus*)
Ac 19:29 caught *G*· and Aristarchus, 1050
20: 4 and *G*· of Derbe, and Timotheus; "
Ro 16:23 *G*· mine host, and of the whole "
1Co 1:14 none of you, but Crispus and *G*·; "
3Jo 1 The elder unto the wellbeloved *G*·, "

Galal (*ga'-lal*)
1Ch 9:15 Heresh, and *G*·, and Mattaniah 1559
16 the son of *G*·, the son of Jeduthun, "
Ne 11:17 Shammua, the son of *G*·, the son of "

Galatia (*ga-la'-she-ah*) See also GALATIANS.
Ac 16: 6 Phrygia and the region of *G*·, 1054
18:23 country of *G*· and Phrygia in order, "
1Co 16: 1 given order to the churches of *G*·, 1053
Ga 1: 2 with me unto the churches of *G*·: "
2Ti 4:10 Crescens to *G*·, Titus unto "
1Pe 1: 1 Pontus, *G*·, Cappadocia, Asia, "

Galatians (*ga-la'-she-uns*)
Ga 3: 1 O foolish *G*·, who hath bewitched 1052
subscr. Unto the *G*· written from Rome. "

galbanum (*gal'-ba-num*)
Ex 30:34 onycha, and *g*·; these sweet spices 2464

Galeed (*gal'-le-ed*) See also JAGAR-SAHADUTHA.
Ge 31:47 but Jacob called it *G*·. 1567
48 was the name of it called *G*·; "

Galilæan (*gal-i-le'-un*) See also GALILÆANS.
M'r 14:70 for thou art a *G*·, and thy speech 1057
Lu 22:59 also was with him: for he is a *G*·. "
23: 6 asked whether the man were a *G*·. "

Galilæans (*gal-i-le'-uns*)
Lu 13: 1 some that told him of the *G*·, 1057
2 Suppose ye that these *G*· were "
2 sinners above all the *G*·, "
Joh 4:45 the *G*· received him, having seen "
Ac 2: 7 are not all these which speak *G*·? "

Galilee (*gal'-i-lee*) See also GALILÆAN.
Jos 20: 7 Kedesh in *G*· in mount Naphtali, 1551
21:32 Kedesh in *G*· with her suburbs, "
1Ki 9:11 twenty cities in the land of *G*·. "
2Ki 15:29 Hazor, and Gilead, and *G*·, all the "
1Ch 6:76 Kedesh in *G*· with her suburbs, "
Isa 9: 1 beyond Jordan, in *G*· of the nations. "
M't 2:22 he turned aside in the parts of *G*·: 1056
3:13 cometh Jesus from *G*· to Jordan "
4:12 into prison, he departed into *G*·; "
15 beyond Jordan, *G*· of the Gentiles; "
18 Jesus, walking by the sea of *G*·, "
23 And Jesus went about all *G*·, "
25 great multitudes of people from *G*·, "
15:29 came nigh unto the sea of *G*·; "
17:22 while they abode in *G*·, Jesus said "
19: 1 he departed from *G*·, and came "
21:11 the prophet of Nazareth of *G*·. "
26:32 I will go before you into *G*·. "
69 Thou also wast with Jesus of *G*·. * "
27:55 which followed Jesus from *G*·, "
28: 7 he goeth before you into *G*·; "
10 that they go into *G*·, and there "
16 eleven disciples went away into *G*·, "
M'r 1: 9 Jesus came from Nazareth of *G*·, "
14 Jesus came into *G*·, preaching the "
16 Now as he walked by the sea of *G*·, "
28 all the region round about *G*·. "
39 synagogues throughout all *G*·, "
3: 7 multitude from *G*· followed him, "
6:21 captains, and chief estates of *G*·; "
7:31 he came unto the sea of *G*·, "
9:30 thence, and passed through *G*·; "
14:28 I will go before you into *G*·. "
15:41 when he was in *G*·, followed him, "
16: 7 that he goeth before you into *G*·: "
Lu 1:26 unto a city of *G*·, named Nazareth, "
2: 4 And Joseph also went up from *G*·, "
39 they returned into *G*·, to their own "
3: 1 and Herod being tetrarch of *G*·, "
4:14 in the power of the Spirit into *G*·: "
31 down to Capernaum, a city of *G*·, "
44 preached in the synagogues of *G*·. "
5:17 were come out of every town of *G*·, "
8:26 which is over against *G*·. "
17:11 the midst of Samaria and *G*·. "
23: 5 beginning from *G*· to this place. "
6 When Pilate heard of *G*·, he asked "
49 women that followed him from *G*·, "
55 which came with him from *G*·, "
24: 6 unto you when he was yet in *G*·. "
Joh 1:43 Jesus would go forth into *G*·, "
2: 1 there was a marriage in Cana of *G*·; "
11 miracles did Jesus in Cana of *G*·, "
4: 3 Judea, and departed again into *G*·. "
43 departed thence, and went into *G*·. "
45 Then when he was come into *G*·, "
46 Jesus came again into Cana of *G*·, "
47 was come out of Judæa into *G*·, he "
54 he was come out of Judæa into *G*·. "
6: 1 Jesus went over the sea of *G*·, "
7: 1 these things Jesus walked in *G*·: "
9 unto them, he abode still in *G*·. "
41 said, Shall Christ come out of *G*·? "
52 Art thou also of *G*·? Search, and "
52 for out of *G*· ariseth no prophet. "
12:21 which was of Bethsaida of *G*·, "
21: 2 and Nathanael of Cana in *G*·, "
Ac 1:11 Ye men of *G*·, why stand ye gazing "
5:37 After this man rose up Judas of *G*· "
9:31 all Judæa and *G*· and Samaria, "
10:37 began from *G*·, after the baptism "
13:31 which came up with him from *G*· "

gall
De 29:18 that beareth *g*· and wormwood; 7219
32:32 their grapes are grapes of *g*·, "
Job 16:13 out my *g*· upon the ground. 4845
20:14 it is the *g*· of asps within him. 4846
25 sword cometh out of his *g*·: "
Ps 69:21 gave me also *g*· for my meat; 7219
Jer 8:14 given us water of *g*· to drink, "
9:15 give them water of *g*· to drink. "
23:15 make them drink the water of *g*·: "
La 3: 5 compassed me with *g*· and travel. "
19 misery, the wormwood and the *g*·. "
Am 6:12 ye have turned judgment into *g*·, "
M't 27:34 vinegar to drink mingled with *g*·: 5521
Ac 8:23 thou art in the *g*· of bitterness, "

gallant
Isa 33:21 neither shall *g*· ship pass thereby. 117

galleries
Ca 7: 5 the king is held in the *g*·. *7298
Eze 41:15 and the *g*· thereof on the one side 862
41:16 windows, and the *g*· round about 862
42: 5 for the *g*· were higher than these, "

gallery See also GALLERIES.
Eze 42: 3 *g*· against *g*· in three stories. 862

galley
Isa 33:21 wherein shall go no *g*· with oars, 590

Gallim (*gal'-lim*)
1Sa 25:44 son of Laish, which was of *G*·. 1554
Isa 10:30 Lift up thy voice, O daughter of *G*·: "

Gallio (*gal'-le-o*)
Ac 18:12 *G*· was the deputy of Achaia, 1058
14 *G*· said unto the Jews, If it were a "
17 And *G*· cared for none of those "

gallows
Es 5:14 a *g*· be made of fifty cubits high, 6086
14 he caused the *g*· to be made. "
6: 4 to hang Mordecai on the *g*· that he "
7: 9 Behold also, the *g*· fifty cubits high, "
10 So they hanged Haman on the *g*· "
8: 7 they have hanged upon the *g*·, "
9:13 ten sons be hanged upon the *g*·. "
25 his sons should be hanged on the *g*·. "

Gamaliel (*gam-a'-le-el*)
Nu 1:10 Manasseh; *G*· the son of Pedahzur. 1583
2:20 of Manasseh shall be *G*· the son of "
7:54 offered *G*· the son of Pedahzur "
59 this was the offering of *G*· the son "
10:23 of the children of Manasseh was *G*· "
Ac 5:34 a Pharisee, named *G*·, a doctor of 1059
22: 3 in this city at the feet of *G*·, "

Gammadims (*gam'-ma-dims*)
Eze 27:11 and the *G*· were in thy towers: *1575

Gamul (*ga'-mul*) See also BETH-GAMUL.
1Ch 24:17 the two and twentieth to *G*·. 1577

Gannim See EN-GANNIM.

gaoler See JAILER.

gap See also GAPED; GAPS.
Eze 22:30 and stand in the *g*· before me 6556

gaped
Job 16:10 *g*· upon me with their mouth; 6473
Ps 22:13 *g*· upon me with their mouths. *6475

gaps
Eze 13: 5 Ye have not gone up into the *g*·. 6556

garden See also GARDENS.
Ge 2: 8 And the Lord God planted a *g*· 1588
9 also in the midst of the *g*·, "
10 out of Eden to water the *g*·; "
15 put him into the *g*· of Eden "
16 of the *g*· thou mayest freely eat: "
3: 1 shall not eat of every tree of the *g*·? "
2 the fruit of the trees of the *g*·: "
3 which is in the midst of the *g*·, "
8 the Lord God walking in the *g*· "
8 amongst the trees of the *g*·. "
10 I heard thy voice in the *g*·, "
23 sent him forth from the *g*· of Eden, "
24 at the east of the *g*· of Eden "
13:10 even as the *g*· of the Lord, "
De 11:10 with thy foot, as a *g*· of herbs: "
1 Ki 21: 2 that I may have it for a *g*· of herbs, "
2 Ki 9:27 he fled by the way of the *g*· house. "
21:18 buried in the *g*· of his own house, "
18 in the *g*· of Uzza: and Amon his "
26 his sepulchre in the *g*· of Uzza: "
25: 4 which is by the king's *g*·: "
Ne 3:15 the pool of Siloah by the king's *g*·, "
Es 1: 5 court of the *g*· of the king's palace; 1594
7: 7 his wrath went into the palace *g*·: "
8 king returned out of the palace *g*· "
Job 8:16 his branch shooteth forth in his *g*·. 1593
Ca 4:12 A *g*· inclosed is my sister, my 1588
16 thou south; blow upon my *g*·, "
16 Let my beloved come into his *g*·, "
5: 1 I am come into my *g*·, my sister, "
6: 2 beloved is gone down into his *g*·, "
11 I went down into the *g*· of nuts 1594
Isa 1: 8 as a lodge in a *g*· of cucumbers, "
30 and as a *g*· that hath no water. 1593
51: 3 her desert like the *g*· of the Lord; 1588
58:11 thou shalt be like a watered *g*·, "
61:11 and as the *g*· causeth the things 1593
Jer 31:12 their soul shall be as a watered *g*·; 1588
39: 4 by the way of the king's *g*·, "
52: 7 walls, which was by the king's *g*·; "
La 2: 6 as if it were of a *g*·: "
Eze 28:13 been in Eden the *g*· of God; "
31: 8 The cedars in the *g*· of God "
8 nor any tree in the *g*· of God "
9 that were in the *g*· of God. "
36:35 is become like the *g*· of Eden; "
Joe 2: 3 the land is as the *g*· of Eden "
Lu 13:19 a man took, and cast into his *g*·; 2779
Joh 18: 1 where was a *g*·, into the which "
26 Did not I see thee in the *g*· "
19:41 a *g*·; and in the *g*· a new sepulchre, "

gardener
Joh 20:15 She, supposing him to be the *g*·, 2780

garden-house See GARDEN and HOUSE.

gardens
Nu 24: 6 forth, as *g*· by the river's side, 1593
Ec 2: 5 I made me *g*· and orchards, "
Ca 4:15 of *g*·, a well of living waters, 1588
6: 2 in the *g*·, and to gather lilies. "
8:13 Thou that dwellest in the *g*·, "
Isa 1:29 for the *g*· that ye have chosen. 1593
65: 3 that sacrificeth in *g*·, and burneth "
66:17 the *g*· behind one tree in the midst, "
Jer 29: 5 plant *g*·, and eat the fruit of them; "

Jer 29:28 plant *g*. and eat the fruit of them.1593
Am 4: 9 when your *g*. and your vineyards "
9:14 make *g*. and eat the fruit of them. "

Gareb (*ga'-reb*)
2Sa 23:38 Ira an Ithrite, *G*. an Ithrite, 1619
1Ch 11:40 Ira the Ithrite, *G*. the Ithrite, "
Jer 31:39 upon the hill *G*. and shall compass"

garlands
Ac 14:13 brought oxen and *g*. unto the gates.4725

garlick
Nu 11: 5 leeks, and the onions, and the *g*.: 7762

garment See also GARMENTS.
Ge 9:23 And Shem and Japheth took a *g*. 8071
25:25 red, all over like an hairy *g*.; 155
39:12 she caught him by his *g*., saying, 899
12 he left his *g*. in her hand, "
13 she saw that he had left his *g*. "
15 that he left his *g*. with me, "
16 she laid up his *g*. by her, "
18 he left his *g*. with me, and fled "
Le 6:10 the priest shall put on his linen *g*.,4055
27 of the blood thereof upon any *g*., 899
13:47 *g*. also that the plague of leprosy "
47 it be a woollen *g*., or a linen *g*.; "
49 be greenish or reddish in the *g*., "
51 plague be spread in the *g*., "
52 He shall therefore burn that *g*., "
53 be not spread in the *g*., "
56 he shall rend it out of the *g*., "
57 if it appear still in the *g*., "
58 And the *g*., either warp, or woof, "
59 in a *g*. of woollen or linen, "
14:55 And for the leprosy of a *g*., "
15:17 And every *g*., and every skin, "
19:19 neither shall a *g*. mingled of linen "
De 22: 5 shall a man put on a woman's *g*.: 8071
11 *g*. of divers sorts, as of woollen *8162
Jos 7:21 Babylonish *g*., and two hundred *155
24 silver, and the *g*., and the wedge "
J'g 8:25 they spread a *g*., and did cast 8071
2Sa 13:18 she had a *g*. of divers colours 3801
19 and rent her *g*. of divers colours "
20: 8 Joab's *g*. that he had put on *4055
1Ki 11:29 he had clad himself with a new *g*.;8008
30 caught the new *g*. that was on him, "
2Ki 9:13 hasted, and took every man his *g*., 899
Ezr 9: 3 I rent my *g*. and my mantle, "
5 having rent my *g*. and my mantle, "
Es 8:15 and with a *g*. of fine linen *8509
Job 13:28 as a *g*. that is moth eaten. 899
30:18 of my disease is my *g*. changed: 3830
38: 9 I made the cloud the *g*. thereof, "
14 and they stand as a *g*. "
41:13 Who can discover the face of his *g*.?"
Ps 69:11 I made sackcloth also my *g*.; * "
73: 6 violence covereth them as a *g*. 7897
102:26 all of them shall wax old like a *g*.; 899
104: 2 thyself with light as with a *g*.: 8008
6 with the deep as with a *g*.: *3830
109:18 with cursing like as with his *g*., 4055
19 Let it be unto him as the *g*. * 899
Pr 20:16 his *g*. that is surety for a stranger: "
25:20 As he that taketh away a *g*. "
27:13 Take his *g*. that is surety "
30: 4 who hath bound the waters in a *g*.?8071
Isa 50: 9 they all shall wax old as a *g*.; 899
51: 6 the earth shall wax old like a *g*., "
8 shall eat them up like a *g*., "
61: 3 the *g*. of praise for the spirit of 4594
Jer 43:12 as a shepherd putteth on his *g*.; 899
Eze 18: 7 hath covered the naked with a *g*.; "
16 hath covered the naked with a *g*.; "
Da 7: 9 whose *g*. was white as snow, *3831
Mic 2: 8 ye pull off the robe with the *g*. 8008
Hag 2:12 holy flesh in the skirt of his *g*., 899
Zec 13: 4 wear a rough *g*. to deceive: *155
Mal 2:16 one covereth violence with his *g*., *3830
M't 9:16 piece of new cloth unto an old *g*., *2440*
16 to fill it up taketh from the *g*., "
20 and touched the hem of his *g*.: "
21 If I may but touch his *g*., "
14:36 only touch the hem of his *g*.: "
22:11 which had not on a wedding *g*.: *1742*
12 in hither not having a wedding *g*.? "
M'r 2:21 piece of new cloth on an old *g*.: *2440*
5:27 press behind, and touched his *g*. "
6:56 it were but the border of his *g*.: "
10:50 And he, casting away his *g*., rose, "
13:16 back again for to take up his *g*. * "
16: 5 clothed in a long white *g*.; and *4749*
Lu 5:36 a piece of a new *g*. upon an old; *2440*
8:44 and touched the border of his *g*.: "
22:36 let him sell his *g*., and buy one. * "
Ac 12: 8 Cast thy *g*. about thee, "
He 1:11 all shall wax old as doth a *g*.; "
Jude 23 hating even the *g*. spotted by the *5509*
Re 1:13 clothed with a *g*. down to the foot, *4158*

garments
Ge 35: 2 change your *g*.: 8071
38:14 she put her widow's *g*. off from 899
19 put on the *g*. of her widowhood. "
49:11 he washed his *g*. in wine, and his 3830
Ex 28: 2 thou shalt make holy *g*. for Aaron 899
3 that they may make Aaron's *g*. "
4 these are the *g*. which they shall "
4 they shall make holy *g*. for Aaron "
29: 5 thou shalt take the *g*., and put upon "
21 and upon his *g*. and upon his sons, "
21 and upon the *g*. of his sons with him: "
21 he shall be hallowed, and his *g*., and"
21 his sons, and his sons' *g*. with him. "
29 And the holy *g*. of Aaron shall be "
31:10 the holy *g*. for Aaron the priest, "

Ex 31:10 the *g*. of his sons, to minister in 899
35:19 the holy *g*. for Aaron the priest, "
19 the *g*. of his sons, to minister in "
21 service, and for the holy *g*. "
39: 1 and made the holy *g*. for Aaron; "
41 the holy *g*. for Aaron the priest, "
41 and his sons, *g*., to minister in the "
40:13 put upon Aaron the holy *g*., "
Le 6:11 put off his *g*., and put on other *g*., "
8: 2 the *g*., and the anointing oil, "
30 upon Aaron, and upon his *g*., and "
30 and upon his sons' *g*. with him; "
30 Aaron, and his *g*., and his sons, "
30 and his sons' *g*. with him. "
16: 4 these are holy *g*.; therefore shall "
23 and shall put off the linen *g*., "
24 put on his *g*., and come forth, "
32 the linen clothes, even the holy *g*.: "
21:10 is consecrated to put on the *g*., "
Nu 15:38 fringes in the borders of their *g*. "
20:26 strip Aaron of his *g*., and put them "
28 And Moses stripped Aaron of his *g*., "
Jos 9: 5 and old *g*. upon them; and all the 8008
13 these our *g*. and our shoes "
J'g 14:12 and thirty changes of *g*.: * 899
13 sheets and thirty change of *g*.: * "
19 gave change of *g*. unto them * "
1Sa 18: 4 and his *g*., even to his sword, *4055
2Sa 10: 4 cut off their *g*. in the middle, 4063
13:31 the king arose, and tare his *g*., 899
1Ki 10:25 vessels of gold, and *g*., and *8008
2Ki 5:22 of silver, and two changes of *g*.. * 899
23 two bags, with two changes of *g*..* "
26 and to receive *g*., and oliveyards, "
7:15 all the way was full of *g*. "
25:29 And changed his prison *g*.: and he "
1Ch 19: 4 and cut off their *g*. in the midst 4063
Ezr 2:69 and one hundred priests' *g*. 3801
Ne 7:70 five hundred and thirty priests' *g*. "
72 threescore and seven priests' *g*. "
Job 37:17 How thy *g*. are warm, when he 899
Ps 22:18 They part my *g*. among them, "
45: 8 All thy *g*. smell of myrrh, and aloes, "
133: 2 went down to the skirts of his *g*.; 4060
Ec 9: 8 Let thy *g*. be always white; 899
Ca 4:11 the smell of thy *g*. is like the smell 8008
Isa 9: 5 noise, and *g*. rolled in blood; 8071
52: 1 on thy beautiful *g*., O Jerusalem, 899
59: 6 Their webs shall not become *g*., "
17 he put on the *g*. of vengeance "
61:10 clothed me with the *g*. of salvation, "
63: 1 Edom, with dyed *g*. from Bozrah? "
2 and thy *g*. like him that treadeth "
3 shall be sprinkled upon my *g*., "
Jer 36:24 were not afraid, nor rent their *g*., "
52:33 And changed his prison *g*.: and he "
La 4:14 that men could not touch their *g*. 3830
Eze 16:16 And of thy *g*. thou didst take, 899
18 And tookest thy broidered *g*., "
26:16 robes, and put off their broidered *g*.: "
42:14 but there they shall lay their *g*. "
14 and shall put on other *g*., "
44:17 they shall be clothed with linen *g*.; "
19 they shall put off their *g*. wherein "
19 and they shall put on other *g*.; "
19 sanctify the people with their *g*.. "
Da 3:21 and their other *g*., and were cast 3831
Joe 2:13 rend your heart, and not your *g*., 899
Zec 3: 3 Joshua was clothed with filthy *g*., "
4 Take away the filthy *g*. from him. "
5 his head, and clothed him with *g*. "
M't 21: 8 spread their *g*. in the way; *2440*
23: 5 enlarge the borders of their *g*., "
27:35 and parted his *g*., casting lots: "
35 They parted my *g*. among them, * "
M'r 11: 7 and cast their *g*. on him; and he "
8 many spread their *g*. in the way; "
15:24 they parted his *g*., casting lots "
Lu 19:35 they cast their *g*. upon the colt, "
24: 4 men stood by them in shining *g*.:*2067*
Joh 13: 4 from supper, and laid aside his *g*.;*2440*
12 and had taken his *g*., and was set "
19:23 took his *g*. and made four parts, "
Ac 9:39 shewing the coats and *g*. which "
Jas 5: 2 and your *g*. are motheaten. "
Re 3: 4 which have not defiled their *g*.; "
16:15 that watcheth, and keepeth his *g*., "

Garmite (*gar'-mite*)
1Ch 4:19 Keilah the *G*., and Eshtemoa the 1636

garner See also GARNERS.
M't 3:12 and gather his wheat into the *g*.; *596*
Lu 3:17 will gather the wheat into his *g*.; "

garners
Ps 144:13 That our *g*. may be full, affording 4200
Joe 1:17 the *g*. are laid desolate, the barns 214

garnish See also GARNISHED.
M't 23:29 and *g*. the sepulchres of the *2885*

garnished
2Ch 3: 6 And he *g*. the house with precious6823
Job 26:13 his spirit he hath *g*. the heavens; 8235
M't 12:44 he findeth it empty, swept, and *g*. *2885*
Lu 11:25 he findeth it swept and *g*. "
Re 21:19 of the wall of the city were *g*. * "

garrison See also GARRISONS.
1Sa 10: 5 where is the *g*. of the Philistines: 5333
13: 3 Jonathan smote the *g*. of the "
4 had smitten a *g*. of the Philistines, "
23 the *g*. of the Philistines went out 4673
14: 1 let us go over to the Philistines' *g*., "
4 to go over unto the Philistines' *g*., "
6 Come, and let us go over unto the *g*. "
11 unto the *g*. of the Philistines; and "
12 men of the *g*. answered Jonathan 4675

1Sa 14:15 people, the *g*., and the spoilers, 4673
2Sa 23:14 and the *g*. of the Philistines was "
1Ch 11:16 the Philistines' *g*. was then at 5333
2Co 11:32 king kept the city of...with a *g*. *5432*

garrisons
2Sa 8: 6 Then David put *g*. in Syria of 5333
14 And he put *g*. in Edom; "
14 throughout all Edom put he *g*., "
1Ch 18: 6 Then David put *g*. in Syria-damascus;
13 And he put *g*. in Edom; and all 5333
2Ch 17: 2 and set *g*. in the land of Judah, "
Eze 26:11 and thy strong *g*. shall go down *4676

Gashmu (*gash'-mu*) See also GESHEM.
Ne 6: 6 and *G*. saith it, that thou and the 1654

gat See also BEGAT; FORGAT; GOT.
Ge 19:27 And Abraham *g*. up early in the
Ex 24:18 and *g*. him up into the mount: *5927
Nu 11:30 And Moses *g*. him into the camp, 622
14:40 and *g*. them up into the top of the 5927
16:27 so they *g*. up from the tabernacle "
J'g 9:48 Abimelech *g*. him up to mount "
51 and *g*. them up to the top of the "
19:28 the man rose up, and *g*. him unto 3212
1Sa 13:15 And Samuel arose, and *g*. him up 5927
24:22 David and his men *g*. them up unto"
26:12 and they *g*. them away, and no 3212
2Sa 4: 7 and *g*. them away through the * "
8:13 And David *g*. him a name when 6213
13:29 every man *g*. him up upon his 7392
17:23 and *g*. him home to his house, 3212
19: 3 And the people *g*. them by stealth 935
1Ki 1: 1 him with clothes, but he *g*. no heat.
Ps 116: 3 the pains of hell *g*. hold upon me:
Ec 2: 8 I *g*. me men singers and women 6213
La 5: 9 We *g*. our bread with the peril of *935

Gatam (*ga'-tam*)
Ge 36:11 Omar, Zepho, and *G*., and Kenaz. 1609
16 Duke Korah, duke *G*., and duke "
1Ch 1:36 Omar, Zephi, and *G*., Kenaz, and "

gate See also GATES.
Ge 19: 1 Lot sat in the gate of Sodom: 8179
22:17 possess the *g*. of his enemies; "
23:10 all that went in at the *g*. of his city, "
18 that went in at the *g*. of his city. "
24:60 let thy seed possess the *g*. of those "
28:17 and this is the *g*. of heaven. "
34:20 came unto the *g*. of their city, "
24 went out of the *g*. of his city; "
24 that went out of the *g*. of his city. "
Ex 27:14 The hangings of one side of the *g*. "
16 And for the *g*. of the court 8179
32:26 Moses stood in the *g*. of the camp, "
27 from *g*. to *g*. throughout the camp, "
38:14 The hangings of the one side of the *g*. "
38:15 for the other side of the court *g*., 8179
18 the hanging for the *g*. of the court "
31 and the sockets of the court *g*., "
39:40 and the hanging for the court *g*., "
40: 8 hang up the hanging at the court *g*. "
33 set up the hanging of the court *g*. "
Nu 4:26 the hanging for the door of the *g*. "
De 21:19 and unto the *g*. of his place; "
22:15 unto the elders of the city in the *g*.: "
24 bring them both out unto the *g*. "
25: 7 go up to the *g*. unto the elders, "
Jos 2: 5 about the time of shutting of the *g*., "
7 were gone out, they shut the *g*. "
7: 5 chased them from before the *g*. "
8:29 cast it at the entering of the *g*. "
20: 4 stand at the entering of the *g*. "
J'g 9:35 stood in the entering of the *g*. "
40 even unto the entering of the *g*. "
44 stood in the entering of the *g*.: "
16: 2 laid wait for him all night in the *g*. "
3 took the doors of the *g*. of the city, "
18:16 stood by the entering of the *g*. "
17 stood in the entering of the *g*. "
Ru 4: 1 Then went Boaz up to the *g*., "
10 and from the *g*. of his place: "
11 all the people that were in the *g*., "
1Sa 4:18 seat backward by the side of the *g*., "
9:18 Saul drew near to Samuel in the *g*., "
21:13 scrabbled on the doors of the *g*., "
2Sa 3:27 Joab took him aside in the *g*. "
10: 8 at the entering in of the *g*.: "
11:23 even unto the entering of the *g*. "
15: 2 stood beside the way of the *g*.: "
18: 4 the king stood by the *g*. side, "
24 went up to the roof over the *g*. "
33 up to the chamber over the *g*., "
19: 8 the king arose, and sat in the *g*. "
8 the king doth sit in the *g*. "
23:15 of Beth-lehem, which is by the *g*.! "
16 that was by the *g*., and took it, "
1Ki 17:10 when he came to the *g*. of the city,6607
22:10 the entrance of the *g*. of Samaria;8179
2Ki 7: 1 a shekel, in the *g*. of Samaria.
3 at the entering of the *g*.: "
17 to have the charge of the *g*.: "
17 the people trode upon him in the *g*., "
18 about this time in the *g*. of Samaria: "
20 the people trode upon him in the *g*., "
9:31 as Jehu entered in at the *g*., "
10: 8 entering in of the *g*. until the "
11: 6 third part shall be at the *g*. of Sur; "
6 part at the *g*. behind the guard: "
19 the way of the *g*. of the guard "
14:13 *g*. of Ephraim unto the corner *g*., "
15:35 built the higher *g*. of the house "
23: 8 the *g*. of Joshua the governor of "
8 left hand at the *g*. of the city. "
25: 4 way of the *g*. between two walls, "

1Ch 9:18 hitherto waited in the king's g' 8179
11:17 well of Beth-lehem, that is at the g'! "
18 that was by the g', and took it, "
19: 9 array before the g' of the city: 6607
26:13 house of their fathers, for every g'.8179
16 with the g' Shallecheth, by the "
2Ch 8:14 also by their courses at every g': "
18: 9 the entering in of the g' of Samaria;"
23: 5 part at the g' of the foundation: "
15 to the entering of the horse g' "
20 and they came through the high g' "
24: 8 set it without at the g' of the house"
25:23 the g' of Ephraim to the corner g', "
26: 9 the corner g', and at the valley g' "
27: 3 He built the high g' of the house "
32: 6 the street of the g' of the city, "
33:14 the entering in at the fish g', "
35:15 and the porters waited at every g'; "
Ne 2:13 by night by the g' of the valley, "
14 I went on to the g' of the fountain, "
15 entered by the g' of the valley, "
3: 1 they builded the sheep g'; they "
3 fish g' did the sons of Hassenaah "
6 the old g' repaired Jehoiada "
13 The valley g' repaired Hanun, "
13 on the wall unto the dung g'. "
14 the dung g' repaired Malchiah "
15 g' of the fountain repaired Shallun "
26 place over against the water g' "
28 the horse g' repaired the priests, "
29 the keeper of the east g'. "
31 over against the g' Miphkad, "
32 unto the sheep g' repaired the "
8: 1 street that was before the water g';"
3 street that was before the water g' "
16 and in the street of the water g', "
16 in the street of the g' of Ephraim. "
12:31 upon the wall toward the dung g': "
37 And at the fountain g', which was "
37 even unto the water g' eastward. "
39 from above the g' of Ephraim, "
39 the old g', and above the fish g', "
39 even unto the sheep g': "
39 they stood still in the prison g'. "
Es 2:19 then Mordecai sat in the king's g'. "
21 while Mordecai sat in the king's g'. "
3: 2 servants, that were in the king's g'."
3 which were in the king's g', "
4: 2 And came even before the king's g':"
2 more might enter into the king's g' "
6 which was before the king's g'. "
5: 1 over against the g' of the house. *6607
9 saw Mordecai in the king's g', 8179
13 the Jew sitting at the king's g'. "
6:10 Jew, that sitteth at the king's g': "
12 came again to the king's g'. "
Job 5: 4 and they are crushed in the g', "
29: 7 When I went out to the g' "
31:21 when I saw my help in the g': "
Ps 69:12 They that sit in the g' speak "
118:20 This g' of the Lord, into which the "
127: 5 speak with the enemies in the g'. "
Pr 17:19 he that exalteth his g' seeketh 6607
22:22 oppress the afflicted in the g': 8179
24: 7 he openeth not his mouth in the g'. "
Ca 7: 4 Heshbon, by the g' of Bath-rabbim: "
Isa 14:31 Howl, O g'; cry, O city; thou, "
22: 7 set themselves in array at the g'. "
24:12 the g' is smitten with destruction. "
28: 6 them that turn the battle to the g'. "
29:21 for him that reproveth in the g', "
Jer 7: 2 Stand in the g' of the Lord's house, "
17:19 and stand in the g' of the children "
19: 2 which is by the entry of the east g', "
20: 2 were in the high g' of Benjamin, "
26:10 down in the entry of the new g' "
31:38 Hananeel unto the g' of the corner."
40 unto the corner of the horse g' "
36:10 at the entry of the new g' of the "
37:13 he was in the g' of Benjamin, "
38: 7 the king then sitting in the g' "
39: 3 came in, and sat in the middle g', "
4 by the g' betwixt the two walls: "
52: 7 of the g' between the two walls, "
La 5:14 elders have ceased from the g', "
Eze 8: 3 to the door of the inner g' that "
5 at the g' of the altar this image "
14 brought me to the door of the g' of "
9: 2 from the way of the higher g', "
10:19 stood at the door of the east g' "
11: 1 unto the east g' of the Lord's house."
1 behold at the door of the g' "
40: 3 seed; he stood in the g'. "
6 Then came he unto the g' which "
6 measured the threshold of the g', "
6 and the other threshold of the g',*
7 and the threshold of the g' by the 8179
7 by the porch of the g' within was "
8 measured also the porch of the g' "
9 measured he the porch of the g', "
9 the porch of the g' was inward. "
10 little chambers of the g' eastward "
11 breadth of the entry of the g', ten "
11 and the length of the g', thirteen "
13 measured then the g' from the roof"
14 post of the court round about the g'."
15 the face of the g' of the entrance "
15 porch of the inner g' were fifty "
16 posts within the g' round about, "
19 from the forefront of the lower g' "
20 And the g' of the outward court "
21 after the measure of the first g': "
22 the measure of the g' that looketh "
23 And the g' of the inner court was "
23 against the g' toward the north, "
23 from g' to g' an hundred cubits. "

Eze 40:24 behold a g' toward the south: 8179
27 there was a g' in the inner court "
27 he measured from g' to g' toward "
28 to the inner court by the south g': "
28 and he measured the south g' "
32 he measured the g' according to "
35 And he brought me to the north g', "
39 And in the porch of the g' were two "
40 up to the entry of the north g', "
40 at the porch of the g', were two "
41 by the side of the g'; eight tables, "
44 And without the inner g' were the "
44 was at the side of the north g'; "
44 one at the side of the east g' having "
48 and the breadth of the g' was three "
42:15 forth toward the g' whose prospect "
43: 1 to the g', even the g' that looketh "
4 the house by the way of the g' "
44: 1 the way of the g' whose prospect "
2 This g' shall be shut, it shall not "
3 by the way of the porch of that g', "
4 brought...the way of the north g' "
45:19 posts of the g' of the inner court. "
46: 1 g' of the inner court that looketh "
2 way of the porch of that g' without, "
2 and shall stand by the post of the g', "
2 worship at the threshold of the g': "
2 but the g' shall not be shut until "
3 shall worship at the door of this g' "
8 by the way of the porch of that g', "
9 the way of the north g' to worship "
9 go out by the way of the south g'; "
9 entereth by the way of the south g' "
9 go forth by the way of the north g' "
9 shall not return by the way of the g' "
12 the g' that looketh toward the east, "
12 going forth one shall shut the g'. "
19 which was at the side of the g', "
47: 2 he me out of the way of the g' "
2 the way without unto the utter g' "
48:31 gates northward; one g' of Reuben, "
31 one g' of Judah, one g' of Levi. "
32 and three gates; one g' of Joseph, "
32 one g' of Benjamin, one g' of Dan. "
33 and three gates: one g' of Simeon, "
33 g' of Issachar, one g' of Zebulun. "
34 their three gates; one g' of Gad, "
34 g' of Asher, one g' of Naphtali. "
Da 2:49 Daniel sat in the g' of the king. 8651
Am 5:10 hate him that rebuketh in the g', 8179
12 they turn aside the poor in the g' "
15 and establish judgment in the g': "
Ob 13 not have entered into the g' of "
Mic 1: 9 he is come unto the g' of my people, "
12 the Lord unto the g' of Jerusalem. "
2:13 have passed through the g', and are "
Zep 1:10 the noise of a cry from the fish g', "
Zec 14:10 from Benjamin's g' unto the place "
10 of the first g', unto the corner g', "
M't 7:13 Enter ye in at the strait g': 4439
13 for wide is the g', and broad is the "
14 Because strait is the g', and narrow "
Lu 7:12 he came nigh to the g' of the city, "
13:24 Strive to enter in at the strait g': * "
16:20 which was laid at his g', full of 4440
Ac 3: 2 the g' of the temple which is called*2374
10 at the Beautiful g' of the temple: 4439
10:17 house, and stood before the g', 4440
12:10 they came unto the iron g' that 4439
13 knocked at the door of the g', 4440
14 she opened not the g' for gladness, "
14 told how Peter stood before the g'. "
Heb 13:12 own blood, suffered without the g'. 4439

gates
Ex 20:10 thy stranger that is within thy g': 8179
De 3: 5 with high walls, g', and bars; 1817
5:14 thy stranger that is within thy g'; 8179
6: 9 posts of thy house, and on thy g'. "
11:20 of thine house, and upon thy g': "
12:12 the Levite that is within your g'; "
15 kill and eat flesh in all thy g', "
17 Thou mayest not eat within thy g' "
18 and the Levite that is within thy g':"
21 and thou shalt eat in thy g' "
14:21 unto the stranger that is in thy g', "
27 the Levite that is within thy g'; "
28 and shalt lay it up within thy g': "
29 which are within thy g', shall come, "
15: 7 of thy brethren within any of thy g' "
22 Thou shalt eat it within thy g': "
16: 5 the passover within any of thy g', "
11 and the Levite that is within thy g', "
14 widow, that are within thy g'. "
18 shalt thou make thee in all thy g', "
17: 2 among you, within any of thy g' "
5 that wicked thing, unto thy g', "
8 of controversy within thy g': "
18: 6 if a Levite come from any of thy g' "
23:16 he shall choose in one of thy g', "
24:14 that are in thy land within thy g': "
26:12 that they may eat within thy g', "
28:52 he shall besiege thee in all thy g', "
55 shall distress thee in all thy g'. "
57 enemy shall distress thee in thy g'. "
31:12 thy stranger that is within thy g', "
Jos 6:26 son shall he set up the g' of it. 1817
J'g 5: 8 then was war in the g': was there 8179
11 people of the Lord go down to the g'."
1Sa 17:52 the valley, and to the g' of Ekron. "
23: 7 into a town that hath g' and bars. 1817
2Sa 18:24 David sat between the two g': and 8179
1Ki 16:34 up the g' thereof in his youngest 1817
2Ki 23: 8 down the high places of the g' 8179
1Ch 9:19 keepers of the g' of the tabernacle: 5592
22 were chosen to be porters in the g' "
23 oversight of the g' of the house 8179

1Ch 22: 3 for the nails for the doors of the g',8179
2Ch 8: 5 cities, with walls, g', and bars; 1817
14: 7 walls, and towers, g', and bars, "
23:19 And he set the porters at the g' 8179
31: 2 to praise in the g' of the tents "
Ne 1: 3 the g' thereof are burned with fire. "
2: 3 g' thereof are consumed with fire? "
8 beams for the g' of the palace "
13 g' thereof were consumed with fire. "
17 the g' thereof are burned with fire: "
6: 1 not set up the doors upon the g';) "
7: 3 Let not the g' of Jerusalem be "
11:19 and their brethren that kept the g', "
12:25 ward at the thresholds of the g' "
30 the people, and the g', and the wall."
13:19 when the g' of Jerusalem began to "
19 that the g' should be shut, *1817
19 some of my servants set I at the g',8179
22 they should come and keep the g', "
Job 38:17 Have the g' of death been opened "
Ps 9:13 liftest me up from the g' of death: "
14 in the g' of the daughter of Zion: "
24: 7 your heads, O ye g'; and be ye lift up"
9 your heads, O ye g'; even lift them "
87: 2 The Lord loveth the g' of Zion "
100: 4 Enter into his g' with thanksgiving, "
107:16 he hath broken the g' of brass, 1817
18 draw near unto the g' of death. 8179
118:19 Open to me the g' of righteousness: "
122: 2 Our feet shall stand within thy g', "
147:13 strengthened the bars of thy g'; "
Pr 1:21 in the openings of the g': in the "
8: 3 She crieth at the g', at the entry of "
34 watching daily at my g', waiting 1817
14:19 wicked at the g' of the righteous. 8179
31:23 Her husband is known in the g', "
31 her own works praise her in the g'. "
Ca 7:13 our g' are all manner of pleasant*6607
Isa 3:26 her g' shall lament and mourn; "
13: 2 go into the g' of the nobles. "
26: 2 Open ye the g', that the righteous 8179
38:10 I shall go to the g' of the grave: "
45: 1 before him the two-leaved g'; *1817
1 and the g' shall not be shut; 8179
2 break in pieces the g' of brass, *1817
54:12 and thy g' of carbuncles, and all 8179
60:11 thy g' shall be open continually; "
18 walls Salvation, and thy g' Praise. "
62:10 through the g'; prepare ye the way "
Jer 1:15 the entering of the g' of Jerusalem, "
7: 2 that enter in at these g' to worship "
14: 2 Judah mourneth, and the g' thereof "
15: 7 I will fan them with a fan in the g' "
17:19 and in all the g' of Jerusalem; "
20 that enter in by these g': "
21 bring it in by the g' of Jerusalem; "
24 bring in no burden through the g' "
25 Then shall there enter into the g' "
27 entering in at the g' of Jerusalem "
27 I kindle a fire in the g' thereof, "
22: 2 thy people that enter in by these g':"
4 enter in by the g' of this house "
19 forth beyond the g' of Jerusalem. "
49:31 which have neither g' nor bars 1817
51:58 and her high g' shall be burned 8179
La 1: 4 g' are desolate: her priests sigh, "
2: 9 Her g' are sunk into the ground; "
4:12 entered into the g' of Jerusalem. "
Eze 21:15 the sword against all their g', "
22 battering rams against the g', "
26: 2 that was the g' of the people: 1817
10 when he shall enter into thy g', 8179
38:11 and having neither bars nor g', 1817
40:18 pavement by the side of the g' over 8179
18 over against the length of the g' "
38 thereof were by the posts of the g', "
44:11 charge at the g' of the house, "
17 in at the g' of the inner court, "
17 they minister in the g' of the inner "
48:31 And the g' of the city shall be "
31 g' northward; one gate of Reuben, "
32 three g'; and one gate of Joseph, "
33 three g'; and one gate of Simeon, "
34 their three g'; and one of Gad, "
Ob 11 foreigners entered into his g', "
Na 2: 6 g' of the rivers shall be opened, "
3:13 g' of thy land shall be set wide open"
Zec 8:16 truth and peace in your g': "
M't 16:18 the g' of hell shall not prevail 4439
Ac 9:24 they watched the g' day and night "
14:13 oxen and garlands unto the g', 4440
Re 21:12 and had twelve g', "
12 and at the g' twelve angels, "
13 On the east three g'; "
13 on the north three g'; "
13 on the south three g'; "
13 and on the west three g'. "
15 and the g' thereof, and the wall "
21 the twelve g' were twelve pearls; "
25 And the g' of it shall not be shut "
22:14 enter in through the g' into the city."

Gath (*gath*) See also GATH-HEPHER; GATH-RIMMON; GITTITE; MORESHETH-GATH.
Jos 11:22 only in Gaza, in G', and Ashdod, 1661
1Sa 5: 8 of Israel be carried about unto G'. "
6:17 Ashkelon one, for G' one, for Ekron"
7:14 to Israel, from Ekron even unto G'; "
17: 4 Goliath, of G', whose height was "
23 Philistine of G', Goliath by name, "
52 Shaaraim, even unto G', and unto "
21:10 and went to Achish the king of G'. "
12 afraid of Achish the king of G'. "
27: 2 Achish, the son of Maoch, king of G'."
3 David dwelt with Achish at G', he "
4 told Saul that David was fled to G': "
11 woman alive, to bring tidings to G',"

2Sa 1:20 Tell it not in G·, publish it not in 1661
15:18 men which came after him from G·, "
21:20 was yet a battle in G·, where was a "
22 four were born to the giant in G·, "
1Ki 2:39 Achish son of Maachah king of G·. "
39 Behold, thy servants be in G·. "
40 saddled his ass, and went to G· to "
40 and brought his servants from G·. "
41 had gone from Jerusalem to G·, and "
2Ki 12:17 went up, and fought against G·, "
1Ch 7:21 and Elead, whom the men of G· that "
8:13 drove away the inhabitants of G·: "
18: 1 subdued them, and took G· and "
20: 6 war at G·, where was a man of "
8 were born unto the giant in G·; "
2Ch 11: 8 And G·, and Mareshah, and Ziph, "
26: 6 and brake down the wall of G·, and "
Ps 56:*title* the Philistines took him in G·. "
Am 6: 2 go down to G· of the Philistines: "
Mi 1:10 Declare ye it not at G·, weep ye not "

gather See also GATHERED; GATHEREST; GATHERETH; GATHERING; TOGETHER.
Ge 6:21 and thou shalt g· it to thee; 622
31:46 said unto his brethren, G· stones; 3950
34:30 g· themselves together against me, 622
41:35 And let them g· all the food 6908
49: 1 G· yourselves together, that I may 622
2 G· yourselves together, and hear,*6908
Ex 3:16 Go, and g· the elders of Israel 622
5: 7 and g· straw for themselves, 7197
12 to g· stubble instead of straw. "
9:19 therefore now, and g· thy cattle, *5756
16: 4 the people shall go out and g· 3950
5 twice as much as they g· daily. "
16 G· of it every man according to his "
26 Six days ye shall g· it; but on the "
27 on the seventh day for to g·, "
23:10 shalt g· in the fruits thereof: 622
Le 8: 3 g· thou all the congregation *6950
19: 9 shalt thou g· the gleanings 3950
10 neither shalt thou g· every grape "
23:22 neither shalt thou g· any gleaning "
25: 3 prune thy vineyard, and g· in the 622
5 neither g· the grapes of thy vine 1219
11 nor g· the grapes in it of thy vine "
20 not sow, nor g· in our increase: 622
Nu 8: 9 shalt g· the whole assembly of the*6950
10: 4 of Israel, shall g· themselves 3259
11:16 G· unto me seventy men of the 622
19: 9 And a man that is clean shall g· "
20: 8 g· thou the assembly together, *6950
21:16 G· the people together, and I will 622
De 4:10 G· me the people together, and I *6950
11:14 that thou mayest g· in thy corn, 622
13:16 thou shalt g· all the spoil of it 6908
24:21 thou g· the grapes of thy vineyard, 1219
28:30 shalt not g· the grapes thereof. *2490
38 shalt g· but little in; for the locust 622
39 nor g· the grapes; for the worm 103
30: 3 and g· thee from all the nations, 6908
4 will the Lord thy God g· thee, "
31:12 G· the people together, men, and *6950
28 G· unto me all the elders of your * "
Ru 2: 7 me glean and g· after the reapers 622
1Sa 7: 5 said, G· all Israel to Mizpeh, 6908
2Sa 3:21 and will g· all Israel unto my lord "
12:28 g· the rest of the people together, 622
1Ki 18:19 g· to me all Israel unto mount 6908
2Ki 4:39 went out into the field to g· herbs, 3950
22:20 I will g· thee unto thy fathers, 622
1Ch 13: 2 they may g· themselves unto us: 6908
16:35 and g· us together, and deliver us "
22: 2 David commanded to g· together 3664
2Ch 24: 5 g· of all Israel money to repair 6908
34:28 I will g· thee to thy fathers, 622
Ezr 10: 7 they should g· themselves together 6908
Ne 1: 9 yet will I g· them from thence, "
7: 5 to g· together the nobles, and the "
12:44 to g· into them out of the fields 3664
Es 2: 3 may g· together all the fair young 6908
4:16 g· together all the Jews that are 3664
8:11 to g· themselves together, and to 6950
Job 11:10 and shut up, or g· together, * "
24: 6 they g· the vintage of the wicked. *3953
34:14 if he g· unto himself his spirit 622
39:12 thy seed, and g· it into thy barn? "
Ps 26: 9 G· not my soul with sinners, "
39: 6 and knoweth not who shall g· them. "
50: 5 G· my saints together unto me; "
56: 6 They g· themselves together, 1481
94:21 g· themselves together against 1413
104:22 they g· themselves together, and * 622
28 That thou givest them they g·: 3950
106:47 g· us from among the heathen, 6908
Pr 28: 8 g· it for him that will pity the poor.* "
Ec 2:26 to g· and to heap up, that he may 622
3: 5 and a time to g· stones together; 3664
Ca 6: 2 in the gardens, and to g· lilies. 3950
Isa 10:31 the inhabitants of Gebim g· ‡5756
11:12 g· together the dispersed of Judah 6908
34:15 hatch, and g· under her shadow: 1716
40:11 shall g· the lambs with his arm, 6908
43: 5 and g· thee from the west; "
49:18 all these g· themselves together, "
54: 7 with great mercies will I g· thee. "
15 they shall surely g· together, 1481
15 whosoever shall g· together against "
56: 8 Yet will I g· others to him, 6908
60: 4 all they g· themselves together, "
62:10 g· out the stones; lift up a 5619
66:18 I will g· all nations and tongues; 6908
Jer 4: 5 the trumpet in the land: cry, g· *4390
6: 1 ye children of Benjamin, g· *5756
7:18 children g· wood, and the fathers 3950
9:22 and none shall g· them. 622
10:17 G· up thy wares out of the land,

Jer 23: 3 I will g· the remnant of my flock 6908
29:14 I will g· you from all the nations, "
31: 8 g· them from the coasts of the earth, "
10 He that scattered Israel will g· him, "
32:37 I will g· them out of all countries, "
40:10 ye, g· ye wine, and summer fruits, 622
49: 5 shall g· up him that wandereth. 6908
14 G· ye together, and come against "
51:11 the arrows; g· the shields: *4390
Eze 11:17 I will even g· you from the people,6908
16:37 therefore I will g· all thy lovers, "
37 will even g· them round about "
20:34 and will g· you out of the countries "
41 and g· you out of the countries "
22:19 g· you into the midst of Jerusalem. "
20 they g· silver, and brass, and iron,6910
20 so will I g· you in mine anger 6908
21 Yea, I will g· you, and blow upon 3664
24: 4 G· the pieces thereof into it, 622
29:13 At the end of forty years will I g· 6908
34:13 and g· them from the countries, "
36:24 and g· you out of all countries, "
37:21 and will g· them on every side, "
39:17 g· yourselves on every side to my 622
Da 3: 2 sent to g· together the princes, 3673
Ho 8:10 now will I g· them, and they shall 6908
9: 6 Egypt shall g· them up, Memphis "
Joe 1:14 g· the elders and all the 622
2: 6 all faces shall g· blackness. *6908
16 G· the people, sanctify the 622
16 assemble the elders, g· the children, "
3: 2 I will also g· all nations, and will 6908
11 g· yourselves together round about: "
Mic 2:12 surely g· the remnant of Israel; "
4: 6 I will g· her that is driven out, * "
12 for he shall g· them as the sheaves "
5: 1 g· thyself in troops, O daughter 1413
Na 2:10 the faces of them all g· blackness.*6908
Hab 1: 9 shall g· the captivity as the sand. 622
15 and g· them in their drag: * "
Zep 2: 1 G· yourselves together, yea, 7197
1 g· together, O nation not desired; "
3: 8 to g· the nations, that I may 622
18 I will g· them that are sorrowful "
19 and g· her that was driven out; 6908
20 even in the time that I g· you: "
Zec 10: 8 and g· them; for I have redeemed "
10 and g· them out of Assyria; and I "
14: 2 g· all nations against Jerusalem 622
M't 3:12 and g· his wheat into the garner; 4863
6:26 do they reap, nor g· into barns; "
7:16 Do men g· grapes of thorns, 4816
13:28 that we go and g· them up? "
29 Nay; lest while ye g· up the tares, "
30 G· ye together first the tares, "
30 but g· the wheat into my barn. 4863
41 they shall g· out of his kingdom 4816
24:31 they shall g· together his elect 1996
25:26 and g· where I have not strawed: 4863
M'r 13:27 and shall g· together his elect 1996
Lu 3:17 will g· the wheat into his garner; 4863
6:44 of thorns men do not g· figs, 4816
44 of a bramble bush g· they grapes. 5166
13:34 as a hen doth g· her brood under *
Joh 6:12 G· up the fragments that remain, 4863
11:52 also he should g· together in one "
15: 6 and men g· them, and cast them "
Eph 1:10 he might g· together in one all * 346
Re 14:18 g· the clusters of the vine of the 5166
16:14 to g· them to battle of that great 4863
19:17 Come and g· yourselves together * "
20: 8 to g· them together to battle: "

gathered
Ge 1: 9 be g· together unto one place, 6960
12: 5 their substance that they had g·, 7408
25: 8 of years; and was g· to his people. 622
17 died; and was g· unto his people. "
29: 3 And thither were all the flocks g·: "
7 the cattle should be g· together: "
8 until all the flocks be g· together, "
22 And Laban g· together all the men "
35:29 died, and was g· unto his people, "
41:48 he g· up all the food of the seven 6908
49 And Joseph g· corn as the sand *6651
47:14 And Joseph g· up all the money 3950
49:29 I am to be g· unto my people: 622
33 he g· up his feet into the bed, "
33 and was g· unto his people. "
Ex 4:29 g· together all the elders of Israel: "
8:14 g· them together upon heaps: 6651
15: 8 the waters were g· together, the *6192
16:17 and g·, some more, some less. 3950
18 he that g· much had nothing over, "
18 and he that g· little had no lack; "
18 they g· every man according to his 3950
21 they g· it every morning, every man "
22 the sixth day they g· twice as much "
23:16 when thou hast g· in thy labours * 622
32: 1 g· themselves together unto Aaron,6950
26 g· themselves together unto him. 622
35: 1 Moses g· all the congregation *6950
Le 8: 4 and the assembly was g· together* "
23:39 ye have g· in the fruit of the land, 622
26:25 and when ye are g· together within "
Nu 10: 7 congregation is to be g· together, 6950
11: 8 the people went about, and g· it, 3950
22 all the fish of the sea be g· together 622
24 and g· the seventy men of the elders "
32 and they g· the quails: "
32 he that g· least...ten homers: "
32 he that...least g· ten homers: 622
14:35 that are g· together against me: 3259
15:32 they found a man that g· sticks *7197
16: 3 And they g· themselves together *6950
11 are g· together against the Lord: 3259

Nu 16:19 And Korah g· all the congregation*6950
42 the congregation was g· against * "
20: 2 And they g· themselves together * "
10 And Moses and Aaron g· the "
24 Aaron shall be g· unto his people: 622
26 Aaron shall be g· unto his people, "
21:23 but Sihon g· all his people together, "
27: 3 them that g· themselves together 3259
13 also shalt be g· unto thy people, 622
13 as Aaron thy brother was g·. "
31: 2 shalt thou be g· unto thy people. "
De 16:13 after that thou hast g· in thy corn "
32:50 and be g· unto thy people; as Aaron "
50 and was g· unto his people: "
33: 5 the tribes of Israel were g· together. "
Jos 9: 2 That they g· themselves together, 6908
10: 5 g· themselves together, and went 622
6 in the mountains are g· together 6908
22:12 g· themselves together at Shiloh, 6950
24: 1 Joshua g· all the tribes of Israel 622
J'g 1: 7 g· their meat under my table: 3950
2:10 were g· unto their fathers: 622
3:13 And he g· unto him the children "
4:13 Sisera g· together all his chariots, 2199
6:33 were g· together, and went over, * 622
34 and Abi-ezer was g· after him. 2199
35 Manasseh; who also was g· after "
7:23 the men of Israel g· themselves 6817
24 of Ephraim g· themselves together, "
9: 6 the men of Shechem g· together, * 622
27 and g· their vineyards, and trode 1219
47 of Shechem were g· together. 6908
10:17 the children of Ammon were g· 6817
11: 3 were g· vain men to Jephthah, 3950
20 Sihon g· all his people together, 622
12: 1 the men of Ephraim g· themselves 6817
4 Jephthah g· together all the men 6908
16:23 of the Philistines g· them together "
18:22 to Micah's house were g· together, 2199
20: 1 the congregation was g· together*6950
11 So all the men of Israel were g· 622
14 children of Benjamin g· themselves "
1Sa 5: 8 sent therefore and g· all the lords "
11 sent and g· together all the lords "
7: 6 And they g· together to Mizpeh, 6908
7 children of Israel were g· together "
8: 4 of Israel g· themselves together, "
13: 5 Philistines g· themselves together* 622
11 Philistines g· themselves together * "
14:48 And he g· an host, and smote the *6213
15: 4 And Saul g· the people together, *8085
17: 1 Philistines g· together their armies 622
1 and were g· together at Shochoh, "
2 the men of Israel were g· together, "
20:38 Jonathan's lad g· up the arrows, 3950
22: 2 was discontented, g· themselves 6908
25: 1 all the Israelites were g· together, "
28: 1 that the Philistines g· their armies "
4 Philistines g· themselves together, "
4 and Saul g· all Israel together, and "
29: 1 Now the Philistines g· together all "
2Sa 2:25 And the children of Benjamin g· "
30 he had g· all the people together, "
6: 1 David g· together all the chosen 3254
10:15 were smitten before Israel, they g· 622
17 told David, he g· all Israel together, "
12:29 And David g· all the people together, "
14:14 which cannot be g· up again; "
17:11 all Israel be generally g· unto thee, "
20:14 and they were g· together, and 7035
21:13 and they g· the bones of them 622
23: 9 that were there g· together to battle, "
11 the Philistines were g· together into "
1Ki 10:26 And Solomon g· together chariots "
11:24 he g· men unto him, and became 6908
18:20 and g· the prophets together unto "
20: 1 of Syria g· all his host together: "
22: 6 of Israel g· the prophets together, "
2Ki 3:21 they g· all that were able to put on 6817
4:39 and g· thereof wild gourds his lap 3950
6:24 Ben-hadad king of Syria g· all his 6908
10:18 And Jehu g· all the people together, "
22: 4 of the door have g· of the people: 622
9 Thy servants have g· the money *5413
20 and thou shalt be g· into thy grave 622
23: 1 and they g· unto him all the elders "
1Ch 11: 1 all Israel g· themselves to David 6908
13 the Philistines were g· together to 622
13: 5 So David g· all Israel together, *6950
15: 3 And David g· all Israel together * "
19: 7 of Ammon g· themselves together 622
17 and he g· all Israel, and passed over "
23: 2 And he g· together all the princes "
2Ch 1:14 And Solomon g· chariots and "
11: 1 he g· of the house of Judah and *6950
12: 5 that were g· together to Jerusalem 622
13: 7 there are g· unto him vain men, 6908
15: 9 And he g· all Judah and Benjamin, "
10 So they g· themselves together at "
18: 5 Therefore the king of Israel g· "
20: 4 And Judah g· themselves together, "
23: 2 g· the Levites out of all the cities "
24: 5 And he g· together the priests "
11 day, and g· money in abundance. 622
25: 5 Amaziah g· Judah together, and 6908
28:24 And Ahaz g· together the vessels 622
29: 4 g· them together into the east street, "
15 And they g· their brethren, and "
20 and g· the rulers of the city, "
30: 3 the people g· themselves together "
32: 4 was g· much people together, 6908
6 and g· them together to him in the "
34: 9 had g· of the hand of Manasseh 622
17 they have g· together the money *5413
28 and thou shalt be g· to thy grave 622

2Ch 34:29 the king sent and g' together all the 622
Ezr 3: 1 the people g' themselves together "
7:28 and I g' together out of Israel 6908
8:15 And I g' them together to the river "
10: 9 the men of Judah and Benjamin g' "
Ne 5:16 all my servants were g' thither "
8: 1 the people g' themselves together 622
13 on the second day were g' together "
12:28 the singers g' themselves together, "
13:11 I g' them together, and set them 6908
Es 2: 8 and when many maidens were g' "
19 when the virgins were g' together "
9: 2 The Jews g' themselves together 6950
15 the Jews that were in Shushan g' "
16 g' themselves together, and stood "
Job 16:10 they have g' themselves together *4390
27:19 lie down, but he shall not be g': 622
30: 7 the nettles they were g' together. 5596
Ps 35:15 and g' themselves together: yea, 622
15 the abjects g' themselves together "
47: 9 The princes of the people are g' "
59: 3 the mighty are g' against me; *1481
102:22 When the people are g' together, 6908
107: 3 And g' them out of the lands, "
140: 2 are they g' together for war. *1481
Pr 27:25 and herbs of the mountains are g'. 622
30: 4 who hath g' the winds in his fists? "
Ec 2: 8 I g' me also silver and gold, 3664
Ca 5: 1 I have g' my myrrh with my spice; 717
Isa 5: 2 it, and g' out the stones thereof,
10:14 are left, have I g' all the earth; 622
13: 4 kingdoms of nations g' together: "
22: 9 and ye g' together the waters 6908
24:22 And they shall be g' together, 622
22 as prisoners are g' in the pit, 626
27:12 ye shall be g' one by one, 3950
33: 4 spoil shall be g' like the gathering 622
34:15 there shall the vultures also be g', 6908
16 and his spirit it hath g' them. "
43: 9 Let all the nations be g' together, "
44:11 let them all be g' together, let them "
49: 5 Though Israel be not g', yet shall 622
56: 8 beside those that are g' unto him, 6908
60: 7 All the flocks of Kedar shall be g' "
62: 9 they that have g' it shall eat it, * 622
Jer 3:17 all the nations shall be g' unto it, 6960
8: 2 they shall not be g', nor be buried; 622
25:33 shall not be lamented, neither g', "
26: 9 people were g' against Jeremiah 6950
40:12 and g' wine and summer fruits 622
15 g' unto thee should be scattered, 6908
Eze 28:25 I shall have g' the house of Israel "
29: 5 not be brought together, nor g': "
38: 8 and is g' out of many people, "
12 upon the people that are g' out 622
13 g' thy company to take a prey? *6950
39:27 and g' them out of their enemies' 6908
28 have g' them unto their own land, 3664
Da 3: 3 g' together unto the dedication 3673
27 being g' together, saw these men, "
Ho 1:11 and the children of Israel be g' 6908
10:10 people shall be g' against them, 622
Mic 1: 7 she g' it of the hire of an harlot, 6908
4:11 many nations are g' against thee,* 622
7: 1 they have g' the summer fruits, "
Zec 12: 3 people of the earth be g' together "
14:14 round about shall be g' together, "
M't 2: 4 he had g' all the chief priests *4863
13: 2 great multitudes were g' together "
40 As therefore the tares are g' and 4816
47 into the sea, and g' of every kind: 4863
48 and g' the good into vessels, 4816
18:20 three are g' together in my name, 4863
22:10 and g' together all as many as they "
34 to silence, they were g' together. "
41 the Pharisees were g' together, "
23:37 often would I have g' thy children 1996
24:28 will the eagles be g' together. 4863
25:32 before him shall be g' all nations: "
27:17 they were g' together, Pilate said "
27 and g' unto him the whole band "
M'r 1:33 city was g' together at the door. 1996
2: 2 many were g' together, insomuch 4863
4: 1 was g' unto him a great multitude, "
5:21 much people g' unto him: and he "
6:30 the apostles g' themselves together "
Lu 8: 4 much people were g' together, *4896
11:29 people were g' thick together. *1865
12: 1 when there were g' together an 1996
13:34 how often would I have g' thy "
15:13 the younger son g' all together, 4863
17:37 will the eagles be g' together. "
24:33 and found the eleven g' together. 4867
Joh 6:13 Therefore they g' them together, 4863
11:47 Then g' the chief priests and the "
Ac 4: 6 were g' together at Jerusalem. "
26 rulers were g' together against the "
27 and the people of Israel, were g' "
12:12 many were g' together praying. "
14:27 and had g' the church together, "
15:30 had g' the multitude together, "
17: 5 g' a company, and set all the city *3792
20: 8 where there they were g' together.4863
28: 3 And when Paul had g' a bundle 4962
1Co 5: 4 when ye are g' together, and my 4863
2Co 8:15 He that had g' much had nothing
15 and he that had g' little had no lack.
Re 14:19 and g' the vine of the earth, 5166
16:16 And he g' them together into a 4863
19:19 and their armies, g' together to "

gatherer
Am 7:14 and a g' of sycomore fruit: *1103

gatherest
De 24:21 When thou g' the grapes of thy 1219

gathereth
Nu 19:10 he that g' the ashes of the heifer 622
Ps 33: 7 he g' the waters of the sea 3664
41: 6 his heart g' iniquity to itself; 6908
147: 2 g' together the outcasts of Israel. 3664
Pr 6: 8 and g' her food in the harvest. 103
10: 5 He that g' in summer is a wise son: "
13:11 but he that g' by labour shall 6908
Isa 10:14 and as one g' eggs that are left, 622
17: 5 when the harvestman g' the corn, "
5 as he that g' ears in the valley *3950
56: 8 which g' the outcasts of Israel 6908
Na 3:18 mountains, and no man g' them. * "
Hab 2: 5 but g' unto him all nations, 622
M't 12:30 he that g' not with me scattereth 4863
23:37 even as a hen g' her chickens 1996
Lu 11:23 he that g' not with me scattereth. 4863
Joh 4:36 and g' fruit unto life eternal: "

gathering See also GATHERINGS.
Ge 1:10 and the g' together of the waters 4723
49:10 him shall the g' of the people be. *3349
Nu 15:33 they that found him g' sticks 7197
1Ki 17:10 widow woman was there g' of sticks: "
12 and, behold, I am g' two sticks, "
2Ch 20:25 were three days in g' of the spoil, *962
Isa 32:10 shall fail, the g' shall not come. *625
33: 4 the gathering of the caterpiller: * "
M't 25:24 g' where thou hast not strawed: 4863
Ac 16:10 assuredly g' that the Lord had *4822
2Th 2: 1 by our g' together unto him, 1997

gatherings
1Co 16: 2 that there be no g' when I come. *3048

Gath-hepher (gath-he'-fer) See also GITTAH-HEPHER.
2Ki 14:25 the prophet, which was of G'. 1662

Gath-rimmon (gath-rim'-mon)
Jos 19:45 Jehud, and Bene-berak, and G', 1667
21:24 her suburbs, G' with her suburbs; "
25 suburbs, and G' with her suburbs; "
1Ch 6:69 suburbs, and G' with her suburbs: "

gave See also FORGAVE; GAVEST.
Ge 2:20 And Adam g' names to all cattle, 7121
3: 6 and g' also unto her husband 5414
12 to be with me, she g' me of the tree, "
14:20 And he g' him tithes of all. "
16: 3 g' her to her husband Abram to be "
18: 7 and g' it unto a young man; and he "
20:14 and g' them unto Abraham, and "
21:14 and g' it unto Hagar, putting it on "
19 with water, and g' the lad drink. "
27 and g' them unto Abimelech; and 5414
24:18 upon her hand, and g' him drink. "
32 and g' straw and provender for 5414
53 and g' them to Rebekah: he g' also "
25: 5 And Abraham g' all that he had "
6 Abraham g' gifts, and sent them "
8 Then Abraham g' up the ghost, and "
17 and he g' up the ghost and died; "
34 Jacob g' Esau bread and pottage 5414
27:17 And she g' the savoury meat and "
28: 4 which God g' unto Abraham. "
6 he g' him a charge, saying, Thou "
29:24 And Laban g' unto his daughter 5414
28 and he g' him Rachel his daughter "
29 Laban g' to Rachel his daughter "
30: 4 she g' him Bilhah her handmaid "
9 and g' her Jacob to wife. "
35 and g' them into the hand of his "
35: 4 And they g' unto Jacob all the "
12 the land which I g' Abraham and "
29 And Isaac g' up the ghost, and died, "
38:18 And he g' it her, and came in unto5414
26 I g' her not to Shelah my son. "
39:21 and g' him favour in the sight of "
40:11 and I g' the cup into Pharaoh's "
21 and he g' the cup into Pharaoh's "
41:45 and he g' him to wife Asenath the "
43:24 g' them water, and they washed "
24 their feet; and he g' their asses "
45:21 Joseph g' them wagons, according "
21 and g' them provision for the way. "
22 he g' each man changes of raiment; "
22 to Benjamin he g' three hundred "
46:18 Zilpah, whom Laban g' to Leah "
25 Bilhah, which Laban g' unto "
47:11 and g' them a possession in the "
17 Joseph g' them bread in exchange "
22 eat their portion which Pharaoh g' "
Ex 2:21 and he g' Moses Zipporah his "
6:13 and g' them a charge unto the "
11: 3 And the Lord g' the people favour 5414
12:36 the Lord g' the people favour in "
14:20 but it g' light by night to these: "
31:18 And he g' unto Moses, when he 5414
32:24 So they g' it me: then I cast it "
34:32 and he g' them in commandment "
36: 6 And Moses g' commandment, and "
Nu 3:51 And Moses g' the money of them 5414
7: 6 and g' them unto the Levites. "
7 four oxen he g' unto the sons of "
8 eight oxen he g' unto the sons of "
9 unto the sons of Kohath he g' none: "
11:25 and g' it unto the seventy elders: * "
17: 6 every one of their princes g' him a "
27:23 and g' him a charge, as the Lord "
31:41 And Moses g' the tribute, which 5414
47 and g' them unto the Levites, "
32:33 And Moses g' unto them, even to "
38 and g' other names unto the cities 7121
40 And Moses g' Gilead unto Machir 5414
De 2:12 his possession, which the Lord g' "
3:12 the cities thereof, g' I unto the "
13 the kingdom of Og, g' I unto the "
De 3:15 And I g' Gilead unto Machir. 5414
16 g' from Gilead even unto the river "
9:11 the Lord g' me the two tables "
10: 4 and the Lord g' them unto me. "
22:16 I g' my daughter unto this man "
29: 8 and g' it for an inheritance unto "
31:23 And he g' Joshua the son of Nun charge, "
Jos 1:14 the land which Moses g' you on 5414
15 which Moses the Lord's servant g' "
11:23 and Joshua g' it for an inheritance "
12: 6 Moses the servant of the Lord g' "
7 which Joshua g' unto the tribes "
13: 8 their inheritance, which Moses g' "
8 Moses the servant of the Lord g' "
14 tribe of Levi he g' none inheritance; "
15 And Moses g' unto the tribe of the "
24 g' inheritance unto the tribe of Gad, "
29 g' inheritance unto the half tribe of "
33 the tribe of Levi Moses g' not any "
14: 3 but unto the Levites he g' none "
4 they g' no part unto the Levites "
13 and g' unto Caleb the son of "
15:13 Caleb, the son of Jephunneh he g' "
17 and he g' him Achsah his daughter "
19 And he g' her the upper springs, "
17: 4 he g' them an inheritance among "
18: 7 the servant of the Lord g' them. "
19:49 children of Israel g' an inheritance "
50 they g' him the city which he asked, "
21: 3 of Israel g' unto the Levites out of "
8 And the children of Israel g' by lot "
9 And they g' out of the tribe of the "
11 And they g' them the city of Arba "
12 villages thereof, g' they to Caleb "
13 they g' to the children of Aaron "
21 For they g' them Shechem with her "
27 tribe of Manasseh they g' Golan in "
43 And the Lord g' unto Israel all 5414
44 Lord g' them rest round about, "
22: 4 the servant of the Lord g' you 5414
7 g' Joshua among their brethren on "
24: 3 his seed, and g' him Isaac. "
4 I g' unto Isaac Jacob and Esau: "
4 and I g' unto Esau mount Seir, "
8 and I g' them into your hand, "
J'g 1:13 and he g' him Achsah his daughter "
15 And Caleb g' her the upper springs "
20 And they g' Hebron unto Caleb, as "
3: 6 and g' their daughters to their sons, "
4:19 bottle of milk, and g' him drink, "
5:25 water, and she g' him milk; 5414
6: 9 and g' you their land; "
9: 4 g' him threescore and ten pieces "
14: 9 and he g' them, and they did eat: "
19 g' change of garments unto them "
15: 2 I g' her to thy companion: "
17: 4 and g' them to the founder, who "
19:21 and g' provender unto the asses: and
20:36 for the men of Israel g' place to 5414
21:14 and they g' them wives which they "
Ru 2:18 and g' to her that she had reserved "
3:17 six measures of barley g' he me; "
4: 7 his shoe, and g' it to his neighbour: "
13 her, the Lord g' her conception, "
17 her neighbours g' it a name, 7121
1Sa 1: 4 he g' to Peninnah his wife, and to 5414
5 Hannah he g' a worthy portion; "
23 and g' her son suck until she weaned
9:23 Bring the portion which I g' thee, 5414
10: 9 Samuel, God g' him another heart: "
18: 4 that was upon him, and g' it 5414
27 and they g' them in full tale to the king
27 Saul g' him Michal his daughter 5414
20:40 And Jonathan g' his artillery unto "
21: 6 the priest g' him hallowed bread: "
22:10 g' him victuals, and g' him the "
27: 6 Achish g' him Ziklag that day: "
30:11 and g' him bread, and he did eat; "
12 they g' him a piece of a cake of figs, "
2Sa 12: 8 And I g' thee thy master's house, "
8 and g' thee the house of Israel "
18: 5 the king g' all the captains charge
24: 9 And Joab g' up the sum of the 5414
1Ki 4:29 And God g' Solomon wisdom and "
5:10 Hiram g' Solomon cedar trees and "
11 And Solomon g' Hiram twenty "
11 g' Solomon to Hiram year by year. "
12 the Lord g' Solomon wisdom, as "
9:11 Solomon g' Hiram twenty cities "
10:10 And she g' the king an hundred "
10 queen of Sheba g' to king Solomon. "
13 king Solomon g' unto the queen of "
13 Solomon g' her of his royal bounty. "
11:18 of Egypt; which g' him an house, "
18 him victuals, and g' him land. "
19 that he g' him to wife the sister "
12:13 men's counsel that they g' him; *3289
13: 3 And he g' a sign the same day, 5414
14: 8 the house of David, and g' it thee: "
15 land which he g' to their fathers, "
19:21 and g' unto the people, and they "
2Ki 10:15 And he g' him his hand; and he "
11:12 upon him, and g' him the testimony; "
12:11 And they g' the money, being told,5414
14 But they g' that to the workmen, "
13: 5 (And the Lord g' Israel a saviour, "
15:19 and Menahem g' Pul a thousand "
17: 3 his servant, and g' him presents. *7725
18:15 And Hezekiah g' him all the silver5414
16 and g' it to the king of Assyria. "
21: 8 land which I g' their fathers; "
22: 8 Hilkiah g' the book to Shaphan, * "
23:35 Jehoiakim g' the silver and the "
25: 6 and they g' judgment upon him. 1696
1Ch 2:35 Sheshan g' his daughter to Jarha 5414

1Ch 6:55 they g' them Hebron in the land 5414
56 they g' to Caleb the son of "
57 Aaron they g' the cities of Judah, "
64 of Israel g' to the Levites "
65 And they g' by lot out of the tribe "
67 And they g' unto them, of the cities"
67 g' also Gezer with her suburbs, * "
14:12 David g' a commandment, and they "
21: 5 Joab g' the sum of the number 5414
25 So David g' to Ornan for the place "
25: 5 God g' to Heman fourteen sons "
28:11 Then David g' to Solomon his son "
14 He g' of gold by weight for things*
16 he g' gold for the tables of *
17 for the gold basons he g' gold by *
29: 7 g' for the service of the house 5414
8 precious stones were found g' them "
2Ch 9: 9 And she g' the king an hundred "
9 queen of Sheba g' king Solomon. "
12 Solomon g' to the queen of Sheba "
10: 8 counsel which the old men g' him,*3289
11:23 he g' them victual in abundance. 5414
13: 5 God of Israel g' the kingdom over "
15 Then the men of Judah g' a shout:
15:15 and the Lord g' them rest round about.
20:30 for his God g' him rest round about.
21: 3 their father g' them great gifts 5414
3 but the kingdom g' he to Jehoram; "
23:11 the crown, and g' him the testimony,
24:12 And the king and Jehoiada g' it 5414
26: 8 the Ammonites g' gifts to Uzziah: "
27: 5 And the children of Ammon g' him "
28:15 and g' them to eat and to drink,
21 and g' it unto the king of Assyria:5414
30: 7 therefore g' them up to desolation, "
24 the princes g' to the congregation 7311
32:24 unto him, and he g' him a sign. 5414
34:10 and they g' it to the workmen "
11 artificers and builders g' they it, "
35: 7 And Josiah g' to the people, of the 7311
8 g' willingly unto the people, "
8 g' unto the priests for the passover5414
9 of the Levites, g' unto the Levites 7311
36:17 he g' them all into his hand. 5414
Ezr 2:69 They g' after their ability unto "
3: 7 g' money also unto the masons, "
5:12 he g' them into the hand of 3052
7:11 the king Artaxerxes g' unto Ezra 5414
10:19 And they g' their hands that they "
Ne 2: 1 I took up the wine, and g' it "
9 river, and g' them the king's letters."
7: 2 That I g' my brother Hanani,...charge
70 of the fathers g' unto the work. 5414
70 The Tirshatha g' to the treasure "
71 the chief of the fathers g' to the "
72 which the rest of the people g' "
8: 8 God distinctly, and g' the sense, 7760
12:31 companies of them that g' thanks,
38 other company of them that g' thanks
40 companies of them that g' thanks
47 g' the portions of the singers 5414
Es 1: 7 And they g' them drink in vessels of
2: 9 and he speedily g' her things for 5414
18 and g' gifts, according to the state "
3:10 his hand, and g' it unto Haman "
4: 5 and g' him a commandment to *
8 he g' him the copy of the writing 5414
10 and g' him commandment unto "
8: 2 Haman, and g' it unto Mordecai. 5414
Job 1:21 Lord g', and the Lord hath taken "
19:16 servant, and he g' me no answer;*
29:11 the eye saw me, it g' witness to me:
21 Unto me men g' ear, and waited,
32:11 I g' ear to your reasons, whilst *
42:10 also the Lord g' Job twice as much 3254
11 man also g' him a piece of money,5414
15 their father g' them inheritance "
Ps 18:13 and the Highest g' his voice; * "
68:11 The Lord g' the word: great was * "
69:21 They g' me also gall for my meat; "
21 in my thirst they g' me vinegar to drink.
77: 1 and he g' ear unto me. *
78:15 and g' them drink as out of the great
29 for he g' them their own desire; 935
46 He g' also their increase unto the 5414
48 g' up their cattle also to the hail, 5462
50 g' their life over to the pestilence; "
62 g' his people over also unto the "
81:12 So I g' them up unto their own *7971
99: 7 the ordinance that he g' them. 5414
105:32 g' them hail for rain, and flaming "
44 g' them the lands of the heathen: "
106:15 And he g' them their request; "
41 he g' them into the hand of the "
135:12 And g' their land for an heritage, "
136:21 And g' their land for an heritage: "
Pr 8:29 When he g' to the sea his decree, 7760
Ec 1:13 g' my heart to seek and search *5414
17 I g' my heart to know wisdom, * "
12: 7 spirit shall return unto God who g' "
9 yea, he g' good heed, and sought *
Ca 5: 6 him, but he g' me no answer.
Isa 41: 2 g' the nations before him, and *5414
2 g' them as the dust to his sword. * "
42:24 Who g' Jacob for a spoil, and "
43: 3 I g' Egypt for thy ransom, * "
50: 6 I g' my back to the smiters, "
Jer 7: 7 the land that I g' to your fathers, "
14 the place which I g' to you and to "
16:15 land that I g' unto their fathers. "
17: 4 from thine heritage that I g' thee; "
23:39 that I g' you and your fathers, "
24:10 the land that I g' unto them and to "
30: 3 the land that I g' to their fathers, "
32:12 I g' the evidence of the purchase* "
36:32 and g' it to Baruch the scribe.

Jer 39: 5 where he g' judgment upon him. 1696
10 and g' them vineyards and fields 5414
11 king of Babylon g' charge
40: 5 the captain of the guard g' him 5414
44:30 as I g' Zedekiah king of Judah "
52: 9 where he g' judgment upon him. 1696
La 1:19 and mine elders g' up the ghost
Eze 16:19 My meat also which I g' thee, 5414
20:11 And I g' them my statutes, and "
12 also I g' them my sabbaths, "
25 Wherefore I g' them also statutes "
36:28 the land that I g' to your fathers; "
39:23 and g' them into the hand of their "
Da 1: 2 And the Lord g' Jehoiakim king of "
7 prince of the eunuchs g' names: 7760
7 for he g' unto Daniel the name "
16 should drink; and g' them pulse. 5414
17 God g' them knowledge and skill "
2:48 and g' him many great gifts, and 3052
5:18 most high God g' Nebuchadnezzar "
19 for the majesty that he g' him,
6:10 and g' thanks before his God, as he did
Ho 2: 8 I g' her corn, and wine, and oil, 5414
13:11 I g' thee a king in mine anger, * "
Am 2:12 ye g' the Nazarites wine to drink;
Mal 2: 5 and I g' them to him for the fear 5414
M't 8:18 he g' commandment to depart 2753
10: 1 g' them power against unclean 1325
14:19 and g' the loaves to his disciples, "
15:36 and g' thanks, and brake them, "
36 and g' to his disciples, "
21:23 who g' thee this authority? "
25:15 unto one he g' five talents, to "
35 an hungred, and ye g' me meat: "
35 was thirsty, and ye g' me drink: 4222
37 or thirsty, and g' thee drink? "
42 an hungred, and ye g' me no meat:1325
42 thirsty, and ye g' me no drink: 4222
26:26 brake it, and g' it to the disciples, 1325
27 g' thanks, and g' it to them, saying, "
48 that betrayed him g' them a sign, "
27:10 and g' them for the potter's field, "
34 g' him vinegar to drink mingled "
48 on a reed, and g' him to drink. 4222
28:12 g' large money unto the soldiers, 1325
M'r 2:26 g' also to them which were with "
5:13 forthwith Jesus g' them leave. 2010
6: 7 and g' them power over unclean 1325
28 a charger, and g' it to the damsel: "
28 and the damsel g' it to her mother. "
41 g' them to his disciples to set "
8: 6 loaves and g' thanks, and brake, * "
6 and g' to his disciples to set before "
11:28 who g' thee this authority to do "
13:34 and g' authority to his servants, * "
14:22 brake it, and g' to them, and said, "
23 had given thanks, he g' it to them: "
15:23 And they g' him to drink wine * "
36 and g' him to drink, saying, Let 4222
37 with a loud voice, and g' up the ghost,
39 so cried out, and g' up the ghost,
45 he g' the body to Joseph. *1433
Lu 2:38 g' thanks likewise unto the Lord, 437
4:20 he g' it again to the minister, and 591
6: 4 g' also to them that were with him; 1325
7:21 many that were blind he g' sight. *5483
9: 1 g' them power and authority over 1325
16 g' to the disciples to set before the "
10:35 two pence, and g' them to the host, "
15:16 and no man g' unto him. "
18:43 they saw it, g' praise unto God. "
20: 2 who is he that g' thee this authority?"
22:17 g' thanks, and said, Take this, *
19 and g' thanks, and brake it, *
19 and g' unto them, saying, This is 1325
23:24 Pilate g' sentence that it should be
29 and the paps which never g' suck.
46 having said thus, he g' up the ghost.
24:30 blessed it, and brake and g' to them, 1929
42 they g' him a piece of a broiled fish, "
Joh 1:12 g' he power to become the sons 1325
3:16 that he g' his only begotten Son, "
4: 5 that Jacob g' to his son Joseph. "
12 Father Jacob, which g' us the well, "
6:31 g' them bread from heaven to eat. "
32 Moses g' you not that bread from "
7:22 Moses...g' unto you circumcision;* "
10:29 Father, which g' them me, is * "
12:49 he g' me a commandment, what I* "
13:26 the sop, he g' it to Judas Iscariot, "
14:31 Father g' me commandment, even 1781
18:14 Caiaphas was he, which g' counsel 4823
19: 9 thou? But Jesus g' him no answer. 1325
30 his head, and g' up the ghost. 3860
38 and Pilate g' him leave. He came 2010
Ac 1:26 they g' forth their lots; and the lot 1325
2: 4 as the Spirit g' them utterance. "
3: 5 he g' heed unto them, expecting to 1907
4:33 g' the apostles witness of the 591
5: 5 fell down, and g' up the ghost:
7: 5 he g' him none inheritance in it, 1325
8 g' him the covenant of circumcision: "
10 g' him favour and wisdom in the "
42 g' them up to worship the host of 3860
8: 6 g' heed unto these things which 4337
10 To whom they all g' heed, from the "
9:41 he g' her his hand, and lifted her 1325
10: 2 which g' much alms to the people, 4160
11:17 God g' them the like gift as he did 1325
12:22 And the people g' a shout, saying,*
23 because he g' not God the glory: 1325
23 eaten of worms, and g' up the ghost
13:20 after that he g' unto them judges 1325
21 God g' unto them Saul the son of "
22 to whom also he g' testimony, and*3140
14: 3 which g' testimony unto the word * "

Ac 14:17 and g' us rain from heaven, and 1325
15:12 g' audience to Barnabas and *
24 we g' no such commandment: 1291
22:22 g' him audience unto this word,
23:30 g' commandment to his accusers*
26:10 I g' my voice against them. 2702
27: 3 g' him liberty to go unto his 2010
35 g' thanks to God in presence of them
Ro 1:24 Wherefore God also g' them up to 3860
26 g' them up unto vile affections: "
28 God g' them over to a reprobate "
1Co 3: 5 even as the Lord g' to every man? 1325
6 but God g' the increase.
2Co 8: 5 g' their own selves to the Lord, 1325
Ga 1: 4 Who g' himself for our sins, that "
2: 5 whom we g' place by subjection, 1502
9 g' to me and Barnabas the right 1325
20 loved me, and g' himself for me. 3860
3:18 God g' it to Abraham by promise.* 5483
Eph 1:22 g' him to be the head over all 1325
4: 8 captive, and g' gifts unto men. "
11 he g' some, apostles; and some, "
5:25 the church, and g' himself for it; 3860
1Th 4: 2 we g' you by the Lord Jesus. 1325
1Ti 2: 6 Who g' himself a ransom for all, "
Tit 2:14 Who g' himself for us, that he might "
Heb 7: 2 Abraham g' a tenth part of all; *
4 Abraham g' the tenth of the spoils.1325
13 no man g' attendance at the altar,*4337
11:22 g' commandment concerning his
12: 9 we g' them reverence: shall we not 1788
Jas 5:18 the heaven g' rain, and the earth 1325
1Pe 1:21 from the dead, and g' him glory; "
1Jo 3:23 another as he g' us commandment. "
5:10 the record that God g' of his Son. *3140
Jude 3 when I g' all diligence to write *4160
Re 1: 1 which God g' unto him, to shew 1325
2:21 I g' her space to repent of her "
11:13 and g' glory to the God of heaven. "
13: 2 the dragon g' him his power, "
4 which g' power unto the beast: "
15: 7 g' unto the seven angels seven "
20:13 sea g' up the dead which were in it; "

gavest See also FORGAVEST.
Ge 3:12 woman whom thou g' to be with 5414
1Ki 8:34 unto the land which thou g' unto "
40 in the land which thou g' unto our "
48 their land, which thou g' unto their "
2Ch 6:25 the land which thou g' to them "
31 in the land which thou g' unto our "
38 toward their land, which thou g' "
20: 7 and g' it to the seed of Abraham "
Ne 9: 7 and g' him the name of Abraham; 7760
13 g' them right judgments, and true 5414
15 g' them bread from heaven for "
20 g' also thy good spirit to instruct "
20 and g' them water for their thirst. "
22 thou g' them kingdoms and nations,"
24 g' them into their hands, with their "
27 g' them saviours, who saved them "
30 therefore g' thou them into the hand"
35 great goodness that thou g' them, "
35 fat land which thou g' before them."
36 land that thou g' unto our fathers "
Job 39:13 G' thou the goodly wings unto *
Ps 21: 4 life of thee, and thou g' it him, 5414
74:14 g' him to be meat to the people "
Lu 7:44 g' me no water for my feet: 1325
45 Thou g' me no kiss: but this woman"
15:29 and yet thou never g' me a kid, "
19:23 Wherefore then g' thou not my "
Joh 17: 4 the work which thou g' me to do. * "
6 which thou g' me out of the world: "
6 they were, and thou g' them me: "
8 them the words which thou g' me; "
12 those that thou g' me I have kept,* "
22 glory which thou g' me I have * "
18: 9 which thou g' me have I lost none.* "

gay
Jas 2: 3 the g' clothing, and say unto him,*2986

Gaza (ga'-zah) See also AZZAH; GAZITES.
Ge 10:19 as thou comest to Gerar, unto G'; 5804
Jos 10:41 from Kadesh-barnea even unto G', "
11:22 only in G', in Gath, and in Ashdod, "
15:47 G' with her towns and her villages,"
J'g 1:18 Also Judah took G' with the coast "
6: 4 till thou come unto G'; and left no "
16: 1 Then went Samson to G', and saw "
21 and brought him down to G', and "
1Sa 6:17 for Ashdod one, for G' one, for "
2Ki 18: 8 the Philistines, even unto G', "
1Ch 7:28 unto G' and the towns thereof: * "
Jer 47: 1 before that Pharaoh smote G'. "
5 is come upon G'; Ashkelon is cut "
Am 1: 6 transgressions of G', and for four, "
7 will send a fire on the wall of G'. "
Zep 2: 4 For G' shall be forsaken, and "
Zec 9: 5 G' also shall see it, and be very "
5 and the king shall perish from G', "
Ac 8:26 down from Jerusalem unto G'. 1048

Gazathites (ga'-zath-ites) See also GAZITES.
Jos 13: 3 lords of the Philistines; the G', *5841

gaze See also GAZING.
Ex 19:21 break through unto the Lord to g',7200

Gazer (ga'-zur) See also GEZER.
2Sa 5:25 from Geba until thou come to G'.*1507
1Ch 14:16 Philistines from Gibeon even to G'.* "

gazers See STARGAZERS.

Gazez (ga'-zez)
1Ch 2:46 Moza, and G': and Haran begat G'.1495

gazing See also GAZINGSTOCK.
Ac 1:11 why stand ye g' up into heaven? *1689

gazingstock
Na 3: 6 and will set thee as a *g*·. 7210
Heb 10:33 whilst ye were made a *g*· both by *2301*

Gazites (*ga'-zites*) See also GAZATHITES.
J'g 16: 2 it was told the *G*·, saying, Samson 5841

Gazzam (*gaz'-zam*)
Ezr 2:48 of Nekoda, the children of *G*·, 1502
Ne 7:51 The children of *G*·, the children of "

Geba (*ghe'-bah*) See also GABA; GIBEAH; GIBEON.
Jos 21:17 her suburbs, *G*· with her suburbs, 1387
1Sa 13: 3 of the Philistines that was in *G*·, "
2Sa 5:25 Philistines from *G*· until thou come "
1Ki 15:22 built with them *G*· of Benjamin, "
2Ki 23: 8 incense, from *G*· to Beer-sheba, and "
1Ch 6:60 Benjamin; *G*· with her suburbs, "
8: 6 fathers of the inhabitants of *G*·, "
2Ch 16: 6 he built therewith *G*· and Mizpah. "
Ne 11:31 of Benjamin from *G*· dwelt at "
12:29 Gilgal, and out of the fields of *G*· "
Isa 10:29 have taken up their lodging at *G*·; "
Zec 14:10 turned as a plain from *G*· to "

Gebal (*ghe'-bal*) See also GIBLITES.
Ps 83: 7 *G*·, and Ammon, and Amalek; the 1381
Eze 27: 9 The ancients of *G*· and the wise "

Geber See also EZION-GEBER.
1Ki 4: 13 The son of *G*·, in Ramoth-gilead:*1398
19 *G*· the son Uri was in the country "

Gebim (*ghe'-bim*)
Isa 10:31 the inhabitants of *G*· gather 1374

Gedaliah (*ghed-a-li'-ah*)
2Ki 25:22 *G*· the son of Ahikam, the son of 1436
23 *G*· governor, there came to *G*· to "
24 *G*· sware to them, and to their men, "
25 smote *G*·, that he died, and the "
1Ch 25: 3 sons of Jeduthun; *G*·, and Zeri, "
9 the second to *G*·, who with his "
Ezr 10:18 and Eliezer, and Jarib, and *G*·. "
Jer 38: 1 *G*· the son of Pashur, and Jucal the "
39:14 committed him unto *G*· the son of "
40: 5 Go back to *G*· the son of Ahikam "
6 *G*· the son of Ahikam to Mizpah; "
7 had made *G*· the son of Ahikam "
8 came to *G*· to Mizpah, even Ishmael "
9 And *G*· the son of Ahikam the son "
11 over them *G*· the son of Ahikam "
12 Judah, to *G*·, unto Mizpah, and "
13 that were in the fields, came to *G*· "
14 But *G*· the son of Ahikam believed "
15 spake to *G*· in Mizpah secretly, "
16 *G*· the son of Ahikam said unto "
41: 1 ten men with him, came unto *G*· the "
2 smote *G*· the son of Ahikam the "
3 even with *G*·, at Mizpah, and the "
4 second day after he had slain *G*·, "
6 unto them, Come to *G*· the son of "
9 had slain because of *G*·, was it "
10 committed to *G*· the son of Ahikam; "
16 slain *G*· the son of Ahikam, even "
18 of Nehemiah had slain *G*· the son of "
43: 6 guard had left with *G*· the son of "
Zep 1: 1 Cushi, the son of *G*·, the son of "

Gedeon (*ghed'-e-on*) See also GIDEON.
He 11:32 time would fail me to tell of *G*·, *1066

Geder (*ghe'-dur*) See also BETH-GADER; GEDERITE; GEDOR.
Jos 12:13 Debir, one; the king of *G*·, one; 1445

Gederah (*ghed'-e-rah*) See also GEDERATHITE.
Jos 15:36 and Adithaim, and *G*·, and 1449

Gederathite (*ghed'-e-rath-ite*)
1Ch 12: 4 Johanan, and Josabad the *G*·, 1452

Gederite (*ghed'-e-rite*)
1Ch 27:28 low plains was Baal-hanan the *G*·:1451

Gederoth (*ghed'-e-roth*)
Jos 15:41 And *G*·, Beth-dagon, and Naamah,1450
2Ch 28:18 Ajalon, and *G*·, and Shocho with the "

Gederothaim (*ghed-e-ro-tha'-im*)
Jos 15:36 Adithaim, and Gederah, and *G*·; 1453

Gedi See EN-GEDI.

Gedor (*ghe'-dor*) See also GEDER.
Jos 15:58 Halhul, Beth-zur, and *G*·, 1446
1Ch 4: 4 Penuel the father of *G*·, Ezer the "
18 Jered the father of *G*·, and Heber "
39 entrance of *G*·, even unto the east "
8:31 And *G*·, and Ahio, and Zacher. "
9:37 *G*·, and Ahio, and Zechariah, and "
12: 7 the sons of Jeroham of *G*·. "

Gehazi (*ghe-ha'-zi*)
2Ki 4:12 said to *G*· his servant, Call this ‡1522
14 *G*· answered, Verily she hath no "
25 to *G*· his servant, Behold, yonder is "
27 *G*· came near to thrust her away. "
29 said to *G*·, Gird up thy loins, and "
31 And *G*· passed on before them, "
36 And he called *G*·, and said, Call "
5:20 But *G*·, the servant of Elisha the "
21 So *G*· followed after Naaman. "
25 Whence comest thou, *G*·? And he "
8: 4 *G*· the servant of the man of God, "
5 *G*· said, My lord, O king, this is the "

Geliloth (*ghel'-il-oth*)
Jos 18:17 went forth toward *G*·, which is 1553

Gemalli (*ghe-mal'-li*)
Nu 13:12 of Dan, Ammiel the son of *G*·. 1582

Gemariah (*ghem-a-ri'-ah*)
Jer 29: 3 and *G*· the son of Hilkiah, (whom 1587
36:10 in the chamber of *G*· the son of "
11 Michaiah the son of *G*·, the son of "
12 Elnathan the son of Achbor, and *G*· "
25 Elnathan and Delaiah and *G*· had "

gender See also GENDERED; GENDERETH.
Le 19:19 Thou shalt not let thy cattle *g*· 7250
2Ti 2:23 knowing that they do *g*· strifes. *1080*

gendered
Job 38:29 frost of heaven, who hath *g*· it? 3205

gendereth
Job 21:10 Their bull *g*·, and faileth not; 5674
Ga 4:24 *g*· to bondage, which is Agar. **1080*

genealogies
1Ch 5:17 All these were reckoned by *g*· in 3187
7: 5 reckoned in all by their *g*· * "
7 and were reckoned by their *g*· * "
9: 1 all Israel were reckoned by *g*·; "
2Ch 12:15 and of Iddo the seer concerning *g*·? "
31:19 to all that were reckoned by *g*· * "
1Ti 1: 4 give heed to fables and endless *g*·, *1076*
Tit 3: 9 But avoid foolish questions, and *g*·, "

genealogy See also GENEALOGIES.
1Ch 4:33 their habitations, and their *g*·. 3188
5: 1 and the *g*· is not to be reckoned "
7 when the *g*· of their generations "
7: 9 after their *g*· by their generations, "
40 throughout the *g*· of them that "
9:22 These were reckoned by their *g*· in "
2Ch 31:16 Beside their *g*· of males, from three "
17 the *g*· of the priests by the house "
18 And to the *g*· of all their little ones, "
Ezr 2:62 those that were reckoned by *g*·. "
8: 1 and this is the *g*· of them that went "
3 were reckoned by *g*· of the males "
Ne 7: 5 that they might be reckoned by *g*·. "
5 And I found a register of the *g*. of "
64 those that were reckoned by *g*·. "

general
1Ch 27:34 and the *g*· of the king's army *8269
Heb 12:23 To the *g*· assembly and church of *3831*

generally
2Sa 17:11 that all Israel be *g*· gathered *
Jer 48:38 There shall be lamentation *g*· *3605

generation See also GENERATIONS.
Ge 7: 1 righteous before me in this *g*·. 1755
15:16 But in the fourth *g*· they shall come "
50:23 Ephraim's children of the third *g*·: "
Ex 1: 6 and all his brethren, and all that *g*·.1755
17:16 war with Amalek from *g*· to *g*·. "
20: 5 unto the third and fourth *g*· of them "
34: 7 unto the third and to the fourth *g*·. "
Nu 14:18 children unto the third and fourth *g*·. "
32:13 until all the *g*·, that had done evil 1755
De 1:35 one of these men of this evil *g*· "
2:14 all the *g*· of the men of war "
5: 9 unto the third and fourth *g*· of them "
23: 2 even to his tenth *g*· shall he not 1755
3 even to their tenth *g*· shall they not "
8 of the Lord in their third *g*·. "
29:22 So that the *g*· to come of your "
32: 5 they are a perverse and crooked *g*·. "
20 for they are a very froward *g*·, "
J'g 2:10 also all that *g*· were gathered unto "
10 there arose another *g*· after them, "
2Ki 10:30 thy children of the fourth *g*· shall sit "
15:12 throne of Israel unto the fourth *g*·. "
Es 9:28 kept throughout every *g*·, every 1755
Ps 12: 7 preserve them from this *g*· for ever. "
14: 5 God is in the *g*· of the righteous. "
22:30 be accounted to the Lord for a *g*·. "
24: 6 is the *g*· of them that seek him, "
48:13 ye may tell it to the *g*· following. "
49:19 He shall go to the *g*· of his fathers; "
71:18 shewed thy strength unto this *g*·, "
73:15 against the *g*· of thy children. "
78: 4 shewing to the *g*· to come the "
6 That the *g*· to come might know "
8 a stubborn and rebellious *g*·; "
8 a *g*· that set not their heart aright, "
95:10 long was I grieved with this *g*·, "
102:18 shall be written for the *g*· to come: "
109:13 in the *g*· following let their name "
112: 2 *g*· of the upright shall be blessed. "
145: 4 One *g*· shall praise thy works to "
Pr 27:24 doth the crown endure to every *g*·? "
30:11 is a *g*· that curseth their father, "
12 a *g*· that are pure in their own eyes, "
13 is a *g*·, O how lofty are their eyes! "
14 is a *g*·, whose teeth are as swords, "
Ec 1: 4 One *g*· passeth away, and another *g*· "
Isa 13:20 shall it be dwelt in from *g*· to *g*·: "
34:10 from *g*· to *g*· it shall lie waste; "
17 from *g*· to *g*· shall they dwell therein. "
51: 8 my salvation from *g*· to *g*·. "
53: 8 and who shall declare his *g*·? for he "
Jer 2:31 O *g*·, see ye the word of the Lord. "
7:29 and forsaken the *g*· of his wrath. "
50:39 shall it be dwelt in from *g*· to *g*·. "
La 5:19 thy throne from *g*· to *g*·. "
Da 4: 3 his dominion is from *g*· to *g*·. 1859
34 his kingdom is from *g*· to *g*·: "
Joe 1: 3 and their children another *g*·. 1755
3:20 and Jerusalem from *g*· to *g*·. "
M't 1: 1 the book of the *g*· of Jesus Christ, *1078*
3: 7 O *g*· of vipers, who hath warned *1081*
11:16 whereunto shall I liken this *g*·? *1074*
12:34 O *g*· of vipers, how can ye, *1081*
39 An evil and adulterous *g*· seeketh *1074*
41 shall rise in judgment with this *g*·, "
42 rise up in the judgment with this *g*·, "
45 shall it be also unto this wicked *g*·. "
16: 4 wicked and adulterous *g*· seeketh "
17:17 O faithless and perverse *g*·, how "
23:33 Ye serpents, ye *g*· of vipers, how *1081*
36 things shall come upon this *g*·. *1074*
24:34 This *g*· shall not pass, till all these "

M'r 8:12 Why doth this *g*· seek after a sign? *1074*
12 shall no sign be given unto this *g*·. "
38 in this adulterous and sinful *g*·; "
9:19 O faithless *g*·, how long shall I be "
13:30 that this *g*· shall not pass, till all "
Lu 1:50 on them that fear him from *g*· to *g*·.* "
3: 7 O *g*· of vipers, who hath warned *1081
7:31 shall I liken the men of this *g*·? *1074*
9:41 O faithless and perverse *g*·, how "
11:29 he began to say, This is an evil *g*·: "
30 also the Son of man be to this *g*·. "
31 the men of this *g*·, and condemn "
32 with this *g*·, and shall condemn it: "
50 may be required of this *g*·; "
51 It shall be required of this *g*·. "
16: 8 in their *g*· wiser than the children "
17:25 and be rejected of this *g*·. "
21:32 This *g*· shall not pass away, till "
Ac 2:40 yourselves from this untoward *g*·. "
8:33 who shall declare his *g*·? for his "
13:36 he had served his own *g*· by the "
Heb 3:10 I was grieved with that *g*·, "
1Pe 2: 9 a chosen *g*·, a royal priesthood, **1085*

generations
Ge 2: 4 These are the *g*· of the heavens 8435
5: 1 This is the book of the *g*· of Adam. "
6: 9 These are the *g*· of Noah: Noah was "
9 a just man and perfect in his *g*·, "
9:12 is with you, for perpetual *g*·: 1755
10: 1 These are the *g*· of the sons of 8435
32 after their *g*·, in their nations: "
11:10 These are the *g*· of Shem: Shem was "
27 Now these are the *g*· of Terah: "
17: 7 thy seed after thee in their *g*· for 1755
9 and thy seed after thee in their *g*·. "
12 every man child in your *g*·, he that "
25:12 Now these are the *g*· of Ishmael, 8435
13 their names, according to their *g*·: "
19 And these are the *g*· of Isaac, "
36: 1 Now these are the *g*· of Esau, who "
9 And these are the *g*· of Esau the "
37: 2 These are the *g*· of Jacob. "
Ex 3:15 this is my memorial unto all *g*·. 1755
6:16 sons of Levi according to their *g*·;8435
19 families of Levi according to their *g*·. "
12:14 throughout your *g*·; ye shall keep 1755
17 ye observe this day in your *g*· "
42 the children of Israel in their *g*·. "
16:32 to be kept for your *g*·; that they "
33 the Lord, to be kept for your *g*·. "
27:21 a statute for ever unto their *g*· "
29:42 burnt offering throughout your *g*· "
30: 8 before the Lord throughout your *g*·. "
10 upon it throughout your *g*·: "
21 to his seed throughout their *g*·. "
31 oil unto me throughout your *g*·. "
31:13 me and you throughout your *g*·; "
16 the sabbath throughout their *g*·, "
40:15 priesthood throughout their *g*·. "
Le 3:17 perpetual statute for your *g*· "
6:18 a statute for ever in your *g*· "
7:36 for ever throughout their *g*·. "
10: 9 for ever throughout your *g*·: "
17: 7 unto them throughout their *g*·. "
21:17 he be of thy seed in their *g*· "
22: 3 all your seed among your *g*·, "
23:14 for ever throughout your *g*· in all "
21 your dwellings throughout your *g*·. "
31 for ever throughout your *g*· "
41 a statute for ever in your *g*·: "
43 That your *g*· may know that I "
24: 3 a statute for ever in your *g*·. "
25:30 that bought it throughout his *g*·: "
Nu 1:20 Israel's eldest son, by their *g*·, 8435
22 children of Simeon, by their *g*·, after "
24 children of Gad, by their *g*·, after "
26 children of Judah, by their *g*·, after "
28 children of Issachar, by their *g*·, "
30 children of Zebulun, by their *g*·, "
32 children of Joseph, by their *g*·, by "
34 children of Manasseh, by their *g*·, "
36 children of Benjamin, by their *g*·, "
38 children of Dan, by their *g*·, after "
40 children of Asher, by their *g*·, after "
42 Naphtali, throughout their *g*·, after "
3: 1 These also are the *g*· of Aaron "
10: 8 for ever throughout your *g*·. 1755
15:14 be among you in your *g*·, "
15 an ordinance for ever in your *g*·: "
21 Lord an heave offering in your *g*·. "
23 and henceforward among your *g*·; "
38 garments throughout their *g*·, "
18:23 for ever throughout your *g*·, "
35:29 throughout your *g*· in all your "
De 7: 9 commandments to a thousand *g*·; "
32: 7 consider the years of many *g*·: "
Jos 22:27 us, and you, and our *g*· after us, "
28 to us or to our *g*· in time to come, "
J'g 3: 2 Only that the *g*· of the children "
Ru 4:18 Now these are the *g*· of Pharez: 8435
1Ch 1:29 These are their *g*·: The firstborn "
5: 7 genealogy of their *g*· was reckoned, "
7: 2 valiant men of might in their *g*·; "
4 And with them, by their *g*·, after "
9 after their genealogy by their *g*·, "
8:28 the fathers, by their *g*·, chief men. "
9: 9 brethren, according to their *g*·, "
34 were chief throughout their *g*·; "
16:15 he commanded to a thousand *g*·; 1755
26:31 according to the *g*· of his fathers. 8435
Job 42:16 and his sons' sons, even four *g*·. 1755
Ps 33:11 the thoughts of his heart to all *g*·. "
45:17 name to be remembered in all *g*·: "
49:11 and their dwelling places to all *g*·; "
61: 6 and his years as many *g*·. "
72: 5 moon endure, throughout all *g*·. "

Ps 79:13 will shew forth thy praise to all g'.1755
85: 5 draw out thine anger to all g'? "
89: 1 known thy faithfulness to all g'. "
4 aud build up thy throne to all g'. "
90: 1 been our dwelling place in all g'. "
100: 5 and his truth endureth to all g'. "
102:12 and thy remembrance unto all g'. "
24 thy years are throughout all g'. "
105: 8 he commanded to a thousand g'. "
106:31 him for righteousness unto all g' "
119:90 Thy faithfulness is unto all g': "
135:13 memorial, O Lord, throughout all g'. "
145:13 endureth throughout all g'. "
146:10 thy God, O Zion, unto all g'. "
Isa 41: 4 calling the g' from the beginning? "
51: 9 in the ancient days, in the g' of old. "
58:12 up the foundations of many g'; "
60:15 excellency, a joy of many g'. "
61: 4 cities, the desolations of many g'. "
Joe 2: 2 even to the years of many g'. "
M't 1:17 So all the g' from Abraham to 1074
17 Abraham to David are fourteen g'; "
17 away into Babylon are fourteen g'; "
17 Babylon unto Christ are fourteen g'. "
Lu 1:48 all g' shall call me blessed. "
Col 1:26 hid from ages and from g', "

Gennesaret (ghen-nes'-a-ret) See also CHINNERETH.
M't 14:34 they came into the land of G'. 1082
M'r 6:53 into the land of G', and drew to "
Lu 5: 1 he stood by the lake of G', "

Gentile (jen'-tile) See also GENTILES.
Ro 2: 9 the Jew first, and also of the G'; *1672
10 the Jew first, and also to the G': * "

Gentiles (jen'-tiles)
Ge 10: 5 By these were the isles of the G' *1471
J'g 4: 2 dwelt in Harosheth of the G'. "
13 from Harosheth of the G' unto the "
16 the host, unto Harosheth of the G': "
Isa 11:10 to it shall the G' seek: and his * "
42: 1 bring forth judgment to the G'. "
6 of the people, for a light of the G'; "
49: 6 give thee for a light to the G', "
22 I will lift up mine hand to the G',* "
54: 3 and thy seed shall inherit the G',* "
60: 3 the G' shall come to thy light, * "
5 the forces of the G' shall come * "
11 unto thee the forces of the G', * "
16 shalt also suck the milk of the G',* "
61: 6 ye shall eat the riches of the G', * "
9 shall be known among the G', * "
62: 2 G' shall see thy righteousness, * "
66:12 of the G' like a flowing stream: * "
19 declare my glory among the G'. * "
Jer 4: 7 destroyer of the G' is on his way;* "
14:22 among the vanities of the G' * "
16:19 the G' shall come unto thee * "
46: 1 the prophet against the G'; * "
La 2: 9 her princes are among the G': * "
Eze 4:13 their defiled bread among the G',* "
Ho 8: 8 shall they be among the G' as a * "
Joe 3: 9 Proclaim ye this among the G'; * "
Mic 5: 8 of Jacob shall be among the G' * "
Zec 1:21 to cast out the horns of the G', * "
Mal 1:11 name shall be great among the G'; "
M't 4:15 beyond Jordan, Galilee of the G'; 1484
6:32 all these things do the G' seek:) "
10: 5 Go not into the way of the G', "
18 testimony against them and the G'. "
12:18 he shall shew judgment to the G'. "
21 in his name shall the G' trust. "
20:19 they shall deliver him to the G' "
25 the princes of the G' exercise "
M'r 10:33 and shall deliver him to the G': "
42 are accounted to rule over the G' "
Lu 2:32 A light to lighten the G', and the "
18:32 he shall be delivered unto the G', "
21:24 shall be trodden down of the G', "
24 the times of the G' be fulfilled. "
22:25 kings of the G' exercise lordship "
Joh 7:35 the dispersed among the G', *1672
35 and teach the G'? * "
Ac 4:27 the G', and the people of Israel, 1484
7:45 into the possession of the G', * "
9:15 to bear my name before the G', "
10:45 on the G' also was poured out "
11: 1 the G' had also received the word "
18 hath God also to the G' granted "
13:42 the G' besought that these words * "
46 lo, we turn to the G'. "
47 set thee to be a light of the G', "
48 the G' heard this, they were glad, "
14: 2 Jews stirred up the G', "
5 of the G', and also of the Jews "
27 the door of faith unto the G'. "
15: 3 declaring the conversion of the G': "
7 the G' by my mouth should hear "
12 wrought among the G' by them. "
14 did visit the G', to take out of them "
17 all the G', upon whom my name "
19 from among the G' are turned "
23 the brethren which are of the G' "
18: 6 henceforth I will go unto the G'. "
21:11 him into the hands of the G'. "
19 God had wrought among the G' "
21 the Jews which are among the G' "
25 As touching the G' which believe, "
22:21 send thee far hence unto the G'. "
26:17 from the people, and from the G', "
20 to the G', that they should repent "
23 light unto the people, and to the G'. "
28:28 salvation of God is sent unto the G', "
Ro 1:13 you also, even as among other G'. "
2:14 the G', which have not the law, "
24 God is blasphemed among the G' "
Ro 3: 9 before proved both Jews and G', *1672
29 of the G'? Yes, of the G' also: 1484
9:24 the Jews only, but also of the G'? "
30 That the G', which followed not "
11:11 salvation is come unto the G', "
12 of them the riches of the G'; "
13 For I speak to you G', inasmuch as "
13 I am the apostle of the G', "
25 until the fulness of the G' be come "
15: 9 And that the G' might glorify God "
9 I will confess to thee among the G', "
10 he saith, Rejoice, ye G', with his "
11 Praise the Lord, all ye G'; and "
12 shall rise to reign over the G'; "
12 in him shall the G' trust. "
16 minister of Jesus Christ to the G', "
16 the offering up of the G' might be "
18 to make the G' obedient, by word "
27 if the G' have been made partakers "
16: 4 but also all the churches of the G'. "
1Co 5: 1 so much as named among the G', "
10:20 the things which the G' sacrifice, "
32 neither to the Jews, nor to the G',*1672
12: 2 Ye know that ye were G', carried 1484
13 whether we be Jews or G', *1672
Ga 2: 2 which I preach among the G', 1484
8 was mighty in me toward the G':) "
12 he did eat with the G': but when "
14 livest after the manner of G', 1483
14 the G' to live as do the Jews? 1484
15 nature, and not sinners of the G', "
3:14 come on the G' through Jesus "
Eph 2:11 being in time past G' in the flesh, "
3: 1 prisoner of Jesus Christ for you G', "
6 That the G' should be fellowheirs, "
8 that I should preach among the G' "
4:17 walk not as other G' walk, in the "
Col 1:27 of this mystery among the G'; "
1Th 2:16 Forbidding us to speak to the G' "
4: 5 as the G' which know not God: "
1Ti 2: 7 a teacher of the G' in faith and "
3:16 preached unto the G', believed * "
2Ti 1:11 apostle, and a teacher of the G'. * "
4:17 and that all the G' might hear: "
1Pe 2:12 conversation honest among the G': "
4: 3 to have wrought the will of the G', "
3Jo 7 forth, taking nothing of the G'. "
Re 11: 2 for it is given unto the G': * "

gentle
1Th 2: 7 But we were g' among you, even 2261
2Ti 2:24 not strive; but be g' unto all men, "
Tit 3: 2 to be no brawlers, but g', shewing 1933
Jas 3:17 g', and easy to be intreated, "
1Pe 2:18 not only to the good and g', but also "

gentleness
2Sa 22:36 and thy g' hath made me great. 6031
Ps 18:35 and thy g' hath made me great. 6038
2Co 10: 1 by the meekness and g' of Christ, 1932
Ga 5:22 longsuffering, g', goodness, faith,*5544

gently
2Sa 18: 5 Deal g' for my sake with the 3814
Isa 40:11 g' lead those that are with young.

Genubath (ghen'-u-bath)
1Ki 11:20 Tahpenes bare him G' his son, 1592
20 and G' was in Pharaoh's household "

Gera (ghe'-rah)
Ge 46:21 and Becher, and Ashbel, G', and 1617
J'g 3:15 Ehud the son of G', a Benjamite, "
2Sa 16: 5 name was Shimei, the son of G': "
19:16 Shimei the son of G', a Benjamite, "
18 Shimei the son of G' fell down "
1Ki 2: 8 hast with thee Shimei the son of G', "
1Ch 8: 3 Addar, and G', and Abihud, "
5 G', and Shephuphan, and Huram. "
7 Ahiah, and G', he removed them, "

gerahs (ghe'-rahs)
Ex 30:13 shekel is twenty g':) an half shekel1626
Le 27:25 twenty g' shall be the shekel. "
Nu 3:47 take them: (the shekel is twenty g':) "
18:16 the sanctuary, which is twenty g'. "
Eze 45:12 the shekel shall be twenty g': "

Gerar (ghe'-rar)
Ge 10:19 as thou comest to G', unto Gaza; 1642
20: 1 and Shur, and sojourned in G'. "
2 and Abimelech king of G' sent, "
26: 1 king of the Philistines unto G'. "
6 And Isaac dwelt in G': "
17 pitched his tent in the valley of G', "
20 herdmen of G' did strive with "
26 Abimelech went to him from G', "
2Ch 14:13 with him pursued them unto G': "
14 smote all the cities round about G'; "

Gergesenes (ghur''-ghes-enes')
M't 8:28 side into the country of the G', *1086

Gerizim (gher'-iz-im)
De 11:29 put the blessing upon mount G', 1630
27:12 upon mount G' to bless the people, "
Jos 8:33 against mount G', and half of them "
J'g 9: 7 in the top of mount G', and lifted "

Gershom (ghur'-shom) See also GERSHON.
Ex 2:22 son, and he called his name G': 1648
18: 3 which the name of the one was G'; "
J'g 18:30 and Jonathan, the son of G', the "
1Ch 6:16 The sons of Levi; G', Kohath, and "
17 the sons of G'; Libni, and Shimei. "
20 G'; Libni his son, Jahath his son, "
43 The son of Jahath, the son of G', "
62 of G' throughout their families "
71 the sons of G' were given out of "
15: 7 Of the sons of G'; Joel the chief, "
23:15 sons of Moses were, G', and Eliezer. "
16 sons of G', Shebuel was the chief. "
1Ch 26:24 And Shebuel the son of G', the son 1648
Ezr 8: 2 Of the sons of Phinehas; G': of the "

Gershon (ghur'-shon) See also GERSHOM; GERSHONITE.
Ge 46:11 sons of Levi; G', Kohath, and 1647
Ex 6:16 G', and Kohath, and Merari: and "
17 sons of G', Libni, and Shimi, "
Nu 3:17 by their names; G', and Kohath, "
18 the sons of G' by their families; "
21 Of G was the family of the Libnites, "
25 charge of the sons of G' in the "
4:22 sum of the sons of G', throughout "
28 the sons of G' in the tabernacle "
38 were numbered of the sons of G', "
41 of the families of the sons of G', "
7: 7 oxen he gave unto the sons of G', 1647
10:17 sons of G' and the sons of Merari "
26:57 G', the family of the Gershonites: "
Jos 21: 6 G' had by lot out of the families "
27 unto the children of G', of the "
1Ch 6: 1 The sons of Levi; G', Kohath, and "
23: 6 sons of Levi, namely G', Kohath, "

Gershonite (ghur'-shon-ite) See also GERSHONITES.
1Ch 26:21 the sons of the G' Laadam, chief 1649
21 even of Laadan the G', were "
29: 8 Lord, by the hand of Jehiel the G'. "

Gershonites (ghur'-shon-ites)
Nu 3:21 these are the families of the G'. 1649
23 The families of the G' shall pitch "
3:24 father of the G' shall be Eliasaph "
4:24 service of the families of the G', "
27 service of the sons of the G', in all "
26:57 of Gershon, the family of the G': "
Jos 21:33 the cities of the G' according to "
1Ch 23: 7 Of the G' were, Laadan, and "
2Ch 29:12 and of the G'; Joah the son of "

Gesham (ghe'-sham)
1Ch 2:47 Regem, and Jotham, and G', and 1529

Geshem (ghe'-shem) See also GASHMU.
Ne 2:19 and G' the Arabian, heard it, 1654
6: 1 Tobiah, and G' the Arabian, and "
2 Sanballat and G' sent unto me, "

Geshur (ghe'-shur) See also GESHURITES.
2Sa 3: 3 the daughter of Talmai king of G'; 1650
13:37 the son of Ammihud, king of G'. "
38 Absalom fled, and went to G', "
14:23 Joab arose and went to G', and "
32 Wherefore am I come from G'? "
15: 8 vow while I abode at G' in Syria, "
1Ch 2:23 And he took G', and Aram, with "
3: 2 daughter of Talmai king of G': "

Geshuri (ghesh'-u-ri) See also GESHURITES.
De 3:14 the coasts of G' and Maachathi; 1651
Jos 13: 2 of the Philistines, and all G', "

Geshurites (ghesh'-u-rites)
Jos 12: 5 of the G' and the Maachathites, 1651
13:11 border of the G' and Maachathites, "
13 Israel expelled not the G', nor the "
13 the G' and the Maachathites dwell "
1Sa 27: 8 invaded the G', and the Gezrites, "

get See also BEGET; FORGET; GAT; GETTETH; GETTING; GOT.
Ge 12: 1 G' thee out of thy county, and 3212
19:14 said, Up, g' you out of this place; 3318
22: 2 g' thee into the land of Moriah; 3212
31:13 g' thee out from this land, and 3318
34: 4 saying, G' me this damsel to wife. 3947
10 therein, and g' you possessions therein.
42: 2 g' you down thither, and buy for 3381
44:17 g' you up in peace unto your 5927
45:17 g' you unto the land of Canaan; 935
Ex 1:10 and so g' them up out of the land. 5927
5: 4 g' you unto your burdens. 3212
11 g' you straw where ye can find it: 3947
7:15 G' thee unto Pharaoh in the 3212
10:28 G' thee from me, take heed to
11: 8 G' thee out, and all the people 3318
12:31 g' you forth from among my people, "
14:17 I will g' me honour upon Pharaoh, 3513
19:24 Away, g' thee down, and thou 3381
32: 7 Go, g' thee down; for thy people, "
Le 14:21 he be poor, and cannot g' so much; 5381
22 such as he is able to g'; "
30 young pigeons, such as he can g'; "
31 Even such as he is able to g', "
32 whose hand is not able to g' that "
Nu 6:21 that that his hand shall g': "
13:17 G' you up this way southward, 5927
14:25 and g' you into the wilderness by 5265
16:24 G' you up from about the 5927
45 G' you up from among this 7426
22:13 G' you into your land: for the 3212
34 I will g' me back again.
27:12 G' thee up into this mount 5927
De 2:13 and g' you over the brook Zered. 5674
3:27 G' thee up into the top of Pisgah, 5927
5:30 G' you into your tents again. *7725
8:18 that giveth the power to g' wealth, 6213
9:12 g' thee down quickly from hence; 3381
17: 8 and get thee up into the place 5927
28:43 is within thee shall g' up above * "
32:49 G' thee up into this mountain "
Jos 2:16 G' you to the mountain, lest the 3212
7:10 G' thee up; wherefore liest thou 6965
17:15 g' thee up to the wood country, 5927
22: 4 and g' you unto your tents, and 3212
J'g 7: 9 Arise, g' thee down unto the host; 3381
14: 2 therefore g' her for me to wife. 3947
3 G' her for me; for she pleaseth me "
19: 9 to morrow g' you early on your way,
Ru 3: 3 and g' thee down to the floor: 3381
1Sa 9:13 Now therefore g' you up; for 5927
15: 6 g' you down from among the 3381

1Sa 20:29 let me g' away, I pray thee, and 4422
22: 5 and g' thee into the land of Judah. 935
23:26 David made haste to g' away for 3212
25: 5 G' you up to Carmel, and go to 5927
2Sa 20: 6 lest he g' him fenced cities, and 4672
1Ki 1: 2 that my lord the king may g' heat.
13 Go and g' thee in unto king David, 935
2:26 G' thee to Anathoth, unto thine 3212
12:18 Rehoboam made speed to g' him 5927
14: 2 g' thee to Shiloh: behold, there is 1980
12 Arise thou therefore, g' thee to 3212
17: 3 G' thee hence, and turn the "
9 Arise, g' thee to Zarephath, which "
18:41 G' thee up, eat and drink; for 5927
44 Prepare thy chariot, and g' thee 3381
2Ki 3:13 g' thee to the prophets of thy 3212
7:12 shall catch them alive, and g' into 935
2Ch 10:18 Rehoboam made speed to g' him 5927
Ne 9:10 So didst thou g' thee a name, as it 6213
Ps 119:104 thy precepts I g' understanding:
Pr 4: 5 G' wisdom, g' understanding: 7069
7 therefore g' wisdom: and with all "
7 thy getting g' understanding. "
6:33 wound and dishonour shall he g'; 4672
16:16 better is it to g' wisdom than gold! 7069
16 to g' understanding rather to be "
17:16 the hand of a fool to g' wisdom, * "
22:25 learn his ways, and g' a snare to 3947
Ec 3: 6 A time to g', and a time to lose; *1245
Ca 4: 6 I will g' me to the mountain of 3212
7:12 Let us g' up early to the vineyards;
Isa 22:15 Go, g' thee unto this treasurer, 935
30:11 G' you out of the way, turn aside
22 shalt say unto it, G' thee hence. 3318
40: 9 g' thee up into the high mountain;5927
47: 5 g' thee into darkness, O daughter 935
Jer 5: 5 I will g' me unto the great men, 3212
13: 1 Go and g' thee a linen girdle, *7069
19: 1 and g' a potter's earthen bottle, * "
46: 4 g' up, ye horsemen, and stand 5927
48: 9 that it may flee and g' away: for 3318
49:30 Flee, g' you far off, dwell deep, *5110
31 Arise, g' you up unto the wealthy 5927
La 3: 7 me about, that I cannot g' out: *3318
Eze 3: 4 go, g' thee unto the house of Israel, 935
11 go, g' thee to them of the captivity, "
11:15 G' you far from the Lord: unto us
22:27 to destroy souls, to g' dishonest 1214
Da 4:14 let the beasts g' away from under 5111
Joe 3:13 come, g' you down; for the press *3381
Zep 3:19 and I will g' them praise and * 776
Zec 6: 7 G' you hence, walk to and fro 3212
M't 4:10 G' thee hence, Satan: for it is 5217
14:22 his disciples to g' into a ship, *1684
16:23 unto Peter, G' thee behind me, 5217
M'r 6:45 his disciples to g' into the ship, *1684
8:33 G' thee behind me, Satan: for 5217
Lu 4: 8 G' thee behind me, Satan: for it "
9:12 and lodge, and g' victuals: for we 2147
13:31 G' thee out, and depart hence: 1831
Ac 7: 3 G' thee out of thy country, and "
10:20 g' thee down, and go with them, 2597
22:18 g' thee quickly out of Jerusalem: 1831
27:43 first into the sea, and g' to land: 1826
2Co 2:11 Lest Satan should g' an advantage*4122
Jas 4:13 and buy and sell, and g' gain:

Gether (*ghe'-ther*)
Ge 10:23 of Aram; Uz, and Hul, and G', 1666
1Ch 1:17 Aram, and Uz, and Hul, and G', "

Gethsemane (*gheth-sem'-a-ne*)
M't 26:36 with them unto a place called G', 1068
M's 14:32 to a place which was named G': "

getteth See also BEGETTETH; FORGETTETH.
2Sa 5: 8 Whosoever g' up to the gutter, *5060
Pr 3:13 the man that g' understanding. 6329
9: 7 a scorner g' to himself shame: 3947
7 rebuketh a wicked man g' himself a
15:32 heareth reproof g' understanding.7069
18:15 heart of the prudent g' knowledge; "
19: 8 He that g' wisdom loveth his own "
Jer 17:11 he that g' riches, and not by right, 6213
48:44 and he that g' up out of the pit 5927

getting See also FORGETTING.
Ge 31:18 the cattle of his g', which he had 7075
Pr 4: 7 with all thy g' get understanding.7069
21: 6 g' of treasures by a lying tongue 6467

Geuel (*ghe-u'-el*)
Nu 13:15 Of the tribe of Gad, G' the son of 1345

Gezer (*ghe'-zur*) See also GAZER; GEZRITES.
Jos 10:33 Horam king of G' came up to 1507
12:12 Eglon, one; the king of G', one; "
16: 3 Beth-horon the nether, and to G': "
10 Canaanites that dwelt in G': but "
21:21 of refuge for the slayer; and G' "
J'g 1:29 G'; but the Canaanites dwelt in G' "
1Ki 9:15 and Hazor, and Megiddo, and G'. "
16 gone up, and taken G', and burnt "
17 Solomon built G', and Beth-horon "
1Ch 6:67 they gave also G' with her suburbs,"
7:28 eastward Naaran, and westward G'," "
20: 4 a war at G' with the Philistines; "

Gezrites (*ghez'-rites*)
1Sa 27: 8 Geshurites, and the G', and the *1511

ghost [or GHOST].
Ge 25: 8 Then Abraham gave up the g', 1478
17 and he gave up the g' and died; "
35:29 And Isaac gave up the g', and died,"
49:33 and yielded up the g', and was "
Job 3:11 why did I not give up the g' when "
10:18 Oh that I had given up the g', "
11:20 shall be as the giving up of the g'.5315
13:19 tongue, I shall give up the g'. 1478
14:10 yea, man giveth up the g', and "
Jer 15: 9 she hath given up the g'; her sun 5315
La 1:19 mine elders gave up the g' in the 1478
M't 1:18 found with child of the Holy G'. ‡4151
20 in her is of the Holy G'. ‡ "
3:11 with the Holy G', and with fire: ‡ "
12:31 blasphemy against the Holy G' * "
32 speaketh against the Holy G', * "
27:50 yielded up the g'. * "
28:19 of the Son, and of the Holy G': ‡ "
M'r 1: 8 baptize you with the Holy G'. ‡ "
3:29 blaspheme against the Holy G' * "
12:36 himself said by the Holy G', * "
13:11 ye that speak, but the Holy G'. ‡ "
15:37 a loud voice, and gave up the g'. 1606
39 so cried out, and gave up the g', "
Lu 1:15 be filled with the Holy G', ‡4151
35 Holy G' shall come upon thee, ‡ "
41 was filled with the Holy G': ‡ "
67 was filled with the Holy G', ‡ "
2:25 and the Holy G' was upon him, * "
26 unto him by the Holy G', * "
3:16 baptize you with the Holy G' ‡ "
22 And the Holy G' descended in ‡ "
4: 1 Jesus being full of the Holy G' * "
12:10 against the Holy G' * "
12 For the Holy G' shall teach * "
23:46 said thus, he gave up the g'. 1606
Joh 1:33 baptizeth with the Holy G' *4151
7:39 for the Holy G' was not yet * "
14:26 Holy G', whom the Father * "
19:30 his head, and gave up the g'. "
20:22 them, Receive ye the Holy G': ‡ "
Ac 1: 2 he through the Holy G' had ‡ "
5 be baptized with the Holy G' ‡ "
8 after that the Holy G' is come ‡ "
16 which the Holy G' by the mouth ‡ "
2: 4 were all filled with the Holy G', * "
33 the promise of the Holy G', ‡ "
38 receive the gift of the Holy G'. ‡ "
4: 8 Peter, filled with the Holy G', ‡ "
31 were all filled with the Holy G', ‡ "
5: 3 to lie to the Holy G', and to keep ‡ "
5 fell down, and gave up the g': 1634
10 at his feet and yielded up the g': "
32 and so is also the Holy G', ‡4151
6: 3 full of the Holy G' and wisdom, * "
5 of faith and of the Holy G', * "
7:51 do always resist the Holy G': ‡ "
55 he, being full of the Holy G', ‡ "
8:15 they might receive the Holy G': ‡ "
17 they received the Holy G'. ‡ "
18 Holy G' was given, he offered ‡ "
19 he may receive the Holy G'. ‡ "
9:17 and be filled with the Holy G'. ‡ "
31 in the comfort of the Holy G', ‡ "
10:38 the Holy G' and with power: ‡ "
44 the Holy G' fell on all them ‡ "
45 out the gift of the Holy G'. ‡ "
47 have received the Holy G' as ‡ "
11:15 the Holy G' fell on them, as on ‡ "
16 be baptized with the Holy G'. ‡ "
24 man, and full of the Holy G' ‡ "
12:23 of worms and gave up the g'. 1634
13: 2 the Holy G' said, Separate me ‡4151
4 being sent forth by the Holy G', ‡ "
9 Paul,) filled with the Holy G', ‡ "
52 with joy, and with the Holy G'. ‡ "
15: 8 giving them the Holy G', even ‡ "
28 it seemed good to the Holy G', ‡ "
16: 6 were forbidden of the Holy G' ‡ "
19: 2 Have ye received the Holy G' ‡ "
2 whether there be any Holy G'. ‡ "
6 the Holy G' came on them; and ‡ "
20:23 that the Holy G' witnesseth ‡ "
28 Holy G' hath made you overseers,‡ "
21:11 Thus saith the Holy G', So ‡ "
28:25 spake the Holy G' by Esaias ‡ "
Ro 5: 5 by the Holy G' which is given ‡ "
9: 1 me witness in the Holy G', ‡ "
14:17 peace, and joy in the Holy G'. ‡ "
15:13 the power of the Holy G'. ‡ "
16 being sanctified by the Holy G'. ‡ "
1Co 2:13 the Holy G' teacheth; * "
6:19 the temple of the Holy G' ‡ "
12: 3 the Lord, but by the Holy G'. * "
2Co 6: 6 the Holy G', by love unfeigned, ‡ "
13:14 the communion of the Holy G', ‡ "
1Th 1: 5 in power, and in the Holy G', ‡ "
6 with joy of the Holy G': ‡ "
2Ti 1:14 by the Holy G' which dwelleth ‡ "
Tit 3: 5 and renewing of the Holy G'; ‡ "
Heb 2: 4 gifts of the Holy G', according ‡ "
3: 7 (as the Holy G' saith, To day if ‡ "
6: 4 made partakers of the Holy G', ‡ "
9: 8 The Holy G' this signifying, ‡ "
10:15 Holy G' also is a witness to us: ‡ "
1Pe 1:12 Holy G' sent down from heaven; ‡ "
2Pe 1:21 were moved by the Holy G'. ‡ "
1Jo 5: 7 Holy G': and these three are one.* "
Jude 20 praying in the Holy G', * "

Giah (*ghi'-ah*)
2Sa 2:24 G' by the way of the wilderness 1520

giant See also GIANTS.
2Sa 21:16 which was of the sons of the g', 7497
18 which was of the sons of the g'. "
20 and he also was born to the g'. "
22 four were born to the g' in Gath, "
1Ch 20: 4 that was of the children of the g': "
6 and he also was the son of the g'. "
8 were born unto the g' in Gath; "
Job 16:14 he runneth upon me like a g'. 1368

giants
Ge 6: 4 were g' in the earth in those days;*5303
Nu 13:33 And there we saw the g', the sons* "
13:33 of Anak, which come of the g': *1368
De 2:11 accounted g', as the Anakims; *7497
20 accounted a land of g': g' dwelt * "
3:11 remained of the remnant of g'; * "
13 which was called the land of g'. * "
Jos 12: 4 was of the remnants of the g', * "
13:12 remained of the remnant of the g':* "
15: 8 at the end of the valley of the g' * "
17:15 of the Perizzites and of the g', * "
18:16 which is in the valley of the g' * "

Gibbar (*ghib'-bar*) See also GIBEON.
Ezr 2:20 children of G', ninety and five. 1402

Gibbethon (*ghib'-be-thon*)
Jos 19:44 Eltekeh, and G', and Baalath, 1405
21:23 Eltekeh with her suburbs, G' with "
1Ki 15:27 and Baasha smote him at G', "
27 and all Israel laid siege to G'. "
16:15 encamped against G', which "
17 Omri went up from G', and all "

Gibea (*ghib'-e-ah*) See also GIBEAH.
1Ch 2:49 Machbenah, and the father of G': 1388

Gibeah (*ghib'-e-ah*) See also GIBEA; GIBEATH; GIBEON.
Jos 15:57 Cain, G', and Timnah; ten cities 1390
J'g 19:12 of Israel; we will pass over to G'. "
13 lodge all night, in G', or in Ramah. "
14 G', which belongeth to Benjamin. "
15 thither, to go in and to lodge in G': "
16 he sojourned in G': but the men "
20: 4 answered and said, I came into G' "
5 And the men of G' rose against me,"
9 the thing which we will do to G'; "
10 when they come to G' of Benjamin,"
13 of Belial, which are in G', that we "
14 out of the cities unto G', to go out "
15 beside the inhabitants of G', "
19 morning, and encamped against G'."
20 array to fight against them at G'. "
21 Benjamin came forth out of G', "
25 at G' the second day, and destroyed "
29 set liers in wait round about G'. "
30 put themselves in array against G'," "
31 God, and the other to G' in the field,"
33 even out of the meadows of G'. * "
34 came against G' ten thousand "
36 wait which they had set beside G'. "
37 wait hasted, and rushed upon G'; "
43 down with ease over against G' "
1Sa 10:26 Saul also went home to G'; and "
11: 4 came the messengers to G' of Saul,"
13: 2 thousand were with Jonathan in G' "
15 and gat him up from Gilgal unto G' "
16 them, abode in G' of Benjamin: "
14: 2 tarried in the uttermost part of G' "
5 other southward over against G'.* "
16 of Saul in G' of Benjamin looked; "
15:34 went up to his house to G' of Saul. "
22: 6 in G' under a tree in Ramah, "
23:19 came up the Ziphites to Saul to G'," "
26: 1 the Ziphites came unto Saul to G', "
2Sa 6: 3 of Abinadab that was in G': * "
4 of Abinadab which was at G', * "
21: 6 unto the Lord in G' of Saul, whom "
23:29 of G' of the children of Benjamin, "
1Ch 11:31 Ithai the son of Ribai of G', that "
2Ch 13: 2 the daughter of Uriel of G'. "
Isa 10:29 Ramah is afraid; G' of Saul is fled. "
Ho 5: 8 Blow ye the cornet in G', and the "
9: 9 themselves, as in the days of G': "
10: 9 hast sinned from the days of G': "
9 battle in G' against the children of "

Gibeath (*ghib'-e-ath*) See also GIBEAH; GIBEATHITE.
Jos 18:28 Jebusi, which is in Jerusalem, G', 1394

Gibeathite (*ghib'-e-ath-ite*)
1Ch 12: 3 of Shemaah the G'; and Jeziel, 1395

Gibeon (*ghib'-e-on*) See also GEBA; GIBEAH; GIBEONITE.
Jos 9: 3 G' heard what Joshua had done 1391
17 cities were G', and Chephirah, "
10: 1 inhabitants of G' had made peace "
2 because G' was a great city, as "
4 help me, that we may smite G': "
5 and encamped before G', and made "
6 men of G' sent unto Joshua to the "
10 great slaughter at G', and chased "
12 Sun, stand thou still upon G'; and "
41 country of Goshen, even unto G'. "
11:19 the Hivites the inhabitants of G': "
18:25 G', and Ramah, and Beeroth, "
21:17 of Benjamin, G' with her suburbs, "
2Sa 2:12 went out from Mahanaim to G'. "
13 and met together by the pool of G': "
16 Helkath-hazzurim, which is in G'. "
24 by the way of the wilderness of G'. "
3:30 brother Asahel at G' in the battle. "
20: 8 at the great stone which is in G', "
1Ki 3: 4 king went to G' to sacrifice there; "
5 In G' the Lord appeared to "
9: 2 as he had appeared unto him at G'. "
1Ch 8:29 And at G' dwelt the father...whose "
29 And at...dwelt the father of G'; whose25
9:35 And in G' dwelt...Jehiel, whose 1391
35 And...dwelt the father of G', Jehiel, 25
14:16 Philistines from G' even to Gazer.1391
16:39 in the high place that was at G', "
21:29 that season in the high place at G'."
2Ch 1: 3 to the high place that was at G'; "
13 from...the high place that was at G' "
Ne 3: 7 the men of G', and of Mizpah, unto "
7:25 The children of G', ninety and five. "
Isa 28:21 shall be wroth as in the valley of G'. "
Jer 28: 1 Azur the prophet, which was of G'."

Jer 41:12 by the great waters that are in G'.1391
16 he had brought again from G':

Gibeonite (*ghib'-e-on-ite*) See also GIBEONITES.
1Ch 12: 4 Ismaiah the G', a mighty man 1393
Ne 3: 7 Melatiah the G', and Jadon the "

Gibeonites (*ghib'-e-on-ites*)
2Sa 21: 1 house, because he slew the G'. 1393
2 G' and said unto them; (now the G' "
3 David said unto the G', What shall "
4 the G' said unto him, We will have "
9 them into the hands of the G', "

Giblites (*ghib'-lites*)
Jos 13: 5 And the land of the G', *1382

Giddalti (*ghid-dal'-ti*)
1Ch 25: 4 Hanani, Eliathah, G', and 1437
29 and twentieth to G', he, his sons, "

Giddel (*ghid'-del*)
Ezr 2:47 The children of G', the children 1435
56 of Darkon, the children of G', "
Ne 7:49 of Hanan, the children of G', the "
58 of Darkon, the children of G', "

Gideon (*ghid'-e-on*) See also GEDEON; JERUBBAAL.
J'g 6:11 his son G' threshed wheat by the 1439
13 G' said unto him, O my Lord, if the "
19 G' went in, and made ready a kid, "
22 G' perceived that he was an angel "
22 G' said, Alas, O Lord God! for "
24 G' built an altar there unto the "
27 G' took ten men of his servants, "
29 G' the son of Joash hath done this "
34 Spirit of the Lord came upon G', "
36 G' said unto God, If thou wilt save "
39 G' said unto God, Let not thine "
7: 1 who is G', and all the people that "
2 said unto G', The people that are "
4 said unto G', The people are yet "
5 said unto G', Every one that "
7 said unto G', By the three hundred "
13 when G' was come, behold, there "
14 save the sword of G' the son of "
15 G' heard the telling of the dream, "
18 The sword of the Lord, and of G'. "
19 So G', and the hundred men that "
20 The sword of the Lord, and of G'. "
24 G' sent messengers throughout all "
25 to G' on the other side Jordan. "
8: 4 G' came to Jordan, and passed "
7 G' said, Therefore when the Lord "
11 And G' went up by the way of them "
13 G' the son of Joash returned from "
21 G' arose, and slew Zebah and "
22 Israel said unto G', Rule thou over "
23 G' said unto them, I will not rule "
24 G' said unto them, I would desire "
27 G' made an ephod thereof, and put "
27 thing became a snare unto G', and "
28 forty years in the days of G'. "
30 G' had threescore and ten sons of "
32 G' the son of Joash died in a good "
33 as G' was dead, that the children of "
35 house of Jerubbaal, namely, G', "

Gideoni (*ghid-e-o'-ni*)
Nu 1:11 Benjamin; Abidan, the son of G'. 1441
2:22 shall be Abidan the son of G'. "
7:60 Abidan the son of G', prince of the "
65 offering of Abidan the son of G'. "
10:24 Benjamin was Abidan the son of G'. "

Gidom (*ghi'-dom*)
J'g 20:45 pursued hard after them unto G', 1440

gier (*jeer*)
Le 11:18 the pelican, and the g' eagle, *7360
De 14:17 the pelican, and the g' eagle, and * "

gier-eagle See GIER and EAGLE.

gift See also GIFTS.
Ge 34:12 me never so much dowry and g', 4976
Ex 23: 8 And thou shalt take no g': 7810
8 for the g' blindeth the wise, "
Nu 8:19 I have given the Levites as a g'
18: 6 are given as a g' for the Lord, 4979
7 office unto you as a service of g': "
11 the heave offering of their g', 4976
De 16:19 neither take a g': for a g' doth 7810
2Sa 19:42 or hath he given us any g'? 5379
Ps 45:12 of Tyre shall be there with a g'; 4503
Pr 17: 8 A g' is as a precious stone in the 7810
23 A wicked man taketh a g' out of "
18:16 A man's g' maketh room for him, 4976
21:14 A g' in secret pacifieth anger: "
25:14 boasteth himself of a false g' *4991
Ec 3:13 of all his labour, it is the g' of God. "
5:19 in his labour; this is the g' of God. "
7: 7 a g' destroyeth the heart. 4979
Eze 46:16 prince give a g' unto any of his sons, "
17 if he give a g' of his inheritance "
M't 5:23 if thou bring thy g' to the altar, 1435
24 Leave there thy g' before the altar, "
24 and then come and offer thy g'. "
8: 4 offer the g' that Moses commanded, "
15: 5 It is a g', by whatsoever thou * "
23:18 sweareth by the g' that is upon it, "
19 for whether is greater, the g', or "
19 or the altar that sanctifieth the g'? * "
M'r 7:11 Corban, that is to say, a g', by "
Joh 4:10 If thou knewest the g' of God, 1431
Ac 2:38 receive the g' of the Holy Ghost. "
8:20 hast thought that the g' of God "
10:45 poured out the g' of the Holy Ghost. "
11:17 God gave them the like g' as he did "
Ro 1:11 impart unto you some spiritual g', 5486
5:15 as the offence, so also is the free g'. "

Ro 5:15 grace of God, and the g' by grace, 1431
16 by one that sinned, so is the g': 1434
16 the free g' is of many offences 5486
17 the g' of righteousness shall reign 1431
18 the free g' came upon all men unto
6:23 but the g' of God is eternal life 5486
1Co 1: 7 So that ye come behind in no g'; "
7: 7 every man hath his proper g' of God, "
13: 2 though I have the g' of prophecy,
2Co 1:11 for the g' bestowed upon us by 5486
8: 4 that we would receive the g', and *5485
9:15 unto God for his unspeakable g'. 1431
Eph 2: 8 of yourselves: it is the g' of God: 1435
3: 7 according to the g' of the grace of 1431
4: 7 the measure of the g' of Christ. "
Ph'p 4:17 Not because I desire a g': but I 1390
1Ti 4:14 Neglect not the g' that is in thee, 5486
2Ti 1: 6 stir up the g' of God, which is in "
Heb 6: 4 have tasted of the heavenly g', 1431
Jas 1:17 Every good g' and every perfect g' †1394
1Pe 4:10 As every man hath received the g', 5486

gifts
Ge 25: 6 Abraham gave g', and sent them 4979
Ex 28:38 Israel shall hallow all their holy g'; "
Le 23:38 beside your g', and beside all your "
Nu 18:29 Out of all your g' ye shall offer "
2Sa 8: 2 David's servants, and brought g'.*4503
6 to David, and brought g'. * "
1Ch 18: 2, 6 servants and brought g'. * "
2Ch 19: 7 of persons, nor taking of g'. 7810
21: 3 their father gave them great g' 4979
26: 8 Ammonites gave g' to Uzziah: 4503
32:23 many brought g' unto the Lord "
Es 2:18 to the provinces, and gave g', 4864
9:22 portions one to another, and g' 4979
Ps 68:18 thou hast received g' for men; "
72:10 of Sheba and Seba shall offer g'. 814
Pr 6:35 though thou givest many g'. 7810
15:27 but he that hateth g' shall live. 4979
19: 6 is a friend to him that giveth g'. 4976
29: 4 that receiveth g' overthroweth it. 8641
Isa 1:23 every one loveth g', and followeth 7810
Eze 16:33 They give g' to all whores: 5078
33 but thou givest thy g' to all thy 5083
20:26 I polluted them in their own g', 4979
31 when ye offer your g', when ye "
39 holy name no more with your g', "
22:12 have they taken g' to shed blood;*7810
Da 2: 6 shall receive of me g' and rewards4978
48 and gave him many great g', and "
5:17 Let thy g' be to thyself, and give "
M't 2:11 they presented unto him g'; gold, 1435
7:11 give good g' unto your children, "
Lu 11:13 give good g' unto your children: 1390
21: 1 casting their g' into the treasury. 1435
5 with goodly stones and g', * 334
Ro 11:29 For the g' and calling of God are 5486
12: 6 Having then g' differing according "
1Co 12: 1 concerning spiritual g', brethren,
4 there are diversities of g', but the 5486
9 to another the g' of healing by the "
28 g' of healings, helps, governments, "
30 Have all the g' of healing? do all "
31 covet earnestly the best g': and "
14: 1 desire spiritual g', but rather that
12 as ye are zealous of spiritual g',
Eph 4: 8 captive, and gave g' unto men. 1390
Heb 2: 4 miracles, and g' of the Holy Ghost,3311
5: 1 may offer both g' and sacrifices 1435
8: 3 ordained to offer g' and sacrifices: "
4 that there are priests that offer g' "
9: 9 were offered both g' and sacrifices, "
11: 4 God testifying of his g': and by it "
Re 11:10 shall send g' one to another;

Gihon (*ghi'-hon*)
Ge 2:13 the name of the second river is G':1521
1Ki 1:33 mule, and bring him down to G': "
38 mule, and brought him to G'. "
45 have anointed him king in G': "
2Ch 32:30 the upper watercourse of G', "
33:14 of David, on the west side of G', "

Gilalai (*ghil'-a-lahee*)
Ne 12:36 Milalai, G', Maai, Nethaneel, and 1562

Gilboa (*ghil-bo'-ah*)
1Sa 28: 4 together, and they pitched in G'. 1533
31: 1 and fell down slain in mount G'. "
8 his three sons fallen in mount G'. "
2Sa 1: 6 happened by chance upon mount G', "
21 Ye mountains of G', let there be no "
21:12 Philistines had slain Saul in G': "
1Ch 10: 1 and fell down slain in mount G'. "
8 and his sons fallen in mount G'. "

Gilead (*ghil'-e-ad*) See also GILEADITE; GILEAD'S; JABESH-GILEAD; RAMOTH-GILEAD.
Ge 31:21 set his face toward the mount G'. 1568
23 they overtook him in the mount G'. "
25 brethren pitched in the mount of G'. "
37:25 of Ishmaelites came from G' "
Nu 26:29 Machir begat G': of G' come the "
30 These are the sons of G': of Jeezer, "
27: 1 Hepher, the son of G', the son of "
32: 1 and the land of G', that, behold, "
26 shall be there in the cities of G'; "
29 ye shall give them the land of G' "
39 son of Manasseh went to G', and "
40 Moses gave G' unto Machir the son "
36: 1 families of the children of G', "
De 2:36 by the river, even unto G', there "
3:10 cities of the plain, and all G', and "
12 and half mount G', and the cities "
13 rest of G', and all Bashan, being "
15 And I gave G' unto Machir. "
16 Gadites I gave from G' even unto "
4:43 and Ramoth in G', of the Gadites; "

De 34: 1 shewed him all the land of G', 1568
Jos 12: 2 and from half G', even unto the "
5 and half G', the border of Sihon "
13:11 and G', and the border of the "
25 and all the cities of G', and half "
31 half G', and Ashtaroth, and Edrei, "
17: 1 the father of G': because he "
1 therefore he had G' and Bashan. "
3 the son of G', the son of Machir, "
5 besides the land of G' and Bashan, "
6 Manasseh's sons had the land of G'. "
20: 8 Ramoth in G' out of the tribe of "
21:38 Ramoth in G' with her suburbs, "
22: 9 to go into the country of G', to the "
13 the land of G', Phinehas the son "
15 unto the land of G', and they spake "
32 Gad, out of the land of G', unto the "
J'g 5:17 G' abode beyond Jordan: and why "
7: 3 depart early from mount G'. "
10: 4 day, which are in the land of G'. "
8 of the Amorites, which is in G'. "
17 together, and encamped in G'. "
18 princes of G' said to one another, "
18 head over all the inhabitants of G'. "
11: 1 and G' begat Jephthah. "
5 elders of G' went to fetch Jephthah "
7 Jephthah said unto the elders of G', "
8 elders of G' said unto Jephthah, "
8 head over all the inhabitants of G'. "
9 Jephthah said unto the elders of G', "
10 the elders of G' said unto Jephthah, "
11 with the elders of G', and the people "
29 he passed over G', and Manasseh, "
29 and passed over Mizpeh of G', "
29 and from Mizpeh of G' he passed "
12: 4 gathered together all the men of G', "
4 and the men of G' smote Ephraim, "
5 that the men of G' said unto him, "
7 buried in one of the cities of G'. "
20: 1 with the land of G', unto the Lord "
1Sa 13: 7 Jordan to the land of Gad and G'. "
2Sa 2: 9 made him king over G', and over "
17:26 Absalom pitched in the land of G'. "
24: 6 they came to G', and to the land of "
1Ki 4:13 son of Manasseh, which are in G'; "
19 son of Uri was in the country of G', "
17: 1 who was of the inhabitants of G', "
22: 3 Know ye that Ramoth in G' is * "
2Ki 10:33 all the land of G', the Gadites, "
33 river Arnon, even G' and Bashan. "
15:29 and Hazor, and G', and Galilee, "
1Ch 2:21 the father of G', whom he married "
22 and twenty cities in the land of G'. "
23 sons of Machir the father of G'. "
5: 9 were multiplied in the land of G'. "
10 throughout all the east land of G'. "
14 the son Jaroah, the son of G', the "
16 and they dwelt in G', in Bashan, "
6:80 Ramoth in G' with her suburbs, "
7:14 bare Machir the father of G': "
17 the sons of G', the son of Machir, "
26:31 men of valour at Jazer of G'. "
27:21 tribe of Manasseh in G', Iddo the "
Ps 60: 7 G' is mine, and Manasseh is mine; "
108: 8 G' is mine, Manasseh is mine; "
Ca 4: 1 goats, that appear from mount G': "
6: 5 of goats that appear from G': "
Jer 8:22 Is there no balm in G'; is there no "
22: 6 Thou art G' unto me, and the head "
46:11 Go up into G', and take balm, "
50:19 upon mount Ephraim and G'. "
Eze 47:18 and from Damascus, and from G', "
Ho 6: 8 G' is a city of them that work "
12:11 Is there iniquity in G'? surely "
Am 1: 3 because they have threshed G' "
13 the women with child of G', "
Ob 1:19 and Benjamin shall possess G'. "
Mic 7:14 in Bashan and G', as in the days of "
Zec 10:10 into the land of G' and Lebanon: "

Gileadite (*ghil'-e-ad-ite*) See also GILEADITES.
J'g 10: 3 after him arose Jair, a G', and 1569
11: 1 Jephthah the G' was a mighty "
40 the daughter of Jephthah the G' "
12: 7 Then died Jephthah the G', and "
2Sa 17:27 and Barzillai the G' of Rogelim, "
19:31 And Barzillai the G' came down "
1Ki 2: 7 of Barzillai the G', and let them be "
Ezr 2:61 daughters of Barzillai the G', and "
Ne 7:63 daughters of Barzillai the G' to "

Gileadites (*ghil'-e-ad-ites*)
Nu 26:29 Gilead come the family of the G'. 1569
J'g 12: 4 Ye G' are fugitives of Ephraim "
5 the G' took the passages of Jordan "
2Ki 15:25 and with him fifty men of the G': "

Gilead's (*ghil'-e-ads*)
J'g 11: 2 And G' wife bare him sons; 1568

Gilgal (*ghil'-gal*)
De 11:30 the champaign over against G', 1537
Jos 4:19 and encamped in G', in the east "
20 of Jordan, did Joshua pitch in G'. "
5: 9 place is called G' unto this day. "
10 Israel encamped in G', and kept "
9: 6 to Joshua unto the camp at G', "
10: 6 to the camp to G', saying, Slack "
7 Joshua ascended from G', he, and "
9 and went up from G' all night. "
15, 43 with him, unto the camp to G'. "
12:23 the king of the nations of G', one; "
14: 6 came unto Joshua in G': and "
15: 7 looking toward G', that is before "
J'g 2: 1 Lord came up from G' to Bochim, "
3:19 quarries that were by G', and said, "
1Sa 7:16 year in circuit to Beth-el, and G', "
10: 8 shalt go down before me to G';

1Sa 11:14 Come, and let us go to G', and 1537
15 And all the people went to G'; "
15 Saul king before the Lord in G'; "
13: 4 called together after Saul to G'. "
7 As for Saul, he was yet in G', and "
8 but Samuel came not to G'; and "
12 come down now upon me to G', "
15 gat him up from G' unto Gibeah of "
15:12 passed on, and gone down to G'. "
21 unto the Lord thy God in G'. "
33 in pieces before the Lord in G'. "
2Sa 19:15 And Judah came to G', to go to "
40 king went on to G', and Chimham "
2Ki 2: 1 Elijah went with Elisha from G'. "
4:38 And Elisha came again to G': and "
Ne 12:29 Also from the house of G', and out "
Ho 4:15 and come not ye unto G', neither "
9:15 All their wickedness is in G': for "
12:11 they sacrifice bullocks in G'; yea, "
Am 4: 4 at G' multiply transgression; "
5: 5 nor enter into G', and pass not to "
5 G' shall surely go into captivity, "
Mic 6: 5 him, from Shittim unto G'; "

Giloh (*ghi'-loh*) See also GILONITE.
Jos 15:51 Goshen, and Holon, and G'; 1542
2Sa 15:12 city, even from G', while he offered "

Gilonite (*ghi'-lo-nite*)
2Sa 15:12 Ahithophel the G', David's 1526
23:34 Eliam the son of Ahithophel the G'. "

Gimzo (*ghim'-zo*)
2Ch 28:18 G' also and the villages thereof: 1579

gin See also GINS.
Job 18: 9 The g' shall take him by the heel, 6341
Isa 8:14 for a g' and for a snare to the "
Am 3: 5 where no g' is for him? shall 4170

Ginath (*ghi'-nath*)
1Ki 16:21 Tibni the son of G', to make him 1527
22 Tibni the son of G': so Tibni died, "

Ginnetho (*ghin'-ne-tho*) See also GINNETHON.
Ne 12: 4 Iddo, G', Abijah, 1599

Ginnethon (*ghin'-ne-thon*) See also GINNETHO.
Ne 10: 6 Daniel, G', Baruch, 1599
12:16 Iddo, Zechariah; of G', Meshullam; "

gins
Ps 140: 5 wayside; they have set g' for me. 4170
141: 9 the g' of the workers of iniquity. "

gird See also GIRDED; GIRDETH; GIRDING; GIRT.
Ex 29: 5 and g' him with the curious girdle 640
9 thou shalt g' them with girdles, 2296
J'g 3:16 he did g' it under his raiment * "
1Sa 25:13 G' ye on every man his sword. "
2Sa 3:31 g' you with sackcloth, and mourn "
2Ki 4:29 G' up thy loins, and take my staff "
9: 1 G' up thy loins, and take this box "
Job 38: 3 G' up now thy loins like a man; 247
40: 7 G' up thy loins now like a man: "
Ps 45: 3 G' thy sword upon thy thigh, O 2296
Isa 8: 9, 9 g' yourselves, and ye shall be 247
15: 3 g' themselves with sackcloth: 2296
32:11 and g' sackcloth upon your loins. 2290
Jer 1:17 Thou therefore g' up thy loins, 2296
4: 8 For this g' you with sackcloth, "
6:26 g' thee with sackcloth, and wallow "
49: 3 g' you with sackcloth; lament, and "
Eze 7:18 They shall also g' themselves "
27:31 and g' them with sackcloth, and "
44:18 they shall not g' themselves with "
Joe 1:13 G' yourselves, and lament, ye "
Lu 12:37 that he shall g' himself, and make *4024*
17: 8 and g' thyself, and serve me, till "
Joh 21:18 another shall g' thee, and carry *2224*
Ac 12: 8 G' thyself, and bind on thy "
1Pe 1:13 Wherefore g' up the loins of your* *328*

girded See also GIRDEDST; GIRT; UNGIRDED.
Ex 12:11 shall ye eat it; with your loins g', 2296
Le 8: 7 and g' him with the girdle, and "
7 he g' him with the curious girdle "
13 them, and g' them with girdles, "
16: 4 and shall be g' with a linen girdle, "
De 1:41 And when ye had g' on every man "
1Sa 2: 4 stumbled are g' with strength. 247
18 a child, g' with a linen ephod. 2296
17:39 And David g' his sword upon his "
25:13 they g' on every man his sword; "
13 and David also g' on his sword: "
2Sa 6:14 David was g' with a linen ephod. "
20: 8 garment that he had put on was g' "
21:16 he being g' with a new sword, "
22:40 For thou hast g' me with strength 247
1Ki 18:46 and he g' up his loins, and ran 8151
20:32 So they g' sackcloth on their loins, 2296
Ne 4:18 one had his sword g' by his side, 631
Ps 18:39 For thou hast g' me with strength 247
30:11 sackcloth, and g' me with gladness; "
65: 6 mountains; being g' with power: "
93: 1 wherewith he hath g' himself: "
109:19 wherewith he is g' continually. 2296
Isa 45: 5 I g' thee, though thou hast not * 247
La 2:10 they have g' themselves with 2296
Eze 16:10 and I g' thee about with fine linen, 2280
23:15 G' with girdles upon their loins, 2289
Da 10: 5 whose loins were g' with fine gold 2296
Joe 1: 8 like a virgin g' with sackcloth "
Lu 12:35 Let your loins be g' about, *4024*
Joh 13: 4 and took a towel, and g' himself. *1241*
5 the towel wherewith he was g'. "
Re 15: 6 breasts g' with golden girdles. **4024*

girdedst
Joh 21:18 thou wast young, thou g' thyself *2224*

girdeth
1Ki 20:11 Let not him that g' on his harness 2296
Job 12:18 and g' their loins with a girdle. * 631
Ps 18:32 It is God that g' me with strength, 247
Pr 31:17 She g' her loins with strength, 2296

girding See also UNDERGIRDING.
Isa 3:24 of a stomacher a g' of sackcloth; 4228
22:12 baldness, and to g' with sackcloth: 2296

girdle See also GIRDLES.
Ex 28: 4 broidered coat, a mitre, and a g': 73
8 And the curious g' of the ephod, *2805
27 above the curious g' of the ephod.* "
28 above the curious g' of the ephod.* "
39 shalt make the g' of needlework. 73
29: 5 with the curious g' of the ephod: *2805
39: 5 And the curious g' of his ephod, * "
20 above the curious g' of the ephod.* "
21 above the curious g' of the ephod,* "
29 a g' of fine twined linen, and blue, 73
Le 8: 7 and girded him with the g', and "
7 with the curious g' of the ephod, *2805
16: 4 and shall be girded with a linen g', 73
1Sa 18: 4 sword, and to his bow, and to his g'. 2290
2Sa 18:11 ten shekels of silver, and a g'. "
20: 8 upon it a g' with a sword fastened "
1Ki 2: 5 put the blood of war upon his g' "
2Ki 1: 8 girt with a g' of leather about his 232
Job 12:18 and girdeth their loins with a g'. "
Ps 109:19 and for a g' wherewith he is girded 4206
Isa 3:24 and instead of a g' a rent; and 2290
5:27 shall the g' of their loins be loosed, 232
11: 5 righteousness shall be the g' of his "
5 loins, and faithfulness the g' of his "
22:21 strengthen him with thy g', and I 73
Jer 13: 1 Go and get thee a linen g', and put 232
2 So I got a g' according to the word "
4 Take the g' that thou hast got, "
6 take the g' from thence, which I "
7 took the g' from the place where I "
7 g' was marred, it was profitable for "
10 even be as this g', which is good for "
11 For as the g' cleaveth to the loins "
M't 3: 4 and a leathern g' about his loins; *2223*
M'r 1: 6 with a g' of a skin about his loins; "
Ac 21:11 he took Paul's g', and bound his "
11 bind the man that owneth this g', "
Re 1:13 about the paps with a golden g'. "

girdles
Ex 28:40 shalt make for them g', and bonnets 73
29: 9 And thou shalt gird them with g', "
Le 8:13 girded them with g', and put "
Pr 31:24 delivereth g' unto the merchant. 2289
Eze 23:15 with g' upon their loins, exceeding 232
Re 15: 6 breasts girded with golden g'. *2223*

Girgashite (*ghur'-gash-ite*) See also GIRGASHITES; GIRGASITE.
1Ch 1:14 also, and the Amorite, and the G', 1622

Girgashites (*ghur'-gash-ites*)
Ge 15:21 the Canaanites, and the G', and *1622
De 7: 1 the Hittites, and the G', and the * "
Jos 3:10 the Perizzites, and the G', and * "
24:11 and the G', the Hivites, and the * "
Ne 9: 8 Jebusites, and the G', to give it, I* "

Girgasite (*ghur'-ga-site*) See also GIRGASHITE.
Ge 10:16 and the Amorite, and the G', *1622

girl See also GIRLS.
Joe 3: 3 and sold a g' for wine, that they 3207

girls
Zec 8: 5 boys and g' playing in the streets 3207

girt See also GIRDED.
2Ki 1: 8 and g' with a girdle of leather about 247
Joh 21: 7 he g' his fisher's coat unto him, *1241*
Eph 6:14 your loins g' about with truth, **4024*
Re 1:13 and g' about the paps with a golden "

Gispa (*ghis'-pah*)
Ne 11:21 and Ziha and G' were over the *1658

Gittah-hepher (*ghit''-tah-he'-fer*) See also GATH-HEPHER.
Jos 19:13 on the east to G', to Ittah-kazin, *1662

Gittaim (*ghit-ta'-im*)
2Sa 4: 3 Beerothites fled to G', and were 1664
Ne 11:33 Hazor, Ramah, G', "

Gittite (*ghit'-tite*) See also GITTITES; GITTITH.
2Sa 6:10 the house of Obed-edom the G'. 1663
11 house of Obed-edom the G' three "
15:19 the king to Ittai the G', Wherefore "
22 Ittai the G' passed over, and all his "
18: 2 under the hand of Ittai the G'. "
21:19 slew the brother of Goliath the G', "
1Ch 13:13 the house of Obed-edom the G'. "
20: 5 the brother of Goliath the G', "

Gittites (*ghit'-tites*)
Jos 13: 3 the G', and the Ekronites; also the 1663
2Sa 15:18 and all the G', six hundred men "

Gittith (*ghit'-tith*)
Ps 8:*title* To the chief Musician upon G', 1665
81:*title* To the chief Musician upon G'. "
84:*title* To the chief Musician upon G'. "

give See also FORGIVE; GAVE; GIVEN; GIVEST; GIVETH; GIVING.
Ge 1:15, 17 heaven to g' light upon the earth, "
12: 7 Unto thy seed will I g' this land; 5414
13:15 to thee will I g' it, and to thy seed "
17 for will I g' it unto thee. "
14:21 G' me the persons, and take the "
15: 2 what wilt thou g' me, seeing I go "
7 to g' thee this land to inherit it. "
17: 8 will g' unto thee, and to thy seed "
16 I will bless her, and g' thee a son "
23: 4 g' me a possession of a...with you, "
9 may g' me the cave of Machpelah, "
23: 9 he shall g' it me for a possession 5414
11 the field g' I thee, and the cave "
11 that is therein, I g' it thee; in the "
11 sons of my people g' I it thee: "
13 But if thou wilt g' it, I pray thee,*
13 I will g' thee money for the field; 5414
24: 7 Unto thy seed will I g' this land: "
14 I will g' thy camels drink also: "
41 if they g' not thee one, thou shalt 5414
43 G' me, I pray thee, a little...to drink; "
46 I will g' thy camels drink also: "
26: 3 seed, I will g' all these countries, 5414
4 g' unto thy seed all these countries; "
27:28 God g' thee of the dew of heaven, "
28: 4 g' thee the blessing of Abraham, "
13 to thee will I g' it, and to thy seed; "
20 and will g' me bread to eat, and "
22 and of all that thou shalt g' me "
22 I will surely g' the tenth unto thee. "
29:19 better that I g' her to thee, than 5414
19 I should g' her to another man: "
21 G' me my wife, for my days are 3051
26 g' the younger before the firstborn. 5414
27 and we will g' thee this also for "
30: 1 G' me children, or else I die. 3051
14 G' me, I pray thee, of thy son's 5414
26 G' me my wives and my children, "
28 me thy wages, and I will g' it. "
31 And he said, What shall I g' thee? "
31 Thou shalt not g' me any thing: "
34: 8 I pray you g' her him to wife. "
9 g' your daughters unto us, and "
11 what ye shall say unto me I will g'. "
12 I will g' according as ye shall say "
12 but g' me the damsel to wife. "
14 to g' our sister to one that is "
16 will we g' our daughters unto you, "
21 and let us g' them our daughters. "
35:12 Isaac, to thee will I g' it, and to thy "
12 seed after thee will I g' the land. "
38: 9 he should g' seed to his brother. "
16 What wilt thou g' me, that thou "
17 Wilt thou g' me a pledge, till thou "
18 What pledge shall I g' thee? And "
41:16 God shall g' Pharaoh an answer of "
42:25 to g' them provision for the way: 5414
27 to g' his ass provender in the inn, "
43:14 God Almighty g' you mercy before "
45:18 I will g' you the good of the land "
47:15 Joseph, and said, G' us bread: 3051
16 And Joseph said, G' your cattle; "
16 I will g' you for your cattle, 5414
19 and g' us seed, that we may live, "
24 shall g' the fifth part unto Pharaoh, "
48: 4 and will g' this land to thy seed "
Ex 2: 9 and I will g' thee thy wages. "
3:21 g' this people favour in the sight "
5: 7 shall no more g' the people straw "
10 Pharaoh, I will not g' you straw. "
6: 4 to g' them the land of Canaan, "
8 to g' it to Abraham, to Isaac, and "
8 and I will g' it you for an heritage: "
10:25 Thou must g' us also sacrifices "
12:25 the land which the Lord will g' you, "
13: 5 sware unto thy fathers to g' thee, "
11 to thy fathers, and shall g' it thee, "
21 a pillar of fire, to g' them light; "
15:26 and wilt g' ear to his commandments, "
16: 8 Lord shall g' you in the evening 5414
17: 2 G' us water that we may drink. "
18:19 I will g' thee counsel, and God shall "
21:23 then thou shalt g' life for life, 5414
30 then he shall g' for the ransom "
32 g' unto their master thirty shekels "
34 shall make it good, and g' money 7725
22:17 utterly refuse to g' her unto him, 5414
29 thy sons shalt thou g' unto me. "
30 the eighth day thou shalt g' it me. "
24:12 and I will g' thee tables of stone, "
25:16 the testimony which I shall g' thee. "
21 the testimony that I shall g' thee. "
22 I will g' thee in commandment unto "
37 that they may g' light over against it. "
30:12 shall they g' every man a ransom 5414
13 This they shall g', every one that "
14 shall g' an offering unto the Lord. "
15 The rich shall not g' more, "
15 shall not g' less than half a shekel, "
15 when they g' an offering unto the 5414
32:13 will I g' unto your seed, and they "
33: 1 Unto thy seed will I g' it: "
14 go with thee, and I will g' thee rest. "
Le 5:16 thereto, and g' it unto the priest: 5414
6: 5 g' it unto him to whom it "
7:32 shoulder shall ye g' unto the priest "
14:34 land of Canaan, which I g' to you "
15:14 and g' them unto the priest: "
20:24 I will g' it unto you to possess it, "
22:14 and shall g' it unto the priest "
23:10 the land which I g' unto you, "
38 offerings, which ye g' unto the Lord. "
25: 2 come into the land which I g' you, "
37 Thou shalt not g' him thy money "
38 to g' you the land of Canaan, "
51 shall g' again the price of his 7725
52 years shall he g' him again the "
26: 4 I will g' you rain in due season, 5414
6 And I will g' peace in the land, "
27:23 and he shall g' thine estimation "
Nu 3: 9 shalt g' the Levites unto Aaron "
48 And thou shalt g' the money, "
5: 7 and g' it unto him against whom he "
6:26 upon thee, and g' thee peace. 7760
7: 5 shalt g' them unto the Levites, 5414
8: 2 the seven lamps shall g' light over "
10:29 the Lord said, I will g' it you: 5414

Nu 11: 4 Who shall g' us flesh to eat?
13 flesh to g' unto all this people? 5414
13 G' us flesh, that we may eat. "
18 Who shall g' us flesh to eat?
18 therefore the Lord will g' you flesh, 5414
21 will g' them flesh, that they may eat "
13: 2 the land of Canaan, which I g' unto "
14: 8 bring us into this land, and g' it us; "
15: 2 habitations, which I g' unto you, "
21 the first of your dough ye shall g' "
18:28 and ye shall g' thereof the Lord's "
19: 3 And ye shall g' her unto Eleazar "
20: 8 and it shall g' forth his water, "
8 thou shalt g' the congregation...drink.
21 Thus Edom refused to g' Israel 5414
21:16 I will g' them water. "
22:13 the Lord refuseth to g' me leave "
18 If Balak would g' me his house full "
24:13 If Balak would g' me his house full "
25:12 I g' unto him my covenant of peace: "
26:54 thou shalt g' the more inheritance, "
54 thou shalt g' the less inheritance: "
27: 4 G' unto us therefore a possession? 5414
7 shalt surely g' them a possession "
9, 10, 11 ye shall g' his inheritance "
19 and g' him a charge in their sight. "
31:29 and g' it unto Eleazar the priest, 5414
30 and g' them unto the Levites, "
32:29 ye shall g' them the land of Gilead "
33:54 more ye shall g' the more inheritance, "
54 fewer ye shall g' the less inheritance: "
34:13 to g' unto the nine tribes, and to 5414
35: 2 that they g' unto the Levites of the "
2 ye shall g' also unto the Levites "
4, 6 which ye shall g' unto the Levites "
7 which ye shall g' to the Levites "
7 them shall ye g' with their suburbs. "
8 shall g' shall be of the possession 5414
8 that have many ye shall g' many;*
8 that have few ye shall g' few: *
8 every one shall g' of his cities 5414
13 cities which ye shall g' six cities "
14 Ye shall g' three cities on this side "
14 three cities shall ye g' in the land "
36: 2 to g' the land for an inheritance "
2 to g' the inheritance of Zelophehad "
De 1: 8 to g' unto them and to their seed "
20 Lord our God doth g' unto us. * "
25 the Lord our God doth g' us. * "
35 I sware to g' unto your fathers, "
36 to him will I g' the land that he "
39 unto them will I g' it, and they shall "
45 to your voice, nor g' ear unto you.*
2: 5 I will not g' you of their land, 5414
9 I will not g' thee of their land "
19 I will not g' thee of the land of the "
28 g' me water for money, that I may "
31 Behold, I have begun to g' Sihon * "
4:38 to g' thee their land for an "
5:31 the land which I g' them to possess "
6:10 to g' thee great and goodly cities, "
23 to g' us the land which he sware "
7: 3 thy daughter thou shalt not g' unto "
13 he sware unto thy fathers to g' "
10:11 I sware unto their fathers to g' "
11: 9 to g' unto them and to their seed, "
14 I will g' you the rain of your land "
21 Lord sware unto your fathers to g' "
14:21 thou shalt g' it unto the stranger "
15:10 Thou shalt surely g' him, and thine "
14 blessed thee thou shalt g' unto him. "
16:10 shalt g' unto the Lord thy God, "
17 Every man shall g' as he is able, "
18: 3 g' unto the priest the shoulder, 5414
4 fleece of thy sheep, shalt thou g' "
19: 8 and g' thee all the land which "
8 the land which he promised to g' "
20:16 the Lord thy God doth g' thee * "
22:14 g' occasions of speech against *7760
19 and g' them unto the father of the 5414
29 shall g' unto the damsel's father "
23:14 to g' up thine enemies before thee; "
24: 1 her a bill of divorcement, and g' it "
15 his day thou shalt g' him his hire, "
25: 3 Forty stripes he may g' him, and "
26: 3 sware unto our fathers for to g' 5414
28:11 Lord sware unto thy fathers to g' "
12 g' the rain unto thy land in his "
55 So that he will not g' to any of them "
65 but the Lord shall g' thee there a "
30:20 to Isaac, and to Jacob, to g' them. "
31: 5 And the Lord shall g' them up * "
7 hath sworn unto their fathers to g' "
14 that I may g' him a charge. "
32: 1 G' ear, O ye heavens, and I will speak;
49 the land of Canaan, which I g' 5414
52 which I g' the children of Israel. "
34: 4 I will g' it unto thy seed: I have "
Jos 1: 2 the land which I do g' to them, "
6 I sware unto their fathers to g' "
2:12 and g' me a true token: "
5: 6 unto their fathers that he would g' "
7:19 g', I pray thee, glory to the Lord 7760
8:18 for I will g' it into thine hand. 5414
9:24 Moses to g' you all the land, and "
14:12 g' me this mountain, whereof the "
15:16 I g' Achsah my daughter to wife. "
19 G' me a blessing; for thou hast "
19 g' me also springs of water. "
17: 4 to g' us an inheritance among our "
18: 4 G' out from among you three *3051
20: 4 and g' him a place, that he may 5414
21: 2 to g' us cities to dwell in, with the "
43 the land which he sware to g' "
J'g 1:12 him will I g' Achsah my daughter "
15 G' me a blessing: for thou hast 3051

J'g 1:15 land; g' me also springs of water. 5414
4:19 G' me, I pray thee, a little...to drink; "
5: 3 g' ear, O ye princes; I, even I, "
7: 2 for me to g' the Midianites into 5414
8: 5 G', I pray you, loaves of bread "
6 should g' bread unto thine army? "
15 we should g' bread unto thy men "
24 that ye would g' me every man the "
25 We will willingly g' them. "
14:12 then I will g' you thirty sheets and "
13 then shall ye g' me thirty sheets "
16: 5 we will g' thee every one of us "
17:10 I will g' thee ten shekels of silver "
20: 7 g' here your advice and counsel. 3051
21: 1 shall not any of us g' his daughter 5414
7 will not g' them of our daughters "
18 g' them wives of our daughters: "
22 ye did not g' unto them at this time, "
Ru 4:12 seed which the Lord shall g' thee "
1Sa 1:11 wilt g' unto thine handmaid a man "
11 then I will g' him unto the Lord "
2:10 he shall g' strength unto his king, "
15 G' flesh to roast for the priest; "
16 but thou shalt g' it me now: "
20 Lord g' thee seed of this woman 7760
28 I g' unto the house of thy father 5414
32 wealth which God shall g' Israel: 3190
6: 5 g' glory unto the God of Israel: 5414
8: 6 said, G' us a king to judge us. "
14 them, and g' them to his servants. "
15 and g' to his officers, and to his "
9: 8 that will I g' to the man of God, "
10: 4 and g' thee two loaves of bread; "
11: 3 G' us seven days' respite, that we "
14:41 G' a perfect lot. And Saul and *3051
17:10 g' me a man, that we may fight 5414
25 will g' him his daughter, and make "
44 I will g' thy flesh unto the fowls "
46 I will g' the carcases of the host "
47 and he will g' you into our hands. "
18:17 Merab, her will I g' thee to wife: "
21 g' him her, that she may be a snare "
21: 3 g' me five loaves of bread in mine "
9 There is none like that; g' it me. "
22: 7 will the son of Jesse g' every one "
25: 8 g', I pray thee, whatsoever cometh "
11 and g' it unto men, whom I know "
27: 5 them g' me a place in some town "
30:22 will not g' them ought of the spoil "
2Sa 12:11 wives before thine eyes, and g' them "
13: 5 come, and g' me meat, and dress 1262
14: 8 and I will g' charge concerning thee. "
16:20 G' counsel among you what we 3051
21: 6 And the king said, I will g' them. 5414
22:50 Therefore I will g' thanks unto thee, "
23:15 one would g' me drink of the water "
24:23 things did Araunah, as a king, g' 5414
1Ki 1:12 let me, I pray thee, g' thee counsel, "
2:17 he g' me Abishag the Shunammite 5414
3: 5 God said, Ask what I shall g' thee. "
9 G' therefore thy servant an "
21 in the morning to g' my child suck, "
25 and g' half to the one, and half to 5414
26 g' her the living child, and in no "
27 G' her the living child, and in no "
5: 6 thee will I g' hire for thy servants "
8:32 to g' him according to his "
36 g' rain upon thy land, which thou * "
39 g' to every man according to his * "
50 g' them compassion before them "
11:11 and will g' it to thy servant. "
13 g' one tribe to thy son for David "
31 and will g' ten tribes to thee: "
35 will g' it unto thee, even ten tribes. "
36 unto his son will I g' one tribe, "
38 and will g' Israel unto thee. "
12: 9 counsel g' ye that we may answer "
13: 7 and I will g' thee a reward. 5414
8 If thou wilt g' me half thine house, "
14:16 g' Israel up because of the sins "
15: 4 did the Lord his God g' him a lamp "
17:19 he said unto her, G' me thy son. "
18:23 them therefore g' us two bullocks; "
21: 2 G' me thy vineyard, that I may "
2 will g' thee for it a better vineyard "
2 g' thee the worth of it in money. "
3 g' the inheritance of my fathers "
4 I will not g' thee the inheritance "
6 G' me thy vineyard for money; or "
6 I will g' thee another vineyard "
6 I will not g' thee my vineyard. "
7 will g' thee the vineyard of Naboth "
15 he refused to g' thee for money; "
2Ki 4:42 G' unto the people, that they may "
43 G' the people, that they may eat: "
5:22 g' them, I pray thee, a talent of "
6:28 G' thy son, that we may eat him to "
29 G' thy son, that we may eat him: "
8:19 to g' him alway a light, and to his "
10:15 g' me thine hand. And he gave "
11:10 over hundreds did the priest g' * "
14: 9 G' thy daughter to my son to wife: "
15:20 silver, to g' to the king of Assyria. "
18:23 g' pledges to my lord the king of "
22: 5 and let them g' it to the doers of 5414
23:35 to g' the money according to the "
35 to g' it unto Pharaoh-nechoh. "
1Ch 11:17 Oh that one would g' me drink of the "
16: 8 G' thanks unto the Lord, call upon "
18 thee will I g' the land of Canaan, 5414
28 G' unto the Lord, ye kindreds of 3051
28 g' unto the Lord glory and strength. "
29 G' unto the Lord the glory due "
34 O g' thanks unto the Lord; for he is "
35 that we may g' thanks to thy holy "
41 to g' thanks to the Lord, because his "

1Ch 21:23 I g' thee the oxen also for burnt 5414
23 for the meat offering; I g' it all. "
22: 9 g' him rest from all his enemies "
9 and I will g' peace and quietness 5414
12 the Lord g' thee wisdom and "
12 g' thee charge concerning Israel, "
25: 3 g' thanks and to praise the Lord. *
29:12 make great, and to g' strength unto all.
19 g' unto Solomon my son a perfect 5414
2Ch 1: 7 Ask what I shall g' thee. "
10 G' me now wisdom and knowledge, "
12 I will g' thee riches, and wealth, "
2:10 I will g' to thy servants, the hewers "
10: 6 What counsel g' ye me to return
9 What advice g' ye that we may return
21: 7 to g' a light to him and to his sons 5414
24:19 them: but they would not g' ear.
25: 9 The Lord is able to g' thee much 5414
18 G' thy daughter to my son to wife: "
30:12 to g' them one heart to do the "
24 Hezekiah king of Judah did g' to 7311
31: 2 to minister, and to g' thanks, and to
4 to g' the portion of the priests 5414
15 to g' to their brethren by courses, "
19 to g' portions to all the males "
32:11 g' over yourselves to die by famine "
35:12 that they might g' according to "
Ezr 4:21 G' ye now commandment *7761
9: 8 to g' us a nail in his holy place, 5414
8 and g' us a little reviving in our "
9 to g' us a reviving, to set up the "
9 and to g' us a wall in Judah "
12 g' not your daughters unto their "
Ne 2: 8 may g' me timber to make beams "
4: 4 and g' them for a prey in the land "
9: 8 to g' the land of the Canaanites, "
8 to g' it, I say, to his seed, "
12 fire, to g' them light in the way "
15 thou hadst sworn to g' them. 5414
30 yet would they not g' ear:
10:30 we would not g' our daughters 5414
12:24 to praise and to g' thanks, according
13:25 Ye shall not g' your daughters 5414
Es 1:19 and let the king g' her royal estate "
20 the wives shall g' to their husbands "
8: 1 that day did the king Ahasuerus g' "
Job 2: 4 all that a man hath will he g' for "
3:11 why did I not g' up the ghost 1478
6:22 G' a reward for me of your substance?
13:19 tongue, I shall g' up the ghost. 1478
32:21 neither let me g' flattering titles
22 For I know not to g' flattering titles;
34: 2 and g' ear unto me, ye that have
Ps 2: 8 and I shall g' thee the heathen for 5415
5: 1 G' ear to my words, O Lord,
6: 5 in the grave who shall g' thee thanks?
17: 1 g' ear unto my prayer, that goeth
18:49 Therefore will I g' thanks unto thee,
28: 4 G' them according to their deeds, 5414
4 g' them after the work of their "
29: 1 G' unto the Lord, O ye mighty, 3051
1 g' unto the Lord glory and strength. "
2 G' unto the Lord the glory due "
11 The Lord will g' strength unto his 5414
30: 4 and g' thanks at the remembrance
12 I will g' thanks unto thee for ever.
35:18 I will g' thee thanks in the great
37: 4 and he shall g' thee the desires of 5414
39:12 g' ear unto my cry; hold not thy
49: 1 g' ear, all ye inhabitants of the
7 nor g' to God a ransom for him: 5414
51:16 not sacrifice; else would I g' it:
54: 2 g' ear to the words of my mouth,
55: 1 G' ear to my prayer, O God;
57: 7 I will sing and g' praise. *
60:11 G' us help from trouble: for vain 3051
72: 1 G' the king thy judgments, O God, 5414
75: 1 Unto thee, O God, do we g' thanks,
1 unto thee do we g' thanks:
78: 1 G' ear, O my people, to my law;
20 he g' bread also? can he provide 5414
79:13 pasture will g' thee thanks for ever:
80: 1 G' ear, O Shepherd of Israel,
84: 8 g' ear, O God of Jacob. Selah.
11 the Lord will g' grace and glory: 5414
85:12 Lord shall g' that which is good; "
86: 6 G' ear, O Lord, unto my prayer;
16 g' thy strength unto thy servant, 5414
91:11 he shall g' his angels charge over
92: 1 It is a good thing to g' thanks
94:13 That thou mayest g' him rest
96: 7 G' unto the Lord, O ye kindreds 3051
7 g' unto the Lord glory and strength. "
8 G' unto the Lord the glory due "
97:12 and g' thanks at the remembrance of
104:11 g' drink to every beast of the field:
27 that thou mayest g' them their 5414
105: 1 g' thanks unto the Lord; call upon
11 Unto thee will I g' the land of 5414
39 and fire to g' light in the night.
106: 1 O g' thanks unto the Lord; for he is
47 to g' thanks unto thy holy name, and
107: 1 g' thanks unto the Lord; for he is
108: 1 I will sing and g' praise, even *
12 G' us help from trouble: for vain 3051
109: 4 but I g' myself unto prayer.
111: 6 that he may g' them the heritage *5441
115: 1 but unto thy name g' glory, for thy
118: 1, 29 O g' thanks unto the Lord; for he
119:34 G' me understanding, and I shall keep
62 I will rise to g' thanks unto thee
73 g' me understanding, that I may learn
125 g' me understanding, that I may know
144 g' me understanding, and I shall live.
169 g' me understanding according to thy
122: 4 g' thanks unto the name of the Lord.

Ps 132: 4 I will not g' sleep to mine eyes, 5414
136: 1 O g' thanks unto the Lord; for he is
2 O g' thanks unto the God of gods:
3 O g' thanks to the Lord of lords:
26 O g' thanks unto the God of heaven:
140:13 Surely the righteous shall g' thanks
141: 1 g' ear unto my voice, when I cry
143: 1 g' ear to my supplications: in thy
Pr 1: 4 To g' subtilty to the simple, and 5414
3:28 to morrow I will g'; when thou hast "
4: 2 I g' you good doctrine, forsake ye "
9 shall g' to thine head an ornament "
5: 9 thou g' thine honour unto others, "
6: 4 G' not sleep to thine eyes, nor "
31 he shall g' all the substance of his "
9: 9 G' instruction to a wise man and "
23:26 My son, g' me thine heart, and let "
25:21 enemy be hungry, g' him bread to
21 if he be thirsty, g' him water to drink:
29:15 The rod and reproof g' wisdom: 5414
17 correct thy son, and he shall g' thee
17 he shall g' delight unto thy soul. 5414
30: 8 g' me neither poverty nor riches; "
15 hath two daughters, crying, G', g'. 3051
31: 3 G' not thy strength unto women, 5414
6 G' strong drink unto him that is "
31 G' her of the fruit of her hands; "
Ec 2: 3 heart to g' myself unto wine. *4900
26 that he may g' to him that is good 5414
5: 1 to hear, than to g' the sacrifice of "
11: 2 G' a portion to seven, and also to "
Ca 2:13 the tender grape g' a good smell. "
7:12 there wi'l I g' thee my loves. "
13 The mandrakes g' a smell, and at "
8: 7 if a man would g' all the substance "
Isa 1: 2 Hear, O heavens, and g' ear, O earth; "
10 g' ear unto the law of our God,
3: 4 And I will g' children to be their 5414
7:14 Lord himself shall g' you a sign, "
22 of milk that they shall g', 6213
8: 9 and g' ear, all ye of far countries:
10: 6 of my wrath will I g' him a charge,
13:10 thereof shall not g' their light:
14: 3 day that the Lord shall g' thee rest
19: 4 And the Egyptians will I g' over 5534
28:23 G' ye ear, and hear my voice;
30:20 the Lord g' you the bread of 5414
23 Then shall he g' the rain of thy "
32: 9 daughters; g' ear unto my speech.
36: 8 g' pledges, I pray thee, to my
8 and I will g' thee two thousand 5414
41:27 g' to Jerusalem one that bringeth "
42: 6 and g' thee for a covenant of the "
8 my glory will I not g' to another, "
12 Let them g' glory unto the Lord, 7760
23 Who among you will g' ear to this?
43: 4 therefore will I g' men for thee, 5414
6 I will say to the north, G' up; "
20 I g' waters in the wilderness, and "
20 desert, to g' drink to my people, "
45: 3 And I will g' thee the treasures of 5414
48:11 I will not g' my glory unto another. "
49: 6 I will also g' thee for a light "
8 and g' thee for a covenant of the "
20 g' place to me that I may dwell. 5066
51: 4 g' ear unto me, O my nation: for a
55:10 that it may g' seed to the sower, *5414
56: 5 Even unto them will I g' in mine "
5 I will g' them an everlasting name, "
60:19 shall the moon g' light unto thee:
61: 3 to g' unto them beauty for ashes, 5414
62: 7 And g' him no rest, till he establish, "
8 I will no more g' thy corn to be "
Jer 3:15 And I will g' you pastors according "
19 and g' thee a pleasant land, a "
4:12 will I g' sentence against them. *1696
16 and g' out their voice against 5414
6:10 shall I speak, and g' warning, *
8:10 Therefore will I g' their wives 5414
9:15 and g' them water of gall to drink. "
11: 5 to g' them a land flowing with 5414
13:15 Hear ye, and g' ear; be not proud:
16 G' glory to the Lord your God, 5414
14:13 I will g' you assured peace in this "
22 or can the heavens g' showers? "
15:13 thy treasures will I g' to the spoil "
16: 7 shall men g' them the cup...to drink "
17: 3 I will g' thy substance and all thy 5414
10 g' every man according to his ways, "
18:18 let us not g' heed to any of his words.
19 G' heed to me, O Lord, and hearken
19: 7 their carcases will I g' to be meat 5414
20: 4 I will g' all Judah into the hand "
5 the kings of Judah will I g' into "
22:25 And I will g' thee into the hand of "
24: 7 will g' them an heart to know me, "
8 I g' Zedekiah the king of Judah, "
25:30 he shall g' a shout, as they that tread
31 he will g' them that are wicked 5414
26:24 should not g' him into the hand "
29: 6 g' your daughters to husbands, "
11 of evil, to g' you an expected end. "
30:16 upon thee will I g' for a prey. "
32: 3 Behold, I will g' this city into the "
19 to g' every one according to his "
22 to g' them, a land flowing with milk "
28 the Lord; Behold, I will g' this city "
39 And I will g' them one heart, and "
34: 2 I will g' this city into the hand of "
18 g' the men that have transgressed "
20 I will even g' them into the hand "
21 Judah and his princes will I g' into "
35: 2 and g' them wine to drink. "
37:21 g' him daily a piece of bread out *5414
38:15 if I g' thee counsel, wilt thou not
16 neither will I g' thee into the 5414

Jer 44:30 I will g' Pharaoh-hophra king of 5414
45: 5 life will I g' unto thee for a prey "
48: 9 G' wings unto Moab, that it may "
50:34 that he may g' rest to the land,
La 2:18 g' thyself no rest; let not the 5414
3:65 G' them sorrow of heart, thy "
4: 3 they g' suck to their young ones: the
Eze 2: 8 thy mouth, and eat that I g' thee. 5414
3: 3 bowels with this roll that I g' thee. "
17 and g' them warning from me.
7:21 And I will g' it into the hands of 5414
11: 2 and g' wicked counsel in this city:
17 I will g' you the land of Israel. 5414
19 And I will g' them one heart, "
19 and will g' them an heart of flesh: "
15: 6 fuel, so will I g' the inhabitants of "
16:33 They g' gifts to all whores: but "
36 which thou didst g' unto them; "
38 and I will g' thee blood in fury * "
39 I will also g' thee into their hand, "
41 also shalt g' no hire any more. "
61 g' them unto thee for daughters, "
17:15 that they might g' him horses and "
20:28 lifted up mine hand to g' it to them, "
42 mine hand to g' it to your fathers. "
21:11 to g' it into the hand of the slayer. "
27 right it is; and I will g' it him. "
23:31 will I g' her cup into thine hand. "
46 and will g' them to be removed "
25:10 and will g' them in possession, "
29:19 I will g' the land of Egypt unto "
21 g' thee the opening of the mouth "
32: 7 the moon shall not g' her light.
33:15 g' again that he had robbed, walk 7999
27 open field will I g' to the beasts 5414
36:26 A new heart also will I g' you, "
26 and I will g' you an heart of flesh. "
39: 4 will g' thee unto the ravenous birds "
11 I will g' unto Gog a place there "
43:19 shalt g' to the priests the Levites "
44:28 g' them no possession in Israel: "
30 ye shall also g' unto the priest the "
45: 8 the rest of the land shall they g' "
13 ye shall g' the sixth part of an ephah
16 land shall g' this oblation 1961, 413
17 prince's part to g' burnt offerings
46: 5 the lambs as he shall be able to g'. 4991
11 and to the lambs as he is able to g'. "
16 If the prince g' a gift unto any of 5414
17 if he g' a gift of his inheritance "
18 he shall g' his sons inheritance out of
47:14 hand to g' it unto your fathers: 5414
23 shall ye g' him his inheritance, "
Da 1:12 let them g' us pulse to eat, and "
2:16 king that he would g' him time, *5415
5:17 and g' thy rewards to another; 3052
6: 2 might g' accounts unto them,
8:13 to g' both the sanctuary and the 5414
9:22 g' thee skill and understanding. *
11:17 g' him the daughter of women, 5414
21 they shall not g' the honour of the "
Ho 2: 5 g' me my bread and my water, "
15 And I will g' her her vineyards "
4:18 rulers with shame do love, G' ye. *3051
5: 1 g' ye ear, O house of the king;
9:14 G' them, O Lord: 5414
14 what wilt thou g'? "
14 g' them a miscarrying womb "
11: 8 How shall I g' thee up, Ephraim? "
13:10 saidst, G' me a king and princes? "
Joe 1: 2 Hear this, ye old men, and g' ear,
2:17 g' not thine heritage to reproach, 5414
Mic 1:14 g' presents to Moresheth-gath: "
5: 3 Therefore will he g' them up, "
6: 7 shall I g' my firstborn for my "
14 which thou deliverest will I g' up "
Hag 2: 9 will I g' peace, saith the Lord "
Zec 3: 7 and I will g' thee places to walk "
8:12 the vine shall g' her fruit, and the "
12 ground shall g' her increase, and "
12 the heavens shall g' their dew; "
10: 1 and g' them showers of rain, to "
11:12 If ye think good, g' me my price; 3051
Mal 2: 2 to g' glory unto my name, saith 5414
M't 4: 6 He shall g' his angels charge
9 All these things will I g' thee, 1325
5:31 g' her a writing of divorcement: "
42 G' to him that asketh thee, and "
6:11 G' us this day our daily bread. "
7: 6 G' not that which is holy unto the "
9 ask bread, will he g' him a stone? 1929
10 a fish, will he g' him a serpent? "
11 g' good gifts unto your children, 1325
11 Father which is in heaven g' good "
9:24 He said unto them, G' place: for the 402
10: 8 freely ye have received, freely g'. 1325
42 whosoever shall g' to drink unto 4222
11:28 heavy laden, and I will g' you rest.
12:36 shall g' account thereof in the day 591
14: 7 g' her whatsoever she would ask. 1325
8 G' me here John Baptist's head in "
16 need not depart; g' ye them to eat. "
16:19 I will g' unto thee the keys of the "
26 a man g' in exchange for his soul? "
17:27 and g' unto them for me and thee. "
19: 7 to g' a writing of divorcement, "
21 g' to the poor, and thou shalt have "
20: 4 whatsoever is right I will g' you.
8 labourers, and g' them their hire, * 591
14 g' unto this last, even as unto thee. 1325
23 and on my left, is not mine to g', "
28 to g' his life a ransom for many. "
22:17 Is it lawful to g' tribute unto "
24:19 them that g' suck in those days!
29 the moon shall not g' her light, 1325
45 to g' them meat in due season? "

M't 25: 8 G' us of your oil; for our lamps 1325
28 g' it unto him which hath ten "
26:15 said unto them, What will ye g' me, "
53 he shall presently g' me more *3936
M'r 6:22 whatsoever thou wilt, and I will g' 1325
23 I will g' it thee, unto the half "
25 I will that thou g' me by and by "
37 G' ye them to eat. And they say "
37 of bread, and g' them to eat? "
8:37 Or what shall a man g' in exchange "
9:41 g' you a cup of water to drink 4222
10:21 g' to the poor, and thou shalt have 1325
40 on my left hand is not mine to g'; "
45 to g' his life a ransom for many. "
12: 9 will g' the vineyard unto others. "
14 Is it lawful to g' tribute to Cæsar, "
15 Shall we g', or shall we not g'? "
13:17 to them that g' suck in those days!
24 the moon shall not g' her light, 1325
14:11 and promised to g' him money. "
Lu 1:32 the Lord God shall g' unto him the "
77 To g' knowledge of salvation unto "
79 To g' light to them that sit in *2014
4: 6 All this power will I g' thee, 1325
6 and to whomsoever I will I g' it. "
10 shall g' his angels charge over thee,
6:30 G' to every man that asketh of 1325
38 G', and it shall be given unto you; "
38 shall men g' into your bosom. "
8:55 he commanded to g' her meat. * "
9:13 said unto them, G' ye them to eat. "
10: 7 drinking such things as they g': 3844
19 I g' unto you power to tread on *1325
11: 3 G' us day by day our daily bread. "
7 I cannot rise and g' thee. "
8 Though he will not rise and g' him, "
8 he will rise and g' him as many "
11 will he g' him a stone? or if he ask 1929
11 will he for a fish g' him a serpent? "
13 g' good gifts unto your children: 1325
13 your heavenly Father g' the Holy "
36 of a candle doth g' thee light. 5461
41 g' alms of such things as ye have; 1325
12:32 Father's good pleasure to g' you "
33 Sell that ye have, and g' alms; "
42 to g' them their portion of meat "
51 I am come to g' peace on earth? "
58 g' diligence that thou mayest be "
14: 9 say to thee, G' this man place; "
15:12 Father, g' me the portion of goods "
16: 2 g' an account of thy stewardship; * 591
12 g' you that which is your own? 1325
17:18 that returned to g' glory to God,
18:12 I g' tithes of all that I possess.
19: 8 half of my goods I g' to the poor; 1325
24 g' it to him that hath ten pounds. "
20:10 they should g' him of the fruit "
16 and shall g' the vineyard to others. "
22 Is it lawful for us to g' tribute "
21:15 I will g' you a mouth and wisdom, "
23 to them that g' suck, in those days!
22: 5 covenanted to g' him money. 1325
23: 2 forbidding to g' tribute to Cæsar, "
Joh 1:22 g' an answer to them that sent us. "
4: 7 saith unto her, G' me to drink. "
10 saith to thee, G' me to drink; "
14 the water that I shall g' him shall "
14 water that I shall g' him shall be in "
15 g' me this water, that I thirst not, "
6:27 the Son of man shall g' unto you: "
34 Lord, evermore g' us this bread. "
51 bread that I will g' is my flesh, "
51 I will g' for the life of the world. * "
52 How can this man g' us his flesh "
7:19 Did not Moses g' you the law, "
9:24 said unto him, G' God the praise: "
10:28 And I g' unto them eternal life; "
11:22 ask of God, God will g' it thee. "
13:26 to whom I shall g' a sop, when I 1929
29 should g' something to the poor. 1325
34 A new commandment I g' unto you, "
14:16 he shall g' you another Comforter, "
27 my peace I g' unto you: not as the "
27 as the world giveth, g' I unto you. "
15:16 in my name, he may g' it you. "
16:23 in my name, he will g' it you. "
17: 2 he should g' eternal life to as many "
Ac 3: 6 but such as I have g' I thee: In the "
5:31 for to g' repentance to Israel, and "
6: 4 g' ourselves continually to prayer, *4342
7: 5 promised that he would g' it to 1325
38 the lively oracles to g' unto us: "
8:19 Saying, G' me also this power, that "
10:43 g' all the prophets witness, that *
13:16 and ye that fear God, g' audience.
34 g' you the sure mercies of David. 1325
19:40 g' an account of this concourse. 591
20:32 to g' you an inheritance among all 1325
35 more blessed to g' than to receive. "
Ro 8:32 him also freely g' us all things? 5483
12:19 but rather g' place unto wrath:
20 if he thirst, g' him drink: for in so 4222
14:12 shall g' account of himself to God. 1325
16: 4 I g' thanks, but also all the churches
1Co 7: 5 ye may g' yourselves to fasting 4980
25 yet I g' my judgment, as one that 1325
10:30 for that for which I g' thanks?
32 G' none offence, neither to the 1096
12: 3 I g' you to understand, that no man
13: 3 though I g' my body to be burned, 3860
14: 7 they g' a distinction in the sounds, 1325
8 the trumpet g' an uncertain sound, "
2Co 4: 6 shined in our hearts, to g' the light
5:12 g' you occasion to glory on our *1325
8:10 herein I g' my advice: for this is "
9: 7 in his heart, so let him g': not *

Eph 1:16 Cease not to g' thanks for you.
17 g' unto you the spirit of wisdom 1325
4:27 Neither g' place to the devil.
28 have to g' to him that needeth. 3330
5:14 and Christ shall g' thee light. *
Col 1: 3 We g' thanks to God and the Father
4: 1 g' unto your servants that which * 3930
1Th 1: 2 We g' thanks to God always for
5:18 In everything g' thanks: for this is the
2Th 2:13 bound to g' thanks alway to God
3:16 g' you peace always by all means. 1325
1Ti 1: 4 Neither g' heed to fables and endless
4:13 I come, g' attendance to reading, to
15 things; g' thyself wholly to them; 2468
5: 7 these things g' in charge, that *
14 g' none occasion to the adversary 1325
6:13 g' thee charge in the sight of God,*
2Ti 1:16 the Lord g' mercy unto the house * 1325
2: 7 Lord g' thee understanding in all "
25 if God peradventure will g' them "
4: 8 judge, shall g' me at that day: 591
Heb 2: 1 to g' the more earnest heed to the
13:17 they that must g' account, that 591
Jas 2:16 notwithstanding ye g' them not 1325
1Pe 3:15 be ready always to g' an answer
4: 5 Who shall g' account to him that is 591
2Pe 1:10 g' diligence to make your calling
1Jo 5:16 he shall g' him life for them that 1325
Re 2: 7 will I g' to eat of the tree of life, "
10 and I will g' thee a crown of life. "
17 him that overcometh will I g' to eat "
17 and will g' him a white stone, "
23 and I will g' unto every one of you "
26 to him will I g' power over the "
28 And I will g' him the morning star. "
4: 9 those beasts g' glory and honour "
10: 9 said unto him, G' me the little book. "
11: 3 will g' power unto my two witnesses, "
17 We g' thee thanks, O Lord God
18 g' reward unto thy servants the 1325
13:15 g' life unto the image of the beast,* "
14: 7 Fear God, and g' glory to him; "
16: 9 they repented not to g' him glory. "
19 to g' unto her the cup of the wine "
17:13 g' their power and strength unto 1239
17 g' their kingdom unto the beast, 1325
18: 7 much torment and sorrow g' her: "
19: 7 and rejoice, an g' honour to him: "
21: 6 I will g' unto him that is athirst "
22:12 g' every man according as his work 591

given See also FORGIVEN.
Ge 1:29 g' you every herb bearing seed, 5414
30 I have g' every green herb for meat: "
9: 3 as the green herb have I g' you 5414
15: 3 Behold, to me thou hast g' no seed: "
18 Unto thy seed have I g' this land, "
16: 5 I have g' my maid into thy bosom; "
20:16 I have g' thy brother a thousand "
21: 7 should have g' children suck? *
24:35 he hath g' him flocks, and herds, 5414
36 and unto him hath he g' all "
27:37 all his brethren have I g' to him "
29:33 he hath therefore g' me this son "
30: 6 and hath g' me a son: therefore "
18 God hath g' me my hire, "
18 because I have g' my maiden "
31: 9 cattle of your father, and g' them "
33: 5 hath graciously g' thy servant. 2603
38:14 she was not g' unto him to wife. 5414
43:23 the God of your father, hath g' you "
48: 9 my sons, whom God hath g' me "
22 I have g' to thee one portion above "
Ex 5:16 is no straw g' unto thy servants, "
18 for there shall no straw be g' you, "
16:15 bread which the Lord hath g' you "
29 the Lord hath g' you the sabbath, "
21: 4 If his master have g' him a wife, * "
31: 6 I have g' with him Aholiab, * "
Le 6:17 g' it unto them for their portion "
7:34 have g' them unto Aaron the priest "
36 the Lord commanded to be g' them "
10:14 are g' out of the sacrifices of peace "
17 God hath g' it you to bear the "
17:11 I have g' it to you upon the altar "
19:20 not at all redeemed, nor freedom g' "
20: 3 he hath g' of his seed unto Molech, "
Nu 3: 9 they are wholly g' unto him out of "
8:16 they are wholly g' unto me from "
19 And I have g' the Levites as a gift "
16:14 or g' us inheritance of fields and "
18: 6 they are g' as a gift for the Lord, * "
7 g' your priest's office unto you "
8 also have g' thee the charge of mine "
8 unto thee have I g' them by reason "
11 I have g' them unto thee, and to thy "
12 unto the Lord, them have I g' thee. "
19 have I g' thee, and thy sons and "
21 I have g' the children of Levi all "
24 I have g' to the Levites to inherit: "
26 the tithes which I have g' you from "
20:12 the land which I have g' them. "
24 which I have g' unto the children "
21:29 he hath g' his sons that escaped, "
26:54 every one shall his inheritance be g' "
62 there was no inheritance g' them "
27:12 the land which I have g' unto the "
32: 5 this land be g' unto thy servants "
7 land which the Lord hath g' them? "
9 land which the Lord had g' them. "
33:53 I have g' you the land to possess it. "
De 1: 3 Lord had g' him in commandment
2: 5 I have g' mount Seir unto Esau 5414
9 have g' Ar unto the children of Lot "
19 I have g' it unto the children of Lot "
24 I have g' into thine hand Sihon "
9:18 Lord your God hath g' you this

De 3:19 your cities which I have g' you; 5414
20 have g' rest unto your brethren, *
20 the Lord your God hath g' them 5414
20 possession, which I have g' you. "
8:10 good land which he hath g' thee. "
9:23 the land which I have g' you; "
12:15 blessing...which he hath g' thee: "
21 flock, which the Lord hath g' thee, "
13:12 God hath g' thee to dwell there, * "
16:17 blessing...which he hath g' thee. "
20:14 the spoil...thy God hath g' thee. "
22:17 g' occasions of speech against *7760
25:19 the Lord thy God hath g' thee rest
26: 9 hath g' us this land, even a land 5414
10 which thou, O Lord, hast g' me. "
11 the Lord thy God hath g' unto thee, "
12 and hast g' it unto the Levite, * "
13 also have g' them unto the Levite, "
14 nor g' ought thereof for the dead: "
15 the land which thou hast g' us, "
28:31 shall be g' unto thine enemies, "
32 daughters shall be g' unto another "
52 land...Lord thy God hath g' thee. "
53 daughters...thy God hath g' thee, "
29: 4 the Lord hath not g' you an heart "
26 whom he had not g' unto them: 2505
Jos 1: 3 that have I g' unto you, as I said 5414
13 Lord your God hath g' you rest, *
13 and hath g' you this land. *5414
15 the Lord have g' your brethren
15 rest, as he hath g' you,
2: 9 the Lord hath g' you the land, 5414
14 when the Lord hath g' us the land,* "
6: 2 I have g' into thine hand Jericho, "
16 the Lord hath g' you the city. "
8: 1 g' into thy hand the king of Ai, "
14: 3 Moses had g' the inheritance of two "
15:19 thou hast g' me a south land; * "
17:14 Why hast thou g' me but one lot "
18: 3 Lord God of your fathers hath g' "
22: 4 the Lord your God hath g' rest
7 had g' possession in Bashan: 5414
23: 1 the Lord had g' rest unto Israel
13, 15 the Lord your God hath g' you. 5414
16 land which he hath g' unto you. "
24:13 And I have g' you a land for * "
33 was g' him in mount Ephraim. "
J'g 1:15 for thou hast g' me a south land;* "
14:20 Samson's wife was g' to his companion,
15: 6 wife, and g' her to his companion. 5414
18 Thou hast g' this great deliverance "
18:10 God hath g' it into your hands; "
Ru 2:12 full reward be g' thee of the Lord
1Sa 1:27 the Lord hath g' me my petition 5414
15:28 hath g' it to a neighbour of thine. "
18:19 Saul's daughter should have been g' "
19 David, that she was g' unto Adriel "
22:13 in that thou hast g' him bread, "
25:27 it even be g' unto the young men "
44 Saul had g' Michal his daughter, "
28:17 and g' it to thy neighbour, even to "
30:23 that which the Lord hath g' us, "
2Sa 4:10 I would have g' him a reward * "
7: 1 Lord had g' him rest round about
9: 9 I have g' unto thy master's son 5414
12: 8 would moreover have g' unto thee*3254
14 hast g' great occasion to the enemies
17: 7 Ahithophel hath g' is not good 3289
18:11 I would have g' thee ten shekels 5414
19:42 or hath he g' us any gift? 5375
22:36 Thou hast also g' me the shield 5414
41 g' me the necks of mine enemies,* "
1Ki 1:48 hath g' one to sit on my throne "
2:21 Let Abishag the Shunammite be g' "
3: 6 g' him a son to sit on his throne, "
12 I have g' thee a wise and an "
13 also g' thee that which thou hast "
5: 4 the Lord my God hath g' me rest
7 day, which hath g' unto David 5414
8:36 thy land, which thou hast g' to thy "
56 the Lord, that hath g' rest unto his "
9: 7 out of the land which I have g' "
12 cities which Solomon had g' him; "
13 cities are these which thou hast g' "
16 and g' it for a present unto his "
12: 8 old men, which they had g' him, 3289
13: 5 sign which the man of God had g' 5414
18:26 the bullock which was g' them, "
2Ki 5: 1 had g' deliverance unto Syria: "
17 I pray thee, be g' to thy servant "
8:29 wounds which the Syrians had g' 5221
9:15 wounds which the Syrians had g' "
23:11 kings of Judah had g' to the sun, 5414
25:30 allowance g' him of the king, "
1Ch 5: 1 was g' unto the sons of Joseph
6:61 cities g' out of the half tribe,
63 Unto the sons of Merari were g' by
71 Unto the sons of Gershom were g'
77 the children of Merari were g' out of
78 g' them out of the tribe of Reuben,
22:18 he not g' you rest on every side?
18 for he hath g' the inhabitants *5414
23:25 The Lord God of Israel hath g' rest
28: 5 the Lord hath g' me many sons,) 5414
29: 3 gold and silver, which I have g', "
14 and of thine own have we g' thee. "
2Ch 2:12 g' to David the king a wise son, "
6:27 upon thy land, which thou hast g', "
7:20 out of my land which I have g' "
14: 6 because the Lord had g' him rest.
7 he hath g' us rest on every side.
20:11 which thou hast g' us to inherit.
21: 6 the wounds which were g' him at 5221
25: 9 hundred talents which I have g' 5414
32:29 God had g' him substance very "
34:14 the law of the Lord g' by Moses.

2Ch 34:18 the priest hath g' me a book. *5414
36:23 hath the Lord God of heaven g' me; "
Ezr 1: 2 The Lord God of heaven hath g' me "
4:21 commandment shall be g' from *7761
6: 4 expences be g' out of the king's 3052
8 expences be g' unto these men,
9 be g' them day by day without fail: "
7: 6 the Lord God of Israel had g': 5414
19 The vessels also that are g' thee 3052
9:13 g' us such deliverance as this; 5414
Ne 2: 7 letters be g' me to the governors "
10:29 God's law, which was g' by Moses "
13: 5 commanded to be g' to the Levites,
10 the Levites had not been g' them. 5414
Es 2: 3 their things for purification be g' "
9 which were meet to be g' her, "
13 whatsoever she desired was g' her "
3:11 silver is g' to thee, the people also, "
14 a commandment to be g' in every "
15 was g' in Shushan the palace. "
4: 8 the decree that was g' at Shushan "
5: 3 it shall be even g' thee to the half "
7: 3 let my life be g' me at my petition, "
8: 7 have g' Esther the house of Haman, "
13 a commandment to be g' in every "
14 was g' at Shushan the palace. "
9:14 and the decree was g' at Shushan; "
Job 3:20 is light g' to him that is in misery, "
23 Why is light g' to a man whose way
9:24 is g' into the hand of the wicked: 5414
10:18 O that I had g' up the ghost, 1478
15:19 unto whom alone the earth was g',5414
22: 7 not g' water to the weary to drink,
24:23 Though it be g' him to be in safety,*5414
33: 4 of the Almighty hath g' me life. *
34:13 g' him a charge over the earth? *
37:10 By the breath of God frost is g': 5414
38:36 g' understanding to the heart? "
39:19 Hast thou g' the horse strength? "
Ps 16: 7 the Lord, who hath g' me counsel:
18:35 Thou hast also g' me the shield 5414
40 g' me the necks of mine enemies;* "
21: 2 hast g' him his heart's desire, "
44:11 g' us like sheep appointed for "
60: 4 hast g' a banner to them that fear "
61: 5 thou hast g' me the heritage of "
71: 3 hast g' commandment to save me; "
72:15 and to him shall be g' of the gold 5414
78:24 had g' them of the corn of heaven.* "
63 maidens were not g' to marriage.*
79: 2 bodies of thy servants have they g' 5414
111: 5 g' meat unto them that fear him: "
112: 9 g' to the poor; his righteousness "
115:16 earth hath he g' to the children "
118:18 he hath not g' me over unto death. "
120: 3 What shall be g' unto thee? or what "
124: 6 who hath not g' us as a prey "
Pr 19:17 that which he hath g' will he pay *1576
23: 2 if thou be a man g' to appetite. 1167
24:21 not with them that are g' to change:
Ec 1:13 sore travail hath God g' to the sons 5414
3:10 travail, which God hath g' to the "
5:19 to whom God hath g' riches and
19 and hath g' him power to eat
6: 2 man to whom God hath g' riches, 5414
8: 8 deliver those that are g' to it. 1167
9: 9 thy vanity, which he hath g' thee 5414
12:11 which are g' from one shepherd.
Isa 3:11 reward of his hands shall be g' him.6213
8:18 children whom the Lord hath g' 5414
9: 6 a child is born, unto us a son is g': "
23:11 the Lord hath g' a commandment
33:16 bread shall be g' him; his waters 5414
35: 2 glory of Lebanon shall be g' unto "
37:10 Jerusalem shall not be g' into the "
43:28 and have g' Jacob to the curse, * "
47: 6 and g' them into thine hand: * "
8 thou that art g' to pleasures, that
50: 4 Lord God hath g' me the tongue 5414
55: 4 Behold, I have g' him for a witness "
Jer 3: 8 away, and g' her a bill of divorce; "
18 I have g' for an inheritance unto your
6:13 every one is g' to covetousness;
8:10 the greatest is g' to covetousness,
13 the things that I have g' them 5414
14 and g' us water of gall to drink,
11:18 the Lord hath g' me knowledge *
12: 7 g' the dearly beloved of my soul 5414
13:20 where is the flock that was g' thee, "
15: 9 she hath g' up the ghost; her sun 5301
21:10 shall be g' into the hand of the king 5414
25: 5 land that the Lord hath g' unto you "
27: 5 g' it unto whom it seemed meet "
6 now have I g' all these lands "
6 beasts of the field have I g' him "
28:14 g' him the beasts of the field also. "
32:22 g' them this land, which thou didst "
24 and the city is g' into the hand of "
25 for the city is g' into the hand of the "
43 it is g' into the hand of the "
35:15 the land which I have g' to you "
38: 3 This city shall surely be g' into the "
18 shall this city be g' into the hand "
39:17 thou shalt not be g' into the hand "
44:20 people which had g' him that answer,
47: 7 the Lord hath g' it a charge against
50:15 hath g' her hand: her foundations *5414
52:34 continual diet g' him of the king "
La 1:11 g' their pleasant things for meat "
2: 7 g' up into the hand of the enemy 5462
5: 6 have g' the hand to the Egyptians, 5414
Eze 3:20 because thou hast not g' him warning, "
4:15 g' thee cow's dung for man's dung,5414
11:15 unto us is this land g' in possession. "
15: 6 which I have g' to the fire for fuel. "
16:17 of my silver, which I had g' thee

Eze 16:34 and no reward is g' unto thee. 5414
17:18 he had g' his hand, and hath done "
18: 7 hath g' his bread to the hungry, "
8 that hath not g' forth upon usury, "
13 Hath g' forth upon usury, and hath "
16 hath g' his bread to the hungry, "
20:15 into the land which I had g' them, "
21:11 And he hath g' it to be furbished, "
28:25 land that I have g' to my servant* "
29: 5 have g' thee for meat to the beasts "
20 I have g' him the land of Egypt "
33:24 the land is g' us for inheritance. "
35:12 desolate, they are g' us to consume. "
37:25 the land that I have g' unto Jacob "
47:11 they shall be g' to salt. "
Da 2:23 who hast g' me wisdom and might, 3052
37 for the God of heaven hath g' thee "
38 heaven hath he g' into thine hand, "
4:16 let a beast's heart be g' unto him; "
5:28 and g' to the Medes and Persians. "
7: 4 and a man's heart was g' to it. "
6 and dominion was g' to it. "
11 and g' to the burning flame. "
14 And there was g' him dominion, "
22 and judgment was g' to the saints "
25 and they shall be g' into his hand "
27 be g' to the people of the saints of "
8:12 host was g' him against the daily 5414
11: 6 she shall be g' up, and they that "
11 multitude shall be g' into his hand. "
Ho 2: 9 flax g' to cover her nakedness. *
12 rewards that my lovers have g' me:5414
Joe 2:23 he hath g' you the former rain * "
3: 3 and have g' a boy for an harlot, "
Am 4: 6 have g' you cleanness of teeth "
9:15 their land which I have g' them, "
Na 1:14 And the Lord hath g' a commandment "
M't 7: 7 Ask, and it shall be g' you: seek, 1325
9: 8 glorified God, which had g' such "
10:19 it shall be g' you in that same hour "
12:39 and there shall no sign be g' to it, "
13:11 g' unto you to know the mysteries "
11 but to them it is not g'. "
12 whosoever hath, to him shall be g'. "
14: 9 he commanded it to be g' her. "
11 in a charger, and g' to the damsel: "
16: 4 there shall no sign be g' unto it, "
19:11 save they to whom it is g'. "
20:23 it shall be g' to them for whom it* "
21:43 taken from you, and g' to a nation 1325
22:30 marry, nor are g' in marriage, 1547
25:29 every one that hath shall be g', 1325
26: 9 sold for much, and g' to the poor. "
28:18 All power is g' unto me in heaven "
M'r 4:11 you it is g' to know the mystery "
24 you that hear shall more be g'. 4369
25 he that hath, to him shall be g': 1325
5:43 something should be g' her to eat. "
6: 2 this which is g' unto him, that even "
8:12 no sign be g' unto this generation. "
10:40 but it shall be g' to them for whom "
12:25 neither marry, nor are g' in marriage; "
13:11 shall be g' you in that hour, 1325
14: 5 and have been g' to the poor. "
23 cup, and when he had g' thanks, "
44 him had g' them a token, saying, 1325
Lu 6:38 Give, and it shall be g' unto you; "
8:10 you it is g' to know the mysteries "
18 whosoever hath, to him shall be g'; "
11: 9 Ask, and it shall be g' you; seek, "
29 there shall no sign be g' it, but the "
12:48 unto whomsoever much is g', of "
17:27 they were g' in marriage, until the day "
19:15 whom he had g' the money, that 1325
26 every one which hath shall be g'; "
20:34 marry, and are g' in marriage; but "
35 neither marry, nor are g' in marriage: "
22:19 This is my body which is g' for you:1325
Joh 1:17 law was g' by Moses, but grace "
3:27 except it be g' him from heaven. "
35 hath g' all things into his hand. "
4:10 he would have g' thee living water. "
5:26 so hath he g' to the Son to have * "
27 hath g' him authority to execute * "
36 which the Father hath g' me "
6:11 when he had g' thanks, he distributed
23 after that the Lord had g' thanks:) "
39 that of all which he hath g' me 1325
65 it were g' unto him of my Father. "
7:39 for the Holy Ghost was not yet g'; "
11:57 Pharisees had g' a commandment, 1325
12: 5 hundred pence, and g' to the poor? "
13: 3 the Father had g' all things into his "
15 For I have g' you an example, "
17: 2 thou hast g' him power over all * "
2 to as many as thou hast g' him. "
7 whatsoever thou hast g' me are of "
8 have g' unto them the words which "
9 for them which thou hast g' me; "
11 those whom thou hast g' me, that "
14 I have g' them thy word; and the "
22 thou gavest me I have g' them; that "
24 they also, whom thou hast g' me, "
24 my glory, which thou hast g' me: "
18:11 cup which my Father hath g' me, "
19:11 except it were g' thee from above: "
Ac 1: 2 Holy Ghost had g' commandments "
3:16 hath g' him this perfect soundness 1325
4:12 name under heaven g' among men, "
5:32 whom God hath g' to them that "
8:18 the Holy Ghost was g', he offered "
17:16 saw the city wholly g' to idolatry.* "
31 whereof he hath g' assurance unto3930
20: 2 and had g' them much exhortation, "
21:40 And when he had g' him licence, Paul "
24:26 money should have been g' him of 1325
Ac 27:24 God hath g' thee all them that *5483
Ro 5: 5 by the Holy Ghost which is g' unto1325
11: 8 hath g' them the spirit of slumber.* "
35 Or who hath first g' to him, and it 4272
12: 3 say through the grace g' unto me, 1325
6 the grace that is g' to us, whether "
13 necessity of saints; g' to hospitality.1377
15:15 the grace that is g' to me of God, 1325
1Co 1: 4 the grace of God which is g' you by "
2:12 know the things that are freely g' 5483
3:10 the grace of God which is g' unto 1325
11:15 for her hair is g' her for a covering. "
24 And when he had g' thanks, he
12: 7 manifestation of the Spirit is g' 1325
8 to one is g' by the Spirit the word "
24 having g' more abundant honour* "
16: 1 as I have g' order to the churches
2Co 1:11 thanks may be g' by many on our
22 and g' the earnest of the Spirit *1325
5: 5 also hath g' unto us the earnest of* "
18 and hath g' to us the ministry * "
9: 9 g' to the poor: his righteousness "
10: 8 the Lord hath g' us for edification,* "
12: 7 there was g' to me a thorn in the "
13:10 power which the Lord hath g' me* "
Ga 2: 9 the grace that was g' unto me, they "
3:21 for if there had been a law g' "
21 which could have g' life, *2227
22 might be g' to them that believe. 1325
4:15 own eyes, and have g' them to me. "
Eph 3: 2 which is g' me to you-ward: "
7 the grace of God g' unto me by the "
8 is this grace g', that I should preach "
4: 7 unto every one of us is g' grace "
19 past feeling have g' themselves *3860
5: 2 hath loved us, and hath g' himself* "
6:19 that utterance may be g' unto me, 1325
Ph'p 1:29 you it is g' in the behalf of Christ,*5483
2: 9 and g' him a name which is above* "
Col 1:25 of God which is g' to me for you, 1325
1Th 4: 8 also g' unto us his holy Spirit. * "
2Th 2:16 hath g' us everlasting consolation* "
1Ti 3: 2 g' to hospitality, apt to teach;
3 g' to wine, no striker, not greedy *3943
8 not g' to much wine, not greedy 4337
4:14 which was g' thee by prophecy, 1325
2Ti 1: 7 For God hath not g' us the spirit * "
9 grace, which was g' us in Christ "
3:16 All scripture is g' by inspiration *
Tit 1: 7 not soon angry, not g' to wine, *3943
7 not g' to filthy lucre; *
2: 3 not g' to much wine, teachers of *1402
Ph'm 22 prayers I shall be g' unto you. *5483
Heb 2:13 the children which God hath g' 1325
4: 8 For if Jesus had g' them rest, then
Jas 1: 5 upbraideth not; and it shall be g' 1325
2Pe 1: 3 power hath g' unto us all things *1433
4 Whereby are g' unto us exceeding* "
3:15 according to the wisdom g' unto 1325
1Jo 3:24 by the Spirit which he hath g' us.* "
4:13 because he hath g' us of his Spirit. "
5:11 that God hath g' to us eternal life,* "
20 and hath g' us an understanding, "
Re 6: 2 and a crown was g' unto him: "
4 power was g' to him that sat thereon "
4 and there was g' unto him a great "
8 power was g' unto them over the "
11 white robes were g' unto every one "
7: 2 to whom it was g' to hurt the earth "
8: 2 to them were g' seven trumpets. "
3 there was g' unto him much incense, "
9: 1 was g' the key of the bottomless pit. "
3 unto them was g' power, as the "
5 to them it was g' that they should "
10: 9 unto him, G' me the little book.
11: 1 there was g' me a reed like unto a "
2 for it is g' unto the Gentiles: "
12:14 to the woman were g' two wings "
13: 5 there was g' unto him a mouth "
5 power was g' unto him to continue "
7 it was g' unto him to make war "
7 power was g' him over all kindreds, "
16: 6 thou hast g' them blood to drink; "
8 power was g' unto him to scorch "
20: 4 and judgment was g' unto them: "

giver See also LAWGIVER.
Isa 24: 2 so with the g' of usury to him.
2Co 9: 7 for God loveth a cheerful g'. 1395

givest
De 15: 9 thou g' him nought; and he cry *5414
10 grieved when thou g' unto him: "
Job 35: 7 what g' thou him? or what "
Ps 50:19 Thou g' thy mouth to evil, and 7971
80: 5 and g' them tears to drink in great
104:28 That thou g' them they gather: 5414
145:15 thou g' them their meat in due "
Pr 6:35 content, though thou g' many gifts.
Eze 3:18 thou g' him not warning, nor speakest
16:33 thou g' thy gifts to all thy lovers, 5414
34 in that thou g' a reward, and no "
1Co 14:17 For thou verily g' thanks well,

giveth See also FORGIVETH.
Ge 49:21 hind let loose: he g' goodly words.5414
Ex 16:29 therefore he g' you on the sixth "
20:12 the land which the Lord thy God g' "
25: 2 every man that g' it willingly "
Le 20: 2 g' any of his seed unto Molech; 5414
4 when he g' of his seed unto Molech, "
27: 9 all that any man g' such unto the "
Nu 5:10 whatsoever any man g' the priest, "
De 2:29 the land which the Lord our God g' "
4: 1 the Lord God of your fathers g' "
21 the Lord thy God g' thee for an "
40 the land which the Lord thy God g' "
De 5:16 the land which the Lord thy God g'5414
8:18 it is he that g' thee power to get "
9: 6 Lord thy God g' thee not this land "
11:17 the good land which the Lord g' "
31 land which the Lord your God g' "
12: 1 God of thy fathers g' thee to * "
9 which the Lord your God g' you. "
10 Lord your God g' you to inherit, *
10 and when he g' you rest from all
13: 1 and g' thee a sign or a wonder, *5414
15: 4 which the Lord thy God g' thee "
7 God g' thee, thou shalt not harden "
16: 5 which the Lord thy God g' thee: "
18 thy God g' thee, throughout thy "
20 the land which the Lord thy God g' "
17: 2 the Lord thy God g' thee, man or "
14 which the Lord thy God g' thee, "
18: 9 which the Lord thy God g' thee, "
19: 1 whose land the Lord thy God g' "
2 which the Lord thy God g' thee to "
3 God g' thee to inherit, into three*
10 thy God g' thee for an inheritance, 5414
14 Lord thy God g' thee to possess "
21: 1 which the Lord thy God g' thee to "
23 the Lord thy God g' thee for an "
24: 3 a bill of divorcement, and g' it * "
4 which the Lord thy God g' thee for "
25:15 which the Lord thy God g' thee. "
19 the land which the Lord thy God g' "
26: 1 thy God g' thee for an inheritance, "
2 that the Lord thy God g' thee, and "
27: 2 the Lord thy God g' thee, that thou "
3 thy God g' thee, a land that floweth "
28: 8 which the Lord thy God g' thee. "
Jos 1:11 which the Lord your God g' you "
15 which the Lord your God g' them: "
J'g 11:24 Chemosh thy god g' thee to possess?
21:18 Cursed be he that g' a wife to 5414
Job 5:10 Who g' rain upon the earth, and
14:10 yea, man g' up the ghost, and 1478
32: 8 the Almighty g' them understanding.
33:13 g' not account of any of his matters.
34:29 When he g' quietness, who then
35:10 who g' songs in the night; 5414
12 There they cry, but none g' answer,
36: 6 but g' right to the poor. 5414
31 he g' meat in abundance.
Ps 18:50 Great deliverance g' he to his king;
37:21 righteous sheweth mercy, and g'. 5414
68:35 he that g' strength and power "
119:130 The entrance of thy words g' light;
130 it g' understanding unto the simple.
127: 2 for so he g' his beloved sleep. 5414
136:25 Who g' food to all flesh: for his "
144:10 is he that g' salvation unto kings: "
146: 7 which g' food to the hungry. "
147: 9 He g' to the beast his food, "
16 He g' snow like wool: he "
Pr 2: 6 For the Lord g' wisdom: out of his "
3:34 but he g' grace unto the lowly. "
13:15 Good understanding g' favour; "
17: 4 A wicked doer g' heed to false lips;
4 and a liar g' ear to a naughty tongue.
19: 6 is a friend to him that g' gifts.
21:26 the righteous g' and spareth not. 5414
22: 9 he g' of his bread to the poor. "
16 he that g' to the rich, shall surely "
23:31 when it g' his colour in the cup, "
24:26 kiss his lips that g' a right answer.
26: 8 so is he that g' honour to a fool. 5414
28:27 that g' unto the poor shall not lack: "
31:15 and g' meat to her household, and "
Ec 2:26 For God g' to a man that is good "
26 but to the sinner he g' travail, to "
5:18 days of his life, which God g' him:* "
6: 2 God g' him not power to eat thereof, "
7:12 wisdom g' life to them that have *
8:15 which God g' him under the sun.*5414
Isa 40:29 He g' power to the faint; and to "
42: 5 that g' breath unto the people "
Jer 5:24 the Lord our God, that g' rain, "
22:13 and g' him not for his work; "
31:35 Lord, which g' the sun for a light "
La 3:30 g' his cheek to him that smiteth * "
Da 2:21 he g' wisdom unto the wise, and 3052
4:17 and g' it to whomsoever he will, 5415
25, 32 and g' it to whomsoever he will. "
Hab 2:15 him that g' his neighbour drink,
M't 5:15 and it g' light unto all that are in *
Joh 3:34 God g' not the Spirit by measure 1325
6:32 my Father g' you the true bread "
33 and g' life unto the world. "
37 All that the Father g' me shall "
10:11 good shepherd g' his life for the *5087
14:27 not as the world g', give I unto you.1325
21:13 taketh bread, and g' them, and fish "
Ac 17:25 seeing he g' to all life, and breath, "
Ro 12: 8 he that g', let him do it with 3330
14: 6 for he g' God thanks; and he that
6 eateth not, and g' God thanks.
1Co 3: 7 but God that g' the increase.
7:38 he that g' her in marriage doeth well;
38 but he that g' her not in marriage
15:38 God g' it a body as it hath pleased 1325
57 God which g' us the victory through "
2Co 3: 6 killeth, but the Spirit g' life.
1Ti 6:17 g' us richly all things to enjoy; 3930
Jas 1: 5 ask of God, that g' to all men 1325
4: 6 But he g' more grace. Wherefore "
6 but g' grace unto the humble. "
1Pe 4:11 it as of the ability which God g': *5524
5: 5 proud, and g' grace to the humble.1325
Re 22: 5 for the Lord God g' them light: *

giving See also FORGIVING; THANKSGIVING.
Ge 24:19 when she had done g' him drink.

De 10:18 in g' him food and raiment. 5414
21:17 by g' him a double portion of all "
Ru 1: 6 visited his people in g' them bread." "
1Ki 5: 9 in g' food for my household. "
2Ch 6:23 by g' him according to his * "
Ezr 3:11 praising and g' thanks unto the Lord; "
Job 11:20 shall be as the g' up of the ghost. 4646
M't 24:38 marrying and g' in marriage, "
Lu 17:16 at his feet, g' him thanks: and he was "
Ac 8: 9 g' out that himself was some *3004*
15: 8 g' them the Holy Ghost, even as *1325*
Ro 4:20 strong in faith, g' glory to God; "
9: 4 covenants, and the g' of the law, *3548*
1Co 14: 7 even things without life g' sound, *1325*
16 say Amen at thy g' of thanks, "
2Co 6: 3 G' no offence in any thing, that *1325*
Eph 5: 4 but rather g' of thanks. "
20 G' thanks always for all things "
Ph'p 4:15 concerning g' and receiving, but *1394*
Col 1:12 G' thanks unto the Father, which "
3:17 g' thanks to God and the Father "
1Ti 2: 1 intercessions, and g' of thanks, * "
4: 1 g' heed to seducing spirits, and "
Tit 1:14 Not g' heed to Jewish fables, and "
Heb 13:15 of our lips g' thanks to his name.* "
1Pe 3: 7 g' honour unto the wife, as unto *632*
2Pe 1: 5 g' all diligence, add to your faith *3923*
Jude 7 g' themselves over to fornication.* "

Gizonite (*ghi'-zo-nite*)
1Ch 11:34 sons of Hashem the G', Jonathan 1493

glad
Ex 4:14 thee, he will be g' in his heart. 8056
J'g 18:20 And the priest's heart was g', 3190
1Sa 11: 9 men of Jabesh; and they were g'. 8056
1Ki 8:66 joyful and g' of heart for all the 2896
1Ch 16:31 Let the heavens be g', and let 8056
2Ch 7:10 g' and merry in heart for the "
Es 5: 9 day joyful and with a g' heart: 2896
8:15 of Shushan rejoiced and was g'. 8056
Job 3:22 rejoice exceedingly, and are g', 7797
22:19 The righteous see it, and are g': 8056
Ps 9: 2 I will be g' and rejoice in thee: "
14: 7 rejoice, and Israel shall be g'. "
16: 9 heart is g', and my glory rejoiceth: "
21: 6 thou hast made him exceeding g' 2302
31: 7 be g' and rejoice in thy mercy: 1523
32:11 Be g' in the Lord, and rejoice, 8056
34: 2 shall hear thereof, and be g'. "
35:27 Let them shout for joy, and be g'. "
40:16 rejoice and be glad in thee
45: 8 whereby they have made thee g'. "
46: 4 shall make g' the city of God, "
48:11 let the daughters of Judah be g', *1523
53: 6 rejoice, and Israel shall be g'. 8056
64:10 righteous shall be g' in the Lord, "
67: 4 O let the nations be g' and sing "
68: 3 But let the righteous be g'; let "
69:32 humble shall see this, and be g': "
70: 4 seek thee rejoice and be g' in thee: "
90:14 that we may rejoice and be g' all "
15 Make us g' according to the days "
92: 4 hast made me g' through thy work: "
96:11 and let the earth be g'; let the sea1523
97: 1 let the multitude of isles be g' 8056
8 Zion heard, and was g'; and the "
104:15 wine that maketh g' the heart of "
34 I will be g' in the Lord. * "
105:38 Egypt was g' when they departed: "
107:30 Then are they g' because they be "
118:24 we will rejoice and be g' in it. "
119:74 They that fear thee will be g' "
122: 1 I was g' when they said unto me, "
126: 3 things for us; whereof we are g'. "
Pr 10: 1 A wise son maketh a g' father: "
12:25 but a good word maketh it g'. "
15:20 A wise son maketh a g' father: "
17: 5 and he that is g' at calamities "
23:25 father and thy mother shall be g', "
24:17 let not thine heart be g' when he 1523
27:11 be wise, and make my heart g', 8056
Ca 1: 4 we will be g' and rejoice in thee, 1523
Isa 25: 9 we will be g' and rejoice in his "
35: 1 solitary place shall be g' for them;7796
39: 2 And Hezekiah was g' of them, 8056
65:18 be ye g' and rejoice for ever 7796
66:10 and be g' with her, all ye that love 1523
Jer 20:15 unto thee; making him very g'. 8056
41:13 were with him, then they were g'. "
50:11 Because ye were g', because ye "
La 1:21 they are g' that thou hast done it:7796
4:21 Rejoice and be g', O daughter of 8056
Da 6:23 was the king exceeding g' for him,2868
Ho 7: 3 They make the king g' with their 8056
Joe 2:21 Fear not, O land; be g' and rejoice:1523
23 Be g' then, ye children of Zion, "
Jon 4: 6 So Jonah was exceeding g' of the 8056
Hab 1:15 therefore they rejoice and are g'. 1523
Zep 3:14 be g' and rejoice with all the 8056
Zec 10: 7 shall see it, and be g'; their heart "
M't 5:12 Rejoice, and be exceeding g': for *21*
M'r 14:11 when they heard it, they were g', *5463*
Lu 1:19 to shew thee these g' tidings. **2097*
8: 1 the g' tidings of the kingdom "
15:32 we should make merry, and be g':*5463*
22: 5 And they were g', and covenanted "
23: 8 saw Jesus, he was exceeding g': "
Joh 8:56 and he saw it, and was g'. "
11:15 And I am g' for your sakes that "
20:20 Then were the disciples g', when "
Ac 2:26 rejoice, and my tongue was g'; * *21*
11:23 was g', and exhorted them all, *5463*
13:32 we declare unto you g' tidings, **2097*
48 Gentiles heard this, they were g', *5463*
Ro 10:15 of peace, and bring g' tidings *2097*
16:19 I am g' therefore on your behalf: **5463*

1Co 16:17 am g' of the coming of Stephanas * "
2Co 2: 2 who is he then that maketh me g', *2165*
13: 9 For we are g', when we are weak, **5463*
1Pe 4:13 be g' also with exceeding joy. * "
Re 19: 7 Let us be g' and rejoice, and we * "

gladly
M'r 6:20 many things, and heard him g'. *2234*
12:37 the common people heard him g'. "
Lu 8:40 the people g' received him: "
Ac 2:41 they that g' received his word * *780*
21:17 the brethren received us g'. "
2Co 11:19 For ye suffer fools g', seeing ye *2234*
12: 9 Most g' therefore will I rather *2236*
15 I will very g' spend and be spent "

gladness
Nu 10:10 Also in the day of your g', 8057
De 28:47 joyfulness, and with g' of heart, 2898
2Sa 6:12 into the city of David with g'. *8057
1Ch 16:27 strength and g' are in his place. 2304
29:22 Lord on that day with great g'. 8057
2Ch 29:30 they sang praises with g', and "
30:21 bread seven days with great g': "
23 kept other seven days with g'. "
Ne 8:17 And there was very great g'. "
12:27 to keep the dedication with g', "
Es 8:16 The Jews had light, and g', and joy," "
17 Jews had joy and g', a feast 8342
9:17, 18 made it a day of feasting and g'.8057
19 day of the month Adar a day of g' "
Ps 4: 7 Thou hast put g' in my heart, "
30:11 sackcloth, and girded me with g'; "
45: 7 anointed thee with the oil of g' 8342
15 With g' and rejoicing shall they 8057
51: 8 Make me to hear joy and g'; "
97:11 and g' for the upright in heart. "
100: 2 Serve the Lord with g': come "
105:43 joy, and his chosen with g': *7440
106: 5 rejoice in the g' of thy nation, 8057
Pr 10:28 hope of the righteous shall be g': "
Ca 3:11 in the day of the g' of his heart. "
Isa 16:10 And g' is taken away, and joy out "
22:13 behold joy and g', slaying oxen, "
30:29 and g' of heart, as when one goeth "
35:10 they shall obtain joy and g , and "
51: 3 joy and g' shall be found therein, "
11 they shall obtain g' and joy; and "
Jer 7:34 voice of mirth, and the voice of g', "
16: 9 voice of mirth, and the voice of g', "
25:10 voice of mirth, and the voice of g', "
31: 7 Sing with g' for Jacob, and shout "
33:11 The voice of joy, and the voice of g'," "
48:33 And joy and g' is taken from the "
Joe 1:16 and g' from the house of our God?1524
Zec 8:19 to the house of Judah joy and g', 8057
M'r 4:16 immediately receive it with g'; **5479*
Lu 1:14 And thou shalt have joy and g'; *20*
Ac 2:46 with g' and singleness of heart, "
12:14 she opened not the gate for g', **5479*
14:17 filling our hearts with food and g'.*2167*
Ph'p 2:29 therefore in the Lord with all g'; **5479*
Heb 1: 9 hath anointed thee with the oil of g' *20*

glass See also GLASSES.
Job 37:18 and as a molten looking g'? *7209
1Co 13:12 now we see through a g' darkly; **2072*
2Co 3:18 beholding as in a g' the glory of **2734*
Jas 1:23 beholding his natural face in a g':**2072*
Re 4: 6 was a sea of g' like unto crystal: **5193*
15: 2 a sea of g' mingled with fire: "
2 sea of g', having the harps of God.* "
21:18 was pure gold, like unto clear g'. *5194*
21 gold, as it were transparent g'. "

glasses See also LOOKINGGLASSES.
Isa 3:23 The g', and the fine linen, and *1549

glean See also GLEANED; GLEANING.
Le 19:10 thou shalt not g' thy vineyard, 5953
De 24:21 thou shalt not g' it afterward: "
Ru 2: 2 and g' ears of corn after him 3950
7 let me g' and gather after the "
8 Go not to g' in another field, "
15 when she was risen up to g', "
15 Let her g' even among the sheaves," "
16 that she may g' them, and rebuke "
23 to g' unto the end of barley harvest" "
Jer 6: 9 shall thoroughly g' the remnant 5953

gleaned
J'g 20:45 they g' of them in the highways 5953
Ru 2: 3 g' in the field after the reapers: 3950
17 So she g' in the field until even, "
17 and beat out that she had g': "
18 mother in law saw what she had g':" "
19 Where hast thou g' to day? "

gleaning See also GLEANINGS.
Le 23:22 shalt thou gather any g' of thy 3951
J'g 8: 2 the g' of the grapes of Ephraim 5955
Isa 17: 6 Yet g' grapes shall be left in it, * "
24:13 as the g' grapes when the vintage* "
Jer 49: 9 they not leave some g' grapes? "

gleaning-grapes See GLEANING and GRAPES.

gleanings
Le 19: 9 shalt thou gather the g' of thy *3951

glede
De 14:13 And the g', and the kite, and the 7201

glistering See also GLITTERING.
1Ch 29: 2 g' stones, and of divers colours, *6320
Lu 9:29 his raiment was white and g'. **1823*

glitter See also GLITTERING.
Eze 21:10 it is furbished that it may g': *1300

glittering See also GLISTERING.
De 32:41 If I whet my g' sword, and mine 1300
Job 20:25 yea, the g' sword cometh out of "
39:23 the g' spear and the shield. *3851

Eze 21:28 to consume because of the g': *1300
Na 3: 3 the bright sword and the g' spear: "
Hab 3:11 at the shining of thy g' spear. "

gloominess
Joe 2: 2 A day of darkness and of g', a day 653
Zep 1:15 a day of darkness and g', a day of "

gloriest
Jer 49: 4 Wherefore g' thou in the valleys, 1984

glorieth
Jer 9:24 But let him that g' glory in this, 1984
1Co 1:31 that g', let him glory in the Lord. *2744*
2Co 10:17 that g', let him glory in the Lord. "

glorified
Le 10: 3 before all the people I will be g'. 3513
Isa 26:15 increased the nation: thou art g': "
44:23 Jacob, and g' himself in Israel. *6286
49: 3 O Israel, in whom I will be g'. "
55: 5 One of Israel; for he hath g' thee. "
60: 9 of Israel, because he hath g' thee. "
21 of my hands, that I may be g'. "
61: 3 of the Lord, that he might be g'. "
66: 5 Let the Lord be g': but he shall 3513
Eze 28:22 I will be g' in the midst of thee: "
39:13 that I shall be g', saith the Lord "
Da 5:23 are all thy ways, hast thou not g': 1922
Hag 1: 8 and I will be g', saith the Lord. 3513
M't 9: 8 they marvelled, and g' God, which *1392*
15:31 and they g' the God of Israel. "
M'r 2:12 then were all amazed, and g' God, "
Lu 4:15 their synagogues, being g' of all. "
5:26 were all amazed, and they g' God, "
7:16 they g' God, saying, That a great "
13:13 she was made straight, and g' God. "
17:15 and with a loud voice g' God. "
23:47 saw what was done, he g' God, "
Joh 7:39 because that Jesus was not yet g'.) "
11: 4 Son of God might be g' thereby. "
12:16 but when Jesus was g', then "
23 that the Son of man should be g'. "
28 I have both g' it, and will glorify "
13:31 Now is the Son of man g', "
31 and God is g' in him. "
32 If God be g' in him, God shall * "
14:13 the Father may be g' in the Son. "
15: 8 Herein is my Father g', that ye bear "
17: 4 I have g' thee on the earth: I "
10 and am g' in them. "
Ac 3:13 hath g' his Son Jesus; "
4:21 for all men g' God for that which "
11:18 they held their peace, and g' God, "
13:48 and g' the word of the Lord: and "
21:20 they g' the Lord, and said unto him," "
Ro 1:21 they g' him not as God, neither "
8:17 that we may be also g' together. *4888*
30 whom he justified, them he also g'.*1392*
Ga 1:24 And they g' God in me. "
2Th 1:10 shall come to be g' in his saints, *1740*
12 of our Lord Jesus Christ may be g' "
3: 1 may have free course and be g', *1392*
Heb 5: 5 Christ g' not himself to be made "
1Pe 4:11 may be g' through Jesus Christ, "
14 but on your part he is g'. * "
Re 18: 7 How much she hath g' herself, "

glorifieth
Ps 50:23 Whoso offereth praise g' me: and 3513

glorify See also GLORIFIED; GLORIFIETH; GLORIFYING.
Ps 22:23 all ye the seed of Jacob, g' him; 3513
50:15 deliver thee, and thou shalt g' me. "
86: 9 O Lord; and shall g' thy name. "
12 I will g' thy name for evermore. "
Isa 24:15 Wherefore g' ye the Lord in the "
25: 3 shall the strong people g' thee, "
60: 7 I will g' the house of my glory. 6286
Jer 30:19 I will also g' them, and they shall 3513
M't 5:16 see your good works, and g' your *1392*
Joh 12:28 Father, g' thy name. Then came "
28 have both glorified it, and will g' it "
13:32 God shall also g' him in himself, "
32 and shall straightway g' him. "
16:14 He shall g' me: for he shall receive "
17: 1 g' thy Son, that thy Son also "
1 that thy Son also may g' thee: "
5 O Father, g' thou me with thine "
21:19 by what death he should g' God. "
Ro 15: 6 one mind and one mouth g' God. "
9 the Gentiles might g' God for his "
1Co 6:20 therefore g' God in your body, "
2Co 9:13 they g' God for your professed "
1Pe 2:12 g' God in the day of visitation. "
4:16 let him g' God on this behalf. "
Re 15: 4 fear thee, O Lord, and g' thy name?" "

glorifying
Lu 2:20 g' and praising God for all things *1392*
5:25 departed to his own house, g' God. "
18:43 and followed him, g' God: "

glorious
Ex 15: 6 O Lord, is become g' in power: 142
11 who is like thee, g' in holiness, "
De 28:58 fear this g' and fearful name, 3513
2Sa 6:20 How g' was the king of Israel to day," "
1Ch 29:13 thank thee, and praise thy g' name.8597
Ne 9: 5 blessed be thy g' name, which is 3519
Es 1: 4 shewed the riches of his g' kingdom "
Ps 45:13 king's daughter is all g' within: 3520
66: 2 of his name: make his praise g'. 3519
72:19 And blessed be his g' name for ever: "
76: 4 Thou art more g' and excellent 215
87: 3 G' things are spoken of thee, O 3513
111: 3 His work is honourable and g': *1926
145: 5 I will speak of the g' honour of thy 3519
12 and the g' majesty of his kingdom.* "

Isa 4: 2 of the Lord be beautiful and g'. 3519
11:10 and his rest shall be g'.
22:23 and he shall be for a g' throne * "
28: 1 whose g' beauty is a fading flower, 6643
4 the g' beauty, which is on the head "
30:30 the Lord shall cause his g' voice 1935
33:21 But there the g' Lord will be * 117
49: 5 I be g' in the eyes of the Lord, *3513
60:13 I will make the place of my feet g'. "
63: 1 g' in his apparel, travelling in the 1921
12 with his g' arm, dividing the water 8597
14 people, to make thyself a g' name. "
Jer 17:12 A g' high throne from the 3519
Eze 27:25 wast replenished, and made very g'"
Da 11:16 and he shall stand in the g' land, 6643
41 He shall enter also into the g' land, "
45 the seas in the g' holy mountain; "
Lu 13:17 g' things that were done by him. 1741
Ro 8:21 g' liberty of the children of God. *1391
2Co 3: 7 engraven in stones, was g'. *1722,
8 of the spirit be rather g'? * "
10 which was made g' had no glory 1392
11 which is done away was g'. *1223, 1391
11 that which remaineth is g'. *1722 "
4: 4 the light of the g' gospel of Christ,* "
Eph 5:27 present it to himself a g' church, 1741
Ph'p 3:21 fashioned like unto his g' body, *1391
Col 1:11 according to his g' power, unto * "
1Ti 1:11 the g' gospel of the blessed God, * "
Tit 2:13 the g' appearing of the great God * "

gloriously
Ex 15: 1 the Lord, for he hath triumphed g':
21 to the Lord, for he hath triumphed g':
Isa 24:23 and before his ancients g'. 3519

glory See also GLORIEST; GLORIETH; GLORYING; VAINGLORY.
Ge 31: 1 hath he gotten all this g'. 3519
45:13 ye shall tell my father of all my g' "
Ex 8: 9 Moses said unto Pharaoh, G' over 6286
16: 7 ye shall see the g' of the Lord; 3519
10 g' of the Lord appeared in a cloud. "
24:16 g' of the Lord abode upon mount "
17 g' of the Lord was like devouring "
28: 2 thy brother for g' and for beauty. "
40 for them, for g' and for beauty. "
29:43 shall be sanctified by my g'. "
33:18 I beseech thee, shew me thy g'. "
22 while my g' passeth by, I will put "
40:34, 35 g' of the...filled the tabernacle. "
Le 9: 6 g' of the Lord shall appear unto you."
23 the g' of the Lord appeared unto all "
Nu 14:10 the g' of the Lord appeared in the "
21 be filled with the g' of the Lord. "
22 those men which have seen my g', "
16:19 the g' of the Lord appeared unto all "
42 and the g' of the Lord appeared. "
20: 6 g' of the Lord appeared unto them. "
De 5:24 Lord our God hath shewed us his g' "
33:17 His g' is like the firstling of his *1926
Jos 7:19 thee, g' to the Lord God of Israel, 3519
1Sa 2: 8 make them inherit the throne of g': "
4:21, 22 The g' is departed from Israel: "
6: 5 shall give g' unto the God of Israel: "
1Ki 8:11 g' of the Lord had filled the house "
2Ki 14:10 g' of this, and tarry at home: 3513
1Ch 16:10 G' ye in his holy name: let the 1984
24 Declare his g' among the heathen; 3519
27 G' and honour are in his presence;*1935
28 give unto the Lord g' and strength.3519
29 the Lord the g' due unto his name: "
35 holy name, and g' in thy praise. *7623
22: 5 and of g' throughout all countries:8597
29:11 and the power, and the g', "
2Ch 5:14 g' of the Lord had filled the house 3519
7: 1 the g' of the Lord filled the house. "
2 g' of the Lord had filled the Lord's "
3 the g' of the Lord upon the house, "
Es 5:11 Haman told them of the g' of his "
Job 19: 9 He hath stripped me of my g', "
29:20 My g' was fresh in me, and my "
39:20 the g' of his nostrils is terrible. 1935
40:10 array thyself with g' and beauty. * "
Ps 3: 3 my g', and the lifter up of mine 3519
4: 2 long will ye turn my g' into shame? "
8: 1 hast set thy g' above the heavens. 1935
5 crowned him with g' and honour. 3519
16: 9 and my g' rejoiceth: my flesh also "
19: 1 The heavens declare the g' of God; "
21: 5 His g' is great in thy salvation: "
24: 7 and the King of g' shall come in. "
8 Who is this King of g'? The Lord "
9 and the King of g' shall come in. "
10 Who is this King of g'? The Lord "
10 of hosts, he is the King of g'. "
29: 1 give unto the Lord g' and strength."
2 the Lord the g' due unto his name; "
3 the God of g' thundereth: the Lord "
9 doth every one speak of his g'. "
30:12 that my g' may sing praise to thee. "
45: 3 with thy g' and thy majesty. 1935
49:16 the g' of his house is increased; 3519
17 his g' shall not descend after him. "
57: 5 let thy g' be above all the earth. "
8 Awake up, my g'; awake, psaltery "
11 let thy g' be above all the earth. "
62: 7 In God is my salvation and my g': "
63: 2 To see thy power and thy g', "
11 one that sweareth by him shall g': 1984
64:10 all the upright in heart shall g'. "
72:19 whole earth be filled with his g'; 3519
73:24 and afterward receive me to g'. "
78:61 and his g' into the enemy's hand. 8597
79: 9 Help us...for the g' of thy name: 3519
84:11 the Lord will give grace and g': "
85: 9 that g' may dwell in our land. "

Ps 89:17 thou art the g' of their strength: 8597
44 Thou hast made his g' to cease, *2892
90:16 and thy g' unto their children. 1926
96: 3 Declare his g' among the heathen, 3519
7 give unto the Lord g' and strength. "
8 the Lord the g' due unto his name: "
97: 6 and all the people see his g'. "
102:15 and all the kings of the earth thy g'."
16 he shall appear in his g'. "
104:31 g' of the Lord shall endure for ever:"
105: 3 G' ye in his holy name: let the 1984
106: 5 I may g' with thine inheritance. "
20 Thus they changed their g' into 3519
108: 1 and give praise, even with my g'. "
5 and thy g' above all the earth; "
113: 4 and his g' above the heavens. "
115: 1 but unto thy name give g', for thy "
138: 5 for great is the g' of the Lord. "
145:11 speak of the g' of thy kingdom, "
148:13 g' is above the earth and heaven. 1935
149: 5 Let the saints be joyful in g': 3519
Pr 3:35 The wise shall inherit g': but "
4: 9 a crown of g' shall she deliver *8597
16:31 The hoary head is a crown of g', "
17: 6 the g' of children are their fathers. "
19:11 his g' to pass over a transgression. "
20:29 g' of young men is their strength: "
25: 2 the g' of God to conceal a thing: 3519
27 to search their own g' is not g'. "
28:12 men do rejoice, there is great g': 8597
Isa 2:10 and for the g' of his majesty. 1926
19, 21 and for the g' of his majesty, "
3: 8 to provoke the eyes of his g'. 3519
4: 5 upon all the g' shall be a defence. "
5:14 and their g', and their multitude, 1926
6: 3 the whole earth is full of his g'. 3519
8: 7 the king of Assyria, and all his g': "
10: 3 and where will ye leave your g'? "
12 and the g' of his high looks. 8597
16 and under his g' he shall kindle 3519
18 shall consume the g' of his forest, "
13:19 Babylon, the g' of kingdoms, the 6643
14:18 nations, even all of them, lie in g',3519
16:14 the g' of Moab shall be contemned, "
17: 3 shall be as the g' of the children "
4 the g' of Jacob shall be made thin, "
20: 5 expectation, and of Egypt their g'. 8597
21:16 and all the g' of Kedar shall fail: 3519
22:18 the chariots of thy g' shall be the "
24 him all the g' of his father's house, "
23: 9 to stain the pride of all g', and to 6643
24:16 songs, even g' to the righteous. "
28: 5 Lord of hosts be for a crown of g', "
35: 2 g' of Lebanon shall be given unto 3519
2 they shall see the g' of the Lord, "
40: 5 the g' of the Lord shall be revealed,"
41:16 shalt g' in the Holy One of Israel. 1984
42: 8 my g' will I not give to another, 3519
12 Let them give g' unto the Lord, "
43: 7 for I have created him for my g', "
45:25 of Israel be justified, and shall g'. 1984
46:13 salvation in Zion for Israel my g'.8597
48:11 I will not give my g' unto another.3519
58: 8 g' of the...shall be thy rereward. "
59:19 his g' from the rising of the sun. "
60: 1 and the g' of the Lord is risen upon"
2 and his g' shall be seen upon thee. "
7 I will glorify the house of my g'. 8597
13 The g' of Lebanon shall come 3519
19 light, and thy God thy g'. 8597
61: 6 and in their g' shall ye boast 3519
62: 2 and all kings thy g': and thou shalt"
3 Thou shalt also be a crown of g' *8597
63:15 of thy holiness and of thy g': "
66:11 with the abundance of her g'. 3519
12 the g' of the Gentiles like a flowing "
18 they shall come, and see my g'. "
19 neither have seen my g'; and they "
19 declare my g' among the Gentiles. "
Jer 2:11 my people have changed their g' "
4: 2 and in him shall they g'. 1984
9:23 Let not the wise man g' in his "
23 let the mighty man g' in his might,"
23 let not the rich man g' in his riches:"
24 But let him that glorieth g' in this, "
13:11 and for a praise, and for a g': 8597
16 Give g' to the Lord your God, 3519
18 down, even the crown of your g'. 8597
14:21 not disgrace the throne of thy g': 3519
22:18 saying, Ah Lord! or, Ah his g'! 1935
48:18 come down from thy g', and sit in 3519
Eze 1:28 the likeness of the g' of the Lord. "
3:12 Blessed be the g' of the Lord from "
23 the g' of the Lord stood there, "
23 as the g' which I saw by the river "
8: 4 the g' of the God of Israel was there,"
9: 3 the g' of the God of Israel was gone"
10: 4 the g' of the Lord went up from the"
4 of the brightness of the Lord's g'. "
18 the g' of the Lord departed from off"
19 the g' of the God of Israel was over "
11:22 the g' of the God of Israel was over "
23 the g' of the Lord went up from the"
20: 6 honey, which is the g' of all lands; 6643
15 honey, which is the g' of all lands; "
24:25 the joy of their g', the desire of 8597
25: 9 his frontiers, the g' of the country. 6643
26:20 I shall set g' in the land of the "
31:18 To whom art thou thus like in g' 3519
39:21 I will set my g' among the heathen, "
43: 2 g' of the God of Israel came from "
2 and the earth shined with his g'. "
4 And the g' of the Lord came into "
5 the g' of the Lord filled the house. "
44: 4 the g' of the Lord filled the house "
Da 2:37 power, and strength, and g'. 3367

Da 4:36 and for the g' of my kingdom, 3367
5:18 a kingdom, and majesty, and g', "
20 and they took his g' from him: "
7:14 was given him dominion, and g', "
11:20 of taxes in the g' of the kingdom: 1925
39 acknowledge and increase with g':3519
Hos 4: 7 therefore will I change their g' "
9:11 their g' shall fly away like a bird, "
10: 5 that rejoiced in it, for the g' thereof,"
Mic 1:15 come unto Adullam the g' of Israel."
2: 9 have ye taken away my g' for ever.1926
Na 2: 9 is none end of the store and g' 3519
Hab 2:14 with the knowledge of the g' of the "
16 Thou art filled with shame for g': "
16 shameful spewing shall be on thy g'."
3: 3 His g' covered the heavens, and 1935
Hag 2: 3 that saw this house in her first g'?3519
7 I will fill this house with g', saith "
9 The g' of this latter house shall be "
Zec 2: 5 will be the g' in the midst of her. "
8 After the g' hath he sent me unto "
6:13 he shall bear the g', and shall sit 1935
11: 3 for their g' is spoiled: a voice of 155
12: 7 that the g' of the house of David 8597
7 and the g' of the inhabitants of "
Mal 2: 2 give g' unto my name, saith the 3519
M't 4: 8 of the world, and the g' of them; 1391
6: 2 that they may have g' of men. 1392
13 the power, and the g', for ever. *1391
29 even Solomon in all his g' was not "
16:27 come in the g' of his Father with his "
19:28 also shall sit in the throne of his g', "
24:30 with power and great g'. "
25:31 the Son of man shall come in his g',"
31 shall he sit upon the throne of his g':"
M'r 8:38 cometh in the g' of his Father with "
10:37 other on thy left hand, in thy g'. "
13:26 the clouds with great power and g'. "
Lu 2: 9 and the g' of the Lord shone round "
14 G' to God in the highest, and on "
32 and the g' of thy people Israel. "
4: 6 will I give thee, and the g' of them:"
9:26 when he shall come in his own g', "
31 Who appeared in g', and spake of "
32 they saw his g', and the two men "
12:27 that Solomon in all his g' was not "
17:18 returned to give g' to God, save "
19:38 peace in heaven, and g' in the "
21:27 in a cloud with power and great g'. "
24:26 things, and to enter into his g'? "
Joh 1:14 we beheld his g', the g' as of the "
2:11 and manifested forth his g'; "
7:18 of himself seeketh his own g': but "
18 he that seeketh his g' that sent him,"
8:50 I seek not mine own g': there is "
11: 4 but for the g' of God, that the Son "
40 thou shouldest see the g' of God? "
12:41 said Esaias, when he saw his g', "
17: 5 with the g' which I had with thee "
22 And the g' which thou gavest me "
24 that they may behold my g', "
Ac 7: 2 The God of g' appeared unto our "
55 and saw the g' of God, and Jesus "
12:23 because he gave not God the g': "
22:11 could not see for the g' of that light, "
Ro 1:23 the g' of the uncorruptible God into "
2: 7 well doing seek for g' and honour "
10 g', honour, and peace, to every man"
3: 7 through my lie unto his g'; "
23 and come short of the g' of God; "
4: 2 he hath whereof to g'; but not 2745
20 strong in faith, giving g' to God; 1391
5: 2 and rejoice in hope of the g' of God."
3 but we g' in tribulations also: *2744
6: 4 the dead by the g' of the Father, 1391
8:18 the g' which shall be revealed in us."
9: 4 the adoption, and the g', and the "
23 make known the riches of his g' on "
23 he had afore prepared unto g', "
11:36 to whom be g' for ever. Amen. "
15: 7 also received us to the g' of God. "
17 I have therefore whereof I may g'*2746
16:27 To God only wise, be g' through 1391
1Co 1:29 no flesh should g' in his presence.2744
31 that glorieth, let him g' in the Lord."
2: 7 before the world unto our g': 1391
8 not have crucified the Lord of g'. "
3:21 Therefore let no man g' in men. 2744
4: 7 why dost thou g', as if thou hadst "
9:16 I have nothing to g' of: for 2745
10:31 ye do, do all to the g' of God. 1391
11: 7 as he is the image and g' of God: "
7 but the woman is the g' of the man."
15 have long hair, it is a g' to her: "
15:40 but the g' of the celestial is one, "
40 the g' of the terrestial is another. "
41 There is one g' of the sun, and "
41 and another g' of the moon, and "
41 and another g' of the stars: for "
41 differeth from another star in g'. "
43 sown in dishonour; it is raised in g':"
2Co 1:20 Amen, unto the g' of God by us. "
3: 7 g' of his countenance; which g' was"
9 ministration of condemnation be g',"
9 of righteousness exceed in g'. "
10 which was made glorious had no g'*1392
10 by reason of the g' that excelleth. 1391
18 as in a glass the g' of the Lord, "
18 into the same image from g' to g', "
4: 6 the knowledge of the g' of God "
15 of many redound to the g' of God. "
17 exceeding and eternal weight of g'; "
5:12 you occasion to g' on our behalf, *2745
12 them which g' in appearance, 2744
8:19 by us to the g' of the same Lord, 1391
23 the churches, and the g' of Christ. "

2Co 10:17 glorieth, let him g· in the Lord. 2744
11:12 that wherein they g·, they may be "
18 Seeing that many g· after the flesh, "
18 after the flesh, I will g· also. "
30 If I must needs g·, I will g· of the "
12: 1 expedient for me doubtless to g·. "
5 Of such an one will I g·: "
5 yet of myself I will not g·, "
6 For though I would desire to g·, "
9 will I rather g· in my infirmities, "
Ga 1: 5 To whom be g· for ever and ever. 1391
5:26 Let us not be desirous of vain g·, *2755
6:13 that they may g· in your flesh. 2744
14 But God forbid that I should g·, "
Eph 1: 6 To the praise of the g· of his grace, 1391
12 should be to the praise of his g·, "
14 possession unto the praise of his g·. "
17 the Father of g·, may give unto you "
18 riches of the g· of his inheritance "
3:13 tribulations for you, which is your g·. "
16 according to the riches of his g·, "
21 Unto him be g· in the church by "
Ph'p 1:11 unto the g· and praise of God. "
2:11 is Lord, to the g· of God the Father. "
3:19 and whose g· is in their shame, "
4:19 to his riches in g· by Christ Jesus. "
20 our Father be g· for ever and ever. "
Col 1:27 the riches of the g· of this mystery "
27 is Christ in you, the hope of g·: "
3: 4 shall ye also appear with him in g·. "
1Th 2: 6 Nor of men sought we g·, neither "
12 called you unto his kingdom and g·. "
20 For ye are our g· and joy. "
2Th 1: 4 So that we ourselves g· in you 2744
9 and from the g· of his power; 1391
2:14 of the g· of our Lord Jesus Christ. "
1Ti 1:17 be honour and g· for ever and ever. "
3:16 in the world, received up into g·. "
2Ti 2:10 is in Christ Jesus with eternal g·. "
4:18 to whom be g· for ever and ever. "
Heb 1: 3 Who being the brightness of his g·, "
2: 7 crownedst him with g· and honour, "
9 suffering of death, crowned with g· "
10 in bringing many sons unto g·, "
3: 3 worthy of more g· than Moses, "
9: 5 it the cherubims of g· shadowing "
13:21 to whom be g· for ever and ever. "
Jas 2: 1 Lord Jesus Christ, the Lord of g·, "
3:14 g· not, and lie not against the 2620
1Pe 1: 7 honour and g· at the appearing of 1391
8 joy unspeakable and full of g·: 1392
11 and the g· that should follow. *1391
21 up from the dead, and gave him g·; "
24 the g· of man as the flower of grass. "
2:20 For what g· is it, if, when ye be 2811
4:13 when his g· shall be revealed, 1391
14 the spirit of g· and of God resteth "
5: 1 a partaker of the g· that shall be "
4 ye shall receive a crown of g· that "
10 hath called us unto his eternal g· "
11 him be g· and dominion for ever * "
2Pe 1: 3 that hath called us to g· and virtue: "
17 from God the Father honour and g·, "
17 voice to him from the excellent g·, "
3:18 To him be g· both now and for ever. "
Jude 24 before the presence of his g· with "
25 our Saviour, be g· and majesty, "
Re 1: 6 to him be g· and dominion for ever "
4: 9 those beasts give g· and honour "
11 receive g· and honour and power: "
5:12 and honour, and g·, and blessing. "
13 Blessing, and honour, and g·, and "
7:12 Saying, Amen: Blessing, and g·, "
11:13 and gave g· to the God of heaven. "
14: 7 Fear God, and give g· to him; "
15: 8 with smoke from the g· of God, "
16: 9 they repented not to give him g·. "
18: 1 the earth was lightened with his g·. "
19: 1 Salvation, and g·, and honour, and "
21:11 Having the g· of God: and her light "
23 for the g· of God did lighten it, and "
24 bring their g· and honour into it. "
26 they shall bring the g· and honour "

glorying
1Co 5: 6 Your g· is not good. Know ye not 2745
9:15 any man should make my g· void. "
2Co 7: 4 great is my g· of you: 2746
12:11 I am become a fool in g·; ye have *2744

glutton
De 21:20 he is a g·, and a drunkard. *2151
Pr 23:21 the drunkard and the g· shall come "

gluttonous
M't 11:19 a man g·, and a winebibber, a 5314
Lu 7:34 Behold a g· man, and a winebibber.

gnash See also GNASHED; GNASHETH; GNASHING.
Ps 112:10 he shall g· with his teeth, and 2786
La 2:16 they hiss and g· the teeth: they "

gnashed
Ps 35:16 they g· upon me with their teeth. 2786
Ac 7:54 they g· on him with their teeth. 1031

gnasheth
Job 16: 9 he g· upon me with his teeth; *2786
Ps 37:12 and g· upon him with his teeth. "
M'r 9:18 foameth, and g· with his teeth, *5149

gnashing
M't 8:12 shall be weeping and g· of teeth. 1030
13:42, 50 shall be wailing and g· of teeth. "
22:13 shall be weeping and g· of teeth. "
24:51 shall be weeping and g· of teeth. "
25:30 shall be weeping and g· of teeth. "
Lu 13:28 shall be weeping and g· of teeth, "

gnat
M't 23:24 which strain at a g·, and swallow 2971

gnaw See also GNAWED.
Zep 3: 3 they g· not the bones till the *1633

gnawed
Re 16:10 and they g· their tongues for pain, 3145

go See also AGO; GOEST; GOETH; GOING; GONE; WENT.
Ge 3:14 upon thy belly shalt thou g·, and 3212
8:16 G· forth of the ark, thou, and thy 3318
9:10 g· out of the ark, to every beast "
11: 3 G· to, let us make brick, and burn 3051
4 G· to, let us build us a city and a "
7 G· to, let us...down, and there "
7 let us g· down, and there confound 3381
31 to g· into the land of Canaan; 3212
12: 5 forth to g· into the land of Canaan; "
19 thy wife, take her, and g· thy way. "
13: 9 then I will g· to the right; or if thou "
9 right hand, then I will g· to the left. "
15: 2 seeing I g· childless, and the 1980
15 shalt g· to thy fathers in peace; 935
16: 2 I pray thee, g· in unto my maid; "
8 whither wilt thou g·? And she *3212
18:21 I will g· down now, and see 3381
19: 2 rise up early, and g· on your ways. 1980
34 and g· thou in, and lie with him. 935
22: 5 I and the lad will g· yonder and 3212
24: 4 But thou shalt g· unto my country, "
11 that women g· out to draw water. 3318
38 shalt g· unto my father's house, 3212
42 do prosper my way which I g·: 1980
51 is before thee, take her, and g·, 3212
55 at least ten; after that she shall g·. "
56 away that I may g· to my master. "
58 Wilt thou g· with this man? "
58 And she said, I will g·. "
26: 2 G· not down into Egypt; dwell in 3381
16 said unto Isaac, G· from us; 3212
27: 3 and g· out to the field, and take 3318
9 G· now to the flock, and fetch me 3212
13 my voice, and g· fetch me them. "
28: 2 Arise, g· to Padan-aram, to the "
20 in this way that I g·, and will give 1980
29: 7 ye the sheep, and g· and feed 3212
21 that I may g· in unto her. 935
30: 3 g· in unto her; and she shall bear "
25 I may g· unto mine own place, 3212
26 I have served thee, and let me g·: "
31:18 for to g· to Isaac his father in the 935
32:26 And he said, Let me g·, for the day 7971
26 let thee g·, except thou bless me. "
33:12 take our journey, and let us g·, 3212
12 and I will g· before thee. "
35: 1 unto Jacob, Arise, g· up to Beth-el, 5927
3 let us arise, and g· up to Beth-el; "
37:14 he said to him, G·, I pray thee, 3212
17 Let us g· to Dothan. And Joseph "
30 is not; and I, whither shall I g·? 935
35 I will g· down into the grave unto 3381
38: 8 G· in unto thy brother's wife, and 935
16 G· to, I pray thee, let me come in 3051
41:55 said unto all the Egyptians, G· 3212
42:15 ye shall not g· forth hence, except 3318
19 g· ye, carry corn for the famine 3212
38 My son shall not g· down with you; 3381
38 the way in which ye g·, 3212
43: 2 father said unto them, G· again, 7725
4 will g· down and buy thee food: 3381
5 not send him, we will not g· down: "
8 we will arise and g·; that we may 3212
13 your brother, and arise, g· again 7725
44:25 our father said, G· again, and buy "
26 And we said, We cannot g· down: 3381
26 be with us, then will we g· down: "
33 the lad g· up with his brethren. 5927
34 For how shall I g· up to my father, "
45: 1 Cause every man to g· out from 3318
9 Haste ye, and g· up to my father, 5927
17 and g·, get you unto the land of 3212
28 I will g· and see him before I die. "
46: 3 fear not to g· down into Egypt; 3381
4 I will g· down with thee into Egypt; "
31 I will g· up, and shew Pharaoh, 5927
50: 5 let me g· up, I pray thee, and bury "
6 said, G· up, and bury thy father, "
Ex 2: 7 Shall I g· and call to thee a nurse 3212
8 Pharaoh's daughter said to her, G·. "
3:11 am I, that I should g· unto Pharaoh, "
16 G·, and gather the elders of Israel "
18 now let us g·, we beseech thee, "
19 king of Egypt will not let you g·, 1980
20 and after that he will let you g·. 7971
21 come to pass, that when ye g·, 3212
21 ye shall not g· empty: "
4:12 Now therefore g·, and I will be with "
18 Let me g·, I pray thee, and return "
18 Jethro said to Moses, G· in peace. "
19 G·, return into Egypt: for all the "
21 that he shall not let the people g·. 7971
23 Let my son g·, that he may serve "
23 if thou refuse to let him g·, behold, "
26 So he let him g·: then she said, *7503
27 G· into the wilderness to meet 3212
5: 1 Let my people g·, that they may 7971
2 obey his voice to let Israel g·? "
2 neither will I let Israel g·. "
3 let us g·, we pray thee, three days' 3212
7 g· and gather straw for themselves. "
8 Let us g· and sacrifice to our God. "
11 G· ye, get you straw where ye can "
17 Let us g· and do sacrifice to the Lord. "
18 G· therefore now, and work; for "
6: 1 a strong hand shall he let them g·, 7971
Ex 6:11 G· in, speak unto Pharaoh king of 935
11 that he let the children of Israel g· 7971
7:14 he refuseth to let the people g·. "
16 unto thee, saying, Let my people g·, "
8: 1 G· unto Pharaoh, and say unto 935
1 Let my people g·, that they may 7971
2 if thou refuse to let them g·, "
3 g· up and come into thine house, 5927
8 and I will let the people g·, that 7971
20 Let my people g·, that they may "
21 if thou wilt not let my people g·, "
25 G· ye, sacrifice to your God in the 3212
27 We will g· three days' journey into "
28 said, I will let you g·, that ye may 7971
28 only ye shall not g· very far away: 3212
29 Behold, I g· out from thee, and I 3318
29 letting the people g· to sacrifice 7971
32 neither would he let the people g·. "
9: 1 G· in unto Pharaoh, and tell him, 935
1 Let my people g·, that they may 7971
2 For if thou refuse to let them g·, "
7 and he did not let the people g·. "
13 Let my people g·, that they may "
28 and I will let you g·, and ye shall "
35 he let the children of Israel g·; "
10: 1 G· in unto Pharaoh, for I have 935
3 let my people g·, that they may 7971
4 if thou refuse to let my people g·, "
7 let the men g·, that they may serve "
8 G·, serve the Lord your God: 3212
8 but who are they that shall g·? 1980
9 We will g· with our young and 3212
9 and with our herds will we g·; "
10 as I will let you g·, and your little 7971
11 g· now ye that are men, and serve 3212
20 not let the children of Israel g·. 7971
24 G· ye, serve the Lord; and let 3212
24 let your little ones also g· with you. "
26 Our cattle also shall g· with us; "
27 and he would not let them g·. 7971
11: 1 afterwards he will let you g· hence: "
1 when he shall let you g·, he shall "
4 About midnight will I g· out into 3318
8 after that I will g· out. And he "
10 not let the children of Israel g· 7971
12:22 none of you shall g· out at the 3318
31 and g·, serve the Lord, as ye have 3212
13:15 Pharaoh would hardly let us g·, 7971
17 Pharaoh had let the people g·, "
21 light; to g· by day and night: 3212
14: 5 that we have let Israel g· from 7971
15 of Israel, that they g· forward: 5265
16 children of Israel shall g· on dry 935
21 Lord caused the sea to g· back 3212
16: 4 the people shall g· out and gather 3318
29 let no man g· of his place on the "
17: 5 G· on before the people, and *5674
5 take in thine hand, and g·. 1980
9 Choose us out men, and g· out, 3318
18:23 all this people shall also g· to 935
19:10 G· unto the people, and sanctify 3212
12 that ye g· not up into the mount, 5927
21 G· down, charge the people, lest 3381
20:26 Neither shalt thou g· up by steps 5927
21: 2 he shall g· out free for nothing. 3318
3 he shall g· out by himself: if he "
3 then his wife shall g· out with him. "
4 and he shall g· out by himself. "
5 my children; I will not g· out free: "
7 not g· out as the menservants do. "
11 then shall she g· out free without "
26 let him g· free for his eye's sake. 7971
27 he shall let him g· free for his "
23:23 mine Angel shall g· before thee, 3212
24: 2 shall the people g· up with him. 5927
30:20 When they g· into the tabernacle 935
32: 1 us gods, which shall g· before us; 3212
7 said unto Moses, G·, get thee down: "
23 us gods, which shall g· before us: "
27 his sword by his side, and g· in 5674
30 now I will g· up unto the Lord; 5927
34 Therefore now g·, lead the people 3212
34 mine Angel shall g· before thee: "
33: 1 unto Moses, Depart, and g· up 5927
3 I will not g· up in the midst of thee; "
14 My presence shall g· with thee, 3212
15 If thy presence g· not with me, 1980
34: 9 Lord, I pray thee, g· among us; 3212
15 g· a whoring after their gods, ‡
16 their daughters g· a whoring ‡
16 and make thy sons g· a whoring ‡
24 when thou shalt g· up to appear *5927
Le 6:13 on the altar; it shall never g· out. 3518
8:33 ye shall not g· out of the door 3318
9: 7 G· unto the altar, and offer thy *7126
10: 7 ye shall not g· out from the door 3318
9 when ye g· into the tabernacle of 935
11:27 that g· on all four, those are 1980
14: 3 And the priest shall g· forth out 3318
36 before the priest g· into it to see 935
36 the priest shall g· in to see the house: "
38 priest shall g· out of the house 3318
53 But he shall let g· the living bird 7971
15:16 man's seed of copulation g· out 3318
16:10 to let him g· for a scapegoat *7971
18 And he shall g· out unto the altar 3318
22 and he shall let g· the goat in the 7971
26 he that let g· the goat for the "
19:16 g· up and down as a talebearer 3212
20: 5 all that g· a whoring after him, ‡
6 wizards, to g· a whoring after ‡
21:11 shall he g· in to any dead body. 935
12 shall he g· out of the sanctuary, 3318
23 he shall not g· in unto the vail, 935
25:28 and in the jubile it shall g· out, 3318
30 it shall not g· out in the jubile. "

Le 25:31 and they shall g' out in the jubile. 3318
33 shall g' out in the year of jubile: "
54 he shall g' out in the year of jubile. "
26: 6 the sword g' through your land. 5674
13 yoke, and made you g' upright. 3212
Nu 1: 3 all that are able to g' forth to war 3318
20, 22, 24, 26, 30, 32, 34, 36, 38, 40, 42 all
that were able to g' forth to war: "
45 all that were able to g' forth to war "
2:24 shall g' forward in the third rank.*5265
31 g' hindmost with their standards.* "
4:19 Aaron and his sons shall g' in, 935
20 But they shall not g' in to see when "
5:12 man's wife g' aside, and commit a 7847
22 causeth the curse shall g' into thy 935
8:15 the Levites g' in to do the service "
24 shall g' in to wait upon the service "
10: 5 the east parts shall g' forward. *5265
9 And if ye g' to war in your land 935
30 he said unto him, I will not g'; but 3212
32 if thou g' with us, yea, it shall be, "
13:17 and g' up into the mountain: 5927
30 Let us g' up at once, and possess it: "
31 We be not able to g' up against the "
14:40 g' up unto the place which the Lord "
42 G' not up, for the Lord is not among "
44 presumed to g' up unto the hill top: "
15:39 which ye use to g' a whoring: ‡
16:30 they g' down quick into the pit; 3381
46 g' quickly unto the congregation, *3212
20:17 we will g' by the king's high way, "
19 him, We will g' by the high way: 5927
19 doing anything else, g' through *5674
20 said, Thou shalt not g' through. * "
21:22 g' along by the king's high way, 3212
22:12 Thou shalt not g' with them; thou "
13 to give me leave to g' with you. 1980
18 cannot g' beyond the word of the 5674
20 thee, rise up, and g' with them; 3212
35 G' with the men: but only the word "
23: 3 by thy burnt offering, and I will g': "
16 G' again unto Balak, and say thus.7725
24:13 g' beyond the commandment of 5674
14 now, behold, I g' unto my people: 1980
26: 2 all that are able to g' to war in 3318
27:17 Which may g' out before them, "
17 which may g' in before them, * 935
21 at his word shall they g' out, and 3318
31: 3 let them g' against the Midianites,1961
23 shall make it g' through the fire, 5674
23 ye shall make g' through the water. "
32: 6 Shall your brethren g' to war, 935
9 that they should not g' into the land "
17 ourselves will g' ready armed before
20 if ye will g' armed before the Lord
21 g' all of you armed over Jordan *5674
34: 4 and shall g' on to Hazar-addar, 3318
9 the border shall g' on to Ziphron, "
11 coast shall g' down from Shepham,3381
12 the border shall g' down to Jordan, "
De 1: 7 g' to the mount of the Amorites, 935
8 g' in and possess the land which "
21 before thee: g' up and possess it, 5927
22 by what way we must g' up, and "
26 ye would not g' up, but rebelled "
28 Whither shall we g' up? our "
33 you by what way ye should g', 3212
37 Thou also shalt not g' in thither. 935
38 he shall g' in thither: encourage "
39 they shall g' in thither, and unto "
41 we will g' up and fight, according 5927
41 ye were ready to g' up into the hill. "
42 G' not up, neither fight; for I am "
2:27 I will g' along by the high way, 3212
3:25 I pray thee, let me g' over, and 5674
27 thou shalt not g' over this Jordan. "
28 he shall g' over before this people, "
4: 1 and g' in and possess the land 935
5 the land whither ye g' to possess it. "
14 them in the land whither ye g' over 5674
21 that I should not g' over Jordan, "
21 and that I should not g' in unto that935
22 land, I must not g' over Jordan: 5674
22 but ye shall g' over, and possess "
26 ye g' over Jordan to possess it; "
34 hath God assayed to g' and take him 935
40 that it may g' well with thee, and with
5:16 that it may g' well with thee, in the
27 G' thou near, and hear all that 7126
30 G' say to them, Get you into your 3212
6: 1 the land whither ye g' to possess 5674
14 Ye shall not g' after other gods, 3212
18 that thou mayest g' in and possess 935
8: 1 and g' in and possess the land which "
9: 1 to g' in to possess nations greater "
5 dost thou g' to possess their land; "
23 G' up and possess the land which 5927
10:11 may g' in and possess the land, 935
11: 8 and g' in and possess the land "
8 land, whither ye g' to possess it; 5674
10 whither thou goest in to possess it, 935
28 to g' after other gods, which ye 3212
31 Jordan to g' in to possess the land 935
12:10 when ye g' over Jordan, and dwell5674
25 that it may g' well with thee, and with
26 g' unto the place which the Lord 935
28 that it may g' well with thee, and with
13: 2 Let us g' after other gods, which 3212
6 g' and serve other gods, which thou "
13 g' and serve other gods, which ye "
14:25 g' unto the place which the Lord 1980
15:12 shalt let him g' free from thee. 7971
13 shalt not let him g' away empty: "
16 I will not g' away from thee; 3318
16: 7 morning, and g' unto thy tents. 1980
19:13 that it may g' well with thee.

De 19:21 life shall g' for life, eye for eye, tooth
20: 5 let him g' and return to his house, 3212
6 also g' and return unto his house, "
7, 8 him g' and return unto his house, "
21:13 after that thou shalt g' in unto her, 935
14 shalt let her g' whither she will; 7971
22: 1 brother's ox or his sheep g' astray,
7 shalt in any wise let the dam g', 7971
13 and g' in unto her, and hate her, 935
23:10 shall he g' abroad out of the camp, 3318
12 whither thou shalt g' forth abroad: "
24: 2 out of his house, she may g' and be 1980
5 he shall not g' out to war, neither 3318
10 thou shalt not g' into his house 935
15 shall the sun g' down upon it;
19 thou shalt not g' again to fetch it: 7725
20 shalt not g' over the boughs again:
25: 5 brother shall g' in unto her, and 935
7 then let his brother's wife g' up 5927
26: 2 and shalt g' unto the place which 1980
3 And thou shalt g' unto the priest * 935
27: 3 that thou mayest g' in unto the land "
28:14 thou shalt not g' aside from any *5493
14 g' after other gods to serve them. 3212
25 shalt g' out one way against them,3318
41 for they shall g' into captivity. 3212
29:18 to g' and serve the gods of these "
30:12 Who shall g' up for us to heaven, 5927
13 Who shall g' over the sea for us, 5674
18 over Jordan to g' to possess it. 935
31: 2 I can no more g' out and come in: 3318
2 Thou shalt not g' over this Jordan. 5674
3 he will g' over before thee, and he "
3 Joshua, he shall g' over before thee, "
6 he it is that doth g' with thee; 1980
7 for thou must g' with this people 935
8 he it is that doth g' before thee; 1980
13 ye g' over Jordan to possess it. 5674
16 and g' a whoring after the gods ‡
16 whither they g' to be among them, 935
21 imagination which they g' about,‡6213
32:47 ye g' over Jordan to possess it. 5674
52 but thou shalt not g' thither unto 935
34: 4 but thou shalt not g' over thither. 5674
Jos 1: 2 therefore arise, g' over this Jordan, "
11 to g' in to possess the land, which 935
16 thou sendest us, we will g'. 3212
2: 1 G' view the land, even Jericho. "
16 afterward may ye g' your way. "
19 that whosoever shall g' out of the 3318
3: 3 from your place, and g' after it. 1980
4 the way by which ye must g': 3212
6: 3 and g' round about the city once. *5362
22 G' into the harlot's house, and 935
7: 2 G' up and view the country. 5927
3 Let not all the people g' up; but let "
3 about two or three thousand g' up "
8: 1 g' up to Ai: see, I have given into "
3 people of war, to g' up against Ai: "
4 g' not very far from the city, 7368
9:11 and g' to meet them, and say unto 3212
12 day we came forth to g' unto you; "
10:13 hasted not to g' down about a 935
14:11 both to g' out, and to come in. 3318
18: 3 ye slack to g' to possess the land, 935
4 rise, and g' through the land, *1980
8 G' and walk through the land, 3212
22: 9 to g' unto the country of Gilead, "
12 to g' up to war against them. 5927
33 not intend to g' up against them * "
23:12 if ye do in any wise g' back, and 7725
12 g' in unto them, and they to you: 935
J'g 1: 1 Who shall g' up for us against 5927
2 the Lord said, Judah shall g' up: "
3 will g' with thee into thy lot. 1980
25 let g' the man and all his family. 7971
2: 1 I made you to g' up out of Egypt, 5927
6 Joshua had let the people g', *7971
4: 6 G' and draw toward mount Tabor, 3212
8 unto her, If thou wilt g' with me, "
8 then I will g': but if thou 1980
8 but if thou wilt not g' with me, 3212
8 with me, then I will not g'. "
9 she said, I will surely g' with thee: "
5:11 the people of the Lord g' down *3381
6:14 G' in this thy might, and thou 3212
7: 3 g' to, proclaim in the ears of the 4994
4 unto thee, This shall g' with thee, 3212
4 the same shall g' with thee; "
4 thee, This shall not g' with thee, "
4 with thee, the same shall not g'. "
7 all the other people g' every man "
10 But if thou fear to g' down, 3381
10 g' thou with Phurah...down to "
11 hands be strengthened to g' down "
9: 9, 11, 13 g' to be promoted over the 1980
38 g' out, I pray now, and fight with 3318
10:14 G' and cry unto the gods which 3212
11: 8 that thou mayest g' with us, and 1980
35 and I cannot g' back. 7725
37 two months, that I may g' up 3212
38 And he said, G'. And he sent her "
12: 1 didst not call us to g' with thee? "
5 escaped said, Let me g' over; 5674
15: 1 g' in to my wife into the chamber. 935
1 father would not suffer him to g' in. "
5 the brands on fire, he let them g' 7971
16:17 then my strength will g' from me,5493
20 g' out as at other times before, 3318
17: 9 I g' to sojourn where I may find 1980
18: 2 G', search the land: who when 3212
5 which we g' shall be prosperous. 1980
6 said unto them, G' in peace: 3212
6 Lord is your way wherein ye g'. "
9 that we may g' up against them: 5927
9 be not slothful to g', and to enter 3212

J'g 18:10 ye g', ye shall come unto a people 935
19 g' with us, and be to us a father 3212
19: 5 and afterward g' your way. "
9 way, that thou mayest g' home. 1980
15 to g' in and to lodge in Gibeah: 935
25 began to spring, they let her g'. 7971
27 went out to g' his way: and, 3212
20: 8 We will not any of us g' to his tent, "
14 to g' out to battle against the 3318
18 of us shall g' up first to the battle 5927
23 Shall I g' up again to battle *5066
23 And the Lord, G' up against him. 5927
28 Shall I yet again g' out to battle 3318
28 And the Lord said, G' up; for to 5927
21:10 G' and smite the inhabitants of 3212
20 G' and lie in wait in the vineyards; "
21 and g' to the land of Benjamin. 1980
Ru 1: 8 G', return each to her mother's 3212
11 why will ye g' with me? are there "
12 again, my daughters, g' your way; "
16 for whither thou goest, I will g'; "
18 stedfastly minded to g' with her, "
2: 2 Let me now g' to the field, "
2 she said unto her, G', my daughter. "
8 G' not to glean in another field, "
8 neither g' from hence, but abide *5674
9 and g' thou after them: have I not 1980
9 art athirst, g' unto the vessels, "
22 that thou g' out with his maidens,3318
3: 4 shalt g' in, and uncover his feet, 935
17 G' not empty unto thy mother in "
1Sa 1:17 Eli answered and said, G' in peace:3212
22 I will not g' up until the child be
3: 9 Eli said unto Samuel, G', lie down:3212
5:11 let it g' again to his own place, 7725
6: 6 did they not let the people g', 7971
8 and send it away, that it may g'. 1980
20 to whom shall he g' up from us? 5927
8:20 g' out before us, and fight our 3318
22 G' ye every man unto his city. 3212
9: 3 and arise, g' seek the asses. "
6 let us g' thither; peradventure he "
6 shew us our way that we should g'.1980
7 we g', what shall we bring the man?3212
9 Come, and let us g' to the seer: "
10 Well said; come, let us g'. So they "
13 he g' up to the high place to eat: 5927
14 for to g' up to the high place. "
19 g' up before me unto the high place; "
19 and to morrow I will let thee g', 7971
10: 3 thou g' on forward from thence, 2498
8 shalt g' down before me to Gilgal; 3381
9 turned his back to g' from Samuel, 3212
11:14 Come, and let us g' to Gilgal, "
14: 1 let us g' over to the Philistines, 5674
4 Jonathan sought to g' over unto the "
6 and let us g' over unto the garrison "
9 still in our place, and will not g' up 5927
10 up unto us; then we will g' up: "
36 Let us g' down after the Philistines 3381
37 I g' down after the Philistines?
15: 3 Now g' and smite Amalek, and 3212
6 G', depart, get you down from "
18 G' and utterly destroy the sinners "
27 Samuel turned about to g' away, "
16: 1 fill thine horn with oil, and g', "
2 And Samuel said, How can I g'? "
17:32 g' and fight with this Philistine. "
33 not able to g' against this Philistine "
37 Saul said unto David, G', and the "
39 he assayed to g'; for he had not "
39 I cannot g' with these; for I have "
55 Saul saw David g' forth against 3318
18: 2 g' no more home to his father's 7725
19: 3 g' out and stand beside my father 3318
17 He said unto me, Let me g'; 7971
20: 5 but let me g', that I may hide "
11 and let us g' out into the field. 3318
13 that thou mayest g' in peace: and 1980
19 thou shalt g' down quickly, 3381
21 saying, G', find out the arrows. 3212
22 g' thy way: for the Lord hath sent "
28 asked leave of me to g' to Bethlehem:
29 he said, Let me g', I pray thee; 7971
40 him, G', carry them to the city. 3212
42 Jonathan said to David, G' in peace, "
23: 2 I g' and smite these Philistines? "
2 G', and smite the Philistines, and "
4 Arise, g' down to Keilah; for I will 3381
8 people together to war, to g' down "
13 went whithersoever they could g'. 1980
13 he forbare to g' forth. 3318
22 G', I pray you, prepare yet, and 3212
23 I will g' with you: and it shall 1980
24:19 will he let him g' well away? 7971
25: 5 g' to Nabal, and greet him 935
19 her servants, G' on before me; 5674
35 G' up in peace to thine house; 5927
26: 6 will g' down with me to Saul to 3381
6 And Abishai said, I will g' down "
11 the cruse of water, and let us g'. 3212
19 saying, G', serve other gods. "
28: 1 shalt g' out with me to battle, 3318
7 I may g' to her, and enquire of her.3212
29: 4 that he may g' again to his place 7725
4 him not g' down with us to battle, 3381
7 now return, and g' in peace, 3212
8 not g' fight against the enemies 935
9 not g' up with us to the battle. 5927
30:10 they could not g' over the brook 5674
2Sa 1:15 G' near, and fall upon him. 5066
2: 1 Shall I g' up into any of the cities 5927
1 And the Lord said unto him, G' up. "
1 David said, Whither shall I g' up? "
3:16 said Abner unto him, G', return. 3212
21 I will arise and g', and will gather "

2Sa 5:19 Shall I g' up to the Philistines? 5927
19 Lord said unto David, G' up: for "
23 Thou shalt not g' up; but fetch a "
24 shall the Lord g' out before thee, *3318
7: 3 G', do all that is in thine heart; 3212
5 G' and tell thy servant David, "
11: 1 time when kings g' forth to battle, 3318
8 G' down to thy house, and wash 3381
10 not g' down unto thine house? "
11 shall I then g' into mine house, 935
12:23 I shall g' to him, but he shall not 1980
13: 7 G' now to thy brother Amnon's 3212
13 shall I cause my shame to g'? * "
24 his servants g' with thy servant. "
25 Nay, my son, let us not all now g'. "
25 he would not g', but blessed him. "
26 let my brother Amnon g' with us. "
26 Why should he g' with thee? "
27 Amnon and all the king's sons g' 7971
39 longed to g' forth unto Absalom: 3318
14: 8 unto the woman, G' to thine house,3212
21 g' therefore, bring the young man "
30 g' and set it on fire. And Absalom's"
15: 7 let me g' and pay my vow, "
9 the king said unto him, G' in peace."
20 should I this day make thee g' up "
20 seeing I g' whither I may, 1980
22 David said to Ittai, G' and pass 3212
16: 9 let me g' over, I pray thee, and 5674
21 G' in unto thy father's concubines,935
17:11 that thou g' to battle in thine own 1980
18: 2 surely g' forth with you myself 3318
3 Thou shalt not g' forth: for if we "
21 G' tell the king what thou hast 3212
19: 7 Now therefore arise, g' forth, and 3318
7 by the Lord, if thou g' not forth, "
15 to g' down to meet the king, to conduct 3212
20 g' down to meet my lord the king.3381
26 and g' to the king; because thy 3212
34 that I should g' up with the king 5927
36 servant will g' a little way over 5674
37 servant Chimham; let him g' over "
38 Chimham shall g' over with me, "
20:11 that is for David, let him g' after *
21:17 Thou shalt g' no more out with 3318
24: 1 G', number Israel and Judah. 3212
2 G' now through all the tribes of 7751
12 G' and say unto David, Thus saith 1980
18 G' up, rear an altar unto the Lord 5927
1Ki 1:13 G' and get thee in unto king 3212
53 Solomon said unto him, G' to thine "
2: 2 I g' the way of all the earth; 1980
6 let not his hoar head g' down to 3381
29 saying, G', fall upon him. 3212
36 g' not forth thence any whither. 3318
3: 7 know not how to g' out or come in. "
8:44 If thy people g' out to battle "
9: 6 but g' and serve other gods, 1980
11: 2 Ye shall not g' in to them, neither 935
10 that he should not g' after other 3212
17 servants with him, to g' into Egypt;935
21 that I may g' to mine own country.3212
22 thou seekest to g' to thine own "
22 Nothing: howbeit let me g' in any*7971
12:24 saith the Lord, Ye shall not g' up, 5927
27 this people g' up to do sacrifice "
28 much for you to g' up to Jerusalem: "
13: 8 I will not g' in with thee, neither 935
16 nor g' in with thee: neither will I "
17 turn again to g' by the way that 3212
14: 3 and g' to him: he shall tell thee 935
7 G', tell Jeroboam, Thus saith the 3212
15:17 he might not suffer any to g' out 3318
17:12 that I may g' in and dress it for 935
13 Fear not; g' and do as thou hast "
18: 1 G', show thyself unto Ahab; and 3212
5 G' into the land, unto all fountains "
8 I am: g', tell thy lord, Behold, Elijah "
11, 14 sayest, G', tell thy lord, Behold, "
43 G' up now, look toward the sea. 5927
43 he said, G' again seven times. 7725
44 G' up, say unto Ahab, Prepare 5927
19:11 G' forth, and stand upon the 3318
15 G', return on thy way to the 3212
20 he said unto him, G' back again: "
20:22 G', strengthen thyself, and mark, "
31 and g' out to the king of Israel: 3318
33 Then he said, G' ye, bring him. 935
34 Because thou hast let g' out of 7971
42 therefore thy life shall g' for his 1961
21:16 Ahab rose up to g' down to the 3381
18 Arise, g' down to meet Ahab king "
22: 4 Wilt thou g' with me to battle to 3212
6 Shall I g' against Ramoth-gilead "
6 G' up; for the Lord shall deliver it5927
12 G' up to Ramoth-gilead, and "
15 shall we g' against Ramoth-gilead 3212
15 G', and prosper: for the Lord 5927
20 persuade Ahab, that he may g' up "
22 will g' forth, and I will be a lying 3318
22 and prevail also: g' forth, and do "
25 when thou shalt g' into an inner 935
48 ships of Tharshish to g' to Ophir 3212
49 my servants g' with thy servants "
2Ki 1: 2 G', enquire of Baal-zebub the god "
3 g' up to meet the messengers of 5927
3 ye g' to enquire of Baal-zebub 1980
6 G', turn again unto the king that 3212
15 G' down with him: be not afraid 3381
2:16 let them g', we pray thee, and seek 3212
18 Did I not say unto you, G' not? "
23 G' up, thou bald head; g' up, thou 5927
3: 7 wilt thou g' with me against Moab 3212
7 And he said, I will g' up: I am as 5927
8 Which way shall we g' up? And he "
4: 3 he said, G', borrow thee vessels 3212

2Ki 4: 7 G', sell the oil, and pay thy debt, 3212
23 Wherefore wilt thou g' to him 1980
24 Drive, and g' forward; slack not 3212
29 take my staff in thine hand, and g' "
5: 5 And the king of Syria said, G' to, "
5 g', and I will send a letter 935
10 G' and wash in Jordan seven 1980
19 And he said unto him, G' in peace.3212
24 and he let the men g', and they 7971
6: 2 us g', we pray thee, unto Jordan, 3212
2 And he answered, G' ye. "
3 I pray thee, and g' with thy servants."
3 And he answered, I will g'. "
13 he said, G' and spy where he is, "
22 and drink, and g' to their master. "
7: 5 g' unto the camp of the Syrians: 935
9 that we may g' and tell the king's "
14 the Syrians, saying, G' and see. 3212
8: 1 and g' thou and thine household, "
8 and g', meet the man of God, and "
10 G', say unto him, Thou mayest "
9: 1 thine hand and g' to Ramoth-gilead: "
2 and g' in, and make him arise up 935
15 let none g' forth nor escape out 3318
15 of the city, to g' to tell it in Jezreel.3212
34 G', see now this cursed woman, *6485
10:13 and we g' down to salute the 3381
24 he that letteth him g', his life shall be
25 G' in, and slay them; let none 935
11: 7 you that g' forth on the sabbath, 3318
9 that should g' out on the sabbath, "
12:17 Hazael set his face to g' up to 5927
17:27 and let them g' and dwell there, 3212
18:21 a man lean, it will g' into his hand,935
25 said to me, G' up against this land,5927
19:31 shall g' forth a remnant, and they 3318
20: 5 on the third day thou shalt g' up 5927
8 shall g' into the house of the Lord "
9 shall the shadow g' forward ten 1980
9 degrees, or g' back ten degrees? 7725
10 shadow to g' down ten degrees: *5186
22: 4 G' up to Hilkiah the high priest, 5927
13 G' ye, enquire of the Lord for me,3212
1Ch 7:11 fit to g' out for war and battle. 3318
14:10 I g' up against the Philistines? 5927
10 the Lord said unto him, G' up; "
14 God said unto him, G' not up after "
15 then thou shalt g' out to battle: 3318
17: 4 G' and tell David my servant, 3212
11 must g' to be with thy fathers, "
20: 1 time that kings g' out to battle, 3318
21: 2 G', number Israel from Beer-sheba3212
10 G' and tell David, saying, Thus "
18 that David should g' up, and set 5927
30 David could not g' before it to 3212
2Ch 1:10 that I may g' out and come in 3318
6:34 If thy people g' out to war against "
7:19 and shall g' and serve other gods, 1980
11: 4 Ye shall not g' up, nor fight against 5927
14:11 we g' against this multitude. * 935
16: 1 he might let none g' out or come in 3318
3 g', break thy league with Baasha 3212
18: 2 persuaded him to g' up with him 5927
3 g' with me to Ramoth-gilead? 3212
5 Shall we g' to Ramoth-gilead to "
5 G' up; for God will deliver it into 5927
11 G' up to Ramoth-gilead, and "
14 Shall we g' to Ramoth-gilead to 3212
14 G' ye up, and prosper, and they 5927
19 that he may g' up and fall at "
21 I will g' out, and be a lying spirit 3318
21 also prevail: g' out, and do even so."
24 that day when thou shalt g' into 935
29 and will g' to the battle; but put "
20:16 morrow g' ye down against them: 3381
17 to morrow g' out against them: 3318
27 to g' again to Jerusalem with joy; 7725
36 to make ships to g' to Tarshish: 3212
37 were not able to g' to Tarshish, "
21:13 of Jerusalem to g' a whoring, ‡
23: 6 shall g' in, for they are holy: * 935
8 were to g' out on the sabbath: 3318
24: 5 G' out unto the cities of Judah, "
25: 5 able to g' forth to war, that could "
7 the army of Israel g' with thee; 935
8 But if thou wilt g', do it, be strong "
10 out of Ephraim, to g' home again: 3212
13 should not g' with him to battle, "
26:18 g' out of the sanctuary; for thou 3318
20 yea, himself hasted also to g' out, "
34:21 G', enquire of the Lord for me, 3212
36:23 be with him, and let him g' up. 5927
Ezr 1: 3 be with him, and let him g' up to "
5 to g' up to build the house of the "
5:15 g', carry them into the temple 236
7: 9 the first month began he to g' up 4609
13 to g' to Jerusalem, g' with thee. 1946
28 chief men to g' up with me. 5927
8:31 to g' unto Jerusalem: and the 3212
9:11 unto which ye g' to possess it, 935
Ne 3:15 stairs that g' down from the city 3381
4: 3 if a fox g' up, he shall even break 5927
6:11 g' into the temple to save his life? 935
11 to save his life? I will not g' in. "
8:10 G' your way, eat the fat, and drink 3212
15 G' forth unto the mount, and 3318
9:12 the way wherein they should g'. 3212
15 they should g' in to possess the land 935
19 the way wherein they should g'. 3212
23 that they should g' in to possess it. 935
Es 1:19 let there g' a royal commandment3318
2:12 maid's turn was come to g' into 935
13 was given her to g' with her out "
15 was come to g' in unto the king, "
4: 8 that she should g' in unto the king, "
16 G', gather together all the Jews 3212

Es 4:16 and so will I g' in unto the king, 935
5:14 g' thou in merrily with the king "
Job 4:21 which is in them g' away? they *5265
6:18 they g' to nothing, and perish. 5927
10:21 I g' whence I shall not return, 3212
15:13 such words g' out of thy mouth? 3318
30 of his mouth shall he g' away. 5493
16:22 then I shall g' the way whence 1980
17:16 They shall g' down to the bars of 3381
20:26 it shall g' ill with him that is left *
21:13 in a moment g' down to the grave.5181
29 asked them that g' by the way? 5674
23: 8 Behold, I g' forward, but he is 1980
24: 5 asses in the desert, g' they forth 3318
10 They cause him to g' naked 1980
27: 6 hold fast, and will not let it g': 7503
31:37 prince would I g' near unto him. 7126
37: 8 Then the beasts g' into dens, and 935
38:35 send lightnings, that they may g',3212
39: 4 they g' forth, and return not 3318
41:19 of his mouth g' burning lamps, 1980
42: 8 and g' to my servant Job, and 3212
Ps 22:29 all they that g' down to the dust 3381
26: 4 will I g' in with dissemblers. 935
28: 1 them that g' down into the pit. 3381
30: 3 that I should not g' down to the pit."
9 when I g' down to the pit? shall "
32: 8 the way hich thou shalt g': 3212
38: 6 I g' mourning all the day long. 1980
39:13 before I g' hence, and be no more.3212
42: 9 why g' I mourning because of the "
43: 2 why g' I mourning because of the 1980
4 will I g' unto the altar of God, 935
48:12 Zion, and g' round about her: 5362
49:19 He shall g' to the generation of 935
55:10 Day and night they g' about it 5437
15 let them g' down quick into hell: 3381
58: 3 they g' astray as soon as they be 8582
59: 6, 14 and g' round about the city. 5437
60:10 didst not g' out with our armies?*3318
63: 9 shall g' into the lower parts of the 935
66:13 I will g' into thy house with * "
71:16 I will g' in the strength of the * "
73:27 that g' a whoring from thee. ‡
78:52 made his own people to g' forth *5265
80:18 So will not we g' back from thee: 5472
84: 7 They g' from strength to strength, 3212
85:13 Righteousness shall g' before him;1980
88: 4 them that g' down into the pit: 3381
89:14 and truth shall g' before thy face, 6923
104: 8 They g' up by the mountains; †‡5927
8 they g' down by the valleys †‡3381
26 There g' the ships: there is that 1980
105:20 of the people, and let him g' free. "
107: 7 that they might g' to a city of 3212
23 They that g' down to the sea in 3381
26 they g' down again to the depths: "
108:11 wilt not thou, O God, g' forth with 3318
115:17 any that g' down into silence. 3381
118:19 I will g' into them, and I will * 935
119:35 Make me to g' in the path of thy 1869
122: 1 Let us g' into the house of the 3212
4 Whither the tribes g' up, the 5927
129: 8 Neither do they which g' by say, 5674
132: 3 my house, nor g' up into my bed; 5927
7 We will g' into his tabernacles: 935
139: 7 Whither shall I g' from thy spirit?3212
143: 7 them that g' down into the pit. 3381
Pr 1:12 as those that g' down into the pit: "
2:19 None that g' unto her return again, 935
3:28 Say not unto thy neighbour, G', 3212
4:13 hold of instruction; let her not g':7503
14 g' not in the way of evil men. * 833
5: 5 Her feet g' down to death; her 3381
23 of his folly he shall g' astray. 7686
6: 3 g', humble thyself, and make sure 3212
6 G' to the ant, thou sluggard; "
28 Can one g' upon hot coals, and *1980
7:25 g' not astray in her paths. 8582
9: 6 g' in the way of understanding. * 833
15 To call passengers who g' right on
14: 7 G' from the presence of a foolish 3212
15:12 neither will he g' unto the wise. "
18: 8 they g' down into the innermost 3381
19: 7 do his friends g' far from him? 7368
22: 6 a child in the way he should g': 6310
10 and contention shall g' out; yea, 3318
24 a furious man thou shalt not g': 935
23:30 they that g' to seek mixed wine. "
25: 8 G' not forth hastily to strive, 3318
26:22 they g' down into the innermost 3381
27:10 neither g' into thy brother's house 935
28:10 causeth the righteous to g' astray 7686
30:27 yet g' they forth all of them by 3318
29 three things which g' well, yea, *6806
Ec 2: 1 I said in mine heart, G' to now, 3212
3:20 All g' unto one place; all are of 1980
5:15 shall he return to g' as he came, 3212
16 so shall he g': and what profit hath "
6: 6 do not all g' to one place? 1980
7: 2 to g' to the house of mourning, 3212
2 than to g' to the house of feasting: "
8: 3 Be not hasty to g' out of his sight: "
9: 3 and after that they g' to the dead. "
7 G' thy way, eat thy bread with 3212
10:15 knoweth not how to g' to the city. "
12: 5 the mourners g' about the streets: 5437
Ca 1: 8 g' thy way forth by the footsteps 3318
3: 2 I will rise now, and g' about the 5437
3 watchmen that g' about the city "
4 him, and would not let him g', 7503
11 G' forth, O ye daughters of Zion, 3318
6: 6 as a flock of sheep which g' up *5927
7: 8 said, I will g' up to the palm tree,* "
11 let us g' forth into the field; let 3318
Isa 2: 3 And many people shall g' and say,1980

Isa 2: 3 and let us g' up to the mountain 5927
3 out of Zion shall g' forth the law, 3318
19 And they shall g' into the holes 935
21 To g' into the clefts of the rocks, "
3:16 walking and mincing as they g', 3212
5: 5 And now g' to; I will tell you what
24 their blossom shall g' up as dust: 5927
6: 8 who will g' for us? Then said I, 3212
9 he said, G', and tell this people, "
7: 3 G' forth now to meet Ahaz, thou, 3318
6 Let us g' up against Judah, and 5927
8: 6 waters of Shiloah that g' softly, 1980
7 channels, and g' over all his banks:"
8 he shall overflow and g' over, *5674
11:15 and make men g' over dryshod. *1869
13: 2 that they may g' into the gates 935
14:19 g' down to the stones of the pit; 3381
15: 5 with weeping shall they g' it up; 5927
18: 2 G', ye swift messengers, to a 3212
20: 2 G' and loose the sackcloth from off "
21: 2 G' up, O Elam: besiege, O Media: 5927
6 G', set a watchman, let him 3212
22:15 G', get thee unto this treasurer, "
23:16 Take an harp, g' about the city, 5437
27: 4 I would g' through them, I would *6585
28:13 they might g', and fall backward, 3212
30: 2 That walk to g' down into Egypt, 3381
8 g', write it before them in a table, 935
31: 1 to them that g' down to Egypt 3381
33:21 shall g' no galley with oars, 3212
34:10 smoke thereof shall g' up for ever:5927
35: 9 ravenous beast shall g' up thereon,"
36: 6 man lean, it will g' into his hand, 935
10 G' up against this land, and 5927
37:32 out of Jerusalem shall g' forth a 3318
38: 5 G', and say to Hezekiah, Thus 1980
10 shall g' to the gates of the grave: 3212
15 I shall g' softly all my years in 1718
18 they that g' down into the pit 3381
22 What is the sign that I shall g' up 5927
42:10 ye that g' down to the sea, and all 3381
13 Lord shall g' forth as a mighty 3318
45: 2 I will g' before thee, and make 3212
13 he shall let g' my captives, not 7971
16 shall g' to confusion together 1980
48:17 by the way that thou shouldest g'.3212
20 G' ye forth of Babylon, flee ye 3318
49: 9 say to the prisoners, G' forth; "
17 that made thee waste shall g' forth "
51:23 Bow down, that we may g' over: 5674
52:11 g' ye out from thence, touch no 3318
11 g' ye out of the midst of her; "
12 ye shall not g' out with haste, "
12 with haste, nor g' by flight: 3212
12 for the Lord will g' before you; 1980
54: 9 should no more g' over the earth; 5674
55:12 For ye shall g' out with joy, and 3318
58: 6 and to let the oppressed g' free, 7971
8 righteousness shall g' before thee;1980
60:20 Thy sun shall no more g' down; 935
62: 1 thereof g' forth as brightness, 3318
10 G' through, g' through the gates; 5674
66:24 And they shall g' forth, and look 3318
Jer 1: 7 shalt g' to all that I shall send 3212
2: 2 G' and cry in the ears of 1980
25 strangers, and after them will I g'.3212
37 Yea, thou shalt g' forth from him, 3318
3: 1 and she g' from him, and become 1980
12 G' and proclaim these words "
4: 5 let us g' into the defenced cities. 935
29 shall g' into thickets, and climb up "
5:10 G' ye up upon her walls, and 5927
6: 4 arise, and let us g' up at noon. "
5 Arise, and let us g' by night, "
25 G' not forth into the field, nor 3318
7:12 g' ye now unto my place which 3212
9: 2 and g' from them! for they be all "
10: 5 be borne, because they cannot g'. 6805
11:12 and inhabitants of Jerusalem g', 1980
13: 1 G' and get thee a linen girdle, "
4 and arise, g' to Euphrates, and 3212
6 Arise, g' to Euphrates, and take "
14:18 If I g' forth into the field, then 3318
18 the prophet and the priest g' about 5503
15: 1 my sight, and let them g' forth. 3318
2 Whither shall we g' forth? then "
5 g' aside to ask how thou doest? *5493
16: 5 g' to lament nor bemoan them: 3212
8 also g' into the house of feasting, 935
17:19 G' and stand in the gate of the 1980
19 by the which they g' out, and in 3318
18: 2 Arise, and g' down to the potter's 3381
11 g' to, speak to the men of Judah, 4994
19: 1 G' and get a potter's earthen 1980
2 g' forth unto the valley of the son 3318
10 sight of the men that g' with thee, 1980
20: 6 that dwell in thine house shall g' 3212
21: 2 that he may g' up from us. 5927
12 lest my fury g' out like fire, and 3318
22: 1 G' down to the house of the king 3381
20 G' up to Lebanon, and cry; and 5927
22 thy lovers shall g' into captivity: 3212
25: 6 g' not after other gods to serve "
32 evil shall g' forth from nation to 3318
27:18 at Jerusalem, g' not to Babylon. 935
28:13 G' and tell Hananiah, saying, 1980
29:12 and ye shall g' and pray unto me, "
30:16 of them, shall g' into captivity; 3212
31: 4 and shalt g' forth in the dances of 3318
6 Arise ye, and let us g' up to Zion 5927
22 How long wilt thou g' about, O 2559
24 and they that g' forth with flocks. 5265
39 measuring line shall yet g' forth 3318
34: 2 G' and speak to Zedekiah king of 1980
3 thou shalt g' to Babylon. 935
9 an Hebrewess, g' free; that none 7971

Jer 34:10 every one his maidservant, g' free;7971
10 then they obeyed, and let them g'. "
11 whom they had let g' free, to return,"
14 let ye g' every man his brother an "
14 thou shalt let him g' free from "
35: 2 G' unto the house of the 1980
11 and let us g' to Jerusalem for fear 935
13 G' and tell the men of Judah and 1980
15 g' not after other gods to serve 3212
36: 5 I cannot g' into the house of the 935
6 Therefore g' thou, and read in the "
19 G', hide thee, thou and Jeremiah;3212
37:12 to g' into the land of Benjamin, "
38:17 thou wilt assuredly g' forth unto 3318
18 if thou wilt not g' forth to the king "
21 if thou refuse to g' forth, this is the"
39:16 G' and speak to Ebed-melech the 1980
40: 1 guard had let him g' from Ramah,7971
4 convenient for thee to g', thither g'. 3212
5 G' back also to Gedaliah the son 7725
5 or g' wheresoever it seemeth 3212
5 convenient unto thee to g'. "
5 and a reward, and let him g'. 7971
15 Let me g', I pray thee, and I will 3212
41:10 and departed to g' over to the 5674
17 to g' to enter into Egypt, 3212
42:14 we will g' into the land of Egypt, 935
15 into Egypt, and g' to sojourn there; "
17 that set their faces to g' into Egypt "
19 G' ye not into Egypt: know "
22 the place whither ye desire to g' "
43: 2 G' not into Egypt to sojourn there: "
12 and he shall g' forth from thence 3318
44:12 have set their faces to g' into the 935
46: 8 and he saith, I will g' up, and *5927
11 G' up into Gilead, and take balm, "
16 let us g' again to our own people, 7725
22 The voice thereof shall g' like a 3212
48: 5 continual weeping shall g' up; 5927
7 and Chemosh shall g' forth into 3318
49: 3 their king shall g' into captivity, 3212
12 that shall altogether g' unpunished? "
28 g' up to Kedar, and spoil the men 5927
50: 4 they shall g', and seek the Lord 3212
6 have caused them to g' astray, 8582
8 g' forth out of the land of the 3318
21 G' up against the land of 5927
27 them g' down to the slaughter: 3381
33 fast; they refused to let them g'. 7971
51: 9 and let us g' every one into his 3212
45 people, g' ye out of the midst of 3318
50 have escaped the sword, g' away, 1980
La 4:18 that we cannot g' in our streets: 3212
Eze 1:12 whither the spirit was to g', they "
20 Whithersoever the spirit was to g', "
20 thither was their spirit to g'; "
3: 1 g' speak unto the house of Israel. "
4 of man, g', get thee unto the house "
11 And g', get thee to them of the "
22 Arise, g' forth into the plain, 3318
24 G', shut thyself within thine house.935
25 and thou shalt not g' out among 3318
6: 9 g' a whoring after their idols: ‡
8: 6 that I should g' far off from my 7368
9 G' in, and behold the wicked 935
9: 4 G' through the midst of the city, 5674
5 G' ye after him through the city, "
7 g' ye forth. And they went forth, 3318
10: 2 G' in between the wheels, even 935
12: 4 thou shalt g' forth at even in their 3318
4 as they that g' forth into captivity. 4161
11 shall remove and g' into captivity. 3212
12 and shall g' forth: they shall dig 3318
13:20 and will let the souls g', even the 7971
14:11 Israel may g' no more astray from 8582
17 Sword, g' through the land; so 5674
15: 7 they shall g' out from one fire, 3318
20:10 I caused them to g' forth out of the "
29 is the high place whereunto ye g'? 935
39 G' ye, serve ye every one his idols,3212
21: 4 therefore shall my sword g' forth 3318
16 G' thee one way or other, either on 258
23:44 as they g' in unto a woman that 935
24:14 I will not g' back, neither will I 6544
26:11 thy strong garrisons shall g' down 3381
20 with them that g' down to the pit, "
30: 9 that day shall messengers g' forth 3318
17 these cities shall g' into captivity.3212
18 daughters shall g' into captivity. "
31:14 with them that g' down to the pit. 3381
32:18 with them that g' down into the pit."
19 g' down, and be thou laid with the "
24 with them that g' down to the pit. "
25 with them that g' down to the pit: "
29, 30 them that g' down to the pit. "
38:11 I will g' up to the land of unwalled 5927
11 I will g' to them that are at rest, 935
39: 9 the cities of Israel shall g' forth, 3318
40:26 there were seven steps to g' up to 5930
42:14 shall they not g' out of the holy 3318
44: 3 shall g' out by the way of the same."
19 And when they g' forth into the "
46: 2 then he shall g' forth; but the gate"
8 shall g' in by the way of the porch 935
8 shall g' forth by the way thereof. 3318
9 g' out by the way of the south gate; "
9 shall g' forth by the way of the "
9 but he shall g' forth over against it."
10 when they g' in, shall g' in; 935
10 when they g' forth, shall g' forth. 3318
12 then he shall g' forth; and after "
47: 8 and g' down into the desert, 3381
8 and g' into the sea: which being 935
15 of Hethlon, as men g' to Zedad; * "
Da 11:44 therefore he shall g' forth with 3318
12: 9 he said, G' thy way, Daniel: for 3212

Da 12:13 g' thou thy way till the end be: 3212
Ho 1: 2 G', take unto thee a wife of "
2: 5 I will g' after my lovers, that give "
7 g' and return to my first husband; "
3: 1 G' yet, love a woman beloved of "
4:15 neither g' ye up to Beth-aven, nor 5927
5: 6 They shall g' with their flocks 3212
14 I, even I, will tear and g' away; "
15 I will g' and return to my place, "
7:11 call to Egypt, they g' to Assyria. 1980
12 When they shall g', I will spread 3212
11: 3 taught Ephraim also to g', taking 8637
Joe 2:16 let the bridegroom g' forth of his 3318
Am 1: 5 people of Syria shall g' into captivity
15 their king shall g' into captivity, 1980
2: 7 his father will g' in unto the same 3212
4: 3 ye shall g' out at the breaches, 3318
5: 5 Gilgal shall surely g' into captivity,
27 will I cause you to g' into captivity
6: 2 and from thence g' ye to Hamath 3212
2 then g' down to Gath of the 3381
7 Therefore now shall they g' captive
7 with the first that g' captive, and the
7:12 g', flee thee away into the land of 3212
15 G', prophesy unto my people Israel."
17 Israel shall surely g' into captivity*
8: 9 cause the sun to g' down at noon 935
9: 4 though they g' into captivity 3212
Jon 1: 2 Arise, g' to Nineveh, that great city,"
3 to g' with them unto Tarshish 935
3: 2 Arise, g' unto Nineveh, that great 3212
Mic 1: 8 I will g' stripped and naked: I will "
2: 3 neither shall ye g' haughtily: for * "
3: 6 and the sun shall g' down over the 935
4: 2 and let us g' up to the mountain 5927
2 the law shall g' forth of Zion, 3318
10 now shalt thou g' forth out of the "
10 and thou shalt g' even to Babylon;*935
5: 8 if he g' through, both treadeth 5674
Na 3:14 g' into clay, and tread the morter, 935
Hab 1: 4 judgment doth never g' forth: for 3318
Hag 1: 8 G' up to the mountain, and bring 5927
Zec 6: 5 which g' forth from standing 3318
6 g' forth into the north country; * "
6 white g' forth after them; and * "
6 grisled g' forth toward the south* "
7 bay went forth, and sought to g' 3212
8 that g' toward the north country 3318
10 thou the same day, and g' into the 935
8:21 inhabitants of one city shall g' 1980
21 Let us g' speedily to pray before 3212
21 the Lord of hosts: I will g' also. "
23 We will g' with you: for we have "
9:14 and his arrow shall g' forth as the 3318
14 and shall g' with whirlwinds of 1980
14: 2 and half of the city shall g' forth 3318
3 Then shall the Lord g' forth, and "
8 that living waters shall g' out from "
16 shall even g' up from year to year 5927
18 if the family of Egypt g' not up, "
Mal 4: 2 and ye shall g' forth, and grow up 3318
M't 2: 8 G' and search diligently for the 4198
20 and g' into the land of Israel: for "
22 he was afraid to g' thither: 565
5:24 before the altar, and g' thy way; 5217
41 shall compel thee to g' a mile, "
41 a mile, g' with him twain. 5217
7:13 there be which g' in thereat: *1525
8: 4 but g' thy way, shew thyself to 5217
9 I say to this man, G', and he goeth; 4198
13 G' thy way; and as thou hast 5217
21 suffer me first to g' and bury my 565
31 suffer us to g' away into the herd * "
32 And he said unto them, G'. And 5217
9: 6 thy bed, and g' unto thine house. "
13 But g' ye and learn what that 4198
10: 5 G' not into the way of the Gentiles, 565
6 But g' rather to the lost sheep 4198
7 And as ye g', preach, saying, "
11 and there abide till ye g' thence. 1831
11: 4 G' and shew John again those 4198
13:28 that we g' and gather them up? 565
14:15 that they may g' into the villages, "
22 g' before him unto the other side, 4254
29 on the water, to g' to Jesus. *2064
16:21 that he must g' unto Jerusalem, 565
17:27 g' thou to the sea, and cast an 4198
18:15 g' and tell him his fault between 5217
19:21 g' and sell that thou hast, and give "
24 for a camel to g' through the eye 1330
20: 4 G' ye also into the vineyard, and 5217
7 G' ye also into the vineyard; and "
14 Take that thine is, and g' thy way: "
18 Behold, we g' up to Jerusalem; 305
21: 2 G' into the village over against 4198
28 g' work to day in my vineyard. 5217
30 And he answered and said I g', sir: 565
31 g' into the kingdom of God before 4254
22: 9 G' ye therefore into the highways, 4198
23:13 ye neither g' in yourselves, *1525
13 ye them that are entering to g' in. "
24:26 he is in the desert; g' not forth: 1831
25: 6 cometh; g' ye out to meet him. * "
9 but g' ye rather to them that sell, 4198
46 these shall g' away into everlasting 565
26:18 G' into the city to such a man, 5217
32 I will g' before you into Galilee. 4254
36 here, while I g' and pray yonder. 565
27:65 g' your way, make it as sure as ye 5217
28: 7 g' quickly, and tell his disciples 4198
10 Be not afraid: g' tell my brethren 565
10 brethren that they g' into Galilee,*5217
19 G' ye therefore, and teach all 4198
M'r 1:38 Let us g' into the next towns, 71
44 but g' thy way, shew thyself to 5217
2:11 and g' thy way into thine house. "

M'r 5:19 G' home to thy friends, and tell 5217
34 g' in peace, and be whole of thy "
6:36 that they may g' into the country 565
37 Shall we g' and buy two hundred "
38 many loaves have ye? g' and see. 5217
45 to g' to the other side before unto 4254
7:29 For this saying g' thy way; the 5217
8:26 Neither g' into the town, nor *1525
9:43 having two hands to g' into hell, 565
10:21 g' thy way, sell whatsoever thou 5217
25 to g' through the eye of a needle, 1525
33 Behold, we g' up to Jerusalem; 305
52 G' thy way; thy faith hath made 5217
11: 2 G' your way into the village over "
6 commanded: and they let them g'. 863
12:38 which love to g' in long clothing, *4043
13:15 not g' down into the house, 2597
14:12 wilt thou that we g' and prepare 565
13 G' ye into the city, and there 5217
14 wheresoever he shall g' in, say *1525
28 I will g' before you into Galilee. 4254
42 Rise up, let us g'; lo, he that 71
16: 7 But g' your way, tell his disciples 5217
15 he said unto them, G' ye into all 4198
Lu 1:17 shall g' before him in the spirit 4281
76 g' before the face of the Lord 4313
2:15 us now g' even unto Bethlehem, 1330
5:14 g', and shew thyself to the priest, 565
24 couch, and g' unto thine house. 4198
7: 8 I say unto one, G', and he goeth; "
22 G' your way, and tell John what "
50 faith hath saved thee; g' in peace. "
8:14 g' forth, and are choked with cares "
22 Let us g' over unto the other side 1330
31 them to g' out into the deep. * 565
48 made thee whole; g' in peace. 4198
51 he suffered no man to g' in, save *1525
9: 5 when ye g' out of that city, *1831
12 that they may g' into the towns 565
13 except we should g' and buy meat 4198
51 set his face to g' to Jerusalem, "
53 though he would g' to Jerusalem.* "
59 me first to g' and bury my father. 565
60 g' thou and preach the kingdom "
61 let me first g' bid them farewell, *
10: 3 G' your ways; Behold, I send you 4198
7 G' not from house to house. 3327
10 g' your ways out into the streets 1831
37 unto him, G', and do thou likewise.4198
11: 5 and shall g' unto him at midnight, "
13:32 G' ye, and tell that fox, Behold, I "
14: 4 and healed him, and let him g'; 630
10 g' and sit down in the lowest 4198
10 Friend, g' up higher: then shalt 4320
18 and I must needs g' and see it: 1831
19 I g' to prove them: I pray thee 4198
21 G' out quickly into the streets 1831
23 G' out into the highways and "
15: 4 and g' after that which is lost, 4198
18 I will arise and g' to my father, "
28 was angry, and would not g' in: 1525
17: 7 G' and sit down to meat? *3928
14 G' shew yourselves unto the 4198
19 Arise, g' thy way: thy faith hath "
23 g' not after them, nor follow them. 565
18:25 camel to g' through a needle's eye,*1525
31 we g' up to Jerusalem, and all 305
19:30 G' ye into the village over against 5217
21: 8 g' ye not therefore after them. 4198
22: 8 G' and prepare us the passover, "
33 am ready to g' with thee, both "
68 not answer me, nor let me g'. * 630
23:22 chastise him, and let him g'. * "
Joh 1:43 Jesus would g' forth into Galilee, 1831
4: 4 must needs g' through Samaria. *1330
16 G', call thy husband, and come 5217
50 G' thy way; thy son liveth. And 4198
6:67 Will ye also g' away? 5217
68 Lord, to whom shall we g'? thou 565
7: 3 Depart hence, and g' into Judæa, 5217
8 G' ye up unto this feast: I g' not up 305
19 Why g' ye about to kill me? *2212
33 then I g' unto him that sent me. 5217
35 Whither will he g', that we shall 4198
35 will he g' unto the dispersed "
8:11 do I condemn thee: g', and sin no "
14 whence I came, and whither I g'; 5217
14 whence I come, and whither I g'. "
21 I g' my way, and ye shall seek me, "
21 whither I g', ye cannot come. "
22 Whither I g', ye cannot come. "
9: 7 G', wash in the pool of Siloam, "
11 G' to the pool of Siloam, and wash: "
10: 9 be saved, and shall g' in and 1525
11: 7 Let us g' into Judæa again. 71
11 but I g', that I may awake him 4198
15 nevertheless let us g' unto him. 71
16 Let us also g', that we may die with "
44 them, Loose him, and let him g'. 5217
13:33 Whither I g', ye cannot come; so "
36 Whither I g', thou canst not follow "
14: 2 I g' to prepare a place for you. 4198
3 if I g' and prepare a place for you, "
4 whither I g' ye know, and the way 5217
12 do; because I g' unto my Father. 4198
28 I g' away, and come again unto 5217
28 I said, I g' unto the Father: 4198
31 even so I do. Arise, let us g' hence. 71
15:16 ye should g' and bring forth fruit, 5217
16: 5 I g' my way to him that sent me; "
7 expedient for you that I g' away: 565
7 for if I g' not away, the Comforter "
10 because I g' to my Father, and ye 5217
16 see me, because I g' to my Father. "
17 and, Because I g' to the F'? "
28 the world, and g' to the Father. 4198

Joh 18: 8 ye seek me, let these g' their way: 5217
19:12 thou let this man g', thou art not * 630
20:17 but g' to my brethren, and say 4198
21: 3 Peter saith unto them, I g' a fishing.5217
3 unto him, We also g' with thee. *2064
Ac 1:11 ye have seen him g' into heaven. *4198
25 that he might g' to his own place. "
3: 3 Peter and John about to g' into 1524
13 he was determined to let him g'. * 630
4:15 commanded them to g' aside out 565
21 they let them g', finding nothing 630
23 And being let g', they went to their 630
5:20 G', stand and speak in the temple 4198
40 name of Jesus, and let them g'. 630
7:40 Make us gods to g' before us: for 4313
8:26 Arise, and g' toward the south 4198
29 G' near, and join thyself to this 4334
9: 6 Arise, and g' into the city, and it * 1525
11 Arise, and g' into the street which 4198
15 G' thy way: for he is a chosen "
10:20 get thee down, and g' with them, "
11:12 the spirit bade me g' with them, 4905
22 he should g' as far as Antioch. *1330
12:17 he said, G' shew these things *
15: 2 should g' up to Jerusalem unto the 305
33 let g' in peace from the brethren * 630
36 g' again and visit our brethren * 1994
16: 3 Paul have to g' forth with him; 1831
7 they assayed to g' into Bithynia: 4198
10 endeavoured to g' into Macedonia, 1831
35 serjeants, saying, Let those men g'.630
36 sent to let you g': now therefore "
36 therefore depart, and g' in peace. 4198
17: 9 and of the other, they let them g'. 630
14 Paul to g' as it were to the sea: 4198
18: 6 I will g' unto the Gentiles. "
19:21 to g' to Jerusalem, saying, After I "
20: 1 departed for to g' into Macedonia. "
13 appointed, minding himself to g' afoot. "
22 behold, I g' bound in the spirit 4198
21: 4 he should not g' up to Jerusalem.* 305
12 besought him not to g' up to "
22:10 Arise, and g' into Damascus; and 4198
23:10 commanded the soldiers to g' 2597
23 hundred soldiers to g' to Cæsarea, 4198
32 left the horsemen to g' with him, "
24:25 G' thy way for this time; when I "
25: 5 g' down with me, and accuse this 4782
9 said, Wilt thou g' up to Jerusalem, 305
12 Cæsar? unto Cæsar shalt thou g'. 4198
20 whether he would g' to Jerusalem, "
27: 3 him liberty to g' unto his friends "
28:18 would have let me g', because * 630
26 G' unto this people, and say, 4198
Ro 15:25 now I g' unto Jerusalem to minister "
1Co 5:10 must ye needs g' out of the world. 1831
6: 1 another, g' to law before the unjust, "
7 ye g' to law one with another. *
10:27 ye be disposed to g'; whatsoever 4198
16: 4 it be meet that I g' also, they shall g' "
6 on my journey whithersoever I g'. 4198
2Co 9: 5 they would g' before unto you, 4281
Ga 2: 9 that we should g' unto the heathen, "
Eph 4:26 let not the sun g' down upon your 1931
Ph'p 2:23 I shall see how it will g' with me. "
1Th 4: 6 no man g' beyond and defraud * 5233
Heb 6: 1 let us g' on unto perfection; not * 5342
11: 8 he was called to g' out into a place 1831
13:13 Let us g' forth therefore unto him "
Jas 4:13 G' to now, ye that say, To day or 33
13 we will g' into such a city, 4198
5: 1 G' to now, ye rich men, weep and 33
Re 3:12 and he shall g' no more out: 1831
10: 8 G' and take the little book which 5217
13:10 captivity shall g' into captivity: * "
16: 1 G' your ways, and pour out the vials "
14 g' forth unto the kings of the earth 1607
17: 8 pit, and g' into perdition: 5217
20: 8 shall g' out to deceive the nations* 1831

goad See also GOADS.
J'g 3:31 six hundred men with an ox g': 4451

goads
1Sa 13:21 for the axes, and to sharpen the g'.1861
Ec 12:11 The words of the wise are as g', "

goat See also GOATS; GOATSKINS; SCAPEGOAT.
Ge 15: 9 and a she g' of three years old, 5795
Le 3:12 if his offering be a g', then he shall "
4:24 his hand upon the head of the g', 8163
7:23 fat, of ox, or of sheep, or of g'. 5795
9:15 and took the g', which was the sin 8163
10:16 Moses diligently sought the g' of "
16: 9 Aaron shall bring the g' upon which "
10 But the g', on which the lot fell to be "
15 Then shall he kill the g' of the sin "
18 and of the blood of the g', and put it "
20 he shall bring the live g': "
21 hands upon the head of the live g', "
21 putting them upon the head of the g', "
22 the g' shall bear upon him all their "
22 shall let go the g' in the wilderness. "
26 that let go the g' for the scapegoat "
27 and the g' for the sin offering, "
17: 3 that killeth an ox, or lamb, or g', 5795
22:27 When a bullock, or a sheep, or a g', "
Nu 15:27 he shall bring a she g' of the first "
18:17 or the firstling of a g', thou shalt "
28:22 And one g' for a sin offering, to *8163
29:22, 28, 31, 34, 38 one g' for a sin * "
De 14: 4 eat: the ox, the sheep, and the g', 5795
5 and the wild g', and the pygarg, 689
Pr 30:31 A greyhound; an he g' also; and 8495
Eze 43:25 every day a g' for a sin offering: 8163
Da 8: 5 an he g' came from the west 5795
5 and the g' had a notable horn 6842
8 Therefore the he g' waxed very

Da 8:21 the rough g' is the king of Grecia: 6842

Goath (*go'-ath*)
Jer 31:39 and shall compass about to G'. 1601

goats See also GOATS'.
Ge 27: 9 thence two good kids of the g'; 5795
16 put the skins of the kids of the g' "
30:32 spotted and speckled among the g': "
33 speckled and spotted among the g', "
35 he removed that day the he g' 8495
35 the she g' that were speckled and 5795
31:38 thy ewes and thy she g' have not "
32:14 Two hundred she g', and twenty "
14 and twenty he g', two hundred 8495
37:31 killed a kid of the g', and dipped *5795
Ex 12: 5 out from the sheep, or from the g': "
Le 1:10 of the sheep, or of the g', "
4:23, 28 his offering, a kid of the g', * "
5: 6 a lamb or a kid of the g', for a sin* "
9: 3 Take ye a kid of the g' for a sin * "
16: 5 two kids of the g' for a sin offering, "
7 shall take the two g', and present 8163
8 shall cast lots upon the two g'; "
22:19 beeves, of the sheep, or of the g'. 5795
23:19 kid of the g' for a sin offering, * "
Nu 7:16 One kid of the g' for a sin offering: "
17 five rams, five he g', five lambs of 6260
22 One kid of the g' for a sin offering: 5795
23 five he g', five lambs of the first 6260
28 One kid of the g' for a sin offering: 5795
29 five he g', five lambs of the first 6260
34 One kid of the g' for a sin offering: 5795
35 five he g', five lambs of the first 6260
40 One kid of the g' for a sin offering: 5795
41 five he g', five lambs of the first 6260
46 One kid of the g' for a sin offering. 5795
47 five he g', five lambs of the first 6260
52 One kid of the g' for a sin offering: 5795
53 five he g', five lambs of the first 6260
58 One kid of the g' for a sin offering: 5795
59 five he g', five lambs of the first 6260
64 One kid of the g' for a sin offering: 5795
65 five he g', five lambs of the first 6260
70 One kid of the g' for a sin offering: 5795
71 five he g', five lambs of the first 6260
76 One kid of the g' for a sin offering: 5795
77 five he g', five lambs of the first 6260
82 One kid of the g' for a sin offering: 5795
83 five he g', five lambs of the first 6260
87 the kids of the g' for sin offering 5795
88 the rams sixty, the he g' sixty, 6260
15:24 one kid of the g' for a sin offering.*5795
28:15 one kid of the g' for a sin offering* "
30 And one kid of the g', to make * "
29: 5 one kid of the g' for a sin offering,* "
11 One the g' for a sin offering; * "
16, 19, 25 And one kid of the g' for a * "
De 32:14 of the breed of Bashan, and g', 6260
1Sa 24: 2 men upon the rocks of the wild g'. 3277
25: 2 sheep, and a thousand g': 5795
2Ch 17:11 thousand and seven hundred he g'. 8495
29:21 seven lambs, and seven he g', 5795
23 they brought forth the he g' for 8163
Ezr 6:17 offering for all Israel, twelve he g', 5796
8:35 twelve he g' for a sin offering: 6842
Job 39: 1 wild g' of the rock bring forth? 3277
Ps 50: 9 house, nor he g' out of thy folds. 6260
13 of bulls, or drink the blood of g'? "
66:15 I will offer bullocks with g'. "
104:18 hills are a refuge for the wild g'; 3277
Pr 27:26 and the g' are the price of the field. 6260
Ca 4: 1 thy hair is as a flock of g', that 5795
6: 5 thy hair is as a flock of g' that "
Isa 1:11 the blood of bullocks,...or of he g'. 6260
34: 6 and with the blood of lambs and g', "
Jer 50: 8 as the he g' before the flocks. "
51:40 slaughter like rams with he g'. "
Eze 27:21 thee in lambs, and rams, and g': "
34:17 between the rams and the he g'. "
39:18 of rams, of lambs, and of g', of "
43:22 shalt offer a kid of the g' without *5795
45:23 a kid of the g' daily for a sin * "
Zec 10: 3 I punished the g': for the Lord 6260
M't 25:32 divideth his sheep from the g': 2056
33 right hand, but the g' on the left. 2055
Heb 9:12 Neither by the blood of g' and 5131
13 For if the blood of bulls and of g', "
19 took the blood of calves and of g', "
10: 4 that the blood of bulls and of g' "

goats'
Ex 25: 4 scarlet, and fine linen, and g' hair, 5795
26: 7 thou shalt make curtains of g' hair "
35: 6, 23 scarlet, and fine linen, and g' hair, "
26 them up in wisdom spun g' hair. "
36:14 And he made curtains of g' hair "
Nu 31:20 all work of g' hair, and all things "
1Sa 19:13 put a pillow of g' hair for his bolster, "
16 with a pillow of g' hair for his bolster, "
Pr 27:27 thou shalt have g' milk enough for "

goats'-hair See GOATS' and HAIR.

goatskins
Heb 11:37 about in sheepskins and g'; 122, 1192

Gob (*gob*)
2Sa 21:18 a battle with the Philistines at G': 1359
19 a battle in G' with the Philistines, "

goblet
Ca 7: 2 Thy navel is like a round g', 101

God [*or* GOD] See also GODDESS; GODHEAD; GOD'S; GODS; GOD-WARD.
Ge 1: 1 G' created the heaven and the 430
2 Spirit of G' moved upon the face "
3 And G' said, Let there be light: "
4 And G' saw the light, that it was "

Ge 1: 4 and G· divided the light from the 430
5 And G· called the light Day, and the "
6 G· said, Let there be a firmament "
7 G· made the firmament, and divided "
8 G· called the firmament Heaven. "
9 G· said, Let the waters under the "
10 And G· called the dry land Earth; "
10 and G· saw that it was good. "
11 G· said, Let the earth bring forth "
12 and G· saw that it was good. "
14 And G· said, Let there be lights "
16 And G· made two great lights; the "
17 And G· set them in the firmament "
18 and G· saw that it was good. "
20 G· said, Let the waters bring forth "
21 G· created great whales, and every "
21 and G· saw that it was good. "
22 And G· blessed them, saying, Be "
24 G· said, Let the earth bring forth "
25 G· made the beast of the earth after "
25 and G· saw that it was good. "
26 And G· said, Let us make man in "
27 G· created man in his own image, "
27 in the image of G· created he him; "
28 G· blessed them, and G· said unto "
29 And G· said, Behold, I have given "
31 And G· saw everything that he had "
2: 2 the seventh day G· ended his work "
3 And G· blessed the seventh day, and "
3 his work which G· created and made. "
4 day that the Lord G· made the earth "
5 for the Lord G· had not caused it to "
7 the Lord G· formed man of the dust "
8 Lord G· planted a garden eastward "
9 the Lord G· to grow every tree that "
15 Lord G· took the man, and put him "
16 the Lord G· commanded the man, "
18 And the Lord G· said, It is not good "
19 the Lord G· formed every beast of "
21 the Lord G· caused a deep sleep to "
22 the Lord G· had taken from man, "
3: 1 field which the Lord G· had made. "
1 hath G· said, Ye shall not eat of every "
3 G· hath said, Ye shall not eat of it, "
5 For G· doth know that in the day "
8 they heard the voice of the Lord G· "
8 from the presence of the Lord G· "
9 And the Lord G· called unto Adam, "
13 the Lord G· said unto the woman, "
14 the Lord G· said unto the serpent, "
21 did the Lord G· make coats of skins, "
22 Lord G· said, Behold, the man is "
23 Therefore the Lord G· sent him forth "
4:25 For G·, said she, hath appointed me "
5: 1 In the day that G· created man, "
1 in the likeness of G· made he him. "
22 And Enoch walked with G·, after he "
24 And Enoch walked with G·: and he "
24 And he was not; for G· took him. "
6: 2 the sons of G· saw the daughters "
4 when the sons of G· came in unto "
5 And G· saw that the wickedness of *3068
9 and Noah walked with G·. 430
11 earth also was corrupt before G·, "
12 And G· looked upon the earth, and, "
13 G· said unto Noah, The end of all "
22 according to all that G· commanded "
7: 9 female, as G· had commanded Noah. "
16 as G· had commanded him: and the "
8: 1 And G· remembered Noah, and every "
1 and G· made a wind to pass over the "
15 And G· spake unto Noah, saying, "
9: 1 and G· blessed Noah and his sons, "
6 in the image of G· made he man. "
8 G· spake unto Noah, and to his sons "
12 And G· said, This is the token of "
16 between G· and every living creature "
17 G· said unto Noah, This is the token "
26 Blessed be the Lord G· of Shem; "
27 G· shall enlarge Japheth, and he "
14:18 was the priest of the most high G·. 410
19 Blessed be Abram of the most high G·, "
20 blessed be the most high G·, which "
22 unto the Lord, the most high G·, "
15: 2 Abram said, Lord G·, what wilt ‡3069
8 he said, Lord G·, whereby shall I ‡ "
16:13 Thou G· seest me: for she said, 410
17: 1 I am the Almighty G·; walk before "
3 and G· talked with him, saying, 430
7 to be a G· unto thee, and to thy seed "
8 possession; and I will be their G·. "
9 G· said unto Abraham, Thou shalt "
15 G· said unto Abraham, As for Sarai "
18 And Abraham said unto G·, O that "
19 G· said, Sarah thy wife shall bear "
22 and G· went up from Abraham. "
23 selfsame day, as G· had said unto "
19:29 when G· destroyed the cities of the "
29 that G· remembered Abraham, "
20: 3 G· came to Abimelech in a dream "
6 And G· said unto him in a dream, "
11 the fear of G· is not in this place; "
13 G· caused me to wander from my "
17 So Abraham prayed unto G·: and G· "
21: 2 time of which G· had spoken to him. "
4 old, as G· had commanded him. "
6 G· hath made me to laugh, so that "
12 G· said unto Abraham, Let it not be "
17 And G· heard the voice of the lad; "
17 and the angel of G· called to Hagar "
17 G· hath heard the voice of the lad "
19 G· opened her eyes, and she saw "
20 G· was with the lad; and he grew, "
22 G· is with thee in all that thou doest: "
23 therefore swear unto me here by G· "
33 of the Lord, the everlasting G·. 410

Ge 22: 1 G· did tempt Abraham, and said 430
3 the place of which G· had told him. "
8 G· will provide himself a lamb for a "
9 to the place which G· had told him of "
12 now I know that thou fearest G·, "
24: 3 G· of heaven, and the G· of the earth, "
7 Lord G· of heaven, which took me "
12 O Lord G· of my master Abraham, "
27 the Lord G· of my master Abraham, "
42 O Lord G· of my master Abraham, "
48 the Lord G· of my master Abraham, "
25:11 G· blessed his son Isaac; and Isaac "
26:24 I am the G· of Abraham thy father: "
27:20 the Lord thy G· brought it to me. "
28 G· give thee of the dew of heaven, "
28: 3 G· Almighty bless thee, and make 410
4 which G· gave unto Abraham. 430
12 the angels of G· ascending and "
13 said, I am the Lord G· of Abraham "
13 thy father, and the G· of Isaac: "
17 is none other but the house of G·, "
20 If G· will be with me, and will keep "
21 then shall the Lord be my G·: "
30: 6 Rachel said, G· hath judged me, and "
17 G· hearkened unto Leah, and she "
18 G· hath given me my hire, because "
20 G· hath endued me with a good "
22 G· remembered Rachel, and G· "
23 G· hath taken away my reproach: "
31: 5 but the G· of my father hath been "
7 G· suffered him not to hurt me. "
9 Thus G· hath taken away the cattle "
11 the angel of G· spake unto me in a "
13 I am the G· of Beth-el, where thou 410
16 all the riches which G· hath taken 430
16 whatsoever G· hath said unto thee, "
24 G· came to Laban the Syrian in a "
29 the G· of your father spake unto me "
42 G· of my father, the G· of Abraham, "
42 G· hath seen mine affliction and the "
50 G· is witness betwixt me and thee. "
53 The G· of Abraham, and the G· of "
53 Nahor, the G· of their father, "
32: 1 and the angels of G· met him. "
9 O G· of my father Abraham, "
9 and G· of my father Isaac, "
28 as a prince hast thou power with G· "
30 for I have seen G· face to face, "
33: 5 which G· hath graciously given "
10 as though I had seen the face of G·, "
11 G· hath dealt graciously with me, "
35: 1 G· said unto Jacob, Arise, go up to "
1 and make there an altar unto G·, 410
3 I will make there an altar unto G·, "
5 terror of G· was upon the cities † 430
7 there G· appeared unto him, "
9 And G· appeared unto Jacob again "
10 And G· said unto him, Thy name is "
11 G· said unto him, I am...Almighty: "
11 said unto him, I am G· Almighty: 410
13 G· went up from him in the place 430
15 the place where G· spake with him, "
39: 9 wickedness, and sin against G·? "
40: 8 Do not interpretations belong to G·? "
41:16 G· shall give Pharaoh an answer of "
25 G· hath shewed Pharaoh what he is "
28 What G· is about to do he sheweth "
32 the thing is established by G·, "
32 and G· will shortly bring it to pass. "
38 a man in whom the Spirit of G· is? "
39 as G· hath shewed thee all this, "
51 the firstborn Manasseh: For G·, "
52 G· hath caused me to be fruitful "
42:18 This do, and live; for I fear G·: "
28 What is this that G· hath done "
43:14 And G· Almighty give you mercy 410
23 your G·, and the G· of your father, 430
29 G· be gracious unto thee, my son. "
44: 7 G· forbid that thy servants should ‡
16 G· hath found out the iniquity of 430
17 G· forbid that I should so: ‡
45: 5 for G· did send me before you to 430
7 G· sent me before you to preserve "
8 not you that sent me hither, but G·: "
9 G· hath made me lord of all Egypt: "
46: 1 unto the G· of his father Isaac. "
2 G· spake unto Israel in the visions "
3 And he said, I am G·, 410
3 the G· of thy father: fear not to 430
48: 3 G· Almighty appeared unto me at 410
9 G· hath given me in this place. 430
11 G· hath shewed me also thy seed. "
15 G·, before whom my fathers "
15 G· which fed me all my life long "
20 G· make thee as Ephraim and "
21 but G· shall be with you, and bring "
49:24 by the hands of the mighty G· *
25 Even by the G· of thy father, 410
50:17 the servants of the G· of thy father. 430
19 for am I in the place of G·? "
20 G· meant it unto good, to bring to "
24 and G· will surely visit you, and "
25 saying, G· will surely visit you, and "
Ex 1:17 But the midwives feared G·, and did "
20 G· dealt well with the midwives: "
21 because the midwives feared G·, "
2:23 their cry came up unto G· by reason "
24 And G· heard their groaning, and "
24 and G· remembered his covenant "
25 And G· looked upon the children of "
25 and G· had respect unto them. "
3: 1 the mountain of G·, even to Horeb. "
4 G· called unto him out of the midst "
6 I am the G· of thy father, "
6 the G· of Abraham, the G· of Isaac, "
6 and the G· of Jacob. "

Ex 3: 6 for he was afraid to look upon G·. 430
11 And Moses said unto G·, Who am I; "
12 shall serve G· upon this mountain. "
13 Moses said unto G·, Behold, when "
13 The G· of your fathers hath sent me "
14 G· said unto Moses, I Am that I Am: "
15 And G· said moreover unto Moses, "
15 The Lord G· of your fathers, "
15 the G· of Abraham, the G· of Isaac, "
15 and the G· of Jacob, "
16 The Lord G· of your fathers, "
16 the G· of Abraham, of Isaac, and "
18 The Lord G· of the Hebrews hath "
18 we may sacrifice to the Lord our G·. "
4: 5 the Lord G· of their fathers, "
5 the G· of Abraham, the G· of Isaac, "
5 and the G· of Jacob, hath appeared "
16 thou shalt be to him instead of G·. "
20 Moses took the rod of G· in his hand. "
27 in the mount of G·, and kissed him. "
5: 1 Thus saith the Lord G· of Israel, "
3 G· of the Hebrews hath met with us: "
3 and sacrifice unto the Lord our G·; "
8 Let us go and sacrifice to our G·. "
6: 2 G· spake unto Moses, and said "
3 by the name of G· Almighty, but 410
7 and I will be to you a G·: 430
7 know that I am the Lord your G·, "
7: 1 I have made thee a g· to Pharaoh: "
16 Lord G· of the Hebrews hath sent "
8:10 none like unto the Lord our G·. "
19 This is the finger of G·: and "
25 sacrifice to your G· in the land. "
26 of the Egyptians to the Lord our G·: "
27 sacrifice to the Lord our G·, as he "
28 sacrifice to the Lord your G· in the "
9: 1, 13 saith the Lord G· of the Hebrews, "
30 ye will not yet fear the Lord G·. "
10: 3 saith the Lord G· of the Hebrews, "
7 they may serve the Lord their G·: "
8 Go, serve the Lord your G·: but who "
16 sinned against the Lord your G·, "
17 intreat the Lord your G·, that he "
25 may sacrifice unto the Lord our G·. "
26 we take to serve the Lord our G·; "
13:17 G· led them not through the way "
17 G· said, Lest peradventure the "
18 But G· led the people about, "
19 G· will surely visit you; and ye "
14:19 the angel of G·, which went before "
15: 2 become my salvation: he is my G·, 410
2 father's G·, and I will exalt him. 430
26 to the voice of the Lord thy G·, "
16: 3 Would to G· we had died by the hand of *
12 know that I am the Lord your G·. 430
17: 9 with the rod of G· in mine hand. "
18: 1 of all that G· had done for Moses, "
4 for the G· of my father, said he, "
5 he encamped at the mount of G·: "
12 burnt offering and sacrifices for G·: "
12 with Moses' father in law before G·. "
15 come unto me to enquire of G·: "
16 make them know the statutes of G·, "
19 counsel, and G· shall be with thee: "
19 mayest bring the causes unto G·: "
21 able men, such as fear G·, men of "
23 this thing, and G· command thee so, "
19: 3 Moses went up unto G·, and the "
17 out of the camp to meet with G·; "
19 and G· answered him by a voice. "
20: 1 G· spake all these words, saying, "
2 I am the Lord thy G·, which have "
5 serve them; for I the Lord thy G· "
5 a jealous G·, visiting the iniquity 410
7 name of the Lord thy G· in vain; 430
10 is the sabbath of the Lord thy G·: "
12 which the Lord thy G· giveth thee. "
19 let not G· speak with us, lest we die. "
20 G· is come to prove you, and that "
21 the thick darkness where G· was. "
21:13 but G· deliver him into his hand; "
22:20 He that sacrificeth unto any g·, "
23:17 shall appear before the Lord G·. ‡3068
19 into the house of the Lord thy G·. 430
25 ye shall serve the Lord your G·, "
24:10 they saw the G· of Israel: and there "
11 they saw G·, and did eat and drink. "
13 Moses went up into the mount of G·. "
29:45 of Israel, and will be their G·. "
46 know that I am the Lord their G·, "
46 among them: I am the Lord their G·. "
31: 3 have filled him with the spirit of G·, "
18 stone, written with the finger of G·. "
32:11 Moses besought the Lord his G·, "
16 And the tables were the work of G·, "
16 the writing was the writing of G·, "
27 Thus saith the Lord G· of Israel, "
34: 6 Lord G·, merciful and gracious, 410
14 For thou shalt worship no other g·: "
14 name is Jealous, is a jealous G·: "
23 appear before the Lord G·. †‡3068
23 appear before...the G· of Israel, 430
24 appear before the Lord thy G· "
26 unto the house of the Lord thy G·. "
35:31 hath filled him with the spirit of G· "
Le 2:13 the salt of the covenant of thy G· "
4:22 commandments of the Lord his G· "
10:17 G· hath given it you to bear *
11:44 For I am the Lord your G·: 430
45 of the land of Egypt, to be your G·: "
18: 2 unto them I am the Lord your G·. "
4 therein: I am the Lord your G·. "
21 thou profane the name of thy G·: "
30 therein: I am the Lord your G·. "
19: 2 for I the Lord your G· am holy. "
3 am the Lord your G·. "

Le 19: 4 molten gods, I am the Lord your G·. 430
10 stranger: I am the Lord your G·. "
12 thou profane the name of thy G·: "
14 shalt fear thy G·: I am the Lord. "
25 thereof: I am the Lord your G·. "
31 by them: I am the Lord your G·. "
32 and fear thy G·: I am the Lord. "
34 of Egypt: I am the Lord your G·. "
36 the Lord your G·, which brought "
20: 7 be ye holy, for I am the Lord your G·. "
24 I am the Lord your G·, which have "
21: 6 They shall be holy unto their G·, "
6 not profane the name of their G·: "
6 the bread of their G·, they do offer: "
7 for he is holy unto his G·. "
8 for he offereth the bread of thy G·: "
12 profane the sanctuary of his G·; for "
12 of the anointing oil of his G· is upon "
17 approach to offer the bread of his G·. "
21 nigh to offer the bread of his G·. "
22 He shall eat the bread of his G·, "
22:25 shall ye offer the bread of your G· "
33 the land of Egypt, to be your G·: "
23:14 brought an offering unto your G·: "
22 the stranger: I am the Lord your G·. "
28 for you before the Lord your G·. "
40 rejoice before the Lord your G· "
43 land of Egypt: I am the Lord your G·. "
24:15 Whosoever curseth his G· shall "
22 country: for I am the Lord your G·. "
25:17 but thou shalt fear thy G·: "
17 for I am the Lord your G·. "
36 but fear thy G·; that thy brother "
38 I am the Lord your G·, which "
38 land of Canaan, and to be your G·. "
43 with rigour; but shalt fear thy G·. "
55 land of Egypt; I am the Lord your G·. "
26: 1 down into it: I am the Lord your G·. "
12 among you, and will be your G·, "
13 am the Lord your G·, which brought "
44 them: for I am the Lord their G·. "
45 that I might be their G·: I am the "
Nu 6: 7 consecration of his G· is upon his "
10: 9 remembered before...Lord your G·. "
10 you for a memorial before your G·: "
10 I am the Lord your G·. "
11:29 would G· that all the Lord's people "
12:13 Heal her now, O G·, I beseech thee. 410
14: 2 Would G· that we had died in ‡
2 would G· we had died in this ‡
15:40 and be holy unto your G·. 430
41 am the Lord your G·, which brought "
41 the land of Egypt, to be your G·: "
41 I am the Lord your G·. "
16: 9 the G· of Israel hath separated "
22 upon their faces, and said, O G·, 410
22 the G· of the spirits of all flesh, 430
20: 3 Would G· that we had died when ‡
21: 5 the people spake against G·, and 430
22: 9 G· came unto Baalam, and said, "
10 Balaam said unto G·, Balak the "
12 G· said unto Balaam, Thou shalt "
18 beyond the word of the Lord my G·, "
20 G· came unto Balaam at night, "
38 word that G· putteth in my mouth, "
23: 4 And G· met Balaam: and he said "
8 How shall I curse, whom G· hath 410
19 G· is not a man, that he should "
21 the Lord his G· is with him, and 430
22 G· brought them out of Egypt; he 410
23 What hath G· wrought! "
27 peradventure it will please G· 430
24: 2 the spirit of G· came upon him. "
4 which heard the words of G·, which 410
8 G· brought him forth out of Egypt; "
16 which heard the words of G·, and "
23 who shall live when G· doeth this! "
25:13 because he was zealous for his G·, 430
27:16 the G· of the spirits of all flesh, "
De 1: 6 The Lord our G· spake unto us "
10 Lord your G· hath multiplied you, "
11 Lord G· of your fathers make you "
19 as the Lord our G· commanded us; "
20 the Lord our G· doth give unto us. "
21 the Lord thy G· hath set the land "
21 Lord G· of thy fathers hath said "
25 which the Lord our G· doth give us. "
26 commandment of the Lord your G·: "
30 Lord your G· which goeth before "
31 the Lord thy G· bare thee, as a man "
32 ye did not believe the Lord your G·, "
41 that the Lord our G· commanded us. "
2: 7 the Lord thy G· hath blessed thee "
7 Lord thy G· hath been with thee; "
29 which the Lord our G· giveth us. "
30 the Lord thy G· hardened his spirit, "
33 our G· delivered him before us; "
36 Lord our G· delivered all unto us: "
37 whatsoever the Lord our G· forbad "
3: 3 So the Lord our G· delivered into "
18 The Lord your G· hath given you "
20 the Lord your G· hath given them "
21 that the Lord your G· hath done "
22 Lord your G· he shall fight for you. "
24 O Lord G·, thou hast begun to ‡3069
24 G· is there in heaven or in earth. 410
4: 1 which the Lord G· of your fathers 430
2 commandments of the Lord your G· "
3 Lord thy G· hath destroyed them "
4 did cleave unto the Lord your G· "
5 as the Lord my G· commanded me, "
7 who hath G· so nigh unto them, "
7 as the Lord our G· is in all things "
10 before the Lord thy G· in Horeb, "
19 which the Lord thy G· hath divided "
21 which the Lord thy G· giveth thee "

De 4:23 the covenant of the Lord your G·, 430
23 the Lord thy G· hath forbidden thee. "
24 the Lord thy G· is a consuming fire, "
24 consuming fire, even a jealous G·. 410
25 evil in the sight of the Lord thy G·, 430
29 thou shalt seek the Lord thy G·, "
30 days, if thou turn to the Lord thy G·, "
31 (For the Lord thy G· is a merciful 430
31 (For the Lord...is a merciful G·;) 410
32 since the day that G· created man 430
33 Did ever people hear the voice of G· "
34 hath G· assayed to go and take him "
34 all that the Lord your G· did for you "
35 know that the Lord he is G·; there "
39 the Lord he is G· in heaven above, "
40 which the Lord thy G· giveth thee, "
5: 2 The Lord our G· made a covenant "
6 am the Lord thy G·, which brought "
9 for I the Lord thy G· am a jealous "
9 a jealous G·, visiting the iniquity 410
11 the name of the Lord thy G· in vain: 430
12 as the Lord thy G· hath commanded "
14 is the sabbath of the Lord thy G·: "
15 the Lord thy G· brought thee out "
15 the Lord thy G· commanded thee "
16 Lord thy G· hath commanded thee, "
16 which the Lord thy G· giveth thee, "
24 the Lord our G· hath shewed us his "
24 that G· doth talk with man, and he "
25 we hear the voice of the Lord our G· "
26 hath heard the voice of the living G· "
27 all that the Lord our G· shall say; "
27 all that the Lord our G· shall speak "
32 Lord your G· hath commanded you: "
33 Lord your G· hath commanded you, "
6: 1 Lord your G· commanded to teach "
2 thou mightest fear the Lord thy G·, "
3 G· of thy fathers hath promised thee, "
4 The Lord our G· is one Lord: "
5 And thou shalt love the Lord thy G· "
10 when the Lord thy G· shall have into "
13 Thou shalt fear the Lord thy G·, "
15 (For the Lord thy G· is a jealous "
15 Lord...is a jealous G· among you) 410
15 lest the anger of the Lord thy G· 430
16 Ye shall not tempt the Lord your G·, "
17 commandments of the Lord your G·, "
20 Lord our G· hath commanded you? "
24 to fear the Lord our G·, for our good "
25 before the Lord our G·, as he hath "
7: 1 When the Lord thy G· shall bring "
2 the Lord thy G· shall deliver them "
6 holy people unto the Lord thy G·: "
6 the Lord thy G· hath chosen thee "
9 that the Lord thy G·, he is G·, "
9 the faithful G·, which keepeth 410
12 Lord thy G· shall keep unto thee 430
16 the Lord thy G· shall deliver thee; "
18 the Lord thy G· did unto Pharaoh, "
19 the Lord thy G· brought thee out: "
19 so shall the Lord thy G· do unto all "
20 Lord thy G· will send the hornet "
21 for the Lord thy G· is among you, "
21 you, a mighty G· and terrible. 410
22 the Lord thy G· will put out those 430
23 the Lord thy G· shall deliver them "
25 an abomination to the Lord thy G·. "
8: 2 way which the Lord thy G· led thee "
5 so the Lord thy G· chasteneth thee. "
6 commandments of the Lord thy G·, "
7 Lord thy G· bringeth thee into a "
10 thou shalt bless the Lord thy G· for "
11 that thou forget not the Lord thy G·, "
14 up, and thou forget the Lord thy G·, "
18 shalt remember the Lord thy G·: "
19 at all forget the Lord thy G·, and "
20 unto the voice of the Lord your G·. "
9: 3 Lord thy G· is he which goeth over "
4 that the Lord thy G· hath cast them "
5 the Lord thy G· doth drive them out "
6 the Lord thy G· giveth thee not this "
7 thou provokedst the Lord thy G· to "
10 stone written with the finger of G·; "
16 had sinned against the Lord your G·, "
23 commandment of the Lord your G·, "
26 O Lord G·, destroy not thy people ‡3069
10: 9 as the Lord thy G· promised him. 430
12 what doth the Lord thy G· require "
12 of thee, but to fear the Lord thy G·, "
12 and to serve the Lord thy G· with all "
14 of heavens is the Lord's thy G·, the "
17 For the Lord your G·, is G· of gods, "
17 a great G·, and mighty, and a 410
20 Thou shalt fear the Lord thy G·; 430
21 He is thy praise, and he is thy G·, "
22 Lord thy G· hath made thee as the "
11: 1 thou shalt love the Lord thy G·, and "
2 chastisement of the Lord your G·, "
12 which the Lord thy G· careth for: "
12 eyes of the Lord thy G· are always "
13 to love the Lord your G·, and to "
22 to love the Lord your G·, to walk "
25 the Lord your G· shall lay the fear "
27 if ye obey the...of the Lord your G·, "
28 not obey the...of the Lord your G·, "
29 when the Lord thy G· hath brought "
31 land which the Lord your G· giveth "
12: 1 land which the Lord G· of thy fathers "
4 shall not do so unto the Lord your G·. "
5 the place which the Lord your G· "
7 ye shall eat before the Lord your G·, "
7 the Lord thy G· hath blessed thee. "
9 inheritance...Lord your G· giveth "
10 land which the Lord your G· giveth "
11 Lord your G· shall choose to cause "
12 shall rejoice before the Lord your G·. "

De 12:15 to the blessing of the Lord thy G· 430
18 must eat them before the Lord thy G· "
18 in the place which the Lord thy G· "
18 shalt rejoice before the Lord thy G· "
20 When the Lord thy G· shall enlarge "
21 which the Lord thy G· hath chosen "
27 upon the altar of the Lord thy G·: "
27 upon the altar of the Lord thy G·, "
28 right in the sight of the Lord thy G·. "
29 Lord thy G· shall cut off the nations "
31 shall not do so unto the Lord thy G·: "
13: 3 for the Lord your G· proveth you, "
3 whether ye love the Lord your G· "
4 shall walk after the Lord your G·, "
5 you away from the Lord your G·, "
5 which the Lord thy G· commanded "
10 thee away from the Lord thy G·, "
12 which the Lord thy G· hath given "
16 every whit, for the Lord thy G·: "
18 to the voice of the Lord thy G·, "
18 right in the eyes of the Lord thy G·. "
14: 1 are the children of the Lord your G·: "
2 an holy people unto the Lord thy G·, "
21 an holy people unto the Lord thy G·. "
23 shalt eat before the Lord thy G·, "
23 mayest learn to fear the Lord thy G· "
24 which the Lord thy G· shall choose "
24 when the Lord thy G· hath blessed "
25 which the Lord thy G· shall choose: "
26 eat there before the Lord thy G·, "
29 that the Lord thy G· may bless thee "
15: 4 which the Lord thy G· giveth thee "
5 unto the voice of the Lord thy G·, "
6 For the Lord thy G· blesseth thee, "
7 land which the Lord thy G· giveth "
10 the Lord thy G· shall bless thee in "
14 the Lord thy G· hath blessed thee "
15 and the Lord thy G· redeemed thee: "
18 and the Lord thy G· shall bless thee. "
19 shalt sanctify unto the Lord thy G·: "
20 shalt eat it before the Lord thy G· "
21 not sacrifice it unto the Lord thy G·. "
16: 1 the passover unto the Lord thy G·: "
1 the Lord thy G· brought thee forth "
2 the passover unto the Lord thy G·, "
5 which the Lord thy G· giveth thee: "
6 which the Lord thy G· shall choose "
7 which the Lord thy G· shall choose: "
8 solemn assembly to the Lord thy G·: "
10 feast of weeks unto the Lord thy G· "
10 shalt give unto the Lord thy G·, *
10 according as the Lord thy G· hath 430
11 shalt rejoice before the Lord thy G·, "
11 which the Lord thy G· hath chosen "
15 a solemn feast unto the Lord thy G· "
15 the Lord thy G· shall bless thee in "
16 appear before the Lord thy G· in the "
17 to the blessing of the Lord thy G· "
18 gates, which the Lord thy G· giveth "
20 land which the Lord thy G· giveth "
21 unto the altar of the Lord thy G·, "
22 which the Lord thy G· hateth. "
17: 1 not sacrifice unto the Lord thy G· "
1 abomination unto the Lord thy G·. "
2 gates which the Lord thy G· giveth "
2 in the sight of the Lord thy G·, in "
8 which the Lord thy G· shall choose; "
12 minister...before the Lord thy G·, "
14 land which the Lord thy G· giveth "
15 whom the Lord thy G· shall choose: "
19 may learn to fear the Lord his G·, "
18: 5 the Lord thy G· hath chosen him "
7 in the name of the Lord his G·, "
9 land which the Lord thy G· giveth "
12 the Lord thy G· doth drive them out "
13 shalt be perfect with the Lord thy G·. "
14 the Lord thy G· hath not suffered "
15 The Lord thy G· will raise up unto "
16 thou desiredst of the Lord thy G· in "
16 again the voice of the Lord my G·, "
19: 1 When the Lord thy G· hath cut off "
1 whose land the Lord thy G· giveth "
2 Lord thy G· giveth thee to possess "
3 Lord thy G· giveth thee to inherit "
8 if the Lord thy G· enlarge thy "
9 to love the Lord thy G·, and to "
10 land, which the Lord thy G· giveth "
14 land that the Lord thy G· giveth "
20: 1 for the Lord thy G· is with thee, "
4 the Lord your G· is he that goeth "
13 the Lord thy G· hath delivered it "
14 which the Lord thy G· hath given "
16 land which the Lord thy G· doth give "
17 the Lord thy G· hath commanded "
18 ye sin against the Lord your G·. "
21: 1 land which the Lord thy G· giveth "
5 them the Lord thy G· hath chosen "
10 Lord thy G· hath delivered them "
23 he that is hanged is accursed of G·;) "
23 which the Lord thy G· giveth thee "
22: 5 abomination unto the Lord thy G·. "
23: 5 Nevertheless the Lord thy G· would "
5 but the Lord thy G· turned the curse "
5 because the Lord thy G· loved thee. "
14 For the Lord thy G· walketh in the "
18 into the house of the Lord thy G· for "
18 abomination unto the Lord thy G·. "
20 that the Lord thy G· may bless thee "
21 vow a vow unto the Lord thy G·, "
21 the Lord thy G· will surely require "
23 hast vowed unto the Lord thy G·, "
24: 4 which the Lord thy G· giveth thee "
9 Remember what the Lord thy G· did "
13 unto thee before the Lord thy G·. "
18 and the Lord thy G· redeemed thee "
19 that the Lord thy G· may bless thee "

De 25:15 land which the Lord thy G' giveth 430
16 abomination unto the Lord thy G'. "
18 and he feared not G'. "
19 Lord thy G' hath given thee rest "
19 land which the Lord thy G' giveth "
26: 1 land which the Lord thy G giveth "
2 land that the Lord thy G' giveth "
2 the Lord thy G' shall choose to place "
3 this day unto the Lord thy G', that "
4 before the altar of the Lord thy G'. "
5 say before the Lord thy G', A Syrian "
7 unto the Lord G' of our fathers, "
10 shalt set it before the Lord thy G', "
10 and worship before the Lord thy G': "
11 thing which the Lord thy G' hath "
13 say before the Lord thy G', I have "
14 to the voice of the Lord my G', and "
16 Lord thy G' hath commanded thee "
17 the Lord this day to be thy G', "
19 an holy people unto the Lord thy G'. "
27: 2 Lord thy G' giveth thee, that thou "
3 Lord thy G' giveth thee, a land that "
3 Lord G' of thy fathers hath promised "
5 build an altar unto the Lord thy G', "
6 build the altar of the Lord thy G' of "
6 thereon unto the Lord thy G': "
7 and rejoice before the Lord thy G'. "
9 the people of the Lord thy G'. "
10 obey the voice of the Lord thy G', "
28: 1 unto the voice of the Lord thy G', "
1 Lord thy G' will set thee on high "
2 unto the voice of the Lord thy G'. "
8 land which the Lord thy G' giveth "
9 shalt keep the...of the Lord thy G', "
13 hearken unto the...of the Lord thy G', "
15 unto the voice of the Lord thy G', to "
45 unto the voice of the Lord thy G', "
47 thou servedst not the Lord thy G' "
52 which the Lord thy G' hath given "
53 daughters...the Lord thy G' hath "
58 fearful name, The Lord thy G'; ‡ "
62 obey the voice of the Lord thy G'. "
67 shalt say, Would G' it were even! ‡
67 shalt say, Would G' it were morning! ‡
29: 6 know that I am the Lord your G'. 430
10 all of you before the Lord your G'; "
12 covenant with the Lord thy G', "
12 the Lord thy G' maketh with thee "
13 and that he may be unto thee a G', "
15 us this day before the Lord our G', "
18 away this day from the Lord our G', "
25 of the Lord G' of their fathers, "
29 things belong unto the Lord our G': "
30: 1 the Lord thy G' hath driven thee, "
2 shalt return unto the Lord thy G', "
3 Lord thy G' will turn thy captivity "
3 the Lord thy G' hath scattered thee. "
4 will the Lord thy G' gather thee, "
5 the Lord thy G' will bring thee into "
6 Lord thy G' will circumcise thine "
6 love the Lord thy G' with all thine "
7 the Lord thy G' will put all these "
9 the Lord thy G' will make thee "
10 unto the voice of the Lord thy G', "
10 if thou turn unto the Lord thy G' "
16 to love the Lord thy G', to walk in "
16 and the Lord thy G' shall bless thee "
20 thou mayest love the Lord thy G', "
31: 3 The Lord thy G', he will go before "
6 Lord thy G', he it is that doth go "
11 to appear before the Lord thy G' "
12 learn, and fear the Lord your G', "
13 and learn to fear the Lord your G', "
17 because our G' is not among us? "
26 the covenant of the Lord your G', "
32: 3 ascribe ye greatness unto our G'. "
4 a G' of truth and without iniquity, 410
12 there was no strange g' with him. "
15 he forsook G' which made him, 433
17 sacrificed unto devils, not to G'; "
18 hast forgotten G' that formed thee. 410
21 jealousy with that which is not G'; "
39 and there is no g' with me: 430
33: 1 Moses the man of G' blessed the "
26 none like unto the G' of Jeshurun, 410
27 The eternal G' is thy refuge, and 430
Jos 1: 9 for the Lord thy G' is with thee "
11 land, which the Lord your G' giveth "
13 Lord your G' hath given you rest, "
15 land which the Lord your G' giveth "
17 the Lord thy G' be with thee, "
2:11 the Lord your G', he is G' in heaven "
3: 3 the covenant of the Lord your G', "
9 hear the words of the Lord your G'. "
10 know that the living G' is among 410
4: 5 before the ark of the Lord your G' 430
23 Lord your G' dried up the waters "
23 Lord your G' did to the Red sea, "
24 fear the Lord your G' for ever. "
7: 7 Joshua said, Alas, O Lord G', ‡3069
7 would to G' we had been content.* "
13 thus saith the Lord G' of Israel, 430
19 glory to the Lord G' of Israel, "
20 sinned against the Lord G' of Israel, "
8: 7 the Lord your G' will deliver it into "
30 Lord G' of Israel in mount Ebal, "
9: 9 of the name of the Lord thy G': for "
18 had sworn unto them by the Lord G' "
19 sworn unto them by the Lord G' of "
23 of water for the house of my G'. "
24 that the Lord thy G' commanded "
10:19 Lord your G' hath delivered them "
40 the Lord G' of Israel commanded. "
42 Lord G' of Israel fought for Israel. "
13:14 sacrifices of the Lord G' of Israel "
33 the Lord G' of Israel was their "

Jos 14: 6 Lord said unto Moses the man of G' 430
8 I wholly followed the Lord my G'. "
9 wholly followed the Lord my G'. "
14 he wholly followed the Lord G' of "
18: 3 land, which the Lord G' of your "
6 for you here before the Lord our G'. "
22: 3 commandment of the Lord your G'. "
4 now the Lord your G' hath given "
5 love the Lord your G', and to walk "
16 committed against the G' of Israel, "
19 beside the altar of the Lord our G'. "
22 Lord G' of gods, the Lord G' of ‡ 410
24 to do with the Lord G' of Israel? 430
29 G' forbid that we should rebel ‡
29 beside the altar of the Lord our G' 430
33 the children of Israel blessed G', "
34 between us that the Lord is G'. "
23: 3 that the Lord your G' hath done "
3 for the Lord your G' is he that hath "
5 And the Lord your G', he shall expel "
5 as the Lord your G' hath promised "
8 But cleave unto the Lord your G', "
10 for the Lord your G', he it is that "
11 that ye love the Lord your G'. "
13 Lord your G' will no more drive "
13 the Lord your G' hath given you. "
14 things which the Lord your G' spake "
15 the Lord your G' promised you; "
15 the Lord your G' hath given you. "
16 the covenant of the Lord your G', "
24: 1 presented themselves before G'. "
2 Thus saith the Lord G' of Israel, "
16 G' forbid that we should forsake ‡
17 For the Lord our G', he it is that 430
18 also serve the Lord; for he is our G'. "
19 the Lord: for he is an holy G'; "
19 he is a jealous G'; he will forgive 410
23 heart unto the Lord G' of Israel. 430
24 The Lord our G' will we serve, "
26 words in the book of the law of G', "
27 unto you, lest ye deny your G'. "
J'g 1: 7 have done, so G' had requited me. "
2:12 forsook the Lord G' of their fathers, "
3: 7 forgat the Lord their G', and served "
20 have a message from G' unto thee. "
4: 6 the Lord G' of Israel commanded "
23 So G' subdued on that day Jabin "
5: 3 sing praise to the Lord G' of Israel. "
5 from before the Lord G' of Israel. "
6: 8 Thus saith the Lord G' of Israel, "
10 I am the Lord your G'; fear not "
20 And the angel of G' said unto him, "
22 Gideon said, Alas, O Lord G'! for ‡3069
26 build an altar unto the Lord thy G' 430
31 if he be a g', let him plead for "
36 Gideon said unto G', If thou wilt "
39 Gideon said unto G', Let not thine "
40 G' did so that night: for it was dry "
7:14 his hand hath G' delivered Midian, "
8: 3 G' hath delivered into your hands "
33 and made Baal-berith their g'. "
34 remembered not the Lord their G', "
9: 7 that G' may hearken unto you. "
9 by me they honour G' and man, "
13 which cheereth G' and man, and go "
23 Then G' sent an evil spirit between "
27 and went into the house of their g', "
29 would to G' this people were under my ‡
46 hold of the house of the g' Berith.* 410
56 G' rendered the wickedness of 430
57 did G' render upon their heads: "
10:10 because we have forsaken our G', "
11:21 Lord G' of Israel delivered Sihon "
23 So now the Lord G' of Israel hath "
24 which Chemosh thy g' giveth thee to "
24 the Lord our G' shall drive out from "
13: 5 a Nazarite unto G' from the womb: "
6 A man of G' came unto me, "
6 the countenance of an angel of G', "
7 be a Nazarite to G' from the womb "
8 the man of G' which thou didst send "
9 G' hearkened to the voice of Manoah; "
9 and the angel of G' came again unto "
22 surely die, because we have seen G'. "
15:19 G' clave an hollow place that was "
16:17 Nazarite unto G' from my mother's "
23 great sacrifice unto Dagon their g', "
23 Our g' hath delivered Samson our "
24 praised their g': for they said, Our g' "
28 O Lord G', remember me, I pray ‡3069
28 only this once, O G' that I may, 430
18: 5 Ask counsel, we pray thee, of G', "
10 G' hath given it into your hands; "
31 all the time that the house of G' was "
20: 2 in the assembly of the people of G', "
18 and went up to the house of G', *1008
18 and asked counsel of G', and said 430
26 came into the house of G', and *1008
27 the ark of the covenant of G' 430
31 one goeth up to the house of G', *1008
21: 2 people came to the house of G', * "
2 and abode there till even before G'. 430
3 And said, O Lord G' of Israel, "
Ru 1:16 my people, and thy G' my G': "
2:12 given thee of the Lord G' of Israel, "
1Sa 1:17 G' of Israel grant thee thy petition "
2: 2 neither is there any rock like our G'. "
3 the Lord is a G' of knowledge, 410
27 there came a man of G' unto Eli, 430
30 Wherefore the Lord G' of Israel "
32 the wealth which G' shall give Israel: "
3: 3 And ere the lamp of G' went out in 430
3 Lord, where the ark of G' was, and "
17 G' do so to thee, and more also, "
4: 4 with the ark of the covenant of G'. "
7 they said, G' is come into the camp. "

1Sa 4:11 And the ark of G' was taken; and 430
13 his heart trembled for the ark of G'. "
17 are dead, and the ark of G' is taken. "
18 he made mention of the ark of G', "
19 that the ark of G' was taken, and "
21 because the ark of G' was taken, "
22 for the ark of G' is taken. "
5: 1, 2 the Philistines took the ark of G', "
7 The ark of the G' of Israel shall not "
7 upon us, and upon Dagon our g'. "
8 with the ark of the G' of Israel? "
8 Let the ark of the G' of Israel be "
8 carried the ark of the G' of Israel "
10 they sent the ark of G' to Ekron. "
10 as the ark of G' came to Ekron, "
10 brought about the ark of the G' of "
11 Send away the ark of the G' of Israel, "
11 hand of G' was very heavy there. "
6: 3 send away the ark of the G' of Israel, "
5 give glory unto the G' of Israel: "
20 to stand before this holy Lord G'? "
7: 8 to cry unto the Lord our G' for us, "
9: 6 now, there is in this city a man of G', "
7 present to bring to the man of G': "
8 that will I give to the man of G', "
9 when a man went to inquire of G', "
10 the city where the man of G' was. "
27 I may shew thee the word of G'. "
10: 3 meet thee three men going up to G' "
5 thou shalt come to the hill of G', "
7 serve thee, for G' is with thee. "
9 G' gave him another heart: and all "
10 and the Spirit of G' came upon him, "
18 Thus saith the Lord G' of Israel, "
19 ye have this day rejected your G', "
24 and said, G' save the king. ‡
26 men, whose hearts G' had touched. 430
11: 6 And the Spirit of G' came upon Saul "
12: 9 when they forgat the Lord their G', "
12 the Lord your G' was your king. "
14 continue following the Lord your G': "
19 thy servants unto the Lord thy G', "
23 G' forbid that I should sin against ‡
13:13 commandment of the Lord thy G', 430
14:18 Bring hither the ark of G'. "
18 For the ark of G' was at that time "
36 Let us draw near hither unto G'. "
37 And Saul asked counsel of G', "
41 Saul said unto the Lord G' of Israel, "
44 G' do so and more also: for thou "
45 G' forbid: as the Lord liveth, ‡
45 he hath wrought with G' this day. 430
15:15 sacrifice unto the Lord thy G'; "
21 sacrifice unto the Lord thy G' in "
30 that I may worship the Lord thy G'. "
16:15 evil spirit from G' troubleth thee. "
16 when the evil spirit from G' is upon "
23 evil spirit from G' was upon Saul, "
17:26 defy the armies of the living G'? "
36 defied the armies of the living G'. "
45 the G' of the armies of Israel, whom "
46 know that there is a G' in Israel. "
18:10 evil spirit from G' came upon Saul, "
19:20 Spirit of G' was upon the messengers "
23 the Spirit of G' was upon him also, "
20: 2 he said unto him, G' forbid; thou ‡
12 O Lord G' of Israel, when I have 430
22: 3 till I know what G' will do for me. "
13 and hast enquired of G' for him, "
15 then begin to enquire of G' for him? "
23: 7 G' hath delivered him into mine "
10 Then said David, O Lord G' of Israel, "
11 O Lord G' of Israel, I beseech thee, "
14 G' delivered him not into his hand. "
16 and strengthened his hand in G'. "
25:22 do G' unto the enemies of David, "
29 bundle of life with the Lord thy G'; "
32 Blessed be the Lord G' of Israel, "
34 Lord G' of Israel liveth, which hath "
26: 8 G' hath delivered thine enemy into "
28:15 and G' is departed from me, and "
29: 9 good in my sight, as an angel of G': "
30: 6 himself in the Lord his G'. "
15 Swear unto me by G', that thou wilt "
2Sa 2:27 Joab said, As G' liveth, unless thou "
3: 9 So do G' to Abner, and more also, "
35 So do G' to me, and more also, "
5:10 the Lord G' of hosts was with him. "
6: 2 bring up from thence the ark of G', "
3 set the ark of G' upon a new cart "
4 accompanying the ark of G': and "
6 put forth his hand to the ark of G', "
7 G' smote him there for his error; "
7 and there he died by the ark of G'. "
12 unto him, because of the ark of G'. "
12 went and brought up the ark of G' "
7: 2 ark of G' dwelleth within curtains. "
18 he said, Who am I, O Lord G'? ‡3069
19 thing in thy sight, O Lord G'; ‡ "
19 the manner of man, O Lord G'? ‡ "
20 Lord G', knowest thy servant. ‡ "
22 thou art great, O Lord G': for there 430
22 neither is there any G' beside thee, "
23 G' went to redeem for a people to "
24 and thou, Lord, art become their G'. "
25 Lord G', the word that thou hast "
26 Lord of hosts is the G' over Israel: "
27 thou, O Lord of hosts, G' of Israel, "
28 And now O Lord G', thou art ‡3069
28 thou art that G', and thou hast 430
29 thou, O Lord G', hast spoken it: ‡3069
9: 3 shew the kindness of G' unto him? 430
10:12 people, and for the cities of our G': "
12: 7 Thus saith the Lord G' of Israel, "
16 David therefore besought G' for the "
22 whether G' will be gracious to †‡3068

2Sa 14:11 king remember the Lord thy G'. 430
13 a thing against the people of G'? "
14 neither doth G' respect any person: "
16 out of the inheritance of G'. "
17 for as an angel of G', so is my lord "
17 therefore the Lord thy G' will be "
20 to the wisdom of an angel of G'. "
15:24 the ark of the covenant of G': "
24 and they set down the ark of G'; "
25 back the ark of G' into the city: "
29 carried the ark of G' again to "
32 the mount, where he worshipped G'. "
16:16 G' save the king, G' save the ‡
23 had enquired at the oracle of G': 430
18:28 Blessed be the Lord thy G', "
33 would G' I...died for thee, O Absalom, "
19:13 G' do so to me, and more also, if 430
27 my lord the king is as an angel of G': "
21:14 that G' was intreated for the land. "
22: 3 G' of my rock; in him will I trust: "
7 and cried to my G': and he did hear "
22 not wickedly departed from my G'. "
30 by my G' have I leaped over a wall. "
31 As for G', his way is perfect; 410
32 For who is G', save the Lord? "
32 and who is a rock, save our G'? 430
33 G' is my strength and power: 410
47 the G' of the rock of my salvation. 430
48 It is G' that avengeth me, and 410
23: 1 the anointed of the G' of Jacob, 430
3 The G' of Israel said, the Rock of "
3 must be just, ruling in the fear of G'. "
5 my house be not so with G'; yet 410
24: 3 Now the Lord thy G' add unto the 430
23 The Lord thy G' accept thee. "
24 burnt offerings unto the Lord my G' "
1Ki 1:17 thou swarest by the Lord thy G' "
25 and say, G' save king Adonijah. ‡
30 unto thee by the Lord G' of Israel, 430
34 and say, G' save king Solomon. ‡
36 the Lord G' of my lord the king 430
39 said, G' save king Solomon. ‡
47 G' make the name of Solomon 430
48 Blessed be the Lord G' of Israel, "
2: 3 keep the charge of the Lord thy G', "
23 G' do so to me, and more also, if "
26 thou barest the ark of the Lord G' ‡3069
3: 5 G' said, Ask what I shall give thee. 430
7 O Lord my G', thou hast made thy "
11 And G' said unto him, Because thou "
28 that the wisdom of G' was in him, "
4:29 And G' gave Solomon wisdom and "
5: 3 unto the name of the Lord his G' "
4 But now the Lord my G' hath given "
5 unto the name of the Lord my G', "
8:15 Blessed be the Lord G' of Israel, "
17 the name of the Lord G' of Israel. "
23 And he said, Lord G' of Israel, "
23 there is no G' like thee, in heaven "
25 now, Lord G' of Israel, keep with thy "
26 And now, O G' of Israel, let thy word, "
27 will G' indeed dwell on the earth? "
28 to his supplication, O Lord my G', "
53 fathers out of Egypt, O Lord G'. ‡3069
57 The Lord our G' be with us, 430
59 be nigh unto the Lord our G' by day "
60 earth may know that the Lord is G', "
61 be perfect with the Lord our G', to "
65 before the Lord our G', seven days "
9: 9 they forsook the Lord their G', who "
10: 9 Blessed be the Lord thy G', which "
24 which G' had put in his heart. "
11: 4 was not perfect with the Lord his G', "
9 turned from the Lord G' of Israel, "
23 G' stirred him up another adversary, "
31 thus saith the Lord, the G' of Israel, "
33 Chemosh the g' of the Moabites, "
33 and Milcom the g' of the children "
12:22 But the word of G' came unto "
22 unto Shemaiah the man of G', "
13: 1 there came a man of G' out of Judah "
4 heard the saying of the man of G', "
5 which the man of G' had given by "
6 and said unto the man of G', Intreat "
6 now the face of the Lord thy G', "
6 the man of G' besought the Lord, "
7 the king said unto the man of G', "
8 the man of G' said unto the king, "
11 works that the man of G' had done "
12 seen what way the man of G' went, "
14 And went after the man of G', "
14 man of G' that camest from Judah? "
21 And he cried unto the man of G' "
21 which the Lord thy G' commanded "
26 he said, It is the man of G', who "
29 up the carcase of the man of G', "
31 wherein the man of G' is buried; "
14: 7 Thus saith the Lord G' of Israel, "
13 the Lord G' of Israel in the house "
15: 3 not perfect with the Lord his G', "
4 for David's sake did the Lord his G' "
30 he provoked the Lord G' of Israel "
16:13 in provoking the Lord G' of Israel "
26, 33 to provoke the Lord G' of Israel "
17: 1 As the Lord G' of Israel liveth, "
12 she said, As the Lord thy G' liveth, "
14 thus saith the Lord G' of Israel, "
18 to do with thee, O thou man of G'? "
20 the Lord, and said, O Lord my G', "
21 said, O Lord my G', I pray thee, "
24 I know that thou art a man of G', "
18:10 the Lord thy G' liveth, there is no "
21 If the Lord be G', follow him: but "
24 and the G' that answereth by fire, "
24 answereth by fire, let him be G'. "
27 and said, Cry aloud: for he is a g'; "

1Ki 18:36 Lord G' of Abraham, Isaac, and of 430
36 be known this day that thou art G' "
37 know that thou art the Lord G', "
39 they said, The Lord, he is the G'; "
39 the Lord, he is the G'. "
19: 8 nights unto Horeb the mount of G'. "
10, 14 jealous for the Lord G' of hosts: "
20:28 there came a man of G', and spake "
28 said, The Lord is G' of the hills, "
28 but he is not G' of the valleys, "
21:10 didst blaspheme G' and the king. "
13 did blaspheme G' and the king. "
22:53 provoked to anger the Lord G' of "
2Ki 1: 2 of Baal-zebub the g' of Ekron "
3 is not a G' in Israel, that ye go to "
3 of Baal-zebub the g' of Ekron? "
6 not a G' in Israel, that thou sendest "
6 to enquire of Baal-zebub the g' of "
9 he spake unto him, Thou man of G', "
10 If I be a man of G', then let the fire "
11 and said unto him, O man of G', "
12 If I be a man of G', let fire come "
12 fire of G' came down from heaven, "
13 and said unto him, O man of G', "
16 of Baal-zebub the g' of Ekron, is it "
16 not because there is no G' in Israel "
2:14 Where is the Lord G' of Elijah? "
4: 7 she came and told the man of G'. "
9 that this is an holy man of G', which "
16 Nay, my lord, thou man of G', do not "
21 laid him on the bed of the man of G', "
22 that I may run to the man of G', "
25 unto the man of G' to mount Carmel. "
25 when the man of G' saw her afar off, "
27 when she came to the man of G' "
27 the man of G' said, Let her alone; "
40 O thou man of G', there is death "
42 and brought the man of G' bread "
5: 3 Would G' my lord were with the ‡
7 Am I G', to kill and to make alive, 430
8 Elisha the man of G' had heard "
11 call on the name of the Lord his G', "
14 to the saying of the man of G': "
15 And he returned to the man of G', "
15 now I know that there is no G' in "
20 the servant of Elisha the man of G', "
6: 6 the man of G' said, Where fell it? "
9 the man of G' sent unto the king "
10 place which the man of G' told him "
15 servant of the man of G' was risen "
31 G' do so and more also to me, if "
7: 2 answered the man of G', and said, "
17 he died, as the man of G' had said, "
18 as the man of G' had spoken to "
19 answered the man of G', and said, "
8: 2 after the saying of the man of G': "
4 servant of the man of G', saying "
7 The man of G' is come hither. "
8 meet the man of G', and enquire "
11 and the man of G' wept. "
9: 6 Thus saith the Lord G' of Israel, "
10:31 in the law of the Lord G' of Israel "
11:12 hands, and said, G' save the king. ‡
13:19 the man of G' was wroth with him, 430
14:25 to the word of the Lord G' of Israel, "
16: 2 right in the sight of the Lord his G', "
17: 7 sinned against the Lord their G', "
9 not right against the Lord their G', "
14 did not believe in the Lord their G'. "
16 left all the...of the Lord their G', "
19 kept not the...of the Lord their G', "
26 not the manner of the G' of the land: "
26 not the manner of the G' of the land. "
27 the manner of the G' of the land. "
39 But the Lord your G' ye shall fear; "
18: 5 He trusted in the Lord G' of Israel; "
12 not the voice of the Lord their G', "
22 We trust in the Lord our G': "
19: 4 It may be the Lord thy G' will hear "
4 hath sent to reproach the living G'; "
4 words which the Lord thy G' hath "
10 not thy G' in whom thou trustest "
15 O Lord G' of Israel, which dwellest "
15 thou art the G', even thou alone, "
16 sent him to reproach the living G'. "
19 Now therefore, O Lord our G', "
19 thou art the Lord G', even thou only. "
20 Thus saith the Lord G' of Israel, "
37 in the house or Nisroch his g', "
20: 5 Lord, the G' of David thy father, "
21:12 thus saith the Lord G' of Israel, "
22 forsook the Lord G' of his fathers, "
22:15 unto them, Thus saith the Lord G' "
18 say to him, Thus saith the Lord G' "
23:16 which the man of G' proclaimed, "
17 It is the sepulchre of the man of G', "
21 the passover unto the Lord your G', "
1Ch 4:10 Jabez called on the G' of Israel, "
10 And G' granted him that which he "
5:20 for they cried to G' in the battle, "
22 slain, because the war was of G'. "
25 against the G' of their fathers, and "
25 whom G' destroyed before them. "
26 the G' of Israel stirred up the spirit "
6:48 the tabernacle of the house of G'. "
49 the servant of G' had commanded. "
9:11 the ruler of the house of G'; "
13 of the service of the house of G'. "
26 and treasuries of the house of G'. "
27 lodged round about the house of G', "
11: 2 and the Lord thy G' said unto thee, "
19 My G' forbid it me, that I should "
12:17 the G' of our fathers look thereon, "
18 helpers; for thy G' helpeth thee, "
22 was a great host, like the host of G'. "
13: 2 and that it be of the Lord our G', "

1Ch 13: 3 let us bring again the ark of our G' 430
5 the ark of G' from Kirjath-jearim. "
6 up thence the ark of G' the Lord, "
7 they carried the ark of G' in a new "
8 all Israel played before G' with "
10 and there he died before G'. "
12 David was afraid of G' that day, "
12 How shall I bring the ark of G' "
14 ark of G' remained with the family "
14:10 And David enquired of G', saying, "
11 said, G' hath broken in upon mine "
14 David enquired again of G'; and G' "
15 for G' is gone forth before thee to "
16 therefore did as G' commanded "
15: 1 prepared a place for the ark of G', "
2 None ought to carry the ark of G' "
2 Lord chosen to carry the ark of G', "
12 up the ark of the Lord G' of Israel "
13 Lord our G' made a breach upon us, "
14 up the ark of the Lord G' of Israel. "
15 the Levites bare the ark of G' upon "
24 the trumpets before the ark of G': "
26 when G' helped the Levites that "
16: 1 So they brought the ark of G', "
1 and peace offerings before G'. "
4 and praise the Lord G' of Israel: "
6 before the ark of the covenant of G'. "
14 is the Lord our G'; his judgments "
35 Save us, O G' of our salvation, "
36 Blessed be the Lord G' of Israel "
42 and with musical instruments of G'. "
17: 2 thine heart; for G' is with thee. "
3 that the word of G' came to Nathan, "
16 Who am I, O Lord G', and what is "
17 a small thing in thine eyes, O G'; "
17 a man of high degree, O Lord G'. "
20 neither is there any G' beside thee, "
21 whom G' went to redeem to be his "
22 and thou, Lord, becamest their G'. "
24 The Lord of hosts is the G' of Israel, "
24 even a G' to Israel: and let the "
25 For thou, O my G', hast told thy "
26 And now, Lord, thou art G', "
19:13 people, and for the cities of our G': "
21: 7 G' was displeased with this thing; "
8 David said unto G', I have sinned "
15 G' sent an angel unto Jerusalem to "
17 And David said unto G', Is it not I "
17 O Lord my G', be on me, and on my "
30 not go before it to enquire of G': "
22: 1 This is the house of the Lord G', "
2 stones to build the house of G'. "
6 an house for the Lord G' of Israel. "
7 unto the name of the Lord my G': "
11 build the house of the Lord thy G', "
12 keep the law of the Lord thy G'. "
18 Is not the Lord your G' with you? "
19 your soul to seek the Lord your G'; "
19 ye the sanctuary of the Lord G', "
19 holy vessels of G', into the house "
23:14 concerning Moses the man of G', "
25 The Lord G' of Israel hath given "
28 of the service of the house of G'; "
24: 5 and governors of the house of G', "
19 Lord G' of Israel had commanded "
25: 5 the king's seer in the words of G', "
5 G' gave to Heman fourteen sons "
6 for the service of the house of G', "
26: 5 the eighth; for G' blessed him. "
20 over the treasures of the house of G', "
32 for every matter pertaining to G', "
28: 2 and for the footstool of our G', "
3 But G' said unto me, Thou shalt "
4 Howbeit the Lord G' of Israel chose "
8 and in the audience of our G', keep "
8 commandments of the Lord your G': "
9 know thou the G' of thy father, "
12 of the treasuries of the house of G', "
20 nor be dismayed: for the Lord G', "
20 even my G', will be with thee; "
21 for all the service of the house of G': "
29: 1 my son, whom alone G' hath chosen, "
1 not for man, but for the Lord G'. "
2 all my might for the house of my G' "
3 my affection to the house of my G', "
3 I have given to the house of my G', "
7 for the service of the house of G' "
10 Blessed be thou, Lord G' of Israel "
13 Now therefore, our G', we thank "
16 O Lord our G', all this store that "
17 I know also, my G', that thou triest "
18 O Lord G' of Abraham, Isaac, and "
20 Now bless the Lord your G'. And "
20 blessed the Lord G' of their fathers, "
2Ch 1: 1 and the Lord his G' was with him, "
3 tabernacle of the congregation of G', "
4 the ark of G' had David brought "
7 In that night did G' appear unto "
8 Solomon said unto G', Thou hast "
9 Lord G', let thy promise unto David "
11 G' said to Solomon, Because this "
2: 4 to the name of the Lord my G', "
4 solemn feasts of the Lord our G'. "
5 for great is our G' above all gods. "
12 Blessed be the Lord G' of Israel, "
3: 3 for the building of the house of G'. "
4:11 king Solomon for the house of G'; "
19 vessels that were for the house of G', "
5: 1 the treasures of the house of G'. "
14 the Lord had filled the house of G'. "
6: 4 Blessed be the Lord G' of Israel, "
7, 10 name of the Lord G' of Israel. "
14 G' of Israel, there is no G' like thee "
16 Now therefore, O Lord G' of Israel, "
17 Now then, O Lord G' of Israel, "
18 But will G' in very deed dwell with "

2Ch 6:19 to his supplication, O Lord my G·. 430
40 Now, my G·, let, I beseech thee, "
41 Now therefore arise, O Lord G·, "
41 thy priests, O Lord G·, be clothed "
42 O Lord G·, turn not away the face "
7: 5 people dedicated the house of G·. "
22 Because they forsook the Lord G· "
8:14 David the man of G· commanded. "
9: 8 Blessed be the Lord thy G·, which "
8 Lord thy G·: because thy G· loved "
23 wisdom, that G· had put in his heart. "
10:15 for the cause was of G·, that the "
11: 2 to Shemaiah the man of G·, saying "
16 hearts to seek the Lord G· of Israel "
16 unto the Lord G· of their fathers. "
13: 5 to know that the Lord G· of Israel "
10 But as for us, the Lord is our G·, "
11 keep the charge of the Lord our G·; "
12 G· himself is with us for our captain, "
12 fight ye not against the Lord G· of "
15 to pass, that G· smote Jeroboam "
16 G· delivered them into their hand. "
18 they relied upon the Lord G· of "
14: 2 right in the eyes of the Lord his G·: "
4 to seek the Lord G· of their fathers, "
7 we have sought the Lord our G·, "
11 And Asa cried unto the Lord his G·, "
11 help us, O Lord our G·; for we rest "
11 O Lord, thou art our G·; let not "
15: 1 the Spirit of G· came upon Azariah "
3 Israel hath been without the true G·, "
4 did turn unto the Lord G· of Israel, "
6 G· did vex them with all adversity. "
9 that the Lord his G· was with him. "
12 a covenant to seek the Lord G· of "
13 would not seek the Lord G· of Israel "
18 And he brought into the house of G· "
16: 7 and not relied on the Lord thy G·. "
17: 4 sought to the Lord G· of his father, "
18: 5 for G· will deliver it into the king's "
13 even what my G· saith, that will I "
31 G· moved them to depart from him. "
19: 3 hast prepared thine heart to seek G·. "
4 unto the Lord G· of their fathers. "
7 is no iniquity with the Lord our G·, "
20: 6 And said, O Lord G· of our fathers, "
6 art not thou G· in heaven? "
7 Art not thou our G·, who didst drive "
12 O our G·, wilt thou not judge them? "
19 to praise the Lord G· of Israel with "
20 Believe in the Lord your G·, so shall "
29 fear of G· was on all the kingdoms "
30 his G· gave him rest round about. "
33 hearts unto the G· of their fathers. "
21:10 forsaken the Lord G· of his fathers. "
12 Thus saith the Lord G· of David thy "
22: 7 destruction of Ahaziah was of G· by "
12 was hid in the house of G· six years: "
23: 3 with the king in the house of G·. "
9 which were in the house of G·. "
11 him, and said, G· save the king. ‡
24: 5 repair the house of your G· from 430
7 had broken up the house of G·; "
9 Moses the servant of G· laid upon "
13 they set the house of G· in his state, "
16 toward G·, and toward his house. "
18 house of the Lord G· of their fathers. "
20 Spirit of G· came upon Zechariah "
20 Thus saith G·, Why transgress ye "
24 had forsaken the Lord G· of their "
27 and the repairing of the house of G·, "
25: 7 But there came a man of G· to him, "
8 G· shall make thee fall before the "
8 for G· hath power to help, and to "
9 And Amaziah said to the man of G·, "
9 the man of G· answered, The Lord "
16 I know that G· hath determined to "
20 would not hear; for it came of G·, "
24 the house of G· with Obed-edom, "
26: 5 sought G· in the days of Zechariah, "
5 understanding in the visions of G·: "
5 the Lord, G· made him to prosper. "
7 And G· helped him against the "
16 against the Lord his G·, and went "
18 for thine honour from the Lord G·. "
27: 6 his ways before the Lord his G·. "
28: 5 the Lord his G· delivered him into "
6 had forsaken the Lord G· of their "
9 because the Lord G· of your fathers "
10 you, sins against the Lord your G·? "
24 the vessels of the house of G·, and "
24 pieces the vessels of the house of G·, "
25 provoked to anger the Lord G· of "
29: 5 house of the Lord G· of your fathers, "
6 evil in the eyes of the Lord our G·, "
7 holy place unto the G· of Israel. "
10 covenant with the Lord G· of Israel, "
36 that G· had prepared the people: "
30: 1 passover unto the Lord G· of Israel. "
5 passover unto the Lord G· of Israel "
6 again unto the Lord G· of Abraham, "
7 against the Lord G· of their fathers, "
8 serve the Lord your G·, that the "
9 for the Lord your G· is gracious and "
12 the hand of G· was to give them one "
16 to the law of Moses the man of G·: "
19 That prepareth his heart to seek G·, "
19 the Lord G· of his fathers, though he "
22 to the Lord G· of their fathers. "
31: 6 consecrated unto the Lord their G·, "
13 Azariah the ruler of the house of G·, "
14 was over the freewill offerings of G·, "
20 and truth before the Lord his G·. "
21 in the service of the house of G·, "
21 the commandments, to seek his G·, "
32: 8 but with us is the Lord our G· to "

2Ch 32:11 The Lord our G· shall deliver us 430
14 your G· should be able to deliver "
15 for no g· of any nation or kingdom 433
15 much less shall your G· deliver 430
16 spake yet more against the Lord G·, "
17 to rail on the Lord G· of Israel, "
17 so shall not the G· of Hezekiah "
19 spake against the G· of Jerusalem, "
21 he was come to the house of his g·, "
29 for G· had given him substance "
31 G· left him, to try him, that he "
33: 7 in the house of G·, of which G· had "
12 he besought the Lord his G·, and "
12 greatly before the G· of his fathers, "
13 knew that the Lord he was G·. "
16 Judah to serve the Lord G· of Israel. "
17 yet unto the Lord their G· only. "
18 and his prayer unto his G·, and the "
18 the name of the Lord G· of Israel, "
19 and how G· was intreated of him, "
34: 3 began to seek after the G· of David 430
8 repair the house of the Lord his G·. "
9 was brought into the house of G·, "
23 Thus saith the Lord G· of Israel, "
26 Thus saith the Lord G· of Israel "
27 thou didst humble thyself before G·, "
32 according to the covenant of G·, "
32 the G· of their fathers. "
33 even to serve the Lord their G·. "
33 following the Lord, the G· of their "
35: 3 serve now the Lord your G·, and "
8 rulers of the house of G·, gave unto "
21 G· commanded me to make haste: "
21 forbear thee from meddling with G·, "
22 words of Necho from the mouth of G·, "
36: 5 evil in the sight of the Lord his G·. "
12 evil in the sight of the Lord his G·, "
13 who had made him swear by G·: "
13 turning unto the Lord G· of Israel. "
15 the Lord G· of their fathers sent "
16 they mocked the messengers of G·, "
18 all the vessels of the house of G·, "
19 And they burnt the house of G·, "
23 hath the Lord G· of heaven given me; "
23 The Lord his G· be with him, "
Ezr 1: 2 The Lord G· of heaven hath given "
3 his G· be with him, and let him go "
3 the house of the Lord G· of Israel, "
3 (he is the G·,) which is in "
4 freewill offering for the house of G· "
5 them whose spirit G· hath raised, "
2:68 offered freely for the house of G· to "
3: 2 builded the altar of the G· of Israel, "
2 in the law of Moses the man of G·. "
8 their coming unto the house of G· "
9 the workmen in the house of G·: "
4: 1 temple unto the Lord G· of Israel; "
2 for we seek your G·, as ye do; "
3 to build an house unto our G·; "
3 will build unto the Lord G· of Israel, "
24 ceased the work of the house of G· 426
5: 1 in the name of the G· of Israel, "
2 and began to build the house of G· "
2 with them were the prophets of G· "
5 But the eye of their G· was upon "
8 to the house of the great G·, which "
11 are the servants of the G· of heaven "
12 had provoked the G· of heaven unto "
13 a decree to build this house of G·. "
14 gold and silver of the house of G·, "
15 and let the house of G· be builded "
16 the foundation of the house of G· "
17 build this house of G· at Jerusalem, "
6: 3 the house of G· at Jerusalem, Let "
5 and silver vessels of the house of G·, "
5 and place them in the house of G·. "
7 the work of this house of G· alone; "
7 build this house of G· in his place. "
8 for the building of this house of G·: "
9 burnt offerings of the G· of heaven, "
10 savours unto the G· of heaven, "
12 the G· that hath caused his name "
12 to destroy this house of G· which is "
14 commandment of the G· of Israel, "
16 dedication of this house of G· with "
17 at the dedication of this house of G· "
18 for the service of G·, which is at "
21 to seek the Lord G· of Israel, did 430
22 of the house of G·, the G· of Israel. "
7: 6 the Lord G· of Israel had given: "
6 to the hand of the Lord his G· upon "
9 according to the good hand of his G· "
12 of the law of the G· of heaven, 426
14 according to the law of thy G· which "
15 freely offered unto the G· of Israel, "
16 willingly for the house of their G· "
17 the altar of the house of your G· "
18 that do after the will of your G·. "
19 the service of the house of thy G·, "
19 those deliver thou before the G· of "
20 be needful for the house of thy G·, "
21 scribe of the law of the G· of heaven, "
23 commanded by the G· of heaven, "
23 for the house of the G· of heaven: "
24 or ministers of this house of G·, "
25 Ezra, after the wisdom of thy G·, "
25 such as know the laws of thy G·; "
26 will not do the law of thy G·, and "
27 Blessed be the Lord G· of our 430
28 as the hand of the Lord my G· was "
8:17 ministers for the house of our G·. "
18 And by the good hand of our G· upon "
21 might afflict ourselves before our G·, "
22 The hand of our G· is upon all them "
23 fasted and besought our G· for this: "
25 the offering of the house of our G·, "

Ezr 8:28 unto the Lord G· of your fathers. 430
30 unto the house of our G·. "
31 and the hand of our G· was upon us, "
33 weighed in the house of our G· by "
35 burnt offerings unto the G· of "
36 the people, and the house of G·. "
9: 4 at the words of the G· of Israel, "
5 my hands unto the Lord my G·, "
6 O my G·, I am ashamed and blush "
6 to lift up my face to thee, my G·: "
8 been shewed from the Lord our G·, "
8 that our G· may lighten our eyes, "
9 yet our G· hath not forsaken us "
9 to set up the house of our G·, and "
10 our G·, what shall we say after this? "
13 seeing that thou our G· hast "
15 O Lord G· of Israel, thou art "
10: 1 down before the house of G·, there "
2 We have trespassed against our G·, "
3 make a covenant with our G· to put "
3 at the commandment of our G·; "
6 before the house of G·, and went "
9 sat in the street of the house of G·, "
11 make confession unto the Lord G· "
14 until the fierce wrath of our G· for "
Ne 1: 4 and prayed before the G· of heaven, "
5 I beseech thee, O Lord G· of heaven, "
5 the great and terrible G·, that 410
2: 4 So I prayed to the G· of heaven. 430
8 to the good hand of my G· upon me. "
12 what my G· had put in my heart "
18 I told them of the hand of my G· to "
20 The G· of heaven, he will prosper us; "
4: 4 Hear, O our G·; for we are despised: "
9 we made our prayer unto our G·, "
15 and G· had brought their counsel to "
20 unto us: our G· shall fight for us. "
5: 9 walk in the fear of our G· because "
13 So G· shake out every man from "
15 did not I, because of the fear of G·. "
19 Think upon me, my G·, for good, "
6: 9 therefore, O G·, strengthen my hands. "
10 meet together in the house of G·, 430
12 perceived that G· had not sent him; "
14 My G·, think thou upon Tobiah and "
16 this work was wrought of our G·. "
7: 2 a faithful man, and feared G· above "
5 G· put into mine heart to gather "
8: 6 Ezra blessed the Lord, the great G·. "
8 they read in the book in the law of G· "
9 day is holy unto the Lord your G·; "
16 and in the courts of the house of G·, "
18 he read in the book of the law of G·. "
9: 3 book of the law of the Lord their G· "
3 and worshipped the Lord their G·. "
4 a loud voice unto the Lord their G·. "
5 and bless the Lord your G· for ever "
7 Thou art the Lord the G·, who didst "
17 but thou art a G· ready to pardon, 433
18 This is thy G· that brought thee up 430
31 thou art a gracious and merciful G·. 410
32 our G·, the great, the mighty, and 430
32 terrible G·, who keepest covenant 410
10:28 of the lands unto the law of G·, 430
29 given by Moses the servant of G·, "
32 the service of the house of our G·; "
33 all the work of the house of our G·. "
34 bring it into the house of our G·, "
34 upon the altar of the Lord our G·, "
36 to bring to the house of our G·, "
36 that minister in the house of our G·: "
37 chambers of the house of our G·; "
38 the tithes unto the house of our G·, "
39 will not forsake the house of our G·. "
11:11 was the ruler of the house of G·. "
16 outward business of the house of G·. "
22 over the business of the house of G·. "
12:24 of David the man of G·, ward "
36 instruments of David the man of G·, "
40 that gave thanks in the house of G·, "
43 for G· had made them rejoice with "
45 porters kept the ward of their G·, "
46 praise and thanksgiving unto G·. "
13: 1 the congregation of G· for ever; "
2 howbeit our G· turned the curse "
4 the chamber of the house of our G·, "
7 in the courts of the house of G·. "
9 again the vessels of the house of G·, "
11 Why is the house of G· forsaken? "
14 Remember me, O my G·, concerning "
14 I have done for the house of my G·, "
18 did not our G· bring all this evil "
22 Remember me, O my G·, concerning "
25 made them swear by G·, saying, "
26 like him, who was beloved of his G·, "
26 and G· made him king over all "
27 to transgress against our G· in "
29 Remember them, O my G·, because "
31 Remember me, O my G·, for good. "
Job 1: 1 that feared G·, and eschewed evil. "
5 and cursed G· in their hearts. "
6 when the sons of G· came to present "
8 that feareth G·, and escheweth evil? "
9 said, Doth Job fear G· for nought? "
16 The fire of G· is fallen from heaven, "
22 sinned not, nor charged G· foolishly. "
2: 1 a day when the sons of G· came "
3 upright man, one that feareth G·, "
9 retain thine integrity? curse G·, "
10 we receive good at the hand of G·, "
3: 4 let not G· regard it from above, 433
23 and whom G· hath hedged in? "
4: 9 By the blast of G· they perish, "
17 mortal man be more just than G·? "
5: 8 I would seek unto G·, and unto 410
8 and unto G· would I commit my 430

Job 5:17 is the man whom G· correcteth: 433
6: 4 the terrors of G· do set themselves "
8 that G· would grant me the thing "
9 that it would please G· to destroy "
8: 3 Doth G· pervert judgment? or doth 410
5 thou wouldest seek unto G· betimes, "
13 are the paths of all that forget G·; "
20 G· will not cast away a perfect man, "
9: 2 how should man be just with G·? "
13 G· will not withdraw his anger, 433
10: 2 I will say unto G·, Do not condemn "
11: 5 But oh that G· would speak, and "
6 Know therefore that G· exacteth of "
7 Canst thou by searching find out G·? "
12: 4 who calleth upon G·, and he "
6 they that provoke G· are secure; 410
6 into whose hand G· bringeth 433
13: 3 and I desire to reason with G·. 410
7 Will ye speak wickedly for G·? "
8 will ye contend for G·? "
15: 4 and restrainest prayer before G·. "
8 Hast thou heard the secret of G·? 433
11 consolations of G· small with thee? 410
13 thou turnest thy spirit against G·, "
25 stretcheth out his hand against G·, "
16:11 G· hath delivered me to the ungodly, "
20 eye poureth out tears unto G·. 433
21 one might plead for a man with G·, "
18:21 place of him that knoweth not G·. 410
19: 6 now that G· hath overthrown me, 433
21 the hand of G· hath touched me. "
22 Why do ye persecute me as G·, 410
26 yet in my flesh shall I see G·: 433
20:15 G· shall cast them out of his belly. 410
23 G· shall cast the fury of his wrath upon
29 portion of a wicked man from G·, 430
29 heritage appointed unto him by G·. 410
21: 9 neither is the rod of G· upon them. 433
14 Therefore they say unto G·, 410
17 G· distributeth sorrows in his anger. "
19 G· layeth up his iniquity for his 433
22 Shall any teach G· knowledge? 410
22: 2 Can a man be profitable unto G·, "
12 Is not G· in the height of heaven? 433
13 thou sayest, How doth G· know? 410
17 said unto G·, Depart from us: "
26 and shalt lift up thy face unto G·. 433
23:16 For G· maketh my heart soft, and 410
24:12 yet G· layeth not folly to them. 433
25: 4 then can man be justified with G·? 410
27: 2 As G· liveth, who hath taken away "
3 the spirit of G· is in my nostrils; 433
5 G· forbid that I should justify ‡
8 when G· taketh away his soul? 433
9 Will G· hear his cry when trouble 410
10 will he always call upon G·? 433
11 I will teach you by the hand of G·: 410
13 the portion of a wicked man with G·, "
22 For G· shall cast upon him, and not "
28:23 G· understandeth the way thereof, 430
29: 2 in the days when G· preserved me; 433
4 when the secret of G· was upon my "
31: 2 portion of G· is there from above? "
6 that G· may know mine integrity. "
14 then shall I do when G· riseth up? 410
23 destruction from G· was a terror "
28 have denied the G· that is above. "
32: 2 he justified himself rather than G·. 430
13 G· thrusteth him down, not man. 410
33: 4 The Spirit of G· hath made me, "
12 thee, that G· is greater than man. 433
14 For G· speaketh once, yea twice, 410
26 He shall pray unto G·, and he will 433
29 worketh G· oftentimes with man, 410
34: 5 G· hath taken away my judgment. "
9 he should delight himself with G·. 430
10 far be it from G·, that he should do 410
12 Yea, surely G· will not do wickedly, "
23 should enter into judgment with G·. "
31 Surely it is meet to be said unto G·, "
37 multiplieth his words against G·. "
35:10 Where is G· my maker, who giveth 433
13 Surely G· will not hear vanity, 410
36: 5 G· is mighty, and despiseth not any: "
22 Behold, G· exalteth by his power: "
26 G· is great, and we know him not, "
37: 5 G· thundereth marvellously with "
10 By the breath of G· frost is given: "
14 consider the wondrous works of G·. "
15 thou know when G· disposed them, 433
22 with G· is terrible majesty. "
38: 7 all the sons of G· shouted for joy? 430
41 when his young ones cry unto G·. 410
39:17 G· hath deprived her of wisdom. 433
40: 2 that reproveth G·, let him answer "
9 Hast thou an arm like G·? or canst 410
19 He is the chief of the ways of G·: "
Ps 3: 2 There is no help for him in G·. 430
7 Arise, O Lord; save me, O my G·: "
4: 1 O G· of my righteousness: thou "
5: 2 my King, and my G·: for unto thee "
4 art not a G· that hath pleasure in 410
10 Destroy thou them, O G·; let them 430
7: 1 my G·, in thee do I put my trust; "
3 O Lord my G·, if I have done this; "
9 the righteous G· trieth the hearts "
10 My defence is of G·, which saveth "
11 G· judgeth the righteous, "
11 and G· is angry with the wicked 410
9:17 and all the nations that forget G·. 430
10: 4 countenance, will not seek after G·: *
4 G· is not in all his thoughts. 430
11 in his heart, G· hath forgotten: 410
12 O G·, lift up thine hand: forget not "
13 doth the wicked contemn G·? he 430
13: 3 and hear me, O Lord my G·: "

Ps 14: 1 said in his heart, There is no G·. 430
2 that did understand, and seek G·. "
5 for G· is in the generation of the "
16: 1 Preserve me, O G·: for in thee do 410
4 that hasten after another g·: their
17: 6 for thou wilt hear me, O G·: 410
18: 2 my G·, my strength, in whom I will "
6 and cried unto my G·: he heard my 430
21 not wickedly departed from my G·. "
28 my G· will enlighten my darkness. "
29 and by my G· have I leaped over a "
30 As for G·, his way is perfect: 410
31 For who is G· save the Lord? 433
31 or who is a rock save our G·? 430
32 G· that girdeth me with strength, 410
46 the G· of my salvation be exalted. 430
47 It is G· that avengeth me, and 410
19: 1 heavens declare the glory of G·; "
20: 1 of the G· of Jacob defend thee; 430
5 in the name of our G· we will set "
7 the name of the Lord our G·. "
22: 1 My G·, my G·, why hast thou 410
2 O my G·, I cry in the daytime, 430
10 art my G· from my mother's belly. 410
24: 5 from the G· of his salvation. 430
25: 2 O my G·, I trust in thee: let me not "
5 for thou art the G· of my salvation; "
22 Israel, O G·, out of all his troubles. "
27: 9 forsake me, O G· of my salvation. "
29: 3 G· of glory thundereth: the Lord 410
30: 2 O Lord my G·, I cried unto thee, 430
12 O Lord my G·, I will give thanks "
31: 5 redeemed me, O Lord G· of truth. 410
14 I said, Thou art my G·. 430
33:12 is the nation whose G· is the Lord; "
35:23 unto my cause, my G· and my Lord. "
24 Judge me, O Lord my G·, according "
36: 1 is no fear of G· before his eyes. "
7 is thy lovingkindness, O G·! "
37:31 The law of his G· is in his heart; "
38:15 thou wilt hear, O Lord my G·. "
21 O my G·, be not far from me. "
40: 3 even praise unto our G·: many shall "
5 O Lord my G·, are thy wonderful "
8 I delight to do thy will, O my G·: "
17 make no tarrying, O my G·. "
41:13 Blessed be the Lord G· of Israel "
42: 1 so panteth my soul after thee, O G·. "
2 My soul thirsteth for G·, 430
2 for the living G·: when shall 410
2 I come and appear before G·? 430
3 say unto me, Where is thy G·? "
4 I went with them to the house of G·, "
5 hope thou in G·: for I shall yet "
6 O my G·, my soul is cast down "
8 my prayer unto the G· of my life. 410
9 I will say unto G· my rock, Why "
10 daily unto me, Where is thy G·? 430
11 hope thou in G·: for I shall yet "
11 of my countenance, and my G·. "
43: 1 Judge me, O G·, and plead my "
2 For thou art the G· of my strength: "
4 Then will I go unto the altar of G·, "
4 unto G· my exceeding joy: 410
4 will I praise thee, O G· my G·. 430
5 hope in G·: for I shall yet praise "
5 of my countenance, and my G·. "
44: 1 We have heard with our ears, O G·, "
4 Thou art my King, O G·: command "
8 In G· we boast all the day long, "
20 have forgotten the name of our G·. "
20 out our hands to a strange g·: 410
21 Shall not G· search this out? 430
45: 2 therefore G· hath blessed thee for "
6 Thy throne, O G·, is for ever and "
7 therefore G·, thy G·, hath anointed "
46: 1 G· is our refuge and strength, a "
4 shall make glad the city of G·, "
5 G· is in the midst of her; she shall "
5 not be moved: G· shall help her, "
7 the G· of Jacob is our refuge. "
10 and know that I am G·: I will be "
11 the G· of Jacob is our refuge. "
47: 1 unto G· with the voice of triumph. "
5 G· is gone up with a shout, the "
6 Sing praises to G·, sing praises: "
7 G· is the King of all the earth: "
8 G· reigneth over the heathen: "
8 G· sitteth upon the throne of his "
9 the people of the G· of Abraham: "
9 shields of the earth belong unto G·: "
48: 1 the city of our G·, in the mountain "
3 G· is known in her palaces for a "
8 Lord of hosts, in the city of our G·: "
8 G· will establish it for ever. "
9 lovingkindness, O G·, in the midst "
10 According to thy name, O G·, so is "
14 this G· is our G· for ever and ever: "
49: 7 nor give to G· a ransom for him: "
15 But G· will redeem my soul from "
50: 1 The mighty G·, even the Lord, "
2 perfection of beauty, G· hath shined. "
3 Our G· shall come, and shall not "
6 for G· is judge himself. Selah. "
7 I am G·, even thy G·. "
14 Offer unto G· thanksgiving; and "
16 But unto the wicked G· saith, What "
22 ye that forget G·, lest I tear you 433
23 will I shew the salvation of G·. 430
51: 1 Have mercy upon me, O G·, "
10 Create in me a clean heart, O G·; "
14 me from bloodguiltiness, O G·, "
14 thou G· of my salvation: "
17 sacrifices of G· are a broken spirit: "
17 a broken and a contrite heart, O G·, "
52: 1 of G· endureth continually. 410

Ps 52: 5 G· shall likewise destroy thee for 410
7 man that made not G· his strength; 430
8 green olive tree in the house of G·: "
8 I trust in the mercy of G· for ever "
53: 1 said in his heart, There is no G·. "
2 G· looked down from heaven upon "
2 did understand, that did seek G·. "
4 they have not called upon G·. "
5 G· hath scattered the bones of him "
5 because G· hath despised them. "
6 G· bringeth back the captivity of "
54: 1 Save me, O G·, by thy name, "
2 Hear my prayer, O G·; give ear "
3 they have not set G· before them. "
4 Behold, G· is mine helper: the Lord "
55: 1 Give ear to my prayer, O G·; "
14 unto the house of G· in company. "
16 As for me, I will call upon G·; "
19 G· shall hear, and afflict them, 410
19 therefore they fear not G·. 430
23 But thou, O G·, shalt bring them "
56: 1 Be merciful unto me, O G·: for man "
4 In G· I will praise his word, "
4 in G· I have put my trust; "
7 anger cast down the people, O G·. "
9 this I know; for G· is for me. "
10 In G· will I praise his word: "
11 In G· have I put my trust: "
12 Thy vows are upon me, O G·: "
13 I may walk before G· in the light "
57: 1 Be merciful unto me, O G·, be "
2 I will cry unto G· most high; "
2 unto G· that performeth all 410
3 G· shall send forth his mercy and 430
5 exalted, O G·, above the heavens; "
7 My heart is fixed, O G·, my heart is "
11 Be thou exalted, O G·, above "
58: 6 Break their teeth, O G·, in their "
11 he is a G· that judgeth in the earth. "
59: 1 me from mine enemies, O my G·: "
5 Thou therefore, O Lord G· of hosts, "
5 the G· of Israel, awake to visit "
9 upon thee: for G· is my defence. "
10 The G· of my mercy shall prevent "
10 G· shall let me see my desire "
13 them know that G· ruleth in Jacob "
17 will I sing: for G· is my defence, "
17 my defence, and the G· of my mercy. "
60: 1 O G·, thou hast cast us off, "
6 G· hath spoken in his holiness; "
10 Wilt not thou, O G·, which hadst "
10 and thou, O G·, which didst not go "
12 Through G· we shall do valiantly: "
61: 1 Hear my cry, O G·; attend unto my "
5 For thou, O G·, hast heard my vows: "
7 He shall abide before G· for ever: "
62: 1 Truly my soul waiteth upon G·: "
5 My soul, wait thou only upon G·; "
7 In G· is my salvation and my glory: "
7 strength, and my refuge, is in G·. "
8 before him: G· is a refuge for us. "
11 G· hath spoken once; twice have I "
11 that power belongeth unto G·. "
63: 1 O G·, thou art my...; early will I "
1 thou art my G·; early will I 410
11 But the king shall rejoice in G·; 430
64: 1 Hear my voice, O G·, in my prayer: "
7 But G· shall shoot at them with an "
9 and shall declare the work of G·; "
65: 1 waiteth for thee, O G·, in Sion: "
5 answer us, O G· of our salvation; "
9 enrichest it with the river of G·, "
66: 1 Make a joyful noise unto G·, all ye "
3 Say unto G·, How terrible art thou "
5 Come and see the works of G·: "
8 O bless our G·, ye people, and make "
10 For thou, O G·, hast proved us: "
16 Come and hear, all ye that fear G·, "
19 But verily G· hath heard me; "
20 Blessed be G·, which hath not "
67: 1 G· be merciful unto us, and bless "
3, 5 Let the people praise thee, O G·; "
6 G·, even our own G·, shall bless us. "
7 G· shall bless us; and all the ends "
68: 1 Let G· arise, let his enemies be "
2 wicked perish at the presence of G·. "
3 let them rejoice before G·: yea, "
4 Sing unto G·, sing praises to his "
5 widows, is G· in his holy habitation. "
6 G· setteth the solitary in families: "
7 O G·, when thou wentest forth "
8 dropped at the presence of G·: "
8 the presence of G·, the G· of Israel. "
9 O G·, didst send a plentiful rain, "
10 thou, O G·, hast prepared of thy "
15 hill of G· is as the hill of Bashan; "
16 the hill which G· desireth to dwell "
17 The chariots of G· are twenty "
18 Lord G· might dwell among them. "
19 even the G· of our salvation. 410
20 that is our G· is the G· of salvation; "
20 G· the Lord belong the issues *3069
21 G· shall wound the head of his 430
24 They have seen thy goings, O G·; "
24 even the goings of my G·, my 410
26 Bless ye G· in the congregations, 430
28 G· hath commanded thy strength: "
28 strengthen, O G·, that which thou "
31 soon stretch out her hands unto G·. "
32 Sing unto G·, ye kingdoms of the "
34 Ascribe ye strength unto G·: "
35 O G·, thou art terrible out of thy "
35 the G· of Israel is he that giveth 410
35 unto his people. Blessed be G·. 430
69: 1 Save me, O G·; for the waters are "
3 eyes fail while I wait for my G·. "

Ps 69: 5 O G·, thou knowest my foolishness; 430
6 wait on thee, O Lord G· of hosts, ‡3069
6 for my sake, O G· of Israel. 430
13 O G·, in the multitude of thy mercy "
29 thy salvation, O G·, set me up on "
30 I will praise the name of G· "
32 your heart shall live that seek G·. "
35 For G· will save Zion, and will build "
70: 1 Make haste, O G·, to deliver me; "
4 continually, Let G· be magnified. "
5 make haste unto me, O G·: thou "
71: 4 Deliver me, O my G·, out of the "
5 thou art my hope, O Lord G·: ‡3069
11 Saying, G· hath forsaken him: 430
12 O G·, be not far from me: O my G·, "
16 go in the strength of the Lord G·: ‡3069
17 O G·, thou hast taught me from 430
18 O G·, forsake me not; until I have "
19 Thy righteousness also, O G·, is "
19 O G·, who is like unto thee! "
22 even thy truth, O my G·: unto thee "
72: 1 Give the king thy judgments, O G·, "
18 be the Lord G·, the G· of Israel, "
73: 1 Truly G· is good to Israel, "
11 they say, How doth G· know? 410
17 I went into the sanctuary of G·; "
26 but G· is the strength of my heart, 430
28 is good for me to draw near to G·: "
28 have put my trust in the Lord G·, ‡3069
74: 1 O G·, why hast thou cast us off 430
8 burned up all the synagogues of G· 410
10 O G·, how long shall the adversary 430
12 For G· is my King of old, working "
22 Arise, O G·, plead thine own cause: "
75: 1 Unto thee, O G·, do we give thanks, "
7 But G· is the judge: he putteth "
9 will sing praises to the G· of Jacob. "
76: 1 In Judah is G· known: his name is "
6 At thy rebuke, O G· of Jacob, "
9 When G· arose to judgment, to save "
11 and pay unto the Lord your G·: "
77: 1 G· with my voice, even unto G· with "
3 I remembered G·, and was troubled: "
9 Hath G· forgotten to be gracious? 410
13 Thy way, O G·, is in the sanctuary: 430
13 sanctuary: who is so great a G· as 410
13 who is so great...as our G·? 430
14 Thou art the G· that doest wonders: 410
16 waters saw thee, O G·, the waters 430
78: 7 they might set their hope in G·, "
7 and not forget the works of G·, 410
8 whose spirit was not stedfast with G·. "
10 They kept not the covenant of G·, 430
18 they tempted G· in their heart by 410
19 Yea, they spake against G·; 430
19 they said, Can G· furnish a table 410
22 Because they believed not in G·, 430
31 The wrath of G· came upon them, "
34 and enquired early after G·. 410
35 they remembered that G· was their 430
35 and the high G· their redeemer. 410
41 they turned back and tempted G·, "
56 and provoked the most high G·, 430
59 When G· heard this, he was wroth, "
79: 1 O G·, the heathen are come into "
9 Help us, O G· of our salvation, "
10 the heathen say, Where is their G·? "
80: 3 Turn us again, O G·, and cause thy "
4 O Lord G· of hosts, how long wilt "
7 Turn us again, O G· of hosts, "
14 Return, we beseech thee, O G· of "
19 Turn us again, O Lord G· of hosts, "
81: 1 Sing aloud unto G· our strength: "
1 make a joyful noise unto the G· of "
4 and a law of the G· of Jacob. "
9 There shall no strange g· be in thee: 410
9 shalt thou worship any strange g·. "
10 am the Lord thy G·, which brought 430
82: 1 G· standeth in the congregation of "
8 Arise, O G·, judge the earth: for "
83: 1 Keep not thou silence, O G·: "
1 not thy peace, and be not still, O G·. 410
12 the houses of G· in possession. "
13 O my G·, make them like a wheel; "
84: 2 flesh crieth out for the living G·. 410
3 Lord of hosts, my King, and my G·. 430
7 them in Zion appeareth before G·. "
8 O Lord G· of hosts, hear my prayer: "
8 give ear, O G· of Jacob. "
9 Behold, O G· our shield, and look "
10 doorkeeper in the house of my G·, "
11 For the Lord G· is a sun and shield: "
85: 4 Turn us, O G· of our salvation, "
8 I will hear what G· the Lord will 410
86: 2 O thou my G·, save thy servant 430
10 wondrous things: thou art G· alone. "
12 I will praise thee, O Lord my G·, "
14 O G·, the proud are risen against "
15 O Lord, art a G· full of compassion, 410
87: 3 are spoken of thee, O city of G·. 430
88: 1 O Lord G· of my salvation, I have "
89: 7 G· is greatly to be feared in the 410
8 O Lord G· of hosts, who is a strong 430
26 Thou art my father, my G·, and 410
90: *title* Prayer of Moses the man of G·. 430
2 to everlasting, thou art G·. 410
17 let the beauty of the Lord our G· 430
91: 2 fortress: my G·; in him will I trust. "
92: 13 shall flourish in the courts of our G·. "
94: 1 O Lord G·, to whom vengeance 410
1 O G·, to whom vengeance belongeth, "
7 neither shall the G· of Jacob regard 430
22 and my G· is the rock of my refuge. "
23 the Lord our G· shall cut them off. "
95: 3 For the Lord is a great G·, and a 410
7 For he is our G·; and we are the 430

Ps 98: 3 have seen the salvation of our G·. 430
99: 5 exalt ye the Lord our G·, and "
8 answeredst them, O Lord our G·: "
8 thou wast a G· that forgavest them, 410
9 the Lord our G·, and worship at 430
9 hill; for the Lord our G· is holy. "
100: 3 Know ye that the Lord he is G·: "
102: 24 O my G·, take me not away in the 410
104: 1 O Lord my G·, thou art very great; 430
21 and seek their meat from G·. 410
33 I will sing praise to my G· while I 430
105: 7 He is the Lord our G·: his "
106: 14 and tempted G· in the desert. 410
21 They forgat G· their saviour, which "
47 Save us, O Lord our G·, and gather 430
48 Blessed be the Lord G· of Israel "
107: 11 rebelled against the words of G·, 410
108: 1 O G·, my heart is fixed; I will sing 430
5 Be thou exalted, O G·, above the "
7 G· hath spoken in his holiness; "
11 O G·, who hast cast us off? and "
11 wilt not thou, O G·, go forth with "
13 Through G· we shall do valiantly: "
109: 1 Hold not thy peace, O G· of my "
21 But do thou for me, O G· the Lord, ‡3069
26 Help me, O Lord my G·: O save 430
113: 5 Who is like unto the Lord our G·, "
114: 7 at the presence of the G· of Jacob; 433
115: 2 heathen say, Where is now their G·? 430
3 But our G· is in the heavens: he "
116: 5 yea, our G· is merciful. "
118: 27 G· is the Lord, which hath shewed 410
28 art my G· and I will praise thee: "
28 thou art my G·, I will exalt thee. 430
119: 115 keep the commandments of my G·. "
122: 9 of the house of the Lord our G· I "
123: 2 our eyes wait upon the Lord our G·, "
132: 2 unto the mighty G· of Jacob; *
5 for the mighty G· of Jacob. *
135: 2 the courts of the house of our G·, 430
136: 2 unto the G· of Gods; for his mercy "
26 give thanks unto the G· of heaven: 410
139: 17 are thy thoughts unto me, O G·! "
19 thou wilt slay the wicked, O G·: 433
23 Search me, O G·, and know my 410
140: 6 unto the Lord, Thou art my G·: "
141: 8 eyes are unto thee, O G· the Lord: ‡3069
143: 10 for thou art my G·: thy spirit 430
144: 9 sing a new song unto thee, O G·: "
15 that people whose G· is the Lord. "
145: 1 I will extol thee, my G·, O king; "
146: 2 I will sing praises unto my G· while "
5 Happy is he that hath the G· of 410
5 whose hope is in the Lord his G·: 430
10 thy G·, O Zion, unto all generations. "
147: 1 good to sing praises unto our G·; "
7 praise upon the harp unto our G·: "
12 Jerusalem; praise thy G·, O Zion. "
149: 6 the high praises of G· be in their 410
150: 1 Praise G· in his sanctuary: praise "
Pr 2: 5 and find the knowledge of G·. 430
17 forgetteth the covenant of her G·. "
3: 4 understanding in the sight of G· and "
21: 12 but G· overthroweth the wicked *
25: 2 the glory of G· to conceal a thing: 430
26: 10 great G· that formed all things *
30: 5 Every word of G· is pure: he is a 433
9 take the name of my G· in vain. 430
Ec 1: 13 this sore travail hath G· given to "
2: 24 that it was from the hand of G·. "
26 For G· giveth to a man that is good in "
26 to him that is good before G·. 430
3: 10 G· hath given to the sons of men "
11 find out the work that G· maketh "
13 all his labour, it is the gift of G·. "
14 whatsoever G· doeth, it shall be for "
14 G· doeth it, that men should fear "
15 and G· requireth that which is past. "
17 G· shall judge the righteous and the "
18 that G· might manifest them, and "
5: 1 when thou goest to the house of G·, "
2 utter anything before G·: for G· is "
4 When thou vowest a vow unto G·, "
6 wherefore should G· be angry at "
7 vanities: but fear thou G·. "
18 of his life, which G· giveth him: "
19 to whom G· hath given riches and "
19 his labour; this is the gift of G·. "
20 G· answereth him in the joy of his "
6: 2 man to whom G· hath given riches, "
2 yet G· giveth him not power to eat "
7: 13 Consider the work of G·: for who "
14 G· also hath set the one over "
18 he that feareth G· shall come forth "
26 pleaseth G· shall escape from her; "
29 that G· hath made man upright; "
8: 2 and that in regard of the oath of G·. "
12 shall be well with them that fear G·, "
13 because he feareth not before G·. "
15 which G· giveth him under the sun. "
17 Then I beheld all the work of G·, "
9: 1 their works, are in the hand of G·: "
7 for G· now accepteth thy works. "
11: 5 thou knowest not the works of G· "
9 G· will bring thee into judgment. "
12: 7 shall return unto G· who gave it. "
13 matter: Fear G·, and keep his "
14 For G· shall bring every work into "
Isa 1: 10 give ear unto the law of our G·, "
2: 3 to the house of the G· of Jacob; "
3: 15 of the poor? saith the Lord G· ††3069
5: 16 G· that is holy shall be sanctified 410
7: 7 Thus saith the Lord G·, It shall ‡3069
11 Ask thee a sign of the Lord thy G·; 430
13 but will ye weary my G· also? "
8: 10 it shall not stand: for G· is with us. 410

Isa 8: 19 not a people seek unto their G·? 430
21 and curse their king and their G·, "
9: 6 The mighty G·, The everlasting 410
10: 21 of Jacob, unto the mighty G·. "
23 the Lord G· of hosts shall make ††3069
24 saith the Lord G· of hosts, O my †‡
12: 2 Behold, G· is my salvation: I will 410
13: 19 be as when G· overthrew Sodom 430
14: 13 my throne above the stars of G·: 410
17: 6 thereof, saith the Lord G· of Israel. 430
10 forgotten the G· of thy salvation, "
13 but G· shall rebuke them, and *
21: 10 the Lord of hosts, the G· of Israel, 430
17 the Lord G· of Israel hath spoken "
22: 5 by the Lord G· of hosts in the ††3069
12 day did the Lord G· of hosts call †‡
14 you till ye die, saith the Lord G·†‡ "
15 saith the Lord G· of hosts, Go, †‡ "
24: 15 the name of the Lord G· of Israel 430
25: 1 O Lord, thou art my G·; I will exalt "
8 the Lord G· will wipe away tears ‡3069
9 in that day, Lo, this is our G·; 430
26: 1 salvation will G· appoint for *
13 O Lord our G·, other lords beside 430
28: 16 the Lord G·, Behold, I lay in Zion ‡3069
22 heard from the Lord G· of hosts †‡
26 G· doth instruct him to discretion, 430
29: 23 and shall fear the G· of Israel. "
30: 15 saith the Lord G·, the Holy One ‡3069
18 for the Lord is a G· of judgment: 430
31: 3 Egyptians are men, and not G·; 410
35: 2 and the excellency of our G·. 430
4 your G· will come with vengeance, "
4 even G· with a recompence; "
36: 7 We trust in the Lord our G·: is it "
37: 4 It may be the Lord thy G· will hear "
4 hath sent to reproach the living G·, "
4 which the Lord thy G· hath heard: "
10 Let not thy G·, in whom thou "
16 O Lord of hosts, G· of Israel, "
16 thou art the G·, even thou alone, "
17 hath sent to reproach the living G·. "
20 Now therefore, O Lord our G·, save "
21 Thus saith the Lord G· of Israel, "
38 in the house of Nisroch his g·, "
38: 5 the G· of David thy father, I have "
40: 1 comfort ye my people, saith your G·. "
3 in the desert a highway for our G·. "
8 but the word of our G· shall stand "
9 the cities of Judah, Behold your G·! "
10 Lord G· will come with strong ‡3069
18 To whom then will ye liken G·? 410
27 is passed over from my G·? 430
28 G·, the Lord, the Creator "
41: 10 be not dismayed; for I am thy G·: "
13 I the Lord thy G· will hold thy "
17 the G· of Israel will not forsake "
42: 5 Thus saith G· the Lord, he that 410
43: 3 For I am the Lord thy G·, the Holy 430
10 before me there was no G· formed, 410
12 there was no strange g· among you: "
12 saith the Lord, that I am G·. 410
44: 6 and beside me there is no G·. 430
8 Is there a G· beside me? yea, 433
8 there is no G·; I know not any. *6697
10 Who hath formed a g·, or molten 410
15 he maketh a g·, and worshippeth it; "
17 the residue thereof he maketh a g·, "
17 Deliver me; for thou art my g·. "
45: 3 by thy name, am the G· of Israel. 430
5 there is no G· beside me: I girded "
14 Surely G· is in thee; and there is 410
14 there is none else, there is no G·. 430
15 Verily thou art a G· that hidest 410
15 thyself, O G· of Israel, the Saviour. 430
18 G· himself that formed the earth "
20 pray unto a g· that cannot save. 410
21 there is no G· else beside me; 430
21 a just G· and a Saviour; 410
22 for I am G·, and there is none else. "
46: 6 he maketh it a g·: they fall down "
9 for I am G·, and there is none else; "
9 I am G·, and there is none like me, 430
48: 1 make mention of the G· of Israel, "
2 themselves upon the G· of Israel; "
16 now the Lord G·, and his Spirit, ‡3069
17 I am the Lord thy G· which 430
49: 4 and my work with my G·. "
5 and my G· shall be my strength. "
22 saith the Lord G·, Behold, I will ‡3069
50: 4 The Lord G· hath given me the ‡ "
5 Lord G· hath opened mine ear, ‡ "
7 the Lord G· will help me; ‡ "
9 the Lord G· will help me; who is ‡ "
10 and stay upon his G·. 430
51: 15 But I am the Lord thy G·, "
20 of the Lord, the rebuke of thy G·. "
22 and thy G· that pleadeth the cause "
52: 4 saith the Lord G·, My people ‡3069
7 saith unto Zion, Thy G· reigneth! 430
10 shall see the salvation of our G·. "
12 and the G· of Israel will be your "
53: 4 stricken, smitten of G·, and afflicted. "
54: 5 The G· of the whole earth shall he "
6 thou wast refused, saith thy G·. "
55: 5 because of the Lord thy G·, and for "
7 and to our G·, for he will abundantly "
56: 8 The Lord G· which gathereth ‡3069
57: 21 peace, saith my G·, to the wicked. 430
58: 2 not the ordinance of their G·: "
2 take delight in approaching to G·. "
59: 2 separated between you and your G·, "
13 and departing away from our G·, "
60: 9 unto the name of the Lord thy G·, "
19 and thy G· thy glory. "
61: 1 Spirit of the Lord G· is upon me; ‡3069

Isa 61: 2 the day of vengeance of our G'; 430
6 call you the Ministers of our G': "
10 my soul shall be joyful in my G'; "
11 Lord G' will cause righteousness ‡3069
62: 3 royal diadem in the hand of thy G'. 430
5 so shall thy G' rejoice over thee. "
64: 4 neither hath the eye seen, O G', "
65:13 saith the Lord G', Behold, my ‡3069
15 the Lord G' shall slay thee, and ‡ "
16 bless himself in the G' of truth; 430
16 shall swear by the G' of truth; "
66: 9 and shut the womb? saith thy G'. "
Jer 1: 6 Lord G'! behold, I cannot speak: ‡3069
2:17 forsaken the Lord thy G', when 430
19 hast forsaken the Lord thy G', "
19 is not in thee, saith the Lord G'. †‡3069
22 before me, saith the Lord G'. ‡ "
3:13 against the Lord thy G', 430
21 have forgotten the Lord their G'. "
22 for thou art the Lord our G'. "
23 our G' is the salvation of Israel. "
25 sinned against the Lord our G', "
25 the voice of the Lord our G'. "
4:10 Then said I, Ah, Lord G'! ‡3069
5: 4 nor the judgment of their G'. 430
5 and the judgment of their G': but "
14 thus saith the Lord G' of hosts, "
19 Wherefore doeth the Lord our G' "
24 Let us now fear the Lord our G', "
7: 3 the Lord of hosts, the G' of Israel, "
20 saith the Lord G'; Behold, mine ‡3069
21 the Lord of hosts, the G' of Israel; 430
23 my voice, and I will be your G', "
28 not the voice of the Lord their G', "
8:14 for the Lord our G' hath put us "
9:15 the Lord of hosts, the G' of Israel; "
10:10 But the Lord is the true G', "
10 he is the living G', and an "
11: 3 saith the Lord G' of Israel; Cursed "
4 my people, and I will be your G': "
13:12 saith the Lord G' of Israel, Every "
16 Give glory to the Lord your G', "
14:13 Ah, Lord G'! behold, the prophets ‡3069
22 art not thou he, O Lord our G'? 430
15:16 by thy name, O Lord G' of hosts. "
16: 9 the Lord of hosts, the G' of Israel; "
10 committed against the Lord our G'? "
19: 3, 15 Lord of hosts, the G' of Israel; "
21: 4 saith the Lord G' of Israel; Behold, "
22: 9 the covenant of the Lord their G', "
23: 2 saith the Lord G' of Israel against "
23 Am I a G' at hand, saith the Lord, "
23 and not a G' afar off? "
36 perverted the words of the living G'," "
36 of the Lord of hosts our G'. "
24: 5 saith the Lord, the G' of Israel; Like "
7 and I will be their G': for they shall "
25:15 saith the Lord, G' of Israel unto me; "
27 the Lord of hosts, the G' of Israel; "
26:13 obey the voice of the Lord your G'; "
16 in the name of the Lord our G'. "
27: 4 the Lord of hosts, the G' of Israel; "
21 the Lord of hosts, the G' of Israel, "
28: 2 speaketh the Lord of hosts, the G' "
14 the Lord of hosts, the G' of Israel; "
29: 4 the Lord of hosts, the G' of Israel, "
8 the Lord of hosts, the G' of Israel; "
21 the Lord of hosts, the G' of Israel, "
25 speaketh the Lord of hosts, the G' "
30: 2 speaketh the Lord G' of Israel, "
9 they shall serve the Lord their G', "
22 my people, and I will be your G'. "
31: 1 will I be the G' of all the families "
6 up to Zion unto the Lord our G'. "
18 for thou art the Lord my G'. "
23 the Lord of hosts, the G' of Israel; "
33 and will be their G', and they shall "
32:14 the Lord of hosts, the G' of Israel; "
15 the Lord of hosts, the G' of Israel; "
17 Ah, Lord G'! behold, thou hast ‡3069
18 the Great, the Mighty G', the Lord 410
25 hast said unto me, O Lord G', ‡3069
27 I am the Lord, the G' of all flesh: 430
36 thus saith the Lord, the G' of Israel," "
38 my people, and I will be their G': "
33: 4 thus saith the Lord, the G' of Israel," "
34: 2 saith the Lord, the G' of Israel; Go "
13 saith the Lord, the G' of Israel; I "
35: 4 the son of Igdaliah, a man of G', "
13 the Lord of hosts, the G' of Israel; "
17 thus saith the Lord G' of hosts, "
17 the G' of Israel; Behold, I will "
18, 19 Lord of hosts, the G' of Israel; "
37: 3 Pray now unto the Lord our G' for "
7 the Lord, the G' of Israel; Thus "
38:17 thus saith the Lord, the G' of hosts," "
17 the G' of Israel; If thou wilt "
39:16 the Lord of hosts, the G' of Israel; "
40: 2 The Lord thy G' hath pronounced "
42: 2 pray for us unto the Lord thy G', "
3 That the Lord thy G' may shew us "
4 I will pray unto the Lord your G' "
5 the Lord thy G' shall send thee "
6 obey the voice of the Lord our G', "
6 obey the voice of the Lord our G'. "
9 saith the Lord, the G' of Israel, unto "
13 obey the voice of the Lord your G', "
15, 18 Lord of hosts, the G' of Israel; "
20 ye sent me unto the Lord your G', "
20 Pray for us unto the Lord our G'; "
20 unto all that the Lord our G' shall "
21 the voice of the Lord your G', "
43: 1 all the words of the Lord their G', "
1 the Lord their G' had sent him to "
2 the Lord our G' hath not sent thee "
10 the Lord of hosts, the G' of Israel; "

Jer 44: 2 the Lord of hosts, the G' of Israel; 430
7 thus saith the Lord, the G' of hosts, "
7 the G' of Israel; Wherefore "
11 the Lord of hosts, the G' of Israel; "
25 the Lord of hosts, the G' of Israel, "
26 Egypt, saying, The Lord G' liveth. ‡3069
45: 2 Lord, the G' of Israel, unto thee, 430
46:10 the day of the Lord G' of hosts, †‡3069
10 for the Lord G' of hosts hath a †‡ "
25 The Lord of hosts, the G' of Israel, 430
48: 1 the Lord of hosts, the G' of Israel; "
49: 5 upon thee, saith the Lord G' of †‡3069
50: 4 go, and seek the Lord their G'. 430
18 the Lord of hosts, the G' of Israel; "
25 work of the Lord G' of hosts, †‡3069
28 vengeance of the Lord our G', 430
31 most proud, saith the Lord G' of †‡3069
40 As G' overthrew Sodom and 430
51: 5 nor Judah of his G', of the Lord of "
10 Zion the work of the Lord our G'. "
33 the Lord of hosts, the G' of Israel; "
56 for the Lord G' of recompences 410
La 3:41 our heart with our hands unto G' "
Eze 1: 1 opened, and I saw visions of G'. 430
2: 4 them, Thus saith the Lord G'. ‡3069
3:11 saith the Lord G'; whether they ‡ "
27 saith the Lord G'; He that ‡ "
4:14 Ah Lord G'! behold, my soul ‡ "
5: 5 saith the Lord G'; This is ‡ "
7 saith the Lord G'; Because ye ‡ "
8 saith the Lord G'; Behold, I, ‡ "
11 as I live, saith the Lord G'; ‡ "
6: 3 hear the word of the Lord G'; ‡ "
3 Thus saith the Lord G' to the ‡ "
11 saith the Lord G'; Smite with ‡ "
7: 2 of man, thus saith the Lord G' ‡ "
5 saith the Lord G'; An evil, an ‡ "
8: 1 the hand of the Lord G' fell there ‡ "
3 in the visions of G' to Jerusalem, 430
4 glory of the G' of Israel was there, "
9: 3 glory of the G' of Israel was gone "
8 Ah Lord G'! wilt thou destroy ‡3069
10: 5 as the voice of the Almighty G' 410
19 glory of the G' of Israel was over 430
20 I saw under the G' of Israel by the "
11: 7 saith the Lord G'; Your slain ‡3069
8 sword upon you, saith the Lord G'. ‡ "
13 loud voice, and said, Ah Lord G'! ‡ "
16 saith the Lord G'; Although I ‡ "
17 saith the Lord G'; I will even ‡ "
20 my people, and I will be their G'. 430
21 own heads, saith the Lord G'. ‡3069
22 the glory of the G' of Israel 430
24 in a vision by the Spirit of G' "
12:10 saith the Lord G'; This burden ‡3069
19 the Lord G' of the inhabitants of ‡ "
23 saith the Lord G'; I will make ‡ "
25 will perform it, saith the Lord G'. ‡ "
28 saith the Lord G'; There shall ‡ "
28 shall be done, saith the Lord G'. ‡ "
13: 3 said the Lord G'; Woe unto the ‡ "
8 saith the Lord G'; Because ye ‡ "
8 against you, saith the Lord G'. ‡ "
9 shall know that I am the Lord G'. ‡ "
13 saith the Lord G'; I will even ‡ "
16 is no peace, saith the Lord G'. ‡ "
18 saith the Lord G'; Woe to the ‡ "
20 saith the Lord G'; Behold, I am ‡ "
14: 4 saith the Lord G'; Every man of ‡ "
6 saith the Lord G'; Repent, and ‡ "
11 I may be their G', saith the Lord 430
11 may be their..., saith the Lord G'. ‡3069
14 righteousness, saith the Lord G'. ‡ "
16 saith the Lord G', they shall ‡ "
18 as I live, saith the Lord G', they ‡ "
20 in it, as I live, saith the Lord G', ‡ "
21 saith the Lord G'; How much ‡ "
23 have done in it, saith the Lord G'. ‡ "
15: 6 saith the Lord G'; As the vine ‡ "
8 a trespass, saith the Lord G'. ‡ "
16: 3 saith the Lord G' unto Jerusalem; ‡ "
8 saith the Lord G', and thou ‡ "
14 put upon thee, saith the Lord G'. ‡ "
19 thus it was, saith the Lord G'. ‡ "
23 woe unto thee! saith the Lord G';) ‡ "
30 is thine heart, saith the Lord G', ‡ "
36 saith the Lord G'; Because thy ‡ "
43 thine head, saith the Lord G': ‡ "
48 saith the Lord G', Sodom thy ‡ "
59 saith the Lord G'; I will even deal ‡ "
63 thou hast done, saith the Lord G'. ‡ "
17: 3 saith the Lord G'; A great eagle ‡ "
9 saith the Lord G'; Shall it prosper? ‡ "
16 saith the Lord G', surely in the ‡ "
19 saith the Lord G'; As I live, ‡ "
22 saith the Lord G'; I will also ‡ "
18: 3 saith the Lord G', ye shall not ‡ "
9 surely live, saith the Lord G'. ‡ "
23 should die? saith the Lord G': ‡ "
30 to his ways, saith the Lord G'. ‡ "
32 that dieth, saith the Lord G': ‡ "
20: 3 saith the Lord G'; Are ye come ‡ "
3 saith the Lord G', I will not be ‡ "
5 saith the Lord G'; In the day ‡ "
5 saying, I am the Lord your G'; 430
7 of Egypt: I am the Lord your G'. "
19 I am the Lord your G'; walk in my "
20 know that I am the Lord your G'. "
27 saith the Lord G'; Yet in this ‡3069
30 saith the Lord G'; Are ye polluted ‡ "
31 As I live, saith the Lord G', I will ‡ "
33 saith the Lord G', surely with a ‡ "
36 plead with you, saith the Lord G'. ‡ "
39 saith the Lord G'; Go ye, serve ‡ "
40 height of Israel, saith the Lord G', ‡ "
44 house of Israel, saith the Lord G'. ‡ "

Eze 20:47 saith the Lord G'; Behold, I will ‡3069
49 Ah Lord G'! they say of me, Doth ‡ "
21: 7 to pass; saith the Lord G'. ‡ "
13 be no more, saith the Lord G'. ‡ "
24 saith the Lord G'; Because ye ‡ "
26 saith the Lord G'; Remove the ‡ "
28 saith the Lord G' concerning the ‡ "
22: 3 saith the Lord G', The city ‡ "
12 forgotten me, saith the Lord G'. ‡ "
19 saith the Lord G'; Because ye are ‡ "
28 saith the Lord G', when the Lord ‡ "
31 their heads, saith the Lord G'. ‡ "
23:22, 28 saith the Lord G'; Behold, I ‡ "
32 saith the Lord G'; Thou shalt ‡ "
34 have spoken it, saith the Lord G'. ‡ "
35 saith the Lord G'; Because thou ‡ "
46 saith the Lord G'; I will bring up ‡ "
49 shall know that I am the Lord G'. ‡ "
24: 3 saith the Lord G'; Set on a pot, ‡ "
6, 9 saith the Lord G'; Woe to the ‡ "
14 judge thee, saith the Lord G'. ‡ "
21 saith the Lord G'; Behold, I will ‡ "
24 shall know that I am the Lord G'. ‡ "
25: 3 Hear the word of the Lord G'; ‡ "
3 the Lord G'; Because thou saidst, ‡ "
6 the Lord G'; Because thou hast ‡ "
8 the Lord G'; Because that Moab ‡ "
12 the Lord G'; Because that Edom ‡ "
13 saith the Lord G'; I will also ‡ "
14 my vengeance, saith the Lord G'. ‡ "
15 saith the Lord G'; Because the ‡ "
16 saith the Lord G'; Behold, I will ‡ "
26: 3 saith the Lord G'; Behold, I am ‡ "
5 have spoken it, saith the Lord G'; ‡ "
7 saith the Lord G'; Behold, I will ‡ "
14 have spoken it, saith the Lord G'. ‡ "
15 saith the Lord G' to Tyrus; Shall ‡ "
19 saith the Lord G'; When I shall ‡ "
21 found again, saith the Lord G'. ‡ "
27: 3 saith the Lord G'; O Tyrus, thou ‡ "
28: 2 saith the Lord G'; Because thine ‡ "
2 and thou hast said, I am a G', 410
2 I sit in the seat of G', in the midst 430
2 thou art a man, and not G', though 410
2 set thine heart as the heart of G': 430
6 saith the Lord G'; Because thou ‡3069
6 set thine heart as the heart of G'; 430
9 him that slayeth thee, I am G'? "
9 but thou shalt be a man, and no G', 410
10 have spoken it, saith the Lord G' ‡3069
12 said the Lord G'; Thou sealest ‡ "
13 been in Eden the garden of G'; 430
14 wast upon the holy mountain of G'; "
16 profane out of the mountain of G': "
22 saith the Lord G'; Behold, I am ‡3069
24 shall know that I am the Lord G'. ‡ "
25 saith the Lord G'; When I shall ‡ "
26 know that I am the Lord their G'. 430
29: 3 saith the Lord G'; Behold, I am ‡3069
8 saith the Lord G'; Behold, I will ‡ "
13 saith the Lord G'; At the end of ‡ "
16 shall know that I am the Lord G'. ‡ "
19 saith the Lord G'; Behold, I will ‡ "
20 wrought for me, saith the Lord G'. ‡ "
30: 2 saith the Lord G'; Howl ye, Woe ‡ "
6 by the sword, saith the Lord G'. ‡ "
10 the Lord G'; I will also make ‡ "
13 the Lord G'; I will also destroy ‡ "
22 saith the Lord G'; Behold, I am ‡ "
31: 8 The cedars in the garden of G' 430
8 nor any tree in the garden of G' "
9 that were in the garden of G', "
10 said the Lord G'; Because thou ‡3069
15 saith the Lord G'; In the day ‡ "
18 his multitude, saith the Lord G'. ‡ "
32: 3 Thus saith the Lord G'; I will ‡ "
8 upon thy land, saith the Lord G'. ‡ "
11 saith the Lord G'; The sword of ‡ "
14 to run like oil, saith the Lord G'. ‡ "
16 her multitude, saith the Lord G'. ‡ "
31 by the sword, saith the Lord G'. ‡ "
32 his multitude, saith the Lord G'. ‡ "
33:11 As I live, saith the Lord G', I ‡ "
25 thus saith the Lord G'; Ye eat ‡ "
27 saith the Lord G'; As I live, ‡ "
34: 2 the Lord G' unto the shepherds; ‡ "
8 As I live, saith the Lord G', surely ‡ "
10 Lord G'; Behold, I am against ‡ "
11 the Lord G'; Behold, I, even I, ‡ "
15 to lie down, saith the Lord G'. ‡ "
17 saith the Lord G'; Behold, I judge ‡ "
20 saith the Lord G' unto them; ‡ "
24 And I the Lord will be their G', 430
30 they know that I the Lord their G' "
30 are my people, saith the Lord G'. ‡3069
31 are men, and I am your G', 430
31 and I am...saith the Lord G'. ‡3069
35: 3 saith the Lord G'; Behold, O ‡ "
6 saith the Lord G', I will prepare ‡ "
11 saith the Lord G', I will even do ‡ "
14 saith the Lord G'; When the ‡ "
36: 2 saith the Lord G'; Because the ‡ "
3 saith the Lord G'; Because they ‡ "
4 hear the word of the Lord G'; ‡ "
4 the Lord G' to the mountains ‡ "
5 saith the Lord G'; Surely in the ‡ "
6 saith the Lord G'; Behold, I have ‡ "
7 saith the Lord G'; I have lifted ‡ "
13 saith the Lord G'; Because they ‡ "
14 nations...more, saith the Lord G'. ‡ "
15 fall any more, saith the Lord G'. ‡ "
22 saith the Lord G'; I do not this ‡ "
23 am the Lord, saith the Lord G', ‡ "
28 my people, and I will be your G'. 430
32 sakes do I this, saith the Lord G', ‡3069
33 saith the Lord G'; In the day ‡ "

Eze 36:37 saith the Lord G·; I will yet ‡3069
37: 3 And I answered, O Lord G·, ‡ "
5 the Lord G· unto these bones; ‡ "
9 saith the Lord G·; Come from ‡ "
12 saith the Lord G·; Behold, O ‡ "
19 saith the Lord G·; Behold, I will ‡ "
21 saith the Lord G·; Behold, I will ‡ "
23 my people, and I will be their G·. 430
27 I will be their G·, and they shall be "
38: 3 saith the Lord G·; Behold, I am ‡3069
10 saith the Lord G·; It shall also ‡ "
14 saith the Lord G·; In that day ‡ "
17 saith the Lord G·; Art thou he ‡ "
18 land of Israel, saith the Lord G·, ‡ "
21 my mountains, saith the Lord G·: ‡ "
39: 1 saith the Lord G·; Behold I am ‡ "
5 have spoken it, saith the Lord G·. ‡ "
8 and it is done, saith the Lord G·; ‡ "
10 robbed them, saith the Lord G·. ‡ "
13 be glorified, saith the Lord G·. ‡ "
17 saith the Lord G·; Speak unto ‡ "
20 all men of war, saith the Lord G·. ‡ "
22 I am the Lord their G· from that 430
25 saith the Lord G·; Now will I ‡3069
28 I am the Lord their G·, which 430
29 house of Israel, saith the Lord G·. ‡3069
40: 2 In the visions of G· brought he me 430
43: 2 glory of the G· of Israel came from "
18 saith the Lord G·; These are the ‡3069
19 minister unto me, saith the Lord G· ‡ "
27 accept you, saith the Lord G·. ‡ "
44: 2 because the Lord, the G· of Isreel, 430
6 saith the Lord G·; O ye house of ‡3069
9 saith the Lord G·; No stranger, ‡ "
12 against them, saith the Lord G·, ‡ "
15 and the blood, saith the Lord G·: ‡ "
27 sin offering, saith the Lord G·. ‡ "
45: 9 saith the Lord G·; Let it suffice ‡ "
9 my people, saith the Lord G·. ‡ "
15 for them, saith the Lord G·. ‡ "
18 saith the Lord G·; In the first ‡ "
46: 1 saith the Lord G·; The gate of ‡ "
16 saith the Lord G·; If the prince ‡ "
47:13 saith the Lord G·; This shall be ‡ "
23 inheritance, saith the Lord G·. ‡ "
48:29 their portions, saith the Lord G·. ‡ "
Da 1: 2 the vessels of the house of G·: 430
2 of Shinar to the house of his g·; "
2 into the treasure house of his g·. "
9 G· had brought Daniel into favour "
17 G· gave them knowledge and skill "
2:18 desire mercies of the G· of heaven 426
19 Daniel blessed the G· of heaven. "
20 Blessed be the name of G· for ever "
23 O thou G· of my fathers, who hast "
28 is a G· in heaven that revealeth "
37 the G· of heaven hath given thee "
44 the G· of heaven set up a kingdom, "
45 G· hath made known to the king "
47 that your G· is a G· of gods, "
3:15 who is that G· that shall deliver you "
17 G· whom we serve is able to deliver "
25 the fourth is like the Son of G·. "
26 ye servants of the most high G·, "
28 Blessed be the G· of Shadrach, "
28 worship any g·, except their own G·. "
29 against the G· of Shadrach, "
29 is no other G· that can deliver "
4: 2 and wonders that the high G· hath "
8 according to the name of my g·, and "
5: 3 of the temple of the house of G· "
18 most high G· gave Nebuchadnezzar "
21 knew that the most high G· ruled "
23 the G· in whose hand thy breath is, "
26 G· hath numbered thy kingdom, "
6: 5 concerning the law of his G·. "
7 shall ask a petition of any G· or "
10 gave thanks before his G·, as he did "
11 making supplication before his G·. "
12 that shall ask a petition of any G· "
16 G· whom thou servest continually, "
20 servant of the living G·, is thy G·, "
22 My G· hath sent his angel, and "
23 him, because he believed in his G·. "
26 and fear before the G· of Daniel: "
26 for he is the living G·, and stedfast "
9: 3 And I set my face unto the Lord G·, 430
4 I prayed unto the Lord my G·, "
4 O Lord, the great and dreadful G·, 410
9 To the Lord our G· belong mercies 430
10 obeyed the voice of the Lord our G·, "
11 law of Moses the servant of G·, "
13 prayer before the Lord our G·, "
14 for the Lord our G· is righteous "
15 now, O Lord our G·, thou hast "
17 Now therefore, O our G·, hear "
18 O my G·, incline thine ear, and hear; "
19 for thine own sake, O my G·: "
20 supplication before the Lord my G· "
20 for the holy mountain of my G·; "
10:12 to chasten thyself before thy G·, "
11:32 do know their G· shall be strong, "
36 magnify himself above every g·, 410
36 things against the G· of gods, "
37 he regard the G· of his fathers, 430
37 nor regard any g·: for he shall 433
38 the G· of forces: and a g· whom his "
39 most strong holds with a strange g·. "
Ho 1: 6 And G· said unto him, Call her †‡
7 save them by the Lord their G·, 430
9 said, Call his name Lo-ammi: †‡
9 my people, and I will not be your G·. "
10 Ye are the sons of the living G·. 410
2:23 they shall say, Thou art my G·. 430
3: 5 seek the Lord their G·, and David "
4: 1 nor knowledge of G· in the land. "

Ho 4: 6 hast forgotten the law of thy G·, 430
12 a whoring from under their G·. "
5: 4 doings to turn unto their G·: "
6: 6 the knowledge of G· more than "
7:10 return to the Lord their G·, "
8: 2 Israel shall cry unto me, My G·, "
6 therefore it is not G·: but the calf "
9: 1 hast gone a whoring from thy G·, "
8 of Ephraim was with my G·: but "
8 and hatred in the house of his G·. "
17 My G· will cast them away, because "
11: 9 for I am G·, and not man; 410
12 but Judah yet ruleth with G·, and 430
12: 3 his strength he had power with G·: "
5 Even the Lord G· of hosts; the Lord "
6 therefore turn thou to thy G·: keep "
6 and wait on thy G· continually. "
9 And I that am the Lord thy G· from "
13: 4 Yet I am the Lord thy G· from the "
4 and thou shalt know no g· but me: "
16 she hath rebelled against her G·: "
14: 1 return unto the Lord thy G·; for "
Joe 1:13 ye ministers of my G·: for the meat "
13 withholden from the house of your G·. "
14 into the house of the Lord your G·, "
16 gladness from the house of our G·? "
2:13 and turn unto the Lord your G·: "
14 offering unto the Lord your G·? "
17 the people, Where is their G·? "
23 and rejoice in the Lord your G·: "
26 praise the name of the Lord your G·, "
27 am the Lord your G·, and none else: "
3:17 I am the Lord your G· dwelling "
Am 1: 8 shall perish, saith the Lord G·. ‡3069
2: 8 condemned in the house of their g·. 430
3: 7 the Lord G· will do nothing, but ‡3069
8 the Lord G· hath spoken, who ‡ "
11 saith the Lord G·; An adversary ‡ "
13 of Jacob, saith the Lord G·, ‡ "
13 saith the...the G· of hosts, 430
4: 2 The Lord G· hath sworn by his ‡3069
5 of Israel, saith the Lord G·. ‡ "
11 as G· overthrew Sodom and 430
12 prepare to meet thy G·, O Israel. "
13 The G· of hosts, is his name. "
5: 3 saith the Lord G·; The city that ‡3069
14 the G· of hosts, shall be with you, 430
15 Lord G· of hosts will be gracious "
16 Therefore the Lord, the G· of hosts, "
26 the star of your g·, which ye made "
27 whose name is The G· of hosts. "
6: 8 Lord G· hath sworn by himself, ‡3069
8 saith the Lord the G· of hosts, 430
14 saith the Lord the G· of hosts; "
7: 1 the Lord G· shewed unto me; ‡3069
2 then I said, O Lord G·, forgive, ‡ "
4 the Lord G· shewed unto me: ‡ "
4 the Lord G· called to contend by ‡ "
5 Then said I, O Lord G·, cease, ‡ "
6 shall not be, saith the Lord G·. ‡ "
8: 1 the Lord G· shewed unto me: ‡ "
3 that day, saith the Lord G·: there ‡ "
9 that day, saith the Lord G·, that ‡ "
11 days come, saith the Lord G·, ‡ "
14 and say, Thy g·, O Dan, liveth; 430
9: 5 the Lord G· of hosts is he that ‡3069
8 the eyes of the Lord G· are upon ‡ "
15 given them, saith the Lord thy G·. 430
Ob 1 the Lord G· concerning Edom; ‡3069
Jon 1: 5 cried every man unto his g·, 430
6 call upon thy G·, if so be that G· "
9 I fear the Lord, the G· of heaven, "
2: 1 Jonah prayed unto the Lord his G· "
6 from corruption, O Lord my G·. "
3: 5 the people of Nineveh believed G·, "
8 cry mightily unto G·: yea, "
9 Who can tell if G· will turn and "
10 G· saw their works, that they "
10 G· repented of the evil, that he "
4: 2 I knew that thou art a gracious G·, 410
6 the Lord G· prepared a gourd, 430
7 But G· prepared a worm when the "
8 G· prepared a vehement east wind; "
9 G· said to Jonah, Doest thou well "
Mic 1: 2 Lord G· be witness against you, ‡3069
3: 7 for there is no answer of G·. 430
4: 2 to the house of the G· of Jacob; "
5 of the name of his g·, and we will "
5 in the name of the Lord our G· "
5: 4 of the name of the Lord his G·; "
6: 6 and bow myself before the high G·? "
8 and to walk humbly with thy G·? "
7: 7 will wait for the G· of my salvation: "
7 salvation: my G· will hear me. "
10 Where is the Lord thy G·? mine "
17 shall be afraid of the Lord our G·, "
18 Who is a G· like unto thee, that 410
Na 1: 2 G· is jealous, and the Lord "
Hab 1:11 imputing this his power unto his g·. 430
12 from everlasting, O Lord my G·, "
12 mighty G·, thou hast established *6697
3: 3 G· came from Teman, and the 433
18 joy in the G· of my salvation. 430
19 The Lord G· is my strength, and* 136
Zep 1: 7 at the presence of the Lord G·: ‡3069
2: 7 the Lord their G· shall visit them, 430
9 the Lord of hosts, the G· of Israel, "
3: 2 she drew not near to her G·. "
17 The Lord thy G· in the midst of thee "
Hag 1:12 the voice of the Lord their G·, "
12 as the Lord their G· had sent him, "
14 house of the Lord of hosts, their G·, "
Zec 6:15 obey the voice of the Lord your G·. "
7: 2 unto the house of G· Sherezer *1008
8: 8 I will be their G·, in truth 430
23 we have heard that G· is with you. "

Zec 9: 7 even he, shall be for our G·, 430
14 Lord G· shall blow the trumpet, ‡3069
16 the Lord their G· shall save them 430
10: 6 for I am the Lord their G·, and will "
11: 4 Thus saith the Lord my G·; Feed "
12: 5 strength in the Lord of hosts their G·. "
8 the house of David shall be as G·, "
13: 9 they shall say, The Lord is my G·. "
14: 5 and the Lord my G· shall come, "
Mal 1: 9 beseech G· that he will be gracious 410
2:10 hath not one G· created us? why "
11 married the daughter of a strange g·. "
16 For the Lord, the G· of Israel, saith 430
17 Where is the G· of judgment? "
3: 8 Will a man rob G·? Yet ye have "
14 It is vain to serve G·: and what "
15 that tempt G· are even delivered. "
18 between him that serveth G· and "
M't 1:23 being interpreted is, G· with us. 2316
2:12 being warned of G· in a dream that "
22 warned of G· in a dream, he turned "
3: 9 G· is able of these stones to raise 2316
16 he saw the Spirit of G· descending "
4: 3 If thou be the Son of G·, command "
4 proceedeth out of the mouth of G·. "
6 If thou be the Son of G·, cast "
7 shalt not tempt the Lord thy G·. "
10 Thou shalt worship the Lord thy G·, "
5: 8 pure in heart: for they shall see G·. "
9 shall be called the children of G·. "
6:24 Ye cannot serve G· and mammon. "
30 G· so clothe the grass of the field, "
33 seek ye first the kingdom of G·, * "
8:29 Jesus, thou Son of G·? art thou "
9: 8 and glorified G·, which had given "
12: 4 he entered into the house of G·, "
28 cast out devils by the Spirit of G·, "
28 the kingdom of G· is come unto "
14:33 Of a truth thou art the Son of G·. "
15: 3 the commandment of G· by your "
4 For G· commanded, saying, Honour "
6 the commandment of G· of none "
31 and they glorified the G· of Israel. "
16:16 Christ, the Son of the living G·. "
23 not the things that be of G·, "
19: 6 therefore G· hath joined together, "
17 none good but one, that is, G·: "
24 to enter into the kingdom of G·. "
26 but with G· all things are possible. "
21:12 into the temple of G·, and cast out "
31 into the kingdom of G· before you. "
43 The kingdom of G· shall be taken "
22:16 and teachest the way of G· in truth, "
21 and unto G· the things that are "
29 the scriptures, nor the power of G·. "
30 but are as the angels of G· in * "
31 which was spoken unto you by G·, "
32 I am the G· of Abraham, "
32 the G· of Isaac, and the G· of Jacob? "
32 G· is not the G· of the dead, "
37 Thou shalt love the Lord thy G· "
23:22 sweareth by the throne of G·, and "
26:61 to destroy the temple of G·, and to "
63 I adjure thee by the living G·, "
63 thou be the Christ, the Son of G·. "
27:40 thou be the Son of G·, come down "
43 He trusted in G·; let him deliver "
43 for he said, I am the Son of G·. "
46 My G·, my G·, why hast thou "
54 Truly this was the Son of G·. "
M'r 1: 1 of Jesus Christ, the Son of G·; "
14 the gospel of the kingdom of G·, "
15 the kingdom of G· is at hand: "
24 who thou art, the Holy One of G·. "
2: 7 who can forgive sins but G· only? "
12 and glorified G·, saying, We never "
26 he went into the house of G· "
3:11 saying, Thou art the Son of G·. "
35 shall do the will of G·, the same "
4:11 the mystery of the kingdom of G·: "
26 So is the kingdom of G·, as if "
30 shall we liken the kingdom of G·? "
5: 7 thou Son of the most high G·? "
7 adjure thee by G·, that thou torment "
7: 8 aside the commandment of G·, "
9 ye reject the commandment of G·, "
13 Making the word of G· of none "
8:33 not the things that be of G·, but "
9: 1 they have seen the kingdom of G· "
47 to enter into the kingdom of G· "
10: 6 G· made them male and female. * "
9 therefore G· hath joined together, "
14 for of such is the kingdom of G·. "
15 shall not receive the kingdom of G· "
18 is none good but one, that is, G·. "
23 riches enter into the kingdom of G·! "
24 to enter into the kingdom of G·! "
25 to enter into the kingdom of G·. "
27 impossible, but not with G·: "
27 for with G· all things are possible. "
11:22 saith unto them, Have faith in G·. "
12:14 teachest the way of G· in truth: "
17 and to G· the things that are God's. "
24 scriptures, neither the power of G·? "
26 how in the bush, G· spake unto him, "
26 saying, I am the G· of Abraham, "
26 the G· of Isaac, and the G· of Jacob? "
27 He is not the G· of the dead, "
27 but the G· of the living: * "
29 The Lord our G· is one Lord: "
30 thou shalt love the Lord thy G· "
32 for there is one G·; and there is * "
34 not far from the kingdom of G·. "
13:19 which G· created unto this time, "
14:25 drink it new in the kingdom of G·. "
15:34 My G·, my G·, why hast thou "

M'r 15:39 Truly this man was the Son of G·. 2316
43 also waited for the kingdom of G·. "
16:19 and sat on the right hand of G·. "
Lu 1: 6 they were both righteous before G·, "
8 before G· in the order of his course, "
16 shall he turn to the Lord their G·. "
19 that stand in the presence of G·; "
26 Gabriel was sent from G· unto a "
30 for thou hast found favour with G·. "
32 the Lord G· shall give unto him "
35 of thee shall be called the Son of G·. "
37 G· nothing shall be impossible. "
47 hath rejoiced in G· my Saviour. "
64 and he spake, and praised G·. "
68 Blessed be the Lord G· of Israel; "
78 the tender mercy of our G·; "
2:13 of the heavenly host praising G·, "
14 Glory to G· in the highest, and on "
20 and praising G· for all the things "
28 arms, and blessed G·, and said, "
37 G· with fastings and prayers *
40 and the grace of G· was upon him. 2316
52 and in favour with G· and man. "
3: 2 the word of G· came unto John "
6 flesh shall see the salvation of G·. "
8 G· is able of these stones to raise "
38 of Adam, which was the son of G·. "
4: 3 If thou be the Son of G·, command "
4 alone, but by every word of G·. * "
8 Thou shalt worship the Lord thy G·, "
9 thou be the Son of G·, cast thyself "
12 shalt not tempt the Lord thy G·. "
34 who thou art, the Holy One of G·. "
41 Thou art Christ the Son of G·. "
43 kingdom of G· to other cities also: "
5: 1 upon him to hear the word of G·, "
21 Who can forgive sins, but G· alone? "
25 to his own house, glorifying G·. "
26 and they glorified G·, and were filled "
6: 4 How he went into the house of G·, "
12 continued all night in prayer to G·. "
20 for yours is the kingdom of G·. "
7:16 and they glorified G·, saying, That "
16 G· hath visited his people. "
28 in the kingdom of G· is greater "
29 justified G·, being baptized with "
30 council of G· against themselves, "
8: 1 glad tidings of the kingdom of G·: "
10 the mysteries of the kingdom of G·: "
11 The seed is the word of G·. "
21 which hear the word of G·, and do "
28 Son of G· most high? I beseech "
39 how great things G· hath done unto "
9: 2 to preach the kingdom of G·, and "
11 unto them of the kingdom of G·, "
20 answering said, The Christ of G·. "
27 till they see the kingdom of G·. "
43 amazed at the mighty power of G·. "
60 thou and preach the kingdom of G·. "
62 back, is fit for the kingdom of G·. "
10: 9 The kingdom of G· is come nigh "
11 that the kingdom of G· is come nigh "
27 Thou shalt love the Lord thy G· "
11:20 But if I with the finger of G· cast "
20 no doubt the kingdom of G· is come "
28 are they that hear the word of G·, "
42 judgment and the love of G·: "
49 said the wisdom of G·, I will send "
12: 6 one of them is forgotten before G·? "
8 also confess before the angels of G·: "
9 be denied before the angels of G·. "
20 But G· said unto him, Thou fool, "
21 and is not rich toward G·. "
24 G· feedeth them: how much more "
28 G· so clothed the grass, which is "
31 rather seek ye the kingdom of G·;* "
13:13 was made straight, and glorified G·. "
18 what is the kingdom of G· like? "
20 shall I liken the kingdom of G·? "
28 the prophets, in the kingdom of G·, "
29 shall sit down in the kingdom of G·. "
14:15 eat bread in the kingdom of G·. "
15:10 in the presence of the angels of G· "
16:13 Ye cannot serve G· and mammon. "
15 but G· knoweth your hearts: for "
15 is abomination in the sight of G·. "
16 the kingdom of G· is preached, and "
17:15 and with a loud voice glorified G·, "
18 give glory to G·, save this stranger. "
20 when the kingdom of G· should "
20 kingdom of G· cometh not with "
21 the kingdom of G· is within you. "
18: 2 feared not G·, neither regarded "
4 Though I fear not G·, nor regard "
7 And shall not G· avenge his own "
11 G·, I thank thee, that I am not as "
13 G· be merciful to me a sinner. "
16 for of such is the kingdom of G·. "
17 shall not receive the kingdom of G· "
19 None is good, save one, that is, G·. "
24 riches enter into the kingdom of G·! "
25 man to enter into the kingdom of G·. "
27 with men are possible with G·. "
43 followed him, glorifying G·: and all "
43 they saw it, gave praise unto G·. "
19:11 kingdom of G· should immediately "
37 and praise G· with a loud voice for "
20:16 heard it, they said, G· forbid. 3361, 1096
21 but teachest the way of G· truly: 2316
25 and unto G· the things which be "
36 and are the children of G·, being "
37 calleth the Lord the G· of Abraham, "
37 the G· of Isaac, and the G· of Jacob. "
38 For he is not a G· of the dead, but "
21: 4 cast in unto the offerings of G·: * "
31 the kingdom of G· is nigh at hand. "
Lu 22:16 be fulfilled in the kingdom of G·. 2316
18 until the kingdom of G· shall come. "
69 the right hand of the power of G·. "
70 Art thou then the Son of G·? "
23:35 if he be Christ, the chosen of G·. "
40 Dost not thou fear G·, seeing thou "
47 he glorified G·, saying, Certainly "
51 waited for the kingdom of G·. "
24:19 word before G· and all the people: "
53 temple, praising and blessing G·. "
Joh 1: 1 was with G·, and the Word was G·. "
2 same was in the beginning with G·. "
6 There was a man sent from G·, "
12 power to become the sons of G·, "
13 nor of the will of man, but of G·. "
18 No man hath seen G· at any time; "
29 and saith, Behold the Lamb of G·, "
34 record that this is the Son of G·. "
36 he saith, Behold the Lamb of G·! "
49 Rabbi, thou art the Son of G·; "
51 and the angels of G· ascending and "
3: 2 thou art a teacher, come from G·: "
2 thou doest, except G· be with him. "
3 he cannot see the kingdom of G·. "
5 cannot enter into the kingdom of G·. "
16 G· so loved the world, that he gave "
17 G· sent not his Son into the world "
18 name of the only begotten Son of G·. "
21 that they are wrought in G·. "
33 hath set to his seal that G· is true. "
34 For he whom G· hath sent speaketh "
34 words of G·: for G· giveth not the "
36 the wrath of G· abideth on him. "
4:10 If thou knewest the gift of G·, and "
24 G· is a Spirit: and they that worship "
5:18 said also that G· was his Father, "
18 making himself equal with G·. "
25 shall hear the voice of the Son of G·: "
42 ye have not the love of G· in you. "
44 honour that cometh from G· only? "
6:27 for him hath G· the Father sealed. "
28 we might work the works of G·? "
29 This is the work of G·, that ye "
33 For the bread of G· is he which "
45 And they shall be all taught of G·. "
46 save he which is of G·, he hath seen "
69 that Christ, the Son of the living G·. "
7:17 whether it be of G·, or whether I "
8:40 the truth which I have heard of G·: "
41 we have one Father, even G·. "
42 If G· were your Father, ye would "
42 proceeded forth, and came from G·; "
47 that is of G· heareth God's words: "
47 them not, because ye are not of G·. "
54 of whom ye say, that he is your G·: "
9: 3 that the works of G· should be made "
16 This man is not of G·, because he "
24 Give G· the praise: we know that "
29 know that G· spake unto Moses: "
31 know that G· heareth not sinners: "
31 if any man be a worshipper of G·, 2318
33 If this man were not of G·, he 2316
35 Dost thou believe on the Son of G·? "
10:33 being a man, makest thyself G·. "
35 unto whom the word of G· came, "
36 because I said, I am the Son of G·? "
11: 4 unto death, but for the glory of G·, "
4 the Son of G· might be glorified "
22 whatsoever thou wilt ask of G·, "
22 G· will give it thee. "
27 thou art the Christ, the Son of G·, "
40 thou shouldest see the glory of G·? "
52 children of G· that were scattered "
12:43 of men more than the praise of G·. "
13: 3 was come from G·, and went to G·; "
31 glorified, and G· is glorified in him. "
32 If G· be glorified in him, *
32 G· shall also glorify him in "
14: 1 ye believe in G·, believe also in me. "
16: 2 think that he doeth G· service. "
27 believed that I came out from G·.* "
30 that thou camest forth from G·. "
17: 3 might know thee the only true G·, "
19: 7 he made himself the Son of G·. "
20:17 and to my G·, and your G·. "
28 said unto him, My Lord and my G·. "
31 Jesus is the Christ, the Son of G·; "
21:19 by what death he should glorify G·. "
Ac 1: 3 pertaining to the kingdom of G·: "
2:11 tongue the wonderful works of G·. "
17 saith G·, I will pour out of my "
22 a man approved of G· among you "
22 G· did by him in the midst of you, "
23 counsel and foreknowledge of G·, "
24 Whom G· hath raised up, having "
30 G· had sworn with an oath to him, "
32 This Jesus hath G· raised up, "
33 by the right hand of G· exalted "
36 that G· hath made that same Jesus, "
39 many as the Lord our G· shall call. "
47 Praising G·, and having favour "
3: 8 and leaping, and praising G·. "
9 saw him walking and praising G·. "
13 The G· of Abraham, and of Isaac, "
13 and of Jacob, the G· of our fathers, "
15 whom G· hath raised from the dead; "
18 things, which G· before had shewed "
21 which G· hath spoken by the mouth "
22 the Lord your G· raise up unto you "
25 covenant which G· made with our "
26 G·, having raised up his Son Jesus, "
4:10 whom G· raised from the dead, "
19 right in the sight of G· to hearken "
19 unto you more than unto G·, "
21 all men glorified G· for that which "
24 they lifted up their voice to G· "
Ac 4:24 art G·, which hast made heaven, *2316
31 they spake the word of G· with "
5: 4 not lied unto men, but unto G·. "
29 ought to obey G· rather than men. "
30 The G· of our fathers raised up "
31 Him hath G· exalted with his "
32 G· hath given to them that obey "
39 But if it be of G·, ye cannot "
39 be found even to fight against G·. 2314
6: 2 we should leave the word of G·, 2316
7 And the word of G· increased; and "
11 against Moses, and against G·. "
7: 2 The G· of glory appeared unto our "
6 And G· spake on this wise, That "
7 in bondage will I judge, said G·: "
9 into Egypt; but G· was with him, "
17 which G· had sworn to Abraham, "
25 how that G· by his hand would "
32 Saying, I am the G· of thy fathers, "
32 thy fathers, the G· of Abraham, "
32 G· of Isaac, and the G· of Jacob. * "
35 the same did G· send to be a ruler "
37 the Lord your G· raise up unto you "
42 Then G· turned, and gave them up "
43 and the star of your g· Remphan, "
45 whom G· drave out before the face "
46 favour before G·, and desired to "
46 a tabernacle for the G· of Jacob. "
55 and saw the glory of G·, and Jesus "
55 standing on the right hand of G·, "
56 standing on the right hand of G·. "
59 stoned Stephen calling upon G·, *
8:10 This man is the great power of G·. 2316
12 concerning the kingdom of G·, "
14 had received the word of G·, "
20 hast thought that the gift of G· may "
21 heart is not right in the sight of G·. "
22 pray G·, if perhaps the thought * "
37 that Jesus Christ is the Son of G·.* "
9:20 synagogues, that he is the Son of G·. "
10: 2 that feared G· with all his house, "
2 people, and prayed to G· alway. "
3 an angel of G· coming in to him, "
4 come up for a memorial before G·. "
15 What G· hath cleansed, that call not "
22 and one that feareth G·, and of good "
22 was warned from G· by an holy angel
28 G· hath shewed me that I should 2316
31 in remembrance in the sight of G·. "
33 are we all here present before G·, "
33 that are commanded thee of G·. * "
34 that G· is no respecter of persons: "
36 The word which G· sent unto the*
38 G· anointed Jesus of Nazareth 2316
38 of the devil; for G· was with him. "
40 Him G· raised up the third day, "
41 witnesses chosen before of G·, even "
42 was ordained of G· to be the Judge "
46 speak with tongues, and magnify G·. "
11: 1 had also received the word of G·. "
9 What G· hath cleansed, that call "
17 G· gave them the like gift as he did "
17 was I, that I could withstand G·? "
18 and glorified G·, saying, Then hath "
18 G· also to the Gentiles granted "
23 had seen the grace of G·, was glad, "
12: 5 of the church unto G· for him. "
22 the voice of a g·, and not of a man. "
23 because he gave not G· the glory: "
24 word of G· grew and multiplied. "
13: 5 they preached the word of G· in the "
7 and desired to hear the word of G·. "
16 ye that fear G·, give audience. "
17 The G· of this people of Israel "
21 G· gave unto them Saul the son of "
23 this man's seed hath G· according "
26 whosoever among you feareth G·, "
30 But G· raised him from the dead: "
33 G· hath fulfilled the same unto us "
36 by the will of G·, fell on sleep, and "
37 But he, whom G· raised again, saw "
43 to continue in the grace of G·. "
44 together to hear the word of G·. "
46 the word of G· should first have "
14:15 unto the living G·, which made "
22 enter into the kingdom of G·. "
26 to the grace of G· for the work "
27 all that G· had done with them, "
15: 4 things that G· had done with them. "
7 G· made choice among us, that the "
8 And G·, which knoweth the hearts, "
10 Now therefore why tempt ye G·, "
12 miracles and wonders G· had "
14 how G· at the first did visit the "
18 Known unto G· are all his works* "
19 the Gentiles are turned to G·: "
40 brethren unto the grace of G·. * "
16:14 which worshipped G·, heard us: "
17 the servants of the most high G·, "
25 and sang praises unto G·: and "
34 believing in G· with all his house. "
17:13 word of G· was preached of Paul "
23 To The Unknown G·. Whom "
24 G· that made the world and all "
29 then as we are the offspring of G·, "
30 ignorance G· winked at; but now "
18: 7 one that worshipped G·, whose "
11 the word of G· among them. "
13 to worship G· contrary to the law. "
21 return again unto you, if G· will. "
26 him the way of G· more perfectly. "
19: 8 concerning the kingdom of G·. "
11 G· wrought special miracles by the "
20 mightily grew the word of G· and* 2962
20:21 repentance toward G·, and faith 2316
24 the gospel of the grace of G·. "

Ac 20:25 preaching the kingdom of G'. *2316
27 unto you all the counsel of G'. "
28 to feed the church of G', which ‡ "
32 I commend you to G', and to "
21:19 things G' had wrought among the "
22: 3 and was zealous toward G', as ye "
14 G' of our fathers hath chosen thee, "
23: 1 in all good conscience before G' "
3 G' shall smite thee, thou whited "
9 let us not fight against G'. *2318
24:14 worship I the G' of my fathers, 2316
15 And have hope toward G', which "
16 void of offence toward G', "
26: 6 made of G' unto our fathers: "
7 instantly serving G' day and night, "
8 that G' should raise the dead? 2316
18 from the power of Satan unto G', "
20 repent and turn to G', and do "
22 therefore obtained help of G', I "
29 I would to G', that not only thou, "
27:23 the angel of G', whose I am, and "
24 G' hath given thee all them that "
25 for I believe G', that it shall be "
35 and gave thanks to G' in presence "
28: 6 minds, and said that he was a g'. "
15 he thanked G', and took courage. "
23 and testified the kingdom of G', "
28 the salvation of G' is sent unto "
31 Preaching the kingdom of G', and "
Ro 1: 1 separated unto the gospel of G', "
4 And declared to be the Son of G' "
7 be in Rome, beloved of G', called "
7 from G' our Father, and the Lord "
8 thank my G' through Jesus Christ "
9 For G' is my witness, whom I serve "
10 by the will of G' to come unto you. "
16 for it is the power of G' unto "
17 therein is the righteousness of G' "
18 For the wrath of G' is revealed "
19 may be known of G' is manifest "
19 for G' hath shewed it unto them. "
21 Because that, when they knew G', "
21 they glorified him not as G', "
23 the glory of the uncorruptible G' "
24 Wherefore G' also gave them up to "
25 changed the truth of G' into a lie, "
26 cause G' gave them up unto vile "
28 to retain G' in their knowledge, "
28 G' gave them over to a reprobate "
30 haters of G', despiteful, proud, 2319
32 Who knowing the judgment of G', 2316
2: 2 the judgment of G' is according "
3 shalt escape the judgment of G'? "
4 the goodness of G' leadeth thee to "
5 of the righteous judgment of G'; "
11 is no respect of persons with G'. "
13 are just before G', but the doers "
16 G' shall judge the secrets of men "
17 and makest thy boast of G', "
23 the law dishonourest thou G'? "
24 For the name of G' is blasphemed "
29 praise is not of men, but of G'. "
3: 2 were committed the oracles of G'. "
3 the faith of G' without effect? "
4 G' forbid: yea, let 3361, 1096
4 let G' be true, but every man a 2316
5 commend the righteousness of G', "
5 Is G' unrighteous who taketh "
6 G' forbid: for then 3361, 1096
6 how shall G' judge the world? 2316
7 truth of G' hath more abounded "
11 there is none that seeketh after G'. "
18 is no fear of G' before their eyes. "
19 may become guilty before G'. "
21 righteousness of G' without the law "
22 Even the righteousness of G' which "
23 and come short of the glory of G'; "
25 Whom G' hath set forth to be a "
25 through the forbearance of G'; "
29 Is he the G' of the Jews only? "
30 Seeing it is one G', which shall "
31 G' forbid: yea, we establish 3336, 1096
4: 2 to glory; but not before G'. 2316
3 Abraham believed G', and it was "
6 whom G' imputeth righteousness "
17 even G', who quickeneth the dead, "
20 promise of G' through unbelief; "
20 strong in faith, giving glory to G'; "
5: 1 we have peace with G' through our "
2 rejoice in hope of the glory of G'. "
5 the love of G' is shed abroad in our "
8 G' commendeth his love toward us, "
10 were reconciled to G' by the death "
11 we also joy in G' through our Lord "
15 much more the grace of G', and the "
6: 2 G' forbid. How shall we, 3361, 1096
10 that he liveth, he liveth unto G'. 2316
11 alive unto G' through Jesus Christ "
13 yield yourselves unto G', as those "
13 of righteousness unto G'. "
15 but under grace? G' forbid. 3361, 1096
17 But G' be thanked, that ye were 2316
22 and become servants to G', ye have "
23 but the gift of G' is eternal life "
7: 4 should bring forth fruit unto G'. "
7 G' forbid. Nay, I had not 3361, 1096
13 G' forbid. But sin, that it "
22 For I delight in the law of G' 2316
25 I thank G' through Jesus Christ "
25 then I myself serve the law of G'; "
8: 3 G' sending his own Son in the "
7 carnal mind is enmity against G': "
7 for it is not subject to the law of G', "
8 are in the flesh cannot please G'. "
9 if so be that the Spirit of G' dwell "
14 many as are led by the Spirit of G': "

Ro 8:14 they are the sons of G'. 2316
16 that we are the children of G': "
17 heirs of G', and joint-heirs with "
19 the manifestation of the sons of G'. "
21 liberty of the children of G'. "
27 saints according to the will of G'. "
28 for good to them that love G', to "
31 If G' be for us, who can be against "
33 God's elect? It is G' that justifieth. "
34 who is even at the right hand of G', "
39 to separate us from the love of G', "
9: 4 the service of G', and the promises; "
5 who is over all, G' blessed forever. 2316
6 word of G' hath taken none effect. "
8 these are not the children of G': "
11 purpose of G' according to election "
14 Is there unrighteousness with G'? "
14 unrighteousness...? G' forbid. 3361, 1096
16 but of G' that sheweth mercy. 2316
20 art thou that repliest against G'? "
22 if G', willing to shew his wrath, "
26 called the children of the living G'. "
10: 1 and prayer to G' for Israel is, that "
2 have a zeal of G', but not according "
3 unto the righteousness of G'. "
9 G' hath raised him from the dead, "
17 and hearing by the word of G'. * "
11: 1 Hath G' cast away his people? "
1 away his people? G' forbid. 3361, 1096
2 G' hath not cast away his people 2316
2 how he maketh intercession to G' "
4 what saith the answer of G' unto him? "
8 G' hath given them the spirit of 2316
11 they should fall? G' forbid. 3361, 1096
21 For if G' spared not the natural 2316
22 the goodness and severity of G': "
23 for G' is able to graff them in "
29 For the gifts and calling of G' "
30 times past have not believed G', "
32 For G' hath concluded them all in "
33 the wisdom and knowledge of G'! "
12: 1 the mercies of G', that ye present "
1 acceptable unto G', which is your "
2 acceptable, and perfect, will of G'. "
3 according as G' hath dealt to every "
13: 1 For there is no power but of G': "
1 powers that be are ordained of G'. "
2 resisteth the ordinance of G': and "
4 For he is the minister of G' to thee "
4 for he is the minister of G', "
14: 3 for G' hath received him. "
4 for G' is able to make him stand.* "
6 the Lord, for he giveth G' thanks; "
6 eateth not, and giveth G' thanks. "
11 every tongue shall confess to G'. "
12 shall give account of himself to G'. "
17 For the kingdom of G' is not meat "
18 serveth Christ is acceptable to G', "
20 meat destroy not the work of G'. "
22 faith? have it to thyself before G'. "
15: 5 the G' of patience and consolation "
6 mind and one mouth glorify G', "
7 also received us to the glory of G'. "
8 for the truth of G', to confirm the "
9 Gentiles might glorify G' for his "
13 Now the G' of hope fill you with "
15 the grace that is given to me of G', "
16 ministering the gospel of G', that "
17 in those things which pertain to G'. "
19 by the power of the Spirit of G'; "
30 in your prayers to G' for me; "
32 unto you with joy by the will of G', "
33 Now the G' of peace be with you "
16:20 And the G' of peace shall bruise "
26 of the everlasting G', made known "
27 To G' only wise, be glory through "
1Co 1: 1 apostle...through the will of G', "
2 Unto the church of G' which is at "
3 and peace, from G' our Father, and "
4 I thank my G' always on your "
4 behalf, for the grace of G' which "
9 G' is faithful, by whom ye were "
14 I thank G' that I baptized none of "
18 are saved it is the power of G'. "
20 not G' made foolish the wisdom "
21 For after that in the wisdom of G' "
21 the world by wisdom knew not G', "
21 it pleased G' by the foolishness * "
24 power of G', and the wisdom of G'. "
25 the foolishness of G' is wiser than "
25 men; and the weakness of G' is "
27 G' hath chosen the foolish things "
27 G' hath chosen the weak things "
28 are despised, hath G' chosen, "
30 who of G' is made unto us wisdom, "
2: 1 unto you the testimony of G'. "
5 of men, but in the power of G'. "
7 the wisdom of G' in a mystery, * "
7 G' ordained before the world unto "
9 which G' hath prepared for them "
10 But G' hath revealed them unto us "
10 things, yea, the deep things of G'. "
11 even so the things of G' knoweth "
11 no man, but the Spirit of G'. "
12 but the spirit which is of G'; that "
12 that are freely given to us of G'. "
14 not the things of the Spirit of G': "
3: 6 watered; but G' gave the increase. "
7 but G' that giveth the increase. "
9 are labourers together with G': * "
10 According to the grace of G' which "
16 that ye are the temple of G', and "
16 that the Spirit of G' dwelleth in "
17 If any man defile the temple of G', "
17 him shall G' destroy; "
17 for the temple of G' is holy, which "

1Co 3:19 this world is foolishness with G'. 2316
4: 1 stewards of the mysteries of G'. "
5 shall every man have praise of G'. "
8 and I would to G' ye did reign, *
9 G' hath set forth us the apostles 2316
20 the kingdom of G' is not in word, "
5:13 them that are without G' judgeth. "
6: 9 not inherit the kingdom of G'? "
10 shall inherit the kingdom of G'. "
11 Jesus, and by the Spirit of our G'. "
13 G' shall destroy both it and them. "
14 G' hath both raised up the Lord, "
15 of an harlot? G' forbid. 3361, 1096
19 which ye have of G', and ye are 2316
20 therefore glorify G' in your body, "
7: 7 man hath his proper gift of G', "
15 but G' hath called us to peace. "
17 G' hath distributed to every man, "
19 of the commandments of G'. "
24 he is called, therein abide with G'. "
40 also that I have the Spirit of G'. "
8: 3 But if any man love G', the same "
4 there is none other G' but one. "
6 there is but one G', the Father, "
8 meat commendeth us not to G': "
9: 9 Doth G' take care of oxen? "
21 (being not without law to G', but "
10: 5 of them G' was not well pleased: "
13 G' is faithful, who will not suffer "
20 sacrifice to devils, and not to G': "
31 ye do, do all to the glory of G'. "
32 Gentiles, nor to the church of G': "
11: 3 and the head of Christ is G'. "
7 as he is the image and glory of G': "
12 by the woman; but all things of G'. "
13 woman pray unto G' uncovered? "
16 custom, neither the churches of G'. "
22 or despise ye the church of G', and "
12: 3 speaking by the Spirit of G' calleth "
6 it is the same G' which worketh "
18 But now hath G' set the members "
24 but G' hath tempered the body "
28 G' hath set some in the church, "
14: 2 not unto men, but unto G': "
18 thank my G', I speak with tongues "
25 he will worship G', and report "
25 report that G' is in you of a truth. "
28 let him speak to himself, and to G'. "
33 G' is not the author of confusion, "
36 came the word of G' out from you? "
15: 9 I persecuted the church of G'. "
10 But by the grace of G' I am what "
10 but the grace of G' which was "
15 are found false witnesses of G'; "
15 have testified of G' that he raised "
24 delivered up the kingdom to G', "
28 that G' may be all in all. "
34 some have not the knowledge of G': "
38 But G' giveth it a body as it hath "
50 cannot inherit the kingdom of G'; "
57 But thanks be to G', which giveth "
16: 2 in store, as G' has prospered him,*
2Co 1: 1 an apostle...by the will of G', and 2316
1 unto the church of G' which is at "
2 and peace from G' our Father, and "
3 Blessed be G', even the Father "
3 and the G' of all comfort; "
4 we ourselves are comforted of G'. "
9 but in G' which raiseth the dead: "
12 but by the grace of G', we have "
18 But as G' is true, our word toward "
19 For the Son of G', Jesus Christ, "
20 For all the promises of G' in him "
20 unto the glory of G' by us. "
21 and hath anointed us, is G'; "
23 call G' for a record upon my soul, "
2:14 Now thanks be unto G', which "
15 we are unto G' a sweet savour of "
17 many, which corrupt the word of G': "
17 but as of G', in the sight of G' "
3: 3 with the Spirit of the living G'; "
5 but our sufficiency is of G'; "
4: 2 handling the word of G' deceitfully; "
2 man's conscience in the sight of G'. "
4 the g' of this world hath blinded "
4 who is the image of G', should "
6 For G', who commanded the light "
6 of the knowledge of the glory of G' "
7 of the power may be of G', and not "
15 many redound to the glory of G'. "
5: 1 we have a building of G', an house "
5 us for the selfsame thing is G', "
11 but we are made manifest unto G'; "
13 we be beside ourselves, it is to G': "
18 And all things are of G', who hath "
19 To wit, that G' was in Christ, "
20 though G' did beseech you by us: "
20 Christ's stead, be ye reconciled to G'. "
21 the righteousness of G' in him. "
6: 1 receive not the grace of G' in vain, "
4 ourselves as the ministers of G', "
7 by the power of G', by the armour "
16 hath the temple of G' with idols? "
16 ye are the temple of the living G'; "
16 as G' hath said, I will be their G', "
7: 1 perfecting holiness in the fear of G'. "
6 G', that comforteth those that are "
12 care for you in the sight of G' "
8: 1 of the grace of G' bestowed on the "
5 and unto us by the will of G'. "
16 But thanks be to G', which put the "
9: 7 for G' loveth a cheerful giver. "
8 And G' is able to make all grace "
11 through us thanksgiving to G'. "
12 by many thanksgivings unto G'; "
13 they glorify G' for your professed "

2Co 9:14 the exceeding grace of G· in you. 2316
15 Thanks be unto G· for his...gift. "
10: 4 mighty through G· to the pulling "
5 itself against the knowledge of G·. "
13 G· hath distributed to us, a "
11: 1 Would to G· ye could bear with *
7 preached to you the gospel of G· 2316
11 I love you not? G· knoweth. "
31 G· and Father of our Lord Jesus "
12: 2 I cannot tell: G· knoweth;) such "
3 I cannot tell: G· knoweth;) "
19 we speak before G· in Christ: but "
21 my G· will humble me among you, "
13: 4 yet he liveth by the power of G·. "
4 him by the power of G· toward you. "
7 Now I pray to G· that ye do no evil; "
11 and the G· of love and peace shall "
14 the love of G·, and the communion "
Ga 1: 1 and G· the Father, who raised him "
3 and peace from G· the Father, and "
4 according to the will of G· and our "
10 For do I now persuade men, or G·? "
13 I persecuted the church of G·, "
15 when it pleased G·, who separated "
20 behold, before G·, I lie not. "
24 And they glorified G· in me. "
2: 6 G· accepteth no man's person:) "
17 minister of sin? G· forbid. 3361, 1096
19 the law, that I might live unto G·. 2316
20 live by the faith of the Son of G·, "
21 I do not frustrate the grace of G·: "
3: 6 Even as Abraham believed G·, and "
8 that G· would justify the heathen "
11 by the law in the sight of G·, it is "
17 that was confirmed before of G· in "
18 G· gave it to Abraham by promise. "
20 not a mediator of one, but G· is one. "
21 law then against the promises of G·? "
21 G· forbid: for if there had 3361, 1096
26 For ye are all the children of G· 2316
4: 4 G· sent forth his Son, made of a "
6 G· hath sent forth the Spirit of his "
7 then an heir of G· through Christ. "
8 Howbeit then, when ye knew not G·, "
9 now, after that ye have known G·, "
9 or rather are known of G·, "
14 but received me as an angel of G·, "
5:21 shall not inherit the kingdom of G·. "
6: 7 G· is not mocked: for whatsoever "
14 But G· forbid that I should *3361, 1096
16 and upon the Israel of G·. 2316
Eph 1: 1 an apostle ... by the will of G·, to "
2 and peace from G· our Father, and "
3 Blessed be the G· and Father of "
17 the G· of our Lord Jesus Christ, "
2: 4 But G·, who is rich in mercy, for his "
8 of yourselves: it is the gift of G·: "
10 which G· hath before ordained that "
12 hope, and without G· in the world: 112
16 unto G· in one body by the cross, 2316
19 saints, and of the household of G·; "
22 for an habitation of G· through the "
3: 2 of the grace of G· which is given me "
7 gift of the grace of G· given unto me "
9 of the world hath been hid in G·, "
10 church the manifold wisdom of G·, "
19 be filled with all the fulness of G·. "
4: 6 One G· and Father of all, who is "
13 of the knowledge of the Son of G·, "
18 alienated from the life of G· through "
24 after G· is created in righteousness "
30 And grieve not the holy Spirit of G·, "
32 even as G· for Christ's sake hath "
5: 1 followers of G·, as dear children; "
2 sacrifice to G· for a sweetsmelling "
5 in the kingdom of Christ and of G·. "
6 cometh the wrath of G· upon the "
20 thanks...unto G· and the Father "
21 one to another in the fear of G·. *
6: 6 the will of G· from the heart; "
11 Put on the whole armour of G·, "
13 unto you the whole armour of G·, "
17 the Spirit which is the word of G·: "
23 from G· the Father and the Lord "
Ph'p 1: 2 and peace, from G· our Father, and "
3 I thank my G· upon every "
8 For G· is my record, how greatly I "
11 unto the glory and praise of G·. "
28 you of salvation, and that of G·. "
2: 6 Who, being in the form of G·, "
6 it not robbery to be equal with G·: "
9 G· also hath highly exalted him, "
11 to the glory of G· the Father. "
13 For it is G· which worketh in you "
15 the sons of G·, without rebuke, "
27 but G· had mercy on him; and not "
3: 3 which worship G· in the spirit, and "
9 the righteousness which is of G· by "
14 the prize of the high calling of G· "
15 G· shall reveal even this unto you. "
19 whose G· is their belly, and whose "
4: 6 requests be made known unto G·. "
7 And the peace of G·, which passeth "
9 and the G· of peace shall be with "
18 acceptable, wellpleasing to G·. "
19 my G· shall supply all your need "
20 unto G· and our Father be glory "
Col 1: 1 an apostle...by the will of G·, and "
2 and peace, from G· our Father and "
3 give thanks to G· and the Father "
6 and knew the grace of G· in truth: "
10 increasing in the knowledge of G·; "
15 is the image of the invisible G·, "
25 dispensation of G· which is given "
25 for you, to fulfil the word of G·; "
27 G· would make known what is the "

Col 2: 2 mystery of G·, and of the Father, 2316
12 of G·, who hath raised him from the "
19 increaseth with the increase of G·. "
3: 1 sitteth on the right hand of G·. "
3 your life is hid with Christ in G·. "
6 wrath of G· cometh on the children "
12 as the elect of G·, holy and beloved, "
15 And let the peace of G· rule in *
17 giving thanks to G· and the Father "
22 in singleness of heart, fearing G·:* "
4: 3 that G· would open unto us a door "
11 unto the kingdom of G·, which "
12 and complete in all the will of G·. "
1Th 1: 1 which is in G· the Father and in the "
1 and peace, from G· our Father, * "
2 We give thanks to G· always for "
3 in the sight of G· and our Father; "
4 knowing...your election of G·. "
9 and how ye turned to G· from idols "
9 to serve the living and true G·; "
2: 2 were bold in our G· to speak unto "
2 to speak unto you the gospel of G· "
4 we were allowed of G· to be put "
4 not as pleasing men, but G·, which "
5 of covetousness; G· is witness: "
8 gospel of G· only, but also our own "
9 preached unto you the gospel of G·. "
10 Ye are witnesses, and G· also, "
12 That ye would walk worthy of G·, "
13 also thank we G· without ceasing, "
13 the word of G· which ye heard of "
13 but as it is in truth, the word of G·, "
14 the churches of G· which in Judæa "
15 please not G·, and are contrary "
3: 2 and minister of G·, and our * "
9 can we render to G· again for you, "
9 joy for your sakes before our G·; "
11 Now G· himself and our Father, "
13 in holiness before G·, even our "
4: 1 ought to walk and to please G·, "
3 For this is the will of G·, even "
5 as the Gentiles which know not G·: "
7 For G· hath not called us unto "
8 despiseth not man, but G·, who "
9 are taught of G· to love one 2312
14 which sleep in Jesus will G· bring 2316
16 and with the trump of G·: and the "
5: 9 G· hath not appointed us to wrath, "
18 for this is the will of G· in Christ "
23 the very G· of peace sanctify you "
23 and I pray G· your whole spirit *
2Th 1: 1 church...in G· our Father and the 2316
2 peace, from G· our Father and the "
3 We are bound to thank G· always "
4 churches of G· for your patience "
5 of the righteous judgment of G·, "
5 worthy of the kingdom of G·, for "
6 it is a righteous thing with G· to "
8 on them that know not G·, "
11 our G· would count you worthy of "
12 according to the grace of our G· "
2: 4 is called G·, or that is worshipped; "
4 he as G· sitteth in the temple of G·, "
4 shewing himself that he is G·. "
11 G· shall send them strong delusion, "
13 to give thanks alway to G· for you, "
13 G· hath from the beginning chosen "
16 G·, even our Father, which hath "
3: 5 into the love of G·, and into the "
1Ti 1: 1 commandment of G· our Saviour, "
2 peace, from G· our Father and Jesus "
11 glorious gospel of the blessed G·, "
17 the only wise G·, be honour and "
2: 3 in the sight of G· our Saviour; "
5 For there is one G·, and one "
5 one mediator between G· and men, "
3: 5 he take care of the church of G·?) "
15 behave thyself in the house of G·, "
15 which is the church of the living G·, "
16 G· was manifest in the flesh, * "
4: 3 G· hath created to be received with "
4 For every creature of G· is good, "
5 sanctified by the word of G· and "
10 because we trust in the living G·, "
5: 4 is good and acceptable before G·. "
5 trusteth in G·, and continueth in "
21 I charge thee before G·, and the "
6: 1 the name of G· and his doctrine "
11 But thou, O man of G·, flee these "
13 give thee charge in the sight of G·, "
17 but in the living G·, who giveth us "
2Ti 1: 1 an apostle ... by the will of G·, "
2 peace, from G· the Father and Christ "
3 I thank G·, whom I serve from my "
6 that thou stir up the gift of G·, "
7 For G· hath not given us the spirit "
8 according to the power of G·; "
2: 9 but the word of G· is not bound. "
15 to shew thyself approved unto G·, "
19 the foundation of G· standeth sure, "
25 if G· peradventure will give them "
3: 4 of pleasure more than lovers of G·; 5377
16 is given by inspiration of G·, 2315
17 That the man of G· may be perfect, 2316
4: 1 G·, and the Lord Jesus Christ, "
16 I pray G· that it may not be laid *
Tit 1: 1 Paul, a servant of G·, and an 2316
2 which G·, that cannot lie, promised "
3 commandment of G· our Saviour; "
4 peace, from G· the Father and the "
7 blameless, as the steward of G·; "
16 They profess that they know G·; "
2: 5 the word of G· be not blasphemed. "
10 the doctrine of G· our Saviour "
11 For the grace of G· that bringeth "
13 appearing of the great G· and our "

Tit 3: 4 kindness and love of G· our Saviour 2316
8 they which have believed in G· "
Ph'm 3 peace, from G· our Father and the "
4 I thank my G·, making mention of "
Heb 1: 1 G·, who at sundry times and in "
6 all the angels of G· worship him. "
8 Thy throne, O G·, is for ever and "
9 G·, even thy G·, hath anointed thee "
2: 4 G· also bearing them witness, both "
9 that he by the grace of G· should "
13 children which G· hath given me. "
17 in things pertaining to G·, to make "
3: 4 but he that built all things is G·. "
12 in departing from the living G·. "
4: 4 G· did rest the seventh day from "
9 therefore a rest to the people of G·. "
10 his own works, as G· did from his. "
12 For the word of G· is quick, and "
14 high priest...Jesus the Son of G·, "
5: 1 in things pertaining to G·, that he "
4 that is called of G·, as was Aaron. "
10 called of G· an high priest after "
12 be principles of the oracles of G·; "
6: 1 dead works, and of faith toward G·, "
3 And this will we do, if G· permit. "
5 have tasted the good word of G·, "
6 to themselves the Son of G· afresh, "
7 receiveth blessing from G·: "
10 For G· is not unrighteous to forget "
13 when G· made promise to Abraham, "
17 Wherein G·, willing more "
18 it was impossible for G· to lie, "
7: 1 priest of the most high G·, who "
3 but made like unto the Son of G·; "
19 the which we draw nigh unto G·. "
25 that come unto G· by him, seeing "
8: 5 as Moses was admonished of G· 5537
10 I will be to them a G·, and they 2316
9: 6 accomplishing the service of G·. *
14 without spot to G·, purge your 2316
14 dead works to serve the living G·? "
20 G· hath injoined unto you. "
24 appear in the presence of G· for us: "
10: 7 written of one,) to do thy will, O G·. "
9 Lo, I come to do thy will, O G·. * "
12 sat down on the right hand of G·; "
21 highpriest over the house of G·; "
29 trodden under foot the Son of G·, "
31 fall into the hands of the living G·. "
36 after ye have done the will of G·, "
11: 3 were framed by the word of G·, "
4 faith Abel offered unto G· a more "
4 righteous, G· testifying of his gifts: "
5 G· had translated him: for before "
5 this testimony, that he pleased G·. "
6 he that cometh to G· must believe "
7 Noah, being warned of G· of things
10 whose builder and maker is G·. 2316
16 wherefore G· is not ashamed to be "
16 ashamed to be called their G·: "
19 G· was able to raise him up, even "
25 affliction with the people of G·, "
40 G· having provided some better "
12: 2 the right hand of the throne of G·. "
7 G· dealeth with you as with sons; "
15 any man fail of the grace of G·; "
22 and unto the city of the living G·, "
23 and to G· the Judge of all, and to "
28 serve G· acceptably with reverence "
29 for our G· is a consuming fire. "
13: 4 and adulterers G· will judge. "
7 spoken unto you the word of G·: "
15 sacrifice of praise to G· continually, "
16 such sacrifices G· is well pleased. "
20 Now the G· of peace, that brought "
Jas 1: 1 James, a servant of G· and of the "
5 let him ask of G·, that giveth to all "
13 he is tempted, I am tempted of G·: "
13 for G· cannot be tempted with evil, "
20 worketh not the righteousness of G·. "
27 religion and undefiled before G· "
2: 5 Hath not G· chosen the poor of this "
19 Thou believest that there is one G·; "
23 Abraham believed G·, and it was "
23 and he was called the Friend of G·. "
3: 9 Therewith bless we G·, even the * "
9 are made after the similitude of G·. "
4: 4 of the world is enmity with G·? "
4 of the world is the enemy of G·. "
6 G· resisteth the proud, but giveth "
7 Submit yourselves therefore to G·. "
8 Draw nigh to G·, and he will draw "
1Pe 1: 2 foreknowledge of G· the Father, "
3 Blessed be the G· and Father of "
5 Who are kept by the power of G· "
21 do believe in G·, that raised him "
21 your faith and hope might be in G·. "
23 by the word of G·, which liveth and "
2: 4 but chosen of G·, and precious, "
5 acceptable to G· by Jesus Christ. "
10 but are now the people of G·: "
12 glorify G· in the day of visitation. "
15 For so is the will of G·, that with "
16 but as the servants of G·. "
17 Fear G·. Honour the king. "
19 if a man for conscience toward G· "
20 patiently, this is acceptable with G·. "
3: 4 is in the sight of G· of great price. "
5 holy women also, who trusted in G·, "
15 the Lord G· in your hearts: and * "
17 it is better, if the will of G· be so, "
18 that he might bring us to G·, being "
20 the longsuffering of G· waited in "
21 of a good conscience toward G·,) "
22 and is on the right hand of G·; "
4: 2 lusts of men, but to the will of G·. "

1Pe 4: 6 live according to G· in the spirit. 2316
10 of the manifold grace of G·. "
11 let him speak as the oracles of G·; "
11 as of the ability which G· giveth: "
11 G· in all things may be glorified "
14 the spirit of glory and of G· resteth "
16 let him glorify G· on this behalf. "
17 must begin at the house of G·: "
17 that obey not the gospel of G·? "
19 according to the will of G· commit "
5: 2 Feed the flock of G· which is among "
5 G· resisteth the proud, and giveth "
6 under the mighty hand of G·, "
10 But the G· of all grace, who hath "
12 the true grace of G· wherein ye "
2Pe 1: 1 through the righteousness of G· "
2 through the knowledge of G·, and of "
17 For he received from G· the Father "
21 holy men of G· spake as they were "
2: 4 For if G· spared not the angels that "
3: 5 that by the word of G· the heavens "
12 unto the coming of the day of G·, "
1Jo 1: 5 that G· is light, and in him is no "
2: 5 verily is the love of G· perfected: "
14 and the word of G· abideth in you, "
17 doeth the will of G· abideth for ever. "
3: 1 should be called the sons of G·: "
2 now are we the sons of G·, and "
8 Son of G· was manifested, that he "
9 is born of G· doth not commit sin; "
9 sin, because he is born of G·. "
10 the children of G· are manifest, "
10 doeth not righteousness is not of G·, "
16 Hereby perceive we the love of G·,* "
17 how dwelleth the love of G· in him? 2316
20 G· is greater than our heart, and "
21 then have we confidence toward G·. "
4: 1 the Spirits whether they are of G·: "
2 Hereby know ye the Spirit of G·: "
2 Christ is come in the flesh is of G·: "
3 is come in the flesh is not of G·: "
4 Ye are of G·, little children, and "
6 We are of G·: he that knoweth G· "
6 he that is not of G· heareth not us. "
7 for love is of G·; and every one that "
7 loveth is born of G·, and knoweth G·. "
8 knoweth not G·; for G· is love. "
9 manifested the love of G· toward us, "
9 G· sent his only begotten Son into "
10 not that we loved G·, but that he "
11 if G· so loved us, we ought also to "
12 No man hath seen G· at any time. "
12 G· dwelleth in us, and his love is "
15 that Jesus Christ is the Son of G·, "
15 G· dwelleth in him, and he in G·. "
16 love that G· hath to us. G· is love; "
16 dwelleth in G·, and G· in him. "
20 If a man say, I love G·, and hateth "
20 G· whom he hath not seen? "
21 he who loveth G· love his brother "
5: 1 Jesus is the Christ is born of G·: "
2 the children of G·, when we love G·, "
3 For this is the love of G·, that "
4 is born of G· overcometh the world: "
5 that Jesus is the Son of G·? "
9 men, the witness of G· is greater: "
9 for this is the witness of G· which "
10 He that believeth on the Son of G· "
10 he that believeth not G· hath made "
10 the record that G· gave of his Son. "
11 G· hath given to us eternal life, "
12 hath not the Son of G· hath not life. "
13 on the name of the Son of G·; * "
13 believe on the name of the Son of G·. "
18 whosoever is born of G· sinneth "
18 but he that is begotten of G· "
19 And we know that we are of G·, and "
20 we know that the Son of G· is come, "
20 This is the true G·, and eternal life. "
2Jo 3 peace, from G· the Father, and from "
9 the doctrine of Christ, hath not G·. "
10 house, neither bid him G· speed: *
11 he that biddeth him G· speed is *
3Jo 11 He that doeth good is of G·: but 2316
11 he that doeth evil hath not seen G·. "
Jude 1 that are sanctified by G· the Father, "
4 grace of our G· into lasciviousness, "
4 and denying the only Lord G·, "
21 Keep yourselves in the love of G·, "
25 To the only wise G· our Saviour, "
Re 1: 1 which G· gave unto him, to shew "
2 Who bare record the word of G·, and "
6 made us kings and priests unto G· "
9 for the word of G·, and for the "
2: 7 in the midst of the paradise of G·. "
18 These things saith the Son of G·, "
3: 1 that hath the seven Spirits of G·, "
2 found thy works perfect before G·. "
12 a pillar in the temple of my G·, and "
12 write upon him the name of my G·, "
12 and the name of the city of my G·, "
12 down out of heaven from my G·: "
14 the beginning of the creation of G·; "
4: 5 which are the seven Spirits of G·. "
8 Lord G· Almighty, which was, and "
5: 6 the seven Spirits of G· sent forth "
9 and hast redeemed us to G· by thy "
10 hast made us unto our G· kings "
6: 9 that were slain for the word of G·, "
7: 2 having the seal of the living G·: "
3 sealed the servants of our G· in "
10 Salvation to our G· which sitteth "
11 on their faces, and worshipped G·, "
12 and might, be unto our G· for ever "
15 are they before the throne of G·, "
Re 7:17 G· shall wipe away all tears from 2316
8: 2 seven angels which stood before G·; "
4 before G· out of the angel's hand. "
9: 4 not the seal of G· in their foreheads. "
13 the golden altar which is before G·, "
10: 7 mystery of G· should be finished. "
11: 1 and measure the temple of G·, and "
4 standing before the G· of the * "
11 the Spirit of life from G· entered "
13 and gave glory to the G· of heaven. "
16 which sat before G· on their seats "
16 their faces, and worshipped G·, "
17 O Lord G· Almighty, which art, and "
19 temple of G· was opened in heaven, "
12: 5 was caught up unto G·, and to his "
6 she hath a place prepared of G·, "
10 kingdom of our G·, and the power "
10 accused them before our G· day "
17 keep the commandments of G·, "
13: 6 mouth in blasphemy against G·, "
14: 4 firstfruits unto G· and to the Lamb. "
5 fault before the throne of G·. * "
7 Fear G·, and give glory to him; "
10 drink of the wine of the wrath of G·, "
12 that keep the commandments of G·, "
19 great winepress of the wrath of G·. "
15: 1 in them is filled up the wrath of G·. "
2 sea of glass, having the harps of G·. "
3 the song of Moses the servant of G·, "
3 are thy works, Lord G· Almighty; "
7 vials full of the wrath of G·, who "
8 smoke from the glory of G·, and "
16: 1 out the vials of the wrath of G· "
7 say, Even so, Lord G· Almighty, "
9 and blasphemed the name of G·, "
11 And blasphemed the G· of heaven "
14 of that great day of G· Almighty. "
19 came in remembrance before G·, "
21 men blasphemed G· because of the "
17:17 For G· hath put in their hearts "
17 the words of G· shall be fulfilled. "
18: 5 G· hath remembered her iniquities. "
8 is the Lord G· who judgeth her. "
20 for G· hath avenged you on her. "
19: 1 and power, unto the Lord our G·: "
4 and worshipped G· that sat on the "
5 Praise our G·, all ye his servants, "
6 the Lord G· omnipotent reigneth. "
9 These are the true sayings of G·. "
10 worship G·: for the testimony of "
13 his name is called The Word of G·. "
15 fierceness and wrath of Almighty G·. "
17 unto the supper of the great G·; "
20: 4 and for the word of G·, and which "
6 shall be priests of G· and of Christ, "
9 came down from G· out of heaven,* "
12 small and great, stand before G·;* "
21: 2 coming down from G· out of heaven, "
3 the tabernacle of G· is with men, "
3 and G· himself shall be with them, "
3 be with them, and be their G·. "
4 And G· shall wipe away all tears * "
7 and I will be his G·, and he shall be "
10 descending out of heaven from G·, "
11 Having the glory of G·: and her "
22 Lord G· Almighty and the Lamb "
23 for the glory of G· did lighten it, "
22: 1 the throne of G· and of the Lamb. "
3 the throne of G· and of the Lamb "
5 for the Lord G· giveth them light: "
6 the Lord G· of the holy prophets "
9 sayings of this book: worship G·. "
18 G· shall add unto him the plagues "
19 G· shall take away his part out of "

goddess
1Ki 11: 5 went after Ashtoreth the g· 430
33 Ashtoreth the g· of the Zidonians, "
Ac 19:27 the temple of the great g· Diana 2299
35 worshipper of the great g· Diana, * "
37 nor yet blasphemers of your g·. "

Godhead
Ac 17:29 think that the G· is like unto gold, 2304
Ro 1:20 even his eternal power and G·; *2305
Col 2: 9 all the fulness of the G· bodily. 2320

godliness See also UNGODLINESS.
1Ti 2: 2 life in all g· and honesty. 2150
10 becometh women professing g·) 2317
3:16 great is the mystery of g·: God 2150
4: 7 and exercise thyself rather unto g·. "
8 but g· is profitable unto all things, "
6: 3 doctrine which is according to g·; "
5 supposing that gain is g·: from such "
6 g· with contentment is great gain. "
11 follow after righteousness, g·, faith, "
2Ti 3: 5 Having a form of g·, but denying "
Tit 1: 1 of the truth which is after g·; "
2Pe 1: 3 pertain unto life and g·, through "
6 patience; and to patience g·; "
7 And to g· brotherly kindness; "
3:11 in all holy conversation and g·, "

godly See also UNGODLY.
Ps 4: 3 apart him that is g· for himself: 2623
12: 1 Help, Lord; for the g· man ceaseth; "
32: 6 this shall every one that is g· pray "
Mal 2:15 That he might seek a g· seed. 430
2Co 1:12 simplicity and g· sincerity, not *2316
7: 9 made sorry after a g· manner, 2596, "
10 g· sorrow worketh repentance "
11 that ye sorrowed after a g· sort, "
11: 2 jealous over you with g· jealousy: "
1Ti 1: 4 questions, rather than g· edifying* "
2Ti 3:12 all that will live g· in Christ Jesus 2153
Tit 2:12 live soberly, righteously, and g·, 2153
Heb 12:28 with reverence and g· fear: *
2Pe 2: 9 knoweth how to deliver the g· out 2152
3Jo 6 their journey after a g· sort,* 516, 2316

God's
Ge 28:22 set for a pillar, shall be G· house: 430
30: 2 I in G· stead, who hath withheld "
32: 2 he said, This is G· host: and he "
Nu 22:22 And G· anger was kindled because "
De 1:17 the judgment is G·: and the cause "
2Ch 20:15 for the battle is not your's, but G·. "
Ne 10:29 to walk in G· law, which was given "
Job 33: 6 according to thy wish in G· stead:* 410
35: 2 My righteousness is more than G·? "
36: 2 I have yet to speak on G· behalf. 433
M't 5:34 by heaven; for it is G· throne: *2316
22:21 unto God the things that are G·. "
M'r 12:17 and to God the things that are G·. "
Lu 18:29 for the kingdom of G· sake, "
20:25 unto God the things which be G·. "
Joh 8:47 that is of God heareth G· words: * "
Ac 23: 4 said, Revilest thou G· high priest? "
Ro 8:33 thing to the charge of G· elect? "
10: 3 being ignorant of G· righteousness, "
13: 6 they are G· ministers, attending "
1Co 3: 9 Ye are G· husbandry, "
9 ye are G· building. "
23 ye are Christ's; and Christ is G·. "
6:20 and in your spirit, which are G·. * "
Tit 1: 1 according to the faith of G· elect, "
1Pe 5: 3 as being lords over G· heritage, * "

Gods [or GODS]
Ge 3: 5 ye shall be as g·, knowing good * 430
31:30 wherefore hast thou stolen my g·? "
32 whomsoever thou findest thy g·, "
35: 2 the strange g· that are among you, "
4 gave unto Jacob all the strange g· "
Ex 12:12 all the g· of Egypt I will execute "
15:11 unto thee, O Lord, among the g·? 410
18:11 the Lord is greater than all g·: 430
20: 3 shalt have no other g· before me. "
23 not make with me g· of silver, "
23 shall ye make unto you g· of gold. "
22:28 Thou shalt not revile the g·, nor * "
23:13 mention of the name of other g·, "
24 Thou shalt not bow down to their g·, "
32 with them, nor with their g·. "
33 if thou serve their g·, it will surely "
32: 1 make us g·, which shall go before us; "
4 be thy g·, O Israel, which brought "
8 be thy g·, O Israel, which have "
23 Make us g·, which shall go before "
31 and have made them g· of gold. "
34:15 and they go a whoring after their g·, "
15 and do sacrifice unto their g·, "
16 and they go a whoring after their g·, "
16 thy sons go a whoring after their g·. "
17 Thou shalt make thee no molten g·. "
Le 19: 4 nor make to yourselves molten g·: "
Nu 25: 2 unto the sacrifices of their g·: "
2 did eat, and bowed down to their g·. "
33: 4 upon their g· also the Lord executed "
De 4:28 there ye shall serve g·, the work of "
5: 7 Thou shalt have none other g· before "
6:14 Ye shall not go after other g·, of the "
14 the g· of the people which are round "
7: 4 that they may serve other g·: "
16 neither shalt thou serve their g·; "
25 The graven images of their g· shall "
8:19 walk after other g·, and serve them, "
10:17 is God of g·, and Lord of lords, "
11:16 and serve other g·, and worship "
28 to go after other g·, which ye have "
12: 2 ye shall possess served their g·, "
3 down the graven images of their g·, "
30 enquire not after their g·, saying, "
30 did these nations serve their g·? "
31 hateth, have they done unto their g·; "
31 have burnt in the fire to their g·. "
13: 2 Let us go after other g·, which thou "
6 Let us go and serve other g·, which "
7 the g· of the people which are round "
13 Let us go and serve other g·, which "
17: 3 And hath gone and served other g·, "
18:20 shall speak in the name of other g·, "
20:18 which they have done unto their g·; "
28:14 to go after other g· to serve them. "
36 there shalt thou serve other g·, wood "
64 there thou shalt serve other g·, which "
29:18 go and serve the g· of these nations; "
26 For they went and served other g·, "
26 them, g· whom they knew not, and "
30:17 drawn away, and worship other g·, "
31:16 whoring after the g· of the strangers "
18 they are turned unto other g·. "
20 then will they turn unto other g·, "
32:16 him to jealousy with strange g·, "
17 to g· whom they knew not, 430
17 to new g· that came newly up, "
37 he shall say, Where are their g·, 430
Jos 22:22 Lord God of g·, the Lord God of g·,‡ "
23: 7 make mention of the name of their g·, "
16 and have gone and served other g·, "
24: 2 and they served other g·. "
14 put away the g· which your fathers "
15 whether the g· which your fathers "
15 or the g· of the Amorites, in whose "
16 forsake the Lord, to serve other g·; "
20 and serve strange g·, then he will "
23 strange g· which are among you. "
J'g 2: 3 their g· shall be a snare unto you. "
12 and followed other g·, of the g· of the "
17 they went a whoring after other g·, "
19 in following other g· to serve them, "

J'g 3: 6 their sons, and served their g'. 430
5: 8 They chose new g'; then was war "
6:10 fear not the g' of the Amorites, "
10: 6 the g' of Syria, and the g' of Zidon, "
6 and the g' of Moab, and the g' of the "
6 Ammon, and the g' of the Philistines, "
13 forsaken me, and served other g': "
14 unto the g' which ye have chosen; "
16 And they put away the strange g' "
17: 5 the man Micah had an house of g', "
18:24 taken away my g' which I made, "
Ru 1:15 unto her people, and unto her g': * "
1Sa 4: 8 out of the hand of these mighty G'? "
8 these are the G' that smote the "
6: 5 from off you, and from off your g', "
7: 3 away the strange g' and Ashtaroth "
8: 8 forsaken me, and served other g', "
17:43 Philistine cursed David by his g'. "
26:19 saying, Go, serve other g'. "
28:13 saw g' ascending out of the earth.* "
2Sa 7:23 from the nations and their g'? "
1Ki 9: 6 go and serve other g', and worship "
9 and have taken hold upon other g', "
11: 2 turn away your heart after their g': "
4 turned away his heart after other g': "
8 incense and sacrificed unto their g'. "
10 that he should not go after other g': "
12:28 behold thy g', O Israel, which "
14: 9 hast gone and made thee other g', "
18:24 call ye on the name of your g', * "
25 and call on the name of your g', * "
19: 2 So let the g' do to me, and more "
20:10 The g' do so unto me, and more "
23 Their g' are g' of the hills; * "
2Ki 5:17 nor sacrifice unto other g', but unto "
17: 7 and had feared other g', "
29 every nation made g' of their own, "
31 Anammelech, the g' of Sepharvaim. "
33 served their own g', after the manner "
35 Ye shall not fear other g', nor bow "
37 and ye shall not fear other g'. "
38 neither shall ye fear other g'. "
18:33 Hath any of the g' of the nations "
34 Where are the g' of Hamath, and of "
34 where are the g' of Sepharvaim, "
35 among all the g' of the countries, "
19:12 Have the g' of the nations delivered "
18 And have cast their g' into the fire: "
18 for they were no g', but the work "
22:17 have burned incense unto other g', "
1Ch 5:25 a whoring after the g' of the people "
10:10 his armour in the house of their g', "
14:12 And when they had left their g' there, "
16:25 he also is to be feared above all g'. "
26 For all the g' of the people are idols: "
2Ch 2: 5 for great is our God above all g'. "
7:19 go and serve other g', and worship "
22 and laid hold on other g', and "
13: 8 which Jeroboam made you for g'. "
9 be a priest of them that are no g'. "
14: 3 away the altars of the strange g'.* "
25:14 he brought the g' of the children of 430
14 Seir, and set them up to be his g', "
15 thou sought after the g' of the people, "
20 they sought after the g' of Edom. "
28:23 sacrificed unto the g' of Damascus, "
23 g' of the kings of Syria help them, "
25 to burn incense unto other g', and "
32:13 were the g' of the nations of those "
14 Who was there among all the g' of "
17 the g' of the nations of other lands "
19 as against the g' of the people of the "
33:15 And he took away the strange g', "
34:25 have burned incense unto other g', "
Ez 1: 7 had put them in the house of his g': "
Ps 82: 1 mighty; he judgeth among the g'. "
6 I have said, Ye are g'; and all of you "
86: 8 Among the g' there is none like unto "
95: 3 and a great King above all g'. "
96: 4 he is to be feared above all g'. "
5 all the g' of the nations are idols: "
97: 7 worship him, all ye g'. "
9 thou art exalted far above all g'. "
135: 5 and that our Lord is above all g'. "
136: 2 O give thanks unto the God of g': "
138: 1 before the g' will I sing praise unto "
Isa 21: 9 images of her g' he hath broken unto "
36:18 Hath any of the g' of the nations "
19 Where are the g' of Hamath and "
19 where are the g' of Sepharvaim? "
20 they among all the g' of these lands, "
37:12 Have the g' of the nations delivered "
19 And have cast their g' into the fire: "
19 for they were no g': "
41:23 that we may know that ye are g': "
42:17 the molten images, Ye are our g'. "
Jer 1:16 have burned incense unto other g', "
2:11 changed their g', which are yet no g'? "
28 But where are thy g' that thou hast "
28 the number of thy cities are thy g', "
5: 7 and sworn by them that are no g': "
19 and served strange g' in your land, "
7: 6 walk after other g' to your hurt: "
9 after other g' whom ye know not; "
18 pour out... offerings unto other g', "
10:11 g' that have not made the heavens 426
11:10 went after other g' to serve them: 430
12 go, and cry unto the g' unto whom "
13 the number of thy cities were thy g'; "
13:10 and walk after other g', to serve "
16:11 and have walked after other g', and "
13 there shall ye serve other g' day and "
20 Shall a man make g' unto himself, "
20 unto himself, and they are no g'? "
19: 4 burned incense in it unto other g' "

Jer 19:13 out drink offerings unto other g'. 430
22: 9 and worshipped other g', and served "
25: 6 And go not after other g' to serve "
32:29 out drink offerings unto other g', "
35:15 and go not after other g' to serve "
43:12 in the houses of the g' of Egypt; "
13 the houses of the g' of the Egyptians "
44: 3 and to serve other g', whom they "
5 to burn no incense unto other g'. "
8 burning incense unto other g' in the "
15 had burned incense unto other g', "
46:25 Pharaoh, and Egypt, with their g', "
48:35 him that burneth incense to his g'. "
Da 2:11 except the g', whose dwelling is not 426
47 your God is a God of g', and a Lord "
3:12 they serve not thy g', nor worship "
14 do not ye serve my g', nor worship "
18 we will not serve thy g', nor worship "
4: 8 in whom is the spirit of the holy g': "
9 the spirit of the holy g' is in thee, "
18 the spirit of the holy g' is in thee. "
5: 4 praised the g' of gold, and of silver, "
11 in whom is the spirit of the holy g'; "
11 like the wisdom of the g', was found "
14 that the spirit of the g' is in thee, "
23 thou hast praised the g' of silver, "
11: 8 carry captives into Egypt their g', 430
36 things against the God of g', and 410
Hos 3: 1 look to other g', and love flagons 430
14: 3 work of our hands, Ye are our g': "
Na 1:14 out of the house of thy g' will I "
Zep 2:11 will famish all the g' of the earth; "
Joh 10:34 in your law, I said, Ye are g'? 2316
35 If he called them g', unto whom "
Ac 7:40 Make us g' to go before us: for as "
14:11 The g' are come down to us in the "
17:18 to be a setter forth of strange g': 1140
19:26 that they be no g', which are made 2316
1Co 8: 5 though there be that are called g', "
5 (as there be g' many, and lords "
Ga 4: 8 them which by nature are no g'. "

God-ward

Ex 18:19 Be thou for the people to G'. 4136, 430
2Co 3: 4 have we through Christ to G': 4314, 2316
1Th 1: 8 your faith to G' is spread "

goest

Ge 10:19 Gaza; as thou g', unto Sodom, 935
30 as thou g', unto Sephar a mount "
25:18 as thou g' toward Assyria: and he "
28:15 thee in all places whither thou g', 3212
32:17 Whose art thou? and whither g' "
Ex 4:21 When thou g' to return into Egypt, "
33:16 is it not in that thou g' with us? "
34:12 the land whither thou g', lest it be 935
Nu 14:14 and that thou g' before them, 1980
De 7: 1 land whither thou g' to possess it, 935
11:10 land, whither thou g' in to possess "
29 land whither thou g' to possess it, "
12:29 before thee, whither thou g' to "
20: 1 When thou g' out to battle against 3318
21:10 When thou g' forth to war against "
23:20 land whither thou g' to possess it. 935
28: 6 shalt thou be when thou g' out. 3318
19 shalt thou be when thou g' out. "
21 land, whither thou g' to possess it. 935
63 land whither thou g' to possess it. "
30:16 land whither thou g' to possess it. "
32:50 in the mount whither thou g' up, 5927
Jos 1: 7 prosper whithersoever thou g'. 3212
9 with thee whithersoever thou g'. "
J'g 14: 3 that thou g' to take a wife of the 1980
19:17 old man said, Whither g' thou? 3212
Ru 1:16 for whither thou g', I will go; "
1Sa 27: 8 as thou g' to Shur, even unto the 935
28:22 strength, when thou g' on thy way. 3212
2Sa 15:19 Wherefore g' thou also with us? "
1Ki 2:37 the day thou g' out, and passest 3318
42 the day thou g' out, and walkest "
Ps 44: 9 and g' not forth with our armies. "
Pr 4:12 When thou g', thy steps shall not 3212
6:22 When thou g', it shall lead thee; *1980
Ec 5: 1 when thou g' to the house of God, 3212
9:10 in the grave, whither thou g'. 1980
Jer 45: 5 prey in all places whither thou g'. 3212
Zec 2: 2 Whither g' thou? And he said 1980
Lu 9:57 follow thee whithersoever thou g'. 565
12:58 When thou g' with thine adversary *5217
Joh 11: 8 and g' thou thither again? "
13:36 Lord, whither g' thou? Jesus "
14: 5 Lord, we know not whither thou g': "
16: 5 you asketh me, Whither g' thou? "

goeth

Ge 2:14 is it which g' toward the east of 1980
32:20 with the present that g' before me, "
33:14 as the cattle that g' before me * "
38:13 father in law g' up to Timnath 5927
Ex 7:15 he g' out unto the water; and thou 3318
22:26 him by that the sun g' down: 935
28:29 when he g' in unto the holy place, "
30 when he g' in before the Lord: "
35 when he g' in unto the holy place "
Le 11:21 that g' upon all four, which *1980
27 And whatsoever g' upon his paws, "
42 Whatsoever g' upon the belly, and "
42 and whatsoever g' upon all four, "
14:46 that g' into the house all the while 935
15:32 of him whose seed g' from him, 3318
16:17 he g' in to make an atonement 935
22: 3 that g' unto the holy things, *7126
4 a man whose seed g' from him; 3318
27:21 when it g' out in the jubile, "
Nu 5:29 when a wife g' aside to another 7847

Nu 21:15 stream of the brooks that g' down *5186
De 1:30 your God which g' before you, 1980
9: 3 is he which g' over before thee; 5674
11:30 where the sun g' down, in the *3996
19: 5 As when a man g' into the wood 935
20: 4 God is he that g' with you, to 1980
23: 9 When the host g' forth against *3318
24:13 when the sun g' down, that he may 935
Jos 10:10 way that g' up to Beth-horon, *4609
11:17 mount Halak, that g' up to Seir, 5927
12: 7 mount Halak, that g' up to Seir; "
16: 1 wilderness... g' up from Jericho * "
2 And g' out from Beth-el to Luz, *3318
3 g' down westward to the coast *3381
19:12 and then g' out to Daberath, *3318
12 and g' up to Japhia, *5927
13 and g' out to Remmon-methoar *3318
27 and g' out to Cabul on the left * "
34 g' out from thence to Hukkok, * "
J'g 5:31 sun when he g' forth in his might. "
20:31 one g' up to the house of God, 5927
21:19 highway that g' up from Beth-el "
1Sa 6: 9 it g' up by the way of his own coast "
22:14 in law, and g' at thy bidding, *5493
30:24 part is that g' down to the battle, 3381
2Ki 5:18 when my master g' into the house 935
11: 8 be ye with the king as he g' out 3318
12:20 of Millo, which g' down to Silla. 3381
2Ch 23: 7 he cometh in, and when he g' out. 3318
Ezr 5: 8 and this work g' fast on, and 5648
Job 7: 9 so he that g' down to the grave 3381
9:11 Lo, he g' by me, and I see him 5674
34: 8 g' in company with the workers of 732
37: 2 the sound that g' out of his mouth. 3318
39:21 he g' on to meet the armed men. "
41:20 Out of his nostrils g' smoke, as out "
21 and a flame g' out of his mouth. "
Ps 17: 1 prayer, that g' not out of feigned "
41: 6 when he g' abroad, he telleth it. 3318
68:21 such an one as g' on still in his 1980
88:16 Thy fierce wrath g' over me; *5674
97: 3 A fire g' before him, and burneth 3212
104:23 Man g' forth unto his work and to 3318
126: 6 He that g' forth and weepeth, 3212
146: 4 His breath g' forth, he returneth 3318
Pr 6:29 that g' in to his neighbour's wife; 935
7:22 He g' after her straightway, 1980
22 as an ox g' to the slaughter, 925
11:10 When it g' well with the righteous, "
16:18 Pride g' before destruction, and an "
20:19 He that g' about as a talebearer 1980
26: 9 g' up into the hand of a drunkard, 5927
20 no wood is, there the fire g' out: 3518
31:18 her candle g' not out by night. "
Ec 1: 5 and the sun g' down, and hasteth 935
6 The wind g' toward the south, and 1980
3:21 the spirit of man that g' upward, 5927
21 of the beast that g' downward 3381
12: 5 because man g' to his long home, 1980
Ca 7: 9 that g' down sweetly, causing the "
Isa 28:19 From the time that it g' forth *5674
30:29 as when one g' with a pipe to 1980
55:11 So shall my word be that g' forth 3318
59: 8 whosoever g' therein shall not 1869
63:14 a beast g' down into the valley, *3318
Jer 5: 6 every one that g' out thence shall "
6: 4 the day g' away, for the shadows *6437
21: 9 but he that g' out, and falleth to 3318
22:10 weep sore for him that g' away: 1980
30:23 whirlwind of the Lord g' forth *3318
38: 2 he that g' forth to the Chaldeans "
44:17 whatsoever thing g' forth out of * "
49:17 every one that g' by it shall be *5674
50:13 every one that g' by Babylon shall "
Eze 7:14 but none g' to the battle: for my 1980
33:31 heart g' after their covetousness. "
40:40 one g' up to the entry of the north 5927
42: 9 as one g' into them from the utter 935
44:27 in the day that he g' into the "
48: 1 one g' to Hamath, Hazar-enan, * "
Hos 6: 4 as the early dew it g' away. 1980
5 are as the light that g' forth. 3318
Zec 5: 3 This is the curse that g' forth "
5 see what is this that g' forth. "
6 This is an ephah that g' forth. "
M't 8: 9 say to this man; Go, and he g': 4198
12:45 Then g' he, and taketh with himself "
13:44 and for joy thereof g' and selleth 5217
15:11 that which g' into the mouth *1525
17 g' into the belly, and is cast out *5562
17:21 this kind g' not out but by prayer *1607
18:12 and g' into the mountains, and *4198
26:24 The Son of man g' as it is written 5217
28: 7 he g' before you into Galilee; 4254
M'r 3:13 And he g' up into a mountain, and 305
7:19 g' out into the draught, purging 1607
14:21 The Son of man indeed g', as it is 5217
45 he g' straightway to him, and *4334
16: 7 that he g' before you into Galilee: 4254
Lu 7: 8 I say unto one, Go, and he g'; 4198
11:26 Then g' he, and taketh to him seven "
22:22 the Son of man g', as it was "
Joh 3: 8 it cometh, and whither it g': 5217
7:20 devil: who g' about to kill thee? *2212
10: 4 he g' before them, and the sheep 4198
11:31 She g' unto the grave to weep *5217
12:35 knoweth not whither he g'. "
Ac 8:26 unto the way that g' down from 2597
1Co 6: 6 But brother g' to law with brother, "
9: 7 Who g' a warfare at any time at * "
Jas 1:24 beholdeth himself, and g' his way, 565
1Jo 2:11 and knoweth not whither he g', 5217
Re 14: 4 the Lamb whithersoever he g'. "
17:11 and g' into perdition. "
19:15 his mouth g' a sharp sword, *1607

Gog See also HAMON-GOG; MAGOG.
1Ch 5: 4 Shemaiah his son, G' his son, 1463
Eze 38: 2 Son of man, set thy face against G', "
3 I am against thee, O G', the chief "
14 prophesy and say unto G', Thus "
16 I shall be sanctified in thee, O G', "
18 G' shall come against the land "
39: 1 prophesy against G', and say, "
1 I am against thee, O G', the chief "
11 that I will give unto G' a place "
11 and there shall they bury G' and "
Re 20: 8 G' and Magog, to gather them 1136

going See also GOINGS.
Ge 12: 9 Abram journeyed, g' on ... toward 1980
15:12 And when the sun was g' down, 935
37:25 g' to carry it down to Egypt. 1980
Ex 17:12 until the g' down of the sun. 935
23: 4 enemy's ox or his ass g' astray, 8582
37:18 six branches g' out of the sides 3318
19 branches g' out of the candlestick. "
21 to the six branches g' out of it. "
Le 11:20 that creep, g' upon all four, *1980
Nu 32: 7 children of Israel from g' over 5674
34: 4 the g' forth thereof shall be from*8444
De 16: 6 at the g' down of the sun, at the 935
33:18 Rejoice, Zebulun, in thy g' out; 3318
Jos 1: 4 toward the g' down of the sun, 3996
6: 9 after the ark, the priests g' on, *1980
11 g' about it once: and they came 5362
13 the priests g' on, and blowing *1980
7: 5 and smote them in the g' down: 4174
10:11 were in the g' down to Beth-horon, "
27 the time of the g' down of the sun, 935
15: 7 is before the g' up to Adummim, *4608
18:17 against the g' up of Adummim, * "
23:14 I am g' the way of all the earth: 1980
J'g 1:36 from the g' up to Akrabbim, *4608
19:18 now g' to the house of the Lord; 1980
28 said unto her, Up, and let us be g'. 3212
1Sa 9:11 they found young maidens g' out 3318
27 were g' down to the end of the city, 3381
10: 3 meet thee three men g' up to God 5927
17:20 the host was g' forth to the fight, 3318
29: 6 thy g' out and thy coming in with "
2Sa 2:19 in g' he turned not to the right 3212
3:25 know thy g' out and thy coming in, 4161
5:24 thou hearest the sound of a g' *6807
1Ki 17:11 as she was g' to fetch it, he called 3212
22:36 about the g' down of the sun. 935
2Ki 2:23 as he was g' up by the way, 5927
9:27 at the g' up to Gur, which is by *4608
19:27 I know thy abode, and thy g' out, 3318
1Ch 14:15 thou shalt hear a sound of g' *6807
26:16 by the causeway of the g' up, *5927
2Ch 11: 4 from g' against Jeroboam. 3212
18:34 the time of the sun g' down he 935
Ne 3:19 against the g' up to the armoury ‡5927
31 to the g' up of the corner. *5944
32 g' up of the corner unto the sheep* "
12:37 at the g' up of the wall, above the ‡4608
Job 1: 7 From g' to and fro in the earth, 7751
2: 2 From g' to and fro in the earth, and "
33:24 Deliver him from g' down to the 3381
28 his soul from g' into the pit, 5674
Ps 19: 6 His g' forth is from the end of 4161
50: 1 the sun unto the g' down thereof. 3996
104:19 the sun knoweth his g' down. "
113: 3 unto the g' down of the same "
121: 8 The Lord shall preserve thy g' out 3318
144:14 there be no breaking in, nor g' out; "
Pr 7:27 g' down to the chambers of death. 3381
14:15 man looketh well to his g'. 838
30:29 four are comely in g': 3212
Isa 13:10 shall be darkened in his g' forth, 3318
37:28 I know thy abode, and thy g' out, "
Jer 48: 5 in the g' up of Luhith continual *4608
5 in the g' down of Horonaim the 4174
50: 4 g' and weeping: they shall go, *1980
Eze 27:19 and Javan g' to and fro occupied * 235
40:31, 34, 37 g' up to it had eight steps. ‡4608
44: 5 every g' forth of the sanctuary. 4161
46:12 after his g' forth one shall shut 3318
Da 6:14 laboured till the g' down of the sun 4606
9:25 the g' forth of the commandment 4161
Ho 6: 3 his g' forth is prepared as the "
Jon 1: 3 he found a ship g' to Tarshish: 935
Mal 1:11 unto the g' down of the same 3996
M't 4:21 And g' on from thence, he saw *4260*
20:17 Jesus g' up to Jerusalem took the *305*
26:46 Rise, let us be g': behold, he *71*
28:11 Now when they were g', behold *4108*
M'r 6:31 there were many coming and g', *5217*
10:32 in the way g' up to Jerusalem; *305*
Lu 14:31 g' to make war against another **4198*
Joh 4:51 And as he was now g' down, *2597*
8:59 g' through the midst of them, **1330*
Ac 9:28 coming in and g' out at Jerusalem. *1607*
20: 5 These g' before tarried for us at **4281*
Ro 10: 3 and g' about to establish their **2212*
1Ti 5:24 g' before to judgment; and some *4254*
Heb 7:18 of the commandment g' before * "
1Pe 2:25 ye were as sheep g' astray; *4105*
Jude 7 g' after strange flesh, are set * *565*

goings See also OUTGOINGS.
Nu 33: 2 And Moses wrote their g' out 4161
2 journeys according to their g' out, "
34: 5 g' out of it shall be at the sea. 8444
8 the g' forth of the border shall be "
9 g' out of it shall be at Hazar-enan: "
12 g' out of it shall be at the salt sea: "
Jos 15: 4 the g' out of that coast were at the "
7 g' out thereof were at En-rogel: "
11 the g' out of the border were at the "
16: 3 the g' out thereof are at the sea. "
8 the g' out thereof were at the sea. "
Jos 18:12 g' out...at the wilderness 8444
14 g' out...at Kirjath-baal, "
Job 34:21 man; and he seeth all his g'. 6806
Ps 17: 5 Hold up my g' in thy paths, * 838
40: 2 a rock, and established my g'. "
68:24 They have seen thy g', O God; 1979
24 even the g' of my God, my King, "
140: 4 purposed to overthrow my g' *6471
Pr 5:21 and he pondereth all his g'. *4570
20:24 Man's g' are of the Lord; how 4703
Isa 59: 8 there is no judgment in their g': 4570
Eze 42:11 their g' out were both according 4161
43:11 thereof, and the g' out thereof, "
48:30 these are the g' out of the city 8444
Mic 5: 2 whose g' forth have been from of 4163

Golan (*go'-lan*)
De 4:43 G' in Bashan of the Manassites. 1474
Jos 20: 8 G' in Bashan out of the tribe of "
21:27 of Manasseh they gave G' in "
1Ch 6:71 Manasseh, G' in Bashan with her "

gold See also GOLDSMITH.
Ge 2:11 land of Havilah, where there is g'; 2091
12 And the g' of that land is good: "
13: 2 in cattle, in silver, and in g'. "
24:22 hands of ten shekels weight of g'; "
35 flocks, and herds, and silver, and g', "
53 jewels of silver, and jewels of g', "
41:42 put a g' chain about his neck; "
44: 8 out of thy lord's house silver or g'? "
Ex 3:22 jewels of silver, and jewels of g', "
11: 2 jewels of silver, and jewels of g', "
12:35 jewels of silver, and jewels of g', "
20:23 shall ye make unto you gods of g'. "
25: 3 take of them; g', and silver, and "
11 overlay it with pure g', within and "
11 make upon it a crown of g' round "
12 thou shalt cast four rings of g' "
13 wood, and overlay them with g'. "
17 make a mercy seat of pure g': "
18 cherubims of g', of beaten work "
24 thou shalt overlay it with pure g', "
24 and make thereto a crown of g' "
26 shalt make for it four rings of g', "
28 overlay them with g', that the table "
29 of pure g' shalt thou make them. "
31 shalt make a candlestick of pure g': "
36 shall be one beaten work of pure g'. "
38 thereof, shall be of pure g'. "
39 talent of pure g' shall he make it, "
26: 6 thou shalt make fifty taches of g', "
29 shalt overlay the boards with g', "
29 and make their rings of g' "
29 thou shalt overlay the bars with g'. "
32 of shittim wood overlaid with g': "
32 their hooks shall be of g', upon the "
37 and overlay them with g', "
37 and their hooks shall be of g': "
28: 5 shall take g', and blue, and purple, "
6 they shall make the ephod of g', "
8 g', of blue, and purple, and scarlet, "
11 them to be set in ouches of g'. "
13 thou shalt make ouches of g'; "
14 two chains of pure g' at the ends; "
15 even of g', of blue, and of purple, "
20 they shall be set in g' in their "
22 ends of wreathen work of pure g'. "
23 upon the breastplate two rings of g', "
24 put the two wreathen chains of g' "
26 And thou shalt make two rings of g', "
27 And two other rings of g' thou shalt "
33 and bells of g' between them round "
36 thou shalt make a plate of pure g', "
30: 3 thou shalt overlay it with pure g', "
3 make unto it a crown of g' round "
5 and overlay them with g'. "
31: 4 to work in g', and in silver, and in "
32:24 Whosoever hath any g', let them "
31 and have made them gods of g'. "
35: 5 offering of the Lord; g', and silver, "
22 rings, and tablets, all jewels of g': "
22 an offering of g' unto the Lord. "
32 to work in g', and in silver, and in "
36:13 And he made fifty taches of g', "
34 And he overlaid the boards with g', "
34 and made their rings of g' "
34 and overlaid the bars with g'. "
36 and overlaid them with g': "
36 their hooks were of g'; and he cast "
38 chapiters and their fillets with g': "
37: 2 he overlaid it with pure g' within "
2 and made a crown of g' to it round "
3 And he cast for it four rings of g', "
4 and overlaid them with g'. "
6 he made the mercy seat of pure g': "
7 And he made two cherubims of g', "
11 And he overlaid it with pure g', "
11 and made thereunto a crown of g' "
12 made a crown of g' for the border* "
13 And he cast for it four rings of g', "
15 and overlaid them with g', to bear "
16 covers to cover withal, of pure g'. "
17 he made the candlestick of pure g': "
22 it was one beaten work of pure g'. "
23 and his snuffdishes of pure g'. "
24 Of a talent of pure g' made he it, "
26 And he overlaid it with pure g', "
26 also he made unto it a crown of g' "
27 And he made two rings of g' for it* "
28 and overlaid them with g'. "
38:24 g' that was occupied for the work "
24 the g' of the offering, was twenty "
39: 2 And he made the ephod of g', blue, "
3 they did beat the g' into thin plates, "
5 of g', blue, and purple, and scarlet, "
6 inclosed in ouches of g', graven, as "
Ex 39: 8 the ephod; of g', blue, and purple, 2091
13 inclosed in ouches of g', in their "
15 ends, of wreathen work of pure g'. "
16 two ouches of g', and two g' rings, "
17 put the two wreathen chains of g' "
19 they made two rings of g', and put "
25 and they made bells of pure g', and "
30 of the holy crown of pure g', "
40: 5 thou shalt set the altar of g' for * "
Nu 7:14 One spoon of ten shekels of g', * "
20 One spoon of g' of ten shekels, * "
84 silver bowls, twelve spoons of g':* "
86 g' of the spoons was an hundred "
8: 4 the candlestick was of beaten g', "
22:18 me his house full of silver and g', "
24:13 me his house full of silver and g', "
31:22 Only the g', and the silver, the "
50 gotten of jewels of g', chains, and "
51 Eleazar the priest took the g' of "
52 all the g' of the offering that they "
54 priest took the g' of the captains "
De 7:25 shalt not desire the silver or g' that "
8:13 thy silver and thy g' is multiplied, "
17:17 multiply to himself silver and g'. "
29:17 idols, wood and stone, silver and g', "
Jos 6:19 all the silver, and g', and vessels "
24 only the silver, and the g', and the "
7:21 and a wedge of g' of fifty shekels "
24 the garment, and the wedge of g', "
22: 8 silver, and with g', and with brass, "
J'g 8:26 and seven hundred shekels of g'; "
1Sa 6: 8 the jewels of g', which ye return "
11 and the coffer with the mice of g' "
15 wherein the jewels of g' were, and "
2Sa 1:24 ornaments of g' upon your apparel. "
8: 7 And David took the shields of g' "
10 vessels of g', and vessels of brass: "
11 silver and g' that he had dedicated "
12:30 weight whereof was a talent of g' "
21: 4 We will have no silver nor g' of "
1Ki 6:20 and he overlaid it with pure g'; "
21 the house within with pure g': "
21 the chains of g' before the oracle; "
21 and he overlaid it with g'. "
22 he overlaid with g', until he had "
22 oracle he overlaid with g'. "
28 he overlaid the cherubims with g'. "
30 of the house he overlaid with g', "
32 and overlaid them with g', and "
32 and spread g' upon the cherubims, "
35 and covered them with g' fitted "
7:48 the altar of g', and the table of g',* "
49 the candlesticks of pure g', five on "
49 the lamps, and the tongs of g', "
50 spoons, and the censers of pure g'; "
50 and the hinges of g', both for the "
51 silver, and the g', and the vessels, "
9:11 trees and fir trees, and with g', "
14 to the king sixscore talents of g'. "
28 from thence g', four hundred and "
10: 2 that bare spices, and very much g', "
10 hundred and twenty talents of g', "
11 that brought g' from Ophir, brought "
14 weight of g' that came to Solomon "
14 threescore and six talents of g', "
16 two hundred targets of beaten g': "
16 six hundred shekels of g' went to "
17 three hundred shields of beaten g': "
17 three pound of g' went to one shield: "
18 and overlaid it with the best g'. "
21 drinking vessels were of g', and all "
21 forest of Lebanon were of pure g'; "
22 the navy of Tharshish, bringing g', "
25 vessels of silver, and vessels of g', "
12:28 made two calves of g', and said "
14:26 he took away all the shields of g' "
15:15 Lord, silver, and g', and vessels. "
18 Asa took all the silver and the g' "
19 thee a present of silver and g'; "
20: 3 Thy silver and thy g' is mine; thy "
5 silver, and thy g', and thy wives, "
7 and for my silver, and for my g'; "
22:48 of Tharshish to go to Ophir for g': "
2Ki 5: 5 six thousand pieces of g', and ten "
7: 8 thence silver, and g', and raiment, "
12:13 vessels of g', or vessels of silver. "
18 g' that was found in the treasures "
14:14 And he took all the g' and silver, "
16: 8 Ahaz took the silver and g' that "
18:14 of silver and thirty talents of g'. "
16 Hezekiah cut off the g' from the "
20:13 silver, and the g', and the spices, 2091
23:33 talents of silver, and a talent of g'. "
35 the silver, and the g' to Pharaoh; "
35 he exacted the silver and the g' "
24:13 cut in pieces all the vessels of g' "
25:15 such things as were of g', in g', "
1Ch 18: 7 And David took the shields of g' "
10 manner of vessels of g' and silver "
11 and the g' that he brought from all "
20: 2 and found it to weigh a talent of g', "
21:25 hundred shekels of g' by weight. "
22:14 an hundred thousand talents of g', "
16 Of the g', the silver, and the brass, "
28:14 He gave of g' by weight for things "
14 by weight for things of g', for all "
15 weight for the candlesticks of g', "
15 and for their lamps of g', "
16 by weight he gave g' for the tables "
17 Also pure g' for the fleshhooks, "
17 for the golden basons he gave g' * "
18 the altar of incense refined g' 2091
18 g' for the pattern of the chariot "
29: 2 the g' for things to be made of g', "
3 own proper good, of g' and silver, "
4 Even three thousand talents of g', "

1Ch 29: 4 of the g' of Ophir, and seven 2091
5 The g' for things of g', and the silver "
7 of g' five thousand talents and ten "
2Ch 1:15 made silver and g' at Jerusalem "
2: 7 a man cunning to work in g', and in "
14 skilful to work in g', and in silver, "
3: 4 he overlaid it within with pure g'. "
5 which he overlaid with fine g', and "
6 and the g' was g' of Parvaim. "
7 and the doors thereof, with g'; and "
8 and overlaid it with fine g', "
9 of the nails was fifty shekels of g'. "
9 the upper chambers with g'. "
10 and overlaid them with g'. "
4: 7 And he made ten candlesticks of g' "
8 he made an hundred basons of g'. "
20 before the oracle, of pure g'; "
21 made he of g', and that perfect g'; "
22 spoons, and the censers, of pure g': "
22 the house of the temple, were of g'. "
5: 1 the silver, and the g', and all the "
8:18 four hundred and fifty talents of g', "
9: 1 bare spices, and g' in abundance, "
9 hundred and twenty talents of g', "
10 which brought g' from Ophir, "
13 Now the weight of g' that came "
13 threescore and six talents of g'; "
14 brought g' and silver to Solomon. "
15 two hundred targets of beaten g': "
15 six hundred shekels of beaten g' "
16 shields made he of beaten g': "
16 three hundred shekels of g' went "
17 ivory, and overlaid it with pure g'. "
18 with a footstool of g', which were "
20 vessels of king Solomon were of g', "
20 forest of Lebanon were of pure g': "
21 bringing g', and silver, ivory, "
24 vessels of silver, and vessels of g', "
12: 9 carried away also the shields of g' "
13:11 candlestick of g' with the lamps "
15:18 himself had dedicated, silver, and g', "
16: 2 Then Asa brought out silver and g' "
3 I have sent thee silver and g'; go "
21: 3 them great gifts of silver, and of g', "
24:14 spoons, and vessels of g' and silver. "
25:24 he took all the g' and the silver, "
32:27 treasuries for silver, and for g', "
36: 3 talents of silver and a talent of g'. "
Ezr 1: 4 help him with silver, and with g', "
6 hands with vessels of silver, with g', "
9 thirty chargers of g', a thousand "
10 Thirty basons of g', silver basons "
11 All the vessels of g' and of silver "
2:69 and one thousand drams of g', "
5:14 the vessels also of g' and silver 1722
7:15 And to carry the silver and g' "
16 silver and g' that thou canst find "
18 the rest of the silver and the g', "
8:25 unto them the silver, and the g', 2091
26 and of g' an hundred talents; "
27 Also twenty basons of g', of a "
27 vessels of fine copper, precious as g'. "
28 the silver and the g' are a freewill "
30 silver, and the g', and the vessels, "
33 and the g' and the vessels weighed "
Ne 7:70 thousand drams of g', fifty basons, "
71 twenty thousand drams of g', and "
72 was twenty thousand drams of g', "
Es 1: 6 the beds were of g' and silver, "
7 gave them drink in vessels of g', "
8:15 with a great crown of g', and with "
Job 3:15 Or with princes that had g', who "
22:24 Then shalt thou lay up g' as dust,*1220
24 and the g' of Ophir as the stones "
23:10 tried me, I shall come forth as g'. 2091
28: 1 a place for g' where they fine it. "
6 sapphires: and it hath dust of g'. "
15 It cannot be gotten for g', 5458
16 be valued with the g' of Ophir, 3800
17 g' and the crystal cannot equal it: 2091
17 shall not be for jewels of fine g'. 6337
19 shall it be valued with pure g'. 3800
31:24 If I have made g' my hope, 2091
24 or have said to the fine g', Thou 3800
36:19 no, not g', nor all the forces of *1222
42:11 and every one an earring of g'. 2091
Ps 19:10 More to be desired are they than g', "
10 yea, than much fine g': 6337
21: 3 thou settest a crown of pure g' on "
45: 9 did stand the queen in g' of Ophir. 3800
13 her clothing is of wrought g'. 2091
68:13 and her feathers with yellow g'. 2742
72:15 shall be given of the g' of Sheba: 2091
105:37 them forth also with silver and g': "
115: 4 Their idols are silver and g', the "
119:72 better unto me than thousands of g' "
127 love thy commandments above g'; "
127 yea, above fine g'. 6337
135:15 of the heathen are silver and g', 2091
Pr 3:14 and the gain thereof than fine g'. 2742
8:10 knowledge rather than choice g'. "
19 My fruit is better than g'; "
19 yea, than fine g'; and my 6337
11:22 a jewel of g' in a swine's snout, 2091
16:16 better is it to get wisdom than g'! 2742
17: 3 the furnace for g': but the Lord 2091
20:15 There is g', and a multitude of "
22: 1 favour rather than silver and g'. "
25:11 apples of g' in pictures of silver. "
12 As an earring of g', and "
12 an ornament of fine g', so is a 3800
27:21 the furnace for g'; so is a man 2091
Ec 2: 8 I gathered me also silver and g', "
Ca 1:10 jewels, thy neck with chains of g'.*
11 We will make thee borders of g' 2091
3:10 bottom thereof of g', the covering "
Ca 5:11 His head is as the most fine g', 6337
14 are as g' rings set with the beryl: 2091
15 marble, set upon sockets of fine g': 6337
Isa 2: 7 land also is full of silver and g', 2091
20 his idols of g', which they made "
13:12 a man more precious than fine g'; 6337
17 as for g', they shall not delight 2091
30:22 of thy molten images of g': "
31: 7 idols of silver, and his idols of g', "
39: 2 silver, and the g', and the spices, "
40:19 spreadeth it over with g', and "
46: 6 They lavish g' out of the bag, "
60: 6 they shall bring g' and incense; "
9 their silver and their g' with them, "
17 For brass I will bring g', and for "
Jer 4:30 deckest thee with ornaments of g', "
10: 4 They deck it with silver and with g'; "
9 and g' from Uphaz, the work of the "
52:19 cups; that which was of g' in g', "
La 4: 1 How is the g' become dim! "
1 how is the most fine g' changed! 3800
2 sons of Zion, comparable to fine g', 6337
Eze 7:19 and their g' shall be removed: 2091
19 their silver and their g' shall not "
16:13 wast thou decked with g' and silver; "
17 fair jewels of my g' and of my silver, "
27:22 with all precious stones, and g'. "
28: 4 g' and silver into thy treasures: "
13 emerald, and the carbuncle, and g': "
38:13 to carry away silver and g', to take "
Da 2:32 This image's head was of fine g', 1722
35 the brass, the silver, and the g', "
38 Thou art this head of g'. "
45 brass, the clay, the silver, and the g'; "
3: 1 the king made an image of g', whose "
5: 4 and praised the gods of g', and of "
7 have a chain of g' about his neck, "
16 have a chain of g' about thy neck, "
23 praised the gods of silver, and g', "
29 and put a chain of g' about his neck, "
10: 5 were girded with fine g' of Uphaz: 3800
11: 8 precious vessels of silver and of g'; 2091
38 shall he honour with g', and silver, "
43 have power over the treasures of g' "
Hos 2: 8 multiplied her silver and g', which "
8: 4 their silver and their g' have they "
Joe 3: 5 ye have taken my silver and my g', "
Na 2: 9 take the spoil of g': for there is "
Hab 2:19 it is laid over with g' and silver, "
Zep 1:18 Neither their silver nor their g' "
Hag 2: 8 The silver is mine, and the g' "
Zec 4: 2 a candlestick all of g', with a bowl "
6:11 Then take silver and g', and make "
9: 3 fine g' as the mire of the streets. 2742
13: 9 and will try them as g' is tried: 2091
14:14 shall be gathered together, g', and "
Mal 3: 3 and purge them as g' and silver, "
M't 2:11 him gifts; g', and frankincense, 5557
10: 9 Provide neither g', nor silver, nor "
23:16 shall swear by the g' of the temple, "
17 whether is greater, the g', or the "
17 temple that sanctifieth the g'? "
Ac 3: 6 said, Silver and g' have I none; 5553
17:29 that the Godhead is like unto g', 5557
20:33 have coveted no man's silver, or g', 5553
1Co 3:12 upon this foundation g', silver, 5557
1Ti 2: 9 not with broidered hair, or g', or "
2Ti 2:20 not only vessels of g' and of silver, 5552
Heb 9: 4 overlaid round about with g', 5553
Jas 2: 2 with a g' ring, in goodly apparel, 5554
5: 3 Your g' and silver is cankered; 5557
1Pet 1: 7 much more precious than of g' 5553
18 corruptible things, as silver and g', "
3: 3 the hair, and of wearing of g', "
Re 3:18 to buy of me g' tried in the fire, "
4: 4 had on their heads crowns of g'. 5552
9: 7 were as it were crowns like g', 5557
20 devils, and idols of g', and 5552
17: 4 decked with g' and precious 5557
18:12 The merchandise of g', and silver, "
16 decked with g', and precious stones, "
21:18 and the city was pure g', like unto 5553
21 the street of the city was pure g', "

golden
Ge 24:22 the man took a g' earring of half a 2091
Ex 25:25 thou shalt make a g' crown to the "
28:34 g' bell and a pomegranate, a g' bell "
30: 4 And two g' rings shalt thou make "
32: 2 Break off the g' earrings, which are "
3 the people brake off the g' earrings "
39:20 And they made two other g' rings,* "
38 the g' altar, and the anointing oil, "
40:26 he put the g' altar in the tent "
Lev 8: 9 did he put the g' plate, the holy "
Nu 4:11 upon the g' altar they shall spread "
7:26, 32, 38, 44, 50, 56, 62, 68, 74, 80 One
g' spoon of ten shekels, full of 2091
86 The g' spoons were twelve, full of "
J'g 8:24 (For they had g' earrings, because "
26 the weight of the g' earrings that he "
1Sa 6: 4 Five g' emerods, and five g' mice, "
17 these are the g' emerods which the "
18 And the g' mice, according to the "
2Ki 10:29 the g' calves that were in Beth-el, "
1Ch 28:17 and for the g' basons he gave gold "
2Ch 4:19 the g' altar also, and the tables "
13: 8 and there are with you g' calves, "
Ezr 6: 5 also let the g' and silver vessels *1722
Es 4:11 king shall hold out the g' sceptre, 2091
5: 2 held out to Esther the g' sceptre "
8: 4 out the g' sceptre toward Esther. "
Ec 12: 6 or the g' bowl be broken, or the "
Isa 13:12 a man than the g' wedge of Ophir.*3800
14: 4 the oppressed ceased! the g' city 4062
Jer 51: 7 Babylon hath been a g' cup in the 2091
Da 3: 5 down and worship the g' image 1722
Da 3: 7 down and worshipped the g' image 1722
10 fall down and worship the g' image: "
12 worship the g' image which thou "
14 nor worship the g' image which I "
18 worship the g' image which thou "
5: 2 commanded to bring the g' and "
3 they brought the g' vessels that "
Zec 4:12 which through the two g' pipes 2091
12 empty the g' oil ... of themselves? "
Heb 9: 4 Which had the g' censer, and the 5552
4 wherein was the g' pot that had "
Re 1:12 turned, I saw seven g' candlesticks; "
13 about the paps with a g' girdle. "
20 and the seven g' candlesticks. "
2: 1 midst of the seven g' candlesticks; "
5: 8 harps, and g' vials full of odours, "
8: 3 having a g' censer; and there was "
3 upon the g' altar which was before "
9:13 from the four horns of the g' altar "
14:14 having on his head a g' crown, "
15: 6 their breasts girded with g' girdles. "
7 seven g' vials full of the wrath of "
17: 4 having a g' cup in her hand full "
21:15 had a g' reed to measure the city, "

goldsmith See also GOLDSMITH'S; GOLDSMITHS.
Isa 40:19 and the g' spreadeth it over with 6884
41: 7 the carpenter encouraged the g', "
46: 6 and hire a g'; and he maketh it "

goldsmith's
Ne 3:31 repaired Malchiah the g' son unto*6885

goldsmiths
Ne 3: 8 the son of Harhaiah, of the g'. 6884
32 repaired the g' and the merchants. "

Golgotha (*gol'-go-thah*) See also CALVARY.
M't 27:33 were come unto a place called G', 1115
M'r 15:22 they bring him unto the place G', "
Joh 19:17 which is called in the Hebrew G': "

Goliath (*go-li'-ath*)
1Sa 17: 4 named G', of Gath, whose height 1555
23 Gath, G' by name, out of the armies "
21: 9 sword of G' the Philistine, whom "
22:10 and gave him the sword of G' the "
2Sa 21:19 slew the brother of G' the Gittite, "
1Ch 20: 5 slew...the brother of G' the Gittite, "

Gomer (*go'-mer*)
Ge 10: 2 sons of Japheth; G', and Magog, 1586
3 And the sons of G'; Ashkenaz, "
1Ch 1: 5 sons of Japheth; G', and Magog, "
6 the sons of G'; Ashchenaz, and "
Ez 38: 6 G', and all his bands; the house of "
Hos 1: 3 went and took G' the daughter of "

Gomorrah (*go-mor'-rah*) See also GOMORRHA.
Ge 10:19 thou goest, unto Sodom, and G', 6017
13:10 the Lord destroyed Sodom and G', "
14: 2 and with Birsha king of G', Shinab "
8 and the king of G', and the king of "
10 and the kings of Sodom and G' fled, "
11 took all the goods of Sodom and G', "
18:20 Because the cry of Sodom and G' is "
19:24 rained upon Sodom and upon G', "
28 he looked toward Sodom and G', "
De 29:23 like the overthrow of Sodom, and G', "
32:32 of Sodom, and of the fields of G': "
Isa 1: 9 we should have been like unto G'. "
10 the law of our God, ye people of G'. "
13:19 when God overthrew Sodom and G'. "
Jer 23:14 and the inhabitants thereof as G'. "
49:18 in the overthrow of Sodom and G', "
50:40 As God overthrew Sodom and G' "
Am 4:11 as God overthrew Sodom and G', "
Zep 2: 9 and the children of Ammon as G', "

Gomorrha (*go-mor'-rah*) See also GOMORRAH.
M't 10:15 for the land of Sodom and G' in *1116
M'r 6:11 more tolerable for Sodom and G' * "
Ro 9:29 and been made like unto G'. * "
2Pe 2: 6 turning the cities of ... and G' * "
Jude 7 Even as Sodom and G', and the * "

gone See also AGONE.
Ge 27:30 Jacob was yet scarce g' out from 3318
28: 7 and was g' to Padan-aram; 3212
31:30 though thou wouldest needs be g', 1980
34:17 our daughter, and we will be g'. "
42:33 of your households, and be g': *3212
44: 4 when they were g' out of the city, 3318
49: 9 the prey, my son, thou art g' up: 5927
Ex 9:29 As soon as I am g' out of the city, 3318
12:32 herds, as ye have said, and be g': 3212
16:14 when the dew that lay was g' up, 5927
19: 1 the children of Israel were g' forth 3318
33: 8 until he was g' into the tabernacle. 935
Le 17: 7 whom they have g' a whoring. *
Nu 5:19 hast not g' aside to uncleanness 7847
20 if thou hast g' aside to another "
7:89 And when Moses was g' into the *935
13:32 land, through which we have g' 5674
16:46 is wrath g' out from the Lord; 3318
21:28 there is a fire g' out of Heshbon, "
De 9: 9 When I was g' up into the mount 5927
13:13 the children of Belial, are g' out 3318
17: 3 hath g' and served other gods, 3212
23:23 That which is g' out of thy lips 4161
27: 4 when ye be g' over Jordan, that *5674
32:36 he seeth that their power is g'. 235
Jos 2: 7 pursued after them were g' out, 3318
4:23 before us, until we were g' over: *5674
23:16 have g' and served other gods, *1980
J'g 3:24 When he was g' out, his servants 3318
4:12 the son of Abinoam was g' up 5927
14 is not the Lord g' out before thee? 3318
18:24 and ye are g' away: and what 3212
20: 3 the children of Israel were g' up 5927

Ru 1:13 hand of the Lord is g' out against 3318
15 thy sister in law is g' back unto 7725
1Sa 14: 3 knew not that Jonathan was g'. 1980
17 now, and see who is g' from us. "
15:12 him up a place, and is g' about, 5437
12 passed on, and g' down to Gilgal. 3381
20 g' the way which the Lord sent 3212
20:41 And as soon as the lad was g', 935
25:37 when the wine was g' out of Nabal, 3318
2Sa 2:27 the people had g' up every one 5927
3: 7 Wherefore hast thou g' in unto 935
22 him away, and he was g' in peace. 3212
23 him away, and he is g' in peace. "
24 sent him away, and he is quite g'? "
6:13 bare the ark of the Lord had g' six 6805
13:15 Amnon said unto her, Arise, be g'. 3212
17:20 They be g' over the brook of water. 5674
22 one of them that was not g' over "
23: 9 the men of Israel were g' away: 5927
24: 8 So when they had g' through all 7751
1Ki 1:25 he is g' down this day, and hath 3381
2:41 Shimei had g' from Jerusalem to 1980
9:16 Pharaoh king of Egypt had g' up, 5927
11:15 the captain of the host was g' up "
13:24 when he was g', a lion met him 3212
14: 9 for thou hast g' and made thee "
10 taketh away dung, till it be all g'. "
18:12 as soon as I am g' from thee, 3212
20:40 was busy here and there, he was g'. 369
21:18 whither he is g' down to possess it. 3381
22:13 the messenger that was g' to call *1980
2Ki 1: 4, 6, 16 bed on which thou art g' up, 5927
2: 9 when they were g' over, that Elijah 5674
5: 2 Syrians had g' out by companies, 3318
6:15 God was risen early, and g' forth, "
7:12 therefore are they g' out of the "
20: 4 afore Isaiah was g' out into the "
11 had g' down in the dial of Ahaz. 3381
1Ch 14:15 God is g' forth before thee to smite 3318
17: 5 but have g' from tent to tent, and 1961
Job 1: 5 the days of their feasting were g' 5362
7: 4 shall I arise, and the night be g'? †4059
19:10 and I am g': and mine hope hath 3212
23:12 Neither have I g' back from the 4185
24:24 but are g' and brought low; 369
28: 4 they are g' away from men. *5128
Ps 14: 3 They are all g' aside, they are 5493
19: 4 line is g' out through all the earth, 3318
38: 4 mine iniquities are g' over mine 5674
10 mine eyes, it also is g' from me. 369
42: 4 I had g' with the multitude, *5674
7 and thy billows are g' over me. "
47: 5 God is g' up with a shout, the Lord 5927
51: *title* after he had g' in to Bath-sheba. 935
53: 3 Every one of them is g' back: they 5472
73: 2 as for me, my feet were almost g': 5186
77: 8 Is his mercy clean g' for ever? 656
89:34 nor alter the thing that is g' out 4161
103:16 wind passeth over it, and it is g': 369
109:23 I am g' like the shadow when it 1980
119:176 I have g' astray like a lost sheep; 8582
124: 4 the stream had g' over our soul: 5674
5 proud waters had g' over our soul. "
Pr 7:19 he is g' a long journey: 1980
20:14 but when he is g' his way, then he 235
Ec 8:10 and g' from the place of the holy, *1980
Ca 2:11 is past, the rain is over and g'; "
5: 6 withdrawn himself, and was g': 5674
6: 1 Whither is thy beloved g', O thou 1980
2 beloved is g' down into his garden, 3381
Isa 1: 4 they are g' away backward. 2114
5:13 my people are g' into captivity, "
10:29 They are g' over the passage: they 5674
15: 2 He is g' up to Bajith, and to Dibon, 5927
8 cry is g' round about the borders 5362
16: 8 they are g' over the sea. *5674
22: 1 art wholly g' up to the housetops? 5927
24:11 the mirth of the land is g'. 1540
38: 8 is g' down in the sun dial of Ahaz, 3381
8 by which degrees it was g' down. "
41: 3 that he had not g' with his feet. 935
45:23 the word is g' out of my mouth 3318
46: 2 themselves are g' into captivity. 1980
51: 5 my salvation is g' forth, and mine 3318
53: 6 All we like sheep have g' astray; 8582
57: 8 to another than me, and art g' up; 5927
Jer 2: 5 they are g' far from me, and have
23 I have not g' after Baalim? see 1980
3: 6 is g' up upon every high mountain "
4: 7 is g' forth from his place to make 3318
5:23 they are revolted and g'. 3212
9:10 and the beast are fled; they are g'. 1980
10:20 my children are g' forth of me, 3318
14: 2 and the cry of Jerusalem is g' up. 5927
15: 6 thou art g' backward: therefore 3212
9 her sun is g' down while it was 935
23:15 Jerusalem is profaneness g' forth 3318
19 a whirlwind of the Lord is g' forth "
29:16 your brethren that are not g' forth "
34:21 army, which are g' up from you. 5927
40: 5 while he was not yet g' back, he 7725
44: 8 land of Egypt, whither ye be g' 935
14 which are g' into the land of Egypt "
28 that are g' into the land of Egypt "
48:11 neither hath he g' into captivity: 1980
15 Moab is spoiled, and g' up out of 5927
15 his chosen young men are g' down 3381
32 thy plants are g' over the sea, *5674
50: 6 have g' from mountain to hill, 1980
La 1: 3 Judah is g' into captivity because
5 her children are g' into captivity 1980
6 and they are g' without strength 3212
18 young men are g' into captivity. 1980
Eze 7:10 the morning is g' forth; the rod 3318
9: 3 glory of the God of Israel was g' 5927
13: 5 Ye have not g' up into the gaps. "

Eze 19:14 And fire is g' out of a rod of her 3318
23:30 because thou hast g' a whoring ‡
24: 6 and whose scum is not g' out of it! 3318
31:12 people of the earth are g' down 3381
32:21 g' down, they lie uncircumcised, "
24 which are g' down uncircumcised "
27 g' down to hell with their weapons "
30 which are g' down with the slain; "
36:20 and are g' forth out of his land. 3318
37:21 whither they be g', and will 1980
44:10 the Levites that are g' away far *
Da 2: 5 The thing is g' from me: if ye will 230
8 ye see the thing is g' from me. "
14 which was g' forth to slay the wise 5312
10:20 when I am g' forth, lo, the prince *3318
Ho 4:12 and they have g' a whoring from ‡
8: 9 For they are g' up to Assyria, 5927
9: 1 for thou hast g' a whoring from ‡
6 they are g' because of destruction: 1980
Am 8: 5 When will the new moon be g', 5674
Jon 1: 5 Jonah was g' down into the sides 3381
Mic 1:16 for they are g' into captivity from thee.
2:13 the gate, and are g' out by it: 3318
Mal 3: 7 g' away from mine ordinances, *5493
M't 10:23 shall not have g' over the cities *5055*
12:43 unclean spirit is g' out of a man, *1831*
14:34 when they were g' over, they *1276*
18:12 and one of them be g' astray, *4105*
12 seeketh that which is g' astray? *
25: 8 oil; for our lamps are g' out. **4570*
26:71 when he was g' out into the porch, *1831*
M'r 1:19 he had g' a little farther thence, **4260*
5:30 that virtue had g' out of him, *1831*
7:29 the devil is g' out of thy daughter. "
30 she found the devil g' out, and her "
10:17 when he was g' forth ... the way, **1607*
Lu 2:15 as the angels were g' away from * *565*
5: 2 the fishermen were g' out of them, *576*
8:46 that virtue is g' out of me. *1831*
11:14 when the devil was g' out, the "
24 the unclean spirit is g' out of a man, "
19: 7 he was g' to be guest with a man *1525*
24:28 though he would have g' further. **4198*
Joh 4: 8 For his disciples were g' away unto *565*
6:22 that his disciples were g' away * "
7:10 when his brethren were g' up, then *305*
12:19 behold, the world is g' after him. *565*
13:31 Therefore, when he was g' out, *1831*
Ac 13: 6 when they had g' through the isle *1330*
42 were g' out of the synagogue, **1826*
16: 6 when they had g' through Phrygia **1330*
19 the hope of their gains was g', *1831*
18:22 landed at Cæsarea, and g' up, * *305*
20: 2 when he had g' over those parts, *1330*
25 among whom I have g' preaching* "
24: 6 Who also hath g' about to profane **3985*
26:31 when they were g' aside, they * *402*
27:28 when they had g' a little further, **1339*
Ro 3:12 They are all g' out of the way, **1578*
1Pe 3:22 Who is g' into heaven, and is on *4198*
2Pe 2:15 and are g' astray, following the **4105*
1Jo 4: 1 false prophets are g' out into the *1831*
Jude 11 they have g' in the way of Cain, **4198*

good See also BEST; BETTER; GOODMAN; GOODS.
Ge 1: 4 God saw the light, that it was g': 2896
10, 12, 18, 21, 25 God saw that it was g'. "
31 made, and, behold, it was very g'. "
2: 9 pleasant to the sight and g' for food; "
9 tree of knowledge of g' and evil. "
12 And the gold of that land is g': "
17 tree of the knowledge of g' and evil, "
18 not g' that the man should be alone; "
3: 5 be as gods, knowing g' and evil. "
6 saw that the tree was g' for food, "
22 to know g' and evil: and now, lest "
15:15 shalt be buried in a g' old age. "
18: 7 fetcht a calf tender and g', and "
19: 8 do ye to them as is g' in your eyes; "
21 16 down over against him a g' way 7368
24:12 thee, send me g' speed this day, "
50 cannot speak unto thee bad or g'. 2896
25: 8 died in a g' old age, an old man, "
26:29 done unto thee nothing but g', "
27: 9 fetch me from thence two g' kids "
46 what g' shall my life do me? "
30:20 endued me with a g' dowry; 2896
31:24, 29 not to Jacob either g' or bad. "
32:12 saidst, I will surely do thee g', 3190
40:16 that the interpretation was g', 2896
41: 5 up upon one stalk, rank and g'. "
22 came up in one stalk, full and g': "
24 thin ears devoured the seven g' "
26 The seven g' kine are seven years; "
26 and the seven g' ears are seven "
35 food of those g' years that come, "
37 was g' in the eyes of Pharaoh, 3190
43:28 servant our father is in g' health, *7965
44: 4 have ye rewarded evil for g'? 2896
45:18 I will give you the g' of the land 2898
20 for the g' of all the land of Egypt "
23 laden with the g' things of Egypt, "
46:29 and wept on his neck a g' while. 5750
49:15 he saw that rest was g', and the 2896
50:20 God meant it unto g', to bring to "
Ex 3: 8 unto a g' land and a large, unto "
18:17 The thing that thou doest is not g'. "
21:34 owner of the pit shall make it g', 7999
22:11 and he shall not make it g'. * "
13 not make g' that which was torn. "
14 he shall surely make it g'. * "
15 he shall not make it g'. "
Le 5: 4 to do evil, or to do g', whatsoever 3190
24:18 killeth a beast shall make it g'; 7999
27:10 nor change it, a g' for a bad, 2896
10 or a bad for a g': "

Le 27:12 value it, whether it be g' or bad; 2896
14 estimate it, whether it be g' or bad: "
33 not search whether it be g' or bad, "
Nu 10:29 with us, and we will do thee g': 2895
29 for the Lord hath spoken g' 2896
13:19 whether it be g' or bad; and what "
20 And be ye of g' courage, and bring "
14: 7 search it, is an exceeding g' land. 2896
23:19 and shall he not make it g'? 6965
24:13 to do either g' or bad of mine own 2896
De 1:14 thing which thou hast spoken is g' "
25 a g' land which the Lord our God "
35 evil generation see that g' land, "
39 no knowledge between g' and evil, "
2: 4 take ye g' heed unto yourselves 3966
3:25 the g' land that is beyond Jordan, 2896
4:15 therefore g' heed unto yourselves; 3966
21 should not go in unto that g' land, 2896
22 go over, and possess that g' land. "
6:11 And houses full of all g' things, 2898
18 and g' in the sight of the Lord: 2896
18 possess the g' land which the Lord "
24 for our g' always, that he might "
8: 7 God bringeth thee into a g' land, "
10 for the g' land which he hath given "
16 to do thee g' at thy latter end; 3190
9: 6 God giveth thee not this g' land 2896
10:13 command thee this day for thy g'? "
11:17 perish quickly from off the g' land "
12:28 doest that which is g' and right "
26:11 And thou shalt rejoice in every g' "
28:12 open unto thee his g' treasure, "
63 rejoiced over you to do you g', 3190
30: 5 he will do thee g', and multiply "
9 in the fruit of thy land, for g': 2896
9 again rejoice over thee for g', "
15 before thee this day life and g', "
31: 6 Be strong and of a g' courage, fear not
7, 23 Be strong and of a g' courage: for
33:16 for the g' will of him that dwelt 7522
Jos 1: 6 Be strong and of a g' courage: for unto
8 then thou shalt have g' success.
9 Be strong and of g' courage; be not
18 only be strong, and of a g' courage;
9:25 it seemeth g' and right unto thee 2896
10:25 be strong and of g' courage: for thus
21:45 failed not ought of any g' thing 2896
23:11 Take g' heed therefore unto 3966
13 perish from off this g' land which 2896
14 hath failed of all the g' things "
15 as all g' things are come upon you, "
15 destroyed you from off this g' land "
16 perish quickly from off the g' land "
24:20 after that he hath done you g'. 3190
J'g 8:32 died in a g' old age, and was 2896
9:11 my sweetness, and my g' fruit, "
10:15 whatsoever seemeth g' unto thee: "
17:13 I that the Lord will do me g', 3190
18: 9 the land, and, behold, it is very g': 2896
22 a g' way from the house of Micah, 7368
19:24 them what seemeth g' unto you: 2896
Ru 2:22 It is g', my daughter, that thou go "
1Sa 1:23 Do what seemeth thee g'; tarry "
2:24 for it is no g' report that I hear: "
3:18 let him do what seemeth him g'. "
11:10 all that seemeth g' unto you. "
12:23 teach you the g' and the right way: "
14:36 whatsoever seemeth g' unto thee. "
40 Do what seemeth g' unto thee. "
15: 9 all that was g', and would not "
19: 4 Jonathan spake g' of David unto "
4 have been to thee-ward very g': "
20:12 behold, if there be g' toward David. "
24: 4 do to him as it shall seem g' 3190
17 for thou hast rewarded me g', 2896
19 the Lord reward thee g' for that "
25: 3 was a woman of g' understanding, "
8 for we come in a g' day: give, I "
15 But the men were very g' unto us, "
21 and he hath requited me evil for g'. "
30 according to all the g' that he hath "
26:16 This thing is not g' that thou hast "
29: 6 coming in with me in the host is g' "
9 know that thou art g' in my sight, "
2Sa 3:19 all that seemed g' to Israel, "
19 that seemed g' to the whole house* "
4:10 to have brought g' tidings, 1319
6:19 a g' piece of flesh, and a flagon *
10:12 Be of g' courage, and let us play
12 do that which seemeth him g'. 2896
13:22 brother Amnon neither g' nor bad: "
14:17 the king to discern g' and bad: "
32 been g' for me to have been there* "
15: 3 See, thy matters are g' and right; "
26 let him do to me as seemeth g' "
16:12 will requite me g' for his cursing "
17: 7 Ahithophel hath given is not g' "
14 appointed to defeat the g' counsel "
18:27 He is a g' man, and cometh with g' "
19:18 and to do what he thought g'. "
27 do therefore what is g' in thine "
35 can I discern between g' and evil? "
37 what shall seem g' unto thee. "
38 that which shall seem g' unto thee: "
24:22 offer up what seemeth g' unto him: "
1Ki 1:42 man, and bringest g' tidings. "
2:38 The saying is g': as my lord the "
42 The word that I have heard is g'. "
3: 9 may discern between g' and bad: "
8:36 teach them the g' way wherein they "
56 one word of all his g' promise, "
12: 7 and speak g' words to them, then "
14:13 him there is found some g' thing "
15 root up Israel out of this g' land, "
21: 2 than it; or, if it seem g' to thee, "
22: 8 not prophesy g' concerning me, "

1Ki 22:13 prophets declare g· unto the king 2896
13 and speak that which is g·. "
18 prophesy no g· concerning me, "
2Ki 3:19 and shall fell every g· tree, and stop "
19 and mar every g· piece of land with "
25 on every g· piece of land cast every "
25 and felled all the g· trees: only in "
7: 9 this day is a day of g· tidings, and "
8: 9 of every g· thing of Damascus, 2898
10: 5 that which is g· in thine eyes. 2896
20: 3 have done that which is g· in thy "
19 G· is the word of the Lord which "
19 And he said, Is it not g·, if peace * "
1Ch 4:40 they found fat pasture and g·, 2896
13: 2 If it seem g· unto you, and that it 2895
16: 3 of bread, and a g· piece of flesh, * "
34 thanks unto the Lord; for he is g·; 2896
19:13 Be of g· courage, and let us behave "
13 do that which is g· in his sight. 2896
21:23 do that which is g· in his eyes: "
22:13 be strong, and of g· courage; dread not "
28: 8 that ye may possess this g· land, 2896
20 Be strong, and of g· courage; and do it: "
29: 3 I have of mine own proper g·, * "
28 died in a g· old age, full of days, 2896
2Ch 5:13 For he is g·; for his mercy endureth "
6:27 thou hast taught them the g· way, "
7: 3 For he is g·; for his mercy endureth "
10: 7 speak g· words to them, they will "
14: 2 And Asa did that which was g· and "
18: 7 for he never prophesied g· unto me, "
12 prophets declare g· to the king "
12 one of theirs, and speak thou g·. "
17 he would not prophesy g· unto me, "
19: 3 there are g· things found in thee, "
11 and the Lord shall be with the g·. "
24:16 because he had done g· in Israel, "
30:18 The g· Lord pardon every one "
22 that taught the g· knowledge of † "
31:20 wrought that which was g· and right "
Ezr 3:11 because he is g·, for his mercy "
5:17 therefore, if it seem g· to the king, 2869
7: 9 according to the g· hand of his God 2896
18 whatsoever shall seem g· to thee, 3191
8:18 And by the g· hand of our God 2896
22 all them for g· that seek him; "
9:12 eat the g· of the land, and leave it 2898
10: 4 be of g· courage, and do it. "
Ne 2: 8 to the g· hand of my God upon me. 2896
18 my God which was g· upon me; "
18 their hands for this g· work. "
5: 9 I said, It is not g· that ye do: "
19 Think upon me, my God, for g·, "
6:19 reported his g· deeds before me, "
9:13 g· statutes and commandments: "
20 Thou gavest also thy g· spirit to "
36 fruit thereof and the g· thereof, 2898
13:14 and wipe not out my g· deeds 2617
31 Remember me, O my God, for g·. 2896
Es 3:11 do with them as it seemeth g· "
5: 4 If it seem g· unto the king, 2895
7: 9 who had spoken g· for the king, 2896
8:17 gladness, a feast and a g· day. "
9:19 gladness and feasting, and a g· day, "
22 and from mourning into a g· day: "
Job 2:10 we receive g· at the hand of God, "
5:27 hear it, and know thou it for thy g·. "
7: 7 mine eye shall no more see g·. 2896
9:25 they flee away, they see no g·. "
10: 3 Is it g· unto thee that thou shouldest "
13: 9 g· that he should search you out? "
15: 3 wherewith he can do no g·? 3276
21:16 their g· is not in their hand: *2898
22:18 filled their house with g· things: 2896
21 thereby g· shall come unto thee. "
24:21 and doeth not g· to the widow. 3190
30:26 I looked for g·, then evil came 2896
34: 4 know among ourselves what is g·. "
39: 4 Their young ones are in g· liking, 2492
Ps 4: 6 Who will shew us any g·? Lord, 2896
14: 1 works, there is none that doeth g·. 2896
3 filthy: there is none that doeth g·, "
25: 8 G· and upright is the Lord: "
27:14 be of g· courage, and he shall * "
31:24 Be of g· courage, and he shall * "
34: 8 taste and see that the Lord is g·: 2896
10 Lord shall not want any g· thing. "
12 many days, that he may see g·? "
14 Depart from evil, and do g·; seek "
35:12 They rewarded me evil for g· to the "
36: 3 hath left off to be wise, and to do g·. 3190
4 himself in a way that is not g·; 2896
37: 3 Trust in the Lord, and do g·; "
23 The steps of a g· man are ordered * "
27 Depart from evil, and do g·; and 2896
38:20 They also that render evil for g· "
20 because I follow the thing that g· is. "
39: 2 I held my peace, even from g·; "
45: 1 My heart is inditing a g· matter: * "
51:18 Do g· in thy...pleasure unto Zion: 3190
18 Do...in thy g· pleasure unto Zion: "
52: 3 Thou lovest evil more than g·; 2896
9 for it is g· before thy saints. "
53: 1 iniquity: there is none that doeth g·. "
3 filthy; there is none that doeth g·. "
54: 6 thy name, O Lord; for it is g·. "
69:16 Lord; for thy lovingkindness is g·: "
73: 1 Truly God is g· to Israel, "
28 But it is g· for me to draw near "
84:11 no g· thing will be withhold from "
85:12 Lord shall give that which is g·; "
86: 5 For thou, Lord, art g·, and ready to "
17 Shew me a token for g·; that they "
92: 1 It is a g· thing to give thanks "
100: 5 For the Lord is g·; his mercy is "
103: 5 thy mouth with g· things; so that "
Ps 104:28 thine hand, they are filled with g·. 2896
106: 1 for he is g·: for his mercy endureth "
5 That I may see the g· of thy chosen, * "
107: 1 for he is g·: for his mercy endureth "
109: 5 have rewarded me evil for g·, "
21 because thy mercy is g·, deliver thou "
111:10 a g· understanding have all they "
112: 5 a g· man sheweth favour, and * "
118: 1 for he is g·: because his mercy "
29 for he is g·: for his mercy endureth "
119:39 I fear: for thy judgments are g·. "
66 Teach me g· judgment and 2898
68 Thou art g·, and doest 2896
68 Thou art..., and doest g·; 2895
71 It is g· for me that I have been 2896
122 Be surety for thy servant for g·: "
122: 9 the Lord our God I will seek thy g·. "
125: 4 Do g·, O Lord, unto those that be 2895
4 unto those that be g·, and to them 2896
128: 5 thou shalt see the g· of Jerusalem 2898
133: 1 how g· and how pleasant it is for 2896
135: 3 for the Lord is g·; sing praises unto "
136: 1 for he is g·: for his mercy endureth "
143:10 thy spirit is g·; lead me into the "
145: 9 The Lord is g· to all: and his tender "
147: 1 for it is g· to sing praises unto our "
Pr 2: 9 and equity; yea, every g· path. "
20 mayest walk in the way of g· men, "
3: 4 find favour and g· understanding "
27 Withhold not g· from them to "
4: 2 For I give you g· doctrine, "
11:17 The merciful man doeth g· to his 1580
23 desire of the righteous is only g·: 2896
27 diligently seeketh g· procureth "
12: 2 A g· man obtaineth favour of the "
14 A man shall be satisfied with g· "
25 but a g· word maketh it glad. "
13: 2 A man shall eat g· by the fruit "
15 G· understanding giveth favour: "
21 to the righteous g· shall be repayed. "
22 A g· man leaveth an inheritance "
14:14 and a g· man shall be satisfied "
19 The evil bow before the g·; and the "
22 shall be to them that devise g·. "
15: 3 beholding the evil and the g·. "
23 word spoken in due season, how g· "
30 a g· report maketh the bones fat. "
16:20 a matter wisely shall find g·: "
29 him into the way that is not g·. "
17:13 Whoso rewarded evil for g·, evil "
20 hath a froward heart findeth no g·: "
22 A merry heart doeth g· like a 3190
26 Also to punish the just is not g·, 2896
18: 5 It is not g· to accept the person of "
22 findeth a wife findeth a g· thing, "
19: 2 without knowledge, it is not g·; "
8 keepeth understanding shall find g·. "
20:18 and with g· advice make war. * "
23 and a false balance is not g·. 2896
22: 1 g· name is rather to be chosen than "
24:13 eat thou honey, because it is g·; 2896
23 It is not g· to have respect of "
25 a g· blessing shall come upon them. "
25:25 so is g· news from a far country. "
27 It is not g· to eat much honey: "
28:21 To have respect of persons is not g·: "
31:12 She will do him g· and not evil "
18 that her merchandise is g·: * "
Ec 2: 3 was that g· for the sons of men, "
24 he should make his soul enjoy g· "
26 God giveth to a man that is g· in * "
26 he may give to him that is g· * "
3:12 I know that there is no g· in them, * "
12 rejoice, and to do g· in his life. "
13 and enjoy the g· of all his labour, "
4: 8 and bereave my soul of g·? "
9 have a g· reward for their labour. "
5:11 what g· is there to the owners *3788
18 it is g· and comely for one to eat 2896
18 to enjoy the g· of all his labour "
6: 3 and his soul be not filled with g·, "
6 yet hath he seen no g·: do not all go "
12 who knoweth what is g· for man "
7: 1 a g· name is better than precious "
11 Wisdom is g· with an inheritance: 2896
18 is g· that thou shouldest take hold "
20 just man upon earth, that doeth g·, "
9: 2 to the g· and to the clean, and to the "
2 as is the g·, so is the sinner; "
18 but one sinner destroyeth much g·. "
11: 6 whether they both shall be alike g·. "
12: 9 yea, he gave g· heed, and sought * "
14 whether it be g·, or whether it be 2896
Ca 1: 3 of the savour of thy g· ointments * "
2:13 tender grape give a g· smell. * "
Isa 1:19 ye shall eat the g· of the land: 2898
5:20 them that call evil g·, and g· evil; 2896
7:15 to refuse the evil, and choose the g·. "
16 to refuse the evil, and choose the g·, "
38: 3 and have done that which is g· "
39: 8 G· is the word of the Lord which "
40: 9 O Zion, that bringest g· tidings, get 1319
9 Jerusalem, that bringest g· tidings, "
41: 6 said to his brother, Be of g· courage. "
23 do g·, or do evil, that we may be 3190
27 one that bringeth g· tidings. 1319
52: 7 feet of him that bringeth g· tidings, "
7 him that bringeth...tidings of g·, 2896
55: 2 and eat ye that which is g·, "
61: 1 preach g· tidings unto the meek; 1319
65: 2 walketh in a way that was not g·, 2896
Jer 4:22 to do g· they have no knowledge. 3190
5:25 withholden g· things from you. 2896
6:16 is the g· way, and walk therein, "
8:15 looked for peace, but no g· came; "
10: 5 neither also is it in them to do g·. 3190
Jer 13:10 this girdle, which is g· for nothing. *6743
23 then may ye also do g·, that are 3190
14:11 not for this people for their g·. 2896
19 and there is no g·; and for the time "
17: 6 and shall not see when g· cometh; "
18: 4 seemed g· to the potter to make it. 3474
10 I will repent of the g·, wherewith 2896
11 your ways and your doings g·. *3190
20 Shall evil be recompensed for g·? 2896
20 I stood before thee to speak g· "
21:10 this city for evil, and not for g·, "
24: 2 One basket had very g· figs, even "
3 I said, Figs; the g· figs, very g·; "
5 these g· figs, so will I acknowledge "
5 land of the Chaldeans for their g·. "
6 will set mine eyes upon them for g·. "
26:14 as seemeth g· and meet unto you. "
29:10 perform my g· word toward you, "
32 shall he behold the g· that I will do "
32:39 the g· of them, and of their children "
40 away from them, to do them g·; 3190
41 rejoice over them to do them g·, 2895
42 bring upon them all the g· that I 2896
33: 9 hear all the g· that I do unto them: "
11 for the Lord is g·; for his mercy "
14 I will perform that g· thing which "
39:16 this city for evil, and not for g·; "
40: 4 If it seem g· unto thee to come "
4 whither it seemeth g· and "
42: 6 Whether it be g·, or whether it be "
44:27 over them for evil, and not for g·: "
La 3:25 The Lord is g· unto them that wait "
26 It is g· that a man should both hope "
27 It is g· for a man that he bear the "
38 High proceedeth not evil and g·? "
Ez 16:50 I took them away as I saw g·. "
17: 8 was planted in a g· soil by great 2896
18:18 and did that which is not g· among "
20:25 them also statutes that were not g·, "
24: 4 even every g· piece, the thigh, and "
34:14 I will feed them in a g· pasture, "
14 there shall they lie in a g· fold, "
18 to have eaten up the g· pasture, "
36:31 your doings that were not g·, "
Da 4: 2 I thought it g· to shew the signs 8232
Ho 4:13 because the shadow thereof is g·: 2896
8: 3 cast off the thing that is g·: "
Am 5:14 Seek g·, and not evil, that ye may "
15 Hate the evil, and love the g·, "
9: 4 upon them for evil, and not for g· "
Mic 1:12 Maroth waited carefully for g·: "
2: 7 do not my words do g· to him 3190
3: 2 Who hate the g·, and love the evil: 2896
6: 8 shewed thee, O man, what is g·; "
7: 2 The g· man is perished out of the *2623
Na 1: 7 The Lord is g·, a strong hold 2896
15 of him that bringeth g· tidings, 1319
Zep 1:12 heart, The Lord will not do g·, 3190
Zec 1:13 g· words and comfortable words. 2896
11:12 If ye think g·, give me my price; "
Mal 2:13 or receiveth it with g· will 7522
17 Every one that doeth evil is g· in 2896
M't 3:10 which bringeth not forth g· fruit 2570
5:13 it is henceforth g· for nothing, 2480
16 that they may see your g· works, 2570
44 do g· to them that hate you, and *2573
45 sun to rise on the evil and on the g·, 18
7:11 to give g· gifts unto your children, "
11 which is in heaven give g· things "
17 Even so every g· tree bringeth forth "
17 tree bringeth forth g· fruit; but a 2570
18 A g· tree cannot bring forth evil 18
18 a corrupt tree bring forth g· fruit. 2570
19 that bringeth not forth g· fruit "
8:30 there was a g· way off from them *3112
9: 2 be of g· cheer; thy sins be forgiven "
22 Daughter, be of g· comfort; thy faith "
11:26 for so it seemed g· in thy sight. *2107
12:33 make the tree g·, and his fruit g·; 2570
34 can ye, being evil, speak g· things? 18
35 A g· man out of the g· treasure of "
35 the heart bringeth forth g· things: "
13: 8 fell into g· ground, and brought, 2570
23 received seed into the g· ground "
24 a man which sowed g· seed in his "
27 Sir, didst thou not sow g· seed in "
37 He that soweth the g· seed is the "
38 the g· seed are the children of the "
48 and gathered the g· into vessels, "
14:27 of g· cheer; it is I; be not afraid. "
17: 4 Lord, it is g· for us to be here: 2570
19:10 with his wife, it is not g· to marry. *4851
16 G· Master, what...thing shall I do, * 18
16 what g· thing shall I do, that I may "
17 callest thou me g·? there is none g· "
20:15 Is thine eye evil, because I am g·? "
22:10 many as they found, both bad and g·: "
25:21 done, thou g· and faithful servant: "
23 Well done, g· and faithful servant; "
26:10 she hath wrought a g· work upon "
24 it had been g· for that man if he had "
M'r 3: 4 to do g· on the sabbath days, or to 15
4: 8 And other fell on g· ground, and 2570
20 they which are sown on g· ground; "
6:50 Be of g· cheer: it is I; be not afraid. "
9: 5 Master, it is g· for us to be here: 2570
50 Salt is g·: but if the salt have lost "
10:17 G· Master, what shall I do that I 18
18 callest thou me g·? there is none g· "
49 Be of g· comfort, rise; he calleth thee. "
14: 6 hath wrought a g· work on me. 2570
7 ye will ye may do them g·: but 2095
21 g· were it for that man if he had 2570
Lu 1: 3 It seemed g· to me also, having had "
53 He hath filled the hungry with g· 18
2:10 bring you g· tidings of great joy, 2097

Lu 2:14 earth peace, g' will toward men. *2107
3: 9 not forth g' fruit is hewn down, 2570
6: 9 on the sabbath days to do g', or to 15
27 do g' to them which hate you, 2573
33 ye do g' to them which do g' to you, 15
35 do g', and lend, hoping for nothing "
38 g' measure, pressed down, and 2570
43 For a g' tree bringeth not forth
43 a corrupt tree bring forth g' fruit. "
45 A g' man out of the g' treasure of 18
45 heart bringeth forth that which is g'; "
8: 8 And other fell on g' ground, and
15 But that on the g' ground are they 2570
15 which in an honest and g' heart, 18
48 Daughter, be of g' comfort: thy *
9:33 it is g' for us to be here: and let 2570
10:21 for so it seemed g' in thy sight. *
42 and Mary hath chosen that g' part, 18
11:13 know how to give g' gifts unto your "
12:32 your Father's g' pleasure to give you
14:34 Salt is g': but if the salt have lost 2570
16:25 thy lifetime receivedst thy g' things, 18
18:18 G' Master, what shall I do to inherit "
19 Why callest thou me g'? none is g'. "
19:17 Well, thou g' servant: because thou "
23:50 and he was a g' man, and a just: "
Joh 1:46 Can there any g' thing come out "
2:10 doth set forth g' wine; and when 2570
10 but thou hast kept the g' wine "
5:29 they that have done g', unto the 18
7:12 some said, He is a g' man: others "
10:11 the g' shepherd: the g' shepherd 2570
14 I am the g' shepherd, and know "
32 Many g' works have I shewed you "
33 For a g' work we stone thee not; "
16:33 but be of g' cheer; I have overcome
Ac 4: 9 g' deed done to the impotent man, 2108
9:36 this woman was full of g' works 18
10:22 of g' report among all the nation * "
38 went about doing g', and healing 2109
11:24 For he was a g' man, and full of the 18
14:17 in that he did g', and gave us 15
15: 7 that a g' while ago God made choice
25 It seemed g' unto us, being assembled
28 For it seemed g' to the Holy Ghost,
38 Paul thought not g' to take him 515
18:18 this tarried there yet a g' while, *2425
22:12 having a g' report of all the Jews *
23: 1 I have lived in all g' conscience until 18
11 Be of g' cheer, Paul: for as thou hast
27:22 And now I exhort you to be of g' cheer:
25 Wherefore, sirs, be of g' cheer: for I
36 Then were they all of g' cheer, and
Ro 2:10 peace to every man the worketh g', 18
3: 8 Let us do evil, that g' may come? "
12 there is none that doeth g', no, not 5544
5: 7 for a g' man some would even dare 18
7:12 commandment holy, and just, and g'. "
13 Was then that which is g' made "
13 death in me by that which is g'; "
16 I consent unto the law that it is g'. 2570
18 in my flesh,) dwelleth no g' thing: 18
18 how to perform that which is g' I 2570
19 For the g' that I would I do not: 18
21 a law, that when I would do g', 2570
8:28 all things work together for g' to 18
9:11 neither having done any g' or evil, "
10:15 and bring glad tidings of g' things! "
11:24 contrary to nature into a g' olive 2565
12: 2 that ye may prove what is that g', 18
9 is evil; cleave to that which is g'. "
21 of evil, but overcome evil with g'. "
13: 3 rulers are not a terror to g' works, "
3 do that which is g', and thou shalt "
4 the minister of God to thee for g'. "
14:16 Let not then your g' be evil spoken "
21 It is g' neither to eat flesh, nor to 2570
15: 2 please his neighbour for his g' to 18
16:18 by g' words and fair speeches *5542
19 have you wise unto that which is g', 18
1Co 5: 6 Your glorying is not g'. Know ye 2570
7: 1 It is g' for a man not to touch a "
8 It is g' for them if they abide even as "
26 that this is g' for the present "
26 that it is g' for a man so to be. "
15:33 evil communications corrupt g' 5543
2Co 5:10 hath done, whether it be g' or bad. 18
6: 8 by evil report and g' report: as 2162
9: 8 may abound to every g' work: 18
13:11 Be perfect, be of g' comfort, be *
Ga 4:18 But it is g' to be zealously 2570
18 affected always in a g' thing, "
6: 6 him that teacheth in all g' things. 18
10 let us do g' unto all men, especially "
Eph 1: 5 according to the g' pleasure of his
9 according to his g' pleasure which
2:10 created in Christ Jesus unto g' 18
4:28 his hands the thing which is g', "
29 but that which is g' to the use of "
6: 7 With g' will doing service, as to 2133
8 whatsoever g' thing any man doeth, 18
Ph'p 1: 6 he which hath begun a g' work in "
15 and some also of g' will: 2107
2:13 to will and to do of his g' pleasure.
19 that I also may be of g' comfort,
4: 8 whatsoever things are of g' report; 2163
Col 1:10 being fruitful in every g' work. 18
1Th 3: 1 thought it g' to be left at Athens 2106
6 brought us g' tidings of your faith *2097
6 have g' remembrance of us always, 18
5:15 but ever follow that which is g', "
21 things; hold fast that which is g'. 2570
2Th 1:11 the g' pleasure of his goodness, *
2:16 and g' hope through grace, 18
17 you in every g' word and work. "
1Ti 1: 5 a pure heart, and of a g' conscience, "
1Ti 1: 8 But we know that the law is g', 2570
18 them mightest war a g' warfare; "
19 Holding faith, and a g' conscience; 18
2: 3 For this is g' and acceptable in 2570
10 professing godliness) with g' works. 18
3: 1 of a bishop, he desireth a g' work. 2570
2 vigilant, sober, of g' behaviour, *
7 he must have a g' report of them 2570
13 purchase to themselves a g' degree, "
4: 4 For every creature of God is g', "
6 thou shalt be a g' minister of Jesus "
6 of faith and of g' doctrine, "
5: 4 for that is g' and acceptable * "
10 Well reported of for g' works; "
10 diligently followed every g' work. 18
25 the g' works of some are manifest 2570
6:12 Fight the g' fight of faith, lay hold "
12 and hast professed a g' profession "
13 Pilate witnessed a g' confession; "
18 That they do g', that they be 14
18 that they be rich in g' works, 2570
19 a g' foundation against the time "
2Ti 1:14 That g' thing which was committed "
2: 3 as a g' soldier of Jesus Christ. "
21 and prepared unto every g' work. 18
3: 3 despisers of those that are g', 865
17 furnished unto all g' works. 18
4: 7 I have fought a g' fight, I have 2570
Tit 1: 8 of hospitality, a lover of g' men, 5358
16 and unto every g' work reprobate. 18
2: 3 much wine, teachers of g' things; 2567
5 keepers at home, g', obedient to * 18
7 thyself a pattern of g' works: 2570
10 shewing all g' fidelity; that they 18
14 peculiar people, zealous of g' 2570
3: 1 to be ready to every g' work, 18
8 be careful to maintain g' works. 2570
8 These things are g' and profitable "
14 also learn to maintain g' works for "
Ph'm 6 the acknowledging of every g' thing 18
Heb 5:14 to discern both g' and evil, 2570
6: 5 And have tasted the g' word "
9:11 an high priest of g' things to come, 18
10: 1 a shadow of g' things to come, "
24 provoke unto love and to g' works: 2570
11: 2 the elders obtained a g' report. *
12 of one, and him as g' as dead,
39 a g' report through faith, *
13: 9 it is a g' thing that the heart be 2570
16 But to do g' and to communicate 2140
18 we trust we have a g' conscience, 2570
21 Make you perfect in every g' work 18
Jas 1:17 Every g' gift and every perfect gift "
2: 3 Sit thou here in a g' place; 2573
3:13 out of a g' conversation his works 2570
17 full of mercy and g' fruits, 18
4:17 to him that knoweth to do g', 2570
1Pe 2:12 they may by your g' works, which "
18 not only to the g' and gentle, but 18
3:10 he that will love life, and see g' days, "
11 Let him eschew evil, and do g'; "
13 be followers of that which is g'? "
16 Having a g' conscience; that, "
16 falsely accuse your g' conversation "
21 answer of a g' conscience toward "
4:10 as g' stewards of the manifold 2570
1Jo 3:17 whoso hath this world's g', and * 979
3Jo 11 which is evil, but that which is g'. 18
11 He that doeth g' is of God: 15
12 hath g' report of all men, and of *

goodlier
1Sa 9: 2 of Israel a g' person than he: from 2896

goodliest
1Sa 8:16 your g' young men, and your asses, 2896
1Ki 20: 3 thy children, even the g', are mine. "

goodliness
Isa 40: 6 all the g' thereof is as the flower 2617

goodly See also GOODLIER; GOODLIEST.
Ge 27:15 Rebekah took g' raiment of her 2530
39: 6 Joseph was a g' person, *3303, 8389
49:21 hind let loose; he giveth g' words. 8233
Ex 2: 2 saw him that he was a g' child, 2896
39:28 and g' bonnets of fine linen, and 6287
Le 23:40 the boughs of g' trees, branches 1926
Nu 24: 5 How g' are thy tents, O Jacob, 2896
31:10 and all their g' castles, with fire. *
De 3:25 that g' mountain, and Lebanon. 2896
6:10 to give thee great and g' cities, "
8:12 and hast built g' houses, and dwelt "
Jos 7:21 among the spoils a g' Babylonish "
1Sa 9: 2 a choice young man, and a g': "
16:12 countenance, and g' to look to. "
2Sa 23:21 he slew an Egyptian, a g' man; 4758
1Ki 1: 6 he also was a very g' man; 2896
2Ch 36:10 with the g' vessels of the house 2532
19 destroyed all the g' vessels thereof, 4261
Job 39:13 the g' wings unto the peacocks? ††7443
Ps 16: 6 yea, I have a g' heritage. 8231
80:10 thereof were like the g' cedars. * 410
Jer 3:19 a g' heritage of the hosts of 6643
11:16 fair, and of g' fruit: with 3303, 8389
Eze 17: 8 that it might be a g' vine. 155
23 and bear fruit, and be a g' cedar: 117
Ho 10: 1 land they have made g' images. 2896
Joe 3: 5 temples my g' pleasant things:
Zec 10: 3 as his g' horse in the battle. 1935
11:13 a g' price that I was prised at of 145
M't 13:45 merchant man, seeking g' pearls: 2573
Lu 21: 5 adorned with g' stones and gifts, "
Jas 2: 2 in g' apparel, and there come *2986
Re 18:14 were dainty and g' are departed * "

goodman
Pr 7:19 For the g' is not at home, 376
M't 20:11 against the g' of the house, *3611
24:43 if the g' of the house had known * "
M'r 14:14 say ye to the g' of the house, "
Lu 12:39 g' of the house had known what * "
22:11 shall say unto the g' of the house, "

goodness See also GOODNESS'.
Ex 18: 9 And Jethro rejoiced for all the g' 2896
33:19 make all my g' pass before thee, 2898
34: 6 and abundant in g' and truth, †‡2617
Nu 10:32 g' the Lord shall do unto us, *2896
J'g 8:35 all the g' which he had shewed "
2Sa 7:28 promised this g' unto thy servant: * "
1Ki 8:66 and glad of heart for all the g' "
1Ch 17:26 promised this g' unto thy servant;* "
2Ch 6:41 and let thy saints rejoice in g'. "
7:10 glad and merry in heart for the g' "
32:32 the acts of Hezekiah, and his g', *2617
35:26 the acts of Josiah, and his g', * "
Ne 9:25 themselves in thy great g'. 2898
35 and in thy great g' that thou gavest "
Ps 16: 2 my g' extendeth not to thee; *2896
21: 3 him with the blessings of g': thou "
23: 6 Surely g' and mercy shall follow me "
27:13 see the g' of the Lord in the land 2898
31:19 how great is thy g', which thou "
33: 5 earth is full of the g' of the Lord. *2617
52: 1 g' of God endureth continually. †‡ "
65: 4 satisfied with the g' of thy house, 2898
11 crownest the year with thy g'; 2896
68:10 hast prepared of thy g' for the poor. "
107: 8 would praise the Lord for his g', ‡2617
9 filleth the hungry soul with g'. *2896
15, 21, 31 praise the Lord for his g', ‡2617
144: 2 My g', and my fortress; my high * "
145: 7 utter the memory of thy great g', 2898
Pr 20: 6 proclaim every one his own g': *2617
Isa 63: 7 great g' toward the house of Israel, 2898
Jer 2: 7 the fruit thereof and the g' thereof; "
31:12 flow together to the g' of the Lord, "
14 people shall be satisfied with my g', "
33: 9 fear and tremble for all the g' *2896
Ho 3: 5 fear the Lord and his g' in the 2898
6: 4 your g' is as a morning cloud, 2617
10: 1 according to the g' of his land 2896
Zec 9:17 For how great is his g', and how 2898
Ro 2: 4 despisest thou the riches of his g' 5544
4 not knowing that the g' of God 5543
11:22 the g' and severity of God: 5544
22 but toward thee, g', if thou "
22 if thou continue in his g': "
15:14 ye also are full of g', filled with all 19
Ga 5:22 longsuffering, gentleness, g', faith, "
Eph 5: 9 the fruit of the Spirit is in all g' "
2Th 1:11 all the good pleasure of his g', "

goodness'
Ps 25: 7 remember thou me for thy g' sake, 2898

goods
Ge 14:11 they took all the g' of Sodom 7399
12 Sodom, and his g', and departed. "
16 he brought back all the g', and also "
16 again his brother Lot, and his g', "
21 persons, and take the g' to thyself. "
24:10 g' of his master were in his hand: *2898
31:18 all his g' which he had gotten, *7399
46: 6 they took their cattle, and their g', "
Ex 22: 8 his hand unto his neighbour's g' 4399
11 his hand unto his neighbour's g'; "
Nu 16:32 unto Korah, and all their g'. 7399
31: 9 all their flocks, and all their g'. 2428
35: 3 for their cattle, and for their g', *7399
De 28:11 thee plenteous in g', in the fruit *2896
2Ch 21:14 and thy wives, and all thy g': *7399
Ezr 1: 4 silver, and with gold, and with g', "
6 vessels of silver, with gold, with g', "
6: 8 the king's g', even of the tribute 5232
7:26 or to confiscation of g', or to
Ne 9:25 houses full of all g', wells digged, *2898
Job 20:10 his hands shall restore their g'. * 202
21 shall no man look for his g'. *2898
28 and his g' shall flow away in the
Ec 5:11 g' increase, they are increased 2896
Eze 38:12 which have gotten cattle and g', 7075
13 to take away cattle and g', to take "
Zep 1:13 their g' shall become a booty, *2428
M't 12:29 and spoil his g', except he first 4632
24:47 make him ruler over all his g'. *5224
25:14 and delivered unto them his g'. "
M'r 3:27 and spoil his g', except he will first 4632
Lu 6:30 away thy g' ask them not again. 4674
11:21 his palace, his g' are in peace: 5224
12:18 I bestow all my fruits and my g'. 18
19 thou hast much g' laid up for many "
15:12 me the portion of g' that falleth *3776
16: 1 unto him that he had wasted his g'. 5224
19: 8 Lord, the half of my g' I give to the "
Ac 2:45 And sold their possessions and g', 5223
1Co 13: 3 though I bestow all my g' to feed 5224
Heb 10:34 joyfully the spoiling of your g', * "
Re 3:17 I am rich, and increased with g', *4147

gopher
Ge 6:14 Make thee an ark of g' wood; 1613

gopher-wood See GOPHER and WOOD.

gore See also GORED.
Ex 21:28 If an ox g' a man or a woman, 5055

gored
Ex 21:31 Whether he have g' a son, 5055
31 or have g' a daughter, "

gorgeous
Lu 23:11 arrayed him in a g' robe, and sent 2986

gorgeously
Eze 23:12 and rulers clothed most g', 4358
Lu 7:25 they which are g' apparelled, 1741

Goshen (*go'-shen*)
Ge 45:10 dwell in the land of G·, and thou 1657
46:28 Joseph, to direct his face unto G·; "
28 and they came into the land of G·. "
29 meet Israel his father, to G·, and "
34 that ye may dwell in the land of G·; "
47: 1 behold, they are in the land of G·. "
4 servants dwell in the land of G·. "
6 in the land of G· let them dwell: "
27 land of Egypt, in the country of G·; "
50: 8 herds, they left in the land of G·. "
Ex 8:22 sever in that day the land of G·, in "
9:26 Only in the land of G·, where the "
Jos 10:41 and all the country of G·, even "
11:16 and all the land of G·, and the "
15:51 And G·, and Holon, and Giloh; "

gospel See also GOSPEL'S.
M't 4:23 preaching the g· of the kingdom, 2098
9:35 preaching the g· of the kingdom, "
11: 5 have the g· preached to them. *2097
24:14 this g· of the kingdom shall be 2098
26:13 Wheresoever this g· shall be "
M'r 1: 1 beginning of the g· of Jesus Christ, "
14 preaching the g· of the kingdom of "
15 repent ye, and believe the g·. "
13:10 the g· must first be published "
14: 9 this g· shall be preached throughout "
16:15 preach the g· to every creature. "
Lu 4:18 to preach the g· to the poor; *2097
7:22 to the poor the g· is preached. * "
9: 6 preaching the g·, and healing every "
20: 1 in the temple, and preached the g·, "
Ac 8:25 preached the g· in many villages "
14: 7 And there they preached the g·. "
21 And when they had preached the g· "
15: 7 should hear the word of the g·, 2098
16:10 to preach the g· unto them. 2097
20:24 testify the g· of the grace of God. 2098
Ro 1: 1 separated unto the g· of God, "
9 my spirit in the g· of his Son, "
15 to preach the g· to you that are 2097
16 For I am not ashamed of the g· 2098
2:16 by Jesus Christ according to my g·. "
10:15 them that preach the g· of peace, *2097
16 they have not all obeyed the g·. *2098
11:28 As concerning the g·, they are "
15:16 ministering the g· of God, that the "
19 have fully preached the g· of Christ. "
20 have I strived to preach the g·, 2097
29 of the blessing of the g· of Christ. *2098
16:25 stablish you according to my g·, "
1Co 1:17 but I preach the g·: not with 2097
4:15 have begotten you through the g·. 2098
9:12 we should hinder the g· of Christ. "
14 that they which preach the g· "
14 should live of the g·. "
16 For though I preach the g·, I have 2097
16 is unto me, if I preach not the g·! "
17 a dispensation of the g· is *
18 that, when I preach the g·, I may 2097
18 I may make the g· of Christ of no 2098
18 that I abuse not my power in the g·. "
15: 1 the g· which I preached unto you, "
2Co 2:12 to preach Christ's g·, and a door "
4: 3 But if our g· be hid, it is hid to them "
4 lest the light of the glorious g· of "
8:18 whose praise is in the g· "
9:13 subjection unto the g· of Christ, "
10:14 in preaching the g· of Christ: "
16 To preach the g· in the regions 2097
11: 4 or another g·, which ye have not 2098
7 have preached to you the g· of God "
Ga 1: 6 grace of Christ unto another g·: "
7 and would pervert the g· of Christ. "
8 preach any other g· unto you than 2097
9 if any man preach any other g· "
11 that the g· which was preached 2098
2: 2 communicated unto them that g· "
5 the truth of the g· might continue "
7 the g· of the uncircumcision was "
7 as the g· of the circumcision was "
14 according to the truth of the g·, 2098
3: 8 before the g· unto Abraham, 4283
4:13 I preached the g· unto you 2097
Eph 1:13 of truth the g· of your salvation: 2098
3: 6 promise in Christ by the g·: "
6:15 the preparation of the g· of peace; "
19 make known the mystery of the g·, "
Ph'p 1: 5 For your fellowship in the g· "
7 and confirmation of the g·, ye all "
12 unto the furtherance of the g·; "
17 I am set for the defence of the g·.* "
27 be as it becometh the g· of Christ: "
27 together for the faith of the g·; "
2:22 he hath served with me in the g·. "
4: 3 which laboured with me in the g·, "
15 that in the beginning of the g·, "
Col 1: 5 in the word of the truth of the g·; "
23 away from the hope of the g·, "
1Th 1: 5 For our g· came not unto you "
2: 2 to speak unto you the g· of God "
4 to be put in trust with the g·, "
8 not the g· of God only, but also our "
9 we preached unto you the g· of God. "
3: 2 fellowlabourer in the g· of Christ, "
2Th 1: 8 and that obey not the g· of our "
2:14 he called you by our g·, to the "
1Ti 1:11 According to the glorious g· of the "
2Ti 1: 8 partaker of the afflictions of the g· "
10 immortality to light through the g·: "
2: 8 from the dead according to my g·: "
Ph'm 13 unto me in the bonds of the g·: "
Heb 4: 2 For unto us was the g· preached, *2097
1Pe 1:12 by them that have preached the g· "
25 by the g· is preached unto you * "
1Pe 4: 6 was the g· preached also to them 2097
17 them that obey not the g· of God? 2098
Re 14: 6 the everlasting g· to preach ‡ "

gospel's
M'r 8:35 his life for my sake and the g·, 2098
10:29 or lands, for my sake, and the g·, "
1Co 9:23 And this I do for the g· sake, "

got See also FORGOT; GAT; GOTTEN.
Ge 36: 6 which he had g· in the land *7408
39:12 her hand, and fled, and g· him out. 3318
15 with me, and fled, and g· him out. "
Ps 44: 3 they g· not the land in possession *3423
Ec 2: 7 I g· me servants and maidens, *7069
Jer 13: 2 So I g· a girdle according to the * "
4 Take the girdle that thou hast g·,* "

gotten See also BEGOTTEN; FORGOTTEN; GOT.
Ge 4: 1 I have g· a man from the Lord. 7069
12: 5 souls that they had g· in Haran; 6213
31: 1 our father's hath he g· all this glory. "
18 all his goods which he had g·, *7408
18 of his getting, which he had g· * "
46: 6 their goods, which they had g· "
Ex 14:18 when I have g· me honour upon
Le 6: 4 thing which he hath deceitfully g·,
Nu 31:50 what every man hath g·, of 4672
De 8:17 mine hand hath g· me this 6213
2Sa 17:13 Moreover, if he be g· into a city, 622
Job 28:15 It cannot be g· for gold, neither 5414
31:25 because mine hand hath g· much;4672
Ps 98: 1 arm, hath g· him the victory. *
Pr 13:11 Wealth g· by vanity shall be
20:21 inheritance may be g· hastily
Ec 1:16 and have g· more wisdom than 3254
Isa 15: 7 the abundance they have g·, 6213
Jer 48:36 riches that he hath g· are perished. "
Eze 28: 4 thou hast g· thee riches, "
4 and hast g· gold and silver "
38:12 which have g· cattle and goods, "
Da 9:15 and hast g· thee renown, as at this "
Ac 21: 1 after we were g· from them, * 645
Re 15: 2 them that had g· the victory *

gourd See also GOURDS.
Jon 4: 6 And the Lord God prepared a g·, 7021
6 Jonah was exceeding glad of the g·. "
7 it smote the g· that it withered. "
9 thou well to be angry for the g·? "
10 Thou hast had pity on the g·, "

gourds
2Ki 4:39 gathered thereof wild g· his lap 6498

govern
1Ki 21: 7 Dost thou now g· the kingdom 6213
Job 34:17 Shall even he that hateth right g·? 2280
Ps 67: 4 and g· the nations upon earth. 5148

government See also GOVERNMENTS.
Isa 9: 6 the g· shall be upon his shoulder: 4951
7 Of the increase of his g· and peace "
22:21 and I will commit thy g· into his 4475
2Pe 2:10 of uncleanness, and despise g·. *2963

governments
1Co 12:28 helps, g·, diversities of tongues. 2941

governor See also GOVERNOR'S; GOVERNORS.
Ge 42: 6 Joseph was the g· over the land, 7989
45:26 he is g· over all the land *4910
1Ki 18: 3 Obadiah, which was g· of the 5921
22:26 Amon the g· of the city, and to 8269
2Ki 23: 8 gate of Joshua the g· of the city, "
25:23 of Babylon had made Gedaliah g·, 6485
1Ch 29:22 unto the Lord to be the chief g·, *5057
2Ch 1: 2 every g· in all Israel, the chief *5387
18:25 back to Amon the g· of the city, 8269
28: 7 and Azrikam the g· of the house, *5057
34: 8 Maaseiah the g· of the city, 8269
Ezr 5: 3 them Tatnai, g· on this side the 6347
6 that Tatnai, g· on this side the "
14 Sheshbazzar, whom he had made g·; "
6: 6 Tatnai, g· beyond the river, "
7 the g· of the Jews and the elders "
13 Tatnai, g· on this side the river, "
Ne 3: 7 the throne of the g· on this side 6346
5:14 I was appointed to be their g· "
14 have not eaten the bread of the g·. "
18 required not I the bread of the g·, "
12:26 in the days of Nehemiah the g·, "
Ps 22:28 he is the g· among the nations. *4910
Jer 20: 1 chief g· in the house of the Lord, *5057
30:21 and their g· shall proceed from *4910
40: 5 made g· over the cities of Judah, 6485
7 has made Gedaliah...g· in the land, "
41: 2 Babylon had made g· over the land. "
18 of Babylon made g· in the land. "
Hag 1: 1, 14 son of Shealtiel, g· of Judah, 6346
2: 2, 21 the son of Shealtiel, g· of Judah, "
Zec 9: 7 he shall be as a g· in Judah, * 441
Mal 1: 8 offer it now unto thy g·; will he 6346
M't 2: 6 shall come a G·, that shall rule 2233
27: 2 him to Pontius Pilate the g·. 2232
11 And Jesus stood before the g·: "
11 and the g· asked him, saying, "
14 that the g· marvelled greatly. "
15 the g· was wont to release unto "
21 g· answered and said unto them, "
23 And the g· said, Why, what evil * "
27 the soldiers of the g· took Jesus "
Lu 2: 2 when Cyrenius was g· of Syria.) 2230
3: 1 Pontius Pilate being g· of Judæa, "
20:20 the power and authority of the g·. 2232
Joh 2: 8 And bear unto the g· of the feast. * 755
9 the g· of the feast called the * "
Ac 7:10 and he made him g· over Egypt 2233
23:24 bring him safe unto Felix the g·. *2232
26 unto the most excellent g· Felix "
33 and delivered the epistle to the g·, "
Ac 23:34 when the g· had read the letter, 2232
24: 1 who informed the g· against Paul. "
10 after that the g· had beckoned unto "
26:30 the king rose up, and the g·, "
2Co 11:32 the g· under Aretas the king kept 1481
Jas 3: 4 whithersoever the g· listeth. *2116

governor's
M't 28:14 And if this come to the g· ears, 2232

governors
J'g 5: 9 My heart is toward the g· of Israel. 2710
14 out of Machir came down g·, "
1Ki 10:15 and of the g· of the country. 6346
1Ch 24: 5 the g· of the sanctuary, and g· of *8269
2Ch 9:14 g· of the country brought gold 6346
23:20 and the g· of the people, and all the 4910
Ezr 8:36 and to the g· on this side the river: 6346
Ne 2: 7 given me to the g· beyond the river, "
9 Then I came to the g· beyond the "
5:15 But the former g· that had been "
Es 3:12 and to the g· that were over every "
Da 2:48 and chief of the g· over all the *5461
3: 2 gather together the princes, the g·, "
3 Then the princes, the g·, and "
27 And the princes, g·, and captains, "
6: 7 kingdom, the g· and the princes, the "
Zec 12: 5 And the g· of Judah shall say in * 441
6 day will I make the g· of Judah * "
M't 10:18 And ye shall be brought before g· 2232
Gal 4: 2 But is under tutors and g· until *3623
1Pe 2:14 Or unto g·, as unto them that are 2232

Gozan (*go'-zan*)
2Ki 17: 6 and in Habor by the river of G·, 1470
18:11 and in Habor by the river of G·, "
19:12 my fathers have destroyed; as G·,* "
1Ch 5:26 and Hara, and to the river G·, "
Isa 37:12 my fathers have destroyed, as G·, "

grace See also DISGRACE.
Ge 6: 8 Noah found g· in the eyes of ‡2580
19:19 now, thy servant hath found g· in ‡ "
32: 5 that I may find g· in thy sight. ‡ "
33: 8 to find g· in the sight of my lord. ‡ "
10 now I have found g· in thy sight, ‡ "
15 let me find g· in the sight of my ‡ "
34:11 Let me find g· in your eyes, ‡ "
39: 4 And Joseph found g· in his sight, ‡ "
47:25 us find g· in the sight of my lord, ‡ "
29 now I have found g· in thy sight, ‡ "
50: 4 now I have found g· in your eyes, ‡ "
Ex 33:12 hast also found g· in my sight. ‡ "
13 if I have found g· in thy sight, ‡ "
13 that I may find g· in thy sight: ‡ "
16 people have found g· in thy sight? ‡ "
17 thou hast found g· in my sight, ‡ "
34: 9 now I have found g· in thy sight, ‡ "
Nu 32: 5 if we have found g· in thy sight, ‡ "
J'g 6:17 now I have found g· in thy sight, ‡ "
Ru 2: 2 him in whose sight I shall find g·. ‡ "
10 Why have I found g· in thine eyes, ‡ "
1Sa 1:18 handmaid find g· in thy sight. ‡ "
20: 3 knoweth that I have found g· in ‡ "
27: 5 I have now found g· in thine eyes, ‡ "
2Sa 14:22 knoweth that I have found g· in ‡ "
16: 4 that I may find g· in thy sight, my* "
Ezr 9: 8 a little space g· hath been shewed 8467
Es 2:17 she obtained g· and favour in his ‡2580
Ps 45: 2 men: g· is poured into thy lips: "
84:11 the Lord will give g· and glory: "
Pr 1: 9 an ornament of g· unto thy head, "
3:22 unto thy soul, and g· to thy neck. "
34 but he giveth g· unto the lowly. "
4: 9 to thine head an ornament of g·: "
22:11 for the g· of his lips the king shall "
Jer 31: 2 found g· in the wilderness; ‡ "
Zec 4: 7 shoutings, crying, G·, g· unto it. "
12:10 spirit of g· and of supplications: "
Lu 2:40 and the g· of God was upon him. 5485
Joh 1:14 of the Father,) full of g· and truth. "
16 have all we received, and g· for g·. "
17 g· and truth came by Jesus Christ. "
Ac 4:33 and great g· was upon them all. "
11:23 had seen the g· of God, was glad, "
13:43 them to continue in the g· of God. "
14: 3 testimony unto the word of his g·, "
26 recommended to the g· of God for "
15:11 through the g· of the Lord Jesus "
40 by the brethren unto the g· of God. "
18:27 which had believed through g·: "
20:24 testify the gospel of the g· of God. "
32 to God, and to the word of his g·, "
Ro 1: 5 By whom we have received g· and "
7 G· to you and peace from God our "
3:24 Being justified freely by his g· "
4: 4 not reckoned of g·, but of debt. "
16 of faith, that it might be by g·; "
5: 2 faith into this g· wherein we stand, "
15 the g· of God, and the gift by g·, "
17 they which receive abundance of g· "
20 g· did much more abound: "
21 even so might g· reign through "
6: 1 continue in sin, that g· may abound? "
14 are not under the law, but under g·. "
15 not under the law, but under g·? "
11: 5 according to the election of g·. "
6 if by g·, then is it no more of works: "
6 otherwise g· is no more g·. "
6 of works, then it is no more g·: * "
12: 3 through the g· given unto me, to "
6 according to the g· that is given to "
15:15 because of the g· that is given to "
16:20 The g· of our Lord Jesus Christ be "
24 The g· of our Lord Jesus Christ * "
1Co 1: 3 G· be unto you, and peace, from "
4 for the g· of God which is given you "
3:10 According to the g· of God which "

1Co 10:30 For if I by g' be a partaker, why am 5485
15:10 by the g' of God I am what I am: "
10 and his g' which was bestowed upon "
10 the g' of God which was with me. "
16:23 The g' of our Lord Jesus Christ be "
2Co 1: 2 G' be to you and peace from God "
12 by the g' of God, we have had our "
4:15 the abundant g' might through the "
6: 1 ye receive not the g' of God in vain. "
8: 1 you to wit of the g' of God bestowed "
6 also finish in you the same g' also. "
7 see that ye abound in this g' also. "
9 ye know the g' of our Lord Jesus "
19 to travel with us with this g', which "
9: 8 God is able to make all g' abound "
14 for the exceeding g' of God in you. "
12: 9 My g' is sufficient for thee: for my "
13:14 The g' of the Lord Jesus Christ, "
Ga 1: 3 G' be to you and peace from God "
6 that called you into the g' of Christ "
15 womb, and called me by his g', "
2: 9 perceived the g' that was given unto "
21 I do not frustrate the g' of God: "
5: 4 by the law; ye are fallen from g'. "
6:18 the g' of our Lord Jesus Christ be "
Eph 1: 2 G' be to you, and peace, from God "
6 To the praise of the glory of his g', "
7 according to the riches of his g'; "
2: 5 with Christ, (by g' ye are saved;) "
7 the exceeding riches of his g' "
8 by g' are ye saved through faith; "
3: 2 the dispensation of the g' of God "
7 according to the gift of the g' of God "
8 is this g' given, that I should preach "
4: 7 unto every one of us is given g' "
29 it may minister g' unto the hearers. "
6:24 G' be with all them that love our "
Ph'p 1: 2 G' be unto you, and peace, from "
7 ye all are partakers of my g'. "
4:23 The g' of our Lord Jesus Christ be "
Col 1: 2 G' be unto you, and peace, from "
6 and knew the g' of God in truth: "
3:16 singing with g' in your hearts to "
4: 6 your speech be always with g', "
18 my bonds. G' be with you. Amen. "
1Th 1: 1 G' be unto you, and peace, from "
5:28 The g' of our Lord Jesus Christ be "
2Th 1: 2 G' unto you, and peace, from God "
12 according to the g' of our God and "
2:16 and good hope through g', "
3:18 The g' of our Lord Jesus Christ be "
1Ti 1: 2 G', mercy, and peace, from God "
14 the g' of our Lord was exceeding "
6:21 the faith. G' be with thee. Amen. "
2Ti 1: 2 G', mercy, and peace, from God the "
9 to his own purpose and g', "
2: 1 be strong in the g' that is in Christ "
4:22 thy spirit. G' be with you. Amen. "
Tit 1: 4 G', mercy, and peace, from God the "
2:11 For the g' of God that bringeth "
3: 7 That being justified by his g', we "
15 faith. G' be with you all. Amen. "
Ph'm 3 G' to you, and peace, from God our "
25 The g' of our Lord Jesus Christ be "
Heb 2: 9 he by the g' of God should taste "
4:16 come boldly unto the throne of g', "
16 and find g' to help in time of need. "
10:29 done despite unto the Spirit of g'? "
12:15 lest any man fail of the g' of God; "
28 let us have g', whereby we may "
13: 9 the heart be established with g'; "
25 G' be with you all. Amen. "
Jas 1:11 g' of the fashion of it perisheth: 2143
4: 6 But he giveth more g'. Wherefore 5485
6 but giveth g' unto the humble. "
1Pe 1: 2 G' unto you, and peace, be "
10 the g' that should come unto you: "
13 for the g' that is to be brought "
3: 7 heirs together of the g' of life; "
4:10 stewards of the manifold g' of God. "
5: 5 proud, and giveth g' to the humble. "
10 But the God of all g', who hath "
12 true g' of God wherein ye stand. "
2Pe 1: 2 G' and peace be multiplied unto "
3:18 grow in g', and in the knowledge "
2Jo 3 G' be with you, mercy, and peace, "
Jude 4 turning the g' of our God into "
Re 1: 4 G' be unto you, and peace, from "
22:21 The g' of our Lord Jesus Christ be "

gracious
Ge 43:29 God be g' unto thee, my son. 2603
Ex 22:27 that I will hear; for I am g'. 2587
33:19 g' to whom I will be g', and will 2603
34: 6 The Lord God, merciful and g', 2587
Nu 6:25 upon thee, and be g' unto thee: 2603
2Sa 12:22 God will be g' to me, that the child "
2Ki 13:23 And the Lord was g' unto them, "
2Ch 30: 9 Lord your God is g' and merciful, 2587
Ne 9:17 ready to pardon, g' and merciful, "
31 thou art a g' and merciful God. "
Job 33:24 Then he is g' unto him, and saith, 2603
Ps 77: 9 Hath God forgotten to be g'? 2589
86:15 a God full of compassion, and g', 2587
103: 8 The Lord is merciful and g', slow to "
111: 4 Lord is g' and full of compassion. "
112: 4 he is g', and full of compassion, "
116: 5 G' is the Lord, and righteous; yea, "
145: 8 Lord is g', and full of compassion; "
Pr 11:16 A g' woman retaineth honour: 2580
Ec 10:12 of a wise man's mouth are g': "
Isa 30:18 that he may be g' unto you, and 2603
19 he will be very g' unto thee at the "
33: 2 O Lord, be g' unto us; we have "
Jer 22:23 g' shalt thou be when pangs come* "
Joe 2:13 is g' and merciful, slow to anger, 2587
Am 5:15 the Lord God of hosts will be g' "
Jon 4: 2 I knew that thou art a g' God, "
Mal 1: 9 God that he will be g' unto us: 2603
Lu 4:22 wondered at the g' words which *5485
1Pe 2: 3 ye have tasted that the Lord is g'. 5543

graciously
Ge 33: 5 God hath g' given thy servant, 2603
11 God hath dealt g' with me, and "
Ps 119:29 lying: and grant me thy law g'. "
Ho 14: 2 receive us g': so will we render *2896

graff
Ro 11:23 God is able to g' them in again. *1461

graffed See also UNGRAFFED.
Ro 11:17 wert g' in among them, and with *1461
19 broken off, that I might be g' in. * "
23 not still in unbelief, shall be g' in:* "
24 and wert g' contrary to nature * "
24 be g' into their own olive tree? * "

graft See GRAFF.

grain
Am 9: 9 yet shall not the least g' fall ‡6872
M't 13:31 like to a g' of mustard seed, which 2848
17:20 faith as a g' of mustard seed, ye "
M'r 4:31 It is like a g' of mustard seed, "
Lu 13:19 It is like a g' of mustard seed, "
17: 6 faith as a g' of mustard seed, ye "
1Co 15:37 body that shall be, but bare g', "
37 of wheat, or of some other g': * "

grandmother
2Ti 1: 5 which dwelt first in thy g' Lois, 3125

grant See also GRANTED.
Le 25:24 shall g' a redemption for the land. 5414
Ru 1: 9 Lord g' you that ye may find rest, "
1Sa 1:17 God of Israel g' thee thy petition "
1Ch 21:22 G' me the place of this * "
22 shalt g' it me for the full price: * "
2Ch 12: 7 I will g' them some deliverance; "
Ezr 3: 7 according to the g' that they had 7558
Ne 1:11 and g' him mercy in the sight of 5414
Es 5: 8 it please the king to g' my petition, "
Job 6: 8 and that God would g' me the thing "
Ps 20: 4 G' thee according to thine own "
85: 7 O Lord, and g' us thy salvation. "
119:29 and g' me thy law graciously. "
140: 8 G' not, O Lord, the desires of the 5414
M't 20:21 G' that these my two sons may *2036
M'r 10:37 G' unto us that we may sit, one 1325
Lu 1:74 That he would g' unto us, that we "
Ac 4:29 g' unto thy servants, that with all "
Ro 15: 5 g' you to be likeminded one toward "
Eph 3:16 That he would g' you, according to "
2Ti 1:18 Lord g' unto him that he may find "
Re 3:21 that overcometh will I g' to sit "

granted
1Ch 4:10 And God g' him that which he 935
2Ch 1:12 and knowledge is g' unto thee; 5414
Ezr 7: 6 and the king g' him all his request, "
Ne 2: 8 And the king g' me, according to "
Es 5: 6 petition? and it shall be g' thee: "
7: 2 Esther? and it shall be g' thee: "
8:11 the king g' the Jews which were in "
9:12 petition? and it shall be g' thee: "
13 let it be g' to the Jews which are in "
Job 10:12 Thou hast g' me life and favour, 6213
Pr 10:24 desire of the righteous shall be g'. 5414
Ac 3:14 a murderer to be g' unto you; 5483
11:18 Gentiles g' repentance unto life. 1325
14: 3 g' signs and wonders to be done * "
Re 19: 8 to her was g' that she should "

grape See also GRAPEGATHERER; GRAPEGLEANINGS; GRAPES.
Le 19:10 neither shalt thou gather every g' *6528
De 32:14 drink the pure blood of the g'. 6025
Job 15:33 He shall shake off his unripe g' 1154
Ca 2:13 the vines with the tender g' give *5563
7:12 whether the tender g' appear, * "
Isa 18: 5 and the sour g' is ripening in 1155
Jer 31:29 The fathers have eaten a sour g',* "
30 every man that eateth the sour g',* "

grapegatherer See also GRAPEGATHERERS.
Jer 6: 9 turn back thine hand as a g' into 1219

grapegatherers
Jer 49: 9 If g' come to thee, would they not 1219
Ob 5 if the g' came to thee, would they "

grapegleanings
Mic 7: 1 as the g' of the vintage: 5955

grapes
Ge 40:10 thereof brought forth ripe g': 6025
11 and I took the g', and pressed them "
49:11 and his clothes in the blood of g': "
Le 25: 5 neither gather the g' of thy vine "
11 nor gather the g' in it of thy vine "
Nu 6: 3 shall he drink any liquor of g', 6025
3 nor eat moist g', or dried. "
13:20 was the time of the firstripe g'. "
23 a branch with one cluster of g', "
24 because of the cluster of g' "
De 23:24 thou mayest eat g' thy fill at thine 6025
24:21 When thou gatherest the g' of thy "
28:30 shalt not gather the g' thereof. * "
39 nor gather the g': for the worms "
32:32 their g' are g' of gall, their clusters 6025
J'g 8: 2 the gleaning of the g' of Ephraim "
9:27 and trode the g', and made merry, "
Ne 13:15 also wine, g', and figs, and all 6025
Ca 2:15 for our vines have tender g'. *5563
7: 7 and thy breasts to clusters of g'. ‡
Isa 5: 2 that it should bring forth g', and 6025
Isa 5: 2 it brought forth wild g'. 891
4 looked that it should bring forth g', 6025
4 brought it forth wild g'? 891
17: 6 gleaning g' shall be left in it, as *
24:13 the gleaning g' when the vintage *
Jer 8:13 there shall be no g' on the vine, 6025
25:30 as they that tread the g', against "
49: 9 they not leave some gleaning g'? "
Eze 18: 2 The fathers have eaten sour g', 1154
Ho 9:10 Israel like g' in the wilderness; 6025
Am 9:13 the treader of g' him that soweth "
Ob 5 would they not leave some g'? "
M't 7:16 Do men gather g' of thorns, or figs 4718
Lu 6:44 of a bramble bush gather they g'. "
Re 14:18 the earth; for her g' are fully ripe. "

grass See also GRASSHOPPER.
Ge 1:11 Let the earth bring forth g', the 1877
12 earth brought forth g', and herb "
Nu 22: 4 ox licketh up the g' of the field. 3418
De 11:15 I will send g' in thy fields 6212
29:23 nor any g' groweth therein, like "
32: 2 and as the showers upon the g': "
2Sa 23: 4 g' springing out of the earth by 1877
1Ki 18: 5 peradventure we may find g' to 2682
2Ki 19:26 they were as the g' of the field, 6212
26 herb, as the g' on the house tops, 2682
Job 5:25 offspring as the g' of the earth. 6212
6: 5 the wild ass bray when he hath g'? 1877
40:15 with thee; he eateth g' as an ox. 2682
Ps 37: 2 shall soon be cut down like the g', "
72: 6 upon the mown g': as showers that "
16 of the city shall flourish like g' of 6212
90: 5 in the morning they are like g' 2682
92: 7 When the wicked spring as the g', 6212
102: 4 is smitten, and withered like g'; "
11 and I am withered like g'. "
103:15 As for man, his days are as g': 2682
104:14 the g' to grow for the cattle, "
106:20 similitude of an ox that eateth g'. 6212
129: 6 as the g' upon the housetops, 2682
147: 8 g' to grow upon the mountains. "
Pr 19:12 his favour is as dew upon the g'. 6212
27:25 the tender g' sheweth itself, and 1877
Isa 15: 6 the g' faileth, there is no green * "
35: 7 shall be g' with reeds and rushes. 2682
37:27 they were as the g' of the field, 6212
27 as the g' on the housetops, and as 2682
40: 6 What shall I cry? All flesh is g', "
7 The g' withereth, the flower fadeth: "
7 upon it: surely the people is g'. "
8 The g' withereth, the flower fadeth: "
44: 4 shall spring up as among the g', "
51:12 man which shall be made as g'; "
Jer 14: 5 forsook it, because there was no g'. 1758
6 did fail, because there was no g'. *6212
50:11 as the heifer at g', and bellow *1877
Da 4:15 in the tender g' of the field; and 1883
15 the beasts in the g' of the earth: 6211
23 brass, in the tender g' of the field; 1883
25 and they shall make thee to eat g' 6211
32 they shall make thee to eat g' as "
33 did eat g' as oxen, and his body "
5:21 they fed him with g' like oxen, "
Am 7: 2 make an end of eating the g' of 6212
Mic 5: 7 as the showers upon the g', that "
Zec 10: 1 of rain, to every one g' in the field. "
M't 6:30 God so clothe the g' of the field, 5528
14:19 to sit down on the g', and took "
M'r 6:39 by companies upon the green g'. "
Lu 12:28 If then God so clothe the g', "
Joh 6:10 there was much g' in the place. "
Jas 1:10 as the flower of the g' he shall pass "
11 it withereth the g', and the flower "
1Pe 1:24 For all flesh is as g', and all the "
24 glory of man as the flower of g'. "
24 The g' withereth, and the flower "
Re 8: 7 and all green g' was burnt up. "
9: 4 should not hurt the g' of the earth, "

grasshopper See also GRASSHOPPERS.
Le 11:22 kind, and the g' after his kind. 2284
Job 39:20 thou make him afraid as a g'? * 697
Ec 12: 5 the g' shall be a burden, and desire 2284

grasshoppers
Nu 13:33 we were in our own sight as g', 2284
J'g 6: 5 they came as g' for multitude; * 697
7:12 lay along in the valley like g' * "
Isa 40:22 the inhabitants thereof are as g'; 2284
Jer 46:23 because they are more than the g',* 697
Am 7: 1 he formed g' in the beginning of *1462
Na 3:17 as the great g', which camp in the "

grate
Ex 27: 4 shalt make for it a g' of network *4345
35:16 with his brasen g', his staves, * "
38: 4 he made for the altar a brasen g' * "
5 the four ends of the g' of brass, * "
30 and the brasen g' for it, and all * "
39:39 brasen altar, and his g' of brass, * "

grave See also ENGRAVE; GRAVECLOTHES; GRAVED; GRAVEN; GRAVE'S; GRAVES; GRAVETH; GRAVING.
Ge 35:20 Jacob set a pillar upon her g': 6900
20 that is the pillar of Rachel's g' "
37:35 go down into the g' unto my son ‡7585
42:38 gray hairs with sorrow to the g'. ‡
44:29 gray hairs with sorrow to the g'. ‡
31 our father with sorrow to the g'. ‡
50: 5 Lo, I die: in my g' which I have 6913
Ex 28: 9 and g' on them the names of 6605
36 and g' upon it, like the engravings *
Nu 19:16 a g', shall be unclean seven days. 6913
18 or one slain, or one dead, or a g': "
1Sa 2: 6 he bringeth down to the g', and ‡7585

2Sa 3:32 and wept at the g' of Abner; 6913
19:37 be buried by the g' of my father "
1Ki 2: 6 head go down to the g' in peace. ‡7585
9 head bring thou down to the g' ‡ "
13:30 he laid his carcase in his own g': 6913
14:13 of Jeroboam shall come to the g'. "
2Ki 22:20 thou shalt be gathered into thy g' "
2Ch 2: 7 to g' with the cunning men that 6603
14 also to g' any manner of graving, 6605
34:28 be gathered to thy g' in peace, 6913
Job 3:22 are glad, when they can find the g'? "
5:26 Thou shalt come to thy g' in a full "
7: 9 goeth down to the g' shall come *7585
10:19 carried from the womb to the g'. 6913
14:13 wouldest hide me in the g', that *7585
17:13 g' is mine house: I have made * "
21:13 in a moment go down to the g'. * "
32 he be brought to the g', and shall 6913
24:19 so doth the g' those which have *7585
30:24 stretch out his hand to the g'. *1164
33:22 soul draweth near unto the g'. *7845
Ps 6: 5 in the g' who shall give thee *7585
30: 3 brought up my soul from the g': * "
31:17 let them be silent in the g'. * "
49:14 sheep they are laid in the g'; * "
14 beauty shall consume in the g' * "
15 my soul from the power of the g': * "
88: 3 my life draweth nigh unto the g'. * "
5 like the slain that lie in the g'. 6913
11 be declared in the g'? or thy "
89:48 his soul from the hand of the g'? *7585
Pr 1:12 swallow them up alive as the g'; * "
30:16 The g'; and the barren womb; ‡ "
Ec 9:10 knowledge, nor wisdom, in the g', ‡ "
Ca 8: 6 death; jealousy is cruel as the g': ‡ "
Isa 14:11 pomp is brought down to the g', †‡ "
19 thou art cast out of thy g' like an *6913
38:10 I shall go to the gates of the g': ‡7585
18 the g' cannot praise thee, death ‡ "
53: 9 he made his g' with the wicked, 6913
Jer 20:17 my mother might have been my g', "
Eze 31:15 when he went down to the g' I ‡7585
32:23 company is round about her g': 6900
24 her multitude round about her g', "
Ho 13:14 them from the power of the g'; ‡7585
14 O g', I will be thy destruction: ‡ "
Na 1:14 make thy g'; for thou art vile. 6913
Joh 11:17 he had lain in the g' four days *3419
31 She goeth unto the g' to weep * "
38 in himself cometh to the g'. * "
12:17 he called Lazarus out of his g', * "
1Co 15:55 sting? O g', where is thy victory? * 86
1Ti 3: 8 Likewise must the deacons be g', 4586
11 Even so must their wives be g', "
Tit 2: 2 aged men be sober, g', temperate, "

graveclothes
Joh 11:44 bound hand and foot with g': 2750

graved See also GRAVEN.
1Ki 7:36 he g' cherubims, lions, and palm 6605
2Ch 3: 7 and g' cherubims on the walls. "

gravel
Pr 20:17 his mouth shall be filled with g'. 2687
Isa 48:19 offspring of thy bowels like the g' *4579
La 3:16 broken my teeth with g' stones, 2687

graven See also GRAVED; ENGRAVEN.
Ex 20: 4 not make unto thee any g' image, 6459
32:16 of God, g' upon the tables. 2801
39: 6 g', as signets are g', with the *6605
Le 26: 1 make you no idols nor g' image, 6459
De 4:16 and make you a g' image, "
23 you, and make you a g' image, or "
25 yourselves, and make a g' image, "
5: 8 shalt not make thee any g' image, "
7: 5 burn their g' images with fire. 6456
25 The g' images of their gods shall "
12: 3 ye shall hew down the g' images "
27:15 maketh any g' or molten image, 6459
J'g 17: 3 to make a g' image and a molten "
4 who made thereof a g' image and "
18:14 and teraphim, and a g' image, and "
17 took the g' image, and the ephod, "
20 the teraphim, and the g' image, "
30 children of Dan set up the g' image: "
31 they set them up Micah's g' image, "
2Ki 17:41 and served their g' images, both 6456
21: 7 he set a g' image of the grove 6459
2Ch 33:19 up groves and g' images, before 6456
34: 7 and had beaten the g' images into "
Job 19:24 they were g' with an iron pen 2672
Ps 78:58 to jealousy with their g' images. 6456
97: 7 they that serve g' images, that 6459
Isa 10:10 and whose g' images did excel 6456
21: 9 all the g' images of her gods "
30:22 the covering of thy g' images of "
40:19 workman melteth a g' image, ‡6459
20 to prepare a g' image, that shall "
42: 8 neither my praise to g' images. 6456
17 that trust in g' images, that say 6459
44: 9 They that make a g' image are all "
10 or molten a g' image that is ‡ "
15 maketh it a g' image, and falleth "
17 maketh a god, even his g' image: "
45:20 the wood of their g' image, and "
48: 5 done them, and my g' image, and "
49:16 I have g' thee upon the palms 2710
Jer 8:19 me to anger with their g' images, 6456
10:14 is confounded by the g' image: 6459
17: 1 g' upon the table of their heart, 2790
50:38 the land of g' images, and they 6456
51:17 is confounded by the g' image: 6459
47 the g' images of Babylon: and her 6456
52 do judgment upon her g' images: "
Ho 11: 2 and burned incense to g' images. "
Mic 1: 7 all the g' images thereof shall be 6456
5:13 Thy g' images also will I cut off, "
Na 1:14 will I cut off the g' image and the 6459
Hab 2:18 What profiteth the g' image that "
18 the maker thereof hath g' it; 6458
Ac 17:29 stone, g' by art and man's device. 5480

grave's
Ps 141: 7 are scattered at the g' mouth. ‡7585

graves
Ex 14:11 Because there were no g' in Egypt, 6913
2Ki 23: 6 the powder thereof upon the g' of "
2Ch 34: 4 strowed it upon the g' of them "
Job 17: 1 extinct, the g' are ready for me. * "
Isa 65: 4 Which remain among the g', and "
Jer 8: 1 of Jerusalem, out of their g': "
26:23 cast his dead body into the g' of "
Eze 32:22 company: his g' are about him: "
23 Whose g' are set in the sides of the "
25, 26 her g' are round about him: "
37:12 I will open your g', and cause you "
12 you to come up out of your g', "
13 when I have opened your g', O my "
13 and brought you up out of your g', "
39:11 give unto Gog a place there of g' * "
M't 27:52 the g' were opened; and many *3419
53 And came out of the g' after his * "
Lu 11:44 for ye are as g' which appear not, * "
Joh 5:28 that are in the g' shall hear his * "
Re 11: 9 their dead bodies to be put in g'. *3418

graveth
Isa 22:16 and that g' an habitation for *2710

graving See also GRAVINGS.
Ex 32: 4 fashioned it with a g' tool, 2747
2Ch 2:14 also to grave any manner of g', 6603
Zec 3: 9 I will engrave the g' thereof, "

gravings
1Ki 7:31 also upon the mouth of it were g' 4734

graving-tool See GRAVING and TOOL.

gravity
1Ti 3: 4 children in subjection with all g'; 4587
Tit 2: 7 uncorruptness, g', sincerity, "

gray See also GRAYHEADED; GREY.
Ge 42:38 down my g' hairs with sorrow 7872
44:29 bring down my g' hairs with sorrow "
31 g' hairs of thy servant our father "
De 32:25 also with the man of g' hairs. "
Ho 7: 9 g' hairs are here and there upon "

grayheaded See also GREYHEADED.
1Sa 12: 2 I am old and g'; and, behold, my 7867
Job 15:10 the g' and very aged men, much "
Ps 71:18 Now also when I am old and g', 7872

grease
Ps 119:70 Their heart is as fat as g'; 2459

great See also GREATER; GREATEST.
Ge 1:16 And God made two g' lights; the 1419
21 God created g' whales, and every "
6: 5 that the wickedness of man was g' 7227
7:11 fountains of the g' deep broken up, "
10:12 and Calah: the same is a g' city. 1419
12: 2 I will make of thee a g' nation, and "
2 bless thee, and make thy name g'; 1431
17 with g' plagues because of Sarai 1419
13: 6 for their substance was g', so that 7227
15: 1 and thy exceeding g' reward. 7235
12 horror of g' darkness fell upon 1419
14 they come out with g' substance. "
18 the g' river, the river Euphrates: "
17:20 and I will make him a g' nation. "
18:18 become a g' and mighty nation, "
20 cry of Sodom and Gomorrah is g', 7227
19:11 with blindness, both small and g': 1419
13 the cry of them is waxen g' before 1431
20: 9 and on my kingdom a g' sin? 1419
21: 8 Abraham made a g' feast the same "
18 for I will make him a g' nation. "
24:35 and he is become g': and he hath 1431
26:13 And the man waxed g', and "
13 and grew until he became very g': "
14 of herds, and g' store of servants: 7227
27:34 a g' and exceeding bitter cry, and 1419
29: 2 g' stone was upon the well's mouth. "
30: 8 g' wrestlings have I wrestled * 430
39: 9 then can I do this g' wickedness, 1419
41:29 years of g' plenty throughout "
45: 7 save your lives by a g' deliverance. "
46: 3 will there make of thee a g' nation: "
48:19 and he also shall be g': but truly 1431
50: 9 and it was a very g' company. 3515
10 a g' and very sore lamentation: 1419
Ex 3: 3 and see this g' sight, why the bush "
6: 6 out arm, and with g' judgments: "
7: 4 the land of Egypt by g' judgments. "
11: 3 the man Moses was very g' in the "
6 there shall be a g' cry throughout "
8 out from Pharaoh in a g' anger. *2750
12:30 and there was a g' cry in Egypt; 1419
14:31 Israel saw that g' work which the "
18:22 every g' matter they shall bring "
29:20 and upon the g' toe of their right foot, "
32:10 I will make of thee a g' nation. 1419
11 of Egypt with g' power, and with "
21 brought so g' a sin upon them? "
30 Ye have sinned a g' sin: and now "
31 this people have sinned a g' sin, "
Le 8:23 upon the g' toe of his right foot, "
24 upon the g' toes of their right feet: "
11:17 and the cormorant, and the g' owl, 3244
14:14 upon the g' toe of his right foot: "
17 his right hand, and upon the g' toe "
25 upon the g' toe of his right foot: "
28 upon the g' toe of his right foot, "
Nu 11:33 the people with a very g' plague. 7227
13:28 walled, and very g': and moreover 1419
32 we saw in it are men of a g' stature. "
14:17 let the power of my Lord be g', 1431
18 of g' mercy, forgiving iniquity †‡7227
22:17 promote thee unto very g' honour, "
23:24 people shall rise up as a g' lion, *3833
24: 9 down as a lion, and as a g' lion: * "
11 to promote thee unto g' honour; "
32: 1 of Gad had a very g' multitude 6099
34: 6 have the g' sea for a border: 1419
7 from the g' sea ye shall point "
De 1: 7 the g' river, the river Euphrates. "
17 hear the small as well as the g'; "
19 all that g' and terrible wilderness, "
28 the cities are g' and walled up to "
2: 7 walking through this g' wilderness: "
10 a people g', and many, and tall, "
21 A people g', and many, and tall, "
3: 5 beside unwalled towns a g' many. 3966
4: 6 Surely this g' nation is a wise and 1419
7 For what nation is there so g', who "
8 And what nation is there so g', that "
32 any such thing as this g' thing is, "
34 and by g' terrors, according to all "
36 earth he shewed thee his g' fire; "
5:22 with a g' voice: and he added no "
25 for this g' fire will consume us: if "
6:10 to give thee g' and goodly cities, "
22 wonders, g' and sore, upon Egypt, "
7:19 g' temptations which thine eyes "
8:15 that g' and terrible wilderness, "
9: 1 cities g' and fenced up to heaven, "
2 A people g' and tall, the children "
10:17 a g' God, a mighty, and a terrible, "
21 thee these g' and terrible things, "
11: 7 eyes have seen all the g' acts of the "
14:16 and the g' owl, and the swan, 3244
18:16 let me see this g' fire any more 1419
25:13 bag divers weights, a g' and a small. "
14 divers measures, a g' and a small. "
26: 5 nation, g', mighty, and populous: "
8 with g' terribleness, and with signs, "
27: 2 thou shalt set thee up g' stones, "
28:59 even g' plagues, and of long "
29: 3 The g' temptations which thine "
3 the signs, and those g' miracles: "
24 meaneth the heat of this g' anger? "
28 and in g' indignation, and cast "
34:12 in all the g' terror which Moses "
Jos 1: 4 even unto the g' river, the river "
4 unto the g' sea toward the going "
6: 5 people shall shout with a g' shout; "
20 people shouted with a g' shout, "
7: 9 what wilt thou do unto thy g' name? "
26 raised over him a g' heap of stones "
8:29 raise thereon a g' heap of stones, "
9: 1 the g' sea over against Lebanon, "
10: 2 Gibeon was a g' city, as one of "
10 slew them with a g' slaughter at "
11 the Lord cast down g' stones from "
18 Roll g' stones upon the mouth of "
20 them with a very g' slaughter, "
27 laid g' stones in the cave's mouth, "
11: 8 chased them unto g' Zidon, and 7227
14:12 that the cities were g' and fenced: 1419
15 a g' man among the Anakims. * "
15:12 border was to the g' sea, and the "
47 and the g' sea, and the border "
17:14 I am a g' people, forasmuch as 7227
15 If thou be a g' people, then get thee "
17 saying, Thou art a g' people, "
17 and hast g' power: thou shalt not 1419
19:28 and Kanah, even unto g' Zidon; 7227
22:10 by Jordan, a g' altar to see to. 1419
23: 4 even unto the g' sea westward. "
9 before you g' nations and strong: "
24:17 which did those g' signs in our "
26 and took a g' stone, and set it up "
J'g 1: 6 cut off his thumbs and his g' toes. "
7 their thumbs and their g' toes cut "
2: 7 who had seen all the g' works of 1419
5:15 there were g' thoughts of heart. "
16 there were g' searchings of heart. "
11:33 vineyards, with a very g' slaughter. "
12: 2 I and my people were at g' strife 3966
15: 8 hip and thigh with a g' slaughter: 1419
18 hast given this g' deliverance into "
16: 5 see wherein his g' strength lieth, "
6 thee, wherein thy g' strength lieth, "
15 me wherein thy g' strength lieth. "
23 to offer a g' sacrifice unto Dagon "
20:38 that they should make a g' flame 7235
21: 5 For they had made a g' oath 1419
1Sa 2:17 men was very g' before the Lord: "
4: 5 all Israel shouted with a g' shout, "
6 the noise of this g' shout in the "
10 and there was a very g' slaughter; "
17 there hath been also a g' slaughter "
5: 9 city with a very g' destruction: "
9 of the city, both small and g', "
6: 9 then he hath done us this g' evil: "
14 where there was a g' stone: and "
15 and put them on the g' stone: and "
18 even unto the g' stone of Abel, "
19 of the people with a g' slaughter. "
7:10 Lord thundered with a g' thunder "
12:16 stand and see this g' thing, which "
17 see that your wickedness is g', 7227
22 his people for his g' name's sake: 1419
24 how g' things he hath done for you. 1431
14:15 so it was a very g' trembling. 430
20 there was a very g' discomfiture. 1419
33 roll a g' stone unto me this day. "
45 who hath wrought this g' salvation "
15:22 Hath the Lord as g' delight in burnt

1Sa 17:25 king will enrich him with g' riches, 1419
19: 5 Lord wrought a g' salvation for all "
8 and slew them with a g' slaughter; "
22 came to a g' well that is in Sechu: "
20: 2 will do nothing either g' or small, "
23: 5 and smote them with a g' slaughter, "
25: 2 and the man was very g', and he had "
26:13 a g' space being between them: 7227
25 thou shalt both do g' things, and *
30: 2 slew not any, either g' or small, 1419
16 because of all the g' spoil that they "
19 to them, neither small nor g', "
2Sa 3:22 brought in a g' spoil with them: 7227
38 and a g' man fallen this day in 1419
5:10 David went on, and grew g', and * "
7: 9 and have made thee a g' name, like "
9 like unto the name of the g' men "
19 house for a g' while to come. 7350
21 hast done all these g' things, to *1420
22 Wherefore thou art g', O Lord 1431
23 to do for you g' things and terrible,1420
12:14 thou hast given g' occasion to the 5006
30 spoil of the city in g' abundance, *3966
18: 7 and there was there a g' slaughter 1419
9 under the thick boughs of a g' oak, "
17 cast him into a g' pit in the wood, "
17 and laid a very g' heap of stones "
29 I saw a g' tumult, but I knew not "
19:32 for he was a very g' man. "
20: 8 they were at the g' stone which is "
21:20 Gath, where was a man of g' stature, "
22:36 thy gentleness hath made me g'. 7235
23:10 wrought a g' victory that day; 1419
12 and the Lord wrought a g' victory. "
24:14 I am in a g' strait: let us all 3966
14 for his mercies are g': and let me 7227
1Ki 1:40 and rejoiced with g' joy, so that 1419
3: 4 for that was the g' high place: "
6 servant David my father g' mercy, "
6 hast kept for him this g' kindness, "
8 a g' people, that cannot be 7227
9 to judge this thy so g' a people? 3515
4:13 threescore g' cities with walls and1419
5: 7 a wise son over this g' people. 7227
17 and they brought g' stones, costly 1419
7: 9 on the outside toward the g' court. "
10 even g' stones, stones of ten cubits, "
12 the g' court round about was with "
8:42 they shall hear of thy g' name, "
65 with him, a g' congregation, from "
10: 2 to Jerusalem with a very g' train, 3515
10 and of spices very g' store, and 7235
11 in from Ophir g' plenty of almug 3966
18 king made a g' throne of ivory, 1419
11:19 And Hadad found g' favour in the3966
18:32 g' as would contain two measures 1004
45 and wind, and there was a g' rain.1419
19: 7 the journey is too g' for thee. 7227
11 and a g' and strong wind rent the 1419
20:13 thou seen all this g' multitude? 1419
21 slew the Syrians with a g' slaughter."
28 deliver all this g' multitude into "
22:31 Fight neither with small nor g', "
2Ki 3:27 was g' indignation against Israel: "
4: 8 where was a g' woman; and she "
38 Set on the g' pot, and seethe "
5: 1 was a g' man with his master, and "
13 had bid thee do some g' thing, "
6:14 and chariots, and a g' host: and 3515
23 And he prepared g' provision for 1419
25 there was a g' famine in Samaria: "
7: 6 horses, even the noise of a g' host: "
8: 4 the g' things that Elisha hath done."
13 that he should do this g' thing? "
10: 6 were with the g' men of the city, "
11 all his g' men, and his kinsfolks, "
19 I have a g' sacrifice to do to Baal; "
16:15 Upon the g' altar burn the morning"
17:21 Lord, and made them sin a g' sin. "
36 of the land of Egypt with g' power "
18:17 with a g' host against Jerusalem. 3515
19 Thus saith the g' king, the king 1419
28 Hear the word of the g' king, "
22:13 for g' is the wrath of the Lord "
23: 2 all the people, both small and g': "
26 from the fierceness of his g' wrath, "
25: 9 every g' man's house burnt he "
26 all the people, both small and g', "
1Ch 11:14 saved them by a g' deliverance. "
23 slew an Egyptian, a man of g' stature, "
12:22 until it was a g' host, like the 1419
16:25 For g' is the Lord, and greatly to be"
17: 8 like the name of the g' men that "
17 house for a g' while to come, 7350
19 making known all these g' things.1420
20: 6 where was a man of g' stature, "
21:13 I am in a g' strait: let me fall 3966
13 Lord; for very g' are his mercies: 7227
22: 8 hast made g' wars: thou shalt not1419
25: 8 ward, as well the small as the g', "
26:13 lots, as well the small as the g', "
29: 1 and the work is g': for the palace is "
9 the king also rejoiced with g' joy. "
12 and in thine hand it is to make g', 1431
22 Lord on that day with g' gladness.1419
2Ch 1: 8 hast shewed g' mercy unto David "
10 this thy people, that is so g'? "
2: 5 the house which I build is g': "
5 for g' is our God above all gods. "
9 about to build shall be wonderful g'."
4: 9 and the g' court, and doors for the "
18 all these vessels in g' abundance: 3966
6:32 for thy g' name's sake, and thy 1419
7: 8 a very g' congregation, from the "
9: 1 with a very g' company, and 3515
9 and of spices g' abundance, and *3966

2Ch 9:17 the king made a g' throne of ivory,1419
13: 8 and ye be a g' multitude, and there7227
17 slew them with a g' slaughter: "
15: 5 but g' vexations were upon all the "
13 put to death, whether small or g',1419
16:12 until his disease was exceeding g': "
14 made a very g' burning for him. 1419
17:12 And Jehoshaphat waxed g' 1432
18:30 Fight ye not with small or g', 1419
20:12 this g' company that cometh 7227
15 by reason of this g' multitude; for "
21: 3 their father gave them g' gifts of "
14 a g' plague will the Lord smite 1419
15 shalt have g' sickness by disease 7227
24:24 the Lord delivered a very g' host 7230
25 (for they left him in g' diseases,) 7227
25:10 they returned home in g' anger. *2750
26:15 shoot arrows and g' stones withal.1419
28: 5 a g' multitude of them captives, "
5 who smote him with a g' slaughter."
13 for our trespass is g', and there is 7227
30:13 month, a very g' congregation. 7230
21 bread seven days with g' gladness:1419
24 and a g' number of priests 7230
26 So there was g' joy in Jerusalem: 1419
31:10 and that which is left is this g' store. "
15 as well to the g' as to the small: 1419
33:14 and raised it up a very g' height, and "
34:21 for g' is the wrath of the Lord 1419
30 all the people, g' and small: and "
36:18 g' and small, and the treasures of "
Ezr 3:11 the people shouted with a g' shout, "
4:10 the g' and noble Asnapper brought7229
5: 8 to the house of the g' God, which "
8 which is builded with g' stones, 1560
11 which a g' king of Israel builded 7229
6: 4 With three rows of g' stones, and 1560
9: 7 in a g' trespass unto this day; *1419
13 and for our g' trespass, seeing that "
10: 1 a very g' congregation of men and 7227
9 of this matter, and for the g' rain. "
Ne 1: 3 are in g' affliction and reproach: 1419
5 the g' and terrible God, that keepeth"
10 thou hast redeemed by thy g' power,"
3:27 against the g' tower that lieth out, "
4: 1 took g' indignation, and mocked 7235
14 the Lord, which is g' and terrible, 1419
19 The work is g' and large, and we 7235
5: 1 there was a g' cry of the people 1419
7 I set a g' assembly against them. "
6: 3 I am doing a g' work, so that I "
7: 4 Now the city was large and g': * "
8: 6 Ezra blessed the Lord, the g' God. "
12 to make g' mirth, because they had"
17 And there was very g' gladness. "
9:17 slow to anger, and of g' kindness,††7227
18 and had wrought g' provocations;1419
25 themselves in thy g' goodness. "
26 and they wrought g' provocations. "
31 thy g' mercies' sake thou didst *7227
32 our God, the g', the mighty, and 1419
35 and in thy g' goodness that thou 7227
37 pleasure, and we are in g' distress.1419
11:14 the son of one of the g' men. * "
12:31 appointed two g' companies of "
43 they offered g' sacrifices, and "
43 God made them rejoice with g' joy: "
13: 5 had prepared for him a g' chamber, "
27 to do all this g' evil, to transgress "
Es 1: 5 the palace, both unto g' and small, "
20 all his empire, (for it is g',) all the 7227
20 honour, both to g' and small. 1419
2:18 the king made a g' feast unto all "
4: 3 was g' mourning among the Jews, "
8:15 with the g' crown of gold, and with "
9: 4 g' in the king's house, and his fame"
10: 3 g' among the Jews, and accepted "
Job 1: 3 a very g' household; so that this 7227
19 a g' wind from the wilderness, 1419
2:13 saw that his grief was very g'. 1431
3:19 The small and g' are there; and 1419
5: 9 doeth g' things and unsearchable; "
25 also that thy seed shall be g', and 7227
9:10 Which doeth g' things past 1419
22: 5 Is not thy wickedness g'? and 7227
23: 6 against me with his g' power? * "
30:18 By the g' force of my disease "
31:25 because my wealth was g', "
34 Did I fear a g' multitude, or did "
32: 9 G' men are not always wise: "
35:15 knoweth it not in g' extremity: *3966
36:18 a g' ransom cannot deliver thee. *7227
26 God is g', and we know him not, 7689
37: 5 g' things doeth he, which we 1419
6 small rain, and of the g' rain of *4306
38:21 the number of thy days is g'? 7227
39:11 him, because his strength is g'? "
Ps 14: 5 There were they in g' fear: for God 6343
18:35 thy gentleness hath made me g' 7235
50 G' deliverance giveth he to his 1431
19:11 keeping of them there is g' reward.7227
13 innocent from the g' transgression."
21: 5 His glory is g' in thy salvation: 1419
22:25 be of thee in the g' congregation: 7227
25:11 pardon mine iniquity; for it is g'. "
31:19 how g' is thy goodness, which thou "
32: 6 in the floods of g' waters they shall "
33:17 he deliver any by his g' strength. 7230
35:18 thee thanks in the g' congregation:7227
36: 6 is like the g' mountains; * 410
6 thy judgments are a g' deep: 7227
37:35 have seen the wicked in g' power, "
40: 9 preached righteousness in the g' 7227
10 thy truth from the g' congregation. "
47: 2 he is a g' king over all the earth, 1419
48: 1 G' is the Lord, and greatly to be "

Ps 48: 2 the north, the city of the g' King. 7227
53: 5 were they in g' fear, where no fear was: "
57:10 thy mercy is g' unto the heavens, 1419
58: 6 break out the g' teeth of the young 4459
68:11 g' was the company of those that 7227
71:19 who hast done g' things: O God, 1419
20 shewed me g' and sore troubles, 7229
76: 1 known: his name is g' in Israel. 1419
77:13 who is so g' a God as our God? "
19 the sea, thy path in the g' waters, 7227
78:15 drink as out of the g' depths. * "
71 following the ewes g' with young†‡
80: 5 tears to drink in g' measure. *7991
86:10 thou art g', and doest wondrous 1419
13 g' is thy mercy toward me: and "
92: 5 how g' are thy works! and thy 1431
95: 3 the Lord is a g' God, and a g' King 1419
96: 4 the Lord is g', and greatly to be "
99: 2 The Lord is g' in Zion; and he is "
3 praise thy g' and terrible name; "
103:11 g' is his mercy toward them that 1396
104: 1 thou art very g'; thou art clothed 1431
25 So is this g' and wide sea, wherein 1419
25 innumerable, both small and g' "
106:21 which had done g' things in Egypt; "
107:23 that do business in g' waters; 7227
108: 4 thy mercy is g' above the heavens: 1419
111: 2 The works of the Lord are g', "
115:13 fear the Lord, both small and g'. "
117: 2 merciful kindness is g' toward us: 1396
119:156 G' are thy tender mercies, O 7227
162 word, as one that findeth g' spoil. "
165 G' peace have they which love thy"
126: 2 Lord hath done g' things for them. 1431
3 Lord hath done g' things for us; "
131: 1 do I exercise myself in g' matters, 1419
135: 5 I know that the Lord is g', and "
10 Who smote g' nations, and slew *7227
136: 4 him who alone doeth g' wonders: 1419
7 To him that made g' lights: for his "
17 To him which smote g' kings: for "
138: 5 for g' is the glory of the Lord. "
139:17 O God! how g' is the sum of them! 6105
144: 7 deliver me out of g' waters, from 7227
145: 3 G' is the Lord, and greatly to be 1419
7 memory of thy g' goodness, and 7227
8 slow to anger, and of g' mercy. 1419
147: 5 G' is our Lord, and of...power: "
5 is our Lord, and of g' power: his *7227
Pr 13: 7 himself poor, yet hath g' riches. "
14:29 to wrath is of g' understanding: "
15:16 Lord than g' treasure and trouble "
16: 8 than g' revenues without right. 7230
18: 9 brother to him that is a g' waster. *1167
16 and bringeth him before g' men. 1419
19:19 A man of g' wrath shall suffer "
22: 1 rather to be chosen than g' riches, 7227
25: 6 stand not in the place of g' men: 1419
26:10 The g' God that formed all things *7227
28:12 men do rejoice, there is g' glory: "
16 is also a g' oppressor: but he that "
Ec 1:16 I am come to g' estate, and have 1431
16 heart had g' experience of wisdom 7235
2: 4 I made me g' works; I builded me 1431
7 house; also I had g' possessions of 7235
7 possessions of g' and small cattle *1241
9 I was g', and increased more than 1431
21 This also is vanity and a g' evil 7227
8: 6 the misery of man is g' upon him. "
9:13 the sun, and it seemed g' unto me: 1419
14 there came a g' king against it, and "
14 and built g' bulwarks against it: "
10: 4 for yielding pacifieth g' offences. "
6 Folly is set in g' dignity, and the 7227
Ca 2: 3 down under his shadow with g' delight,
Isa 2: 9 and the g' man humbleth himself:
5: 9 g' and fair, without inhabitant: 1419
6:12 and there be a g' forsaking in the *7227
8: 1 Take thee a g' roll, and write in it 1419
9: 2 in darkness have seen a g' light: "
12: 6 for g' is the Holy One of Israel "
13: 4 mountains, like as of a g' people; 7227
16:14 with all that g' multitude; and the "
19:20 send them a saviour, and a g' one, * "
23: 3 And by g' waters the seed of Sihor, "
27: 1 his sore and g' and strong sword 1419
13 that the g' trumpet shall be blown, "
29: 6 and with earthquake, and g' noise, "
30:25 in the day of the g' slaughter, 7227
32: 2 the shadow of a g' rock in a weary 3515
33:23 is the prey of a g' spoil divided; 4766
34: 6 g' slaughter in the land of Idumea. 1419
15 shall the g' owl make her nest, *7091
36: 2 King Hezekiah with a g' army. 3515
4 the g' king, the king of Assyria, 1419
13 Hear ye the words of the g' king, "
38:17 for peace I had g' bitterness:
47: 9 for the g' abundance of thine 3966
51:10 the sea, the waters of the g' deep; 7227
53:12 divide him a portion with the g', "
54: 7 with g' mercies will I gather thee. 1419
13 and g' shall be the peace of thy 7227
63: 7 the g' goodness toward the house "
Jer 4: 6 the north, and a g' destruction. 1419
5: 5 me unto the g' men, and will speak "
27 therefore they are become g', and 1431
6: 1 of the north, and g' destruction. 1419
22 and a g' nation shall be raised "
10: 6 Lord; thou art g', and thy name is g' "
22 and a g' commotion out of the north "
11:16 with the noise of a g' tumult he "
13: 9 and the g' pride of Jerusalem. 7227
14:17 people is broken with a g' breach, 1419
16: 6 the g' and the small shall die in "
10 pronounced all this g' evil against "
20:17 womb to be always g' with me. 2030

Jer 21: 5 and in fury, and in g' wrath. 1419
6 they shall die of a g' pestilence. "
22: 8 Lord done thus unto this g' city? "
25:14 g' kings shall serve themselves of "
32 a g' whirlwind shall be raised up "
26:19 procure g' evil against our souls. "
27: 5 g' power and by my outstretched "
7 many nations and g' kings shall "
28: 8 against g' kingdoms, of war, and of "
30: 7 Alas! for that day is g', so that "
31: 8 a g' company shall return thither. "
32:17 heaven and the earth by thy g' "
18 the G', the Mighty God, the Lord "
19 G' in counsel, and mighty in work: "
21 out arm, and with g' terror; "
37 and in my fury, and in g' wrath; "
42 all this g' evil upon this people, "
33: 3 shew thee g' and mighty things, "
36: 7 for g' is the anger and the fury "
41:12 the g' waters that are in Gibeon. 7227
43: 9 Take g' stones in thine hand, and 1419
44: 7 ye this g' evil against your souls, "
15 a g' multitude, even all the people "
26 I have sworn by my g' name, saith "
45: 5 seekest thou g' things for thyself? "
48: 3 spoiling and g' destruction. "
50: 9 an assembly of g' nations from the "
22 in the land, and of g' destruction. "
41 and a g' nation, and many kings "
51:54 g' destruction from the land of the "
55 destroyed out of her the g' voice; "
55 her waves do roar like g' waters. *7227
52:13 all the houses of the g' men, 1419
La 1: 1 that was g' among the nations, 7227
3 and because of g' servitude: 7230
2:13 thy breach is g' like the sea: who 1419
3:23 morning: g' is thy faithfulness. 7227
Eze 1: 4 came out of the north, a g' cloud, 1419
24 like the noise of g' waters, as the 7227
3:12 behind me a voice of a g' rushing, 1419
13 them, and a noise of a g' rushing. "
8: 6 the g' abominations that the house "
9: 9 Judah is exceeding g', and the land "
13:11 O g' hailstones, shall fall; and a 417
13 g' hailstones in my fury to consume "
16: 7 thou hast increased and waxen g', 1431
26 thy neighbours, g' of flesh; and 1432
17: 3 saith the Lord God; A g' eagle 1419
3 eagle with g' wings, full of "
5 he placed it by g' waters, and set *7227
7 There was also another g' eagle 1419
7 with g' wings and many feathers, "
8 in a good soil by g' waters, that *7227
9 even without g' power or many ‡1419
17 mighty army and g' company 7227
21:14 it is the sword of the g' men that 1419
23:23 g' lords and renowned, all of them *7991
24: 9 will even make the pile for fire g'. 1431
12 her g' scum went not forth out of 7227
25:17 I will execute g' vengeance upon 1419
26:19 and g' waters shall cover thee; 7227
27:26 have brought thee into g' waters: "
28: 5 By thy g' wisdom and by thy 7230
29: 3 g' dragon that lieth in the midst 1419
18 to serve a g' service against Tyrus: "
30: 4 g' pain shall be in Ethiopia, when* "
9 g' pain shall come upon them, as* "
16 Sin shall have g' pain, and No 2342
31: 4 The waters made him g', the *1431
6 his shadow dwelt all g' nations. 7227
7 for his root was by g' waters. * "
15 the g' waters were stayed: and I "
32:13 from beside the g' waters; * "
36:23 I will sanctify my g' name, which 1419
37:10 their feet, an exceeding g' army. "
38: 4 a g' company with bucklers and 7227
13 and goods, to take a g' spoil? 1419
15 a g' company, and a mighty army: "
19 there shall be a g' shaking in the "
22 g' hailstones, fire, and brimstone. 417
39:17 a g' sacrifice upon the mountains 1419
41: 8 were a full reed of six g' cubits. 679
47: 9 shall be a very g' multitude of fish, 7227
10 as the fish of the g' sea, exceeding 1419
15 from the g' sea, the way of Hethlon, "
19 in Kadesh, the river to the g' sea. "
20 the g' sea from the border, till a "
48:28 and to the river toward the g' sea. "
Da 2: 6 and rewards and g' honour: 7690
31 and behold a g' image. "
31 This g' image, whose brightness *7229
35 became a g' mountain, and filled "
45 the g' God hath made known to "
48 the king made Daniel a g' man, 7236
48 and gave him many g' gifts, 7260
4: 3 How g' are his signs! and how "
10 and the height thereof was g'. 7690
30 Is not this g' Babylon, that I 7227
5: 1 the king made a g' feast to a "
7: 2 the heavens strove upon the g' sea. "
3 And four g' beasts came up from 7260
7 and it had g' iron teeth: "
8 and a mouth speaking g' things. "
11 because of the voice of the g' words "
17 These g' beasts, which are four, "
20 a mouth that spake very g' things, "
25 And he shall speak g' words *
8: 4 to his will, and became g'. *1431
8 the he goat waxed very g': and * "
8 the g' horn was broken; 1419
9 exceeding g', toward the south, 1431
10 And it waxed g', even to the host "
21 the g' horn that is between his 1419
9: 4 the g' and dreadful God, keeping "
12 by bringing upon us a g' evil: "
18 but for thy g' mercies. 7227

Da 10: 4 I was by the side of the g' river, 1419
7 a g' quaking fell upon them, so "
8 this g' vision, and there remained "
11: 3 that shall rule with g' dominion, 7227
5 dominion shall be a g' dominion. "
10 a multitude of g' forces: and one "
11 he shall set forth a g' multitude; "
13 with a g' army and with much 1419
25 with a g' army; and the king of the "
25 with a very g' and mighty army; "
28 return into his land with g' riches; "
44 go forth with g' fury to destroy, "
12: 1 the g' prince which standeth for "
Ho 1: 2 hath committed g' whoredom, "
11 for g' shall be the day of Jezreel. 1419
8:12 written to him the g' things of *7239
9: 7 thine iniquity, and the g' hatred. 7227
10:15 because of your g' wickedness: 7451
13: 5 in the land of g' drought. 8514
Joe 1: 6 hath the cheek teeth of a g' lion. 3833
2: 2 a g' people and a strong; there 7227
11 for his camp is very g': for he is "
11 of the Lord is g' and very terrible; 1419
13 to anger, and of g' kindness, ††7227
20 because he hath done g' things. 1431
21 for the Lord will do g' things. "
25 g' army which I sent among you. 1419
31 the g' and the terrible day of the "
3:13 for their wickedness is g'. 7227
Am 3: 9 g' tumults in the midst thereof, "
15 the g' houses shall have an end, "
6: 2 go ye to Hamath the g': then go "
11 and he will smite the g' house 1419
7: 4 it devoured the g' deep, and did 7227
8: 5 and the shekel g', and falsifying 1431
Jon 1: 2 go to Nineveh, that g' city, and cry 1419
4 the Lord sent out a g' wind into "
12 this g' tempest is upon you. "
17 prepared a g' fish to swallow up "
3: 2 go unto Nineveh, that g' city, and "
3 g' city of three days' journey. "
4: 2 to anger, and of g' kindness, ††7227
11 spare Nineveh, that g' city, 1419
Mic 2:12 they shall make g' noise by reason of
5: 4 now shall he be g' unto the ends 1431
7: 3 and the g' man, he uttereth his 1419
Na 1: 3 and g' in power, and will not 1431
3: 3 and a g' number of carcases; and 3514
10 her g' men were bound in chains. 1419
17 as the g' grasshoppers, which *1462
Hab 3:15 through the heap of g' waters. *7227
Zep 1:10 and a g' crashing from the hills. 1419
14 The g' day of the Lord is near, "
Zec 1:14 and for Zion with a g' jealousy. "
4: 7 Who art thou, O g' mountain? "
7:12 came a g' wrath from the Lord "
8: 2 for Zion with g' jealousy, and I "
2 I was jealous for her with g' fury. "
9:17 how g' is his goodness, and how g' is
12:11 In that day shall there be a g' 1431
14: 4 a very g' valley; and half of the 1419
13 a g' tumult from the Lord shall 7227
14 and apparel, in g' abundance. 3966
Mal 1:11 shall be g' among the Gentiles; 1419
11 shall be g' among the heathen, "
14 for I am a g' King, saith the Lord "
4: 5 coming of the g' and dreadful day "
M't 2:10 rejoiced with exceeding g' joy. 3173
18 and g' mourning, Rachel weeping 4183
4:16 which sat in darkness saw g' light; 3173
25 him g' multitudes of people from 4183
5:12 for g' is your reward in heaven: "
19 shall be called g' in the kingdom 3173
35 for it is the city of the g' King. "
6:23 how g' is that darkness! 4214
7:27 and g' was the fall of it. 3173
8: 1 g' multitudes followed him. 4183
10 I have not found so g' faith, no, 5118
18 Jesus saw g' multitudes about 4183
24 arose a g' tempest in the sea, 3173
26 the sea; and there was a g' calm. "
12:15 and g' multitudes followed him, *4183
13: 2 And g' multitudes were gathered "
46 found one pearl of g' price, went 4186
14:14 and saw a g' multitude, and was 4183
15:28 O woman, g' is thy faith: be it 3173
30 And g' multitudes came unto him, 4183
33 as to fill so g' a multitude? 5118
19: 2 And g' multitudes followed him; 4183
22 sorrowful: for he had g' possessions. "
20:25 that are g' exercise authority 3171
26 whosoever will be g' among you, 3173
29 a g' multitude followed him. 4183
21: 8 And a very g' multitude spread *4118
22:36 which is the g' commandment in 3173
38 is the first and g' commandment. "
24:21 then shall be g' tribulation, such "
24 shall shew g' signs and wonders; "
30 of heaven with power and g' glory. 4183
31 with a g' sound of a trumpet, and 3173
26:47 and with him a g' multitude with 4183
27:60 he rolled a g' stone to the door 3173
28: 2 there was a g' earthquake: for the "
8 with fear and g' joy; and did run "
M'r 1:35 rising up a g' while before day, 3029
3: 7 and a g' multitude from Galilee 4183
8 a g' multitude, when they had "
8 heard what g' things he did 3745
4: 1 gathered unto him a g' multitude, 4183
32 and shooteth out g' branches; so 3173
37 there arose a g' storm of wind, "
39 ceased; and there was a g' calm. "
5:11 a g' herd of swine feeding. "
19 tell them how g' things the Lord 3745
20 how g' things Jesus had done for "
42 astonished with a g' astonishment. 3173

M'r 7:36 so much the more a g' deal they 3123
8: 1 the multitude being very g', and 3827
9:14 saw a g' multitude about them, 4183
10:22 grieved: for he had g' possessions. "
42 their g' ones exercise authority 3173
43 whosoever will be g' among you, "
46 his disciples and a g' number of 2425
48 but he cried the more a g' deal, 4183
13: 2 Seest thou these g' buildings? 3173
26 clouds with g' power and glory. 4183
14:43 and with him a g' multitude * "
16: 4 rolled away: for it was very g'. 3173
Lu 1:15 For he shall be g' in the sight of "
32 He shall be g', and shall be called "
49 hath done to me g' things; and 3167
58 had shewed g' mercy upon her; *3170
2: 5 his espoused wife, being g' with child.
10 I bring you good tidings of g' joy, 3173
36 she was of a g' age, and had lived 4183
4:25 when g' famine was throughout 3173
38 was taken with a g' fever; and "
5: 6 inclosed a g' multitude of fishes: 4183
15 and g' multitudes came together "
29 Levi made him a g' feast in his 3173
29 and there was a g' company 4183
6:17 a g' multitude of people out of all "
23 your reward is g' in heaven: for "
35 and your reward shall be g', and "
49 and the ruin of that house was g'. 3173
7: 9 I have not found so g' faith, no, 5118
16 That a g' prophet is risen up 3173
8:37 they were taken with g' fear: and "
39 how g' things God hath done 3745
39 how g' things Jesus had done unto "
9:48 you all, the same shall be g'. 3173
10: 2 The harvest truly is g', but the *4183
13 they had a g' while ago repented, *3819
13:19 and waxed a g' tree; and the *3173
14:16 A certain man made a g' supper, "
25 there went g' multitudes with him: 4183
32 while the other is yet a g' way off, "
15:20 when he was yet a g' way off, *3112
16:26 there is a g' gulf fixed: so that 3173
21:11 g' earthquakes shall be in divers "
11 and g' signs shall there be "
23 shall be g' distress in the land, "
27 cloud with power and g' glory. 4183
22:44 as it were g' drops of blood
23:27 a g' company of people, and of 4183
24:52 to Jerusalem with g' joy: 3173
Joh 5: 3 a g' multitude of impotent folk, *4183
6: 2 And a g' multitude followed him, "
5 saw a g' company come unto him, "
18 by reason of a g' wind that blew. 3173
7:37 that g' day of the feast, Jesus "
21:11 the net to land full of g' fishes, "
Ac 2:20 before that g' and notable day of "
4:33 with g' power gave the apostles "
33 and g' grace was upon them all. "
5: 5 and g' fear came on all them that "
11 And g' fear came upon all the "
6: 7 and a g' company of the priests 4183
8 g' wonders and miracles among 3173
7:11 and Chanaan, and g' affliction: and "
8: 1 there was a g' persecution against "
2 and made g' lamentation over him. "
8 And there was g' joy in that city. * "
9 that himself was some g' one: "
10 This man is the g' power of God. "
27 an eunuch of g' authority under "
9:16 how g' things he must suffer for *3745
10:11 as it had been a g' sheet knit at 3173
11: 5 as it had been a g' sheet, let down "
21 and a g' number believed, and 4183
28 that there should be g' dearth 3173
14: 1 a g' multitude both of the Jews 4183
15: 3 they caused g' joy unto all the 3173
16:26 there was a g' earthquake, so that "
17: 4 devout Greeks a g' multitude, and 4183
19:27 of the g' goddess Diana should be 3173
28 G' is Diana of the Ephesians. "
34 out, G' is Diana of the Ephesians. "
35 of the g' goddess Diana, and of the "
21:40 there was made a g' silence, he 4183
22: 6 shone from heaven a g' light round 2425
28 With a g' sum obtained I this 4183
23: 9 And there arose a g' cry: and the 3173
10 there arose a g' dissension, the 4183
14 bound ourselves under a g' curse, "
24: 2 by thee we enjoy g' quietness, *4183
7 with g' violence took him away * "
25:23 and Bernice, with g' pomp, and "
26:22 witnessing both to small and g', 3173
28: 6 after they had looked a g' while, *4183
29 g' reasoning among themselves. * "
Ro 9: 2 That I have g' heaviness and 3173
15:23 a g' desire these many years *1974
1Co 9:11 it is a g' thing if we shall reap 3173
16: 9 a g' door and effectual is opened "
2Co 1:10 delivered us from so g' a death, 5082
3:12 we use g' plainness of speech: 4183
7: 4 G' is my boldness of speech toward "
4 you, g' is my glorying of you: "
8: 2 How that in a g' trial of affliction* "
22 diligent, upon the g' confidence "
11:15 it is no g' thing if his ministers 3173
Eph 2: 4 for his g' love wherewith he loved 4183
5:32 This is a g' mystery: but I speak 3173
Col 2: 1 ye knew what g' conflict I have *2245
4:13 that he hath a g' zeal for you, *4183
1Th 2:17 to see your face with g' desire. "
1Ti 3:13 and g' boldness in the faith which "
16 g' is the mystery of godliness: 3173
6: 6 with contentment is g' gain. "
2Ti 2:20 But in a g' house there are not "
Tit 2:13 glorious appearing of the g' God "

Ph'm 7 have g' joy and consolation in *4183
Heb 2: 3 if we neglect so g' salvation; 5082
4:14 that we have a g' high priest, 3173
7: 4 consider how g' this man was, 4080
10:32 ye endured a g' fight of afflictions; 4183
35 hath g' recompence of reward. 3173
12: 1 with so g' a cloud of witnesses, 5118
13:20 that g' shepherd of the sheep, 3173
Jas 3: 4 which though they be so g', and 5082
5 member, and boasteth g' things. 3166
5 g' a matter a little fire kindleth! *2245
1Pe 3: 4 in the sight of God of g' price. 4185
2Pe 1: 4 g' and precious promises: 3176
2:18 speak g' swelling words of vanity 5246
3:10 shall pass away with a g' noise, "
Jude 6 unto the judgment of the g' day, 3173
16 mouth speaketh g' swelling words, 5246
Re 1:10 and heard behind me a g' voice, 3173
2:22 into g' tribulation, except they "
6: 4 was given unto him a g' sword. "
12 and, lo, there was a g' earthquake; "
15 kings of the earth, and the g' men, *3173
17 the g' day of his wrath is come; 3173
7: 9 and, lo, a g' multitude, which no 4183
14 which came out of g' tribulation, 3173
8: 8 as it were a g' mountain burning "
10 there fell a g' star from heaven, "
9: 2 as the smoke of a g' furnace; and "
14 are bound in the g' river Euphrates. "
11: 8 in the street of the g' city, which "
11 g' fear fell upon them which saw "
12 they heard a g' voice from heaven "
13 hour was there a g' earthquake, "
15 there were g' voices in heaven, "
17 hast taken to thee thy g' power, "
18 that fear thy name, small and g'; "
19 and an earthquake, and g' hail. "
12: 1 a g' wonder in heaven; a woman "
3 g' red dragon, having seven heads "
9 And the g' dragon was cast out, "
12 having g' wrath, because he "
14 two wings of a g' eagle, that she "
13: 2 and his seat, and g' authority. "
5 a mouth speaking g' things and "
13 he doeth g' wonders, so that he "
16 he causeth all, both small and g', "
14: 2 as the voice of a g' thunder: "
8 that g' city, because she made "
19 into the g' winepress of the wrath "
15: 1 g' and marvellous, seven angels "
3 G' and marvelous are thy works, "
16: 1 I heard a g' voice out of the temple "
9 men were scorched with g' heat, "
12 vial upon the g' river Euphrates; "
14 of that g' day of God Almighty. "
17 came a g' voice out of the temple "
18 there was a g' earthquake, such as "
18 mighty an earthquake, and so g'. "
19 the g' city was divided into three "
19 g' Babylon came in remembrance "
21 upon men a g' hail out of heaven, "
21 plague thereof was exceeding g'. "
17: 1 judgment of the g' whore that "
5 Mystery, Babylon The G', The "
6 I wondered with g' admiration. "
18 is that g' city, which reigneth over "
18: 1 from heaven, having g' power; "
2 Babylon the g' is fallen, is fallen, "
10 Alas, alas that g' city Babylon, that "
16 Alas, alas that g' city, that was "
17 so g' riches is come to nought. 5118
18 What city is like unto this g' 3173
19 Alas, alas that g' city, wherein "
21 took up a stone like a g' millstone, "
21 shall that g' city Babylon be thrown "
23 thy merchants were the g' men *3173
19: 1 I heard a g' voice of much people 3173
2 hath judged the g' whore, which "
5 that fear him, both small and g'. "
6 the voice of a g' multitude, and 4183
17 unto the supper of the g' God; 3173
18 free and bond, both small and g'. "
20: 1 and a g' chain in his hand. "
11 I saw a g' white throne, and him "
12 I saw the dead, small and g', "
21: 3 I heard a g' voice out of heaven "
10 spirit to a g' and high mountain, * "
10 and shewed me that g' city, "
12 had a wall g' and high, and had "

greater
Ge 1:16 the g' light to rule the day, and 1419
4:13 punishment is g' than I can bear. "
39: 9 none g' in this house than I; "
41:40 throne will I be g' than thou. 1431
48:19 shall be g' than he, and his seed "
Ex 18:11 the Lord is g' than all gods: 1419
Nu 14:12 make of thee a g' nation and "
De 1:28 The people is g' and taller than "
4:38 thee g' and mightier than thou art. "
7: 1 seven nations g' and mightier 7227
9: 1 nations g' and mightier than 1419
14 nation mightier and g' than they. 7227
11:23 ye shall possess g' nations and 1419
Jos 10: 2 because it was g' than Ai, and all "
1Sa 14:30 not been now a much g' slaughter *7235
2Sa 13:15 g' than the love wherewith he had 1419
16 g' than the other that thou didst * "
1Ki 1:37 and make his throne g' than thee "
47 and make his throne g' than thy "
1Ch 11: 9 So David waxed g' and...: for the 1980
9 and g': for the Lord of hosts was 1419
2Ch 3: 5 And the g' house he cieled with "
Es 9: 4 this man Mordecai waxed g' and "
4 this man Mordecai waxed...and g'. "
Job 33:12 thee, that God is g' than man. 7235
La 4: 6 people is g' than the punishment 1431
Eze 8: 6 thou shalt see g' abominations. *1419
13 shalt see g' abominations that * "
15 shalt see g' abominations than "
43:14 lesser settle even to the g' settle "
Da 11:13 a multitude g' than the former, 7227
Am 6: 2 their border g' than your border? "
Hag 2: 9 house shall be g' than the former, 1419
M't 11:11 hath not risen a g' than John the 3187
11 kingdom of heaven is g' than he. "
12: 6 place is one g' than the temple. "
41 behold, a g' than Jonas is here. 4119
42 behold, a g' than Solomon is here. "
23:14 ye shall receive the g' damnation. *4055
17 for whether is g', the gold, or the 3187
19 whether is g', the gift, or the "
M'r 4:32 becometh g' than all herbs, and "
12:31 none other commandment g' than "
40 these shall receive g' damnation. 4055
Lu 7:28 there is not a g' prophet than 3187
28 is g' than he. "
11:31 behold, a g' than Solomon is here. 4119
32 and, behold, a g' than Jonas is here. "
12:18 pull down my barns, and build g'; 3187
20:47 same shall receive g' damnation. 4055
22:27 For whether is g', he that sitteth 3187
Joh 1:50 thou shalt see g' things than these. "
4:12 Art thou g' than our father Jacob, "
5:20 g' works than these, that ye may "
36 But I have g' witness than that "
8:53 thou g' than our father Abraham, "
10:29 gave them me, is g' than all; and no "
13:16 The servant is not g' than his lord; "
16 neither he that is sent g' than he "
14:12 g' works than these shall he do; "
28 for my Father is g' than I. "
15:13 G' love hath no man than this, "
20 The servant is not g' than his "
19:11 me unto thee hath the g' sin. "
Ac 15:28 to lay upon you no g' burden than 4119
1Co 14: 5 for g' is he that prophesieth than 3187
15: 6 g' part remain unto this present, 4119
Heb 6:13 could swear by no g', he sware by 3187
16 for men verily swear by the g': "
9:11 a g' and more perfect tabernacle, "
11:26 reproach of Christ g' riches than "
Jas 3: 1 shall receive the g' condemnation. * "
2Pe 2:11 which are g' in power and might, "
1Jo 3:20 God is g' than our heart, and "
4: 4 because g' is he that is in you, than "
5: 9 of men, the witness of God is g': "
3Jo 4 I have no g' joy than to hear that 3186

greatest
1Ch 12:14 an hundred, and the g' over a 1419
29 the g' part of them had kept the 4768
Job 1: 3 was the g' of all the men of the 1419
Jer 6:13 the least even unto the g' of them "
8:10 the least even unto the g' is given "
31:34 least of them unto the g' of them, "
42: 1 the least even unto the g', came "
8 people from the least even to the g'. "
44:12 the least even unto the g', by the "
Jon 3: 5 the g' of them even to the least of "
M't 13:32 g' among herbs, and becometh *3187
18: 1 Who is the g' in the kingdom of "
4 the same is g' in the kingdom of "
23:11 But he that is g' among you shall "
M'r 9:34 themselves, who should be the g'. "
Lu 9:46 which of them should be g'. "
22:24 of them should be accounted the g'. "
26 but he that is g' among you, let * "
Ac 8:10 heed, from the least to the g', 3173
1Co 13:13 but the g' of these is charity. 3187
Heb 8:11 know me, from the least to the g'. 3173

greatly
Ge 3:16 I will g' multiply thy sorrow and
7:18 were increased g' upon the earth; 3966
19: 3 pressed upon them g'; and they "
24:35 Lord hath blessed my master g'; "
32: 7 Jacob was g' afraid and distressed: "
Ex 19:18 and the whole mount quaked g'. "
Nu 11:10 anger of the Lord was kindled g'; "
14:39 Israel: and the people mourned g'. "
De 15: 4 for the Lord shall g' bless thee *
17:17 neither shall he g' multiply to 3966
Jos 10: 2 they feared g', because Gibeon * "
J'g 2:15 and they were g' distressed. * "
6: 6 And Israel was g' impoverished * "
1Sa 11: 6 and his anger was kindled g'. "
15 all the men of Israel rejoiced g'. "
12:18 all the people g' feared the Lord "
16:21 he loved him g'; and he became "
17:11 they were dismayed, and g' afraid. "
28: 5 afraid, and his heart g' trembled. "
30: 6 And David was g' distressed; for "
2Sa 10: 5 because the men were g' ashamed: "
12: 5 anger was g' kindled against the "
24:10 have sinned g' in that I have done: "
1Ki 2:12 his kingdom was established g'. "
5: 7 of Solomon, that he rejoiced g'. "
18: 3 (Now Obadiah feared the Lord g': "
1Ch 4:38 house of their fathers increased g'. 7230
16:25 and g' to be praised: he also is *3966
19: 5 for the men were g' ashamed. "
21: 8 said unto God, I have sinned g', "
2Ch 25:10 was g' kindled against Judah, and "
33:12 and humbled himself g' before the "
Job 3:25 thing which I g' feared is come *
8: 7 thy latter end should g' increase. 3966
Ps 21: 1 salvation how g' shall he rejoice! "
28: 7 therefore my heart g' rejoiceth; and
38: 6 I am bowed down g'; I go 3966
45:11 So shall the king g' desire thy *
47: 9 belong unto God: he is g' exalted. 3966
48: 1 and g' to be praised in the city *3966
62: 2 defence; I shall not be g' moved. 7227
65: 9 thou g' enrichest it with the "
71:23 My lips shall g' rejoice when I
78:59 wroth, and g' abhorred Israel: 3966
89: 7 God is g' to be feared in the *7227
96: 4 and g' to be praised: he is to *3966
105:24 And he increased his people g'; "
107:38 so that they are multiplied g'; "
109:30 I will g' praise the Lord with my * "
112: 1 delighteth g' in his commandments. "
116:10 have I spoken: I was g' afflicted: "
119:51 have had me g' in derision: yet "
145: 3 the Lord, and g' to be praised; * "
Pr 23:24 father of the righteous shall g' rejoice:
Isa 42:17 they shall be g' ashamed, that ‡
Jer 3: 1 shall not that land be g' polluted?
4:10 surely thou hast g' deceived this
9:19 we are g' confounded, because we 3966
20:11 they shall be g' ashamed; for ‡ "
Eze 20:13 and my sabbaths they g' polluted:
25:12 vengeance, and hath g' offended,
Da 5: 9 was king Belshazzar g' troubled, 7690
9:23 for thou art g' beloved: therefore
10:11 man g' beloved, understand the word
19 O man g' beloved, fear not:
Ob 2 the heathen: thou art g' despised. 3966
Zep 1:14 it is near, and hasteth g', even "
Zec 9: 9 Rejoice g', O daughter of Zion; "
M't 27:14 that the governor marvelled g'. 3029
54 they feared g', saying, Truly this *4970
M'r 5:23 And besought him g', saying, My *4183
38 and them that wept and wailed g'. "
9:15 were g' amazed, and running to 1568
12:27 the living: ye therefore do g' err. 4183
Joh 3:29 rejoiceth g' because of the 5479
Ac 3:11 is called Solomon's, g' wondering. 1569
6: 7 multiplied in Jerusalem g'; *4970
1Co 16:12 g' desired him to come unto you *4183
Ph'p 1: 8 how g' I long after you all in the *1971
4:10 I rejoiced in the Lord g', that now 3171
1Th 3: 6 desiring g' to see us, as we also *1971
2Ti 1: 4 G' desiring to see thee, being * "
4:15 he hath g' withstood our words. 3029
1Pe 1: 6 Wherein ye g' rejoice, though now for
2Jo 4 I rejoiced g' that I found of thy 3029
3Jo 3 I rejoiced g', when the brethren "

greatness
Ex 15: 7 And in the g' of thine excellency 7230
16 by the g' of thine arm they 1419
Nu 14:19 unto the g' of thy mercy. 1433
De 3:24 shew thy servant thy g', and thy "
5:24 his glory and his g', and we "
9:26 redeemed through thy g', which "
11: 2 his g', his mighty hand, and his "
32: 3 Lord: ascribe ye g' unto our God. "
1Ch 17:19 hast thou done all this g', in 1420
21 a name of g' and terribleness, * "
29:11 Thine, O Lord, is the g', and "
2Ch 9: 6 the g' of thy wisdom was not 4768
24:27 and the g' of the burdens laid 7230
Ne 13:22 according to the g' of thy mercy. "
Es 10: 2 the g' of Mordecai, whereunto the 1420
Ps 66: 3 through the g' of thy power shall 7230
71:21 Thou shalt increase my g', and 1420
79:11 according to the g' of thy power 1433
145: 3 and his g' is unsearchable. 1420
6 acts: and I will declare thy g'. "
150: 2 according to his excellent g'. 1433
Pr 5:23 and in the g' of his folly he shall 7230
Isa 40:26 by the g' of his might, for that "
57:10 wearied in the g' of thy way; * "
63: 1 travelling in the g' of his strength? "
Jer 13:22 For the g' of thine iniquity are "
Eze 31: 2 Whom art thou like in thy g'? 1433
7 Thus was he fair in his g', in the "
18 in glory and in g' among the trees "
Da 4:22 for thy g' is grown, and reacheth 7238
7:27 and the g' of the kingdom under "
Eph 1:19 g' of his power to us-ward who 3174

great-owl See GREAT and OWL.

greaves
1Sa 17: 6 he had g' of brass upon his legs. 4697

Grecia See also GRECIANS; GREECE.
Da 8:21 the rough goat is the king of G': *3120
10:20 forth, lo, the prince of G' shall * "
11: 2 stir up all against the realm of G'. * "

Grecians See also GREEKS.
Joe 3: 6 have ye sold unto the G', that 3125
Ac 6: 1 arose a murmuring of the G' *1675
9:29 disputed against the G': but * "
11:20 spake unto the G', preaching * "

Greece See also GRECIA.
Zec 9:13 O Zion, against thy sons, O G', 3120
Ac 20: 2 exhortation, he came into G', 1671

greedily
Pr 21:26 He coveteth g' all the day long: 8378
Eze 22:12 and thou hast g' gained of thy
Jude 11 ran g' after the error of Balaam *1632

greediness
Eph 4:19 to work all uncleanness with g'. 4124

greedy
Ps 17:12 as a lion that is g' of his prey, 3700
Pr 1:19 every one that is g' of gain; 1214
15:27 He that is g' of gain troubleth his "
Isa 56:11 they are g' dogs which can 5794, 5315
1Ti 3: 3 no striker, not g' of filthy lucre; * 866
8 much wine, not g' of filthy lucre; 146

Greek See also GREEKS.
M'r 7:26 woman was a G', a Syrophenician 1674

Lu 23:38 of G', and Latin, and Hebrew, *1673
Joh 19:20 in Hebrew, and G', and Latin. 1676
Ac 16: 1 believed; but his father was a G': 1672
3 knew all that his father was a G'. "
21:37 Who said, Canst thou speak G'? 1676
Ro 1:16 the Jew first, and also to the G'. 1672
10:12 between the Jew and the G': for "
Ga 2: 3 who was with me, being a G', "
3:28 There is neither Jew nor G', there "
Col 3:11 there is neither G' nor Jew, "
Re 9:11 in the G' tongue hath his name 1673

Greeks See also GRECIANS.
Joh 12:20 there were certain G' among 1672
Ac 14: 1 Jews and also of the G' believed. "
17: 4 the devout G' a great multitude, "
12 women which were G', and of *1674
18: 4 persuaded the Jews and the G'. 1672
17 the G' took Sosthenes, the chief * "
19:10 the Lord Jesus, both Jews and G'. "
17 known to all the Jews and G' also "
20:21 to the Jews, and also to the G', "
21:28 brought G' also into the temple, "
Ro 1:14 I am debtor both to the G', and to "
1Co 1:22 and the G' seek after wisdom: "
23 and unto the G' foolishness; * "
24 which are called, both Jews and G'," "

green See also GREENISH.
Ge 1:30 have given every g' herb for meat:3418
9: 3 even as the g' herb have I given "
30:37 Jacob took him rods of g' poplar, *3892
Ex 10:15 there remained not any g' thing 3418
Le 2:14 of thy firstfruits g' ears of corn *
23:14 parched corn, nor g' ears, until *
De 12: 2 the hills, and under every g' tree: 7488
J'g 16: 7 seven g' withs that were never 3892
8 seven g' withs which had not been "
1Ki 14:23 high hill, and under every g' tree. 7488
2Ki 16: 4 the hills, and under every g' tree. "
17:10 high hill, and under every g' tree: "
19:26 and as the g' herb, as the grass on 3419
2Ch 28: 4 the hills, and under every g' tree. 7488
Es 1: 6 white, g', and blue, hangings, 3768
Job 8:16 He is g' before the sun, and his 7373
15:32 and his branch shall not be g'. 7488
39: 8 he searcheth after every g' thing. 3387
Ps 23: 2 me to lie down in g' pastures: 1877
37: 2 grass, and wither as the g' herb. 3418
35 himself like a g' bay tree. 7488
52: 8 am like a g' olive tree in the house "
Ca 1:16 yea, pleasant: also our bed is g'. "
2:13 fig tree putteth forth her g' figs, 6291
Isa 15: 6 grass faileth, there is no g' thing. 3418
37:27 and as the g' herb, as the grass 3419
57: 5 under every g' tree, slaying the 7488
Jer 2:20 under every g' tree thou wanderest, "
3: 6 under every g' tree, and there hath "
13 under every g' tree, and ye have "
11:16 A g' olive tree, fair, and of goodly "
17: 2 the g' trees upon the high hills. "
8 cometh, but her leaf shall be g'; "
Eze 6:13 under every g' tree, and under "
17:24 have dried up the g' tree, and 3892
20:47 shall devour every g' tree in thee, "
Ho 14: 8 him: I am like a g' fir tree. 7488
M'r 6:39 by companies upon the g' grass. 5515
Lu 23:31 they do these things in a g' tree, 5200
Re 8: 7 and all g' grass was burnt up. 5515
9: 4 neither any g' thing, neither any "

greenish
Le 13:49 if the plague be g' or reddish in 3422
14:37 hollow strakes, g' or reddish, which "

greenness
Job 8:12 Whilst it is yet in his g', and not cut 3

greet See also GREETETH; GREETING.
1Sa 25: 5 go to Nabal, and g' him in 7592, 7965
Ro 16: 3 G' Priscilla and Aquila my * 782
5 Likewise g' the church that is in * "
6 G' Mary; who bestowed much * 782
8 G' Amplias my beloved in the * "
11 G' them that be of the household * "
1Co 16:20 All the brethren g' you. G' ye * "
2Co 13:12 G' one another with an holy kiss.* "
Ph'p 4:21 which are with me g' you. * "
Col 4:14 physician, and Demas, g' you. * "
1Th 5:26 G' all the brethren with an holy * "
Tit 3:15 G' them that love us in the faith.* "
1Pe 5:14 G' ye one another with a kiss of * "
2Jo 13 of thy elect sister g' thee. * "
3Jo 14 thee. G' the friends by name. * "

greeteth
2Ti 4:21 Eubulus g' thee, and Pudens, * 782

greeting See also GREETINGS.
Ac 15:23 send g' unto the brethren which 5463
23:26 excellent governor Felix sendeth g'. "
Jas 1: 1 which are scattered abroad, g'. "

greetings
M't 23: 7 And g' in the markets, and to be * 783
Lu 11:43 synagogues and g' in the markets.* "
20:46 love g' in the markets, and the * "

grew
Ge 2: 5 herb of the field before it g': *6779
19:25 that which g' upon the ground. 6780
21: 8 the child g', and was weaned: 1431
20 God was with the lad; and he g', "
25:27 And the boys g': and Esau was "
26:13 g' until he became very great: 1432
47:27 had possession therein, and g', *6509
Ex 1:12 the more they multiplied and g'. *6555
2:10 And the child g', and she brought 1431
J'g 11: 2 and his wife's sons g' up, and they "
13:24 and the child g', and the Lord "

1Sa 2:21 child Samuel g' before the Lord. 1431
26 the child Samuel g' on, and was 1432
3:19 And Samuel g', and the Lord was 1431
2Sa 5:10 And David went on and g' great, *
12: 3 it g' up together with him, and 1431
Eze 17: 6 g', and became a spreading vine 6779
10 wither in the furrows where it g'. 6780
Da 4:11 The tree g', and was strong, and 7236
20 tree that thou sawest, which g', "
M'r 4: 7 thorns g' up, and choked it, and it 305
5:26 bettered, but rather g' worse, 2064
Lu 1:80 And the child g', and waxed strong 837
2:40 And the child g', and waxed strong "
13:19 it g', and waxed a great tree; "
Ac 7:17 people g' and multiplied in Egypt, "
12:24 the word of God g' and multiplied. "
19:20 So mightily g' the word of God "

grey [so most editions here] See also GRAY; GREYHEADED; GREYHOUND.
Pr 20:29 beauty of old men is the g' head. *7872

greyheaded [so most editions here]
Ps 71:18 Now also when I am old and g', *7872

greyhound
Pr 30:31 A g'; an he goat also; and a 2223, 4975

grief See also GRIEFS.
Ge 26:35 Which were a g' of mind unto Isaac 4786
1Sa 1:16 complaint and g' have I spoken *3708
25:31 this shall be no g' unto thee, nor 6330
2Ch 6:29 his own sore and his own g', *4341
Job 2:13 saw that his g' was very great. 3511
6: 2 my g' were thoroughly weighed, *3708
16: 5 of my lips should asswage your g'. "
6 I speak, my g' is not asswaged: 3511
Ps 6: 7 eye is consumed because of g'; 3708
31: 9 mine eye is consumed with g', yea, "
10 For my life is spent with g', *3015
69:26 they talk to the g' of those whom*4341
Pr 17:25 A foolish son is a g' to his father, 3708
Ec 1:18 For in much wisdom is much g': "
2:23 days are sorrows, and his travail g'; "
Isa 17:11 shall be a heap in the day of g' 2470
53: 3 sorrows, and acquainted with g': 2483
10 he hath put him to g': when thou 2470
Jer 6: 7 before me continually is g' and *2483
10:19 Truly this is a g', and I must bear "
45: 3 Lord hath added g' to my sorrow; *3015
La 3:32 though he cause g', yet will he 3013
Jon 4: 6 head, to deliver him from his g'. *7451
2Co 2: 5 if any have caused g', he hath * 3076
Heb 13:17 do it with joy, and not with g': 4727
1Pe 2:19 conscience toward God endure g', 3077

griefs
Isa 53: 4 hath borne our g', and carried our 2483

grievance
Hab 1: 3 and cause me to behold g'? *5999

grieve See also GRIEVED; GRIEVETH; GRIEVING.
1Sa 2:33 thine eyes, and to g' thine heart: 109
1Ch 4:10 from evil, that it may not g' me! *6087
Ps 78:40 wilderness, and g' him in the desert! "
La 3:33 willingly nor g' the children of 3013
Eph 4:30 And g' not the holy spirit of God, 3076

grieved
Ge 6: 6 and it g' him at his heart, 6087
34: 7 and the men were g', and they were "
45: 5 be not g', nor angry with yourselves, "
49:23 The archers have sorely g' him, 4843
Ex 1:12 And they were g' because of the 6973
De 15:10 thine heart shall not be g' when 7489
J'g 10:16 soul was g' for the misery of Israel.7114
1Sa 1: 8 thou not? and why is thy heart g'? 7489
15:11 it g' Samuel; and he cried unto *2734
20: 3 Jonathan know this, lest he be g': 6087
34 was g' for David, because his father "
30: 6 the soul of all the people was g', 4784
2Sa 19: 2 the king was g' for his son. *6087
Ne 2:10 it g' them exceedingly that there 7489
8:11 the day is holy; neither be ye g'. 6087
13: 8 And it g' me sore: therefore I cast 7489
Es 4: 4 was the queen exceedingly g'; 2342
Job 4: 2 with thee, wilt thou be g'? 3811
30:25 was not my soul g' for the poor? 5701
Ps 73:21 Thus my heart was g', and I was 2556
95:10 Forty years long was I g' with 6962
112:10 The wicked shall see it, and be g';3707
119:158 the transgressors, and was g'; 6962
139:21 am not I g' with those that rise up "
Isa 54: 6 thee as a woman forsaken and g' 6087
57:10 hand; therefore thou wast not g'. *2470
Jer 5: 3 have not g'; thou hast consumed 2342
Da 7:15 I Daniel was g' in my spirit 3735
11:30 he shall be g', and return, 3512
Am 6: 6 they are not g' for the affliction 2470
M'r 3: 5 g' for the hardness of their hearts,4818
10:22 at that saying, and went away g': *3076
Joh 21:17 Peter was g' because he said unto "
Ac 4: 2 g' that they taught the people, * 1278
16:18 Paul, being g', turned and said to * "
Ro 14:15 if thy brother be g' with thy meat, 3076
2Co 2: 4 not that ye should be g', but that * "
5 he hath not g' me, but in part: * "
Heb 3:10 I was g' with that generation, * 4360
17 with whom was he g' forty years? * "

grieveth
Ru 1:13 for it g' me much for your sakes 4843
Pr 26:15 it g' him to bring it again to his *3811

grieving
Eze 28:24 nor any g' thorn of all that are 3510

grievous
Ge 12:10 the famine was g' in the land. *3515
18:20 and because their sin is very g'; 3513

Ge 21:11 the thing was very g' in Abraham's 7489
12 Let it not be g' in thy sight because "
41:31 following; for it shall be very g'. 3515
50:11 is a g' mourning to the Egyptians: "
Ex 8:24 there came a g' swarm of flies "
9: 3 there shall be a very g' murrain. "
18 will cause it to rain a very g' hail, "
24 fire mingled with the hail, very g', "
10:14 coasts of Egypt: very g' were they; "
1Ki 2: 8 cursed me with a g' curse in the 4834
12: 4 Thy father made our yoke g': 7185
4 thou the g' service of thy father, 7186
2Ch 10: 4 Thy father made our yoke g': now 7185
4 the g' servitude of thy father, 7186
Ps 10: 5 His ways are always g'; thy *2342
31:18 be put to silence; which speak g' *6277
Pr 15: 1 wrath: but g' words stir up anger.6089
10 Correction is g' unto him that 7451
Ec 2:17 under the sun is g' unto me: for "
Isa 15: 4 out; his life shall be g' unto him. *3415
21: 2 A g' vision is declared unto me; 7186
Jer 6:28 They are all g' revolters, 5493
10:19 for my hurt! my wound is g': 2470
14:17 a great breach, with a very g' blow. "
16: 4 They shall die of g' deaths; they 8463
23:19 in fury, even a g' whirlwind: *2342
30:12 incurable, and thy wound is g'. 2470
Na 3:19 thy wound is g': all that hear "
M't 23: 4 heavy burdens and g' to be borne, 1418
Lu 11:46 with burdens g' to be borne, and ye "
Ac 20:29 shall g' wolves enter in among you,926
25: 7 and g' complaints against Paul, "
Ph'p 3: 1 to me indeed is not g', but for * 3636
Heb 12:11 seemeth to be joyous, but g': 3077
1Jo 5: 3 and his commandments are not g'. 926
Re 16: 2 noisome and g' sore upon the men 4190

grievously
Isa 9: 1 afterward did more g' afflict her *3513
Jer 23:19 whirlwind: it shall fall g' upon *2342
La 1: 8 Jerusalem hath g' sinned; 2399
20 for I have g' rebelled: abroad the 4784
Eze 14:13 against me by trespassing g', *4604
M't 8: 6 sick of the palsy, g' tormented. 1171
15:22 daughter is g' vexed with a devil. 2560

grievousness
Isa 10: 1 that write g' which they have *5999
21:15 bent bow, and from the g' of war. 3514

grind See also GRINDING; GROUND.
J'g 16:21 and he did g' in the prison house. 2912
Job 31:10 Then let my wife g' unto another, "
Isa 3:15 pieces, and g' the faces of the poor? "
47: 2 Take the millstones, and g' meal: "
La 5:13 They took the young men to g'. *2911
M't 21:44 shall fall, it will g' him to powder.*3039
Lu 20:18 shall fall, it will g' him to powder.* "

grinders
Ec 12: 3 the g' cease because they are few, 2912

grinding
Ec 12: 4 when the sound of the g' is low, 2913
M't 24:41 Two women shall be g' at the mill; 229
Lu 17:35 Two women shall be g' together; "

grisled
Ge 31:10 ringstraked, speckled, and g'. 1261
12 are ringstraked, speckled, and g': "
Zec 6: 3 fourth chariot g' and bay horses. "
6 the g' go forth toward the south "

groan See also GROANED; GROANETH; GROANING.
Job 24:12 Men g' from out of the city, 5008
Jer 51:52 all her land the wounded shall g'. 602
Eze 30:24 he shall g' before him with the 5008
Joe 1:18 How do the beasts g'! the herds 584
Ro 8:23 we ourselves g' within ourselves, 4727
2Co 5: 2 in this we g', earnestly desiring to "
4 we that are in this tabernacle do g'. "

groaned
Joh 11:33 g' in the spirit, and was troubled, 1690

groaneth
Ro 8:22 g' and travaileth in pain together 4959

groaning See also GROANINGS.
Ex 2:24 And God heard their g', and God 5009
6: 5 And I have also heard the g' of the "
Job 23: 2 my stroke is heavier than my g'. 585
Ps 6: 6 I am weary with my g'; all the "
38: 9 and my g' is not hid from thee. "
102: 5 By reason of the voice of my g' my "
20 To hear the g' of the prisoner; * 603
Joh 11:38 therefore again g' in himself 1690
Ac 7:34 and I have heard their g', and 4726

groanings
J'g 2:18 because of their g' by reason of *5009
Eze 30:24 the g' of a deadly wounded man. "
Ro 8:26 with g' which cannot be uttered. 4726

grope See also GROPETH.
De 28:29 thou shalt g' at noonday, as the 4959
Job 5:14 g' in the noonday as in the night. "
12:25 They g' in the dark without light, "
Isa 59:10 We g' for the wall like the blind, 1659
10 and we g' as if we had no eyes: "

gropeth
De 28:29 as the blind g' in darkness, and 4959

gross
Isa 60: 2 earth, and g' darkness the people: 6205
Jer 13:16 of death, and make it g' darkness. "
M't 13:15 For this people's heart is waxed g',3975
Ac 28:27 the heart of this people is waxed g'. "

ground See also AGROUND; GROUNDED.
Ge 2: 5 there was not a man to till the g'. 127
6 and watered the whole face of the g'. "

Ge 2: 7 formed man of the dust of the g'. 127
9 out of the g' made the Lord God to "
19 out of the g' the Lord God formed "
3:17 cursed is the g' for thy sake; "
19 bread, till thou return unto the g'; "
23 to till the g' from whence he was "
4: 2 but Cain was a tiller of the g'. "
3 Cain brought of the fruit of the g' "
10 blood crieth unto me from the g'. "
12 When thou tillest the g', it shall "
5:29 the g' which the Lord hath cursed. "
7:23 which was upon the face of the g', "
8: 8 abated from off the face of the g'; "
13 behold, the face of the g' was dry. "
21 I will not again curse the g' any "
18: 2 and bowed himself toward the g',* 776
19: 1 with his face toward the g'; * "
25 and that which grew upon the g'. 127
33: 3 himself to the g' seven times, 776
38: 9 he spilled it on the g', lest that he "
44:11 down every man his sack to the g', "
14 and they fell before him on the g'. "
Ex 3: 5 whereon thou standest is holy g'. 127
4: 3 And he said, Cast it on the g'. 776
3 And he cast it on the g', "
8:21 and also the g' whereon they are. 127
9:23 the fire ran along upon the g'; * 776
14:16 shall go on dry g' through the "
22 midst of the sea upon the dry g' "
16:14 as small as the hoar frost on the g'.776
32:20 the fire, and g' it to powder, 2912
Le 20:25 that creepeth on the g', which I 127
Nu 11: 8 gathered it, and g' it in mills, 2912
16:31 g' clave asunder that was under 127
De 4:18 anything that creepeth on the g', "
9:21 g' it very small, even until it was *2912
15:23 shalt pour it upon the g' as water. 776
22: 6 in any tree, or on the g', whether "
28: 4 the fruit of thy g', and the fruit 127
11 the fruit of thy g', in the land "
56 the sole of her foot upon the g' 776
Jos 3:17 stood firm on dry g' in the midst "
17 Israelites passed over on dry g', "
24:32 a parcel of g' which Jacob bought 7704
J'g 4:21 fastened it into the g': for he was 776
6:39 and upon all the g' let there be dew. "
40 and there was dew on all the g'. "
13:20 and fell on their faces to the g'. "
20:21 Gibeah, and destroyed down to the g' "
25 day, and destroyed down to the g' "
Ru 2:10 bowed herself to the g', and said "
1Sa 3:19 let none of his words fall to the g'. "
5: 4 was fallen upon his face to the g' "
8:12 and will set them to ear his g', 2758
14:25 and there was honey upon the g'. 7704
32 calves, and slew them on the g': 776
45 one hair of his head fall to the g'; "
20:31 the son of Jesse liveth upon the g', 127
41 fell on his face to the g', and bowed 776
25:23 face, and bowed herself to the g', "
26: 7 and his spear stuck in the g' at his "
28:14 and stooped with his face to the g', "
2Sa 2:22 should I smite thee to the g'? "
8: 2 casting them down to the g'; even "
14: 4 she fell on her face to the g', and did "
14 water spilt on the g', which cannot "
22 Joab fell to the g' on his face, "
33 bowed himself on his face to the g' "
17:12 as the dew falleth on the g': 127
19 and spread g' corn thereon; *7383
18:11 thou not smite him there to the g'? 776
20:10 and shed out his bowels to the g', "
23:11 a piece of g' full of lentiles: and 7704
12 stood in the midst of the g', and *2513
24:20 the king on his face upon the g'. 776
1Ki 1:23 the king with his face to the g'. "
7:46 cast them, in the clay g' between 127
2Ki 2: 8 so that they two went over on dry g'. "
15 themselves to the g' before him. 776
19 is naught, and the g' barren. "
4:37 bowed herself to the g', and took "
9:26 and cast him into the plat of g', "
13:18 Smite upon the g'. And he smote 776
1Ch 11:13 was a parcel of g' full of barley; 7704
21:21 to David with his face to the g'. 776
27:26 the field for tillage of the g' was 127
2Ch 4:17 king cast them, in the clay g' "
7: 3 with their faces to the g' upon the 776
20:18 his head with his face to the g': "
Ne 8: 6 the Lord with their faces to the g'. "
10:35 to bring the firstfruits of our g', 127
37 the tithes of our g' unto the Levites, "
Job 1:20 down upon the g', and worshipped, 776
2:13 they sat down with him upon the g' "
5: 6 doth trouble spring out of the g'; 127
14: 8 the stock thereof die in the g'; 6083
16:13 poureth out my gall upon the g'. 776
18:10 The snare is laid for him in the g', "
38:27 To satisfy the desolate and waste g'; "
39:24 swalloweth the g' with fierceness 776
Ps 74: 7 dwelling place of thy name to the g'. "
89:39 his crown by casting it to the g'. "
44 cast his throne down to the g'. "
105:35 and devoured the fruit of their g'. 127
107:33 and the watersprings into dry g'; "
35 and dry g' into watersprings. * 127
143: 3 hath smitten my life down to the g'; 776
147: 6 casteth the wicked down to the g'. "
Isa 3:26 being desolate shall sit upon the g'. "
14:12 how art thou cut down to the g', "
21: 9 her gods he hath broken unto the g'. "
25:12 bring to the g', even to the dust. "
26: 5 he layeth it low, even to the g'; "
28:24 and break the clods of his g'? 127
29: 4 shalt speak out of the g', and thy 776

Isa 29: 4 familiar spirit, out of the g', and 776
30:23 thou shalt sow the g' withal; 127
24 young asses that ear the g' shall eat "
35: 7 parched g' shall become a pool, *
44: 3 and floods upon the dry g':
47: 1 sit on the g': there is no throne, 776
51:23 thou hast laid thy body as the g', "
53: 2 plant, and as a root out of a dry g': "
Jer 4: 3 Break up your fallow g', and sow
7:20 and upon the fruit of the g'; 127
14: 2 they are black unto the g'; 776
4 Because the g' is chapt, for there 127
25:33 they shall be dung upon the g'. "
27: 5 the beast that are upon the g', * 776
La 2: 2 hath brought them down to the g': "
9 Her gates are sunk into the g'; "
10 sit upon the g', and keep silence: "
10 hang down their heads to the g'. "
21 the old lie on the g' in the streets: "
Eze 12: 6 thy face, that thou see not the g': "
12 that he see not the g' with his eyes. "
13:14 bring it down to the g', so that "
19:12 she was cast down to the g', and the "
13 wilderness, in a dry and thirsty g'.* "
24: 7 she poured it not upon the g', "
26:11 garrisons shall go down to the g'. "
16 they shall sit upon the g', and "
28:17 I will cast thee to the g', "
38:20 every wall shall fall to the g'. "
41:16 and from the g' up to the windows, "
20 From the g' unto above the door "
42: 6 and the middlemost from the g'. "
43:14 from the bottom upon the g' even "
Da 8: 5 earth, and touched not the g': "
7 he cast him down to the g', and "
10 the host and of the stars to the g', "
12 it cast down the truth to the g'; "
18 sleep on my face toward the g': "
10: 9 my face, and my face toward the g'. "
15 I set my face toward the g', "
Ho 2:18 with the creeping things of the g': 127
10:12 mercy; break up your fallow g': "
Am 3:14 be cut off, and fall to the g'. 776
Ob 3 shall bring me down to the g'? "
Hag 1:11 upon that which the g' bringeth 127
Zec 8:12 and the g' shall give her increase, 776
Mal 3:11 not destroy the fruits of your g'; 127
M't 10:29 shall not fall on the g' without 1093
13: 8 But other fell into good g', and "
23 received seed into the good g' is he "
15:35 multitude to sit down on the g'. "
M'r 4: 5 And some fell on stony g', where it "
8 other fell on good g', and did 1093
16 which are sown on stony g', who, * "
20 they which are sown on good g'; 1093
26 man should cast seed into the g';* "
8: 6 people to sit down on the g': "
9:20 he fell on the g', and wallowed "
14:35 fell on the g', and prayed that, if it "
Lu 8: 8 other fell on good g', and sprang "
15 But that on the good g' are they, "
12:16 g' of a certain rich man brought 5561
13: 7 down; why cumbereth it the g'? 1093
14:18 I have bought a piece of g', and I,* 68
19:44 shall lay thee even with the g', 1474
22:44 of blood falling down to the g'. 1093
Joh 4: 5 near to the parcel of g' that Jacob 5564
8: 6 with his finger wrote on the g', 1093
8 stooped down, and wrote on the g'. "
9: 6 he spat on the g', and made clay 5476
12:24 a corn of wheat fall into the g' *1093
18: 6 went backward, and fell to the g'. 5476
Ac 7:33 where thou standest is holy g'. 1093
22: 7 I fell unto the g', and heard 1475
1Ti 3:15 the pillar and g' of the truth. 1477

grounded
Isa 30:32 every place where the g' staff *4145
Eph 3:17 ye, being rooted and g' in love, 2311
Col 1:23 continue in the faith g' and settled, "

grove See also GROVES.
Ge 21:33 And Abraham planted a g' in * 815
De 16:21 Thou shalt not plant thee a g' * 842
J'g 6:25 cut down the g' that is by it: * "
26 the wood of the g' which thou * "
28 the g' was cut down that was * "
30 he hath cut down the g' that was * "
1Ki 15:13 she had made an idol in a g'; * "
16:33 Ahab made a g'; and Ahab did * "
2Ki 13: 6 remained the g' also in Samaria.)* "
17:16 even two calves, and made a g', * "
21: 3 and made a g', as did Ahab king * "
7 set a graven image of the g' that * "
23: 4 for Baal, and for the g', and for * "
6 he brought out the g' from the * "
7 women wove hangings for the g'.* "
15 to powder, and burned the g'. * "
2Ch 15:16 she had made an idol in a g': * "

groves
Ex 34:13 images, and cut down their g': * 842
De 7: 5 images, and cut down their g', * "
12: 3 and burn their g' with fire; * "
J'g 3: 7 and served Baalim and the g'. * "
1Ki 14:15 because they have made their g', * "
23 and g', on every high hill, and * "
18:19 prophets of the g' four hundred * "
2Ki 17:10 and g' in every high hill, and * "
18: 4 the images, and cut down the g', * "
23:14 the images, and cut down the g', * "
2Ch 14: 3 the images, and cut down the g': * "
17: 6 took away the high places and g' * "
19: 3 thou hast taken away the g' * "
24:18 fathers, and served g' and idols: * "
31: 1 in pieces, and cut down the g', * "
33: 3 and made g', and worshipped all * "

2Ch 33:19 and set up g' and graven images,* 842
34: 3, 4 the g', and the carved images, * "
7 altars and the g', and had beaten* "
Isa 17: 8 either the g', or the images, * "
27: 9 the g' and images shall not stand* "
Jer 17: 2 their altars and their g' by the * "
Mic 5:14 I will pluck up thy g' out of the * "

grow See also GREW; GROWETH; GROWN.
Ge 2: 9 the Lord God to g' every tree 6779
48:16 and let them g' into a multitude 1711
Nu 6: 5 locks of the hair of his head g'. 1431
J'g 16:22 the hair of his head began to g' 6779
2Sa 23: 5 although he make it not to g'. "
2Ki 19:29 such things as g' of themselves, *5599
Ezr 4:22 why should damage g' to the hurt 7680
Job 8:11 Can the rush g' up without mire? 1342
19 out of the earth shall others g'. *6779
14:19 washest away the things which g'*5599
31:40 Let thistles g' instead of wheat, 3318
39: 4 good liking, they g' up with corn; 7235
Ps 92:12 shall g' like a cedar in Lebanon. 7685
104:14 causeth the grass to g' for the 6779
147: 8 who maketh grass to g' upon the "
Ec 11: 5 how the bones do g' in the womb of her
Isa 11: 1 Branch shall g' out of his roots: *6509
17:11 shalt thou make thy plant to g', *7735
53: 2 For he shall g' up before him *5927
Jer 12: 2 they have taken root: they g', yea, 3212
33:15 Branch of righteousness to g' up 6779
Eze 44:20 nor suffer their locks to g' long; 7971
47:12 this side and on that side, shall g'5927
Ho 14: 5 he shall g' as the lily, and cast *6524
7 as the corn, and g' as the vine: * "
Jon 4:10 neither madest it g'; which came 1431
Zec 6:12 he shall g' up out of his place, 6779
Mal 4: 2 and g' up as calves of the stall. *6335
M't 6:28 the lilies of the field, how they g'; 837
13:30 both g' together until the harvest: 4886
21:19 no fruit g' on thee henceforward *1096
M'r 4:27 the seed should spring and g' up, 3373
Lu 12:27 Consider the lilies how they g': 837
Ac 5:24 of them whereunto this would g'. 1096
Eph 4:15 may g' up into him in all things, 837
1Pe 2: 2 the word, that ye may g' thereby: "
2Pe 3:18 g' in grace, and in the knowledge "

groweth
Ex 10: 5 every tree which g' for you out of 6779
Le 13:39 freckled spot that g' in the skin; *6524
25: 5 That which g' of its own accord 5599
11 reap that which g' of itself in it, "
De 29:23 beareth, nor any grass g' therein, 5927
J'g 19: 9 the day g' to an end, lodge here, 2583
Job 38:38 When the dust g' into hardness, *3332
Ps 90: 5 they are like grass which g' up. 2498
6 morning it flourisheth, and g' up; "
129: 6 which withereth afore it g' up: 8025
Isa 37:30 eat this year such as g' of itself; 5599
M'r 4:32 when it is sown, it g' up, and 305
Eph 2:21 g' unto an holy temple in the Lord: 837
2Th 1: 3 that your faith g' exceedingly, 5232

grown
Ge 38:11 house, till Shelah my son be g': 1431
14 she saw that Shelah was g', and "
Ex 2:11 when Moses was g', that he went "
9:32 smitten: for they were not g' up. 648
Le 13:37 there is black hair g' up therein; 6779
De 32:15 thou art waxen fat, thou art g' thick,
Ru 1:13 tarry for them till they were g'? 1431
2Sa 10: 5 until your beards be g', and then 6779
1Ki 12: 8 that were g' up with him, and 1431
10 that were g' up with him spake "
2Ki 4:18 And when the child was g', it fell "
19:26 as corn blasted before it be g' up. 6965
1Ch 19: 5 at Jericho until your beards be g', 6779
Ezr 9: 6 our trespass is g' up unto the 1431
Ps 144:12 as plants g' up in their youth; "
Pr 24:31 it was all g' over with thorns, 5927
Isa 37:27 as corn blasted before it be g' up. 6965
Jer 50:11 are g' fat as the heifer at grass, *6335
Eze 16: 7 are fashioned, and thine hair is g', 6779
Da 4:22 that are g' and become strong: 7236
22 for thy greatness is g', "
33 till his hairs were g' like eagles' "
M't 13:32 when it is g', it is the greatest 837

growth
Am 7: 1 the shooting up of the latter g'; 3954
1 and, lo, it was the latter g' after "

grudge See also GRUDGING.
Le 19:18 bear any g' against the children 5201
Ps 59:15 and g' if they be not satisfied. *3885
Jas 5: 9 G' not one against another, *4727

grudging
1Pe 4: 9 one to another without g'. *1112

grudgingly
2Co 9: 7 not g', or of necessity: 1537, 3077

guard See also GUARDS; SAFEGUARD.
Ge 37:36 Pharaoh's, and captain of the g'. 2876
39: 1 of Pharaoh, captain of the g', an "
40: 3 the house of the captain of the g', "
4 the g' charged Joseph with them, "
41:12 servant to the captain of the g'; "
2Sa 23:23 And David set him over his g'. 4928
1Ki 14:27 the hands of the chief of the g', 7323
28 that the g' bare them, and brought "
28 them back into the g' chamber. "
2Ki 10:25 that Jehu said to the g' and to the "
25 the g' and the captains cast them "
11: 4 with the captains and the g', and "
6 third part at the gate behind the g': "
11 And the g' stood, every man with "
13 Athaliah heard the noise of the g' "

1Ki 11:19 the captains, and the *g*', and all 7323
19 gate of the *g*' to the king's house. "
25: 8 Nebuzar-adan, captain of the *g*', 2876
10 that were with the captain of the *g*'."
11 the captain of the *g*' carry away. "
12 the captain of the *g*' left of the poor"
15 the captain of the *g*' took away. "
18 the captain of the *g*' took Seraiah "
20 captain of the *g*' took these, and "
1Ch 11:25 and David set him over his *g*', 4928
2Ch 12:10 the chief of the *g*', that kept the 7323
11 the *g*' came and fetched them, "
11 them again into the *g*' chamber. "
Ne 4:22 in the night they may be a *g*' to us,4929
23 men of the *g*' which followed me, "
Jer 39: 9 the captain of the *g*' carried away 2876
10 the captain of the *g*' left of the poor"
11 Nebuzar-adan the captain of the *g*',"
13 the captain of the *g*' sent, and "
40: 1 the captain of the *g*' had let him go"
2 the captain of the *g*' took Jeremiah,"
5 captain of the *g*' gave him victuals "
41:10 captain of the *g*' had committed "
43: 6 the captain of the *g*' had left with "
52:12 the captain of the *g*', which served "
14 the captain of the *g*', brake down "
15 the captain of the *g*' carried away "
16 the captain of the *g*' left certain of "
19 took the captain of the *g*' away. "
24 the captain of the *g*' took Seraiah "
26 the captain of the *g*' took them, "
30 the captain of the *g*' carried away "
Eze 38: 7 thee, and be thou a *g*' unto them 4929
Da 2:14 Arioch the captain of the king's *g*',2877
Ac 28:16 prisoners to the captain of the *g*':*4759

guard's
Ge 41:10 in the captain of the *g*' house, *2876

Gudgodah (*gud-go'-dah*) See also HOR-HAGID-GAD.
De 10: 7 unto *G*'; and from *G*' to Jotbath, 1412

guest See also GUESTCHAMBER; GUESTS.
Lu 19: 7 gone to be *g*' with a man that is *2647*

guestchamber
M'r 14:14 The Master saith, Where is the *g*',*2646*
Lu 22:11 saith unto thee, Where is the *g*', "

guests
1Ki 1:41 Adonijah and all the *g*' that were 7121
49 the *g*' that were with Adonijah "
Pr 9:18 her *g*' are in the depths of hell. "
Zep 1: 7 a sacrifice, he hath bid his *g*'. "
M't 22:10 the wedding was furnished with *g*'.*345*
11 when the king came to see the *g*', "

guide See also GUIDED; GUIDES; GUIDING.
Job 38:32 canst thou *g*' Arcturus with his 5148
Ps 25: 9 The meek will he *g*' in judgment: 1869
31: 3 name's sake lead me, and *g*' me. 5095
32: 8 I will *g*' thee with mine eye. *3289
Ps 48:14 he will be our *g*' even unto death. 5090
55:13 my *g*', and mine acquaintance. * 441
73:24 Thou shalt *g*' me with thy counsel,5148
112: 5 will *g*' his affairs with discretion.*3557
Pr 2:17 forsaketh the *g*' of her youth, * 441
6: 7 having no *g*', overseer, or ruler, *7101
11: 3 of the upright shall *g*' them: 5148
23:19 and *g*' thine heart in the way. 833
Isa 49:10 springs of water shall he *g*' them.5095
51:18 There is none to *g*' her among all "
58:11 And the Lord shall *g*' thee 5148
Jer 3: 4 thou art the *g*' of my youth? 441
Mic 7: 5 put ye not confidence in a *g*': "
Lu 1:79 *g*' our feet into the way of peace. *2720*
Joh 16:13 he will *g*' you into all truth: *3594*
Ac 1:16 was *g*' to them that took Jesus. *3595*
8:31 except some man should *g*' me? *3594*
Ro 2:19 art a *g*' of the blind, a light of *3595*
1Ti 5:14 *g*' the house, give none occasion *3616*

guided
Ex 15:13 thou hast *g*' them in thy strength 5095
2Ch 32:22 other, and *g*' them on every side. "
Job 31:18 a father, and I have *g*' her from ‡5148
Ps 78:52 and *g*' them in the wilderness 5090
72 *g*' them by the skilfulness of his 5148

guides
M't 23:16 Woe unto you, ye blind *g*', which *3595*
24 Ye blind *g*', which strain at a gnat "

guiding
Ge 48:14 Manasseh's head, *g*' his hands

guile See also BEGUILE.
Ex 21:14 to slay him with *g*'; thou shalt 6195
Ps 32: 2 in whose spirit there is no *g*'. 7423
34:13 and thy lips from speaking *g*'. 4820
55:11 deceit and *g*' depart not from her "
Joh 1:47 Israelite indeed, in whom is no *g*'!*1388*
2Co 12:16 being crafty, I caught you with *g*'. "
1Th 2: 3 nor of uncleanness, nor in *g*': "
1Pe 2: 1 laying aside all malice, and all *g*', "
22 neither was *g*' found in his mouth: "
3:10 his lips that they speak no *g*': "
Re 14: 5 in their mouth was found no *g*': * "

guilt See also GUILTLESS.
De 19:13 shalt put away the *g*' of innocent *
21: 9 put away the *g*' of innocent blood *

guiltiness See also BLOODGUILTINESS.
Ge 26:10 shouldest have brought *g*' upon us.817

guiltless
Ex 20: 7 the Lord will not hold him *g*' 5352
Nu 5:31 the man be *g*' from iniquity, * "
32:22 be *g*' before the Lord, and before 5355
De 5:11 the Lord will not hold him *g*' 5352
Jos 2:19 upon his head, and we will be *g*: 5355
1Sa 26: 9 the Lord's anointed, and be *g*'? 5352
2Sa 3:28 I and my kingdom are *g*' 5355
14: 9 the king and his throne be *g*'. "
1Ki 2: 9 hold him not *g*': for thou art 5352
M't 12: 7 would not have condemned the *g*'. *338*

guilty
Ge 42:21 verily *g*' concerning our brother, 816
Le 4:13 should not be done, and are *g*'; "
22 should not be done, and is *g*'; "
27 ought not to be done, and be *g*'; "
5: 2 he also shall be unclean, and *g*'. "
3 knoweth of it, then he shall be *g*'. "
4 then he shall be *g*' in one of these. "
5 he shall be *g*' in one of these things," "
17 he wist it not, yet is he *g*', "
6: 4 he hath sinned, and is *g*', that he "
Nu 5: 6 the Lord, and that person be *g*'; "
14:18 and by no means clearing the *g*',
35:27 he shall not be *g*' of blood:
31 a murderer, which is *g*' of death: 7563
J'g 21:22 at this time, that ye should be *g*'. 816
Ezr 10:19 wives; and being *g*', they offered "
Pr 30:10 curse thee, and thou be found *g*'. "
Eze 22: 4 Thou art become *g*' in thy blood. "
Zec 11: 5 hold themselves not *g*': and they "
M't 23:18 gift that is upon it, he is *g*'. *3784*
26:66 and said, He is *g*' of death. *1777*
M'r 14:64 condemned him to be *g*' of death.* "
Ro 3:19 world may become *g*' before God. *5267*
1Co 11:27 shall be *g*' of the body and blood *1777*
Jas 2:10 offend in one point, he is *g*' of all. "

gulf
Lu 16:26 and you there is a great *g*' fixed: *5490*

Guni (*gu'-ni*) See also GUNITES.
Ge 46:24 Jahzeel, and *G*', and Jezer, and 1476
Nu 26:48 of *G*', the family of the Gunites: "
1Ch 5:15 the son of *G*', chief of the house of "
7:13 Jahziel, and *G*', and Jezer, and "

Gunites (*gu'-nites*)
Nu 26:48 of Guni, the family of the *G*': 1477

Gur (*gur*) See also GUR-BAAL.
2Ki 9:27 they did so at the going up to *G*', 1483

Gur-baal (*gur-ba'-al*)
2Ch 26: 7 the Arabians that dwelt in *G*'. 1485

gush See also GUSHED.
Jer 9:18 our eyelids *g*' out with waters. 5140

gushed
1Ki 18:28 till the blood *g*' out upon them. 8210
Ps 78:20 that the waters *g*' out, and the 2100
105:41 and the waters *g*' out; they ran in "
Isa 48:21 rock also, and the waters *g*' out. "
Ac 1:18 midst, and all his bowels *g*' out. *1632*

gutter See also GUTTERS.
2Sa 5: 8 Whosoever getteth up to the *g*', *6794

gutters
Ge 30:38 pilled before the flocks in the *g*' 7298
41 the eyes of the cattle in the *g*'. "

H

ha See also AHA.
Job 39:25 *H*', *h*.; and he smelleth the *1889

Haahashtari (*ha-a-hash'-te-ri*)
1Ch 4: 6 Hepher, and Temeni, and *H*'. 326

Haammonai See CHEPHAR-HAAMMONAI.

Habaiah (*hab-ah'-yah*)
Ezr 2:61 the children of *H*', the children of 2252
Ne 7:63 the children of *H*', the children of * "

Habakkuk (*hab'-ak-kuk*)
Hab 1: 1 The burden which *H*' the prophet 2265
3: 1 A prayer of *H*' the prophet upon "

Habaziniah (*hab-az-in-i'-ah*)
Jer 35: 3 Jeremiah, the son of *H*', and his *2262

habergeon See also HABERGEONS.
Ex 28:32 as it were the hole of an *h*', *8473
39:23 robe, as the hole of an *h*', * "
Job 41:26 the spear, the dart, nor the *h*'. *8302

habergeons
2Ch 26:14 helmets, and *h*', and bows, and *8302
Ne 4:16 shields, and the bows, and the *h*';* "

habitable
Pr 8:31 in the *h*' part of his earth; 8398

habitation See also HABITATIONS.
Ex 15: 2 and I will prepare him an *h*'; *5115
13 in thy strength unto thy holy *h*'. 5116
Le 13:46 without the camp shall his *h*' be. *4186
De 12: 5 even unto his *h*' shall ye seek, 7933
26:15 Look down from thy holy *h*', 4583
1Sa 2:29 I have commanded in my *h*'; "
32 shalt see an enemy in my *h*', "
2Sa 15:25 shew me both it, and his *h*': 5116
2Ch 6: 2 have built an house of *h*' for thee, 2073
29: 6 their faces from the *h* of the Lord, 4908
Ez 7:15 Israel, whose *h*' is in Jerusalem, 4907
Job 5: 3 root: but suddenly I cursed his *h*'.5116
24 thou shalt visit thy *h*', and shalt * "
8: 6 *h*' of thy righteousness prosperous."
18:15 shall be scattered upon his *h*. "
Ps 26: 8 I have loved the *h*' of thy house, 4583
33:14 From the place of his *h*' he looketh 3427
68: 5 the widows, is God in his holy *h*'. 4583
69:25 Let their *h*' be desolate; and let 2918
71: 3 Be thou my strong *h*', whereunto 4583
89:14 judgment... the *h*' of thy throne: *4349
91: 9 refuge, even the most High, thy *h*';4583
Ps 97: 2 judgment are the *h*' of his throne. *4349
104:12 fowls of the heaven have their *h*', 7931
107: 7 that they might go to a city of *h*', 4186
36 that they may prepare a city for *h*'; "
132: 5 *h*' for the mighty God of Jacob. *4908
13 he hath desired it for his *h*'. 4186
Pr 3:33 but he blesseth the *h*' of the just. 5116
Isa 22:16 graveth an *h*' for himself in a rock? 4908
27:10 and the *h*' forsaken, and left like 5116
32:18 people shall dwell in a peaceable *h*'," "
33:20 eyes shall see Jerusalem a quiet *h*'," "
34:13 and it shall be an *h*' of dragons, "
35: 7 in the *h*' of dragons, where each "
63:15 behold from the *h*' of thy holiness 2073
Jer 9: 6 Thine *h*' is in the midst of deceit; 3427
10:25 and have made his *h*' desolate. 5116
25:30 utter his voice from his holy *h*'; 4583
30 shall mightily roar upon his *h*'; *5116
31:23 O *h*' of justice, and mountain of "
33:12 an *h*' of shepherds causing their "
41:17 dwell in the *h*' of Chimham, *1628
49:19 against the *h*' of the strong: 5116
50: 7 the *h*' of justice, even the Lord, "
19 I will bring Israel again to his *h*',* "
44 Jordan unto the *h*' of the strong: "
45 he shall make their *h*' desolate "
Eze 29:14 Pathros, into the land of their *h*';*4351
Da 4:21 fowls of the heaven had their *h*': 7932
Ob 3 whose *h*' is high; that saith in his3427
Hab 3:11 and moon stood still in their *h*': 2073
Zec 2:13 is raised up out of his holy *h*'. 4583
Ac 1:20 Let his *h*' be desolate, and let no *1886*
17:26 and the bounds of their *h*'; *2733*
Eph 2:22 for an *h*' of God through the *2732*
Jude 6 but left their own *h*', he hath *3613*
Re 18: 2 and is become the *h*' of devils, *2732*

habitations
Ge 36:43 according to their *h*' in the land of4186
49: 5 of cruelty are in their *h*'. *4380
Ex 12:20 in all your *h*' shall ye eat 4186
35: 3 kindle no fire throughout your *h*' "
Le 23:17 Ye shall bring out of your *h*' two "
Nu 15: 2 the land of your *h*', which I give "
1Ch 4:33 These were their *h*', and their "
41 the *h*' that were found there. *4583
7:28 possessions and *h*' were, Beth-el 4186
Ps 74:20 are full of the *h*' of cruelty. 4999
78:28 their camp, round about their *h*'. 4908
Isa 54: 2 forth the curtains of thine *h*': 4908
Jer 9:10 and for the *h*' of the wilderness *4999
21:13 or who shall enter into our *h*'? 4585
25:37 the peaceable *h*' are cut down *4999
49:20 he shall make their *h*' desolate *5116
La 2: 2 swallowed up all the *h*' of Jacob, 4999
Eze 6:14 toward Diblath, in all their *h*': 4186
Am 1: 2 *h*' of the shepherds shall mourn, *4999
Lu 16: 9 receive you into everlasting *h*'. *4638*

Habor (*Ha'-bor*)
2Ki 17: 6 placed him in Halah and in *H*' 2249
18:11 put them in Halah and in *H*' by "
1Ch 5:26 brought them unto Halah, and *H*', "

Haccerem See BETH-HACCEREM.

Hachaliah (*hak-a-li'-ah*)
Ne 1: 1 words of Nehemiah the son of *H*'.*2446
10: 1 the Tirshatha, the son of *H*', * "

Hachilah (*hak'-i-lah*)
1Sa 23:19 in the hill of *H*', which is on the 2444
26: 1 David hide himself in the hill of *H*',"
3 Saul pitched in the hill of *H*', "

Hachmoni (*hak'-mo-ni*) See also HACHMONITE.
1Ch 27:32 of *H*' was with the king's sons; 2453

Hachmonite (*hak'-mo-nite*) See also TACHMONITE.
1Ch 11:11 Jashobeam, an *H*', the chief of 2453

had See also HADST.
Ge 1:31 every thing that he *h*' made, and
2: 2 ended his work which he *h*' made;
2 from all his work which he *h*' made.
3 in it he *h*' rested from all his work*
5 the Lord God *h*' not caused it to rain
8 put the man whom he *h*' formed
22 which the Lord God *h*' taken from
3: 1 which the Lord God *h*' made.
4: 4 And the Lord *h*' respect unto Abel
5 Cain and his offering he *h*' not respect.
5: 4 after he *h*' begotten Seth were *
6: 6 that he *h*' made man on the earth,
12 for all flesh *h*' corrupted his way upon
7: 9 and the female, as God *h*' commanded
16 of all flesh, as God had commanded
8: 6 window of the ark which he *h*' made:
9:24 what his younger son *h*' done unto
11: 3 *h*' brick for stone, and slime *h*' 1961
30 But Sarai was barren; she *h*' no child.

Ge 12: 1 Now the Lord h' said unto Abram.*
4 departed, as the Lord h' spoken unto
5 their substance that they h' gathered
5 and all the souls that they h' gotten
16 and he h' sheep, and oxen, and 1961
20 away, and his wife, and all that he h'.
13: 1 and all that he h', and Lot with him,
3 his tent h' been at the beginning,
4 the altar, which he h' made there at
5 And Lot also,...h' flocks,and herds,1961
14:13 there came one that h' escaped,
16: 1 and she h' an handmaid, an Egyptian,
3 after Abram h' dwelt ten years in the
4, 5 when she saw that she h' conceived,
17:23 selfsame day, as God h' said unto him.
18: 8 and the calf which he h' dressed, and
33 as soon as he h' left communing with
19:17 when they h' brought them forth
20: 4 But Abimelech h' not come near
18 For the Lord God h' fast closed up all
21: 1 Lord visited Sarah as he h' said, and
1 Lord did unto Sarah as he h' spoken.
2 the set time of which God h' spoken
4 days old, as God h' commanded him.
9 which she h' born unto Abraham,
25 which Abimelech's servants h' violently
22: 3 the place of which God h' told him.
9 to the place which God h' told him of;
23:16 the silver which he h' named in the
24: 1 and the Lord h' blessed Abraham in
2 house, that ruled over all that he h',
15 before he h' done speaking, that,
16 virgin, neither h' any man known her;
19 And when she h' done giving him
21 whether the Lord h' made his journey
22 as the camels h' done drinking, that
29 And Rebekah h' a brother, and his
45 And before I h' done speaking in
48 which h' led me in the right way to
65 For she h' said unto the servant,
65 the servant h' said, It is my master
66 told Isaac all things that he h' done.
25: 5 Abraham gave all that he h' unto Isaac.
6 of the concubines, which Abraham h',
26: 8 when he h' been there a long time,
14 For he h' possession of flocks, and
15 his father's servants h' digged in the
15 Philistines h' stopped them, and filled
18 which they h' digged in the days of
18 names by which his father h' called
32 concerning the well which they h'
27:17 and the bread, which she h' prepared,
30 as soon as Isaac h' made an end of
31 And he also h' made savoury meat,
28: 6 Esau saw that Isaac h' blessed Jacob,
9 unto the wives which he h', Mahalath
18 took the stone that he h' put for his
29:16 Laban h' two daughters: the name of
20 a few days, for the love he h' to her.
30: 9 Leah saw that she h' left bearing,
25 Rachel h' borne Joseph,that Jacob said
35 and every one that h' some white in it,
38 which he h' pilled before the flocks
43 exceedingly, and h' much cattle, 1961
31:18 all his goods which he h' gotten,
18 which he h' gotten in Padan-aram,
19 Rachel h' stolen the images that *
21 he fled with all that he h'; and he rose
25 Jacob h' pitched his tent in the mount:
32 knew not that Rachel h' stolen them.
34 Now Rachel had taken the images,
42 fear of Isaac, h' been with me, surely
32:23 the brook, and sent over that he h'.
33:10 though I h' seen the face of God, *
19 a field, where he h' spread his tent,
34: 5 Jacob heard that he h' defiled Dinah
7 because he h' wrought folly in Israel
13 and said, because he h' defiled Dinah
19 thing, because he h' delight in Jacob's
27 spoiled the city, because they h' defiled
35:16 Rachel travailed, and she h' hard
36: 6 his substance, which he h' got in the
38:15 to be an harlot, because she h' covered
30 his brother, that h' the scarlet thread
39: 1 the Ishmeelites, which h' brought him
4 all that he h' he put into his hand. 3426
5 the time he h' made him overseer* "
5 his house, and over all that he h', "
5 the Lord was upon all that he h' in "
6 he left all that he h' in Joseph's hand;
6 he knew not ought he h', save the *
13 saw that he h' left his garment in her
40: 1 and his baker h' offended their lord
16 I h' three white baskets on my *
22 as Joseph h' interpreted to them.
41:21 And when they h' eaten them up, it
21 not be known that they h' eaten them;
43 ride in the second chariot which he h';
54 to come, according as Joseph h' said:
43: 2 when they h' eaten up the corn which
2 h' brought out of Egypt, their father
6 the man whether ye h' yet a brother?
10 h' lingered, surely now we h' returned
23 in your sacks: I h' your money. 935
44: 2 to the word that Joseph h' spoken.
45:27 the words of Joseph, which he h' said
27 wagons which Joseph h' sent to carry
46: 1 took his journey with all that he h',
5 wagons which Pharaoh h' sent to
6 their goods which they h' gotten in
47:11 Rameses, as Pharaoh h' commanded.
22 the priests h' a portion assigned them
27 h' possessions therein, and grew, *
48:11 I h' not thought to see thy face:
49:33 when Jacob h' made an end of *
50:14 returned...after he h' buried his

Ex 2: 6 And she h' compassion on him, and*
16 priest of Midian h' seven daughters:
25 children of Israel, and God h' respect*
4:28 words of the Lord who h' sent him,
28 signs which he h' commanded him.
30 all the words which the Lord h' spoken
31 they heard that the Lord h' visited the
31 that he h' looked upon their affliction,
5:14 Pharaoh's taskmasters h' set over
7:10 they did so as the Lord h' commanded:
13 hearkened not,... as the Lord h' said.
22 hearken unto them; as the Lord h' said.
25 after that the Lord h' smitten the river.
8:12 of the frogs which he h' brought
15 hearkened not...as the Lord h' said.
19 hearkened not...as the Lord h' said,
9:12 hearkened not...as the Lord h' spoken
35 as the Lord h' spoken by Moses.
10:15 fruit of the trees which the hail h' left:
23 children of Israel h' light in their 1961
12:28 as the Lord h' commanded Moses
39 h' they prepared for themselves any
13:17 when Pharaoh h' let the people go,
19 for he h' straitly sworn the children
14:12 it h' been better for us to serve *
15:25 when he h' cast into the waters, *
16: 3 would to God we h' died by the hand
18 that gathered much h' nothing over,
18 he that gathered little h' no lack; they
17:10 Joshua did as Moses h' said to him,
18: 1 Jethro...heard of all that God h' done
1 that the Lord h' brought Israel out of
2 after he h' sent her back, and her
8 all that the Lord h' done unto Pharaoh
8 all the travail that h' come upon them
9 the goodness which the Lord h' done
9 whom he h' delivered out of the hand
24 hearkened...and did all that he h' said.
19: 2 desert of Sinai, and h' pitched in *
31:18 Moses, when he h' made an end of
32: 4 a graving tool, after he h' made *
20 he took the calf which they h' made,
25 (for Aaron h' made them naked
29 For Moses h' said, Consecrate *
33: 5 the Lord h' said unto Moses, Say *
34: 4 Sinai, as the Lord h' commanded
32 all that the Lord h' spoken with him
33 And till Moses h' done speaking with
35:25 and brought that which they h' spun,
29 the Lord h' commanded to be made
36: 1 to all that the Lord h' commanded.
2 heart the Lord h' put wisdom, even
3 the children of Israel h' brought for
7 stuff they h' was sufficient for all 1961
22 board h' two tenons, equally distant
39:43 h' done it as the Lord h' commanded,
43 so h' they done it: and Moses blessed
40:23 the Lord; as the Lord h' commanded

Le 10: 5 out of the camp; as Moses h' said,
19 if I h' eaten the sin offering to day,
21: 3 unto him, which h' no husband; 1961
24:23 bring forth him that h' cursed out of

Nu 1:48 the Lord h' spoken unto Moses: *
3: 4 of Sinai, and they h' no children: 1961
7: 1 on the day that Moses h' fully set up
1 and h' anointed them, and sanctified
8: 4 the pattern which the Lord h' shewed
22 as the Lord h' commanded Moses
12: 1 Ethiopian woman whom he h' married:
1 for he h' married an Ethiopian woman.
14 If her father h' but spit in her face,
13:32 of the land which they h' searched
14: 2 Would God that we h' died in the
2 would God we h' died in this
24 he h' another spirit with him, 1961
16:31 as he h' made an end of speaking *
39 they that were burnt h' offered;
20: 3 Would God that we h' died when our
21: 9 if a serpent h' bitten any man,
26 who h' fought against the former king
22: 2 saw all that Israel h' done to the
33 unless she h' turned from me, surely
33 now also I h' slain thee, and saved
23 2 Balak did as Balaam h' spoken;
30 did as Balaam h' said, and offered
26:33 the son of Hepher h' no sons, 1961
65 For the Lord h' said of them, They
27: 3 in his own sin, and h' no sons. 1961
31:32 which the men of war h' caught, *
35 that h' not known man by lying
53 (For the men of war h' taken spoil,
32: 1 the children of Gad h' a very great 1961
9 land which the Lord h' given them.
13 all the generation, that h' done evil
33: 4 firstborn, which the Lord h' smitten

De 1: 3 all that the Lord h' given him in
4 After he h' slain Sihon the king
39 h' no knowledge between good *
41 when ye h' girded on every man
2:12 when they h' destroyed them *
7: 8 the oath which he h' sworn unto *
9:16 behold, ye h' sinned against the Lord
16 and h' made you a molten calf:
10: 5 tables in the ark which I h' made;
15 the Lord h' a delight in thy fathers
19:19 as he h' thought to have done unto
29:26 whom he h' not given unto them:
31:24 Moses h' made an end of writing
32:30 except their Rock h' sold them,
30 and the Lord h' shut them up?
34: 9 Moses h' laid his hands upon him:

Jos 2: 6 she h' brought them up to the roof
6 she h' laid in order upon the roof.
11 as soon as we h' heard these things,
4: 4 twelve men, whom he h' prepared of
5: 1 Lord h' dried up the waters of Jordan

Jos 5: 5 them they h' not circumcised.
7 because they h' not circumcised
8 when they h' done circumcising all
12 after they h' eaten of the old corn
12 neither h' the children of Israel 1961
6: 8 Joshua h' spoken unto the people,
10 And Joshua h' commanded the people,*
22 Joshua h' said unto the two men *
22 that h' spied out the country, Go into
23 and her brethren, and all that she h';
25 father's household, and all that she h';
7: 7 we h' been content, and dwelt on the
24 and his tent, and all that he h':
25 they h' stoned them with stones. *
8:13 And when they h' set the people, *
18 stretched out the spear that he h' *
19 soon as he h' stretched out his hand:
20 and they h' no power to flee this way
21 that the ambush h' taken the city,
24 Israel h' made an end of slaying
26 until he h' utterly destroyed all the
33 as Moses...h' commanded before.
9: 3 Joshua h' done unto Jericho and to Ai,
4 made as if they h' been ambassadors,
16 they h' made a league with them,
18 h' sworn unto them by the Lord God
21 as the princes h' promised them.
10: 1 h' heard how Joshua h' taken Ai,
13 the people h' avenged themselves
20 children of Israel h' made an end of
27 the cave wherein they h' been hid,
32 all that he h' done to Libnah.
33 until he h' left none remaining.
35 to all which he h' done to Lachish.
37 to all that he h' done to Eglon;
39 as he h' done to Hebron, so he did to
39 as he h' done also to Libnah, and to
11: 1 Jabin king of Hazor h' heard those*
14 until they h' destroyed them, neither
14: 3 For Moses h' given the inheritance of
15 And the land h' rest from war.
17: 1 man of war, therefore he h' Gilead 1961
3 the son of Manasseh, h' no sons, "
6 daughters of Manasseh h'...inheritance
6 of Manasseh's sons h' the land *1961
8 Manasseh h' the...of Tappuah: * "
11 Manasseh h' in Issachar and in "
18: 2 seven tribes, which h' not yet received
19: 2 h' in their inheritance Beer-sheba,1961
9 of Simeon h' their inheritance
49 they h' made an end of dividing *
21: 4 h' by lot out of the tribe of Judah, 1961
5 children of Kohath h' by lot out of
6 And the children of Gershon h' by lot
7 Merari by their families h' out of the
10 were of the children of Levi, h': *1961
20 of Kohath, even they h' the cities
45 the Lord h' spoken unto the house of
22: 7 Moses h' given possession in Bashan:
23: 1 the Lord h' given rest unto Israel
24:31 h' known all the works of the Lord,
31 Lord, that he h' done for Israel.

J'g 1: 8 children of Judah h' fought *
8 Jerusalem, and h' taken it, and *
19 because they h' chariots of iron.
2: 6 And when Joshua h' let the people go,
7 who h' seen all the great works of the
10 the works which he h' done for Israel.
15 Lord h' said, and as the Lord h' sworn
3: 1 as h' not known all the wars of
11 And the land h' rest forty years.
12 because they h' done evil in the sight
16 him a dagger which h' two edges,
18 And when he h' made an end to
20 a summer parlour, which he h' *
30 And the land h' rest fourscore years.
4: 3 he h' nine hundred chariots of iron;
11 h' severed himself from the Kenites
18 when he h' turned in unto her *
24 until they h' destroyed Jabin king of
5:26 When she h' pierced and stricken*
31 And the land h' rest forty years.
6: 3 Israel h' sown, that the Midianites
27 and did as the Lord h' said unto him:
7:19 and they h' but newly set the watch:
8: 3 abated toward him, when he h' said
8 the men of Succoth h' answered him.
19 if ye h' saved them alive, I would not
24 (For they h' golden earrings, because
30 Gideon h' threescore and ten sons of
30 begotten: for he h' many wives. 1961
34 their God, who h' delivered them out
35 which he h' shewed unto Israel.
9:22 Abimelech h' reigned three years*
10: 4 And he h' thirty sons that rode on 1961
4 and they h' thirty cities, which are
11:34 her he h' neither son nor daughter.
39 to his vow which he h' vowed:
12: 9 And he h' thirty sons, and thirty 1961
14 h' forty sons, and thirty nephews, "
14: 4 Philistines h' dominion over Israel.
6 a kid, and he h' nothing in his hand:
6 father or his mother what he h' done.
9 that he h' taken the honey out of the
18 h' not plowed with my heifer,
18 ye h' not found out my riddle.
20 whom he h' used as his friend.
15: 5 And when he h' set the brands on fire,
6 because he h' taken his wife, and *
17 when he h' made an end of speaking,
19 and when he h' drunk, his spirit came
16: 8 which h' not been dried, and she
18 saw that he h' told her all his heart,
17: 3 he h' restored the eleven hundred*
3 I h' wholly dedicated the silver *
5 the man Micah h' an house of gods,

J'g 18: 1 all their inheritance *h*' not fallen
7 Zidonians, and *h*' no business with any
27 took the things which Micah *h*' made,
27 and the priest which he *h*', 1961
28 they *h*' no business with any man;
19: 6 damsel's father *h*' said unto the man,*
17 And when he *h*' lifted up his eyes,*
20:36 liers in wait which they *h*' set beside
21: 1 men of Israel *h*' sworn in Mizpeh,
5 they *h*' made a great oath concerning
12 virgins that *h*' known no man by lying
14 they *h*' saved alive of the women
15 because that the Lord *h*' made a breach
Ru 1: 6 she *h*' heard in the country of Moab
6 Lord *h*' visited his people in giving
2: 1 Naomi *h*' a kinsman of her husband's,
17 beat out that she *h*' gleaned:
18 in law saw what she *h*' gleaned:
18 she *h*' reserved after she was sufficed.
19 with whom she *h*' wrought, and said,
3: 7 And when Boaz *h*' eaten and drunk,
16 all that the man *h*' done to her.
1Sa 1: 2 he *h*' two wives; the name of the one
2 Peninnah *h*' children, but Hannah 1961
2 children, but Hannah *h*' no children.
5 but the Lord *h*' shut up her womb.
6 because the Lord *h*' shut up her womb.
9 rose up after they *h*' eaten in Shiloh,
9 and after they *h*' drunk.
13 Eli thought she *h*' been drunken.
20 after Hannah *h*' conceived, that she*
24 And when she *h*' weaned him, she
3: 8 that the Lord *h*' called the child.
4:18 And he *h*' judged Israel forty years.
5: 9 after they *h*' carried it about, the
9 they *h*' emerods in their secret parts. *
6: 6 he *h*' wrought wonderfully among
16 lords of the Philistines *h*' seen it,
19 because they *h*' looked into the ark
19 because the Lord *h*' smitten many of
7:14 cities which the Philistines *h*' taken
9: 2 he *h*' a son, whose name was Saul, 1961
15 Now the Lord *h*' told Samuel in his
10: 9 when he *h*' turned his back to go
13 And when he *h*' made an end of
20 Samuel *h*' caused all the tribes *
21 he *h*' caused the tribe of Benjamin *
26 of men, whose hearts God *h*' touched.
13: 1 and when he *h*' reigned two years *
4 that Saul *h*' smitten a garrison of
4 that Israel also was *h*' in abomination
8 set time that Samuel *h*' appointed:
10 soon as he *h*' made an end of offering
21 Yet they *h*' a file for the mattocks,
14:11 out of the holes where they *h*' hid.
17 And when they *h*' numbered, behold
22 which *h*' hid themselves in mount
24 Saul *h*' adjured the people, saying, †
30 the people *h*' eaten freely to day
30 for *h*' there not been now a much *
17: 5 he *h*' an helmet of brass upon his head,
6 And he *h*' greaves of brass upon his
12 name was Jesse; and he *h*' eight sons:
20 and went, as Jesse *h*' commanded him;
21 the Philistines *h*' put the battle in*
39 assayed to go; for he *h*' not proved it.
40 in a shepherd's bag which he *h*', even
18: 1 when he *h*' made an end of speaking
19:18 told him all that Saul *h*' done to him.
20:34 because his father *h*' done him shame.
37 of the arrow which Jonathan *h*' shot,
22:21 that Saul *h*' slain the Lord's priests.
24: 5 because he *h*' cut off Saul's skirt.
10 the Lord *h*' delivered thee to day into
16 when David *h*' made an end of speaking
18 when the Lord *h*' delivered me into
25: 2 great, and he *h*' three thousand sheep,
34 there *h*' not been left unto Nabal
35 received...that which she *h*' brought
37 and his wife *h*' told him these things,*
44 But Saul *h*' given Michal his daughter,
26: 5 to the place where Saul *h*' pitched:
28: 3 was dead, and all Israel *h*' lamented
3 And Saul *h*' put away those that
3 those that *h*' familiar spirits,
20 for he *h*' eaten no bread all the day,
24 And the woman *h*' a fat calf in the
30: 1 the Amalekites *h*' invaded the land
2 And *h*' taken the women captives, that
4 wept, until they *h*' no more power to
12 and when he *h*' eaten, his spirit came
12 for he *h*' eaten no bread, nor drunk
16 And when he *h*' brought him down,
16 spoil that they *h*' taken out of the land
18 that the Amalekites *h*' carried away:
19 any thing that they *h*' taken to them:
21 whom they *h*' made also to abide at the
31:11 which the Philistines *h*' done to Saul;
2Sa 1: 1 and David *h*' abode two days in Ziklag;
21 as though he *h*' not been anointed *
27 the people *h*' gone up every one from
30 and when he *h*' gathered all the people
31 servants of David *h*' smitten of
3: 7 And Saul *h*' a concubine, whose name
17 And Abner *h*' communication with the
22 for he *h*' sent him away, and he was
30 because he *h*' slain their brother
4: 2 And Saul's son *h*' two men that 1961
4 Saul's son, *h*' a son that was lame of
5:12 that the Lord *h*' established him king
12 and that he *h*' exalted his kingdom for
17 heard that they *h*' anointed David
25 so, as the Lord *h*' commanded him;*
6: 8 because the Lord *h*' made a breach
13 the ark of the Lord *h*' gone six paces,
17 the tabernacle that David *h*' pitched
2Sa 6: 18 as David *h*' made an end of offering
22 of them shall I be *h*' in honour.
23 the daughter of Saul *h*' no child unto
7: 1 and the Lord *h*' given him rest round
8:10 because he *h*' fought against
10 for Hadadezer *h*' wars with Toi.
11 silver and gold that he *h*' dedicated *
9: 2 And when they *h*' called him unto *
10 Now Ziba *h*' fifteen sons and twenty
12 And Mephibosheth *h*' a young son,
11:10 And when they *h*' told David, saying,
13 And when David *h*' called him, he did
22 David all that Joab *h*' sent him for.
27 that David *h*' done displeased the
12: 2 The rich man *h*' exceeding many 1961
3 But the poor man *h*' nothing, save one
6 this thing, and because he *h*' no pity.
8 if that *h*' been too little, I would
13: 1 the son of David *h*' a fair sister
3 But Amnon *h*' a friend, whose name
10 took the cakes which she *h*' made,
11 And when she *h*' brought them unto
15 the love wherewith he *h*' loved her.
18 And she *h*' a garment of divers colours
22 because he *h*' forced his sister Tamar.
23 that Absalom *h*' sheepshearers in
28 Now Absalom *h*' commanded his *
29 Amnon as Absalom *h*' commanded.
36 as he *h*' made an end of speaking,
14: 2 woman that *h*' a long time mourned
6 and thy handmaid *h*' two sons, and
32 it *h*' been good for me to have been *
33 and when he *h*' called for Absalom,
15: 2 any man that *h*' a controversy 1961
24 until all the people *h*' done passing
30 and *h*' his head covered, and he went
16:23 as if a man *h*' enquired at the oracle *
17:14 For the Lord *h*' appointed to defeat
18 which *h*' a well in his court; whither
20 And when they *h*' sought and could
18:18 Absalom...*h*' taken and reared up
33 would God I *h*' died for thee, O
19: 6 perceive, that if Absalom *h*' lived,
6 and all we *h*' died this day,
6 then it *h*' pleased thee well.
8 for Israel *h*' fled every man to his tent.
24 and *h*' neither dressed his feet, nor
32 and he *h*' provided the king of
43 our advice should not be first *h*' in
20: 3 whom he *h*' left to keep the house,
5 the set time which he *h*' appointed
8 garment that he *h*' put on was girded
21: 2 children of Israel *h*' sworn unto them;
11 Aiah, the concubine of Saul, *h*' done.
12 which *h*' stolen them from the street
12 where the Philistines *h*' hanged them,*
15 the Philistines *h*' yet war again 1961
20 that *h*' on every hand six fingers, and
22: 1 the day that the Lord *h*' delivered him*
38 turned not again until I *h*' consumed*
23: 8 the mighty men whom David *h*': the
18 and slew them, and *h*' the name among
20 who *h*' done many acts, he slew two
21 the Egyptian *h*' a spear in his hand;
22 and *h*' the name among three mighty
24: 8 So when they *h*' gone through all the
10 after that he *h*' numbered the people,
1Ki 1: 6 And his father *h*' not displeased him
41 heard it as they *h*' made an end of
2: 28 for Joab *h*' turned after Adonijah,
41 that Shimei *h*' gone from Jerusalem to
3: 1 until he *h*' made an end of building
10 Pleased...that Solomon *h*' asked this
21 but when I *h*' considered it in the
28 judgment which the king *h*' judged;
4: 2 these were the princes which he *h*':
7 And Solomon *h*' twelve officers over
11 which *h*' Taphath the daughter of
14 the son of Iddo *h*' Mahanaim: *
24 For he *h*' dominion over all the region
24 and he *h*' peace on all sides 1961
26 And Solomon *h*' forty thousand stalls
34 earth which *h*' heard of his wisdom.
5:15 And Solomon *h*' three score and 1961
7: 8 house where he dwelt *h*' another *
20 pillars *h*' pomegranates also above, *
28 they *h*' borders, and the borders were
30 And every base *h*' four brazen wheels,
30 four corners thereof *h*' undersetters
37 all of them *h*' one casting, one
51 which David his father *h*' dedicated;
8:11 glory of the Lord *h*' filled the house *
54 Solomon *h*' made an end of praying
66 that the Lord *h*' done for David his
9: 1 when Solomon *h*' finished the building
2 as he *h*' appeared unto him at Gibeon.
10 when Solomon *h*' built two houses, the
11 Hiram...*h*' furnished Solomon with
12 see the cities which Solomon *h*' given
16 Pharaoh...*h*' gone up, and taken
19 the cities of stone that Solomon *h*',1961
24 her house which Solomon *h*' built for
27 shipmen that *h*' knowledge of the sea,
10: 4 when the queen of Sheba *h*' seen all
4 and the house that he *h*' built,
7 until I came, and mine eyes *h*' seen it:
15 Beside ... he *h*' of the merchantmen, *
19 The throne *h*' six steps, and the *
22 For the king *h*' at sea a navy of
24 wisdom, which God *h*' put in his heart
26 and he *h*' a thousand and four
27 And Solomon *h*' horses brought out of
11: 3 And he *h*' seven hundred wives, 1961
9 God of Israel, which *h*' appeared unto
10 And *h*' commanded him concerning
15 after he *h*' smitten every male in
1Ki 11: 16 until he *h*' had cut off every male in
29 *h*' clad himself with a new garment;
12: 8 counsel...which they *h*' given him
12 as the king *h*' appointed, saying, *
32 unto the calves that he *h*' made:
32 the high places which he *h*' made.
33 upon the altar which he *h*' made in
33 the month which he *h*' devised of his
13: 4 which *h*' cried against the altar in *
5 the sign which the man of God *h*' given
11 the man of God *h*' done that day in
11 the words which he *h*' spoken unto the
12 For his sons *h*' seen what way the man
23 came to pass, after he *h*' eaten bread,
23 and after he *h*' drunk, that he saddled
28 the lion *h*' not eaten the carcase, nor
31 after he *h*' buried him, that he spake
14: 22 with their sins ... they *h*' committed,*
22 above all that their fathers *h*' done.
26 shields of gold ... Solomon *h*' made.
15: 3 which he *h*' done before him: and his
12 the idols that his fathers *h*' made.
13 because she *h*' made an idol in a
15 things which his father *h*' dedicated,
15 which himself *h*' dedicated, into the
20 the captains of the hosts which he *h*'*
22 timber ... wherewith Baasha *h*' built:
29 until he *h*' destroyed him, according
16: 31 as if it *h*' been a light thing for him
32 house of Baal, which he *h*' built in
17: 7 because there *h*' been no rain in * 1961
19: 1 told Jezebel all that Elijah *h*' done,
1 how he *h*' slain all the prophets
21: 1 Naboth the Jezreelite *h*' a vineyard 1961
4 which Naboth...*h*' spoken to him:
4 for he *h*' said, I will not give thee the
11 did as Jezebel *h*' sent unto them, and
11 the letters which she *h*' sent unto them,
22: 31 that *h*' rule over his chariots, saying, *
53 according to all that his father *h*' done.
2Ki 1: 17 word of the Lord ... Elijah *h*' spoken.
17 of Judah; because he *h*' no son. 1961
2: 14 when he also *h*' smitten the waters,
3: 2 image of Baal that his father *h*' made.
4: 12, 15 when he *h*' called her, she stood
17 season that Elijah *h*' said unto her.
20 And when he *h*' taken him,
5: 2 the Syrians *h*' gone out by companies,
2 and *h*' brought away captive out of the
7 king of Israel *h*' read the letter,
8 Elisha the man of God *h*' heard *
8 that the king of Israel *h*' rent his
13 if the prophet *h*' bid thee do some
6: 23 when they *h*' eaten and drunk,
30 he *h*' sackcloth upon his flesh.
7: 6 For the Lord *h*' made the host
15 which the Syrians *h*' cast away
17 as the man of God *h*' said,
18 as the man of God *h*' spoken
8: 1 woman, whose son he *h*' restored
5 how he *h*' restored a dead body
5 whose son he *h*' restored to life,
29 wounds which the Syrians *h*' given him
9: 14 Now Joram *h*' kept Ramoth-gilead,*
15 wounds which the Syrians *h*' given him,
31 she said, *H*' Zimri peace, who slew his*
10: 1 And Ahab *h*' seventy sons in Samaria,
17 till he *h*' destroyed him, according to
25 soon as he *h*' made an end of offering
11: 15 For the priest *h*' said, Let her not *
12: 6 the priests *h*' not repaired the
11 that *h*' the oversight of the house of
18 his fathers, kings of Judah, *h*' dedicated,
13: 7 king of Syria *h*' destroyed them,*
7 and *h*' made them like the dust *
23 and *h*' compassion on them, and
23 *h*' respect unto them, because of his
25 which he *h*' taken out of the hand
14: 5 servants which *h*' slain the king
15: 3 his father Amaziah *h*' done;
9 as his fathers *h*' done:
34 that his father Uzziah *h*' done.
16: 11 that king Ahaz *h*' sent from Damascus
18 that they *h*' built in the house,
17: 4 for he *h*' sent messengers to So king
4 as he *h*' done year by year:
7 children of Israel *h*' sinned against
7 which *h*' brought them up out of
7 and *h*' feared other gods, *
8 which they *h*' made.
12 whereof the Lord *h*' said unto them,
15 concerning whom the Lord *h*' charged
20 until he *h*' cast them out
23 as he *h*' said by all his servants *
28 priests whom they *h*' carried away
29 which the Samaritans *h*' made,
35 the Lord *h*' made a covenant,
18: 4 serpent that Moses *h*' made:
16 Hezekiah king of Judah *h*' overlaid,
18 when they *h*' called to the king,
19: 8 for he *h*' heard that he was departed
20: 11 by which it *h*' gone down in the dial
12 for he *h*' heard that Hezekiah
12 heard that Hezekiah *h*' been sick.
21: 3 Hezekiah his father *h*' destroyed;
7 of the grove that he *h*' made
16 till he *h*' filled Jerusalem
24 slew all them that *h*' conspired
22: 11 when the king *h*' heard the words of
23: 5 whom the kings of Judah *h*' ordained
8 where the priests *h*' burned incense,
11 kings of Judah *h*' given to the sun,
12 which the kings of Judah *h*' made,
12 altars which Manasseh *h*' made
13 Solomon ... king of Israel *h*' builded
15 Nebat, who made Israel to sin, *h*' made,

2Ki 23: 19 kings of Israel h· made to provoke
19 acts that he h· done in Beth-el.
26 Manasseh h· provoked him
29 slew him...when he h· seen him.
32, 37 all that his fathers h· done.
24: 7 king of Babylon h· taken from the
9 all that his father h· done.
13 Solomon king of Israel h· made
13 As the Lord h· said.
19 all that Jehoiakim h· done,
20 until he h· cast them out
25: 16 bases which Solomon h· made
17 and like unto these h· the second pillar
22 king of Babylon h· left,
23 king of Babylon h· made Gedaliah
1Ch 2: 22 begat Jair, who h· three and 1961
26 Jerahmeel h· also another wife, whose
34 Now Sheshan h· no sons, but 1961
34 Sheshan h· a servant, an Egyptian,
52 Kirjath-jearim h· sons; Haroeh, and
4: 5 Ashur the father of Tekoa h· two 1961
22 and Saraph, who h· the dominion in
27 And Shimei h· sixteen sons and six
27 but his brethren h· not many children,
40 they of Ham h· dwelt there of old.*
6: 31 the Lord, after that the ark h· rest.
32 until Solomon h· built the house
49 the servant of God h· commanded.
66 the sons of Kohath h· cities of 1961
7: 4 for they h· many wives and sons.
15 and Zelophehad h· daughters. 1961
8: 8 after he h· sent them away;
38 And Azel h· six sons, whose names are
40 and h· many sons, and sons' sons, an
9: 23 they and their children h· the
28 And certain of them h· the charge of
31 the Korahite, h· the set office over the
44 And Azel h· six sons, whose names are
10: 9 when they h· stripped him, *
11 Philistines h· done to Saul,
13 counsel of one that h· a familiar
11: 10 mighty men whom David h·, who
11 the mighty men whom David h·;
20 he slew them, and h· a name 1961
22 who h· done many acts;
24 and h· the name among the three
12: 15 when it h· overflown all his banks;
29 greatest part of them h· kept the ward
32 were men that h· understanding of
39 their brethren h· prepared for them.
13: 11 because the Lord h· made a breach
14 house of Obed-edom, and all that he h·.
14: 2 that the Lord h· confirmed him
4 his children which he h· in 1961
12 when they h· left their gods *
15: 3 which he h· prepared for it.
27 David also h· upon him an ephod of
16: 1 that David h· pitched for it:
2 when David h· made an end
18: 9 how David h· smitten all
10 because he h· fought against
10 (for Hadarezer h· war with Tou;) 1961
19: 6 they h· made themselves odious
17 when David h· put the battle
21: 28 Lord h· answered him
23: 11 but Jeush and Beriah h· not many
17 And Eliezer h· none other sons; 1961
22 And Eliezer died, and h· no sons, "
24: 2 died before their father, and h· no "
19 God of Israel h· commanded him.
28 Of Mahli came Eleazar, who h· no 1961
26: 9 And Meshelemiah h· sons and
10 of the children of Merari, h· sons;
26 captain of the host, h· dedicated.
28 Joab the son of Zeruiah, h· dedicated;
28 and whosoever h· dedicated
27: 23 because the Lord h· said
28: 2 As for me, I h· in mine heart to *
2 and h· made ready for the building:
12 of all that he h· by the spirit, of the
29: 25 majesty as h· not been on any 1961
2Ch 1: 3 servant of the Lord h· made "
4 ark of God h· David brought
4 place which David h· prepared
4 for he h· pitched a tent
5 the son of Hur, h· made,
12 such as none of the kings have h· 1961
14 and he h· a thousand and four "
16 Solomon h· horses brought
2: 17 David his father h· numbered
3: 1 that David h· prepared
5: 1 David his father h· dedicated:
14 glory of the Lord h· filled *
6: 13 Solomon h· made a brasen
13 and h· set it in the midst
7: 2 glory of the Lord h· filled *
6 the king h· made to praise
7 altar which Solomon h· made
10 the Lord h· shewed unto David,
8: 1 wherein Solomon h· built
2 which Huram h· restored
6 store cities that Solomon h·, 1961
11 house that he h· built for her:
12 which he h· built before the porch,
14 for so h· David the man of God
18 ships, and servants that h· knowledge
9: 3 queen of Sheba h· seen the wisdom
3 and the house that he h· built,
6 and mine eyes h· seen it:
12 which she h· brought unto the king
23 that God h· put into his heart.
25 And Solomon h· four thousand 1961
10: 2 whither he h· fled from
6 the old men that h· stood before 1961
11: 14 his sons h· cast them off *
15 calves which he h· made.

2Ch 12: 1 when Rehoboam h· established *
1 the kingdom, and h· strengthened *
2 they h· transgressed against the Lord,
9 which Solomon h· made.
13 city which the Lord h· chosen
14: 6 for the land h· rest, and *
6 he h· no war in those years;
6 because the Lord h· given him rest.
8 And Asa h· an army of men that 1961
15: 8 which he h· taken from mount
11 spoil which they h· brought,
15 for they h· sworn with all their hearts
16 she h· made an idol in a grove:
18 things that his father h· dedicated,
18 and that he himself h· dedicated,
16: 14 which he h· made for himself
17: 2 which Asa his father h· taken.
5 and he h· riches and honour in 1961
9 taught in Judah, and h· the book *
13 And he h· much business in the 1961
18: 1 Now Jehoshaphat h· riches and "
2 and for the people that he h· with*
10 son of Chenaanah h· made him horns*
30 king of Syria h· commanded
20: 21 when he h· consulted with
23 when they h· made an end
27 the Lord h· made them to rejoice
29 when they h· heard that the Lord *
33 the people h· not prepared
21: 2 And he h· brethren the sons of
6 for he h· the daughter of Ahab to 1961
7 that he h· made with David,
10 because he h· forsaken the Lord
22: 1 to the camp h· slain all the eldest.
7 whom the Lord h· anointed to cut
9 and when they h· slain him, *
9 So the house of Ahaziah h· no power
23: 8 Jehoiada the priest h· commanded,*
9 that h· been king David's,
23: 18 whom David h· distributed in the
21 that they h· slain Athaliah *
24: 7 wicked woman, h· broken up
10 until they h· made an end.
14 And when they h· finished it,
16 because he h· done good in Israel,
22 his father h· done to him,
24 because they h· forsaken the Lord
25: 3 servants that h· killed the king
26: 5 Zechariah, who h· understanding
10 for he h· much cattle, both in the 1961
11 Moreover Uzziah h· an host of fighting
19 and h· a censer in his hand to burn
20 because the Lord h· smitten him.
28: 3 whom the Lord h· cast out *
6 they h· forsaken the Lord God
17 the Edomites h· come and smitten
18 Philistines also h· invaded
18 and h· taken Beth-shemesh,
29: 2 that David his father h· done.
22 when they h· killed the rams, *
29 when they h· made an end
34 other priests h· sanctified themselves:
36 that God h· prepared the people:
30: 2 for the king h· taken counsel,
3 the priests h· not sanctified
3 neither h· the people gathered
5 for they h· not done it of a long
17 therefore the Levites h· the charge of
18 Zebulun, h· not cleansed themselves,
31: 1 until they h· utterly destroyed
10 we have h· enough to eat, and have
32: 27 And Hezekiah h· exceeding much 1961
29 for God h· given him substance
33: 2 whom the Lord h· cast out *
3 his father h· broken down,
4 whereof the Lord h· said, *
7 the idol which he h· made,
7 of which God h· said to David, *
9 whom the Lord h· destroyed *
15 altars that he h· built in the mount
22 Manasseh his father h· made,
23 Manasseh his father h· humbled
25 all them that h· conspired against
34: 4 that h· sacrificed unto them.
7 when he h· broken down the altars*
7 and h· beaten the graven images *
8 when he h· purged the land,
9 Levites that kept the doors h· gathered
10 the workmen that h· the oversight of
11 kings of Judah h· destroyed.
19 when the king h· heard the words
22 they that the king h· appointed,
35: 20 when Josiah h· prepared the temple,
24 in the second chariot that he h·;
36: 13 who h· made him swear
14 the Lord which he h· hallowed
15 because he h· compassion on his people,
17 and h· no compassion upon young man
20 And them that h· escaped from
21 until the land h· enjoyed
Ezr 1: 5 whose spirit God h· raised,
7 which Nebuchadnezzar h· brought
7 and h· put them in the house
2: 1 those which h· been carried away,
1 king of Babylon h· carried away
3: 7 the grant that they h· of Cyrus king of
12 that h· seen the first house,
5: 12 our fathers h· provoked the God
14 whom he h· made governor;
6: 13 which Darius the king h· sent,
21 all such as h· separated themselves
22 the Lord h· made them joyful,
7: 6 Lord God of Israel h· given:
10 For Ezra h· prepared his heart
20 the princes h· appointed for the
22 because we h· spoken unto the

Ezr 8: 25 all Israel there present, h· offered:
35 of those that h· been carried away,*
9: 4 of those that h· been carried away;*
10: 1 Now when Ezra h· prayed, *
1 and when he h· confessed, *
6 of them that h· been carried away.*
8 of those that h· been carried away.*
17 the men that h· taken strange
18 were found that h· taken strange
44 All these h· taken strange wives:
44 and some of them h· wives 3426
44 by whom they h· children. 7760
Ne 1: 2 the Jews that h· escaped,
2: 1 Now I h· not been beforetime
9 Now the king h· sent captains
12 what my God h· put in my heart *
16 neither h· I as yet told it
18 words that he h· spoken unto me.
4: 6 for the people h· a mind to work. 1961
15 and God h· brought their counsel
18 every one h· his sword girded by
5: 15 governors that h· been before me*
15 and h· taken of them bread and *
6: 1 heard that I h· builded the wall,
1 at that time I h· not set up the doors
12 that God h· not sent him;
12 and Sanballat h· hired him.
18 Johanan h· taken the daughter
7: 1 and I h· set up the doors,
6 of those that h· been carried away,
6 king of Babylon h· carried away,
67 and they h· two hundred forty and five
8: 1 which the Lord h· commanded
4 which they h· made for the purpose;
12 because they h· understood
14 law which the Lord h· commanded
17 unto that day h· not the children
9: 18 when they h· made them a molten
18 and h· wrought great provocations;
28 But after they h· rest, they did evil
28 so that they h· the dominion over them:
11: 16 the Levites, h· the oversight of the*
12: 29 the singers h· builded them
43 for God h· made them rejoice
13: 3 when they h· heard the law,
5 And he h· prepared for him
10 of the Levites h· not been given
23 Jews that h· married wives
Es 1: 8 for so the king h· appointed
2: 1 and what she h· done,
6 Who h· been carried away from
6 which h· been carried away
6 king of Babylon h· carried away.
7 for she h· neither father nor mother.
10 Esther h· not shewed her people
10 Mordecai h· charged her that she
12 After that she h· been twelve months.
15 who h· taken her for his daughter,
20 Esther h· not yet shewed her
20 as Mordecai h· charged her:
3: 2 for the king h· so commanded
4 for he h· told them that he was
6 for they h· shewed him the people
12 to all that Haman h· commanded*
4: 5 whom he h· appointed to attend
7 of all that h· happened unto him,
7 that Haman h· promised to pay
17 to all that Esther h· commanded
5: 5 that Esther h· prepared.
11 wherein the king h· promoted him,
11 and how he h· advanced him
12 that she h· prepared but myself;
6: 2 that Mordecai h· told of Bigthana
4 gallows that he h· prepared for him.
13 every thing that h· befallen him.
14 banquet that Esther h· prepared.
7: 4 But if we h· been sold for bondmen
4 I h· held my tongue,
9 which Haman h· made for *
9 Mordecai, who h· spoken good *
10 that he h· prepared for Mordecai.
8: 1 for Esther h· told what he was unto
2 which he h· taken from Haman,
3 that he h· devised against the Jews.
16 The Jews h· light, and gladness, and
17 the Jews h· joy and gladness, a feast
9: 1 that the Jews h· rule over them that
16 stood for their lives, and h· rest from
23 to do as they h· begun,
23 as Mordecai h· written unto them;
24 all the Jews, h· devised against
24 and h· cast Pur, that is, the lot,
26 which they h· seen concerning
26 and which h· come unto them,
31 Esther the queen h· enjoined them,
31 and as they h· decreed for themselves
Job 2: 11 for they h· made an appointment*
3: 13 then h· I been at rest,
15 Or with princes that h· gold, who
16 untimely birth I h· not been;
26 neither h· I rest, neither was I quiet;*
6: 20 confounded because they h· hoped;
9: 16 If I h· called, and he h· answered me;
16 that he h· hearkened unto my voice. *
10: 18 Oh that I h· given up the ghost,
18 and no eye h· seen me!
19 as though I h· not been;
22: 8 as for the mighty man, he h· the earth
24: 16 which they h· marked for *
29: 12 and him that h· none to help him.
31: 25 because mine hand h· gotten
31 Oh that we h· of his flesh! we cannot*
35 mine adversary h· written a book.*
32: 3 because they h· found no answer,
3 and yet h· condemned Job.
4 Now Elihu h· waited

Job 32: 4 till Job *h* spoken, *
16 When I *h* waited, *
38: 8 as if it *h* issued out of the womb?
42: 7 after the Lord *h* spoken these words
10 gave Job twice as much as he *h* before.
11 they that *h* been of his acquaintance
11 that the Lord *h* brought upon him:
12 for he *h* fourteen thousand sheep, 1961
13 He *h* also seven sons and three "
Ps 27: 13 I *h* fainted, unless I *h* believed to see
35: 14 as though he *h* been my friend
42: 4 for I *h* gone with the multitude, *
55: 6 Oh that I *h* wings like a dove! for then
73: 2 my steps *h* well nigh slipped.
74: 5 according as he *h* lifted up *
78: 11 wonders that he *h* shewed them.
23 Though he *h* commanded the *
24 And *h* rained down manna *
24 and *h* given them of the corn *
43 How he *h* wrought his signs *
44 And *h* turned their rivers into *
54 which his right hand *h* purchased.
81: 13 that my people *h* hearkened unto me, *
13 and Israel *h* walked in my ways? *
84: 10 I *h* rather be a doorkeeper in the
89: 7 and to be *h* in reverence of all them *
94: 17 Unless the Lord *h* been my help,
17 my soul *h* almost dwelt in silence.
105: 26 and Aaron whom he *h* chosen.
106: 21 which *h* done great things
23 destroy them, *h* not Moses his 3884
119: 51 The proud have *h* me greatly in
56 This I *h*, because I kept thy 1961
87 They *h* almost consumed me
92 Unless thy law *h* been my delights,
124: 1 If it *h* not been the Lord
2 If it *h* not been the Lord
3 Then they *h* swallowed us up
4 Then the waters *h* overwhelmed us,
4 the stream *h* gone over our soul:
5 Then the proud waters *h*
Pr 8: 26 While as yet he *h* not made
24: 31 and nettles *h* covered the face *
Ec 1: 16 yea, my heart *h* great experience of
2: 7 and *h* servants born in my house; 1961
7 also I *h* great possessions of "
11 that my hands *h* wrought,
11 labour that I *h* laboured to do:
18 which I *h* taken under the sun: *
4: 1 and they *h* no comforter;
1 but they *h* no comforter.
8: 10 who *h* come and gone from
10 city where they *h* so done: *
Ca 3: 4 until I *h* brought him
5: 6 but my beloved *h* withdrawn
8: 11 Solomon *h* a vineyard at Baal-hamon;
Isa 1: 9 Except the Lord of hosts *h* left unto
6: 2 each one *h* six wings;
6 which he *h* taken with the tongs
22: 11 neither *h* respect unto him that
26: 13 lords beside thee have *h* dominion
29: 16 He *h* no understanding? *
37: 8 for he *h* heard that he was
38: 9 when he *h* been sick,
17 Behold, for peace I *h* great bitterness:
21 For Isaiah *h* said, Let them take
22 Hezekiah also *h* said,
39: 1 for he *h* heard that he *
1 *h* been sick, and was recovered.
41: 3 way that he *h* not gone with
48: 18 then *h* thy peace been as a river,
19 Thy seed also *h* been as the
49: 21 these, where *h* they been? *
52: 15 for that which *h* not been told
15 and that which they *h* not heard
53: 9 because he *h* done no violence,
59: 10 and we grope as if we *h* no eyes: *
60: 10 but in my favour have I *h* mercy on
Jer 2: 21 Yet I *h* planted thee a noble
3: 7 after she *h* done all these things,
8 adultery I *h* put her away,
4: 23 and the heavens, and they *h* no light.
5: 7 when I *h* fed them to the full,
6: 15 ashamed when they *h* committed
8: 12 ashamed when they *h* committed
9: 2 Oh that I *h* in the wilderness a lodging
11: 19 I knew not that they *h* devised
13: 7 the place where I *h* hid it:
16: 15 the lands whither he *h* driven them:
19: 14 whither the Lord *h* sent him
23: 8 whither I *h* driven them;
22 But if they *h* stood in my counsel, *
22 and *h* caused my people to hear my
24: 1 king of Babylon *h* carried away
1 from Jerusalem, and *h* brought them
2 One basket *h* very good figs, even like
2 the other basket *h* very naughty figs,
25: 17 unto whom the Lord *h* sent me:
26: 8 when Jeremiah *h* made an end
8 all that the Lord *h* commanded
19 evil which he *h* pronounced
28: 12 the prophet *h* broken the yoke
29: 1 Nebuchadnezzar *h* carried away
32: 3 king of Judah *h* shut him up,
16 Now when I *h* delivered the evidence
34: 8 king Zedekiah *h* made a covenant
10 which *h* entered into the covenant,
11 whom they *h* let go free,
15 turned, and *h* done right in my
15 and ye *h* made a covenant
16 whom he *h* set at liberty
18 which they *h* made before me,
36: 4 which he *h* spoken unto him,
11 the son of Shaphan, *h* heard out
13 all the words that he *h* heard,
16 when they *h* heard all the words,

Jer 36: 23 Jehudi *h* read three or four leaves,
25 and Gemariah *h* made intercession
27 after that the king *h* burned the
32 king of Judah *h* burned in the fire:
37: 4 for they *h* not put him into prison.
10 though ye *h* smitten the whole
15 for they *h* made that the prison.
16 Jeremiah *h* remained there
38: 1 that Jeremiah *h* spoken unto all *
7 that they *h* put Jeremiah in the
27 that the king *h* commanded.
39: 5 when they *h* taken him,
10 poor of the people, which *h* nothing,
40: 1 of the guard *h* let him go from
1 Ramah, when he *h* taken him
7 king of Babylon *h* made Gedaliah
7 and *h* committed unto him
11 king of Babylon *h* left a remnant
11 and that he *h* set over them
41: 2 king of Babylon *h* made governor
4 after he *h* slain Gedaliah,
9 wherein Ishmael *h* cast all the dead *
9 whom he *h* slain because
10 captain of the guard *h* committed
11 the son of Nethaniah *h* done,
14 that Ishmael *h* carried away captive
16 whom he *h* recovered from
16 after that he *h* slain Gedaliah
16 whom he *h* brought again
18 son of Nethaniah *h* slain Gedaliah
43: 1 when Jeremiah *h* made an end
5 whither they *h* been driven,
6 of the guard *h* left with Gedaliah
44: 15 that their wives *h* burned incense *
17 for then *h* we plenty of victuals, 1961
20 which *h* given him that answer,
45: 1 when he *h* written these words *
52: 2 to all that Jehoiakim *h* done.
3 till he *h* cast them out from
20 which king Solomon *h* made
La 1: 7 pleasant things that she *h* in the *1961
9 wonderfully: she *h* no comforter. *
2: 17 that which he *h* devised; *
17 his word that he *h* commanded *
Eze 1: 5 they *h* the likeness of a man.
6 And every one *h* four faces,
6 and every one *h* four wings.
8 And they *h* the hands of a man under
8 and they four *h* their faces and their
10 they four *h* the face of a man, and the
10 they four *h* the face of an ox on the
10 they four also *h* the face of an eagle
16 and they four *h* one likeness: and
23 every one *h* two, which covered on this
23 every one *h* two, which covered on that
25 when they stood, and *h* let down *
27 and it *h* brightness round about. *
3: 6 Surely, *h* I sent thee to them, *
8: 8 and when I *h* digged in the wall,
9: 3 which *h* the writer's inkhorn by his
11 which *h* the inkhorn by his side,
10: 6 when he *h* commanded the man *
10 they four *h* one likeness, as if a 1961
10 as if a wheel *h* been in the midst
12 even the wheels that the four *h*.
14 and every one *h* four faces: the first
21 Every one *h* four faces apiece, and
11: 24 vision that I *h* seen went up
25 things that the Lord *h* shewed me.
16: 14 which I *h* put upon thee,
17 which I *h* given thee,
17: 3 full of feathers, which *h* divers colours,
18 lo, he *h* given his hand,
19: 5 she saw that she *h* waited,
11 And she *h* strong rods for the 1961
20: 6 a land that I *h* espied for them,
15 which I *h* given them, flowing
24 they *h* not executed my judgments,
24 but *h* despised my statutes,
24 and *h* polluted my sabbaths,
28 when I *h* brought them into
23: 10 for they *h* executed judgment *
19 wherein she *h* played the harlot
32 laughed to scorn and *h* in derision;
39 when they *h* slain their children
29: 18 yet *h* he no wages, nor his army, 1961
18 service that he *h* served against
33: 15 give again that he *h* robbed,
21 that one that *h* escaped out of
22 and *h* opened my mouth,
35: 5 Because thou hast *h* a perpetual 1961
5 their iniquity *h* an end: *
36: 18 the blood that they *h* shed
18 wherewith they *h* polluted it:
21 But I *h* pity for mine holy name,
21 house of Israel *h* profaned
40: 10 and the posts *h* one measure on this
26 and it *h* palm trees, one on this side,
31, 34, 37, the going up to it *h* eight steps.
41: 6 but they *h* not hold in the wall *1961
18 and every cherub *h* two faces;
23 and the sanctuary *h* two doors.
24 And the doors *h* two leaves apiece,
42: 6 but *h* not pillars as the pillars of the
15 Now when he *h* made an end of
20 it *h* a wall round about, five hundred
44: 22 a widow that *h* a priest before. *1961
25 for sister that hath *h* no husband, "
47: 3 the man that *h* the line in his hand *
7 Now when I *h* returned, behold,
Da 1: 4 and such as *h* ability in them to
9 Now God *h* brought Daniel into *
11 prince of the eunuchs *h* set over
17 Daniel *h* understanding in all visions
18 the king *h* said he should bring
2: 24 whom the king *h* ordained to

Da 3: 2 Nebuchadnezzar the king *h* set up.
3 Nebuchadnezzar the king *h* set up;
3 image that Nebuchadnezzar *h* set up.
7 Nebuchadnezzar the king *h* set up:
27 upon whose bodies the fire *h* no power,
27 smell of fire *h* passed on them.
4: 12 the beasts of the field *h* shadow under
21 fowls of the heaven *h* their habitation;
5: 2 Nebuchadnezzar *h* taken out
6: 24 those men which *h* accused Daniel,
24 and the lions *h* the mastery of them
7: 1 Daniel *h* a dream and visions of 2370
4 and *h* eagle's wings: I beheld till
5 and it *h* three ribs in the mouth *
6 which *h* upon the back of it four
6 the beast *h* also four heads;
7 and it *h* great iron teeth:
7 and it *h* ten horns.
12 they *h* their dominion taken away: *
20 even of that horn that *h* eyes, and a
8: 3 a ram which *h* two horns: and the
5 and the goat *h* a notable horn
6 to the ram that *h* two horns
6 which I *h* seen standing before *
15 even I Daniel, *h* seen the vision,
9: 21 whom I *h* seen in the vision
10: 1 and *h* understanding of the vision.
11 And when he *h* spoken this word
15 And when he *h* spoken such words
19 And when he *h* spoken unto me, *
Ho 1: 8 when she *h* weaned Lo-ruhamah,
2: 23 upon her that *h* not obtained
12: 3 his strength he *h* power with God:
4 Yea, he *h* power over the angel,
Am 7: 2 when they *h* made an end *
Ob 1: 5 have stolen till they *h* enough?
16 as though they *h* not been.
Jon 1: 10 because he *h* told them.
17 the Lord *h* prepared a great fish *
3: 10 that he *h* said that he would *
4: 10 Thou hast *h* pity on the gourd, for
Na 3: 8 the rivers, that *h* the waters round
Hab 3: 4 he *h* horns coming out of his 1961
Hag 1: 12 their God *h* sent him,
Zec 1: 12 against which thou hast *h* indignation
5: 9 for they *h* wings like the wings of a
7: 2 When they *h* sent unto the
10: 6 as though I *h* not cast them off:
11: 10 which I *h* made with all the people.
Mal 2: 15 Yet *h* he the residue of the spirit.
M't 1: 6 Solomon of her that *h* been the wife
24 angel of the Lord *h* bidden him, *
25 till she *h* brought forth her firstborn
2: 3 Herod the king *h* heard these things, *
4 when he *h* gathered all the chief *
7 when he *h* privily called the wise
9 When they *h* heard the king,
11 when they *h* opened their treasures, *
16 time which he *h* diligently enquired
3: 4 And the same John *h* his raiment 2192
4: 2 when he *h* fasted forty days
12 when Jesus *h* heard that John *
24 lunatick, and those that *h* the palsy; *
7: 28 when Jesus *h* ended these sayings, *
9: 8 which *h* given such power
10: 1 And when he *h* called unto him *
11: 1 when Jesus *h* made an end
2 Now when John *h* heard in the prison *
21 done in you, *h* been done in Tyre
23 done in thee, *h* been done in Sodom,
12: 7 But if ye *h* known what this
10 a man which *h* his hand withered. *2192
13: 5 where they *h* not much earth: "
5 they *h* no deepness of earth: "
6 they *h* no root, they withered "
46 when he *h* found one pearl *
46 sold all that he *h*, and bought 2192
53 when Jesus *h* finished these
14: 3 For Herod *h* laid hold on John,
13 when the people *h* heard thereof, *
21 And they that *h* eaten were about *
23 And when he *h* sent the multitudes
35 the men of that place *h* knowledge *
16: 5 they *h* forgotten to take bread. *
17: 8 when they *h* lifted up their eyes, *
18: 24 And when he *h* begun to reckon,
25 forasmuch as he *h* not to pay, his 2192
25 and children, and all that he *h*, "
32 after that he *h* called him, *
33 not thou also have *h* compassion
33 fellowservant, even as I *h* pity on thee?
19: 1 when Jesus *h* finished these sayings,
22 sorrowful: for he *h* great 2258, 2192
20: 2 And when he *h* agreed with the
11 when they *h* received it, *
34 So Jesus *h* compassion on them, and *
21: 28 A certain man *h* two sons; and he 2192
32 when ye *h* seen it, *
45 and Pharisees *h* heard his parables, *
22: 11 a man which *h* not on a wedding 1746
22 When they *h* heard these words, *
25 when he *h* married a wife, *
28 be of the seven? for they all *h* her. 2192
34 But when the Pharisees *h* heard *
34 that he *h* put the Sadducees to silence,
23: 30 If we *h* been in the days of our
24: 43 of the house *h* known in what hour
25: 16 Then he that *h* received the five *
17 likewise he that *h* received two, *
18 But he that *h* received one went *
20 so he that *h* received five talents, *
22 He also that *h* received two *
24 Then he that *h* received the one
26: 1 when Jesus *h* finished all these
8 they *h* indignation, saying, To what
19 as Jesus *h* appointed them; *

M't 26: 24 it h' been good for that man *
24 if he h' not been born.
30 And when they h' sung an hymn,
57 they that h' laid hold on Jesus led
27: 2 And when they h' bound him, *
3 Then Judas, which h' betrayed him,*
16 they h' then a notable prisoner, 2192
18 that for envy they h' delivered him.
26 when he h' scourged Jesus, *
29 they h' platted a crown of thorns, *
31 after that they h' mocked him,
34 and when he h' tasted thereof,
50 Jesus, when he h' cried again
59 when Joseph h' taken the body, *
60 which he h' hewn out in the rock:
28: 12 with the elders, and h' taken counsel,
16 a mountain where Jesus h' appointed
M'r 1: 19 when he h' gone a little farther *
22 as one that h' authority, and not *2192
26 when the unclean spirit h' torn him,*
37 And when they h' found him, *
42 as soon as he h' spoken, *
2: 4 and when they h' broken it up,
25 what David did, when he h' need, 2192
3: 1 a man there which h' a withered "
3 the man which h' the withered "
5 And when he h' looked round
10 For he h' healed many;
10 touch him, as many as h' plagues. 2192
4: 5 where it h' not much earth; and "
5 sprang up, because it h' no depth "
6 because it h' no root, it withered "
36 when they h' sent away the *
5: 3 Who h' his dwelling among the 2192
4 Because that he h' been often bound
4 and the chains h' been plucked
15 with the devil, and h' the legion, *2192
18 he that h' been possessed with the
19 and hath h' compassion on thee.
20 how great things Jesus h' done for
25 h' an issue of blood twelve years, 1510
26 And h' suffered many things
26 of many physicians, and h' spent
26 all that she h', and was nothing 3844
27 When she h' heard of Jesus, *
30 that virtue h' gone out of him,
32 to see her that h' done this thing.
40 But when he h' put them all out,*
6: 17 Herod himself h' sent forth
17 for he h' married her.
18 For John h' said unto Herod, *
19 Therefore Herodias h' a quarrel *
30 both what they h' done,
30 and what they h' taught.
31 and they h' no leisure so much as to
41 when he h' taken the five loaves *
46 And when he h' sent them away,
49 they supposed it h' been a spirit,*
53 And when they h' passed over,
7: 14 when he h' called all the people *
25 whose young daughter h' an 2192
32 that was deaf, and h' an impediment
8: 7 And they h' a few small fishes: 2192
9 they that h' eaten were about four*
14 Now the disciples h' forgotten to*
14 neither h' they in the ship with 2192
23 and when he h' spit on his eyes,
33 But when he h' turned about *
34 and when he h' called the people*
9: 8 when they h' looked round about,*
9 tell no man what things they h' seen,
34 they h' disputed among themselves,
36 and when he h' taken him in his *
10: 22 away grieved: for he h' great 2258,2192
11: 6 even as Jesus h' commanded:
11 and when he h' looked round about
12: 12 knew that he h' spoken the parable*
22 And the seven h' her, and left no * 2983
23 for the seven h' her to wife. 2192
28 perceiving that he h' answered
44 all that she h', even all her living. 2192
13: 20 except that the Lord h' shortened
14: 4 there were some that h' indignation
16 and found as he h' said unto them:
21 if he h' never been born.
23 and when he h' given thanks,
26 And when they h' sung an hymn,
44 he that betrayed him h' given them
15: 7 with them that h' made insurrection
7 who h' committed murder in
8 to do as he h' ever done unto them.*
10 chief priests h' delivered him
15 when he h' scourged him,
20 And when they h' mocked him,
24 And when they h' crucified him,*
44 whether he h' been any while dead.
16: 1 and Salome h' bought sweet spices,*
9 out of whom he h' cast seven devils.
10 told them that h' been with him,
11 when they h' heard that he was alive,*
11 and h' been seen of her,
14 believed not them which h' seen him
19 after the Lord h' spoken unto them,
Lu 1: 3 having h' perfect understanding *
7 And they h' no child, because that 1510
22 that he h' seen a vision in the temple:
58 how the Lord h' shewed great mercy
2: 17 And when they h' seen it, *
20 things that they h' heard and seen,
26 before he h' seen the Lord's Christ.
36 great age, and h' lived with an *
39 when they h' performed all things
43 when they h' fulfilled the days,
3: 19 evils which Herod h' done,
4: 13 when the devil h' ended all the
16 where he h' been brought up:

Lu 4: 17 And when he h' opened the book.*
33 a man, which h' a spirit of an 2192
35 when the devil h' thrown him
40 all they that h' any sick with 2192
5: 4 Now when he h' left speaking,
6 And when they h' this done,
9 of the fishes which they h' taken:
11 And when they h' brought their ships
6: 8 the man which h' the withered 2192
7: 1 Now when he h' ended all his
10 servant whole that h' been sick.*
13 saw her, he h' compassion on her, and
39 which h' bidden him saw it,
41 a certain creditor which h' two 1510
42 And when they h' nothing to pay, 2192
8: 2 certain women, which h' been healed
8 And when he h' said these things,*
27 which h' devils long time, and 2192
29 For he h' commanded the unclean*
29 For oftentimes it h' caught him:
39 how great things Jesus h' done unto
42 For he h' one only daughter, 1510
43 which h' spent all her living
47 for what cause she h' touched him,*
9: 8 some, that Elias h' appeared;
10 told him what they h' done.
11 and healed them that h' need of 2192
36 any of those things which they h' seen.
10: 13 if the mighty works h' been done
13 they h' a great while ago repented,*
33 he saw him, he h' compassion
39 And she h' a sister called Mary, 1510
11: 38 marvelled that he h' not first washed
13: 1 whose blood Pilot h' mingled with
6 A certain man h' a fig tree 2192
11 a woman which h' a spirit of "
14 because that Jesus h' healed on the
17 And when he h' said these things,*
14: 2 before him which h' the dropsy.
15: 9 found the piece which I h' lost.
11 And he said, A certain man h' two 2192
14 And when he h' spent all,
20 father saw him, and h' compassion*
16: 1 rich man, which h' a steward; 2192
1 that he h' wasted his goods. *
8 because he h' done wisely:
17: 6 If ye h' faith as a grain of mustard†2192
19: 15 to whom he h' given the money,
15 how much every man h' gained
28 And when he h' thus spoken,
32 and found even as he h' said
37 the mighty works that they h' seen;
20: 19 that he h' spoken this parable *
33 of them is she? for seven h' her 2192
21: 4 cast in all the living that she h'. "
22: 13 and found as he h' said unto them:
55 And when they h' kindled a fire
61 how he h' said unto him, *
64 And when they h' blindfolded him,*
23: 8 because he h' heard many things
13 when he h' called together the *
25 whom they h' desired; *
46 And when Jesus h' cried with a loud ‡
51 The same h' not consented to the
24: 1 the spices which they h' prepared,
14 all these things which h happened.
21 we trusted that it h' been he *
23 they h' also seen a vision of angels,
24 even so as the women h' said:
37 supposed that they h' seen a spirit.*
40 And when he h' thus spoken,
Joh 2: 9 ruler of the feast h' tasted the *
15 And when he h' made a scourge *
22 remembered that he h' said this*
22 and the word which Jesus h' said.
4: 1 how the Pharisees h' heard
18 For thou hast h' five husbands; 2192
50 the word that Jesus h' spoken *
5: 4 whole of whatsoever disease he h'.*2722
5 which h' an infirmity thirty and 2192
6 and knew that he h' been now
13 for Jesus h' conveyed himself away,
15 was Jesus, which h' made him whole.
16 because he h' done these things *
18 he not only h' broken the sabbath,*
46 For h' ye believed Moses, ye *
6: 11 and when he h' given thanks, *
13 unto them that h' eaten.
14 when they h' seen the miracle *
19 So when they h' rowed about
23 after that the Lord h' given thanks:
25 And when they h' found him *
60 when they h' heard this, said, *
7: 9 When he h' said these words *
8: 3 when they h' set her in the midst,*
10 When Jesus h' lifted up himself,*
19 if ye h' known me, ye should *
9: 6 When he h' thus spoken,
8 they which before h' seen him *
15 asked him how he h' received his*
18 that he h' been blind,
18 that h' received his sight.
22 for the Jews h' agreed already,
35 that they h' cast him out;
35 and when he h' found him, *
11: 6 When he h' heard therefore *
13 they thought that he h' spoken *
17 that he h' lain in the grave
21 my brother h' not died.
28 And when she h' so said,
32 my brother h' not died.
43 And when he thus h' spoken,
45 came to Mary, and h' seen the *
46 what things Jesus h' done.
57 and the Pharisees h' given a
12: 1 Lazarus was which h' been dead,*

Joh 12: 6 he was a thief, and h' the bag, *2192
9 whom he h' raised from the dead.
14 when he h' found a young ass, *
16 that they h' done these things
18 that he h' done this miracle.
37 But though he h' done so many
13: 3 the Father h' given all things into
12 So after he h' washed their feet,
12 and h' taken his garments, *
21 When Jesus h' thus said,
26 And when he h' dipped the sop,
29 because Judas h' the bag, that 2192
29 that Jesus h' said unto him, *
14: 7 If ye h' known me, ye should
15: 22 If I h' not come and spoken
22 they h' not...sin, but now they
22 they...not h' sin: but now they 2192
24 If I h' not done among them
24 they h' not...sin, but now have
24 they...not h' sin: but now have 2192
17: 5 the glory which I h' with thee "
18: 1 When Jesus h' spoken these words,
6 as he h' said unto them, *
18 who h' made a fire of coals; *
22 And when he h' thus spoken,
24 Now Annas h' sent him bound *
38 And when he h' said this,
19: 23 when they h' crucified Jesus,
30 When Jesus therefore h' received the
20: 12 where the body of Jesus h' lain.
14 And when she h' thus said,
18 that she h' seen the Lord, *
18 and that he h' spoken these things
20 And when he h' so said,
22 And when he h' said this,
21: 15 So when they h' dined, Jesus
19 And when he h' spoken this,
Ac 1: 2 Holy Ghost h' given commandments
2 unto the apostles whom he h' chosen:
9 And when he h' spoken these things,
17 and h' obtained part of this ministry.*
2: 30 and knowing that God h' sworn *
44 were together, and h' all things 2192
45 to all men, as every man h' need. "
3: 10 at that which h' happened
12 or holiness we h' made this man
18 which God before h' shewed *
4: 7 And when they h' set them in the
13 that they h' been with Jesus.
15 But when they h' commanded
21 when they h' further threatened
23 and elders h' said unto them.
31 And when they h' prayed,
32 but they h' all things common. 1510
35 every man according as he h' need. 2192
5: 23 but when we h' opened, we found
27 And when they h' brought them,
34 a doctor of the law, h' in reputation
40 when they h' called the apostles,
6: 6 and when they h' prayed,
15 As it h' been the face of an angel.
7: 5 when as yet he h' no child. 5607
17 which God h' sworn to Abraham,*
36 after that he h' shewed wonders *
44 Our fathers h' the tabernacle of 1510
44 as he h' appointed, speaking *
44 to the fashion that he h' seen.
60 And when he h' said this,
8: 11 And to him they h' regard, *
11 that of long time he h' bewitched them
14 heard that Samaria h' received the
25 when they h' testified and preached
27 who h' the charge of all her treasure,*
27 and h' come to Jerusalem ... to worship,
9: 18 fell from his eyes as it h' been scales:*
19 And when he h' received meat, *
27 how he h' seen the Lord in the way,
27 and that he h' spoken to him,
27 and how he h' preached boldly
31 Then h' the churches rest 2192
33 which h' kept his bed eight years,
37 whom when they h' washed,
38 the disciples h' heard that Peter *
41 and when he h' called the saints *
10: 8 when he h' declared all these things*
11 as it h' been a great sheet *
17 which he h' seen should mean
24 and h' called together his *
31 and thine alms are h' in remembrance
11: 1 the Gentiles h' also received
5 as it h' been a great sheet, *
6 when I h' fastened mine eyes,
13 how he h' seen an angel
23 and h' seen the grace of God,
26 And when he h' found him,
12: 4 And when he h' apprehended him,
12 And when he h' considered the thing,
16 and when they h' opened the door,
17 how the Lord h' brought him out
19 And when Herod h' sought for him,
25 when they h' fulfilled their ministry,
13: 1 which h' been brought up with *
3 And when they h' fasted and
5 and they h' also John to their 2192
6 when they h' gone through
19 when he h' destroyed seven nations
22 And when he h' removed him,
24 When John h' first preached
29 And when they h' fulfilled all that
36 after he h' served his own
14: 8 who never h' walked:
9 perceiving that he h' faith to be 2192
11 people saw what Paul h' done,
18 that they h' not done sacrifice *
19 supposing he h' been dead. *
21 when they h' preached the gospel

Ac 14:21 to that city, and h' taught many,
23 when they h' ordained them elders
23 in every church, and h' prayed
24 And after they h' passed throughout *
25 And when they h' preached
26 from whence they h' been
27 and h' gathered the church
27 all that God h' done with them, *
27 and how he h' opened the door
15: 2 Paul and Barnabas h' no small 1096
4 that God h' done with them.
7 when there h' been much disputing,
12 God h' wrought among the Gentiles
13 And after they h' held their peace,
30 and when they h' gathered the *
31 Which when they h' read,
33 And after they h' tarried there
16: 6 Now when they h' gone throughout *
10 And after he h' seen the vision,
10 that the Lord h' called us for to
23 when they h' laid many stripes
27 that the prisoners h' been fled.
34 when he h' brought them into *
40 and when they h' seen the brethren,
17: 1 when they h' passed through
9 when they h' taken security of Jason,
13 Jews of Thessalonica h' knowledge
18: 2 Claudius h' commanded all
18 in Cenchrea: for he h' a vow. 2192
22 when he h' landed at Cæsarea,
23 after he h' spent some time there,*
26 Aquila and Priscilla h' heard, *
27 which h' believed through grace:
19: 6 when Paul h' laid his hands
13 over them which h' evil spirits 2192
21 when he h' passed through
35 townclerk h' appeased the people,
41 And when he h' thus spoken,
20: 2 when he h' gone over those parts,
2 and h' given them much
11 come up again, and h' broken bread,
13 for so he h' appointed,
16 For Paul h' determined to sail
36 And when he h' thus spoken,
21: 1 gotten from them, and h' launched,
3 when we h' discovered Cyprus,
5 when we h' accomplished those
6 when we h' taken our leave *
7 when we h' finished our course
9 the same man h' four daughters, 1510
19 And when he h' saluted them,
19 what things God h' wrought among
29 For they h' seen before with him
29 supposed that Paul h' brought into
33 who he was, and what he h' done.
40 And when he h' given him licence,
22:29 and because he h' bound him.
23: 7 And when he h' so said, there arose a
12 eat nor drink till they h' killed Paul.
13 than forty which h' made this
30 say before thee what they h' against *
34 And when the governor h' read the
24:10 after that the governor h' beckoned
19 and object, if they h' ought 2192
25: 6 And when he h' tarried among them
12 Festus, when he h' conferred with the
14 And when they h' been there many *
19 But h' certain questions against 2192
21 But when Paul h' appealed to be
25 when I found that he h' committed
26 after examination h', I might 1096
26:30 And when he h' thus spoken, *
32 if he h' not appealed unto Cæsar.
27: 4 And when we h' launched from *
5 And when we h' sailed over the sea
7 And when we h' sailed slowly many
13 supposing that they h' obtained their
16 we h' much work to come by the *
17 Which when they h' taken up, they
28 and when they h' gone a little further,*
30 when they h' let down the boat into
35 And when he h' thus spoken,
35 and when he h' broken it, he began *
38 And when they h' eaten enough,
40 And when they h' taken up the *
28: 3 And when Paul h' gathered a bundle
6 but after they h' looked a great while,*
9 others also, which h' diseases in 2192
11 which h' wintered in the isle,
18 Who, when they h' examined me,
19 not that I h' ought to accuse my 2192
23 And when they h' appointed him a
25 after that Paul h' spoken one word,
29 And when he h' said these words,*
29 and h' great reasoning among *2192
Ro 1: 2 Which he h' promised afore by his *
4:11 faith which he h' yet being
12 which he h' being yet uncircumcised.
21 persuaded that, what he h' promised,
5:14 even over them that h' not sinned
6:21 What fruit h' ye then in those 2192
7: 7 Nay, I h' not known sin, but by the
7 for I h' not known lust, except the
7 law h' said, Thou shalt not covet.
9:10 but when Rebecca also h' conceived *
23 which he h' afore prepared unto glory,*
29 Except the Lord of Sabaoth h' left us
29 we h' been as Sodoma,
1Co 1:15 say that I h' baptized in mine own *
2: 8 for h' they known it, they would not
7:29 be as though they h' none; and 2192
11:24 And when he h' given thanks, he brake
25 took the cup, when he h' supped,*
14:19 Yet in the church I h' rather speak five
2Co 1: 9 But we h' the sentence of death in 2192
12 we have h' our conversation in the *

2Co 2:13 I h' no rest in my spirit, because 2192
3:10 which was made glorious h' no glory
7: 5 our flesh h' no rest, but we were 2192
12 for his cause that h' done the wrong,*
8: 6 we desired Titus, that as he h' begun
15 He that h' gathered *
15 much h' nothing over;
15 and he that h' gathered *
15 gathered little h' no lack.
9: 5 whereof ye h' notice before, that the *
11:21 reproach, as though we h' been weak,
Ga 1:23 But they h' heard only, That he which *
2: 2 by any means I should run, or h' run,
3:21 for if there h' been a law given which
4:15 that, if it h' been possible, ye would *
22 Abraham h' two sons, the one by 2192
Eph 2: 3 Among whom also we all h' our *
Ph'p 2:26 because that ye h' heard
26 that he h' been sick. *
27 but God h' mercy on him; and not on
3:12 Not as though I h' already attained *
1Th 1: 9 what manner of entering in we h' 2192
2: 2 even after that we h' suffered before,*
2Th 2:12 believed not the truth, but h' pleasure
Tit 1: 5 elders in every city, as I h' appointed *
Heb 1: 3 when he h' by himself purged our sins,
2:14 he might destroy him that h' the 2192
3:16 For some, when they h' heard, did *
17 was it not with them that h' sinned,*
4: 8 For if Jesus h' given them rest,
5: 7 when he h' offered up prayers and *
6:15 And so, after he h' patiently endured,*
7: 6 blessed him that h' the promises,*2192
8: 7 if that first covenant h' been faultless,
9: 1 verily the first covenant h' also 2192
4 Which h' the golden censer, and * "
4 the golden pot that h' manna, *2192
19 when Moses h' spoken every precept
10: 2 once purged should have h' no 2192
6 sacrifices for sin thou hast h' no *
12 But this man, after he h' offered one
15 for after that he h' said before,*
34 ye h' compassion of me in my bonds,
11: 5 because God h' translated him:*
5 before his translation he h' this
11 judged him faithful who h' promised.
15 if they h' been mindful of that country
15 they might have h' opportunity 2192
17 and he that h' received the promises
26 for he h' respect unto the recompence *
31 she h' received the spies with peace.*
36 others h' trial of cruel mockings 2983
12: 9 we have h' fathers of our flesh 2192
Jas 2:21 when he h' offered Isaac his son *
25 when she h' received the messengers,*
25 and h' sent them out another way?*
1Pe 2:10 people of God: which h' not obtained
2Pe 2:21 For it h' been better for them not *
1Jo 2: 7 an old commandment which ye h' 2192
19 for if they h' been of us, they would
2Jo 1: 5 but that which we h' from the 2192
3Jo 1:13 I h' many things to write, but I "
Re 1:16 And he h' in his right hand seven "
4: 4 and they h' on their heads crowns *"
7 and the third beast h' a face as a "
8 And the four beasts h' each of * "
5: 6 stood a Lamb as it h' been slain,
8 and when he h' taken the book,
6: 2 and he that sat on him h' a bow; 2192
3 And when he h' opened the second *
5 And when he h' opened the third *
5 and he that sat on him h' a pair 2192
7 And when he h' opened the fourth *
9 And when he h' opened the fifth seal,*
12 And I beheld when he h' opened the *
8: 1 And when he h' opened the seventh *
6 seven angels which h' the seven 2192
9 were in the sea, and h' life, died; "
9: 8 And they h' hair as the hair of "
9 And they h' breastplates, as it "
10 they h' tails like unto scorpions, *"
11 And they h' a king over them, *"
14 the sixth angel which h' the "
19 like unto serpents, and h' heads, *"
10: 2 And he h' in his hand a little book "
3 when he h' cried, seven thunders *
4 when the seven thunders h' uttered *
10 as soon as I h' eaten it, my belly was
13:11 and he h' two horns like a lamb, 2192
14 miracles which he h' power to do *
14 the beast, which h' the wound *2192
15 And he h' power to give life unto *
17 save he that h' the mark, or the *2192
14:18 another angel...which h' power *
18 with a cry to him that h' the sharp 2192
15: 2 them that h' gotten the victory over*
16: 2 the men which h' the mark of 2192
17: 1 of the seven angels which h' the "
18:19 were made rich all that h' ships in "
19:12 and he h' a name written, that no *"
20 he deceived them that h' received
20: 4 and which h' not worshipped the *
4 neither h' received his mark "
21: 9 seven angels which h' the seven 2192
12 And h' a wall great and high * "
12 and h' twelve gates, and at the * "
14 And the wall of the city h' twelve "
15 And he that talked with me h' a "
23 And the city h' no need of the sun *"
22: 8 And when I h' heard and seen,

Hadad (ha'-dad) See also BEN-HADAD; HADAD-RIMMON; HADAR.
Ge 36:35 And Husham died, and H' the son 1908
36 And H' died, and Samlah of "
1Ki 11:14 an adversary unto Solomon, H' "
17 That H' fled, he and certain "

1Ki 11:17 H' being yet a little child. 1908
19 H' found great favour in the sight "
21 when H' heard in Egypt that "
21 H' said to Pharaoh, Let me depart, "
25 besides the mischief that H' did: "
1Ch 1:30 Mishma, and Dumah, Massa, H', "
46 H' the son of Bedad, which smote "
47 when H' was dead, Samlah of "
50 Baal-hanan was dead, H' reigned "
51 H' died also. And the dukes of "

Hadadezer (had-a-de'-zer) See also HADAREZER.
2Sa 8: 3 David smote also H', the son of 1909
5 came to succour H' king of Zobah, "
7 that were on the servants of H', "
8 Betah, and...Berothai, cities of H', "
9 had smitten all the host of H', "
10 because he had fought against H', "
10 for H' had wars with Toi. "
12 and of the spoil of H', son of "
1Ki 11:23 which fled from his lord H' "

Hadadrimmon (ha''-dad-rim'-mon)
Zec 12:11 as the mourning of H' in the 1910

Hadar (ha'-dar) See also HADAD.
Ge 25:15 H', and Tema, Jetur, Naphish, 1924
36:39 and H' reigned in his stead: "

Hadarezer (had-a-re'-zer) See also HADADEZER.
2Sa 10:16 And H' sent, and brought out 1928
16 the captain of the host of H' "
19 the kings that were servants to H' "
1Ch 18: 3 David smote H' king of Zobah "
5 came to help H' king of Zobah, "
7 that were on the servants of H', "
8 and from Chun, cities of H', "
9 had smitten all the host of H' "
10 because he had fought against H', "
10 for H' had war with Tou; "
19:16 the captain of the host of H' "
19 when the servants of H' saw that "

Hadashah (had'-a-shah)
Jos 15:37 Zenan, and H', and Migdal-gad, 2322

Hadassah (ha-das'-sah) See also ESTHER.
Es 2: 7 he brought up H', that is, Esther, 1919

Hadattah (ha-dat'-tah) See also HAZOR-HADATTAH.
Jos 15:25 Hazor, H', and Kerioth, *2675

Haddah See EN-HADDAH.

Haddon See ESAR-HADDON.

Hadid (ha'-did)
Ezr 2:33 The children of Lod, H', and Ono, 2307
Ne 7:37 of Lod, H', and Ono, seven "
11:34 H', Zeboim, Neballat, "

Hadlai (had'-la-i)
2Ch 28:12 and Amasa the son of H', stood 2311

Hadoram (ha-do'-ram) See also ADORAM.
Ge 10:27 And H', and Uzal, and Diklah, 1913
1Ch 1:21 H' also, and Uzal, and Diklah, "
18:10 He sent H' his son to king David, "
2Ch 10:18 Then king Rehoboam sent H' "

Hadrach (ha'-drak)
Zec 9: 1 word of the Lord in the land of H',2317

hadst
Ge 30:30 For it was little which thou h' before I
31:42 with me, surely thou h' sent me away
J'g 15: 2 thought that thou h' utterly hated
1Sa 25:34 except thou h' hasted and come to
2Sa 2:27 As God liveth, unless thou h' spoken,
2Ki 13:19 then h' thou smitten Syria till thou h',
Ezr 9:14 be angry with us till thou h' consumed
Ne 9:15 land which thou h' sworn to give them.
23 concerning which thou h' promised *
Ps 44: 3 because thou h' a favour unto them.
60:10 O God, which h' cast us off? *
90: 2 or ever thou h' formed the earth
Isa 26:15 thou h' removed it far unto all the *
48:18 O that thou h' hearkened to my
Jer 3: 3 and thou h' a whore's forehead,
Jon 2: 3 For thou h' cast me into the deep,*
Lu 19:42 Saying, If thou h' known, even thou
Jo 11:21 unto Jesus, Lord, if thou h' been here
32 unto him, Lord, if thou h' been here,
1Co 4: 7 glory, as if thou h' not received it?
Heb 10: 8 not, neither h' pleasure therein;

haft See also HANDLE.
J'g 3:22 the h' also went in after the blade; 5325

Hagab (ha'-gab) See also HAGABA.
Ezr 2:46 The children of H', the children 2285

Hagaba (hag'-a-bah) See also HAGAB; HAGABAH.
Ne 7:48 the children of H', the children of 2286

Hagabah (hag'-a-bah) See also HAGABA.
Ezr 2:45 the children of H', the children of 2286

Hagar (ha'-gar) See also AGAR; HAGARITES.
Ge 16: 1 an Egyptian, whose name was H'.1904
3 Sarai, Abram's wife, took H' her "
4 he went in unto H', and she "
8 he said, H', Sarai's maid, whence "
15 H' bare Abram a son: and Abram "
15 called his son's name, which H' bare, "
16 when H' bare Ishmael to Abram. "
21: 9 Sarah saw the son of H' the "
14 and gave it unto H', putting it "
17 and the angel of God called to H' "
17 unto her, What aileth thee, H'? "
25:12 Ishmael, Abraham's son, whom H' "

Hagarenes (haga-renes') See also HAGARITES.
Ps 83: 6 Ishmaelites; of Moab, and the H';1905

Hagarites (hag'-a-rites) See also HAGARENES; HAGERITE.
1Ch 5:10 they made war with the H', who *1905

1Ch 5:19 they made war with the *H'*, with *1905
20 and the *H'* were delivered into * "

Hagerite (*hag'-e-rite*) See also HAGARITES; HAGGERI.
1Ch 27:31 over the flocks was Jaziz the *H'*. *1905

Haggai (*hag'-ga-i*)
Ezr 5: 1 the prophets, *H'* the prophet, and 2292
6:14 through the prophesying of *H'* the "
Hag 1: 1 the Lord by *H'* the prophet unto "
3 the Lord by *H'* the prophet, saying, "
12 and the words of *H'* the prophet, as "
13 Then spake *H'* the Lord's "
2: 1, 10 of the Lord by the prophet *H'*, "
13 Then said *H'*, If one that is unclean "
14 Then answered *H'*, and said, So is "
20 came unto *H'* in the four and "

Haggeri (*hag'-gher-i*) See also HAGERITE.
1Ch 11:38 Mibhar the son of *H'*, *1905

Haggi (*hag'-ghi*) See also HAGGITES.
Ge 46:16 Ziphion, and *H'*, Shuni, and 2291
Nu 26:15 of *H'*, the family of the Haggites: "

Haggiah (*hag-ghi'-ah*)
1Ch 6:30 Shimea his son, *H'* his son, 2293

Haggites (*hag'-ghites*) See also HAGGI.
Nu 26:15 of Haggi, the family of the *H'*: 2291

Haggith (*hag'-ghith*)
2Sa 3: 4 fourth, Adonijah the son of *H'*; 2294
1Ki 1: 5 Adonijah the son of *H'* exalted "
11 the son of *H'* doth reign, and "
2:13 the son of *H'* came to Bath-sheba "
1Ch 3: 2 the fourth, Adonijah the son of *H'*: "

Hahiroth See PI-HAHIROTH.

Hai (*ha'-i*) See also AI.
Ge 12: 8 Beth-el on the west, and *H'* on *5857
13: 3 between Beth-el and *H'*; * "

hail See also HAILSTONES.
Ex 9:18 to rain a very grievous *h'*, such as 1259
19 the *h'* shall come down upon them, "
22 that there may be *h'* in all the "
23 the Lord sent thunder and *h'*, and "
23 rained *h'* upon the land of Egypt. "
24 was *h'*, and fire mingled with the *h'*, "
25 the *h'* smote throughout all the "
25 the *h'* smote every herb of the field, "
26 of Israel were, was there no *h'*. "
28 more mighty thunderings and *h'*; "
29 neither shall there be any more *h'*; "
33 the thunders and *h'* ceased, and "
34 saw that the rain and the *h'* and "
10: 5 remaineth unto to you from the *h'*, "
12 even all that the *h'* hath left. "
15 of the trees which the *h'* had left: "
Job 38:22 thou seen the treasures of the *h'*, "
Ps 18:12 thick clouds passed, *h'* stones and "
13 his voice; *h'* stones and coals of "
78:47 He destroyed their vines with *h'*, "
48 He gave up their cattle...to the *h'*, "
105:32 He gave them *h'* for rain, and "
148: 8 Fire, and *h'*; snow, and vapours; "
Isa 28: 2 as a tempest of *h'* and a destroying "
17 the *h'* shall sweep away the refuge "
32:19 When it shall *h'*, coming down on 1258
Hag 2:17 with mildew and with *h'* in all the 1259
M't 26:49 and said, *H'*, master; and kissed *5463*
27:29 mocked him, saying, *H'*, King of the "
28: 9 Jesus met them, saying, All *h'*. "
M'r 15:18 salute him, *H'*, King of the Jews! "
Lu 1:28 *H'*, thou that art highly favoured, "
Joh 19: 3 And said, *H'*, King of the Jews! "
Re 8: 7 followed *h'* and fire mingled with *5464*
11:19 and an earthquake, and great *h'*. "
16:21 there fell upon men a great *h'* out "
21 because of the plague of the *h'*; "

Hail See BEN-HAIL.

hailstones See also HAIL and STONES.
Jos 10:11 more which died with *h'* than 68, 1259
Isa 30:30 scattering, and tempest, and *h'*." "
Eze 13:11 ye, O great *h'*, shall fall; and a 68, 417
13 and great *h'* in my fury to "
38:22 and great *h'*, fire, and brimstone." "

hair See also HAIRS.
Ex 25: 4 scarlet, and fine linen, and goats' *h'*,
26: 7 shalt make curtains of goats' *h'* to
35: 6 scarlet, and fine linen, and goats *h'*,
23 and goats' *h'*, and red skins of rams,
26 them up in wisdom spun goats' *h'*.
36:14 And he made curtains of goats' *h'*
Le 13: 3 and when the *h'* in the plague is 8181
4 and the *h'* thereof be not turned "
10 it have turned the *h'* white, and "
20 and the *h'* thereof be turned white; "
25 the *h'* in the bright spot be turned "
26 no white *h'* in the bright spot, "
30 there be in it a yellow thin *h'*; "
31 and that there is no black *h'*. "
32 there be in it no yellow *h'*, "
36 priest shall not seek for yellow *h'*; "
37 and that there is black *h'* grown up "
40 whose *h'* is fallen off his head, he 4803
41 he that hath his *h'* fallen off from "
14: 8 shave off all his *h'*, and wash 8181
9 he shall shave all his *h'* off his head "
9 eyebrows, even all his *h'* he shall "
Nu 6: 5 let the locks of the *h'* of his head "
18 shall take the *h'* of the head "
19 of the Nazarite, after the *h'* of his *
31:20 of goats' *h'*, and all things made of "
J'g 16:22 the *h'* of his head began to grow 8181
20:16 could sling stones at an *h'* breadth, 8185
1Sa 14:45 there shall not one *h'* of his head "
19:13 put a pillow of goats' *h'* for his bolster.
1Sa 19:16 a pillow of goats' *h'* for his bolster.
2Sa 14:11 there shall not one *h'* of thy son 8185
26 because the *h'* was heavy on him, ‡
26 he weighed the *h'* of his head 8181
1Ki 1:52 there shall not an *h'* of him fall 8185
Ezr 9: 3 plucked off the *h'* of my head 8181
Ne 13:25 and plucked off their *h'*, and made
Job 4:15 the *h'* of my flesh stood up: 8185
Ca 4: 1 thy *h'* is as a flock of goats, 8181
6: 5 thy *h'* is as a flock of goats "
7: 5 and the *h'* of thine head like 1803
Isa 3:24 instead of well set *h'* baldness; 4748
7:20 head, and the *h'* of the feet: 8181
50: 6 to them that plucked off the *h'*:
Jer 7:29 Cut off thine *h'*, O Jerusalem, and 5145
Eze 5: 1 balances to weigh and divide the *h'*.
16: 7 and thine *h'* is grown, whereas 8181
Da 3:27 nor was an *h'* of their head singed, 8177
7: 9 and the *h'* of his head like the pure "
M't 3: 4 John had his raiment of camel's *h'*, *2359*
5:36 canst not make one *h'* white or "
M'r 1: 6 John was clothed with camel's *h'*, "
Lu 21:18 But there shall not an *h'* of your "
Joh 11: 2 and wiped his feet with her *h'*, "
12: 3 wiped his feet with her *h'*: "
Ac 27:34 an *h'* fall from the head "
1Co 11:14 if a man have long *h'*, it is a *2863*
15 But if a woman have long *h'*, it is a "
15 for her *h'* is given her for a *2864*
1Ti 2: 9 not with broided *h'*, or gold, or *4117*
1Pet 3: 3 of plaiting the *h'*, and of wearing *2359*
Re 6:12 black as sackcloth of *h'*, *5155*
9: 8 And they had *h'* as the *h'* of *2359*

hair-breadth See HAIR and BREADTH.

hairs
Ge 42:38 bring down my gray *h'* with sorrow
44:29 bring down my gray *h'* with sorrow
31 the gray *h'* of thy servant our father
Le 13:21 no white *h'* therein, and if it be 8181
De 32:25 suckling also with the man of gray *h'*.
Ps 40:12 they are more than the *h'* of mine 8185
69: 4 cause are more than the *h'* of mine "
Isa 46: 4 even to hoar *h'* will I carry you:
Da 4:33 his *h'* were grown like eagles' *8177
Ho 7: 9 gray *h'* are here and there upon him,
M't 10:30 the very *h'* of your head are all *2359*
Lu 7:38 wipe them with the *h'* of her head,* "
44 wiped them with the *h'* of her head.* "
12: 7 But even the very *h'* of your head "
Re 1:14 His head and his *h'* were white * "

hairy
Ge 25:25 red, all over like an *h'* garment; 8181
27:11 Esau my brother is a *h'* man, and 8163
23 because his hands were *h'*, as his "
2Ki 1: 8 answered him, He was an *h'* 1167, 8181
Ps 68:21 the *h'* scalp of such an one as goeth "

Hakkatan (*hak'-ka-tan*)
Ezr 8:12 Johannan the son of *H'*, and with 6997

Hakkore See EN-HAKKORE.

Hakkoz (*hak'-koz*) See also KOZ.
1Ch 24:10 The seventh to *H'*, the eighth to 6976

Hakupha (*ha-ku'-fah*)
Ezr 2:51 the children of *H'*, the children of 2709
Ne 7:53 the children of *H'*, the children of "

Halah (*ha'-lah*)
2Ki 17: 6 and placed them in *H'* and in 2477
18:11 and put them in *H'* and in Habor "
1Ch 5:26 and brought them unto *H'*, and "

Halak (*ha'-lak*)
Jos 11:17 mount *H'*, that goeth up to Seir, 2510
12: 7 mount *H'*, that goeth up to Seir; "

hale See also HALING.
Lu 12:58 lest he *h'* thee to the judge, ‡*2694*

half
Ge 24:22 a golden earring of *h'* a shekel 1235
Ex 24: 6 Moses took *h'* of the blood, and 2677
6 and *h'* of the blood he sprinkled "
25:10 two cubits and a *h'* shall be the "
10 and a cubit and a *h'* the breadth "
10 thereof, and a cubit and a *h'* "
10 cubit and a *h'* the height "
17 two cubits and a *h'* shall be the "
17 thereof, and a cubit and a *h'* "
23 cubit and a *h'* the height thereof. "
26:12 the *h'* curtain that remaineth, shall "
16 a cubit and a *h'* shall be the "
30:13 *h'* a shekel after the shekel of the 4276
13 an *h'* shekel shall be the offering "
15 give less than *h'* a shekel, "
23 sweet cinnamon *h'* so much, even "
36:21 a board one cubit and a *h'*. 2677
37: 1 two cubits and a *h'* was the length "
1 and a cubit and a *h'* the breadth of "
1 and a cubit and a *h'* the height of "
6 two cubits and a *h'* was the length "
6 one cubit and a *h'* the breadth "
10 a cubit and a *h'* the height thereof: "
38:26 *h'* a shekel, after the shekel of 4276
Le 6:20 *h'* of it in the morning, and *h'* "
Nu 12:12 of whom the flesh is *h'* consumed 2677
15: 9 mingled with *h'* an hin of oil. "
10 for a drink offering *h'* an hin "
28:14 their drink offerings shall be *h'* an "
31:29 Take it of their *h'*, and give it unto 4276
30 And of the children of Israel's *h'*, "
36 the *h'*, which was the portion 4275
42 And of the children of Israel's *h'*, 4276
43 the *h'* that pertained unto the 4275
47 Even of the children of Israel's *h'*, 4276
32:33 and unto *h'* the tribe of Manasseh 2677
34:13 nine tribes, and to the *h'* tribe: "
14 and *h'* the tribe of Manasseh have "
Nu 34:15 The two tribes and the *h'* tribe 2677
De 3:12 *h'* mount Gilead, and the cities "
13 gave I unto the *h'* tribe of "
16 unto the river Arnon *h'* the *8432
29: 8 and to the *h'* tribe of Manasseh. 2677
Jos 1:12 and to *h'* the tribe of Manasseh, "
4:12 and *h'* the tribe of Manasseh, "
8:33 *h'* of them over against mount "
33 Gerizim, and *h'* of them over "
12: 2 and from *h'* Gilead, even unto the "
5 Maachathites, and *h'* Gilead, the "
6 Gadites, and the *h'* tribe of "
13: 7 nine tribes, and the *h'* tribe of "
25 and *h'* the land of the children "
29 unto the *h'* tribe of Manasseh: and "
29 was the possession of the *h'* tribe "
31 And *h'* Gilead, and Ashtaroth, and "
31 to the one *h'* of the children of "
14: 2 nine tribes, and for the *h'* tribe. "
3 two tribes and an *h'* tribe on the "
18: 7 Reuben, and *h'* the tribe of "
21: 5 and out of the *h'* tribe of Manasseh, "
6 and out of the *h'* tribe of Manasseh "
25 And out of the *h'* tribe of 4276
27 out of the other *h'* tribe of 2677
22: 1 the Gadites, and the *h'* tribe of "
7 Now to the one *h'* of the tribe of "
7 but unto the other *h'* thereof gave "
9 the children of Gad and the *h'* tribe "
10 Gad and the *h'* tribe of Manasseh "
11 the children of Gad and the *h'* tribe "
13, 15, and to the *h'* tribe of Manasseh, "
21 and the *h'* tribe of Manasseh "
1Sa 14:14 within as it were an *h'* acre of land, "
2Sa 10: 4 shaved off the one *h'* of their beards, "
18: 3 neither if *h'* of us die, will they "
19:40 and also *h'* the people of Israel. "
1Ki 3:25 give *h'* to the one, and *h'* to the "
7:31 a cubit and an *h'*: and also upon "
32 a wheel was a cubit and *h'* a cubit. "
35 a round compass of *h'* a cubit high: "
10: 7 the *h'* was not told me: thy wisdom "
13: 8 If thou wilt give me *h'* thine house, "
16: 9 Zimri, captain of *h'* his chariots, 4276
21 *h'* of the people followed Tibni 2677
21 and *h'* followed Omri. "
1Ch 2:52 Haroeh, and *h'* of the Manahethites.* "
54 Joab, and *h'* of the Manahethites, * "
5:18 and *h'* the tribe of Manasseh, of "
23 the children of the *h'* tribe of "
26 and the *h'* tribe of Manasseh, and "
6:61 out of the *h'* tribe, namely, out "
61 of the *h'* tribe of Manasseh, 4276
70 And out of the *h'* tribe of Manasseh; "
71 the *h'* tribe of Manasseh, Golan in 2677
12:31 And of the *h'* tribe of Manasseh "
37 and of the *h'* tribe of Manasseh, "
26:32 and the *h'* tribe of Manasseh, for "
27:20 of the *h'* tribe of Manasseh, Joel "
21 Of the *h'* tribe of Manasseh in "
2Ch 9: 6 the one *h'* of the greatness of thy "
Ne 3: 9 ruler of the *h'* part of Jerusalem. "
12 ruler of the *h'* part of Jerusalem, "
16 the ruler of the *h'* part of Beth-zur, "
17 the ruler of the *h'* part of Keilah. "
18 the ruler of the *h'* part of Keilah. "
4: 6 joined together unto the *h'* thereof: "
16 the *h'* of my servants wrought in "
16 and the other *h'* of them held "
21 *h'* of them held the spears "
12:32 and *h'* of the princes of Judah, "
38 and the *h'* of the people upon the "
40 I, and the *h'* of the rulers with me: "
13:24 their children spake *h'* in the "
Es 5: 3 given thee to the *h'* of the kingdom. "
6 the *h'* of the kingdom it shall be "
7: 2 even to the *h'* of the kingdom. "
Ps 55:23 shall not live out *h'* their days; 2673
Eze 16:51 Neither hath Samaria committed *h'* 2677
40:42 a cubit and an *h'* long, and "
42 a cubit and an *h'* broad, "
43:17 border about it shall be *h'* a cubit; "
Da 12: 7 for a time, times, and an *h'*; and "
Ho 3: 2 of barley, and an *h'* homer of "
Zec 14: 2 *h'* of the city shall go forth into 2677
4 *h'* of the mountain shall remove "
4 and *h'* of it toward the south. "
8 *h'* of them toward the former sea, "
8 *h'* of them toward the hinder sea: "
M'r 6:23 it thee, unto the *h'* of my kingdom. *2255*
Lu 10:30 departed, leaving him *h'* dead. *2253*
19: 8 the *h'* of my goods I give to the *2255*
Re 8: 1 about the space of *h'* an hour. *2256*
11: 9 three days and an *h'*, and shall not *2255*
11 three days and an *h'* the Spirit of life "
12:14 a time, and times, and *h'* a time,

half-dead See HALF and DEAD.

half-homer See HALF and HOMER.

Halhul (*hal'-hul*)
Jos 15:58 *H'*, Beth-zur, and Gedor, 2478

Hali (*ha'-li*)
Jos 19:25 their border was Helkath, and *H'*, 2482

haling
Ac 8: 3 *h'* men and women committed ‡*4951*

hall
M't 27:27 took Jesus into the common *h'*, †‡*4232*
M'r 15:16 led him away into the *h'*, * *833*
Lu 22:55 a fire in the midst of the *h'*, * "
Joh 18:28 led...unto the *h'* of judgment: *4232*
28 went not into the judgment *h'*, †‡ "
33 Pilate entered...the judgment *h'* †‡ "
19: 9 went again into the judgment *h'*, †‡ "
Ac 23:35 to be kept in Herod's judgment *h'*. * "

Hallelujah See ALLELUIA.
Hallohesh (*hal-lo'-hesh*) See also HALOHESH.
Ne 10:24 H', Pileha, Shobek, 3873
hallow See also HALLOWED.
Ex 28:38 the children of Israel shall h' in 6942
29: 1 to h' them, to minister unto me "
40: 9 and shalt h' it, and all the vessels "
Le 16:19 cleanse it, and h' it from the "
22: 2 those things which they h' unto me: "
3 which the children of Israel h' unto "
32 I am the Lord which h' you, "
25:10 And ye shall h' the fiftieth year, "
Nu 6:11 and shall h' his head that same day. "
1Ki 8:64 same day did the king h' the middle "
Jer 17:22 but h' ye the sabbath day, as I "
24 but h' the sabbath day, to do no "
27 to h' the sabbath day, and not to "
Eze 20:20 h' my sabbaths; and they shall be "
44:24 and they shall h' my sabbaths. "
hallowed
Ex 20:11 blessed the sabbath day, and h' it. 6942
29:21 and he shall be h', and his garments, "
Le 12: 4 she shall touch no h' thing, nor 6944
19: 8 profaned the h' thing of the Lord: * "
22:32 I will be h' among the children 6942
Nu 3:13 I h' unto me all the firstborn "
5:10 every man's h' things shall be his: 6944
16:37 the fire yonder; for they are h'. *6942
38 therefore they are h': and they * "
18: 8 all the h' things of the children of 6944
29 even the h' part thereof out of it. 4720
De 26:13 I have brought away the h' things 6944
1Sa 21: 4 there is h' bread; if the young * "
6 the priest gave him h' bread: for * "
1Ki 9: 3 I have h' this house, which thou 6942
7 which I have h' for my name, "
2Ki 12:18 all the h' things that Jehoshaphat, 6944
18 and his own h' things, and all "
2Ch 7: 7 Moreover Solomon h' the middle 6942
36:14 of the Lord which he had h' in "
M't 6: 9 in heaven, H' be thy name. 37
Lu 11: 2 in heaven, H' be thy name. "
Halohesh (*ha-lo'-hesh*) See also HALLOHESH.
Ne 3:12 repaired Shallum the son of H'. *3873
halt See also HALTED; HALTETH; HALTING.
1Ki 18:21 How long h' ye between two ‡6452
Ps 38:17 I am ready to h', and my sorrow ‡6761
M't 18: 8 to enter into life h' or maimed, 5560
M'r 9:45 better for thee to enter h' into life,* "
Lu 14:21 the maimed, and the h', and the* "
Joh 5: 3 of blind, h', withered, waiting for "
halted
Ge 32:31 him, and he h' upon his thigh. ‡6761
Mic 4: 7 I will make her that h' a remnant, ‡"
halteth
Mic 4: 6 will I assemble her that h', and ‡6761
Zep 3:19 I will save her that h', and gather ‡"
halting
Jer 20:10 my familiars watched for my h'. ‡6761
Ham (*ham*)
Ge 5:32 Noah begat Shem, H', and 2526
6:10 Noah begat three sons, Shem, H', "
7:13 Noah, and Shem, and H', and "
9:18 were Shem, and H', and Japheth: "
18 and H' is the father of Caanan. "
22 And H', the father of Caanan, saw "
10: 1 Shem, H', and Japheth: and unto "
6 the sons of H'; Cush, and Mizraim, "
20 These are the sons of H', after their "
14: 5 and the Zuzims in H', and the 1990
1Ch 1: 4 Noah, Shem, H', and Japheth. 2526
8 The sons of H'; Cush, and "
4:40 for they of H' had dwelt there of "
Ps 78:51 strength in the tabernacles of H': "
105:23 Jacob sojourned in the land of H'. "
27 and wonders in the land of H'. "
106:22 Wondrous works in the land of H', "
Haman (*ha'-man*) See also HAMAN'S.
Es 3: 1 H' the son of Hammedatha 2001
2 bowed, and reverenced H': for the "
4 they told H', to see whether "
5 when H' saw that Mordecai bowed "
5 then was H' full of wrath. "
6 wherefore H' sought to destroy all "
7 that is, the lot, before H' from day "
8 H' said unto king Ahasuerus, "
10 and gave it unto H' the son of "
11 the king said unto H', The silver "
12 according to all that H' had "
15 the king and H' sat down to drink; "
4: 7 of the money that H' had promised "
5: 4 let the king and H' come this day "
5 Cause H' to make haste, that he "
5 So the king and H' came to the "
8 let the king and H' come to the "
9 Then went H' forth that day joyful "
9 but when H' saw Mordecai in the "
10 Nevertheless H' refrained himself: "
11 H' told them of the glory of his "
12 H' said moreover, Yea, Esther the "
14 And the thing pleased H'; and he "
6: 4 Now H' was come into the outward "
5 Behold, H' standeth in the court. "
6 So H' came in. And the king "
6 Now H' thought in his heart, To "
7 H' answered the king, For the "
10 Then the king said to H', Make "
11 Then took H' the apparel and the "
12 But H' hasted to his house "
13 And H' told Zeresh his wife "
14 And hasted to bring H' unto the "
7: 1 So the king and H' came to "
6 and enemy is this wicked H'. "
Es 7: 6 Then H' was afraid 2001
7 and H' stood up to make request "
8 and H' was fallen upon the bed "
9 which H' had made for Mordecai, "
9 standeth in the house of H'. Then "
10 So they hanged H' on the gallows "
8: 1 give the house of H' the Jews' "
2 which he had taken from H', and "
2 Mordecai over the house of H'. "
3 to put away the mischief of H' the "
5 to reverse the letters devised by H', "
7 I have given Esther...house of H', "
9:10 The ten sons of H' the son of "
12 the palace, and the ten sons of H'; "
24 Because H' the son of "
Haman's (*Ha'-mans*)
Es 7: 8 they covered H' face. 2001
9:13 and let H' ten sons be hanged "
14 and they hanged H' ten sons. "
Hamath (*ha'-math*) See also HAMATHITE; HAMATH-ZOBAH; HEMATH.
Nu 13:21 unto Rehob, as men come to H'. 2574
34: 8 your border unto...entrance of H'; "
Jos 13: 5 Hermon unto the entering into H'. "
J'g 3: 3 Baal-hermon...entering in of H'. "
2Sa 8: 9 When Toi king of H' heard that "
1Ki 8:65 from the entering in of H' unto the "
2Ki 14:25 from the entering of H' unto the "
28 and H', which belonged to Judah, "
17:24 and from H', and from Sepharvaim, "
30 and the men of H' made Ashima, "
18:34 Where are the gods of H', and of "
19:13 Where is the king of H', and the "
23:33 at Riblah in the land of H', that he "
25:21 slew them at Riblah...land of H'. "
1Ch 18: 3 Hadarezer king of Zobah unto H'. "
9 when Tou king of H' heard how "
2Ch 7: 8 of H' unto the river of Egypt. "
8: 4 store cities, which he built in H'. "
Isa 10: 9 is not H' as Arpad? is not "
11:11 from H', and from the islands "
36:19 Where are the gods of H' and "
37:13 Where is the king of H', and the "
Jer 39: 5 H', where he gave judgment upon "
49:23 H' is confounded, and Arpad: "
52: 9 to Riblah in the land of H'; "
27 to death in Riblah in the land of H'. "
Eze 47:16 H', Berothah, Sibraim, which is "
16 of Damascus and the border of H'; "
17 northward, and the border of H'. "
20 till a man come over against H'. "
48: 1 of Hethlon, as one goeth to H', "
1 Damascus northward...coast of H'; "
Am 6: 2 from thence go ye to H' the great 2579
Zec 9: 2 H' also shall border thereby; 2574
Hamathite (*ham'-a-thite*)
Ge 10:18 the Zemarite, and the H': and 2577
1Ch 1:16 the Zemarite, and the H'. "
Hamath-zobah (*ha''-math-zo'-bah*)
2Ch 8: 3 And Solomon went to H', and 2578
Hammahlekoth See SELA-HAMMAHLEKOTH.
Hammath (*ham'-math*)
Jos 19:35 and H', Rakkath, and 2575
Hammedatha (*ham-med'-a-thah*)
Es 3: 1 the son of H' the Agagite, 4099
10 Haman the son of H' the Agagite, "
8: 5 by Haman the son of H' the "
9:10 sons of Haman the son of H', the "
24 son of H', the Agagite, the enemy "
Hammelech (*ham'-me-lek*)
Jer 36:26 Jerahmeel the son of H', and *4429
38: 6 Malchiah the son of H', that was* "
hammer See also HAMMERS.
J'g 4:21 took an h' in her hand, and went 4718
5:26 right hand to the workmen's h'; 1989
26 and with the h' she smote "
1Ki 6: 7 neither h' nor axe nor any tool of 4717
Isa 41: 7 he that smootheth with the h' 6360
Jer 23:29 and like a h' that breaketh "
50:23 the h' of the whole earth "
hammers.
Ps 74: 6 work...at once with axes and h'. 3597
Isa 44:12 and fashioneth it with h', and 4717
Jer 10: 4 fasten it with nails and with h', "
Hammoleketh (*ham-mol'-e-keth*)
1Ch 7:18 And his sister H' bare Ishod, 4447
Hammon (*ham'-mon*)
Jos 19:28 Hebron, and Rehob, and H', 2540
1Ch 6:76 and H' with her suburbs, and "
Hammoth-dor (*ham''-moth-dor'*)
Jos 21:32 and H' with her suburbs, 2576
Hamon See BAAL-HAMON; HAMON-GOG.
Hamonah (*ha-mo'-nah*)
Eze 39:16 the name of the city shall be H'. 1997
Hamon-gog (*ha''-mon-gog'*)
Eze 39:11 shall call it The valley of H'. 1996
15 have buried it in the valley of H'. "
Hamor (*ha'-mor*) See also EMMOR; HAMOR'S.
Ge 33:19 at the hand of the children of H', 2544
34: 2 when Shechem the son of H' the "
4 Shechem spake unto his father H', "
6 H' the father of Shechem went "
8 And H' communed with them, "
13 answered Shechem and H' his "
18 And their words pleased H' "
20 H' and Shechem his son came "
24 And unto H' and unto Shechem "
26 they slew H' and Shechem his son "
Jos 24:32 Jacob bought of the sons of H' "
J'g 9:28 serve the men of H' the father of "
Hamor's (*ha'-mors*)
Ge 34:18 and Shechem H' son. 2544
Hamuel (*ha-mu'-el*)
1Ch 4:26 H' his son, Zacchur his son, *2536
Hamul (*ha'-mul*) See also HAMULITES.
Gen 46:12 sons of Pharez...Hezron and H'. 2538
Nu 26:21 of H', the family of the Hamulites. "
1Ch 2: 5 sons of Pharez; Hezron, and H' "
Hamulites (*ha'-mu-lites*)
Nu 26:21 of Hamul, the family of the H'. 2539
Hamutal (*ha-mu'-tal*)
2Ki 23:31 his mother's name was H', 2537
24:18 H', the daughter of Jeremiah "
Jer 52: 1 his mother's name was H' "
Hanameel (*ha-nam'-e-el*)
Jer 32: 7 Behold, H' the son of Shallum *2601
8 So H' mine uncle's son came* "
9 And I bought the field of H' * "
12 in the sight of H' mine uncle's * "
Hanan (*ha'-nan*) See also BAAL-HANAN; BEN-HANAN; ELON-BETH-HANAN
1Ch 8:23 And Abdon, and Zichri, and H', 2605
38 Sheariah, and Obadiah, and H'. "
9:44 Obadiah, and H': these were the "
11:43 H' the son of Maachah, and "
Ezr 2:46 of Shalmai, the children of H', "
Ne 7:49 The children of H', the children "
8: 7 Azariah, Jozabad, H', Pelaiah, "
10:10 Kelita, Pelaiah, H', "
22 Pelatiah, H', Anaiah, "
26 And Ahijah, H', Anan, "
13:13 and next to them was H' the son "
Jer 35: 4 into the chamber of the sons of H', "
Hananeel (*ha-nan'-e-el*)
Ne 3: 1 sanctified it unto the tower of H'. 2606
12:39 the tower of H', and the tower of* "
Jer 31:38 the tower of H' unto the gate * "
Zec 14:10 the tower of H' unto the king's * "
Hanani (*ha-na'-ni*)
1Ki 16: 1 came to Jehu the son of H' 2607
7 of the prophet Jehu, the son of H' "
1Ch 25: 4 Hananiah, H', Eliathah, Giddalti, "
25 The eighteenth to H', he, his sons, "
2Ch 16: 7 at that time H' the seer came to "
19: 2 Jehu the son of H' the seer went "
20:34 in the book of Jehu the son of H', "
Ezr 10:20 of the sons of Immer; H', and "
Ne 1: 2 That H', one of my brethren, "
7: 2 That I gave my brother H', and "
12:36 and Judah, H', with the musical "
Hananiah (*han-a-ni'-ah*) See also SHADRACH.
1Ch 3:19 Meshullam, and H', and 2608
21 the sons of H'; Pelatiah, and "
8:24 H', and Elam, and Antothijah, "
25: 4 Jerimoth, H', Hanani, "
25:23 The sixteenth to H', he, his sons, "
2Ch 26:11 H', one of the king's captains. "
Ezr 10:28 Jehohanan, H', Zabbai, "
Ne 3: 8 repaired H' the son of one of the "
30 repaired H', the son of Shelemiah, "
7: 2 and H' the ruler of the palace, "
10:23 Hoshea, H', Hashub, "
12:12 of Jeremiah, H'; "
41 Zechariah, and H', with trumpets; "
Jer 28: 1 H' the son of Azur the prophet, "
5 Jeremiah said unto the prophet H' "
10 Then H' the prophet took the "
11 H' spake in the presence of all the "
12 after that H' the prophet had "
13 Go and tell H', saying, Thus saith "
15 Then said...Jeremiah unto H' "
15 the prophet, Hear now, H'; "
17 So H' the prophet died the same "
36:12 and Zedekiah the son of H', and "
37:13 Shelemiah the son of H'; and he "
Da 1: 6 Daniel, H', Mishael, and Azariah: "
7 and to H', of Shadrach; and to "
11 over Daniel, H', Mishael, and "
19 none like Daniel, H', Mishael, "
2:17 and made the thing known to H', "
hand See also AFOREHAND; BEFOREHAND; HANDBREADTH; HANDED; HANDFUL; HANDKERCHIEFS HANDMAID; HANDS; HANDSTAVES; HANDWRITING; HANDYWORK
Ge 3:22 now, lest he put forth his h', and 3027
4:11 thy brother's blood from thy h'; "
8: 9 then he put forth his h', and took "
9: 2 fishes of the sea; into your h' are "
5 at the h' of every beast will I "
5 require it, and at the h' of man; "
5 at the h' of every man's "
13: 9 if thou wilt take the left h', 8041
9 or if thou depart to the right h', 3225
14:15 which is on the left h' of Damascus. 8040
20 thine enemies into thy h'. 3027
22 I have lift up mine h' unto the "
16: 6 Behold, thy maid is in thy h'; "
12 his h' will be against every man, "
12 and every man's h' against him; "
19:10 the men put forth their h', and "
16 the men laid hold upon his h', and "
16 upon the h' of his wife, and upon "
16 the h' of his two daughters; "
21:18 hold him in thine h'; for I will "
30 lambs shalt thou take of my h', "
22: 6 he took the fire in his h', and a "
10 Abraham stretched forth his h', "
12 Lay not thine h' upon the lad, "
24: 2 Put, I pray thee, thy h' under my "
9 the servant put his h' under the "
10 goods of his master were in his h': "
18 let down her pitcher upon her h', "
49 that I may turn to the right h'. 3225

Ge 25:26 and his h' took hold on Esau's heel:3027
27:17 into the h' of her son Jacob. "
41 mourning for my father are at h'; 7126
30:35 gave them into the h' of his sons. 3027
31:29 It is in the power of my h' to do "
39 of my h' didst thou require it, "
32:11 Deliver me, I pray thee, from the h' "
11 of my brother, from the h' of Esau: "
13 that which came to his h' a present "
16 delivered them into the h' of his * "
33:10 then receive my present at my h': "
19 at the h' of the children of Hamor, "
35: 4 strange gods which were in their h', "
37:22 and lay no h' upon him; that he "
27 and let not our h' be upon him; "
38:18 thy staff that is in thine h'. "
20 sent the kid by the h' of his friend "
20 his pledge from the woman's h': "
28 put out his h': and the midwife "
28 took and bound upon his h' a "
29 as he drew back his h', that, "
30 had the scarlet thread upon his h': "
39: 3 that he did to prosper in his h'. "
4 all that he had he put into his h'. "
6 left all that he had in Joseph's h'; "
8 committed all that he hath to my h'; "
12 left his garment in her h', and fled, "
13 he had left his garment in her h', "
22 committed to Joseph's h' all the "
23 any thing that was under his h'; "
40:11 Pharaoh's cup was in my h': and I "
11 I gave the cup into Pharaoh's h'. 3709
13 deliver Pharaoh's cup into his h', 3027
21 he gave the cup into Pharaoh's h':3709
41:35 lay up corn under the h' of 3027
42 took off his ring from his h', and "
42 put it upon Joseph's h', and "
44 shall no man lift up his h' "
42:37 deliver him into my h', and I will "
43: 9 of my h' shalt thou require him: "
12 take double money in your h'; and "
12 sacks, carry it again in your h'; "
15 they took double money in their h', "
21 have brought it again in our h'. "
26 present which was in their h' into "
44:17 in whose h' the cup is found, he "
46: 4 Joseph shall put his h' upon thine "
47:29 put, I pray thee, thy h' under my "
48:13 them both, Ephraim in his right h' 3225
13 toward Israel's left h', 8040
13 and Manasseh in his left h' "
13 toward Israel's right h', 3225
14 Israel stretched out his right h', "
14 his left h' upon Manasseh's head, 8040
17 laid his right h' upon the head 3027
17 he held up his father's h', to remove "
18 put thy right h' upon his head. 3225
22 which I took out of the h' of the 3027
49: 8 thy h' shall be in the neck of thine "
Ex 2:19 delivered us out of the h' of the "
3: 8 deliver them out of the h' of the "
19 let you go, no, not by a mighty h'. "
20 I will stretch out my h', and smite "
4: 2 What is that in thine h'? And he "
4 Put forth thine h', and take it by "
4 And he put forth his h', and "
4 it became a rod in his h': 3709
6 Put now thine h' into thy bosom. 3027
6 And he put his h' into his bosom: "
6 behold, his h' was leprous as snow. "
7 Put thine h' into thy bosom again. "
7 And he put his h' into his bosom "
13 send, I pray thee, by the h' of him "
17 shalt take this rod in thine h', "
20 took the rod of God in his h'. "
21 which I have put in thine h': "
5:21 to put a sword in their h' to slay us. "
6: 1 for with a strong h' shall he let "
1 and with a strong h' shall he drive "
7: 4 that I may lay my h' upon Egypt, "
5 when I stretch forth mine h' upon "
15 serpent shalt thou take in thine h'. "
17 with the rod that is in mine h' "
19 stretch out thine h' upon the "
8: 5 Stretch forth thine h' with thy rod "
6 Aaron stretched out his h' over the "
17 Aaron stretched out his h' with his "
9: 3 the h' of the Lord is upon thy "
15 now I will stretch out my h', that I "
22 Stretch forth thine h' toward "
10:12 Stretch out thine h' over the land "
21 Stretch out thine h' toward heaven, "
22 Moses stretched forth his h' "
12:11 your staff in your h'; and ye "
13: 3 for by strength of h' the Lord "
9 a sign unto thee upon thine h', "
9 for with a strong h' hath the Lord "
14 By strength of h' the Lord brought "
16 for a token upon thine h', and for "
16 for by strength of h' the Lord "
14: 8 of Israel went out with an high h'. "
16 stretch out thine h' over the sea, "
21 Moses stretched out his h' over the "
22 on their right h', and on their left. 3225
26 Stretch out thine h' over the sea, 3027
27 Moses stretched forth his h' over "
29 a wall unto them on their right h',3225
30 saved Israel that day out of the h'3027
15: 6 Thy right h', O Lord, is become 3225
6 thy right h', O Lord, hath dashed "
9 my sword, my h' shall destroy 3027
12 Thou stretchedst out thy right h',3225
20 took a timbrel in her h'; and all 3027
16: 3 we had died by the h' of the Lord "
17: 5 the river, take in thine h', and go. "
9 with the rod of God in mine h'. "
Ex 17:11 Moses held up his h', that Israel 3027
11 and when he let down his h', "
18: 9 delivered out of the h' of the "
10 delivered you out of the h' of the "
10 and out of the h' of Pharaoh, "
10 from under the h' of the Egyptians. "
19:13 There shall not an h' touch it, "
21:13 God deliver him into his h'; then I "
16 him, or if he be found in his h', "
20 and he die under his h'; he shall be "
24 tooth for tooth, h' for h', foot "
22: 4 the theft be certainly found in his h' "
8 put his h' unto his neighbour's "
11 he hath not put his h' unto his "
23: 1 put not thine h' with the wicked "
31 inhabitants of the land into your h'; "
24:11 of Israel he laid not his h': "
25:25 a border of an h' breadth 2948
29:20 upon the thumb of their right h', 3027
32: 4 he received them at their h', and "
11 great power, and with a mighty h'? "
15 of the testimony were in his h': "
33:22 and will cover thee with my h' 3709
23 And I will take away mine h', "
34: 4 took in his h' the two tables of 3027
29 tables of testimony in Moses' h', "
35:29 commanded to be made by the h' "
38:15 court gate, on this h' and that h', "
21 by the h' of Ithamar, son to Aaron 3027
Le 1: 4 he shall put his h' upon the head "
3: 2, 8, 13 shall lay his h' upon the head "
4: 4 shall lay his h' upon the bullock's "
24 lay his h' upon the head of the goat "
29, 33 lay his h' upon the...sin "
8:23 upon the thumb of his right h', "
36 the Lord commanded by the h' of "
9:22 Aaron lifted up his h' toward the * "
10:11 spoken unto them by the h' of "
14:14 upon the thumb of his right h', "
15 it into the palm of his own left h': 8042
16 the oil that is in his left h', and 3709
17 the rest of the oil that is in his h' "
17 upon the thumb of his right h', 3027
18 the oil that is in the priest's h' 3709
25 upon the thumb of his right h', 3027
26 oil into the palm of his own left h': 8042
27 the oil that is in his left h' seven 3709
28 the oil that is in his h' upon the "
28 upon the thumb of his right h', 3027
29 the oil that is in the priest's h' he 3709
32 leprosy, whose h' is not able to get*3027
16:21 send him away by the h' of a fit "
22:25 Neither from a stranger's h' shall "
25:14 ought of thy neighbour's h', "
28 shall remain in the h' of him that "
26:25 ye shall be delivered into the h' of "
46 in mount Sinai by the h' of Moses. "
Nu 4:28 charge shall be under the h' of "
33 congregation, under the h' of "
37 commandment...by the h' of Moses. "
45 word of...by the h' of Moses. "
49 were numbered by the h' of Moses. "
5:18 and the priest shall have in his h' "
25 offering out of the woman's h', "
6:21 beside that that his h' shall get: * "
7: 8 under the h' of Ithamar the son of "
9:23 of the Lord by the h' of Moses. "
10:13 of the Lord by the h' of Moses. "
11:15 kill me, I pray thee, out of h', 2026
23 Is the Lord's h' waxed short? 3027
15:23 by the h' of Moses, from the day "
16:40 Lord said to him by the h' of Moses. "
20:11 Moses lifted up his h', and with "
17 we will not turn to the right h' nor 3225
20 much people, and with a strong h'. 3027
21: 2 deliver this people into my h', then "
26 taken all his land out of his h', "
34 I have delivered him into thy h', "
22: 7 rewards of divination in their h'; "
23 his sword drawn in his h': and "
26 to the right h' or to the left. 3325
29 there were a sword in mine h', 3027
31 sword drawn in his h': and he "
25: 7 and took a javelin in his h'; "
27:18 spirit, and lay thine h' upon him; "
23 commanded by the h' of Moses. "
31: 6 the trumpets to blow in his h'. "
33: 1 under the h' of Moses and Aaron. "
3 of Israel went out with an high h' "
35:18 if he smite him with an h' weapon "
21 in enmity smite him with his h', "
25 out of the h' of the revenger of "
36:13 by the h' of Moses unto the "
De 1:27 deliver us into the hand of the "
2: 7 the works of thy h': he knoweth "
15 the h' of the Lord was against "
24 I have given into thine h' Sihon "
27 I will neither turn unto the right h'3225
30 deliver him into thy h', as 3027
3: 2 and his land, into thy h'; and thou "
8 out of the h' of the two kings of the "
24 thy mighty h': for what God "
4:34 and by a mighty h', and by a "
5:15 through a mighty h' and by a "
32 turn aside to the right h' or to the 3225
6: 8 a sign upon thine h', and they 3027
21 out of Egypt with a mighty h': "
7: 8 you out with a mighty h', and "
8 from the h' of Pharaoh king of "
19 and the mighty h', and the "
24 deliver their kings into thine h', "
8:17 the might of mine h' hath gotten "
9:26 out of Egypt, with a mighty h'. "
10: 3 having the two tables in mine h'. "
11: 2 his mighty h', and his stretched "
18 a sign upon your h', that they may "
De 12: 6 heave offerings of your h', and 3027
7 all that ye put your h' unto, ye "
11 the heave offering of your h', "
17 or heave offering of thine h': "
13: 9 thine h' shall be first upon him to "
9 and afterwards the h' of all the "
17 the cursed thing to thine h': that "
14:25 bind up the money in thine h', "
29 the work of thine h' which thou "
15: 3 thy brother thine h' shall release; "
7 nor shut thine h' from thy poor "
8 thou shalt open thine h' wide unto "
9 the year of release, is at h'; 7126
10 all that thou puttest thine h' unto. 3027
11 Thou shalt open thine h' wide unto "
16:10 a freewill offering of thine h', "
17:11 to the right h', nor to the left. 3225
20 to the right h', or to the left: to the "
19: 5 his h' fetcheth a stroke with the 3027
12 into the h' of the avenger of blood, "
21 for tooth, h' for h', foot for foot. "
23:20 all that thou settest thine h' to in "
25 pluck the ears with thine h'; "
24: 1 give it in her h', and send her "
3 giveth it in her h', and sendeth "
25:11 out of the h' of him that smiteth "
11 and putteth forth her h', "
12 Then thou shalt cut off her h', 3709
26: 4 take the basket out of thine h', 3027
8 with a mighty h', and with "
28: 8 all that thou settest thine h' unto; "
12 bless all the work of thine h': "
14 to the right h', or to the left, 3225
20 all that thou settest thine h' unto 3027
32 shall be no might in thine h'. "
30: 9 every work of thine h', in the "
32:27 Our h' is high, and the Lord "
35 the day of their calamity is at h', 7138
39 that can deliver out of my h'. 3027
40 I lift up my h' to heaven, and say, "
41 mine h' take hold on judgment; "
33: 2 from his right h' went a fiery law 3225
3 all his saints are in thy h': and 3027
34:12 in all that mighty h', and in all "
Jos 1: 7 to the right h' or to the left, 3225
2:19 our head, if any h' be upon him. 3027
4:24 the h' of the Lord, that it is "
5:13 his sword drawn in his h': and "
6: 2 I have given into thine h' Jericho, "
7: 7 into the h' of the Amorites, to "
8: 1 I have given into thy h' the king "
7 God will deliver it into your h'. "
18 the spear that is in thy h' toward "
18 for I will give it into thine h'. "
18 the spear that he had in his h' "
19 he had stretched out his h': and "
26 Joshua drew not his h' back, "
9:25 we are in thine h': as it "
26 out of the h' of the children of "
10: 6 Slack not thy h' from thy servants; "
8 delivered them into thine h'; * "
19 hath delivered them into your h'. "
30 the king thereof, into the h' of "
32 Lachish into the h' of Israel, which "
11: 8 Lord delivered them into the h' "
14: 2 by the h' of Moses, for the nine "
17: 7 border went along on the right h' 3225
19:27 goeth out to Cabul on the left h', 8040
20: 2 I spake unto you by the h' of Moses:3027
5 deliver the slayer up into his h'; "
9 by the h' of the avenger of blood, "
21: 2 by the h' of Moses to give us "
8 commanded by the h' of Moses. "
44 all their enemies into their h'. "
22: 9 of the Lord by the h' of Moses. "
31 out of the h' of the Lord. "
23: 6 turn not aside...to the right h' 3225
24: 8 I gave them into your h', that ye 3027
10 I delivered you out of his h'. "
11 and I delivered them into your h'. "
J'g 1: 2 I have delivered the land into his h'. "
4 the Perizzites into their h': and "
35 the h' of the house of Joseph "
2:15 the h' of the Lord was against them "
16 out of the h' of those that spoiled "
18 out of the h' of their enemies all "
23 them into the h' of Joshua. "
3: 4 their fathers by the h' of Moses. "
8 into the h' of Chushan-rishathaim "
10 into his h'; and his h' prevailed "
21 Ehud put forth his left h', and took "
28 enemies the Moabites into your h'. "
30 that day under the h' of Israel. "
4: 2 Lord sold them into the h' of Jabin "
7 I will deliver him into thine h'. "
9 Sisera into the h' of a woman. "
14 hath delivered Sisera into thine h': "
21 took an hammer in her h', and "
24 the h' of the children of Israel "
5:26 She put her h' to the nail, "
26 and her right h' to the workmen's 3225
6: 1 Lord delivered them into the h' of 3027
2 the h' of Midian prevailed against "
9 out of the h' of the Egyptians, "
9 out of the h' of all that oppressed "
14 from the h' of the Midianites: 3709
21 the staff that was in his h', 3027
36 If thou wilt save Israel by mine h', "
37 thou wilt save Israel by mine h'. "
7: 2 Mine own h' hath saved me. "
6 putting their h' to their mouth, "
7 deliver the Midianites into thine h': "
8 the people took victuals in their h', "
9 I have delivered it into thine h'. "
14 into his h' hath God delivered "
15 Lord hath delivered into your h' "

J'g 7:16 put a trumpet in every man's h'. *3027
8: 6 and Zalmunna now in thine h'. "
7 and Zalmunna into mine h', then "
15 and Zalmunna now in thine h', "
22 thou hast delivered us from the h' "
9:17 delivered you out of the h' of "
29 this people were under my h'! then "
48 Abimelech took an axe in his h', "
10:12 I delivered you out of their h'. "
11:21 into the h' of Israel, and they "
12: 3 the Lord delivered them into my h': "
13: 1 delivered them into the h' of "
5 out of the h' of the Philistines. "
14: 6 he had nothing in his h': "
15:12 deliver thee into the h' of the "
13 deliver thee into their h': but "
15 put forth his h', and took it, "
17 cast away the jawbone out of his h', "
18 into the h' of thy servant: and now "
18 into the h' of the uncircumcised? "
16:18 and brought money in their h'. "
23 Samson our enemy into our h'. "
26 the lad that held him by the h', "
29 the one with his right h', and of the 3225
17: 3 from my h' for my son, to make 3027
18:19 lay thine h' upon thy mouth, and "
20:28 I will deliver them into thine h'. "
48 all that came to h': also they *4672
Ru 1:13 the h' of the Lord is gone out 3027
4: 5 thou buyest the field of the h' of "
9 and Mahlon's, of the h' of Naomi. "
1Sa 2:13 a fleshhook of three teeth in his h'; "
4: 3 out of the h' of our enemies. 3709
8 out of the h' of these mighty Gods? 3027
5: 6 the h' of the Lord was heavy upon "
7 his h' is sore upon us, and upon "
9 the h' of the Lord was against the "
11 h' of God was very heavy there. "
6: 3 why his h' is not removed from "
5 peradventure he will lighten his h' "
9 we shall know that it is not his h' "
12 turned not aside to the right h' 3225
7: 3 he will deliver you out of the h' of 3027
8 he will save us out of the h' of the "
13 the h' of the Lord was against the "
9: 8 I have here at h' the fourth part "
16 out of the h' of the Philistines: "
10:18 the h' of the Egyptians, and...the h' "
12: 3 or of whose h' have I received any "
4 taken ought of any man's h'. "
5 ye have not found ought in my h'. "
9 he sold them into the h' of Sisera, "
9 and into the h' of the Philistines, "
9 and into the h' of the king of Moab, "
10 deliver us out of the h' of our "
11 delivered you out of the h' of your "
15 then shall the h' of the Lord be "
13:22 in the h' of any of the people "
14:10 hath delivered them into our h': "
12 hath delivered them into the h' of "
19 unto the priest; Withdraw thine h'. "
26 no man put his h' to his mouth: "
27 rod that was in his h', and dipped "
27 and put his h' to his mouth; "
37 wilt thou deliver them into the h' "
43 the rod that was in mine h', "
16:16 he shall play with his h', and thou "
23 took an harp, and played with his h': "
17:22 David left his carriage in the h' of "
37 me out of the h' of this Philistine. "
40 took his staff in his h', and "
40 his sling was in his h': "
46 the Lord deliver thee into mine h'; "
49 David put his h' in his bag, and "
50 there was no sword in the h' of "
57 the head of the Philistine in his h'. "
18:10 David played with his h', as at "
10 there was a javelin in Saul's h'. "
17 Let not mine h' be upon him, but "
17 the h' of the Philistines be upon "
21 that the h' of the Philistines may be "
25 fall by the h' of the Philistines. "
19: 5 he did put his life in his h', and 3709
9 with his javelin in his h': 3027
9 and David played with his h'. "
20:16 at the h' of David's enemies. "
19 when the business was in h', and "
21: 3 what is under thine h'? give me 3027
3 five loaves of bread in mine h', "
4 no common bread under mine h', "
8 is there not here under thine h' "
22: 6 having his spear in his h', and all "
17 their h' also is with David, and "
17 king would not put forth their h' "
23: 4 deliver the Philistines into thine h'. "
6 came down with an ephod in his h'. "
7 hath delivered him into mine h'; "
11 Keilah deliver me up into his h'? "
12 me and my men into the h' of Saul? "
14 God delivered him not into his h'. "
16 and strengthened his h' in God. "
17 h' of Saul my father shall not find "
20 to deliver him into the king's h'. "
24: 4 deliver thine enemy into thine h', "
6 to stretch forth mine h' against "
10 delivered thee to day into mine h' "
10 I will not put forth mine h' "
11 see the skirt of thy robe in my h': "
11 nor transgression in mine h', "
12, 13 mine h' shall not be upon thee. "
15 and deliver me out of thine h'. "
18 had delivered me into thine h', "
20 shall be established in thine h'. "
25: 8 whatsoever cometh to thine h' "
26 avenging thyself with thine own h', "
33 avenging myself with mine own h'. "
1Sa 25:35 David received of her h' that which 3027
39 cause of my reproach from the h' "
26: 8 thine enemy into thine h' this day: "
9 can stretch forth his h' against "
11 that I should stretch forth mine h' "
18 or what evil is in mine h'? "
23 delivered thee into my h' to day, "
23 I would not stretch forth mine h' "
27: 1 perish one day by the h' of Saul: "
1 so shall I escape out of his h'. "
28:17 rent the kingdom out of thine h', "
19 into the h' of the Philistines: "
19 Israel into the h' of the Philistines. "
21 I have put my life in my h', 3709
30:23 that came against us into our h'. 3027
2Sa 1:14 not afraid to stretch forth thine h' "
2:19 he turned not to the right h' 3225
21 Turn thee aside to thy right h' "
3: 8 not delivered thee into the h' of 3027
12 behold, my h' shall be with thee, "
18 By the h' of my servant David I "
18 save my people Israel out of the h' "
18 Philistines, and out of the h' of all "
4:11 require his blood of your h', and "
5:19 thou deliver them into mine h'? "
6: 6 Uzzah put forth his h' to the ark "
19 deliver the Philistines into thine h'. 3027
8: 1 out of the h' of the Philistines. "
10: 2 to comfort him by the h' of his "
10 he delivered into the h' of Abishai "
11:14 sent it by the h' of Uriah. "
12: 7 I delivered thee out of the h' of "
25 he sent by the h' of Nathan the "
13: 5 I may see it, and eat it at her h'. "
6 my sight, that I may eat at her h'. "
10 chamber, that I may eat of thine h'. "
19 laid her h' on her head, and went "
14:16 out of the h' of the man that 3709
19 Is not the h' of Joab with thee 3027
19 none can turn to the right h' 3231
15: 5 he put forth his h', and took him, 3027
16: 6 mighty men were on his right h' 3225
8 into the h' of Absalom thy son: 3027
18: 2 under the h' of Joab, and a third "
2 under the h' of Abishai the son of "
2 third part under the h' of Ittai "
12 shekels of silver in mine h', "
12 yet would I not put forth mine h' "
28 that lifted up their h' against my "
19: 9 out of the h' of our enemies, and 3709
9 he delivered us out of the h' of the "
20: 9 by the beard with the right h' 3027
10 the sword that was in Joab's h': "
21 hath lifted up his h' against the "
21:20 that had on every h' six fingers, "
22 the h' of David, and by the h' of his "
22: 1 out of the h' of all his enemies, 3709
1 enemies, and out of the h' of Saul: "
23:10 smote the Philistines until his h' 3027
10 was weary, and his h' clave unto "
21 the Egyptian had a spear in his h'; "
21 the spear out of the Egyptian's h', "
24:14 fall now into the h' of the Lord; "
14 let me not fall into the h' of man. "
16 the angel stretched out his h' "
16 It is enough: stay now thine h'. "
17 let thine h', I pray thee, be against "
1Ki 2:19 and she sat on his right h'. 3225
25 king Solomon sent by the h' of 3027
46 kingdom was established in the h' "
7:26 it was an h' breadth thick, and 2947
8:15 and hath with his h' fulfilled it, 3027
24 and hast fulfilled it with thine h', "
42 thy strong h', and of thy stretched "
53 by the h' of Moses thy servant, "
56 by the h' of Moses his servant. "
11:12 I will rend it out of the h' of thy "
26 he lifted up his h' against the king. "
27 the cause that he lifted up his h' "
31 rend the kingdom out of the h' of "
34 the whole kingdom out of his h': "
35 the kingdom out of his son's h', "
13: 4 he put forth his h' from the altar, "
4 And his h', which he put forth "
6 that my h' may be restored me "
6 the king's h' was restored him "
14:18 by the h' of his servant Ahijah "
15:18 delivered them into the h' of his "
16: 7 by the h' of the prophet Jehu "
17:11 a morsel of bread in thine h'. "
18: 9 deliver thy servant into the h' of "
44 out of the sea, like a man's h'. 3709
46 the h' of the Lord was on Elijah; 3027
20: 6 they shall put it in their h', "
13 I will deliver it into thine h'. "
28 this great multitude into thine h', "
42 thou hast let go out of thy h' "
22: 3 take it not out of the h' of the king "
6 deliver it into the h' of the king. "
12 shall deliver it into the king's h'. "
15 deliver it into the h' of the king. "
19 on his right h' and on his left. 3225
34 Turn thine h', and carry me out 3027
2Ki 3:10 deliver them into the h' of Moab! "
13 to deliver them into the h' of "
15 the h' of the Lord came upon him. "
18 the Moabites also into your h'. "
4:29 take my staff in thine h', and go "
5:11 strike his h' over the place, and "
18 he leaneth on my h', and I bow "
24 he took them from their h', "
6: 7 he put out his h', and took it. "
7: 2 a lord on whose h' the king leaned "
17 the lord on whose h' he leaned "
8: 8 Take a present in thine h', and go, "
20 under the h' of Judah, and made a "
2Ki 8:22 revolted from under the h' of Judah 3027
9: 1 take this box of oil in thine h', "
7 the Lord, at the h' of Jezebel. "
10:15 If it be, give me thine h'. "
15 And he gave him his h'; "
11: 8 his weapons in his h': and he that "
12:15 into whose h' they delivered the "
13: 3 into the h' of Hazael king of Syria, "
3 and into the h' of Ben-hadad "
5 from under the h' of the Syrians: "
16 Put thine h' upon the bow. "
16 And he put his h' upon it: and "
25 took again out of the h' of "
25 which he had taken out of the h' of "
14: 5 kingdom was confirmed in his h', "
25 by the h' of his servant Jonah, "
27 by the h' of Jeroboam the son of "
15:19 that his h' might be with him to "
19 confirm the kingdom in his h'. "
16: 7 out of the h' of the king of Syria, 3709
7 out of the h' of the king of Israel, "
17: 7 from under the h' of Pharaoh, 3027
20 delivered them into the h' of "
39 out of the h' of all your enemies. "
18:21 if a man lean, it will go into his h', 3709
29 to deliver you out of his h': 3027
30 delivered into the h' of the king "
33 out of the h' of the king of Assyria? "
34 delivered Samaria out of mine h'? "
35 their country out of mine h', that "
35 deliver Jerusalem out of mine h'? "
19:10 delivered into the h' of the king "
14 letter of the h' of the messengers, "
19 save thou us out of his h', "
20: 6 thee and this city out of the h' of 3709
21:14 into the h' of their enemies; 3027
22: 2 turned not aside to the right h' 3225
5 let them deliver it into the h' of 3207
7 them into their h', because they "
9 the h' of them that do the work, "
23:13 on the right h' of the mount 3225
1Ch 4:10 that thine h' might be with me, 3027
5:10 who fell by their h': and they "
20 were delivered into their h', "
6:15 and Jerusalem by the h' of "
39 who stood on his right h', even 3225
44 sons of Merari stood on the left h': 8040
11:23 in the Egyptian's h' was a spear 3027
23 the spear out of the Egyptian's h', "
12: 2 could use both the right h' and the 3231
13: 9 Uzza put forth his h' to hold the 3027
10 because he put his h' to the ark: "
14:10 wilt thou deliver them into mine h'? "
10 I will deliver them into thine h'. "
11 by mine h' like the breaking forth "
16: 7 into the h' of Asaph and his "
18: 1 out of the h' of the Philistines. "
19:11 delivered unto the h' of Abishai his "
20: 6 six on each h', and six on each foot: "
8 they fell by the h' of David, and 3027
8 and by the h' of his servants. "
21:13 me fall now into the h' of the Lord; "
13 but let me not fall into the h' of man. "
15 It is enough, stay now thine h'. "
16 having a drawn sword in his h' "
17 let thine h', I pray thee, O Lord my "
22:18 inhabitants of the land into mine h'; "
26:28 it was under the h' of Shelomith, "
28:19 in writing by his h' upon me, "
29: 8 by the h' of Jehiel the Gershonite. "
12 and in thine h' is power and might; "
12 and in thine h' it is to make great, "
16 cometh of thine h', and is all thine "
2Ch 3:17 one on the right h', and the other 3225
17 the name of that on the right h' "
4: 5 thickness of it was an h' breadth, 2947
6 put five on the right h', and five 3225
7 in the temple, five on the right h', "
6:15 and hast fulfilled it with thine h', 3027
32 and thy mighty h', and thy "
10:15 he spake by the h' of Ahijah "
12: 5 I also left you in the h' of Shishak. "
7 upon Jerusalem by the h' of "
13: 8 in the h' of the sons of David; "
16 God delivered them into their h'. "
16: 7 the king...escaped out of thine h'. "
8 he delivered them into thine h'. "
17: 5 stablished the kingdom in his h'; "
18: 5 God will deliver it into the king's h'. "
11 the Lord shall deliver it into the h' "
14 they shall be delivered into your h'. "
18 of heaven standing on his right h' 3225
33 Turn thine h', that thou mayest 3027
20: 6 and in thine h' is there not power "
21:10 from under the h' of Judah unto "
10 Libnah revolt from under his h'; "
23: 7 man with his weapons in his h'; "
10 man having his weapon in his h', "
18 by the h' of the priests the Levites, "
24:11 by the h' of the Levites, and when "
24 a very great host into their h', "
25:15 their own people out of thine h'? "
20 into the h' of their enemies, *"
26:11 by the h' of Jeiel the scribe "
11 under the h' of Hananiah, one of "
13 under their h' was an army, three "
19 and had a censer in his h' "
28: 5 into the h' of the king of Syria; "
5 into the h' of the king of Israel, "
9 he hath delivered them into your h', "
30: 6 of the h' of the kings of Assyria. 3709
12 the h' of God was to give them 3027
16 they received of the h' of the "
31:13 under the h' of Cononiah and "
32:11 out of the h' of the king of 3709
13 deliver their lands out of mine h'? 3027

2Ch 32: 14 deliver his people out of mine h'. 3027
14 able to deliver you out of mine h'? "
15 deliver his people out of mine h', "
15 and out of the h' of my fathers: "
15 God deliver you out of mine h'? "
17 delivered their peopleout of mine h'," "
17 deliver his people out of mine h'. "
22 from the h' of Sennacherib the "
22 and from the h' of all other, "
33: 8 the ordinances by the h' of Moses. "
34: 2 to the right h', nor to the left. 3225
9 gathered of the h' of Manasseh 3027
10 put it in the h' of the workmen "
17 into the h' of the overseers, and "
17 to the h' of the workmen. "
35: 6 word of the Lord by the h' of Moses." "
36: 17 he gave them all into his h'. "
Ezr 1: 8 by the h' of Mithredath the "
5: 12 he gave them into the h' of 3028
6: 12 that shall put to their h' to alter "
7: 6 according to the h' of the Lord 3027
9 according to the good h' of his God "
14 of thy God which is in thine h'; 3028
25 of thy God, that is in thine h', "
28 as the h' of the Lord my God was 3027
8: 18 by the good h' of our God upon us "
22 The h' of our God is upon all "
26 I even weighed unto their h' six "
31 and the h' of our God was upon us, "
31 and he delivered us from the h' of 3709
33 by the h' of Meremoth the son of 3027
9: 2 yea, the h' of the princes and "
7 into the h' of the kings of the lands," "
Ne 1: 10 great power, and by thy strong h'. "
2: 8 according to the good h' of my God "
18 Then I told them of the h' of my "
4: 17 and with the other h' held a weapon.*
6: 5 with an open letter in his h'; 3027
8: 4 Hilkiah, and Maaseiah...right h'; 3225
4 and on his left h', Pedaiah, and 8040
9: 14 by the h' of Moses thy servant: 3027
27 into the h' of their enemies, who "
27 out of the h' of their enemies. "
28 in the h' of their enemies, so that "
30 into the h' of the people of the "
11: 24 son of Judah, was at the king's h' "
12: 31 one went on the right h' upon the 3225
Es 2: 21 sought to lay h' on the king *3027
3: 10 the king took his ring from his h'. "
5: 2 golden sceptre that was in his h'. "
6: 2 who sought to lay h' on the king * "
9 the h' of one of the king's most "
8: 7 he laid his h' upon the Jews. "
9: 2 to lay h' on such as sought their "
10 on the spoil laid they not their h'. "
15 on the prey they laid not their h'. "
Job 1: 11 put forth thine h' now, and touch "
2: 5 put forth thine h' now, and touch "
6 Behold, he is in thine h'; but save "
10 we receive good at the h' of God, 854
5: 15 and from the h' of the mighty. 3027
6: 9 that he would let loose his h', "
23 Deliver me from the enemy's h'? or," "
23 Redeem me from the h' of the "
9: 24 The earth is given into the h' of "
33 that might lay his h' upon us both. "
10: 7 none that can deliver out of thine h'." "
11: 14 If iniquity be in thine h', put it far "
12: 6 into whose h' God bringeth "
9 the h' of the Lord hath wrought "
10 In whose h' is the soul of every "
13: 14 and put my life in mine h'? 3709
21 Withdraw thine h' far from me: "
15: 23 day of darkness is ready at his h'. 3027
25 stretcheth out his h' against God, "
19: 21 the h' of God hath touched me. "
20: 22 every h' of the wicked shall come "
21: 5 lay your h' upon your mouth. "
16 their good is not in their h': "
23: 9 the left h', where he doth work, 8040
9 he hideth himself on the right h', 3225
26: 13 his h' hath formed the crooked 3027
27: 11 I will teach you by the h' of God: "
22 he would fain flee out of his h'. "
28: 9 He putteth forth his h' upon the "
29: 9 and laid their h' on their mouth. 3709
20 and my bow was renewed in my h'. 3027
30: 12 Upon my right h' rise the youth; 3225
21 with thy strong h' thou opposest 3027
24 not stretch out his h' to the grave, "
31: 21 have lifted up my h' against the "
25 and because mine h' had gotten "
27 or my mouth hath kissed my h': "
33: 7 neither shall my h' be heavy upon*405
34: 20 shall be taken away without h'. 3027
35: 7 or what receiveth he of thine h'? "
37: 7 He sealeth up the h' of every man; "
40: 4 I will lay mine h' upon my mouth. "
14 thine own right h' can save thee. 3225
41: 8 Lay thine h' upon him, remember 3709
Ps 10: 12 O God, lift up thine h': forget not 3027
14 spite, to requite it with thy h': "
16: 8 he is at my right h', I shall not be 3225
11 at thy right h' there are pleasures "
17: 7 O thou that savest by thy right h' "
14 From men which are thy h', O 3027
18: *title* delivered him from the h' of all 3709
title enemies, and from the h' of Saul: 3027
35 and thy right h' hath holden me 3225
20: 6 the saving strength of his right h'. "
21: 8 Thine h' shall find out all thine 3027
8 thy right h' shall find out those 3225
26: 10 and their right h' is full of bribes. "
31: 5 Into thine h' I commit my spirit: 3027
8 me up into the h' of the enemy: "
15 My times are in thy h': deliver me "

Ps 31: 15 from the h' of mine enemies, 3027
32: 4 day and night thy h' was heavy "
36: 11 and let not the h' of the wicked "
37: 24 Lord upholdeth him with his h'. "
33 The Lord will not leave him in his h'," "
38: 2 in me, and thy h' presseth me sore." "
39: 10 consumed by the blow of thine h'. "
44: 2 drive out the heathen with thy h', "
3 but thy right h', and thine arm, 3225
45: 4 thy right h' shall teach thee terrible" "
9 upon thy right h' did stand the "
48: 10 thy right h' is full of righteousness." "
60: 5 save with thy right h', and hear me." "
63: 8 thee: thy right h' upholdeth me. "
71: 4 God, out of the h' of the wicked, 3027
4 out of the h' of the unrighteous 3709
73: 23 hast holden me by my right h'. 3027
74: 11 Why withdrawest thou thy h', "
11 even thy right h'? pluck it out 3225
75: 8 in the h' of the Lord there is a 3027
77: 10 the right h' of the most High. 3225
20 by the h' of Moses and Aaron. 3027
78: 42 They remembered not his h', nor "
54 mountain, which his right h' had 3225
61 his glory into the enemy's h'. 3027
80: 15 which thy right h' hath planted, 3225
17 Let thy h' be upon the man of thy 3027
17 upon the man of thy right h', 3225
81: 14 turned my h' against their 3027
82: 4 rid them out of the h' of the wicked." "
88: 5 they are cut off from thy h'. "
89: 13 mighty arm: strong is thy h', "
13 and high is thy right h'. 3225
21 my h' shall be established: mine 3027
25 I will set his h' also in the sea, "
25 and his right h' in the rivers. 3225
42 Thou hast set up the right h' of his "
48 his soul from the h' of the grave?*3027
91: 7 ten thousand at thy right h'; but 3225
95: 4 In his h' are the deep places 3027
7 pasture, and the sheep of his h'. "
97: 10 them out of the h' of the wicked. "
98: 1 his right h', and his holy arm, 3225
104: 28 thou openest thine h', they are 3027
106: 10 from the h' of him that hated them," "
10 and redeemed them from the h' of "
26 he lifted up his h' against them, "
41 into the h' of the heathen; and "
42 into subjection under their h'. "
107: 2 redeemed from the h' of the enemy;" "
108: 6 save with thy right h', and answer 3225
109: 6 let Satan stand at his right h'. "
27 know that this is thy h'; that thou, 3027
31 at the right h' of the poor, to save 3225
110: 1 Sit thou at my right h', until I make" "
5 The Lord at thy right h' shall strike" "
118: 15 right h' of the Lord doeth valiantly. "
16 The right h' of the Lord is exalted: "
16 right h' of the Lord doeth valiantly. "
119: 109 My soul is continually in my h': 3709
173 Let thine h' help me; for I have 3027
121: 5 Lord is thy shade upon thy right h'. "
123: 2 the h' of their masters, and as the "
2 eyes of a maiden unto the h' of her "
127: 4 As arrows are in the h' of a mighty "
129: 7 the mower filleth not his h'; 3709
136: 12 With a strong h', and with a 3027
137: 5 let my right h' forget her cunning. 3225
138: 7 stretch forth thine h' against the 3027
7 thy right h' shall save me. 3225
139: 5 and before, and laid thine h' upon 3709
10 there shall thy h' lead me, and 3027
10 thy right h' shall hold me. 3225
142: 4 I looked on my right h', and "
144: 7 Send thine h' from above; rid me, 3027
7 from the h' of strange children; "
8 and their right h' is a right h' of 3225
11 from the h' of strange children; 3027
11 and their right h' is a right h' of 3225
145: 16 Thou openest thine h', and 3027
149: 6 a twoedged sword in their h'; "
Pr 1: 24 I have stretched out my h', and no "
3: 16 Length of days is in her right h'; 3225
16 in her left h' riches and honour. 8040
27 the power of thine h' to do it. 3027
4: 27 Turn not to the right h' nor to the 3227
6: 1 thou hast stricken thine h' with * 3709
3 art come into the h' of thy friend; 3027
5 as a roe from the h' of the hunter, 3027
5 and as a bird from the h' of the "
10: 4 poor that dealeth with a slack h': 3709
4 but the h' of the diligent maketh 3027
11: 21 Though h' join in h', the wicked "
12: 24 The h' of the diligent shall bear "
16: 5 though h' join in h', he shall not "
17: 16 is there a price in the h' of a fool "
19: 24 A slothful man hideth his h' in his "
21: 1 The king's heart is in the h' of the "
26: 6 a message by the h' of a fool "
9 into the h' of a drunkard, so is a "
15 The slothful hideth his h' in his "
27: 16 and the ointment of his right h', 3225
30: 32 lay thine h' upon thy mouth. 3027
31: 20 She stretcheth out her h' to the 3709
Ec 2: 24 that it was from the h' of God. 3027
5: 14 and there is nothing in his h', "
15 which he may carry away in his h'. "
7: 18 from this withdraw not thine h': "
9: 1 their works, are in the h' of God: "
10 Whatsoever thy h' findeth to do, "
10: 2 wise man's heart is at his right h': 3225
11: 6 evening withhold not thine h': 3027
Ca 2: 6 His left h' is under my head, 8040
6 and his right h' doth embrace me. 3225
5: 4 My beloved put in his h' by the 3027
8: 3 His left h' should be under my 8040

Ca 8: 3 his right h' should embrace me. 3225
Isa 1: 12 who hath required this at your h', 3027
25 I will turn my h' upon thee, "
3: 6 let this ruin be under thy h': "
5: 25 he hath stretched forth his h' "
25 but his h' is stretched out still. "
6: 6 having a live coal in his h', "
8: 11 with a strong h', and instructed me "
9: 12, 17 but his h' is stretched out still. "
20 he shall snatch on the right h', 3225
20 and he shall eat on the left h', 8040
21 but his h' is stretched out still. 3027
10: 4 but his h' is stretched out still. "
5 the staff in their h' is mine "
10 my h' hath found the kingdoms "
13 the strength of mine h' I have done "
14 my h' hath found as a nest "
32 he shall shake his h' against the "
11: 8 put his h' on the cockatrice' den. "
11 the Lord shall set his h' again "
14 they shall lay their h' upon Edom "
15 shall he shake his h' over the river," "
13: 2 shake the h', that they may go "
6 the day of the Lord is at h'; 7138
14: 26 this is the h' that is stretched out 3027
27 and his h' is stretched out, and who" "
19: 4 into the h' of a cruel lord; "
16 the shaking of the h' of the Lord "
22: 21 commit thy government into his h': "
23: 11 He stretched out his h' over the sea," "
25: 10 mountain shall the h' of the Lord "
26: 11 when thy h' is lifted up, they will "
28: 2 cast down to the earth with the h'. "
4 while it is yet in his h' he eateth it 3709
31: 3 the Lord shall stretch out his h', 3027
34: 17 and his h' hath divided it unto "
36: 6 it will go into his h', and pierce 3709
15 into the h' of the king of Assyria. 3027
18 out of the h' of the king of Assyria? "
19 delivered Samaria out of my h'? "
20 delivered their land out of my h', "
20 deliver Jerusalem out of my h'? "
37: 10 into the h' of the king of Assyria. "
14 from the h' of the messengers, "
20 save us from his h', that all the "
38: 6 thee and this city out of the h' 3709
40: 2 received of the Lord's h' double 3027
10 Lord God will come with strong h',*
12 the waters in the hollow of his h', "
41: 10 right h' of my righteousness. 3225
13 thy God will hold thy right h', "
20 the h' of the Lord hath done this, 3027
42: 6 will hold thine h', and will keep "
43: 13 none that can deliver out of my h': "
44: 5 another shall subscribe with his h' "
20 Is there not a lie in my right h'? 3225
45: 1 whose right h' I have holden, to "
47: 6 and given them into thine h': 3027
48: 13 Mine h' also hath laid the "
13 and my right h' hath spanned the 3225
49: 2 in the shadow of his h' hath he 3027
22 I will lift up mine h' to the "
50: 2 Is my h' shortened at all, that it "
11 This shall ye have of my h'; ye "
51: 16 the shadow of mine h', that I may "
17 hast drunk at the h' of the Lord "
18 that taketh her by the h' of all the "
22 I have taken out of thine h' the cup "
23 into the h' of them that afflict "
53: 10 of the Lord shall prosper in his h'. "
54: 3 shalt break forth on the right h' 3225
56: 2 keepeth his h' from doing...evil. 3027
57: 10 thou hast found...life of thine h'; * "
59: 1 the Lord's h' is not shortened, "
62: 3 crown of glory in the h' of the Lord, "
3 royal diadem in the h' of thy God. 3709
8 Lord hath sworn by his right h', 3225
63: 12 That led them by the right h' of "
64: 8 we all are the work of thy h'. 3027
66: 2 all those things hath mine h' "
14 the h' of the Lord shall be known "
Jer 1: 9 the Lord put forth his h', and "
6: 9 turn back thine h' as a "
12 I will stretch out my h' upon the "
11: 21 that thou die not by our h': "
12: 7 soul into the h' of her enemies. 3709
15: 6 therefore will I stretch out my h' 3027
17 I sat alone because of thy h': "
21 thee out of the h' of the wicked, "
21 thee out of the h' of the terrible. 3709
16: 21 I will cause them to know mine h' 3027
18: 4 marred in the h' of the potter: "
6 as the clay is in the potter's h', "
6 so are ye in mine h', O house "
20: 4 into the h' of the king of Babylon, "
5 into the h' of their enemies, which "
13 the poor from the h' of evildoers. "
21: 5 with an outstretched h' and with a "
7 into the h' of Nebuchadrezzar "
7 and into the h' of their enemies, "
7 h' of those that seek their life: "
10 into the h' of the king of Babylon, "
12 out of the h' of the oppressor, "
22: 3 out of the h' of the oppressor: "
24 the signet upon my right h', yet "
25 the h' of them that seek thy life, "
25 h' of them whose face thou fearest, "
25 even into the h' of Nebuchadrezzar "
25 and into the h' of the Chaldeans "
23: 23 Am I a God at h', saith the Lord, 7138
25: 15 the wine cup of this fury at my h', 3027
17 the cup at the Lord's h', and made "
28 take the cup at thine h' to drink, "
26: 14 I am in your h': do with me "
24 the h' of Ahikam the son of "
24 give him into the h' of the people "

Jer 27: 3 by the h· of the messengers which 3027
6 into the h· of Nebuchadnezzar the "
8 I have consumed them by his h·. "
29: 3 By the h· of Elasah the son of "
21 into the h· of Nebuchadrezzar king "
31: 11 the h· of him that was stronger "
32 the day that I took them by the h· "
32: 3 into the h· of the king of Babylon, "
4 out of the h· of the Chaldeans, "
4 into the h· of the king of Babylon, "
21 and with a strong h·, and with a "
24 and the city is given into the h· of "
25 for the city is given into the h· of "
28 h· of the Chaldeans, and into the h· "
36 It shall be delivered into the h· of "
43 it is given into the h· of the "
34: 2 into the h· of the king of Babylon, "
3 thou shalt not escape out of his h·, "
3 and delivered into his h·; "
20 into the h· of their enemies, and "
20 the h· of them that seek their life: "
21 give into the h· of their enemies, "
21 h· of them that seek their life, "
21 and into the h· of the king of "
36: 14 Take in thine h· the roll wherein "
14 took the roll in his h·, and came "
37: 17 into the h· of the king of Babylon. "
38: 3 into the h· of the king of Babylon's "
5 he is in your h·: for the king is not "
16 into the h· of these men that seek "
18 into the h· of the Chaldeans, and "
18 shalt not escape out of their h·, "
19 lest they deliver me into their h·, "
23 not escape out of their h·, "
23 shalt be taken by the h· of the king "
39: 17 into the h· of the men of whom "
40: 4 the chains...were upon thine h·. "
41: 5 offerings and incense in their h·, "
42: 11 and to deliver you from his h·. "
43: 3 into the h· of the Chaldeans, "
9 Take great stones in thine h·, and "
44: 25 and fulfilled with your h·, saying, * "
30 into the h· of his enemies, "
30 the h· of them that seek his life; "
30 into the h· of Nebuchadrezzar king "
46: 24 into the h· of the people of the north. "
26 the h· of those that seek their lives, "
26 into the h· of Nebuchadrezzar king "
26 and into the h· of his servants: "
50: 15 she hath given her h·: her * "
51: 7 a golden cup in the Lord's h·, "
25 I will stretch out mine h· upon "
La 1: 7 her people fell into the h· of the "
10 The adversary...spread out his h· "
14 transgressions is bound by his h·: "
2: 3 he hath drawn back his right h· 3225
4 stood with his right h· as an "
7 into the h· of the enemy the walls 3027
8 he hath not withdrawn his h· from "
3: 3 he turneth his h· against me all "
5: 6 We have given the h· to the "
8 that doth deliver us out of their h·. "
12 Princes are hanged up by their h·: "
Eze 1: 3 the h· of the Lord was there upon "
2: 9 an h· was sent unto me; and, lo, "
3: 14 but the h· of the Lord was strong "
18, 20 blood will I require at thine h·. "
22 the h· of the Lord was there upon "
6: 11 Smite with thine h·, and stamp 3709
14 So will I stretch out my h· upon 3027
8: 1 the h· of the Lord God fell there "
3 he put forth the form of an h·, "
11 every man his censer in his h·; "
9: 1 his destroying weapon in his h·. "
2 a slaughter weapon in his h·; "
10: 2 fill thine h· with coals of fire *2651
7 one cherub stretched forth his h· 3027
8 the form of a man's h· under their "
12: 7 I digged...the wall with mine h·; "
23 The days are at h·, and the effect 7126
13: 9 mine h· shall be upon the prophets 3027
21 deliver my people out of your h·, "
21 and they...be no more in your h· "
23 deliver my people out of your h·: "
14: 9 I will stretch out my h· upon him, "
13 will I stretch out mine h· upon it, "
16: 27 I have stretched out my h· over "
39 I will also give thee into their h·, "
46 daughters that dwell at thy left h·: 8040
46 sister that dwelleth at thy right h·, 3225
49 neither did she strengthen the h· 3027
17: 18 he had given his h·, and hath "
18: 8 hath withdrawn his h· from "
17 hath taken off his h· from the poor, "
20: 5 and lifted up mine h· unto the seed "
5 when I lifted up mine h· unto them, "
6 that I lifted up mine h· unto them, "
15 also I lifted up my h· unto them in "
22 I withdrew mine h·, and wrought "
23 I lifted up mine h· unto them also in "
28 for the which I lifted up mine h· to "
33 a mighty h·, and with a stretched "
34 ye are scattered, with a mighty h·, "
42 for the which I lifted up mine h· to "
21: 11 to give it into the h· of the slayer. "
16 either on the right h·, or on...left,* 3221
22 At his right h· was the divination 3225
24 ye shall be taken with the h·. 3079
31 deliver thee into the h· of brutish 3027
22: 13 I have smitten mine h· at thy 3079
23: 9 I have delivered her into the h· 3027
9 of her lovers, into the h· of the "
28 the h· of them whom thou hatest, "
28 h· of them from whom thy mind "
31 will I give her cup into thine h·. "
25: 7 I will stretch out mine h· upon "

Eze 25: 13 I will also stretch out mine h· upon 3027
14 by the h· of my people Israel: "
16 I will stretch out mine h· upon "
27: 15 the merchandise of thine h·: they "
28: 9 in the h· of him that slayeth thee. "
10 by the h· of strangers: for I have "
29: 7 they took hold of thee by thy h·, 3709
30: 10 by the h· of Nebuchadrezzar king 3027
12 the land into the h· of the wicked: "
12 is therein, by the h· of strangers: "
22 the sword to fall out of his h·. "
24 and put my sword in his h·: "
25 into the h· of the king of Babylon, "
31: 11 into the h· of the mighty one "
33: 6 will I require at the watchman's h·. "
8 his blood will I require at thine h·. "
22 Now the h· of the Lord was upon "
34: 10 I will require my flock at their h·, "
27 out of the h· of those that served "
35: 3 I will stretch out mine h· against "
36: 7 I have lifted up mine h·, Surely the "
8 Israel; for they are at h· to come. 7126
37: 1 The h· of the Lord was upon me, 3027
17 they shall become one in thine h·. "
19 which is in the h· of Ephraim, and "
19 they shall be one in mine h·. "
20 writest shall be in thine h· before "
38: 12 turn thine h· upon the desolate "
39: 3 smite the bow out of thy left h·, "
3 thine arrows to fall out of...right h·. "
21 my h· that I have laid upon them. "
23 them into the h· of their enemies: "
40: 1 the h· of the Lord was upon me, "
3 a line of flax in his h·, and a "
5 and in the man's h· a measuring "
5 by the cubit and an h· breath 2948
43 hooks, an h· broad, fastened * "
43: 13 cubit is a cubit and an h· breadth; "
44: 12 I lifted up mine h· against them, 3027
46: 7 according as his h· shall attain * "
47: 3 man that had the line in his h· "
14 I lifted up mine h· to give it unto "
Da 1: 2 into his h·, with part of the vessels "
2: 38 hath he given into thine h·, 3028
3: 17 he will deliver us out of thine h·, "
4: 35 none can stay his h·, or say "
5: 5 came forth fingers of a man's h·, "
5 saw the part of the h· that wrote. "
23 and the God in whose h· thy breath "
24 Then was the part of the h· sent "
7: 25 and they shall be given into his h· "
8: 4 that could deliver out of his h·; 3027
7 deliver the ram out of his h·. "
25 cause craft to prosper in his h·; "
25 but he shall be broken without h·. "
9: 15 land of Egypt with a mighty h·, "
10: 10 an h· touched me, which set me "
11: 11 multitude shall be given into his h·. "
16 which by his h· shall be consumed. "
41 escape out of his h·, even Edom, "
42 He shall stretch forth his h· also "
12: 7 he held up his right h· 3225
7 and his left h· unto heaven, 8040
Ho 2: 10 shall deliver her out of mine h·. 3027
7: 5 stretched out his h· with scorners. "
12: 7 the balances of deceit are in his h·: "
Joe 1: 15 the day of the Lord is at h·, 7138
2: 1 the day of the Lord...is nigh at h·; "
3: 8 into the h· of the children of 3027
Am 1: 8 I will turn mine h· against Ekron: "
5: 19 leaned his h· on the wall, and a "
7: 7 with a plumbline in his h·. "
9: 2 hell, thence shall mine h· take "
Jon 4: 11 cannot discern between...right h· 3235
11 between their right...and...left h·. 8040
Mic 2: 1 it is in the power of their h·. 3027
4: 10 thee from the h· of thine enemies. 3709
5: 9 Thine h· shall be lifted up upon 3027
12 cut off witchcrafts out of thine h·; "
7: 16 lay their h· upon their mouth, "
Hab 2: 16 the Lord's right h· shall be turned 3225
3: 4 he had horns coming out of his h·: 3027
Zep 1: 4 I will also stretch out mine h· "
7 the day of the Lord is at h·: 7138
2: 13 he will stretch out his h· against 3027
15 by her shall hiss, and wag his h·. "
Zec 2: 1 with a measuring line in his h·. "
9 I will shake mine h· upon them, "
3: 1 Satan standing at his right h· to 3225
4: 10 plummet in the h· of Zerubbabel 3027
8: 4 his staff in his h· for very age. "
11: 6 every one into his neighbour's h·, "
6 and into the h· of his king: "
6 out of their h· I will not deliver "
12: 6 on the right h· and on the left: 3225
13: 7 I will turn mine h· upon the little 3027
14: 13 shall lay hold every one on the h· "
13 of his neighbour, and...h· shall rise "
13 up against the h· of his neighbour. "
Mal 1: 10 will I accept an offering at your h·. "
13 should I accept this of your h·? "
2: 13 receiveth it with good will at your h·. "
M't 3: 2 for the kingdom of heaven is at h·. 1448
12 Whose fan is in his h·, and he will 5495
4: 17 for the kingdom of heaven is at h·. 1448
5: 30 if thy right h· offend thee, cut it 5495
6: 3 doest alms, let not thy left h· "
3 know what thy right h· doeth. "
8: 3 Jesus put forth his h·, and touched 5495
15 he touched her h·, and the fever "
9: 18 lay thy h· upon her, and she shall "
25 took her by the h·, and the maid "
10: 7 The kingdom of heaven is at h·. 1448
12: 10 a man which had his h· withered. 5495
13 to the man, Stretch forth thine h·. "
49 he stretched forth his h· toward his "

M't 14: 31 Jesus stretched forth his h·, and 5495
18: 8 if thy h· or thy foot offend thee, "
20: 21 may sit, the one on thy right h·, and "
23 to sit on my right h·, and on my "
22: 13 Bind him h· and foot, and take 5495
44 Sit thou on my right h·, till I make "
25: 33 shall set the sheep on his right h·, "
34 say unto them on his right h·, Come "
41 unto them on the left h·, Depart "
26: 18 The Master saith, My time is at h·; 1451
23 He that dippeth his h· with me 5495
45 behold, the hour is at h·, and the 1448
46 he is at h· that doth betray me. "
51 stretched out his h·, and drew his 5495
64 sitting on the right h· of power, "
27: 29 his head, and a reed in his right h·: "
38 one on the right h·, and another on "
M'r 1: 15 the kingdom of God is at h·: 1448
31 and took her by the h·, and lifted 5495
41 put forth his h·, and touched "
3: 1 man there which had a withered h·. "
3 had the withered h·, Stand forth. "
5 Stretch forth thine h·. And he "
5 and his h· was restored whole as the "
5: 41 took the damsel by the h·, and said "
7: 32 beseech him to put his h· upon "
8: 23 he took the blind man by the h·, "
9: 27 took him by the h·, and lifted him "
43 if thy h· offend thee, cut it off: "
10: 37 we may sit, one on thy right h·, and "
37 the other on thy left h·, in thy glory. "
40 to sit on my right h· and on my left h·. "
12: 36 Sit thou on my right h·, till I make "
14: 42 lo, he that betrayeth me is at h·. 1448
62 sitting on the right h· of power, and "
15: 27 the one on his right h·, and the other "
16: 19 and sat on the right h· of God. "
Lu 1: 1 many have taken in h· to set 2021
66 And the h· of the Lord was with 5495
71 and from the h· of all that hate us; "
74 being delivered out of the h· of our "
3: 17 Whose fan is in his h·, and he will "
5: 13 he put forth his h·, and touched "
6: 6 man whose right h· was withered. "
8 which had the withered h·, Rise up, "
10 Stretch forth thy h·. And he did so. "
10 his h· was restored whole as...other "
8: 54 and took her by the h·, and called, "
9: 62 No man, having put his h· to the "
15: 22 and put a ring on his h·, and shoes "
20: 42 my Lord, Sit thou on my right h·, "
21: 30 that summer is now nigh at h·. *
31 kingdom of God is nigh at h·. *
22: 21 the h· of him that betrayeth me 5495
69 sit on the right h· of the power of "
23: 33 one on the right h·, and the other on "
Joh 2: 13 the Jews' passover was at h·, and 1451
3: 35 hath given all things into his h·. 5495
7: 2 feast of tabernacles was at h·. 1451
10: 28 any man pluck them out of my h·. 5495
29 to pluck them out of my Father's h·. "
39 him: but he escaped out of their h·. "
11: 44 h· and foot with graveclothes; "
55 Jews' passover was nigh at h·: and "
18: 22 struck Jesus with the palm of his h·, "
42 for the sepulchre was nigh at h·. "
20: 25 and thrust my h· into his side, I 5495
27 and reach hither thy h·, and thrust "
Ac 2: 25 for he is on my right h·, that "
33 being by the right h· of God exalted, "
34 my Lord, Sit thou on my right h·, "
3: 7 took him by the right h·, and 5495
4: 28 whatsoever thy h· and thy counsel "
30 stretching forth thine h· to heal; "
5: 31 hath God exalted with his right h· "
7: 25 God by his h· would deliver them: 5495
35 by the h· of the angel which "
50 Hath not my h· made all these "
55 Jesus standing on the right h· of God, "
56 man standing on the right h· of God. "
9: 8 they led him by the h·, and 5496
12 coming in, and putting his h· on *5495
41 he gave her his h·, and lifted "
11: 21 And the h· of the Lord was with "
12: 11 delivered me out of the h· of Herod, "
17 beckoning unto them with the h· to "
13: 11 behold, the h· of the Lord is upon "
11 seeking some to lead him by the h·. 5497
16 beckoning with his h· said, Men of 5495
19: 33 Alexander beckoned with the h·, "
21: 3 Cyprus, we left it on the left h·, "
40 beckoned with the h· unto the 5495
22: 11 being led by the h· of them that 5496
23: 19 captain took him by the h·, and 5495
26: 1 Paul stretched forth the h·, and "
28: 3 of the heat, and fastened on his h·. "
4 beast hang on his h·, they said "
Ro 8: 34 even at the right h· of God, who also "
13: 12 night is far spent, the day is at h·: 1448
1Co 12: 15 Because I am not the h·, I am not 5495
21 And the eye cannot say unto the h·, "
16: 21 of me Paul with mine own h·. "
2Co 6: 7 on the right h· and on the left, "
10: 16 of things made ready to our h·. "
Ga 3: 19 by angels in the h· of a mediator. 5495
6: 11 written unto you with mine own h·. "
Eph 1: 20 set him at his own right h· in the "
Ph'p 4: 5 unto all men. The Lord is at h·. 1451
Col 3: 1 Christ sitteth on the right h· of God. "
4: 18 salutation by the h· of me Paul. 5495
2Th 2: 2 as that the day of Christ is at h·. †1764
3: 17 of Paul with mine own h·, 5495
2Ti 4: 6 the time of my departure is at h·. *2186
Ph'm 19 written it with mine own h·, 5495
Heb 1: 3 the right h· of the Majesty on high; "
13 Sit on my right h·, until I make "

Heb 8: 1 set on the right h' of the throne
9 when I took them by the h' to lead 5495
10:12 sat down on the right h' of God;
12: 2 is set down at the right h' of the
1Pet 3:22 is on the right h' of God; angels, and
4: 7 the end of all things is at h'. 1448
5: 6 under the mighty h' of God, that 5495
Re 1: 3 therein: for the time is at h'. 1451
16 he had in his right h' seven stars: 5495
17 he laid his right h' upon me, "
20 which thou sawest in my right h', and
2: 1 the seven stars in his right h',
5: 1 I saw in the right h' of him that sat
7 took the book out of the right h'
6: 5 him had a pair of balances in his h'. 5495
8: 4 up before God out of the angel's h'. "
10: 2 he had in his h' a little book "
5 the earth lifted up his h' to heaven, "
8 which is open in the h' of the angel "
10 book out of the angel's h', and ate "
13:16 to receive a mark in their right h', "
14: 9 mark in his forehead, or in his h', "
14 and in his h' a sharp sickle. "
17: 4 having a golden cup in her h' full of "
19: 2 the blood of his servants at her h'. "
20: 1 pit and a great chain in his h'. "
22:10 of this book: for the time is at h'. 1451

handbreadth See also HAND and BREADTH.
Ex 37:12 a border of an h' round about; 2948
2Ch 4: 5 And the thickness of it was an h', 2947
Ps 39: 5 thou hast made my days as an h';* "

handed See also BROKENHANDED; LEFTHANDED.
2Sa 17: 2 he is weary and weak h', and will 3027

handful See also HANDFULS.
Le 2: 2 shall take thereout his h' of 4393,7062
5:12 priest shall take his h' of it, "
6:15 shall take of it his h', of the flour 7062
9:17 took an h' thereof, and burnt *4390,3709
Nu 5:26 And the priest shall take an h' 7061
1Ki 17:12 an h' of meal in a barrel, 4393, 3709
Ps 72:16 There shall be an h' of corn *6451
Ec 4: 6 Better is an h' with quietness, 4393,3709
Jer 9:22 as the h' after the harvestman, 5995

handfuls
Ge 41:47 the earth brought forth by h'. 7062
Ex 9: 8 Take to you h' of ashes of 4393, 2651
Ru 2:16 let fall also some of the h' *6653
1Ki 20:10 Samaria shall suffice for h' for all 8168
Eze 13:19 my people for h' of barley and for "

handiwork See HANDYWORK.

handkerchiefs
Ac 19:12 brought unto the sick h' or aprons, 4676

handle See also HAFT; HANDLED; HANDLES; HANDLETH; HANDLING.
Ge 4:21 father of all such as h' the harp 8610
J'g 5:14 they that h' the pen of the writer. 4900
1Ch 12: 8 that could h' shield and buckler, 6186
2Ch 25: 5 that could h' spear and shield. 270
Ps 115: 7 They have hands, but they h' not: 4184
Jer 2: 8 and they that h' the law knew 8610
46: 9 the Libyans, that h' the shield; and "
9 the Lydians, that h' and bend the "
Eze 27:29 all that h' the oar, the mariners, "
Lu 24:39 h' me, and see; for a spirit 5584
Col 2:21 touch not; taste not; h' not; 2345

handled
Eze 21:11 furbished, that it may be h': 8610,3709
M'r 12: 4 and sent him away shamefully h'. 821
1Jo 1: 1 looked upon, and...hands have h', 5584

handles
Ca 5: 5 upon the h' of the lock. 3709

handleth
Pr 16:20 He that h' a matter wisely shall * 5921
Jer 50:16 and him that h' the sickle 8610
Am 2:15 shall he stand that h' the brow; "

handling
Eze 38: 4 shields, all of them h' swords: 8610
2Co 4: 2 h' the word of God deceitfully; 1389

handmaid See also HANDMAIDEN; HANDMAIDS.
Ge 16: 1 she had an h', an Egyptian, 8198
25:12 the Egyptian, Sarah's h', bare unto "
29:24 Leah Zilpah his maid for an h'. "
29 Bilhah his h' to be her maid. "
30: 4 she gave him Bilhah her h' to wife "
35:25 the sons of Bilhah, Rachel's h'; "
26 And the sons of Zilpah, Leah's h'; "
Ex 23:12 the son of thy h', and the stranger, 519
J'g 19:19 also for me, and for thy h', "
Ru 2:13 spoken friendly unto thine h', 8198
3: 9 I am Ruth thine h': spread 519
9 therefore thy skirt over thine h'; "
1Sa 1:11 the affliction of thine h', and "
11 me, and not forget thine h', "
11 but wilt give unto thine h' "
16 Count not thine h' for a daughter "
18 Let thine h' find grace in thy sight.*8198
25:24 let thine h', I pray thee, speak in 519
24 and hear the words of thine h'. "
25 but I thine h' saw not the young "
27 which thine h' hath brought unto 8198
28 forgive the trespass of thine h'. 519
31 my lord, then remember thine h'. "
41 let thine h' be a servant "
28:21 thine h' hath obeyed thy voice, 8198
22 also unto the voice of thine h', "
2Sa 14: 6 And thy h' had two sons, and they "
7 family is risen against thine h', "
12 woman said, Let thine h', I pray "
15 and thy h' said, I will now speak "
15 perform the request of his h'. * 519
16 to deliver his h' out of the hand * "
17 Then thine h' said, The word of 8198
2Sa 14:19 words in the mouth of thine h': 8198
20:17 Hear the words of thine h'. And 519
1Ki 1:13 O king, swear unto thine h', "
17 the Lord thy God unto thine h', "
3:20 while thine h' slept, and laid it "
2Ki 4: 2 Thine h' hath not any thing in the 8198
16 man of God, do not lie unto thine h'. "
Ps 86:16 and save the son of thine h'. 519
116:16 servant, and the son of thine h': "
Pr 30:23 and an h' that is heir to her 8198
Jer 34:16 every man his h', whom he had "
Lu 1:38 Behold the h' of the Lord; be it 1399

handmaiden See also HANDMAIDENS.
Lu 1:48 regarded the low estate of his h': 1399

handmaidens
Ge 33: 6 Then the h' came near, they and *8198
Ru 2:13 like unto one of thine h'. "
Ac 2:18 on my servants and on my h' 1399

handmaids
Ge 33: 1 Rachel, and unto the two h'. 8198
2 he put the h' and their children "
2Sa 6:20 eyes of the h' of his servants, 519
Isa 14: 2 them...for servants and h': and *8198
Jer 34:11 the servants and the h', whom "
11 subjection for servants and for h'. "
16 you for servants and for h'. "
Joe 2:29 upon the h' in those days will I "

hands
Ge 5:29 our work and toil of our h', 3027
16: 9 and submit thyself under her h'. "
20: 5 innocency of my h' have I done 3709
24:22 two bracelets for her h' of ten 3027
30 bracelets upon his sister's h', and "
47 and the bracelets upon her h'. "
27:16 of the kids of the goats upon his h', "
22 but the h' are the h' of Esau. "
23 him not, because his h' were hairy "
23 hairy, as his brother Esau's h': "
31:42 the labour of my h', and rebuked 3709
37:21 delivered him out of their h'; * 3027
22 rid him out of their h', to deliver * "
39: 1 bought him out of the h' of the * "
43:22 have we brought down in our h' * "
48:14 guiding his h' wittingly; for "
49:24 the arms of his h' were made "
24 strong by the h' of the mighty God "
Ex 9:29 I will spread abroad my h' 3709
33 spread abroad his h' unto the "
15:17 Sanctuary, O Lord, which thy h' 3027
17:12 But Moses' h' were heavy; and "
12 Hur stayed up his h', the one on the "
12 his h' were steady until the going "
29:10 h' upon the head of the bullock. "
15, 19 h' upon the head of the ram. "
24 the h' of Aaron, and in the h' of 3709
25 shalt receive them of their h', 3027
30:19 sons shall wash their h' and their "
21 they shall wash their h' and their "
32:19 he cast the tables out of his h', "
35:25 did spin with their h', and brought "
40:31 washed their h' and their feet "
Le 4:15 lay their h' upon the head of the "
7:30 His own h' shall bring the offerings "
8:14 their h' upon the head of the "
18 laid their h' upon...of the bullock "
22 laid their h' upon the...of the ram. "
24 upon the thumbs of their right h', * "
27 he put all upon Aaron's h', and 3709
27 and upon his sons' h', and "
28 Moses took them from off their h', "
15:11 and hath not rinsed his h' in water, 3027
16:12 his h' full of sweet incense beaten 2651
21 Aaron shall lay both his h' upon 3027
24:14 lay their h' upon his head, and let "
Nu 5:18 the offering of memorial in her h', 3709
6:19 upon the h' of the Nazarite, after "
8:10 put their h' upon the Levites: 3027
12 the Levites shall lay their h' upon "
24:10 he smote his h' together: and 3709
27:23 he laid his h' upon him, and gave 3027
De 1:25 of the fruit of the land in their h', "
3: 3 God delivered into our h' Og also, * "
4:28 the work of men's h', wood and "
9:15 of the covenant were in my two h'. "
17 cast them out of my two h', "
12:18 in all that thou puttest thine h' * "
16:15 all the works of thine h', therefore "
17: 7 The h' of the witnesses shall be * "
7 afterward the h' of all the people. * "
20:13 delivered it into thine h', thou * "
21: 6 shall wash their h' over the "
7 Our h' have not shed this blood, "
10 delivered them into thine h', "
24:19 bless thee in all the work of thine h'. "
27:15 work of the h' of the craftsman, "
31:29 anger through the work of your h'. "
33: 7 let his h' be sufficient for him; "
11 accept the work of his h': smite "
34: 9 Moses had laid his h' upon him: "
Jos 2:24 the Lord hath delivered into our h' "
J'g 2:14 he delivered them into the h' of "
14 sold them into the h' of their "
6:13 us into the h' of the Midianites. *3709
7: 2 give the Midianites into their h', * 3027
11 shall thine h' be strengthened to go "
19 the pitchers that were in their h'. "
20 held the lamps in their left h', and "
20 the trumpets in their right h' "
8: 3 God hath delivered into your h' * "
6, 15 said, Are the h' of Zebah and 3709
34 out of the h' of all their enemies * 3027
9:16 according to...deserving of his h'; "
10: 7 into the h' of the Philistines, and * "
7 into the h' of the children of "
11:30 children of Ammon into mine h', * "
J'g 11:32 Lord delivered them into his h'. * 3027
12: 2 ye delivered me not out of their h'.* "
3 I put my life in my h', and 3709
13:23 a meat offering at our h', neither* 3027
14: 9 he took thereof in his h', and 3709
15:14 his bands loosed from off his h'. 3027
16:24 hath delivered into our h' our * "
18:10 hath given it into your h'; a * "
19:27 her h' were upon the threshold. "
1Sa 5: 4 both the palms of his h' were cut "
7:14 out of the h' of the Philistines. * "
10: 4 thou shalt receive of their h'. * "
11: 7 by the h' of messengers, saying, * "
14:13 Jonathan climbed up upon his h' "
48 out of the h' of them that spoiled "
17:47 and he will give you into our h'. * "
21:13 feigned himself mad in their h', "
30:15 deliver me into the h' of my master, "
2Sa 2: 7 now let your h' be strengthened, "
3:34 Thy h' were not bound, nor thy "
4: 1 his h' were feeble, and all the "
12 cut off their h' and their feet, "
16:21 the h' of all that are with thee "
21: 9 he delivered them into the h' of "
22:21 the cleanness of my h' hath he "
35 He teacheth my h' to war; so that "
23: 6 they cannot be taken with h': * "
1Ki 8:22 spread forth his h' toward heaven: "
38 spread forth his h' toward this "
54 with his h' spread up to heaven. "
14:27 the h' of the chief of the guard, 3027
16: 7 the work of his h', in being like "
2Ki 3:11 poured water on the h' of Elijah. "
4:34 and his h' upon his h': 3709
5:20 in not receiving at his h' that 3027
9:23 Joram turned his h', and fled, and "
35 the feet, and the palms of her h'. "
10:24 whom I have brought into your h' "
11:12 they clapped their h', and said, 3709
16 they laid h' on her; and she went *3027
12:11 the h' of them that did the work, "
13:16 put his h' upon the king's h'. "
19:18 the work of men's h', wood and "
22:17 the works of their h'; therefore "
1Ch 12:17 there is no wrong in mine h', the 3709
25: 2 under the h' of Asaph, which *3027
3 under the h' of their father "
6 the h' of their father for song in "
29: 5 to be made by the h' of artificers. "
2Ch 6: 4 who hath with his h' fulfilled that "
12 of Israel, and spread forth his h': 3709
13 and spread forth his h' toward "
29 and shall spread forth his h' in "
8:18 by the h' of his servants ships, 3027
12:10 the h' of the chief of the guard, "
15: 7 let not your h' be weak: for your "
23:15 they laid h' on her; and when * "
29:23 they laid their h' upon them: "
32:19 which were the work of the h' of "
34:25 the works of their h'; therefore "
35:11 sprinkled the blood from their h',* "
Ezr 1: 6 about them strengthened their h' "
4: 4 weakened the h' of the people of "
5: 8 and prospereth in their h'. 3028
6:22 to strengthen their h' in the 3027
9: 5 and spread out my h' unto the 3709
10:19 gave their h' that they would *3027
Ne 2:18 they strengthened their h' for "
4:17 one of his h' wrought in the work, "
6: 9 Their h' shall be weakened from "
9 O God, strengthen my h'. "
8: 6 with lifting up their h': and they "
9:24 and gavest them into their h', "
13:21 ye do so again, I will lay h' on you. "
Es 3: 6 he thought scorn to lay h' on "
9 the h' of those that have the charge "
9:16 but they laid not their h' on the * "
Job 1:10 hast blessed the work of his h', "
4: 3 hast strengthened the weak h'. "
5:12 their h' cannot perform their "
18 woundeth, and his h' make whole. "
9:30 and make my h' never so clean; 3709
10: 3 despise the work of thine h', and "
8 Thine h' have made me and 3027
11:13 stretch out thine h' toward him; 3709
14:15 desire to the work of thine h'. 3027
16:11 me over into the h' of the wicked. "
17 any injustice in mine h': also 3709
17: 3 who is he that will strike h' 3027
9 he that hath clean h' shall be "
20:10 and his h' shall restore their "
22:30 by the pureness of thine h'. 3709
27:23 Men shall clap their h' at him, "
30: 2 the strength of their h' profit me, 3027
31: 7 if any blot hath cleaved to mine h'; 3709
34:19 they all are the work of his h'. 3027
37 he clappeth his h' among us, and "
Ps 7: 3 if there be iniquity in my h'; 3709
8: 6 over the works of thy h'; 3027
9:16 snared in the work of his own h'. 3709
18:20 the cleanness of my h' hath he 3027
24 the cleanness of my h' in his "
34 He teacheth my h' to war, so that "
22:16 they pierced my h' and my feet. "
24: 4 He that hath clean h', and a pure 3709
26: 6 I will wash mine h' in innocency: "
10 In whose h' is mischief, and their 3027
28: 2 when I lift up my h' toward thy "
4 them after the work of their h'; "
5 the operation of his h', he shall "
44:20 stretched out our h' to a strange 3709
47: 1 O clap your h', all ye people; "
55:20 He hath put forth his h' against 3027
58: 2 the violence of your h' in the earth. "
63: 4 I will lift up my h' in thy name. 3709
68:31 Ethiopia shall...stretch out her h' 3027

Ps 73:13 and washed my h' in innocency. 3709
76: 5 men of might have found their h'. 3027
78:72 them by the skilfulness of his h'. 3709
81: 6 his h' were delivered from the "
88: 9 I have stretched out my h' unto "
90:17 the work of our h' upon us; yea, 3027
17 the work of our h' establish thou "
91:12 shall bear thee up in their h', 3709
92: 4 triumph in the works of thy h'. 3027
95: 5 his h' formed the dry land. "
98: 8 Let the floods clap their h': let 3709
102:25 heavens are the work of thy h'. 3027
111: 7 The works of his h' are verity "
115: 4 and gold, the work of men's h'. "
7 They have h', but they handle not: "
119:48 My h' also will I lift up unto thy 3709
73 Thy h' have made me and 3027
125: 3 the righteous put forth their h'. "
128: 2 shalt eat the labour of thine h': 3709
134: 2 Lift up your h' in the sanctuary, 3027
135:15 and gold, the work of men's h'. "
138: 8 not the works of thine own h'. "
140: 4 Lord, from the h' of the wicked; "
141: 2 the lifting up of my h' as the 3709
143: 5 I muse on the work of thy h'. 3027
6 I stretch forth my h' unto thee: "
144: 1 teacheth my h' to war, and my "
Pr 6:10 a little folding of the h' to sleep: "
17 and h' that shed innocent blood, "
12:14 the recompence of a man's h' shall "
14: 1 plucketh it down with her h'. * "
17:18 void of understanding striketh h', 3709
21:25 him; for his h' refuse to labour. 3027
22:26 one of them that strike h', or of 3709
24:33 a little folding of the h' to sleep: 3027
30:28 The spider taketh hold with her h', "
31:13 worketh willingly with her h'. 3709
16 the fruit of her h' she planteth "
19 She layeth her h' to the spindle, 3027
19 and her h' hold the distaff. 3709
20 reacheth forth her h' to the needy. 3027
31 Give her of the fruit of her h'; "
Ec 2:11 the works that my h' had wrought, "
4: 5 The fool foldeth his h' together, "
6 than both the h' full with travail *2651
5: 6 destroy the work of thine h'? 3027
7:26 her h' as bands: whoso pleaseth "
10:18 through idleness of the h' the "
Ca 5: 5 and my h' dropped with myrrh, "
14 His h' are as gold rings set with "
7: 1 the work of the h' of a cunning "
Isa 1:15 when ye spread forth your h', I 3709
15 your h' are full of blood. 3027
2: 8 worship the work of their own h', "
3:11 the reward of his h' shall be given "
5:12 consider the operation of his h'. "
13: 7 Therefore shall all h' be faint, and "
17: 8 the work of his h', neither shall "
19:25 and Assyria the work of my h', "
25:11 And he shall spread forth his h' "
11 swimmeth spreadeth forth his h'. "
11 together with the spoils of their h'. 3027
29:23 the work of mine h', in the midst "
31: 7 your own h' have made unto you "
33:15 shaketh his h' from holding of 3709
35: 3 Strengthen ye the weak h', and 3027
37:19 the work of men's h', wood and "
45: 9 or thy work, He hath no h'? "
11 the work of my h' command ye me. "
12 I, even my h', have stretched out "
49:16 thee upon the palms of my h'; 3709
55:12 of the field shall clap their h'. "
59: 3 your h' are defiled with blood, and "
6 the act of violence is in their h'. "
60:21 the work of my h', that I may 3027
65: 2 I have spread out my h' all the "
22 long enjoy the work of their h'. "
Jer 1:16 the works of their own h'. "
2:37 and thine h' upon thine head: for "
4:31 that spreadeth her h', saying, 3709
6:24 our h' wax feeble: anguish hath 3027
10: 3 the work of the h' of the workman, "
9 and of the h' of the founder: "
19: 7 and by the h' of them that seek* "
21: 4 weapons of war that are in your h', "
23:14 they strengthen also the h' of "
25: 6 anger with the works of your h'; "
7 works of your h' to your own hurt. "
14 the works of their own h'. "
30: 6 his h' on his loins, as a woman "
32:30 the work of their h', saith the Lord. "
33:13 the h' of him that telleth them, "
38: 4 he weakeneth the h' of the men "
4 and the h' of all the people, "
44: 8 the works of your h', burning "
47: 3 their children for feebleness of h'; "
48:37 upon all the h' shall be cuttings, "
50:43 his h' waxed feeble: anguish took "
La 1:14 hath delivered me into their h', "
17 Zion spreadeth forth her h', and "
2:15 All that pass by clap their h' 3709
19 lift up thy h' toward him for the "
3:41 lift up our heart with our h' "
64 according to the work of their h'. 3027
4: 2 the work of the h' of the potter! "
6 moment, and no h' stayed on her. "
10 The h' of the pitiful women have "
Eze 1: 8 And they had the h' of a man "
7:17 All h' shall be feeble, and all knees "
21 into the h' of the strangers for a "
27 and the h' of the people of the "
10: 7 and put it into the h' of him 2651
12 and their h', and their wings, 3027
21 h' of a man was under their wings. "
11: 9 into the h' of strangers, and will "
13:22 strengthened the h' of the wicked, "

Eze 16:11 I put bracelets upon thy h', and 3027
21: 7 all h' shall be feeble, and every "
14 smite thine h' together, and let 3709
17 I will also smite mine h' together "
22:14 can thine h' be strong, in the days 3027
23:37 blood is in their h', and with "
42 which put bracelets upon their h', "
45 adulteresses, and blood is in her h'. "
25: 6 thou hast clapped thine h', and "
Da 2:34 a stone was cut out without h', 3028
45 cut out of the mountain without h', "
3:15 that shall deliver you out of my h'? "
10:10 and upon the palms of my h'. 3027
Ho 14: 3 any more to the work of our h', "
Ob 1:13 laid h' on their substance in the "
Jon 3: 8 the violence that is in their h'. 3709
Mic 5:13 worship the work of thine h'. 3027
7: 3 they may do evil with both h' 3709
Na 3:19 thee shall clap the h' over thee: "
Hab 3:10 and lifted up his h' on high. 3027
Zep 3:16 Zion, Let not thine h' be slack. "
Hag 1:11 upon all the labour of the h'. 3709
2:14 so is every work of their h'; 3027
17 in all the labours of your h'; "
Zec 4: 9 The h' of Zerubbabel have laid "
9 his h' shall also finish it; "
8: 9 Let your h' be strong, ye that "
13 fear not, but let your h' be strong. "
13: 6 are these wounds in thine h'? * "
M't 4: 6 in their h' they shall bear thee up, 5495
15: 2 for they wash not their h' when "
20 but to eat with unwashen h' "
17:22 shall be betrayed into the h' of "
18: 8 rather than having two h' or two "
28 and he laid h' on him, and took *2902
19:13 should put his h' on them, and 5495
15 he laid his h' on them, and "
21:46 when they sought to lay h' on *2902
26:45 is betrayed into the h' of sinners. 5495
50 laid h' on Jesus, and took him. "
67 smote him with the palms of their h', "
27:24 washed his h' before the multitude, 5495
M'r 5:23 come and lay thy h' on her, that "
6: 2 works are wrought by his h'? "
5 laid his h' upon a few sick folk, "
7: 2 with unwashen, h', they found "
3 except they wash their h' oft, eat "
5 but eat bread with unwashen h'? "
8:23 his eyes, and put his h' upon him, "
25 he put his h' again upon his eyes, "
9:31 is delivered into the h' of men, "
43 than having two h' to go into hell, "
10:16 in his arms, put his h' upon them, "
14:41 is betrayed into the h' of sinners. "
46 laid their h' on him, and took him. "
58 this temple that is made with h', 5499
58 will build another made without h'. 886
65 strike him with the palms of their h'.
16:18 they shall lay h' on the sick, and 5495
Lu 4:11 And in their h' they shall bear thee "
40 laid his h' on every one of them, "
6: 1 did eat, rubbing them in their h'. "
9:44 shall be delivered into the h' of "
13:13 And he laid his h' on her: "
20:19 hour sought to lay h' on him; "
21:12 they shall lay their h' on you, "
22:53 ye stretched forth no h' against me: "
23:46 into thy h' I commend my spirit: "
24: 7 be delivered into the h' of sinful "
39 Behold my h' and my feet, that it "
40 he shewed them his h' and his "
50 he lifted up his h', and blessed "
Joh 7:30 but no man laid h' on him, because* "
44 him; but no man laid h' on him. "
8:20 and no man laid h' on him; for *4084
13: 3 given all things into his h', and 5495
9 but also my h' and my head. "
19: 3 and they smote him with their h'. 4475
20:20 shewed unto them his h' and his 5495
25 I shall see in his h' the print of the "
27 hither thy finger, and behold my h'; "
21:18 thou shalt stretch forth thy h', "
Ac 2:23 by wicked h' have crucified and * "
4: 3 they laid h' on them, and put "
5:12 by the h' of the apostles were "
18 laid their h' on the apostles, and "
6: 6 prayed, they laid their h' on them. "
7:41 in the works of their own h'. "
48 not in temples made with h'; 5499
8:17 Then laid they their h' on them, 5495
18 laying on of the apostles' h' "
19 that on whomsoever I lay h', he "
9:17 and putting his h' on him said, "
11:30 by the h' of Barnabas and Saul. * "
12: 1 the king stretched forth his h' to "
7 And his chains fell off from his h'. "
13: 3 prayed, and laid their h' on them, "
14: 3 and wonders to be done by their h'. "
17:24 not in temples made with h'; 5499
25 is worshipped with men's h', 5495
19: 6 when Paul had laid his h' upon "
11 special miracles by the h' of Paul: "
26 no gods, which are made with h': "
20:34 these h' have ministered unto my "
21:11 bound his own h' and feet, "
11 shall deliver him into the h' of the "
27 all the people, and laid h' on him, "
24: 7 took him away out of our h', * "
27:19 out with our own h' the tackling 849
28: 8 laid his h' on him, and healed him. 5495
17 into the h' of the Romans. "
Ro 10:21 I have stretched forth my h' unto "
1Co 4:12 labour, working with our own h': "
2Co 5: 1 an house not made with h', eternal 886
11:33 by the wall, and escaped his h'. 5495
Ga 2: 9 the right h' of fellowship; that "

Eph 2:11 Circumcision in...flesh made by h'; 5499
4:28 working with his h' the thing 5495
Col 2:11 the circumcision made without h', 886
1Th 4:11 and to work with your own h', 5495
1Ti 2: 8 lifting up holy h', without wrath "
4:14 with the laying on of the h' of the "
5:22 Lay h' suddenly on no man, neither "
2Ti 1: 6 in thee by the putting on of my h'. "
Heb 1:10 heavens are the works of thine h': "
2: 7 set him over the works of thy h': "
6: 2 of baptisms, and of laying on of h', "
9:11 tabernacle, not made with h', that 5499
24 into the holy places made with h', "
10:31 to fall into the h' of the living God. 5495
12:12 lift up the h' which hang down, "
Jas 4: 8 Cleanse your h', ye sinners; and "
1Jo 1: 1 and our h' have handled, of the "
Re 7: 9 white robes, and palms in their h'; "
9:20 not of the works of their h', that "
20: 4 upon their foreheads, or in their h'; * "

handstaves
Eze 39: 9 the arrows, and the h', and 4731,3027

hand-weapon See HAND and WEAPON.

handwriting
Col 2:14 Blotting out the h' of ordinances *5498

handywork
Ps 19: 1 firmament sheweth his h'. 4639,3027

Hanes (ha'-nees) See also TAHPANES.
Isa 30: 4 and his ambassadors came to H'. 2609

hang See also HANGED; HANGETH; HANGING.
Ge 40:19 and shall h' thee on a tree; 8518
Ex 26:12 shall h' over the backside of the 5628
13 it shall h' over the sides of the 1961,
32 And thou shalt h' it upon four 5414
33 And thou shalt h' up the vail under "
40: 8 and h' up the hanging at the "
Nu 25: 4 and h' them up before the Lord 3363
De 21:22 and thou h' him on a tree: 8518
28:66 thy life shall h' in doubt before 8511
2Sa 21: 6 and we will h' them up unto the 3363
Es 6: 4 to h' Mordecai on the gallows 8518
7: 9 Then the king said, H' him thereon. "
Ca 4: 4 whereon there h' a thousand "
Isa 22:24 And they shall h' upon him all the "
La 2:10 the virgins of Jerusalem h' down 3381
Eze 15: 3 will men take a pin of it to h' 8518
M't 22:40 h' all the law and the prophets. *2910
Ac 28: 4 venomous beast h' on his hand, * "
Heb 12:12 lift up the hands which h' down, 3935

hanged See also HANGETH; HANGING; HUNG.
Ge 40:22 But he h' the chief baker: 8518
41:13 unto mine office, and him he h'. "
De 21:23 he that is h' is accursed of God; "
Jos 8:29 the king of Ai he h' on a tree "
10:26 them: and h' them on five trees: "
2Sa 4:12 and h' them up over the pool "
17:23 and h' himself, and died, and was 2614
18:10 I saw Absalom h' in an oak. *8518
21: 9 and they h' them in the hill 3363
12 where the Philistines had h' them, 8511
13 the bones of them that were h'. 3363
Ezr 6:11 let him be h' thereon; and let his *4223
Es 2:23 therefore they were both h' on a 8518
5:14 king that Mordecai may be h' "
7:10 So they h' Haman on the gallows "
8: 7 him they have h' upon the gallows, "
9:13 let Haman's ten sons be h' upon "
14 and they h' Haman's ten sons. "
25 that he and his sons should be h' "
Ps 137: 2 We h' our harps upon the willows "
La 5:12 Princes are h' up by their hand: "
Eze 27:10 they h' the shield and helmet in "
11 they h' their shields upon thy walls "
M't 18: 6 that a millstone were h' about his 2910
27: 5 departed, and went and h' himself. 519
M'r 9:42 that a millstone were h' about his 4029
Lu 17: 2 that a millstone were h' about his "
23:39 of the malefactors which were h' 2910
Ac 5:30 whom ye slew and h' on a tree. * "
10:39 whom they slew and h' on a tree: * "

hangeth
Job 26: 7 and h' the earth upon nothing. 8518
Ga 3:13 Cursed is every one that h' on a 2910

hanging See also HANGINGS.
Ex 26:36 shalt make an h' for the door *4539
37 thou shalt make for the h' five * "
27:16 gate of the court shall be an h' * "
35:15 and the h' for the door at the * "
17 the h' for the door of the court, * "
36:37 he made an h' for the tabernacle * "
38:18 And the h' for the gate of the court * "
39:38 and the h' for the tabernacle door, * "
40 the h' for the court gate, his cords, * "
40: 5 the h' of the door to the tabernacle. * "
8 hang up the h' at the court gate. * "
28 he set up the h' at the door of the * "
33 and set up the h' of the court gate. * "
Nu 3:25 h' for the door of the tabernacle * "
31 and the h', and all the service * "
4:25 h' for the door of the tabernacle * "
26 and the h' for the door of the gate * "
Jos 10:26 they were h' upon the trees until 8518

hangings
Ex 27: 9 side southward there shall be h' 7050
11 side in length there shall be h' "
12 west side shall be h' of fifty "
14 The h' of one side of the gate "
15 on the other side shall be h' "
35:17 The h' of the court, his pillars, "
38: 9 the h' of the court were of fine "
11 side the h' were an hundred cubits, * "
12 for the west side were h' 7050
14 The h' of the one side of the gate

Ex 38: 15 that hand, were h· of fifteen cubits; 7050
16 All the h· of the court round about "
18 answerable to the h· of the court. "
39: 40 The h· of the court, his pillars, "
Nu 3: 26 And the h· of the court, and the "
4: 26 And the h· of the court, and the "
2Ki 23: 7 where the women wove h· for the 1004
Es 1: 6 were white, green, and blue, h·.
Haniel (*ha'-ne-el*) See also HANNIEL.
1Ch 7: 39 sons of Ulla; Arah, and H·, *2592
Hannah (*han'-nah*)
1Sa 1: 2 the name of the one was H·, 2584
2 but H· had no children. "
5 unto H· he gave a worthy portion; "
5 for he loved H·: but the Lord "
8 H·, why weepest thou? and why "
9 So H· rose up after they had eaten "
13 Now H·, she spake in her heart; "
15 H· answered and said, No, my lord, "
19 and Elkanah knew H· his wife; "
20 about after H· had conceived, "
22 But H· went not up; for she said "
2: 1 H· prayed, and said, My heart "
21 the Lord visited H·, so that she "
Hannathon (*han'-na-thon*)
Jos 19: 14 it on the north side to H·: 2615
Hanniel (*han'-ne-el*) See also HANIEL.
Nu 34: 23 Manasseh, H· the son of Ephod. 2592
Hanoch (*ha'-nok*) See also HANOCHITES; HENOCH.
Ge 25: 4 Ephah, and Epher, and H·, and 2585
46: 9 of Reuben; H·, and Phallu, and "
Ex 6: 14 H·, and Pallu, Hezron, and Carmi: "
Nu 26: 5 H·, of whom cometh the family of "
1Ch 5: 3 H·, and Pallu, Hezron, and Carmi. "
Hanochites (*ha'-nok-ites*)
Nu 26: 5 cometh the family of the H·: 2599
Hanun (*ha'-nun*)
2Sa 10: 1 H· his son reigned in his stead. 2586
2 I will shew kindness unto H· the "
3 of Ammon said unto H· their lord, "
4 Wherefore H· took David's "
1Ch 19: 2 said, I will shew kindness unto H· "
2 of the children of Ammon to H·, "
3 said to H·, Thinkest thou that "
4 H· took David's servants, and "
6 H· and the children of Ammon "
Ne 3: 13 The valley gate repaired H·, and "
30 and H· the sixth son of Zalaph, "
hap See also PERHAPS.
Ru 2: 3 her h· was to light on a part of 4745
Haphraim (*haf-ra'-im*)
Jos 19: 19 And H·, and Shihon, and *2663
haply
1Sa 14: 30 if h· the people had eaten freely 3863
M'r 11: 13 if h· he might find any thing 686
Lu 14: 29 Lest h·, after he hath laid the 3379
Ac 5: 39 lest h· ye be found even to fight "
17: 27 if h· they might feel after him, 686
2Co 9: 4 Lest h· if they of Macedonia come *3381
happen See also HAPPENED; HAPPENETH.
1Sa 28: 10 there shall no punishment h· to 7136
Pr 12: 21 There shall no evil h· to the just: 579
Isa 41: 22 shew us what shall h·: let them 7136
M'r 10: 32 what things should h· unto him, 4819
happened
1Sa 6: 9 it was a chance that h· to us. 1961
2Sa 1: 6 As I h· by chance upon mount 7136
20: 1 there h· to be there a man of 7122
Es 4: 7 all that had h· unto him, and of 7136
Jer 44: 23 therefore this evil is h· unto you, 7122
Lu 24: 14 of all these things which had h·. 4819
Ac 3: 10 at that which had h· unto him. "
Ro 11: 25 blindness in part is h· to Israel, *1096
1Co 10: 11 all these things h· unto them for 4819
Ph'p 1: 12 that the things which h· unto me "
1Pe 4: 12 as though some strange thing h· 4819
2Pe 2: 22 But it is h· unto them according to "
happeneth
Ec 2: 14 that one event h· to them all. 7136
15 As it h· to the fool, 4745
15 so it h· even to me: 7136
8: 14 men, unto whom it h· according 5060
14 wicked men, to whom it h· "
9: 11 time and chance h· to them all. 7136
happier
1Co 7: 40 But she is h· if she so abide, 3107
Happuch See KEREN-HAPPUCH.
happy See also HAPPIER.
Ge 30: 13 Leah said, H· am I, for the 837
De 33: 29 H· art thou, O Israel: who is like 835
1Ki 10: 8 H· are thy men, h· are these thy "
2Ch 9: 7 H· are thy men, and h· are these "
Job 5: 17 h· is the man whom God correcteth: "
Ps 127: 5 H· is the man that hath his quiver "
128: 2 h· shalt thou be, and it shall be "
137: 8 h· shall he be, that rewardeth thee "
9 H· shall he be, that taketh and "
144: 15 H· is that people, that is in such a "
15 h· is that people, whose God is the "
146: 5 H· is he that hath the God "
Pr 3: 13 H· is the man that findeth wisdom, "
18 h· is every one that retaineth her. 833
14: 21 hath mercy on the poor, h· is he. 835
16: 20 trusteth in the Lord, h· is he. "
28: 14 H· is the man that feareth alway: "
29: 18 he that keepeth the law, h· is he. "
Jer 12: 1 are all they h· that deal very *7951
Mal 3: 15 And now we call the proud h·; 833
Joh 13: 17 h· are ye if ye do them. *3107
Ac 26: 2 I think myself h·, king Agrippa, "
Ro 14: 22 H· is he that condemneth not *3107
Jas 5: 11 we count them h· which endure. *3106
1Pe 3: 14 for righteousness' sake, h· are ye: *3107
4: 14 for the name of Christ, h· are ye; * "
Hara (*ha'-rah*)
1Ch 5: 26 Habor, and H·, and to the river 2024
Haradah (*har'-a-dah*)
Nu 33: 24 Shapher, and encamped in H·. 2732
25 And they removed from H·, and "
Haran (*ha'-ran*) See also BETH-HARAN; CHARRAN.
Ge 11: 26 begat Abram, Nahor, and H·. 2039
27 Nahor, and H·; and H· begat "
28 H· died before his father Terah "
29 Milcah, the daughter of H·, the "
31 Lot the son of H· his son's son, "
31 they came unto H·, and dwelt 2771
32 five years: and Terah died in H·. "
12: 4 when he departed out of H·. "
5 souls that they had gotten in H·; "
27: 43 thou to Laban my brother to H·; "
28: 10 Beer-sheba, and went toward H·. "
29: 4 And they said, Of H· are we. "
2Ki 19: 12 as Gozan, and H·, and Rezeph, "
1Ch 2: 46 Caleb's concubine, bare H·, and "
46 and Gazez: and H· begat Gazez. "
23: 9 Shelomith, and Haziel, and H·, 2039
Isa 37: 12 H·, and Rezeph, and the children 2771
Eze 27: 23 H·, and Canneh, and Eden, the "
Hararite (*har'-a-rite*)
2Sa 23: 11 Shammah the son of Agee the H·. 2043
33 Shammah the H·, Ahiam the son of "
33 Ahiam the son of Sharar the H·, "
1Ch 11: 34 Jonathan the son of Shage the H·, "
35 Ahiam the son of Sacar the H·, "
Harbona (*har-bo'-nah*) See also HARBONAH.
Es 1: 10 Biztha, H·, Bigtha, and Abagtha, 2726
Harbonah (*har-bo'-nah*) See also HARBONA.
Es 7: 9 H·, one of the chamberlains, 2726
hard See also HARDER; HARDHEARTED.
Ge 18: 14 Is any thing too h· for the Lord? 6381
35: 16 travailed, and she had h· labour. 7185
17 when she was in h· labour, that "
Ex 1: 14 their lives bitter with h· bondage, 7186
18: 26 the h· causes they brought unto "
Lev 3: 9 he take off h· by the backbone; 5980
De 1: 17 the cause that is too h· for you, 7185
15: 18 It shall not seem h· unto thee, "
17: 8 If there arise a matter too h· for 6381
26: 6 us, and laid upon us h· bondage: 7186
J'g 9: 52 and went h· unto the door of the ‡5066
20: 45 and pursued h· after them unto "
1Sa 14: 22 even they also followed h· after 1692
31: 2 the Philistines followed h· upon "
2Sa 1: 6 and horsemen followed h· after "
3: 39 the sons of Zeruiah be too h· for 7186
13: 2 and Amnon thought it h· for him 6381
1Ki 10: 1 to prove him with h· questions. 2420
21: 1 h· by the palace of Ahab king of 681
2Ki 2: 10 Thou hast asked a h· thing: 7185
1Ch 10: 2 the Philistines followed h· after 5221
19: 4 in the midst h· by their buttocks, *
2Ch 9: 1 prove Solomon with h· questions 2420
Job 41: 24 h· as a piece of the nether *3332
Ps 60: 3 hast shewed thy people h· things: 7186
63: 8 My soul followeth h· after thee: 1692
88: 7 Thy wrath lieth h· upon me, and 5564
94: 4 they utter and speak h· things? *6277
Pr 13: 15 the way of transgressors is h·. *386
Isa 14: 3 the h· bondage wherein thou 7186
Jer 32: 17 and there is nothing too h· for thee: 6381
27 is there any thing too h· for me? "
Eze 3: 5 and of an h· language, but to the 3515
6 and of an h· language, whose words "
Da 5: 12 and shewing of h· sentences, and *280
Jon 1: 13 men rowed h· to bring it to the land; "
M't 25: 24 that thou art an h· man, reaping 4642
M'r 10: 24 how h· is it for them that trust 1422
Joh 6: 60 This is an h· saying; who can 4642
Ac 9: 5 h· for thee to kick against the * "
18: 7 house joined h· to the synagogue. 4927
26: 14 it is h· for thee to kick against 4642
Heb. 5: 11 things to say, and h· to be uttered, 1421
2Pe 3: 16 some things h· to be understood, 1425
Jude 15 and of all their h· speeches which 4642
harden See also HARDENED.
Ex 4: 21 but I will h· his heart, that he 2388
7: 3 I will h· Pharaoh's heart, and 7185
14: 4 I will h· Pharaoh's heart, that he 2388
17 will h· the hearts of the Egyptians, "
De 15: 7 thou shalt not h· thine heart, nor 553
Jos 11: 20 was of the Lord to h· their hearts, 2388
1Sa 6: 6 Wherefore then do ye h· your 5513
Job 6: 10 yea, I would h· myself in sorrow: *5339
Ps 95: 8 H· not your heart, as in the 7185
Heb 3: 8 H· not your hearts, as in the 4645
15 voice, h· not your hearts, as in the "
4: 7 his voice, h· not your hearts. "
hardened
Ex 7: 13 And he h· Pharaoh's heart, that 2388
14 Pharaoh's heart is h·, he refuseth *3515
22 Pharaoh's heart was h·, neither 2388
8: 15 he h· his heart, and hearkened not 3513
19 and Pharaoh's heart was h·, and 2388
32 And Pharaoh h· his heart at this 3513
9: 7 And the heart of Pharaoh was h·, *3515
12 the Lord h· the heart of Pharaoh, 2388
34 sinned yet more, and h· his heart, 3513
35 And the heart of Pharaoh was h·, 2388
10: 1 I have h· his heart, and the heart 3513
20 the Lord h· Pharaoh's heart, so 2388
27 the Lord h· Pharaoh's heart, and "
11: 10 the Lord h· Pharaoh's heart, so "
Ex 14: 8 the Lord h· the heart of Pharaoh 2388
De 2: 30 the Lord thy God h· his spirit, 7185
1Sa 6: 6 and Pharaoh h· their hearts? 3513
2Ki 17: 14 would not hear, but h· their necks, 7185
2Ch 36: 13 and h· his heart from turning 553
Ne 9: 16 h· their necks, and hearkened not 7185
17 but h· their necks, and in their "
29 h· their neck, and would not hear. "
Job 9: 4 who hath h· himself against him, "
39: 16 She is h· against her young ‡7188
Isa 63: 17 from thy ways, and h· our heart * "
Jer 7: 26 but h· their neck: they did worse *7185
19: 15 they have h· their necks, that * "
Dan 5: 20 up, and his mind h· in pride, 8631
M'r 6: 52 loaves: for their heart was h·. 4456
8: 17 have ye your heart yet h·? "
Joh 12: 40 blinded their eyes, and h· their "
Ac 19: 9 But when divers were h·, and 4645
Heb 3: 13 h· through the deceitfulness of sin. "
hardeneth
Pr 21: 29 A wicked man h· his face: but as 5810
28: 14 but he that h· his heart shall fall 7185
29: 1 being often reproved h· his neck, "
Rom 9: 18 mercy, and whom he will he h·. 4645
harder
Pr 18: 19 A brother offended is h· to be won
Jer 5: 3 made their faces h· than a rock; 2388
Eze 3: 9 As an adamant h· than flint 2389
hardhearted
Eze 3: 7 Israel are impudent and h·. *7186, 3820
hardly
Ge 16: 6 And when Sarai dealt h· with her, 6031
Ex 13: 15 Pharaoh would h· let us go, 7185
Isa 8: 21 through it, h· bestead and hungry: ‡ "
M't 19: 23 a rich man shall h· enter into *1423
M'r 10: 23 How h· shall they that have riches "
Lu 9: 39 bruising him h· departeth from 3425
18: 24 How h· shall they that have riches 1423
Ac 27: 8 And, h· passing it, came unto a *3433
hardness
Job 38: 38 the dust groweth into h·, and *4165
M't 19: 8 because of the h· of your hearts 4641
M'r 3: 5 grieved for the h· of their hearts, *4457
10: 5 For the h· of your heart he wrote 4641
16: 14 their unbelief and h· of heart, "
Ro 2: 5 thy h· and impenitent heart 4643
2Ti 2: 3 therefore endure h·, as a good *2553
hare
Le 11: 6 the h·, because he cheweth the cud, 768
De 14: 7 the camel, and the h·, and the "
Hareph (*ha'-ref*)
1Ch 2: 51 H· the father of Beth-gader. 2780
Haresha See TEL-HARESHA.
Hareth (*ha'-reth*)
1Sa 22: 5 and came into the forest of H·. *2802
Harhaiah (*har-ha-i'-ah*)
Ne 3: 8 the son of H·, of the goldsmiths. 2736
Harhas (*har'-has*) See also HASRAH.
2Ki 22: 14 the son of H·, keeper of the 2745
Harhur (*har'-hur*)
Ezr 2: 51 of Hakupha, the children of H·, 2744
Ne 7: 53 of Hakupha, the children of H·, "
Harim (*ha'-rim*)
1Ch 24: 8 The third to H·, the fourth to 2766
Ezr 2: 32 The children of H·, three hundred "
39 The children of H·, a thousand and "
10: 21 the sons of H·; Maaseiah, and "
31 of the sons of H·; Eliezer, Ishijah, "
Ne 3: 11 Malchijah the son of H·, and "
7: 35 The children of H·, three hundred "
42 The children of H·, a thousand "
10: 5 H·, Meremoth, Obadiah, "
27 Malluch, H·, Baanah. "
12: 15 Of H·, Adna; of Meraioth, Helkai; "
Hariph (*ha'-rif*) See also JORAH.
Ne 7: 24 The children of H·, an hundred 2756
10: 19 H·, Anathoth, Nebai, "
harlot See also HARLOT'S; HARLOTS.
Ge 34: 31 with our sister as with an h·? 2181
38: 15 he thought her to be an h·; "
21 Where is the h·, that was openly 6948
21 There was no h· in this place. "
22 there was no h· in this place. "
24 daughter in law hath played the h·; 2181
Le 21: 14 or profane, or an h·, these shall "
Jos 6: 17 only Rahab the h· shall live, she "
25 Joshua saved Rahab the h· alive, "
J'g 11: 1 he was the son of an h·: "
16: 1 saw there an h·, and went "
Pr 7: 10 a woman with the attire of an h·, "
Isa 1: 21 the faithful city become an h·! "
23: 15 years shall Tyre sin as an h·. "
16 thou h· that hast been forgotten; "
Jer 2: 20 tree thou wanderest, playing the h·. "
3: 1 played the h· with many lovers; "
6 tree, and there hath played the h·. "
8 but went and played the h· also. "
Eze 16: 15 and playedst the h· because of thy "
16 and playedst the h· thereupon: "
28 yea, thou hast played the h· with "
31 hast not been as an h·, in that thou "
35 O h·, hear the word of the Lord: "
41 thee to cease from playing the h·, "
23: 5 And Aholah played the h· when she "
19 wherein she had played the h· in "
44 unto a woman that playeth the h·: "
Hos 2: 5 their mother hath played the h·: "
3: 3 thou shalt not play the h·, and "
4: 15 Though thou, Israel, play the h·, "
Joe 3: 3 have given a boy for an h·, "
Am 7: 17 Thy wife shall be an h· in the city, "

Mic 1: 7 she gathered it of the hire of an h·, 2181
7 shall return to the hire of an h·. "
Na 3: 4 of the wellfavoured h·, the mistress "
1Co 6:15 make them the members of an h·? 4204
16 is joined to an h· is one body? "
Heb 11:31 By faith the h· Rahab perished not "
Jas 2:25 was not Rahab the h· justified by "

harlot's
Jos 2: 1 came into an h· house, named *2181
6:22 Go into the h· house, and bring "

harlots See also HARLOTS'.
1Ki 3:16 two women, that were h·, unto the 2181
Pr 29: 3 he that keepeth company with h· "
Ho 4:14 they sacrifice with h·: therefore 6948
M't 21:31 and the h· go into the kingdom 4204
32 and the h· believed him: and ye, "
Lu 15:30 devoured thy living with h·, thou "
Re 17: 5 mother of h· and abominations "

harlots'
Jer 5: 7 by troops in the h· houses. 2181

harm See also HARMFUL.
Ge 31:52 and this pillar unto me, for h·. 7451
Le 5:16 for the h· that he hath done in *2398
Nu 35:23 his enemy, neither sought his h·: 7451
1Sa 26:21 I will no more do thee h·, 7489
2Sa 20: 6 the son of Bichri do us more h· 3415
2Ki 4:41 there was no h· in the pot. 1697,7451
1Ch 16:22 and do my prophets no h·. 7489
Ps 105:15 and do my prophets no h·. "
Pr 3:30 if he have done thee no h·. 7451
Jer 39:12 look well to him, and do him no h·; "
Ac 16:28 Do thyself no h·: for we are all 2556
27:21 to have gained this h· and loss. *5196
28: 5 into the fire, and felt no h·. 2556
6 saw no h· come to him, they *824
21 shewed or spake any h· of thee. 4190
1Pe 3:13 who is he that will h· you, 2559

harmless
M't 10:16 wise as serpents, and h· as doves. 185
Ph'p 2:15 That ye may be blameless and h·, "
Heb 7:26 who is holy, h·, undefiled, * 172

Harnepher (*har-ne'-fur*)
1Ch 7:36 Suah, and H·, and Shual, 2774

harness See also HARNESSED.
1Ki 20:11 him that girdeth on his h· boast *
22:34 between the joints of the h·: ‡8302
2Ch 9:24 raiment, h·, and spices, horses, *5402
18:33 between the joints of the h·: ‡8302
Jer 46: 4 H· the horses; and get up, ye 631

harnessed
Ex 13:18 the children of Israel went up h·* 2571

Harod (*ha'-rod*) See also HARODITE.
J'g 7: 1 and pitched beside the well of H·: 5878

Harodite (*ha'-ro-dite*) See also HARORITE.
2Sa 23:25 Shammah the H·, Elika the H·, 2733

Haroeh (*ha-ro'-eh*) See also REAIAH.
1Ch 2:52 H·, and half of the Manahethites. 7204

Harorite (*ha'-ro-rite*) See also HARODITE.
1Ch 11:27 Shammoth the H·, Helez the 2033

Harosheth (*har'-o-sheth*)
J'g 4: 2 which dwelt in H· of the Gentiles. 2800
13 from H· of the Gentiles unto the "
16 the host, unto H· of the Gentiles: "

harp See also HARPED; HARPING; HARPS.
Ge 4:21 such as handle the h· and organ. 3658
31:27 songs, with tabret, and with h·? "
1Sa 10: 5 a pipe, and a h·, before them; "
16:16 a cunning player on an h·: "
23 David took an h·, and played "
1Ch 25: 3 who prophesied with a h·, to give "
Job 21:12 They take the timbrel and h·, and "
30:31 My h· also is turned to mourning "
Ps 33: 2 Praise the Lord with h·: sing unto "
43: 4 upon the h· will I praise thee, "
49: 4 open my dark saying upon the h·. "
57: 8 awake, psaltery and h·: I myself "
71:22 unto thee will I sing with the h·, "
81: 2 the pleasant h· with the psaltery. "
92: 3 upon the h· with a solemn sound. "
98: 5 Sing unto the Lord with the h·; "
5 with the h·, and the voice of a "
108: 2 Awake, psaltery and h·: I myself "
147: 7 sing praise upon the h· unto our "
149: 3 unto him with the timbrel and h·. "
150: 3 praise him with the psaltery and h·. "
Isa 5:12 the h·, and the viol, the tabret, and "
16:11 my bowels shall sound like an h· "
23:16 Take an h·, go about the city, "
24: 8 endeth, the joy of the h· ceaseth. "
Da 3: 5, 7, 10, 15 flute, h·, sackbut, 7030
1Co 14: 7 giving sound, whether pipe or h·, 2788

harped
1Co 14: 7 be known what is piped or h·? 2789

harpers
Re 14: 2 I heard the voice of h· harping 2790
18:22 And the voice of h·, and musicians, "

harping
Re 14: 2 voice of harpers h· with their 2789

harps
2Sa 6: 5 even on h·, and on psalteries, and 3658
1Ki 10:12 h· also and psalteries for singers: "
1Ch 13: 8 and with h·, and with psalteries, "
15:16 psalteries and h· and cymbals "
21 with h· on the Sheminith "
28 a noise with psalteries and h·. "
16: 5 Jeiel with psalteries and with h·; "
25: 1 who should prophesy with h·, with "
6 with cymbals, psalteries, and h·, for "
2Ch 5:12 cymbals and psalteries and h·, "
9:11 and h· and psalteries for singers: 3658
20:28 with psalteries and h· and "
29:25 with psalteries, and with h·, "
Ne 12:27 cymbals, psalteries, and with h·. "
Ps 137: 2 We hanged our h· upon the willows "
Isa 30:32 it shall be with tabrets and h·: "
Eze 26:13 sound of thy h· shall no more be "
Re 5: 8 having every one of them h·, *2788
14: 2 of harpers harping with their h·: "
15: 2 sea of glass, having the h· of God. "

harrow See also HARROWS.
Job 39:10 will he h· the valleys after thee? 7702

harrows
2Sa 12:31 saws, and under h· of iron, and 2757
1Ch 20: 3 and with h· of iron, and with axes "

Harsa See TEL-HARSA.

Harsha (*har'-shah*)
Ezr 2:52 of Mehida, the children of H·, 2797
Ne 7:54 of Mehida, the children of H·, "

hart See also HARTS.
De 12:15 the roebuck, and as of the h·. 354
22 as the roebuck and the h· is eaten, "
14: 5 The h·, and the roebuck, and the "
15:22 as the roebuck, and as the h·. "
Ps 42: 1 As the h· panteth after the water "
Ca 2: 9 is like a roe or a young h·: "
17 or a young h· upon the mountains "
8:14 to a young h· upon the mountains "
Isa 35: 6 shall the lame man leap as an h·, "

harts
1Ki 4:23 an hundred sheep, beside h·, 354
La 1: 6 her princes are become like h· "

Harum (*ha'-rum*)
1Ch 4: 8 families of Aharhel the son of H·. 2037

Harumaph (*ha-ru'-maf*)
Ne 3:10 repaired Jedaiah the son of H·, 2739

Haruphite (*ha'-ru-fite*)
1Ch 12: 5 Shemariah, and Shephatiah the H·, 2741

Haruz (*ha'-ruz*)
2Ki 21:19 Meshullemeth, the daughter of H· 2743

harvest See also HARVESTMAN.
Ge 8:22 seedtime and h·, and cold and 7105
30:14 in the days of wheat h·, and found "
45: 6 there shall neither be earing nor h·. "
Ex 23:16 the feast of h·, the firstfruits of "
34:21 in earing time and in h· thou shalt "
22 the firstfruits of wheat h·, and the "
Le 19: 9 when ye reap the h· of your land, "
9 thou gather the gleanings of thy h·. "
23:10 shall reap the h· thereof, then ye "
10 a sheaf of the firstfruits of your h· "
22 when ye reap the h· of your land, "
22 thou gather any gleaning of thy h·: "
25: 5 groweth of its own accord of thy h· "
De 24:19 When thou cuttest down thine h· "
Jos 3:15 all his banks all the time of h·, "
J'g 15: 1 in the time of wheat h·, "
Ru 1:22 in the beginning of barley h·. "
2:21 until they have ended all my h·. "
23 end of barley h· and of wheat h·; "
1Sa 6:13 their wheat h· in the valley: "
8:12 to reap his h·, and to make his "
12:17 Is it not wheat h· to day? "
2Sa 21: 9 were put to death in the days of h·, "
9 in the beginning of barley h·. "
10 from the beginning of h· until "
23:13 came to David in the h· time "
Job 5: 5 Whose h· the hungry eateth up, "
Pr 6: 8 and gathereth her food in the h·. "
10: 5 he that sleepeth in h· is a son "
20: 4 therefore shall he beg in h·, and "
25:13 the cold of snow in the time of h·, "
26: 1 as rain in h·, so honour is not "
Isa 9: 3 according to the joy in h·, and as "
16: 9 thy summer fruits and for thy h· "
17:11 the h· shall be a heap in the day of "
18: 4 like a cloud of dew in the heat of h·. "
5 For afore the h·, when the bud is "
23: 3 the h· of the river, is her revenue; "
Jer 5:17 they shall eat up thine h·, and thy "
24 us the appointed weeks of the h·. "
8:20 The h· is past, the summer is "
50:16 the sickle in the time of h·: "
51:33 the time of her h· shall come. "
Ho 6:11 he hath set an h· for thee, "
Joe 1:11 the h· of the field is perished. "
3:13 the sickle, for the h· is ripe: "
Am 4: 7 were yet three months to the h·: "
M't 9:37 The h· truly is plenteous, but the 2326
38 Lord of the h·, that he will send "
38 send forth labourers into his h·. "
13:30 both grow together until the h·: "
30 and in the time of h· I will say "
39 the h· is the end of the world; "
M'r 4:29 the sickle, because the h· is come. "
Lu 10: 2 The h· truly is great, but the "
2 ye therefore the Lord of the h·, "
2 send forth labourers into his h·. "
Joh 4:35 four months, and then cometh h·? "
35 for they are white already to h·. "
Re 14:15 the h· of the earth is ripe. "

harvestman
Isa 17: 5 when the h· gathereth the corn, 7105
Jer 9:22 as the handful after the h·, 7114

has See HATH.

Hasadiah (*has-a-di'-ah*)
1Ch 3:20 and H·, Jushab-hesed, five. 2619

Hasenuah (*has-e-nu'-ah*) See also SENUAH.
1Ch 9: 7 son of Hodaviah, the son of H·, *5574

Hash See MAHER-SHALAL-HASH-BAZ.

Hashabiah (*hash-a-bi'-ah*)
1Ch 6:45 The son of H·, the son of Amaziah, 2811
9:14 son of H·, of the sons of Merari; "
25: 3 Jeshaiah, H·, and Mattithiah, "
19 The twelfth, to H·, he, his sons, "
26:30 Hebronites, H· and his brethren, "
27:17 Of the Levites, H· the son of "
2Ch 35: 9 his brethren, and H· and Jeiel "
Ezr 8:19 H·, and with him Jeshaiah of "
24 H· and ten of their brethren "
Ne 3:17 Next unto him repaired H·, "
10:11 Micha, Rehob, H·, "
11:15 the son of H·, the son of Bunni; "
22 the son of Bani, the son of H·, "
12:21 Of Hilkiah, H·; of Jedaiah, "
24 chief of the Levites: H·, Sherebiah, "

Hashabnah (*hash-ab'-nah*)
Ne 10:25 Rehum, H·, Maaseiah, 2812

Hashabniah (*hash-ab-ni'-ah*)
Ne 3:10 repaired Hattush the son of H·. *2813
9: 5 Bani, H·, Sherebiah, Hadijah, * "

Hashbadana (*hash-bad'-a-nah*)
Ne 8: 4 Hashum, and H·, Zechariah, *2806

Hashem (*ha'-shem*)
1Ch 11:34 The sons of H· the Gizonite, 2044

Hashmonah (*hash-mo'-nah*)
Nu 33:29 from Mithcah, and pitched in H·. 2832
30 And they departed from H·, and "

Hashub (*ha'-shub*) See also HASSHUB.
Ne 3:11 and H· the son of Pahath-moab, *2815
23 him repaired Benjamin and H· * "
10:23 Hoshea, Hananiah, H·, * "
11:15 Shemaiah the son of H·, the son * "

Hashubah (*hash-u'-bah*)
1Ch 3:20 H·, and Ohel, and Berechiah, 2807

Hashum (*ha'-shum*)
Ezr 2:19 The children of H·, two hundred 2828
10:33 Of the sons of H·; Mattenai, "
Ne 7:22 The children of H·, three hundred "
8: 4 and Malchiah, and H·, and "
10:18 Hodijah, H·, Bezai, "

Hashupha (*hash-u'-fah*) See also HASUPHA.
Ne 7:46 the children of H·, the children *2817

Hasrah (*has'-rah*) See also HARHAS.
2Ch 34:22 the son of H· keeper of the 2641

Hassenaah (*has-se-na'-ah*) See also SENAAH.
Ne 3: 3 fish gate did the sons of H· build, 5574

Hasshub (*hash'-ub*) See also HASHUB.
1Ch 9:14 Shemaiah the son of H·, the son 2815

hast
Ge 3:11 H· thou eaten of the tree,
13 What is this that thou h· done?
14 Because thou h· done this, thou art
17 Because thou h· hearkened unto the
17 and h· eaten of the tree, of which I
4:10 And he said, What h· thou done?
14 Behold, thou h· driven me out this
12:18 What is this that thou h· done unto
15: 3 Behold, to me thou h· given no seed:
18: 5 And they said, so do, as thou h· said.
19:12 unto Lot, H· thou here any besides?
12 whatsoever thou h· in the city, bring
19 and thou h· magnified thy mercy,
19 which thou h· shewed unto me in
21 this city, for the which thou h· spoken.
20: 3 woman which thou h· taken; for she
9 and said unto him, What h· thou done
9 that thou h· brought on me and my
9 thou h· done deeds unto me that ought
10 What sawest thou, that thou h· done
21:23 the land wherein thou h· sojourned.
29 ewe lambs which thou h· set by
22:12 seeing thou h· not withheld thy son,
16 for because thou h· done this thing,
16 and h· not withheld thy son, thine
18 because thou h· obeyed my voice.
24:14 same be she that thou h· appointed
14 I know that thou h· shewed kindness
26:10 What is this thou h· done unto us?
27:20 How is it that thou h· found it so
36 H· thou not reserved a blessing for
38 H· thou but one blessing, my father?
45 forget that which thou h· done to
29:25 What is this that thou h· done unto
25 wherefore then h· thou beguiled me?
30:15 Is it a small matter that thou h· taken
31:26 said to Jacob, What h· thou done,
26 that thou h· stolen away unawares to
28 And h· not suffered me to kiss my
28 thou h· now done foolishly in so doing.
30 yet wherefore h· thou stolen my gods?
36 my sin, that thou h· so hotly pursued
37 Whereas thou h· searched all my stuff,
37 what h· thou found of all thy
41 and thou h· changed my wages ten
32:10 which thou h· shewed unto thy
28 for as a prince h· thou power with
28 God and with men, and h· prevailed.
33: 9 my brother; keep that thou h· unto
37:10 is this dream that thou h· dreamed?
38:23 this kid, and thou h· not found her.
29 she said, How h· thou broken forth?
39:17 servant, which thou h· brought
45:10 and thy herds, and all that thou h·:
11 and thy household, and all that thou h·.
47:25 And they said, Thou h· saved our lives:
30 And he said, I will do as thou h· said.
Ex 3:12 When thou h· brought forth the people
4:10 nor since thou h· spoken unto thy
5:22 h· thou so evil entreated this
22 why is it that thou h· sent me?

Ex 5:23 neither *h'* thou delivered thy people
9:19 gather thy cattle, and all that thou *h'*
10:29 And Moses said, Thou *h'* spoken well,
12:44 when thou *h'* circumcised him, then
13:12 cometh of a beast which thou *h'*; 1961
14:11 *h'* thou taken us away to die in the
11 wherefore *h'* thou dealt thus
15: 7 thou *h'* overthrown them that rose *
13 Thou in thy mercy *h'* led forth the
13 the people which thou *h'* redeemed:
13 thou *h'* guided them in thy strength
16 pass over, which thou *h'* purchased.
17 O Lord, which thou *h'* made for
17: 3 this that thou *h'* brought us up
20:25 thy tool upon it, thou *h'* polluted it.
23:16 thy labours, which thou *h'* sown *
16 when thou *h'* gathered in thy *
29:36 when thou *h'* made an atonement *
32:11 which thou *h'* brought forth out of the
21 that thou *h'* brought so great a sin
32 of thy book which thou *h'* written.
33: 1 people which thou *h'* brought up
12 and thou *h'* not let me know whom
12 Yet thou *h'* said, I know thee by
12 and thou *h'* also found grace in my
17 this thing also that thou *h'* spoken:
17 for thou *h'* found grace in my sight,
Nu 5:19 and if thou *h'* not gone aside to
20 But if thou *h'* gone aside to another
11:11 Wherefore *h'* thou afflicted thy
21 and thou *h'* said, I will give them
14:17 be great, according as thou *h'* spoken,
19 and as thou *h'* forgiven this people,
16:13 a small thing that thou *h'* brought us
14 Moreover thou *h'* not brought us into
22:28 that thou *h'* smitten me these three
29 Because thou *h'* mocked me: I would
30 thine ass, upon which thou *h'* ridden
32 Wherefore *h'* thou smitten thine ass
23:11 What *h'* thou done unto me? I took
11 and, behold, thou *h'* blessed them
24:10 thou *h'* altogether blessed them these
27:13 And when thou *h'* seen it, thou also
De 1:14 The thing...thou *h'* spoken is good
31 where thou *h'* seen how that the Lord
2: 7 with thee; thou *h'* lacked nothing.
3:24 O Lord God, thou *h'* begun to shew thy
4:33 the midst of the fire, as thou *h'* heard,
8:10 When thou *h'* eaten and art full, *
12 Lest when thou *h'* eaten and art full,
12 and *h'* built goodly houses, and dwelt
13 and all that thou *h'* is multiplied;
9: 2 thou *h'* heard say, Who can stand
12 for thy people which thou *h'* brought
26 inheritance, which thou *h'* redeemed:
26 which thou *h'* brought forth out of
12:26 Only thy holy things which thou *h'*, 1961
13: 2 which thou *h'* not known, and let us
6 which thou *h'* not known, thou, nor
16:13 after that thou *h'* gathered in thy corn
17: 4 and thou *h'* heard of it, and enquired
21: 8 people Israel, whom thou *h'* redeemed,
10 and thou *h'* taken them captive, *
11 a beautiful woman, and *h'* a desire
14 of her, because thou *h'* humbled her.
22: 3 which he hath lost, and thou *h'* found,
9 fruit of thy seed which thou *h'* sown,
23:23 according as thou *h'* vowed unto the
23 which thou *h'* promised with thy
24:19 harvest in thy field, and *h'* forgot a
26:10 land, which thou, O Lord, *h'* given me.
12 When thou *h'* made an end of tithing
12 and *h'* given it unto the Levite, the *
13 which thou *h'* commanded me:
14 to all that thou *h'* commanded me.
15 the land which thou *h'* given us, as
17 Thou *h'* avouched the Lord this day
28:20 doings, whereby thou *h'* forsaken me:
32:18 art unmindful, and *h'* forgotten God
Jos 2:17 this thine oath...*h'* made us swear.
20 of thine oath...*h'* made us to swear.
7: 7 wherefore *h'* thou at all brought
19 and tell me now what thou *h'* done;
25 And Joshua said, Why *h'* thou troubled
14: 9 because thou *h'* wholly followed the
15:19 for thou *h'* given me a south land;
17:14 Why *h'* thou given me but one lot and
17 Thou art a great people, and *h'* great
J'g 1:15 Give me a blessing: for thou *h'* given
5:21 O my soul, thou *h'* trodden down *
6:36 Israel by mine hand, as thou *h'* said,
37 Israel by mine hand, as thou *h'* said.
8: 1 said unto him, Why *h'* thou served us
22 for thou *h'* delivered us from the hand
9:38 the people that thou *h'* despised?
11:12 saying, What *h'* thou to do with me,
35 Alas, my daughter! thou *h'* brought
36 My father, if thou *h'* opened thy mouth
14:16 thou *h'* put forth a riddle unto the
16 children of my people, and *h'* not told
15:11 what is this that thou *h'* done unto
18 Thou *h'* given this great deliverance
16:10 Behold, thou *h'* mocked me, and told
13 Hitherto thou *h'* mocked me, and
15 thou *h'* mocked me these three times,
15 and *h'* not told me wherein thy great
18: 3 in this place? and what *h'* thou here?
Ru 2:11 thou *h'* done unto thy mother in
11 and how thou *h'* left thy father and
13 for that thou *h'* comforted me, and
19 Where *h'* thou gleaned to-day?
3:10 for thou *h'* shewed more kindness
15 Bring the vail that thou *h'* upon thee, *
1Sa 1:17 thy petition that thou *h'* asked of him.
4:20 fear not; for thou *h'* born a son.
12: 4 And they said, Thou *h'* not defrauded

1Sa 12: 4 neither *h'* thou taken ought of any
13:11 And Samuel said, What *h'* thou done?
13 said to Saul, Thou *h'* done foolishly:
13 thou *h'* not kept the commandment
14 because thou *h'* not kept that...the Lord
14:43 Tell me what thou *h'* done. And
15:23 Because thou *h'* rejected the word of
26 for thou *h'* rejected the word of the
17:28 and with whom *h'* thou left those few
45 armies of Israel, whom thou *h'* defied.
20: 8 for thou *h'* brought thy servant into a
19 And when thou *h'* stayed three days,
30 do not I know that thou *h'* chosen the
22:13 in that thou *h'* given him bread, and a
13 and a sword, and *h'* enquired of God
24:17 for thou *h'* rewarded me good,
18 And thou *h'* shewed this day how
18 how that thou *h'* dealt well with me:
19 good for that thou *h'* done unto me
25: 6 and peace be upon all that thou *h'*.
7 I have heard that thou *h'* shearers:
31 either that thou *h'* shed blood
33 be thou which *h'* kept me this day
26:15 wherefore then *h'* thou not kept thy
16 thing is not good that thou *h'* done
28:12 Why *h'* thou deceived me? for thou
15 Why *h'* thou disquieted me, to bring
29: 4 place which thou *h'* appointed him,
6 as the Lord liveth, thou *h'* been
8 and what *h'* thou found in thy servant
2Sa 1:26 very pleasant *h'* thou been unto me:
3: 7 Wherefore *h'* thou gone in unto my
24 the king, and said, What *h'* thou done?
24 why is it that thou *h'* sent him away,
6:22 maidservants which thou *h'* spoken of,
7:18 my house, that thou *h'* brought me
19 but thou *h'* spoken also of thy
21 to thine own heart, *h'* thou done all
24 For thou *h'* confirmed to thyself thy *
25 the word that thou *h'* spoken
25 it forever, and do as thou *h'* said.
27 God of Israel, *h'* revealed to thy
28 and thou *h'* promised this goodness
29 for thou, O Lord God, *h'* spoken it:
11:19 When thou *h'* made an end of telling
12: 9 Wherefore *h'* thou despised the
9 thou *h'* killed Uriah the Hittite with
9 and *h'* taken his wife to be thy wife,
9 and *h'* slain him with the sword of
10 because thou *h'* despised me,
10 and *h'* slain with the sword of the
14 by this deed thou *h'* given great
21 What thing is this that thou *h'* done?
14:13 Wherefore then *h'* thou thought such
15:35 And *h'* thou not there with thee Zadok
16: 8 Saul, in whose stead thou *h'* reigned:
10 say, Wherefore *h'* thou done so?
18:21 Go tell the king what thou *h'* seen.
22 son, seeing that thou *h'* no tidings *
19: 5 Thou *h'* shamed this day the faces of
6 For thou *h'* declared this day, that
22:36 Thou *h'* also given me the shield of
37 Thou *h'* enlarged my steps under me;
40 for thou *h'* girded me with strength to
40 rose up against me *h'* thou subdued
41 Thou *h'* also given me the necks of
44 Thou also *h'* delivered me from the
44 thou *h'* kept me to be the head of the
49 thou also *h'* lifted me up on high *
49 thou *h'* delivered me from the violent *
1Ki 1:11 *H'* thou not heard that Adonijah the
24 my Lord, O king, *h'* thou said,
27 and thou *h'* not shewed it unto thy
2: 8 And behold, thou *h'* with thee *
26 and because thou *h'* been afflicted in *
43 Why then *h'* thou not kept the oath of
3: 6 Thou *h'* shewed unto thy servant
6 and thou *h'* kept for him this great
6 that thou *h'* given him a son to sit on
7 O Lord my God, thou *h'* made thy
8 thy people which thou *h'* chosen,
11 Because thou *h'* asked this thing, and
11 and *h'* not asked for thyself long life;
11 neither *h'* asked riches for thyself,
11 nor *h'* asked the life of thine enemies;
11 but *h'* asked for thyself understanding
13 which thou *h'* not asked, both riches,
8:24 Who *h'* kept with thy servant David
24 and *h'* fulfilled it with thine hand,
25 walk before me as thou *h'* walked
29 the place of which thou *h'* said, My
36 which thou *h'* given to thy people for
44 toward the city which thou *h'* chosen,
48 the city which thou *h'* chosen, and the
9: 3 thy supplication, that thou *h'* made
3 this house, which thou *h'* built, to put
13 cities are these which thou *h'* given
11:11 and thou *h'* not kept my covenant and
22 But what *h'* thou lacked with me,
13:21 forasmuch as thou *h'* disobeyed the
21 and *h'* not kept the commandment
22 But camest back, and *h'* eaten bread
14: 8 and yet thou *h'* not been as my
9 But *h'* done evil above all that were
9 for thou *h'* gone and made thee other
9 to provoke me to anger, and *h'* cast
16: 2 and thou *h'* walked in the way of
2 and *h'* made my people Israel to sin,
17:13 Fear not; go and do as thou *h'* said:
20 *h'* thou also brought evil upon the
18:18 of the Lord, and thou *h'* followed
37 and that thou *h'* turned their heart
20:13 *H'* thou seen all this great multitude?
25 like the army that thou *h'* lost, horse
36 Because thou *h'* not obeyed the voice
40 judgment be; thyself *h'* decided it.

1Ki 20:42 Because thou *h'* let go out of thy hand
21:19 *H'* thou killed, and also taken
20 said to Elijah, *H'* thou found me, O
20 because thou *h'* sold thyself to work
22 wherewith thou *h'* provoked me to
2Ki 1:16 Forasmuch as thou *h'* sent messengers
2:10 Thou *h'* asked a hard thing:
4: 2 tell me, what *h'* thou in the house? 3426
13 thou *h'* been careful for us with all
5: 8 Wherefore *h'* thou rent thy clothes?
6:22 smite those whom thou *h'* taken
9:18 said, What *h'* thou to do with peace?
19 answered, What *h'* thou to do with
10:30 Because thou *h'* done well in
30 and *h'* done unto the house of Ahab
14:10 Thou *h'* indeed smitten Edom, and
17:26 The nations which thou *h'* removed,
19: 6 of the words which thou *h'* heard,
11 Behold, thou *h'* heard what the kings
15 thou *h'* made heaven and earth.
20 That which thou *h'* prayed to me
22 Whom *h'* thou reproached and
22 and against whom *h'* thou exalted thy
23 By thy messengers thou *h'* reproached
23 and *h'* said, With the multitude of my
25 *H'* thou not heard long ago how I
20:19 word of the Lord which thou *h'* spoken.
22:18 the words which thou *h'* heard;
19 and thou *h'* humbled thyself *
19 and *h'* rent thy clothes, and wept
23:17 that thou *h'* done against the altar of
1Ch 17: 8 thee whithersoever thou *h'* walked, *
16 that thou *h'* brought me hitherto?
17 for thou *h'* also spoken of thy servant's
17 and *h'* regarded me according to the
19 to thine own heart, *h'* thou done all
21 thy people, whom thou *h'* redeemed *
23 let the thing that thou *h'* spoken
23 forever, and do as thou *h'* said.
25 For thou, O my God, *h'* told thy
26 Lord, thou art God, and *h'* promised
22: 8 saying, Thou *h'* shed blood
8 and *h'* made great wars: thou shalt
8 because thou *h'* shed much blood
28: 3 because thou *h'* been a man of war, *
3 a man of war, and *h'* shed blood.
20 until thou *h'* finished all the work *
29:17 triest the heart, and *h'* pleasure in
2Ch 1: 8 Thou *h'* shewed great mercy unto
8 and *h'* made me to reign in his stead.
9 for thou *h'* made me king over a
11 and thou *h'* not asked riches, wealth,
11 neither yet *h'* asked long life;
11 but *h'* asked wisdom and knowledge
6:15 Thou which *h'* kept with thy servant
15 that which thou *h'* promised him;
15 and *h'* fulfilled it with thine hand
16 that which thou *h'* promised him,
16 walk in my law, as thou *h'* walked
17 which thou *h'* spoken unto thy *
20 the place whereof thou *h'* said that
27 when thou *h'* taught them the good *
27 which thou *h'* given unto thy people
34 this city which thou *h'* chosen, and
38 the city which thou *h'* chosen, and
16: 7 Because thou *h'* relied on the king of
9 Herein thou *h'* done foolishly:
19: 3 in that thou *h'* taken away the groves
3 and *h'* prepared thine heart to seek
20:11 which thou *h'* given us to inherit.
37 Because thou *h'* joined thyself with
21:12 Because thou *h'* not walked in the
13 But *h'* walked in the way of the kings
13 and *h'* made Judah...to go a whoring,
13 and also *h'* slain thy brethren of thy
24: 6 Why *h'* thou not required of the
25:15 Why *h'* thou sought after the gods of
16 destroy thee, because thou *h'* done
16 and *h'* not hearkened unto my counsel.
19 Thou sayest, Lo, thou *h'* smitten the
26:18 sanctuary; for thou *h'* trespassed;
34:26 the words which thou *h'* heard;
Ezr 9:11 Which thou *h'* commanded by thy
13 that thou our God *h'* punished us
13 and *h'* given us such deliverance as
10:12 As thou *h'* said, so must we do.
Ne 1:10 whom thou *h'* redeemed by thy great
6: 7 And thou *h'* also appointed prophets
9: 6 thou *h'* made heaven, the heaven of
8 to his seed, and *h'* performed thy
33 for thou *h'* done right, but we have
37 whom thou *h'* set over us because of
Es 6:10 and the horse, as thou *h'* said,
10 nothing fail of all that thou *h'* spoken.
13 before whom thou *h'* begun to fall,
Job 1: 8 *H'* thou considered my servant Job,
10 *H'* not thou made an hedge about
10 thou *h'* blessed the work of his hands,
2: 3 *H'* thou considered my servant Job,
4: 3 Behold, thou *h'* instructed many, and
3 and thou *h'* strengthened the weak
4 and thou *h'* strengthened the feeble
7:20 why *h'* thou set me as a mark against
10: 4 *H'* thou eyes of flesh? or seest thou as
9 that thou *h'* made me as the clay;
10 *H'* thou not poured me out as milk,
11 Thou *h'* clothed me with skin and
11 and *h'* fenced me with bones and *
12 Thou *h'* granted me life and favour,
13 And these things *h'* thou hid in *
18 Wherefore then *h'* thou brought me
11: 4 For thou *h'* said, My doctrine is *
14: 5 thou *h'* appointed his bounds that he
15: 8 *H'* thou heard the secret of God?
16: 7 thou *h'* made desolate all my
8 And thou *h'* filled me with wrinkles,

Job 17: 4 For thou h· hid their heart from
22: 6 For thou h· taken a pledge from thy
7 Thou h· not given water to the weary
7 and thou h· withholden bread from
9 Thou h· sent widows away empty,
15 H· thou marked the old way which*
26: 2 How h· thou helped him that is
3 How h· thou counselled him that hath
3 and how h· thou plentifully declared*
4 To whom h· thou uttered words? and
33: 32 If thou h· anything to say, answer 3426
34: 16 If now thou h· understanding, hear
36: 17 But thou h· fulfilled the judgment of*
21 for this h· thou chosen rather than
23 can say, Thou h· wrought iniquity?
37: 18 H· thou with him spread out the sky,*
38: 4 declare if thou h· understanding.
12 H· thou commanded the morning
16 H· thou entered into the springs of
16 or h· thou walked in the search of the
17 h· thou seen the doors of the shadow
18 H· thou perceived the breadth of the
22 H· thou entered into the treasures of
22 h· thou seen the treasures of the hail,
39: 19 H· thou given the horse strength?
19 h· thou clothed his neck with
40: 9 H· thou an arm like God? or canst
Ps 3: 7 for thou h· smitten all mine enemies
4: 1 thou h· enlarged me when I was in
7 Thou h· put gladness in my heart,
7: 6 judgment that thou h· commanded.
8: 1 who h· set thy glory above the heavens.
2 babes and sucklings h· thou ordained
3 the stars, which thou h· ordained;
5 For thou h· made him a little lower
5 and h· crowned him with glory and*
6 thou h· put all things under his feet:
9: 4 For thou h· maintained my right and
5 Thou h· rebuked the heathen,
5 thou h· destroyed the wicked,
5 thou h· put out their name for ever
6 end: and thou h· destroyed cities;
10 for thou, Lord, h· not forsaken them
10: 14 Thou h· seen it; for thou beholdest
17 Lord, thou h· heard the desire of the
16: 2 O my soul, thou h· said unto the Lord,†
17: 3 Thou h· proved mine heart; thou
3 mine heart; thou h· visited me in the
3 thou h· tried me, and shalt find
18: 35 Thou h· also given me the shield of
36 Thou h· enlarged my steps under me,
39 For thou h· girded me with strength
39 thou h· subdued under me those that
40 Thou h· also given me the necks of
43 Thou h· delivered me from the
43 and thou h· made me the head of the
48 thou h· delivered me from the *
21: 2 Thou h· given him his heart's desire,
2 and h· not withholden the request of
5 honour and majesty h· thou laid upon*
6 For thou h· made him most blessed*
6 thou h· made him exceeding glad with*
22: 1 My God, my God, why h· thou forsaken
15 and thou h· brought me into the dust
21 for thou h· heard me from the horns
27: 9 thou h· been my help; leave me
30: 1 O Lord, for thou h· lifted me up,
1 and h· not made my foes to rejoice
2 I cried unto thee, and thou h· healed
3 thou h· brought up my soul from the
3 thou h· kept me alive, that I should not
7 thou h· made my mountain to stand*
11 Thou h· turned for me my mourning
11 thou h· put off my sackcloth, and
31: 5 thou h· redeemed me, O Lord God of
7 in thy mercy: for thou h· considered
7 thou h· known my soul in adversities;
19 which thou h· laid up for them that
19 which thou h· wrought for them that
35: 22 This thou h· seen, O Lord: keep not
39: 5 Behold, thou h· made my days as an
40: 5 wonderful works which thou h· done,
6 desire; mine ears h· thou opened:
6 and sin-offering h· thou not required.
42: 9 Why h· thou forgotten me? why go I
44: 7 But thou h· saved us from our enemies,
7 and h· put them to shame that hated
9 But thou h· cast off, and put us to
11 Thou h· given us like sheep appointed
11 and h· scattered us among the
19 Though thou h· sore broken us in the
50: 16 What h· thou to do to declare my
18 and h· been partaker with adulterers.
21 These things h· thou done and I kept
51: 8 that the bones which thou h· broken
52: 9 because thou h· done it: and I will
53: 5 thou h· put them to shame, because
56: 13 For thou h· delivered my soul from
59: 16 for thou h· been my defence and
60: 1 O God, thou h· cast us off, thou
1 cast us off, thou h· scattered us, thou
1 thou h· been displeased; O turn
2 Thou h· made the earth to tremble;
2 thou h· broken it: heal the breaches
3 Thou h· shewed thy people hard
3 thou h· made us to drink the wine of
4 Thou h· given a banner to them that
61: 3 For thou h· been a shelter for me,
5 For thou, O God, h· heard my vows:
5 thou h· given me the heritage of those
63: 7 Because thou h· been my help,
65: 9 them corn, when thou h· so provided
66: 10 For thou, O God, h· proved us: thou
10 thou h· tried us as silver is tried.
12 Thou h· caused men to ride over our
68: 10 thou, O God, h· prepared of thy *

Ps 68: 18 Thou h· ascended on high, thou
18 on high, thou h· led captivity captive:
18 thou h· received gifts for men; yea,
28 that which thou h· wrought for us.
69: 19 Thou h· known my reproach, and my*
26 persecute him whom thou h· smitten;
26 grief of those whom thou h· wounded.
71: 3 thou h· given commandment to save
17 O God, thou h· taught me from my
19 is very high, who h· done great things:
20 Thou, which h· shewed me great
23 and my soul, which thou h· redeemed.
73: 23 thou h· holden me by my right hand.
27 thou h· destroyed all them that go a
74: 1 O God, why h· thou cast us off for ever?
2 which thou h· purchased of old; the
2 inheritance, which thou h· redeemed;
2 mount Zion, wherein thou h· dwelt.
16 thou h· prepared th light and the sun.
17 Thou h· set all the borders of the
17 thou h· made summer and winter.
77: 14 thou h· declared thy strength among
15 Thou h· with thin arm redeemed thy
80: 8 Thou h· brought a vine out of Egypt:*
8 thou h· cast out the heathen and*
12 Why h· thou then broken down her
85: 1 Lord, thou h· been favourable unto thy
1 thou h· brought back the captivity of
2 Thou h· forgiven the iniquity of thy
2 people, thou h· covered all their sins.
3 Thou h· taken away all thy wrath: thou
3 thou h· turned thyself from the
86: 9 All nations whom thou h· made shall
13 and thou h· delivered my soul from
17 because thou, O Lord, h· holpen me,
88: 6 Thou h· laid me in the lowest pit,
7 thou h· afflicted me with all thy waves.
8 Thou h· put away mine acquaintance
8 thou h· made me an abomination
18 Lover and friend h· thou put far from
89: 10 Thou h· broken Rahab in pieces, as
10 thou h· scattered thine enemies with
11 the fulness thereof, thou h· founded
12 north and the south thou h· created
13 Thou h· a mighty arm: strong is thy
38 But thou h· cast off and abhorred,
38 thou h· been wroth with thine
39 Thou h· made void the covenant of thy
39 thou h· profaned his crown by casting
40 Thou h· broken down all his hedges;
40 thou h· brought his strong holds to
42 Thou h· set up the right hand of his
42 thou h· made all his enemies to rejoice.
43 Thou h· also turned the edge of his*
43 and h· not made him to stand in the
44 Thou h· made his glory to cease, and
45 days of his youth h· thou shortened:
45 thou h· covered him with shame.
47 wherefore h· thou made...men in vain?
90: 1 thou h· been our dwelling place
8 Thou h· set our iniquities before thee,
15 wherein thou h· afflicted us, and the
91: 9 Because thou h· made the Lord, which
92: 4 For thou, Lord, h· made me glad
102: 10 for thou h· lifted me up, and cast me
25 Of old h· thou laid the foundation of
104: 8 the place which thou h· founded for*
9 Thou h· set a bound that they may not
24 in wisdom h· thou made them all:
26 whom thou h· made to play therein.
108: 11 Wilt not thou, O God, who h· cast us
109: 27 thy hand; that thou, Lord, h· done it.
110: 3 morning: thou h· the dew of thy youth.
116: 8 For thou h· delivered my soul from
16 handmaid: thou h· loosed my bonds.
118: 13 Thou h· thrust sore at me that I might*
21 for thou h· heard me, and art become
119: 4 Thou h· commanded us to keep thy
21 Thou h· rebuked the proud that are
49 upon which thou h· caused me to hope.
65 Thou h· dealt well with thy servant,
75 thou in faithfulness h· afflicted me.
90 thou h· established the earth, and it
93 for with them thou h· quickened me.
98 commandments h· made me wiser
102 judgments: for thou h· taught me.
118 Thou h· trodden down all them that
138 testimonies that thou h· commanded
152 that thou h· founded them for ever.
171 when thou h· taught me thy statutes.*
137: 8 rewardeth thee as thou h· served us.
138: 2 for thou h· magnified thy word above
139: 1 O Lord, thou h· searched me, and
5 Thou h· beset me behind and before,
13 For thou h· possessed my reins: thou ‡
13 thou h· covered me in my mother's ‡
140: 7 thou h· covered my head in the day of
Pr 3: 28 will give; when thou h· it by thee. 3426
6: 1 if thou h· stricken thy hand with a
22: 27 If thou h· nothing to pay, why should
23: 8 The morsel which thou h· eaten shalt
24: 14 when thou h· found it, then there shall
25: 16 H· thou found honey? eat so much as
30: 32 If thou h· done foolishly in lifting up
32 or if thou h· thought evil, lay thine
Ec 5: 4 pay that which thou h· vowed. *
7: 22 that thou thyself likewise h· cursed
Ca 1: 15 thou art fair; thou h· doves' eyes.*
4: 1 thou h· doves' eyes within thy locks:*
9 Thou h· ravished my heart, my sister,
9 thou h· ravished my heart with one of
Isa 2: 6 Therefore thou h· forsaken thy people
3: 6 Thou h· clothing, be thou our ruler,
9: 3 Thou h· multiplied the nation, and
4 For thou h· broken the yoke of his
14: 13 For thou h· said in thine heart, I will*

Isa 14: 20 because thou h· destroyed thy land,
17: 10 Because thou h· forgotten the God of
10 and h· not been mindful of the rock
22: 16 What h· thou here? and whom *
16 here? and whom h· thou here, that
16 that thou h· hewed thee out a
23: 16 thou harlot that h· been forgotten;
25: 1 for thou h· done wonderful things; thy
2 For thou h· made of a city an heap; of
4 For thou h· been a strength to the
26: 12 for thou also h· wrought all our works
14 therefore h· thou visited and destroyed
15 Thou h· increased the nation, O Lord,
15 O Lord, thou h· increased the nation:
37: 6 words that thou h· heard, wherewith
11 Behold, thou h· heard what the kings
16 thou h· made heaven and earth.
21 Israel, Whereas thou h· prayed to me
23 Whom h· thou reproached and
23 and against whom h· thou exalted thy
24 By thy servants h· thou reproached
24 and h· said, By the multitude of my
26 H· thou not heard long ago, how I
38: 17 but thou h· in love to my soul
17 for thou h· cast all my sins behind
39: 8 of the Lord which thou h· spoken.
40: 28 H· thou not known? h· thou not heard,
43: 4 thou h· been honourable, and I have
22 But thou h· not called upon me, O
22 but thou h· been weary of me, O Israel.
23 Thou h· not brought me the small
23 neither h· thou honoured me with thy
24 Thou h· bought me no sweet cane with
24 neither h· thou filled me with the fat
24 but thou h· made me to serve with
24 thou h· wearied me with thine
45: 4 thee, though thou h· not known me.
5 thee, though thou h· not known me:
10 woman, What h· thou brought forth?*
47: 6 upon the ancient h· thou very heavily
10 For thou h· trusted in thy wickedness:
10 thou h· said, None seeth me. Thy
10 and thou h· said in thine heart, I am,
12 wherein thou h· laboured from thy
15 with whom thou h· laboured, even thy
48: 6 Thou h· heard, see all this; and will
49: 20 after thou h· lost the other, shall say*
51: 13 and h· feared continually every day*
17 which h· drunk at the hand of the Lord
17 thou h· drunken the dregs of the cup
23 and thou h· laid thy body as the
57: 6 even to them h· thou poured a drink
6 offering, thou h· offered a meat offering.
7 and high mountain h· thou set thy bed:
8 h· thou set up thy remembrance:
8 for thou h· discovered thyself to
8 thou h· enlarged thy bed, and made
10 thou h· found the life of thine hand;*
11 and of whom h· thou been afraid or
11 afraid or feared, that thou h· lied,*
11 and h· not remembered me, nor laid
60: 15 Whereas thou h· been forsaken
62: 8 for the which thou h· laboured:
63: 17 O Lord, why h· thou made us to err*
64: 7 for thou h· hid thy face from us,
7 and h· consumed us, because of our
Jer 1: 12 Thou h· well seen: for I will hasten
2: 17 H· thou not procured this unto thyself,
17 in that thou h· forsaken the Lord thy
18 h· thou to do in the way of Egypt,
18 h· thou to do in the way of Assyria,
19 that thou h· forsaken the Lord thy God,
23 know what thou h· done: thou art a
27 Thou h· brought me forth: for they
28 are thy gods that thou h· made thee?
33 therefore h· thou also taught the
3: 1 but thou h· played the harlot with
2 and see where thou h· not been lien
2 In the ways h· thou sat for them,
2 and thou h· polluted the land with
5 Behold, thou h· spoken and done evil
6 H· thou seen that which backsliding
13 that thou h· transgressed against the
13 and h· scattered thy ways to the
4: 10 surely thou h· greatly deceived this
19 because thou h· heard, O my soul, the
5: 3 thou h· stricken them, but they have
3 thou h· consumed them, but they have
12: 2 Thou h· planted them, yea, they have
3 thou h· seen me, and tried mine heart*
5 If thou h· run with the footmen,
13: 4 Take the girdle that thou h· got,
21 thou h· taught them to be captains,
25 because thou h· forgotten me, and
14: 19 H· thou utterly rejected Judah? hath
19 why h· thou smitten us, and there is
22 for thou h· made all these things.
15: 6 Thou h· forsaken me, saith the Lord,
10 thou h· borne me a man of strife
17 for thou h· filled me with indignation.
20: 6 friends, to whom thou h· prophesied
7 O Lord, thou h· deceived me, and I
7 art stronger than I, and h· prevailed:
26: 9 Why h· thou prophesied in the name
28: 6 thy words which thou h· prophesied,
13 Thou h· broken the yokes of wood; but
16 because thou h· taught rebellion
29: 25 Because thou h· sent letters in thy
27 therefore why h· thou not reproved
30: 13 thou h· no healing medicines.
31: 18 Thou h· chastised me, and I was
32: 17 thou h· made the heaven and the earth
20 Which h· set signs and wonders in*
20 and h· made thee a name, as at this*
21 And h· brought forth thy people Israel*
22 And h· given them this land, which*

Jer 32: 23 therefore thou h' caused all this evil
24 and what thou h' spoken is come to
25 And thou h' said unto me, O Lord
36: 6 which thou h' written from my mouth,
14 wherein thou h' read in the ears of
29 Thus saith the Lord; Thou h' burned
29 Why h' thou written therein, saying,
38: 25 now what thou h' said unto the king,
39: 18 because thou h' put thy trust in me,
44: 16 As for the word that thou h' spoken
48: 7 For because thou h' trusted in thy
50: 24 caught, because thou h' striven
51: 62 O Lord, thou h' spoken against this
63 when thou h' made an end of reading
La 1: 21 they are glad that thou h' done it:
21 the day that thou h' called, and
22 unto them, as thou h' done unto me
2: 20 and consider to whom thou h' done
21 thou h' slain them in the day of thine
21 thine anger; thou h' killed, and not
22 Thou h' called as in the solemn day
3: 17 And thou h' removed my soul far off
42 have rebelled: thou h' not pardoned.
43 Thou h' covered with anger, and
43 thou h' slain, thou h' not pitied.
44 Thou h' covered thyself with a cloud,
45 Thou h' made us as the offscouring
56 Thou h' heard my voice: hide not *
58 O Lord, thou h' pleaded the causes of
58 of my soul; thou h' redeemed my life.
59 O Lord, thou h' seen my wrong:
60 Thou h' seen all their vengeance and
61 Thou h' heard their reproach, O Lord,
5: 22 But thou h' utterly rejected us; thou
Eze 3: 19 but thou h' delivered thy soul.
20 thou h' not given him warning,
21 also thou h' delivered thy soul.
4: 6 And when thou h' accomplished them,
8 till thou h' ended the days of thy
5: 11 because thou h' defiled my sanctuary
8: 12 Son of man, h' thou seen what the
15, 17 H' thou seen this, O son of man?
9: 11 I have done as thou h' commanded
16: 7 and thou h' increased and waxen*
17 Thou h' also taken thy fair jewels of*
18 and thou h' set mine oil and mine *
19 I fed thee, thou h' even set it before *
20 Moreover thou h' taken thy sons and
20 whom thou h' borne unto me, and
20 and these h' thou sacrificed unto
21 That thou h' slain my children and
22 whoredoms thou h' not remembered
24 That thou h' also built unto thee an
25 Thou h' built thy high place at every
25 and h' made thy beauty to be
25 and h' opened thy feet to every one
26 Thou h' also committed fornication
26 and h' increased thy whoredoms, to
28 Thou h' played the whore also with
28 yea, thou h' played the harlot with
29 Thou h' moreover multiplied thy
31 and h' not been as an harlot, in
37 with whom thou h' taken pleasure,
37 and all them that thou h' loved, with
37 with all them that thou h' hated; I
43 Because thou h' not remembered the
43 but h' fretted me in all these things;
47 Yet h' thou not walked after their
48 as thou h' done, thou and thy
51 thou h' multiplied thine abominations
51 and h' justified thy sisters in all
51 abominations which thou h' done.
52 Thou also, which h' judged thy sisters,
52 that thou h' committed more
52 in that thou h' justified thy sisters.
54 all that thou h' done, in that thou art
58 Thou h' borne thy lewdness and
59 even deal with thee as thou h' done,
59 which h' despised the oath in
63 for all that thou h' done, saith the Lord
22: 4 guilty in thy blood that thou h' shed;
4 and h' defiled thyself in thine idols*
4 thine idols which thou h' made; and
4 and thou h' caused thy days to draw
8 Thou h' despised mine holy things,
8 and h' profaned my sabbaths.
12 to shed blood; thou h' taken usury
12 and thou h' greedily gained of thy
12 and h' forgotten me, saith the Lord
13 gain which thou h' made, and at thy
23: 30 because thou h' gone a whoring after
31 Thou h' walked in the way of thy
35 Because thou h' forgotten me, and
41 whereupon thou h' set mine incense*
25: 6 Because thou h' clapped thine hands,
27: 3 O Tyrus, thou h' said, I am of perfect
28: 2 and thou h' said, I am a god, I sit in
4 understanding thou h' gotten thee
4 and h' gotten gold and silver into thy
5 and by thy traffick h' thou increased
6 Because thou h' set thine heart as
13 Thou h' been in Eden the garden*
14 thou h' walked up and down in the
16 and thou h' sinned: therefore I will
17 thou h' corrupted thy wisdom by
18 Thou h' defiled thy sanctuaries by the
31: 10 Because thou h' lifted up thyself in*
32: 9 countries which thou h' not known.
33: 9 but thou h' delivered thy soul.
35: 5 Because thou h' had a perpetual
5 and h' shed the blood of the children
6 thou h' not hated blood, even blood
10 Because thou h' said, These two
11 which thou h' used out of thy hatred
12 which thou h' spoken against the
36: 13 up men, and h' bereaved thy nations;
Eze 38: 13 h' thou gathered thy company to take
43: 23 When thou h' made an end of cleansing
47: 6 Son of man, h' thou seen this? Then
Da 2: 23 my fathers, who h' given me wisdom
23 and h' made known unto me now
23 for thou h' now made known unto
3: 10 Thou, O king, h' made a decree, that
12 certain Jews whom thou h' set over
12, 18 golden image which thou h' set up.
5: 22 h' not humbled thine heart, though
23 But h' lifted up thyself against the
23 and thou h' praised the gods of silver,
6: 12 H' thou not signed a decree, that
13 the decree that thou h' signed, but
9: 7 whither thou h' driven them, because
15 that h' brought thy people forth out
15 and h' gotten thee renown, as at this
10: 19 speak; for thou h' strengthened me.
Ho 4: 6 because thou h' rejected knowledge,
6 seeing thou h' forgotten the law of
9: 1 for thou h' gone a whoring from thy
1 thou h' loved a reward upon every
10: 9 O Israel, thou h' sinned from the
13: 9 O Israel, thou h' destroyed thyself;*
14: 1 thy God; for thou h' fallen by thine
Ob 15 as thou h' done, it shall be done unto
Jon 1: 10 Why h' thou done this? For the men
14 for thou, O Lord, h' done as it pleased
2: 6 yet h' thou brought up my life from
4: 10 Then said the Lord, Thou h' had pity
10 for the which thou h' not laboured,
Mic 7: 20 which thou h' sworn unto our fathers
Na 3: 16 Thou h' multiplied thy merchants
Hab 1: 12 O Lord, thou h' ordained him for
2: 8 Because thou h' spoiled many nations,
10 Thou h' consulted shame to thy house
Zep 3: 11 thou h' transgressed against me: for
Zec 1: 12 thou h' had indignation these
Mal 1: 2 Wherein h' thou loved us? Was not
2: 14 against whom thou h' dealt
M't 5: 26 thou h' paid the uttermost farthing.*
6: 6 and when thou h' shut thy door, pray*
8: 13 and as thou h' believed, so be it done
11: 25 because thou h' hid these things*
25 and h' revealed them unto babes.
17: 27 and when thou h' opened his mouth
18: 15 if he shall hear thee thou h' gained
19: 21 go and sell that thou h', and give 5224
20: 12 and thou h' made them equal unto us,
21: 16 babes and sucklings thou h' perfected
25: 21, 23 thou h' been faithful over a few
24 reaping where thou h' not sown,*
24 gathering where thou h' not strawed:*
25 lo, there thou h' that is thine. 2192
26: 25 He said unto him, Thou h' said.
64 Jesus saith unto him, Thou h' said:
27: 46 my God, why h' thou forsaken me?
M'k 10: 21 sell whatsoever thou h', and give 2192
12: 32 Well, Master, thou h' said the truth:
15: 34 my God, why h' thou forsaken me?
Lu 1: 4 wherein thou h' been instructed. *
30 Fear not, Mary: for thou h' found
2: 31 Which thou h' prepared before the
48 Son, why h' thou thus dealt with us?
7: 43 unto him, Thou h' rightly judged.
10: 21 earth, that thou h' hid these things*
21 and h' revealed them unto babes: *
28 Thou h' answered right: this do,
11: 27 and the paps which thou h' sucked.*
12: 19 Soul, thou h' much goods laid up 2192
20 things be, which thou h' provided?
59 thence, till thou h' paid the very last*
13: 26 and thou h' taught in our streets.*
14: 22 it is done as thou h' commanded, and*
15: 30 thou h' killed for him the fatted calf.*
18: 22 sell all that thou h', and distribute 2192
19: 17 because thou h' been faithful in a *
20: 39 said, Master, thou h' well said.
24: 18 and h' not known the things which*
Joh 2: 10 but thou h' kept the good wine until
4: 11 Sir, thou h' nothing to draw with, 2192
11 from whence then h' thou that "
17 Thou h' well said, I have no *
18 For thou h' had five husbands; 2192
6: 68 thou h' the words of eternal life. "
7: 20 Thou h' a devil: who goeth about "
8: 48 art a Samaritan, and h' a devil? "
52 Now we know that thou h' a devil. "
57 years old, and h' thou seen Abraham?
9: 37 Thou h' both seen him, and it is he
11: 41 I thank thee that thou h' heard me.*
42 may believe that thou h' sent me.*
13: 8 If I wash thee not, thou h' no part 2192
38 crow, till thou h' denied me thrice.
14: 9 and yet h' thou not known me,*
17: 2 As thou h' given him power over all*
2 life to as many as thou h' given him.
3 and Jesus Christ, whom thou h' sent.*
7 whatsoever thou h' given me are of
9 but for them which thou h' given me;
11 name those whom thou h' given me,
18 As thou h' sent me into the world,*
21 world may believe that thou h' sent*
23 world may know that thou h' sent me,*
23 h' loved them, as thou h' loved me.*
24 whom thou h' given me, be with me
24 glory which thou h' given me: for
25 these have known that thou h' sent*
26 thou h' loved me may be in them, and*
18: 35 thee unto me: what h' thou done?
20: 15 tell me where thou h' laid him, and I
29 Thomas, because thou h' seen me,
29 thou h' believed: blessed are they that
Ac 1: 24 whether of these two thou h' chosen,
2: 28 Thou h' made known to me the ways*
4: 24 which h' made heaven, and earth,*
Ac 4: 25 by the mouth of David h' said, Why*
27 child Jesus whom thou h' anointed,*
5: 4 why h' thou conceived this thing in
4 thou h' not lied unto men, but unto
8: 20 because thou h' thought that the gift
21 Thou h' neither part nor lot in this 2076
10: 33 and thou h' well done that thou art
22: 15 unto all men of what thou h' seen and
23: 11 for as thou h' testified of me in
19 What is that thou h' to tell me? 2192
24: 10 I know that thou h' been of many
25: 12 H' thou appealed unto Cæsar? unto
26: 16 of these things which thou h' seen,
Ro 2: 20 which h' the form of knowledge *2192
9: 20 formed it, Why h' thou made me thus?*
14: 22 H' thou faith? have it to thyself 2192
1Co 4: 7 and what h' thou that thou didst "
7: 28 and if thou marry, thou h' not sinned;
8: 10 see thee which h' knowledge sit 2192
Col 4: 17 the ministry which thou h' received
1Ti 4: 6 doctrine, whereunto thou h' attained.
6: 12 and h' professed a good profession*
2Ti 1: 13 which thou h' heard of me, in faith and
2: 2 And the things that thou h' heard of
3: 10 But thou h' fully known my doctrine,*
14 in the things which thou h' learned
14 learned and h' been assured of,
14 knowing of whom thou h' learned
15 And that from a child thou h' known
Ph'm 1: 5 which thou h' toward the Lord 2192
Heb 1: 9 Thou h' loved righteousness, and
10 Thou, Lord, in the beginning h' laid
2: 8 Thou h' put all things in subjection*
10: 5 not, but a body h' thou prepared me:
6 for sin thou h' had no pleasure.*
Jas 2: 18 Thou h' faith, and I have works: 2192
Re 1: 19 Write the things which thou h' seen,*
2: 2 thou h' tried them which say they are*
2 and are not, and h' found them liars:*
3 And h' borne, and...patience,
3 borne, and h' patience, and for *2192
3 and for my name's sake h' laboured,*
3 laboured, and h' not fainted.
4 thee, because thou h' left thy first*
6 But this thou h', that thou hatest 2192
13 and h' not denied my faith, even in*
14 because thou h' there them that 2192
15 So h' thou also them that hold the "
3: 1 that thou h' a name that thou "
3 therefore how thou h' received
4 Thou h' a few names even in 2192
8 for thou h' a little strength,
8 strength, and h' kept my word *
8 my word, and h' not denied my name.*
10 Because thou h' kept the word of my*
11 hold that fast which thou h', that 2192
4: 11 for thou h' created all things, and*
5: 9 for thou wast slain, and h' redeemed*
10 And h' made us unto our God kings*
11: 17 because thou h' taken to thee thy
17 thee thy great power, and h' reigned.*
16: 5 shalt be, because thou h' judged thus.*
6 thou h' given them blood to drink;

haste See also HASTED; HASTETH; HASTING.
Ge 19: 22 H' thee, escape thither; for I 4116
24: 46 And she made h', and let down her "
43: 30 And Joseph made h'; for his "
45: 9 H' ye, and go up to my father, "
13 and ye shall h' and bring down "
Ex 10: 16 called for Moses and Aaron in h'; "
12: 11 ye shall eat it in h': it is the 2649
33 send them out of the land in h'; 4116
34: 8 And Moses made h', and bowed "
De 16: 3 out of the land of Egypt in h': 2649
32: 35 shall come upon them make h'. 2363
J'g 9: 48 make h', and do as I have done. 4116
13: 10 And the woman made h', and ran, "
1Sa 9: 12 make h' now, for he came to day "
20: 38 Make speed, h', stay not. And 2363
21: 8 the king's business required h'. 5169
23: 26 David made h' to get away for 2648
27 H' thee, and come; for the 4116
25: 18 Then Abigail made h', and took "
2Sa 4: 4 as she made h' to flee, that he 2648
2Ki 7: 15 Syrians had cast away in their h'. "
2Ch 35: 21 God commanded me to make h': 926
Ezr 4: 23 they went up in h' to Jerusalem 924
Es 5: 5 Cause Haman to make h', that 4116
6: 10 Make h', and take the apparel "
Job 20: 2 answer, and for this I make h'. *2363
Ps 22: 19 my strength, h' thee to help me. "
31: 22 For I said in my h', I am cut 2648
38: 22 Make h' to help me, O Lord 2363
40: 13 O Lord, make h' to help me. "
70: 1 Make h', O God, to deliver me; "
1 make h' to help me, O Lord. 2363
5 make h' unto me, O God: thou "
71: 12 my God, make h' for my help. 2439
116: 11 I said in my h', All men are liars. 2648
119: 60 I made h', and delayed not to keep 2363
141: 1 I cry unto thee: make h' unto me; "
Pr 1: 16 evil, and make h' to shed blood. 4116
28: 20 but he that maketh h' to be rich 213
Ca 8: 14 Make h', my beloved, and be 1272
Isa 28: 16 that believeth shall not make h'. 2363
49: 17 Thy children shall make h'; thy 4116
52: 12 ye shall not go out with h', 2649
59: 7 they make h' to shed innocent 4116
Jer 9: 18 And let them make h', and take "
Da 2: 25 in Daniel before the king in h', 927
3: 24 was astonied, and rose up in h', "
6: 19 and went in h' unto the den of lions. "
Na 2: 5 they shall make h' to the wall 4116
M'r 6: 25 she came in straightway with h' 4710
Lu 1: 39 went into the hill country with h', "
2: 16 And they came with h', and found 4692

Lu 19: 5 Zacchæus, make h·, and come 4692
6 And he made h·, and came down, "
Ac 22:18 Make h·, and get thee quickly out "

hasted See also HASTENED.
Ge 18: 7 young man; and he h· to dress it. 4116
24:18 and she h·, and let down her "
20 And she h·, and emptied her "
Ex 5:13 the taskmasters h· them, saying, *213
Jos 4:10 and the people h· and passed over. 4116
8:14 that they h· and rose up early, "
19 and h· and set the city on fire. "
10:13 h· not to go down about a whole 213
J'g 20:37 the liers in wait h·, and rushed 2363
1Sa 17:48 that David h·, and ran toward *4116
25:23 when Abigail saw David, she h·, "
34 except thou hadst h· and come to "
42 And Abigail h·, and arose, and "
28:24 and she h·, and killed it, and took "
2Sa 19:16 was of Bahurim, h· and came "
1Ki 20:41 And he h·, and took the ashes "
2Ki 9:13 Then they h·, and took every man "
2Ch 26:20 himself h· also to go out, because 1765
Es 6:12 h· to his house mourning, and "
14 and h· to bring Haman unto the 926
Job 31: 5 or if my foot hath h· to deceit; 2363
Ps 48: 5 they were troubled, and h· away. 2648
104: 7 voice of thy thunder they h· away. "
Ac 20:16 for he h·, if it were possible for *4692

hasten See also HASTENED; HASTENETH.
1Ki 22: 9 H· hither Micaiah the son of *4116
2Ch 24: 5 and see that ye h· the matter. "
Ps 16: 4 be multiplied that h· after ††
55: 8 I would h· my escape from the *2363
Ec 2:25 or who else can h· hereunto, more*"
Isa 5:19 Let him make speed, and h· "
60:22 I the Lord will h· it in his time. "
Jer 1:12 I will h· my word to perform it, *8245

hastened See also HASTED.
Ge 18: 6 And Abraham h· into the tent 4116
19:15 then the angels h· Lot, saying, 213
2Ch 24: 5 Howbeit the Levites h· it not. 4116
Es 3:15 The posts went out, being h· *1765
8:14 being h· and pressed on by the 926
Jer 17:16 I have not h· from being a pastor 213

hasteneth See also HASTETH.
Isa 51:14 The captive exile h· that he may *4116

hasteth See also HASTENETH.
Job 9:26 as the eagle that h· to the prey. *2907
40:23 drinketh up a river, and h· not: *2648
Pr 7:23 as a bird h· to the snare, 4116
19: 2 and he that h· with his feet sinneth. 213
28:22 He that h· to be rich hath an evil 926
Ec 1: 5 the sun goeth down, and h· to his 7602
Jer 48:16 to come, and his affliction h· fast. 4116
Hab 1: 8 fly as the eagle that h· to eat. 2363
Zep 1:14 is near, it is near, and h· greatly, 4116

hastily
Ge 41:14 and they brought him h· out of 7323
J'g 2:23 without driving them out h·; 4118
9:54 he called h· unto the young man 4120
1Sa 4:14 And the man came in h·, and told *4116
1Ki 20:33 and did h· catch it: and they said,* "
Pr 20:21 inheritance may be gotten h· at 926
25: 8 Go not forth h· to strive, lest thou 4118
Joh 11:31 that she rose up h· and went out,* 5030

hasting
Isa 16: 5 judgment, and h· righteousness. *4106
2Pe 3:12 h· unto the coming of the day of *4692

hasty
Pr 14:29 but he that is h· of spirit exalteth 7116
21: 5 every one that is h· only to want. *213
29:20 Seest thou a man that is h· in his "
Ec 5: 2 let not thine heart be h· to utter 4116
7: 9 Be not h· in thy spirit to be 926
8: 3 Be not h· to go out of his sight: "
Isa 28: 4 the h· fruit before the summer; *1061
Dan 2:15 Why is the decree so h· from the *2685
Hab 1: 6 that bitter and h· nation, which 4116

Hasupha (*has'-u-fah*) See also HASHUPHA.
Ezr 2:43 the children of H·, the children 2817

Hatach (*ha'-tak*)
Es 4: 5 called Esther for H·, one of the *2047
6 So H· went forth to Mordecai unto*"
9 And H· came and told Esther the * "
10 Esther spake unto H·, and gave * "

hatch See also HATCHETH.
Isa 34:15 make her nest, and lay, and h·, 1234
59: 5 They h· cockatrice' eggs, and "

hatcheth
Jer 17:11 partridge sitteth on eggs, and h· ††3205

hate See also HATED; HATEFUL; HATEST; HATETH; HATING.
Ge 24:60 the gate of those which h· them. 8130
26:27 come ye to me, seeing ye h· me, "
50:15 Joseph will peradventure h· us, 7852
Ex 20: 5 fourth generation of them that h· 8130
Le 19:17 Thou shalt not h· thy brother in "
26:17 they that h· you shall reign over "
Nu 10:35 let them that h· thee flee before "
De 5: 9 fourth generation of them that h· "
7:10 repayeth them that h· him to their "
15 them upon all them that h· thee. "
19:11 But if any man h· his neighbour, "
22:13 go in unto her, and h· her, "
24: 3 And if the latter husband h· her, "
30: 7 on them that h· thee, which "
32:41 and will reward them that h· me. "
33:11 and of them that h· him, that they "
J'g 11: 7 Did not ye h· me, and expel me out "
14:16 Thou dost but h· me, and lovest me "
2Sa 22:41 that I might destroy them that h· "
1Ki 22: 8 but I h· him; for he doth not "
2Ch 18: 7 but I h· him; for he never 8130
19: 2 and love them that h· the Lord? "
Job 8:22 They that h· thee shall be clothed "
Ps 9:13 of them that h· me, thou that liftest "
18:40 that I might destroy them that h· "
21: 8 shall find out those that h· thee. "
25:19 they h· me with cruel hatred. "
34:21 and they that h· the righteous "
35:19 eye that h· me without a cause. "
38:19 they that h· me wrongfully are "
41: 7 All that h· me whisper together "
44:10 and they which h· us spoil for "
55: 3 me, and in wrath they h· me. *7852
68: 1 let them also that h· him flee 8130
69: 4 They that h· me without a cause "
14 delivered from them that h· me, "
83: 2 and they that h· thee have lifted up "
86:17 that they which h· me may see "
89:23 face, and plague them that h· him. "
97:10 Ye that love the Lord, h· evil: "
101: 3 I h· the work of them that turn "
105:25 turned their heart to h· his people, "
118: 7 see my desire upon them that h· "
119:104 therefore I h· every false way. "
113 I h· vain thoughts: but thy law "
128 right; and I h· every false way. "
163 I h· and abhor lying: but thy law "
129: 5 and turned back that h· Zion. "
139:21 I h· them, O Lord, that h· thee? "
22 I h· them with perfect hatred: "
Pr 1:22 scorning, and fools h· knowledge? "
6:16 These six things doth the Lord h·:* "
8:13 The fear of the Lord is to h· evil: "
13 and the froward mouth, do I h·. "
36 all they that h· me love death. "
9: 8 Reprove not a scorner, lest he h· "
19: 7 the brethren of the poor do h· him: "
25:17 he be weary of thee, and so h· thee. "
29:10 The bloodthirsty h· the upright: "
Ec 3: 8 A time to love, and a time to h·; "
Isa 61: 8 I h· robbery for burnt offering; and "
Jer 44: 4 this abominable thing that I h·. "
Eze 16:27 unto the will of them that h· thee, "
Da 4:19 the dream be to them that h· thee, 8131
Am 5:10 They h· him that rebuketh in the 8130
15 H· the evil, and love the good, "
21 I h·, I despise your feast days, "
6: 8 and h· his palaces: therefore will I "
Mic 3: 2 Who h· the good, and love the evil; "
Zec 8:17 for all these are things that I h·, "
M't 5:43 shalt love thy neighbour, and h· 3404
44 do good to them that h· you, * "
6:24 for either he will h· the one, "
24:10 another, and shall h· one another. "
Lu 1:71 from the hand of all that h· us; "
6:22 when men shall h· you, and when "
27 enemies, do good to them which h· "
14:26 and h· not his father, and mother,* "
16:13 either he will h· the one, and love "
Joh 7: 7 cannot h· you; but me it hateth, "
15:18 If the world h· you, ye know that * "
Ro 7:15 do I not; but what I h·, that do I. "
1Jo 3:13 my brethren, if the world h· you.* "
Re 2: 6 of the Nicolaitanes, which I also h·. "
15 the Nicolaitanes, which thing I h·.* "
17:16 these shall h· the whore, and shall "

hated
Ge 27:41 And Esau h· Jacob because of the 7852
29:31 the Lord saw that Leah was h·, 8130
33 the Lord hath heard that I was h·, "
37: 4 than all his brethren, they h· him, "
5 and they h· him yet the more. "
8 they h· him yet the more for his "
49:23 and shot at him, and h· him: *7852
De 1:27 Because the Lord h· us, he hath 8135
4:42 h· him not in times past; 8130
9:28 and because he h· them, he hath 8135
19: 4 whom he h· not in times past; 8130
6 as he h· him not in time past, "
21:15 one beloved, and another h·, and "
15 both the beloved and the h·; "
15 firstborn son be her's that was h·: 8146
16 firstborn before the son of the h·, 8130
17 acknowledge the son of the h· for "
Jos 20: 5 neighbour unwittingly, and h· him "
J'g 15: 2 thought that thou hadst utterly h· "
2Sa 5: 8 that are h· of David's soul, he shall "
13:15 Then Amnon h· her exceedingly; so "
15 the hatred wherewith he h· her was "
22 for Absalom h· Amnon, because he "
22:18 enemy, and from them that h· me: "
Es 9: 1 Jews had rule over them that h· "
5 what they would unto those that h·* "
Job 31:29 the destruction of him that h· me, "
Ps 18:17 enemy, and from them which h· me "
26: 5 I have h· the congregation of evil * "
31: 6 I have h· them that regard lying * "
44: 7 hast put them to shame that h· us.*"
55:12 neither was it he that h· me that "
Pr 1:29 For that they h· knowledge, and "
5:12 How have I h· instruction, and my "
14:17 a man of wicked devices is h·. "
20 The poor is h· even of his own "
Ec 2:17 Therefore I h· life; because the "
18 Yea, I h· all my labour which I had "
Isa 60:15 thou hast been forsaken and h·, so "
66: 5 Your brethren that h· you, that * "
Jer 12: 8 against me: therefore have I h· it. "
Eze 16:37 with all them that thou hast h·; "
35: 6 sith thou hast not h· blood, even "
Ho 9:15 for there I h· them: for the "
Mal 1: 3 I h· Esau, and laid his mountains "
24: 9 and ye shall be h· of all nations for "
M't 10:22 ye shall be h· of all men for my 3404
M'r 13:13 And ye shall be h· of all men for my "
Lu 19:14 But his citizens h· him, and sent a "
Lu 21:17 And ye shall be h· of all men for my 3404
Joh 15:18 ye know that it h· me before it "
18 me before it h· you. "
24 they both seen and h· both me 3404
25 They h· me without a cause. "
17:14 the world hath h· them, because "
Ro 9:13 I loved, but Esau have I h·. "
Eph 5:29 no man ever yet h· his own flesh; "
Heb 1: 9 loved righteousness, and h· iniquity;"

hateful
Ps 36: 2 his iniquity be found to be h·. *8130
Tit 3: 3 envy, h·, and hating one another. 4767
Re 18: 2 of every unclean and h· bird. 3404

hatefully
Eze 23:29 they shall deal with thee h·, *8135

haters
Ps 81:15 The h· of the Lord should have 8130
Ro 1:30 h· of God, despiteful, proud, *2319

hatest
2Sa 19: 6 thine enemies, and h· thy friends. 8130
Ps 5: 5 thou h· all workers of iniquity. "
45: 7 righteousness, and h· wickedness:*"
50:17 Seeing thou h· instruction, and "
Eze 23:28 the hand of them whom thou h·, "
Re 2: 6 thou h· the deeds of...Nicolaitanes, 3404

hateth
Ex 23: 5 see the ass of him that h· thee 8130
De 7:10 will not be slack to him that h· him, "
12:31 which he h·, have they done unto "
16:22 image; which the Lord thy God h·. "
22:16 unto this man to wife, and he h· her;"
Job 16: 9 teareth me in his wrath, who h· me:*7852
34:17 even he that h· right govern? 8130
Ps 11: 5 him that loveth violence his soul h·. "
120: 6 long dwelt with him that h· peace. "
Pr 11:15 and he that h· suretiship is sure. "
12: 1 but he that h· reproof is brutish. "
13: 5 A righteous man h· lying: but a "
24 He that spareth his rod h· his son: "
15:10 and he that h· reproof shall die. "
27 but he that h· gifts shall live. "
26:24 He that h· dissembleth with his lips,"
28 A lying tongue h· those that are "
28:16 he that h· covetousness shall "
29:24 partner with a thief h· his own soul:"
Isa 1:14 your appointed feasts my soul h·: "
Mal 2:16 saith that he h· putting away: * "
Joh 3:20 h· the light, neither cometh to the 3404
7: 7 cannot hate you; but me it h·, "
12:25 he that h· his life in this world "
15:19 world, therefore the world h· you. "
23 He that h· me h· my Father also. "
1Jo 2: 9 is in the light, and h· his brother, "
11 But he that h· his brother is in "
3:15 Whosoever h· his brother, is a "
4:20 and h· his brother, he is a liar: "

hath
Ge 1:20 the moving creature that h· life,
3: 1 Yea, h· God said, Ye shall not eat of
3 God h· said, Ye shall not eat of it,
4:11 earth, which h· opened her mouth to
25 For God, said she, h· appointed me
5:29 ground which the Lord h· cursed.
14:20 the most high God, which h· delivered
16: 2 Behold now, the Lord h· restrained
11 because the Lord h· heard thy
17:14 people; he h· broken my covenant.
18:19 Abraham that which he h· spoken
19:13 and the Lord h· sent us to destroy it.
19 thy servant h· found grace in thy
21: 6 Sarah said, God h· made me to laugh,
12 in all that Sarah h· said unto thee,*
17 for God h· heard the voice of the lad
26 I wot not who h· done this thing:
22:20 Behold, Milcah, she h· also born
23: 9 me the cave of Machpelah, which he h·.
24:27 who h· not left destitute my master
35 And the Lord h· blessed my master
35 and he h· given him flocks,
36 unto him h· he given all that he h·.
44 woman whom the Lord h· appointed
51 son's wife, as the Lord h· spoken
56 seeing the Lord h· prospered my way;
26:22 For now the Lord h· made room for
27:27 of a field which the Lord h· blessed:
33 where is he that h· taken venison,
35 came with subtilty, and h· taken
36 for he h· supplanted me these two
36 behold, now he h· taken away my
29:32 Surely the Lord h· looked upon my
33 Because the Lord h· heard that I was
33 he h· therefore given me this son
30: 2 who h· withheld from thee the fruit
6 And Rachel said, God h· judged me,
6 and h· also heard my voice, and
6 voice, and h· given me a son:
18 Leah said, God h· given me my hire,
20 God h· endued me with a good dowry;
23 and said, God h· taken away my
27 the Lord h· blessed me for thy sake.
30 and the Lord h· blessed thee since
31: 1 saying, Jacob h· taken away all that
1 which was our father's h· he gotten
5 the God of my father h· been with me.
7 And your father h· deceived me,
9 Thus God h· taken away the cattle of
15 of him strangers? for he h· sold us,
15 and h· quite devoured also our
16 riches which God h· taken from
16 whatsoever God h· said unto thee,
42 God h· seen mine affliction and the
33: 5 which God h· graciously given thy
11 because God h· dealt graciously with
37:20 Some evil beast h· devoured him:

Ge 37:33 an evil beast h' devoured him;
38:24 Tamar thy daughter in law h' played
26 She h' been more righteous than I; *
39: 8 me in the house, and he h' committed
8 all that he h' to my hands; 3426
9 neither h' he kept back any thing from
14 See, he h' brought in an Hebrew unto
41:25 God h' shewed Pharaoh what he is
39 Forasmuch as God h' shewed thee all
51 For God, said he, h' made me forget
52 For God h' caused me to be fruitful
42:28 What is this that God h' done unto us?
43:23 God of your father, h' given you
44:16 God h' found out the iniquity of thy
45: 6 For these two years h' the famine been
8 but God: and he h' made me a father
9 God h' made me lord of all Egypt:
46:32 their trade h' been to feed cattle; *
34 Thy servants' trade h' been about *
47:18 my lord also h' our herds of cattle; *413
48: 9 my sons, whom God h' given me
11 and, lo, God h' shewed me also thy
Ex 3:13 The God of your fathers h' sent me
14 I Am h' sent me unto you.
15 the God of Jacob, h' sent me unto you:
18 The Lord God of the Hebrews h' met
4: 1 The Lord h' not appeared unto thee.
5 the God of Jacob, h' appeared unto
11 unto him, Who h' made man's mouth?
5: 3 The God of the Hebrews h' met with
23 to speak in thy name, he h' done evil
7:16 Lord God of the Hebrews h' sent me
9:18 hail, such as h' not been in Egypt
10:12 even all that the hail h' left.
12:25 give you, according as he h' promised,
13: 9 strong hand h' the Lord brought thee
14: 3 the wilderness h' shut them in.
15: 1 unto the Lord, for he h' triumphed
1 the horse and his rider h' he thrown
4 and his host h' he cast into the sea:
6 thy right hand, O Lord, h' dashed in*
21 ye to the Lord, for he h' triumphed
21 the horse and his rider h' he thrown
16: 6 that the Lord h' brought you out
9 for he h' heard your murmurings.
15 bread which the Lord h' given you to
16 thing which the Lord h' commanded,
23 This is that which the Lord h' said,
29 See, for that the Lord h' given you the
17:16 Because the Lord h' sworn that
18:10 who h' delivered you out of the hand of
10 who h' delivered the people from under
19: 8 All that the Lord h' spoken we will do.
21: 8 her master, who h' betrothed her to
8 seeing he h' dealt deceitfully with
29 and it h' been testified to his owner,
29 and he h' not kept him in, but
29 that he h' killed a man or a woman;
36 that the ox h' used to push in time *
36 and his owner h' not kept him in;
22:11 that he h' not put his hand unto his
24: 3 All the words which the Lord h' said
7 All that the Lord h' said will we do,
8 which the Lord h' made with you
32:24 Whosoever h' any gold, let them
33 Whosoever h' sinned against me,
35: 1 words which the Lord h' commanded,
10 make all that the Lord h' commanded;
30 See, the Lord h' called by name
31 And he h' filled him with the spirit
34 And he h' put in his heart that he
35 Them h' he filled with wisdom of
Le 4: 3 bring for his sin, which he h' sinned,
22 When a ruler h' sinned, and done *
23 Or if his sin, wherein he h' sinned,
28 Or if his sin, which he h' sinned
28 blemish, for his sin which he h' sinned.
35 for his sin which he h' committed,
5: 1 whether he h' seen or known of it;
5 shall confess that he h' sinned in
6 Lord for his sin which he h' sinned,
7 his trespass, which he h' committed,
10 for him for his sin which he h' sinned,
13 that he h' sinned in one of these,
16 the harm that he h' done in the ho'y
19 he h' certainly trespassed against *
6: 2 or h' oppressed his neighbour; *
4 Then it shall be, because he h' sinned,
4 thing which he h' deceitfully gotten,
5 all that about which he h' sworn
7 for any thing of all that he h' done*
10 the ashes which the fire h' consumed
7: 8 the burnt-offering which he h' offered.
8:34 As he h' done this day, so the Lord
34 h' commanded to do, to make an
10: 6 burning which the Lord h' kindled.
11 statutes which the Lord h' spoken
15 for ever; as the Lord h' commanded.
17 and God h' given it you to bear the
11: 9 whatsoever h' fins and scales in the
12 Whatsoever h' no fins nor scales in
42 whatsoever h' more feet among all
12: 7 the law for her that h' born a male *
13: 4 shut up him that h' the plague seven
7 after that he h' been seen of the
12 skin of him that h' the plague from
13 him clean that h' the plague: it is
17 him clean that h' the plague: he is
31 shall shut up him that h' the plague
33 shall shut up him that h' the scall
41 And he that h' his hair fallen off *
50 shut up it that h' the plague seven
14:43 after that he h' taken away the stones,
43 and after he h' scraped the house,
48 behold, the plague h' not spread in
15: 2 When any man h' a running issue 1961

Le 15:4 bed, whereon he lieth that h' the issue,
6 whereon he sa' that h' the issue
7 the flesh of him that h' the issue
8 And if he that h' the issue spit upon
9 he rideth upon that h' the issue
11 he toucheth that h' the issue,
11 and h' not rinsed his hands in water, *
12 that he toucheth which h' the issue,
13 And when he that h' an issue is
32 This is the law of him that h' an issue,
33 and of him that h' an issue, of the
16:20 when he h' made an end of reconciling
17: 2 thing which the Lord h' commanded,
4 unto that man; he h' shed blood;
19: 8 because he h' profaned the hallowed
22 for his sin which he h' done:
22 and the sin which he h' done shall be
20: 3 because he h' given of his seed unto
9 he h' cursed his father or his mother;
11 with his father's wife h' uncovered
17 he h' uncovered his sister's nakedness;
18 he h' discovered her fountain,
18 and she h' uncovered the fountain
20 he h' uncovered his uncle's nakedness:
21 he h' uncovered his brother's
27 also or woman that h' a familiar 1961
21: 3 him, which h' had no husband;
17 generations that h' any blemish, 1961
18 man he be that h' a blemish,
18 or a lame, or that he h' a flat nose,
20 or a dwarf, or that h' a blemish in his
20 or scabbed, or h' his stones broken;
21 No man that h' a blemish of the seed
21 he h' a blemish; he shall not come
23 unto the altar, because he h' a blemish;
22: 4 is a leper, or h' a running issue;
5 whatsoever uncleanness he h';
6 The soul which h' touched any such *
20 But whatsoever h' a blemish, that
23 bullock or a lamb that h' any thing
24:14 Bring forth him that h' cursed
19 as he h' done, so shall it be done
20 as he h' caused a blemish in a man,
25:25 brother be waxen poor, and h' sold*
28 hand of him that h' bought it until
27:22 the Lord a field which he h' bought,
28 devote unto the Lord of all that he h',
Nu 5: 2 leper, and every one that h' an issue,
7 him against whom he h' trespassed.
27 And when he h' made her to drink
6: 9 and he h' defiled the head of his*
21 law of the Nazarite who h' vowed,*
10:29 the Lord h' spoken good concerning
12: 2 H' the Lord indeed spoken only by
2 h' he not spoken also by us?
14: 3 And wherefore h' the Lord brought*
16 therefore he h' slain them in the
24 and h' followed me fully, him will
40 the place which the Lord h' promised:
15:22 which the Lord h' spoken unto
23 Even all that the Lord h' commanded
31 Because he h' despised the word of the
31 and h' broken his commandment,
16: 5 whom he h' chosen will he cause to*
9 that the God of Israel h' separated
10 And he h' brought thee near to him,
28 shall know that the Lord h' sent me
29 then the Lord h' not sent me.
19: 2 law which the Lord h' commanded,
15 open vessel, which h' no covering
20 because he h' defiled the sanctuary
20 of separation h' not been sprinkled
20:14 all the travel that h' befallen us;
16 and h' brought us forth out of Egypt:*
21:28 it h' consumed Ar of Moab, and
29 he h' given his sons that escaped,
22:10 king of Moab, h' sent unto me, saying,
23: 7 Balak the king of Moab h' brought me
8 I curse, whom God h' not cursed?
8 whom the Lord h' not defied?
12 that which the Lord h' put in my*
17 him, What h' the Lord spoken?
19 h' he said, and shall he not do it?
19 or h' he spoken, and shall he not
20 and he h' blessed; and I cannot
21 He h' not beheld iniquity in Jacob,
21 neither h' he seen perverseness in
22 he h' as it were the strength of an
23 and of Israel, What h' God wrought!
24: 3 said, Balaam the son of Beor h' said,*
3 man whose eyes are open h' said:*
4 He h' said, which heard the words of*
6 aloes which the Lord h' planted,
8 he h' as it were the strength of an
11 the Lord h' kept thee back from
15 Balaam the son of Beor h' said,*
15 man whose eyes are open h' said:*
16 He h' said, which heard the words of*
25:11 son of Aaron the priest, h' turned my
27: 4 his family, because he h' no son?*
30: 1 thing which the Lord h' commanded.
4 her bond wherewith she h' bound
4 every bond wherewith she h' bound
5 her bonds wherewith she h' bound
12 if her husband h' utterly made them*
12 her husband h' made them void;
15 them void after that he h' heard them;
31:17 kill every woman that h' known man
19 whosoever h' killed any person,
19 and whosoever h' touched any slain,
50 what every man h' gotten, of jewels
32: 7 the land which the Lord h' given
21 until he h' driven out his enemies
24 that which h' proceeded out of your
31 As the Lord h' said unto thy servants,
36: 5 of the sons of Joseph h' said well.*

De 1:10 The Lord your God h' multiplied you,
11 and bless you, as he h' promised you!
21 the Lord thy God h' set the land
21 as the Lord God of thy fathers h' said
27 hated us, he h' brought us forth
36 I give the land that he h' trodden
36 because he h' wholly followed the
2: 7 For the Lord thy God h' blessed thee
7 the Lord thy God h' been with thee;
3:18 The Lord your God h' given you this
20 the Lord your God h' given them*
21 all that the Lord your God h' done
4: 3 the Lord thy God h' destroyed them
7 great, who h' God so nigh unto them,
8 that h' statutes and judgments
19 which the Lord thy God h' divided
20 But the Lord h' taken you, and
23 which the Lord thy God h' forbidden
32 whether there h' been any such thing
32 as this great thing is, or h' been heard
34 Or h' God assayed to go and take him
5:12 as the Lord...God h' commanded thee.*
16 as the Lord...God h' commanded thee;*
24 Lord our God h' shewed us his glory
26 of all flesh, that h' heard the voice
32 as the Lord...God h' commanded you:
33 which the Lord...God h' commanded
6: 3 Lord God of thy fathers h' promised
17 his statutes, which he h' commanded
19 before thee, as the Lord h' spoken.
20 the Lord our God h' commanded
25 as he h' commanded us.
7: 1 and h' cast out many nations before*
6 the Lord thy God h' chosen thee to be
8 unto your fathers, h' the Lord brought
8:10 for the good land which he h' given
17 the might of mine hand h' gotten me
9: 3 them quickly, as the Lord h' said
4 after that the Lord thy God h' cast
4 the Lord h' brought me in to possess
28 he h' brought them out to slay them
10: 9 Levi h' no part nor inheritance 1961
21 he is thy God, that h' done for thee
22 now the Lord thy God h' made thee as
11: 4 and how the Lord h' destroyed them
25 ye shall tread upon, as he h' said unto
29 when the Lord thy God h' brought*
12: 7 wherein the Lord thy God h' blessed
12 forasmuch as he h' no part nor
15 of the Lord thy God which he h' given
20 enlarge thy border, as he h' promised
21 the Lord thy God h' chosen to put*
13: 5 because he h' spoken to turn you
10 because he h' sought to thrust thee
12 which the Lord thy God h' given thee*
17 as he h' sworn unto thy fathers;
14: 2 and the Lord h' chosen thee to be a
10 And whatsoever h' not fins and scales
24 when the Lord thy God h' blessed*
27 he h' no part nor inheritance with
29 And the Levite, (because he h' no part
15:14 wherewith the Lord thy God h' blessed
18 for he h' been worth a double hired
16:10 as the Lord thy God h' blessed thee:
11 which the Lord thy God h' chosen to*
17 of the Lord thy God which he h' given
17: 2 man or woman, that h' wrought*
3 And h' gone and served other gods,
16 forasmuch as the Lord h' said unto
18: 2 is their inheritance, as he h' said unto
5 For the Lord thy God h' chosen him
14 the Lord thy God h' not suffered thee
21 word which the Lord h' not spoken?
22 thing which the Lord h' not spoken,
22 but the prophet h' spoken it
19: 1 When the Lord thy God h' cut off the*
8 enlarge thy coast, as he h' sworn unto
18 a false witness, and h' testified falsely
20: 5 What man is there that h' built a new
5 house, and h' not dedicated it?
6 what man is he that h' planted a
6 vineyard, and h' not yet eaten of it?
7 what man is there that h' betrothed
7 a wife, and h' not taken her?
13 when the Lord thy God h' delivered it*
14 which the Lord thy God h' given thee.
17 as the Lord thy God h' commanded
21: 1 and it be not known who h' slain him:
3 which h' not been wrought with,
3 and which h' not drawn in the yoke;
5 the Lord thy God h' chosen to minister
10 the Lord thy God h' delivered them *
16 sons to inherit that which he h', 1961
17 a double portion of all that he h': 4672
22: 3 which he h' lost, and thou hast found,
17 And, lo, he h' given occasions of
19 because he h' brought up an evil
21 because she h' wrought folly in Israel,
24 because he h' humbled his neighbour's
29 because he h' humbled her, he may
23: 1 or h' his privy member cut off, shall
24: 1 When a man h' taken a wife, *
1 because he h' found some uncleanness
5 When a man h' taken a new wife,*
5 cheer up his wife which he h' taken.
25:10 house of him that h' his shoe loosed.
19 when the Lord thy God h' given thee
26: 9 And he h' brought us into this place,
9 and h' given us this land,
11 which the Lord thy God h' given unto
16 day the Lord thy God h' commanded*
18 And the Lord h' avouched thee this
18 peculiar people, as he h' promised
19 above all nations which he h' made,
19 the Lord thy God, as he h' spoken.
27: 3 Lord God of thy fathers h' promised

De 28: 9 people unto himself, as he h' sworn
52 which the Lord thy God h' given thee.
53 which the Lord thy God h' given thee,
55 because he h' nothing left him in the
29: 4 Yet the Lord h' not given you an
13 be unto thee a God, as he h' said unto*
13 and as he h' sworn unto thy fathers,*
22 sicknesses which the Lord h' laid
24 Wherefore h' the Lord done thus
30: 1 whither the Lord thy God h' driven
3 whither the Lord thy God h' scattered
31: 2 also the Lord h' said unto me, Thou
3 go before thee, as the Lord h' said.
7 land which the Lord h' sworn unto
32: 6 is not he thy father that h' bought
6 h' he not made thee, and established
27 and the Lord h' not done all this.
Jos 1: 13 The Lord your God h' given you rest,*
13 and h' given you this land. *
15 your brethren rest, as he h' given you,
2: 9 I know that the Lord h' given you the
14 it shall be, when the Lord h' given us*
24 Truly the Lord h' delivered into our
6: 16 Shout; for the Lord h' given you the
22 thence the woman, and all that she h',
7: 11 Israel h' sinned, and they have also
15 burnt with fire, he and all that he h':
15 because he h' transgressed the
15 and because he h' wrought folly in
8: 31 over which no man h' lift up any iron:*
10: 4 for it h' made peace with Joshua
19 the Lord your God h' delivered them
14: 10 behold, the Lord h' kept me alive,
17: 14 forasmuch as the Lord h' blessed me
18: 3 the Lord God of your fathers h' given
22: 4 now the Lord your God h' given rest
25 For the Lord h' made Jordan a border
23: 3 all that the Lord your God h' done
3 the Lord your God is he that h' fought
5 as the Lord your God h' promised*
9 For the Lord h' driven out from before
9 but as for you, no man h' been able to
10 fighteth for you as he h' promised*
13 which the Lord your God h' given you.
14 that not one thing h' failed of all the
14 and not one thing h' failed thereof.
15 which the Lord your God h' given you.
16 off the good land which he h' given
24: 20 after that he h' done you good.
27 for it h' heard all the words of the
J'g 1: 7 as I have done, so God h' requited me.
2: 20 that this people h' transgressed *
3: 28 for the Lord h' delivered your enemies
4: 6 said unto him, H' not the Lord God of
14 day in which the Lord h' delivered
6: 13 but now the Lord h' forsaken us,
25 the altar of Baal that thy father h',
29 to another, Who h' done this thing?
29 Gideon the son of Joash h' done this
30 because he h' cast down the altar of
30 and because he h' cut down the grove
31 because one h' cast down his altar.
32 because he h' thrown down his altar.
7: 2 saying, Mine own hand h' saved me.
14 into his hand h' God delivered Midian,
15 for the Lord h' delivered into your
8: 3 God h' delivered into your hands
7 Therefore when the Lord h' delivered
11: 23 the Lord God of Israel h' dispossessed
36 according to that which h' proceeded
36 as the Lord h' taken vengeance
13: 10 Behold, the man h' appeared unto me,
15: 6 the Philistines said, Who h' done this?
10 up, to do to him as he h' done to us.
16: 17 There h' not come a razor upon mine
18 for he h' shewed me all his heart.
23 Our god h' delivered Samson our
24 Our god h' delivered into our hands
18: 4 Micah with me, and h' hired me,
10 for God h' given it into your hands;
21: 11 and every woman that h' lain by man.
Ru 1: 20 for the Almighty h' dealt very bitterly
21 and the Lord h' brought me home
21 seeing the Lord h' testified against
21 and the Almighty h' afflicted me?
2: 7 so she came, and h' continued even
11 unto her, It h' fully been shewed me,
20 Blessed be he of the Lord, who h' not
4: 14 Blessed be the Lord, which h' not left
15 to thee than seven sons, h' born him.
1Sa 1: 27 and the Lord h' given me my petition
2: 5 so that the barren h' born seven;
5 she that h' many children is waxed
8 and he h' set the world upon them.
3: 17 the thing that the Lord h' said unto
4: 3 Wherefore h' the Lord smitten us
7 for there h' not been such a thing
17 and there h' been also a great
6: 7 on which there h' come no yoke,
9 then he h' done us this great evil:
7: 12 saying, Hitherto h' the Lord helped
9: 24 for unto this time h' it been kept
10: 1 Is it not because the Lord h' anointed
2 lo, thy father h' left the care of
22 Behold, he h' hid himself among the
24 See ye him whom the Lord h' chosen,
11: 13 to day the Lord h' wrought salvation
12: 13 behold, the Lord h' set a king over you.
22 because it h' pleased the Lord to make
24 consider how great things he h' done
13: 14 the Lord h' sought him a man after
14 and the Lord h' commanded him
14: 10 the Lord h' delivered them into our
12 the Lord h' delivered them into the
29 My father h' troubled the land: see
38 and see wherein this sin h' been

1Sa 14: 45 Shall Jonathan die, who h' wrought
45 for he h' wrought with God this day.
15: 11 h' not performed my commandments.
16 I will tell thee what the Lord h' said
22 said, H' the Lord as great delight
23 he h' also rejected thee from being
26 the Lord h' rejected thee from being
28 the Lord h' rent the kingdom of
28 and h' given it to a neighbour of
33 As thy sword h' made women
16: 8, 9 Neither h' the Lord chosen this.
10 Jesse, The Lord h' not chosen these.
22 for he h' found favour in my sight,
17: 36 seeing he h' defied the armies of the
18: 7 Saul h' slain his thousands, and David
22 Behold, the king h' delight in thee,
19: 4 because he h' not sinned against thee,
20: 13 as he h' been with my father.
15 not when the Lord h' cut off the
22 go thy way: for the Lord h' sent thee
26 for he thought, Something h' befallen
29 for our family h' a sacrifice in the city;
29 my brother, he h' commanded me
32 shall he be slain? what h' he done?
21: 2 The king h' commanded me a
2 and h' said unto me, Let no man
11 Saul h' slain his thousands, and David
22: 8 my son h' made a league with the *
8 that my son h' stirred up my
23: 7 God h' delivered him into mine hand;
7 entering into a town that h' gates and
10 thy servant h' certainly heard that
11 come down, as thy servant h' heard?
22 where his haunt is, and who h' seen
25: 21 all that this fellow h' in the wilderness,
26 seeing the Lord h' withholden thee
27 thine handmaid h' brought unto my
28 and evil h' not been found in thee*
30 all the good that he h' spoken
31 or that my lord h' avenged himself:
34 which h' kept me back from hurting
39 the Lord, that h' pleaded the cause of
39 and h' kept his servant from evil:
26: 8 God h' delivered thine enemy into
27: 12 saying, He h' made his people Israel
28: 7 a woman that h' a familiar spirit, 1172
7 a woman that h' a familiar spirit "
9 thou knowest what Saul h' done,
9 how he h' cut off those that have
17 And the Lord h' done to him, as he
17 for the Lord h' rent the kingdom
18 therefore h' the Lord done this thing
21 Behold thine handmaid h' obeyed thy
29: 3 which h' been with me these days,
30: 23 with that which the Lord h' given us,
23 who h' preserved us and delivered
2Sa 1: 16 for thy mouth h' testified against thee,
3: 9 as the Lord h' sworn to David, even so
18 for the Lord h' spoken of David,
23 and he h' sent him away, and he is
29 one that h' an issue, or that is a leper,
4: 8 and the Lord h' avenged my lord the
9 As the Lord liveth, who h' redeemed
5: 20 The Lord h' broken forth upon mine
6: 12 The Lord h' blessed the house of
7: 27 therefore h' thy servant found in his
9: 3 Jonathan h' yet a son, which is lame
11 that my lord the king h' commanded*
10: 3 that he h' sent comforters unto thee?
3 h' not David rather sent his servants
12: 5 the man that h' done this thing
13 The Lord also h' put away thy sin;
13: 20 H' Amnon thy brother been with
24 thy servant h' sheepshearers; let the
32 of Absalom this h' been determined
14: 19 that my lord the king h' spoken:
20 h' thy servant Joab done this thing:
22 in that the king h' fulfilled the request
30 field is near mine, and he h' barley
15: 4 that every man which h' any suit or
16: 8 The Lord h' returned upon thee all the
8 and the Lord h' delivered the
10 because the Lord h' said unto him,
11 let him curse; for the Lord h' bidden
21 which he h' left to keep the house;
17: 6 Ahithophel h' spoken after this
7 that Ahithophel h' given is not good
21 for thus h' Ahithophel counselled
18: 19 how that the Lord h' avenged him of
28 the Lord thy God, which h' delivered
31 for the Lord h' avenged thee this day
19: 27 And he h' slandered thy servant unto
42 or h' he given us any gift?
20: 21 Bichri by name, h' lifted up his hand
22: 21 of my hands h' he recompensed me.
25 Therefore the Lord h' recompensed
36 and thy gentleness h' made me great.
23: 5 yet he h' made with me an everlasting
1Ki 1: 19 And he h' slain oxen and fat cattle
19 and h' called all the sons of the king,
19 Solomon thy servant h' he not called.
25 gone down this day, and h' slain oxen
25 and h' called all the king's sons,
26 thy servant Solomon, h' he not called.
29 As the Lord liveth, that h' redeemed
37 As the Lord h' been with my lord
43 lord king David h' made Solomon king.
44 And the king h' sent with him Zadok
48 which h' given one to sit on my throne
51 lo, he h' caught hold on the horns of
2: 24 the Lord liveth, which h' established
24 and who h' made me an house,
31 Do as he h' said, and fall upon him,
38 as my lord the king h' said, so will
5: 4 the Lord my God h' given me rest
7 the Lord this day, which h' given unto

1Ki 8: 15 and h' with his hand fulfilled it,
20 And the Lord h' performed his word
56 Blessed be the Lord, that h' given rest
56 there h' not failed one word of all his
9: 8 Why h' the Lord done thus unto this
9 therefore h' the Lord brought upon
12: 11 father h' chastised you with whips, *
13: 3 is the sign which the Lord h' spoken;
26 therefore the Lord h' delivered him
26 unto the lion, which h' torn him,
14: 11 the air eat: for the Lord h' spoken it.
16: 16 Zimri h' conspired, and h' also slain
18: 10 whither my Lord h' not sent to seek
19: 18 and every mouth which h' not kissed
22: 23 behold, the Lord h' put a lying spirit
23 and the Lord h' spoken evil concerning
28 the Lord h' not spoken by me.
2Ki 1: 9 Thou man of God, the king h' said,
11 O man of God, thus h' the king said,
2: 2 for the Lord h' sent me to Beth-el.
4 for the Lord h' sent me to Jericho.
6 for the Lord h' sent me to Jordan.
16 the Spirit of the Lord h' taken him up,
3: 7 The king of Moab h' rebelled against
10 that the Lord h' called these three
13 for the Lord h' called these three
4: 2 Thine handmaid h' not any thing in
14 Verily she h' no child, and her
27 and the Lord h' hid it from me,
27 hid it from me, and h' not told me.
5: 20 Behold, my master h' spared Naaman
22 My master h' sent me, saying,
6: 29 eat him: and she h' hid her son.
32 this son of a murderer h' sent to take
7: 6 Lo, the king of Israel h' hired against
8: 1 for the Lord h' called for a famine;
4 the great things that Elisha h' done.
9 king of Syria h' sent me to thee,
10 the Lord h' shewed me that he shall
13 The Lord h' shewed me that thou shalt
10: 10 for the Lord h' done that which he
14: 10 and thine heart h' lifted thee up:
17: 26 therefore he h' sent lions among
18: 22 and whose altars Hezekiah h' taken
22 and h' said to Judah and Jerusalem,
27 H' my master sent me to thy master,
27 h' he not sent me to the men which
33 H' any of the gods of the nations
19: 4 king of Assyria his master h' sent to
4 which the Lord thy God h' heard:
16 which h' sent him to reproach the
21 the word that the Lord h' spoken
21 the daughter of Zion h' despised thee,
21 the daughter of Jerusalem h' shaken
20: 9 will do the thing that he h' spoken:
21: 11 Manasseh king of Judah h' done these
11 abominations, and h' done wickedly
11 and h' made Judah also to sin
22: 10 Hilkiah the priest h' delivered
16 book which the king of Judah h' read:
1Ch 14: 11 God h' broken in upon mine enemies
15: 2 for them h' the Lord chosen to carry
16: 12 his marvellous works that he h' done,
17 And h' confirmed the same to Jacob *
17: 25 therefore thy servant h' found in his
19: 3 that he h' sent comforters unto thee?
22: 11 house of the Lord thy God, as he h' said
18 and h' he not given you rest on every
18 for he h' given the inhabitants of the
23: 25 The Lord God of Israel h' given rest
28: 4 for he h' chosen Judah to be the ruler;
5 for the Lord h' given me many sons,
5 he h' chosen Solomon my son to sit
10 for the Lord h' chosen thee to build an
29: 1 whom alone God h' chosen, is yet
2Ch 2: 11 Because the Lord h' loved his people,*
11 he h' made thee king over them.
12 who h' given to David the king a wise
15 which my lord h' spoken of, let him
6: 1 The Lord h' said that he would dwell
4 who h' with his hands fulfilled that
10 The Lord therefore h' performed his
10 that he h' spoken: for I am risen *
7: 21 Why h' the Lord done thus unto this
22 therefore h' he brought all this evil
8: 11 the ark of the Lord h' come.
13: 6 is risen up, and h' rebelled against*
14: 7 we have sought him, and he h' given
15: 3 long season Israel h' been without
18: 22 the Lord h' put a lying spirit in the
22 and the Lord h' spoken evil against
27 in peace, then h' not the Lord spoken
20: 37 the Lord h' broken thy works.
23: 3 as the Lord h' said of the sons of
24: 20 forsaken the Lord, he h' also forsaken
25: 8 for God h' power to help, and to 3426
16 I know that God h' determined to
28: 9 he h' delivered them into your hand,
29: 8 and he h' delivered them to trouble,
11 for the Lord h' chosen you to stand
30: 8 his sanctuary, which he h' sanctified
31: 10 for the Lord h' blessed his people;
32: 12 H' not the same Hezekiah taken
34: 18 Hilkiah the priest h' given me a book.
36: 23 kingdoms of the earth h' the Lord
23 heaven given me; and he h' charged
Ezr 1: 2 The Lord God of heaven h' given me
2 and he h' charged me to build him
4: 3 the king of Persia h' commanded us.
18 ye sent unto us h' been plainly read
19 commanded, and search h' been made,
19 this city of old time h' made
5: 3 Who h' commanded you to build this*
16 even until now h' it been in building
6: 12 the God that h' caused his name to
7: 27 which h' put such a thing as this in

Ezr 7:28 And h' extended mercy unto me
9: 2 princes and rulers h' been chief
8 little space grace h' been shewed
9 yet our God h' not forsaken us in our
9 but h' extended mercy unto us in the
Es 1:15 because she h' not performed the
16 Vashti the queen h' not done wrong
5: 5 that he may do as Esther h' said.
8 will do to morrow as the king h' said.
6: 3 What honour and dignity h' been done
Job 1:10 about all that he h' on every side?
11 touch all that he h', and he will curse
12 all that he h' is in thy power; only
16 and h' burned up the sheep, and the
21 the Lord gave, and the Lord h' taken
2: 4 all that a man h' will he give for his
3:23 and whom God h' hedged in?
5:16 So the poor h' hope, and iniquity 1961
6: 5 the wild ass bray when he h' grass?
7: 8 The eye of him that h' seen me shall *
9: 4 who h' hardened himself against him,
4 against him and h' prospered? *
10:12 and thy visitation h' preserved my
12: 9 the hand of the Lord h' wrought this?
13 and strength, he h' counsel and
13: 1 Lo, mine eye h' seen all this,
1 mine ear h' heard and understood it.
16: 7 But now he h' made me weary:
12 I was at ease, but he h' broken me *
12 he h' also taken me by my neck,
17: 6 He h' made me also a byword of the
9 and he that h' clean hands shall
19: 6 Know now that God h' overthrown
6 and h' compassed me with his net.
8 He h' fenced up my way that I cannot
8 pass, and he h' set darkness in my
9 He h' stripped me of my glory,
10 He h' destroyed me on every side,
10 and mine hope h' he removed like a
11 He h' also kindled his wrath against
13 He h' put my brethren far from me,
21 for the hand of the Lord h' touched
20:15 He h' swallowed down riches, and
19 Because he h' oppressed and
19 oppressed and h' forsaken the poor; *
19 he h' violently taken away an house,
21:21 For what pleasure h' he in his house
31 shall repay him what he h' done?
23:10 when he h' tried me, I shall come
11 My foot h' held his steps, his way
17 neither h' he covered the darkness *
26: 2 the arm that h' no strength?
3 counselled him that h' no wisdom?
6 and destruction h' no covering.
10 He h' compassed the waters with
13 By his spirit he h' garnished the *
13 his hand h' formed the crooked
27: 2 As God liveth, who h' taken away my
2 the Almighty, who h' vexed my soul;
8 the hypocrite, though he h' gained, *
28: 6 of sapphires: and it h' dust of gold.
7 which the vulture's eye h' not seen:
30:11 Because he h' loosed my cord, and
19 He h' cast me into the mire, and I
31: 5 or my foot h' hasted to deceit;
7 If my step h' turned out of the way,
7 and if any blot h' cleaved to mine
17 the fatherless h' not eaten thereof;
27 my heart h' been secretly enticed,
27 or my mouth h' kissed my hand:
32:14 Now he h' not directed his words
19 my belly is as wine which h' no vent;
33: 2 my tongue h' spoken in my mouth.
4 The Spirit of God h' made me,
4 breath of the Almighty h' given me *
34: 5 For Job h' said, I am righteous:
5 and God h' taken away my judgment.
9 For he h' said, It profiteth a man
13 Who h' given him a charge over the *
13 or who h' disposed the whole world? *
35 Job h' spoken without knowledge, *
35:15 it is not so, he h' visited in his anger;
36:23 Who h' enjoined him his way?
38: 5 Who h' laid the measures thereof, *
5 or who h' stretched the line upon it? *
25 Who h' divided a watercourse for the
28 H' the rain a father? or who 3426
28 h' begotten the drops of dew?
29 hoary frost of heaven, who h' gendered
36 Who h' put wisdom in the inward
36 or who h' given understanding to the
39: 5 Who h' sent out the wild ass free?
5 or who h' loosed the bands of the
17 Because God h' deprived her of
17 neither h' he imparted to her
41:11 Who h' prevented me, that I should
42: 7 that is right as my servant Job h'.
Ps 2: 7 the Lord h' said unto me, Thou art *
4: 3 know that the Lord h' set apart him
5: 4 thou art not a God that h' pleasure in
6: 8 for the Lord h' heard the voice of my
9 The Lord h' heard my supplication;
7:12 he h' bent his bow, and made it ready.
13 He h' also prepared for him the
14 iniquity, and h' conceived mischief,
9: 7 he h' prepared his throne for
10: 6 He h' said in his heart, I shall not *
11 He h' said in his heart, God *
11 said in his heart, God h' forgotten:
13 he h' said in his heart, Thou wilt *
13: 6 because he h' dealt bountifully with
14: 1 The fool h' said in his heart, There is
16: 7 bless the Lord, who h' given me
18:20 of my hands h' he recompensed me.
24 Therefore h' the Lord recompensed
35 and thy right hand h' holden me

Ps 18:35 and thy gentleness h' made me great.
19: 4 In them h' he set a tabernacle for the
22:24 For he h' not despised nor abhorred
24 neither h' he hid his face from him;
31 shall be born, that he h' done this.
24: 2 For he h' founded it upon the seas,
4 He that h' clean hands, and a pure
4 who h' not lifted up his soul unto
28: 6 because he h' heard the voice
31:21 for he h' shewed me his marvellous
33:12 and the people whom he h' chosen
35: 8 let his net that he h' hid catch
21 Aha, aha, our eye h' seen it.
27 which h' pleasure in the prosperity
36: 3 he h' left off to be wise, and to do
37:16 little that a righteous man h' is better
40: 3 And he h' put a new song in my
41: 9 which did eat of my bread, h' lifted up
44:15 and the shame of my face h' covered
45: 2 therefore God h' blessed thee for ever.
7 thy God, h' anointed thee with the oil
46: 8 what desolations he h' made in the
50: 1 even the Lord, h' spoken, and called
2 perfection of beauty, God h' shined.
53: 1 The fool h' said in his heart, There is
5 for God h' scattered the bones of
5 because God h' despised them.
54: 7 For he h' delivered me out of all my
7 and mine eye h' seen his desire upon
55: 5 and horror h' overwhelmed me.
18 He h' delivered my soul in peace
20 He h' put forth his hands against
20 with him: he h' broken his covenant.
60: 6 God h' spoken in his holiness;
62:11 God h' spoken once; twice have I
66:14 have uttered, and my mouth h' spoken,
16 I will declare what he h' done for my
19 But verily God h' heard me;
19 he h' attended to the voice of my
20 Blessed be God, which h' not turned
68:10 Thy congregation h' dwelt therein: *
28 Thy God h' commanded thy strength:
69: 7 borne reproach; shame h' covered my
9 zeal of thine house h' eaten me up;
20 Reproach h' broken my heart; and I
31 an ox or bullock that h' horns and
71:11 saying, God h' forsaken him:
72:12 poor also, and him that h' no helper.
74: 3 all that the enemy h' done wickedly
18 that the enemy h' reproached, O Lord,
77: 9 H' God forgotten to be gracious?
9 h' he in anger shut up his tender
78: 4 his wonderful works that he h' done.
69 like the earth which he h' established
80:15 which thy right hand h' planted,
84: 3 Yea, the sparrow h' found an house,
88: 4 I am as a man that h' no strength:
91:14 Because he h' set his love upon me,
93: 1 wherewith he h' girded himself: the
98: 1 for he h' done marvellous things: his
1 his holy arm, h' gotten him the victory.
2 The Lord h' made known his
2 his righteousness h' he openly shewed
3 He h' remembered his mercy and his
100: 3 it is he that h' made us, and not we
101: 5 him that h' an high look and a proud
102:19 For he h' looked down from the
103:10 He h' not dealt with us after our sins;
12 far h' he removed our transgressions
19 The Lord h' prepared his throne in
104:16 of Lebanon, which he h' planted;
105: 5 his marvellous works that he h' done;
8 He h' remembered his covenant
107: 2 whom he h' redeemed from the hand
16 For he h' broken the gates of brass,
108: 7 God h' spoken in his holiness;
109:11 Let the extortioner catch all that he h';
110: 4 The Lord h' sworn, and will not
111: 4 He h' made his wonderful works to be
5 He h' given meat unto them that fear
6 He h' shewed his people the power
9 he h' commanded his covenant
112: 9 He h' dispersed, he h' given to the
115: 3 God is in the heavens: he h' done
3 done whatsoever he h' pleased. *–
12 The Lord h' been mindful of us:
16 but the earth h' he given to the
116: 1 I love the Lord, because he h' heard ‡
2 Because he h' inclined his ear unto
7 for the Lord h' dealt bountifully with
118:18 The Lord h' chastened me sore:
18 but he h' not given me over unto
24 is the day which the Lord h' made;
27 God is the Lord, which h' shewed us
119:20 the longing that it h' unto thy
50 for thy word h' quickened me.
53 Horror h' taken hold upon me because
139 My zeal h' consumed me, because
167 My soul h' kept thy testimonies;
120: 6 My soul h' long dwelt with him that
124: 6 who h' not given us as a prey to their
126: 2 Lord h' done great things for them.
3 The Lord h' done great things for us;
127: 5 Happy is the man that h' his quiver
129: 4 he h' cut asunder the cords of the
132:11 The Lord h' sworn in truth unto
135: 4 For the Lord h' chosen Jacob unto
136:24 And h' redeemed us from our
138: 6 Lord be high, yet h' he respect unto
143: 3 For the enemy h' persecuted my soul;
3 he h' smitten my life down to the
3 he h' made me to dwell in darkness,
146: 5 Happy is he that h' the God of Jacob
147:13 For he h' strengthened the bars of thy
13 he h' blessed thy children within thee.
20 He h' not dealt so with any nation:

Ps 148: 6 He h' also stablished them for ever
6 he h' made a decree which shall not
150: 6 Let every thing that h' breath praise
Pr 3:19 The Lord by wisdom h' founded the *
19 by understanding h' he established *
7:20 He h' taken a bag of money with him,
26 For she h' cast down many wounded:
9: 1 Wisdom h' builded her house,
1 she h' hewn out her seven pillars:
2 She h' killed her beasts;
2 she h' mingled her wine;
2 she h' also furnished her table.
3 She h' sent forth her maidens:
10:13 the lips of him that h' understanding
23 a man of understanding h' wisdom. *
12: 9 He that is despised, and h' a servant,
13: 4 the sluggard desireth, and h' nothing:
7 maketh himself rich, yet h' nothing:
7 himself poor, yet h' great riches.
14:20 but the rich h' many friends.
21 but he that h' mercy on the poor,
31 but he that honoureth him h' mercy on
32 but the righteous h' hope in his death.
33 heart of him that h' understanding:
15:14 the heart of him that h' understanding
15 a merry heart h' a continual feast.
23 A man h' joy by the answer of his
16: 4 The Lord h' made all things for
22 of life unto him that h' it. 1167
17: 8 stone in the eyes of him that h' it: "
16 seeing he h' no heart to it?
20 He that h' a froward heart findeth no
20 and he that h' a perverse tongue
21 and the father of a fool h' no joy.
24 is before him that h' understanding;
27 He that h' knowledge spareth his
18: 2 A fool h' no delight in understanding,
24 A man that h' friends must shew *
19:17 He that h' pity upon the poor lendeth
17 that which he h' given will he pay *
23 and he that h' it shall abide satisfied;
25 reprove one that h' understanding,
20:12 the Lord h' made even both of them.
22: 9 He that h' a bountiful eye shall be
23: 6 the bread of him that h' an evil eye,
29 Who h' woe? who h' sorrow?
29 who h' contentions? who h' babbling?
29 who h' wounds without cause?
29 who h' redness of eyes?
24:29 I will do so to him as he h' done to me:
25: 8 thy neighbour h' put thee to shame.
28 He that h' no rule over his own *
28:11 but the poor that h' understanding
22 He that hasteth to be rich h' an evil
30: 4 Who h' ascended up into heaven, or
15 The horseleach h' two daughters,
Ec 1: 3 What profit h' a man of all his labour
9 The thing that h' been, it is that which
10 it h' been already of old time,
13 this sore travail h' God given to the
2:12 even that which h' been already done.
21 yet to a man that h' not laboured
22 For what h' man of all his labour, 1933
22 he h' laboured under the sun? *
3: 9 What profit h' he that worketh in that
10 the travail, which God h' given to the
11 He h' made every thing beautiful in
11 also he h' set the world in their heart,
15 That which h' been is now; and
15 that which is to be h' already been;
19 so that a man h' no preeminence
4: 3 both they, which h' not yet been,
3 who h' not seen the evil work that
8 yea, he h' neither child nor brother:
10 for he h' not another to help him up.
5:16 so shall he go: and what profit h' he
16 he that h' laboured for the wind? *
17 and he h' much sorrow and wrath
19 to whom God h' given riches and
19 and h' given him power to eat thereof,
6: 2 A man to whom God h' given riches, *
5 Moreover he h' not seen the sun,
5 this h' more rest than the other.
6 years twice told, yet h' he seen no *
8 For what h' the wise more than the
8 what h' the poor, that knoweth to
10 That which h' been is named
7:13 straight, which he h' made crooked?
14 God also h' set the one over against
29 found, that God h' made man upright; *
8: 8 There is no man that h' power over the
8 neither h' he power in the day of
15 because a man h' no better thing
9: 9 which he h' given thee under the sun,
10:20 and that which h' wings shall tell 1167
Ca 1: 4 the king h' brought me into his
6 because the sun h' looked upon me:
3: 8 every man h' his sword upon his
8: 6 which h' a most vehement flame. *
8 little sister, and she h' no breasts:
Isa 1: 2 O earth: for the Lord h' spoken, I
12 who h' required this at your hand,
20 for the mouth of the Lord h' spoken it.
30 and as a garden that h' no water.
5: 1 My wellbeloved h' a vineyard in a *
14 Therefore hell h' enlarged herself,
25 and he h' stretched forth his hand
25 them, and h' smitten them:
6: 7 and said, Lo, this h' touched thy lips;
8:18 children whom the Lord h' given me
9: 2 death, upon them h' the light shined.
8 word into Jacob, and it h' lighted upon
10:10 As my hand h' found the kingdoms of
12 when the Lord h' performed his whole
14 And my hand h' found as a nest the
28 at Michmash he h' laid up his *

Isa 12: 5 the Lord; for he h' done excellent
14: 5 The Lord h' broken the staff of the
9 it h' raised up from their thrones all
24 The Lord of hosts h' sworn, saying,
27 For the Lord of hosts h' purposed, and
32 That the Lord h' founded Zion,
16: 13 the word that the Lord h' spoken *
14 But now the Lord h' spoken, saying,
19: 12 what the Lord of hosts h' purposed
14 The Lord h' mingled a perverse spirit
17 which he h' determined against it.*
20: 3 Like as my servant Isaiah h' walked
21: 4 the night of my pleasure h' he turned
6 For thus h' the Lord said unto me, Go,
9 images of her gods he h' broken unto*
16 For thus h' the Lord said unto me,
17 for the Lord God of Israel h' spoken it.
22: 25 shall be cut off: for the Lord h' spoken
23: 4 O Zidon: for the sea h' spoken,
8 Who h' taken this counsel against
9 The Lord of hosts h' purposed it, to
11 the Lord h' given a commandment
24: 3 for the Lord h' spoken this word.
6 Therefore h' the curse devoured the
25: 8 all the earth: for the Lord h' spoken it.
27: 7 H' he smitten him, as he smote those
28: 2 the Lord h' a mighty and strong one,
25 When he h' made plain the face
29: 4 as of one that h' a familiar spirit,
8 he is faint, and his soul h' appetite:
10 For the Lord h' poured out upon you
10 of deep sleep, and h' closed your eyes:
10 your rulers, the seers h' he covered.
30: 24 which h' been winnowed with the
33 it is prepared; he h' made it deep and
31: 4 For thus h' the Lord spoken unto me,*
33: 5 he h' filled Zion with judgment and
8 he h' broken the covenant,
8 he h' despised the cities, he regardeth
14 fearfulness h' surprised the
34: 2 he h' utterly destroyed them,
2 he h' delivered them to the slaughter.
6 for the Lord h' a sacrifice in Bozrah,
16 for my mouth it h' commanded, and
16 his spirit it h' gathered them.
17 And he h' cast the lot for them, and
17 his hand h' divided it unto them by
36: 7 whose altars Hezekiah h' taken away,
12 said, H' my master sent me to thy
12 h' he not sent me to the men that sit
18 H' any of the gods of the nations
37: 4 his master h' sent to reproach the
4 which the Lord thy God h' heard:
17 which h' sent to reproach the living
22 the word which the Lord h' spoken
22 the daughter of Zion, h' despised thee,
22 the daughter of Jerusalem h' shaken
38: 7 will do this thing that he h' spoken;
15 he h' both spoken unto me,
15 and himself h' done it: I shall go
40: 2 for she h' received of the Lord's hand
5 for the mouth of the Lord h' spoken
12 Who h' measured the waters in the
13 Who h' directed the Spirit of the Lord,
13 or being his counsellor h' taught him?
20 impoverished that he h' no oblation *
21 h' it not been told you from the
26 and behold who h' created these
41: 4 Who h' wrought and done it, calling
20 the hand of the Lord h' done this, and
20 the Holy One of Israel h' created it.
26 Who h' declared from the beginning,
42: 25 Therefore he h' poured upon him the *
25 and it h' set him on fire round about, *
43: 27 Thy first father h' sinned, and thy *
44: 10 who h' formed a god, or molten a
18 for he h' shut their eyes, that they
20 a deceived heart h' turned him aside,
23 O ye heavens; for the Lord h' done it:
23 for the Lord h' redeemed Jacob, and
45: 9 or thy work, He h' no hands?
18 he h' established it, he created it not *
21 counsel together: who h' declared this
21 from ancient time? who h' told it
47: 10 thy knowledge, it h' perverted thee;
48: 5 Mine idol h' done them, and my
5 molten image, h' commanded
13 Mine hand also h' laid the foundation
13 and my right hand h' spanned the
14 which among them h' declared these
14 The Lord h' loved him: he will do
16 the Lord God, and his Spirit, h' sent
20 The Lord h' redeemed his servant
49: 1 The Lord h' called me from the womb;
1 of my mother h' he made mention of
2 And he h' made my mouth like a sharp
2 in the shadow of his hand h' he hid
2 in his quiver h' he hid me;
10 for he that h' mercy on them shall
13 for the Lord h' comforted his people,
14 But Zion said, The Lord h' forsaken
14 and my Lord h' forgotten me.
21 Who h' begotten me these, seeing I
21 and who h' brought up these?
50: 4 The Lord God h' given me the tongue
5 The Lord God h' opened mine ear,
10 walketh in darkness, and h' no light?
51: 9 Art thou not it that h' cut Rahab, *
10 Art thou not it which h' dried the sea,*
10 that h' made the depths of the sea*
13 that h' stretched forth the heavens,*
18 all the sons whom she h' brought forth;
18 of all the sons that she h' brought up.
52: 9 for the Lord h' comforted his people,
9 he h' redeemed Jerusalem.
10 The Lord h' made bare his holy arm

Isa 53: 1 Who h' believed our report?
2 he h' no form nor comeliness;
4 Surely he h' borne our griefs, and
6 and the Lord h' laid on him the
10 bruise him; he h' put him to grief:
12 because he h' poured out his soul *
54: 6 For the Lord h' called thee as a
10 saith the Lord that h' mercy on thee.
55: 1 the waters, and he that h' no money;
5 Holy One of Israel; for he h' glorified
56: 3 stranger, that h' joined himself to
3 The Lord h' utterly separated me *
58: 14 for the mouth of the Lord h' spoken it.
59: 3 your tongue h' muttered perverseness.*
60: 9 because he h' glorified thee.
61: 1 because the Lord h' anointed me to
1 he h' sent me to bind up the
9 the seed which the Lord h' blessed.
10 for he h' clothed me with the garments
10 he h' covered me with the robe of
62: 8 The Lord h' sworn by his right hand,
11 Behold, the Lord h' proclaimed unto
63: 7 to all that the Lord h' bestowed on us,
7 which he h' bestowed on them
64: 4 by the ear, neither h' the eye seen,
4 beside thee, what he h' prepared for *
65: 20 nor an old man that h' not filled his
66: 2 all those things h' mine hand made,
8 Who h' heard such a thing?
8 who h' seen such things?
Jer 2: 11 H' a nation changed their gods,
30 your own sword h' devoured your
37 the Lord h' rejected thy confidences,
3: 3 and there h' been no latter rain;
6 which backsliding Israel h' done?
6 and there h' played the harlot.
10 Judah h' not turned unto me with
11 backsliding Israel h' justified herself
24 For shame h' devoured the labour of
4: 17 because she h' been rebellious against
27 For thus h' the Lord said, The whole *
5: 23 But this people h' a revolting and a
6: 6 For thus h' the Lord of hosts said,
24 anguish h' taken hold of us, and pain,
30 because the Lord h' rejected them.
7: 29 for the Lord h' rejected and forsaken
8: 14 the Lord our God h' put us to silence,
21 astonishment h' taken hold on me.
9: 12 whom the mouth of the Lord h' spoken,
10: 12 He h' made the earth by his power,
12 he h' established the world by his
12 and h' stretched out the heavens by
11: 15 What h' my beloved to do in mine
15 seeing she h' wrought lewdness
16 of a great tumult he h' kindled fire
17 that planted thee, h' pronounced evil
18 And the Lord h' given me knowledge*
13: 15 not proud: for the Lord h' spoken.
14: 19 Judah? h' thy soul lothed Zion?
15: 9 She that h' borne seven languisheth:
9 she h' given up the ghost;
9 she h' been ashamed and confounded:
16: 10 Wherefore h' the Lord pronounced all
18: 13 heathen, who h' heard such things:
13 of Israel h' done a very horrible thing.
15 Because my people h' forgotten me,
20: 3 The Lord h' not called thy name
13 for he h' delivered the soul of the poor
22: 8 Wherefore h' the Lord done thus unto
21 This h' been thy manner from thy
23: 9 like a man whom wine h' overcome,
17 The Lord h' said, Ye shall have peace;
18 For who h' stood in the counsel of the
18 and h' perceived and heard his word?*
18 who h' marked his word, and heard it?
28 The prophet that h' a dream, let him
28 a dream; and he that h' my word, let
35 What h' the Lord answered?
35 and, What h' the Lord spoken?
37 What h' the Lord answered thee?
37 and, What h' the Lord spoken?
25: 3 the word of the Lord h' come unto me,
4 And the Lord h' sent unto you all
5 in the land that the Lord h' given
13 Jeremiah h' prophesied against all
31 for the Lord h' a controversy with the
36 for the Lord h' spoiled their pasture.*
38 He h' forsaken his covert, as the lion:
26: 11 for he h' prophesied against this city,
13 him of the evil that he h' pronounced
15 for of a truth the Lord h' sent me
16 for he h' spoken to us in the name of
27: 13 as the Lord h' spoken against the
28: 9 that the Lord h' truly sent him.
15 The Lord h' not sent thee; but thou
29: 15 The Lord h' raised us up prophets in
26 The Lord h' made thee priest in the
31 Because that Shemaiah h' prophesied
32 because he h' taught rebellion
31: 3 The Lord h' appeared of old unto me,*
11 For the Lord h' redeemed Jacob,
22 for the Lord h' created a new thing in
32: 31 For this city h' been to me as a
33: 24 families which the Lord h' chosen, *
24 he h' even cast them off?
34: 14 an Hebrew, which h' been sold unto
14 and when he h' served thee six years,
35: 8 our father in all that he h' charged us,*
16 but this people h' not hearkened unto
18 unto all that he h' commanded you: *
36: 7 the Lord h' pronounced against this
28 Jehoiakim the king of Judah h' burned.
38: 21 the word that the Lord h' shewed me:
40: 2 The Lord thy God h' pronounced this*
3 Now the Lord h' brought it, and done
3 done according as he h' said: *

Jer 40: 5 the king of Babylon h' made governor
14 king of the Ammonites h' sent Ishmael
42: 18 anger and my fury h' been poured
19 The Lord h' said concerning you,
21 for the which he h' sent me unto you.
43: 2 the Lord our God h' not sent thee to
45: 3 for the Lord h' added grief to my
46: 10 God of hosts h' a sacrifice in the north
12 and thy cry h' filled the land: *
12 for the mighty man h' stumbled
17 he h' passed the time appointed.
47: 7 seeing the Lord h' given it a charge
7 the sea shore? there h' he appointed
48: 8 be destroyed, as the Lord h' spoken.
11 Moab h' been at ease from his youth,
36 because the riches that he h' gotten
39 how h' Moab turned the back with
42 because he h' magnified himself
49: 1 H' Israel no sons? h' he no heir?
16 Thy terribleness h' deceived thee,
20 that he h' taken against Edom;
20 and his purposes, that he h' purposed
24 to flee, and fear h' seized on her:
30 king of Babylon h' taken counsel
30 you, and h' conceived a purpose
50: 6 My people h' been lost sheep:
14 for she h' sinned against the Lord.
15 she h' given her hand: her foundations
15 as she h' done, do unto her.
17 king of Assyria h' devoured him;
17 king of Babylon h' broken his bones.
25 The Lord h' opened his armoury,
25 and h' brought forth the weapons
29 according to all that she h' done, do
29 she h' been proud against the Lord,
43 The king of Babylon h' heard the
45 the Lord, that he h' taken against
45 and his purposes, that he h' purposed
51: 5 For Israel h' not been forsaken, *
7 Babylon h' been a golden cup in the
10 The Lord h' brought forth our
11 the Lord h' raised up the spirit of the
12 for the Lord h' both devised and done
14 The Lord of hosts h' sworn by himself,
15 He h' made the earth by his power,
15 he h' established the world by his
15 and h' stretched out the heaven by his
30 their might h' failed; they became as
34 the king of Babylon h' devoured me,
34 he h' crushed me,
34 he h' made me an empty vessel,
34 he h' swallowed me up like a dragon,
34 he h' filled his belly with my delicates,
34 he h' cast me out.
44 that which he h' swallowed up:
49 As Babylon h' caused the slain of
51 shame h' covered our faces:
55 Because the Lord h' spoiled Babylon,*
La 1: 2 among all her lovers she h' none to
8 Jerusalem h' grievously sinned;
9 for the enemy h' magnified himself.
10 The adversary h' spread out his hand
10 she h' seen that the heathen entered
12 the Lord h' afflicted me in the day
13 From above h' he sent fire into my
13 he h' spread a net for my feet,
13 he h' turned me back:
13 he h' made me desolate and faint all
14 he h' made my strength to fall,
15 The Lord h' trodden under foot all my
15 he h' called an assembly against me
15 the Lord h' trodden the virgin, the
17 Lord h' commanded concerning Jacob,
2: 1 How h' the Lord covered the daughter
2 The Lord h' swallowed up all the
2 of Jacob, and h' not pitied:
2 he h' thrown down in his wrath the
2 h' brought them down to the ground:
2 he h' polluted the kingdom and
3 He h' cut off in his fierce anger all the
3 he h' drawn back his right hand
4 He h' bent his bow like an enemy:
5 an enemy: he h' swallowed up Israel,
5 he h' swallowed up all her palaces:
5 he h' destroyed his strong holds,
5 and h' increased in the daughter of
6 and he h' violently taken away his
6 he h' destroyed his places of the
6 the Lord h' caused the solemn feasts
6 and h' despised in the indignation of
7 The Lord h' cast off his altar,
7 he h' abhorred his sanctuary,
7 he h' given up into the hand of the
8 The Lord h' purposed to destroy the
8 he h' stretched out a line,
8 he h' not withdrawn his hand from
9 he h' destroyed and broken her bars:
17 The Lord h' done that which he had
17 he h' fulfilled his word that he had
17 he h' thrown down, and h' not pitied:
17 and he h' caused thine enemy to
17 he h' set up the horn of thine
22 up h' mine enemy consumed.
3: 1 I am the man that h' seen affliction by
2 He h' led me, and brought me into
4 My flesh and my skin h' he made old;
4 he h' broken my bones.
5 He h' builded against me, and
6 He h' set me in dark places,
7 He h' hedged me about, that I cannot
7 he h' made my chain heavy.
9 He h' inclosed my ways with hewn
9 he h' made my paths crooked.
11 He h' turned aside my ways,
11 he h' made me desolate.
12 He h' bent his bow, and set me as

La 3:13 He h' caused the arrows of his quiver
15 He h' filled me with bitterness,
15 he h' made me drunken with
16 He h' also broken my teeth with gravel
16 he h' covered me with ashes.
20 My soul h' them still in remembrance,
28 because he h' borne it upon him.
4:11 The Lord h' accomplished his fury;
11 he h' poured out his fierce anger,
11 and h' kindled a fire in Zion,
11 and it h' devoured the foundations
16 The anger of the Lord h' divided them;
Eze 2: 3 to a rebellious nation that h' rebelled*
5 that there h' been a prophet
3:20 his righteousness which he h' done
4:14 behold, my soul h' not been polluted:
5: 6 And she h' changed my judgments
6: 9 whorish heart, which h' departed
7:10 the rod h' blossomed, pride h' budded.
8:12 not; the Lord h' forsaken the earth.
9: 9 The Lord h' forsaken the earth, and
12: 9 h' not the house of Israel...said
13: 6 and the Lord h' not sent them:
14: 9 be deceived when he h' spoken a*
15: 5 when the fire h' devoured it, and it is
16:48 Sodom thy sister h' not done, she nor
51 Neither h' Samaria committed half
17:12 come to Jerusalem, and h' taken the
13 And h' taken of the king's seed, *
13 and h' taken an oath of him: *
13 he h' also taken the mighty of the *
18 given his hand, and h' done all these
19 surely mine oath that he h' despised,
19 and my covenant that he h' broken,
20 his trespass that he h' trespassed
6 And h' not eaten upon the mountains,
6 neither h' lifted up his eyes to the idols
6 neither h' defiled his neighbour's wife
6 neither h' come near to a menstruous
7 And h' not oppressed any,
7 but h' restored to the debtor his
7 h' spoiled none by violence,
7 h' given his bread to the hungry,
7 and h' covered the naked with a
8 He that h' not given forth upon usury,
8 neither h' taken any increase,
8 that h' withdrawn his hand from
8 h' executed true judgment between
9 H' walked in my statutes,
9 and h' kept my judgments, to deal
11 but even h' eaten upon the mountains,
12 H' oppressed the poor and needy,
12 h' spoiled by violence,
12 h' not restored the pledge, and
12 h' not lifted up his eyes to the idols
12 h' committed abomination,
13 H' given forth upon usury,
13 and h' taken increase:
13 he h' done all these abominations;
14 all his father's sins which he h' done,
15 That h' not eaten upon the mountains,
15 neither h' lifted up his eyes to the idols
15 h' not defiled his neighbour's wife,
16 Neither h' oppressed any,
16 h' not withholden the pledge,
16 neither h' spoiled by violence,
16 but h' given his bread to the hungry,
16 h' covered the naked with a garment,
17 That h' taken off his hand from the
17 that h' not received usury nor increase,
17 h' executed my judgments,
17 h' walked in my statutes;
19 When the son h' done that which is
19 and right, and h' kept all my statutes,
19 and h' done them, he shall surely live.
21 from all his sins that he h' committed,
22 transgressions that he h' committed,
22 in his righteousness that he h' done
24 righteousness that he h' done shall not
24 in his trespass that he h' trespassed,
24 and in his sin that he h' sinned,
26 for his iniquity that he h' done shall
27 his wickedness that he h' committed,
28 transgressions that he h' committed,
19:14 her branches, which h' devoured her
14 so that she h' no strong rod to be a*
21:11 And he h' given it to be furbished,*
22:11 And one h' committed abomination
11 and another h' lewdly defiled his
11 and another in thee h' humbled his
13 thy blood which h' been in the midst
28 God, when the Lord h' not spoken.
24:12 She h' wearied herself with lies,
24 according to all that he h' done shall
25:12 Because that Edom h' dealt against
12 and h' greatly offended, and revenged
26: 2 because that Tyrus h' said against
27:26 east wind h' broken thee in the midst
29: 3 which h' said, My river is mine own,
9 because he h' said, The river is mine,
31:10 and he h' shot up his top among the
33:13 for his iniquity that he h' committed,
16 sins that he h' committed shall be
16 he h' done that which is lawful and
32 song of one that h' a pleasant voice,
33 a prophet h' been among them
36: 2 Because the enemy h' said against
44: 2 the God of Israel, h' entered in by it,
25 or for sister that h' had no husband,
Da 1:10 who h' appointed your meat and your
2:27 secret which the king h' demanded
37 for the God of heaven h' given thee a
38 fowls of the heaven h' he given into
38 hand, and h' made thee ruler over
45 the great God h' made known to the
5 Nebuchadnezzar the king h' set up;

Da 3:28 who h' sent his angel, and delivered
4: 2 that the high God h' wrought toward
5:26 God h' numbered thy kingdom, and
6:22 My God h' sent his angel, and
22 h' shut the lions' mouths,
27 who h' delivered Daniel from the
9:12 And he h' confirmed his words, which
12 the whole heaven h' not been done
12 as h' been done upon Jerusalem.
14 Therefore h' the Lord watched upon
11:12 And when he h' taken away the *
Ho 1: 2 for the land h' committed great *
2: 5 For their mother h' played the harlot:
5 conceived them h' done shamefully:
12 whereof she h' said, These are my
4: 1 for the Lord h' a controversy with the
12 for the spirit of whoredoms h' caused
19 The wind h' bound her up in her
5: 6 he h' withdrawn himself from them.
6: 1 for he h' torn, and he will heal us;
1 he h' smitten, and he will bind us up.
11 Also, O Judah, he h' sent an harvest*
7: 4 after he h' kneaded the dough, until*
8 Ephraim, he h' mixed himself among*
12 them, as their congregation h' heard.
8: 3 Israel h' cast off the thing that is good:
5 Thy calf, O Samaria, h' cast thee off;
7 it h' no stalk: the bud shall yield no
9 alone by himself: Ephraim h' hired
11 Because Ephraim h' made many altars
14 For Israel h' forgotten his Maker,
14 and Judah h' multiplied fenced cities:
10: 1 multitude of his fruit he h' increased
12: 2 The Lord h' also a controversy with
13:16 for she h' rebelled against her God:
Joe 1: 2 H' this been in your days, or
4 That which the palmerworm h' left
4 h' the locust eaten; and that
4 and that which the locust h' left
4 left h' the cankerworm eaten;
4 and that which the cankerworm h' left
4 left h' the caterpiller eaten.
6 and he h' the cheek teeth of a great
7 He h' laid my vine waste, and barked
7 he h' made it clean bare, and cast it
19 for the fire h' devoured the pastures
19 and the flame h' burned all the trees
20 and the fire h' devoured the pastures
2: 2 there h' not been ever the like,
20 because he h' done great things.
23 for he h' given you the former rain*
25 you the years that the locust h' eaten,
26 that h' dealt wondrously with you:
32 as the Lord h' said, and in the
3: 8 people far off: for the Lord h' spoken
Am 3: 1 word that the Lord h' spoken against
4 when he h' no prey? will a young lion
6 evil in a city, and the Lord h' not done
8 The lion h' roared, who will not fear?
8 the Lord God h' spoken, who can but
4: 2 The Lord God h' sworn by his holiness,
6: 8 The Lord God h' sworn by himself,
7:1,4 Thus h' the Lord God shewed unto*
10 Amos h' conspired against thee in
8: 1 Thus h' the Lord God shewed unto*
7 The Lord h' sworn by the excellency
9: 6 and h' founded his troop in the
Ob 1: 3 The pride of thine heart h' deceived
18 house of Esau; for the Lord h' spoken
Jon 1: 9 which h' made the sea and the dry
Mic 2: 4 he h' changed the portion of my *
4 how h' he removed it from me! *
4 turning away he h' divided our fields.*
4: 4 mouth of the Lord of hosts h' spoken
5: 1 daughter of troops: he h' laid siege
3 which travaileth h' brought forth:
6: 2 for the Lord h' a controversy with his
8 He h' shewed thee, O man, what is
9 ye the rod, and who h' appointed it.
Na 1: 3 the Lord h' his way in the whirlwind
14 the Lord h' given a commandment
2: 2 For the Lord h' turned away the *
3:19 whom h' not thy wickedness passed
Hab 2:18 that the maker thereof h' graven it;
Zep 1: 7 for the Lord h' prepared a sacrifice,
7 he h' bid his guests.
3:15 Lord h' taken away thy judgments,
15 he h' cast out thine enemy:
Hag 2:19 the olive tree, h' not brought forth:
Zec 1: 2 The Lord h' been sore displeased
6 according to our doings, so h' he dealt
10 they whom the Lord h' sent to walk to
2: 8 After the glory h' he sent me unto the
9 that the Lord of hosts h' sent me.
11 the Lord of hosts h' sent me unto thee.
3: 2 the Lord that h' chosen Jerusalem
4: 9 the Lord of hosts h' sent me unto you.
10 For who h' despised the day of small
6:15 the Lord of hosts h' sent me unto you.
7: 7 words which the Lord h' cried by the
12 which the Lord of hosts h' sent in his*
10: 3 the Lord of hosts h' visited his flock
3 and h' made them as his goodly horse*
13: 4 of his vision, when he h' prophesied;*
Mal 1: 4 against whom the Lord h' indignation
9 this h' been by your means: will
14 the deceiver, which h' in his flock a
2:10 all one father? h' not one God created
11 Judah h' dealt treacherously, and an
11 Judah h' profaned the holiness of the
11 and h' married the daughter of a
14 Because the Lord h' been witness
M't 3: 7 who h' warned you to flee from the*
5:23 that thy brother h' ought against 2192
28 to lust after her h' committed
31 It h' been said, Whosoever shall put*

M't 5:33 ye have heard that it h' been said by*
38, 43 Ye have heard that it h' been said,*
8:20 the Son of man h' not where to lay 2192
9: 6 the Son of man h' power on earth "
22 comfort; thy faith h' made thee whole.
11:11 born of women there h' not risen a
15 He that h' ears to hear, let him 2192
18 and they say, He h' a devil. "
13: 9 Who h' ears to hear, let him hear. "
12 For whosoever h', to him shall be "
12 but whosoever h' not, from him "
12 shall be taken away even that he h'."
21 Yet h' he not root in himself, but "
27 from whence then h' it tares? "
28 unto them, An enemy h' done this.
43 Who h' ears to hear, let him hear. 2192
44 the which when a man h' found,*
44 goeth and selleth all that he h', 2192
54 Whence h' this man this wisdom,
56 Whence then h' this man all these
16:17 for flesh and blood h' not revealed it
19: 6 What therefore God h' joined together,
29 And every one that h' forsaken houses,
20: 7 Because no man h' hired us.
21: 3 ye shall say, The Lord h' need of 2192
24:45 whom his lord h' made ruler over his
25:28 unto him which h' ten talents. 2192
29 every one that h' shall be given, "
29 from him that h' not shall be "
29 taken away even that which he h'. "
26:10 for she h' wrought a good work upon
12 For in that she h' poured this *
13 that this woman h' done, be told
65 saying, He h' spoken blasphemy;
27:23 Why, what evil h' he done?
M'r 2:10 the Son of man h' power on earth 2192
3:22 He h' Beelzebub, and by the prince "
26 he cannot stand, but h' an end. "
29 Holy Ghost h' never forgiveness, "
30 they said, He h' an unclean spirit. "
4: 9 He that h' ears to hear, let him "
25 he that h', to him shall be given: "
25 and he that h' not, from him shall "
25 be taken even that which he h'. "
5:19 great things the Lord h' done for thee,
19 and h' had compassion on thee. *
34 thy faith h' made thee whole;
6: 2 From whence h' this man these
7: 6 Well h' Esaias prophesied of you*
37 He h' done all things well: he maketh
9:17 my son, which h' a dumb spirit; 2192
22 And ofttimes it h' cast him into the
10: 9 What therefore God h' joined together.
29 There is no man that h' left house,
52 thy way; thy faith h' made thee whole.
11: 3 ye that the Lord h' need of him; 2192
12:43 That this poor widow h' cast more in,*
13:20 the elect's sake, whom he h' chosen,*
20 he h' shortened the days. *
14: 6 she h' wrought a good work on me.
8 She h' done what she could: she is
9 this also that she h' done shall be
15:14 Why, what evil h' he done?
Lu 1:25 Thus h' the Lord dealt with me
36 she h' also conceived a son in her old
47 And my spirit h' rejoiced in God my
48 For he h' regarded the low estate of
49 he that is mighty h' done to me great
51 He h' shewed strength with his arm;
51 he h' scattered the proud in the
52 He h' put down the mighty from
53 He h' filled the hungry with good
53 and the rich he h' sent empty away.
54 He h' holpen his servant Israel,
68 for he h' visited and redeemed his
69 And h' raised up an horn of salvation
78 the dayspring from on high h' visited*
2:15 the Lord h' made known unto us.
3: 7 who h' warned you to flee from the*
11 He that h' two coats, let him 2192
11 impart to him that h' none; "
11 and he that h' meat, let him do "
4:18 because he h' anointed me to preach*
18 h' sent me to heal the brokenhearted,
5:24 Son of man h' power upon earth 2192
7: 5 and he h' built us a synagogue. *
16 That God h' visited his people.
20 they said, John Baptist h' sent us unto
33 wine; and ye say, He h' a devil. 2192
44 but she h' washed my feet with tears,
45 the time I came in h' not ceased to
46 but this woman h' anointed my feet
50 Thy faith h' saved thee; go in peace.
8: 8 He that h' ears to hear, let him 2192
16 No man, when he h' lighted a candle,
18 whosoever h', to him shall be 2192
18 and whosoever h' not, from him "
39 great things God h' done unto thee.
46 said, Somebody h' touched me: *
48 thy faith h' made thee whole;
9:58 the Son of man h' not where to 2192
10:40 that my sister h' left me to serve *
42 and Mary h' chosen that good part,
12: 5 Fear him, which after he h' killed
5 h' power to cast into hell; 2192
44 make him ruler over all that he h'.5224
13:16 of Abraham, whom Satan h' bound,*
25 is risen up, and h' shut to the door,
14:29 after he h' laid the foundation,
33 that forsaketh not all that he h', 5224
35 He that h' ears to hear, let him 2192
15: 5 And when he h' found it, he layeth it
9 And when she h' found it, she calleth
27 and thy father h' killed the fatted
27 because he h' received him safe and
30 which h' devoured thy living with

Lu 17:19 way: thy faith h' made thee whole.
18:29 no man that h' left house, or parents,
42 thy sight: thy faith h' saved thee.
19:16 Lord, thy pound h' gained ten pounds.
18 Lord, thy pound h' gained five pounds.
24 give it to him that h' ten pounds. 2192
25 unto him, Lord, he h' ten pounds. "
26 every one which h' shall be given; "
26 from him that h' not, even that "
26 he h' shall be taken away from "
31 Because the Lord h' need of him. "
34 they said, The Lord h' need of him. "
20:24 image and superscription h' it?
21: 3 this poor widow h' cast in more than *
4 of her penury h' cast in all the *
22:29 as my Father h' appointed unto me;*
31 behold, Satan h' desired to have you,*
36 he that h' a purse, let him take it, 2192
36 his scrip: and he that h' no sword, "
23:22 Why, what evil h' he done?
41 but this man h' done nothing amiss.
24:34 is risen indeed, and h' appeared to
39 for a spirit h' not flesh and bones, 2192
Joh 1:18 No man h' seen God at any time;
18 of the Father, he h' declared him.
2:17 zeal of thine house h' eaten me up.*
3:13 And no man h' ascended up to heaven,
18 because he h' not believed in the
29 He that h' the bride is the 2192
32 And what he h' seen and heard,
33 He that h' received his testimony
33 h' set to his seal that God is true.
34 For he whom God h' sent speaketh
35 and h' given all things into his hand.
36 believeth on the Son h' everlasting 2192
4:33 H' any man brought him ought to
44 a prophet h' no honour in his own 2192
5:22 judgeth no man, but h' committed
23 not the Father which h' sent him.*
24 him that sent me, h' everlasting 2192
26 For as the Father h' life in himself;"
26 so h' he given to the Son to have life *
27 And h' given him authority to *
30 will of the Father which h' sent me.*
36 the Father h' given me to finish,
36 of me, that the Father h' sent me.
37 the Father himself, which h' sent me,*
37 h' borne witness of me.
38 whom he h' sent, him ye believe not.*
6: 9 here, which h' five barley loaves, 2192
27 for him h' God the Father sealed.
29 ye believe on him whom he h' sent.*
39 the Father's will which h' sent me,*
39 that of all which he h' given me
44 except the Father which h' sent me *
45 Every man therefore that h' heard,
45 and h' learned of the Father, cometh
46 Not that any man h' seen the Father,
46 he which is of God, he h' seen the
47 believeth on me h' everlasting 2192
54 and drinketh my blood, h' eternal "
57 As the living Father h' sent me, *
7:29 for I am from him, and he h' sent me.*
31 than these which this man h' done?
38 on me as the scripture h' said,
42 H' not the scripture said, That Christ
8:10 accusers? h' no man condemned *
28 but as my Father h' taught me, I*
29 the Father h' not left me alone; for I
37 because my word h' no place in you.
40 a man that h' told you the truth,
9: 3 Neither h' this man sinned, nor his*
17 that he h' opened thine eyes? *
21 or who h' opened his eyes, we know*
30 whence he is, and yet he h' opened*
10:20 He h' a devil, and is mad; 2192
21 not the words of him that h' a devil.*
36 whom the Father h' sanctified, and*
11:39 for he h' been dead four days.
12: 7 the day of my burying h' she kept*
38 Lord, who h' believed our report?
38 and to whom h' the arm of the Lord
40 He h' blinded their eyes, and
48 not my words, h' one that judgeth 2192
13:18 eateth bread with me h' lifted up his*
14: 9 Philip? he that h' seen me
9 seen me h' seen the Father;
21 He that h' my commandments, 2192
30 of this world cometh, and h' nothing "
15: 9 As the Father h' loved me, so have I
13 Greater love h' no man than this, 2192
16: 6 unto you, sorrow h' filled your heart.
15 All things that the Father h' are 2192
21 when she is in travail h' sorrow, "
17:14 and the world h' hated them,
25 Father, the world h' not known thee:*
18:11 the cup which my Father h' given me,
19:11 me unto thee h' the greater sin. 2192
20:21 as my Father h' sent me, even so send
Ac 1: 7 which the Father h' put in his own
2:24 Whom God h' raised up, having *
32 This Jesus h' God raised up, whereof*
33 he h' shed forth this, which ye now
36 that God h' made that same Jesus,
3:13 God of our fathers, h' glorified his Son
15 whom God h' raised from the dead;*
16 in his name h' made this man strong,
16 faith which is by him h' given him
18 should suffer, he h' so fulfilled. *
21 which God h' spoken by the mouth of*
4:16 a notable miracle h' been done by
5: 3 why h' Satan filled thine heart to lie
31 Him h' God exalted with his right*
32 whom God h' given to them that obey
7:50 H' not my hand made all these*
9:12 And h' seen in a vision a man named

Ac 9:13 much evil he h' done to thy saints*
14 And here he h' authority from 2192
17 way as thou camest, h' sent me,
10:15 What God h' cleansed, that call not
28 but God h' shewed me that I should
11: 8 or unclean h' at any time entered
9 What God h' cleansed, that call not
18 h' God also to the Gentiles granted
12:11 that the Lord h' sent his angel,
11 and h' delivered me out of the hand*
13:23 Of this man's seed h' God...raised
33 God h' fulfilled the same unto us
33 in that he h' raised up Jesus again;*
47 For so h' the Lord commanded us,
15:14 Simeon h' declared how God at the
21 For Moses of old time h' in every 2192
17: 7 Whom Jason h' received: and these
26 And h' made of one blood all nations*
26 face of the earth, and h' determined*
31 Because he h' appointed a day, in
31 by that man whom he h' ordained;
31 whereof he h' given assurance unto
31 in that he h' raised him from the
19:26 this Paul h' persuaded and turned
20:28 the Holy Ghost h' made you overseers,
28 which he h' purchased with his own*
21:28 and h' polluted this holy place.
22:14 The God of our fathers h' chosen
23: 9 but if a spirit or an angel h' spoken to
17 he h' a certain thing to tell him. 2192
18 who h' something to say unto thee. "
25:25 and that he himself h' appealed to*
27:24 lo, God h' given thee all them that sail
28: 4 whom, though he h' escaped the sea,
Ro 1:19 for God h' shewed it unto them. *
3: 1 What advantage then h' the Jew?
7 if the truth of God h' more abounded*
25 Whom God h' set forth to be *
4: 1 as pertaining to the flesh, h' found?
2 he h' whereof to glory; but not 2192
5:15 Jesus Christ, h' abounded unto many.*
21 That as sin h' reigned unto death,*
6: 9 death h' no more dominion over him.
7: 1 how that the law h' dominion over a
2 the woman which h' an husband 5220
8: 2 in Christ Jesus h' made me free *
20 of him who h' subjected the same in*
9: 6 the word of God h' taken none effect.
18 Therefore h' he mercy on whom he
19 For who h' resisted his will? *
21 H' not the potter power over the 2192
24 Even us, whom he h' called, not of*
31 of righteousness, h' not attained to*
10: 9 that God h' raised him from the dead,*
16 Lord, who h' believed our report?
11: 1 H' God cast away his people? *
2 God h' not cast away his people. *
7 Israel h' not obtained that which*
7 but the election h' obtained it, *
8 God h' given them the spirit of *
32 For God h' concluded them all in
34 For who h' known the mind of the
34 or who h' been his counsellor?
35 Or who h' first given to him,
12: 3 according as God h' dealt to every
13: 8 for he that loveth another h' fulfilled
14: 3 that eateth: for God h' received him.
15:18 things which Christ h' not wrought*
26 For it h' pleased them of Macedonia
27 It h' pleased them verily; and their
16: 2 whatsoever business she h' need of*
2 for she h' been a succourer of many,
1Co 1:11 For it h' been declared unto me of
20 h' not God made foolish the wisdom
27 But God h' chosen the foolish things*
27 and God h' chosen the weak things*
28 which are despised, h' God chosen,*
2: 9 But as it is written, Eye h' not seen,*
9 the things which God h' prepared for*
10 But God h' revealed them unto us by*
16 For who h' known the mind of the
3:14 man's work abide which he h' built*
4: 9 I think that God h' set forth us the
5: 2 that he that h' done this deed might*
3 concerning him that h' so done this
6:14 And God h' both raised up the Lord,*
7: 4 The wife h' not power of her own
4 also the husband h' not power of
7 But every man h' his proper gift 2192
12 If any brother h' a wife that "
13 the woman which h' an husband "
15 but God h' called us to peace.
17 But as God h' distributed to every
17 as the Lord h' called every one, so let
25 as one that h' obtained mercy of the
28 if a virgin marry, she h' not sinned.
37 no necessity, but h' power over his 2192
37 and h' so decreed in his heart that he
9:14 Even so h' the Lord ordained that*
10:13 There h' no temptation taken you but
12:12 body is one, and h' many members,2192
18 But now h' God set the members every
18 in the body, as it h' pleased him. *
24 but God h' tempered the body *
28 And God h' set some in the church,
14:26 one of you h' a psalm, h' a doctrine,2192
26 h' a tongue, h' a revelation, "
26 h' an interpretation. Let all things "
15:25 he must reign, till he h' put all
27 he h' put all things under his feet.*
38 God giveth it a body as it h' pleased*
16: 2 as God h' prospered him, that there*
2Co 1:21 you in Christ, and h' anointed us,*
22 Who h' also sealed us, and given the*
2: 5 he h' not grieved me, but in part:
3: 6 Who also h' made us able ministers*

2Co 4: 4 the god of this world h' blinded the
6 out of darkness, h' shined in our *
5: 5 Now he that h' wrought us for the*
5 who also h' given unto us the earnest*
10 according to that he h' done, whether
18 are of God, who h' reconciled us to*
18 by Jesus Christ, and h' given to us*
19 and h' committed unto us the word*
21 For he h' made him to be sin for us,*
6:14 fellowship h' righteousness with *
14 communion h' light with darkness?
15 concord h' Christ with Belial?
15 h' he that believeth with an infidel?
16 And what agreement h' the temple of
16 as God h' said, I will dwell in them,*
7: 8 that the same epistle h' made you*
8:12 according to that a man h', and 2192
12 not according to that he h' not. "
9: 2 and your zeal h' provoked very many.
9 As it is written, He h' dispersed
9 he h' given to the poor:
10: 8 which the Lord h' given us for *
13 of the rule which God h' distributed*
13:10 power which the Lord h' given me to*
Ga 3: 1 foolish Galatians, who h' bewitched*
1 Christ h' been evidently set forth,*
13 Christ h' redeemed us from the curse*
22 But the scripture h' concluded all ‡
4: 6 God h' sent forth the Spirit of his Son*
27 for the desolate h' many more *
27 than she which h' an husband. 2192
5: 1 liberty wherewith Christ h' made us*
Eph 1: 3 who h' blessed us with all spiritual
4 According as he h' chosen us in him*
6 wherein he h' made us accepted *
8 Wherein he h' abounded toward us*
9 good pleasure which he h' purposed*
22 And h' put all things under his feet,*
2: 1 And you h' he quickened, who were*
5 dead in sins, h' quickened us together*
6 And h' raised us up together, and*
10 which God h' before ordained that we*
14 he is our peace, who h' made both*
14 one, and h' broken down the middle*
3: 9 beginning of the world h' been hid in
4:32 as God for Christ's sake h' forgiven*
5: 2 as Christ also h' loved us, and *
2 h' given himself for us an offering*
5 an idolater, h' any inheritance 2192
Ph'p 1: 6 that he which h' begun a good work*
2: 9 God also h' highly exalted him, and*
22 he h' served with me in the gospel.*
3: 4 thinketh that he h' whereof he might*
4:10 last your care of me h' flourished*
Col 1:12 the Father, which h' made us meet*
13 Who h' delivered us from the power*
13 of darkness, and h' translated us*
21 works, yet now h' he reconciled
26 Even the mystery which h' been hid
2:12 who h' raised him from the dead.*
13 h' he quickened together with him,*
18 into those things which he h' not seen,
3:25 for the wrong which he h' done:
4:13 I bear him record, that he h' a zeal 2192
1Th 2:12 who h' called you unto his kingdom*
4: 7 For God h' not called us unto
8 but God, who h' also given unto us*
5: 9 For God h' not appointed us to wrath,*
2Th 2:13 God h' from the beginning chosen*
16 even our Father, which h' loved us,*
16 and h' given us everlasting *
1Ti 1:12 Jesus our Lord, who h' enabled me,*
4: 3 which God h' created to be received*
5: 8 those of his own house, he h' denied
6:16 Who only h' immortality, dwelling 2192
16 whom no man h' seen, nor can see:
2Ti 1: 7 For God h' not given us the spirit of*
9 Who h' saved us, and called us with*
10 Jesus Christ, who h' abolished *
10 and h' brought life and immortality*
2: 4 may please him who h' chosen him*
4:10 For Demas h' forsaken me, having*
15 for he h' greatly withstood our words.*
Tit 1: 3 But h' in due times manifested *
9 faithful word as he h' been taught, *
2:11 that bringeth salvation h' appeared
Ph'm 18 If he h' wronged thee, or oweth thee
Heb 1: 2 H' in these last days spoken unto
2 whom he h' appointed heir of all*
4 as he h' by inheritance obtained a
9 even thy God, h' anointed thee with
2: 5 unto the angels h' he not put in *
13 the children which God h' given me.
18 in that he himself h' suffered being
3: 3 as he who h' builded the house *
3 h' more honour than the house. 2192
4:10 he also h' ceased from his own works,
7:24 h' an unchangeable priesthood. 2192
8: 6 But now h' he obtained a more
13 new covenant, he h' made the first old.
9:20 testament which God h' enjoined *
26 end of the world h' he appeared to put
10:14 by one offering he h' perfected for
20 living way, which he h' consecrated*
29 who h' trodden under foot the Son of
29 and h' counted the blood of the
29 and h' done despite unto the Spirit
30 we know him that h' said, Vengeance*
35 which h' great recompence of 2192
11:10 for a city which h' foundations,
16 for he h' prepared for them a city.
12:26 but now he h' promised, saying,
13: 5 for he h' said, I will never leave thee,
Jas 1:12 which the Lord h' promised to them*
15 Then when lust h' conceived, it
2: 5 H' not God chosen the poor of this*

Jas 2: 5 of the kingdom which he h' promised*
13 without mercy, that h' shewed no
14 though a man say he h' faith, and 2192
17 faith, if it h' not works, is dead, " "
3: 7 is tamed, and h' been tamed of
5: 7 of the earth, and h' long patience *
1Pe 1: 3 to his abundant mercy h' begotten *
15 But as he which h' called you is holy,*
2: 9 the praises of him who h' called you *
3: 18 For Christ also h' once suffered for *
4: 1 Forasmuch then as Christ h' suffered *
1 for he that h' suffered in the flesh
1 in the flesh h' ceased from sin;
10 As every man h' received the gift,
5: 10 who h' called us unto his eternal glory *
2Pe 1: 3 as his divine power h' given unto us
3 knowledge of him that h' called us to*
9 and h' forgotten that he was purged *
14 our Lord Jesus Christ h' shewed me.*
3: 15 wisdom given unto him h' written*
1Jo 2: 11 because that darkness h' blinded
23 Son, the same h' not the Father: 2192
23 acknowledgeth the Son h' the Father "
25 is the promise that he h' promised*
27 as it h' taught you, ye shall abide*
3: 1 of love the Father h' bestowed upon
3 every man that h' this hope in 2192
6 whosoever sinneth h' not seen him,
15 no murderer h' eternal life 2192
17 But whoso h' this world's good, and "
24 by the Spirit which he h' given us.*
4: 12 No man h' seen God at any time.
13 because he h' given us of his Spirit.
16 believed the love that God h' to us. 2192
18 out fear: because fear h' torment. "
20 his brother whom he h' seen, how
20 can he love God whom he h' not seen?
5: 9 witness of God which he h' testified of
10 on the Son of God h' the witness 2192
10 believeth not God h' made him a liar;
11 that God h' given to us eternal life,*
12 He that h' the Son h' life; and he 2192
12 that h' not the Son of God h' not life. "
20 and h' given us an understanding, that
2Jo 9 the doctrine of Christ, h' not God. 2192
9 of Christ, he h' both the Father "
3Jo 11 he that doeth evil h' not seen God.
12 Demetrius h' good report of all men,
Jude 6 he h' reserved in everlasting chains
Re 1: 6 And h' made us kings and priests*
2: 7, 11 He that h' an ear, let him hear 2192
12 saith he which h' the sharp sword "
17 He that h' an ear, let him hear "
18 who h' his eyes like unto a flame of "
29 He that h' an ear, let him hear "
3: 1 saith he that h' the seven Spirits "
6 He that h' an ear, let him hear "
7 he that is true, he that h' the key of "
13, 22 He that h' an ear, let him hear "
5: 5 the Root of David, h' prevailed to open
9: 11 in the Greek tongue h' his name 2192
10: 7 as he h' declared to his servants the*
12: 6 where she h' a place prepared of 2192
12 knoweth that he h' but a short "
13: 18 Let him that h' understanding "
16: 9 the name of God, which h' power "
17: 7 which h' the seven heads and ten "
9 here is the mind which h' wisdom. "
17 For God h' put in their hearts to fulfil*
18: 5 and God h' remembered her iniquities.
6 in the cup which she h' filled fill to*
7 How much she h' glorified herself,*
20 for God h' avenged you on her.
19: 2 for he h' judged the great whore,
2 and h' avenged the blood of his
7 and his wife h' made herself ready.
16 And he h' on his vesture and on 2192
20: 6 Blessed and holy is he that h' part "
6 such the second death h' no power, "

Hathath (*ha'-thath*)
1Ch 4: 13 and the sons of Othniel; H'. 2867

hating
Ex 18: 21 men of truth, h' covetousness; 8130
Tit 3: 3 envy, hateful, and h' one another. 3404
Jude 23 h' even the garment spotted by the "

Hatipha (*hat'-if-ah*)
Ezr 2: 54 of Neziah, the children of H'. 2412
Ne 7: 56 of Neziah, the children of H'. "

Hatita (*hat'-it-ah*)
Ezr 2: 42 the children of H', the children 2410
Ne 7: 45 the children of H', the children "

hatred
Nu 35: 20 But if he thrust him of h', 8135
2Sa 13: 15 that the h' wherewith he hated her "
Ps 25: 19 and they hate me with cruel h'. "
109: 3 me about also with words of h'; "
5 for good, and h' for my love. "
139: 22 I hate them with perfect h': "
Pr 10: 12 H' stirreth up strifes: but love "
18 He that hideth h' with lying lips, "
15: 17 than a stalled ox and h' therewith. "
26: 26 Whose h' is covered by deceit, his "
Ec 9: 1 no man knoweth either love or h' "
6 Also their love, and their h', and "
Eze 25: 15 to destroy it for the old h'; * 342
35: 5 thou hast had a perpetual h', and* "
11 which thou hast used out of thy h' 8135
Ho 9: 7 thine iniquity, and the great h'. * 4895
8 h' in the house of his God. "
Ga 5: 20 h', variance, emulations, wrath, * 2189

hats
Da 3: 21 their hosen, and their h', and *3737

Hattaavah See KIBROTH-HATTAAVAH.

Hatticon See HAZAR-HATTICON.

Hattil (*hat'-til*)
Ezr 2: 57 the children of H', the children 2411
Ne 7: 59 of Shephatiah, the children of H'. "

Hattush (*hat'-tush*)
1Ch 3: 22 H', and Igeal, and Bariah, and 2407
Ezr 8: 2 Daniel: of the sons of David; H'. "
Ne 3: 10 And next unto him repaired H' the "
10: 4 H', Shebaniah, Malluch, "
12: 2 Amariah, Malluch, H', "

haughtily
Mic 2: 3 necks; neither shall ye go h': 7317

haughtiness
Isa 2: 11 the h' of men shall be bowed 7312
17 the h' of men shall be made low: "
13: 11 will lay low the h' of the terrible 1346
16: 6 his h', and his pride, and his * "
Jer 48: 29 and the h' of his heart. 7312

haughty
2Sa 22: 28 thine eyes are upon the h', that 7311
Ps 131: 1 my heart is not h', nor mine eyes 1361
Pr 16: 18 and an h' spirit before a fall. 1363
18: 12 destruction the heart of man is h', 1361
21: 24 Proud and h' scorner is his name, 3093
Isa 3: 16 the daughters of Zion are h', 1361
10: 33 and the h' shall be humbled. *1364
24: 4 h' people of the earth do languish.* 4791
Eze 16: 50 And they were h', and committed 1361
Zep 3: 11 shalt no more be h' because of my "

haul See HALE.

haunt
1Sa 23: 22 his place where his h' is, and 7272
30: 31 and his men were wont to h'. 1980
Eze 26: 17 terror to be on all that h' it! 3427

Hauran (*haw'-ran*)
Eze 47: 16 which is by the coast of H'. 2362
18 ye shall measure from H', and "

have See also HAD; HAST; HATH; HAVING.
Ge 1: 26 let them h' dominion over the fish
28 and h' dominion over the fish of
29 And God said, Behold, I h' given you
30 I h' given every green herb for meat:
4: 20 in tents, and of such as h' cattle.
23 for I h' slain a man to my wounding,
6: 7 whom I h' created from the face of
7 it repenteth me that I h' made
7: 1 for thee h' I seen righteous before me
4 that I h' made will I destroy from
8: 21 more every thing living, as I h' done.
9: 3 as the green herb h' I given you
17 which I h' established between me
11: 6 and they h' all one language; and
6 from them, which they h' imagined *
12: 19 so I might h' taken her to me to *
14: 22 I h' lift up mine hand unto the Lord,
23 shouldest say, I h' made Abram rich:
24 the young men h' eaten, and the
15: 18 Unto thy seed h' I given this land,
16: 5 I h' given my maid into thy bosom;*
13 H' I also here looked after him that
17: 5 father of many nations h' I made
20 as for Ishmael, I h' heard thee:
18: 3 My Lord, if now I h' found favour in
10 and lo, Sarah thy wife shall h' a son.
12 am waxed old shall I h' pleasure, 1961
14 time of life, and Sarah shall h' a son.
21 they h' done altogether according to
27 Behold now, I h' taken upon me to
31 now, I h' taken upon me to speak unto
19: 8 Behold now, I h' two daughters
8 which h' not known man; let me, I
21 See, I h' accepted thee concerning
20: 5 and innocency of my hands h' I done
9 and what h' I offended thee, that
16 Behold, I h' given thy brother a
21: 7 And she said, Who would h' said unto
7 that Sarah should h' given children*
23 kindness that I h' done unto thee,
30 witness unto me, that I h' digged this
22: 16 By myself h' I sworn, saith the Lord,
24: 19 also, until they h' done drinking.
25 We h' both straw and provender
31 for I h' prepared the house, and
33 I will not eat, until I h' told mine
26: 10 might lightly h' lien with thy wife,
27 seeing ye hate me, and h' sent me
29 do us no hurt, as we h' not touched
29 and as we h' done unto thee nothing
32 said unto him, We h' found water.
27: 19 I h' done according as thou badest
33 and I h' eaten of all before thou
37 Behold, I h' made him thy lord, and
37 all his brethren h' I given to him
37 and with corn and wine h' I sustained
40 when thou shalt h' the dominion,*
28: 15 I will not leave thee, until I h' done
15 that which I h' spoken to thee of.
22 And this stone, which I h' set for a
29: 34 because I h' born him three sons:
30: 3 that I may also h' children by her.*
8 with my sister, and I h' prevailed:
16 for surely I h' hired thee with my
18 because I h' given my maiden to my *
20 because I h' born him six sons: and
26 for whom I h' served thee, and let me
26 knowest my service which I h' done
27 if I h' found favour in thine eyes,
27 I h' learned by experience that the
29 Thou knowest how I h' served thee,
31: 6 with all my power I h' served your
12 for I h' seen all that Laban doeth unto
27 that I might h' sent thee away with
38 This twenty years h' I been with thee;
38 ewes and thy she goats h' not cast
Ge 31: 38 the rams of thy flock h' I not eaten.
41 Thus h' I been twenty years in thy
43 their children which they h' born?
51 which I h' cast betwixt me and thee;
32: 4 I h' sojourned with Laban and
5 And I h' oxen, and asses, flocks, 1961
30 for I h' seen God face to face, and my
33: 9 And Esau said, I h' enough, my 3426
10 if now I h' found grace in thy sight,
10 for therefore I h' seen thy face, as
11 and because I h' enough. And he 3426
34: 30 Ye h' troubled me to make me to
35: 17 Fear not; thou shalt h' this son also.
37: 6 you, this dream which I h' dreamed:
8 or shalt thou indeed h' dominion
9 Behold, I h' dreamed a dream more;
32 and said, This h' we found: know
40: 8 We h' dreamed a dream, and there is
15 and here also h' I done nothing that
41: 15 I h' dreamed a dream, and there is
15 and I h' heard say of thee, that thou
28 This is the thing which I h' spoken*
41 See, I h' set thee over all the land
42: 2 I h' heard that there is corn in Egypt:
36 Me h' ye bereaved of my children:
43: 7 yet alive? h' ye another brother? 3426
21 and we h' brought it again in our
22 And other money h' we brought
44: 4 Wherefore h' ye rewarded evil for
5 indeed he divineth? ye h' done evil
15 What deed is this that ye h' done?
19 saying, H' ye a father, or a 3426
20 We h' a father, an old man, and a "
45: 13 and of all that ye h' seen; and ye
46: 30 let me die, since I h' seen thy face,
32 and they h' brought their flocks, and
47: 1 and all that they h', are come out of
4 for thy servants h' no pasture for*
9 evil h' the days of the years of my life*
9 and h' not attained unto the days of
23 Behold, I h' bought you this day and
26 that Pharaoh should h' the fifth part;
29 If now I h' found grace in thy sight,
48: 22 Moreover I h' given to thee one
49: 18 I h' waited for thy salvation, O Lord.
23 The archers h' sorely grieved him,
26 blessings of thy father h' prevailed
50: 4 If now I h' found grace in your eyes,
5 in my grave which I h' digged for
Ex 1: 18 and said unto them, Why h' ye done
18 and h' saved the men children alive?
2: 20 why is it that ye h' left the man?
22 he said, I h' been a stranger
3: 7 I h' surely seen the affliction of my
7 and h' heard their cry by reason of
9 and I h' also seen the oppression
12 that I h' sent thee: When thou hast
16 I h' surely visited you, and seen that
17 And I h' said, I will bring you up out
4: 11 or the seeing, or the blind? h' not I*
21 which I h' put in thine hand: but I
5: 14 Wherefore h' ye not fulfilled your
21 ye h' made our savour to be abhorred
6: 4 And I h' also established my
5 And I h' also heard the groaning of
5 and I h' remembered my covenant.
12 the children of Israel h' not hearkened
7: 1 See, I h' made thee a god to Pharaoh:
9: 16 for this cause h' I raised thee up,
27 I h' sinned this time: the Lord is
10: 1 for I h' hardened his heart, and the
2 what things I h' wrought in Egypt,
2 and my signs which I h' done among
6 nor thy fathers' fathers h' seen, since
16 I h' sinned against the Lord your
12: 17 for in this selfsame day h' I brought
31 and go, serve the Lord, as ye h' said.
32 and your herds, as ye h' said, and be
14: 5 and they said, Why h' we done this,
5 that we h' let Israel go from serving
13 whom ye h' seen to day, ye shall see
18 when I h' gotten me honour upon
15: 5 The depths h' covered them: they*
17 which thy hands h' established.
26 which I h' brought upon the
16: 3 for ye h' brought us forth into this
12 I h' heard the murmurings of the
32 I h' fed you in the wilderness, when*
17: 16 sworn that the Lord will h' war
18: 3 I h' been an alien in a strange
16 When they h' a matter, they come 1961
19: 4 Ye h' seen what I did unto the
20: 2 which h' brought thee out of the land*
3 Thou shalt h' no other gods before
22 unto the children of Israel, Ye h' seen*
22 that I h' talked with you from heaven.
21: 4 If his master h' given him a wife, and*
4 she h' born him sons or daughters;*
8 he shall h' no power, seeing he
9 And if he h' betrothed her unto his*
31 Whether he h' gored a son, or
31 or h' gored a daughter, according to
22: 3 if he h' nothing, then he shall be
8 he h' put his hand unto his neighbour's
23: 13 And in all things that I h' said unto
20 into the place which I h' prepared.
24: 12 commandments which I h' written;
14 if any man h' any matters to do, let*
26: 2 every one of the curtains shall h' one
28: 3 whom I h' filled with the spirit of
7 It shall h' the two shoulderpieces 1961
32 shall h' a binding of woven work "
29: 35 to all things which I h' commanded
31: 2 See, I h' called by name Bezaleel the
3 And I h' filled him with the spirit
6 And I, behold, I h' given with him

Ex 31: 6 that are wise hearted I *h'* put wisdom,
6 may make all that I *h'* commanded
11 according to all that I *h'* commanded
32: 7 of Egypt, *h'* corrupted themselves.
8 They *h'* turned aside quickly out of
8 they *h'* made them a molten calf,
8 a molten calf, and *h'* worshipped it,
8 and *h'* sacrificed thereunto, and
8 which *h'* brought thee up out of the *
9 I *h'* seen this people, and, behold, it is
13 and all this land that I *h'* spoken of
30 Ye *h'* sinned a great sin: and now I
31 and said, Oh, this people *h'* sinned a
31 a great sin, and *h'* made them gods
34 the place of which I *h'* spoken unto
33: 13 if I *h'* found grace in thy sight,
16 I and thy people *h'* found grace in thy
34: 9 If now I *h'* found grace in thy sight,
10 do marvels, such as *h'* not been done
27 I *h'* made a covenant with thee and
Le 4: 13 and they *h'* done somewhat against
14 When the sin, which they *h'* sinned
6: 3 Or *h'* found that which was lost, and
17 I *h'* given it unto them for their
7: 7 atonement therewith shall *h'* it. 1961
8 even the priest shall *h'* to himself "
10 shall all the sons of Aaron *h'*, one "
33 fat, shall *h'* the right shoulder "
34 and the heave shoulder *h'* I taken of
34 and *h'* given them unto Aaron the
10: 17 Wherefore *h'* ye not eaten the sin
18 ye should indeed *h'* eaten it in the
19 Behold, this day *h'* they offered their
19 and such things *h'* befallen me: *
19 should it *h'* been accepted in the
11: 10 And all that *h'* not fins and scales in
11 shall *h'* their carcases in abomination.
13 which ye shall *h'* in abomination
21 which *h'* legs above their feet, to leap
23 which *h'* four feet, shall be an
12: 2 If a woman *h'* conceived seed, and*
13: 2 When a man shall *h'* in the skin 1961
10 and it *h'* turned the hair white, and
13 if the leprosy *h'* covered all his flesh,
24 burneth *h'* a white bright spot, *1961
29 If a man or a woman *h'* a plague* "
38 If a man also or a woman *h'* in * "
55 if the plague *h'* not changed his
15: 19 And if a woman *h'* an issue, and 1961
25 And if a woman *h'* an issue of her "
16: 4 and he shall *h'* the linen breeches "
17: 7 after whom they *h'* gone a whoring.*
11 and I *h'* given it to you upon the
18: 27 abominations *h'* the men of the land
19: 23 and shall *h'* planted all manner of
31 Regard not them that *h'* familiar
36 ephah, and a just hin, shall ye *h'*: 1961
20: 6 after such as *h'* familiar spirits, and
12 they *h'* wrought confusion; their
13 both of them *h'* committed an
24 But I *h'* said unto you, Ye shall
24 which *h'* separated you from other
25 on the ground, which I *h'* separated
26 Lord am holy, and *h'* severed you
22: 13 and *h'* no child, and is returned unto
23: 7 ye shall *h'* an holy convocation: 1961
14 the selfsame day that ye *h'* brought
23 shall ye *h'* a sabbath, a memorial *1961
39 when ye *h'* gathered in the fruit of
24: 22 Ye shall *h'* one manner of law, as 1961
25: 26 And if the man *h'* none to redeem "
31 the villages which *h'* no wall round
44 bondmaids, which thou shalt *h'*, 1961
26: 9 For I will *h'* respect unto you, and
13 and I *h'* broken the bands of your
26 And when I *h'* broken the staff of your*
37 and ye shall *h'* no power to stand 1961
40 and that also they *h'* walked contrary
41 And that I also *h'* walked contrary *
41 and *h'* brought them into the land of *
27: 20 or if he *h'* sold the field to another
Nu 3: 12 And I, behold, I *h'* taken the Levites
32 and *h'* the oversight of them that
4: 15 Aaron and his sons *h'* made an
5: 7 confess their sin which they *h'* done:
8 But if the man *h'* no kinsman to
18 the priest shall *h'* in his hand 1961
19 If no man *h'* lain with thee, and if
20 and some man *h'* lain with thee
27 and *h'* done trespass against her
8: 16 of Israel, *h'* I taken them unto me.
18 And I *h'* taken the Levites for all the
19 And I *h'* given the Levites as a gift to
9: 14 ye shall *h'* one ordinance, both for 1961
11: 11 and wherefore *h'* I not found favour
12 *H'* I conceived all this people?
12 *h'* I begotten them, that thou
13 Whence should I *h'* flesh to give unto
15 if I *h'* found favour in thy sight; and
18 for ye *h'* wept in the ears of the Lord,
20 because that ye *h'* despised the Lord
20 and *h'* wept before him, saying, Why
12: 11 us, wherein we *h'* done foolishly,
11 foolishly, and wherein we *h'* sinned.
13: 32 The land, through which we *h'* gone
14: 11 for all the signs which I *h'* shewed
14 for they *h'* heard that thou Lord art
15 then the nations which *h'* heard the
22 Because all those men which *h'* seen
22 in the wilderness, and *h'* tempted me
22 these ten times, and *h'* not hearkened
27 I *h'* heard the murmurings of the
28 as ye *h'* spoken in mine ears, so will I
29 and upward, which *h'* murmured
31 know the land which ye *h'* despised.
35 I the Lord *h'* said, I will surely do it
Nu 14: 40 Lord hath promised: for we *h'* sinned.
15: 22 And if ye *h'* erred, and not observed *
29 Ye shall *h'* one law for him that 1961
16: 15 I *h'* not taken one ass from them,
15 from them, neither *h'* I hurt one of
28 for I *h'* not done them of mine own
30 that these men *h'* provoked the Lord.
41 saying, Ye *h'* killed the people of the
18: 6 And I, behold, I *h'* taken your
7 I *h'* given your priest's office unto you*
8 Behold, I also *h'* given thee the charge
8 unto thee *h'* I given them by reason of
11 I *h'* given them unto thee, and to thy
12 offer unto the Lord, them *h'* I given
19 unto the Lord, *h'* I given thee, and
20 Thou shalt *h'* no inheritance in their
20 neither shalt thou *h'* any part 1961
21 And, behold, I *h'* given the children of
23 of Israel they *h'* no inheritance.
24 I *h'* given to the Levites to inherit:
24 therefore I *h'* said unto them, Among
26 which I *h'* given you from them for
30 When ye *h'* heaved the best thereof *
32 when ye *h'* heaved from it the best of
20: 4 And why *h'* ye brought up the
5 And wherefore *h'* ye made us to come
12 into the land which I *h'* given them.
15 and we *h'* dwelt in Egypt a long time;*
17 nor to the left, until we *h'* passed thy
24 into the land which I *h'* given unto
21: 5 Wherefore *h'* ye brought us up out of
7 came to Moses, and said, We *h'* sinned,
7 we *h'* spoken against the Lord, and
30 We *h'* shot at them; Heshbon is
30 and we *h'* laid them waste even unto
34 Fear him not: for I *h'* delivered him
22: 28 What *h'* I done unto thee, that thou
34 I *h'* sinned; for I knew not that thou
38 *h'* I now any power at all to say
23: 4 him, I *h'* prepared seven altars,
4 and I *h'* offered upon every altar a
20 Behold, I *h'* received commandment
24: 19 come he that shall *h'* dominion,
25: 13 And he shall *h'* it, and his seed *1961
18 they *h'* beguiled you in the matter of
27: 8 If a man die, and *h'* no son, then ye
9 And if he *h'* no daughter, then ye
10 And if he *h'* no brethren, then ye
11 And if his father *h'* no brethren, then
12 which I *h'* given unto the children of
17 be not as sheep which *h'* no shepherd.
28: 25, 26 ye shall *h'* an holy convocation; 1961
29: 1 ye shall *h'* an holy convocation; "
7 And ye shall *h'* on the tenth day "
12 ye shall *h'* an holy convocation; "
35 ye shall *h'* a solemn assembly: "
30: 9 they *h'* bound their souls, shall stand*
31: 15 him, *H'* ye saved all the women alive?
18 children, that *h'* not known a man
49 Thy servants *h'* taken the sum of the
50 We *h'* therefore brought an oblation
32: 4 for cattle, and thy servants *h'* cattle:
5 if we *h'* found grace in thy sight, let
11 because they *h'* not wholly followed
12 for they *h'* wholly followed the Lord.
17 until we *h'* brought them unto their
18 until the children of Israel *h'* inherited
23 behold, ye *h'* sinned against the Lord:
30 they shall *h'* possessions among 270
33: 53 for I *h'* given you the land to possess
34: 6 ye shall even *h'* the great sea for 1961
14 fathers, *h'* received their inheritance;
14 Manasseh *h'* received...inheritance:
15 half tribe *h'* received their inheritance
35: 8 from them that *h'* many ye shall *
8 but from them that *h'* few ye shall *
13 six cities shall ye *h'* for refuge. *1961
22 or *h'* cast upon him any thing without*
28 Because he should *h'* remained in the
De 1: 6 in Horeb, saying, Ye *h'* dwelt long
8 Behold, I *h'* set the land before you:
28 our brethren *h'* discouraged our
28 and moreover we *h'* seen the sons of
41 We *h'* sinned against the Lord, we
2: 3 Ye *h'* compassed this mountain long
5 because I *h'* given mount Seir unto
9 because I *h'* given Ar unto the
19 because I *h'* given it unto the
24 behold, I *h'* given into thine hand
31 Behold, I *h'* begun to give Sihon and
3: 19 (for I know that ye *h'* much cattle,)
19 in your cities which I *h'* given you;
20 Until the Lord *h'* given rest unto your*
20 his possession, which I *h'* given you.
21 Thine eyes *h'* seen all that the Lord
4: 3 Your eyes *h'* seen what the Lord did
5 Behold, I *h'* taught you statutes and
9 things which thine eyes *h'* seen, *
25 and ye shall *h'* remained long in the
5: 7 Thou shalt *h'* none other gods 1961
24 and we *h'* heard his voice out of the
24 we *h'* seen this day that God doth talk
26 out of the midst of the fire, as we *h'*,
28 and the Lord said unto me, I *h'* heard
28 of this people, which they *h'* spoken
28 spoken unto thee: they *h'* well said
28 well said all that they *h'* spoken.
6: 10 Lord thy God shall *h'* brought thee*
11 when thou shalt *h'* eaten and be full;*
7: 16 thine eye shall *h'* no pity upon
24 thee, until thou *h'* destroyed them.
9: 7 ye *h'* been rebellious against the
8 angry with you to *h'* destroyed you.
12 forth out of Egypt *h'* corrupted
12 they *h'* made them a molten image.
13 I *h'* seen this people, and, behold, it is
De 9: 20 very angry with Aaron to *h'* destroyed
23 which I *h'* given you; then ye rebelled
24 Ye *h'* been rebellious against the
10: 21 things, which thine eyes *h'* seen.
11: 2 your children which *h'* not known,
2 *h'* not seen the chastisement
7 But your eyes *h'* seen all the great
28 other gods, which ye *h'* not known.
12: 21 as I *h'* commanded thee, and thou
31 which he hateth, *h'* they done unto
31 they *h'* burnt in the fire to their gods.*
13: 13 and *h'* withdrawn the inhabitants of
13 other gods, which ye *h'* not known;
17 and *h'* compassion upon thee, and
14: 9 all that *h'* fins and scales shall ye *
15: 21 or *h'* any ill blemish, thou shalt not*
17: 3 heaven, which I *h'* not commanded;
5 woman which *h'* committed that
18: 1 the tribe of Levi, shall *h'* no part nor
2 Therefore shall they *h'* no inheritance
8 They shall *h'* like portions to eat,
17 said unto me, They *h'* well spoken
17 well spoken that which they *h'* spoken.
20 which I *h'* not commanded him to
19: 14 which they of old time *h'* set in thine
19 as he had thought to *h'* done unto his*
20: 9 when the officers *h'* made an end of
18 which they *h'* done unto their gods;
21: 7 and say, Our hands *h'* not shed this
7 this blood, neither *h'* our eyes seen it.
11 that thou wouldest *h'* her to thy *
14 And it shall be, if thou *h'* no delight in
15 If a man *h'* two wives, one beloved, 1961
15 and they *h'* born him children, both
18 If a man *h'* a stubborn and 1961
18 and that, when they *h'* chastened him,*
22 And if a man *h'* committed a sin
23: 12 Thou shalt *h'* a place also without 1961
13 And thou shalt *h'* a paddle upon thy "
25: 5 and one of them die, and *h'* no child,
13 Thou shalt not *h'* in thy bag divers 1961
14 Thou shalt not *h'* in thine house "
15 But thou shalt *h'* a perfect and just "
15 and just measure shalt thou *h'*: "
26: 10 And now, behold, I *h'* brought the
13 before the Lord thy God, I *h'* brought
13 out of mine house, and also *h'* given
13 me: I *h'* not transgressed thy
13 neither *h'* I forgotten them:
14 I *h'* not eaten thereof in my mourning,
14 neither *h'* I taken away ought thereof
14 but I *h'* hearkened to the voice of
14 and *h'* done according to all that thou
28: 21 until he *h'* consumed thee from off the
31 and thou shalt *h'* none to rescue them.
36 thou nor thy fathers *h'* known; *
51 of thy sheep, until he *h'* destroyed
64 nor thy fathers *h'* known, even wood *
65 shall the sole of thy foot *h'* rest: *1961
66 and shalt *h'* none assurance of thy life:
29: 2 Ye *h'* seen all that the Lord did before
3 which thine eyes *h'* seen, the *
5 And I *h'* led you forty years in the
6 Ye *h'* not eaten bread, neither
6 *h'* ye drunk wine or strong drink: that
16 For ye know how we *h'* dwelt in the *
17 And ye *h'* seen their abominations, and
19 I shall *h'* peace, though I walk in the
25 Because they *h'* forsaken the covenant*
30: 1 curse, which I *h'* set before thee,
3 and *h'* compassion upon thee, and
15 See, I *h'* set before thee this day life
19 that I *h'* set before you life and death,
31: 5 which I *h'* commanded you.
13 which *h'* not known any thing, may
16 break my covenant which I *h'* made
18 which they shall *h'* wrought, in that
20 For when I shall *h'* brought them into
20 and they shall *h'* eaten and filled
21 I *h'* brought them into the land which
27 ye *h'* been rebellious against the
29 the way which I *h'* commanded you;
32: 5 They *h'* corrupted themselves, their
21 They *h'* moved me to jealousy with
21 they *h'* provoked me to anger with
33: 9 I *h'* not seen him; neither did he
9 for they *h'* observed thy word, and
34: 4 I *h'* caused thee to see it with thine
Jos 1: 3 that *h'* I given unto you, as I said unto
8 and then thou shalt *h'* good success.
9 *H'* not I commanded thee? Be strong
15 Until the Lord *h'* given your brethren
15 and they also *h'* possessed the land
2: 10 For we *h'* heard how the Lord dried
12 since I *h'* shewed you kindness, that
13 and all that they *h'*, and deliver our
3: 4 for ye *h'* not passed this way
5: 9 This day *h'* I rolled away the reproach
6: 2 I *h'* given into thine hand Jericho, and
7: 11 and they *h'* also transgressed my
11 for they *h'* even taken of the accursed
11 and *h'* also stolen, and dissembled
11 and they *h'* put it even among their
20 Indeed I *h'* sinned against the Lord
20 of Israel, and thus and thus *h'* I done:
8: 1 see, I *h'* given into thy hand the
6 till we *h'* drawn them from the city;
8 And it shall be, when ye *h'* taken the
8 shall ye do. See, I *h'* commanded you.
9: 9 for we *h'* heard the fame of him, and
19 We *h'* sworn unto them by the Lord
22 Wherefore *h'* ye beguiled us, saying,
24 lives because of you, and *h'* done this
10: 8 Fear them not: for I *h'* delivered them
11: 20 and that they might *h'* no favour, 1961
13: 6 for an inheritance, as I *h'* commanded

Jos 13: 8 and the Gadites h' received their *
14: 9 land whereon thy feet h' trodden *
17: 16 in the land of the valley h' chariots of
17 thou shalt not h' one lot only: 1961
18 though they h' iron chariots, and
18: 7 But the Levites h' no part among you;
22: 2 And said unto them, Ye h' kept all
2 and h' obeyed my voice in all that I
3 Ye h' not left your brethren these
3 but h' kept the charge of the
11 tribe of Manasseh h' built an altar
16 trespass is this that ye h' committed
16 in that ye h' builded you an altar, that
23 That we h' built us an altar to turn
24 And if we h' not rather done it for fear
25 ye h' no part in the Lord: so shall
27 in time to come, Ye h' no part in the
31 because ye h' not committed this
31 now ye h' delivered the children of
23: 3 And ye h' seen all that the Lord your
4 Behold, I h' divided unto you by lot
4 with all the nations that I h' cut off,
8 your God, as ye h' done unto this day.
15 until he h' destroyed you from off this
16 When ye h' transgressed the *
16 and h' gone and served other gods,*
24: 7 them; and your eyes h' seen *
7 what I h' done in Egypt: and ye dwelt*
13 And I h' given you a land for which *
22 that ye h' chosen you the Lord, to
J'g 1: 2 behold, I h' delivered the land into his
7 as I h' done, so God hath requited me.
2: 1 and h' brought you unto the land
2 but ye h' not obeyed my voice:
2 my voice: why h' ye done this?
20 their fathers, and h' not hearkened
3: 19 and said, I h' a secret errand unto
20 And Ehud said, I h' a message from
5: 13 that remaineth h' dominion *
13 the Lord made me h' dominion *
30 H' they not sped?
30 h' they not divided the prey; to every
6: 10 but ye h' not obeyed my voice.
14 of the Midianites: h' not I sent thee?
17 If now I h' found grace in thy sight,
22 for because I h' seen an angel of the
7: 9 unto the host; for I h' delivered it into
8: 2 What h' I done now in comparison of
9: 16 Now therefore, if ye h' done truly and
16 in that ye h' made Abimelech king,
16 and if ye h' dealt well with Jerubbaal
16 and h' done unto him according to the
18 and h' slain his sons, threescore and
18 and h' made Abimelech, the son of his
19 If ye then h' dealt truly and sincerely
48 What ye h' seen me do, make haste,
48 me do, make haste, and do as I h' done.
10: 10 unto the Lord, saying, We h' sinned
10 because we h' forsaken our God, and
13 Yet ye h' forsaken me, and served
14 unto the gods which ye h' chosen;
15 We h' sinned: do thou unto us
11: 27 Wherefore I h' not sinned against
35 for I h' opened my mouth unto the
13: 15 until we shall h' made ready a kid for*
22 surely die, because we h' seen God.
23 he would not h' received a burnt
23 neither would he h' shewed us all
23 nor would as at this time h' told us
14: 2 and said, I h' seen a woman in
6 and he rent him as he would h' rent a
15 house with fire: h' ye called us to
15 ye called us to take that we h'? is it*
16 Behold, I h' not told it my father nor
15: 7 Though ye h' done this, yet will I be*
11 As they did unto me, so h' I done unto
16 with the jaw of an ass h' I slain a
16: 17 for I h' been a Nazarite unto God from
17: 13 good, seeing I h' a Levite to my 1961
18: 9 for we h' seen the land, and, behold, it
14 therefore consider what ye h' to do.
24 And he said, Ye h' taken away my gods
24 are gone away: and what h' I more?
20: 5 night, and thought to h' slain me:
5 and my concubine h' they forced, *
6 for they h' committed lewdness and
10 all the folly that they h' wrought in
21: 7 seeing we h' sworn by the Lord that
18 for the children of Israel h' sworn.*
Ru 1: 8 as ye h' dealt with the dead, and with
12 for I am too old to h' an husband.
12 If I should say, I h' hope,
12 if I should h' an husband also to night,
2: 9 h' I not charged the young men that
9 which the young men h' drawn.
10 Why h' I found grace in thine eyes,
21 until they h' ended all my harvest.
3: 3 until he shall h' done eating and
18 until he h' finished the thing this day.
4: 9 witnesses this day, that I h' bought all
10 the wife of Mahlon, h' I purchased to
1Sa 1: 15 I h' drunk neither wine nor strong
15 but h' poured out my soul before the*
16 of my complaint and grief h' I spoken
20 Because I h' asked him of the Lord.
23 tarry until thou h' weaned him; only
28 Therefore also I h' lent him to the
2: 5 They that were full h' hired out
15 he will not h' sodden flesh of thee, 3947
29 mine offering, which I h' commanded
3: 12 all things which I h' spoken concerning
13 For I h' told him that I will judge his
14 And therefore I h' sworn unto the
4: 9 as they h' been to you: quit yourselves
5: 10 They h' brought about the ark of the
6: 21 The Philistines h' brought again the

1Sa 7: 6 We h' sinned against the Lord. And
8: 7 thee: for they h' not rejected thee,
7 but they h' rejected me, that I should
8 all the works which they h' done since
8 wherewith they h' forsaken me, and
18 your king which ye shall h' chosen
19 Nay; but we will h' a king over us; 1961
9: 7 bring to the man of God: what h' we?
8 Behold, I h' here at hand the 4672
16 for I h' looked upon my people,
24 I h' invited the people. So Saul did
10: 19 And ye h' this day rejected your God,
19 and ye h' said unto him, Nay, but set a
12: 1 Israel, Behold, I h' hearkened unto
1 me, and h' made a king over you.
2 and I h' walked before you from my
3 his anointed: whose ox h' I taken?
3 I taken? or whose ass h' I taken?
3 I taken? or whom h' I defrauded?
3 I defrauded? whom h' I oppressed?
3 whose hand h' I received any bribe
5 that ye h' not found ought in my hand.
10 unto the Lord, and said, We h' sinned,
10 because we h' forsaken the Lord,
10 and h' served Baalim and Ashtaroth:
13 behold the king whom ye h' chosen,
13 and whom ye h' desired! and, behold,
17 which ye h' done in the sight of the
19 for we h' added unto all our sins this
20 Fear not: ye h' done all this
13: 12 and I h' not made supplication unto
13 for now would the Lord h' established
14: 29 how mine eyes h' been enlightened,
33 And he said, Ye h' transgressed:
15: 3 destroy all that they h', and spare
11 repenteth me that I h' set up Saul to
13 I h' performed the commandment of
15 Saul said, They h' brought them from
15 and the rest we h' utterly destroyed.
20 I h' obeyed the voice of the Lord,
20 and h' gone the way which the Lord
20 and h' brought Agag the king of
20 and h' utterly destroyed the
21 should h' been utterly destroyed *
24 Saul said unto Samuel, I h' sinned:
24 I h' transgressed the commandment
30 Then he said, I h' sinned: yet honour
16: 1 for Saul, seeing I h' rejected him
1 for I h' provided me a king among
7 because I h' refused him: for the
18 Behold, I h' seen a son of Jesse the
17: 25 men of Israel said, H' ye seen this
29 David said, What h' I now done? Is
39 these; for I h' not proved them.
18: 8 They h' ascribed unto David ten
8 and to me they h' ascribed but
19 should h' been given to David, that
20: 1 What h' I done? what is mine
7 is well; thy servant shall h' peace:
12 when I h' sounded my father about
23 thou and I h' spoken of, behold, the
29 and now, if I h' found favour in thine
42 forasmuch as we h' sworn both of us
21: 2 thee, and what I h' commanded thee:
2 I h' appointed my servants to such
4 if the young men h' kept themselves
5 Of a truth women h' been kept from
8 for I h' neither brought my sword
14 wherefore then h' ye brought him
15 H' I need of mad men, that ye *
15 that ye h' brought this fellow to play
22: 8 That all of you h' conspired against
13 Why h' ye conspired against me, thou
22 I h' occasioned the death of all the
23: 21 Lord; for ye h' compassion on me.
27 for the Philistines h' invaded the
24: 10 Behold, this day thine ey s h' seen
11 and I h' not sinned again t thee; yet
17 me good, whereas I h' rewarded
25: 7 And now I h' heard that tho hast
11 and my flesh that I h' killed for my
21 Surely in vain h' I kept all th t this
30 when the Lord shall h' done to my
30 and shall h' appointed thee ruler over
31 when the Lord shall h' dealt well with
35 see, I h' harkened to thy voice,
35 thy voice, and h' accepted thy person.
26: 16 because ye h' not kept your master,
18 for what h' I done? or what evil is in
19 If the Lord h' stirred thee up against*
19 for they h' driven me ou this day
21 Then said Saul, I h' sinned: return,
21 this day: behold, I h' played the fool,
21 the fool, and h' erred exceedingly.
27: 5 If I h' now found grace in thine
10 Whither h' ye made a road to day?
28: 9 cut off those that h' familiar spirits,
15 therefore I h' called thee, that thou
21 obeyed thy voice, and I h' put my life
21 and h' hearkened unto thy words
22 and eat, that th'u mayest h' strength,
29: 3 and I h' found no fault in him since
6 for I h' not found evil in thee since
8 But what h' I done? and what hast
8 I h' been with thee unto this day,
9 the Philistines h' said, He shall not
10 up early in the morning, and h' light,
30: 22 of the spoil that we h' recovered, save
2Sa 1: 10 was on his arm, and h' brought them
16 against thee, saying, I h' slain the
2: 5 that ye h' shewed this kindness unto
5 even unto Saul, and h' buried him.
6 because ye h' done this thing.
7 also the house of Judah h' anointed
3: 8 and h' not delivered thee into the
4: 6 as though they would h' fetched

2Sa 4: 10 Saul is dead, thinking to h' brought
10 who thought that I would h' given *
11 much more, when wicked men h' slain
7: 6 Whereas I h' not dwelt in any house
6 but h' walked in a tent and in a
7 all the places wherein I h' walked
9 and h' cut off all thine enemies out
9 and h' made thee a great name, like*
11 and h' caused thee to rest from all*
22 according to all that we h' heard
9: 9 I h' given unto thy master's son all
10 that thy master's son may h' food 1961
12: 8 I would moreover h' given unto thee
13 David said unto Nathan, I h' sinned
27 to David, and said, I h' fought against
27 against Rabbah, and h' taken the city
13: 9 And Amnon said, H' out all men 3318
28 h' not I commanded you? be
32 not my lord suppose that they h' slain
14: 15 because the people h' made me afraid:
21 Behold now, I h' done this thing: go
22 that I h' found grace in thy sight, my
29 to h' sent him to the king; but he *
31 h' thy servants set my field on fire?
32 good for me to h' been there still:*
15: 7 pay my vow, which I h' vowed unto
26 But if he thus say, I h' no delight in
34 as I h' been thy father's servant
36 Behold, they h' there with them their
16: 10 What h' I to do with you, ye sons of
19 as I h' served in thy father's presence,
17: 15 and thus and thus h' I counselled.
18: 11 and I would h' given thee ten shekels
13 Otherwise I should h' wrought *
13 thyself wouldest h' set thyself against
18 I h' no son to keep my name in
19: 5 this day h' saved thy life, and the
20 I h' sinned: therefore, behold, I am
22 What h' I to do with you, ye sons of
28 What right therefore h' I yet to 3426
29 I h' said, Thou and Ziba divide the*
34 How long h' I to live, that I should*
41 Why h' our brethren...stolen thee
41 and h' brought the king, and his *
42 h' we eaten at all of the king's cost?
43 said, We h' ten parts in the king,
43 and we h' also more right in David
20: 1 and said, We h' no part in David,
1 neither h' we inheritance in the son
21: 4 We will h' no silver nor gold of Saul,*
16 sword, thought to h' slain David.
22: 22 for I h' kept the ways of the Lord,
22 and h' not wickedly departed from
24 h' kept myself from mine iniquity.*
30 for by thee I h' run through a troop:*
30 by my God h' I leaped over a wall. *
38 I h' pursued mine enemies, and
39 And I h' consumed them, and
24: 10 David said unto the Lord, I h' sinned
10 sinned greatly in that I h' done:
10 servant; for I h' done very foolishly.
17 the people, and said, Lo, I h' sinned,
17 and I h' done wickedly: but these
17 what h' they done? let thine hand,
1Ki 1: 35 and I h' appointed him to be ruler
44 and they h' caused him to ride upon
45 h' anointed him king in Gihon:
2: 14 said moreover, I h' somewhat to say
23 if Adonijah h' not spoken this word
42 The word that I h' heard is good.
43 commandment that I h' charged thee
3: 12 Behold, I h' done according to thy
12 lo, I h' given thee a wise and
13 And I h' also given thee that which
5: 8 I h' considered the things which thou
8: 13 I h' surely built thee an house to
20 and h' built an house for the name
21 And I h' set there a place for the ark.
27 less this house that I h' builded?
28 Yet h' thou respect unto the prayer
33 because they h' sinned against thee,
35 because they h' sinned against thee;
43 this house, which I h' builded, is
44 and toward the house that I h' built
47 them captives, saying, We h' sinned,
47 sinned, and h' done perversely, we
47 we h' committed wickedness;
48 the house which I h' built for thy
50 And forgive thy people that h' sinned
50 wherein they h' transgressed against
50 that they may h' compassion on
59 wherewith I h' made supplication
9: 3 I h' heard thy prayer and thy
3 I h' hallowed this house, which thou
4 to all that I h' commanded thee, and
6 my statutes which I h' set before you,
7 out of the land which I h' given them;
7 and this house, which I h' hallowed for
9 and h' taken hold on other gods, *
9 and h' worshipped them, and served*
11: 11 my statutes, which I h' commanded
13 for Jerusalem's sake which I h' chosen.
32 But he shall h' one tribe for my 1961
32 the city which I h' chosen out of all
33 Because that they h' forsaken me,
33 and h' worshipped Ashtoreth the
33 and h' not walked in my ways, to do
36 the city which I h' chosen me to put
12: 9 people, who h' spoken to me, saying,
16 saying, What portion h' we in David?
16 neither h' we inheritance in the son
14: 15 because they h' made their groves,
15: 19 behold, I h' sent unto thee a present
17: 4 and I h' commanded the ravens to
9 I h' commanded a widow woman
12 thy God liveth, I h' not a cake, 3426

1Ki 17:18 What h' I to do with thee, O thou man
18: 9 And he said, What h' I sinned, that
18 answered, I h' not troubled Israel;
18 ye h' forsaken the commandments
36 and that I h' done all these things at
19:10 And he said, I h' been very jealous
10 for the children of Israel h' forsaken
14 And he said, I h' been very jealous
14 the children of Israel h' forsaken
18 Yet I h' left me seven thousand in *
18 all the knees which h' not bowed
20 Go back again: for what h' I done to
20: 4 saying, I am thine, and all that I h'.
5 Although I h' sent unto thee, saying,*
28 Because the Syrians h' said, The
31 Behold now, we h' heard that the
21: 2 thy vineyard, that I may h' it for 1961
20 he answered, I h' found thee: because
22:11 Syrians, until thou h' consumed them.*
17 as sheep that h' not a shepherd:
17 These h' no master: let them return
2Ki 2:21 Thus saith the Lord, I h' healed these
3:13 What h' I to do with thee? get thee to
23 and they h' smitten one another: now
27 eldest son that should h' reigned in
5: 6 behold, I h' therewith sent Naaman
13 wouldest thou not h' done it? how
7:12 shew you what the Syrians h' done to
17 whose hand he leaned to h' the charge
9: 3 I h' anointed thee king over Israel.
5 and he said, I h' an errand to thee, O
6 I h' anointed thee king over the
12 saith the Lord, I h' anointed thee king
26 Surely I h' seen yesterday the blood
10: 8 They h' brought the heads of the
19 wanting: for I h' a great sacrifice to
24 any of the men whom I h' brought *
11:15 H' her forth without the ranges: 3318
13:17 in Aphek, till thou h' consumed
19 Thou shouldest h' smitten five or six
17:38 And the covenant that I h' made with
18:14 saying, I h' offended; return from me:
20 I h' counsel and strength for the war.*
34 h' they delivered Samaria out of
35 that h' delivered their country out of
19: 6 of the king of Assyria h' blasphemed
11 the kings of Assyria h' done to all
12 H' the gods of the nations delivered
12 which my fathers h' destroyed; as
17 the kings of Assyria h' destroyed the
18 And h' cast their gods into the fire:
18 and stone: therefore they h' destroyed
20 Sennacherib king of Assyria I h' heard.
24 h' digged and drunk strange waters,
24 and with the sole of my feet h' I dried*
25 not heard long ago how I h' done it,
25 of ancient times that I h' formed it?*
25 now h' I brought it to pass, that
20: 3 remember now how I h' walked before
3 and h' done that which is good in
5 thy father, I h' heard thy prayer,
5 I h' seen thy tears: behold, I will heal
9 This sign shalt thou h' of the Lord,*
15 And he said, What h' they seen in
15 that are in mine house h' they seen:
15 my treasures that I h' not shewed
17 and that which thy fathers h' laid up
21: 7 and in Jerusalem, which I h' chosen
8 according to all that I h' commanded
15 Because they h' done that which was
15 and h' provoked me to anger, since the
22: 4 keepers of the door h' gathered of the
5 that h' the oversight of the house of
8 I h' found the book of the law in the
9 Thy servants h' gathered the money
9 and h' delivered it into the hand of
9 that h' the oversight of the house of
13 because our fathers h' not hearkened
17 Because they h' forsaken me, and
17 and h' burned incense unto other
19 I also h' heard thee, saith the Lord.
23:27 as I h' removed Israel, and will cast
27 city Jerusalem which I h' chosen,
1Ch 11:19 blood of these men that h' put their
15:12 unto the place that I h' prepared for
17: 5 For I h' not dwelt in an house since the
5 but h' gone from tent to tent, and
6 Wheresoever I h' walked with all
6 Why h' ye not built me an house of
8 I h' been with thee whithersoever
8 and h' cut off all thine enemies from
8 and h' made thee a name like the*
20 to all that we h' heard with our ears.
21: 8 And David said unto God, I h' sinned
8 because I h' done this thing: but now,
8 servant; for I h' done very foolishly.
17 even I it is that h' sinned and done
17 as for these sheep, what h' they done?
22:14 behold, in my trouble I h' prepared
14 and stone h' I prepared; and thou
28: 6 for I h' chosen him to be my son, and
29: 2 Now I h' prepared with all my might
3 because I h' set my affection to thee
3 I h' of mine own proper good, of 3426
3 I h' given to the house of my God,*
3 all that I h' prepared for the holy
14 and of thine own h' we given thee.
16 all this store that we h' prepared to
17 I h' willingly offered all these things:
17 and now h' I seen with joy thy people,
19 for the which I h' made provision.
2Ch 1:11 over whom I h' made thee king:
12 such as none of the kings h' had
12 that h' been before thee, either shall
12 there any after thee h' the like, 1961
2:13 And now I h' sent a cunning man,

2Ch 6: 2 But I h' built an house of habitation
6 But I h' chosen Jerusalem, that my
6 and h' chosen David to be over my
10 and h' built the house for the name of
11 And in it h' I put the ark, wherein is
18 much less this house which I h' built!
19 H' respect therefore to the prayer of
24,26 because they h' sinned against thee;
33 this house which I h' built is called by
34 the house which I h' built for thy
37 their captivity, saying, We h' sinned,
37 sinned, we h' done amiss, and
37 done amiss, and h' dealt wickedly;
38 whither they h' carried them captives,
38 and toward the house which I h' built
39 forgive thy people which h' sinned
7:12 and said unto him, I h' heard thy
12 and h' chosen this place to myself for
16 For now I h' chosen and sanctified
17 according to all that I h' commanded
18 according as I h' covenanted with *
19 which I h' set before you, and shall go
20 out of my land which I h' given them;
20 and this house, which I h' sanctified
10: 9 answer to this people, that h' spoken
16 saying, What portion h' we in David?
16 and we h' none inheritance in the son
12: 5 saith the Lord, Ye h' forsaken me,
5 and therefore h' I also left you in
7 They h' humbled themselves;
13: 7 h' strengthened themselves against*
9 H' ye not cast out the priests of the
9 and h' made you priests after the
10 our God, and we h' not forsaken him;
11 our God; but ye h' forsaken him.
14: 7 because we h' sought the Lord our
7 we h' sought him, and he hath given
11 or with them that h' no power: help*
16: 3 behold, I h' sent thee silver and gold;
9 henceforth thou shalt h' wars. 3426
18:16 as sheep that h' no shepherd:
16 and the Lord said, These h' no master;
20: 8 they dwelt therein, and h' built thee
12 for we h' no might against this great
21:15 And thou shalt h' great sickness by
23:14 them, H' her forth of the ranges: 3318
24:20 because ye h' forsaken the Lord, he
25: 9 hundred talents which I h' given to
28: 9 and ye h' slain them in a rage that
11 which ye h' taken captive of your
13 for whereas we h' offended against *
29: 6 For our fathers h' trespassed, and
6 Lord our God, and h' forsaken him,
6 and h' turned away their faces from
7 Also they h' shut up the doors of the
7 and h' not burned incense nor offered
9 For, lo, our fathers h' fallen by the
18 We h' cleansed all the house of the
19 h' we prepared and sanctified
31 Now ye h' consecrated yourselves unto
31:10 of the Lord, we h' had enough to eat,
10 and h' left plenty: for the Lord hath
32:13 what I and my fathers h' done unto all
17 h' not delivered their people out of
33: 7 which I h' chosen before all the tribes
8 land which I h' appointed for your
8 to do all that I h' commanded them,
34:15 I h' found the book of the law in the
17 And they h' gathered together the
17 and h' delivered it into the hand of the
21 because our fathers h' not kept the
24 book which they h' read before the
25 Because they h' forsaken me, and
25 and h' burned incense unto other gods,
27 I h' even heard thee also, saith the
35:21 What h' I to do with thee, thou king of
21 against the house wherewith I h' war:
23 H' me away; for I am sore 5674
Ezr 4: 3 Ye h' nothing to do with us to build
12 and h' set up the walls thereof, and
14 Now because we h' maintenance *
15 and that they h' moved sedition within
16 thou shalt h' no portion on this 383
19 rebellion and sedition h' been made
20 There h' been mighty kings also 1934
20 which h' ruled over all countries
6: 9 And that which they h' need of, both
11 Also I h' made a decree, that whosoever
12 I Darius h' made a decree; let it be
7:15 and his counsellors h' freely offered
20 which thou shalt h' occasion to bestow,
9: 1 and the Levites, h' not separated
2 For they h' taken of their daughters
2 so that the holy seed h' mingled
7 h' we been in a great trespass
7 iniquities h' we...been delivered
10 for we h' forsaken thy commandments,
11 which h' filled it from one end to
10: 2 said unto Ezra, We h' trespassed
2 and h' taken strange wives of the
10 said unto them, Ye h' transgressed,
10 and h' taken strange wives, to increase
13 we are many that h' transgressed in
14 let all them which h' taken strange
Ne 1: 6 which we h' sinned against thee: both
6 I and my father's house h' sinned.
7 We h' dealt very corruptly against
7 and h' not kept the commandments,
9 the place that I h' chosen to set my
2: 5 and if thy servant h' found favour in
20 but ye h' no portion, nor right, nor
4: 5 for they h' provoked thee to anger
5: 3 We h' mortgaged our lands, *
4 We h' borrowed money for the king's
5 for other men h' our lands and
8 after our ability h' redeemed our

Ne 5:14 I and my brethren h' not eaten the
19 according to all that I h' done for
6:13 and that they might h' matter for an
14 the prophets, that would h' put me in
9:33 thou hast done right, but we h' done
34 Neither h' our kings...kept thy law,
35 For they h' not served thee in their
37 also they h' dominion over our bodies,
10:37 same Levites might h' the tithes
13:14 that I h' done for the house of my God,
29 because they h' defiled the priesthood,
Es 1:18 which h' heard of the deed of the
3: 9 of those that h' the charge of the
4:11 but I h' not been called to come in
5: 4 the banquet that I h' prepared for
8 If I h' found favour in the sight of the
7: 3 If I h' found favour in thy sight, O
8: 5 and if I h' found favour in his sight
7 Behold, I h' given Esther the house of
7 and him they h' hanged upon the
9: 1 enemies of the Jews hoped to h' power
12 The Jews h' slain and destroyed five
12 what h' they done in the rest of the
Job 1: 5 It may be that my sons h' sinned, and
15 yea, they h' slain the servants with
17 fell upon the camels, and h' carried
3: 9 let it look for light, but h' none;
13 For now should I h' lain still and
13 I should h' slept: then had I been at
4: 4 Thy words h' upholden him that was
8 Even as I h' seen, that they plow
5: 3 I h' seen the foolish taking root: but
27 Lo this, we h' searched it, so it is;
6: 8 Oh that I might h' my request; 935
10 Then should I yet h' comfort; *1961
10 for I h' not concealed the words of
15 My brethren h' dealt deceitfully as a
24 me to understand wherein I h' erred.
7:20 I h' sinned; what shall I do unto
8: 4 If thy children h' sinned against him,
4 and he h' cast them away for their
18 deny him, saying, I h' not seen thee.
10: 8 Thine hands h' made me and
19 I should h' been as though I had
19 I should h' been carried from the
12: 3 But I h' understanding as well as
14:15 thou wilt h' a desire to the work
22 his flesh upon him shall h' pain, *
15:17 and that which I h' seen I will
18 Which wise men h' told from their
18 from their fathers, and h' not hid it:
16: 2 I h' heard many such things:
3 Shall vain words h' an end? or what
10 They h' gaped upon me with their
10 they h' smitten me upon the cheek
10 they h' gathered themselves together*
15 I h' sewed sackcloth upon my skin,
18 blood, and let my cry h' no place. 1961
17:13 I h' made my bed in the darkness.
14 I h' said to corruption, Thou art my
18:17 the earth, and he shall h' no name in
19 He shall neither h' son nor nephew
19: 3 These ten times h' ye reproached me:
4 And be it indeed that I h' erred, mine
14 my kinsfolk h' failed, and my
14 and my familiar friends h' forgotten
21 H' pity upon me, h' pity upon me,
20: 3 I h' heard the check of my reproach,
7 they which h' seen him shall say,
21: 3 and after that I h' spoken, mock on.
15 what profit should we h', if we pray
29 H' ye not asked them that go by the
22: 9 of the fatherless h' been broken.
15 way which wicked men h' trodden?
25 and thou shalt h' plenty of silver. *
26 then shalt thou h' thy delight in the*
23:11 hath held his steps, his way h' I kept,
12 Neither h' I gone back from the
12 I h' esteemed the words of his mouth
24: 7 clothing, that they h' no covering
19 the grave those which h' sinned.
27:12 Behold, all ye yourselves h' seen it;
28: 8 The lion's whelps h' not trodden it,
22 We h' heard the fame thereof with
30: 1 are younger than I h' me in derision,
1 whose fathers I would h' disdained *
1 to h' set with the dogs of my flock. *
13 my calamity, they h' no helper.
16 the days of affliction h' taken hold
31: 5 If I h' walked with vanity, or if my
9 If mine heart h' been deceived by a
9 or if I h' laid wait at my neighbour's
16 If I h' withheld the poor from their
16 or h' caused the eyes of the widow to
17 Or h' eaten my morsel myself alone,
18 and I h' guided her from my mother's
19 If I h' seen any perish for want of
20 If his loins h' not blessed me, and if
21 If I h' lifted up my hand against the
24 If I h' made gold my hope, or
24 or h' said to the fine gold, Thou art
28 for I should h' denied the God that is
30 Neither h' I suffered my mouth to *
39 If I h' eaten the fruits thereof without
39 or h' caused the owners thereof to
32:13 should say, We h' found out wisdom:
33: 2 Behold, now I h' opened my mouth,
8 and I h' heard the voice of thy words,
24 to the pit: I h' found a ransom.
27 and if any say, I h' sinned, and
34: 2 ear unto me, ye that h' knowledge.
31 I h' borne chastisement, I will not
32 if I h' done iniquity, I will do no more
35: 3 What profit shall I h', if I be cleansed
36: 2 that I h' yet to speak on God's behalf.
9 transgressions that they h' exceeded.

Job 36:16 Even so would he *h'* removed thee out
38:17 *H'* the gates of death been opened
23 Which I *h'* reserved against tne time
39: 6 Whose house I *h'* made the wilderness,
40: 5 Once *h'* I spoken; but I will not
42: 3 therefore *h'* I uttered that I
5 I *h'* heard of thee by the hearing of *
7 for ye *h'* not spoken of me the thing
8 in that ye *h'* not spoken of me the thing
Ps 2: 4 the Lord shall *h'* them in derision.
6 Yet *h'* I set my king upon my holy
7 art my Son; this day *h'* I begotten
3: 6 that *h'* set themselves against me
4: 1 *h'* mercy upon me, and hear my
5:10 transgressions; for they *h'* rebelled
6: 2 *H'* mercy upon me, O Lord; for I
7: 3 O Lord my God, if I *h'* done this; if
4 If I *h'* rewarded evil unto him that
4 yea, I *h'* delivered him that without
8: 6 madest him to *h'* dominion over
9:13 *H'* mercy upon me, O Lord;
10: 2 in the devices that they *h'* imagined.
12: 4 Who *h'* said, With our tongue will we
13: 4 Lest mine enemy say, I *h'* prevailed
5 But I *h'* trusted in thy mercy; my
14: 1 they *h'* done abominable works,
4 *H'* all...of iniquity no knowledge?
6 Ye *h'* shamed the counsel of the *
16: 6 places; yea, I *h'* a goodly heritage.5921
8 I *h'* set the Lord always before me:
17: 4 I *h'* kept me from the paths of the
6 I *h'* called upon thee, for thou wilt
11 They *h'* now compassed us in our
11 they *h'* set their eyes bowing down *
14 which *h'* their portion in this life, *
18:21 For I *h'* kept the ways of the Lord,
21 and *h'* not wickedly departed from
29 For by thee I *h'* run through a troop;*
29 and by my God *h'* I leaped over a *
37 I *h'* pursued mine enemies, and *
38 I *h'* wounded them that they were *
43 a people whom I *h'* not known shall
19:13 let them not *h'* dominion over me:
22:12 Many bulls *h'* compassed me: strong
12 strong bulls of Bashan *h'* beset me
16 For dogs *h'* compassed me: the
16 assembly of the wicked *h'* inclosed
25: 6 for they *h'* been ever of old.
16 thee unto me, and *h'* mercy upon
26: 1 Judge me, O Lord; for I *h'* walked in
1 I *h'* trusted also in the Lord;
3 before mine eyes: and I *h'* walked in
4 I *h'* not sat with vain persons, neither
5 I *h'* hated the congregation of evil *
8 Lord, I *h'* loved the habitation of thy*
27: 4 One thing *h'* I desired of the Lord,
7 *h'* mercy also upon me, and
30:10 Hear, O Lord, and *h'* mercy upon
31: 4 me out of the net that they *h'* laid
6 I *h'* hated them that regard lying *
9 *H'* mercy upon me, O Lord, for I
13 For I *h'* heard the slander of many:
17 for I *h'* called upon thee: let the
32: 5 thee, and mine iniquity *h'* I not hid.
9 the mule, which *h'* no understanding:
33:21 because we *h'* trusted in his holy
35: 7 For withou cause *h'* they hid for me
7 without cause they *h'* digged for my
25 Ah, so would we *h'* it: let them not
25 say, We *h'* swal owed him up.
37:14 The wicked *h'* drawn out the sword,
14 and *h'* bent their bow, to cast down
25 I *h'* been young, and now am old;
25 yet *h'* I not seen the righteous
35 I *h'* seen the wicked in great power,
38: 8 I *h'* roared by reason of...disquietness
40: 9 I *h'* preached righteousness in the
9 lo, I *h'* not refrained my lips, O Lord,*
10 I *h'* not hid thy ighteousness within
10 I *h'* declared thy faithfulness and thy
10 I *h'* not conce ed thy l vingkindn ss
12 For innumerable vils *h'* compass d
12 mine iniquities *h'* taken hold upon
41: 4 heal my soul; for I *h'* sinned against
42: 3 My tears *h'* been my meat day
44: 1 We *h'* heard with our ears, O God, our
1 our fathers *h'* told us, what work
17 come upon us; yet *h'* we no forgotten
17 neither *h'* we dealt falsely in thy
18 neither *h'* our steps declined from
20 If we *h'* forgotten the name f our
45: 1 which I *h'* made touching the king:
8 whereby they *h'* made thee gla .
48: 8 As we *h'* heard, so *h'* we se n in the
9 We *h'* thought of hy lovingkindness,
49:14 the upright shall *h'* dominion
50: 5 those that *h'* made a covenant with
8 to *h'* been continually before me.*
51: 1 *H'* mercy upon me, O God,
4 Against thee, thee only, *h'* I sinned,
53: 1 and *h'* done abominable iniquity:
4 *H'* the...of iniquity no knowledge?
4 as they eat bread: they *h'* not called*
54: 3 after my soul: they *h'* not set God
55: 9 for I *h'* seen violence and strife in the
12 then I could *h'* borne it: neither was it
12 against me; then I would *h'* hid
19 Because they *h'* no changes, therefore
56: 4 in God I *h'* put my trust; I will not fear
11 In God *h'* I put my trust: I will not be
57: 6 They *h'* prepared a net for my steps;
6 they *h'* digged a pit before me, into
59: 8 shalt *h'* all the heathen in derision.
62:11 hath spoken once; twice *h'* I heard
63: 2 thy glory, so as I *h'* seen thee in the
66:14 Which my lips *h'* uttered, and my

Ps 68:13 Though ye *h'* lien among the pots, *
24 They *h'* seen thy goings, O God;
69: 7 for thy sake I *h'* borne reproach;
22 should *h'* been for their welfare, *
35 there, and *h'* it in possession.
71: 6 By thee *h'* I been holden up from the
17 and hitherto *h'* I declared thy
18 until I *h'* shewed thy strength unto
72: 8 He shall *h'* dominion also from sea to
73: 7 with fatness: they *h'* more than heart
13 Verily I *h'* cleansed my heart in vain,
14 For all the day long *h'* I been plagued,
25 Whom *h'* I in heaven but thee? and
28 I *h'* put my trust in the Lord God, that
74: 7 They *h'* cast fire into thy sanctuary,
7 they *h'* defiled by casting down the
8 they *h'* burned up all the synagogues
18 that the foolish people *h'* blasphemed
20 *H'* respect unto the covenant: for the
76: 5 are spoiled, they *h'* slept their sleep:
5 none of the men of might *h'* found
77: 5 I *h'* considered the days of old, the
78: 3 Which we *h'* heard and known, and
3 known, and our fathers *h'* told us.
79: 1 thy holy temple *h'* they defiled;
1 they *h'* laid Jerusalem on heaps.
2 thy servants *h'* they given to be meat
3 Their blood *h'* they shed like water
6 the heathen that *h'* not known thee,*
6 the kingdoms that *h'* not called upon*
7 For they *h'* devoured Jacob, and laid
12 wherewith they *h'* reproached thee,
81:14 I should soon *h'* subdued their *
15 of the Lord should *h'* submitted *
15 but their time should *h'* endured *
16 He should *h'* fed them also with the*
16 the rock should I *h'* satisfied thee. *
82: 6 I *h'* said, Ye are gods; and all of you*
83: 2 and they that hate thee *h'* lifted up
3 They *h'* taken crafty counsel against*
4 They *h'* said, Come, and let us cut
5 For they *h'* consulted together with
8 they *h'* holpen the children of Lot.
85:10 righteousness and peace *h'* kissed
86:14 of violent men *h'* sought after my
14 and *h'* not set thee before them.
16 O turn unto me, and *h'* mercy
88: 1 I *h'* cried day and night before thee:
9 Lord, I *h'* called daily upon thee, I
9 I *h'* stretched out my hands unto thee.
13 But unto thee *h'* I cried, O Lord; and
16 over me; thy terrors *h'* cut me off.
89: 2 For I *h'* said, Mercy shall be built up
3 I *h'* made a covenant with my chosen,
3 I *h'* sworn unto David my servant,
19 I *h'* laid help upon one that is mighty;
19 I *h'* exalted one chosen out f the
20 I *h'* found David my servant; with my
20 with my holy oil *h'* I anointed him:
35 Once *h'* I sworn by my h liness that
51 thine enemies *h'* reproached, O
51 wherewith they *h'* reproached the
90:15 and the years wherein we *h'* seen evil.
93: 3 The floods *h'* lifted up, O Lord, the
3 the floods *h'* lifted up the r voice;
94:20 the throne of iniquity *h'* fellowship
95:10 and they *h'* not known my ways:
98: all the ends of the earth *h'* seen the
102: For I *h'* eaten ashes like bread, and
13 Thou shall arise, and *h'* mercy
27 s me, an thy years shall *h'* no end.
104:1 fowls f the heaven their habitation,
33 praise my God while I *h'* my being.
106: 6 We sinned with ou thers, we
6 we committed iniquity, we
iniquity, we *h'* done wickedly.
109: they *h'* p ken against m with a
And hey rewarded m evil for
111: 2 sought out f all them that *h'* pleasure
10 a good understanding *h'* all they that
115: 5 They *h'* mouths, but th y speak not:
5 eye *h'* they, bu they s e not:
The *h'* ears, but they he r not: noses
6 noses y, but they smell not:
7 They *h'* hands, but they handle not:
7 feet *h'* the , bu they walk not:
116:10 I belie ed, th refore *h'* I spoken: I *
118:26 we *h'* blessed you out of the house of
119: 6 when I *h'* resp un all thy
wh I shall *h'* learne thy righteous*
10 Wi my whole heart *h'* I sought thee:
11 Thy w d hid in mine heart, that
13 With lip *h'* I eclared all the
1 I *h'* r oiced i the way thy
15 and *h'* espect unto th ways.
22 for I *h'* kept thy tes nies.
26 I *h'* declared my ways, and thou *
30 I ch sen the way f truth: thy
30 thy judgments *h'* I laid before me.
31 I *h'* stuck un o hy testimon es: O*
40 Behold, I longed after thy recepts:
42 So hal wherewith answer him
43 for I *h'* ed in t y j gments.
47 in y commandmen ...I loved.
48 unto thy mmandments,...I *h'* loved;
51 proud had m greatly derision:
51 yet *h'* I not declined from thy law.
52 O Lord; and *h'* comforted myself.
54 Thy statutes *h'* been my songs in
55 I *h'* remembered thy name, O Lord, in
55 in the ni t, and k t thy law.
57 I *h'* said that I would keep thy words.
61 Tho bands of the wicked *h'* robbed me:
61 but I *h'* not forgotten thy law.
66 for I *h'* believed thy commandments.
67 astray: but now *h'* I kept thy word.*

Ps 119:69 The proud *h'* forged a lie against me:
71 good for me that I *h'* been afflicted;
73 Thy hands *h'* made me and fashioned
74 me; because I *h'* hoped in thy word.
79 that *h'* known thy testimonies. *
85 The proud *h'* digged pits for me,
92 I should then *h'* perished in mine
94 me; for I *h'* sought thy precepts.
95 The wicked *h'* waited for me to
96 I *h'* seen an end of all perfection:
99 I *h'* more understanding than all my
101 I *h'* refrained my feet from every evil
102 I *h'* not departed from thy judgments:
106 I *h'* sworn, and I will perform it, that
110 The wicked *h'* laid a snare for me:
111 Thy testimonies *h'* I taken as an
112 I *h'* inclined mine heart to perform
117 and I will *h'* respect unto thy statutes
121 I *h'* done judgment and justice:
126 work: for they *h'* made void thy law.
133 let not any iniquity *h'* dominion
139 mine enemies *h'* forgotten thy words.
143 Trouble and anguish *h'* taken hold on
152 I *h'* known of old that thou hast
161 Princes *h'* persecuted me without a
165 Great peace *h'* they which love thy
166 Lord, I *h'* hoped for thy salvation,
168 I *h'* kept thy precepts and thy
173 help me; for I *h'* chosen thy precepts.
174 I *h'* longed for thy salvation, O Lord;
176 I *h'* gone astray like a lost sheep;
123: 2 until that he *h'* mercy upon us.
3 *H'* mercy upon us, O Lord, *h'* mercy
129: 1,2 Many a time *h'* they afflicted me
2 yet they *h'* not prevailed against me.
130: 1 Out of the depths *h'* I cried unto thee
131: 2 Surely I *h'* behaved and quieted
132:14 here will I dwell; for I *h'* desired it.
17 I *h'* ordained a lamp for mine
135:16 They *h'* mouths, but they speak not;
16 eyes *h'* they, but they see not;
17 They *h'* ears, but they hear not;
140: 3 They *h'* sharpened their tongues like
4 who *h'* purposed to overthrow my
5 The proud *h'* hid a snare for me, and
5 they *h'* spread a net by the wayside;
5 wayside; they *h'* set gins for me.
141: 9 the snares which they *h'* laid for me,
142: 3 I walked *h'* they privily laid a snare
143: 3 as those that *h'* been long dead.
146: 2 unto my God while I *h'* any being.
147:20 judgments, they *h'* not known them.
149: 9 this honour *h'* all his saints. Praise
Pr 1:14 among us; let us all *h'* one purse: 1961
24 Because I *h'* called, and ye refused;
24 I *h'* stretched out my hand, and no
25 But ye *h'* set at nought all my counsel,
3:30 cause, if he *h'* done thee no harm.
4:11 I *h'* taught thee in the way of wisdom;
11 of wisdom; I *h'* led thee in right paths.
16 sleep not, except they *h'* done mischief;
5:12 And say, How *h'* I hated instruction,
13 And *h'* not obeyed the voice of my
7:14 I *h'* peace offerings with me; this day*
14 with me; this day *h'* I paid my vows.
15 to seek thy face, and I *h'* found thee.
16 I *h'* decked my bed with coverings of
17 I *h'* perfumed my bed with myrrh,
26 yea, many strong men *h'* been slain *
8:14 I am understanding; I *h'* strength.
9: 5 drink of the wine which I *h'* mingled.
13: 3 wide his lips shall *h'* destruction.
14:26 his children shall *h'* a place of 1961
17: 2 A wise servant shall *h'* rule over a son
2 shall *h'* part of the inheritance
19:10 much less for a servant to *h'* rule over
20: 4 shall he beg in harvest, and *h'* nothing.
9 Who can say, I *h'* made my heart clean,
22:19 I *h'* made known to thee this day, even
20 *H'* not I written to thee excellent
28 landmark, which thy fathers *h'* set.
23:24 begetteth a wise child shall *h'* joy
35 They *h'* stricken me, shalt thou say,
24:23 It is not good to *h'* respect of persons
25: 7 of the prince whom thine eyes *h'* seen
27:27 And thou shalt *h'* goats' milk *
28:10 but the upright shall *h'* good things*
13 forsaketh them shall *h'* mercy. *
19 tilleth his land shall *h'* plenty of
19 after vain persons shall *h'* poverty
21 To *h'* respect of persons is not good:
27 hideth his eyes shall *h'* many a curse.
29:21 shall *h'* him become his son at the
30: 2 *h'* not the understanding of a man.
3 wisdom, nor *h'* the knowledge of
7 Two things *h'* I required of thee; deny
20 and saith, I *h'* done no wickedness.
27 The locusts *h'* no king, yet go they
31:11 so that he shall *h'* no need of spoil.
29 Many daughters *h'* done virtuously,
Ec 1:14 I *h'* seen all the works that are done
16 and *h'* gotten more wisdom than all
16 that *h'* been before me in Jerusalem:*
2:19 yet shall he *h'* rule over all my
19 all my labour wherein I *h'* laboured,
19 and wherein I *h'* shewed myself wise
3:10 I *h'* seen the travail, which God hath
19 yea, they *h'* all one breath; so that a
4: 9 because they *h'* a good reward for 3426
11 if two lie together, then they *h'* heat:
16 even of all that *h'* been before them:*
5:13 There is a sore evil which I *h'* seen
18 Behold that which I *h'* seen: it is good
6: 1 There is an evil which I *h'* seen under
3 and also that he *h'* no burial; I 1961
7:12 giveth life to them that *h'* it. *1167

Ec 7:15 All things h' I seen in the days of my
23 All this h' I proved by wisdom: I
27 Behold, this h' I found, saith the
28 one man among a thousand h' I found;
28 among all those h' I not found.
29 Lo, this only h' I found, that God hath
29 they h' sought out many inventions.
8: 9 All this h' I seen, and applied my heart
9: 5 neither h' they any more a reward;
6 neither h' they any more a portion for
13 This wisdom h' I seen also under the
10: 5 There is an evil which I h' seen under
7 I h' seen servants upon horses, and
12: 1 when thou shalt say, I h' no pleasure
Ca 1: 6 but mine own vineyard h' I not kept.
9 I h' compared thee, O my love, to a
2:15 for our vines h' tender grapes. *
5: 1 I h' gathered my myrrh with my spice;
1 I h' eaten my honeycomb with my
1 I h' drunk my wine with my milk:
3 I h' put off my coat; how shall I
3 I h' washed my feet; how shall I
6: 5 for they h' overcome me: thy hair is
7:13 which I h' laid up for thee, O my
8: 8 We h' a little sister, and she hath no
12 thou, O Solomon, must h' a thousand,
Isa 1: 2 I h' nourished and brought up
2 children, and they h' rebelled against
4 that are corrupters: they h' forsaken
4 they h' provoked the Holy One of
6 they h' not been closed, neither
9 remnant, we should h' been as
9 we should h' been like unto Gomorrah.
29 of the oaks which ye h' desired,
29 for the gardens that ye h' chosen.
2: 8 that which their own fingers h' made:
3: 9 for they h' rewarded evil unto
14 for ye h' eaten up the vineyard; the
4: 4 When the Lord shall h' washed away
4 and shall h' purged the blood of
5: 4 What could h' been done more to my
4 that I h' not done in it? wherefore
13 because they h' no knowledge: and*
24 because they h' cast away the law of
6: 5 for mine eyes h' seen the King, the
12 the Lord h' removed men far away,
7: 5 h' taken evil counsel against thee,*
17 days that h' not come, from the day
8: 4 the child shall h' knowledge
19 unto them that h' familiar spirits,
9: 2 walked in darkness h' seen a great
17 the Lord shall h' no joy in their *
17 neither shall h' mercy on their
10: 1 which they h' prescribed; *
11 Shall I not, as I h' done unto Samaria
13 the strength of my hand I h' done it,
13 and I h' removed the bounds of the
13 people, and h' robbed their treasures,
13 and I h' put down the inhabitants
14 that are left, h' I gathered all the
29 they h' taken up their lodging at
13: 3 I h' commanded my sanctified ones,
3 I h' also called my mighty ones for
18 and they shall h' no pity on the fruit
14: 1 For the Lord will h' mercy on
24 Surely as I h' thought, so shall it
15: 7 the abundance they h' gotten, and
7 and that which they h' laid up, shall
16: 6 We h' heard of the pride of Moab; he
8 lords of the heathen h' broken down
10 I h' made their vintage shouting to
17: 7 and his eyes shall h' respect to the
8 which his fingers h' made, either the
18: 2 whose land the rivers h' spoiled! *
7 whose land the rivers h' spoiled, to *
19: 3 to them that h' familiar spirits, and
13 they h' also seduced Egypt, even they
14 and they h' caused Egypt to err in
21: 2 the sighing thereof h' I made to cease.
3 pangs h' taken hold upon me, as the
10 that which I h' heard of the Lord of
10 of Israel, h' I declared unto you.
22: 3 are bound together, which h' fled *
9 Ye h' seen also the breaches of the*
10 And ye h' numbered the houses of*
10 and the houses h' ye broken down to*
11 but ye h' not looked unto the maker*
23: 2 that pass over the sea, h' replenished.
12 there also shalt thou h' no rest.
24: 5 because they h' transgressed
16 part of the earth h' we heard songs,
16 me! the treacherous dealers h' dealt
16 yea, the treacherous dealers h' dealt
25: 9 we h' waited for him, and he will save
9 we h' waited for him, we will be glad
26: 1 We h' a strong city; salvation will
8 O Lord, h' we waited for thee; the
9 With my soul h' I desired thee in the
13 lords beside thee h' had dominion
16 Lord, in trouble h' they visited thee,
17 so h' we been in thy sight, O Lord.
18 We h' been with child, we
18 with child, we h' been in pain, we
18 we h' as it were brought forth wind;
18 we h' not wrought any deliverance in
18 h' the inhabitants of the world fallen.
27:11 made them will not h' mercy on
28: 7 But they also h' erred through wine,*
7 the priest and the prophet h' erred*
15 ye h' said, We h' made a covenant
15 for we h' made lies our refuge, and
15 under falsehood h' we hid ourselves:
22 I h' heard from the Lord God of hosts
29:13 but h' removed their heart far from
30: 2 and h' not asked at my mouth; to
7 therefore h' I cried concerning this,

Isa 30:18 that he may h' mercy upon you:
29 Ye shall h' a song, as in the night 1961
31: 6 children of Israel h' deeply revolted.
7 which your own hands h' made unto
33: 2 unto us; we h' waited for thee:
13 ye that are far off, what I h' done;
36: 5 I h' counsel and strength for war:*
19 and h' they delivered Samaria out of
20 that h' delivered their land out of my
37: 6 the king of Assyria h' blasphemed me.
11 the kings of Assyria h' done to all
12 H' the gods of the nations delivered
12 my fathers h' destroyed, as Gozan,
18 the kings of Assyria h' laid waste all
19 And h' cast their gods into the fire:
19 and stone: therefore they h' destroyed
25 I h' digged, and drunk water; and
25 the sole of my feet h' I dried up all*
26 heard long ago, how I h' done it;
26 of ancient times, that I h' formed it?*
26 now h' I brought it to pass, that thou
38: 3 I beseech thee, how I h' walked before
3 and h' done that which is good in thy
5 thy father, I h' heard thy prayer,
5 I h' seen thy tears: behold, I will add
12 I h' cut off like a weaver my life: he
39: 4 Then said he, What h' they seen in
4 All that is in mine house h' they seen:
4 treasures that I h' not shewed them.
6 and that which thy fathers h' laid up
40:21 H' ye not known? h' ye not heard?
21 h' ye not understood from the
29 to them that h' no might he increaseth*
41: 8 Jacob whom I h' chosen, the seed of
9 Thou whom I h' taken from the ends
9 I h' chosen thee, and not cast thee
25 I h' raised up one from the north, and
42: 1 I h' put my spirit upon him: he shall
4 till he h' set judgment in the earth:
6 I the Lord h' called thee in
14 I h' long time holden my peace; I
14 I h' been still, and refrained myself:
16 in paths that they h' not known: *
24 he against whom we h' sinned? for
43: 1 O Israel, Fear not: for I h' redeemed
1 I h' called thee by thy name; thou art
4 and I h' loved thee: therefore will I
7 by my name: for I h' created him
7 for my glory, I h' formed him;
7 formed him; yea, I h' made him.
8 the blind people that h' eyes, 3426
8 eyes, and the deaf that h' ears.
12 I h' declared, and h' saved, and I
12 and I h' shewed them, when there was
14 For your sake I h' sent to Babylon,
14 and h' brought down all their nobles,
21 This people h' I formed for myself;*
23 I h' not caused thee to serve with an
27 and thy teachers h' transgressed
28 Therefore I h' profaned the princes*
28 and h' given Jacob to the curse, and*
44: 1 servant; and Israel, whom I h' chosen:
2 thou, Jesurun, whom I h' chosen.
8 h' not I told thee from that time,
8 and h' declared it? ye are even my*
16 Aha, I am warm, I h' seen the fire:
18 They h' not known nor understood:*
19 to say, I h' burned part of it in the
19 yea, also I h' baked bread upon the
19 I h' roasted flesh, and eaten it: and
21 I h' formed thee; thou art my
22 I h' blotted out, as a thick cloud, thy
22 return unto me; for I h' redeemed
45: 1 whose right hand I h' holden, to
4 I h' even called thee by thy name; I
4 I h' surnamed thee, though thou hast
8 up together; I the Lord h' created it.
12 I h' made the earth, and created man
12 I, even my hands, h' stretched out the
12 all their host h' I commanded.
13 I h' raised him up in righteousness,
19 I h' not spoken in secret, in a dark
20 they h' no knowledge that set up
21 h' not I the Lord? and there is no
23 I h' sworn by myself, the word is gone
24 in the Lord h' I righteousness and †
46: 4 I h' made, and I will bear; even I will
11 yea, I h' spoken it, I will also bring it
11 I h' purposed it, I will also do it.
47: 6 I h' polluted mine inheritance, and *
48: 3 I h' declared the former things from
5 h' even from the beginning declared
6 I h' shewed thee new things from this
10 Behold, I h' refined thee, but not with
10 I h' chosen thee in the furnace of
15 I, even I, h' spoken; yea, I h' called
15 I h' brought him, and he shall make
16 I h' not spoken in secret from the
19 his name should not h' been cut off*
49: 4 Then I said, I h' laboured in vain,
4 I h' spent my strength for nought,
8 In an acceptable time h' I heard thee,
8 and in a day of salvation h' I helped
13 will h' mercy upon his afflicted.
15 that she should not h' compassion
16 Behold, I h' graven thee upon the
20 children which thou shalt h', after*
50: 1 whom I h' put away? or which of
1 creditors is it to whom I h' sold you?
1 Behold, for your iniquities h' ye sold*
2 or h' I no power to deliver? behold,
7 therefore h' I set my face like a flint,
11 and in the sparks that ye h' kindled.
11 This shall ye h' of mine hand; ye 1961
51:16 And I h' put my words in thy mouth,
16 and I h' covered thee in the shadow

Isa 51:20 Thy sons h' fainted, they lie at the
22 Behold, I h' taken out of thine hand
23 which h' said to thy soul, Bow down,
52: 3 Ye h' sold yourselves for nought;*
5 Now therefore, what h' I here, saith*
53: 6 All we like sheep h' gone astray; we
6 we h' turned every one to his own
54: 7 For a small moment h' I forsaken
8 kindness will I h' mercy on thee,
9 for as I h' sworn that the waters of
9 so h' I sworn that I would not be
16 Behold, I h' created the smith that
16 and I h' created the waster to destroy.
55: 4 Behold, I h' given him for a witness
7 and he will h' mercy upon him;
56:11 dogs which can never h' enough, 3045
57:11 h' not I held my peace even of old,
18 I h' seen his ways, and will heal him:
58: 3 Wherefore h' we fasted, say they, and
3 wherefore h' we afflicted our soul,
5 Is it such a fast that I h' chosen?
6 Is not this the fast that I h' chosen?
59: 2 But your iniquities h' separated
2 and your sins h' hid his face from
3 your lips h' spoken lies, your tongue
8 they h' made them crooked paths:
21 and my words which I h' put in thy
60:10 but in my favour h' I had mercy
61: 7 For your shame ye shall h' double;
62: 6 I h' set watchmen upon thy walls, O
9 But they that h' gathered it shall eat
9 and they that h' brought it together
63: 3 I h' trodden the winepress alone;
18 of thy holiness h' possessed it *
18 our adversaries h' trodden down thy
64: 4 men h' not heard, nor perceived by
5 for we h' sinned: in those is*
6 iniquities, like the wind, h' taken us'
65: 2 I h' spread out my hands all the day
7 which h' burned incense upon the
10 in, for my people that h' sought me.
66: 2 all those things h' been, saith*
3 Yea, they h' chosen their own ways,
19 afar off, that h' not heard my fame,
19 neither h' seen my glory; and they
24 of the men that h' transgressed
Jer 1: 9 Behold, I h' put my words in thy
10 See, I h' this day set thee over the
16 all their wickedness, who h' forsaken
16 and h' burned incense unto other
18 For, behold, I h' made thee this day a
2: 5 What iniquity h' your fathers found in
5 and h' walked after vanity, and are
11 but my people h' changed their glory
13 For my people h' committed two evils;
13 they h' forsaken me the fountain of
16 and Tahapanes h' broken the crown
20 For of old time I h' broken thy yoke,
23 I am not polluted, I h' not gone after
25 for I h' loved strangers, and after
27 for they h' turned their back unto me,
29 ye all h' transgressed against me,
30 In vain h' I smitten your children;
31 H' I been a wilderness unto
32 yet my people h' forgotten me days
34 I h' not found it by secret search, ‡
35 because thou sayest, I h' not sinned.
3: 3 the showers h' been withholden,
13 and ye h' not obeyed my voice, saith
18 I h' given for an inheritance unto*
20 so h' ye dealt treacherously with me,
21 of Israel: for they h' perverted their
21 and they h' forgotten the Lord their
25 for we h' sinned against the Lord our
25 and h' not obeyed the voice of the
4:10 Ye shall h' peace; whereas the 1961
18 Thy way and thy doings h' procured
22 is foolish, they h' not known me;*
22 and they h' none understanding: they
22 to do good they h' no knowledge.
28 be black: because I h' spoken it, I
28 I h' purposed it, and will not repent,
31 For I h' heard a voice as of a woman
5: 3 them, but they h' not grieved; *
3 but they h' refused to receive
3 they h' made their faces harder than
3 than a rock; they h' refused to return.
5 for they h' known the way of the Lord*
5 but these h' altogether broken the
7 thy children h' forsaken me, and
11 and the house of Judah h' dealt very
12 They h' belied the Lord, and said, It
19 Like as ye h' forsaken me, and served
21 which h' eyes, and see not; *
21 see not; which h' ears, and hear not:
22 which h' placed the sand for the
25 Your iniquities h' turned away these
25 and your sins h' withholden good
31 and my people love to h' it so: and
6: 2 I h' likened the daughter of Zion to*
10 they h' no delight in it.
14 They h' healed also the hurt of the
19 because they h' not hearkened unto
23 they are cruel, and h' no mercy;
24 We h' heard the fame thereof: our
27 I h' set thee for a tower and a fortress
7:11 Behold, even I h' seen it, saith the
13 And now, because ye h' done all these
14 and to your fathers, as I h' done to
15 as I h' cast out all your brethren, even
23 in all the ways that I h' commanded*
25 unto this day I h' even sent unto you
30 For the children of Judah h' done evil
30 they h' set their abominations in the
31 And they h' built the high places of
8: 2 host of heaven, whom they h' loved.

Jer 8: 2 loved, and whom they h' served, and
2 and after whom they h' walked, and
2 walked, and whom they h' sought, and
2 and whom they h' worshipped: they
3 whither I h' driven them, saith the
6 What h' I done? every one turned to
9 lo, they h' rejected the word of the
11 For they h' healed the hurt of the
13 and the things that I h' given them
14 because we h' sinned against the
16 for they are come, and h' devoured the
19 Why h' they provoked me to anger
9: 5 they h' taught their tongue to speak
13 Because they h' forsaken my law
13 and h' not obeyed my voice, neither
14 But h' walked after the imagination
16 they nor their fathers h' known:
16 sword after them, till I h' consumed
19 confounded, because we h' forsaken
19 land, because our dwellings h' cast us
10: 11 The gods that h' not made the heavens
21 are become brutish, and h' not sought
25 for they h' eaten up Jacob, and
25 and h' made his habitation desolate.
11: 5 which I h' sworn unto your fathers,*
10 and the house of Judah h' broken my
13 streets of Jerusalem h' ye set up altars
17 which they h' done against themselves
20 for unto thee h' I revealed my cause.
12: 2 yea, they h' taken root: they grow,
5 and they h' wearied thee, then how
6 even they h' dealt treacherously with
6 yea, they h' called a multitude after
7 I h' forsaken mine house, I h' left
7 I h' given the dearly beloved of my
8 out against me: therefore h' I hated it.
10 Many pastors h' destroyed my
10 they h' trodden my portion under foot,
10 they h' made my pleasant portion a
11 They h' made it desolate, and being
12 end of the land: no flesh shall h' peace.*
13 They h' sown wheat, but shall reap
13 they h' put themselves to pain, but
14 inheritance which I h' caused my
15 after that I h' plucked them out I will
15 and h' compassion on them, and
13: 11 so h' I caused to cleave unto me the
14 pity, nor spare, nor h' mercy,
27 I h' seen thine adulteries, and thy
14: 3 And their nobles h' sent their little*
7 are many; we h' sinned against thee.
10 people, Thus h' they loved to wander,
10 they h' not refrained their feet,
14 not, neither h' I commanded them,
16 and they shall h' none to bury them,
20 our fathers: for we h' sinned against
15: 5 For who shall h' pity upon thee,
8 I h' brought upon them against the
8 h' caused him to fall upon it suddenly,
10 I h' neither lent on usury, nor men
10 nor men h' lent to me on usury; yet
15 for thy sake I h' suffered rebuke.
16: 2 neither shalt thou h' sons or
5 for I h' taken away my peace from this
10 what is our sin that we h' committed
11 Because your fathers h' forsaken me,
11 Lord, and h' walked after other gods,
11 after other gods, and h' served them,
11 served them, and h' worshipped them,
11 worshipped them, and h' forsaken me,
11 forsaken me, and h' not kept my law;
12 And ye h' done worse than your
18 sin double; because they h' defiled my
18 they h' filled mine inheritance with
19 Surely our fathers h' inherited lies,
17: 4 for ye h' kindled a fire in mine anger,
13 because they h' forsaken the Lord, the
16 As for me, I h' not hastened from
16 neither h' I desired the woeful day;
18: 8 nation, against whom I h' pronounced,
15 hath forgotten me, they h' burned
15 and they h' caused them to stumble in
20 for they h' digged a pit for my soul.
22 for they h' digged a pit to take me,
19: 4 Because they h' forsaken me, and
4 me, and h' estranged this place, and
4 and h' burned incense in it unto other
4 they nor their fathers h' known *
4 and h' filled this place with the blood
5 They h' built also the high places of
13 upon whose roofs they h' burned
13 and h' poured out drink offerings
15 all the evil that I h' pronounced
15 because they h' hardened their necks,
20: 12 for unto thee h' I opened my cause.
17 mother might h' been my grave,
21: 7 neither h' pity, nor h' mercy.
10 For I h' set my face against this city
22: 9 Because they h' forsaken the covenant*
12 in the place whither they h' led him
23: 2 Ye h' scattered my flock, and driven
2 them away, and h' not visited them:
3 whither I h' driven them, and will
11 yea, in my house h' I found their
13 And I h' seen folly in the prophets of
14 I h' seen also in the prophets of
17 Ye shall h' peace; and they say 1961
20 shall not return, until he h' executed,
20 and till he h' performed the thoughts
21 I h' not sent these prophets, yet they*
21 I h' not spoken to them, yet they *
22 then they should h' turned them from*
25 I h' heard what the prophets said,
25 saying, I h' dreamed, I h' dreamed.
27 as their fathers h' forgotten my name*
36 for ye h' perverted the words of the

Jer 23: 38 and I h' sent unto you, saying, Ye shall
24: 5 whom I h' sent out of this place into
25: 3 and I h' spoken unto you, rising
3 and speaking; but ye h' not hearkened.
4 but ye h' not hearkened, nor inclined
7 Yet ye h' not hearkened unto me, saith
8 Because ye h' not heard my words,
13 my words which I h' pronounced
26: 4 to walk in my law, which I h' set before
5 them, but ye h' not hearkened;
11 this city, as ye h' heard with your ears.
12 this city all the words that ye h' heard.
27: 5 I h' made the earth, the man and the
5 and h' given it unto whom it seemed*
6 And now h' I given all these lands
6 and the beasts of the field h' I given
8 until I h' consumed them by his hand.
15 For I h' not sent them, saith the Lord,
28: 2 I h' broken the yoke of the king of
8 The prophets that h' been before me
14 I h' put a yoke of iron upon the neck
14 and I h' given him the beasts of the
29: 4 whom I h' caused to be carried away
7 I h' caused you to be carried away
9 I h' not sent them, saith the Lord.
14 whither I h' driven you, saith the
15 Because ye h' said, The Lord hath
18 the nations whither I h' driven them:
19 Because they h' not hearkened to my
20 whom I h' sent from Jerusalem to
23 Because they h' committed villany in
23 and h' committed adultery with their
23 and h' spoken lying words in my
23 which I h' not commanded them;*
32 shall not h' a man to dwell among 1961
30: 2 the words that I h' spoken unto thee
5 We h' heard a voice of trembling, of
14 All thy lovers h' forgotten thee; they
14 for I h' wounded thee with the wound
15 increased, I h' done these things unto
18 and h' mercy on his dwellingplaces;
24 shall not return, until he h' done it,
24 and until he h' performed the intents
31: 3 Yea, I h' loved thee with an
3 with lovingkindness h' I drawn thee.
18 I h' surely heard Ephraim bemoaning
20 I will surely h' mercy upon him,
25 For I h' satiated the weary soul, and
25 and I h' replenished every sorrowful
28 that like as I h' watched over them,
29 The fathers h' eaten a sour grape,
37 for all that they h' done, saith the
32: 23 they h' done nothing of all that thou
29 upon whose roofs they h' offered
30 children of Judah h' only done evil
30 children of Israel h' only provoked
32 which they h' done to provoke me to
33 And they h' turned unto me the back,
33 yet they h' not hearkened to receive
37 whither I h' driven them in mine
42 Like as I h' brought all this great
42 all the good that I h' promised them.
33: 5 whom I h' slain in mine anger and in
5 wickedness I h' hid my face from this
8 whereby they h' sinned against
8 iniquities, whereby they h' sinned,
8 whereby they h' transgressed against
14 which I h' promised unto the house
21 he should not h' a son to reign 1961
24 thou not what this people h' spoken,
24 thus they h' despised my people, that*
25 if I h' not appointed the ordinances
26 to return, and h' mercy on them.
34: 5 for I h' pronounced the word, saith
17 Ye h' not hearkened unto me, in
18 will give the men that h' transgressed
18 which h' not performed the words of
35: 7 seed, nor plant vineyard, nor h' any:
8 Thus h' we obeyed the voice of
9 neither h' we vineyard, nor field, 1961
10 we h' dwelt in tents, and h' obeyed,
14 notwithstanding I h' spoken unto
15 I h' sent also unto you all my
15 which I h' given to you and to your
15 but ye h' not inclined your ear, nor
16 the son of Rechab h' performed the
17 all the evil that I h' pronounced
17 because I h' spoken unto them, but
17 unto them, but they h' not heard;
17 and I h' called unto them, but they
17 unto them, but they h' not answered.
18 ye h' obeyed the commandment
36: 2 all the words that I h' spoken unto
30 He shall h' none to sit upon the 1961
31 all the evil that I h' pronounced
37: 18 What h' I offended against thee, or
18 people, that ye h' put me in prison?
38: 2 for he shall h' his life for a prey. *
9 lord the king, these men h' done evil
9 in all that they h' done to Jeremiah
9 whom they h' cast into the dungeon;
22 shall say, Thy friends h' set thee on,
22 set thee on, and h' prevailed against
25 the princes hear that I h' talked
40: 3 because ye h' sinned against the
3 and h' not obeyed his voice, therefore
10 dwell in your cities that ye h' taken.
41: 8 Slay us not: for we h' treasures 3426
42: 4 prophet said unto them, I h' heard
10 repent me of the evil that I h' done
12 that he may h' mercy upon you,
14 the trumpet, nor h' hunger of bread
19 know certainly that I h' admonished
21 And now I h' this day declared it to
21 but ye h' not obeyed the voice of the
43: 10 throne upon these stones that I h' hid;

Jer 44: 2 God of Israel; Ye h' seen all the evil
2 that I h' brought upon Jerusalem,
3 they h' committed to provoke me to
9 H' ye forgotten the wickedness of
9 which they h' committed in the land*
10 neither h' they feared, nor walked in
12 that h' set their faces to go into the
13 as I h' punished Jerusalem, by the
14 they h' a desire to return 5375
17 as we h' done, we, and our fathers,
18 unto her, we h' wanted all things,
18 and h' been consumed by the sword
22 abominations which you h' committed;
23 Because ye h' burned incense, and
23 because ye h' sinned against the
23 and h' not obeyed the voice of the
25 Ye and your wives h' both spoken
25 perform our vows that we h' vowed,
26 Behold, I h' sworn by my great name,
45: 4 Behold, that which I h' built will I
4 and that which I h' planted I will
46: 5 Wherefore h' I seen them dismayed
12 The nations h' heard of thy shame,
28 the nations whither I h' driven thee:
48: 2 in Heshbon they h' devised evil
5 the enemies h' heard a cry of
29 We h' heard the pride of Moab,
33 and I h' caused wine to fail from the
34 Jahaz, h' they uttered their voice,
38 for I h' broken Moab like a vessel
49: 9 they will destroy till they h' enough. *
10 I h' made Esau bare, I h' uncovered
12 drink of the cup h' assuredly drunken;*
13 For I h' sworn by myself, saith the
14 I h' heard a rumour from the Lord,
23 for they h' heard evil tidings: they are
24 anguish and sorrows h' taken her, as
31 which h' neither gates nor bars
37 sword after them, till I h' consumed
50: 6 their shepherds h' caused them to go
6 they h' turned them away on the
6 they h' gone from mountain to hill,
6 they h' forgotten their restingplace.
7 that found them h' devoured them:
7 because they h' sinned against the
17 the lions h' driven him away: first
18 as I h' punished the king of Assyria.
21 to all that I h' commanded thee.
24 I h' laid a snare for thee, and thou
51: 7 the nations h' drunken of her wine;
9 We would h' healed Babylon, but she
24 their evil that they h' done in Zion
30 mighty men of Babylon h' foreborn to
30 they h' remained in their holds: *
30 they h' burned her dwellingplaces;*
32 the reeds they h' burned with fire,
50 Ye that h' escaped the sword, go
51 because we h' heard reproach:
La 1: 2 all her friends h' dealt treacherously
8 because they h' seen her nakedness:
11 they h' given their pleasant things
18 for I h' rebelled against his
20 for I h' grievously rebelled: abroad
21 They h' heard that I sigh: there is
21 all mine enemies h' heard of my
2: 7 they h' made a noise in the house of
10 they h' cast up dust upon their heads;
10 they h' girded themselves with
14 Thy prophets h' seen vain and foolish
14 and they h' not discovered thine
14 but h' seen for thee false burdens and
16 All thine enemies h' opened their
16 We h' swallowed her up: certainly
16 looked for; we h' found, we h' seen it.
22 those that I h' swaddled and brought
3: 21 recall to my mind, therefore h' I hope.
32 yet will he h' compassion according
42 We h' transgressed and h' rebelled:
46 All our enemies h' opened their
53 They h' cut off my life in the dungeon,
4: 10 the pitiful women h' sodden their own
12 would not h' believed that the *
12 the enemy should h' entered into*
13 that h' shed the blood of the just in
14 They h' wandered as blind men in*
14 they h' polluted themselves with *
17 in our watching we h' watched for a
5: 4 We h' drunken our water for money;
5 persecution: we labour, and h' no rest.
6 We h' given the hand to the Egyptians,
7 Our fathers h' sinned, and are not;
7 and we h' borne their iniquities.
8 Servants h' ruled over us: there is*
14 The elders h' ceased from the gate,
16 woe unto us, that we h' sinned!
Eze 2: 3 they and their fathers h' transgressed
3: 6 they would h' hearkened unto thee.*
8 Behold, I h' made thy face strong
9 adamant harder than flint h' I made
17 Son of man, I h' made thee a
4: 5 For I h' laid upon thee the years of
6 I h' appointed thee each day for a
14 till now h' I not eaten of that which
15 Lo, I h' given thee cow's dung for
5: 5 I h' set it in the midst of the nations
6 for they h' refused my judgments and
6 statutes, they h' not walked in them.
7 and h' not walked in my statutes,
7 neither h' kept my judgments,
7 neither h' done according to the
9 do in thee that which I h' not done,
11 eye spare, neither will I h' any pity.
13 that I the Lord h' spoken it in my
13 when I h' accomplished my fury in
15 furious rebukes. I the Lord h' spoken
17 upon thee. I the Lord h' spoken it.

Eze 6: 8 that ye may h' some that shall 1961
9 for the evils which they h' committed
10 that I h' not said in vain that I would
7: 4 neither will I h' pity: but I will
9 will I h' pity: I will recompense thee
14 They h' blown the trumpet, even to
20 therefore h' I set far from them.
8: 17 they h' filled the land with violence,
17 and h' returned to provoke me to
18 neither will I h' pity: and though
9: 1 Cause them that h' charge over
5 your eye spare, neither h' ye pity:
10 neither will I h' pity, but I will
11 saying, I h' done as thou hast
11: 5 Thus h' ye said, O house of Israel:
6 Ye h' multiplied your slain in this
6 ye h' filled the streets thereof with the
7 Your slain whom ye h' laid in the
8 Ye h' feared the sword; and I will
12 for ye h' not walked in my statutes,
12 but h' done after the manners of the
15 of Jerusalem h' said, Get you far from
16 I h' cast them far off among the
16 and although I h' scattered them
17 countries where ye h' been scattered.
12: 2 which h' eyes to see, and see not;
2 they h' ears to hear, and hear not:
6 for I h' set thee for a sign unto the
11 like as I h' done, so shall it be done
22 proverb that ye h' in the land of
28 but the word which I h' spoken shall *
13: 3 their own spirit, and h' seen nothing!
5 Ye h' not gone up into the gaps,
6 They h' seen vanity and lying
6 and they h' made others to hope that
7 H' ye not seen a vain vision, and
7 h' ye not spoken a lying divination,
7 Lord saith it; albeit I h' not spoken?
8 Because ye h' spoken vanity, and
10 because they h' seduced my people,
12 the daubing wherewith ye h' daubed
14 the wall that ye h' daubed with
15 and upon them that h' daubed it with
22 ye h' made the heart of the righteous
22 sad, whom I h' not made sad;
14: 3 Son of man, these men h' set up their
9 I the Lord h' deceived that prophet,
22 the evil that I h' brought upon
22 even concerning all that I h' brought
23 and ye shall know that I h' not done
23 all that I h' done in it, saith the Lord
15: 6 which I h' given to the fire for fuel,
8 because they h' committed a trespass,
16: 5 to h' compassion upon thee; but thou
7 I h' caused thee to multiply as the *
27 Behold, therefore I h' stretched out
27 and h' diminished thine ordinary food,
17: 21 know that I the Lord h' spoken it.
24 I the Lord h' brought down the high
24 high tree, h' exalted the low tree,
24 h' dried up the green tree, and
24 and h' made the dry tree to flourish:
24 I the Lord h' spoken and h' done it.
18: 2 The fathers h' eaten sour grapes, and
3 ye shall not h' occasion any more to
23 H' I any pleasure at all that the
31 whereby ye h' transgressed; and
32 For I h' no pleasure in the death
20: 27 Yet in this your fathers h' blasphemed
27 in that they h' committed a trespass
41 wherein ye h' been scattered; and I
43 doings, wherein ye h' been defiled;
43 for all your evils that ye h' committed.
44 when I h' wrought with you for my
48 I the Lord h' kindled it: it shall not
21: 5 that I the Lord h' drawn forth my
15 I h' set the point of the sword against
17 fury to rest: I the Lord h' said it.
23 to them that h' sworn oaths: but he
24 Because ye h' made your iniquity to
25 when iniquity shall h' an end, *
29 when their iniquity shall h' an end.*
32 for I the Lord h' spoken it.
22: 4 therefore h' I made thee a reproach
7 In thee h' they set light by father
7 in the midst of thee h' they dealt by
7 in thee h' they vexed the fatherless
10 In thee h' they discovered their
10 in thee h' they humbled her that was
12 In thee h' they taken gifts to shed
13 Behold, therefore I h' smitten mine
14 I the Lord h' spoken it, and will do it.
22 that I the Lord h' poured out my
25 the prey; they h' devoured souls;
25 they h' taken the treasure and *
25 they h' made her many widows in
26 Her priests h' violated my law, and
26 law, and h' profaned mine holy things:
26 they h' put no difference between the
26 neither h' they shewed difference
26 and h' hid their eyes from my
28 And her prophets h' daubed them
29 The people of the land h' used
29 and h' vexed the poor and needy:
29 yea, they h' oppressed the stranger
31 Therefore h' I poured out mine
31 I h' consumed them with the fire of
31 their own way h' I recompensed upon
23: 9 Wherefore I h' delivered her into the *
37 That they h' committed adultery, and
37 and with their idols h' they committed
37 h' also caused their sons...to pass
38 Moreover this they h' done unto me:
38 they h' defiled my sanctuary in the
38 day, and h' profaned my sabbaths.
39 thus h' they done in the midst of

Eze 23: 40 furthermore, that ye h' sent for men
24: 8 I h' set her blood upon the top of a
13 because I h' purged thee, and thou
13 till I h' caused my fury to rest upon
14 I the Lord h' spoken it: it shall come
21 whom ye h' left shall fall by the
22 And ye shall do as I h' done: ye shall
25: 15 Because the Philistines h' dealt by
15 and h' taken vengeance with a
26: 5 for I h' spoken it, saith the Lord God:
14 for I the Lord h' spoken it, saith the
27: 4 thy builders h' perfected thy beauty.
5 They h' made all thy ship boards of
5 they h' taken cedars from Lebanon
6 Of the oaks of Bashan h' they made
6 the company of the Ashurites h' made
11 they h' made thy beauty perfect.
26 Thy rowers h' brought thee into great
28: 10 strangers: for I h' spoken it, saith the
14 and I h' set thee so: thou wast upon *
16 merchandise they h' filled the midst *
22 when I shall h' executed judgments
25 When I shall h' gathered the house of
25 land that I h' given to my servant *
29: 3 own, and I h' made it for myself.
5 I h' given thee for meat to the beasts
6 because they h' been a staff of reed to
9 The river is mine, and I h' made it.
20 I h' given him the land of Egypt for
30: 8 when I h' set a fire in Egypt, and
12 strangers: I the Lord h' spoken it.
16 Sin shall h' great pain, and No shall *
16 and Noph shall h' distresses daily.
21 Son of man, I h' broken the arm of
31: 9 I h' made him fair by the multitude *
11 I h' therefore delivered him into the *
11 I h' driven him out for his wickedness.
12 h' cut him off, and h' left him:
12 from his shadow, and h' left him.
32: 24 yet h' they borne their shame with
25 They h' set her a bed in the midst of
25 yet h' they borne their shame with
27 and they h' laid their swords under
32 For I h' caused my terror in the land
33: 7 I h' set thee a watchman unto the
11 I h' no pleasure in the death of
29 when I h' laid the land most desolate
29 abominations...they h' committed.
34: 4 The diseased h' ye not strengthened,
4 neither h' ye healed that which was
4 neither h' ye bound up that which
4 neither h' ye brought again that
4 neither h' ye sought that which was
4 and with cruelty h' ye ruled them.
12 they h' been scattered in the cloudy
18 to h' eaten up the good pasture,
18 and to h' drunk of the deep waters,
19 they eat that which ye h' trodden
19 drink that which ye h' fouled with
21 Because ye h' thrust with side and *
21 with your horns, till ye h' scattered
24 among them; I the Lord h' spoken it.
27 when I h' broken the bands of their
35: 11 among them, when I h' judged thee.*
12 and that I h' heard all thy blasphemies
13 your mouth ye h' boasted against me,
13 and h' multiplied your words against
13 words against me: I h' heard them.
36: 3 Because they h' made you desolate,
5 of my jealousy h' I spoken against
5 which h' appointed my land into
6 Behold, I h' spoken in my jealousy
6 because ye h' borne the shame of the
7 I h' lifted up mine hand, Surely the
22 which ye h' profaned among the
23 which ye h' profaned in the midst of
33 In the day that I shall h' cleansed *
36 I the Lord h' spoken it, and I will
37: 13 when I h' opened your graves, O my
14 that I the Lord h' spoken it, and
23 wherein they h' sinned, and will
24 and they all shall h' one shepherd: 1961
25 land that I h' given unto Jacob my
25 wherein your fathers h' dwelt; and *
38: 8 which h' been always waste: but it is
12 which h' gotten cattle and goods,
17 Art thou he of whom I h' spoken in *
19 in the fire of my wrath h' I spoken,
39: 5 the open field: for I h' spoken it,
8 this is the day whereof I h' spoken.
15 till the buriers h' buried it in the
19 sacrifice which I h' sacrificed for
21 see my judgment that I h' executed,
21 and my hand that I h' laid upon
24 their transgressions h' I done unto *
25 and h' mercy upon the whole
26 After that they h' borne their shame,*
26 they h' trespassed against me, when
27 When I h' brought them again from
28 but I h' gathered them unto their
28 and h' left none of them any more *
41: 6 that they might h' hold, but they 1961
43: 8 they h' even defiled my holy name by
8 abominations that they h' committed:
8 wherefore I h' consumed them in
11 ashamed of all that they h' done,
44: 7 In that ye h' brought into my
7 and they h' broken my covenant
8 And ye h' not kept the charge of
8 but ye h' set keepers of my charge in
12 therefore h' I lifted up mine hand
13 abominations...they h' committed.
18 They shall h' linen bonnets upon 1961
18 and shall h' linen breeches upon * "
45: 5 house, h' for themselves, for a * "
10 Ye shall h' just balances, and a just "

Eze 45: 21 ye shall h' the passover, a feast of 1961
47: 13 Israel: Joseph shall h' two portions.
22 they shall h' inheritance with you 5307
48: 11 which h' kept my charge, which went
13 the Levites shall h' five and twenty
23 side, Benjamin shall h' a portion.*
24 west side, Simeon shall h' a portion.*
Da 2: 3 I h' dreamed a dream, and my spirit
9 for ye h' prepared lying and corrupt
25 I h' found a man of the captives of
26 unto me the dream which I h' seen,
30 that I h' more than any living, 383
3: 12 these men, O king, h' not regarded
14 the golden image which I h' set up?
15 worship the image which I h' made;
25 of the fire, and they h' no hurt; 383
28 and h' changed the king's word,
4: 9 my dream that I h' seen, and the
18 dream I king Nebuchadnezzar h' seen.
26 after that thou shalt h' known that
30 that I h' built for the house of the
5: 7 and h' a chain of gold about his neck,
14 I h' even heard of thee, that the spirit
15 the astrologers, h' been brought in
16 And I h' heard of thee, that thou canst
16 and h' a chain of gold about thy neck,
23 and they h' brought the vessels of his
23 and thy concubines, h' drunk wine in
6: 2 the king should h' no damage. 1934
7 and the captains, h' consulted
22 mouths, that they h' not hurt me:
22 before thee, O king, h' I done no hurt.
9: 5 We h' sinned, and h' committed
5 and h' done wickedly, and h' rebelled,
6 Neither h' we hearkened unto thy
7 trespass that they h' trespassed
8 to our fathers, because we h' sinned
9 forgivenesses, though we h' rebelled
10 Neither h' we obeyed the voice of the
11 Yea, all Israel h' trangressed thy law,
11 of God, because we h' sinned against
15 we h' sinned, we h' done wickedly.
10: 16 me, and I h' retained no strength.*
11: 5 and h' dominion; his dominion shall
24 his fathers h' not done, nor his fathers'
30 and h' indignation against the
30 and h' intelligence with them that
43 he shall h' power over the treasures
12: 7 and when he shall h' accomplished to
Ho 1: 6 for I will no more h' mercy upon
7 But I will h' mercy upon the house
2: 4 And I will not h' mercy upon her
12 rewards that my lovers h' given me:
23 and I will h' mercy upon her that
4: 10 For they shall eat, and not h' enough:
10 because they h' left off to take heed to
12 they h' gone a whoring from under
18 they h' committed whoredom *
5: 1 because ye h' been a snare on Mizpah,
2 though I h' been a rebuker of them *
4 and they h' not known the Lord.*
7 They h' dealt treacherously against
7 for they h' begotten strange children:
9 the tribes of Israel h' I made known
6: 5 Therefore h' I hewed them by the
5 I h' slain them by the words of my
7 But they like men h' transgressed the
7 there h' they dealt treacherously
10 I h' seen an horrible thing in the
7: 1 When I would h' healed Israel, then *
2 now their own doings h' beset them
5 the princes h' made him sick with *
6 For they h' made ready their heart
7 and h' devoured their judges;*
9 Strangers h' devoured his strength,
13 Woe unto them! for they h' fled from
13 because they h' transgressed against
13 though I h' redeemed them, yet they *
13 yet they h' spoken lies against me.
14 And they h' not cried unto me with
15 Though I h' bound and strengthened
8: 1 because they h' transgressed my
4 They h' set up kings, but not by me:
4 they h' made princes, and I knew it not:
4 their gold h' they made them idols,
7 For they h' sown the wind, and they *
10 Yea, though they h' hired among the *
12 I h' written to him the great things of *
9: 9 They h' deeply corrupted themselves,
10: 1 of his land they h' made goodly images.
3 We h' no king, because we feared not
4 They h' spoken words, swearing *
13 Ye h' plowed wickedness, ye h' reaped
13 ye h' eaten the fruit of lies: because
12: 8 rich, I h' found me out substance:
10 I h' also spoken by the prophets, and
10 and I h' multiplied visions, and used
13: 2 and h' made them molten images of
6 therefore h' they forgotten me.
14: 8 What h' I to do any more with idols?
8 I h' heard him, and observed him: I
Joe 1: 18 because they h' no pasture;
3: 2 whom they h' scattered among the
3 And they h' cast lots for my people;
3 and h' given a boy for an harlot, and
4 Yea, and what h' ye to do with me, *
5 Because ye h' taken my silver and
5 and h' carried into your temples my
6 Jerusalem h' ye sold unto the Grecians,
7 out of the place whither ye h' sold
19 because they h' shed innocent blood
21 their blood that I h' not cleansed:
Am 1: 3 because they h' threshed Gilead with
13 because they h' ripped up the women
2: 4 because they h' despised the law of
4 and h' not kept his commandments,

Am 2: 4 the which their fathers h' walked: *
3: 2 You only h' I known of all the families
4 out of his den, if he h' taken nothing?
5 from the earth, and h' taken nothing
15 great houses shall h' an end, saith
4: 6 And I also h' given you cleanness of
6 yet h' ye not returned unto me, saith
7 And also I h' withholden the rain
8 yet h' ye not returned unto me, saith
9 I h' smitten you with blasting and
9 yet h' ye not returned unto me, saith
10 I h' sent among you the pestilence
10 your young men h' I slain with sword,
10 and h' taken away your horses; and
10 I h' made the stink of your camps to
10 yet h' ye not returned unto me, saith
11 I h' overthrown some of you, as God
11 yet h' ye not returned unto me, saith
5:11 ye h' built houses of hewn stone, but
11 ye h' planted pleasant vineyards, but
14 shall be with you, as ye h' spoken.*
25 H' ye offered unto me sacrifices and*
26 But ye h' borne the tabernacle of
6:12 for ye h' turned judgment into gall,
13 H' we not taken to us horns by our
9: 7 H' not I brought up Israel out of the
15 of their land which I h' given them,
Ob 1 We h' heard a rumour from the Lord,
2 Behold, I h' made thee small among
5 would they not h' stolen till they had*
7 thy confederacy h' brought thee even
7 h' deceived thee, and prevailed
12 thou shouldest not h' looked on the*
12 neither shouldest thou h' rejoiced*
12 thou h' spoken proudly in the day of*
13 Thou shouldest not h' entered into *
13 thou shouldest not h' looked on their*
13 nor h' laid hands on their substance*
14 Neither shouldest thou h' stood in *
14 thou h' delivered up those of his that*
16 For as ye h' drunk upon my holy
Jon 2: 9 I will pay that that I h' vowed.
Mic 2: 5 Therefore thou shalt h' none that 1961
9 The women of my people h' ye cast*
9 from their children h' ye taken away*
13 up before them: they h' broken up,
13 and h' passed through the gate, and *
3: 4 as they h' behaved themselves ill in
6 that ye shall not h' a vision; and it
4: 6 driven out, and her that I h' afflicted;
9 for pangs h' taken thee as a woman in
5: 2 whose goings forth h' been from of *
12 shalt h' no more soothsayers: 1961
15 heathen, such as they h' not heard. *
6: 3 O my people, what h' I done unto
3 and wherein h' I wearied thee? testify
12 and the inhabitants thereof h' spoken
7: 1 for I am as when they h' gathered the
9 because I h' sinned against him, until
19 he will h' compassion upon us;
Na 1:12 Though I h' afflicted thee, I will afflict
2: 2 for the emptiers h' emptied them out,
Hab 1:14 creeping things, that h' no ruler over
3: 2 O Lord, I h' heard thy speech, and
Zep 1: 6 and those that h' not sought the
17 because they h' sinned against the
2: 3 which h' wrought his judgment;
8 I h' heard the reproach of Moab,
8 whereby they h' reproached my people,
10 This shall they h' for their pride,
10 because they h' reproached and
3: 4 her priests h' polluted the sanctuary,
4 they h' done violence to the law.
6 I h' cut off the nations: their towers
19 every land where they h' been put to*
Hag 1: 6 Ye h' sown much, and bring in little;
6 ye eat, but ye h' not enough; ye drink,
Zec 1: 4 former prophets h' cried, saying, *
11 We h' walked to and fro through the
12 how long wilt thou not h' mercy
19 These are the horns which h' scattered
21 These are the horns which h' scattered*
2: 6 for I h' spread you abroad as the four
3: 4 I h' caused thine iniquity to pass
9 For behold the stone that I h' laid
4: 2 I h' looked, and behold a candlestick
9 h' laid the foundations of this house;
6: 8 toward the north country h' quieted
7: 3 as I h' done these so many years?
8:15 So again h' I thought in these days
23 for we h' heard that God is with you.
9: 8 any more: for now h' I seen with
11 I h' sent forth thy prisoners out of the
13 When I h' bent Judah for me, filled
10: 2 For the idols h' spoken vanity, and the
2 vanity, and the diviners h' seen a lie,
2 and h' told false dreams; they comfort
6 for I h' mercy upon them: and
8 gather them; for I h' redeemed them:
8 shall increase as they h' increased.
12:10 look upon me whom they h' pierced,
14:12 will smite all the people that h' fought
18 and come not, that h' no rain; there*
Mal 1: 2 I h' loved you, saith the Lord. Yet ye
6 And ye say, Wherein h' we despised
7 and ye say, Wherein h' we polluted
10 I h' no pleasure in you, saith the Lord
12 But ye h' profaned it, in that ye say,*
13 and ye h' snuffed at it, saith the
2: 2 yea, I h' cursed them already, because
4 And ye shall know that I h' sent this
8 ye h' caused many to stumble at the
8 ye h' corrupted the covenant of Levi,
9 Therefore h' I also made you
9 according as ye h' not kept my ways,
9 ways, but h' been partial in the law.
Mal 2:10 H' we not all one father? hath not one
13 And this h' ye done again, covering *
17 Ye h' wearied the Lord with your
17 Yet ye say, Wherein h' we wearied
3: 7 ordinances, and h' not kept them.
8 man rob God? Yet ye h' robbed me.*
8 ye say, Wherein h' we robbed thee?
9 for ye h' robbed me, even this whole*
13 Your words h' been stout against me,
13 What h' we spoken so much against
14 Ye h' said, It is vain to serve God:
14 and what profit is it that we h' kept
14 and that we h' walked mournfully
M't 2: 2 for we h' seen his star in the east,*
8 and when ye h' found him, bring me
15 Out of Egypt h' I called my son. *
3: 9 We h' Abraham to our father: for 2192
14 I h' need to be baptized of thee, "
5:13 but if the salt h' lost his savour,
21, 27 Ye h' heard that it was said by
33 Again, ye h' heard that it hath been
38 Ye h' heard that it hath been said,
40 thy coat, let him h' thy cloke also.
43 Ye h' heard that it hath been said,
46 what reward h' ye? do not even 2192
6: 1 otherwise ye h' no reward of your "
2 that they may h' glory of men.
2, 5 unto you, They h' their reward.* 568
8 what things ye h' need of, before 2192
16 unto you, They h' their reward. * 568
32 knoweth that ye h' need of all these
7:22 Lord, h' we not prophesied in thy *
22 and in thy name h' cast out devils? *
8:10 I h' not found so great faith, no, not in
20 unto him, The foxes h' holes, 2192
20 and the birds of the air h' nests; but
29 What h' we to do with thee,
9:13 I will h' mercy, and not sacrifice: *
27 Thou son of David, h' mercy on us.
10: 8 freely ye h' received, freely give. *
23 Ye shall not h' gone over the cities
25 If they h' called the master of the house
11: 5 and the poor h' the gospel preached
17 We h' piped unto you, and ye *
17 piped unto you, and ye h' not danced; *
17 we h' mourned unto you, and ye *
17 unto you, and ye h' not lamented. *
21 they would h' repented long ago in
23 mighty works, which h' been done in*
23 it would h' remained until this day.
12: 3 H' ye not read what David did, when
5 Or h' ye not read in the law, how that
7 meaneth, I will h' mercy, and not *
7 ye would not h' condemned the
11 that shall h' one sheep, and if it fall 2192
18 Behold my servant, whom I h' chosen;
13:12 and he shall h' more abundance: but
15 and their eyes they h' closed; lest at
17 righteous men h' desired to see *
17 which ye see, and h' not seen them; *
35 things which h' been kept secret *
51 H' ye understood all these things?
14: 4 It is not lawful for thee to h' her. 2192
5 when he would h' put him to death,
17 We h' here but five loaves, and two 2192
15: 6 Thus h' ye made the commandment
22 H' mercy on me, O Lord, thou son
32 I h' compassion on the multitude,
32 three days, and h' nothing to eat: 2192
33 Whence should we h' so much bread
34 How many loaves h' ye? And they 2192
16: 7 It is because we h' taken no bread.*
8 because ye h' brought no bread?
17:12 but h' done unto him whatsoever they*
15 Lord, h' mercy on my son: for he is
20 If ye h' faith as a grain of mustard 2192
18:12 if a man h' an hundred sheep, and 1099
26 Lord, h' patience with me, and I will
29 H' patience with me, and I will pay
33 not thou also h' had compassion
19: 4 H' ye not read, that he which made
12 which h' made themselves eunuchs *
16 shall I do, that I may h' eternal 2192
20 All these things h' I kept from my
21 and thou shalt h' treasure in 2192
27 Behold, we h' forsaken all, and followed
27 thee; what shall we h' therefore? 2701
28 That ye which h' followed me, in the
20:10 that they should h' received more; *
12 These last h' wrought but one hour,
12 which h' borne the burden and heat of
30 cried out saying, H' mercy on us,
31 cried the more, saying, H' mercy on
21:13 but ye h' made it a den of thieves. *
16 h' ye never read, Out of the mouth *
21 If ye h' faith, and doubt not, ye 2192
22: 4 I h' prepared my dinner: my oxen and
31 h' ye not read that which was spoken
23:23 and h' omitted the weightier matters of
23 these ought ye to h' done, and not to
30 we would not h' been partakers with
37 how often would I h' gathered thy
24:25 Behold, I h' told you before.
43 would come, he would h' watched,
43 and would not h' suffered his house
25:20 I h' gained beside them five talents
22 I h' gained two other talents beside
26 and gather where I h' not strawed: *
27 to h' put my money to the exchangers,
27 I should h' received mine own with
29 and he shall h' abundance: but from
40 Inasmuch as ye h' done it unto one of*
40 my brethren, ye h' done it unto me. *
26: 9 For this ointment might h' been sold
11 For ye h' the poor always with you; 2192
11 with you; but me ye h' not always. "
M't 26:65 further need h' we of witnesses? 2192
65 behold, now ye h' heard his blasphemy.
27: 4 Saying, I h' sinned in that I
4 that I h' betrayed the innocent blood.*
19 H' thou nothing to do with that just
19 for I h' suffered many things this day
43 deliver him now, if he will h' him: *
65 said unto them, Ye h' a watch: 2192
28: 7 there shall ye see him: lo, I h' told you.
20 whatsoever I h' commanded you: *
M'r 1: 8 I indeed h' baptized you with water: *
24 what h' we to do with thee,
2:17 They that are whole h' no need 2192
19 as long as they h' the bridegroom "
25 H' ye never read what David did, *
3:15 And to h' power to heal sicknesses, 2192
4:15 but when they h' heard, Satan cometh
16 who, when they h' heard the word,
17 And h' no root in themselves, and 2192
23 If any man h' ears to hear, let him * "
40 how is it that ye h' no faith?
5: 7 What h' I to do with thee,
6:18 for thee to h' thy brother's wife, 2192
19 and would h' killed him; but she *
36 for they h' nothing to eat. *2192
38 How many loaves h' ye? go and see.*
48 the sea, and would h' passed by them.
7: 4 which they h' received to hold, as the
13 tradition, which ye h' delivered: and
16 If any man h' ears to hear, let *2192
24 and would h' no man know it: but he
8: 2 I h' compassion on the multitude,
2 because they h' now been with me *
2 three days, and h' nothing to eat: 2192
5 How many loaves h' ye? And they "
16 It is because we h' no bread. "
17 reason ye, because ye h' no bread? "
17 h' ye your heart yet hardened? "
9: 1 till they h' seen the kingdom of God*
13 and they h' done unto him whatsoever
17 Master, I h' brought unto thee my son.*
22 h' compassion on us, and help us.
50 but if the salt h' lost his saltness,
50 ye season it? H' salt in yourselves 2192
50 and h' peace with one another. *
10:20 Master, all these h' I observed from
21 and thou shalt h' treasure in 2192
23 How hardly shall they that h' riches "
28 we h' left all, and h' followed thee.
47 Jesus, thou son of David, h' mercy
48 Thou son of David, h' mercy on me.
11:17 but ye h' made it a den of thieves.
22 saith unto them, H' faith in God. 2192
23 he shall h' whatsoever he saith. 2071
24 receive them, and ye shall h' them. "
25 forgive, if ye h' ought against any: 2192
12:10 And h' ye not read this scripture; The
26 h' ye not read in the book of Moses,
43 than all they which h' cast into the*
13:23 But take ye heed: behold, I h' foretold
14: 5 For it might h' been sold for more
5 and h' been given to the poor. And*
7 For ye h' the poor with you 2192
7 good: but me ye h' not always. "
64 Ye h' heard the blasphemy: what
Lu 1: 1 Forasmuch as many h' taken in hand
14 And thou shalt h' joy and gladness; 2071
62 father, how he would h' him called.
70 holy prophets, which h' been since the
2:30 For mine eyes h' seen thy salvation,
44 they, supposing him to h' been in the*
48 and I h' sought thee sorrowing. *
3: 8 We h' Abraham to our father: 2192
4:23 whatsoever we h' heard done in
34 What h' we to do with thee,
5: 5 Master, we h' toiled all the night, and*
5 and h' taken nothing: nevertheless *
26 saying, We h' seen strange things
6: 3 H' ye not read so much as this, what
24 for ye h' received your consolation.
32 which love you, what thank h' ye? 2076
33 do good to you, what thank h' ye? "
34 hope to receive, what thank h' ye? "
7: 9 I h' not found so great faith, no, not
22 tell John what things ye h' seen and
32 and saying, We h' piped unto you,*
32 unto you, and ye h' not danced; *
32 danced; we h' mourned to you, *
32 mourned to you, and ye h' not wept, *
39 would h' known who and what manner
40 I h' somewhat to say unto thee. 2192
8:13 and these h' no root, which for a "
14 when they h' heard, go forth, and are
18 even that which he seemeth to h'. *2192
28 What h' I to do with thee,
9: 3 neither h' two coats apiece. 2192
9 And Herod said, John h' I beheaded: *
13 We h' no more but five loaves 2076
58 said unto him, Foxes h' holes, 2192
58 and birds of the air h' nests; but
10:13 which h' been done in you, they had*
24 many prophets and kings h' desired *
24 which ye see, and h' not seen them; *
24 ye hear, and h' not heard them. *
11: 5 Which of you shall h' a friend, 2192
6 and I h' nothing to set before him? "
41 give alms of such things as ye h'; 1751
42 these ought ye to h' done, and not to
52 for ye h' taken away the key of *
12: 3 Therefore whatsoever ye h' spoken in
3 and that which ye h' spoken in the
4 that h' no more that they can do. 2192
17 because I h' no room where to
24 which neither h' storehouse nor 2076
30 knoweth that ye h' need of these
33 Sell that ye h', and give alms; 5224

Lu 12:39 would h' watched, and not h' suffered
48 to whom men h' committed much.*
50 But I h' a baptism to be baptized 2192
13:26 h' eaten and drunk in thy presence, *
34 how often would I h' gathered thy
14: 5 Which of you shall h' an ass or an ox
10 then shalt thou h' worship in the 2071
18 him, I h' bought a piece of ground,
18 see it: I pray thee h' me excused. 2192
19 And another said, I h' bought five yoke
19 them: I pray thee h' me excused. 2192
20 And another said, I h' married a wife,
28 the cost, whether he h' sufficient 2192
34 Salt is good: but if the salt h' lost
15: 6 for I h' found my sheep which was
9 for I h' found the piece which I
16 And he would fain h' filled his belly
17 h' bread enough and to spare, and I
18 Father, I h' sinned against heaven,
21 I h' sinned against heaven, and in
31 with me, and all that I h' is thine. 1699
16:11 If therefore ye h' not been faithful in
12 And if ye h' not been faithful in that
24 Father Abraham, h' mercy on me,
28 For I h' five brethren; that he 2192
29 They h' Moses and the prophets; "
17: 8 serve me, till I h' eaten and drunken;
10 when ye shall h' done all those things
10 we h' done that which was our duty to
13 and said, Jesus, Master, h' mercy
18:21 And he said, All these h' I kept from
22 thou shalt h' treasure in heaven: 2192
24 hardly shall they that h' riches "
28 Then Peter said, Lo, we h' left all, and
38 Jesus, thou son of David, h' mercy
39 Thou son of David, h' mercy on
19: 8 and if I h' taken any thing from any
14 We will not h' this man to reign over *
17 h' thou authority over ten cities. 2192
20 here is thy pound, which I h' kept*
23 I might h' required mine own with
46 but ye h' made it a den of thieves.
21: 4 all these h' of their abundance cast*
22:15 With desire I h' desired to eat this
28 Ye are they which h' continued
31 Satan hath desired to h' you, that he
32 But I h' prayed for thee, that thy *
37 things concerning me h' an end. *2192
71 for we ourselves h' have heard of his
23: 8 and he hoped to h' seen some miracle*
14 Ye h' brought this man unto me, as *
14 h' found no fault in this man "
22 I h' found no cause of death in him:
24:17 that ye h' one to another, as ye 474
20 condemned to death, and h' crucified *
21 he which should h' redeemed Israel:*
25 believe all that the prophets h' spoken:
26 Ought not Christ to h' suffered these*
28 made as though he would h' gone *
39 flesh and bones, as ye see me h'. *2192
41 unto them, H' ye here any meat? "
Joh 1:16 And of his fulness h' all we received,*
41 We h' found the Messias, which is,
45 We h' found him, of whom Moses in
2: 3 saith unto him, They h' no wine. 2192
4 Woman, what h' I to do with thee?
10 and when men h' well drunk, then
3:11 and testify that we h' seen; and ye
12 If I h' told you earthly things, and ye*
15 not perish, but h' eternal life. 2192
16 not perish, but h' everlasting life.
4: 9 the Jews h' no dealings with the
10 drink; thou wouldest h' asked of him,
10 and he would h' given thee living
17 and said, I h' no husband. 2192
17 hast well said, I h' no husband. "
32 I h' meat to eat that ye know not "
42 for we h' heard him ourselves, and
5: 7 Sir, I h' no man, when the water 2192
26 given to the Son to h' life in himself;"
29 they that h' done good, unto the
29 they that h' done evil, unto the
36 But I h' greater witness than that 2192
37 Ye h' neither heard his voice at any
38 And ye h' not his word abiding in 2192
39 in them ye think ye h' eternal life: "
40 come to me, that we might h' life. "
42 that ye h' not the love of God in "
46 Moses, ye would h' believed me: *
6:36 ye also h' seen me, and believe not.
40 may h' everlasting life: and I will 2192
53 drink his blood, ye h' no life in you."
70 H' not I chosen you twelve, and one *
7:21 I h' done one work, and ye all marvel.*
23 because I h' made a man every whit *
44 some of them would h' taken him;
45 them, Why h' ye not brought him.*
48 H' any of the rulers...believed on him?*
8: 6 that they might h' to accuse him. *2192
12 but shall h' the light of life.
19 ye should h' known my Father also.*
26 I h' many things to say and to 2192
26 those things which I h' heard of him.*
28 When ye h' lifted up the Son of man,
38 I speak that which I h' seen with
38 that which ye h' seen with your *
40 the truth, which I h' heard of God: *
41 we h' one Father, even God. "
49 Jesus answered, I h' not a devil; "
55 Yet ye h' not known him; but I know
9:27 He answered them, I h' told you *
41 were blind, ye should h' no sin: 2192
10:10 I am come that they might h' life, "
10 and that they might h' it more "
16 And other sheep I h', which are not "
18 I h' power to lay it down, and I

Joh 10:18 and I h' power to take it again. 2192
18 This commandment h' I received of *
32 Many good works h' I shewed you
11:34 And said, Where h' ye laid him? They
37 blind, h' caused that even this man
37 even this man should not h' died. *
12: 8 the poor always ye h' with you; 2192
8 you; but me ye h' not always. "
28 I h' both glorified it, and will glorify
34 We h' heard out of the law that
35 Walk while ye h' the light, lest 2192
36 While ye h' light, believe in the "
48 the word that I h' spoken, the same*
49 For I h' not spoken of myself; but*
13:12 them, Know ye what I h' done to you?
14 Lord and Master, h' washed your feet;
15 For I h' given you an example, that ye
15 that ye should do as I h' done to you.
18 I know whom I h' chosen: but that
26 I shall give a sop, when I h' dipped it.*
29 Buy those things that we h' need 2192
34 as I h' loved you, that ye also love
35 ye are my disciples, if ye h' love 2192
14: 2 if it were not so, I would h' told you.
7 ye should h' known my Father also:
7 henceforth ye know him, and h' seen
9 H' I been so long time with you, and
25 These things h' I spoken unto you,
26 remembrance, whatsoever I h' said *
28 Ye h' heard how I said unto you, I *
29 And now I h' told you before it come
15: 3 the word which I h' spoken unto
9 so h' I loved you: continue ye in my
10 even as I h' kept my Father's
11 These things h' I spoken unto you,
12 love one another, as I h' loved you.
15 doeth: but I h' called you friends.
15 for all things that I h' heard of my
15 Father I h' made known to you.
16 h' not chosen me, but I h' chosen you,*
19 but I h' chosen you out of the world,*
20 If they h' persecuted me, they will*
20 if they h' kept my saying, they will*
22 now they h' no cloke for their sin. 2192
24 but now h' they both seen and hated
27 because ye h' been with me from the
16: 1 These things h' I spoken unto you,
3 because they h' not known the Father,
4 But these things h' I told you, that
6 But because I h' said these things unto
12 I h' yet many things to say unto 2192
22 And ye now therefore h' sorrow: "
24 Hitherto h' ye asked nothing in my
25 These things h' I spoken unto you,
27 because ye h' loved me, and h' believed
33 These things I h' spoken unto you
33 you, that in me ye might h' peace. 2192
33 In the world ye shall h' tribulation: "
33 good cheer; I h' overcome the world.
17: 4 I h' glorified thee on the earth: *
4 I h' finished the work which thou*
6 I h' manifested thy name unto the*
6 them me; and they h' kept thy word.
7 Now they h' known that all things*
8 For I h' given unto them the words
8 they h' received them, and h' known *
8 and they h' believed that thou didst *
12 those that thou gavest me I h' kept,*
13 that they might h' my joy fulfilled 2192
14 I h' given them thy word; and the
18 even so h' I also sent them into *
22 which thou gavest me I h' given them;
25 I h' known thee, and these h' known *
26 And I h' declared unto them thy name,*
18: 8 Jesus answered, I h' told you that I *
9 which thou gavest me h' I lost none.*
20 and in secret h' I said nothing,
21 them which heard me, what I h' said *
23 If I h' spoken evil, bear witness of the
30 we would not h' delivered him up unto
35 chief priests h' delivered thee unto*
39 But ye h' a custom, that I should 2076
19: 7 We h' a law, and by our law he 2192
10 knowest thou not that I h' power "
10 crucify thee, and h' power to "
11 Thou couldest h' no power at all "
15 answered, we h' no king but Cæsar."
22 What I h' written I h' written.
20: 2 They h' taken away the Lord out of the
2 and we know not where they h' laid
13 Because they h' taken away my Lord,
13 I know not where they h' laid him.
15 if thou h' borne him hence, tell me*
25 said unto him, We h' seen the Lord.
29 that h' not seen, and yet h' believed.
31 that believing ye might h' life 2192
21: 5 Children, h' ye any meat? They
10 of the fish which ye h' now caught.
Ac 1: 1 The former treatise h' I made, O *
4 which, saith he, ye h' heard of me.*
11 come in like manner as ye h' seen him*
16 must needs h' been fulfilled,
21 men which h' companied with us all
2:23 Him, being delivered...ye h' taken,*
23 by wicked hands h' crucified and *
36 whom ye h' crucified, both Lord and*
3: 6 silver and gold h' I none; 5225
6 but such as I h' give I thee: 2192
24 follow after, as many as h' spoken,
24 h' likewise foretold of these days.*
4: 7 or by what name h' ye done this?
20 speak the things which we h' seen*
5: 9 How is it that ye h' agreed together
9 the feet of them which h' buried thy
21 sent to the prison to h' them brought.
26 lest they should h' been stoned. *

Ac 5:28 and, behold, ye h' filled Jerusalem
6:11 We h' heard him speak blasphemous
14 For we h' heard him say, that this
7:25 his brethren would h' understood*
26 and would h' set them at one again,
34 I h' seen, I...the affliction of my
34 I h' seen the affliction of my people*
34 and I h' heard their groaning, and am
42 h' ye offered to me slain beasts and*
52 h' not your fathers persecuted? *
52 and they h' slain them which shewed*
52 of whom ye h' been now the betrayers
53 Who h' received the law by the *
53 disposition of angels, and h' not kept*
8:24 these things which ye h' spoken come
9: 6 said, Lord, what wilt thou h' me to *
13 Lord, I h' heard by many of this man,
10:10 very hungry, and would h' eaten:*
14 for I h' never eaten any thing that is
20 doubting nothing: for I h' sent them.
29 for what intent ye h' sent for me? *
47 which h' received the Holy Ghost as
12: 6 And when Herod would h' brought*
13: 2 Saul for the work whereunto I h' called
15 if ye h' any word of exhortation 2076
22 I h' found David the son of Jesse, a
27 they h' fulfilled them in condemning *
33 Thou art my Son, this day h' I begotten
46 should first h' been spoken to you: *
47 I h' set thee to be a light of the Gentiles,
14:13 and would h' done sacrifice with the
15:24 Forasmuch as we h' heard, that certain
24 out from us h' troubled you with words,
26 Men that h' hazarded their lives for the
27 We h' sent therefore Judas and Silas,
36 in every city where we h' preached *
16: 3 Him would Paul h' to go forth with
15 If ye h' judged me to be faithful to the
27 and would h' killed himself,
36 The magistrates h' sent to let you go:
37 h' beaten us openly uncondemned,
37 Romans, and h' cast us into prison;
17: 3 that Christ must needs h' suffered, *
6 These that h' turned the world upside
28 we live, and move, and h' our being;
18:10 for I h' much people in this city. 2076
19: 2 H' ye received the Holy Ghost since*
2 We h' not so much as heard whether *
21 After I h' been there, I must also see
25 by this craft we h' our wealth. 2076
30 And when Paul would h' entered in*
33 and would h' made his defence unto
37 For ye h' brought hither these men,
38 h' a matter against any man, the 2192
20:18 after what manner I h' been with you*
20 but h' shewed you, and h' taught *
24 which I h' received of the Lord Jesus,*
25 among whom I h' gone preaching the*
27 For I h' not shunned to declare *
33 I h' coveted no man's silver, or gold, *
34 that these hands h' ministered unto*
35 I h' shewed you all things, how *
21:23 We say to thee, We h' four men 1526
23 four men which h' a vow on them; 2192
25 we h' written and concluded that they*
22:29 from him which should h' examined*
30 he would h' known the certainty *
23: 1 I h' lived in all good conscience before
10 Paul should h' been pulled in pieces *
14 We h' bound ourselves under a great
14 eat nothing until we h' slain Paul.
20 The Jews h' agreed to desire thee that
21 which h' bound themselves with an
21 neither eat nor drink till they h' killed
27 and should h' been killed of them:*
28 when I would h' known the cause*
29 to h' nothing laid to his charge 2192
24: 5 For we h' found this man a pestilent
6 and would h' judged according to*
15 And h' hope toward God, which *2192
16 to h' always a conscience void of "
19 Who ought to h' been here before thee,
20 if they h' found any evil doing in me,*
23 and to let him h' liberty, and 2192
25 when I h' a convenient season, 3335
26 that money should h' been given *
25: 8 against Cæsar, h' I offended any thing
10 to the Jews h' I done no wrong, as
11 For if I be an offender, or h' committed
15 desiring to h' judgment against him.*
16 h' the accusers face to face, 2192
16 and h' licence to answer for himself 2983
24 multitude of the Jews h' dealt with me,*
25 to Augustus, I h' determined to send*
26 Of whom I h' no certain thing to 2192
26 I h' brought him forth before you,
26 had, I might h' somewhat to write. 2192
26:16 for I h' appeared unto thee for this
32 This man might h' been set at liberty,
27:21 Sirs, ye should h' hearkened unto me,
21 unto me, and not h' loosed from Crete,
21 and to h' gained this harm and loss.
29 lest we should h' fallen upon rocks,*
30 they would h' cast anchors out of the*
33 that ye h' tarried and continued*
28: 6 when he should h' swollen, or fallen
17 I h' committed nothing against *
18 would h' let me go, because there*
20 For this cause therefore h' I called*
27 and their eyes h' they closed; lest
Ro 1: 5 By whom we h' received grace and*
10 I might h' a prosperous journey by*
13 Now I would not h' you ignorant,
13 that I might h' some fruit among 2192
32 h' pleasure in them that do them.*
2:12 For as many as h' sinned without law

Ro 2:12 and as many as h' sinned in the law
14 the Gentiles, which h' not the law; 2192
3: 9 for we h' before proved both Jews *
13 with their tongues they h' used deceit;
17 the way of peace h' they not known:
23 For all h' sinned, and come short of
4:17 I h' made thee a father of many
5: 1 we h' peace with God through *2192
2 By whom also we h' access by faith "
11 by whom we h' now received the
12 upon all men, for that all h' sinned: *
6: 5 For if we h' been planted together in
14 For sin shall not h' dominion over you:
17 but ye h' obeyed from the heart *
19 for as ye h' yielded your members *
22 ye h' your fruit unto holiness, 2192
8: 9 if any man h' not the Spirit of * "
15 For ye h' not received the spirit of *
15 ye h' received the Spirit of adoption,
23 which h' the firstfruits of the 2192
9: 2 That I h' great heaviness and 2076
9 I come, and Sarah shall h' a son. 2071
13 Jacob h' I loved, but Esau h' I hated.*
15 saith to Moses, I will h' mercy on whom
15 mercy on whom I will h' mercy, and
15 and I will h' compassion on whom
15 on whom I will h' compassion.
17 for this same purpose h' I raised thee
18 mercy on whom he will h' mercy. *
30 h' attained to righteousness, even *
10: 2 record that they h' a zeal of God, 2192
3 h' not submitted themselves unto the *
14 on him in whom they h' not believed?
14 in him of whom they h' not heard?
16 But they h' not all obeyed the gospel.*
18 But I say, H' they not heard? Yes*
21 All day long I h' stretched forth *
11: 3 Lord, they h' killed thy prophets, and
4 I h' reserved to myself seven thousand
4 who h' not bowed the knee to the
11 I say then, H' they stumbled that*
30 in times past h' not believed God,*
30 yet h' now obtained mercy through
31 so h' these also now not believed, *
32 that he might h' mercy upon all.
12: 4 For as we h' many members in 2192
4 members h' not the same office: "
13: 3 thou shalt h' praise of the same: "
14:22 Hast thou faith? h' it to thyself "
15: 4 of the scriptures might h' hope. "
15 I h' written the more boldly unto you*
17 I h' therefore whereof I may glory 2192
19 I h' fully preached the gospel of Christ.
20 Yea, so I h' strived to preach the *
21 and they that h' not heard shall
22 I h' been much hindered from coming*
27 if the Gentiles h' been made partakers
28 I h' performed this, and h' sealed to
31 my service which I h' for Jerusalem
16: 4 Who h' for my life laid down their*
17 to the doctrine which ye h' learned;*
19 but yet I would h' you wise unto that
1Co 2: 8 they would not h' crucified the Lord of
9 neither h' entered into the heart of *
12 Now we h' received, not the spirit of*
16 But we h' the mind of Christ. 2192
3: 2 I h' fed you with milk, and not with*
6 I h' planted, Apollos watered; but*
10 I h' laid the foundation, and another*
4: 5 shall every man h' praise of God. 1096
6 I h' in a figure transferred to myself
8 ye h' reigned as kings without us:
11 and h' no certain dwellingplace;
15 ye h' ten thousand instructors in 2192
15 yet h' ye not many fathers: for in
17 For this cause h' I sent unto you
5: 1 one should h' his father's wife. *2192
2 puffed up, and h' not rather mourned,*
3 h' judged already, as though I were
11 But now I h' written unto you not to*
12 For what h' I to do to judge them also
6: 4 If then ye h' judgments of things 2192
19 which ye h' of God, and ye are not "
7: 2 let every man h' his own wife, "
2 every woman h' her own husband. "
25 virgins I h' no commandment of "
28 Nevertheless such shall h' trouble "
29 that both they that h' wives be as "
32 I would h' you without carefulness.
40 I think also that I h' the Spirit 2192
8: 1 we know that we all h' knowledge. "
9: 1 h' I not seen Jesus Christ our Lord? "
4 H' we not power to eat and to 2192
5 H' we not power to lead about a "
6 h' not power to forbear "
11 If we h' sown unto you spiritual †
12 we h' not used this power; *
15 But I h' used none of these things; *
15 neither h' I written these things, *
16 gospel, I h' nothing to glory of: 2076
17 thing willingly, I h' a reward: 2192
19 yet h' I made myself servant unto *
27 when I h' preached to others, I
10:20 that ye should h' fellowship with
11: 3 But I would h' you know, that the
10 to h' power on her head because 2192
14 if a man h' long hair, it is a shame
15 But if a woman h' long hair, it is a
16 we h' no such custom, neither the 2192
22 h' ye not houses to eat and to "
22 and shame them that h' not? "
23 For I h' received of the Lord that *
12: 1 I would not h' you ignorant.
13 and h' been all made to drink into *
21 unto the hand, I h' no need of thee: 2192
21 to the feet, I h' no need of you. "

1Co 12:23 parts h' more abundant comeliness. 2192
24 For our comely parts h' no need: "
25 members should h' the same care "
30 H' all the gifts of healing? do all 2192
13: 1 and of angels, and h' not charity "
2 though I h' the gift of prophecy, "
2 and though I h' all faith, so that "
2 mountains, and h' not charity, "
3 to be burned, and h' not charity, "
15: 1 which also ye h' received, and wherein *
2 unto you, unless ye h' believed in vain.*
15 because we h' testified of God that *
19 If in this life only we h' hope in 2070
24 when he shall h' delivered up the *
24 when he shall h' put down all rule
31 which I h' in Christ Jesus our 2192
32 I h' fought with beasts at Ephesus,*
34 for some h' not the knowledge of 2192
49 And as we h' borne the image of the
54 this corruptible shall h' put on
54 and this mortal shall h' put on
16: 1 as I h' given order to the churches of*
12 when he shall h' convenient time.
15 and that they h' addicted themselves
17 lacking on your part they h' supplied.*
18 For they h' refreshed my spirit and *
2Co 1: 8 h' you ignorant of our trouble which
12 we h' had our conversation in the *
14 As also ye h' acknowledged us in *
15 that ye might h' a second benefit; 2192
24 Not for that we h' dominion over
2: 3 I should h' sorrow for them of 2192
4 the love which I h' more "
5 But if any h' caused grief, he hath *
3: 4 And such trust h' we through 2192
12 Seeing then that we h' such hope,* "
4: 1 Therefore seeing we h' this "
1 as we h' received mercy, we faint *
2 But h' renounced the hidden things
7 But we h' this treasure in earthen 2192
13 and therefore h' I spoken; we *
5: 1 we h' a building of God, an house 2192
12 that ye may h' somewhat to answer "
16 yea, though we h' known Christ after
6: 2 For he saith, I h' heard thee in a *
2 of salvation h' I succoured thee: *
7: 2 we h' wronged no man, *
2 we h' corrupted no man, *
2 we h' defrauded no man. *
3 for I h' said before, that ye are in
11 things ye h' approved yourselves *
14 For if I h' boasted any thing to him
16 rejoice therefore that I h' confidence*
8:10 who h' begun before, not only to do,*
11 also out of that which ye h'. *2192
18 And we h' sent with him the brother,
22 And we h' sent with him our brother,
22 whom we h' oftentimes proved
22 great confidence which I h' in you.*
9: 3 Yet h' I sent the brethren, lest our
11: 2 I h' espoused you to one husband, *
4 Christ, whom we h' not preached, *
4 spirit, which ye h' not received, *
4 gospel, which ye h' not accepted, *
6 h' been thoroughly made manifest
7 H' I committed an offence in abasing*
7 because I h' preached to you the *
9 and in all things I h' kept myself*
25 and a day I h' been in the deep;
12:11 in glorifying; ye h' compelled me: *
11 for I ought to h' been commended
21 many which h' sinned already,
21 h' not repented of the uncleanness *
21 which they h' committed.*
13: 2 which heretofore h' sinned, and to
Ga 1: 8 than that which we h' preached unto*
9 than that ye h' received, let him be *
13 For ye h' heard of my conversation
2: 4 liberty which we h' in Christ 2192
16 even we h' believed in Jesus Christ,*
3: 4 H' ye suffered so many things in *
21 a law given which could h' given life,*
21 righteousness should h' been by the
27 as many of you as h' been baptized *
27 into Christ h' put on Christ.*
4: 9 But now, after that ye h' known God,
11 I am afraid of you, lest I h' bestowed
12 for I am as ye are: ye h' not injured *
15 would h' plucked out your own eyes,
15 own eyes, and h' given them to me.*
5:10 I h' confidence in you through the
13 For, brethren, ye h' been called unto*
21 as I h' also told you in time past, *
24 And they that are Christ's h' crucified
6: 4 and then shall he h' rejoicing in 2192
10 As we h' therefore opportunity, let "
11 Ye see how large a letter I h' written ‡
13 but desire to h' you circumcised, that
Eph 1: 7 In whom we h' redemption 2192
11 In whom also we h' obtained an *
2:18 For through him we both h' access 2192
3: 2 If ye h' heard of the dispensation of
12 In whom we h' boldness and 2192
4:19 past feeling h' given themselves *
20 But ye h' not so learned Christ; *
21 ye h' heard him, and h' been taught*
28 that he may h' to give to him *2192
5:11 And h' no fellowship with the
6:22 Whom I h' sent unto you for the
Ph'p 1: 7 because I h' you in my heart; 2192
12 which happened unto me h' fallen out
2:12 as ye h' always obeyed, not as in my
16 that I h' not run in vain, neither *
20 For I h' no man likeminded, who 2192
27 lest I should h' sorrow upon "
3: 3 and h' no confidence in the flesh.

Ph'p 3:4 Though I might also h' confidence 2192
8 for whom I h' suffered the loss of all *
13 I count not myself to h' apprehended:
16 whereto we h' already attained, let
17 so as ye h' us for an ensample. 2192
18 of whom I h' told you often, and now *
4: 9 things, which ye h' both learned, and *
11 for I h' learned, in whatsoever state
14 ye h' well done, that ye did *
18 But I h' all, and abound: I am full, 568
Col 1: 4 and of the love which ye h' to all the
14 In whom we h' redemption 2192
18 things he might h' the preeminence.
23 gospel, which ye h' heard, and which*
2: 1 what great conflict I h' for you, *2192
1 and for as many as h' not seen my
6 As ye h' therefore received Christ*
7 in the faith, as ye h' been taught, *
23 Which things h' indeed a shew 2192
3: 9 seeing that ye h' put off the old man
10 And h' put on the new man, which is
13 if any man h' a quarrel against 2192
4: 1 that ye also h' a Master in heaven. "
8 Whom I h' sent unto you for the
11 of God, which h' been a comfort unto
1Th 2: 6 when we might h' been burdensome,
8 we were willing to h' imparted unto *
14 for ye also h' suffered like things of *
14 even as they h' of the Jews: *
15 and h' persecuted us; and they *
18 Wherefore we would h' come unto
3: 5 the tempter h' tempted you, and our*
6 and that ye h' good remembrance 2192
4: 1 that as ye h' received of us how ye*
6 as we also h' forewarned you and *
12 and that ye may h' lack of nothing. 2192
13 But I would not h' you to be ignorant,
13 even as others which h' no hope. 2192
5: 1 brethren, ye h' no need that I write "
2Th 2:15 traditions which ye h' been taught,*
3: 1 word of the Lord may h' free course,*
2 wicked men: for all men h' not faith.
4 And we h' confidence in the Lord
9 Not because we h' not power, but 2192
14 and h' no company with him, that*
1Ti 1: 6 some having swerved h' turned aside
19 concerning faith h' made shipwreck: *
20 whom I h' delivered unto Satan, that*
2: 4 Who will h' all men to be saved, and †
3: 7 he must h' a good report of them 2192
13 For they that h' used the office of a
5: 4 But if any widow h' children or *2192
10 if she h' brought up children, *
10 if she h' lodged strangers, *
10 if she h' washed the saints' feet, *
10 if she h' relieved the afflicted, *
10 if she h' diligently followed every *
11 for when they h' begun to wax
12 because they h' cast off their first
16 woman that believeth h' widows, *2192
6: 2 And they that h' believing masters, "
10 after, they h' erred from the faith,
21 Which some professing h' erred
2Ti 1: 3 ceasing I h' remembrance *2192
12 for I know whom I h' believed, and
12 keep that which I h' committed unto
2:18 Who concerning the truth h' erred,
4: 7 I h' fought a good fight, I h' finished
7 finished my course, I h' kept the faith:
12 And Tychicus h' I sent to Ephesus.*
20 but Trophimus h' I left at Miletum*
Tit 3: 5 righteousness which we h' done, *
8 that they which h' believed in God
12 for I h' determined there to winter.
Ph'm 7 we h' great joy and consolation *2192
10 Onesimus, whom I h' begotten in my
12 Whom I h' sent again: thou therefore
13 Whom I would h' retained with me,
13 in thy stead he might h' ministered*
19 I Paul h' written it with mine own *
20 Yea, brother, let me h' joy of thee in
Heb 1: 5 my Son, this day h' I begotten thee?
2: 1 to the things which we h' heard, *
3:10 and they h' not known my ways. *
4: 3 For we which h' believed do enter
3 As I h' sworn in my wrath, if they*
8 he not afterward h' spoken of
13 eyes of him with whom we h' to do.
14 that we h' a great high priest, *2192
15 For we h' not an high priest which "
5: 2 Who can h' compassion on the *
5 Thou art my Son, to day h' I begotten
11 Of whom we h' many things to say,
12 ye h' need that one teach you 2192
12 and are become such as h' need of "
14 of use h' their senses exercised to "
6: 4 and h' tasted of the heavenly gift, *
5 And h' tasted the good word of God,*
10 labour of love, which ye h' shewed*
10 in that ye h' ministered to the saints, *
18 we might h' a strong consolation, 2192
18 who h' fled for refuge to lay hold
19 Which hope we h' as an anchor of 2192
7: 5 h' a commandment to take tithes "
28 high priests which h' infirmity; * *
8: 1 the things which we h' spoken *
1 We h' such an high priest, who is 2192
3 that this man h' somewhat also to "
7 then should no place h' been sought
9:26 For then must he often h' suffered
10: 2 For then would they not h' ceased
2 should h' had no more conscience 2192
26 that we h' received the knowledge
34 that ye h' in heaven a better and 2192
36 For ye h' need of patience,
36 that, after ye h' done the will of God,*

Heb10: 38 my soul shall h' no pleasure *
11: 15 they might h' had opportunity 2192
15 opportunity to h' returned. *
12: 4 Ye h' not yet resisted unto blood,
5 And ye h' forgotten the exhortation
9 Furthermore we h' had fathers *2192
17 when he would h' inherited the *
28 let us h' grace, whereby we may 2192
13: 2 for thereby some h' entertained
5 content with such things as ye h': 3918
7 Remember them which h' the rule*
7 who h' spoken unto you the word of*
9 not with meats, which h' not profited*
9 them that h' been occupied therein.*
10 We h' an altar, whereof they 2192
10 they h' no right to eat which serve "
14 For here we h' no continuing city, "
17 Obey them that h' the rule over you,
18 trust we h' a good conscience, 2192
22 for I h' written a letter unto you in
24 Salute all them that h' the rule over
Jas 1: 4 But let patience h' her perfect 2192
2: 1 My brethren, h' not the faith of * "
3 ye h' respect to him that weareth
6 But ye h' despised the poor. Do not
9 But if ye h' respect to persons, ye
13 For he shall h' judgment without*
14 he hath faith, and h' not works? 2192
18 Thou hast faith, and I h' works: shew
3: 14 But if ye h' bitter envying and 2192
4: 2 Ye lust, and h' not: ye kill, and "
2 desire to h', and cannot obtain: * "
2 ye fight and war, yet ye h' not, "
5: 3 Ye h' heaped treasure together for the
4 hire of the labourers who h' reaped*
4 the cries of them which h' reaped*
5 Ye h' lived in pleasure on the earth,
5 ye h' nourished your hearts, as in a
6 Ye h' condemned and killed the just;
10 h' spoken in the name of the Lord,*
11 Ye h' heard of the patience of Job,
11 and h' seen the end of the Lord; that
15 and if he h' committed sins, they shall
1Pe 1: 10 prophets h' enquired and searched*
12 by them that h' preached the gospel*
22 Seeing ye h' purified your souls in
2: 3 If so be ye h' tasted that the Lord is
10 mercy, but now h' obtained mercy.
4: 3 may suffice us to h' wrought the will
8 all things h' fervent charity *2192
5: 10 after that ye h' suffered a while, make
12 as I suppose, I h' written briefly,
2Pe 1: 1 to them that h' obtained like precious
15 to h' these things in remembrance.*
16 For we h' not followed cunningly*
19 We h' also a more sure word of 2192
2: 14 an heart they h' exercised with * "
15 Which h' forsaken the right way, and*
20 For if after they h' escaped the
21 better for them not to h' known the
21 than, after they h' known it, to turn*
1Jo 1: 1 which we h' heard, which we h' seen
1 which we h' looked upon, and *
1 our hands h' handled of the Word*
2 and we h' seen it, and bear witness,
3 That which we h' seen and heard
3 that ye also may h' fellowship 2192
5 message which we h' heard of him,
6 If we say that we h' fellowship 2192
7 as he is in the light, we h' fellowship"
8 If we say that we h' no sin, we "
10 we say that we h' not sinned, we
2: 1 any man sin, we h' an advocate 2192
7 the word which ye h' heard from the*
13 because ye h' known him that is from*
13 because ye h' overcome the wicked
13 because ye h' known the Father.*
14 I h' written unto you, fathers, because
14 because ye h' known him that is from*
14 I h' written unto you, young men,
14 and ye h' overcome the wicked one.
18 and as ye h' heard that antichrist
19 they would no doubt h' continued
20 But ye h' an unction from the Holy2192
21 I h' not written unto you because ye
24 which ye h' heard from the beginning.*
24 If that which ye h' heard from the*
26 These things h' I written unto you
27 the anointing which ye h' received*
28 we may h' confidence, and not be 2192
3: 14 We know that we h' passed from
17 and seeth his brother h' need, *2192
21 then h' we confidence toward God. "
4: 3 whereof ye h' heard that it should
4 and h' overcome them: because
14 And we h' seen and do testify that the
16 And we h' known and believed the*
17 that we may h' boldness in the 2192
21 this commandment h' we from him."
5: 13 These things h' I written unto you
13 may know that ye h' eternal life, 2192
14 the confidence that we h' in him," "
15 we know that we h' the petitions "
2Jo 1 also all they that h' known the truth;*
4 as we h' received a commandment*
6 That, as ye h' heard from the
8 those things which we h' wrought,
3Jo 4 I h' no greater joy than to hear 2192
6 Which h' borne witness of thy charity*
9 who loveth to h' the preeminence
Jude 11 for they h' gone in the way of Cain,*
15 which they h' ungodly committed, and
15 which ungodly sinners h' spoken
22 And of some h' compassion, making a
Re 1: 18 Amen; and h' the keys of hell and 2192
2: 4 Nevertheless I h' somewhat against"
Re 2: 10 and ye shall h' tribulation ten days:2192
14 But I h' a few things against thee, "
20 I h' a few things against thee, "
24 as many as h' not this doctrine, "
24 and which h' not known the depths*
25 But that which ye h' already hold 2192
3: 2 for I h' not found thy works perfect
4 in Sardis which h' not defiled their*
8 behold, I h' set before thee an open
9 and to know that I h' loved thee.
17 goods, and h' need of nothing; 2192
7: 3 till we h' sealed the servants of our
14 and h' washed their robes, and made*
9: 3 scorpions of the earth h' power. 2192
4 men which h' not the seal of God "
11: 6 These h' power to shut heaven, "
6 and h' power over waters to turn "
7 And when they shall h' finished their
12: 17 and h' the testimony of Jesus *2192
13: 9 If any man h' an ear, let him hear.*"
14: 11 and they h' no rest day nor night, "
16: 6 For they h' shed the blood of saints*
17: 2 the earth h' committed fornication,*
2 the earth h' been made drunk with*
12 which h' received no kingdom as yet;
13 These h' one mind, and shall give 2192
18: 3 For all nations h' drunk of the wine*
3 the earth h' committed fornication.*
5 For her sins h' reached unto heaven,
9 who h' committed fornication and*
19: 10 brethren that h' the testimony *2192
21: 8 shall h' their part in the lake which*
22: 14 that they may h' right to the tree 2071
16 I Jesus h' sent mine angel to testify

haven See also HAVENS.
Ge 49: 13 shall dwell at the h' of the sea 2348
13 and he shall be for an h' of ships; "
Ps 107: 30 them unto their desired h'. 4231
Ac 27: 12 the h' was not commodious 3040
12 which is an h' at Crete, and lieth "

havens
Ac 27: 8 place which is called The fair h'; 2568

Havilah (hav'-il-ah)
Ge 2: 11 compasseth the whole land of H',2341
10: 7 of Cush; Seba, and H', and Sabtah,"
29 Ophir, and H', and Jobab: all these"
25: 18 they dwelt from H' unto Shur, that"
1Sa 15: 7 from H' until thou comest to "
1Ch 1: 9 Cush; Seba, and H', and Sabta, "
23 And Ophir, and H', and Jobab. All "

having
Ge 12: 8 and pitched his tent, h' Bethel on the
Le 7: 20 h' his uncleanness upon him, even
20: 18 lie with a woman h' her sickness,
22: 3 the Lord, h' his uncleanness upon
22 or maimed, or h' a wen, or scurvy,
Nu 24: 4, 16 a trance, but h' his eyes open:
De 10: 3 the mount, h' the two tables in mine
J'g 1: 7 h' their thumbs and their toes cut off,
19: 3 h' his servant with him, and a couple
Ru 1: 13 ye stay for them from h' husbands?
1Sa 22: 6 in Ramah, h' his spear in his hand,*
26: 2 of Ziph, h' three thousand chosen men
1Ki 22: 10 on his throne, h' put on their robes,*
1Ch 4: 42 h' for their captains Pelatiah, and
21: 16 and the heaven, h' a drawn sword in
26: 12 men, h' wards one against another,
2Ch 5: 12 h' cymbals and psalteries and harps,*
11: 12 h' Judah and Benjamin on his *
23: 10 every man h' his weapon in his hand,*
Ezr 9: 5 and h' rent my garment and my *
Ne 10: 28 h' knowledge, and h' understanding;*
13: 4 the priest, h' the oversight of *5414
Es 6: 12 mourning, and h' his head covered.
Ps 13: 2 in my soul, h' sorrow in my heart
Pr 6: 7 Which h' no guide, overseer, or ruler,
18: 1 desire a man, h' separated himself,*
Isa 6: 6 h' a live coal in his hand,
41: 15 threshing instrument h' teeth: 1167
Jer 41: 5 h' their beards shaven, and their
5 and h' cut themselves, with offerings
Eze 38: 11 and h' neither bars nor gates,
40: 44 the east gate h' the prospect toward
44: 11 my sanctuary, h' charge at the gates
Da 8: 20 which thou sawest h' two horns *1167
Mic 1: 11 of Saphir, h' thy shame naked: *
Zec 9: 9 he is just, and h' salvation;
M't 7: 29 them as one h' authority, 2192
8: 9 authority, h' soldiers under me: "
9: 36 as sheep h' no shepherd. "
15: 30 h' with them those that were lame, "
18: 8 rather than h' two hands or two "
9 rather than h' two eyes to be cast "
22: 12 in hither not h' a wedding garment?"
24 If a man die, h' no children, his "
25 deceased, and, h' no issue, left his "
26: 7 a woman h' an alabaster box of "
M'r 6: 34 were as sheep not h' a shepherd: "
8: 1 and h' nothing to eat, Jesus called*"
18 H' eyes, see ye not? and h' ears, "
9: 43 than h' two hands to go into hell, "
45 than h' two feet to be cast into hell, "
47 than h' two eyes to be cast into hell "
11: 13 a fig tree afar off h' leaves, he came, "
12: 6 H' yet therefore one son, his * "
28 h' heard them reasoning together,*
14: 3 a woman h' an alabaster box of 2192
51 young man, h' a linen cloth cast about
Lu 1: 3 h' had perfect understanding of all
5: 39 No man also h' drunk old wine
7: 8 authority, h' under me soldiers, 2192
8: 15 heart, h' heard the word, keep it,
43 a woman h' an issue of blood 5607,1722
9: 62 No man, h' put his hand to the plough,
11: 36 full of light, h' no part dark, the 2192
Lu 15: 4 man of you, h' an hundred sheep, 2192
8 what woman h' ten pieces of silver,"
17: 7 h' a servant plowing or feeding 2192
19: 15 returned, h' received the kingdom,
20: 28 If any man's brother die, h' a wife, 2192
23: 14 h' examined him before you, have
46 and h' said thus, he gave up the ghost.
Joh 4: 45 h' seen all the things that he did at
5: 2 tongue Bethesda, h' five porches. 2192
7: 15 this man letters, h' never learned?
13: 1 h' loved his own which were in the
2 the devil now h' put into the heart of
30 He then h' received the sop went
18: 3 Judas then, h' received a band of men
10 Simon Peter h' a sword drew it, 2192
Ac 2: 24 raised up, h' loosed the pains of death
33 h' received of the Father the promise
47 and h' favour with all the people, 2192
3: 26 God, h' raised up his Son Jesus, sent
4: 37 H' land, sold it, and brought 5225,846
12: 20 h' made Blastus...their friend,
14: 19 h' stoned Paul, drew him out of the*
16: 24 Who, h' received such a charge,
18: 18 h' shorn his head in Cenchrea: for he
19: 1 Paul h' passed through the upper
29 and h' caught Gaius and Aristarchus,
22: 12 h' a good report of all the Jews *
23: 27 h' understood that he was a Roman.
24: 22 h' more perfect knowledge of that
26: 10 h' received authority from the chief
22 H' therefore obtained help of God, I
27: 33 continued fasting, h' taken nothing.
Ro 2: 14 h' not the law, are a law unto 2192
9: 11 neither h' done any good or evil, that
12: 6 H' then gifts differing according 2192
15: 23 But now h' no more place in these "
1Co 6: 1 h' a matter against another, go "
7: 37 h' no necessity, but hath power "
11: 4 prophesying, h' his head covered, "
12: 24 h' given more abundant honour to*
2Co 2: 3 h' confidence in you all, that my joy
4: 13 We h' the same spirit of faith, 2192
6: 10 as h' nothing, and yet possessing "
7: 1 H' therefore these promises, "
9: 8 that ye, always h' all sufficiency "
10: 6 And h' in a readiness to revenge * "
15 but h' hope, when your faith is "
Ga 3: 3 h' begun in the Spirit, are ye now
Eph 1: 5 H' predestinated us unto the
9 H' made known unto us the mystery
2: 12 h' no hope, and without God in 2192
15 H' abolished in his flesh the enmity,
16 cross, h' slain the enmity thereby:
4: 18 H' the understanding darkened,*
5: 27 not h' spot, or wrinkle, or any 2192
6: 13 the evil day, and h' done all, to stand,
14 Stand therefore, h' your loins girt
14 and h' on the breastplate of 1746
Ph'p 1: 23 h' a desire to depart, and to be 2192
25 And h' this confidence, I know that I
30 H' the same conflict which ye 2192
2: 2 h' the same love, being of one "
3: 9 not h' mine own righteousness, "
4: 18 h' received of Epaphroditus the
Col 1: 20 h' made peace through the blood of
2: 13 him, h' forgiven you all trespasses;
15 h' spoiled principalities and powers,
19 body h'... nourishment ministered,*
1Th 1: 6 h' received the word in much
1Ti 1: 6 From which some h' swerved have
19 some h' put away concerning faith
3: 4 h' his children in subjection with 2192
4: 2 h' their conscience seared with a hot*
8 h' promise of the life that now is, 2192
5: 9 years old, h' been the wife of one man,
12 H' damnation, because they have 2192
6: 8 And h' food and raiment let us be "
2Ti 2: 19 of God standeth sure, h' this seal, "
3: 5 H' a form of godliness, but "
4: 3 themselves teachers, h' itching ears;
10 h' loved this present world, and is
Tit 1: 6 h' faithful children not accused 2192
2: 8 h' no evil thing to say of you. "
Ph'm 21 H' confidence in thy obedience I
Heb 7: 3 h' neither beginning of days, nor 2192
9: 12 h' obtained eternal redemption for us,
10: 1 For the law h' a shadow of good 2192
19 H' therefore, brethren, boldness to "
21 And h' an high priest over the house
22 h' our hearts sprinkled from an evil
11: 13 not h' received the promises, but
39 all, h' obtained a good report through
40 God h' provided some better thing for
1Pe 1: 8 Whom h' not seen, ye love;
2: 12 H' your conversation honest 2192
3: 8 h' compassion one of another, *
16 H' a good conscience; that, 2192
2Pe 1: 4 h' escaped the corruption that is in
2: 14 H' eyes full of adultery, and that 2192
2Jo 12 H' many things to write unto you, "
Jude 5 h' saved the people out of the land of
16 h' men's persons in admiration *
19 sensual, h' not the Spirit. 2192
Re 5: 6 h' seven horns and seven eyes, "
8 h' every one of them harps, and "
7: 2 h' the seal of the living God: "
8: 3 at the altar, h' a golden censer; "
9: 17 h' breastplates of fire, and of "
12: 3 h' seven heads and ten horns, and "
12 down unto you, h' great wrath, "
13: 1 h' seven heads and ten horns, and "
14: 1 h' his Father's name written in "
6 h' the everlasting gospel to preach "
14 h' on his head a golden crown, and "
17 heaven, he also h' a sharp sickle. "
15: 1 angels h' the seven last plagues; "

Re 15: 2 sea of glass, h' the harps of God. 2192
6 the temple, h' the seven plagues, * "
6 h' their breasts girded with * "
17: 3 h' seven heads and ten horns. "
4 h' a golden cup in her hand full of "
18: 1 from heaven, h' great power; "
20: 1 h' the key of the bottomless pit "
21: 11 H' the glory of God: and her light "

havock
Ac 8: 3 Saul, he made h' of the church. *3075

Havoth-jair (*ha"-voth-ja'-ir*) See also BASHAN-HAVOTH.
Nu 32: 41 thereof, and called them H'. *2334
J'g 10: 4 which are called H' unto this day.* "

hawk
Le 11: 16 the owl, and the night h', and the 8464
16 cuckow, and the h' after his kind, 5322
De 14: 15 the owl, and the night h', and the 8464
15 cuckow, and the h' after his kind, 5322
Job 39: 26 Doth the h' fly by thy wisdom, "

hay
Pr 27: 25 The h' appeareth, and the tender 2682
Isa 15: 6 for the h' is withered away, the * "
1Co 3: 12 silver, precious stones, wood, h', 5528

Hazael (*ha'-za-el*)
1Ki 19: 15 anoint H' to be king over Syria: 2371
17 that escapeth the sword of H' shall "
2Ki 8: 8 the king said unto H', Take a "
9 So H' went to meet him, and took "
12 And H' said, Why weepeth my "
13 And H' said, But what, is thy "
15 and H' reigned in his stead. "
28 of Ahab to war against H' king of "
29 Ramah, when he fought against H' "
9: 14 and all Israel, because of H' king "
15 when he fought with H' king of "
10: 32 and H' smote them in all the "
12: 17 Then H' king of Syria went up, "
17 and H' set his face to go up to "
18 and sent it to H' king of Syria: "
13: 3 into the hand of H' king of Syria, "
3 hand of Ben-hadad the son of H', "
22 But H' king of Syria oppressed "
24 So H' king of Syria died; and "
25 hand of Ben-hadad the son of H' "
2Ch 22: 5 to war against H' king of Syria "
6 Ramah, when he fought with H' "
Am 1: 4 send a fire into the house of H', "

Hazaiah (*ha-za-i'-ah*)
Ne 11: 5 Col-hozeh, the son of H', the son 2382

Hazar See HAZAR-ADDAR; HAZAR-ENAN; HAZAR-GADDAH; HAZAR-HATTICON; HAZAR-SHUAL; HAZAR-SUSAH; HAZAR-SUSIM.

Hazar-addar (*ha"-zar-ad'-dar*) See also ADDAR.
Nu 34: 4 and shall go on to H', and pass 2692

hazarded
Ac 15: 26 Men that have h' their lives for 3860

Hazar-enan (*ha"-zar-e'-nan*)
Nu 34: 9 goings out of it shall be at H': 2704
10 east border from H' to Shepham: "
Eze 47: 17 border from the sea shall be H', *2703
48: 1 as one goeth to Hamath, H'. 2704

Hazar-gaddah (*ha"-zar-gad'-dah*)
Jos 15: 27 H', and Heshmon, and Beth-palet, 2693

Hazar-hatticon (*ha"-zar-hat'-ti-con*)
Eze 47: 16 H', which is by the coast of *2694

Hazarmaveth (*ha-zar-ma'-veth*)
Ge 10: 26 Sheleph, and H', and Jerah, 2700
1Ch 1: 20 Sheleph, and H', and Jerah, "

Hazar-shual (*ha"-zar-shoo'-al*)
Jos 15: 28 And H', and Beer-sheba, and 2705
19: 3 H', and Balah, and Azem, "
1Ch 4: 28 Beer-sheba, and Moladah, and H', "
Ne 11: 27 at H', and at Beer-sheba, and in "

Hazar-susah (*ha"-zar-soo'-sah*) See also HAZAR-SUSIM.
Jos 19: 5 and Beth-marcaboth, and H', 2701

Hazar-susim (*ha"-zar-soo'-sim*) See also HAZAR-SUSAH.
1Ch 4: 31 at Beth-marcaboth, and H', 2702

Hazazon-tamar (*haz"-a-zon-ta'-mar*) See also HAZEZON-TAMAR.
2Ch 20: 2 they be in H', which is Engedi. 2688

hazel
Ge 30: 37 and of the h' and chestnut tree; *3869

Hazelelponi (*haz-el-el-po'-ni*)
1Ch 4: 3 the name of their sister was H': *6753

Hazerim (*haz'-e-rim*)
De 2: 23 the Avims which dwelt in H', *2699

Hazeroth (*haz'-e-roth*)
Nu 11: 35 from Kibroth-hattaavah unto H'; 2698
35 and abode at H'. "
12: 16 the people removed from H', "
33: 17 and encamped at H'. "
18 And they departed from H', and "
De 1: 1 Laban, and H', and Dizahab. "

Hazezon-tamar (*haz"-e-zon-ta'-mar*) See also EN-GEDI; HAZAZON-TAMAR.
Ge 14: 7 the Amorites, that dwelt in H'. *2688

Haziel (*ha'-ze-el*)
1Ch 23: 9 Shelomith, and H', and Haran, 2381

Hazo (*ha'-zo*)
Ge 22: 22 Chesed, and H', and Pildash, 2375

Hazor (*ha'-zor*) See also BAAL-HAZOR; EN-HAZOR; HEZRON.
Jos 11: 1 when Jabin king of H' had heard 2674
10 and took H', and smote the king "
10 for H' beforetime was the head "
11 and he burnt H' with fire. 2674
13 Israel burned none of them, save H' "
12: 19 Madon, one; the king of H', one; "
15: 23 And Kedesh, and H', and Ithnan, "
25 And H', Hadattah, and *2675
25 Kerioth, and Hezron, which is H'. 2674
19: 36 And Adamah, and Ramah, and H', "
J'g 4: 2 king of Canaan, that reigned in H'; "
17 peace between Jabin the king of H' "
1Sa 12: 9 of Sisera, captain of the host of H', "
1Ki 9: 15 and H', and Megiddo, and Gezer. "
2Ki 15: 29 Kedesh, and H', and Gilead, "
Ne 11: 33 H', Ramah, Gittaim, "
Jer 49: 28 and concerning the kingdoms of H', "
30 dwell deep, O ye inhabitants of H', "
33 H' shall be a dwelling for dragons, "

Hazor-hadattah See HAZOR and HADATTAH.

Hazzurim See HELKATH-HAZZURIM.

he See in the APPENDIX; also HIM; HIS.

head See also BEHEADED; FOREHEAD; GODHEAD; GRAYHEADED; HEADBANDS; HEADLONG; HEADS; HEADSTONE.
Ge 3: 15 it shall bruise thy h', and thou 7218
24: 26 And the man bowed down his h', and "
48 And I bowed down my h', and "
40: 13 shall Pharaoh lift up thine h', and 7218
16 I had three white baskets on my h': "
17 them out of the basket upon my h'. "
19 shall Pharaoh lift up thy h' from off "
20 he lifted up the h' of the chief "
47: 31 bowed himself upon the bed's h'. "
48: 14 laid it upon Ephraim's h', who was "
14 his left hand upon Manasseh's h', "
17 hand upon the h' of Ephraim, "
17 Ephraim's h' unto Manasseh's h'. "
18 put thy right hand upon his h'. "
49: 26 they shall be on the h' of Joseph, "
26 and on the crown of the h' of him 6936
Ex 12: 9 his h' with his legs, and with the 7218
27 And the people bowed the h' and "
26: 24 coupled together above the h' of *7218
29: 6 put the mitre upon his h', and put "
7 oil, and pour it upon his h', and "
10 hands upon the h' of the bullock. "
15 their hands upon the h' of the ram. "
17 unto his pieces, and unto his h'. "
19 their hands upon the h' of the ram. "
34: 8 Moses made haste, and bowed his h' "
36: 29 coupled together at the h' thereof, *7218
Le 1: 4 upon the h' of the burnt offering; "
8 the parts, the h', and the fat. "
12 pieces, with his h' and his fat: "
15 wring off his h', and burn it on the "
3: 2, 8 hand upon the h' of his offering, "
13 lay his hand upon the h' of it, "
4: 4 lay his hand upon the bullock's h', "
11 with his h', and with his legs, "
15 hands upon the h' of the bullock "
24 his hand upon the h' of the goat, "
29, 33 upon the h' of the sin offering, "
5: 8 wring off his h' from his neck, "
8: 9 And he put the mitre upon his h'; "
12 the anointing oil upon Aaron's h', "
14 upon the h' of the bullock for the "
18 their hands upon the h' of the ram. "
20 Moses burnt the h', and the pieces, "
22 hands upon the h' of the ram. "
9: 13 with the pieces thereof, and the h': "
13: 12 plague from his h' even to his foot, "
29 a plague upon the h' or the beard; "
30 a leprosy upon the h' or beard. "
40 whose hair is fallen off his h', "
41 the part of his h' toward his face, "
42 if there be in the bald h', or bald "
42 leprosy sprung up in his bald h', "
43 sore be white reddish in his bald h', "
44 unclean; his plague is in his h'. 7218
45 shall be rent, and his h' bare, "
14: 9 shall shave all his hair off his h' "
18 the h' of him that is to be cleansed: "
29 the h' of him that is to be cleansed, "
16: 21 hands upon the h' of the live goat, "
21 them upon the h' of the goat, "
19: 32 rise up before the hoary h', and "
21: 5 not make baldness upon their h', 7218
10 upon whose h' the anointing oil "
10 shall not uncover his h', nor rend "
24: 14 lay their hands upon his h', and "
Nu 1: 4 one h' of the house of his fathers. "
5: 18 uncover the woman's h', and put * "
6: 5 shall no rasor come upon his h': "
5 the locks of the hair of his h' grow. "
7 of his God is upon his h'. "
9 defiled the h' of his consecration; "
9 shall shave his h' in the day "
11 and shall hallow his h' that same "
18 Nazarite shall shave the h' of his "
18 the hair of the h' of his separation, "
17: 3 h' of the house of their fathers. "
22: 31 and he bowed down his h', and fell "
25: 15 he was h' over a people, and of a 7218
De 19: 5 the h' slippeth from the helve, and 1270
21: 12 she shall shave her h', and pare 7218
28: 13 the Lord shall make thee the h', "
23 thy heaven that is over thy h' "
35 of thy foot unto the top of thy h'. 6936
44 he shall be the h', and thou shalt 7218
33: 16 come upon the h' of Joseph, "
16 and upon the top of the h' of him 6936
20 the arm with the crown of the h'. "
Jos 2: 19 his blood shall be upon his h', 7218
19 his blood shall be on our h', "
11: 10 was the h' of all those kingdoms. "
22: 14 each one was an h' of the house of "
J'g 5: 26 Sisera, she smote off his h', "
9: 53 of a millstone upon Abimelech's h', 7218
10: 18 h' over all the inhabitants of "
11: 8 be our h' over all the inhabitants "
9 before me, shall I be your h'? "
11 the people made him h' and captain "
13: 5 no rasor shall come on his h': "
16: 13 weavest the seven locks of my h' "
17 hath not come a rasor upon mine h'; "
19 shave off the seven locks of his h'; "
22 the hair of his h' began to grow "
1Sa 1: 11 shall no rasor come upon his h'. "
4: 12 rent, and with earth upon his h'. "
5: 4 and the h' of Dagon and both the "
10: 1 vial of oil, and poured it upon his h', "
14: 45 one hair of his h' fall to the ground; "
15: 17 made the h' of the tribes of Israel, "
17: 5 had an helmet of brass upon his h', "
7 and his spear's h' weighed six 3852
38 an helmet of brass upon his h'; 7218
46 take thine h' from thee; and I will "
51 him, and cut off his h' therewith. "
54 David took the h' of the Philistine, "
57 with the h' of the Philistine in his "
25: 39 of Nabal upon his own h'. "
28: 2 thee keeper of mine h' for ever. "
31: 9 they cut off his h', and stripped off "
2Sa 1: 2 rent, and earth upon his h': and so "
10 the crown that was upon his h', "
16 Thy blood be upon thy h'; for "
2: 16 every one his fellow by the h', "
3: 8 Am I a dog's h', which against "
29 Let it rest on the h' of Joab "
4: 7 beheaded him, and took his h', "
8 they brought the h' of Ish-bosheth "
8 Behold the h' of Ish-bosheth the "
12 they took the h' of Ish-bosheth, "
12: 30 their king's crown from off his h', "
30 and it was set on David's h'. "
13: 19 Tamar put ashes on her h', and "
19 laid her hand on her h', and went "
14: 25 his foot even to the crown of his h' 6936
26 And when he polled his h', (for it 7218
26 he weighed the hair of his h' at two "
15: 30 and had his h' covered, and he "
30 covered every man his h', and they "
32 coat rent, and earth upon his h': "
16: 9 I pray thee, and take off his h'. "
18: 9 and his h' caught hold of the oak, "
20: 21 his h' shall be thrown to thee over "
22 they cut off the h' of Sheba "
22: 44 kept me to be h' of the heathen: "
1Ki 2: 6 let not his hoar h' go down to the grave "
9 his hoar h' bring thou down to the "
32 return his blood upon his own h', 7218
33 return upon the h' of Joab, and "
33 and upon the h' of his seed for ever; "
37 blood shall be upon thine own h'. "
44 thy wickedness upon thine own h'; "
8: 32 to bring his way upon his h'; "
19: 6 and a cruse of water at his h'. 4763
2Ki 2: 3, 5 thy master from thy h' to-day? 7218
23 thou bald h'; go up, thou bald h'. "
4: 19 said unto his father, My h', my h'. 7218
6: 5 the axe h' fell into the water: 1270
25 an ass's h' was sold for fourscore 7218
31 the h' of Elisha the son of Shaphat "
32 hath sent to take away mine h'? "
9: 3 the box of oil, and pour it on his h', "
6 he poured the oil on his h', "
30 painted her face, and tired her h', "
19: 21 Jerusalem hath shaken her h' at "
25: 27 did lift up the h' of Jehoiachin "
1Ch 10: 9 they took his h', and his armour, "
10 fastened his h' in the temple of 1538
20: 2 crown of their king from off his h', 7218
2 and it was set upon David's h': "
29: 11 thou art exalted as h' above all. "
2Ch 6: 23 his way upon his own h'; "
20: 18 And Jehoshaphat bowed his h' with "
Ezr 9: 3 plucked off the hair of my h' and 7218
6 iniquities are increased over our h', "
Ne 4: 4 their reproach upon their own h', "
Es 2: 17 he set the royal crown upon her h', "
6: 8 royal which is set upon his h': "
12 and having his h' covered. "
9: 25 should return upon his own h', "
Job 1: 20 rent his mantle, and shaved his h', "
10: 15 yet will I not lift up my h'. "
16: 4 you, and shake mine h' at you. "
19: 9 and taken the crown from my h'. "
20: 6 and his h' reach unto the clouds; "
29: 3 When his candle shined upon my h', "
41: 7 irons? or his h' with fish spears? "
Ps 3: 3 glory, and the lifter up of mine h'. "
7: 16 shall return upon his own h', "
18: 43 made me the h' of the heathen: "
21: 3 a crown of pure gold on his h'. "
22: 7 the lip, they shake the h', saying, "
23: 5 thou anointest my h' with oil; "
27: 6 now shall mine h' be lifted up "
38: 4 iniquities are gone over mine h': "
40: 12 more than the hairs of mine h': "
44: 14 shaking of the h' among the people. "
60: 7 also is the strength of mine h'; "
68: 21 shall wound the h' of his enemies, "
69: 4 more than the hairs of mine h': "
83: 2 that hate thee have lifted up the h'. "
108: 8 also is the strength of mine h'; "
110: 7 therefore shall he lift up the h'. "
118: 22 become the h' stone of the corner. "
133: 2 the precious ointment upon the h', "
140: 7 covered my h' in the day of battle. "
9 the h' of those that compass me "
141: 5 oil, which shall not break my h': "
Pr 1: 9 an ornament of grace unto thy h', "
4: 9 shall give to thine h' an ornament "

Pr 10: 6 Blessings are upon the h' of the 7218
11:26 blessing shall be upon the h' of him "
16:31 The hoary h' is a crown of glory, "
20:29 the beauty of old men is the gray h'. "
25:22 heap coals of fire upon his h'. 7218
Ec 2:14 The wise man's eyes are in his h'; "
9: 8 and let thy h' lack no ointment. "
Ca 2: 6 His left hand is under my h', "
5: 2 for my h' is filled with dew, "
11 His h' is as the most fine gold, "
7: 5 Thine h' upon thee is like Carmel, "
5 and the hair of thine h' like purple; "
8: 3 left hand should be under my h', "
Isa 1: 5 the whole h' is sick, and the whole "
6 the sole of the foot even unto the h' "
3:17 with a scab the crown of the h' of 6936
7: 8 the h' of Syria is Damascus, and 7218
8 the h' of Damascus is Rezin; "
9 And the h' of Ephraim is Samaria, "
9 the h' of Samaria is Remaliah's son. "
20 the h', and the hair of the feet: "
9:14 will cut off from Israel h' and tail, "
15 ancient and honourable, he is the h'; "
19:15 the h' or tail, branch or rush, "
28: 1 are on the h' of the fat valleys "
4 which is on the h' of the fat valley, "
37:22 of Jerusalem hath shaken her h' "
51:11 joy shall be upon their h': * "
20 they lie at the h' of all the streets,* "
58: 5 to bow down his h' as a bulrush, "
59:17 an helmet of salvation upon his h': "
Jer 2:16 have broken the crown of thy h'. 6936
37 and thine hands upon thine h'. 7218
9: 1 Oh that my h' were waters, "
18:16 shall be astonished, and wag his h'. "
22: 6 unto me, and the h' of Lebanon: "
23:19 grievously upon the h' of the wicked. "
30:23 with pain upon the h' of the wicked. "
48:37 every h' shall be bald, and every "
45 of the h' of the tumultuous ones. 6936
52:31 h' of Jehoiachin king of Judah, 7218
La 2:15 they hiss and wag their h' at the "
3:54 Waters flowed over mine h'; then I "
5:16 The crown is fallen from our h': "
Eze 5: 1 upon thine h' and upon thy beard: "
8: 3 took me by a lock of mine h'; "
9:10 recompense their way upon their h'. "
10: 1 above the h' of the cherubims there "
11 whither the h' looked they followed "
13:18 upon the h' of every stature to hunt "
16:12 a beautiful crown upon thine h'. "
25 high place at every h' of the way, "
31 eminent place the h' of every way, "
43 recompense thy way upon thine h', "
17:19 will I recompense upon his own h'. "
21:19 at the h' of the way to the city. "
21 at the h' of the two ways, "
24:17 bind the tire of thine h' upon thee, "
29:18 every h' was made bald, and every 7218
33: 4 his blood shall be upon his own h'. "
42:12 was a door in the h' of the way, "
Da 1:10 me endanger my h' to the king. "
2:28 the visions of thy h' upon thy bed 7217
32 This image's h' was of fine gold, "
38 Thou art this h' of gold. "
3:27 nor was an hair of their h' singed, "
4: 5 the visions of my h' troubled me. "
10 the visions of mine h' in my bed; "
13 I saw in the visions of my h' upon "
7: 1 and visions of his h' upon his bed: "
9 hair of his h' like the pure wool: "
15 the visions of my h' troubled me. "
20 of the ten horns that were in his h', "
Ho 1:11 and appoint themselves one h', 7218
Joe 3: 4 recompence upon your own h'; "
7 your recompence upon your own h': "
Am 2: 7 of the earth on the h' of the poor, "
8:10 loins, and baldness upon every h'; "
9: 1 cut them in the h', all of them; "
Ob 15 shall return upon thine own h'. "
Jon 2: 5 weeds were wrapped about my h'. "
4: 6 a shadow over his h', to deliver "
8 the sun beat upon the h' of Jonah, "
Mic 2:13 and the Lord on the h' of them. "
Hab 3:13 woundedst the h' out of the house "
14 his staves the h' of his villages: "
Zec 1:21 so that no man did lift up his h': "
3: 5 men set a fair mitre upon his h'. "
5 they set a fair mitre upon his h', "
6:11 set them upon the h' of Joshua "
M't 5:36 Neither shalt thou swear by thy h',2776
6:17 when thou fastest, anoint thine h'. "
8:20 hath not where to lay his h'. "
10:30 hairs of your h' are all numbered. "
14: 8 Give me here John Baptist's h' in "
11 And his h' was brought in a "
21:42 is become the h' of the corner: "
26: 7 ointment, and poured it on his h', "
27:29 of thorns, they put it upon his h', "
30 the reed, and smote him on the h'. "
37 set up over his h' his accusation "
M'r 6:24 she said, The h' of John the Baptist. "
25 in a charger the h' of John the "
27 commanded his h' to be brought: "
28 brought his h' in a charger, and "
12: 4 and wounded him in the h', and 2775
10 is become the h' of the corner: 2776
14: 3 the box, and poured it on his h'. "
15:17 thorns, and put it about his h', * "
19 they smote him on the h' with a 2776
Lu 7:38 wipe them with the hairs of her h', "
44 wiped them with the hairs of her h'.* "
46 My h' with oil thou didst not "
9:58 hath not where to lay his h'. "
12: 7 hairs of your h' are all numbered. "
20:17 is become the h' of the corner? "
Lu 21:18 shall not an hair of your h' perish. 2776
Jo 13: 9 but also my hands and my h'. "
19: 2 of thorns, and put it on his h', and "
30 and he bowed his h', and gave up "
20: 7 the napkin, that was about his h', "
12 the one at the h', and the other "
Ac 4:11 is become the h' of the corner. "
18:18 having shorn his h' in Cenchrea: "
27:34 shall not an hair fall from the h' of "
Ro 12:20 shalt heap coals of fire on his h'. "
1Co 11: 3 the h' of every man is Christ; and "
3 the h' of the woman is the man; "
3 and the h' of Christ is God. "
4 prophesying, having his h' covered, "
4 covered, dishonoureth his h'. "
5 prophesieth with her h' uncovered "
5 uncovered dishonoureth her h': "
7 indeed ought not to cover his h', "
10 woman to have power on her h' "
12:21 nor again the h' to the feet, I have "
Eph 1:22 gave him to be h' over all things "
4:15 which is the h', even Christ: "
5:23 the husband is the h' of the wife, "
23 as Christ is the h' of the church: "
Col 1:18 he is the h' of the body, the church: "
2:10 the h' of all principality and power: "
19 And not holding the H', from "
1Pe 2: 7 same is made the h' of the corner, "
Re 1:14 His h' and his hairs were white "
10: 1 and a rainbow was upon his h', "
12: 1 her h' a crown of twelve stars: "
14:14 having on his h' a golden crown, "
19:12 and on his h' were many crowns; "

headbands
Isa 3:20 and the h', and the tablets, and *7196

headed See BEHEADED; GRAYHEADED.

headlong
Job 5:13 counsel of the froward is carried h'.
Lu 4:29 that they might cast him down h'. 2630
Ac 1:18 of iniquity; and falling h', he burst 4248

heads
Ge 2:10 parted, and became into four h'. 7218
43:28 And they bowed down their h', and*
Ex 4:31 then they bowed their h' and
6:14 the h' of their fathers' houses: 7218
25 the h' of the fathers of the Levites "
18:25 and made them h' over the people, "
Le 10: 6 Uncover not your h', neither rend "
19:27 not round the corners of your h', "
Nu 1:16 fathers, h' of thousands in Israel. "
7: 2 h' of the house of their fathers, "
8:12 hands upon the h' of the bullocks: "
10: 4 are h' of the thousands of Israel, "
13: 3 were h' of the children of Israel. "
25: 4 Take all the h' of the people. * "
30: 1 spake unto the h' of the tribes "
De 1:15 and made them h' over you, "
5:23 even all the h' of your tribes, and "
33: 5 when the h' of the people and the "
21 he came with the h' of the people, "
Jos 7: 6 Israel, and put dust upon their h'. 7218
14: 1 the h' of the fathers of the tribes "
19:51 the h' of the fathers of the tribes "
21: 1 the h' of the fathers of the Levites "
1 the h' of the fathers of the tribes "
22:21 the h' of the thousands of Israel, "
30 and h' of the thousands of Israel "
23: 2 for their h', and for their judges, "
24: 1 for their h', and for their judges, "
J'g 7:25 brought the h' of Oreb and Zeeb to "
8:28 they lifted up their h' no more. "
9:57 did God render upon their h': "
1Sa 29: 4 it not be with the h' of these men? "
1Ki 8: 1 all the h' of the tribes, the chief of "
20:31 on our loins, and ropes upon our h', "
32 and put ropes on their h', and came "
2Ki 10: 6 take ye the h' of the men your "
7 put their h' in baskets, and sent "
8 have brought the h' of the king's "
1 Ch 5:24 h' of the house of their fathers, "
7: 2 h' of their father's house, to wit, of "
7, 9 h' of the house of their fathers, "
11 by the h' of their fathers, mighty "
40 h' of their father's house, choice "
8: 6 the h' of the fathers of the "
10 were his sons, h' of the fathers. "
13 h' of the fathers of the inhabitants "
28 These were h' of the fathers, by "
9:13 h' of the house of their fathers, "
12:19 Saul to the jeopardy of our h'. "
32 the h' of them were two hundred; "
29:20 and bowed down their h', and
2 Ch 3:16 put them on the h' of the pillars;*7218
5: 2 all the h' of the tribes, the chief of "
28:12 the h' of the children of Ephraim, "
29:30 bowed their h', and worshipped. "
Ne 8: 6 bowed their h', and worshipped
Job 2:12 sprinkled dust upon their h' 7218
Ps 24: 7 Lift up your h', O ye gates; and "
9 Lift up your h', O ye gates; even "
66:12 caused men to ride over our h'; "
74:13 thou brakest the h' of the dragons "
14 Thou brakest the h' of leviathan "
109:25 upon me they shaked their h'. "
110: 6 wound the h' over many countries.* "
Isa 15: 2 on all their h' shall be baldness, "
35:10 and everlasting joy upon their h': "
Jer 14: 3 confounded, and covered their h'. "
4 ashamed, they covered their h'. "
La 2:10 have cast up dust upon their h'; "
10 of Jerusalem hang down their h' "
Eze 1:22 upon the h' of the living creature * "
22 stretched forth over their h' above. "
25 firmament that was over their h', "
26 firmament that was over their h' "
Eze 7:18 and baldness upon all their h'. 7218
11:21 their way upon their own h', saith "
22:31 have I recompensed upon their h', "
23:15 in dyed attire upon their h', all of "
42 beautiful crowns upon their h'. "
24:23 your tires shall be upon your h', "
27:30 shall cast up dust upon their h', "
32:27 laid their swords under their h', "
44:18 have linen bonnets upon their h', "
20 Neither shall they shave their h', "
20 they shall only poll their h'. "
Da 7: 6 the beast had also four h'; and 7217
Mic 3: 1 Hear, I pray you, O h' of Jacob, 7218
9 ye h' of the house of Jacob, "
11 The h' thereof judge for reward, "
M't 27:39 by reviled him, wagging their h', 2776
M'r 15:29 railed on him, wagging their h', "
Lu 21:28 look up, and lift up your h'; "
Ac 18: 6 Your blood be upon your own h'; "
21:24 that they may shave their h': "
Re 4: 4 they had on their h' crowns of gold. "
9: 7 on their h' were as it were crowns "
17 and the h' of the horses were as the "
17 horses were as the h' of lions; "
19 like unto serpents, and had h', "
12: 3 having seven h' and ten horns, and "
3 and seven crowns upon his h'. "
13: 1 having seven h' and ten horns, "
1 upon his h' the name of blasphemy. "
3 And I saw one of his h' as it were "
17: 3 having seven h' and ten horns. "
7 hath the seven h' and ten horns. "
9 The seven h' are seven mountains, "
18:19 they cast dust on their h', and cried, "

headstone See also HEAD and STONE.
Zec 4: 7 he shall bring forth the h' ‡68,7222

heady
2 Ti 3: 4 Traitors, h', highminded, lovers *4312

heal See also HEALED; HEALETH; HEALING.
Nu 12:13 H' her now, O God, I beseech 7495
De 32:39 I make alive; I wound, and I h': "
2 Ki 20: 5 I will h' thee: on the third day "
8 the sign that the Lord will h' me, "
2 Ch 7:14 their sin, and will h' their land. "
Ps 6: 2 O Lord, h' me; for my bones are "
41: 4 be merciful unto me: h' my soul; "
60: 2 h' the breaches thereof; for it "
Ec 3: 3 A time to kill, and a time to h'; "
Isa 19:22 he shall smite and h' it: and they* "
22 of them, and shall h' them. "
57:18 I have seen his ways, and will h' "
19 saith the Lord; and I will h' him. "
Jer 3:22 and I will h' your backslidings. "
17:14 H' me, O Lord, and I shall be "
30:17 I will h' thee of thy wounds, "
La 2:13 great like the sea: who can h' thee? "
Ho 5:13 yet could he not h' you, nor cure "
6: 1 he hath torn, and he will h' us; he "
14: 4 I will h' their backsliding, I will "
Zec 11:16 nor h' that that is broken, "
M't 8: 7 unto him, I will come and h' him. 2323
10: 1 and to h' all manner of sickness "
8 H' the sick, cleanse the lepers, "
12:10 lawful to h' on the sabbath days? "
13:15 converted, and I should h' them. 2390
M'r 3: 2 he would h' on the sabbath day; 2323
15 to have power to h' sicknesses, * "
Lu 4:18 sent me to h' the brokenhearted, *2390
23 proverb, Physician, h' thyself: 2323
5:17 the Lord was present to h' them. 2390
6: 7 he would h' on the sabbath day; 2323
7: 3 would come and h' his servant. *1295
9: 2 of God, and to h' the sick. 2390
10: 9 h' the sick that are therein, and 2323
14: 3 lawful to h' on the sabbath day? "
Jo 4:47 would come down, and h' his son: 2390
12:40 be converted, and I should h' them. "
Ac 4:30 stretching forth thine hand to h'; 2392
28:27 be converted, and I should h' them. "

healed
Ge 20:17 and God h' Abimelech, and his 7495
Ex 21:19 cause him to be thoroughly h'. "
Le 13:18 skin thereof, was a boil, and is h', "
37 the scall is h', he is clean: "
14: 3 if the plague of leprosy be h' in "
48 clean, because the plague is h'. "
De 28:27 itch, whereof thou canst not be h'. "
35 a sore botch that cannot be h', "
1 Sa 6: 3 then ye shall be h', and it shall be "
2 Ki 2:21 the Lord, I have h' these waters; "
22 So the waters were h' unto this "
8:29 king Joram went back to be h' in "
9:15 king Joram was returned to be h' "
2Ch 22: 6 he returned to be h' in Jezreel "
30:20 to Hezekiah, and h' the people. "
Ps 30: 2 cried unto thee, and thou hast h' me. "
107:20 He sent his word, and h' them, * "
Isa 6:10 their heart, and convert, and be h'. "
53: 5 and with his stripes we are h'. "
Jer 6:14 They have h' also the hurt of the "
8:11 For they have h' the hurt of the "
15:18 incurable, which refuseth to be h'? "
17:14 Heal me, O Lord, and I shall be h'; "
51: 8 her pain, if so be she may be h'. "
9 We would have h' Babylon, "
9 Babylon, but she is not h': "
Eze 30:21 not be bound up to be h', *5414,7499
34: 4 have ye h' that which was sick, 7495
47: 8 the sea, the waters shall be h'. "
9 for they shall be h'; and every "
11 marishes thereof shall not be h'; "
Ho 7: 1 When I would have h' Israel, then* "
11: 3 they knew not that I h' them. "
M't 4:24 had the palsy; and he h' them. 2323
8: 8 only, and my servant shall be h'. 2390

M't 8:13 servant was h· in the selfsame 2390
16 his word, and h· all that were sick: 2323
12:15 followed him, and he h· them all; "
22 blind, and dumb: and he h· him, "
14:14 toward them, and he h· their sick. "
15:30 at Jesus' feet; and he h· them: "
19: 2 followed him; and he h· them there. "
21:14 him in the temple; add he h· them. "
M'r 1:34 he h· many that were sick of "
3:10 For he had h· many; insomuch "
5:23 hands on her, that she may be h·; *4982
29 that she was h· of that plague. 2390
6: 5 upon a few sick folk, and h· them. 2323
13 many that were sick, and h· them. "
Lu 4:40 on every one of them, and h· them. "
5:15 hear, and to be h· by him of their "
6:17 and to be h· of their diseases; 2390
18 unclean spirits: and they were h·. 2323
19 virtue out of him, and h· them all. 2390
7: 7 word, and my servant shall be h·. "
8: 2 women, which had been h· of evil "
36 possessed of the devils was h·. *4982
43 neither could be h· of any, 2323
47 and how she was h· immediately. 2390
9:11 h· them that had need of healing. "
42 and h· the child, and delivered "
13:14 Jesus had h· on the sabbath day, 2323
14 in them therefore come and be h·, "
14: 4 him, and h· him, and let him go; "
17:15 when he saw that he was h·, 2390
22:51 he touched his ear, and h· him. "
Joh 5:13 And he that was h· wist not who "
Ac 3:11 man which was h· held Peter and* "
4:14 beholding the man which was h· 2323
5:16 and they were h· every one. "
8: 7 and that were lame, were h·. "
14: 9 that he had faith to be h·, *4982
28: 8 his hands on him and h· him. 2390
9 in the island, came, and were h·: *2323
Heb 12:13 the way; but let it rather be h·. 2390
Jas 5:16 one for another, that ye may be h·. "
1Pe 2:24 by whose stripes ye were h·. "
Re 13: 3 his deadly wound was h·: and all 2323
12 beast, whose deadly wound was h·. "

healer
Isa 3: 7 swear, saying, I will not be an h·; 2280

healeth
Ex 15:26 for I am the Lord that h· thee. 7495
Ps 103: 3 iniquities; who h· all thy diseases; "
147: 3 He h· the broken in heart, and "
Isa 30:26 and h· the stroke of their wound. "

healing See also HEALINGS.
Jer 14:19 us, and there is no h· for us? 4832
19 and for the time of h·, and behold "
30:13 up: thou hast no h· medicines. 8585
Na 3:19 There is no h· of thy bruise; *3545
Mal 4: 2 arise with h· in his wings; 4832
M't 4:23 h· all manner of sickness and all 2323
9:35 h· every sickness and every disease "
Lu 9: 6 the gospel, and h· every where. "
11 healed them that had need of h·. 2322
Ac 4:22 this miracle of h· was shewed. 2392
10:38 and h· all that were oppressed of 2390
1Co 12: 9 gifts of h· by the same Spirit; *2386
30 Have all the gifts of h·? do all ‡ "
Re 22: 2 were for the h· of the nations. 2322

healings
1Co 12:28 miracles, then gift of h·, helps, 2386

health
Ge 43:28 servant our father is in good h·, *7965
2Sa 20: 9 Art thou in h·, my brother? * "
Ps 42:11 who is the h· of my countenance, ‡3444
43: 5 who is the h· of my countenance, ‡ "
67: 2 thy saving h· among all nations. ‡
Pr 3: 8 It shall be h· to thy navel, and 7500
4:22 find them, and h· to all their flesh. 4832
12:18 but the tongue of the wise is h·. "
13:17 but a faithful ambassador is h·. "
16:24 the soul, and h· to the bones. "
Isa 58: 8 and thine h· shall spring forth * 724
Jer 8:15 and for a time of h·, and behold *4832
22 the h· of the daughter of my 724
30:17 For I will restore h· unto thee, "
33: 6 I will bring it h· and cure, and I "
Ac 27:34 some meat: for this is for your h·: *4991
3Jo 2 thou mayest prosper and be in h·, 5198

heap See also HEAPED; HEAPETH; HEAPS.
Ge 31:46 they took stones, and made an h·: 1530
46 they did eat there upon the h·. "
48 This h· is a witness between me "
51 Behold this h·, and behold this "
52 This h· be witness, and this pillar "
52 I will not pass over this h· to thee, "
52 thou shalt not pass over this h· and "
Ex 15: 8 the floods stood upright as an h·, 5067
De 13:16 and it shall be an h· for ever; 8510
32:23 I will h· mischiefs upon them; 5595
Jos 3:13 and they shall stand upon an h·. 5067
16 rose up upon an h· very far from "
7:26 over him a great h· of stones 1530
8:28 Ai, and made it an h· for ever, even 8510
29 raise thereon a great h· of stones, 1530
Ru 3: 7 down at the end of the h· of corn: 6194
2Sa 18:17 very great h· of stones upon him: 1530
Job 8:17 roots are wrapped about the h·, "
16: 4 I could h· up words against you, *2266
27:16 Though he h· up silver as the dust, 6651
36:13 hypocrites in heart h· up wrath: *7760
Ps 33: 7 waters of the sea together as an h·: 5067
78:13 made the waters to stand as an h·. "
Pr 25:22 shalt h· coals of fire upon his head, 2846
Ec 2:26 gather and to h· up, that he may 3664
Ca 7: 2 thy belly is like an h· of wheat 6194
Isa 17: 1 city, and it shall be a ruinous h·. 4596
Isa 17:11 the harvest shall be a h· in the day *5067
25: 2 thou hast made of a city an h·; 1530
Jer 30:18 shall be builded on her own h·, 8510
49: 2 it shall be a desolate h·, and her "
Eze 24:10 H· on wood, kindle the fire, 7235
Mic 1: 6 make Samaria as an h· of the field, 5856
Hab 1:10 for they shall h· dust, and take it. *6651
3:15 through the h· of great waters. 2563
Hag 2:16 came to an h· of twenty measures, 6194
Ro 12:20 shalt h· coals of fire on his head. 4987
2Ti 4: 3 they h· to themselves teachers, 2002

heaped
Zec 9: 3 and h· up silver as the dust, and 6651
Jas 5: 3 Ye have h· treasures together for *2343

heapeth
Ps 39: 6 he h· up riches, and knoweth not 6651
Hab 2: 5 and h· unto him all people: 6908

heaps
Ex 8:14 gathered them together upon h·: 2563
J'g 15:16 the jawbone of an ass, h· upon h·, 2565
2Ki 10: 8 Lay ye them in two h· at the 6652
19:25 waste fenced cities into ruinous h·. 1530
2Ch 31: 6 their God, and laid them by h·. 6194
7 to lay the foundation of the h·, "
8 the princes came and saw the h·, "
9 and the Levites concerning the h·. "
Ne 4: 2 stones out of the h· of the rubbish "
Job 15:28 which are ready to become h·. 1530
Ps 79: 1 they have laid Jerusalem on h·. 5856
Isa 37:26 defenced cities into ruinous h·. 1530
Jer 9:11 I will make Jerusalem h·, and a "
26:18 Jerusalem shall become h·, and 5856
31:21 up waymarks, make thee high h·: *8564
50:26 cast her up as h·, and destroy her 6194
51:37 And Babylon shall become h·, a 1530
Ho 12:11 their altars are as h· in the furrows "
Mic 3:12 Jerusalem shall become h·, and 5856

hear See also HEARD; HEAREST; HEARETH; HEARING.
Ge 4:23 H· my voice; ye wives of Lamech, 8085
21: 6 that all that h· will laugh with me.* "
23: 6 H· us, my lord: thou art a mighty "
8 h· me, and intreat for me to Ephron "
11 Nay, my lord, h· me: the field give "
13 I pray thee, h· me: I will give thee "
37: 6 H·, I pray you, this dream which "
42:21 besought us, and we would not h·; "
22 the child; and ye would not h·? "
49: 2 together, and h·, ye sons of Jacob; "
Ex 6:12 how then shall Pharaoh h· me, "
7:16 hitherto thou wouldest not h·. * "
15:14 The people shall h·, and be afraid:* "
19: 9 the people may h· when I speak "
20:19 Speak thou with us, and we will h·: "
22:23 unto me, I will surely h· their cry; "
27 he crieth unto me, that I will h·; "
32:18 the noise of them that sing do I h·. "
Le 5: 1 sin and h· the voice of swearing, * "
Nu 9: 8 h· what the Lord will command "
12: 6 H· now my words: If there be a "
14:13 Then the Egyptians shall h· it, "
16: 8 H·, I pray you, ye sons of Levi: "
20:10 said unto them, H· now, ye rebels; "
23:18 Rise up, Balak, and h·; hearken "
30: 4 And her father h· her vow, and * "
De 1:16 H· the causes between your "
17 ye shall h· the small as well as the "
17 bring it unto me, and I will h· it. "
43 and ye would not h·, but rebelled * "
2:25 who shall h· report of thee, and "
3:26 your sakes, and would not h· me: * "
4: 6 which shall h· all these statutes, "
10 and I will make them h· my words, "
28 which neither see, nor h·, nor eat, "
33 Did ever people h· the voice of God "
36 of heaven he made thee to h· his "
5: 1 H·, O Israel, the statutes and "
25 if we h· the voice of the Lord our "
27 and h· all that the Lord our God "
27 thee; and we will h· it, and do it. "
6: 3 H· therefore, O Israel, and observe "
4 H·, O Israel: The Lord our God is "
9: 1 H·, O Israel: Thou art to pass over "
12:28 Observe and h· all these words "
13:11 all Israel shall h·, and fear, and "
12 shalt h· say in one of thy cities, "
17:13 all the people shall h·, and fear "
18:16 Let me not h· again the voice of "
19:20 which remain shall h·, and fear, "
20: 3 H·, O Israel, ye approach this day "
21:21 and all Israel shall h·, and fear. "
29: 4 eyes to see, and ears to h·, unto this "
30:12, 13 that we may h· it, and do it? "
17 turn away, so that thou wilt not h·, "
31:12 that they may h·, and that they may "
13 may h·, and learn to fear the "
32: 1 and h·, O earth, the words of my "
33: 7 said, H·, Lord, the voice of Judah, "
Jos 3: 9 hither, and h· the words of the Lord "
6: 5 ye h· the sound of the trumpet, "
7: 9 inhabitants of the land shall h· of "
J'g 5: 3 H·, O ye kings; give ear, O ye "
16 to h· the bleatings of the flocks? "
7:11 And thou shalt h· what they say; "
14:13 forth thy riddle, that we may h· it. "
1Sa 2:23 I h· of your evil dealings by all "
24 for it is no good report that I h·: "
8:18 the Lord will not h· you in that *6030
13: 3 land, saying, Let the Hebrews h·. 8085
15:14 the lowing of the oxen which I h·? "
16: 2 can I go? if Saul h· it, he will kill me. "
22: 7 H· now, ye Benjamites; will the "
12 said, H· now, thou son of Ahitub. "
25:24 h· the words of thine handmaid. * "
26:19 let my lord the king h· the words "
2Sa 14:16 For the king will h·, to deliver his 8085
15: 3 man deputed of the king to h· thee. "
10 as ye h· the sound of the trumpet, "
35 thing soever thou shalt h· out of the "
36 unto me every thing that ye can h·. "
16:21 shall h· that thou art abhorred of "
17: 5 let us h· likewise what he saith. "
19:35 I h· any more the voice of singing "
20:16 H·, h·; say, I pray you, unto Joab, "
17 H· the words of thine handmaid. "
17 And he answered, I do h·. "
22: 7 did h· my voice out of his temple, * "
45 as soon as they h·, they shall be * "
1Ki 4:34 people to h· the wisdom of Solomon, "
8:30 and h· thou in heaven thy dwelling "
32 Then h· thou in heaven, and do, "
34, 36 h· thou in heaven, and forgive "
39 Then h· thou in heaven thy "
42 For they shall h· of thy great name, "
43 H· thou in heaven thy dwelling "
45 h· thou in heaven their prayer "
49 Then h· thou their prayer and "
10: 8 before thee, and that h· thy wisdom. "
24 sought to Solomon, to h· his wisdom, "
18:26 O Baal, h· us. But there was no 6030
37 H· me, O Lord, h· me, that this "
22:19 H· thou therefore the word of 8085
2Ki 7: 1 said, H· ye the word of the Lord; "
6 Syrians to h· a noise of chariots, "
14:11 But Amaziah would not h·. "
17:14 they would not h·, but hardened "
18:12 would not h· them, nor do them. "
28 H· the word of the great king, the "
19: 4 thy God will h· all the words of "
7 and he shall h· a rumour, and shall "
16 Lord, bow down thine ear, and h·: "
16 and h· the words of Sennacherib, "
20:16 Hezekiah, H· the word of the Lord. "
1Ch 14:15 thou shalt h· a sound of going * "
28: 2 H· me, my brethren, and my "
2Ch 6:21 h· thou from thy dwelling place, "
23 Then h· thou from heaven, and "
25 Then h· thou from the heavens, "
27 Then h· thou from heaven, and "
30 Then h· thou from heaven thy "
33 Then h· thou from the heavens, "
35 Then h· thou from the heavens "
39 Then h· thou from the heavens, "
7:14 then will I h· from heaven, and "
9: 7 before thee, and h· thy wisdom. "
23 Solomon, to h· his wisdom, that "
13: 4 H· me, thou Jeroboam, and all "
15: 2 H· ye me, Asa, and all Judah and "
18:18 Therefore h· the word of the Lord; "
20: 9 then thou wilt h· and help. "
20 and said, H· me, O Judah, and ye "
25:20 But Amaziah would not h·; for it "
28:11 Now h· me therefore, and deliver "
29: 5 H· me, ye Levites, sanctify now "
Ne 1: 6 that thou mayest h· the prayer of * "
4: 4 H·, O our God: for we are despised: "
20 ye h· the sound of the trumpet, "
8: 2 that could h· with understanding, "
9:29 their neck, and would not h·. "
Job 3:18 h· not the voice of the oppressor. "
5:27 h· it, and know thou it for thy good. "
13: 6 H· now my reasoning, and hearken "
17 H· diligently my speech, and my "
15:17 I will shew thee, h· me; and that "
21: 2 H· diligently my speech, and let "
22:27 prayer unto him, and he shall h· "
27: 9 Will God h· his cry when trouble "
30:20 thee, and thou dost not h· me: *6030
31:35 Oh that one would h· me! behold *8085
33: 1 Job, I pray thee, h· my speeches, "
34: 2 H· my words, O ye wise men; "
16 thou hast understanding, h· this: "
35:13 God will not h· vanity, neither will "
37: 2 H· attentively the noise of his † "
42: 4 H·, I beseech thee, and I will speak: "
Ps 4: 1 H· me when I call, O God of my *6030
1 mercy upon me, and h· my prayer. 8085
3 the Lord will h· when I call unto "
5: 3 voice shalt thou h· in the morning, "
10:17 thou wilt cause thine ear to h·: 7181
13: 3 Consider and h· me, O Lord my *6030
17: 1 H· the right, O Lord, attend unto 8085
6 for thou wilt h· me, O God: *6030
6 ear unto me, and h· my speech. 8085
18:44 As soon as they h· of me, they "
20: 1 h· thee in the day of trouble; *6030
6 will h· him from his holy heaven * "
9 let the king h· us when we call. "
27: 7 H·, O Lord, when I cry with my 8085
28: 2 H· the voice of my supplications, "
30:10 H·, O Lord, and have mercy upon "
34: 2 the humble shall h· thereof, and be "
38:15 thou wilt h·, O Lord my God. *6030
16 For I said, H· me, lest otherwise * "
39:12 H· my prayer, O Lord, and give 8085
49: 1 H· this, all ye people; give ear, "
50: 7 H·, O my people, and I will speak; "
51: 8 Make me to h· joy and gladness; "
54: 2 H· my prayer, O God; give ear to "
55: 2 Attend unto me, and h· me: *6030
17 aloud: and he shall h· my voice. 8085
19 God shall h·, and afflict them, even "
59: 7 lips: for who, say they, doth h·? "
60: 5 with thy right hand, and h· me. *6030
61: 1 H· my cry, O God; attend unto my 8085
64: 1 H· my voice, O God, in my prayer: "
66:16 Come and h·, all ye that fear God, "
18 in my heart, the Lord will not h· me: "
69:13 the multitude of thy mercy h· me, *6030
16 H· me, O Lord; for thy "
17 I am in trouble: h· me speedily. * "

Ps 81: 8 H', O my people, and I will testify 8085
84: 8 O Lord God of hosts, h' my prayer: "
85: 8 h' what God the Lord will speak: "
86: 1 down thine ear, O Lord, h' me: *6030
92: 11 shall h' my desire of the wicked *8085
94: 9 planted the ear, shall he not h'? "
95: 7 To day if ye will h' his voice, "
102: 1 H' my prayer, O Lord, and let my "
20 To h' the groaning of the prisoner; "
115: 6 They have ears, but they h' not: "
119: 145 my whole heart; h' me, O Lord: *6030
149 H' my voice according unto thy 8085
130: 2 Lord, h' my voice: let thine ears "
135: 17 They have ears, but they h' not; 238
138: 4 they h' the words of thy mouth. *8085
140: 6 h' the voice of my supplications. * 238
141: 6 h' my words; for they are sweet. 8085
143: 1 H' my prayer, O Lord, give ear to "
7 H' me speedily, O Lord: my *6030
8 Cause me to h' thy lovingkindness 8085
145: 19 he also will h' their cry, and will "
Pr 1: 5 wise man will h', and will increase "
8 h' the instruction of thy father, "
4: 1 H', ye children, the instruction of a "
10 H', O my son, and receive my "
5: 7 H' me now therefore, O ye * "
8: 6 H'; for I will speak of excellent "
33 H' instruction, and be wise, and "
19: 20 H' counsel, and receive instruction, "
27 Cease, my son, to h' the instruction "
22: 17 ear, and h' the words of the wise, "
23: 19 H' thou, my son, and be wise, "
Ec 5: 1 be more ready to h', than to give "
7: 5 better to h' the rebuke of the wise, "
5 for a man to h' the song of fools. "
21 lest thou h' thy servant curse thee: "
12: 13 us h' the conclusion of the whole * "
Ca 2: 14 let me h' thy voice; for sweet is thy "
8: 13 to thy voice: cause me to h' it. "
Isa 1: 2 H', O heavens, and give ear, O "
10 H' the word of the Lord, ye rulers "
15 make many prayers, I will not h': "
6: 9 H' ye indeed, but understand not; "
10 h' with their ears, and understand "
7: 13 said, H' ye now, O house of David; "
18: 3 when he bloweth a trumpet, h' ye. "
28: 12 refreshing: yet they would not h'. "
14 h' the word of the Lord, ye scornful "
23 Give ye ear, and h' my voice; "
23 voice; hearken, and h' my speech. "
29: 18 And in that day shall the deaf h' the "
30: 9 children that will not h' the law of "
19 when he shall h' it, he will answer "
21 ears shall h' a word behind thee, "
32: 3 ears of them that h' shall hearken. "
9 h' my voice, ye careless daughters; "
33: 13 H', ye that are far off, what I have "
34: 1 Come near, ye nations, to h'; and "
1 the earth h', and all that is therein; "
36: 13 H' ye the words of the great king, "
37: 4 the Lord thy God will h' the words "
7 and he shall h' a rumour, and "
17 Incline thine ear, O Lord, and h'; "
17 and h' all the words of Sennacherib, "
39: 5 H' the word of the Lord of hosts: "
41: 17 I the Lord will h' them, I the God *6030
42: 18 H', ye deaf; and look, ye blind, 8085
23 and h' for the time to come? "
43: 9 or let them h', and say, It is truth. "
44: 1 Yet now h', O Jacob my servant; "
47: 8 Therefore h' now this, thou that art "
48: 1 H' ye this, O house of Jacob, which "
14 All ye, assemble yourselves, and h'; "
16 Come ye near unto me, h' ye this; "
50: 4 mine ear to h' as the learned. "
51: 21 Therefore h' now this, thou afflicted, "
55: 3 h', and your soul shall live; and I "
59: 1 his ear heavy, that it cannot h': "
2 face from you, that he will not h'. "
65: 12 when I spake, ye did not h'; but "
24 while they are yet speaking, I will h'. "
66: 4 when I spake, they did not h': but "
5 H' the word of the Lord, ye that "
Jer 2: 4 H' ye the word of the Lord, O house "
4: 21 and h' the sound of the trumpet? "
5: 21 H' now this, O foolish people, and "
21 which have ears, and h' not: "
6: 10 and give warning, that they may h'? "
18 Therefore h', ye nations, and know, "
19 H', O earth: behold, I will bring "
7: 2 H' the word of the Lord, all ye of "
16 to me: for I will not h' thee. "
9: 10 can men h' the voice of the cattle; "
20 h' the word of the Lord, O ye women, "
10: 1 H' ye the word which the Lord "
11: 2, 6 H' ye the words of this covenant, "
10 which refused to h' my words, "
14 for I will not h' them in the time "
13: 10 people, which refuse to h' my words, "
11 for a glory: but they would not h'. "
15 H' ye, and give ear; be not proud: "
17 But if ye will not h' it, my soul shall "
14: 12 they fast, I will not h' their cry; "
17: 20 H' ye the word of the Lord, ye kings "
23 neck stiff, that they might not h', "
18: 2 I will cause thee to h' my words. "
19: 3 H' ye the word of the Lord, O kings "
15 that they might not h' my words. "
20: 16 let him h' the cry in the morning, "
21: 11 say, H' ye the word of the Lord; "
22: 2 H' the word of the Lord, O king of "
5 But if ye will not h' these words, "
21 but thou saidst, I will not h'. "
29 O earth, earth, earth, h' the word "
23: 22 caused my people to h' my words, "
25: 4 nor inclined your ear to h'. "
Jer 28: 7 h' thou now this word that I speak 8085
15 H' now, Hananiah; the Lord hath "
29: 19 but ye would not h', saith the Lord. "
20 H' ye therefore the word of the "
31: 10 H' the word of the Lord, O ye "
33: 9 which shall h' all the good that I do "
34: 4 Yet h' the word of the Lord, O "
36: 3 Judah will h' all the evil which I "
25 the roll: but he would not h' them. "
37: 20 h' now, I pray thee, O my lord the "
38: 25 if the princes h' that I have talked "
42: 14 nor h' the sound of the trumpet, "
15 therefore h' the word of the Lord, "
44: 24 H' the word of the Lord, all Judah "
26 h' ye the word of the Lord, all "
49: 20 h' the counsel of the Lord, that the "
50: 45 h' ye the counsel of the Lord, that "
La 1: 18 h', I pray you, all people, and "
Eze 2: 5, 7 whether they will h', or whether "
8 h' what I say unto thee; Be not "
3: 10 thine heart, and h' with thine ears. "
11 whether they will h', or whether "
17 therefore h' the word at my mouth, "
27 He that heareth, let him h'; and he "
6: 3 h' the word of the Lord God; Thus "
8: 18 a loud voice, yet will I not h' them. "
12: 2 they have ears to h', and h' not: "
13: 2 hearts, H' ye the word of the Lord; "
19 lying to my people that h' your lies? * "
16: 35 O harlot, h' the word of the Lord: "
18: 25 H' now, O house of Israel; Is not "
20: 47 H' the word of the Lord; Thus "
24: 26 to cause thee to h' it with thine 2045
25: 3 H' the word of the Lord God; 8085
33: 7 thou shalt h' the word at my mouth, "
30 h' what is the word that cometh "
31 and they h' thy words, but they will "
32 for they h' thy words, but they do "
34: 7, 9 ye shepherds, h' the word of the "
36: 1 Ye mountains of Israel, h' the word "
4 h' the word of the Lord God; Thus "
15 Neither will I cause men to h' in "
37: 4 O ye dry bones, h' the word of the "
40: 4 h' with thine ears, and set thine "
44: 5 h' with thine ears all that I say unto "
Da 3: 5 time ye h' the sound of the cornet, 8086
10 shall h' the sound of the cornet, "
15 time ye h' the sound of the cornet, "
5: 23 which see not, nor h', nor know: "
9: 17 h' the prayer of thy servant, and *8085
18 O my God, incline thine ear, and h'; "
19 O Lord, h'; O Lord, forgive; O Lord, "
Ho 2: 21 to pass in that day, I will h', saith *6030
21 the Lord, I will h' the heavens, * "
21 and they shall h' the earth; * "
22 And the earth shall h' the corn, * "
22 the oil; and they shall h' Jezreel. * "
4: 1 H' the word of the Lord, ye 8085
5: 1 H' ye this, O priests; and hearken, "
Joe 1: 2 H' this, ye old men, and give ear, "
Am 3: 1 H' this word that the Lord hath "
13 H' ye, and testify in the house of "
4: 1 H' this word, ye kine of Bashan, "
5: 1 H' ye this word which I take up "
23 I will not h' the melody of thy viols, "
7: 16 h' thou the word of the Lord: Thou "
8: 4 H' this, O ye that swallow up the "
Mic 1: 2 H', all ye people; hearken, O earth, "
3: 1 H', I pray you, O heads of Jacob, "
4 the Lord, but he will not h' them: *6030
9 H' this, I pray you, ye heads of 8085
6: 1 H' ye now what the Lord saith; "
1 and let the hills h' thy voice. "
2 H' ye, O mountains, the Lord's "
9 h' ye the rod, and who hath "
7: 7 my salvation: my God will h' me. "
Na 3: 19 all that h' the bruit of thee shall "
Hab 1: 2 shall I cry, and thou wilt not h'! "
Zec 1: 4 but they did not h', nor hearken "
3: 8 H' now, O Joshua the high priest, "
7: 7 Should ye not h' the words which "
11 their ears, that they should not h'. 8085
12 lest they should h' the law, and the "
13 as he cried, and they would not h'; "
13 so they cried, and I would not h', "
8: 9 be strong, ye that h' in these days "
10: 6 Lord their God, and will h' them. 6030
13: 9 call on my name, and I will h' them: "
Mal 2: 2 If ye will not h', and if ye will not 8085
M't 10: 14 not receive you, nor h' your words, 191
27 what ye h' in the ear, that preach "
11: 4 those things which ye do h' and see: "
5 lepers are cleansed, and the deaf h', "
15 He that hath ears to h', let him h'. "
12: 19 any man h' his voice in the streets. "
42 to h' the wisdom of Solomon; and, "
13: 9 Who hath ears to h', let him * "
9 Who hath ears...let him h'. "
13 see not; and hearing they h' not, "
14 By hearing ye shall h', and shall not "
15 their eyes, and h' with their ears, "
16 they see: and your ears, for they h'. "
17 and to h' those things which ye h', "
18 H' ye therefore the parable of the "
43 Who hath ears to h', let him * "
43 Who hath ears...let him h'. "
15: 10 said unto them, H', and understand: "
17: 5 whom I am well pleased; h' ye him. "
18: 15 if he shall h' thee, thou hast gained "
16 if he will not h' thee, then take with "
17 And if he shall neglect to h' them, 3878
17 but if he neglect to h' the church, "
21: 33 H' another parable: There was a 191
24: 6 ye shall h' of wars and rumours of "
M'r 4: 9 He that hath ears to h', let him h'. "
12 they may h', and not understand; "
M'r 4: 18 among thorns; such as h' the word, *191
20 such as h' the word, and receive it, "
23 any man have ears to h', let him h'. "
24 Take heed what ye h': with what "
24 you that h' shall more be given. * "
33 unto them, as they were able to h' it. "
6: 11 shall not receive you, nor h' you, "
7: 16 any man have ears to h', let him h'. * "
37 he maketh both the deaf to h', and "
8: 18 see ye not? having ears, h' ye not? "
9: 7 This is my beloved Son: h' him. "
12: 29 H', O Israel; the Lord our God is one "
13: 7 ye shall h' of wars and rumours of "
Lu 5: 1 upon him to h' the word of God, * "
15 multitudes came together to h', and "
6: 17 came to h' him, and to be healed of "
27 I say unto you which h', Love your "
7: 22 lepers are cleansed, the deaf h', the "
8: 8 He that hath ears to h', let him h'. "
12 by the way side are they that h'; * "
13 they h', receive the word with "
18 Take heed therefore how ye h': for "
21 which h' the word of God, and do it. "
9: 9 is this, of whom I h' such things? "
35 This is my beloved Son: h' him. "
10: 24 to h' those things which ye h', and "
11: 28 blessed are they that h' the word of "
31 to h' the wisdom of Solomon; and, "
14: 35 He that hath ears to h', let him h'. "
15: 1 publicans and sinners for to h' him. "
16: 2 him, How is it that I h' this of thee? "
29 and the prophets; let them h' them. "
31 they h' not Moses and the prophets, "
18: 6 said, H' what the unjust judge saith. "
19: 48 people were very attentive to h' him. * "
21: 9 ye shall h' of wars and commotions, "
38 to him in the temple, for to h' him. "
Joh 5: 25 the dead shall h' the voice of God: "
25 God: and they that h' shall live. "
28 are in the graves shall h' his voice, "
30 as I h', I judge; and my judgment is "
6: 60 This is an hard saying; who can h' it? "
7: 51 law judge any man, before it h' him, "
8: 43 even because ye cannot h' my word. "
47 ye therefore h' them not, because ye "
9: 27 told you already, and ye did not h': "
27 wherefore would ye h' it again? "
10: 3 and the sheep h' his voice: and he "
8 but the sheep did not h' them. "
16 and they shall h' my voice; and they "
20 a devil, and is mad; why h' ye him? "
27 My sheep h' my voice, and I know "
12: 47 if any man h' my words, and believe "
14: 24 the word which ye h' is not mine, "
16: 13 whatsoever he shall h', that shall he "
Ac 2: 8 h' we every man in our own tongue, "
11 we do h' them speak in our tongues, "
22 Ye men of Israel, h' these words; "
33 forth this, which ye now see and h'. "
3: 22 shall ye h' in all things whatsoever * "
23 which will not h' that prophet, * "
7: 37 like unto me; him shall ye h'. * "
10: 22 his house, and to h' words of thee. "
33 to h' all things that are commanded "
13: 7 and desired to h' the word of God. "
44 city together, to h' the word of God. "
15: 7 should h' the word of the gospel, "
17: 21 either to tell, or to h' some new thing. "
32 We will h' thee again of this matter. "
19: 26 see and h', that not alone at Ephesus, "
21: 22 for they will h' that thou art come. "
22: 1 h' ye my defence which I make "
14 shouldest h' the voice of his mouth. "
23: 35 I will h' thee, said he, when thine 1251
24: 4 wouldest h' us of thy clemency a 191
25: 22 I would also h' the man myself. "
22 morrow, said he, thou shalt h' him. "
26: 3 I beseech thee to h' me patiently. "
29 thou, but also all that h' me this day, "
28: 22 to h' of thee what thou thinkest: "
26 Hearing ye shall h', and shall not "
27 their eyes, and h' with their ears, "
28 the Gentiles, and that they will h' it. "
Ro 10: 14 shall they h' without a preacher? "
11: 8 see, and ears that they should not h'; "
1Co 11: 18 I h' that there be divisions among "
14: 21 yet for all that will they not h' me, 1522
Ga 4: 21 under the law, do ye not h' the law? 191
Ph'p 1: 27 be absent, I may h' of your affairs, "
30 saw in me, and now h' to be in me. "
2Th 3: 11 h' that there are some which walk "
1Ti 4: 16 save thyself, and them that h' thee. "
2Ti 4: 17 and that all the Gentiles might h': "
Heb 3: 7, 15 To day if ye will h' his voice, "
4: 7 said, To day if ye will h' his voice, "
Jas 1: 19 let every man be swift to h', slow to "
1Jo 5: 15 that he h' us, whatsoever we ask, * "
3Jo 4 no greater joy than to h' that my "
Re 1: 3 that h' the words of this prophecy, "
2: 7, 11, 17, 29 that hath an ear, let him h' "
3: 6, 13 He that hath an ear, let him h' "
20 if any man h' my voice, and open "
22 He that hath an ear, let him h' "
9: 20 neither can see, nor h', nor walk: "
13: 9 If any man have an ear, let him h'. "

heard See also HEARDEST.
Ge 3: 8 And they h' the voice of the Lord 8085
10 I h' thy voice in the garden, and I "
14: 14 Abraham h' that his brother was "
16: 11 the Lord hath h' thy affliction. "
17: 20 And as for Ishmael, I have h' thee: "
18: 10 Sarah h' it in the tent door, which "
21: 17 And God h' the voice of the lad; "
17 God hath h' the voice of the lad "
26 thou tell me, neither yet h' I of it, "
24: 30 when he h' the words of Rebekah "

Ge 24:52 Abraham's servant h' their words, 8085
27: 5 Rebekah h' when Isaac spake to "
6 I h' thy father speak unto Esau thy "
34 And when Esau h' the words of his "
29:13 when Laban h' the tidings of Jacob "
33 the Lord hath h' that I was hated, "
30: 6 and hath also h' my voice, and hath "
31: 1 he h' the words of Laban's sons, "
34: 5 And Jacob h' that he had defiled "
7 came out of the field when they h' it: "
35:22 father's concubine: and Israel h' it. "
37:17 I h' them say, Let us go to Dothan. "
21 And Reuben h' it, and he delivered "
39:15 when he h' that I lifted up my voice "
19 his master h' the words of his wife, "
41:15 have h' say of thee, that thou canst "
42: 2 have h' that there is corn in Egypt: "
43:25 they h' that they should eat bread "
45: 2 and the house of Pharaoh h'. "
16 fame thereof was h' in Pharaoh's "
Ex 2:15 Now when Pharaoh h' this thing, he "
24 And God h' their groaning, and "
3: 7 have h' their cry by reason of their "
4:31 they h' that the Lord had visited "
6: 5 I have also h' the groaning of the "
16: 9 for he hath h' your murmurings. "
12 I have h' the murmurings of the "
18: 1 Midian, Moses' father in law, h' of all "
23:13 neither let it be h' out of thy mouth. "
28:35 be h' when he goeth into the holy "
32:17 Joshua h' the noise of the people "
33: 4 the people h' these evil tidings, "
Le 10:20 when Moses h' that, he was content. "
24:14 let all that h' him lay their hands "
Nu 7:89 then he h' the voice of one speaking "
11: 1 and the Lord h' it; and his anger "
10 Then Moses h' the people weep "
12: 2 also by us? And the Lord h' it. "
14:14 have h' that thou Lord art seen face "
15 the nations which have h' the fame "
27 I have h' the murmurings of the "
16: 4 Moses h' it, he fell upon his face: "
20:16 he h' our voice, and sent an angel, "
21: 1 h' tell that Israel came by the way "
22:36 Balak h' that Balaam was come, "
24: 4 which h' the words of God, which * "
16 which h' the words of God, and * "
30: 7 husband h' it, and held his peace * "
7 at her in the day that he h' it: * "
8 the day that he h' it; then he shall* "
11 husband h' it, and held his peace "
12 them void on the day he h' them; "
14 at her in the day that he h' them. "
30:15 void after that he hath h' them; "
33:40 h' of the coming of the children of "
De 1:34 the Lord h' the voice of your words, "
4:12 ye h' the voice of the words, but saw "
12 no similitude; only ye h' a voice. "
32 thing is, or hath been h' like it? "
33 of the fire, as thou hast h', and live? "
5:23 ye h' the voice out of the midst "
24 have h' his voice out of the midst "
26 hath h' the voice of the living God "
28 the Lord h' the voice of your words, "
28 I have h' the voice of the words of "
9: 2 and of whom thou hast h' say, "
17: 4 be told thee, and thou hast h' of it, "
26: 7 the Lord h' our voice, and looked "
Jos 2:10 we have h' how the Lord dried up "
11 as soon as we had h' these things, "
5: 1 h' that the Lord had dried up "
6:20 people h' the sound of the trumpet, "
9: 1 Hivite, and the Jebusite, h' thereof; "
3 when the inhabitants of Gibeon h' "
9 for we have h' the fame of him, "
16 h' that they were their neighbours, "
10: 1 had h' how Joshua had taken Ai, "
11: 1 when Jabin king of Hazor had h'; "
22:11 And the children of Israel h' say, "
12 when the children of Israel h' of it, "
30 h' the words that the children of "
24:27 it hath h' all the words of the Lord "
J'g 7:15 Gideon h' the telling of the dream, "
9:30 ruler of the city h' the words of Gaal "
46 the men of the tower of Shechem h' "
18:25 Let not thy voice be h' among us, "
20: 3 Now the children of Benjamin h' "
Ru 1: 6 she had h' in the country of Moab "
1Sa 1:13 lips moved, but her voice was not h': "
2:22 and h' all that his sons did unto all "
4: 6 Philistines h' the noise of the shout, "
14 when Eli h' the noise of the crying, "
19 h' the tidings that the ark of God "
7: 7 when the Philistines h' that the "
7 when the children of Israel h' it, "
9 for Israel; and the Lord h' him. *6030
8:21 And Samuel h' all the words of the 8085
11: 6 upon Saul when he h' those tidings, "
13: 3 in Geba, and the Philistines h' of it. "
4 Israel h' say that Saul had smitten "
14:22 they h' that the Philistines fled, "
27 Jonathan h' not when his father "
17:11 Saul and all Israel h' those words "
23 the same words: and David h' them. "
28 And Eliab his eldest brother h' "
31 And when the words were h' "
22: 1 all his father's house h' it, they "
6 Saul h' that David was discovered, "
23:10 hath certainly h' that Saul seeketh "
11 come down, as thy servant hath h'? "
25 And when Saul h' that, he pursued "
25: 4 And David h' in the wilderness "
7 I have h' that thou hast shearers: "
39 David h' that Nabal was dead, "
31:11 inhabitants of Jabesh-gilead h' of "
2Sa 3:28 afterward when David h' it, he "

2Sa 4: 1 Saul's son h' that Abner was dead 8085
5:17 Philistines h' that they had anointed "
17 and David h' of it, and went down "
7:22 to all that we have h' with our ears. "
8: 9 Toi king of Hamath h' that David "
10: 7 when David h' of it, he sent Joab, "
11:26 the wife of Uriah h' that Uriah "
13:21 But when king David h' of all these "
18: 5 the people h' when the king gave "
19: 2 people h' say that day how the king "
1Ki 1:11 Hast thou not h' that Adonijah "
41 h' it as they had made an end of "
41 Joab h' the sound of the trumpet, "
45 This is the noise that ye have h'. "
2:42 The word that I have h' is good. "
3:28 And all Israel h' of the judgment "
4:34 earth, which had h' of his wisdom. "
5: 1 he had h' that they had anointed "
7 Hiram h' the words of Solomon, "
6: 7 nor any tool of iron h' in the house, "
9: 3 I have h' thy prayer and thy "
10: 1 the queen of Sheba h' of the fame "
6 report that I h' in mine own land "
7 exceedeth the fame which I h'. "
11:21 when Hadad h' in Egypt that David "
12: 2 Jeroboam the son of Nebat,...h' of it, "
20 when all Israel h' that Jeroboam "
13: 4 when king Jeroboam h' the saying "
26 him back from the way h' thereof, "
14: 6 Ahijah h' the sound of her feet, "
15:21 when Baasha h' thereof, that he "
16:16 people that were encamped h' say, "
17:22 the Lord h' the voice of Elijah; * "
19:13 when Elijah h' it, that he wrapped "
20:12 when Ben-hadad h' this message, "
31 we have h' that the kings of the "
21:15 Jezebel h' that Naboth was stoned, "
16 when Ahab h' that Naboth was dead, "
27 to pass, when Ahab h' those words, "
2Ki 3:21 Moabites h' that the kings were "
5: 8 when Elisha the man of God had h' "
6:30 the king h' the words of the woman, "
9:30 come to Jezreel, Jezebel h' of it; "
11:13 Athaliah h' the noise of the guard "
19: 1 to pass, when king Hezekiah h' it, "
4 which the Lord thy God hath h': "
6 of the words which thou hast h', "
8 for he had h' that he was departed "
9 And when he h' say of Tirhakah "
11 hast h' what the kings of Assyria "
20 king of Assyria I have h'. * "
25 Hast thou not h' long ago how I "
20: 5 h' thy prayer, I have seen thy tears, "
12 had h' that Hezekiah had been sick. "
22:11 king had h' the words of the book "
18 the words which thou hast h'; "
19 I also have h' thee, saith the Lord. "
25:23 h' that the king of Babylon had "
1Ch 10:11 when all Jabesh-gilead h' all that "
14: 8 h' that David was anointed king "
8 David h' of it, and went out against "
17:20 to all that we have h' with our ears. "
18: 9 Tou king of Hamath h' how David "
19: 8 when David h' of it, he sent Joab, "
2Ch 5:13 make one sound to be h' in praising "
7:12 have h' thy prayer, and have chosen "
9: 1 the queen of Sheba h' of the fame "
5 report which I h' in mine own land "
6 thou exceedest the fame that I h'. "
10: 2 Jeroboam the son of Nebat,...h' it, "
15: 8 And when Asa h' these words, and "
16: 5 when Baasha h' it, that he left off "
20:29 they had h' that the Lord fought "
23:12 Athaliah h' the noise of the people "
30:27 and their voice was h', and their "
33:13 and h' his supplication, and brought "
34:19 king had h' the words of the law, "
26 the words which thou hast h'; "
27 I have even h' thee also, saith the "
Ezr 3:13 shout, and the noise was h' afar off. "
4: 1 of Judah and Benjamin h' that the "
9: 3 And when I h' this thing, I rent my "
Ne 1: 4 when I h' these words, that I sat "
2:10 Ammonite, h' of it, it grieved them "
19 Arabian, h' it, they laughed us to "
4: 1 when Sanballat h' that we builded "
7 h' that the walls of Jerusalem were "
15 our enemies h' that it was known "
5: 6 I was very angry when I h' their cry "
6: 1 h' that I had builded the wall, * "
16 when all our enemies h' thereof, "
8: 9 when they h' the words of the law. "
12:43 joy of Jerusalem was h' even afar off. "
13: 3 when they had h' the law, that they "
Es 1:18 have h' of the deed of the queen. "
2: 8 commandment and...decree was h', "
Job 2:11 when Job's three friends h' of all "
4:16 there was silence, and I h' a voice, "
13: 1 mine ear hath h' and understood it. "
15: 8 Hast thou h' the secret of God? "
16: 2 I have h' many such things: "
19: 7 I cry out of wrong, but I am not h':6030
20: 3 have h' the check of my reproach, 8085
26:14 how little a portion is h' of him? * "
28:22 We have h' the fame thereof with "
29:11 When the ear h' me, then it blessed "
33: 8 and I have h' the voice of thy words, "
37: 4 not stay them when his voice is h'. "
42: 5 I have h' of thee by the hearing of "
Ps 3: 4 and he h' me out of his holy hill. *6030
6: 8 hath h' the voice of my weeping. 8085
9 The Lord hath h' my supplication; "
10:17 hast h' the desire of the humble: "
18: 6 he h' my voice out of his temple, "
19: 3 language, where their voice is not h'. "
22:21 thou hast h' me from the horns of *6030

Ps 22:24 when he cried unto him, he h'. 8085
28: 6 h' the voice of my supplications. "
31:13 For I have h' the slander of many: "
34: 4 I sought the Lord, and he h' me, *6030
6 poor man cried, and the Lord h' 8085
38:13 But I, as a deaf man, h' not; * "
40: 1 he inclined unto me, and h' my cry "
44: 1 We have h' with our ears, O God, "
48: 8 As we have h', so have we seen in "
61: 5 For thou, O God, hast h' my vows: "
62:11 twice have I h' this; that power "
66: 8 make the voice of his praise to be h': "
19 But verily God hath h' me; he hath "
76: 8 didst cause judgment to be h' from "
78: 3 Which we have h' and known, and "
21 the Lord h' this, and was wroth: "
59 When God h' this, he was wroth, "
81: 5 h' a language that I understood not. "
97: 8 Zion h', and was glad; and the "
106:44 their affliction, when he h' their cry: "
116: 1 because he hath h' my voice and ‡ "
118:21 h' me, and...become my salvation. *6030
120: 1 cried unto the Lord, and he h' me. * "
132: 6 Lo, we h' of it at Ephratah: 8085
Pr 21:13 cry himself, but shall not be h'. 6030
Ec 9:16 despised, and his words are not h'. 8085
17 words of wise men are h' in quiet "
Ca 2:12 voice of the turtle is h' in our land; "
Isa 6: 8 Also I h' the voice of the Lord, "
10:30 cause it to be h' unto Laish, *7181
15: 4 voice shall be h' even unto Jahaz: 8085
16: 6 We have h' of the pride of Moab; "
21:10 that which I have h' of the Lord of "
24:16 part of the earth have we h' songs, "
28:22 for I have h' from the Lord of hosts "
30:30 cause his glorious voice to be h', "
37: 1 to pass, when king Hezekiah h' it, "
4 which the Lord thy God hath h': "
6 afraid of the words that thou hast h', "
8 he had h' that he was departed "
9 And he h' say concerning Tirhakah "
9 when he h' it, he sent messengers "
11 hast h' what the kings of Assyria "
26 Hast thou not h' long ago, how I "
38: 5 I have h' thy prayer, I have seen "
39: 1 for he had h' that he had been sick, "
40:21 have ye not known? have ye not h'? "
28 hast thou not h', that the everlasting "
42: 2 cause his voice to be h' in the street. "
48: 6 Thou hast h', see all this; and will "
49: 8 In an acceptable time have I h' *6030
52:15 had not h' shall they consider. 8085
58: 4 to make your voice to be h' on high. "
60:18 Violence shall no more be h' in thy "
64: 4 men have not h', nor perceived by "
65:19 voice of weeping shall be no more h' "
66: 8 Who hath h' such a thing? who "
19 isles...that have not h' my fame, "
Jer 3:21 voice was h' upon the high places, "
4:19 thou hast h', O my soul, the sound "
31 For I have h' a voice as of a woman "
6: 7 violence and spoil is h' in her; "
24 We have h' the fame thereof: our "
7:13 early and speaking, but ye h' not; "
8: 6 I hearkened and h', but they spake "
16 The snorting of his horses was h' "
9:19 a voice of wailing is h' out of Zion, "
18:13 heathen, who hath h' such things; "
22 Let a cry be h' from their houses, "
20: 1 h' that Jeremiah prophesied these "
10 For I h' the defaming of many, "
23:18 hath perceived and h' his word? * "
18 hath marked his word, and h' it? "
25 I have h' what the prophets said, "
25: 8 Because ye have not h' my words, "
36 principal of the flock, shall be h': * "
26: 7 the prophets and all the people h' "
10 When the princes of Judah h' these "
11 city, as ye have h' with your ears. "
12 all the words that ye have h'. "
21 and all the princes, h' his words, "
21 but when Urijah h' it, he was afraid, "
30: 5 We have h' a voice of trembling, "
31:15 voice was h' in Ramah, lamentation, "
18 have surely h' Ephraim bemoaning "
33:10 Again there shall be h' in this place, "
34:10 h' that every one should let his * "
35:17 unto them, but they have not h'; "
36:11 had h' out of the book all the words "
13 them all the words that he had h', "
16 pass, when they had h' all the words, "
24 his servants that h' all these words. "
37: 5 that besieged Jerusalem h' tidings "
38: 1 h' the words that Jeremiah had "
7 h' that they had put Jeremiah in "
40: 7 h' that the king of Babylon had "
11 h' that the king of Babylon had left "
41:11 h' of all the evil that Ishmael "
42: 4 said unto them, I have h' you; "
46:12 The nations have h' of thy shame, "
48: 4 little ones have caused a cry to be h'. "
5 enemies have h' a cry of destruction. "
29 We have h' the pride of Moab, "
49: 2 will cause an alarm of war to be h' "
14 I have h' a rumour from the Lord, "
21 noise thereof was h' in the Red sea. "
23 for they have h' evil tidings; "
50:43 king of Babylon hath h' the report "
46 and the cry is h' among the nations. "
51:46 rumour that shall be h' in the land: "
51 because we have h' reproach: "
La 1:21 They have h' that I sigh: there is "
21 mine enemies have h' of my trouble; "
3:56 Thou hast h' my voice; hide not * "
61 Thou hast h' their reproach, O Lord, "
Eze 1:24 went, I h' the noise of their wings, "

Eze 1:28 and I h' a voice of one that spake. 8085
2: 2 that I h' him that spake unto me. "
3:12 I h' behind me a voice of a great "
13 I h' also the voice of the wings of "
10: 5 the cherubims' wings was h' even 8085
19: 4 The nations also h' of him; he was "
9 no more be h' upon the mountains "
26:13 of thy harps shall be no more h'. "
27:30 And shall cause their voice to be h' "
33: 5 He h' the sound of the trumpet, "
35:12 I have h' all thy blasphemies which "
13 words against me: I have h' them. "
43: 6 And I h' him speaking unto me out "
Da 3: 7 people h' the sound of the cornet, 8086
5:14 have even h' of thee, that the spirit "
16 I have h' of thee, that thou canst "
6:14 the king, when he h' these words, "
8:13 Then I h' one saint speaking, and 8085
16 And I h' a man's voice between the "
10: 9 Yet h' I the voice of his words: "
9 and when I h' the voice of his words, "
12 thy words were h', and I am come "
12: 7 And I h' the man clothed in linen, "
8 And I h', but I understood not: "
Ho 7:12 them, as their congregation hath h'. "
14: 8 I have h' him, and observed him: *6030
Ob 1 We have h' a rumour from the 8085
Jon 2: 2 unto the Lord, and he h' me; *6030
Mic 5:15 heathen, such as they have not h'.*8085
Na 2:13 thy messengers shall no more be h'. "
Hab 3: 2 O Lord, I have h' thy speech, and "
16 When I h', my belly trembled; my "
Zep 2: 8 I have h' the reproach of Moab, "
Zec 8:23 for we have h' that God is with you "
Mal 3:16 and the Lord hearkened, and h' it, "
M't 2: 3 When Herod the king had h' these 191
9 When they had h' the king, they "
18 In Rama was there a voice h', "
2:22 when he h' that Archelaus did reign "
4:12 Jesus had h' that John was cast into "
5:21, 27 Ye have h' that it was said by "
33 ye have h' that it hath been said by "
38, 43 Ye have h' that it hath been said. "
6: 7 shall be h' for their much speaking. 1522
8:10 When Jesus h' it, he marvelled, and 191
9:12 But when Jesus h' that, he said unto "
11: 2 when John had h' in the prison the "
12:24 when the Pharisees h' it, they said, "
13:17 which ye hear, and have not h' them. "
14: 1 Herod the tetrarch h' of the fame of "
13 When Jesus h' of it, he departed "
13 people had h' thereof, they followed "
15:12 offended, after they h' this saying? "
17: 6 when the disciples h' it, they fell on "
19:22 when the young man h' that saying, "
25 When his disciples h' it, they were "
20:24 when the ten h' it, they were moved "
30 when they h' that Jesus passed by, "
21:45 chief priests and Pharisees had h' "
22: 7 the king h' thereof, he was wroth: * "
22 had h' these words, they marvelled, "
33 when the multitude h' this, they were "
34 had h' that he had put the Sadducees "
26:65 now ye have h' his blasphemy. "
27:47 they h' that, said, This man calleth "
M'r 2:17 When Jesus h' it, he saith unto them, "
3: 8 when they had h' what great things* "
21 when his friends h' of it, they went "
4:15 when they have h', Satan cometh "
16 who, when they have h' the word, "
5:27 When she had h' of Jesus, came "
36 As soon as Jesus h' the word that * "
6:14 king Herod h' of him; for his name "
16 Herod h' thereof, he said, It is John, "
20 when he h' him, he did many things, "
20 did many things, and h' him gladly. "
29 when his disciples h' of it, they came "
55 that were sick, where they h' he was. "
7:25 had an unclean spirit, h' of him, "
10:41 when the ten h' it, they began to be "
47 when he h' that it was Jesus of "
11:14 for ever. And his disciples h' it. "
18 the scribes and chief priests h' it, "
12:28 having h' them reasoning together, "
37 the common people h' him gladly. "
14:11 And when they h' it, they were glad, "
58 We h' him say, I will destroy this "
64 Ye have h' the blasphemy: what "
15:35 h' it, said, Behold, he calleth Elias. "
16:11 when they had h' that he was alive, "
Lu 1:13 for thy prayer is h'; and thy wife 1522
41 when Elisabeth h' the salutation of 191
58 cousins h' how the Lord had shewed "
66 h' them laid them up in their hearts, "
2:18 all they that h' it, wondered at those "
20 things that they had h' and seen, "
47 all that h' him were astonished at his "
4:23 we have h' done in Capernaum, do "
28 when they h' these things, were filled "
7: 3 when he h' of Jesus, he sent unto "
9 Jesus h' these things, he marvelled "
22 what things ye have seen and h'; "
29 all the people that h' him, and the "
8:14 which, when they have h', go forth, "
15 having h' the word, keep it, and bring "
50 when Jesus h' it, he answered him,* "
9: 7 Herod the tetrarch h' of all that was "
10:24 which ye hear, and have not h' them. "
39 sat at Jesus' feet, and h' his word. "
12: 3 in darkness shall be h' in the light; "
14:15 sat at meat with him h' these things, "
15:25 house, he h' musick and dancing. "
16:14 were covetous, h' all these things: "
18:22 when Jesus h' these things, he said "
23 he h' this, he was very sorrowful: "
26 h' it said, Who then can be saved? "

Lu 19:11 as they h' these things, he added 191
20:16 they h' it, they said, God forbid. "
22:71 ourselves have h' of his own mouth. "
23: 6 When Pilate h' of Galilee, he asked "
8 he had h' many things of him; "
Jo 1:37 the two disciples h' him speak, and "
40 One of the two which h' John speak, "
3:32 hath seen and h', that he testifieth; "
4: 1 Pharisees had h' that Jesus made "
42 for we have h' him ourselves, and "
47 When he h' that Jesus was come out "
5:37 Ye have neither h' his voice at any "
6:45 Every man therefore that hath h', "
60 disciples, when they had h' this, said, "
7:32 The Pharisees h' that the people "
40 when they h' this saying, said, Of a "
8: 6 the ground, as though he h' them not.* "
9 they which h' it, being convicted by 191
26 those things which I have h' of him. "
40 the truth, which I have h' of God: "
9:32 world began was it not h' that any "
35 Jesus h' that they had cast him out; "
40 Pharisees which were with him h' "
11: 4 Jesus h' that, he said, This sickness "
6 had h' therefore that he was sick, "
20 soon as she h' that Jesus was coming, "
29 As soon as she h' that, she arose "
41 I thank thee that thou hast h' me.* "
12:12 when they h' that Jesus was coming "
18 h' that he had done this miracle. "
29 and h' it, said that it thundered: "
34 have h' out of the law that Christ "
14:28 Ye have h' how I said unto you, I go "
15:15 things that I have h' of my Father "
18:21 ask them which h' me, what I have "
19: 8 When Pilate...h' that saying, he was "
13 Pilate...h' that saying, he brought "
21: 7 Simon Peter h' that it was the Lord, "
Ac 1: 4 which, saith he, ye have h' of me. "
2: 6 every man h' them speak in his own "
37 when they h' this, they were pricked "
4: 4 of them which h' the word believed; "
20 things which we have seen and h'. "
24 they h' that, they lifted up their voice "
5: 5 fear came on all them that h' these "
11 upon as many as h' these things. "
21 when they h' that, they entered into "
24 priests h' these things, they doubted "
33 When they h' that, they were cut to "
6:11 We have h' him speak blasphemous "
14 have h' him say, that this Jesus "
7:12 when Jacob h' that there was corn in "
34 have h' their groaning, and am come "
54 they h' these things, they were cut "
8:14 at Jerusalem h' that Samaria had "
30 and h' him read the prophet Esaias, "
9: 4 he fell to the earth, and h' a voice "
13 I have h' by many of this man, how "
21 all that h' him were amazed, and "
38 the disciples had h' that Peter was * "
10:31 said, Cornelius, thy prayer is h', 1522
44 fell on all them which h' the word. 191
46 they h' them speak with tongues, "
11: 1 in Judæa h' that the Gentiles had "
7 I h' a voice saying unto me, Arise, "
18 When they h' these things, they held "
13:48 the Gentiles h' this, they were glad "
14: 9 The same h' Paul speak: who "
14 Barnabas and Paul, h' of, they rent "
15:24 Forasmuch as we have h', that "
16:14 which worshipped God, h' us: whose "
25 God: and the prisoners h' them. *1874
38 when they h' that they were Romans. 191
17: 8 of the city, when they h' these things. "
32 when they h' of the resurrection of "
18:26 when Aquila and Priscilla had h', "
19: 2 We have not so much as h' whether* "
5 they h' this, they were baptized "
10 dwelt in Asia h' the word of the Lord "
28 h' these sayings, they were full of "
21:12 when we h' these things, both we, "
20 when they h' it, they glorified the "
22: 2 they h' that he spake in the Hebrew "
7 h' a voice saying unto me, Saul, Saul, "
9 h' not the voice of him that spake to "
15 men of what thou hast seen and h'. "
26 When the centurion h' that, he went "
23:16 Paul's sister's son h' of their lying "
24:22 when Felix h' these things, having * "
24 sent for Paul, and h' him concerning "
26:14 I h' a voice speaking unto me, and "
28:15 brethren h' of us, they came to meet "
Ro 10:14 in him of whom they have not h'? "
18 I say, Have they not h'? Yes verily,* "
15:21 that have not h' shall understand. "
1Co 2: 9 Eye hath not seen, nor ear h', "
2Co 6: 2 I have h' thee in a time accepted, *1873
12: 4 into paradise, and h' unspeakable 191
Ga 1:13 ye have h' of my conversation in "
23 h' only, That he which persecuted * "
Eph 1:13 after that ye h' the word of truth, "
15 after I h' of your faith in the Lord * "
3: 2 If ye have h' of the dispensation of "
4:21 If so be that ye have h' him, and "
Ph'p 2:26 that ye had h' that he had been sick "
4: 9 both learned, and received, and h', "
Col 1: 4 Since we h' of your faith in Christ "
5 whereof ye h' before in the word of 4257
6 since the day ye h' of it, and knew 191
9 since the day we h' it, do not cease "
23 the gospel, which ye have h', and "
1Th 2:13 the word of God which ye h' of us,* 189
2Ti 1:13 words, which thou hast h' of me, 191
2: 2 the things that thou hast h' of me "
Heb 2: 1 heed to the things which we have h', "
3 confirmed unto us by them that h' "

Heb 3:16 when they had h', did provoke: 191
4: 2 mixed with faith in them that h' it. "
5: 7 and was h' in that he feared; 1522
12:19 which voice they that h' intreated 191
Jas 5:11 Ye have h' of the patience of Job, "
2Pe 1:18 voice which came from heaven we h', "
1Jo 1: 1 which we have h', which we have seen "
3 we have seen and h' declare we "
5 message which we have h' of him, "
2: 7 the word which ye have h' from * "
18 have h' that antichrist shall come, "
24 which ye have h' from the beginning. "
24 which ye have h' from the beginning "
3:11 that ye h' from the beginning, "
4: 3 ye have h' that it should come; "
2Jo 6 as ye have h' from the beginning, "
Re 1:10 h' behind me a great voice, as of a "
3: 3 how hast thou received and h', and* "
4: 1 first voice which I h' was as it were "
5:11 I h' the voice of many angels round "
13 and all that are in them, h' I saying, "
6: 1 I h', as it were, the noise of thunder, "
3 I h' the second beast say, Come "
5 I h' the third beast say, Come and "
6 I h' a voice in the midst of the four "
7 I h' the voice of the fourth beast say, "
7: 4 I h' the number of them which were "
8:13 I beheld, and h' an angel flying "
9:13 I h' a voice from the four horns of "
16 and I h' the number of them. "
10: 4 I h' a voice from heaven saying unto "
8 the voice which I h' from heaven "
11:12 they h' a great voice from heaven "
12:10 I h' a loud voice saying in heaven, "
14: 2 I h' a voice from heaven, as the voice "
2 I h' the voice of harpers harping "
13 I h' a voice from heaven saying unto "
16: 1 I h' a great voice out of the temple "
5 I h' the angel of the waters say, "
7 I h' another out of the altar say, "
18: 4 I h' another voice from heaven, "
22 trumpeters, shall be h' no more at all "
22 millstone shall be h' no more at all "
23 the bride shall be h' no more at all "
19: 1 I h' a great voice of much people "
6 I h', as it were, the voice of a great "
21: 3 I h' a great voice out of heaven "
22: 8 I John saw these things, and h' "
8 them. And when I had h' and seen, "

heardest
De 4:36 thou h' his words out of the midst 8085
Jos 14:12 thou h' in that day how the Anakims "
2Ki 22:19 h' what I spake against this place, "
2Ch 34:27 thou h' his words against this place, "
Ne 9: 9 and h' their cry by the Red sea; "
27, 28 thee, thou h' them from heaven; "
Ps 31:22 thou h' the voice of my supplications "
119:26 declared my ways, and thou h' me: *6030
Isa 48: 7 the day when thou h' them not; 8085
8 Yea, thou h' not; yea, thou knewest "
Jon 2: 2 hell cried I, and thou h' my voice. "

hearer See also HEARERS.
Jas 1:23 if any be a h' of the word, and not 202
25 he being not a forgetful h', but "

hearers
Ro 2:13 For not the h' of the law are just 202
Eph 4:29 may minister grace unto the h'. * 191
2Ti 2:14 but to the subverting of the h'. * "
Jas 1:22 doers of the word, and not h' only, 202

hearest
Ru 2: 8 Boaz unto Ruth, H' thou not, my 8085
1Sa 24: 9 Wherefore h' thou men's words, * "
2Sa 5:24 when thou h' the sound of a going "
1Ki 8:30 and when thou h', forgive. "
2Ch 6:21 and when thou h', forgive. "
Ps 22: 2 in the daytime, but thou h' not; *6030
65: 2 O thou that h' prayer, unto thee 8085
M't 21:16 unto him, H' thou what these say? 191
27:13 H' thou not how many things they "
Joh 3: 8 and thou h' the sound thereof, but "
11:42 I knew that thou h' me always: "

heareth
Ex 16: 7 for that he h' your murmurings 8085
8 that the Lord h' your murmurings "
Nu 30: 5 disallow her in the day that he h'; "
De 29:19 when he h' the words of this curse, "
1Sa 3: 9 Speak, Lord; for thy servant h'. "
10 answered, Speak; for thy servant h'. "
11 of every one that h' it shall tingle. "
2Sa 17: 9 first, that whosoever h' it will say, "
2Ki 21:12 that whosoever h' of it, both his ears "
Job 34:28 and he h' the cry of the afflicted. * "
Ps 34:17 and the Lord h' and delivereth * "
38:14 I was as a man that h' not, "
69:33 for the Lord h' the poor, and "
Pr 8:34 Blessed is the man that h' me, "
13: 1 wise son h' his father's instruction: "
1 but a scorner h' not rebuke. "
8 riches: but the poor h' not rebuke. "
15:29 he h' the prayer of the righteous. "
31 The ear that h' the reproof of life * "
32 h' reproof getteth understanding.* "
18:13 answereth a matter before he h' it, "
21:28 man that h' speaketh constantly. "
25:10 Lest he that h' it put thee to shame, "
29:24 he h' cursing, and bewrayeth it not. "
Isa 41:26 there is none that h' your words. "
42:20 opening the ears, but he h' not. "
Jer 19: 3 whosoever h', his ears shall tingle. "
Eze 3:27 He that h', let him hear; and he "
33: 4 Then whosoever h' the sound of the "
M't 7:24 whosoever h' these sayings of mine, 191
26 every one that h' these sayings of "
13:19 any one h' the word of the kingdom, "
20 the same is he that h' the word, "

M't 13:22 the thorns is he that h' the word; 191
23 good ground is he that h' the word, "
Lu 6:47 cometh to me, and h' my sayings, "
49 he that h', and doeth not, is like "
10:16 He that h' you h' me; and he that "
Joh 3:29 bridegroom, which standeth and h' "
5:24 He that h' my word, and believeth "
8:47 He that is of God h' God's words: "
9:31 we know that God h' not sinners: "
31 of God, and doeth his will, him he h'. "
18:37 one that is of the truth h' my voice. "
2Co 12: 6 seeth me to be, or that he h' of me. "
1Jo 4: 5 of the world, and the world h' them. "
6 he that knoweth God h' us; he that "
6 he that is not of God h' not us. "
5:14 thing according to his will, he h' us: "
Re 22:17 And let him that h' say, Come. "
18 that h' the words of the prophecy of "

hearing
De 31:11 this law before all Israel in their h'. 241
2Sa 18:12 for in our h' the king charged thee "
2Ki 4:31 there was neither voice, nor h'. 7182
Job 33: 8 Surely thou hast spoken in mine h', 241
42: 5 heard of thee by the h' of the ear: 8088
Pr 20:12 The h' ear, and the seeing eye, 8085
28: 9 turneth away his ear from h' the law, "
Ec 1: 8 seeing, nor the ear filled with h'. "
Isa 11: 3 reprove after the h' of his ears: 4926
21: 3 I was bowed down at the h' of it; *8085
33:15 stoppeth his ears from h' of blood, "
Eze 9: 5 to the others he said in mine h', 241
10:13 it was cried unto them in my h', "
Am 8:11 but of h' the words of the Lord: 8085
M't 13:13 seeing see not; and h' they hear not, 191
14 By h' ye shall hear, and shall not 189
15 and their ears are dull of h', 191
M'r 6: 2 and many h' him were astonished, "
Lu 2:46 both h' them, and asking them "
8:10 and h' they might not understand. "
18:36 h' the multitude pass by, he asked "
Ac 5: 5 Ananias h' these words fell down, "
8: 6 Philip spake, h' and seeing the * "
9: 7 h' a voice, but seeing no man. "
18: 8 many of the Corinthians h' believed, "
25:21 reserved unto the h' of Augustus, *1233
23 and was entered into the place of h', 201
28:26 H' ye shall hear, and shall not 189
27 and their ears are dull of h', 191
Ro 10:17 So then faith cometh by h', 189
17 and h' by the word of God. "
1Co 12:17 body were an eye, where were the h'? "
17 whole were h', where...the smelling? "
Ga 3: 2, 5 of the law, or by the h' of faith? "
Ph'm 5 H' of thy love and faith, which thou 191
Heb 5:11 to be uttered, seeing ye are dull of h'. 189
2Pe 2: 8 them, in seeing and h', vexed his "

hearken See also HEARKENED; HEARKENETH; HEARKENING.
Ge 4:23 wives of Lamech, h' unto...speech: 238
21:12 said unto thee, h' unto her voice; 8085
23:15 My lord, h' unto me: the land is "
34:17 not h' unto us, to be circumcised; "
49: 2 and h' unto Israel your father. "
Ex 3:18 And they shall h' to thy voice: "
4: 1 they will not believe me, nor h' unto "
8 neither h' to the voice of the first, "
9 two signs, neither h' unto thy voice, "
6:30 and how shall Pharaoh h' unto me? "
7: 4 But Pharaoh shall not h' unto you, "
22 neither did he h' unto them; as * "
11: 9 Pharaoh shall not h' unto you; "
15:26 If thou wilt diligently h' to the voice "
18:19 H' now unto my voice, I will give "
Le 26:14 But if ye will not h' unto me, "
18 ye will not yet for all this h' unto "
21 will not h' unto me; I will bring "
27 if ye will not for all this h' unto me, "
Nu 23:18 h' unto me, thou son of Zippor: 238
De 1:45 Lord would not h' to your voice, *8085
4: 1 Now therefore h', O Israel, unto the "
7:12 if ye h' to these judgments, and "
11:13 if ye shall h' diligently unto my "
13: 3 Thou shalt not h' unto the words "
8 consent unto him, nor h' unto him; "
18 shalt h' to the voice of the Lord "
15: 5 if thou carefully h' unto the voice "
17:12 h' unto the priest that standeth * "
18:15 like unto me; unto him ye shall h'; "
19 whosoever will not h' unto my words "
21:18 chastened him, will not h' unto "
23: 5 thy God would not h' unto Balaam; "
26:17 judgments, and to h' unto his voice: "
27: 9 Take heed, and h', O Israel; this day "
28: 1 shalt h' diligently unto the voice of "
2 if thou shalt h' unto the voice of the "
13 thou h' unto the commandments "
15 if thou wilt not h' unto the voice of "
30:10 If thou shalt h' unto the voice of * "
Jos 1:17 in all things, so will we h' unto thee: "
18 will not h' unto thy words in all that "
24:10 But I would not h' unto Balaam; "
J'g 2:17 would not h' unto their judges, * "
3: 4 would h' unto the commandments "
9: 7 H' unto me, ye men of Shechem, "
7 Shechem, that God may h' unto you. "
11:17 king of Edom would not h' thereto.* "
19:25 But the men would not h' to him: "
20:13 Benjamin would not h' to the voice "
1Sa 8: 7 H' unto the voice of the people in all "
9 Now therefore h' unto their voice: "
22 H' unto their voice, and make them "
15: 1 therefore h' thou unto the voice of "
22 better...to h' than the fat of rams. 7181
28:22 h' thou also unto the voice of thine 8085
30:24 For who will h' unto you in this "

2Sa 12:18 he would not h' unto our voice: *8085
13:14 he would not h' unto her voice: "
16 But he would not h' unto her. "
1Ki 8:28 to h' unto the cry and to the prayer, "
29 that thou mayest h' unto the prayer, "
30 And h' thou to the supplication of "
52 to h' unto them in all that they call "
11:38 thou wilt h' unto all that I command "
20: 8 H' not unto him, nor consent. "
22:28 H', O people, every one of you. * "
2Ki 10: 6 if ye will h' unto my voice, take ye "
17:40 Howbeit they did not h', but they "
18:31 H' not to Hezekiah: for thus saith "
32 and h' not unto Hezekiah, when he "
2Ch 6:19 to h' unto the cry and the prayer "
20 to h' unto the prayer which thy "
21 H' therefore unto the supplications "
10:16 the king would not h' unto them, * "
18:27 And he said, H', all ye people. * "
20:15 H' ye, all Judah, and ye 7181
33:10 his people: but they would not h'.* "
Ne 13:27 Shall we then h' unto you to do all 8085
Job 13: 6 and h' to the pleadings of my lips. 7181
32:10 H' to me; I also will shew mine 8085
33: 1 speeches, and h' to all my words. 238
31 Mark well, O Job, h' unto me: 8085
33 If not, h' unto me: hold thy peace, "
34:10 Therefore h' unto me, ye men of "
16 this; h' to the voice of my words. 238
34 and let a wise man h' unto me. *8085
37:14 H' unto this, O Job: stand still, 238
Ps 5: 2 H' unto the voice of my cry, 7181
34:11 Come, ye children, h' unto me: I 8085
45:10 H', O daughter, and consider, and "
58: 5 not h' to the voice of charmers, * "
81: 8 O Israel, if thou wilt h' unto me; "
11 But my people would not h' to my * "
Pr 7:24 H' unto me now therefore, O ye "
8:32 Now therefore h' unto me, O ye "
23:22 H' unto thy father that begat thee, "
29:12 If a ruler h' to lies, all his servants*7181
Ca 8:13 the companions h' to thy voice: "
Isa 28:23 my voice; h', and hear my speech. "
32: 3 the ears of them that hear shall h'. "
34: 1 h', ye people: let the earth hear, "
36:16 H' not to Hezekiah: for thus saith 8085
42:23 who will h' and hear for the time 7181
46: 3 H' unto me, O house of Jacob, 8085
12 H' unto me, ye stouthearted, that "
48:12 H' unto me, O Jacob and Israel, "
49: 1 and h', ye people, from far; The 7181
51: 1 H' to me, ye that follow after 8085
4 H' unto me, my people; and give *7181
7 H' unto me, ye that know 8085
55: 2 h' diligently unto me, and eat ye "
Jer 6:10 uncircumcised, and they cannot h': 7181
17 H' to the sound of the trumpet. But "
17 But they said, We will not h'. "
7:27 but they will not h' to thee: thou 8085
11:11 cry unto me, I will not h' unto them. "
16:12 heart, that they may not h' unto me: "
17:24 to pass, if ye diligently h' unto me, "
27 h' unto me to hallow the sabbath "
18:19 h' to the voice of them that contend "
23:16 H' not unto the words of the "
26: 3 If so be they will h', and turn every "
4 If ye will not h' to me, to walk in "
5 To h' to the words of my servants "
27: 9 h' not ye to your prophets, nor to "
14 h' not unto the words of the "
16 H' not to the words of your "
17 H' not unto them; serve the king of "
29: 8 neither h' to your dreams which ye "
12 pray unto me, and I will h' unto you. "
35:13 Will ye not receive instruction to h' "
37: 2 did h' unto the words of the Lord, "
38:15 counsel, wilt thou not h' unto me? "
44:16 of the Lord, we will not h' unto thee. "
Eze 3: 7 the house of Israel will not h' unto "
7 thee; for they will not h' unto me: "
20: 8 me, and would not h' unto me: they "
39 also, if ye will not h' unto me: "
Da 9:19 O Lord, h' and do; defer not, 7181
Ho 5: 1 h', ye house of Israel; and give ye "
9:17 because they did not h' unto him: 8085
Mic 1: 2 h', O earth, and all that therein is: 7181
Zec 1: 4 did not hear, nor h' unto me, "
7:11 they refused to h', and pulled away "
M'k 4: 3 H'; Behold, there went out a sower 191
7:14 H' unto me every one of you, "
Ac 2:14 unto you, and h' to my words: *1801
4:19 right in the sight of God to h' unto 191
7: 2 Men, brethren, and fathers, h'; The "
12:13 damsel came to h', named Rhoda, *5219
15:13 Men and brethren, h' unto me: 191
Jas 2: 5 H', my beloved brethren, Hath not "

hearkened See also HEARKENEDST.
Ge 3:17 hast h' unto the voice of thy wife, 8085
16: 2 And Abram h' to the voice of Sarai. "
23:16 And Abraham h' unto Ephron; and "
30:17 And God h' unto Leah, and she "
22 and God h' to her, and opened her "
34:24 and unto Shechem his son h' all "
39:10 that he h' not unto her, to lie by her, "
Ex 6: 9 they h' not unto Moses for anguish "
12 Israel have not h' unto me; how "
7:13 Pharaoh's heart, that he h' not "
8:15 hardened his heart, and h' not "
19 heart was hardened, and he h' not "
9:12 heart of Pharaoh, and he h' not "
16:20 they h' not unto Moses; but some "
18:24 So Moses h' to the voice of his father "
Nu 14:22 and have not h' to my voice; "
21: 3 the Lord h' to the voice of Israel, "
De 9:19 Lord h' unto me at that time also. "
23 believed him not, nor h' to his voice. "

De 10:10 Lord h' unto me at that time also. 8085
18:14 h' unto observers of times, and unto* "
26:14 I have h' to the voice of the Lord "
34: 9 the children of Israel h' unto him, "
Jos 1:17 as we h' unto Moses in all things, "
10:14 the Lord h' unto the voice of a man: "
J'g 2:20 and have not h' unto my voice; "
11:28 Ammon h' not unto the words of "
13: 9 And God h' to the voice of Manoah; "
1Sa 2:25 h' not unto the voice of their father, "
12: 1 I have h' unto your voice in all that "
19: 6 Saul h' unto the voice of Jonathan: "
25:35 I have h' to thy voice, and have "
28:21 and have h' unto thy words which "
23 him; and he h' unto their voice. "
1Ki 12:15 the king h' not unto the people; "
16 Israel saw that the king h' not "
24 They h' therefore to the word of the "
15:20 So Ben-hadad h' unto king Asa, "
2Ki 13: 4 and the Lord h' unto him: for he saw "
16: 9 And the king of Assyria h' unto him: "
20:13 And Hezekiah h' unto them, and "
21: 9 But they h' not: and Manasseh "
22:13 because our fathers have not h' unto "
2Ch 10:15 So the king h' not unto the people: "
16: 4 And Ben-hadad h' unto king Asa, "
24:17 Then the king h' unto them. "
25:16 and hast not h' unto my counsel. "
30:20 Lord h' to Hezekiah, and healed "
35:22 and h' not unto the words of Necho "
Ne 9:16 and h' not to thy commandments, "
29 h' not unto thy commandments, but "
34 nor h' unto thy commandments 7181
Es 3: 4 unto him, he h' not unto them, that 8085
Job 9:16 that he had h' unto my voice. 238
Ps 81:13 Oh that my people had h' unto me,*8085
106:25 h' not unto the voice of the Lord. "
Isa 21: 7 he h' diligently with much heed: *7181
48:18 hadst h' to my commandments! "
Jer 6:19 they have not h' unto my words, "
7:24 But they h' not, nor inclined their 8085
26 Yet they h' not unto me, nor inclined "
8: 6 I h' and heard, but they spake not "
25: 3 and speaking; but ye have not h'. "
4 but ye have not h', nor inclined "
7 Yet ye have not h' unto me, saith "
26: 5 sending them, but ye have not h'; "
29:19 they have not h' to my words, saith "
32:33 have not h' to receive instruction. "
34:14 but your fathers h' not unto me, "
17 have not h' unto me, in proclaiming "
35:14 speaking; but ye h' not unto me. "
15 inclined your ear, nor h' unto me. "
16 but this people hath not h' unto me: "
36:31 against them; but they h' not. "
37:14 But he h' not to him: so Irijah took "
44: 5 But they h' not, nor inclined their "
Eze 3: 6 them, they would have h' unto thee.* "
Da 9: 6 have we h' unto thy servants the "
Mal 3:16 and the Lord h', and heard it, and 7181
Ac 27:21 Sirs, ye should have h' unto me, 3980

hearkenedst
De 28:45 because thou h' not unto the voice 8085

hearkeneth
Pr 1:33 But whoso h' unto me shall dwell 8085
12:15 but he that h' unto counsel is wise. "

hearkening
Ps 103:20 h' unto the voice of his word. 8085

heart See also HEARTED; HEART'S; HEARTS.
Ge 6: 5 thoughts of his h' was only evil 3820
6 earth, and it grieved him at his h'. "
8:21 Lord said in his h', I will not again "
21 the imagination of man's h' is evil "
17:17 said in his h', Shall a child be born "
20: 5 integrity of my h' and innocency 3824
6 didst this in the integrity of thy h'; "
24:45 I had done speaking in mine h', 3820
27:41 Esau said in his h', The days of "
42:28 their h' failed them, and they were "
45:26 Jacob's h' fainted, for he believed "
Ex 4:14 seeth thee, he will be glad in his h'. "
21 I will harden his h', that he shall "
7: 3 harden Pharaoh's h', and multiply "
13 hardened Pharaoh's h', that he "
14 Pharaoh's h' is hardened, he "
22 Pharaoh's h' was hardened, neither "
23 neither did he set his h' to this also. "
8:15 was respite, he hardened his h', "
19 and Pharaoh's h' was hardened, "
32 Pharaoh hardened his h' at this "
9: 7 the h' of Pharaoh was hardened, "
12 Lord hardened the h' of Pharaoh, "
14 send all my plagues upon thine h', "
34 and hardened his h', he and his "
35 the h' of Pharaoh was hardened, "
10: 1 for I have hardened his h', and "
1 and the h' of his servants, that I "
20 hardened Pharaoh's h', so that he "
27 Lord hardened Pharaoh's h', and he "
11:10 hardened Pharaoh's h', so that he "
14: 4 will harden Pharaoh's h', that he "
5 h' of Pharaoh and of his servants 3824
8 Lord hardened the h' of Pharaoh 3820
15: 8 were congealed in the h' of the sea. "
23: 9 for ye know the h' of a stranger, 5315
25: 2 giveth it willingly with his h' ye 3820
28:29 breastplate of judgment upon his h', "
30 and they shall be upon Aaron's h', "
30 Israel upon his h' before the Lord "
35: 5 whosoever is of a willing h', let him "
21 every one whose h' stirred him up, "
26 the women whose h' stirred them up "
29 whose h' made them willing to bring "
34 hath put in his h' that he may teach, "
35 hath he filled with wisdom of h', "

Ex 36: 2 whose h' the Lord had put wisdom, 3820
2 every one whose h' stirred him up "
Le 19:17 not hate thy brother in thine h': 3824
26:16 the eyes, and cause sorrow of h': * 5315
Nu 15:39 that ye seek not after your own h' 3824
32: 7 discourage ye the h' of the children 3820
9 discouraged the h' of the children "
De 1:28 brethren have discouraged our h', 3824
2:30 spirit, and made his h' obstinate, "
4: 9 lest they depart from thy h' all the "
29 if thou seek him with all thy h' and "
39 consider it in thine h', that the Lord "
5:29 that there were such an h' in them, "
6: 5 the Lord thy God with all thine h', "
6 thee this day, shall be in thine h': "
7:17 say in thine h', These nations are "
8: 2 to know what was in thine h': "
5 Thou shalt also consider in thine h', "
14 thine h' be lifted up, and thou forget "
17 And thou say in thine h', My power "
9: 4 Speak not thou in thine h', after "
5 or for the uprightness of thine h', "
10:12 the Lord thy God with all thy h' and "
16 the foreskin of your h', and be no "
11:13 serve him with all your h' and with "
16 that your h' be not deceived, and ye "
18 lay up these my words in your h' "
13: 3 the Lord your God with all your h' "
15: 7 thou shalt not harden thine h', nor "
9 be not a thought in thy wicked h', "
10 thine h' shall not be grieved when "
17:17 that his h' turn not away: neither "
20 That his h' be not lifted up above "
18:21 if thou say in thine h', How shall we "
19: 6 the slayer, while his h' is hot, and "
20: 8 brethren's h' faint as well as his h'. "
24:15 he is poor, ... setteth his h' upon it: 5315
26:16 keep and do them with all thine h', 3824
28:28 blindness, and astonishment of h': "
47 joyfulness, and with gladness of h', "
65 a trembling h', and failing of eyes, 3820
67 for the fear of thine h' wherewith 3824
29: 4 not given you an h' to perceive, 3820
18 whose h' turneth away this day 3824
19 he bless himself in his h', saying, I "
19 walk in the imagination of mine h', 3820
30: 2 all thine h', and with all thy soul; 3824
6 thy God will circumcise thine h', "
6 and the h' of thy seed, to love the "
6 Lord thy God with all thine h', and "
10 the Lord thy God with all thine h', "
14 thy mouth, and in thy h', that thou "
17 if thine h' turn away, so that thou "
Jos 5: 1 their h' melted, neither was there "
14: 7 word again as it was in mine h'. "
8 made the h' of the people melt: 3820
22: 5 to serve him with all your h' and 3824
24:23 incline your h' unto the Lord God "
J'g 5: 9 My h' is toward the governors of 3820
15 there were great thoughts of h'. "
16 there were great searchings of h'. "
16:15 thee, when thine h' is not with me? "
17 That he told her all his h', and said "
18 saw that he had told her all his h', "
18 for he hath shewed me all his h'. "
18:20 the priest's h' was glad, and he took "
19: 5 Comfort thine h' with a morsel of "
6 all night, and let thine h' be merry. "
8 said, Comfort thine h', I pray thee. 3824
9 here, that thine h' may be merry; "
Ru 3: 7 his h' was merry, he went to lie 3820
1Sa 1: 8 not? and why is thy h' grieved? 3824
13 Now Hannah, she spake in her h'; 3820
2: 1 My h' rejoiceth in the Lord, mine "
33 thine eyes, and to grieve thine h': 5315
35 is in mine h' and in my mind: 3824
4:13 his h' trembled for the ark of God. 3820
9:19 will tell thee all that is in thine h'. 3824
10: 9 Samuel, God gave him another h': 3820
12:20 serve the Lord with all your h'; 3824
24 serve him in truth with all your h': "
13:14 sought him a man after his own h', "
14: 7 Do all that is in thine h': turn thee; "
7 I am with thee according to thy h'. "
16: 7 but the Lord looketh on the h'. "
17:28 the naughtiness of thine h'; for thou "
32 Let no man's h' fail because of 3820
21:12 David laid up these words in his h', 3824
24: 5 David's h' smote him, because he 3820
25:31 nor offence of h' unto my lord, "
36 and Nabal's h' was merry within "
37 that his h' died within him, and he "
27: 1 David said in his h', I shall now "
28: 5 afraid, and his h' greatly trembled. "
2Sa 3:21 over all that thine h' desireth. *5315
6:16 and she despised him in her h'. 3820
7: 3 king, Go, do all that is in thine h'; 3824
21 to thine own h', hast thou done 3820
27 thy servant found in his h' to pray "
13:28 when Amnon's h' is merry with wine, "
33 the king take the thing to his h', "
14: 1 the king's h' was toward Absalom. "
17:10 whose h' is as the h' of a lion, "
18:14 them through the h' of Absalom, "
19:14 the h' of all the men of Judah, 3824
14 of Judah, even as the h' of one man; "
19 the king should take it to his h'. 3820
24:10 David's h' smote him after that he "
1Ki 2: 4 all their h' and with all their soul, 3824
44 wickedness which thine h' is privy to, "
3: 6 and in uprightness of h' with thee; "
9 an understanding h' to judge thy 3820
12 wise and an understanding h'; "
4:29 largeness of h', even as the sand "
8:17 the h' of David my father to build 3824
18 it was in thine h' to build an house "

1Ki 8:18 didst well that it was in thine h'. 3824
23 walk before thee with all their h': "
38 every man the plague of his own h', "
39 to his ways, whose h' thou knowest; "
48 return unto thee with all their h', "
61 Let your h' therefore be perfect "
66 and glad of h' for all the goodness "
9: 3 mine eyes and mine h' shall be there "
4 integrity of h', and in uprightness, "
10: 2 with him of all that was in her h'. "
24 wisdom...God had put in his h'. 3820
11: 2 they will turn away your h' after 3824
3 and his wives turned away his h'. 3820
4 wives turned away his h' after 3824
4 and his h' was not perfect with "
4 was the h' of David his father. "
9 his h' was turned from the Lord "
12:26 And Jeroboam said in his h', 3820
27 the h' of this people turn again "
33 which he had devised of his own h'; "
14: 8 followed me with all his h', to do 3824
15: 3 his h' was not perfect with the Lord "
3 God, as the h' of David his father. "
14 Asa's h' was perfect with the Lord "
18:37 hast turned their h' back again. 3820
21: 7 eat bread, and let thine h' be merry: "
2Ki 5:26 Went not mine h' with thee, when "
6:11 the h' of the king of Syria was sore "
9:24 and the arrow went out at his h', "
10:15 h' right, as my h' is with thy h'? 3824
30 according to all that was in mine h', "
31 Lord God of Israel with all his h': "
12: 4 cometh into any man's h' to bring 3820
14:10 and thine h' hath lifted thee up: "
20: 3 in truth and with a perfect h', 3824
22:19 thine h' was tender, and thou hast "
23: 3 with all their h' and all their soul, 3820
25 turned to the Lord with all his h', 3824
1Ch 12:17 mine h' shall be knit unto you; "
33 rank: they were not of double h'. 3820
38 came with a perfect h' to Hebron, "
38 were of one h' to make David king. 3824
15:29 and she despised him in her h'. 3820
16:10 the h' of them rejoice that seek the "
17: 2 David, Do all that is in thine h'; 3824
19 according to thine own h', hast thou 3820
25 found in his h' to pray before thee. "
22:19 set your h' and your soul to seek 3824
28: 2 I had in mine h' to build an house "
9 serve him with a perfect h' and 3820
29: 9 with perfect h' they offered willingly "
17 triest the h', and hast pleasure in 3824
17 the uprightness of mine h' I have "
18 the thoughts of the h' of thy people, "
18 and prepare their h' unto thee: "
19 give...Solomon my son a perfect h', "
2Ch 1:11 Because this was in thine h', and "
6: 7 was in the h' of David my father "
8 as it was in thine h' to build an "
8 didst well in that it was in thine h': "
30 his ways, whose h' thou knowest; "
38 they return to thee with all their h' 3820
7:10 and merry in h' for the goodness "
11 came into Solomon's h' to make in "
16 mine eyes and mine h' shall be there "
9: 1 with him of all that was in her h'. 3824
23 wisdom, that God had put in his h'. 3820
12:14 prepared not his h' to seek the Lord. "
15:12 all their h' and with all their soul; 3824
15 for they had sworn with all their h', "
17 h' of Asa was perfect all his days. "
16: 9 whose h' is perfect toward him. "
17: 6 his h' was lifted up in the ways 3820
19: 3 hast prepared thine h' to seek God. 3824
9 faithfully, and with a perfect h'. "
22: 9 who sought the Lord with all his h'. "
25: 2 the Lord, but not with a perfect h'. "
19 thine h' lifteth thee up to boast: 3820
26:16 h' was lifted up to his destruction: * "
29:10 it is in mine h' to make a covenant 3824
31 as many as were of a free h' burnt 3820
34 Levites were more upright in h' 3824
30:12 one h' to do the commandment of 3820
19 That prepareth his h' to seek God, 3824
31:21 did it with all his h', and prospered. "
32:25 for his h' was lifted up: therefore 3820
26 himself for the pride of his h', "
31 might know all that was in his h'. 3824
34:27 Because thine h' was tender, and "
31 and his statutes, with all his h', "
36:13 hardened his h' from turning unto "
Ezr 6:22 turned the h' of the king of Assyria 3820
7:10 Ezra had prepared his h' to seek 3824
27 a thing as this in the king's h', 3820
Ne 2: 2 nothing else but sorrow of h'. "
12 had put in my h' to do at Jerusalem: "
6: 8 feignest them out of thine own h'. "
7: 5 my God put into mine h' to gather "
9: 8 foundest his h' faithful before thee, 3824
Es 1:10 the h' of the king was merry with 3820
5: 9 that day joyful and with a glad h': "
6: 6 Haman thought in his h', For whom "
7: 5 durst presume in his h' to do so? "
Job 7:17 shouldest set thine h' upon him? ‡
8:10 and utter words out of their h'? "
9: 4 He is wise in h', and mighty in 3824
10:13 things hast thou hid in thine h': "
11:13 thou prepare thine h', and stretch 3820
12:24 the h' of the chief of the people ‡
15:12 Why doth thine h' carry thee away? "
17: 4 hid their h' from understanding: "
11 off, even the thoughts of my h'. 3824
22:22 and lay up his words in thine h'. "
23:16 God maketh my h' soft, and the 3820
27: 6 my h' shall not reproach me so "
29:13 and I caused the widow's h' to sing 3820

Job 31: 7 mine h' walked after mine eyes, 3820
9 If mine h' have been deceived by a "
27 my h' hath been secretly enticed, "
33: 3 be of the uprightness of my h': "
34:14 If he set his h' upon man, "
36:13 hypocrites in h' heap up wrath: "
37: 1 At this also my h' trembleth, and is "
24 not any that are wise of h'. "
38:36 given understanding to the h'? *7907
41:24 His h' is as firm as a stone; 3820
Ps 4: 4 commune with your own h' upon 3824
7 Thou hast put gladness in my h', 3820
7:10 God, which saveth the upright in h'. "
9: 1 thee, O Lord, with my whole h'; "
10: 6 said in his h', I shall not be moved: "
11 said in his h', God hath forgotten: "
13 said in his h', Thou wilt not require "
17 thou wilt prepare their h', thou wilt "
11: 2 privily shoot at the upright in h'. "
12: 2 and with a double h' do they speak. "
13: 2 soul, having sorrow in my h' daily? 3824
5 h' shall rejoice in thy salvation. 3820
14: 1 The fool hath said in his h', There "
15: 2 and speaketh the truth in his h'. 3824
16: 9 Therefore my h' is glad, and my 3820
17: 3 Thou hast proved mine h'; thou "
19: 8 Lord are right, rejoicing the h': "
14 mouth, and the meditation of my h', "
20: 4 thee according to thine own h', *3824
22:14 my h' is like wax; it is melted in 3820
26 him: your h' shall live for ever. 3824
24: 4 hath clean hands, and a pure h'; "
25:17 The troubles of my h' are enlarged: "
26: 2 prove me; try my reins and my h'. 3820
27: 3 against me, my h' shall not fear: "
8 my h' said unto thee, Thy face, "
14 and he shall strengthen thine h': "
28: 7 h' trusted in him, and I am helped: "
7 therefore my h' greatly rejoiceth; "
31:24 he shall strengthen your h', all ye 3824
32:11 joy, all ye that are upright in h'. 3820
33:11 of his h' to all generations. "
21 our h' shall rejoice in him, because "
34:18 unto them that are of a broken h'; "
36: 1 saith within my h', that there is no "
10 righteousness to the upright in h'. "
37: 4 give thee the desires of thine h'. "
15 sword shall enter into their own h', "
31 The law of his God is in his h'; "
38: 8 reason of the disquietness of my h'. "
10 My h' panteth, my strength faileth "
39: 3 My h' was hot within me, while I "
40: 8 God: yea, thy law is within my h'. 4578
10 thy righteousness within my h'; 3820
12 head: therefore my h' faileth me. "
41: 6 his h' gathereth iniquity to itself; "
44:18 Our h' is not turned back, neither "
21 he knoweth the secrets of the h'. "
45: 1 My h' is inditing a good matter: "
5 in the h' of the king's enemies; "
49: 3 the meditation of my h' shall be of "
51:10 Create in me a clean h', O God; "
17 a broken and a contrite h', O God, "
53: 1 The fool hath said in his h', There "
55: 4 My h' is sore pained within me: "
21 than butter, but war was in his h': "
57: 7 My h' is fixed, O God, my h' is fixed: "
58: 2 in h' ye work wickedness; ye weigh "
61: 2 thee, when my h' is overwhelmed: "
62: 8 pour out your h' before him: 3824
10 increase, set not your h' upon them. 3820
64: 6 one of them, and the h', is deep. "
10 and all the upright in h' shall glory. "
66:18 I regard iniquity in my h', the Lord "
69:20 Reproach hath broken my h'; and "
32 your h' shall live that seek God. 3824
73: 1 even to such as are of a clean h'. "
7 they have more than h' could wish. "
13 I have cleansed my h' in vain, "
21 Thus my h' was grieved, and I was "
26 My flesh and my h' faileth: but God "
26 but God is the strength of my h', "
77: 6 I commune with mine own h': and "
78: 8 that set not their h' aright, and 3820
18 they tempted God in their h' by 3824
37 their h' was not right with him, 3820
72 to the integrity of his h'; and 3824
84: 2 my h' and my flesh crieth out for 3820
5 in whose h' are the ways of them. 3824
86:11 truth: unite my h' to fear thy name. "
12 O Lord my God, with all my h': "
94:15 all the upright in h' shall follow it. 3820
95: 8 Harden not your h', as in the 3824
10 It is a people that do err in their h', "
97:11 and gladness for the upright in h'. 3820
101: 2 within my house with a perfect h'. 3824
4 A froward h' shall depart from me: 3820
5 hath an high look and a proud h' 3824
102: 4 My h' is smitten, and withered like "
104:15 that maketh glad the h' of man, "
15 which strengtheneth man's h'. "
105: 3 let the h' of them rejoice that seek 3820
25 turned their h' to hate his people, "
107:12 brought down their h' with labour; "
108: 1 O God, my h' is fixed; I will sing "
109:16 might even slay the broken in h'. 3824
22 and my h' is wounded within me. 3820
111: 1 praise the Lord with my whole h', 3824
112: 7 his h' is fixed, trusting in the Lord. 3820
8 His h' is established, he shall not "
119: 2 that seek him with the whole h'. "
7 praise thee with uprightness of h', 3824
10 With my whole h' have I sought 3820
11 Thy word have I hid in mine h', "
32 when thou shalt enlarge my h'. "
34 I shall observe it with my whole h'. "

Ps 119: 36 Incline my h· unto thy testimonies, 3820
58 thy favour with my whole h·: but "
69 keep thy precepts with my whole h·. "
70 Their h· is as fat as grease; but I "
80 Let my h· be sound in thy statutes; "
111 for they are the rejoicing of my h·. "
112 I have inclined mine h· to perform "
145 I cried with my whole h·; hear me, "
161 my h· standeth in awe of thy word. "
131: 1 my h· is not haughty, nor mine eyes "
138: 1 will praise thee with my whole h·: "
139: 23 Search me...and know my h·: 3824
140: 2 imagine mischiefs in their h·; 3820
141: 4 Incline not my h· to any evil thing, "
143: 4 me; my h· within me is desolate. "
147: 3 He healeth the broken in h·, and "
Pr 2: 2 apply thine h· to understanding; "
10 wisdom entereth into thine h·, and "
3: 1 thine h· keep my commandments: "
3 them upon the table of thine h·: "
5 Trust in the Lord with all thine h·; "
4: 4 Let thine h· retain my words: keep "
21 keep them in the midst of thine h·. 3824
23 Keep thy h· with all diligence; for 3820
5: 12 and my h· despised reproof; "
6: 14 Frowardness is in his h·, he deviseth "
18 An h· that deviseth wicked "
21 Bind them continually upon thine h·, "
25 not after her beauty in thine h·; 3824
7: 3 them upon the table of thine h·. 3820
10 attire of an harlot, and subtil of h·. "
25 Let not thine h· decline to her ways, "
8: 5 fools, be ye of an understanding h·. "
10: 8 The wise in h· will receive "
20 the h· of the wicked is little worth. "
11: 20 They that are of a froward h· are "
29 shall be servant to the wise of h·. "
12: 8 of a perverse h· shall be despised. "
20 Deceit is in the h· of them that "
23 but the h· of fools proclaimeth "
25 Heaviness in the h· of man maketh "
13: 12 Hope deferred maketh the h· sick: "
14: 10 The h· knoweth his own bitterness; "
13 in laughter the h· is sorrowful; "
14 The backslider in h· shall be filled "
30 A sound h· is the life of the flesh: "
33 Wisdom resteth in the h· of him "
15: 7 the h· of the foolish doeth not so. "
13 A merry h· maketh a cheerful "
13 but by sorrow of the h· the spirit "
14 h· of him that hath understanding "
15 is of a merry h· hath a continual "
28 The h· of the righteous studieth to "
30 The light of the eyes rejoiceth the h·: "
16: 1 The preparations of the h· in man, "
5 Every one that is proud in h· is an "
9 A man's h· deviseth his way; but "
21 wise in h· shall be called prudent: "
23 h· of the wise teacheth his mouth, "
17: 16 wisdom, seeing he hath no h· to it? * "
20 He that hath a froward h· findeth "
22 A merry h· doeth good like a "
18: 2 but that his h· may discover itself. "
12 the h· of man is haughty, and "
15 The h· of the prudent getteth "
19: 3 his h· fretteth against the Lord. "
21 are many devices in a man's h·; "
20: 5 Counsel in the h· of man is like "
9 I have made my h· clean, I am pure "
21: 1 The king's h· is in the hand of the "
4 An high look, and a proud h· "
22: 11 He that loveth pureness of h·, "
15 Foolishness is bound in the h· of a "
17 apply thine h· unto my knowledge. "
23: 7 as he thinketh in his h·, so is he: *5315
7 but his h· is not with thee. 3820
12 Apply thine h· unto instruction, "
15 thine h· be wise, my h· shall rejoice, "
17 Let not thine h· envy sinners: "
19 wise, and guide thine h· in the way. "
26 My son, give me thine h·, and "
33 and thine h· shall utter perverse "
24: 2 For their h· studieth destruction, "
12 he that pondereth the h· consider *3826
17 let not thine h· be glad when he 3820
25: 3 the h· of kings is unsearchable. "
20 he that singeth songs to an heavy h·. "
26: 23 Burning lips and a wicked h· are "
25 are seven abominations in his h·. "
27: 9 Ointment...perfume rejoice the h·: "
11 son, be wise, and make my h· glad, "
19 to face, so the h· of man to man. "
28: 14 he that hardeneth his h· shall fall "
25 He that is of a proud h· stirreth up *5315
26 trusteth in his own h· is a fool: 3820
31: 11 The h· of her husband doth safely "
Ec 1: 13 I gave my h· to seek and search out "
16 I communed with mine own h·, "
16 yea, my h· had great experience of "
17 And I gave my h· to know wisdom, "
2: 1 I said in mine h·, Go to now, I will "
3 I sought in mine h· to give myself * "
3 acquainting mine h· with wisdom; "
10 I withheld not my h· from any joy; "
10 for my h· rejoiced in all my labour: "
15 said I in my h·, As it happeneth "
15 Then I said in my h·, that this also "
20 to cause my h· to despair of all the "
22 labour, and of the vexation of his h·, "
23 his h· taketh not rest in the night. "
3: 11 he hath set the world in their h·, "
17 I said in mine h·, God shall judge "
18 in mine h· concerning the estate of "
5: 2 and let not thine h· be hasty to utter "
20 answereth him in the joy of his h·. "
7: 2 and the living will lay it to his h·. "

Ec 7: 3 countenance the h· is made better. 3820
4 The h· of the wise is in the house of "
4 h· of fools is in the house of mirth. "
7 mad; and a gift destroyeth the h·. * "
22 oftentimes...thine own h· knoweth "
25 I applied mine h· to know, and to "
26 woman, whose h· is snares and nets, "
8: 5 wise man's h· discerneth both time "
9 and applied my h· unto every work "
11 the h· of the sons of men is fully set "
16 I applied mine h· to know wisdom, "
9: 1 For all this I considered in my h· "
3 the h· of the sons of men is full of "
3 and madness is in their h· while 3824
7 drink thy wine with a merry h·; 3820
10: 2 wise man's h· is at his right hand; "
2 hand; but a fool's h· at his left. "
11: 9 let thy h· cheer thee in the days of "
9 and walk in the ways of thine h·, "
10 remove sorrow from thy h·, and put "
Ca 3: 11 in the day of the gladness of his h·. "
4: 9 Thou hast ravished my h·, my 3823
9 thou hast ravished my h· with one "
5: 2 I sleep, but my h· waketh: it is 3820
8: 6 Set me as a seal upon thine h·, "
Isa 1: 5 head is sick, and the whole h· faint. 3824
6: 10 Make the h· of this people fat, 3820
10 and understand with their h·, and 3824
7: 2 And his h· was moved, and the h· of "
9: 9 say in the pride and stoutness of h·, "
10: 7 neither doth his h· think so; "
7 but it is in his h· to destroy and "
12 the stout h· of the king of Assyria, "
13: 7 faint, and every man's h· shall melt: "
14: 13 hast said in thine h·, I will ascend "
15: 5 My h· shall cry out for Moab; 3820
19: 1 and the h· of Egypt shall melt in 3824
21: 4 h· panted, fearfulness affrighted "
29: 13 have removed their h· far from me, 3820
30: 29 gladness of h·, as when one goeth 3824
32: 4 The h· also of the rash shall "
6 and his h· shall work iniquity, to 3820
33: 18 Thine h· shall meditate terror. "
35: 4 Say to them that are of a fearful h·, "
38: 3 in truth and with a perfect h·, "
42: 25 burned him, yet he laid it not to h·. "
44: 19 none considereth in his h·, neither * "
20 deceived h· hath turned him aside, "
47: 7 didst not lay these things to thy h·, "
8 that sayest in thine h·, I am, and 3824
10 thou hast said in thine h·, I am 3820
49: 21 Then shalt thou say in thine h·, 3824
51: 7 the people in whose h· is my law; 3820
57: 1 and no man layeth it to h·: "
11 remembered...nor laid it to thy h·? "
15 revive the h· of the contrite ones. "
17 on frowardly in the way of his h·. "
59: 13 from the h· words of falsehood. "
60: 5 and thine h· shall fear, and be 3824
63: 4 the day of vengeance is in mine h·, 3820
17 and hardened our h· from thy fear? "
65: 14 my servants shall sing for joy of h·, "
14 but ye shall cry for sorrow of h·, "
66: 14 ye see this, your h· shall rejoice, "
Jer 3: 10 turned unto me with her whole h·, "
15 you pastors according to mine h·, "
17 the imagination of their evil h·, "
4: 4 take away the foreskins of your h·, 3824
9 that the h· of the king shall perish, 3820
9 perish, and the h· of the princes; "
14 wash thine h· from wickedness, "
18 because it reacheth unto thine h·. "
19 I am pained at my very h·; "
19 my h· maketh a noise in me; "
5: 23 hath a revolting and a rebellious h·; "
24 Neither say they in their h·, Let 3824
7: 24 in the imagination of their evil h·, 3820
31 not, neither came it into my h·. * "
8: 18 against sorrow, my h· is faint in me. "
9: 8 but in h· he layeth his wait. 7130
14 the imagination of their own h·, 3820
26 Israel are uncircumcised in the h·. "
11: 8 in the imagination of their evil h·: "
20 that triest the reins and the h·, "
12: 3 and tried mine h· toward thee: "
11 because no man layeth it to h·. "
13: 10 walk in the imagination of their h·, "
22 if thou say in thine h·, Wherefore 3824
14: 14 nought, and the deceit of their h·. 3820
15: 16 me the joy and rejoicing of mine h·: 3824
16: 12 after the imagination of his evil h·, 3820
17: 1 graven upon the table of their h·, "
5 whose h· departeth from the Lord. "
9 The h· is deceitful above all things, "
10 I the Lord search the h·, I try the "
18: 12 do the imagination of his evil h·. "
20: 9 word was in mine h· as a burning "
12 seest the reins and the h·, let me see "
22: 17 thine eyes and thine h· are not but "
23: 9 Mine h· within me is broken "
16 they speak a vision of their own h·, "
17 after the imagination of his own h·, "
20 performed the thoughts of his h·: "
26 the h· of the prophets that prophesy "
26 of the deceit of their own h·; "
24: 7 I will give them an h· to know me, "
7 return unto me with their whole h·. "
29: 13 shall search for me with all your h·. 3824
30: 21 engaged his h· to approach unto *3820
24 performed the intents of his h·: "
31: 21 set thine h· toward the highway, "
32: 39 will give them one h·, and one way, "
41 with my whole h· and with my whole "
48: 29 pride, and the haughtiness of his h·. "
31 mine h· shall mourn for the men * "
36 mine h· shall sound for Moab like 3820

Jer 48: 36 and mine h· shall sound like pipes 3820
41 as the h· of a woman in her pangs. "
49: 16 the pride of thine h·, O thou that "
22 the h· of the mighty men of Edom "
22 as the h· of a woman in her pangs. "
51: 46 And lest your h· faint, and ye fear 3824
La 1: 20 mine h· is turned within me; for I 3820
22 my sighs are many, and my h· is "
2: 18 Their h· cried unto the Lord, O wall "
19 pour out thine h· like water before "
3: 41 Let us lift up our h· with our hands 3824
51 eye affecteth mine h· because of *5315
65 Give them sorrow of h·, thy curse 3820
5: 15 The joy of our h· is ceased; our "
17 For this our h· is faint; for these "
Eze 3: 10 receive in thine h·, and hear with 3824
6: 9 am broken with their whorish h·, 3820
11: 19 I will give them one h·, and I will "
19 I will take the stony h· out of their "
19 and will give them an h· of flesh: "
21 But as for them whose h· walketh "
21 after the h· of their detestable things "
13: 17 which prophesy out of their own h·; "
22 have made the h· of the righteous "
14: 3 have set up their idols in their h·, "
4 that setteth up his idols in his h·, "
5 the house of Israel in their own h·, "
7 and setteth up his idols in his h·, "
16: 30 weak is thine h·, saith the Lord 3826
18: 31 and make you a new h· and a new 3820
20: 16 for their h· went after their idols. "
21: 7 every h· shall melt, and all hands "
15 that their h· may faint, and their "
22: 14 Can thine h· endure, or can thine "
25: 6 rejoiced in h· with all thy despite *5315
15 vengeance with a despiteful h·, * "
27: 31 weep for thee with bitterness of h· * "
28: 2 thine h· is lifted up, and thou hast 3820
2 thou set thine h· as the h· of God: "
5 thine h· is lifted up because of thy 3824
6 set thine h· as the h· of God; 3820
17 Thine h· was lifted up because of "
31: 10 his h· is lifted up in his height; 3824
33: 31 h· goeth after their covetousness. 3820
36: 5 with the joy of all their h·, 3824
26 A new h· also will I give you, and 3820
26 I will take away the stony h· out of "
26 and I will give you an h· of flesh. "
40: 4 set thine h· upon all that I shall "
44: 7 strangers, uncircumcised in h·, and "
9 No stranger, uncircumcised in h·, "
Da 1: 8 Daniel purposed in his h· that he "
2: 30 know the thoughts of thy h·. 3825
4: 16 Let his h· be changed from man's, "
16 let a beast's h· be given unto him; "
5: 20 But when his h· was lifted up, "
21 and his h· was made like the beasts, "
22 hast not humbled thine h·, though "
6: 14 set his h· on Daniel to deliver him: 1079
7: 4 and a man's h· was given to it. 3825
28 but I kept the matter in my h·. 3821
8: 25 he shall magnify himself in his h·, 3824
10: 12 didst set thine h· to understand, 3820
11: 12 multitude, his h· shall be lifted up; 3824
28 and his h· shall be against the holy "
Ho 4: 8 they set their h· on their iniquity. 5315
11 and new wine take away the h·. *3820
7: 6 made ready their h· like an oven, "
11 is like a silly dove without h·: * "
14 have not cried unto me with their h·, "
10: 2 Their h· is divided; now shall they 3820
11: 8 mine h· is turned within me, my "
13: 6 were filled, and their h· was exalted; "
8 and will rend the caul of their h·, "
Joe 2: 12 turn ye even to me with all your h·, 3824
13 And rend your h·, and not your "
Ob 3 The pride of thine h· hath deceived 3820
3 that saith in his h·, Who shall "
Na 2: 10 and the h· melteth, and the knees "
Zep 1: 12 that say in their h·, The Lord will 3824
2: 15 that said in her h·, I am, and there "
3: 14 be glad and rejoice with all the h·, 3820
Zec 7: 10 evil against his brother in your h·. 3824
10: 7 h· shall rejoice as through wine: 3820
7 their h· shall rejoice in the Lord. "
12: 5 of Judah shall say in their h·, "
Mal 2: 2 if ye will not lay it to h·, to give glory "
2 because ye do not lay it to h·. "
4: 6 he shall turn the h· of the fathers to "
6 and the h· of the children to their "
M't 5: 8 Blessed are the pure in h·: for they 2588
28 adultery with her already in his h·. "
6: 21 treasure is, there will your h· be "
11: 29 for I am meek and lowly in h·: "
12: 34 the abundance of the h· the mouth "
35 out of the good treasure of the h· * "
40 three nights in the h· of the earth. "
13: 15 this people's h· is waxed gross, and "
15 should understand with their h·, "
19 away that which was sown in his h·. "
15: 8 lips; but their h· is far from me. "
18 the mouth come forth from the h·; "
19 out of the h· proceed evil thoughts, "
22: 37 the Lord thy God with all thy h·, "
24: 48 that evil servant shall say in his h·, "
M'r 6: 52 loaves: for their h· was hardened. "
7: 6 lips, but their h· is far from me. "
19 Because it entereth not into his h·, "
21 out of the h· of men, proceed evil "
8: 17 have ye your h· yet hardened? "
10: 5 the hardness of your h· he wrote 4641
11: 23 and shall not doubt in his h·, but 2588
12: 30 the Lord thy God with all thy h·, "
33 And to love him with all the h·, "
16: 14 their unbelief and hardness of h·, 4641
Lu 2: 19 and pondered them in her h·. 2588

Lu 2:51 kept all these sayings in her h'. 2588
6:45 out of the good treasure of his h' "
45 out of the evil treasure of his h' * "
45 abundance of the h' his mouth "
8:15 which in an honest and good h', "
9:47 perceiving the thought of their h', "
10:27 the Lord thy God with all thy h', "
12:34 treasure is, there will your h' be "
45 But and if that servant say in his h', "
24:25 and slow of h' to believe all that the "
32 Did not our h' burn within us, while "
Joh 12:40 their eyes, and hardened their h'; "
40 eyes, nor understand with their h', "
13:2 having now put into the h' of Judas "
14:1 Let not your h' be troubled: ye "
27 Let not your h' be troubled, neither "
16:6 unto you, sorrow hath filled your h'. "
22 and your h' shall rejoice, and your "
Ac 2:26 Therefore did my h' rejoice, and my "
37 they were pricked in their h', and "
46 with gladness and singleness of h', "
4:32 were of one h', and of one soul: "
5:3 why hath Satan filled thine h' to lie "
4 conceived this thing in thine h'? "
33 heard that, they were cut to the h', "
7:23 into his h' to visit his brethren 2588
51 and uncircumcised in h' and ears, "
54 they were cut to the h', and they "
8:21 thy h' is not right in the sight of "
22 the thought of thine h' may be "
37 If thou believest with all thine h', * "
11:23 with purpose of h' they would cleave "
13:22 Jesse, a man after mine own h', "
16:14 whose h' the Lord opened, that she "
21:13 ye to weep and to break mine h'? "
28:27 For the h' of this people is waxed "
27 understand with their h', and should "
Ro 1:21 and their foolish h' was darkened. "
2:5 after thy hardness and impenitent h' "
29 and circumcision is that of the h', "
6:17 have obeyed from the h' that form "
9:2 and continual sorrow in my h'. "
10:6 Say not in thine h', Who shall ascend "
8 even in thy mouth, and in thy h': "
9 shalt believe in thine h' that God "
10 For with the h' man believeth unto "
1Co 2:9 have entered into the h' of man, "
7:37 he that standeth stedfast in his h', "
37 and hath so decreed in his h' that "
14:25 the secrets of his h' made manifest; "
2Co 2:4 and anguish of h' I wrote unto you "
3:3 stone, but in fleshy tables of the h'.* "
15 is read, the vail is upon their h'. "
5:12 glory in appearance, and not in h'. "
6:11 open unto you, our h' is enlarged. "
8:16 care into the h' of Titus for you. "
9:7 as he purposeth in his h', so let him "
Eph 4:18 because of the blindness of their h': "
5:19 making melody in your h' to the "
6:5 in singleness of your h', as unto "
6 doing the will of God from the h'; 5590
Ph'p 1:7 all, because I have you in my h'; 2588
Col 3:22 but in singleness of h', fearing God: "
1Th 2:17 short time in presence, not in h', "
1Ti 1:5 is charity out of a pure h', and of a "
2Ti 2:22 call on the Lord out of a pure h'. "
Heb 3:10 They do alway err in their h'; "
12 be in any of you an evil h' of "
4:12 of thoughts and intents of the h'. "
10:22 Let us draw near with a true h' in "
13:9 thing that the h' be established "
Jas 1:26 his tongue, but deceiveth his own h'," "
1Pe 1:22 ye love one another with a pure h' "
3:4 let it be the hidden man of the h', "
2Pe 2:14 an h' they have exercised with "
1Jo 3:20 For if our h' condemn us, God is "
20 God is greater than our h', and "
21 if our h' condemn us not, then have "
Re 18:7 for she saith in her h', I sit a queen, "

hearted See also BROKENHEARTED; FAINTHEARTED; HARDHEARTED; MERRYHEARTED; STIFFHEARTED; STOUTHEARTED; TENDERHEARTED.
Ex 28:3 speak unto all that are wise h', 3820
31:6 in the hearts of all that are wise h' "
35:10 And every wise h' among you shall "
22 as many as were willing h', and "
25 And all the women that were wise h' "
36:1 and every wise h' man, in whom "
2 and every wise h' man, in whose "
8 And every wise h' man among them "

hearth
Ge 18:6 knead it and make cakes upon the h'.*
Ps 102:3 my bones are burned as an h'. *4168
Isa 30:14 a sherd to take fire from the h', or 3344
Jer 36:22 fire on the h' burning before him.* 254
23 it into the fire that was on the h', * "
23 in the fire that was on the h'. * "
Zec 12:6 like an h' of fire among the wood,*3595

heartily
Col 3:23 whatsoever ye do, do it h', as to 1537,5590

heart's
Ps 10:3 wicked boasteth of his h' desire, 5315
21:2 Thou hast given him his h' desire, 3820
Ro 10:1 my h' desire and prayer to God 2588

hearts
Ge 18:5 of bread, and comfort ye your h';*3820
Ex 14:17 will harden the h' of the Egyptians, "
31:6 the h' of all that are wise hearted "
Le 26:36 will send a faintness into their h' *3824
41 uncircumcised h' be humbled, * "
De 20:3 let not your h' faint, fear not, and* "
32:46 Set your h' unto all the words "
Jos 2:11 our h' did melt, neither did there "
7:5 the h' of the people melted, and "
11:20 was of the Lord to harden their h', 3820
23:14 ye know in all your h' and in all 3824
J'g 9:3 h' inclined to follow Abimelech; 3820
16:25 to pass, when their h' were merry, "
19:22 they were making their h' merry, "
1Sa 6:6 then do ye harden your h', as the 3824
6 and Pharaoh hardened their h'? 3820
7:3 unto the Lord with all your h', *3824
3 and prepare your h' unto the Lord, "
10:26 men, whose h' God had touched. 3820
2Sa 15:6 Absalom stole the h' of the men of "
13 The h' of the men of Israel are "
1Ki 8:39 thou only, knowest the h' of all 3824
58 he may incline our h' unto him, "
1Ch 28:9 for the Lord searcheth all h', and "
2Ch 6:14 walk before thee with all their h': *3820
30 for thou only knowest the h' of the 3824
11:16 such as set their h' to seek the Lord "
20:33 the people had not prepared their h' "
Job 1:5 sinned, and cursed God in their h'. "
Ps 7:9 the righteous God trieth the h' and 3826
28:3 but mischief is in their h'. 3824
33:15 He fashioneth their h' alike; he 3820
35:25 Let them not say in their h', Ah, so "
74:8 said in their h', Let us destroy * "
90:12 may apply our h' unto wisdom. *3824
125:4 them that are upright in their h'. 3826
Pr 15:11 then the h' of the children of men? "
17:3 for gold: but the Lord trieth the h'. "
21:2 eyes: but the Lord pondereth the h'." "
31:6 unto those that be of heavy h'. *5315
Isa 44:18 see; and their h', that they cannot 3826
Jer 31:33 and write it in their h'; and will *3820
32:40 but I will put my fear in their h', 3824
42:20 ye dissembled in your h', when ye*5315
48:41 the mighty men's h' in Moab at 3820
Eze 13:2 that prophesy out of their own h', "
32:9 will also vex the h' of many people, "
Da 11:27 both these kings' h' shall be to do 3824
Ho 7:2 they consider not in their h' that I "
Zec 7:12 they made their h' as an adamant 3820
8:17 none of you imagine evil in your h' "
M't 9:4 Wherefore think ye evil in your h'? 2588
18:35 from your h' forgive not every one "
19:8 because of the hardness of your h' *4641
M'r 2:6 there, and reasoning in their h', 2588
8 reason ye these things in your h'? "
3:5 grieved for the hardness of their h',* "
4:15 word that was sown in their h'. * "
Lu 1:17 to turn the h' of the fathers to the "
51 in the imagination of their h'. * "
66 laid them up in their h', saying, * "
2:35 the thoughts of many h' may be "
3:15 all men mused in their h' of John, "
5:22 them, What reason ye in your h'? "
8:12 away the word out of their h', * "
16:15 but God knoweth your h': for that "
21:14 Settle it therefore in your h', not to "
26 Men's h' failing them for fear, and *674
34 any time your h' be overcharged 2588
24:38 why do thoughts arise in your h'?* "
Ac 1:24 which knowest the h' of all men, 2589
7:39 in their h' turned back again into 2588
14:17 filling our h' with food and gladness," "
15:8 And God, which knoweth the h', *2589
9 them, purifying their h' by faith. 2588
Ro 1:24 through the lusts of their own h', "
2:15 work of the law written in their h', "
5:5 love of God is shed abroad in our h' "
8:27 he that searcheth the h' knoweth "
16:18 deceive the h' of the simple. "
1Co 4:5 manifest the counsels of the h': "
2Co 1:22 the earnest of the Spirit in our h'. "
3:2 written in our h', known and read "
4:6 hath shined in our h', to give the "
7:3 that ye are in our h' to die and live "
Ga 4:6 the Spirit of his Son into your h', "
Eph 3:17 That Christ may dwell in your h' by "
6:22 and that he might comfort your h'. "
Ph'p 4:7 shall keep your h' and minds "
Col 2:2 That their h' might be comforted, "
3:15 let the peace of God rule in your h', "
16 singing with grace in your h' to the "
4:8 your estate, and comfort your h'; "
1Th 2:4 men, but God, which trieth our h'. "
3:13 he may stablish your h' unblamable "
2Th 2:17 Comfort your h', and stablish you "
3:5 And the Lord direct your h' into the "
Heb 3:8 Harden not your h', as in the "
15 voice, harden not your h', as in the "
4:7 hear his voice, harden not your h'. "
8:10 mind, and write them in their h': * "
10:16 I will put my laws into their h', "
22 having our h' sprinkled from an evil "
Jas 3:14 envying and strife in your h', * "
4:8 purify your h', ye double minded. "
5:5 ye have nourished your h', as in a "
8 ye also patient; stablish your h': "
1Pe 3:15 sanctify the Lord God in your h': "
2Pe 1:19 and the day star arise in your h': "
1Jo 3:19 and shall assure our h' before him.* "
Re 2:23 which searcheth the reins and h': "
17:17 God hath put in their h' to fulfil "

hearts'
Ps 81:12 them up unto their own h' lust: 3820

hearty
Pr 27:9 of a man's friend by h' counsel. 5315

he-asses See ASSES.

heat See also HEATED.
Ge 8:22 and cold and h', and summer and 2527
18:1 in the tent door in the h' of the day; "
De 29:24 meaneth the h' of this great anger? 2750
32:24 devoured with burning h', and 7565
1Sa 11:11 Ammonites until the h' of the day: 2527
2Sa 4:5 came about the h' of the day to her "
1Ki 1:1 him with clothes, but he gat no h'. 3179
2 that my lord the king may get h'. 2552
Job 24:19 Drought and h' consume the snow 2527
30:30 and my bones are burned with h'. 2721
Ps 19:6 nothing hid from the h' thereof. 2535
Ec 4:11 lie together, then they have h': *2552
Isa 4:6 shadow in the daytime from the h', 2721
18:4 like a clear h' upon herbs, and like 2527
4 a cloud of dew in the h' of harvest. "
25:4 the storm, a shadow from the h', 2721
5 strangers, as the h' in a dry place; "
5 the h' with the shadow of a cloud: "
49:10 neither shall the h' nor sun smite 8273
Jer 17:8 and shall not see when h' cometh, 2527
36:30 be cast out in the day to the h', 2721
51:39 their h' I will make their feasts. *2527
Eze 3:14 bitterness, in the h' of my spirit; 2534
Da 3:19 that they should h' the furnace 228
M't 20:12 borne the burden and h' of the 2742
Lu 12:55 ye say, There will be h'; and it "
Ac 28:3 there came a viper out of the h', 2329
Jas 1:11 no sooner risen with a burning h', *2742
2Pe 3:10 elements shall melt with fervent h', 2741
12 elements shall melt with fervent h'? "
Re 7:16 the sun light on them, nor any h'. 2738
16:9 men were scorched with great h', "

heated
Da 3:19 more than it was wont to be h'. 228
Ho 7:4 as an oven h' by the baker, 1197

heath
Jer 17:6 shall be like the h' in the desert, 6176
48:6 be like the h' in the wilderness. "

heathen
Le 25:44 the h' that are round about you; *1471
26:33 I will scatter you among the h', * "
38 And ye shall perish among the h', * "
45 land of Egypt in the sight of the h',* "
De 4:27 left few in number among the h', * "
2Sa 22:44 hast kept me to be head of the h': * "
50 unto thee, O Lord, among the h', * "
2Ki 16:3 to the abominations of the h', * "
17:8 walked in the statutes of the h', * "
11 did the h' whom the Lord carried* "
15 went after the h' that were round* "
21:2 after the abominations of the h', "
1Ch 16:24 Declare his glory among the h'; * "
35 deliver us from the h', that we may* "
2Ch 20:6 over all the kingdoms of the h'? * "
28:3 after the abominations of the h' "
33:2 unto the abominations of the h', "
9 to do worse than the h', whom the* "
36:14 all the abominations of the h'; "
Ezr 6:21 the filthiness of the h' of the land, "
Ne 5:8 Jews, which were sold unto the h'; "
9 because of the reproach of the h' "
17 came unto us from among the h' "
6:6 It is reported among the h', and * "
16 all the h' that were about us saw "
Ps 2:1 Why do the h' rage, and the people* "
8 I shall give thee the h' for thine * "
9:5 Thou hast rebuked the h', thou * "
15 The h' are sunk down in the pit * "
19 let the h' be judged in thy sight. * "
10:16 the h' are perished out of his land.* "
18:43 hast made me the head of the h': * "
49 unto thee, O Lord, among the h', * "
33:10 the counsel of the h' to nought: * "
44:2 thou didst drive out the h' with * "
11 hast scattered us among the h'. * "
14 us a byword among the h', a * "
46:6 The h' raged, the kingdoms were* "
10 I will be exalted among the h', * "
47:8 God reigneth over the h': God * "
59:5 of Israel, awake to visit all the h': * "
8 shalt have all the h' in derision. * "
78:55 cast out the h' also before them, * "
79:1 h' are come into thine inheritance; "
6 Pour out thy wrath upon the h' that "
10 Wherefore should the h' say, Where "
10 let him be known among the h' in "
80:8 hast cast out the h', and planted * "
94:10 He that chastiseth the h', shall not* "
96:3 Declare his glory among the h', * "
10 Say among the h' that the Lord * "
98:2 shewed in the sight of the h'. * "
102:15 So the h' shall fear the name of * "
105:44 And gave them the lands of the h': * "
106:35 But were mingled among the h', * "
41 gave them into the hand of the h'; * "
47 and gather us from among the h', * "
110:6 He shall judge among the h', he * "
111:6 give them the heritage of the h'. * "
115:2 Wherefore should the h' say, * "
126:2 then said they among the h', The* "
135:15 The idols of the h' are silver and * "
149:7 To execute vengeance upon the h',* "
Isa 16:8 lords of the h' have broken down * "
Jer 9:16 scatter them also among the h', * "
10:2 Learn not the way of the h', and * "
2 for the h' are dismayed at them. * "
25 Pour out thy fury upon the h' that "
18:13 Ask ye now among the h', who * "
49:14 an ambassador is sent unto the h', * "
15 make thee small among the h', * "
La 1:3 she dwelleth among the h', she * "
10 she hath seen that the h' entered * "
4:15 they said among the h', They shall* "
20 shadow we shall live among the h'.* "
Eze 7:24 I will bring the worst of the h', * "
11:12 after the manners of the h' that * "
16 cast them far off among the h', and* "
12:16 their abominations among the h' * "
16:14 renown went forth among the h' * "
20:9 be polluted before the h', among * "
14 be polluted before the h', in "

Eze 20:22 be polluted in the sight of the h'. *1471
23 would scatter them among the h', * "
32 say, We will be as the h', as the* "
41 be sanctified in you before the h'.* "
22: 4 made thee a reproach unto the h',* "
15 will scatter thee among the h', * "
16 in thyself in the sight of the h', * "
23:30 hast gone a whoring after the h', * "
25: 7 deliver thee for a spoil to the h'; * "
8 of Judah is like unto all the h'; * "
28:25 sanctified...in the sight of the h', * "
30: 3 it shall be the time of the h'. * "
31:11 hand of the mighty one of the h';* "
17 shadow in the midst of the h'. * "
34:28 shall no more be a prey to the h', * "
29 neither bear the shame of the h' * "
36: 3 unto the residue of the h', and ye* "
4 to the residue of the h' that are * "
5 against the residue of the h', and* "
6 ye have born the shame of the h': * "
7 Surely the h' that are about you, * "
15 the shame of the h' any more, * "
19 I scattered them among the h', * "
20 And when they entered unto the h',* "
21 Israel had profaned among the h',* "
22 ye have profaned among the h', * "
23 which was profaned among the h',* "
23 h' shall know that I am the Lord,* "
24 will take you from among the h', * "
30 reproach of famine among the h'.* "
36 Then the h' that are left round * "
37:21 Israel from among the h', whither* "
28 h' shall know that I the Lord do * "
38:16 that the h' may know me, when * "
39: 7 h' shall know that I am the Lord,* "
21 I will set my glory among the h' * "
21 all the h' shall see my judgment * "
23 the h' shall know that the house * "
28 led into captivity among the h': * "
Joe 2:17 that the h' should rule over them:* "
19 you a reproach among the h': * "
3:11 and come, all ye h', and gather * "
12 Let the h' be wakened, and come * "
12 to judge all the h' round about. * "
Am 9:12 of all the h', which are called by * "
Ob 1 ambassador is sent among the h',* "
2 made thee small among the h': * "
15 the Lord is near upon all the h': * "
16 shall all the h' drink continually, * "
Mic 5:15 in anger and fury upon the h', * "
Hab 1: 5 Behold ye among the h', and * "
3:12 thou didst thresh the h' in anger.* "
Zep 2:11 even all the isles of the h'. * "
Hag 2:22 of the kingdoms of the h'; and I * "
Zec 1:15 sore displeased with the h' that * "
8:13 as ye were a curse among the h', * "
9:10 he shall speak peace unto the h':* "
14:14 the wealth of all the h' round * "
18 smite the h' that come not up * "
Mal 1:11 name shall be great among the h',* "
14 name is dreadful among the h'. * "
M't 6: 7 not vain repetitions, as the h' do: *1482
18:17 let him be unto thee as an h' man* "
Ac 4:25 Why did the h' rage, and the *1484
2Co 11:26 in perils by the h', in perils in the * "
Ga 1:16 I might preach him among the h'; * "
2: 9 that we should go unto the h', and* "
3: 8 that God would justify the h' * "

heave See also HEAVED.
Ex 29:27 the shoulder of the h' offering, 8641
28 for it is an h' offering: and it shall "
28 be an h' offering from the children "
28 their h' offering unto the Lord. "
Le 7:14 an h' offering unto the Lord, and it "
32 an h' offering of the sacrifices of "
34 and the h' shoulder have I taken of "
10:14 the wave breast and h' shoulder "
15 The h' shoulder and the wave "
Nu 6:20 the wave breast and h' shoulder: "
15:19 shall offer up an h' offering unto the "
20 of your dough for an h' offering: "
20 h' offering of the threshingfloor, "
20 threshingfloor, so shall ye h' it. 7311
21 the Lord an h' offering in your 8641
18: 8 the charge of mine h' offerings of "
11 the h' offering of their gift, with all "
19 the h' offerings of the holy things, "
24 which they offer as an h' offering "
26 ye shall offer up an h' offering of "
27 your h' offering shall be reckoned "
28 offer an h' offering unto the Lord "
28 the Lord's h' offering to Aaron the "
29 offer every h' offering of the Lord, "
31:29 for an h' offering of the Lord. "
41 which was the Lord's h' offering, "
De 12: 6 h' offerings of your hand, and your "
11 and the h' offering of your hand, "
17 or h' offering of thine hand: "

heaved
Ex 29:27 is waved, and which is h' up, of 7311
Nu 18:30 When ye have h' the best thereof * "
32 when ye have h' from it the best of * "

heaven See also HEAVEN'S; HEAVENS.
Ge 1: 1 the beginning God created the h' 8064
8 And God called the firmament H'. "
9 waters under the h' be gathered "
14, 15 lights in the firmament of the h' "
17 set them in the firmament of the h' "
20 earth in the open firmament of h'. "
6:17 the breath of life, from under h'; "
7:11 and the windows of h' were opened. "
19 hills, that were under the whole h', "
23 things, and the fowl of the h'; and "
8: 2 the windows of h' were stopped, and "
2 the rain from h' was restrained; "
Ge 11: 4 whose top may reach unto h'; and 8064
14:19 high God, possessor of h' and earth: "
22 God, the possessor of h' and earth, "
15: 5 Look now toward h', and tell the "
19:24 and fire from the Lord out of h'; "
21:17 of God called to Hagar out of h', "
22:11 the Lord called unto him out of h', "
15 Lord called unto Abraham out of h' "
17 thy seed as the stars of the h', "
24: 3 the Lord, the God of h', and the God "
7 The Lord God of h', which took me "
26: 4 seed to multiply as the stars of h', "
27:28 God give thee of the dew of h', and "
39 and of the dew of h' from above; "
28:12 and the top of it reached to h': and "
17 of God, and this is the gate of h'. "
49:25 bless thee with blessings of h' above, "
Ex 9: 8 sprinkle it toward the h' in the sight "
10 Moses sprinkled it up toward h'; "
22 Stretch forth thine hand toward h', "
23 stretched forth his rod toward h': "
10:21 Stretch out thine hand toward h', "
22 stretched forth his hand toward h'; "
16: 4 I will rain bread from h' for you; "
17:14 of Amalek from under h'. "
20: 4 likeness of any thing that is in h' "
11 days the Lord made h' and earth, "
22 that I have talked with you from h'. "
24:10 were the body of h' in his clearness. "
31:17 days the Lord made h' and earth, "
32:13 multiply your seed as the stars of h', "
Le 26:19 and I will make your h' as iron, and "
De 1:10 as the stars of h' for multitude. "
28 cities are great and walled up to h'; "
2:25 nations that are under the whole h', "
3:24 what God is there in h' or in earth, "
4:11 with fire unto the midst of h', with "
19 lest thou lift up thine eyes unto h', "
19 and the stars, even all the host of h', "
19 unto all nations under the whole h'. "
26 I call h' and earth to witness against "
32 the one side of h' unto the other, "
36 Out of h' he made thee to hear his "
39 he is God in h' above, and upon the "
5: 8 likeness of any thing that is in h' "
7:24 destroy their name from under h': "
9: 1 cities great and fenced up to h', "
14 blot out their name from under h': "
10:14 the h' and the h' of heavens is the "
22 thee as the stars of h' for multitude. "
11:11 and drinketh water of the rain of h': "
17 and he shut up the h', that there be "
21 as the days of h' upon the earth. * "
17: 3 or moon, or any of the host of h', "
25:19 of Amalek from under h'; thou "
26:15 from thy holy habitation, from h', "
28:12 the h' to give the rain unto thy land "
23 thy h' that is over thy head shall be "
24 h' shall it come down upon thee, "
62 as the stars of h' for multitude; "
29:20 blot out his name from under h'. "
30: 4 out unto the uttermost parts of h', "
12 It is not in h', that thou shouldest "
12 say, Who shall go up for us to h', "
19 I call h' and earth to record this day "
31:28 call h' and earth to record against "
32:40 For I lift up my hand to h', and say, "
33:13 precious things of h', for the dew, "
26 who rideth upon the h' in thy help, "
Jos 2:11 he is God in h' above, and in earth "
8:20 smoke of the city ascended up to h', "
10:11 Lord cast down great stones from h' "
13 the sun stood still in the midst of h', "
J'g 5:20 They fought from h'; the stars in "
13:20 the flame went up toward h' from "
20:40 flame of the city ascended up to h'. "
1Sa 2:10 of h' shall he thunder upon them: "
5:12 the cry of the city went up to h'. "
2Sa 18: 9 taken up between the h' and the "
21:10 water dropped upon them out of h', "
22: 8 foundations of h' moved and shook, "
14 The Lord thundered from h', and "
1Ki 8:22 spread forth his hands toward h': "
23 is no God like thee, in h' above, or "
27 h' and h' of heavens cannot contain "
30 hear thou in h' thy dwelling place: "
32 hear thou in h', and do, and judge "
34 Then hear thou in h', and forgive "
35 When h' is shut up, and there is no "
36 Then hear thou in h', and forgive "
39, 43 hear thou in h' thy dwelling place, "
45 hear thou in h' their prayer and "
49 in h' thy dwelling place, and "
54 with his hands spread up to h'. "
18:45 that the h' was black with clouds "
22:19 all the host of h' standing by him "
2Ki 1:10 then let fire come down from h', "
10 And there came down fire from h', "
12 of God, let fire come down from h', "
12 the fire of God came down from h', "
14 came fire down from h', and burnt "
2: 1 Lord would take up Elijah into h' "
11 went up by a whirlwind into h'. "
7: 2 Lord would make windows in h', "
19 Lord should make windows in h', "
14:27 the name of Israel from under h': "
17:16 and worshipped all the host of h', "
19:15 thou hast made h' and earth. "
21: 3 all the host of h', and served them. "
5 he built altars for all the host of h' "
23: 4 the grove, and for all the host of h': "
5 planets, and to all the host of h'. "
1Ch 21:16 stand between the earth and the h', "
26 he answered him from h' by fire "
29:11 all that is in the h' and in the earth "
2Ch 2: 6 h' and h' of heavens cannot contain "
2Ch 2:12 of Israel, that made h' and earth, 8064
6:13 spread forth his hands toward h', "
14 no God like thee in the h', nor in the "
18 h' and the h' of heavens cannot "
21 thy dwelling place, even from h'; "
23 Then hear thou from h', and do, and "
26 the h' is shut up, and there is no "
27 hear thou from h', and forgive the "
30 hear thou from h' thy dwelling "
7: 1 the fire came down from h', and "
13 If I shut up h' that there be no rain, "
14 then will I hear from h', and will "
18:18 the host of h' standing on his right "
20: 6 our fathers, art not thou God in h'? "
28: 9 in a rage that reacheth up unto h'. "
30:27 holy dwelling place, even unto h'. "
32:20 son of Amoz, prayed and cried to h'. "
33: 3 and worshipped all the host of h', "
5 he built altars for all the host of h' "
36:23 hath the Lord God of h' given me; "
Ezr 1: 2 The Lord God of h' hath given me "
5:11 We are the servants of the God of h' 8065
12 fathers had provoked the God of h' "
6: 9 the burnt offerings of the God of h', "
10 sweet savours unto the God of h', "
7:12, 21 scribe of the law of the God of h', "
23 is commanded by the God of h', let "
23 done for the house of the God of h': "
Ne 1: 4 and prayed before the God of h', 8064
5 O Lord God of h', the great and "
9 unto the uttermost part of the h', "
2: 4 So I prayed to the God of h'. "
20 The God of h', he will prosper us; "
9: 6 thou hast made h', the h' of heavens, "
6 and the host of h' worshippeth thee. "
13 and spakest with them from h', "
15 gavest them bread from h' for their "
23 multipliedst thou as the stars of h', "
27, 28 thou heardest them from h'; and "
Job 1:16 The fire of God is fallen from h', "
2:12 dust upon their heads toward h'. "
11: 8 It is as high as h'; what canst thou "
16:19 behold, my witness is in h', and my "
20:27 The h' shall reveal his iniquity; * "
22:12 Is not God in the height of h'? "
14 and he walketh in the circuit of h'. "
26:11 The pillars of h' tremble and are "
28:24 earth, and seeth under the whole h'; "
35:11 maketh us wiser than the fowls of h'? "
37: 3 He directeth it under the whole h', "
38:29 and the hoary frost of h', who hath "
33 Knowest thou the ordinances of h'?* "
37 or who can stay the bottles of h', "
41:11 is under the whole h' is mine. "
Ps 11: 4 temple, the Lord's throne is in h': "
14: 2 The Lord looked down from h' upon "
19: 6 forth is from the end of the h', and "
20: 6 he will hear him from his holy h' "
33:13 Lord looketh from h'; he beholdeth "
53: 2 God looked down from h' upon the "
57: 3 He shall send from h', and save me "
69:34 Let the h' and earth praise him, "
73:25 Whom have I in h' but thee? and "
76: 8 judgment to be heard from h'; "
77:18 of thy thunder was in the h'; the *1534
78:23 above, and opened the doors of h', 8064
24 had given them of the corn of h'. "
26 an east wind to blow in the h': "
79: 2 be meat unto the fowls of the h', "
80:14 look down from h', and behold, and "
85:11 righteousness shall look...from h'. "
89: 6 who in the h' can be compared *7834
29 and his throne as the days of h'. 8064
37 and as a faithful witness in h'. *7834
102:19 from h' did the Lord behold the 8064
103:11 as the h' is high above the earth, "
104:12 shall the fowls of the h' have their "
105:40 them with the bread of h'. "
107:26 They mount up to the h', they go "
113: 6 the things that are in h', and in the "
115:15 the Lord which made h' and earth. "
16 The h', even the heavens, are the "
119:89 O Lord, thy word is settled in h'. "
121: 2 the Lord, which made h' and earth. "
124: 8 the Lord, who made h' and earth. "
134: 3 The Lord that made h' and earth "
135: 6 the Lord pleased, that did he in h', "
136:26 O give thanks unto the God of h': "
139: 8 If I ascend up into h', thou art there: "
146: 6 Which made h', and earth, the sea, "
147: 8 Who covereth the h' with clouds, "
148:13 his glory is above the earth and h'. "
Pr 23: 5 they fly away as an eagle toward h'. "
25: 3 The h' for height, and the earth for "
30: 4 Who hath ascended up into h', or "
Ec 1:13 all things that are done under h': "
2: 3 should do under the h' all the days "
3: 1 time to every purpose under the h': "
5: 2 God is in h', and thou upon earth: "
Isa 13: 5 a far country, from the end of h', "
10 the stars of h' and the constellations "
14:12 How art thou fallen from h', O "
13 I will ascend into h', I will exalt "
34: 4 all the host of h' shall be dissolved, "
5 for my sword shall be bathed in h': "
37:16 earth: thou hast made h' and earth. "
40:12 and meted out h' with the span, "
55:10 cometh down, and the snow from h', "
63:15 Look down from h', and behold "
66: 1 The h' is my throne, and the earth "
Jer 7:18 to make cakes to the queen of h', "
33 shall be meat for the fowls of the h', "
8: 2 the moon, and all the host of h', "
7 Yea, the stork in the h' knoweth her "
10: 2 be not dismayed at the signs of h'; "
15: 3 the fowls of the h', and the beasts "

Jer 16: 4 shall be meat for the fowls of h·. 8064
19: 7 to be meat for the fowls of the h·, "
13 incense unto all the host of h·, and "
23: 24 Do not I fill h· and earth? saith "
31: 37 If h· above can be measured, and "
32: 17 thou hast made the h· and the earth "
33: 22 the host of h· cannot be numbered, "
25 the ordinances of h· and earth; "
34: 20 be for meat unto the fowls of the h·, "
44: 17 burn incense unto the queen of h·, "
18 to burn incense to the queen of h·, "
19 burned incense to the queen of h·, "
25 to burn incense to the queen of h·, "
49: 36 winds from the four quarters of h·, "
51: 9 for her judgment reacheth unto h·, "
15 hath stretched out the h· by his * "
48 the h· and the earth, and all that is "
53 Babylon should mount up to h·, "
La 2: 1 cast down from h· unto the earth "
3: 50 Lord look down, and behold from h·. "
4: 19 swifter than the eagles of the h·: "
Eze 8: 3 up between the earth and the h·, "
29: 5 of the field and to the fowls of the h·. "
31: 6 All the fowls of h· made their nests "
13 shall all the fowls of the h· remain, "
32: 4 all the fowls of the h· to remain "
7 I will cover the h·, and make the "
8 All the bright lights of h· will I "
38: 20 the fowls of the h·, and the beasts "
Da 2: 18 desire mercies of the God of h· 8065
19 Then Daniel blessed the God of h·. "
28 there is a God in h· that revealeth "
37 for the God of h· hath given thee a "
38 the fowls of the h· hath he given "
44 shall the God of h· set up a kingdom, "
4: 11 height thereof reached unto h·, and * "
12 and the fowls of the h· dwelt in the "
13 and an holy one came down from h·; "
15 let it be wet with the dew of h·, and "
20 whose height reached unto the h·, "
21 branches the fowls of the h· had "
22 is grown, and reacheth unto h·, and "
23 an holy one coming down from h·, "
23 and let it be wet with the dew of h·, "
25 shall wet thee with the dew of h·, "
31 there fell a voice from h·, saying, "
33 his body was wet with the dew of h·, "
34 lifted up mine eyes unto h·, and "
35 to his will in the army of h·, and "
37 and extol and honour the King of h·, "
5: 21 his body was wet with the dew of h·; "
23 up thyself against the Lord of h·; "
6: 27 he worketh signs and wonders in h· "
7: 2 the four winds of the h· strove "
13 of man came with the clouds of h·, "
27 of the kingdom under the whole h·, "
8: 8 ones toward the four winds of h·. 8064
10 waxed great, even to the host of h·; "
9: 12 under the whole h· hath not been "
11: 4 divided toward the four winds of h·; "
12: 7 right hand and his left hand unto h·, "
Ho 2: 18 and with the fowls of h·, and with "
4: 3 the field, and with the fowls of h·; "
7: 12 them down as the fowls of the h·. "
Am 9: 2 though they climb up to h·, thence "
6 that buildeth his stories in the h·, "
Jon 1: 9 the Lord, the God of h·, which hath "
Na 3: 16 thy merchants above the stars of h·: "
Zep 1: 3 I will consume the fowls of the h·, "
5 them that worship the host of h· "
Hag 1: 10 the h· over you is stayed from dew, "
Zec 2: 6 abroad as the four winds of the h·, "
5: 9 ephah between the earth and the h·. "
Mal 3: 10 will not open you the windows of h·, "
M't 3: 2 for the kingdom of h· is at hand. 3772
17 And lo a voice from h·, saying, * "
4: 17 for the kingdom of h· is at hand. "
5: 3, 10 for theirs is the kingdom of h·. "
12 for great is your reward in h·: for so "
16 glorify your Father which is in h·. "
18 Till h· and earth pass, one jot or one "
19 called the least in the kingdom of h·: "
19 be called great in the kingdom of h·. "
20 case enter into the kingdom of h·. "
34 Swear not at all; neither by h·; for "
5: 45 of your Father which is in h·: * "
48 your Father which is in h· is perfect. "
6: 1 reward of your Father which is in h·. "
9 pray ye: Our Father which art in h·, "
10 will be done in earth, as it is in h·. "
20 up for yourselves treasures in h·, "
7: 11 your Father which is in h· give good "
21 shall enter into the kingdom of h·; "
21 the will of my Father which is in h·. "
8: 11 and Jacob, in the kingdom of h·. "
10: 7 saying, The kingdom of h· is at hand. "
32 also before my Father which is in h·. "
33 deny before my Father which is in h·. "
11: 11 he that is least in the kingdom of h· "
12 the kingdom of h· suffereth violence, "
23 which art exalted unto h·, shalt be "
25 O Father, Lord of h· and earth, "
12: 50 will of my Father which is in h·, the "
13: 11 the mysteries of the kingdom of h·, "
24 kingdom of h· is likened unto a man "
31 The kingdom of h· is like to a grain "
33 kingdom of h· is like unto leaven, "
44, 45 Again, the kingdom of h· is like "
47 the kingdom of h· is like unto a net, "
52 instructed unto the kingdom of h· is "
14: 19 and looking up to h·, he blessed, and "
16: 1 he would shew them a sign from h·. "
17 thee, but my Father which is in h·. "
19 thee the keys of the kingdom of h·: "
19 bind on earth shall be bound in h·: "
19 loose on earth shall be loosed in h·. "

M't 18: 1 the greatest in the kingdom of h·? 3772
3 not enter into the kingdom of h·. "
4 is greatest in the kingdom of h·. "
10 in h· their angels do always behold "
10 the face of my Father which is in h·. "
14 of your Father which is in h·, that "
18 bind on earth shall be bound in h·: "
18 loose on earth shall be loosed in h·. "
19 them of my Father which is in h·. "
23 the kingdom of h· is likened unto a "
19: 14 me: for of such is the kingdom of h·. "
21 and thou shalt have treasure in h·: "
23 hardly enter into the kingdom of h·. "
20: 1 the kingdom of h· is like unto a man "
21: 25 whence was it? from h·, or of men? "
25 If we shall say, From h·; he will say "
22: 2 The kingdom of h· is like unto a "
30 but are as the angels of God in h·. "
23: 9 one is your Father, which is in h·. "
13 shut up the kingdom of h· against "
22 that shall swear by h·, sweareth by "
24: 29 the stars shall fall from h·, and the "
30 the sign of the Son of man in h·: "
30 Son of man coming in the clouds of h· "
31 from one end of h· to the other. "
35 H· and earth shall pass away, but "
36 not the angels of h·, but my Father "
25: 1 the kingdom of h· be likened unto "
14 For the kingdom of h· is as a man* "
26: 64 and coming in the clouds of h·. 3772
28: 2 of the Lord descended from h·, and "
18 is given unto me in h· and in earth. "
M'r 1: 11 there came a voice from h·, saying,* "
6: 41 he looked up to h·, and blessed, and "
7: 34 And looking up to h·, he sighed, and "
8: 11 him, seeking of him a sign from h·, "
10: 21 and thou shalt have treasure in h·: "
11: 25 your Father also which is in h· may "
26 your Father which is in h· forgive* "
30 John, was it from h·, or of men? "
31 If we shall say, From h·; he will say, "
12: 25 are as the angels which are in h·. "
13: 25 the stars of h· shall fall, and the "
25 the powers that are in h· shall be * "
27 earth to the uttermost part of h·. "
31 H· and earth shall pass away: but "
32 no, not the angels which are in h·, "
14: 62 and coming in the clouds of h·. "
16: 19 he was received up into h·, and sat "
Lu 2: 15 were gone away from them into h·, "
3: 21 and praying, the h· was opened, And "
22 and a voice came from h·, which "
4: 25 when the h· was shut up three years "
6: 23 your reward is great in h·: for in "
9: 16 and looking up to h·, he blessed "
54 command fire to come down from h·, "
10: 15 which art exalted to h·, shalt be "
18 Satan as lightning fall from h·. "
20 your names are written in h·. "
21 O Father, Lord of h· and earth, that "
11: 2 say, Our Father which art in h·, * "
2 will be done as in h·, so in earth. * "
16 him, sought of him a sign from h·. "
15: 7 joy shall be in h· over one sinner "
18 I have sinned against h·, and before "
21 Father, I have sinned against h·, "
16: 17 it is easier for h· and earth to pass, "
17: 24 out of the one part under h·, shineth "
24 unto the other part under h·; "
29 rained fire and brimstone from h·, "
18: 13 lift up so much as his eyes unto h·, "
22 and thou shalt have treasure in h·: "
19: 38 peace in h·, and glory in the highest "
20: 4 baptism of John, was it from h·, or "
5 If we shall say, From h·; he will "
21: 11 great signs shall there be from h·. "
26 the powers of h· shall be shaken. * "
33 H· and earth shall pass away: but "
22: 43 appeared an angel unto him from h·, "
24: 51 from them, and carried up into h·. "
Jo 1: 32 descending from h· like a dove, and "
51 Hereafter ye shall see h· open, and "
3: 13 And no man hath ascended up to h·, "
13 but he that came down from h·, even "
13 even the Son of man which is in h·. "
27 except it be given him from h·. "
31 he that cometh from h· is above all. "
6: 31 He gave them bread from h· to eat "
32 gave you not that bread from h·; "
32 giveth you the true bread from h·. "
33 is he which cometh down from h·, "
38 I came down from h·, not to do mine "
41 the bread which came down from h·. "
42 that he saith, I came down from h·? "
50 bread which cometh down from h·, "
51, 58 bread which came down from h·: "
12: 28 Then came there a voice from h·, "
17: 1 and lifted up his eyes to h·, and said, "
Ac 1: 10 looked stedfastly toward h· as he "
11 why stand ye gazing up into h·? "
11 which is taken up from you into h·, "
11 as ye have seen him go into h·. "
2: 2 there came a sound from h· as of a "
5 men, out of every nation under h·. "
19 I will shew wonders in h· above, and "
3: 21 Whom the h· must receive until the "
4: 12 none other name under h· given "
24 which hast made h·, and earth, and "
7: 42 them up to worship the host of h·; "
49 H· is my throne, and earth is my "
55 looked up stedfastly into h·, and saw "
9: 3 round about him a light from h·: "
10: 11 And saw h· opened, and a certain "
16 vessel was received up again into h·. "
11: 5 let down from h· by four corners; "
9 voice answered me again from h·. "

Ac 11: 10 and all were drawn up again into h·. 3772
14: 15 which made h·, and earth, and the "
17 gave us rain from h·, and fruitful 3771
17: 24 that he is Lord of h· and earth, 3772
22: 6 there shone from h· a great light "
26: 13 I saw in the way a light from h·, 3771
Ro 1: 18 wrath of God is revealed from h· 3772
10: 6 heart, Who shall ascend into h·? "
1Co 8: 5 gods, whether in h· or in earth, as "
15: 47 the second man is the Lord from h·. "
2Co 5: 2 with our house which is from h·: "
12: 2 an one caught up to the third h·. "
Ga 1: 8 we, or an angel from h·, preach any "
Eph 1: 10 both which are in h·, and which * "
3: 15 family in h· and earth is named, "
6: 9 your Master also is in h·; neither "
Ph'p 2: 10 of things in h·, and things in earth 2032
3: 20 For our conversation is in h·; from 3772
Col 1: 5 hope which is laid up for you in h·,* "
16 that are in h·, and that are in earth,* "
20 be things in earth, or things in h·. * "
23 every creature which is under h·; "
4: 1 knowing ye also have a Master in h·. "
1Th 1: 10 And to wait for his Son from h·, "
4: 16 shall descend from h· with a shout, "
2Th 1: 7 Jesus shall be revealed from h· "
Heb 9: 24 but into h· itself, now to appear in "
10: 34 that ye have in h· a better and an * "
12: 23 firstborn, which are written in h·, "
25 from him that speaketh from h·: "
26 shake not the earth only, but also h·. "
Jas 5: 12 swear not neither by h·, neither "
18 and the h· gave rain, and the earth "
1Pet 1: 4 not away, reserved in h· for you, "
12 the Holy Ghost sent down from h·; "
3: 22 Who is gone into h·, and is on the "
2Pe 1: 18 this voice which came from h· we "
1Jo 5: 7 are three that bear record in h·, the* "
Re 3: 12 cometh down out of h· from my God: "
4: 1 behold, a door was opened in h·: "
2 a throne was set in h·, and one sat "
5: 3 And no man in h·, nor in earth, "
13 every creature which is in h·, and "
6: 13 the stars of h· fell unto the earth, "
14 And the h· departed as a scroll when "
8: 1 was silence in h· about the space of "
10 and there fell a great star from h·, "
13 flying through the midst of h·, 3321
9: 1 I saw a star fall from h· unto the 3772
10: 1 angel come down from h·, clothed "
4 I heard a voice from h· saying unto "
5 the earth lifted up his hand to h·, "
6 who created h·, and the things that "
8 voice which I heard from h· spake "
11: 6 These have power to shut h·, that it "
12 heard a great voice from h· saying "
12 they ascended up to h· in a cloud; "
13 and gave glory to the God of h·. "
15 were great voices in h·, saying, The "
19 the temple of God was opened in h·, "
12: 1 appeared a great wonder in h·; "
3 appeared another wonder in h·; "
4 third part of the stars of h·, and did "
7 And there was war in h·: Michael "
8 was their place found any more in h·. "
10 heard a loud voice saying in h·, Now "
13: 6 and them that dwell in h·. "
13 fire come down from h· on the earth "
14: 2 I heard a voice from h·, as the voice "
6 another angel fly in the midst of h·, 3321
7 that made h·, and earth, and the 3772
13 I heard a voice from h· saying unto "
17 out of the temple which is in h·, he "
15: 1 I saw another sign in h·, great and "
5 the tabernacle of the testimony in h· "
16: 11 blasphemed the God of h· because "
17 great voice out of the temple of h·, * "
21 fell upon men a great hail out of h·, "
18: 1 another angel come down from h·, "
4 and I heard another voice from h·, "
5 For her sins have reached unto h·, "
20 Rejoice over her, thou h·, and ye "
19: 1 a great voice of much people in h·, "
11 And I saw h· opened, and behold a "
14 armies which were in h· followed "
17 the fowls that fly in the midst of h·, 3321
20: 1 angel come down from h·, having 3772
9 fire came down from God out of h·, "
11 face the earth and the h· fled away; "
21: 1 I saw a new h· and a new earth: "
1 for the first h· and the first earth "
2 coming down from God out of h·, "
3 heard a great voice out of h· saying,* "
10 holy Jerusalem, descending out of h· "

heavenly

M't 6: 14 your h· Father will also forgive 3770
26 yet your h· Father feedeth them. "
32 h· Father knoweth that ye have need "
15: 13 my h· Father hath not planted, "
18: 35 shall my h· Father do also unto 2032
Lu 2: 13 a multitude of the h· host praising 3770
11: 13 your h· Father give the Holy 1537, 3772
Joh 3: 12 believe, if I tell you of h· things? 2032
Ac 26: 19 disobedient unto the h· vision: 3770
1Co 15: 48 and as is the h·, such are they also 2032
48 such are they also that are h·. "
49 shall also bear the image of the h·. "
Eph 1: 3 spiritual blessings in h· places in "
20 own right hand in the h· places, "
2: 6 together in h· places in Christ Jesus: "
3: 10 powers in h· places might be known "
2Ti 4: 18 preserve me unto his h· kingdom: "
Heb 3: 1 brethren, partakers of the h· calling, "
6: 4 tasted of the h· gift, and were made "
8: 5 example and shadow of h· things, "
9: 23 but the h· things themselves with "

Heb11:16 a better country, that is, an h': 2032
12:22 of the living God, the h' Jerusalem, "

heaven's
M't 19:12 eunuchs for the kingdom of h' sake. 3772

heavens
Ge 2: 1 the h' and the earth were finished,*8064
4 the generations of the h' and of * "
4 God made the earth and the h', * "
De 10:14 and the heaven of h' is the Lord's "
32: 1 Give ear, O ye h', and I will speak; "
33:28 also his h' shall drop down dew. "
J'g 5: 4 and the h' dropped, the clouds also "
2Sa 22:10 He bowed the h' also, and came "
1Ki 8:27 heaven of h' cannot contain thee; "
1Ch 16:26 are idols: but the Lord made the h'. "
31 Let the h' be glad, and let the earth "
27:23 Israel like to the stars of the h'. * "
2Ch 2: 6 heaven of h' cannot contain him? "
6:18 heaven of h' cannot contain thee; "
25 Then hear thou from the h', and * "
33 Then hear thou from the h', even * "
35 hear thou from the h' their prayer * "
39 Then hear thou from the h', even * "
Ezr 9: 6 our trespass is grown up unto the h'. "
Ne 9: 6 hast made heaven, the heaven of h', "
Job 9: 8 Which alone spreadeth out the h', "
14:12 till the h' be no more, they shall not "
15:15 yea, the h' are not clean in his sight. "
20: 6 his excellency mount up to the h', "
26:13 his spirit he hath garnished the h'; "
35: 5 Look unto the h', and see; and "
Ps 2: 4 He that sitteth in the h' shall laugh: "
8: 1 who hast set thy glory above the h'. "
3 When I consider thy h', the work of "
18: 9 He bowed the h' also, and came "
13 The Lord also thundered in the h', "
19: 1 The h' declare the glory of God; "
33: 6 word of the Lord were the h' made; "
36: 5 Thy mercy, O Lord, is in the h'; "
50: 4 He shall call to the h' from above, "
6 h' shall declare his righteousness: "
57: 5 Be thou exalted, O God, above the h'; "
10 For thy mercy is great unto the h', "
11 Be thou exalted, O God, above the h': "
68: 4 extol him that rideth upon the h' *6160
8 h' also dropped at the presence 8064
33 To him that rideth upon the h' of h', "
73: 9 They set their mouth against the h', "
89: 2 shalt thou establish in the very h'. "
5 And the h' shall praise thy wonders, "
11 The h' are thine, the earth also is "
96: 5 are idols: but the Lord made the h'. "
11 Let the h' rejoice, and let the earth "
97: 6 The h' declare his righteousness, "
102:25 and the h' are the work of thy hands. "
103:19 hath prepared his throne in the h'; "
104: 2 stretchest out the h' like a curtain: "
108: 4 For thy mercy is great above the h': "
5 Be thou exalted, O God, above the h': "
113: 4 nations, and his glory above the h'. "
115: 3 our God is in the h': he hath done "
16 heaven, even the h', are the Lord's: "
123: 1 eyes, O thou that dwellest in the h'. "
136: 5 To him that by wisdom made the h': "
144: 5 Bow thy h', O Lord, and come down: "
148: 1 Praise ye the Lord from the h': "
4 Praise him, ye h' of h', and ye waters "
4 and ye waters that be above the h'. "
Pr 3:19 hath he established the h'. "
8:27 he prepared the h', I was there: "
Isa 1: 2 Hear, O h', and give ear, O earth: "
5:30 light is darkened in the h' thereof. *6183
13:13 Therefore I will shake the h', and 8064
34: 4 the h' shall be rolled together as a "
40:22 stretcheth out the h' as a curtain, "
42: 5 he that created the h', and stretched "
44:23 Sing, O ye h'; for the Lord hath "
24 that stretcheth forth the h' alone; "
45: 8 Drop down, ye h', from above, and "
12 have stretched out the h', and all "
18 saith the Lord that created the h'; "
48:13 my right hand hath spanned the h': "
49:13 Sing, O h'; and be joyful, O earth; "
50: 3 I clothe the h' with blackness, and "
51: 6 Lift up your eyes to the h', and look "
6 the h' shall vanish away like smoke, "
13 hath stretched forth the h', and laid "
16 that I may plant the h', and lay the "
55: 9 as the h' are higher than the earth, "
64: 1 Oh that thou wouldest rend the h', "
65:17 I create new h' and a new earth: "
66:22 as the new h' and the new earth, "
Jer 2:12 Be astonished, O ye h', at this, and "
4:23 and the h', and they had no light. "
25 and all the birds of the h' were fled. "
28 mourn, and the h' above be black: "
9:10 the fowl of the h' and the beast are "
10:11 gods that have not made the h' 8065
11 the earth, and from under these h'. "
12 hath stretched out the h' by his 8064
13 is a multitude of waters in the h', "
14:22 rain? or can the h' give showers? "
51:16 is a multitude of waters in the h'; "
La 3:41 with our hands unto God in the h'. "
66 in anger from under the h' of the "
Eze 1: 1 that the h' were opened, and I saw "
Da 4:26 have known that the h' do rule. 8065
Ho 2:21 I will hear the h', and they shall 8064
Joe 2:10 the h' shall tremble: the sun and "
30 I will shew wonders in the h' and in "
3:16 the h' and the earth shall shake: "
Hab 3: 3 His glory covered the h', and the "
Hag 2: 6 I will shake the h', and the earth, "
21 I will shake the h' and the earth; "
Zec 6: 5 These the four spirits of the h', * "
Zec 8:12 and the h' shall give their dew: 8064
12: 1 stretcheth forth the h', and layeth "
M't 3:16 lo, the h' were opened unto him, 3772
24:29 powers of the h' shall be shaken: "
M'r 1:10 he saw the h' opened, and the Spirit "
Lu 12:33 a treasure in the h' that faileth not, "
Ac 2:34 David is not ascended into the h': "
7:56 Behold, I see the h' opened, and the "
2Co 5: 1 made with hands, eternal in the h'. "
Eph 4:10 that ascended up far above all h', "
Heb 1:10 and the h' are the works of thine "
4:14 priest, that is passed into the h', "
7:26 and made higher than the h'; "
8: 1 the throne of the Majesty in the h'; "
9:23 patterns of things in the h' should "
2Pe 3: 5 the word of God the h' were of old, "
7 But the h' and the earth, which are "
10 the h' shall pass away with a great "
12 h' being on fire shall be dissolved, "
13 look for new h' and a new earth, "
Re 12:12 Therefore rejoice, ye h', and ye that "

heave-offering See HEAVE and OFFERING.
heave-shoulder See HEAVE and SHOULDER.

heavier
Job 6: 3 now it would be h' than the sand 3513
23: 2 my stroke is h' than my groaning. "
Pr 27: 3 a fool's wrath is h' than them both. "

heavily
Ex 14:25 wheels, that they drave them h': 3517
Ps 35:14 I bowed down h', as one that *6957
Isa 47: 6 hast thou very h' laid thy yoke. 3513

heaviness
Ezr 9: 5 sacrifice I arose up from my h'; *8589
Job 9:27 I will leave off my h', and comfort *6440
Ps 69:20 and I am full of h': and I looked 5136
119:28 My soul melteth for h': strengthen 8424
Pr 10: 1 foolish son is the h' of his mother. "
12:25 H' in the heart of man maketh it 1674
14:13 but the end of that mirth is h'. 8424
Isa 29: 2 and there shall be h' and sorrow: *8386
61: 3 of praise for the spirit of h'; 3544
Ro 9: 2 great h' and continual sorrow *3077
2Co 2: 1 would not come again to you in h'.* "
Ph'p 2:26 and was full of h', because that * 85
Jas 4: 9 to mourning, and your joy to h'. 2726
1Pe 1: 6 ye are in h' through manifold *3076

heavy See also HEAVIER.
Ex 17:12 Moses' hands were h'; and they 3515
18:18 for this thing is too h' for thee; "
Nu 11:14 alone, because it is too h' for me. "
1Sa 4:18 for he was an old man, and h'. 3513
5: 6 But the hand of the Lord was h' "
11 the hand of God was very h' there. "
2Sa 14:26 because the hair was h' on him, "
1Ki 12: 4 his h' yoke which he put upon us, 3515
10 Thy father made our yoke h', but 3513
11 father did lade you with a h' yoke, 3515
11 My father made your yoke h', and 3513
14: 6 I am sent to thee with h' tidings. 7186
20:43 went to his house h' and displeased, 5620
21: 4 Ahab came into his house h' and "
2Ch 10: 4 his h' yoke that he put upon us, 3515
10 Thy father made our yoke h', but 3513
11 my father put a h' yoke upon you, 3515
14 My father made your yoke h', but 3513
Ne 5:18 bondage was h' upon this people. "
Job 33: 7 neither shall my hand be h' upon "
Ps 32: 4 night thy hand was h' upon me: "
38: 4 over mine head: as an h' burden 3515
4 burden they are too h' for me. 3513
Pr 25:20 that singeth songs to an h' heart. 7451
27: 3 stone is h', and the sand weighty; 3514
31: 6 unto those that be of h' hearts. *4751
Isa 6:10 make their ears h', and shut their 3513
24:20 transgression thereof shall be h' "
30:27 and the burden thereof is h': *3514
46: 1 your carriages were h' loaden: * "
58: 6 to undo the h' burdens, and to let *4133
59: 1 neither his ear h', that it cannot 3513
La 3: 7 get out: he hath made my chain h'. "
M't 11:28 all ye that labour and are h' laden, "
23: 4 For they bind h' burdens and 926
26:37 began to be sorrowful and very h'. * 85
43 asleep again: for their eyes were h'. 916
M'r 14:33 be sore amazed, and to be very h';* 85
40 asleep again, for their eyes were h', 916
Lu 9:32 were with him were h' with sleep: "

Heber (*he'-bur*) See also EBER; HEBER'S; HEBERITES.
Ge 46:17 and the sons of Beriah; H', and 2268
Nu 26:45 the sons of Beriah: of H', the "
J'g 4:11 Now H' the Kenite, which was of "
17 the tent of Jael the wife of H' the "
17 and the house of H' of Kenite. "
5:24 Jael the wife of H' the Kenite be, "
1Ch 4:18 and H' the father of Socho, and "
5:13 Jachan, and Zia and H', seven. 5677
7:31 And the sons of Beriah; H', 2268
32 And H' begat Japhlet, and Shomer, "
8:17 Meshullam, and Hezeki, and H', "
22 And Ishpan, and H', and Eliel, *5677
Lu 3:35 Phalec, which was the son of H', *1443

Heberites (*he'-bur-ites*)
Nu 26:45 of Heber, the family of the H': of 2277

Heber's (*he'-burs*)
J'g 4:21 Then Jael H' wife took a nail of 2268

Hebrew (*he'-broo*) See also HEBREWESS; HEBREWS.
Ge 14:13 escaped, and told Abram the H'; 5680
39:14 he hath brought in a H' unto us "
17 The H' servant, which thou hast "
41:12 with us a young man, an H', "
Ex 1:15 Egypt spake to the H' midwives, "
Ex 1:16 of a midwife to the H' women, 5680
19 Because the H' women are not as "
2: 7 to thee a nurse of the H' women, "
11 spied an Egyptian smiting a H', "
21: 2 If thou buy an H' servant, six years "
De 15:12 an H' man, or an H' woman, "
Jer 34: 9 being an H' or an Hebrewess, go "
14 every man his brother an H', which "
Jon 1: 9 And he said unto them, I am a H'; "
Lu 23:38 of Greek, and Latin, and H', *1444
Joh 5: 2 called in the H' tongue Bethesda, 1447
19:13 Pavement, but in the H', Gabbatha. "
17 which is called in the H' Golgotha: "
20 written in H', and Greek, and Latin. "
Ac 21:40 spake unto them in the H' tongue, 1446
22: 2 that he spake in the H' tongue to "
26:14 saying in the H' tongue, Saul, Saul, "
Ph'p 3: 5 of Benjamin, an H' of the Hebrews; "
Re 9:11 name in the H' tongue is Abaddon, 1447
16:16 in the H' tongue Armageddon. "

Hebrewess (*he'-broo-ess*)
Jer 34: 9 being an Hebrew or an H', go free; 5680

Hebrews (*he'-brooz*) See also HEBREWS'.
Ge 40:15 away out of the land of the H': 5680
43:32 might not eat bread with the H'; "
Ex 2:13 two men of the H' strove together: "
3:18 God of the H' hath met with us: "
5: 3 God of the H' hath met with us: "
7:16 The Lord God of the H' hath sent "
9: 1, 13 saith the Lord God of the H', "
10: 3 Thus saith the Lord God of the H', "
1Sa 4: 6 great shout in the camp of the H'? "
9 that ye be not servants unto the H' "
13: 3 all the land, saying, Let the H' hear. "
7 some of the H' went over Jordan "
19 the H' make them swords or spears: "
14:11 the H' come forth out of the holes "
21 H' that were with the Philistines "
29: 3 What do these H' here? And "
Ac 6: 1 of the Grecians against the H', 1445
2Co 11:22 Are they H'? so am I. Are they "
Ph'p 3: 5 of Benjamin, an Hebrew of the H'; "
Heb *subscr.* Written to the H' from Italy

Hebrews' (*he'-brooz*)
Ex 2: 6 This is one of the H' children. 5680

Hebron (*he'-brun*) See also HEBRONITES.
Ge 13:18 plain of Mamre, which is in H', 2275
23: 2 same is H' in the land of Canaan: "
19 same is H' in the land of Canaan. "
35:27 unto the city of Arbah, which is H', "
37:14 So he sent him out of the vale of H', "
Ex 6:18 Amram, and Izhar, and H', and "
Nu 3:19 Amram, and Izehar, H', and Uzziel. "
13:22 by the south, and came unto H'; "
22 Now H' was built seven years before "
Jos 10: 3 sent unto Hoham king of H', and "
5 king of Jerusalem, the king of H', "
23 king of Jerusalem the king of H', "
36 and all Israel with him, unto H'; "
39 as he had done to H', so he did to "
11:21 from the mountains, from H', from "
12:10 Jerusalem, one; the king of H', one; "
14:13 Jephunneh H' for an inheritance. "
14 H' therefore became the "
15 name of H' before was Kirjath-arba; "
15:13 father of Anak, which city is H'. "
54 and Kirjath-arba, which is H', and "
19:28 And H', and Rehob, and Hammon, "
20: 7 and Kirjath-arba, which is H', "
21:11 H', in the hill country of Judah, "
13 H' with her suburbs, to be a city "
J'g 1:10 the Canaanites that dwelt in H', "
10 now the name of H' before was "
20 And they gave H' unto Caleb, as "
16: 3 the top of an hill that is before H'. "
1Sa 30:31 to them which were in H', and to "
2Sa 2: 1 I go up? And he said, Unto H'. "
3 and they dwelt in the cities of H'. "
11 David was king in H' over the house "
32 they came to H' at break of day. "
3: 2 unto David were sons born in H': "
5 These were born to David in H'. "
19 to speak in the ears of David in H' "
20 So Abner came to David to H', and "
22 Abner was not with David in H'; "
27 when Abner was returned to H', "
32 And they buried Abner in H': and "
4: 1 heard that Abner was dead in H', "
8 of Ish-bosheth unto David to H', "
12 hanged them up over the pool in H'. "
12 it in the sepulchre of Abner in H'. "
5: 1 tribes of Israel to David unto H', "
3 of Israel came to the king to H'; "
3 made a league with them in H' "
5 In H' he reigned over Judah seven "
13 after he was come from H'; and "
15: 7 I have vowed unto the Lord, in H'. "
9 peace. So he arose, and went to H'. "
10 shall say, Absalom reigneth in H'. "
1Ki 2:11 seven years reigned he in H', and "
1Ch 2:42 sons of Mareshah the father of H'. "
43 And the sons of H'; Korah, and "
3: 1 which were born unto him in H'; "
4 These six were born unto him in H'; "
6: 2 Kohath; Amram, Izhar, and H', and "
18 were, Amram, and Izhar, and H', "
55 gave them H' in the land of Judah, "
57 namely, H', the city of refuge, "
11: 1 themselves to David unto H', "
3 elders of Israel to the king to H'; "
3 made a covenant with them in H' "
12:23 came to David to H', to turn the "
38 came with a perfect heart to H', to "
15: 9 Of the sons of H'; Eliel the chief, "

1Ch 23:12 Amram, Izhar, H', and Uzziel, four. 2275
19 Of the sons of H'; Jeriah the first, "
24:23 And the sons of H'; Jeriah the
29:27 seven years reigned he in H', and 2275
2Ch 11:10 Zorah, and Aijalon, and H', which "

Hebronites (*he'-brun-ites*)
Nu 3:27 and the family of the H', and the 2276
26:58 the family of the H', the family of "
1Ch 26:23 and the Izharites, the H', and the "
30 And of the H', Hashabiah and his "
31 Among the H' was Jerijah the chief, "
31 even among the H', according to "

hedge See also HEDGED; HEDGES.
Job 1:10 not thou made an h' about him, 7753
Pr 15:19 slothful man is as an h' of thorns: 4881
Ec 10: 8 whoso breaketh an h', a serpent *1447
Isa 5: 5 I will take away the h' thereof, 4881
Eze 13: 5 the h' for the house of Israel ††1447
22:30 them, that should make up the h',†‡ "
Ho 2: 6 I will h' up thy way with thorns, 7753
Mic 7: 4 upright is sharper than a thorn h': 4534
M'r 12: 1 and set an h' about it, and digged 5418

hedged
Job 3:23 is hid, and whom God hath h' in? 5526
La 3: 7 He hath h' me about, that I cannot *1443
M't 21:33 a vineyard, and h' it round *5418, 4060

hedges
1Ch 4:23 that dwelt among plants and h': *1448
Ps 80:12 thou then broken down her h', *1447
89:40 Thou hast broken down all his h'; 1448
Jer 49: 3 and run to and fro by the h'; for * "
Na 3:17 which camp in the h' in the cold "
Lu 14:23 Go out into the highways and h', 5418

heed
Ge 31:24 Take h' that thou speak not to 8104
29 Take thou h' that thou speak not "
Ex 10:28 Get thee from me, take h' to thyself, "
19:12 Take h' to yourselves, that ye go not "
34:12 Take h' to thyself, lest thou make "
Nu 23:12 Must I not take h' to speak that "
De 2: 4 take ye good h' unto yourselves "
4: 9 Only take h' to thyself, and keep thy "
15 Take ye therefore good h' unto "
23 Take h' unto yourselves, lest ye "
11:16 Take h' to yourselves, that your "
12:13 Take h' to thyself that thou offer not "
19 Take h' to thyself that thou forsake "
30 Take h' to thyself that thou be not "
24: 8 Take h' in the plague of leprosy, "
27: 9 Take h', and hearken, O Israel; *5535
Jos 22: 5 But take diligent h' to do the 8104
23:11 Take good h' therefore unto your "
1Sa 19: 2 take h' to thyself until the morning, "
2Sa 20:10 Amasa took no h' to the sword that "
1Ki 2: 4 If thy children take h' to their way, "
8:25 thy children take h' to their way, "
2Ki 10:31 Jehu took no h' to walk in the law * "
1Ch 22:13 prosper if thou takest h' to fulfil * "
28:10 Take h' now; for the Lord hath 7200
2Ch 6:16 thy children take h' to their way 8104
19: 6 Take h' what ye do: for ye judge *7200
7 take h' and do it: for there is no 8104
33: 8 so that they will take h' to do all "
Ezr 4:22 Take h' now that ye fail not to do 2095
Job 36:21 Take h', regard not iniquity: for 8104
Ps 39: 1 I said, I will take h' to my ways, "
119: 9 by taking h' thereto according to "
Pr 17: 4 wicked doer giveth h' to false lips; 7181
Ec 7:21 Also take no h' unto all words 5414, 3820
12: 9 he gave good h', and sought out, * 238
Isa 7: 4 Take h', and be quiet; fear him, 8104
21: 7 hearkened diligently with much h': 7182
Jer 9: 4 Take ye h' every one of his 8104
17:21 Take h' to yourselves, and bear no "
18:18 us not give h' to any of his words. 7181
19 Give h' to me, O Lord, and hearken "
Ho 4:10 have left off to take h' to the Lord. 8104
Mal 2:15 Therefore take h' to your spirit, and "
16 therefore take h' to your spirit, that "
M't 6: 1 Take h' that ye do not your alms 4337
16: 6 Take h' and beware of the leaven 3708
18:10 Take h' that ye despise not one of * "
24: 4 Take h' that no man deceive you. 991
M'r 4:24 Take h' what ye hear: with what "
8:15 Take h', beware of the leaven of 3708
13: 5 Take h' lest any man deceive you: 991
9 take h' to yourselves: for they shall "
23 take ye h': behold, I have foretold "
33 Take ye h', watch and pray: for ye "
Lu 8:18 Take h' therefore how ye hear: for "
11:35 Take h' therefore that the light *4648
12:15 Take h',... beware of covetousness: 3708
17: 3 Take h' to yourselves: If thy 4337
21: 8 Take h' that ye be not deceived: 991
34 take h' to yourselves, lest at any 4337
Ac 3: 5 he gave h' unto them, expecting to 1907
5:35 take h' to yourselves what ye 4337
8: 6 accord gave h' unto those things "
10 To whom they all gave h', from the "
20:28 Take h' therefore unto yourselves, "
22:26 Take h' what thou doest: for this *3708
Ro 11:21 take h' lest he also spare not thee.*
1Co 3:10 every man take h' how he buildeth 991
8: 9 But take h' lest by any means this "
10:12 thinketh he standeth take h' lest he "
Ga 5:15 take h' that ye be not consumed one "
Col 4:17 Take h' to the ministry which thou "
1Ti 1: 4 give h' to fables and endless 4337
4: 1 giving h' to seducing spirits, and "
16 Take h' unto thyself, and unto the 1907
Tit 1:14 Not giving h' to Jewish fables, and 4337
Heb 2: 1 the more earnest h' to the things "
3:12 Take h' brethren, lest there be in 991
2Pe 1:19 ye do well that ye take h', as unto 4337

heel See also HEELS.
Ge 3:15 head, and thou shalt bruise his h'. 6119
25:26 his hand took hold on Esau's h'; "
Job 18: 9 The gin shall take him by the h', "
Ps 41: 9 hath lifted up his h' against me. "
Ho 12: 3 He took his brother by the h' in the 6117
Joh 13:18 hath lifted up his h' against me. 4418

heels
Ge 49:17 adder ...that biteth the horse h', 6119
Job 13:27 thou settest a print upon the h' of *8328
Ps 49: 5 iniquity of my h' shall compass 6120
Jer 13:22 discovered, and thy h' made bare. 6119

Hegai (*he'-gahee*) See also HEGE.
Es 2: 8 the palace, to the custody of H', 1896
8 custody of H', keeper of the women. "
15 H' the king's chamberlain, the "

Hege (*he'-ghe*) See also HEGAI.
Es 2: 3 unto the custody of H' the king's *1896

heifer See also HEIFER'S.
Ge 15: 9 Take me an h' of three years old, 5697
Nu 19: 2 bring thee a red h' without spot, 6510
5 one shall burn the h' in his sight; "
6 the midst of the burning of the h'. "
9 shall gather up the ashes of the h', "
10 gathereth the ashes of the h' shall "
17 ashes of the burnt h' of purification "
De 21: 3 elders of that city shall take an h', 5697
4 down the h' unto a rough valley, "
6 shall wash their hands over the h' "
J'g 14:18 If ye had not plowed with my h', ye "
1Sa 16: 2 Take an h' with thee, and say, I am "
Isa 15: 5 unto Zoar, an h' of three years old: * "
Jer 46:20 Egypt is like a very fair h', but "
48:34 voice,...as an h' of three years old: * "
50:11 ye are grown fat as the h' at grass, "
Ho 4:16 slideth back as a backsliding h': 6510
10:11 Ephraim is as an h' that is taught, 5697
Heb 9:13 the ashes of an h' sprinkling the 1151

heifer's
De 21: 4 shall strike off the h' neck there 5697

height See also HEIGHTS.
Ge 6:15 and the h' of it thirty cubits. 6967
Ex 25:10, 23 a cubit and a half the h' thereof. "
27: 1 the h' thereof shall be three cubits. "
18 and the h' five cubits of fine twined "
30: 2 two cubits shall be the h' thereof: "
37: 1 and a cubit and a half the h' of it: "
10 a cubit and a half the h' thereof: "
25 and two cubits was the h' of it; the "
38: 1 and three cubits the h' thereof. "
18 the h' in the breadth was five cubits "
1Sa 16: 7 or on the h' of his stature; 1364
17: 4 whose h' was six cubits and a span. 1363
1Ki 6: 2 and the h' thereof thirty cubits. 6967
20 and twenty cubits in the h' thereof: "
26 The h' of the one cherub was ten "
7: 2 the h' thereof thirty cubits, upon "
16 the h' of the one chapiter was five "
16 the h' of the other chapiter was five "
23 all about, his h' was five cubits: and "
27 thereof, and three cubits the h' of it. "
32 the h' of a wheel was a cubit and "
2Ki 19:23 come up to the h' of the mountains, 4791
25:17 h' of the one pillar was eighteen 6967
17 the h' of the chapiter three cubits; "
2Ch 3: 4 the h' was an hundred and twenty: 1363
4: 1 and ten cubits the h' thereof. 6967
2 and five cubits the h' thereof; and a "
33:14 and raised it up a very great h', 1361
Ezr 6: 3 the h' thereof threescore cubits, 7312
Job 22:12 Is not God in the h' of heaven? and 1363
12 behold the h' of the stars, how high 7218
Ps 102:19 down from the h' of his sanctuary; 4791
Pr 25: 3 The heaven for h', and the earth 7312
Isa 7:11 in the depth; or in the h' above. 1361
37:24 come up to the h' of the mountains, 4791
24 will enter into the h' of his border, "
Jer 31:12 come and sing in the h' of Zion, and "
49:16 rock, that holdest the h' of the hill; "
51:53 should fortify the h' of her strength, "
52:21 the h' of one pillar was eighteen 6967
22 and the h' of one chapiter was five "
Eze 17:23 In the mountain of the h' of Israel 4791
19:11 and she appeared in her h' with the 1363
20:40 in the mountain of the h' of Israel, 4791
31: 5 his h' was exalted above all the *6967
10 thou hast lifted up thyself in h', * "
10 and his heart is lifted up in his h'; 1363
14 exalt themselves for their h', *6967
14 their trees stand up in their h', 1363
32: 5 and fill the valleys with thy h'. 7419
40: 5 one reed; and the h', one reed. 6967
41: 8 I saw also the h' of the house *1364
Da 3: 1 whose h' was threescore cubits, 7314
4:10 earth, and the h' thereof was great. "
11 the h' thereof reached unto heaven, "
20 whose h' reached unto the heaven, "
Am 2: 9 Amorite before them, whose h' was 1363
9 was like the h' of the cedars, and "
Ro 8:39 Nor h', nor depth, nor any other 5313
Eph 3:18 and length, and depth, and h'; 5311
Re 21:16 breadth and the h' of it are equal. "

heights
Ps 148: 1 the heavens: praise him in the h'. 4791
Isa 14:14 ascend above the h' of the clouds: 1116

heinous
Job 31:11 For this is an h' crime; yea, it is an 2154

heir See also HEIRS.
Ge 15: 3 one born in my house is mine h'. 3423
4 This shall not be thine h'; but he "
4 thine own bowels shall be thine h'. "
21:10 of this bondwoman shall not be h' "
2Sa 14: 7 and we will destroy the h' also: "
Pr 30:23 handmaid that is h' to her mistress. 3423
Jer 49: 1 Hath Israel no sons? hath he no h'? "
2 then shall Israel be h' unto them * "
Mic 1:15 Yet will I bring an h' unto thee, * "
M't 21:38 This is the h'; come, let us kill him, 2818
M'r 12: 7 This is the h'; come, let us kill him, "
Lu 20:14 This is the h'; come, let us kill him, "
Ro 4:13 he should be the h' of the world, "
Ga 4: 1 That the h', as long as he is a child, "
7 then an h' of God through Christ. "
30 shall not be h' with the son of the *2816
Heb 1: 2 whom...appointed h' of all things, 2818
11: 7 and became h' of the righteousness "

heirs See also FELLOWHEIRS; JOINT-HEIRS.
Jer 49: 2 unto them that were his h', saith *3423
Ro 4:14 if they which are of the law be h', 2818
8:17 And if children, then h'; h' of God, "
Ga 3:29 and h' according to the promise. "
Tit 3: 7 by his grace, we should be made h' "
Heb 1:14 them who shall be h' of salvation? *2816
6:17 to shew unto the h' of promise 2818
11: 9 h' with him of the same promise: 4789
Jas 2: 5 rich in faith, and h' of the kingdom 2818
1Pe 3: 7 h' together of the grace of life; *4789

Helah (*he'-lah*)
1Ch 4: 5 had two wives, H', and Naarah. 2458
7 the sons of H' were, Zereth, and "

Helam (*he'-lam*)
2Sa 10:16 the river: and they came to H': and 2431
17 passed over Jordan, and came to H'. "

Helbah (*hel'-bah*)
J'g 1:31 nor of H', nor of Aphik, nor of 2462

Helbon (*hel'-bon*)
Eze 27:18 in the wine of H', and white wool. 2463

held See also BEHELD; HOLDEN; UPHELD; WITHHELD.
Ge 24:21 wondering at her h' his peace, to *2790
34: 5 and Jacob h' his peace until they "
48:17 and he h' up his father's hand, to 8557
Ex 17:11 when Moses h' up his hand, that 7311
36:12 the loops h' one curtain to another. *6901
Le 10: 3 glorified. And Aaron h' his peace. 1826
Nu 30: 7 and h' his peace at her in the day *2790
11 heard it, and h' his peace at her, "
14 he h' his peace at her in the day he "
J'g 7:20 h' the lamps in their left hands, 2388
16:26 unto the lad that h' him by the hand, "
Ru 3:15 And when she h' it, he measured 270
1Sa 10:27 no presents. But he h' his peace. 2790
25:36 behold, he h' a feast in his house, "
2Sa 18:16 Israel: for Joab h' back the people. 2820
1Ki 8:65 at that time Solomon h' a feast, 6213
2Ki 18:36 But the people h' their peace, and 2790
2Ch 4: 5 received and h' three thousand 3557
Ne 4:16 half of them h' both the spears, 2388
17 with the other hand h' a weapon. "
21 half of them h' the spears from "
5: 8 Then h' they their peace, and 2790
Es 5: 2 king h' out to Esther the golden 3447
7: 4 I had h' my tongue, although 2790
8: 4 the king h' out the golden sceptre 3447
Job 23:11 My foot hath h' his steps, his 270
29:10 The nobles h' their peace, and *2244
Ps 32: 9 whose mouth must be h' in with *1102
39: 2 I h' my peace, even from good; 2814
94:18 thy mercy, O Lord, h' me up. 5582
Ca 3: 4 I h' him, and would not let him go, 270
7: 5 the king is h' in the galleries. * 631
Isa 36:21 they h' their peace, and answered 2790
57:11 have not I h' my peace even of old, 2814
Jer 50:33 took them captives h' them fast; *2388
Da 12: 7 when he h' up his right hand and 7311
M't 12:14 and h' a council against him, how *2983
26:63 But Jesus h' his peace. And the 4623
28: 9 they came and h' him by the feet, *2902
M'k 3: 4 or to kill? But they h' their peace. 4623
9:34 But they h' their peace: for by the "
14:61 But he h' his peace, and answered "
15: 1 the chief priests h' a consultation 4160
Lu 14: 4 And they h' their peace. And he 2270
20:26 at his answer, and h' their peace. 4601
22:63 the men that h' Jesus mocked him, 4912
Ac 3:11 man which was healed h' Peter 2902
11:18 they h' their peace, and glorified 2270
14: 4 and part h' with the Jews, and part 2258
15:13 and after they had h' their peace, 4601
Ro 7: 6 being dead wherein we were h'. *2722
Re 6: 9 for the testimony which they h': 2192

Heldai (*hel'-dahee*) See also HELED; HELEM.
1Ch 27:15 H' the Netophathite, of Othniel: 2469
Zec 6:10 of them of the captivity, even of H', "

heldest See WITHHELDEST.

Heleb (*he'-leb*) See also HELED.
2Sa 23:29 H' the son of Baanah, a 2460

Heled (*he'-led*) See also HELEB; HELDAI.
1Ch 11:30 H' the son of Baanah the 2466

Helek (*he'-lek*) See also HELEKITES.
Nu 26:30 of Helek, the family of the Helekites: 2507
Jos 17: 2 and for the children of H', and for "

Helekites (*he'-lek-ites*)
Nu 26:30 of Helek, the family of the H': 2516

Helem (*he'-lem*) See also HELDAI.
1Ch 7:35 And the sons of his brother H'; 2494
Zec 6:14 And the crowns shall be to H', "

Heleph (*he'-lef*)
Jos 19:33 And their coast was from H', 2501

Helez (*he'-lez*)
2Sa 23:26 H' the Paltite, Ira the son of 2503
1Ch 2:39 Azariah begat H', and H' begat "
11:27 the Harorite, H' the Pelonite, "
27:10 seventh month was H' the Pelonite, "

Heli (*he'-li*) See also ELI.
Lu 3:23 Joseph, which was the son of *H'*. *2242*
Helkai (*hel'-kahee*)
Ne 12:15 Of Harim, Adna; of Meraioth, *H'*; 2517
Helkath (*hel'-kath*) See also HELKATH-HAZZURIM; HUKOK.
Jos 19:25 their border was *H'*, and Hali, and 2520
21:31 *H'* with her suburbs, and Rehob "
Helkath-hazzurim (*hel''-kath-haz'-zu-rim*)
2Sa 2:16 that place was called *H'*, which is 2521
hell
De 32:22 shall burn unto the lowest *h'*, †‡7585
2Sa 22: 6 The sorrows of *h'* compassed me * "
Job 11: 8 deeper than *h'*; what canst thou * "
26: 6 *H'* is naked before him, and * "
Ps 9:17 The wicked shall be turned into *h'*,* "
16:10 thou wilt not leave my soul in *h'*; * "
18: 5 The sorrows of *h'* compassed me * "
55:15 let them go down quick into *h'*: †‡ "
86:13 my soul from the lowest *h'*. †‡ "
116: 3 the pains of *h'* gat hold upon me: * "
139: 8 if I make my bed in *h'*, behold, * "
Pr 5: 5 death; her steps take hold on *h'*. * "
7:27 Her house is the way to *h'*, going * "
9:18 her guests are in the depths of *h'*.* "
15:11 *H'* and destruction are before the * "
24 he may depart from *h'* beneath. * "
23:14 and shalt deliver his soul from *h'*.* "
27:20 *H'* and destruction are never full; * "
Isa 5:14 Therefore *h'* hath enlarged herself,‡ "
14: 9 *H'* from beneath is moved for thee ‡ "
15 thou shalt be brought down to *h'*, ‡ "
28:15 and with *h'* are we at agreement; ‡ "
18 agreement with *h'* shall not stand; ‡ "
57: 9 didst debase thyself even unto *h'*. ‡ "
Eze 31:16 I cast him down to *h'* with them ‡ "
17 They also went down into *h'* with ‡ "
32:21 speak to him out of the midst of *h'*‡ "
27 gone down to *h'* with their weapons‡ "
Am 9: 2 Though they dig into *h'*, thence ‡ "
Jon 2: 2 out of the belly of *h'* cried I, and ‡ "
Hab 2: 5 who enlargeth his desire as *h'*, and‡ "
M't 5:22 fool, shall be in danger of *h'* fire. *1067*
29, 30 body should be cast into *h'*. "
10:28 to destroy both soul and body in *h'*. "
11:23 shalt be brought down to *h'*: for if* *86*
16:18 and the gates of *h'* shall not prevail* "
18: 9 two eyes to be cast into *h'* fire. *1067*
23:15 more the child of *h'* than yourselves. "
33 can ye escape the damnation of *h'*? "
M'r 9:43 than having two hands to go into *h'*, "
45 having two feet to be cast into *h'*, "
47 having two eyes to be cast into *h'* fire "
Lu 10:15 heaven, shalt be thrust down to *h'*.* *86*
12: 5 killed hath power to cast into *h'*; *1067*
16:23 in *h'* he lift up his eyes, being in * *86*
Ac 2:27 thou wilt not leave my soul in *h'*, * "
31 that his soul was not left in *h'*, * "
Jas 3: 6 nature; and it is set on fire of *h'*. *1067*
2Pe 2: 4 sinned, but cast them down to *h'*, *5020*
Re 1:18 have the keys of *h'* and of death.* *86*
6: 8 Death, and *H'* followed with him.* "
20:13 death and *h'* delivered up the dead* "
14 death and *h'* were cast into the lake* "
hell-fire See HELL and FIRE.
helm
Jas 3: 4 turned about with a very small *h'*,*4079*
helmet See also HELMETS.
1Sa 17: 5 had an *h'* of brass upon his head, 3553
38 put an *h'* of brass upon his head; 6959
Isa 59:17 an *h'* of salvation upon his head; 3553
Eze 23:24 buckler and shield and *h'* round 6959
27:10 hanged the shield and *h'* in thee; 3553
38: 5 all of them with shield and *h'*: "
Eph 6:17 And take the *h'* of salvation, and *4030*
1Th 5: 8 and for an *h'*, the hope of salvation. "
helmets
2Ch 26:14 spears, and *h'*, and habergeons, 3553
Jer 46: 4 stand forth with your *h'*; furbish "
Helon (*he'-lon*)
Nu 1: 9 Of Zebulun; Eliab the son of *H'*. 2497
2: 7 Eliab the son of *H'* shall be captain "
7:24 Eliab the son of *H'*, prince of the "
29 the offering of Eliab the son of *H'*. "
10:16 of Zebulun was Eliab the son of *H'*. "
help See also HELPED; HELPETH; HELPING; HELPS; HOLPEN.
Ge 2:18 will make him an *h'* meet for him. 5828
20 was not found an *h'* meet for him. "
49:25 of thy father, who shall *h'* thee; 5826
Ex 18: 4 of my father, said he, was mine *h'*, 5828
23: 5 and wouldest forbear to *h'* him, †5800
5 thou shalt surely *h'* with him. ‡ "
De 22: 4 shalt surely *h'* him to lift them up 6965
32:38 let them rise up and *h'* you, and 5826
33: 7 an *h'* to him from his enemies. 5828
26 rideth upon the heaven in thy *h'*, "
29 Lord, the shield of thy *h'*, and who is "
Jos 1:14 men of valour, and *h'* them; 5826
10: 4 Come up unto me, and *h'* me, that "
6 us quickly, and save us, and *h'* us: "
33 of Gezer came up to *h'* Lachish; "
J'g 5:23 came not to the *h'* of the Lord, 5833
23 *h'* of the Lord against the mighty. "
1Sa 11: 9 the sun be hot, ye shall have *h'*. *8668
2Sa 10:11 for me, then thou shalt *h'* me: 3447
11 thee, then I will come and *h'* thee. 3467
19 Syrians feared to *h'* the children of "
14: 4 did obeisance, and said, *H'*, O king. "
2Ki 6:26 him, saying, *H'*, my lord, O king. "
27 not *h'* thee, whence shall I *h'* thee? "
1Ch 12:17 come peaceably unto me to *h'* me, 5826
22 day there came to David to *h'* him, "
1Ch 18: 5 Syrians of Damascus came to *h'* *5826
19:12 for me, then thou shalt *h'* me: but 8668
12 strong for thee, then I will *h'* thee. 3467
19 Syrians *h'* the children of Ammon "
22:17 princes of Israel to *h'* Solomon 5826
2Ch 14:11 Lord, it is nothing with thee to *h'*, "
11 no power: *h'* us, O Lord our God; "
19: 2 Shouldest thou *h'* the ungodly, "
20: 4 together, to ask *h'* of the Lord: even "
9 then thou wilt hear and *h'*. *3467
25: 8 God hath power to *h'*, and to cast 5826
26:13 to *h'* the king against the enemy. "
28:16 unto the kings of Assyria to *h'* him. "
23 the gods of the kings of Syria to *h'** "
23 I sacrifice to them, that they may *h'* "
29:34 brethren the Levites did *h'* them, 2388
32: 3 the city: and they did *h'* him. *5826
8 with us is the Lord our God to *h'* us, "
Ezr 1: 4 of his place *h'* him with silver, 5375
8:22 of soldiers and horsemen to *h'* us 5826
Job 6:13 Is not my *h'* in me? and is wisdom 5833
8:20 neither will he *h'* the evil doers: *2388
29:12 and him that had none to *h'* him. 5826
31:21 when I saw my *h'* in the gate: 5833
Ps 3: 2 soul, There is no *h'* for him in God. 3444
12: 1 *H'*, Lord; for the godly man 3467
20: 2 Send thee *h'* from the sanctuary, 5828
22:11 trouble is near; there is none to *h'*. 5826
19 O my strength, haste thee to *h'* me. 5833
27: 9 thou hast been my *h'*; leave me not, "
33:20 Lord: he is our *h'* and our shield. 5828
35: 2 buckler, and stand up for mine *h'*. 5833
37:40 And the Lord shall *h'* them, and *5826
38:22 Make haste to *h'* me, O Lord my 5833
40:13 me: O Lord, make haste to *h'* me. "
17 thou art my *h'* and my deliverer; "
42: 5 for the *h'* of his countenance. †3444
44:26 Arise for our *h'*, and redeem us 5833
46: 1 a very present *h'* in trouble. "
5 God shall *h'* her, and that right 5826
59: 4 fault: awake to *h'* me, and behold. 7125
60:11 Give us *h'* from trouble: for vain 5833
11 trouble: for vain is the *h'* of man. 8668
63: 7 Because thou hast been my *h'*, 5833
70: 1 me; make haste to *h'* me, O Lord. "
5 thou art my *h'* and my deliverer; 5828
71:12 O my God, make haste for my *h'*. 5833
79: 9 *H'* us, O God of our salvation, for 5826
89:19 I have laid *h'* upon one that is 5828
94:17 Unless the Lord had been my *h'*, 5833
107:12 fell down, and there was none to *h'*. 5826
108:12 Give us *h'* from trouble: for vain 5833
12 trouble: for vain is the *h'* of man. 8668
109:26 *H'* me, O Lord my God: O save me 5826
115: 9, 10, 11 is their *h'* and their shield. 5828
118: 7 my part with them that *h'* me: 5826
119:86 persecute me wrongfully; *h'* thou "
173 Let thine hand *h'* me; for I have * "
175 thee; and let thy judgments *h'* me. "
121: 1 hills, from which cometh my *h'*. 5828
2 My *h'* cometh from the Lord, which "
124: 8 Our *h'* is in the name of the Lord, "
146: 3 son of man, in whom there is no *h'*. 8668
5 hath the God of Jacob for his *h'*, 5828
Ec 4:10 he hath not another to *h'* him up.* 6965
Isa 10: 3 to whom will ye flee for *h'*? and 5833
20: 6 whither we flee for *h'* to be delivered* "
30: 5 be an *h'* nor profit, but a shame, 5828
7 For the Egyptians shall *h'* in vain, *5826
31: 1 them that go down to Egypt for *h'*; 5833
2 the *h'* of them that work iniquity. "
41:10 I will *h'* thee; yea, I will uphold 5826
13 unto thee, Fear not; I will *h'* thee. "
14 I will *h'* thee, saith the Lord, and "
44: 2 from the womb, which will *h'* thee; "
50: 7 the Lord God will *h'* me; therefore "
9 Behold, the Lord God will *h'* me; "
63: 5 I looked, and there was none to *h'*; "
Jer 37: 7 which is come forth to *h'* you, 5833
La 1: 7 the enemy, and none did *h'* her: 5826
4:17 eyes as yet failed for our vain *h'*: 5833
Eze 12:14 all that are about him to *h'* him, 5828
32:21 midst of hell with them that *h'* him: 5826
Da 10:13 of the chief princes, came to *h'* me; "
11:34 they shall be holpen with a little *h'*: 5828
45 to his end, and none shall *h'* him. 5826
Ho 13: 9 thyself; but in me is thine *h'*. 5828
M't 15:25 worshipped him, saying, Lord, *h'* me. *997*
M'r 9:22 have compassion on us, and *h'* us. "
24 I believe; *h'* thou mine unbelief. "
Lu 5: 7 that they should come and *h'* them. *4815*
10:40 bid her therefore that she *h'* me. *4878*
Ac 16: 9 over into Macedonia, and *h'* us. *997*
21:28 Crying out, Men of Israel, *h'*: This "
26:22 Having therefore obtained *h'* of *1947*
Ph'p 4: 3 *h'* those women which laboured *4815*
Heb 4:16 find grace to *h'* in time of need. *996*
helped See also HOLPEN.
Ex 2:17 Moses stood up and *h'* them, and 3467
1Sa 7:12 Hitherto hath the Lord *h'* us. 5826
1Ki 1: 7 and they following Adonijah *h'* him. "
20:16 the thirty and two kings that *h'* him. "
1Ch 5:20 And they were *h'* against them, and "
12:19 Saul to battle: but they *h'* them not: "
21 And they *h'* David against the band "
15:26 when God *h'* the Levites that bare "
2Ch 18:31 cried out, and the Lord *h'* him; and "
20:23 every one *h'* to destroy another. "
26: 7 God *h'* him against the Philistines, "
15 marvellously *h'*, till he was strong. "
28:21 king of Assyria: but he *h'* him not. 5833
Ezr 10:15 and Shabbethai the Levite *h'* them. 5826
Es 9: 3 officers of the king, *h'* the Jews; 5375
Job 26: 2 thou *h'* him that is without power? 5826
Ps 28: 7 heart trusted in him, and I am *h'*: "
116: 6 I was brought low, and he *h'* me. *3467
Ps 118:13 I might fall: but the Lord *h'* me. 5826
Isa 41: 6 They *h'* every one his neighbour; "
49: 8 in a day of salvation have I *h'* thee: "
Zec 1:15 and they *h'* forward the affliction. "
Ac 18:27 *h'* them much which had believed *4820*
Re 12:16 the earth *h'* the woman, and the *997*
helper See also HELPERS.
2Ki 14:26 nor any left, nor any *h'* for Israel. 5826
Job 30:13 my calamity, they have no *h'*. "
Ps 10:14 thou art the *h'* of the fatherless. "
30:10 upon me: Lord, be thou my *h'*. "
54: 4 Behold, God is mine *h'*: the Lord is "
72:12 poor also, and him that hath no *h'*. "
Jer 47: 4 and Zidon every *h'* that remaineth: "
Ro 16: 9 Salute Urbane, our *h'* in Christ, *4904*
Heb 13: 6 Lord is my *h'*, and I will not fear *998*
helpers See also FELLOWHELPERS.
1Ch 12: 1 the mighty men, *h'* of the war. 5826
18 unto thee, and peace be to thine *h'*; "
Job 9:13 the proud *h'* do stoop under him. "
Eze 30: 8 when all her *h'* shall be destroyed. "
Na 3: 9 Put and Lubim were thy *h'*. 5833
Ro 16: 3 and Aquila my *h'* in Christ Jesus: *4904*
2Co 1:24 your faith, but are *h'* of your joy: "
helpeth
1Ch 12:18 thine helpers; for thy God *h'* thee. 5826
Isa 31: 3 both he that *h'* shall fall, and he "
Ro 8:26 the Spirit also *h'* our infirmities: *4878*
1Co 16:16 and to every one that *h'* with us, *4903*
helping
Ezr 5: 2 were the prophets of God *h'* them. 5582
Ps 22: 1 why art thou so far from *h'* me, 3467
2Co 1:11 Ye also *h'* together by prayer for us, *4943*
helps
Ac 27:17 they used *h'*, undergirding the ship; *996*
1Co 12:28 gifts of healings, *h'*, governments, *484*
helve
De 19: 5 and the head slippeth from the *h'*, 6086
hem See also HEMS.
Ex 28:33 upon the *h'* of it thou shalt make *7757
33 scarlet, round about the *h'* thereof; * "
34 upon the *h'* of the robe round * "
39:25 upon the *h'* of the robe, round * "
26 round about the *h'* of the robe to * "
M't 9:20 touched the *h'* of his garment: *2899
14:36 only touch the *h'* of his garment: * "
Hemam (*he'-mam*) See also HOMAM.
Ge 36:22 of Lotan were Hori and *H'*; 1967
Heman (*he'-man*)
1Ki 4:31 than Ethan the Ezrahite, and *H'*, 1968
1Ch 2: 6 of Zerah; Zimri, and Ethan, and *H'*, "
6:33 *H'* a singer, the son of Joel, the son "
15:17 So the Levites appointed *H'* the son "
19 the singers, *H'*, Asaph, and Ethan, "
16:41 And with them *H'* and Jeduthun, "
42 *H'* and Jeduthun with trumpets "
25: 1 of the sons of Asaph, and of *H'*, and "
4 Of *H'*: the son of *H'*; Bukkiah, "
5 *H'* the king's seer in the words of "
5 And God gave to *H'* fourteen sons "
6 order to Asaph, Jeduthun, and *H'*. "
2Ch 5:12 of Asaph, of *H'*, of Jeduthun, with "
29:14 the sons of *H'*; Jehiel, and Shimei: "
35:15 and Asaph, and *H'*, and Jeduthun "
Ps 88: *title* Maschil of *H'* the Ezrahite. "
Hemath (*he'-math*) See also HAMATH.
1Ch 2:55 the Kenites that came of *H'*, the *2574
13: 5 even unto the entering of *H'*, * "
Am 6:14 the entering in of *H'* unto the * "
Hemdan (*hem'-dan*) See also AMRAM.
Ge 36:26 *H'*, and Eshban, and Ithran, and 2533
hemlock
Ho 10: 4 as *h'* in the furrows of the field, 7219
Am 6:12 the fruit of righteousness into *h'*: *3939
hems
Ex 39:24 they made upon the *h'* of the robe *7757
hen
M't 23:37 even as a *h'* gathereth her chickens *3733*
Lu 13:34 as a *h'* doth gather her brood under "
Hen (*hen*)
Zec 6:14 and to *H'* the son of Zephaniah, 2581
Hena (*he'-nah*)
2Ki 18:34 gods of Sepharvaim, *H'*, and Ivah? 2012
19:13 city of Sepharvaim, of *H'*, and Ivah? "
Isa 37:13 city of Sepharvaim, *H'*, and Ivah? "
Henadad (*hen'-a-dad*)
Ezr 3: 9 the sons of *H'*, with their sons and 2582
Ne 3:18 Bavai the son of *H'*, the ruler of the "
24 him repaired Binnui the son of *H'* "
10: 9 Binnui of the sons of *H'*, Kadmiel; "
hence See also HENCEFORTH; HENCEFORWARD.
Ge 37:17 They are departed *h'*; for I heard 2088
42:15 ye shall not go forth *h'*, except your "
50:25 ye shall carry up my bones from *h'*. "
Ex 11: 1 afterwards he will let you go *h'*: "
1 surely thrust you out *h'* altogether. "
13:19 carry up my bones away *h'* with you. "
33: 1 and go up *h'*, thou and the people "
15 go not with me, carry us not up *h'*. "
De 9:12 Arise, get thee down quickly from *h'*, "
Jos 4: 3 you *h'* out of the midst of Jordan, "
J'g 6:18 Depart not *h'*, I pray thee, until I "
Ru 2: 8 neither go from *h'*, but abide here "
1Ki 17: 3 Get thee *h'*, and turn thee eastward, "
Ps 39:13 strength, before I go *h'*, and be no more.
Isa 30:22 thou shalt say unto it, Get thee *h'*. 3318
Jer 38:10 Take from *h'* thirty men with thee, 2088
Zec 6: 7 Get you *h'*, walk to and fro through 3212
M't 4:10 Get thee *h'*, Satan: for it is written, *5217*
17:20 Remove *h'* to yonder place; and it *1782*

Lu 4: 9 of God, cast thyself down from *h*: 1782
13: 31 Get thee out, and depart *h*: for "
16: 26 would pass from *h*' to you cannot; "
Joh 2: 16 Take these things *h*; make not my "
7: 3 Depart *h*', and go into Judæa, that "
14: 31 even so I do. Arise, let us go *h*'. "
18: 36 but now is my kingdom not from *h*'. "
20: 15 Sir, if thou have borne him *h*', tell me "
Ac 1: 5 Holy Ghost not many days *h*'.3326, 5025
22: 21 send thee far *h*' unto the Gentiles. 1821
Jas 4: 1 come they not *h*', even of your lusts 1782

henceforth
Ge 4: 12 it shall not *h*' yield unto thee her 3254
Nu 18: 22 Israel *h*' come nigh the tabernacle 5750
De 17: 16 Ye shall *h*' return no more that 3254
19: 20 shall *h*' commit no more any such "
J'g 2: 21 will not *h*' drive out any from before "
2Ki 5: 17 for thy servant will *h*' offer neither 5750
2Ch 16: 9 from *h*' thou shalt have wars. 6258
Ps 125: 2 his people from *h*' even for ever. * "
131: 3 in the Lord from *h*' and for ever. * "
Isa 9: 7 with justice from *h*' even for ever. "
52: 1 for *h*' there shall no more come into "
59: 21 saith the Lord, from *h*' and for ever. 3254
Eze 36: 12 shalt no more *h*' bereave them of men.
M't 23: 39 Ye shall not see me *h*', till ye 575,737
26: 29 I will not drink *h*' of this fruit of " "
Lu 1: 48 from *h*' all generations shall call me 3568
5: 10 not; from *h*' thou shalt catch men. "
12: 52 *h*' there shall be five in one house "
Joh 14: 7 from *h*' ye know him, and have seen 737
15: 15 *H*' I call you not servants; for the *3765
Ac 4: 17 speak *h*' to no man in this name. 3371
18: 6 from *h*' I will go unto the Gentiles. 3568
Ro 6: 6 that *h*' we should not serve sin. *3371
2Co 5: 15 should not *h*' live unto themselves,* "
16 *h*' know we no man after 575,3588,3568
16 yet now *h*' know we him no more. *2089
Ga 6: 17 From *h*' let no man trouble me: 3063
Eph 4: 14 That we *h*' be no more children, * "
17 ye *h*' walk not as other Gentiles *3371
2Ti 4: 8 *H*' there is laid up for me a crown 3063
Heb10: 13 From *h*' expecting till his enemies "
Re 14: 13 dead which die in the Lord from *h*': 534

henceforward
Nu 15: 23 and *h*' among your generations; *1973
M't 21: 19 no fruit grow on thee *h*' for ever. 3371

Henoch (*he'-nok*) See also ENOCH.
1Ch 1: 3 *H*', Methuselah, Lamech, Noah 2585
33 Epher, and *H*', and Abido, and "

Hepher (*he'-fer*) See also GATH-HEPHER; HEPHERITES.
Nu 26: 32 of *H*', the family of the Hepherites.2660
33 Zelophehad the son of *H*' had no "
27: 1 the son of *H*', the son of Gilead, "
Jos 12: 17 Tappuah, one; the king of *H*', one; "
17: 2 for the children of *H*', and for the "
3 But Zelophehad, the son of *H*', the "
1Ki 4: 10 Sochoh, and all the land of *H*': "
1Ch 4: 6 Naarah bare him Ahuzam, and *H*', "
11: 36 *H*' the Mecherathite, Ahijah the "

Hepherites (*he'-fer-ites*)
Nu 26: 32 of Hepher, the family of the *H*'. 2662

Hephzi-bah (*hef'-zi-bah*)
2Ki 21: 1 And his mother's name was *H*'. 2657
Isa 62: 4 but thou shalt be called *H*', and "

her See in the APPENDIX; also HERS; HERSELF.

herald
Da 3: 4 Then an *h*' cried aloud, To you it is 3744

herb See also HERBS.
Ge 1: 11 the *h*' yielding seed, and the fruit 6212
12 *h*' yielding seed after his kind, and "
29 I have given you every *h*' bearing "
30 have given every green *h*' for meat: "
2: 5 every *h*' of the field before it grew: "
3: 18 and thou shalt eat the *h*' of the field; "
9: 3 even as the green *h*' have I given "
Ex 9: 22 every *h*' of the field, throughout "
25 the hail smote every *h*' of the field, "
10: 12 and eat every *h*' of the land, even all "
15 and they did eat every *h*' of the land, "
De 32: 2 the small rain upon the tender *h*', 1877
2Ki 19: 26 and as the green *h*', as the grass on "
Job 8: 12 it withereth before any other *h*'. 2682
38: 27 the bud of the tender *h*' to spring *1877
Ps 37: 2 grass, and wither as the green *h*'. "
104: 14 and *h*' for the service of man: that 6212
Isa 37: 27 of the field, and as the green *h*', as 1877
66: 14 your bones shall flourish like an *h*':* "

herbs
Ex 10: 15 the trees, or in the *h*' of the field. *6212
12: 8 and with bitter *h*' they shall eat it. "
Nu 9: 11 with unleavened bread and bitter *h*'. "
De 11: 10 it with thy foot, as a garden of *h*': 3419
1Ki 21: 2 I may have it for a garden of *h*', "
2Ki 4: 39 went out into the field to gather *h*', 219
Ps 105: 35 did eat up all the *h*' in their land, *6212
Pr 15: 17 Better is a dinner of *h*' where love 3419
27: 25 *h*' of the mountains are gathered. 6212
Isa 18: 4 like a clear heat upon *h*', and like * 216
26: 19 thy dew is as the dew of *h*', and the 219
42: 15 and hills, and dry up all their *h*'; 6212
Jer 12: 4 and the *h*' of every field wither, for "
M't 13: 32 grown, it is the greatest among *h*', 3001
M'r 4: 32 up, and becometh greater than all *h*', "
Lu 11: 42 mint and rue and all manner of *h*'.* "
Ro 14: 2 another, who is weak, eateth *h*'. "
Heb 6: 7 and bringeth forth *h*' meet for them 1008

herd See also HERDMAN; HERDS; SHEPHERD.
Ge 18: 7 And Abraham ran unto the *h*', 1241
Le 1: 2 even of the *h*', and of the flock. "
3 offering be a burnt sacrifice of the *h*'. "
Le 3: 1 peace offering, if he offer it of the *h*'; 1241
27: 32 concerning the tithe of the *h*', or of "
Nu 15: 3 the Lord, of the *h*', or of the flock: "
De 12: 21 shalt kill of thy *h*' and of thy flock, "
15: 19 that come of thy *h*' and of thy flock "
16: 2 of the flock and the *h*', in the place "
1Sa 11: 5 came after the *h*' out of the field * "
2Sa 12: 4 of his own flock and of his own *h*', "
Jer 31: 12 the young of the flock and of the *h*': "
Jon 3: 7 man nor beast, *h*' nor flock, taste "
Hab 3: 17 and there shall be no *h*' in the stalls: "
M't 8: 30 them an *h*' of many swine feeding. 34
31 us to go away into the *h*' of swine. "
32 they went into the *h*' of swine: and, * "
32 the whole *h*' of swine ran violently "
M'r 5: 11 mountains a great *h*' of swine feeding. "
13 the *h*' ran violently down a steep place "
Lu 8: 32 an *h*' of many swine feeding on the "
33 the *h*' ran violently down a steep place "

herdman See also HERDMEN.
Am 7: 14 but I was an *h*', and a gatherer of 951

herdmen
Ge 13: 7 between the *h*' of Abram's cattle 7462
7 cattle and the *h*' of Lot's cattle: "
8 between my *h*' and thy *h*'; for we be "
26: 20 And the *h*' of Gerar did strive with "
20 of Gerar did strive with Isaac's *h*', "
1Sa 21: 7 the chiefest of the *h*' that belonged to "
Am 1: 1 who was among the *h*' of Tekoa, 5349

herds See also SHEPHERDS.
Ge 13: 5 with Abram, had flocks, and *h*', and 1241
24: 35 hath given him flocks, and *h*', and "
26: 14 and possession of *h*', and great store "
32: 7 the flocks, and *h*', and the camels, "
33: 13 and the flocks and *h*' with young are "
45: 10 and thy *h*', and all that thou hast: "
46: 32 and their *h*', and all that they have. "
47: 1 and their *h*', and all that they have, "
17 for the cattle of the *h*', and for the "
18 my lord also hath our *h*' of cattle; 4735
50: 8 their flocks, and their *h*', they left 1241
Ex 10: 9 flocks and with our *h*' will we go; "
24 your flocks and your *h*' be stayed: "
12: 32 take your flocks and your *h*', as ye "
38 flocks, and *h*', even very much cattle "
34: 3 flocks nor *h*' feed before that mount. "
Nu 11: 22 Shall the flocks and the *h*' be slain "
De 8: 13 when thy *h*' and thy flocks multiply, "
12: 6 firstlings of your *h*' and of your * "
17 firstlings of thy *h*' or of thy flock, * "
14: 23 the firstlings of thy *h*' and of thy * "
1Sa 30: 20 David took all the flocks and the *h*', "
2Sa 12: 2 had exceeding many flocks and *h*': "
1Ch 27: 29 And over the *h*' that fed in Sharon "
29 over the *h*' that were in the valleys "
2Ch 32: 29 and possessions of flocks and *h*' in "
Ne 10: 36 firstlings of our *h*' and of our flocks, "
Pr 27: 23 thy flocks, and look well to thy *h*'. 5739
Isa 65: 10 a place for the *h*' to lie down in, 1241
Jer 3: 24 their flocks and their *h*', their sons "
5: 17 shall eat up thy flocks and thine *h*': "
Hos 5: 6 and with their *h*' to seek the Lord; "
Joe 1: 18 the *h*' of cattle are perplexed, 5739

here See also HEREAFTER; HEREBY; HEREIN; HEREOF; HERETOFORE; HEREUNTO; HEREWITH.
Ge 16: 13 Have I also *h*' looked after him that 1988
19: 12 unto Lot, Hast thou *h*' any besides? 6311
15 thy two daughters, which are *h*'; 4672
21: 23 swear unto me *h*' by God that thou 2008
22: 1 Abraham: and he said, Behold, *h*' I am.
5 Abide ye *h*' with the ass; and I and 6311
7 and he said, *H*' am I, my son. 2009
11 Abraham: and he said, *H*' am I. "
24: 13 Behold, I stand *h*' by the well of water;*
27: 1 and he said unto him, Behold, *h*' am I.
18 *H*' am I; who art thou, my son? 2009
31: 11 saying, Jacob: And I said, *H*' am I. "
37 set it *h*' before my brethren and thy 3541
37: 13 And he said to him, *H*' am I. 2009
40: 15 and *h*' also have I done nothing 6311
42: 33 leave one of your brethren *h*' with me,*
46: 2 Jacob, Jacob. And he said, *H*' am I. 2009
47: 23 *h*' is seed for you, and ye shall sow the
Ex 3: 4 Moses. And he said, *H*' am I. 2009
24: 14 Tarry ye *h*' for us, until we come 2088
33: 16 wherein shall it be known *h*' that I*645
Nu 14: 40 Lo we be *h*', and will go up unto the
22: 8 said unto them, Lodge *h*' this night.6311
19 pray you, tarry ye also *h*' this night,2088
23: 1 unto Balak, Build me *h*' seven altars, "
1 and prepare me *h*' seven oxen and "
15 Stand *h*' by thy burnt-offering, 3541
29 Balak, Build me *h*' seven altars, 2088
29 and prepare me *h*' seven bullocks "
32: 6 go to war, and shall ye sit *h*'? 6311
16 will build sheepfolds *h*' for our cattle, "
De 5: 3 who are all of us *h*' alive this day. "
31 But as for thee, stand thou *h*' by me, "
12: 8 the things that we do *h*' this day, "
29: 15 him that standeth *h*' with us this day "
15 him that is not *h*' with us this day: "
Jos 18: 6 cast lots for you *h*' before the Lord "
8 that I may *h*' cast lots for you before "
21: 9 cities which are *h*' mentioned by name,
J'g 4: 20 thee, and say, Is there any man *h*'? 6311
18: 3 this place? and what hast thou *h*'? "
19: 9 lodge *h*', that thine heart may be "
24 Behold, *h*' is my daughter a maiden,
20: 7 give *h*' your advice and counsel. 1988
Ru 2: 8 but abide *h*' fast by my maidens: 3541
4: 1 turn aside, sit down *h*'. And he 6311
2 Sit ye down *h*'. And they sat down. "
1Sa 1: 26 the woman that stood by thee *h*', 2088
3: 4 Samuel: and he answered, *H*' am I.2009
5 he said, *H*' am I; for thou calledst 2005
1Sa 3: 6, 8 *H*' am I; for thou didst call me. 2005
16 my son. And he answered, *H*' am I.2009
9: 8 I have *h*' at hand the fourth part of*
11 and said unto them, Is the seer *h*'?2088
12: 3 behold, *h*' I am: witness against me
14: 34 sheep, and slay them *h*', and eat; 2088
16: 11 Jesse, Are *h*' all thy children? 8552
21: 8 not *h*' under thine hand spear or 6311
9 behold, it is *h*' wrapped in a cloth
9 for there is no other save that *h*'. 2088
22: 12 he answered, *H*' I am, my lord. 2005
23: 3 Behold, we be afraid *h*' in Judah: 6311
29: 3 What do these Hebrews *h*'? And
2Sa 1: 7 And I answered, *H*' am I. 2009
11: 12 Tarry *h*' to day also, and to-morrow 2088
15: 26 behold, *h*' am I, let him do to me as
18: 30 Turn aside, and stand *h*'. And he 3541
20: 4 three days, and be thou *h*' present.6311
24: 22 behold, *h*' be oxen for burnt sacrifice, *
1Ki 2: 30 And he said, Nay; but I will die *h*'. 6311
18: 8, 11 tell thy lord, Behold, Elijah is *h*'.
14 tell thy lord, Behold, Elijah is *h*'.
19: 9, 13 What doest thou *h*', Elijah? 6311
20: 40 thy servant was busy *h*' and there, 2008
22: 7 Is there not *h*' a prophet of the 6311
2Ki 2: 2 Tarry *h*', I pray thee; for the Lord "
4 tarry *h*', I pray thee; for the Lord "
6 Tarry, I pray thee, *h*'; for the Lord "
3: 11 Is there not *h*' a prophet of the Lord, "
11 *H*' is Elisha, the son of Shaphat, "
7: 3 Why sit we *h*', until we die? "
4 and if we sit still *h*', we die also. "
10: 23 be *h*' with you none of the servants "
1Ch 29: 17 joy thy people, which are present *h*', "
Job 38: 11 *h*' shall thy proud waves be stayed?"
35 and say unto thee, *H*' we are? 2009
Ps 132: 14 *h*' will I dwell; for I have desired it. 6311
Isa 6: 8 Then said I, *H*' am I; send me. 2005
21: 9 behold, *h*' cometh a chariot of men, 2088
22: 16 What hast thou *h*'? and whom 6311
16 and whom hast thou *h*', that thou "
16 hast hewed thee out a sepulchre *h*', "
28: 10 line; *h*' a little, and there a little: 8033
13 line; *h*' a little, and there a little; "
52: 5 what have I *h*', saith the Lord, that 6311
58: 9 shalt cry, and he shall say, *H*' I am. 2009
Eze 8: 6 house of Israel committeth *h*', 6311
9 wicked abominations that they do *h*'. "
17 abominations which they commit *h*'? "
Ho 7: 9 gray hairs are *h*' and there upon 2236
M't 12: 41 behold, a greater than Jonas is *h*'. 5602
42 behold, a greater than Solomon is *h*'. "
14: 8 Give me *h*' John Baptist's head in a "
17 We have *h*' but five loaves, and two "
16: 28 standing *h*', which shall not taste "
17: 4 Lord, it is good for us to be *h*': "
4 let us make *h*' three tabernacles; "
20: 6 Why stand ye *h*' all the day idle? "
24: 2 shall not be left *h*' one stone upon "
23 unto you, Lo, *h*' is Christ, or there; "
26: 36 Sit ye *h*', while I go and pray yonder. 848
38 tarry ye *h*', and watch with me. 5602
28: 6 He is not *h*': for he is risen, as "
M'r 6: 3 and are not his sisters *h*' with us? "
8: 4 with bread *h*' in the wilderness? "
9: 1 there be some of them that stand *h*', "
5 Master, it is good for us to be *h*': "
13: 1 of stones and what buildings are *h*'!*
21 Lo, *h*' is Christ; or, lo, he is there; 5602
14: 32 Sit ye *h*', while I shall pray. "
34 unto death: tarry ye *h*', and watch. "
16: 6 he is risen; he is not *h*': behold the "
Lu 4: 23 Capernaum, do...*h*' in thy country. "
9: 12 for we are *h*' in a desert place. "
27 standing *h*', which shall not taste "
33 Master, it is good for us to be *h*': "
11: 31 behold, a greater than Solomon is *h*'. "
32 behold, a greater than Jonas is *h*'. "
17: 21 shall they say, Lo *h*'! or, lo there! "
23 And they shall say to you, See *h*'; or "
19: 20 Lord, behold, *h*' is thy pound, which I
22: 38 Lord, behold, *h*' are two swords. 5602
24: 6 He is not *h*', but is risen: remember "
41 unto them, Have ye *h*' any meat? 1759
Joh 6: 9 There is a lad *h*', which hath five 5602
11: 21, 32 if thou hadst been *h*', my brother "
Ac 4: 10 doth this man stand *h*' before you 3936
9: 10 And he said, Behold, I am *h*', Lord.
14 And *h*' he hath authority from the 5602
10: 33 Now therefore are we all *h*' present 3918
16: 28 thyself no harm: for we are all *h*'. 1759
24: 19 ought to have been *h*' before thee, 3918
20 Or else let these same *h*' say, if they*
25: 24 men which are *h*' present with us, 4840
24 me, both at Jerusalem, and also *h*', 1759
Col 4: 9 you all things which are done *h*'. 5602
Heb 7: 8 And *h*' men that die receive tithes; "
13: 14 For *h*' have we no continuing city, "
Jas 2: 3 unto him, Sit thou *h*' in a good place; "
3 there, or sit *h*' under my footstool:* "
1Pe 1: 17 the time of your sojourning *h*' in fear.*
Re 13: 10 *H*' is the patience and the faith of 5602
18 *H*' is wisdom. Let him that hath "
14: 12 *H*' is the patience of the saints: "
12 *h*' are they that keep the * "
17: 9 *h*' is the mind which hath wisdom. "

hereafter
Isa 41: 23 Shew the things that are to come *h*', 268
Eze 20: 39 and *h*' also, if ye will not hearken 310
Da 2: 29 what should come to pass *h*': 311,1836
45 what shall come to pass *h*': " "
M't 26: 64 *H*' shall ye see the Son of man *575,737
M'r 11: 14 man eat fruit of thee *h*' for ever. *3370
Lu 22: 69 *H*' shall the Son of man sit on *575,3568
Joh 1: 51 *H*' ye shall see heaven open, * 737
13: 7 now; but thou shalt know *h*'. 3326,5023

Joh 14:30 H· I will not talk much with you:*2089
1Ti 1:16 should h· believe on him to life ‡3195
Re 1:19 the things which shall be h·; 3326,5023
4: 1 thee things which must be h·. " "
9:12 there come two woes more h·. " "
hereby
Ge 42:15 H· ye shall be proved: By the life 2063
33 H· shall I know that ye are true men; "
Nu 16:28 And Moses said, H· ye shall know "
Jos 3:10 And Joshua said, H· ye shall know "
1Co 4: 4 yet am I not h· justified: but 1722,5129
1Jo 2: 3 And h· we do know that we do " "
5 h· know we that we are in him. " "
3:16 H· perceive we the love of God, " "
19 And h· we know that we are of " "
24 h· we know that he abideth in " "
4: 2 H· know ye the Spirit of God: " "
6 H· know we the spirit of truth,*1537,5124
13 H· know we that we dwell in 1722,5129
herein
Ge 34:22 Only h· will the men consent unto*2063
2Ch 16: 9 H· thou hast done foolishly: 5921,
Joh 4:37 And h· is that saying true, One 1722,5129
9:30 Why h· is a marvellous thing, " "
15: 8 H· is my Father glorified, that " "
Ac 24:16 And h· do I exercise myself, to " "
2Co 8:10 And h· I give my advice: for " "
1Jo 4:10 H· is love, not that we loved God, " "
17 H· is our love made perfect, " "
hereof
M't 9:26 the fame h· went abroad into all 3778
Heb 5: 3 And by reason h· he ought, as for *5026
Heres (he'-res) See also KIR-HERES; TIMMATH-HERES.
J'g 1:35 Amorites would dwell in mount H· 2776
Heresh (he'-resh)
1Ch 9:15 Bakbakkar, H·, and Galal, and 2792
heresies
1Co 11:19 there must be also h· among you, ‡ 139
Ga 5:20 wrath, strife, seditions, h·, envyings, "
2Pe 2: 1 shall bring in damnable h·, even "
heresy See also HERESIES.
Ac 24:14 after the way which they call h·, so* 139
heretick
Tit 3:10 A man that is an h· after the first†‡ 141
heretofore
Ex 4:10 not eloquent, neither h·, nor since 8543
5: 7 people straw to make brick, as h·: "
8 the bricks, which they did make h·, "
14 both yesterday and to day, as h·? "
Jos 3: 4 for ye have not passed this way h·. "
Ru 2:11 a people which thou knewest not h·. "
1Sa 4: 7 hath not been such a thing h·. 865
2Co 13: 2 write to them which h· have sinned,4258
hereunto
Ec 2:25 who else can hasten h·, more than I?*
1Pe 2:21 For even h· were ye called: 1519,5124
herewith
Eze 16:29 and yet thou wast not satisfied h·. 2063
Mal 3:10 prove me now h·, saith the Lord of "
heritage See also HERITAGES.
Ex 6: 8 and I will give it you for an h·: 4181
Job 20:29 the h· appointed unto him by God. 5159
27:13 and the h· of oppressors, which they "
Ps 16: 6 places; yea, I have a goodly h·. "
61: 5 the h· of those that fear thy name. 3425
94: 5 people, O Lord, and afflict thine h·. 5159
111: 6 may give them the h· of the heathen. "
119:111 testimonies have I taken as an h· 5157
127: 3 Lo, children are an h· of the Lord: 5159
135:12 And gave their land for an h·, "
12 an h· unto Israel his people. "
136:21 And gave their land for an h·: for his "
22 Even an h· unto Israel his servant: "
Isa 54:17 the h· of the servants of the Lord, "
58:14 thee with the h· of Jacob thy father: "
Jer 2: 7 and made mine h· an abomination. "
3:19 a goodly h· of the hosts of nations? "
12: 7 I have left mine h·; I have given the "
8 Mine h· is unto me as a lion in the "
9 Mine h· is unto me as a speckled "
15 every man to his h·, and every man "
17: 4 discontinue from thine h· that I gave "
50:11 O ye destroyers of mine h·, because "
Joe 2:17 give not thine h· to reproach, that "
3: 2 for my people and for my h· Israel, "
Mic 2: 2 his house, even a man and his h·. "
7:14 the flock of thine h·, which dwell "
18 the remnant of his h·? he retaineth "
Mal 1: 3 laid his mountains and his h· waste "
1Pe 5: 3 as being lords over God's h·, but *2819
heritages
Isa 49: 8 to cause to inherit the desolate h·; 5159
Hermas (her'-mas)
Ro 16:14 Phlegon, H·, Patrobas, Hermes, 2057
Hermes (her'-mees)
Ro 16:14 H·, and the brethren which are 2060
Hermogenes (her-moj'-e-nees)
2Ti 1:15 of whom are Phygellus and H·. 2061
Hermon (her'-mon) See also BAAL-HERMON; HERMONITES.
De 3: 8 the river of Arnon unto mount H·; 2768
9 which H· the Sidonians call Sirion; "
4:48 even unto mount Sion, which is H·. "
Jos 11: 3 under H· in the land of Mizpeh. "
17 valley of Lebanon under mount H·: "
12: 1 unto mount H·, and all the plain on "
5 And reigned in mount H·, and in "
13: 5 from Baal-gad under mount H· unto "
11 and all mount H·, and all Bashan "
1Ch 5:23 and Senir, and unto mount H·. "
Ps 89:12 Tabor and H· shall rejoice in thy 2768
133: 3 As the dew of H·, and as the dew "
Ca 4: 8 from the top of Shenir and H·, "
Hermonites (her'-mon-ites) See also HERMON.
Ps 42: 6 land of Jordan, and of the H·, *2769
Herod (her'-od) See also HERODIANS; HEROD'S.
M't 2: 1 in the days of H· the king, behold, 2264
3 When H· the king had heard these "
7 Then H·, when he had privily "
12 that they should not return to H·, "
13 for H· will seek the young child to "
15 was there until the death of H·: "
16 Then H·, when he saw that he was "
19 But when H· was dead, behold, an "
22 in the room of his father H·, he "
14: 1 At that time H· the tetrarch heard "
3 For H· had laid hold on John, and "
6 danced before them, and pleased H·. "
M'k 6:14 king H· heard of him; for his name "
16 But when H· heard thereof, he said, "
17 H· himself had sent forth and laid "
18 For John had said unto H·, It is not "
20 For H· feared John, knowing that "
21 H· on his birthday made a supper "
22 came in, and danced, and pleased H· "
8:15 Pharisees, and of the leaven of H·. "
Lu 1: 5 There was in the days of H·, the "
3: 1 and H· being tetrarch of Galilee, "
19 H· the tetrarch, being reproved "
19 for all the evils which H· had done, "
9: 7 H· the tetrarch heard of all that was "
9 And H· said, John have I beheaded: "
13:31 depart hence: for H· will kill thee. "
23: 7 he sent him to H·, who himself also "
8 And when H· saw Jesus, he was "
11 And H· with his men of war set him "
12 Pilate and H· were made friends "
15 nor yet H·: for I sent you to him; "
Ac 4:27 whom thou hast anointed, both H· "
12: 1 Now about that time H· the king "
6 H· would have brought him forth, "
11 delivered me out of the hand of H·, "
19 And when H· had sought for him, "
20 H· was highly displeased with them "
21 And upon a set day H·, arrayed in "
13: 1 brought up with H· the tetrarch, "
Herodians (he-ro'-de-uns)
M't 22:16 their disciples with the H·, saying, 2265
M'k 3: 6 took counsel with the H· against "
12:13 of the Pharisees and of the H·, to "
Herodias (he-ro'-de-as) See also HERODIAS'.
M't 14: 6 the daughter of H· danced before 2266
M'k 6:19 Therefore H· had a quarrel against "
22 when the daughter of the said H· "
Lu 3:19 being reproved by him for H· his "
Herodias' (he-ro'-de-as)
M't 14: 3 and put him in prison for H· sake,*2266
M'k 6:17 bound him in prison for H· sake, * "
Herodion (he-ro'-de-on)
Ro 16:11 Salute H· my kinsman. Greet 2267
Herod's (her'-ods)
M't 14: 6 when H· birthday was kept, the 2264
Lu 8: 3 the wife of Chuza H· steward, and "
23: 7 he belonged unto H· jurisdiction, "
Ac 23:35 him to be kept in H· judgment hall. "
heron
Le 11:19 stork, the h· after her kind, and the 601
De 14:18 and the h· after her kind, and the "
hers See also HERSELF.
De 21:15 if the firstborn be h· that was hated:
1Sa 25:42 with five damsels of h· that went after
2Ki 8: 6 Restore all that was h·, and all the
Job 39:16 ones, as though they were not h·: her
herself
Ge 18:12 Therefore Sarah laughed within h·,
20: 5 even she h·, said, He is my brother:
24:65 she took a vail, and covered h·.
38:14 covered...with a vail, and wrapped h·,
Ex 2: 5 came down to wash h· at the river;*
Le 15:28 she shall number to h· seven days,
21: 9 if she profane h· by playing the whore,
Nu 22:25 she thrust h· unto the wall: and
30: 3 and bind h· by a bond, being in her
J'g 5:29 her, yea, she returned answer to h·,
Ru 2:10 her face, and bowed h· to the ground,
1Sa 4:19 husband were dead, she bowed h· and
25:23 on her face, and bowed h· to the ground,
41 she arose, and bowed h· on her face
2Sa 11: 2 the roof he saw a woman washing h·;*
1Ki 14: 5 she shall feign h· to be another woman.
2Ki 4:37 and bowed h· to the ground, and took
Job 39:18 What time she lifteth up h· on high,
Ps 84: 3 and the swallow a nest for h·, where
Pr 31:22 She maketh h· coverings of tapestry;
Isa 5:14 Therefore hell hath enlarged h·, *5315
34:14 there, and find for h· a place of rest. *
61:10 as a bride adorneth h· with her jewels.
Jer 3:11 backsliding Israel hath justified h·
4:31 Zion, that bewaileth h·, that spreadeth*
49:24 and turneth h· to flee, and fear hath
Eze 22: 3 maketh idols against h· to defile
3 maketh idols against..., to defile h·.*
23: 7 with all their idols she defiled h·.
24:12 She hath wearied h· with lies, and her
Ho 2:13 she decked h· with her earrings and
Zec 9: 3 And Tyrus did build h· a strong hold,
M't 9:21 For she said within h·, If I may but 1438
M'r 4:28 the earth bringeth forth fruit of h·; 844
Lu 1:24 and hid h· five months, saying, 1438
13:11 together, and could in no wise lift up h·.
Joh 20:14 she turned h· back, and saw Jesus
16 She turned h·, and saith unto him,
Heb 11:11 Through faith also Sara h· received 846
Re 2:20 woman Jezebel, which calleth h· a 1438
18: 7 How much she hath glorified h·, and "
19: 7 and his wife hath made h· ready. "
Hesed (he'-sed) See also JUSHAB-HESED.
1Ki 4:10 The son of H·, in Aruboth; to him*2618
Heshbon (hesh'-bon)
Nu 21:25 in H·, and in all the villages thereof.2809
26 For H· was the city of Sihon the king "
27 Come into H·, let the city of Sihon "
28 For there is a fire gone out of H·, "
30 H· is perished even unto Dibon, and "
34 of the Amorites, which dwelt at H·. "
32: 3 Nimrah, and H·, and Elealeh, and "
37 the children of Reuben built H·, "
De 1: 4 of the Amorites, which dwelt in H·, "
2:24 hand Sihon the Amorite, king of H·, "
26 unto Sihon king of H· with words "
30 Sihon king of H· would not let us "
3: 2 of the Amorites, which dwelt at H·. "
6 as we did unto Sihon king of H·, "
4:46 of the Amorites, who dwelt at H·, "
29: 7 unto this place, Sihon the king of H·, "
Jos 9:10 beyond Jordan, to Sihon king of H·, "
12: 2 of the Amorites, who dwelt in H·, "
5 the border of Sihon king of H·. "
13:10 the Amorites, which reigned in H·, "
17 H·, and all her cities that are in the "
21 the Amorites, which reigned in H·, "
26 And from H· unto Ramath-mizpeh, "
27 the kingdom of Sihon king of H·, "
21:39 H· with her suburbs, Jazer with her "
J'g 11:19 of the Amorites, the king of H·; "
26 While Israel dwelt in H· and her "
1Ch 6:81 H· with her suburbs, and Jazer with "
Ne 9:22 and the land of the king of H·, and "
Ca 7: 4 thine eyes like the fishpools in H·, "
Isa 15: 4 And H· shall cry, and Elealeh: their "
16: 8 fields of H· languish, and the vine "
9 will water thee with my tears, O H·: "
Jer 48: 2 in H· they have devised evil against "
34 the cry of H·, even unto Elealeh, "
45 fled stood under the shadow of H· "
45 but a fire shall come forth out of H·, "
49: 3 Howl, O H·, for Ai is spoiled: cry, "
Heshmon (hesh'-mon) See also AZMON.
Jos 15:27 And Hazar-gaddah, and H·, and 2829
Heth (heth)
Ge 10:15 begat Sidon his firstborn, and H·, 2845
23: 3 spake unto the sons of H·, saying, "
5 And the children of H· answered "
7 the land, even to the children of H·. "
10 dwelt among the children of H·: "
10 the audience of the children of H·, "
16 in the audience of the sons of H·, "
18 the presence of the children of H·, "
20 of a buryingplace by the sons of H·. "
25:10 purchased of the sons of H·: "
27:46 because of the daughters of H·: "
46 take a wife of the daughters of H·, "
49:32 therein was from the children of H·. "
1Ch 1:13 begat Zidon his firstborn, and H·, "
Hethlon (heth'-lon)
Eze 47:15 way of H·, as men go to Zedad; 2855
48: 1 end to the coast of the way of H·, "
hew See also HEWED; HEWETH; HEWN.
Ex 34: 1 H· thee two tables of stone like 6458
De 10: 1 H· thee two tables of stone like "
12: 3 shall h· down the graven images of 1438
19: 5 with his neighbour to h· wood, and 2404
1Ki 5: 6 that they h· me cedar trees out of 3772
6 to h· timber like unto the Sidonians. "
18 and Hiram's builders did h· them,*6458
1Ch 22: 2 set masons to h· wrought stones 2672
2Ch 2: 2 thousand to h· in the mountain, * "
Jer 6: 6 H· ye down trees, and cast them 3772
Da 4:14 H· down the tree, and cut off his 1414
23 H· the tree down, and destroy it; "
hewed See also HEWN.
Ex 34: 4 And he h· two tables of stone like 6458
De 10: 3 and h· two tables of stone like unto "
1Sa 11: 7 of oxen, and h· them in pieces, *5408
15:33 And Samuel h· Agag in pieces 8158
1Ki 5:17 costly stones, and h· stones, to lay*1496
6:36 with three rows of h· stone, and a * "
7: 9 to the measures of h· stones, sawed* "
11 after the measures of h· stones, * "
12 with three rows of h· stones, and a* "
2Ki 12:12 and to buy timber and h· stone to *4274
Isa 22:16 thou hast h· thee out a sepulchre 2672
Jer 2:13 and h· them out cisterns, broken "
Ho 6: 5 have I h· them by the prophets; "
hewer See also HEWERS.
De 29:11 the h· of thy wood unto the drawer 2404
hewers
Jos 9:21 let them be h· of wood and drawers 2404
23 bondmen, and h· of wood and "
27 make them that day h· of wood and "
1Ki 5:15 thousand h· in the mountains; *2672
2Ki 12:12 masons, and h· of stone, and to buy "
1Ch 22:15 h· and workers of stone and timber, "
2Ch 2:10 thy servants, the h· that cut timber,2404
18 thousand to be h· in the mountain*2672
Jer 46:22 her with axes, as h· of wood. 2404
heweth
Isa 10:15 axe boast itself against him that h·2672
22:16 as he that h· him out a sepulchre * "
44:14 He h· him down cedars, and taketh 3772
hewn See also HEWED.
Ex 20:25 thou shalt not build it of h· stone: 1496
2Ki 22: 6 timber and h· stone to repair the 4274
2Ch 34:11 to buy h· stone, and timber for "
Pr 9: 1 she hath h· out her seven pillars: 2672
Isa 9:10 but we will build with h· stones: 1496

Isa 10 33 ones of stature shall be *h'* down. 1438
33: 9 Lebanon is ashamed and *h'* down:*7060
51: 1 unto the rock whence ye are *h'*, 2672
La 3: 9 inclosed my ways with *h'* stone, 1496
Eze 40: 42 four tables were of *h'* stone for the "
Am 5: 11 ye have built houses of *h'* stone, "
M't 3: 10 is *h'* down, and cast into the fire. *1581*
7: 19 is *h'* down, and cast into the fire. "
27: 60 which he had *h'* out in the rock; *2998*
M'r 15: 46 in a sepulchre which was *h'* out of a"
Lu 3: 9 is *h'* down, and cast into the fire. *1581*
23: 53 a sepulchre that was *h'* in stone, *2991*

Hezeki (*hez'-e-ki*)
1Ch 8: 17 and Meshullam, and *H'*, and *2395

Hezekiah (*hez-e-ki'-ah*) See also EZEKIAS; HIZKIAH.
2Ki 16: 20 *H'* his son reigned in his stead. 2396
18: 1 that *H'* the son of Ahaz king of "
9 pass in the fourth year of king *H'*, "
10 even in the sixth year of *H'*, that "
13 fourteenth year of king *H'* did "
14 And *H'* king of Judah sent to the "
14 king of Assyria appointed unto *H'* "
15 And *H'* gave him all the silver that "
16 At that time did *H'* cut off the gold "
16 pillars which *H'* king of Judah had "
17 from Lachish to king *H'* with a "
19 Speak ye now to *H'*, Thus saith "
22 whose altars *H'* hath taken away, "
29 saith the king, Let not *H'* deceive "
30 Neither let *H'* make you trust in the"
31 Hearken not to *H'*: for thus saith "
32 and hearken not unto *H'*, when he "
37 to *H'* with their clothes rent, and "
19: 1 when king *H'* heard it, that he rent "
3 Thus saith *H'*, This day is a day of "
5 servants of king *H'* came to Isaiah. "
9 he sent messengers again unto *H'*, "
10 Thus shall ye speak to *H'* king of "
14 And *H'* received the letter of the "
14 and *H'* went up into the house of "
15 And *H'* prayed before the Lord, "
20 Isaiah the son of Amoz sent to *H'*, "
20: 1 those days was *H'* sick unto death. "
3 in thy sight. And *H'* wept sore. "
5 Turn again, and tell *H'* the captain "
8 And *H'* said unto Isaiah, What "
10 *H'* answered, It is a light thing for "
12 sent letters and a present unto *H'*: "
12 he had heard that *H'* had been sick. "
13 And *H'* hearkened unto them, and "
13 dominion, that *H'* shewed them not. "
14 Isaiah the prophet unto king *H'*, "
14 And *H'* said, They are come from "
15 And *H'* answered, All the things "
16 Isaiah said unto *H'*, Hear the word "
19 Then said *H'* unto Isaiah, Good is "
20 And the rest of the acts of *H'*, and "
21 And *H'* slept with his fathers: and "
21: 3 high places which *H'* his father had "
1Ch 3: 13 Ahaz his son, *H'* his son, Manasseh "
23 of Neariah: Elioenai, and *H'*, and * "
4: 41 came in the days of *H'* king of "
2Ch 28: 27 *H'* his son reigned in his stead. "
29: 1 *H'* began to reign when he was five "
18 Then they went into *H'* the king, "
20 Then *H'* the king rose early, and "
27 And *H'* commanded to offer the "
30 *H'* the king and the princes "
31 Then *H'* answered and said, Now "
36 And *H'* rejoiced, and all the people, "
30: 1 And *H'* sent to all Israel and Judah, "
18 But *H'* prayed for them, saying, The "
20 Lord hearkened to *H'*, and healed "
22 *H'* spake comfortably unto all the "
24 For *H'* king of Judah did give to "
31: 2 *H'* appointed the courses of the "
8 when *H'* and the princes came and "
9 *H'* questioned with the priests "
11 Then *H'* commanded to prepare "
13 the commandment of *H'* the king, "
20 thus did *H'* throughout all Judah. "
32: 2 when *H'* saw that Sennacherib was "
8 themselves upon the words of *H'* "
9 unto *H'* king of Judah, and unto all "
11 Doth not *H'* persuade you to give "
12 Hath not the same *H'* taken away "
15 therefore let not *H'* deceive you, "
16 God, and against his servant *H'*. "
17 so shall not the God of *H'* deliver "
20 And for this cause *H'* the king, "
22 Lord saved *H'* and the inhabitants "
23 and presents to *H'* king of Judah: "
24 those days *H'* was sick to the death, "
25 *H'* rendered not again according "
26 *H'* humbled himself for the pride "
26 not upon them in the days of *H'*. "
27 *H'* had exceeding much riches and "
30 same *H'* also stopped the upper "
30 And *H'* prospered in all his works. "
32 the rest of the acts of *H'*, and his "
33 *H'* slept with his fathers, and they "
33: 3 high places which *H'* his father had "
Ezr 2: 16 The children of Ater of *H'*, ninety "
Ne 7: 21 The children of Ater of *H'*, ninety "
Pr 25: 1 men of *H'* king of Judah copied out. "
Isa 1: 1 Ahaz, and *H'*, kings of Judah. "
36: 1 in the fourteenth year of king *H'*, "
2 unto king *H'* with a great army. "
4 Say ye now to *H'*, Thus saith the "
7 whose altars *H'* hath taken away, "
14 saith the king, Let not *H'* deceive "
15 Neither let *H'* make you trust in the "
16 Hearken not to *H'*: for thus saith "
18 Beware lest *H'* persuade you, "

Isa 36: 22 to *H'* with their clothes rent, and 2396
37: 1 when king *H'* heard it, that he rent "
3 Thus saith *H'*, This day is a day of "
5 servants of king *H'* came to Isaiah. "
9 he sent messengers to *H'*, saying, "
10 Thus shall ye speak to *H'* king of "
14 And *H'* received the letter from the "
14 and *H'* went up unto the house of "
15 *H'* prayed unto the Lord, saying, "
21 Isaiah the son of Amoz sent unto *H'*, "
38: 1 those days was *H'* sick unto death. "
2 Then *H'* turned his face toward the "
3 in thy sight. And *H'* wept sore. "
5 Go, and say to *H'*, Thus saith the "
9 The writing of *H'* king of Judah, "
22 *H'* also had said, What is the sign "
39: 1 sent letters and a present to *H'*: "
2 *H'* was glad of them, and shewed "
2 dominion, that *H'* shewed them not "
3 Isaiah the prophet unto king *H'*, "
3 And *H'* said, They are come from "
4 And *H'* answered, All that is in mine "
5 Then said Isaiah to *H'*, Hear the "
8 Then said *H'* to Isaiah, Good is the "
Jer 15: 4 because of Manasseh the son of *H'* "
26: 18 prophesied in the days of *H'* king "
19 Did *H'* king of Judah and all Judah "
Ho 1: 1 Uzziah, Jotham, Ahaz, and *H'*, kings "
Mic 1: 1 the days of Jotham, Ahaz, and *H'* "

Hezion (*he'-zi-on*)
1Ki 15: 18 the son of *H'*, king of Syria, that 2383

Hezir (*he'-zur*)
1Ch 24: 15 seventeenth to *H'*, the eighteenth 2387
Ne 10: 20 Magpiash, Meshullam, *H'*, "

Hezrai (*hez'-rahee*) See also HEZRO.
2Sa 23: 35 *H'* the Carmelite, Paarai the *2695

Hezro (*hez'-ro*) See also HEZRAI.
1Ch 11: 37 *H'* the Carmelite, Naarai the son 2695

Hezron (*hez'-ron*) See also HAZOR; HEZRONITES; HEZRON'S.
Ge 46: 9 Hanoch, and Phallu, and *H'*, and 2696
12 sons of Pharez were *H'* and Hamul. "
Ex 6: 14 Hanoch, and Pallu, *H'*, and Carmi: "
Nu 26: 6 Of *H'*, the family of the Hezronites: "
21 of *H'*, the family of the Hezronites: "
Jos 15: 3 and passed along to *H'*, and went "
25 Kerioth, and *H'*, which is Hazor, * "
Ru 4: 18 of Pharez: Pharez begat *H'*, "
19 And *H'* begat Ram, and Ram begat "
1Ch 2: 5 The sons of Pharez; *H'*, and Hamul. "
9 The sons also of *H'*, that were born "
18 Caleb the son of *H'* begat children "
21 *H'* went in to the daughter of Machir "
24 And after that *H'* was dead in "
25 Jerahmeel the firstborn of *H'* were, "
4: 1 The sons of Judah; Pharez, *H'*, and "
5: 3 were, Hanoch, and Pallu, *H'*, and "

Hezronites (*hez'-ron-ites*)
Nu 26: 6 Of Hezron, the family of the *H'*: 2697
21 of Hezron, the family of the *H'*: "

Hezron's (*hez'-ronz*)
1Ch 2: 24 Abiah *H'* wife bare him Ashur 2696

hid See also HIDDEN.
Ge 3: 8 Adam and his wife *h'* themselves 2244
10 I was naked; and I *h'* myself. "
4: 14 and from thy face shall I be *h'*; 5641
35: 4 and Jacob *h'* them under the oak 2934
Ex 2: 2 child, she *h'* him three months. 6845
12 Egyptian, and *h'* him in the sand. 2934
3: 6 And Moses *h'* his face; for he was 5641
Le 4: 13 and the thing be *h'* from the eyes 5956
5: 3 defiled withal, and it be *h'* from him; "
4 with an oath, and it be *h'* from him; "
Nu 5: 13 be *h'* from the eyes of her husband, "
De 33: 19 and of treasures *h'* in the sand. *2934
Jos 2: 4 took the two men, and *h'* them, 6845
6 *h'* them with the stalks of flax, 2934
6: 17 because she *h'* the messengers 2244
25 because she *h'* the messengers, "
7: 21 are *h'* in the earth in the midst 2934
22 behold, it was *h'* in his tent, and the "
10: 16 five kings fled, and *h'* themselves 2244
17 five kings are found *h'* in a cave "
27 cave wherein they had been *h'*, * "
J'g 9: 5 Jerubbaal was left; for he *h'* himself. "
1Sa 3: 18 whit, and *h'* nothing from him. 3582
10: 22 hath *h'* himself among the stuff. 2244
14: 11 holes where they had *h'* themselves. "
22 which had *h'* themselves in mount "
20: 24 So David *h'* himself in the field: 5641
2Sa 17: 9 he is *h'* now in some pit, or in some 2244
18: 13 there is no matter *h'* from the king, 3582
1Ki 10: 3 was not any thing *h'* from the king, 5956
18: 4 and *h'* them by fifty in a cave, and 2244
13 how I *h'* an hundred men of the "
2Ki 4: 27 and the Lord hath *h'* it from me, 5956
6: 29 eat him: and she hath *h'* her son. 2244
7: 8 and raiment, and went and *h'* it; 2934
8 thence also, and went and *h'* it. "
11: 2 and they *h'* him, even him and his 5641
3 he was with her *h'* in the house of 2244
1Ch 21: 20 four sons with him *h'* themselves. "
2Ch 9: 2 nothing *h'* from Solomon which 5956
22: 9 for he was *h'* in Samaria, and *2244
11 of Ahaziah, *h'* him from Athaliah, 5641
12 *h'* in the house of God six years: 2244
Job 3: 10 nor *h'* sorrow from mine eyes. 5641
21 for it more than for *h'* treasures; 4301
23 given to a man whose way is *h'*, 5641
5: 21 Thou shalt be *h'* from the scourge 2244
6: 16 ice, and wherein the snow is *h'*: *5956
10: 13 things hast thou *h'* in thine heart: *6845
15: 18 their fathers, and have not *h'* it: 3582
17: 4 For thou hast *h'* their heart from 6845

Job 20: 26 darkness shall be *h'* in his secret *2244
28: 11 thing that is *h'* bringeth he forth 8587
21 Seeing it is *h'* from the eyes of all 5956
29: 8 men saw me, and *h'* themselves: 2244
38: 30 The waters are *h'* as with a stone, †‡ "
Ps 9: 15 net which they *h'* is their own foot 2934
17: 14 thou fillest with thy *h'* treasure: *6845
19: 6 there is nothing *h'* from the heat 5641
22: 24 neither hath he *h'* his face from him; "
32: 5 and mine iniquity have I not *h'*. 3680
35: 7 have they *h'* for me their net in a 2934
8 net that he hath *h'* catch himself: "
38: 9 my groaning is not *h'* from thee. 5641
40: 10 I have not *h'* thy righteousness 3680
55: 12 then I would have *h'* myself from 5641
69: 5 and my sins are not *h'* from thee. 3582
119: 11 Thy word have I *h'* in mine heart, *6845
139: 15 My substance was not *h'* from *3582
140: 5 The proud have *h'* a snare for me, 2934
Pr 2: 4 for her as for *h'* treasures; 4301
Isa 28: 15 falsehood have we *h'* ourselves: 5641
29: 14 of their prudent men shall be *h'*. "
40: 27 My way is *h'* from the Lord, and my "
42: 22 and they are *h'* in prison houses: 2244
49: 2 shadow of his hand hath he *h'* me, "
2 in his quiver hath he *h'* me; *5641
50: 6 I *h'* not my face from shame and "
53: 3 and we *h'* as it were our faces from* "
54: 8 In a little wrath I *h'* my face from "
57: 17 I *h'* me, and was wroth, and he went "
59: 2 your sins have *h'* his face from you, "
64: 7 for thou hast *h'* thy face from us, "
65: 16 because they are *h'* from mine eyes. "
Jer 13: 5 So I went, and *h'* it by Euphrates, 2934
7 from the place where I had *h'* it: "
16: 17 they are not *h'* from my face, 5641
17 is their iniquity *h'* from mine eyes. *6845
18: 22 take me, and *h'* snares for my feet. 2934
33: 5 I have *h'* my face from this city. 5641
36: 26 the prophet: but the Lord *h'* them. "
43: 10 upon these stones that I have *h'*; 2934
Eze 22: 26 *h'* their eyes from my sabbaths, 5956
39: 23 therefore *h'* I my face from them, 5641
24 them, and *h'* my face from them. "
Ho 5: 3 and Israel is not *h'* from me: 3582
13: 12 is bound up; his sin is *h'*. *6845
14 repentance shall be *h'* from mine 5641
Am 9: 3 be *h'* from my sight in the bottom "
Na 3: 11 thou shalt be *h'*, thou also shalt 5956
Zep 2: 3 it may be ye shall be *h'* in the day 5641
M't 5: 14 that is set on an hill cannot be *h'*. *2928*
10: 26 and *h'*, that shall not be known. *2927*
11: 25 because thou hast *h'* these things* *613*
13: 33 and *h'* in three measures of meal, *1470*
44 is like unto treasure *h'* in a field; **2928*
25: 18 the earth, and *h'* his lord's money. *613*
25 went and *h'* thy talent in the earth: *2928*
M'r 4: 22 For there is nothing *h'*, which shall *2927*
7: 24 know it: but he could not be *h'*. *2990*
Lu 1: 24 and *h'* herself five months, saying, *4032*
8: 17 neither any thing *h'*, that shall not* *614*
47 saw that she was not *h'*, she came *2990*
9: 45 and it was *h'* from them, that they* *3871*
10: 21 that thou hast *h'* these things from* *613*
12: 2 neither *h'*, that shall not be known. *2927*
13: 21 and *h'* in three measures of meal, *1470*
18: 34 and this saying was *h'* from them, *2928*
19: 42 now they are *h'* from thine eyes. "
Joh 8: 59 but Jesus *h'* himself, and went out "
2Co 4: 3 if our gospel be *h'*, it is *h'* to them *2572*
Eph 3: 9 hath been *h'* in God, who created *613*
Col 1: 26 which hath been *h'* from ages and "
2: 3 In whom are *h'* all the treasures * *614*
3: 3 your life is *h'* with Christ in God. *2928*
1Ti 5: 25 that are otherwise cannot be *h'*. "
Heb 11: 23 was *h'* three months of his parents, "
Re 6: 15 *h'* themselves in the dens and in "

Hiddai (*hid'-dahee*) See also HURAI.
2Sa 23: 30 *H'* of the brooks of Gaash, 1914

Hiddekel (*hid'-de-kel*)
Ge 2: 14 the name of the third river is *H'*: 2313
Da 10: 4 side of the great river, which is *H'*. "

hidden See also HID.
Le 5: 2 and if it be *h'* from him; he also 5956
De 30: 11 it is not *h'* from thee, neither is *6381
Job 3: 16 Or as an *h'* untimely birth I had 2934
15: 20 of years is *h'* to the oppressor. *6845
24: 1 times are not *h'* from the Almighty, * "
Ps 51: 6 in the *h'* part thou shalt make me 5640
83: 3 and consulted against thy *h'* ones. 6845
Pr 28: 12 when the wicked rise, a man is *h'*. *2664
Isa 45: 3 and *h'* riches of secret places, that 4301
48: 6 from this time, even *h'* things, and 5341
Ob 6 how are his *h'* things sought up! 4710
Ac 26: 26 none of these things are *h'* from *2990*
1Co 2: 7 the *h'* wisdom, which God ordained *613*
4: 5 bring to the light the *h'* things of *2927*
2Co 4: 2 the *h'* things of dishonesty, not "
1Pe 3: 4 But let it be the *h'* man of the heart, "
Re 2: 17 will I give to eat of the *h'* manna, *2928*

hide See also HID; HIDDEN; HIDEST; HIDETH; HIDING.
Ge 18: 17 Shall I *h'* from Abraham that thing 3680
47: 18 We will not *h'* it from my lord, how 3582
Ex 2: 3 when she could not longer *h'* him, 6845
Le 8: 17 the bullock, and his *h'*, his flesh, *5785
9: 11 flesh and the *h'* he burnt with fire* "
20: 4 ways *h'* their eyes from the man, 5956
De 7: 20 left, and *h'* themselves from thee, 5641
22: 1 astray, and *h'* myself from them: 5956
3 likewise thou mayest not *h'* thyself. "
4 the way, and *h'* thyself from them: "
31: 17 and I will *h'* my face from them, 5641
18 I will surely *h'* my face in that day "
32: 20 said, I will *h'* my face from them. "

Jos 2:16 *h·* yourselves there three days, 2247
7:19 thou hast done; *h·* it not from me. 3582
J'g 6:11 to *h·* it from the Midianites. 5127
1Sa 3:17 I pray thee *h·* it not from me: God 3582
17 if thou *h·* any thing from me of all "
13: 6 people did *h·* themselves in caves, 2244
19: 2 in a secret place, and *h·* thyself: "
20: 2 why should my father *h·* this thing 5641
5 that I may *h·* myself in the field "
19 the place where thou didst *h·* thyself "
23:19 Doth not David *h·* himself with us "
26: 1 Doth not David *h·* himself in the "
2Sa 14:18 *H·* not from me, I pray thee, the 3582
1Ki 17: 3 *h·* thyself by the brook Cherith, 5641
22:25 an inner chamber to *h·* thyself. 2247
2Ki 7:12 out of the camp to *h·* themselves "
2Ch 18:24 an inner chamber to *h·* thyself. 2244
Job 13:20 then will I not *h·* myself from thee. 5641
14:13 thou wouldest *h·* me in the grave, 6845
20:12 though he *h·* it under his tongue; 3582
24: 4 poor of the earth *h·* themselves 2244
33:17 purpose, and *h·* pride from man. 3680
34:22 of iniquity may *h·* themselves. 5641
40:13 *H·* them in the dust together; 2934
Ps 13: 1 how long wilt thou *h·* thy face 5641
17: 8 *h·* me under the shadow of thy "
27: 5 the time of trouble he shall *h·* me *6845
5 of his tabernacle shall he *h·* me; 5641
9 *H·* not thy face far from me; put "
30: 7 thou didst *h·* thy face, and I was "
31:20 Thou shalt *h·* them in the secret "
51: 9 *H·* thy face from my sins, and blot "
54 *title* Doth not David *h·* himself with
55: 1 O God, and *h·* not thyself from my 5956
56: 6 they *h·* themselves, they mark my 6845
64: 2 *H·* me from the secret counsel of 5641
69:17 *h·* not thy face from thy servant; "
78: 4 not *h·* them from their children, 3582
89:46 Lord? wilt thou *h·* thyself for ever? 5641
102: 2 *H·* not thy face from me in the day "
119:19 *h·* not thy commandments from me. "
143: 7 *h·* not thy face from me, lest I be "
9 enemies: I flee unto thee to *h·* me. 3680
Pr 2: 1 *h·* my commandments with thee; *6845
28:28 wicked rise, men *h·* themselves: 5641
Isa 1:15 I will *h·* mine eyes from you: yea, 5956
2:10 and *h·* thee in the dust, for fear of 2934
3: 9 their sin as Sodom, they *h·* it not. 3582
16: 3 *h·* the outcasts; bewray not him 5641
26:20 *h·* thyself as it were for a little 2247
29:15 that seek deep to *h·* their counsel 5641
58: 7 thou *h·* not thyself from thine own 5956
Jer 13: 4 Euphrates, and *h·* it there in a hole 2934
6 which I commanded thee to *h·* there. "
23:24 Can any *h·* himself in secret places 5641
36:19 Go, *h·* thee, thou and Jeremiah; and "
38:14 thee a thing; *h·* nothing from me. 3582
25 *h·* it not from us, and we will not "
43: 9 and *h·* them in the clay in the 2934
49:10 he shall not be able to *h·* himself: 2247
La 3:56 *h·* not thine ear at my breathing, 5956
Eze 28: 3 no secret that they can *h·* from ‡6004
31: 8 the garden of God could not *h·* him: "
39:29 Neither will I *h·* my face any more 5641
Da 10: 7 so that they fled to *h·* themselves. 2244
Am 9: 3 they *h·* themselves in the top "
Mic 3: 4 he will even *h·* his face from them 5641
Joh 12:36 and did *h·* himself from them. *2928
Jas 5:20 and shall *h·* a multitude of sins. *2572
Re 6:16 *h·* us from the face of him that 2928

hidest
Job 13:24 Wherefore *h·* thou thy face, and 5641
Ps 10: 1 why *h·* thou thyself in times of 5956
44:24 Wherefore *h·* thou thy face, and 5641
88:14 why *h·* thou thy face from me? "
104:29 Thou *h·* thy face, they are troubled: "
Isa 45:15 thou art a God that *h·* thyself, O

hideth
1Sa 23:23 places where he *h·* himself, and 2244
Job 23: 9 he *h·* himself on the right hand, 5848
34:29 and when he *h·* his face, who then 5641
42: 3 Who is he that *h·* counsel without 5956
Ps 10:11 he *h·* his face; he will never see it. 5641
139:12 the darkness *h·* not from thee; 2821
Pr 10:18 He that *h·* hatred with lying lips, 3680
19:24 man *h·* his hand in his bosom, *2934
22: 3 foreseeth the evil, and *h·* himself: 5641
26:15 slothful *h·* his hand in his bosom; *2934
27:12 foreseeth the evil, and *h·* himself; 5641
16 Whosoever *h·* her *h·* the wind, and *6845
28:27 that *h·* his eyes shall have many a 5956
Isa 8:17 that *h·* his face from the house of 5641
M't 13:44 when a man hath found, he *h·*, *2928

hiding
Job 31:33 by *h·* mine iniquity in my bosom: 2934
Ps 32: 7 Thou art my *h·* place; thou shalt 5643
119:114 art my *h·* place and my shield: "
Isa 28:17 waters shall overflow the *h·* place. "
32: 2 be as an *h·* place from the wind, 4224
Hab 3: 4 and there was the *h·* of his power. 2253

hiding-place See HIDING and PLACE.

Hiel (*hi'-el*)
1Ki 16:34 *H·* the Beth-elite build Jericho: 2419

Hierapolis (*hi-e-rap'-o-lis*)
Col 4:13 are in Laodicea, and them in *H·*. 2404

Higgaion (*hig-gah'-yon*)
Ps 9:16 work of his own hands. *H·*. Selah. 1902

high See also HIGHER; HIGHEST; HIGHMINDED; HIGHWAY.
Ge 7:19 all the *h·* hills, that were under the 1364
14:18 was the priest of the most *h·* God. 5945
19 be Abram of the most *h·* God, "
20 And blessed be the most *h·* God, "
Ge 14:22 unto the Lord, the most *h·* God, 5945
29: 7 Lo, it is yet *h·* day, neither is it 1419
Ex 14: 8 of Israel went out with an *h·* hand. 7311
25:20 stretch forth their wings on *h·*, 4605
37: 9 spread out their wings on *h·*, and "
39:31 to fasten it on *h·* upon the mitre; * "
Le 21:10 And he that is the *h·* priest among 1419
26:22 and your *h·* ways shall be desolate.*
30 I will destroy your *h·* places, and 1116
Nu 11:31 it were two cubits *h·* upon the face of *
20:17 we will go by the king's *h·* way,
19 We will go by the *h·* way: and if I 4546
21:22 we will go along by the king's *h·* way,
28 the lords of the *h·* places of Arnon. 1116
22:41 him up into the *h·* places of Baal, "
23: 3 thee. And he went to an *h·* place. *8205
24:16 the knowledge of the most *H·*, 5945
33: 3 of Israel went out with an *h·* hand 7311
52 pluck down all their *h·* places: 1116
35:25 in it unto the death of the *h·* priest, 1419
28 until the death of the *h·* priest: but "
28 after the death of the *h·* priest the "
De 2:27 I will go along by the *h·* way, I will 1870
3: 5 cities were fenced with *h·* walls, 1364
12: 2 upon the *h·* mountains, and upon 7311
26:19 to make thee *h·* above all nations 5945
28: 1 thy God will set thee on *h·* above all "
43 shall get up above thee very *h·*; *4605
52 thy *h·* and fenced walls come down, 1364
32: 8 When the most *H·* divided to the 5945
13 He made him ride on the *h·* places 1116
27 Our hand is *h·*, and the Lord hath *7311
33:29 shalt tread upon their *h·* places. 1116
Jos 20: 6 and until the death of the *h·* priest 1419
J'g 5:18 death in the *h·* places of the field. 4791
1Sa 9:12 of the people to day in the *h·* place: 1116
13 before he go up to the *h·* place to eat; "
14 them, for to go up to the *h·* place. "
19 go up before me unto the *h·* place; "
25 from the *h·* place into the city, "
10: 5 coming down from the *h·* place with "
13 prophesying, he came to the *h·* place. "
13: 6 in rocks, and in *h·* places, and in *6877
2Sa 1:19 Israel is slain upon thy *h·* places: 1116
25 thou wast slain in thine *h·* places. "
22: 3 my *h·* tower, and my refuge, my 4869
14 and the most *H·* uttered his voice. 5945
34 and setteth me upon my *h·* places. 1116
49 hast lifted me up on *h·* above them *7311
23: 1 the man who was raised up on *h·*, 5920
1Ki 3: 2 the people sacrificed in *h·* places, 1116
3 and burnt incense in *h·* places. "
4 for that was the great *h·* place: "
6:10 all the house, five cubits *h·*: and 6967
23 of olive tree, each ten cubits *h·*. "
7:15 brass, of eighteen cubits *h·* apiece: "
35 a round compass of half a cubit *h·*: "
9: 8 this house, which is *h·*, every one 5945
11: 7 Solomon build an *h·* place for 1116
12:31 he made an house of *h·* places, and "
32 the priests of the *h·* places which "
13: 2 he offer the priests of the *h·* places "
32 all the houses of the *h·* places which "
33 the people priests of the *h·* places: "
33 one of the priests of the *h·* places. "
14:23 For they also built them *h·* places, 1364
23 on every *h·* hill, and under every "
15:14 the *h·* places were not removed: 1116
21: 9 set Naboth on *h·* among the people: 7218
12 set Naboth on *h·* among the people. "
22:43 the *h·* places were not taken away; 1116
43 burnt incense yet in the *h·* places. "
2Ki 12: 3 the *h·* places were not taken away: "
3 and burnt incense in the *h·* places. "
10 scribe and the *h·* priest came up, 1419
14: 4 Howbeit the *h·* places were not 1116
4 and burnt incense on the *h·* places. "
15: 4 the *h·* places were not removed: the "
4 burnt incense still on the *h·* places. "
35 the *h·* places were not removed: the "
35 burned incense still in the *h·* places. "
16: 4 burnt incense in the *h·* places, and "
17: 9 they built them *h·* places in all their "
10 groves in every *h·* hill, and under 1364
11 burnt incense in all the *h·* places, 1116
29 them in the houses of the *h·* places "
32 of them priests of the *h·* places, "
32 them in the houses of the *h·* places. "
18: 4 He removed the *h·* places, and brake "
22 whose *h·* places and whose altars "
19:22 and lifted up thine eyes on *h·*? 4791
21: 3 For he built up again the *h·* places 1116
22: 4 Go up to Hilkiah the *h·* priest, that 1419
8 And Hilkiah the *h·* priest said unto "
23: 4 commanded Hilkiah the *h·* priest, "
5 to burn incense in the *h·* places in 1116
8 and defiled the *h·* places where the "
8 down the *h·* places of the gates "
9 the priests of the *h·* places came not "
13 And the *h·* places that were before "
15 and the *h·* place which Jeroboam "
15 both that altar and the *h·* place he "
15 brake down, and burned the *h·* place, "
19 all the houses also of the *h·* places "
20 slew all the priests of the *h·* places "
1Ch 14: 2 his kingdom was lifted up on *h·*, 4605
16:39 in the *h·* place that was at Gibeon, 1116
17:17 to the estate of a man of *h·* degree, 4608
21:29 season in the *h·* place at Gibeon. 1116
2Ch 1: 3 to the *h·* place that was at Gibeon; "
13 to the *h·* place that was at Gibeon "
3:15 pillars of thirty and five cubits *h·*, 753
6:13 and three cubits *h·*, and had set it 6967
7:21 this house, which is *h·*, shall be *5945
11:15 priests for the *h·* places, and for 1116
14: 3 and the *h·* places, and brake down "
2Ch 14: 5 the *h·* places and the images: and 1116
15:17 the *h·* places were not taken away "
17: 6 took away the *h·* places and groves "
20:19 of Israel with a loud voice on *h·*. *4605
33 the *h·* places were not taken away: 1116
21:11 made *h·* places in the mountains "
23:20 through the *h·* gate into the king's *5945
24:11 and the *h·* priest's officer came and 7218
27: 3 He built the *h·* gate of the house *5945
28: 4 and burnt incense in the *h·* places, 1116
25 he made *h·* places to burn incense "
31: 1 threw down the *h·* places and the "
32:12 taken away his *h·* places and his "
33: 3 he built again the *h·* places which "
17 did sacrifice still in the *h·* places, "
19 places wherein he built *h·* places, "
34: 3 Jerusalem from the *h·* places, and "
4 the images, that were on *h·* above 4605
9 they came to Hilkiah the *h·* priest, 1419
Ne 3: 1 Eliashib the *h·* priest rose up with "
20 the house of Eliashib the *h·* priest. "
25 lieth out from the king's *h·* house, *5945
13:28 the son of Eliashib the *h·* priest, 1419
Es 5:14 gallows be made of fifty cubits *h·*, 1364
7: 9 the gallows fifty cubits *h·*, which "
Job 5:11 To set up on *h·* those that be low; 4791
11: 8 It is as *h·* as heaven; what canst 1363
16:19 in heaven, and my record is on *h·*. 4791
21:22 seeing he judgeth those that are *h·*. 7311
22:12 height of the stars, how *h·* they are! "
25: 2 he maketh peace in his *h·* places. 4791
31: 2 of the Almighty from on *h·*? "
38:15 and the *h·* arm shall be broken. 7311
39:18 time she lifteth up herself on *h·*, 4791
27 command, and make her nest on *h·*? 7311
41:34 He beholdeth all *h·* things: he is 1364
Ps 7: 7 sakes therefore return thou on *h·*. 4791
17 to the name of the Lord most *h·*. 5945
9: 2 praise to thy name, O thou most *H·*. "
18: 2 of my salvation, and my *h·* tower. 4869
27 but wilt bring down *h·* looks. *7311
33 and setteth me upon my *h·* places. 1116
21: 7 through the mercy of the most *H·* 5945
46: 4 of the tabernacles of the most *H·*. "
47: 2 the Lord most *h·* is terrible; he is "
49: 2 Both low and *h·*, rich and poor, 376
50:14 pay thy vows unto the most *H·*: 5945
56: 2 fight against me, O thou most *H·*. *4791
57: 2 I will cry unto God most *h·*; unto 5945
62: 9 and men of *h·* degree are a lie: 376
68:15 an *h·* hill as the hill of Bashan. 1386
16 Why leap ye, ye *h·* hills? this is the "
18 Thou hast ascended on *h·*, thou 4791
69:29 salvation, O God, set me up on *h·*. 7682
71:19 also, O God, is very *h·*, who hast 4791
73:11 is there knowledge in the most *H·*? 5945
75: 5 Lift not up your horn on *h·*: speak 4791
77:10 of the right hand of the most *H·*. 5945
78:17 by provoking the most *H·* in the "
35 and the *h·* God their redeemer. "
56 and provoked the most *h·* God, and "
58 to anger with their *h·* places, and 1116
69 built his sanctuary like *h·* palaces, *7311
82: 6 of you are children of the most *H·*. 5945
83:18 art the most *h·* over all the earth. "
89:13 thy hand, and *h·* is thy right hand. 7311
91: 1 in the secret place of the most *H·* 5945
9 even the most *H·*, thy habitation; "
14 I will set him on *h·*, because he 7682
92: 1 praises unto thy name, O most *H·*: 5945
8 Lord, art most *h·* for evermore. 4791
93: 4 The Lord on *h·* is mightier than the "
97: 9 Lord, art *h·* above all the earth: 5945
99: 2 and he is *h·* above all the people. 7311
101: 5 hath an *h·* look and a proud heart 1362
103:11 the heaven is *h·* above the earth, 1361
104:18 The *h·* hills are a refuge for the 1364
107:11 the counsel of the most *H·*: 5945
41 Yet setteth he the poor on *h·* from 7682
113: 4 The Lord is *h·* above all nations, 7311
5 our God, who dwelleth on *h·*, 1361
131: 1 matters, or in things too *h·* for me. *6381
138: 6 Though the Lord be *h·*, yet hath 7311
139: 6 it is *h·*, I cannot attain unto it. 7682
144: 2 my *h·* tower, and my deliverer; 4869
149: 6 the *h·* praises of God be in their 7319
150: 5 him upon the *h·* sounding cymbals. 8643
Pr 8: 2 standeth in the top of the *h·* places, 4791
9:14 a seat in the *h·* places of the city. "
18:11 as an *h·* wall in his own conceit. 7682
21: 4 An *h·* look, and a proud heart, and 7312
24: 7 Wisdom is too *h·* for a fool: he 7311
Ec 12: 5 shall be afraid of that which is *h·*, 1364
Isa 2:13 the cedars of Lebanon, that are *h·* 7311
14 upon all the *h·* mountains, and upon "
15 upon every *h·* tower, and upon *1364
6: 1 upon a throne, *h·* and lifted up, 7311
10:12 and the glory of his *h·* looks. 7312
33 the *h·* ones of stature shall be hewn "
13: 2 a banner upon the *h·* mountain, *8192
14:14 clouds; I will be like the most *H·*. 5945
15: 2 gone up to...the *h·* places, to weep: 1116
16:12 that Moab is weary on the *h·* place, "
22:16 heweth him out a sepulchre on *h·*, 4791
24:18 the windows from on *h·* are open, "
21 the host of the *h·* ones that are on *h·*, "
25:12 fortress of the *h·* fort of thy walls 4869
26: 5 down them that dwell on *h·*; the 4791
30:13 swelling out in a *h·* wall, whose 7682
25 upon every *h·* mountain, and upon *1364
26 and upon every *h·* hill, rivers and 4791
32:15 spirit be poured upon us from on *h·*, "
33: 5 is exalted; for he dwelleth on *h·*: "
16 He shall dwell on *h·*: his place of "
36: 7 whose *h·* places and whose altars 1111
37:23 and lifted up thine eyes on *h·*? even 4796

Isa 40: 9 get thee up into the h' mountain; 1364
26 Lift up your eyes on h', and behold 4791
41: 18 I will open rivers in h' places, and*8203
49: 9 pastures shall be in all h' places. * "
52: 13 and extolled, and be very h'. 1361
57: 7 Upon a lofty and h' mountain hast 5375
15 the h' and lofty One that inhabiteth 7311
15 I dwell in the h' and holy place, 4791
58: 4 make your voice to be heard on h'. "
14 ride upon the h' places of the earth, 1116
Jer 2: 20 when upon every h' hill and under 1364
3: 2 up thine eyes unto the h' places, *8205
6 upon every h' mountain and under 1364
21 was heard upon the h' places, *8205
4: 11 A dry wind of the h' places in the* "
7: 29 take up a lamentation on h' places;*"
31 have built the h' places of Tophet, 1116
12: 12 are come upon all h' places *8205
14: 6 asses did stand in the h' places, * "
17: 2 by the green trees upon the h' hills. 1364
3 thy h' places for sin, throughout 1116
12 A glorious h' throne from the *4791
19: 5 built also the h' places of Baal, 1116
20: 2 were in the h' gate of Benjamin, *5945
25: 30 The Lord shall roar from on h', 4791
26: 18 house as the h' places of a forest. 1116
31: 21 up waymarks, make thee h' heaps: *8564
32: 35 they built the h' places of Baal, 1116
48: 35 him that offereth in the h' places, "
49: 16 make thy nest as h' as the eagle, 1361
51: 58 her h' gates shall be burned with 1364
La 3: 35 before the face of the most H'. 5945
38 Out of the mouth of the most H' "
Eze 1: 18 were so h' that they were dreadful; 1362
6: 3 and I will destroy your h' places. 1116
6 and the h' places shall be desolate; "
13 upon every h' hill, in all the tops 7311
16: 16 deckedst thy h' places with divers 1116
24 thee an h' place in every street. *7413
25 built thy h' place at every head of* "
31 and makest thine h' place in every* "
39 shall break down thy h' places: * "
17: 22 highest branch of the h' cedar, *7311
22 will plant it upon an h' mountain 1364
24 Lord have brought down the h' tree, "
20: 28 then they saw every h' hill, and all 7311
29 What is the h' place whereunto ye 1116
21: 26 is low, and abase him that is h'. 1364
31: 3 and of an h' stature; and his top 1362
4 the deep set him up on h' with her*7311
34: 6 mountains, and upon every h' hill: "
14 the h' mountains of Israel shall *4791
36: 2 even the ancient h' places are ours 1116
40: 2 set me upon a very h' mountain, 1364
42 and one cubit h': whereupon also 1363
41: 22 altar of wood was three cubits h', 1364
43: 7 of their kings in their h' places. 1116
Da 3: 26 ye servants of the most h' God, 5943
4: 2 and wonders that the h' God hath "
17 the most H' ruleth in the kingdom "
24 this is the decree of the most H', "
32 most H' ruleth in the kingdom "
34 and I blessed the most H', and I "
5: 18 most h' God gave Nebuchadnezzar "
21 most h' God ruled in the kingdom "
7: 18 But the saints of the most H' shall 5946
22 given to the saints of the most H'; "
25 great words against the most H'. 5943
25 wear out the saints of the most H', 5946
27 people of the saints of the most H', "
8: 3 and the two horns were h'; but one 1364
Ho 7: 16 return, but not to the most H': 5920
10: 8 The h' places also of Aven, the sin 1116
11: 7 they called them to the most H', 5920
Am 4: 13 treadeth upon the h' places of the 1116
7: 9 h' places of Isaac shall be desolate, "
Ob 3 whose habitation is h'; that saith 4791
Mic 1: 3 and tread upon the h' places of the 1116
5 what are the h' places of Judah? "
3: 12 house as the h' places of the forest. "
6: 6 and bow myself before the h' God? 4791
Hab 2: 9 that he may set his nest on h', that "
3: 10 voice, and lifted up his hands on h'. 7315
19 me to walk upon mine h' places. 1116
Zep 1: 16 cities, and against the h' towers. 1364
Hag 1: 1, 12, 14, of Josedech, the h' priest, 1419
2: 2 the son of Josedech, the h' priest, "
4 the son of Josedech, the h' priest; "
Zec 3: 1 he shewed me Joshua the h' priest "
8 Hear now, O Joshua the h' priest, "
6: 11 the son of Josedech, the h' priest; "
M't 4: 8 up into an exceeding h' mountain, 5308
17: 1 them up into an h' mountain apart, "
26: 3 the palace of the h' priest, who was 749
51 struck a servant of the h' priest's, "
57 him away to Caiaphas the h' priest, "
58 afar off unto the h' priest's palace, "
62 And the h' priest arose, and said unto "
63 And the h' priest answered and said "
65 Then the h' priest rent his clothes, "
M'r 2: 26 days of Abiathar the h' priest, and "
5: 7 Jesus, thou Son of the most h' God? 5310
6: 21 supper to his lords, h' captains, and
9: 2 them up into an h' mountain apart 5308
14: 47 and smote a servant of the h' priest, 749
53 led Jesus away to the h' priest: and "
54 into the palace of the h' priest: and "
60 the h' priest stood up in the midst, "
61 Again the h' priest asked him, and "
63 Then the h' priest rent his clothes, "
66 one of the maids of the h' priest: "
Lu 1: 78 dayspring from on h' hath visited 5311
3: 2 and Caiaphas being the h' priests,* 749
4: 5 taking him up into an h' mountain,*5308
8: 28 Jesus, thou Son of God most h'? 5310
22: 50 smote the servant of the h' priest, 749
Lu 22: 54 him into the h' priest's house. And 749
24: 49 be endued with power from on h'. 5311
Joh 11: 49 being the h' priest that same year, 749
51 but being h' priest that year, he "
18: 10 and smote the h' priest's servant, and "
13 which was the h' priest that same "
15 was known unto the h' priest, and "
15 Jesus into the palace of the h' priest. "
16 which was known unto the h' priest, "
19 The h' priest then asked Jesus of his "
22 Answerest thou the h' priest so? "
24 bound unto Caiaphas the h' priest. "
26 of the servants of the h' priest, "
19: 31 that sabbath day was an h' day, 3173
Ac 4: 6 Annas the h' priest, and Caiaphas, 749
6 were of the kindred of the h' priest, "
5: 17 the h' priest rose up, and all they "
21 But the h' priest came, and they that "
24 the h' priest and the captain of the*2409
27 and the h' priest asked them, 749
7: 1 said the h' priest, Are these things "
48 most H' dwelleth not in temples 5310
9: 1 And Saul...went unto the h' priest, 749
13: 17 with an h' arm brought he them 5308
16: 17 are the servants of the most h' God, 5310
22: 5 the h' priest doth bear me witness, 749
23: 2 the h' priest Ananias commanded "
4 said, Revilest thou God's h' priest? "
5 wist not...that he was the h' priest: "
24: 1 Ananias the h' priest descended with "
25: 2 Then the h' priest and the chief of * "
Ro 12: 16 Mind not h' things, but condescend 5308
13: 11 it is h' time to awake out of sleep:
2Co 10: 5 and every h' thing that exalteth 5313
Eph 4: 8 When he ascended up on h', he led 5311
6: 12 spiritual wickedness in h' places.* 2032
Ph'p 3: 14 the prize of the h' calling of God in 507
Heb 1: 3 the right hand of the Majesty on h'; 5308
2: 17 a merciful and faithful h' priest in 749
3: 1 consider the Apostle and H' Priest of "
4: 14 that we have a great h' priest, that is "
15 we have not an h' priest which cannot "
5: 1 For every h' priest taken from among "
5 not himself to be made an h' priest; "
10 of God an h' priest after the order of "
6: 20 an h' priest for ever after the order "
7: 1 of Salem, priest of the most h' God, 5310
26 For such an h' priest became 749
27 not daily, as those h' priests, to offer "
28 the law maketh men h' priests which "
8: 1 We have such an h' priest, who is set "
3 every h' priest is ordained to offer "
9: 7 went the h' priest alone once every "
11 an h' priest of good things to come, "
25 as the h' priest entereth into the holy "
10: 21 having an h' priest over the house*3173
13: 11 sanctuary by the h' priest for sin, 749
Re 21: 10 spirit to a great and h' mountain, 5308
12 And had a wall great and h', and had "

higher
Nu 24: 7 and his king shall be h' than Agag, 7311
1Sa 9: 2 he was h' than any of the people. 1364
10: 23 he was h' than any of the people 1361
2Ki 15: 35 He built the h' gate of the house *5945
Ne 4: 13 the wall, and on the h' places, I *6706
Job 35: 5 the clouds which are h' than thou. 1361
Ps 61: 2 me to the rock that is h' than I. 7311
89: 27 h' than the kings of the earth. *5945
Ec 5: 8 for he that is h' than the highest 1364
8 and there be h' than they.
Isa 55: 9 the heavens are h' than the earth, 1361
9 so are my ways h' than your ways, "
Jer 36: 10 in the h' court, at the entry of the *5945
Eze 9: 2 came from the way of the h' gate, * "
42: 5 the galleries were h' than these, *3201
43: 13 shall be the h' place of the altar. *1354
Da 8: 3 but one was h' than the other, and 1364
3 the other, and the h' came up last. "
Lu 14: 10 may say unto thee, Friend, go up h': 511
Ro 13: 1 soul be subject unto the h' powers. 5242
Heb 7: 26 and made h' than the heavens; 5308

highest
Ps 18: 13 and the H' gave his voice; *5945
87: 5 the h' himself shall establish her. * "
Pr 8: 26 h' part of the dust of the world. *7218
9: 3 upon the h' places of the city, 4791
Ec 5: 8 for he that is higher than the h' *1364
Eze 17: 3 took the h' branch of the cedar: *6788
22 of the h' branch of the high cedar,* "
41: 7 from the lowest chamber to the h' 5945
M't 21: 9 of the Lord; Hosanna in the h'. 5310
M'r 11: 10 of the Lord: Hosanna in the h'. "
Lu 1: 32 shall be called the Son of the H': * "
35 power of the H' shall overshadow * "
76 be called the prophet of the H': * "
2: 14 Glory to God in the h', and on earth "
6: 35 ye shall be the children of the H': * "
14: 8 sit not down in the h' room; lest *4411
19: 38 peace in heaven, and glory in the h'. 5310
20: 46 the h' seats in the synagogues, *4410

highly
Lu 1: 28 said, Hail, thou that art h' favoured,
16: 15 which is h' esteemed among men *5308
Ac 12: 20 Herod was h' displeased with them 2371
Ro 12: 3 not to think of himself more h' than 5252
Ph'p 2: 9 God also hath h' exalted him, and 5251
1Th 5: 13 to esteem them very h' in love 1537,4053

highminded
Ro 11: 20 by faith. Be not h', but fear: 5309
1Ti 6: 17 they be not h', nor trust in uncertain "
2Ti 3: 4 heady, h', lovers of pleasures more *5187

highness
Job 31: 23 by reason of his h' I could not †‡7613
Isa 13: 3 even them that rejoice in my h'. *1346

high-place See HIGH and PLACE.

high-priest See HIGH and PRIEST.

highway See also HIGH; HIGHWAYS.
J'g 21: 19 on the east side of the h' that goeth 4546
1Sa 6: 12 went along the h', lowing as they "
2Sa 20: 12 in blood in the midst of the h'. And "
12 he removed Amasa out of the h' into "
13 When he was removed out of the h', "
2Ki 18: 17 which is in the h' of the fuller's field. "
Pr 16: 17 The h' of the upright is to depart "
Isa 7: 3 pool in the h' of the fuller's field; "
11: 16 there shall be an h' for the remnant "
19: 23 day shall there be a h' out of Egypt "
35: 8 And an h' shall be there, and a way, 4547
36: 2 pool in the h' of the fuller's field. 4546
40: 3 in the desert a h' for our God. "
62: 10 cast up, cast up the h'; gather out "
Jer 31: 21 set thine heart toward the h', even "
M'r 10: 46 Timæus, sat by the h' side begging.*3598

highways
J'g 5: 6 the h' were unoccupied, and the 734
20: 31 in the h', of which one goeth up 4546
32 draw them from the city unto the h'. "
45 they gleaned of them in the h' five "
Isa 33: 8 The h' lie waste, the wayfaring man "
49: 11 a way, and my h' shall be exalted. "
Am 5: 16 they shall say in all the h', Alas! *2351
M't 22: 9 Go ye therefore into the h', *1327,3598
10 servants went out into the h', and "
Lu 14: 23 Go out into the h' and hedges, and "

Hilen (*hi'-len*) See also HOLON.
1Ch 6: 58 And H' with her suburbs, Debir 2432

Hilkiah (*hil-ki'-ah*) See also HELKAI; HILKIAH'S.
2Ki 18: 18 out to them Eliakim the son of H', 2518
26 Then said Eliakim the son of H', "
37 Then came Eliakim the son of H', "
22: 4 Go up to H' the high priest, that he "
8 And H' the high priest said unto "
8 And H' gave the book to Shaphan, "
10 H' the priest hath delivered me a "
12 the king commanded H' the priest, "
14 So H' the priest, and Ahikam, and "
23: 4 the king commanded H' the high "
24 the book that H' the priest found in "
1Ch 6: 13 Shallum begat H', and H' begat "
45 the son of Amaziah, the son of H', "
9: 11 Azariah the son of H', the son of "
26: 11 H' the second, Tebaliah the third, "
2Ch 34: 9 they came to H' the high priest, "
14 H' the priest found a book of the "
15 H' answered and said to Shaphan "
15 H' delivered the book to Shaphan. "
18 H' the priest hath given me a book. "
20 And the king commanded H', and "
22 H',...went to Huldah the prophetess, "
35: 8 H' and Zechariah and Jehiel, rulers "
Ezr 7: 1 the son of Azariah, the son of H', "
Ne 8: 4 and Urijah, and H', and Maaseiah, "
11: 11 Seraiah the son of H', the son of "
12: 7 Sallu, Amok, H', Jedaiah. These "
21 Of H', Hashabiah; of Jedaiah. "
Isa 22: 20 my servant Eliakim the son of H': "
22 Then came Eliakim, the son of H', "
Jer 1: 1 words of Jeremiah the son of H', "
29: 3 and Gemariah the son of H', whom "

Hilkiah's (*hil-ki'-ahs*)
Isa 36: 3 H' son, which was over the house,*2518

hill See also DUNGHILL; HILL'S; HILLS.
Ex 17: 9 I will stand on the top of the h' with 1389
10 and Hur went up to the top of the h'. "
24: 4 builded an altar under the h', and*2022
Nu 14: 44 presumed to go up unto the h' top:* "
45 which dwelt in that h', and smote * "
De 1: 41 ye were ready to go up into the h'. * "
43 went presumptuously up into the h'. * "
Jos 5: 3 of Israel at the h' of the foreskins. 1389
13: 6 the inhabitants of the h' country 2022
15: 9 drawn from the top of the h' unto * "
17: 16 The h' is not enough for us: and * "
18: 13 near the h' that lieth on the south * "
14 the h' that lieth before Beth-horon * "
21: 11 Hebron, in the h' country of Judah, * "
24: 30 on the north side of the h' of Gaash.* "
33 buried him in a h' that pertained *1389
J'g 2: 9 on the north side of the h' Gaash. *2022
7: 1 by the h' of Moreh, in the valley. 1389
16: 3 carried them up to the top of an h' *2022
1Sa 7: 1 the house of Abinadab in the h', 1389
9: 11 they went up to the h' to the city, *4608
10: 5 thou shalt come to the h' of God, 1389
10 they came thither to the h', behold, "
23: 19 in the h' of Hachilah, which is on "
25: 20 came down by the covert of the h', *2022
26: 1 not David hide himself in the h' of 1389
3 Saul pitched in the h' of Hachilah, "
13 stood on the top of an h' afar off; *2022
2Sa 2: 24 they were come to the h' of Ammah, 1389
25 troop, and stood on the top of an h'. "
13: 34 the way of the h' side behind him. 2022
16: 1 was a little past the top of the h', *
21: 9 they hanged them in the h' before*2022
1Ki 11: 7 in the h' that is before Jerusalem,* "
14: 23 groves, on every high h', and under 1389
16: 24 bought the h' Samaria of Shemer 2022
24 and built on the h', and called the "
24 of Shemer, owner of the h', Samaria. "
2Ki 1: 9 behold, he sat on the top of an h'. "
4: 27 she came to the man of God to the h', "
17: 10 groves in every high h', and under 1389
Ps 2: 6 my king upon my holy h' of Zion. 2022
3: 4 and he heard me out of his holy h'. "
15: 1 who shall dwell in thy holy h'? "
24: 3 Who shall ascend into the h' of the "

Ps 42: 6 the Hermonites, from the h· Mizar. 2022
43: 3 let them bring me unto thy holy h·, "
68: 15 h· of God is as the h· of Bashan; * "
15 an high h· as the h· of Bashan. * "
16 this is the h· which God desireth to* "
99: 9 our God, and worship at his holy h·; "
Ca 4: 6 and to the h· of frankincense. 1389
Isa 5: 1 a vineyard in a very fruitful h·: 7161
10: 32 of Zion, the h· of Jerusalem. 1389
30: 17 mountain, and as an ensign on an h·. "
25 and upon every high h·, rivers and "
31: 4 mount Zion, and for the h· thereof. "
40: 4 mountain and h· shall be made low: "
Jer 2: 20 when upon every high h· and under "
16: 16 from every h·, and out of the holes "
31: 39 over against it upon the h· Gareb, "
49: 16 that holdest the height of the h·: "
50: 6 they have gone from mountain to h·, "
Eze 6: 13 altars, upon every high h·, in all the "
20: 28 they saw every high h·, and all the "
34: 6 mountains, and upon every high h·: "
26 round about my h· a blessing; "
M't 5: 14 A city that is set on an h· cannot 3735
Lu 1: 39 went into the h· country with haste, 3714
65 throughout all the h· country of "
3: 5 mountain and h· shall be brought 1015
4: 29 led him unto the brow of the h· 3735
9: 37 they were come down from the h·,* "
Ac 17: 22 Paul stood in the midst of Mars' h·,*697
hill-country See HILL and COUNTRY.
Hillel (*hil'-lel*)
J'g 12: 13 And after him Abdon the son of H·, 1985
15 the son of H· the Pirathonite died, "
hill's
2Sa 16: 13 Shimei went along on the h· side *2022
hills
Ge 7: 19 all the high h·, that were under *2022
49: 26 utmost bound of the everlasting h·: 1389
Nu 23: 9 him, and from the h· I behold him: "
De 1: 7 in the h·, and in the vale, and in *2022
8: 7 that spring out of valleys and h·; "
9 out of whose h· thou mayest dig 2042
11: 11 it, is a land of h· and valleys, and 2022
12: 2 upon the h·, and under every green 1389
33: 15 the precious things of the lasting h·. "
Jos 9: 1 on this side Jordan, in the h·, and *2022
10: 40 smote all the country of the h·, and* "
11: 16 the h·, and all the south country, * "
1Ki 20: 23 Their gods are gods of the h·; "
28 The Lord is God of the h·, but he is "
22: 17 saw all Israel scattered upon the h·,* "
2Ki 16: 4 on the h·, and under every green 1389
2Ch 28: 4 on the h·, and under every green "
Job 15: 7 wast thou made before the h·? "
Ps 18: 7 foundations also of the h· moved *2022
50: 10 and the cattle upon a thousand h·. 2042
65: 12 and the little h· rejoice on every 1389
68: 16 Why leap ye, ye high h·? this is *2022
72: 3 and the little h·, by righteousness.*1389
80: 10 The h· were covered with the *2022
95: 4 the strength of the h· is his also. * "
97: 5 h· melted like wax at the presence ‡ "
98: 8 hands: let the h· be joyful together "
104: 10 valleys, which run among the h·. * "
13 watereth the h· from his chambers:* "
18 The high h· are a refuge for the * "
32 he toucheth the h·, and they smoke.* "
114: 4 rams, and the little h· like lambs. 1389
6 rams; and ye little h·, like lambs? "
121: 1 I will lift up mine eyes unto the h·,*2022
148: 9 Mountains, and all h·; fruitful 1389
Pr 8: 25 before the h· was I brought forth: "
Ca 2: 8 mountains, skipping upon the h·. "
Isa 2: 2 shall be exalted above the h·; and "
14 upon all the h· that are lifted up, "
5: 25 the h· did tremble, and their 2022
7: 25 all h· that shall be digged with the "
40: 12 in scales, and the h· in a balance? 1389
41: 15 and shalt make the h· as chaff. "
42: 15 make waste mountains and h·, and "
54: 10 depart, and the h· be removed; but "
55: 12 the mountains and the h· shall break "
65: 7 and blasphemed me upon the h·: "
Jer 3: 23 salvation is hoped for from the h·, "
4: 24 and all the h· moved lightly "
13: 27 abominations on the h· in the fields. "
17: 2 by the green trees upon the high h·. "
Eze 6: 3 and to the h·, to the rivers, and to "
35: 8 in thy h·, and in thy valleys, and in "
36: 4, 6 and to the h·, to the rivers, and to "
Ho 4: 13 and burn incense upon the h·, under "
10: 8 Cover us; and to the h·, Fall on us. "
Joe 3: 18 and the h· shall flow with milk, and "
Am 9: 13 sweet wine, and all the h· shall melt. "
Mic 4: 1 it shall be exalted above the h·; and "
6: 1 and let the h· hear thy voice. "
Na 1: 5 the h· melt, and the earth is burned "
Hab 3: 6 the perpetual h· did bow: his ways "
Zep 1: 10 and a great crashing from the h·. "
Lu 23: 30 Fall on us; and to the h·, Cover us. 1015
hill-top See HILL and TOP.
him See in the APPENDIX; also HIMSELF.
himself
Ge 14: 15 And he divided h· against them, he
18: 2 door, and bowed h· toward the ground,
19: 1 and he bowed h· with his face toward
22: 8 My son, God will provide h· a lamb for
23: 7 And Abraham stood up, and bowed h·
12 And Abraham bowed down h· before
24: 52 worshipped the Lord, bowing h· to the
27: 42 doth comfort h·, purposing to kill
30: 36 three days' journey betwixt h· and
32: 21 h· lodged that night in...company. 1931
33: 3 bowed h· to the ground seven times,
41: 14 shaved h·, and changed his raiment,
42: 7 but made h· strange unto them,
24 And he turned h· about from them,
43: 31 refrained h·, and said, Set on bread.
32 And they set on for him by h·, and for
45: 1 Then Joseph could not refrain h· before
1 while Joseph made h· known unto his
46: 29 to Goshen, and presented h· unto him;
47: 31 Israel bowed h· upon the bed's head.
48: 2 and Israel strengthened h·, and sat
12 and he bowed h· with his face to the
Ex 10: 6 and he turned h·, and went out from *
21: 3 If he came in by h·, he shall go out 1610
3 he shall go out by h·: if he were "
4 master's, and he shall go out by h·. "
8 master, who hath betrothed her to h·,
Le 7: 8 the priest shall have to h· the skin of
9: 8 of the sin offering, which was for h·.
14: 8 wash h· in water, that he may be clean:
15: 5, 6, 7, 8, 10, 11, 22, 27 bathe h· in water,
16: 6 of the sin offering, which is for h·,
6 and make an atonement for h·, and for
11 of the sin offering, which is for h·,
11 and shall make an atonement for h·,
11 of the sin offering which is for h·:
17 and have made an atonement for h·,
24 an atonement for h·, and for the people,
17: 15 and bathe h· in water, and be unclean
21: 4 he shall not defile h·, being a chief
4 man among his people, to profane h·.
11 nor defile h· for his father, or for his
22: 8 he shall not eat to defile h· therewith:
25: 26 it, and h· be able to redeem it; *3027
47 wax poor, and sell h· unto the stranger
49 or if he be able, he may redeem h·. 3027
27: 8 then he will present h· before the *
Nu 6: 3 He shall separate h· from wine and
5 in the which he separateth h· unto the
6 All the days that he separateth h· unto
7 He shall not make h· unclean for his
16: 9 bring you near to h· to do the service
19: 12 shall purify h· with it on the third 1931
12 but if he purify not h· the third day,
13 purifieth not h·, defileth the tabernacle
19 on the seventh day he shall purify h·, *
19 wash his clothes, and bathe h· in water,
20 and shall not purify h·, that soul shall
23: 24 lion, and lift up h· as a young lion:
25: 3 And Israel, joined h· unto Baal-peor:
31: 53 war had taken spoil, every man for h·.
35: 19 revenger of blood h· shall slay the 1931
36: 7 Israel shall keep h· to the inheritance*
9 shall keep h· to his own inheritance.*
De 7: 6 thee to be a special people unto h·,‡
14: 2 thee to be a peculiar people unto h·,‡
17: 16 But he shall not multiply horses to h·,
17 Neither shall he multiply wifes to h·,
17 shall he greatly multiply to h· silver
23: 11 cometh on, he shall wash h· with water:
28: 9 establish thee a holy people unto h·,
29: 13 thee to day for a people unto h·, and
19 that he bless h· in his heart, saying, I
32: 36 and repent h· for his servants, when he
33: 21 And he provided the first part for h·,
Jos 22: 23 thereon, let the Lord h· require it;
J'g 3: 19 he h· turned again from the quarries 1931
20 parlour, which he had for h· alone.
4: 11 in law of Moses, had severed h· from
6: 31 if he be a god, let him plead for h·,
7: 5 a dog lappeth, him shalt thou set by h·;
9: 5 son of Jerubbaal was left; for he hid h·.
16: 30 And he bowed h· with all his might;
Ru 3: 8 the man was afraid, and turned h·:
1Sa 2: 14 brought up the priest took for h·. *
3: 21 Lord revealed h· to Samuel in Shiloh
8: 11 your sons, and appoint them for h·,*
10: 19 your God, who h· saved you out of all
22 he hath hid h· among the stuff. 1931
14: 47 whithersoever he turned h·, he vexed
17: 16 evening, and presented h· forty days.
18: 4 And Jonathan stripped h· of the robe
5 Saul sent him, and behaved h· wisely:
14 And David behaved h· wisely in all his
15 Saul saw that he behaved h· very wisely,
30 that David behaved h· more wisely than
20: 24 So David hid h· in the field: and when
41 the ground, and bowed h· three times:
21: 13 and feigned h· mad in their hands, and
23: 19 Doth not David hide h· with us in the
23 the lurking places where he hideth h·,
24: 8 with his face to the earth, and bowed h·.
25: 31 or that my lord hath avenged h·: but
26: 1 Doth not David hide h· in the hill of
28: 8 And Saul disguised h·, and put on other
14 his face to the ground, and bowed h·.*
29: 4 he reconcile h· unto his master?
30: 6 but David encouraged h· in the Lord
31 David h· and his men were wont to
2Sa 3: 6 Abner made h· strong for the house
31 And king David h· followed the bier. *
6: 20 who uncovered h· to day in the eyes of
20 fellows shamelessly uncovereth h·!
7: 23 God went to redeem for a people to h·,
9: 8 And he bowed h·, and said, What is thy
12: 18 how will he then vex h·, if we tell him
20 anointed h·, and changed his apparel,
13: 6 Amnon lay down, and made h· sick:
14: 22 and bowed h·, and thanked the king:*
33 bowed h· on his face to the ground
15: 23 the king also h· passed over the brook
17: 23 hanged h·, and died, and was buried
18: 21 And Cushi bowed h· unto Joab, and ran.
24: 20 bowed h· before the king on his face
1Ki 1: 5 the son of Haggith exalted h·, saying, I
23 he bowed h· before the king with his
47 And the king bowed h· upon the bed.
1Ki 1: 52 said, If he will shew h· a worthy man,
53 and bowed h· to king Solomon: and *
2: 19 and bowed h· unto her, and sat down
11: 29 he had clad h· with a new garment; 1931
15: 15 and the things which h· had dedicated,
16: 9 drinking h· drunk in the house of Azra
17: 21 And he stretched h· upon the child
18: 2 And Elijah went to shew h· unto Ahab.
6 Ahab went one way by h·, and Obadiah
6 and Obadiah went another way by h·.
42 And he cast h· down upon the earth,
19: 4 But he h· went a day's journey into 1931
4 requested for h· that he might die; 5315
20: 11 that girdeth on his harness boast h· as
16 Ben-hadad was drinking h· drunk in
38 disguised h· with ashes upon his face.
21: 25 which did sell h· to work wickedness
29 how Ahab humbleth h· before me?
29 he humbleth h· before me, I will not
22: 30 king of Israel disguised h·, and went
2Ki 4: 34 and he stretched h· upon the child;
35 and stretched h· upon him: and the
5: 14 and dipped h· seven times in Jordan,
6: 10 and saved h· there, not once nor twice.
19: 1 covered h· with sackcloth, and went
23: 16 And as Josiah turned h·, he spied the
1Ch 12: 1 he yet kept h· close because of Saul
13: 13 brought not the ark home to h· to *
21: 21 and bowed h· to David with his face to
2Ch 12: 1 and had strengthened h·, he forsook *
12 And when he humbled h·, the wrath of
13 So king Rehoboam strengthened h· in
13: 9 cometh to consecrate h· with a 3027
12 God h· is with us for our captain, and*
15: 18 and that he h· had dedicated, silver,
16: 9 to shew h· strong in the behalf of them
14 sepulchres, which he had made for h·
17: 1 and strengthened h· against Israel
16 Zichri, who willingly offered h· unto
18: 29 So the king of Israel disguised h·; and
34 of Israel stayed h· up in his chariot
20: 3 and set h· to seek the Lord, and 6440
35 Jehoshaphat king of Judah join h· with
36 he joined h· with him to make ships
21: 4 he strengthened h·, and slew all his
23: 1 Jehoiada strengthened h·, and took
25: 11 And Amaziah strengthened h·, and *
14 and bowed down h· before them, and
26: 8 for he strengthened h· exceedingly.*
20 yea, h· hasted also to go out, 1931
32: 1 cities, and thought to win them for h·.
5 Also he strengthened h·, and built up*
9 he h· laid siege against Lachish, *1931
26 Hezekiah humbled h· for the pride of
27 he made h· treasuries for silver, and *
33: 12 and humbled h· greatly before the God
23 And humbled not h· before the Lord,
23 Manasseh his father had humbled h·;
35: 22 but disguised h·, that he might fight
36: 12 and humbled not h· before Jeremiah
Ezr 10: 1 weeping and casting h· down before
8 forfeited, and h· separated from 1931
Es 5: 10 Nevertheless Haman refrained h·: and
Job 1: 12 only upon h· put not forth thine hand.
2: 1 among them to present h· before the
8 a potsherd to scrape h· withal; and he
4: 2 who can withhold h· from speaking?
9: 4 who hath hardened h· against him,
15: 25 strengtheneth h· against the Almighty.
17: 8 shall stir up h· against the hypocrite.
18: 4 He teareth h· in his anger: shall *5315
22: 2 that is wise may be profitable unto h·?
23: 9 he hideth h· on the right hand, that I
27: 10 Will he delight h· in the Almighty?
32: 2 he justified h· rather than God. 5315
34: 9 that he should delight h· with God.
14 gather unto h· his spirit and his breath;
41: 25 When he raiseth up h·, the mighty are
Ps 4: 3 hath set apart him that is godly for h·:
10: 10 He croucheth, and humbleth h·, that*
14 the poor committeth h· unto thee; thou
35: 8 let his net that he hath hid catch h·:
36: 2 For he flattereth h· in his own eyes,
4 he setteth h· in a way that is not good;
37: 35 and spreading h· like a green bay tree.
50: 6 righteousness: for God is judge h·. 1931
52: 7 and strengthened h· in his wickedness.
54: *title* Doth not David hide h· with us?
55: 12 me that did magnify h· against me;
68: 30 one submit h· with pieces of silver:*
87: 5 the Highest h· shall establish her. 1931
93: 1 strength, wherewith he hath girded h·:
109: 18 As he clothed h· with cursing like as
113: 6 Who humbleth h· to behold the things
132: 18 But upon h· shall his crown flourish.
135: 4 the Lord hath chosen Jacob unto h·,
14 will repent h· concerning his servants.
Pr 5: 22 own iniquities shall take the wicked h·,*
9: 7 a scorner getteth to h· shame: and he
10: 7 a wicked man getteth h· a blot.
11: 25 watereth shall be watered also h·. 1931
12: 9 better than he that honoureth h·, and
13: 7 that maketh h· rich, yet hath nothing:
7 maketh h· poor, yet hath great riches.
14: 14 a good man shall be satisfied from h·.
16: 4 Lord hath made all things for h·: *4617
26 He that laboureth laboureth for h·;*
18: 1 a man, having separated h·, seeketh
24 hath friends must shew h· friendly:*
21: 13 shall cry h·, but shall not be heard.*1931
22: 3 man foreseeth the evil, and hideth h·;
25: 9 Debate thy cause with thy neighbour h·;
14 Whoso boasteth h· of a false gift is
27: 12 man foreseeth the evil, and hideth h·;
28: 10 he shall fall h· into his own pit: 1931
29: 15 child left to h· bringeth his mother to

Ec 5: 9 the king h' is served by the field.
10:12 but the lips of a fool will swallow up h'.
Ca 2: 9 shewing h' through the lattice.
3: 9 King Solomon made h' a chariot of the
5: 6 but my beloved had withdrawn h', and
Isa 2: 9 and the great man humbleth h': *
20 they made each one for h' to worship,*
3: 5 the child shall behave h' proudly
7:14 the Lord h' shall give you a sign; 1931
8:13 Sanctify the Lord of hosts h'; and let*
19:17 mention thereof shall be afraid in h',*
22:16 graveth a habitation for h' in a rock?
28:20 than that a man can stretch h' on it:
20 narrower than that he can wrap h' in
31: 4 nor abase h' for the noise of them:
37: 1 clothes, and covered h' with sackcloth,
38:15 both spoken...and h' hath done it: 1931
44: 5 and another shall call h' by the name
5 and surname h' by the name of Israel.
14 oak, which he strengtheneth for h'
15 for he will take thereof, and warm h';
16 yea, he warmeth h', and saith, Aha,
23 Jacob, and glorified h' in Israel.
45:18 God h' that formed the earth and *1931
56: 3 that hath joined h' to the Lord, speak,
59:15 departeth from evil maketh h' a prey:
61:10 as a bridegroom decketh h' with
63:12 them, to make h' an everlasting name?
64: 7 that stirreth up h' to take hold of thee:
65:16 That he who blesseth h' in the earth
16 shall bless h' in the God of truth; and
Jer 10:23 know that the way of man is not in h':
16:20 Shall a man make gods unto h', and
23:24 Can any hide h' in secret places that I
29:26 that is mad, and maketh h' a prophet,
27 which maketh h' a prophet to you?
31:18 heard Ephraim bemoaning h' thus;
34: 9 none should serve h' of them, to wit, of
37:12 to separate h' thence in the midst of*
43:12 shall array h' with the land of Egypt,
48:26 for he magnified h' against the Lord:
42 because he hath magnified h' against
49:10 he shall not be able to hide h': his seed
51: 3 and against him that lifteth h' up in his
14 The Lord of hosts hath sworn by h',5315
La 1: 9 for the enemy hath magnified h'.
Eze 7:13 neither shall any strengthen h' in the
14: 7 Israel, which separateth h' from me,
24: 2 the king of Babylon set h' against *
25:12 offended, and revenged h' upon them;
45:22 prepare for h' and for all the people
Da 1: 8 not defile h' with the portion of the
8 eunuchs that he might not defile h'.
6:14 was sore displeased with h', and set*
8:11 he magnified h' even to the prince *
25 and he shall magnify h' in his heart,
9:26 Messiah be cut off, but not for h': *
11:36 to his will; and he shall exalt h', and
36 and magnify h' above every god, and
37 for he shall magnify h' above all.
Ho 5: 6 he hath withdrawn h' from them.
7: 8 hath mixed h' among the people; 1931
8: 9 up to Assyria, a wild ass alone by h':
10: 1 vine, he bringeth forth fruit unto h':*
13: 1 he exalted h' in Israel; but when 1931
Am 2:14 neither shall the mighty deliver h':5315
15 is swift of foot shall not deliver h': "
16 he that rideth the horse deliver h'. "
6: 8 The Lord God hath sworn by h', "
Jon 4: 8 he fainted, and wished in h' to die, and
Hab 2: 6 him that ladeth h' with thick clay!
M't 6: 4 secret h' shall reward thee openly.*846
8:17 H' took our infirmities, and bare our "
12:15 knew it, he withdrew h' from thence:*
26 out Satan, he is divided against h';1438
45 taketh with h' seven other spirits "
45 other spirits more wicked than h', "
13:21 Yet hath he not root in h', but "
16:24 will come after me, let him deny h', "
18: 4 shall humble h' as this little child, "
23:12 shall exalt h' shall be abased; and "
12 shall humble h' shall be exalted. "
27: 3 repented h', and brought again the "
5 departed, and went and hanged h'. "
42 He saved others; h' he cannot save.1438
57 who also h' was Jesus' disciple: 846
M'k 3: 7 Jesus withdrew h' with his disciples *
21 on him: for they said, He is beside h'.
26 If Satan rise up against h', and be 1438
5: 5 crying, and cutting h' with stones. "
30 knowing in h' that virtue had gone "
6:17 For Herod h' had sent forth and laid 846
8:34 let him deny h', and take up his 1438
12:33 and to love his neighbour as h', is "
36 David h' said by the Holy Ghost, 846
37 David therefore h' calleth him Lord; "
14:54 the servants, and warmed h' at the fire.
67 saw Peter warming h', she looked upon
15:31 He saved others; h' he cannot save.1438
Lu 3:23 Jesus h' began to be about thirty 846
5:16 And he withdrew h' into the wilderness,
6: 3 David did, when h' was an hungred,*846
7:39 he spake within h', saying, This 1438
9:23 let him deny h', and take up his "
25 world, and lose h', or be cast away? "
10: 1 place, whither he h' would come. 846
29 he, willing to justify h', said unto 1438
11:18 If Satan also be divided against h', "
26 other spirits more wicked than h'; "
12:17 And he thought within h', saying, "
21 layeth up treasure for h', and is not "
37 he shall gird h', and make them to sit
47 will, and prepared not h', neither did *
14:11 whosoever exalteth h' shall be 1438
11 and he that humbleth h' shall be
15:15 And he went and joined h' to a citizen

Lu 15:17 And when he came to h', he said, 1438
16: 3 the steward said within h', What "
18: 4 he said within h', Though I fear not "
11 stood, and prayed thus with h', God, "
14 that exalteth h' shall be abased; "
14 that humbleth h' shall be exalted. "
19:12 to receive for h' a kingdom, and to "
20:42 And David h' saith in the book of 846
23: 2 saying that he h' is Christ a King. 1438
7 who h' also was at Jerusalem at 846
35 let him save h', if he be Christ, the 1438
51 who also h' waited for the kingdom *846
24:12 wondering in h' at that which was *1438
15 Jesus h' drew near, and went with 846
27 the things concerning h'. 1438
36 Jesus h' stood in the midst of them,846
Joh 2:24 Jesus did not commit h' unto them,1438
4: 2 Though Jesus h' baptized not, but 846
12 drank thereof h', and his children, "
44 For Jesus h' testified, that a prophet "
53 and h' believed, and his whole house."
5:13 for Jesus had conveyed h' away, a
18 Father, making h' equal with God. 1438
19 Son can do nothing of h', but what "
20 sheweth him all things that h' doeth:846
26 For as the Father hath life in h'; 1438
26 given to the Son to have life in h'; "
37 And the Father h', which hath sent *846
6: 6 for he h' knew what he would do. "
15 again into a mountain h' alone. "
61 Jesus knew in h' that his disciples 1438
7: 4 he h' seeketh to be known openly. 846
18 He that speaketh of h' seeketh his 1438
8: 7 he lifted up h', and said unto them,
10 When Jesus had lifted up h', and saw
22 Will he kill h'? because he saith, 1438
59 Jesus hid h', and went out of the temple,
9:21 age; ask him; he shall speak for h'. 848
11:38 groaning in h' cometh to the grave.1438
51 this spake he not of h': but being "
12:36 departed, and did hide h' from them.
13: 4 and took a towel, and girded h'. 1438
32 God shall also glorify him in h', and "
16:13 for he shall not speak of h'; but "
27 the Father h' loveth you, because 846
18:18 Peter stood with them, and warmed h'.
25 And Simon Peter stood and warmed h'.
19: 7 because he made h' the Son of God.1438
12 whosoever maketh h' a king 848
21: 1 things Jesus shewed h' again to the 1438
1 and on this wise shewed he h'.
7 naked, and did cast h' into the sea.1438
14 that Jesus shewed h' to his disciples, *
Ac 1: 3 To whom also he shewed h' alive 1438
2:34 he saith h', The Lord said unto my 846
5:13 rest durst no man join h' to them:
36 boasting h' to be somebody; to 1438
7:26 next day he shewed h' unto them as *
8: 9 out that he h' was some great one: 1448
13 Then Simon h' believed also: and 846
34 this? of h', or of some other man? 1438
9:26 he assayed to join h' to the disciples:
10:17 while Peter doubted in h' what this 1438
12:11 when Peter was come to h', he said, "
14:17 he left not h' without witness, in that "
16:27 and would have killed h', supposing "
18:19 he h' entered into the synagogue, 846
19:22 but he h' stayed in Asia for a season. "
31 not adventure h' into the theatre. 1438
20:13 he appointed, minding h' to go afoot.846
21:26 the next day purifying h' with them
25: 4 he h' would depart shortly thither. 1438
8 he answered for h', Neither against*
16 to answer for h' concerning the crime*
25 he h' hath appealed to Augustus, 848
26: 1 forth the hand, and answered for h':*
24 And as he thus spake for h', Festus,*
27: 3 to go unto his friends to refresh h'.
28:16 suffered to dwell by h' with a soldier1438
Ro 12: 3 not to think of h' more highly than he
14: 7 liveth to h', and no man dieth to h'. 1438
12 shall give an account of h' to God.
22 Happy is he that condemneth not h' "
15: 3 For even Christ pleased not h'; but,"
1Co 2:15 things, yet he h' is judged of no man.846
3:15 he h' shall be saved; yet so as by fire."
18 Let no man deceive h'. If any man 1438
7:36 that he behaveth h' uncomely toward
11:28 But let a man examine h', and so 1438
29 eateth and drinketh damnation to h', "
14: 4 in an unknown tongue edifieth h'; "
8 who shall prepare h' to the battle? "
28 and let him speak to h', and to God.1438
37 If any man think h' to be a prophet,
15:28 then shall the Son also h' be subject 846
2Co 5:18 who hath reconciled us to h' by 1438
19 reconciling the world unto h', not "
10: 7 man trust to h' that he is Christ's, "
7 let him of h' think this again, that, "
18 For not he that commendeth h' is "
11:14 Satan h' is transformed into an angel846
20 if a man exalt h', if a man smite you
Ga 1: 4 Who gave h' for our sins, that he 1438
2:12 withdrew and separated h', fearing "
20 who loved me, and gave h' for me.
6: 3 if a man think h' to be something, "
3 when he is nothing, he deceiveth h'.1438
4 shall he have rejoicing in h' alone, "
Eph 1: 5 of children by Jesus Christ to h', 848
9 which he hath purposed in h': *
2:15 make in h' of twain one new man, 1438
20 Jesus Christ h' being the chief corner848
5: 2 loved us, and hath given h' for us 1438
25 loved the church, and gave h' for it; "
27 present it to h' a glorious church, "
28 He that loveth his wife loveth h'. "

Eph 5:33 so love his wife even as h'; and the 1438
Ph'p 2: 7 But made h' of no reputation, and "
8 in fashion as a man, he humbled h', "
3:21 even to subdue all things unto h'. "
Col 1:20 him to reconcile all things unto h'; 848
1Th 3:11 Now God h' and our Father, and 846
4:16 Lord h' shall descend from heaven "
2Th 2: 4 opposeth and exalteth h' above all 1438
4 of God, shewing h' that he is God. "
16 Now our Lord Jesus Christ h', and 846
3:16 Now the Lord of peace h' give you "
1Ti 2: 6 Who gave h' a ransom for all, to be 1438
2Ti 2: 4 No man that warreth entangleth h' "
13 abideth faithful: he cannot deny h'.1438
21 If a man therefore purge h' from "
Tit 2:14 Who gave h' for us, that he might "
14 and purify unto h' a peculiar people, "
3:11 sinneth, being condemned of h'. * 843
Heb 1: 3 when he had by h' purged our sins,*1438
2:14 h' likewise took part of the same; 846
18 For in that he h' hath suffered being "
5: 2 for that he h' is also compassed with "
3 so also for h', to offer for sins. 1438
4 no man taketh this honour unto h', "
5 So also Christ glorified not h' to be "
6:13 swear by no greater, he sware by h', "
7:27 he did once, when he offered up h'. "
9: 7 blood, which he offered for h', and "
14 eternal Spirit offered h' without spot "
25 Nor yet that he should offer h' often, "
26 put away sin by the sacrifice of h'. 848
12: 3 contradiction of sinners against h',† "
Jas 1:24 For he beholdeth h', and goeth his 1438
27 and to keep h' unspotted from the "
1Pe 2:23 but committed h' to him that judgeth
1Jo 2: 6 ought h' also so to walk, even as he 846
3: 3 hath this hope in him purifieth h', 1438
5:10 Son of God hath the witness in h':* "
18 that is begotten of God keepeth h',† "
3Jo 10 doth he h' receive the brethren, 846
Re 19:12 written, that no man knew, but he h'.
21: 3 God h' shall be with them, and be 846

hin
Ex 29:40 fourth part of an h' of beaten oil; 1969
40 the fourth part of an h' of wine for "
30:24 the sanctuary, and of oil olive an h': "
Le 19:36 ephah, and a just h', shall ye have: "
23:13 be of wine, the fourth part of an h'. "
Nu 15: 4 with the fourth part of an h' of oil. "
5 the fourth part of an h' of wine for "
6 with the third part of an h' of oil. "
7 offer the third part of an h' of wine, "
9 flour mingled with half an h' of oil. "
10 half an h' of wine, for an offering "
28: 5 fourth part of an h' of beaten oil. "
7 part of an h' for the one lamb: "
14 be half an h' of wine unto a bullock, "
14 the third part of an h' unto a ram, "
14 a fourth part of an h' unto a lamb: "
Eze 4:11 by measure; the sixth part of an h': "
45:24 for a ram, an h' of oil for an ephah. "
46: 5 to give, and an h' of oil to an ephah. "
7 unto, and an h' of oil to an ephah "
11 to give, and an h' of oil to an ephah. "
14 and the third part of an h' of oil, to "

hind See also BEHIND; HINDER; HINDMOST; HINDS.
Ge 49:21 Naphtali is a h' let loose: he giveth 355
Pr 5:19 Let her be as the loving h' and 365
Jer 14: 5 the h' also calved in the field, and "

hinder See also HINDERED; HINDERETH; HINDERMOST.
Ge 24:56 And he said unto them, H' me not, 309
Nu 22:16 thee, h' thee from coming unto me:4513
2Sa 2:23 the h' end of the spear smote him 310
1Ki 7:25 and all their h' parts were inward. 268
2Ch 4: 4 and all their h' parts were inward. "
Ne 4: 8 against Jerusalem, and to h' *6213,8442
Job 9:12 he taketh away, who can h' him? 7725
11:10 together, then who can h' him? "
Ps 78:66 smote his enemies in the h' parts: *268
Joe 2:20 his h' part toward the utmost sea, 5490
Zec 14: 8 and half of them toward the h' sea:* 314
M'r 4:38 he was in the h' part of the ship, *4403
Ac 8:36 what doth h' me to be baptized? 2967
27:41 but the h' part was broken with *4403
1Co 9:12 we should h' the gospel *5100,1464,1325
Ga 5: 7 did h' you that ye should not obey 848

hindered
Ezr 6: 8 unto these men, that they be not h'.989
Lu 11:52 them that were entering in ye h'. 2967
Ro 15:22 been much h' from coming to you.*1465
1Th 2:18 once and again; but Satan h' us. "
1Pe 3: 7 of life; that your prayers be not h'. 1581

hindereth
Isa 14: 6 anger, is persecuted, and none h'.*2820

hindermost See also HINDMOST.
Ge 33: 2 after, and Rachel and Joseph h'. 314
Jer 50:12 the h' of the nations shall be a 319

hindmost See also HINDERMOST.
Nu 2:31 They shall go h' with their standards.314
De 25:18 and smote the h' of thee, even all 2179
Jos 10:19 enemies, and smite the h' of them; "

hinds See also HINDS'.
Job 39: 1 thou mark when the h' do calve? 355
Ps 29: 9 of the Lord maketh the h' to calve, "
Ca 2: 7 the h' of the field, that ye stir not up, "
3: 5 the h' of the field that ye stir not up, "

hinds'
2Sa 22:34 He maketh my feet like h' feet: 355
Ps 18:33 He maketh my feet like h' feet, and "
Hab 3:19 and he will make my feet like h' feet, "

hinges
1Ki 7:50 and the *h'* of gold, both for the 6596
Pr 26:14 As the door turneth upon its *h'*, so 6735

Hinnom (*hin'-nom*)
Jos 15: 8 up by the valley of the son of *H'* 2011
8 before the valley of *H'* westward, "
18:16 before the valley of the son of *H'*, "
16 and descended to the valley of *H'*, "
2Ki 23:10 in the valley of the children of *H'*, "
2Ch 28: 3 incense in the valley of the son of *H'*, "
33: 6 the fire in the valley of the son of *H'*: "
Ne 11:30 Beer-sheba unto the valley of *H'*. "
Jer 7:31 is in the valley of the son of *H'*, "
32 nor the valley of the son of *H'*, but "
19: 2 forth unto the valley of the son of *H'*, "
6 nor The valley of the son of *H'*, but "
32:35 are in the valley of the son of *H'*, "

hip
J'g 15: 8 he smote them *h'* and thigh with a 7785

Hirah (*hi'-rah*)
Ge 38: 1 Adullamite, whose name was *H'*. 2437
12 he and his friend *H'* the Adullamite. "

Hiram (*hi'-ram*) See also HIRAM'S; HURAM.
2Sa 5:11 *H'* king of Tyre sent messengers 2438
1Ki 5: 1 *H'* king of Tyre sent his servants "
1 for *H'* was ever a lover of David. "
2 And Solomon sent to *H'*, saying, "
7 *H'* heard the words of Solomon, "
8 And *H'* sent to Solomon, saying, "
10 *H'* gave Solomon cedar trees and "
11 Solomon gave *H'* twenty thousand "
11 gave Solomon to *H'* year by year. "
12 was peace between *H'* and Solomon; "
7:13 sent and fetched *H'* out of Tyre. "
40 *H'* made the lavers, and the shovels, "
40 *H'* made an end of...all the work "
45 which *H'* made to king Solomon "
9:11 *H'* the king of Tyre had furnished "
11 king Solomon gave *H'* twenty cities "
12 *H'* came out from Tyre to see the "
14 And *H'* sent to the king sixscore "
27 *H'* sent in the navy his servants, "
10:11 navy also of *H'*, that brought gold "
22 of Tharshish with the navy of *H'*: "
1Ch 14: 1 *H'* king of Tyre sent messengers to "

Hiram's (*hi'-rams*)
1Ki 5:18 Solomon's builders and *H'* builders 2438

hire See also HIRED; HIRES; HIREST.
Ge 30:18 God hath given me my *h'*, because 7939
32 Goats: and of such shall be my *h'*. "
33 shall come for my *h'* before thy face: "
31: 8 The ringstraked shall be thy *h'*; * "
Ex 22:15 an hired thing, it came for his *h'*. "
De 23:18 shalt not bring the *h'* of a whore, 868
24:15 At his day thou shalt give him his *h'*. 7939
1Ki 5: 6 thee will I give *h'* for thy servants "
1Ch 19: 6 to *h'* them chariots and horsemen 7936
Isa 23:17 Tyre, and she shall turn to her *h'*, 868
18 her *h'* shall be holiness to the Lord: "
46: 6 the balance, and *h'* a goldsmith; 7936
Eze 16:31 an harlot, in that thou scornest *h'*; 868
41 thou also shalt give no *h'* any more. "
Mic 1: 7 she gathered it of the *h'* of an harlot, "
7 shall return to the *h'* of an harlot. "
3:11 the priests thereof teach for *h'*, and 4242
Zec 8:10 no *h'* for man, nor any *h'* for beast; 7939
M't 20: 1 to *h'* labourers into his vineyard. *3409*
8 give them their *h'*, beginning from *3408*
Lu 10: 7 for the labourer is worthy of his *h'*. "
Jas 5: 4 *h'* of the labourers who have reaped "

hired
Ge 30:16 surely I have *h'* thee with my son's 7936
Ex 12:45 an *h'* servant shall not eat thereof. 7916
22:15 be an *h'* thing, it came for his hire. "
Le 19:13 the wages of him that is *h'* shall not "
22:10 *h'* servant, shall not eat of the holy "
25: 6 thy *h'* servant and for thy stranger "
40 as an *h'* servant, and as a sojourner, "
50 to the time of an *h'* servant shall it "
53 as a yearly *h'* servant shall he be "
De 15:18 worth a double *h'* servant to thee, * "
23: 4 *h'* against thee Balaam the son of 7936
24:14 oppress an *h'* servant that is poor 7916
J'g 9: 4 wherewith Abimelech *h'* vain and 7936
18: 4 Micah with me, and hath *h'* me, and "
1Sa 2: 5 full have *h'* out themselves for bread; "
2Sa 10: 6 Ammon sent and *h'* the Syrians of "
2Ki 7: 6 Israel hath *h'* against us the kings "
1Ch 19: 7 So they *h'* thirty and two thousand "
2Ch 24:12 *h'* masons and carpenters to repair "
25: 6 He *h'* also an hundred thousand "
Ezr 4: 5 And *h'* counsellers against them, to "
Ne 6:12 for Tobiah and Sanballat had *h'* him. "
13 Therefore was he *h'*, that I should "
13: 2 but *h'* Balaam against them, that he "
Isa 7:20 Lord shave with a rasor that is *h'*, 7917
Jer 46:21 her *h'* men are in the midst of her 7916
Ho 8: 9 himself: Ephraim hath *h'* lovers. 8566
10 they have *h'* among the nations, * "
M't 20: 7 him, Because no man hath *h'* us. *3409*
9 were *h'* about the eleventh hour, "
M'r 1:20 the ship with the *h'* servants, and *3411*
Lu 15:17 many *h'* servants of my father's *3407*
19 make me as one of thy *h'* servants. "
Ac 28:30 whole years in his own *h'* house, *3410*

hireling
Job 7: 1 days also like the days of an *h'*? 7916
2 and as an *h'* looketh for the reward "
14: 6 shall accomplish, as an *h'*, his day. "
Isa 16:14 three years, as the years of an *h'*, "
21:16 year, according to the years of an *h'*, "
Mal 3: 5 that oppress the *h'* in his wages, "
Joh 10:12 is an *h'*, and not the shepherd, *3411*
13 The *h'* fleeth, because he is an **3411*
13 because he is an *h'*, and careth not "

hires
Mic 1: 7 all the *h'* thereof shall be burned 868

hirest
Eze 16:33 gifts to all thy lovers, and *h'* them, *7806

his See in the APPENDIX.

hiss See also HISSING.
1Ki 9: 8 shall be astonished, and shall *h'*; 8319
Job 27:23 and shall *h'* him out of his place. "
Isa 5:26 will *h'* unto them from the end of "
7:18 the Lord shall *h'* for the fly that is "
Jer 19: 8 shall be astonished and *h'* because "
49:17 shall *h'* at all the plagues thereof. "
50:13 astonished and *h'* at all her plagues. "
La 2:15 they *h'* and wag their head at the "
16 they *h'* and gnash the teeth: they "
Eze 27:36 merchants among the people shall *h'* "
Zep 2:15 one that passeth by her shall *h'*, "
Zec 10: 8 I will *h'* for them, and gather them; "

hissing
2Ch 29: 8 to astonishment, and to *h'*, as ye 8322
Jer 18:16 land desolate, and a perpetual *h'*; 8292
19: 8 make this city desolate, and an *h'*; 8322
25: 9 an astonishment, and an *h'*, and "
18 astonishment, an *h'*, and a curse; "
29:18 an astonishment, and an *h'*, and a "
51:37 an astonishment, and an *h'*, without "
Mic 6:16 and the inhabitants thereof an *h'*: "

hit
1Sa 31: 3 Saul, and the archers *h'* him; *4672
1Ch 10: 3 Saul, and the archers *h'* him, * "

hither See also HITHERTO.
Ge 15:16 they shall come *h'* again: for the 2008
42:15 except your youngest brother come *h'*. "
45: 5 with yourselves, that ye sold me *h'*: "
8 was not you that sent me *h'*, but God: "
13 haste and bring down my father *h'*. "
Ex 3: 5 Draw not nigh *h'*: put off thy shoes 1988
Jos 2: 2 Behold, there came men in *h'* to night "
3: 9 Come *h'*, and hear the words of 5066
18: 6 and bring the description *h'* to me, "
J'g 16: 2 Gazites, saying, Samson is come *h'*. "
18: 3 Who brought thee *h'*? and what 1988
19:12 We will not turn aside *h'* into the city * "
Ru 2:14 At mealtime come thou *h'*, and eat 1988
1Sa 13: 9 Bring *h'* a burnt offering to me, 5066
14:18 Bring *h'* the ark of God. For the ark "
34 Bring me *h'* every man his ox, and "
36 Let us draw near *h'* unto God. 1988
38 Draw ye near *h'*, all the chief of the "
15:32 Bring ye *h'* to me Agag the king of 5066
16:11 we will not sit down till he come *h'*. 6311
17:28 he said, Why camest thou down *h'*? * "
23: 9 the priest, Bring *h'* the ephod. 5066
30: 7 I pray thee, bring me *h'* the ephod. "
2Sa 1:10 Have brought them *h'* unto my lord. "
5: 6 the lame, thou shalt not come in *h'*: "
6 thinking, David cannot come in *h'*. "
14:32 Come *h'*, that I may send thee unto the "
20:16 Come near *h'*, that I may speak with "
1Ki 22: 9 Hasten *h'* Micaiah the son of Imlah. * "
2Ki 2: 8 and they were divided *h'* and thither, "
14 the waters, they parted *h'* and thither: "
8: 7 saying, The man of God is come *h'*. 2008
1Ch 11: 5 said to David, Thou shalt not come *h'*. "
2Ch 28:13 Ye shall not bring in the captives *h'*: "
Ezr 4: 2 king of Assur, which brought us up *h'* "
Ps 73:10 Therefore his people return *h'*: 1988
81: 2 Take a psalm, and bring *h'* the timbrel "
Pr 9: 4,16 Whoso is simple, let him turn in *h'*: "
Isa 57: 3 draw near *h'*, ye sons of the sorceress, "
Eze 40: 4 them unto thee art thou brought *h'*: "
Da 3:26 high God, come forth, and come *h'*. "
M't 8:29 art thou come *h'* to torment us *5602*
14:18 He said, Bring them *h'* to me. "
17:17 I suffer you? bring him *h'* to me. "
22:12 thou in *h'* not having a wedding "
M'r 11: 3 and straightway he will send him *h'*. "
Lu 9:41 and suffer you? Bring thy son *h'*. "
14:21 bring in *h'* the poor, and...maimed. "
15:23 And bring *h'* the fatted calf, and kill * "
19:27 bring *h'*, and slay them before me. *5602*
30 man sat: loose him, and bring him *h'*. * "
Joh 4:15 thirst not, neither come *h'* to draw *1759*
16 Go, call thy husband, and come *h'*. "
6:25 him, Rabbi, when camest thou *h'*? *5602*
20:27 Reach *h'* thy finger, and behold my "
27 and reach *h'* thy hand, and thrust "
Ac 9:21 and came *h'* for that intent, that he "
10:32 and call *h'* Simon, whose surname **3333*
17: 6 upside down are come *h'* also; *1759*
19:37 For ye have brought *h'* these men, "
25:17 when they were come *h'*, without **1759*
Re 4: 1 Come up *h'*, and I will shew thee *5602*
11:12 saying unto them, Come up *h'*. And "
17: 1 Come *h'*; I will shew unto thee the *1204*
21: 9 Come *h'*, I will shew thee the bride, "

hitherto
Ex 7:16 *h'* thou wouldest not hear. 5704, 3541
Jos 17:14 as the Lord hath blessed me *h'*? "
J'g 16:13 *H'* thou hast mocked me, and 2008
1Sa 1:16 and grief have I spoken *h'*. 5704, 2008
7:12 *H'* hath the Lord helped us. "
2Sa 7:18 that thou hast brought me *h'*? *1988
15:34 have been thy father's servant *h'*, 227
1Ch 9:18 Who *h'* waited in...king's gate 5704, 2008
12:29 *h'* the greatest part of them had "
17:16 that thou hast brought me *h'*? *1988
Job 38:11 *H'* shalt thou come, but no 5704, 6311
Ps 71:17 *h'* have I declared thy wondrous 2008
Isa 18: 2, 7 terrible from their beginning *h'*; *1973
Da 7:28 *H'* is the end of the matter. *5705, 3542
Joh 5:17 My father worketh *h'*, and I **2193, 737*
16:24 *H'* have ye asked nothing in my "
Ro 1:13 to come unto you, but was let *h'*, *891, 1204*
1Co 3: 2 for *h'* ye were not able to bear it, **3768*

Hittite (*hit'-tite*) See also HITTITES.
Ge 23:10 and Ephron the *H'* answered 2850
25: 9 of Ephron the son of Zohar the *H'*, "
26:34 Judith the daughter of Beeri the *H'*, "
34 the daughter of Elon the *H'*: "
36: 2 Adah the daughter of Elon the *H'*, "
49:29 is in the field of Ephron the *H'*, "
30 with the field of Ephron the *H'* for "
50:13 a buryingplace of Ephron the *H'*. "
Ex 23:28 and the *H'*, from before thee. "
33: 2 Canaanite, the Amorite, and the *H'*, "
34:11 and the Canaanite, and the *H'*, and "
Jos 9: 1 sea over against Lebanon, the *H'*, "
11: 3 and to the Amorite, and the *H'*, and "
1Sa 26: 6 David and said to Ahimelech the *H'*, "
2Sa 11: 3 of Eliam, the wife of Uriah the *H'*? "
6 Joab, saying, Send me Uriah the *H'*. "
17 and Uriah the *H'* died also. "
21, 24 servant Uriah the *H'* is dead also. "
12: 9 killed Uriah the *H'* with the sword, "
10 wife of Uriah the *H'* to be thy wife. "
23:39 Uriah the *H'*: thirty and seven in all. "
1Ki 15: 5 only in the matter of Uriah the *H'*. "
1Ch 11:41 Uriah the *H'*, Zabad the son of "
Eze 16: 3 an Amorite, and thy mother an *H'*. "
45 your mother was an *H'*, and your "

Hittites (*hit'-tites*)
Ge 15:20 And the *H'*, and the Perizzites, *2850
Ex 3: 8 place of the Canaanites, and the *H'*, * "
17 land of the Canaanites, and the *H'*, * "
13: 5 land of the Canaanites, and the *H'*, * "
23:23 in unto the Amorites and the *H'*, * "
Nu 13:29 and the *H'*, and the Jebusites, and * "
De 7: 1 many nations before thee, the *H'*, * "
20:17 destroy them; namely, the *H'*, and * "
Jos 1: 4 all the land of the *H'*, and unto the "
3:10 you the Canaanites, and the *H'*, * "
12: 8 and in the south country; the *H'*, * "
24:11 and the Canaanites, and the *H'*, * "
J'g 1:26 man went into the land of the *H'*, "
3: 5 dwelt among the Canaanites, *H'*, * "
1Ki 9:20 that were left of the Amorites, *H'*, "
10:29 and so for all the kings of the *H'*, "
11: 1 Edomites, Zidonians, and *H'*; "
2Ki 7: 6 hired against us the kings of the *H'*, "
2Ch 1:17 horses for all the kings of the *H'*, "
8: 7 the people that were left of the *H'*, "
Ezr 9: 1 even of the Canaanites, the *H'*, the "
Ne 9: 8 the land of the Canaanites, the *H'*, * "

Hivite (*hi'-vite*) See also HIVITES.
Ge 10:17 And the *H'*, and the Arkite, and 2340
34: 2 Shechem the son of Hamor the *H'*, "
36: 2 Anah the daughter of Zibeon the *H'*; "
Ex 23:28 which shall drive out the *H'*, the "
33: 2 Hittite, and the Perizzite, the *H'*, "
34:11 and the Perizzite, and the *H'*, and "
Jos 9: 1 Perizzite, the *H'*, and the Jebusite, "
11: 3 and to the *H'* under Hermon in the "
1Ch 1:15 And the *H'*, and the Arkite, and "

Hivites (*hi'-vites*)
Ex 3: 8 and the *H'*, and the Jebusites. *2340
17 and the *H'*, and the Jebusites, * "
13: 5 and the *H'*, and the Jebusites, "
23:23 and the Canaanites, the *H'*, and the * "
De 7: 1 and the *H'*, and the Jebusites, * "
20:17 the *H'*, and the Jebusites; as the * "
Jos 3:10 *H'*, and the Perizzites, and the * "
9: 7 the men of Israel said unto the *H'*, "
11:19 Israel, save the *H'* the inhabitants "
12: 8 the Perizzites, the *H'*, and the * "
24:11 and the Girgashites, the *H'*, and * "
J'g 3: 3 *H'* that dwelt in mount Lebanon; "
5 Amorites, and Perizzites, and *H'*, "
2Sa 24: 7 and to all the cities of the *H'*, and "
1Ki 9:20 *H'*, and Jebusites, which were not "
2Ch 8: 7 the *H'*, and the Jebusites, which "

Hizkiah (*hiz-ki'-ah*) See also HEZEKIAH; HIZKIJAH.
Zep 1: 1 the son of *H'*, in the days of Josiah 2396

Hizkijah (*hiz-ki'-jah*) See also HIZKIAH.
Ne 10:17 Ater, *H'*, Azzur, Hodijah, Bani, 2396

ho
Isa 55: 1 *H'*, every one that thirsteth, come 1945
Zec 2: 6 *H'*, *h'*, come forth, and flee from the "

hoar See also HOARFROST; HOARY.
Ex 16:14 small as the *h'* frost on the ground. 3713
1Ki 2: 6 let not his *h'* head go down to the 7872
9 his *h'* head bring thou down to the "
Isa 46: 4 even to *h'* hairs will I carry you: 7872

hoarfrost See also HOAR; HOARY; and FROST.
Ps 147:16 he scattereth the *h'* like ashes. 3713

hoary
Le 19:32 shalt rise up before the *h'* head, 7872
Job 38:29 and the *h'* frost of heaven, who hath 3713
41:32 one would think the deep to be *h'*. 7872
Pr 16:31 The *h'* head is a crown of glory, if "

Hobab (*ho'-bab*) See also JETHRO.
Nu 10:29 And Moses said unto *H'*, the son of 2246
J'g 4:11 the children of *H'* the father in law "

Hobah (*ho'-bah*)
Ge 14:15 and pursued them unto *H'*, which 2327

Hod (*hod*)
1Ch 7:37 Bezer, and *H'*, and Shamma, and 1963

Hodaiah (*ho-da-i'-ah*) See also HODAVIAH.
1Ch 3:24 the sons of Elioenai were, *H'*, and *1939

Hodaviah (*ho-da-vi'ah*) See also HODAIAH; HODEVAH.
1Ch 5:24 and Jeremiah, and H', and Jahdiel, 1938
9: 7 the son of H', the son of Hasenuah, "
Ezr 2:40 children of H', seventy and four. "

Hodesh (*ho'-desh*)
1Ch 8: 9 begat of H' his wife, Jobab, and 2321

Hodevah (*ho-de'-vah*) See also HODAVIAH.
Ne 7:43 children of H', seventy and four. 1937

Hodiah (*ho-di'-ah*) See also HODIJAH.
1Ch 4:19 the sons of his wife H' the sister 1940

Hodijah (*ho-di'-jah*) See also HODIAH.
Ne 8: 7 Shabbethai, H', Maaseiah, Kelita, *1940
9: 5 Sherebiah, H', Shebaniah, and * "
10:10 Shebaniah, H', Kelita, Pelaiah, * "
13 H', Bani, Beninu. * "
18 H', Hashum, Bezai, * "

Hodshi See TAHTIM-HODSHI.

Hoglah (*hog'-lah*) See also BETH-HOGLAH.
Nu 26:33 were Mahlah, and Noah, H', 2295
27: 1 daughters; Mahlah, Noah, and H', "
36:11 and H', and Milcah, and Noah, the "
Jos 17: 3 daughters, Mahlah, and Noah, H', "

Hoham (*ho'-ham*)
Jos 10: 3 sent unto H' king of Hebron, and 1944

hoised
Ac 27:40 and h' up the mainsail to the wind. *1869

hoist See HOISED.

hold See also BEHOLD; HELD; HOLDEN; HOLDEST; HOLDETH; HOLDING; HOLDS; HOUSEHOLD; UPHOLD; WITHHOLD.
Ge 19:16 the men laid h' upon his hand, 2388
21:18 up the lad, and h' him in thine hand; "
25:26 his hand took h' on Esau's heel; 270
Ex 5: 1 that they may h' a feast unto me
9: 2 let them go, and wilt h' them still, 2388
10: 9 we must h' a feast unto the Lord.
14:14 for you, and ye shall h' your peace. 2790
15:14 sorrow shall take h' on the 270
15 trembling shall take h' upon them; "
20: 7 the Lord will not h' him guiltless
26: 5 loops may take h' one of another. *6901
Nu 30: 4 and her father shall h' his peace *2790
14 h' his peace at her from day to day; "
De 5:11 the Lord will not h' him guiltless
21:19 father and his mother lay h' on him, 8610
22:28 and lay h' on her, and lie with her, "
32:41 and mine hand take h' on judgment; 270
J'g 9:46 entered into an h' of the house ‡6877
49 Abimelech, and put them to the h', ‡ "
49 and set the h' on fire upon them; ‡ "
16:29 Samson took h' of the two middle 3943
18:19 they said unto him, H' thy peace, 2790
19:29 knife, and laid h' on his concubine, 2388
Ru 3:15 that thou hast upon thee, and h' it. 270
1Sa 15:27 laid h' upon the skirt of his mantle, 2388
22: 4 the while that David was in the h'. ‡4686
5 said unto David, Abide not in the h' ‡ "
24:22 his men gat them up unto the h'. ‡ "
2Sa 1:11 then David took h' on his clothes, 2388
2:21 lay thee h' on one of the young men, 270
22 I h' up my face to Joab my brother? 5375
4:10 I took h' of him, and slew him in 270
5: 7 David took the strong h' of Zion: 4686
17 heard of it; and went down to the h'. ‡ "
6: 6 to the ark of God, and took h' of it; 270
13:11 he took h' of her, and said unto her, 2388
20 but h' now thy peace, my sister: 2790
18: 9 and his head caught h' of the oak, 2388
23:14 David was then in an h', and the ‡4686
24: 7 And came to the strong h' of Tyre, 4013
1Ki 1:50 caught h' on the horns of the altar. 2388
51 caught h' on the horns of the altar, 270
2: 9 h' him not guiltless: for thou art
28 caught h' on the horns of the altar. 2388
9: 9 and have taken h' upon other gods, "
13: 4 the altar, saying, Lay h' on him. 8610
2Ki 2: 3, 5 Yea, I know it; h' ye your peace. 2814
12 and he took h' of his own clothes, 2388
6:32 door, and h' him fast at the door: 3905
7: 9 good tidings, and we h' our peace: 2814
1Ch 11:16 David was then in the h', and the ‡4686
12: 8 David into the h' to the wilderness ‡4679
16 and Judah to the h' unto David. ‡ "
13: 9 put forth his hand to h' the ark; 270
2Ch 7:22 Egypt, and laid h' on other gods, 2388
Ne 8:11 saying, H' your peace, for the day 2013
Es 4:11 the king shall h' out the golden 3447
Job 6:24 Teach me, and I will h' my tongue: 2790
8:15 he shall h' it fast, but it shall not 2388
9:28 that thou wilt not h' me innocent.
11: 3 thy lies make men h' their peace? 2790
13: 5 ye would altogether h' your peace! "
13 H' your peace, let me alone, that "
19 for now, if I h' my tongue, I shall "
17: 9 righteous shall also h' on his way, 270
21: 6 am afraid, and trembling taketh h' "
27: 6 My righteousness I h' fast, and 2388
20 Terrors take h' on him as waters, *5381
30:16 days of affliction have taken h' upon 270
33:31 h' thy peace, and I will speak. 2790
33 h' thy peace, and I shall teach thee "
36:17 judgment and justice take h' on 8551
38:13 take h' of the ends of the earth, 270
41:26 him that layeth at him cannot h': *6965
Ps 17: 5 H' up my goings in thy paths, *8551
35: 2 Take h' of shield and buckler, and 2388
39:12 h' not thy peace at my tears: for I 2790
40:12 iniquities have taken h' upon me, *5381
48: 6 Fear took h' upon them there, and 270
69:24 wrathful anger take h' of them. *5381
83: 1 h' not thy peace, and be not still, 2790
Ps 109: 1 H' not thy peace, O God of my 2790
116: 3 the pains of hell gat h' upon me: 4672
119:53 Horror hath taken h' upon me 270
117 H' thou me up, and I shall be safe: 5582
143 and anguish have taken h' on me: 4672
139:10 me, and thy right hand shall h' me. 270
Pr 2:19 neither take they h' of the paths *5381
3:18 life to them that lay h' upon her: 2388
4:13 Take fast h' of instruction; let her "
5: 5 to death; her steps take h' on hell. 8551
30:28 spider taketh h' with her hands, 8610
31:19 and her hands h' the distaff. 8551
Ec 2: 3 and to lay h' on folly, till I might 270
7:18 that thou shouldest take h' of this; "
Ca 3: 8 They all h' swords, being expert * "
7: 8 I will take h' of the boughs thereof: "
Isa 3: 6 a man shall take h' of his brother 8610
4: 1 seven women shall take h' of one 2388
5:29 shall roar, and lay h' of the prey, 270
13: 8 and sorrows shall take h' of them; "
21: 3 pangs have taken h' upon me, as "
27: 5 Or let him take h' of my strength, 2388
31: 9 pass over to his strong h' for fear, *5553
41:13 Lord thy God will h' thy right hand, 2388
42: 6 and will h' thine hand, and will keep "
56: 2 the son of man that layeth h' on it; * "
4 me, and take h' of my covenant; "
6 it, and taketh h' of my covenant; * "
62: 1 Zion's sake will I not h' my peace, 2814
6 never h' their peace day nor night: "
64: 7 stirreth up himself to take h' of 2388
12 wilt thou h' thy peace, and afflict 2814
Jer 2:13 cisterns, that can h' no water. 3557
4:19 I cannot h' my peace, because thou 2790
6:23 They shall lay h' on bow and spear; 2388
24 anguish hath taken h' of us, and "
8: 5 h' fast deceit, they refuse to return. "
21 astonishment hath taken h' on me. "
50:42 They shall h' the bow and the lance: "
43 feeble: anguish took h' of him, "
Eze 29: 7 they took h' of thee by thy hand, 8610
30:21 to make it strong to h' the sword. "
41: 6 round about that they might have h', 270
6 had not h' in the wall of the house. "
Am 6:10 Then shall he say, H' thy tongue: 2013
Mic 4: 8 strong h' of the daughter of Zion, *6076
6:14 take h', but shalt not deliver; *5253
Na 1: 7 a strong h' in the day of trouble; 4581
Hab 1:10 they shall deride every strong h'; 4013
Zep 1: 7 H' thy peace at the presence of the
Zec 1: 6 they not take h' of your fathers? *5381
8:23 ten men shall take h' out of all 2388
23 even shall take h' of the skirt of "
9: 3 Tyrus did build herself a strong h', 4692
12 Turn you to the strong h', ye 1225
11: 5 and h' themselves not guilty; and 816
14:13 shall lay h' every one on the hand 2388
M't 6:24 or else he will h' to the one, and 472
12:11 he not lay h' on it, and lift it out? 2902
14: 3 For Herod had laid h' on John, and "
20:31 because they should h' their peace: 4623
21:26 for all h' John as a prophet. 2192
26:48 kiss, that same is he: h' him fast. *2902
55 temple, and ye laid no h' on me. * "
57 they that had laid h' on Jesus led * "
M'r 1:25 H' thy peace, and come out of him. 5392
3:21 they went out to lay h' on him: 2902
6:17 and laid h' upon John, and bound "
7: 4 which they have received to h', as "
8 ye h' the tradition of men, as the "
10:48 that he should h' his peace: but 4623
12:12 and they sought to lay h' on him, 2902
14:51 and the young men laid h' on him: "
Lu 4:35 H' thy peace, and come out of him. 5392
16:13 or else he will h' to the one, and 472
18:39 him, that he should h' his peace: 4623
19:40 if these should h' their peace, the "
20:20 that they might take h' of his words, 1949
26 they could not take h' of his words "
23:26 they laid h' upon one Simon, a "
Ac 4: 3 put them in h' unto the next day: *5084
12:17 with the hand to h' their peace, 4601
18: 9 but speak, and h' not thy peace: 4623
Ro 1:18 h' the truth in unrighteousness; ‡2722
1Co 14:30 sitteth by, let the first h' his peace. *4601
Ph'p 2:29 gladness; and h' such in reputation. 2192
1Th 5:21 things; h' fast that which is good. 2722
2Th 2:15 stand fast, and h' the traditions 2902
1Ti 6:12 of faith, lay h' on eternal life, 1949
19 that they may lay h' on eternal life. "
2Ti 1:13 H' fast the form of sound words, 2192
Heb 3: 6 if we h' fast the confidence and the 2722
14 Christ, if we h' the beginning of our "
4:14 of God, let us h' fast our profession. 2902
6:18 lay h' upon the hope set before us: "
10:23 Let us h' fast the profession of our 2722
Re 2:14 that h' the doctrine of Balaam, 2902
15 h' the doctrine of the Nicolaitanes, "
25 ye have already h' fast till I come. "
3: 3 and heard, and h' fast, and repent. *5083
11 h' that fast which thou hast, that 2902
18: 2 and the h' of every foul spirit, and 5438
20: 2 And he laid h' on the dragon, that 2902

holden See also HELD; UPHOLDEN; WITHHOLDEN.
2Ki 23:22 there was not h' such a passover *6213
23 this passover was h' to the Lord * "
Job 36: 8 and be h' in cords of affliction; *3920
Ps 18:35 and thy right hand hath h' me up, 5582
71: 6 By thee have I been h' up from the 5564
73:23 thou hast h' me by my right hand. 270
Pr 5:22 be h' with the cords of his sins. 8551
Isa 42:14 I have long time h' my peace; I 2814
45: 1 Cyrus, whose right hand I have h', 2388
Lu 24:16 But their eyes were h' that they 2902
Ac 2:24 possible that he should be h' of it. "
Ro 14: 4 Yea, he shall be h' up: for God is *2476

holder See HOUSEHOLDER.

holdest See also BEHOLDEST; UPHOLDEST.
Es 4:14 if thou altogether h' thy peace at 2790
Job 13:24 face, and h' me for thine enemy? 2803
Ps 77: 4 Thou h' mine eyes waking: I am so 270
Jer 49:16 rock, that h' the height of the hill: 8610
Hab 1:13 h' thy tongue when the wicked 2790
Re 2:13 and thou h' fast my name, and 2902

holdeth See also BEHOLDETH; UPHOLDETH; WITHHOLDETH.
Job 2: 3 and still he h' fast his integrity, 2388
26: 9 He h' back the face of his throne, * 270
Ps 66: 9 Which h' our soul in life, and 7760
Pr 11:12 man of understanding h' his peace. 2790
17:28 a fool, when he h' his peace, "
Da 10:21 none that h' with me in these 2388
Am 1: 5 that h' the sceptre from the house 8551
8 that h' the sceptre from Ashkelon, "
Re 2: 1 saith he that h' the seven stars in 2902

holding See also BEHOLDING; UPHOLDING.
Isa 33:15 his hands from h' of bribes, 8551
Jer 6:11 I am weary with h' in: I will pour 3557
M'r 7: 3 not, h' the tradition of the elders. 2902
Ph'p 2:16 H' forth the word of life; that I 1907
Col 2:19 And not h' the Head, from which 2902
1Ti 1:19 H' faith, and a good conscience; 2192
3: 9 H' the mystery of the faith in a "
Tit 1: 9 H' fast the faithful word as he 472
Re 7: 1 h' the four winds of the earth, 2902

holds See also HOUSEHOLDS.
Nu 13:19 whether in tents, or in strong h'; 4013
J'g 6: 2 mountains...caves, and strong h'. 4679
1Sa 23:14 abode in the wilderness in strong h', "
19 hide himself with us in strong h' "
29 and dwelt in strong h' at En-gedi. "
2Ki 8:12 their strong h' wilt thou set on fire, 4013
2Ch 11:11 he fortified the strong h', and put 4694
Ps 89:40 hast brought his strong h' to ruin. 4013
Isa 23:11 to destroy the strong h' thereof. 4581
Jer 48:18 and he shall destroy thy strong h'. 4013
41 and the strong h' are surprised, 4679
51:30 they have remained in their h': "
La 2: 2 strong h' of the daughter of Judah; 4013
5 he hath destroyed his strong h', "
Eze 19: 9 they brought him into h', that his 4686
Da 11:24 his devices against the strong h', 4013
39 shall he do in the most strong h' * "
Mic 5:11 and throw down all thy strong h': * "
Na 3:12 All thy strong h' shall be like fig * "
14 fortify thy strong h': go into clay, * "

hole See also HOLE'S; HOLES.
Ex 28:32 there shall be an h' in the top of it, 6310
32 woven work round about the h' of it, "
32 as it were the h' of an habergeon, "
39:23 And there was an h' in the midst of "
23 the robe, as the h' of an habergeon, "
23 with a band round about the h', "
2Ki 12: 9 a chest, bored a h' in the lid of it, 2356
Ca 5: 4 put in his hand by the h' of the door, "
Isa 11: 8 shall play on the h' of the asp, "
51: 1 h' of the pit whence ye are digged. 4718
Jer 13: 4 and hid it there in a h' of the rock. 5357
Eze 8: 7 I looked, behold a h' in the wall. 2356

hole's
Jer 48:28 nest in the sides of the h' mouth. ‡6354

holes See also ARMHOLES.
1Sa 14:11 Hebrews come forth out of the h' 2356
Isa 2:19 shall go into the h' of the rocks, 4631
7:19 valleys, and in the h' of the rocks, 5357
42:22 all of them snared in h', and they 2356
Jer 16:16 hill, and out of the h' of the rocks. 5357
Mic 7:17 they shall move out of their h' *4526
Na 2:12 filled his h' with prey, and his dens *2356
Hag 1: 6 wages to put it into a bag with h'. 5344
Zec 14:12 shall consume away in their h', *2356
M't 8:20 The foxes have h', and the birds 5454
Lu 9:58 Foxes have h', and the birds of the "

holiday See HOLYDAY.

holier
Isa 65: 5 near to me; for I am h' than thou. 6942

holiest
Heb 9: 3 which is called the H' of all: * 39
8 the way into the h' of all was not * "
10:19 into the h' by the blood of Jesus, * "

holily
1Th 2:10 how h' and justly and unblameably 3743

holiness
Ex 15:11 who is like thee, glorious in h', 6944
28:36 of a signet, H' to the Lord. "
39:30 of a signet, H' to the Lord. "
1Ch 16:29 worship the Lord in the beauty of h'. "
2Ch 20:21 that should praise the beauty of h', "
31:18 they sanctified themselves in h': "
Ps 29: 2 worship the Lord in the beauty of h'. "
30: 4 at the remembrance of his h'. * "
47: 8 sitteth upon the throne of his h'. "
48: 1 our God, in the mountain of his h'. * "
60: 6 God hath spoken in his h'; I will "
89:35 Once have I sworn by my h' that I "
93: 5 h' becometh thine house, O Lord, "
96: 9 worship the Lord in the beauty of h': "
97:12 thanks at the remembrance of his h'. * "
108: 7 God hath spoken in his h'; I will "
110: 3 in the beauties of h' from the "
Isa 23:18 and her hire shall be h' to the Lord: "
35: 8 and it shall be called The way of h'; "
62: 9 shall drink it in the courts of my h'. * "
63:15 behold from the habitation of thy h' "
18 people of thy h' have possessed it "
Jer 2: 3 Israel was h' unto the Lord, and the "
23: 9 and because of the words of his h'. * "
31:23 of justice, and mountain of h'.

Am 4: 2 The Lord God hath sworn by his h' 6944
Ob 17 deliverance, and there shall be h' ;* "
Zec 14: 20 of the horses, H' unto the Lord; * "
21 shall be h' unto the Lord of hosts:* "
Mal 2: 11 Judah hath profaned the h' of the "
Lu 1: 75 In h' and righteousness before him, 3742
Ac 3: 12 though by our own power or h' we *2150
Ro 1: 4 power, according to the spirit of h', 42
6: 19 servants to righteousness unto h'. * 38
22 have your fruit unto h', and the end* "
2Co 7: 1 perfecting h' in the fear of God. 42
Eph 4: 24 in righteousness and true h'. 3742
1Th 3: 13 hearts unblameable in h' before God, 42
4: 7 us unto uncleanness, but unto h'. * 38
1Ti 2: 15 faith ... charity and h' with sobriety.* "
Tit 2: 3 be in behaviour as becometh h', *2412
Heb 12: 10 that we might be partakers of his h'. 41
14 Follow peace with all men, and h', * 38

hollow
Ge 32: 25 him, he touched the h' of his thigh; 3709
25 and the h' of Jacob's thigh was out "
32 the h' of the thigh, unto this day: "
32 because he touched the h' of Jacob's "
Ex 27: 8 H' with boards shalt thou make it: 5014
38: 7 he made the altar h' with boards. "
Le 14: 37 walls of the house with h' strakes, 8258
J'g 15: 19 God clave an h' place that was *4388
Isa 40: 12 the waters in the h' of his hand, 8168
Jer 52: 21 thereof was four fingers: it was h'. 5014

Holon (ho'-lon) See also HILEN.
Jos 15: 51 And Goshen, and H', and Giloh; 2473
21: 15 And H' with her suburbs, and Debir "
Jer 48: 21 upon H', and upon Jahazah, and "

holpen See also HELPED.
Ps 83: 8 they have h' the children of Lot. ‡2220
86: 17 because thou, Lord, has h' me, ‡5826
Isa 31: 3 he that is h' shall fall down, and ‡
Da 11: 34 they shall be h' with a little help: ‡
Lu 1: 54 He hath h' his servant Israel, in 482

holy See also HOLIER; HOLIEST; HOLYDAY; UNHOLY.
Ex 3: 5 whereon thou standest is h' ground. 6944
12: 16 there shall be an h' convocation, "
16 shall be an h' convocation to you; "
15: 13 thy strength unto thy h' habitation. "
16: 23 of the h' sabbath unto the Lord: "
19: 6 of priests, and an h' nation. 6918
20: 8 the sabbath day, to keep it h'. 6942
22: 31 And ye shall be h' men unto me: 6944
26: 33 between the h' place and the most h'. "
34 of the testimony in the most h' place. "
28: 2 shalt make h' garments for Aaron "
4 shall make h' garments for Aaron "
29 when he goeth in unto the h' place, "
35 when he goeth in unto the h' place "
38 bear the iniquity of the h' things, "
38 shall hallow in all their h' gifts; "
43 the altar to minister in the h' place; "
29: 6 and put the h' crown upon the mitre. "
29 the h' garments of Aaron shall be "
30 cometh...to minister in the h' place. "
31 seethe his flesh in the h' place. ‡6918
33 eat thereof, because they are h'. 6944
34 shall not be eaten, because it is h'. "
37 it; and it shall be an altar most h': "
37 toucheth the altar shall be h'. "
30: 10 it is most h' unto the Lord. "
25 shalt make it an oil of h' ointment, "
25 it shall be an h' anointing oil. "
29 them, that they may be most h': "
29 whatsoever toucheth them...be h'. 6942
31 This shall be an h' anointing oil 6944
32 it is h', and it shall be h' unto you. "
35 tempered together, pure and h': "
36 thee: it shall be unto you most h'. "
37 shall be unto thee h' for the Lord. "
31: 10 the h' garments for Aaron the priest, "
11 and sweet incense for the h' place: "
14 sabbath therefore; for it is h' unto "
15 sabbath to rest, h' to the Lord: "
35: 2 day there shall be to you an h' day, "
19 service, to do service in the h' place, "
19 the h' garments for Aaron the priest, "
21 service, and for the h' garments. "
37: 29 And he made the h' anointing oil, "
38: 24 work in all the work of the h' place,* "
39: 1 to do service in the h' place, and "
1 made the h' garments for Aaron; "
30 plate of the h' crown of pure gold, "
41 to do service in the h' place, and "
41 the h' garments for Aaron the priest, "
40: 9 vessels thereof: and it shall be h'. "
10 altar: and it shall be an altar most h'. "
13 put upon Aaron the h' garments, "
Le 2: 3, 10 is a thing most h' of the offerings "
5: 15 in the h' things of the Lord; then "
16 that he hath done in the h' thing, "
6: 16 shall it be eaten in the h' place; *6918
17 it is most h', as is the sin offering, 6944
18 one that toucheth them shall be h'. 6942
25 before the Lord: it is most h'. 6944
26 in the h' place shall it be eaten, in 6918
27 touch the flesh thereof shall be h': 6942
27 it was sprinkled in the h' place. 6918
29 shall eat thereof: it is most h'. 6944
30 to reconcile withal in the h' place, "
7: 1 trespass offering: it is most h'. "
6 it shall be eaten in the h' place: 6918
6 eaten in the...place: it is most h'. 6944
8: 9 put the golden plate, the h' crown; "
10: 10 difference between h' and unholy, "
12 beside the altar: for it is most h': 6944
13 And ye shall eat it in the h' place, 6918
17 have ye not eaten...in the h' place, *6944

Le 10: 17 seeing it is most h', and God hath 6944
18 not brought in within the h' place:* "
18 indeed have eaten it in the h' place,* "
11: 44 and ye shall be h'; for I am h': 6918
45 ye shall therefore be h', for I am h'. "
14: 13 the burnt offering, in the h' place: *6944
13 the trespass offering: it is most h': "
16: 2 not at all times into the h' place "
3 shall Aaron come into the h' place: "
4 He shall put on the h' linen coat, "
4 these are h' garments; be attired: "
16 make an atonement for the h' place, "
17 make an atonement in the h' place, "
20 an end of reconciling the h' place, "
23 when he went into the h' place, "
24 his flesh with water in the h' place, 6918
27 to make atonement in the h' place, 6944
32 linen clothes, even the h' garments: "
33 an atonement for the h' sanctuary, "
19: 2 and say unto them, Ye shall be h': 6918
2 for I the Lord your God am h'. "
24 fruit thereof shall be h' to praise 6944
20: 3 and to profane my h' name. "
7 be ye h': for I am the Lord your 6918
26 be h' unto me: for I the Lord am h', "
21: 6 They shall be h' unto their God, and "
6 do offer: therefore they shall be h'. 6944
7 husband: for he is h' unto his God. 6918
8 thy God: he shall be h' unto thee: "
8 the Lord which sanctify you, am h'. "
22 both of the most h', and of the h'. 6944
22: 2 themselves from the h' things of "
2 that they profane not my h' name "
3 that goeth unto the h' things, which "
4 he shall not eat of the h' things, "
6 and shall not eat of the h' things, "
7 shall afterward eat of the h' things; "
10 shall no stranger eat of the h' thing: "
10 servant, shall not eat of the h' thing. "
12 eat of an offering of the h' things. "
14 man eat of the h' thing unwittingly, "
14 it unto the priest with the h' thing. "
15 they shall not profane the h' things "
16 when they eat their h' things: for "
32 Neither shall ye profane my h' name; "
23: 2 which ye shall proclaim to be h' "
3 sabbath of rest, an h' convocation; "
4 even h' convocations, which ye "
7 day ye shall have an h' convocation: "
8 seventh day is an h' convocation: "
20 shall be h' to the Lord for the priest. "
21 may be an h' convocation unto you: "
24 of trumpets, an h' convocation. "
27 shall be an h' convocation unto you; "
35 first day shall be an h' convocation: "
36 eighth day shall be an h' convocation "
37 shall proclaim to be h' convocations, "
24: 9 and they shall eat it in the h' place: 6918
9 is most h' unto him of the offerings 6944
25: 12 it shall be h' unto you: ye shall eat "
27: 9 of such unto the Lord shall be h'. "
10 and the exchange thereof shall be h'. "
14 man shall sanctify his house to be h' "
21 shall be h' unto the Lord, as a field "
23 that day, as a h' thing unto the Lord. "
28 every devoted thing is most h' unto "
30 is the Lord's: it is h' unto the Lord. "
32 the tenth shall be h' unto the Lord. "
33 it the change thereof shall be h'; "
Nu 4: 4 about the most h' things: "
15 they shall not touch any h' thing, * "
19 approach unto the most h' things: "
20 see when the h' things are covered,* "
5: 9 every offering of the h' things of the "
17 the priest shall take h' water in an 6918
6: 5 he shall be h', and shall let the locks "
8 separation he is h' unto the Lord. "
20 this is h' for the priest, with the 6944
15: 40 and be h' unto your God. 6918
16: 3 seeing all the congregation are h', "
5 will shew who are his, and who is h'; "
7 Lord doth choose, he shall be h': "
18: 9 shall be thine of the most h' things, 6944
9 be most h' for thee and for thy sons. "
10 In the most h' place shalt thou eat "
10 shall eat it: it shall be h' unto thee. "
17 they are h': thou shalt sprinkle "
19 the heave offerings of the h' things, "
32 neither shall ye pollute the h' things "
28: 7 in the h' place shalt thou cause the "
18 first day shall be an h' convocation; "
25, 26 ye shall have an h' convocation; "
29: 1 ye shall have an h' convocation; "
7 seventh month an h' convocation; "
12 ye shall have an h' convocation; ye "
31: 6 to the war, with the h' instruments,* "
35: 25 which was anointed with the h' oil. "
De 7: 6 thou art an h' people unto the Lord 6918
12: 26 Only thy h' things which thou hast, 6944
14: 2 for thou art an h' people unto the 6918
21 For thou art an h' people unto the "
23: 14 therefore shall thy camp be h': that "
26: 15 Look down from thy h' habitation, 6944
19 thou mayest be an h' people unto 6918
28: 9 shall establish thee an h' people "
33: 8 Urim be with thy h' one, whom *2623
Jos 5: 15 place whereon thou standest is h'. 6944
24: 19 serve the Lord: for he is an h' God; 6918
1Sa 2: 2 There is none h' as the Lord: for "
6: 20 to stand before this h' Lord God? "
21: 5 vessels of the young men are h', 6944
1Ki 6: 16 oracle, even for the most h' place. "
7: 50 the inner house, the most h' place, "
8: 4 all the h' vessels that were in the "
6 of the house, to the most h' place, "
8 out in the h' place before the oracle, "

1Ki 8: 10 priests were come out of the h' place, 6944
2Ki 4: 9 I perceive that this is an h' man 6918
19: 22 even against the H' One of Israel. "
1Ch 6: 49 all the work of the place most h', 6944
16: 10 Glory ye in his h' name: let the "
35 we may give thanks to thy h' name, "
22: 19 the h' vessels of God, into the house "
23: 13 should sanctify the most h' things, "
28 in the purifying of all h' things, "
32 and the charge of the h' place, "
29: 3 I have prepared for the h' house, "
16 build thee an house for thine h' name "
2Ch 3: 8 and he made the most h' house, the "
10 in the most h' house he made two "
4: 22 doors thereof for the most h' place, "
5: 5 all the h' vessels that were in the "
7 into the most h' place, even under "
11 were come out of the h' place: "
8: 11 of Israel, because the places are h'. "
23: 6 they shall go in, for they are h': but "
29: 5 the filthiness out of the h' place. "
7 burnt offerings in the h' place unto "
30: 27 came up to his h' dwelling place, "
31: 6 the tithe of h' things which were * "
14 of the Lord, and the most h' things. "
35: 3 which were h' unto the Lord, 6918
3 Put the h' ark in the house which 6944
5 stand in the h' place according to "
13 but the other h' offerings sod they "
Ezr 2: 63 should not eat of the most h' things, "
8: 28 unto them, Ye are h' unto the Lord; "
28 Lord; the vessels are h' also; and "
9: 2 h' seed have mingled themselves "
8 to give us a nail in his h' place, "
Ne 7: 65 should not eat of the most h' things, "
8: 9 This day is h' unto the Lord your 6918
10 for this day is h' unto our Lord: "
11 Hold your peace, for the day is h'; "
9: 14 known unto them thy h' sabbath, 6944
10: 31 on the sabbath, or on the h' day: "
33 the set feasts, and for the h' things, "
11: 1 to dwell in Jerusalem the h' city, "
18 All the Levites in the h' city "
12: 47 and they sanctified h' things unto "
Job 6: 10 concealed the words of the H' One. 6918
Ps 2: 6 my king upon my h' hill of Zion. 6944
3: 4 and he heard me out of his h' hill. "
5: 7 will I worship toward thy h' temple. "
11: 4 The Lord is in his h' temple, the "
15: 1 who shall dwell in thy h' hill? "
16: 10 thou suffer thine H' One to see 2623
20: 6 will hear him from his h' heaven 6944
22: 3 thou art h', O thou that inhabitest 6918
24: 3 or who shall stand in his h' place? 6944
28: 2 up my hands toward thy h' oracle. "
33: 21 we have trusted in his h' name. "
43: 3 let them bring me unto thy h' hill, "
46: 4 the h' place of the tabernacles of 6918
51: 11 take not thy h' spirit from me. 6944
65: 4 thy house, even of thy h' temple. †6918
68: 5 widows, is God in his h' habitation. 6944
17 them, as in Sinai, in the h' place. * "
35 art terrible out of thy h' places: 4720
71: 22 the harp, O thou H' One of Israel. 6918
78: 41 and limited the H' One of Israel. "
79: 1 thy h' temple have they defiled; 6944
86: 2 Preserve my soul; for I am h': O *2623
87: 1 foundation is in the h' mountains. 6944
89: 18 the H' One of Israel is our king. 6918
19 spakest in vision to thy h' one, *2623
20 with my h' oil have I anointed him: 6944
98: 1 his right hand, and his h' arm, "
99: 3 and terrible name; for it is h'. 6918
5 at his footstool; for he is h'. "
9 our God, and worship at his h' hill; 6944
9 hill; for the Lord our God is h'. 6918
103: 1 is within me, bless his h' name. 6944
105: 3 Glory ye in his h' name: let the "
42 For he remembered his h' promise, "
106: 47 to give thanks unto thy h' name, "
111: 9 ever: h' and reverend is his name. 6918
138: 2 will worship toward thy h' temple, 6944
145: 17 his ways, and h' in all his works. *2623
21 bless his h' name for ever and ever. 6944
Pr 9: 10 and the knowledge of the h' is 6918
20: 25 who devoureth that which is h', 6944
30: 3 nor have the knowledge of the h'. 6918
Ec 8: 10 and gone from the place of the h', "
Isa 1: 4 have provoked the H' One of Israel "
4: 3 in Jerusalem, shall be called h', "
5: 16 God that is h' shall be sanctified "
19 counsel of the H' One of Israel draw "
24 despised the word of the H' One "
6: 3 said, H', h', h', is the Lord of hosts: "
13 the h' seed shall be the substance 6944
10: 17 fire, and his H' One for a flame: 6918
20 stay upon the Lord, the H' One of "
11: 9 nor destroy in all my h' mountain: 6944
12: 6 great is the H' One of Israel in the 6918
17: 7 shall have respect to the H' One "
27: 13 worship the Lord in the h' mount 6944
29: 19 rejoice in the H' One of Israel. 6918
23 sanctify the H' One of Jacob, and "
30: 11 cause the H' One of Israel to cease "
12 thus saith the H' One of Israel, "
15 the Lord God, the H' One of Israel; "
29 night when a h' solemnity is kept; 6942
31: 1 look not unto the H' One of Israel, 6918
37: 23 even against the H' One of Israel. "
40: 25 shall I be equal? saith the H' One. "
41: 14 thy redeemer, the H' One of Israel. "
16 shalt glory in the H' One of Israel. "
20 the H' One of Israel hath created it. "
43: 3 Lord thy God, the H' One of Israel, "
14 your redeemer, the H' One of Israel; "
15 I am the Lord, your H' One, the

Isa 45: 11 saith the Lord, the H· One of Israel. 6918
47: 4 is his name, the H· One of Israel. "
48: 2 they call themselves of the h· city, 6944
17 Redeemer, the H· One of Israel; 6918
49: 7 Redeemer of Israel, and his H· One, "
7 the H· One of Israel, and he shall "
52: 1 garments, O Jerusalem, the h· city: 6944
10 The Lord hath made bare his h· arm "
54: 5 Redeemer the H· One of Israel; 6918
55: 5 God, and for the H· One of Israel; "
56: 7 will I bring to my H· mountain, 6944
57: 13 and shall inherit my h· mountain; "
15 eternity, whose name is H·; I dwell 6918
15 I dwell in the high and h· place, "
58: 13 doing thy pleasure on my h· day; 6944
13 the h· of the Lord, honourable; 6918
60: 9 God, and to the H· One of Israel, "
14 The Zion of the H· One of Israel. "
62: 12 they shall call them, The h· people, 6944
63: 10 rebelled, and vexed his h· Spirit: "
11 he that put his h· Spirit within him? "
64: 10 Thy h· cities are a wilderness, Zion "
11 Our h· and our beautiful house, "
65: 11 Lord, that forget my h· mountain, "
25 nor destroy in all my h· mountain, "
66: 20 to my h· mountain Jerusalem, saith "
Jer 11: 15 the h· flesh is passed from thee? "
25: 30 his voice from his h· habitation; "
31: 40 shall be h· unto the Lord; it shall "
50: 29 Lord, against the H· One of Israel. "
51: 5 sin against the H· One of Israel. 6918
Eze 7: 24 and their h· places shall be defiled. 6942
20: 39 but pollute ye my h· name no more 6944
40 mine h· mountain, in the mountain "
40 oblations, with all your h· things. "
21: 2 drop thy word toward the h· place, *4720
22: 8 Thou hast despised mine h· things, 6944
26 and have profaned mine h· things, "
26 between the h· and profane, "
28: 14 thou wast upon the h· mountain "
36: 20 they profaned my h· name, when "
21 I had pity for mine h· name, which "
22 but for mine h· name's sake, which "
38 As the h· flock, as the flock of * "
39: 7 So will I make my h· name known "
7 will not let them pollute my h· name "
7 I am the Lord, the H· One in Israel. 6918
25 will be jealous for my h· name; 6944
41: 4 unto me, This is the most h· place. "
42: 13 separate place, they be h· chambers, "
13 shall eat the most h· things: "
13 shall they lay the most h· things, "
13 trespass offering...the place is h·. 6918
14 shall they not go out of the h· place 6944
14 wherein they minister; for they are h·; "
43: 7 and my h· name, shall the house of 6944
8 they have even defiled my h· name "
12 round about shall be most h·. "
44: 8 kept the charge of mine h· things: "
13 to come near to any of my h· things, "
13 in the most h· place: but they shall "
19 lay them in the h· chambers, and "
23 between the h· and profane, "
45: 1 the Lord, an h· portion of the land: "
1 This shall be h· in all the borders "
3 sanctuary and the most h· place. "
4 The h· portion of the land shall be "
4 and an h· place for the sanctuary. 4720
6 the oblation of the h· portion: 6944
7 of the oblation of the h· portion, "
7 before the oblation of the h· portion, "
46: 19 into the h· chambers of the priests, "
48: 10 the priests, shall be this h· oblation; "
12 shall be unto them a thing most h· "
14 the land: for it is h· unto the Lord. "
18 the oblation of the h· portion shall "
18 the oblation of the h· portion; "
20 ye shall offer the h· oblation "
21 and on the other of the h· oblation, "
21 and it shall be the h· oblation; "
Da 4: 8 in whom is the spirit of the h· gods: 6922
9 the spirit of the h· gods is in thee, "
13 a watcher and an h· one came down "
17 demand by the word of the h· ones: "
18 the spirit of the h· gods is in thee. "
23 a watcher and an h· one coming "
5: 11 whom is the spirit of the h· gods; "
8: 24 destroy the mighty...h· people. 6918
9: 16 city Jerusalem, thy h· mountain: 6944
20 God for the h· mountain of my God; "
24 thy people and upon thy h· city, "
24 prophecy, and to anoint the most H·. "
11: 28 shall be against the h· covenant; "
30 indignation against the h· covenant: "
30 them that forsake the h· covenant. "
45 seas in the glorious h· mountain; "
12: 7 scatter the power of the h· people, "
Ho 11: 9 the H· One in the midst of thee: 6918
Joe 2: 1 sound an alarm in my h· mountain: 6944
3: 17 dwelling in Zion, my h· mountain: "
17 then shall Jerusalem be h·, and "
Am 2: 7 same maid, to profane my h· name: "
Ob 16 have drunk upon my h· mountain, "
Jon 2: 4 look again toward thy h· temple. "
7 unto thee, into thine h· temple. "
Mic 1: 2 you, the Lord from his h· temple. "
Hab 1: 12 O Lord my God, mine H· One? 6918
2: 20 but the Lord is in his h· temple: 6944
3: 3 and the H· One from mount Paran. 6918
Zep 3: 11 because of my h· mountain. 6944
Hag 2: 12 If one bear h· flesh in the skirt of "
12 oil, or any meat, shall it be h·? 6942
Zec 2: 12 Judah his portion in the h· land, 6944
13 raised up out of his h· habitation. "
8: 3 the Lord of hosts the h· mountain. "
M't 1: 18 found with child of the H· Ghost. 40

M't 1: 20 in her is of the H· Ghost. 40
3: 11 baptize you with the H· Ghost, "
4: 5 devil taketh him up into the h· city, "
7: 6 not that which is h· unto the dogs, "
12: 31 the blasphemy against the H· Ghost* "
32 speaketh against the H· Ghost, * 40
24: 15 of desolation,...stand in the h· place, "
25: 31 glory, and all the h· angels with him, * "
27: 53 went into the h· city, and appeared "
28: 19 of the Son, and of the H· Ghost: "
M'r 1: 8 baptize you with the H· Ghost. "
24 who thou art, the H· One of God. "
3: 29 blaspheme against the H· Ghost "
6: 20 that he was a just man and an h·, "
8: 38 of his Father with the h· angels. "
12: 36 himself said by the H· Ghost, "
13: 11 not ye that speak, but the H· Ghost. "
Lu 1: 15 shall be filled with the H· Ghost, "
35 The H· Ghost shall come upon "
35 that h· thing which shall be born "
41 was filled with the H· Ghost: "
49 great things; and h· is his name. "
67 was filled with the H· Ghost, "
70 the mouth of his h· prophets, which "
72 and to remember his h· covenant; "
2: 23 womb shall be called h· to the Lord; "
25 and the H· Ghost was upon him. "
26 unto him by the H· Ghost, that "
3: 16 baptize you with the H· Ghost "
22 the H· Ghost descended in a bodily "
4: 1 Jesus being full of the H· Ghost "
34 who thou art; the H· One of God. "
9: 26 in his Father's, and of the h· angels. "
11: 13 give the H· Spirit to them that ask "
12: 10 against the H· Ghost it shall "
12 For the H· Ghost shall teach you "
Jo 1: 33 which baptizeth with the H· Ghost. "
7: 39 for the H· Ghost was not yet given; * "
14: 26 Comforter, which is the H· Ghost, "
17: 11 H· Father, keep through thine own "
20: 22 them, Receive ye the H· Ghost: "
Ac 1: 2 he through the H· Ghost had given "
5 be baptized with the H· Ghost not "
8 that the H· Ghost is come upon "
16 the H· Ghost by the mouth of David "
2: 4 were all filled with the H· Ghost, "
27 thine H· One to see corruption. 3741
33 the promise of the H· Ghost, he 40
38 receive the gift of the H· Ghost. "
3: 14 ye denied the H· One and the Just, "
21 by the mouth of all his h· prophets "
4: 8 Peter, filled with the H· Ghost, said "
27 of a truth against thy h· child Jesus, "
30 by the name of thy h· child Jesus. "
31 were all filled with the H· Ghost, "
5: 3 heart to lie to the H· Ghost, and "
32 so is also the H· Ghost, whom "
6: 3 full of the H· Ghost and wisdom, * "
5 full of faith and of the H· Ghost, "
13 words against this h· place, and the "
7: 33 where thou standest is h· ground. "
51 do always resist the H· Ghost: "
55 he, being full of the H· Ghost, "
8: 15 they might receive the H· Ghost: "
17 and they received the H· Ghost. "
18 hands the H· Ghost was given, he "
19 he may receive the H· Ghost. "
9: 17 and be filled with the H· Ghost. "
31 in the comfort of the H· Ghost, "
10: 22 was warned from God by an h· angel "
38 with the H· Ghost and with power: "
44 the H· Ghost fell on all them "
45 out the gift of the H· Ghost "
47 have received the H· Ghost as well "
11: 15 the H· Ghost fell on them, as on "
16 shall be baptized with the H· Ghost. "
24 full of the H· Ghost and of faith: "
13: 2 the H· Ghost said, Separate me "
4 being sent forth by the H· Ghost, "
9 filled with the H· Ghost, set his "
35 thine H· One to see corruption. 3741
52 with joy, and with the H· Ghost. 40
15: 8 giving them the H· Ghost, even "
28 it seemed good to the H· Ghost, "
16: 6 were forbidden of the H· Ghost "
19: 2 Have ye received the H· Ghost "
2 whether there be any H· Ghost. "
6 the H· Ghost came on them; "
20: 23 Save that the H· Ghost witnesseth "
28 H· Ghost hath made you overseers, "
21: 11 said, Thus saith the H· Ghost, So "
28 and hath polluted this h· place. "
28: 25 Well spake the H· Ghost by Esaias "
Ro 1: 2 by his prophets in the h· scriptures, "
5: 5 in our hearts by the H. Ghost "
7: 12 law is h·, and the commandment h·, "
9: 1 me witness in the H· Ghost, "
11: 16 For if the firstfruit be h·, the lump is "
16 the lump is also h·: and if the lump "
16 if the root be h·, so are the branches. "
12: 1 a living sacrifice, h·, acceptable unto "
14: 17 peace, and joy in the H· Ghost. "
15: 13 through the power of the H· Ghost. "
16 being sanctified by the H· Ghost. "
16: 16 Salute one another with an h· kiss. "
1Co 2: 13 which the H· Ghost teacheth; * "
3: 17 for the temple of God is h·, which "
6: 19 is the temple of the H· Ghost "
7: 14 children unclean; but now are they h·. "
34 may be h· both in body and in spirit: "
9: 13 which minister about h· things *2413
12: 3 is the Lord, but by the H· Ghost. 40
16: 20 Greet ye one another with an h· kiss. "
2Co 6: 6 by kindness, by the H· Ghost, by "
13: 12 Greet one another with an h· kiss. "
14 communion of the H· Ghost, be "

Eph 1: 4 we should be h· and without blame 40
13 sealed with that h· Spirit of promise, "
2: 21 groweth unto an h· temple in the "
3: 5 unto his h· apostles and prophets "
4: 30 And grieve not the h· Spirit of God, "
5: 27 it should be h· and without blemish. "
Col 1: 22 to present you h· and unblameable "
3: 12 as the elect of God, h· and beloved, "
1Th 1: 5 in power, and in the H· Ghost, "
6 affliction with joy of the H· Ghost: "
4: 8 hath also given unto us his h· Spirit. "
5: 26 Greet all the brethren with an h· kiss. "
27 be read unto all the h· brethren. * "
1Ti 2: 8 lifting up h· hands, without wrath 3741
2Ti 1: 9 us, and called us with an h· calling, 40
14 by the H· Ghost which dwelleth "
3: 15 thou hast known the h· scriptures, *2413
Tit 1: 8 sober, just, h·, temperate; Holding 3741
3: 5 and renewing of the H· Ghost; 40
Heb 2: 4 miracles and gifts of the H· Ghost, "
3: 1 Wherefore, h· brethren, partakers of "
7 as the H· Ghost saith, To day if "
6: 4 made partakers of the H· Ghost, "
7: 26 who is h·, harmless, undefiled, 3741
9: 8 The H· Ghost this signifying, 40
12 he entered in once into the h· place, 39
24 into the h· places made with hands, "
25 entereth into the h· place every year "
10: 15 the H· Ghost also is a witness to 40
1Pe 1: 12 you with the H· Ghost sent down "
15 hath called you is h·, so be ye h· in all "
16 it is written, Be ye h·; for I am h·. "
2: 5 spiritual house, an h· priesthood, to "
9 a royal priesthood, an h· nation, a "
3: 5 in the old time the h· women also, "
2Pe 1: 18 we were with him in the h· mount. "
21 h· men of God spake as they were * "
21 were moved by the H· Ghost. "
2: 21 from the h· commandment delivered "
3: 2 spoken before by the h· prophets, "
11 in all h· conversation and godliness, "
1Jo 2: 20 ye have an unction from the H· One, "
5: 7 the Word, and the H· Ghost: * "
Jude 20 yourselves in your most h· faith, "
20 faith, praying in the H· Ghost, "
Re 3: 7 saith he that is h·, he that is true, "
4: 8 night, saying, H·, h·, h·, Lord God "
6: 10 How long, O Lord, h· and true, dost "
11: 2 the h· city shall they tread under foot "
14: 10 the presence of the h· angels, and in "
15: 4 for thou only art h·: for all nations 3741
18: 20 and ye h· apostles and prophets; * 40
20: 6 Blessed and h· is he that hath part "
21: 2 John saw the h· city, new Jerusalem, "
10 me that great city, the h· Jerusalem, "
22: 6 God of the h· prophets sent his angel* "
11 and that is h·, let him be...still. "
11 and he that is..., let him be h· still. 37
19 book of life, and out of the h· city, 40

holyday See also HOLY and DAY.
Ps 42: 4 with a multitude that kept h·. 2287
Col 2: 16 in respect of an h·, or of the new *1859

Holy Ghost See HOLY and GHOST.

Holy One See HOLY and ONE.

Holy place See HOLY and PLACE.

Holy Spirit See HOLY and SPIRIT.

Homam (*ho'-mam*) See also HEMAM.
1Ch 1: 39 the sons of Lotan; Hori and H·: 1950

home See also HOMEBORN.
Ge 39: 16 by her, until his lord came h·. 1004
43: 16 Bring these men h·, and slay, and* "
26 And when Joseph came h·, they "
Ex 9: 19 the field, and shall not be brought h·, "
Le 18: 9 she be born at h·, or born abroad, "
De 21: 12 shalt bring her h· to thine house; 8432
24: 5 but he shall be free at h· one year, 1004
Jos 2: 18 father's household, h· unto thee. * "
J'g 11: 9 If ye bring me h· again to fight 7725
19: 9 your way, that thou mayest go h·. 168
Ru 1: 21 hath brought me h· again empty: 7725
1Sa 2: 20 And they went unto their own h·. 4725
6: 7 bring their calves h· from them: 1004
10 cart, and shut up their calves at h·: "
10: 26 And Saul also went h· to Gibeah; * "
18: 2 go no more h· to his father's house. 7725
24: 22 And Saul went h·; but David and 1004
2Sa 13: 7 David sent h· to Tamar, saying, "
14: 13 not fetch h· again his banished. 7725
17: 23 and gat him h· to his house, to his 1004
1Ki 5: 14 in Lebanon, and two months at h·: "
13: 7 Come h· with me, and refresh thyself, "
15 Come h· with me, and eat bread. "
2Ki 14: 10 glory of this, and tarry at h·: for "
1Ch 13: 12 shall I bring the ark of God h· to me? "
13 So David brought not the ark h· to * "
2Ch 25: 10 out of Ephraim, to go h· again: 4725
10 and they returned h· in great anger. "
19 abide now at h·; why shouldest 1004
Es 5: 10 and when he came h·, he sent and "
Job 39: 12 him, that he will bring h· thy seed, 7725
Ps 68: 12 that tarried at h· divided the spoil. 1004
Pr 7: 19 For the goodman is not at h·, he is "
20 will come h· at the day appointed. "
Ec 12: 5 man goeth to his long h·, and the "
Jer 39: 14 that he should carry him h·: so he "
La 1: 20 bereaveth, at h· there is as death. "
Hab 2: 5 proud man, neither keepeth at h·, 5115
Hag 1: 9 when ye brought it h·, I did blow 1004
M't 8: 6 my servant lieth at h· sick of the *3614
M'r 5: 19 Go h· to thy friends, and tell them *3624
Lu 9: 61 bid them farewell, which are at h· at* "
15: 6 And when he cometh h·, he calleth 3624
Joh 19: 27 that disciple took her unto his own h·. "
20: 10 went away again unto their own h·. 1438

Ac 21: 6 ship; and they returned h' again. 2398
1Co 11:34 any man hunger, let him eat at h'; 3624
14:35 let them ask their husbands at h': "
2Co 5: 6 whilst we are at h' in the body, we 1736
1Ti 5: 4 learn first to shew piety at h', and *2398
Tit 2: 5 be discreet, chaste, keepers at h', 3626

homeborn
Ex 12:49 One law shall be to him that is h', 249
Jer 2:14 Israel a servant? is he a h' slave? 1004

homer (*ho'-mer*) See also HOMERS.
Le 27:16 an h' of barley seed shall be valued 2563
Isa 5:10 seed of an h' shall yield an ephah. "
Eze 45:11 may contain the tenth part of an h', "
11 the ephah the tenth part of an h': "
11 measure thereof shall be after the h'. "
13 part of an ephah of an h' of wheat, "
13 part of an ephah of an h' of barley: "
14 the cor, which is an h' of ten baths; "
14 ten baths; for ten baths are an h': "
Ho 3: 2 of silver, and for an h' of barley, "
2 of barley, and an half h' of barley: 3963

homers (*ho'-mers*)
Nu 11:32 gathered least gathered ten h': 2563

honest See also DISHONEST.
Lu 8:15 they, which in an h' and good heart, 2570
Ac 6: 3 you seven men of h' report, full of the *
Ro 12:17 things h' in the sight of all men. *2570
2Co 8:21 Providing for h' things, not only in* "
13: 7 but ye should do that which is h', * "
Ph'p 4: 8 are true, whatsoever things are h', *4586
1Pe 2:12 your conversation h' among the *2570

honestly
Ro 13:13 Let us walk h', as in the day; not 2156
1Th 4:12 That ye may walk h' toward them † "
Heb 13:18 in all things willing to live h'. ‡2573

honesty See also DISHONESTY.
1Ti 2: 2 quiet...life in all godliness and h'. *4587

honey See also HONEYCOMB.
Ge 43:11 a little balm, and a little h', spices, 1706
Ex 3: 8 a land flowing with milk and h'; "
17 a land flowing with milk and h'. "
13: 5 a land flowing with milk and h', "
16:31 of it was like wafers made with h'. "
33: 3 a land flowing with milk and h': "
Le 2:11 burn no leaven, nor any h', in any "
20:24 land that floweth with milk and h': "
Nu 13:27 surely it floweth with milk and h'; "
14: 8 land which floweth with milk and h'. "
16:13, 14 that floweth with milk and h', "
De 6: 3 land that floweth with milk and h'. "
8: 8 a land of oil olive, and h'; "
11: 9 land that floweth with milk and h'. "
26: 9, 15 that floweth with milk and h'. "
27: 3 land that floweth with milk and h'; "
31:20 that floweth with milk and h'; and "
32:13 made him to suck h' out of the rock, "
Jos 5: 6 land that floweth with milk and h'. "
J'g 14: 8 was a swarm of bees and h' in the "
9 had taken the h' out of the carcase "
18 What is sweeter than h'? and what "
1Sa 14:25 and there was h' upon the ground. "
26 the h' dropped; but no man put his "
29 because I tasted a little of this h'. "
43 I did but taste a little h' with the "
2Sa 17:29 And h', and butter, and sheep, and "
1Ki 14: 3 and cracknels, and a cruse of h', "
2Ki 18:32 a land of oil olive and of h', that ye "
2Ch 31: 5 wine, and oil, and h', and of all the "
Job 20:17 floods, the brooks of h' and butter. "
Ps 19:10 gold: sweeter also than h' and the "
81:16 and with h' out of the rock should I "
119:103 yea, sweeter than h' to my mouth! "
Pr 24:13 son, eat thou h', because it is good; "
25:16 Hast thou found h'? eat so much as "
27 It is not good to eat much h': so for "
Ca 4:11 h' and milk are under thy tongue; "
5: 1 eaten my honeycomb with my h'; "
Isa 7:15 Butter and h' shall he eat, that he "
22 for butter and h' shall every one eat "
Jer 11: 5 a land flowing with milk and h', as "
32:22 a land flowing with milk and h'; "
41: 8 and of barley, and of oil, and of h'. "
Eze 3: 3 in my mouth as h' for sweetness. "
16:13 didst eat fine flour, and h', and oil: "
19 gave thee, fine flour, and oil, and h', "
20: 6, 15 flowing with milk and h', which "
27:17 Pannag, and h', and oil, and balm. "
M't 3: 4 his meat was locusts and wild h'. 3192
M'r 1: 6 and he did eat locusts and wild h'; "
Re 10: 9 it shall be in thy mouth sweet as h'. "
10 it was in my mouth sweet as h': "

honeycomb
1Sa 14:27 and dipped it in an h', and put 3295,1706
Ps 19:10 also than honey and the h'. 5317,6688
Pr 5: 3 a strange woman drop as an h', *5317
16:24 Pleasant words are as an h', 6688,1706
24:13 the h', which is sweet to thy taste: 5317
27: 7 The full soul loatheth an h'; but to "
Ca 4:11 lips, O my spouse, drop as the h': "
5: 1 have eaten my h' with my honey; 3293
Lu 24:42 a broiled fish, and of an h'. *3193,2781

honour See also DISHONOUR; HONOURABLE; HONOURED; HONOUREST; HONOURETH; HONOURS.
Ge 49: 6 mine h', be not thou united: for *3519
Ex 14:17 and I will get me h' upon Pharaoh, 3513
18 I have gotten me h' upon Pharaoh, "
20:12 H' thy father and thy mother: that "
Le 19:15 nor h' the person of the mighty: 1921
32 and h' the face of the old man, and "
Nu 22:17 promote thee unto very great h', 3513
37 able indeed to promote thee to h'? "
24:11 to promote thee unto great h': but, "
Nu 24:11 Lord hath kept thee back from h'. 3519
27:20 put some of thine h' upon him, 1935
De 5:16 H' thy father and thy mother, as 3513
26:19 in praise, and in name, and in h'; 8597
J'g 4: 9 thou takest shall not be for thine h'; "
9: 9 by me they h' God and man, and 3513
13:17 come to pass we may do thee h'? "
1Sa 2:30 them that h' me I will h', and they "
15:30 sinned: yet h' me now, I pray thee, "
2Sa 6:22 of, of them shall I be had in h'. "
10: 3 thou that David doth h' thy father, "
1Ki 3:13 hast not asked, both riches, and h': 3519
1Ch 16:27 Glory and h' are in his presence; 1926
17:18 to thee, for the h' of thy servant? 3519
19: 3 thou that David doth h' thy father, 3513
29:12 Both riches and h' come of thee, 3519
28 old age, full of days, riches, and h': "
2Ch 1:11 hast not asked riches, wealth, or h', "
12 give thee riches, and wealth, and h', "
17: 5 he had riches and h' in abundance. "
18: 1 had riches and h' in abundance, and "
26:18 neither shall it be for thine h' from "
32:27 exceeding much riches and h': and "
33 inhabitants of Jerusalem did him h' "
Es 1: 4 and the h' of his excellent majesty 3366
20 shall give to their husbands h', both "
6: 3 What h' and dignity hath been done "
6 whom the king delighteth to h'? "
6 would the king delight to do h' more "
7, 9 whom the king delighteth to h', "
9, 11 whom the king delighteth to h'. "
8:16 light, and gladness, and joy, and h'. "
Job 14:21 sons come to h', and he knoweth 3513
Ps 7: 5 earth, and lay mine h' in the dust. *3519
8: 5 crowned him with glory and h'. 1926
21: 5 h' and majesty hast thou laid upon 1935
26: 8 the place where thine h' dwelleth. *3519
49:12 man being in h' abideth not: he is 3366
20 that is in h', and understandeth not, "
66: 2 Sing forth the h' of his name: *3519
71: 8 praise and with thy h' all the day. 8597
91:15 I will deliver him, and h' him. 3515
96: 6 H' and majesty are before him: 1935
104: 1 art clothed with h' and majesty. "
112: 9 his horn shall be exalted with h'. 3519
145: 5 the glorious h' of thy majesty, and 1926
149: 9 written: this h' have all his saints. "
Pr 3: 9 H' the Lord with thy substance, 3513
16 and in her left hand riches and h'. 3519
4: 8 she shall bring thee to h', when 3513
5: 9 Lest thou give thine h' unto others, 1935
8:18 Riches and h' are with me; yea, 3519
11:16 A gracious woman retaineth h': "
14:28 multitude of people is the king's h': *1927
15:33 wisdom; and before h' is humility. 3519
18:12 haughty, and before h' is humility. "
20: 3 It is an h' for a man to cease from "
21:21 findeth life, righteousness, and h'. "
22: 4 the Lord are riches, and h', and life. "
25: 2 but the h' of kings is to search out* "
26: 1 harvest, so h' is not seemly for a fool. "
8 so is he that giveth h' to a fool. "
29:23 h' shall uphold the humble in spirit. "
31:25 Strength and h' are her clothing; *1926
Ec 6: 2 riches, wealth, and h', so that he 3519
10: 1 is in reputation for wisdom and h'. "
Isa 29:13 with their lips do h' me, but have 3513
43:20 The beast of the field shall h' me, "
58:13 and shalt h' him, not doing thine "
Jer 33: 9 a praise and an h' before all the *8597
Da 2: 6 me gifts and rewards and great h': 3367
4:30 of my power, and for the h' of my * "
36 mine h' and brightness returned *1923
37 extol and h' the King of heaven, all 1922
5:18 and majesty, and glory, and h': *1923
11:21 not give the h' of the kingdom: 1935
38 shall he h' the God of forces: and 3513
38 his fathers knew not shall he h' "
Mal 1: 6 I be a father, where is mine h'? 3519
M't 13:57 A prophet is not without h', save in 820
15: 4 H' thy father and mother: and he 5091
6 h' not his father or his mother, he "
19:19 H' thy father and thy mother: and, "
M'r 6: 4 A prophet is not without h', but in 820
7:10 H' thy father and thy mother; 5091
10:19 not; H' thy father and mother. "
Lu 18:20 h' thy father and thy mother. "
Joh 4:44 hath no h' in his own country. 5092
5:23 that all men should h' the Son, 5091
23 the Son, even as they h' the Father. "
41 I receive not h' from men. *1391
44 which receive h' one of another, * "
44 the h' that cometh from God only? * "
8:49 but I h' my Father, and ye do 5091
54 Jesus answered, If I h' myself, *1392
54 If I...myself, my h' is nothing: *1391
12:26 serve me, him will my Father h'. 5091
Ro 2: 7 for glory and h' and immortality, 5092
10 But glory, h', and peace, to every "
9:21 to make one vessel unto h', and "
12:10 love; in h' preferring one another; "
13: 7 fear to whom fear; h' to whom h'. "
1Co 12:23 these we bestow more abundant h'; "
24 given more abundant h' to that "
2Co 6: 8 h' and dishonour, by evil report *1391
Eph 6: 2 H' thy father and mother; which 5091
Col 2:23 not in any h' to the satisfying of *5092
1Th 4: 4 his vessel in sanctification and h'; "
1Ti 1:17 be h' and glory for ever and ever. "
5: 3 H' widows that are widows indeed. 5091
17 be counted worthy of double h', 5092
6: 1 their own masters worthy of all h', "
16 whom be h' and power everlasting: "
2Ti 2:20 some to h', and some to dishonour. "
21 be a vessel unto h', sanctified, and "
Heb 2: 7 crownedst him with glory and h'. "
Heb 2: 9 death, crowned with glory and h'; 5092
3: 3 builded the house hath more h' "
5: 4 no man taketh this h' unto himself, "
1Pe 1: 7 might be found unto praise and h' "
2:17 H' all men. Love the brotherhood. 5091
17 Fear God. H' the king. "
3: 7 giving h' unto the wife, as unto 5092
2Pe 1:17 from God the Father h' and glory, "
Re 4: 9 beasts give glory and h' and thanks "
11 to receive glory and h' and power: "
5:12 and h', and glory, and blessing. "
13 Blessing, and h', and glory, and "
7:12 h', and power, and might, be unto "
19: 1 Salvation, and glory, and h', and * "
7 and rejoice, and give h' to him: *1391
21:24 do bring their glory and h' into it. *5092
26 bring the glory and h' of the nations "

honourable
Ge 34:19 was more h' than all the house of *3513
Nu 22:15 more, and more h' than they. "
1Sa 9: 6 man of God, and he is an h' man; * "
22:14 bidding, and is h' in thine house? "
2Sa 23:19 Was he not most h' of three? "
23 He was more h' than the thirty, "
2Ki 5: 1 man with his master, and h', 5375, 6440
1Ch 4: 9 was more h' than his brethren: 3513
11:21 three, he was more h' than the two; "
25 he was h' among the thirty, but "
Job 22: 8 and the h' man dwelt in it. 5375,6440
Ps 45: 9 were among thy h' women: upon 3368
111: 3 His work is h' and glorious: and *1935
Isa 3: 3 of fifty, and the h' man, and 5375,6440
5 ancient, and...base against the h'. 3519
5:13 and their h' men are famished, and "
9:15 ancient and h', he is the head; 5375,6440
23: 8 traffickers are the h' of the earth? 1935
9 contempt all the h' of the earth. 3513
42:21 magnify the law, and make it h'. 142
43: 4 thou hast been h', and I have loved 3513
58:13 delight, the holy of the Lord, h'; and "
Na 3:10 and they cast lots for her h' men, "
M'r 15:43 of Arimathæa, an h' counsellor, 2158
Lu 14: 8 more h' man than thou be bidden 1784
Ac 13:50 up the devout and h' women, 2158
17:12 of h' women which were Greeks, "
1Co 4:10 ye are h', but we are despised. *1741
12:23 body, which we think to be less h', 820
Heb 13: 4 Marriage is h' in all, and the bed *5093

honoured
Ex 14: 4 and I will be h' upon Pharaoh, *3513
Pr 13:18 that regardeth reproof shall be h'. "
27:18 waiteth on his master shall be h'. "
Isa 43:23 hast thou h' me with thy sacrifices. "
La 1: 8 all that h' her despise her, because "
5:12 the faces of elders were not h'. 1921
Da 4:34 and h' him that liveth for ever, 1922
Ac 28:10 also h' us with many honours; 5092
1Co 12:26 one member be h', all the members 1392

honourest See also DISHONOUREST.
1Sa 2:29 and h' thy sons above me, to make 3513

honoureth See also DISHONOURETH.
Ps 15: 4 but he h' them that fear the Lord. 3513
Pr 12: 9 better than he that h' himself, and "
14:31 that h' him hath mercy on the poor. "
Mal 1: 6 A son h' his father, and a servant "
M't 15: 8 mouth, and h' me with their lips; 5091
M'r 7: 6 This people h' me with their lips, "
Joh 5:23 that h' not the Son h' not the Father "
8:54 it is my Father that h' me; of *1392

honours
Ac 28:10 also honoured us with many h'; 5091

hoods
Isa 3:23 linen, and the h', and the vails. *6797

hoof See also HOOFS.
Ex 10:26 shall not an h' be left behind; 6541
Le 11: 3 Whatsoever parteth the h', and is "
4 cud, or of them that divide the h': "
4, 5, 6 cud, but divideth not the h'; "
7 the swine, though he divide the h' "
26 every beast which divideth the h', "
De 14: 6 And every beast that parteth the h', "
7 of them that divide the cloven h'; "
7 chew the cud, but divide not the h'; "
8 swine, because it divideth the h', "

hoofs See also HORSEHOOFS.
Ps 69:31 or bullock that hath horns and h'. 6536
Isa 5:28 horses' h' shall be counted like 6541
Jer 47: 3 the noise of the stamping of the h' "
Eze 26:11 the h' of his horses shall he tread "
32:13 nor the h' of beasts trouble them. "
Mic 4:13 iron, and I will make thy h' brass: "

hook See also HOOKS.
2Ki 19:28 I will put my h' in thy nose, 2397
Job 41: 1 draw out leviathan with an h'? 100
2 thou put an h' into his nose? *2443
Isa 37:29 will I put my h' in thy nose, 2397
M't 17:27 go thou to the sea, and cast an h', 44

hooks See also FISHHOOKS; PRUNINGHOOKS.
Ex 26:32 their h' shall be of gold, upon the 2053
37 gold, and their h' shall be of gold: "
27:10, 11 h' of the pillars and their fillets "
17 their h' shall be of silver, and their "
36:36 with gold: their h' were of gold; "
38 the five pillars of it with their h': "
38:10, 11, 12, 17, the h' of the pillars and "
19 their h' of silver, and the overlaying "
28 shekels he made h' for the pillars, "
Isa 18: 5 cut off the sprigs with pruning h', "
Eze 29: 4 But I will put h' in thy jaws, and 2397
38: 4 thee back, and put h' into thy jaws, "
40:43 And within were h', an hand broad, 8240
Am 4: 2 that he will take you away with h', 6793

hope See also HOPED; HOPE'S; HOPETH; HOPING.
Ru 1:12 If I should say, I have h', if I 8615
Ezr 10: 2 yet now there is h' in Israel 4723
Job 4: 6 thy fear, thy confidence, thy h'. 8615
5:16 So the poor hath h', and iniquity "
6:11 is my strength, that I should h'? *3176
7: 6 shuttle, and are spent without h'. 8615
8:13 and the hypocrite's h' shall perish: "
14 Whose h' shall be cut off; and *3689
11:18 be secure, because there is h': 8615
20 their h' shall be as the giving up "
14: 7 there is h' of a tree, if it be cut down, "
19 and thou destroyest the h' of man. "
17:15 And where is now my h'? as for "
15 as for my h', who shall see it? "
19:10 mine h' hath he removed like a tree. "
27: 8 For what is the h' of the hypocrite, "
31:24 If I have made gold my h', or have 3689
41: 9 Behold, the h' of him is in vain: 8431
Ps 16: 9 my flesh also shall rest in h'. * 983
22: 9 didst make me h' when I was upon *982
31:24 heart, all ye that h' in the Lord. 3176
33:18 upon them that h' in his mercy; "
22 upon us, according as we h' in thee.* "
38:15 in thee, O Lord, do I h': thou wilt "
39: 7 what wait I for? my h' is in thee. 8431
42: 5 disquieted in me? h' thou in God: 3176
11 within me? h' thou in God: "
43: 5 disquieted within me? h' in God: "
71: 5 For thou art my h', O Lord God: 8615
14 But I will h' continually, and will 3176
78: 7 they might set their h' in God. 3689
119:49 which thou hast caused me to h'. 3176
81 salvation: but I h' in thy word. "
114 and my shield: I h' in thy word. "
116 let me not be ashamed of my h'. 7664
130: 5 doth wait, and in his word do I h'. 3176
7 Let Israel h' in the Lord: for with "
131: 3 Let Israel h' in the Lord from "
146: 5 whose h' is in the Lord his God: 7664
147:11 him, in those that h' in his mercy. 3176
Pr 10:28 The h' of the righteous shall be 8431
11: 7 and the h' of unjust men perisheth. "
13:12 H' deferred maketh the heart sick: "
14:32 the righteous hath h' in his death. 2620
19:18 Chasten thy son while there is h', 8615
26:12 is more h' of a fool than of him. "
29:20 is more h' of a fool than of him. "
Ec 9: 4 joined to all the living there is h': 986
Isa 38:18 into the pit cannot h' for thy truth. 7663
57:10 saidst thou not, There is no h': 2976
Jer 2:25 but thou saidst, There is no h': "
14: 8 O the h' of Israel, the saviour 4723
17: 7 Lord, and whose h' the Lord is. 4009
13 O Lord, the h' of Israel, all that 4723
17 thou art my h' in the day of evil. *4268
18:12 And they said, There is no h': 2976
31:17 And there is h' in thine end, saith 8615
50: 7 the Lord, the h' of their fathers. 4723
La 3:18 strength and my h' is perished *8431
21 to my mind, therefore have I h'. 3176
24 soul; therefore will I h' in him. "
26 good that a man should both h' 2342
29 the dust; if so be there may be h'. 8615
Eze 13: 6 and they have made others to h' 3176
19: 5 had waited, and her h' was lost, 8615
37:11 bones are dried, and our h' is lost: "
Ho 2:15 the valley of Achor for a door of h': "
Joe 3:16 Lord will be the h' of his people, *4268
Zec 9:12 the strong hold, ye prisoners of h': 8615
Lu 6:34 to them of whom ye h' to receive. 1679
Ac 2:26 also my flesh shall rest in h': 1680
16:19 that the h' of their gains was gone, "
23: 6 the h' and resurrection of the dead "
24:15 And have h' toward God, which "
26: 6 am judged for the h' of the promise "
7 God day and night, h' to come. 1679
27:20 all h' that we should be saved was 1680
28:20 that for the h' of Israel I am bound "
Ro 4:18 Who against h' believed in h', that "
5: 2 and rejoice in h' of the glory of God. "
4 experience; and experience, h': "
5 And h' maketh not ashamed: "
8:20 who hath subjected the same in h', "
24 for we are saved by h': "
24 but h' that is seen is not h': "
24 man seeth, why doth he yet h' for? *1679
25 But if we h' for that we see not, "
12:12 Rejoicing in h'; patient in 1680
15: 4 of the scriptures might have h'. "
13 the God of h' fill you with all joy and "
13 that ye may abound in h', through "
1Co 9:10 he that ploweth should plow in h'; "
10 and that he that thresheth in h' * "
10 should be partaker of his h'. "
13:13 And now abideth faith, h', charity, "
15:19 If in this life only we have h' in *1679
2Co 1: 7 And our h' of you is stedfast, 1680
3:12 Seeing then that we have such h', "
10:15 but having h', when your faith is "
Ga 5: 5 wait for the h' of righteousness by "
Eph 1:18 know what is the h' of his calling, "
2:12 having no h', and without God in "
4: 4 are called in one h' of your calling; "
Ph'p 1:20 my earnest expectation and my h', "
2:23 Him therefore I h' to send 1679
Col 1: 5 the h' which is laid up for you in 1680
23 away from the h' of the gospel, "
27 Christ in you, the h' of glory: "
1Th 1: 3 patience of h' in our Lord Jesus "
2:19 For what is our h', or joy, or crown "
4:13 even as others which have no h'. "
5: 8 for an helmet, the h' of salvation. "
2Th 2:16 and good h' through grace, "
1Ti 1: 1 Lord Jesus Christ, which is our h'; "
Tit 1: 2 In h' of eternal life, which God,
Tit 2:13 Looking for that blessed h', and 1680
3: 7 according to the h' of eternal life. "
Heb 3: 6 confidence and rejoicing of the h' "
6:11 full assurance of h' unto the end: "
18 lay hold upon the h' set before us: "
19 which h' we have as an anchor of "
7:19 the bringing in of a better h' did; 1680
1Pe 1: 3 begotten us again unto a lively h' "
13 and h' to the end for the grace that 1679
21 your faith and h' might be in God. 1680
3:15 a reason of the h' that is in you "
1Jo 3: 3 every man that hath this h' in him "

hoped
Es 9: 1 the enemies of the Jews h' to have 7663
Job 6:20 confounded because they had h'; 982
Ps 119:43 for I have h' in thy judgments. 3176
74 because I have h' in thy word. "
147 and cried: I h' in thy word. "
166 Lord, I have h' for thy salvation, 7663
Jer 3:23 Truly in vain is salvation h' for from* "
Lu 23: 8 he h' to have seen some miracle 1679
Ac 24:26 He h' also that the money should "
2Co 8: 5 And this they did, not as we h', but "
Heb 11: 1 is the substance of things h' for, "

hope's
Ac 26: 7 For which h' sake, king Agrippa, I*1679

hopeth
1Co 13: 7 believeth all things, h' all things, 1679

Hophni (*hof'-ni*)
1Sa 1: 3 two sons of Eli, H' and Phinehas, 2652
2:34 thy two sons, on H' and Phinehas; "
4: 4 H' and Phinehas, were there with "
11 two sons of Eli, H' and Phinehas, "
17 H' and Phinehas are dead, and "

Hophra See PHARAOH-HOPHRA.

hoping
Lu 6:35 and lend, h' for nothing again; * 560
1Ti 3:14 thee, h' to come unto thee shortly: 1679

hopper See GRASSHOPPER.

Hor (*hor*) See also HOR-HAGIDGAD.
Nu 20:22 Kadesh, and came unto mount H'. 2023
23 unto Moses and Aaron in mount H', "
25 and bring them up unto mount H': "
27 and they went up into mount H' "
21: 4 And they journeyed from mount H' "
33:37 Kadesh, and pitched in mount H', "
38 the priest went up into mount H', "
39 years old when he died in mount H'. "
41 And they departed from mount H', "
34: 7 ye shall point out for you mount H': "
8 From mount H' ye shall point out "
De 32:50 thy brother died in mount H', and "

Horam (*ho'-ram*)
Jos 10:33 Then H' king of Gezer came up 2036

Horeb (*ho'-reb*) See also SINAI.
Ex 3: 1 the mountain of God, even to H'. 2722
17: 6 thee there upon the rock in H'; "
33: 6 their ornaments by the mount H'. "
De 1: 2 are eleven days' journey from H' "
6 Lord our God spake unto us in H', "
19 And when we departed from H', we "
4:10 before the Lord thy God in H', "
15 Lord spake unto you in H' out of "
5: 2 God made a covenant with us in H'. "
9: 8 Also in H' ye provoked the Lord to "
18:16 desiredst of the Lord thy God in H' "
29: 1 which he made with them in H'. "
1Ki 8: 9 stone, which Moses put there at H', "
19: 8 nights unto H' the mount of God. "
2Ch 5:10 which Moses put therein at H', "
Ps 106:19 made a calf in H', and worshipped "
Mal 4: 4 which I commanded unto him in H' "

Horem (*ho'-rem*)
Jos 19:38 And Iron, and Migdal-el, H', and 2765

Hor-hagidgad (*hor-hag-id'-gad*) See also GUDGODAH.
Nu 33:32 Bene-jaakan, and encamped at H'. *2735
33 they went from H', and pitched * "

Hori (*ho'-ri*) See also HORITE.
Ge 36:22 of Lotan were H' and Hemam; 2753
30 are the dukes that came of H', * "
Nu 13: 5 of Simeon, Shaphat, the son of H'. "
1Ch 1:39 the sons of Lotan; H', and Homam: "

Horims (*ho'-rims*) See also HORITES.
De 2:12 The H' also dwelt in Seir *2752
22 when he destroyed the H' from * "

Horite (*ho'-rite*) See also HORI; HORITES.
Ge 36:20 These are the sons of Seir the H', 2752

Horites (*ho'-rites*) See also HORIMS.
Ge 14: 6 And the H' in their mount Seir, 2752
36:21 these are the dukes of the H', the "
29 are the dukes that came of the H'; "

Hormah (*hor'-mah*) See also ZEPHATH.
Nu 14:45 discomfited them, even unto H'. 2767
21: 3 he called the name of the place H'. "
De 1:44 destroyed you in Seir, even unto H'. "
Jos 12:14 The king of H', one; the king of "
15:30 And Eltolad, and Chesil, and H', "
19: 4 And Eltolad, and Bethul, and H', "
J'g 1:17 the name of the city was called H'. "
1Sa 30:30 And to them which were in H', "
1Ch 4:30 And at Bethuel, and at H', and at "

horn See also HORNS; INKHORN.
Ex 21:29 ox were wont to push with his h' *
Jos 6: 5 a long blast with the ram's h', 7161
1Sa 2: 1 mine h' is exalted in the Lord: my "
10 and exalt the h' of his anointed. "
16: 1 fill thine h' with oil, and go, I will "
13 Then Samuel took the h' of oil, and "
2Sa 22: 3 shield, and the h' of my salvation,
1Ki 1:39 Zadok the priest took an h' of oil 7161
1Ch 25: 5 the words of God, to lift up the h'. "
Job 16:15 skin, and defiled my h' in the dust. "
Ps 18: 2 buckler, and the h' of my salvation, "
75: 4 to the wicked, Lift not up the h': "
5 Lift not up your h' on high: speak "
89:17 thy favour our h' shall be exalted. "
24 in my name shall his h' be exalted. "
92:10 But my h' shalt thou exalt like "
10 thou exalt like the h' of an unicorn: "
112: 9 his h' shalt be exalted with honour. 7161
132:17 will I make the h' of David to bud: "
148:14 also exalteth the h' of his people, "
Jer 48:25 The h' of Moab is cut off, and his "
La 2: 3 his fierce anger all the h' of Israel: "
17 set up the h' of thine adversaries. "
Eze 29:21 the h' of the house of Israel to bud "
Da 7: 8 up among them another little h', 7162
8 in this h' were eyes like the eyes of "
11 great words which the h' spake: "
20 even of that h' that had eyes, and "
21 same h' made war with the saints, "
8: 5 the goat had a notable h' between 7161
8 strong, the great h' was broken; "
9 one of them came forth a little h', "
21 great h' that is between his eyes "
Mic 4:13 I will make thine h' iron, and I will "
Zec 1:21 the Gentiles, which lifted up their h' "
Lu 1:69 hath raised up an h' of salvation 2768

hornet See also HORNETS.
De 7:20 God will send the h' among them, 6880
Jos 24:12 I sent the h' before you, which drave "

hornets
Ex 23:28 And I will send h' before thee, *6880

horns
Ge 22:13 ram caught in a thicket by his h': 7161
Ex 27: 2 And thou shalt make the h' of it "
2 his h' shall be of the same: and "
29:12 and put it upon the h' of the altar "
30: 2 the h' thereof shall be of the same. "
3 round about, and the h' thereof: "
10 an atonement upon the h' of it once "
37:25 the h' thereof were of the same. "
26 round about, and the h' of it: also "
38: 2 he made the h' thereof on the four "
2 it; the h' thereof were of the same: "
Le 4: 7 blood upon the h' of the altar of "
18 blood upon the h' of the altar which "
25, 30, 34 upon the h' of the altar of "
8:15 and put it upon the h' of the altar "
9: 9 and put it upon the h' of the altar, "
16:18 and put it upon the h' of the altar "
De 33:17 his h' are like the h' of unicorns: "
Jos 6: 4 ark seven trumpets of rams' h': 3104
6 bear seven trumpets of rams' h' "
13 seven trumpets of rams' h' before "
1Ki 1:50 caught hold on the h' of the altar. 7161
51 caught hold on the h' of the altar. "
2:28 caught hold on the h' of the altar. "
22:11 And Zedekiah...made him h' of iron: "
2Ch 18:10 And Zedekiah...made him h' of iron, "
Ps 22:21 me from the h' of the unicorns. "
69:31 or bullock that hath h' and hoofs. 7160
75:10 the h' of the wicked also will I cut 7161
10 h' of the righteous shall be exalted. "
118:27 even unto the h' of the altar. "
Jer 17: 1 and upon the h' of your altars; "
Eze 27:15 for a present h' of ivory and ebony. "
34:21 pushed all the diseased with your h', "
43:15 altar and upward shall be four h'. "
20 thereof, and on the four h' of it, "
Da 7: 7 were before it; and it had ten h'. 7162
8 I considered the h', and, behold, "
8 three of the first h' plucked up by "
20 the ten h' that were in his head, "
24 And the ten h' out of this kingdom "
8: 3 the river a ram which had two h': 7161
3 and the two h' were high; but one "
6 came to the ram that had two h', "
7 smote the ram, and brake his two h': "
20 sawest having two h' are the kings "
Am 3:14 the h' of the altar shall be cut off, "
6:13 Have we not taken to us h' by our "
Hab 3: 4 he had h' coming out of his hand:* "
Zec 1:18 eyes, and saw, and behold four h'. "
19, 21 h' which have scattered Judah, "
21 to cast out the h' of the Gentiles, "
Re 5: 6 having seven h' and seven eyes, 2768
9:13 from the four h' of the golden altar "
12: 3 having seven heads and ten h', "
13: 1 sea, having seven heads and ten h', "
1 and upon his h' ten crowns, and "
11 he had two h' like a lamb, and he "
17: 3 having seven heads and ten h'. "
7 hath the seven heads and ten h'. "
12 the ten h' which thou sawest are "
16 the ten h' which thou sawest upon "

Horon See BETH-HORON; HORONITE.

Horonaim (*hor-o-na'-im*) See also HOLON.
Isa 15: 5 in the way of H' they shall raise 2773
Jer 48: 3 A voice of crying shall be from H', "
5 for in the going down of H' the "
34 voice, from Zoar even unto H', "

Horonite (*ho'-ron-ite*)
Ne 2:10 When Sanballat the H', and 2772
19 But when Sanballat the H', and "
13:28 was son in law to Sanballat the H': "

horrible
Ps 11: 6 brimstone, and an h' tempest: *2152
40: 2 brought me up also out of an h' pit, 7588
Jer 5:30 A wonderful and h' thing is 8186
18:13 Israel hath done a very h' thing. "
23:14 prophets of Jerusalem an h' thing: "
Ho 6:10 I have seen an h' thing in the house "

horribly
Jer 2:12 heavens, at this, and be h' afraid, 8175
Eze 32:10 their kings shall be h' afraid for 8178
horror
Ge 15:12 an h' of great darkness fell upon 367
Ps 55: 5 and h' hath overwhelmed me. 6427
119:53 H' hath taken hold upon me *2152
Eze 7:18 h' shall cover them; and shame 6427
horse See also HORSEBACK; HORSEHOOFS; HORSELEACH; HORSEMAN; HORSES.
Ge 49:17 the path, that biteth the h' heels, *5483
Ex 15: 1 the h' and his rider hath he thrown "
19 For the h' of Pharaoh went in with* "
21 the h' and his rider hath he thrown "
1Ki 10:29 and an h' for an hundred and fifty: "
20:20 king of Syria escaped on an h' with "
25 h' for h', and chariot for chariot: "
2Ch 1:17 and an h' for an hundred and fifty: "
23:15 come to the entering of the h' gate "
Ne 3:28 From above the h' gate repaired "
Es 6: 8 the h' that the king rideth upon, "
9 this apparel and h' be delivered "
10 and take the apparel and the h', "
11 took Haman the apparel and the h', "
Job 39:18 she scorneth the h' and his rider. "
19 Hast thou given the h' strength? "
Ps 32: 9 Be ye not as the h', or as the mule, "
33:17 An h' is a vain thing for safety: "
76: 6 both the chariot and h' are cast "
147:10 not in the strength of the h': "
Pr 21:31 The h' is prepared against the day "
26: 3 A whip for the h', a bridle for the "
Isa 43:17 bringeth forth the chariot and h', "
63:13 the deep, as an h' in the wilderness, "
Jer 8: 6 as the h' rusheth into the battle. "
31:40 unto the corner of the h' gate toward "
51:21 break in pieces the h' and his rider; "
Am 2:15 he that rideth the h' deliver himself. "
Zec 1: 8 behold a man riding upon a red h', "
9:10 and the h' from Jerusalem, "
10: 3 them as his goodly h' in the battle. "
12: 4 smite every h' with astonishment, "
4 smite every h' of the people with "
14:15 And so shall be the plague of the h', "
Re 6: 2 I saw, and behold a white h': and 2462
4 went out another h' that was red: "
5 I beheld, and lo a black h'; and he "
8 And I looked, and behold a pale h': "
14:20 winepress, even unto the h' bridles,* "
19:11 opened, and behold a white h'; "
19 war against him that sat on the h', "
21 sword of him that sat upon the h', "
horseback
2Ki 9:18 there went one on h' to meet 7392,5483
19 Then he sent out a second on h'," "
Es 6: 9 on h' through the street of the 7392
11 on h' through the street of the city,* "
8:10 and sent letters by posts on h', 5483
horse-gate See HORSE and GATE.
horse-heels See HORSE and HEELS.
horsehoofs
J'g 5:22 Then were the h' broken by 6119,5483
horseleach
Pr 30:15 the h' hath two daughters, 5936
horseman See also HORSEMEN.
2Ki 9:17 Joram said, Take an h', and send 7395
Na 3: 3 The h' lifteth up both the bright 6571
horsemen
Ge 50: 9 up with him both chariots and h': 6571
Ex 14: 9 chariots of Pharaoh, and his h', "
17, 18 his chariots, and upon his h'. "
23 horses, his chariots, and his h'. "
26 their chariots, and upon their h'. "
28 covered the chariots, and the h', "
15:19 in with his chariots and with his h' "
Jos 24: 6 with chariots and h' unto the Red "
1Sa 8:11 for his chariots, and to be his h'; "
13: 5 chariots, and six thousand h', "
2Sa 1: 6 h' followed hard after him. 1167, "
8: 4 chariots, and seven hundred h', "
10:18 the Syrians, and forty thousand h', "
1Ki 1: 5 he prepared him chariots and h', "
4:26 chariots, and twelve thousand h'. "
9:19 for his chariots, and cities for his h'," "
22 rulers of his chariots, and his h'. "
10:26 gathered together chariots and h': "
26 chariots, and twelve thousand h', "
20:20 escaped on an horse with the h'. "
2Ki 2:12 chariot of Israel, and the h' thereof." "
13: 7 he leave of the people...but fifty h', "
14 chariot of Israel, and the h' thereof. "
18:24 on Egypt for chariots and for h'? "
1Ch 18: 4 chariots, and seven thousand h', "
19: 6 silver to hire them chariots and h' "
2Ch 1:14 Solomon gathered chariots and h': "
14 chariots, and twelve thousand h', "
8: 6 cities, and the cities of the h', and "
9 and captains of his chariots and h'. "
9:25 chariots, and twelve thousand h'; "
12: 3 and threescore thousand h': "
16: 8 with very many chariots and h'? "
Ezr 8:22 a band of soldiers and h' to help us "
Ne 2: 9 had sent captains of the army and h' "
Isa 21: 7 he saw a chariot with a couple of h', "
9 chariot of men, with a couple of h', "
22: 6 quiver with chariots of men and h', "
7 the h' shall set themselves in array "
28:28 his cart, nor bruise it with his h'.* "
31: 1 in h', because they are very strong "
36: 9 on Egypt for chariots and for h'? "
Jer 4:29 for the noise of the h' and bowmen; "
46: 4 get up, ye h', and stand forth with "
Eze 23: 6 young men, h' riding upon horses. "
Eze 23:12 h' riding upon horses, all of them 6571
26: 7 with chariots, and with h', and "
10 shall shake at the noise of the h', "
27:14 in thy fairs with horses and h' and* "
38: 4 and all thine army, horses and h', "
Da 11:40 with chariots, and with h', and with "
Ho 1: 7 nor by battle, by horses, nor by h'. "
Joe 2: 4 and as h', so shall they run. "
Hab 1: 8 their h' shall spread themselves, "
8 and their h' shall come from far; "
Ac 23:23 and h' threescore and ten, and 2460
32 they left the h' to go with him, "
Re 9:16 the number of the army of the h' 2461
horses See also HORSES'.
Ge 47:17 them bread in exchange for h', 5483
Ex 9: 3 field, upon the h', upon the asses, "
14: 9 all the h' and chariots of Pharaoh, "
23 even all Pharaoh's h', his chariots, "
De 11: 4 unto their h', and to their chariots; "
17:16 he shall not multiply h' to himself, "
16 the end that he should multiply h': "
20: 1 and seest h', and chariots, and a "
Jos 11: 4 with h' and chariots very many. "
6 thou shalt hough their h', and burn "
9 he houghed their h', and burnt "
2Sa 15: 1 prepared him chariots and h', "
1Ki 4:26 had forty thousand stalls of h' for "
28 Barley also and straw for the h' and "
10:25 armour, and spices, h', and mules, "
28 had h' brought out of Egypt, * "
18: 5 grass to save the h' and mules alive, "
20: 1 with him, and h', and chariots: "
21 and smote the h' and chariots, and "
22: 4 people as thy people, my h' as thy h'. "
2Ki 2:11 a chariot of fire, and h' of fire, and "
3: 7 as thy people, and my h' as thy h'. "
5: 9 Naaman came with his h' and with "
6:14 sent he thither h', and chariots, "
15 the city both with h' and chariots. "
17 was full of h' and chariots of fire "
7: 6 noise of chariots, and a noise of h', "
7 left their tents, and their h', and "
10 but h' tied, and asses tied, and the "
13 five of the h' that remain, which "
14 They took therefore two chariot h'; "
9:33 sprinkled on the wall, and on the h': "
10: 2 there are with you chariots and h', "
11:16 way by the which the h' came into* "
14:20 And they brought him on h': and "
18:23 I will deliver thee two thousand h', "
23:11 he took away the h' that the kings "
1Ch 18: 4 also houghed all the chariot h', but "
2Ch 1:16 had h' brought out of Egypt, *5483
17 so brought they out h' for all the * "
9:24 harness, and spices, h', and mules, "
25 had four thousand stalls for h' and "
28 unto Solomon h' out of Egypt, "
25:28 And they brought him upon h', and "
Ezr 2:66 Their h' were seven hundred thirty "
Ne 7:68 Their h', seven hundred thirty and "
Ps 20: 7 trust in chariots, and some in h': "
Ec 10: 7 I have seen servants upon h', and "
Ca 1: 9 to a company of h' in Pharaoh's *5484
Isa 2: 7 their land is also full of h', neither5483
30:16 said, No; for we will flee upon h'; "
31: 1 stay on h', and trust in chariots, "
3 and their h' flesh, and not spirit. "
36: 8 I will give thee two thousand h', "
66:20 the Lord out of all nations upon h', "
Jer 4:13 his h' are swifter than eagles. "
5: 8 They were as fed h' in the morning: "
6:23 they ride upon h', set in array as "
8:16 The snorting of his h' was heard "
12: 5 how canst thou contend with h'? "
17:25 riding in chariots and on h', they, "
22: 4 riding in chariots and on h', he, "
46: 4 Harness the h'; and get up, ye "
9 Come up, ye h'; and rage, ye "
47: 3 stamping of...hoofs of his strong h',* "
50:37 A sword is upon their h', and upon5483
42 they shall ride upon h', every one "
51:27 cause the h' to come up as the rough "
Eze 17:15 that they might give him h' and "
23: 6 men, horsemen riding upon h'. "
12 horsemen riding upon h', all of "
20 whose issue is like the issue of h'. "
23 renowned, all of them riding upon h'. "
26: 7 with h', and with chariots, and with "
10 By reason of the abundance of his h' "
11 the hoofs of his h' shall he tread "
27:14 with h' and horsemen and mules. "
38: 4 all thine army, h' and horsemen, "
15 all of them riding upon h', a great "
39:20 at my table with h' and chariots, "
Ho 1: 7 by battle, by h', nor by horsemen. "
14: 3 save us; we will not ride upon h': "
Joe 2: 4 of them is as the appearance of h'; "
Am 4:10 and have taken away your h'; "
6:12 Shall h' run upon the rock? will one "
Mic 5:10 that I will cut off thy h' out of the "
Na 3: 2 of the wheels and of the pransing h', "
Hab 1: 8 Their h' are also swifter than the "
3: 8 that thou didst ride upon thine h' "
15 walk through the sea with thine h', "
Hag 2:22 the h' and their riders shall come "
Zec 1: 8 and behind him were there red h', "
6: 2 In the first chariot were red h'; "
2 and in the second chariot black h'; "
3 And in the third chariot white h'; "
3 fourth chariot grisled and bay h'. "
6 The black h' which are therein go "
10: 5 riders on h' shall be confounded. "
14:20 there be upon the bells of the h', "
Re 9: 7 of the locusts were like unto h' 2462
9 the chariots of many h' running to "
17 And thus I saw the h' in the vision. "
Re 9:17 heads of the h' were as the heads 2462
18:13 and h', and chariots, and slaves, * "
19:14 heaven followed him upon white h'. "
18 of mighty men, and the flesh of h', "
horses'
Isa 5:28 their h' hoofs shall be counted 5483
Jas 3: 3 we put bits in the h' mouths, that 2462
Hosah (*ho'-sah*)
Jos 19:29 and the coast turneth to H'; 2621
1Ch 16:38 of Jeduthun and H' to be porters: "
26:10 Also H', of the children of Merari, "
11 and brethren of H' were thirteen. "
16 To Shuppim and H' the lot came "
hosanna (*ho-zan'-nah*)
M't 21: 9 H' to the son of David: Blessed 5614
9 name of the Lord; H' in the highest." "
15 and saying, H' to the son of David; "
M'r 11: 9 H'; Blessed is he that cometh in "
10 name of the Lord; H' in the highest." "
Joh 12:13 H': Blessed is the King of Israel "
Hosea (*ho-se'-ah*) See also HOSHEA; OSEE; OSHEA.
Ho 1: 1 of the Lord that came unto H', 1954
2 of the word of the Lord by H'. "
2 Lord said to H', Go, take unto thee "
hosen
Da 3:21 were bound in their coats, their h',6361
Hoshaiah (*ho-sha-i'-ah*)
Ne 12:32 And after them went H', and half 1955
Jer 42: 1 and Jezaniah the son of H', "
43: 2 Then spake Azariah the son of H', "
Hoshama (*ho-sha'-mah*)
1Ch 3:18 Jecamiah, H', and Nedabiah. 1953
Hoshea (*ho-she'-ah*) See also HOSEA.
De 32:44 people, he, and H' the son of Nun.1954
2Ki 15:30 And H' the son of Elah made a "
17: 1 began H' the son of Elah to reign "
3 and H' became his servant, and "
4 of Assyria found conspiracy in H': "
6 In the ninth year of H' the king of "
18: 1 in the third year of H' son of Elah "
9 which was the seventh year of H' "
10 that is the ninth year of H' king of "
1Ch 27:20 of Ephraim, H' the son of Azaziah: "
Ne 10:23 H', Hananiah, Hashub, "
hospitality
Ro 12:13 necessity of saints; given to h'. 5381
1Ti 3: 2 given to h', apt to teach; 5382
Tit 1: 8 But a lover of h', a lover of good "
1Pe 4: 9 Use h' one to another without "
host See also HOSTS.
Ge 2: 1 finished, and all the h' of them. 6635
21:22 chief captain of his h' spake unto "
32 Phichol the chief captain of his h', "
32: 2 them, he said, This is God's h': 4264
Ex 14: 4 upon Pharaoh, and upon all his h';2428
17 upon Pharaoh, and upon all his h', "
24 unto the h' of the Egyptians, 4264
24 troubled the h' of the Egyptians, "
28 all the h' of Pharaoh that came 2428
15: 4 Pharaoh's chariots and his h' hath "
16:13 the dew lay round about the h'. *4264
Nu 2: 4, 6, 8, 11, 13, 15, 19, 21, 23, 26, 28,
30 And his h', and those that were 6635
4: 3 all that enter into the h', to do the "
10:14 and over his h' was Nahshon the son of
15, 16 over the h' of the tribe of the 6635
18 and over his h' was Elizur the son "
19, 20 over the h' of the tribe of the "
22 and over his h' was Elishama the "
23, 24 over the h' of the tribe of the "
25 and over his h' was Ahiezer the "
26, 27 over the h' of the tribe of the "
31:14 wroth with the officers of the h', 2428
48 were over thousands of the h', 6635
De 2:14 wasted out from among the h', *4264
15 destroy them from among the h',* "
4:19 stars, even all the h' of heaven, 6635
17: 3 moon, or any of the h' of heaven, "
23: 9 When the h' goeth forth against *4264
Jos 1:11 Pass through the h', and command* "
3: 2 the officers went through the h'; * "
5:14 captain of the h' of the Lord am 6635
15 captain of the Lord's h' said unto "
8:13 all the h' that was on the north of 4264
18: 9 came again to Joshua to the h' at* "
J'g 4: 2 captain of whose h' was Sisera, 6635
15 all his chariots, and all his h', 4264
16 after the chariots, and after the h', "
16 all the h' of Sisera fell upon the "
7: 1 so that the h' of the Midianites "
8 and the h' of Midian was beneath* "
9 Arise, get thee down unto the h';* "
10 thy servant down to the h': * "
11 strengthened to go...unto the h': * "
11 armed men that were in the h'. * "
13 bread tumbled into the h' of "
14 delivered Midian, and all the h'. "
15 and returned into the h' of Israel,* "
15 into your hand the h' of Midian. "
21 the h' ran, and cried, and fled. "
22 even throughout all the h': and the "
22 and the h' fled to Beth-shittah in "
8:11 smote the h': for the h' was secure. "
12 Zalmunna, discomfited all the h'. "
1Sa 11:11 came into the midst of the h' * "
12: 9 captain of the h' of Hazor, and 6635
14:15 there was trembling in the h', in *4264
19 the noise that was in the h' of the* "
48 And he gathered an h', and smote*2428
50 the captain of his h' was Abner, 6635
17:20 as the h' was going forth to the 2428
46 the carcases of the h' of the 4264

1Sa 17: 55 unto Abner, the captain of the *h'*. 6635
26: 5 son of Ner, the captain of his *h'*: "
28: 5 Saul saw the *h'* of the Philistines, 4264
19 also shall deliver the *h'* of Israel "
29: 6 thy coming in with me in the *h'* is "
2Sa 2: 8 Son of Ner, captain of Saul's *h'*, 6635
3: 23 Joab and all the *h'* that was with "
5: 24 to smite the *h'* of the Philistines. 4264
8: 9 David had smitten all the *h'* of 2428
16 son of Zeruiah was over the *h'*; 6635
10: 7 and all the *h'* of the mighty men. "
16 Shobach the captain of the *h'* of "
18 Shobach the captain of their *h'*, "
17: 25 Amasa captain of the *h'* instead of "
19: 13 be not captain of the *h'* before me "
20: 23 Joab was over all the *h'* of Israel: "
23: 16 through the *h'* of the Philistines, 4264
24: 2 said to Joab the captain of the *h'*, 2428
4 and against the captains of the *h'*. "
4 and the captain of the *h'* went "
1Ki 1: 19 Joab the captain of the *h'*: 6635
25 and the captains of the *h'*, and "
2: 32 of Ner, captain of the *h'* of Israel, "
32 Jether, captain of the *h'* of Judah. "
35 Jehoiada in his room over the *h'*: "
4: 4 son of Jehoiada was over the *h'*: "
11: 15 and Joab the captain of the *h'* was "
21 Joab the captain of the *h'* was "
16: 16 made Omri, the captain of the *h'*, "
20: 1 Syria gathered all his *h'* together: 2428
22: 34 hand, and carry me out of the *h'*; 4264
36 a proclamation throughout the *h'* "
2Ki 3: 9 there was no water for the *h'*, and "
4: 13 king, or to the captain of the *h'*? 6635
5: 1 Naaman, captain of the *h'* of the "
6: 14 and chariots, and a great *h'*: 2428
15 an *h'* compassed the city both with "
24 king of Syria gathered all his *h'*,
7: 4 let us fall unto the *h'* of the 4264
6 had made the *h'* of the Syrians "
6 even the noise of a great *h'*: 2428
14 sent after the *h'* of the Syrians, 4264
9: 5 the captains of the *h'* were sitting; 2428
11: 15 the hundreds, the officers of the *h'*, "
17: 16 worshipped all the *h'* of heaven, 6635
18: 17 Hezekiah with a great *h'* against *2426
21: 3 worshipped all the *h'* of heaven, 6635
5 built altars for all the *h'* of heaven "
23: 4 grove, and for all the *h'* of heaven: "
5 planets, and to all the *h'* of heaven. "
25: 1 Babylon came, he, and all his *h'*, *2428
19 the principal scribe of the *h'*, 6635
1Ch 9: 19 being over the *h'* of the Lord, *4264
11: 15 the *h'* of the Philistines encamped "
18 brake through the *h'* of the "
12: 14 sons of Gad, captains of the *h'*: 6635
21 valour, and were captains in the *h'*. "
22 was a great *h'*, like the *h'* of God. 4264
14: 15 to smite the *h'* of the Philistines. "
16 they smote the *h'* of the Philistines "
18: 9 smitten all the *h'* of Hadarezer 2428
15 the son of Zeruiah was over the *h'*; 6635
19: 8 and all the *h'* of the mighty men, "
16 Shophach the captain of the *h'* of "
18 Shophach the captain of the *h'*. "
25: 1 David and the captains of the *h'* "
26: 26 captains of the *h'*, had dedicated, "
27: 3 of all the captains of the *h'* for the "
5 The third captain of the *h'* for the "
2Ch 14: 9 an *h'* of a thousand thousand, *2428
13 before the Lord, and before his *h'*; 4264
16: 7 the *h'* of the king of Syria escaped 2428
8 and the Lubims a huge *h'*, "
18: 18 all the *h'* of heaven standing on 6635
33 thou mayest carry me out of the *h'*; "
23: 14 hundreds that were set over the *h'*, 2428
24: 23 the *h'* of Syria came up against * "
24 the Lord delivered a very great *h'* "
26: 11 Uzziah had an *h'* of fighting men,* "
14 for them throughout all the *h'* 6635
28: 9 before the *h'* that came to Samaria, "
33: 3 worshipped all the *h'* of heaven, "
5 built altars for all the *h'* of heaven "
11 the captains of the *h'* of the king of "
Ne 9: 6 heaven of heavens, with all their *h'*, "
6 the *h'* of heaven worshippeth thee. "
Ps 27: 3 Though an *h'* should encamp 4264
33: 6 and all the *h'* of them by the 6635
16 saved by the multitude of an *h'*: 2428
136: 15 overthrew Pharaoh and his *h'* in "
Isa 13: 4 mustereth the *h'* of the battle. 6635
24: 21 shall punish the *h'* of the high ones "
34: 4 all the *h'* of heaven shall be "
4 all their *h'* shall fall down, as the "
40: 26 bringeth out their *h'* by number: "
45: 12 and all their *h'* have I commanded. "
Jer 8: 2 the moon, and all the *h'* of heaven, "
19: 13 incense unto all the *h'* of heaven, "
33: 22 *h'* of heaven cannot be numbered, "
51: 3 men; destroy ye utterly all her *h'*. "
52: 25 the principal scribe of the *h'*, who "
Eze 1: 24 of speech, as the noise of an *h'*: 4264
Da 8: 10 great, even to the *h'* of heaven; 6635
10 some of the *h'* and of the stars "
11 himself even to the prince of the *h'*, "
12 And an *h'* was given him against "
13 give both the sanctuary and the *h'* "
Ob 20 captivity of this *h'* of the children 2426
Zep 1: 5 that worship the *h'* of heaven 6635
Lu 2: 13 a multitude of the heavenly *h'* *4756*
10: 35 pence, and gave them to the *h'*, *3830*
Ac 7: 42 up to worship the *h'* of heaven; *4756*
Ro 16: 23 Gaius mine *h'*, and of the whole *3581*

hostages
2Ki 14: 14 house, and *h'*, and returned 1121,8594
2Ch 25: 24 house, the *h'* also, and returned " "

hosts
Ex 12: 41 the *h'* of the Lord went out from 6635
Nu 1: 52 standard, throughout their *h'*. "
2: 32 of the camps throughout their *h'* "
10: 25 all the camps throughout their *h'*: "
Jos 10: 5 and went up, they and all their *h'*, 4264
11: 4 went out, they and all their *h'* with "
J'g 8: 10 in Karkor, and their *h'* with them, "
10 that were left of all the *h'* of the * "
1Sa 1: 3 unto the Lord of *h'* in Shiloh. 6635
11 O Lord of *h'*, if thou wilt indeed "
4: 4 of the covenant of the Lord of *h'*, "
15: 2 Thus saith the Lord of *h'*, I "
17: 45 thee in the name of the Lord of *h'*, "
2Sa 5: 10 the Lord God of *h'* was with him. "
6: 2 called by the name of the Lord of *h'* "
18 in the name of the Lord of *h'*. "
7: 8 Thus saith the Lord of *h'*, I took "
26 The Lord of *h'* is the God over "
27 For thou, O Lord of *h'*, God of "
1Ki 2: 5 did to the two captains of the *h'* of "
15: 20 sent the captains of the *h'* which *2428
18: 15 As the Lord of *h'* liveth, before 6635
19: 10, 14 jealous for the Lord God of *h'*: "
2Ki 3: 14 As the Lord of *h'* liveth, before "
19: 31 zeal of the Lord of *h'* shall do this.*
1Ch 11: 9 and greater: for the Lord of *h'* 6635
17: 7 Thus saith the Lord of *h'*, I took "
24 The Lord of *h'* is the God of Israel, "
Ps 24: 10 Lord of *h'*, he is the King of glory. "
46: 7, 11 The Lord of *h'* is with us; the "
48: 8 seen in the city of the Lord of *h'*, "
59: 5 O Lord God of *h'*, the God of Israel, "
69: 6 that wait on thee, O Lord God of *h'*, "
80: 4 O Lord God of *h'*, how long wilt "
7 Turn us again, O God of *h'*, and "
14 we beseech thee, O God of *h'*: "
19 Turn us again, O Lord God of *h'*, "
84: 1 are thy tabernacles, O Lord of *h'*! "
3 O Lord of *h'*, my King, and my God. "
8 O Lord God of *h'*, hear my prayer: "
12 O Lord of *h'*, blessed is the man "
89: 8 O Lord God of *h'*, who is a strong "
103: 21 Bless ye the Lord, all ye his *h'*; ye "
108: 11 thou, O God, go forth with our *h'*? "
148: 2 angels: praise ye him, all his *h'*. * "
Isa 1: 9 Except the Lord of *h'* had left unto "
24 saith the Lord, the Lord of *h'*, "
2: 12 For the day of the Lord of *h'* shall "
3: 1 the Lord, the Lord of *h'*, doth take "
15 the poor? saith the Lord God of *h'*. "
5: 7 For the vineyard of the Lord of *h'* "
9 In mine ears said the Lord of *h'*, "
16 But the Lord of *h'* shall be exalted "
24 cast away the law of the Lord of *h'*, "
6: 3 Holy, holy, holy, is the Lord of *h'*: "
5 have seen the King, the Lord of *h'*. "
8: 13 Sanctify the Lord of *h'* himself; "
18 in Israel from the Lord of *h'*, which "
9: 7 The zeal of the Lord of *h'* will "
13 neither do they seek the Lord of *h'*. "
19 Through the wrath of the Lord of *h'* "
10: 16 shall the Lord, the Lord of *h'*, "
23 For the Lord God of *h'* shall make "
24 thus saith the Lord God of *h'*, O my "
26 And the Lord of *h'* shall stir up a "
33 Behold, the Lord, the Lord of *h'*, "
13: 4 the Lord of *h'* mustereth the *h'* of "
13 in the wrath of the Lord of *h'*, and "
14: 22 against them, saith the Lord of *h'*, "
23 of destruction, saith the Lord of *h'*. "
24 The Lord of *h'* hath sworn, saying, "
27 For the Lord of *h'* hath purposed, "
17: 3 of Israel, saith the Lord of *h'*. "
18: 7 be brought unto the Lord of *h'* "
7 place of the name of the Lord of *h'*, "
19: 4 saith the Lord, the Lord of *h'*. "
12 what the Lord of *h'* hath purposed "
16 of the hand of the Lord of *h'*, which "
17 of the counsel of the Lord of *h'*, "
18 and swear to the Lord of *h'*; one "
20 for a witness unto the Lord of *h'* "
25 Whom the Lord of *h'* shall bless, "
21: 10 I have heard of the Lord of *h'*, the "
22: 5 perplexity by the Lord God of *h'* "
12 that day did the Lord God of *h'* call "
14 in mine ears by the Lord of *h'*, "
14 till ye die, saith the Lord God of *h'*. "
15 Thus saith the Lord God of *h'*, Go, "
25 In that day, saith the Lord of *h'*, "
23: 9 The Lord of *h'* hath purposed it, to "
24: 23 Lord of *h'* shall reign in mount Zion, "
25: 6 this mountain shall the Lord of *h'* "
28: 5 Lord of *h'* be for a crown of glory, "
22 have heard from the Lord God of *h'* "
29 cometh forth from the Lord of *h'*, "
29: 6 be visited of the Lord of *h'* with "
31: 4 the Lord of *h'* come down to fight "
5 the Lord of *h'* defend Jerusalem; "
37: 16 O Lord of *h'*, God of Israel, that "
32 zeal of the Lord of *h'* shall do this. "
39: 5 Hear the word of the Lord of *h'*: "
44: 6 and his redeemer the Lord of *h'*; "
45: 13 nor reward, saith the Lord of *h'*. "
47: 4 the Lord of *h'* is his name, the "
48: 2 Israel; the Lord of *h'* is his name. "
51: 15 roared: The Lord of *h'* is his name. "
54: 5 husband; the Lord of *h'* is his name; "
Jer 2: 19 in thee, saith the Lord God of *h'*. "
3: 19 goodly heritage of the *h'* of nations? "
5: 14 thus saith the Lord God of *h'*, "
6: 6 For thus hath the Lord of *h'* said "
9 Thus saith the Lord of *h'*, They "
7: 3 the Lord of *h'*, the God of Israel, "
21 the Lord of *h'*, the God of Israel; "
8: 3 driven them, saith the Lord of *h'*. "
Jer 9: 7 Therefore saith the Lord of *h'*, 6635
15 the Lord of *h'*, the God of Israel; "
17 Thus saith the Lord of *h'*, Consider "
10: 16 The Lord of *h'* is his name. "
11: 17 For the Lord of *h'*, that planted "
20 Lord of *h'*, that judgest righteously, "
22 Therefore thus saith the Lord of *h'*, "
15: 16 by thy name, O Lord God of *h'*. "
16: 9 the Lord of *h'*, the God of Israel; "
19: 3 the Lord of *h'*, the God of Israel; "
11 Thus saith the Lord of *h'*; Even so "
15 the Lord of *h'*, the God of Israel; "
20: 12 Lord of *h'*, that triest the righteous, "
23: 15 Therefore thus saith the Lord of *h'* "
16 Thus saith the Lord of *h'*, Hearken "
36 living God, of the Lord of *h'* our God. "
25: 8 Therefore thus saith the Lord of *h'*; "
27 the Lord of *h'*, the God of Israel; "
28 Thus saith the Lord of *h'*; Ye shall "
29 of the earth, saith the Lord of *h'*. "
32 Thus saith the Lord of *h'*, Behold, "
26: 18 Thus saith the Lord of *h'*; Zion "
27: 4 the Lord of *h'*, the God of Israel; "
18 make intercession to the Lord of *h'*, "
19 For thus saith the Lord of *h'* "
21 the Lord of *h'*, the God of Israel, "
28: 2 the Lord of *h'*, the God of Israel, "
14 the Lord of *h'*, the God of Israel; "
29: 4 the Lord of *h'*, the God of Israel, "
8 the Lord of *h'*, the God of Israel; "
17 Thus saith the Lord of *h'*; Behold, "
21, 25 the Lord of *h'*, the God of Israel, "
30: 8 saith the Lord of *h'*, that I will break "
31: 23 the Lord of *h'*, the God of Israel; "
35 The Lord of *h'* is his name: "
32: 14, 15 the Lord of *h'*, the God of Israel; "
18 the Mighty God, the Lord of *h'*, is "
33: 11 Praise the Lord of *h'*: for the Lord "
12 Thus saith the Lord of *h'*; Again "
35: 13, 17, 18, 19, the Lord of *h'*, the God of "
38: 17 the God of *h'*, the God of Israel; "
39: 16 the Lord of *h'*, the God of Israel; "
42: 15, 18 the Lord of *h'*, the God of Israel; "
43: 10 the Lord of *h'*, the God of Israel; "
44: 2 the Lord of *h'*, the God of Israel; "
7 thus saith the Lord, the God of *h'*, "
11 the Lord of *h'*, the God of Israel; "
25 the Lord of *h'*, the God of Israel, "
46: 10 is the day of the Lord God of *h'*, "
10 the Lord God of *h'* hath a sacrifice "
18 King, whose name is the Lord of *h'*, "
25 The Lord of *h'*, the God of Israel, "
48: 1 the Lord of *h'*, the God of Israel; "
15 King, whose name is the Lord of *h'*. "
49: 5 upon thee, saith the Lord God of *h'*, "
7 Edom, thus saith the Lord of *h'*; "
26 off in that day, saith the Lord of *h'*. "
35 Thus saith the Lord of *h'*; Behold, "
50: 18 the Lord of *h'*, the God of Israel; "
25 the work of the Lord God of *h'* in "
31 proud, saith the Lord God of *h'*: "
33 Thus saith the Lord of *h'*; The "
34 strong; the Lord of *h'* is his name: "
51: 5 Judah of his God, of the Lord of *h'*; "
14 The Lord of *h'* hath sworn by "
19 the Lord of *h'* is his name. "
33 the Lord of *h'*, the God of Israel; "
57 King, whose name is the Lord of *h'*. "
58 Thus saith the Lord of *h'*; The "
Ho 12: 5 Even the Lord God of *h'*; the Lord "
Am 3: 13 saith the Lord God, the God of *h'*, "
4: 13 Lord, the God of *h'*, is his name. "
5: 14 the Lord, the God of *h'*, shall be "
15 Lord God of *h'* will be gracious "
16 Therefore the Lord, the God of *h'*, "
27 Lord, whose name is The God of *h'*. "
6: 8 saith the Lord the God of *h'*, I "
14 Israel, saith the Lord the God of *h'*; "
9: 5 Lord God of *h'* is he that toucheth "
Mic 4: 4 of the Lord of *h'* hath spoken it. "
Na 2: 13 against thee, saith the Lord of *h'*, "
3: 5 against thee, saith the Lord of *h'*; "
Hab 2: 13 not of the Lord of *h'* that the people "
Zep 2: 9 the Lord of *h'*, the God of Israel, "
10 against the people of the Lord of *h'*. "
Hag 1: 2 Thus speaketh the Lord of *h'*, "
5 therefore thus saith the Lord of *h'*; "
7 saith the Lord of *h'*; Consider your "
9 Why? saith the Lord of *h'*. Because "
14 work in the house of the Lord of *h'*, "
2: 4 I am with you, saith the Lord of *h'*: "
6 For thus saith the Lord of *h'*; Yet "
7 with glory, saith the Lord of *h'*. "
8 gold is mine, saith the Lord of *h'*. "
9 of the former, saith the Lord of *h'*: "
9 I give peace, saith the Lord of *h'*. "
11 Thus saith the Lord of *h'*; Ask now "
23 In that day, saith the Lord of *h'*, "
23 chosen thee, saith the Lord of *h'*. "
Zec 1: 3 them, Thus saith the Lord of *h'*; "
3 ye unto me, saith the Lord of *h'*, "
3 turn unto you, saith the Lord of *h'*. "
4 Thus saith the Lord of *h'*; Turn ye "
6 Like as the Lord of *h'* thought to do "
12 O Lord of *h'*, how long wilt thou not "
14 Thus saith the Lord of *h'*; I am "
16 be built in it, saith the Lord of *h'*, "
17 Thus saith the Lord of *h'*; My cities "
2: 8 For thus saith the Lord of *h'*; "
9 that the Lord of *h'* hath sent me. "
11 that the Lord of *h'* hath sent me unto "
3: 7 Thus saith the Lord of *h'*; If thou "
9 thereof, saith the Lord of *h'*, "
10 In that day, saith the Lord of *h'*, "
4: 6 by my spirit, saith the Lord of *h'*. "
9 that the Lord of *h'* hath sent me unto "

Zec 5: 4 bring it forth, saith the Lord of *h*·, 6635
6:12 Thus speaketh the Lord of *h*·, "
15 that the Lord of *h*· hath sent me unto "
7: 3 were in the house of the Lord of *h*·, "
4 came the word of the Lord of *h*· "
9 Thus speaketh the Lord of *h*·, "
12 which the Lord of *h*· hath sent in "
12 a great wrath from the Lord of *h*·. "
13 would not hear, saith the Lord of *h*·: "
8: 1 the word of the Lord of *h*· came to "
2 Thus saith the Lord of *h*·; I was "
3 the mountain of the Lord of *h*· the "
4 Thus saith the Lord of *h*·; There "
6 Thus saith the Lord of *h*·; If it be "
6 in mine eyes? saith the Lord of *h*·. "
7 Thus saith the Lord of *h*·; Behold, "
9 Thus saith the Lord of *h*·; Let your "
9 the house of the Lord of *h*· was laid, "
11 former days, saith the Lord of *h*·. "
14 For thus saith the Lord of *h*·; As I "
14 saith the Lord of *h*·, and I repented "
18 the word of the Lord of *h*· came "
19 Thus saith the Lord of *h*·; The fast "
20 Thus saith the Lord of *h*·; It shall "
21 and to seek the Lord of *h*·: I will "
22 shall come to seek the Lord of *h*· in "
23 Thus saith the Lord of *h*·; In those "
9:15 The Lord of *h*· shall defend them; "
10: 3 the Lord of *h*· hath visited his flock "
12: 5 strength in the Lord of *h*· their God. "
13: 2 in that day, saith the Lord of *h*·, "
7 is my fellow, saith the Lord of *h*·: "
14:16, 17 worship the King, the Lord of *h*·, "
21 be holiness unto the Lord of *h*·: "
21 in the house of the Lord of *h*·. "
Mal 1: 4 thus saith the Lord of *h*·, They "
6 saith the Lord of *h*· unto you, O "
8 thy person? saith the Lord of *h*·. "
9 your persons? saith the Lord of *h*·. "
10 pleasure in you, saith...Lord of *h*·, "
11 the heathen, saith the Lord of *h*·. "
13 snuffed at it, saith the Lord of *h*·; "
14 a great King, saith the Lord of *h*·, "
2: 2 unto my name, saith the Lord of *h*·, "
4 be with Levi, saith the Lord of *h*·. "
7 is the messenger of the Lord of *h*·. "
8 of Levi, saith the Lord of *h*·. "
12 an offering unto the Lord of *h*·. "
16 his garment, saith the Lord of *h*·: "
3: 1 he shall come, saith the Lord of *h*·. "
5 fear not me, saith the Lord of *h*·. "
7 unto you, saith the Lord of *h*·. "
10 now herewith, saith the Lord of *h*·, "
11 in the field, saith the Lord of *h*·. "
12 delightsome land, saith...Lord of *h*·. "
14 mournfully before the Lord of *h*·? "
17 shall be mine, saith the Lord of *h*·, "
4: 1 burn them up, saith the Lord of *h*·, "
3 I shall do this, saith the Lord of *h*·. "

hot See also HOTTEST.
Ex 16:21 when the sun waxed *h*·, it melted. 2552
22:24 And my wrath shall wax *h*·, and I 2734
32:10 that my wrath may wax *h*· against "
11 why doth thy wrath wax *h*· against "
19 and Moses' anger waxed *h*·, and he "
22 not the anger of my lord wax *h*·: "
Le 13:24 skin whereof there is a *h*· burning,*784
De 9:19 of the anger and *h*· displeasure, 2534
19: 6 the slayer, while his heart is *h*·, 3179
Jos 9:12 This our bread we took *h*· for our 2525
J'g 2:14, 20 the anger of the Lord was *h*· *2734
3: 8 anger of the Lord was *h*· against * "
6:39 Let not thine anger be *h*· against * "
10: 7 anger of the Lord was *h*· against * "
1Sa 11: 9 by that time the sun be *h*·, ye shall 2527
21: 6 to put *h*· bread in the day when it "
Ne 7: 3 be opened until the sun be *h*·; "
Job 6:17 when it is *h*·, they are consumed "
Ps 6: 1 chasten me in thy *h*· displeasure. 2534
38: 1 chasten me in thy *h*· displeasure. "
39: 3 My heart was *h*· within me, while 2552
78:48 their flocks to *h*· thunderbolts. 7565
Pr 6:28 Can one go upon *h*· coals, and his feet
Eze 24:11 that the brass of it may be *h*·, and 3179
Da 3:22 and the furnace exceeding *h*·, the 228
Ho 7: 7 They are all *h*· as an oven, and 2552
1Ti 4: 2 conscience seared with a *h*· iron; *2748*
Re 3:15 that thou art neither cold nor *h*·: *2200*
15 I would thou wert cold or *h*·. "
16 lukewarm, and neither cold nor *h*·, "

Hotham (*ho'-tham*) See also HOTHAN.
1Ch 7:32 Japhlet, and Shomer, and *H*·, 2369

Hothan (*ho'-than*) See also HOTHAM.
1Ch 11:44 Shama and Jehiel the sons of *H*· 2369

Hothir (*ho'-thir*)
1Ch 25: 4 Mallothi, *H*·, and Mahazioth: 1956
28 The one and twentieth to *H*·, he, "

hotly
Ge 31:36 thou hast so *h*· pursued after me? 1814

hottest
2Sa 11:15 in the forefront of the *h*· battle, 2389

hough See also HOUGHED.
Jos 11: 6 shalt *h*· their horses, and burn 6131

houghed
Jos 11: 9 he *h*· their horses, and burnt their 6131
2Sa 8: 4 David *h*· all the chariot horses, but "
1Ch 18: 4 David also *h*· all the chariot horses, "

hound See GREYHOUND.

hour See also HOURS.
Da 3: 6 the same *h*· be cast into the midst 8160
15 be cast the same *h*· into the midst "
4:19 was astonied for one *h*·, and his * "
33 The same *h*· was the thing fulfilled "
5: 5 In the same *h*· came forth fingers 8160
M't 8:13 was healed in the selfsame *h*·. *5610*
9:22 was made whole from that *h*·. "
10:19 that same *h*· what ye shall speak. "
15:28 was made whole from that very *h*·. "
17:18 child was cured from that very *h*·. "
20: 3 he went out about the third *h*·, and "
5 out about the sixth and ninth *h*·, "
6 about the eleventh *h*· he went out, "
9 were hired about the eleventh *h*·, "
12 These last have wrought but one *h*·, "
24:36 of that day and *h*· knoweth no man, "
42 not what *h*· your Lord doth come.* "
44 such an *h*· as ye think not the Son "
50 and in an *h*· that he is not aware of, "
25:13 ye know neither the day nor the *h*· "
26:40 could ye not watch with me one *h*·? "
45 the *h*· is at hand, and the Son of "
55 In that same *h*· said Jesus to the "
27:45 the sixth *h*· there was darkness "
45 over all the land unto the ninth *h*·. "
46 about the ninth *h*· Jesus cried with "
M'r 13:11 given you in that *h*·, that speak ye: "
32 day and that *h*· knoweth no man, "
14:35 possible, the *h*· might pass from "
37 couldest not thou watch one *h*·? "
41 it is enough, the *h*· is come; behold, "
15:25 was the third *h*·, and they crucified "
33 And when the sixth *h*· was come, "
33 the whole land until the ninth *h*·. "
34 the ninth *h*· Jesus cried with a loud "
Lu 7:21 And in that same *h*· he cured many "
10:21 In that *h*· Jesus rejoiced in spirit, "
12:12 in the same *h*· what ye ought to say. "
39 known what *h*· the thief would "
40 cometh at an *h*· when ye think not. "
46 at an *h*· when he is not aware, and "
20:19 the same *h*· sought to lay hands "
22:14 when the *h*· was come, he sat down, "
53 but this is your *h*·, and the power of "
59 And about the space of one *h*· after "
23:44 it was about the sixth *h*·, and there "
44 over all the earth until the ninth *h*·. "
24:33 rose up the same *h*·, and returned "
Joh 1:39 day: for it was about the tenth *h*·. "
2: 4 with thee? mine *h*· is not yet come. "
4: 6 well: and it was about the sixth *h*·. "
21 Woman, believe me, the *h*· cometh, "
23 the *h*· cometh, and now is, when the "
52 enquired he of them the *h*· when he "
52 Yesterday at the seventh *h*· the "
53 knew that it was at the same *h*·, "
5:25 The *h*· is coming, and now is, when "
28 the *h*· is coming, in the which all "
7:30 because his *h*· was not yet come. "
8:20 on him; for his *h*· was not yet come. "
12:23 The *h*· is come, that the Son of man "
27 I say? Father, save me from this *h*·: "
27 for this cause came I unto this *h*·. "
13: 1 when Jesus knew that his *h*· was "
16:21 sorrow, because her *h*· is come: "
32 the *h*· cometh, yea, is now come, "
17: 1 and said, Father, the *h*· is come; "
19:14 the passover, and about the sixth *h*·: "
27 from that *h*· that disciple took her "
Ac 2:15 seeing it is but the third *h*· of the "
3: 1 into the temple at the *h*· of prayer, "
1 of prayer, being the ninth *h*·. "
10: 3 the ninth *h*· of the day an angel *5610*
9 housetop to pray about the sixth *h*·: "
30 days ago I was fasting until this *h*·; "
30 the ninth *h*· I prayed in my house, "
16:18 her. And he came out the same *h*·. "
33 took them the same *h*· of the night, "
22:13 And the same *h*· I looked up upon "
23:23 hundred, at the third *h*· of the night; "
1Co 4:11 this present *h*· we both hunger, "
8: 7 of the idol unto this *h*· eat it as a * *734*
15:30 stand we in jeopardy every *h*·? *5610*
Ga 2: 5 by subjection, no, not for an *h*·; "
Re 3: 3 shalt not know what *h*· I will come "
10 keep thee from the *h*· of temptation, "
8: 1 about the space of half an *h*·. *2256*
9:15 prepared for an *h*·, and a day, and *5610*
11:13 same *h*· was there a great "
14: 7 for the *h*· of his judgment is come: "
17:12 power as kings one *h*· with the "
18:10 for in one *h*· is thy judgment come. "
17 in one *h*· so great riches is come "
19 for in one *h*· is she made desolate. "

hours
Joh 11: 9 Are there not twelve *h*· in the *5610*
Ac 5: 7 about the space of three *h*· after, "
19:34 about the space of two *h*· cried out, "

house See also HOUSEHOLD; HOUSES; HOUSE-TOP; STOREHOUSES.
Ge 7: 1 thou and all thy *h*· into the ark; 1004
12: 1 kindred, and from thy father's *h*·, "
15 woman was taken into Pharaoh's *h*·. "
17 plagued Pharaoh and his *h*· with "
14:14 trained servants, born in his own *h*·, "
15: 2 the steward of my *h*· is this Eliezer "
3 one born in my *h*· is mine heir. "
17:12 he that is born in the *h*·, or bought "
13 He that is born in thy *h*·, and he "
23 son, and all that were born in his *h*·, "
23 among the men of Abraham's *h*·; "
27 all the men of his *h*·, born in the *h*·, "
19: 2 I pray you, into your servant's *h*·, "
3 unto him, and entered into his *h*·; "
4 of Sodom, compassed the *h*· round, "
10 pulled Lot into the *h*· to them, "
11 at the door of the *h*· with blindness, "
20:13 me to wander from my father's *h*·, "
18 the wombs of the *h*· of Abimelech, "
24: 2 unto his eldest servant of his *h*·. "
7 which took me from my father's *h*·, 1004
23 is there room in thy father's *h*· for "
27 to the *h*· of my master's brethren. "
28 told them of her mother's *h*· these "
31 for I have prepared the *h*·, and room "
32 the man came into the *h*·: and he "
38 go unto my father's *h*·, and to my "
40 my kindred, and of my father's *h*·: "
27:15 which were with her in the *h*·, "
28: 2 to the *h*· of Bethuel thy mother's "
17 none other but the *h*· of God, and "
21 again to my father's *h*· in peace; "
22 set for a pillar, shall be God's *h*·: "
29:13 him, and brought him to his *h*·. "
30:30 I provide for mine own *h*· also? "
31:14 inheritance for us in our father's *h*·? "
30 sore longedst after thy father's *h*·, "
41 have I been twenty years in thy *h*·; "
33:17 built him an *h*·, and made booths "
34:19 than all the *h*· of his father. "
26 took Dinah out of Shechem's *h*·, "
29 spoiled even all that was in the *h*·. "
30 I shall be destroyed, I and my *h*·. "
36: 6 and all the persons of his *h*·, "
38:11 Remain a widow at thy father's *h*·, "
11 went and dwelt in her father's *h*·. "
39: 2 he was in the *h*· of his master the "
4 he made him overseer over his *h*·, "
5 he had made him overseer in his *h*·, "
5 Lord blessed the Egyptian's *h*· "
5 was upon all that he had in the *h*·, "
8 not what is with me in the *h*·, "
9 is none greater in this *h*· than I; "
11 that Joseph went into the *h*· to do "
11 was none of the men of the *h*· there "
14 she called unto the men of her *h*·, "
40: 3 in ward in the *h*· of the captain of "
7 with him in the ward of his lord's *h*·, "
14 and bring me out of this *h*·: "
41:10 in the captain of the guard's *h*·, "
40 Thou shalt be over my *h*·, and "
51 all my toil, and all my father's *h*·. "
42:19 be bound in the *h*· of your prison: "
43:16 he said to the ruler of his *h*·, "
17 brought the men into Joseph's *h*·. "
18 they were brought into Joseph's *h*·; "
19 near to the steward of Joseph's *h*·, "
19 with him at the door of the *h*·, "
24 brought the men into Joseph's *h*·, "
26 which was in their hand into the *h*·, "
44: 1 commanded the steward of his *h*·, "
8 should we steal out of thy lord's *h*· "
14 his brethren came to Joseph's *h*·; "
45: 2 and the *h*· of Pharaoh heard. "
8 to Pharaoh, and lord of all his *h*·, "
16 thereof was heard in Pharaoh's *h*·, "
46:27 all the souls of the *h*· of Jacob, "
31 brethren, and unto his father's *h*·, "
31 My brethren, and my father's *h*·, "
47:14 the money into Pharaoh's *h*·. "
50: 4 spake unto the *h*· of Pharaoh, "
7 the elders of his *h*·, and all the "
8 and all the *h*· of Joseph, and his "
8 and his father's *h*·: only their little "
22 in Egypt, he, and his father's *h*·: "
Ex 2: 1 there went a man of the *h*· of Levi, "
3:22 of her that sojourneth in her *h*·, "
7:23 Pharaoh turned and went into his *h*·, "
8: 3 shall go up and come into thine *h*·, "
3 and into the *h*· of thy servants, and "
24 of flies into the *h*· of Pharaoh, "
12: 3 according to the *h*· of their fathers,* "
3 of their fathers, a lamb for an *h*·: * "
4 and his neighbour next unto his *h*· "
22 go out at the door of his *h*· until "
30 there was not a *h*· where there was "
46 In one *h*· shall it be eaten; thou "
46 of the flesh abroad out of the *h*·; "
13: 3 Egypt, out of the *h*· of bondage; "
14 Egypt, from the *h*· of bondage: "
16:31 the *h*· of Israel called the name "
19: 3 shalt thou say to the *h*· of Jacob, "
20: 2 Egypt out of the *h*· of bondage. "
17 shalt not covet thy neighbour's *h*·, "
22: 7 and it be stolen out of the man's *h*·; "
8 then the master of the *h*· shall be "
23:19 bring into the *h*· of the Lord thy "
34:26 bring unto the *h*· of the Lord thy "
40:38 in the sight of all the *h*· of Israel, "
Le 10: 6 the whole *h*· of Israel, bewail the "
14:34 the plague of leprosy in a *h*· of the "
35 And he that owneth the *h*· shall "
35 is as it were a plague in the *h*·: "
36 that they empty the *h*·, before the "
36 all that is in the *h*· be not made "
36 priest shall go in to see the *h*·: "
37 in the walls of the *h*· with hollow "
38 out of the *h*· to the door of the *h*·, "
38 and shut up the *h*· seven days: "
39 be spread in the walls of the *h*·; "
41 shall cause the *h*· to be scraped "
42 mortar, and shall plaister the *h*·. "
43 again, and break out in the *h*·, "
43 and after he hath scraped the *h*·, "
44 if the plague be spread in the *h*·, "
44 it is a fretting leprosy in the *h*·: "
45 he shall break down the *h*·, the "
45 thereof, and all the mortar of the *h*·; "
46 he that goeth into the *h*· all the "
47 he that lieth in the *h*· shall wash "
47 he that eateth in the *h*· shall wash "
48 plague hath not spread in the *h*·, "
48 after the *h*· was plaistered: then the "
48 priest shall pronounce the *h*· clean, "
49 take to cleanse the *h*· two birds, "
51 water, sprinkle the *h*· seven times: "

Le 14:52 cleanse the h' with the blood of the 1004
53 make an atonement for the h': and "
55 leprosy of a garment, and of a h', "
16: 6 atonement for himself, and for his h'."
11 atonement for himself, and for his h'."
17: 3 be of the h' of Israel, that killeth "
8 the h' of Israel, or of the strangers "
10 man there be of the h' of Israel, "
22: 11 of it, and he that is born in his h': "
13 is returned unto her father's h', as "
18 he be of the h' of Israel, or of the "
25: 29 if a man sell a dwelling h' in a "
30 then the h' that is in the walled city "
33 then the h' that was sold, and the "
27: 14 man shall sanctify his h' to be holy "
15 that sanctified it will redeem his h', "
Nu 1: 2 families, by the h' of their fathers,* "
4 every one head of the h' of his "
18, 20, 22, 24, 26, 28, 30, 32, 34, 36, 38,
40, 42, by the h' of their fathers, * "
44 one was for the h' of his fathers. "
45 Israel, by the h' of their fathers, * "
2: 2 the ensign of their father's h': * "
32 Israel by the h' of their fathers: * "
34 according to the h' of their fathers.* "
3: 15 after the h' of their fathers, by * "
20 according to the h' of their fathers.* "
24 the chief of the h' of the father of "
30 the h' of the father of the families "
35 the chief of the h' of the father of "
4: 2 families, by the h' of their fathers, * "
29 families, by the h' of their fathers;* "
34 and after the h' of their fathers, * "
38 and by the h' of their fathers, * "
40, 42 families, by the h' of...fathers, * "
46 and after the h' of their fathers, * "
7: 2 heads of the h' of their fathers, * "
12: 7 so, who is faithful in all mine h'. "
17: 2 according to the h' of their fathers, "
2 according to the h' of their fathers * "
3 head of the h' of their fathers. * "
8 the rod of Aaron for the h' of Levi "
18: 1 and thy sons, and thy father's h' "
11 every one that is clean in thy h' "
13 every one that is clean in thine h' "
20: 29 thirty days, even all the h' of Israel. "
22: 18 give me his h' full of silver and gold, "
24: 13 give me his h' full of silver and gold, "
25: 14 a prince of a chief h' among the "
15 people, and of a chief h' in Midian. "
26: 2 throughout their fathers' h', all * "
30: 3 in her father's h' in her youth; "
10 if she vowed in her husband's h', "
16 yet in her youth in her father's h'. "
34: 14 according to the h' of their fathers,* "
14 according to the h' of their fathers.* "
De 5: 6 of Egypt, from the h' of bondage. "
21 thou covet thy neighbour's h', his "
6: 7 when thou sittest in thine h', and "
9 write them upon the posts of thy h', "
12 of Egypt, from the h' of bondage. "
7: 8 you out of the h' of bondmen, "
26 bring an abomination into thine h', "
8: 14 of Egypt, from the h' of bondage; "
11: 19 them when thou sittest in thine h', "
20 upon the door posts of thine h', "
13: 5 you out of the h' of bondage, "
10 of Egypt, from the h' of bondage. "
15: 16 because he loveth thee and thine h', "
20: 5 is there that hath built a new h', "
5 let him go and return to his h', lest "
6 him also go and return unto his h', "
7, 8 let him go and return unto his h'. "
21: 12 shalt bring her home to thine h'; "
13 shall remain in thine h', and bewail "
22: 2 shalt bring it unto thine own h', "
8 When thou buildest a new h', then "
8 thou bring not blood upon thine h', "
21 damsel to the door of her father's h', "
21 to play the whore in her father's h': "
23: 18 into the h' of the Lord thy God "
24: 1 hand, and send her out of his h'. "
2 when she is departed out of his h', "
3 hand, and sendeth her out of his h'; "
10 not go into his h' to fetch his pledge. "
25: 9 will not build up his brother's h'. "
10 The h' of him that hath his shoe "
14 Thou shalt not have in thine h' "
26: 11 given unto thee, and unto thine h', "
13 the hallowed things out of mine h', "
28: 30 thou shalt build an h', and thou "
Jos 2: 1 went, and came into an harlot's h', "
3 which are entered into thine h': "
6 brought them up to the roof o. the h',* "
12 shew kindness unto my father's h',1004
15 for her h' was upon the town wall, "
19 shall go out of the doors of thy h' "
19 shall be with thee in the h', "
6: 17 and all that are with her in the h', "
22 Go into the harlot's h', and bring "
24 the treasury of the h' of the Lord. "
9: 23 of water for the h' of my God. "
17: 17 Joshua spake unto the h' of Joseph, "
18: 5 and the h' of Joseph shall abide in "
20: 6 his own city, and unto his own h', "
21: 45 had spoken unto the h' of Israel; "
22: 14 of each chief h' a prince throughout "
14 an head of the h' of their fathers * "
24: 15 as for me and my h', we will serve "
17 of Egypt, from the h' of bondage, "
J'g 1: 22 the h' of Joseph, they also went up "
23 And the h' of Joseph sent to descry "
35 hand of the h' of Joseph prevailed, "
4: 17 and the h' of Heber the Kenite. "
6: 8 you forth out of the h' of bondage; "
15 I am the least in my father's h'. "

J'g 8: 27 a snare unto Gideon, and to his h'. 1004
29 Joash went and dwelt in his own h'. "
35 kindness to the h' of Jerubbaal, "
9: 1 of the h' of his mother's father, "
4 silver out of the h' of Baal-berith, "
5 And he went unto his father's h' "
6 all the h' of Millo, and went, and "
16 well with Jerubbaal and his h', "
18 are risen up against my father's h' "
19 with Jerubbaal and with his h' this "
20 of Shechem, and the h' of Millo; "
20 Shechem, and from the h' of Millo, "
27 and went into the h' of their god, "
46 an hold of the h' of the god Berith. "
10: 9 and against the h' of Ephraim; "
11: 2 shalt not inherit in our father's h'; "
7 and expel me out of my father's h'? "
31 cometh forth of the doors of my h' "
34 came to Mizpeh unto his h', and, "
12: 1 we will burn thine h' upon thee "
14: 15 we burn thee and thy father's h' "
19 and he went up to his father's h'. "
16: 21 and he did grind in the prison h'. "
25 for Samson out of the prison h'; "
26 pillars whereupon the h' standeth, "
27 Now the h' was full of men and "
29 pillars upon which the h' stood, "
30 and the h' fell upon the lords, and "
31 and all the h' of his father came "
17: 4 and they were in the h' of Micah. "
5 the man Micah had an h' of gods, "
8 to the h' of Micah, as he journeyed. "
12 priest, and was in the h' of Micah. "
18: 2 to the h' of Micah, they lodged "
3 When they were by the h' of Micah, "
13 and came unto the h' of Micah. "
15 came to the h' of the young man "
15 Levite, even unto the h' of Micah, "
18 these went into Micah's h', and "
19 be a priest unto the h' of one man, "
22 good way from the h' of Micah, "
22 in the houses near to Micah's h' "
26 turned and went back unto his h'. "
31 that the h' of God was in Shiloh. "
19: 2 away from him unto her father's h' "
3 brought him into her father's h': "
15 took them into his h' to lodging. "
18 am now going to the h' of the Lord; "
18 is no man that receiveth me to h'. "
21 So he brought him into his h', and "
22 of Belial, beset the h' round about, "
22 spake to the master of the h', the "
22 the man that came into thine h', "
23 man, the master of the h', went out "
23 that this man is come into mine h', "
26 fell down at the door of the man's h' "
27 opened the doors of the h', and "
27 fallen down at the door of the h'. "
29 when he was come into his h', he "
20: 5 beset the h' round about upon me "
8 will we any of us turn into his h'. "
18 and went up to the h' of God, *1008
26 came unto the h' of God, and wept,* "
31 one goeth up to the h' of God, * "
21: 2 the people came to the h' of God, * "
Ru 1: 8 Go, return each to her mother's h': 1004
9 each of you in the h' of her husband. "
2: 7 that she tarried a little in the h'. "
4: 11 is come into thine h' like Rachel "
11 which two did build the h' of Israel: "
12 let thy h' be like the h' of Pharez, "
1Sa 1: 7 she went up to the h' of the Lord, "
19 and came to their h' to Ramah: "
21 the man Elkanah, and all his h', "
24 unto the h' of the Lord in Shiloh: "
2: 11 Elkanah went to Ramah to his h'. "
27 appear unto the h' of thy father, "
27 were in Egypt in Pharaoh's h'? "
28 I give unto the h' of thy father all "
30 that thy h', and the h' of thy father, "
31 and the arm of thy father's h', "
31 shall not be an old man in thine h'. "
32 an old man in thine h' for ever. "
33 the increase of thine h' shall die in "
35 I will build him a sure h'; and he "
36 every one that is left in thine h' "
3: 12 I have spoken concerning his h': "
13 that I will judge his h' for ever for "
14 I have sworn unto the h' of Eli, "
14 iniquity of Eli's h' shall not be "
15 the doors of the h' of the Lord. "
5: 2 brought it into the h' of Dagon, "
5 nor any that come into Dagon's h', "
7: 1 brought it into the h' of Abinadab "
2 all the h' of Israel lamented after "
3 spake unto all the h' of Israel, "
17 for there was his h'; and there he "
9: 18 I pray thee, where the seer's h' is. "
20 on thee, and on all thy father's h'? "
25 with Saul upon the top of the h'. * "
26 called Saul to the top of the h'. * "
10: 25 people away, every man to his h'. 1004
15: 34 Saul went up to his h' to Gibeah "
17: 25 make his father's h' free in Israel. "
18: 2 go no more home to his father's h'. "
10 prophesied in the midst of the h': "
19: 9 he sat in his h' with his javelin in "
11 sent messengers unto David's h', "
20: 15 thy kindness from my h' for ever: "
16 a covenant with the h' of David, "
21: 15 shall this fellow come into my h'? "
22: 1 and all his father's h' heard it, "
11 son of Ahitub, and all his father's h', "
14 and is honourable in thine h'? "
15 nor to all the h' of my father: "
16 thou, and all thy father's h'. "

1Sa 22: 22 of all the persons of thy father's h'. 1004
23: 18 wood, and Jonathan went to his h'. "
24: 21 my name out of my father's h'. "
25: 1 and buried him in his h' at Ramah. "
3 and he was of the h' of Caleb. "
6 to thee, and peace be to thine h', "
28 certainly make my lord a sure h'; "
35 unto her, Go up in peace to thine h'; "
36 he held a feast in his h', like the "
28: 24 the woman had a fat calf in the h'; "
31: 9 to publish it in the h' of their idols, "
10 his armour in the h' of Ashtaroth: "
2Sa 1: 12 the Lord, and for the h' of Israel; "
2: 4 David king over the h' of Judah. "
7 the h' of Judah have anointed me "
10 But the h' of Judah followed David. "
11 king in Hebron over the h' of Judah "
3: 1 the h' of Saul and the h' of David: "
1 the h' of Saul waxed weaker and "
6 the h' of Saul and the h' of David, "
6 himself strong for the h' of Saul. "
8 day unto the h' of Saul thy father, "
10 the kingdom from the h' of Saul, "
19 good to the whole h' of Benjamin. "
29 of Joab, and on all his father's h'; "
29 there not fail from the h' of Joab "
4: 5 of the day to the h' of Ish-bosheth, "
6 thither into the midst of the h', "
7 For when they came into the h', he "
11 a righteous person in his own h' "
5: 8 the lame shall not come into the h'. "
5: 11 masons: and they built David an h'. "
6: 3, 4 it out of the h' of Abinadab "
5 and all the h' of Israel played "
10 aside into the h' of Obed-edom "
11 continued in the h' of Obed-edom "
12 hath blessed the h' of Obed-edom, "
12 ark of God from the h' of Obed-edom "
15 David and all the h' of Israel "
19 people departed every one to his h'. "
21 thy father, and before all his h', "
7: 1 to pass, when the king sat in his h', "
2 I dwell in an h' of cedar, but the ark "
5 Shalt thou build me an h' for me "
6 I have not dwelt in any h' since "
7 Why build ye not me an h' of cedar? "
11 thee that he will make thee an h'. "
13 He shall build an h' for my name, "
16 And thine h' and thy kingdom shall "
18 and what is my h', that thou hast "
19 hast spoken also of thy servant's h', "
25 thy servant, and concerning his h', "
26 and let the h' of thy servant David "
27 saying, I will build thee an h': "
29 thee to bless the h' of thy servant, "
29 let the h' of thy servant be blessed "
9: 1 any that is left of the h' of Saul, "
2 there was of the h' of Saul a servant "
3 there not yet any of the h' of Saul, "
4 Behold, he is in the h' of Machir, "
5 fetched him out of the h' of Machir, "
9 pertained to Saul and to all his h'. "
12 in the h' of Ziba were servants "
11: 2 upon the roof of the king's h': "
4 and she returned unto her h'. "
8 Go down to thy h', and wash thy "
8 Uriah departed out of the king's h', "
9 slept at the door of the king's h' "
9 lord, and went not down to his h'. "
10 Uriah went not down unto his h', "
10 thou not go down unto thine h'? "
11 shall I then go into mine h', to eat "
13 lord, but went not down to his h'. "
27 David sent and fetched her to his h', "
12: 8 I gave thee thy master's h', and "
8 and gave thee the h' of Israel and "
10 shall never depart from thine h'; "
11 against thee out of thine own h', "
15 And Nathan departed unto his h'. "
17 And the elders of his h' arose, "
20 came into the h' of the Lord, and "
20 then he came to his own h'; and "
13: 7 Go now to thy brother Amnon's h', "
8 went to her brother Amnon's h'; "
20 in her brother Absalom's h'. "
14: 8 Go to thine h', and I will give "
9 be on me, and on my father's h': "
24 Let him turn to his own h', and "
24 So Absalom returned to his own h', "
31 and came to Absalom unto his h', "
15: 16 were concubines, to keep the h'. "
35 thou shalt hear out of the king's h', "
16: 3 To day shall the h' of Israel restore "
5 man of the family of the h' of Saul, "
8 thee all the blood of the h' of Saul, "
21 which he hath left to keep the h'; "
22 a tent upon the top of the h'; "
17: 18 quickly, and came to a man's h' in "
20 came to the woman to the h', "
23 arose, and gat him home to his h',* "
19: 5 Joab came into the h' to the king, "
11 to bring the king back to his h'? "
11 is come to the king, even to his h'. "
17 Ziba the servant of the h' of Saul, "
20 of all the h' of Joseph to go down "
28 my father's h' were but dead men "
30 again in peace unto his own h'. "
20: 3 David came to his h' at Jerusalem; "
3 whom he had left to keep the h', "
21: 1 It is for Saul, and for his bloody h', "
4 silver nor gold of Saul, nor of his h'; "
23: 5 Although my h' be not so with God; "
24: 17 me, and against my father's h'. "
1Ki 1: 53 said unto him, Go to thine h'. "
2: 24 and who hath made me an h', as "
27 he spake concerning the h' of Eli "

1Ki 2:31 me, and from the h' of my father. 1004
33 upon his h', and upon his throne, "
34 he was buried in his own h' in the "
36 Build thee an h' in Jerusalem, "
3: 1 made an end of building his own h', "
1 the h' of the Lord, and the wall of "
2 because there was no h' built unto "
17 I and this woman dwell in one h'; "
17 delivered of a child...in the h'. "
18 us in the h', save we two in the h'. "
5: 3 my father could not build an h' "
5 I purpose to build an h' unto the "
5 he shall build an h' unto my name. "
17 to lay the foundation of the h'. "
18 timber and stones to build the h'. "
6: 1 he began to build the h' of the Lord. "
2 the h' which king Solomon built "
3 porch before the temple of the h', "
3 according to the breadth of the h'; "
3 the breadth thereof before the h'. "
4 for the h' he made windows of "
5 And against the wall of the h' he "
5 against the walls of the h' round "
6 wall of the h' he made narrowed "
6 not be fastened in the wall of the h'. "
7 And the h', when it was in building, "
7 nor any tool of iron heard in the h', "
8 was in the right side of the h': "
9 So he built the h', and finished it; "
9 covered the h' with beams and "
10 he built chambers against all the h', "
10 rested on the h' with timber of cedar. "
12 this h' which thou art in building, "
14 built the h', and finished it. "
15 he built the walls of the h' within "
15 floor of the h', and the walls of the "
15 covered the floor of the h' with "
16 twenty cubits on the sides of the h', "
17 And the h', that is, the temple "
18 And the cedar of the h' within "
19 the oracle he prepared in the h' "
21 overlaid the h' within with pure "
22 the whole h' he overlaid with gold, "
22 until he had finished all the h': "
27 the cherubims within the inner h': "
27 one another in the midst of the h'. "
29 And he carved all the walls of the h' "
30 the floor of the h' he overlaid with "
37 the foundation of the h' of the Lord "
38 was the h' finished throughout "
7: 1 Solomon was building his own h' "
1 years, and he finished all his h'. "
2 He built also the h' of the forest "
8 And his h' where he dwelt had "
8 also an h' for Pharaoh's daughter, "
12 inner court of the h' of the Lord, "
12 and for the porch of the h'. "
39 bases on the right side of the h', "
39 and five on the left side of the h': "
39 set the sea on the right side of the h' "
40 king Solomon for the h' of the Lord: "
45 vessels...for the h' of the Lord, "
48 pertained unto the h' of the Lord: "
50 of the inner h', the most holy place, "
50 and for the doors of the h', to wit, "
51 all the work...for the h' of the Lord. "
51 the treasures of the h' of the Lord. "
8: 6 into the oracle of the h', to the "
10 the cloud filled the h' of the Lord, "
11 glory of the Lord had filled the h' "
13 surely built thee an h' to dwell in, "
16 all the tribes of Israel to build an h', "
17 David my father to build an h' for "
18 heart to build an h' unto my name, "
19 thou shalt not build the h'; but thy "
19 of thy loins, he shall build the h' "
20 built an h' for the name of the Lord "
27 how much less this h' that I have "
29 eyes may be open toward this h' "
31 come before thine altar in this h': "
33 supplication unto thee in this h': "
38 forth his hands toward this h': "
42 shall come and pray toward this h'; "
43 that this h', which I have builded, "
44 toward the h' that I have built "
48 and the h' which I have built for "
63 Israel, dedicated the h' of the Lord. "
64 that was before the h' of the Lord: "
9: 1 had finished the building of the h' "
1 king's h', and all Solomon's desire "
3 I have hallowed this h', which thou "
7 and this h', which I have hallowed "
8 And at this h', which is high, every "
8 thou unto this land, and to this h'? "
10 the h' of the Lord, and the king's h', "
15 the h' of the Lord, and his own h', "
24 unto her h' which Solomon had "
25 the Lord. So he finished the h'. "
10: 4 wisdom, and the h' that he had built, "
5 he went up unto the h' of the Lord; "
12 trees pillars for the h' of the Lord, "
12 and for the king's h', harps also "
17 in the h' of the forest of Lebanon. "
21 of the h' of the forest of Lebanon "
11: 18 which gave him an h', and appointed "
20 Tahpenes weaned in Pharaoh's h': "
28 all the charge of the h' of Joseph. "
38 with thee, and build thee a sure h', "
12: 16 now see to thine own h', David. "
19 rebelled against the h' of David "
20 none that followed the h' of David, "
21 he assembled all the h' of Judah, "
21 to fight against the h' of Israel, "
23 all the h' of Judah and Benjamin, "
24 return every man to his h'; for this "
26 kingdom return to the h' of David: "

1Ki 12:27 sacrifice in the h' of the Lord at 1004
31 he made an h' of high places, and* "
13: 2 shall be born unto the h' of David, "
8 If thou wilt give me half thine h', "
18 him back with thee into thine h', "
19 eat bread in his h', and drank water, "
34 became sin unto the h' of Jeroboam, "
14: 4 and came to the h' of Ahijah. "
8 kingdom away from the h' of David, "
10 bring evil upon the h' of Jeroboam, "
10 remnant of the h' of Jeroboam, "
12 get thee to thine own h': and "
13 God of Israel in the h' of Jeroboam. "
14 cut off the h' of Jeroboam that day: "
26 the treasures of the h' of the Lord, "
26 and the treasures of the king's h'; "
27 which kept the door of the king's h'. "
28 king went into the h' of the Lord, "
15: 15 into the h' of the Lord, silver, and "
18 the treasures of the h' of the Lord, "
18 and the treasures of the king's h', "
27 son of Ahijah, of the h' of Issachar, "
29 he smote all the h' of Jeroboam; "
16: 3 and the posterity of his h'; and will "
3 make thy h' like the h' of Jeroboam "
7 against Baasha, and against his h', "
7 in being like the h' of Jeroboam; "
9 drinking himself drunk in the h' of "
9 of Arza steward of his h' in Tirzah.* "
11 that he slew all the h' of Baasha: "
12 Zimri destroy all the h' of Baasha, "
18 went into the palace of the king's h', "
18 burnt the king's h' over him with "
32 an altar to Baal in the h' of Baal. "
17: 15 he and her h', did eat many days. "
17 the mistress of the h', fell sick; "
23 down out of the chamber into the h', "
18: 3 which was the governor of his h'. * "
18 but thou, and thy father's h', in that "
20: 6 they shall search thine h', and the "
31 the h' of Israel are merciful kings: "
43 king of Israel went to his h' heavy "
21: 2 because it is near unto my h': "
4 And Ahab came into his h' heavy "
22 make thine h' like the h' of Jeroboam "
22 and like the h' of Baasha the son of "
29 will I bring the evil upon his h'. "
22: 17 return every man to his h' in peace. "
39 and the ivory h' which he made, "
2Ki 4: 2 tell me, what hast thou in the h'? "
2 hath not any thing in the h', save "
32 Elisha was come into the h', behold, "
35 and walked in the h' to and fro; "
5: 9 stood at the door of the h' of Elisha. "
18 into the h' of Rimmon to worship "
18 I bow myself in the h' of Rimmon: "
18 down myself in the h' of Rimmon, "
24 hand, and bestowed them in the h': "
6: 32 But Elisha sat in his h', and the "
7: 11 they told it to the king's h' within.* "
8: 3 to cry unto the king for her h' and "
5 cried to the king for her h' and for "
18 of Israel, as did the h' of Ahab: "
27 walked in the way of the h' of Ahab, "
27 of the Lord, as did the h' of Ahab: "
27 was the son in law of the h' of Ahab. "
9: 6 And he arose, and went into the h'; "
7 smite the h' of Ahab thy master, "
8 the whole h' of Ahab shall perish: "
9 h' of Ahab like the h' of Jeroboam "
9 and like the h' of Baasha the son "
27 he fled by the way of the garden h'. "
10: 3 and fight for your master's h'. "
5 And he that was over the h', and * "
10 spake concerning the h' of Ahab: "
11 all that remained of the h' of Ahab "
12 was at the shearing h' in the way, "
14 them at the pit of the shearing h', "
21 And they came into the h' of Baal; "
21 and the h' of Baal was full from "
23 And Jehu went...into the h' of Baal, "
25 went to the city of the h' of Baal. "
26 images out of the h' of Baal, and "
27 and brake down the h' of Baal, "
27 and made it a draught h' unto this day. "
30 eyes, hast done unto the h' of Ahab 1004
11: 3 hid in the h' of the Lord six years. "
4 them to him into the h' of the Lord, "
4 oath of them in the h' of the Lord, "
5 of the watch of the king's h'; "
6 so shall ye keep the watch of the h', "
7 keep the watch of the h' of the Lord "
15 not be slain in the h' of the Lord. "
16 the horses came into the king's h': "
18 went into the h' of Baal, and brake "
18 officers over the h' of the Lord. "
19 the king from the h' of the Lord, "
19 gate of the guard to the king's h'. "
20 with the sword beside the king's h'. "
12: 4 is brought into the h' of the Lord, "
4 to bring into the h' of the Lord, "
5 them repair the breaches of the h', "
6 not repaired the breaches of the h'. "
7 repair ye not the breaches of the h'? "
7 deliver it for the breaches of the h'. "
8 to repair the breaches of the h'. "
9 one cometh into the h' of the Lord: "
9 was brought into the h' of the Lord. "
10 was found in the h' of the Lord. "
11 the oversight of the h' of the Lord: "
11 wrought upon the h' of the Lord, "
12 the breaches of the h' of the Lord, "
12 was laid out for the h' to repair it. "
13 the h' of the Lord bowls of silver, "
13 was brought into the h' of the Lord: "
14 repaired therewith the h' of the "

2Ki 12:16 not brought into the h' of the Lord: 1004
18 the treasures of the h' of the Lord, "
18 and in the king's h', and sent it "
20 and slew Joash in the h' of Millo, "
13: 6 from the sins of the h' of Jeroboam, "
14: 14 were found in the h' of the Lord. "
14 in the treasures of the king's h', "
15: 5 his death, and dwelt in a several h' "
5 the king's son was over the h', "
25 in the palace of the king's h', with "
35 higher gate of the h' of the Lord, "
16: 8 gold that was found in the h' of "
8 in the treasures of the king's h', "
14 Lord, from the forefront of the h', "
14 the altar and the h' of the Lord, "
18 sabbath that they had built in the h', "
18 turned he from the h' of the Lord "
17: 21 rent Israel from the h' of David; "
18: 15 silver that was found in the h' of "
15 in the treasures of the king's h'. "
19: 1 and went into the h' of the Lord. "
14 went up into the h' of the Lord, "
26 as the grass on the h' tops, and as corn
30 that is escaped of the h' of Judah 1004
37 worshipping in the h' of Nisroch "
20: 1 Set thine h' in order; for thou shalt "
5 shalt go up unto the h' of the Lord. "
8 I shall go up into the h' of the Lord "
13 and all the h' of his precious things, "
13 and all the h' of his armour, and all "
13 there was nothing in his h', nor in "
15 What have they seen in thine h'? "
15 that are in mine h' have they seen: "
17 that all that is in thine h', and that "
21: 4 he built altars in the h' of the Lord, "
5 the two courts of the h' of the Lord. "
7 grove that he had made in the h', "
7 In this h', and in Jerusalem, which "
13 and the plummet of the h' of Ahab: "
18 buried in the garden of his own h', "
23 and slew the king in his own h'. "
22: 3 the scribe, to the h' of the Lord, "
4 is brought into the h' of the Lord, "
5 the oversight of the h' of the Lord: "
5 work which is in the h' of the Lord, "
5 to repair the breaches of the h', "
6 and hewn stone to repair the h'. "
8 found the book of the law in the h' "
9 the money that was found in the h', "
9 the oversight of the h' of the Lord. "
23: 2 king went up into the h' of the Lord, "
2 was found in the h' of the Lord. "
6 the grove from the h' of the Lord, "
7 that were by the h' of the Lord, "
11 entering in of the h' of the Lord, "
12 the two courts of the h' of the Lord, "
24 priest found in the h' of the Lord. "
27 and the h' of which I said, My name "
24: 13 the treasures of the h' of the Lord, "
13 and the treasures of the king's h', "
25: 9 the h' of the Lord, and the king's h', "
9 great man's h' burnt he with fire. "
13 brass that were in the h' of the "
13 sea that was in the h' of the Lord, "
16 had made for the h' of the Lord; "
1Ch 2: 54 Ataroth, the h' of Joab, and half *5854
55 the father of the h' of Rechab. 1004
4: 21 the families of the h' of them that "
21 fine linen, of the h' of Ashbea, "
38 the h' of their fathers increased * "
5: 13 brethren of the h' of their fathers * "
15 Guni, chief of the h' of their * "
24 heads of the h' of their fathers, * "
24 heads of the h' of their fathers. * "
6: 31 service of song in the h' of the Lord, "
32 Solomon had built the h' of the "
48 of the tabernacle of the h' of God. "
7: 2 heads of their father's h', to wit, * "
4 generations, after the h' of their * "
7, 9 heads of the h' of their fathers, * "
23 because it went evil with his h'. "
40 heads of their fathers' h', choice * "
9: 9 fathers in the h' of their fathers. * "
11 Ahitub, the ruler of the h' of God; "
13 heads of the h' of their fathers, * "
13 work of the service of the h' of God. "
19 his brethren, of the h' of his father, "
23 of the gates of the h' of the Lord, "
23 namely, the h' of the tabernacle, by "
26 and treasuries of the h' of God. "
27 lodged round about the h' of God. "
10: 6 sons, and all his h' died together. "
10 his armour in the h' of their gods, "
12: 28 of his father's h' twenty and two "
29 had kept the ward of the h' of Saul. "
30 famous throughout the h' of their* "
13: 7 new cart out of the h' of Abinadab: "
13 it aside into the h' of Obed-edom "
14 Obed-edom in his h' three months. "
14 Lord blessed the h' of Obed-edom, "
14: 1 and carpenters, to build him an h'. "
15: 25 out of the h' of Obed-edom with joy. "
16: 43 departed every man to his h': "
43 and David returned to bless his h'. "
17: 1 came to pass, as David sat in his h', "
1 Lo, I dwell in an h' of cedars, but "
4 Thou shalt not build me an h' to "
5 For I have not dwelt in an h' since "
6 ye not built me an h' of cedars? "
10 that the Lord will build thee an h'. "
12 He shall build me an h', and I will "
14 But I will settle him in mine h' and "
16 I, O Lord God, and what is mine h', "
17 spoken of thy servant's h' for a "
23 thy servant and concerning his h' "
24 and let the h' of David thy servant "

1Ch 17: 25 that thou wilt build him an h': 1004
27 thee to bless the h' of thy servant, "
21: 17 be on me, and on my father's h'; "
22: 1 said, This is the h' of the Lord God, "
2 stones to build the h' of God. "
5 the h' that is to be builded for the "
6 him to build an h' for the Lord God "
7 it was in my mind to build an h' "
8 shalt not build an h' unto my name, "
10 He shall build an h' for my name; "
11 build the h' of the Lord thy God, "
14 I have prepared for the h' of the "
19 into the h' that is to be built to the "
23: 4 to set forward the work of the h' of "
11 according to their father's h'. "
24 Levi after the h' of their fathers; * "
24 for the service of the h' of the Lord, "
28 for the service of the h' of the Lord, "
28 work of the service of the h' of God; "
32 in the service of the h' of the Lord, "
24: 4 chief men of the h' of their fathers, * "
4 acording to the h' of their fathers. * "
5 and governors of the h' of God, * "
19 to come into the h' of the Lord, 1004
30 after the h' of their fathers. * "
25: 6 for song in the h' of the Lord, "
6 for the service of the h' of God, "
26: 6 ruled throughout the h' of their "
12 to minister in the h' of the Lord. "
13 according to the h' of their * "
15 and to his sons the h' of Asuppim. * "
20 over the treasures of the h' of God, "
22 the treasures of the h' of the Lord. "
27 to maintain the h' of the Lord. "
28: 2 to build an h' of rest for the ark "
3 shalt not build an h' for my name, "
4 chose me before all the h' of my "
4 the h' of Judah, the h' of my father; "
6 thy son, he shall build my h' and "
10 to build an h' for the sanctuary: "
12 of the courts of the h' of the Lord, "
12 of the treasuries of the h' of God, "
13 of the service of the h' of the Lord, "
13 of service in the h' of the Lord. "
20 for the service of the h' of the Lord. "
21 for all the service of the h' of God: "
29: 2 for the h' of my God the gold for "
3 my affection to the h' of my God, "
3 which I have given to the h' of God, "
3 all I have prepared for the holy h', "
7 gave for the service of the h' of God "
8 to the treasure of the h' of the Lord, "
16 have prepared to build thee an h' "
2Ch 2: 1 Solomon determined to build an h' "
1 Lord, and an h' for his kingdom. "
3 to build him an h' to dwell therein, "
4 build an h' to the name of the Lord "
5 And the h' which I build is great: "
6 But who is able to build him an h', "
6 then, that I should build him an h', "
9 the h' which I am about to build "
12 that might build an h' for the Lord, "
12 Lord, and an h' for his kingdom. "
3: 1 began to build the h' of the Lord "
3 for the building of the h' of God. "
4 porch that was in front of the h', "
4 according to the breadth of the h', 1004
5 And the greater h' he cieled with "
6 he garnished the h' with precious "
7 He overlaid also the h', the beams, "
8 he made the most holy h', the length "
8 according to the breadth of the h', "
10 in the most holy h' he made two "
11, 12 reaching to the wall of the h': "
15 he made before the h' two pillars "
4: 11 king Solomon for the h' of God; "
16 Solomon for the h' of the Lord of "
19 all the vessels that were for the h' "
22 the entry of the h', the inner doors "
22 the doors of the h' of the temple, "
5: 1 Solomon made for the h' of the "
1 among the treasures of the h' of "
7 to the oracle of the h', into the most "
13 h' was filled with a cloud, even the h' "
14 glory of the Lord had filled the h' of "
6: 2 I have built an h' of habitation for "
5 the tribes of Israel to build an h' in, "
7 David my father to build an h' for "
8 heart to build an h' for my name, "
9 thou shalt not build the h'; but thy "
9 he shall build the h' for my name. "
10 have built the h' for the name of "
18 how much less this h' which I have "
20 eyes may be open upon this h' day "
22 come before thine altar in this h'; "
24 supplication before thee in this h'; "
29 spread forth his hands in this h': "
32 if they come and pray in this h'; "
33 may know that this h' which I have "
34 and the h' which I have built for "
38 toward the h' which I have built for "
7: 1 the glory of the Lord filled the h'. "
2 priests could not enter into the h' "
2 of the Lord had filled the Lord's h'. "
3 the glory of the Lord upon the h', "
5 the people dedicated the h' of God. "
7 that was before the h' of the Lord: "
11 the h' of the Lord, and the king's h': "
11 the h' of the Lord, and in his own h', "
12 place to myself for an h' of sacrifice. "
16 have I chosen and sanctified this h', "
20 and this h', which I have sanctified "
21 And this h', which is high, shall be "
21 unto this land, and unto this h'? "
8: 1 the h' of the Lord, and his own h', "
11 unto the h' that he had built for her: "

2Ch 8: 11 My wife shall not dwell in the h' of 1004
16 the foundation of the h' of the Lord. "
16 So the h' of the Lord was perfected. "
9: 3 Solomon, and the h' that he had "
4 he went up into the h' of the Lord; "
11 trees terraces to the h' of the Lord, "
16 in the h' of the forest of Lebanon. "
20 of the h' of the forest of Lebanon "
10: 16 and now, David, see to thine own h'. "
19 rebelled against the h' of David "
11: 1 he gathered of the h' of Judah and "
4 return every man to his h': for "
12: 9 the treasures of the h' of the Lord, "
9 and the treasures of the king's h'; "
10 kept the entrance of the king's h'. "
11 king entered into the h' of the Lord, "
15: 18 he brought into the h' of God the "
16: 2 h' of the Lord, and of the king's h', "
10 seer, and put him in a prison h'; "
17: 14 according to the h' of their fathers: * "
18: 16 every man to his h' in peace. "
19: 1 Judah returned to his h' in peace "
11 the ruler of the h' of Judah, "
20: 5 in the h' of the Lord, before the new "
9 we stand before this h', and in thy "
9 for thy name is in this h', and cry "
28 trumpets unto the h' of the Lord. "
21: 6 of Israel, like as did the h' of Ahab: "
7 would not destroy the h' of David, "
13 to the whoredoms of the h' of Ahab, "
13 slain thy brethren of thy father's h', "
17 that was found in the king's h', "
22: 3 also in the ways of the h' of Ahab: "
4 of the Lord like the h' of Ahab: "
7 anointed to cut off the h' of Ahab. "
8 judgment upon the h' of Ahab, "
9 So the h' of Ahaziah had no power "
10 all the seed royal of the h' of Judah. "
12 them hid in the h' of God six years: "
23: 3 with the king in the h' of God. "
5 third part shall be at the king's h'; "
5 in the courts of the h' of the Lord. "
6 none come into the h' of the Lord, "
7 cometh into the h', he shall be put "
9 David's, which were in the h' of God. "
12 the people into the h' of the Lord: "
14 Slay her not in the h' of the Lord. "
15 of the horse gate by the king's h', "
17 went to the h' of Baal, and brake it "
18 the offices of the h' of the Lord "
18 distributed in the h' of the Lord, "
19 at the gates of the h' of the Lord, "
20 the king from the h' of the Lord: "
20 the high gate into the king's h', "
24: 4 minded to repair the h' of the Lord. "
5 repair the h' of your God from year "
7 had broken up the h' of God; and "
7 dedicated things of the h' of the "
8 at the gate of the h' of the Lord. "
12 of the service of the h' of the Lord, "
12 to repair the h' of the Lord, "
12 brass to mend the h' of the Lord. "
13 they set the h' of God in his state, "
14 made vessels for the h' of the Lord, "
14 burnt offerings in the h' of the Lord "
16 both toward God, and toward his h'. "
18 And they left the h' of the Lord God "
21 in the court of the h' of the Lord. "
27 and the repairing of the h' of God, "
25: 24 that were found in the h' of God "
24 and the treasures of the king's h', "
26: 19 before the priests in the h' of the "
21 dwelt in a several h', being a leper; "
21 was cut off from the h' of the Lord: "
21 his son was over the king's h', "
27: 3 the high gate of the h' of the Lord, "
28: 7 Azrikam the governor of the h', and "
21 a portion out of the h' of the Lord, "
21 and out of the h' of the king, and of "
24 together the vessels of the h' of God, "
24 pieces the vessels of the h' of God, "
24 up the doors of the h' of the Lord, "
29: 3 the doors of the h' of the Lord, "
5 sanctify the h' of the Lord God of "
15 Lord, to cleanse the h' of the Lord. "
16 the inner part of the h' of the Lord, "
16 into the court of the h' of the Lord. "
17 so they sanctified the h' of the Lord "
18 We have cleansed all the h' of the "
20 and went up to the h' of the Lord. "
25 set the Levites in the h' of the Lord "
31 offerings into the h' of the Lord. "
35 the service of the h' of the Lord was "
30: 1 should come to the h' of the Lord "
15 offerings into the h' of the Lord. "
31: 10 the chief priest of the h' of Zadok "
10 the offerings into the h' of the Lord, "
11 chambers in the h' of the Lord; "
13 Azariah the ruler of the h' of God. "
16 that entereth into the h' of the Lord, "
17 priests by the h' of their fathers, * "
21 began in the service of the h' of God, "
32: 21 he was come into the h' of his god, "
33: 4 he built altars in the h' of the Lord, "
5 the two courts of the h' of the Lord. "
7 idol...he had made, in the h' of God, "
7 In this h', and in Jerusalem, which "
15 the idol out of the h' of the Lord, "
15 in the mount of the h' of the Lord, "
20 and they buried him in his own h': "
24 him, and slew him in his own h'. "
34: 8 he had purged the land, and the h', "
8 to repair the h' of the Lord his God. "
9 that was brought into the h' of God, "
10 the oversight of the h' of the Lord, "
10 workmen that wrought in the h' of "

2Ch 34: 10 Lord, to repair and amend the h': 1004
14 was brought into the h' of the Lord, "
15 book of the law in the h' of the Lord. "
17 money that was found in the h' of "
30 king went up into the h' of the Lord, "
30 that was found in the h' of the Lord. "
35: 2 to the service of the h' of the Lord, "
3 Put the holy ark in the h' which "
8 and Jehiel, rulers of the h' of God, "
21 against the h' wherewith I have war: "
36: 7 of the vessels of the h' of the Lord "
10 goodly vessels of the h' of the Lord, "
14 polluted the h' of the Lord which "
17 sword in the h' of their sanctuary, "
18 all the vessels of the h' of God, "
18 the treasures of the h' of the Lord, "
19 And they burnt the h' of God, and "
23 charged me to build him an h' in "
Ezr 1: 2 charged me to build him an h' at "
3 and build the h' of the Lord God of "
4 freewill offering for the h' of God "
5 to go up to build the h' of the Lord "
7 the vessels of the h' of the Lord, "
7 had put them in the h' of his gods; "
2: 36 of the h' of Jeshua, nine hundred "
59 could not shew their father's h', * "
68 when they came to the h' of the Lord "
68 offered freely for the h' of God "
3: 8 of their coming unto the h' of God "
8 the work of the h' of the Lord. "
9 the workmen in the h' of God: "
11 foundation of the h' of the Lord was "
12 men, that had seen the first h', "
12 the foundation of this h' was laid "
4: 3 nothing to do with us to build an h' "
24 ceased the work of the h' of God 1005
5: 2 and began to build the h' of God "
3 commanded you to build this h', "
8 to the h' of the great God, which is "
9 commanded you to build this h', "
11 and build the h' that was builded "
12 who destroyed this h', and carried "
13 a decree to build this h' of God. "
14 of gold and silver of the h' of God, "
15 let the h' of God be builded in his "
16 laid the foundation of the h' of God "
17 made in the king's treasure h', "
17 to build this h' of God at Jerusalem, "
6: 1 was made in the h' of the rolls, "
3 a decree concerning the h' of God "
3 Let the h' be builded, the place "
4 be given out of the king's h': "
5 and silver vessels of the h' of God, "
5 and place them in the h' of God. "
7 Let the work of this h' of God alone; "
7 elders of the Jews build this h' of "
8 for the building of this h' of God: "
11 timber be pulled down from his h', "
11 and let his h' be made a dunghill "
12 alter and to destroy this h' of God "
15 And this h' was finished on the "
16 kept the dedication of this h' of God "
17 at the dedication of this h' of God "
22 hands in the work of the h' of God, 1004
7: 16 willingly for the h' of their God 1005
17 upon the altar of the h' of your God "
19 for the service of the h' of thy God, "
20 be needful for the h' of thy God, "
20 it out of the king's treasure h'. "
23 done for the h' of the God of heaven: "
24 or ministers of this h' of God, "
27 to beautify the h' of the Lord 1004
8: 17 us ministers for the h' of our God. "
25 the offering of the h' of our God, "
29 the chambers of the h' of the Lord. "
30 to Jerusalem unto the h' of our God. "
33 vessels weighed in the h' of our God "
36 the people, and the h' of God. "
9: 9 reviving, to set up the h' of our God, "
10: 1 himself down before the h' of God, "
6 rose up from before the h' of God, "
9 sat in the street of the h' of God, "
16 after the h' of their fathers, and all * "
Ne 1: 6 I and my father's h' have sinned. "
2: 8 palace which appertained to the h', "
8 and for the h' that I shall enter into. "
3: 10 Harumaph, even over against his h'. "
16 and unto the h' of the mighty. "
20 unto the door of the h' of Eliashib "
21 from the door of the h' of Eliashib "
21 even to the end of the h' of Eliashib. "
23 and Hashub over against their h'. "
23 the son of Ananiah by his h'. "
24 from the h' of Azariah unto the "
25 lieth out from the king's high h', "
28 every one over against his h'. "
29 son of Immer over against his h'. "
4: 16 were behind all the h' of Judah. "
5: 13 shake out every man from his h', "
6: 10 I came unto the h' of Shemaiah "
10 us meet together in the h' of God, "
7: 3 every one to be over against his h'. "
39 of the h' of Jeshua, nine hundred "
61 could not shew their father's h', * "
8: 16 every one upon the roof of his h', "
16 and in the courts of the h' of God, 1004
10: 32 for the service of the h' of our God; "
33 for all the work of the h' of our God. "
34 to bring it into the h' of our God, "
35 by year, unto the h' of the Lord: "
36 flocks, to bring to the h' of our God, "
36 that minister in the h' of our God: "
37 the chambers of the h' of our God; "
38 of the tithes unto the h' of our God, "
38 the chambers, into the treasure h'. "
39 will not forsake the h' of our God. "

Ne 11:11 was the ruler of the h' of God. 1004
12 brethren that did the work of the h' "
16 outward business of the h' of God. "
22 over the business of the h' of God. "
12:29 Also from the h' of Gilgal, and out* "
37 above the h' of David, even unto "
40 that gave thanks in the h' of God, "
13: 4 the chamber of the h' of our God, "
7 in the courts of the h' of God. "
9 again the vessels of the h' of God, "
11 Why is the h' of God forsaken? "
14 I have done for the h' of my God, "
Es 1: 8 appointed to all the officers of his h', "
9 feast for the women in the royal h' "
22 man should bear rule in his own h', "
2: 3 the palace, to the h' of the women, "
8 was brought also unto the king's h', "
9 be given her, out of the king's h': "
9 best place of the h' of the women. "
11 before the court of the women's h', "
13 her out of the h' of the women "
13 of the women unto the king's h'. "
14 into the second h' of the women, "
16 king Ahasuerus into his h' royal "
4:13 thou shalt escape in the king's h', "
14 thy father's h' shall be destroyed: "
5: 1 in the inner court of the king's h', "
1 over against the king's h': "
1 upon his royal throne in the royal h', "
1 over against the gate of the h'. "
6: 4 the outward court of the king's h', "
12 Haman hasted to his h' mourning, "
7: 8 the queen also before me in the h'? "
9 king, standeth in the h' of Haman. "
8: 1 give the h' of Haman the Jews' "
2 set Mordecai over the h' of Haman. "
7 have given Esther the h' of Haman, "
9: 4 Mordecai was great in the king's h', "
Job 1:10 hedge about him, and about his h', "
13, 18 wine in their eldest brother's h': "
19 smote the four corners of the h', "
7:10 He shall return no more to his h', "
8:15 He shall lean upon his h', but it "
17:13 If I wait, the grave is mine h': "
19:15 They that dwell in mine h', and my "
20:19 violently taken away an h' which "
28 The increase of his h' shall depart, "
21:21 pleasure hath he in his h' after him, "
28 say, Where is the h' of the prince? "
27:18 He buildeth his h' as a moth, and as "
30:23 to the h' appointed for all living. "
38:20 know the paths to the h' thereof? "
39: 6 h' I have made the wilderness, "
42:11 did eat bread with him in his h': "
Ps 5: 7 as for me, I will come into thy h' in "
23: 6 dwell in the h' of the Lord for ever. "
26: 8 have loved the habitation of thy h', "
27: 4 I may dwell in the h' of the Lord all "
30 *title* at the dedication of the h' of David. "
31: 2 for an h' of defence to save me. "
36: 8 satisfied with the fatness of thy h'; "
42: 4 I went with them to the h' of God, "
45:10 own people, and thy father's h'; "
49:16 the glory of his h' is increased; "
50: 9 I will take no bullock out of thy h', "
52 *title* come to the h' of Abimelech. "
8 a green olive tree in the h' of God: "
55:14 and walked unto the h' of God in "
59 *title* they watched the h' to kill him. "
65: 4 satisfied with the goodness of thy h', "
66:13 I will go into thy h' with burnt "
69: 9 the zeal of thine h' hath eaten me "
84: 3 the sparrow hath found an h', and "
4 are they that dwell in thy h': they "
10 a doorkeeper in the h' of my God, "
92:13 be planted in the h' of the Lord "
93: 5 holiness becometh thine h', O Lord, "
98: 3 his truth toward the h' of Israel: "
101: 2 walk within my h' with a perfect "
7 deceit shall not dwell within my h': "
102: 7 a sparrow alone upon the h' top. "
104:17 the stork, the fir trees are her h'. 1004
105:21 He made him lord of his h', and "
112: 3 Wealth and riches shall be in his h': "
113: 9 the barren woman to keep h', and "
114: 1 the h' of Jacob from a people of "
115:10 O h' of Aaron, trust in the Lord: "
12 he will bless the h' of Israel; "
12 he will bless the h' of Aaron. "
116:19 In the courts of the Lord's h', in "
118: 3 Let the h' of Aaron now say, that "
26 blessed you out of the h' of the "
119:54 songs in the h' of my pilgrimage. "
122: 1 Let us go into the h' of the Lord. "
5 the thrones of the h' of David. "
9 Because of the h' of the Lord our "
127: 1 Except the Lord build the h', they "
128: 3 vine by the sides of thine h': "
132: 3 come into the tabernacle of my h', "
134: 1 night stand in the h' of the Lord. "
135: 2 Ye that stand in the h' of the Lord, "
2 in the courts of the h' of our God, "
19 Bless the Lord, O h' of Israel: "
19 bless the Lord, O h' of Aaron: "
20 Bless the Lord, O h' of Levi: ye "
Pr 2:18 For her h' inclineth unto death, "
3:33 the Lord is in the h' of the wicked: "
5: 8 come not nigh the door of her h': "
10 labours be in the h' of a stranger; "
6:31 give all the substance of his h'. "
7: 6 For at the window of my h' I looked "
8 he went the way to her h', and "
11 her feet abide not in her h': "
27 Her h' is the way to hell, going "
9: 1 Wisdom hath builded her h', she "
14 she sitteth at the door of her h', "

Pr 11:29 He that troubleth his own h' shall 1004
12: 7 the h' of the righteous shall stand. "
14: 1 wise woman buildeth her h': but "
11 The h' of the wicked shall be "
15: 6 In the h' of the righteous is much "
25 will destroy the h' of the proud: "
27 greedy of gain troubleth his own h'; "
17: 1 than an h' full of sacrifices with "
13 evil shall not depart from his h'. "
19:14 H' and riches are the inheritance "
21: 9 a brawling woman in a wide h'. "
12 considereth the h' of the wicked: "
24: 3 Through wisdom is an h' builded; "
27 and afterwards build thine h'. "
25:17 thy foot from thy neighbour's h'; "
24 brawling woman and in a wide h'. "
27:10 neither go into thy brother's h' in "
Ec 2: 7 and had servants born in my h'; "
5: 1 when thou goest to the h' of God, "
7: 2 better to go to the h' of mourning, "
2 than to go to the h' of feasting: "
4 the wise is in the h' of mourning; "
4 heart of fools is in the h' of mirth. "
10:18 of the hands the h' droppeth "
12: 3 the keepers of the h' shall tremble, "
Ca 1:17 The beams of our h' are cedar, and "
2: 4 brought me to the banqueting h', "
3: 4 brought him into my mother's h', "
8: 2 bring thee into my mother's h', "
7 all the substance of his h' for love, "
Isa 2: 2 the mountain of the Lord's h' shall "
3 Lord, to the h' of the God of Jacob; "
5 O h' of Jacob, come ye, and let us "
6 forsaken thy people the h' of Jacob, "
3: 6 his brother of the h' of his father, "
7 for in my h' is neither bread nor "
5: 7 Lord of hosts is the h' of Israel, "
8 Woe unto them that join h' to h', "
6: 4 and the h' was filled with smoke. "
7: 2 it was told the h' of David, saying, "
13 said, Hear ye now, O h' of David; "
17 and upon thy father's h', days that "
8:17 hideth his face from the h' of Jacob, "
10:20 as are escaped of the h' of Jacob, "
14: 1 they shall cleave to the h' of Jacob. "
2 the h' of Israel shall possess them "
17 opened not the h' of his prisoners?* "
18 in glory, every one in his own h'. "
22: 8 the armour of the h' of the forest. "
15 Shebna, which is over the h', and "
18 shall be the shame of thy Lord's h'. "
21 Jerusalem, and to the h' of Judah. "
22 the key of the h' of David will I lay "
23 a glorious throne to his father's h'. "
24 him all the glory of his father's h', "
23: 1 is laid waste, so that there is no h', "
24:10 every h' is shut up, that no man "
29:22 concerning the h' of Jacob, Jacob "
31: 2 arise against the h' of the evildoers, "
36: 3 son, which was over the h', and * "
37: 1 and went into the h' of the Lord. "
14 went up unto the h' of the Lord, "
31 escaped of the h' of Judah shall "
38 worshipping in the h' of Nisroch "
38: 1 Set thine h' in order: for thou shalt "
20 days of our life in the h' of the Lord. "
22 I shall go up to the h' of the Lord? "
39: 2 them the h' of his precious things, "
2 and all the h' of his armour, and all "
2 there was nothing in his h', nor in "
4 What have they seen in thy h'? And "
4 All that is in mine h' have they "
6 all that is in thine h', and that "
42: 7 in darkness out of the prison h'. "
44:13 man; that it may remain in the h'. "
46: 3 Hearken unto me, O h' of Jacob, "
3 all the remnant of the h' of Israel, "
48: 1 Hear ye this, O h' of Jacob, which "
56: 5 will I give in mine h' and within "
7 them joyful in my h' of prayer: "
7 mine h' shall be called an h' of "
58: 1 and the h' of Jacob their sins. "
7 the poor that are cast out to thy h'? "
60: 7 I will glorify the h' of my glory. "
63: 7 goodness toward the h' of Israel, "
64:11 Our holy and our beautiful h', "
66: 1 where is the h' that ye build unto "
20 clean vessel into the h' of the Lord. "
Jer 2: 4 word of the Lord, O h' of Jacob, "
4 all the families of the h' of Israel: "
26 so is the h' of Israel ashamed; they, "
3:18 In those days the h' of Judah shall "
18 walk with the h' of Israel, and they "
20 with me, O h' of Israel, "
5:11 the h' of Israel and the h' of Judah "
15 upon you from far, O h' of Israel, "
20 Declare this in the h' of Jacob, "
7: 2 Stand in the gate of the Lord's h', "
10 come and stand before me in this h', "
11 Is this h', which is called by my "
14 will I do unto this h', which is "
30 the h' which is called by my name, "
9:26 h' of Israel are uncircumcised in "
10: 1 speaketh unto you, O h' of Israel: "
11:10 the h' of Israel and the h' of Judah "
15 hath my beloved to do in mine h', "
17 h' of Israel and of the h' of Judah, "
12: 6 brethren, and the h' of thy father, "
7 I have forsaken mine h', I have left "
14 pluck out the h' of Judah from "
13:11 to cleave unto me the whole h' of "
11 whole h' of Judah, saith the Lord; "
16: 5 Enter not into the h' of mourning, "
8 not also go into the h' of feasting, "
17:26 of praise, unto the h' of the Lord. "
18: 2 go down to the potter's h', and "

Jer 18: 3 Then I went down to the potter's h', 1004
6 O h' of Israel, cannot I do with you "
6 are ye in mine hand, O h' of Israel. "
19:14 stood in the court of the Lord's h'; "
20: 1 chief governor in the h' of the Lord, "
2 which was by the h' of the Lord. "
6 all that dwell in thine h' shall go "
21:11 And touching the h' of the king of "
12 O h' of David, thus saith the Lord; "
22: 1 down to the h' of the king of Judah, "
4 enter in by the gates of this h' "
5 Lord, that this h' shall become a "
6 Lord unto the king's h' of Judah; "
13 buildeth his h' by unrighteousness, "
14 I will build me a wide h' and large "
23: 8 led the seed of the h' of Israel out "
11 in my h' have I found their "
34 will even punish the man and his h'. "
26: 2 Stand in the court of the Lord's h', "
2 come to worship in the Lord's h', "
6 Then will I make this h' like Shiloh, "
7 these words in the h' of the Lord. "
9 saying, This h' shall be like Shiloh, "
9 Jeremiah in the h' of the Lord. "
10 from the king's h' unto the h' of the "
10 entry of the new gate of the Lord's h'. "
12 to prophesy against this h' and "
18 h' as the high places of a forest. "
27:16 the vessels of the Lord's h' shall "
18 which are left in the h' of the Lord, "
18 and in the h' of the king of Judah, "
21 that remain in the h' of the Lord, "
21 and in the h' of the king of Judah "
28: 1 spake unto me in the h' of the Lord, "
3 place all the vessels of the Lord's h', "
5 that stood in the h' of the Lord, "
6 again the vessels of the Lord's h', "
29:26 officers in the h' of the Lord, for "
31:27 that I will sow the h' of Israel "
27 and the h' of Judah with the seed "
31 new covenant with the h' of Israel, "
31 and with the h' of Judah: "
33 I will make with the h' of Israel; "
32: 2 which was in the king of Judah's h'. "
34 set their abominations in the h', "
33:11 of praise into the h' of the Lord. "
14 the h' of Israel...to the h' of Judah. "
17 upon the throne of the h' of Israel; "
34:13 out of the h' of bondmen, saying, "
15 before me in the h' which is called "
35: 2 Go unto the h' of the Rechabites, "
2 bring them into the h' of the Lord, "
3 and the whole h' of the Rechabites; "
4 brought them into the h' of the Lord, "
5 the sons of the h' of the Rechabites "
7 shall ye build h', nor sow seed, nor "
18 said unto the h' of the Rechabites, "
36: 3 that the h' of Judah will hear all the "
5 cannot go into the h' of the Lord: "
6 in the Lord's h' upon the fasting "
8 words of the Lord in the Lord's h'. "
10 of Jeremiah in the h' of the Lord, "
10 the new gate of the Lord's h', in "
12 he went down into the king's h', "
37:15 in prison in the h' of Jonathan the "
17 king asked him secretly in his h', "
20 not to return to the h' of Jonathan "
38: 7 eunuchs which was in the king's h', "
8 went forth out of the king's h', and "
11 went into the h' of the king under "
14 the third entry that is in the h' of "
17 and thou shalt live, and thine h': "
22 are left in the king of Judah's h' "
26 to return to Jonathan's h', to die "
39: 8 Chaldeans burned the king's h', "
41: 5 bring them to the h' of the Lord. "
43: 9 at the entry of Pharaoh's h' in "
48:13 as the h' of Israel was ashamed of "
51:51 the sanctuaries of the Lord's h'. "
52:13 the h' of the Lord, and the king's h'; "
17 brass that were in the h' of the Lord, "
17 sea that was in the h' of the Lord, "
20 had made in the h' of the Lord: "
La 2: 7 made a noise in the h' of the Lord, "
Eze 2: 5 for they are a rebellious h', yet "
6 looks, though they be a rebellious h. "
8 rebellious like that rebellious h': "
3: 1 and go speak unto the h' of Israel. "
4 go, get thee unto the h' of Israel, "
5 language, but to the h' of Israel; "
7 the h' of Israel will not hearken "
7 all the h' of Israel are impudent "
9 though they be a rebellious h'. "
17 a watchman unto the h' of Israel: "
24 me, Go, shut thyself within thine h'. "
26 reprover: for they are a rebellious h'. "
27 forbear: for they are a rebellious h'. "
4: 3 shall be a sign to the h' of Israel. "
4 iniquity of the h' of Israel upon it: "
5 bear the iniquity of the h' of Israel. "
6 the iniquity of the h' of Judah forty "
5: 4 come forth into all the h' of Israel. "
6:11 abominations of the h' of Israel! "
8: 1 I sat in mine h', and the elders of "
6 that the h' of Israel committeth "
10 and all the idols of the h' of Israel, "
11 of the ancients of the h' of Israel, "
12 the ancients of the h' of Israel do "
14 door of the gate of the Lord's h' "
16 the inner court of the Lord's h', * "
17 Is it a light thing to the h' of Judah "
9: 3 he was, to the threshold of the h'. "
6 men which were before the h'. "
7 Defile the h', and fill the courts "
9 The iniquity of the h' of Israel and "
10: 3 stood on the right side of the h'. "

Eze 10: 4 stood over the threshold of the *h'*; 1004
4 the *h'* was filled with the cloud, "
18 from off the threshold of the *h'*, "
19 of the east gate of the Lord's *h'*; "
11: 1 unto the east gate of the Lord's *h'*, "
5 Thus have ye said, O *h'* of Israel: "
15 and all the *h'* of Israel wholly, are "
12: 2 in the midst of a rebellious *h'*, "
2 not: for they are a rebellious *h'*. "
3 though they be a rebellious *h'*. "
6 thee for a sign unto the *h'* of Israel. "
9 the *h'* of Israel, the rebellious *h'*, "
10 all the *h'* of Israel that are among "
24 divination within the *h'* of Israel. "
25 O rebellious *h'*, will I say the word, "
27 they of the *h'* of Israel say, The "
13: 5 hedge for the *h'* of Israel to stand "
9 in the writing of the *h'* of Israel, "
14: 4 Every man of the *h'* of Israel that "
5 I may take the *h'* of Israel in their "
6 say unto the *h'* of Israel, Thus saith "
7 every one of the *h'* of Israel, or of "
11 That the *h'* of Israel may go no "
17: 2 a parable unto the *h'* of Israel; "
12 Say now to the rebellious *h'*, Know "
18: 6, 15 to the idols of the *h'* of Israel, "
25 Hear now, O *h'* of Israel; Is not my "
29 Yet saith the *h'* of Israel, The way "
29 O *h'* of Israel, are not my ways "
30 I will judge you, O *h'* of Israel, "
31 for why will ye die, O *h'* of Israel? "
20: 5 unto the seed of the *h'* of Jacob, "
13 But the *h'* of Israel rebelled against "
27 speak unto the *h'* of Israel, and say "
30 Wherefore say unto the *h'* of Israel, "
31 enquired of by you, O *h'* of Israel? "
39 As for you, O *h'* of Israel, thus "
40 there shall all the *h'* of Israel, all of "
44 corrupt doings, O ye *h'* of Israel, "
22: 18 the *h'* of Israel is to me become "
23: 39 they done in the midst of mine *h'*. "
24: 3 a parable unto the rebellious *h'*, "
21 Speak unto the *h'* of Israel, Thus "
25: 3 against the *h'* of Israel, when they "
8 the *h'* of Judah is like unto all the "
12 against the *h'* of Judah by taking "
27: 14 They of the *h'* of Togarmah traded "
28: 24 pricking brier unto the *h'* of Israel, "
25 shall have gathered the *h'* of Israel "
29: 6 a staff of reed to the *h'* of Israel. "
16 the confidence of the *h'* of Israel, "
21 the horn of the *h'* of Israel to bud "
33: 7 watchman unto the *h'* of Israel; "
10 man, speak unto the *h'* of Israel; "
11 for why will ye die, O *h'* of Israel? "
20 O ye *h'* of Israel, I will judge you "
34: 30 the *h'* of Israel, are my people, "
35: 15 the inheritance of the *h'* of Israel, "
36: 10 all the *h'* of Israel, even all of it: "
17 when the *h'* of Israel dwelt in their "
21 the *h'* of Israel had profaned among "
22 say unto the *h'* of Israel, Thus saith "
22 this for your sakes, O *h'* of Israel, "
32 for your own ways, O *h'* of Israel. "
37 be enquired of by the *h'* of Israel, "
37: 11 bones are the whole *h'* of Israel: "
16 all the *h'* of Israel his companions: "
38: 6 the *h'* of Togarmah of the north "
39: 12 shall the *h'* of Israel be burying of "
22 So the *h'* of Israel shall know that "
23 the *h'* of Israel went into captivity "
25 mercy upon the whole *h'* of Israel, "
29 out my spirit upon the *h'* of Israel, "
40: 4 that thou seest to the *h'* of Israel. "
5 wall on the outside of the *h'* round "
45 the keepers of the charge of the *h'*. "
47 the altar that was before the *h'*. "
48 brought me to the porch of the *h'*, "
41: 5 he measured the wall of the *h'*, six "
6 round about the *h'* on every side. "
6 into the wall which was of the *h'* "
6 had not hold in the wall of the *h'*. "
7 the winding about of the *h'* went "
7 still upward round about the *h'*: "
7 breadth of the *h'* was still upward, "
8 I saw also the height of the *h'* round "
10 round about the *h'* on every side. "
13 So he measured the *h'*, an hundred "
14 the breadth of the face of the *h'*, "
17 the door, even unto the inner *h'*, "
19 through all the *h'* round about. "
26 the side chambers of the *h'*, and "
42: 15 an end of measuring the inner *h'*, "
43: 4 glory of the Lord came into the *h'* "
5 the glory of the Lord filled the *h'*. "
6 speaking unto me out of the *h'*; "
7 shall the *h'* of Israel no more defile "
10 shew the *h'* to the *h'* of Israel, that "
11 shew them the form of the *h'*, and "
12 This is the law of the *h'*; upon the "
12 Behold, this is the law of the *h'*. "
21 it in the appointed place of the *h'*, "
44: 4 way of the north gate before the *h'*: "
4 the Lord filled the *h'* of the Lord: "
5 ordinances of the *h'* of the Lord, "
5 mark well the entering in of the *h'*, "
6 rebellious, even to the *h'* of Israel, "
6 the Lord God; O ye *h'* of Israel, "
7 sanctuary, to pollute it, even my *h'*, "
11 having charge at the gates of the *h'*, "
11 and ministering to the *h'*: "
12 the *h'* of Israel to fall into iniquity; "
14 keepers of the charge of the *h'*, "
22 of the seed of the *h'* of Israel, "
30 the blessing to rest in thine *h'*. "
45: 5 the Levites, the ministers of the *h'*, "

Eze 45: 6 shall be for the whole *h'* of Israel. 1004
8 shall they give to the *h'* of Israel "
17 all solemnities of the *h'* of Israel: "
17 reconciliation for the *h'* of Israel. "
19 upon the posts of the *h'*, and upon "
20 so shall ye reconcile the *h'*. "
46: 24 the ministers of the *h'* shall boil the "
47: 1 me again unto the door of the *h'*; "
1 the threshold of the *h'* eastward: "
1 forefront of the *h'* stood toward the "
1 under from the right side of the *h'*, "
48: 21 the sanctuary of the *h'* shall be in "
Da 1: 2 part of the vessels of the *h'* of God: "
2 land of Shinar to the *h'* of his god; "
2 into the treasure *h'* of his god. "
2: 17 Daniel went to his *h'*, and made 1005
4: 4 was at rest in mine *h'*, "
30 built for the *h'* of the kingdom * "
5: 3 out of the temple of the *h'* of God "
10 his lords came into the banquet *h'*: "
23 brought the vessels of his *h'* before "
6: 10 was signed, he went into his *h'*; "
Ho 1: 4 of Jezreel upon the *h'* of Jehu, 1004
4 the kingdom of the *h'* of Israel. "
6 have mercy upon the *h'* of Israel; "
7 have mercy upon the *h'* of Judah, "
5: 1 and hearken, ye *h'* of Israel; "
1 and give ye ear, O *h'* of the king; "
12 to the *h'* of Judah as rottenness. "
14 as a young lion to the *h'* of Judah: "
6: 10 horrible thing in the *h'* of Israel: "
8: 1 an eagle against the *h'* of the Lord, "
9: 4 not come into the *h'* of the Lord. "
8 and hatred in the *h'* of his God. "
15 I will drive them out of mine *h'*, "
11: 12 and the *h'* of Israel with deceit: "
Joe 1: 9 is cut off from the *h'* of the Lord; "
13 withholden from the *h'* of your God. "
14 into the *h'* of the Lord your God, "
16 gladness from the *h'* of our God? "
3: 18 come forth of the *h'* of the Lord, "
Am 1: 4 will send a fire into the *h'* of Hazael, "
5 the sceptre from the *h'* of Eden: "
2: 8 condemned in the *h'* of their god. "
3: 13 ye, and testify in the *h'* of Jacob, "
15 the winter *h'* with the summer *h'*; "
5: 1 even a lamentation, O *h'* of Israel. "
3 shall leave ten, to the *h'* of Israel. "
4 saith the Lord unto the *h'* of Israel, "
6 out like fire in the *h'* of Joseph, "
19 or went into the *h'*, and leaned his "
25 forty years, O *h'* of Israel? "
6: 1 to whom the *h'* of Israel came! "
9 remain ten men in one *h'*, that they "
10 to bring out the bones out of the *h'*, "
10 him that is by the sides of the *h'*, "
11 smite the great *h'* with breaches, "
11 and the little *h'* with clefts. "
14 against you a nation, O *h'* of Israel, "
7: 9 will rise against the *h'* of Jeroboam "
10 thee in the midst of the *h'* of Israel: "
16 not thy word against the *h'* of Isaac. "
9: 8 not utterly destroy the *h'* of Jacob, "
9 I will sift the *h'* of Israel among all "
Ob 17 and the *h'* of Jacob shall possess "
18 And the *h'* of Jacob shall be a fire, "
18 and the *h'* of Joseph a flame, "
18 and the *h'* of Esau for stubble, "
18 be any remaining of the *h'* of Esau; "
Mic 1: 5 and for the sins of the *h'* of Israel, "
10 in the *h'* of Aphrah roll thyself in* 1035
2: 2 so they oppress a man and his *h'*, 1004
7 thou that art named the *h'* of Jacob, "
3: 1 and ye princes of the *h'* of Israel; "
9 and you, ye heads of the *h'* of Jacob, "
9 and princes of the *h'* of Israel, that "
12 mountain of the *h'* as the high "
4: 1 the mountain of the *h'* of the Lord "
2 and to the *h'* of the God of Jacob; "
6: 4 thee out of the *h'* of servants; "
10 wickedness in the *h'* of the wicked, "
16 all the works of the *h'* of Ahab, and "
7: 6 enemies are the men of his own *h'*. "
Na 1: 14 out of the *h'* of thy gods will I cut "
Hab 2: 9 an evil covetousness to his *h'*, "
10 hast consulted shame to thy *h'* by "
3: 13 head out of the *h'* of the wicked, by "
Zep 2: 7 for the remnant of the *h'* of Judah; "
Hag 1: 2 that the Lord's *h'* should be built. "
4 cieled houses, and this *h'* lie waste? "
8 and bring wood, and build the *h'*; "
9 Because of mine *h'* that is waste, "
9 ye run every man unto his own *h'*. "
14 work in the *h'* of the Lord of hosts, "
2: 3 among you that saw this *h'* in her "
7 and I will fill this *h'* with glory, "
9 The glory of this latter *h'* shall be "
Zec 1: 16 my *h'* shall be built in it, saith the "
3: 7 thou shalt also judge my *h'*, and "
4: 9 have laid the foundation of this *h'*; "
5: 4 shall enter into the *h'* of the thief, "
4 the *h'* of him that sweareth falsely "
4 shall remain in the midst of his *h'*, "
11 build it an *h'* in the land of Shinar: "
6: 10 go into the *h'* of Josiah the son of "
7: 2 they had sent unto the *h'* of God *1008
3 priests which were in the *h'* of the 1004
8: 9 the foundation of the *h'* of the Lord "
13 O *h'* of Judah, and *h'* of Israel; "
15 Jerusalem and to the *h'* of Judah: "
19 to the *h'* of Judah joy and gladness, "
9: 8 And I will encamp about mine *h'* "
10: 3 visited his flock the *h'* of Judah, "
6 I will strengthen the *h'* of Judah, "
6 and I will save the *h'* of Joseph, "
11: 13 to the potter in the *h'* of the Lord. "

Zec 12: 4 mine eyes upon the *h'* of Judah, 1004
7 that the glory of the *h'* of David "
8 and the *h'* of David shall be as God, "
10 I will pour upon the *h'* of David, "
12 the family of the *h'* of David apart, "
12 family of the *h'* of Nathan apart, "
13 The family of the *h'* of Levi apart, "
13: 1 fountain opened to the *h'* of David "
6: 1 wounded in the *h'* of my friends. "
14: 20 the pots in the Lord's *h'* shall be "
21 in the *h'* of the Lord of hosts. "
Mal 3: 10 there may be meat in mine *h'*, and "
M't 2: 11 when they were come into the *h'*, 3614
5: 15 light unto all that are in the *h'*. "
7: 24 which built his *h'* upon a rock: "
25 winds blew, and beat upon that *h'*; "
26 which built his *h'* upon the sand: "
27 winds blew, and beat upon that *h'*; "
8: 14 Jesus was come into Peter's *h'*, he "
9: 6 up thy bed, and go unto thine *h'*. 3624
7 he arose, and departed to his *h'*. "
10 as Jesus sat at meat in the *h'*, 3614
23 when Jesus came into the ruler's *h'*, "
28 And when he was come into the *h'*, "
10: 6 the lost sheep of the *h'* of Israel. 3624
12 when ye come into an *h'*, salute it. 3614
13 And if the *h'* be worthy, let your "
14 when ye depart out of that *h'* or "
25 call the master of the *h'* Beelzebub, 3617
12: 4 How he entered into the *h'* of God, 3624
25 city or *h'* divided against itself 3614
29 one enter into a strong man's *h'*, "
29 man? and then he will spoil his *h'*. "
44 return into my *h'* from whence I 3624
13: 1 same day went Jesus out of the *h'*, 3614
36 away, and went into the *h'*: "
57 his own country, and in his own *h'*. "
15: 24 the lost sheep of the *h'* of Israel. 3624
17: 25 And when he was come into the *h'*, 3614
20: 11 against the goodman of the *h'*, *3617
21: 13 My *h'* shall be called the *h'* 3624
23: 38 your *h'* is left unto you desolate. "
24: 17 to take any thing out of his *h'*: 3614
43 goodman of the *h'* had known in 3617
43 suffered his *h'* to be broken up. 3614
26: 6 in the *h'* of Simon the leper, "
18 I will keep the passover at thy *h'* "
M'r 1: 29 entered into the *h'* of Simon and 3614
2: 1 was noised that he was in the *h'*. 3624
11 bed, and go thy way into thine *h'*. "
15 that, as Jesus sat at meat in his *h'*, 3614
26 How he went into the *h'* of God in 3624
3: 19 him: and they went into an *h'*. "
25 And if a *h'* be divided against itself, 3614
25 itself, that *h'* cannot stand. "
27 can enter into a strong man's *h'*, "
27 man; and then he will spoil his *h'*. "
5: 35 from the ruler of the synagogue's *h'* "
38 cometh to the *h'* of the ruler of the 3624
6: 4 his own kin, and in his own *h'*. 3614
10 ye enter into a *h'*, there abide till ye "
7: 17 when he was entered into the *h'* 3624
24 and Sidon, and entered into an *h'*, 3614
30 when she was come to her *h'*, she 3624
8: 26 And he sent him away to his *h'*, * "
9: 28 when he was come into the *h'*, his "
33 and being in the *h'* he asked them, 3614
10: 10 And in the *h'* his disciples asked "
29 There is no man that hath left *h'*, or "
11: 17 not written, My *h'* shall be called 3624
17 of all nations the *h'* of prayer? "
13: 15 housetop not go down into the *h'*, *3614
15 to take any thing out of his *h'*: "
34 taking a far journey, who left his *h'*, "
35 when the master of the *h'* cometh, "
14: 3 Bethany in the *h'* of Simon the leper, "
14 say ye to the goodman of the *h'*, 3617
Lu 1: 23 he departed to his own *h'*. 3624
27 was Joseph, of the *h'* of David; "
33 reign over the *h'* of Jacob for ever; "
40 entered into the *h'* of Zacharias, "
56 months, and returned to her own *h'*. "
69 us in the *h'* of his servant David; "
2: 4 was of the *h'* and lineage of David: "
4: 38 and entered into Simon's *h'*. 3614
5: 24 up thy couch, and go into thine *h'*. 3624
25 he lay, and departed to his own *h'*. "
29 him a great feast in his own *h'*: 3614
6: 4 How he went into the *h'* of God, 3624
48 He is like a man which built an *h'*, 3614
48 beat vehemently upon that *h'*, "
49 built an *h'* upon the earth; against "
49 and the ruin of that *h'* was great. "
7: 6 he was now not far from the *h'*, "
10 that were sent, returning to the *h'*, 3624
36 he went into the Pharisee's *h'*, and 3614
37 sat at meat in the Pharisee's *h'*, "
44 I entered into thine *h'*, thou gavest "
8: 27 neither abode in any *h'*, but in the "
39 Return to thine own *h'*, and shew 3624
41 him that he would come into his *h'*: "
49 from the ruler of the synagogue's *h'*, "
51 And when he came into the *h'*, he 3614
9: 4 whatsoever *h'* ye enter into, there "
61 which are at home at my *h'*. 3624
10: 5 into whatsoever *h'* ye enter, first 3614
5 first say, Peace be to this *h'*. 3624
7 in the same *h'* remain, eating and 3614
7 of his hire. Go not from *h'* to *h'*. "
38 Martha received him into her *h'*. 3624
11: 17 and a *h'* divided against a *h'* falleth. "
24 I will return unto my *h'* whence I "
12: 39 the goodman of the *h'* had known 3617
39 have suffered his *h'* to be broken 3624
52 there shall be five in one *h'* divided. "
13: 25 the master of the *h'* is risen up, 3617

Lu 13:35 your h' is left unto you desolate: 3624
14: 1 the h' of one of the chief Pharisees "
21 the master of the h' being angry 3617
23 to come in, that my h' may be filled. 3624
15: 8 sweep the h', and seek diligently 3614
25 he came and drew nigh to the h', "
16:27 send him to my father's h': 3624
17:31 housetop, and his stuff in the h', 3614
18:14 man went down to his h' justified 3624
29 no man that hath left h', or parents, 3614
19: 5 for to day I must abide at thy h'. 3624
9 This day is salvation come to this h'."
46 written, My h' is the h' of prayer: "
22:10 follow him into the h' where he 3614
11 say unto the goodman of the h', "
54 him into the high priest's h'. 3624
Joh 2:16 Father's h' an h' of merchandise. "
17 zeal of thine h' hath eaten me up. "
4:53 himself believed, and his whole h'. 3614
7:53 every man went unto his own h'. 3624
8:35 abideth not in the h' for ever: 3614
11:20 him: but Mary sat still in the h'. 3624
31 which were with her in the h', 3614
12: 3 the h' was filled with the odour of "
14: 2 my Father's h' are many mansions: "
Ac 2: 2 all the h' where they were sitting. 3624
36 let all the h' of Israel know "
46 breaking bread from h' to h', * "
5:42 in the temple, and in every h', * "
7:10 governor over Egypt and all his h'. "
20 up in his father's h' three months: "
42 O ye h' of Israel, have ye offered to "
47 But Solomon built him an h'. "
49 what h' will ye build me? saith * "
8: 3 entering into every h', and "
9:11 enquire in the h' of Judas for one 3614
17 his way, and entered into the h'; "
10: 2 one that feared God with all his h', 3624
6 tanner, whose h' is by the sea side: 3614
17 had made enquiry for Simon's h', "
22 angel to send for thee into his h', 3624
30 ninth hour I prayed in my h', and, "
32 he is lodged in the h' of one Simon 3614
11:11 three men already come unto the h' "
12 and we entered into the man's h': 3624
13 how he had seen an angel in his h', "
14 thou and all thy h' shall be saved. "
12:12 came to the h' of Mary the mother 3614
16:15 Lord, come into my h', and abide 3624
31 and thou shalt be saved, and thy h'. "
32 Lord, and to all that were in his h'. 3614
34 he had brought them into his h', 3624
34 believing in God with all his h'. 3832
40 and entered into the h' of Lydia: "
17: 5 and assaulted the h' of Jason, 3614
18: 7 a certain man's h', named Justus, "
7 h' joined hard to the synagogue. "
8 believed on the Lord with all his h'; 3624
19:16 they fled out of that h' naked and "
20:20 you publickly, and from h' to h', "
21: 8 we entered into the h' of Philip the "
28:30 whole years in his own hired h', * "
Ro 16: 5 greet the church that is in their h'. 3624
1Co 1:11 them which are of the h' of Chloe,* "
16:15 ye know the h' of Stephanas, that 3614
19 with the church that is in their h'. 3624
2Co 5: 1 we know that if our earthly h' of 3614
1 an h' not made with hands, eternal "
2 with our h' which is from heaven: *3613
Col 4:15 and the church which is in his h'. 3624
1Ti 3: 4 One that ruleth well his own h', "
5 know not how to rule his own h', "
15 to behave thyself in the h' of God, "
5: 8 specially for those of his own h', *3609
13 wandering about from h' to h'; 3614
14 bear children, guide the h', give *3616
2Ti 1:16 mercy unto the h' of Onesiphorus; 3624
2:20 But in a great h' there are not only 3614
Ph'm 2 and to the church in thy h': 3624
Heb 3: 2 also Moses was faithful in all his h'. "
3 as he who hath builded the h' "
3 hath more honour than the h'. "
4 every h' is builded by some man; "
5 verily was faithful in all his h', "
6 But Christ as a son over his own h'; "
6 whose h' are we, if we hold fast the "
8: 8 h' of Israel and with the h' of Judah: "
10 I will make with the h' of Israel "
10:21 an high priest over the h' of God; "
11: 7 an ark to the saving of his h'; "
1Pe 2: 5 stones, are built up a spiritual h', "
4:17 must begin at the h' of God: "
2Jo 10 receive him not into your h', 3614

house-full See HOUSE and FULL.

household See also HOUSEHOLDS.
Ge 18:19 his children and his h' after him. 1004
31:37 hast thou found of all thy h' stuff? "
35: 2 Jacob said unto his h', and to all "
45:11 lest thou, and thy h', and all that "
47:12 and all his father's h', with bread, "
Ex 1: 1 man and his h' came with Jacob. "
12: 4 if the h' be too little for the lamb, "
Le 16:17 for himself, and for his h', and for "
De 6:22 upon Pharaoh, and upon all his h',* "
14:26 thou shalt rejoice, thou, and thine h', "
15:20 Lord shall choose, thou and thy h'. "
Jos 2:18 all thy father's h', home unto thee. "
6:25 harlot alive, and her father's h', "
7:14 the h' which the Lord shall take "
18 And he brought his h' man by man; "
J'g 6:27 because he feared his father's h', "
18:25 lose thy life, with the lives of thy h'. "
1Sa 25:17 our master, and against all his h':* "
27: 3 and his men, every man with his h', "
2Sa 2: 3 bring up, every man with his h': "
2Sa 6:11 blessed Obed-edom, and all his h'. *1004
20 Then David returned to bless his h'. "
15:16 went forth, and all his h' after him. "
16: 2 asses be for the king's h' to ride on; "
17:23 put his h' in order, and hanged * "
19:18 ferry boat to carry over the king's h', "
41 have brought the king, and his h', "
1Ki 4: 6 Ahishar was over the h': and "
7 victuals for the king and his h': "
5: 9 my desire, in giving food for my h'. "
11 measures of wheat for food to his h', "
11:20 and Genubath was in Pharaoh's h'* "
2Ki 7: 9 we may go and tell the king's h'. "
8: 1 go thou and thine h', and sojourn "
2 she went with her h', and sojourned "
18:18, 37 Hilkiah, which was over the h', "
19: 2 sent Eliakim, which was over the h', "
1Ch 24: 6 one principal h' being taken for * "
Ne 13: 8 I cast forth all the h' stuff of Tobiah "
Job 1: 3 she asses, and a very great h'; 5657
Pr 27:27 for the food of thy h', and for the 1004
31:15 giveth meat to her h', and a portion "
21 not afraid of the snow for her h': "
21 for all her h' are clothed with scarlet. "
27 looketh well to the ways of her h', "
Isa 36:22 son of Hilkiah, that was over the h', "
37: 2 sent Eliakim, who was over the h', "
M't 10:25 more shall they call them of his h'? 3615
36 man's foes shall be they of his own h'. "
24:45 his lord hath made ruler over his h', 2322
Lu 12:42 his lord shall make ruler over his h', "
Ac 10: 7 he called two of his h' servants, 3610
16:15 when she was baptized, and her h', 3624
Ro 16:10 them which are of Aristobulus' h'. "
11 them that be of the h' of Narcissus, "
1Co 1:16 baptized also the h' of Stephanas: 3624
Ga 6:10 unto them who are of the h' of faith. 3609
Eph 2:19 with the saints, and of the h' of God; "
Ph'p 4:22 chiefly they that are of Cæsar's h'. 3614
2Ti 4:19 and the h' of Onesiphorus. *3624

householder
M't 13:27 servants of the h' came and said 3617
52 is like unto a man that is an h', "
20: 1 is like unto a man that is an h', "
21:33 was a certain h', which planted a "

households
Ge 42:33 food for the famine of your h', *1004
45:18 take your father and your h', and "
47:24 your food, and for them of your h', "
Nu 18:31 eat it in every place, ye and your h': "
De 11: 6 swallowed them up, and their h', "
12: 7 put your hand unto, ye and your h', "
Jos 7:14 Lord shall take shall come by h'; "

houses See also STOREHOUSES.
Ge 42:19 corn for the famine of your h': 1004
Ex 1:21 feared God, that he made them h'.‡ "
6:14 be the heads of their fathers' h': "
8: 9 the frogs from thee and thy h', "
11 depart from thee, and from thy h', "
13 the frogs died out of the h', out of "
21 upon thy people, and into thy h': "
21 h' of the Egyptians shall be full of "
24 into his servants' h', and into all the "
9:20 and his cattle flee into the h': "
10: 6 And they shall fill thy h', and the "
6 and the h' of all thy servants, and "
6 and the h' of all the Egyptians; "
12: 7 on the upper door post of the h', "
13 for a token upon the h' where ye are: "
15 put away leaven out of your h': "
19 be no leaven found in your h': for "
23 destroyer to come in unto your h' to "
27 over the h' of the children of Israel "
27 the Egyptians, and delivered our h'. "
Le 25:31 But the h' of the villages which no "
32 and the h' of the cities of their "
33 the h' of the cities of the Levites "
Nu 4:22 throughout the h' of their fathers, "
16:32 swallowed them up, and their h', * "
17: 6 according to their fathers' h', even "
32:18 We will not return unto our h', until "
De 6:11 and h' full of all good things, which "
8:12 and hast built goodly h', and dwelt "
19: 1 in their cities, and in their h'; "
Jos 9:12 hot for our provision out of our h' "
J'g 18:14 that there is in these h' an ephod, "
22 that were in the h' near to Micah's "
1Ki 9:10 Solomon had built the two h', the "
13:32 against all the h' of the high places "
20: 6 house, and the h' of thy servants; "
2Ki 17:29 for them in the h' of the high places "
32 for them in the h' of the high places. "
23: 7 brake down the h' of the sodomites, "
19 all the h' also of the high places "
25: 9 and all the h' of Jerusalem, and "
1Ch 15: 1 David made him h' in the city of "
29: 4 to overlay the walls of the h' withal: "
2Ch 25: 5 according to the h' of their fathers, "
34:11 floor the h' which the kings of Judah "
35: 4 yourselves by the h' of your fathers, "
Ne 4:14 daughters, your wives, and your h'. "
5: 3 our lands, vineyards, and h', that "
11 their oliveyards, and their h', also "
9:25 and possessed h' full of all goods, "
10:34 our God, after the h' of our fathers, "
Job 1: 4 sons went and feasted in their h', * "
3:15 gold, who filled their h' with silver: "
4:19 less in them that dwell in h' of clay, "
15:28 and in h' which no man inhabiteth, "
21: 9 Their h' are safe from fear, neither "
22:18 he filled their h' with good things: "
24:16 In the dark they dig through h', "
Ps 49:11 that their h' shall continue for ever, "
83:12 us take to ourselves the h' of God *4999
Pr 1:13 we shall fill our h' with spoil: 1004
Ec 2: 4 I builded me h'; I planted me 1004
Isa 3:14 the spoil of the poor is in your h'. "
5: 9 a truth many h' shall be desolate, "
6:11 and the h' without man, and the "
8:14 of offence to both the h' of Israel, "
13:16 their h' shall be spoiled, and their "
21 and their h' shall be full of doleful "
22 shall cry in their desolate h', * 490
15: 3 on the tops of their h', and in their* "
22:10 numbered the h' of Jerusalem, 1004
10 h' have ye broken down to fortify "
32:13 upon all the h' of joy in the joyous "
42:22 and they are hid in the prison h': "
65:21 And they shall build h', and inhabit "
Jer 5: 7 by troops in the harlots' h'. "
27 birds, so are their h' full of deceit: "
6:12 their h' shall be turned unto others, "
17:22 carry forth a burden out of your h' "
18:22 Let a cry be heard from their h', "
19:13 And the h' of Jerusalem, and the h' "
13 because of all the h' upon whose "
29: 5 Build ye h', and dwell in them; and "
28 build ye h', and dwell in them; and "
32:15 H' and fields and vineyards shall be "
29 on this city, and burn it with the h', "
33: 4 concerning the h' of this city, and "
4 the h' of the kings of Judah, which "
35: 9 Nor to build h' for us to dwell in: "
39: 8 and the h' of the people, with fire, "
43:12 fire in the h' of the gods of Egypt; "
13 the h' of the gods of the Egyptians "
52:13 and all the h' of Jerusalem, and all "
13 the h' of the great men, burned he* "
La 5: 2 turned to strangers, our h' to aliens. "
Eze 7:24 then, and they shall possess their h': "
11: 3 say, It is not near; let us build h': "
16:41 they shall burn thine h' with fire, "
23:47 and burn up their h' with fire. "
26:12 walls and destroy thy pleasant h': "
28:26 therein, and shall build h', and plant "
33:30 the walls and in the doors of the h', "
45: 4 It shall be a place for their h', and "
Da 2: 5 your h' shall be made a dunghill. 1005
3:29 their h' shall be made a dunghill: "
Ho 11:11 I will place them in their h', saith 1004
Joe 2: 9 they shall climb up upon the h'; "
Am 3:15 and the h' of ivory shall perish, and "
15 and the great h' shall have an end, "
5:11 ye have built h' of hewn stone, but "
Mic 1:14 the h' of Achzib shall be a lie to the "
2: 2 and h', and take them away: so they "
9 cast out from their pleasant h'; "
Zep 1: 9 fill their master's h' with violence * "
13 a booty, and their h' a desolation: "
13 they shall also build h', but not "
2: 7 in the h' of Ashkelon shall they lie "
Hag 1: 4 to dwell in your cieled h', and this "
Zec 14: 2 city shall be taken, and the h' rifled, "
M't 11: 8 wear soft clothing are in kings' h'. 3624
19:29 that hath forsaken h', or brethren, 3614
23:14 ye devour widows' h', and for a * "
M'r 8: 3 away, fasting to their own h', they* 3624
10:30 h', and brethren, and sisters, and 3614
12:40 Which devour widows' h', and for a "
Lu 16: 4 they may receive me into their h'. 3624
20:47 Which devour widows' h', and for 3614
Ac 4:34 possessors of lands or h' sold them, "
1Co 11:22 ye not h' to eat and to drink in? "
1Ti 3:12 their children and their own h' well. 3624
2Ti 3: 6 sort are they which creep into h', 3614
Tit 1:11 who subvert whole h', teaching 3624

housetop See also HOUSE and TOP; HOUSETOPS.
Pr 21: 9 better to dwell in a corner of the h', 1406
25:24 better to dwell in the corner of the h', "
M't 24:17 Let him which is on the h' not 1430
M'r 13:15 let him that is on the h' not go down "
Lu 5:19 they went upon the h', and let him "
17:31 he which shall be upon the h', and "
Ac 10: 9 Peter went up upon the h' to pray "

housetops
Ps 129: 6 them be as the grass upon the h', 1406
Isa 22: 1 thou art wholly gone up to the h'? "
37:27 as the grass on the h', and as corn "
Jer 48:38 upon all the h' of Moab, and in the "
Zep 1: 5 the host of heaven upon the h'; "
M't 10:27 the ear, that preach ye upon the h'. 1430
Lu 12: 3 shall be proclaimed upon the h'. "

houshold See HOUSEHOLD.

how See also HOWBEIT; HOWSOEVER.
Ge 26: 9 h' saidst thou, She is my sister? 349
27:20 H' is it that thou hast found it so 4100
28:17 H' dreadful is this place! this is "
30:29 knowest h' I have served thee, 854,834
29 and h' thy cattle was with me. "
38:29 said, H' hast thou broken forth? *4100
39: 9 his wife: h' then can I do this great 349
44: 8 h' then should we steal out of thy "
16 or h' shall we clear ourselves? 4100
34 h' shall I go up to my father, and 349
47: 8 said unto Jacob, H' old art thou? 4100
18 lord, h' that our money is spent; "
Ex 2:18 H' is it that ye are come so soon 4069
6:30 h' shall Pharaoh hearken unto me? 349
9:29 h' that the earth is the Lord's. "
10: 2 may know h' that I am the Lord. * "
3 H' long wilt thou refuse to humble 5704
16:28 H' long refuse ye to keep my "
18: 8 way, and h' the Lord delivered them. "
19: 4 h' I bare you on eagles' wings, and "
36: 1 know h' to work all manner of work "
Nu 10:31 h' we are to encamp in the wilderness, "
14:11 H' long will this people provoke 5704
11 h' long will it be ere they believe "
27 H' long shall I bear with this evil "

Nu 20:15 *H'* our fathers went down into Egypt,
23: 8 *H'* shall I curse, whom God hath 4100
8 *h'* shall I defy, whom the Lord hath "
24: 5 *H'* goodly are thy tents, O Jacob,
De 1:12 *H'* can I myself alone bear your 349
31 *h'* that the Lord thy God bare thee,
7:17 than I; *h'* can I dispossess them? 349
9: 7 not, *h'* thou provokedst the Lord 834
11: 4 *h'* he made the water of the Red "
4 and *h'* the Lord hath destroyed them
6 *h'* the earth opened her mouth, and,834
12:30 *H'* did these nations serve their 349
18:21 *H'* shall we know the word which "
25:18 *H'* he met thee by the way, and 834
29:16 *h'* we have dwelt in the land of "
16 and *h'* we came through the nations "
31:27 and *h'* much more after my death? 637
32:30 *H'* should one chase a thousand, 349
Jos 2:10 *h'* the Lord dried up the water of 834
9: 7 *h'* shall we make a league with you? 349
24 *h'* that the Lord...commanded his
10: 1 *h'* Joshua had taken Ai, and had 3588
1 *h'* the inhabitants of Gibeon had "
14:12 that day *h'* the Anakims were there, "
18: 3 *H'* long are ye slack to go to 5704
J'g 13:12 *H'* shall we order the child, and *4100
12 and *h'* shall we do unto him? †
16:15 *H'* canst thou say, I love thee, 349
18: 7 *h'* they dwelt careless, after the
20: 3 Tell us, *h'* was this wickedness? 349
21: 7,16 *H'* shall we do for wives for 4100
Ru 1: 6 *h'* that the Lord had visited his
2:11 *h'* thou hast left thy father and thy
3:18 thou know *h'* the matter will fall 5704
1Sa 1:14 *H'* long wilt thou be drunken? put "
2:22 *h'* they lay with the women that 434
10:27 said, *H'* shall this man save us? 4100
12:24 *h'* great things he hath done for 834
14:29 *h'* mine eyes have been enlightened3588
30 *H'* much more, if haply the 637
15: 2 *h'* he laid wait for him in the way, 834
16: 1 *H'* long wilt thou mourn for Saul, 5704
2 *H'* can I go? if Saul hear it, he will349
17:18 and look *h'* thy brethren fare, and
23: 3 *h'* much more then if we come to 637
24:10 *h'* that the Lord had delivered thee 834
18 *h'* that thou hast dealt well with
28: 9 *h'* he hath cut off those that have
2Sa 1: 4 unto him, *H'* went the matter? 4100
5 *H'* knowest thou that Saul and 349
14 *H'* wast thou not afraid to stretch "
19 places: *h'* are the mighty fallen! "
25 *H'* are the mighty fallen in the "
27 *H'* are the mighty fallen, and the "
2:22 *h'* then should I hold up my face to "
26 *h'* long shall it be then, ere thou 5704
4:11 *H'* much more, when wicked men 637
6:20 *H'* glorious was the king of Israel4100
11: 7 demanded of him *h'* Joab did, and
7 and *h'* the people did, and *h'* the war
12:18 *h'* will he then vex himself, if we 349
16:11 *h'* much more now may this 637
18:19 *h'* that the Lord hath avenged him
19: 2 *h'* the king was grieved for his son.*
34 *H'* long have I to live, that I should4100
24: 3 people, *h'* many soever they be, an
1Ki 3: 7 I know not *h'* to go out or come in.
5: 3 *h'* that David my father could not
8:27 *h'* much less this house that I 637
12: 6 *H'* do ye advise that I may answer*349
14:19 *h'* he warred, and *h'* he reigned,
18:13 *h'* I hid an hundred men of the Lord's
21 *H'* long halt ye between two 5704
19: 1 *h'* he had slain all the prophets 834
20: 7 see *h'* this man seeketh mischief: 3588
21:29 thou *h'* Ahab humbleth himself
22:16 *H'* many times shall I adjure 5704
45 of Jehoshaphat,...and *h'* he warred, 834
2Ki 5: 7 *h'* he seeketh a quarrel against me. 3588
13 *h'* much rather then, when he 637
6:15 Alas, my master! *h'* shall we do? 349
32 *h'* this son of a murderer hath sent 3588
8: 5 *h'* he had restored a dead body to 834
9:25 *h'* that, when I and thou rode together
10: 4 before him: *h'* then shall we stand? 349
14:15 *h'* he fought with Amaziah king of 834
28 *h'* he warred, and *h'* he recovered "
17:28 them *h'* they should fear the Lord. 349
18:24 *H'* then wilt thou turn away the face"
19:25 not heard long ago *h'* I have done it,
20: 3 *h'* I have walked before thee in 834
20 and *h'* he made a pool, and a conduit,"
1Ch 13:12 *H'* shall I bring the ark of God 1963
18: 9 *h'* David had smitten all the host*3588
2Ch 6:18 *h'* much less this house which I 637
7: 3 saw *h'* the fire came down, and the *
18:15 *H'* many times shall I adjure 5704
20:11 Behold, I say, *h'* they reward us,
32:15 *h'* much less shall your God 637
33:19 also, and *h'* God was intreated of him,
Ezr 7:22 and salt without prescribing *h'* much.
Ne 2: 6 For *h'* long shall thy journey be? 5704
17 *h'* Jerusalem lieth waste, and the 834
Es 2:11 to know *h'* Esther did, and what should
5:11 *h'* the king had advanced him above the 834
8: 6 *h'* can I endure to see the evil that 346
6 *h'* can I endure to see the destruction"
Job 4:19 *H'* much less in them that dwell in 637
6:25 *H'* forcible are right words! but 4100
7:19 *H'* long wilt thou not depart 5704
8: 2 *H'* long wilt thou speak these "
2 *h'* long shall the words of thy mouth
9: 2 *h'* should man be just with God? 4100
14 *H'* much less shall I answer him, 637
13:23 *H'* many are mine iniquities and 4100
15:16 *H'* much more abominable 637
Job 18: 2 *H'* long will it be ere ye make 5704
19: 2 *H'* long will ye vex my soul, and "
21:17 *H'* oft is the candle of the wicked 4100
17 and *h'* oft cometh their destruction *
34 *H'* then comfort ye me in vain, 349
22:12 the height of the stars, *h'* high 3588
13 thou sayest, *H'* doth God know? *4100
25: 4 *H'* then can man be justified with "
4 or *h'* can he be clean that is born of "
6 *H'* much less man, that is a 637
26: 2 *H'* hast thou helped him that is 4100
2 *h'* savest thou the arm that hath no
3 *H'* hast thou counselled him that 4100
3 *h'* hast thou plentifully declared the*
14 *h'* little a portion is heard of him? 4100
34:19 *H'* much less to him that accepted 834
37:17 *H'* thy garments are warm, when he "
Ps 3: 1 *h'* are they increased that trouble 4100
4: 2 *h'* long will ye turn my glory 5704
2 *h'* long will ye love vanity, and seek
6: 3 vexed: but thou, O Lord, *h'* long? 5704
8: 1,9 *h'* excellent is thy name in all the 4100
11: 1 *h'* say ye to my soul, Flee as a bird 349
13: 1 *H'* long wilt thou forget me, O 5704
1 *h'* long wilt thou hide thy face from "
2 *H'* long shall I take counsel in my "
2 *h'* long shall mine enemy be exalted "
21: 1 *h'* greatly shall he rejoice! 4100
31:19 Oh *h'* great is thy goodness, which "
35:17 Lord, *h'* long wilt thou look on? "
36: 7 *H'* excellent is thy lovingkindness, "
39: 4 it is; that I may know *h'* frail I am. "
44: 2 *H'* thou didst drive out the heathen*
2 *h'* thou didst afflict the people, and*
62: 3 *H'* long will ye imagine mischief 5704
66: 3 *H'* terrible art thou in thy works! 4100
73:11 *H'* doth God know? and is there 349
19 *H'* are they brought into desolation, "
74: 9 us any that knoweth *h'* long. 5704
10 God, *h'* long shall the adversary
22 *h'* the foolish man reproacheth thee
78:40 *H'* oft did they provoke him in the 4101
43 *H'* he had wrought his signs in 834
79: 5 *H'* long, Lord? wilt thou be angry 5704
80: 4 hosts, *h'* long wilt thou be angry "
82: 2 *H'* long will ye judge unjustly, and "
84: 1 *H'* amiable are thy tabernacles, O 4100
89:46 *H'* long, Lord? wilt thou hide 5704
47 Remember *h'* short my time is: 4100
50 *h'* I do bear in my bosom the reproach
90:13 Return, O Lord, *h'* long? and let it 5704
92: 5 O Lord, *h'* great are thy works! 4100
94: 3 *h'* long shall the wicked, *h'* long 5704
4 *H'* long shall they utter and speak hard
104:24 *h'* manifold are thy works! in 4100
119:84 *H'* many are the days of thy "
97 O *h'* love I thy law! it is my "
103 *H'* sweet are thy words unto my "
159 Consider *h'* I love thy precepts: 3588
132: 2 *H'* he sware unto the Lord, and 834
133: 1 *h'* good and *h'* pleasant it is for 4100
137: 4 *H'* shall we sing the Lord's song in 349
139:17 *H'* precious also are thy thoughts 4100
17 O God! *h'* great is the sum of them! "
Pr 1:22 *H'* long, ye simple ones, will ye 5704
5:12 *H'* have I hated instruction, and 349
6: 9 *H'* long wilt thou sleep, O 5704
15:11 *h'* much more then the hearts 637
23 spoken in due season, *h'* good is it! 4100
16:16 *H'* much better is it to get wisdom "
19: 7 *h'* much more do his friends 637
20:24 *h'* can a man then understand his 4100
21:27 *h'* much more, when he 637
30:13 O *h'* lofty are their eyes! 4100
Ec 2:16 And *h'* dieth the wise man? as the 349
4:11 but *h'* can one be warm alone? "
10:15 he knoweth not *h'* to go to the city. 834
11: 5 *h'* the bones do grow in the womb of
Ca 4:10 *H'* fair is thy love, my sister, my 4100
10 *h'* much better is thy love than
5: 3 off my coat; *h'* shall I put it on? 349
3 my feet; *h'* shall I defile them? "
7: 1 *H'* beautiful are thy feet with 4100
6 *H'* fair and *h'* pleasant art thou,
Isa 1:21 *H'* is the faithful city become an 349
6:11 Then said I, Lord, *h'* long? And 5704
14: 4 *H'* hath the oppressor ceased! the 349
12 *H'* art thou fallen from heaven, O "
19:11 *h'* say ye unto Pharaoh, I am the son "
20: 6 Assyria: and *h'* shall we escape? "
36: 9 *H'* then wilt thou turn away the face "
37:26 heard long ago, *h'* I have done it;
38: 3 *h'* I have walked before thee in 834
48:11 *h'* should my name be polluted? 349
50: 4 know *h'* to speak a word in season
52: 7 *H'* beautiful upon the mountains 4100
Jer 2:21 *h'* then art thou turned into the 349
23 *H'* canst thou say, I am not polluted,"
3:19 *H'* shall I put thee among the "
4:14 *H'* long shall thy vain thoughts 5704
21 *H'* long shall I see the standard, "
5: 7 *H'* shall I pardon thee for this? 335
8: 8 *H'* do ye say, We are wise, and the 349
9: 7 *h'* shall I do for the daughter of my "
19 *H'* are we spoiled! we are greatly "
12: 4 *H'* long shall the land mourn, and 5704
5 *h'* canst thou contend with horses? 349
5 *h'* wilt thou do in the swelling of "
15: 5 shall go aside to ask *h'* thou doest?*
22:23 *h'* gracious shalt thou be when 4100
23:26 *H'* long shall this be in the heart 5704
31:22 *H'* long wilt thou go about, O thou "
36:17 *H'* didst thou write all these words 349
46:13 *h'* Nebuchadrezzar king of Babylon
47: 6 *h'* long will it be ere thou be quiet?5704
7 *H'* can it be quiet, seeing the Lord 349
Jer 48:14 *H'* say ye, We are mighty and strong349
17 *H'* is the strong staff broken, and "
39 howl, saying, *H'* is it broken down! "
39 *h'* hath Moab turned the back "
49:25 *H'* is the city of praise not left, the "
50:23 *H'* is the hammer of the whole earth "
23 *h'* is Babylon become a desolation "
51:41 *H'* is Sheshach taken! and "
41 *h'* is the praise of the whole earth *
41 *h'* is Babylon...an astonishment 349
La 1: 1 *H'* doth the city sit solitary, that "
1 *h'* is she become as a widow! she that
1 provinces, *h'* is she become tributary!
2: 1 *H'* hath the Lord covered the 349
4: 1 *H'* is the gold become dim!
1 *h'* is the fine gold changed!
Eze 14:21 *H'* much more when I send 637
15: 5 *h'* much less shall it be meet
16:30 *H'* weak is thine heart, saith the 4100
26:17 *H'* art thou destroyed, that wast 349
33:10 in them, *h'* should we then live? "
Da 4: 3 *H'* great are his signs! and 4101
3 and how mighty are his wonders!
8:13 *H'* long shall be the vision 5704
10:17 For *h'* can the servant of this my 1963
12: 6 *H'* long shall it be to the end of 5704
Ho 8: 5 *h'* long will it be ere they attain to 349
11: 8 *H'* shall I give thee up, Ephraim? "
8 *h'* shall I deliver thee, Israel? "
8 *h'* shall I make thee as Adinah? 349
8 *h'* shall I set thee as Zeboim? mine
Joe 1:18 *H'* do the beasts groan! the 4100
Ob 5 *h'* art thou cut off! would they not 349
6 *H'* are the things of Esau searched "
6 *h'* are his hidden things sought up!
Mic 2: 4 *h'* hath he removed it from me! 349
Hab 1: 2 O Lord, *h'* long shall I cry, and 5704
2: 6 that which is not his! *h'* long?
Zep 2:15 *h'* is she become a desolation, a 349
Hag 2: 3 and *h'* do ye see it now? is it not 4100
Zec 1:12 *h'* long wilt thou not have mercy 5704
9:17 For *h'* great is his goodness, and 4100
17 and *h'* great is his beauty!
M't 6:23 *h'* great is that darkness! *4214*
28 lilies of the field, *h'* they grow; *4459*
7: 4 Or *h'* wilt thou say to thy brother, "
11 *h'* to give good gifts unto your
11 *h'* much more shall your Father *4214*
10:19 thought *h'* or what ye shall speak: *4459*
25 *h'* much more shall they call them *4214*
12: 4 *H'* he entered into the house of *4459*
5 *h'* that on the sabbath days the
12 *H'* much then is a man better *4214*
14 him, *h'* they might destroy him. *3704*
29 *h'* shall then his kingdom stand? *4459*
29 *h'* can one enter into a strong man's"
34 *h'* can ye, being evil, speak good "
15:34 them, *H'* many loaves have ye? *4214*
16: 9,10 and *h'* many baskets ye took up? "
11 *H'* is it that ye do not understand *4459*
12 *H'* that he bade them not beware
21 *h'* that he must go unto Jerusalem,
17:17 *h'* long shall I be with you? *2193*
17 *h'* long shall I suffer you? bring *4219*
18:12 *H'* think ye? if a man have an *5101*
21 Lord, *h'* oft shall my brother sin *4212*
21:20 *H'* soon is the fig tree withered *4459*
22:12 *h'* camest thou in hither not having"
15 *h'* they might entangle him in his *3704*
43 *H'* then doth David in spirit call *4459*
45 then call him Lord, *h'* is he his son? "
23:33 *h'* can ye escape the damnation "
37 *h'* often would I have gathered thy
26:54 *h'* then shall the scriptures be *4459*
27:13 not *h'* many things they witness *4214*
M'r 2:16 *H'* is it that he eateth and *5101
26 *H'* he went into the house of God *4459*
3: 6 him, *h'* they might destroy him. *3704*
23 *H'* can Satan cast out Satan? *4459*
4:13 *h'* then will ye know all parables? "
27 and grow up, he knoweth not *h'*. *5613*
40 *h'* is it that ye have no faith? *4459
5:16 *h'* it befell to him that was possessed"
19 *h'* great things the Lord hath done*3745*
20 *h'* great things Jesus had done for "
6:38 *H'* many loaves have ye? go and *4214*
8: 5 *H'* many loaves have ye? And they"
19,20 *h'* many baskets full of fragments"
21 *H'* is it that ye do not understand?*4459*
9:12 *h'* it is written of the Son of man,
19 *h'* long shall I be with you? *2193*
19 *h'* long shall I suffer you? bring
21 *H'* long is it ago since this came *4214*
10:23 *H'* hardly shall they that have *4459*
24 *h'* hard is it for them that trust in "
11:18 sought *h'* they might destroy him: "
12:26 *h'* in the bush God spake unto *5613*
35 *H'* say the scribes that Christ is *4459*
41 *h'* the people cast money into the "
14: 1 *h'* they might take him by craft, "
11 *h'* he might conveniently betray "
15: 4 *h'* many things they witness *4214*
Lu 1:34 *H'* shall this be, seeing I know not*4459*
58 *h'* the Lord had shewed great *3754*
62 *h'* he would have him called. *5101*
2:49 them, *H'* is it that ye sought me? "
6: 4 *H'* he went into the house of God, *5613*
42 *h'* canst thou say to thy brother, "
7:22 *h'* that the blind see, the lame *3754*
8:18 Take heed therefore *h'* ye hear: *4459*
39 *h'* great things God hath done *3745*
39 *h'* great things Jesus had done "
47 *h'* she was healed immediately. *5613*
9:41 *h'* long shall I be with you, *2193*
10:26 written in the law? *h'* readest thou?*4459*
11:13 *h'* to give good gifts unto your

Lu 11:13 h' much more shall your heavenly 4214
18 h' shall his kingdom stand? 4459
12:11 h' or what thing ye shall answer, "
24 h' much more are ye better than 4214
27 Consider the lilies h' they grow: 4459
28 h' much more will he clothe you, 4214
50 and h' am I straitened till it be 4459
56 h' is it that ye do not discern this "
13:34 h' often would I have gathered 4212
14: 7 h' they chose out the chief rooms; 4459
15:17 H' many hired servants of my 4214
16: 2 H' is it that I hear this of thee? *5101
5 H' much owest thou unto my lord?4214
7 another, And h' much owest thou? "
18:24 H' hardly shall they that have 4459
19:15 h' much every man had gained by*5101
20:41 H' say they that Christ is David's 4459
44 him Lord, h' is he then his son? "
21: 5 h' it was adorned with goodly 3754
22: 2 scribes sought h' they might kill 4459
4 h' he might betray him unto them. "
61 h' he had said unto him, Before 5613
23:55 sepulchre, and h' his body was laid."
24: 6 h' he spake unto you when he was "
20 h' the chief priests and our rulers 3704
35 and h' he was known of them in 5613
Joh 3: 4 H' can a man be born when he is 4459
9 unto him, H' can these things be? "
12 h' shall ye believe, if I tell you of "
4: 1 h' the Pharisees had heard that 3754
9 H' is it that thou, being a Jew, 4459
5:44 H' can ye believe, which receive "
47 h' shall ye believe my words? "
6:42 h' is it then that he saith, I came "
52 H' can this man give us of his flesh "
7:15 H' knoweth this man letters, "
8:33 h' sayest thou, Ye shall be made "
9:10 him, H' were thine eyes opened? "
15 him h' he had received his sight. "
16 H' can a man that is a sinner do "
19 blind? h' then doth he now see? "
26 to thee? h' opened he thine eyes? "
10:24 H' long dost thou make us to 2193
11:36 the Jews, Behold h' he loved him! 4459
12:19 Perceive ye h' ye prevail nothing? 3754
34 h' sayest thou, The Son of man 4459
14: 5 goest; and h' can we know the way?"
9 h' sayest thou then, Shew us the "
22 h' is it that thou wilt manifest *5101
28 h' I said unto you, I go away, and 3754
Acts 2: 8 h' hear we every man in our own 4459
4:21 nothing h' they might punish them,"
5: 9 H' is it that ye have agreed 5101
7:25 h' that God by his hand would "
8:31 H' can I, except some man should4459
9:13 h' much evil he hath done to thy 3745
16 him h' great things he must suffer "
27 h' he had seen the Lord in the way,4459
27 and h' he had preached boldly at "
10:28 h' that it is an unlawful thing for 5613
38 H' God anointed Jesus of Nazareth"
11:13 h' he had seen an angel in his 4459
16 h' that he said, John indeed 5613
12:14 h' Peter stood before the gate. *
17 h' the Lord had brought him out 4459
13:32 h' that the promise which was "
14:27 h' he had opened the door of faith "
15: 7 h' that a good while ago God made "
14 h' God at the first did visit the 2531
36 of the Lord, and see h' they do. 4459
20:20 And h' I kept back nothing that 5613
35 h' that so labouring ye ought to "
35 h' he said, It is more blessed to 3754
21:20 h' many thousands of Jews there 4214
23:30 h' that the Jews laid wait for the *
Ro 3: 6 h' then shall God judge the world?4459
4:10 H' was it then reckoned? when "
6: 2 H' shall we, that are dead to sin, * "
7: 1 h' that the law hath dominion over "
18 h' to perform that which is good *
8:32 h' shall he not with him also freely4459
10:14 H' then shall they call on him in "
14 h' shall they believe in him of whom"
14 h' shall they hear without a "
15 h' shall they preach, except they 5618
15 H' beautiful are the feet of them "
11: 2 h' he maketh intercession to God 5613
12 h' much more their fulness? 4214
24 h' much more shall these, which "
33 h' unsearchable are his judgments, 5613
1Co 1:26 h' that not many wise men after "
3:10 heed h' he buildeth thereupon. 4459
6: 3 h' much more things that pertain 3386
7:16 or h' knowest thou, O man, 5101
32 Lord, h' he may please the Lord: 4459
33 world, h' he may please his wife. "
34 h' she may please her husband. "
10: 1 h' that all our fathers were under "
14: 7 h' shall it be known what is piped 4459
9 h' shall it be known what is spoken?"
16 h' shall he that occupieth the room "
26 H' is it then, brethren? when ye *5101
15: 3 h' that Christ died for our sins "
12 h' say some among you that there 4459
35 H' are the dead raised up? and "
2Co 3: 8 H' shall not the ministration of the"
7:15 h' with fear and trembling ye 5613
8: 2 H' that in a great trial of affliction "
12: 4 H' that he was caught up into "
13: 5 h' that Jesus Christ is in you, *
Ga 1:13 h' that beyond measure I persecuted "
4: 9 h' turn ye again to the weak and 4459
13 h' through infirmity of the flesh *3754
6:11 Ye see h' large a letter I have 4080
Eph 3: 3 H' that by revelation he made "
6:21 may know my affairs, and h' I do, 5101

Ph'p 1: 8 h' greatly I long after you all in 5613
2:23 as I shall see h' it will go with me. 4012
4:12 h' to be abased, and I know how to "
Col 4: 6 h' ye ought to answer every man. 4459
1Th 1: 9 h' ye turned to God from idols to "
2:10 God also, h' holily and justly and 5613
11 h' we exhorted and comforted and "
4: 1 h' ye ought to walk and to please 4459
4 know h' to possess his vessel in "
2Th 3: 7 know h' ye ought to follow us: 4459
1Ti 3: 5 know not h' to rule his own house, "
5 h' shall he take care of the church 4459
15 h' thou oughtest to behave thyself "
2Ti 1:18 h' many things he ministered unto 3745
Ph'm 16 me, but h' much more unto thee, 4214
19 h' thou owest unto me even thine 3754
Heb 2: 3 H' shall we escape, if we neglect 4459
7: 4 consider h' great this man was, 4080
8: 6 by h' much also he is the mediator 3745
9:14 H' much more shall the blood of 4214
10:29 Of h' much sorer punishment, 4214
12:17 For ye know h' that afterward, *3754
Jas 2:22 h' faith wrought with his works, * "
24 h' that by works a man is justified,*
3: 5 h' great a matter a little fire 2245
2Pe 2: 9 knoweth h' to deliver the godly out
1Jo 3:17 h' dwelleth the love of God in him? 4459
4:20 h' can he love God whom he hath * "
Jude 5 h' that the Lord, having saved the
18 H' that they told you there should
Re 2: 2 h' thou canst not bear them which*3754
3: 3 h' thou hast received and heard, 4459
6:10 H' long, O Lord, holy and 2193
18: 7 H' much she hath glorified herself,3745

howbeit
J'g 4:17 H' Sisera fled away on his feet to the
11:28 H' the king of the children of Ammon
16:22 H' the hair of his head began to grow
18:29 h' the name of the city was Laish 199
21:18 H' we may not give them wives of our
Ru 3:12 h' there is a kinsman nearer than I.
1Sa 8: 9 h' yet protest solemnly unto them 389
2Sa 2:23 H' he refused to turn aside: wherefore
12:14 H', because by this deed thou hast 657
13:14 H' he would not hearken unto her
25 h' he would not go, but blessed him.
23:19 h' he attained not unto the first three.
1Ki 2:15 h' the kingdom is turned about, and is
10: 7 H' I believed not the words, until I
11:13 H' I will not rend away all the 7535
22 Nothing: h' let me go in any wise.
34 H' I will not take the whole kingdom
2Ki 3:25 h' the slingers went about it, and
8:10 h' the Lord hath shewed me that he
10:29 H' from the sins of Jeroboam the son
12:13 H' there were not made for the house*
14: 4 H' the high places were not taken
15:35 H' the high places were not removed:
17:29 H' every nation made gods of their
40 H' they did not hearken, but they did
22: 7 H' there was no reckoning made with
1Ch 11:21 h' he attained not to the first three.
28: 4 H' the Lord God of Israel chose me
2Ch 9: 6 H' I believed not their words, until I
18:34 h' the king of Israel stayed himself up
20:33 H' the high places were not taken
21: 7 H' the Lord would not destroy the
20 H' they buried him in the city of *
24: 5 H' the Levites hastened it not.
27: 2 h' he entered not into the temple of
32:31 H' in the business of the 3651
Ne 9:33 H' thou art just in all that is brought
13: 2 h' our God turned the curse into a
Job 30:24 H' he will not stretch out his hand to*
Isa 10: 7 H' he meaneth not so, neither doth his
Jer 44: 4 H' I sent unto you all my servants the
M't 17:21 H' this kind goeth not out but by*
M'r 5:19 H' Jesus suffered him not, but saith*
7: 7 H' in vain do they worship me, *
Joh 6:23 H' there came other boats from 1161
7:13 H' no man spake openly of him 3305
27 H' we know this man whence he is:235
11:13 H' Jesus spake of his death: but they*
16:13 H' when he, the Spirit of truth, is
Ac 4: 4 H' many of them which heard the*
7:48 H' the most High dwelleth not in 235
14:20 H', as the disciples stood round *
17:34 H' certain men clave unto him, and*
27:26 H' we must be cast upon a certain
28: 6 H' they looked when he should have*
1Co 2: 6 H' we speak wisdom among them
8: 7 H' there is not in every man that 235
14: 2 h' in the spirit he speaketh mysteries.*
20 h' in malice be ye children, but in 235
15:46 H' that was not first which is
2Co 11:21 H' whereinsoever any is bold, *
Ga 4: 8 H' then, when ye know not God, 235
1Ti 1:16 h' for this cause I obtained mercy,
Heb 3:16 h' not all that came out of Egypt * "

howl See also HOWLED; HOWLING.
Isa 13: 6 H' ye; for the day of the Lord ‡3213
14:31 H', O gate; cry, O city; thou, ‡ "
15: 2 Moab shall h' over Nebo, and ‡‡ "
3 every one shall h', weeping ‡‡ "
16: 7 h' for Moab, every one shall h': ‡ "
23: 1 H', ye ships of Tarshish; for it ‡ "
6 h', ye inhabitants of the isle. ‡ "
14 H', ye ships of Tarshish, for your ‡ "
52: 5 rule over them make them to h', ‡ "
65:14 and shall h' for vexation of spirit. ‡ "
Jer 4: 8 you with sackcloth, lament and h': ‡ "
25:34 H', ye shepherds, and cry; and ‡ "
47: 2 the inhabitants of the land shall h'.‡ "
48:20 h' and cry; tell ye it in Arnon, ‡ "
31 Therefore will I h' for Moab, and ‡ "

Jer 48:39 They shall h', saying, How is it ‡3213
49: 3 H', O Heshbon, for Ai is spoiled: ‡ "
51: 8 fallen and destroyed: h' for her: ‡ "
Eze 21:12 Cry and h', son of man: for it ‡ "
30: 2 Thus saith the Lord God; H' ye, ‡ "
Joe 1: 5 and h', all ye drinkers of wine, ‡ "
11 h', O ye vinedressers, for the ‡ "
13 h', ye ministers of the altar; come‡ "
Mic 1: 8 I will wail and h', I will go stripped ‡ "
Zep 1:11 H', ye inhabitants of Maktesh, ‡ "
Zec 11: 2 H', fir tree; for the cedar is fallen; ‡ "
2 h', O ye oaks of Bashan; for the "
Jas 5: 1 weep and h' for your miseries that 3649

howled
Ho 7:14 when they h' upon their beds: *3213

howling See also HOWLINGS.
De 32:10 and in the waste h' wilderness; he 3214
Isa 15: 8 Moab; the h' thereof unto Eglaim,‡3213
8 and the h' thereof unto Beer-elim.‡ "
Jer 25:36 an h' of the principal of the flock, "
Zep 1:10 and an h' from the second, and ‡ "
Zec 11: 3 voice of the h' of the shepherds; ‡ "

howlings
Am 8: 3 songs of the temple shall be h' ‡3213

howsoever
J'g 19:20 h' let all thy wants lie upon me; 7535
2Sa 18:22 h', let me, I pray thee, also *1961,4101
23 But h', said he, let me run. And he*
Zep 3: 7 be cut off, h' I punished them: *3605,834

Hozeh See COL-HOZEH.

huge
2Ch 16: 8 and the Lubims a h' host, with 7230

Hukkok (*huk'-kok*) See also HELKATH; HUKOK.
Jos 19:34 and goeth out from thence to H', 2712

Hukok (*hu'-kok*) See also HUKKOK.
1Ch 6:75 And H' with her suburbs, and 2712

Hul (*hul*)
Ge 10:23 Uz, and H', and Gether, and Mash.2343
1Ch 1:17 and Aram, Uz, and H', and Gether, "

Huldah (*hul'-dah*)
2Ki 22:14 went unto H' the prophetess, the 2468
2Ch 34:22 went to H' the prophetess, the "

humble See also HUMBLED; HUMBLETH.
Ex 10: 3 long wilt thou refuse to h' thyself 6031
De 8: 2 to h' thee, and to prove thee, "
16 that he might h' thee, and that he "
J'g 19:24 and h' ye them, and do with them "
2Ch 7:14 If my people,...shall h' themselves,3665
34:27 thou didst h' thyself before God, "
Job 22:29 and he shall save the h' 7807,5869
Ps 9:12 he forgetteth not the cry of the h'. *6041
10:12 up thine hand: forget not the h'. * "
17 hast heard the desire of the h': * "
34: 2 the h' shall hear thereof, and be * "
69:32 The h' shall see this, and be glad * "
Pr 6: 3 go, h' thyself, and make sure thy 7511
16:19 Better it is to be of an h' spirit *8213
29:23 but honour shall uphold the h' in *8217
Isa 57:15 that is of a contrite and h' spirit, "
15 to revive the spirit of the h', and "
Jer 13:18 the queen, H' yourselves, sit down:8213
M't 18: 4 Whosoever therefore shall h' 5013
23:12 and he that shall h' himself shall "
2Co 12:21 my God will h' me among you, "
Jas 4: 6 but giveth grace unto the h'. 5011
10 H' yourselves in the sight of the 5013
1Pe 5: 5 proud, and giveth grace to the h'. 5011
6 H' yourselves therefore under 5013

humbled See also HUMBLEDST.
Le 26:41 their uncircumcised hearts be h', 3665
De 8: 3 And he h' thee, and suffered thee 6031
21:14 her, because thou hast h' her. "
22:24 he hath h' his neighbour's wife: "
29 because he hath h' her, he may not "
2Ki 22:19 and thou hast h' thyself before *3665
2Ch 12: 6 Israel and the king h' themselves; "
7 Lord saw that they h' themselves: "
7 saying, They have h' themselves; "
12 And when he h' himself, the wrath "
30:11 and of Zebulun h' themselves, and "
32:26 Hezekiah h' himself for the pride "
33:12 h' himself greatly before the "
19 graven images, before he was h': "
23 And h' not himself before the Lord, "
23 Manasseh his father had h' himself;"
36:12 h' not himself before Jeremiah "
Ps 35:13 I h' my soul with fasting; and *6031
Isa 2:11 The lofty looks of man shall be h',*8213
5:15 and the mighty man shall be h', "
15 the eyes of the lofty shall be h': "
10:33 down, and the haughty shall be h'.*"
Jer 44:10 They are not h' even unto this 1792
La 3:20 remembrance, and is h' in me. *7743
Eze 22:10 thee have they h' her that was set 6031
11 another in thee hath h' his sister, "
Da 5:22 Belshazzar, hast not h' thine heart,8214
Ph'p 2: 8 he h' himself, and became obedient 5013

humbledst
2Ch 34:27 and h' thyself before me, and *3665

humbleness
Col 3:12 kindness, h' of mind, meekness, *5012

humbleth
1Ki 21:29 how Ahab h' himself before me? 3665
29 because he h' himself before me, "
Ps 10:10 He croucheth, and h' himself, *7817
113: 6 Who h' himself to behold the 8213
Isa 2: 9 and the great man h' himself: * "
Lu 14:11 that h' himself shall be exalted. 5013
18:14 that h' himself shall be exalted. "

humbly
2Sa 16: 4 I h' beseech thee that I may find *7812
Mic 6: 8 love mercy, and to walk h' with 6800
humiliation
Ac 8:33 In his h' his judgment was taken 5014
humility
Pr 15:33 wisdom; and before honour is h'. 6038
18:12 haughty, and before honour is h'. "
22: 4 By h' and the fear of the Lord are "
Ac 20:19 Serving the Lord with all h' of *5012
Col 2:18 your reward in a voluntary h' and "
23 and h', and neglecting of the body; "
1Pe 5: 5 another and be clothed with h': "
Humtah (*hum'-tah*)
Jos 15:54 And H', and Kirjath-arba, which 2547
hundred See also HUNDREDFOLD; HUNDREDS.
Ge 5: 3 Adam lived an h' and thirty years. 3967
4 begotten Seth were eight h' years: "
5 lived were nine h' and thirty years: "
6 And Seth lived an h' and five years, "
7 Enos eight h' and seven years, "
8 were nine h' and twelve years: "
10 Cainan eight h' and fifteen years, "
11 Enos were nine h' and five years: "
13 Mahalaleel eight h' and forty years, "
14 Cainan were nine h' and ten years: "
16 Jared eight h' and thirty years, "
17 were eight h' ninety and five years: "
18 Jared lived an h' sixty and two "
19 he begat Enoch eight h' years, "
20 were nine h' sixty and two years: "
22 he begat Methuselah three h' years, "
23 were three h' sixty and five years: "
25 Methuselah lived an h' eighty and "
26 seven h' eighty and two years, "
27 were nine h' sixty and nine years: "
28 Lamech lived an h' eighty and two "
30 Noah five h' ninety and five years, "
31 seven h' seventy and seven years: "
32 And Noah was five h' years old: "
6: 3 his days shall be an h' and twenty "
15 of the ark shall be three h' cubits, "
7: 6 And Noah was six h' years old "
24 upon the earth an h' and fifty days "
8: 3 after the end of the h' and fifty days "
9:28 flood three h' and fifty years. "
29 of Noah nine h' and fifty years: "
11:10 Shem was an h' years old, and "
11 he begat Arphaxad five h' years, "
13 begat Salah four h' and three years, "
15 begat Eber four h' and three years, "
17 begat Peleg four h' and thirty years, "
19 begat Reu two h' and nine years, "
21 begat Serug two h' and seven years. "
23 after he begat Nahor two h' years, "
25 Terah an h' and nineteen years, "
32 Terah were two h' and five years: "
14:14 own house, three h' and eighteen, "
15:13 shall afflict them four h' years; "
17:17 unto him that is an h' years old? "
21: 5 Abraham was an h' years old, "
23: 1 an h' and seven and twenty years "
15 land is worth four h' shekels of "
16 four h' shekels of silver, current "
25: 7 an h' threescore and fifteen years. "
17 an h' and thirty and seven years: "
32: 6 thee, and four h' men with him. "
14 Two h' she goats and twenty he "
14 two h' ewes, and twenty rams, "
33: 1 Esau came, and with him four h' "
19 father, for an h' pieces of money. "
35:28 Isaac were an h' and fourscore "
45:22 gave three h' pieces of silver, "
47: 9 of my pilgrimage are an h' and "
28 was an h' forty and seven years. "
50:22 Joseph lived an h' and ten years. "
26 being an h' and ten years old: "
Ex 6:16 were an h' thirty and seven years. "
18 were an h' thirty and three years. "
20 Amram were an h' and thirty and "
12:37 about six h' thousand on foot that "
40 was four h' and thirty years. "
41 end of the four h' and thirty years, "
14: 7 And he took six h' chosen chariots, "
27: 9 fine twined linen of an h' cubits "
11 be hangings of an h' cubits long, "
18 the court shall be an h' cubits, "
30:23 of pure myrrh five h' shekels, and "
23 two h' and fifty shekels, and of "
23 calamus two h' and fifty shekels, "
24 And of cassia five h' shekels, "
38: 9 fine twined linen, an h' cubits: "
11 the hangings were an h' cubits, "
24 seven h' and thirty shekels, after "
25 congregation was an h' talents, "
25 seven h' and threescore and fifteen "
26 old and upward, for six h' thousand "
26 thousand and five h' and fifty men "
27 of the h' talents of silver were cast "
27 an h' sockets of the h' talents, "
28 seven h' seventy and five shekels "
29 two thousand and four h' shekels. "
Le 26: 8 five of you shall chase an h', and an "
8 h' of you shall put ten thousand to "
Nu 1:21 forty and six thousand and five h'. "
23 fifty and nine thousand and three h'. "
25 and five thousand six h' and fifty. "
27 and fourteen thousand and six h'. "
29 fifty and four thousand and four h'. "
31 and seven thousand and four h'. "
33 were forty thousand and five h'. "
35 thirty and two thousand and two h'. "
37 and five thousand and four h'. "
39 and two thousand and seven h'. "
Nu 1:41 forty and one thousand and five h'. 3967
43 fifty and three thousand and four h'. "
46 numbered were six h' thousand and "
46 three thousand and five h' and fifty. "
2: 4 and fourteen thousand and six h'. "
6 fifty and four thousand and four h'. "
8 and seven thousand and four h'. "
9 an h' thousand and fourscore "
9 and four h', throughout their armies. "
11 forty and six thousand and five h'. "
13 fifty and nine thousand and three h'. "
15 forty and five thousand and six h' "
16 of Reuben were an h' thousand "
16 one thousand and four h' and fifty, "
19 were forty thousand and five h'. "
21 thirty and two thousand and two h'. "
23 thirty and five thousand and four h'. "
24 of Ephraim were an h' thousand "
24 and eight thousand and an h', "
26 and two thousand and seven h'. "
28 forty and one thousand and five h'. "
30 fifty and three thousand and four h'. "
31 camp of Dan were an h' thousand "
31 fifty and seven thousand and six h'. "
32 their hosts were six h' thousand "
32 three thousand and five h' and fifty. "
3:22 were seven thousand and five h'. "
28 eight thousand and six h', keeping "
34 were six thousand and two h'. "
43 two thousand two h' and threescore "
46 two h' and threescore and thirteen "
50 a thousand three h' and threescore "
4:36 two thousand seven h' and fifty. "
40 two thousand and six h' and thirty. "
44 were three thousand and two h'. "
48 thousand and five h' and fourscore. "
7:13, 19, 25, 31, 37, 43, 49, 55, 61, 67, 73,
79, 85 an h' and thirty shekels, "
85 two thousand and four h' shekels, "
86 spoons was an h' and twenty shekels. "
11:21 I am, are six h' thousand footmen; "
16: 2 two h' and fifty princes of the "
17 his censer, two h' and fifty censers; "
35 consumed the two h' and fifty men "
49 were fourteen thousand and seven h', "
26: 7 thousand and seven h' and thirty. "
10 fire devoured two h' and fifty men: "
14 twenty and two thousand and two h'. "
18 of them, forty thousand and five h'. "
22 and sixteen thousand and five h'. "
25 and four thousand and three h'. "
27 threescore thousand and five h'. "
34 fifty and two thousand and seven h'. "
37 thirty and two thousand and five h'. "
41 forty and five thousand and six h'. "
43 and four thousand and four h'. "
47 fifty and three thousand and four h'. "
50 forty and five thousand and four h'. "
51 children of Israel, six h' thousand "
51 and a thousand seven h' and thirty. "
31:28 one soul of five h', both of the "
32 six h' thousand and seventy "
36 number three h' thousand and seven "
36 thirty thousand and five h' sheep: "
37 six h' and threescore and fifteen. "
39 were thirty thousand and five h'; "
43 three h' thousand and thirty "
43 seven thousand and five h' sheep, "
45 thirty thousand asses and five h', "
52 thousand seven h' and fifty shekels. "
33:39 Aaron was an h' and twenty and "
De 22:19 amerce him in an h' shekels of "
31: 2 I am an h' and twenty years "
34: 7 Moses was an h' and twenty years "
Jos 7:21 and two h' shekels of silver, "
24:29 died, being an h' and ten years old. "
32 Shechem for an h' pieces of silver: "
J'g 2: 8 died, being an h' and ten years old. "
3:31 slew of the Philistines six h' men "
4: 3 for he had nine h' chariots of iron; "
13 nine h' chariots of iron, and all the "
7: 6 to their mouth, were three h' men: "
7 By the three h' men that lapped will "
8 and retained those three h' men: "
16 he divided the three h' men into "
19 Gideon, and the h' men that were "
22 And the three h' blew the trumpets, "
8: 4 three h' men that were with him, "
10 an h' and twenty thousand men that "
26 a thousand and seven h' shekels of "
11:26 coasts of Arnon, three h' years? "
15: 4 went and caught three h' foxes, "
16: 5 one of us eleven h' pieces of silver "
17: 2 The eleven h' shekels of silver that "
3 restored the eleven h' shekels of "
4 his mother took two h' shekels of "
18:11 six h' men appointed with weapons "
16 six h' men appointed with their "
17 six h' men that were appointed with "
20: 2 four h' thousand footmen that drew "
10 And we will take ten men of an h' "
10 of Israel, and an h' of a thousand, "
15 numbered seven h' chosen men. "
16 there were seven h' chosen men "
17 four h' thousand men that drew "
35 and five thousand and an h' men: "
47 But six h' men turned and fled to "
21:12 four h' young virgins, that had "
1Sa 11: 8 of Israel were three h' thousand, "
13:15 present with him, about six h' men. "
14: 2 with him were about six h' men; "
15: 4 Telaim, two h' thousand footmen, "
17: 7 weighed six h' shekels of iron: "
18:25 an h' foreskins of the Philistines, "
27 slew of the Philistines two h' men; "
22: 2 were with him about four h' men. "
1Sa 23:13 his men, which were about six h', 3967
25:13 up after David about four h' men; "
13 and two h' abode by the stuff. "
18 made haste, and took two h' loaves, "
18 corn, and an h' clusters of raisins, "
18 and two h' cakes of figs, and laid "
27: 2 he passed over with the six h' men "
30: 9 David went, he and the six h' men "
10 David pursued, he and four h' men: "
10 for two h' abode behind, which were "
17 four h' young men, which rode upon "
21 And David came to the two h' men, "
2Sa 2:31 three h' and threescore men died. "
3:14 I espoused to me for an h' foreskins "
8: 4 chariots, and seven h' horsemen, "
4 reserved of them for an h' chariots. "
10:18 slew the men of seven h' chariots "
14:26 hair of his head at two h' shekels "
15:11 with Absalom went two h' men out "
18 six h' men which came after him "
16: 1 upon them two h' loaves of bread, "
1 and an h' bunches of raisins, "
1 and an h' of summer fruits, and a "
21:16 weighed three h' shekels of brass "
23: 8 lift up his spear against eight h', "
18 lifted up his spear against three h', "
24: 9 Israel eight h' thousand valiant men "
9 of Judah were five h' thousand men. "
1Ki 4:23 and an h' sheep, beside harts, and "
5:16 three thousand and three h', which "
6: 1 in the four h' and eightieth year "
7: 2 the length thereof was an h' cubits, "
20 the pomegranates were two h' in "
42 And four h' pomegranates for the "
8:63 an h' and twenty thousand sheep. "
9:23 five h' and fifty, which bare rule "
28 gold, four h' and twenty talents, "
10:10 an h' and twenty talents of gold, "
14 six h' threescore and six talents of "
16 six h' shekels of gold went to one "
16 made two h' targets of beaten gold: "
17 he made three h' shields of beaten "
26 had a thousand and four h' chariots, "
29 of Egypt for six h' shekels of silver, "
29 and an horse for an h' and fifty: and "
11: 3 he had seven h' wives, princesses, "
3 and three h' concubines: and his "
12:21 an h' and fourscore thousand chosen "
18: 4 Obadiah took an h' prophets, and "
13 how I hid an h' men of the Lord's "
19 prophets of Baal four h' and fifty, "
19 the prophets of the groves four h', "
22 prophets are four h' and fifty men. "
20:15 and they were two h' and thirty two: "
29 an h' thousand footmen in one day. "
22: 6 the prophets together, about four h' "
2Ki 3: 4 of Israel an h' thousand lambs, and "
4 an h' thousand rams, with the wool. "
26 he took with him seven h' men "
4:43 should I set this before an h' men? "
14:13 unto the corner gate, four h' cubits. "
18:14 of Judah three h' talents of silver "
19:35 an h' fourscore and five thousand: "
23:33 a tribute of an h' talents of silver, "
1Ch 4:42 of the sons of Simeon, five h' men, "
5:18 thousand seven h' and threescore, "
21 of sheep two h' and fifty thousand, "
21 and of men an h' thousand. "
7: 2 two and twenty thousand and six h'. "
9 was twenty thousand and two h'. "
11 thousand and two h' soldiers, fit to "
8:40 sons, and sons' sons, an h' and fifty. "
9: 6 their brethren, six h' and ninety. "
9 generations, nine h' and fifty and six. "
13 and seven h' and threescore; "
22 in the gates were two h' and twelve. "
11:11 up his spear against three h' slain "
20 lifting up his spear against three h', "
12:14 one of the least was over an h', and "
24 six thousand and eight h', ready "
25 the war, seven thousand and one h'. "
26 of Levi four thousand and six h'. "
27 were three thousand and seven h'; "
30 twenty thousand and eight h', "
32 the heads of them were two h'; and "
35 and eight thousand and six h'. "
37 battle, an h' and twenty thousand. "
15: 5 and his brethren an h' and twenty: "
6 and his brethren two h' and twenty: "
7 his brethren an h' and thirty: "
8 the chief, and his brethren two h': "
10 his brethren an h' and twelve, and "
18: 4 but reserved of them an h' chariots. "
21: 3 Lord make his people an h' times "
5 an h' thousand men that drew "
5 Judah was four h' threescore and "
25 for the place six h' shekels of gold "
22:14 Lord an h' thousand talents of gold, "
25: 7 was two h' fourscore and eight. "
26:30 of valour, a thousand and seven h', "
32 thousand and seven h' chief fathers, "
29: 7 and one h' thousand talents of iron. "
2Ch 1:14 had a thousand and four h' chariots, "
17 a chariot for six h' shekels of silver, "
17 and an horse for an h' and fifty: "
2: 2 three thousand and six h' to oversee "
17 were found an h' and fifty thousand "
17 and three thousand and six h'. "
18 thousand and six h' overseers to set "
3: 4 the height was an h' and twenty: "
8 gold, amounting to six h' talents. "
16 and made an h' pomegranates, and "
4: 8 And he made an h' basons of gold. "
13 four h' pomegranates on the two "
5:12 an h' and twenty priests sounding "
7: 5 an h' and twenty thousand sheep: "

2Ch 8:10 officers, even two h' and fifty, that 3967
18 four h' and fifty talents of gold, "
9: 9 an h' and twenty talents of gold, "
13 six h' and threescore and six talents "
15 Solomon made two h' targets of "
15 six h' shekels of beaten gold went "
16 three h' shields made he of beaten "
16 three h' shekels of gold went to one "
11: 1 an h' and fourscore thousand "
12: 3 With twelve h' chariots, and "
13: 3 even four h' thousand chosen men: "
3 with eight h' thousand chosen men, "
17 Israel five h' thousand chosen men. "
14: 8 out of Judah three h' thousand; "
8 two h' and fourscore thousand: "
9 thousand, and three h' chariots; "
15:11 brought, seven h' oxen and seven "
17:11 seven thousand and seven h' rams, "
11 thousand and seven h' he goats. "
14 men of valour three h' thousand. "
15 him two h' and fourscore thousand. "
16 him two h' thousand mighty men "
17 bow and shield two h' thousand. "
18 an h' and fourscore thousand ready "
18: 5 together of prophets four h' men, "
24:15 an h' and thirty years old was he "
25: 5 three h' thousand choice men, able "
6 hired...an h' thousand mighty men "
6 of Israel for an h' talents of silver. "
9 the h' talents which I have given to "
23 to the corner gate, four h' cubits. "
26:12 valour were two thousand and six h'. "
13 army, three h' thousand and seven "
13 thousand and five h', that made war "
27: 5 same year an h' talents of silver, "
28: 6 an h' and twenty thousand in one "
8 of their brethren two h' thousand, "
29:32 an h' rams, and two h' lambs: "
33 consecrated things were six h' oxen "
35: 8 thousand and six h' small cattle, "
8 small cattle, and three h' oxen. "
9 small cattle, and five h' oxen. "
36: 3 condemned the land in an h' talents "
Ezr 1:10 of a second sort four h' and ten, "
11 were five thousand and four h'. "
2: 3 thousand an h' seventy and two. "
4 Shephatiah, three h' seventy and "
5 of Arah, seven h' seventy and five. "
6 two thousand eight h' and twelve. "
7 a thousand two h' fifty and four. "
8 of Zattu, nine h' forty and five. "
9 of Zaccai, seven h' and threescore. "
10 children of Bani, six h' forty and two. "
11 of Bebai, six h' twenty and three. "
12 a thousand two h' twenty and two. "
13 of Adonikam, six h' sixty and six. "
15 of Adin, four h' fifty and four. "
17 of Bezai, three h' twenty and three. "
18 children of Jorah, an h' and twelve. "
19 of Hashum, two h' twenty and three. "
21 Beth-lehem, an h' twenty and three. "
23 of Anathoth, an h' twenty and eight. "
25 Beeroth, seven h' and forty and three. "
26 and Gaba, six h' twenty and one. "
27 of Michmas, an h' twenty and two. "
28 and Ai, two h' twenty and three. "
30 of Magbish, an h' fifty and six. "
31 a thousand two h' fifty and four. "
32 of Harim, three h' and twenty. "
33 and Ono, seven h' twenty and five. "
34 of Jericho, three h' forty and five. "
35 three thousand and six h' and thirty. "
36 of Jeshua, nine h' seventy and three. "
38 a thousand two h' forty and seven. "
41 of Asaph, an h' twenty and eight. "
42 Shobai, in all an h' thirty and nine. "
58 were three h' ninety and two. "
60 of Nekoda, six h' fifty and two. "
64 thousand three h' and threescore. "
65 thousand three h' thirty and seven: "
65 two h' singing men and singing "
66 horses were seven h' thirty and six; "
66 their mules, two h' forty and five; "
67 their camels, four h' thirty and five; "
67 six thousand seven h' and twenty. "
69 silver, and one h' priests' garments. "
6:17 an h' bullocks, two h' rams, four h' 3969
7:22 Unto an h' talents of silver, "
22 and to an h' measures of wheat, "
22 and to an h' baths of wine, "
22 and to an h' baths of oil, and salt "
8: 3 of the males an h' and fifty. 3967
4 and with him two h' males. "
5 and with him three h' males. "
9 with him two h' and eighteen males. "
10 him an h' and threescore males. "
12 and with him an h' and ten males. "
20 two h' and twenty Nethinims: all of "
26 six h' and fifty talents of silver, "
26 and silver vessels an h' talents, "
26 and of gold an h' talents; "
Ne 5:17 my table an h' and fifty of the Jews "
7: 8 thousand an h' seventy and two. "
9 three h' seventy and two. "
10 of Arah, six h' fifty and two. "
11 thousand and eight h' and eighteen. "
12 a thousand two h' fifty and four. "
13 of Zattu, eight h' forty and five. "
14 of Zaccai, seven h' and threescore. "
15 of Binnui, six h' forty and eight. "
16 of Bebai, six h' twenty and eight. "
17 thousand three h' twenty and two. "
18 six h' threescore and seven. "
20 children of Adin, six h' fifty and five. "
22 Hashum, three h' twenty and eight. "
23 of Bezai, three h' twenty and four. "

Ne 7:24 children of Hariph, an h' and twelve. 3967
26 an h' fourscore and eight. "
27 Anathoth, an h' twenty and eight. "
29 Beeroth, seven h' forty and three. "
30 and Gaba, six h' twenty and one. "
31 Michmas, an h' and twenty and two. "
32 and Ai, an h' twenty and three. "
34 a thousand two h' fifty and four. "
35 of Harim, three h' and twenty. "
36 of Jericho, three h' forty and five. "
37 and Ono, seven h' twenty and one. "
38 three thousand nine h' and thirty. "
39 Jeshua, nine h' seventy and three. "
41 a thousand two h' forty and seven. "
44 of Asaph, an h' forty and eight. "
45 of Shobai, an h' thirty and eight. "
60 were three h' ninety and two. "
62 of Nekoda, six h' forty and two. "
66 thousand three h' and threescore, "
67 thousand three h' thirty and seven: "
67 two h' forty and five singing men "
68 horses, seven h' thirty and six: "
68 their mules, two h' forty and five: "
69 their camels, four h' thirty and five: "
69 thousand seven h' and twenty asses. "
70 five h' and thirty priests' garments. "
71 thousand and two h' pound of silver. "
11: 6 four h' threescore and eight valiant "
8 Sallai, nine h' twenty and eight. "
12 were eight h' twenty and two: "
13 of the fathers, two h' forty and two: "
14 of valour, an h' twenty and eight: "
18 city were two h' fourscore and two: "
19 gates, were an h' seventy and two. "
Es 1: 1 h' and seven and twenty provinces: "
4 days, even an h' and fourscore days "
8: 9 an h' twenty and seven provinces, "
9: 6 Jews slew and destroyed five h' men. "
12 have slain and destroyed five h' men "
15 and slew three h' men at Shushan; "
30 the h' twenty and seven provinces "
Job 1: 3 five h' yoke of oxen, and five h' she "
42:16 this lived Job an h' and forty years, "
Pr 17:10 man than an h' stripes into a fool. "
Ec 6: 3 If a man beget an h' children, and "
8:12 Though a sinner do evil an h' times, "
Ca 8:12 that keep the fruit thereof two h'. "
Isa 37:36 a h' and fourscore and five thousand: "
65:20 the child shall die an h' years old; "
20 sinner being an h' years old shall "
Jer 52:23 upon the network were an h' round "
29 eight h' thirty and two persons: "
30 seven h' forty and five persons: "
30 were four thousand and six h'. "
Eze 4: 5 the days, three h' and ninety days: "
9 three h' and ninety days shalt thou "
40:19 h' cubits eastward and northward. "
23 from gate to gate an h' cubits. "
27 gate toward the south an h' cubits. "
47 an h' cubits long, and an h' cubits "
41:13 the house, an h' cubits long; "
13 the walls thereof, an h' cubits long; "
14 place toward the east, an h' cubits. "
15 and on the other side, an h' cubits, "
42: 2 length of an h' cubits was the north "
8 before the temple were an h' cubits. "
16 measuring reed, five h' reeds, 520
17 the north side, five h' reeds, 3967
18 the south side, five h' reeds, "
19 and measured five h' reeds with the "
20 five h' reeds long, and five h' broad, "
45: 2 for the sanctuary five h' in length, "
2 with five h' in breadth, square round "
15 lamb out of the flock, out of two h', "
48:16 north side four thousand and five h', "
16 south side four thousand and five h', "
16 east side four thousand and five h', "
16 west side four thousand and five h'. "
17 toward the north two h' and fifty, "
17 toward the south two h' and fifty, "
17 toward the east two h' and fifty, "
17 toward the west two h' and fifty. "
30 four thousand and five h' measures. "
32 east side four thousand and five h': "
33 four thousand and five h' measures: "
34 west side four thousand and five h', "
Da 6: 1 kingdom an h' and twenty princes, 3969
8:14 two thousand and three h' days; 3967
12:11 a thousand two h' and ninety days. "
12 three h' and five and thirty days. "
Am 5: 3 out by a thousand shall leave an h', "
3 went forth by an h' shall leave ten, "
M't 18:12 if a man have an h' sheep, and one 1540
28 which owed him an h' pence: "
M'r 4: 8 and some sixty, and some an h'. * "
20 some sixty, and some an h'. * "
6:37 buy two h' pennyworth of bread, 1250
14: 5 sold for more than three h' pence, 5145
Lu 7:41 the one owed five h' pence, and 4001
15: 4 man of you, having an h' sheep, 1540
16: 6 And he said, An h' measures of oil. "
7 he said, An h' measures of wheat. "
Joh 6: 7 Two h' pennyworth of bread is not 1250
12: 5 ointment sold for three h' pence, 5145
19:39 aloes, about an h' pound weight. 1540
21: 8 land, but as it were two h' cubits, 1250
11 great fishes, an h' and fifty and 1540
Ac 1:15 were about an h' and twenty, "
5:36 a number of men, about four h', 5071
7: 6 and entreat them evil four h' years. "
13:20 the space of four h' and fifty years, "
23:23 Make ready two h' soldiers to go 1250
23 and spearmen two h', at the third "
27:37 two h' threescore and sixteen souls. "
Ro 4:19 when he was about an h' years old, 1541
1Co 15: 6 of above five h' brethren at once; 4001

Ga 3:17 was four h' and thirty years after, 5071
Re 7: 4 an h' and forty and four thousand 1540
9:16 were two h' thousand thousand: *3461
11: 3 a thousand two h' and threescore 1250
12: 6 a thousand two h' and threescore "
13:18 number is Six h' threescore and six. 5516
14: 1 him an h' forty and four thousand, 1540
3 the h' and forty and four thousand, "
20 of a thousand and six h' furlongs. 5516
21:17 an h' and forty and four cubits, 1540

hundredfold
Ge 26:12 in the same year an h': 3967,8180
2Sa 24: 3 many soever they be, an h', " 6471
M't 13: 8 some an h', some sixtyfold, some 1540
23 bringeth forth, some an h', some "
19:29 shall receive an h', and shall 1542
M'r 10:30 he shall receive an h' now in this "
Lu 8: 8 sprang up, and bare fruit an h'. "

hundreds
Ex 18:21, 25 rulers of h', rulers of fifties, 3967
Nu 31:14 thousands, and captains over h'. "
48 and captains of h', came near unto "
52 thousands, and of the captains of h'. "
54 the captains of thousands and of h', "
De 1:15 captains over h', and captains over "
1Sa 22: 7 of thousands, and captains of h'; "
29: 2 of the Philistines passed on by h', "
2Sa 18: 1 thousands and captains of h' over "
4 all the people came out by h' and "
2Ki 11: 4 sent and fetched the rulers over h', "
9 captains over the h' did according "
10 the captains over h' did the priest "
15 commanded the captains of the h', "
19 he took the rulers over h', and the "
1Ch 13: 1 the captains of thousands and h', "
26:26 the captains over thousands and h', "
27: 1 and captains of thousands and h', "
28: 1 captains over the h', and the "
29: 6 the captains of thousands and of h', "
2Ch 1: 2 the captains of thousands and of h', "
23: 1 himself, and the captains of h', "
9 to the captains of h' spears, and "
14 the captains of h' that were set "
20 And he took the captains of h', and "
25: 5 captains over h', according to the "
M'r 6:40 in ranks, by h', and by fifties. 1540

hundredth
Ge 7:11 In the six h' year of Noah's life, in 3967
8:13 in the six h' and first year, in the * "
Ne 5:11 also the h' part of the money, and "

hundred thousand See HUNDRED and THOUSAND.

hung See HANGED.

hunger See also HUNGERBITTEN; HUNGERED.
Ex 16: 3 to kill the whole assembly with h'. 7457
De 8: 3 thee, and suffered thee to h', 7456
28:48 in h', and in thirst, and in 7457
32:24 They shall be burnt with h', and "
Ne 9:15 bread from heaven for their h', "
Ps 34:10 young lions do lack, and suffer h': 7456
Pr 19:15 sleep; an idle soul shall suffer h'. "
Isa 49:10 They shall not h' nor thirst; "
Jer 38: 9 he is like to die for h' in the place *7457
42:14 trumpet, nor have h' of bread; 7456
La 2:19 young children, that faint for h' 7457
4: 9 than they that be slain with h': "
Eze 34:29 shall be no more consumed with h' * "
M't 5: 6 Blessed are they which do h' and 3983
Lu 6:21 Blessed are ye that h' now: for ye "
25 you that are full! for ye shall h'. "
15:17 and to spare, and I perish with h'! 3042
Joh 6:35 that cometh to me shall never h'; 3983
Ro 12:20 Therefore if thine enemy h', feed "
1Co 4:11 we both h', and thirst, and are "
11:34 And if any man h', let him eat at * "
2Co 11:27 often, in h' and thirst, in fastings 3042
Re 6: 8 to kill with sword, and with h', * "
7:16 They shall h' no more, neither 3983

hungerbitten
Job 18:12 His strength shall be h', and 7457

hungered See also HUNGRED; HUNGRY.
M't 21:18 as he returned into the city, he h'. 3983
Lu 4: 2 they were ended, he afterward h'. "

hungred See also HUNGERED.
M't 4: 2 nights, he was afterward an h'. *3983
12: 1 his disciples were an h', and began "
3 what David did, when he was an h', "
25:35 I was an h', and ye gave me meat: "
37 when saw we thee an h', and fed "
42 For I was an h', and ye gave me no "
44 Lord, when saw we thee an h', or "
M'r 2:25 when he had need, and was an h', "
Lu 6: 3 David did, when himself was an h', "

hungry See also HUNGERED.
1Sa 2: 5 and they that were h' ceased: 7456
2Sa 17:29 The people is h', and weary, and "
2Ki 7:12 They know that we be h'; therefore "
Job 5: 5 Whose harvest the h' eateth up, "
22: 7 hast withholden bread from the h'. "
24:10 take away the sheaf from the h'; * "
Ps 50:12 If I were h', I would not tell thee: "
107: 5 H' and thirsty, their soul fainted "
9 filleth the h' soul with goodness. "
36 there he maketh the h' to dwell, "
146: 7 which giveth food to the h'. "
Pr 6:30 to satisfy his soul when he is h'; "
25:21 If thine enemy be h', give him bread "
27: 7 to the h' soul every bitter thing is "
Isa 8:21 through it, hardly bestead and h': "
21 that when they shall be h', they "
9:20 snatch on the right hand, and be h'; "
29: 8 be as when an h' man dreameth, "

Isa 32: 6 to make empty the soul of the h·, 7456
44: 12 he is h·, and his strength faileth: "
58: 7 Is it not to deal thy bread to the h·, "
10 if thou draw out thy soul to the h·, "
65: 13 servants shall eat, but ye shall be h·: "
Eze 18: 7, 16 hath given his bread to the h·, "
M'r 11: 12 come from Bethany, he was h·: *3983
Lu 1: 53 He hath filled the h· with good "
Ac 10: 10 And he became very h·, and would 4361
1Co 11: 21 one is h·, and another is drunken. 3983
Ph'p 4: 12 both to be full and to be h·, both "

hunt See also HUNTED; HUNTEST; HUNTETH; HUNTING.
Ge 27: 5 went to the field to h· for venison, 6679
1Sa 26: 20 h· a partridge in the mountains. 7291
Job 38: 39 Wilt thou h· the prey for the lion? 6679
Ps 140: 11 evil shall h· the violent man to "
Pr 6: 26 adulteress will h· for the precious* "
Jer 16: 16 shall h· them from every mountain, "
La 4: 18 They h· our steps, that we cannot "
Eze 13: 18 head of every stature to h· souls! "
18 Will ye h· the souls of my people, "
20 wherewith ye there h· the souls to "
20 even the souls that ye h· to make "
Mic 7: 2 they h· every man his brother with "

hunted
Eze 13: 21 be no more in your hand to be h·; 4686

hunter See also HUNTERS.
Ge 10: 9 was a mighty h· before the Lord: 6718
9 Even as Nimrod the mighty h· "
25: 27 Esau was a cunning h·, a man of "
Pr 6: 5 as a roe from the hand of the h·, "

hunters
Jer 16: 16 and after will I send for many h·, 6719

huntest
1Sa 24: 11 thee; yet thou h· my soul to take it. 6658
Job 10: 16 Thou h· me as a fierce lion: and 6679

hunteth
Le 17: 13 which h· and catcheth any beast *6679

hunting
Ge 27: 30 his brother came in from his h·. 6718
Pr 12: 27 roasteth not that...he took in h·: "

Hupham (*hu'-fam*) See also HUPPIM; HUPHAMITES.
Nu 26: 39 H·, the family of the Huphamites. 2349

Huphamites (*hu'-fam-ites*)
Nu 26: 39 of Hupham, the family of the H·. 2350

Huppah (*hup'-pah*)
1Ch 24: 13 thirteenth to H·, the fourteenth 2647

Huppim (*hup'-pim*) See also HUPHAM.
Ge 46: 21 Rosh, Muppim, and H·, and Ard. 2650
1Ch 7: 12 Shuppim also, and H·, the children "
15 Machir took to wife the sister of H· "

Hur (*hur*)
Ex 17: 10 Moses, Aaron, and H· went up to 2354
12 Aaron and H· stayed up his hands, "
24: 14 behold, Aaron and H· are with you: "
31: 2 the son of Uri, the son of H·, of the "
35: 30 the son of Uri, the son of H·, of the "
38: 22 the son of Uri, the son of H·, of the "
Nu 31: 8 Zur, and H·, and Reba, five kings "
Jos 13: 21 Zur, and H·, and Reba, which were "
1Ki 4: 8 The son of H·, in mount Ephraim:* "
1Ch 2: 19 him Ephrath, which bare him H·. "
20 And H· begat Uri, and Uri begat "
50 were the sons of Caleb the son of H·, "
4: 1 and Carmi, and H·, and Shobal. "
4 are sons of H·, the firstborn of "
2Ch 1: 5 the son of Uri, the son of H·, had "
Ne 3: 9 repaired Rephaiah the son of H·, "

Hurai (*hu'-rahee*) See also HIDDAI.
1Ch 11: 32 H· of the brooks of Gaash, Abiel 2360

Huram (*hu'-ram*) See also HIRAM.
1Ch 8: 5 Gera, and Shephuphan, and H·. 2361
2Ch 2: 3 Solomon sent to H· the king of Tyre, "
11 H· the king of Tyre answered 2438
12 H· said moreover, Blessed be the 2361
13 understanding, of H· my father's, 2438
4: 11 And H· made the pots, and the 2361
11 And H· finished the work that he "
16 did H· his father make to king "
8: 2 cities which H· had restored to 2438
18 And H· sent him by the hands of "
9: 10 And the servants also of H·, and "
21 to Tarshish with the servants of H·: "

Huri (*hu'-ri*)
1Ch 5: 14 Abihail the son of H·, the son of 2359

hurl See also HURLETH; HURLING.
Nu 35: 20 or h· at him by laying of wait, *7993

hurleth
Job 27: 21 as a storm h· him out of his place. *8175

hurling
1Ch 12: 2 in h· stones and shooting arrows out*

hurt See also HURTFUL; HURTING.
Ge 4: 23 and a young man to my h·. *2250
26: 29 That thou wilt do us no h·, as we 7451
31: 7 but God suffered him not to h me. 7489
29 the power of my hand to do you h·: 7451
Ex 21: 22 strive, and h· a woman with child, 5062
35 if one man's ox h· another's, that he "
22: 10 and it die, or be h·, or driven away, 7665
14 ought of his neighbour, and it be h·, "
Nu 16: 15 neither have I h· one of them. 7489
Jos 24: 20 then he will turn and do you h·, * "
1Sa 20: 21 there is peace to thee, and no h·; 1697
24: 9 Behold, David seeketh thy h·? 7451
25: 7 which were with us, we h· them not, 3637
15 good unto us, and we were not h·, "
2Sa 18: 32 rise against thee to do thee h·, 7451
2Ki 14: 10 shouldest thou meddle to thy h·, 7451
2Ch 25: 19 shouldest thou meddle to thine h·, "
Ezr 4: 22 grow to the h· of the kings? 5142
Es 9: 2 hand on such as sought their h·: 7451
Job 35: 8 Thy wickedness may h· a man as thou
Ps 15: 4 He that sweareth to his own h·, 7489
35: 4 to confusion that devise my h·. 7451
26 together that rejoice at mine h·: "
38: 12 that seek my h· speak mischievous "
41: 7 against me do they devise my h·. "
70: 2 put to confusion, that desire my h·. "
71: 13 and dishonour that seek my h·. "
24 unto shame, that seek my h·. "
105: 18 Whose feet they h· with fetters: 6031
Ec 5: 13 for the owners thereof to their h·. 7451
8: 9 ruleth over another to his own h·. "
10: 9 Whoso removeth stones shall be h· 6087
Isa 11: 9 They shall not h· nor destroy in all 7489
27: 3 lest any h· it, I will keep it night 6485
65: 25 They shall not h· nor destroy in all 7489
Jer 6: 14 healed also the h· of the daughter 7667
7: 6 walk after other gods to your h·: 7451
8: 11 healed the h· of the daughter of 7667
21 the h· of the daughter of my people "
21 the daughter of my people am I h·; 7665
10: 19 Woe is me for my h·! my wound is 7667
24: 9 kingdoms of the earth for their h·, *7451
25: 6 hands; and I will do you no h·. 7489
7 works of your hands to your own h·. 7451
38: 4 the welfare of this people, but the h·. "
Da 3: 25 of the fire, and they have no h·; 2257
6: 22 mouths, that they have not h· me: 2255
22 thee, O king, have I done no h·. 2248
23 no manner of h· was found upon 2257
M'r 16: 18 deadly thing, it shall not h· them; 984
Lu 4: 35 he came out of him, and h· him not. "
10: 19 nothing shall by any means h· you. 91
Ac 18: 10 no man shall set on thee to h· thee: *2559
27: 10 will be with h· and much damage, *5196
Re 2: 11 shall not be h· of the second death. 91
6: 6 see thou h· not the oil and the wine. "
7: 2 it was given to h· the earth and the "
3 H· not the earth, neither the sea, "
9: 4 should not h· the grass of the earth, "
10 power was to h· men five months. "
19 had heads, and with them they do h·. "
11: 5 any man will h· them, fire proceedeth "
5 if any man will h· them, he must in "

hurtful
Ezr 4: 15 rebellious city, and h· unto kings 5142
Ps 144: 10 his servant from the h· sword. 7451
1Ti 6: 9 and into many foolish and h· lusts, 983

hurting
1Sa 25: 34 hath kept me back from h· thee. 7489

husband See also HUSBANDMAN; HUSBAND'S; HUSBANDS.
Ge 3: 6 and gave also unto her h· with her; 376
16 and thy desire shall be to thy h·, "
16: 3 gave her to her h· Abram to be his "
29: 32 now therefore my h· will love me. "
34 time will my h· be joined unto me, "
30: 15 matter that thou hast taken my h·? "
18 I have given my maiden to my h·: "
20 now will my h· dwell with me, "
Ex 4: 25 Surely a bloody h· art thou to me. *2860
26 A bloody h· thou art, because of * "
21: 22 as the woman's h· will lay upon 1167
Le 19: 20 is a bondmaid, betrothed to an h·, 376
21: 3 nigh unto him, which hath had no h·; "
7 take a woman put away from her h·: "
Nu 5: 13 and it be hid from the eyes of her h·, "
19 with another instead of thy h·; "
20 aside to another, instead of thy h·, "
20 have lain with thee beside thine h·: "
27 have done trespass against her h·, "
29 aside to another instead of her h·, "
30: 6 had at all an h·, when she vowed, "
7 her h· heard it, and held his peace "
8 if her h· disallowed her on the day "
11 her h· heard it, and held his peace "
12 if her h· hath utterly made them void "
12 her h· hath made them void; "
13 afflict the soul, her h· may establish "
13 it, or her h· may make it void. "
14 if her h· altogether hold his peace "
De 21: 13 and be her h·, and she shall be thy 1167
22: 22 with a woman married to an h·, then "
23 is a virgin be betrothed unto an h·, 376
24: 3 if the latter h· hate her, and write "
3 or if the latter h· die, which took her "
4 former h·, which sent her away, 1167
25: 11 to deliver her h· out of the hand of 376
28: 56 be evil toward the h· of her bosom, "
J'g 13: 6 the woman came and told her h·, "
9 but Manoah her h· was not with her. "
10 haste, and ran, and shewed her h·, "
14: 15 Entice thy h·, that he may declare "
19: 3 And her h· arose, and went after her, "
20: 4 And the Levite, the h· of the woman "
Ru 1: 3 Elimelech Naomi's h· died; and she "
5 was left of her two sons and her h·. "
9 each of you in the house of her h·. "
12 way; for I am too old to have a h·. "
12 I should have an h· also to night, "
2: 11 in law since the death of thine h·: "
1Sa 1: 8 Then said Elkanah her h· to her, "
22 for she said unto her h·, I will not "
23 And Elkanah her h· said unto her, "
2: 19 she came up with her h· to offer "
4: 19 father in law and her h· were dead, "
21 of her father in law and her h·. "
25: 19 But she told not her h· Nabal. "
2Sa 3: 15 and took her from her h·, even from "
16 her h· went with her along weeping "
11: 26 heard that Uriah her h· was dead, "
26 was dead, she mourned for her h·. 1167
14: 5 widow woman, and mine h· is dead. 376
7 shall not leave to my h· neither name "
2Ki 4: 1 Thy servant my h· is dead; and thou "
9 she said unto her h·, Behold now, I "
14 she hath no child, and her h· is old. "
22 And she called unto her h·, and said, "
26 Is it well with thy h·? is it well with "
Pr 12: 4 woman is a crown to her h·: 1167
31: 11 The heart of her h· doth safely trust "
23 Her h· is known in the gates, "
28 her h· also, and he praiseth her. "
Isa 54: 5 For thy Maker is thine h·; the Lord "
Jer 3: 20 treacherously departeth from her h·, "
6: 11 the h· with the wife shall be taken, 376
31: 32 an h· unto them, saith the Lord: 1167
Eze 16: 32 taketh strangers instead of her h·! 376
45 that lotheth her h· and her children; "
44: 25 or for sister that hath had no h·, "
Ho 2: 2 is not my wife, neither am I her h·: "
7 I will go and return to my first h·; "
Joe 1: 8 sackcloth for the h· of her youth. 1167
M't 1: 16 begat Joseph the h· of Mary, of 435
19 Then Joseph her h·, being a just man, "
M'r 10: 12 a woman shall put away her h·, and "
Lu 2: 36 had lived with an h· seven years "
16: 18 her that is put away from her h· "
Joh 4: 16 Go, call thy h·, and come hither. "
17 answered and said, I have no h·. "
17 Thou hast well said, I have no h·: "
18 whom thou now hast is not thy h·: "
Ac 5: 9 which have buried thy h· are at the "
10 her forth, buried her by her h·. "
Ro 7: 2 woman which hath an h· is bound 5220
2 by the law to her h· so long as he 435
2 if the h· be dead, she is loosed from "
2 she is loosed from the law of her h·. "
3 while her h· liveth, she be married "
3 if her h· be dead, she is free from "
1Co 7: 2 let every woman have her own h·. "
3 Let the h· render unto the wife due "
3 likewise also the wife unto the h·. "
4 power of her own body, but the h·: "
4 likewise also the h· hath not power "
10 Let not the wife depart from her h·: "
11 or be reconciled to her h·: and let "
11 and let not the h· put away his wife. "
13 which hath an h· that believeth not, "
14 the unbelieving h· is sanctified by "
14 wife is sanctified by the h·: * "
16 whether thou shalt save thy h·? or "
34 world, how she may please her h·. "
39 by the law as long as her h· liveth; "
39 if her h· be dead, she is at liberty "
2Co 11: 2 for I have espoused you to one h·, "
Ga 4: 27 children than she which hath an h·. "
Eph 5: 23 For the h· is the head of the wife, "
33 wife see that she reverence her h·. "
1Ti 3: 2 the h· of one wife, vigilant, sober, "
Tit 1: 6 the h· of one wife, having faithful "
Re 21: 2 as a bride adorned for her h·. "

husbandman See also HUSBANDMEN.
Ge 9: 20 Noah began to be an h·, and he 376,127
Jer 51: 23 I break in pieces the h· and his yoke 406
Am 5: 16 they shall call the h· to mourning, "
Zec 13: 5 I am no prophet, I am an h·; *5647
Joh 15: 1 true vine, and my Father is the h·. 1092
2Ti 2: 6 The h· that laboureth must be first "
Jas 5: 7 the h· waiteth for the precious fruit "

husbandmen
2Ki 25: 12 the land to be vine dressers and h·. 1461
2Ch 26: 10 h· also, and vine dressers in the 406
Jer 31: 24 h·, and they that go with flocks. "
52: 16 land for vinedressers and for h·. 3009
Joe 1: 11 Be ye ashamed, O ye h·; howl, O 406
M't 21: 33 let it out to h·, and went into a far 1092
34 he sent his servants to the h·, that "
35 the h· took his servants, and beat "
38 when the h· saw the son, they said "
40 what will he do unto those h·? "
41 let out his vineyard unto other h·, "
M'r 12: 1 let it out to h·, and went into a far "
2 he sent to the h· a servant, that he "
2 receive from the h· of the fruit of "
7 those h· said among themselves, "
9 will come and destroy the h·, and "
Lu 20: 9 a vineyard and let it forth to h·, "
10 sent a servant to the h·, that they "
10 the h· beat him, and sent him away "
14 when the h· saw him, they reasoned "
16 shall come and destroy these h·, "

husbandry
2Ch 26: 10 and in Carmel: for he loved h·. 127
1Co 3: 9 with God: ye are God's h·, ye are 1091

husband's
Nu 30: 10 vowed in her h· house, or bound 376
De 25: 5 her h· brother shall go in unto her, 2993
5 perform the duty of an h· brother 2992
7 My h· brother refuseth to raise up 2993
7 perform the duty of my h· brother. 2992
Ru 2: 1 kinsman of her h·, a mighty man 376

husbands
Ru 1: 11 womb, that they may be your h·? 582
13 ye stay for them from having h·? 376
Es 1: 17 they shall despise their h· in their 1167
20 wives shall give to their h· honour, "
Jer 29: 6 and give your daughters to h·, that 582
Eze 16: 45 lothed their h· and their children: "
Joh 4: 18 For thou hast had five h·; and he 435
1Co 14: 35 let them ask their h· at home: for it "
Eph 5: 22 submit yourselves unto your own h·, "
24 be to their own h· in every thing. "
25 H·, love your wives, even as Christ "
Col 3: 18 submit yourselves unto your own h·, "

Col 3:19 H', love your wives, and be not bitter 435
1Ti 3:12 deacons be the h' of one wife, ruling "
Tit 2: 4 love their h', to love their children, 5362
5 obedient to their own h', that the 435
1Pe 3: 1 wives, in subjection to your own h'; "
5 in subjection unto their own h': "
7 Likewise, ye h', dwell with them "

Hushah (*hu'-shah*) See also HUSHATHITE; SHUAH.
1Ch 4: 4 Gedor, and Ezer the father of H'. 2364

Hushai (*hu'-shahee*)
2Sa 15:32 H' the Archite came to meet him 2365
37 So H' David's friend came into the "
16:16 when H' the Archite, David's friend, "
16 that H' said unto Absalom, God "
17 Absalom said to H', Is this thy "
18 H' said unto Absalom, Nay; but "
17: 5 Call now H' the Archite also, and "
6 when H' was come to Absalom, "
7 And H' said unto Absalom, The "
8 For, said H', thou knowest thy "
14 The counsel of H' the Archite is "
15 Then said H' unto Zadok and to "
1Ki 4:16 Baanah the son of H' was in Asher "
1Ch 27:33 and H' the Archite was the king's "

Husham (*hu'-sham*)
Ge 36:34 and H' of the land of Temani 2367
35 And H' died, and Hadad the son of "
1Ch 1:45 H' of the land of the Temanites "
46 when H' was dead, Hadad the son "

Hushathite (*hu'-shath-ite*)
2Sa 21:18 then Sibbechai the H' slew Saph, 2843
23:27 the Anethothite, Mebunnai the H', "
1Ch 11:29 Sibbecai the H', Ilai the Ahohite, "
20: 4 time Sibbechai the H' slew Sippai, "
27:11 eighth month was Sibbecai the H', "

Hushim (*hu'-shim*) See also SHUHAM.
Ge 46:23 And the sons of Dan; H'. 2366
1Ch 7:12 the children of Ir, and H', the sons "
8: 8 H' and Baara were his wives. "
11 And of H' he begat Abitub, and "

husk See also HUSKS.
Nu 6: 4 from the kernels even to the h'. 2085
2Ki 4:42 ears of corn in the h' thereof. *6861

husks
Lu 15:16 filled his belly with the h' that 2769

Huz (*huz*)
Ge 22:21 H' his firstborn, and Buz his *5780

Huzoth See KIRJATH-HUZOTH.

Huzzab (*huz'-zab*)
Na 2: 7 And H' shall be led away captive, ‡5324

hyacinth See JACINTH.

Hymenæus (*hy-men-e'-us*)
1Ti 1:20 Of whom is H' and Alexander; 5211
2Ti 2:17 Of whom is H' and Philetus; "

hymn See also HYMNS.
M't 26:30 they had sung an h', they went out 5214
M'r 14:26 they had sung an h', they went out

hymns
Eph 5:19 in psalms and h' and spiritual 5215
Col 3:16 in psalms and h' and spiritual "

hypocrisies
1Pe 2: 1 and all guile, and h', and envies, 5272

hypocrisy See also HYPOCRISIES.
Isa 32: 6 work iniquity, to practise h', and *2612
M't 23:28 within ye are full of h' and 5272
M'r 12:15 knowing their h', said unto them, "
Lu 12: 1 leaven of the Pharisees, which is h'. "
1Ti 4: 2 Speaking lies in h'; having their "
Jas 3:17 without partiality, and without h'. 505

hypocrite See also HYPOCRITE'S; HYPOCRITES.
Job 13:16 for an h' shall not come before *2611
17: 8 stir up himself against the h'. * "
20: 5 the joy of the h' but for a moment? * "
27: 8 For what is the hope of the h', * "
34:30 That the h' reign not, lest *120, "
Pr 11: 9 An h' with his mouth destroyeth * "
Isa 9:17 for every one is a h' and an *2611
M't 7: 5 Thou h', first cast out the beam 5273
Lu 6:42 Thou h', cast out first the beam "
13:15 Thou h', doth not each one of you * "

hypocrite's
Job 8:13 and the h' hope shall perish: *2611

hypocrites
Job 15:34 the congregation of h' shall be *2611
36:13 But the h' in heart heap up wrath: * "
Isa 33:14 hath surprised the h'. *120,
M't 6: 2 as the h' do in the synagogues 5273
5 thou shalt not be as the h' are: for "
16 when ye fast, be not, as the h', of "
15: 7 Ye h', well did Esaias prophesy of "
16: 3 O ye h', ye can discern the face * "
22:18 and said, Why tempt ye me, ye h'? "
23:13 scribes and Pharisees, h'! for ye "
14 scribes and Pharisees, h'! for ye * "
15, 23, 25, 27 scribes and Pharisees, h'! "
29 scribes and Pharisees, h'! because "
24:51 appoint him his portion with the h': "
M'r 7: 6 Esaias prophesied of you h', as it is "
Lu 11:44 scribes and Pharisees, h'! for ye * "
12:56 Ye h', ye can discern the face of the "

hypocritical
Ps 35:16 With h' mockers in feasts, they *2611
Isa 10: 6 will send him against an h' nation, * "

hyssop
Ex 12:22 ye shall take a bunch of h', and dip 231
Le 14: 4 cedar wood, and scarlet, and h': "
6 wood, and the scarlet, and the h', "
49 cedar wood, and scarlet, and h': "
51 the cedar wood, and the h', and the "
52 cedar wood, and with the h', and "
Nu 19: 6 cedar wood, and h', and scarlet, "
18 a clean person shall take h', and "
1Ki 4:33 the h' that springeth out of the "
Ps 51: 7 Purge me with h', and I shall be "
Joh 19:29 with vinegar, and put it upon h', 5301
Heb 9:19 water, and scarlet wool, and h', and "

I.

I See in the APPENDIX; also I-CHABOD; ME; MY.

I Am See AM.

Ibhar (*ib'-har*)
2Sa 5:15 I' also, and Elishua, and Nepheg, 2984
1Ch 3: 6 I' also, and Elishama, and "
14: 5 And I', and Elishua, and Elpalet, "

Ibleam (*ib'-le-am*)
Jos 17:11 and I' and her towns, and the 2991
J'g 1:27 nor the inhabitants of I' and her "
2Ki 9:27 going up to Gur, which is by I'. "

Ibneiah (*ib-ne-i'-ah*)
1Ch 9: 8 And I' the son of Jeroham, and 2997

Ibnijah (*ib-ni'-jah*)
1Ch 9: 8 the son of Reuel, the son of I'; 2998

Ibri (*ib'-ri*)
1Ch 24:27 and Shoham, and Zaccur, and I'. 5681

Ibzan (*ib'-zan*)
J'g 12: 8 And after him I' of Bethlehem 78
10 Then died I', and was buried at "

ice
Job 6:16 are blackish by reason of the i', 7140
38:29 Out of whose womb came the i'? "
Ps 147:17 He casteth forth his i' like morsels: "

I-chabod (*ik'-a-bod*) See also I-CHABOD'S.
1Sa 4:21 she named the child I', saying, 350

I-chabod's (*ik'-a-bods*)
1Sa 14: 3 the son of Ahitub, I' brother, 350

Iconium (*i-co'-ne-um*)
Ac 13:51 against them, and came unto I'. 2430
14: 1 And it came to pass in I', that they "
19 certain Jews from Antioch and I', "
21 to Lystra, and to I', and Antioch, "
16: 2 brethren that were at Lystra and I'. "
2Ti 3:11 unto me at Antioch, at I', at Lystra; "

Idalah (*id'-a-lah*)
Jos 19:15 and Shimron, and I', and 3030

Idbash (*id'-bash*)
1Ch 4: 3 Jezreel, and Ishma, and I': and 3031

Iddo (*id'-do*)
1Ki 4:14 Ahinadab the son of I' had 5714
1Ch 6:21 Joah his son, I' his son, Zerah his "
27:21 I' the son of Zechariah: of 3035
2Ch 9:29 and in the visions of I' the seer 3260
12:15 and of I' the seer concerning 5714
13:22 written in the story of the prophet I'. "
Ezr 5: 1 and Zechariah the son of I', "
6:14 and Zechariah the son of I'. "
8:17 with commandment unto I' the 112
17 what they should say unto I', and "
Ne 12: 4 I', Ginnetho, Abijah, 5714
16 Of I', Zechariah; of Ginnethon, "
Zec 1: 1 the son of Berechiah, the son of I' "
7 the son of I' the prophet, saying, "

idle
Ex 5: 8 for they be i'; therefore they cry, 7504
17 But he said, Ye are i', ye are i': "
Pr 19:15 and an i' soul shall suffer hunger. 7423
M't 12:36 That every i' word that men shall 692
20: 3 and saw others standing i' in the "
6 found others standing i', and saith* "
6 Why stand ye here all the day i'? "
Lu 24:11 words seemed to them as i' tales, 3026
1Ti 5:13 And withal they learn to be i', 692
13 not only i', but tattlers also and "

idleness
Pr 31:27 and eateth not the bread of i'. 6104
Ec 10:18 and through i' of the hands the 8220
Eze 16:49 and abundance of i' was in her *8252

idol See also IDOL'S; IDOLS.
1Ki 15:13 she had made an i' in a grove; *4656
13 Asa destroyed her i', and burnt it* "
2Ch 15:16 because she had made an i' in a * "
16 grove: and Asa cut down her i', * "
33: 7 image, the i' which he had made, 5566
15 the i' out of the house of the Lord, "
Isa 48: 5 Mine i' hath done them, and my 6090
66: 3 incense, as if he blessed an i'. 205
Jer 22:28 man Coniah a despised broken i'? *6089
Zec 11:17 Woe to the i' shepherd that leaveth *457
Ac 7:41 and offered a sacrifice unto the i', 1497
1Co 8: 4 we know that an i' is nothing in "
7 with conscience of the i' unto this "
7 eat it as a thing offered unto an i'; 1494
10:19 say I then? that the i' is any thing, 1497

idolater See also IDOLATERS.
1Co 5:11 a fornicator, or covetous, or an i', 1496
Eph 5: 5 nor covetous man, who is an i', "

idolaters
1Co 5:10 or extortioners, or with i'; 1496
6: 9 neither fornicators, nor i', nor "
10: 7 Neither be i', as were some of "
Re 21: 8 i', and all liars, shall have their "
22:15 and murderers, and i', and "

idolatries
1Pe 4: 3 banquetings, and abominable i': 1495

idolatrous
2Ki 23: 5 he put down the i' priests, whom 3649

idolatry See also IDOLATRIES.
1Sa 15:23 stubbornness is as iniquity and i'. 8655
Ac 17:16 he saw the city wholly given to i'. *2712
1Co 10:14 my dearly beloved, flee from i'. 1495
Ga 5:20 I', witchcraft, hatred, variance, "
Col 3: 5 and covetousness, which is i': "

idol's
1Co 8:10 sit at meat in the i' temple, shall 1493

idols
Le 19: 4 Turn ye not unto i', nor make 457
26: 1 Ye shall make you no i' nor graven "
30 upon the carcases of your i', 1544
De 29:17 and their i', wood and stone, silver "
1Sa 31: 9 publish it in the house of their i', 6091
1Ki 15:12 and removed all the i' that his 1544
21:26 did very abominably in following i', "
2Ki 17:12 For they served i', whereof the "
21:11 made Judah also to sin with his i': "
21 served the i' that his father served, "
23:24 and the images, and the i', and all "
1Ch 10: 9 to carry tidings unto their i', and 6091
16:26 all the gods of the people are i': 457
2Ch 15: 8 put away the abominable i' out *8251
24:18 and served groves and i': and 6091
34: 7 cut down all the i' throughout all *2553
Ps 96: 5 the gods of the nations are i': but 457
97: 7 that boast themselves of i': worship "
106:36 And they served their i': which 6091
38 sacrificed unto the i' of Canaan: 6091
115: 4 Their i' are silver and gold, the "
135:15 The i' of the heathen are silver and "
Isa 2: 8 Their land also is full of i'; they 457
18 and the i' he shall utterly abolish. "
20 day a man shall cast his i' of silver, "
20 and his i' of gold, which they made "
10:10 hath found the kingdoms of the i', "
11 have done unto Samaria and her i', "
11 so do to Jerusalem and her i'? 6091
19: 1 the i' of Egypt shall be moved at 457
3 and they shall seek to the i', and to "
31: 7 man shall cast away his i' of silver, "
7 and his i' of gold, which your own "
45:16 together that are makers of i'. 6736
46: 1 their i' were upon the beasts, and 6091
57: 5 Enflaming yourselves with i' under *410
Jer 50: 2 her i' are confounded, her images 6091
38 and they are mad upon their i'. 367
Eze 6: 4 your slain men before your i'. 1544
5 children of Israel before their i'; "
6 your i' may be broken and cease, "
9 which go a whoring after their i': "
13 shall be among their i' round about "
13 offer sweet savour to all their i'. "
8:10 and all the i' of the house of Israel, "
14: 3 man, these men have set up their i' "
4 that setteth up his i' in his heart, "
4 according to the multitude of his i'; "
5 estranged from me through their i'. "
6 turn yourselves from your i'; and "
7 setteth up his i' in his heart, and "
16:36 with all the i' of thy abominations, "
18: 6 eyes to the i' of the house of Israel, "
12 hath lifted up his eyes to the i', "
15 eyes to the i' of the house of Israel, "
20: 7 not yourselves with the i' of Egypt: "
8 did they forsake the i' of Egypt: "
16 for their heart went after their i'. "
18 nor defile yourselves with their i': "
24 eyes were after their fathers' i'. "
31 pollute yourselves with all your i', "
39 Go ye, serve ye every one his i', and "
39 with your gifts, and with your i'. "
22: 3 maketh i' against herself to defile "
4 defiled thyself in thine i' which "
23: 7 with all their i' she defiled herself. "
30 thou art polluted with their i'. "
37 with their i' have they committed "
39 had slain their children to their i', "
49 you, and ye bear the sins of your i': "
30:13 I will also destroy the i', and I will "
33:25 lift up your eyes toward your i', "
36:18 shed upon the land, and for their i' "
25 from all your i', will I cleanse you. "
37:23 themselves any more with their i', "
44:10 astray away from me after their i'; "
12 unto them before their i', and "
Ho 4:17 Ephraim is joined to i': let him 6091
8: 4 their gold have they made them i', "
13: 2 and i' according to their own "
14: 8 have I to do any more with i'? I "
Mic 1: 7 all the i' thereof will I lay desolate: "
Hab 2:18 trusteth therein, to make dumb i'? 457
Zec 10: 2 For the i' have spoken vanity, *8655
13: 2 cut off the names of the i' out of 6091
Ac 15:20 they abstain from pollutions of i', 1497

Ac 15:29 abstain from meats offered to i', 1494
21:25 from things offered to i', and from "
Ro 2:22 thou that abhorrest i', dost thou 1497
1Co 8: 1 as touching things offered to i', we 1494
4 that are offered in sacrifice unto i', "
10 those things which are offered to i'; "
10:19 which is offered in sacrifice to i' is "
28 offered in sacrifice unto i', eat not "
12: 2 carried away unto these dumb i', 1497
2Co 6:16 hath the temple of God with i'? "
1Th 1: 9 ye turned to God from i' to serve "
1Jo 5:21 children, keep yourselves from i'. "
Re 2:14 eat things sacrificed unto i', and 1494
20 and to eat things sacrificed unto i'. "
9:20 i' of gold, and silver, and brass, 1497

Idumæa (*i-doo-me'-ah*) See also IDUMEA.
M'r 3: 8 from Jerusalem, and from I', and 2401

Idumea (*i-doo-me'-ah*) See also EDOM; IDUMÆA.
Isa 34: 5 it shall come down upon I', and * 123
6 great slaughter in the land of I'. * "
Eze 35:15 O Mount Seir, and all I', even all * "
36: 5 of the heathen, and against all I',* "

if
Ge 4: 7 I' thou doest well, shalt thou not 518
7 i' thou doest not well, sin lieth at "
24 I' Cain should be avenged 3588
8: 8 to see i' the waters were abated from "
13: 9 i' thou wilt take the left hand, then 518
9 or i' thou depart to the right hand, "
16 so that i' a man can number the "
15: 5 i' thou be able to number them: "
18: 3 My Lord, i' now I have found favour "
21 unto me; and i' not, I will know. "
26 I' I find in Sodom fifty righteous "
28 I' I find there forty and five, I will "
30 I will not do it, i' I find thirty there. "
20: 7 and i' thou restore her not, know "
24:41 and i' they give not thee one, thou "
42 i' now thou do prosper my way "
49 i' ye will deal kindly and truly with "
49 and i' not, tell me; that I may turn "
25:22 I' it be so, why am I thus! And she "
27:46 i' Jacob take a wife of the daughters "
28:20 I' God will be with me, and will "
30:27 i' I have found favour in thine eyes, "
31 i' thou wilt do this thing for me, I "
31: 8 I' he said thus, The speckled shall "
8 and i' he said thus, The ringstraked "
50 I' thou shalt afflict my daughters, "
50 or i' thou shalt take other wives "
32: 8 I' Esau come to the one company, "
33:10 i' now I have found grace in thy "
13 and i' men shall overdrive them one "
34:15 I' ye will be as we be, that every "
17 But i' ye will not hearken unto us, "
22 i' every male among us be "
37:26 What profit is it i' we slay our 3588
42:19 I' ye be true men, let one of your 518
38 i' mischief befall him by the way in "
43: 4 I' thou wilt send our brother with 518
5 But i' thou wilt not send him, we "
9 i' I bring him not unto thee, and set "
11 I' it must be so now, do this; take "
14 I' I be bereaved of my children, I 834
44:22 for i' he should leave his father, his "
26 i' our youngest brother be with us, 518
29 And i' ye take this also from me, "
32 I' I bring him not unto thee, then "
47: 6 and i' thou knowest any man of "
16 you for your cattle, i' money fail. "
29 I' now I have found grace in thy "
50: 4 I' now I have found grace in your "
Ex 4: 8 i' they will not believe thee, neither "
9 i' they will not believe also these "
23 and i' thou refuse to let him go, *
8: 2 and i' thou refuse to let them go, "
21 Else, i' thou wilt not let my people 518
9: 2 For i' thou refuse to let them go, "
10: 4 Else, i' thou refuse to let my people "
12: 4 And i' the household be too little for "
13:13 i' thou wilt not redeem it, then thou "
15:26 I' thou wilt diligently hearken to "
18:23 I' thou shalt do this thing, and God "
19: 5 i' ye will obey my voice indeed, and "
20:25 And i' thou wilt make me an altar "
25 for i' thou lift up thy tool upon it, "
21: 2 I' thou buy an Hebrew servant, 3588
3 I' he came in by himself, he shall 518
3 i' he were married, then his wife "
4 I' his master have given him a wife, "
5 i' the servant shall plainly say, I "
7 i' a man sell his daughter to be a 3588
8 I' she please not her master, who 518
9 And i' he have betrothed her unto "
10 I' he take him another wife; her "
11 i' he do not these three unto her, "
13 i' a man lie not in wait, but God 834
14 i' a man come presumptuously 3588
16 i' he be found in his hand, he shall "
18 i' men strive together, and one 3588
19 I' he rise again, and walk abroad 518
20 i' a man smite his servant, or his 3588
21 i' he continue a day or two, he 518
22 I' men strive, and hurt a woman "
23 i' any mischief follow, then thou "
26 i' any man smite the eye of his 3588
27 i' he smite out his manservant's 518
28 I' an ox gore a man or a woman, 3588
29 i' the ox were wont to push with 518
30 I' there be laid on him a sum of "
32 I' the ox shall push a manservant "
33 i' a man shall open a pit, or i' a man "
35 i' one man's ox hurt another's, 3588
22: 1 I' a man shall steal an ox, or a "
2 I' a thief be found breaking up, 518
Ex 22: 3 I' the sun be risen upon him, there 518
3 i' he have nothing, then he shall be "
4 I' the theft be certainly found in "
5 I' a man shall cause a field or "
6 I' fire break out, and catch in 3588
7 I' a man shall deliver unto his "
7 i' the thief be found, let him pay 518
8 I' the thief be not found, then the "
10 I' a man deliver unto his 3588
12 i' it be not stolen from him, he 518
13 I' it be torn in pieces, then let him "
14 And i' a man borrow ought of his 3588
15 i' the owner thereof be with it, he 518
15 i' it be an hired thing, it came for "
16 i' a man entice a maid that is not 3588
17 I' her father utterly refuse to give 518
23 I' thou afflict them in any wise, "
25 I' thou lend money to any of my "
26 I' thou at all take thy neighbour's "
23: 4 I' thou meet thine enemy's ox or 3588
5 I' thou see the ass of him that "
22 i' thou shalt indeed obey his voice, 518
33 i' thou serve their gods, it will surely "
24:14 i' any man have any matters to do,*
29:34 And i' ought of the flesh of the 518
32:32 now, i' thou wilt forgive their sin; "
32 and i' not, blot me, I pray thee, out "
33:13 i' I have found grace in thy sight, "
15 I' thy presence go not with me, "
34: 9 I' now I have found grace in thy "
20 and i' thou redeem him not, then "
40:37 But i' the cloud were not taken up "
Le 1: 2 I' any man of you bring an *3588
3 I' his offering be a burnt sacrifice 518
10 And i' his offering be of the flocks, "
14 And i' the burnt sacrifice for his "
2: 4 And i' thou bring an oblation of * "
5, 7 And i' thy oblation be a meat "
14 And i' thou offer a meat offering of "
3: 1 And i' his oblation be a sacrifice of "
1 i' he offer it of the herd; whether it "
6 And i' his offering for a sacrifice of "
7 I' he offer a lamb for his offering, "
12 And i' his offering be a goat, then "
4: 2 I' a soul shall sin through 3588
3 I' the priest that is anointed do 518
13 And i' the whole congregation of "
23 Or i' his sin, wherein he hath "
27 And i' any one of the common 518
28 Or i' his sin, which he hath sinned, 176
32 And i' he bring a lamb for a sin 518
5: 1 And i' a soul sin, and hear the 3588
1 i' he do not utter it, then he shall 518
2 Or i' a soul touch any unclean 834
3 Or i' he touch the uncleanness of 3588
4 Or i' a soul swear, pronouncing "
7 And i' he be not able to bring a 518
11 But i' he be not able to bring two "
15 I' a soul commit a trespass, and 3588
17 And i' a soul sin, and commit any "
6: 2 I' a soul sin, and commit a "
28 and i' it be sodden in a brasen pot, 518
7:12 I' he offer it for a thanksgiving, "
16 But i' the sacrifice of his offering "
18 And i' any of the flesh of the "
10:19 and i' I had eaten the sin offering "
11:37 And i' any part of their carcase 3588
38 But i' any water be put upon the "
39 And i' any beast, of which ye may "
12: 2 I' a woman have conceived seed, "
5 But i' she bear a maid child, then 518
8 And i' she be not able to bring a "
13: 4 I' the bright spot be white in the "
5 behold, i' the plague in his sight be at "
6 behold, i' the plague be somewhat "
7 But i' the scab spread much abroad 518
8 And i' the priest see that, behold, the "
10 behold, i' the rising be white in the "
12 And i' a leprosy break out abroad 518
13 i' the leprosy have covered all his "
16 Or i' the raw flesh turn again, 3588
17 i' the plague be turned into white; "
20 And i', when the priest seeth it, "
21 But i' the priest look on it, and, 518
21 and i' it be not lower than the skin, "
22 And i' it spread much abroad in "
23 But i' the bright spot stay in his "
24 Or i' there be any flesh, in the *3588
25 behold, i' the hair in the bright spot "
26 But i' the priest look on it, and, "
27 and i' it be spread much abroad in 518
28 And i' the bright spot stay in his "
29 I' a man or woman have a *3588
30 behold, i' it be in sight deeper than "
31 And i' the priest look on the 3588
32 i' the scall spread not, and there be in "
34 i' the scall be not spread in the skin, "
35 But i' the scall spread much in 3588
36 i' the scall be spread in the skin, the "
37 But i' the scall be in his sight at a 518
38 I' a man also or a woman have in the*
39 behold, i' the bright spots in the skin, "
42 And i' there be in the bald head, 3588
43 i' the rising of the sore be white "
49 And i' the plague be greenish or "
51 i' the plague be spread in the 3588
53 And i' the priest shall look, and, 518
55 i' the plague have not changed his "
56 And i' the priest look, and, behold, "
57 And i' it appear still in the 518
14: 3 i' the plague of leprosy be healed in "
21 And i' he be poor, and cannot get 518
37 i' the plague be in the walls of the "
39 i' the plague be spread in the walls of "
43 And i' the plague come again, and 518
44 i' the plague be spread in the house, it "
Le 14:48 And i' the priest shall come in, and 518
15: 8 And i' he that hath the issue spit 3588
16 And i' any man's seed of copulation "
19 And i' a woman have an issue, and "
23 And i' it be on her bed, or on 518
24 And i' any man lie with her at all, "
25 And i' a woman have an issue of 3588
25 or i' it run beyond the time of her "
28 But i' she be cleansed of her issue, 518
17:16 But i' he wash them not, nor bathe "
18: 5 which i' a man do, he shall live in
19: 5 And i' ye offer a sacrifice of peace*3588
6 and i' ought remain until the third
7 And i' it be eaten at all on the third 518
33 And i' a stranger sojourn with 3588
20: 4 And i' the people of the land do 518
12 And i' a man lie with his daughter 834
13 I' a man also lie with mankind, as "
14 And i' a man take a wife and her "
15 And i' a man lie with a beast, he "
16 And i' a woman approach unto any "
17 And i' a man shall take his sister, "
18 And i' a man shall lie with a woman "
20 And i' a man shall lie with his "
21 And i' a man shall take his brother's "
21: 9 i' she profane herself by playing 3588
22: 9 i' they profane it: I the Lord do "
11 But i' the priest buy any soul with "
12 I' the priest's daughter also be "
13 But i' the priest's daughter be a "
14 And i' a man eat of the holy thing "
24:19 And i' a man cause a blemish in "
25:14 And i' thou sell ought unto thy "
20 And i' ye shall say, What shall we "
25 I' thy brother be waxen poor, and "
25 and i' any of his kin come to redeem*
26 And i' the man have none to 3588
28 But i' he be not able to restore it 518
29 And i' a man sell a dwelling house 3588
30 And i' it be not redeemed within 518
33 And i' a man purchase of the 834
35 And i' thy brother be waxen poor, 3588
39 And i' thy brother that dwelleth by "
47 And i' a sojourner or stranger wax "
49 or i' he be able, he may redeem
51 I' there be yet many years behind, 518
52 And i' there remain but few years "
54 And i' he be not redeemed in these "
26: 3 I' ye walk in my statutes, and keep "
14 But i' ye will not hearken unto me, "
15 And i' ye shall despise my statutes, "
18 And i' ye will not yet for all this "
21 And i' ye walk contrary unto me, "
23 And i' ye will not be reformed by "
27 And i' ye will not for all this "
40 I' they shall confess their iniquity,*
41 i' then their uncircumcised hearts 176
27: 4 And i' it be a female, then thy 518
5 i' it be from five years old even unto "
6 i' it be from a month old even unto "
7 i' it be from sixty years old and "
7 i' it be a male, then thy estimation "
8 i' he be poorer than thy estimation "
9 i' it be a beast, whereof men bring "
10 i' he shall at all change beast for "
11 And i' it be any unclean beast, of "
13 But i' he will at all redeem it, then "
15 And i' he that sanctified it will "
16 And i' a man shall sanctify unto "
17 I' he sanctify his field from the "
18 But i' he sanctify his field after "
19 And i' he that sanctified the field "
20 And i' he will not redeem the field, "
20 i' he have sold the field to another "
22 And i' a man sanctify unto the "
27 And i' it be of an unclean beast, "
27 or i' it be not redeemed, then it "
31 And i' a man will at all redeem "
33 and i' he change it all, then both it "
Nu 5: 8 But i' the man have no kinsman "
12 I' any man's wife go aside, and 3588
14 or i' the spirit of jealousy come upon
19 I' no man have lain with thee, 518
19 and i' thou hast not gone aside to "
20 But i' thou hast gone aside to 3588
20 and i' thou be defiled, and some
27 i' she be defiled, and have done 518
28 And i' the woman be not defiled, "
6: 9 And i' any man die very suddenly 3588
9:10 I' any man of you or your posterity "
14 And i' a stranger shall sojourn
10: 4 And i' they blow but with one 518
9 And i' ye go to war in your land 3588
32 i' thou go with us, yea, it shall be, "
11:15 And i' thou deal thus with me, 518
15 i' I have found favour in thy sight; "
12: 6 i' there be a prophet among you, "
14 I' her father had but spit in her face, "
14: 8 I' the Lord delight in us, then 518
15 Now i' thou shalt kill all this people as "
15:14 And i' a stranger sojourn with *3588
22 And i' ye have erred, and not "
24 i' ought be committed by ignorance 518
27 i' any soul sin through ignorance, "
16:29 I' these men die the common death "
29 or i' they be visited after the visitation "
30 But i' the Lord make a new thing 518
20:19 and i' I and my cattle drink of thy "
21: 2 I' thou wilt indeed deliver this "
9 that i' a serpent had bitten any man, "
22:18 I' Balak would give me his house "
20 I' the men come to call thee, rise "
34 i' it displease thee, I will get me "
24:13 I' Balak would give me his house "
27: 8 I' a man die, and have no son, 3588
9 And i' he have no daughter, then 518

Nu 27:10 And i' he have no brethren, then 518
11 And i' his father have no brethren, "
30: 2 I' a man vow a vow unto the *3588
3 I' a woman also vow a vow unto the*
5 But i' her father disallow her in 518
6 And i' she had at all an husband, "
8 But i' her husband disallowed her "
10 And i' she vowed in her husband's "
12 But i' her husband hath utterly "
14 But i' her husband altogether hold "
15 i' he shall any ways make them void"
32: 5 i' we have found grace in thy sight, "
15 For i' ye turn away from after
20 I' ye will do this thing, i' ye will go518
23 But i' ye will not do so, behold, ye "
29 I' the children of Gad and the "
30 But i' they will not pass over with "
33:55 But i' ye will not drive out the "
35:16 i' he smite him with an instrument "
17 And i' he smite him with throwing "
18 Or i' he smite him with an hand "
20 But i' he thrust him of hatred, or "
22 But i' he thrust him suddenly "
26 But i' the slayer shall at any time "
36: 3 And i' they be married to any of the "
De 4:29 But i' from thence thou shalt seek the‡
29 i' thou seek him with all thy heart ‡3588
30 i' thou turn to the Lord thy God, and*
5:25 i' we hear the voice of the Lord 518
6:25 i' we observe to do all these 3588
7:12 i' ye hearken to these judgments,*6112
17 I' thou shalt say in thine heart, 3588
8:19 i' thou do at all forget the Lord 518
11:13 i' ye shall hearken diligently unto "
22 For i' ye shall diligently keep all 518
27 i' ye obey the commandments of 834
28 i' ye will not obey the 518
12:21 I' the place which the Lord thy 3588
13: 1 I' there arise among you a prophet,"
6 I' thy brother, the son of thy "
12 I' thou shalt hear say in one of thy "
14 i' it be truth, and the thing certain, "
14:24 i' the way be too long for thee, 3588
24 or i' the place be too far from thee* "
15: 5 Only i' thou carefully hearken 518
7 I' there be among you a poor man3588
12 And i' thy brother, an Hebrew man, "
16 i' he say unto thee, I will not go "
21 And i' there be any blemish therein,"
21 as i' it be lame, or blind, or have any
17: 2 I' there be found among you, 3588
8 I' there arise a matter too hard for "
18: 6 And i' a Levite come from any of "
21 And i' thou say in thine heart, "
22 i' the thing follow not, nor come to
19: 8 And i' the Lord thy God enlarge 518
9 I' thou shalt keep all these 3588
11 But i' any man hate his neighbour, "
16 I' a false witness rise up against "
18 and, behold, i' the witness be a false
20:11 i' it make thee answer of peace, and518
12 And i' it will make no peace with "
21: 1 I' one be found slain in the land 3588
14 i' thou have no delight in her, then 518
15 I' a man have two wives, one 3588
15 and i' the firstborn son be hers that
18 I' a man have a stubborn and 3588
22 And i' a man have committed a sin "
22: 2 And i' thy brother be not nigh 518
2 or i' thou know him not, then thou
6 I' a bird's nest chance to be 3588
8 house, i' any man fall from thence. "
13 I' any man take a wife, and go in "
20 But i' this thing be true, and the 518
22 I' a man be found lying with a 3588
23 I' a damsel that is a virgin be "
25 But i' a man find a betrothed 518
28 I' a man find a damsel that is a 3588
23:10 I' there be among you any man, "
22 But i' thou shalt forbear to vow, it "
24: 3 And i' the latter husband hate her,
3 or i' the latter husband die, 3588
7 I' a man be found stealing any of "
12 And i' the man be poor, thou shalt 518
25: 1 I' there be a controversy between3588
2 i' the wicked man be worthy to be 518
3 lest, i' he should exceed, and beat
5 I' brethren dwell together, and 3588
7 And i' the man like not to take 518
8 and i' he stand to it, and say, I like
28: 1 i' thou shalt hearken diligently 518
2 i' thou shalt hearken unto the 3588
9 i' thou shalt keep...commandments"
13 i' that thou hearken unto the "
15 i' thou wilt not hearken unto the 518
58 I' thou wilt not observe to do all "
30: 4 I' any of thine be driven out unto "
10 I' thou shalt hearken unto the 3588
10 and i' thou turn unto the Lord thy "
32:41 I' I whet my glittering sword, and 518
Jos 2:14 i' ye utter not this our business. "
19 our head, i' any hand be upon him. "
20 And i' thou utter this our business, "
8:15 as i' they were beaten before them,
9: 4 as i' they had been ambassadors, and
14:12 i' so be the Lord will be with me, * 194
17:15 I' thou be a great people, then 518
15 i' mount Ephraim be too narrow *3588
20: 5 And i' the avenger of blood pursue "
22:19 i' the land of your possession be 518
22 i' it be in rebellion, or i' in
23 or i' to offer thereon burnt offering "
23 or i' to offer peace offerings thereon,"
24 And i' we have not rather done it for"
24:15 And i' it seem evil unto you to serve"
20 I' ye forsake the Lord, and serve 3588

J'g 4: 8 I' thou wilt go with me, then I 518
8 but i' thou wilt not go with me, "
6:13 i' the Lord be with us, why then is all
17 I' now I have found grace in thy 518
31 i' he be a god, let him plead for "
36 I' thou wilt save Israel by mine "
37 and i' the dew be on the fleece "
7:10 But i' thou fear to go down, go thou "
8:19 i' ye had saved them alive, I would3863
9:15 I' in truth ye anoint me king over 518
15 and i' not, let fire come out of the "
16 i' ye have done truly and sincerely, "
16 and i' ye have dealt well with "
19 I' ye then have dealt truly and "
20 But i' not, let fire come out from "
36 of the mountains as i' they were men.
11: 9 I' ye bring me home again to fight 518
10 i' we do not so according to thy * "
30 I' thou shalt without fail deliver "
36 i' thou hast opened thy mouth unto*
12: 5 thou an Ephraimite? I' he said, Nay;
13:16 i' thou wilt offer a burnt offering, 518
23 I' the Lord were pleased to kill 3863
14:12 i' ye can certainly declare it me 518
13 i' ye cannot declare it me, then "
18 I' ye had not ploughed with my 3883
16: 7 I' they bind me with seven green 518
11 I' they bind me fast with new ropes "
13 I' thou weavest the seven locks of "
17 i' I be shaven, then my strength will"
21:21 i' the daughters of Shiloh come out
Ru 1:12 I' I should say, I have hope, i' I 3588
1:17 also, i' ought but death part thee "
3:13 that i' he will perform unto thee 518
13 but i' he will not do the part of a "
4: 4 I' thou wilt redeem it, redeem it: "
4 but i' thou wilt not redeem it, then "
1Sa 1:11 i' thou wilt indeed look on the "
2:16 And i' any man said unto him, Let
16 me now: and i' not, I will take it 518
25 I' one man sin against another, the "
25 but i' a man sin against the Lord, "
3: 9 i' he call thee, that thou shalt say, "
17 also, i' thou hide anything from me "
6: 3 I' ye send away the ark of the God "
9 i' it goeth up by the way of his own "
9 but i' not, then we shall know that "
7: 3 I' ye do return unto the Lord with "
9: 7 behold, i' we go, what shall we
10:22 i' the man should yet come thither.*
11: 3 i' there be no man to save us, we 518
12:14 I' ye will fear the Lord, and serve "
15 But i' ye will not obey the voice of "
25 But i' ye shall still do wickedly, ye "
14: 9 I' they say thus unto us, Tarry "
10 But i' they say thus, Come up unto "
30 i' haply the people had eaten freely 3863
16: 2 i' Saul hear it, he will kill me. And the
17: 9 I' he be able to fight with me, and 518
9 but i' I prevail against him, and kill "
19:11 saying, I' thou save not thy life "
20: 6 I' thy father at all miss me, then "
7 I' he say thus, It is well; thy "
7 but i' he be very wroth, then be sure "
8 i' there be in me iniquity, slay me "
9 for i' I knew certainly that evil "
10 or what i' thy father answer thee *176
12 behold, i' there be good toward
13 but i' it please my father to do 3588
21 I' I expressly say unto the lad, 518
22 But i' I say thus unto the young "
29 i' I have found favour in thine eyes, "
21: 4 i' the young men have kept "
9 i' thou wilt take that, take it; for "
23: 3 i' we come to Keilah against the 3588
23 i' he be in the land, that I will 518
24:19 For i' a man find his enemy, will 3588
25:22 i' I leave of all that pertain to him 518
26:19 I' the Lord have stirred thee up "
19 but i' they be the children of men, "
27: 5 I' I have now found grace in thine "
2Sa 3:35 i' I taste bread, or ought else, 3588, "
7:14 I' he commit iniquity, I will chasten834
10:11 I' the Syrians be too strong for 518
11 i' the children of Ammon be too "
11:20 And i' so be that the king's wrath "
12: 8 and i' that had been too little, I
18 i' we tell him that the child is dead?
13:26 I' not, I pray thee, let my brother 3808
14:32 and i' there be any iniquity in me, 518
15: 8 I' the Lord shall bring me again "
26 But i' he thus say, I have no delight "
33 I' thou passest on with me, then "
34 But i' thou return to the city, and "
16:23 was as i' a man had enquired at
17: 3 whom thou seekest is as i' all returned:
6 after his saying? i' not; speak thou.518
13 Moreover, i' he begotten into a city, "
18: 3 for i' we flee away, they will not "
3 neither i' half of us, will they care "
25 I' he be alone, there is tidings in "
19: 6 that i' Absalom had lived, and all 3863
7 i' thou go not forth, there will not 3588
13 i' thou be not captain of the host 518
1Ki 1:52 I' he will shew himself a worthy "
52 i' wickedness shall be found in him, "
2: 4 I' thy children take heed to their "
23 i' Adonijah have not spoken this 3588
3:14 And i' thou wilt walk in my ways, 518
6:12 i' thou wilt walk in my statutes, "
8:31 I' any man trespass against his "
35 i' they pray toward this place, and "
37 I' there be in the land famine, 3588
37 i' there be pestilence, blasting, "
37 or i' there be caterpiller; i' their "
44 I' thy people go out to battle "

1Ki 8:46 I' they sin against thee, (for there 3588
9: 4 And i' thou wilt walk before me, as 518
6 But i' ye shall at all turn from "
11:38 i' thou wilt hearken unto all that I "
12: 7 I' thou wilt be a servant unto this "
27 I' this people go up to do sacrifice "
13: 8 I' thou wilt give me half thine "
16:31 as i' it had been a light thing for him to
18:21 i' the Lord be God, follow him: but 518
21 but i' Baal, then follow him. And "
19: 2 i' I make not thy life as the life of one
20:39 i' by any means he be missing, 518
21: 2 or, i' it seem good to thee, I will "
6 or else, i' it please thee, I will give "
22:28 I' thou return at all in peace, the "
2Ki 1:10 I' I be a man of God, then let fire "
12 I' I be a man of God, let fire come "
2:10 i' thou see me when I am taken "
10 unto thee; but i' not, it shall not be "
4:29 i' thou meet any man, salute him 3588
29 and i' any salute thee, answer him "
5:13 i' the prophet had bid thee do some
6:27 I' the Lord do not help thee, whence
31 i' the head of Elisha the son of 518
7: 2 i' the Lord would make windows
4 I' we say, We will enter into the 518
4 and i' we sit still here, we die also. "
4 i' they save us alive, we shall live; "
4 and i' they kill us, we shall but die: "
9 i' we tarry till the morning light,
19 i' the Lord shall make windows in
9:15 I' it be your minds, then let none 518
10: 6 time to them, saying, I' ye be mine, "
6 and i' ye will hearken unto my voice,
15 I' it be, give me thine hand. And he
24 I' any of the men whom I have
18:21 on which i' a man lean, it will go 834
22 But i' ye say unto me, We trust in 3588
23 i' thou be able on thy part to set 518
20:19 i' peace and truth be in my days?
21: 8 only i' they will observe to do
1Ch 12:17 I' ye be come peaceably unto me to "
17 but i' ye be come to betray me to "
13: 2 I' it seem good unto you, and that "
19:12 he said, I' the Syrians be too strong "
12 but i' the children of Ammon be too "
22:13 i' thou takest heed to fulfill the "
28: 7 i' he be constant to do my "
9 i' thou seek him, he will be found "
9 but i' thou forsake him, he will cast "
2Ch 6:22 I' a man sin against his neighbour, "
24 And i' thy people Israel be put to "
28 I' there be a dearth in the land, 3588
28 I' there be pestilence, i' there be "
28 i' their enemies besiege them in "
32 i' they come and pray in this house;*
34 I' thy people go out to war against3588
36 I' they sin against thee, (for there "
37 Yet i' they bethink themselves in the
38 I' they return to thee with all their
7:13 I' I shut up heaven that there be 2005
13 or i' I command the locust to "
13 or i' I send pestilence among my 518
14 I' my people, which are called by my
17 i' thou wilt walk before me, as 518
19 But i' ye turn away, and forsake my "
10: 7 I' thou be kind to this people, and "
15: 2 and i' ye seek him, he will be found "
2 but i' ye forsake him, he will forsake "
18:27 I' thou certainly return in peace, "
20: 9 I', when evil cometh upon us, as the "
25: 8 But i' thou wilt go, do it, be strong "
30: 9 For i' ye turn again unto the Lord,
9 from you, i' ye return unto him. 518
Ezr 4:13 i' this city be builded, and the 2006
16 i' this city be builded again, and "
5:17 i' it seem good to the king, let there "
Ne 1: 8 I' ye transgress, I will scatter you
9 But i' ye turn unto me, and keep my
2: 5 I' it please the king, and if thy 518
7 I' it please the king, let letters be "
4: 3 i' a fox go up, he shall even break 518
9:29 (which i' a man do, he shall live in
10:31 And i' the people of the land bring
13:21 i' ye do so again, I will lay hands 518
Es 1:19 I' it please the king, let there go a "
3: 9 I' it please the king, let it be "
4:14 For i' thou altogether holdest thy "
16 the law: and i' I perish, I perish. 834
5: 4 I' it seem good unto the king, let 518
8 I' I have found favour in the sight "
8 and i' it please the king to grant my "
6:13 I' Mordecai be of the seed of the "
7: 3 and said, I' I have found favour in "
3 and i' it please the king, let my life "
4 But i' we had been sold for 432
8: 5 I' it please the king, and i' I have 518
9:13 I' it please the king, let it be "
Job 4: 2 I' we assay to commune with thee,
5: 1 i' there be any that will answer thee;*
6:28 for it is evident unto you i' I lie. *518
8: 4 I' thy children have sinned against "
5 I' thou wouldest seek unto God "
6 I' thou wert pure and upright; "
18 I' he destroy him from his place, "
9: 3 I' he will contend with him, he "
13 I' God will not withdraw his anger,*
16 I' I had called, and he had 518
19 I' I speak of strength, lo, he is "
19 and i' of judgment, who shall set "
20 I' I justify myself, mine own mouth*"
20 i' I say, I am perfect, it shall also *
23 I' the scourge slay suddenly, he 518
24 thereof; i' not, where, and who is he? "
27 I' I say, I will forget my complaint, "
29 I' I be wicked, why then labour I in*

Job 9:30 I' I wash myself with snow water, 518
10:14 I' I sin, then thou markest me, and "
15 I' I be wicked, woe unto me; "
15 and i' I be righteous, yet will I not "
11:10 I' he cut off, and shut up, or gather "
13 I' thou prepare thine heart, and "
14 I' iniquity be in thine hand, put it "
13:10 i' ye do secretly accept persons. "
19 now, i' I hold my tongue, I shall *3588
14:14 I' a man die, shall he live again? 518
16: 4 i' your soul were in my soul's 3863
17:13 I' I wait, the grave is mine house: 518
19: 5 I' indeed ye will magnify yourselves "
21: 4 and i' it were so, why should not my* "
22:23 I' thou return to the Almighty, "
24:17 i' one know them, they are in the *3588
25 And i' it be not so now, who will 518
27:14 I' his children be multiplied, it is "
29:24 I' I laughed on them, they believed
31: 5 I' I have walked with vanity, 518
5 or i' my foot hath hasted to deceit; *
7 I' my step hath turned out of the 518
7 and i' any blot hath cleaved to mine
9 I' mine heart have been deceived 518
9 or i' I have laid wait at my neighbour's*
13 I' I did despise the cause of my 518
16 I' have withheld the poor from their "
19 I' I have seen any perish for want "
20 I' his loins have not blessed me, "
20 and i' he were not warmed with the
21 I' I have lifted up my hand against 518
24 I' I have made gold my hope, or "
25 I' I rejoiced because my wealth was "
26 I' I beheld the sun when it shined, "
29 I' I rejoiced at the destruction of "
31 I' the men of my tabernacle said "
33 I' I covered my transgressions as "
38 I' my land cry against me, or that "
39 I' I have eaten the fruits thereof "
33: 5 I' thou canst answer me, set thy "
23 I' there be a messenger with him, "
27 and i' any say, I have sinned, and
32 I' thou hast anything to say, 518
33 I' not, hearken unto me: hold thy "
34:14 I' he set his heart upon man, "
14 i' he gather unto himself his spirit
16 I' now thou hast understanding, 518
32 i' I have done iniquity, I will do no "
35: 3 I have, i' I be cleansed from my sin? "
6 I' thou sinnest, what doest thou 518
6 or i' thy transgressions be multiplied,
7 I' thou be righteous, what givest 518
36: 8 And i' they be bound in fetters, and "
11 I' they obey and serve him, they "
12 But i' they obey not, they shall "
37:20 i' a man speak, surely he shall be * "
38: 5 measures therof, i' thou knowest? 3588
8 as i' it had issued out of the womb?
18 the earth? declare i' thou knowest 518
Ps 7: 3 O Lord my God, i' I have done this; "
3 i' there be iniquity in my hands; "
4 I' I have rewarded evil unto him "
12 I' he turn not, he will whet his "
11: 3 I' the foundations be destroyed, 3588
14: 2 to see i' there were any that did "
28: 1 i' thou be silent to me, I become like "
40: 5 i' I would declare and speak of them, "
41: 6 And i' he come to see me, he 518
44:20 I' we have forgotten the name of "
50:12 I' I were hungry, I would not tell "
59:15 and grudge i' they be not satisfied. "
66:18 I' I regard iniquity in my heart, the "
73:15 I' I say, I will speak thus; behold, "
81: 8 Israel, i' thou wilt hearken unto me; "
89:30 I' his children forsake my law, and "
31 I' they break my statutes, and keep "
90:10 and i' by reason of strength they be* "
95: 7 To day i' ye will hear his voice, * "
124: 1, 2 I' it had not been the Lord who 3884
130: 3 I' thou, Lord, shouldest mark 518
132:12 I' thy children will keep my "
137: 5 I' I forget thee, O Jerusalem, let my "
6 I' I do not remember thee, let my "
6 i' I prefer not Jerusalem above my "
139: 8 I' I ascend up into heaven, thou art "
8 i' I make my bed in hell, behold,
9 I' I take the wings of the morning,
11 I' I say, Surely the darkness shall
18 I' I should count them, they are more
24 And see i' there be any wicked way 518
Pr 1:10 i' sinners entice thee, consent thou "
11 I' they say, Come with us, let us lay "
2: 1 i' thou wilt receive my words, and "
3 Yea, i' thou criest after knowledge, "
4 I' thou seekest her as silver, and "
3:30 without cause, i' he have done thee "
6: 1 i' thou be surety for thy friend, "
1 i' thou hast stricken thy hand with
31 But i' he be found, he shall restore
9:12 I' thou be wise, thou shalt be wise 518
12 but i' thou scornest, thou alone shall
16:31 i' it be found in...way of righteousness.*
19:19 for i' thou deliver him, yet thou 518
22:18 pleasant thing i' thou keep them 3588
27 I' thou hast nothing to pay, why 518
23: 2 i' thou be a man given to appetite. "
15 i' thine heart be wise, my heart shall "
24:10 I' thou faint in the day of adversity, "
11 I' thou forbear to deliver them that *
12 I' thou sayest, Behold, we knew it 3588
25:21 I' thine enemy be hungry, give 518
21 and i' he be thirsty, give him water "
30:32 I' thou hast done foolishly in lifting "
32 or i' thou hast thought evil, lay thine "
Ec 4:10 For i' they fall, the one will lift up "
5: 8 I' thou seest the oppression of the "
Ec 6: 3 I' a man beget an hundred children, 518
10:10 I' the iron be blunt, and he do not "
11: 3 I' the clouds be full of rain, they "
Ca 1: 8 I' thou know not, O thou fairest "
8: 7 i' a man would give all the substance "
9 I' she be a wall, we will build upon "
Isa 1:19 I' ye be willing and obedient, ye "
20 But i' ye refuse and rebel, ye shall "
5:30 and i' one look unto the land, behold
7: 9 I' ye will not believe, surely ye 518
8:20 i' they speak not according to this "
10:15 as i' the rod should shake itself
15 or as i' the staff should lift up itself
15 itself, as i' it were no wood. *
21:12 i' ye will enquire, enquire ye: 518
36: 6 whereon i' a man lean, it will go
8 i' thou be able on thy part to set 518
47:12 i' so be thou shalt be able to profit, 194
12 i' so be thou mayest prevail. "
58: 9 I' thou take away from the midst of
10 And i' thou draw out thy soul to the
13 I' thou turn away thy foot from 518
59:10 and we grope as i' we had no eyes:*
66: 3 killeth an ox is as i' he slew a man;*
3 lamb, as i' he cut off a dog's neck; *
3 as i' he offered swine's blood; he *
3 incense, as i' he blessed an idol. *
Jer 4: 1 I' thou wilt return, O Israel, saith 518
5: 1 places thereof, i' ye can find a man, "
1 i' there be any that executeth "
7: 5 For i' ye throughly amend your "
5 i' ye throughly execute judgment "
6 I' ye oppress not the stranger, the
12: 5 I' thou hast run with thy footmen, 3588
5 i' in the land of peace, wherein thou*
16 i' they will diligently learn the 518
17 But i' they will not obey, I will "
13:17 But i' ye will not hear it, my soul "
22 And i' thou say in thine heart, 3588
14:18 I' I go forth into the field, then 518
18 and i' I enter into the city, then "
15: 2 i' they say unto thee, Whither *3588
19 I' thou return, then will I bring 518
19 and i' thou take forth the precious "
17:24 i' ye diligently hearken unto me, "
27 But i' ye will not hearken unto me "
18: 8 I' that nation, against whom I have
10 I' it do evil in my sight, that it obey
21: 2 i' so be that the Lord will deal * 194
22: 4 For i' ye do this thing indeed, then 518
5 But i' ye will not hear these words, "
26: 3 I' so be they will hearken, and * 194
4 I' ye will not hearken to me, 518
15 that i' ye put me to death, ye shall "
27:18 But i' they be prophets, and i' the "
31:36 I' those ordinances depart from "
37 I' heaven above can be measured, "
33:20 I' ye can break my covenant of the 518
25 I' my covenant be not with day "
25 and i' I have not appointed the
38:15 I' I declare it unto thee, wilt thou 518
15 i' I give thee counsel, wilt thou not "
17 I' thou wilt assuredly go forth unto "
18 But i' thou wilt not go forth to "
25 But i' the princes hear that I 3588
40: 4 I' it seem good unto thee to come 518
4 but i' it seem ill unto thee to come "
42:10 I' ye will still abide in this land, "
13 But i' ye say, We will not dwell in "
15 I' ye wholly set your faces to enter "
49: 9 I' grapegatherers come to thee, "
9 i' thieves by night, they will destroy "
51: 8 pain, i' so be she may be healed. 194
La 1:12 and see i' there be any sorrow like 518
2: 6 tabernacle, as i' it were of a garden:
3:29 dust; i' so be there may be hope. 194
Eze 3:19 Yet i' thou warn the wicked, and 3588
21 Nevertheless i' thou warn the "
10:10 as i' a wheel had been in the 834
14: 9 And i' the prophet be deceived 3588
15 I' I cause noisome beasts to pass 3863
17 Or i' I bring a sword upon that land,
19 Or i' I send a pestilence into that
16:47 but, as i' that were a very little thing,
18: 5 But i' a man be just, and do that 3588
10 I' he beget a son that is a robber,
14 Now, lo, i' he beget a son, that
20:11, 13, 21 which i' a man do, he shall
39 i' ye will not hearken unto me: 518
21:13 and what i' the sword contemn
33: 2 i' the people of the land take a man
3 I' when he seeth the sword come
4 i' the sword come, and take him
6 But i' the watchman see the 3588
6 i' the sword come, and take any *
8 i' thou dost not speak to warn the*
9 i' thou warn the wicked of his 3588
9 i' he do not turn from his way, *
10 I' our transgressions and our *3588
13 i' he trust to his own righteousness,
14 i' he turn from his sin, and do that
15 I' the wicked restore the pledge,
19 But i' the wicked turn from his *
43:11 And i' they be ashamed of all that 518
46:16 I' the prince give a gift unto any 3588
17 But i' he give a gift of his "
Da 2: 5 i' ye will not make known unto 2006
6 But i' ye shew the dream, and the "
9 But i' ye will not make known "
3:15 Now i' ye be ready that at what "
15 but i' ye worship not, ye shall be "
17 I' it be so, our God whom we serve "
4:27 i' it may be the lengthening of thy "
5:16 now i' thou canst read the writing, "
Ho 6: 3 i' we follow on to know the Lord:*
8: 7 i' so be it yield, the strangers shall 194
Joe 2:14 Who knoweth i' he will return and*
3: 4 and i' ye recompense me, swiftly 518
Am 3: 4 out of his den, i' he have taken "
5:19 As i' a man did flee from a lion, 834
6: 9 i' there remain ten men in one 518
Ob 5 I' thieves came to thee, "
5 i' robbers by night, how art thou "
5 i' the grapegatherers came to thee, "
Jon 1: 6 i' so be that God will think upon 194
3: 9 Who can tell i' God will turn and *
Mic 2:11 I' a man walking in the spirit 3863
5: 8 who, i' he go through, both 518
Na 3:12 i' they be shaken, they shall even "
Hag 2:12 I' one bear holy flesh in the skirt 2005
13 I' one that is unclean by a dead 518
Zec 3: 7 I' thou wilt walk in my ways, and "
7 and i' thou wilt keep my charge, "
8: 6 I' it be marvellous in the eyes of 3588
11:12 I' ye think good, give me my price; 518
12 and i' not forbear. So they weighed "
Mal 1: 6 i' then I be a father, where is mine "
6 and i' I be a master, where is my "
8 And i' ye offer the blind for *3588
8 and i' ye offer the lame and sick, * "
2: 2 I' ye will not hear, and i' ye will 518
3:10 i' I will not open you the windows of
M't 4: 3 I' thou be the Son of God, command 1487
6 I' thou be the Son of God, cast "
9 i' thou wilt fall down and worship 1487
5:13 but i' the salt have lost his savour, "
23 Therefore i' thou bring thy gift to the
29 And i' thy right eye offend thee, 1487
30 And i' thy right hand offend thee, cut
46 For i' ye love them which love you, 1487
47 And i' ye salute your brethren only, "
6:14 For i' ye forgive men their "
15 But i' ye forgive not men their "
22 i' therefore thine eye be single, "
23 But i' thine eye be evil, thy whole 1487
23 I' therefore the light that is in "
30 Wherefore, i' God so clothed the "
7: 9 i' his son ask bread, will he give 1487
10 Or i' he ask a fish, will he give him "
11 I' ye then, being evil, know how to 1487
8: 2 i' thou wilt, thou canst make me 1487
31 I' thou cast us out, suffer us to 1487
9:21 I' I may but touch his garment, 1487
10:13 And i' the house be worthy, let "
13 but i' it be not worthy, let your "
25 I' they have called the master of 1487
11:14 And i' ye will receive it, this is "
21 for i' the mighty works, which "
23 for i' the mighty works, which "
12: 7 But i' ye had known what this "
11 and i' it fall into a pit on the 1487
26 And i' Satan cast out Satan, he 1487
27 And i' I by Beelzebub cast out "
28 But i' I cast out devils by the Spirit "
14:28 Lord, i' it be thou, bid me come "
15:14 And i' the blind lead the blind, 1487
16:24 I' any man will come after me, let 1487
17: 4 i' thou wilt, let us make here three "
20 I' ye have faith as a grain of 1487
18: 8 Wherefore i' thy hand or thy foot 1487
9 And i' thine eye offend thee, pluck "
12 i' a man have an hundred sheep, 1487
13 And i' so be that he find it, verily "
15 Moreover i' thy brother shall "
15 i' he shall hear thee, thou hast "
16 But i' he will not hear thee, then "
17 And i' he shall neglect to hear them, "
17 but i' he neglect to hear the church, "
19 That i' two of you shall agree on "
35 i' ye from your hearts forgive not "
19:10 I' the case of the man be so with 1487
17 but i' thou wilt enter into life, keep "
21 I' thou wilt be perfect, go and sell "
21: 3 And i' any man say ought unto 1487
21 I' ye have faith, and doubt not, ye "
21 but also i' ye shall say unto this 2579
24 which i' ye tell me, I in like wise 1487
25 I' we shall say, From heaven; he "
26 But i' we shall say, Of men; we "
22:24 Moses said, I' a man die, having "
45 I' David then call him Lord, how 1487
23:30 I' we had been in the days of our "
24:23 Then i' any man shall say unto 1487
24 i' it were possible, they shall 1487
26 Wherefore i' they shall say unto 1487
43 that i' the goodman of the house 1487
48 But and i' that evil servant shall 1487
26:24 good for that man i' he had not 1487
39 i' it be possible, let this cup pass "
42 i' this cup may not pass away from "
27:40 I' thou be the Son of God, come "
42 I' he be the King of Israel, let * "
43 i' he will have him: for he said, I "
28:14 And i' this come to the governor's 1487
M'r 1:40 I' thou wilt, thou canst make me "
3:24 i' a kingdom be divided against "
25 And i' a house be divided against "
26 i' Satan rise up against himself, 1487
4:23 I' any man have ears to hear, let him
26 as i' a man should cast seed into 1487
5:28 I' I may touch but his clothes, I 2579
6:56 touch i' it were but the border of "
7:11 I' a man shall say to his father or 1487
8: 3 And i' I send them away fasting to "
36 i' he shall gain the whole world, * "
9:23 I' thou canst believe, all things 1487
35 I' any man desire to be first, the "
43 i' thy hand offend thee, cut it off: 1487
45 And i' thy foot offend thee, cut it off: "
47 i' thine eye offend thee, pluck it out: "
50 i' the salt have lost his saltness, "
10:12 And i' a woman shall put away her "

M'r 11: 3 *i*· any man say unto you, Why do 1487
13 *i*· haply he might find any thing 1487
25 forgive, *i*· ye have ought against "
26 But *i*· ye do not forgive, neither * "
31 *I*· we shall say, From heaven; he 1487
32 *i*· we shall say, Of men; they feared* "
12: 19 *I*· a man's brother die, and leave "
13: 21 then *i*· any man shall say to you, "
22 to seduce, *i*· it were possible, even 1487
14: 21 that man *i*· he had never been born. "
31 *I*· I should die with thee, I will not 1487
35 and prayed that, *i*· it were possible, 1487
15: 44 marvelled *i*· he were already dead: "
16: 18 and *i*· they drink any deadly thing, 2579
Lu 4: 3 *I*· thou be the Son of God, 1487
7 *I*· thou therefore wilt worship me, 1487
9 *I*· thou be the Son of God, cast 1487
5: 12 *i*· thou wilt, thou canst make me 1487
36 *i*· otherwise, then both the new *1490
6: 32 For *i*· ye love them which love you, 1487
33 And *i*· ye do good to them which 1487
34 *i*· ye lend to them of whom ye hope "
7: 39 This man, *i*· he were a prophet, 1487
9: 23 *I*· any man will come after me, let "
25 *i*· he gain the whole world, and lose "
10: 6 And *i*· the son of peace be there, 1487
6 *i*· not, it shall turn to you again. 1490
13 *i*· the mighty works had been done 1487
11: 11 *I*· a son shall ask bread of any of you *
11 *i*· he ask a fish, will he for a fish give*
12 *i*· he shall ask an egg, will he offer 1487
13 *I*· ye then, being evil, know how to 1487
18 *I*· Satan also be divided against 1499
19 *i*· I by Beelzebub cast out devils, by 1487
20 But *i*· I with the finger of God cast "
36 *I*· thy whole body therefore be full "
12: 26 *I*· ye then be not able to do that "
28 *I*· then God so clothe the grass, "
38 And *i*· he shall come in the second 1487
39 that *i*· the goodman of the house 1487
45 But and *i*· that servant say in his 1487
49 will I, *i*· it be already kindled? 1487
13: 9 And *i*· it bear fruit, well: and 2579
9 and *i*· not, then after that thou 1487
14: 34 but *i*· the salt have lost his savour, 1487
15: 4 *i*· he lose one of them, doth not leave*
8 *i*· she lose one piece, doth not light 1487
16: 11 *I*· therefore ye have not been 1487
12 And *i*· ye have not been faithful in "
30 but *i*· one went unto them from the 1487
31 *I*· they hear not Moses and the 1487
17: 3 *I*· thy brother trespass against 1487
3 and *i*· he repent, forgive him. "
4 *i*· he trespass against thee seven "
6 *I*· ye had faith as a grain of 1487
19: 8 and *i*· I have taken any thing from "
31 And *i*· any man ask you, Why do "
40 *i*· these should hold their peace, the "
42 *I*· thou hadst known, even thou, 1487
20: 5 *I*· we shall say, From heaven; he 1487
6 But and *i*· we say, Of men; all the "
28 *I*· any man's brother die, having a "
22: 42 *i*· thou be willing, remove this cup 1487
67 *I*· I tell you, ye will not believe: 1487
68 And *i*· I also ask you, ye will not "
23: 31 *i*· they do these things in a green "
35 himself, *i*· he be Christ, the chosen "
37 *I*· thou be the king of the Jews, save "
39 *I*· thou be Christ, save thyself and* "
Joh 1: 25 *i*· thou be not that Christ, nor Elias, "
3: 12 *I*· I have told you earthly things, "
12 *i*· I tell you of heavenly things? 1487
4: 10 *I*· thou knewest the gift of God, 1487
5: 31 *I*· I bear witness of myself, my 1487
43 *i*· another shall come in his own "
47 But *i*· ye believe not his writings, 1487
6: 51 *i*· any man eat of this bread, he 1487
62 What and *i*· ye shall see the Son "
7: 4 *I*· thou do these things, shew 1487
17 *I*· any man will do his will, he 1487
23 *I*· a man on the sabbath day 1487
37 *I*· any man thirst, let him come 1487
8: 16 And yet *i*· I judge, my judgment is "
19 *i*· ye had known me, ye should 1487
24 for *i*· ye believe not that I am he, 1487
31 *I*· ye continue in my word, then "
36 *I*· the Son therefore shall make you "
39 *I*· ye were Abraham's children, 1487
42 *I*· God were your Father, ye would "
46 *i*· I say the truth, why do ye not "
51, 52 *I*· a man keep my saying, he 1437
54 *I*· I honour myself, my honour is "
55 and *i*· I should say, I know him not, "
9: 22 that *i*· any man did confess that he "
31 but *i*· any man be a worshipper of "
33 *I*· this man were not of God, he 1487
41 *I*· ye were blind, ye should have "
10: 9 by me *i*· any man enter in, he shall 1487
24 *I*· thou be the Christ, tell us 1487
35 *I*· he called them gods, unto whom "
37 *I*· I do not the works of my Father, "
38 But *i*· I do, though ye believe not "
11: 9 *I*· any man walk in the day, he 1487
10 But *i*· a man walk in the night, he "
12 Lord, *i*· he sleep, he shall do well. 1487
21, 32 *i*· thou hadst been here, my brother "
40 *i*· thou wouldest believe, thou 1487
48 *I*· we let him thus alone, all men "
57 *i*· any man knew where he were, he "
12: 24 but *i*· it die, it bringeth forth much "
26 *I*· any man serve me, let him follow "
26 *i*· any man serve me, him will my "
32 I, *i*· I be lifted up from the earth, "
47 And *i*· any man hear my words, and "
13: 8 *I*· I wash thee not, thou hast no part "
14 *I*· I then, your Lord and Master, 1487
Joh 13: 17 *I*· ye know these things, 1487
17 happy are ye *i*· ye do them. 1487
32 *I*· God be glorified in him, God *1487
35 disciples, *i*· ye have love one to 1487
14: 2 *i*· it were not so, I would have told 1490
3 And *i*· I go and prepare a place 1487
7 *I*· ye had known me, ye should 1487
14 *I*· ye shall ask any thing in my 1487
15 *I*· ye love me, keep my "
23 *I*· a man love me, he will keep my "
28 *I*· ye loved me, ye would rejoice, 1487
15: 6 *I*· a man abide not in me, he is cast 1487
7 *I*· ye abide in me, and my words "
10 *I*· ye keep my commandments, ye "
14 my friends, *i*· ye do whatsoever I "
18 *I*· the world hate you, ye know 1487
19 *I*· ye were of the world, the world "
20 *I*· they have persecuted me, they "
20 *i*· they have kept my saying, they "
22 *I*· I had not come and spoken unto "
24 *I*· I had not done among them the "
16: 7 for *i*· I go not away, the Comforter 1487
7 *i*· I depart, I will send him unto "
18: 8 *i*· therefore ye seek me, let these go 1487
23 *I*· I have spoken evil, bear witness "
23 but *i*· well, why smitest thou me? "
30 *I*· he were not a malefactor, we "
36 *i*· my kingdom were of this world, "
19: 12 *I*· thou let this man go, thou art 1487
20: 15 *i*· thou have borne him hence, tell 1487
21: 22 *I*· I will that he tarry till I come, 1487
23 but, *I*· I will that he tarry till I "
25 *i*· they should be written every one, "
Ac 4: 9 *I*· we this day be examined of the 1487
5: 38 for *i*· this counsel or this work be 1487
39 But *i*· it be of God, ye cannot 1487
8: 22 *i*· perhaps the thought of thine "
37 *I*· thou believest with all thine * "
9: 2 that *i*· he found any of this way, 1487
13: 15 *i*· ye have any word of exhortation 1487
15: 29 from which *i*· ye keep yourselves, ye "
16: 15 *I*· ye have judged me to be faithful 1487
17: 27 *i*· haply they might feel after him, "
18: 14 *I*· it were a matter of wrong or "
15 But *i*· it be a question of words and "
21 will return again unto you, *i*· God will.
19: 38 Wherefore *i*· Demetrius, and the 1487
39 *i*· ye enquire any thing concerning "
20: 16 *i*· it were possible for him, to be at "
23: 9 *i*· a spirit or an angel hath spoken "
24: 19 *i*· they had ought against me. "
20 *i*· they have found any evil doing * "
25: 5 *i*· there be any wickedness in him. "
11 For *i*· I be an offender, or have 1487
11 but *i*· there be none of these things "
26: 5 *i*· they would testify, that after 1487
32 *i*· he had not appealed unto Cæsar. "
27: 12 *i*· by any means they might attain 1513
39 *i*· it were possible, to thrust in *1487
Ro 1: 10 *i*· by any means now at length I 1513
2: 25 profiteth, *i*· thou keep the law: 1487
25 but *i*· thou be a breaker of the law, "
26 Therefore *i*· the uncircumcision "
27 *i*· it fulfil the law, judge thee, who "
3: 3 For what *i*· some do not believe? 1487
5 *i*· our unrighteousness commend "
7 For *i*· the truth of God hath more "
4: 2 For *i*· Abraham were justified by "
14 For *i*· they which are of the law be "
24 *i*· we believe on him that raised up*
5: 10 For *i*·, when we were enemies, we 1487
15 For *i*· through the offence of one "
17 For *i*· by one man's offence death "
6: 5 *i*· we have been planted together "
8 Now *i*· we be dead with Christ, we "
7: 2 but *i*· the husband be dead, she 1487
3 So then *i*·, while her husband liveth, "
3 but *i*· her husband be dead, she is "
16 *I*· then I do that which I would 1487
20 Now *i*· I do that I would not, it is "
8: 9 *i*· so be that the Spirit of God 1512
9 Now *i*· any man have not the Spirit 1487
10 And *i*· Christ be in you, the body "
11 But *i*· the Spirit of him that raised 1487
13 For *i*· ye live after the flesh, ye "
13 but *i*· ye through the Spirit do 1487
17 And *i*· children, then heirs; heirs "
17 *i*· so be that we suffer with him, 1512
25 But *i*· we hope for that we see not, 1487
31 *I*· God be for us, who can be "
9: 22 What *i*· God, willing to shew his "
10: 9 That *i*· thou shalt confess with 1487
11: 6 And *i*· by grace, then is it no more 1487
6 But *i*· it be of works, then is it no* "
12 Now *i*· the fall of them be the riches "
14 *I*· by any means I may provoke 1513
15 For *i*· the casting away of them be 1487
16 For *i*· the firstfruit be holy, the "
16 and *i*· the root be holy, so are the "
17 And *i*· some of the branches be "
18 But *i*· thou boast, thou bearest "
21 For *i*· God spared not the natural "
22 *i*· thou continue in his goodness: 1487
23 *i*· they abide not still in unbelief, "
24 For *i*· thou wert cut out of the 1487
12: 18 *I*· it be possible, as much as lieth "
20 Therefore *i*· thine enemy hunger, 1487
20 *i*· he thirst, give him drink: for in "
13: 4 But *i*· thou do that which is evil, "
9 and *i*· there be any other 1487
14: 15 But *i*· thy brother be grieved with "
23 is damned *i*· he eat, because he 1487
15: 24 *i*· first I be somewhat filled with "
27 For *i*· the Gentiles have been made 1487
1Co 3: 12 Now *i*· any man build upon this "
14 *I*· any man's work abide which "
1Co 3: 15 *I*· any man's work shall be burned, 1487
17 *I*· any man defile the temple of "
18 *I*· any man among you seemeth to "
4: 7 now *i*· thou didst receive it, why 1499
7 glory, as *i*· thou hadst not received it?
19 to you shortly, *i*· the Lord will, 1487
5: 11 *i*· any man that is called a brother "
6: 2 and *i*· the world shall be judged 1487
4 *I*· then ye have judgments of 1487
7: 8 It is good for them *i*· they abide "
9 But *i*· they cannot contain, let 1487
11 But and *i*· she depart, let her 1487
12 *i*· any brother hath a wife that 1487
13 and *i*· he be pleased to dwell with her, *
15 But *i*· the unbelieving depart, let 1487
21 but *i*· thou mayest be made free, 1499
28 But and *i*· thou marry, thou hast 1487
28 and *i*· a virgin marry, she hath not "
36 But *i*· any man think that he 1487
36 *i*· she pass the flower of her age, 1487
39 but *i*· her husband be dead, she is "
40 But she is happier *i*· she so abide, "
8: 2 And *i*· any man think that he 1487
3 But *i*· any man love God, the same "
8 for neither, *i*· we eat, are we the 1487
8 neither, *i*· we eat not, are we the "
10 For *i*· any man see thee which hast "
13 *i*· meat make my brother to offend, 1487
9: 2 *I*· I be not an apostle unto others, "
11 *I*· we have sown unto you spiritual "
11 *i*· we shall reap your carnal things? "
12 *I*· others be partakers of this "
16 unto me, *i*· I preach not the gospel! 1487
17 For *i*· I do this thing willingly, I 1487
17 *i*· against my will, a dispensation "
10: 27 *I*· any of them that believe not 1487
28 But *i*· any man say unto you, This 1487
30 For *i*· I by grace be a partaker, 1487
11: 5 is even all one as *i*· she were shaven.
6 For *i*· the woman be not covered, 1487
6 but *i*· it be a shame for a woman "
14 *i*· a man have long hair, it is a 1487
15 But *i*· a woman have long hair, it is "
16 But *i*· any man seem to be 1487
31 For *i*· we would judge ourselves, "
34 *i*· any man hunger, let him eat at "
12: 15 *I*· the foot shall say, Because I 1487
16 And *i*· the ear shall say, Because I "
17 *I*· the whole body were an eye, 1487
17 *I*· the whole were hearing, where "
19 And *i*· they were all one member, "
14: 6 *i*· I come unto you speaking with *1487
8 *i*· the trumpet give an uncertain "
11 Therefore *i*· I know not the meaning "
14 For *i*· I pray in an unknown tongue, "
23 *I*· therefore the whole church be "
24 But *i*· all prophesy, and there come "
27 *I*· any man speak in an unknown 1535
28 But *i*· there be no interpreter, 1487
30 *I*· any thing be revealed to another "
35 And *i*· they will learn any thing, 1487
37 *I*· any man think himself to be a "
38 But *i*· any man be ignorant, "
15: 2 saved, *i*· ye keep in memory what I "
12 Now *i*· Christ be preached that he "
13 But *i*· there be no resurrection of "
14 And *i*· Christ be not risen, then is "
15 *i*· so be that the dead rise not. 1512
16 For *i*· the dead rise not, then is 1487
17 And *i*· Christ be not raised, your "
19 *I*· in this life only we have hope in "
29 the dead, *i*· the dead rise not at all? "
32 *I*· after the manner of men I have "
32 what advantageth it me, *i*· the dead "
16: 4 And *i*· it be meet that I go also, 1487
7 while with you, *i*· the Lord permit. "
10 Now *i*· Timotheus come, see that "
22 *I*· any man love not the Lord Jesus 1487
2Co 2: 2 For *i*· I make you sorry, who is he "
5 But *i*· any have caused grief, "
10 for *i*· I forgave any thing, to whom "
3: 7 But *i*· the ministration of death, "
9 For *i*· the ministration of "
11 For *i*· that which is done away was "
4: 3 But *i*· our gospel be hid, it is hid 1499
5: 1 For we know that *i*· our earthly 1487
3 *I*· so be that being clothed we 1489
14 that *i*· one died for all, then were *1487
17 Therefore *i*· any man be in Christ, "
7: 14 For *i*· I have boasted any thing to "
8: 12 For *i*· there be first a willing mind, "
9: 4 Lest haply *i*· they of Macedonia 1437
10: 2 as *i*· we walked according to the flesh.
7 *I*· any man trust to himself that 1487
9 as *i*· I would terrify you by letters.
11: 4 For *i*· he that cometh preacheth 1487
4 or *i*· ye receive another spirit, which "
15 *i*· his ministers also be transformed 1499
16 *i*· otherwise, yet as a fool receive 1490
20 *i*· a man bring you into bondage, 1487
20 *i*· a man devour you, *i*· a man take "
20 *i*· a man exalt himself, *i*· a man "
30 *I*· I must needs glory, I will glory "
13: 2 as *i*· I were present, the second *1487
2 that, *i*· I come again, I will not spare:
Ga 1: 9 *I*· any man preach any other gospel 1487
10 for *i*· I yet pleased men, I should "
2: 14 *I*· thou, being a Jew, livest after "
17 But *i*·, while we seek to be justified "
18 For *i*· I build again the things which "
21 *i*· righteousness come by the law, "
3: 4 in vain? *i*· it be yet in vain. 1489
15 yet *i*· it be confirmed, no man *
18 For *i*· the inheritance be of the law 1487
21 for *i*· there had been a law given "
29 And *i*· ye be Christ's, then are ye "

Ga 4: 7 and i' a son, then an heir of God 1487
15 that, i' it had been possible, ye "
5: 2 that i' ye be circumcised, Christ 1487
11 i' I yet preach circumcision, why 1487
15 But i' ye bite and devour one "
18 But i' ye be led of the Spirit, ye are "
25 I' we live in the Spirit, let us also "
6: 1 i' a man be overtaken in a fault, 1487
3 For i' a man think himself to be 1487
9 season we shall reap, i' we faint not.
Eph 3: 2 I' ye have heard of the 1489
4: 21 I' so be that ye have heard him,
Ph'p 1: 22 But i' I live in the flesh, this is 1487
2: 1 I' there be...any consolation in "
1 i' any comfort of love, "
1 i' any fellowship of the Spirit, "
1 i' any bowels and mercies, "
17 Yea, and i' I be offered upon the "
3: 4 I' any other man thinketh that he "
11 I' by any means I might attain 1513
12 i' that I may apprehend that for 1499
15 i' in any thing ye be otherwise 1487
4: 8 good report; i' there be any virtue, "
8 and i' there be any praise, think on "
Col 1: 23 I' ye continue in the faith 1489
2: 20 Wherefore i' ye be dead with 1487
3: 1 I' ye then be risen with Christ, "
13 i' any man have a quarrel against 1437
4: 10 i' he come unto you, receive him; "
1Th 3: 8 For now we live, i' ye stand fast in "
4: 14 For i' we believe that Jesus died 1487
2Th 3: 10 that i' any would not work, neither "
14 And i' any man obey not our word "
1Ti 1: 8 is good, i' a man use it lawfully: 1487
10 and i' there be any other thing 1487
2: 15 i' they continue in faith and 1487
3: 1 I' a man desire the office of a 1487
5 For i' a man know not how to "
15 But i' I tarry long, that thou mayest 1487
4: 4 i' it be received with thanksgiving: "
6 I' thou put the brethren in "
5: 4 i' any widow have children or 1487
8 But i' any provide not for his own, "
10 i' she have brought up children "
10 i' she have lodged strangers, "
10 i' she have washed the saints' feet, "
10 i' she have relieved the afflicted, "
10 i' she have diligently followed every "
16 I' any man or woman that "
6: 3 I' any man teach otherwise, and "
2Ti 2: 5 i' a man also strive for masteries, 1487
11 For i' we be dead with him, we 1487
12 I' we suffer, we shall also reign "
12 i' we deny him, he also will deny "
13 I' we believe not, yet he abideth "
21 I' a man therefore purge himself 1487
25 i' God peradventure will give them 3379
Tit 1: 6 I' any be blameless, the husband of 1487
Ph'm 17 I' thou count me therefore a "
18 I' he hath wronged thee, or oweth "
Heb 2: 2 For i' the word spoken by angels "
3 i' we neglect so great salvation; "
3: 6 i' we hold fast the confidence and 1487
7 To day i' ye will hear his voice, "
14 i' we hold the beginning of our "
15 To day i' ye will hear his voice, "
4: 3 i' they shall enter into my rest: *1487
5 I' they shall enter into my rest. * "
7 To day i' ye will hear his voice, 1487
8 For i' Jesus had given them rest, 1487
6: 3 And this will we do, i' God permit. 1487
6 I' they shall fall away, to renew "
7: 11 I' therefore perfection were by 1487
8: 4 For i' he were on earth, he should "
7 For i' that first covenant had been "
9: 13 For i' the blood of bulls and of "
10: 26 For i' we sin wilfully after that we "
38 but i' any man draw back, my soul 1487
11: 15 i' they had been mindful of that 1487
12: 7 I' ye endure chastening, God * "
8 But i' ye be without chastisement, "
20 And i' so much as a beast touch the "
25 for i' they escaped not who refused 1487
25 i' we turn away from him that *
13: 23 i' he come shortly, I will see you. 1487
Jas 1: 5 I' any of you lack wisdom, let him 1487
23 For i' any be a hearer of the word, "
26 I' any man among you seem to be "
2: 2 i' there come unto your assembly 1487
8 I' ye fulfil the royal law according 1487
9 But i' ye have respect to persons, "
11 Now i' thou commit no adultery, "
11 yet i' thou kill, thou art become a*
15 I' a brother or sister be naked, 1487
17 i' it hath not works, is dead, "
3: 2 I' any man offend not in word, 1487
14 But i' ye have bitter envying and "
4: 11 but i' thou judge the law, thou art "
15 I' the Lord will, we shall live, and 1487
5: 15 and i' he have committed sins, they "
19 Brethren, i' any of you do err from 1487
1Pe 1: 6 i' need be, ye are in heaviness 1487
17 And i' ye call on the Father, who "
2: 3 I' so be ye have tasted that the 1512
19 i' a man for conscience toward God 1487
20 i', when ye be buffeted for your "
20 i', when ye do well, and suffer for "
3: 1 that, i' any obey not the word, they "
13 i' ye be followers of that which is 1487
14 and i' ye suffer for righteousness' sake, "
17 i' the will of God be so, that ye 1487
4: 11 I' any man speak, let him speak "
11 i' any man minister, let him do it "
14 I' ye be reproached for the name "
16 Yet i' any man suffer as a Christian, "
17 and i' it first begin at us, what "
1Pe 4: 18 And i' the righteous scarcely be 1487
2Pe 1: 8 For i' these things be in you, and
10 for i' ye do these things, ye shall never
2: 4 For i' God spared not the angels 1487
20 For i' after they have escaped the "
1Jo 1: 6 I' we say that we have fellowship 1487
7 But i' we walk in the light, as he is "
8 I' we say that we have no sin, we "
9 I' we confess our sins, he is "
10 I' we say that we have not sinned, "
2: 1 And i' any man sin, we have an "
3 i' we keep his commandments. "
15 I' any man love the world, the love "
19 for i' they had been of us, they 1487
24 I' that which ye have heard from 1487
29 I' ye know that he is righteous, ye "
3: 13 my brethren, i' the world hate you 1487
20 For i' our heart condemn us, God †1437
21 i' our heart condemn us not, "
4: 11 Beloved, i' God so loved us, we 1487
12 I' we love one another, God 1487
20 I' a man say, I love God, and "
5: 9 I' we receive the witness of men, 1487
14 i' we ask any thing according to 1437
15 And i' we know that he hear us, "
16 I' any man see his brother sin a "
2Jo 10 I' there come any unto you, and 1487
3Jo 6 whom i' thou bring forward on their*
10 i' I come, I will remember his 1437
Re 1: 15 brass, as i' they burned in a furnace;
3: 3 I' therefore thou shalt not 1487
20 i' any man hear my voice, and open "
11: 5 And i' any man will hurt them, 1487
5 and i' any man will hurt them, he "
13: 9 I' any man have an ear, let him "
14: 9 I' any man worship the beast and "
22: 18 I' any man shall add unto these 1487
19 And i' any man shall take away "

Igal (i'-gal) See also IGEAL.
Nu 13: 7 Issachar, I' the son of Joseph. 3008
2Sa 23: 36 I' the son of Nathan of Zobah, "

Igdaliah (ig-da-li'-ah)
Jer 35: 4 of I', a man of God, which was 3012

Igeal (ig'-e-al) See also IGAL.
1Ch 3: 22 Hattush, and I', and Bariah, and*3008

ignominy
Pr 18: 3 contempt, and with i' reproach. *7036

ignorance
Le 4: 2 If a soul shall sin through i' *7684
13 of Israel sin through i', *7686
22 done somewhat through i' *7684
27 common people sin through i', * "
5: 15 a trespass, and sin through i', * "
18 his i' wherein he erred and wist it* "
Nu 15: 24 if ought be committed by i' * "
25 shall be forgiven them; for it is i': * "
25 before the Lord, for their i': * "
26 seeing all the people were in i'. * "
27 if any soul sin through i', then he* "
28 he sinneth by i' before the Lord, * "
29 for him that sinneth through i', * "
Ac 3: 17 brethen, I wot that through i' ye did 52
17: 30 the times of this i' God winked at; "
Eph 4: 18 God through the i' that is in them, "
1Pe 1: 14 to the former lusts in your i': "
2: 15 to silence the i' of foolish men: 56

ignorant
Ps 73: 22 So foolish was I, and i': I was 3808, 3045
Isa 56: 10 they are all i', they are all * "
63: 16 though Abraham be i' of us, * "
Ac 4: 13 they were unlearned and i' men, 2399
Ro 1: 13 Now I would not have you i', 50
10: 3 For they being i' of God's "
11: 25 that ye should be i' of this mystery, "
1Co 10: 1 I would not that ye should be i', "
12: 1 brethren, I would not have you i'. "
14: 38 if any man be i', let him be i'. "
2Co 1: 8 would not, brethren, have you i' of "
2: 11 of us: for we are not i' of his devices. "
1Th 4: 13 But I would not have you to be i', "
Heb 5: 2 Who can have compassion on the i', "
2Pe 3: 5 For this they willingly are i' of *2990
8 beloved, be not i' of this one thing, * "

ignorantly
Nu 15: 28 for the soul that sinneth i', when *7683
De 19: 4 Whoso killeth...neighbour i', *1097, 1847
Ac 17: 23 Whom therefore ye i' worship, him *50
1Ti 1: 13 mercy, because I did it i' in unbelief. "

Iim (i'-im) See also IJE-ABARIM.
Nu 33: 45 And they departed from I', and *5864
Jos 15: 29 Baalah, and I', and Azem,

Ije-abarim (i'-je-ab'-a-rim) See also IIM.
Nu 21: 11 and pitched at I', in the 5863
33: 44 and pitched in I', in the border "

Ijon (i'-jon)
1Ki 15: 20 and smote I', and Dan, and 5859
2Ki 15: 29 took I', and Abel-beth-maachah, "
2Ch 16: 4 and they smote I', and Dan, and "

Ikkesh (ik'-kesh)
2Sa 23: 26 Ira the son of I' the Tekoite, 6142
1Ch 11: 28 Ira the son of I' the Tekoite, "
27: 9 sixth month was Ira the son of I' "

Ilai (i'-lahee) See also ZALMON.
1Ch 11: 29 the Hushathite, I' the Ahohite, 5866

ill
Ge 41: 3 them out of the river, i' favoured 7451
4 the i' favoured and leanfleshed kine "
19 up after them, poor and very i' "
20 the lean and the i' favoured kine "
Ge 41: 21 they were still i' favoured, as at 7451
27 the seven thin and i' favoured kine "
43: 6 dealt so i' with me, as to tell 7489
De 15: 21 blind, or have any i' blemish, 7451
Job 20: 26 it shall go i' with him that is left *3415
Ps 106: 32 so that it went i' with Moses for "
Isa 3: 11 it shall be i' with him: for the 7451
Jer 40: 4 if it seem i' unto thee to come 7489
Joel 2: 20 and his i' savour shall come up, 6709
Mic 3: 4 they have behaved themselves i' *7489
Ro 13: 10 Love worketh no i' to his 2556

ill-favoured See ILL and FAVOURED.

illuminated
Heb 10: 32 in which, after ye were i', ye *5461

Illyricum (il-lir'-ic-um)
Ro 15: 19 and round about unto I', I have 2437

image See also IMAGE'S; IMAGES.
Ge 1: 26 said, Let us make man in our i', 6754
27 God created man in his own i', "
27 in the i' of God created he him; "
5: 3 in his own likeness, after his i'; "
9: 6 for in the i' of God made he man. "
Ex 20: 4 not make unto thee any graven i',
Le 26: 1 make you no idols nor graven i',
1 neither rear you up a standing i', *6676
1 neither shall ye set up any i' of *4906
De 4: 16 and make you a graven i', the
23 and make you a graven i', or the
25 and make a graven i', or the
5: 8 shalt not make thee any graven i',
9: 12 they have made them a molten i'.
16: 22 shalt thou set thee up any i'; *4676
27: 15 maketh any graven or molten i',
J'g 17: 3 for my son, to make a graven i'
3 and a molten i': now therefore I
4 thereof a graven i', and a molten i':
18: 14 and a graven i' and a molten i'?
17 and took the graven i', and the
17 teraphim, and the molten i': and the
18 and fetched the carved i', the ephod,
18 the teraphim, and the molten i'.
25 the teraphim, and the graven i',
30 children of Dan set up the graven i':
31 them up Micah's graven i', which
1Sa 19: 13 Michal took an i', and laid it in *8655
16 behold, there was an i' in the bed, * "
2Ki 3: 2 he put away the i' of Baal that *4676
10: 27 they brake down the i' of Baal, and* "
21: 7 he set a graven i' of the grove that he
2Ch 3: 10 he made two cherubims of i' work, 6816
33: 7 And he set a carved i', the idol
Job 4: 16 an i' was before mine eyes, there *8544
Ps 73: 20 thou shalt despise their i'. 6754
106: 19 Horeb, and worshipped the molten i'.
Isa 40: 19 The workman melteth a graven i',
20 workman to prepare a graven i',
44: 9 They that make a graven i' are all
10 formed a god, or molten a graven i'
15 he maketh it a graven i', and falleth
17 he maketh a god, even his graven i':
45: 20 set up the wood of their graven i',
48: 5 hath done them, and my graven i',
5 and my molten i', hath commanded
Jer 10: 14 is confounded by the graven i': 6459
14 for his molten i' is falsehood, and
51: 17 is confounded by the graven i': 6459
17 for his molten i' is falsehood, and
Eze 8: 3 was the seat of the i' of jealousy, 5566
5 altar this i' of jealousy in the entry. "
Da 2: 31 king, sawest, and behold a great i'. 6755
31 This great i', whose brightness was "
34 which smote the i' upon his feet, "
35 and the stone that smote the i' "
3: 1 the king made an i' of gold, whose "
2 to the dedication of the i' which "
3 unto the dedication of the i' that "
3 set up; and they stood before the i' "
5 fall down and worship the golden i' "
7 down and worshipped the golden i' "
10 fall down and worship the golden i': "
12 nor worship the golden i' which "
14 nor worship the golden i' which I "
15 fall down and worship the i' which "
18 nor worship the golden i' which "
Ho 3: 4 and without an i', and without an * "
Na 1: 14 cut off the graven i' and the molten i':
Hab 2: 18 What profiteth the graven i' that
18 the molten i', and a teacher of lies,
M't 22: 20 Whose is this i' and superscription? 1504
M'r 12: 16 Whose is this i' and superscription? "
Lu 20: 24 Whose i' and superscription hath "
Ac 19: 35 i' which fell down from Jupiter? "
Ro 1: 23 into an i' made like to corruptible 1504
8: 29 conformed to the i' of his Son, that "
11: 4 not bowed the knee to the i' of Baal.
1Co 11: 7 as he is the i' and glory of God: 1504
15: 49 as we have borne the i' of the earthy, "
49 also bear the i' of the heavenly. "
2Co 3: 18 changed into the same i' from glory 1504
4: 4 gospel of Christ, who is the i' of God, "
Col 1: 15 Who is the i' of the invisible God, "
3: 10 after the i' of him that created him: "
Heb 1: 3 and the express i' of his person, 5481
10: 1 not the very image of the things, 1504
Re 13: 14 they should make an i' to the beast, "
15 to give life unto the i' of the beast, "
15 i' of the beast should both speak, "
15 not worship the i' of the beast "
14: 9 man worship the beast and his i', "
11 who worship the beast and his i', "
15: 2 victory over the beast, and over his i', "
16: 2 upon them which worshipped his i'. "
19: 20 and them that worshipped his i'. "
20: 4 worshipped the beast, neither his i', "

imagery
Eze 8:12 man in the chambers of his i·? 4906
image's
Da 2:32 This i· head was of fine gold, *6755
images
Ge 31:19 Rachel had stolen the i· that were*8655
34 Rachel had taken the i·, and put * "
35 he searched, but found not the i·.* "
Ex 23:24 and quite break down their i·. *4676
34:13 break their i·, and cut down their* "
Le 26:30 cut down your i·, and cast your *2553
Nu 33:52 destroy all their molten i·, and
De 7: 5 and break down their i·, and cut *4676
5 and burn their graven i· with fire.
25 The graven i· of their gods shall ye
12: 3 ye shall hew down the graven i· of
1Sa 6: 5 ye shall make i· of your emerods, 6754
5 and i· of your mice that mar the "
11 of gold and the i· of their emerods, "
2Sa 5:21 And there they left their i·, and 6091
1Ki 14: 9 made thee other gods, and molten i·,
23 built them high places, and i·, *4676
2Ki 10:26 forth the i· out of the house of Baal,*"
11:18 and his i· brake they in pieces 6754
17:10 they set them up i· and groves *4676
16 made them molten i·, even two calves,
41 and served their graven i·, both
18: 4 brake the i·, and cut down the *4676
23:14 And he brake in pieces the i·, * "
24 wizards, and the i·, and the idols, *8655
2Ch 14: 3 and brake down the i·, and cut *4676
5 away...the high places and the i·:* "
23:17 his altars and his i· in pieces, 6754
28: 2 and made also molten i· for Baalim.
31: 1 Judah, and brake the i· in pieces,*4676
33:19 and set up groves and graven i·,
22 sacrificed unto all the carved i·
34: 3 and the groves, and the carved i·,
3 the groves,...and the molten i·,
4 and the i·, that were on high above*2553
4 and the groves, and the carved i·,
4 the groves,...and the molten i·.
7 beaten the graven i· into powder, 6456
Ps 78:58 him to jealousy with their graven i·."
97: 7 be all they that serve graven i·,
Isa 10:10 and whose graven i· did excel
17: 8 made, either the groves, or the i·.*2553
21: 9 and all the graven i· of her gods
27: 9 the groves and i· shall not stand *2553
30:22 covering of thy graven i· of silver,
22 ornament of thy molten i· of gold:
41:29 their molten i· are wind and confusion.
42: 8 neither my praise to graven i·.
17 ashamed, that trust in graven i·,
17 that say to the molten i·, Ye are our
Jer 8:19 me to anger with their graven i·,
43:13 He shall break also the i· of *4676
50: 2 confounded, her i· are broken in *1544
38 for it is the land of graven i·, and
51:47 upon the graven i· of Babylon:
52 do judgment upon her graven i·:
Eze 6: 4 your i· shall be broken: and I will*2553
6 and your i· may be cut down, and* "
7:20 made the i· of their abominations 6754
16:17 and madest to thyself i· of men, and"
21:21 he consulted with i·, he looked in *8655
23:14 the i· of the Chaldeans pourtrayed 6754
30:13 cause their i· to cease out of Noph; 457
Ho 10: 1 his land they have made goodly i·.*4676
2 their altars, he shall spoil their i·.* "
11: 2 and burned incense to graven i·.
13: 2 and have made them molten i· of their
Am 5:26 Moloch and Chiun your i·, the 6754
Mic 1: 7 all the graven i· thereof shall be
5:13 Thy graven i· also will I cut off, 4676
13 and thy standing i· out of the midst*
image-work See IMAGE and WORK.
imagination See also IMAGINATIONS.
Ge 6: 5 every i· of the thoughts of his 3336
8:21 the i· of man's heart is evil from "
De 29:19 I walk in the i· of mine heart, *8307
31:21 for I know their i· which they go 3336
1Ch 29:18 keep this for ever in the i· of the "
Jer 3:17 after the i· of their evil heart. *8307
7:24 and in the i· of their evil heart, * "
9:14 the i· of their own heart, and after* "
11: 8 one in the i· of their evil heart: * "
13:10 walk in the i· of their heart, and * "
16:12 one after the i· of his evil heart, * "
18:12 every one do the i· of his evil heart.*"
23:17 after the i· of his own heart, * "
Lu 1:51 proud in the i· of their hearts. *1271*
imaginations
1Ch 28: 9 all the i· of the thoughts: if thou 3336
Pr 6:18 An heart that deviseth wicked i·, 4284
La 3:60 and all their i· against me. * "
61 Lord, and all their i· against me;* "
Ro 1:21 became vain in their i·, and their **1261*
2Co 10: 5 Casting down i·, and every high *3053*
imagine See also IMAGINED; IMAGINETH.
Job 6:26 Do ye i· to reprove words, and ‡2803
21:27 the devices which ye wrongfully i· 2554
Ps 2: 1 and the people i· a vain thing? ‡1897
38:12 and i· deceits all the day long. ‡ "
62: 3 will ye i· mischief against a man?*2050
140: 2 Which i· mischiefs in their heart; ‡2803
Pr 12:20 in the heart of them that i· evil: *2790
Ho 7:15 yet do they i· mischief against ‡2803
Na 1: 9 What do ye i· against the Lord? ‡ "
Zec 7:10 you i· evil against his brother ‡ "
8:17 none of you i· evil in your hearts ‡
Ac 4:25 rage, and the people i· vain things? *3191*
imagined
Ge 11: 6 them, which they have i· to do. *2161
Ps 10: 2 in the devices that they have i·. ‡2803
21:11 they i· a mischievous device, ‡ "
imagineth
Na 1:11 that i· evil against the Lord, ‡2803
Imla (*im'-lah*) See also IMLAH.
2Ch 18: 7 the same is Micaiah the son of I·. 3229
8 quickly Micaiah the son of I·. "
Imlah (*im'-lah*) See also IMLA.
1Ki 22: 8 one man, Micaiah the son of I·, 3229
9 hither Micaiah the son of I·.
Immanuel (*im-man'-u-el*) See also EMMANUEL.
Is 7:14 a son, and shall call his name I· 6005
8: 8 fill the breadth of the land, O I·.
immediately
M't 4:22 And they i· left the ship, and **2112*
8: 3 And i· his leprosy was cleansed. * "
14:31 And i· Jesus stretched forth his * "
20:34 i· their eyes received sight, and * "
24:29 i· after the tribulation of those * "
26:74 the man. And i· the cock crew. * "
M'k 1:12 i· the spirit driveth him into the **2117*
28 i· his fame spread abroad *
31 i· the fever left her, and she **2112*
42 i· the leprosy departed from him,* "
2: 8 i· when Jesus perceived in his * "
12 And i· he arose, took up the bed, * "
4: 5 and i· it sprang up, because it * "
15 Satan cometh i·, and taketh away* "
16 word, i· receive it with gladness;* "
17 word's sake, i· they are offended.* "
29 i· he putteth in the sickle, * "
5: 2 i· there met him out of the tombs* "
30 Jesus, i· knowing in himself that * "
6:27 i· the king sent an executioner, * "
50 i· he talked with them, and saith * "
10:52 And i· he received his sight, and * "
14:43 And i·, while he yet spake, * "
Lu 1:64 And his mouth was opened i·, and *3916*
4:39 i· she arose and ministered unto "
5:13 i· the leprosy departed from him.**2112*
25 And i· he rose up before them, *3916*
6:49 beat vehemently, and i· it fell; **2112*
8:44 and i· her issue of blood stanched.*3916*
47 him, and how she was healed i·. "
12:36 they may open unto him i·. **2112*
13:13 and i· she was made straight, *3916*
18:43 And i· he received his sight, and "
19:11 kingdom of God should i· appear. "
40 peace, the stones would i· cry out.*
22:60 And i·, while he yet spake, the *3916*
Joh 5: 9 i· the man was made whole, and **2112*
6:21 i· the ship was at the land * "
13:30 received the sop went i· out: * "
18:27 again: and i· the cock crew. * "
21: 3 forth, and entered into a ship i·; **2117*
Ac 3: 7 and i· his feet and ancle bones *3916*
9:18 i· there fell from his eyes as it **2112*
34 make thy bed. And he arose i·. * "
10:33 I· therefore I sent to thee; and **1824*
11:11 i· there were three men already * "
12:23 And i· the angel of the Lord smote *3916*
13:11 And i· there fell on him a mist and "
16:10 i· we endeavoured to go into **2112*
26 and i· all the doors were opened, *3916*
17:10 the brethren i· sent away Paul *2112*
14 i· the brethren sent away Paul "
21:32 Who i· took soldiers and **1824*
Ga 1:16 i· I conferred not with flesh and *2112*
Re 4: 2 And i· I was in the spirit: and * "
Immer (*im'-mur*)
1Ch 9:12 son of Meshillemith, the son of I·; 564
24:14 to Bilgah, the sixteenth to I·, "
Ezr 2:37 The children of I·, a thousand fifty "
59 Tel-harsa, Cherub, Addan, and I·: "
10:20 of the sons of I·; Hanani, and "
Ne 3:29 them repaired Zadok the son of I· "
7:40 The children of I·, a thousand fifty "
61 Tel-haresha, Cherub, Addon, and I·;"
11:13 son of Meshillemoth, the son of I·, "
Jer 20: 1 Now Pashur the son of I· the priest, "
immortal
1Ti 1:17 Now unto the King eternal, i·, **862*
immortality
Ro 2: 7 glory and honour and i·, eternal **861*
1Co 15:53 and this mortal must put on i·. *110*
54 this mortal shall have put on i·, "
1Ti 6:16 Who only hath i·, dwelling in the "
2Ti 1:10 hath brought life and i· to light ‡*861*
immovable See UNMOVABLE.
immutability
Heb 6:17 the i· of his counsel, confirmed it *276*
immutable
Heb 6:18 That by two i· things, in which it *276*
Imna (*im'-nah*) See also IMNAH; JIMNA.
1Ch 7:35 Zophah, and I·, and Shelesh, and 3234
Imnah (*im'-nah*) See also IMNA; JIMNAH.
1Ch 7:30 sons of Asher; I·, and Ishuah, 3232
2Ch 31:14 And Kore the son of I· the Levite, "
impart See also IMPARTED.
Lu 3:11 let him i· to him that hath none; *3330*
Ro 1:11 i· unto you some spiritual gift, "
imparted
Job 39:17 hath he i· to her understanding. 2505
1Th 2: 8 were willing to have i· unto you, **3330*
impediment
M'r 7:32 deaf, and had an i· in his speech; *3424*
impenitent
Ro 2: 5 But, after thy hardness and i· heart *279*
imperfect See UNPERFECT.
imperious
Eze 16:30 the work of an i· whorish woman; 7986
implacable
Ro 1:31 without natural affection, i·, * *786*
implead
Ac 19:38 deputies: let them i· one another.**1458*
importunity
Lu 11: 8 yet because of his i· he will rise *335*
impose See also IMPOSED.
Ezr 7:24 it shall not be lawful to i· toll, 7412
imposed
Heb 9:10 i· on them until the time of *1945*
impossible
M't 17:20 and nothing shall be i· unto you. *101*
19:26 With men this is i·; but with God *102*
M'r 10:27 With men it is i·, but not with God: "
Lu 1:37 with God nothing shall be i·. * *101*
17: 1 is i· but that offences will come: *418*
18:27 things which are i· with men are *102*
Heb 6: 4 For it is i· for those who were once* "
18 in which it was i· for God to lie, "
11: 6 without faith it is i· to please him: "
impotent
Joh 5: 3 lay a great multitude of i· folk, * *770*
7 The i· man answered him, Sir, I * "
Ac 4: 9 the good deed done to the i· man, *772*
14: 8 certain man at Lystra, i· in his feet, *102*
impoverish See also IMPOVERISHED.
Jer 5:17 they shall i· thy fenced cities, *7567
impoverished
J'g 6: 6 And Israel was greatly i· because*1809
Isa 40:20 is so i· that he hath no oblation 5533
Mal 1: 4 Whereas, Edom saith, We are i·, *7567
imprisoned
Ac 22:19 know that I i· and beat in every *5439*
imprisonment See also IMPRISONMENTS.
Ezr 7:26 or to confiscation of goods, or to i·. 613
Heb 11:36 yea, moreover of bonds and i·: *5438*
imprisonments
2Co 6: 5 In stripes, in i·, in tumults, in *5438*
impudent
Pr 7:13 kissed him, and with an i· face 5810
Eze 2: 4 i· children and stiffhearted. 7186, 6440
3: 7 all the house of Israel are i·*2389, 4696
impute See also IMPUTED; IMPUTETH; IMPUTING.
1Sa 22:15 king i· any thing unto his servant,7760
2Sa 19:19 Let not my lord i· iniquity unto 2803
Ro 4: 8 to whom the Lord will not i· sin. **3049*
imputed
Le 7:18 it be i· unto him that offereth it: 2803
17: 4 blood shall be i· unto that man; he "
Ro 4:11 might be i· unto them also: **3049*
22 therefore it was i· to him for * "
23 sake alone, that it was i· to him; * "
24 to whom it shall be i·, if we believe*"
5:13 sin is not i· when there is no law. **1677*
Jas 2:23 and it was i· unto him for **3049*
imputeth
Ps 32: 2 whom the Lord i· not iniquity, 2803
Ro 4: 6 unto whom God i· righteousness **3049*
imputing
Hab 1:11 offend, i· this his power unto his God. *
2Co 5:19 not i· their trespasses unto them; **3049*
Imrah (*im'-rah*)
1Ch 7:36 and Shual, and Beri, and I·, 3236
Imri (*im'-ri*)
1Ch 9: 4 the son of I·, the son of Bani, 556
Ne 3: 2 them builded Zaccur the son of I·. "
in See in the APPENDIX; also INASMUCH; INDEED; INGATHERING; INNER; INSIDE; INSOMUCH; INTO; INWARD; HEREIN; THEREIN; WHEREIN; WITHIN.
inasmuch
De 19: 6 of death, i· as he hated him not 3588
Ru 3:10 i· as thou followedst not young 1115
M't 25:40 I· as ye have done it unto one*1909,3745*
45 I· as ye did it not to one of the " "
Ro 11:13 i· as I am the apostle of the " "
Ph'p 1: 7 i· as both in my bonds, and in " "
Heb 3: 3 i· as he who hath builded the**2596,* "
7:20 And i· as not without an oath " "
1Pe 4:13 i· as ye are partakers of Christ's **2526*
incense See also FRANKINCENSE; INCENSED.
Ex 25: 6 for anointing oil, and for sweet i·, 7004
30: 1 make an altar to burn i· upon: "
7 shall burn thereon sweet i· every "
7 the lamps, he shall burn i· upon it.*
8 at even, he shall burn i· upon it, *6999
8 a perpetual i· before the Lord 7004
9 Ye shall offer no strange i· thereon, "
27 and his vessels, and the altar of i·, "
31: 8 all his furniture, and the altar of i·, "
11 and sweet i· for the holy place: "
35: 8 anointing oil, and for the sweet i·, "
15 And the i· altar, and his staves, "
15 the anointing oil, and the sweet i·, "
28 anointing oil, and for the sweet i·. "
37:25 made the i· altar of shittim wood: "
29 and the pure i· of sweet spices, "
39:38 the anointing oil, and the sweet i·, "
40: 5 altar of gold for the i· before the ark"
27 And he burnt sweet i· thereon; as "
Le 4: 7 the horns of the altar of sweet i· "

Le 10: 1 put fire therein, and put *i* thereon, 7004
16:12 and his hands full of sweet *i* beaten "
13 he shall put the *i* upon the fire "
13 of the *i* may cover the mercy seat "
Nu 4:16 light, and the sweet *i*, and the daily "
7:14 of ten shekels of gold, full of *i*: "
20 of gold of ten shekels, full of *i*: "
26, 32, 38, 44, 50, 56, 62, 68, 74, 80 One golden spoon of ten shekels, full of *i*: "
86 golden spoons were twelve, full of *i*, "
16: 7 put *i* in them before the Lord to "
17 man his censer, and put *i* in them, "
18 fire in them, and laid *i* thereon, "
35 hundred and fifty men that offered *i*. "
40 near to offer *i* before the Lord; "
46 from off the altar, and put on *i*, "
47 put on *i*, and made an atonement "
De 33:10 they shall put *i* before thee, and "
1Sa 2:28 to burn *i*, to wear an ephod before "
1Ki 3: 3 he sacrificed and burnt *i* in high 6999
9:25 and he burnt *i* upon the altar that "
11: 8 wives, which burnt *i* and sacrificed "
12:33 offered upon the altar, and burnt *i*. "
13: 1 stood by the altar to burn *i*. "
2 high places that burn *i* upon thee, "
22:43 the people offered and burnt *i* yet "
2Ki 12: 3 people still sacrificed and burnt *i* "
14: 4 people did sacrifice and burnt *i* on "
15: 4 people sacrificed and burnt *i* still "
35 and burned *i* still in the high "
16: 4 and burnt *i* in the high places, "
17:11 they burnt *i* in all the high places, "
18: 4 children of Israel did burn *i* to it: "
22:17 and have burned *i* unto other gods, "
23: 5 had ordained to burn *i* in the high "
5 them also that burned *i* unto Baal, "
8 where the priests had burned *i*, "
1Ch 6:49 offering, and on the altar of *i*, 7004
23:13 for ever, to burn *i* before the Lord, 6999
28:18 for the altar of *i* refined gold by 7004
2Ch 2: 4 and to burn before him sweet *i*, "
13:11 burnt sacrifices and sweet *i*: "
25:14 before them, and burned *i* to them. 6999
26:16 to burn *i* upon the altar of "
16 to burn...upon the altar of *i*. 7004
18 Uzziah, to burn *i* unto the Lord, 6999
18 that are consecrated to burn *i*: "
19 had a censer in his hand to burn *i*: "
19 the Lord, from beside the *i* altar. 7004
28: 3 he burnt *i* in the valley of the son 6999
4 also and burnt *i* in the high places, "
25 places to burn *i* unto other gods, "
29: 7 not burned *i* nor offered burnt 7004
11 minister unto him, and burn *i*. 6999
30:14 all the altars for *i* took they away, "
32:12 one altar, and burn *i* upon it? "
34:25 and have burned *i* unto other gods, "
Ps 66:15 of fatlings, with the *i* of rams; 7004
141: 2 prayer be set forth before thee as *i*; "
Isa 1:13 *i* is an abomination unto me; "
43:23 offering, nor wearied thee with *i*. *3828
60: 6 they shall bring gold and *i*; and * "
65: 3 burneth *i* upon altars of brick; 6999
7 burned *i* upon the mountains, * "
66: 3 he that burneth *i*, as if he blessed *3828
Jer 1:16 have burned *i* unto other gods, 6999
6:20 cometh there to me *i* from Sheba, *3828
7: 9 and burn *i* unto Baal, and walk 6999
11:12 the gods unto whom they offer *i*: "
13 even altars to burn *i* unto Baal. "
17 me to anger in offering *i* unto Baal. "
17:26 and meat offerings, and *i*, and 3828
18:15 they have burned *i* to vanity, and 6999
19: 4 have burned *i* in it unto other gods, "
13 *i* unto all the host of heaven, "
32:29 roofs they have offered *i* unto Baal, "
41: 5 with offerings and *i* in their hand, *3828
44: 3 in that they went to burn *i*, and 6999
5 to burn no *i* unto other gods. "
8 burning *i* unto other gods in the "
15 wives had burned *i* unto other gods, "
17 to burn *i* unto the queen of "
18 to burn *i* to the queen of heaven, "
19 burned *i* to the queen of heaven, "
21 The *i* that ye burned in the cities 7002
23 Because ye have burned *i*, and 6999
25 to burn *i* to the queen of heaven, "
48:35 and him that burneth *i* to his gods. "
Eze 8:11 and a thick cloud of *i* went up. 7004
16:18 set mine oil and mine *i* before "
23:41 thou hast set mine *i* and mine oil. "
Ho 2:13 wherein she burned *i* to them, 6999
4:13 burn *i* upon the hills, under oaks "
11: 2 and burned *i* to graven images. "
Hab 1:16 and burn *i* unto their drag; "
Mal 1:11 in every place *i* shall be offered "
Lu 1: 9 his lot was to burn *i* when he went 2370
10 praying without at the time of *i*. 2368
11 on the right side of the altar of *i*. "
Re 8: 3 there was given unto him much *i*, "
4 the smoke of the *i*, which came "

incensed
Isa 41:11 all they that were *i* against thee 2734
45:24 and all that are *i* against him shall "

incline See also INCLINED; INCLINETH.
Jos 24:23 and *i* your heart unto the Lord 5186
1Ki 8:58 That he may *i* our hearts unto him, "
Ps 17: 6 *i* thine ear unto me, and hear my "
45:10 and consider, and *i* thine ear; "
49: 4 I will *i* mine ear to a parable: "
71: 2 escape: *i* thine ear unto me, and * "
78: 1 *i* your ears to the words of my "
88: 2 thee: *i* thine ear unto my cry; "
102: 2 *i* thine ear unto me: in the day "
119:36 *I* my heart unto thy testimonies, "
Ps 141: 4 *I* not my heart to any evil thing, 5186
Pr 2: 2 thou *i* thine ear unto wisdom, 7181
4:20 *i* thine ear unto my sayings. 5186
Isa 37:17 *I* thine ear, O Lord, and hear; "
55: 3 *I* your ear, and come unto me: "
Da 9:18 O my God, *i* thine ear, and hear; "

inclined
J'g 9: 3 and their hearts *i* to follow 5186
Ps 40: 1 and he *i* unto me, and heard my "
116: 2 Because he hath *i* his ear unto me, "
119:112 I have *i* mine heart to perform "
Pr 5:13 nor *i* mine ear to them that "
Jer 7:24 hearkened not, nor *i* their ear, "
26 not unto me, nor *i* their ear, "
11: 8 they obeyed not, nor *i* their ear, "
17:23 obeyed not, neither *i* their ear, "
25: 4 hearkened, nor *i* your ear to hear. "
34:14 not unto me, neither *i* their ear. "
35:15 ye have not *i* your ear, nor "
44: 5 nor *i* their ear to turn from their "

inclineth
Pr 2:18 her house *i* unto death, and her 7743

inclose See also INCLOSED; INCLOSINGS.
Ca 8: 9 we will *i* her with boards of cedar. 6696

inclosed
Ex 39: 6 onyx stones *i* in ouches of gold, 4142
13 they were *i* in ouches of gold in "
J'g 20:43 Thus they *i* the Benjamites 3803
Ps 17:10 They are *i* in their own fat: with 5462
22:16 assembly of the wicked have *i* me: 5362
Ca 4:12 A garden *i* is my sister, my *5274
La 3: 9 He hath *i* my ways with hewn *1443
Lu 5: 6 they *i* a great multitude of fishes: *4788*

inclosings
Ex 28:20 shall be set in gold in their *i*. *4396
39:13 in ouches of gold in their *i*. * "

incontinency
1Co 7: 5 Satan tempt you not for your *i*. *192*

incontinent
2Ti 3: 3 false accusers, *i*, fierce, despisers* *193*

incorruptible See also UNCORRUPTIBLE.
1Co 9:25 corruptible crown; but we an *i*. *862*
15:52 and the dead shall be raised *i*, "
1Pe 1: 4 To an inheritance *i*, and undefiled, "
23 corruptible seed, but of *i*, "

incorruption
1Co 15:42 in corruption; it is raised in *i*: *861*
50 neither doth corruption inherit *i*. "
53 must put on *i*, and this mortal "
54 corruptible shall have put on *i*, "

increase See also INCREASED; INCREASEST; INCREASETH; INCREASING.
Ge 47:24 to pass in the *i*, that ye shall give *8393
Le 19:25 may yield unto you the *i* thereof: "
25: 7 shall all the *i* thereof be meat. "
12 ye shall eat the *i* thereof out of "
16 thou shalt *i* the price thereof, and 7235
20 shall not sow, nor gather in our *i*: 8393
36 Take thou no usury of him, or *i*: 8635
37 nor lend him thy victuals for *i*. 4768
26: 4 the land shall yield her *i*, and the 2981
20 your land shall not yield her *i*, "
Nu 18:30 as the *i* of the threshingfloor, 8393
30 and as the *i* of the winepress. "
32:14 an *i* of sinful men, to augment 8635
De 6: 3 that ye may *i* mightily, as the 7235
7:13 the *i* of thy kine, and the flocks 7698
22 once, lest the beasts of the field *i* 7235
14:22 truly tithe all the *i* of thy seed, 8393
28 bring forth all the tithe of thine *i* "
16:15 God shall bless thee in all thine *i*, "
26:12 tithing all the tithes of thine *i* the "
28: 4 thy cattle, the *i* of thy kine, 7698
18 the *i* of thy kine, and the flocks of "
51 or the *i* of thy kine, or flocks of thy "
32:13 he might eat the *i* of the fields; 8570
22 consume the earth with her *i*, 2981
J'g 6: 4 and destroyed the *i* of the earth, "
9:29 *I* thine army, and come out. 7239
1Sa 2:33 all the *i* of thine house shall die 4768
1Ch 27:23 Lord had said he would *i* Israel 7235
27 over the *i* of the vineyards for the "
2Ch 31: 5 and of all the *i* of the field; 8393
32:28 Storehouses also for the *i* of corn, "
Ezr 10:10 wives, to *i* the trespass of Israel. 3254
Ne 9:37 yieldeth much *i* unto the kings 8393
Job 8: 7 thy latter end should greatly *i*. 7685
20:28 The *i* of his house shall depart, 2981
31:12 and would root out all mine *i*. 8393
Ps 44:12 not *i* thy wealth by their price. 7235
62:10 if riches *i*, set not your heart upon 5107
67: 6 Then shall the earth yield her *i*; 2981
71:21 Thou shalt *i* my greatness, and 7235
73:12 in the world; they *i* in riches. 7685
78:46 also their *i* unto the caterpiller, 2981
85:12 and our land shall yield her *i*. "
107:37 which may yield fruits of *i*. 8393
115:14 The Lord shall *i* you more and 3254
Pr 1: 5 man will hear, and will *i* learning; "
3: 9 with the firstfruits of all thine *i*: 8393
9: 9 man, and he will *i* in learning. 3254
13:11 that gathereth by labour shall *i*. 7235
14: 4 much *i* is by the strength of the ox. 8393
18:20 the *i* of his lips shall he be filled "
22:16 oppresseth the poor to *i* his riches, 7235
28:28 when they perish, the righteous *i*. "
Ec 5:10 he that loveth abundance with *i*: 8393
11 When goods *i*, they are increased 7235
6:11 there be many things that *i* vanity, "
Isa 9: 7 Of the *i* of his government and 4768
29:19 The meek also shall *i* their joy 3254
30:23 and bread of the *i* of the earth, 8393
Isa 57: 9 and didst *i* thy perfumes, and 7235
Jer 2: 3 and the firstfruits of his *i*: all that 8393
23: 3 and they shall be fruitful and *i*. *7235
Eze 5:16 I will *i* the famine upon you, and 3254
18: 8 usury, neither hath taken any *i*, 8635
13 upon usury, and hath taken *i*: "
17 that hath not received usury nor *i*, "
22:12 thou hast taken usury and *i*, and "
34:27 and the earth shall yield her *i*, 2981
36:11 and they shall *i* and bring fruit: 7235
29 I will call for the corn, and will *i* it,* "
30 of the tree, and the *i* of the field, 8570
37 I will *i* them with men like a flock. 7235
48:18 and the *i* thereof shall be for food 8393
Da 11:39 acknowledge and *i* with glory: 7235
Ho 4:10 whoredom, and shall not *i*: 6555
Zec 8:12 and the ground shall give her *i*, 2981
10: 8 shall *i* as they have increased. 7235
Lu 17: 5 said unto the Lord, *I* our faith. *4369*
Joh 3:30 He must *i*, but I must decrease. *837*
1Co 3: 6 Apollos watered; but God gave the *i*. "
7 watereth; but God that giveth the *i*. "
2Co 9:10 *i* the fruits of your righteousnesss; "
Eph 4:16 of the body unto the edifying *838*
Col 2:19 increaseth with the *i* of God. "
1Th 3:12 the Lord make you to *i* and abound *4121*
4:10 that ye *i* more and more; **4052*
2Ti 2:16 they will *i* unto more ungodliness. **4298*

increased
Ge 7:17 and the waters *i*, and bare up the 7235
18 and were *i* greatly upon the earth; "
30:30 and it is now *i* unto a multitude; 6555
43 And the man *i* exceedingly, and "
Ex 1: 7 were fruitful, and *i* abundantly, 8317
23:30 thou be *i*, and inherit the land. 6509
1Sa 14:19 of the Philistines went on and *i*: 7227
2Sa 15:12 for the people *i* continually with "
1Ki 22:35 And the battle *i* that day: and 5927
1Ch 4:38 house of their fathers *i* greatly. 6555
5:23 they *i* from Bashan unto 7235
2Ch 18:34 And the battle *i* that day: howbeit 5927
Ezr 9: 6 for our iniquities are *i* over our 7235
Job 1:10 and his substance is *i* in the land. 6555
Ps 3: 1 Lord, how are they *i* that trouble 7231
4: 7 that their corn and their wine *i*. "
49:16 when the glory of his house is *i*; 7235
105:24 And he *i* his people greatly; and 6509
Pr 9:11 and the years of thy life shall be *i*. 3254
Ec 2: 9 So I was great, and *i* more than "
5:11 increase, they are *i* that eat them: 7231
Isa 9: 3 the nation, and not *i* the joy: 1431
26:15 Thou hast *i* the nation, O Lord, 3254
15 thou hast *i* the nation: thou art "
51: 2 and blessed him, and *i* him. *7235
Jer 3:16 ye be multiplied and *i* in the land, 6509
5: 6 and their backslidings are *i*. 6105
15: 8 Their widows are *i* to me above "
29: 6 that ye may be *i* there, and not *7235
30:14 iniquity; because thy sins were *i*. 6105
15 because thy sins were *i*, I have "
La 2: 5 hath *i* in the daughter of Judah *7235
Eze 16: 7 and thou hast *i* and waxen great, * "
26 and hast *i* thy whoredoms, to "
23:14 And that she *i* her whoredoms: 3254
28: 5 thy traffick hast thou *i* thy riches, 7235
41: 7 so *i* from the lowest chamber *5927
Da 12: 4 and fro, and knowledge shall be *i*. 7235
Ho 4: 7 As they were *i*, so they sinned *7230
10: 1 of his fruit he hath *i* the altars; *7235
Am 4: 9 fig trees and your olive trees *i*, "
Zec 10: 8 they shall increase as they have *i*. "
M'r 4: 8 yield fruit that sprang up and *i*, * *837*
Lu 2:52 Jesus *i* in wisdom and stature, **4298*
Ac 6: 7 And the word of God *i*; and the *837*
9:22 Saul *i* the more in strength, and *1743*
16: 5 the faith, and *i* in number daily. *4052*
2Co 10:15 having hope, when your faith is *i*,* *837*
Re 3:17 I am rich, and *i* with goods, and **4147*

increasest
Job 10:17 and *i* thine indignation upon me; 7235

increaseth
Job 10:16 For it *i*. Thou huntest me as a *1342
12:23 He *i* the nations, and destroyeth 7679
Ps 74:23 rise up against thee *i* continually. *5927
Pr 11:24 is that scattereth, and yet *i*; 3254
16:21 sweetness of the lips *i* learning. "
23:28 *i* the transgressors among men. "
24: 5 yea, a man of knowledge *i* strength. 553
28: 8 that by usury and unjust gain *i* *7235
29:16 are multiplied, transgression *i*: "
Ec 1:18 he that *i* knowledge, *i* sorrow. 3254
Isa 40:29 that have no might he *i* strength. 7235
Ho 12: 1 he daily *i* lies and desolation; * "
Hab 2: 6 to him that *i* that which is not his "
Col 2:19 together, *i* with the increase of God. *837*

increasing
Col 1:10 and *i* in the knowledge of God; *837*

incredible
Ac 26: 8 it be thought a thing *i* with you, *571*

incurable
2Ch 21:18 his bowels with an *i* disease. 369,4832
Job 34: 6 wound is *i* without transgression. 605
Jer 15:18 my wound *i*, which refuseth to be "
30:12 Thy bruise is *i*, and thy wound is "
15 thy sorrow is *i* for the multitude "
Mic 1: 9 For her wound is *i*; for it is come "

indebted
Lu 11: 4 forgive every one that is *i* to us. *3784*

indeed
Ge 17:19 thy wife shall bear thee a son *i*; *61
20:12 And yet *i* she is my sister; she is 546
37: 8 to him, Shalt thou *i* reign over us?
8 or shalt thou *i* have dominion over us?

Ge 37:10 thy brethren i' come to bow down
40:15 For i' I was stolen away out of the
43:20 And said, O sir, we came i' down at
44: 5 drinketh, and whereby i' he divineth?
Ex 19: 5 If ye will obey my voice i', and keep
23:22 But if thou shalt i' obey his voice, and
Le 10:18 ye should i' have eaten it in the holy *
Nu 12: 2 Hath the Lord i' spoken only by
21: 2 If thou wilt i' deliver this people 389
22:37 am I not able i' to promote thee to 552
De 2:15 For i' the hand of the Lord was *1571
21:16 of the hated, which is i' the firstborn:*
Jos 7:20 I' I have sinned against the Lord *546
1Sa 1:11 if thou wilt i' look on the affliction of
2:30 I said i' that thy house, and the house
2Sa 14: 5 I am i' a widow woman, and mine* 61
15: 8 shall bring me again i' to Jerusalem,
1Ki 8:27 But will God i' dwell on the earth? *552
2Ki 14:10 Thou hast i' smitten Edom, and thine
1Ch 4:10 Oh that thou wouldest bless me i', and
21:17 I it is that have sinned and done evil i';*
Job 19: 4 And be it i' that I have erred, 551
5 If i' ye will magnify yourselves
Ps 58: 1 Do ye i' speak righteousness, O 552
Isa 6: 9 people, Hear ye i', but understand not;
9 and see ye i', but perceive not.
Jer 22: 4 For if ye do this thing i', then shall
M't 3:11 I i' baptize you with water unto 3303
13:32 Which i' is the least of all seeds: "
20:23 them, Ye shall drink i' of my cup, "
23:27 which i' appear beautiful outward,* "
26:41 the spirit i' is willing, but the flesh "
M'r 1: 8 I i' have baptized you with water: "
9:13 That Elias is i' come, and they *2532
10:39 Ye shall i' drink of the cup that *3303
11:32 John, that he was a prophet i'. *3689
14:21 The Son of man i' goeth, as it is *3303
Lu 3:16 I i' baptize you with water; but "
11:48 for they i' killed them, and ye build* "
23:41 And we i' justly; for we receive the "
24:34 Saying, The Lord is risen i', and 3689
Joh 1:47 Behold an Israelite i', in whom is 230
4:42 this is i' the Christ, the Saviour of "
6:55 For my flesh is meat i', "
55 and my blood is drink i'. "
7:26 know i' that this is the very Christ? "
8:31 word, then are ye my disciples i'; * "
36 make you free, ye shall be free i'. 3689
Ac 4:16 for that i' a noble miracle hath 3303
11:16 John i' baptized with water; but ye "
22: 9 that were with me saw i' the light, "
Ro 6:11 to be dead i' unto sin, but alive * "
8: 7 the law of God, neither i' can be. 1063
14:20 All things i' are pure; but it is evil3303
1Co 11: 7 For a man i' ought not to cover his "
2Co 8:17 For i' he accepted the exhortation; "
11: 1 in my folly: and i' bear with me. 235
Ph'p 1:15 Some i' preach Christ even of envy3303
2:27 For i' he was sick nigh unto death:2532
3: 1 to me i' is not grievous, but for you3303
Col 2:23 Which things have i' a shew of "
1Th 4:10 And i' ye do it toward all the 1063
1Ti 5: 3 Honour widows that are widows i'.3689
5 Now she that is a widow i', and "
16 relieve them that are widows i'. "
1Pe 2: 4 disallowed i' of men, but chosen of 3303

India (*in'-de-ah*)
Es 1: 1 from I' even unto Ethiopia, 1912
8: 9 which are from I' unto Ethiopia, "

indignation
De 29:28 and in wrath, and in great i', and 7110
2Ki 3:27 there was great i' against Israel: * "
Ne 4: 1 was wroth, and took great i', and 3707
Es 5: 9 he was full of i' against Mordecai.*2534
Job 10:17 and increasest thine i' upon me; 3708
Ps 69:24 Pour out thine i' upon them, and 2195
78:49 anger, wrath, and i', and trouble, "
102:10 Because of thine i' and thy wrath: "
Isa 10: 5 the staff in their hand is mine i'. "
25 the i' shall cease, and mine anger "
13: 5 the weapons of his i', to destroy the "
26:20 moment, until the i' be overpast. "
30:27 his lips are full of i', and his tongue "
30 with the i' of his anger, and with 2197
34: 2 i' of the Lord is upon all nations, 7110
66:14 and his i' toward his enemies. 2194
Jer 10:10 shall not be able to abide his i'. 2195
15:17 hand: for thou hast filled me with i'. "
50:25 brought forth the weapons of his i':"
La 2: 6 hath despised in the i' of his anger "
Eze 21:31 I will pour out mine i' upon thee, "
22:24 nor rained upon in the day of i'. "
31 I poured out mine i' upon them; "
Da 8:19 shall be in the last end of the i': "
11:30 have i' against the holy covenant: 2194
36 prosper till the i' be accomplished:2195
Mic 7: 9 I will bear the i' of the Lord, 2197
Na 1: 6 Who can stand before his i'? and 2195
Hab 3:12 didst march through the land in i', "
Zep 3: 8 to pour upon them mine i', even all "
Zec 1:12 hast had i' these threescore and 2194
Mal 1: 4 whom the Lord hath i' for ever. "
M't 20:24 were moved with i' against the two 23
26: 8 they had i', saying, To what purpose "
M'r 14: 4 some that had i' within themselves, "
Lu 13:14 of the synagogue answered with i', "
Ac 5:17 Sadducees, and were filled with i', 2205
Ro 2: 8 unrighteousness, i', and wrath, 2372
2Co 7:11 yea, what i', yea, what fear, yea, 24
Heb 10:27 of judgment and fiery i', which *2205
Re 14:10 mixture into the cup of his i'; *3709

inditing
Ps 45: 1 My heart is i' a good matter: I *7370

industrious
1Ki 11:28 young man that he was i', he 6213,4399

inexcusable
Ro 2: 1 Therefore thou art i', O man, * 379

infallible
Ac 1: 3 by many i' proofs, being seen of them*

infamous
Eze 22: 5 shall mock thee, which art i' 2931,8034

infamy
Pr 25:10 shame, and thine i' turn not away.1681
Eze 36: 3 talkers, and are an i' of the people:* "

infant See also INFANTS.
1Sa 15: 3 slay both man and woman, i' and 5768
Isa 65:20 be no more thence an i' of days, 5764

infants
Job 3:16 been; as i' which never saw light. 5768
Ho 13:16 their i' shall be dashed in pieces, "
Lu 18:15 they brought unto him also i', that1025

inferior
Job 12: 3 I am not i' to you: yea, who 5307
13: 2 I know also: I am not i' unto you. "
Da 2:39 arise another kingdom i' to thee, 772
2Co 12:13 you were i' to other churches, 2274

infidel
2Co 6:15 hath he that believeth with an i'? *571
1Ti 5: 8 the faith, and is worse than an i'. * "

infinite
Job 22: 5 great? and thine iniquities i'?*369,7093
Ps 147: 5 power: his understanding is i'. " 4557
Na 3: 9 her strength, and it was i'; 7097

infirmities
M't 8:17 Himself took our i', and bare our 769
Lu 5:15 and to be healed by him of their i'. "
7:21 cured many of their i' and plagues,*3554
8: 2 been healed of evil spirits and i', 769
Ro 8:26 the Spirit also helpeth our i': for * "
15: 1 to bear the i' of the weak, and not 771
2Co 11:30 of the things which concern my i'. *769
12: 5 I will not glory, but in mine i'. * "
9 will I rather glory in my i', that the* "
10 Therefore I take pleasure in i', in * "
1Ti 5:23 stomach's sake and thine often i'. "
Heb 4:15 touched with the feeling of our i'; "

infirmity See also INFIRMITIES.
Le 12: 2 days of the separation for her i' *1738
Ps 77:10 And I said, This is my i': but I 2470
Pr 18:14 spirit of a man will sustain his i'; 4245
Lu 13:11 a woman which had a spirit of i' 769
12 thou art loosed from thine i'. "
Joh 5: 5 had an i' thirty and eight years. "
Ro 6:19 men because of the i' of your flesh: "
Ga 4:13 Ye know how through i' of the flesh "
Heb 5: 2 himself also is compassed with i'. "
7:28 men high priests which have i'; "

inflame See also ENFLAME.
Isa 5:11 until night, till wine i' them! 1814

inflammation
Le 13:28 clean: for it is an i' of the burning.*6867
De 28:22 and with a fever, and with an i', 1816

inflicted
2Co 2: 6 this punishment, which was i' of many.

influences
Job 38:31 bind the sweet i' of Pleiades, *4575

infolding
Eze 1: 4 a fire i' itself, and a brightness 3947

inform See also INFORMED.
De 17:10 according to all that they i' thee: *3384

informed
Da 9:22 And he i' me, and talked with me,* 995
Ac 21:21 are i' of thee, that thou teachest 2727
24 they were i' concerning thee, "
24: 1 who i' the governor against Paul. 1718
25: 2 of the Jews i' him against Paul, "
15 and the elders of the Jews i' me, "

ingathering
Ex 23:16 and the feast of i', which is in the 614
34:22 the feast of i' at the year's end. "

inhabit See also INHABITED; INHABITEST; INHABITETH; INHABITING.
Nu 35:34 the land which ye shall i', wherein 3427
Pr 10:30 the wicked shall not i' the earth. *7931
Isa 42:11 the villages that Kedar doth i': 3427
65:21 shall build houses, and i' them; "
22 shall not build and another i'; they "
Jer 17: 6 but shall i' the parched places in 7931
48:18 Thou daughter that dost i' Dibon,*3427
Eze 33:24 they that i' those wastes of the land "
Am 9:14 build the waste cities, and i' them; "
Zep 1:13 also build houses, but not i' them; "

inhabitant See also INHABITANTS.
Job 28: 4 flood breaketh out from the i'; *1481
Isa 5: 9 even great and fair, without i'. 3427
6:11 Until the cities be wasted without i', "
9: 9 and the i' of Samaria that say in "
12: 6 Cry out and shout, thou i' of Zion: "
20: 6 And the i' of this isle shall say in "
24:17 are upon thee, O i' of the earth. "
33:24 And the i' shall not say, I am sick:7934
Jer 2:15 his cities are burned without i'. 3427
4: 7 shall be laid waste, without an i'. "
9:11 of Judah desolate, without an i'. "
10:17 out of the land, O i' of the fortress.* "
21:13 I am against thee, O i' of the valley, "
22:23 O i' of Lebanon, that makest thy "
26: 9 city shall be desolate without an i'? "
33:10 without man, and without i', and "
34:22 of Judah a desolation without an i'. "
44:22 and a curse, without an i', as at "
46:19 waste and desolate without an i'. "
48:19 O i' of Aroer, stand by the way, and "
43 thee, O i' of Moab, saith the Lord. "
51:29 Babylon a desolation without an i'. "
Jer 51:35 Babylon, shall the i' of Zion say; 3427
37 and an hissing, without an i'. "
Am 1: 5 cut off the i' from the plain of Aven, "
8 I will cut off the i' from Ashdod, "
Mic 1:11 Pass ye away, thou i' of Saphir, "
11 the i' of Zaanan came not forth in "
12 the i' of Maroth waited carefully for "
13 O thou i' of Lachish, bind the "
15 heir unto thee, O i' of Mareshah: "
Zep 2: 5 thee, that there shall be no i'. "
3: 6 is no man, that there is none i'. "

inhabitants See also INHABITERS.
Ge 19:25 and all the i' of the cities, and all 3427
34:30 to stink among the i' of the land, "
50:11 the i' of the land, the Canaanites, "
Ex 15:14 take hold on the i' of Palestina. "
15 all the i' of Canaan shall melt away. "
23:31 I will deliver the i' of the land into "
34:12 with the i' of the land whither thou "
15 a covenant with the i' of the land, "
Le 18:25 the land itself vomiteth out her i'. "
25:10 all the land unto all the i' thereof: "
Nu 13:32 land that eateth up the i' thereof; "
14:14 they will tell it to the i' of this land: "
32:17 cities because of the i' of the land. "
33:52 ye shall drive out the i' of the land "
53 ye shall dispossess the i' of the land,*
55 will not drive out the i' of the land3427
De 13:13 have withdrawn the i' of their city, "
15 shalt surely smite the i' of that city "
Jos 2: 9 all the i' of the land faint because "
24 all the i' of the country do faint "
7: 9 all the i' of the land shall hear of it, "
8:24 of slaying all the i' of Ai in the field, "
26 had utterly destroyed all the i' of Ai. "
9: 3 And when the i' of Gibeon heard "
11 all the i' of our country spake to us, "
24 to destroy all the i' of the land from "
10: 1 the i' of Gibeon had made peace "
11:19 save the Hivites the i' of Gibeon: "
13: 6 All the i' of the hill country from "
15:15 he went up thence to the i' of Debir: "
63 the Jebusites the i' of Jerusalem, "
17: 7 hand unto the i' of En-tappuah. "
11 and the i' of Dor and her towns, "
11 and the i' of En-dor and her towns, "
11 the i' of Taanach and her towns, "
11 the i' of Megiddo and her towns, "
12 not drive out the i' of those cities; "
J'g 1:11 he went against the i' of Debir: 3427
19 he drave out the i' of the mountain;
19 not drive out the i' of the valley, 3427
27 of Beth-shean and her towns,
27 nor the i' of Dor and her towns, 3427
27 nor the i' of Ibleam and her towns, "
27 the i' of Megiddo and her towns: "
30 Zebulun drive out the i' of Kitron, "
30 nor the i' of Nahalol; but the "
31 did Asher drive out the i' of Accho, "
31 nor the i' of Zidon, nor of Ahlab, "
32 the Canaanites, the i' of the land: "
33 drive out the i' of Beth-shemesh, "
33 nor the i' of Beth-anath; "
33 the Canaanites, the i' of the land: "
33 nevertheless the i' of Beth-shemesh "
2: 2 no league with the i' of this land; "
5: 7 The i' of the villages ceased, they * "
11 toward the i' of his villages in Israel:
23 curse ye bitterly the i' thereof; 3427
10:18 be head over all the i' of Gilead. "
11: 8 our head over all the i' of Gilead. "
21 the Amorites, the i' of that country. "
20:15 i' of Gibeah, which were numbered "
21: 9 none of the i' of Jabesh-gilead there. "
10 Go and smite the i' of Jabesh-gilead "
12 found among the i' of Jabesh-gilead "
Ru 4: 4 Buy it before the i', and before the* "
1Sa 6:21 to the i' of Kirjath-jearim, saying, "
23: 5 So David saved the i' of Keilah. "
27: 8 nations were of old the i' of the land, "
31:11 when the i' of Jabesh-gilead heard "
2Sa 5: 6 the Jebusites, the i' of the land: "
1Ki 17: 1 who was of the i' of Gilead, *8453
21:11 nobles who were the i' in his city,*3427
2Ki 19:26 their i' were of small power, "
22:16 this place, and upon the i' thereof, "
19 place, and against the i' thereof, "
23: 2 and all the i' of Jerusalem with him, "
1Ch 8: 6 of the fathers of the i' of Geba, and "
13 of the fathers of the i' of Aijalon, "
13 who drove away the i' of Gath: "
9: 2 Now the first i' that dwelt in their "
11: 4 Jebusites were, the i' of the land. "
5 And the i' of Jebus said to David, "
22:18 the i' of the land into mine hand; "
2Ch 15: 5 were upon all the i' of the countries. "
20: 7 the i' of this land before thy people "
15 all Judah, and ye i' of Jerusalem, "
18 and the i' of Jerusalem fell before "
20 O Judah, and ye i' of Jerusalem; "
23 up against the i' of mount Seir, "
23 had made an end of the i' of Seir, "
21:11 caused the i' of Jerusalem to commit "
13 the i' of Jerusalem to go a whoring, "
22: 1 i' of Jerusalem made Ahaziah king "
32:22 the i' of Jerusalem from the hand of "
26 both he and the i' of Jerusalem, so "
33 the i' of Jerusalem did him honour "
33: 9 Judah and the i' of Jerusalem to err, "
34:24 this place, and upon the i' thereof, "
27 place, and against the i' thereof, "
28 place, and upon the i' of the same. "
30 of Judah, and the i' of Jerusalem, "
32 the i' of Jerusalem did according to "
35:18 present, and the i' of Jerusalem. "
Ezr 4: 6 the i' of Judah and Jerusalem. "

Ne 3:13 and the i' of Zanoah; they built it. 3427
7: 3 watches of the i' of Jerusalem, "
9:24 the i' of the land, the Canaanites, "
Job 26: 5 the waters, and the i' thereof. 7934
Ps 33: 8 all the i' of the world stand in awe 3427
14 looketh upon all the i' of the earth. "
49: 1 give ear, all ye i' of the world: "
75: 3 and all the i' thereof are dissolved: "
83: 7 the Philistines with the i' of Tyre; "
Isa 5: 3 O i' of Jerusalem, and men of Judah, "
8:14 for a snare to the i' of Jerusalem. "
10:13 have put down the i' like a valiant* "
31 the i' of Gebim gather themselves "
18: 3 All ye i' of the world, and dwellers "
21:14 The i' of the land of Tema brought "
22:21 be a father to the i' of Jerusalem, "
23: 2 Be still, ye i' of the isle; thou whom "
6 to Tarshish; howl, ye i' of the isle. "
24: 1 scattereth abroad the i' thereof. "
5 also is defiled under the i' thereof; "
6 the i' of the earth are burned, and "
26: 9 the i' of the world will learn "
18 have the i' of the world fallen. "
21 to punish the i' of the earth for "
37:27 their i' were of small power, "
38:11 no more with the i' of the world. "
40:22 the i' thereof are as grasshoppers; "
42:10 therein; the isles, and the i' thereof. "
11 let the i' of the rock sing, let them "
49:19 be too narrow by reason of the i', "
Jer 1:14 forth upon all the i' of the land. "
4: 4 men of Judah and i' of Jerusalem: "
6:12 out my hand upon the i' of the land, "
8: 1 the bones of the i' of Jerusalem, "
10:18 I will sling out the i' of the land "
11: 2 Judah, and to the i' of Jerusalem; "
9 and among the i' of Jerusalem. "
12 of Judah and i' of Jerusalem go, "
13:13 I will fill all the i' of this land even "
13 prophets, and all the i' of Jerusalem, "
17:20 Judah, and all the i' of Jerusalem, "
25 of Judah, and the i' of Jerusalem: "
18:11 Judah, and to the i' of Jerusalem, "
19: 3 of Judah, and i' of Jerusalem; "
12 this place,...and to the i' thereof, "
21: 6 I will smite the i' of this city, both "
23:14 and the i' thereof as Gomorrah. "
25: 2 Judah, and to all the i' of Jerusalem, "
9 against the i' thereof, and against "
29 sword upon all the i' of the earth, "
30 grapes, against all the i' of the earth. "
26:15 this city, and upon the i' thereof: "
32:32 of Judah, and the i' of Jerusalem. "
35:13 of Judah and the i' of Jerusalem, "
17 all the i' of Jerusalem all the evil "
36:31 upon the i' of Jerusalem, and upon "
42:18 forth upon the i' of Jerusalem; "
46: 8 I will destroy the city and the i' "
47: 2 and all the i' of the land shall howl. "
49: 8 back, dwell deep, O i' of Dedan; "
20 purposed against the i' of Teman: "
30 far off, dwell deep, O ye i' of Hazor, "
50:21 it, and against the i' of Pekod: "
34 and disquiet the i' of Babylon. "
35 upon the i' of Babylon, and upon "
51:12 he spake against the i' of Babylon. "
24 to all the i' of Chaldea all their evil "
35 my blood upon the i' of Chaldea, "
La 4:12 the earth and all the i' of the world, "
Eze 11:15 whom the i' of Jerusalem have said, "
12:19 Lord God of the i' of Jerusalem, "
15: 6 so will I give the i' of Jerusalem. "
26:17 she and her i', which cause their "
27: 8 The i' of Zidon and Arvad were thy "
35 the i' of the isles shall be astonished "
29: 6 all the i' of Egypt shall know that I "
Da 4:35 all the i' of the earth are reputed 1753
35 and among the i' of the earth: and "
9: 7 Judah, and to the i' of Jerusalem, 3427
Ho 4: 1 controversy with the i' of the land, "
10: 5 The i' of Samaria shall fear 7934
Joe 1: 2 and give ear, all ye i' of the land. 3427
14 the i' of the land into the house of "
2: 1 let all the i' of the land tremble: "
Mic 6:12 and the i' thereof have spoken lies, "
16 and the i' thereof an hissing: "
Zep 1: 4 and upon all the i' of Jerusalem; "
11 Howl, ye i' of Maktesh, for all the "
2: 5 Woe unto the i' of the sea coast, "
Zec 8:20 people, and the i' of many cities: "
21 the i' of one city shall go to another, "
11: 6 I will no more pity the i' of the land, "
12: 5 The i' of Jerusalem shall be my "
7 the i' of Jerusalem do not magnify "
8 the Lord defend the i' of Jerusalem; "
10 David, and upon the i' of Jerusalem, "
13: 1 of David and to the i' of Jerusalem "
Re 17: 2 the i' of the earth have been made 2730

inhabited
Ge 36:20 of Seir the Horite, who i' the land;*3427
Ex 16:35 years, until they came to a land i'; "
Le 16:22 their iniquities unto a land not i':*1509
J'g 1:17 the Canaanites that i' Zephath, 3427
21 out the Jebusites that i' Jerusalem; "
1Ch 5: 9 eastward he i' unto the entering in* "
Isa 13:20 It shall never be i', neither shall it "
44:26 saith to Jerusalem, Thou shalt be i'; "
45:18 it not in vain, he formed it to be i': "
54: 3 make the desolate cities to be i'. "
Jer 6: 8 make thee desolate, a land not i'. "
17: 6 wilderness, in a salt land and not i'. "
22: 6 and cities which are not i'. "
46:26 and afterward it shall be i', as in 7931
50:13 it shall not be i', but it shall be 3427
39 it shall be no more i' for ever; "
Eze 12:20 cities that are i' shall be laid waste, "
26:17 that wast i' of seafaring men, 3427
19 city, like the cities that are not i'; "
20 down to the pit, that thou be not i'; "
29:11 it, neither shall it be i' forty years. "
34:13 in all the i' places of the country. 4186
36:10 and the cities shall be i', and the 3427
35 cities are become fenced, and are i'. "
38:12 the desolate places that are now i', "
Zec 2: 4 Jerusalem shall be i' as towns "
7: 7 when Jerusalem was i' and in "
7 men i' the south and the plain? "
9: 5 Gaza, and Ashkelon shall not be i'. "
12: 6 and Jerusalem shall be i' again in* "
14:10 be lifted up, and i' in her place, * "
11 but Jerusalem shall be safely i'. * "

inhabiters See also INHABITANTS.
Re 8:13 woe, woe, to the i' of the earth *2730
12:12 Woe to the i' of the earth and of * "

inhabitest
Ps 22: 3 O thou that i' the praises of Israel. 3427

inhabiteth
Job 15:28 and in houses which no man i', *3427
Isa 57:15 high and lofty One that i' eternity, 7931

inhabiting
Ps 74:14 to the people i' the wilderness. 6728

inherit See also DISINHERIT; INHERITED; INHERITETH.
Ge 15: 7 to give thee this land to i' it. 3423
8 shall I know that I shall i' it? "
28: 4 that thou mayest i' the land "
Ex 23:30 thou be increased, and i' the land. 5157
32:13 seed, and they shall i' it for ever. "
Le 20:24 Ye shall i' their land, and I will 3423
25:46 you, to i' them for a possession; * "
Nu 18:24 I have given to the Levites to i': *5159
26:55 tribes of their fathers they shall i'. 5157
32:19 we will not i' with them on yonder "
33:54 the tribes of your fathers ye shall i'. "
34:13 is the land which ye shall i' by lot, "
De 1:38 for he shall cause Israel to i' it. "
2:31 that thou mayest i' his land. 3423
3:28 he shall cause them to i' the land 5157
12:10 the Lord your God giveth you to i', "
16:20 thou mayest live, and i' the land 3423
19: 3 the Lord thy God giveth thee to i', 5157
14 which thou shalt i' in the land that "
21:16 his sons to i' that which he hath, "
31: 7 and thou shalt cause them to i' it. "
Jos 17:14 but one lot and one portion to i', *5159
J'g 11: 2 shalt not i' in our father's house, 5157
1Sa 2: 8 to make them i' the throne of glory: "
2Ch 20:11 which thou hast given us to i'. 3423
Ps 25:13 and his seed shall i' the earth. "
37: 9 the Lord, they shall i' the earth. "
11 But the meek shall i' the earth; "
22 blessed of him shall i' the earth; "
29 The righteous shall i' the land, "
34 he shall exalt thee to i' the land: "
69:36 seed also of his servants shall i' it:5157
82: 8 earth: for thou shalt i' all nations. "
Pr 3:35 The wise shall i' glory: but shame "
8:21 those that love me to i' substance; "
11:29 his own house shall i' the wind: "
14:18 The simple i' folly: but the prudent "
Isa 49: 8 to cause to i' the desolate heritages; "
54: 3 and thy seed shall i' the Gentiles,*3423
57:13 and shall i' my holy mountain; "
60:21 they shall i' the land for ever, the "
65: 9 and mine elect shall i' it, and my "
Jer 8:10 fields to them that shall i' them: * "
12:14 caused my people Israel to i'; 5157
49: 1 why then doth their king i' Gad, *3423
Eze 47:13 whereby ye shall i' the land *5157
14 shall i' it, one as well as another: 3423
Zec 2:12 And the Lord shall i' Judah his 5157
M't 5: 5 meek: for they shall i' the earth. 2816
19:29 and shall i' everlasting life. "
25:34 i' the kingdom prepared for you "
M'r 10:17 shall I do that I may i' eternal life? "
Lu 10:25 what shall I do to i' eternal life? "
18:18 what shall I do to i' eternal life? "
1Co 6: 9 shall not i' the kingdom of God? "
10 shall i' the kingdom of God. "
15:50 and blood cannot i' the kingdom "
50 doth corruption i' incorruption. "
Ga 5:21 shall not i' the kingdom of God. "
Heb 6:12 faith and patience i' the promises. "
1Pe 3: 9 called, that ye should i' a blessing. "
Rev 21: 7 that overcometh shall i' all things; "

inheritance See also INHERITANCES.
Ge 31:14 yet any portion or i' for us in our 5159
48: 6 name of their brethren in their i'. "
Ex 15:17 in the mountain of thine i', in the "
34: 9 our sin, and take us for thine i'. 5157
Le 25:46 them as an i' for your children "
Nu 16:14 given us i' of fields and vineyards:5159
18:20 Thou shalt have no i' in their land,5157
20 I am thy part and thine i' among 5159
21 Levi all the tenth in Israel for an i', "
23 children of Israel they have no i'. "
24 of Israel they shall have no i'. "
26 given you from them for your i', "
26:53 the land shall be divided for an i', "
54 many thou shalt give the more i', "
54 and to few thou shalt give the less i' "
56 to every one shall his i' be given "
62 because there was no i' given "
27: 7 an i' among their father's brethren; "
7 i' of their father to pass unto them. "
8 his i' to pass unto his daughter. "
9 shall give his i' unto his brethren. "
10 his i' unto his father's brethren. "
11 shall give his i' unto his kinsman "
32:18 have inherited every man his i'. "
19 our i' is fallen to us on this side 5159
32 the possession of our i' on this side "
33:54 divide the land by lot for an i' *5157
54 the more ye shall give the more i',5159
54 to the fewer ye shall give the less i': "
54 every man's i' shall be in the place*
34: 2 that shall fall unto you for an i', 5159
14 fathers, have received their i'; "
14 of Manasseh have received their i':5159
15 have received their i' on this side "
18 every tribe, to divide the land by i'.5157
29 Lord commanded to divide the i' "
35: 2 the i' of their possession cities to 5159
8 to his i' which he inheriteth. "
36: 2 to give the land for an i' by lot to "
2 the i' of Zelophehad our brother "
3 their i' be taken from the i' of our "
3 shall be put to the i' of the tribe "
3 it be taken from the lot of our i'. "
4 their i' be put unto the i' of the "
4 their i' be taken away from the i' "
7 not the i' of the children of Israel "
7 to the i' of the tribe of his fathers. "
8 daughter, that possesseth an i' in "
8 enjoy every man the i' of his fathers. "
9 Neither shall the i' remove from "
9 shall keep himself to his own i'. "
12 and their i' remained in the tribe "
De 4:20 to be unto him a people of i', as ye "
21 Lord thy God giveth thee for an i': "
38 to give thee their land for an i', as it "
9:26 destroy not thy people and thine i', "
29 they are thy people and thine i', "
10: 9 no part nor i' with his brethren; "
9 the Lord is his i', according as the "
12: 9 as yet come to the rest and to the i', "
12 as he hath no part nor i' with you. "
14:27 for he hath no part nor i' with thee. "
29 he hath no part nor i' with thee, "
15: 4 Lord thy God giveth thee for an i' "
18: 1 have no part nor i' with Israel: "
1 the Lord made by fire, and his i'. "
2 Therefore shall they have no i' "
2 the Lord is their i', as he hath said "
19:10 Lord thy God giveth thee for an i', "
14 they of old time have set in thine i', "
20:16 thy God doth give thee for an i', "
21:23 Lord thy God giveth thee for an i'. "
24: 4 Lord thy God giveth thee for an i'. "
25:19 giveth thee for an i' to possess it, "
26: 1 Lord thy God giveth thee for an i', "
29: 8 it for an i' unto the Reubenites, "
32: 8 divided to the nations their i', 5157
9 people; Jacob is the lot of his i'. 5159
33: 4 the i' of the congregation of Jacob.4181
Jos 1: 6 shalt thou divide for an i' the land,5157
11:23 and Joshua gave it for an i' unto 5159
13: 6 by lot unto the Israelites for an i', "
7 land for an i' unto the nine tribes, "
8 the Gadites have received their i', "
14 the tribe of Levi he gave none i'; "
14 of Israel made by fire are their i', "
15 the children of Reuben i' according*
23 the i' of the children of Reuben 5159
24 Moses gave i' unto the tribe of Gad
28 is the i' of the children of Gad 5159
29 And Moses gave the i' unto the half
32 which Moses did distribute for i' *5157
33 of Levi Moses gave not any i': 5159
33 the Lord God of Israel was their i', "
14: 1 Israel, distributed for i'. *5157
2 By lot was their i', as the Lord 5159
3 Moses had given the i' of two tribes "
3 unto the Levites he gave none i' "
9 feet have trodden shall be thine i', "
13 son of Jephunneh Hebron for an i'. "
14 Hebron therefore became the i' of "
15:20 i' of the tribe of...children of Judah "
16: 4 and Ephraim, took their i'. 5157
5 the border of their i' on the east 5159
8 the i' of the tribe of the children of "
9 the i' of the children of Manasseh, "
17: 4 to give us an i' among our brethren. "
4 them an i' among the brethren of "
6 daughters of Manasseh had an i' 5157
18: 2 which had not yet received their i'.5159
4 it according to the i' of them; "
7 priesthood of the Lord is their i': "
7 received their i' beyond Jordan "
20 the i' of the children of Benjamin, "
28 the i' of the children of Benjamin "
19: 1 i' was within the i' of the children "
2 and they had in their i' Beer-sheba, "
8 This is the i' of the tribe of the "
9 the i' of the children of Simeon: "
9 the children of Simeon had their i'5157
9 had their...within the i' of them. 5159
10 border of their i' was unto Sarid: "
16 is the i' of the children of Zebulun "
23, 31, 39 This is the i' of the tribe of "
41 And the coast of their i' was Zorah, "
48 This is the i' of the tribe of the "
49 an end of dividing the land for i' 5157
49 of Israel gave an i' to Joshua the 5157
51 divided for an i' by lot in Shiloh 5157
21: 3 unto the Levites out of their i', 5159
23: 4 to be an i' for your tribes, from "
24:28 depart, every man unto his i'. "
30 buried him in the border of his i' "
32 the i' of the children of Joseph. "
J'g 2: 6 every man unto his i' to possess "
9 buried him in the border of his i' "
18: 1 the Danites sought them an i' to "
1 all their i' had not fallen unto them. "
20: 6 all the country of the i' of Israel: "
21:17 There must be an i' for them that 3425

J'g 21:23 went and returned unto their i', 5159
24 from thence every man unto his i'. "
Ru 4: 5 up the name of the dead upon his i'. "
6 for myself, lest I mar mine own i': "
10 up the name of the dead upon his i', "
1Sa 10: 1 thee to be captain over his i'? "
26:19 from abiding in the i' of the Lord, "
2Sa 14:16 my son together out of the i' of God. "
20: 1 have we i' in the son of Jesse: "
19 thou swallow up the i' of the Lord? "
21: 3 ye may bless the i' of the Lord? "
1Ki 8:36 hast given to thy people for an i'. "
51 For they be thy people, and thine i'. "
53 people of the earth to be thine i', "
12:16 have we i' in the son of Jesse: "
21: 3 I should give the i' of my fathers "
4 not give thee the i' of my fathers. "
2Ki 21:14 will forsake the remnant of mine i', "
1Ch 16:18 land of Canaan, the lot of your i'; "
28: 8 leave it for an i' for your children 5157
2Ch 6:27 given unto thy people for an i'. 5159
10:16 we have none i' in the son of Jesse: "
Ezr 9:12 leave it for an i' to your children 3423
Ne 11:20 cities of Judah, every one in his i'. 5159
Job 31: 2 i' of the Almighty from on high? * "
42:15 gave them i' among their brethren. "
Ps 2: 8 give thee the heathen for thine i', "
16: 5 The Lord is the portion of mine i' 2506
28: 9 Save thy people, and bless thine i': 5159
33:12 whom he hath chosen for his own i'. "
37:18 and their i' shall be for ever. "
47: 4 He shall choose our i' for us, "
68: 9 whereby thou didst confirm thine i', "
74: 2 the rod of thine i', which thou hast "
78:55 and divided them an i' by line, and "
62 and was wroth with his i'. "
71 Jacob his people, and Israel his i'. "
79: 1 the heathen are come into thine i'; "
94:14 people, neither will he forsake his i'. "
105:11 land of Canaan, the lot of your i': "
106: 5 that I may glory with thine i'. "
40 that he abhorred his own i'. "
Pr 13:22 A good man leaveth an i' to his 5157
17: 2 part of the i' among the brethren 5159
19:14 and riches are the i' of fathers: "
20:21 An i' may be gotten hastily at the "
Ec 7:11 Wisdom is good with an i': and by "
Isa 19:25 of my hands, and Israel mine i'. "
47: 6 I have polluted mine i', and given "
63:17 servants' sake, the tribes of thine i'. "
Jer 3:18 given for an i' unto your fathers. 5157
10:16 and Israel is the rod of his i': The 5159
12:14 evil neighbours, that touch the i' "
16:18 filled mine i' with the carcases of "
32: 8 for the right of i' is thine, and the 3425
51:19 and Israel is the rod of his i': The 5159
La 5: 2 Our i' is turned to strangers, our "
Eze 22:16 And thou shalt take thine i' in *2490
33:24 many; the land is given us for i'. 4181
35:15 at the i' of the house of Israel, 5159
36:12 and thou shalt be their i', and thou "
44:28 be unto them for an i': I am their i': "
45: 1 shall divide by lot the land for i', "
46:16 the i' thereof shall be his sons'; "
16 it shall be their possession by i'. "
17 gift of his i' to one of his servants, "
17 his i' shall be to his sons' for them. "
18 shall not take of the people's i' by "
18 shall give his sons i' out of his own 5157
47:14 this land shall fall unto you for i'. 5159
22 divide it by lot for an i' unto you, "
22 they shall have i' with you among "
23 there shall ye give him his i', saith "
48:29 lot unto the tribes of Israel for i', "
M't 21:38 kill him, and let us seize on his i'. 2817
M'r 12: 7 kill him, and the i' shall be ours. "
Lu 12:13 that he divide the i' with me. "
20:14 kill him, that the i' may be ours. "
Ac 7: 5 And he gave him none i' in it, "
20:32 to give you an i' among all them "
26:18 i' among them which are sanctified 2819
Ga 3:18 if the i' be of the law, it is no more 2817
Eph 1:11 In whom...we...obtained an i', *2820
14 is the earnest of our i' until the 2817
18 of the glory of his i' in the saints. "
5: 5 hath any i' in the kingdom of Christ "
Col 1:12 be partakers of the i' of the saints 2819
3:24 shall receive the reward of the i': 2817
Heb 1: 4 as he hath by i' obtained a more *2820
9:15 receive the promise of eternal i'. 2817
11: 8 he should after receive for an i', "
1Pe 1: 4 an i' incorruptible, and undefiled, "

inheritances
Jos 19:51 These are the i', which Eleazer 5159

inherited
Nu 32:18 have i' every man his inheritance. 5157
Jos 14: 1 of Israel i' in the land of Canaan, "
Ps 105:44 they i' the labour of the people; *3423
Jer 16:19 Surely our fathers have i' lies, 5157
Eze 33:24 and he i' the land: but we are 3423
Heb 12:17 he would have i' the blessing, *2816

inheriteth
Nu 35: 8 to his inheritance which he i'. 5157

inheritor
Isa 65: 9 of Judah an i' of my mountains: 3423

iniquities
Le 16:21 all the i' of the children of Israel, 5771
22 goat shall bear upon him all their i' "
26:39 i' of their fathers shall they pine "
Nu 14:34 day for a year, shall ye bear your i', "
Ezr 9: 6 our i' are increased over our head, "
7 for our i' have we, our kings, and "
13 punished us less than our i' deserve, "
Ne 9: 2 sins, and the i' of their fathers. "
Job 13:23 How many are mine i' and sins? 5771
26 me to possess the i' of my youth. "
22: 5 great? and thine i' infinite? "
Ps 38: 4 mine i' are gone over mine head: as "
40:12 mine i' have taken hold upon me, "
51: 9 my sins, and blot out all mine i'. "
64: 6 They search out i'; they 5766
65: 3 I' prevail against me: as for 1647,5771
79: 8 remember not against us former i': "
90: 8 Thou hast set our i' before thee, "
103: 3 Who forgiveth all thine i'; who "
10 rewarded us according to our i'. "
107:17 and because of their i', are afflicted. "
130: 3 If thou, Lord, shouldest mark i', O "
8 shall redeem Israel from all his i'. "
Pr 5:22 His own i' shall take the wicked "
Isa 43:24 thou hast wearied me with thine i'. "
50: 1 for your i' have ye sold yourselves, "
53: 5 he was bruised for our i': "
11 many; for he shall bear their i'. "
59: 2 But your i' have separated between "
12 and as for our i', we know them; "
64: 6 our i', like the wind, have taken "
7 consumed us, because of our i'. "
65: 7 Your i', and the i' of your fathers "
Jer 5:25 Your i' have turned away these "
11:10 back to the i' of their forefathers, "
14: 7 though our i' testify against us, "
33: 8 and I will pardon all their i', "
La 4:13 the i' of her priests, that have shed "
5: 7 not; and we have borne their i'. "
Eze 24:23 but ye shall pine away for your i', "
28:18 by the multitude of thine i', by the "
32:27 their i' shall be upon their bones, "
36:31 in your own sight for your i' and "
33 have cleansed you from all your i' "
43:10 they may be ashamed of their i': "
Da 4:27 and thine i' by shewing mercy to 5758
9:13 that we might turn from our i', 5771
16 sins, and for the i' of our fathers, "
Am 3: 2 I will punish you for all your i'. "
Mic 7:19 he will subdue our i'; and thou "
Ac 3:26 away every one of you from his i'. 4189
Ro 4: 7 are they whose i' are forgiven, 458
Heb 8:12 their i' will I remember no more. * "
10:17 sins and i' will I remember no more. "
Re 18: 5 and God hath remembered her i'. 92

iniquity See also INIQUITIES.
Ge 15:16 i' of the Amorites is not yet full. 5771
19:15 be consumed in the i' of the city. "
44:16 found out the i' of thy servants: "
Ex 20: 5 visiting the i' of the fathers upon "
28:38 may bear the i' of the holy things, "
43 that they bear not i', and die: "
34: 7 forgiving i' and transgression and "
7 visiting the i' of the fathers upon "
9 and pardon our i' and our sin, and "
Le 5: 1 utter it, then he shall bear his i'. "
17 is he guilty, and shall bear his i'. "
7:18 that eateth of it shall bear his i'. "
10:17 to bear the i' of the congregation, "
17:16 his flesh; then he shall bear his i'. "
18:25 I do visit the i' thereof upon it, "
19: 8 one that eateth it shall bear his i', "
20:17 nakedness; he shall bear his i'. "
19 near kin: they shall bear their i'. "
22:16 them to bear the i' of trespass, "
26:39 of you shall pine away in their i' in "
40 confess their i', and the i' of their "
41:43 of the punishment of their i': "
Nu 5:15 bringing i' to remembrance. "
31 shall the man be guiltless from i', "
31 and this woman shall bear her i'. "
14:18 forgiving i' and transgression, "
18 visiting the i' of the fathers upon "
19 I beseech thee, the i' of this people "
15:31 cut off; his i' shall be upon him. "
18: 1 shall bear the i' of the sanctuary: "
1 shall bear the i' of your priesthood. "
23 and they shall bear their i': it shall "
23:21 He hath not beheld i' in Jacob, 205
30:15 them; then he shall bear her i'. 5771
De 5: 9 visiting the i' of the fathers upon "
19:15 not rise up against a man for any i'. "
32: 4 a God of truth and without i', 5766
Jos 22:17 Is the i' of Peor too little for us, 5771
20 man perished not alone in his i'. "
1Sa 3:13 ever for the i' which he knoweth; "
14 i' of Eli's house shall not be purged "
15:23 stubbornness is as i' and idolatry. *205
20: 1 have I done? what is mine i'? 5771
8 if there be in me i', slay me "
25:24 me, my lord, upon me let this i' be; "
2Sa 7:14 If he commit i', I will chasten him 5753
14: 9 the i' be on me, and on my father's 5771
32 if there be any i' in me, let him kill "
19:19 Let not my lord impute i' unto me, "
22:24 and have kept myself from mine i'. "
24:10 take away the i' of thy servant; "
1Ch 21: 8 do away the i' of thy servant; for "
2Ch 19: 7 is no i' with the Lord our God, 5766
Ne 4: 5 And cover not their i', and let not 5771
Job 4: 8 that plow i', and sow wickedness, 205
5:16 hope, and i' stoppeth her mouth. 5766
6:29 Return, I pray you, let it not be i'; * "
30 Is there i' in my tongue? cannot * "
7:21 and take away mine i'? 5771
10: 6 That thou enquirest after thine i', "
14 wilt not acquit me from mine i'. "
11: 6 thee less than thine i' deserveth. "
14 If i' be in thine hand, put it far 205
14:17 a bag, and thou sewest up mine i'. 5771
15: 5 thy mouth uttereth thine i', and "
16 man, which drinketh i' like water? 5766
20:27 The heaven shall reveal his i'; and 5771
21:19 God layeth up his i' for his children: 205
Job 22:23 away i' far from thy tabernacles. 5766
31: 3 punishment to the workers of i'? 205
11 an i' to be punished by the judges. 5771
28 an i' to be punished by the judge: "
33 by hiding mine i' in my bosom: "
33: 9 innocent; neither is there i' in me. "
34: 8 in company with the workers of i', 205
10 that he should commit i'. 5766
22 where the workers of i' may hide 205
32 if I have done i', I will do no more. 5766
36:10 that they return from i'. 205
21 Take heed, regard not i': for this "
23 can say, Thou hast wrought i'? *5766
Ps 5: 5 sight: thou hatest all workers of i'. 205
6: 8 Depart from me, all ye workers of i'; "
7: 3 this; if there be i' in my hands; 5766
14 Behold, he travaileth with i', and 205
14: 4 all the workers of i' no knowledge? "
18:23 and I kept myself from mine i'. 5771
25:11 O Lord, pardon mine i'; for it is "
28: 3 with the workers of i', which speak 205
31:10 strength faileth because of mine i', 5771
32: 2 whom the Lord imputeth not i', "
5 thee, and mine i' have I not hid. "
5 and thou forgavest the i' of my sin. "
36: 2 until his i' be found to be hateful. "
3 The words of his mouth are i' and 205
12 There are the workers of i' fallen: "
37: 1 envious against the workers of i'. *5766
38:18 For I will declare mine i'; I will 5771
39:11 with rebukes dost correct man for i', "
41: 6 his heart gathereth i' to itself; 205
49: 5 the i' of my heels shall compass 5771
51: 2 Wash me thoroughly from mine i', "
5 I was shapen in i'; and in sin "
53: 1 and have done abominable i': 5766
4 the workers of i' no knowledge? 205
55: 3 for they cast i' upon me, and in "
56: 7 Shall they escape by i'? in thine "
59: 2 Deliver me from the workers of i', "
64: 2 insurrection of the workers of i': "
66:18 If I regard i' in my heart, the Lord "
69:27 Add i' unto their i': and let them 5771
78:38 full of compassion, forgave their i', "
85: 2 hast forgiven the i' of thy people, "
89:32 the rod, and their i' with stripes. "
92: 7 all the workers of i' do flourish; 205
9 the workers of i' shall be scattered. "
94: 4 the workers of i' boast themselves. "
16 up for me against the workers of i'? "
20 the throne of i' have fellowship *1942
23 shall bring upon them their own i', 205
106: 6 we have committed i', we have 5753
43 and were brought low for their i'. 5771
107:42 and all i' shall stop her mouth. 5766
109:14 i' of his fathers be remembered 5771
119: 3 They also do no i': they walk in *5766
133 let not any i' have dominion over 205
125: 3 put forth their hands unto i'. 5766
5 them forth with the workers of i': 205
141: 4 wicked works with men that work i': "
9 and the gins of the workers of i'. "
Pr 10:29 shall be to the workers of i'. "
16: 6 By mercy and truth i' is purged: 5771
19:28 mouth of the wicked devoureth i'. 205
21:15 shall be to the workers of i'. "
22: 8 that soweth i' shall reap vanity: 5766
Ec 3:16 righteousness, that i' was there. *7562
Isa 1: 4 nation, a people laden with i', 5771
13 it is i', even the solemn meeting. 205
5:18 unto them that draw i' with cords 5771
6: 7 thine i' is taken away, and thy sin "
13:11 evil, and the wicked for their i'; and "
14:21 children for the i' of their fathers; "
22:14 Surely this i' shall not be purged "
26:21 inhabitants of the earth for their i': "
27: 9 shall the i' of Jacob be purged; "
29:20 all that watch for i' are cut off: 205
30:13 this i' shall be to you as a breach 5771
31: 2 the help of them that work i'. 205
32: 6 his heart will work i', to practise "
33:24 therein shall be forgiven their i'. 5771
40: 2 her i' is pardoned: for she hath "
53: 6 hath laid on him the i' of us all. "
57:17 For the i' of his covetousness was I "
59: 3 with blood, and your fingers with i'; "
4 conceive mischief, and bring forth i'. 205
6 their works are works of i', and the "
7 their thoughts are thoughts of i'; "
64: 9 neither remember i' for ever: 5771
Jer 2: 5 What i' have your fathers found *5766
22 yet thine i' is marked before me, 5771
3:13 Only acknowledge thine i', that "
9: 5 weary themselves to commit i'. 5753
13:22 For the greatness of thine i' are 5771
14:10 he will now remember their i', "
20 wickedness, and the i' of our fathers: "
16:10 or what is our i'? or what is our sin "
17 neither is their i' hid from mine "
18 I will recompense their i' and their "
18:23 forgive not their i', neither blot out "
25:12 nation, saith the Lord, for their i', "
30:14 for the multitude of thine i'; "
15 for the multitude of thine i': "
31:30 every one shall die for his own i': "
34 for I will forgive their i', and I will "
32:18 recompensest the i' of the fathers "
33: 8 I will cleanse them from all their i', "
36: 3 I may forgive their i' and their sin. "
31 seed and his servants for their i'; "
50:20 the i' of Israel shall be sought for, "
51: 6 be not cut off in her i'; for this "
La 2:14 they have not discovered thine i', "
4: 6 punishment of the i' of the daughter "
22 The punishment of thine i' is "
22 he will visit thine i', O daughter of "

Eze 3:18 same wicked man shall die in his i';5771
19 wicked way, he shall die in his i'; "
20 his righteousness, and commit i', 5766
4: 4 lay the i' of the house of Israel 5771
4 lie upon it thou shalt bear their i'. "
5 laid upon thee the years of their i', "
5 shalt thou bear the i' of the house "
6 thou shalt bear the i' of the house "
17 and consume away for their i'. "
7:13 himself in the i' of his life, "
16 mourning, every one for his i'. "
19 it is the stumblingblock of their i'. "
9: 9 i' of the house of Israel and Judah "
14: 3 the stumblingblock of their i' "
4, 7 the stumblingblock of his i' "
10 bear the punishment of their i': "
16:49 this was the i' of thy sister Sodom, "
18: 8 hath withdrawn his hand from i', 5766
17 not die for the i' of his father, he 5771
18 lo, even he shall die in his i' "
19 not the son bear the i' of the father? "
20 shall not bear the i' of the father, "
20 the father bear the i' of the son: "
24 and committeth i', and doeth 5766
26 committeth i', and dieth in them; "
26 his i' that he hath done shall he die. "
30 so i' shall not be your ruin. 5771
21:23 he will call to remembrance the i', "
24 made your i' to be remembered, "
25 is come, when i' shall have an end, "
29 when their i' shall have an end. "
28:15 created, till i' was found in thee. *5766
18 by the i' of thy traffick; * "
29:16 bringeth their i' to remembrance, 5771
33: 6 them, he is taken away in his i'; "
8 that wicked man shall die in his i'; "
9 from his way, he shall die in his i'; "
13 own righteousness, and commit i', 5766
13 for his i' that he hath committed, "
15 of life, without committing i'; "
18 righteousness, and committeth i', "
35: 5 the time that their i' had an end: 5771
39:23 went into captivity for their i': "
44:10 idols; they shall even bear their i'. "
12 the house of Israel to fall into i'; "
12 God, and they shall bear their i'. "
Da 9: 5 sinned, and have committed i', *5753
24 and to make reconciliation for i', 5771
Ho 4: 8 and they set their heart on their i'. "
5: 5 Israel and Ephraim fall in their i'; "
6: 8 Gilead is a city of them that work i',205
7: 1 the i' of Ephraim was discovered, 5771
8:13 now will he remember their i', "
9: 7 for the multitude of thine i', and "
9 he will remember their i', he will "
10: 9 battle...against the children of i' 5932
13 wickedness, ye have reaped i'; ye 5766
12: 8 find none i' in me that were sin. 5771
11 Is there i' in Gilead? surely they 205
13:12 The i' of Ephraim is bound up; 5771
14: 1 for thou hast fallen by thine i'. "
2 Take away all i', and receive us "
Mic 2: 1 Woe to them that devise i', and 205
3:10 with blood, and Jerusalem with i'. 5766
7:18 like unto thee, that pardoneth i', 5771
Hab 1: 3 Why dost thou shew me i', and 205
13 evil, and canst not look on i': *5999
2:12 blood, and stablisheth a city by i'! 5766
Zep 3: 5 the midst thereof; he will not do i': "
13 remnant of Israel shall not do i', "
Zec 3: 4 I have caused thine i' to pass 5771
9 will remove the i' of that land in one "
Mal 2: 6 and i' was not found in his lips: 5766
6 and did turn many away from i'. 5771
M't 7:23 depart from me, ye that work i'. 458
13:41 that offend, and them which do i'; "
23:28 within ye are full of hypocrisy and i'. "
24:12 because i' shall abound, the love of "
Lu 13:27 depart from me, all ye workers of i'. 93
Ac 1:18 a field with the reward of i'; "
8:23 of bitterness, and in the bond of i'. "
Ro 6:19 to uncleanness and to i' unto i'; 458
1Co 13: 6 Rejoiceth not in i', but rejoiceth in * 93
2Th 2: 7 mystery of i' doth already work: *458
2Ti 2:19 the name of Christ depart from i'. * 93
Tit 2:14 might redeem us from all i', and 458
Heb 1: 9 loved righteousness, and hated i'; "
Jas 3: 6 And the tongue is a fire, a world of i': 93
2Pe 2:16 But was rebuked for his i': the *3892

injoin See ENJOIN.

injured
Ga 4:12 as ye are: ye have not i' me at all.* 91

injurious
1Ti 1:13 and a persecutor, and i': but I 5197

injustice
Job 16:17 Not for any i' in mine hands: also *2555

ink See also INKHORN.
Jer 36:18 and I wrote them with i' in the 1773
2Co 3: 3 written not with i', but with the 3188
2Jo 12 would not write with paper and i': "
3Jo 13 I will not with i' and pen write unto "

inkhorn
Eze 9: 2 with a writer's i' by his side: 7083
3 had the writer's i' by his side; "
11 linen, which had the i' by his side, "

inn
Ge 42:27 to give his ass provender in the i', *4411
43:21 when we came to the i', that we * "
Ex 4:24 came to pass by the way in the i', * "
Lu 2: 7 was no room for them in the i'. 2646
10:34 and brought him to an i', and took 3829

inner See also INNERMOST.
1Ki 6:27 the cherubims within the i' house: 6442
6:36 he built the i' court with three rows 6442
7:12 for the i' court of the house of the "
50 the doors of the i' house, the most "
20:30 into the city, into an i' chamber. 2315
22:25 shalt go into an i' chamber to hide "
2Ki 9: 2 and carry him to an i' chamber; "
1Ch 28:11 and of the i' parlours thereof, and 6442
2Ch 4:22 the i' doors thereof for the most "
18:24 shalt go into an i' chamber to hide 2315
29:16 went into the i' part of the house 6441
Es 4:11 unto the king into the i' court, 6442
5: 1 stood in the i' court of the king's "
Eze 8: 3 the door of the i' gate that looketh "
16 he brought me into the i' court "
10: 3 and the cloud filled the i' court. "
40:15 the porch of the i' gate were fifty "
19 unto the forefront of the i' court "
23 the gate of the i' court was over "
27 a gate in the i' court toward the "
28 he brought me to the i' court by "
32 he brought me into the i' court "
44 the i' gate were the chambers "
44 of the singers in the i' court, which "
41:15 with the i' temple, and the porches "
17 the door, even unto the i' house, "
42: 3 cubits which were for the i' court, "
15 an end of measuring the i' house, "
43: 5 and brought me into the i' court; "
44:17 enter in at the gates of the i' court, "
17 minister in the gates of the i' court, "
21 when they enter into the i' court. "
27 into the sanctuary, unto the i' court, "
45:19 the posts of the gate of the i' court. "
46: 1 The gate of the i' court that looketh "
Ac 16:24 thrust them into the i' prison, and 2082
Eph 3:16 might by his Spirit in the i' man; *2080

innermost
Pr 18: 8 down into the i' parts of the belly. 2315
26:22 down into the i' parts of the belly. "

innocency
Ge 20: 5 and i' of my hands have I done 5356
Ps 26: 6 I will wash mine hands in i': so will "
73:13 in vain, and washed my hands in i'. "
Da 6:22 as before him i' was found in me; 2136
Ho 8: 5 long will it be ere they attain to i'? 5356

innocent See also INNOCENTS.
Ex 23: 7 the i' and righteous slay thou not: 5355
De 19:10 That i' blood be not shed in thy "
13 the guilt of i' blood from Israel, "
21: 8 and lay not i' blood unto thy people "
9 put away the guilt of i' blood from "
27:25 taketh reward to slay an i' person. "
1Sa 19: 5 then wilt thou sin against i' blood, "
1Ki 2:31 mayest take away the i' blood, *2600
2Ki 21:16 Manasseh shed i' blood very much, 5355
24: 4 also for the i' blood that he shed: "
4 he filled Jerusalem with i' blood; "
Job 4: 7 thee, who ever perished, being i'? "
9:23 he will laugh at the trial of the i'. "
28 know that thou wilt not hold me i'. 5352
17: 8 the i' shall stir up himself against 5355
22:19 and the i' laugh them to scorn. "
30 He shall deliver the island of the i': "
27:17 on, and the i' shall divide the silver. "
33: 9 without transgression, I am i'; 2643
Ps 10: 8 places doth he murder the i': 5355
15: 5 nor taketh reward against the i'. "
19:13 i' from the great transgression. *5352
94:21 and condemn the i' blood. 5355
106:38 And shed i' blood, even the blood "
Pr 1:11 let us lurk privily for the i' without "
6:17 and hands that shed i' blood, "
29 toucheth her shall not be i'. *5352
28:20 haste to be rich shall not be i'. * "
Isa 59: 7 they make haste to shed i' blood: 5355
Jer 2:35 Yet thou sayest, Because I am i', 5352
7: 6 and shed not i' blood in this place, 5355
22: 3 neither shed i' blood in this place. "
17 and for to shed i' blood, and for "
26:15 ye shall surely bring i' blood upon "
Joe 3:19 they have shed i' blood in their land. "
Jon 1:14 and lay not upon us i' blood: for "
M't 27: 4 in that I have betrayed the i' blood. 121
24 I am i' of the blood of this just "

innocents
Jer 2:34 blood of the souls of the poor i': *5355
19: 4 filled this place with the blood of i'; "

innumerable
Job 21:33 as there are i' before him. 369,4557
Ps 40:12 For i' evils have compassed me " "
104:25 wherein are things creeping i', " "
Jer 46:23 the grasshoppers, and are i'. "
Lu 12: 1 an i' multitude of people; *3461
Heb 11:12 sand which is by the sea shore i'. 382
12:22 and to an i' company of angels, 3461

inordinate
Eze 23:11 was more corrupt in her i' love *5691
Col 3: 5 uncleanness, i' affection, evil *3806

inquire See ENQUIRE.

inquisition
De 19:18 the judges shall make diligent i': 1875
Es 2:23 when i' was made of the matter, 1245
Ps 9:12 When he maketh i' for blood, he 1875

insatiable See UNSATIABLE.

inscription
Ac 17:23 altar with this i', To The Unknown 1924

inside
1Ki 6:15 covered them on the i' with wood, 1004

insomuch See also FORASMUCH; INASMUCH.
Mal 2:13 i' that he regardeth not the offering
M't 8:24 i' that the ship was covered with 5620
12:22 i' that the blind and dumb both "
13:54 i' that they were astonished, and 5620
15:31 I' that the multitude wondered, "
24:24 i' that, if it were possible, they shall* "
27:14 i' that the governor marvelled "
M'r 1:27 i' that they questioned among "
45 i' that Jesus could no more openly "
2: 2 i' that there was no room to receive * "
12 i' that they were all amazed, and "
3:10 i' that they pressed upon him for to "
9:26 dead: i' that many said, He is dead. "
Lu 12: 1 i' that they trode one upon another, "
Ac 1:19 i' as that field is called in their "
5:15 I' that they brought forth the sick "
2Co 1: 8 i' that we despaired even of life: "
8: 6 I' that we desired Titus, that as 1519
Ga 2:13 i' that Barnabas also was carried 5620

inspiration
Job 32: 8 the i' of the Almighty giveth them *5397
2Ti 3:16 scripture is given by i' of God, *2315

instant
Isa 29: 5 yea, it shall be at an i' suddenly. 6621
30:13 breaking cometh suddenly at an i'. "
Jer 18: 7 At what i' I shall speak concerning 7281
9 at what i' I shall speak concerning "
Lu 2:38 she coming in that i' gave thanks *5610
23:23 And they were i' with loud voices, ‡1945
Ro 12:12 continuing i' in prayer; *4342
2Ti 4: 2 be i' in season, out of season; 2186

instantly
Lu 7: 4 they besought him i', saying, *4705
Ac 26: 7 i' serving God day and night, *1722,1616

instead
Ge 2:21 and closed up the flesh i' thereof; 8478
4:25 me another seed instead of Abel, "
44:33 let thy servant abide i' of the lad a "
Ex 4:16 even he shall be to thee i' of a mouth, *
16 and thou shalt be to him i' of God.*
5:12 of Egypt to gather stubble i' of straw.*
Nu 3:12 of Israel i' of all the firstborn 8478
41 i' of all the firstborn among the "
41 i' of all the firstlings among the "
45 the Levites i' of all the firstborn "
45 of the Levites i' of their cattle; "
5:19 with another i' of thy husband, * "
20 aside to another i' of thy husband, * "
29 aside to another i' of her husband, * "
8:16 i' of such as open every womb, "
16 even i' of the firstborn of all the *
10:31 thou mayest be to us i' of eyes. 8478
J'g 15: 2 she? take her, I pray thee, i' of her. "
2Sa 17:25 captain of the host i' of Joab: "
1Ki 3: 7 made thy servant king i' of David "
2Ki 14:21 him king i' of his father Amaziah.* "
17:24 of Samaria i' of the children of "
1Ch 29:23 as king i' of David his father, and "
2Ch 12:10 I' of which king Rehoboam made * "
Es 2: 4 the king be queen i' of Vashti. "
17 and made her queen i' of Vashti. "
Job 31:40 i' of wheat, and cockle i' of barley. "
Ps 45:16 I' of thy fathers shall be thy "
Isa 3:24 i' of sweet smell there shall be "
24 stink; and i' of a girdle a rent; "
24 and i' of well set hair baldness; "
24 and i' of a stomacher a girding of "
24 sackcloth; and burning i' of beauty. "
55:13 I' of the thorn shall come up the fir "
13 i' of the brier shall come up the "
Jer 22:11 which reigned i' of Josiah his father, "
37: 1 son of Josiah reigned i' of Coniah "
Eze 16:32 taketh strangers i' of her husband! "

instruct See also INSTRUCTED; INSTRUCTING.
De 4:36 his voice, that he might i' thee: 3256
Ne 9:20 also thy good spirit to i' them, 7919
Job 40: 2 with the Almighty i' him? *3250
Ps 16: 7 my reins also i' me in the night 3256
32: 8 I will i' thee and teach thee in the 7919
Ca 8: 2 mother's house, who would i' me: 3925
Isa 28:26 his God doth i' him to discretion, 3256
Da 11:33 among the people shall i' many: 995
1Co 2:16 of the Lord, that he may i' him? 4822

instructed
De 32:10 he i' him, he kept him as the * 995
2Ki 12: 2 Jehoiada the priest i' him. 3384
1Ch 15:22 he i' about the song, because he 3256
25: 7 brethren that were i' in the songs 3925
2Ch 3: 3 Solomon was i' for the building *3245
Job 4: 3 Behold, thou hast i' many, and 3256
Ps 2:10 be i', ye judges of the earth. "
Pr 5:13 mine ear to them that i' me! 3925
21:11 when the wise is i', he receiveth 7919
Isa 8:11 and i' me that I should not walk 3256
40:14 and who i' him, and taught him 995
Jer 6: 8 Be thou i', O Jerusalem, lest my 3256
31:19 and after that I was i', I smote 3045
M't 13:52 is i' unto the kingdom of heaven *3100
14: 8 being before i' of her mother, *4264
Lu 1: 4 things, wherein thou hast been i'. 2727
Ac 18:25 man was i' in the way of the Lord; "
Ro 2:18 excellent, being i' out of the law; "
Ph'p 4:12 all things I am i' both to be full *3453

instructer See also INSTRUCTERS; INSTRUCTOR.
Ge 4:22 an i' of every artificer in brass *3913

instructers
1Co 4:15 ye have ten thousand i' in Christ, *3807

instructing
2Ti 2:25 In meekness i' those that oppose *3811

instruction
Job 33:16 ears of men, and sealeth their i', 4561
Ps 50:17 Seeing thou hatest i', and castest 4148
Pr 1: 2 To know wisdom and i'; to "
3 To receive the i' of wisdom, "
7 but fools despise wisdom and i'. "

Pr 1: 8 My son, hear the i' of thy father, 4148
4: 1 Hear, ye children, the i' of a father, "
13 Take fast hold of i'; let her not go: "
5: 12 How have I hated i', and my heart "
23 He shall die without i'; and in the "
6: 23 reproofs of i' are the way of life: "
8: 10 Receive my i', and not silver; and "
33 Hear i', and be wise, and refuse it "
9: 9 Give i' to a wise man, and he will be
10: 17 in the way of life that keepeth i': *4148
12: 1 Whoso loveth i' loveth knowledge:* "
13: 1 A wise son heareth his father's i': "
18 shall be to him that refuseth i': * "
15: 5 A fool despiseth his father's i': * "
32 refuseth i' despiseth his own soul:* "
33 fear of the Lord is the i' of wisdom: "
16: 22 hath it: but the i' of fools is folly.* "
19: 20 Hear counsel, and receive i', that "
27 to hear the i' that causeth to err "
23: 12 Apply thine heart unto i', and "
23 wisdom, and i', and understanding." "
24: 32 I looked upon it, and received i'. "
Jer 17: 23 they might not hear, nor receive i'. "
32: 33 have not hearkened to receive i'. "
35: 13 Will ye not receive i' to hearken to "
Eze 5: 15 an i' and an astonishment unto "
Zep 3: 7 wilt fear me, thou wilt receive i';* "
2Ti 3: 16 correction, for i' in righteousness: *3809*

instructor See also INSTRUCTER.
Ro 2: 20 An i' of the foolish, a teacher of *3810*

instrument See also INSTRUMENTS.
Nu 35: 16 if he smite him with an i' of iron, *3627
Ps 33: 2 the psaltery and an i' of ten strings.* "
92: 3 Upon an i' of ten strings, and upon "
144: 9 upon a psaltery and an i' of ten strings* "
Isa 28: 27 are not threshed with a threshing i', "
41: 15 make thee a new sharp threshing i' "
54: 16 bringeth forth an i' for his work;* 3627
Eze 33: 32 voice, and can play well on an i': "

instruments
Ge 49: 5 i' of cruelty are in their *3627
Ex 25: 9 the pattern of all the i' thereof, * "
Nu 3: 8 keep all the i' of the tabernacle * "
4: 12 shall take all the i' of ministry, * "
26 cords, and all the i' of their service, " "
32 with all their i', and with all their "
32 ye shall reckon the i' of the charge "
7: 1 sanctified it, and all the i' thereof,* "
31: 6 with the holy i', and the trumpets* "
1Sa 8: 12 his i' of war, and i' of his chariots. "
18: 6 with joy, and with i' of musick. 7991
2Sa 6: 5 on all manner of i' made of fir wood, "
24: 22 burnt sacrifice, and threshing i' "
22 and other i' of the oxen for wood. *3627
1Ki 19: 21 their flesh with the i' of the oxen, * "
1Ch 9: 29 and all the i' of the sanctuary, * "
12: 33 with all i' of war, fifty thousand, "
37 with all manner of i' of war for the "
15: 16 to be the singers with i' of musick, "
16: 42 sound, and with musical i' of God. "
21: 23 and the threshing i' for wood, and the "
23: 5 Lord with the i' which I made, 3627
28: 14 for all i' of all manner of service; * "
14 silver also for all i' of silver by * "
14 for all i' of every kind of service: * "
2Ch 4: 16 and all their i', did Huram his * "
5: 1 and all the i', put he among the * "
13 and cymbals and i' of musick, and "
7: 6 also with i' of musick of the Lord, "
23: 13 the singers with i' of musick, and "
29: 26 Levites stood with the i' of David, "
27 with the i' ordained by David king "
30: 21 singing with loud i' unto the Lord. "
34: 12 all that could skill of i' of musick. "
Ne 12: 36 with the musical i' of David the "
Ps 7: 13 prepared for him the i' of death; "
68: 25 the players on i' followed after; * "
87: 7 as the players on i' shall be there:* "
150: 4 him with stringed i' and organs. 4482
Ec 2: 8 as musical i', and that of all sorts.†
Isa 32: 7 The i' also of the churl are evil: 3627
38: 20 sing my songs to the stringed i' "
Eze 40: 42 i' wherewith they slew the burnt 3627
Da 6: 18 neither were i' of musick brought 1761
Am 1: 3 Gilead with threshing i' of iron: "
6: 5 invent to themselves i' of musick, 3627
Hab 3: 19 chief singer on my stringed i'. "
Zec 11: 15 yet the i' of a foolish shepherd. 3627
Ro 6: 13 as i' of unrighteousness unto sin: *3696*
13 as i' of righteousness unto God. "

insurrection
Ezr 4: 19 time hath made i' against kings, 5376
Ps 64: 2 the i' of the workers of iniquity: *7285
M'r 15: 7 bound with them that had made i' *4955*
7 had committed murder in the i'. *4714*
Ac 18: 12 the Jews made i' with one accord *2721*

intangle See ENTANGLE.

integrity
Ge 20: 5 the i' of my heart and innocency 8537
6 didst this in the i' of thy heart; "
1Ki 9: 4 thy father walked, in i' of heart, "
Job 2: 3 and still he holdeth fast his i', 8538
9 him, Dost thou still retain thine i'? "
27: 5 till I die I will not remove mine i' "
31: 6 that God may know mine i'. "
Ps 7: 8 according to mine i' that is in me. 8537
25: 21 Let i' and uprightness preserve "
26: 1 Lord; for I have walked in mine i': "
11 as for me, I will walk in mine i': "
41: 12 me, thou upholdest me in mine i', "
78: 72 according to the i' of his heart; "
Pr 11: 3 The i' of the upright shall guide 8538
19: 1 is the poor that walketh in his i', 8537
20: 7 The just man walketh in his i': his "

intelligence
Da 11: 30 and have i' with them that forsake *995

intend See also INTENDED; INTENDEST; INTENDING.
Jos 22: 33 and did not i' to go up against *559
2Ch 28: 13 ye i' to add more to our sins and to* "
Ac 5: 28 and i' to bring this man's blood *1014*
35 what ye i' to do as touching these *3195*

intended
Ps 21: 11 For they i' evil against thee: they 5186

intendest
Ex 2: 14 i' thou to kill me, as thou killedst* 559

intending
Lu 14: 28 which of you, i' to build a tower, *2309*
Ac 12: 4 i' after Easter to bring him forth *1011*
20: 13 Assos, there i' to take in Paul: *3195*

intent See also INTENTS.
2Sa 17: 14 i' that the Lord might bring evil 5668
2Ki 10: 19 to the i' that he might destroy the 4616
2Ch 16: 1 to the i' that he might let none go out* "
Eze 40: 4 the i' that I might shew them unto* 4616
Da 4: 17 to the i' that the living may know 1701
Joh 11: 15 not there, to the i' ye may believe; *2443*
13: 28 for what i' he spake this unto
Ac 9: 21 and came hither for that i',
10: 29 for what i' ye have sent for me? *3056*
1Co 10: 6 to the i' we should not lust after
Eph 3: 10 To the i' that now unto the *2443*

intents
Jer 30: 24 have performed the i' of his heart: 4209
Heb 4: 12 of the thoughts and i' of the heart. *1771*

intercession See also INTERCESSIONS.
Isa 53: 12 and made i' for the transgressors. 6293
Jer 7: 16 for them, neither make i' to me: "
27: 18 let them now make i' to the Lord "
36: 25 Gemariah had made i' to the king "
Ro 8: 26 the Spirit itself maketh i' for us *5241*
27 maketh i' for the saints according *1793*
34 of God, who also maketh i' for us. "
11: 2 he maketh i' to God against Israel,* "
Heb 7: 25 he ever liveth to make i' for them. "

intercessions
1Ti 2: 1 prayers, i', and giving of thanks, *1783*

intercessor
Isa 59: 16 wondered that there was no i': 6293

intermeddle See also INTERMEDDLETH.
Pr 14: 10 a stranger doth not i' with his joy. 6148

intermeddleth
Pr 18: 1 seeketh and i' with all wisdom. *1566

intermission
La 3: 49 and ceaseth not, without any i', 2014

interpret See also INTERPRETED; INTERPRETING.
Ge 41: 8 there was none that could i' them 6622
12 according to his dream he did i'. * "
15 and there is none that can i' it: "
15 canst understand a dream to i' it. "
1Co 12: 30 all speak with tongues? do all i'? *1329*
14: 5 speaketh with tongues, except he i', "
13 tongue pray that he may i'. "
27 and that by course; and let one i'. "

interpretation See also INTERPRETATIONS.
Ge 40: 5 according to the i' of his dream, 6623
12 This is the i' of it: The three "
16 baker saw that the i' was good, "
18 This is the i' thereof: The three "
41: 11 according to the i' of his dream. "
J'g 7: 15 of the dream, and the i' therof, 7667
Pr 1: 6 understand a proverb, and the i'; *4426
Ec 8: 1 who knoweth the i' of a thing? 6592
Da 2: 4 the dream, and we will shew the i'. 6591
5 me the dream, with the i' thereof, "
6 shew the dream and the i' thereof, "
6 me the dream, and the i' thereof. "
7 dream, and we will shew the i' of it. "
9 that ye can shew me the i' thereof. "
16 that he would shew the king the i'. "
24 I will shew unto the king the i'. "
25 make known unto the king the i'. "
26 I have seen, and the i' thereof? "
30 make known the i' to the king, "
36 and we will tell the i' thereof before "
45 is certain, and the i' thereof sure. "
4: 6 known unto me the i' of the dream. "
7 make known unto me the i' thereof. "
9 that I have seen, and the i' thereof. "
18 declare the i' thereof, forasmuch "
18 able to make known unto me the i': "
19 dream, or the i' thereof, trouble "
19 and the i' thereof to thine enemies. "
24 This is the i', O king, and this is "
5: 7 writing, and shew me the i' thereof, "
8 known to the king the i' thereof. "
12 be called, and he will shew the i'. "
15 make known unto me the i' thereof: "
15 could not shew the i' of the thing: "
16 known to me the i' thereof, thou "
17 and make known to him the i'. "
26 This is the i' of the thing: Mene; "
7: 16 made me know the i' of the things. "
Joh 1: 42 Cephas, which is by i', A stone. *2059*
9: 7 pool of Siloam, which is by i', Sent. "
Ac 9: 36 which by i' is called Dorcas: this *1329*
13: 8 sorcerer (for so is his name by i') *3177*
1Co 12: 10 to another the i' of tongues: *2058*
14: 26 tongue, hath a revelation, hath an i'. "
Heb 7: 2 being by i' King of righteousness, *2059*
2Pe 1: 20 the scripture is of any private i'. *1955*

interpretations
Ge 40: 8 Do not i' belong to God? tell me 6623
Da 5: 16 that thou canst make i', and 6591

interpreted
Ge 40: 22 baker: as Joseph had i' to them. 6622
41: 12 him, and he i' to us our dreams; "
13 to pass, as he i' to us, so it was; "
Ezr 4: 7 and i' in the Syrian tongue. *8638
M't 1: 23 which being i' is, God with us. *3177*
M'r 5: 41 cumi; which is, being i', Damsel, "
15: 22 is, being i', The place of a skull. "
34 which is, being i', My God, my God, "
Joh 1: 38 which is to say, being i', Master, *2059*
41 which is, being i', the Christ. *3177*
Ac 4: 36 being i', The son of consolation, "

interpreter
Ge 40: 8 a dream, and there is no i' of it. *6622
42: 23 for he spake unto them by an i'. 3887
Job 33: 23 an i', one among a thousand, to "
1Co 14: 28 if there be no i', let him keep *1328*

interpreting
Da 5: 12 understanding, i' of dreams, and 6591

into See also THEREINTO.
Ge 2: 7 breathed i' his nostrils the breath of
10 parted, and became i' four heads. *
15 and put him i' the garden of Eden
6: 18 and thou shalt come i' the ark, 413
19 sort shalt thou bring i' the ark, "
7: 1 thou and all thy house i' the ark; "
7 his sons' wives with him, i' the ark, "
9 two and two unto Noah i' the ark, "
13 of his sons with them, i' the ark, "
15 went in unto Noah i' the ark, two "
8: 9 she returned unto him i' the ark; "
9 pulled her in unto him i' the ark. "
9: 2 sea; i' your hands are they delivered.
11: 31 Chaldees, to go i' the land of Canaan;
12: 5 went forth to go i' the land of Canaan;
5 and i' the land of Canaan they came.
10 Abram went down i' Egypt to sojourn
11 he was come near to enter i' Egypt, 935
14 that, when Abram was come i' Egypt,
15 woman was taken i' Pharaoh's house.
13: 1 he had, and Lot with him, i' the south.
14: 20 delivered thine enemies i' thy hand.
16: 5 I have given my maid i' thy bosom;
18: 6 And Abraham hastened i' the tent
19: 2 I pray you, i' your servant's house, 413
3 unto him, and entered i' his house; "
10 and pulled Lot i' the house to them,
23 the earth when Lot entered i' Zoar.*
21: 32 i' the land of the Philistines. 413
22: 2 and get thee i' the land of Moriah; "
24: 20 emptied her pitcher i' the trough, "
32 And the man came i' the house: and
67 Isaac brought her i' his mother
26: 2 Go not down i' Egypt; dwell in the
27: 17 prepared, i' the hand of her son Jacob.
28: 15 will bring thee again i' this land; 413
29: 1 came i' the land of the people of the*
30: 35 gave them i' the hand of his sons.
31: 33 went i' Jacob's tent, and i' Leah's tent,
33 and i' the two maidservants' tents;
33 tent, and entered i' Rachel's tent.
32: 17 herds, and the camels, i' two bands;
6 delivered them i' the hand of his
36: 6 went i' the country from the face 413
37: 20 us slay him, and cast him i' some pit,
22 cast him i' this pit that is in the 413
24 they took him, and cast him i' a pit:
28 and they brought Joseph i' Egypt.
35 I will go down i' the grave unto my*
36 Midianites sold him i' Egypt unto 413
39: 4 and all that he had he put i' his hand.
11 that Joseph went i' the house to do
20 took him, and put him i' the prison, 413
40: 3 i' the prison, the place where Joseph "
11 and pressed them i' Pharaoh's cup, "
11 I gave the cup i' Pharaoh's hand. 5921
13 deliver Pharaoh's cup i' his hand,
15 they should put me i' the dungeon.
21 gave the cup i' Pharaoh's hand: 5921
41: 57 And all countries came i' Egypt to
42: 17 all together i' ward three days. 413
25 every man's money i' his sack, "
37 deliver him i' my hand, and I will 5921
43: 17 brought the men i' Joseph's house.
18 they were brought i' Joseph's
24 brought the men i' Joseph's house,
26 which was in their hand i' the house,
30 he entered i' his chamber, and wept
45: 4 your brother, whom ye sold i' Egypt.
25 and came i' the land of Canaan unto
46: 3 fear not to go down i' Egypt; for I will
4 I will go down with thee i' Egypt; for
6 and came i' Egypt, Jacob, and all his
7 seed brought he with him i' Egypt.
8 of Israel, which came i' Egypt,
27 house of Jacob, which came i' Egypt,
28 they came i' the land of Goshen.
47: 14 brought the money i' Pharaoh's house.
48: 5 I came unto thee i' Egypt, are mine;
16 let them grow i' a multitude in the
49: 6 my soul, come not thou i' their secret;
33 he gathered up his feet i' the bed, 413
50: 13 his sons carried him i' the land of
14 And Joseph returned i' Egypt, he, and
Ex 1: 1 of Israel, which came i' Egypt;
22 son that is born ye shall cast i' the
3: 18 three days' journey i' the wilderness,
4: 6 him, Put now thine hand i' thy bosom.
6 he put his hand i' his bosom: and
7 Put thine hand i' thy bosom again. 413
7 put his hand i' his bosom again; "
19 Moses in Midian, Go, return i' Egypt:
21 When thou goest to return i' Egypt,
27 Go i' the wilderness to meet Moses.

Ex 5: 3 thee, three days' journey i' the desert,
7:23 turned and went i' his house, 413
8: 3 shall go up and come i' thine house,
3 and i' thy bedchamber, and upon thy
3 and i' the house of thy servants, and
3 upon thy people and i' thine ovens,
3 and i' thy kneading troughs:
21 upon thy people, and i' thy houses:
24 grievous swarm of flies i' the house of
24 i' his servants' houses, and i' all the
27 three days' journey i' the wilderness,
9:20 and his cattle flee i' the houses: 413
10: 4 will I bring the locusts i' thy coast:
19 locusts, and cast them i' the Red sea;
11: 4 midnight will I go out i' the midst
13: 5, 11 thee i' the land of the Canaanites,413
14:22 of Israel went i' the midst of the sea
28 that came i' the sea after them;
15: 1 his rider hath he thrown i' the sea.
4 and his host hath he cast i' the sea:
5 they sank i' the bottom as a stone.
19 and with his horsemen i' the sea,
21 his rider hath he thrown i' the sea.
22 went out i' the wilderness of Shur; 413
25 when he had cast i' the waters, "
16: 3 brought us forth i' this wilderness, "
18: 5 his wife unto Moses i' the wilderness,"
7 welfare; and they came i' the tent.
27 he went his way i' his own land. 413
19: 1 came they i' the wilderness of Sinai.
12 that ye go not up i' the mount, or
21:13 but God deliver him i' his hand;
23:19 shalt bring i' the house of the Lord thy
20 bring thee i' the place which I have 413
31 inhabitants of the land i' your hand;
24:12 Come up to me i' the mount, and be
13 Moses went up i' the mount of God.413
15 Moses went up i' the mount, and a "
18 Moses went i' the midst of the cloud,
18 and gat him i' the mount: and 413
25:14 thou shalt put the staves i' the rings
16 shalt put i' the ark the testimony 413
26:11 put the taches i' the loops, and couple
27: 7 the staves shall be put i' the rings, and
29: 3 thou shalt put them i' one basket, 5921
30 i' the tabernacle of...congregation 413
30:20 i' the tabernacle of the congregation,"
32:24 then I cast it i' the fire, and there
33: 5 I will come up i' the midst of thee
8 until he was gone i' the tabernacle.
9 as Moses entered i' the tabernacle,
11 And he turned again i' the camp: 413
37: 5 And he put the staves i' the rings by
38: 7 And he put the staves i' the rings on
39: 3 did beat the gold i' thin plates,
3 and cut it i' wires, to work it in the
40:20 and put the testimony i' the ark, 413
21 brought the ark i' the tabernacle, "
32 went i' the tent of the congregation, "
35 was not able to enter i' the tent "
Le 1: 6 burnt offering, and cut it i' his pieces.
12 And he shall cut it i' his pieces, with
6:30 blood is brought i' the tabernacle 413
8:20 he cut the ram i' pieces; and Moses
9:23 and Aaron went i' the tabernacle 413
10: 9 with ye, when ye go i' the tabernacle "
11:32 it must be put i' water, and it shall
12: 4 thing, nor come i' the sanctuary, 413
13:17 if the plague be turned i' white;
14: 7 living bird loose i' the open field. 5921
8 that he shall come i' the camp, 413
15 pour it i' the palm of his own left 5921
26 oil i' the palm of his own left hand: "
34 ye be come i' the land of Canaan, 413
36 the priest go i' it to see the plague,*
40 shall cast them i' an unclean place 413
41 without the city i' an unclean place: "
45 out of the city i' an unclean place. "
46 he that goeth i' the house all the "
53 bird out of the city i' the open fields,"
16: 2 not at all times i' the holy place "
3 shall Aaron come i' the holy place: "
10 go for a scapegoat i' the wilderness.
21 hand of a fit man i' the wilderness:
23 Aaron shall come i' the tabernacle 413
23 on when he went i' the holy place, "
26 and afterward come i' the camp. "
28 afterward he shall come i' the camp."
19:23 when ye shall come i' the land, and "
23:10 ye be come i' the land which I give "
25: 2 ye come i' the land which I give you,"
26:25 be delivered i' the hand of the enemy.
32 will bring the land i' desolation:
36 send a faintness i' their hearts in the
41 them i' the land of their enemies;
Nu 4:30, 35, 39, 43 that entereth i' the service,*
5:17 shall take, and put it i' the water: 413
27 causeth the curse shall enter i' her,
7:89 Moses was gone i' the tabernacle 413
11:30 Moses gat him i' the camp, he and "
13:17 and go up i' the mountain:
14: 3 it not better for us to return i' Egypt?
4 captain, and let us return i' Egypt.
8 he will bring us i' this land, and 413
16 able to bring this people i' the land "
24 him will I bring i' the land whereinto"
25 get you i' the wilderness by the way
30 ye shall not come i' the land, 413
40 them up i' the top of the mountain,*"
15: 2 come i' the land of your habitations, "
18 ye come i' the land whither I bring "
16:14 i' a land that floweth with milk and
30 they go down quick i' the pit; then ye
33 went down alive i' the pit, and the
47 ran i' the midst of the congregation;413
17: 8 went i' the tabernacle of witness; "
Nu 19: 6 i' the midst of the burning of the 413
7 he shall come i' the camp, and the "
14 all that come i' the tent, and all that "
20: 1 congregation, i' the desert of Zin in the
4 of the Lord i' this wilderness, 413
12 i' the land which I have given them. "
15 How our fathers went down i' Egypt,
24 he shall not enter i' the land which 413
27 they went up i' mount Hor in the "
21: 2 indeed deliver this people i' my hand,
22 turn i' the fields, or i' the vineyards;
23 out against Israel i' the wilderness:
27 Come i' Heshbon, let the city of Sihon*
29 i' captivity unto Sihon king of the
34 I have delivered him i' thy hand, and
22:13 Get you i' your land: for the Lord 413
23 out of the way, and went i' the field:
23 smote the ass, to turn her i' the way.
41 brought him up i' the high places of
23:14 he brought him i' the field of Zophim,
24: 4, 16 falling i' a trance, but having his *
25: 8 after the man of Israel i' the tent, 413
27:12 Get thee up i' this mount Abarim,
31:24 afterward ye shall come i' the camp.
27 And divide the prey i' two parts; 413
54 brought it i' the tabernacle of the "
32: 7 from going over i' the land which "
9 they should not go i' the land which "
32 before the Lord i' the land of Canaan,
33: 8 midst of the sea i' the wilderness,
38 the priest went up i' mount Hor 413
51 over Jordan i' the land of Canaan; "
34: 2 ye come i' the land of Canaan; "
35:10 over Jordan i' the land of Canaan;
28 slayer shall return i' the land of his413
36:12 married i' the families of the sons of
De 1:22 and i' what cities we shall come. *
24 turned and went up i' the mountain,
27 deliver us i' the hand of the Amorites,
31 went, until ye came i' this place. 5704
40 take your journey i' the wilderness
41 war, ye were ready to go up i' the hill.
43 went presumptuously up i' the hill.
2: 1 took our journey i' the wilderness by
24 behold, I have given i' thine hand Sihon
29 i' the land which the Lord our God 413
30 that he might deliver him i' thy hand,
3: 2 his people, and his land, i' thy hand;
3 God delivered i' our hands Og also,
27 Get thee up i' the top of Pisgah, and
5: 5 and went not up i' the mount: saying,
30 to them, Get you i' your tents again.*
6:10 i' the land which he sware unto thy413
7: 1 thy God shall bring thee i' the land "
24 shall deliver their kings i' thine hand,
26 an abomination i' thine house, 413
8: 7 God bringeth thee i' a good land, "
9: 9 i' the mount to receive the tables of
21 I cast the dust thereof i' the brook 413
28 not able to bring them i' the land "
10: 1 and come up unto me i' the mount,
3 and went up i' the mount, having the
22 Thy fathers went down i' Egypt with
11: 5 until ye came i' this place; *5704
13:16 spoil of it i' the midst of the street 413
14: 6 and cleaveth the cleft i' two claws,*
25 turn it i' money, and bind up the
17: 8 get thee up i' the place which the *413
18: 9 thou art come i' the land which "
19: 3 i' three parts, that every slayer may
5 i' the wood with his neighbour to
11 die, and fleeth i' one of these cities:413
12 deliver him i' the hand of the avenger
20:13 thy God hath delivered it i' thine hands,
21:10 God hath delivered them i' thine hands,
23: 1 off, shall not enter i' the congregation
2 shall not enter i' the congregation of
2 shall he not enter i' the congregation
3 shall not enter i' the congregation of
3 they not enter i' the congregation of
5 turned the curse i' a blessing unto
8 shall enter i' the congregation of the
11 he shall come i' the camp again. *8432
18 i' the house of the Lord thy God for
24 When thou comest i' thy neighbour's
25 When thou comest i' the standing corn
24:10 not go i' his house to fetch his 413
26: 5 he went down i' Egypt, and sojourned
9 and he hath brought us i' this land,413
28:25 shalt be removed i' all the kingdoms?*
38 shalt carry much seed out i' the field,
41 them; for they shall go i' captivity.
68 Lord shall bring thee i' Egypt again
29:12 enter i' covenant with the Lord thy
12 i' his oath, which the Lord thy God
28 and cast them i' another land, 413
30: 5 thy God will bring thee i' the land "
31:20 shall have brought them i' the land "
21 them i' the land which I sware. "
23 the children of Israel i' the land "
32:26 I said, I would scatter them i' corners,*
49 Get thee up i' this mountain 413
Jos 2: 1 and came i' an harlot's house, named
3 thee, which are entered i' thine house:
18 when we come i' the land, thou shalt
19 of the doors of thy house i' the street,
24 Lord hath delivered i' our hands all
3:11 passeth over before you i' Jordan.
4: 5 your God i' the midst of Jordan, 413
6: 2 I have given i' thine hand Jericho,
11 and they came i' the camp, and
14 city once, and returned i' the camp.
19 shall come i' the treasury of the Lord.
20 so that the people went up i' the city,
22 Go i' the harlot's house, and bring out
24 put i' the treasury of the house of the
Jos 7: 7 deliver us i' the hand of the Amorites,
8: 1 given i' thy hand the king of Ai, and
7 your God will deliver it i' your hand.
13 Joshua went that night i' the midst of
18 Ai; for I will give it i' thine hand.
19 and they entered i' the city, and took
10: 8 for I have delivered them i' thine hand;
19 suffer them not to enter i' their 413
19 God hath delivered them i' your hand.
20 of them entered i' fenced cities. 413
27 and cast them i' the cave wherein "
30 king thereof, i' the hand of Israel;
32 delivered Lachish i' the hand of Israel.
11: 8 delivered them i' the hand of Israel,
13: 5 Hermon unto the entering i' Hamath.
18: 5 shall divide it i' seven parts: Judah
6 describe the land i' seven parts,
9 described it by cities i' seven parts
20: 4 take him i' the city unto them, and
5 not deliver the slayer up i' his hand;
21:44 delivered all their enemies i' their
22:13 of Manasseh, i' the land of Gilead, 413
24: 4 and his children went down i' Egypt.
8 And I brought you i' the land of the
8 and I gave them i' your hand, that ye
11 and I delivered them i' your hand.
J'g 1: 2 I have delivered the land i' his hand.
3 Come up with me i' my lot, that we
3 I likewise will go with thee i' thy lot.
4 and the Perizzites i' their hand:
16 of Judah i' the wilderness of Judah,
24 we pray thee, the entrance i' the city.
25 he shewed them the entrance i' the
26 man went i' the land of the Hittites,
34 the children of Dan i' the mountain:
2:14 he delivered them i' the hands of
14 he sold them i' the hands of their
23 he them i' the hand of Joshua.
3: 8 and he sold them i' the hand of
10 king of Mesopotamia i' his hand; and
21 right thigh, and thrust it i' his belly:
28 your enemies the Moabites i' your
4: 2 sold them i' the hand of Jabin king of
7 and I will deliver him i' thine hand.
9 sell Sisera i' the hand of a woman.
14 hath delivered Sisera i' thine hand:
18 had turned in unto her i' the tent, she
21 and smote the nail i' his temples,
21 fastened it i' the ground: for he was
22 And when he came i' her tent, behold,*
5:15 he was sent on foot i' the valley. *
6: 1 delivered them i' the hand of Midian
5 they entered i' the land to destroy it.
13 delivered us i' the hands of the
7: 2 to give the Midianites i' their hands,
7 deliver the Midianites i' thine hand:
9 for I have delivered it i' thine hand.
13 of barley bread tumbled i' the host
14 for i' his hand hath God delivered
15 returned i' the host of Israel, and 413
15 delivered i' your hand the host of
16 three hundred men i' three companies,
8: 3 delivered i' your hands the princes
7 Zebah and Zalmunna i' mine hand,
9:27 And they went out i' the fields, and
27 and went i' the house of their God,
42 that the people went out i' the field;
43 and divided them i' three companies,
46 entered i' an hold of the house of 413
10: 7 them i' the hands of the Philistines,
7 i' the hands of the children of Ammon.
11:19 thee, through my land i' my place.*5704
21 and all his people i' the hand of Israel,
30 the children of Ammon i' mine hands,
32 the Lord delivered them i' his hands.
12: 3 the Lord delivered them i' my hand:
13: 1 them i' the hand of the Philistines
15: 1 I will go in to my wife i' the chamber.
5 them go i' the standing corn of the
12 thee i' the hand of the Philistines.
13 fast, and deliver thee i' their hand:
18 deliverance i' the hand of thy servant:
18 fall i' the hand of the uncircumcised?
16:23 Samson our enemy i' our hand.
24 hath delivered i' our hands our enemy,
18:10 for God hath given it i' your hands;
18 these went i' Micah's house, and
19: 3 she brought him i' her father's house:
11 turn in i' this city of the Jebusites, 413
12 aside hither i' the city of a stranger, "
15 took them i' his house to lodging.
21 So he brought him i' his house, and
22 the man that came i' thine house, 413
23 that this man is come i' mine house, "
29 when he was come i' his house, he "
29 with her bones, i' twelve pieces,
29 and sent her i' all the coasts of Israel.*
20: 4 i' Gibeah that belongeth to Benjamin,
8 will we any of us turn i' his house.*
28 I will deliver them i' thine hand.
Ru 1: 2 And they came i' the country of Moab,
2:18 she took it up, and went i' the city:
3:14 known that a woman came i' the floor.*
15 it on her: and she went i' the city.
4:11 woman that is come i' thine house 413
1Sa 2:14 And he struck it i' the pan, or kettle, or
36 thee, i' one of the priests' offices, 413
4: 3 the people were come i' the camp, "
5 ark...of the Lord came i' the camp, "
6 of the Lord was come i' the camp. "
7 they said, God is come i' the camp. "
10 and they fled every man i' his tent:*
13 when the man came i' the city, and
5: 2 they brought it i' the house of Dagon,
5 nor any that come i' Dagon's house,
6:14 the cart came i' the field of Joshua, 413

1Sa 6:19 they had looked i' the ark of the Lord,
7: 1 brought it i' the house of Abinadab 413
13 came no more i' the coast of Israel:*
9:13 As soon as ye be come i' the city, ye
14 And they went up i' the city: *8432
14 and when they were come i' the city,*
22 and brought them i' the parlour, and
25 down from the high place i' the city,
10: 6 and shalt be turned i' another man.
11:11 they came i' the midst of the host in
12: 8 When Jacob was come i' Egypt, and
9 he sold them i' the hand of Sisera,
9 and i' the hand of the Philistines,
9 and i' the hand of the king of Moab,
14:10 Lord hath delivered them i' our hand:
12 delivered them i' the hand of Israel.
21 went up with them i' the camp from
26 the people were come i' the wood, *413
37 deliver them i' the hand of Israel?
17:22 and ran i' the army, and came and*
46 the Lord deliver thee i' mine hand;
47 and he will give you i' our hands.
49 that the stone sunk i' his forehead;
19:10 and he smote the javelin i' the wall:
20: 8 hast brought thy servant i' a covenant
11 Come, and let us go out i' the field.
35 that Jonathan went out i' the field at
42 and Jonathan went i' the city.
21:15 shall this fellow come i' my house? 413
22: 5 and get thee i' the land of Judah.
5 and came i' the forest of Hareth.
23: 4 deliver the Philistines i' thine hand.
7 God hath delivered him i' mine hand;
7 by entering i' a town that hath gates
11 of Keilah deliver me up i' his hand?
12 me and my men i' the hand of Saul?
14 but God delivered him not i' his hand.
16 and went to David i' the wood, and
20 be to deliver him i' the king's hand.
25 he came down i' a rock, and abode in*
24: 4 deliver thine enemy i' thine hand,
10 thee to day i' mine hand in the cave:
18 Lord had delivered me i' thine hand,
26: 3 Saul came after him i' the wilderness.
8 thine enemy i' thine hand this day:
10 or he shall descend i' battle, and
23 Lord delivered thee i' my hand to day,
27: 1 i' the land of the Philistines; 413
28:19 with thee i' the hand of the Philistines:
19 of Israel i' the hand of the Philistines.
29:11 return i' the land of the Philistines. 413
30:15 deliver me i' the hands of my master,
23 that came against us i' our hand.
31: 9 and sent i' the land of the Philistines
2Sa 2: 1 I go up i' any of the cities of Judah?
3: 8 delivered thee i' the hand of David,
34 not bound, nor thy feet put i' fetters:
4: 6 thither i' the midst of the house, 5704
7 For when they came i' the house, he
5: 8 lame shall not come i' the house. 413
19 wilt thou deliver them i' mine hand?
19 deliver the Philistines i' thine hand.
6:10 Lord unto him i' the city of David:5921
10 it aside i' the house of Obed-edom
12 the house of Obed-edom i' the city of
16 of the Lord came i' the city of David,
10: 2 servants came i' the land of the
10 he delivered i' the hand of Abishai
14 before Abishai, and entered i' the city.
11:11 I then go i' mine house, to eat and to413
23 us, and came out unto us i' the field,
12: 8 and thy master's wives i' thy bosom,
20 came i' the house of the Lord, and
13:10 Bring the meat i' the chamber, that I
10 brought them i' the chamber to Amnon
15:25 Carry back the ark of God i' the city:
27 return i' the city in peace, and your
31 the counsel of Ahithophel i' foolishness.
37 Hushai David's friend came i' the city,
37 and Absalom came i' Jerusalem.
16: 8 the kingdom i' the hand of Absalom
17:13 if he be gotten i' a city, then shall 413
13 and we will draw it i' the river, 5704
17 might not be seen to come i' the city:
18: 6 went out i' the field against Israel:
17 cast him i' a great pit in the wood, 413
19: 2 that day was turned i' mourning
3 them by stealth that day i' the city,
5 Joab came i' the house to the king,
20:12 Amasa out of the highway i' the field,
21: 9 them i' the hands of the Gibeonites,
22: 7 temple, and my cry did enter i' his ears.
20 brought me forth also i' a large place:
23:11 were gathered together i' a troop,
24:14 let us fall now i' the hand of the Lord;
14 and let me not fall i' the hand of man.
1Ki 1:15 went in unto the king i' the chamber:
28 she came i' the king's presence, and,
3: 1 brought her i' the city of David, 413
6: 8 with winding stairs i' the middle 5921
8 and out of the middle i' the third. "
8: 6 i' the oracle of the house, to the "
11:17 servants with him, to go i' Egypt;
40 and fled i' Egypt, unto Shishak king of
13:18 him back with thee i' thine house, 413
14:12 and when thy feet enter i' the city, the
28 the king went i' the house of the Lord,
28 them back i' the guard chamber. 413
15:15 dedicated, i' the house of the Lord,
18 them i' the hand of his servants:
16:18 i' the palace of the king's house, 413
21 the people of Israel divided i' two parts:
17:19 and carried him up i' a loft, where 413
21 this child's soul come i' him again.5921
22 soul of the child came i' him again, "
23 down out of the chamber i' the house,

1Ki 18: 5 Go i' the land, unto all fountains of *
9 deliver thy servant i' the hand of Ahab,
19: 4 went a day's journey i' the wilderness,
20: 2 to Ahab king of Israel i' the city, and
13 I will deliver it i' thine hand this day;
28 all this great multitude i' thine hand,
30 the rest fled to Aphek, i' the city; 413
30 Ben-hadad fled and came i' the city, "
30 fled, and came...i' an inner chamber. "
33 him to come up i' the chariot. 5921
39 went out i' the midst of the battle;
21: 4 Ahab came i' his house heavy and 413
22: 6 shall deliver it i' the hand of the king.
12 Lord shall deliver it i' the king's hand.
15 shall deliver it i' the hand of the king.
25 shalt go i' an inner chamber to hide
30 thyself, and enter i' the battle;
30 himself, and went i' the battle.
35 wound i' the midst of the chariot. 413
2Ki 2: 1 up Elijah i' heaven by a whirlwind,
11 went up by a whirlwind i' heaven.
16 upon some mountain, or i' some valley.
3:10 to deliver them i' the hand of Moab!
13 to deliver them i' the hand of Moab.
18 deliver the Moabites also i' your hand.
4: 4 shalt pour out i' all those vessels, 5921
11 and he turned i' the chamber, and 413
32 when Elisha was come i' the house,
39 went out i' the field to gather herbs,413
39 shred them i' the pot of pottage: "
41 bring meal. And he cast it i' the pot:"
5:18 master goeth i' the house of Rimmon
6: 5 the axe head fell i' the water: and 413
20 when they were come i' Samaria, that
23 came no more i' the land of Israel.
7: 4 If we say, We will enter i' the city,
8 they went i' one tent, and did eat 413
8 and entered i' another tent, and "
12 catch them alive, and get i' the city."
8:21 and the people fled i' their tents. *
9: 6 And he arose, and went i' the house;
26 and cast him i' the plat of ground,
10:15 took him up to him i' the chariot. 413
21 And they came i' the house of Baal;
23 son of Rechab, i' the house of Baal,
24 I have brought i' your hands 5921
11: 4 them to him i' the house of the Lord,
13 the people i' the temple of the Lord.
16 the horses came i' the king's house: *
18 of the land went i' the house of Baal,*
12: 4 is brought i' the house of the Lord,
4 that cometh i' any man's heart 5921
4 to bring i' the house of the Lord,
9 one cometh i' the house of the Lord:
9 brought i' the house of the Lord.
11 i' the hands of them that did the 5921
13 brought i' the house of the Lord:
15 i' whose hand they delivered the 5921
16 brought i' the house of the Lord:
13: 3 delivered them i' the hand of Hazael
3 and i' the hand of Ben-hadad the son
21 the man i' the sepulchre of Elisha:
17: 6 and carried Israel away i' Assyria,*
20 them i' the hand of spoilers,
18:21 if a man lean, it will go i' his hand,
30 be delivered i' the hand of the king
19: 1 and went i' the house of the Lord.
10 be delivered i' the hand of the king
14 went up i' the house of the Lord, *
18 And have cast their gods i' the fire:
23 enter i' the lodgings of his borders,
23 and i' the forest of his Carmel. *
25 waste fenced cities i' ruinous heaps.
28 the tumult is come up i' mine ears,
32 He shall not come i' this city, nor *413
33 and shall not come i' this city, * "
37 they escaped i' the land of Armenia.
20: 4 was gone out i' the middle court,
8 I shall go up i' the house of the Lord*
20 conduit, and brought water i' the city,
21:14 them i' the hand of their enemies;
22: 4 brought i' the house of the Lord,
5 deliver it i' the hand of the doers 5921
7 that was delivered i' their hand, "
9 delivered it i' the hand of them that"
20 be gathered i' thy grave in peace; *413
23: 2 went up i' the house of the Lord, *
12 dust of them i' the brook Kidron. 413
24:15 carried he i' captivity from Jerusalem
1Ch 5:20 Hagarites were delivered i' their hand,
6:15 And Jehozadak went i' captivity,
10: 9 and sent i' the land of the Philistines
11:15 to David, i' the cave of Adullam; 413
12: 8 David i' the hold to the wilderness*
13:13 it aside i' the house of Obed-edom 413
14:10 wilt thou deliver them i' mine hand?
10 for I will deliver them i' thine hand.
17 fame of David went out i' all lands;
16: 7 i' the hand of Asaph and his brethren.*
19: 2 i' the land of the children of Ammon 413
15 his brother, and entered i' the city.
21:13 let me fall now i' the hand of the Lord;
13 but let me not fall i' the hand of man.
27 up his sword again i' the sheath 413
22:18 inhabitants of the land i' mine hand;
19 i' the house that is to be built to the
23: 6 David divided them i' courses among
24:19 service to come i' the house of the Lord,
2Ch 5: 7 the house, i' the most holy place, *413
6:41 arise, O Lord God, i' thy resting place,
7: 2 not enter i' the house of the Lord, 413
10 he sent the people away i' their tents,*
11 all that came i' Solomon's heart 5921
9: 4 he went up i' the house of the Lord;*
12:11 king entered i' the house of the Lord,
11 them again i' the guard chamber. 413

2Ch 13:16 and God delivered them i' their hand.
15:12 And they entered i' a covenant to seek
18 And he brought i' the house of God
16: 8 Lord, he delivered them i' thine hand.
18: 5 for God will deliver it i' the king's hand.
11 shall deliver it i' the hand of the king.
14 they shall be delivered i' your hand.
24 shalt go i' an inner chamber to hide
20:20 went forth i' the wilderness of Tekoa:
21:17 And they came up i' Judah, *
17 and brake i' it, and carried away
23: 1 the son of Zichri, i' covenant with him.
6 none come i' the house of the Lord,
7 whosoever else cometh i' the house,
12 to the people i' the house of the Lord:
20 the high gate i' the king's house, *
24:10 and cast i' the chest, until they had
24 a very great host i' their hand, because
25:20 them i' the hand of their enemies,
26:16 and went i' the temple of the Lord 413
27: 2 not i' the temple of the Lord. And "
28: 5 him i' the hand of the king of Syria;
5 i' the hand of the king of Israel.
9 he hath delivered them i' your hand,
27 they brought him not i' the sepulchres
29: 4 them together i' the east street,
16 i' the inner part of the house of the *
16 i' the court of the house of the Lord.
16 it out abroad i' the brook Kidron. *
31 offerings i' the house of the Lord.
30: 8 enter i' his sanctuary, which he hath
9 that they shall come again i' this land:
14 and cast them i' the brook Kidron.
15 offerings i' the house of the Lord.
31: 1 to his possession, i' their own cities.
10 the offerings i' the house of the Lord,
16 that entereth i' the house of the Lord,
32: 1 and entered i' Judah, and encamped
21 he was come i' the house of his god,
33:13 again to Jerusalem i' his kingdom.
34: 7 beaten the graven images i' powder,
9 was brought i' the house of God,
14 brought i' the house of the Lord,
17 it i' the hand of the overseers, 5921
30 king went up i' the house of the Lord.*
36:17 for age: he gave them all i' his hand.
Ezr 5: 8 we went i' the province of Judea, to
12 them i' the hand of Nebuchadnezzar
12 carried the people away i' Babylon.
14 brought them i' the temple of Babylon,
15 carry them i' the temple that is in*
9: 7 delivered i' the hand of the kings of
10: 6 went i' the chamber of Johanan 413
Ne 2: 7 convey me over till I come i' Judah;*"
8 for the house that I shall enter i'. 5921
5: 5 we bring i' bondage our sons and
6:11 go i' the temple to save his life? 413
7: 5 my God put i' mine heart to gather "
8: 1 as one man i' the street that was "
9:11 persecutors thou threwest i' the deeps,
11 as a stone i' the mighty waters.
22 and didst divide them i' corners: so*
23 and broughtest them i' the land, 413
24 and gavest them i' their hands, with
27 them i' the hands of their enemies,
30 i' the hand of the people of the lands.
10:29 their nobles, and entered i' a curse,
29 and i' an oath, to walk in God's law,
34 to bring it i' the house of our God,
38 the chambers, i' the treasure-house.
12:44 to gather i' them out of the fields of
13: 1 not come i' the congregation of God
2 our God turned the curse i' a blessing.
15 i' Jerusalem on the sabbath day:
Es 1:22 letters i' all the king's provinces, 413
22 i' every province according to the
2:14 she returned i' the second house 413
16 Ahasuerus i' his house royal in the "
3: 9 to bring it i' the king's treasuries. "
13 by posts i' all the king's provinces, "
4: 1 out i' the midst of the city, and
2 none might enter i' the king's gate*413
11 unto the king i' the inner court, "
6: 4 Haman was come i' the outward court
7: 7 wrath went i' the palace garden: 413
8 the palace garden i' the place of the "
9:22 and from mourning i' a good day:
Job 3: 6 come i' the number of the months.
9:24 is given i' the hand of the wicked:
10: 9 wilt thou bring me i' dust again? 413
12: 6 i' whose hand God bringeth
14: 3 bringest me i' judgment with thee?
16:11 me over i' the hands of the wicked.413
17:12 They change the night i' day: the
18: 8 For he is cast i' a net by his own feet,
18 shall be driven from light i' darkness,
22: 4 will he enter with thee i' judgment?
30: 3 fleeing i' the wilderness in former *
19 He hath cast me i' the mire, and I am
31 and my organ i' the voice of them that
33:28 deliver his soul from going i' the pit,
36:16 thee out of the strait i' a broad place,
37: 8 Then the beasts go i' dens, and 1119
38:16 Hast thou entered i' the springs of5704
22 Hast thou entered i' the treasures*413
38 When the dust groweth i' hardness,
39:12 thy seed, and gather it i' thy barn?
40:23 can draw up Jordan i' his mouth. *413
41: 2 Canst thou put a hook i' his nose?
22 sorrow is turned i' joy before him. *
28 are turned with him i' stubble.
Ps 4: 2 long will ye turn my glory i' shame?
5: 7 I will come i' thy house in the
7:15 and is fallen i' the ditch which he
9:17 The wicked shall be turned i' hell, *
10: 9 poor, when he draweth him i' his net.*

Ps 16: 4 take up their names i' my lips. *5921
18: 6 cry came before him, even i' his ears.
19 brought me forth also i' a large place;
22:15 hast brought me i' the dust of death.
24: 3 shall ascend i' the hill of the Lord?
28: 1 like them that go down i' the pit.
30:11 for me my mourning i' dancing:
31: 5 I' thine hand I commit my spirit:
8 not shut me up i' the hand of the
32: 4 is turned i' the drought of summer.*
35: 8 i' that very destruction let him fall.*
13 my prayer returned i' mine own 5921
37:15 sword shall enter i' their own heart,
20 i' smoke shall they consume away.*
45: 2 grace is poured i' thy lips: therefore
15 they shall enter i' the King's palace.
46: 2 be carried i' the midst of the sea;*
55:15 and let them go down quick i' hell:
23 them down i' the pit of destruction:
56: 8 put thou my tears i' thy bottle: are
57: 6 i' the midst whereof they are fallen
60: 9 Who will bring me i' the strong city?
9 who will lead me i' Edom? *5704
63: 9 shall go i' the lower parts of the earth.
66: 6 He turned the sea i' dry land: they
11 Thou broughtest us i' the net; thou
12 broughtest us out i' a wealthy place.
13 go i' thy house with burnt offerings:
69: 2 I am come i' deep waters, where the
27 them not come i' thy righteousness.
73:17 I went i' the sanctuary of God; 413
18 castedst them down i' destruction.*
19 How are they brought i' desolation, *
74: 7 They have cast fire i' thy sanctuary,*
76: 6 and horse are cast i' a dead sleep.
78:44 And had turned their rivers i' blood;
61 And delivered his strength i' captivity,
61 his glory i' the enemy's hand.
79: 1 heathen are come i' thine inheritance:
12 neighbours sevenfold i' their bosom413
88: 4 with them that go down i' the pit:
18 and mine acquaintance i' darkness.
95:11 they should not enter i' my rest. 413
96: 8 an offering, and come i' his courts.
100: 4 Enter i' his gates with thanksgiving,
4 and i' his courts with praise: be
104:10 He sendeth the springs i' the valleys,
105:23 Israel also came i' Egypt; and Jacob
29 He turned their waters i' blood, and
106:15 but sent leanness i' their soul.
20 changed their glory i' the similitude*
41 And he gave them i' the hand of the
42 they were brought i' subjection
107:33 He turneth rivers i' a wilderness, and
33 the watersprings i' dry ground;
34 A fruitful land i' barrenness, for the
35 the wilderness i' a standing water,
35 and dry ground i' watersprings.
108:10 Who will bring me i' the strong city?
10 who will lead me i' Edom? *5704
109:18 let it come i' his bowels like water,
18 and like oil i' his bones.
114: 8 turned the rock i' a standing water,
8 the flint i' a fountain of waters.
115:17 neither any that go down i' silence.
118:19 I will go i' them, and I will praise the
20 i' which the righteous shall enter.
122: 1 Let us go i' the house of the Lord. *
132: 3 I will not come i' the tabernacle of
3 of my house, nor go up i' my bed; 5921
7 We will go i' his tabernacles: we will
8 Arise, O Lord, i' thy rest; thou, and
135: 9 and wonders i' the midst of thee,
136:13 which divided the Red sea i' parts:*
139: 8 If I ascend up i' heaven, thou art
140:10 them: let them be cast i' the fire;
10 i' deep pits, that they rise not up
141:10 Let the wicked fall i' their own nets,
143: 2 not i' judgment with thy servant:
7 unto them that go down i' the pit.
10 lead me i' the land of uprightness.*
Pr 1:12 as those that go down i' the pit:
2:10 wisdom entereth i' thine heart,
4:14 Enter not i' the path of the wicked,
6: 3 art come i' the hand of thy friend;
13:17 wicked messenger falleth i' mischief:
16:29 him i' the way that is not good. *
33 The lot is cast i' the lap; but the
17:10 reproof entereth more i' a wise man
10 than an hundred stripes i' a fool.
20 a perverse tongue falleth i' mischief.
18: 6 A fool's lips enter i' contention, and
8 i' the innermost parts of the belly.
10 righteous runneth i' it, and is safe.
19:15 Slothfulness casteth i' a deep sleep;
23:10 enter not i' the fields of the fatherless:
24:16 but the wicked shall fall i' mischief.*
26: 9 goeth up i' the hand of a drunkard,
22 i' the innermost parts of the belly.
27:10 neither go i' thy brother's house in*
28:10 he shall fall himself i' his own pit:
14 his heart shall fall i' mischief.
29: 8 men bring a city i' a snare: *
30: 4 Who hath ascended up i' heaven,
Ec 1: 7 All the rivers run i' the sea; yet 413
10: 8 He that diggeth a pit shall fall i' it;
11: 9 God will bring thee i' judgment.
12:14 shall bring every work i' judgment,
Ca 1: 4 hath brought me i' his chambers:
3: 4 brought him i' my mother's house, 413
4 i' the chamber of her that conceived "
4:16 Let my beloved come i' his garden,
5: 1 I am come i' my garden, my sister, my
6: 2 beloved is gone down i' his garden,*
11 I went down i' the garden of nuts 413
7:11 beloved, let us go forth i' the field;
Ca 8: 2 bring thee i' my mother's house, 413
Isa 2: 4 beat their swords i' plowshares,
4 and their spears i' pruninghooks:
10 Enter i' the rock, and hide thee in the
19 they shall go i' the holes of the rocks,
19 and i' the caves of the earth, for fear
21 To go i' the clefts of the rocks,
21 and i' the tops of the ragged rocks,
3:14 The Lord will enter i' judgment with
5:13 my people are gone i' captivity,
14 he that rejoiceth, shall descend i' it.
9: 8 The Lord sent a word i' Jacob, and it
10 but we will change them i' cedars.‡
13: 2 they may go i' the gates of the nobles.
14 and flee every one i' his own land.* 413
14: 7 quiet: they break forth i' singing.
13 I will ascend i' heaven, I will exalt my
19: 1 swift cloud, and shall come i' Egypt:*
4 I give over i' the hand of a cruel lord;
8 they that cast angle i' the brooks
23 the Assyrian shall come i' Egypt,
23 and the Egyptian i' to Assyria, and the
21: 4 of my pleasure hath he turned i' fear
22:18 thee like a ball i' a large country: 413
21 commit thy government i' his hand:
23: 9 i' contempt all the honourable
24:18 noise of the fear shall fall i' the pit; 413
26:20 my people, enter thou i' thy chambers,
29:17 shall be turned i' a fruitful field,
30: 2 That walk to go down i' Egypt, and
6 i' the land of trouble and anguish,*
20 be removed i' a corner any more,*
29 to come i' the mountain of the Lord,
34: 9 thereof shall be turned i' pitch,
9 and the dust thereof i' brimstone,
36: 6 it will go i' his hand, and pierce it:
15 be delivered i' the hand of the king
37: 1 and went i' the house of the Lord.
10 not be given i' the hand of the king
19 And have cast their gods i' the fire:
24 I will enter i' the height of his border,
26 waste defenced cities i' ruinous heaps.
29 thy tumult, is come up i' mine ears,
33 He shall not come i' this city, *413
34 shall not come i' this city, saith the* "
38 they escaped i' the land of Armenia:
38:18 go down i' the pit cannot hope for thy
40: 9 get thee up i' the high mountain; 5921
44:23 break forth i' singing, ye mountains,
46: 2 but themselves are gone i' captivity.
47: 5 thou silent, and get thee i' darkness,
6 and given them i' thine hand:
49:13 break forth i' singing, O mountains:
51:23 put it i' the hand of them that afflict
52: 1 there shall no more come i' thee the
4 people went down aforetime i' Egypt
9 Break forth i' joy, sing together,
54: 1 break forth i' singing, and cry aloud,
55:12 shall break forth before you i' singing,
57: 2 He shall enter i' peace: they shall
59: 5 is crushed breaketh out i' a viper.
63:14 As a beast goeth down i' the valley,
65: 6 even recompense i' their bosom, 5921
7 their former work i' their bosom. "
17 be remembered, nor come i' mind. "
66:20 offering in a clean vessel i' the house
Jer 2: 7 brought you i' a plentiful country, 413
21 art thou turned i' the degenerate plant
4: 5 and let us go i' the defenced cities. 413
29 they shall go i' thickets, and climb
6: 9 as a grapegatherer i' the baskets. 5921
25 Go not forth i' the field, nor walk by
7:31 not, neither came it i' my heart. 5921
8: 6 as the horse rusheth i' the battle.*
14 let us enter i' the defenced cities, 413
9:21 For death is come up i' our windows,
21 and is entered i' our palaces, to cut off
10: 9 Silver spread i' plates is brought
12: 7 of my soul i' the hand of her enemies.
13:16 he turn it i' the shadow of death,
14:18 If I go forth i' the field, then behold
18 and if I enter i' the city, then behold
18 about i' a land that they know not.* 413
15: 4 removed i' all kingdoms of the earth,*
14 i' a land which thou knowest not:
16: 5 Enter not i' the house of mourning,
8 not also go i' the house of feasting,
13 land i' a land that ye know not, 5921
15 i' their land that I gave unto their "
17:25 there enter i' the gates of this city*
19: 5 neither came it i' my mind: 5921
20: 4 all Judah i' the hand of the king
4 shall carry them captive i' Babylon,*
5 I give i' the hand of their enemies,
6 in thine house, shall go i' captivity:
21: 4 them i' the midst of this city. 413
7 i' the hand of Nebuchadrezzar king
7 and i' the hand of their enemies,
7 and i' the hand of those that seek
10 i' the hand of the king of Babylon,
13 or who shall enter i' our habitations?
22: 7 cedars, and cast them i' the fire. 5921
22 and thy lovers shall go i' captivity:
25 i' the hand of them that seek thy life,
25 and i' the hand of them whose face
25 even i' the hand of Nebuchadrezzar
25 and i' the hand of the Chaldeans.
26 i' another country, where ye were 5921
28 cast i' a land which they know not? "
23:15 profaneness gone forth i' all the land.
24: 5 this place i' the land of the Chaldeans,
9 to be removed i' all the kingdoms of
26:21 was afraid, and fled, and went i' Egypt;
22 the king sent men i' Egypt, namely,
22 and certain men with him i' Egypt. 413
23 i' the graves of the common people. "
Jer 26:24 not give him i' the hand of the people
27: 6 lands i' the hand of Nebuchadnezzar 413
28: 3 again i' this place all the vessels of
4 of Judah, that went i' Babylon, saith*
6 captive, from Babylon i' this place.* 413
29:14 bring you again i' the place whence* "
16 are not gone forth with you i' captivity;
21 them i' the hand of Nebuchadrezzar
30: 6 and all faces are turned i' paleness?
16 every one of them, shall go i' captivity;
31:13 for I will turn their mourning i' joy,
32: 3 give this city i' the hand of the king of
4 be delivered i' the hand of the king of
18 of the fathers i' the bosom of their 413
24 is given i' the hand of the Chaldeans,
25 is given i' the hand of the Chaldeans.
28 this city i' the hand of the Chaldeans,
28 and i' the hand of Nebuchadrezzar
35 neither came it i' my mind, that 5921
36 be delivered i' the hand of the king of
43 it is given i' the hand of the Chaldeans.
33:11 of praise i' the house of the Lord.
34: 2 give this city i' the hand of the king
3 be taken, and delivered i' his hand;
10 which had entered i' the covenant,
11 and brought them i' subjection for
16 and brought them i' subjection, to be
17 to be removed i' all the kingdoms of*
20 give them i' the hand of their enemies,
20 and i' the hand of them that seek their
21 I give i' the hand of their enemies,
21 and i' the hand of them that seek their
21 and i' the hand of the king of Babylon's
35: 2 bring them i' the house of the Lord,
2 i' one of the chambers, and give 413
4 brought them i' the house of the Lord,
4 i' the chamber of the sons of Hanan,413
11 king of Babylon came up i' the land,"
36: 5 I cannot go i' the house of the Lord:
12 Then he went down i' the king's house,
12 i' the scribe's chamber: and, lo, 5921
20 they went in to the king i' the court,
23 i' the fire that was on the hearth, 413
37: 4 for they had not put him i' prison.
7 return to Egypt i' their own land.
12 to go i' the land of Benjamin,
16 was entered i' the dungeon, and 413
16 and i' the cabins, and Jeremiah "
17 be delivered i' the hand of the king
21 Jeremiah i' the court of the prison.
38: 3 be given i' the hand of the king surely
6 him i' the dungeon of Malchiah 413
9 whom they have cast i' the dungeon;"
11 and went i' the house of the king
11 down by cords i' the dungeon 413
14 prophet unto him i' the third entry "
16 I give thee i' the hand of these men
18 be given i' the hand of the Chaldeans,
19 lest they deliver me i' their hand, and
39: 9 carried away captive i' Babylon the
17 given i' the hand of the men of whom
40: 4 good...to come with me i' Babylon,
4 ill...to come with me i' Babylon,
41: 7 they came i' the midst of the city, 413
7 and cast them i' the midst of the pit,"
17 Beth-lehem, to go to enter i' Egypt,
42:14 we will go i' the land of Egypt, where
15 set your faces to enter i' Egypt,
17 to go i' Egypt to sojourn there; 935
18 when ye shall enter i' Egypt: "
19 Go ye not i' Egypt: know certainly
43: 2 to say, Go not i' Egypt to sojourn there:
3 carry us away captives i' Babylon.*
7 So they came i' the land of Egypt: for
44:12 faces to go i' the land of Egypt
14 gone i' the land of Egypt to sojourn
14 should return i' the land of Judah,
21 them, and came it not i' his mind? 5921
28 the land of Egypt i' the land of Judah,
28 gone i' the land of Egypt to sojourn
30 of Egypt i' the hand of his enemies,
30 i' the hand of them that seek his life;
30 Judah i' the hand of Nebuchadrezzar
46:11 Go up i' Gilead, and take balm, O
19 furnish thyself to go i' captivity: for
24 i' the hand of the people of the north.
26 them i' the hand of those that seek
26 and i' the hand of Nebuchadrezzar
26 and i' the hand of his servants: and
47: 6 put up thyself i' thy scabbard, 413
48: 7 Chemosh shall go forth i' captivity
11 neither hath he gone i' captivity:
44 from the fear shall fall i' the pit; 413
49: 3 for their king shall go i' captivity, and
32 I will scatter i' all winds them that*
51: 9 us go every one i' his own country:
50 let Jerusalem come i' your mind. 5921
51 come i' the sanctuaries of the Lord's"
59 Zedekiah the king of Judah i' Babylon*
63 cast it i' the midst of Euphrates: 413
52:12 the king of Babylon, i' Jerusalem,
La 1: 3 Judah is gone i' captivity because 1473
5 her children are gone i' captivity
7 people fell i' the hand of the enemy,
10 the heathen entered i' her sanctuary,
10 should not enter i' thy congregation.
13 above hath he sent fire i' my bones,
14 Lord hath delivered me i' their hands,
18 my young men are gone i' captivity.
2: 7 given up i' the hand of the enemy the
9 Her gates are sunk i' the ground; he
12 poured out i' their mothers' bosom. 413
3: 2 and brought me i' darkness, but not*
13 of his quiver to enter i' my reins.
4:12 entered i' the gates of Jerusalem.
22 more carry thee away i' captivity:

La 5:15 our dance is turned i' mourning.
Eze 2: 2 the spirit entered i' me when he spake
3:22 Arise, go forth i' the plain, and I 413
23 I arose, and went forth i' the plain: "
24 the spirit entered i' me, and set me
4:14 there abominable flesh i' my mouth.
5: 4 cast them i' the midst of the fire,
4 come forth i' all the house of Israel."
6 changed my judgments i' wickedness*
10 of thee will I scatter i' all the winds.*
12 scatter a third part i' all the winds.*
7:11 is risen up i' a rod of wickedness:
21 will give it i' the hands of the strangers
22 for the robbers shall enter i' it, and
8:16 he brought me i' the inner court 413
10: 7 and put it i' the hands of him that "
11: 5 the things that come i' your mind,
9 deliver you i' the hands of strangers,
24 vision by the Spirit of God i' Chaldea,
12: 4 as they that go forth i' captivity.
13: 5 Ye have not gone up i' the gaps,
9 shall they enter i' the land of Israel;
14:19 Or if I send a pestilence i' that land,413
15: 4 Behold, it is cast i' the fire for fuel;
16: 8 and entered i' a covenant with thee,
13 and thou didst prosper i' a kingdom.*
39 And I will also give thee i' their hand,
17: 4 and carried it i' a land of traffick; he
15 in sending his ambassadors i' Egypt,
19: 9 they brought him i' holds, that his
20: 6 i' a land that I had espied for them, 413
10 and brought them i' the wilderness."
15 not bring them i' the land which I "
28 when I had brought them i' the land, "
32 that which cometh i' your mind 5921
35 I will bring you i' the wilderness 413
37 bring you i' the bond of the covenant:
38 shall not enter i' the land of Israel: 413
42 shall bring you i' the land of Israel, "
42 i' the country for the which I lifted "
21:11 to give it i' the hand of the slayer.
14 which entereth i' their privy chambers.
30 I cause it to return i' his sheath?
31 thee i' the hand of brutish men,
22:19 you i' the midst of Jerusalem. 413
20 i' the midst of the furnace, to blow "
23: 9 delivered her i' the hand of her lovers,
9 i' the hand of the Assyrians, upon
16 messengers unto them i' Chaldea.
17 came to her i' the bed of love,
28 deliver thee i' the hand of them whom
28 i' the hand of them from whom thy
31 will I give her cup i' thine hand.
39 the same day i' my sanctuary 413
24: 3 set it on, and also pour water i' it:
4 Gather the pieces thereof i' it, even
25: 3 Judah, when they went i' captivity;
26:10 when he shall enter i' thy gates,
10 as men enter i' a city wherein is
20 with them that descend i' the pit,
27:26 have brought thee i' great waters:
27 shall fall i' the midst of the seas in
28: 4 gold and silver i' thy treasures:
23 For I will send i' her pestilence, and
23 and blood i' her streets; and the *
29: 5 leave thee thrown i' the wilderness,
14 them to return i' the land of Pathros,
14 i' the land of their habitation, 5921
30:12 the land i' the hand of the wicked:
17 and these cities shall go i' captivity.
18 her daughters shall go i' captivity.
25 put my sword i' the hand of the king
31:11 him i' the hand of the mighty one
16 hell with them that descend i' the pit:
17 They also went down i' hell with him
32: 9 i' the countries which thou hast 5921
18 with them that go down i' the pit.
24 down uncircumcised i' the nether 413
36: 5 my land i' their possession with the*
24 will bring you i' your own land. 413
37: 5 I will cause breath to enter i' you,
10 and the breath came i' them, and they
12 and bring you i' the land of Israel. 413
17 join them one to another i' one stick;
21 and bring them i' their own land: 413
22 be divided i' two kingdoms any more
38: 4 and put hooks i' thy jaws, and I will
8 thou shalt come i' the land that is 413
10 shall things come i' thy mind, 5921
39:23 went i' captivity for their iniquity:
23 them i' the hand of their enemies:
28 them to be led i' captivity among
40: 2 brought he me i' the land of Israel,413
17 brought he me i' the outward court, "
32 he brought me i' the inner court "
41: 6 they entered i' the wall which was of
42: 1 brought me forth i' the utter court,413
1 and he brought me i' the chamber
9 as one goeth i' them from the utter
12 the east, as one entereth i' them.
14 of the holy place i' the utter court, 413
43: 4 Lord came i' the house by the way "
5 brought me i' the inner court; and, "
44: 7 brought i' my sanctuary strangers*
9 shall enter i' my sanctuary, of any413
12 the house of Israel to fall i' iniquity;*
16 They shall enter i' my sanctuary, 413
19 they go forth i' the utter court, even "
19 even i' the utter court to the people, "
21 when they enter i' the inner court.
27 day that he goeth i' the sanctuary,
46:19 i' the holy chambers of the priests,
20 they bear them not out i' the utter
21 brought me forth i' the utter court,
47: 8 country, and go down i' the desert,5921
8 the desert, and go down i' the sea:*

Eze 47: 8 which being brought forth i' the sea,
Da 1: 2 Jehoiakim king of Judah i' his hand,
2 i' the land of Shinar to the house of
2 brought the vessels i' the treasure
9 brought Daniel i' favour and tender*
2:29 came i' thy mind upon thy bed,
38 heaven hath he given i' thine hand,
3: 6, 11, 15 i' the midst of a burning fiery
20 cast them i' the burning fiery furnace.
21 cast i' the midst of the burning fiery
23 bound i' the midst of the burning fiery
24 men bound i' the midst of the fire?
5:10 his lords came i' the banquet house:
6: 7 he shall be cast i' the den of lions.
10 was signed, he went i' his house; and his
12 king, shall be cast i' the den of lions?
16 and cast him i' the den of lions.
24 they cast them i' the den of lions.
7:25 they shall be given i' his hand until
10: 8 was turned in me i' corruption, and
11: 7 shall enter i' the fortress of the king
8 also carry captives i' Egypt their gods,
9 the south shall come i' his kingdom,
9 and shall return i' his own land. 413
11 multitude shall be given i' his hand.
28 he return i' his land with great riches;
40 and he shall enter i' the countries,
41 He shall enter also i' the glorious land,
Ho 2:14 her, and bring her i' the wilderness,
4: 7 will I change their glory i' shame.
9: 4 not come i' the house of the Lord.
11: 5 not return i' the land of Egypt, 413
9 thee: and I will not enter i' the city.
12: 1 Assyrians, and oil is carried i' Egypt.
12 And Jacob fled i' the country of Syria,
Joe 1:14 land i' the house of the Lord your God,*
2:20 will drive him i' a land barren and 413
31 The sun shall be turned i' darkness,
31 and the moon i' blood, before the
3: 2 bring them down i' the valley of 413
5 and have carried i' your temples my
8 daughters i' the hand of the children
10 Beat your plowshares i' swords,
10 and your pruninghooks i' spears;
Am 1: 4 send a fire i' the house of Hazael,
5 Syria shall go i' captivity unto Kir,
15 their king shall go i' captivity, he and
2: 1 the bones of the king of Edom i' lime:
4: 3 ye shall cast them i' the palace, saith
5: 5 seek not Beth-el, nor enter i' Gilgal,
5 Gilgal shall surely go i' captivity,
8 the shadow of death i' the morning,
19 or went i' the house, and leaned his
27 will I cause you to go i' captivity
6:12 ye have turned judgment i' gall, and
12 the fruit of righteousness i' hemlock:
7:12 flee thee away i' the land of Judah, 413
17 Israel shall surely go i' captivity *
8:10 I will turn your feasts i' mourning,
10 all your songs i' lamentation; and I
9: 2 Though they dig i' hell, thence shall
4 though they go i' captivity before
Ob 11 and foreigners entered i' his gates,
13 shouldest not have entered i' the gate
Jon 1: 3 and went down i' it, to go with them
4 sent out a great wind i' the sea, 413
5 that were in the ship i' the sea, to "
5 gone down i' the sides of the ship; "
12 me up, and cast me forth i' the sea; "
15 Jonah, and cast him forth i' the sea:"
2: 3 For thou hadst cast me i' the deep,
7 in unto thee, i' thine holy temple. 413
3: 4 to enter i' the city a day's journey,
Mic 1: 6 down the stones thereof i' the valley,
16 for they are gone i' captivity from
3: 5 that putteth not i' their mouths, 5921
4: 3 shall beat their swords i' plowshares,
3 and their spears i' pruninghooks:
12 gather them as the sheaves i' the floor.*
5: 5 the Assyrian shall come i' our land:
6 when he cometh i' our land, and when
7:19 all their sins i' the depths of the sea.
Na 3:10 carried away, she went i' captivity:
12 fall i' the mouth of the eater. 5921
14 go i' clay, and tread the morter, make
Hab 3:16 rottenness entered i' my bones, and I
Hag 1: 6 wages to put it i' a bag with holes. 413
Zec 5: 4 shall enter i' the house of the thief, "
4 i' the house of him that sweareth "
8 he cast it i' the midst of the ephah; "
6: 6 go forth i' the north country; * "
10 and go i' the house of Josiah the son
10:10 bring them i' the land of Gilead 413
11: 6 men every one i' his neighbour's hand,
6 and i' the hand of his king: and they
14: 2 of the city shall go forth i' captivity,
Mal 3:10 all the tithes i' the storehouse, 413
M't 1:17 until the carrying away i' Babylon* 3350
17 from the carrying away i' Babylon* "
2:11 when they were come i' the house, 1519
12 departed i' their own country "
13 and his mother, and flee i' Egypt, "
14 by night, and departed i' Egypt: "
20 mother, and go i' the land of Israel:"
21 and came i' the land of Israel. "
22 turned aside i' the parts of Galilee:"
3:10 is hewn down, and cast i' the fire. "
12 gather his wheat i' the garner; "
4: 1 i' the wilderness to be tempted of "
5 devil taketh him up i' the holy city, "
8 up i' an exceeding high mountain,* "
12 that John was cast i' prison, *
12 prison, he departed i' Galilee; 1519
18 casting a net i' the sea: for they "
5: 1 he went up i' a mountain: and "
20 in no case enter i' the kingdom * "

M't 5:25 officer, and thou be cast i' prison. 1519
29, 30 whole body should be cast i' hell. "
6: 6 thou prayest, enter i' thy closet, "
13 lead us not i' temptation, but "
26 do they reap, nor gather i' barns; "
30 and to morrow is cast i' the oven, "
7:19 is hewn down, and cast i' the fire. "
21 enter i' the kingdom of heaven; "
8: 5 Jesus was entered i' Capernaum, "
12 shall be cast out i' outer darkness: "
14 Jesus was come i' Peter's house, "
23 And when he was entered i' a ship, "
28 i' the country of the Gergesenes, "
31 us to go away i' the herd of swine, "
32 out, they went i' the herd of swine: "
32 down a steep place i' the sea, "
33 fled, and went their ways i' the city, "
9: 1 And he entered i' a ship, and passed "
1 over, and came i' his own city. "
17 do men put new wine i' old bottles: "
17 they put new wine i' new bottles, "
23 Jesus came i' the ruler's house, and "
26 hereof went abroad i' all that land. "
28 when he was come i' the house, the "
38 send forth labourers i' his harvest "
10: 5 Go not i' the way of the Gentiles, "
5 i' any city of the Samaritans enter "
11 And i' whatsoever city or town ye "
12 when ye come i' an house, salute it. "
23 you in this city, flee ye i' another: "
11: 7 went ye out i' the wilderness to see? "
12: 4 How he entered i' the house of God, "
9 thence, he went i' their synagogue: "
11 if it fall i' a pit on the sabbath day, "
29 one enter i' a strong man's house, "
44 I will return i' my house from "
13: 2 so that he went i' a ship, and sat; "
8 But other fell i' good ground, and *1909
20 received the seed i' stony places, * "
23 received seed i' the good ground is* "
30 but gather the wheat i' my barn. 1519
36 away, and went i' the house: "
42 shall cast them i' a furnace of fire: "
47 unto a net, that was cast i' the sea, "
48 and gathered the good i' vessels, "
50 cast them i' the furnace of fire: "
54 he was come i' his own country, he "
14:13 thence by ship i' a desert place * "
15 that they may go i' the villages, "
22 his disciples to get i' a ship, and to "
23 up i' a mountain apart to pray: and "
32 when they were come i' the ship, "
34 came i' the land of Gennesaret. * "
35 they sent out i' all that country "
15:11 Not that which goeth i' the mouth "
14 blind, both shall fall i' the ditch. "
17 in at the mouth goeth i' the belly, "
17 and is cast out i' the draught? "
21 i' the coasts of Tyre and Sidon. "
29 and went up i' a mountain, and sat "
39 and came i' the coasts of Magdala. "
16:13 When Jesus came i' the coasts of "
17: 1 them up i' an high mountain apart, "
15 for ofttimes he falleth i' the fire, "
15 and oft i' the water. "
22 be betrayed i' the hands of men: "
25 when he was come i' the house, "
18: 3 shall not enter i' the kingdom of "
8 thee to enter i' life halt or maimed, "
8 two feet to be cast i' everlasting fire. "
9 thee to enter i' life with one eye, "
9 two eyes to be cast i' hell fire. "
12 and goeth i' the mountains, and *1909
30 but went and cast him i' prison, 1519
19: 1 and came i' the coasts of Judæa "
17 if thou wilt enter i' life, keep the "
23 enter i' the kingdom of heaven. "
24 man to enter i' the kingdom of God. "
20: 1 to hire labourers i' his vineyard. "
2 a day, he sent them i' his vineyard. "
4 Go ye also i' the vineyard, and "
7 them, Go ye also i' the vineyard; and "
21: 2 Go i' the village over against you, "
10 when he was come i' Jerusalem, "
12 Jesus went i' the temple of God, "
17 went out of the city i' Bethany; "
18 as he returned i' the city, he * "
21 removed, and be thou cast i' the sea; "
23 when he was come i' the temple, "
31 harlots go i' the kingdom of God "
33 to husbandmen, and went i' a far "
22: 9 Go ye therefore i' the highways, *1909
10 servants went out i' the highways, 1519
13 cast him i' outer darkness; there "
24:16 be in Judæa flee i' the mountains:*1909
38 day that Noe entered i' the ark. 1519
25:14 as a man travelling i' a far country, "
21, 23 enter thou i' the joy of thy lord. 1519
30 ye the unprofitable servant i' outer "
41 me, ye cursed, i' everlasting fire, "
46 go away i' everlasting punishment: "
46 but the righteous i' life eternal. "
26:18 Go i' the city to such a man, and "
30 they went out i' the mount of Olives.* "
32 again, I will go before you i' Galilee. "
41 that ye enter not i' temptation: "
45 is betrayed i' the hands of sinners.† "
52 Put up again thy sword i' his place: "
71 when he was gone out i' the porch, "
27: 6 for to put them i' the treasury, "
27 took Jesus i' the common hall, "
53 and went i' the holy city, and "
28: 7 he goeth before you i' Galilee; "
10 my brethren that they go i' Galilee, "
11 some of the watch came i' the city, "
16 disciples went away i' Galilee. "

M't 28:16 *i'* a mountain where Jesus had *1519
M'r 1:12 spirit driveth him *i'* the wilderness. “
14 Jesus came *i'* Galilee, preaching “
16 brother casting a net *i'* the sea: *1722
21 And they went *i'* Capernaum; and 1519
21 day he entered *i'* the synagogue, “
29 they entered *i'* the house of Simon “
35 and departed *i'* a solitary place, “
38 Let us go *i'* the next towns, that I “
45 no more openly enter *i'* the city, “
2: 1 again he entered *i'* Capernaum after “
11 and go thy way *i'* thine house. * “
22 putteth new wine *i'* old bottles: “
22 wine must be put *i'* new bottles. “
26 he went *i'* the house of God in the “
3: 1 he entered again *i'* the synagogue; “
13 he goeth up *i'* a mountain, and “
19 him: and they went *i'* an house. “
27 can enter *i'* a strong man's house, “
4: 1 that he entered *i'* a ship, and sat “
26 should cast seed *i'* the ground; *1909
37 the waves beat *i'* the ship, so that 1519
5: 1 *i'* the country of the Gadarenes. “
12 him, saying, Send us *i'* the swine, “
12 that we may enter *i'* them. “
13 went out, and entered *i'* the swine: “
13 down a steep place *i'* the sea, “
18 And when he was come *i'* the ship, “
6: 1 and came *i'* his own country; and “
10 place soever ye enter *i'* an house, “
31 yourselves apart *i'* a desert place, “
32 *i'* a desert place by ship privately. “
36 may go *i'* the country round about, “
36 and *i'* the villages, and buy * “
45 his disciples to get *i'* the ship, and “
46 he departed *i'* a mountain to pray. “
51 went up unto them *i'* the ship; and “
53 came *i'* the land of Gennesaret, 1909
56 he entered, *i'* villages, or cities, or 1519
7: 15 that entering *i'* him can defile him: “
17 And when he was entered *i'* the “
18 from without entereth *i'* the man, “
19 not *i'* his heart, but *i'* the belly “
19 and goeth out *i'* the draught, “
24 *i'* the borders of Tyre and Sidon, “
24 and entered *i'* a house, and would “
33 and put his fingers *i'* his ears, and “
8: 10 entered *i'* a ship with his disciples, “
10 came *i'* the parts of Dalmanutha. “
13 and entering *i'* the ship again “
26 Neither go *i'* the town, nor tell it to “
27 *i'* the towns of Cæsarea Philippi: “
9: 2 up *i'* a high mountain apart by “
22 ofttimes it hath cast him *i'* the fire, “
22 and *i'* the waters, to destroy him: “
25 of him, and enter no more *i'* him. “
28 when he was come *i'* the house, his “
31 is delivered *i'* the hands of men, “
42 neck, and he were cast *i'* the sea. “
43 for thee to enter *i'* life maimed, “
43 than having two hands to go *i'* hell, “
43 *i'* the fire that never shall be “
45 better for thee to enter halt *i'* life, “
45 having two feet to be cast *i'* hell, “
45 *i'* the fire that never shall be * “
47 to enter *i'* the kingdom of God “
47 having two eyes to be cast *i'* hell “
10: 1 *i'* the coast of Judæa by the farther “
17 when he was gone forth *i'* the way, “
23 have riches enter *i'* the kingdom of “
24 to enter *i'* the kingdom of God! “
25 man to enter *i'* the kingdom of God. “
11: 2 way *i'* the village over against you: “
2 as soon as ye be entered *i'* it, ye “
11 And Jesus entered *i'* Jerusalem, “
11 and *i'* the temple: and when he “
15 and Jesus went *i'* the temple, and “
23 be thou cast *i'* the sea: and shall “
12: 1 husbandmen, and went *i'* a far country. “
41 people cast money *i'* the treasury: 1519
43 which have cast *i'* the treasury: “
13: 15 housetop not go down *i'* the house,* “
14: 13 Go ye *i'* the city, and there shall “
16 came *i'* the city, and found as he “
26 they went out *i'* the mount of Olives.* “
28 risen, I will go before you *i'* Galilee. “
38 pray, lest ye enter *i'* temptation. “
41 is betrayed *i'* the hands of sinners. “
54 *i'* the palace of the high priest: 2080,
68 he went out *i'* the porch: and the “
15: 16 soldiers led him away *i'* the hall, *2080
16: 5 And entering *i'* the sepulchre, they 1519
7 that he goeth before you *i'* Galilee: “
12 walked, and went *i'* the country. “
15 Go ye *i'* all the world, and preach “
19 he was received up *i'* heaven, and “
Lu 1: 9 he went *i'* the temple of the Lord. “
39 went *i'* the hill country with haste, “
39 with haste, *i'* a city of Juda; “
40 entered *i'* the house of Zacharias, “
79 guide our feet *i'* the way of peace. “
2: 3 be taxed, every one *i'* his own city.* “
4 *i'* Judæa, unto the city of David “
15 gone away from them *i'* heaven, “
27 he came by the Spirit *i'* the temple:* “
39 they returned *i'* Galilee, to their “
3: 3 he came *i'* all the country about “
9 is hewn down, and cast *i'* the fire. “
17 will gather the wheat *i'* his garner; “
4: 1 led by the Spirit *i'* the wilderness,* “
5 taking him up *i'* a high mountain,* “
14 the power of the Spirit *i'* Galilee: “
16 *i'* the synagogue on the sabbath “
37 out *i'* every place of the country “
38 and entered *i'* Simon's house. And “
42 departed and went *i'* a desert place: “

Lu 5: 3 And he entered *i'* one of the ships, 1519
4 Launch out *i'* the deep, and let “
16 withdrew himself *i'* the wilderness,*1722
19 couch *i'* the midst before Jesus. 1519
24 up thy couch, and go *i'* thine house.* “
37 putteth new wine *i'* old bottles; “
38 wine must be put *i'* new bottles; “
6: 4 How he went *i'* the house of God, “
6 he entered *i'* the synagogue and “
12 he went out *i'* a mountain to pray, “
38 over, shall men give *i'* your bosom. “
39 shall they not both fall *i'* the ditch? “
7: 1 people, he entered *i'* Capernaum. “
11 that he went *i'* a city called Nain;* “
24 ye out *i'* the wilderness for to see? “
36 he went *i'* the Pharisee's house, “
44 I entered *i'* thine house, thou “
8: 22 went *i'* a ship with his disciples: “
29 driven of the devil *i'* the wilderness. “
30 many devils were entered *i'* him. “
31 command them to go out *i'* the deep. “
32 would suffer them to enter *i'* them. “
33 the man, and entered *i'* the swine: “
33 down a steep place *i'* the lake, “
37 and he went up *i'* the ship, and “
41 that he would come *i'* his house: “
51 And when he came *i'* the house, he* “
9: 4 whatsoever house ye enter *i'*, there “
10 aside privately *i'* a desert place * “
12 may go *i'* the towns and country “
28 and went up *i'* a mountain to pray. “
34 feared as they entered *i'* the cloud. “
44 sayings sink down *i'* your ears: “
44 be delivered *i'* the hands of men. “
52 *i'* a village of the Samaritans, “
10: 1 two before his face *i'* every city “
2 send forth labourers *i'* his harvest. “
5 And *i'* whatsoever house ye enter, “
8 And *i'* whatsoever city ye enter, “
10 But *i'* whatsoever city ye enter, “
10 ways out *i'* the streets of the same, “
38 that he entered *i'* a certain village: “
38 Martha received him *i'* her house. “
11: 4 And lead us not *i'* temptation; but “
12: 5 killed hath power to cast *i'* hell; “
28 and to morrow is cast *i'* the oven; “
58 and the officer cast thee *i'* prison. “
13: 19 a man took, and cast *i'* his garden; “
14: 1 *i'* the house of one of the chief “
5 have an ass or an ox fallen *i'* a pit, “
21 out quickly *i'* the streets and lanes “
23 Go out *i'* the highways and hedges, “
15: 13 took his journey *i'* a far country, “
15 sent him *i'* his fields to feed swine. “
16: 4 they may receive me *i'* their houses. “
9 you *i'* everlasting habitations. “
16 and every man presseth *i'* it. “
22 by the angels *i'* Abraham's bosom: “
28 also come *i'* this place of torment. “
17: 2 his neck, and he cast *i'* the sea, “
12 as he entered *i'* a certain village, “
27 the day that Noe entered *i'* the ark, “
18: 10 men went up *i'* the temple to pray; “
24 riches enter *i'* the kingdom of God! “
25 man to enter *i'* the kingdom of God. “
19: 4 up *i'* a sycomore tree to see him: 1909
12 nobleman went *i'* a far country 1519
23 not thou my money *i'* the bank, 1909
30 ye *i'* the village over against you; 1519
45 And he went *i'* the temple, and “
20: 9 went *i'* a far country for a long time. “
21: 1 casting their gifts *i'* the treasury. 1519
12 up to the synagogues, and *i'* prisons,* “
24 be led away captive *i'* all nations: 1519
22: 3 Satan *i'* Judas surnamed Iscariot, “
10 when ye are entered *i'* the city, “
10 him *i'* the house where he entereth “
33 thee, both *i'* prison, and to death.* “
40 that ye enter not *i'* temptation. “
46 pray, lest ye enter *i'* temptation. “
54 him *i'* the high priest's house. “
66 and led him *i'* their council, saying, “
23: 19 and for murder, was cast *i'* prison. “
25 and murder, was cast *i'* prison, “
42 when thou comest *i'* thy kingdom.*1722
46 *i'* thy hands I commend my spirit: 1519
24: 7 delivered *i'* the hands of sinful men, “
26 things, and to enter *i'* his glory? “
51 them, and carried up *i'* heaven. “
Joh 1: 9 every man that cometh *i'* the world. “
43 Jesus would go forth *i'* Galilee, “
3: 4 second time *i'* his mother's womb, “
5 cannot enter *i'* the kingdom of God. “
17 not his Son *i'* the world to condemn “
19 that light is come *i'* the world, and “
22 his disciples *i'* the land of Judæa; “
24 For John was not yet cast *i'* prison. “
35 hath given all things *i'* his hand. 1722
4: 3 and departed again *i'* Galilee. 1519
14 springing up *i'* everlasting life. * “
28 went her way *i'* the city, and saith “
38 and ye are entered *i'* their labours. “
43 thence, and went *i'* Galilee. “
45 Then when he was come *i'* Galilee, “
46 Jesus came again *i'* Cana of Galilee,* “
47 was come out of Judæa *i'* Galilee, “
54 was come out of Judæa *i'* Galilee. “
5: 4 down at a certain season *i'* the pool,*1722
7 is troubled, to put me *i'* the pool: 1519
24 shall not come *i'* condemnation; “
6: 3 And Jesus went up *i'* a mountain, “
14 that should come *i'* the world. “
15 again *i'* a mountain himself alone. “
17 And entered *i'* a ship, and went “
21 willingly received him *i'* the ship: “
22 not with his disciples *i'* the boat, “

Joh 7: 3 and go *i'* Judæa, that thy disciples 1519
14 feast Jesus went up *i'* the temple, “
8: 2 he came again *i'* the temple, “
9: 39 judgment I am come *i'* this world, “
10: 1 not by the door *i'* the sheepfold, “
36 sanctified, and sent *i'* the world, “
40 Jordan *i'* the place where John “
11: 7 disciples, Let us go *i'* Judæa again. “
27 which should come *i'* the world. “
30 Jesus was not yet come *i'* the town, “
54 wilderness, *i'* a city called Ephraim, “
12: 24 a corn of wheat fall *i'* the ground “
46 I am come a light *i'* the world, that “
13: 2 having now put *i'* the heart of Judas “
3 had given all things *i'* his hands, “
5 that he poureth water *i'* a bason, “
27 after the sop Satan entered *i'* him. “
15: 6 them, and cast them *i'* the fire, “
16: 13 come, he will guide you *i'* all truth: “
20 your sorrow shall be turned *i'* joy. “
21 joy that a man is born *i'* the world. “
28 Father, and am come *i'* the world: “
17: 18 As thou hast sent me *i'* the world, “
18 have I also sent them *i'* the world. “
18: 1 a garden, *i'* the which he entered, “
11 Put up thy sword *i'* the sheath: “
15 *i'* the palace of the high priest. “
28 went not *i'* the judgment hall, lest “
33 entered *i'* the judgment hall again, “
37 for this cause came I *i'* the world, “
19: 9 went again *i'* the judgment hall, “
17 cross went forth *i'* a place called * “
20: 6 and went *i'* the sepulchre, and seeth “
11 down, and looked *i'* the sepulchre, “
25 my finger *i'* the print of the nails, “
25 and thrust my hand *i'* his side, I will “
27 thy hand, and thrust it *i'* my side: “
21: 3 and entered *i'* a ship immediately; “
7 and did cast himself *i'* the sea. “
Ac 1: 11 why stand ye gazing up *i'* heaven? “
11 is taken up from you *i'* heaven, “
11 as ye have seen him go *i'* heaven. “
13 they went up *i'* an upper room, “
2: 20 The sun shall be turned *i'* darkness, “
20 and the moon *i'* blood, before that “
34 is not ascended *i'* the heavens: “
3: 1 *i'* the temple at the hour of prayer, “
2 of them that entered *i'* the temple; “
3 and John about to go *i'* the temple, “
8 entered with them *i'* the temple, “
5: 15 brought forth the sick *i'* the streets, 2596
21 *i'* the temple early in the morning, 1519
7: 3 *i'* the land which I shall shew thee. “
4 removed him *i'* this land, wherein “
6 they should bring them *i'* bondage, “
9 with envy, sold Joseph *i'* Egypt: 1519
15 Jacob went down *i'* Egypt, and died, “
16 were carried over *i'* Sychem, and * “
23 *i'* his heart to visit his brethren 1909
34 come, I will send thee *i'* Egypt. 1519
39 hearts turned back again *i'* Egypt,* “
45 *i'* the possession of the Gentiles, *1722
55 looked up stedfastly *i'* heaven, 1519
8: 3 entering *i'* every house, and haling 1531
38 they went down both *i'* the water, 1519
9: 6 Arise, and go *i'* the city, and it shall “
8 and brought him *i'* Damascus. “
11 *i'* the street...called Straight. *1909
17 his way, and entered *i'* the house; 1519
39 brought him *i'* the upper chamber: “
10: 10 they made ready, he fell *i'* a trance, 1909
16 was received up again *i'* heaven. 1519
22 angel to send for thee *i'* his house, “
24 after they entered *i'* Cæsarea. “
11: 8 at any time entered *i'* my mouth. “
10 all were drawn up again *i'* heaven. “
12 and we entered *i'* the man's house: “
12: 17 departed, and went *i'* another place:* “
13: 14 *i'* the synagogue on the sabbath “
14: 1 *i'* the synagogue of the Jews, “
20 he rose up, and came *i'* the city: “
22 enter *i'* the kingdom of God. “
25 Perga, they went down *i'* Attalia:* “
16: 7 they assayed to go *i'* Bithynia: 2596
9 Come over *i'* Macedonia, and help 1519
10 endeavoured to go *i'* Macedonia, “
15 Lord, come *i'* my house, and abide “
19 *i'* the marketplace unto the rulers, “
23 they cast them *i'* prison, charging “
24 thrust them *i'* the inner prison, “
34 he had brought them *i'* his house, “
37 Romans, and have cast us *i'* prison; “
40 and entered *i'* the house of Lydia: “
17: 10 went *i'* the synagogue of the Jews. “
18: 7 entered *i'* a certain man's house, “
18 sailed thence *i'* Syria, and with him* “
19 he himself entered *i'* the synagogue, “
27 he was disposed to pass *i'* Achaia, “
19: 8 he went *i'* the synagogue, and spake “
22 he sent *i'* Macedonia two of them “
29 with one accord *i'* the theatre. “
31 adventure himself *i'* the theatre. “
20: 1 departed for to go *i'* Macedonia. “
2 exhortation, he came *i'* Greece, “
3 as he was about to sail *i'* Syria, * “
4 accompanied him *i'* Asia Sopater * 891
9 Eutychus, being fallen *i'* a deep sleep:*
18 the first day that I came *i'* Asia, *1519
21: 3 sailed *i'* Syria, and landed at Tyre:* “
8 entered *i'* the house of Philip the “
11 him *i'* the hands of the Gentiles. “
26 with them entered *i'* the temple, “
28 brought Greeks also *i'* the temple, “
29 that Paul had brought *i'* the temple. “
34 him to be carried *i'* the castle. “
37 as Paul was to be led *i'* the castle, “

Ac 21:38 and leddest out i' the wilderness 1519
22: 4 i' prisons both men and women. "
10 Arise, and go i' Damascus; and "
11 were with me, I came i' Damascus. "
23 clothes, and threw dust i' the air, "
24 him to be brought i' the castle. "
23:10 them, and to bring him i' the castle. "
16 he went and entered i' the castle, "
20 down Paul to morrow i' the council,* "
28 brought him forth i' their council:* "
24:27 Porcius Festus came i' Felix' room:*
25: 1 when Festus was come i' the province,
23 was entered i' the place of hearing, 1519
27: 1 determined...we should sail i' Italy,* "
2 entering i' a ship of Adramyttium,*
6 ship of Alexandria sailing i' Italy;* 1519
15 and could not bear up i' the wind,*
17 they should fall i' the quicksands,* 1519
30 had let down the boat i' the sea, "
38 and cast out the wheat i' the sea. "
39 i' the which they were minded, * "
41 i' a place where two seas met, * "
43 should cast themselves first i' the sea,*
28: 5 he shook off the beast i' the fire, 1519
17 i' the hands of the Romans: "
23 came many to him i' his lodging; "
Ro 1:23 i' an image made like to corruptible* 1722
25 changed the truth of God i' a lie, * "
26 i' that which is against nature: 1519
5: 2 faith i' this grace wherein we stand, "
12 one man sin entered i' the world, "
6: 3 us as were baptized i' Jesus Christ "
3 were baptized i' his death? "
4 with him by baptism i' death: "
7:23 me i' captivity to the law of sin "
8:21 i' the glorious liberty of the 1519
10: 6 Who shall ascend i' heaven? that is, "
7 Or, Who shall descend i' the deep? "
18 their sound went i' all the earth, "
11:24 to nature i' a good olive tree: "
24 be graffed i' their own olive tree? "
15:24 I take my journey i' Spain, I will *1519
28 fruit, I will come by you i' Spain.* "
1Co 2: 9 have entered i' the heart of man, 1909
4:17 bring you i' remembrance of my ways*
9:27 my body, and bring it i' subjection: "
11:20 together therefore i' one place, *1909
12:13 are we all baptized i' one body, 1519
13 been all made to drink i' one Spirit.* "
14: 9 spoken? for ye shall speak i' the air. "
23 be come together i' one place, *1909
2Co 1:16 And to pass by you i' Macedonia, 1519
2:13 I went from thence i' Macedonia. "
3:18 i' the same image from glory to glory, "
7: 5 when we were come i' Macedonia, 1519
8:16 earnest care i' the heart of Titus 1722
10: 5 bringing i' captivity every thought to "
11:13 themselves i' the apostles of Christ. 1519
14 is transformed i' an angel of light. "
20 if a man bring you i' bondage, "
12: 4 that he was caught up i' paradise, 1519
Ga 1: 6 called you i' the grace of Christ *1722
17 but I went i' Arabia, and returned 1519
21 i' the regions of Syria and Cilicia; "
2: 4 they might bring us i' bondage: "
3:27 baptized i' Christ have put on 1519
4: 6 the Spirit of his Son i' your hearts, "
Eph 4: 9 i' the lower parts of the earth? "
15 may grow up i' him in all things, "
Col 1:13 translated us i' the kingdom of his "
2:18 intruding i' those things which *
2Th 3: 5 direct your hearts i' the love of God, 1519
5 and i' the patient waiting for Christ. "
1Ti 1: 3 when I went i' Macedonia, that "
12 faithful, putting me i' the ministry;* "
15 came i' the world to save sinners; "
3: 6 i' the condemnation of the devil. "
7 he fall i' reproach and the snare of "
16 in the world, received up i' glory. *1722
5: 9 not a widow be taken i' the number*
6: 7 we brought nothing i' this world, 1519
9 rich fall i' temptation and a snare, "
9 i' many foolish and hurtful lusts,* "
2Ti 3: 6 are they which creep i' houses, "
Heb 1: 6 in the firstbegotten i' the world, he "
3:11 They shall not enter i' my rest. "
18 they should not enter i' his rest, "
4: 1 being left us of entering i' his rest, "
3 which have believed do enter i' rest, "
3 wrath, if they shall enter i' my rest: "
5 again, If they shall enter i' my rest. "
10 For he that is entered i' his rest, he "
11 labour therefore to enter i' that rest, "
14 priest, that is passed i' the heavens,*
6:19 entereth i' that within the veil; 1519
8:10 I will put my laws i' their mind, "
9: 6 went always i' the first tabernacle, "
7 i' the second went the high priest "
8 the way i' the holiest of all was not yet
12 he entered in once i' the holy place, 1519
24 is not entered i' the holy places "
24 but i' heaven itself, now to appear "
25 entereth i' the holy place every "
10: 5 when he cometh i' the world, he "
16 I will put my laws i' their hearts,* 1909
19 i' the holiest by the blood of Jesus, "
31 fall i' the hands of the living God. 1519
11: 8 i' a place which he should after "
13:11 blood is brought i' the sanctuary by "
Jas 1: 2 joy when ye fall i' divers temptations; "
25 looketh i' the perfect law of liberty, 1519
4:13 to morrow we will go i' such a city, "
5: 4 i' the ears of the Lord of sabaoth. "
12 lest ye fall i' condemnation. *5259
1Pe 1:12 things the angels desire to look i'. 1519
2: 9 darkness i' his marvellous light: "
1Pe 3:22 Who is gone i' heaven, and is on 1519
2Pe 1:11 i' the everlasting kingdom of our "
2: 4 delivered them i' chains of darkness,*
6 of Sodom and Gomorrha i' ashes
1Jo 4: 1 prophets are gone out i' the world. 1519
9 his only begotten Son i' the world, "
2Jo 7 deceivers are entered i' the world, "
10 receive him not i' your house, "
Jude 4 grace of our God i' lasciviousness, "
Re 2:10 shall cast some of you i' prison, "
22 Behold, I will cast her i' a bed, "
22 with her i' great tribulation, "
5: 6 of God sent forth i' all the earth. "
8: 5 the altar, and cast it i' the earth: * "
8 with fire was cast i' the sea: "
11:11 of life from God entered i' them, 1909
12: 6 the woman fled i' the wilderness, 1519
9 he was cast out i' the earth, and * "
14 she might fly i' the wilderness, "
14 i' her place, where she is nourished* "
13:10 He that leadeth i' captivity shall *
10 captivity shall go i' captivity: 1519
14:10 i' the cup of his indignation; *1722
19 thrust in his sickle i' the earth, 1519
19 i' the great winepress of the wrath "
15: 8 man was able to enter i' the temple, "
16:16 gathered them together i' a place "
17 angel poured out his vial i' the air;* "
19 great city was divided i' three parts, "
17: 3 away in the spirit i' the wilderness: "
8 bottomless pit, and go i' perdition: "
11 of the seven, and goeth i' perdition. "
18:21 millstone, and cast it i' the sea, "
19:20 alive i' a lake of fire burning with "
20: 3 And cast him i' the bottomless pit, "
10 was cast i' the lake of fire and "
14 and hell were cast i' the lake of fire. "
15 of life was cast i' the lake of fire. "
21:24 bring their glory and honour i' it. "
26 and honour of the nations i' it. "
27 enter i' it any thing that defileth, "
22:14 in through the gates i' the city. "

intreat See also ENTREAT; INTREATED.
Ge 23: 8 i' for me to Ephron the son of 6293
Ex 8: 8 I' the Lord, that he may take 6279
9 when shall I i' for thee, and for thy "
28 not go very far away: i' for me. "
29 i' the Lord that the swarms of flies "
9:28 I' the Lord (for it is enough) that "
10:17 once, and i' the Lord your God, "
Ru 1:16 Ruth said, I' me not to leave thee, 6293
1Sa 2:25 the Lord, who shall i' for him? 6419
1Ki 13: 6 I' now the face of the Lord thy 2470
Ps 45:12 the people shall i' thy favour. "
Pr 19: 6 will i' the favour of the prince: "
1Co 4:13 Being defamed, we i': we are 3870
Ph'p 4: 3 I i' thee also, true yokefellow, *2065
1Ti 5: 1 an elder, but i' him as a father; *3870

intreated See also ENTREATED.
Ge 25:21 Isaac i' the Lord for his wife, 6279
21 and the Lord was i' of him, and "
Ex 8:30 out from Pharaoh, and i' the Lord. "
10:18 out from Pharaoh, and i' the Lord. "
J'g 13: 8 Then Manoah i' the Lord, and said, "
2Sa 21:14 after that God was i' for the land. "
24:25 So the Lord was i' for the land, and "
1Ch 5:20 in the battle, and he was i' of them; "
2Ch 33:13 and he was i' of him, and heard "
19 also, and how God was i' of him, "
Ezr 8:23 God for this: and he was i' of us. "
Job 19:16 answer; I i' him with my mouth.* 2603
17 I i' for the children's sake of *2589
Ps 119:58 I i' thy favour with my whole 2470
Isa 19:22 Lord, and he shall be i' of them. 6279
Lu 15:28 came his father out, and i' him. 3870
Heb 12:19 i' that the word should not be 3868
Jas 3:17 and easy to be i', full of mercy and 2138

intreateth See ENTREATETH.

intreaties
Pr 18:23 The poor useth i'; but the rich 8469

intreaty See also INTREATIES.
2Co 8: 4 Praying us with much i' that we 3874

intruding
Col 2:18 i' into those things which he hath *1687

invade See also INVADED.
2Ch 20:10 thou wouldest not let Israel i', 935
Hab 3:16 he will i' them with his troops. *1464

invaded
1Sa 23:27 for the Philistines have i' the land.* 6584
27: 8 went up, and i' the Geshurites, * "
30: 1 the Amalekites had i' the south, * "
2Ki 13:20 bands of the Moabites i' the land 935
2Ch 28:18 Philistines also had i' the cities 6584

invasion
1Sa 30:14 We made an i' upon the south of *6584

invent See also INVENTED.
Am 6: 5 i' to themselves instruments of *2803

invented
2Ch 26:15 engines, i' by cunning men, 2803

inventions
Ps 99: 8 thou tookest vengeance of their i'. *5949
106:29 provoked him to anger with their i' *4611
39 went a whoring with their own i'.* "
Pr 8:12 and find out knowledge of witty i'. *4209
Ec 7:29 but they have sought out many i'. 2810

inventors
Ro 1:30 i' of evil things, disobedient to 2182

invisible
Ro 1:20 For the i' things of him from the 517
Col 1:15 Who is the image of the i' God, "
16 and that are in earth, visible and i', "
1Ti 1:17 unto the King eternal, immortal, i', 517
Heb 11:27 endured, as seeing him who is i'. "

invited
1Sa 9:24 since I said, I have i' the people. 7121
2Sa 13:23 and Absalom i' all the king's sons. "
Es 5:12 am I i' unto her also with the king. "

inward See also INWARDS.
Ex 28:26 is in the side of the ephod i'. 1004
39:19 was on the side of the ephod i'. "
Le 13:55 it is fret i', whether it be bare *
2Sa 5: 9 round about from Millo and i'. 1004
1Ki 7:25 and all their hinder parts were i'. "
2Ch 3:13 their feet, and their faces were i'.* "
4: 4 and all their hinder parts were i'. "
Job 19:19 All my i' friends abhorred me: 5475
38:36 hath put wisdom in the i' parts? 2910
Ps 5: 9 their i' part is very wickedness; 7130
49:11 Their i' thought is, that their "
51: 6 thou desirest truth in the i' parts: 2910
64: 6 i' thought of every one of them, 7130
Pr 20:27 all the i' parts of the belly. *2315
30 do stripes the i' parts of the belly.* "
Isa 16:11 and mine i' parts for Kir-haresh. 7130
Jer 31:33 I will put my law in their i' parts, "
Eze 40: 9 and the porch of the gate was i'. *1004
16 and windows were round about i': 6441
41: 3 Then went he i', and measured the "
42: 4 a walk of ten cubits breadth i', 6442
Lu 11:39 your i' part is full of ravening and 2081
Ro 7:22 the law of God after the i' man: 2080
2Co 4:16 the i' man is renewed day by day. 2081
7:15 his i' affection is more abundant 4698

inwardly
Ps 62: 4 their mouth, but they curse i'. 7130
M't 7:15 but i' they are ravening wolves. 2081
Ro 2:29 he is a Jew, which is one i'; 1722,2927

inwards
Ex 29:13 all the fat that covereth the i', 7130
17 in pieces, and wash the i' of him, "
22 and the fat that covereth the i', and "
Le 1: 9 his i' and his legs shall he wash in "
13 he shall wash the i' and the legs "
3: 3 the fat that covereth the i', "
3 and all the fat that is upon the i', "
9 and the fat that covereth the i', "
9 and all the fat that is upon the i', "
14 the fat that covereth the i', "
14 and all the fat that is upon the i', "
4: 8 the fat that covereth the i', "
8 and all the fat that is upon the i', "
11 and with his legs, and his i', and his "
7: 3 and the fat that covereth the i', "
8:16 took all the fat that was upon the i', "
21 And he washed the i' and the legs "
25 and all the fat that was upon the i', "
9:14 he did wash the i' and the legs, "
19 and that which covereth the i', and

Iphedeiah (if-e-di'-ah)
1Ch 8:25 And I', and Penuel, the sons of *3301

Ir (ur) See also IR-NAHASH; IR-SHEMESH.
1Ch 7:12 and Huppim, the children of I'. 5893

Ira (i'-rah)
2Sa 20:26 I' also the Jairite was a chief 5896
23:26 I' the son of Ikkesh the Tekoite, "
38 I' an Ithrite, Gareb an Ithrite, "
1Ch 11:28 I' the son of Ikkesh the Tekoite, "
40 I' the Ithrite, Gareb the Ithrite, "
27: 9 I' the son of Ikkesh the Tekoite: "

Irad (i'-rad)
Ge 4:18 And unto Enoch was born I': 5897
18 I' begat Mehujael: and Mehujael "

Iram (i'-ram)
Ge 36:43 Duke Magdiel, duke I': these be 5902
1Ch 1:54 Duke Magdiel, duke I'. These are "

Iri (i'-ri)
1Ch 7: 7 and I', five; heads of the house 5901

Irijah (i-ri'-jah)
Jer 37:13 whose name was I', the son of 3376
14 I' took Jeremiah, and brought him "

Ir-nahash (ur-na'-hash)
1Ch 4:12 and Tehinnah, the father of I'. 5904

iron See also IRONS.
Ge 4:22 of every artificer in brass and i': 1270
Le 26:19 I will make your heaven as i', and "
Nu 31:22 the silver, the brass, the i', the tin, "
35:16 smite him with an instrument of i', "
De 3:11 his bedstead was a bedstead of i'; "
4:20 you forth out of the i' furnace, even "
8: 9 a land whose stones are i', and out "
27: 5 thou shalt not lift up any i' tool "
28:23 earth that is under thee shall be i'. "
48 shall put a yoke of i' upon thy neck, "
33:25 Thy shoes shall be i' and brass; "
Jos 6:19 gold, and vessels of brass and i', "
24 and the vessels of brass and of i', "
8:31 which no man hath lift up any i': "
17:16 of the valley have chariots of i', "
18 though they have i' chariots, and "
22: 8 gold, and with brass, and with i', "
J'g 1:19 because they had chariots of i'. "
4: 3 he had nine hundred chariots of i'; "
13 even nine hundred chariots of i', "
1Sa 17: 7 weighed six hundred shekels of i': "
2Sa 12:31 saws, and under harrows of i', "
31 and under axes of i', and made "
23: 7 be fenced with i' and the staff of a "
1Ki 6: 7 any tool of i' heard in the house, "
8:51 from the midst of the furnace of i'. "
22:11 Chenaanah made him horns of i': "
2Ki 6: 6 it in thither; and the i' did swim. "
1Ch 20: 3 with harrows of i', and with axes. "

1Ch 22: 3 David prepared *i'* in abundance 1270
14 and of brass and *i'* without weight; "
16 the brass, and the *i'*, there is no "
29: 2 of brass, the *i'* for things of *i'*, "
7 one hundred thousand talents of *i'*. "
2Ch 2: 7 in brass, and in *i'*, and in purple, "
14 in silver, in brass, in *i'*, in stone, "
18: 10 had made him horns of *i'*, "
24: 12 also such as wrought *i'* and brass "
Job 19: 24 they were graven with an *i'* pen "
20: 24 He shall flee from the *i'* weapon, "
28: 2 *I'* is taken out of the earth, and "
40: 18 brass; his bones are like bars of *i'*. "
41: 27 He esteemeth *i'* as straw, and brass "
Ps 2: 9 shalt break them with a rod of *i'*; "
105: 18 hurt with fetters: he was laid in *i'*: "
107: 10 being bound in affliction and *i'*; "
16 and cut the bars of *i'* in sunder. "
149: 8 and their nobles with fetters of *i'*; "
Pr 27: 17 *I'* sharpeneth *i'*; so a man "
Ec 10: 10 If the *i'* be blunt, and he do not "
Isa 10: 34 the thickets of the forest with *i'*, "
45: 2 and cut in sunder the bars of *i'*: "
48: 4 thy neck is as an *i'* sinew, and thy "
60: 17 gold, and for *i'* I will bring silver, "
17 for wood brass, and for stones *i'*: "
Jer 1: 18 and an *i'* pillar, and brasen walls "
6: 28 they are brass and *i'*; they are all "
11: 4 land of Egypt, from the *i'* furnace, "
15: 12 Shall *i'* break the northern *i'* and "
17: 1 of Judah is written with a pen of *i'*, "
28: 13 shalt make for them yokes of *i'*. "
14 have put a yoke of *i'* upon the neck "
Eze 4: 3 take thou unto thee an *i'* pan, "
3 and set it for a wall of *i'* between "
22: 18 are brass, and tin, and *i'*, and lead, "
20 silver, and brass, and *i'*, and lead, "
27: 12 with silver, *i'*, tin, and lead, they "
19 bright *i'*, cassia, and calamus, were "
Da 2: 33 His legs of *i'*, his feet part of *i'* and 6523
34 image upon his feet that were of *i'* "
35 Then was the *i'*, the clay, the brass, "
40 kingdom shall be strong as *i'*: "
40 *i'* breaketh in pieces and subdueth "
40 and as *i'* that breaketh all these, "
41 part of potters' clay, and part of *i'*, "
41 be in it of the strength of the *i'*, "
41 sawest the *i'* mixed with miry clay. "
42 the toes of the feet were part of *i'*, "
43 sawest *i'* mixed with miry clay, "
43 even as *i'* is not mixed with clay. "
45 it brake in pieces the *i'*, the brass, "
4: 15, 23 even with a band of *i'* and brass, "
5: 4 of gold, and of silver, of brass, of *i'*, "
23 gods of silver, and gold, of brass, *i'*, "
7: 7 it had great *i'* teeth: it devoured "
19 whose teeth were of *i'*, and his nails "
Am 1: 3 with threshing instruments of *i'*: 1270
Mic 4: 13 for I will make thine horn *i'*, and I "
Ac 12: 10 they came unto the *i'* gate that *4603*
1Ti 4: 2 conscience seared with a hot *i'*; "
Re 2: 27 he shall rule them with a rod of *i'*; *4603*
9: 9 as it were breastplates of *i'*; "
12: 5 to rule all nations with a rod of *i'*: "
18: 12 and of brass, and *i'*, and marble, *4604*
19: 15 he shall rule them with a rod of *i'*: *4603*

Iron (*i'-ron*)
Jos 19: 38 And *I'*, and Migdal-el, Horem, 3375

irons
Job 41: 7 thou fill his skin with barbed *i'*? 7905

Irpeel (*ur'-pe-el*)
Jos 18: 27 Rekem, and *I'*, and Taralah, 3416

Ir-shemesh (*ur-she'-mesh*)
Jos 19: 41 was Zorah, and Eshtaol, and *I'*, 5905

Iru (*i'-ru*)
1Ch 4: 15 Caleb the son of Jephunneh; *I'*, 5902

is See in the APPENDIX.

Isaac (*i'-za-ak*) See also ISAAC'S.
Ge 17: 19 and thou shalt call his name *I'*: 3327
21 covenant will I establish with *I'*, "
21: 3 him, whom Sarah bare to him, *I'*. "
4 Abraham circumcised his son *I'* "
5 when his son *I'* was born unto him. "
8 the same day that *I'* was weaned. "
10 be heir with my son, even with *I'*. "
12 for in *I'* shall thy seed be called. "
22: 2 Take now thy son, thine only son *I'* "
3 men with him, and *I'* his son, "
6 offering, and laid it upon *I'* his son; "
7 and *I'* spake unto Abraham his "
9 and bound *I'* his son, and laid him "
24: 4 and take a wife unto my son *I'*. "
14 hast appointed for thy servant *I'*; "
62 *I'* came from the way of the well "
63 *I'* went out to meditate in the field "
64 saw *I'*, she lighted off the camel. "
66 told *I'* all things that he had done. "
67 *I'* brought her into his mother "
67 *I'* was comforted after his mother's "
25: 5 gave all that he had unto *I'*. "
6 sent them away from *I'* his son, "
9 his sons *I'* and Ishmael buried him "
11 that God blessed his son *I'*; "
11 and *I'* dwelt by the well Lahai-roi. "
19 these are the generations of *I'*, "
19 Abraham's son: Abraham begat *I'*: "
20 *I'* was forty years old when he took "
21 *I'* entreated the Lord for his wife, "
26 *I'* was threescore years old when "
28 *I'* loved Esau, because he did eat "
26: 1 *I'* went unto Abimelech king of "
6 And *I'* dwelt in Gerar: "
8 *I'* was sporting with Rebekah his "
9 Abimelech called *I'*, and said, "
Ge 26: 9 *I'* said unto him, Because I said, 3327
12 *I'* sowed in that land, and received "
16 Abimelech said unto *I'*, Go from "
17 *I'* departed thence, and pitched "
18 *I'* digged again the wells of water, "
27 *I'* said unto them, Wherefore come "
31 *I'* sent them away, and they "
35 which were a grief of mind unto *I'* "
27: 1 when *I'* was old, and his eyes were "
5 when *I'* spake to Esau his son. "
20 *I'* said unto his son, How is it that "
21 *I'* said unto Jacob, Come near, I "
22 Jacob went near unto *I'* his father; "
26 his father *I'* said unto him, Come "
30 *I'* had made an end of blessing "
30 gone out from the presence of *I'* "
32 *I'* his father said unto him, Who "
33 *I'* trembled very exceedingly, and "
37 *I'* answered and said unto Esau, "
39 *I'* his father answered and said "
46 Rebekah said to *I'*, I am weary of "
28: 1 *I'* called Jacob, and blessed him, "
5 *I'* sent away Jacob: and he went "
6 saw that *I'* had blessed Jacob, "
8 daughters of Canaan pleased not *I'* "
13 thy father, and the God of *I'*: "
31: 18 for to go to *I'* his father in the land "
42 Abraham, and the fear of *I'*, had "
53 sware by the fear of his father *I'*. "
32: 9 and God of my father *I'*, the Lord "
35: 12 land which I gave Abraham and *I'*, "
27 Jacob came unto *I'* his father unto "
27 where Abraham and *I'* sojourned. "
28 *I'* were a hundred and fourscore "
29 And *I'* gave up the ghost, and died, "
46: 1 unto the God of his father *I'*. "
48: 15 fathers Abraham and *I'* did walk, "
16 of my fathers Abraham and *I'*; "
49: 31 buried *I'* and Rebekah his wife; "
50: 24 to Abraham, to *I'*, and to Jacob. "
Ex 2: 24 Abraham, with *I'*, and with Jacob. "
3: 6 Abraham, the God of *I'*, and the "
15 the God of *I'*, and the God of Jacob, "
16 God of Abraham, of *I'*, and of "
4: 5 the God of *I'*, and the God of Jacob, "
6: 3 I appeared unto Abraham, unto *I'*, "
8 give it to Abraham, to *I'*, and to "
32: 13 Remember Abraham, *I'*, and Israel, "
33: 1 swear unto Abraham, to *I'*, and to "
Le 26: 42 and also my covenant with *I'*, "
Nu 32: 11 swear unto Abraham, unto *I'*, and "
De 1: 8 your fathers, Abraham, *I'*, and "
6: 10 to Abraham, to *I'*, and to Jacob, "
9: 5 fathers, Abraham, *I'*, and Jacob. "
27 servants, Abraham, *I'*, and Jacob; "
29: 13 to Abraham, to *I'*, and to Jacob. "
30: 20 to Abraham, to *I'*, and to Jacob, "
34: 4 I sware unto Abraham, unto *I'*, "
Jos 24: 3 multiplied his seed, and gave him *I'*. "
4 I gave unto *I'* Jacob and Esau: "
1Ki 18: 36 God of Abraham, *I'*, and of Israel, "
2Ki 13: 23 his covenant with Abraham, *I'*, and "
1Ch 1: 28 sons of Abraham; *I'*, and Ishmael. "
34 And Abraham begat *I'*. "
34 The sons of *I'*; Esau and Israel. "
16: 16 Abraham, and of his oath unto *I'*; "
29: 18 God of Abraham, *I'*, and of Israel, "
2Ch 30: 6 God of Abraham, *I'*, and Israel, "
Ps 105: 9 Abraham, and his oath unto *I'*; 3446
Jer 33: 26 seed of Abraham, *I'*, and Jacob: "
Am 7: 9 high places of *I'* shall be desolate, "
16 thy word against the house of *I'*. "
M't 1: 2 begat *I'*; and *I'* begat Jacob; *2664*
8: 11 sit down with Abraham, and *I'*, "
22: 32 God of *I'*, and the God of Jacob? "
M'r 12: 26 God of Abraham, and the God of *I*, "
Lu 3: 34 which was the son of *I'*, which was "
13: 28 see Abraham, and *I'*, and Jacob, "
20: 37 and the God of *I'*, and the God of "
Ac 3: 13 The God of Abraham, and of *I'*, "
7: 8 Abraham begat *I'*, and circumcised "
8 and *I'* begat Jacob; and Jacob "
32 God of Abraham, and the God of *I'*, "
Ro 9: 7 but, In *I'* shall thy seed be called. "
10 by one, even by our father *I'*; "
Ga 4: 28 Now we, brethren, as *I'* was, are "
Heb 11: 9 dwelling in tabernacles with *I'* and "
17 when he was tried, offered up *I'*: "
18 That in *I'* shall thy seed be called: "
20 By faith *I'* blessed Jacob and Esau "
Jas 2: 21 offered *I'* his son upon the altar? "

Isaac's (*i'-za-aks*)
Ge 26: 19 *I'* servants digged in the valley, 3327
20 Gerar did strive with *I'* herdmen, "
25 and there *I'* servants digged a well. "
32 *I'* servants came, and told him "

Isaiah (*i-za'-yah*) See also ESAIAS.
2Ki 19: 2 to *I'* the prophet the son of Amoz. 3470
5 of king Hezekiah came to *I'*. "
6 And *I'* said unto them, Thus shall "
20 Then *I'* the son of Amoz sent to "
20: 1 *I'* the son of Amoz came to him, "
4 *I'* was gone out into the middle "
7 And *I'* said, Take a lump of figs. "
8 Hezekiah said unto *I'*, What shall "
9 *I'* said, This sign shalt thou have of "
11 *I'* the prophet cried unto the Lord: "
14 *I'* the prophet unto king Hezekiah, "
16 *I'* said unto Hezekiah, Hear the "
19 said Hezekiah unto *I'*, Good is the "
2Ch 26: 22 did *I'* the prophet, the son of Amoz, "
32: 20 *I'* the son of Amoz, prayed and "
32 in the vision of *I'* the prophet, "
Isa 1: 1 The vision of *I'* the son of Amoz, "
2: 1 word that *I'* the son of Amoz saw "
Isa 7: 3 Then said the Lord unto *I'*, Go 3470
13: 1 which *I'* the son of Amoz did see. "
20: 2 the same time spake the Lord by *I'* "
3 my servant *I'* hath walked naked "
37: 2 unto *I'* the prophet the son of Amoz. "
5 of king Hezekiah came to *I'*. "
6 *I'* said unto them, Thus shall ye say "
21 Then *I'* the son of Amoz sent unto "
38: 1 *I'* the prophet the son of Amoz "
4 came the word of the Lord to *I'*, "
21 *I'* had said, Let them take a lump "
39: 3 *I'* the prophet unto king Hezekiah, "
5 Then said *I'* to Hezekiah, Hear the "
8 Then said Hezekiah to *I'*, Good is "

Iscah (*is'-cah*) See also SARAH.
Ge 11: 29 of Milcah, and the father of *I'*. 3252

Iscariot (*is-car'-e-ot*) See also JUDAS.
M't 10: 4 Judas *I'*, who also betrayed him. *2469*
26: 14 one of the twelve, called Judas *I'*, "
M'r 3: 19 Judas *I'*, which also betrayed him: "
14: 10 And Judas *I'*, one of the twelve, "
Lu 6: 16 Judas *I'*, which also was the traitor. "
22: 3 Satan into Judas surnamed *I'*, "
Joh 6: 71 spake of Judas *I'* the son of Simon: "
12: 4 one of his disciples, Judas *I'*, "
13: 2 now put it into the heart of Judas *I'*, "
26 the sop, he gave it to Judas *I'*, the* "
14: 22 Judas saith unto him, not *I'*, Lord, "

Ish See ISH-BOSHETH; ISH-TOB.

Ishbah (*ish'-bah*)
1Ch 4: 17 and *I'* the father of Eshtemoa. 3431

Ishbak (*ish'-bak*)
Ge 25: 2 and Midian, and *I'*, and Shuah. 3435
1Ch 1: 32 and Midian, and *I'*, and Shuah. "

Ishbi-benob (*ish''-bi-be'-nob*)
2Sa 21: 16 And *I'*, which was of the sons of 3430

Ish-bosheth (*ish-bo'-sheth*) See also ESH-BAAL.
2Sa 2: 8 took *I'* the son of Saul, and 378
10 *I'* Saul's son was forty years old "
12 the servants of *I'* the son of Saul, "
15 pertained to *I'* the son of Saul, "
3: 7 *I'* said to Abner, Wherefore hast "
8 very wroth for the words of *I'*, 378
14 David sent messengers to *I'* Saul's "
15 *I'* sent, and took her from her "
4: 5 heat of the day to the house of *I'*, "
8 brought the head of *I'* unto David "
8 Behold the head of *I'* the son of "
12 they took the head of *I'*, and buried "

Ishi (*i'-shi*)
1Ch 2: 31 of Appaim; *I'*. And the sons of *I'*; 3469
4: 20 the sons of *I'* were, Zoheth, and "
42 and Uzziel, the sons of *I'*. "
5: 24 of their fathers, even Epher, and *I'*, "
Ho 2: 16 Lord, that thou shalt call me *I'*; 376

Ishiah (*i-shi'-ah*) See also ISHIJAH; ISSHIAH.
1Ch 7: 3 and Obadiah, and Joel, *I'*, five: *3449

Ishijah (*i-shi'-jah*) See also ISHIAH; JESIAH.
Ezr 10: 31 the sons of Harim; Eliezer, *I'*, *3449

Ishma (*ish'-mah*)
1Ch 4: 3 Jezreel, and *I'*, and Idbash: and 3457

Ishmael (*ish'-ma-el*) See also ISHMAELITE; ISHMAEL'S.
Ge 16: 11 a son, and shalt call his name *I'*; 3458
15 son's name, which Hagar bare, *I'*. "
16 old, when Hagar bare *I'* to Abram. "
17: 18 O that *I'* might live before thee! "
20 And as for *I'*, I have heard thee: "
23 And Abraham took *I'* his son, and "
25 *I'* his son was thirteen years old, "
26 circumcised, and *I'* his son. "
25: 9 his sons Isaac and *I'* buried him "
12 these are the generations of *I'*, "
13 are the names of the sons of *I'*, "
13 the firstborn of *I'*, Nebajoth; and "
16 These are the sons of *I'*, and these "
17 these are the years of the life of *I'*, "
28: 9 Then went Esau unto *I'*, and took "
9 Mahalath the daughter of *I'*, "
2Ki 25: 23, 25 even *I'* the son of Nethaniah, "
1Ch 1: 28 sons of Abraham; Isaac, and *I'*. "
29 The firstborn of *I'*, Nebaioth; then "
31 Kedemah. These are the sons of *I'*. "
8: 38 *I'*, and Sheariah, and Obadiah, and "
9: 44 *I'*, and Sheariah, and Obadiah, and "
2Ch 19: 11 Zebadiah the son of *I'*, the ruler "
23: 1 *I'* the son of Jehohanan, and "
Ezr 10: 22 Pashur; Elioenai, Maaseiah, *I'*, "
Jer 40: 8 even *I'* the son of Nethaniah, and "
14 hath sent *I'* the son of Nethaniah "
15 I will slay *I'* the son of Nethaniah, "
16 for thou speakest falsely of *I'*. "
41: 1 month, that *I'* the son of Nethaniah "
2 Then arose *I'* the son of Nethaniah, "
3 *I'* also slew all the Jews that were "
6 And *I'* the son of Nethaniah went "
7 *I'* the son of Nethaniah slew them, "
8 among them that said unto *I'*, "
9 *I'* had cast all the dead bodies "
9 *I'* the son of Nethaniah filled it with "
10 *I'* carried away captive all the "
10 *I'* the son of Nethaniah carried "
11 *I'* the son of Nethaniah had done, "
12 fight with *I'* the son of Nethaniah, "
13 which were with *I'* saw Johanan "
14 people that *I'* had carried away "
15 But *I'* the son of Nethaniah escaped "
16 he had recovered from *I'* the son of "
18 *I'* the son of Nethaniah had slain "

Ishmaelite (*ish'-ma-el-ite*) See also ISHMAELITES; ISHMEELITE.
1Ch 27: 30 the camels also was Obil the *I'*: 3459

Ishmaelites (*ish'-ma-el-ites*) See also ISHMEELITES.
J'g 8:24 earrings, because they were I·. 3459
Ps 83: 6 tabernacles of Edom, and the I·; "
Ishmael's (*ish'-ma-els*)
Ge 36: 3 And Bashemath I· daughter, sister 3458
Ishmaiah (*ish-ma-i'-ah*) See also ISMAIAH.
1Ch 27:19 Zebulun, I· the son of Obadiah: 3460
Ishmeelite (*ish'-me-el-ite*) See also ISHMAELITE; ISHMEELITES.
1Ch 2:17 of Amasa was Jether the I·. *3459
Ishmeelites (*ish'-me-el-ites*) See also ISHMAELITES.
Ge 37:25 I· came from Gilead, with their *3459
27 Come, and let us sell him to the I·,* "
28 sold Joseph to the I· for twenty * "
39: 1 bought him of the hands of the I·,* "
Ishmerai (*ish'-me-rahee*)
1Ch 8:18 I· also, and Jezliah, and Jobab, 3461
Ishod (*i'-shod*)
1Ch 7:18 his sister Hammoleketh bare I·, *379
Ishpan (*ish'-pan*)
1Ch 8:22 And I·, and Heber, and Eliel, 3473
Ish-tob (*ish'-tob*)
2Sa 10: 6 and of I· twelve thousand men. *382
8 of Zoba, and of Rehob, and I·, * "
Ishuah (*ish'-u-ah*) See also ISUAH.
Ge 46:17 and I·, and Isui, and Beriah, *3438
Ishuai (*ish'-u-ahee*) See also ISHUI.
1Ch 7:30 and Isuah, and I·, and Beriah, *3440
Ishui (*ish'-u-i*) See also ISHUAI; JESUI.
1Sa 14:49 Saul were Jonathan, and I·, and *3440
island See also ISLANDS; ISLE.
Job 22:30 shall deliver the i· of the innocent, *336
Isa 34:14 meet with the wild beasts of the i·,*338
Ac 27:16 a certain i· which is called Clauda, 3519
26 we must be cast upon a certain i·. 3520
28: 1 knew that the i· was called Melita. "
7 the chief man of the i·, whose name "
9 which had diseases in the i·, came, "
Re 6:14 every mountain and i· were moved "
16:20 And every i· fled away, and the "
islands See also ISLES.
Isa 11:11 Hamath, and from the i· of the sea. 339
13:22 the wild beasts of the i· shall cry in *338
41: 1 Keep silence before me, O i·; and 339
42:12 and declare his praise in the i·. "
15 I will make the rivers i·, and I will "
59:18 to the i· he will repay recompence. "
Jer 50:39 beasts of the i· shall dwell there, * "
isle See also ISLAND; ISLES.
Isa 20: 6 inhabitants of this i· shall say in *339
23: 2 Be still, ye inhabitants of the i·; "
6 howl, ye inhabitants of the i·. "
Ac 13: 6 gone through the i· unto Paphos, *3520
28:11 which had wintered in the i·, whose* "
Re 1: 9 was in the i· that is called Patmos, "
isles See also ISLANDS.
Ge 10: 5 were the i· of the Gentiles divided 339
Es 10: 1 the land, and upon the i· of the sea. "
Ps 72:10 and of the i· shall bring presents: "
97: 1 the multitude of i· be glad thereof. "
Isa 24:15 God of Israel in the i· of the sea. "
40:15 taketh up the i· as a very little thing. "
41: 5 The i· saw it, and feared; the ends "
42: 4 and the i· shall wait for his law. "
10 the i·, and the inhabitants thereof. "
49: 1 Listen, O i·, unto me; and hearken, "
51: 5 the i· shall wait upon me, and on "
60: 9 Surely the i· shall wait for me, and "
66:19 to Tubal, and Javan, to the i· afar off, "
Jer 2:10 pass over the i· of Chittim, and see; "
25:22 the i· which are beyond the sea, "
31:10 declare it in the i· afar off, and say, "
Eze 26:15 the i· shake at the sound of thy fall, "
18 the i· tremble in the day of thy fall; "
18 the i· that are in the sea shall be "
27: 3 merchant of the people for many i·, "
6 brought out of the i· of Chittim. "
7 and purple from the i· of Elishah "
15 many i· were the merchandise of "
35 All the inhabitants of the i· shall be "
39: 6 them that dwell carelessly in the i·: "
Da 11:18 shall he turn his face unto the i·, "
Zep 2:11 place, even all the i· of the heathen. "
Ismachiah (*is-ma-ki'-ah*)
2Ch 31:13 and Jozabad, and Eliel, and I·, 3253
Ismaiah (*is-ma-i'-ah*) See also ISHMAIAH.
1Ch 12: 4 And I· the Gibeonite, a mighty *3460
Ispah (*is'-pah*)
1Ch 8:16 And Michael, and I·, and Joha, *3472
Israel (*iz'-ra-el*) See also EL-ELOHE-ISRAEL; ISRAELITE; ISRAEL'S; JACOB; JESHURUN.
Ge 32:28 be called no more Jacob, but I·: 3478
32 children of I· eat not of the sinew "
34: 7 because he had wrought folly in I· "
35:10 Jacob, but I· shall be thy name; "
10 and he called his name I·. "
21 I· journeyed, and spread his tent "
22 when I· dwelt in that land, that "
22 father's concubine: and I· heard it. "
36:31 any king over the children of I·. "
37: 3 I· loved Joseph more than all his "
13 I· said unto Joseph, Do not thy "
42: 5 the sons of I· came to buy corn "
43: 6 I· said, Wherefore dealt ye so ill "
8 Judah said unto I· his father, "
11 I· said unto them, If it must be so "
Ge 45:21 And the children of I· did so: and 3478
28 I· said, It is enough; Joseph my "
46: 1 I· took his journey with all that he "
2 God spake unto I· in the visions of "
5 the sons of I· carried Jacob their "
8 are the names of the children of I·, "
29 went up to meet I· his father, to "
30 I· said unto Joseph, Now let me die "
47:27 And I· dwelt in the land of Egypt, "
29 time drew nigh that I· must die: "
31 I· bowed himself upon the bed's "
48: 2 I· strengthened himself, and sat "
8 I· beheld Joseph's sons, and said, "
10 the eyes of I· were dim for age, "
11 I· said unto Joseph, I had not "
14 And I· stretched out his right hand, "
20 In thee shall I· bless, saying, God "
21 I· said unto Joseph, Behold, I die: "
49: 2 and hearken unto I· your father. "
7 in Jacob, and scatter them in I·. "
16 people, as one of the tribes of I·. "
24 is the shepherd, the stone of I·: "
28 these are the twelve tribes of I·: "
50: 2 and the physicians embalmed I·. "
25 took an oath of the children of I·, "
Ex 1: 1 are the names of the children of I·, "
7 the children of I· were fruitful, and "
9 the children of I· are more and "
12 because of the children of I·. "
13 children of I· to serve with rigour: "
2:23 of I· sighed by reason of bondage, "
25 God looked upon the children of I·, "
3: 9 the cry of the children of I· is come "
10 forth my people the children of I· "
11 bring forth the children of I· out of "
13 when I come unto the children of I·, "
14, 15 thou say unto the children of I·, "
16 gather the elders of I· together, "
18 come, thou and the elders of I·, "
4:22 Thus saith the Lord, I· is my son, "
29 all the elders of the children of I·: "
31 Lord had visited the children of I·, "
5: 1 Thus saith the Lord God of I·, Let "
2 should obey his voice to let I· go? "
2 the Lord, neither will I let I· go. "
14 the officers of the children of I·, "
15 officers of the children of I· came "
19 officers of the children of I· did see "
6: 5 the groaning of the children of I·, "
6 say unto the children of I·, I am "
9 spake so unto the children of I·: "
11 children of I· go out of his land. "
12 of I· have not hearkened unto me; "
13 a charge unto the children of I·, "
13 the children of I· out of the land of "
14 sons of Reuben the firstborn of I·; "
26 Bring out the children of I· from "
27 to bring out the children of I· from "
7: 2 that he send the children of I· out "
4 and my people the children of I·, "
5 and bring out the children of I· "
9: 4 shall sever between the cattle of I· "
4 die of all that is the children's of I·. "
6 cattle of the children of I· died not "
26 where the children of I· were, was "
35 would he let the children of I· go; "
10:20 would not let the children of I· go. "
23 of I· had light in their dwellings. "
11: 7 children of I· shall not a dog move "
7 between the Egyptians and I·. "
10 the children of I· go out of his land. "
12: 3 ye unto all the congregation of I·, "
6 assembly of the congregation of I· "
15 that soul shall be cut off from I·. "
19 cut off from the congregation of I·, "
21 Moses called for all the elders of I·, "
27 the houses of the children of I· in "
28 And the children of I· went away, "
31 both ye and the children of I·; "
35 of I· did according to the word of "
37 And the children of I· journeyed "
40 the sojourning of the children of I·, "
42 children of I· in their generations. "
47 the congregation of I· shall keep it. "
50 Thus did all the children of I·; as "
51 bring the children of I· out of the "
13: 2 womb among the children of I·, "
18 children of I· went up harnessed "
19 straitly sworn the children of I·, "
14: 2 Speak unto the children of I·, that "
3 will say of the children of I·, They "
5 we have let I· go from serving us? "
8 he pursued after the children of I·: "
8 of I· went out with an high hand. "
10 children of I· lifted up their eyes "
10 of I· cried out unto the Lord. "
15 Speak unto the children of I·, that "
16 of I· shall go on dry ground "
19 which went before the camp of I·, "
20 the Egyptians and the camp of I·; "
22 of I· went into the midst of the sea "
25 Let us flee from the face of I·; for "
29 children of I· walked upon dry land "
30 the Lord saved I· that day out of "
30 I· saw the Egyptians dead upon "
31 I· saw that great work which the "
15: 1 sang Moses and the children of I· "
19 the children of I· went on dry land "
22 Moses brought I· from the Red sea, "
16: 1 congregation of the children of I· "
2 children of I· murmured against "
3 the children of I· said unto them, "
6 said unto all the children of I·, "
9 all the congregation of the...of I·, "
10 whole congregation of the...of I·, "
12 murmurings of the children of I·: "
Ex 16:15 when the children of I· saw it, they 3478
17 And the children of I· did so, and "
31 I· called the name thereof Manna: "
35 children of I· did eat manna forty "
17: 1 I· journeyed from the wilderness "
5 take with thee of the elders of I·; "
6 so in the sight of the elders of I·. "
7 the chiding of the children of I·, "
8 and fought with I· in Rephidim. "
11 held up his hand, that I· prevailed: "
18: 1 for Moses, and for I· his people, "
1 Lord had brought I· out of Egypt; "
9 which the Lord had done to I·, "
12 Aaron came, and all the elders of I·, "
25 Moses chose able men out of all I·, "
19: 1 children of I· were gone forth out "
2 there I· camped before the mount. "
3 Jacob, and tell the children of I·; "
6 shalt speak unto the children of I·. "
20:22 shalt say unto the children of I·, "
24: 1 and seventy of the elders of I·; "
4 according to the twelve tribes of I·. "
5 young men of the children of I·, "
9 and seventy of the elders of I·: "
10 And they saw the God of I·: and "
11 the nobles of the children of I· he "
17 in the eyes of the children of I·. "
25: 2 Speak unto the children of I·, that "
22 unto the children of I·. "
27:20 shalt command the children of I·, "
21 on the behalf of the children of I·. "
28: 1 from among the children of I·, that "
9, 11 the names of the children of I·: "
12 memorial unto the children of I·: "
21 the names of the children of I·, "
29 bear the names of the children of I· "
30 the judgment of the children of I· "
38 I· shall hallow in all their holy "
29:28 for ever from the children of I·: "
28 offering from the children of I· "
43 will meet with the children of I·, "
45 will dwell among the children of I·, "
30:12 takest the sum of the children of I· "
16 money of the children of I·, "
16 memorial unto the children of I· "
31 shalt speak unto the children of I·, "
31:13 thou also unto the children of I·, "
16 of I· shall keep the sabbath, "
17 between me and the children of I· "
32: 4, 8 These be thy gods, O I·, which "
13 Remember Abraham, Isaac, and I·, "
20 made the children of I· drink of it. "
27 Thus saith the Lord God of I·, Put "
33: 5 Say unto the children of I·, Ye are "
6 of I· stripped themselves of their "
34:23 before the Lord God, the God of I·. "
27 covenant with thee and with I·. "
30 all the children of I· saw Moses, "
32 all the children of I· came nigh: "
34 and spake unto the children of I· "
35 children of I· saw the face of Moses, "
35: 1 congregation of the children of I· "
4 congregation of the children of I·, "
20 children of I· departed from "
29 of I· brought a willing offering unto "
30 Moses said unto the children of I·, "
36: 3 of I· had brought for the service "
39: 6 the names of the children of I·. "
7 a memorial to the children of I·; "
14 to the names of the children of I·, "
32 children of I· did according to all "
42 children of I· made all the work. "
40:36 of I· went onward in all their "
38 in the sight of all the house of I·, "
Le 1: 2 Speak unto the children of I·, and "
4: 2 Speak unto the children of I·, "
13 congregation of I· sin through "
7:23, 29 Speak unto the children of I·, "
34 have I taken of the children of I· "
34 ever from among the children of I·. "
36 be given them of the children of I·. "
38 the children of I· to offer their "
9: 1 and his sons, and the elders of I·; "
3 the children of I· thou shalt speak, "
10: 6 brethren, the whole house of I·, "
11 that ye may teach the children of I· "
14 peace offerings of the children of I·. "
11: 2 Speak unto the children of I·, "
12: 2 Speak unto the children of I·, "
15: 2 Speak unto the children of I·, and "
31 shall ye separate the children of I· "
16: 5 of I· two kids of the goats for a sin "
16 uncleanness of the children of I·, "
17 and for all the congregation of I·. "
19 uncleanness of the children of I·. "
21 the iniquities of the children of I·, "
34 the children of I· for all their sins "
17: 2 unto all the children of I·, and say "
3 soever there be of the house of I·, "
5 of I· may bring their sacrifices, "
8, 10 man there be of the house of I· "
12 I said unto the children of I·, No "
13 man there be of the children of I·, "
14 I said unto the children of I·, Ye "
18: 2 Speak unto the children of I·, and "
19: 2 congregation of the children of I·, "
20: 2 shalt say to the children of I·, "
2 he be of the children of I·, or of the "
2 strangers that sojourn in I·, that "
21:24 and unto all the children of I·. "
22: 2 holy things of the children of I·, "
3 children of I· hallow unto the Lord, "
15 holy things of the children of I·, "
18 and unto all the children of I·, "
18 Whatsoever he be of the house of I·, "
18 the strangers in I·, that will offer "

Le 22: 32 hallowed among the children of I':3478
23: 2, 10 Speak unto the children of I', and "
24, 34 Speak unto the children of I', "
43 children of I' to dwell in booths, "
44 unto the children of I' the feasts of "
24: 2 Command the children of I', that "
8 being taken from the children of I': "
10 went out among the children of I': "
10 of I' strove together in the camp; 3481
15 speak unto the children of I', 3478
23 Moses spake to the children of I', "
23 of I' did as the Lord commanded "
25: 2 Speak unto the children of I', and "
33 possession among the children of I'. "
46 your brethren the children of I', "
55 me the children of I' are servants; "
26: 46 between him and the children of I' "
27: 2 Speak unto the children of I', and "
34 Moses for the children of I' in "
Nu 1: 2 congregation of the children of I', "
3 are able to go forth to war in I': "
16 fathers, heads of thousands in I'. "
44 the princes of I', being twelve men: "
45 numbered of the children of I', "
45 were able to go forth to war in I'; "
49 of them among the children of I': "
52 children of I' shall pitch their tents, "
53 congregation of the children of I': "
54 children of I' did according to all "
2: 2 children of I' shall pitch by his own "
32 were numbered of the children of I' "
33 numbered among the children of I'; "
34 children of I' did according to all "
3: 8 the charge of the children of I', to "
9 unto him out of the children of I'. "
12 from among the children of I' "
12 matrix among the children of I': "
13 unto me all the firstborn in I', "
38 for the charge of the children of I'; "
40 of the males of the children of I' "
41 firstborn among the children of I'; "
41 the cattle of the children of I'. "
42 firstborn among the children of I', "
45 firstborn among the children of I', "
46 the firstborn of the children of I', "
50 the firstborn of the children of I' "
4: 46 Aaron and the chief of I' numbered, "
5: 2 Command the children of I', that "
4 the children of I' did so, and put "
4 unto Moses, so did the children of I'. "
6 Speak unto the children of I', When "
9 holy things of the children of I', "
12 Speak unto the children of I', and "
6: 2 Speak unto the children of I', and "
23 ye shall bless the children of I', "
27 my name upon the children of I'; "
7: 2 That the princes of I', heads of the "
84 was anointed, by the princes of I': "
8: 6 from among the children of I', "
9 whole assembly of the children of I' "
10 children of I' shall put their hands "
11 for an offering of the children of I', "
14 from among the children of I': "
16 me from among the children of I'; "
16 firstborn of all the children of I', "
17 firstborn of the children of I' are "
18 the firstborn of the children of I'. "
19 sons from among the children of I', "
19 do the service of the children of I' "
19 atonement for the children of I': "
19 no plague among the children of I', "
19 the children of I' come nigh unto "
20 congregation of the children of I', "
20 so did the children of I' unto them. "
9: 2 children of I' also keep the passover "
4 Moses spake unto the children of I', "
5 Moses, so did the children of I'. "
7 season among the children of I'? "
10 Speak unto the children of I', "
17 that the children of I' journeyed: "
17 children of I' pitched their tents. "
18 Lord the children of I' journeyed, "
19 of I' kept the charge of the Lord, "
22 children of I' abode in their tents, "
10: 4 are heads of the thousands of I', "
12 children of I' took their journeys "
28 journeyings of the children of I' "
29 hath spoken good concerning I'. "
36 unto the many thousands of I'. "
11: 4 the children of I' also wept again, "
16 me seventy men of the elders of I', "
30 the camp, he and the elders of I'. "
13: 2 which I give unto the children of I': "
3 were heads of the children of I'. "
24 which the children of I' cut down "
26 congregation of the children of I', "
32 had searched unto the children of I', "
14: 2 of I' murmured against Moses and "
5 congregation of the children of I'. "
7 the company of the children of I', "
10 before all the children of I'. "
27 murmurings of the children of I', "
39 sayings unto all the children of I': "
15: 2, 18 Speak unto the children of I', "
25, 26 congregation of the children of I', "
29 is born among the children of I', "
32 of I' were in the wilderness, "
38 Speak unto the children of I', and "
16: 2 with certain of the children of I', "
9 the God of I' hath separated you "
9 you from the congregation of I', to "
25 and the elders of I' followed him. "
34 all I' that were round about them "
38 be a sign unto the children of I': "
40 memorial unto the children of I', "
41 children of I' murmured against "

Nu 17: 2 Speak unto the children of I', and 3478
5 murmurings of the children of I', "
6 Moses spake unto the children of I', "
9 Lord unto all the children of I': "
12 the children of I' spake unto Moses, "
18: 5 any more upon the children of I'. "
6 from among the children of I': "
8 hallowed things of the children of I'; "
11 wave offerings of the children of I': "
14 Every thing devoted in I' shall be "
19 which the children of I' offer unto "
20 inheritance among the children of I'. "
21 the tenth in I' for an inheritance, "
22 children of I' henceforth come nigh "
23 of I' they have no inheritance. "
24 But the tithes of the children of I', "
24 of I' they shall have no inheritance. "
26 take of the children of I' the tithes "
28 ye receive of the children of I'; "
32 the holy things of the children of I', "
19: 2 Speak unto the children of I', that "
9 congregation of the children of I' "
10 it shall be unto the children of I', "
13 that soul shall be cut off from I': "
20: 1 Then came the children of I', even "
12 me in the eyes of the children of I', "
13 children of I' strove with the Lord, "
14 Thus saith thy brother I', Thou "
19 the children of I' said unto him, "
21 Edom refused to give I' passage "
21 wherefore I' turned away from him. "
22 the children of I', even the whole "
24 I have given unto the children of I', "
29 thirty days, even all the house of I'. "
21: 1 I' came by the way of the spies; "
1 he fought against I', and took some "
2 And I' vowed a vow unto the Lord, "
3 Lord hearkened to the voice of I', "
6 people; and much people of I' died. "
10 the children of I' set forward, and "
17 I' sang this song, Spring up, O "
21 I' sent messengers unto Sihon "
23 suffer I' to pass through his border: "
23 out against I' into the wilderness: "
23 to Jahaz, and fought against I'. "
24 I' smote him with the edge of the "
25 And I' took all these cities: "
25 and I' dwelt in all the cities of the "
31 I' dwelt in the land of the Amorites. "
22: 1 the children of I' set forward, and "
2 that I' had done to the Amorites. "
3 because of the children of I'. "
23: 7 curse me Jacob, and come, defy I'. "
10 number of the fourth part of I'? "
21 hath he seen perverseness in I': "
23 is there any divination against I': "
23 it shall be said of Jacob and of I', "
24: 1 that it pleased the Lord to bless I', "
2 and he saw I' abiding in his tents "
5 O Jacob, and thy tabernacles, O I'! "
17 a Sceptre shall rise out of I', and "
18 enemies; and I' shall do valiantly. "
25: 1 And I' abode in Shittim, and the "
3 I' joined himself unto Baal-peor: "
3 of the Lord was kindled against I'. "
4 Lord may be turned away from I'. "
5 Moses said unto the judges of I', "
6 behold, one of the children of I' "
6 congregation of the children of I', "
8 after the man of I' into the tent, "
8 the man of I', and the woman "
8 was stayed from the children of I'. "
11 wrath away from the children of I', "
11 the children of I' in my jealousy. "
13 an atonement for the children of I'. "
26: 2 congregation of the children of I', "
2 all that are able to go to war in I'. "
4 Moses and the children of I', "
5 Reuben, the eldest son of I': the "
51 the numbered of the children of I', "
62 numbered among the children of I', "
62 them among the children of I'. "
63 the children of I' in the plains of "
64 the children of I' in the wilderness "
27: 8 shalt speak unto the children of I', "
11 children of I' a statute of judgment, "
12 I have given unto the children of I'. "
20 the children of I' may be obedient. "
21 and all the children of I' with him, "
28: 2 Command the children of I', and "
29: 40 of I' according to all that the Lord "
30: 1 tribes concerning the children of I', "
31: 2 children of I' of the Midianites: "
4 throughout all the tribes of I', shall "
5 delivered out of the thousands of I', "
9 children of I' took all the women "
12 congregation of the children of I', "
16 these caused the children of I', "
54 the children of I' before the Lord. "
32: 4 smote before the congregation of I', "
7 ye the heart of the children of I' "
9 the heart of the children of I', "
13 Lord's anger was kindled against I', "
14 fierce anger of the Lord toward I'. "
17 armed before the children of I', "
18 of I' have inherited every man his "
22 before the Lord, and before I': "
28 of the tribes of the children of I': "
33: 1 the journeys of the children of I', "
3 after the passover the children of I' "
5 of I' removed from Rameses, "
38 of I' were come out of the land of "
40 of the coming of the children of I'. "
51 Speak unto the children of I', and "
34: 2 Command the children of I', and, "
13 commanded the children of I', "

Nu 34: 29 children of I' in the land of Canaan. 3478
35: 2 Command the children of I', that "
8 the possession of the children of I': "
10 Speak unto the children of I', and "
15 both for the children of I', and for "
34 dwell among the children of I'. "
36: 1 chief fathers of the children of I': "
2 by lot to the children of I': "
3 other tribes of the children of I', "
4 jubile of the children of I' shall be, "
5 Moses commanded the children of I' "
7 of I' remove from tribe to tribe: "
7 Every one of the children of I' shall "
8 in any tribe of the children of I', "
8 of I' may enjoy every man the "
9 of I' shall keep himself to his own "
13 children of I' in the plains of Moab "
De 1: 1 words which Moses spake unto all I' "
3 Moses spake unto the children of I', "
38 for he shall cause I' to inherit it. "
2: 12 as I' did unto the land of his "
3: 18 your brethren the children of I', "
4: 1 Now therefore hearken, O I', unto "
44 Moses set before the children of I': "
45 Moses spake unto the children of I', "
46 Moses and the children of I' smote, "
5: 1 Moses called all I', and said unto "
1 Hear, O I', the statutes and "
6: 3 Hear therefore, O I', and observe "
4 Hear, O I': The Lord our God is "
9: 1 Hear, O I': Thou art to pass over "
10: 6 the children of I' took their journey "
12 I', what doth the Lord thy God "
11: 6 possession, in the midst of all I': "
13: 11 And all I' shall hear, and fear, and "
17: 4 such abomination is wrought in I': "
12 shalt put away the evil from I'. "
20 and his children, in the midst of I'. "
18: 1 no part nor inheritance with I': "
6 from any of thy gates out of all I', "
19: 13 guilt of innocent blood from I', "
20: 3 Hear, O I', ye approach this day "
21: 8 merciful, O Lord, unto thy people I', "
21 you; and all I' shall hear, and fear. "
22: 19 an evil name upon a virgin of I': "
21 she hath wrought folly in I', to play "
22 shalt thou put away evil from I'. "
23: 17 be no whore of the daughters of I', "
17 nor a sodomite of the sons of I'. "
24: 7 his brethren of the children of I', "
25: 6 that his name be not put out of I'. "
7 up unto his brother a name in I', "
10 his name shall be called in I', The "
26: 15 and bless thy people I', and the "
27: 1 elders of I' commanded the people, "
9 the Levites spake unto all I', "
9 Take heed, and hearken, O I'; this "
14 and say unto all the men of I' with "
29: 1 children of I' in the land of Moab, "
2 And Moses called unto all I', and "
10 officers, with all the men of I', "
21 unto evil out of all the tribes of I', "
31: 1 and spake these words unto all I'. "
7 said unto him in the sight of all I', "
9 Lord, and unto all the elders of I'. "
11 I' is come to appear before the Lord "
11 law before all I' in their hearing. "
19 and teach it the children of I': put "
19 for me against the children of I'. "
22 and taught it the children of I'. "
23 bring the children of I' into the land "
30 ears of all the congregation of I' "
32: 8 to the number of children of I'. "
45 speaking all these words to all I': "
49 the children of I' for a possession: "
51 against me among the children of I' "
51 in the midst of the children of I'. "
52 which I give the children of I'. "
33: 1 of God blessed the children of I' "
5 of the people and the tribes of I' "
10 thy judgments, and I' thy law, "
21 Lord, and his judgments with I'. "
28 I' then shall dwell in safety alone: "
29 Happy art thou, O I': who is like "
34: 8 of I' wept for Moses in the plains "
9 children of I' hearkened unto him, "
10 prophet since in I' like unto Moses, "
12 Moses shewed in the sight of all I'. "
Jos 1: 2 them, even to the children of I'. "
2: 2 of I' to search out the country. "
3: 1 Jordan, he and all the children of I', "
7 magnify thee in the sight of all I', "
9 Joshua said unto the children of I', "
12 twelve men out of the tribes of I', "
4: 4 had prepared of the children of I', "
5 of the tribes of the children of I': "
7 a memorial unto the children of I' "
8 of I' did so as Joshua commanded, "
8 of the tribes of the children of I', "
12 armed before the children of I', "
14 Joshua in the sight of all I'; "
21 he spake unto the children of I', "
22 I' came over this Jordan on dry "
5: 1 from before the children of I', "
1 more, because of the children of I'. "
2 circumcise again the children of I' "
3 and circumcised the children of I' "
6 children of I' walked forty years "
10 children of I' encamped in Gilgal, "
12 children of I' manna any more; "
6: 1 up because of the children of I': "
18 and make the camp of I' a curse, "
23 left them without the camp of I'. "
25 and she dwelleth in I' even unto "
7: 1 children of I' committed a trespass "
1 kindled against the children of I'. "

Jos 7: 6 he and the elders of I·, and put 3478
8 I say, when I· turneth their backs "
11 I· hath sinned, and they have also "
12 the children of I· could not stand "
13 for thus saith the Lord God of I·, "
13 thing in the midst of thee, O I·: "
15 because he hath wrought folly in I·. "
16 and brought I· by their tribes; "
19 thee, glory to the Lord God of I·, "
20 sinned against the Lord God of I·, "
23 and unto all the children of I·, "
24 And Joshua, and all I· with him, "
25 And all I· stoned him with stones, "
8: 10 and went up, he and the elders of I·, "
14 city went out against I· to battle, "
15 all I· made as if they were beaten "
17 Beth-el, that went not out after I·: "
17 the city open, and pursued after I·. "
21 I· saw that the ambush had taken "
22 so they were in the midst of I·, "
24 when I· had made an end of slaying "
27 and the spoil of that city I· took "
30 an altar unto the Lord God of I· "
31 Lord commanded the children of I·, "
32 the presence of the children of I·. "
33 all I·, and their elders, and officers, "
33 they should bless the people of I·. "
35 before all the congregation of I·, "
9: 2 to fight with Joshua, and with I·, "
6 said unto him, and to the men of I·, "
7 the men of I· said unto the Hivites, "
17 And the children of I· journeyed, "
18 the children of I· smote them not, "
18 unto them by the Lord God of I·. "
19 unto them by the Lord God of I·: "
26 out of the hand of the children of I·, "
10: 1 of Gibeon had made peace with I·, "
4 Joshua and with the children of I·. "
10 Lord discomfited them before I·, "
11 came to pass, as they fled before I·, "
11 children of I· slew with the sword. "
12 Amorites before the children of I·, "
12 he said in the sight of I·, Sun, stand "
14 a man: for the Lord fought for I·. "
15 returned, and all I· with him, "
20 of I· had made an end of slaying "
21 against any of the children of I·. "
24 Joshua called for all the men of I·, "
29 Makkedah, and all I· with him, "
30 king thereof, into the hand of I·; "
31 from Libnah, and all I· with him, "
32 Lachish into the hand of I·, "
34 unto Eglon, and all I· with him; "
36 up from Eglon, and all I· with him, "
38 returned, and all I· with him, to "
40 as the Lord God of I· commanded. "
42 the Lord God of I· fought for I·. "
43 returned, and all I· with him, unto "
11: 5 waters of Merom, to fight against I·. "
6 deliver them up all slain before I·: "
8 delivered them into the hand of I·, "
13 I· burned none of them, save Hazor "
14 the children of I· took for a prey "
16 mountain of I·, and the valley "
19 made peace with the children of I·, "
20 should come against I· in battle, "
21 and from all the mountains of I·: "
22 in the land of the children of I·: "
23 gave it for an inheritance unto I· "
12: 1 which the children of I· smote, and "
6 Lord and the children of I· smite: "
7 of I· smote on this side Jordan on "
7 unto the tribes of I· for a possession "
13: 6 out from before the children of I·: "
13 of I· expelled not the Geshurites, "
14 of the Lord God of I· made by fire "
22 the children of I· slay with sword "
33 God of I· was their inheritance, "
14: 1 which the children of I· inherited "
1 of the tribes of the children of I·, "
5 Moses, so the children of I· did, "
10 of I· wandered in the wilderness: "
14 wholly followed the Lord God of I·. "
17: 13 children of I· were waxen strong, "
18: 1 of I· assembled together at Shiloh, "
2 the children of I· seven tribes, "
3 Joshua said unto the children of I·, "
10 the land unto the children of I· "
19: 49 of I· gave an inheritance to Joshua "
51 of the tribes of the children of I·, "
20: 2 Speak to the children of I·, saying, "
9 appointed for all the children of I·, "
21: 1 of the tribes of the children of I·; "
3 children of I· gave unto the Levites "
8 of I· gave by lot unto the Levites "
41 the possession of the children of I· "
43 the Lord gave unto I· all the land "
45 had spoken unto the house of I·; "
22: 9 departed from the children of I· "
11 children of I· heard say, Behold, "
11 at the passage of the children of I·. "
12 when the children of I· heard of it, "
12 of I· gathered themselves together "
13 I· sent unto the children of Reuben, "
14 throughout all the tribes of I·; "
14 fathers among the thousands of I·. "
16 committed against the God of I·, "
18 with the whole congregation of I·. "
20 fell on all the congregation of I·? "
21 the heads of the thousands of I·, "
22 he knoweth, and I· he shall know; "
24 ye to do with the Lord God of I·? "
30 and heads of the thousands of I· "
31 ye have delivered the children of I· "
32 land of Canaan, to the children of I·, "
33 thing pleased the children of I·; "

Jos 22: 33 and the children of I· blessed God, 3478
23: 1 that the Lord had given rest unto I· "
2 And Joshua called for all I·, and "
24: 1 all the tribes of I· to Shechem, "
1 and called for the elders of I·, and "
2 Thus saith the Lord God of I·, "
9 Moab, arose and warred against I·, "
23 your heart unto the Lord God of I·. "
31 I· served the Lord all the days of "
31 the Lord, that he had done for I·. "
32 of I· brought up out of Egypt, "
J'g 1: 1 the children of I· asked the Lord, "
28 came to pass, when I· was strong, "
2: 4 words unto all the children of I·, "
6 children of I· went every man unto "
7 of the Lord, that he did for I·. "
10 works which he had done for I·. "
11 I· did evil in the sight of the Lord, "
14 of the Lord was hot against I·, "
20 of the Lord was hot against I·; "
22 That through them I may prove I·, "
3: 1 the Lord left, to prove I· by them, "
1 as many of I· as had not known †
2 of the children of I· might know, to 3478
4 And they were to prove I· by them, "
5 of I· dwelt among the Canaanites, "
7 I· did evil in the sight of the Lord, "
8 of the Lord was hot against I·, "
8 the children of I· served...eight "
9 children of I· cried unto the Lord, "
9 up a deliverer to the children of I·, "
10 came upon him, and he judged I·, "
12 I· did evil again in the sight of the "
12 Eglon the king of Moab against I·, "
13 Amalek, and went and smote I·, "
14 children of I· served Eglon the king "
15 children of I· cried unto the Lord, "
15 of I· sent a present unto Eglon the "
27 children of I· went down with him "
30 that day under the hand of I·. "
31 ox goad: and he also delivered I·. "
4: 1 I· again did evil in the sight of the "
3 children of I· cried unto the Lord: "
3 oppressed the children of I·. "
4 she judged I· at that time. "
5 of I· came up to her for judgment. "
6 not the Lord God of I· commanded, "
23 of Canaan before the children of I·. "
24 hand of the children of I· prospered, "
5: 2 ye the Lord for the avenging of I·, "
3 sing praise to the Lord God of I·. "
5 from before the Lord God of I·. "
7 villages ceased, they ceased in I·, "
7 arose, that I arose a mother in I·. "
8 seen among forty thousand in I·? "
9 heart is toward the governors of I·, "
11 the inhabitants of his villages in I·: "
6: 1 I· did evil in the sight of the Lord: "
2 of Midian prevailed against I·: "
2 children of I· made them the dens "
3 I· had sown, that the Midianites "
4 left no sustenance for I·, neither "
6 And I· was greatly impoverished "
6 children of I· cried unto the Lord. "
7 children of I· cried unto the Lord "
8 a prophet unto the children of I·, "
8 Thus saith the Lord God of I·, I "
14 shalt save I· from the hand of the "
15 Lord, wherewith shall I save I·? "
36 said unto God, If thou wilt save I· "
37 shall I know that thou wilt save I· "
7: 2 I· vaunt themselves against me, "
8 rest of I· every man unto his tent, "
14 the son of Joash, a man of I·: "
15 and returned into the host of I·, "
23 I· gathered themselves together "
8: 22 the men of I· said unto Gideon, "
27 I· went thither a whoring after it: "
28 subdued before the children of I·, "
33 the children of I· turned again, "
34 of I· remembered not the Lord "
35 which he had shewed unto I·. "
9: 22 had reigned three years over I·, "
55 of I· saw that Abimelech was dead, "
10: 1 there arose to defend I· Tola the "
2 And he judged I· twenty and three "
3 Jair, a Gileadite, and judged I· "
6 I· did evil again in the sight of the "
7 of the Lord was hot against I·, "
8 and oppressed the children of I·: "
8 of I· that were on the other side "
9 so that I· was sore distressed. "
10 children of I· cried unto the Lord, "
11 Lord said unto the children of I·, "
15 children of I· said unto the Lord, "
16 was grieved for the misery of I·. "
17 I· assembled themselves together, "
11: 4 of Ammon made war against I·. "
5 of Ammon made war against I·, "
13 Because I· took away my land, "
15 I· took not away the land of Moab, "
16 But when I· came up from Egypt, "
17 I· sent messengers unto the king "
17 consent: and I· abode in Kadesh. "
19 I· sent messengers unto Sihon "
19 I· said unto him, Let us pass, we "
20 But Sihon trusted not I· to pass "
20 in Jahaz, and fought against I·. "
21 Lord God of I· delivered Sihon and "
21 all his people into the hand of I·, "
21 so I· possessed all the land of the "
23 God of I· hath dispossessed the "
23 from before his people I·, and "
25 did he ever strive against I·, or did "
26 While I· dwelt in Heshbon and her "
27 between the children of I· and the "

J'g 11: 33 subdued before the children of I·. 3478
39 no man. And it was a custom in I·, "
40 the daughters of I· went yearly to "
12: 7 And Jephthah judged I· six years. "
8 him Ibzan of Beth-lehem judged I·. "
9 And he judged I· seven years. "
11 him Elon, a Zebulonite, judged I·; "
11 and he judged I· ten years. "
13 of Hillel, a Pirathonite, judged I·. "
14 colts: and he judged I· eight years. "
13: 1 I· did evil again in the sight of the "
5 I· out of the hand of the Philistines. "
14: 4 Philistines had dominion over I·. "
15: 20 he judged I· in the days of the "
16: 31 And he judged I· twenty years. "
17: 6 those days there was no king in I·, "
18: 1 those days there was no king in I·: "
1 unto them among the tribes of I·. "
19 unto a tribe and a family in I·? "
29 their father, who was born unto I·: "
19: 1 days, when there was no king in I·, "
12 that is not of the children of I·; "
29 and sent her into all the coasts of I·. "
30 I· came up out of the land of Egypt "
20: 1 Then all the children of I· went out, "
2 even of all the tribes of I·, presented "
3 heard that the children of I· were "
3 Then said the children of I·, Tell "
6 country of the inheritance of I·: "
6 committed lewdness and folly in I·. "
7 Behold, ye are all children of I·; "
10 throughout all the tribes of I·, "
10 folly that they have wrought in I·. "
11 all the men of I· were gathered "
12 tribes of I· sent men through all "
13 death, and put away evil from I·. "
13 of their brethren the children of I·: "
14 to battle against the children of I·. "
17 men of I·, beside Benjamin, were "
18 And the children of I· arose, and "
19 children of I· rose up in the morning, "
20 the men of I· went out to battle "
20 I· put themselves in array to fight "
22 men of I· encouraged themselves, "
23 children of I· went up and wept "
24 children of I· came near against "
25 I· again eighteen thousand men; "
26 Then all the children of I·, and all "
27 children of I· enquired of the Lord, "
29 I· set liers in wait round about "
30 I· went up against the children of "
31 in the field, about thirty men of I·. "
32 the children of I· said, Let us flee, "
33 men of I· rose up out of their place, "
33 liers in wait of I· came forth out of "
34 thousand chosen men out of all I·, "
35 Lord smote Benjamin before I·: "
35 of I· destroyed of the Benjamites "
36 of I· gave place to the Benjamites, "
38 sign between the men of I· and the "
39 the men of I· retired in the battle, "
39 the men of I· about thirty persons: "
41 when the men of I· turned again, "
42 their backs before the men of I· "
48 I· turned again upon the children "
21: 1 men of I· had sworn in Mizpeh, "
3 And said, O Lord God of I·, why is "
3 why is this come to pass in I·, that "
3 be to day one tribe lacking in I·? "
5 And the children of I· said, Who is "
5 all the tribes of I· that came not up "
6 of I· repented them for Benjamin "
6 one tribe cut off from I· this day. "
8 of I· that came not up to Mizpeh to "
15 made a breach in the tribes of I·. "
17 a tribe be not destroyed out of I·. "
18 for the children of I· had sworn, "
24 the children of I· departed thence "
25 those days there was no king in I·: "
Ru 2: 12 be given thee of the Lord God of I·, "
4: 7 the manner in former time in I· "
7 and this was a testimony in I·. "
11 which two did build the house of I·: "
14 that his name may be famous in I·. "
1Sa 1: 17 God of I· grant thee thy petition "
2: 22 all that his sons did unto all I·; "
28 choose him out of all the tribes of I· "
28 made by fire of the children of I·? "
29 all the offerings of I· my people? "
30 Wherefore the Lord God of I· saith, "
32 the wealth which God shall give I·: "
3: 11 Behold, I will do a thing in I·, at "
20 all I· from Dan even to Beer-sheba "
4: 1 the word of Samuel came to all I·. "
1 I· went out against the Philistines "
2 put themselves in array against I·: "
2 I· was smitten before the "
3 I· said, Wherefore hath the Lord "
5 all I· shouted with a great shout, "
10 fought, and I· was smitten, and they "
10 fell of I· thirty thousand footmen. "
17 I· is fled before the Philistines, "
18 And he had judged I· forty years. "
21, 22 The glory is departed from I·: "
5: 7 ark of the God of I· shall not abide "
8 do with the ark of the God of I·? "
8 the ark of the God of I· be carried "
8 they carried the ark of the God of I· "
10 about the ark of the God of I· to us, "
11 Send away the ark of the God of I·, "
6: 3 send away the ark of the God of I·, "
5 shall give glory unto the God of I·: "
7: 2 house of I· lamented after the Lord. "
3 spake unto all the house of I·, "
4 of I· did put away Baalim and "
5 Gather all I· to Mizpeh, and I will "

1Sa 7: 6 judged the children of I' in Mizpeh. 3478
7 of I' were gathered together to "
7 the Philistines went up against I'. "
7 when the children of I' heard it, "
8 the children of I' said to Samuel, "
9 Samuel cried unto the Lord for I'; "
10 drew near to battle against I': "
10 and they were smitten before I'. "
11 the men of I' went out of Mizpeh, "
13 came no more into the coast of I': "
14 taken from I' were restored to I', "
14 I' deliver out of the hands of the "
14 peace between I' and the Amorites. "
15 judged I' all the days of his life. "
16 and judged I' in all those places. "
17 and there he judged I'; and there "
8: 1 he made his sons judges over I'. "
4 elders of I' gathered themselves "
22 Samuel said unto the men of I', "
9: 2 of I' a goodlier person than he: "
9 Beforetime in I', when a man went "
16 to be captain over my people I', "
20 on whom is all the desire of I'? Is "
21 the smallest of the tribes of I'? "
10: 18 And said unto the children of I', "
18 Thus saith the Lord God of I', "
18 I brought up I' out of Egypt, and "
20 all the tribes of I' to come near, "
11: 2 lay it for a reproach upon all I'. "
3 messengers unto all the coasts of I': "
7 them throughout all the coasts of I' "
8 of I' were three hundred thousand, "
13 Lord hath wrought salvation in I'. "
15 all the men of I' rejoiced greatly. "
12: 1 And Samuel said unto all I', "
13: 1 he had reigned two years over I', "
2 chose...three thousand men of I'; "
4 I' heard say that Saul had smitten "
4 that I' also was had in abomination "
5 themselves together to fight with I', "
6 of I' saw that they were in a strait, "
13 thy kingdom upon I' for ever. "
19 found throughout all the land of I': "
14: 12 delivered them into the hand of I'. "
18 at that time with the children of I'. "
22 men of I' which had hid themselves "
23 So the Lord saved I' that day: and "
24 men of I' were distressed that day: "
37 deliver them into the hand of I'? "
39 as the Lord liveth, which saveth I', "
40 Then said he unto all I', Be ye on "
41 Saul said unto the Lord God of I', "
45 wrought this great salvation in I'? "
47 So Saul took the kingdom over I', "
48 and delivered I' out of the hands of "
15: 1 to be king over his people, over I': "
2 that which Amalek did to I', how "
6 kindness to all the children of I', "
17 not made the head of the tribes of I', "
17 the Lord anointed thee king over I'? "
26 thee from being king over I'. "
28 rent the kingdom of I' from thee "
29 Strength of I' will not lie nor repent: "
30 elders of my people, and before I', "
35 that he had made Saul king over I'. "
16: 1 rejected him from reigning over I'? "
17: 2 men of I' were gathered together, "
3 I' stood on a mountain on the other "
8 and cried unto the armies of I', "
10 I defy the armies of I' this day; "
11 Saul and all I' heard those words "
19 and they, and all the men of I', "
21 I' and the Philistines had put the "
24 all the men of I', when they saw "
25 men of I' said, Have ye seen this "
25 surely to defy I' is he come up: "
25 make his father's house free in I'. "
26 taketh away the reproach from I'? "
45 hosts, the God of the armies of I', "
46 may know that there is a God in I'. "
52 the men of I' and of Judah arose, "
53 of I' returned from chasing after "
18: 6 women came out of all cities of I', "
16 But all I' and Judah loved David, "
18 my life, or my father's family in I', "
19: 5 wrought a great salvation for all I': "
20: 12 said unto David, O Lord God of I', "
23: 10 Then said David, O Lord God of I', "
11 O Lord God of I', I beseech thee, "
17 and thou shalt be king over I', and "
24: 2 thousand chosen men out of all I', "
14 whom is the king of I' come out? "
20 kingdom of I' shall be established "
25: 30 have appointed thee ruler over I'; "
32 Blessed be the Lord God of I', "
34 deed, as the Lord God of I' liveth, "
26: 2 three thousand chosen men of I' "
15 man? and who is like to thee in I'? "
20 king of I' is come out to seek a flea, "
27: 1 me any more in any coast of I': "
12 his people I' utterly to abhor him; "
28: 1 for warfare, to fight with I'. "
3 dead, and all I' had lamented him, "
4 Saul gathered all I' together, and "
19 the Lord will also deliver I' with "
19 Lord also shall deliver the host of I' "
29: 3 the servant of Saul the king of I', "
30: 25 a statute and an ordinance for I' "
31: 1 the Philistines fought against I': "
1 I' fled from before the Philistines, "
7 of I' that were on the other side "
7 Jordan, saw that the men of I' fled, "
2Sa 1: 3 Out of the camp of I' am I escaped. "
12 the Lord, and for the house of I'; "
19 beauty of I' is slain upon thy high "
24 Ye daughters of I', weep over Saul, "

2Sa 2: 9 and over Benjamin, and over all I'. 3478
10 old when he began to reign over I', "
17 Abner was beaten, and the men of I', "
28 still, and pursued after I' no more, "
3: 10 set up the throne of David over I' "
12 to bring about all I' unto thee. "
17 communication with the elders of I', "
18 I will save my people I' out of the "
19 Hebron all that seemed good to I', "
21 gather all I' unto my lord the king, "
37 all the people and all I' understood "
38 a great man fallen this day in I'? "
5: 1 came all the tribes of I' to David "
2 leddest out and broughtest in I': "
2 thee, Thou shalt feed my people I', "
2 and thou shalt be a captain over I'. "
3 elders of I' came to the king to "
3 they anointed David king over I'. "
5 thirty and three years over all I' "
12 had established him king over I', "
17 had anointed David king over I', "
6: 1 together all the chosen men of I', "
5 house of I' played before the Lord "
15 the house of I' brought up the ark "
19 among the whole multitude of I', "
20 glorious was the king of I' to day, "
21 over the people of the Lord, over I': "
7: 6 up the children of I' out of Egypt, "
7 walked with all the children of I' "
7 a word with any of the tribes of I', "
7 I commanded to feed my people I', "
8 to be ruler over my people, over I': "
10 appoint a place for my people I', "
11 judges to be over my people I', "
23 is like thy people, even like I', "
24 confirmed to thyself thy people I' "
26 Lord of hosts is the God over I': "
27 For thou, O Lord of hosts, God of I', "
8: 15 And David reigned over all I'; and "
10: 9 he chose of all the choice men of I', "
15 that they were smitten before I', "
17 he gathered all I' together, and "
18 And the Syrians fled before I'; and "
19 that they were smitten before I', "
19 they made peace with I', and served "
11: 1 his servants with him, and all I'; "
11 The ark, and I', and Judah, abide "
12: 7 Thus saith the Lord God of I', "
7 I anointed thee king over I', and "
8 thee the house of I' and of Judah; "
12 I will do this thing before all I', "
13: 12 such thing ought to be done in I': "
13 shalt be as one of the fools in I'. "
14: 25 in all I' there was none to be so "
15: 2 servant is of one of the tribes of I'. "
6 this manner did Absalom to all I' "
6 stole the hearts of the men of I'. "
10 spies throughout all the tribes of I', "
13 hearts of the men of I' are after "
16: 3 house of I' restore me the kingdom "
15 and all the people the men of I', "
18 this people, and all the men of I', "
21 I' shall hear that thou art abhorred "
22 concubines in the sight of all I'. "
17: 4 well, and all the elders of I'. "
10 all I' knoweth that thy father is a "
11 that all I' be generally gathered "
13 shall all I' bring ropes to that city, "
14 Absalom and all the men of I' said, "
15 Absalom and the elders of I'; "
24 he and all the men of I' with him. "
26 I' and Absalom pitched in the land "
18: 6 went out into the field against I': "
7 the people of I' were slain before "
16 returned from pursuing after I': "
17 all I' fled every one to his tent. "
19: 8 I' had fled every man to his tent. "
9 strife throughout all the tribes of I', "
11 speech of all I' is come to the king, "
22 man be put to death this day in I'? "
22 that I am this day king over I'? "
40 king, and also half the people of I'. "
41 all the men of I' came to the king, "
42 of Judah answered the men of I', "
43 the men of I' answered the men of "
43 than the words of the men of I'. "
20: 1 Jesse: every man to his tents, O I'. "
2 man of I' went up from after David, "
14 he went through all the tribes of I' "
19 are peaceable and faithful in I': "
19 destroy a city and a mother in I': "
23 Joab was over all the host of I': "
21: 2 were not of the children of I', but "
2 and the children of I' had sworn "
2 zeal to the children of I' and Judah. "
4 for us shalt thou kill any man in I'. "
5 remaining in any of the coasts of I', "
15 had yet war again with I'; "
17 that thou quench not the light of I'. "
21 when he defied I', Jonathan the "
23: 1 Jacob, and the sweet psalmist of I', "
3 God of I' said, the Rock of I' spake "
9 and the men of I' were gone away: "
24: 1 of the Lord was kindled against I', "
1 to say, Go, number I' and Judah. "
2 Go now through all the tribes of I', "
4 king, to number the people of I'. "
9 were in I' eight hundred thousand "
15 the Lord sent a pestilence upon I' "
25 the plague was stayed from I'. "
1Ki 1: 3 throughout all the coast of I', "
20 the eyes of all I' are upon thee, "
30 unto thee by the Lord God of I', "
34 anoint him there king over I': "
35 appointed him to be ruler over I' "
48 Blessed be the Lord God of I', "

1Ki 2: 4 (said he) a man on the throne of I'. 3478
5 the two captains of the hosts of I', "
11 David reigned over I' were forty "
15 that all I' set their faces on me, "
32 son of Ner, captain of the host of I', "
3: 28 I' heard of the judgment which the "
4: 1 king Solomon was king over all I'. "
7 had twelve officers over all I', "
20 Judah and I' were many, as the "
25 Judah and I' dwelt safely, every "
5: 13 Solomon raised a levy out of all I'; "
6: 1 of I' were come out of the land of "
1 year of Solomon's reign over I', "
13 will dwell among the children of I', "
13 and will not forsake my people I'. "
8: 1 Solomon assembled the elders of I', "
1 the fathers of the children of I', "
2 men of I' assembled themselves "
3 all the elders of I' came, and all the "
5 and all the congregation of I', that "
9 a covenant with the children of I', "
14 blessed all the congregation of I': "
14 all the congregation of I' stood; "
15 Blessed be the Lord God of I', "
16 forth my people I' out of Egypt, "
16 no city out of all the tribes of I' "
16 chose David to be over my people I'. "
17 for the name of the Lord God of I'. "
20 father, and sit on the throne of I', "
20 for the name of the Lord God of I'. "
22 of all the congregation of I', "
23 Lord God of I', there is no God like "
25 Lord God of I', Keep with thy "
25 my sight to sit on the throne of I'; "
26 O God of I', let thy word, I pray "
30 of thy people I', when they shall "
33 people I' be smitten down before "
34 forgive the sin of thy people I', "
36 thy servants, and of thy people I', "
38 any man, or by all thy people I', "
41 stranger, that is not of thy people I', "
43 to fear thee, as do thy people I'; "
52 the supplication of thy people I', "
55 congregation of I' with a loud voice, "
56 hath given rest unto his people I', "
59 cause of his people I' at all times, "
62 And the king, and all I' with him, "
63 I' dedicated the house of the Lord. "
65 held a feast, and all I' with him, "
66 his servant, and for I' his people. "
9: 5 the throne of thy kingdom upon I' "
5 thee a man upon the throne of I'. "
7 I cut off I' out of the land which I "
7 I' shall be a proverb and a byword "
20 which were not of the children of I', "
21 of I' also were not able utterly to "
22 I' did Solomon make no bondmen: "
10: 9 thee, to set thee on the throne of I': "
9 the Lord loved I' forever, therefore "
11: 2 Lord said unto the children of I', "
9 turned from the Lord God of I', "
16 did Joab remain there with all I', "
25 And he was an adversary to I' all "
25 and he abhorred I', and reigned "
31 thus saith the Lord, the God of I', "
32 chosen out of all the tribes of I': "
37 desireth, and shalt be king over I'. "
38 David, and will give I' unto thee. "
42 reigned in Jerusalem over all I' "
12: 1 I' were come to Shechem to make "
3 and all the congregation of I' came, "
16 I' saw that the king hearkened not "
16 to your tents, O I': now see to "
16 So I' departed unto their tents. "
17 children of I' which dwelt in the "
18 all I' stoned him with stones, that "
19 So I' rebelled against the house of "
20 I' heard that Jeroboam was come "
20 and made him king over all I': "
21 to fight against the house of I', "
24 your brethren the children of I': "
28 thy gods, O I', which brought thee "
33 a feast unto the children of I': "
14: 7 thus saith the Lord God of I', "
7 made thee prince over my people I', "
10 him that is shut up and left in I', "
13 I' shall mourn for him, and bury "
13 God of I' in the house of Jeroboam. "
14 shall raise him up a king over I', "
15 the Lord shall smite I', as a reed "
15 he shall root up I' out of this good "
16 give I' up because of the sin of "
16 did sin, and who made I' to sin. "
18 him; and all I' mourned for him, "
19 of the chronicles of the kings of I'. "
21 did choose out of all the tribes of I', "
24 cast out before the children of I'. "
15: 9 year of Jeroboam king of I' reigned "
16 between Asa and Baasha king of I' "
17 king of I' went up against Judah, "
19 thy league with Baasha king of I', "
20 which he had against the cities of I', "
25 Jeroboam began to reign over I' "
25 and reigned over I' two years. "
26 sin wherewith he made I' to sin. "
27 and all I' laid siege to Gibbethon. "
30 and which he made I' sin, by his "
30 provoked the Lord God of I' to "
31 the chronicles of the kings of I'? "
32 Baasha king of I' all their days. "
33 to reign over all I' in Tirzah, "
34 sin wherewith he made I' to sin. "
16: 2 made thee prince over my people I'; "
2 hast made my people I' to sin, to "
5 of the chronicles of the kings of I'? "
8 Baasha to reign over I' in Tirzah, "

1Ki 16:13 by which they made I' to sin, in 3478
13 Lord God of I' to anger with their "
14 of the chronicles of the kings of I'? "
16 wherefore all I' made Omri, the "
16 king over I' that day in the camp. "
17 from Gibbethon, and all I' with him, "
19 which he did, to make I' to sin. "
20 of the chronicles of the kings of I'? "
21 people of I' divided into two parts: "
23 began Omri to reign over I', twelve "
26 his sin wherewith he made I' to sin, "
26 Lord God of I' to anger with their "
27 of the chronicles of the kings of I'? "
29 the son of Omri to reign over I': "
29 Omri reigned over I' in Samaria "
33 provoke the Lord God of I' to anger "
33 kings of I' that were before him. "
17: 1 As the Lord God of I' liveth, before "
14 thus saith the Lord God of I', The "
18:17 him, Art thou he that troubleth I'? "
18 answered, I have not troubled I'; "
19 to me all I' unto mount Carmel, "
20 sent unto all the children of I', "
31 came, saying, I' shall be thy name: "
36 God of Abraham, Isaac, and of I', "
36 this day that thou art God in I', "
19:10, 14 of I' have forsaken thy covenant, "
16 thou anoint to be king over I': "
18 have left me seven thousand in I', "
20: 2 messengers to Ahab king of I' "
4 the king of I' answered and said, "
7 the king of I' called all the elders "
11 the king of I' answered and said, "
13 a prophet unto Ahab, king of I', "
15 even all the children of I', being "
20 Syrians fled; and I' pursued them: "
21 the king of I' went out, and smote "
22 the prophet came to the king of I', "
26 up to Aphek, to fight against I'. "
27 the children of I' were numbered, "
27 of I' pitched before them like two "
28 spake unto the king of I', and "
29 children of I' slew of the Syrians "
31 that the kings of the house of I' "
31 heads, and go out to the king of I': "
32 came to the king of I', and said, "
40 the king of I' said unto him, So "
41 king of I' discerned him that he "
43 king of I' went to his house heavy "
21: 7 thou now govern the kingdom of I'? "
18 go down to meet Ahab king of I', "
21 him that is shut up and left in I', "
22 me to anger, and made I' to sin. "
26 cast out before the children of I'. "
22: 1 without war between Syria and I'. "
2 Judah came down to the king of I'. "
3 king of I' said unto his servants, "
4 Jehoshaphat said to the king of I'. "
5 said unto the king of I', Enquire, "
6 king of I' gathered the prophets "
8 king of I' said unto Jehoshaphat, "
9 king of I' called an officer, and "
10 king of I' and Jehoshaphat the "
17 saw all I' scattered upon the hills, "
18 king of I' said unto Jehoshaphat, "
26 the king of I' said, Take Micaiah, "
29 king of I' and Jehoshaphat the "
30 king of I' said unto Jehoshaphat, "
30 the king of I' disguised himself, "
31 great, save only with the king of I'. "
32 they said, Surely it is the king of I'. "
33 that it was not the king of I', "
34 smote the king of I' between the "
39 of the chronicles of the kings of I'? "
41 the fourth year of Ahab king of I'. "
44 made peace with the king of I'. "
51 son of Ahab began to reign over I' "
51 and reigned two years over I'. "
52 son of Nebat, who made I' to sin: "
53 to anger the Lord God of I', "
2Ki 1: 1 Moab rebelled against I' after the "
3, 6 because there is not a God in I', "
16 not because there is no God in I' to "
18 of the chronicles of the kings of I'? "
2:12 the chariot of I', and the horsemen "
3: 1 son of Ahab began to reign over I' "
3 son of Nebat, which made I' to sin; "
4 of I' an hundred thousand lambs, "
5 Moab rebelled against the king of I'. "
6 the same time, and numbered all I'. "
9 So the king of I' went, and the king "
10 king of I' said, Alas! that the Lord "
12 king of I' and Jehoshaphat and the "
13 And Elisha said unto the king of I', "
13 the king of I' said unto him, Nay: "
24 when they came to the camp of I', "
27 was great indignation against I': "
5: 2 out of the land of I' a little maid; "
4 the maid that is of the land of I'. "
5 send a letter unto the king of I'. "
6 the letter unto the king of I', "
7 the king of I' had read the letter, "
8 the king of I' had rent his clothes, "
8 know that there is a prophet in I'. "
12 better than all the waters of I'? "
15 no God in all the earth, but in I': "
6: 8 king of Syria warred against I', "
9 man of God sent unto the king of I', "
10 king of I' sent to the place which "
11 which of us is for the king of I'? "
12 Elisha, the prophet that is in I', "
12 telleth the king of I' the words that "
21 king of I' said unto Elisha, when "
23 came no more into the land of I'. "
26 king of I' was passing by upon the "
7: 6 king of I' hath hired against us "

2Ki 7:13 they are as all the multitude of I' 3478
8:12 thou wilt do unto the children of I': "
16 fifth year of Joram the...king of I', "
18 walked in the way of the kings of I', "
25 twelfth year of Joram...king of I' "
26 the daughter of Omri king of I'. "
9: 3 I have anointed thee king over I'. "
6 Thus saith the Lord God of I', "
6 the people of the Lord, even over I'. "
8 him that is shut up and left in I'. "
12 I have anointed thee king over I'. "
14 he and all I', because of Hazael "
21 Joram king of I' and Ahaziah king "
10:21 And Jehu sent through all I': and "
28 Thus Jehu destroyed Baal out of I'. "
29 son of Nebat, who made I' to sin, "
30 shall sit on the throne of I'. "
31 walk in the law of the Lord God of I' "
31 of Jeroboam, which made I' to sin. "
32 the Lord began to cut I' short: "
32 smote them in all the coasts of I'; "
34 of the chronicles of the kings of I'? "
36 Jehu reigned over I' in Samaria "
13: 1 son of Jehu began to reign over I' "
2 son of Nebat, which made I' to sin; "
3 of the Lord was kindled against I', "
4 for he saw the oppression of I', "
5 And the Lord gave I' a saviour, so "
5 children of I' dwelt in their tents, "
6 of Jeroboam, who made I' sin, "
8 of the chronicles of the kings of I'? "
10 to reign over I' in Samaria, and "
11 the son of Nebat, who made I' sin: "
12 of the chronicles of the kings of I'? "
13 in Samaria with the kings of I'. "
14 the king of I' came down unto him, "
14 the chariot of I', and the horsemen "
16 And he said to the king of I', Put "
18 he said unto the king of I', Smite "
22 Hazael king of Syria oppressed I' "
25 him, and recovered the cities of I'. "
14: 1 second year of Joash...king of I' "
8 messengers to Joash,...king of I', "
9 the king of I' sent to Amaziah "
11 Jehoash king of I' went up; "
12 was put to the worse before I'; "
13 Jehoash king of I' took Amaziah "
15 of the chronicles of the kings of I'? "
16 in Samaria with the kings of I'; "
17 Jehoahaz king of I' fifteen years. "
23 of Joash king of I' began to reign "
24 son of Nebat, who made I' to sin. "
25 He restored the coast of I' from "
25 to the word of the Lord God of I', "
26 For the Lord saw the affliction of I', "
26 nor any left, nor any helper for I'. "
27 he would blot out the name of I' "
28 which belonged to Judah, for I', "
28 of the chronicles of the kings of I'? "
29 fathers, even with the kings of I'; "
15: 1 year of Jeroboam king of I' began "
8 the son of Jeroboam reigned over I' "
9 son of Nebat, who made I' to sin. "
11 of the chronicles of the kings of I'. "
12 Thy sons shall sit on the throne of I' "
15 of the chronicles of the kings of I'. "
17 the son of Gadi to reign over I', "
18 son of Nebat, who made I' to sin. "
20 Menahem exacted the money of I', "
21 of the chronicles of the kings of I'? "
23 of Menahem began to reign over I' "
24 son of Nebat, who made I' to sin. "
26 of the chronicles of the kings of I'. "
27 of Remaliah began to reign over I' "
28 son of Nebat, who made I' to sin. "
29 In the days of Pekah king of I' "
31 of the chronicles of the kings of I'. "
32 Pekah the son of Remaliah king of I' "
16: 3 walked in the way of the kings of I', "
3 out from before the children of I'. "
5 Pekah son of Remaliah king of I' "
7 out of the hand of the king of I', "
17: 1 of Elah to reign in Samaria over I' "
2 kings of I' that were before him. "
6 and carried I' away into Assyria, "
7 of I' had sinned against the Lord "
8 out from before the children of I', "
8 and of the kings of I', which they "
9 children of I' did secretly those "
13 Yet the Lord testified against I', "
18 the Lord was very angry with I', "
19 walked in the statutes of I' which "
20 the Lord rejected all the seed of I', "
21 he rent I' from the house of David; "
21 Jeroboam drave I' from following "
22 I' walked in all the sins of Jeroboam "
23 Lord removed I' out of his sight, "
23 was I' carried away out of their own "
24 instead of the children of I': "
34 of Jacob, whom he named I'; "
18: 1 of Hoshea son of Elah king of I', "
4 of I' did burn incense to it: "
5 He trusted in the Lord God of I'; "
9 of Hoshea son of Elah king of I', "
10 ninth year of Hoshea king of I', "
11 king of Assyria did carry away I' "
19:15 O Lord God of I', which dwellest "
20 Thus saith the Lord God of I', "
22 even against the Holy One of I'. "
21: 2 cast out before the children of I'. "
3 a grove, as did Ahab king of I'; "
7 have chosen out of all tribes of I', "
8 make the feet of I' move any more "
9 destroyed before the children of I'. "
12 thus saith the Lord God of I', "
22:15, 18 Thus saith the Lord God of I', "

2Ki 23:13 Solomon the king of I' had builded 3478
15 son of Nebat, who made I' to sin, "
19 kings of I' had made to provoke the "
22 days of the judges that judged I', "
22 nor in all the days of the kings of I', "
27 of my sight, as I have removed I', "
24:13 gold which Solomon king of I' had "
1Ch 1:34 The sons of Isaac; Esau and I'. "
43 reigned over the children of I'; "
2: 1 These are the sons of I'; Reuben, "
7 Achar, the troubler of I', who "
4:10 Jabez called on the God of I', "
5: 1 sons of Reuben the firstborn of I', "
1 the sons of Joseph the son of I': "
3 of Reuben the firstborn of I' were, "
17 the days of Jeroboam king of I'. "
26 the God of I' stirred up the spirit "
6:38 the son of Levi, the son of I'. "
49 and to make an atonement for I', "
64 I' gave to the Levites these cities "
7:29 the children of Joseph the son of I'. "
9: 1 I' were reckoned by genealogies; "
1 book of the kings of I' and Judah, "
10: 1 the Philistines fought against I'; "
1 men of I' fled from before the "
7 men of I' that were in the valley "
11: 1 all I' gathered themselves to David "
2 leddest out and broughtest in I': "
2 Thou shalt feed my people I', and "
2 shalt be ruler over my people I'. "
3 came all the elders of I' to the king "
3 they anointed David king over I', "
4 David and all I' went to Jerusalem, "
10 and with all I', to make him king, "
10 the word of the Lord concerning I'. "
12:32 to know what I' ought to do; "
38 to make David king over all I': "
38 all the rest of I' were of one heart "
40 for there was joy in I'. "
13: 2 unto all the congregation of I', "
2 that are left in all the land of I', "
5 So David gathered all I' together, "
6 And David went up, and all I', to "
8 David and all I' played before God "
14: 2 had confirmed him king over I', "
2 on high, because of his people I'. "
8 David was anointed king over all I', "
15: 3 David gathered all I' together to "
12 up the ark of the Lord God of I' "
14 up the ark of the Lord God of I'. "
25 the elders of I', and the captains "
28 Thus all I' brought up the ark of "
16: 3 And he dealt to every one of I', "
4 thank and praise the Lord God of I': "
13 O ye seed of I' his servant, ye "
17 to I' for an everlasting covenant, "
36 Blessed be the Lord God of I' for "
40 the Lord, which he commanded I'; "
17: 5 since the day that I brought up I' "
6 I have walked with all I', spake I "
6 a word to any of the judges of I', "
7 be ruler over my people I': "
9 will ordain a place for my people I', "
10 judges to be over my people I'. "
21 in the earth is like thy people I', "
22 thy people I' didst thou make thine "
24 is the God of I', even a God to I': "
18:14 So David reigned over all I', and "
19:10 he chose out of all the choice of I', "
16 were put to the worse before I', "
17 he gathered all I', and passed over "
18 But the Syrians fled before I'; and "
19 were put to the worse before I', "
20: 7 But when he defied I', Jonathan "
21: 1 And Satan stood up against I', "
1 and provoked David to number I'. "
2 number I' from Beer-sheba even to "
3 will he be a cause of trespass to I'? "
4 and went throughout all I', and "
5 And all they of I' were a thousand "
7 this thing; therefore he smote I'. "
12 throughout all the coasts of I'. "
14 the Lord sent pestilence upon I': "
14 fell of I' seventy thousand men. "
16 Then David and the elders of I', *
22: 1 altar of the burnt offering for I'. 3478
2 the strangers...in the land of I'; "
6 an house for the Lord God of I'. "
9 give peace and quietness unto I' "
10 the throne of his kingdom over I' "
12 give thee charge concerning I', "
13 charged Moses with concerning I': "
17 commanded all the princes of I' to "
23: 1 made Solomon his son king over I'. "
2 together all the princes of I', "
25 Lord God of I' hath given rest unto "
24:19 Lord God of I' had commanded "
26:29 for the outward business over I', "
30 were officers among them of I' on "
27: 1 children of I' after their number, "
16 Furthermore over the tribes of I': "
22 were the princes of the tribes of I'. "
23 would increase I' like to the stars "
24 there fell wrath for it against I'; "
28: 1 assembled all the princes of I', "
4 Lord God of I' chose me before all "
4 of my father to be king over I' "
4 me to make me king over all I': "
5 of the kingdom of the Lord over I'. "
8 sight of all I' the congregation of "
29: 6 and princes of the tribes of I', "
10 thou, Lord God of I' our father, "
18 God of Abraham, Isaac, and of I', "
21 sacrifices in abundance for all I': "
23 prospered; and all I' obeyed him. "
25 exceedingly in the sight of all I', "

1Ch 29:25 been on any king before him in I'. 3478
26 the son of Jesse reigned over all I'. "
27 the time that he reigned over I' was "
30 that went over him, and over I', "
2Ch 1: 2 Then Solomon spake unto all I', "
2 and to every governor in all I', "
13 congregation, and reigned over I'. "
2: 4 This is an ordinance for ever to I'. "
12 Blessed be the Lord God of I', that "
17 all the strangers...in the land of I', "
5: 2 Solomon assembled the elders of I', "
2 of the fathers of the children of I', "
3 men of I' assembled themselves "
4 And all the elders of I' came; and "
6 all the congregation of I' that were "
10 a covenant with the children of I', "
6: 3 the whole congregation of I': "
3 all the congregation of I' stood. "
4 Blessed be the Lord God of I', "
5 no city among all the tribes of I' "
5 man to be a ruler over my people I': "
6 David to be over my people I'. "
7 for the name of the Lord God of I'. "
10 and am set on the throne of I', as "
10 for the name of the Lord God of I'. "
11 he made with the children of I'. "
12 of all the congregation of I', "
13 before all the congregation of I', "
14 God of I', there is no God like thee "
16 God of I', keep with thy servant "
16 sight to sit upon the throne of I'; "
17 O Lord God of I', let thy word be "
21 of thy servant, and of thy people I', "
24 thy people I' be put to the worse "
25 and forgive the sin of my people I', "
27 thy servants, and of thy people I', "
29 of any man, or of all thy people I', "
32 which is not of thy people I', "
33 fear thee, as doth thy people I', "
7: 3 of I' saw how the fire came down, "
6 before them, and all I' stood. "
8 seven days, and all I' with him, "
10 to Solomon, and to I' his people. "
18 not fail thee a man to be ruler in I'. "
8: 2 the children of I' to dwell there. "
7 the Jebusites, which were not of I', "
8 whom the children of I' consumed "
9 children of I' did Solomon make no "
11 in the house of David king of I', "
9: 8 because thy God loved I', to "
30 in Jerusalem over all I' forty years. "
10: 1 for to Shechem were all I' come to "
3 all I' came and spake to Rehoboam, "
16 all I' saw that the king would not "
16 every man to your tents, O I': and "
16 So all I' went to their tents. "
17 I' that dwelt in the cities of Judah "
18 of I' stoned him with stones, that "
19 I' rebelled against the house of "
11: 1 were warriors, to fight against I', "
3 to all I' in Judah and Benjamin, "
13 and the Levites that were in all I' "
16 after them out of all the tribes of I' "
16 hearts to seek the Lord God of I' "
12: 1 law of the Lord, and all I' with him. "
6 princes of I' and the king humbled "
13 chosen out of all the tribes of I', "
13: 4 me, thou Jeroboam, and all I'; "
5 know that the Lord God of I' gave "
5 gave the kingdom over I' to David "
12 children of I', fight ye not against "
15 God smote Jeroboam and all I' "
16 children of I' fled before Judah: "
17 slain of I' five hundred thousand "
18 children of I' were brought under "
15: 3 I' hath been without the true God, "
4 did turn unto the Lord God of I', "
9 fell to him out of I' in abundance, "
13 would not seek the Lord God of I' "
17 were not taken away out of I': "
16: 1 king of I' came up against Judah, "
3 thy league with Baasha king of I', "
4 his armies against the cities of I'; "
11 book of the kings of Judah and I'. "
17: 1 strengthened himself against I'. "
4 and not after the doings of I'. "
18: 3 king of I' said unto Jehoshaphat "
4 Jehoshaphat said unto the king of I', "
5 of I' gathered together of prophets "
7 king of I' said unto Jehoshaphat, "
8 of I' called for one of his officers, "
9 the king of I' and Jehoshaphat king "
16 I' scattered upon the mountains, "
17 the king of I' said to Jehoshaphat, "
19 Who shall entice Ahab king of I', "
25 Then the king of I' said, Take ye "
28 So the king of I' and Jehoshaphat "
29 king of I' said unto Jehoshaphat, I "
29 So the king of I' disguised himself; "
30 great, save only with the king of I'. "
31 that they said, It is the king of I'. "
32 that it was not the king of I', they "
33 smote the king of I' between the "
34 I' stayed himself up in his chariot "
19: 8 and of the chief of the fathers of I', "
20: 7 of this land before thy people I', "
10 thou wouldest not let I' invade, "
19 up to praise the Lord God of I' "
29 fought against the enemies of I'. "
34 in the book of the kings of I'. "
35 himself with Ahaziah king of I', "
21: 2 the sons of Jehoshaphat king of I'. "
4 and divers also of the princes of I'. "
6, 13 in the way of the kings of I', "
22: 5 Ahab king of I' to war against "
23: 2 and the chief of the fathers of I', "
2Ch 24: 5 gather of all I' money to repair the 3478
6 and of the congregation of I', for "
9 the servant of God laid upon I' "
16 he had done good in I', both toward "
25: 6 mighty men of valour out of I' "
7 let not the army of I' go with thee; "
7 for the Lord is not with I', to wit, "
9 which I have given to the army of I'? "
17 the son of Jehu, king of I', saying, "
18 king of I' sent to Amaziah king of "
21 So Joash the king of I' went up; "
22 was put to the worse before I', "
23 king of I' took Amaziah king of "
25 of Joash son of Jehoahaz king of I' "
26 book of the kings of Judah and I'? "
27: 7 book of the kings of I' and Judah. "
28: 2 walked in the ways of the kings of I', "
3 cast out before the children of I'. "
5 into the hand of the king of I', "
8 of I' carried away captive of their "
13 and there is fierce wrath against I'. "
19 low because of Ahaz king of I'; "
23 were the ruin of him, and of all I'. "
26 book of the kings of Judah and I'. "
27 the sepulchres of the kings of I': "
29: 7 the holy place unto the God of I'. "
10 covenant with the Lord God of I', "
24 to make an atonement for all I': "
24 offering should be made for all I'. "
27 ordained by David king of I'. "
30: 1 Hezekiah sent to all I' and Judah, "
1 passover unto the Lord God of I'. "
5 proclamation throughout all I', "
5 passover unto the Lord God of I' "
6 and his princes throughout all I' "
6 Ye children of I', turn again unto "
6 God of Abraham, Isaac, and I', "
21 I' that were present at Jerusalem "
25 congregation that came out of I', "
25 that came out of the land of I', "
26 Solomon the son of David king of I' "
31: 1 all I' that were present went out to "
1 Then all the children of I' returned, "
5 of I' brought in abundance the first "
6 the children of I' and Judah, "
8 blessed the Lord, and his people I'. "
32:17 letters to rail on the Lord God of I', "
32 book of the kings of Judah and I'. "
33: 2 cast out before the children of I'. "
7 chosen before all the tribes of I', "
8 I any more remove the foot of I' "
9 destroyed before the children of I'. "
16 Judah to serve the Lord God of I'. "
18 in the name of the Lord God of I', "
18 in the book of the kings of I'. "
34: 7 idols throughout all the land of I', "
9 and of all the remnant of I', "
21 them that are left in I' and in Judah, "
23 Thus saith the Lord God of I', Tell "
26 of I' concerning the words which "
33 that pertained to the children of I', "
33 all that were present in I' to serve, "
35: 3 unto the Levites that taught all I', "
3 son of David king of I' did build; "
3 Lord your God, and his people I', "
4 to the writing of David king of I', "
17 of I' that were present kept the "
18 no passover like to that kept in I' "
18 kings of I' keep such a passover as "
18 all Judah and I' that were present, "
25 and made them an ordinance in I': "
27 in the book of the kings of I'. "
36: 8 in the book of the kings of I' "
13 turning unto the Lord God of I'. "
Ezr 1: 3 the house of the Lord God of I', "
2: 2 of the men of the people of I': "
59 their seed, whether they were of I': "
70 their cities, and all I' in their cities. "
3: 1 the children of I' were in the cities, "
2 builded the altar of the God of I', "
10 the ordinance of David king of I'. "
11 mercy endureth for ever toward I'. "
4: 1 temple unto the Lord God of I'; "
3 rest of the chief of the fathers of I', "
3 will build unto the Lord God of I', "
5: 1 in the name of the God of I', even 3479
11 which a great king of I' builded "
6:14 the commandment of the God of I', "
16 the children of I', the priests, and "
17 and for a sin offering for all I', "
17 to the number of the tribes of I'. "
21 I', which were come again out of 3478
21 land, to seek the Lord God of I', "
22 of the house of God, the God of I'. "
7: 6 which the Lord God of I' had given: "
7 went up some of the children of I', "
10 teach in I' statutes and judgments. "
11 the Lord, and of his statutes to I'. "
13 that all they of the people of I', 3479
15 freely offered unto the God of I', "
28 out of I' chief men to go up with 3478
8:18 Mahli, the son of Levi, the son of I'; "
25 his lords, and all I' there present, "
29 and chief of the fathers of I', "
35 burnt offerings unto the God of I', "
35 twelve bullocks for all I', ninety "
9: 1 The people of I', and the priests, "
4 at the words of the God of I', "
15 Lord God of I', thou art righteous: "
10: 1 assembled unto him out of I' a "
2 is hope in I' concerning this thing. "
5 all I', to swear that they should do "
10 wives, to increase the trespass of I'. "
25 Moreover of I': of the sons of "
Ne 1: 6 for the children of I' thy servants, "
6 confess the sins of the children of I', "
Ne 2:10 the welfare of the children of I'. 3478
7: 7 say, of the men of the people of I' "
61 their seed, whether they were of I'. "
73 and all I', dwelt in their cities; "
73 children of I' were in their cities. "
8: 1 the Lord had commanded to I'. "
14 children of I' should dwell in booths "
17 had not the children of I' done so. "
9: 1 of I' were assembled with fasting, "
2 I' separated themselves from all "
10:33 to make an atonement for I', "
39 the children of I' and the children "
11: 3 to wit, I', the priests, and the "
20 And the residue of I', of the priests, "
12:47 all I' in the days of Zerubbabel, "
13: 2 of I' with bread and with water, "
3 separated from I' all the mixed "
18 wrath upon I' by profaning the "
26 king of I' sin by these things? "
26 and God made him king over all I': "
Ps 14: 7 salvation of I' were come out of "
7 shall rejoice, and I' shall be glad. "
22: 3 that inhabitest the praises of I'. "
23 and fear him, all ye the seed of I'. "
25:22 Redeem I', O God, out of all his "
41:13 Blessed be the Lord God of I' from "
50: 7 O I', and I will testify against thee: "
53: 6 salvation of I' were come out of "
6 shall rejoice, and I' shall be glad. "
59: 5 Lord God of hosts, the God of I', "
68: 8 the presence of God, the God of I'. "
26 the Lord, from the fountain of I'. "
34 his excellency is over I', and his "
35 God of I' is he that giveth strength "
69: 6 confounded for my sake, O God of I'. "
71:22 the harp, O thou Holy One of I'. "
72:18 be the Lord God, the God of I', "
73: 1 God is good to I', even to such as "
76: 1 God known: his name is great in I'. "
78: 5 Jacob, and appointed a law in I', "
21 and anger also came up against I'; "
31 smote down the chosen men of I'. "
41 and limited the Holy One of I'. "
55 tribes of I' to dwell in their tents. "
59 wroth, and greatly abhorred I': "
71 his people, and I' his inheritance. "
80: 1 Give ear, O Shepherd of I', thou "
81: 4 For this was a statute for I', and "
8 O I', if thou wilt hearken unto me; "
11 voice; and I' would none of me. "
13 me, and I' had walked in my ways! "
83: 4 name of I' may be no more in "
89:18 and the Holy One of I' is our king. "
98: 3 his truth toward the house of I': "
103: 7 his acts unto the children of I'. "
105:10 to I' for an everlasting covenant: "
23 I' also came into Egypt; and Jacob "
106:48 Blessed be the Lord God of I' from "
114: 1 When I' went out of Egypt, the "
2 his sanctuary, and I' his dominion. "
115: 9 O I', trust thou in the Lord: he is "
12 he will bless the house of I'; he "
118: 2 I' now say, that his mercy endureth "
121: 4 keepeth I' shall neither slumber "
122: 4 unto the testimony of I', to give "
124: 1 was on our side, now may I' say; "
125: 5 but peace shall be upon I'. "
128: 6 children, and peace upon I'. "
129: 1 from my youth, may I' now say: "
130: 7 Let I' hope in the Lord: for with "
8 And he shall redeem I' from all "
131: 3 Let I' hope in the Lord from "
135: 4 and I' for his peculiar treasure. "
12 an heritage unto I' his people. "
19 Bless the Lord, O house of I': "
136:11 brought out I' from among them: "
14 made I' to pass through the midst "
22 an heritage unto I' his servant: "
147: 2 together the outcasts of I'. "
19 statutes and his judgments unto I'. "
148:14 the children of I', a people near "
149: 2 Let I' rejoice in him that made "
Pr 1: 1 the son of David, king of I'; "
Ec 1:12 was king over I' in Jerusalem. "
Ca 3: 7 are about it, of the valiant of I'. "
Isa 1: 3 I' doth not know, my people doth "
4 provoked the Holy One of I' unto "
24 Lord of hosts, the Mighty One of I'. "
4: 2 for them that are escaped of I'. "
5: 7 Lord of hosts is the house of I', "
19 of the Holy One of I' draw nigh "
24 the word of the Holy One of I'. "
7: 1 the son of Remaliah, king of I', "
8:14 of offence to both the houses of I', "
18 for signs and for wonders in I' "
9: 8 Jacob, and it hath lighted upon I'. "
12 shall devour I' with open mouth. "
14 Lord will cut off from I' head and "
10:17 the light of I' shall be for a fire, "
20 that the remnant of I', and such as "
20 upon the Lord, the Holy One of I', "
22 people I' be as the sand of the sea, "
11:12 shall assemble the outcasts of I', "
16 like as it was to I' in the day that "
12: 6 great is the Holy One of I' in the "
14: 1 will yet choose I', and set them in "
2 the house of I' shall possess them "
17: 3 be as the glory of the children of I', "
6 thereof, saith the Lord God of I'. "
7 have respect to the Holy One of I'. "
9 left because of the children of I': "
19:24 In that day shall I' be the third "
25 my hands, and I' mine inheritance. "
21:10 of the Lord of hosts, the God of I', "
17 the Lord God of I' hath spoken it. "
24:15 of the Lord God of I' in the isles of "

Isa 27: 6 I' shall blossom and bud, and fill 3478
12 one by one, O ye children of I'. "
29: 19 shall rejoice in the Holy One of I'. "
23 and shall fear the God of I'. "
30: 11 cause the Holy One of I' to cease "
12 thus saith the Holy One of I', "
15 the Lord God, the Holy One of I'; "
29 the Lord, to the mighty One of I'. "
31: 1 look not unto the Holy One of I', "
6 children of I' have deeply revolted. "
37: 16 O Lord of hosts, God of I', that "
21 Thus saith the Lord God of I', "
23 even against the Holy One of I'. "
40: 27 thou, O Jacob, and speakest, O I', "
41: 8 But thou, I', art my servant, Jacob "
14 thou worm Jacob, and ye men of I'; "
14 thy redeemer, the Holy One of I'. "
16 shalt glory in the Holy One of I'. "
17 the God of I' will not forsake them. "
20 the Holy One of I' hath created it. "
42: 24 for a spoil, and I' to the robbers? "
43: 1 and he that formed thee, O I', Fear "
3 Lord thy God, the Holy One of I', "
14 redeemer, the Holy One of I'; "
15 One, the Creator of I', your King. "
22 thou hast been weary of me, O I'. "
28 the curse, and I' to reproaches. "
44: 1 and I', whom I have chosen: "
5 surname himself by the name of I'. "
6 Thus saith the Lord the King of I', "
21 Remember these, O Jacob and I'; "
21 O I', thou shalt not be forgotten of "
23 Jacob, and glorified himself in I'. "
45: 3 thee by thy name, am the God of I'. "
4 servant's sake, and I' mine elect, "
11 saith the Lord, the Holy One of I', "
15 God that hidest thyself, O God of I', "
17 But I' shall be saved in the Lord "
25 shall all the seed of I' be justified, "
46: 3 all the remnant of the house of I', "
13 salvation in Zion for I' my glory. "
47: 4 is his name, the Holy One of I'. "
48: 1 which are called by the name of I', "
1 and make mention of the God of I', "
2 stay themselves upon the God of I'; "
12 Hearken unto me, O Jacob and I', "
17 thy Redeemer, the Holy One of I'; "
49: 3 Thou art my servant, O I', in whom "
5 Though I' be not gathered, yet "
6 and to restore the preserved of I': "
7 Redeemer of I', and his Holy One, "
7 is faithful, and the Holy One of I', "
52: 12 the God of I' will be your rereward. "
54: 5 thy Redeemer the Holy One of I'; "
55: 5 thy God, and for the Holy One of I'; "
56: 8 which gathereth the outcasts of I' "
60: 9 thy God, and to the Holy One of I', "
14 The Zion of the Holy One of I'. "
63: 7 goodness toward the house of I', "
16 of us, and I' acknowledge us not: "
66: 20 of I' bring an offering in a clean "
Jer 2: 3 I' was holiness unto the Lord, and "
4 all the families of the house of I': "
14 Is I' a servant? is he a homeborn "
26 so is the house of I' ashamed, "
31 Have I been a wilderness unto I'? "
3: 6 which backsliding I' hath done? "
8 backsliding I' committed adultery "
11 The backsliding I' hath justified "
12 Return, thou backsliding I', saith "
18 shall walk with the house of I', "
20 dealt treacherously...O house of I', "
21 supplications of the children of I': "
23 Lord our God is the salvation of I'. "
4: 1 wilt return, O I', saith the Lord, "
5: 11 house of I' and the house of Judah "
15 upon you from far, O house of I', "
6: 9 glean the remnant of I' as a vine: "
7: 3 the Lord of hosts, the God of I', "
12 the wickedness of my people I'. "
21 the Lord of hosts, the God of I'; "
9: 15 the Lord of hosts, the God of I'; "
26 the house of I' are uncircumcised "
10: 1 speaketh unto you, O house of I': "
16 and I' is the rod of his inheritance: "
11: 3 Thus saith the Lord God of I'; "
10 house of I' and the house of Judah "
17 for the evil of the house of I' and of "
12: 14 caused my people I' to inherit; "
13: 11 cleave unto me...whole house of I' "
12 Thus saith the Lord God of I', "
14: 8 the hope of I', the saviour thereof "
16: 9 the Lord of hosts, the God of I'; "
14 of I' out of the land of Egypt; "
15 of I' from the land of the north, "
17: 13 O Lord, the hope of I', all that "
18: 6 O house of I', cannot I do with you "
6 are ye in mine hand, O house of I'. "
13 virgin of I' hath done a...horrible "
19: 3, 15 the Lord of hosts, the God of I'; "
21: 4 Thus saith the Lord God of I'; "
23: 2 Lord God of I' against the pastors "
6 be saved, and I' shall dwell safely: "
7 of I' out of the land of Egypt; "
8 which led the seed of the house of I' "
13 and caused my people I' to err. "
24: 5 Thus saith the Lord, the God of I'; "
25: 15 saith the Lord God of I' unto me; "
27 the Lord of hosts, the God of I'; "
27: 4 the Lord of hosts, the God of I'; "
21 the Lord of hosts, the God of I', "
28: 2 the Lord of hosts, the God of I', "
14 the Lord of hosts, the God of I'; "
29: 4 the Lord of hosts, the God of I', "
8 the Lord of hosts, the God of I'; "
21 the Lord of hosts, the God of I', "

Jer 29: 23 they have committed villainy in I', 3478
25 the Lord of hosts, the God of I', "
30: 2 Thus speaketh the Lord God of I', "
3 again the captivity of my people I' "
4 that the Lord spake concerning I' "
10 neither be dismayed, O I': for, lo, "
31: 1 be the God of all the families of I', "
2 even I', when I went to cause him "
4 thou shalt be built, O virgin of I': "
7 save thy people, the remnant of I'. "
9 for I am a father to I', and Ephraim "
10 He that scattered I' will gather "
21 O virgin of I', turn again to these "
23 the Lord of hosts, the God of I'; "
27 I will sow the house of I' and the "
31 new covenant with the house of I', "
33 I will make with the house of I'; "
36 the seed of I' also shall cease from "
37 I will also cast off all the seed of I' "
32: 14, 15 the Lord of hosts, the God of I'; "
20 and in I', and among other men; "
21 people I' out of the land of Egypt "
30 the children of I' and the children "
30 children of I' have only provoked "
32 of all the evil of the children of I' "
36 thus saith the Lord, the God of I', "
33: 4 thus saith the Lord, the God of I', "
7 and the captivity of I' to return, "
14 have promised unto the house of I' "
17 upon the throne of the house of I'; "
34: 2, 13 saith the Lord, the God of I'; "
35: 13 the Lord of hosts, the God of I'; "
17 Lord God of hosts, the God of I'; "
18, 19 the Lord of hosts, the God of I'; "
36: 2 I have spoken unto thee against I', "
37: 7 Thus saith the Lord, the God of I'; "
38: 17 the God of hosts, the God of I'; "
39: 16 the Lord of hosts, the God of I'; "
41: 9 made for fear of Baasha king of I': "
42: 9 Thus saith the Lord, the God of I', "
15, 18 the Lord of hosts, the God of I'; "
43: 10 the Lord of hosts, the God of I'; "
44: 2 the Lord of hosts, the God of I'; "
7 the God of hosts, the God of I'; "
11 the Lord of hosts, the God of I'; "
25 the Lord of hosts, the God of I', "
45: 2 Thus saith the Lord, the God of I', "
46: 25 The Lord of hosts, the God of I', "
27 Jacob, and be not dismayed, O I': "
48: 1 the Lord of hosts, the God of I'; "
13 house of I' was ashamed of Beth-el "
27 For was not I' a derision to thee? "
49: 1 Hath I' no sons? hath he no heir? "
2 shall I' be heir unto them that were "
50: 4 the children of I' shall come, "
17 I' is a scattered sheep; the lions "
18 the Lord of hosts, the God of I'; "
19 will bring I' again to his habitation, "
20 iniquity of I' shall be sought for, "
29 Lord, against the Holy One of I'. "
33 of I' and...Judah were oppressed "
51: 5 For I' hath not been forsaken, nor "
5 with sin against the Holy One of I'. "
33 the Lord of hosts, the God of I'; "
49 hath caused the slain of I' to fall, "
La 2: 1 unto the earth the beauty of I', "
3 his fierce anger all the horn of I': "
5 enemy: he hath swallowed up I', "
Eze 2: 3 I send thee to the children of I', "
3: 1 and go speak unto the house of I'. "
4 go, get thee unto the house of I', "
5 language, but to the house of I'; "
7 of I' will not hearken unto thee; "
7 I' are impudent and hardhearted. "
17 a watchman unto the house of I': "
4: 3 shall be a sign to the house of I'. "
4 iniquity of the house of I' upon it: "
5 bear the iniquity of the house of I'. "
13 children of I' eat their defiled bread "
5: 4 come forth into all the house of I'. "
6: 2 face toward the mountains of I', "
3 Ye mountains of I', hear the word "
5 dead carcases of the children of I' "
11 abominations of the house of I'! "
7: 2 the Lord God unto the land of I'; "
8: 4 glory of the God of I' was there, "
6 that the house of I' committeth "
10 and all the idols of the house of I', "
11 of the ancients of the house of I', "
12 the ancients of the house of I' do in "
9: 3 glory of the Lord of I' was gone up "
8 thou destroy all the residue of I' "
9 The iniquity of the house of I' and "
10: 19 glory of the God of I' was over them "
20 that I saw under the God of I' "
11: 5 Thus have ye said, O house of I': "
10 I will judge you in the border of I'; "
11 I will judge you in the border of I': "
13 a full end of the remnant of I'? "
15 and all the house of I' wholly, "
17 and I will give you the land of I'. "
22 glory of the God of I' was over them "
12: 6 thee for a sign unto the house of I'. "
9 of man, hath not the house of I', "
10 house of I' that are among them. "
19 of Jerusalem, and of the land of I'; "
22 proverb...ye have in the land of I', "
23 no more use it as a proverb in I'; "
24 divination within the house of I'. "
27 behold, they of the house of I' say, "
13: 2 prophesy against the prophets of I' "
4 O I', thy prophets are like the foxes "
5 up the hedge for the house of I' "
9 in the writing of the house of I', "
9 shall they enter into the land of I'; "
16 the prophets of I' which prophesy "

Eze 14: 1 certain of the elders of I' unto me, 3478
4 Every man of the house of I' that "
5 the house of I' in their own heart, "
6 Therefore say unto the house of I', "
7 For every one of the house of I', "
7 the stranger that sojourneth in I', "
9 him from the midst of my people I'. "
11 house of I' may go no more astray "
17: 2 a parable unto the house of I'; "
23 In the mountain of the height of I' "
18: 2 proverb concerning the land of I', "
3 any more to use this proverb in I'. "
6, 15 to the idols of the house of I', "
25 Hear now, O house of I'; Is not my "
29 Yet saith the house of I', The way "
29 O house of I', are not my ways "
30 I will judge you, O house of I', "
31 for why will ye die, O house of I'? "
19: 1 a lamentation for the princes of I', "
9 be heard upon the mountains of I'. "
20: 1 of the elders of I' came to enquire "
3 of man, speak unto the elders of I', "
5 In the day when I chose I', and "
13 the house of I' rebelled against me "
27 of man, speak unto the house of I', "
30 Wherefore say unto the house of I', "
31 enquired of by you, O house of I'? "
38 shall not enter into the land of I': "
39 As for you, O house of I', thus saith "
40 in the mountain of the height of I', "
40 there shall all the house of I', all "
42 shall bring you into the land of I', "
44 corrupt doings, O ye house of I', "
21: 2 prophesy against the land of I', "
3 say to the land of I', Thus saith "
12 shall be upon all the princes of I': "
25 thou, profane wicked prince of I', "
22: 6 Behold, the princes of I', every one "
18 house of I' is to me become dross: "
24: 21 Speak unto the house of I', Thus "
25: 3 against the land of I', when it was "
6 thy despite against the land of I'; "
14 Edom by the hand of my people I': "
27: 17 land of I', they were thy merchants: "
28: 24 pricking brier unto the house of I', "
25 shall have gathered the house of I' "
29: 6 a staff of reed to the house of I'. "
16 the confidence of the house of I', "
21 horn of the house of I' to bud forth, "
33: 7 a watchman unto the house of I'; "
10 of man, speak unto the house of I'; "
11 for why will ye die, O house of I'? "
20 O ye house of I', I will judge you "
24 those wastes of the land of I' "
28 mountains of I' shall be desolate, "
34: 2 against the shepherds of I', "
2 Woe be to the shepherds of I' that "
13 feed them upon the mountains of I' "
14 upon the high mountains of I' shall "
14 they feed upon the mountains of I'. "
30 even the house of I', are my people, "
35: 5 shed blood of the children of I' by "
12 spoken against the mountains of I', "
15 the inheritance of the house of I', "
36: 1 prophesy unto the mountains of I', "
1 Ye mountains of I', hear the word "
4 ye mountains of I', hear the word "
6 therefore concerning the land of I', "
8 But ye, O ye mountains of I', ye "
8 yield your fruit to my people of I'; "
10 all the house of I', even all of it: "
12 walk upon you, even my people I'; "
17 house of I' dwelt in their own land, "
21 which the house of I' had profaned "
22 Therefore say unto the house of I', "
22 this for your sakes, O house of I', "
32 for your own ways, O house of I'. "
37 be enquired of by the house of I', "
37: 11 bones are the whole house of I': "
12 and bring you into the land of I'. "
16 the children of I' his companions: "
16 all the house of I' his companions: "
19 the tribes of I' his fellows, and will "
21 I will take the children of I' from "
22 the land upon the mountains of I'; "
28 know that I the Lord do sanctify I', "
38: 8 people, against the mountains of I': "
14 my people of I' dwelleth safely, "
16 come up against my people of I', "
17 by my servants the prophets of I', "
18 shall come against the land of I', "
19 a great shaking in the land of I'; "
39: 2 thee upon the mountains of I': "
4 shalt fall upon the mountains of I', "
7 known in the midst of my people I'; "
7 I am the Lord, the Holy One in I'. "
9 they that dwell in the cities of I' "
11 Gog a place there of graves in I', "
12 the house of I' be burying of them, "
17 sacrifice upon the mountains of I', "
22 house of I' shall know that I am "
23 house of I' went into captivity for "
25 mercy upon the whole house of I', "
29 out my spirit upon the house of I', "
40: 2 brought he me into the land of I', "
4 that thou seest to the house of I'. "
43: 2 glory of the God of I' came from "
7 in the midst of the children of I' "
7 shall the house of I' no more defile, "
10 shew the house to the house of I', "
44: 2 Lord, the God of I', hath entered in "
6 rebellious, even to the house of I', "
6 O ye house of I', let it suffice you "
9 that is among the children of I'. "
10 far from me, when I' went astray, "
12 the house of I' to fall into iniquity; "

Eze 44:15 children of I· went astray from me,3478
22 take maidens...of the house of I·, "
28 shall give them no possession in I·: "
29 dedicated thing in I· shall be theirs. "
45: 6 shall be for the whole house of I·. "
8 land shall be his possession in I·: "
8 shall they give to the house of I· "
9 Let it suffice you, O princes of I·: "
15 out of the fat pastures of I·; "
16 this oblation for the prince in I·. "
17 all solemnities of the house of I·: "
17 reconciliation for the house of I·. "
47:13 according to the twelve tribes of I·: "
18 and from the land of I· by Jordan, "
21 you according to the tribes of I·. "
22 country among the children of I·; "
22 with you among the tribes of I·. "
48:11 when the children of I· went astray, "
19 serve it out of all the tribes of I·. "
29 unto the tribes of I· for inheritance, "
31 after the names of the tribes of I·: "
Da 1: 3 bring certain of the children of I·, "
9: 7 of Jerusalem, and unto all I·, "
11 all I· have transgressed thy law, "
20 my sin and the sin of my people I·, "
Ho 1: 1 the son of Joash, king of I·. "
4 the kingdom of the house of I·. "
5 break the bow of I· in the valley "
6 have mercy upon the house of I·; "
10 I· shall be as the sand of the sea, "
11 children of I· be gathered together, "
3: 1 Lord toward the children of I·, "
4 I· shall abide many days without a "
5 shall the children of I· return, and "
4: 1 word of the Lord, ye children of I·: "
15 Though thou, I·, play the harlot, yet "
16 I· slideth back as a backsliding "
5: 1 and hearken, ye house of I·; "
3 Ephraim, and I· is not hid from me: "
3 whoredom, and I· is defiled. "
5 pride of I· doth testify to his face: "
5 shall I· and Ephraim fall in their "
9 tribes of I· have I made known that "
6:10 horrible thing in the house of I·: "
10 whoredom of Ephraim, I· is defiled. "
7: 1 When I would have healed I·, then "
10 the pride of I· testifieth to his face: "
8: 2 I· shall cry unto me, My God, we "
3 I· hath cast off the thing that is "
6 from I· was it also: the workman "
8 I· is swallowed up: now shall they "
14 I· hath forgotten his Maker, and "
9: 1 Rejoice not, O I·, for joy, as other "
7 are come; I· shall know it: "
10 I· like grapes in the wilderness; "
10: 1 I· is an empty vine, he bringeth "
6 I· shall be ashamed of his own "
8 the sin of I·, shall be destroyed: "
9 I·, thou hast sinned from the days "
15 shall the king of I· utterly be cut off. "
11: 1 When I· was a child, then I loved "
8 how shall I deliver thee, I·? how "
12 and the house of I· with deceit: "
12:12 I· served for a wife, and for a wife "
13 the Lord brought I· out of Egypt, "
13: 1 trembling, he exalted himself in I·; "
9 O I·, thou hast destroyed thyself; "
14: 1 O I·, return unto the Lord thy God; "
5 I will be as the dew unto I·: he "
Joe 2:27 know that I am in the midst of I·, "
3: 2 my people and for my heritage I·, "
16 the strength of the children of I·. "
Am 1: 1 concerning I· in the days of Uzziah "
1 the son of Joash king of I·, "
2: 6 For three transgressions of I·, and "
11 not even thus, O ye children of I·? "
3: 1 spoken against you, O children of I·, "
12 shall the children of I· be taken out "
14 I shall visit the transgressions of I· "
4: 5 this liketh you, O ye children of I·, "
12 thus will I do unto thee, O I·: "
12 prepare to meet thy God, O I·. "
5: 1 even a lamentation, O house of I·. "
2 The virgin of I· is fallen; she shall "
3 shall leave ten, to the house of I·. "
4 saith the Lord unto the house of I·, "
25 wilderness forty years, O house of I·? "
6: 1 to whom the house of I· came! "
14 against you a nation, O house of I·, "
7: 8 in the midst of my people I·: "
9 sanctuaries of I· shall be laid waste; "
10 Beth-el sent to Jeroboam king of I·, "
10 thee in the midst of the house of I·: "
11 I· shall surely be led away captive "
15 Go, prophesy unto my people I·. "
16 sayest, Prophesy not against I·, "
17 and I· shall surely go into captivity "
8: 2 end is come upon my people of I·; "
9: 7 unto me, O children of I·? "
7 not I brought up I· out of the land "
9 will sift the house of I· among all "
14 the captivity of my people of I·, "
Ob 20 of this host of the children of I· "
Mic 1: 5 and for the sins of the house of I·. "
13 transgressions of I· were found in "
14 shall be a lie to the kings of I·. "
15 come unto Adullam the glory of I·. "
2:12 surely gather the remnant of I·; "
3: 1 and ye princes of the house of I·; "
8 his transgression, and to I· his sin. "
9 and princes of the house of I·, "
5: 1 smite the judge of I· with a rod "
2 unto me that is to be ruler in I·; "
3 shall return unto the children of I·. "
6: 2 people, and he will plead with I·. "
Na 2: 2 of Jacob, as the excellency of I·: "

Zep 2: 9 the Lord of hosts, the God of I·, 3478
3:13 remnant of I· shall not do iniquity, "
14 O daughter of Zion; shout, O I·; be "
15 the king of I·, even the Lord, is in "
Zec 1:19 scattered Judah, I·, and Jerusalem. "
8:13 O house of Judah, and house of I·; "
9: 1 of man, as of all the tribes of I·, "
11:14 brotherhood between Judah and I·. "
12: 1 of the word of the Lord for I·, "
Mal 1: 1 word of the Lord to I· by Malachi. "
5 be magnified from the border of I·. "
2:11 an abomination is committed in I· "
16 the Lord, the God of I·, saith that "
4: 4 unto him in Horeb for all I·, "
M't 2: 6 that shall rule my people I·. 2474
20 mother, and go into the land of I·: "
21 and came into the land of I·. "
8:10 found so great faith, no, not in I·. "
9:33 saying, It was never so seen in I·. "
10: 6 to the lost sheep of the house of I·. "
23 not have gone over the cities of I·, "
15:24 unto the lost sheep of the house of I·. "
31 and they glorified the God of I·. "
19:28 judging the twelve tribes of I·. "
27: 9 they of the children of I· did value; "
42 If he be the King of I·, let him now "
M'r 12:29 the commandments is, Hear, O I·; "
15:32 Let Christ the King of I· descend "
Lu 1:16 of the children of I· shall he turn "
54 He hath holpen his servant I·, "
68 Blessed be the Lord God of I·; for "
80 till the day of his shewing unto I·. "
2:25 waiting for the consolation of I·: "
32 and the glory of thy people I·. "
34 fall and rising again of many in I·; "
4:25 many widows were in I· in the days "
27 many lepers were in I· in the time of "
7: 9 found so great faith, no, not in I·. "
22:30 judging the twelve tribes of I·. "
24:21 he which should have redeemed I·: "
Joh 1:31 he should be made manifest to I·, "
49 Son of God; thou art the King of I·. "
3:10 Art thou a master of I·, and "
12:13 King of I· that cometh in the name "
Ac 1: 6 restore again the kingdom to I·? "
2:22 Ye men of I·, hear these words; 2475
36 all the house of I· know assuredly, 2474
3:12 Ye men of I·, why marvel ye at this? 2475
4: 8 of the people, and elders of I·, *2474
10 you all, and to all the people of I·, "
27 the Gentiles, and the people of I·, "
5:21 all the senate of the children of I·, "
31 for to give repentance to I·, and "
35 Ye men of I·, take heed to 2475
7:23 his brethren the children of I·. 2474
37 which said unto the children of I·, "
42 O ye house of I·, have ye offered to "
9:15 and kings, and the children of I·: "
10:36 God sent unto the children of I·, "
13:16 Men of I·, and ye that fear God, 2475
17 The God of this people of I· chose 2474
23 promise raised unto I· a Saviour, "
24 repentance to all the people of I·. "
21:28 Crying out, Men of I·, help: This 2475
28:20 that for the hope of I· I am bound 2474
Ro 9: 6 they are not all I·, which are of I·: "
27 Esaias also crieth concerning I·, "
27 children of I· be as the sand of the "
31 But I·, which followed after the law "
10: 1 desire and prayer to God for I· is,* "
19 But I say, Did not I· know? "
21 But to I· he saith, All day long I "
11: 2 intercession to God against I·, "
7 I· hath not obtained that which he "
25 blindness in part is happened to I·, "
26 And so all I· shall be saved: as it is "
1Co 10:18 Behold I· after the flesh: are not "
2Co 3: 7 of I· could not stedfastly behold "
13 of I· could not stedfastly look to "
Ga 6:16 and mercy, and upon the I· of God. "
Eph 2:12 aliens from the commonwealth of I·, "
Ph'p 3: 5 of the stock of I·, of the tribe of "
Heb 8: 8 a new covenant with the house of I· "
10 that I will make with the house of I· "
11:22 the departing of the children of I·; "
Re 2:14 cast a stumblingblock before...of I·, "
7: 4 of all the tribes of the children of I·. "
21:12 twelve tribes of the children of I·: "

Israelite (*iz'-ra-el-ite*) See also ISRAELITES; ISRAELITISH.
Nu 25:14 name of the I· that was slain,*1121,3478
2Sa 17:25 son, whose name was Ithra an I·, 3481
Joh 1:47 Behold an I· indeed, in whom is 2475
Ro 11: 1 For I also am an I·, of the seed of "

Israelites (*iz'-ra-el-ites*)
Ex 9: 7 not one of the cattle of the I· dead.3478
Le 23:42 are I· born shall dwell in booths:* "
Jos 3:17 the I· passed over on dry ground,* "
8:24 all the I· returned unto Ai, and * "
13: 6 lot unto the I· for an inheritance,* "
13 dwell among the I· until this day.* "
J'g 20:21 to the ground of the I· that day "
1Sa 2:14 in Shiloh unto all the I· that came "
13:20 the I· went down to the Philistines, "
14:21 be with the I· that were with Saul "
25: 1 all the I· were gathered together,* "
29: 1 I· pitched by a fountain which is "
2Sa 4: 1 feeble, and all the I· were troubled. "
2Ki 3:24 I· rose up and smote the Moabites, "
7:13 even as all the multitude of the I· * "
1Ch 9: 2 the I·, the priests, Levites, and "
Ro 9: 4 Who are I·; to whom pertaineth 2475
2Co 11:22 Are they I·? so am I. Are they "

Israelitish (*iz'-ra-el-i-tish*)
Le 24:10 the son of an I· woman, whose 3482

Le 24:10 this son of the I· woman and a man3482
11 the I· woman's son blasphemed "

Israel's (*iz'-ra-els*)
Ge 48:13 his right hand toward I· left hand,3478
13 his left hand toward I· right hand, "
Ex 18: 8 and to the Egyptians for I· sake, "
Nu 1:20 children of Reuben, I· eldest son, "
31:30 the children of I· half, thou shalt "
42 the children of I· half, which Moses "
47 Even of the children of I· half, "
De 21: 8 blood unto thy people of I· charge.* "
2Sa 5:12 his kingdom for his people I· sake. "
2Ki 3:11 And one of the king of I· servants "

Issachar (*is'-sa-kar*)
Ge 30:18 and she called his name I·. 3485
35:23 and Judah, and I·, and Zebulun: "
46:13 the sons of I·; Tola, and Phuvah, "
49:14 I· is a strong ass couching down "
Ex 1: 3 I·, Zebulun, and Benjamin, "
Nu 1: 8 Of I·; Nethaneel the son of Zuar. "
28 children of I·, by their generations, "
29 of the tribe of I·, were fifty and four "
2: 5 unto him shall be the tribe of I·: "
5 shall be captain of the children of I·. "
7:18 the son of Zuar, prince of I·, "
10:15 host of the tribe of the children of I· "
13: 7 tribe of I·, Igal the son of Joseph. "
26:23 the sons of I· after their families: "
25 These are the families of I· "
34:26 of the tribe of the children of I·, "
De 27:12 Judah, and I·, and Joseph, and "
33:18 thy going out; and, I·, in thy tents. "
Jos 17:10 on the north, and in I· on the east. "
11 Manasseh had in I· and in Asher "
19:17 came out to I·, for the children of I· "
23 of the tribe of the children of I· "
21: 6 out of the families of the tribe of I·, "
28 out of the tribe of I·, Kishon with "
J'g 5:15 of I· were with Deborah; even I·, "
10: 1 Puah, the son of Dodo, a man of I·; "
1Ki 4:17 the son of Paruah, in I·: "
15:27 son of Ahijah, of the house of I·, "
1Ch 2: 1 Simeon, Levi, and Judah, I·, and "
6:62 their families out of the tribe of I·, "
72 And out of the tribe of I·; Kedesh "
7: 1 sons of I· were, Tola, and Puah, "
5 the families of I· were valiant men "
12:32 the children of I·, which were men "
40 that were nigh them, even unto I· "
26: 5 Ammiel the sixth, I· the seventh, "
27:18 of I·, Omri the son of Michael: "
2Ch 30:18 many of Ephraim, and Manasseh, I·, "
Eze 48:25 unto the west side, I· a portion. "
26 And by the border of I·, from the "
33 one gate of I·, one gate of Zebulun. "
Re 7: 7 Of the tribe of I· were sealed 2466

Isshiah (*is-shi'-ah*) See also ISAIAH; JESIAH.
1Ch 24:21 sons of Rehabiah, the first was I·.3449
25 The brother of Michah was I·: "

issue See also ISSUED; ISSUES.
Ge 48: 6 And thy i·, which thou begettest 4138
Le 12: 7 cleansed from the i· of her blood.*4726
15: 2 When any man hath a running i· 2100
2 because of his i· he is unclean. 2101
3 shall be his uncleanness in his i·: "
3 whether his flesh run with his i·, or "
3 his flesh be stopped from his i·, "
4 whereon he lieth that hath the i·, 2100
6 whereon he sat that hath the i· "
7 the flesh of him that hath the i· "
8 if he that hath the i· spit upon him "
9 he rideth upon that hath the i· shall "
11, 12 he toucheth that hath the i·, "
13 And when he that hath an i· "
13 is cleansed of his i·, 2101
15 for him before the Lord for his i·. "
19 And if a woman have an i·, 2100
19 and her i· in her flesh be blood, 2101
25 if a woman have an i· of her blood 2100
25 days of the i· of her uncleanness 2101
26 she lieth all the days of her i· "
28 But if she be cleansed of her i·, "
30 atonement before the Lord for the i· "
32 is the law of him that hath an i·, 2100
33 of him that hath an i·, of the man, "
22: 4 is a leper, or hath a running i·; "
Nu 5: 2 leper, and every one that hath an i·, "
2Sa 3:29 house of Joab one that hath an i·, "
2Ki 20:18 of thy sons that shall i· from thee, 3318
Isa 22:24 house, the offspring and the i·, all 6849
39: 7 thy sons that shall i· from thee, 3318
Eze 23:20 and whose i· is like the i· of horses.2231
47: 8 waters i· out toward the east 3318
M't 9:20 with an i· of blood twelve years, 131
22:25 having no i·, left his wife unto his*4690
M'r 5:25 had an i· of blood twelve years, 4511
Lu 8:43 having an i· of blood twelve years, "
44 and immediately her i· of blood "

issued
Jos 8:22 the other i· out of the city against*3318
Job 38: 8 as if it had i· out of the womb? * "
Eze 47: 1 waters i· out from under the "
12 waters they i· out of the sanctuary:* "
Da 7:10 A fiery stream i· and came forth 5047
Re 9:17 out of their mouths i· fire and *1607
18 which i· out of their mouths. "

issues
Ps 68:20 the Lord belong the i· from death.‡8444
Pr 4:23 for out of it are the i· of life. "

Isuah (*is'-u-ah*) See also ISHUAH.
1Ch 7:30 Imnah, and Isuah, and Ishuai, and *3440

Isui (*is'-u-i*) See also ISHUI.
Ge 46:17 Jimnah, and Ishuah, and I·, and *3440

it See in the APPENDIX; also ALBEIT; HOWBEIT; ITS; ITSELF.

Italian (*it-al'-yan*)
Ac 10: 1 of the band called the I· band. *2483*

Italy (*it'-a-lee*)
Ac 18: 2 in Pontus, lately come from I·, *2482*
27: 1 that we should sail into I·, "
6 ship of Alexandria sailing into I·; "
Heb13: 24 the saints. They of I· salute you. "
subsc. Written to the Hebrews from I·*

itch See also ITCHING.
De 28: 27 and with the scab, and with the i·, 2775

itching
2Ti 4: 3 teachers, having i· ears; *2833*

Ithai (*ith'-a-i*) See also ITTAI.
1Ch 11: 31 I· the son of Ribai of Gibeah, that 2833

Ithamar (*ith'-a-mar*)
Ex 6: 23 Nadab and Abihu, Eleazar, and I·. 385
28: 1 Abihu, Eleazar and I·, Aaron's sons. "
38: 21 by the hand of I·, son to Aaron the "
Le 10: 6 unto Eleazar and unto I·, his sons, "
12 Aaron, unto Eleazar and unto I·, "
16 he was angry with Eleazar and I·, "
Nu 3: 2 firstborn, and Abihu, Eleazar, and I·. "
4 I· ministered in the priest's office "
4: 28 shall be under the hand of I· the "
33 under the hand of I· the son of "
7: 8 under the hand of I· the son of "
26: 60 Nadab, and Abihu, Eleazar, and I·. "
1Ch 6: 3 Nadab, and Abihu, Eleazar, and I·. "
24: 1 Nadab, and Abihu, Eleazar, and I·. "
2 Eleazar and I· executed the priest's "
3 and Ahimelech of the sons of I·, "
4 of Eleazar than of the sons of I·; "
4 and eight among the sons of I·. "
5 of Eleazar, and of the sons of I·. "
6 for Eleazar, and one taken for I·. "
Ezr 8: 2 Gershom: of the sons of I·; Daniel: "

Ithiel (*ith'-e-el*)
Ne 11: 7 son of Maaseiah, the son of I·, the 384
Pr 30: 1 man spake unto I·, even unto I· and"

Ithmah (*ith'-mah*)
1Ch11: 46 of Elnaam, and I· the Moabite, 3495

Ithnan (*ith'-nan*)
Jos 15: 23 And Kedesh, and Hazor, and I·, 3497

Ithra (*ith'-rah*) See also JETHER.
2Sa 17: 25 whose name was I· an Israelite, 3501

Ithran (*ith'-ran*)
Ge 36: 26 Hemdan, and Eshban, and I·. 3506
1Ch 1: 41 Amram, and Eshban, and I·, "
7: 37 and Shilshah, and I·, and Beera. "

Ithream (*ith'-re-am*)
2Sa 3: 5 sixth, I·, by Eglah David's wife. 3507
1Ch 3: 3 the sixth, I· by Eglah his wife. "

Ithrite (*ith'-rite*) See also ITHRITES.
2Sa 23: 38 Ira an I·, Gareb an I·, 3505
1Ch 11: 40 Ira the I·, Gareb the I·, "

Ithrites (*ith'-rites*)
1Ch 2: 53 families of Kirjath-jearim; the I·, 3505

its
Le 25: 5 That which groweth of i· own accord *

itself
Ge 1: 11 whose seed is in i·, upon the earth:*
12 yielding fruit, whose seed was in i·,*
Le 7: 24 fat of the beast that dieth of i·, and
17: 15 soul that eateth that which dieth of i·
18: 25 land i· vomiteth out her inhabitants.*
22: 8 That which dieth of i·, or is torn
25: 11 neither reap that which groweth of i·
De 14: 21 not eat of any thing that died of i·:
1Ki 7: 34 undersetters were of the very base i·.
Job 10: 22 A land of darkness, as darkness i·;*
Ps 41: 6 his heart gathereth iniquity to i·;
68: 8 Sinai i· was moved at the presence*2088
Pr 18: 2 but that his heart may discover i·.
23: 31 in the cup, when it moveth i· aright.*
27: 16 of his right hand, which bewrayeth i·.*
25 and the tender grass sheweth i·,
Isa 10: 15 Shall the axe boast i· against him that
15 shall the saw magnify i· against him
15 rod should shake i· against them that*
15 as if the staff should lift up i·, as if it*
37: 30 eat this year such as groweth of i·; and
55: 2 and let your soul delight i· in fatness.
60: 20 neither shall thy moon withdraw i·:
Jer 31: 24 there shall dwell in Judah i·, and in*
Eze 1: 4 a great cloud, and a fire infolding i·,
4: 14 not eaten of that which dieth of i·,
17: 14 be base, that it might not lift i· up,
29: 15 neither shall it exalt i· any more above
44: 31 eat of any thing that is dead of i·,
Da 7: 5 a bear, and it raised up i· on one side,*
Mt 6: 34 take thought for the things of i·. *1438*
12: 25 Every kingdom divided against i· "
25 city or house divided against i· "
M'r 3: 24 if a kingdom be divided against i·, "
25 if a house be divided against i·, "
Lu 11: 17 Every kingdom divided against i· is "
Jo 15: 4 the branch cannot bear fruit of i·, "
20: 7 wrapped together in a place by i·. *5565*
21: 25 even the world i· could not contain *846*
Ro 8: 16 Spirit i· beareth witness with our * "
21 creature i· also shall be delivered "
26 the Spirit i· maketh intercession for† "
14: 14 there is nothing unclean of i·: but *1438*
1Co 11: 14 Doth not even nature i· teach you, *846*
13: 4 charity vaunteth not i·, is not puffed
5 Doth not behave i· unseemly,
2Co 10: 5 every high thing that exalteth i· *
Eph 4: 16 of the body unto the edifying of i· *1438*
Heb 9: 24 into heaven i·, now to appear in the *846*
3Jo 12 of all men, and of the truth i·;

Ittah-kazin (*it''-tah-ka'-zin*)
Jos 19: 13 the east to Gittah-hepher, to I·. *6278

Ittai (*it'-ta-i*) See also ITHAI.
2Sa 15: 19 said the king to I· the Gittite, 863
21 I· answered the king, and said, "
22 David said to I·, Go and pass over. "
22 And I· the Gittite passed over, "
18: 2 a third part...under the hand of I· "
5 commanded Joab and Abishai and I·,"
12 charged thee and Abishai and I·, "
23: 29 I· the son of Ribai out of Gibeah "

Ituræa (*i-tu-re'-ah*)
Lu 3: 1 his brother Philip tetrarch of I· *2484*

Ivah (*i'-vah*) See also AHAVA; AVA.
2Ki 18: 34 of Sepharvaim, Hena, and I·? *5755
19: 13 of Sepharvaim, of Hena, and I·? * "
Isa 37: 13 city of Sepharvaim, Hena, and I·?* "

ivory
1Ki 10: 18 the king made a great throne of i·, 8127
22 silver, i·, and apes, and peacocks. 8143
22: 39 and the i· house which he made, 8127
2Ch 9: 17 the king made a great throne of i·, "
21 silver, i·, and apes, and peacocks. 8143
Ps 45: 8 and cassia, out of the i· palaces, 8127
Ca 5: 14 his belly is as bright i· overlaid "
7: 4 Thy neck is as a tower of i·; thine "
Eze 27: 6 have made thy benches of i·, "
15 for a present horns of i· and ebony. "
Am 3: 15 houses of i· shall perish, and the "
6: 4 That lie upon beds of i·, and stretch"
Re 18: 12 wood, and all manner vessels of i·, *1661*

Izehar (*iz'-e-har*) See also IZEHARITES; IZHAR.
Nu 3: 19 families; Amram, and I·, Hebron,*3324

Izeharites (*iz'-e-har-ites*) See also IZHARITE.
Nu 3: 27 and the family of the I·, and the *3325

Izhar (*iz'-har*) See also IZEHAR; IZHARITES.
Ex 6: 18 sons of Kohath; Amram, and I·, 3324
21 the sons of I·; Korah, and Nepheg, "
Nu 16: 1 the son of I·, the son of Kohath, "
1Ch 6: 2 the sons of Kohath; Amram, I·, "
18 of Kohath were, Amram, and I·, "
38 The son of I·, the son of Kohath, "
23: 12 of Kohath; Amram, I·, Hebron, "
18 sons of I·; Shelomith the chief: "

Izharites (*iz'-har-ites*) See also IZEHARITES.
1Ch 24: 22 Of the I·; Shelomoth: of the sons 3325
26: 23 Of the Amramites, and the I·, "
29 Of the I·, Chenaniah and his sons "

Izrahiah (*iz-ra-hi'-ah*) See also JEZRAHIAH.
1Ch 7: 3 And the sons of Uzzi; I·: and the 3156
3 sons of I·; Michael, and Obadiah, "

Izrahite (*iz'-ra-hite*) See also EZRAHITE.
1Ch 27: 8 fifth month was Shamhuth the I·: 3155

Izri (*iz'-ri*) See also ZERI.
1Ch 25: 11 fourth to I·, he, his sons, and his 3342

J.

Jaakan (*ja'-a-kan*) See also AKAN; BENE-JAAKAN.
De 10: 6 Beeroth of the children of J· to *3292

Jaakobah (*ja-ak'-o-bah*)
1Ch 4: 36 Elioenai, and J·, and Jeshohaiah, 3291

Jaala (*ja'-a-lah*) See also JAALAH.
Ne 7: 58 The children of J·, the children 3279

Jaalah (*ja'-a-lah*) See also JAALA.
Ezr 2: 56 The children of J·, the children of 3279

Jaalam (*ja'-a-lam*)
Ge 36: 5 Aholibamah bare Jeush, and J·, *3281
14 to Esau Jeush and J·, and Korah* "
18 duke Jeush, duke J·, duke Korah:* "
1Ch 1: 35 and Jeush, and J·, and Korah. * "

Jaan See DAN-JAAN.

Jaanai (*ja'-a-nahee*)
1Ch 5: 12 and J·, and Shaphat in Bashan. *3285

Jaare-oregim (*ja''-a-re-or'-eg-im*) See also JAIR.
2Sa 21: 19 where Elhanan the son of J·, 3296

Jaasau (*ja-a'-saw*)
Ezr 10: 37 Mattaniah, Mattenai, and J·, *3299

Jaasiel (*ja-a'-se-el*)
1Ch 27: 21 of Benjamin, J· the son of Abner: 3300

Jaazaniah (*ja-az-a-ni'-ah*) See also JEZANIAH.
2Ki 25: 23 and J· the son of a Maachathite, 2970
Jer 35: 3 Then I took J· the son of Jeremiah, "
Eze 8: 11 them stood J· the son of Shaphan, "
11: 1 whom I saw J· the son of Azur, "

Jaazer (*ja-a'-zer*) See also JAZER.
Nu 21: 32 And Moses sent to spy out J·, *3270
32: 35 And Atroth, Shophan, and J·, * "

Jaaziah (*ja-a-zi'-ah*)
1Ch 24: 26 and Mushi: the sons of J·; Beno 3269
27 The sons of Merari by J·; Beno, and "

Jaaziel (*ja-a'-ze-el*) See also AZIEL.
1Ch 15: 18 degree, Zechariah, Ben, and J·, 3268

Jabal (*ja'-bal*)
Ge 4: 20 Adah bare J·: he was the father 2989

Jabbok (*jab'-bok*)
Ge 32: 22 and passed over the ford J·. 2999
Nu 21: 24 his land from Arnon unto J·, "
De 2: 37 nor unto any place of the river J·, "
3: 16 the border even unto the river J·, "
Jos 12: 2 half Gilead, even unto the river J·, "
J'g 11: 13 from Arnon even unto J·, and unto "
22 Amorites, from Arnon even unto J·, "

Jabesh (*ja'-besh*) See also JABESH-GILEAD.
1Sa 11: 1 the men of J· said unto Nahash, 3003
3 And the elders of J· said unto him, "
5 him the tidings of the men of J·. "
9 and shewed it to the men of J·; "
10 the men of J· said, To morrow we "
31: 12 and came to J·, and burnt them "
13 and buried them under a tree at J·, "
2Ki 15: 10 the son of J· conspired against him, "
13 the son of J· began to reign "
14 and smote Shallum the son of J· "
1Ch 10: 12 and brought them to J·, and buried "
12 their bones under the oak in J·, "

Jabesh-gilead (*ja''-besh-ghil'-e-ad*)
J'g 21: 8 none to the camp from J· to 3003,1568
9 none of the inhabitants of J· "
10 and smite the inhabitants of J· "
12 among the inhabitants of J· "
14 saved alive of the women of J·: "
1Sa 11: 1 up, and encamped against J·: "
9 shall ye say unto the men of J·, "
31: 11 inhabitants of J· heard of that "
2Sa 2: 4 men of J· were they that buried "
5 messengers unto the men of J·, "
21: 12 his son from the men of J·, "
1Ch 10: 11 J· heard all that the Philistines "

Jabez (*ja'-bez*)
1Ch 2: 55 of the scribes which dwelt at J·; 3258
4: 9 J· was more honourable than his "
9 and his mother called his name J·, "
10 And J· called on the God of Israel, "

Jabin (*ja'-bin*) See also JABIN'S.
Jos 11: 1 when J· king of Hazor had heard 2985
J'g 4: 2 into the hand of J· king of Canaan, "
17 was peace between J· the king of "
23 God subdued on that day J· the "
24 prevailed against J· the king of "
24 until they had destroyed J· king of "
Ps 83: 9 as to J· at the brook of Kison: "

Jabin's (*ja'-bins*)
J'g 4: 7 Sisera, the captain of J· army, 2985

Jabneel (*jab'-ne-el*) See also JABNEH.
Jos 15: 11 mount Baalah, and went unto J·; 2995
19: 33 Adami, Nekeb, and J·, unto Lakum; "

Jabneh (*jab'-neh*) See also JABNEEL.
2Ch 26: 6 wall of Gath, and the wall of J·, 2996

Jachan (*ja'-kan*) See also AKAN.
1Ch 5: 13 Jorai, and J·, and Zia, and Heber.*3275

Jachin (*ja'-kin*) See also JACHINITES; JARIB.
Ge 46: 10 Jamin, and Ohad, and J·, and 3199
Ex 6: 15 Jamin, and Ohad, and J·, and "
Nu 26: 12 of J·, the family of the Jachinites: "
1Ki 7: 21 and called the name thereof J·: "
1Ch 9: 10 Jedaiah, and Jehoiarib, and J·, "
24: 17 The one and twentieth to J·, the "
2Ch 3: 17 name of that on the right hand J·, "
Ne 11: 10 Jedaiah the son of Joiarib, J·. "

Jachinites (*ja'-kin-ites*)
Nu 26: 12 of Jachin, the family of the J·: 3200

jacinth
Re 9: 17 breastplates of fire, and of j·, *5191*
21: 20 the eleventh, a j·; the twelfth, an *5192*

Jacob (*ja'-cub*) See also ISRAEL; JACOB'S; JAMES.
Ge 25: 26 heel; and his name was called J·: 3290
27 J· was a plain man, dwelling in "
28 venison: but Rebekah loved J·. "
29 And J· sod pottage: and Esau came "
30 Esau said to J·, Feed me, I pray "
31 and J· said, Sell me this day thy "
33 And J· said, Swear to me this day; "
33 and he sold his birthright unto J·. "
34 J· gave Esau bread and pottage of "
27: 6 Rebekah spake unto J· her son, "
11 J· said to Rebekah his mother, "
15 put them upon J· her younger son: "
17 into the hand of her son J·. "
19 J· said unto his father, I am Esau "
21 Isaac said unto J·, Come near, I "
22 J· went near unto Isaac his father; "
30 had made an end of blessing J·, "
30 J· was yet scarce gone out from "
36 said, Is not he rightly named J·? "
41 Esau hated J· because of the "
41 then will I slay my brother J·. "
42 sent and called J· her younger son, "
46 if J· take a wife of the daughters of "
28: 1 Isaac called J·, and blessed him, "
5 Isaac sent away J·: and he went "
6 Esau saw that Isaac had blessed J·, "
7 J· obeyed his father and his mother, "
10 J· went out from Beer-sheba, and "
16 J· awaked out of his sleep, and he "
18 J· rose up early in the morning, "
20 J· vowed a vow, saying, If God will "
29: 1 Then J· went on his journey, and "
4 J· said unto them, My brethren, "
10 when J· saw Rachel the daughter "
10 J· went near, and rolled the stone "

Ge 29:11 and J· kissed Rachel, and lifted up 3290
12 J· told Rachel that he was her "
13 when Laban heard the tidings of J· "
15 Laban said unto J·, Because thou "
18 J· loved Rachel; and said, I will "
20 J· served seven years for Rachel; "
21 J· said unto Laban, Give me my "
28 J· did so, and fulfilled her week: "
30: 1 saw that she bare J· no children, "
1 and said unto J·, Give me children, "
4 to wife: and J· went in unto her. "
5 Bilhah conceived, and bare J· a son. "
7 again, and bare J· a second son. "
9 her maid, and gave her J· to wife. "
10 Zilpah Leah's maid bare J· a son. "
12 Leah's maid bare J· a second son. "
16 And J· came out of the field in the "
17 conceived, and bare J· the fifth son. "
19 again, and bare J· the sixth son. "
25 J· said unto Laban, Send me away, "
31 J· said, Thou shalt not give me any "
36 journey betwixt himself and J·: "
36 J· fed the rest of Laban's flocks. "
37 J· took him rods of green poplar, "
40 J· did separate the lambs, and set "
41 that J· laid the rods before the eyes "
31: 1 J· hath taken away all that was our "
2 J· beheld the countenance of "
3 the Lord said unto J·, Return unto "
4 J· sent and called Rachel and Leah "
11 unto me in a dream, saying, J·: "
17 J· rose up, and set his sons and his "
20 J· stole away unawares to Laban "
22 on the third day that J· was fled. "
24 speak not to J· either good or bad. "
25 Then Laban overtook J·. "
25 Now J· had pitched his tent in the "
26 Laban said to J·, What hast thou "
29 speak not to J· either good or bad. "
31 J· answered and said to Laban, "
32 J· knew not that Rachel had stolen "
36 And J· was wroth, and chode with "
36 and J· answered and said to Laban, "
43 Laban answered and said unto J·, "
45 J· took a stone, and set it up for a "
46 J· said unto his brethren, Gather "
47 but J· called it Galeed. "
51 Laban said to J·, Behold this heap, "
53 J· sware by the fear of his father "
54 J· offered sacrifice upon the mount, "
32: 1 J· went on his way, and the angels "
2 when J· saw them, he said, This is "
3 J· sent messengers before him to "
4 Esau; Thy servant J· saith thus, "
6 the messengers returned to J·, "
7 Then J· was greatly afraid and "
9 And J· said, O God of my father "
20 Behold, thy servant J· is behind us. "
24 And J· was left alone; and there "
27 What is thy name? And he said, J·. "
28 name shall be called no more J·, "
29 J· asked him, and said, Tell me, "
30 And J· called the name of the place "
33: 1 J· lifted up his eyes, and looked, "
10 And J· said, Nay, I pray thee, if "
17 J· journeyed to Succoth, and built "
18 And J· came to Shalem, a city of "
34: 1 of Leah, which she bare unto J·, "
3 unto Dinah the daughter of J·, "
5 J· heard that he had defiled Dinah "
5 J· held his peace until they were "
6 out unto J· to commune with him. "
7 the sons of J· came out of the field "
13 the sons of J· answered Shechem "
25 two of the sons of J·, Simeon and "
27 The sons of J· came upon the slain, "
30 J· said to Simeon and Levi, Ye have "
35: 1 God said unto J·, Arise, go up to "
2 J· said unto his household, and to "
4 gave unto J· all the strange gods "
4 J· hid them under the oak which "
5 did not pursue after the sons of J·. "
6 J· came to Luz, which is in the land "
9 God appeared unto J· again, when "
10 said unto him, Thy name is J·: "
10 shall not be called any more J·, "
14 J· set up a pillar in the place where "
15 And J· called the name of the place "
20 And J· set a pillar upon her grave: "
22 Now the sons of J· were twelve: "
26 these are the sons of J·, which were "
27 J· came unto Isaac his father unto "
29 his sons Esau and J· buried him. "
36: 6 from the face of his brother J·. "
37: 1 J· dwelt in the land wherein his "
2 These are the generations of J·. "
34 And J· rent his clothes, and put "
42: 1 when J· saw that there was corn in "
1 J· said unto his sons, Why do ye "
4 J· sent not with his brethren; "
29 they came unto J· their father unto "
36 And J· their father said unto them, "
45:25 into the land of Canaan unto J· "
27 the spirit of J· their father revived: "
46: 2 of the night, and said, J·, J·. "
5 And J· rose up from Beer-sheba: "
5 the sons of Israel carried J· their "
6 came into Egypt, J·, and all his "
8 came into Egypt, J· and his sons: "
15 of Leah, which she bare unto J· in "
18 and these she bare unto J·, even "
22 of Rachel, which were born to J·: "
25 and she bare these unto J·: all the "
26 souls that came with J· into Egypt, "
27 all the souls of the house of J·, "
47: 7 Joseph brought in J· his father. "

Ge 47: 7 Pharaoh: and J· blessed Pharaoh. 3290
8 Pharaoh said unto J·, How old art "
9 J· said unto Pharaoh, The days of "
10 J· blessed Pharaoh, and went out "
28 And J· lived in the land of Egypt "
28 whole age of J· was an hundred "
48: 2 one told J·, and said, Behold, thy "
3 J· said unto Joseph, God Almighty "
49: 1 J· called unto his sons, and said, "
2 together, and hear, ye sons of J·; "
7 I will divide them in J·, and scatter "
24 the hands of the mighty God of J·; "
33 J· had made an end of commanding "
50:24 to Abraham, to Isaac, and to J·. "
Ex 1: 1 and his household came with J·. "
5 that came out of the loins of J·. "
2:24 Abraham, with Isaac, and with J·. "
3: 6, 15 God of Isaac, and the God of J·. "
16 of Abraham, of Isaac, and of J·, "
4: 5 the God of Isaac, and the God of J·, "
6: 3 Abraham, unto Isaac, and unto J·, "
8 to Abraham, to Isaac, and to J·; "
19: 3 shalt thou say to the house of J·, "
33: 1 to Abraham, to Isaac, and to J·, "
Le 26:42 I remember my covenant with J·, "
Nu 23: 7 Come, curse me J·, and come, defy "
10 Who can count the dust of J·, and "
21 He hath not beheld iniquity in J·, "
23 there is no enchantment against J·, "
23 this time it shall be said of J· and "
24: 5 How goodly are thy tents, O J·, "
17 there shall come a Star out of J·, "
19 Out of J· shall come he that shall "
32:11 Abraham, unto Isaac, and unto J·; "
De 1: 8 fathers, Abraham, Isaac, and J·, "
6:10 to Abraham, to Isaac, and to J·, "
9: 5 fathers, Abraham, Isaac, and J·. "
27 servants, Abraham, Isaac, and J·; "
29:13 to Abraham, to Isaac, and to J·. "
30:20 to Abraham, to Isaac, and to J·, "
32: 9 J· is the lot of his inheritance. "
33: 4 inheritance of...congregation of J·. "
10 They shall teach J· thy judgments, "
28 fountain of J· shall be upon a land "
34: 4 Abraham, unto Isaac, and unto J·, "
Jos 24: 4 And I gave unto Isaac J· and Esau: "
4 but J· and his children went down "
32 parcel of ground which J· bought "
1Sa 12: 8 When J· was come into Egypt, and "
2Sa 23: 1 the anointed of the God of J·, and "
1Ki 18:31 of the tribes of the sons of J·, "
2Ki 13:23 with Abraham, Isaac, and J·, and "
17:34 Lord commanded the children of J·, "
1Ch 16:13 ye children of J·, his chosen ones. "
17 confirmed the same to J· for a law, "
Ps 14: 7 J· shall rejoice, and Israel shall be "
20: 1 name of the God of J· defend thee; "
22:23 all ye the seed of J·, glorify him; "
24: 6 seek him, that seek thy face, O J·. "
44: 4 God: command deliverances for J·. "
46: 7, 11 the God of J· is our refuge. "
47: 4 the excellency of J· whom he loved. "
53: 6 J· shall rejoice, and Israel shall be "
59:13 let them know that God ruleth in J· "
75: 9 I will sing praises to the God of J·. "
76: 6 At thy rebuke, O God of J·, both "
77:15 people, the sons of J· and Joseph. "
78: 5 he established a testimony in J·, "
21 so a fire was kindled against J·, "
71 brought him to feed J· his people, "
79: 7 For they have devoured J·, and "
81: 1 a joyful noise unto the God of J·. "
4 Israel, and a law of the God of J·. "
84: 8 my prayer: give ear, O God of J·. "
85: 1 brought back the captivity of J·. "
87: 2 more than all the dwellings of J·. "
94: 7 neither shall the God of J· regard it. "
99: 4 judgment and righteousness in J·. "
105: 6 ye children of J· his chosen. "
10 confirmed the same unto J· for a "
23 J· sojourned in the land of Ham. "
114: 1 house of J· from a people of strange "
7 at the presence of the God of J·; "
132: 2 vowed unto the mighty God of J·; "
5 habitation for the mighty God of J·. "
135: 4 Lord hath chosen J· unto himself, "
146: 5 that hath the God of J· for his help, "
147:19 He sheweth his word unto J·, his "
Isa 2: 3 Lord, to the house of the God of J·; "
5 O house of J·, come ye, and let us "
6 forsaken thy people the house of J·, "
8:17 his face from the house of J·, "
9: 8 The Lord sent a word into J·, and "
10:20 as are escaped of the house of J·, "
21 return, even the remnant of J·, "
14: 1 For the Lord will have mercy on J·, "
1 they shall cleave to the house of J·. "
17: 4 the glory of J· shall be made thin, "
27: 6 them that come of J· to take root: "
9 shall the iniquity of J· be purged; "
29:22 concerning the house of J·, "
22 J· shall not now be ashamed, "
23 and sanctify the Holy One of J·, "
40:27 Why sayest thou, O J·, and "
41: 8 J· whom I have chosen, the seed "
14 Fear not, thou worm J·, and ye "
21 strong reasons, saith the King of J·. "
42:24 Who gave J· for a spoil, and Israel "
43: 1 the Lord that created thee, O J·, "
22 thou hast not called upon me, O J·; "
28 and have given J· to the curse, and "
44: 1 Yet now hear, O J· my servant; "
2 Fear not, O J·, my servant; and "
5 shall call himself by the name of J·; "
21 Remember these, O J· and Israel; "
23 for the Lord hath redeemed J·, "

Isa 45: 4 For J· my servant's sake, and 3290
19 I said not unto the seed of J·, Seek "
46: 3 Hearken unto me, O house of J·, "
48: 1 Hear ye this, O house of J·, which "
12 Hearken unto me, O J· and Israel, "
20 Lord hath redeemed his servant J·. "
49: 5 servant, to bring J· again to him, "
6 servant to raise up the tribes of J·, "
26 thy Redeemer, the mighty One of J·. "
58: 1 and the house of J· their sins. "
14 feed thee with the heritage of J· "
59:20 that turn from transgression in J·, "
60:16 thy Redeemer, the mighty One of J·. "
65: 9 I will bring forth a seed out of J·, "
Jer 2: 4 word of the Lord, O house of J·, "
5:20 Declare this in the house of J·, and "
10:16 The portion of J· is not like them: "
25 for they have eaten up J·, and "
30:10 fear thou not, O my servant J·, "
10 and J· shall return, and shall be in "
31: 7 Sing with gladness for J·, and "
11 For the Lord hath redeemed J·, "
33:26 Then will I cast away the seed of J·, "
26 the seed of Abraham, Isaac, and J·: "
46:27 fear not thou, O my servant J·, "
27 J· shall return, and be in rest and "
28 Fear thou not, O J· my servant, "
51:19 The portion of J· is not like them; "
La 1:17 hath commanded concerning J·, "
2: 2 swallowed...the habitations of J·, "
3 burned against J· like a flaming "
Eze 20: 5 unto the seed of the house of J·, "
28:25 that I have given to my servant J·. "
37:25 the land that I have given unto J· "
39:25 I bring again the captivity of J·, "
Ho 10:11 plow, and J· shall break his clods. "
12: 2 punish J· according to his ways; "
12 J· fled into the country of Syria, "
Am 3:13 ye, and testify in the house of J·, "
6: 8 I abhor the excellency of J·, and "
7: 2, 5 thee: by whom shall J· arise? "
8: 7 hath sworn by the excellency of J·, "
9: 8 not utterly destroy the house of J·, "
Ob 10 thy violence against thy brother J· "
17 J· shall possess their possessions. "
18 And the house of J· shall be a fire, "
Mic 1: 5 the transgression of J· is all this, "
5 What is the transgression of J·? "
2: 7 that art named the house of J·, "
12 surely assemble, O J·, all of thee; "
3: 1 Hear, I pray you, O heads of J·, "
8 declare unto J· his transgression, "
9 you, ye heads of the house of J·, "
4: 2 and to the house of the God of J·; "
5: 7 remnant of J· shall be in the midst "
8 remnant of J· shall be among the "
7:20 Thou wilt perform the truth to J·, "
Na 2: 2 turned away the excellency of J·, "
Mal 1: 2 saith the Lord: yet I loved J·, "
2:12 out of the tabernacles of J·, "
3: 6 ye sons of J· are not consumed. "
M't 1: 2 begat J·; and J· begat Judas 2384
15 Matthan; and Matthan begat J·; "
16 And J· begat Joseph the husband "
8:11 with Abraham, and Isaac, and J·, "
22:32 the God of Isaac, and the God of J·? "
M'r 12:26 the God of Isaac, and the God of J·? "
Lu 1:33 he shall reign over the house of J· "
3:34 Which was the son of J·, which was "
13:28 see Abraham, and Isaac, and J·, "
20:37 the God of Isaac, and the God of J·. "
Joh 4: 5 that J· gave to his son Joseph. "
12 Art thou greater than our father J·, "
Ac 3:13 of Abraham, and of Isaac, and of J·, "
7: 8 begat J·; and J· begat the twelve "
12 when J· heard that there was corn "
14 and called his father J· to him, "
15 J· went down into Egypt, and died, "
32 the God of Isaac, and the God of J·. "
46 find a tabernacle for the God of J·. "
Ro 9:13 J· have I loved, but Esau have I "
11:26 turn away ungodliness from J·: "
Heb11: 9 in tabernacles with Isaac and J·, "
20 By faith, Isaac blessed J· and Esau "
21 By faith J·, when he was a dying, "

Jacob's (ja'-cubs)
Ge 27:22 voice is J· voice, but the hands 3290
28: 5 Rebekah, J· and Esau's mother. "
30: 2 And J· anger was kindled against "
42 were Laban's, and the stronger J·. "
31:33 And Laban went into J· tent, and "
32:18 shalt say, They be thy servant J·; "
25 hollow of J· thigh was out of joint, "
32 he touched the hollow of J· thigh "
34: 7 in Israel in lying with J· daughter; "
19 he had delight in J· daughter: "
35:23 Reuben, J· firstborn, and Simeon, "
45:26 J· heart fainted, for he believed *
46: 8 and his sons: Reuben, J· firstborn. 3290
19 sons of Rachel J· wife; Joseph, and "
26 of his loins, besides J· son's wives, "
Jer 30: 7 it is even the time of J· trouble; "
18 again the captivity of J· tents, "
Mal 1: 2 Was not Esau J· brother? saith "
Joh 4: 6 Now J· well was there. Jesus 2384

Jada (ja'-dah)
1Ch 2:28 of Onam were, Shammai, and J·. 3047
32 And the sons of J· the brother of "

Jadau (ja'-daw)
Ezr 10:43 Zabad, Zebina, J·, and Joel. *3035

Jaddua (jad'-du-ah)
Ne 10:21 Meshezabeel, Zadok, J·, 3037
12:11 Jonathan, and Jonathan begat J·. "
22 Joiada, and Johanan, and J·, "

Jadon (*ja'-don*)
Ne 3: 7 and *J'* the Meronothite, the men 3036
Jael (*ja'-el*)
J'g 4:17 away on his feet to the tent of *J'* 3278
18 And *J'* went out to meet Sisera, and "
21 *J'* Heber's wife took a nail of the "
22 *J'* came out to meet him, and said "
5: 6 in the days of *J'*, the highways were "
24 Blessed above women shall *J'* the "
Jagur (*ja'-gur*)
Jos 15:21 were Kabzeel, and Eder, and *J'*, 3017
Jah (*jah*) See also JEHOVAH.
Ps 68: 4 upon the heavens by his name *J'*,‡3050
Jahath (*ja'-hath*)
1Ch 4: 2 Reaiah the son of Shobal begat *J'*;3189
2 and *J'* begat Ahumai, and Lahad. "
6:20 Libni his son, *J'* his son, Zimmah "
43 The son of *J'*, the son of Gershom, "
23:10 sons of Shimei were, *J'*, Zina, and "
11 And *J'* was the chief, and Zirah the "
24:22 of the sons of Shelomoth; *J'*. "
2Ch 34:12 the overseers of them were *J'* and "
Jahaz (*ja'-haz*) See also JAHAZA; JAHAZAH; JAHZAH.
Nu 21:23 he came to *J'*, and fought against 3096
De 2:32 he and all his people, to fight at *J'*. "
J'g 11:20 pitched in *J'*, and fought against "
Isa 15: 4 voice shall be heard even unto *J'*: "
Jer 48:34 even unto *J'*, have they uttered "
Jahaza (*ja-ha'-zah*) See also JAHAZ.
Jos 13:18 *J'*, and Kedemoth, and Mephaath,*3096
Jahazah (*ja-ha'-zah*) See also JAHAZ.
Jos 21:36 suburbs, and *J'* with her suburbs,*3096
Jer 48:21 and upon *J'*, and upon Mephaath,* "
Jahaziah (*ja-ha-zi'-ah*)
Ezr 10:15 and *J'* the son of Tikvah were *3167
Jahaziel (*ja-ha'-ze-el*)
1Ch 12: 4 Jeremiah, and *J'*, and Johanan, 3166
16: 6 Benaiah also and *J'* the priests "
23:19 *J'* the third, and Jekameam the "
24:23 *J'* the third, Jekameam the fourth. "
2Ch 20:14 Then upon *J'* the son of Zechariah, "
Ezr 8: 5 the son of *J'*, and with him three "
Jahdai (*jah'-dahee*)
1Ch 2:47 sons of *J'*; Regem, and Jotham, 3056
Jahdiel (*jah'-de-el*)
1Ch 5:24 and *J'*, mighty men of valour, 3164
Jahdo (*jah'-do*)
1Ch 5:14 the son of *J'*, the son of Buz; 3163
Jahleel (*jah'-le-el*) See also JAHLEELITES.
Ge 46:14 Zebulun; Sered, and Elon, and *J'*.3177
Nu 26:26 of *J'*, the family of the Jahleelites. "
Jahleelites (*jah'-le-el-ites*)
Nu 26:26 of Jahleel, the family of the *J'*. 3178
Jahmai (*jah'-mahee*)
1Ch 7: 2 and Jeriel, and *J'*, and Jibsam, 3181
Jahzah (*jah'-zah*) See also JAHAZ.
1Ch 6:78 suburbs, and *J'* with her suburbs,3096
Jahzeel (*jah'-ze-el*) See also JAHZEELITES; JAHZIEL.
Ge 46:24 sons of Naphtali; *J'*, and Guni, 3183
Nu 26:48 *J'*, the family of the Jahzeelites: "
Jahzeelites (*jah'-ze-el-ites*)
Nu 26:48 of Jahzeel, the family of the *J'*: of 3184
Jahzerah (*jah'-ze-rah*) See also AHAZAI.
1Ch 9:12 Adiel, the son of *J'*, the son of 3170
Jahziel (*jah'-ze-el*) See also JAHZEEL.
1Ch 7:13 sons of Naphtali; *J'*, and Guni, 3185
jailor
Ac 16:23 charging the *j'* to keep them 1200
Jair (*ja'-ur*) See also HAVOTH-JAIR; JAARE-OREGIM; JAIRITE.
Nu 32:41 *J'* the son of Manasseh went and 2971
Jos 13:30 towns of *J'*, which are in Bashan, "
J'g 10: 3 And after him arose *J'*, a Gileadite, "
5 *J'* died, and was buried in Camon. "
1Ki 4:13 to him pertained the towns of *J'* "
1Ch 2:22 Segub begat *J'*, who had three and "
23 and Aram, with the towns of *J'*, "
20: 5 Elhanan the son of *J'* slew Lahmi3265
Es 2: 5 name was Mordecai, the son of *J'*,2971
Jairite (*ja'-ur-ite*)
2Sa 20:26 Ira also the *J'* was a chief ruler 2972
Jairus (*ja-i'-rus*)
M'r 5:22 of the synagogue, *J'* by name; 2383
Lu 8:41 there came a man named *J'*, and "
Jakan (*ja'-kan*) See also AKAN; JAAKAN.
1Ch 1:42 Ezer; Bilhan, and Zavan, and *J'*.*3292
Jakeh (*ja'-keh*)
Pr 30: 1 The words of Agur the son of *J'*, 3348
Jakim (*ja'-kim*)
1Ch 8:19 And *J'*, and Zichri, and Zabdi, 3356
24:12 to Eliashib, the twelfth to *J'*, "
Jalon (*ja'-lon*)
1Ch 4:17 and Mered, and Epher, and *J'*: 3210
Jambres (*jam'-brees*)
2Ti 3: 8 Jannes and *J'* withstood Moses. 2387
James (*james*) See also JACOB.
M't 4:21 *J'* the son of Zebedee, and John 2385
10: 2 *J'* the son of Zebedee, and John "
3 *J'* the son of Alphæus, and "
13:55 brethren, *J'*, and Joses, and Simon, "
17: 1 Jesus taketh Peter, *J'*, and John his "
27:56 Mary the mother of *J'* and Joses, "
M'r 1:19 *J'* the son of Zebedee, and John "
29 and Andrew, with *J'* and John. "
M'r 3:17 *J'*...and John the brother of *J'*; 2385
18 and *J'* the son of Alphæus, and "
5:37 and *J'*, and John the brother of *J'*. "
6: 3 the brother of *J'*, and Joses, and of "
9: 2 with him Peter, and *J'*, and John, "
10:35 *J'* and John, the sons of Zebedee, "
41 much displeased with *J'* and John. "
13: 3 Peter and *J'* and John and Andrew "
14:33 with him Peter and *J'* and John, "
15:40 Mary the mother of *J'* the less and "
16: 1 Mary the mother of *J'*, and Salome, "
Lu 5:10 *J'*, and John, the sons of Zebedee, "
6:14 Andrew his brother, *J'* and John, "
15 Thomas, *J'* the son of Alphæus, "
16 And Judas the brother of *J'*, and "
8:51 go in, save Peter, and *J'*, and John, "
9:28 he took Peter and John and *J'*, and "
54 his disciples *J'* and John saw this, "
24:10 and Mary the mother of *J'*, and "
Ac 1:13 abode...Peter, and *J'*, and John, "
13 Matthew, *J'* the son of Alphæus, "
13 and Judas the brother of *J'*. "
12: 2 he killed *J'* the brother of John "
17 Go shew these things unto *J'*, and "
15:13 *J'* answered, saying, Men and "
21:18 Paul went in with us unto *J'*; "
1Co 15: 7 After that, he was seen of *J'*; then "
Ga 1:19 I none, save *J'* the Lord's brother. "
2: 9 *J'*, Cephas, and John, who seemed "
12 before that certain came from *J'*, "
Jas 1: 1 *J'*, a servant of God and of the "
Jude 1 of Jesus Christ, and brother of *J'*, "
Jamin (*ja'-min*) See also JAMINITES.
Ge 46:10 Jemuel, and *J'*, and Ohad, and 3226
Ex 6:15 Jemuel, and *J'*, and Ohad, and "
Nu 26:12 of *J'*, the family of the Jaminites: "
1Ch 2:27 of Jerahmeel were, Maaz, and *J'*, "
4:24 of Simeon were, Nemuel, and *J'*, "
Ne 8: 7 Sherebiah, *J'*, Akkub, Shabbethai, "
Jaminites (*ja'-min-ites*)
Nu 26:12 of Jamin, the family of the *J'*: 3228
Jamlech (*jam'-lek*)
1Ch 4:34 Meshobab, and *J'*, and Joshah 3230
jangling
1Ti 1: 6 turned aside unto vain *j'*; have *3150
Janna (*jan'-nah*)
Lu 3:24 Melchi, which was the son of *J'*, *2388
Jannes (*jan'-nees*)
2Ti 3: 8 *J'* and Jambres withstood Moses, 2389
Janoah (*ja-no'-ah*) See also JANOHAH.
2Ki 15:29 *J'*, and Kedesh, and Hazor, and 3239
Janohah (*ja-no'-hah*) See also JANOAH.
Jos 16: 6 and passed by it on the east to *J'*;*3239
7 it went down from *J'* to Ataroth,* "
Janum (*ja'-num*)
Jos 15:53 And *J'*, and Beth-tappuah, and *3241
Japheth (*ja'-feth*)
Ge 5:32 Noah begat Shem, Ham, and *J'*. 3315
6:10 three sons, Shem, Ham, and *J'*. "
7:13 Noah, and Shem, and Ham, and *J'*, "
9:18 ark, were Shem, and Ham, and *J'*: "
23 And Shem and *J'* took a garment, "
27 shall enlarge *J'*, and he shall dwell "
10: 1 sons of Noah, Shem, Ham, and *J'*: "
2 The sons of *J'*; Gomer, and Magog, "
21 of Eber, brother of *J'* the elder, "
1Ch 1: 4 Noah, Shem, Ham, and *J'*. "
5 The sons of *J'*; Gomer, and Magog, "
Japhia (*ja-fi'-ah*)
Jos 10: 3 and unto *J'* king of Lachish, and 3309
19:12 out to Daberath, and goeth up to *J'*, "
2Sa 5:15 and Elishua, and Nepheg, and *J'*, "
1Ch 3: 7 And Nogah, and Nepheg, and *J'*, "
14: 6 And Nogah, and Nepheg, and *J'*, "
Japhlet (*jaf'-let*) See also JAPHLETI.
1Ch 7:32 Heber begat *J'*, and Shomer, and 3310
33 And the sons of *J'*; Pasach, and "
33 These are the children of *J'*. "
Japhleti (*jaf'-let-i*) See also JAPHLET.
Jos 16: 3 down westward to the coast of *J'*,*3311
Japho (*ja'-fo*) See also JOPPA.
Jos 19:46 Rakkon, with the border before *J'*.*3305
Jarah (*ja'-rah*) See also JEHOADAH.
1Ch 9:42 And Ahaz begat *J'*; and *J'* begat 3294
Jareb (*ja'-reb*)
Ho 5:13 the Assyrian, and sent to king *J'*: 3377
10: 6 Assyria for a present to king *J'*: "
Jared (*ja'-red*) See also JERED.
Ge 5:15 sixty and five years, and begat *J'*:3382
16 Mahalaleel lived after he begat *J'* "
18 *J'* lived an hundred sixty and two "
19 And *J'* lived after he begat Enoch "
20 the days of *J'* were nine hundred "
Lu 3:37 Enoch, which was the son of *J'*, 2391
Jaresiah (*ja-re-si'-ah*)
1Ch 8:27 *J'*, and Eliah, and Zichri, the sons*3298
Jarha (*jar'-hah*)
1Ch 2:34 an Egyptian, whose name was *J'*. 3398
35 Sheshan gave his daughter to *J'* "
Jarib (*ja'-rib*) See also JACHIN.
1Ch 4:24 and Jamin, *J'*, Zerah, and Shaul: 3402
Ezr 8:16 for Elnathan, and for *J'*, and for "
10:18 and Eliezer, and *J'*, and Gedaliah. "
Jarkon See ME-JARKON.
Jarmuth (*jar'-muth*) See also REMETH.
Jos 10: 3 unto Piram king of *J'*, and unto 3412
3, 5 king of *J'*, the king of Lachish, "
12:11 The king of *J'*, one; the king of "
Jos 15:35 *J'*, and Adullam, Socoh, and Azekah, 3412
21:29 *J'* with her suburbs, En-gannim "
Ne 11:29 and at Zareah, and at *J'*, "
Jaroah (*ja-ro'-ah*)
1Ch 5:14 the son of Huri, the son of *J'*, 3386
Jashen (*ja'-shen*) See also HASHEM.
2Sa 23:32 the Shaalbonite, of the sons of *J'*, 3464
Jasher (*ja'-shur*)
Jos 10:13 not this written in the book of *J'*?*3477
2Sa 1:18 it is written in the book of *J'*. * "
Jashobeam (*jash-o'-be-am*)
1Ch 11:11 *J'*, an Hachmonite, the chief of the 3434
12: 6 and Joezer, and *J'*, the Korhites, "
27: 2 month was *J'* the son of Zabdiel: "
Jashub (*ja'-shub*) See also JASHUBI-LEHEM; JOB; JASHUBITES; SHEAR-JASHUB.
Nu 26:24 *J'*, the family of the Jashubites: 3437
1Ch 7: 1 Puah, *J'*, and Shimrom, four. "
Ezr 10:29 and Adaiah, *J'*, and Sheal, and "
Jashubi-lehem (*jash''-u-bi-le'-hem*)
1Ch 4:22 had the dominion in Moab, and *J'*.3433
Jashubites (*jash'-u-bites*)
Nu 26:24 Of Jashub, the family of the *J'*: 3432
Jasiel (*ja'-se-el*)
1Ch 11:47 and Obed, and *J'* the Mesobaite. *
Jason (*ja'-sun*)
Ac 17: 5 and assaulted the house of *J'*, and 2394
6 they drew *J'* and certain brethren "
7 Whom *J'* hath received: and these "
9 when they had taken security of *J'*, "
Ro 16:21 Lucius, and *J'*, and Sosipater, my "
jasper
Ex 28:20 a beryl, and an onyx, and a *j'*: 3471
39:13 row, a beryl, an onyx, and a *j'*: "
Eze 28:13 the onyx, and the *j'*, the sapphire, "
Re 4: 3 to look upon like a *j'* and a sardine 2393
21:11 even like a *j'* stone, clear as crystal; "
18 building of the wall of it was of *j'*: "
19 The first foundation was *j'*; the "
Jathniel (*jath'-ne-el*)
1Ch 26: 2 Zebadiah the third, *J'* the fourth, 3496
Jattir (*jat'-tur*)
Jos 15:48 in the mountains, Shamir, and *J'*, 3492
21:14 *J'* with her suburbs, and Eshtemoa "
1Sa 30:27 and to them which were in *J'*, "
1Ch 6:57 Libnah with her suburbs, and *J'*, "
Javan (*ja'-van*)
Ge 10: 2 and *J'*, and Tubal, and Meshech, 3120
4 And the sons of *J'*; Elishah, and "
1Ch 1: 5 and *J'*, and Tubal, and Meshech, "
7 And the sons of *J'*; Elishah, and "
Isa 66:19 that draw the bow, to Tubal, and *J'*, "
Eze 27:13 *J'*, Tubal, and Meshech, they were "
19 Dan also and *J'* going to and fro "
javelin
Nu 25: 7 and took a *j'* in his hand; *7420
1Sa 18:10 and there was a *j'* in Saul's hand.*2595
11 And Saul cast the *j'*; for he said, I* "
19: 9 in his house with his *j'* in his hand:* "
10 David even to the wall with the *j'*;* "
10 and he smote the *j'* into the wall:* "
20:33 Saul cast a *j'* at him to smite him:* "
jaw See also JAWBONE; JAWS.
J'g 15:16 with the *j'* of an ass have I slain a*3895
19 clave an hollow place that in the *j'*,* "
Job 41: 2 or bore his *j'* through with a thorn? "
Pr 30:14 their *j'* teeth as knives, to devour 4973
jawbone
J'g 15:15 he found a new *j'* of an ass, and 3895
16 With the *j'* of an ass, heaps upon "
17 he cast away the *j'* out of his hand, "
jaws
Job 29:17 I brake the *j'* of the wicked, and 4973
Ps 22:15 and my tongue cleaveth to my *j'*; 4455
Isa 30:28 be a bridle in the *j'* of the people, 3895
Eze 29: 4 I will put hooks in thy *j'*, and I will "
38: 4 thee back, and put hooks into thy *j'*, "
Ho 11: 4 that take off the yoke on their *j'*, "
jaw-teeth See JAW and TEETH.
Jazer (*ja'-zur*) See also JAAZER.
Nu 32: 1 and when they saw the land of *J'*, 3270
3 Ataroth, and Dibon, and *J'*, and "
Jos 13:25 their coast was *J'*, and all the cities "
21:39 her suburbs, *J'* with her suburbs; "
2Sa 24: 5 of the river of Gad, and toward *J'*: "
1Ch 6:81 suburbs, and *J'* with her suburbs. "
26:31 them men of valour at *J'* of Gilead. "
Isa 16: 8 they are come even unto *J'*, they "
9 I will bewail with the weeping of *J'* "
Jer 48:32 weep for thee with the weeping of *J'*: "
32 they reach even to the sea of *J'*: "
Jaziz (*ja'-ziz*)
1Ch 27:31 over the flocks was *J'* the Hagerite 3151
jealous
Ex 20: 5 Lord thy God am a *j'* God, visiting 7067
34:14 Lord, whose name is *J'*, is a *j'* God: "
Nu 5:14 and he be *j'* of his wife, and she be 7065
14 he be *j'* of his wife, and she be not "
30 and he be *j'* over his wife, and shall "
De 4:24 is a consuming fire, even a *j'* God. 7067
5: 9 for I the Lord thy God am a *j'* God. "
6:15 Lord thy God is a *j'* God among you) "
Jos 24:19 he is an holy God; he is a *j'* God; 7072
1Ki 19:10,14 I have been very *j'* for the Lord 7065
Eze 39:25 and will be *j'* for my holy name; "
Joe 2:18 Then will the Lord be *j'* for his land. "
Na 1: 2 God is *j'*, and the Lord revengeth; 7072
Zec 1:14 I am *j'* for Jerusalem and for Zion 7065

Zec 8: 2 I was j for Zion with great jealousy,7065
2 and I was j for her with great fury. "
2Co 11: 2 am j over you with godly jealousy:2206

jealousies
Nu 5:29 This is the law of j, when a wife *7068

jealousy See also JEALOUSIES.
Nu 5:14 And the spirit of j come upon him,7068
14 or if the spirit of j come upon him, "
15 for it is an offering of j, an offering "
18 her hands, which is the j offering: "
25 the priest shall take the j offering "
30 the spirit of j cometh upon him, "
25:11 not the children of Israel in my j. "
De 29:20 his j shall smoke against that man, "
32:16 provoked him to j with strange 7065
21 They have moved me to j with that "
21 I will move them to j with those "
1Ki 14:22 provoked him to j with their sins "
Ps 78:58 moved him to j with their graven "
79: 5 for ever? shall thy j burn like fire?7068
Pr 6:34 For j is the rage of a man: "
Ca 8: 6 as death; j is cruel as the grave: "
Isa 42:13 he shall stir up j like a man of war: "
Eze 8: 3 was the seat of the image of j, "
3 which provoketh to j. 7069
5 altar this image of j in the entry. 7068
16:38 I will give thee blood in fury and j. "
42 and my j shall depart from thee, "
23:25 And I will set my j against thee, "
36: 5 in the fire of my j have I spoken "
6 have spoken in my j and in my fury, "
38:19 in my j and in the fire of my wrath "
Zep 1:18 be devoured by the fire of his j: "
3: 8 be devoured with the fire of my j. "
Zec 1:14 jealous...for Zion with a great j. "
8: 2 I was jealous for Zion with great j, "
Ro 10:19 I will provoke you to j by them
11:11 Gentiles, for to provoke them to j.
1Co 10:22 Do we provoke the Lord to j? are we
2Co 11: 2 am jealous over you with godly j: 2205

Jearim (je'-a-rim) See also KIRJATH-JEARIM.
Jos 15:10 along unto the side of mount J·, 3297

Jeaterai (je-at'-e-rahee)
1Ch 6:21 his son, Zerah his son, J· his son.*2979

Jeberechiah (je-ber''-e-ki'-ah)
Isa 8: 2 priest, and Zechariah the son of J·.3000

Jebus (je'-bus) See also JEBUSI; JEBUSITE; JERUSALEM.
J'g 19:10 departed...came over against J·, 2982
11 And when they were by J·, the day "
1Ch 11: 4 went to Jerusalem, which is J·; "
5 the inhabitants of J· said to David, "

Jebusi (jeb'-u-si) See also JEBUSITE.
Jos 18:16 to the side of J· on the south, *2983
28 Eleph, and J·, which is Jerusalem,*"

Jebusite (jeb'-u-site) See also JEBUSITES.
Ge 10:16 the J·, and the Amorite, and the 2983
Ex 33: 2 the Perizzite, the Hivite, and the J·: "
34:11 Perizzite, and the Hivite, and the J·. "
Jos 9: 1 Hivite, and the J·, heard thereof; "
11: 3 and the J· in the mountains, "
15: 8 unto the south side of the J·; "
2Sa 24:16 threshingplace of Araunah the J·. "
18 threshingfloor of Araunah the J·. "
1Ch 1:14 The J· also, and the Amorite, and "
21:15, 18 threshingfloor of Ornan the J·. "
28 the threshingfloor of Ornan the J·, "
2Ch 3: 1 the threshingfloor of Ornan the J·. "
Zec 9: 7 in Judah, and Ekron as a J·. "

Jebusites (jeb'-u-sites)
Ge 15:21 and the Girgashites, and the J·. *2983
Ex 3: 8 and the Hivites, and the J·. * "
17 and the Hivites, and the J·, unto a* "
13: 5 and the Hivites, and the J·, which* "
23:23 Canaanites, the Hivites, and the J·:* "
Nu 13:29 the J·, and the Amorites, dwell in* "
De 7: 1 and the Hivites, and the J·, seven* "
20:17 Perizzites, the Hivites, and the J·;* "
Jos 3:10 and the Amorites, and the J·. * "
12: 8 Perizzites, the Hivites, and the J·:* "
15:63 J· the inhabitants of Jerusalem, "
63 J· dwell with the children of Judah "
24:11 Girgashites, the Hivites, and the J·; "
J'g 1:21 out the J· that inhabited Jerusalem; "
21 the J· dwell with the children of "
3: 5 and Perizzites, and Hivites, and J·:* "
19:11 let us turn in into this city of the J·, "
2Sa 5: 6 men went to Jerusalem unto the J·, "
8 and smiteth the J·, and the lame "
1Ki 9:20 Hittites, Perizzites, Hivites, and J·, "
1Ch 11: 4 where the J· were, the inhabitants "
6 Whosoever smiteth the J· first shall "
2Ch 8: 7 and the Hivites, and the J·, which "
Ezr 9: 1 the Hittites, the Perizzites, the J·, "
Ne 9: 8 and the J·, and the Girgashites, "

Jecamiah (jek-a-mi'-ah) See also JEKAMIAH.
1Ch 3:18 and Shenazar, J·, Hoshama, and *3359

Jecholiah (jek-o-li'-ah) See also JECOLIAH.
2Ki 15: 2 And his mother's name was J· of *3203

Jechonias (jek-o-ni'-as) See also JECONIAH.
M't 1:11 Josias begat J· and his brethren, *2423
12 to Babylon, J· begat Salathiel; * "

Jecoliah (jek-o-li'-ah) See also JECHOLIAH.
2Ch 26: 3 His mother's name also was J· of *3203

Jeconiah (jek-o-ni'-ah) See also CONIAH; JECHONIAS; JEHOIACHIN.
1Ch 3:16 J· his son, Zedekiah his son. 3204
17 the sons of J·; Assir, Salathiel his "
Es 2: 6 which had been carried away with J· "
Jer 24: 1 had carried away captive J· the son "
27:20 when he carried away captive J·
28: 4 I will bring again to this place J· 3204
29: 2 (After that J· the king, and the

Jedaiah (jed-a-i'-ah)
1Ch 4:37 the son of Allon, the son of J·, the 3042
9:10 of the priests; J·, and Jehoiarib, 3048
24: 7 forth to Jehoiarib, the second to J·, "
Ezr 2:36 the children of J·, of the house of "
Ne 3:10 repaired J· the son of Harumaph, 3042
7:39 the children of J·, of the house of 3048
11:10 Of the priests: J· the son of Joiarib, "
12: 6 Shemaiah, and Joiarib, J·, "
7 Sallu, Amok, Hilkiah, J·. "
19 of Joiarib, Mattenai; of J·, Uzzi; "
21 Hashabiah; of Tobijah, J·, Nethaneel. "
Zec 6:10 of Heldai, of Tobijah, and of J·, "
14 Helem, and to Tobijah, and to J·, "

Jediael (jed-e-a'-el)
1Ch 7: 6 Bela, and Becher, and J·, three. 3043
10 The sons also of J·; Bilhan: and "
11 All these the sons of J·, by the "
11:45 J· the son of Shimri, and Joha his "
12:20 and Jozabad, and J·, and Michael, "
26: 2 the firstborn, J· the second, "

Jedidah (je-di'-dah)
2Ki 22: 1 his mother's name was J·, the 3040

Jedidiah (jed-id-i'-ah) See also SOLOMON.
2Sa 12:25 called his name J·, because of the 3041

Jeduthun (jed'-u-thun)
1Ch 9:16 son of Galal, the son of J·, and 3038
16:38 Obed-edom also the son of J· and "
41 And with them Heman and J·, and "
42 And with them Heman and J· with "
42 And the sons of J· were porters. "
25: 1 of Asaph, and of Heman, and of J·, "
3 Of J·: the sons of J·; Gedaliah, and "
3 under the hands of their father J·, "
6 order to Asaph, J·, and Heman. "
2Ch 5:12 of them of Asaph, of Heman, of J·, "
29:14 and of the sons of J·; Shemaiah, "
35:15 and Heman, and J· the king's seer; "
Ne 11:17 the son of Galal, the son J·. "
Ps 39: *title* To the chief Musician, even to J·, "
62: *title* To the chief Musician, to J·, "
77: *title* To the chief Musician, to J·, "

Jeezer (je-e'-zur) See also ABIEZER; JEEZERITES.
Nu 26:30 of J·, the family of the Jeezerites:* 372

Jeezerites (je-e'-zur-ites)
Nu 26:30 of Jeezer, the family of the J·: * 373

Jegar-sahadutha (je''-gar-sa-ha-du'-thah) See also GALEED.
Ge 31:47 And Laban called it J·: but Jacob 3026

Jehaleleel (je-hal-e'-le-el) See also JEHALELEL.
1Ch 4:16 the sons of J·: Ziph, and Ziphah, *3094

Jehalelel (je-hal'-e-lel) See also JEHALELEEL.
2Ch 29:12 and Azariah the son of J·: *3094

Jehdeiah (jeh-di'-ah)
1Ch 24:20 of the sons of Shubael; J·. 3165
27:30 the asses was J· the Meronothite: "

Jehezekel (je-hez'-e-kel) See also EZEKIEL.
1Ch 24:16 to Pethahiah, the twentieth to J·,*3168

Jehiah (je-hi'-ah) See also JEHIEL.
1Ch 15:24 J· were doorkeepers for the ark. 3174

Jehiel (je-hi'-el) See also JEHIAH; JEIEL; JEHIELI.
1Ch 9:35 dwelt the father of Gibeon, J·, *3273
11:44 Shama and J· the sons of Hothan* "
15:18, 20 Shemiramoth, and J·, and Unni,3171
16: 5 and Shemiramoth, and J·, and "
23: 8 the chief was J·, and Zetham, and "
27:32 J· the son of Hachmoni was with the "
29: 8 by the hand of J· the Gershonite. "
2Ch 21: 2 Azariah, and J·, and Zechariah, "
29:14 sons of Heman; J·, and Shimei: * "
31:13 And J·, and Azaziah, and Nahath, "
35: 8 and Zechariah and J·, rulers of the "
Ezr 8: 9 Obadiah the son of J·, and with him "
10: 2 Shechaniah the son of J·, one of the "
21 and Elijah, and Shemaiah, and J·, "
26 Zechariah, and J·, and Abdi, and "

Jehieli (je-hi'-el-i) See also JEHIEL.
1Ch 26:21 Laadan the Gershonite, were J·. 3172
22 The sons of J·; Zetham, and Joel "

Jehizkiah (je-hiz-ki'-ah) See also HEZEKIAH.
2Ch 28:12 J· the son of Shallum, and Amasa 3169

Jehoadah (je-ho'-a-dah) See also JARAH.
1Ch 8:36 Ahaz begat J·; and J· begat *3085

Jehoaddan (je-ho-ad'-dan)
2Ki 14: 2 And his mother's name was J· of 3086
2Ch 25: 1 And his mother's name was J· of "

Jehoahaz (je-ho'-a-haz) See also AHAZIAH; JOAHAZ; SHALLUM.
2Ki 10:35 J· his son reigned in his stead. 3059
13: 1 J· the son of Jehu began to reign "
4 J· besought the Lord, and the Lord "
7 leave of the people to J· but fifty "
8 the rest of the acts of J·, and all "
9 J· slept with his fathers; and they "
10 began Jehoash the son of J· to reign "
22 oppressed Israel all the days of J·. "
25 Jehoash the son of J· took again "
25 he had taken out of the hand of J· "
14: 1 the second year of Joash son of J·*3099
8 Jehoash, the son of J· son of Jehu,3059
17 after the death of Jehoash son of J· "
23:30 the land took J· the son of Josiah, "
31 J· was twenty and three years old "
34 to Jehoiakim, and took J· away: "
2Ch 21:17 save J·, the youngest of his sons. "
25:17 and sent to Joash, the son of J·, "
23 the son of Joash, the son of J·, at 3059
25 after the death of Joash son of J· "
36: 1 the land took J· the son of Josiah, "
2 J· was twenty and three years old* "
4 Necho took J· his brother, and * "

Jehoash (je-ho'-ash) See also JOASH.
2Ki 11:21 Seven years old was J· when he 3060
12: 1 year of Jehu J· began to reign; "
2 J· did that which was right in the "
4 J· said to the priests, All the money "
6 three and twentieth year of king J· "
7 Then king J· called for Jehoiada the "
18 And J· king of Judah took all the "
13:10 began J· the son of Jehoahaz to "
25 J· the son of Jehoahaz took again "
14: 8 Amaziah sent messengers to J·, "
9 J· the king of Israel sent to Amaziah "
11 Therefore J· king of Israel went up; "
13 And J· king of Israel took Amaziah "
13 the son of J· the son of Ahaziah, "
15 rest of the acts of J· which he did, "
16 J· slept with his fathers, and was "
17 the death of J· son of Jehoahaz "

Jehohanan (je-ho'-ha-nan) See also JOHANAN; JOHN.
1Ch 26: 3 J· the sixth, Elioenai the seventh. 3076
2Ch 17:15 And next to him was J· the captain "
23: 1 Jeroham, and Ishmael the son of J·, "
Ezr 10:28 Of the sons also of Bebai; J·, "
Ne 12:13 Ezra, Meshullam; of Amariah, J·; "
42 Uzzi, and J·, and Malchijah, and "

Jehoiachin (je-hoy'-a-kin) See also CONIAH; JECONIAH; JECONIAS; JEHOIACHIN'S.
2Ki 24: 6 J· his son reigned in his stead. 3078
8 J· was eighteen years old when he "
12 J· the king of Judah went out to "
15 he carried away J· to Babylon, and "
25:27 thirtieth year of the captivity of J· "
27 lift up the head of J· king of Judah "
2Ch 36: 8 J· his son reigned in his stead. "
9 J· was eight years old when he "
Jer 52:31 thirtieth year of the captivity of J· "
31 lifted up the head of J· king of "

Jehoiachin's (je-hoy'-a-kins)
Eze 1: 2 fifth year of king J· captivity, 3112

Jehoiada (je-hoy'-a-dah) See also BERECHIAS; JOIADA.
2Sa 8:18 Benaiah the son of J· was over 3111
20:23 Benaiah the son of J· was over the "
23:20 Benaiah the son of J·, the son of a "
22 things did Benaiah the son of J·, "
1Ki 1: 8 and Benaiah the son of J·, and "
26 and Benaiah the son of J·, and thy "
32 prophet, and Benaiah the son of J·. "
36 Benaiah the son of J· answered "
38, 44 and Benaiah the son of J·, and "
2:25 the hand of Benaiah the son of J·; "
29 Solomon sent Benaiah the son of J·, "
34 So Benaiah the son of J· went up, "
35 Benaiah the son of J· in his room "
46 commanded Benaiah the son of J·; "
4: 4 Benaiah the son of J· was over the "
2Ki 11: 4 J· sent and fetched the rulers over "
9 that J· the priest commanded: "
9 sabbath, and came to J· the priest. "
15 But J·...commanded the captains "
17 J· made a covenant between the "
12: 2 J· the priest instructed him. "
7 Jehoash called for J· the priest, "
9 J· the priest took a chest, and bored "
1Ch 11:22 Benaiah the son of J·, the son of "
24 things did Benaiah the son of J·, "
12:27 J· was the leader of the Aaronites, "
18:17 And Benaiah the son of J· was over "
27: 5 month was Benaiah the son of J·, "
34 was J· the son of Benaiah, and "
2Ch 22:11 But Jehoshabeath,...the wife of J· "
23: 1 year J· strengthened himself, "
8 that J· the priest had commanded, "
8 for J·...dismissed not the courses. "
9 J·...delivered to the captains "
11 J· and his sons anointed him, and "
14 Then J·...brought out the captains "
16 J· made a covenant between him, "
18 J· appointed the offices of the house "
24: 2 sight of the Lord all the days of J· "
3 J· took for him two wives; and he "
6 the king called for J· the chief, and "
12 J· gave it to such as did the work "
14 the money before the king and J·, "
14 Lord continually all the days of J·. "
15 J· waxed old, and was full of days "
17 the death of J· came the princes "
20 came upon Zechariah the son of J· "
22 kindness which J· his father had "
25 him for the blood of the sons of J· "
Ne 3: 6 gate repaired J· the son of Paseah,*"
Jer 29:26 made thee priest in the stead of J· "

Jehoiakim (je-hoy'-a-kim) See also ELIAKIM; JOIAKIM.
2Ki 23:34 father, and turned his name to J·,3079
35 J· gave the silver and the gold to "
36 J· was twenty and five years old "
24: 1 J· became his servant three years: "
5 Now the rest of the acts of J·, "
6 So J· slept with his fathers: "
19 according to all that J· had done. "
1Ch 3:15 firstborn Johanan, the second J·, "
16 the sons of J·: Jeconiah his son, "
2Ch 36: 4 and turned his name to J·. "
5 J· was twenty and five years old "
8 Now the rest of the acts of J·, "
Jer 1: 3 It came also in the days of J· "
22:18 thus saith the Lord concerning J·

Jer 22: 24 Coniah the son of J' king of Judah 3079
24: 1 away captive Jeconiah the son of J' "
25: 1 fourth year of J' the son of Josiah "
26: 1 In the beginning of the reign of J' "
21 J' the king, with all his mighty "
22 J' the king sent men into Egypt, "
23 and brought him unto J' the king; "
27: 1 In the beginning of the reign of J' "
20 away captive Jeconiah the son of J' "
28: 4 to this place Jeconiah the son of J' "
35: 1 in the days of J' the son of Josiah "
36: 1 came to pass in the fourth year of J' "
9 came to pass in the fifth year of J' "
28 J' the king of Judah hath burned. "
29 thou shalt say to J' king of Judah, "
30 saith the Lord of J' king of Judah; "
32 which J'...had burned in the fire: "
37: 1 instead of Coniah the son of J', "
45: 1 fourth year of J' the son of Josiah "
46: 2 smote in the fourth year of J' "
52: 2 according to all that J' had done. "
Da 1: 1 In the third year of the reign of J' "
2 the Lord gave J' king of Judah into "

Jehoiarib (*je-hoy'-a-rib*) See also JOIARIB.
1Ch 9: 10 Jedaiah, and J', and Jachin, 3080
24: 7 Now the first lot came forth to J', "

Jehonadab (*je-hon'-a-dab*) See also JONADAB.
2Ki 10: 15 he lighted on J' the son of Rechab 3082
15 thy heart? And J' answered, It is. "
23 went, and J' the son of Rechab, "

Jehonathan (*je-hon'-a-than*) See also JONATHAN.
1Ch 27: 25 castles, was J' the son of Uzziah: *3083
2Ch 17: 8 and Shemiramoth, and J', and "
Ne 12: 18 Shammua; of Shemaiah, J'; "

Jehoram (*je-ho'-ram*) See also HADORAM; JORAM.
1Ki 22: 50 J' his son reigned in his stead. 3088
2Ki 1: 17 And J' reigned in his stead "
17 in the second year of J' the son of "
3: 1 J' the son of Ahab began to reign "
6 And king J' went out of Samaria "
8: 16 J' the son of Jehoshaphat king of "
25 Ahaziah the son of J' king of Judah "
29 son of J' king of Judah went down "
9: 24 and smote J' between his arms, * "
12: 18 J', and Ahaziah, his fathers, kings "
2Ch 17: 8 with them Elishama and J', priests. "
21: 1 And J' his son reigned in his stead. "
3 but the kingdom gave he to J'; "
4 J' was risen up to the kingdom of "
5 J' was thirty and two years old "
9 Then J' went forth with his princes, "
16 Lord stirred up against J' the spirit "
22: 1 Ahaziah the son of J' king of Judah "
5 J' the son of Ahab king of Israel "
6 Azariah the son of J' king of Judah "
6 went down to see J' the son of Ahab "
7 he went out with J' against Jehu "
11 the daughter of king J', the wife of "

Jehoshabeath (*je-ho-shab'-e-ath*) See also JEHOSHEBA.
2Ch 22: 11 But J', the daughter of the king, 3090
11 J', the daughter of king Jehoram, "

Jehoshaphat (*je-hosh'-a-fat*) See also JOSAPHAT; JOSHAPHAT.
2Sa 8: 16 J' the son of Ahilud was recorder; 3092
20: 24 J' the son of Ahilud was recorder: "
1Ki 4: 3 J' the son of Ahilud, the recorder. "
17 J' the son of Paruah, in Issachar: "
15: 24 and J' his son reigned in his stead. "
22: 2 J' the king of Judah came down "
4 he said unto J', Wilt thou go with "
4 J' said to the king of Israel, I am "
5 And J' said unto the king of Israel, "
7 J' said, Is there not here a prophet "
8 said unto J', There is yet one man, "
8 And J' said, Let not the king say so. "
10 and J' the king of Judah sat each "
18 king of Israel said unto J', Did I "
29 and J' the king of Judah went up "
30 king of Israel said unto J', I will "
32 captains of the chariots saw J', that "
32 fight against him: and J' cried out. "
41 J' the son of Asa began to reign "
42 J' was thirty and five years old "
44 J' made peace with the king of "
45 the rest of the acts of J', and his "
48 J' made ships of Tharshish to go "
49 Ahaziah the son of Ahab unto J', "
49 in the ships. But J' would not. "
50 J' slept with his fathers, and was "
51 the seventeenth year of J' king of "
2Ki 1: 17 year of Jehoram the son of J' king "
3: 1 the eighteenth year of J' king of "
7 and sent to J' the king of Judah, "
11 J' said, Is there not here a prophet "
12 J' said, The word of the Lord is "
12 J' and the king of Edom went down "
14 not that I regard the presence of J' "
8: 16 Israel, J' being then king of Judah, "
16 Jehoram the son of J' king of Judah "
9: 2 look out there Jehu the son of J' "
14 Jehu the son of J'...conspired "
12: 18 took all the hallowed things that J', "
1Ch 3: 10 his son, Asa his son, J' his son, "
15: 24 Shebaniah, and J', and Nethaneel, *3046
18: 15 and J' the son of Alihud, recorder. 3092
2Ch 17: 1 And J' his son reigned in his stead, "
3 the Lord was with J', because he "
5 all Judah brought to J' presents; "
10 that they made no war against J'. "
11 the Philistines brought J' presents, "
12 And J' waxed great exceedingly; "
18: 1 Now J' had riches and honour in "
2Ch 18: 3 Ahab king of Israel said unto J' 3092
4 And J' said unto the king of Israel, "
6 J' said, Is there not here a prophet "
7 And the king of Israel said unto J', "
7 And J' said, Let not the king say so. "
9 and J' king of Judah sat either "
17 And the king of Israel said to J', "
28 and J' the king of Judah went up "
29 And the king of Israel said unto J', "
31 the captains of the chariot saw J', "
31 J' cried out, and the Lord helped "
19: 1 J' the king of Judah returned to "
2 to meet him, and said to king J', "
4 And J' dwelt at Jerusalem: and he "
8 Jerusalem did J' set of the Levites, "
20: 1 came against J' to battle. "
2 Then there came some that told J', "
3 J' feared, and set himself to seek "
5 J' stood in the congregation of "
15 of Jerusalem, and thou king J', "
18 J' bowed his head with his face to "
20 J' stood and said, Hear me, O Judah, "
25 J' and his people came to take away "
27 J' in the forefront of them, to go "
30 So the realm of J' was quiet: for "
31 And J' reigned over Judah: he was "
34 Now the rest of the acts of J', first "
35 did J' king of Judah join himself "
37 of Mareshah prophesied against J', "
21: 1 J' slept with his fathers, and was "
2 And he had brethren the sons of J', "
2 all these were the sons of J' king "
12 hast not walked in the ways of J' "
22: 9 said they, he is the son of J', who "
Joe 3: 2 them down into the valley of J', "
12 and come up to the valley of J': "

Jehosheba (*je-hosh'-e-bah*) See also JEHOSHABEATH.
2Ki 11: 2 J', the daughter of king Joram, 3089

Jehoshua (*je-hosh'-u-ah*) See also JEHOSHUAH; JOSHUA.
Nu 13: 16 called Oshea the son of Nun J'. *3091

Jehoshuah (*je-hosh'-u-ah*) See also JEHOSHUA.
1Ch 7: 27 Non his son, J' his son. *3091

Jehovah (*je-ho'-vah*) See also GOD; JAH; JEHOVAH-JIREH; JEHOVAH-NISSI; JEHOVAH-SHALOM; LORD.
Ex 6: 3 name J' was I not known to them. 3068
Ps 83: 18 thou, whose name alone is J', art "
Isa 12: 2 J' is my strength and my song; "
26: 4 the Lord J' is everlasting strength. "

Jehovah-jireh (*je-ho''-vah-ji'-reh*)
Ge 22: 14 called the name of that place J': 3070

Jehovah-nissi (*je-ho''-vah-nis'-si*)
Ex 17: 15 altar, and called the name of it J': 3071

Jehovah-shalom (*je-ho''-vah-sha'-lom*)
J'g 6: 24 unto the Lord, and called it J': 3073

Jehozabad (*je-hoz'-a-bad*) See also JOZABAD.
2Ki 12: 21 J' the son of Shomer, his servants, 3075
1Ch 26: 4 J' the second, Joah the third, "
2Ch 17: 18 next him was J', and with him an "
24: 26 J' the son of Shimrith a Moabitess. "

Jehozadak (*je-hoz'-a-dak*) See also JOZADAK.
1Ch 6: 14 Seraiah, and Seraiah begat J', 3087
15 J' went into captivity, when the "

Jehu (*je-hu*)
1Ki 16: 1 word of the Lord came to J' the 3058
7 also by the hand of the prophet J' "
12 he spake against Baasha by J' the "
19: 16 J'...shalt thou anoint to be king "
17 the sword of Hazael shall J' slay: "
17 that escapeth from the sword of J' "
2Ki 9: 2 there J' the son of Jehoshaphat "
5 And J' said, Unto which of all us? "
11 J' came forth to the servants of his "
13 with trumpets, saying, J' is king. "
14 J' the son of Jehoshaphat the son "
15 And J' said, If it be your minds, "
16 So J' rode in a chariot, and went to "
17 spied the company of J' as he came, "
18 J' said, What hast thou to do with "
19 J' answered, What hast thou to do "
20 the driving is like the driving of J' "
21 they went out against J', and met "
22 it came to pass, when Joram saw J', "
22 that he said, Is it peace, J'? "
24 And J' drew a bow with his full "
25 Then said J' to Bidkar his captain, "
27 J' followed after him, and said, 3058
30 And when J' was come to Jezreel, "
31 as J' entered in at the gate, she "
10: 1 And J' wrote letters, and sent to "
5 up of the children, sent to J', saying, "
11 J' slew all that remained of the "
13 J' met with the brethren of Ahaziah "
18 J' gathered all the people together, "
18 little; but J' shall serve him much. "
19 J' did it in subtilty, to the intent "
20 And J' said, Proclaim a solemn "
21 And J' sent through all Israel: "
23 J' went, and Jehonadab the son of "
24 J' appointed fourscore men without, "
25 And J' said to the guard and to the "
28 J' destroyed Baal out of Israel. "
29 J' departed not from after them, "
30 the Lord said unto J', Because thou "
31 J' took no heed to walk in the law "
34 the rest of the acts of J', and all "
35 And J' slept with his fathers: and "
36 time that J' reigned over Israel "
12: 1 seventh year of J' Jehoash began "
13: 1 Jehoahaz the son of J' began to "
2Ki 14: 8 the son of Jehoahaz son of J', 3058
15: 12 of the Lord which he spake unto J', "
1Ch 2: 38 And Obed begat J', and J' begat "
4: 35 Joel, and J' the son of Josibiah, "
12: 3 Berachah, and J' the Antothite, "
2Ch 19: 2 J' the son of Hanani the seer went "
20: 34 they are written in the book of J' "
22: 7 went out with Jehoram against J' "
8 J' was executing judgment upon "
9 in Samaria,) and brought him to J': "
25: 17 the son of Jehoahaz, the son of J', "
Ho 1: 4 of Jezreel upon the house of J'. "

Jehubbah (*je-hub'-bah*)
1Ch 7: 34 of Shamer; Ahi, and Rohgah, J', 3160

Jehucal (*je-hu'-kal*) See also JUCAL.
Jer 37: 3 king sent J' the son of Shelemiah 3081

Jehud (*je'-hud*)
Jos 19: 45 And J', and Bene-berak, and 3055

Jehudi (*je-hu'-di*)
Jer 36: 14 Therefore all the princes sent J' 3065
21 So the king sent J' to fetch the roll: "
21 J' read it in the ears of the king, "
23 J' had read three or four leaves, he "

Jehudijah (*je-hu-di'-jah*) See also HODIAH.
1Ch 4: 18 And his wife J' bare Jered the *3057

Jehush (*je'-hush*) See also JEUSH.
1Ch 8: 39 J' the second, and Eliphelet the *3266

Jeiel (*je-i'-el*) See also JEHIEL; JEUEL.
1Ch 5: 7 were the chief, J', and Zecariah, 3273
15: 18 Obed-edom, and J', the porters. "
21 Obed-edom, and J', and Azaziah, "
16: 5 and next to him Zechariah, J', and "
5 J' with psalteries and with harps; "
2Ch 20: 14 of Benaiah, the son of J', the son of "
26: 11 account by the hand of J' the scribe "
29: 3 sons of Elizaphan; Shimri, and J':* "
35: 9 Hashabiah and J' and Jozabad, "
Ezr 8: 13 names are these, Eliphelet, J', and* "
10: 43 the sons of Nebo; J', Mattithiah, "

Jekabzeel (*je-kab'-ze-el*) See also KABZEEL.
Ne 11: 25 at J', and in the villages thereof, 3343

Jekameam (*je-kam'-e-am*)
1Ch 23: 19 the third, and J' the fourth. 3360
24: 23 Jahaziel the third, J' the fourth. "

Jekamiah (*jek-a-mi'-ah*) See also JECAMIAH.
1Ch 2: 41 Shallum begat J', and J' begat 3359

Jekuthiel (*je-ku'-the-el*)
1Ch 4: 18 and J' the father of Zanoah. 3354

Jemima (*je-mi'-mah*)
Job 42: 14 he called the name of the first, J'; *3224

Jemuel (*je-mu'-el*) See also NEMUEL.
Ge 46: 10 sons of Simeon; J', and Jamin, 3223
Ex 6: 15 the sons of Simeon; J', and Jamin, "

jeoparded
J'g 5: 18 a people that j' their lives unto the 2778

jeopardy
2Sa 23: 17 the men that went in j' of their lives?
1Ch 11: 19 that have put their lives in j'?
19 for with the j' of their lives they brought
12: 19 master Saul to the j' of our heads.
Lu 8: 23 filled with water, and were in j'. 2793
1Co 15: 30 And why stand we in j' every hour? "

Jephthae (*jef'-thah-e*) See also JEPHTHAH.
Heb 11: 32 Barak, and of Samson, and of J'; *2422

Jephthah (*jef'-thah*) See also JEPHTHAE; JIPHTHAH-EL.
J'g 11: 1 Now J' the Gileadite was a mighty 3316
1 of an harlot: and Gilead begat J'. "
2 they thrust out J', and said unto "
3 Then J' fled from his brethren, "
3 there were gathered vain men to J', "
5 the elders of Gilead went to fetch J' "
6 they said unto J', Come, and be our "
7 J' said unto the elders of Gilead, "
8 the elders of Gilead said unto J', "
9 J' said unto the elders of Gilead, "
10 the elders of Gilead said unto J', "
11 J' went with the elders of Gilead, "
11 J' uttered all his words before the "
12 J' sent messengers unto the king "
13 answered...the messengers of J', "
14 J' sent messengers again unto the "
15 Thus saith J', Israel took not away "
28 hearkened not unto the words of J' "
29 Spirit of the Lord came upon J', "
30 J' vowed a vow unto the Lord, and "
32 J' passed over unto the children of "
34 J' came to Mizpeh unto his house, "
40 yearly to lament the daughter of J' "
12: 1 went northward, and said unto J', "
2 J' said unto them, I and my people "
4 J' gathered together all the men of "
7 And J' judged Israel six years. "
7 Then died J' the Gileadite, and was "
1Sa 12: 11 sent Jerubbaal, and Bedan, and J', "

Jephunneh (*je-fun'-neh*)
Nu 13: 6 tribe of Judah, Caleb the son of J'. 3312
14: 6 son of Nun, and Caleb the son of J', "
30 therein, save Caleb the son of J', "
38 son of Nun, and Caleb the son of J', "
26: 65 of them, save Caleb the son of J', "
32: 12 Save Caleb the son of J' the "
34: 19 tribe of Judah, Caleb the son of J'. "
De 1: 36 Save Caleb the son of J'; he shall "
Jos 14: 6 Caleb the son of J' the Kenezite said "
13 and gave unto Caleb the son of J' "
14 inheritance of Caleb the son of J' "
15: 13 unto Caleb the son of J' he gave a "

Jos 21:12 gave they to Caleb the son of J· 3312
1Ch 4:15 the sons of Caleb the son of J·: Iru, "
6:56 they gave to Caleb the son of J·. "
7:38 the sons of Jether; J·, and Pispah, "

Jerah *(je'-rah)*
Ge 10:26 and Hazarmaveth, and J·, 3392
1Ch 1:20 and Hazarmaveth, and J·, "

Jerahmeel *(je-rah'-me-el)* See also JERAHMEELITES.
1Ch 2: 9 J·, and Ram, and Chelubai. 3396
25 sons of J· the firstborn of Hezron "
26 J· had also another wife, whose "
27 the sons of Ram the firstborn of J· "
33 These were the sons of J·. "
42 sons of Caleb the brother of J· were, "
24:29 Kish: the son of Kish was J·. "
Jer 36:26 J· the son of Hammelech, "

Jerahmeelites *(je-rah'-me-el-ites)*
1Sa 27:10 and against the south of the J·, 3397
30:29 which were in the cities of the J·, "

Jered *(je'-red)* See also JARED.
1Ch 1: 2 Kenan, Mahalaleel, J·, *3382
4:18 wife Jehudijah bare J· the father of "

Jeremai *(jer'-e-mahee)*
Ezr 10:33 Zabad, Eliphelet, J·, Manasseh, 3413

Jeremiah *(jer-e-mi'-ah)* See also JEREMIAH'S; JEREMIAS; JEREMY.
2Ki 23:31 the daughter of J· of Libnah. 3414
24:18 the daughter of J· of Libnah. "
1Ch 5:24 and Azriel, and J·, and Hodaviah, "
12: 4 and J·, and Jahaziel, and Johanan, "
10 the fourth, J· the fifth, "
13 J· the tenth, Machbanai the "
2Ch 35:25 And J· lamented for Josiah: "
36:12 and humbled not himself before J· "
21 word of the Lord by the mouth of J·, "
22 the Lord spoken by the mouth of J· "
Ezr 1: 1 word of the Lord by the mouth of J· "
Ne 10: 2 Seraiah, Azariah, J·, "
12: 1 and Jeshua: Seraiah, J·, Ezra, "
12 Seraiah, Meraiah; of J·, Hananiah; "
34 Benjamin, and Shemaiah, and J·, "
Jer 1: 1 The words of J· the son of Hilkiah, "
11 me, saying, J·, what seest thou? "
7: 1 word that came to J· from the Lord, "
11: 1 word that came to J· from the Lord, "
14: 1 came to J· concerning the dearth. "
18: 1 word which came to J· from the "
18 let us devise devices against J·; "
19:14 Then came J· from Tophet, "
20: 1 heard that J· prophesied these "
2 Then Pashur smote J· the prophet, "
3 brought forth J· out of the stocks. "
3 Then said J· unto him, The Lord "
21: 1 which came unto J· from the Lord, "
3 Then said J· unto them, Thus shall "
24: 3 Lord unto me, What seest thou, J·? "
25: 1 word that came to J· concerning "
2 The which J· the prophet spake "
13 J· hath prophesied against all the "
26: 7 the people heard J· speaking these "
8 J· had made an end of speaking all "
9 people were gathered against J· in "
12 spake J· unto all the princes and "
20 according to all the words of J·: "
24 the son of Shaphan was with J·, "
27: 1 this word unto J· from the Lord, "
28: 5 J· said unto the prophet Hananiah "
6 prophet J· said, Amen: the Lord do "
11 And the prophet J· went his way. "
12 word of the Lord came unto J· the "
12 from off the neck of the prophet J·, "
15 said the prophet J· unto Hananiah "
29: 1 are the words of the letter that J· "
27 why hast thou not reproved J· of "
29 read this letter in the ears of J· "
30 came the word of the Lord unto J·, "
30: 1 word that came to J· from the Lord, "
32: 1 The word that came to J· from the "
2 J· the prophet was shut up in the "
6 J· said, The word of the Lord came "
26 came the word of the Lord unto J·, "
33: 1 Lord came unto J· the second time, "
19 the word of the Lord came unto J·, "
23 the word of the Lord came to J·, "
34: 1 which came unto J· from the Lord, "
6 Then J· the prophet spake all these "
8 that came unto J· from the Lord, "
12 the word of the Lord came to J· "
35: 1 which came unto J· from the Lord, "
3 I took Jaazaniah the son of J·, "
12 came the word of the Lord unto J·, "
18 And J· said unto...the Rechabites, "
36: 1 word came unto J· from the Lord, "
4 J· called Baruch the son of Neriah: "
4 Baruch wrote from the mouth of J· "
5 J· commanded Baruch, saying, I "
8 J· the prophet commanded him, "
10 Baruch in the book the words of J· "
19 Baruch, Go, hide thee, thou and J·; "
26 the scribe and J· the prophet: "
27 the word of the Lord came to J·, "
27 Baruch wrote at the mouth of J·, "
32 Then took J· another roll, and gave "
32 wrote therein from the mouth of J· "
37: 2 which he spake by the prophet J·. "
3 the priest to the prophet J·, saying, "
4 J· came in and went out among "
6 of the Lord unto the prophet J·, "
12 Then J· went forth out of Jerusalem "
13 and he took J· the prophet, saying, "
14 Then said J·, It is false; I fall not "
14 so Irijah took J·, and brought him "
15 the princes were wroth with J·, "
Jer 37:16 J· was entered into the dungeon, 3414
16 J· had remained there many days; "
17 And J· said, There is: for, said he, "
18 J· said unto king Zedekiah, What "
21 should commit J· into the court of "
21 J· remained in the court of the "
38: 1 heard the words that J· had spoken "
6 took they J·, and cast him into the "
6 and they let down J· with cords. "
6 but mire: so J· sunk in the mire. "
7 they had put J· in the dungeon; "
9 evil in all that they have done to J· "
10 J· the prophet out of the dungeon, "
11 by cords into the dungeon to J·. "
12 the Ethiopian said unto J·, Put now "
12 under the cords. And J· did so. "
13 So they drew up J· with cords, and "
13 J· remained in the court of the "
14 and took J· the prophet unto him "
14 the king said unto J·, I will ask "
15 J· said unto Zedekiah, If I declare "
16 the king sware secretly unto J·, "
17 said J· unto Zedekiah, Thus saith "
19 Zedekiah the king said unto J·, I "
20 J· said, They shall not deliver thee. "
24 Then said Zedekiah unto J·, Let no "
27 Then came all the princes unto J·, "
28 J· abode in the court of the prison "
39:11 Babylon gave charge concerning J· "
14 sent, and took J· out of the court "
15 the word of the Lord came unto J·, "
40: 1 that came to J· from the Lord, "
2 the captain of the guard took J·, "
6 Then went J· unto Gedaliah the "
42: 2 And said unto J· the prophet, Let, "
4 J· the prophet said unto them, I "
5 they said to J·, The Lord be a true "
7 the word of the Lord came unto J·. "
43: 1 J· had made an end of speaking "
2 and all proud men, saying unto J·, "
6 J· the prophet and Baruch the son "
8 came the word of the Lord unto J· "
44: 1 word that came to J· concerning "
15 in Pathros, answered J·, saying, "
20 Then J· said unto all the people, to "
24 J· said unto all the people, and to "
45: 1 word that J· the prophet spake unto "
1 words in a book at the mouth of J·, "
46: 1 word of the Lord which came to J· "
13 The word that the Lord spake to J· "
47: 1 word of the Lord that came to J· "
49:34 word of the Lord that came to J· "
50: 1 the land of the Chaldeans by J· "
51:59 which J· the prophet commanded "
60 J· wrote in a book all the evil that "
61 J· said to Seraiah, When thou comest "
64 Thus far are the words of J·. "
52: 1 the daughter of J· of Libnah. "
Da 9: 2 the word of the Lord came to J· the "

Jeremiah's *(jer-e-mi'-ahz)*
Jer 28:10 yoke from off the prophet J· neck, 3414

Jeremias *(jer-e-mi'-as)* See also JEREMIAH.
M't 16:14 others, J·, or one of the prophets. *2408

Jeremoth *(jer'-e-moth)* See also JERIMOTH.
1Ch 8:14 And Ahio, Shashak, and J·, 3406
23:23 Mahli, and Eder, and J·, three. "
25:22 The fifteenth to J·, he, his sons, and "
Ezr 10:26 and Jehiel, and Abdi, and J·, and "
27 Mattaniah, and J·, and Zabad, and "

Jeremy *(jer'-e-mee)* See also JEREMIAH.
M't 2:17 that which was spoken by J· the *2408
27: 9 that which was spoken by J· the * "

Jeriah *(je-ri'-ah)* See also JERIJAH.
1Ch 23:19 Of the sons of Hebron; J· the first, 3404
24:23 J· the first, Amariah the second, "

Jeribai *(jer'-ib-ahee)*
1Ch 11:46 Eliel the Mahavite, and J·, and 3403

Jericho *(jer'-ik-o)*
Nu 22: 1 of Moab on this Jordan by J·. 3405
26: 3 plains of Moab by Jordan near J·, "
63 plains of Moab by Jordan near J·. "
31:12 Moab, which are by Jordan near J·. "
33:48 plains of Moab by Jordan near J·. "
50 plains of Moab by Jordan near J·, "
34:15 this side Jordan near J· eastward, "
35: 1 plains of Moab by Jordan near J·, "
36:13 plains of Moab by Jordan near J·. "
De 32:49 of Moab, that is over against J·; "
34: 1 of Pisgah, that is over against J·. "
3 and the plain of the valley of J·, the "
Jos 2: 1 saying, Go view the land, even J·. "
2 it was told the king of J·, saying, "
3 And the king of J· sent unto Rahab, "
3:16 people passed over right against J·. "
4:13 Lord unto battle, to the plains of J·. "
19 in Gilgal, in the east border of J·. "
5:10 month at even in the plains of J·. "
13 to pass, when Joshua was by J·, "
6: 1 J· was straitly shut up because of "
2 I have given into thine hand J·, "
25 which Joshua sent to spy out J·. "
26 riseth up and buildeth this city J·: "
7: 2 And Joshua sent men from J· to Ai, "
8: 2 as thou didst unto J· and her king: "
9: 3 what Joshua had done unto J· "
10: 1 as he had done to J· and her king, "
28 as he did unto the king of J·. "
30 thereof as he did unto the king of J·. "
12: 9 The king of J·, one; the king of Ai, "
13:32 Moab, on the other side Jordan, by J·, "
16: 1 of Joseph fell from Jordan by J·, "
1 unto the water of J· on the east, "
1 wilderness that goeth up from J· "
7 and to Naarath, and came to J·, "
Jos 18:12 border went up to the side of J· on 3405
21 according to their families were J·, "
20: 8 And on the other side Jordan by J· "
24:11 over Jordan, and came unto J·: "
11 the men of J· fought against you, "
2Sa 10: 5 Tarry at J· until your beards be "
1Ki 16:34 did Hiel the Beth-elite build J·: "
2Ki 2: 4 for the Lord hath sent me to J·. "
4 not leave thee. So they came to J·. "
5 sons of the prophets that were at J· "
15 prophets which were to view at J· "
18 again to him, (for he tarried at J·,) "
25: 5 overtook him in the plains of J·; "
1Ch 6:78 And on the other side Jordan by J·, "
19: 5 Tarry at J· until your beards be "
2Ch 28:15 upon asses, and brought them to J·, "
Ezr 2:34 The children of J·, three hundred "
Ne 3: 2 unto him builded the men of J·. "
7:36 The children of J·, three hundred "
Jer 39: 5 Zedekiah in the plains of J·: "
52: 8 Zedekiah in the plains of J·; "
M't 20:29 And as they departed from J·, a 2410
M'r 10:46 came to J·: and as he went out of J· "
Lu 10:30 went down from Jerusalem to J·, "
18:35 that as he was come nigh unto J·, "
19: 1 entered and passed through J·. "
Heb11:30 By faith the walls of J· fell down, "

Jeriel *(je-ri'-el)*
1Ch 7: 2 Uzzi, and Rephaiah, and J·, and 3400

Jerijah *(je-ri'-jah)* See also JERIAH.
1Ch 26:31 the Hebronites was J· the chief, 3404

Jerimoth *(jer'-im-oth)* See also JEREMOTH.
1Ch 7: 7 Uzzi, and Uzziel, and J·, and Iri, 3406
8 and Elioenai, and Omri, and J·, * "
12: 5 Eluzai, and J·, and Bealiah, and "
24:30 of Mushi; Mahli, and Eder, and J·. "
25: 4 Mattaniah, Uzziel, Shebuel, and J·, "
27:19 of Naphtali, J· the son of Azriel: * "
2Ch 11:18 him Mahalath the daughter of J· "
31:13 and Nahath, and Asahel, and J·, "

Jerioth *(je'-re-oth)*
1Ch 2:18 of Azubah his wife, and of J·: 3408

Jeroboam *(jer-o-bo'-am)* See also JEROBOAM'S.
1Ki 11:26 J· the son of Nebat, an Ephrathite 3379
28 J· was a mighty man of valour: "
29 when J· went out of Jerusalem, "
31 And he said to J·, Take thee ten "
40 Solomon sought therefore to kill J·. "
40 And J· arose, and fled into Egypt, "
12: 2 to pass, when J· the son of Nebat, "
2 Solomon, and J· dwelt in Egypt;) "
3 And J· and all the congregation of "
12 So J· and all the people came to "
15 by Ahijah the Shilonite unto J· "
20 all Israel heard that J· was come "
25 Then J· built Shechem in mount "
26 J· said in his heart, Now shall the "
32 J· ordained a feast in the eighth "
13: 1 and J· stood by the altar to burn "
4 J· heard the saying of the man of * "
33 J· returned not from his evil way, "
34 became sin unto the house of J·, "
14: 1 time Abijah the son of J· fell sick. "
2 J· said to his wife, Arise, I pray "
2 be not known to be the wife of J·; "
5 Behold, the wife of J· cometh to ask "
6 he said, Come in, thou wife of J·; "
7 Go, tell J·, Thus saith the Lord God "
10 will bring evil upon the house of J·, "
10 will cut off from J· him that pisseth "
10 the remnant of the house of J·, "
11 Him that dieth of J· in the city "
13 only of J· shall come to the grave, "
13 God of Israel in the house of J·. "
14 cut off the house of J· that day: "
16 Israel up because of the sins of J·, "
19 the rest of the acts of J·, how he "
20 J· reigned were two and twenty "
30 was war between Rehoboam and J· "
15: 1 in the eighteenth year of king J· "
6 was war between Rehoboam and J· "
7 was war between Abijam and J·. "
9 twentieth year of J· king of Israel "
25 Nadab the son of J· began to reign "
29 that he smote all the house of J·; "
29 he left not to J· any that breathed, "
30 of the sins of J· which he sinned, "
34 walked in the way of J·, and in his "
16: 2 thou hast walked in the way of J·, "
3 make thy house like the house of J· "
7 in being like the house of J·; "
19 in walking in the way of J·, and in "
26 For he walked in all the way of J· "
31 for him to walk in the sins of J· "
21:22 thine house like the house of J· "
22:52 of his mother, and in the way of J· "
2Ki 3: 3 he cleaved unto the sins of J· the "
9: 9 house of Ahab like the house of J· "
10:29 from the sins of J· the son of Nebat, "
31 he departed not from the sins of J·, "
13: 2 and followed the sins of J· the son "
6 not from the sins of the house of J·, "
11 departed not from all the sins of J· "
13 and J· sat upon his throne: "
14:16 and J· his son reigned in his stead. "
23 J· the son of Joash king of Israel "
24 departed not from all the sins of J· "
27 he saved them by the hand of J· "
28 the rest of the acts of J·, and all "
29 J· slept with his fathers, even with "
15: 1 twenty and seventh year of J· king "
8 did Zachariah the son of J· reign "
9 he departed not from the sins of J· "
18 not all his days from the sins of J· "

2Ki 15: 24, 28 departed not from the sins of J· 3379
17: 21 they made J· the son of Nebat king: "
21 J· drave Israel from following the "
22 of Israel walked in all the sins of J· "
23: 15 the high place which J· the son of "
1Ch 5: 17 and in the days of J· king of Israel. "
2Ch 9: 29 visions of Iddo the seer against J· "
10: 2 came to pass, when J·...heard it, "
2 it, that J· returned out of Egypt. "
3 J· and all Israel came and spake to "
12 So J· and all the people came to "
15 hand of Ahijah the Shilonite to J· "
11: 4 returned from going against J·. "
14 J· and his sons had cast them off "
12: 15 wars between Rehoboam and J· "
13: 1 in the eighteenth year of king J· "
2 was war between Abijah and J·. "
3 J· also set the battle in array "
4 Hear me, thou J·, and all Israel; "
6 J· the son of Nebat, the servant of "
8 calves, which J· made you for gods. "
13 J· caused an ambushment to come "
15 God smote J· and all Israel before "
19 Abijah pursued after J·, and took "
20 Neither did J· recover strength "
Ho 1: 1 in the days of J· the son of Joash, "
Am 1: 1 in the days of J· the son of Joash "
7: 9 I will rise against the house of J· "
10 the priest of Beth-el sent to J· king "
11 saith, J· shall die by the sword, "

Jeroboam's (*jer-o-bo'-ams*)
1Ki 14: 4 And J· wife did so, and arose, and 3379
17 J· wife arose, and departed, and "

Jeroham (*je-ro'-ham*)
1Sa 1: 1 name was Elkanah, the son of J·, 3395
1Ch 6: 27 son, J· his son, Elkanah his son. "
34 The son of Elkanah, the son of J·, "
8: 27 Eliah, and Zichri, the sons of J·. "
9: 8 Ibneiah the son of J·, and Elah the "
12 And Adaiah the son of J·, the son of "
12: 7 Zebadiah, the sons of J· of Gedor. "
27: 22 Of Dan, Azareel the son of J·. "
2Ch 23: 1 Azariah the son of J·, and Ishmael "
Ne 11: 12 and Adaiah the son of J·, the son of "

Jerubbaal (*je-rub'-ba-al*) See also GIDEON; JERUBBESHETH.
J'g 6: 32 on that day he called him J·, 3378
7: 1 J·, who is Gideon, and all the people "
8: 29 J· the son of Joash went and dwelt "
35 they kindness to the house of J·, "
9: 1 Abimelech the son of J· went to "
2 that all the sons of J·,...reign over "
5 slew his brethren the sons of J·, "
5 the youngest son of J· was left; "
16 and if ye have dealt well with J· "
19 dealt truly and sincerely with J· "
24 and ten sons of J· might come, "
28 serve him? is not he the son of J·? "
57 the curse of Jotham the son of J·. "
1Sa 12: 11 And the Lord sent J·, and Bedan, "

Jerubbesheth (*je-rub'-be-sheth*) See also JERUBBAAL.
2Sa 11: 21 smote Abimelech the son of J·? 3380

Jeruel (*je-ru'-el*)
2Ch 20: 16 brook, before the wilderness of J·. 3385

Jerusalem (*je-ru'-sa-lem*) See also JERUSALEM'S; SALEM.
Jos 10: 1 king of J· had heard how Joshua 3389
3 king of J· sent unto Hoham king of "
5, 23 king of J·, the king of Hebron, "
12: 10 The king of J·, one; the king of "
15: 8 side of the Jebusite; the same is J·: "
63 the Jebusites the inhabitants of J·, "
63 with the children of Judah at J· "
18: 28 Eleph, and Jebusi, which is J·, "
J'g 1: 7 they brought him to J·, and there "
8 of Judah had fought against J·, "
21 out the Jebusites that inhabited J·; "
21 of Benjamin in J· unto this day. "
19: 10 over against Jebus, which is J·; "
1Sa 17: 54 the Philistine, and brought it to J·; "
2Sa 5: 5 in J· he reigned thirty and three "
6 the king and his men went to J· "
13 concubines and wives out of J·, "
14 those that were born unto him in J·: "
8: 7 Hadadezer, and brought them to J·. "
9: 13 So Mephibosheth dwelt in J·: for "
10: 14 children of Ammon, and came to J·. "
11: 1 But David tarried still at J·. "
12 So Uriah abode in J· that day, and "
12: 31 and all the people returned unto J·. "
14: 23 Geshur, and brought Absalom to J·. "
28 Absalom dwelt two full years in J·, "
15: 8 shall bring me again indeed to J·, "
11 went two hundred men out of J·, "
14 servants that were with him at J·, "
29 carried the ark of God again to J·: "
37 the city, and Absalom came into J·. "
16: 3 the king, Behold, he abideth at J·: "
15 people the men of Israel, came to J·, "
17: 20 not find them, they returned to J·. "
19: 19 that my lord the king went out of J·, "
25 he was come to J· to meet the king, "
33 and I will feed thee with me in J·. "
34 should go up with the king unto J·? "
20: 2 their king, from Jordan even to J·. "
3 And David came to his house at J·; "
7 and they went out of J·, to pursue "
22 Joab returned to J· unto the king. "
24: 8 they came to J· at the end of nine "
16 out his hand upon J· to destroy it, "
1Ki 2: 11 and three years reigned he in J·. "
36 unto him, Build thee an house in J·, "
38 And Shimei dwelt in J· many days. "
1Ki 2: 41 Shimei had gone from J· to Gath, 3389
3: 1 and the wall of J· round about. "
15 he came to J·, and stood before the "
8: 1 of Israel, unto king Solomon in J·, "
9: 15 and the wall of J·, and Hazor, and "
19 Solomon desired to build in J·, "
10: 2 she came to J· with a very great "
26 chariots, and with the king at J·. "
27 made silver to be in J· as stones, "
11: 7 in the hill that is before J·, and for "
29 when Jeroboam went out of J·, "
36 have a light alway before me in J·, "
42 the time that Solomon reigned in J· "
12: 18 him up to his chariot, to flee to J·. "
21 when Rehoboam was come to J·, "
27 in the house of the Lord at J·, "
28 is too much for you to go up to J·: "
14: 21 he reigned seventeen years in J·, "
25 king of Egypt came up against J·: "
15: 2 Three years reigned he in J·. "
4 Lord his God give him a lamp in J·, "
4 son after him, and to establish J·: "
10 forty and one years reigned he in J·. "
22: 42 reigned twenty and five years in J·. "
2Ki 8: 17 and he reigned eight years in J·. "
26 and he reigned one year in J·. "
9: 28 carried him in a chariot to J·, "
12: 1 and forty years reigned he in J·. "
17 Hazael set his face to go up to J·. "
18 of Syria: and he went away from J·. "
14: 2 reigned twenty and nine years in J·. "
2 name was Jehoaddan of J·. "
13 at Beth-shemesh, and came to J·, "
13 and brake down the wall of J· from "
19 a conspiracy against him in J·: "
20 he was buried at J· with his fathers "
15: 2 reigned two and fifty years in J·. "
2 name was Jecholiah of J·. "
33 and he reigned sixteen years in J·. "
16: 2 and reigned sixteen years in J·, "
5 king of Israel came up to J· to war: "
18: 2 reigned twenty and nine years in J·. "
17 with a great host against J·: "
17 And they went up and came to J·. "
22 and hath said to Judah and J·, "
22 worship before this altar in J·? "
35 should deliver J· out of mine hand? "
19: 10 J· shall not be delivered into the "
21 daughter of J· hath shaken her head "
31 out of J· shall go forth a remnant, "
21: 1 reigned fifty and five years in J·. "
4 Lord said, In J· will I put my name. "
7 and in J·, which I have chosen "
12 I am bringing such evil upon J· and "
13 stretch over J· the line of Samaria, "
13 wipe J· as a man wipeth a dish, "
16 filled J· from one end to another; "
19 and he reigned two years in J·. "
22: 1 reigned thirty and one years in J·. "
14 (now she dwelt in J· in the college;) "
23: 1 all the elders of Judah and of J·. "
2 all the inhabitants of J· with him, "
4 he burned them without J· in the "
5 and in the places round about J·; "
6 without J·, unto the brook Kidron, "
9 not up to the altar of the Lord in J·, "
13 the high places that were before J·, "
20 upon them, and returned to J·. "
23 was holden to the Lord in J·. "
24 spied in the land of Judah and in J·, "
27 off this city J· which I have chosen, "
30 brought him to J·, and buried him "
31 and he reigned three months in J·. "
33 that he might not reign in J·; "
36 and he reigned eleven years in J·. "
24: 4 for he filled J· with innocent blood; "
8 and he reigned in J· three months. "
8 the daughter of Elnathan of J·. "
10 king of Babylon came up against J·, "
14 he carried away all J·, and all the "
15 carried he into captivity from J· to "
18 and he reigned eleven years in J·. "
20 it came to pass in J· and Judah, "
25: 1 he, and all his host, against J·, "
8 of the king of Babylon, unto J·: "
9 house, and all the houses of J·, "
10 down the walls of J· round about. "
1Ch 3: 4 in J· he reigned thirty and three "
5 these were born unto him in J·; "
6: 10 temple that Solomon built in J·:) "
15 Lord carried away Judah and J· "
32 built the house of the Lord in J·: "
8: 28 chief men. These dwelt in J·. "
32 dwelt with their brethren in J·, "
9: 3 in J· dwelt of the children of Judah, "
34 their generations; these dwelt at J·. "
38 dwelt with their brethren at J·, "
11: 4 David and all Israel went to J·, "
14: 3 And David took more wives at J·: "
4 of his children which he had in J·; "
15: 3 gathered all Israel together to J·, "
18: 7 Hadarezer, and brought them to J·. "
19: 15 into the city. Then Joab came to J·. "
20: 1 But David tarried at J·. And Joab "
3 and all the people returned to J·. "
21: 4 throughout all Israel, and came to J·. "
15 And God sent an angel unto J· to "
16 in his hand stretched out over J·. "
23: 25 that they may dwell in J· for ever: "
28: 1 with all the valiant men, unto J·. "
29: 27 and three years reigned he in J·. "
2Ch 1: 4 he had pitched a tent for it at J·. "
13 high place that was at Gibeon to J·, "
14 cities, and with the king at J·. "
15 silver and gold at J· as plenteous "
2: 7 are with me in Judah and in J· "
2Ch 2: 16 and thou shalt carry it up to J·. 3389
3: 1 to build the house of the Lord at J· "
5: 2 unto J·, to bring up the ark of "
6: 6 But I have chosen J·, that my name "
8: 6 that Solomon desired to build in J·, "
9: 1 Solomon with hard questions at J·, "
25 cities, and with the king at J·. "
27 king made silver in J· as stones, "
30 And Solomon reigned in J· over all "
10: 18 him up to his chariot, to flee to J·. "
11: 1 when Rehoboam was come to J·, "
5 Rehoboam dwelt in J·, and built "
14 and came to Judah and J·: "
16 the Lord God of Israel came to J·, "
12: 2 king of Egypt came up against J·, "
4 pertained to Judah, and came to J·. "
5 that were gathered together to J· "
7 shall not be poured out upon J· "
9 king of Egypt came up against J·, "
13 strengthened himself in J·, and "
13 he reigned seventeen years in J·. "
13: 2 He reigned three years in J·. His "
14: 15 in abundance, and returned to J·. "
15: 10 gathered themselves together at J· "
17: 13 mighty men of valour, were in J·. "
19: 1 returned to his house in peace to J·. "
4 Jehoshaphat dwelt at J·: and he "
8 in J· did Jehoshaphat set of the "
8 when they returned to J·. "
20: 5 the congregation of Judah and J·, "
15 all Judah, and ye inhabitants of J·, "
17 the Lord with you, O Judah and J·: "
18 the inhabitants of J· fell before the "
20 O Judah, and ye inhabitants of J·; "
27 every man of Judah and J·, "
27 of them, to go again to J· with joy; "
28 they came to J· with psalteries and "
31 reigned twenty and five years in J·. "
21: 5 and he reigned eight years in J·. "
11 the inhabitants of J· to commit "
13 inhabitants of J· to go a whoring, "
20 he reigned in J· eight years, and "
22: 1 inhabitants of J· made Ahaziah his "
2 reign, and he reigned one year in J·. "
23: 2 of Israel, and they came to J·. "
24: 1 and he reigned forty years in J·. "
6 Judah and out of J· the collection, "
9 proclamation through Judah and J·, "
18 wrath came upon Judah and J· for "
23 and they came to Judah and J·, and "
25: 1 reigned twenty and nine years in J·. "
1 mother's name...Jehoaddan of J·. "
23 and brought him to J·, and brake "
23 brake down the wall of J· from the "
27 a conspiracy against him in J·; "
26: 3 he reigned fifty and two years in J·. "
3 name also was Jecoliah of J·. "
9 Moreover Uzziah built towers in J· "
15 he made in J· engines, invented "
27: 1 and he reigned sixteen years in J·. "
8 and reigned sixteen years in J·. "
28: 1 and he reigned sixteen years in J·: "
10 under the children of Judah and J· "
24 him altars in every corner of J·. "
27 buried him in the city, even in J·: "
29: 1 reigned nine and twenty years in J·. "
8 of the Lord was upon Judah and J·, "
30: 1 come to the house of the Lord at J·, "
2 and all the congregation in J·, "
3 gathered themselves together to J·. "
5 unto the Lord God of Israel at J·: "
11 themselves, and came to J·. "
13 there assembled at J· much people "
14 took away the altars that were in J·, "
21 of Israel that were present at J· "
26 So there was great joy in J·: for "
26 Israel there was not the like in J·. "
31: 4 the people that dwelt in J· to give "
32: 2 he was purposed to fight against J·, "
9 of Assyria send his servants to J·, "
9 and unto all Judah that were at J·, "
10 that ye abide in the siege in J·? "
12 and commanded Judah and J·, "
18 people of J· that were on the wall, "
19 they spake against the God of J·, "
22 Hezekiah and the inhabitants of J· "
23 brought gifts unto the Lord to J·: "
25 upon him, and upon Judah and J·. "
26 both he and the inhabitants of J·, "
33 inhabitants of J· did him honour at "
33: 1 he reigned fifty and five years in J·: "
4 In J· shall my name be for ever. "
7 and in J·, which I have chosen "
9 and the inhabitants of J· to err, "
13 him again to J· into his kingdom. "
15 in J·, and cast them out of the city. "
21 reign, and reigned two years in J·. "
34: 1 reigned in J· one and thirty years. "
3 he began to purge Judah and J· "
5 altars, and cleansed Judah and J·. "
7 land of Israel, he returned to J·. "
9 Benjamin; and they returned to J·. "
22 (now she dwelt in J· in the college:) "
29 all the elders of Judah and J·. "
30 of Judah, and the inhabitants of J·, "
32 he caused all that were present in J· "
32 the inhabitants of J· did according "
35: 1 kept a passover unto the Lord in J·: "
18 present, and the inhabitants of J·. "
24 they brought him to J·, and he died, "
24 Judah and J· mourned for Josiah. "
36: 1 him king in his father's stead in J·. "
2 and he reigned three months in J·. "
3 king of Egypt put him down at J·, "
4 his brother king over Judah and J·, "
5 and he reigned eleven years in J·: "

2Ch 36: 9 three months and ten days in J·: 3389
10 his brother king over Judah and J·: "
11 and reigned eleven years in J·. "
14 Lord which he had hallowed in J·. "
19 and brake down the wall of J·, "
23 me to build him an house in J·, "
Ezr 1: 2 me to build him an house at J·, "
3 with him, and let him go up to J·, "
3 (he is the God,) which is in J·. "
4 for the house of God that is in J·. "
5 house of the Lord which is in J·. "
7 had brought forth out of J·, "
11 brought up from Babylon unto J·. "
2: 1 and came again unto J· and Judah, "
68 house of the Lord which is at J·, "
3: 1 together as one man to J·. "
8 coming unto the house of God at J·, "
8 come out of the captivity unto J·; "
4: 6 the inhabitants of Judah and J·. "
8 the scribe wrote a letter against J· 3390
12 from thee to us are come unto J·, "
20 have been mighty kings also over J·, "
23 up in haste to J· unto the Jews, "
24 of the house of God which is at J·. "
5: 1 the Jews that were in Judah and J·: "
2 the house of God which is at J·: "
14 out of the temple that was in J·, "
15 them into the temple that is in J·, "
16 of the house of God which is in J·: "
17 to build this house of God at J·, "
6: 3 concerning the house of God at J·, "
5 out of the temple which is at J·, "
5 again unto the temple which is at J·, "
9 of the priests which are at J·, "
12 this house of God which is at J·. "
18 the service of God, which is at J·; "
7: 7 and the Nethinims, unto J·, 3389
8 he came to J· in the fifth month, "
9 of the fifth month came he to J·, "
13 their own freewill to go up to J·, 3390
14 enquire concerning Judah and J·, "
15 of Israel, whose habitation is in J·, "
16 house of their God which is in J·: "
17 house of your God which is in J·. "
19 deliver thou before the God of J·. "
27 house of the Lord which is in J·: 3389
8: 29 at J·, in the chambers of the house "
30 to bring them to J· unto the house "
31 of the first month, to go unto J·: "
32 And we came to J·, and abode there "
9: 9 give us a wall in Judah and in J·. "
10: 7 made proclamation throughout...J· "
7 gather themselves together unto J·; "
9 together unto J· within three days. "
Ne 1: 2 of the captivity, and concerning J·. "
3 the wall of J· also is broken down, "
2: 11 So I came to J·, and was there three "
12 God had put in my heart to do at J·: "
13 viewed the walls of J·, which were "
17 how J· lieth waste, and the gates "
17 let us build up the wall of J·, that "
20 nor right, nor memorial, in J·. "
3: 8 fortified J· unto the broad wall. "
9 Hur, the ruler of the half part of J·. "
12 the ruler of the half part of J·, "
4: 7 that the walls of J· were made up, "
8 to come and to fight against J·, "
22 with his servant lodge within J·, "
6: 7 prophets to preach of thee at J·, "
7: 2 ruler of the palace, charge over J·: "
3 Let not the gates of J· be opened "
3 watches of the inhabitants of J·, "
6 and came again to J· and to Judah, "
8: 15 proclaim in...their cities, and in J·, "
11: 1 the rulers of the people dwelt at J·: "
1 of ten to dwell in J· the holy city, "
2 offered themselves to dwell at J·. "
3 of the province that dwelt in J·: "
4 at J· dwelt certain of the children "
6 the sons of Perez that dwelt at J· "
22 overseer also of the Levites at J· "
12: 27 at the dedication of the wall of J· "
27 to bring them to J·, to keep the "
28 the plain country round about J·, "
29 them villages round about J·. "
43 the joy of J· was heard even afar off. "
13: 6 But in all this time was not I at J·: "
7 I came to J·, and understood of the "
15 they brought into J· on the sabbath "
16 the children of Judah, and in J·. "
19 the gates of J· began to be dark "
20 all kind of ware lodged without J· "
Es 2: 6 Who had been carried away from J· "
Ps 51: 18 Zion: build thou the walls of J·. "
68: 29 of thy temple at J· shall kings bring "
79: 1 defiled; they have laid J· on heaps. "
3 shed like water round about J·; "
102: 21 Lord in Zion, and his praise in J·; "
116: 19 house, in the midst of thee, O J·. "
122: 2 shall stand within thy gates, O J·. "
3 J· is builded as a city that is "
6 Pray for the peace of J·: they shall "
125: 2 the mountains are round about J·, "
128: 5 thou shalt see the good of J· all the "
135: 21 out of Zion, which dwelleth at J·. "
137: 5 If I forget thee, O J·, let my right "
6 if I prefer not J· above my chief joy. "
7 children of Edom in the day of J·; "
147: 2 The Lord doth build up J·: he "
12 Praise the Lord, O J·; praise thy "
Ec 1: 1 the son of David, king in J·. "
12 Preacher was king over Israel in J·. "
16 they that have been before me in J·: "
2: 7 above all that were in J· before me: "
9 than all that were before me in J·: "
Ca 1: 5 but comely, O ye daughters of J·, "
Ca 2: 7 I charge you, O ye daughters of J·, 3389
3: 5 I charge you, O ye daughters of J·, "
10 with love, for the daughters of J·. "
5: 8 I charge you, O daughters of J·, "
16 this is my friend, O daughters of J·. "
6: 4 O my love, as Tirzah, comely as J·, "
8: 4 I charge you, O daughters of J·, "
Isa 1: 1 he saw concerning Judah and J· "
2: 1 Amoz saw concerning Judah and J·. "
3 and the word of the Lord from J·. "
3: 1 take away from J· and from Judah "
8 J· is ruined, and Judah is fallen: "
4: 3 and he that remaineth in J·, shall be "
3 is written among the living in J·: "
4 shall have purged the blood of J· "
5: 3 now, O inhabitants of J·, and men of "
7: 1 went up toward J· to war against "
8: 14 for a snare to the inhabitants of J·. "
10: 10 graven images did excel them of J· "
11 her idols, so do to J· and her idols? "
12 work upon mount Zion and on J·, "
32 the daughter of Zion, the hill of J·. "
22: 10 ye have numbered the houses of J·, "
21 be a father to the inhabitants of J·, "
24: 23 shall reign in mount Zion, and in J·, "
27: 13 the Lord in the holy mount at J·. "
28: 14 that rule this people which is in J·. "
30: 19 the people shall dwell in Zion at J·: "
31: 5 so will the Lord of hosts defend J·; "
9 fire is in Zion, and his furnace in J·. "
33: 20 eyes shall see J· a quiet habitation, "
36: 2 sent Rabshakeh from Lachish to J· "
7 away, and said to Judah and to J·, "
20 Lord should deliver J· out of my "
37: 10 J· shall not be given into the hand "
22 the daughter of J· hath shaken her "
32 out of J· shall go forth a remnant, "
40: 2 Speak ye comfortably to J·, and cry "
9 O J·, that bringest good tidings, "
41: 27 give to J· one that bringeth good "
44: 26 saith to J·, Thou shalt be inhabited; "
28 saying to J·, Thou shalt be built; "
51: 17 Awake, awake, stand up, O J·, "
52: 1 put on thy beautiful garments, O J·, "
2 arise, and sit down, O J·: loose "
9 sing together, ye waste places of J·: "
9 his people, he hath redeemed J·. "
62: 6 set watchmen upon thy walls, O J·, "
7 till he make J· a praise in the earth. "
64: 10 Zion is a wilderness, J· a desolation. "
65: 18 I create J· a rejoicing, and her "
19 I will rejoice in J·, and joy in my "
66: 10 Rejoice ye with J·, and be glad with "
13 and ye shall be comforted in J·. "
20 beasts, to my holy mountain J·, "
Jer 1: 3 unto the carrying away of J· captive "
15 at the entering of the gates of J·, "
2: 2 Go and cry in the ears of J·, saying, "
3: 17 shall call J· the throne of the Lord; "
17 it, to the name of the Lord, to J·: "
4: 3 Lord to the men of Judah and J·, "
4 men of Judah and inhabitants of J·: "
5 ye in Judah, and publish in J·; "
10 greatly deceived this people and J·, "
11 it be said to this people and to J·, "
14 O J·, wash thine heart from "
16 publish against J·, that watchers "
5: 1 to and fro through the streets of J·, "
6: 1 to flee out of the midst of J·, "
6 trees, and cast a mount against J·: "
8 Be thou instructed, O J·, lest my "
7: 17 of Judah and in the streets of J·? "
29 Cut off thine hair, O J·, and cast it "
34 Judah, and from the streets of J·, 3389
8: 1 the bones of the inhabitants of J·, "
5 is this people of J· slidden back "
9: 11 I will make J· heaps, and a den of "
11: 2 Judah, and to the inhabitants of J·; "
6 of Judah, and in the streets of J·, "
9 and among the inhabitants of J·. "
12 of Judah and inhabitants of J· go, "
13 to the number of streets of J· "
13: 9 of Judah, and the great pride of J·. "
13 all the inhabitants of J·, and "
27 Woe unto thee, O J·! wilt thou not "
14: 2 and the cry of J· is gone up. "
16 shall be cast out in the streets of J· "
15: 4 Judah, for that which he did in J·. "
5 shall have pity upon thee, O J·? "
17: 19 go out, and in all the gates of J·; "
20 all the inhabitants of J·, that enter "
21 nor bring it in by the gates of J·; "
25 Judah, and the inhabitants of J·: "
26 Judah, and from the places about J·, "
27 even entering in at the gates of J· "
27 it shall devour the palaces of J·, "
18: 11 Judah, and to the inhabitants of J·, "
19: 3 of Judah, and inhabitants of J·; "
7 void the counsel of Judah and J· "
13 the houses of J·, and the houses of "
22: 19 cast forth beyond the gates of J·. "
23: 14 have seen also in the prophets of J· "
15 the prophets of J· is profaneness "
24: 1 the carpenters and smiths, from J·, "
8 his princes, and the residue of J·, "
25: 2 to all the inhabitants of J·, saying, "
18 To wit, J·, and the cities of Judah, "
26: 18 a field, and J· shall become heaps, "
27: 3 of the messengers which come to J· "
18 of the king of Judah, and at J·, go "
20 king of Judah from J· to Babylon, "
20 and all the nobles of Judah and J·; "
21 of the king of Judah and of J·; "
29: 1 Jeremiah the prophet sent from J· "
1 away captive from J· to Babylon; "
2 the princes of Judah and J·, and "
Jer 29: 2 the smiths, were departed from J·;) 3389
4 caused to be carried away from J· "
20 I have sent from J· to Babylon: "
25 unto all the people that are at J·, "
32: 2 king of Babylon's army besieged J·: "
32 of Judah, and the inhabitants of J·. "
44 and in the places about J·, and in "
33: 10 the streets of J·, that are desolate, "
13 and in the places about J·, and in "
16 be saved, and J· shall dwell safely: "
34: 1 all the people, fought against J·, "
6 unto Zedekiah king of Judah in J·, "
7 Babylon's army fought against J·, "
8 with all the people which were at J·, "
19 of Judah, and the princes of J·, "
35: 11 Come, and let us go to J· for fear "
11 of the Syrians: so we dwell at J·. "
13 of Judah and the inhabitants of J·, "
17 upon all the inhabitants of J· all "
36: 9 the Lord to all the people in J·, "
9 from the cities of Judah unto J·. "
31 and upon the inhabitants of J·, "
37: 5 Chaldeans that besieged J· heard "
5 of them, they departed from J·. "
11 was broken up from J· for fear of "
12 Jeremiah went forth out of J· to go "
38: 28 until the day that J· was taken: "
28 he was there when J· was taken. "
39: 1 Babylon and all his army against J·, "
8 and brake down the walls of J·. "
40: 1 away captive of J· and Judah, "
42: 18 forth upon the inhabitants of J·; "
44: 2 evil that I have brought upon J·, "
6 of Judah and in the streets of J·; "
9 of Judah, and in the streets of J·? "
13 as I have punished J·, by the sword, "
17 of Judah, and in the streets of J·: "
21 of Judah, and in the streets of J·, "
51: 35 inhabitants of Chaldea, shall J· say. "
50 and let J· come into your mind. "
52: 1 and he reigned eleven years in J·. "
3 it came to pass in J· and Judah, "
4 he and all his army, against J·, "
12 served the king of Babylon, into J·, "
13 and all the houses of J·, and all the "
14 brake down all the walls of J· round "
29 he carried away captive from J· "
La 1: 7 J· remembered in the days of her "
8 J· hath grievously sinned; "
17 J· is as a menstruous woman "
2: 10 virgins of J· hang down their heads "
13 I liken to thee, O daughter of J·? "
15 their head at the daughter of J·, "
4: 12 have entered into the gates of J·. "
Eze 4: 1 pourtray upon it the city, even J·: "
7 set thy face toward the siege of J·, "
16 I will break the staff of bread in J·: "
5: 5 saith the Lord God; This is J·: "
8: 3 me in the visions of God to J·, "
9: 4 of the city, through the midst of J·, "
8 pouring out of thy fury upon J·? "
11: 15 the inhabitants of J· have said, "
12: 10 burden concerneth the prince in J·, "
19 Lord God of the inhabitants of J·, "
13: 16 which prophesy concerning J·, "
14: 21 my four sore judgments upon J·, "
22 evil that I have brought upon J·, "
15: 6 so will I give the inhabitants of J·. "
16: 2 cause J· to know her abominations, "
3 Thus saith the Lord God unto J·; "
17: 12 the king of Babylon is come to J·, "
21: 2 Son of man, set thy face toward J·, "
20 and to Judah in J· the defenced. "
22 right hand was the divination for J·, "
22: 19 will gather you into the midst of J·. "
23: 4 Samaria is Aholah, and J· Aholibah. "
24: 2 of Babylon set himself against J· "
26: 2 that Tyrus hath said against J·, "
33: 21 one that had escaped out of J· came "
36: 38 the flock of J· in her solemn feasts; "
Da 1: 1 came Nebuchadnezzar...unto J·, "
5: 2 out of the temple which was in J·; 3390
3 the house of God which was at J·; "
6: 10 open in his chamber toward J·, "
9: 2 years in the desolations of J·. 3389
7 Judah, and to the inhabitants of J·, "
12 done as hath been done upon J·. "
16 be turned away from thy city J·, "
16 J· and thy people are become a "
25 to restore and to build J· unto the "
Joe 2: 32 Zion and in J· shall be deliverance, "
3: 1 again the captivity of Judah and J·, "
6 the children of J· have ye sold unto "
16 of Zion, and utter his voice from J·; "
17 mountain: then shall J· be holy, "
20 J· from generation to generation. "
Am 1: 2 Zion, and utter his voice from J·; "
2: 5 it shall devour the palaces of J·. "
Ob 11 his gates, and cast lots upon J·, "
20 Zarephath; and the captivity of J·, "
Mic 1: 1 he saw concerning Samaria and J·. "
5 places of Judah? are they not J·? "
9 the gate of my people, even to J·. "
12 from the Lord unto the gate of J·. "
3: 10 with blood, and J· with iniquity. "
12 a field, and J· shall become heaps, "
4: 2 and the word of the Lord from J·. "
8 shall come to the daughter of J·. "
Zep 1: 4 and upon all the inhabitants of J·; "
12 that I will search J· with candles, "
3: 14 with all the heart, O daughter of J·. "
16 In that day it shall be said to J·, "
Zec 1: 12 long wilt thou not have mercy on J· "
14 I am jealous for J· and for Zion "
16 I am returned to J· with mercies: "
16 shall be stretched forth upon J·. "

Zec 1:17 Zion, and shall yet choose *J*. 3389
19 scattered Judah, Israel, and *J*. "
2: 2 he said unto me, To measure *J*, "
4 *J* shall be inhabited as towns "
12 land, and shall choose *J* again. "
3: 2 Lord that hath chosen *J* rebuke "
7: 7 *J* was inhabited and in prosperity, "
8: 3 and will dwell in the midst of *J*: "
3 *J* shall be called a city of truth; "
4 women dwell in the streets of *J*, "
8 they shall dwell in the midst of *J*: "
15 to do well unto *J* and to the house "
22 come to seek the Lord of hosts in *J*, "
9: 9 shout, O daughter of *J*: behold, "
10 Ephraim, and the horse from *J*, "
12: 2 I will make *J* a cup of trembling "
2 both against Judah and against *J*. "
3 make *J* a burdensome stone for all "
5 The inhabitants of *J* shall be my "
6 and *J* shall be inhabited again "
6 in her own place, even in *J*. "
7 the glory of the inhabitants of *J* "
8 Lord defend the inhabitants of *J*; "
9 the nations that come against *J*. "
10 and upon the inhabitants of *J*, the "
11 there be a great mourning in *J*, "
13: 1 and to the inhabitants of *J* for sin "
14: 2 I will gather all nations against *J* "
4 which is before *J* on the east, "
8 living waters shall go out from *J*; "
10 from Geba to Rimmon south of *J*: "
11 but *J* shall be safely inhabited. "
12 people that have fought against *J*; "
14 And Judah also shall fight at *J*; "
16 the nations which came against *J* "
17 earth unto *J* to worship the King, "
21 every pot in *J* and in Judah shall "
Mal 2:11 is committed in Israel and in *J*; "
3: 4 offering of Judah and *J* be pleasant "
M't 2: 1 wise men from the east to *J*, 2414
3 was troubled, and all *J* with him. "
3: 5 went out to him *J*, and all Judæa, "
4:25 from *J*, and from Judæa, and from "
5:35 neither by *J*; for it is the city of "
15: 1 and Pharisees, which were of *J*, "
16:21 how that he must go unto *J*, and "
20:17 And Jesus going up to *J* took the "
18 Behold, we go up to *J*; and the "
21: 1 And when they drew nigh unto *J*, "
10 when he was come into *J*, all the "
23:37 O *J*, *J*, thou that killest the 2419
M'r 1: 5 the land of Judæa, and they of *J*, 2414
3: 8 And from *J*, and from Idumæa, and "
22 scribes which came down from *J* "
7: 1 of the scribes, which came from *J*. "
10:32 were in the way going up to *J*; "
33 Saying, Behold, we go up to *J*; "
11: 1 when they came nigh to *J*, unto 2419
11 Jesus entered into *J*, and into the 2414
15 they come to *J*: and Jesus went "
27 And they come again to *J*: and as "
15:41 which came up with him unto *J*. "
Lu 2:22 they brought him to *J*, to present "
25 there was a man in *J*, whose 2419
38 that looked for redemption in *J*. "
41 his parents went to *J* every year "
42 went up to *J* after the custom *2414
43 child Jesus tarried behind in *J*; 2419
45 not, they turned back again to *J*, "
4: 9 he brought him to *J*, and set him "
5:17 town of Galilee, and Judæa, and *J*: "
6:17 of people out of all Judæa and *J*, "
9:31 which he should accomplish at *J*. "
51 stedfastly set his face to go to *J*, "
53 was as though he would go to *J*. "
10:30 man went down from *J* to Jericho, "
13: 4 above all men that dwelt in *J*? "
22 teaching, and journeying toward *J*. "
33 be that a prophet perish out of *J*. "
34 O *J*, *J*, which killest the prophets, "
17:11 it came to pass, as he went to *J*, "
18:31 unto them, Behold, we go up to *J*, 2414
19:11 parable, because he was nigh to *J*, 2419
28 he went before, ascending up to *J*. 2414
21:20 see *J* compassed with armies, 2419
24 and *J* shall be trodden down of the "
23: 7 himself also was at *J* at that 2414
28 Daughters of *J*, weep not for me, 2419
24:13 from *J* about threescore furlongs. "
18 him, Art thou only a stranger in *J*, "
33 the same hour, and returned to *J*, "
47 among all nations, beginning at *J*. "
49 tarry ye in the city of *J*, until ye * "
52 and returned to *J* with great joy: "
Joh 1:19 sent priests and Levites from *J* 2414
2:13 at hand, and Jesus went up to *J*, "
23 when he was in *J* at the passover, "
4:20 in *J* is the place where men ought "
21 in this mountain, nor yet at *J*, "
45 things that he did at *J* at the feast: "
5: 1 the Jews; and Jesus went up to *J*. "
2 is at *J* by the sheep market a pool, "
7:25 Then said some of them of *J*, Is "
10:22 was at *J* the feast of the dedication, "
11:18 Now Bethany was nigh unto *J*, "
55 went out of the country up to *J* "
12:12 heard that Jesus was coming to *J*, "
Ac 1: 4 they should not depart from *J*, "
8 be witnesses unto me both in *J*, 2419
12 Then returned they unto *J* from "
12 is from *J* a sabbath day's journey. "
19 known unto all the dwellers at *J*; "
2: 5 there were dwelling at *J* Jews, "
14 Judæa, and all ye that dwell at *J*, "
4: 6 were gathered together at *J*. * "
16 to all them that dwell in *J*; "

Ac 5:16 of the cities round about unto *J*, 2419
28 ye have filled *J* with your doctrine, "
6: 7 disciples multiplied in *J* greatly; "
8: 1 the church which was at *J*; 2414
14 the apostles which were at *J* heard "
25 returned to *J*, and preached the 2419
26 that goeth down from *J* unto Gaza, "
27 and had come to *J* for to worship, "
9: 2 might bring them bound unto *J*. "
13 evil he hath done to thy saints at *J*: "
21 which called on this name in *J*, "
26 And when Saul was come to *J*, "
28 them coming in and going out at *J*. "
10:39 in the land of the Jews, and in *J*; "
11: 2 when Peter was come up to *J*, 2414
22 ears of the church which was in *J*: "
27 prophets from *J* unto Antioch. "
12:25 and Saul returned from *J*, 2419
13:13 John departing...returned to *J*. 2414
27 For they that dwell at *J*, and their 2419
31 up with him from Galilee to *J*, "
15: 2 go up to *J* unto the apostles and "
4 And when they were come to *J*, "
16: 4 and elders which were at *J*. "
18:21 keep this feast that cometh in *J*: *2414
19:21 Macedonia and Achaia, to go to *J*, 2419
20:16 to be at *J* the day of Pentecost. 2414
22 I go bound in the spirit unto *J*, 2419
21: 4 that he should not go up to *J*. "
11 So shall the Jews at *J* bind the man "
12 besought him not to go up to *J*. "
13 to die at *J* for the name of the Lord "
15 up our carriages, and went up to *J*. "
17 And when we were come to *J*, 2414
31 band, that all *J* was in an uproar. 2419
22: 5 which were there bound unto *J*, "
17 that, when I was come again to *J*, "
18 and get thee quickly out of *J*: "
23:11 as thou hast testified of me in *J*, "
24:11 since I went up to *J* for to worship. "
25: 1 he ascended from Cæsarea to *J*. 2414
3 that he would send for him to *J*, 2419
7 Jews which came down from *J* 2414
9 Wilt thou go up to *J*, and there be "
15 About whom, when I was at *J*, the "
20 him whether he would go to *J*, 2419
24 dealt with me, both at *J*, and also 2414
26: 4 first among mine own nation at *J*, "
10 Which thing I also did in *J*: "
20 unto them of Damascus, and at *J*, "
28:17 yet was I delivered prisoner from *J* "
Ro 15:19 so that from *J*, and round about 2419
25 But now I go unto *J* to minister "
26 for the poor saints which are at *J*. "
31 that my service which I have for *J* "
1Co 16: 3 to bring your liberality unto *J*. "
Ga 1:17 Neither went I up to *J* to them 2414
18 I went up to *J* to see Peter, "
2: 1 went up again to *J* with Barnabas, "
4:25 and answereth to *J* which now is, 2419
26 But *J* which is above is free, which "
Heb 12:22 of the living God, the heavenly *J*, "
Re 3:12 the city of my God, which is new *J*, "
21: 2 saw the holy city, new *J*, coming "
10 great city, the holy *J*, descending "

Jerusalem's (*je-ru'-sa-lems*)
1Ki 11:13 for *J* sake which I have chosen. 3389
32 David's sake, and for *J* sake, the "
Isa 62: 1 and for *J* sake I will not rest, until "

Jerusha (*je-ru'-shah*) See also JERUSHAH.
2Ki 15:33 And his mother's name was *J*, the 3388

Jerushah (*je-ru'-shah*) See also JERUSHA.
2Ch 27: 1 His mother's name also was *J*, 3388

Jesaiah (*jes-a-i'-ah*) See also ISAIAH; JESHAIAH.
1Ch 3:21 of Hananiah; Pelatiah, and *J*: *3470
Ne 11: 7 the son of Ithiel, the son of *J*. * "

Jeshaiah (*jesh-a-i'-ah*) See also JESAIAH.
1Ch 25: 3 and Zeri, and *J*, Hashabiah, and 3470
15 The eighth to *J*, he, his sons, and "
26:25 Rehabiah his son, and *J* his son, "
Ezr 8: 7 of Elam; *J* the son of Athaliah, "
19 with him *J* of the sons of Merari. "

Jeshanah (*je-sha'-nah*)
2Ch 13:19 and *J* with the towns thereof, and 3466

Jesharelah (*je-shar'-e-lah*) See also ASARELAH.
1Ch 25:14 The seventh to *J*, he, his sons, 3480

Jeshebeab (*je-sheb'-e-ab*)
1Ch 24:13 to Huppah, the fourteenth to *J*, 3434

Jesher (*je'-shur*)
1Ch 2:18 sons are these; *J*, and Shobab, 3475

Jeshimon (*jesh'-im-on*)
Nu 21:20 Pisgah, which looketh toward *J*. *3452
23:28 of Peor, that looketh toward *J*. * "
1Sa 23:19 which is on the south of *J*? * "
24 in the plain on the south of *J*. * "
26: 1 of Hachilah, which is before *J*? * "
3 hill of Hachilah, which is before *J*, * "

Jeshimoth See BETH-JESHIMOTH.

Jeshishai (*jesh'-i-shahee*)
1Ch 5:14 the son of *J*, the son of Jahdo, *3454

Jeshohaiah (*je-sho-ha-i'-ah*)
1Ch 4:36 Elioenai, and Jaakobah, and *J*, 3439

Jeshua (*jesh'-u-ah*) See also JESHUAH; JOSHUA.
2Ch 31:15 were Eden, and Miniamin, and *J*, 3442
Ezr 2: 2 *J*, Nehemiah, Seraiah, Reelaiah, "
6 of the children of *J* and Joab, two "
36 of Jedaiah, of the house of *J*, nine "
40 the children of *J* and Kadmiel, of "
3: 2 stood up *J* the son of Jozadak, "
8 and *J* the son of Jozadak, and the "

Ezr 3: 9 Then stood *J* with his sons and his 3442
4: 3 But Zerubbabel, and *J*, and the rest "
5: 2 and *J* the son of Jozadak, 3443
8:33 them was Jozabad the son of *J*, "
10:18 the sons of *J* the son of Jozadak, 3442
Ne 3:19 to him repaired Ezer the son of *J*, "
7: 7 with Zerubbabel, *J*, Nehemiah, "
11 of the children of *J* and Joab, "
39 of Jedaiah, of the house of *J*, "
43 the children of *J*, of Kadmiel, and "
8: 7 Also *J*, and Bani, and Sherebiah, "
17 since the days of *J* the son of Nun "
9: 4 stairs, of the Levites, *J*, and Bani, "
5 Then the Levites, *J*, and Kadmiel, "
10: 9 both *J* the son of Azaniah, Binnui "
11:26 And at *J*, and at Moladah, and at "
12: 1 the son of Shealtiel, and *J*: "
7 of their brethren in the days of *J*. "
8 the Levites: *J*, Binnui, Kadmiel, "
10 And *J* begat Joiakim, Joiakim also "
24 and *J* the son of Kadmiel, "
26 the days of Joiakim the son of *J*, "

Jeshuah (*jesh'-u-ah*) See also JESHUA.
1Ch 24:11 The ninth to *J*, the tenth to *3442

Jeshurun (*jesh'-u-run*) See also ISRAEL; JESURUN.
De 32:15 But *J* waxed fat, and kicked: 3484
33: 5 he was king in *J*, when the heads "
26 is none like unto the God of *J*, "

Jesiah (*je-si'-ah*) See also ISHIAH.
1Ch 12: 6 Elkanah, and *J*, and Azareel, *3449
23:20 Micah the first, and *J* the second * "

Jesimiel (*je-sim'-e-el*)
1Ch 4:36 and Adiel, and *J*, and Benaiah, 3450

Jesimoth See BETH-JESIMOTH.

Jesse (*jes'-se*)
Ru 4:17 he is the father of *J*, the father 3448
22 Obed begat *J*, and *J* begat David. "
1Sa 16: 1 send thee to *J* the Beth-lehemite: "
3 call *J* to the sacrifice, and I will "
5 And he sanctified *J* and his sons, "
8 *J* called Abinadab, and made him "
9 Then *J* made Shammah to pass "
10 *J* made seven of his sons to pass "
10 Samuel said unto *J*, The Lord hath "
11 Samuel said unto *J*, Are here all "
11 And Samuel said unto *J*, Send and "
18 Behold, I have seen a son of *J* "
19 Saul sent messengers unto *J*, and "
20 *J* took an ass laden with bread, "
22 Saul sent to *J*, saying, Let David, I "
17:12 whose name was *J*; and he had "
13 three eldest sons of *J* went and "
17 *J* said unto David his son, Take "
20 and went, as *J* had commanded "
58 I am the son of thy servant *J* the "
20:27 cometh not the son of *J* to meat, "
30 chosen the son of *J* to thine own "
31 as long as the son of *J* liveth upon "
22: 7 the son of *J* give every one of you "
8 made a league with the son of *J*, "
9 I saw the son of *J* coming to Nob, "
13 against me, thou and the son of *J*, "
25:10 David? and who is the son of *J*? "
2Sa 20: 1 we inheritance in the son of *J*: "
23: 1 David the son of *J* said, and the "
1Ki 12:16 we inheritance in the son of *J*: "
1Ch 2:12 begat Obed, and Obed begat *J*, "
13 And *J* begat his firstborn Eliab, "
10:14 kingdom unto David the son of *J*. "
12:18 and on thy side, thou son of *J*: "
29:26 David the son of *J* reigned over all "
2Ch 10:16 none inheritance in the son of *J*: "
11:18 daughter of Eliab the son of *J*; "
Ps 72:20 The prayers of David the son of *J* "
Isa 11: 1 forth a rod out of the stem of *J*, "
10 that day there shall be a root of *J*, "
M't 1: 5 Obed of Ruth; and Obed begat *J*; 2421
6 And *J* begat David the king; and "
Lu 3:32 Which was the son of *J*, which was "
Ac 13:22 I have found David the son of *J*, "
Ro 15:12 saith, There shall be a root of *J*, "

jesting
Eph 5: 4 nor foolish talking, nor *j*, which 2160

Jesui (*jes'-u-i*) See also ISHUI; JESUITES.
Nu 26:44 of *J*, the family of the Jesuites: *3440

Jesuites (*jes'-u-ites*)
Nu 26:44 of Jesui, the family of the *J*: of *3441

Jesurun (*jes'-u-run*) See also JESHURUN.
Isa 44: 2 thou, *J*, whom I have chosen. *3484

Jesus (*je'-zus*) See also BAR-JESUS; CHRIST; JESUS'; JOSHUA; JUSTUS.
M't 1: 1 book of the generation of *J* Christ, 2424
16 of whom was born *J*, who is called "
18 birth of *J* Christ was on this wise: "
21 son, and thou shalt call his name *J*: "
25 son: and he called his name *J*. "
2: 1 when *J* was born in Bethlehem of "
3:13 cometh *J* from Galilee to Jordan "
15 *J* answering said unto him, Suffer "
16 *J*, when he was baptized, went up "
4: 1 was *J* led up of the spirit into the "
7 *J* said unto him, It is written "
10 saith *J* unto him, Get thee hence, * "
12 *J* had heard that John was cast * "
17 From that time *J* began to preach, "
18 *J*, walking by the sea of Galilee, * "
23 *J* went about all Galilee, teaching "
7:28 when *J* had ended these sayings, "
8: 3 *J* put forth his hand, and touched * "
4 *J* saith unto him, See thou tell no "
5 *J* was entered into Capernaum, * "

M't 8: 7 J' saith unto him, I will come and* 2424
10 When J' heard it, he marvelled, "
13 J' said unto the centurion, Go thy "
14 J' was come into Peter's house, "
18 Now when J' saw great multitudes "
20 J' saith unto him, The foxes have "
22 But J' said unto him, Follow me; "
29 do with thee, J', thou son of God?* "
34 the whole city came out to meet J': "
9: 2 J' seeing their faith said unto the "
4 And J' knowing their thoughts said, "
9 And as J' passed forth from thence, "
10 pass, as J' sat at meat in the house,* "
12 when J' heard that, he said unto * "
15 J' said unto them, Can the children "
19 J' arose, and followed him, and so "
22 J' turned him about, and when he "
23 when J' came into the ruler's house, "
27 when J' departed thence, two blind "
28 J' saith unto them, Believe ye that "
30 and Jesus straitly charged them, "
35 And J' went about all the cities and "
10: 5 These twelve J' sent forth, and "
11: 1 J'...made an end of commanding "
4 J' answered and said unto them, "
7 J' began to say unto the multitudes "
25 J' answered and said, I thank thee, "
12: 1 J' went on the sabbath day through "
15 But when J' knew it, he withdrew "
25 J' knew their thoughts, and said * "
13: 1 same day went J' out of the house, "
34 things spake J' unto the multitudes "
36 Then J' sent the multitude away,* "
51 J' saith....Have ye understood all* "
53 when J' had finished these parables, "
57 But J' said unto them, A prophet is "
14: 1 tetrarch heard of the fame of J', "
12 and buried it, and went and told J'. "
13 When J' heard of it, he departed "
14 J' went forth, and saw a great * "
16 J' said unto them, They need not "
22 J' constrained his disciples to get* "
25 fourth watch of the night J' went* "
27 straightway J' spake unto them, "
29 he walked on the water, to go to J'. "
31 immediately J' stretched forth his "
15: 1 came to J' scribes and Pharisees, "
16 J' said, Are ye also yet without * "
21 J' went thence, and departed into "
28 J' answered and said unto her, O "
29 J' departed from thence, and came "
32 J' called his disciples unto him, "
34 And J' saith unto them, How many "
16: 6 Then J' said unto them, Take heed "
8 Which when J' perceived, he said "
13 When J' came into the coasts of "
17 J' answered and said unto him, "
20 should tell no man that he was J'* "
21 that time forth began J' to shew "
24 said J' unto his disciples, If any "
17: 1 And after six days J' taketh Peter, "
4 and said unto J', Lord, it is good "
7 J' came and touched them, and "
8 they saw no man, save J' only. "
9 the mountain, J' charged them, "
11 J' answered and said unto them, * "
17 J' answered and said, O faithless "
18 and J' rebuked the devil; and he "
19 Then came the disciples to J' apart, "
20 J' said unto them, Because of your* "
22 abode in Galilee, J' said unto them, "
25 into the house, J' prevented him, "
26 J' saith unto him, Then are the "
18: 1 time came the disciples unto J', "
2 J' called a little child unto him, * "
22 J' saith unto him, I say not unto "
19: 1 when J' had finished these sayings, "
14 J' said, Suffer little children, and "
18 J' said, Thou shalt do no murder, "
21 J' said unto him, If thou wilt be "
23 said J' unto his disciples, Verily I "
26 J' beheld them, and said unto them, "
28 J' said unto them, Verily I say unto "
20: 17 J' going up to Jerusalem took the "
22 J' answered and said, Ye know not "
25 J' called them unto him, and said, "
30 when they heard that J' passed by, "
32 J' stood still, and called them, and "
34 J' had compassion on them, and "
21: 1 Olives, then sent J' two disciples, "
6 and did as J' commanded them, "
11 This is J' the prophet of Nazareth "
12 J' went into the temple of God, and "
16 J' said unto them, Yea; have ye "
21 J' answered and said unto them, "
24 J' answered and said unto them, I "
27 they answered J', and said, We "
31 J' saith unto them, Verily I say "
42 J' saith unto them, Did ye never "
22: 1 J' answered and spake unto them "
18 But J' perceived their wickedness, "
29 J' answered and said unto them, "
37 J' said unto him, thou shalt love * "
41 gathered together, J' asked them, "
23: 1 Then spake J' to the multitude, "
24: 1 J' went out, and departed from the "
2 J' said unto them, See ye not all * "
4 J' answered and said unto them, "
26: 1 when J' had finished all these "
4 that they might take J' by subtilty, "
6 J' was in Bethany, in the house of "
10 When J' understood it, he said "
17 bread the disciples came to J', "
19 disciples did as J' had appointed "
26 J' took bread, and blessed it, "
31 saith J' unto them, All ye shall be "

M't 26: 34 J' said unto him, Verily I say unto 2424
36 cometh J' with them unto a place "
49 forthwith he came to J', and said, "
50 J' said unto him, Friend, wherefore "
50 came they, and laid hands on J', "
51 which were with J' stretched out "
52 said J' unto him, Put up again thy "
55 In that same hour said J' to the "
57 they that had laid hold on J' led "
59 sought false witness against J', "
63 J' held his peace. And the high "
64 J' saith unto him, Thou hast said: "
69 Thou also wast with J' of Galilee. "
71 was also with J' of Nazareth. "
75 Peter remembered the word of J', "
27: 1 took counsel against J' to put him "
11 And J' stood before the governor: "
11 J' said unto him, Thou sayest. "
17 or J' which is called Christ? "
20 ask Barabbas, and destroy J'. "
22 then with J' which is called Christ? "
26 he had scourged J', he delivered "
27 soldiers of the governor took J' "
37 This Is J' The King Of The Jews. "
46 ninth hour J' cried with a loud "
50 J', when he had cried again with a "
54 watching J', saw the earthquake, "
55 which followed J' from Galilee, "
58 Pilate, and begged the body of J'. "
28: 5 I know that ye seek J', which was "
9 J' met them, saying, All hail. And "
10 said J' unto them, Be not afraid: "
16 into a mountain where J' had "
18 J' came and spake unto them, "
M'r 1: 1 beginning of the gospel of J' Christ, "
9 J' came from Nazareth of Galilee, "
14 J' came into Galilee, preaching the "
17 J' said unto them, Come ye after "
24 do with thee, thou J' of Nazareth? "
25 J' rebuked him, saying, Hold thy "
41 J', moved with compassion, put * "
45 insomuch that J' could no more "
2: 5 When J' saw their faith, he said "
8 when J' perceived in his spirit "
15 that, as J' sat at meat in his house,* "
15 sat also together with J' and his "
17 When J' heard it, he saith unto "
19 J' said unto them, Can the children "
3: 7 J' withdrew himself with his "
5: 6 when he saw J' afar off, he ran and "
7 What have I to do with thee, J', "
13 And forthwith J' gave them leave. "
15 they come to J', and see him that "
19 Howbeit J' suffered him not, but * "
20 great things J' had done for him: "
21 when J' was passed over again by "
24 J' went with him; and much * "
27 When she had heard of J', came in 2424
30 J', immediately knowing in "
36 As soon as J' heard the word that "
6: 4 J' said unto them, A prophet is not "
30 themselves together unto J', "
34 J', when he came out, saw much* "
7: 27 J' said unto her, Let the children* "
8: 1 J' called his disciples unto him, * "
17 And when J' knew it, he saith unto "
27 And J' went out, and his disciples, "
9: 2 six days J' taketh with him Peter, "
4 and they were talking with J'. "
5 Peter answered and said to J', "
8 more, save J' only with themselves. "
23 J' said unto him, If thou canst "
25 When J' saw that the people came "
27 J' took him by the hand, and lifted "
39 J' said, Forbid him not: for there "
10: 5 J' answered and said unto them, "
14 when J' saw it, he was much "
18 J' said unto him, Why callest thou "
21 Then J' beholding him loved him, "
23 J' looked round about, and saith "
24 J' answereth again, and saith unto "
27 J' looking upon them saith, With "
29 J' answered and said, Verily I say "
32 J' went before them: and they were "
38 J' said unto them, Ye know not "
39 J' said unto them, Ye shall indeed "
42 J' called them to him, and saith "
47 he heard that it was J' of Nazareth, "
47 out, and say, J', thou son of David, "
49 J' stood still, and commanded him "
50 his garment, rose, and came to J'. "
51 J' answered and said unto him, "
52 And J' said unto him, Go thy way; "
52 sight, and followed J' in the way.* "
11: 6 them even as J' had commanded: "
7 they brought the colt to J', and "
11 J' entered into Jerusalem, and into* "
14 J' answered and said unto it, No * "
15 J' went into the temple, and began* "
22 J' answering saith unto them, "
29 J' answered and said unto them, "
33 they answered and said unto J', "
33 J' answering saith unto them, "
12: 17 J' answering said unto them, "
24 J' answering said unto them, Do "
29 J' answered him, The first of all "
34 when J' saw that he answered "
35 J' answered and said, while he "
41 J' sat over against the treasury, * "
13: 2 J' answering said unto him, Seest "
5 J' answering them began to say, "
14: 6 J' said, Let her alone; why trouble "
18 eat, J' said, Verily I say unto you, "
22 J' took bread, and blessed, and * "
27 And J' saith unto them, All ye shall "
30 And J' saith unto him, Verily I say "

M'r 14: 48 J' answered and said unto them, 2424
53 they led J' away to the high priest: "
55 sought for witness against J' to put "
60 and asked J', saying, Answerest "
62 And J' said, I am: and ye shall see "
67 thou also wast with J' of Nazareth. "
72 called to mind the word that J' said "
15: 1 bound J', and carried him away, "
5 J' yet answered nothing; so that "
15 delivered J', when he had scourged "
34 ninth hour J' cried with a loud "
37 and J' cried with a loud voice, and "
43 Pilate, and craved the body of J'. "
16: 6 Ye seek J' of Nazareth, which was "
9 Now when J' was risen early the * "
Lu 1: 31 son, and shalt call his name J'. 2424
2: 21 his name was called J', which was "
27 the parents brought in the child J', "
43 the child J' tarried behind in "
52 And J' increased in wisdom and "
3: 21 pass, that J' also being baptized, "
23 J' himself began to be about thirty "
4: 1 And J' being full of the Holy Ghost "
4 And J' answered him, saying, It is "
8 J' answered and said unto him, "
12 J' answering said unto him, It is "
14 J' returned in the power of the "
34 J' of Nazareth? art thou come to "
35 And J' rebuked him, saying, Hold "
5: 10 And J' said unto Simon, Fear not; "
12 who seeing J' fell on his face, "
19 his couch into the midst before J'. "
22 But when J' perceived their "
31 And J' answering said unto them, "
6: 3 J' answering them said, Have ye "
9 Then said J' unto them, I will ask "
11 another what they might do to J'. "
7: 3 And when he heard of J', he sent "
4 when they came to J', they "
6 Then J' went with them. And "
9 When J' heard these things, he "
19 two of his disciples sent them to J', "
22 Then J' answering said unto them,* "
37 when she knew that J' sat at meat* "
40 And J' answering said unto him, 2424
8: 28 When he saw J', he cried out, and "
28 What have I to do with thee, J', "
30 J' asked him, saying, What is thy "
35 and came to J', and found the man, "
35 sitting at the feet of J', clothed, "
38 be with him: but J' sent him away,* "
39 great things J' had done unto him. "
40 pass, that, when J' was returned, "
45 J' said, Who touched me? When all "
46 J' said, Somebody hath touched "
50 But when J' heard it, he answered "
9: 33 Peter said unto J', Master, it is "
36 voice was past, J' was found alone. "
41 And J' answering said, O faithless "
42 And J' rebuked the unclean spirit, "
43 every one at all things which J' did,* "
47 And J', perceiving the thought of "
50 And J' said unto him, Forbid him "
58 And J' said unto him, Foxes have "
60 J' said unto him, Let the dead bury* "
62 And J' said unto him, No man, "
10: 21 In that hour J' rejoiced in spirit, * "
29 said unto J', And who is my "
30 And J' answering said, A certain "
37 Then said J' unto him, Go, and do "
41 And J' answered and said unto * "
13: 2 And J' answering said unto them,* "
12 And when J' saw her, he called her "
14 J' had healed on the sabbath day, "
14: 3 And J' answering spake unto the "
17: 13 J', Master, have mercy on us. "
17 J' answering said, Were there not "
18: 16 J' called them unto him, and said, "
19 J' said unto him, Why callest thou "
22 Now when J' heard these things, he "
24 when J' saw that he was very "
37 him, that J' of Nazareth passeth by. "
38 saying, J', thou son of David, have "
40 J' stood, and commanded him to be "
42 J' said unto him, Receive thy sight: "
19: 1 J' entered and passed through * "
3 he sought to see J' who he was; 2424
5 And when J' came to the place, he "
9 And J' said unto him, This day is "
35 they brought him to J': and they "
35 the colt, and they set J' thereon. "
20: 8 J' said unto them, Neither tell I "
34 And J' answering said unto them, "
22: 47 and drew near unto J' to kiss him. "
48 J' said unto him, Judas, betrayest "
51 J' answered and said, Suffer ye "
52 Then J' said unto the chief priests, "
63 the men that held J' mocked him, "
23: 8 And when Herod saw J', he was "
20 willing to release J', spake again "
25 but he delivered J' to their will. "
26 cross, that he might bear it after J'. "
28 But J' turning unto them said, "
34 Then said J', Father, forgive them "
42 he said unto J', Lord, remember "
43 J' said unto him, Verily I say unto* "
46 when J' had cried with a loud "
52 Pilate, and begged the body of J'. "
24: 3 found not the body of the Lord J'. "
15 J' himself drew near, and went "
19 Concerning J' of Nazareth, which "
36 J' himself stood in the midst of "
Joh 1: 17 grace and truth came by J' Christ. "
29 John seeth J' coming unto him, "
36 looking upon J' as he walked, he "
37 him speak, and they followed J'. "

Joh 1:38 J· turned, and saw them following,2424
42 And he brought him to J·. "
42 when J· beheld him, he said, Thou "
43 The day following J· would go "
45 prophets, did write, J· of Nazareth, "
47 J· saw Nathanael coming to him, "
48, 50 J· answered and said unto him, "
2: 1 and the mother of J· was there: "
2 J· was called, and his disciples, to "
3 the mother of J· saith unto him, "
4 J· saith unto her, Woman, what "
7 J· saith unto them, Fill the "
11 This beginning of miracles did J· "
13 hand, and J· went up to Jerusalem. "
19 J· answered and said unto them, "
22 and the word which J· had said. "
24 J· did not commit himself unto "
3: 2 The same came to J· by night, and* "
3 J· answered and said unto him, "
5 J· answered, Verily, verily, I say "
10 J· answered and said unto him, "
22 After these things came J· and his "
4: 1 that J· made and baptized more "
2 Though J· himself baptized not, "
6 J· therefore, being wearied with "
7 J· saith unto her, Give me to drink. "
10, 13 J· answered and said unto her, "
16 J· saith unto her, Go, call thy "
17 J· said unto her, Thou hast well "
21 J· saith unto her, Woman, believe "
26 J· saith unto her, I that speak unto "
34 J· saith unto them, My meat is to "
44 J· himself testified, that a prophet "
46 J· came again into Cana of Galilee,* "
47 he heard that J· was come out of "
48 Then said J· unto him, Except ye "
50 J· saith unto him, Go thy way; "
50 man believed the word that J· had "
53 J· said unto him, Thy son liveth: "
54 the second miracle that J· did, "
5: 1 and J· went up to Jerusalem. "
6 When J· saw him lie, and knew "
8 J· saith unto him, Rise, take up "
13 for J· had conveyed himself away, "
14 Afterward J· findeth him in the "
15 told the Jews that it was J·, which "
16 therefore did the Jews persecute J·, "
17 J· answered them, My Father "
19 Then answered J· and said unto "
6: 1 J· went over the sea of Galilee, "
3 J· went up into a mountain, and "
5 When J· then lifted up his eyes, "
10 J· said, Make the men sit down. "
11 J· took the loaves; and when he "
14 had seen the miracle that J· did, * "
15 When J· therefore perceived that "
17 dark, and J· was not come to them. "
19 they see J· walking on the sea, and "
22 that J· went not with his disciples "
24 therefore saw that J· was not there, "
24 came to Capernaum, seeking for J·. "
26 J· answered them and said, Verily, "
29 J· answered and said unto them, "
32 Then J· said unto them, Verily, "
35 J· said unto them, I am the bread "
42 Is not this J·, the son of Joseph, "
43 J· therefore answered and said "
53 Then J· said unto them, Verily, "
61 When J· knew in himself that his "
64 J· knew from the beginning who "
67 Then said J· unto the twelve, Will "
70 J· answered them, Have not I "
7: 1 these things J· walked in Galilee: "
6 Then J· said unto them, My time "
14 feast J· went up into the temple, "
16 J· answered them, and said, My "
21 J· answered and said unto them, "
28 Then cried J· in the temple as he "
33 Then said J· unto them, Yet a little "
37 J· stood and cried, saying, If any "
39 that J· was not yet glorified. "
50 (he that came to J· by night, being*846
8: 1 J· went unto the mount of Olives.2424
6 But J· stooped down, and with his "
9 J· was left alone, and the woman "
10 When J· had lifted up himself, and "
11 And J· said unto her, Neither do I "
12 Then spake J· again unto them, "
14 J· answered and said unto them, "
19 J· answered, Ye neither know me "
20 These words spake J· in the * "
21 Then said J· again unto them, I go* "
25 J· saith unto them, Even the same "
28 Then said J· unto them, When ye "
31 Then said J· to those Jews which "
34 J· answered them, Verily, verily, I "
39 J· saith unto them, If ye were "
42 J· said unto them, If God were "
49 J· answered, I have not a devil; "
54 J· answered, If I honour myself, "
58 J· said unto them, Verily, verily, I "
59 J· hid himself, and went out of the "
9: 1 And as J· passed by, he saw a man* "
3 J· answered, Neither hath this 2424
11 A man that is called J· made clay, "
14 sabbath day when J· made the clay, "
35 J· heard that they had cast him "
37 J· said unto him, Thou hast both "
39 J· said, For judgment I am come "
41 J· said unto them, If ye were blind, "
10: 6 This parable spake J· unto them: "
7 Then said J· unto them again, "
23 J· walked in the temple in "
25 J· answered them, I told you, and "
32 J· answered them, Many good "
34 J· answered them, Is it not written "

Joh 11: 4 When J· heard that, he said, This 2424
5 J· loved Martha, and her sister, "
9 J· answered, Are there not twelve "
13 Howbeit J· spake of his death: but "
14 Then said J· unto them plainly, "
17 when J· came, he found that he had "
20 as soon as she heard that J· was "
21 Then said Martha unto J·, Lord, "
23 J· saith unto her, Thy brother "
25 J· saith...,I am the resurrection, "
30 Now J· was not yet come into the "
32 when Mary was come where J· was, "
33 When J· therefore saw her weeping, "
35 J· wept. "
38 J· therefore again groaning in "
39 J· said, Take ye away the stone. "
40 J· saith unto her, Said I not unto "
41 And J· lifted up his eyes, and said, "
44 J· saith unto them, Loose him, and "
45 had seen the things which J· did, * "
46 told them what things J· had done. "
51 that J· should die for that nation; "
54 J· therefore walked no more openly "
56 Then sought they for J·, and spake "
12: 1 J· six days before the passover "
3 and anointed the feet of J·, and "
7 Then said J·, Let her alone: "
11 Jews went away, and believed on J·. "
12 they heard that J· was coming to "
14 And J·, when he had found a young "
16 but when J· was glorified, then "
21 him, saying, Sir, we would see J·. "
22 again Andrew and Philip tell J·. "
23 And J· answered them, saying, "
30 J· answered and said, This voice "
35 Then J· said unto them, Yet a little "
36 things spake J·, and departed, and "
44 J· cried and said, He that believeth "
13: 1 J· knew that his hour was come "
3 J· knowing that the Father had "
7 J· answered and said unto him, "
8 J· answered him, If I wash thee "
10 J· saith to him, He that is washed "
21 When J· had thus said, he was "
23 one of his disciples, whom J· loved. "
26 J· answered, He it is, to whom I "
27 Then said J· unto him, That thou "
29 J· had said unto him, Buy those "
31 J· said, Now is the Son of man "
36 J· answered him, Whither I go, "
38 J· answered him, Wilt thou lay "
14: 6 J· saith unto him, I am the way, "
9 J· saith unto him, Have I been so "
23 J· answered and said unto him, If "
16:19 J· knew that they were desirous "
31 J· answered...,Do ye now believe? "
17: 1 These words spake J·, and lifted up "
3 J· Christ, whom thou hast sent. "
18: 1 When J· had spoken these words, "
2 for J· ofttimes resorted thither "
4 J· therefore, knowing all things "
5 They answered him, J· of Nazareth. "
5 J· saith unto them, I am he. "
7 And they said, J· of Nazareth. "
8 J· answered, I have told you that "
11 Then said J· unto Peter, Put up thy "
12 and officers of the Jews took J·, "
15 Simon Peter followed J·, and so "
15 went in with J· into the palace of "
19 The high priest then asked J· of "
20 J· answered him, I spake openly to "
22 struck J· with the palm of his hand, "
23 J· answered him, If I have spoken "
28 Then led they J· from Caiaphas "
32 the saying of J· might be fulfilled, "
33 and called J·, and said unto him, "
34 J· answered him, Sayest thou this "
36 J· answered, My kingdom is not of "
37 J· answered, Thou sayest that I "
19: 1 Then Pilate therefore took J·, and "
5 came J· forth, wearing the crown "
9 saith unto J·, Whence art thou? "
9 But J· gave him no answer. "
11 J· answered, Thou couldest have "
13 he brought J· forth, and sat down "
16 they took J·, and led him away. "
18 side one, and J· in the midst. "
19 J· of Nazareth the King of the "
20 the place where J· was crucified "
23 when they had crucified J·, took "
25 stood by the cross of J· his mother, "
26 When J· therefore saw his mother, "
28 J· knowing that all things were "
30 When J· therefore had received "
33 when they came to J·, and saw that "
38 Arimathæa, being a disciple of J·, "
38 he might take away the body of J·: "
38 therefore, and took the body of J·.* "
39 at the first came to J· by night, * "
40 Then took they the body of J·, "
42 There laid they J· therefore "
20: 2 the other disciple, whom J· loved, "
12 where the body of J· had lain. "
14 herself back, and saw J· standing, "
14 and knew not that it was J·. "
15 J· saith unto her, Woman, why "
16 J· saith unto her, Mary. She "
17 J· saith unto her, Touch me not; "
19 came J· and stood in the midst, "
21 Then said J· to them again, Peace "
24 was not with them when J· came. "
26 then came J·, the doors being shut, "
29 J· saith unto him, Thomas, because "
30 many other signs truly did J· in "
31 might believe that J· is the Christ, "
21: 1 J· shewed himself again to his "

Joh 21: 4 now come, J· stood on the shore: 2424
4 disciples knew not that it was J·. "
5 J· saith unto them, Children, have "
7 that disciple whom J· loved saith "
10 J· saith unto them, Bring of the fish "
12 J· saith unto them, Come and dine. "
13 J· then cometh, and taketh bread, "
14 third time that J· shewed himself "
15 J· saith to Simon Peter, Simon, "
17 J· saith unto him, Feed my sheep. "
20 disciple whom J· loved following; "
21 Peter seeing him saith to J·, Lord, "
22 J· saith unto him, If I will that he "
23 yet J· said not unto him, He shall "
25 many other things which J· did, "
Ac 1: 1 that J· began both to do and teach, "
11 this same J·, which is taken up "
14 Mary the mother of J·, and with "
16 was guide to them that took J·. "
21 Lord J· went in and out among us, "
2:22 J· of Nazareth, a man approved of "
32 This J· hath God raised up, "
36 God hath made that same J·, whom "
38 one of you in the name of J· Christ "
3: 6 In the name of J· Christ of "
13 fathers, hath glorified his Son J·; "
20 he shall send J· Christ, which "
26 God, having raised up his Son J·, "
4: 2 preached through J· the "
10 the name of J· Christ of Nazareth, "
13 them, that they had been with J·. "
18 at all nor teach in the name of J·. "
27 a truth against thy holy child J·, "
30 by the name of thy holy child J·. "
33 of the resurrection of the Lord J·: "
5:30 God of our fathers raised up J·, "
40 should not speak in the name of J· "
42 not to teach and preach J· Christ. "
6:14 J· of Nazareth shall destroy this "
7:45 with J· into the possession of the "
55 J· standing on the right hand of "
59 saying, Lord J·, receive my spirit. "
8:12 of God, and the name of J· Christ, "
16 baptized in the name of the Lord J·.) "
35 and preached unto him J·. "
37 that J· Christ is the Son of God. * "
9: 5 I am J· whom thou persecutest: "
17 even J·, that appeared unto thee in "
27 at Damascus in the name of J·. "
29 boldly in the name of the Lord J·,* "
34 J· Christ maketh thee whole: "
10:36 preaching peace by J· Christ: (he is "
38 How God anointed J· of Nazareth "
11:17 who believed on the Lord J· Christ; "
20 Grecians, preaching the Lord J·. "
13:23 raised unto Israel a Saviour, J·: "
33 in that he hath raised up J· again; "
15:11 the grace of the Lord J· Christ we "
26 for the name of our Lord J· Christ. "
16:18 in the name of J· Christ to come out "
31 Believe on the Lord J· Christ, and "
17: 3 this J·, whom I preach unto you, "
7 that there is another king, one J·. "
18 because he preached unto them J·, "
18: 5 to the Jews that J· was Christ. "
28 by the scriptures that J· was Christ. "
19: 4 come after him, that is, on Christ J·. "
5 baptized in the name of the Lord J·. "
10 Asia heard the word of the Lord J·,* "
13 evil spirits the name of the Lord J·, "
13 We adjure you by J· whom Paul "
15 said, J· I know, and Paul I know; "
17 name of the Lord J· was magnified. "
20:21 and faith toward our Lord J· Christ. "
24 which I have received of the Lord J·, "
35 remember the words of the Lord J·, "
21:13 to die...for the name of the Lord J·. "
22: 8 said unto me, I am J· of Nazareth, "
25:19 and of one J·, which was dead, "
26: 9 things contrary to the name of J· of "
15 I am J· whom thou persecutest. "
28:23 persuading them concerning J·, "
31 which concern the Lord J· Christ, "
Ro 1: 1 Paul, a servant of J· Christ, called "
3 concerning his Son J· Christ our * "
6 are ye also the called of J· Christ: "
7 our Father, and the Lord J· Christ. "
8 I thank my God through J· Christ "
2:16 the secrets of men by J· Christ. "
3:22 of God which is by faith of J· Christ "
24 the redemption that is in Christ J·: "
26 of him which believeth in J·. "
4:24 believe on him that raised up J· "
5: 1 God through our Lord J· Christ: "
11 in God through our Lord J· Christ, "
15 which is by one man, J· Christ, "
17 shall reign in life by one, J· Christ.) "
21 unto eternal life by J· Christ our "
6: 3 us as were baptized into J· Christ "
11 unto God through J· Christ our "
23 God is eternal life through J· Christ "
7:25 I thank God through J· Christ our "
8: 1 to them which are in Christ J·, "
2 law of the Spirit of life in Christ J· "
11 if the Spirit of him that raised up J· "
39 God, which is in Christ J· our Lord. "
10: 9 confess with thy mouth the Lord J·, "
13:14 But put ye on the Lord J· Christ, "
14:14 and am persuaded by the Lord J·, "
15: 5 another according to Christ J·: "
6 the Father of our Lord J· Christ. "
8 I say that J· Christ was a minister* "
16 should be the minister of J· Christ "
17 I may glory through J· Christ in "
30 for the Lord J· Christ's sake, "
16: 3 Aquilla my helpers in Christ J·: "

Ro 16:18 such serve not our Lord J' Christ,*2424
20 grace of our Lord J' Christ be with "
24 grace of our Lord J' Christ be with* "
25 and the preaching of J' Christ, "
27 be glory through J' Christ for ever. "
1Co 1: 1 called to be an apostle of J' Christ "
2 them that are sanctified in Christ J', "
2 call upon the name of J' Christ our "
3 Father, and from the Lord J' Christ. "
4 which is given you by J' Christ; "
7 the coming of our Lord J' Christ: "
8 in the day of our Lord J' Christ. "
9 of his Son J' Christ our Lord. "
10 by the name of our Lord J' Christ, "
30 But of him are ye in Christ J', "
2: 2 save J' Christ, and him crucified. "
3:11 than that is laid, which is J' Christ. "
4:15 for in Christ J' I have begotten you "
5: 4 In the name of our Lord J' Christ, "
4 the power of our Lord J' Christ, "
5 be saved in the day of the Lord J'. "
6:11 justified in the name of the Lord J', "
8: 6 and one Lord J' Christ, by whom are "
9: 1 have I not seen J' Christ our Lord? "
11:23 the Lord J' the same night in which "
12: 3 Spirit of God calleth J' accursed: "
3 no man can say that J' is the Lord, "
15:31 rejoicing which I have in Christ J' "
57 victory through our Lord J' Christ. "
16:22 man love not the Lord J' Christ, * "
23 The grace of our Lord J' Christ be "
24 My love be with you all in Christ J'. "
2Co 1: 1 Paul, an apostle of J' Christ by the "
2 Father, and from the Lord J' Christ. "
3 the Father of our Lord J' Christ, "
14 are ours in the day of the Lord J'. "
19 For the Son of God, J' Christ, who "
4: 5 ourselves, but Christ J' the Lord; "
6 glory of God in the face of J' Christ. "
10 the body the dying of the Lord J', "
10, 11 the life also of J' might be made "
14 that he which raised up the Lord J' "
14 shall raise up us also by J', and "
5:18 hath reconciled us...by J' Christ, * "
8: 9 the grace of our Lord J' Christ, "
11: 4 that cometh preacheth another J', "
31 and Father of our Lord J' Christ, "
13: 5 how that J' Christ is in you, except "
14 The grace of the Lord J' Christ, "
Ga 1: 1 neither by man, but by J' Christ, "
3 Father, and from our Lord J' Christ, "
12 but by the revelation of J' Christ. "
2: 4 liberty which we have in Christ J', "
16 law, but by the faith of J' Christ, "
16 even we have believed in J' Christ, "
3: 1 J' Christ hath been evidently set "
14 on the Gentiles through J' Christ; "
22 that the promise by faith of J' Christ "
26 of God by faith in Christ J'. "
28 for ye are all one in Christ J'. "
4:14 an angel of God, even as Christ J'. "
5: 6 in J' Christ neither circumcision "
6:14 in the cross of our Lord J' Christ, "
15 in Christ J' neither circumcision * "
17 my body the marks of the Lord J'. "
18 grace of our Lord J' Christ be with "
Eph 1: 1 Paul, an apostle of J' Christ by the "
1 and to the faithful in Christ J': "
2 Father, and from the Lord J' Christ. "
3 and Father of our Lord J' Christ, "
5 adoption of children by J' Christ "
15 I heard of your faith in the Lord J', "
17 That the God of our Lord J' Christ, "
2: 6 in heavenly places in Christ J': "
7 toward us through Christ J'. "
10 created in Christ J' unto good works, "
13 in Christ J' ye who sometimes were "
20 J' Christ himself being the chief "
3: 1 the prisoner of J' Christ for you "
9 who created all things by J' Christ:* "
11 he purposed in Christ J' our Lord: "
14 the Father of our Lord J' Christ, * "
21 be glory in the church by Christ J' "
4:21 taught by him, as the truth is in J': "
5:20 in the name of our Lord J' Christ; "
6:23 the Father and the Lord J' Christ. "
24 love our Lord J' Christ in sincerity. "
Ph'p 1: 1 the servants of J' Christ, "
1 to all the saints in Christ J' which "
2 Father, and from the Lord J' Christ. "
6 perform it until the day of J' Christ: "
8 you all in the bowels of J' Christ. "
11 which are by J' Christ, unto the "
19 the supply of the Spirit of J' Christ, "
26 may be more abundant in J' Christ "
2: 5 in you, which was also in Christ J': "
10 That at the name of J' every knee "
11 confess that J' Christ is Lord, "
19 But I trust in the Lord J' to send "
21 not the things which are J' Christ's. "
3: 3 the spirit, and rejoice in Christ J', "
8 knowledge of Christ J' my Lord: "
12 also I am apprehended of Christ J'. "
14 the high calling of God in Christ J'. "
20 for the Saviour, the Lord J' Christ: "
4: 7 hearts and minds through Christ J'. "
19 to his riches in glory by Christ J'. "
21 Salute every saint in Christ J'. The "
23 grace of our Lord J' Christ be with "
Col 1: 1 Paul, an apostle of J' Christ by the "
2 our Father and the Lord J' Christ.* "
3 the Father of our Lord J' Christ, "
4 we heard of your faith in Christ J', "
28 every man perfect in Christ J': * "
2: 6 received Christ J' the Lord, so walk "
3:17 do all in the name of the Lord J'. "
Col 4:11 And J', which is called Justus, who 2424
1Th 1: 1 Father and in the Lord J' Christ: "
1 Father, and the Lord J' Christ. * "
3 of hope in our Lord J' Christ, "
10 he raised from the dead, even J', "
2:14 which in Judæa are in Christ J': "
15 Who both killed the Lord J', and "
19 the presence of our Lord J' Christ "
3:11 Father, and our Lord J' Christ, "
13 at the coming of our Lord J' Christ "
4: 1 and exhort you by the Lord J', that "
2 we gave you by the Lord J'. "
14 if we believe that J' died and rose "
14 which sleep in J' will God bring "
5: 9 salvation by our Lord J' Christ, "
18 this is the will of God in Christ J' "
23 the coming of our Lord J' Christ. "
28 grace of our Lord J' Christ be with "
2Th 1: 1 our Father and the Lord J' Christ: "
2 our Father and the Lord J' Christ. "
7 the Lord J' shall be revealed from "
8 not the gospel of our Lord J' Christ: "
12 name of our Lord J' Christ may be "
12 of our God and the Lord J' Christ. "
2: 1 the coming of our Lord J' Christ, "
14 of the glory of our Lord J' Christ. "
16 Now our Lord J' Christ himself, "
3: 6 in the name of our Lord J' Christ, "
12 and exhort by our Lord J' Christ, "
18 grace of our Lord J' Christ be with "
1Ti 1: 1 Paul, an apostle of J' Christ by the "
1 our Saviour, and Lord J' Christ, "
2 our Father and J' Christ our Lord. "
12 And I thank Christ J' our Lord, "
14 faith and love which is in Christ J'. "
15 Christ J' came into the world to save "
16 in me first J' Christ might shew "
2: 5 God and men, the man Christ J'; "
3:13 in the faith which is in Christ J'. "
4: 6 shalt be a good minister of J' Christ, "
5:21 before God, and the Lord J' Christ, "
6: 3 the words of our Lord J' Christ, "
13 all things, and before Christ J', "
14 appearing of our Lord J' Christ: "
2Ti 1: 1 Paul, an apostle of J' Christ by the "
1 promise of life which is in Christ J', "
2 the Father and Christ J' our Lord. "
9 was given us in Christ J' before the "
10 appearing of our Saviour J' Christ, "
13 faith and love which is in Christ J'. "
2: 1 in the grace that is in Christ J'. "
3 as a good soldier of J' Christ. "
8 that J' Christ of the seed of David "
10 the salvation which is in Christ J' "
3:12 all that will live godly in Christ J' "
15 through faith which is in Christ J'. "
4: 1 before God, and the Lord J' Christ, "
22 Lord J' Christ be with thy spirit. "
Tit 1: 1 of God, and an apostle of J' Christ, "
4 and the Lord J' Christ our Saviour. "
2:13 God and our Saviour J' Christ; "
3: 6 through J' Christ our Saviour; "
Ph'm 1 Paul, a prisoner of J' Christ, and "
3 our Father and the Lord J' Christ. "
5 which thou hast toward the Lord J', "
6 thing which is in you in Christ J'. "
9 now also a prisoner of J' Christ. "
23 my fellowprisoner in Christ J'; "
25 grace of our Lord J' Christ be with "
Heb 2: 9 see J', who was made a little lower "
3: 1 Priest of our profession, Christ J'; "
4: 8 For if J' had given them rest, then* "
14 the heavens, J' the Son of God, "
6:20 even J', made an high priest for ever "
7:22 was J' made a surety of a better "
10:10 of the body of J' Christ once for all. "
19 into the holiest by the blood of J' "
12: 2 Looking unto J' the author and "
24 And to J' the mediator of the new "
13: 8 J' Christ the same yesterday, and "
12 Wherefore J' also, that he might "
20 again from the dead our Lord J', "
21 in his sight, through J' Christ; "
Jas 1: 1 of God and of the Lord J' Christ, "
2: 1 not the faith of our Lord J' Christ, "
1Pe 1: 1 Peter, an apostle of J' Christ, to the "
2 sprinkling of the blood of J' Christ: "
3 and Father of our Lord J' Christ, "
3 hope by the resurrection of J' Christ "
7 glory at the appearing of J' Christ: "
13 you at the revelation of J' Christ; "
2: 5 acceptable to God by J' Christ. "
3:21 by the resurrection of J' Christ: "
4:11 may be glorified through J' Christ, "
5:10 unto his eternal glory by Christ J',* "
14 be with you all that are in Christ J'.* "
2Pe 1: 1 servant and an apostle of J' Christ, "
1 of God and our Saviour J' Christ: "
2 the knowledge...of J' our Lord, "
8 knowledge of our Lord J' Christ. "
11 of our Lord and Saviour J' Christ. "
14 our Lord J' Christ hath shewed me. "
16 and coming of our Lord J' Christ, "
2:20 of the Lord and Saviour J' Christ, "
3:18 of our Lord and Saviour J' Christ. "
1Jo 1: 3 Father, and with his Son J' Christ. "
7 blood of J' Christ his Son cleanseth "
2: 1 the Father, J' Christ the righteous: "
22 that denieth that J' is the Christ? "
3:23 on the name of his Son J' Christ, "
4: 2, 3 that J' Christ is come in the flesh "
15 shall confess that J' is the Son of "
5: 1 believeth that J' is the Christ is "
5 believeth that J' is the Son of God? "
6 by water and blood, even J' Christ; "
20 is true, even in his Son J' Christ. "
2Jo 3 from the Lord J' Christ, the Son of 2424
7 that J' Christ is come in the flesh. "
Jude 1 Jude, the servant of J' Christ, and "
1 preserved in J' Christ, and called: "
4 Lord God, and our Lord J' Christ. "
17 the apostles of our Lord J' Christ; "
21 for the mercy of our Lord J' Christ "
Re 1: 1 The Revelation of J' Christ, which "
2 and of the testimony of J' Christ, "
5 from J' Christ, who is the faithful "
9 kingdom and patience of J' Christ, "
9 and for the testimony of J' Christ. "
12:17 and have the testimony of J' Christ. "
14:12 of God, and the faith of J'. "
17: 6 with the blood of the martyrs of J': "
19:10 that have the testimony of J': "
10 the testimony of J' is the spirit of "
20: 4 were beheaded for the witness of J', "
22:16 I J' have sent mine angel to testify "
20 Amen. Even so, come, Lord J'. "
21 grace of our Lord J' Christ be with "

Jesus' (*je'-zus*)
M't 15:30 and cast them down at J' feet; *2424
27:57 who also himself was J' disciple: "
Lu 5: 8 saw it, he fell down at J' knees, "
8:41 fell down at J' feet, and besought "
10:39 Mary, which also sat at J' feet, * "
Joh 12: 9 they came not for J' sake only, but "
13:23 Now there was leaning on J' bosom "
25 He then lying on J' breast saith "
2Co 4: 5 ourselves your servants for J' sake. "
11 delivered unto death for J' sake, "

Jesus Christ See Jesus and Christ.

Jether (*je'-thur*) See also Hobab; Ithra; Ithrites; Jethro; Raguel.
J'g 8:20 he said unto J' his firstborn, Up, 3500
1Ki 2: 5 Ner, and unto Amasa the son of J', "
32 and Amasa the son of J', captain of "
1Ch 2:17 and the father of Amasa was J' the "
32 of Shammai; J', and Jonathan: "
32 and J' died without children. "
4:17 sons of Ezra were, J', and Mered, "
7:38 sons of J'; Jephunneh, and Pispah, "

Jetheth (*je'-theth*)
Ge 36:40 Timnah, duke Alvah, duke J', 3509
1Ch 1:51 Timnah, duke Aliah, duke J', "

Jethlah (*jeth'-lah*)
Jos 19:42 Shaalabbin, and Ajalon, and J', *3494

Jethro (*je'-thro*) See also Jether.
Ex 3: 1 Now Moses kept the flock of J' his 3503
4:18 Moses went and returned to J' his "
18 And J' said to Moses, Go in peace. "
18: 1 When J', the priest of Midian, "
2 Then J', Moses' father in law, took "
5 J', Moses' father in law, came with "
6 father in law J' am come unto thee, "
9 J' rejoiced for all the goodness "
10 J' said, Blessed be the Lord, who "
12 J', Moses' father in law, took a "

Jetur (*je'-tur*)
Ge 25:15 Hadar, and Tema, J', Naphish, 3195
1Ch 1:31 J', Naphish, and Kedemah. These "
5:19 Hagarites, with J', and Nephish, "

Jeuel (*je-u'-el*) See also Jeiel.
1Ch 9: 6 the sons of Zerah; J', and their 3262

Jeush (*je'-ush*) See also Jehush.
Ge 36: 5 Aholibamah bare J', and Jaalam, 3266
14 she bare to Esau J', and Jaalam, "
18 duke J', duke Jaalam, duke Korah: "
1Ch 1:35 Reuel, and J', and Jaalam, and "
7:10 J', and Benjamin, and Ehud, and "
23:10 Jahath, Zina, and J', and Beriah. "
11 J' and Beriah had not many sons; "
2Ch 11:19 J', and Shamariah, and Zaham. "

Jeuz (*je'-uz*)
1Ch 8:10 And J', and Shachia, and Mirma. 3263

Jew (*jew*) See also Jewess; Jewish; Jews.
Es 2: 5 the palace there was a certain J', 3064
3: 4 he had told them that he was a J'. "
5:13 Mordecai the J' sitting at the king's "
6:10 do even so to Mordecai the J', that "
8: 7 the queen and to Mordecai the J', "
9:29 of Abihail, and Mordecai the J', "
31 Mordecai the J' and Esther the "
10: 3 Mordecai the J' was next unto king "
Jer 34: 9 them, to wit, of a J' his brother. "
Zec 8:23 hold of the skirt of him that is a J', "
Joh 4: 9 being a J', askest drink of me, 2453
18:35 Pilate answered, Am I a J'? Thine "
Ac 10:28 man that is a J' to keep company, "
13: 6 a J', whose name was Bar-jesus: "
18: 2 found a certain J' named Aquila, "
24 certain J' named Apollos, born at "
19:14 Sceva, a J', and chief of the priests, "
34 when they knew that he was a J', "
21:39 a man which am a J' of Tarsus, "
22: 3 man which am a J' born in Tarsus, "
Ro 1:16 the J' first, and also to the Greek. "
2: 9 the J' first, and also of the Gentile; "
10 the J' first, and also to the Gentile: "
17 Behold, thou art called a J', and "
28 is not a J', which is one outwardly; "
29 he is a J', which is one inwardly; "
3: 1 What advantage then hath the J'? "
10:12 between the J' and the Greek: "
1Co 9:20 And to the Jews I became as a J', "
Ga 2:14 If thou, being a J', livest after the "
3:28 There is neither J' nor Greek, "
Col 3:11 Where there is neither Greek nor J', "

jewel See also Jewels.
Pr 11:22 As a j' of gold in a swine's snout, 5141

Pr 20:15 lips of knowledge are a precious *j*. 3627
Eze 16:12 I put a *j* on thy forehead, and *5141

jewels
Ge 24:53 servant brought forth *j* of silver, 3627
53 and *j* of gold, and raiment, and "
Ex 3:22 sojourneth in her house, *j* of silver, "
22 and *j* of gold, and raiment: and ye "
11: 2 neighbour, *j* of silver, and *j* of gold. "
12:35 of the Egyptians *j* of silver, "
35 and *j* of gold, and raiment: "
35:22 rings, and tablets, all *j* of gold: "
Nu 31:50 of *j* of gold, chains, and bracelets, "
51 gold of them, even all wrought *j*. "
1Sa 6: 8 put the *j* of gold, which ye return "
15 with it, wherein the *j* of gold were, "
2Ch 20:25 precious *j*, which they stripped off "
32:27 and for all manner of pleasant *j*; * "
Job 28:17 it shall not be for *j* of fine gold. "
Ca 1:10 cheeks are comely with rows of *j*, "
7: 1 joints of thy thighs are like *j*, the 2484
Isa 3:21 The rings, and nose *j*, 5141
61:10 bride adorneth herself with her *j*. 3627
Eze 16:17 Thou hast also taken thy fair *j* of "
39 shall take thy fair *j*, and leave thee "
23:26 clothes, and take away thy fair *j*. "
Ho 2:13 with her earrings and her *j*, 2484
Mal 3:17 that day when I make up my *j*; *5459

Jewess (*jew'-ess*)
Ac 16: 1 certain woman, which was a *J*·, 2453
24:24 his wife Drusilla, which was a *J*·, "

Jewish (*jew'-ish*)
Tit 1:14 Not giving heed to *J*· fables, and 2451

Jewry (*jew'-ree*) See also JUDÆA.
Da 5:13 king my father brought out of *J*·?*3061
Lu 23: 5 people, teaching throughout all *J*·,*2449
Joh 7: 1 he would not walk in *J*·, because * "

Jews (*jews*) See also JEWS'.
2Ki 16: 6 Syria, and drave the *J*· from Elath: 3064
25:25 the *J*· and the Chaldees that were "
Ezr 4:12 the *J*· which came up from thee to 3062
23 in haste to Jerusalem unto the *J*·, "
5: 1 son of Iddo, prophesied unto the *J*· "
5 God was upon the elders of the *J*·, "
6: 7 alone; let the governors of the *J*· "
7 and the elders of the *J*· built this "
8 shall do to the elders of these *J*· "
14 the elders of the *J*· builded, and "
Ne 1: 2 concerning the *J*· that had escaped, 3064
2:16 neither had I as yet told it to the *J*·, "
4: 1 indignation, and mocked the *J*·. "
2 and said, What do these feeble *J*·? "
12 the *J*· which dwelt by them came, "
5: 1 wives against their brethren the *J*·. "
8 have redeemed our brethren the *J*·, "
17 were at my table... *J*· and rulers, "
6: 6 that thou and the *J*· think to rebel: "
13:23 In those days also saw I *J*· that "
Es 3: 6 Haman sought to destroy all the *J*· "
13 kill, and to cause to perish, all *J*·, "
4: 3 was great mourning among the *J*·, "
7 to the king's treasuries for the *J*·, "
13 king's house, more than all the *J*·. "
14 and deliverance arise to the *J*· "
16 gather together all the *J*· that are "
6:13 Mordecai be of the seed of the *J*·, "
8: 3 that he had devised against the *J*·. "
5 which he wrote to destroy the *J*· "
7 he laid his hand upon the *J*·. "
8 Write ye also for the *J*·, as it liketh "
9 Mordecai commanded unto the *J*·, "
9 the *J*· according to their writing, "
11 Wherein the king granted the *J*· "
13 *J*· should be ready against that day "
16 The *J*· had light, and gladness, and "
17 the *J*· had joy and gladness, a feast "
17 the people of the land became *J*·: 3054
17 the fear of the *J*· fell upon them. 3064
9: 1 *J*· hoped to have power over them, "
1 the *J*· had rule over them that "
2 *J*· gathered themselves together "
3 officers of the king, helped the *J*·; "
5 the *J*· smote all their enemies with "
6 Shushan the palace the *J*· slew and "
10 the enemy of the *J*·, slew they; * "
12 The *J*· have slain and destroyed "
13 king, let it be granted to the *J*· "
15 For the *J*· that were in Shushan "
16 *J*· that were in the king's provinces "
18 *J*· that were in Shushan assembled "
19 Therefore the *J*· of the villages, "
20 sent letters unto all the *J*· that "
22 the *J*· rested from their enemies, "
23 the *J*· undertook to do as they had "
24 Agagite, the enemy of all the *J*·, "
24 devised against the *J*· to destroy "
25 which he devised against the *J*·, "
27 *J*· ordained, and took upon them, "
28 should not fail from among the *J*·, "
30 he sent the letters unto all the *J*·, "
10: 3 Ahasuerus, great among the *J*·, "
Jer 32:12 *J*· that sat in the court of the prison. "
38:19 afraid of the *J*· that are fallen to "
40:11 when all the *J*· that were in Moab, "
12 all the *J*· returned out of all places "
15 all the *J*· which are gathered unto "
41: 3 Ishmael also slew all the *J*· that "
44: 1 concerning all the *J*· which dwell "
52:28 the seventh year three thousand *J*· "
30 carried away captive of the *J*· "
Da 3: 8 came near, and accused the *J*·. "
12 certain *J*· whom thou hast set "
M't 2: 2 is he that is born King of the *J*·? 2453
27:11 saying, Art thou the King of the *J*·? "
29 him, saying, Hail, King of the *J*·! "
M't 27:37 This Is Jesus The King Of The *J*·. 2453
28:15 is commonly reported among the *J*· "
M'r 7: 3 For the Pharisees, and all the *J*·, "
15: 2 him, Art thou the King of the *J*·? "
9 release unto you the King of the *J*·? "
12 whom ye call the King of the *J*·? "
18 to salute him, Hail, King of the *J*·! "
26 written over, The King Of The *J*·. "
Lu 7: 3 sent unto him the elders of the *J*·, "
23: 3 saying, Art thou the King of the *J*·? "
37 If thou be the king of the *J*·, save "
38 This Is The King Of The *J*·. "
51 was of Arimathæa, a city of the *J*·: "
Joh 1:19 when the *J*· sent priests and Levites "
2: 6 manner of the purifying of the *J*·,* "
18 Then answered the *J*· and said unto "
20 Then said the *J*·, Forty and six "
3: 1 named Nicodemus, a ruler of the *J*·: "
25 of John's disciples and the *J*· * "
4: 9 the *J*· have no dealings with the "
22 worship: for salvation is of the *J*·. "
5: 1 this there was a feast of the *J*·; "
10 *J*· therefore said unto him that was "
15 and told the *J*· that it was Jesus, "
16 therefore did the *J*· persecute Jesus, "
18 the *J*· sought the more to kill him, "
6: 4 passover, a feast of the *J*·, was nigh. "
41 The *J*· then murmured at him, "
52 The *J*· therefore strove among "
7: 1 because the *J*· sought to kill him. "
11 Then the *J*· sought him at the feast, "
13 openly of him for fear of the *J*·. "
15 And the *J*· marvelled, saying, How "
35 said the *J*· among themselves, "
8:22 said the *J*·, Will he kill himself? "
31 Jesus to those *J*· which believed "
48 Then answered the *J*·, and said "
52 Then said the *J*· unto him, Now we "
57 Then said the *J*· unto him, Thou "
9:18 the *J*· did not believe concerning "
22 parents, because they feared the *J*·: "
22 for the *J*· had agreed already, that "
10:19 was a division...again among the *J*· "
24 Then came the *J*· round about him, "
31 Then the *J*· took up stones again "
33 The *J*· answered him, saying, For "
11: 8 the *J*· of late sought to stone thee; "
19 many of the *J*· came to Martha "
31 The *J*· then which were with her "
33 weeping, and the *J*· also weeping "
36 Then said the *J*·, Behold how he "
45 many of the *J*· which came to Mary, "
54 no more openly among the *J*·; "
12: 9 people of the *J*· therefore knew "
11 of him many of the *J*· went away, "
13:33 as I said unto the *J*·, Whither I go, "
18:12 and officers of the *J*· took Jesus, "
14 he, which gave counsel to the *J*·, "
20 whither the *J*· always resort; "
31 The *J*· therefore said unto him, It "
33 him, Art thou the King of the *J*·? "
36 I should not be delivered to the *J*·: "
38 he went out again unto the *J*·, and "
39 release unto you the King of the *J*·? "
19: 3 And said, Hail, King of the *J*·! and "
7 *J*· answered him, We have a law, "
12 but the *J*· cried out, saying, If thou "
14 he saith unto the *J*·, Behold your "
19 Of Nazareth The King Of The *J*·. "
20 This title then read many of the *J*·: "
21 Then said the chief priests of the *J*· "
21 Write not, The King of the *J*·; but "
21 that he said, I am King of the *J*·. "
31 The *J*· therefore,...besought Pilate "
38 but secretly for fear of the *J*·, "
40 as the manner of the *J*· is to bury. "
20:19 were assembled for fear of the *J*·, "
Ac 2: 5 were dwelling at Jerusalem *J*·, "
10 of Rome, *J*· and proselytes, "
9:22 the *J*· which dwelt at Damascus, "
23 the *J*· took counsel to kill him: "
10:22 among all the nation of the *J*·, "
39 he did both in the land of the *J*·, "
11:19 word to none but unto the *J*· only. "
12: 3 because he saw it pleased the *J*·, "
11 expectation of the people of the *J*·. "
13: 5 of God in the synagogues of the *J*·: "
42 *J*· were gone out of the synagogue,* "
43 many of the *J*· and religious "
45 when the *J*· saw the multitudes, "
50 the *J*· stirred up the devout and "
14: 1 into the synagogue of the *J*·, "
1 great multitude both of the *J*· and "
2 the unbelieving *J*· stirred up the "
4 and part held with the *J*·, and part "
5 and also of the *J*· with their rulers, "
19 thither certain *J*· from Antioch "
16: 3 circumcised him because of the *J*· "
20 being *J*·, do exceedingly trouble "
17: 1 where was a synagogue of the *J*·: "
5 But the *J*· which believed not, "
10 went into the synagogue of the *J*·. "
13 But when the *J*· of Thessalonica "
17 he in the synagogue of the *J*·, "
18: 2 all *J*· to depart from Rome:) "
4 persuaded the *J*· and the Greeks. "
5 testified to the *J*· that Jesus was "
12 the *J*· made insurrection with one "
14 Gallio said unto the *J*·, If it were "
14 O ye *J*·, reason would that I should "
19 and reasoned with the *J*·. "
28 For he mightily convinced the *J*·, "
19:10 Lord Jesus, both *J*· and Greeks. "
13 Then certain of the vagabond *J*·, "
17 And this was known to all the *J*· "
33 the *J*· putting him forward. "
Ac 20: 3 And when the *J*· laid wait for him, 2453
19 me by the lying in wait of the *J*·: "
21 Testifying both to the *J*·, and also "
21:11 So shall the *J*· at Jerusalem bind "
20 how many thousands of *J*· there are "
21 thou teachest all the *J*· which are "
27 the *J*· which were of Asia, when "
22:12 a good report of all the *J*· which "
30 wherefore he was accused of the *J*·, "
23:12 certain of the *J*· banded together, "
20 The *J*· have agreed to desire thee "
27 This man was taken of the *J*·, "
30 that the *J*· laid wait for the man, * "
24: 5 mover of sedition among all the *J*· "
9 the *J*· also assented, saying that "
18 certain *J*· from Asia found me "
27 willing to shew the *J*· a pleasure, "
25: 2 the chief of the *J*· informed him "
7 the *J*· which came down from "
8 Neither against the law of the *J*·, "
9 willing to do the *J*· a pleasure, "
10 to the *J*· have I done no wrong, as "
15 the elders of the *J*· informed me, "
24 the multitude of the *J*· have dealt "
26: 2 whereof I am accused of the *J*·: "
3 questions which are among the *J*·: "
4 at Jerusalem, know all the *J*·; "
7 Agrippa, I am accused of the *J*·. "
21 the *J*· caught me in the temple, "
28:17 days Paul called the chief of the *J*· "
19 But when the *J*· spake against it, "
29 said these words, the *J*· departed, * "
Ro 3: 9 before proved both *J*· and Gentiles, "
29 Is he the God of the *J*· only? "
9:24 called, not of the *J*· only, but also "
1Co 1:22 For the *J*· require a sign, and the "
23 unto the *J*· a stumblingblock, and "
24 are called, both *J*· and Greeks, "
9:20 And unto the *J*· I became as a Jew, "
20 that I might gain the *J*·; to them "
10:32 none offence, neither to the *J*·, nor "
12:13 whether we be *J*· or Gentiles, "
2Co 11:24 Of the *J*· five times received I forty "
Ga 2:13 the other *J*· dissembled likewise "
14 of Gentiles, and not as do the *J*·, 2452
14 the Gentiles to live as do the *J*·? 2450
15 We who are *J*· by nature, and not 2453
1Th 2:14 even as they have of the *J*·: "
Re 2: 9 which say they are *J*·, and are not, "
3: 9 which say they are *J*·, and are not, "

Jews' (*jews*)
2Ki 18:26 talk not with us in the *J*· language 3066
28 a loud voice in the *J*· language, "
2Ch 32:18 with a loud voice in the *J*· speech "
Ne 13:24 not speak in the *J*· language, but "
Es 3:10 the Agagite, the *J*· enemy. 3064
8: 1 the house of Haman the *J*· enemy "
Isa 36:11 speak not to us in the *J*· language, "
13 a loud voice in the *J*· language, "
Joh 2:13 the *J*· passover was at hand, *2453
7: 2 the *J*· feast of tabernacles was at* "
11:55 the *J*· passover was nigh at hand:* "
19:42 because of the *J*· preparation day; "
Ga 1:13 in time past in the *J*· religion, 2454
14 profited in the *J*· religion above "

Jezaniah (*jez-a-ni'-ah*) See also JAAZANIAH.
Jer 40: 8 and *J*· the son of a Maachathite, 3153
42: 1 Kareah, and *J*· the son of Hoshaiah, "

Jezebel (*jez'-e-bel*) See also JEZEBEL'S.
1Ki 16:31 he took to wife *J*· the daughter of 348
18: 4 when *J*· cut off the prophets of the "
13 what I did when *J*· slew the prophets "
19: 1 And Ahab told *J*· all that Elijah had "
2 *J*· sent a messenger unto Elijah, "
21: 5 *J*· his wife came to him, and said "
7 *J*· his wife said unto him, Dost thou "
11 did as *J*· had sent unto them, and "
14 sent to *J*·, saying, Naboth is stoned, "
15 *J*· heard that Naboth was stoned, "
15 that *J*· said to Ahab, Arise, take "
23 And of *J*· also spake the Lord, "
23 The dogs shall eat *J*· by the wall of "
25 Lord, whom *J*· his wife stirred up. "
2Ki 9: 7 of the Lord, at the hand of *J*·. "
10 the dogs shall eat *J*· in the portion "
22 as the whoredoms of thy mother *J*· "
30 was come to Jezreel, *J*· heard of it; "
36 Jezreel shall dogs eat the flesh of *J*·: "
37 the carcase of *J*· shall be as dung "
37 so that they shall not say, This is *J*·. "
Re 2:20 thou sufferest that woman *J*·, 2403

Jezebel's (*jez'-e-bels*)
1Ki 18:19 four hundred which eat at *J*· table. 348

Jezer (*je'-zur*) See also JEZERITES.
Ge 46:24 and Guni, and *J*·, and Shillem, 3337
Nu 26:49 Of *J*·, the family of the Jezerites: "
1Ch 7:13 and Guni, and *J*·, and Shallum, "

Jezerites (*je'-zur-ites*)
Nu 26:49 of Jezer, the family of the *J*·: 3339

Jeziah (*je-zi'-ah*)
Ezr 10:25 Ramiah, and *J*·, and Malchiah, *3150

Jeziel (*je'-ze-el*)
1Ch 12: 3 and *J*·, and Pelet, the sons of 3149

Jezliah (*jez-li'-ah*)
1Ch 8:18 *J*·, and Jobab, the sons of Elpaal;*3152

Jezoar (*je-zo'-ar*) See also ZOAR.
1Ch 4: 7 of Helah were, Zereth, and *J*·, *3328

Jezrahiah (*jez-ra-hi'-ah*) See also IZRAHIAH.
Ne 12:42 sang loud, with *J*· their overseer. 3156

Jezreel (*jez'-re-el*) See also JEZREELITE.
Jos 15:56 *J*·, and Jokdeam, and Zanoah, 3157
17:16 they who are of the valley of *J*·. "

Jos 19:18 And their border was toward J'. 3157
J'g 6:33 and pitched in the valley of J'. "
1Sa 25:43 David also took Ahinoam of J'; "
29: 1 pitched by a fountain which is in J'. "
11 And the Philistines went up to J'. "
2Sa 2: 9 and over J', and over Ephraim, and "
4: 4 of Saul and Jonathan out of J', "
1Ki 4:12 which is by Zartanah beneath J', "
18:45 And Ahab rode, and went to J'. "
46 before Ahab to the entrance of J'. "
21: 1 had a vineyard, which was in J', "
23 shall eat Jezebel by the wall of J'. "
2Ki 8:29 Joram went back to be healed in J' "
29 to see Joram the son of Ahab in J', "
9:10 eat Jezebel in the portion of J', "
15 was returned to be healed in J' "
15 out of the city to go to tell it in J'. "
16 rode in a chariot, and went to J'; "
17 a watchman on the tower of J', "
30 And when Jehu was come to J', "
36 In the portion of J' shall dogs eat "
37 of the field in the portion of J'; "
10: 1 to Samaria, unto the rulers of J', "
6 and come to me to J' by to morrow "
7 baskets, and sent him them to J'. "
11 remained of the house of Ahab in J', "
1Ch 4: 3 Etam; J', and Ishma, and Idbash: "
2Ch 22: 6 he returned to be healed in J' "
6 Jehoram the son of Ahab at J', "
Ho 1: 4 said unto him, Call his name J'; "
4 I will avenge the blood of J' upon "
5 bow of Israel in the valley of J'. "
11 for great shall be the day of J'. "
2:22 the oil; and they shall hear J'. "

Jezreelite (*jez'-re-el-ite*) See also JEZREELITESS.
1Ki 21: 1 that Naboth the J' had a vineyard, 3158
4 Naboth the J' had spoken to him: "
6 Because I spake unto Naboth the J', "
7 thee the vineyard of Naboth the J'. "
15 of the vineyard of Naboth the J', "
16 to the vineyard of Naboth the J', "
2Ki 9:21 him in the portion of Naboth the J'. "
25 of the field of Naboth the J': "

Jezreelitess (*jez'-re-el-i-tess*)
1Sa 27: 3 his two wives, Ahinoam the J', 3159
30: 5 taken captives, Ahinoam the J', "
2Sa 2: 2 two wives also, Ahinoam the J', "
3: 2 was Amnon, of Ahinoam the J'; "
1Ch 3: 1 Amnon, of Ahinoam the J'; "

Jibsam (*jib'-sam*)
1Ch 7: 2 and Jahmai, and J', and Shemuel, 3005

Jidlaph (*jid'-laf*)
Ge 22:22 and Pildash, and J', and Bethuel. 3044

Jimna (*jim'-nah*) See also IMNA; JIMNAH; JIMNITES.
Nu 26:44 of J', the family of the Jimnites: *3232

Jimnah (*jim'-nah*) See also JIMNA.
Ge 46:17 sons of Asher; J', and Ishuah, *3232

Jimnites (*jim'-nites*)
Nu 26:44 of Jimna, the family of the J': *3232

Jiphtah (*jif'-tah*) See also JEPHTHAH; JIPHTHAH-EL.
Jos 15:43 And J', and Ashnah, and Nezib, *3316

Jiphthah-el (*jif'-thah-el*)
Jos 19:14 thereof are in the valley of J': *3317
27 to the valley of J' toward the north* "

Joab (*jo'-ab*) See also ATAROTH; HOUSE; JOAB'S.
1Sa 26: 6 the son of Zeruiah, brother to J', 3097
2Sa 2:13 J' the son of Zeruiah, and the "
14 Abner said to J', Let the young "
14 And J' said, Let them arise. "
18 three sons of Zeruiah there, J', and "
22 should I hold up my face to J' "
24 J' also and Abishai pursued after "
26 Abner called to J', and said, Shall "
27 J' said, As God liveth, unless thou "
28 So J' blew a trumpet, and all the "
30 J' returned from following Abner: "
32 J' and his men went all night, and "
3:22 servants of David and J' came "
23 When J' and all the host that was "
23 they told J', saying, Abner the son "
24 Then J' came to the king, and "
26 when J' was come out from David, "
27 J' took him aside in the gate to "
29 Let it rest on the head of J', and on "
29 not fail from the house of J' one "
30 So J' and Abishai his brother slew "
31 David said to J', and to all the "
8:16 J' the son of Zeruiah was over the "
10: 7 when David heard of it, he sent J', "
9 When J' saw that the front of the "
13 J' drew nigh, and the people that "
14 So J' returned from the children "
11: 1 that David sent J', and his servants "
6 David sent to J', saying, Send me "
6 And J' sent Uriah to David. "
7 David demanded of him how J' did, "
11 and my lord J', and the servants "
14 David wrote a letter to J', and sent "
16 to pass, when J' observed the city, "
17 city went out, and fought with J': "
18 J' sent and told David all the "
22 David all that J' had sent him for. "
25 Thus shalt thou say unto J', Let "
12:26 J' fought against Rabbah of the "
27 J' sent messengers to David, and "
14: 1 J' the son of Zeruiah perceived "
2 J' sent to Tekoah, and fetched "
3 So J' put the words in her mouth. "
19 Is not the hand of J' with thee in "

2Sa 14:19 for thy servant J', he bade me, 3097
20 hath thy servant J' done this thing: "
21 the king said unto J', Behold now, "
22 J' fell to the ground on his face, "
22 J' said, To day thy servant knoweth "
23 J' arose and went to Geshur, and "
29 Absalom sent for J', to have sent "
31 J' arose, and came to Absalom "
32 Absalom answered J', Behold, I "
33 J' came to the king, and told him: "
17:25 captain of the host instead of J': "
18: 2 of the people under the hand of J', "
5 the king commanded J' and "
10 a certain man saw it, and told J', "
11 J' said unto the man that told him, "
12 the man said unto J', Though I "
14 Then said J', I may not tarry thus "
16 J' blew the trumpet, and the people "
16 for J' held back the people. "
20 J' said unto him, Thou shalt not "
21 Then said J' to Cushi, Go tell the "
21 Cushi bowed himself unto J', and "
22 the son of Zadok yet again to J', "
22 J' said, Wherefore wilt thou run, "
29 When J' sent the king's servant, "
19: 1 it was told J', Behold, the king "
5 J' came into the house to the king, "
13 me continually in the room of J'. "
20: 9 J' said to Amasa, Art thou in "
9 J' took Amasa by the beard with "
10 So J' and Abishai his brother "
11 and said, He that favoureth J', "
11 is for David, let him go after J'. "
13 all the people went on after J', to "
15 people that were with J' battered "
16 say, I pray you, unto J', Come near "
17 her, the woman said, Art thou J'? "
20 J' answered and said, Far be it, "
21 the woman said unto J', Behold, "
22 son of Bichri, and cast it out to J'. "
22 J' returned to Jerusalem unto the "
23 J' was over all the host of Israel: "
23:18 Abishai, the brother of J', the son "
24 brother of J' was one of the thirty; "
37 armourbearer to J' the son of "
24: 2 the king said to J' the captain of "
3 J' said unto the king, Now the "
4 king's word prevailed against J', "
4 J' and the captains of the host "
9 J' gave up the sum of the number "
1Ki 1: 7 he conferred with J' the son of "
19 and J' the captain of the host: "
41 J' heard the sound of the trumpet, "
2: 5 J' the son of Zeruiah did to me, "
22 and for J' the son of Zeruiah. "
28 Then tidings came to J': "
28 for J' had turned after Adonijah, "
28 J' fled unto the tabernacle of the "
29 that J' was fled unto the tabernacle "
30 Thus said J', and thus he answered "
31 the innocent blood, which J' shed, "
33 therefore return upon the head of J', "
11:15 J' the captain of the host was gone "
16 For six months did J' remain there "
21 J' the captain of the host was dead, "
1Ch 2:16 sons of Zeruiah; Abishai and J', "
54 Ataroth, the house of J', and half 5854
4:14 Seraiah begat J', the father of 3097
11: 6 So J' the son of Zeruiah went first "
8 J' repaired the rest of the city. "
20 the brother of J', he was chief of "
26 were, Asahel the brother of J', "
39 the armourbearer of J' the son of "
18:15 J' the son of Zeruiah was over the "
19: 8 when David heard of it, he sent J', "
10 when J' saw that the battle was "
14 So J' and the people that were "
15 city. Then J' came to Jerusalem. "
20: 1 J' led forth the power of the army, "
1 J' smote Rabbah, and destroyed it. "
21: 2 David said to J' and to the rulers "
3 And J' answered, The Lord make "
4 king's word prevailed against J'. "
4 Wherefore J' departed, and went "
5 J' gave the sum of the number of "
6 king's word was abominable to J'. "
26:28 and J' the son of Zeruiah, had "
27: 7 month was Asahel the brother of J', "
24 J' the son of Zeruiah began to "
34 general of the king's army was J'. "
Ezr 2: 6 of the children of Jeshua and J', "
8: 9 Of the sons of J'; Obadiah the son "
Ne 7:11 of the children of Jeshua and J', "
Ps 60: *title* when J' returned, and smote of "

Joab's (*jo'-abs*)
2Sa 14:30 J' field is near mine, and he hath 3097
17:25 Nahash, sister to Zeruiah J' mother, "
18: 2 the son of Zeruiah, J' brother, "
15 young men that bare J' armour "
20: 7 there went out after him J' men, "
8 J' garment that he had put on was* "
10 to the sword that was in J' hand: "
11 one of J' men stood by him, and "

Joah (*jo'-ah*) See also ETHAN.
2Ki 18:18 J' the son of Asaph the recorder. 3098
26 Shebna, and J', unto Rab-shakeh, "
37 J' the son of Asaph the recorder, "
1Ch 6:21 J' his son, Iddo his son, Zerah his "
26: 4 J' the third, and Sacar the fourth, "
2Ch 29:12 Gershonites; J' the son of Zimmah, "
12 and Eden the son of J': "
34: 8 J' the son of Joahaz the recorder, "
Isa 36: 3 and J', Asaph's son, the recorder. "
11 Shebna and J' unto Rabshakeh, "
22 J', the son of Asaph, the recorder, "

Joahaz (*jo'-a-haz*) See also JEHOAHAZ.
2Ch 34: 8 Joah the son of J' the recorder, 3098

Joanna (*jo-an'-nah*)
Lu 3:27 Which was the son of J', which *2489
8: 3 And J' the wife of Chuza Herod's "
24:10 It was Mary Magdalene, and J', "

Joash (*jo'-ash*) See also JEHOASH.
J'g 6:11 pertained unto J' the Abi-ezrite: 3101
29 the son of J' hath done this thing. "
30 men of the city said unto J', Bring "
31 J' said unto all that stood against "
7:14 the sword of Gideon the son of J', "
8:13 the son of J' returned from battle "
29 the son of J' went and dwelt in his "
32 Gideon the son of J' died in a good "
32 in the sepulchre of J' his father, "
1Ki 22:26 the city, and to J' the king's son; "
2Ki 11: 2 took J' the son of Ahaziah, and "
12:19 the rest of the acts of J', and all "
20 slew J' in the house of Millo, which "
13: 1 the three and twentieth year of J' "
9 and J' his son reigned in his stead. "
10 the thirty and seventh year of J' "
12 the rest of the acts of J', and all "
13 And J' slept with his fathers; and "
13 J' was buried in Samaria with the "
14 J' the king of Israel came down "
25 Three times did J' beat him, and "
14: 1 second year of J' son of Jehoahaz "
1 the son of J' king of Judah. "
3 to all things as J' his father did. "
17 the son of J' king of Judah "
23 year of Amaziah the son of J' "
23 Jeroboam the son of J' king of "
27 the hand of Jeroboam the son of J'. "
1Ch 3:11 son, Ahaziah his son, J' his son, "
4:22 J', and Saraph, who had the "
7: 8 Zemira, and J', and Eliezer, and 3135
12: 3 The chief was Ahiezer, then J', 3101
27:28 and over the cellars of oil was J': 3135
2Ch 18:25 the city, and to J' the king's son; 3101
22:11 took J' the son of Ahaziah, and "
24: 1 J' was seven years old when he "
2 J' did that which was right in the "
4 J' was minded to repair the house "
22 Thus J' the king remembered not "
24 they executed judgment against J'. "
25:17 Judah took advice, and sent to J', "
18 J' king of Israel sent to Amaziah "
21 so J' the king of Israel went up; "
23 J' the king of Israel took Amaziah "
23 king of Judah, the son of J', the "
25 Amaziah the son of J' king of Judah "
25 death of J' son of Jehoahaz king of "
Ho 1: 1 days of Jeroboam the son of J', "
Am 1: 1 days of Jeroboam the son of J' "

Joatham (*jo'-a-tham*) See also JOTHAM.
M't 1: 9 And Ozias begat J'; and J' begat*2488

Job (*jobe*) See also JASHUB; JOB'S.
Ge 46:13 Tola, and Phuvah, and J', and 3102
Job 1: 1 land of Uz, whose name was J'; 347
5 that J' sent and sanctified them, "
5 J' said, It may be that my sons have "
5 hearts. Thus did J' continually. "
8 Hast thou considered my servant J', "
9 said, Doth J' fear God for nought? "
14 there came a messenger unto J', "
20 Then J' arose, and rent his mantle, "
22 In all this J' sinned not, nor charged "
2: 3 Hast thou considered my servant J', "
7 smote J' with sore boils from the "
10 In all this did not J' sin with his "
3: 1 After this opened J' his mouth, and "
2 And J' spake, and said, "
6: 1 But J' answered, and said, "
9: 1 Then J' answered and said, "
12: 1 And J' answered and said, "
16: 1 Then J' answered and said, "
19: 1 Then J' answered and said, "
21: 1 But J' answered and said, "
23: 1 Then J' answered and said, "
26: 1 But J' answered and said, "
27: 1 Moreover J' continued his parable, "
29: 1 Moreover J' continued his parable, "
31:40 barley. The words of J' are ended. "
32: 1 three men ceased to answer J', "
2 against J' was his wrath kindled, "
3 and yet had condemned J'. "
4 Elihu had waited till J' had spoken, "
12 was none of you that convinced J', "
33: 1 J', I pray thee, hear my speeches, "
31 Mark well, O J', hearken unto me: "
34: 5 For J' hath said, I am righteous: "
7 What man is like J', who drinketh "
35 J' hath spoken without knowledge, "
36 My desire is that J' may be tried "
35:16 doth J' open his mouth in vain; "
37:14 Hearken unto this, O J': stand still, "
38: 1 the Lord answered J' out of the "
40: 1 the Lord answered J', and said, "
3 J' answered the Lord, and said, "
6 answered the Lord unto J' out of "
42: 1 J' answered the Lord, and said, "
7 had spoken these words unto J', "
7 that is right, as my servant J' hath. "
8 go to my servant J', and offer up "
8 my servant J' shall pray for you: "
8 which is right, like my servant J'. "
9 them: the Lord also accepted J'. "
10 the Lord turned the captivity of J', "
10 gave J' twice as much as he had "
12 Lord blessed the latter end of J' "
15 found so fair as the daughter of J': "
16 lived J' a hundred and forty years, "

Job 42:17 So J' died, being old and full of 347
Eze 14:14 three men, Noah, Daniel, and J', "
20 Noah, Daniel, and J', were in it, as "
Jas 5:11 have heard of the patience of J', 2492

Job's (*jobes*)
Job 2:11 when J' three friends heard of all 347

Jobab (*jo'-bab*)
Ge 10:29 And Ophir, and Havilah, and J': 3103
36:33 and J' the son of Zerah of Bozrah "
34 And J' died, and Husham of the "
Jos 11: 1 he sent to J' king of Madon, and "
1Ch 1:23 And Ophir, and Havilah, and J'. "
44 J' the son of Zerah of Bozrah "
45 And when J' was dead, Husham "
8: 9 he begat of Hodesh his wife, J', "
18 Ishmerai also, and Jezliah, and J'. "

Jochebed (*jok'-e-bed*)
Ex 6:20 Amram took him J' his father's 3115
Nu 26:59 the name of Amram's wife was J', "

Joed (*jo'-ed*)
Ne 11: 7 the son of J', the son of Pedaiah, 3133

Joel (*jo'-el*)
1Sa 8: 2 the name of his firstborn was J'; 3100
1Ch 4:35 J', and Jehu the son of Josibiah, "
5: 4 The sons of J'; Shemaiah his son, "
8 the son of J', who dwelt in Aroer, "
12 J' the chief, and Shapham the next, "
6:33 Heman a singer, the son of J', the "
36 Elkanah, the son of J', the son of "
7: 3 and Obadiah, and J', Ishiah, five: "
11:38 J' the brother of Nathan, Mibhar "
15: 7 the sons of Gershom; J' the chief, "
11 Levites, for Uriel, Asaiah, and J', "
17 appointed Heman the son of J'; "
23: 8 Jehiel, and Zatham, and J', three. "
26:22 Zetham, and J' his brother, which "
27:20 Manasseh, J' the son of Pedaiah: "
2Ch 29:12 Amasai, and J' the son of Azariah, "
Ezr 10:43 Zabad, Zebina, Jadau, and J', "
Ne 11: 9 And J' the son of Zichri was their "
Joe 1: 1 word of the Lord that came to J' "
Ac 2:16 was spoken by the prophet J'; 2493

Joelah (*jo-e'-lah*)
1Ch 12: 7 J', and Zebadiah, the sons of 3132

Joezer (*jo-e'-zer*)
1Ch 12: 6 and Jesiah, and Azareel, and J', 3134

Jogbehah (*jog'-be-hah*)
Nu 32:35 Shophan, and Jaazer, and J', 3011
J'g 8:11 tents on the east of Nobah and J', "

Jogli (*jog'-li*)
Nu 34:22 of Dan, Bukki the son of J'. 3020

Joha (*jo'-hah*)
1Ch 8:16 And Michael, and Ispah, and J', 3109
11:45 son of Shimri, and J' his brother, "

Johanan (*jo-ha'-nan*) See also JEHOHANAN; JOHN.
2Ki 25:23 and J' the son of Careah, 3110
1Ch 3:15 sons of Josiah were, the firstborn J', "
24 and J', and Dalaiah, and Anani, "
6: 9 Azariah, and Azariah begat J', "
10 J' begat Azariah, (he it is that "
12: 4 Jahaziel, and J', and Josabad the "
12 J' the eighth, Elzabad the ninth, "
2Ch 28:12 Ephraim, Azariah the son of J', 3076
Ezr 8:12 J' the son of Hakkatan, and with 3110
10: 6 and went into the chamber of J', *3076
Ne 6:18 his son J' had taken the daughter* "
12:22 J', and Jaddua, were recorded 3110
23 even until the days of J' the son of "
Jer 40: 8 and J' and Jonathan the sons of "
13 Moreover J' the son of Kareah, and "
15 Then J' the son of Kareah spake to "
16 the son of Ahikam said unto J' the "
41:11 But when J' the son of Kareah, "
13 which were with Ishmael saw J' "
14 and went unto J' the son of Kareah. "
15 escaped from J' with eight men, "
16 Then took J' the son of Kareah, "
42: 1 the captains of the forces, and J' "
8 Then called he J' the son of Kareah, "
43: 2 J' the son of Kareah, and all the "
4 So J' the son of Kareah, and all "
5 But J' the son of Kareah, and all "

John (*jon*) See also BAPTIST; JEHOHANAN; JOHN'S; MARK.
M't 3: 1 In these days came J' the Baptist, 2491
4 same J' had his raiment of camel's "
13 from Galilee to Jordan unto J', "
14 J' forbade him, saying, I have need "
4:12 heard that J' was cast into prison, "
21 son of Zebedee, and J' his brother, "
9:14 came to him the disciples of J', "
10: 2 son of Zebedee, and J' his brother; "
11: 2 when J' had heard in the prison "
4 Go and shew J' again those things "
7 unto the multitudes concerning J', "
11 risen a greater than J' the Baptist: "
12 from the days of J' the Baptist "
13 and the law prophesied until J'. "
18 J' came neither eating nor drinking, "
14: 2 his servants, This is J' the Baptist; "
3 For Herod had laid hold on J', "
4 J' said unto him, It is not lawful "
8 J' the Baptist's head in a charger. "
10 sent, and beheaded J' in the prison. "
16:14 say that thou art J' the Baptist: "
17: 1 Peter, James, and J' his brother, "
13 spake unto them of J' the Baptist. "
21:25 The baptism of J', whence was it? "
26 people; for all hold J' as a prophet. "
32 J' came unto you in the way of "
M'r 1: 4 J' did baptize in the wilderness, "
6 J' was clothed with camel's hair, "
9 and was baptized of J' in Jordan. 2491
14 Now after that J' was put in prison, "
19 son of Zebedee, and J' his brother, "
29 and Andrew, with James and J'. "
2:18 the disciples of J' and of the * "
18 Why do the disciples of J' and of * "
3:17 and J' the brother of James; "
5:37 James, and J' the brother of James. "
6:14 J' the Baptist was risen from the "
16 he said, It is J', whom I beheaded: "
17 laid hold upon J', and bound him "
18 J' had said unto Herod, It is not "
20 Herod feared J', knowing that he "
24 said, The head of J' the Baptist. "
25 charger the head of J' the Baptist. "
8:28 they answered, J' the Baptist: "
9: 2 with him Peter and James, and J', "
38 J' answered him, saying, Master, "
10:35 James and J', the sons of Zebedee, "
41 much displeased with James and J'. "
11:30 baptism of J', was it from heaven, "
32 all men counted J', that he was a "
13: 3 Peter, and James, and J', and "
14:33 with him Peter and James and J', "
Lu 1:13 and thou shalt call his name J'. "
60 Not so; but he shall be called J'. "
63 and wrote, saying, His name is J'. "
3: 2 the word of God came unto J' the "
15 all men mused in their hearts of J', "
16 J' answered, saying unto them all, "
20 all, that he shut up J' in prison. "
5:10 James, and J', the sons of Zebedee, "
33 Why do the disciples of J' fast often, "
6:14 and J', Philip and Bartholomew, "
7:18 disciples of J' shewed him of all "
19 J' calling unto him two of his "
20 J' the Baptist hath sent us...thee, "
22 tell J' what things ye have seen "
24 messengers of J' were departed, "
24 unto the people concerning J', "
28 greater prophet than J' the Baptist: "
29 baptized with the baptism of J'. "
33 J' the Baptist came neither eating "
8:51 save Peter, and James, and J', "
9: 7 that J' was risen from the dead; "
9 Herod said, J' have I beheaded: "
19 answering said, J' the Baptist; "
28 he took Peter and J' and James, "
49 And J' answered and said, Master, "
54 his disciples James and J' saw this, "
11: 1 as J' also taught his disciples. "
16:16 law and the prophets were until J': "
20: 4 baptism of J', was it from heaven, "
6 be persuaded that J' was a prophet. "
22: 8 he sent Peter and J', saying, Go and "
Joh 1: 6 sent from God, whose name was J'. "
15 J' bare witness of him, and cried, "
19 And this is the record of J', when "
26 J' answered them, saying, I baptize "
28 Jordan, where J' was baptizing. "
29 The next day J' seeth Jesus coming* "
32 And J' bare record, saying, I saw "
35 J' stood, and two of his disciples; "
40 of the two which heard J' speak, "
3:23 And J' also was baptizing in Ænon "
24 For J' was not yet cast into prison. "
26 And they came unto J', and said "
27 J' answered and said, A man can "
4: 1 baptized more disciples than J', "
5:33 sent unto J', and he bare witness "
36 have greater witness than that of J': "
10:40 the place where J' at first baptized; "
41 him, and said, J' did no miracle: "
41 that J' spake of this man were true. "
Ac 1: 5 For J' truly baptized with water; "
13 abode both Peter, and James, and J', "
22 Beginning from the baptism of J', "
3: 1 Peter and J' went up together into "
3 seeing Peter and J' about to go into "
4 fastening his eyes upon him with J', "
11 which was healed held Peter and J', "
4: 6 Caiaphas, and J', and Alexander, "
13 saw the boldness of Peter and J', "
19 But Peter and J' answered and said "
8:14 they sent unto them Peter and J': "
10:37 the baptism which J' preached; "
11:16 J' indeed baptized with water; "
12: 2 killed James the brother of J' with "
12 of J', whose surname was Mark; "
25 them J', whose surname was Mark. "
13: 5 they had also J' to their minister. "
13 J' departing from them returned "
24 When J' had first preached before "
25 And as J' fulfilled his course, he "
15:37 them J', whose surname was Mark. "
18:25 knowing only the baptism of J'. "
19: 4 J' verily baptized with the baptism "
Gal 2: 9 Cephas, and J', who seemed to be "
Re 1: 1 it by his angel unto his servant J': "
4 J' to the seven churches which are "
9 I J', who also am your brother, "
21: 2 And I J' saw the holy city, new * "
22: 8 And I J' saw these things, and "

John's (*jonz*)
Joh 3:25 between some of J' disciples and 2491
Ac 19: 3 And they said, Unto J' baptism. "

Joiada (*joy'-a-dah*) See also JEHOIADA.
Ne 12:10 Eliashib, and Eliashib begat J', 3111
11 J' begat Jonathan, and Jonathan "
22 Levites in the days of Eliashib, J', "
13:28 one of the sons of J', the son of "

Joiakim (*joy'-a-kim*) See also JEHOIAKIM.
Ne 12:10 Jeshua begat J', J' also begat 3113
12 in the days of J' were priests, the "
26 in the days of J' the son of Jeshua, "

Joiarib (*joy'-a-rib*) See also JEHOIARIB.
Ezr 8:16 for J', and for Elnathan, men of 3114
Ne 11: 5 the son of Adaiah, the son of J', "
10 the priests: Jedaiah the son of J', "
12: 6 Shemaiah, and J', Jedaiah, "
19 of J', Mattenai; of Jedaiah, Uzzi; "

join See also JOINED; JOINING.
Ex 1:10 they j' also unto our enemies, and 3254
2Ch 20:35 king of Judah j' himself with 2266
Ezr 9:14 and j' in affinity with the people of 2859
Pr 11:21 Though hand j' in hand, the wicked
16: 5 though hand j' in hand, he shall not be
Isa 5: 8 unto them that j' house to house, 5060
9:11 him, and j' his enemies together; *5526
56: 6 that j' themselves to the Lord, to 3867
Jer 50: 5 let us j' ourselves to the Lord in a "
Eze 37:17 j' them one to another into one 7126
Da 11: 6 they shall j' themselves together 2266
Ac 5:13 durst no man j' himself to them: 2858
8:29 near, and j' thyself to this chariot. "
9:26 assayed to j' himself to the disciples: "

joined See also ENJOINED.
Ge 14: 3 these were j' together in the vale 2266
14: 8 they j' battle with them in the vale *6186
29:34 will my husband be j' unto me, 3867
Ex 28: 7 shoulderpieces thereof j' at the two 2266
7 and so it shall be j' together. "
Nu 18: 2 that they may be j' unto thee, and 3867
4 they shall be j' unto thee, and keep "
25: 3 Israel j' himself unto Baal-peor: 6775
5 men that were j' unto Baal-peor. "
1Sa 4: 2 they j' battle, Israel was smitten 5203
1Ki 7:32 of the wheels were j' to the base: *
20:29 the seventh day the battle was j': 7126
2Ch 18: 1 and j' affinity with Ahab. 2859
20:36 j' himself with him to make ships 2266
37 thou hast j' thyself with Ahaziah, "
Ezr 4:12 thereof, and j' the foundations. * 2338
Ne 4: 6 all the wall was j' together unto 7194
Es 9:27 such as j' themselves unto them, 3867
Job 3: 6 not be j' unto the days of the year, *2302
41:17 They are j' one to another, they 1692
23 flakes of his flesh are j' together: "
Ps 83: 8 Assur also is j' with them: they 3867
106:28 j' themselves also unto Baal-peor, 6775
Ec 9: 4 to him that is j' to all the living 977
Isa 13:15 every one that is j' unto them *5595
14: 1 strangers shall be j' with them, *3867
20 shalt not be j' with them in burial, 3161
56: 3 that hath j' himself to the Lord, 3867
Eze 1: 9 wings were j' one to another; 2266
11 two wings of every one were j' one "
46:22 there were courts j' of forty cubits *7000
Ho 4:17 Ephraim is j' to idols: let him 2266
Zec 2:11 nations shall be j' to the Lord *3867
M't 19: 6 therefore God hath j' together, 4801
M'r 10: 9 therefore God hath j' together, "
Lu 15:15 and j' himself to a citizen of that 2858
Ac 5:36 about four hundred, j' themselves: 4347
18: 7 house j' hard to the synagogue. 4927
1Co 1:10 that ye be perfectly j' together *2675
6:16 that he which is j' to an harlot 2858
17 he that is j' unto the Lord is one "
Eph 4:16 the whole body fitly j' together *4883
5:31 shall be j' unto his wife, and they *4347

joining See also JOININGS.
2Ch 3:12 j' to the wing of the other cherub. 1692

joinings
1Ch 22: 3 doors of the gates, and for the j'; *4226

joint See also JOINT-HEIRS; JOINTS.
Ge 32:25 of Jacob's thigh was out of j'. *3363
Ps 22:14 and all my bones are out of j': 6504
Pr 25:19 broken tooth, and a foot out of j'. 4154
Eph 4:16 by that which every j' supplieth, 860

joint-heirs
Ro 8:17 heirs of God, and j' with Christ; 4789

joints
1Ki 22:34 between the j' of the harness: 1694
2Ch 18:33 between the j' of the harness: "
Ca 7: 1 the j' of thy thighs are like jewels, ‡2542
Da 5: 6 that the j' of his loins were loosed, 7001
Col 2:19 all the body by j' and bands having 860
Heb 4:12 spirit, and of the j' and marrow, 719

Jokdeam (*jok'-de-am*)
Jos 15:56 And Jezreel, and J', and Zanoah, 3347

Jokim (*jo'-kim*)
1Ch 4:22 J', and the men of Chozeba, and 3137

Jokmeam (*jok'-me-am*) See also JOKNEAM.
1Ch 6:68 and J' with her suburbs, and 3361

Jokneam (*jok'-ne-am*) See also JOKMEAM; KIBZAIM.
Jos 12:22 the king of J' of Carmel, one; 3362
19:11 to the river that is before J'; "
21:34 J' with her suburbs, and Kartah "
1Ki 4:12 unto the place that is beyond J': * "

Jokshan (*jok'-shan*)
Ge 25: 2 she bare him Zimran, and J', and 3370
3 And J' begat Sheba, and Dedan. "
1Ch 1:32 she bare Zimran, and J', and "
32 the sons of J'; Sheba, and Dedan. "

Joktan (*jok'-tan*)
Ge 10:25 and his brother's name was J'. 3355
26 J' begat Almodad, and Sheleph, "
29 Jobab: all these were the sons of J'. "
1Ch 1:19 and his brother's name was J'. "
20 J' begat Almodad, and Sheleph, "
23 Joab. All these were the sons of J'. "

Joktheel (*jok'-the-el*) See also SELAH.

Jos 15: 38 and Dilean, and Mizpeh, and J·, 3371
2Ki 14: 7 and called the name of it J· unto "
Jona (*jo'-nah*) See also BAR-JONA; JONAH; JONAS.
Joh 1: 42 Thou art Simon the son of J·: *2495
Jonadab (*jon'-a-dab*) See also JEHONADAB.
2Sa 13: 3 had a friend, whose name was J·, 3122
3 and J· was a very subtle man. "
5 J· said unto him, Lay thee down "
32 and J·, the son of Shimeah David's "
35 And J· said unto the king, Behold, "
Jer 35: 6 for J· the son of Rechab our father "
8 have we obeyed the voice of J· 3082
10 that J· our father commanded us. 3122
14 the words of J· the son of Rechab 3082
16 the sons of J· the son of Rechab "
18 obeyed the commandment of J· "
19 J· the son of Rechab shall not 3122
Jonah (*jo'-nah*) See also JONA; JONAS.
2Ki 14: 25 by the hand of his servant J·, 3124
Jon 1: 1 the word of the Lord came unto J· "
3 J· rose up to flee unto Tarshish "
5 J· was gone down into the sides of "
7 cast lots, and the lot fell upon J·. "
15 took up J·, and cast him forth into "
17 a great fish to swallow up J·. "
17 J· was in the belly of the fish three "
2: 1 J· prayed unto the Lord his God "
10 it vomited out J· upon the dry land. "
3: 1 word of the Lord came unto J· the "
3 So J· arose, and went unto Nineveh, "
4 J· began to enter into the city a "
4: 1 But it displeased J· exceedingly, "
5 J· went out of the city, and sat on "
6 and made it to come up over J·, "
6 J· was exceeding glad of the gourd. "
8 the sun beat upon the head of J·, "
9 God said unto J·, Doest thou well "
Jonan (*jo'-nan*)
Lu 3: 30 Joseph, which was the son of J·, *2494
Jonas (*jo'-nas*) See also JONA; JONAH.
M't 12: 39 it, but the sign of the prophet J·: *2495
40 For as J· was three days and three * "
41 repented at the preaching of J·; * "
41 behold, a greater than J· is here * "
16: 4 it, but the sign of the prophet J·. * "
Lu 11: 29 it, but the sign of J· the prophet. * "
30 J· was a sign unto the Ninevites, * "
32 repented at the preaching of J·; * "
32 behold, a greater than J· is here. * "
Joh 21: 15, 16, 17 Simon, son of J·, lovest thou * "
Jonathan (*jon'-a-than*) See also JEHONATHAN; JONATHAN'S.
J'g 18: 30 J·, the son of Gershom, the son of 3129
1Sa 13: 2 a thousand were with J· in Gibeah "
3 J· smote the garrison of the "
16 Saul, and J· his son, and the people "
22 people that were with Saul and J·: "
22 with J· his son was there found. "
14: 1 J· the son of Saul said unto the "
3 people knew not that J· was gone. "
4 which J· sought to go over unto "
6 J· said to the young man that 3083
8 said J·, Behold, we will pass over "
12 J· and his armourbearer, 3129
12 J· said unto his armourbearer, "
13 J· climbed up upon his hands and "
13 and they fell before J·; and his "
14 which J· and his armourbearer "
17 behold, J· and his armourbearer "
21 that were with Saul and J·. "
27 But J· heard not when his father "
29 said J·, My father hath troubled "
39 it be in J· my son, he shall surely "
40 I and J· my son will be on the "
41 Saul and J· were taken: but the "
42 lots between me and J· my son. "
42 And J· was taken. "
43 Then Saul said to J·, Tell me what "
43 And J· told him, and said, I did but "
44 also: for thou shalt surely die, J·. "
45 people said unto Saul, Shall J· die, "
45 So the people rescued J·, that he "
49 the sons of Saul were J·, and Ishui, "
18: 1 soul of J· was knit with the soul of 3083
1 and J· loved him as his own soul. "
3 J· and David made a covenant, "
4 J· stripped himself of the robe that "
19: 1 Saul spake to J· his son, and to all 3129
2 J· Saul's son delighted much in 3083
2 J· told David, saying, Saul my "
4 J· spake good of David unto Saul "
6 hearkened unto the voice of J·: "
7 J· called David, and J· shewed him "
7 J· brought David to Saul, and he "
20: 1 said before J·, What have I done? "
3 Let not J· know this, lest he be "
4 Then said J· unto David, "
5 And David said to J·, Behold "
9 And J· said, Far be it from thee: "
10 Then said David to J·, Who shall "
11 J· said unto David, Come, and let "
12 J· said unto David, O Lord God of "
13 Lord do so and much more to J·: "
16 J· made a covenant with the house "
17 J· caused David to swear again, "
18 J· said to David, To-morrow is the "
25 J· arose, and Abner sat by Saul's "
27 Saul said unto J· his son, Wherefore "
28 J· answered Saul, David earnestly "
30 Saul's anger was kindled against J·, "
32 J· answered Saul his father, and "
33 J· knew that it was determined "
34 So J· arose from the table in fierce "
1Sa 20: 35 J· went out into the field at the time 3083
37 of the arrow which J· had shot, "
37 J· cried after the lad, and said, Is "
38 J· cried after the lad, Make speed, "
39 only J· and David knew the matter. "
40 J· gave his artillery unto his lad, "
42 And J· said to David, Go in peace, "
42 departed: and J· went into the city. "
23: 16 J· Saul's son arose, and went to "
18 the wood, and J· went to his house. "
31: 2 Philistines slew J·, and Abinadab, "
2Sa 1: 4 Saul and J· his son are dead also. "
5 that Saul and J· his son be dead? "
12 even, for Saul, and for J· his son, "
17 lamentation over Saul and over J· "
22 the bow of J· turned not back, and "
23 Saul and J· were lovely and "
25 O J·, thou wast slain in thine high "
26 distressed for thee, my brother J·: "
4: 4 J·, Saul's son, had a son that was "
4 the tidings came of Saul and J· "
9: 3 J· hath yet a son, which is lame "
6 when Mephibosheth, the son of J·, "
7 kindness for J· thy father's sake, "
15: 27 thy son, and J· the son of Abiathar. "
36 Zadok's son, and J· Abiathar's son; "
17: 17 Now J· and Ahimaaz stayed by "
20 said, Where is Ahimaaz and J·? "
21: 7 spared Mephibosheth, the son of J· "
7 between David and J· the son of "
12 bones of Saul and the bones of J· "
13 Saul and the bones of J· his son; "
14 the bones of Saul and J· his son "
21 J· the son of Shimeah the brother "
23: 32 of the sons of Jashen, J·, "
1Ki 1: 42 J· the son of Abiathar the priest 3129
43 J· answered and said to Adonijah, "
1Ch 2: 32 of Shammai; Jether, and J·: "
33 And the sons of J·; Peleth, and "
8: 33 Saul begat J·, and Malchi-shua, 3083
34 And the son of J· was Merib-baal; "
9: 39 Saul begat J·, and Malchi-shua, "
40 And the son of J· was Merib-baal: "
10: 2 and the Philistines slew J·, and 3129
11: 34 J· the son of Shage the Hararite, "
20: 7 J· the son of Shimea David's 3083
27: 32 J· David's uncle was a counsellor, "
Ezr 8: 6 Ebed the son of J·, and with him "
10: 15 Only J· the son of Asahel and "
Ne 12: 11 And Joiada begat J·, and J· begat "
14 Of Melicu, J·; of Shebaniah, "
35 Zechariah the son of J·, the son of "
Jer 37: 15 prison in the house of J· the scribe: "
20 return to the house of J· the scribe, "
40: 8 Johanan and J· the sons of Kareah, 3129
Jonathan's (*jon'-a-thans*)
1Sa 20: 38 J· lad gathered up the arrows, 3129
2Sa 9: 1 shew him kindness for J· sake? "
Jer 38: 26 to return to J· house, to die there. "
Jonath-elem-rechokim (*jo'''-nath-e''-lem-re-ko'-kim*)
Ps 56: *title* the chief Musician upon J·, *3128
Joppa (*jop'-pah*) See also JAPHO.
2Ch 2: 16 it to thee in floats by sea to J·, 3305
Ezr 3: 7 trees from Lebanon to the sea of J· "
Jon 1: 3 of the Lord, and went down to J·; "
Ac 9: 36 there was at J· a certain disciple 2445
38 as Lydda was nigh to J·, and the "
42 it was known throughout all J·; "
43 he tarried many days in J· with one "
10: 5 now send men to J·, and call for one "
8 unto them, he sent them to J·. "
23 and certain brethren from J· "
32 Send therefore to J·, and call "
11: 5 I was in the city of J· praying: and "
13 Send men to J·, and call for Simon, "
Jorah (*jo'-rah*) See also HARIPH.
Ezr 2: 18 The children of J·, an hundred and 3139
Jorai (*jo'-rahee*)
1Ch 5: 13 Sheba, and J·, and Jachan, and 3140
Joram (*jo'-ram*) See also JEHORAM.
2Sa 8: 10 Toi sent J· his son unto king David, 3141
10 J· brought with him vessels of silver, "
2Ki 8: 16 the fifth year of J· the son of Ahab 3141
21 So J· went over to Zair, and all the "
23 And the rest of the acts of J·, and all "
24 J· slept with his fathers, and was "
25 twelfth year of J· the son of Ahab "
28 he went with J· the son of Ahab to "
28 and the Syrians wounded J·. "
29 And king J· went back to be healed "
29 went down to see J· the son of Ahab "
9: 14 son of Nimshi conspired against J·. "
14 (Now J· had kept Ramoth-gilead, he "
15 king J· was returned to be healed 3188
16 went to Jezreel; for J· lay there. 3141
16 of Judah was come down to see J·. "
17 And J· said, Take an horseman, 3188
21 And J· said, Make ready. And his "
21 J· king of Israel and Ahaziah king "
22 it came to pass, when J· saw Jehu, "
23 And J· turned his hands, and fled, "
29 eleventh year of J· the son of Ahab "
11: 2 Jehosheba, the daughter of king J·, 3141
1Ch 3: 11 J· his son, Ahaziah his son, Joash "
26: 25 J· his son, and Zichri his son, and "
2Ch 22: 5 and the Syrians smote J·. "
7 was of God by coming to J·: "
M't 1: 8 Josaphat begat J·; and J· begat 2496
Jordan (*jor'-dan*)
Ge 13: 10 and beheld all the plain of J·, 3383
11 Lot chose him all the plain of J·; "
32: 10 with my staff I passed over this J·; "
Ge 50: 10 of Atad, which is beyond J·, and 3383
11 Abel-mizraim, which is beyond J·. "
Nu 13: 29 of the sea, and by the coast of J·. "
22: 1 in the plains of Moab on this side J· "
26: 3 them in the plains of Moab by J· "
63 Israel in the plains of Moab by J· "
31: 12 the plains of Moab, which are by J· "
32: 5 possession, and bring us not over J·. "
19 inherit with them on yonder side J·, "
19 fallen to us on this side J· eastward. "
21 And will go all of you armed over J· "
29 Reuben will pass with you over J·, "
32 on this side J· may be ours. "
33: 48 pitched in the plains of Moab by J. "
49 pitched by J·, from Beth-jesimoth "
50 Moses in the plains of Moab by J· "
51 over J· into the land of Canaan; "
34: 12 the border shall go down to J·, and "
15 their inheritance this side J· near "
35: 1 Moses in the plains of Moab by J· "
10 ye be come over J· into the land of "
14 give three cities on this side J·, "
36: 13 Israel in the plains of Moab by J· "
De 1: 1 on this side J· in the wilderness, "
5 On this side J·, in the land of Moab, "
2: 29 until I shall pass over J· into the "
3: 8 the land that was on this side J·, "
17 plain also, and J·, and the coast, "
20 God hath given them beyond J·: "
25 see the good land that is beyond J·, "
27 for thou shalt not go over this J·. "
4: 21 sware that I should not go over J·, "
22 in this land, I must not go over J·: "
26 whereunto ye go over J· to possess "
41 severed three cities on this side J· "
46 On this side J·, in the valley over "
47 this side J· toward the sunrising; "
49 And all the plain on this side J· "
9: 1 Thou art to pass over J· this day, "
11: 30 Are they not on the other side J·, "
31 For ye shall pass over J· to go in to "
12: 10 But when ye go over J·, and dwell "
27: 2 when ye shall pass over J· unto the "
4 shall be when ye be gone over J·, "
12 people, when ye are come over J·; "
30: 18 passest over J· to go to possess it. "
31: 2 Thou shalt not go over this J·. "
13 in the land whither ye go over J· "
32: 47 whither ye go over J· to possess it. "
Jos 1: 2 go over this J·, thou, and all this "
11 days ye shall pass over this J·, "
14 Moses gave you on this side J·; "
15 this side J· toward the sunrising. "
2: 7 them the way to J· unto the fords: "
10 were on the other side J·, Sihon "
3: 1 from Shittim, and came to J·, "
8 to the brink of the water of J·, "
8 ye shall stand still in J·. "
11 passeth over before you into J·. "
13 earth, shall rest in the waters of J·, "
13 the waters of J· shall be cut off "
14 from their tents, to pass over J·, "
15 bare the ark were come unto J·, "
15 J· overfloweth all his banks all the "
17 on dry ground in the midst of J·, "
17 people were passed clean over J·. "
4: 1 people were clean passed over J·, "
3 you hence out of the midst of J·, "
5 Lord your God into the midst of J·, "
7 the waters of J· were cut off before "
7 the Lord; when it passed over J·, "
7 the waters of J· were cut off: and "
8 twelve stones out of the midst of J·, "
9 up twelve stones in the midst of J·, "
10 the ark stood in the midst of J·, "
16 that they come up out of J·. "
17 saying, Come ye up out of J·. "
18 come up out of the midst of J·, "
18 waters of J· returned unto their "
19 came up out of J· on the tenth day "
20 stones, which they took out of J·, "
22 Israel came over this J· on dry "
23 God dried up the waters of J· from "
5: 1 were on the side of J· westward, "
1 Lord had dried up the waters of J· "
7: 7 at all brought this people over J·, "
7 and dwelt on the other side J·! "
9: 1 kings which were on this side J·, "
10 the Amorites, that were beyond J·, "
12: 1 their land on the other side J· "
7 smote on this side J· on the west, "
13: 8 gave them, beyond J· eastward, "
23 And the border...of Reuben was J·, "
27 of Heshbon, J· and his border, "
27 on the other side J· eastward. "
32 plains of Moab, on the other side J·, "
14: 3 an half tribe on the other side J·: "
15: 5 salt sea, even unto the end of J·. "
5 the sea at the uttermost part of J·: "
16: 1 of Joseph fell from J· by Jericho, "
7 to Jericho, and went out at J·. "
17: 5 which were on the other side J·; "
18: 7 received their inheritance beyond J· "
12 on the north side was from J·; "
19 the salt sea at the south end of J·: "
20 J· was the border of it on the east "
19: 22 outgoings of their border were at J·: "
33 the outgoings thereof were at J·: "
34 to Judah upon J· toward the "
20: 8 other side J· by Jericho eastward, "
22: 4 Lord gave you on the other side J·. "
7 brethren on this side J· westward. "
10 they came unto the borders of J·, "
10 Manasseh built there an altar by J·, "
11 in the borders of J·, at the passage "
25 the Lord hath made J· a border "

Jos 23: 4 inheritance for your tribes, from J'.3383
24: 8 which dwelt on the other side J'; "
11 ye went over J', and came unto "
J'g 3: 28 took the fords of J' toward Moab, "
5: 17 Gilead abode beyond J': and why "
7: 24, 24 waters unto Beth-barah and J'. "
25 Zeeb to Gideon on the other side J'. "
8: 4 Gideon came to J', and passed over, "
10: 8 that were on the other side J' in "
9 children of Ammon passed over J' "
11: 13 even unto Jabbok, and unto J': "
22 from the wilderness even unto J'. "
12: 5 Gileadites took the passages of J' "
6 slew him at the passages of J': "
1Sa 13: 7 some of the Hebrews went over J' "
31: 7 they that were on the other side J', "
2Sa 2: 29 passed over J', and went through "
10: 17 Israel together, and passed over J', "
17: 22 with him, and they passed over J': "
22 of them that was not gone over J'. "
24 Absalom passed over J', he and all "
19: 15 the king returned, and came to J'. "
15 king, to conduct the king over J'. "
17 they went over J' before the king. "
18 the king, as he was come over J'; "
31 from Rogelim, and went over J'. "
31 the king, to conduct him over J'. "
36 servant will go a little way over J' "
39 And all the people went over J'. "
41 David's men with him, over J'? "
20: 2 king, from J' even to Jerusalem. "
24: 5 they passed over J', and pitched "
1Ki 2: 8 he came down to meet me at J', "
7: 46 In the plain of J' did the king cast "
17: 3, 5 brook Cherith, that is before J'. "
2Ki 2: 6 for the Lord hath sent me to J'. "
7 afar off: and they two stood by J'. "
13 back, and stood by the bank of J'; "
5: 10 Go and wash in J' seven times, "
14 dipped himself seven times in J', "
6: 2 Let us go, we pray thee, unto J', "
4 when they came to J', they cut "
7: 15 they went after them unto J': and, "
10: 33 From J' eastward, all...Gilead, "
1Ch 6: 78 on the other side J' by Jericho, "
78 on the east side of J', were given "
12: 15 they that went over J' in the first "
37 on the other side of J', of the "
19: 17 all Israel, and passed over J', "
26: 30 among them of Israel on this side J' "
2Ch 4: 17 In the plain of J' did the king cast "
Job 40: 23 he can draw up J' into his mouth. "
Ps 42: 6 remember thee from the land of J', "
114: 3 and fled: J' was driven back. "
5 thou J', that thou wast driven back? "
Isa 9: 1 by the way of the sea, beyond J', "
Jer 12: 5 wilt thou do in the swelling of J'? "
49: 19 like a lion from the swelling of J' "
50: 44 like a lion from the swelling of J' "
Eze 47: 18 and from the land of Israel by J' "
Zec 11: 3 lions; for the pride of J' is spoiled. "
M't 3: 5 and all the region round about J', 2446
6 baptized of him in J', confessing "
13 cometh Jesus from Galilee to J' "
4: 15 by the way of the sea, beyond J', "
25 from Judæa, and from beyond J'. "
19: 1 into the coasts of Judæa beyond J'; "
M'r 1: 5 baptized of him in the river of J', "
9 and was baptized of John in J'. "
3: 8 Idumæa, and from beyond J'; "
10: 1 of Judæa by the farther side of J': "
Lu 3: 3 came into all the country about J', "
4: 1 the Holy Ghost returned from J', "
Joh 1: 28 were done in Bethabara beyond J', "
3: 26 he that was with thee beyond J', "
10: 40 went away again beyond J' into "

Jorim (*jo'-rim*)
Lu 3: 29 Eliezer, which was the son of J'. 2497
Jorkoam (*jor'-ko-am*)
1Ch 2: 44 begat Raham, the father of J': *3421
Josabad (*jos'-a-bad*) See also JOZABAD.
1Ch 12: 4 Johanan, and J' the Gederathite, *3107
Josaphat (*jos'-a-fat*) See also JEHOSHAPHAT.
M't 1: 8 Asa begat J'; and J' begat Joram;*2498
Jose (*jo'-ze*) See also JOSES.
Lu 3: 29 Which was the son of J', which *2499
Josedech (*jos'-e-dek*) See also JOZADAK.
Hag 1: 1 to Joshua the son of J', the high *3087
12 and Joshua the son of J', the high* "
14 spirit of Joshua the son of J', the* "
2: 2 to Joshua the son of J', the high * "
4 Joshua, son of J', the high priest;* "
Zec 6: 11 the head of Joshua the son of J', * "
Joseph (*jo'-zef*) See also BARSABAS; JOSEPH'S.
Ge 30: 24 And she called his name J'; and 3130
25 to pass, when Rachel had borne J', "
33: 2 and Rachel and J' hindermost. "
7 and after came J' near and Rachel, "
35: 24 sons of Rachel; J', and Benjamin: "
37: 2 J', being seventeen years old, was "
2 J' brought unto his father...report. "
3 Israel loved J' more than all his "
5 J' dreamed a dream, and he told "
13 Israel said unto J', Do not thy "
17 J' went after his brethren, and "
23 when J' was come unto his brethren, "
23 that they stript J' out of his coat, "
28 drew and lifted up J' out of the pit, "
28 and sold J' to the Ishmeelites for "
28 and they brought J' into Egypt. "
29 behold, J' was not in the pit; and "
33 J' is without doubt rent in pieces. "
39: 1 J' was brought down to Egypt; "
2 And the Lord was with J', and he "
Ge 39: 4 J' found grace in his sight, and 3130
6 J' was a goodly person, and well "
7 master's wife cast her eyes upon J'; "
10 as she spake to J' day by day, "
11 that J' went into the house to do *
21 But the Lord was with J', and 3130
40: 3 the place where J' was bound. "
4 of the guard charged J' with them, "
6 And J' came in unto them in the "
8 And J' said unto them, Do not "
9 chief butler told his dream to J', "
12 And J' said unto him, This is the "
16 he said unto J', I also was in my "
18 J' answered and said, This is the "
22 as J' had interpreted to them. "
23 not the chief butler remember J', "
41: 14 Pharaoh sent and called J', and "
15 And Pharaoh said unto J', I have "
16 J' answered Pharaoh, saying, It is "
17 Pharaoh said unto J', In my dream, "
25 J' said unto Pharaoh, The dream "
39 Pharaoh said unto J', Forasmuch "
41 Pharaoh said unto J', See, I have "
44 Pharaoh said unto J', I am "
45 And J' went out over all the land of "
46 J' was thirty years old when he "
46 J' went out from the presence of "
49 J' gathered corn as the sand of the "
50 unto J' were born two sons before "
51 J' called the name of the firstborn "
54 to come, according as J' had said: "
55 unto all the Egyptians, Go unto J'; "
56 J' opened all the storehouses, and "
57 came into Egypt to J' for to buy "
42: 6 J' was the governor over the land, "
7 J' saw his brethren, and he knew "
8 J' knew his brethren, but they knew "
9 J' remembered the dreams which "
14 J' said unto them, That is it that I "
18 J' said unto them the third day, "
23 knew not that J' understood them; "
25 J' commanded to fill their sacks "
36 J' is not, and Simeon is not, and ye "
43: 15 down to Egypt, and stood before J'. "
16 when J' saw Benjamin with them, "
17 And the man did as J' bade; and "
25 present against J' came at noon: "
26 when J' came home, they brought "
30 J' made haste; for his bowels did "
44: 2 to the word that J' had spoken. "
4 J' said unto his steward, Up, follow "
15 J' said unto them, What deed is "
45: 1 Then J' could not refrain himself "
1 while J' made himself known unto "
3 J' said unto his brethren, I am J'; "
4 J' said unto his brethren, Come "
4 I am J' your brother, whom ye sold "
9 Thus saith thy son J', God hath "
17 Pharaoh said unto J', Say unto thy "
21 J' gave them wagons, according to "
26 told him, saying, J' is yet alive, "
27 they told him all the words of J', "
27 saw the wagons which J' had sent "
28 It is enough; J' my son is yet alive: "
46: 4 J' shall put his hand upon thine "
19 sons of Rachel Jacob's wife; J', and "
20 unto J' in the land of Egypt were "
27 sons of J', which were born him in "
28 he sent Judah before him unto J', "
29 J' made ready his chariot, and went "
30 Israel said unto J', Now let me die, "
31 J' said unto his brethren, and unto "
47: 1 Then J' came and told Pharaoh, and "
5 And Pharaoh spake unto J', saying, "
7 And J' brought in Jacob his father, "
11 And J' placed his father and his "
12 J' nourished his father, and his "
14 J' gathered up all the money that "
14 J' brought the money into Pharaoh's "
15 the Egyptians came unto J', and "
16 J' said, Give your cattle; and I will "
17 they brought their cattle unto J': "
17 J' gave them bread in exchange for "
20 J' bought all the land of Egypt for "
23 J' said unto the people, Behold, I "
26 J' made it a law over the land of "
29 and he called his son J', and said "
48: 1 told J', Behold, thy father is sick: "
2 thy son J' cometh unto thee: "
3 Jacob said unto J', God Almighty "
9 J' said unto his father, They are "
11 And Israel said unto J', I had not "
12 J' brought them out from between "
13 J' took them both, Ephraim in his "
15 he blessed J', and said, God, before "
17 when J' saw that his father laid his "
18 J' said unto his father, Not so, my "
21 Israel said unto J', Behold, I die: "
49: 22 J' is a fruitful bough, even a fruitful "
26 shall be on the head of J', and on "
50: 1 J' fell upon his father's face, and "
2 J' commanded...the physicians to "
4 J' spake unto the house of Pharaoh, "
7 J' went up to bury his father: and "
8 And all the house of J', and his "
14 J' returned into Egypt, he, and his "
15 said, J' will peradventure hate us, "
16 And they sent a messenger unto J', "
17 So shall ye say unto J', Forgive, I "
17 J' wept when they spake unto him. "
19 J' said unto them, Fear not: for am "
22 And J' dwelt in Egypt, he, and his "
22 J' lived an hundred and ten years. "
23 J' saw Ephraim's children of the "
24 J' said unto his brethren, I die: "
25 J' took an oath of the children of "
Ge 50: 26 J' died, being an hundred and ten 3130
Ex 1: 5 souls: for J' was in Egypt already. "
6 J' died, and all his brethren, and "
8 king over Egypt, which knew not J' "
13: 19 Moses took the bones of J' with "
Nu 1: 10 Of the children of J': of Ephraim: "
32 Of the children of J', namely, of "
13: 7 tribe of Issachar, Igal the son of J'. "
11 Of the tribe of J', namely, of the "
26: 28 The sons of J' after their families "
37 the sons of J' after their families. "
27: 1 families of Manasseh the son of J': "
32: 33 tribe of Manasseh the son of J', "
34: 23 prince of the children of J', for the "
36: 1 of the families of the sons of J', "
5 The tribe of the sons of J' hath said "
12 the sons of Manasseh the son of J', "
De 27: 12 Issachar, and J', and Benjamin: "
33: 13 And of J' he said, Blessed of the "
16 blessing come upon the head of J', "
Jos 14: 4 the children of J' were two tribes, "
16: 1 the children of J' fell from Jordan "
4 So the children of J', Manasseh and "
17: 1 for he was the firstborn of J'; "
2 children of Manasseh the son of J' "
14 children of J' spake unto Joshua, "
16 And the children of J' said, The hill "
17 Joshua spake unto the house of J', "
18: 5 the house of J' shall abide in their "
11 of Judah and the children of J'. "
24: 32 And the bones of J', which the "
32 the inheritance of the children of J'. "
J'g 1: 22 the house of J', they also went up "
23 house of J' sent to descry Beth-el. "
35 hand of the house of J' prevailed, "
2Sa 19: 20 first this day of all the house of J' "
1Ki 11: 28 all the charge of the house of J'. "
1Ch 2: 2 Dan, J', and Benjamin, Naphtali, "
5: 1 was given unto the sons of J' "
7: 29 In these dwelt the children of J' "
25: 2 the sons of Asaph; Zaccur, and J', "
9 first lot came forth for Asaph to J': "
Ezr 10: 42 Shallum, Amariah, and J'. "
Ne 12: 14 Melicu, Jonathan; of Shebaniah, J'; "
Ps 77: 15 thy people, the sons of Jacob and J'. "
78: 67 he refused the tabernacle of J', "
80: 1 thou that leadest J' like a flock; "
81: 5 he ordained in J' for a testimony, 3084
105: 17 sent a man before them, even J', 3130
Eze 37: 16 For J', the stick of Ephraim, and "
19 I will take the stick of J', which is "
47: 13 Israel: J' shall have two portions. "
48: 32 and one gate of J', one gate of "
Am 5: 6 out like fire in the house of J', and "
15 be gracious unto the remnant of J'. "
6: 6 not grieved for the affliction of J'. "
Ob 18 a fire, and the house of J' a flame, "
Zec 10: 6 and I will save the house of J', and "
M't 1: 16 begat J' the husband of Mary, 2501
18 mother Mary was espoused to J', "
19 Then J' her husband, being a just "
20 J', thou son of David, fear not to "
24 J' being raised from sleep did as "
2: 13 Lord appeareth to J' in a dream, "
19 Lord appeareth in a dream to J' "
27: 57 rich man of Arimathæa, named J', "
59 And when J' had taken the body, he "
M'r 15: 43 J' of Arimathæa, an honourable "
45 centurion, he gave the body to J'. "
Lu 1: 27 to a man whose name was J', "
2: 4 And J' also went up from Galilee, "
16 found Mary, and J', and the babe "
33 J' and his mother marvelled at * "
43 J' and his mother knew not of it. * "
3: 23 (as was supposed) the son of J', "
24 of Janna, which was the son of J', "
26 of Semei, which was the son of J',* "
30 of Juda, which was the son of J', "
23: 50 was a man named J', a counsellor; "
Joh 1: 45 Jesus of Nazareth, the son of J'. "
4: 5 that Jacob gave to his son J'. "
6: 42 Is not this Jesus, the son of J', "
19: 38 after this J' of Arimathæa, being a "
Ac 1: 23 J' called Barsabas, who was "
7: 9 with envy, sold J' into Egypt: "
13 J' was made known to his brethren; "
14 Then sent J', and called his father "
18 king arose, which knew not J'. "
Heb 11: 21 dying, blessed both the sons of J'; "
22 By faith J', when he died, made "
Re 7: 8 Of the tribe of J' were sealed "
Joseph's (*jo'-zefs*)
Ge 37: 31 they took J' coat, and killed a kid 3130
39: 5 the Egyptian's house for J' sake; "
6 he left all that he had in J' hand; "
20 J' master took him, and put him "
22 prison committed to J' hand all the "
41: 42 his hand, and put it upon J' hand, "
45 called J' name Zaphnath-paaneah; "
42: 3 J' ten brethren went down to buy "
4 Benjamin, J' brother, Jacob sent "
6 J' brethren came, and bowed down "
43: 17 man brought the men into J' house. "
18 they were brought into J' house; "
19 near to the steward of J' house, "
24 man brought the men into J' house, "
44: 14 and his brethren came to J' house; "
45: 16 house, saying, J' brethren are come: "
48: 8 Israel beheld J' sons, and said, Who "
50: 15 J' brethren saw that their father "
23 were brought up upon J' knees. "
1Ch 5: 2 ruler; but the birthright was J':) "
Lu 4: 22 And they said, Is not this J' son? 2501
Ac 7: 13 J' kindred was made known unto "
Joses (*jo'-zez*) See also JOSE.

M't 13:55 James, and J', and Simon, and *2500
27:56 Mary the mother of James and J', "
M'r 6: 3 the brother of James, and J', and "
15:40 mother of James the less and of J', "
47 Mary the mother of J' beheld where "
Ac 4:36 J', who...was surnamed Barnabas,* "

Joshah (*jo'-shah*)
1Ch 4:34 and J' the son of Amaziah, 3144

Joshaphat (*josh'-a-fat*) See also JEHOSHAPHAT; JOSAPHAT.
1Ch 11:43 Maachah, and J' the Mithnite, 3146

Joshaviah (*josh-a-vi'-ah*)
1Ch 11:46 Jeribai, and J', the sons of Elnaam, 3145

Joshbekashah (*josh-bek'-a-shah*)
1Ch 25: 4 J', Mallothi, Hothir, and 3436
24 The seventeenth to J', he, his sons, "

Joshua (*josh'-u-ah*) See also HOSEA; HOSHEA: JEHOSHUAH; JESHUA; JESHUAH; JESUS; OSEA; OSHEA.
Ex 17: 9 Moses said unto J', Choose us out 3091
10 So J' did as Moses had said to him, "
13 And J' discomfited Amalek and his "
14 and rehearse it in the ears of J': "
24:13 Moses rose up, and his minister J': "
32:17 And when J' heard the noise of the "
33:11 but his servant J', the son of Nun, "
Nu 11:28 J' the son of Nun, the servant of "
14: 6 J' the son of Nun, and Caleb the "
30 Jephunneh, and J' the son of Nun. "
38 But J' the son of Nun, and Caleb "
26:65 Jephunneh, and J' the son of Nun. "
27:18 Take thee J' the son of Nun, a man "
22 and he took J', and set him before "
32:12 the Kenezite, and J' the son of Nun: "
28 J' the son of Nun, and the chief "
34:17 the priest, and J' the son of Nun. "
De 1:38 J' the son of Nun, which standeth "
3:21 And I commanded J' at that time, "
28 But charge J', and encourage him, "
31: 3 and J', he shall go over before thee, "
7 Moses called unto J', and said unto "
14 call J', and present yourselves in "
14 Moses and J' went, and presented "
23 he gave J' the son of Nun a charge, "
34: 9 J' the son of Nun was full of the "
Jos 1: 1 Lord spake unto J' the son of Nun, "
10 Then J' commanded the officers of "
12 half the tribe of Manasseh, spake J', "
16 they answered J', saying, All that "
2: 1 And J' the son of Nun sent out of "
23 came to J' the son of Nun, and told "
24 said unto J', Truly the Lord hath "
3: 1 J' rose early in the morning; and "
5 J' said unto the people, Sanctify "
6 J' spake unto the priests, saying, "
7 the Lord said unto J', This day will "
9 J' said unto the children of Israel, "
10 J' said, Hereby ye shall know that "
4: 1 that the Lord spake unto J', saying, "
4 Then J' called the twelve men, "
5 J' said unto them, Pass over before "
8 of Israel did so as J' commanded, "
8 Jordan, as the Lord spake unto J', "
9 J' set up twelve stones in the midst "
10 Lord commanded J' to speak unto "
10 to all that Moses commanded J': "
14 On that day the Lord magnified J' "
15 And the Lord spake unto J', saying, "
17 J' therefore commanded the priests, "
20 out of Jordan, did J' pitch in Gilgal. "
5: 2 At that time the Lord said unto J', "
3 And J' made him sharp knives, and "
4 the cause why J' did circumcise: "
7 their stead, them J' circumcised: "
9 Lord said unto J', This day have I "
13 to pass, when J' was by Jericho, "
13 J' went unto him, and said unto "
14 J' fell on his face to the earth, and "
15 the Lord's host said unto J', Loose "
15 standest is holy. And J' did so. "
6: 2 Lord said unto J', See, I have given "
6 J' the son of Nun called the priests, "
8 when J' had spoken unto the people, "
10 J' had commanded the people, "
12 J' rose early in the morning, and "
16 J' said unto the people, Shout; for "
22 J' had said unto the two men that "
25 J' saved Rahab the harlot alive, "
25 which J' sent to spy out Jericho. "
26 And J' adjured them at that time, "
27 So the Lord was with J'; and his "
7: 2 J' sent men from Jericho to Ai, "
3 they returned to J', and said unto "
6 J' rent his clothes, and fell to the "
7 J' said, Alas, O Lord God, wherefore "
10 the Lord said unto J', Get thee up; "
16 So J' rose up early in the morning, "
19 J' said unto Achan, My son, give, I "
20 Achan answered J', and said, indeed "
22 So J' sent messengers, and they "
23 brought them unto J', and unto all "
24 J', and all Israel with him, took "
25 J' said, Why hast thou troubled us? "
8: 1 Lord said unto J', Fear not, neither "
3 J' arose, and all the people of war, "
3 J' chose out thirty thousand...men "
9 J' therefore sent them forth: and "
9 J' lodged that night among the "
10 J' rose up early in the morning, "
13 J' went that night into the midst of "
15 J' and all Israel made as if they "
16 they pursued after J', and were "
18 Lord said unto J', Stretch out the "
18 J' stretched out the spear that he "
Jos 8:21 when J' and all Israel saw that 3091
23 took alive, and brought him to J'. "
26 for J' drew not his hand back, "
27 the Lord which he commanded J'. "
28 J' burnt Ai, and made it an heap for "
29 J' commanded that they should "
30 J' built an altar unto the Lord "
35 which J' read not before all the "
9: 2 to fight with J' and with Israel, "
3 Gibeon heard what J' had done "
6 went to J' unto the camp at Gilgal, "
8 And they said unto J', We are thy "
8 And J' said unto them, Who are ye? "
15 J' made peace with them, and "
22 J' called for them, and he spake "
24 they answered J', and said, Because "
27 J' made them that day hewers of "
10: 1 had heard how J' had taken Ai, "
4 it hath made peace with J' and "
6 men of Gibeon sent unto J' to the "
7 So J' ascended from Gilgal, he, and "
8 Lord said unto J', Fear them not: "
9 J' therefore came unto them "
12 Then spake J' to the Lord in the "
15 J' returned, and all Israel with him, "
17 it was told J', saying, the five kings "
18 J' said, Roll great stones upon the "
20 when J' and the children of Israel "
21 people returned to the camp to J' "
22 said J', Open the mouth of the cave, "
24 brought out those kings unto J', "
24 J' called for all the men of Israel, "
25 J' said unto them, Fear not, nor be "
26 afterward J' smote them, and slew "
27 that J' commanded, and they took "
28 that day J' took Makkedah, and "
29 J' passed from Makkedah, and all "
31 J' passed from Libnah, and all "
33 J' smote him and his people, until "
34 from Lachish J' passed unto Eglon, "
36 J' went up from Eglon, and all "
38 J' returned, and all Israel with him, "
40 So J' smote all the country of the "
41 J' smote them from Kadesh-barnea "
42 their land did J' take at one time, "
43 J' returned, and all Israel with him, "
11: 6 Lord said unto J', Be not afraid "
7 J' came, and all the people of war "
9 J' did unto them as the Lord bade "
10 J' at that time turned back, and "
12 all the kings of them, did J' take, "
13 save Hazor only; that did J' burn. "
15 Moses command J', and so did J'; "
16 So J' took all that land, the hills, "
18 J' made war a long time with all "
21 at that time came J', and cut off "
21 J' destroyed them utterly with "
23 So J' took the whole land, according "
23 J' gave it for an inheritance unto "
12: 7 the kings of the country which J' "
7 J' gave unto the tribes of Israel "
13: 1 J' was old and stricken in years; "
14: 1 the priest, and J' the son of Nun, "
6 children of Judah came unto J' "
13 J' blessed him, and gave unto Caleb "
15:13 commandment of the Lord to J', "
17: 4 priest, and before J' the son of Nun, "
14 children of Joseph spake unto J', "
15 J' answered them, If thou be a "
17 J' spake unto the house of Joseph, "
18: 3 J' said unto the children of Israel, "
8 J' charged them that went to "
9 again to J' to the host at Shiloh. "
10 J' cast lots for them in Shiloh "
10 there J' divided the land unto the "
19:49 of Israel gave an inheritance to J' "
51 J' the son of Nun, and the heads of "
20: 1 The Lord also spake unto J', saying, "
21: 1 unto J' the son of Nun, and unto "
22: 1 Then J' called the Reubenites, and "
6 So J' blessed them, and sent them "
7 unto the other half thereof gave J' "
7 when J' sent them away also unto "
23: 1 J' waxed old and stricken in age. "
2 J' called for all Israel, and for their "
24: 1 J' gathered all the tribes of Israel "
2 J' said unto all the people, Thus "
19 J' said unto the people, Ye cannot "
21 And the people said unto J', Nay; "
22 J' said unto the people, Ye are "
24 the people said unto J', The Lord "
25 J' made a covenant with the people "
26 J' wrote these words in the book of "
27 J' said unto all the people, Behold, "
28 So J' let the people depart, every "
29 J' the son of Nun, the servant of "
31 served the Lord all the days of J', "
31 days of the elders that overlived J', "
J'g 1: 1 after the death of J' it came to pass, "
2: 6 when J' had let the people go, the "
7 served the Lord all the days of J', "
7 days of the elders that outlived J', "
8 J' the son of Nun, the servant of "
21 nations which J' left when he died: "
23 he them into the hand of J'. "
1Sa 6:14 the cart came into the field of J', "
18 unto this day in the field of J', the "
1Ki 16:34 he spake by J' the son of Nun. "
2Ki 23: 8 in the entering in of the gate of J' "
Hag 1: 1 and to J' the son of Josedech, the "
12 J' the son of Josedech, the high "
14 the spirit of J' the son of Josedech, "
2: 2 and to J' the son of Josedech, the "
4 be strong, O J', son of Josedech, "
Zec 3: 1 he shewed me J' the high priest "
3 Now J' was clothed with filthy "
Zec 3: 6 angel of the Lord protested unto J', 3091
8 Hear now, O J' the high priest, "
9 stone that I have laid before J'; "
6:11 and set them upon the head of J' "

Josiah (*jo-si'-ah*) See also JOSIAS.
1Ki 13: 2 the house of David, J' by name; 2977
2Ki 21:24 of the land made J' his son king "
26 and J' his son reigned in his stead. "
22: 1 J' was eight years old when he "
3 in the eighteenth year of king J', "
23:16 as J' turned himself, he spied the "
19 J' took away, and did to them "
23 in the eighteenth year of king J', "
24 J' put away, that he might perform "
28 the rest of the acts of J', and all "
29 king J' went against him; and he "
30 land took Jehoahaz the son of J', "
34 the son of J' king in the room of J' "
1Ch 3:14 Amon his son, J' his son. "
15 the sons of J' were, the firstborn "
2Ch 33:25 of the land made J' his son king "
34: 1 J' was eight years old when he "
33 J' took away all the abominations "
35: 1 J' kept a passover unto the Lord in "
7 J' gave to the people, of the flock, "
16 to the commandment of king J'. "
18 keep such a passover as J' kept, "
19 reign of J' was this passover kept. "
20 when J' had prepared the temple, "
20 and J' went out against him. "
22 J' would not turn his face from him, "
23 the archers shot at king J'; and "
24 and Jerusalem mourned for J'. "
25 Jeremiah lamented for J': and all "
25 spake of J' in their lamentations "
26 the rest of the acts of J', and his "
36: 1 land took Jehoahaz the son of J', "
Jer 1: 2 days of J' the son of Amon king of "
3 days of Jehoiakim the son of J' king "
3 year of Zedekiah the son of J' king "
3: 6 said also unto me in the days of J' "
22:11 Lord touching Shallum the son of J' "
11 reigned instead of J' his father, "
18 concerning Jehoiakim the son of J' "
25: 1 year of Jehoiakim the son of J' king "
3 year of J' the son of Amon king of "
26: 1 the reign of Jehoiakim the son of J' "
27: 1 the reign of Jehoiakim the son of J' "
35: 1 the days of Jehoiakim the son of J' "
36: 1 year of Jehoiakim the son of J' "
2 from the days of J', even unto this "
9 year of Jehoiakim the son of J' king "
37: 1 Zedekiah the son of J' reigned "
45: 1 year of Jehoiakim the son of J' king "
46: 2 year of Jehoiakim the son of J' king "
Zep 1: 1 days of J' the son of Amon, king of "
Zec 6:10 house of J' the son of Zephaniah; "

Josias (*jo-si'-as*) See also JOSIAH.
M't 1:10 begat Amon; and Amon begat J'; *2502
11 And J' begat Jechonias and his * "

Josibiah (*jos-ib-i'-ah*)
1Ch 4:35 And Joel, and Jehu the son of J', *3143

Josiphiah (*jos-if-i'-ah*)
Ezr 8:10 sons of Shelomith; the son of J', 3131

jostle See JUSTLE.

jot
M't 5:18 one j' or one tittle shall in no wise 2503

Jotbah (*jot'-bah*)
2Ki 21:19 the daughter of Haruz of J'. 3192

Jotbath (*jot'-bath*) See also JOTBATHAH.
De 10: 7 from Gudgodah to J', a land of 3193

Jotbathah (*jot'-ba-thah*) See also JOTBATH.
Nu 33:33 Hor-hagidgad, and pitched in J'. 3193
34 removed from J', and encamped "

Jotham (*jo'-tham*) See also JOATHAM.
J'g 9: 5 J' the youngest son of Jerubbaal 3147
7 And when they told it to J', he went "
21 J' ran away, and fled, and went to "
57 upon them came the curse of J' "
2Ki 15: 5 And J' the king's son was over the "
7 and J' his son reigned in his stead. "
30 year of J' the son of Uzziah. "
32 J' the son of Uzziah king of Judah "
36 the rest of the acts of J', and all "
38 J' slept with his fathers, and was "
16: 1 Ahaz the son of J' king of Judah "
1Ch 2:47 the sons of Jahdai; Regem, and J', "
3:12 his son, Azariah his son, J' his son, "
5:17 by genealogies in the days of J' "
2Ch 26:21 and J' his son was over the king's "
23 and J' his son reigned in his stead. "
27: 1 J' was twenty and five years old "
6 So J' became mighty, because he "
7 the rest of the acts of J', and all "
9 J' slept with his fathers, and they "
Isa 1: 1 in the days of Uzziah, J', Ahaz, and "
7: 1 in the days of Ahaz the son of J', "
Ho 1: 1 in the days of Uzziah, J', Ahaz, and "
Mic 1: 1 the days of J', Ahaz, and Hezekiah, "

journey See also JOURNEYED; JOURNEYING; JOURNEYS.
Ge 24:21 had made his j' prosperous or not. 1870
29: 1 Jacob went on his j', and 5575,7272
30:36 set three days' j' betwixt himself 1870
31:23 pursued after him seven days' j'; "
33:12 Let us take our j', and let us go, 5265
46: 1 Israel took his j' with all that he "
Ex 3:18 three days' j' into the wilderness, 1870
5: 3 thee, three days' j' into the desert, "
8:27 three days' j' into the wilderness, "
13:20 they took their j' from Succoth, 5265
16: 1 And they took their j' from Elim, "

Nu 9:10 or be in a *j* afar off, yet he shall 1870
13 man that is clean, and is not in a *j*. "
10: 6 the south side shall take their *j*: 5265
13 they first took their *j* according to "
33 mount of the Lord three days' *j*: 1870
33 before them in the three days' *j*, "
11:31 as it were a day's *j* on this side, "
31 it were a day's *j* on the other side, "
33: 8 went three days' *j* in the wilderness "
12 took their *j* out of the wilderness *5265
De 1: 2 eleven days' *j* from Horeb by the way
7 Turn you, and take your *j*, and 5265
40 take your *j* into the wilderness by "
2: 1 took our *j* into the wilderness by "
24 take your *j*, and pass over the river "
10: 6 of Israel took their *j* from Beeroth* "
11 Arise, take thy *j* before the people, 4550
Jos 9:11 Take victuals with you for the *j*, 1870
13 old by reason of the very long *j*. "
J'g 4: 9 the *j* that thou takest shall not be "
1Sa 15:18 the Lord sent thee on a *j*, and said, "
2Sa 11:10 Uriah, Camest thou not from thy *j*? "
1Ki 18:27 or he is pursuing, or he is in a *j*, "
19: 4 went a day's *j* into the wilderness, "
7 because the *j* is too great for thee. "
2Ki 3: 9 fetched a compass of seven days' *j*: "
2Ch 1:13 Solomon came from his *j* to the high
Ne 2: 6 For how long shall thy *j* be? and 4109
Pr 7:19 not at home, he is gone a long *j*: 1870
Jon 3: 3 great city of three days' *j*. 4109
4 to enter into the city a day's *j*, "
M't 10:10 Nor scrip for your *j*, neither two 3598
25:15 ability; and straightway took his *j*. 589
M'r 6: 8 should take nothing for their *j*, 3598
13:34 of man is as a man taking a far *j*,* 590
Lu 2:44 in the company, went a day's *j*; 3598
9: 3 Take nothing for your *j*, neither "
11: 6 a friend of mine in his *j* is come "
15:13 and took his *j* into a far country, 589
Joh 4: 6 therefore, being wearied with his *j*, 3597
Ac 1:12 from Jerusalem a sabbath day's *j*. 3598
10: 9 as they went on their *j*, and drew 3596
22: 6 as I made my *j*, and was come 4198
Ro 1:10 I might have a prosperous *j* by *2137
15:24 I take my *j* into Spain, I will *4198
24 I trust to see you in my *j*, and to 1279
1Co 16: 6 may bring me on my *j* whithersoever
Tit 3:13 and Apollos on their *j* diligently,
3Jo 6 if thou bring forward on their *j*

journeyed
Ge 11: 2 to pass, as they *j* from the east, 5265
12: 9 Abram *j*, going on still toward the "
13:11 and Lot *j* east: and they separated "
20: 1 Abraham *j* from thence toward the "
33:17 Jacob *j* to Succoth, and built him "
35: 5 And they *j*: and the terror of God "
16 they *j* from Beth-el; and there was "
21 And Israel *j*, and spread his tent "
Ex 12:37 children of Israel *j* from Rameses "
17: 1 Israel *j* from the wilderness of Sin, "
40:37 they *j* not till the day that it was "
Nu 9:17 after that the children of Israel *j*: "
18 of the Lord the children of Israel *j*, "
19 the charge of the Lord, and *j* not. "
20 commandment of the Lord they *j*. "
21 up in the morning, then they *j*: "
21 that the cloud was taken up, they *j*. "
22 abode in their tents, and *j* not: "
22 but when it was taken up, they *j*. "
23 commandment of the Lord they *j*: "
11:35 people *j* from Kibroth-hattaavah "
12:15 *j* not till Miriam was brought in "
20:22 whole congregation, *j* from Kadesh, "
21: 4 And they *j* from mount Hor by the "
11 And they *j* from Oboth, and pitched "
33:22 they *j* from Rissah, and pitched in "
De 10: 7 From thence they *j* unto Gudgodah; "
Jos 9:17 children of Israel *j*, and came unto "
J'g 17: 8 the house of Micah, as he *j*. 6213,1870
Lu 10:33 But a certain Samaritan, as he *j*, 3593
Ac 9: 3 as he *j*, he came near Damascus: 4198
7 the men which *j* with him stood 4922
26:13 me and them which *j* with me. 4198

journeying See also JOURNEYINGS.
Nu 10: 2 and for the *j* of the camps. 4550
29 We are *j* unto the place of which 5265
Lu 13:22 and *j* toward Jerusalem. 4197,4160

journeyings
Nu 10:28 the *j* of the children of Israel 4550
2Co 11:26 in *j* often, in perils of waters, 3597

journeys
Ge 13: 3 he went on his *j* from the south 4550
Ex 17: 1 after their *j*, according to the "
40:36 Israel went onward in all their *j*: "
38 of Israel, throughout all their *j*. "
Nu 10: 6 they shall blow an alarm for their *j*. "
12 the children of Israel took their *j* "
33: 1 are the *j* of the children of Israel, "
2 goings out according to their *j* "
2 *j* according to their goings out. "

joy See also ENJOY; JOYED; JOYFUL; JOYING.
1Sa 18: 6 king Saul, with tabrets, with *j*, 8057
1Ki 1:40 rejoiced with great *j*, so that the "
1Ch 12:40 abundantly: for there was *j* in Israel. "
15:16 by lifting up the voice with *j*. "
25 of the house of Obed-edom with *j*. "
29: 9 the king also rejoiced with great *j*. "
17 now have I seen with *j* thy people, "
2Ch 20:27 to go again to Jerusalem with *j*; "
30:26 there was great *j* in Jerusalem: for "
Ezr 3:12 and many shouted aloud for *j*: "
13 discern the noise of the shout of *j* "
6:16 of this house of God with *j*, 2305
Ezr 6:22 kept...bread seven days with *j*: 8057
Ne 8:10 the *j* of the Lord is your strength. 2304
12:43 made them rejoice with great *j*: 8057
43 that the *j* of Jerusalem was heard "
Es 8:16 had light, and gladness, and *j*, 8342
17 the Jews had *j* and gladness, a 8057
9:22 turned unto them from sorrow to *j*,* "
22 make them days of feasting and *j*,* "
Job 8:19 Behold, this is the *j* of his way, 4885
20: 5 and the *j* of the hypocrite but for 8057
29:13 the widow's heart to sing for *j*. 7442
33:26 he shall see his face with *j*: for he 8643
38: 7 all the sons of God shouted for *j*? "
41:22 sorrow is turned into *j* before him. "
Ps 5:11 let them ever shout for *j*, because "
16:11 in thy presence is fulness of *j*; 8057
21: 1 The king shall *j* in thy strength, 8055
27: 6 in his tabernacle sacrifices of *j*; 8643
30: 5 but *j* cometh in the morning. 7440
32:11 shout for *j*, all ye that are upright "
35:27 Let them shout for *j*, and be glad, "
42: 4 with the voice of *j* and praise, 7440
43: 4 God, unto God my exceeding *j*: 1524
48: 2 the *j* of the whole earth, is mount 4885
51: 8 Make me to hear *j* and gladness; 8342
12 unto me the *j* of thy salvation; "
65:13 corn; they shout for *j*, they also sing.
67: 4 let the nations be glad and sing for *j*: "
105:43 brought forth his people with *j*, 8342
126: 5 that sow in tears shall reap in *j*. 7440
132: 9 and let thy saints shout for *j*. 7442
16 her saints shall shout aloud for *j*. "
137: 6 not Jerusalem above my chief *j*. 8057
Pr 12:20 but to the counsellors of peace is *j*. "
14:10 doth not intermeddle with his *j*. "
15:21 Folly is *j* to him that is destitute of "
23 man hath *j* by the answer of his "
17:21 and the father of a fool hath no *j*. 8056
21:15 It is *j* to the just to do judgment: 8057
23:24 begetteth a wise child shall have *j* 8056
Ec 2:10 withheld not my heart from any *j*; 8057
26 wisdom, and knowledge, and *j*: "
5:20 answereth him in the *j* of his heart. "
9: 7 eat thy bread with *j*, and drink thy "
Isa 9: 3 the nation, and not increased the *j*: "
3 they *j* before thee according to 8055
3 according to the *j* in harvest, "
17 shall have no *j* in their young men, "
12: 3 with *j* shall ye draw water out of 8342
16:10 and *j* out of the plentiful field; 1524
22:13 *j* and gladness, slaying oxen, and 8342
24: 8 endeth, the *j* of the harp ceaseth. 4885
11 all *j* is darkened, the mirth of the 8057
29:19 meek also shall increase their *j* "
32:13 yea, upon all the houses of *j* in the 4885
14 a *j* of wild asses, a pasture of "
35: 2 rejoice even with *j* and singing: 1525
10 with songs and everlasting *j* upon 8057
10 they shall obtain *j* and gladness, "
51: 3 *j* and gladness shall be found 8342
11 everlasting *j* shall be upon their 8057
11 they shall obtain gladness and *j*; "
52: 9 Break forth into *j*, sing together, "
55:12 For ye shall go out with *j*, and be 8057
60:15 a *j* of many generations. 4885
61: 3 the oil of *j* for mourning, the 8342
7 everlasting *j* shall be unto them. 8057
65:14 servants shall sing for *j* of heart, 2898
18 a rejoicing, and her people a *j*. 4885
19 Jerusalem, and *j* in my people: 7796
66: 5 he shall appear to your *j*, and 8057
10 love her: rejoice for *j* with her, 4885
Jer 15:16 the *j* and rejoicing of mine heart: 8342
31:13 I will turn their mourning into *j*, "
33: 9 And it shall be to me a name of *j*, "
11 The voice of *j*, and the voice of "
48:27 spakest of him, thou skippedst for *j*. *
33 *j* and gladness is taken from the 8057
49:25 of praise not left, the city of my *j*! 4885
La 2:15 beauty, The *j* of the whole earth? "
5:15 The *j* of our heart is ceased; our "
Eze 24:25 the *j* of their glory, the desire of "
36: 5 with the *j* of all their heart, 8057
Ho 9: 1 Rejoice not, O Israel, for *j*, as 1524
Joe 1:12 *j* is withered away from the sons 8342
16 *j* and gladness from the house of 8057
Hab 3:18 I will *j* in the God of my salvation. 1523
Zep 3:17 he will rejoice over thee with *j*; 8057
17 he will *j* over thee with singing. 1523
Zec 8:19 house of Judah *j* and gladness, 8342
M't 2:10 rejoiced with exceeding great *j*. 5479
13:20 word, and anon with *j* receiveth it; "
44 for *j* thereof goeth and selleth all "
25:21, 23 enter thou into the *j* of thy lord. "
28: 8 sepulchre with fear and great *j*; "
Lu 1:14 thou shalt have *j* and gladness; "
44 the babe leaped in my womb for *j*. 20
2:10 bring you good tidings of great *j*, 5479
6:23 ye in that day, and leap for *j*: "
8:13 they hear, receive the word with *j*; 5479
10:17 the seventy returned again with *j*, "
15: 7 *j* shall be in heaven over one sinner "
10 is *j* in the presence of the angels "
24:41 while they yet believed not for *j*, "
52 returned to Jerusalem with great *j*: "
Joh 3:29 this my *j* therefore is fulfilled. "
15:11 you, that my *j* might remain in you, "
11 and that your *j* might be full. "
16:20 your sorrow shall be turned into *j*. "
21 for *j* that a man is born into the "
22 your *j* no man taketh from you. "
24 receive, that your *j* may be full. "
17:13 have my *j* fulfilled in themselves. "
Ac 2:28 thou shalt make me full of *j* with *2167
8: 8 And there was great *j* in that city. 5479
13:52 the disciples were filled with *j*, and "
Ac 15: 3 caused great *j* unto all the brethren. 5479
20:24 I might finish my course with *j*, * "
Ro 5:11 *j* in God through our Lord Jesus *2744
14:17 peace, and *j* in the Holy Ghost. 5479
15:13 fill you with all *j* and peace in "
32 That I may come unto you with *j* "
2Co 1:24 faith, but are helpers of your *j*: "
2: 3 in you all, that my *j* is...of you all. "
3 in you all, that...is the *j* of you all.
7:13 more joyed we for the *j* of Titus, 5479
8: 2 abundance of their *j* and their deep "
Ga 5:22 fruit of the Spirit is love, *j*, peace, "
Ph'p 1: 4 for you all making request with *j*, "
25 for your furtherance and *j* of faith; "
2: 2 Fulfil ye my *j*, that ye be "
17 faith, I *j*, and rejoice with you all. 5463
18 For the same cause also do ye *j*, "
4: 1 and longed for, my *j* and crown, 5479
1Th 1: 6 affliction, with *j* of the Holy Ghost: "
2:19 what is our hope, or *j*, or crown of "
20 For ye are our glory and *j*. "
3: 9 for all the *j*...for your sakes before "
9 wherewith we *j* for your sakes 5463
2Ti 1: 4 tears, that I may be filled with *j*; 5479
Ph'm 7 we have great *j* and consolation 5485
20 let me have *j* of thee in the Lord: 3685
Heb 12: 2 who for the *j* that was set before 5479
13:17 that they may do it with *j*, and not "
Jas 1: 2 count it all *j* when ye fall into "
4: 9 mourning, and your *j* to heaviness. "
1Pe 1: 8 rejoice with *j* unspeakable and full "
4:13 may be glad also with exceeding *j*. 21
1Jo 1: 4 unto you, that your *j* may be full. 5479
2Jo 12 face to face, that our *j* may be full. "
3Jo 4 I have no greater *j* than to hear "
Jude 24 of his glory with exceeding *j*, 20

joyed
2Co 7:13 the more *j* we for the joy of Titus, 5463

joyful
1Ki 8:66 went unto their tents *j* and glad of 8056
Ezr 6:22 for the Lord had made them *j*, 8055
Es 5: 9 Haman went forth that day *j* and 8056
Job 3: 7 let no *j* voice come therein. 7445
Ps 5:11 them also that love thy name be *j* 5970
35: 9 my soul shall be *j* in the Lord: 1523
63: 5 mouth shall praise thee with *j* lips: 7445
66: 1 Make a *j* noise unto God, all ye
81: 1 make a *j* noise unto the God of
89:15 the people that know the *j* sound: 8643
95: 1 let us make a *j* noise to the rock
2 make a *j* noise unto him with psalms.
96:12 Let the field be *j*, and all that is *5937
98: 4 Make a *j* noise unto the Lord, all
6 make a *j* noise before the Lord, the
8 hands: let the hills be *j* together *7442
100: 1 Make a *j* noise unto the Lord, all
113: 9 and to be a *j* mother of children. 8056
149: 2 children of Zion be *j* in their King. 1523
5 Let the saints be *j* in glory: let *5937
Ec 7:14 In the day of prosperity be *j*, but 2896
Isa 49:13 Sing, O heavens; and be *j*, O earth; 1523
56: 7 them *j* in my house of prayer: 8055
61:10 my soul shall be *j* in my God; 1523
2Co 7: 4 I am exceeding *j* in all our *5479

joyfully
Ec 9: 9 Live *j* with the wife whom thou 2416
Lu 19: 6 came down, and received him *j*. 5463
Heb 10:34 took *j* the spoiling of your 3326,5479

joyfulness
De 28:47 not the Lord thy God with *j*, 8057
Col 1:11 and longsuffering with *j*; *5479

joying
Col 2: 5 spirit, *j* and beholding your order, 5463

joyous
Isa 22: 2 stirs, a tumultuous city, a *j* city: 5947
23: 7 Is this your *j* city, whose antiquity "
32:13 all the houses of joy in the *j* city: "
Heb 12:11 for the present seemeth to be *j*: 5479

Jozabad (*joz'-a-bad*) See also JEHOZABAD; JOSABAD.
1Ch 12:20 *J*, and Jediael, and Michael, and 3107
20 *J*, and Elihu, and Zilthai, captains "
2Ch 31:13 and Jerimoth, and *J*, and Eliel, "
35: 9 Jeiel and *J*, chief of the Levites "
Ezr 8:33 with them was *J* the son of Jeshua, "
10:22 Ishmael, Nethaneel, *J*, and Elasah. "
23 Also of the Levites; *J*, and Shimei, "
Ne 8: 7 Azariah, *J*, Hanan, Pelaiah, and "
11:16 Shabbethai and *J*, of the chief of "

Jozachar (*joz'-a-kar*) See also ZABAD.
2Ki 12:21 For *J* the son of Shimeath, and *3108

Jozadak (*joz'-a-dak*) See also JEHOZADAK; JOSEDECH.
Ezr 3: 2 stood up Jeshua the son of *J*, 3136
8 and Jeshua the son of *J*, and the "
5: 2 and Jeshua the son of *J*, and began "
10:18 of the sons of Jeshua the son of *J*, "
Ne 12:26 the son of Jeshua, the son of *J*, "

Jubal (*ju'-bal*)
Ge 4:21 And his brother's name was *J*: he 3106

jubile (*ju'-bi-lee*)
Le 25: 9 the trumpet of the *j* to sound on *8643
10 it shall be a *j* unto you; and ye 3104
11 A *j* shall that fiftieth year be unto "
12 For it is the *j*; it shall be holy unto "
13 In the year of this *j* ye shall return "
15 after the *j* thou shalt buy of thy "
28 hath bought it until the year of *j*: "
28 in the *j* it shall go out, and he shall "
30 it shall not go out in the *j*. "

Le 25: 31 and they shall go out in the j. 3104
33 shall go out in the year of j: "
40 shall serve thee unto the year of j: "
50 was sold to him unto the year of j: "
52 but few years unto the year of j, "
54 then he shall go out in the year of j, "
27: 17 sanctify his field from the year of j, "
18 if he sanctify his field after the j, "
18 remain, even unto the year of the j, "
21 field, when it goeth out in the j, "
23 even unto the year of the j: "
24 year of the j the field shall return "
Nu 36: 4 when the j of the children of Israel "

jubilee See JUBILE.

Jucal (*ju'-kal*) See also JEHUCAL.
Jer 38: 1 and J· the son of Shelemiah, and 3116

Juda (*ju'-dah*) See also JUDAH.
M't 2: 6 thou Bethlehem, in the land of J·, *2455
6 the least among the princes of J·: * "
M'r 6: 3 of James, and Joses, and of J·, * "
Lu 1: 39 with haste, into a city of J·; *2448
3: 26 of Joseph, which was the son of J·, *2455
30 of Simeon, which was the son of J·, * "
33 Phares, which was the son of J·, * "
Heb 7: 14 that our Lord sprang out of J·; * "
Re 5: 5 behold, the Lion of the tribe of J·, * "
7: 5 Of the tribe of J· were sealed * "

Judæa (*ju-de'-ah*) See also JEWRY; JUDAH; JUDEA.
M't 2: 1 Jesus was born in Bethlehem of J· 2449
5 said unto him, In Bethlehem of J·: "
22 heard that Archelaus did reign in J· "
3: 1 preaching in the wilderness of J·, "
5 out to him Jerusalem, and all J·, "
4: 25 and from Jerusalem, and from J·, "
19: 1 the coasts of J· beyond Jordan; "
24: 16 be in J· flee into the mountains: "
M'r 1: 5 out unto him all the land of J·, "
3: 7 Galilee followed him, and from J·, "
10: 1 and cometh into the coasts of J· "
13: 14 that be in J· flee to the mountains: "
Lu 1: 5 the days of Herod, the king of J·, "
65 all the hill country of J·, "
2: 4 out of the city of Nazareth, into J·, "
3: 1 Pontius Pilate being governor of J·, "
5: 17 out of every town of Galilee, and J·, "
6: 17 multitude of people out of all J· "
7: 17 him went forth throughout all J·, "
21: 21 are in J· flee to the mountains; "
Joh 3: 22 his disciples into the land of J·; "
4: 3 He left J·, and departed again into "
47 that Jesus was come out of J· into "
54 he was come out of J· into Galilee. "
7: 3 Depart hence, and go into J·, that "
11: 7 disciples, Let us go into J· again. "
Ac 1: 8 and in all J·, and in Samaria, and "
2: 9 dwellers in Mesopotamia, and in J·, "
14 Ye men of J·, and all ye that dwell 2453
8: 1 the regions of J· and Samaria, 2449
9: 31 rest throughout all J· and Galilee "
10: 37 was published throughout all J·, "
11: 1 and brethren that were in J· heard "
29 unto the brethren which dwelt in J·: "
12: 19 he went down from J· to Cæsarea, "
15: 1 men which came down from J· "
21: 10 there came down from J· a certain "
26: 20 and throughout all the coasts of J·, "
28: 21 neither received letters out of J· "
Ro 15: 31 from them that do not believe in J·; "
2Co 1: 16 be brought on my way toward J·. "
Ga 1: 22 by face unto the churches of J· "
1Th 2: 14 which in J· are in Christ Jesus: "

Judah (*ju'-dah*) See also BETHLEHEM-JUDAH; JUDA; JUDAH'S; JUDAS; JUDÆA; JUDE.
Ge 29: 35 therefore she called his name J·; 3063
35: 23 and Levi, and J·, and Issachar, and "
37: 26 And J· said unto his brethren, What "
38: 1 J· went down from his brethren, "
2 And J· saw there a daughter of a "
6 J· took a wife for Er his firstborn, "
8 J· said unto Onan, Go in unto thy "
11 said J· to Tamar his daughter in "
12 J· was comforted, and went up unto "
15 When J· saw her, he thought her to "
20 J· sent the kid by the hand of his "
22 And he returned to J·, and said, I "
23 J· said, Let her take it to her, lest "
24 that it was told J·, saying, Tamar "
24 J· said, Bring her forth, and let her "
26 J· acknowledged them, and said, "
43: 3 J· spake unto him, saying, The man "
8 J· said unto Israel his father, Send "
44: 14 And J· and his brethren came to "
16 J· said, What shall we say unto my "
18 J· came near unto him, and said, "
46: 12 the sons of J·; Er, and Onan, and "
28 he sent J· before him unto Joseph, "
49: 8 J·, thou art he whom thy brethren "
9 J· is a lion's whelp: from the prey, "
10 sceptre shall not depart from J·, "
Ex 1: 2 Reuben, Simeon, Levi, and J·, "
31: 2 the son of Hur, of the tribe of J·: "
35: 30 the son of Hur, of the tribe of J·; "
38: 22 the son of Hur, of the tribe of J·, "
Nu 1: 7 J·; Nahshon the son of Amminadab. "
26 children of J·, by their generations, "
27 of them, even of the tribe of J·, "
2: 3 of the standard of the camp of J· "
3 be captain of the children of J·. "
9 numbered in the camp of J· were an "
7: 12 of Amminadab, of the tribe of J·: "
10: 14 of the camp of the children of J· "
13: 6 Of the tribe of J·, Caleb the son of "
26: 19 The sons of J· were Er and Onan: "
20 sons of J· after their families were; "
Nu 26: 22 are the families of J· according to 3063
34: 19 Of the tribe of J·, Caleb the son of "
De 27: 12 and Levi, and J·, and Issachar, and "
33: 7 this is the blessing of J·: and he "
7 said, Hear, Lord, the voice of J·, "
34: 2 all the land of J·, unto the utmost "
Jos 7: 1 son of Zerah, of the tribe of J·, took "
16 and the tribe of J· was taken: "
17 he brought the family of J·; and he "
18 Zerah, of the tribe of J·, was taken. "
11: 21 and from all the mountains of J·, "
14: 6 of J· came unto Joshua in Gilgal: "
15: 1 lot of the tribe of the children of J· "
12 is the coast of the children of J· "
13 a part among the children of J·, "
20, 21 of the tribe of the children of J· "
63 children of J· could not drive them "
63 dwell with the children of J· unto "
18: 5 J· shall abide in their coast on the "
11 forth between the children of J· "
14 a city of the children of J·: "
19: 1 inheritance of the children of J·. "
9 of the portion of the children of J· "
9 part of the children of J· was too "
34 and to J· upon Jordan toward the "
20: 7 is Hebron, in the mountain of J·. "
21: 4 had by lot out of the tribe of J·, "
9 out of the tribe of the children of J·, "
11 is Hebron, in the hill country of J·, "
J'g 1: 2 And the Lord said, J· shall go up: "
3 J· said unto Simeon his brother, "
4 J· went up; and the Lord delivered "
8 J· had fought against Jerusalem, "
9 children of J· went down to fight "
10 And J· went against the Canaanites "
16 of J· into the wilderness of J·, "
17 J· went with Simeon his brother, "
18 J· took Gaza with the coast thereof, "
19 Lord was with J·; and he drave out "
10: 9 over Jordan to fight also against J·, "
15: 9 Philistines went...and pitched in J·, "
10 men of J· said, Why are ye come up "
11 thousand men of J· went to the top "
17: 7 Bethlehem-judah of the family of J·, "
18: 12 pitched in Kirjath-jearim, in J·: "
20: 18 the Lord said, J· shall go up first. "
Ru 1: 7 way to return unto the land of J·. "
4: 12 Pharez, whom Tamar bare unto J·, "
1Sa 11: 8 and the men of J· thirty thousand. "
15: 4 and ten thousand men of J·. "
17: 1 at Shochoh, which belongeth to J·, "
52 the men of Israel and of J· arose, "
18: 16 But all Israel and J· loved David, "
22: 5 and get thee into the land of J·. "
23: 3 Behold, we be afraid here in J·: "
23 throughout all the thousands of J·. "
27: 6 pertaineth unto the kings of J· "
10 David said, Against the south of J·, "
30: 14 the coast which belongeth t J·, "
16 Philistines, and out of the land of J·. "
26 of the spoil unto the elders of J·, "
2Sa 1: 18 children of J· the use of the bow: "
2: 1 I go up into any of the cities of J·? "
4 the men of J· came, and there they "
4 David king over the house of J·. "
7 house of J· have anointed me king "
10 But the house of J· followed David. "
11 king in Hebron over the house of J· "
3: 8 which against J· do shew kindness "
10 of David over Israel and over J·, "
5: 5 he reigned over J· seven years and "
5 three years over all Israel and J·. "
6: 2 were with him from Baale of J·, "
11: 11 and Israel, and J·, abide in tents; "
12: 8 thee the house of Israel and of J·; "
19: 11 Speak unto the elders of J·, saying, "
14 bowed the heart of all the men of J·, "
15 J· came to Gilgal, to go to meet the "
16 the men of J· to meet king David. "
40 the people of J· conducted the king, "
41 the men of J· stolen thee away, "
42 all the men of J· answered the men "
43 of Israel answered the men of J·, "
43 words of the men of J· were fiercer "
20: 2 the men of J· clave unto their king, "
4 Assemble me the men of J· within "
5 went to assemble the men of J·: "
21: 2 zeal to the children of Israel and J·. "
24: 1 to say, Go, number Israel and J·. "
7 they went out to the south of J·, "
9 of J· were five hundred thousand "
1Ki 1: 9 the men of J· the king's servants: "
35 to be ruler over Israel and over J·. "
2: 32 of Jether, captain of the host of J·. "
4: 20 J· and Israel were many, as the "
25 J· and Israel dwelt safely, every "
12: 17 which dwelt in the cities of J·, "
20 of David, but the tribe of J· only. "
21 he assembled all the house of J·, "
23 the son of Solomon, king of J·, "
23 all the house of J· and Benjamin, "
27 even unto Rehoboam king of J·, "
27 go again to Rehoboam king of J·. "
32 like unto the feast that is in J·, "
13: 1 there came a man of God out of J· "
12 of God went, which came from J·. "
14 man of God that camest from J·? "
21 the man of God that came from J·, "
14: 21 the son of Solomon reigned in J·. "
22 J· did evil in the sight of the Lord, "
29 of the chronicles of the kings of J·? "
15: 1 of Nebat reigned Abijam over J·. "
7 of the chronicles of the kings of J·? "
9 king of Israel reigned Asa over J·. "
17 king of Israel went up against J·, "
17 go out or come in to Asa king of J·. "
1Ki 15: 22 a proclamation throughout all J·; 3063
23 of the chronicles of the kings of J·? "
25 the second year of Asa king of J·, "
28, 33 the third year of Asa king of J· "
16: 8 and sixth year of Asa king of J· "
10 and seventh year of Asa king of J·, "
15 and seventh year of Asa king of J· "
23 and first year of Asa king of J·, "
29 and eighth year of Asa king of J· "
19: 3 Beer-sheba, which belongeth to J·, "
22: 2 king of J· came down to the king "
10 and Jehoshaphat the king of J· "
29 Jehoshaphat the king of J· went up "
41 son of Asa began to reign over J· "
45 of the chronicles of the kings of J·? "
51 year of Jehoshaphat king of J·, "
2Ki 1: 17 the son of Jehoshaphat king of J·; "
3: 1 year of Jehoshaphat king of J·, "
7 sent to Jehoshaphat the king of J·, "
9 of Israel went, and the king of J·, "
14 of Jehoshaphat the king of J·, "
8: 16 Jehoshaphat being then king of J·, "
16 son of Jehoshaphat king of J· began "
19 Lord would not destroy J· for David "
20 revolted from under the hand of J·, "
22 revolted from under the hand of J· "
23 of the chronicles of the kings of J·? "
25 Jehoram king of J· begin to reign. "
29 king of J· went down to see Joram "
9: 16 of J· was come down to see Joram. "
21 and Ahaziah king of J· went out, "
27 Ahaziah the king of J· saw this, he "
29 began Ahaziah to reign over J·. "
10: 13 the brethren of Ahaziah king of J·, "
12: 18 Jehoash king of J· took all the "
18 fathers, kings of J·, had dedicated, "
19 of the chronicles of the kings of J·? "
13: 1 Joash the son of Ahaziah king of J· "
10 seventh year of Joash king of J· "
12 fought against Amaziah king of J·, "
14: 1 Amaziah the son of Joash king of J·. "
9 Israel sent to Amaziah king of J·, "
10 fall, even thou, and J· with thee? "
11 he and Amaziah king of J· looked "
11 which belongeth to J·. "
12 And J· was put to the worse before "
13 of Israel took Amaziah king of J·, "
15 he fought with Amaziah king of J·, "
17 the son of Joash king of J· lived "
18 of the chronicles of the kings of J·? "
21 all the people of J· took Azariah, "
22 built Elath, and restored it to J·, "
23 Amaziah the son of Joash king of J·, "
28 and Hamath, which belonged to J·, "
15: 1 son of Amaziah king of J· to reign. "
6 of the chronicles of the kings of J·? "
8 eighth year of Azariah king of J· "
13 thirtieth year of Uzziah king of J·; "
17 thirtieth year of Azariah king of J· "
23 fiftieth year of Azariah king of J· "
27 fiftieth year of Azariah king of J· "
32 son of Uzziah king of J· to reign. "
36 of the chronicles of the kings of J·? "
37 the Lord began to send against J· "
16: 1 Jotham king of J· began to reign. "
19 of the chronicles of the kings of J·? "
17: 1 the twelfth year of Ahaz king of J· "
13 against Israel, and against J·, "
18 none left but the tribe of J· only. "
19 Also J· kept not the commandments "
18: 1 of Ahaz king of J· began to reign. "
5 like him among all the kings of J·, "
13 against all the fenced cities of J·, "
14 Hezekiah king of J· sent to the king "
14 appointed unto Hezekiah king of J· "
16 Hezekiah king of J· had overlaid, "
22 and hath said to J· and Jerusalem, "
19: 10 ye speak to Hezekiah king of J·, "
30 that is escaped of the house of J· "
20: 20 of the chronicles of the kings of J·? "
21: 11 Manasseh king of J· hath done these "
11 made J· also to sin with his idols: "
12 such evil upon Jerusalem and J·, "
16 sin wherewith he made J· to sin, "
17, 25 the chronicles of the kings of J·? "
22: 13 for all J·, concerning the words of "
16 book which the king of J· had read: "
18 king of J· which sent you to inquire "
23: 1 the elders of J· and of Jerusalem. "
2 and all the men of J· and all the "
5 kings of J· had ordained to burn "
5 in the high places in the cities of J·, "
8 the priests out of the cities of J·, "
11 the horses that the kings of J· had "
12 which the kings of J· had made, "
17 man of God, which came from J·, "
22 of Israel, nor of the kings of J·; "
24 that were spied in the land of J· "
26 his anger was kindled against J·, "
27 will remove J· also out of my sight, "
28 of the chronicles of the kings of J·? "
24: 2 sent them against J· to destroy it, "
3 of the Lord came this upon J·, "
5 of the chronicles of the kings of J·? "
12 Jehoiachin the king of J· went out "
20 came to pass in Jerusalem and J·, "
25: 21 J· was carried away out of their "
22 that remained in the land of J·, "
27 captivity of Jehoiachin king of J·, "
27 up the head of Jehoiachin king of J· "
1Ch 2: 1 Simeon, Levi, and J·, Issachar, "
3 the sons of J·; Er, and Onan, and "
3 Er, the firstborn of J·, was evil in "
4 Zerah. All the sons of J· were five. "
10 prince of the children of J·; "
4: 1 The sons of J·; Pharez, Hezron, "

1Ch 4:21 sons of Shelah the son of J· were, 3063
27 multiply, like to the children of J·. "
41 the days of Hezekiah king of J·, "
5: 2 J· prevailed above his brethren, "
17 in the days of Jotham king of J·, "
6:15 Lord carried away J· and Jerusalem "
55 gave them Hebron in the land of J·, "
65 of the tribe of the children of J·, "
9: 1 book of the kings of Israel and J·, "
3 dwelt of the children of J·, and of "
4 children of Pharez the son of J·. "
12:16 of the children of Benjamin and J· "
24 children of J· that bare shield and "
13: 6 which belonged to J·, to bring up "
21: 5 J· was four hundred threescore "
27:18 Of J·, Elihu, one of the brethren of "
28: 4 he hath chosen J· to be the ruler; "
4 of the house of J·, the house of my "
2Ch 2: 7 cunning men that are with me in J· "
9:11 such seen before in the land of J·. "
10:17 Israel that dwelt in the cities of J·, "
11: 1 of the house of J· and Benjamin "
3 the son of Solomon, king of J·, "
3 to all Israel in J· and Benjamin, "
5 and built cities for defence in J·. "
10 Aijalon, and Hebron, which are in J· "
12 having J· and Benjamin on his side. "
14 their possession, and came to J· "
17 strengthened the kingdom of J·, "
23 the countries of J· and Benjamin, "
12: 4 fenced cities which pertained to J·, "
5 Rehoboam, and to the princes of J·, "
12 and also in J· things went well. "
13: 1 began Abijah to reign over J·. "
13 so they were before J·, and the "
14 when J· looked back, behold, the "
15 Then the men of J· gave a shout: "
15 as the men of J· shouted, it came "
15 and all Israel before Abijah and J·. "
16 the children of Israel fled before J·: "
18 children of J· prevailed, because "
14: 4 commanded J· to seek the Lord God "
5 all the cities of J· the high places, "
6 And he built fenced cities in J·: "
7 Therefore he said unto J·, Let us "
8 out of J· three hundred thousand; "
12 before Asa, and before J·; and the "
15: 2 me, Asa, and all J· and Benjamin; "
8 idols out of all the land of J· and "
9 he gathered all J· and Benjamin, "
15 And all J· rejoiced at the oath: "
16: 1 king of Israel came up against J·, "
1 go out or come in to Asa king of J·. "
6 Asa the king took all J·; and they "
7 the seer came to Asa king of J·, "
11 book of the kings of J· and Israel. "
17: 2 forces in all the fenced cities of J·, "
2 set garrisons in the land of J·, and "
5 J· brought to Jehoshaphat presents; "
6 high places and groves out of J·. "
7 to teach in the cities of J·. "
9 they taught in J·, and had the book "
9 throughout all the cities of J·, "
10 the lands that were round about J·, "
12 he built in J· castles, and cities of "
13 much business in the cities of J·: "
14 Of J·, the captains of thousands; "
19 the fenced cities throughout all J·. "
18: 3 said unto Jehoshaphat king of J·, "
9 Israel and Jehoshaphat king of J· "
28 Jehoshaphat the king of J· went up "
19: 1 Jehoshaphat king of J· returned to "
5 all the fenced cities of J·, city by "
11 the ruler of the house of J·, for all "
20: 3 proclaimed a fast throughout all J·. "
4 J· gathered themselves together, to "
4 out of the cities of J· they came to "
5 stood in the congregation of J· and "
13 all J· stood before the Lord, with "
15 he said, Hearken ye, all J·, and ye "
17 Lord with you, O J· and Jerusalem: "
18 all J· and the inhabitants of "
20 stood and said, Hear me, O J·, "
22 Seir, which were come against J·; "
24 when J· came toward the watch "
27 every man of J· and Jerusalem, "
31 Jehoshaphat reigned over J·: he "
35 Jehoshaphat king of J· join himself "
21: 3 things, with fenced cities in J·: "
8 from under the dominion of J·, "
10 revolted from under the hand of J· "
11 high places in the mountains of J·, "
11 and compelled J· thereto. "
12 nor in the ways of Asa king of J·, "
13 hast made J· and the inhabitants "
17 they came up into J·, and brake "
22: 1 son of Jehoram king of J· reigned. "
6 Jehoram king of J· went down to "
8 found the princes of J·, and the "
10 all the seed royal of the house of J·. "
23: 2 they went about in J·, and gathered "
2 the Levites out of all the cities of J·, "
8 Levites and all J· did according to "
24: 5 Go out unto the cities of J·, and "
6 the Levites to bring in out of J· "
9 made a proclamation through J· "
17 Jehoiada came the princes of J·, "
18 wrath came upon J· and Jerusalem "
23 they came to J· and Jerusalem, "
25: 5 Amaziah gathered J· together, and "
5 of their fathers, throughout all J· "
10 was greatly kindled against J·, "
12 children of J· carry away captive, "
13 fell upon the cities of J·, from "
17 Amaziah king of J· took advice, "
18 Israel sent to Amaziah king of J·, "

2Ch 25:19 fall, even thou, and J· with thee? 3063
21 both he and Amaziah king of J·, "
21 which belongeth to J·. "
22 J· was put to the worse before "
23 of Israel took Amaziah king of J·, "
25 son of Joash king of J· lived after "
26 book of the kings of J· and Israel? "
28 with his fathers in the city of J·. "
26: 1 all the people of J· took Uzziah, "
2 built Eloth, and restored it to J·, "
27: 4 built cities in the mountains of J·, "
7 book of the kings of Israel and J·. "
28: 6 slew in J· a hundred and twenty "
9 of your fathers was wroth with J·, "
10 to keep under the children of J· "
17 Edomites had come and smitten J·, "
18 low country, and of the south of J·, "
19 brought J· low because of Ahaz "
19 he made J· naked, and transgressed "
25 city of J· he made high places to "
26 book of the kings of J· and Israel. "
29: 8 the wrath of the Lord was upon J· "
21 and for the sanctuary, and for J·. "
30: 1 Hezekiah sent to all Israel and J·, "
6 throughout all Israel and J·, "
12 in J· the hand of God was to give "
24 Hezekiah king of J· did give to the "
25 the congregation of J·, with the "
25 and that dwelt in J·, rejoiced. "
31: 1 present went out to the cities of J·, "
1 places and the altars out of all J· "
6 the children of Israel and J·, that "
6 dwelt in the cities of J·, they also "
20 did Hezekiah throughout all J·, "
32: 1 entered into J·, and encamped "
8 the words of Hezekiah king of J·. "
9 unto Hezekiah king of J·, and unto "
9 unto all J· that were at Jerusalem, "
12 commanded J· and Jerusalem, "
23 presents to Hezekiah king of J·: "
25 was wrath upon him, and upon J· "
32 book of the kings of J· and Israel. "
33 all J· and the inhabitants of "
33: 9 Manasseh made J· and the "
14 war in all the fenced cities of J·. "
16 commanded J· to serve the Lord "
34: 3 twelfth year he began to purge J· "
5 and cleansed J· and Jerusalem. "
9 the remnant of Israel, and of all J· "
11 which the kings of J· had destroyed. "
21 that are left in Israel and in J·, "
24 have read before the king of J·: "
26 as for the king of J·, who sent you "
29 all the elders of J· and Jerusalem. "
30 the Lord, and all the men of J·, "
35:18 all J· and Israel that was present, "
21 to do with thee, thou king of J·? "
24 all J· and Jerusalem mourned for "
27 book of the kings of Israel and J·. "
36: 4 Eliakim his brother king over J· "
8 book of the kings of Israel and J·: "
10 Zedekiah his brother king over J· "
23 house in Jerusalem, which is in J·. "
Ezr 1: 2 house at Jerusalem, which is in J·. "
3 go up to Jerusalem, which is in J·, "
5 rose up the chief of the fathers of J· "
8 unto Sheshbazzar, the prince of J·. "
2: 1 again unto Jerusalem and J·, "
3: 9 his sons, the sons of J·, together, "
4: 1 the adversaries of J· and Benjamin "
4 the hands of the people of J·, "
6 against the inhabitants of J· and "
5: 1 unto the Jews that were in J· 3061
7:14 to enquire concerning J· and "
9: 9 to give us a wall in J· and in 3063
10: 7 made proclamation throughout J· "
9 men of J· and Benjamin gathered "
23 Kelita,) Pethahiah, J·, and Eliezer. "
Ne 1: 2 came, he and certain men of J·; "
2: 5 thou wouldest send me unto J·, "
7 convey me over till I come into J·; "
4:10 J· said, The strength of the bearers "
16 were behind all the house of J·. "
5:14 be their governor in the land of J·, "
6: 7 saying, There is a king in J·: "
17 nobles of J· sent many letters unto "
18 were many in J· sworn unto him, "
7: 6 came again to Jerusalem and to J·, "
11: 3 in the cities of J· dwelt every one "
4 dwelt certain of the children of J·, "
4 the children of J·; Athaiah the son "
9 J· the son of Senuah was second "
20 Levites, were in all the cities of J·, "
24 the children of Zerah the son of J·, "
25 some of the children of J· dwelt at "
36 the Levites were divisions in J·, "
12: 8 Sherebiah, J·, and Mattaniah, "
31 up the princes of J· upon the wall, "
32 and half of the princes of J·, "
34 J·, and Benjamin, and Shemaiah, "
36 Nethaneel, and J·, Hanani, with "
44 J· rejoiced for the priests and for "
13:12 brought all J· the tithe of the corn "
15 days saw I in J· some treading "
16 the sabbath unto the children of J·, "
17 contended with the nobles of J·, "
Es 2: 6 away with Jeconiah king of J·, "
Ps 48:11 let the daughters of J· be glad, "
60: 7 of mine head; J· is my lawgiver; "
63: *title* he was in the wilderness of J·. "
68:27 the princes of J· and their council, "
69:35 Zion, and will build the cities of J·: "
76: 1 In J· is God known: his name is "
78:68 But chose the tribe of J·, the "
97: 8 the daughters of J· rejoiced "
108: 8 of mine head; J· is my lawgiver; "

Ps 114: 2 J· was his sanctuary, and Israel 3063
Pr 25: 1 men of Hezekiah king of J· copied "
Isa 1: 1 which he saw concerning J· and "
1 Ahaz and Hezekiah, kings of J·. "
2: 1 the son of Amoz saw concerning J· "
3: 1 and from J· the stay and the staff, "
8 Jerusalem is ruined, and J· is fallen: "
5: 3 men of J·, judge, I pray you, "
7 the men of J· his pleasant plant: "
7: 1 the son of Uzziah, king of J·, "
6 Let us go up against J·, and vex it, "
17 that Ephraim departed from J·; "
8: 8 he shall pass through J·; he shall "
9:21 they together shall be against J·. "
11:12 gather together the dispersed of J· "
13 adversaries of J· shall be cut off: "
13 Ephraim shall not envy J·, "
13 and J· shall not vex Ephraim. "
19:17 the land of J· shall be a terror unto "
22: 8 he discovered the covering of J·, "
21 Jerusalem, and to the house of J·. "
26: 1 this song be sung in the land of J·; "
36: 1 against all the defenced cities of J·, "
7 said to J· and to Jerusalem, Ye "
37:10 ye speak to Hezekiah king of J·, "
31 that is escaped of the house of J· "
38: 9 The writing of Hezekiah king of J·, "
40: 9 say unto the cities of J·, Behold "
44:26 to the cities of J·, Ye shall be built, "
48: 1 come forth out of the waters of J·, "
65: 9 J· an inheritor of my mountains: "
Jer 1: 2 Josiah the son of Amon king of J·, "
3 Jehoiakim...of Josiah king of J·, "
3 Zedekiah...of Josiah king of J·, "
15 and against all the cities of J·. "
18 whole land, against the kings of J·, "
2:28 of thy cities are thy gods, O J·. "
3: 7 her treacherous sister J· saw it. "
8 treacherous sister J· feared not, "
10 her treacherous sister J· hath not "
11 herself more than treacherous J·. "
18 the house of J· shall walk with the "
4: 3 saith the Lord to the men of J· "
4 Ye men of J· and inhabitants of "
5 Declare ye in J·, and publish in "
16 their voice against the cities of J·. "
5:11 the house of J· have dealt very "
20 of Jacob, and publish it in J·, "
7: 2 the word of the Lord, all ye of J·, "
17 not what they do in the cities of J· "
30 children of J· have done evil in my "
34 cause to cease from the cities of J·, "
8: 1 out the bones of the kings of J·, "
9:11 will make the cities of J· desolate, "
26 J·, and Edom, and the children of "
10:22 make the cities of J· desolate, and "
11: 2 speak unto the men of J·, and to "
6 all these words in the cities of J·, "
9 is found among the men of J·, "
10 house of J· have broken...covenant "
12 the cities of J· and inhabitants the "
13 of thy cities were thy gods, O J·; "
17 of Israel and of the house of J·, "
12:14 pluck out the house of J· from "
13: 9 manner will I mar the pride of J·, "
11 of Israel and the whole house of J· "
19 J· shall be carried away captive all "
14: 2 J· mourneth, and the gates thereof "
19 Hast thou utterly rejected J·? hath "
15: 4 the son of Hezekiah king of J·, "
17: 1 sin of J· is written with a pen of "
19 the kings of J· come in, and by the "
20 the Lord, ye kings of J·, and all J·, "
25 their princes the men of J·, and "
26 shall come from the cities of J·, "
18:11 go to, speak to the men of J·, "
19: 3 word of the Lord, O kings of J·, "
4 have known, nor the kings of J·, "
7 I will make void the counsel of J· "
13 houses of the kings of J·, shall be "
20: 4 give all J· into the hand of the king "
5 all the treasures of the kings of J· "
21: 7 I will deliver Zedekiah king of J·, "
11 touching the house of the king of J·, "
22: 1 down to the house of the king of J·, "
2 O king of J·, that sitteth upon the "
6 Lord unto the king's house of J·; "
11 Shallum...of Josiah king of J·, "
18 Jehoiakim...of Josiah king of J·; "
24 the son of Jehoiakim king of J· "
30 David, and ruling any more in J·. "
23: 6 In his days J· shall be saved, and "
24: 1 the son of Jehoiakim king of J·, "
1 and the princes of J·, with the "
5 that are carried away captive of J·, "
8 will I give Zedekiah the king of J·, "
25: 1 concerning all the people of J·, "
1 Jehoiakim...of Josiah king of J·, "
2 spake unto all the people of J· "
3 Josiah the son of Amon king of J·, "
18 cities of J·, and the kings thereof, "
26: 1 Jehoiakim...of Josiah king of J· "
2 and speak unto all the cities of J·, "
10 princes of J· heard these things, "
18 in the days of Hezekiah king of J·, "
18 spake to all the people of J·, saying, "
19 Did Hezekiah king of J· and all "
19 and all J· put him at all to death? "
27: 1 Jehoiakim...of Josiah king of J· "
3 come...unto Zedekiah king of J·; "
12 I spake also to Zedekiah king of J· "
18 in the house of the king of J·, and "
20 the son of Jehoiakim king of J· "
20 all the nobles of J· and Jerusalem; "
21 in the house of the king of J·, and "
28: 1 of the reign of Zedekiah king of J·. "

Jer 28: 4 the son of Jehoiakim king of J', 3063
4 with all the captives of J', that went "
29: 2 the princes of J' and Jerusalem, "
3 (whom Zedekiah king of J' sent "
22 up a curse by all the captivity of J' "
30: 3 the captivity of my people...J', "
4 spake concerning Israel and...J'. "
31: 23 use this speech in the land of J' "
24 there shall dwell in J' itself, and in "
27 house of J' with the seed of man, "
31 of Israel, and with the house of J': "
32: 1 tenth year of Zedekiah king of J', "
3 king of J' had shut him up, saying, "
4 king of J' shall not escape out of "
30 children of J' have only done evil "
32 of Israel and of the children of J', "
32 their prophets, and the men of J', "
35 this abomination, to cause J' to sin. "
44 Jerusalem, and in the cities of J', "
33: 4 the houses of the kings of J', "
7 And I will cause the captivity of J' "
10 beast, even in the cities of J', "
13 in the cities of J', shall the flocks "
14 of Israel and to the house of J'. "
16 In those days shall J' be saved, and "
34: 2 speak to Zedekiah king of J', and "
4 of the Lord, O Zedekiah king of J'; "
6 words unto Zedekiah king of J' in "
7 against all the cities of J' that were "
7 cities remained of the cities of J'. "
19 princes of J', and the princes of "
21 Zedekiah king of J' and his princes "
22 make the cities of J' a desolation "
35: 1 Jehoiakim...of Josiah king of J', "
13 Go and tell the men of J' and the "
17 I will bring upon J' and upon all "
36: 1 Jehoiakim...of Josiah king of J', "
2 thee against Israel, and against J', "
3 be that the house of J' will hear all "
6 shalt read them in the ears of all J' "
9 Jehoiakim...of Josiah king of J', "
9 that came from the cities of J' unto "
28 which...the king of J' hath burned. "
29 shalt say to Jehoiakim king of J', "
30 the Lord of Jehoiakim king of J'; "
31 and upon the men of J', all the evil "
32 Jehoiakim king of J' had burned "
37: 1 Babylon made king in the land of J'. "
7 Thus shall ye say to the king of J', "
39: 1 ninth year of Zedekiah king of J', "
4 Zedekiah the king of J' saw them, "
6 of Babylon slew all the nobles of J'. "
10 which had nothing, in the land of J', "
40: 1 away captive of Jerusalem and J', "
5 made governor over the cities of J', "
11 Babylon had left a remnant of J', "
12 driven, and came to the land of J', "
15 and the remnant in J' perish? "
42: 15 word of the Lord, ye remnant of J'; "
19 concerning you, O ye remnant of J'; "
43: 4 the Lord, to dwell in the land of J'. "
5 forces, took all the remnant of J', "
5 driven, to dwell in the land of J': "
9 in the sight of the men of J'; 3064
44: 2 and upon all the cities of J'; 3063
6 and was kindled in the cities of J' "
7 child and suckling, out of J', "
9 the wickedness of the kings of J', "
9 have committed in the land of J', "
11 you for evil, and to cut off all J'. "
12 And I will take the remnant of J', "
14 So that none of the remnant of J', "
14 should return into the land of J', "
17 and our princes, in the cities of J', "
21 that ye burned in the cities of J', "
24 all J' that are in the land of Egypt: "
26 all J' that dwell in the land of Egypt; "
26 in the mouth of any man of J' in all "
27 all men of J' that are in the land of "
28 land of Egypt into the land of J', "
28 all the remnant of J', that are gone "
30 I gave Zedekiah king of J' into the "
45: 1 Jehoiakim...of Josiah king of J', "
46: 2 Jehoiakim...of Josiah king of J', "
49: 34 of the reign of Zedekiah king of J', "
50: 4 they and the children of J' together, "
20 the sins of J', and they shall not be "
33 the children of J' were oppressed "
51: 5 been forsaken, nor J' of his God, "
59 went with Zedekiah the king of J' "
52: 3 came to pass in Jerusalem and J', "
10 he slew also all the princes of J' in "
27 J' was carried away captive out of "
31 captivity of Jehoiachin king of J', "
31 the head of Jehoiachin king of J', "
La 1: 3 J' is gone into captivity because of "
15 the virgin, the daughter of J', as in "
2: 2 strong holds of the daughter of J'; "
5 increased in the daughter of J' "
5: 11 and the maids in the cities of J'. "
Eze 4: 6 bear the iniquity of the house of J' "
8: 1 and the elders of J' sat before me, "
17 Is it a light thing to the house of J' "
9: 9 of Israel and J' is exceeding great, "
21: 20 to J' in Jerusalem the defenced. "
25: 3 and against the house of J', when "
8 of J' is like unto all the heathen; "
12 hath dealt against the house of J' "
27: 17 J', and the land of Israel, they were "
37: 16 For J', and for the children of Israel "
19 with him, even with the stick of J', "
48: 7 unto the west side, a portion for J'. "
8 And by the border of J', from the "
22 between the border of J' and the "
31 one gate of J', one gate of Levi. "
Da 1: 1 of the reign of Jehoiakim king of J' "
Da 1: 2 gave Jehoiakim king of J' into his 3063
6 these were of the children of J', "
2: 25 found a man of the captives of J', 3061
5: 13 the children of the captivity of J', "
6: 13 the children of the captivity of J', "
9: 7 to the men of J', and to the 3063
Ho 1: 1 Ahaz, and Hezekiah, kings of J', "
7 have mercy upon the house of J', "
11 Then shall the children of J' and "
4: 15 the harlot, yet let not J' offend; "
5: 5 J' also shall fall with them. "
10 princes of J' were like them that "
12 to the house of J' as rottenness. "
13 his sickness, and J' saw his wound, "
14 as a young lion to the house of J': "
6: 4 O J', what shall I do unto thee? "
11 O J', he hath set an harvest for thee, "
8: 14 J' hath multiplied fenced cities: "
10: 11 J' shall plow, and Jacob shall break "
11: 12 but J' yet ruleth with God, and is "
12: 2 hath also a controversy with J', "
Joe 3: 1 shall bring again the captivity of J' "
6 children also of J' and the children "
8 into the hand of the children of J', "
18 rivers of J' shall flow with waters, "
19 violence against the children of J', "
20 But J' shall dwell forever, and "
Am 1: 1 in the days of Uzziah king of J', "
2: 4 For three transgressions of J', and "
5 I will send a fire upon J', and it "
7: 12 flee thee away into the land of J', "
Ob 12 rejoiced over the children of J' in "
Mic 1: 1 Ahaz, and Hezekiah, kings of J', "
5 and what are the high places of J'? "
9 is incurable; for it is come unto J'; "
5: 2 be little among the thousands of J', "
Na 1: 15 O J', keep thy solemn feasts, "
Zep 1: 1 Josiah the son of Amon, king of J'. "
4 also stretch out mine hand upon J', "
2: 7 for the remnant of the house of J'; "
Hag 1: 1, 14 son of Shealtiel, governor of J', "
2: 2 the son of Shealtiel, governor of J', "
21 speak to Zerubbabel, governor of J', "
Zec 1: 12 on Jerusalem and on the cities of J', "
19, 21 horns which have scattered J', "
21 horn over the land of J' to scatter "
2: 12 the Lord shall inherit J' his portion "
8: 13 among the heathen, O house of J', "
15 Jerusalem and to the house of J': "
19 to the house of J' joy and gladness, "
9: 7 God, and he be as a governor in J', "
13 have bent J' for me, filled the bow "
10: 3 visited his flock the house of J', "
6 I will strengthen the house of J', "
11: 14 brotherhood between J' and Israel. "
12: 2 be in the siege both against J' and "
4 mine eyes upon the house of J', "
5 governors of J' shall say in their "
6 will I make the governors of J' like "
7 also shall save the tents of J' first, "
7 not magnify themselves against J'. "
14: 5 in the days of Uzziah king of J': "
14 J' also shall fight at Jerusalem; "
21 every pot in Jerusalem and in J' "
Mal 2: 11 J' hath dealt treacherously, and "
11 for J' hath profaned the holiness "
3: 4 shall the offering of J'...be pleasant "
Heb 8: 8 of Israel and with the house of J': 2455

Judah's (*ju'-dahs*)
Ge 38: 7 And Er, J' firstborn, was wicked 3063
12 daughter of Shuah J' wife died; * "
Jer 32: 2 which was in the king of J' house. "
38: 22 that are left in the king of J' house "

Judas (*ju'-das*) See also BARSABAS; ISCARIOT; JUDAH; JUDE; LEBBÆUS; THADDÆUS.
M't 1: 2 Jacob begat J' and his brethren; *2455
3 And J' begat Phares and Zara of * "
10: 4 J' Iscariot, who also betrayed him. "
13: 55 and Joses, and Simon, and J'? "
26: 14 twelve, called J' Iscariot, went "
25 J', which betrayed him, answered "
47 lo, J', one of the twelve, came, "
27: 3 J', which had betrayed him, when "
M'r 3: 19 J' Iscariot, which also betrayed "
14: 10 J' Iscariot, one of the twelve, went "
43 cometh J', one of the twelve, and "
Lu 6: 16 And J' the brother of James, and "
16 J' Iscariot, which...was the traitor. "
22: 3 Satan into J' surnamed Iscariot, "
47 and he that was called J', one of "
48 J', betrayest thou the Son of man "
Joh 6: 71 He spake of J' Iscariot the son of "
12: 4 disciples, J' Iscariot, Simon's son, "
13: 2 put into the heart of J' Iscariot, "
26 the sop, he gave it to J' Iscariot, "
29 thought, because J' had the bag, "
14: 22 J' saith to him, not Iscariot, Lord, "
18: 2 J' also, which betrayed him, knew "
3 J' then having received a band of "
5 J' also, which betrayed him, stood "
Ac 1: 13 and J' the brother of James. "
16 David spake before concerning J', "
25 from which J' by transgression fell, "
5: 37 After this man rose up J' of Galilee "
9: 11 the house of J' for one called Saul, "
15: 22 J' surnamed Barsabas, and Silas, "
27 have sent therefore J' and Silas, "
32 J' and Silas, being prophets also "

Judas-Iscariot See JUDAS and ISCARIOT.

Jude (*jood*) See also JUDAS.
Jude 1 J', the servant of Jesus Christ, †2455

Judea (*ju-de'-ah*) See also JUDÆA.
Ezr 5: 8 we went into the province of J', *3061

judge See also JUDGED; JUDGES; JUDGEST; JUDGETH; JUDGING.
Ge 15: 14 whom they shall serve, will I j': 1777
16: 5 the Lord j' between me and thee. 8199
18: 25 not the J' of all the earth do right? "
19: 9 sojourn, and he will needs be a j': "
31: 37 that they may j' betwixt us both. 3198
53 God of their father, j' betwixt us. 8199
49: 16 Dan shall j' his people, as one of 1777
Ex 2: 14 thee a prince and a j' over us? 8199
5: 21 The Lord look upon you, and j'; "
18: 13 that Moses sat to j' the people: "
16 and I j' between one and another, "
22 let them j' the people at all seasons: "
22 every small matter they shall j': "
Le 19: 15 shalt thou j' thy neighbour. "
Nu 35: 24 the congregation shall j' between "
De 1: 16 j' righteously between every man "
16: 18 and they shall j' the people with just "
17: 9 the j' that shall be in those days, "
12 the Lord thy God, or unto the j', "
25: 1 that the judges may j' them; "
2 the j' shall cause him to lie down, "
32: 36 For the Lord shall j' his people, 1777
J'g 2: 18 Lord was with the j', and delivered 8199
18 their enemies all the days of the j': "
19 the j' was dead, that they returned, "
11: 27 Lord the J' be j' this day between "
1Sa 2: 10 Lord shall j' the ends of the earth; 1777
25 against another, the j' shall...him: *430
25 against another, the...shall j' him: 6419
3: 13 that I will j' his house for ever for 8199
8: 5 make us a king to j' us like all the "
6 they said, Give us a king to j' us. "
20 that our king may j' us, and go out "
24: 12 The Lord j' between me and thee, "
15 The Lord therefore be j', and 1784
15 and j' between me and thee, and *8199
2Sa 15: 4 Oh that I were made j' in the land, "
1Ki 3: 9 understanding heart to j' thy people, "
9 for who is able to j' this thy so great "
7: 7 for the throne where he might j', "
8: 32 heaven, and do, and j' thy servants, "
1Ch 16: 33 because he cometh to j' the earth. "
2Ch 1: 10 who can j' this thy people, that is "
11 that thou mayest j' my people, "
6: 23 heaven, and do, and j' thy servants, "
19: 6 ye j' not for man, but for the Lord, "
20: 12 O our God, wilt thou not j' them? "
Ezr 7: 25 which may j' all the people that 1934,1778
Job 9: 15 would make supplication to my j'. *8199
22: 13 can he j' through the dark cloud? "
23: 7 I be delivered for ever from my j'. "
31: 28 iniquity to be punished by the j': *6416
Ps 7: 8 The Lord shall j' the people: *1777
8 j' me, O Lord, according to my 8199
9: 8 shall j' the world in righteousness, "
10: 18 j' the fatherless and the oppressed, "
26: 1 J' me, O Lord; for I have walked "
35: 24 J' me, O Lord my God, according "
43: 1 J' me, O God, and plead my cause "
50: 4 earth, that he may j' his people. 1777
6 for God is j' himself. 8199
54: 1 name, and j' me by thy strength. 1777
58: 1 do ye j' uprightly, O ye sons of 8199
67: 4 thou shalt j' the people righteously, "
68: 5 a j' of the widows, is God in his 1781
72: 2 j' thy people with righteousness, 1777
4 He shall j' the poor of the people, 8199
75: 2 congregation I will j' uprightly. "
7 God is the j': he putteth down one, "
82: 2 How long will ye j' unjustly, and "
8 Arise, O God, j' the earth: for thou "
94: 2 Lift up thyself, thou j' of the earth: "
96: 10 he shall j' the people righteously. 1777
13 for he cometh to j' the earth: 8199
13 j' the world with righteousness, "
98: 9 for he cometh to j' the earth: "
9 righteousness shall he j' the world, "
110: 6 He shall j' among the heathen, he 1777
135: 14 Lord will j' his people, and he will "
Pr 31: 9 Open thy mouth, j' righteously, 8199
Ec 3: 17 God shall j' the righteous and the "
Isa 1: 17 j' the fatherless, plead for the "
23 they j' not the fatherless, neither "
2: 4 he shall j' among the nations, and "
3: 2 man of war, the j', and the prophet, "
13 and standeth to j' the people. 1777
5: 3 j', I pray you, betwixt me and 8199
11: 3 not j' after the sight of his eyes, "
4 righteousness shall he j' the poor, "
33: 22 the Lord is our j', the Lord is our "
51: 5 and mine arms shall j' the people; "
Jer 5: 28 they j' not the cause, the cause of *1777
28 right of the needy do they not j'. 8199
La 3: 59 seen my wrong: j' thou my cause. "
Eze 7: 3, 8 will j' thee according to thy ways, "
27 to their deserts will I j' them; "
11: 10 I will j' you in the border of Israel; "
11 I will j' you in the border of Israel: "
16: 38 I will j' thee, as women that break "
18: 30 Therefore I will j' you, O house of "
20: 4 Wilt thou j' them, son of man, "
4 wilt thou j' them? cause them to "
21: 30 I will j' thee in the place where thou "
22: 2 Now, thou son of man, wilt thou j', "
2 wilt thou j' the bloody city? yea, "
23: 24 they shall j' thee according to their "
36 Son of man, wilt thou j' Aholah and "
45 they shall j' them after the manner "
24: 14 to thy doings, shall they j' thee, "
33: 20 I will j' you every one after his ways. "
34: 17 I j' between cattle and cattle, "
20 even I, will j' between the fat cattle "
22 I will j' between cattle and cattle. "
44: 24 j' it according to my judgments: "

Joe 3:12 there will I sit to *j* all the heathen 8199
Am 2: 3 cut off the *j* from the midst thereof, "
Ob 21 Zion to *j* the mount of Esau; "
Mic 3:11 heads thereof *j* for reward, and the "
4: 3 And he shall *j* among many people, "
5: 1 shall smite the *j* of Israel with a rod "
7: 3 and the *j* asketh for a reward; "
Zec 3: 7 then thou shalt also *j* my house, 1777
M't 5:25 adversary deliver thee to the *j*, 2923
25 the *j* deliver thee to the officer, "
7: 1 *J* not, that ye be not judged. 2919
2 with what judgment ye *j*, ye shall "
Lu 6:37 *J* not, and ye shall not be judged: "
12:14 made me a *j* or a divider over you? 1348
57 yourselves *j* ye not what is right? 2919
58 him; lest he hale thee to the *j*, 2923
58 and the *j* deliver thee to the officer, "
18: 2 There was in a city a *j*, which "
6 said, Hear what the unjust *j* saith. "
19:22 of thine own mouth will I *j* thee, 2919
Joh 5:30 as I hear, I *j*: and my judgment "
7:24 *J* not according to the appearance, "
24 but *j* righteous judgment. "
51 Doth our law *j* any man, before it "
8:15 Ye *j* after the flesh; I *j* no man. "
16 And yet if I *j*, my judgment is true: "
26 many things to say and to *j* of you: "
12:47 words, and believe not, I *j* him not: "
47 for I came not to *j* the world, but to "
48 the same shall *j* him in the last day. "
18:31 and *j* him according to your law. "
Ac 4:19 you more than unto God, *j* ye. "
7: 7 they shall be in bondage will I *j*, "
27 made thee a ruler and *j* over us? 1348
35 Who made thee a ruler and a *j*? "
10:42 to be the *J* of quick and dead. 2923
13:46 *j* yourselves unworthy of...life, 2919
17:31 will *j* the world in righteousness "
18:15 for I will be no *j* of such matters. 2923
23: 3 sittest thou to *j* me after the law, 2919
24:10 thou hast been of many years a *j* 2923
Ro 2:16 God shall *j* the secrets of men 2919
27 if it fulfil the law, *j* thee, who by "
3: 6 then how shall God *j* the world? "
14: 3 which eateth not *j* him that eateth: "
10 But why dost thou *j* thy brother? "
13 Let us not therefore *j* one another "
13 but *j* this rather, that no man put "
1Co 4: 3 yea, I *j* not mine own self. 350
5 *j* nothing before the time, until 2919
5:12 to *j* them also that are without? * "
12 do not ye *j* them that are within? "
6: 2 that the saints shall *j* the world? "
2 are ye unworthy to *j* the smallest 2922
3 ye not that we shall *j* angels? 2919
4 them to *j* who are least esteemed "
5 be able to *j* between his brethren? *1252
10:15 as to wise men; *j* ye what I say. 2919
11:13 *J* in yourselves: is it comely that "
31 we would *j* ourselves, we should *1252
14:29 two or three, and let the others *j*. * "
2Co 5:14 because we thus *j*, that if one 2919
Col 2:16 Let no man therefore *j* you in "
2Ti 4: 1 who shall *j* the quick and the dead "
8 which the Lord, the righteous *j*, 2923
Heb 10:30 again, The Lord shall *j* his people. 2919
12:23 to God the *J* of all, and to the 2923
13: 4 and adulterers God will *j*. 2919
Jas 4:11 the law: but if thou *j* the law, "
11 art not a doer of the law, but a *j*. 2923
5: 9 the *j* standeth before the door. "
1Pe 4: 5 ready to *j* the quick and the dead. 2919
Re 6:10 thou not *j* and avenge our blood "
19:11 he doth *j* and make war. "

judged

Ge 30: 6 And Rachel said, God hath *j* me, 1777
Ex 18:26 they *j* the people at all seasons: 8199
26 small matter they *j* themselves. "
J'g 3:10 he *j* Israel, and went out to war: "
4: 4 Lapidoth, she *j* Israel at that time. "
10: 2 he *j* Israel twenty and three years, "
3 and *j* Israel twenty and two years. "
12: 7 And Jephthah *j* Israel six years. "
8 him Ibzan of Beth-lehem *j* Israel. "
9 sons. And he *j* Israel seven years. "
11 him Elon, a Zebulonite, *j* Israel; "
11 and he *j* Israel ten years. "
13 of Hillel, a Pirathonite, *j* Israel. "
14 colts: and he *j* Israel eight years. "
15:20 And he *j* Israel in the days of the "
16:31 And he *j* Israel twenty years. "
1Sa 4:18 heavy. And he *j* Israel forty years. "
7: 6 Samuel *j* the children of Israel in "
15 Samuel *j* Israel all the days of his "
16 and *j* Israel in all those places. "
17 there he *j* Israel; and there he "
1Ki 3:28 judgment which the king had *j*; "
2Ki 23:22 days of the judges that *j* Israel, "
Ps 9:19 let the heathen be *j* in thy sight. "
37:33 nor condemn him when he is *j*. "
109: 7 he shall be *j*, let him be condemned: "
Jer 22:16 He *j* the cause of the poor and 1777
Eze 16:38 wedlock and shed blood are *j*; 4941
52 also, which hast *j* thy sisters, *6419
28:23 the wounded shall be *j* in the *5307
35:11 among them, when I have *j* thee. 8199
36:19 according to their doings I *j* them. "
Da 9:12 and against our judges that *j* us, "
M't 7: 1 Judge not, that ye be not *j*. 2919
2 judgment ye judge, ye shall be *j*: "
Lu 6:37 Judge not, and ye shall not be *j*: "
7:43 said unto him, Thou hast rightly *j*. "
Joh 16:11 because the prince of this world is *j*. "
Ac 16:15 If ye have *j* me to be faithful to "
24: 6 would have *j* according to our law.* "
25: 9 be *j* of these things before me? "
Ac 25:10 seat, where I ought to be *j*: to the 2919
20 and there be *j* of these matters. "
26: 6 now I stand and am *j* for the hope "
Ro 2:12 in the law shall be *j* by the law; "
3: 4 mightest overcome when thou art *j**"
7 why yet am I also *j* as a sinner? "
1Co 2:15 things, yet he himself is *j* of no man. 350
4: 3 thing that I should be *j* of you, "
5: 3 present in spirit, have *j* already, 2919
6: 2 if the world shall be *j* by you, are "
10:29 why is my liberty *j* of another "
11:31 ourselves, we should not be *j*. "
32 when we are *j*, we are chastened "
14:24 he is convinced of all, he is *j* of all: 350
Heb 11:11 she *j* him faithful who had *2233
Jas 2:12 as they that shall be *j* by the law 2919
1Pe 4: 6 they might be *j* according to men "
Re 11:18 of the dead, that they should be *j*, "
16: 5 shalt be, because thou hast *j* thus.* "
19: 2 for he hath *j* the great whore, "
20:12 the dead were *j* out of those things "
13 they were *j* every man according to "

judges

Ex 21: 6 master shall bring him unto the *j*; *430
22 he shall pay as the *j* determine. 6414
22: 8 house shall be brought unto the *j*, *430
9 parties shall come before the *j*; * "
9 whom the *j* shall condemn, he shall* "
Nu 25: 5 Moses said unto the *j* of Israel, 8199
De 1:16 And I charged your *j* at that time, "
16:18 *J* and officers shalt thou make "
19:17 before the priests and *j*, which "
18 *j* shall make diligent inquisition: "
21: 2 elders and thy *j* shall come forth, "
25: 1 that the *j* may judge them; then "
32:31 our enemies themselves being *j*. 6414
Jos 8:33 their *j*, stood on this side the ark 8199
23: 2 for their *j*, and for their officers, "
24: 1 for their *j*, and for their officers; "
J'g 2:16 Nevertheless the Lord raised up *j*, "
17 would not hearken unto their *j*, "
18 when the Lord raised them up *j*, "
Ru 1: 1 pass in the days when the *j* ruled, "
1Sa 8: 1 that he made his sons *j* over Israel. "
2 Abiah: they were *j* in Beer-sheba. "
2Sa 7:11 since the time that I commanded *j* "
2Ki 23:22 the days of the *j* that judged Israel, "
1Ch 17: 6 I a word to any of the *j* of Israel, "
10 since the time that I commanded *j* "
23: 4 six thousand were officers and *j*: "
26:29 over Israel, for officers and *j*. "
2Ch 1: 2 to the *j*, and to every governor in "
19: 5 he set *j* in the land throughout all "
6 said to the *j*, Take heed what ye do: "
Ezr 7:25 thine hand, set magistrates and *j*, 1782
10:14 of every city, and the *j* thereof, 8199
Job 9:24 covereth the faces of the *j* thereof; "
12:17 spoiled, and maketh the *j* fools. "
31:11 iniquity to be punished by the *j*. 6414
Ps 2:10 be instructed, ye *j* of the earth. 8199
141: 6 their *j* are overthrown in...places, "
148:11 princes, and all *j* of the earth: "
Pr 8:16 nobles, even all the *j* of the earth. "
Isa 1:26 I will restore thy *j* as at the first, "
40:23 maketh the *j* of the earth as vanity. "
Da 3: 2 governors, and the captains, the *j*, 148
3 the governors, and captains, the *j*, "
9:12 against our *j* that judged us, by 8199
Hos 7: 7 oven, and have devoured their *j*; "
13:10 thy *j* of whom thou saidst, Give me "
Zep 3: 3 her *j* are evening wolves; they "
M't 12:27 therefore they shall be your *j*. 2923
Lu 11:19 therefore shall they be your *j*. "
Ac 13:20 And after that he gave unto them *j* "
Jas 2: 4 And are become *j* of evil thoughts? "

judgest

Ps 51: 4 and be clear when thou *j*. 8199
Jer 11:20 O Lord of hosts, that *j* righteously, "
Ro 2: 1 O man, whosoever thou art that *j*: 2919
1 for wherein thou *j* another, thou "
1 thou that *j* doest the same things. "
3 that *j* them which do such things, "
14: 4 Who art thou that *j* another man's "
Jas 4:12 who art thou that *j* another? "

judgeth

Job 21:22 seeing he *j* those that are high. 8199
36:31 by them *j* he the people; he giveth 1777
Ps 7:11 God *j* the righteous, and God is *8199
58:11 he is a God that *j* in the earth. "
82: 1 the mighty; he *j* among the gods. "
Pr 29:14 The king that faithfully *j* the poor, "
Joh 5:22 the Father *j* no man, but hath *2919
8:50 there is one that seeketh and *j*. "
12:48 not my words, hath one that *j* him: "
1Co 2:15 But he that is spiritual *j* all things, 350
4: 4 but he that *j* me is the Lord. "
5:13 But them that are without God *j*. 2919
Jas 4:11 evil...brother, and *j* his brother, "
11 evil of the law, and *j* the law: "
1Pe 1:17 *j* according to every man's work, "
2:23 himself to him that *j* righteously: "
Re 18: 8 strong is the Lord God who *j* her.* "

judging

2Ki 15: 5 house, *j* the people of the land. 8199
2Ch 26:21 house, *j* the people of the land. "
Ps 9: 4 thou satest in the throne *j* right. "
Isa 16: 5 of David, *j*, and seeking judgment, "
M't 19:28 *j* the twelve tribes of Israel. 2919
Lu 22:30 thrones *j* the twelve tribes of Israel. "

judgment See also JUDGMENTS.

Ge 18:19 of the Lord, to do justice and *j*; ‡4941
Ex 12:12 gods of Egypt I will execute *j*: *8201
21:31 according to this *j* shall it be done 4941
Ex 23: 2 to decline after many to wrest *j*: "
6 shalt not wrest the *j* of thy poor 4941
28:15 make the breastplate of *j* with "
29 the breastplate of *j* upon his heart, "
30 thou shalt put in the breastplate of *j* "
30 Aaron shall bear the *j* of the "
Le 19:15 shall do no unrighteousness in *j*: "
35 shall do no unrighteousness in *j*, "
Nu 27:11 the children of Israel a statute of *j*, "
21 after the *j* of Urim before the Lord: "
35:12 stand before the congregation in *j*. "
29 shall be for a statute of *j* unto you "
De 1:17 ye shall not respect persons in *j*; "
17 for the *j* is God's: and the cause "
10:18 He doth execute the *j* of the "
16:18 shall judge the people with just *j*. "
19 Thou shalt not wrest *j*; thou shalt "
17: 8 a matter too hard for thee in *j*, "
9 shall shew thee the sentence of *j*: "
11 according to the *j* which they shall "
24:17 not pervert the *j* of the stranger, "
25: 1 they come unto *j*, that the judges "
27:19 perverteth the *j* of the stranger, "
32: 4 all his ways are *j*: a God of truth ‡ "
41 and mine hand take hold on *j*; "
Jos 20: 6 stand before the congregation for *j*, "
J'g 4: 5 of Israel came up to her for *j*. "
5:10 ye that sit in *j*, and walk by the *4055
1Sa 8: 3 and took bribes, and perverted *j*. 4941
2Sa 8:15 David executed *j* and justice unto "
15: 2 controversy came to the king for *j*, "
6 Israel that came to the king for *j*: "
1Ki 3:11 thyself understanding to discern *j*; "
28 Israel heard of the *j* which the king "
28 wisdom of God was in him, to do *j*. "
7: 7 might judge, even the porch of *j*: "
10: 9 he thee king, to do *j* and justice. "
20:40 said unto him, So shall thy *j* be; "
2Ki 25: 6 Riblah; and they gave *j* upon him. "
1Ch 18:14 executed *j* and justice among all "
2Ch 9: 8 king over them, to do *j* and justice. "
19: 6 who is with you in the *j*. 1697,
8 for the *j* of the Lord, and for "
20: 9 *j*, or pestilence, or famine, we 8196
22: 8 when Jehu was executing *j* upon 8199
24:24 So they executed *j* against Joash. 8201
Ezr 7:26 let *j* be executed speedily upon 1780
Es 1:13 toward all that knew law and *j*: 1779
Job 8: 3 Doth God pervert *j*? or doth the 4941
9:19 and if of *j*, who shall set me a time "
32 and we should come together in *j*. "
14: 3 and bringest me into *j* with thee? "
19: 7 I cry aloud, but there is no *j*. "
29 that ye may know there is a *j*. 1779
22: 4 will he enter with thee into *j*? 4941
27: 2 liveth, who hath taken away my *j*; * "
29:14 my *j* was as a robe and a diadem. * "
32: 9 neither do the aged understand *j*. "
34: 4 Let us choose to us *j*: let us know* "
5 and God hath taken away my *j*. * "
12 neither will the Almighty pervert *j*. "
23 he should enter into *j* with God. "
35:14 not see him, yet *j* is before him; *1779
36:17 hast fulfilled the *j* of the wicked: "
17 *j* and justice take hold on thee. "
37:23 he is excellent in power, and in *j*, 4941
40: 8 Wilt thou also disannul my *j*? wilt "
Ps 1: 5 ungodly shall not stand in the *j*, "
7: 6 to the *j* that thou hast commanded. "
9: 7 he hath prepared his throne for *j*. "
8 he shall minister *j* to the people 1777
16 by the *j* which he executeth: 4941
25: 9 The meek will he guide in *j*: and "
33: 5 He loveth righteousness and *j*: the "
35:23 awake to my *j*, even with my cause, "
37: 6 the light, and thy *j* as the noonday. "
28 Lord loveth *j*, and forsaketh not "
30 wisdom, and his tongue talketh of *j*. "
72: 2 righteousness, and...poor with *j*. "
76: 8 didst cause *j* to be heard from *1779
9 God arose to *j*, to save all the 4941
89:14 Justice and *j* are the habitation ‡ "
94:15 *j* shall return unto righteousness: "
97: 2 righteousness and *j* are the ‡ "
99: 4 The king's strength also loveth *j*; ‡ "
4 executest *j* and righteousness in ‡ "
101: 1 I will sing of mercy and *j*: unto "
103: 6 and *j* for all that are oppressed. * "
106: 3 Blessed are they that keep *j*, and "
30 up Phinehas, and executed *j*: 6419
111: 7 of his hands are verity and *j*; 4941
119:66 Teach me good *j* and knowledge: 2940
84 when wilt thou execute *j* on them 4941
121 I have done *j* and justice: leave ‡ "
149 quicken me according to thy *j*. * "
122: 5 For there are set thrones of *j*, the "
143: 2 enter not into *j* with thy servant: "
146: 7 executeth *j* for the oppressed: "
149: 9 execute upon them the *j* written: "
Pr 1: 3 wisdom, justice, and *j*, and equity; ‡ "
2: 8 He keepeth the paths of *j*, and ‡ "
9 understand righteousness, and *j*, ‡ "
8:20 in the midst of the paths of *j*: "
13:23 is that is destroyed for want of *j*. * "
16:10 his mouth transgresseth not in *j*. "
17:23 the bosom to pervert the ways of *j*. "
18: 5 to overthrow the righteous in *j*. "
19:28 An ungodly witness scorneth *j*: "
20: 8 that sitteth in the throne of *j* ‡1779
21: 3 To do justice and *j* is more 4941
7 them; because they refuse to do *j*. ‡ "
15 It is joy to the just to do *j*: but ‡ "
24:23 to have respect of persons in *j*. "
28: 5 Evil men understand not *j*: but "
29: 4 king by *j* establisheth the land: "
26 every man's *j* cometh from the "

Pr 31: 5 pervert the j' of any of the afflicted.1779
Ec 3:16 I saw under the sun the place of j'.4941
5: 8 violent perverting of j' and justice "
8: 5 heart discerneth both time and j'. "
6 every purpose there is time and j', "
11: 9 things God will bring thee into j'. "
12:14 God shall bring every work into j', "
Isa 1:17 well; seek j', relieve the oppressed, "
21 it was full of j'; righteousness "
27 Zion shall be redeemed with j', and‡"
3:14 The Lord will enter into j' with the "
4: 4 the midst thereof by the spirit of j', "
5: 7 and he looked for j', but behold ‡ "
16 Lord of hosts shall be exalted in j', "
9: 7 to establish it with j' and with "
10: 2 To turn aside the needy from j', ‡1779
16: 3 Take counsel, execute j'; make 6415
5 and seeking j', and hasting 4941
28: 6 a spirit of j' to him that sitteth in j', "
7 err in vision, they stumble in j'. 6417
17 J' also will I lay to the line, and 4941
30:18 you: for the Lord is a God of j': ‡"
32: 1 and princes shall rule in j'. ‡"
16 j' shall dwell in the wilderness, ‡"
33: 5 filled Zion with j' and righteousness.‡"
34: 5 upon the people of my curse, to j'. "
40:14 and taught him in the path of j', "
27 my j' is passed over from my God? "
41: 1 let us come near together to j'. "
42: 1 shall bring forth j' to the Gentiles. "
3 he shall bring forth j' unto truth. "
4 till he have set j' in the earth: "
49: 4 yet surely my j' is with the Lord, "
51: 4 make my j' to rest for a light of the "
53: 8 was taken from prison and from j': "
54:17 that shall rise against thee in j' "
56: 1 Keep ye j', and do justice: for my "
59: 8 there is no j' in their goings: they ‡"
9 Therefore is j' far from us, neither‡"
11 we look for j', but there is none; ‡"
14 j' is turned away backward, and ‡"
15 displeased him that there was no j'.‡"
61: 8 I the Lord love j', I hate robbery "
Jer 4: 2 in truth, in j', and in righteousness;‡"
5: 1 if there be any that executeth j', *"
4 of the Lord, nor the j' of their God. "
5 of the Lord, and the j' of their God: "
7: 5 if ye thoroughly execute j' between "
8: 7 people know not the j' of the Lord.*"
9:24 j', and righteousness, in the earth:‡"
10:24 O Lord, correct me, but with j'; ‡"
21:12 Execute j' in the morning, and "
22: 3 Execute ye j' and righteousness, "
15 eat and drink, and do j' and justice, "
23: 5 execute j' and justice in the earth. "
33:15 shall execute j' and righteousness "
39: 5 where he gave j' upon him. "
48:21 j' is come upon the plain country; "
47 Lord: Thus far is the j' of Moab. "
49:12 whose j' was not to drink of the cup* "
51: 9 her j' reacheth unto heaven, and is "
47 will do j' upon the graven images 6485
52 will do j' upon her graven images: "
52: 9 where he gave j' upon him. 4941
Eze 18: 8 executed true j' between man and "
23:10 for they had executed j' upon her.*8196
24 I will set j' before them, and they 4941
34:16 the strong; I will feed them with j'. "
39:21 heathen shall see my j' that I have "
44:24 they shall stand in j'; *8199
45: 9 spoil, and execute j' and justice, 4941
Da 4:37 works are truth, and his ways j': 1780
7:10 the j' was set, and the books were "
22 j' was given to the saints of the most "
26 But the j' shall sit, and they shall "
Ho 2:19 and in j', and in lovingkindness, 4941
5: 1 j' is toward you, because ye have "
11 is oppressed and broken in j', "
10: 4 thus j' springeth up as hemlock in "
12: 6 keep mercy and j', and wait on thy ‡
Am 5: 7 Ye who turn j' to wormwood, and "
15 good, and establish j' in the gate: "
24 But let j' run down as waters, and "
6:12 ye have turned j' into gall, and the "
Mic 3: 1 Israel; Is it not for you to know j'? "
8 and of j', and of might, to declare "
9 that abhor j', and pervert all equity. "
7: 9 my cause, and execute j' for me: "
Hab 1: 4 slacked, and j' doth never go forth: "
4 therefore wrong j' proceedeth. "
7 j' and their dignity shall proceed "
12 thou hast ordained them for j'; "
Zep 2: 3 earth, which have wrought his j'; "
3: 5 morning doth he bring his j' to light, "
Zec 7: 9 Execute true j', and shew mercy "
8:16 execute the j' of truth and peace in "
Mal 2:17 them; or, Where is the God of j'? "
3: 5 And I will come near to you to j'; "
M't 5:21 kill shall be in danger of the j': 2920
22 a cause shall be in danger of the j': "
7: 2 with what j' ye judge, ye shall be 2917
10:15 and Gomorrha in the day of j', 2920
11:22 for Tyre and Sidon at the day of j', "
24 the land of Sodom in the day of j', "
12:18 and he shall shew j' to the Gentiles. "
20 till he send forth j' unto victory. "
36 give account thereof in the day of j'. "
41 The men of Nineveh shall rise in j' "
42 of the south shall rise up in the j' "
23:23 of the law, j', mercy, and faith: ‡ "
27:19 he was set down on the j' seat, 968
M'r 6:11 and Gomorrah in the day of j', *2920
Lu 10:14 for Tyre and Sidon at the j', than "
11:31 of the south shall rise up in the j' "
32 of Nineve shall rise up in the j' "
42 pass over j' and the love of God: ‡ "
Joh 5:22 hath committed all j' unto the Son:*2920
27 him authority to execute j' also, "
30 as I hear, I judge: and my j' is just; "
7:24 appearance, but judge righteous j'. "
8:16 And yet if I judge, my j' is true: "
9:39 For j' I am come into this world, 2917
12:31 Now is the j' of this world: now 2920
16: 8 sin, and of righteousness, and of j': "
11 Of j', because the prince of this "
18:28 from Caiaphas unto the hall of j': ‡‡4232
28 went not into the j' hall, lest they ‡‡ "
33 Pilate entered into the j' hall ‡‡ "
19: 9 And went again into the j' hall, ‡‡ "
13 and sat down in the j' seat in a 968
Ac 8:33 humiliation his j' was taken away:2920
18:12 Paul, and brought him to the j' seat,968
16 And he drave them from the j' seat. "
17 and beat him before the j' seat. "
23:35 him to be kept in Herod's j' hall. *4232
24:25 temperance, and j' to come, 2917
25: 6 the next day sitting on the j' seat 968
10 said Paul, I stand at Cæsar's j' seat, "
15 desiring to have j' against him. *1349
17 on the morrow I sat on the j' seat, 968
Ro 1:32 Who knowing the j' of God, that *1345
2: 2 the j' of God is according to truth 2917
3 that thou shalt escape the j' of God? "
5 of the righteous j' of God; 1341
5:16 the j' was by one to condemnation, 2917
18 by the offence of one j' came upon all
14:10 all stand before the j' seat of Christ.968
1Co 1:10 the same mind and in the same j'. 1106
4: 3 be judged of you, or of man's j': 2250
7:25 yet I give my j', as one that hath 1106
40 happier if she so abide, after my j': "
2Co 5:10 appear before the j' seat of Christ; 968
Ga 5:10 that troubleth you shall bear his j',2917
Ph'p 1: 9 more in knowledge and in all j'; * 144
2Th 1: 5 token of the righteous j' of God, 2920
1Ti 5:24 open beforehand, going before to j'; "
Heb 6: 2 of the dead, and of eternal j'. 2917
9:27 once to die, but after this the j': 2920
10:27 certain fearful looking for of j' and "
Jas 2: 6 and draw you before the j' seats? 2922
13 For he shall have j' without mercy, 2920
13 and mercy rejoiceth against j'. "
1Pe 4:17 time is come that j' must begin 2917
2Pe 2: 3 j' now of a long time lingereth * "
4 darkness, to be reserved unto j'; 2920
9 reserve the unjust unto the day of j' "
3: 7 against the day of j' and perdition "
1Jo 4:17 may have boldness in the day of j': "
Jude 6 unto the j' of the great day. "
15 To execute j' upon all, and to "
Re 14: 7 him; for the hour of his j' is come: "
17: 1 thee the j' of the great whore 2917
18:10 for in one hour is thy j' come. 2920
20: 4 them, and j' was given unto them: 2917

judgment-hall See JUDGMENT and HALL.

judgments
Ex 6: 6 out arm, and with great j': 8201
7: 4 out of the land of Egypt by great j'. "
21: 1 are the j' which thou shalt set 4941
24: 3 the words of the Lord, and all the j': "
Le 18: 4 Ye shall do my j', and keep mine "
5 keep my statutes, and my j': "
26 keep my statutes and my j', "
19:37 statutes, and all my j', and do them: "
20:22 keep all my statutes, and all my j', "
25:18 shall do my statutes, and keep my j', "
26:15 statutes, or if your soul abhor my j', "
43 because they despised my j', and "
46 the statutes and j' and laws, which "
Nu 33: 4 gods also the Lord executed j'. 8201
35:24 of blood according to these j': 4941
36:13 are the commandments and the j', "
De 4: 1 unto the statutes and unto the j', "
5 I have taught you statutes and j', "
8 hath statutes and j' so righteous "
14 time to teach you statutes and j', "
45 the statutes, and the j', which Moses "
5: 1 the statutes and j' which I speak in "
31 and the j', which thou shalt teach "
6: 1 and the j', which the Lord your God "
20 and the j', which the Lord our God "
7:11 and the j', which I command thee "
12 if ye hearken to these j', and keep, "
8:11 and his j', and his statutes, which I "
11: 1 charge, and his statutes, and his j', "
32 observe to do all the statutes and j' "
12: 1 These are the statutes and j', which "
26:16 thee to do these statutes and j': "
17 and his commandments, and his j', "
33:10 shall teach Jacob thy j', and Israel "
21 of the Lord and his j' with Israel. "
2Sa 22:23 For all his j' were before me: and as "
1Ki 2: 3 and his j', and his testimonies, "
6:12 and execute my j', and keep all my "
8:58 and his j', which he commanded "
9: 4 wilt keep my statutes and my j': "
11:33 my statutes and my j', as did David "
1Ch 16:12 wonders, and the j' of his mouth; "
14 our God; his j' are in all the earth. "
22:13 to fulfill the statutes and j' which "
28: 7 do my commandments and my j', "
2Ch 7:17 observe my statutes and my j'; "
19:10 and commandment, statutes and j', "
Ezr 7:10 to teach in Israel statutes and j'. "
Ne 1: 7 nor the statutes, nor the j', which "
9:13 gavest them right j', and true laws, "
29 but sinned against thy j', (which if a "
10:29 Lord, and his j' and his statutes; "
Ps 10: 5 thy j' are far above out of his sight: "
18:22 For all his j' were before me, and I "
19: 9 the j' of the Lord are true and "
36: 6 thy j' are a great deep: O Lord, 4941
48:11 Judah be glad, because of thy j'. "
72: 1 Give the king thy j', O God, and thy "
89:30 my law, and walk not in my j'; "
97: 8 of Judah rejoiced because of thy j', "
105: 5 wonders, and the j' of his mouth; "
7 our God: his j' are all in the earth. "
119: 7 shall have learned thy righteous j'. "
13 I declared all the j' of thy mouth. "
20 that it hath unto thy j' at all times. "
30 truth: thy j' have I laid before me. "
39 which I fear: for thy j' are good. "
43 mouth; for I have hoped in thy j'. "
52 I remembered thy j' of old, O Lord; "
62 thee because of thy righteous j'. "
75 know, O Lord, that thy j' are right. "
102 I have not departed from thy j': "
106 that I will keep thy righteous j'. "
108 mouth, O Lord, and teach me thy j'. "
120 of thee; and I am afraid of thy j'. "
137 O Lord, and upright are thy j'. "
156 quicken me according to thy j'. "
160 every one of thy righteous j' "
164 thee because of thy righteous j'. "
175 praise thee; and let thy j' help me. "
147:19 his statutes and his j' unto Israel. "
20 as for his j', they have not known "
Pr 19:29 J' are prepared for scorners, and 8201
Isa 26: 8 Yea, in the way of thy j', O Lord, 4941
9 for when thy j' are in the earth, "
Jer 1:16 And I will utter my j' against them "
12: 1 yet let me talk with thee of thy j':* "
Eze 5: 6 she hath changed my j' into "
6 for they have refused my j' and my "
7 statutes, neither have kept my j', "
7 have done according to the j' of * "
8 will execute j' in the midst of thee "
10 and I will execute j' in thee, 8201
15 when I shall execute j' in thee in "
11: 9 and will execute j' among you. "
12 statutes, neither executed my j', 4941
14:21 my four sore j' upon Jerusalem, 8201
16:41 execute j' upon thee in the sight of "
18: 9 my statutes, and hath kept my j', 4941
17 hath executed my j', hath walked in "
20:11 my statutes, and shewed them my j', "
13 statutes, and they despised my j', "
16 they despised my j', and walked not "
18 neither observe their j', nor defile "
19 walk in my statutes, and keep my j', "
21 neither kept my j' to do them, "
24 they had not executed my j', "
25 and j' whereby they should not live; "
23:24 judge thee according to their j'. "
25:11 And I will execute j' upon Moab; 8201
28:22 when I shall have executed j' in her, "
26 when I have executed j' upon all "
30:14 in Zoan, and will execute j' in No. "
19 Thus will I execute j' in Egypt: "
36:27 ye shall keep my j', and do them. 4941
37:24 also walk in my j', and observe my "
44:24 shall judge it according to my j': "
Da 9: 5 from thy precepts and from thy j': "
Ho 6: 5 thy j' are as the light that goeth "
Zep 3:15 The Lord hath taken away thy j', "
Mal 4: 4 all Israel, with the statutes and j'. "
Ro 11:33 how unsearchable are his j', and 2917
1Co 6: 4 ye have j' of things pertaining to *2922
Re 15: 4 thee; for thy j' are made manifest.*1345
16: 7 true and righteous are thy j'. 2920
19: 2 For true and righteous are his j': "

judgment-seat See JUDGMENT and SEAT.

Judith (*ju'-dith*)
Ge 26:34 Esau...when he took to wife J' 3067

juice
Ca 8: 2 wine of the j' of my pomegranate. 6071

Julia (*ju'-le-ah*)
Ro 16:15 Salute Philologus, and J', Nereus, 2456

Julius (*ju'-le-us*)
Ac 27: 1 unto one named J', a centurion of 2457
3 And J' courteously entreated Paul, "

jumping
Na 3: 2 horses, and of the j' chariots. ‡7540

Junia (*ju'-ne-ah*)
Ro 16: 7 Salute Andronicus and J', my *2458

Junias See JUNIA.

juniper
1Ki 19: 4 and sat down under a j' tree: 7574
5 as he lay and slept under a j' tree, "
Job 30: 4 bushes, and j' roots for their meat.*"
Ps 120: 4 of the mighty, with coals of j'. "

Jupiter (*ju'-pit-ur*)
Ac 14:12 And they called Barnabas, J'; 2203
13 Then the priest of J', which was "
19:35 image which fell down from J'? 1356

jurisdiction
Lu 23: 7 that he belonged unto Herod's j', 1849

Jushab-hesed (*ju''-shab-he'-sed*)
1Ch 3:20 and Berechiah, and Hasadiah, J', 3142

just See also UNJUST.
Ge 6: 9 Noah was a j' man and perfect in *6662
Le 19:36 J' balances, j' weights, a j' ephah, 6664
36 and a j' hin, shall ye have; I am "
De 16:18 judge the people with j' judgment.*"
20 is altogether j' shalt thou follow, "
25:15 shalt have a perfect and j' weight, "
15 a perfect and j' measure shalt thou "
32: 4 without iniquity, j' and right is he. 6662
2Sa 23: 3 He that ruleth over men must be j',*"
Ne 9:33 thou art j' in all that is brought "

Job 4:17 mortal man be more j' than God? 6663
9: 2 how should man be j' with God? "
12: 4 the j' upright man is laughed to 6662
27:17 prepare it, but the j' shall put it on, "
33:12 in this thou art not j': I will 6663
34:17 thou condemn him that is most j'? 6662
Ps 7: 9 establish the j': for the righteous* "
37:12 The wicked plotteth against the j', "
Pr 3:33 he blesseth the habitation of the j'.* "
4:18 path of the j' is as the shining light,* "
9: 9 teach a j' man, and he will increase* "
10: 6 Blessings...upon the head of the j':* "
7 The memory of the j' is blessed: † "
20 tongue of the j' is as choice silver:* "
31 The mouth of the j' bringeth forth* "
11: 1 but a j' weight is his delight. 8003
9 shall the j' be delivered. *6662
12:13 But the j' shall come out of trouble.* "
21 There shall no evil happen to the j':* "
13:22 of the sinner is laid up for the j'. * "
16:11 A j' weight and balance are the 4941
17:15 and he that condemneth the j'. *6662
26 Also to punish the j' is not good, * "
18:17 is first in his own cause seemeth j': "
20: 7 The j' man walketh in his integrity:‡ "
21:15 It is joy to the j' to do judgment: * "
24:16 For a j' man falleth seven times, * "
29:10 upright: but the j' seek his soul. *3477
27 man is an abomination to the j': *6662
Ec 7:15 there is a j' man that perisheth in* "
20 there is not a j' man upon earth, * "
8:14 that there be j' men, unto whom it* "
Isa 26: 7 The way of the j' is uprightness: "
7 dost weigh the path of the j'. "
29:21 aside the j' for a thing of nought. "
45:21 a j' God and a Saviour; there is none "
La 4:13 have shed the blood of the j' in the "
Eze 18: 5 if a man be j', and do that which is "
9 he is j', he shall surely live, saith "
45:10 Ye shall have j' balances, 6664
10 and a j' ephah, and a j' bath. "
Ho 14: 9 right, and the j' shall walk in them: 6662
Am 5:12 they afflict the j', they take a bribe, "
Hab 2: 4 but the j' shall live by his faith. "
Zep 3: 5 The j' Lord is in the midst thereof;* "
Zec 9: 9 he is j', and having salvation; "
M't 1:19 her husband, being a j' man, and *1342
5:45 rain on the j' and on the unjust. "
13:49 sever the wicked from among the j',* "
27:19 nothing to do with that j' man: * "
24 of the blood of this j' person: * "
M'r 6:20 that he was a j' man and an holy, * "
Lu 1:17 disobedient to the wisdom of the j';* "
2:25 the same man was j' and devout, * "
14:14 at the resurrection of the j'. "
15: 7 over ninety and nine j' persons, * "
20:20 should feign themselves j' men, * "
23:50 and he was a good man, and a j': * "
Joh 5:30 I judge: and my judgment is j'; * "
Ac 3:14 ye denied the Holy One and the J',* "
7:52 before of the coming of the J' One;* "
10:22 Cornelius the centurion, a j' man,* "
22:14 know his will, and see that J' One,* "
24:15 the dead, both of the j' and unjust. "
Ro 1:17 written, The j' shall live by faith. * "
2:13 of the law are j' before God, "
3: 8 may come? whose damnation is j'. 1738

Ro 3:26 that he might be j', and the justifier 1342
7:12 commandment holy, and j', and * "
Ga 3:11 for, The j' shall live by faith. * "
Ph'p 4: 8 honest, whatsoever things are j', "
Col 4: 1 servants that which is j' and equal; "
Tit 1: 8 a lover of good men, sober, j', holy, "
Heb 2: 2 a j' recompence of reward; 1738
10:38 Now the j' shall live by faith: but *1342
12:23 the spirits of j' men made perfect, "
Jas 5: 6 have condemned and killed the j';* "
1Pe 3:18 for sins, the j' for the unjust, that * "
2Pe 2: 7 And delivered j' Lot, vexed with * "
1Jo 1: 9 and j' to forgive us our sins, and to* "
Re 15: 3 j' and true are thy ways, thou King* "

justice See also INJUSTICE.
Ge 18:19 the Lord, to do j' and judgment; *6666
De 33:21 he executed the j' of the Lord, "
2Sa 8:15 David executed judgment and j' "
15: 4 unto me, and I would do him j'! 6663
1Ki 10: 9 thee king, to do judgment and j'. 6666
1Ch 18:14 executed judgment and j' among "
2Ch 9: 8 over them, to do judgment and j'. "
Job 8: 3 or doth the Almighty pervert j'? 6664
36:17 judgment and j' take hold on thee.4941
37:23 in judgment, and in plenty of j': 6666
Ps 82: 3 do j' to the afflicted and needy. 6663
89:14 J' and judgment are the *6664
119:121 I have done judgment and j': * "
Pr 1: 3 of wisdom, j', and judgment, and * "
8:15 kings reign, and princes decree j'. "
21: 3 To do j' and judgment is more ‡6666
Ec 5: 8 perverting of judgment and j' in 6664
Isa 9: 7 it with judgment and with j' from*6666
56: 1 Lord, Keep ye judgment, and do j':* "
58: 2 ask of me the ordinances of j'; *6664
59: 4 None calleth for j', nor any pleadeth* "
9 us, neither doth j' overtake us: *6666
14 backward, and j' standeth afar off:* "
Jer 22:15 and drink, and do judgment and j', "
23: 5 shall execute judgment and j' in the "
31:23 O habitation of j', and mountain 6664
50: 7 the habitation of j', even the Lord, "
Eze 45: 9 and execute judgment and j', take6666

justification
Ro 4:25 and was raised again for our j'. 1347
5:16 gift is of many offences unto j'. 1345
18 came upon all men unto j' of life. 1347

justified
Job 11: 2 should a man full of talk be j'? 6663
13:18 cause; I know that I shall be j'. * "
25: 4 How then can man be j' with God?* "
32: 2 he j' himself rather than God. "
Ps 51: 4 mighest be j' when thou speakest, "
143: 2 thy sight shall no man living be j'.‡ "
Isa 43: 9 their witnesses, that they may be j': "
26 declare thou, that thou mayest be j'. "
45:25 shall all the seed of Israel be j', "
Jer 3:11 backsliding Israel hath j' herself * "
Eze 16:51 and hast j' thy sisters in all thine "
52 in that thou hast j' thy sisters. "
M't 11:19 But wisdom is j' of her children. 1344
12:37 For by thy words thou shalt be j', "
Lu 7:29 and the publicans, j' God, being "
35 wisdom is j' of all her children. "
18:14 this man went down to his house j' "

Ac 13:39 that believe are j' from all things, 1344
39 could not be j' by the law of Moses. "
Ro 2:13 but the doers of the law shall be j'. "
3: 4 thou mightest be j' in thy sayings, "
20 shall no flesh be j' in his sight: "
24 Being j' freely by his grace through "
28 that a man is j' by faith without the "
4: 2 For if Abraham were j' by works, "
5: 1 being j' by faith, we have peace "
9 then, being now j' by his blood, "
8:30 whom he called, them he also j': "
30 whom he j', them he also glorified. "
1Co 4: 4 yet am I not hereby j': but he that "
6:11 j' in the name of the Lord Jesus, "
Ga 2:16 is not j' by the works of the law, "
16 might be j' by the faith of Christ, "
16 works of the law shall no flesh be j'. "
17 if, while we seek to be j' by Christ, "
3:11 no man is j' by the law in the sight "
24 Christ, that we might be j' by faith. "
5: 4 whosoever of you are j' by the law; "
1Ti 3:16 manifest in the flesh, j' in the Spirit, "
Tit 3: 7 being j' by his grace, we should be "
Jas 2:21 not Abraham our father j' by works "
24 then how that by works a man is j', "
25 not Rahab the harlot j' by works, "

justifier
Ro 3:26 j' of him which believeth in Jesus. 1344

justifieth
Pr 17:15 He that j' the wicked, and he that 6663
Isa 50: 8 He is near that j' me; who will "
Ro 4: 5 on him that j' the ungodly, 1344
8:33 of God's elect? It is God that j'. "

justify See also JUSTIFIED; JUSTIFIETH; JUSTIFYING.
Ex 23: 7 not: for I will not j' the wicked. 6663
De 25: 1 then they shall j' the righteous, "
Job 9:20 I j' myself, mine own mouth shall* "
27: 5 God forbid that I should j' you: till "
33:32 me: speak, for I desire to j' thee. "
Isa 5:23 Which j' the wicked for reward, "
53:11 shall my righteous servant j' many;* "
Lu 10:29 he, willing to j' himself, said unto 1344
16:15 which j' yourselves before men. "
Ro 3:30 shall j' the circumcision by faith, "
Ga 3: 8 would j' the heathen through faith, "

justifying
1Ki 8:32 and j' the righteous, to give him 6663
2Ch 6:23 by j' the righteous, by giving him "

justle
Na 2: 4 they shall j' one against another ‡8264

justly See also UNJUSTLY.
Mic 6: 8 but to do j', and to love mercy, 4941
Lu 23:41 And we indeed j'; for we receive 1346
1Th 2:10 how holily and j' and unblameably* "

Justus (*jus'-tus*) See also BARSABAS; JESUS.
Ac 1:23 Barsabas, who was surnamed J', 2459
18: 7 J', one that worshipped God, "
Col 4:11 And Jesus, which is called J', who "

Juttah (*jut'-tah*)
Jos 15:55 Maon, Carmel, and Ziph, and J',*3194
21:16 and J' with her suburbs, and "

K.

Kabzeel (*kab'-ze-el*) See also JEKABZEEL.
Jos 15:21 coast of Edom southward were K',6909
2Sa 23:20 the son of a valiant man, of K', "
1Ch 11:22 the son of a valiant man of K', "

Kadesh (*ka'-desh*) See also EN-MISHPAT; KADESH-BARNEA; KEDESH.
Ge 14: 7 came to En-mishpat, which is K', 6946
16:14 behold, it is between K' and Bered." "
20: 1 dwelled between K' and Shur, and "
Nu 13:26 the wilderness of Paran, to K'; "
20: 1 the people abode in K'; and Miriam "
14 Moses sent messengers from K' "
16 behold, we are in K', a city in the "
22 congregation, journeyed from K', "
27:14 that is the water of Meribah in K' "
33:36 the wilderness of Zin, which is K'. "
37 they removed from K', and pitched "
De 1:46 abode in K' many days, according "
J'g 11:16 unto the Red sea, and came to K'; "
17 consent: and Israel abode in K'. "
Ps 29: 8 Lord shaketh the wilderness of K'. "
Eze 47:19 even to the waters of strife in K',* "
48:28 unto the waters of strife in K', "

Kadesh-barnea (*ka''-desh-bar'-ne-ah*) See also KADESH.
Nu 32: 8 sent them from K' to see the land.6947
34: 4 shall be from the south to K', "
De 1: 2 by the way of mount Seir unto K'.) "
19 commanded us; and we came to K'. "
2:14 space in which we came from K', "
9:23 when the Lord sent you from K', "
Jos 10:41 Joshua smote them from K' even "
14: 6 God concerning me and thee in K'. "
7 servant of the Lord sent me from K' "
15: 3 up on the south side unto K', "

Kadmiel (*kad'-me-el*)
Ezr 2:40 the children of Jeshua and K', 6934
3: 9 K' and his sons, the sons of Judah, "
Neh 7:43 the children of Jeshua, of K', and "
9: 4 the Levites, Jeshua, and Bani, K', "
5 the Levites, Jeshua, and K', Bani, "
10: 9 Binnui of the sons of Henadad, K'; "

Neh 12: 8 Binnui, K', Sherebiah, Judah, 6934
24 and Jeshua the son of K', with their "

Kadmonites (*kad'-mo-nites*)
Ge 15:19 and the Kennizzites, and the K', *6935

Kallai (*kal'-la-i*)
Neh 12:20 Of Sallai, K'; of Amok, Eber; 7040

Kanah (*ka'-nah*)
Jos 16: 8 westward into the river K'; 7071
17: 9 coast descended unto the river K', "
19:28 and K', even unto great Zidon; "

Kareah (*ka'-re-ah*) See also CAREAH.
Jer 40: 8 and Jonathan the sons of K', 7143
13 Johanan the son of K', and all the "
15 the son of K' spake to Gedaliah in "
16 said unto Johanan the son of K', "
41:11 when Johanan the son of K', and "
13 Johanan the son of K', and all the "
14 went unto Johanan the son of K'. "
16 took Johanan the son of K', and all "
42: 1 and Johanan the son of K', and "
8 called he Johanan the son of K', "
43: 2 Johanan the son of K', and all the "
4 So Johanan the son of K', and all "
5 But Johanan the son of K', and all "

Karkaa (*kar'-ka-ah*)
Jos 15: 3 and fetched a compass to K': *7173

Karkor (*kar'-kor*)
J'g 8:10 Zebah and Zalmunna were in K', 7174

Kartah (*kar'-tah*) See also KATTATH.
Jos 21:34 suburbs, and K' with her suburbs, 7177

Kartan (*kar'-tan*) See also KIRJATHAIM.
Jos 21:32 K' with her suburbs; three cities. 7178

Kattath (*kat'-tath*) See also KARTAH; KITRON.
Jos 19:15 And K', and Nahallal, and 7005

Kedar (*ke'-dar*)
Ge 25:13 of Ishmael, Nebajoth; and K', 6938
1Ch 1:29 of Ishmael, Nebaioth; then K', "
Ps 120: 5 that I dwell in the tents of K'! "
Ca 1: 5 of Jerusalem, the tents of K', "

Isa 21:16 and all the glory of K' shall fail: 6938
17 mighty men of the children of K', "
42:11 the villages that K' doth inhabit: "
60: 7 the flocks of K' shall be gathered "
Jer 2:10 and send unto K', and consider "
49:28 Concerning K', and concerning the "
28 go up to K', and spoil the men of "
Eze 27:21 Arabia, and all the princes of K', "

Kedemah (*ked'-e-mah*)
Ge 25:15 Tema, Jetur, Naphish, and K': 6929
1Ch 1:31 Jetur, Naphish, K'. These are the "

Kedemoth (*ked'-e-moth*)
De 2:26 out of the wilderness of K' unto 6932
Jos 13:18 Jahaza, and K', and Mephaath, "
21:37 K' with her suburbs, and Mephaath "
1Ch 6:79 K' also with her suburbs, and "

Kedesh (*ke'-desh*) See also KADESH; KEDESH-NAPHTALI; KISHION.
Jos 12:22 The king of K', one; the king of 6943
15:23 And K', and Hazor, and Ithnan, "
19:37 And K', and Edrei, and En-hazor, "
20: 7 And they appointed K' in Galilee "
21:32 K' in Galilee with her suburbs, "
J'g 4: 9 arose, and went with Barak to K'. "
10 Zebulun and Naphtali to K'; "
11 plain of Zaanaim, which is by K'. "
2Ki 15:29 and K', and Hazor, and Gilead, and "
1Ch 6:72 K' with her suburbs, Daberath "
76 K' in Galilee with her suburbs, and "

Kedesh-naphtali (*ke''-desh-naf'-ta-li*)
J'g 4: 6 the son of Abinoam out of K',6943,5321

keep See also KEEPEST; KEEPETH; KEEPING; KEPT.
Ge 2:15 of Eden to dress it and to k' it. 8104
3:24 way, to k' the way of the tree of life. "
6:19 the ark, to k' them alive with thee; "
20 come unto thee, to k' them alive. "
7: 3 to k' seed alive upon the face of "
17: 9 shalt k' my covenant therefore, 8104
10 is my covenant, which ye shall k', "
18:19 they shall k' the way of the Lord, "

Ge 28:15 will k' thee in all places whither 8104
20 and will k' me in this way that I go, "
30:31 I will again feed and k' thy flock. "
33: 9 k' that thou hast unto thyself. *1961
41:35 and let them k' food in the cities. 8104
Ex 6: 5 whom the Egyptians k' in bondage; "
12: 6 shall k' it up until the fourteenth 4931
14 ye shall k' it a feast to the Lord 2287
14 shall k' it a feast by an ordinance "
25 that ye shall k' this service. 8104
47 congregation of Israel shall k' it. 6213
48 and will k' the passover to the Lord, "
48 then let him come near and k' it; "
13: 5 thou shalt k' this service in this 5647
10 shalt therefore k' this ordinance 8104
15:26 and k' all his statutes, I will put "
16:28 refuse ye to k' my commandments "
19: 5 voice indeed, and k' my covenant, "
20: 6 love me, and k' my commandments. "
8 the sabbath day, to k' it holy. 6942
22: 7 neighbour money or stuff to k', 8104
10 ox, or a sheep, or any beast, to k'; "
23: 7 K' thee far from a false matter; 7368
14 Three times thou shalt k' a feast 2287
15 Thou shalt k' the feast of...bread: 8104
20 before thee, to k' thee in the way, "
31:13 Verily my sabbaths ye shall k': "
14 Ye shall k' the sabbath therefore; "
16 of Israel shall k' the sabbath, "
34:18 of unleavened bread shalt thou k'. "
Le 6: 2 which was delivered him to k', *
4 which was delivered him to k', *6485
8:35 k' the charge of the Lord, that ye 8104
18: 4 k' mine ordinances, to walk therein: "
5 Ye shall therefore k' my statutes, "
26 Ye shall therefore k' my statutes "
30 shall ye k' mine ordinance, that "
19: 3 and his father, and k' my sabbaths: "
19 Ye shall k' my statutes. Thou shalt "
30 Ye shall k' my sabbaths, and "
20: 8 ye shall k' my statutes, and do "
22 shall therefore k' all my statutes, "
22: 9 shall therefore k' mine ordinance, "
31 shall ye k' my commandments, "
23:39 ye shall k' a feast unto the Lord 2287
41 ye shall k' it a feast unto the Lord "
25: 2 the land k' a sabbath unto the Lord. "
18 k' my judgments, and do them; 8104
26: 2 Ye shall k' my sabbaths, and "
3 and k' my commandments, and do "
Nu 1:53 k' the charge of the tabernacle of "
3: 7 And they shall k' his charge, and "
8 they shall k' all the instruments of "
32 that k' the charge of the sanctuary. "
6:24 The Lord bless thee, and k' thee: "
8:26 to k' the charge, and shall do no "
9: 2 of Israel also k' the passover at 6213
3 shall k' it in his appointed season. "
3 ceremonies thereof, shall ye k' it. "
4 that they should k' the passover. "
6 not k' the passover on that day: "
10 yet he shall k' the passover unto "
11 month at even they shall k' it, "
12 of the passover they shall k' it. "
13 and forbeareth to k' the passover, "
14 will k' the passover unto the Lord; "
18: 3 they shall k' thy charge, and the 8104
4 k' the charge of the tabernacle of "
5 shall k' the charge of the sanctuary, "
7 with thee shall k' your priest's "
29:12 ye shall k' a feast unto the Lord 2287
31:18 with him, k' alive for yourselves. "
30 k' the charge of the tabernacle 8104
36: 7 k' himself to the inheritance *1692
9 k' himself to his own inheritance. * "
De 4: 2 ye may k' the commandments of 8104
6 K' therefore and do them; for this "
9 and k' thy soul diligently, lest thou "
40 shalt k' therefore his statutes, and "
5: 1 learn them, and k', and do them. * "
10 love me and k' my commandments. "
12 K' the sabbath day to sanctify it,* "
15 commanded thee to k' the sabbath 6213
29 k' all my commandments always, 8104
6: 2 God, to k' all his statutes and his "
17 diligently k' the commandments of "
7: 8 and because he would k' the oath "
9 k' his commandments to a thousand "
11 therefore k' the commandments, "
12 judgments, and k', and do them, "
12 shall k' unto thee the covenant "
8: 2 wouldest k' his commandments, or "
6 thou shalt k' the commandments "
10:13 To k' the commandments of the "
11: 1 and k' his charge, and his statutes, "
8 shall ye k' all the commandments "
22 For if ye shall diligently k' all these "
13: 4 k' his commandments, and obey "
18 to k' all his commandments which "
16: 1 k' the passover unto the Lord 6213
10 k' the feast of weeks unto the Lord "
15 days shalt thou k' a solemn feast 2287
17:19 to k' all the words of this law and 8104
19: 9 shalt k' all these commandments "
23: 9 k' thee from every wicked thing. "
23 out of thy lips thou shalt k' and * "
26:16 k' and do them with all thine heart, "
17 ways, and to k' his statutes, and his "
18 shouldest k' all his commandments; "
27: 1 K' all the commandments which I "
28: 9 k' the commandments of the Lord "
45 to k' his commandments and his "
29: 9 K' ...the words of this covenant, "
30:10, 16 to k' his commandments and his "
Jos 6:18 k' yourselves from the accursed "
10:18 and set men by it for to k' them: "

Jos 22: 5 to k' his commandments, and to 8104
23: 6 to k' and to do all that is written in "
J'g 2:22 will k' the way of the Lord to walk "
22 as their fathers did k' it, or not. "
3:19 thee, O king: who said, K' silence. "
Ru 2:21 shalt k' fast by my young men, 1692
1Sa 2: 9 will k' the feet of his saints, and 8104
7: 1 his son to k' the ark of the Lord. "
2Sa 8: 2 death, and with one full line to k' alive. "
15:16 were concubines, to k' the house. 8104
16:21 which he hath left to k' the house; "
18:18 I have no son to k' my name in "
20: 3 whom he had left to k' the house, 8104
1Ki 2: 3 k' the charge of the Lord thy God, "
3 walk in his ways, to k' his statutes, "
3:14 walk in my ways, to k' my statutes "
6:12 k' all my commandments to walk "
8:25 k' with thy servant David my father "
58 ways, and to k' his commandments, "
61 and to k' his commandments, as at "
9: 4 k' my statutes and my judgments; "
6 and will not k' my commandments "
11:33 to k' my statutes and my judgments, "
38 in my sight, to k' my statutes and 8104
20:39 unto me, and said, K' this man: "
2Ki 11: 6 shall ye k' the watch of the house, "
7 they shall k' the watch of the house "
17:13 and k' my commandments and my "
23: 3 to k' his commandments and his "
21 K' the passover unto the Lord 6213
1Ch 4:10 that thou wouldest k' me from evil, "
12:33 thousand, which could k' rank: *5737
38 men of war, that could k' rank, * "
22:12 mayest k' the law of the Lord thy 8104
23:32 k' the charge of the tabernacle "
28: 8 k' and seek for...the commandments "
29:18 k' this for ever in the imagination "
19 heart, to k' thy commandments, "
2Ch 6:16 k' with thy servant David my father "
13:11 we k' the charge of the Lord our "
22: 9 no power to k' still the kingdom. *6113
23: 6 shall k' the watch of the Lord. 8104
28:10 to k' under the children of Judah 3533
30: 1 to k' the passover unto the Lord 6213
2 to k' the passover in the second "
3 they could not k' it at that time, "
5 to k' the passover unto the Lord "
13 to k' the feast of unleavened bread "
23 took counsel to k' other seven days: "
34:31 Lord, and to k' his commandments, 8104
35:16 the same day, to k' the passover, 6213
18 kings of Israel k' such a passover "
Ezr 8:29 and k' them, until ye weigh them 8104
Ne 1: 9 and k' my commandments, and do "
12:27 to k' the dedic tion with gladness, 6213
13:22 they should come and k' the gates, 8104
Es 3: 8 neither k' they the king's laws: 6213
9:21 k' the fourteen h day of the month "
27 would k' these two days according "
Job 14:13 k' me se ret, until thy wrath be "
20:13 but k' it still within his mouth: 4513
Ps 12: 7 Thou shalt '' them, O Lord, thou 8104
17: 8 K' me as the apple of the eye, "
19:13 K' back thy servant also from 2820
22:29 and none can k' alive his own soul. "
25:10 such as k' his covenant and his 5341
20 O k' my soul, and deliver me: let 8104
31:20 shalt k' them secretly in a pavilion "
33:19 and to k' them alive in famine. "
34:13 K' thy tongue from evil, and thy 5341
35:22 hast seen, O Lord: k' not silence: "
37:34 Wait on the Lord, and k' his way, 8104
39: 1 I will k' my mouth with a bridle, "
41: 2 preserve him, and k' him alive; "
50: 3 come, and shall not k' silence: "
78: 7 God, but k' his commandments: 5341
83: 1 K' not thou silence, O God: hold not "
89:28 My mercy will I k' for him for 8104
31 and k' not my commandments; "
91:11 over thee, to k' thee in all thy ways. "
103: 9 neither will he k' his anger for 5201
18 To such as k' his covenant, and to 8104
105:45 his statutes, and k' his laws. *5341
106: 3 are they that k' judgment, and he 8104
113: 9 the barren woman to k' house, "
119: 2 are they that k' his testimonies, 5341
4 us to k' thy precepts diligently. *8104
5 were directed to k' thy statutes! * "
8 I will k' thy statutes: O forsake * "
17 that I may live, and k' thy word. * "
33 and I shall k' it unto the end. 5341
34 and I shall k' thy law; "
44 So shall I k' thy law continually *8104
57 said that I would k' thy words. * "
60 not to k' thy commandments. * "
63 and of them that k' thy precepts. * "
69 will k' thy precepts with my whole 5341
88 I k' the testimony of thy mouth. *8104
100 because I k' thy precepts. *5341
101 way, that I might k' thy word. *8104
106 I will k' thy righteous judgments.* "
115 I will k' the commandments of my 5341
129 therefore doth my soul k' them. "
134 of man: so will I k' thy precepts. *8104
136 eyes, because they k' not thy law.* "
145 me, O Lord: I will k' thy statutes. 5341
146 me, and I shall k' thy testimonies.*8104
127: 1 except the Lord k' the city, the "
132:12 If thy children will k' my covenant "
140: 4 K' me, O Lord, from the hands of "
141: 3 my mouth; k' the door of my lips. 5341
9 K' me from the snares which they 8104
Pr 2:11 thee, understanding shall k' thee: 5341
20 and k' the paths of the righteous. 8104
3: 1 thine heart k' my commandments: 5341
21 k' sound wisdom and discretion: "

Pr 3:26 shall k' thy foot from being taken. 8104
4: 4 k' my commandments, and live. "
6 love her, and she shall k' thee. 5341
13 instruction; let her not go: k' her; "
21 k' them in the midst of thine heart. 8104
23 K' thy heart with all diligence; 5341
5: 2 that thy lips may k' knowledge. "
6:20 son, k' thy father's commandment, "
22 thou sleepest, it shall k' thee; *8104
24 To k' thee from the evil woman, "
7: 1 My son, k' my words, and lay up "
2 K' my commandments, and live; "
5 k' thee from the strange woman, "
8:32 blessed are they that k' my ways. "
22: 5 he that doth k' his soul shall be far* "
18 thing if thou k' them within thee; "
28: 4 as k' the law contend with them. "
Ec 3: 6 time to k', and a time to cast away; "
7 time to k' silence, and a time to speak; "
5: 1 K' thy foot when thou goest to the 8104
8: 2 to k' the king's commandment, "
12:13 God, and k' his commandments: "
Ca 8:12 those that k' the fruit thereof two 5201
Isa 26: 3 Thou wilt k' him in perfect peace, 5341
27: 3 I the Lord do k' it; I will water it "
3 hurt it, I will k' it night and day. "
41: 1 K' silence before me, O islands; "
42: 6 hold thine hand, and will k' thee, 5341
43: 6 and to the south, K' not back; 3607
56: 1 saith the Lord, K' ye judgment, 8104
4 the eunuchs that k' my sabbaths, "
62: 6 mention of the Lord, k' not silence,* "
65: 6 I will not k' silence, but will "
Jer 3: 5 ever? will he k' it to the end? 8104
12 and I will not k' anger for ever, 5201
31:10 k' him, as a shepherd doth his 8104
42: 4 I will k' nothing back from you. 4513
La 2:10 sit upon the ground, and k' silence: "
Eze 11:20 k' mine ordinances, and do them: 8104
18:21 k' all my statutes, and do that which "
20:19 k' my judgments, and do them; "
36:27 ye shall k' my judgments, and do "
43:11 that they may k' the whole form "
44:16 me, and they shall k' my charge. "
24 and they shall k' my laws and my "
Da 9: 4 them that k' his commandments; "
Ho 12: 6 k' mercy and judgment, and wait "
Am 5:13 the prudent shall k' silence in that "
Mic 7: 5 k' the doors of thy mouth from 8104
Na 1:15 O Judah, k' thy solemn feasts, 2287
2: 1 k' the munition, watch the way, 5341
Hab 2:20 let all the earth k' silence before him. "
Zec 3: 7 if thou wilt k' my charge, then 8104
7 and shalt also k' my courts, "
13: 5 man taught me to k' cattle from *7069
14:16 to k' the feast of tabernacles. 2287
18, 19 up to k' the feast of tabernacles. "
Mal 2: 7 priest's lips should k' knowledge, "
M't 19:17 into life, k' the commandments. 5083
26:18 I will k' the passover at thy house 4160
M'r 7: 9 that ye may k' your own tradition. 5083
Lu 4:10 charge over thee, to k' thee: *1314
8:15 having heard the word, k' it. *2722
11:28 hear the word of God, and k' it. 5442
19:43 and k' thee in on every side, 4912
Joh 8:51, 52 If a man k' my saying, he shall 5083
55 but I know him, and k' his saying. "
12:25 world shall k' it unto life eternal. 5442
14:15 ye love me, k' my commandments. 5083
23 a man love me, he will k' my words: "
15:10 If ye k' my commandments, ye "
20 my saying, they will k' yours also. "
17:11 Holy Father, k' through thine own "
15 shouldest k' them from the evil. "
Ac 5: 3 to k' back part of the price of the 3557
10:28 man that is a Jew to k' company, *2853
12: 4 quaternions of soldiers to k' him; *5442
15: 5 them to k' the law of Moses. 5083
24 be circumcised, and k' the law: * "
29 from which if ye k' yourselves, ye 1301
16: 4 deliver them the decrees for to k', 5442
23 the jailor to k' them safely: 5083
18:21 I must by all means k' this feast 4160
21:25 only that they k' themselves from 5442
24:23 a centurion to k' Paul, and *5083
Ro 2:25 verily profiteth, if thou k' the law: *4238
26 k' the righteousness of the law, 5442
1Co 5: 8 Therefore let us k' the feast, not 1858
11 unto you not to k' company, 4874
7:37 heart that he will k' his virgin, 5083
9:27 I k' under my body, and bring it *5299
11: 2 k' the ordinances, as I delivered *2722
14:28 let him k' silence in the church; 4601
34 women k' silence in the churches: "
15: 2 ye k' in memory what I preached *2722
2Co 11: 9 unto you, and so will I k' myself. *5083
Ga 6:13 who are circumcised k' the law; 5442
Eph 4: 3 to k' the unity of the Spirit in the 5083
Ph'p 4: 7 shall k' your hearts and minds *5432
2Th 3: 3 stablish you, and k' you from evil. *5442
1Ti 5:22 other men's sins: k' thyself pure. 5083
6:14 k' this commandm t without "
20 k' that which is commi ted to thy *5442
2Ti 1:12 k' that which I have committed * "
14 unto thee k' by the Holy Ghost "
Jas 1:27 to k' himself unspotted from the 5083
2:10 whosoever shall k' the whole law, "
1Jo 2: 3 him, if we k' his commandments. "
3:22 because we k' his commandments, "
5: 2 God, and k' his commandments. * "
3 that we k' his commandments: "
21 children, k' yourselves from idols. *5442
Jude 21 K' yourselves in the love of God, 5083
24 that is able to k' you from falling, *5442
Re 1: 3 k' those things which are written 5083
3:10 also will k' thee from the hour of "

Re 12:17 which k' the commandments of 5088
14:12 that k' the commandments of God, "
22: 9 which k' the sayings of this book: "

keeper See also DOORKEEPER; KEEPERS.
Ge 4: 2 Abel was a k' of the sheep, but 7462
9 know not: Am I my brother's k'? 8104
39:21 the sight of the k' of the prison. 8269
22 the k' of the prison committed to "
23 The k' of the prison looked not to "
1Sa 17:20 and left the sheep with a k', 8104
22 carriage in the hand of the k' of "
28: 2 make thee k' of mine head for ever. "
2Ki 22:14 son of Harhas, k' of the wardrobe; "
2Ch 34:22 son of Hasrah, k' of the wardrobe; "
Ne 2: 8 Asaph the k' of the king's forest, "
3:29 Shemaiah...the k' of the east gate. "
Es 2: 3 chamberlain, k' of the women; "
8 custody of Hegai, k' of the women. "
15 chamberlain, the k' of the women, "
Job 27:18 and as a booth that the k' maketh. 5341
Ps 121: 5 The Lord is thy k': the Lord is thy 8104
Ca 1: 6 made me k' of the vineyards; but 5201
Jer 35: 4 Maaseiah...the k' of the door: 8104
Ac 16:27 the k' of the prison awaking out *1200
36 the k' of the prison told this * "

keepers See also DOORKEEPERS.
2Ki 11: 5 even be k' of the watch of the 8104
22: 4 which the k' of the door have "
23: 4 the k' of the door, to bring forth "
25:18 priest, and the three k' of the door: "
1Ch 9:19 k' of the gates of the tabernacle: "
19 of the Lord, were k' of the entry. "
Es 6: 2 chamberlains, the k' of the door, * "
Ec 12: 3 day when the k' of the house shall "
Ca 5: 7 k' of the walls took away any veil "
8:11 he let out the vineyard unto k'; 5201
Jer 4:17 As k' of a field, are they against 8104
52:24 and the three k' of the door: "
Eze 40:45 the k' of the charge of the house. "
46 the k' of the charge of the altar: "
44: 8 ye have set k' of my charge in my "
14 them k' of the charge of the house, "
M't 28: 4 for fear of him the k' did shake, *5083
Ac 5:23 k' standing without before the 5441
12: 6 k' before the door kept the prison.* "
19 him not, he examined the k', and * "
Tit 2: 5 discreet, chaste, k' at home, good,*3626

keepest
1Ki 8:23 who k' covenant and mercy with 8104
2Ch 6:14 which k' covenant, and shewest "
Ne 9:32 who k' covenant and mercy, let not "
Ac 21:24 walkest orderly, and k' the law. *5442

keepeth
Ex 21:18 and he die not, but k' his bed: *5307
De 7: 9 k' covenant and mercy with them 8104
1Sa 16:11 and, behold, he k' the sheep. 7462
Ne 1: 5 that k' covenant and mercy for 8104
Job 33:18 He k' back his soul from the pit, 2820
Ps 34:20 He k' all his bones: not one of 8104
121: 3 he that k' thee will not slumber. "
4 he that k' Israel shall neither "
146: 6 therein is: which k' truth for ever: "
Pr 2: 8 He k' the paths of judgment, and *5341
10:17 the way of life that k' instruction: *8104
13: 3 He that k' his mouth...his life: *5341
3 He that...his mouth k' his life: 8104
6 k' him that is upright in the way: *5341
16:17 he that k' his way preserveth his "
19: 8 he that k' understanding shall 8104
16 k' the commandment k' his own "
21:23 Whoso k' his mouth and his "
23 tongue k' his soul from troubles. "
24:12 he that k' thy soul, doth not he 5341
27:18 Whoso k' the fig tree shall eat the "
28: 7 Whoso k' the law is a wise son: but "
29: 3 he that k' company with harlots
11 a wise man k' it in till afterwards. 7623
18 he that k' the law, happy is he. 8104
Ec 8: 5 Whoso k' the commandment shall "
Isa 26: 2 nation which k' the truth may enter "
56: 2 that k' the sabbath from polluting "
2 k' his hand from doing any evil. "
6 that k' the sabbath from polluting "
Jer 48:10 that k' back his sword from blood. 4513
La 3:28 He sitteth alone and k' silence, *
Hab 2: 5 he is a proud man, neither k' at home,
Lu 11:21 a strong man armed k' his palace, *5442
Joh 7:19 and yet none of you k' the law? *4160
9:16 because he k' not the sabbath day. 5083
14:21 my commandments, and k' them, "
24 loveth me not k' not my sayings: "
1Jo 2: 4 and k' not his commandments, "
5 whoso k' his word, in him verily is "
3:24 And he that k' his commandments "
5:18 that is begotten of God k' himself, "
Re 2:26 and k' my works unto the end, "
16:15 that watcheth, and k' his garments, "
22: 7 blessed is he that k' the sayings of "

keeping
Ex 34: 7 K' mercy for thousands, forgiving 5341
Nu 3:28 k' the charge of the sanctuary. 8104
38 k' the charge of the sanctuary for "
De 8:11 God, in not k' his commandments, "
1Sa 25:16 we were with them k' the sheep. 7462
Ne 12:25 were porters k' the ward at the 8104
Ps 19:11 in k' of them there is great reward. "
Eze 17:14 by k' of his covenant it might stand. "
Da 9: 4 k' the covenant and mercy to them* "
Lu 2: 8 k' watch over their flock by night. 5442
1Co 7:19 k' of the commandments of God. 5084
1Pe 4:19 commit the k' of their souls to him in*

Kehelathah (*ke-hel'-a-thah*)
Nu 33:22 from Rissah, and pitched in K'. 6954
23 they went from K', and pitched in "

Keilah (*ki'-lah*)
Jos 15:44 K', and Achzib, and Mareshah; 7084
1Sa 23: 1 the Philistines fight against K', "
2 smite the Philistines, and save K'. "
3 much more then if we come to K' "
4 and said, Arise, go down to K'; "
5 So David and his men went to K', "
5 David saved the inhabitants of K'. "
6 of Ahimelech fled to David to K', "
7 Saul that David was come to K'. "
8 to go down to K', to besiege David "
10 that Saul seeketh to come to K', "
11 men of K' deliver me up into his "
12 men of K' deliver me and my men "
13 arose and departed out of K', "
13 that David was escaped from K'; "
1Ch 4:19 the father of K' the Garmite, "
Ne 3:17 the ruler of the half part of K', in "
18 the ruler of the half part of K'. "

Kelaiah (*kel-ah'-yah*) See also KELITA.
Ezr 10:23 Jozabad, and Shimei, and K', 7041

Kelita (*kel'-i-tah*) See also KELAIAH.
Ezr 10:23 and Kelaiah, (the same is K',) 7042
Ne 8: 7 Maaseiah, K', Azariah, Jozabad, "
10:10 Hodijah, K', Pelaiah, Hanan, "

Kemuel (*kem-u'-el*)
Ge 22:21 and K' the father of Aram, 7055
Nu 34:24 Ephraim, K' the son of Shiphtan. "
1Ch 27:17 Levites, Hashabiah the son of K': "

Kenan (*ke'-nan*) See also CAINAN.
1Ch 1: 2 K', Mahalaleel, Jered, 7018

Kenath (*ke'-nath*) See also NOBAH.
Nu 32:42 And Nobah went and took K', 7079
1Ch 2:23 with K', and the towns thereof, "

Kenaz (*ke'-naz*) See also KENEZITE.
Ge 36:11 Omar, Zepho, and Gatam, and K'. 7073
15 duke Omar, duke Zepho, duke K', "
42 Duke K', duke Teman, duke "
Jos 15:17 Othniel the son of K', the brother "
J'g 1:13 And Othniel the son of K', Caleb's "
3: 9 even Othniel the son of K', Caleb's "
11 And Othniel the son of K' died. "
1Ch 1:36 Zephi, and Gatam, K', and Timna, "
53 Duke K', duke Teman, duke "
4:13 And the sons of K'; Othniel, and "
15 and the sons of Elah, even K'. "

Kenezite (*ken'-e-zite*) See also KENIZZITES.
Nu 32:12 the son of Jephunneh the K', *7074
Jos 14: 6, 14 the son of Jephunneh the K' * "

Kenite (*ken'-ite*) See also KENITES.
Nu 24:22 the K' shall be wasted, until *7014
J'g 1:16 children of the K', Moses' father 7017
4:11 Now Heber the K', which was of 7014
17 of Jael the wife of Heber the K': 7017
17 and the house of Heber the K'. "
5:24 Jael the wife of Heber the K' be, "

Kenites (*ken'-ites*) See also MIDIANITES.
Ge 15:19 The K', and the Kenizzites, and *7017
Nu 24:21 he looked on the K', and took up* "
J'g 4:11 had severed himself from the K', "
1Sa 15: 6 Saul said unto the K', Go, depart, "
6 So the K' departed from among "
27:10 and against the south of the K'. "
30:29 which were in the cities of the K', "
1Ch 2:55 These are the K' that came of "

Kenizzites (*ken'-iz-zites*) See also KENEZITE.
Ge 15:19 The Kenites, and the K', and the *7074

kept
Ge 26: 5 k' my charge, my commandments, 8104
29: 9 father's sheep: for she k' them. 7462
39: 9 neither hath he k' back any thing 2820
42:16 and ye shall be k' in prison, that * 631
Ex 3: 1 Moses k' the flock of Jethro his *7462
16:23 for you to be k' until the morning. 4931
32 of it to be k' for your generations; "
33 Lord, to be k' for your generations. "
34 up before the Testimony, to be k'. "
21:29 owner, and he hath not k' him in, 8104
36 and his owner hath not k' him in; "
Nu 5:13 of her husband, and be k' close, 5641
9: 5 k' the passover on the fourteenth 6213
7 wherefore are we k' back, that we 1639
19 of Israel k' the charge of the Lord, 8104
23 they k' the charge of the Lord, at "
17:10 k' for a token against the rebels; 4931
19: 9 it shall be k' for the congregation "
24:11 hath k' thee back from honour. 4513
31:47 k' the charge of the tabernacle 8104
De 32:10 he k' him as the apple of his eye. 5341
33: 9 thy word, and k' thy covenant. * "
Jos 5:10 k' the passover on the fourteenth 6213
14:10 behold, the Lord hath k' me alive, "
22: 2 have k' all that Moses the servant 8104
3 k' the charge of the commandment "
Ru 2:23 she k' fast by the maidens of Boaz 1692
1Sa 9:24 this time hath it been k' for thee 8104
13:13 hast not k' the commandment of "
14 hast not k' that which the Lord "
17:34 Thy servant k' his father's sheep, 7462
21: 4 have k' themselves...from women. 8104
6 women have been k' from us 6113
25:21 vain have I k' all that this fellow 8104
33 hast k' me this day from coming 3607
34 k' me back from hurting thee, *4513
39 and hath k' his servant from evil: 2820
26:15 thou not k' thy lord the king? 8104
16 because ye have not k' your master, "
2Sa 13:34 And the young man that k' the watch
22:22 I have k' the ways of the Lord, and 8104
24 have k' myself from mine iniquity. "
44 k' me to be head of the heathen: "
1Ki 2:43 Why then hast thou not k' the oath "
3: 6 hast k' for him this great kindness, 8104
8:24 Who hast k' with thy servant David "
11:10 but he k' not that which the Lord "
11 thou hast not k' my covenant and "
34 because he k' my commandments "
13:21 and hast not k' the commandment "
14: 8 who k' my commandments, and "
27 k' the door of the king's house. "
2Ki 9:14 (Now Joram had k' Ramoth-gilead, "
12: 9 and the priests that k' the door put "
17:19 Judah k' not the commandments of "
18: 6 but k' his commandments, which "
1Ch 10:13 word of the Lord, which he k' not, "
12: 1 k' himself close because of Saul 6113
29 part of them had k' the ward of 8104
2Ch 6:15 hast k' with thy servant David "
7: 8 Solomon k' the feast seven days, *6213
9 they k' the dedication of the altar "
12:10 k' the entrance of the king's house. 8104
30:21 present at Jerusalem k' the feast 6213
23 k' other seven days with gladness. "
34: 9 the Levites that k' the doors had *8104
21 our fathers have not k' the word of "
35: 1 Moreover Josiah k' a passover 6213
17 k' the passover at that time, "
18 no passover like to that k' in Israel "
18 keep such a passover as Josiah k', "
19 reign of Josiah was this passover k'. "
36:21 as she lay desolate she k' sabbath, 7673
Ezr 3: 4 k' also the feast of tabernacles, 6213
6:16 k' the dedication of this house of 5648
19 of the captivity k' the passover 6213
22 k' the feast of unleavened bread "
Ne 1: 7 have not k' the commandments, 8104
8:18 they k' the feast seven days; and 6213
9:34 priests, nor our fathers, k' thy law, "
11:19 brethren that k' the gates, were 8104
12:45 singers and the porters k' the ward "
Es 2:14 which k' the concubines: "
21 of those which k' the door, were "
9:28 days should be remembered and k' 6213
Job 23:11 his way have I k', and not 8104
28:21 k' close from the fowls of the air. 5641
29:21 waited, and k' silence at my counsel.
31:34 I k' silence, and went not out of the
Ps 17: 4 I have k' me from the paths of the 8104
18:21 For I have k' the ways of the Lord, "
23 and I k' myself from mine iniquity. "
30: 3 hast k' me alive, that I should not
32: 3 When I k' silence, my bones 2790
42: 4 with a multitude that k' holyday. *2287
50:21 hast thou done, and I k' silence; 2790
78:10 They k' not the covenant of God, 8104
56 God, and k' not his testimonies: "
99: 7 they k' his testimonies, and the "
119:22 for I have k' thy testimonies. 5341
55 in the night, and have k' thy law. *8104
56 I had, because I k' thy precepts. 5341
67 but now have I k' thy word. *8104
158 because they k' not thy word. "
167 My soul hath k' thy testimonies; * "
168 I have k' thy precepts and thy * "
Ec 2:10 eyes desired I k' not from them. 680
5:13 riches k' for the owners thereof to 8104
Ca 1: 6 mine own vineyard have I not k'. 5201
Isa 30:29 night when a holy solemnity is k'; 6942
Jer 16:11 me, and have not k' my law; 8104
35:18 your father, and k' all his precepts, "
Eze 5: 7 neither have k' my judgments, 6213
18: 9 and hath k' my judgments, to deal 8104
19 hath k' all my statutes, and hath "
20:21 neither k' my judgments to do them, "
44: 8 ye have not k' the charge of mine "
15 that k' the charge of my sanctuary "
48:11 which have k' my charge, which "
Da 5:19 whom he would he k' alive; and
7:28 but I k' the matter in my heart. 5202
Ho 12:12 a wife, and for a wife he k' sheep. 8104
Am 1:11 and he k' his wrath for ever: "
2: 4 have not k' his commandments, "
Mic 6:16 For the statutes of Omri are k', and "
Mal 2: 9 as ye have not k' my ways, but "
3: 7 ordinances, and have not k' them. "
14 is it that we have k' his ordinance, "
M't 8:33 they that k' them fled, and went *1006
13:35 things which have been k' secret *
14: 6 But when Herod's birthday was k',* 71
19:20 things have I k' from my youth up: *5442
M'r 4:22 neither was any thing k' secret, *1096
9:10 k' that saying with themselves, 2902
Lu 2:19 But Mary k' all these things, and 4933
51 his mother k' all these sayings in 1301
8:29 he was k' bound with chains and 5442
9:36 they k' it close, and told no man *4601
18:21 these have I k' from my youth up. *5442
19:20 I have k' laid up in a napkin: 2192
Joh 2:10 hast k' the good wine until now. 5083
12: 7 of my burying hath she k' this. * "
15:10 even as I have k' my Father's "
20 if they have k' my saying, they will "
17: 6 me; and they have k' thy word. "
12 the world, I k' them in thy name: "
12 that thou gavest me I have k', *5442
18:16 and spake unto her that k' the door, 2377
17 saith the damsel that k' the door "
Ac 5: 2 k' back part of the price, his wife 3557
7:53 of angels, and have not k' it. 5442
9:33 which had k' his bed eight years, 2621
12: 5 Peter therefore was k' in prison: 5083
6 before the door k' the prison. "
15:12 Then all the multitude k' silence, 4601
20:20 how I k' back nothing that was *5288
22: 2 them, they k' the more silence: *3930
20 k' the raiment of them that slew *5442
23:35 to be k' in Herod's judgment hall. "
25: 4 Paul should be k' at Cæsarea, and 5083

Ac 25:21 him to be k' till I might send him to 5083
27:43 Paul, k' them from their purpose;*2967
28:16 himself with a soldier that k' him.*5442
Ro 16:25 k' secret since the world began,
2Co 11: 9 k' myself from being burdensome 5083
32 k' the city of the Damascenes *5432
Ga 3:23 we were k' under the law, shut up "
2Ti 4: 7 my course, I have k' the faith: 5083
Heb 11:28 Through faith he k' the passover, 4160
Jas 5: 4 which is of you k' back by fraud, 650
1Pe 1: 5 k' by the power of God through *5432
2Pe 3: 7 by the same word are k' in store, *2343
Jude 6 which k' not their first estate, 5083
Re 3: 8 strength, and hast k' my word, "
10 hast k' the word of my patience, * "

kerchiefs See also HANDKERCHIEFS.
Eze 13:18 make k' upon the head of every 4556
21 Your k' also will I tear, and deliver "

Keren-happuch (*ke''-ren-hap'-puk*)
Job 42:14 and the name of the third, K'. 7163

Kerioth (*ke'-re-oth*) See also ISCARIOT; KIRIOTH.
Jos 15:25 Hadattah, and K', and Hezron, *7152
Jer 48:24 And upon K', and upon Bozrah, "
41 K' is taken, and the strong holds "

kernels
Nu 6: 4 from the k' even to the husk. 2785

Keros (*ke'-ros*)
Ezr 2:44 The children of K', the children 7026
Ne 7:47 The children of K', the children of "

kettle
1Sa 2:14 he struck it into the pan, or k', or 1731

Keturah (*ket-u'-rah*)
Ge 25: 1 took a wife, and her name was K'.6989
4 All these were the children of K'. "
1Ch 1:32 Now the sons of K', Abraham's "
33 All these are the sons of K'. "

key See also KEYS.
J'g 3:25 they took a k', and opened them: 4668
Isa 22:22 the k' of the house of David will I "
Lu 11:52 taken away the k' of knowledge: 2807
Re 3: 7 true, he that hath the k' of David, "
9: 1 given the k' of the bottomless pit. "
20: 1 having the k' of the bottomless pit "

keys
M't 16:19 the k' of the kingdom of heaven: 2807
Re 1:18 have the k' of hell and of death. "

Kezia (*ke-zi'-ah*)
Job 42:14 and the name of the second, K'; *7103

Keziz (*ke'-ziz*)
Jos 18:21 Beth-hoglah, and the valley of K',*7104

Kibroth-hattaavah (*kib''-roth-hat-ta'-a-vah*)
Nu 11:34 called the name of that place K': 6914
35 journeyed from K' unto Hazeroth; "
33:16 desert of Sinai, and pitched at K'. "
17 And they departed from K', and "
De 9:22 and at K', ye provoked the Lord to "

Kibzaim (*kib-za'-im*) See also JOKMEAM.
Jos 21:22 And K' with her suburbs, and 6911

kick See also KICKED.
1Sa 2:29 Wherefore k' ye at my sacrifice 1163
Ac 9: 5 for thee to k' against the pricks. *2979
26:14 for thee to kick against the pricks. "

kicked
De 32:15 Jeshurun waxed fat, and k': thou 1163

kid See also KIDS.
Ge 37:31 killed a k' of the goats, and dipped*8163
38:17 will send thee a k' from the flock. 1423
20 Judah sent the k' by the hand "
23 I sent this k', and thou hast not "
Ex 23:19 seethe a k' in his mother's milk. "
34:26 seethe a k' in his mother's milk. "
Le 4:23 a k' of the goats, a male without *8163
28 his offering, a k' of the goats, *8166
5: 6 a k' of the goats, for a sin offering;* "
9: 3 a k' of the goats for a sin offering;*8163
23:19 shall sacrifice one k' of the goats "
Nu 7:16, 22, 28, 34, 40, 46, 52, 58, 64, 70, 76, 82 One
k' of the goats for a sin offering: *8163
15:11 for one ram, or for a lamb, or a k'.*5795
24 one k' of the goats for a sin *8163
28:15 one k' of the goats for a sin * "
30 one k' of the goats to make an * "
29: 5 one k' of the goats for a sin * "
11 One k' of the goats for a sin * "
16, 19, 25 one k' of the goats for a sin* "
De 14:21 seethe a k' in his mother's milk. 1423
J'g 6:19 went in, and made ready a k',1423,5795
13:15 have made ready a k' for thee. " "
19 took a k' with a meat offering, " "
14: 6 him as he would have rent a k', 1423
15: 1 visited his wife with a k'; 1423,5795
1Sa 16:20 and a bottle of wine, and a k', 1423
Isa 11: 6 leopard shall lie down with the k';1423
Eze 43:22 offer a k' of the goats without *8163
45:23 a k' of the goats daily for a sin "
Lu 15:29 thou never gavest me a k', that I 2056

kidneys
Ex 29:13, 22 the two k', and the fat that is 3629
Le 3: 4 the two k', and the fat that is on "
4 caul above the liver, with the k', "
10 the two k', and the fat that is upon "
10 caul above the liver, with the k', "
15 the two k', and the fat that is upon "
15 caul above the liver, with the k', "
4: 9 the two k', and the fat that is upon "
9 caul above the liver, with the k', "
7: 4 the two k', and the fat that is on "
4 that is above the liver, with the k'. "
8:16, 25 above the liver, and the two k', "

Le 9:10 the fat, and the k', and the caul 3629
19 the k', and the caul above the liver: "
De 32:14 goats, with the fat of k' of wheat; "
Isa 34: 6 goats, with the fat of the k' of rams: "

Kidron (*kid'-ron*) See also CEDRON.
2Sa 15:23 himself passed over the brook K'. 6939
1Ki 2:37 and passest over the brook K', "
15:13 idol, and burnt it by the brook K'. "
2Ki 23: 4 Jerusalem in the fields of K', "
6 Jerusalem, unto the brook K', "
6 and burned it at the brook K', and "
12 dust of them into the brook K'. "
2Ch 15:16 it, and burnt it at the brook K'. "
29:16 it out abroad into the brook K'. "
30:14 and cast them into the brook K'. "
Jer 31:40 all the fields unto the brook of K', "

kids
Ge 27: 9 thence two good k' of the goats; 1423
16 put the skins of the k' of the goats "
Le 16: 5 two kids of the goats for a sin *8163
Nu 7:87 the k' of the goats for sin offering* "
1Sa 10: 3 Beth-el, one carrying three k', 1423
1Ki 20:27 them like two little flocks of k'; 5795
2Ch 35: 7 of the flock, lambs and k', all 1121,5795
Ca 1: 8 feed thy k' beside the shepherds' 1423

kill See also KILLED; KILLEST; KILLETH; KILLING.
Ge 4:15 any finding him should k' him. *5221
12:12 they will k' me, but they will save 2026
26: 7 place should k' me for Rebekah; "
27:42 himself, purposing to k' thee. "
37:21 and said, Let us not k' him. *5221
Ex 1:16 it be a son, then ye shall k' him: 4191
2:14 intendest thou to k' me, as thou 2026
4:24 met him, and sought to k' him. 4191
12: 6 Israel shall k' it in the evening. 7819
21 your families, and k' the passover. "
16: 3 to k' this whole assembly with 4191
17: 3 to k' us and our children and our "
20:13 Thou shalt not k'. *7523
22: 1 ox, or a sheep, and k' it, or sell it; 2873
24 and I will k' you with the sword; 2026
29:11 thou shalt k' the bullock before 7819
20 Then shalt thou k' the ram, and "
Le 1: 5 shall k' the bullock before the Lord: "
11 he shall k' it on the side of the altar "
3: 2 k' it at the door of the tabernacle "
8, 13 k' it before the tabernacle of the "
4: 4 and k' the bullock before the Lord. "
24 and k' it in the place where they "
24 k' the burnt offering before the Lord: "
33 where they k' the burnt offering. "
7: 2 where they k' the burnt offering "
2 shall they k' the trespass offering: "
14:13 where he shall k' the sin offering "
19 he shall k' the burnt offering: "
25 k' the lamb of the trespass offering, "
50 he shall k' the one of the birds in "
16:11 k' the bullock of the sin offering "
15 he k' the goat of the sin offering, "
20: 4 seed unto Molech, and k' him not: 4191
16 thou shalt k' the woman, and the 2026
22:28 ye shall not k' it and her young 7819
Nu 11:15 thus with me, k' me, I pray thee, 2026
14:15 thou shalt k' all this people as one 4191
16:13 to k' us in the wilderness, except "
22:29 hand, for now would I k' thee. *2026
31:17 k' every male among the little ones, "
17 k' every woman that hath known "
35:27 revenger of blood k' the slayer; *7523
De 4:42 should k' his neighbour unawares, "
5:17 Thou shalt not k'. * "
12:15 k' and eat flesh in all thy gates, 2076
21 shalt k' of thy herd and of thy "
13: 9 thou shalt surely k' him; thine 2026
32:39 I k', and I make alive; I wound, 4191
J'g 13:23 If the Lord were pleased to k' us, "
15:13 but surely we will not k' thee. "
16: 2 when it is day, we shall k' him. 2026
20:31 to smite of the people, and k', 2491
39 smite and k' of the men of Israel "
1Sa 16: 2 if Saul hear it, he will k' me. And 2026
17: 9 fight with me, and to k' me, then 5221
9 prevail against him, and k' him, "
19: 1 that they should k' David. *4191
2 Saul my father seeketh to k' thee: * "
17 Let me go; why should I k' thee? "
24:10 some bade me k' thee: but mine 2026
30:15 God, that thou wilt neither k' me, 4191
2Sa 13:28 Amnon; then k' him, fear not: "
14: 7 that we may k' him, for the life of "
32 any iniquity in me, let him k' me. "
21: 4 shalt thou k' any man in Israel. "
1Ki 11:40 sought therefore to k' Jeroboam. "
12:27 they shall k' me, and go again to 2026
2Ki 5: 7 Am I God, to k' and make alive, 4191
7: 4 and if they k' us, we shall but die. "
11:15 followeth her k' with the sword. "
2Ch 35: 6 So k' the passover, and sanctify 7819
Es 3:13 to k', and to cause to perish, all *2026
Ps 59: *title* watched the house to k' him. 4191
Ec 3: 3 A time to k', and a time to heal; 2026
Isa 14:30 I will k' thy root with famine, 4191
29: 1 to year; let them k' sacrifices. *5362
Eze 34: 3 the wool, ye k' them that are fed: 2076
M't 5:21 of old time, Thou shalt not k'; 5407
21 shall k' shall be in danger of the "
10:28 fear not them which k' the body, 615
28 but are not able to k' the soul: "
17:23 they shall k' him, and the third day "
21:38 let us k' him, and let us seize on his "
23:34 some of them ye shall k' and crucify; "
24: 9 up to be afflicted, and shall k' you: "
26: 4 take Jesus by subtilty, and k' him. "
M'r 3: 4 or to do evil? to save life, or to k'? "

M'r 9:31 hands of men, and they shall k' him; 615
10:19 Do not k', Do not steal, Do not 5407
34 spit upon him, and shall k' him: 615
12: 7 let us k' him, and the inheritance "
Lu 12: 4 not afraid of them that k' the body, "
13:31 depart hence: for Herod will k' thee. "
15:23 hither the fatted calf, and k' it; 2380
18:20 Do not commit adultery, Do not k',5407
20:14 is the heir: come, let us k' him, 615
22: 2 sought how they might k' him; * 337
Joh 5:18 the Jews sought the more to k' him,615
7: 1 because the Jews sought to k' him. "
19 the law? Why go ye about to k' me? "
20 devil: who goeth about to k' thee? "
25 Is not this he, whom they seek to k'? "
8:22 said the Jews, Will he k' himself? "
37 ye seek to k' me, because my word "
40 now ye seek to k' me, a man that "
10:10 not, but for to steal, and to k', and 2380
Ac 7:28 Wilt thou k' me, as thou didst the 337
9:23 the Jews took counsel to k' him: "
24 the gates day and night to k' him. "
10:13 to him, Rise, Peter; k', and eat. 2380
21:31 And as they went about to k' him, 615
23:15 he come near, are ready to k' him.* 337
25: 3 laying wait in the way to k' him. "
26:21 temple, and went about to k' me. 1315
27:42 counsel was to k' the prisoners, 615
Ro 13: 9 Thou shalt not k', Thou shalt not 5407
Jas 2:11 adultery, said also, Do not k'. "
11 yet if thou k', thou art become a * "
4: 2 ye k', and desire to have, and "
Re 2:23 I will k' her children with death; 615
6: 4 that they should k' one another: *4969
8 to k' with sword, and with hunger, 615
9: 5 given that they should not k' them, "
11: 7 shall overcome them, and k' them. "

killed See also KILLEDST.
Ge 37:31 k' a kid of the goats, and dipped 7819
Ex 21:29 him in, but that he hath k' a man 4191
Le 4:15 the bullock shall be k' before the 7819
6:25 place where the burnt offering is k' "
25 sin offering be k' before the Lord: "
8:19 And he k' it; and Moses sprinkled "
14: 5 one of the birds be k' in an earthen* "
6 in the blood of the bird that was k' "
Nu 16:41 Ye have k' the people of the Lord. 4191
31:19 whosoever hath k' any person, 2026
1Sa 24:11 skirt of thy robe, and k' thee not, "
25:11 that I have k' for my shearers, 2873
28:24 hasted, and k' it, and took flour, 2076
2Sa 12: 9 hast k' Uriah the Hittite with the*5221
21:17 smote the Philistine, and k' him. 4191
1Ki 16: 7 Jeroboam; and because he k' him.*5221
10 in and smote him, and k' him, 4191
21:19 Hast thou k', and also taken 7523
2Ki 15:25 k' him, and reigned in his room. *4191
1Ch 19:18 k' Shophach the captain of the host. "
2Ch 18: 2 Ahab k' sheep and oxen for him 3076
25: 3 servants that had k' the king his 5221
29:22 So they k' the bullocks, and the 7819
22 when they had k' the rams, they "
22 they k' also the lambs, and they "
24 And the priests k' them, and they "
30:15 k' the passover on the fourteenth "
35: 1 k' the passover on the fourteenth "
11 they k' the passover, and the "
Ezr 6:20 k' the passover for all the children "
Ps 44:22 for thy sake are we k' all the day 2026
Pr 9: 2 She hath k' her beasts; she hath 2873
La 2:21 anger; thou hast k', and not pitied.* "
M't 16:21 be k', and be raised again the third 615
21:35 beat one, and k' another, and stoned "
22: 4 my fatlings are k', and all things 2380
23:31 of them which k' the prophets. *5407
M'r 6:19 him, and would have k' him; * 615
8:31 and be k', and after three days rise "
9:31 after that he is k', he shall rise the "
12: 5 and him they k', and many others; "
8 they took him, and k' him, and cast "
14:12 when they k' the passover, *2380
Lu 11:47 prophets, and your fathers k' them.615
48 for they indeed k' them, and ye build "
12: 5 after he hath k' hath power to cast "
15:27 thy father hath k' the fatted calf, 2380
30 thou hast k' for him the fatted calf.* "
20:15 out of the vineyard, and k' him. 615
22: 7 when the passover must be k'. *2380
Ac 3:15 And k' the Prince of life, whom God 615
12: 2 he k' James the brother of John 337
16:27 sword, and would have k' himself.* "
23:12 eat nor drink till they had k' Paul. 615
21 eat nor drink till they have k' him:*337
27 and should have been k' of them: * 615
Ro 8:36 For thy sake we are k' all the day 2289
11: 3 Lord, they have k' thy prophets, 615
2Co 6: 9 we live; as chastened, and not k'; 2289
1Th 2:15 Who both k' the Lord Jesus, and 615
Jas 5: 6 have condemned and k' the just; 5407
Re 6:11 should be k' as they were, should 615
9:18 three was the third part of men k', "
20 which were not k' by these plagues "
11: 5 them, he must in this manner be k'. "
13:10 sword must be k' with the sword. "
15 the image of the beast should be k'. "

killedst
Ex 2:14 kill me, as thou k' the Egyptian? 2026
1Sa 24:18 me into thine hand, thou k' me not. "

killest
M't 23:37 Jerusalem,...that k' the prophets,* 615
Lu 13:34 Jerusalem, which k' the prophets,* "

killeth
Le 17: 3 of Israel, that k' an ox, or lamb, 7819
3 camp, or that k' it out of the camp. "

Le 24:17 he that k' any man shall surely *5221
18 that k' a beast shall make it good;*"
21 he that k' a beast, he shall restore "
21 he that k' a man, he shall be put to "
Nu 35:11 which k' any person at unawares. "
15 one that k' any person unawares "
30 Whoso k' any person, the murderer"
De 19: 4 Whoso k' his neighbour ignorantly, "
Jos 20: 3 slayer that k' any person unawares "
9 whosoever k' any...at unawares "
1Sa 2: 6 The Lord k', and maketh alive: 4191
17:25 who k' him, the king will enrich 5221
26 to the man that k' this Philistine, "
27 it be done to the man that k' him. "
Job 5: 2 For wrath k' the foolish man, and 2026
24:14 the light k' the poor and needy, 6991
Pr 21:25 The desire of the slothful k' him; 4191
Isa 66: 3 He that k' an ox is as if he slew 7819
Joh 16: 2 whosoever k' you will think that he 615
2Co 3: 6 letter k', but the spirit giveth life. "
Re 13:10 he that k' with the sword must be* "

killing
J'g 9:24 him in the k' of his brethren. *2026
2Ch 30:17 charge of the k' of the passovers 7821
Isa 22:13 slaying oxen, and k' sheep, eating 7819
Ho 4: 2 By swearing, and lying, and k', 7523
M'r 12:5 others; beating some, and k' some. 615

kin See also KINSFOLK; KINSMAN; KINSWOMAN.
Le 18: 6 any that is near of k' to him, 1320
20:19 for he uncovereth his near k': 7607
21: 2 for his k', that is near unto him, "
25:25 if any of his k' come to redeem it,*7138
49 any that is nigh of k' unto him of 1320
Ru 2:20 man is near of k' unto us, one of our
2Sa 19:42 Because the king is near of k' to us:
M'r 6: 4 country, and among his own k', 4773

Kinah (*ki'-nah*)
Jos 15:22 K', and Dimonah, and Adadah, 7016

kind See also KINDS; MANKIND; WOMANKIND.
Ge 1:11 tree yielding fruit after his k', 4327
12 and herb yielding seed after his k', "
12 seed was in itself, after his k': "
21 forth abundantly, after their k', * "
21 every winged fowl after his k': "
24 the living creature after his k', "
24 beast of the earth after his k': and* "
25 the beast of the earth after his k', "
25 and cattle after their k', and every "
25 creepeth upon the earth after his k': "
6:20 Of fowls after their k', "
20 and of cattle after their k', "
20 thing of the earth after his k', "
7:14 They, and every beast after his k', "
14 all the cattle after their k', and "
14 creepeth upon the earth after his k', "
14 and every fowl after his k', every "
Le 11:14 vulture, and the kite after his k'; "
15 Every raven after his k'; "
16 cuckow, and the hawk after his k', "
19 the stork, the heron after her k', "
22 ye may eat; the locust after his k', "
22 and the bald locust after his k', "
22 and the beetle after his k', "
22 and the grasshopper after his k'. "
29 mouse, and the tortoise after his k', "
19:19 thy cattle gender with a diverse k': "
De 14:13 kite, and the vulture after his k', 4327
14 And every raven after his k', "
15 cuckow, and the hawk after his k', "
18 the stork, and the heron after her k', "
1Ch 28:14 instruments of every k' of service: "
2Ch 10: 7 If thou be k' to this people, and 2896
Ne 13:20 merchants and sellers of all k' of ware
Ec 2: 5 trees in them of all k' of fruits: *
Eze 27:12 of the multitude of all k' of riches;
M't 13:47 the sea, and gathered of every k': 1085
17:21 this k' goeth not out but by prayer* "
M'r 9:29 This k' can come forth by nothing, "
Lu 6:35 he is k' unto the unthankful and 5543
1Co 13: 4 Charity suffereth long, and is k'; 5541
15:39 but there is one k' of flesh of men,*
Eph 4:32 And be ye k' one to another, 5543
Jas 1:18 a k' of firstfruits of his creatures. 5100
3: 7 For every k' of beasts, and of 5449

kindle See also KINDLED; KINDLETH.
Ex 35: 3 shall k' no fire throughout your 1197
Pr 26:21 is a contentious man to k' strife. *2787
Isa 9:18 k' in the thickets of the forest, *3341
10:16 k' a burning like the burning of a*3344
30:33 a stream of brimstone, doth k' it. 1197
43: 2 shall the flame k' upon thee. "
50:11 all ye that k' a fire, that compass 6919
Jer 7:18 wood, and the fathers k' the fire, 1197
17:27 then will I k' a fire in the gates 3341
21:14 I will k' a fire in the forest thereof, "
33:18 and to k' meat offerings, and to do*6999
43:12 k' a fire in the houses of the gods 3341
49:27 k' a fire in the wall of Damascus, "
50:32 and I will k' a fire in his cities, "
Eze 20:47 God; Behold, I will k' a fire in thee, "
24:10 k' the fire, consume the flesh, *1814
Am 1:14 k' a fire in the wall of Rabbah, 3341
Ob 18 they shall k' in them, and devour *1814
Mal 1:10 neither do ye k' fire on mine altar 215

kindled
Ge 30: 2 And Jacob's anger was k' against 2734
39:19 to me; that his wrath was k'. "
Ex 4:14 of the Lord was k' against Moses. "
22: 6 he that k' the fire shall surely 1197
Le 10: 6 burning which the Lord hath k'. 8313
Nu 11: 1 heard it; and his anger was k'; 2734
10 anger of the Lord was k' greatly; "
11:33 wrath of the Lord was k' against "
12: 9 and the anger of the Lord was k' "
Nu 22:22 And God's anger was k' because he 2734
27 Balaam's anger was k', and he "
24:10 Balak's anger was k' against "
25: 3 anger of the Lord was k' against "
32:10 Lord's anger was k' the same time, "
13 Lord's anger was k' against Israel, "
De 6:15 anger of the Lord thy God be k' 2734
7: 4 the anger of the Lord be k' against "
11:17 Lord's wrath be k' against you, "
29:27 anger of the Lord was k' against "
31:17 my anger shall be k' against them "
32:22 For a fire is k' in mine anger, and 6919
Jos 7: 1 anger of the Lord was k' against 2734
23:16 shall the anger of the Lord be k' "
J'g 9:30 the son of Ebed, his anger was k'. "
14:19 And his anger was k', and he went "
1Sa 11: 6 and his anger was k' greatly. "
17:28 Eliab's anger was k' against David, "
20:30 Saul's anger was k' against "
2Sa 6: 7 anger of the Lord was k' against "
12: 5 And David's anger was greatly k' "
22: 9 devoured: coals were k' by it. 1197
13 before him were coals of fire k'. "
24: 1 anger of the Lord was k' against 2734
2Ki 13: 3 anger of the Lord was k' against "
22:13 wrath of the Lord that is k' against 3341
17 my wrath shall be k' against this "
23:26 his anger was k' against Judah, 2734
1Ch 13:10 And the anger of the Lord was k' "
2Ch 25:10 wherefore their anger was greatly k'"
15 anger of the Lord was k' against "
Job 19:11 hath also k' his wrath against me, "
32: 2 Then was k' the wrath of Elihu the "
2 against Job was his wrath k', "
3 his three friends was his wrath k', "
5 three men, then his wrath was k'. "
42: 7 My wrath is k' against thee, and "
Ps 2:12 when his wrath is k' but a little. 1197
18: 8 devoured: coals were k' by it. "
78:21 so a fire was k' against Jacob, and 5400
106:18 a fire was k' in their company; 1197
40 was the wrath of the Lord k' 2734
124: 3 their wrath was k' against us: "
Isa 5:25 is the anger of the Lord k' against "
50:11 and in the sparks that ye have k'. 1197
Jer 11:16 tumult he hath k' fire upon it, 3341
15:14 a fire is k' in mine anger, which 6919
17: 4 ye have k' a fire in mine anger, "
44: 6 was k' in the cities of Judah and 1197
La 4:11 hath k' a fire in Zion, and it hath 3341
Eze 20:48 see that I the Lord have k' it: 1197
Ho 8: 5 mine anger is k' against them: 2734
11: 8 me, my repentings are k' together. 3648
Zec 10: 3 was k' against the shepherds, 2734
Lu 12:49 what will I, if it be already k'? 381
22:55 they had k' a fire in the midst of 681
Ac 28: 2 for they k' a fire, and received us 381

kindleth
Job 41:21 His breath k' coals, and a flame 3857
Isa 44:15 yea, he k' it; and baketh bread; 5400
Jas 3: 5 how great a matter a little fire k'!* 381

kindly
Ge 24:49 if ye will deal k' and truly with 2617
34: 3 and spake k' unto the damsel. 5921,3820
47:29 and deal k' and truly with me; 2617
50:21 and spake k' unto them. 5921,3820
Jos 2:14 will deal k' and truly with thee. 2617
Ru 1: 8 Lord deal k' with you, as ye have "
1Sa 20: 8 shalt deal k' with thy servant; "
2Ki 25:28 he spake k' to him, and set his 2896
Jer 52:32 spake k' unto him, and set his "
Ro 12:10 Be k' affectioned one to another *5387

kindly-affectioned See KINDLY and AFFECTIONED.

kindness See also LOVINGKINDNESS.
Ge 20:13 is thy k' which thou shalt shew 2617
21:23 to the k' that I have done unto thee, "
24:12 shew k' unto my master Abraham. "
14 hast shewed k' unto my master. "
40:14 be well with thee, and shew k', "
Jos 2:12 Lord, since I have shewed you k',* "
12 shew k' unto my father's house, * "
J'g 8:35 shewed they k' to the house of "
Ru 2:20 not left off his k' to the living and "
3:10 shewed more k' in the latter end "
1Sa 15: 6 ye shewed k' to all the children of "
20:14 I live shew me the k' of the Lord, "
15 not cut off thy kindness from my "
2Sa 2: 5 have shewed this k' unto your lord, "
6 the Lord shew k' and truth unto "
6 will requite you this k', because 2896
3: 8 Judah do shew k' this day unto 2617
9: 1 shew him k' for Jonathan's sake? "
3 may shew the k' of God unto him? "
7 shew thee k' for Jonathan thy "
10: 2 will shew k' unto Hanun the son of "
2 as his father shewed k' unto me. "
16:17 Hushai, Is this thy k' to thy friend?"
1Ki 2: 7 shew k' unto the sons of Barzillai "
3: 6 hast kept for him this great k', "
1Ch 19: 2 shew k' unto Hanun the son of "
2 because his father shewed k' to me. "
2Ch 24:22 king remembered not the k' which "
Ne 9:17 slow to anger, and of great k', and* "
Es 2: 9 him, and she obtained k' of him; "
Ps 31:21 hath shewed me his marvellous k' "
117: 2 For his merciful k' is great toward* "
119:76 thy merciful k' be for my comfort,* "
141: 5 smite me; it shall be a k': "
Pr 19:22 The desire of a man is his k': and "
31:26 and in her tongue is the law of k'. "
Isa 54: 8 with everlasting k' will I have "
10 my k' shall not depart from thee, "
Jer 2: 2 remember thee, the k' of thy youth, "
Joe 2:13 slow to anger, and of great k', and* "
Jon 4: 2 slow to anger, and of great k', and *2617
Ac 28: 2 people shewed us no little k': 5363
2Co 6: 6 by k', by the Holy Ghost, by love 5544
Eph 2: 7 in his k' toward us through Christ "
Col 3:12 k', humbleness of mind, meekness, "
Tit 3: 4 after that the k' and love of God "
2Pe 1: 7 to godliness brotherly k'; and to *5360
7 and to brotherly k' charity. * "

kindred See also KINDREDS.
Ge 12: 1 of thy country, and from thy k', 4138
24: 4 go unto my country, and to my k', "
7 from the land of my k', and which* "
38 my father's house, and to my k', 4940
40 take a wife for my son of my k', "
41 oath, when thou comest to my k'; "
31: 3 land of thy fathers, and to thy k'; 4138
13 return unto the land of thy k'. * "
32: 9 unto thy country, and to thy k', "
43: 7 straitly of our state, and of our k', "
Nu 10:30 to mine own land, and to my k'. "
Jos 6:23 and they brought out all her k', 4940
Ru 2: 3 who was of the k' of Elimelech. * "
3: 2 And now is not Boaz of our k', *4130
1Ch 12:29 of Benjamin, the k' of Saul, * 250
Es 2:10 not shewed her people nor her k': 4138
20 Esther had not yet shewed her k' "
8: 6 to see the destruction of my k'? "
Job 32: 2 the Buzite, of the k' of Ram: *4940
Eze 11:15 thy brethren, the men of thy k', 1353
Lu 1:61 thy k' that is called by this name. 4772
Ac 4: 6 were of the k' of the high priest, 1085
7: 3 of thy country, and from thy k', 4772
13 Joseph's k' was made known unto*1085
14 all his k', threescore and fifteen 4772
19 same dealt subtilly with our k', *1085
Re 5: 9 blood out of every k', and tongue, *5443
14: 6 every nation, and k', and tongue, * "

kindreds
1Ch 16:28 unto the Lord, ye k' of the people, 4940
Ps 22:27 all the k' of the nations shall "
96: 7 O ye k' of the people, give unto the "
Ac 3:25 all the k' of the earth be blessed. *3965
Re 1: 7 all k' of the earth shall wail *5443
7: 9 of all nations, and k', and people,* "
11: 9 and k' and tongues and nations * "
13: 7 power was given him over all k', * "

kinds
Ge 8:19 upon the earth, after their k', *4940
2Ch 16:14 odours and divers k' of spices 2177
Jer 15: 3 I will appoint over them four k', 4940
Eze 47:10 fish shall be according to their k', 4327
Da 3: 5 dulcimer, and all k' of musick, ye 2177
7 all k' of musick, all the people, the "
10 and all k' of musick, shall fall down"
15 all k' of musick, ye fall down and "
1Co 12:10 another divers k' of tongues; to 1085
14:10 so many k' of voices in the world, "

kine See also COW.
Ge 32:15 forty k', and ten bulls, twenty she 6510
41: 2 river seven well favoured k' and "
3 seven other k' came up after them "
3 the other k' upon the brink of the "
4 ill favoured and leanfleshed k' "
4 the seven well favoured and fat k'. "
18 came up out of the river seven k', "
19 seven other k' came up after them, "
20 the lean and ill favoured k' did eat "
20 did eat up the first seven fat k': "
26 The seven good k' are seven years; "
27 the seven thin and ill favoured k' "
De 7:13 increase of thy k', and the flocks 504
28: 4, 18 increase of thy k', and the flocks "
51 increase of thy k', or flocks of thy "
32:14 Butter of k', and milk of sheep, 1241
1Sa 6: 7 new cart, and take two milch k', 6510
7 no yoke, and tie the k' to the cart, "
10 and took two milch k', and tied "
12 the k' took the straight way to the "
14 and offered the k' a burnt offering "
2Sa 17:29 sheep, and cheese of k', for David, 1241
Am 4: 1 Hear this word, ye k' of Bashan, 6510

king See also KING'S; KINGS.
Ge 14: 1 k' of Shinar, Arioch k' of Ellasar, 4428
1 k' of Elam, and Tidal k' of nations; "
2 made war with Bera k' of Sodom, "
2 and with Birsha k' of Gomorrah, "
2 Shinab k' of Admah, and Shemeber "
2 k' of Zeboiim, and the k' of Bela, "
8 k' of Sodom, and the k' of Gomorrah, "
8 k' of Admah, and the k' of Zeboiim, "
8 and the k' of Bela (the same is Zoar;)"
9 With Chedorlaomer the k' of Elam, "
9 and with Tidal k' of nations, "
9 k' of Shinar, and Arioch k' of "
17 k' of Sodom went out to meet him "
18 k' of Salem brought forth bread "
21 the k' of Sodom said unto Abram, "
22 Abram said to the k' of Sodom, "
20: 2 k' of Gerar sent, and took Sarah. "
26: 1 k' of the Philistines unto Gerar. "
8 k' of the Philistines looked out of "
36:31 reigned any k' over the children "
40: 1 butler of the k' of Egypt and his "
1 offended their lord the k' of Egypt. "
5 and the baker of the k' of Egypt, "
41:46 stood before Pharaoh k' of Egypt. "
Ex 1: 8 there arose up a new k' over Egypt, "
15 k' of Egypt spake to the Hebrew "
17 the k' of Egypt commanded them, "
18 k' of Egypt called for the midwives, "
2:23 of time that the k' of Egypt died: "
3:18 of Israel, unto the k' of Egypt, "
19 the k' of Egypt will not let you go, "
5: 4 And the k' of Egypt said unto them, "

Ex 6:11 speak unto Pharaoh k' of Egypt, 4428
13 and unto Pharaoh k' of Egypt, to "
27 which spake to Pharaoh k' of Egypt, "
29 thou unto Pharaoh k' of Egypt "
14: 5 it was told the k' of Egypt that the "
8 the heart of Pharaoh k' of Egypt, "
Nu 20:14 from Kadesh unto the k' of Edom, "
21: 1 And when k' Arad the Canaanite, "
21 unto Sihon k' of the Amorites, "
26 city of Sihon the k' of the Amorites, "
26 against the former k' of Moab, "
29 unto Sihon k' of the Amorites. "
33 and Og the k' of Bashan went out "
34 didst unto Sihon k' of the Amorites, "
22: 4 of Zippor was k' of the Moabites "
10 k' of Moab, hath sent unto me, "
23: 7 the k' of Moab hath brought me "
21 the shout of a k' is among them. "
24: 7 his k' shall be higher than Agag, "
32:33 kingdom of Sihon k' of the Amorites, "
33 the kingdom of Og k' of Bashan, "
33:40 k' Arad the Canaanite, which dwelt "
De 1: 4 slain Sihon the k' of the Amorites, "
4 Og the k' of Bashan, which dwelt at "
2:24 Sihon the Amorite, k' of Heshbon, "
26 Sihon k' of Heshbon with words of "
30 Sihon k' of Heshbon would not let "
3: 1 and Og the k' of Bashan came out "
2 didst unto Sihon k' of the Amorites, "
3 hands Og also, the k' of Bashan, "
6 we did unto Sihon k' of Heshbon, "
11 only Og k' of Bashan remained of "
4:46 land of Sihon k' of the Amorites, "
47 and the land of Og k' of Bashan, "
7: 8 the hand of Pharaoh k' of Egypt. "
11: 3 unto Pharaoh the k' of Egypt, "
17:14 I will set a k' over me, like as all "
15 set him k' over thee, whom the Lord "
15 brethren shalt thou set k' over thee: "
28:36 k' which thou shalt set over thee, "
29: 7 Sihon the k' of Heshbon, and Og "
7 and Og the k' of Bashan, came out "
33: 5 he was k' in Jeshurun, when the "
Jos 2: 2 was told the k' of Jericho, saying, "
3 the k' of Jericho sent unto Rahab, "
6: 2 hand Jericho, and the k' thereof, "
8: 1 into thy hand the k' of Ai, and his "
2 thou shalt do to Ai and her k' as "
2 thou didst unto Jericho and her k': "
14 when the k' of Ai saw it, that they "
23 k' of Ai they took alive, and brought "
29 k' of Ai he hanged on a tree until "
9:10 Jordan, to Sihon k' of Heshbon, "
10 and to Og k' of Bashan, which was "
10: 1 k' of Jerusalem had heard how "
1 he had done to Jericho and her k', "
1 so he had done to Ai and her k'; "
3 Adoni-zedec k' of Jerusalem "
3 sent unto Hoham k' of Hebron, "
3 and unto Piram k' of Jarmuth, "
3 and unto Japhia k' of Lachish, "
3 and unto Debir k' of Eglon, saying, "
5 k' of Jerusalem, the k' of Hebron, "
5 k' of Jarmuth, the k' of Lachish, "
5 k' of Eglon, gathered themselves "
23 of the cave, the k' of Jerusalem, "
23 k' of Hebron, the k' of Jarmuth, "
23 k' of Lachish, and the k' of Eglon. "
28 the k' thereof he utterly destroyed, "
28 as he did to the k' of Makkedah "
28 as he did unto the k' of Jericho. "
30 delivered it also, and the k' thereof, "
30 but did unto the k' thereof "
30 as he did unto the k' of Jericho. "
33 Horam k' of Gezer came up to help "
37 and the k' thereof, and all the cities "
39 And he took it, and the k' thereof, "
39 did to Debir, and to the k' thereof; "
39 done also to Libnah, and to her k'. "
11: 1 k' of Hazor had heard those things, "
1 that he sent to Jobab k' of Madon, "
1 Madon, and to the k' of Shimron, "
1 and to the k' of Achshaph, "
10 Hazor, and smote the k' thereof "
12: 2 Sihon k' of the Amorites, who "
4 And the coast of Og k' of Bashan, "
5 the border of Sihon k' of Heshbon. "
9 The k' of Jericho, one; "
9 the k' of Ai, which is beside Beth-el, "
10 The k' of Jerusalem, one; "
10 the k' of Hebron, one; "
11 The k' of Jarmuth, one; "
11 the k' of Lachish, one; "
12 The k' of Eglon, one; "
12 the k' of Gezer, one; "
13 The k' of Debir, one; "
13 the k' of Geder, one; "
14 The k' of Hormah, one; "
14 the k' of Arad, one; "
15 The k' of Libnah, one; "
15 the k' of Adullam, one; "
16 The k' of Makkedah, one; "
16 the k' of Beth-el, one; "
17 The k' of Tappuah, one; "
17 the k' of Hepher, one; "
18 The k' of Aphek, one; "
18 the k' of Lasharon, one; "
19 The k' of Madon, one; "
19 the k' of Hazor, one; "
20 The k' of Shimron-meron, one; "
20 the k' of Achshaph, one; "
21 The k' of Taanach, one; "
21 the k' of Megiddo, one; "
22 The k' of Kedesh, one; "
22 the k' of Jokneam of Carmel, one; "
23 The k' of Dor in the coast of Dor, "

Jos 12:23 the k' of the nations of Gilgal, one; 4428
24 The k' of Tirzah, one: all the kings "
13:10 cities of Sihon k' of the Amorites, "
21 kingdom of Sihon k' of the Amorites, "
27 the kingdom of Sihon k' of Heshbon, "
30 all the kingdom of Og k' of Bashan, "
24: 9 Balak the son of Zippor, k' of Moab, "
J'g 3: 8 the hand of ... k' of Mesopotamia: "
10 k' of Mesopotamia into his hand; "
12 strengthened Eglon the k' of Moab "
14 of Israel served the k' of Moab "
15 present unto Eglon the k' of Moab. "
17 the present unto Eglon k' of Moab: "
19 a secret errand unto thee, O k': "
4: 2 into the hand of Jabin k' of Canaan, "
17 between Jabin the k' of Hazor and "
23 on that day Jabin the k' of Canaan "
24 against Jabin the k' of Canaan, "
24 had destroyed Jabin k' of Canaan. "
8:18 one resembled the children of a k'. "
9: 6 and made Abimelech k', "
8 on a time to anoint a k' unto them; "
15 If in truth ye anoint me k' over you, "
16 that ye have made Abimelech k', 4427
18 made...k' over the men of Shechem, "
11:12 sent messengers unto the k' of the 4428
13 the k' of the children of Ammon "
14 sent messengers again unto the k' "
17 messengers unto the k' of Edom, "
17 the k' of Edom would not hearken "
17 they sent unto the k' of Moab: "
19 Sihon k' of the Amorites, the k' of "
25 Balak the son of Zippor, k' of Moab? "
28 the k' of the children of Ammon, "
17: 6 days there was no k' in Israel, "
18: 1 days there was no k' in Israel: "
19: 1 when there was no k' in Israel, "
21:25 days there was no k' in Israel: "
1Sa 2:10 he shall give strength unto his k', "
8: 5 make us a k' to judge us like all "
6 they said, Give us a k' to judge us. "
9 manner of the k' that shall reign "
10 the people that asked of him a k'. "
11 manner of the k' that shall reign "
18 your k' which ye shall have chosen "
19 Nay; but we will have a k' over us; "
20 that our k' may judge us, and go "
22 voice, and make them a k'. "
10:19 unto him, Nay, but set a k' over us. "
24 shouted, and said, God save the k'. "
11:15 they made Saul k' before the Lord 4427
12: 1 and have made a k' over you. 4428
2 behold, the k' walketh before you: "
9 into the hand of the k' of Moab, "
12 the k' of the children of Ammon "
12 Nay; but a k' shall reign over us: "
12 the Lord your God was your k'. "
13 behold the k' whom ye have chosen, "
13 the Lord hath set a k' over you. "
14 also the k' that reigneth over you "
17 sight of the Lord, in asking you a k'. "
19 all our sins this evil, to ask us a k'. "
25 be consumed, both ye and your k'. "
15: 1 anoint thee to be k' over his people, "
8 took Agag the k' of the Amalekites "
11 that I have set up Saul to be k': "
17 Lord anointed thee k' over Israel? "
20 brought Agag the k' of Amalek, "
23 also rejected thee from being k'. "
26 thee from being k' over Israel. "
32 me Agag the k' of the Amalekites. "
35 he had made Saul k' over Israel. 4427
16: 1 provided me a k' among his sons. 4428
17:25 k' will enrich him with great riches, "
55 thy soul liveth, O k', I cannot tell. "
56 the k' said, Enquire thou whose son "
18: 6 and dancing, to meet k' Saul, "
18 I should be son in law to the k'? "
22 Behold, the k' hath delight in thee, "
25 The k' desireth not any dowry, "
27 they gave them in full tale to the k', "
19: 4 not the k' sin against his servant, "
20: 5 not fail to sit with the k' at meat: "
24 the k' sat him down to eat meat. "
25 the k' sat upon his seat, as at other "
21: 2 k' hath commanded me a business, "
10 and went to Achish the k' of Gath. "
11 Is not this David the k' of the land? "
12 sore afraid of Achish the k' of Gath. "
22: 3 and he said unto the k' of Moab, "
4 brought them before the k' of Moab: "
11 k' sent to call Ahimelech the priest, "
11 and they came all of them to the k'. "
14 Then Ahimelech answered the k', "
15 let not the k' impute any thing unto "
16 the k' said, Thou shalt surely die, "
17 k' said unto the footmen that stood "
17 the servants of the k' would not put "
18 k' said to Doeg, Turn thou, and fall "
23:17 and thou shalt be k' over Israel, 4427
20 therefore, O k', come down 4428
24: 8 after Saul, saying, My lord the k'. "
14 After whom is the k' of Israel come "
20 well that thou shalt surely be k', "
25:36 in his house, like the feast of a k'; "
26:14 Who art thou that criest to the k'? "
15 hast thou not kept thy lord the k'? "
15 people in to destroy the k' thy lord. "
17 said, It is my voice, my lord, O k'. "
19 let my lord the k' hear the words of "
20 the k' of Israel is come out to seek "
27: 2 Achish, the son of Maoch, k' of Gath. "
28:13 the k' said unto her, Be not afraid: "
29: 3 the servant of Saul the k' of Israel, "
8 the enemies of my lord the k'? "
2Sa 2: 4 David k' over the house of Judah. "

2Sa 2: 7 of Judah have anointed me k' over 4428
9 And made him k' over Gilead, 4427
11 time that David was k' in Hebron 4428
3: 3 daughter of Talmai k' of Geshur; "
17 for David in times past to be k' over "
21 gather all Israel unto my lord the k', "
23 Abner the son of Ner came to the k', "
24 Then Joab came to the k', and said, "
31 k' David himself followed the bier. "
32 the k' lifted up his voice, and wept "
33 the k' lamented over Abner, and "
36 whatsoever the k' did pleased all "
37 it was not of the k' to slay Abner "
38 And the k' said unto his servants, "
39 this day weak, though anointed k', "
4: 8 and said to the k', Behold the head "
8 Lord hath avenged my lord the k' "
5: 2 when Saul was k' over us, thou wast "
3 the elders of Israel came to the k' "
3 k' David made a league with them "
3 they anointed David k' over Israel. "
6 k' and his men went to Jerusalem "
11 Hiram k' of Tyre sent messengers "
12 had established him k' over Israel, "
17 had anointed David k' over Israel, "
6:12 And it was told k' David, saying, "
16 saw k' David leaping and dancing "
20 How glorious was the k' of Israel "
7: 1 pass, when the k' sat in his house, "
2 the k' said unto Nathan the prophet, "
3 And Nathan said to the k', Go, do all "
18 Then went k' David in, and sat "
8: 3 the son of Rehob, k' of Zobah, "
5 to succour Hadadezer k' of Zobah, "
8 k' David took...much brass. "
9 When Toi k' of Hamath heard that "
10 sent Joram his son unto k' David, "
11 k' David did dedicate unto the Lord, "
12 son of Rehob, k' of Zobah. "
9: 2 the k' said unto him, Art thou Ziba? "
3 And the k' said, Is there not yet any "
3 Ziba said unto the k', Jonathan hath "
4 the k' said unto him, Where is he? "
4 Ziba said unto the k', Behold, he is "
5 Then k' David sent, and fetched "
9 Then the k' called to Ziba, Saul's "
11 said Ziba unto the k', According "
11 my lord the k' hath commanded his "
11 As for Mephibosheth, said the k', "
10: 1 k' of the children of Ammon died, "
5 k' said, Tarry at Jericho until your "
6 and of k' Maacah a thousand men, "
11: 8 him a mess of meat from the k'. "
19 the matters of the war unto the k', "
12: 7 I anointed thee k' over Israel, and I "
13: 6 when the k' was come to see him, "
6 unto the k', I pray thee, let Tamar "
13 I pray thee, speak unto the k'; "
21 when k' David heard of all these "
24 Absalom came to the k', and said, "
24 let the k', I beseech thee, and his "
25 the k' said to Absalom, Nay, my son, "
26 the k' said unto him, Why should "
31 the k' arose, and tare his garments, "
33 let not my lord the k' take the thing "
35 Jonadab said unto the k', Behold, "
36 the k' also and all his servants wept "
37 the son of Ammihud, k' of Geshur. "
39 soul of k' David longed to go forth "
14: 3 come to the k', and speak on this "
4 woman of Tekoah spake to the k', "
4 did obeisance, and said, Help, O k'. "
5 the k' said unto her, What aileth "
8 the k' said unto the woman, Go to "
9 woman of Tekoah said unto the k', "
9 My lord, O k', the iniquity be on me, "
9 the k' and his throne be guiltless. "
10 the k' said, Whosoever saith ought "
11 the k' remember the Lord thy God, "
12 speak one word unto my lord the k'. "
13 the k' doth speak this thing as one "
13 k' doth not fetch home again his "
15 of this thing unto my lord the k', "
15 said, I will now speak unto the k'; "
16 For the k' will hear, to deliver his "
17 The word of my lord the k' shall "
17 so is my lord the k' to discern good "
18 the k' answered and said unto the "
18 said, Let my lord the k' now speak. "
19 the k' said, Is not the hand of Joab "
19 As thy soul liveth, my lord the k', "
19 that my lord the k' hath spoken: "
21 the k' said unto Joab, Behold now, "
22 bowed himself, and thanked the k': "
22 grace in thy sight, my lord, O k', "
22 k' hath fulfilled the request of his "
24 the k' said, Let him turn to his own "
29 Joab, to have sent him to the k'; "
32 that I may send thee to the k', to "
33 Joab came to the k', and told him: "
33 came to the k', and bowed himself "
33 face to the ground before the k': "
33 and the k' kissed Absalom. "
15: 2 came to the k' for judgment, "
3 man deputed of the k' to hear thee. "
6 that came to the k' for judgment: "
7 Absalom said unto the k', I pray "
9 the k' said unto him, Go in peace. "
15 the king's servants said unto the k', "
15 my lord the k' shall appoint. "
16 And the k' went forth, and all his "
16 the k' left ten women, which were "
17 the k' went forth, and all the people "
18 from Gath, passed on before the k'. "
19 Then said the k' to Ittai the Gittite, "
19 thy place, and abide with the k': "

2Sa 15: 21 And Ittai answered the k', and said 4428
21 liveth, and as my lord the k' liveth, "
21 what place my lord the k' shall be, "
23 the k' also himself passed over the "
25 the k' said unto Zadok, Carry back "
27 k' said also unto Zadok the priest, "
34 Absalom, I will be thy servant, O k': "
16: 2 k' said unto Ziba, What meanest "
3 And the k' said, And where is thy "
3 And Ziba said unto the k', Behold, he "
4 Then said the k' to Ziba, Behold, "
4 grace in thy sight, my lord, O k'. "
5 when k' David came to Bahurim, "
6 and at all the servants of k' David: "
9 of Zeruiah unto the k', Why should "
9 this dead dog curse my lord the k'? "
10 And the k' said, What have I to do "
14 And the k', and all the people that "
16 God save the k', God save the k'. "
17: 2 flee; and I will smite the k' only: "
16 lest the k' be swallowed up, and all "
17 and they went and told k' David. "
21 well, and went and told k' David, "
18: 2 the k' said unto the people, I will "
4 k' said unto them, What seemeth "
4 the k' stood by the gate side, and "
5 And the k' commanded Joab and "
5 the k' gave all the captains charge "
12 in our hearing the k' charged thee "
13 there is no matter hid from the k', "
19 now run, and bear the k' tidings, "
21 Go tell the k' what thou hast seen. "
25 watchman cried, and told the k'. "
26 k' said, He also bringeth tidings. "
27 the k' said, He is a good man, and "
28 and said unto the k', All is well. "
28 earth upon his face before the k', "
28 their hand against my lord the k'. "
29 And the k' said, Is the young man "
30 the k' said unto him, Turn aside, "
31 Cushi said, Tidings, my lord the k': "
32 the k' said unto Cushi, Is the young "
32 enemies of my lord the k', and all "
33 the k' was much moved, and went "
19: 1 the k' weepeth and mourneth for "
2 how the k' was grieved for his son. "
4 But the k' covered his face, "
4 and the k' cried with a loud voice, "
5 Joab came into the house to the k', "
8 the k' arose, and sat in the gate. "
8 Behold, the k' doth sit in the gate. "
8 all the people came before the k': "
9 The k' saved us out of the hand of "
10 not a word of bringing the k' back? "
11 And k' David sent to Zadok and to "
11 to bring the k' back to his house? "
11 speech of...Israel is come to the k', "
12 are ye the last to bring back the k'? "
14 they sent this word unto the k', "
15 So the k' returned, and came to "
15 go to meet the k', to conduct the k' "
16 the men of Judah to meet k' David. "
17 they went over Jordan before the k'. "
18 son of Gera fell down before the k', "
19 said unto the k', Let not my lord "
19 lord the k' went out of Jerusalem, "
19 the k' should take it to his heart. "
20 to go down to meet my lord the k'. "
22 that I am this day k' over Israel? "
23 k' said unto Shimei, Thou shalt not "
23 die. And the k' sware unto him. "
24 of Saul came down to meet the k', "
24 from the day the k' departed until "
25 come to Jerusalem to meet the k', "
25 the k' said unto him, Wherefore "
26 lord, O k', my servant deceived me: "
26 may ride thereon, and go to the k'; "
27 thy servant unto my lord the k'; "
27 my lord the k' is as an angel of God: "
28 dead men before my lord the k': "
28 I yet to cry any more unto the k'? "
29 the k' said unto him, Why speakest "
30 And Mephibosheth said unto the k', "
30 lord the k' is come again in peace "
31 and went over Jordan with the k', "
32 had provided the k' of sustenance "
33 the k' said unto Barzillai, Come "
34 Barzillai said unto the k', How long "
34 go up with the k' unto Jerusalem? "
35 yet a burden unto my lord the k'? "
36 little way over Jordan with the k': "
36 why should the k' recompense it me "
37 let him go over with my lord the k'; "
38 the k' answered, Chimham shall go "
39 And when the k' was come over, "
39 the k' kissed Barzillai, and blessed "
40 Then the k' went on to Gilgal, and "
40 people of Judah conducted the k', "
41 all the men of Israel came to the k', "
41 and said unto the k', Why have our "
41 brought the k', and his household, "
42 Because the k' is near of kin to us: "
43 said, We have ten parts in the k', "
43 first had in bringing back our k'? "
20: 2 men of Judah clave unto their k', "
3 and the k' took the ten women his "
4 said the k' to Amasa, Assemble me "
21 lifted up his hand against the k', "
22 returned to Jerusalem unto the k'. "
21: 2 the k' called the Gibeonites, and "
5 they answered the k', The man that "
6 And the k' said, I will give them. "
7 the k' spared Mephibosheth, the son "
8 the k' took the two sons of Rizpah "
14 all that the k' commanded. "
22: 51 is the tower of salvation for his k': "

2Sa 24: 2 the k' said to Joab the captain of 4428
3 Joab said unto the k', Now the Lord "
3 eyes of my lord the k' may see it: "
3 doth my lord the k' delight in this "
4 out from the presence of the k', "
9 number of the people unto the k': "
20 Araunah looked, and saw the k' and "
20 bowed himself before the k' on his "
21 lord the k' come to his servant? "
22 Let my lord the k' take and offer up "
23 Araunah, as a k', give unto the k'. "
23 Araunah said unto the k', The Lord "
24 And the k' said unto Araunah, Nay; "
1Ki 1: 1 Now k' David was old and stricken "
2 for my lord the k' a young virgin: "
2 let her stand before the k', and let "
2 that my lord the k' may get heat. "
3 and brought her to the k'. "
4 was very fair, and cherished the k', "
4 to him: but the k' knew her not. "
5 himself, saying, I will be k': 4427
13 get thee in unto k' David, and say 4428
13 Didst not thou, my lord, O k', swear "
14 thou yet talkest there with the k', "
15 in unto the k' into the chamber: "
15 and the k' was very old; and "
15 Shunammite ministered unto the k'. "
16 and did obeisance unto the k'. "
16 the k' said, What wouldest thou? "
18 my lord the k', thou knowest it not: "
19 hath called all the sons of the k', "
20 O k', the eyes of Israel are upon "
20 on the throne of my lord the k' after "
21 the k' shall sleep with his fathers, "
22 while she yet talked with the k', "
23 told the k', saying, Behold Nathan "
23 when he was come in before the k', "
23 he bowed himself before the k' with "
24 said, My lord, O k', hast thou said, "
25 him, and say, God save k' Adonijah. "
27 Is this thing done by my lord the k', "
27 throne of my lord the k' after him? "
28 k' David answered and said, Call "
28 presence, and stood before the k'. "
29 And the k' sware, and said, As the "
31 earth, and did reverence to the k', "
31 Let my lord k' David live for ever. "
32 k' David said, Call me Zadok the "
32 And they came before the k'. "
33 The k' also said unto them, Take "
34 anoint him there k' over Israel: "
34 and say, God save k' Solomon. "
35 he shall be k' in my stead: for I 4427
36 son of Jehoiada answered the k', 4428
36 Lord God of my lord the k' say so "
37 Lord hath been with my lord the k', "
37 than the throne of my lord k' David. "
38 to ride upon k' David's mule, "
39 people said, God save k' Solomon. "
43 lord k' David hath made Solomon "
43 David hath made Solomon k'. 4427
44 the k' hath sent with him Zadok 4428
45 have anointed him k' in Gihon: "
47 came to bless our lord k' David, "
47 the k' bowed himself upon the bed. "
48 And also thus said the k', Blessed "
51 Adonijah feareth k' Solomon: "
51 k' Solomon swear unto me to day "
53 k' Solomon sent, and they brought "
53 and bowed himself to k' Solomon: "
2: 17 I pray thee, unto Solomon the k', "
18 I will speak for thee unto the k'. "
19 therefore went unto k' Solomon, "
19 And the k' rose up to meet her, and "
20 the k' said unto her, Ask on, my "
22 And k' Solomon answered and said "
23 Then k' Solomon sware by the Lord, "
25 And k' Solomon sent by the hand of "
26 unto Abiathar the priest said the k', "
29 it was told k' Solomon that Joab "
30 him, Thus saith the k', Come forth. "
30 Benaiah brought the k' word again, "
31 the k' said unto him, Do as he hath "
35 k' put Benaiah the son of Jehoiada "
35 the k' put in the room of Abiathar. "
36 the k' sent and called for Shimei, "
38 Shimei said unto the k', The saying "
38 as my lord the k' hath said, so will "
39 Achish son of Maachah k' of Gath. "
42 the k' sent and called for Shimei, "
44 The k' said moreover to Shimei, "
45 k' Solomon shall be blessed, and "
46 the k' commanded Benaiah the son "
3: 1 affinity with Pharaoh k' of Egypt, "
4 the k' went to Gibeon to sacrifice "
7 hast made thy servant k' instead of 4427
16 that were harlots, unto the k', 4428
22 son. Thus they spake before the k'. "
23 Then said the k', The one saith, "
24 And the k' said, Bring me a sword. "
24 they brought a sword before the k'. "
25 the k' said, Divide the living child "
26 the living child was unto the k', "
27 the k' answered and said, Give her "
28 judgment which the k' had judged; "
28 and they feared the k': for they saw "
4: 1 k' Solomon was k' over all Israel. "
7 provided victuals for the k' and his "
19 in the country of Sihon k' of the "
19 Amorites, and of Og k' of Bashan; "
27 provided victual for k' Solomon, "
27 that came unto k' Solomon's table, "
5: 1 Hiram k' of Tyre sent his servants "
1 anointed him k' in the room of his "
13 k' Solomon raised a levy out of all "
17 k' commanded, and they brought "

1Ki 6: 2 house which k' Solomon built for 4428
7: 13 k' Solomon sent and fetched Hiram "
14 he came to k' Solomon, and wrought "
40 work that he made k' Solomon for "
45 which Hiram made to k' Solomon "
46 plain of Jordan did the k' cast them, "
51 work that k' Solomon made for the "
8: 1 unto k' Solomon in Jerusalem, "
2 themselves unto k' Solomon at the "
5 And k' Solomon, and all the "
14 the k' turned his face about, and "
62 And the k', and all Israel with him, "
63 the k' and all the children of Israel "
64 did the k' hallow the middle of the "
66 they blessed the k', and went unto "
9: 11 Hiram the k' of Tyre had furnished "
11 k' Solomon gave Hiram twenty "
14 sent to the k' sixscore talents of "
15 the levy which k' Solomon raised; "
16 Pharaoh k' of Egypt had gone up, "
26 k' Solomon made a navy of ships "
28 and brought it to k' Solomon. "
10: 3 was not any thing hid from the k', "
6 And she said to the k', It was a true "
9 for ever, therefore made he thee k', "
10 And she gave the k' an hundred and "
10 queen of Sheba gave to k' Solomon. "
12 k' made of the almug trees pillars "
13 k' Solomon gave unto the queen of "
16 And k' Solomon made two hundred "
17 the k' put them in the house of the "
18 the k' made a great throne of ivory, "
21 all k' Solomon's drinking vessels "
22 k' had at sea a navy of Tharshish "
23 k' Solomon exceeded all the kings "
26 and with the k' at Jerusalem. "
27 k' made silver to be in Jerusalem as "
11: 1 But k' Solomon loved many strange "
18 Egypt, unto Pharaoh k' of Egypt; "
23 his lord Hadadezer k' of Zobah: "
26 he lifted up his hand against the k'. "
27 he lifted up his hand against the k': "
37 and shalt be k' over Israel. "
40 Egypt, unto Shishak k' of Egypt, "
12: 1 come to Shechem to make him k'. 4427
2 from the presence of k' Solomon, 4428
6 k' Rehoboam consulted with the old "
12 third day, as the k' had appointed, "
13 the k' answered the people roughly, "
15 k' hearkened not unto the people; "
16 the k' hearkened not unto them, "
16 the people answered the k', saying, "
18 k' Rehoboam sent Adoram, who "
18 k' Rehoboam made speed to get him "
20 and made him k' over all Israel: 4427
23 the son of Solomon, k' of Judah, 4428
27 even unto Rehoboam k' of Judah, "
27 go again to Rehoboam k' of Judah. "
28 Whereupon the k' took counsel, "
13: 4 when k' Jeroboam heard the saying "
6 k' answered and said unto the man "
7 the k' said unto the man of God, "
8 the man of God said unto the k', If "
11 which he had spoken unto the k', "
14: 2 I should be k' over this people. "
14 Lord shall raise him up a k' over "
25 that Shishak k' of Egypt came up "
27 k' Rehoboam made in their stead "
28 k' went into the house of the Lord, "
15: 1 eighteenth year of k' Jeroboam "
9 year of Jeroboam k' of Israel "
16 between Asa and Baasha k' of Israel "
17 And Baasha k' of Israel went up "
17 out or come in to Asa k' of Judah. "
18 k' Asa sent them to Ben-hadad, "
18 the son of Hezion, k' of Syria, "
19 thy league with Baasha k' of Israel, "
20 Ben-hadad hearkened unto k' Asa, "
22 Then k' Asa made a proclamation "
22 k' Asa built with them Geba of "
25 the second year of Asa k' of Judah, "
28 the third year of Asa k' of Judah "
32 between Asa and Baasha k' of Israel "
33 the third year of Asa k' of Judah "
16: 8 and sixth year of Asa k' of Judah "
10 seventh year of Asa k' of Judah, "
15 seventh year of Asa k' of Judah "
16 and hath also slain the k': "
16 Israel made Omri...k' over Israel 4427
21 the son of Ginath, to make him k'; "
23 and first year of Asa k' of Judah 4428
29 and eighth year of Asa k' of Judah "
31 of Ethbaal k' of the Zidonians, "
19: 15 anoint Hazael to be k' over Syria: "
16 thou anoint to be k' over Israel: "
20: 1 the k' of Syria gathered all his hosts "
2 to Ahab k' of Israel into the city, "
4 the k' of Israel answered and said, "
4 My lord, O k', according to thy "
7 the k' of Israel called all the elders "
9 Tell my lord the k', All that thou "
11 the k' of Israel answered and said, "
13 a prophet unto Ahab k' of Israel, "
20 the k' of Syria escaped on an horse "
21 the k' of Israel went out, and smote "
22 the prophet came to the k' of Israel, "
22 year the k' of Syria will come up "
23 servants of the k' of Syria said unto "
28 and spake unto the k' of Israel, "
31 and go out to the k' of Israel: "
32 heads, and came to the k' of Israel, "
38 and waited for the k' by the way, "
39 And as the k' passed by, he cried "
39 he cried unto the k': and he said, "
40 k' of Israel said unto him, So shall "
41 k' of Israel discerned him that he "

1Ki 20:43 the k' of Israel went to his house 4428
21: 1 the palace of Ahab k' of Samaria. "
10 didst blaspheme God and the k'. "
13 did blaspheme God and the k'. "
18 go down to meet Ahab k' of Israel, "
22: 2 k' of Judah came down to the k' of "
3 k' of Israel said unto his servants, "
3 out of the hand of the k' of Syria? "
4 Jehoshaphat said to the k' of Israel, "
5 said unto the k' of Israel, I enquire, "
6 k' of Israel gathered the prophets "
6 deliver it into the hand of the k'. "
8 k' of Israel said unto Jehoshaphat, "
8 said, Let not the k' say so. "
9 the k' of Israel called an officer, "
10 And the k' of Israel and "
10 Jehoshaphat the k' of Judah sat "
13 prophets declare good unto the k' "
15 came to the k'. And the k' said "
15 deliver it into the hand of the k'. "
16 the k' said unto him, How many "
18 k' of Israel said unto Jehoshaphat, "
26 And the k' of Israel said, Take "
27 Thus saith the k', Put this fellow "
29 So the k' of Israel and "
29 Jehoshaphat the k' of Judah went "
30 k' of Israel said unto Jehoshaphat, "
30 k' of Israel disguised himself, and "
31 k' of Syria commanded his thirty "
31 save only with the k' of Israel. "
32 said, Surely it is the k' of Israel. "
33 that it was not the k' of Israel, that "
34 smote the k' of Israel between the "
35 the k' was stayed up in his chariot "
37 the k' died, and was brought to "
37 and they buried the k' in Samaria. "
41 the fourth year of Ahab k' of Israel. "
44 made peace with the k' of Israel. "
47 no k' in Edom: a deputy was k'. "
51 year of Jehoshaphat k' of Judah, "
2Ki 1: 3 messengers of the k' of Samaria, "
6 again unto the k' that sent you, "
9 Then the k' sent unto him a captain "
9 Thou man of God, the k' hath said, "
11 the k' said, Come down quickly. "
15 went down with him unto the k'. "
17 the son of Jehoshaphat k' of Judah; "
3: 1 year of Jehoshaphat k' of Judah, "
4 k' of Moab was a sheepmaster, "
4 rendered unto the k' of Israel an "
5 Ahab was dead, that the k' of Moab "
5 rebelled against the k' of Israel. "
6 k' Jehoram went out of Samaria "
7 to Jehoshaphat the k' of Judah, "
7 k' of Moab hath rebelled against "
9 the k' of Israel went, and the k' of "
9 the k' of Edom: and they fetched "
10 k' of Israel said, Alas! that the "
11 one of the k' of Israel's servants "
12 the k' of Israel and Jehoshaphat "
12 the k' of Edom went down to him. "
13 Elisha said unto the k' of Israel, "
13 And the k' of Israel said unto him, "
14 of Jehoshaphat the k' of Judah, "
26 the k' of Moab saw that the battle "
26 through even unto the k' of Edom: "
4:13 thou be spoken for to the k', "
5: 1 of the host of the k' of Syria, "
5 And the k' of Syria said, Go to, go, "
5 send a letter unto the k' of Israel. "
6 the letter to the k' of Israel, saying, "
7 when the k' of Israel had read the "
8 the k' of Israel had rent his clothes, "
8 that he sent to the k', saying, "
6: 8 k' of Syria warred against Israel, "
9 of God sent unto the k' of Israel, "
10 the k' of Israel sent to the place "
11 the heart of the k' of Syria was sore "
11 which of us is for the k' of Israel? "
12 servants said, None, my lord, O k': "
12 telleth the k' of Israel the words "
21 the k' of Israel said unto Elisha, "
24 k' of Syria gathered all his host, "
26 as the k' of Israel was passing by "
26 him, saying, Help, my lord, O k'. "
28 the k' said unto her, What aileth "
30 when the k' heard the words of the "
32 the k' sent a man from before him: "
7: 2 lord on whose hand the k' leaned 4428
6 the k' of Israel hath hired against "
12 the k' arose in the night, and said "
14 the k' sent after the host of the "
15 returned, and told the k'. "
17 the k' appointed the lord on whose "
17 when the k' came down to him. "
18 man of God had spoken to the k', "
8: 3 to cry unto the k' for her house "
4 And the k' talked with Gehazi the "
5 telling the k' how he had restored "
5 cried to the k' for her house and for "
5 My lord, O k', this is the woman, "
6 And when the k' asked the woman, "
6 the k' appointed unto her a certain "
7 Ben-hadad the k' of Syria was sick; "
8 the k' said unto Hazael, Take a "
9 k' of Syria hath sent me to thee, "
13 that thou shalt be k' over Syria. "
16 Joram the son of Ahab k' of Israel, "
16 Jehoshaphat being...k' of Judah, "
16 Jehoram k' of Judah began to reign. "
20 and made a k' over themselves. "
25 Joram the son of Ahab k' of Israel, "
25 the son of Jehoram k' of Judah "
26 the daughter of Omri k' of Israel. "
28 k' of Syria in Ramoth-gilead; "
29 k' Joram went back to be healed in "

2Ki 8:29 fought against Hazael k' of Syria. 4428
29 the son of Jehoshaphat k' of Judah "
9: 3 I have anointed thee k' over Israel. "
6 I have anointed thee k' over the "
12 I have anointed thee k' over Israel. "
13 with trumpets, saying, Jehu is k'. 4427
14 because of Hazael k' of Syria. 4428
15 k' Joram was returned to be healed "
15 he fought with Hazael k' of Syria.) "
16 k' of Judah was come down to see "
18, 19 Thus saith the k', Is it peace? "
21 k' of Israel and Ahaziah k' of Judah "
27 Ahaziah the k' of Judah saw this, "
10: 5 we will not make any k': do thou 4427
13 brethren of Ahaziah k' of Judah, 4428
13 children of the k' and the children "
11: 2 the daughter of k' Joram, sister of "
7 the house of the Lord about the k'. "
8 shall compass the k' round about, "
8 be ye with the k' as he goeth out "
10 give k' David's spears and shields, "
11 in his hand, round about the k', "
12 and they made him k', and anointed 4427
12 hands, and said, God save the k'. 4428
14 the k' stood by a pillar, as the "
14 and the trumpeters by the k', and "
17 between the Lord and the k' and "
17 between the k' also and the people. "
19 they brought down the k' from the "
12: 6 twentieth year of k' Jehoash the "
7 k' Jehoash called for Jehoiada the "
17 Hazael k' of Syria went up, and "
18 Jehoash k' of Judah took all the "
18 and sent it to Hazael k' of Syria: "
13: 1 the son of Ahaziah k' of Judah "
3 into the hand of Hazael k' of Syria, "
4 the k' of Syria oppressed them. "
7 the k' of Syria had destroyed them, "
10 seventh year of Joash k' of Judah "
12 against Amaziah k' of Judah, "
14 Joash the k' of Israel came down "
16 said to the k' of Israel, Put thine "
18 he said unto the k' of Israel, Smite "
22 Hazael k' of Syria oppressed Israel "
24 So Hazael k' of Syria died; and "
14: 1 son of Jehoahaz k' of Israel reigned "
1 the son of Joash k' of Judah. "
5 which had slain the k' his father. "
8 Jehoahaz son of Jehu, k' of Israel, "
9 And Jehoash the k' of Israel sent "
9 sent to Amaziah k' of Judah, saying, "
11 Jehoash k' of Israel went up; "
11 Amaziah k' of Judah looked one "
13 And Jehoash k' of Israel took "
13 Amaziah k' of Judah, the son of "
15 fought with Amaziah k' of Judah, "
17 the son of Joash k' of Judah lived "
17 son of Jehoahaz k' of Israel "
21 made him k' instead of his father 4427
22 that the k' slept with his fathers. 4428
23 the son of Joash k' of Judah "
23 the son of Joash k' of Israel began "
15: 1 year of Jeroboam k' of Israel began "
1 Azariah son of Amaziah k' of Judah "
5 the Lord smote the k', so that he "
8 eighth year of Azariah k' of Judah "
13 nine...year of Uzziah k' of Judah; "
17 year of Azariah k' of Judah began "
19 k' of Assyria came against the land: "
20 of silver, to give to the k' of Assyria. "
20 the k' of Assyria turned back, and "
23 the fiftieth...of Azariah k' of Judah "
27 and fiftieth...of Azariah k' of Judah "
29 In the days of Pekah k' of Israel "
29 Tiglath-pileser k' of Assyria, and "
32 the son of Remaliah k' of Israel "
32 son of Uzziah k' of Judah to reign. "
37 against Judah Rezin the k' of Syria, "
16: 1 Ahaz son of Jotham k' of Judah "
5 Then Rezin k' of Syria and Pekah "
5 son of Remaliah k' of Israel came "
6 Rezin k' of Syria recovered Elath to "
7 to Tiglath-pileser k' of Assyria, "
7 me out of the hand of the k' of Syria, "
7 out of the hand of the k' of Israel, "
8 it for a present to the k' of Assyria. "
9 k' of Assyria hearkened unto him: "
9 the k' of Assyria went up against "
10 And k' Ahaz went to Damascus to "
10 meet Tiglath-pileser k' of Assyria, "
10 k' Ahaz sent to Urijah the priest the "
11 k' Ahaz had sent from Damascus: "
11 k' Ahaz came from Damascus. "
12 the k' was come from Damascus, "
12 the k' saw the altar: "
12 and the k' approached to the altar, "
15 And k' Ahaz commanded Urijah the "
16 to all that k' Ahaz commanded. "
17 k' Ahaz cut off the borders of the "
18 of the Lord for the k' of Assyria. "
17: 1 the twelfth year of Ahaz k' of Judah "
3 came up Shalmaneser k' of Assyria; "
4 the k' of Assyria found conspiracy "
4 sent messengers to So k' of Egypt, "
4 no present to the k' of Assyria, "
4 the k' of Assyria shut him up, "
5 k' of Assyria came up throughout "
6 the k' of Assyria took Samaria, and "
7 the hand of Pharaoh k' of Egypt, "
21 made Jeroboam the son of Nebat k': 4427
24 the k' of Assyria brought men from 4428
26 they spake to the k' of Assyria, "
27 Then the k' of Assyria commanded, "
18: 1 of Hoshea son of Elah k' of Israel, "
1 the son of Ahaz k' of Judah began "
7 rebelled against the k' of Assyria, "

2Ki 18: 9 in the fourth year of k' Hezekiah, 4428
9 of Hoshea son of Elah k' of Israel, "
9 Shalmaneser k' of Assyria came up "
10 the ninth year of Hoshea k' of Israel, "
11 k' of Assyria did carry away Israel "
13 the fourteenth year of k' Hezekiah "
13 Sennacherib k' of Assyria come up "
14 k' of Judah sent to the k' of Assyria "
14 the k' of Assyria appointed unto "
14 Hezekiah k' of Judah three hundred "
16 Hezekiah k' of Judah had overlaid, "
16 and gave it to the k' of Assyria. "
17 the k' of Assyria sent Tartan and "
17 from Lachish to k' Hezekiah with "
18 when they had called to the k', there "
19 saith the great k', the k' of Assyria, "
21 so is Pharaoh k' of Egypt unto all "
23 pledges to my lord the k' of Assyria, "
28 of the great k', the k' of Assyria: "
29 Thus saith the k', Let not Hezekiah "
30 into the hand of the k' of Assyria. "
31 thus saith the k' of Assyria, Make an "
33 out of the hand of the k' of Assyria? "
19: 1 when k' Hezekiah heard it, that he "
4 k' of Assyria his master hath sent "
5 servants of k' Hezekiah came to "
6 servants of the k' of Assyria have "
8 the k' of Assyria warring against "
9 heard say of Tirhakah k' of Ethiopia, "
10 ye speak to Hezekiah k' of Judah, "
10 into the hand of the k' of Assyria. "
13 k' of Hamath, and the k' of Arpad, "
13 and the k' of the city of Sepharvaim, "
20 against Sennacherib k' of Assyria "
32 Lord concerning the k' of Assyria, "
36 Sennacherib k' of Assyria departed, "
20: 6 out of the hand of the k' of Assyria; "
12 k' of Babylon, sent letters and a "
14 Isaiah the prophet unto k' Hezekiah, "
18 in the palace of the k' of Babylon. "
21: 3 a grove, as did Ahab k' of Israel; "
11 Manasseh k' of Judah hath done "
23 and slew the k' in his own house. "
24 had conspired against k' Amon; "
24 made Josiah his son k' in his stead. 4427
22: 3 the eighteenth year of k' Josiah, 4428
3 that the k' sent Shaphan the son of "
9 Shaphan the scribe came to the k', "
9 brought the k' word again, and said, "
10 Shaphan the scribe shewed the k', "
10 And Shaphan read it before the k'. "
11 k' had heard the words of the book "
12 k' commanded Hilkiah the priest, "
16 which the k' of Judah hath read: "
18 to the k' of Judah which sent you to "
20 they brought the k' word again. "
23: 1 the k' sent, and they gathered unto "
2 the k' went up into the house of the "
3 the k' stood by a pillar, and made a "
4 the k' commanded Hilkiah the high "
12 k' beat down, and brake them down "
13 the k' of Israel had builded for "
13 children of Ammon, did the k' defile. "
21 the k' commanded all the people, "
23 in the eighteenth year of k' Josiah, "
25 unto him was there no k' before him, "
29 Pharaoh-nechoh k' of Egypt went up "
29 against the k' of Assyria to the river "
29 k' Josiah went against him; and he "
30 made him k' in his father's stead. 4427
34 made Eliakim the son of Josiah k' "
24: 1 k' of Babylon came up, 4428
7 the k' of Egypt came not again any "
7 the k' of Babylon had taken from "
7 that pertained to the k' of Egypt. "
10 of Nebuchadnezzar k' of Babylon "
11 k' of Babylon came against the city, "
12 Jehoiachin the k' of Judah went "
12 went out to the k' of Babylon, he "
12 the k' of Babylon took him in the "
13 which Solomon k' of Israel had made "
16 the k' of Babylon brought captive "
17 the k' of Babylon made Mattaniah "
17 made...his father's brother k' 4427
20 rebelled against the k' of Babylon. 4428
25: 1 Nebuchadnezzar k' of Babylon came, "
2 the eleventh year of k' Zedekiah. "
4 k' went the way toward the plain. "
5 the Chaldees pursued after the k', 4428
6 they took the k', and brought him "
6 up to the k' of Babylon to Riblah; "
8 k' Nebuchadnezzar k' of Babylon, "
8 a servant of the k' of Babylon, unto "
11 that fell away to the k' of Babylon, "
20 them to the k' of Babylon to Riblah: "
21 And the k' of Babylon smote them, "
22 Nebuchadnezzar k' of Babylon had "
23 heard the k' of Babylon had made "
24 the land, and serve the k' of Babylon; "
27 captivity of Jehoiachin k' of Judah, "
27 Evil-merodach k' of Babylon in the "
27 the head of Jehoiachin k' of Judah "
30 allowance given him of the k', "
1Ch 1:43 before any k' reigned over the "
3: 2 daughter of Talmai k' of Geshur: "
4:23 they dwelt with the k' for his work. "
41 the days of Hezekiah k' of Judah, "
5: 6 k' of Assyria carried away captive: "
17 in the days of Jotham k' of Judah, "
17 in the days of Jeroboam k' of Israel. "
26 up the spirit of Pul k' of Assyria, "
26 of Tilgath-pilneser k' of Assyria, "
11: 2 when Saul was k', thou wast he that "
3 came all the elders of Israel to the k' "
3 they anointed David k' over Israel, "
10 with all Israel, to make him k'. 4427

1Ch 12: 31 name, to come and make David *k*'. 4427
38 to make David *k*' over all Israel: "
38 were of one heart to make David *k*'. "
14: 1 Hiram *k*' of Tyre sent messengers 4428
2 had confirmed him *k*' over Israel, "
8 was anointed *k*' over all Israel, "
15: 29 saw *k*' David dancing and playing: "
17: 16 David the *k*' came and sat before "
18: 3 David smote Hadarezer *k*' of Zobah "
5 came to help Hadarezer *k*' of Zobah, "
9 when Tou *k*' of Hamath heard how "
9 the host of Hadarezer *k*' of Zobah; "
10 sent Hadoram his son to *k*' David, "
11 *k*' David dedicated unto the Lord, "
17 of David were chief about the *k*'. "
19: 1 the *k*' of the children of Ammon "
5 the *k*' said, Tarry at Jericho until "
7 the *k*' of Maachah and his people; "
20: 2 David took the crown of their *k*' "
21: 3 my lord the *k*', are they not all my "
23 let my lord the *k*' do that which is "
24 *k*' David said to Ornan, Nay; but I "
23: 1 made Solomon...*k*' over Israel. 4427
24: 6 Levites, wrote them before the *k*', 4428
31 in the presence of David the *k*', "
25: 2 according to the order of the *k*'. "
26: 26 David the *k*', and the chief fathers, "
30 Lord, and in the service of the *k*'. "
32 whom *k*' David made rulers over "
32 to God, and affairs of the *k*'. "
27: 1 and their officers that served the *k*' "
24 account of the chronicles of *k*' David. "
31 the substance which was *k*' David's. "
28: 1 that ministered to the *k*' by course, "
1 substance and possession of the *k*', "
2 David the *k*' stood up upon his feet, "
4 father to be *k*' over Israel for ever: "
4 me to make me *k*' over all Israel: 4427
29: 1 David the *k*' said unto all the 4428
9 David the *k*' also rejoiced with great "
20 and worshipped the Lord, and the *k*'. "
22 made Solomon the son of David *k*' "
23 sat on the throne of the Lord as *k*' "
24 all the sons likewise of *k*' David, "
24 themselves unto Solomon the *k*'. "
25 been on any *k*' before him in Israel. "
29 the acts of David the *k*', first and "
2Ch 1: 9 hast made me *k*' over a people 4427
11 over whom I have made thee *k*': "
14 and with the *k*' at Jerusalem. 4428
15 And the *k*' made silver and gold at "
2: 3 sent to Huram the *k*' of Tyre, "
11 Huram the *k*' of Tyre answered "
11 he hath made thee *k*' over them. 4427
12 given to David the *k*' a wise son, 4428
4: 11 that he was to make for *k*' Solomon "
16 make to *k*' Solomon for the house "
17 plain of Jordan did the *k*' cast them, "
5: 3 themselves unto the *k*' in the feast "
6 *k*' Solomon, and all the congregation "
6: 3 the *k*' turned his face, and blessed "
7: 4 the *k*' and all the people offered "
5 And *k*' Solomon offered a sacrifice "
5 *k*' and all the people dedicated the "
6 the *k*' had made to praise the Lord, "
8: 10 the chief of *k*' Solomon's officers, "
11 in the house of David *k*' of Israel, "
15 the commandment of the *k*' unto "
18 and brought them to *k*' Solomon. "
9: 5 And she said to the *k*', It was a true "
8 throne, to be *k*' for the Lord thy God: "
8 therefore made he thee *k*' over them, "
9 she gave the *k*' an hundred and "
9 queen of Sheba gave *k*' Solomon. "
11 the *k*' made of the algum trees "
12 *k*' Solomon gave to the queen of "
12 which she had brought unto the *k*'. "
15 *k*' Solomon made two hundred "
16 *k*' put them in the house of the forest "
17 the *k*' made a great throne of ivory, "
20 the drinking vessels of *k*' Solomon "
22 *k*' Solomon passed all the kings of "
25 cities, and with the *k*' at Jerusalem. "
27 *k*' made silver in Jerusalem as "
10: 1 all Israel come to make him *k*'. 4427
2 the presence of Solomon the *k*', 4428
6 *k*' Rehoboam took counsel with the "
12 on the third day, as the *k*' bade, "
13 And the *k*' answered them roughly; "
13 *k*' Rehoboam forsook the counsel of "
15 *k*' hearkened not unto the people: "
16 the *k*' would not hearken unto them, "
16 the people answered the *k*', saying, "
18 Then *k*' Rehoboam sent Hadoram "
18 *k*' Rehoboam made speed to get him "
11: 3 the son of Solomon, *k*' of Judah, "
22 for he thought to make him *k*'. 4427
12: 2 in the fifth year of *k*' Rehoboam 4428
2 Shishak *k*' of Egypt came up against "
6 and the *k*' humbled themselves; "
9 Shishak *k*' of Egypt came up against "
10 *k*' Rehoboam made shields of brass, "
11 *k*' entered into the house of the Lord, "
13 *k*' Rehoboam strengthened himself "
13: 1 the eighteenth year of *k*' Jeroboam "
15: 16 Maachah the mother of Asa the *k*', "
16: 1 Baasha *k*' of Israel came up against "
1 out or come in to Asa *k*' of Judah. "
2 and sent to Ben-hadad *k*' of Syria, "
3 thy league with Baasha *k*' of Israel, "
4 Ben-hadad hearkened unto *k*' Asa, "
6 Then Asa the *k*' took all Judah; "
7 the seer came to Asa *k*' of Judah, "
7 thou hast relied on the *k*' of Syria, "
7 the host of the *k*' of Syria escaped "
17: 19 These waited on the *k*', beside "
2Ch 17: 19 whom the *k*' put in the fenced cities? 4428
18: 3 *k*' of Israel said unto Jehoshaphat "
3 said unto Jehoshaphat *k*' of Judah, "
4 said unto the *k*' of Israel, Enquire, "
5 the *k*' of Israel gathered together "
7 *k*' of Israel said unto Jehoshaphat, "
7 said, Let not the *k*' say so. "
8 *k*' of Israel called for one of his "
9 the *k*' of Israel and Jehoshaphat "
9 the *k*' of Judah sat either of them "
11 deliver it into the hand of the *k*'. "
12 the prophets declare good to the *k*' "
14 come to the *k*', the *k*' said unto him, "
15 the *k*' said to him, how many times "
17 the *k*' of Israel said to Jehoshaphat, "
19 Who shall entice Ahab *k*' of Israel, "
25 *k*' of Israel said, Take ye Micaiah, "
26 Thus saith the *k*', Put this fellow in "
28 the *k*' of Israel and Jehoshaphat "
28 the *k*' of Judah went up to "
29 *k*' of Israel said unto Jehoshaphat, "
29 the *k*' of Israel disguised himself; "
30 the *k*' of Syria had commanded the "
30 save only with the *k*' of Israel. "
31 that they said, It is the *k*' of Israel. "
32 that it was not the *k*' of Israel, "
33 smote the *k*' of Israel between the "
34 the *k*' of Israel stayed himself up in "
19: 1 Jehoshaphat the *k*' of Judah "
2 him, and said to *k*' Jehoshaphat, "
20: 15 and thou *k*' Jehoshaphat, Thus "
35 this did Jehoshaphat *k*' of Judah "
35 himself with Ahaziah *k*' of Israel, "
21: 2 sons of Jehoshaphat *k*' of Israel. "
8 and made themselves a *k*'. "
12 in the ways of Asa *k*' of Judah, "
22: 1 made Ahaziah his...son *k*' in his 4427
1 of Jehoram *k*' of Judah reigned. 4428
5 the son of Ahab *k*' of Israel "
5 to war against Hazael *k*' of Syria at "
6 he fought with Hazael *k*' of Syria. "
6 the son of Jehoram *k*' of Judah "
11 the daughter of the *k*', took Joash "
11 the daughter of *k*' Jehoram, the "
23: 3 made a covenant with the *k*' in the "
7 shall compass the *k*' round about, "
7 be ye with the *k*' when he cometh "
9 shields, that had been *k*' David's, "
10 the temple, by the *k*' round about. "
11 the testimony, and made him *k*'. 4427
11 him, and said, God save the *k*'. 4428
12 people running and praising the *k*', "
13 *k*' stood at his pillar at the entering "
13 princes and the trumpets by the *k*': "
16 all the people, and between the *k*', "
20 the *k*' from the house of the Lord: "
20 the *k*' upon the throne of the kingdom. "
24: 6 the *k*' called for Jehoiada the chief, "
12 the *k*' and Jehoiada gave it to such "
14 the rest of the money before the *k*' "
17 and made obeisance to the *k*'. "
17 Then the *k*' hearkened unto them. "
21 at the commandment of the *k*' in "
22 *k*' remembered not the kindness "
23 of them unto the *k*' of Damascus. "
25: 3 that had killed the *k*' his father. "
7 a man of God to him, saying, O *k*', "
16 with him, that the *k*' said unto him, "
17 Amaziah *k*' of Judah took advice, 4428
17 the son of Jehu, *k*' of Israel, "
18 Joash *k*' of Israel sent to Amaziah "
18 to Amaziah *k*' of Judah, saying, "
21 So Joash the *k*' of Israel went up; "
21 both he and Amaziah *k*' of Judah, "
23 And Joash the *k*' of Israel took "
23 Amaziah *k*' of Judah, the son of "
25 the son of Joash *k*' of Judah lived "
25 Joash son of Jehoahaz *k*' of Israel "
26: 1 sixteen years old, and made him *k*' 4427
2 that the *k*' slept with his fathers. 4428
13 to help the *k*' against the enemy. "
18 And they withstood Uzziah the *k*', "
21 Uzziah the *k*' was a leper unto the "
27: 5 He fought also with the *k*' of the "
28: 5 him into the hand of the *k*' of Syria; "
5 into the hand of the *k*' of Israel, "
7 Elkanah that was next to the *k*'. "
16 *k*' Ahaz send unto the kings of "
19 low because of Ahaz *k*' of Israel; "
20 Tilgath-pilneser *k*' of Assyria came "
21 out of the house of the *k*', and of "
21 and gave it unto the *k*' of Assyria: "
22 the Lord: this is that *k*' Ahaz. "
29: 15 to the commandment of the *k*', "
18 they went in to Hezekiah the *k*', "
19 which *k*' Ahaz in his reign did cast "
20 Then Hezekiah the *k*' rose early, "
23 before the *k*' and the congregation; "
24 the *k*' commanded that the burnt "
27 ordained by David *k*' of Israel. "
29 the *k*' and all that were present "
30 Hezekiah the *k*' and the princes "
30: 2 For the *k*' had taken counsel, and "
4 the thing pleased the *k*' and all the "
6 went with the letters from the *k*', "
6 to the commandment of the *k*', "
12 the commandment of the *k*' and of "
24 Hezekiah *k*' of Judah did give to "
26 the son of David *k*' of Israel their "
31: 13 commandment of Hezekiah the *k*', "
32: 1 Sennacherib *k*' of Assyria came, "
7 nor dismayed for the *k*' of Assyria, "
8 the words of Hezekiah *k*' of Judah. "
9 *k*' of Assyria send his servants to "
9 unto Hezekiah *k*' of Judah, and "
10 saith Sennacherib, *k*' of Assyria, "
2Ch 32: 11 of the hand of the *k*' of Assyria? 4428
20 for this cause Hezekiah the *k*', and "
21 in the camp of the *k*' of Assyria. "
22 of Sennacherib the *k*' of Assyria, "
23 presents to Hezekiah *k*' of Judah "
33: 11 of the host of the *k*' of Assyria, "
25 had conspired against *k*' Amon; "
25 made Josiah his son *k*' in his stead. 4427
34: 16 Shaphan carried the book to the *k*' 4428
16 brought the *k*' word back again, "
18 Shaphan the scribe told the *k*', "
18 And Shaphan read it before the *k*'. "
19 when the *k*' had heard the words of "
20 the *k*' commanded Hilkiah, and "
22 they that the *k*' had appointed, "
24 have read before the *k*' of Judah: "
26 as for the *k*' of Judah, who sent you "
28 So they brought the *k*' word again. "
29 the *k*' sent and gathered together "
30 the *k*' went up into the house of the "
31 the *k*' stood in his place, and made "
35: 3 son of David *k*' of Israel did build; "
4 to the writing of David *k*' of Israel, "
16 to the commandment of *k*' Josiah. "
20 Necho *k*' of Egypt came up to fight "
21 I to do with thee, thou *k*' of Judah? "
23 the archers shot at *k*' Josiah; "
23 *k*' said to his servants, Have me "
36: 1 made him *k*' in his father's stead 4427
3 the *k*' of Egypt put him down at 4428
4 the *k*' of Egypt made Eliakim his "
4 made Eliakim...*k*' over Judah 4427
6 came up Nebuchadnezzar *k*' of 4428
10 *k*' Nebuchadnezzar sent, and "
10 made Zedekiah...*k*' over Judah 4427
13 against *k*' Nebuchadnezzar, 4428
17 upon them the *k*' of the Chaldees, "
18 the treasures of the *k*', and of his "
22 the first year of Cyrus *k*' of Persia, "
22 up the spirit of Cyrus *k*' of Persia, "
23 Thus saith Cyrus *k*' of Persia, All "
Ezr 1: 1 the first year of Cyrus *k*' of Persia, "
1 up the spirit of Cyrus *k*' of Persia, "
2 Thus saith Cyrus *k*' of Persia, The "
7 the *k*' brought forth the vessels "
8 did Cyrus *k*' of Persia bring forth "
2: 1 the *k*' of Babylon had carried away "
3: 7 they had of Cyrus *k*' of Persia. "
10 the ordinance of David *k*' of Israel. "
4: 2 days of Esar-haddon *k*' of Assur, "
3 as *k*' Cyrus the *k*' of Persia hath "
5 all the days of Cyrus *k*' of Persia, "
5 the reign of Darius *k*' of Persia. "
7 unto Artaxerxes *k*' of Persia; "
8 to Artaxerxes the *k*' in this sort: 4430
11 him, even unto Artaxerxes the *k*'; "
12 Be it known unto the *k*', that the "
13 Be it known now unto the *k*', that, "
14 have we sent and certified the *k*'; "
16 We certify the *k*' that, if this city be "
17 sent the *k*' an answer unto Rehum "
23 of *k*' Artaxerxes' letter was read "
24 of the reign of Darius *k*' of Persia. "
5: 6 the river, sent unto Darius the *k*': "
7 thus; Unto Darius the *k*', all peace. "
8 known unto the *k*', that we went "
11 which a great *k*' of Israel builded "
12 Nebuchadnezzar the *k*' of Babylon, "
13 first year of Cyrus the *k*' of Babylon "
13 *k*' Cyrus made a decree to build "
14 the *k*' take out of the temple of "
17 therefore, if it seem good to the *k*', "
17 decree was made of Cyrus the *k*' to "
17 let the *k*' send his pleasure to us "
6: 1 Darius the *k*' made a decree, and "
3 In the first year of Cyrus the *k*' the "
3 same Cyrus the *k*' made a decree "
10 pray for the life of the *k*', and of his "
13 that which Darius the *k*' had sent, "
14 Darius, and Artaxerxes *k*' of Persia. "
15 year of the reign of Darius the *k*'. "
22 heart of the *k*' of Assyria unto 4428
7: 1 reign of Artaxerxes *k*' of Persia, "
6 the *k*' granted him all his request, "
7 seventh year of Artaxerxes the *k*'. "
8 was in the seventh year of the *k*'. "
11 the *k*' Artaxerxes gave unto Ezra "
12 Artaxerxes, *k*' of kings, unto Ezra 4430
14 as thou art sent of the *k*', and of his "
15 *k*' and his counsellors have freely "
21 And I, even I Artaxerxes the *k*', do "
23 wrath against the realm of the *k*' "
26 of thy God, and the law of the *k*', "
28 mercy unto me before the *k*', 4428
8: 1 in the reign of Artaxerxes the *k*'. "
22 require of the *k*' a band of soldiers "
22 we had spoken unto the *k*', saying, "
25 which the *k*', and his counsellors, "
Ne 2: 1 twentieth year of Artaxerxes the *k*', "
1 the wine, and gave it unto the *k*'. "
2 the *k*' said unto me, Why is thy "
3 unto the *k*', Let the *k*' live for ever: "
4 *k*' said unto me, For what dost thou "
5 said unto the *k*', If it please the *k*', "
6 the *k*' said unto me, (the queen also "
6 it pleased the *k*' to send me; and I "
7 said unto the *k*', If it please the *k*', "
8 And the *k*' granted me, according "
9 *k*' had sent captains of the army "
19 ye do? will ye rebel against the *k*'? "
5: 14 thirtieth year of Artaxerxes the *k*'. "
6: 6 thou mayest be their *k*', according "
7 There is a *k*' in Judah: and now "
7 reported to the *k*' according to "
7: 6 the *k*' of Babylon had carried away, "
9: 22 and the land of the *k*' of Heshbon, "

Ne 9:22 and the land of Og k' of Bashan. 4428
13: 6 and thirtieth year of Artaxerxes k' "
6 of Babylon came I unto the k', and "
6 days obtained I leave of the k': "
26 k' of Israel sin by these things? "
26 many nations were there no k' like "
26 God made him k' over all Israel: "
Es 1: 2 the k' Ahasuerus sat on the throne "
5 the k' made a feast unto all the "
7 according to the state of the k'. "
8 for so the k' had appointed to all "
9 which belonged to k' Ahasuerus. "
10 the heart of the k' was merry with "
10 the presence of Ahasuerus the k', "
11 Vashti the queen before the k' "
12 therefore was the k' very wroth, and "
13 the k' said to the wise men, which "
15 the commandment of the k' "
16 Memucan answered before the k' "
16 hath not done wrong to the k' only, "
16 the provinces of the k' Ahasuerus. "
17 The k' Ahasuerus commanded "
19 If it please the k', let there go a "
19 come no more before k' Ahasuerus; "
19 let the k' give her royal estate unto "
21 pleased the k' and the princes; "
21 the k' did according to the word of "
2: 1 the wrath of k' Ahasuerus was "
2 young virgins sought for the k': "
3 let the k' appoint officers in all the "
4 maiden which pleaseth the k' be "
4 the thing pleased the k'; and he "
6 away with Jeconiah k' of Judah, "
6 k' of Babylon had carried away. "
12 was come to go in to k' Ahasuerus, "
13 came every maiden unto the k'; "
14 she came in unto the k' no more, "
14 except the k' delighted in her, and "
15 was come to go in unto the k', she "
16 was taken unto k' Ahasuerus into "
17 the k' loved Esther above all the "
18 the k' made a great feast unto all "
18 according to the state of the k'. "
21 to lay hand on the k' Ahasuerus. "
22 Esther certified the k' thereof in "
23 book of the chronicles before the k'. "
3: 1 did k' Ahasuerus promote Haman "
2 for the k' had so commanded "
7 in the twelfth year of k' Ahasuerus, "
8 And Haman said unto k' Ahasuerus, "
9 If it please the k', let it be written "
10 the k' took his ring from his hand, "
11 k' said unto Haman, The silver is "
12 in the name of k' Ahasuerus was it "
15 k' and Haman sat down to drink; "
4: 8 that she should go in unto the k', "
11 unto the k' into the inner court, "
11 k' shall hold out the golden sceptre, "
11 been called to come in unto the k' "
16 and so will I go in unto the k', "
5: 1 the k' sat upon his royal throne in "
2 k' saw Esther the queen standing "
2 the k' held out to Esther the golden "
3 said the k' unto her, What wilt thou, "
4 If it seem good unto the k', let "
4 the k' and Haman come this day "
5 the k' said, Cause Haman to make "
5 k' and Haman came to the banquet "
6 k' said unto Esther at the banquet "
8 found favour in the sight of the k', "
8 please the k' to grant my petition, "
8 k' and Haman come to the banquet "
8 do to morrow as the king hath said. "
11 wherein the k' had promoted him, "
11 the princes and servants of the k'. "
12 did let no man come in with the k' "
12 I invited unto her also with the k'. "
14 to morrow speak thou unto the k' "
14 then go thou in merrily with the k' "
6: 1 On that night could not the k' sleep, "
1 and they were read before the k'. "
2 to lay hand on the k' Ahasuerus. "
3 k' said, What honour and dignity "
4 And the k' said, Who is in the court? "
4 speak unto the k' to hang Mordecai "
5 And the k' said, Let him come in. "
6 the k' said unto him, What shall be "
6 whom the k' delighteth to honour? "
6 would the k' delight to do honour "
7 Haman answered the k', For the "
7 whom the k' delighteth to honour, "
8 brought which the k' useth to wear, "
8 the horse that the k' rideth upon, "
9 whom the k' delighteth to honour, "
9 whom the k' delighteth to honour. "
10 the k' said to Haman, Make haste, "
11 whom the k' delighteth to honour. "
7: 1 the k' and Haman came to banquet "
2 the k' said again unto Esther on "
3 have found favour in thy sight, O k', "
3 and if it please the k', let my life be "
5 the k' Ahasuerus answered and said "
6 Haman was afraid before the k' and "
7 k' arising from the banquet of wine "
7 determined against him by the k'. "
8 the k' returned out of the palace "
8 said the k', Will he force the queen "
9 chamberlains, said before the k', "
9 who had spoken good for the k', "
9 Then the k' said, Hang him thereon. "
8: 1 did the k' Ahasuerus give the house "
1 And Mordecai came before the k'; "
2 the k' took off his ring, which he "
3 spake yet again before the k', "
4 the k' held out the golden sceptre "
4 arose, and stood before the k', "
Es 8: 5 If it please the k', and if I have 4428
5 the thing seem right before the k', "
7 the k' Ahasuerus said unto Esther "
10 he wrote in the k' Ahasuerus' name, "
11 Wherein the k' granted the Jews "
12 the provinces of the k' Ahasuerus, "
15 went out from the presence of the k' "
9: 2 the provinces of the k' Ahasuerus, "
3 officers of the k', helped the Jews; * "
11 palace was brought before the k'. "
12 the k' said unto Esther the queen, "
13 If it please the k', let it be granted "
14 the k' commanded it so to be done: "
20 the provinces of the k' Ahasuerus, "
25 when Esther came before the k', he "
10: 1 And the k' Ahasuerus laid a tribute "
2 whereunto the k' advanced him, "
3 Jew was next unto k' Ahasuerus, "
Job 15:24 him, as a k' ready to the battle. "
18:14 shall bring him to the k' of terrors. "
29:25 chief, and dwelt as a k' in the army, "
34:18 fit to say to a k', Thou art wicked? "
41:34 a k' over all the children of pride. "
Ps 2: 6 Yet have I set my k' upon my holy "
5: 2 voice of my cry, my K', and my God: "
10:16 The Lord is K' for ever and ever: "
18:50 deliverance giveth he to his k'; "
20: 9 let the k' hear us when we call. "
21: 1 The k' shall joy in thy strength, O "
7 For the k' trusteth in the Lord, "
24: 7 and the K' of glory shall come in. "
8 Who is this K' of glory? The Lord "
9 and the K' of glory shall come in. "
10 Who is this K' of glory? The Lord "
10 Lord of hosts, he is the K' of glory. "
29:10 yea, the Lord sitteth K' for ever. "
33:16 no k' saved by the multitude of an "
44: 4 Thou art my K', O God: command "
45: 1 which I have made touching the k': "
11 the k' greatly desire thy beauty: "
14 be brought unto the k' in raiment "
47: 2 he is a great K' over all the earth. "
6 praises unto our K', sing praises. "
7 For God is the K' of all the earth: "
48: 2 the north, the city of the great K'. "
63:11 But the k' shall rejoice in God; "
68:24 the goings of my God, my K', in the "
72: 1 Give the k' thy judgments, O God, "
74:12 For God is my K' of old, working "
84: 3 O Lord of hosts, my K', and my God. "
89:18 and the Holy One of Israel is our k'. "
95: 3 God, and a great K' above all gods. "
98: 6 joyful noise before the Lord, the K'. "
105:20 The k' sent and loosed him; even "
135:11 Sihon k' of the Amorites, and Og k' "
136:19 Sihon k' of the Amorites: for his "
20 And Og the k' of Bashan: for his "
145: 1 I will extol thee, my God, O k'; and "
149: 2 children of Zion be joyful in their K'. "
Pr 1: 1 the son of David, k' of Israel; "
16:10 sentence is in the lips of the k': "
14 The wrath of a k' is as messengers "
20: 2 The fear of a k' is as the roaring of "
8 A k' that sitteth in the throne of "
26 A wise k' scattereth the wicked, "
28 Mercy and truth preserve the k': "
22:11 of his lips the k' shall be his friend. "
24:21 son, fear thou the Lord and the k': "
25: 1 of Hezekiah k' of Judah copied out. "
5 away the wicked from before the k', "
6 thyself in the presence of the k', "
29: 4 The k' by judgment establisheth "
14 k' that faithfully judgeth the poor, "
30:27 The locusts have no k', yet go they "
31 k' against whom there is no rising "
31: 1 words of k' Lemuel, the prophecy "
Ec 1: 1 the son of David, k' in Jerusalem. "
12 I the Preacher was k' over Israel in "
2:12 man do that cometh after the k'? "
4:13 wise child than an old and foolish k', "
5: 9 the k' himself is served by the field. "
8: 4 Where the word of a k' is, there is * "
9:14 there came a great k' against it, "
10:16 thee, O land, when thy k' is a child, "
17 when thy k' is the son of nobles, "
20 Curse not the k', no not in thy "
Ca 1: 4 the k' hath brought me into his "
12 While the k' sitteth at his table, "
3: 9 K' Solomon made himself a chariot "
11 behold k' Solomon with the crown "
7: 5 the k' is held in the galleries. "
Isa 6: 1 In the year that k' Uzziah died I saw "
5 eyes have seen the K', the Lord of "
7: 1 the son of Uzziah, k' of Judah, "
1 Rezin the k' of Syria, and Pekah "
1 the son of Remaliah, k' of Israel, "
6 and set a k' in the midst of it, even "
17 Judah; even the k' of Assyria. "
20 the river, by the k' of Assyria, "
8: 4 taken away before the k' of Assyria. "
7 k' of Assyria, and all his glory: "
21 and curse their k' and their God, "
10:12 the stout heart of the k' of Assyria, "
14: 4 proverb against the k' of Babylon, "
28 In the year that k' Ahaz died was "
19: 4 and a fierce k' shall rule over them, "
20: 1 Sargon the k' of Assyria sent him,) "
4 So shall the k' of Assyria lead away "
6 be delivered from the k' of Assyria: "
23:15 according to the days of one k': "
30:33 old; yea, for the k' it is prepared; "
32: 1 a k' shall reign in righteousness, "
33:17 eyes shall see the k' in his beauty: "
22 is our lawgiver, the Lord is our k'; "
36: 1 the fourteenth year of k' Hezekiah, "
1 Sennacherib k' of Assyria came up "
Isa 36: 2 the k' of Assyria sent Rabshakeh 4428
2 unto k' Hezekiah with a great army. "
4 saith the great k', the k' of Assyria, "
6 so is Pharaoh k' of Egypt to all that "
8 to my master the k' of Assyria, and "
13 of the great k', the k' of Assyria. "
14 Thus saith the k', Let not Hezekiah "
15 into the hand of the k' of Assyria. "
16 thus saith the k' of Assyria, Make "
18 out of the hand of the k' of Assyria? "
37: 1 when k' Hezekiah heard it, that he "
4 k' of Assyria his master hath sent "
5 the servants of k' Hezekiah came "
6 servants of the k' of Assyria have "
8 the k' of Assyria warring against "
9 concerning Tirhakah k' of Ethiopia, "
10 ye speak to Hezekiah k' of Judah, "
10 into the hand of the k' of Assyria. "
13 k' of Hamath, and the k' of Arphad, "
13 and the k' of the city of Sepharvaim, "
21 against Sennacherib k' of Assyria: "
33 Lord concerning the k' of Assyria, "
37 Sennacherib k' of Assyria departed, "
38: 6 out of the hand of the k' of Assyria: "
9 writing of Hezekiah k' of Judah, "
39: 1 Baladan, k' of Babylon, sent letters "
3 the prophet unto k' Hezekiah, "
7 in the palace of the k' of Babylon. "
41:21 reasons, saith the K' of Jacob. "
43:15 One, the creator of Israel, your K'. "
44: 6 saith the Lord the K' of Israel, "
57: 9 wentest to the k' with ointment, "
Jer 1: 2 Josiah the son of Amon k' of Judah, "
3, 3 the son of Josiah k' of Judah, "
3: 6 unto me in the days of Josiah the k', "
4: 9 that the heart of the k' shall perish, "
8:19 Lord in Zion? is not her k' in her? "
10: 7 not fear thee, O K' of nations? "
10 living God, and an everlasting k': "
13:18 Say unto the k' and to the queen, "
15: 4 the son of Hezekiah k' of Judah, "
20: 4 into the hand of the k' of Babylon, "
21: 1 when k' Zedekiah sent unto him "
2 k' of Babylon maketh war against "
4 ye fight against the k' of Babylon, "
7 I will deliver Zedekiah k' of Judah, "
7 of Nebuchadrezzar k' of Babylon, "
10 into the hand of the k' of Babylon, "
11 the house of the k' of Judah, say, "
22: 1 to the house of the k' of Judah, "
2 the word of the Lord, O k' of Judah, "
11 the son of Josiah k' of Judah, "
18 the son of Josiah k' of Judah; "
24 the son of Jehoiakim k' of Judah "
25 of Nebuchadrezzar k' of Babylon, "
23: 5 and a K' shall reign and prosper, "
24: 1 k' of Babylon had carried away "
1 the son of Jehoiakim k' of Judah, "
8 I give Zedekiah the k' of Judah, "
25: 1 the son of Josiah k' of Judah, "
1 of Nebuchadrezzar k' of Babylon; "
3 Josiah the son of Amon k' of Judah, "
9 the k' of Babylon, my servant, and "
11 shall serve the k' of Babylon seventy "
12 I will punish the k' of Babylon, and "
19 Pharaoh k' of Egypt, and his "
26 the k' of Sheshach shall drink after "
26: 1 son of Josiah k' of Judah came this "
18 the days of Hezekiah k' of Judah, "
19 Did Hezekiah k' of Judah and all "
21 when Jehoiakim the k', with all his "
21 the k' sought to put him to death: "
22 the k' sent men into Egypt, namely, "
23 brought him unto Jehoiakim the k'; "
27: 1 the son of Josiah k' of Judah came "
3 send them to the k' of Edom, and to "
3 and to the k' of Moab, and to the "
3 and to the k' of the Ammonites, "
3 Ammonites, and to the k' of Tyrus, "
3 and to the k' of Zidon, by the hand "
3 unto Zedekiah k' of Judah; "
6, 8 Nebuchadnezzar...k' of Babylon, "
8 under the yoke of the k' of Babylon, "
9 shall not serve the k' of Babylon: "
11 under the yoke of the k' of Babylon, "
12 spake also to Zedekiah k' of Judah "
12 under the yoke of the k' of Babylon, "
13 will not serve the k' of Babylon? "
14 shall not serve the k' of Babylon: "
17 serve the k' of Babylon, and live: "
18 and in the house of the k' of Judah, "
20 k' of Babylon took not, when he "
20 k' of Judah from Jerusalem to "
21 in the house of the k' of Judah and "
28: 1 the reign of Zedekiah k' of Judah, "
2 the yoke of the k' of Babylon. "
3 k' of Babylon took away from this "
4 k' of Judah, with all the captives of "
4 break the yoke of the k' of Babylon. "
11 of Nebuchadnezzar k' of Babylon "
14 Nebuchadnezzar k' of Babylon; "
29: 2 Jeconiah the k', and the queen, and "
3 (whom Zedekiah k' of Judah sent "
3 to Nebuchadnezzar k' of Babylon) "
16 k' that sitteth upon the throne of "
21 of Nebuchadrezzar k' of Babylon; "
22 whom the k' of Babylon roasted in "
30: 9 Lord their God, and David their k', "
32: 1 tenth year of Zedekiah k' of Judah, "
2 king of Babylon's army besieged "
2 was in the k' of Judah's house. "
3 Zedekiah k' of Judah had shut him "
3 into the hand of the k' of Babylon, "
4 k' of Judah shall not escape out of "
4 into the hand of the k' of Babylon, "
28 of Nebuchadrezzar k' of Babylon, "

Jer 32: 36 into the hand of the k' of Babylon 4428
34: 1 k' of Babylon, and all his army, "
2 and speak to Zedekiah k' of Judah, "
2 into the hand of the k' of Babylon, "
3 behold the eyes of the k' of Babylon, "
4 the Lord, O Zedekiah k' of Judah; "
6 words unto Zedekiah k' of Judah in "
7 the k' of Babylon's army fought "
8 k' Zedekiah had made a covenant "
21 And Zedekiah k' of Judah and his "
21 hand of the k' of Babylon's army, "
35: 1 the son of Josiah k' of Judah, "
11 k' of Babylon came up into the land, "
36: 1, 9 the son of Josiah k' of Judah, "
16 We will surely tell the k' of all these "
20 they went in to the k' into the court, "
20 all the words in the ears of the k'. "
21 the k' sent Jehudi to fetch the roll: "
21 Jehudi read it in the ears of the k', "
21 princes which stood beside the k'. "
22 Now the k' sat in the winterhouse "
24 the k', nor any of his servants that "
25 intercession to the k' that he would "
26 the k' commanded Jerahmeel the "
27 that the k' had burned the roll, "
28 the k' of Judah hath burned. "
29 shalt say to Jehoiakim k' of Judah, "
29 The k' of Babylon shall certainly "
30 the Lord of Jehoiakim k' of Judah; "
32 k' of Judah had burned in the fire: "
37: 1 And k' Zedekiah the son of Josiah "
1 Nebuchadrezzar k' of Babylon "
1 made k' in the land of Judah. "
3 Zedekiah the k' sent Jehucal the "
7 Thus shall ye say to the k' of Judah, "
17 Zedekiah the k' sent, and took him "
17 and the k' asked him secretly in his "
17 into the hand of the k' of Babylon. "
18 Jeremiah said unto k' Zedekiah, "
19 The k' of Babylon shall not come "
20 now, I pray thee, O my lord the k': "
21 Zedekiah the k' commanded that "
38: 3 hand of the k' of Babylon's army, "
4 the princes said unto the k', We "
5 Zedekiah the k' said, Behold, he is in "
5 for the k' is not he that can do any "
7 the k' then sitting in the gate of "
8 house, and spake to the k', saying, "
9 My lord the k', these men have done "
10 the k' commanded Ebed-melech "
11 went into the house of the k' under "
14 Then Zedekiah the k' sent, and took "
14 the k' said unto Jeremiah, I will ask "
16 Zedekiah the k' sware secretly unto "
17 unto the k' of Babylon's princes, "
18 forth to the k' of Babylon's princes, "
19 Zedekiah the k' said unto Jeremiah, "
22 are left in the k' of Judah's house "
22 forth to the k' of Babylon's princes, "
23 by the hand of the k' of Babylon: "
25 what thou hast said unto the k', "
25 also what the k' said unto thee: "
26 my supplication before the k', "
27 words that the k' had commanded. "
39: 1 ninth year of Zedekiah k' of Judah, "
1 Nebuchadrezzar k' of Babylon "
3 princes of the k' of Babylon came "
3 of the princes of the k' of Babylon. "
4 Zedekiah the k' of Judah saw them, "
5 to Nebuchadnezzar k' of Babylon "
6 the k' of Babylon slew the sons of "
6 the k' of Babylon slew all the nobles "
11 Nebuchadrezzar k' of Babylon gave "
13 and all the k' of Babylon's princes; "
40: 5 k' of Babylon hath made governor "
7 k' of Babylon had made Gedaliah "
9 land, and serve the k' of Babylon, "
11 k' of Babylon had left a remnant of "
14 Baalis the k' of the Ammonites "
41: 1 the princes of the k', even ten men "
2 k' of Babylon had made governor "
9 which Asa the k' had made for fear "
9 for fear of Baasha k' of Israel "
18 the k' of Babylon made governor "
42: 11 Be not afraid of the k' of Babylon, "
43: 10 Nebuchadrezzar the k' of Babylon, "
44: 30 give Pharaoh-hophra k' of Egypt "
30 Zedekiah k' of Judah into the hand "
30 of Nebuchadrezzar k' of Babylon, "
45: 1 the son of Josiah k' of Judah, "
46: 2 army of Pharaoh-necho k' of Egypt, "
2 Nebuchadrezzar k' of Babylon "
2 the son of Josiah k' of Judah. "
13 k' of Babylon should come and "
17 Pharaoh k' of Egypt is but a noise; "
18 As I live, saith the K', whose name "
26 of Nebuchadrezzar k' of Babylon, "
48: 15 the K', whose name is the Lord of "
49: 1 why then doth their k' inherit Gad,* "
3 their k' shall go into captivity, and* "
28 k' of Babylon shall smite, "
30 k' of Babylon hath taken counsel "
34 the reign of Zedekiah k' of Judah, "
38 thence the k' and the princes, "
50: 17 k' of Assyria hath devoured him; "
17 k' of Babylon hath broken his bones. "
18 I will punish the k' of Babylon and "
18 I have punished the k' of Assyria. "
43 The k' of Babylon hath heard the "
51: 31 shew the k' of Babylon that his city "
34 the k' of Babylon hath devoured me, "
57 the K', whose name is the Lord of "
59 went with Zedekiah the k' of Judah "
52: 3 rebelled against the k' of Babylon. "
4 k' of Babylon came, he and all his "
5 the eleventh year of k' Zedekiah. "

Jer 52: 8 the Chaldeans pursued after the k', 4428
9 they took the k', and carried him up "
9 unto the k' of Babylon to Riblah in "
10 the k' of Babylon slew the sons of "
11 k' of Babylon bound him in chains, "
12 of Nebuchadrezzar k' of Babylon, "
12 which served the k' of Babylon, "
15 that fell to the k' of Babylon, and "
20 k' Solomon had made in the house "
26 brought them to the k' of Babylon "
27 the k' of Babylon smote them, and "
31 captivity of Jehoiachin k' of Judah, "
31 Evil-merodach k' of Babylon, in the "
31 the head of Jehoiachin k' of Judah, "
34 diet given him of the k' of Babylon, "
La 2: 6 of his anger the k' and the priest. "
9 her k' and her princes are among "
Eze 1: 2 year of k' Jehoiachin's captivity, "
7: 27 The k' shall mourn, and the prince "
17: 12 k' of Babylon is come to Jerusalem, "
12 and hath taken the k' thereof, and "
16 surely in the place where the k' "
16 dwelleth that made him k' whose 4427
19: 9 brought him to the k' of Babylon: 4428
21: 19 the sword of the k' of Babylon may "
21 k' of Babylon stood at the parting "
24: 2 k' of Babylon set himself against "
26: 7 k' of Babylon, a k' of kings, "
28: 12 a lamentation upon the k' of Tyrus, "
29: 2 face against Pharaoh k' of Egypt, "
3 against thee, Pharaoh k' of Egypt, "
18 k' of Babylon caused his army to "
19 Nebuchadrezzar k' of Babylon; "
30: 10 of Nebuchadrezzar k' of Babylon. "
21 the arm of Pharaoh k' of Egypt; "
22 I am against Pharaoh k' of Egypt, "
24, 25 the arms of the k' of Babylon, "
25 into the hand of the k' of Babylon, "
31: 2 speak unto Pharaoh k' of Egypt, "
32: 2 lamentation for Pharaoh k' of Egypt, "
11 The sword of the k' of Babylon shall "
37: 22 and one k' shall be k' to them all: "
24 David my servant shall be k' over "
Da 1: 1 the reign of Jehoiakim k' of Judah "
1 Nebuchadnezzar k' of Babylon "
2 Lord gave Jehoiakim k' of Judah "
3 k' spake unto Ashpenaz the master "
5 k' appointed them a daily provision "
5 they might stand before the k'. "
10 unto Daniel, I fear my lord the k', "
10 me endanger my head to the k'. "
18 k' had said he should bring them in, "
19 the k' communed with them; and "
19 therefore stood they before the k'. "
20 the k' enquired of them, he found "
21 even unto the first year of k' Cyrus. "
2: 2 Then the k' commanded to call the "
2 for to shew the k' his dreams. "
2 they came and stood before the k'. "
3 k' said unto them, I have dreamed "
4 Then spake the Chaldeans to the k' "
4 O k', live for ever: tell thy servants 4430
5 The k' answered and said to the "
7 k' tell his servants the dream, and "
8 The k' answered and said, I know of "
10 Chaldeans answered before the k', "
10 there is no k', lord, nor ruler, "
11 is a rare thing that the k' requireth, "
11 other that can shew it before the k', "
12 For this cause the k' was angry and "
15 is the decree so hasty from the k'? "
16 desired of the k' that he would give "
16 shew the k' the interpretation. "
24 k' had ordained to destroy the wise "
24 bring me in before the k', and I will "
24 shew unto the k' the interpretation. "
25 brought in Daniel before the k' in "
25 will make known unto the k' the "
26 The k' answered and said to Daniel, "
27 answered in the presence of the k', "
27 secret which the k' hath demanded "
27 the soothsayers, shew unto the k'; "
28 known to the k' Nebuchadnezzar "
29 As for thee, O k', thy thoughts "
30 known the interpretation to the k', "
31 Thou, O k', sawest, and behold a "
36 interpretation thereof before the k'. "
37 Thou, O k', art a k' of kings: for "
45 known to the k' what shall come "
46 the k' Nebuchadnezzar fell upon his "
47 The k' answered unto Daniel, and "
48 the k' made Daniel a great man, "
49 Then Daniel requested of the k', "
49 but Daniel sat in the gate of the k'. "
3: 1 the k' made an image of gold, "
2 Then Nebuchadnezzar the k' sent to "
2 Nebuchadnezzar the k' had set up. "
3 Nebuchadnezzar the k' had set up; "
5 Nebuchadnezzar the k' hath set up: "
7 Nebuchadnezzar the k' had set up. "
9 They spake and said to the k' "
9 Nebuchadnezzar, O k', live for ever. "
10 Thou, O k', hast made a decree, that "
12 men, O k', have not regarded thee: "
13 brought these men before the k'. "
16 said to the k', O Nebuchadnezzar, "
17 deliver us out of thine hand, O k'. "
18 if not, be it known unto thee, O k', "
24 the k' was astonied, and rose up "
24 and said unto the k', True, O k'. "
30 k' promoted Shadrach, Meshach, "
4: 1 Nebuchadnezzar the k', unto all "
18 This dream I k' Nebuchadnezzar "
19 k' spake, and said, Belteshazzar, "
22 It is thou, O k', that art grown and "
23 And whereas the k' saw a watcher "

Da 4: 24 This is the interpretation, O k', 4430
24 which is come upon my lord the k': "
27 Wherefore, O k', let my counsel be "
28 came upon the k' Nebuchadnezzar. "
30 The k' spake, and said, Is not this "
31 O k' Nebuchadnezzar, to thee it is "
37 extol and honour the K' of heaven, "
5: 1 Belshazzar the k' made a great "
2 that the k', and his princes, his "
3 and the k', and his princes, and "
5 the k' saw the part of the hand that "
7 The k' cried aloud to bring in the "
7 the k' spake, and said to the wise "
8 known to the k' the interpretation "
9 was k' Belshazzar greatly troubled, "
10 by reason of the words of the k' "
10 and the queen spake and said, O k', "
11 the k' Nebuchadnezzar thy father, "
11 k', I say, thy father, made master "
12 whom the k' named Belteshazzar: "
13 Daniel brought in before the k'. "
13 the k' spake and said unto Daniel, "
13 k' my father brought out of Jewry? "
17 answered and said before the k', "
17 I will read the writing unto the k', "
18 O thou k', the most high God gave "
30 was...the k' of the Chaldeans slain. "
6: 2 and the k' should have no damage. "
3 the k' thought to set him over the "
6 assembled together to the k', "
6 unto him, K' Darius, live for ever. "
7 save of thee, O k', he shall be cast "
8 Now, O k', establish the decree, and "
9 k' Darius signed the writing and "
12 spake before the k' concerning the "
12 save of thee, O k', shall be cast into "
12 k' answered and said, The thing is "
13 and said before the k', That Daniel, "
13 regardeth not thee, O k', nor the "
14 Then the k', when he heard these "
15 these men assembled unto the k', "
15 and said unto the k', Know, O k', "
15 statute which the k' establisheth "
16 k' commanded, and they brought "
16 the k' spake and said unto Daniel, "
17 the k' sealed it with his own signet, "
18 Then the k' went to his palace, and "
19 Then the k' arose very early in the "
20 the k' spake and said to Daniel, O "
21 unto the k', O k', live for ever. "
22 before thee, O k', have I done no "
23 was the k' exceeding glad for him "
24 k' commanded, and they brought "
25 k' Darius wrote unto all people, "
7: 1 year of Belshazzar k' of Babylon "
8: 1 year of the reign of k' Belshazzar 4428
21 the rough goat is the k' of Grecia: "
21 is between his eyes is the first k'. "
23 the full, a k' of fierce countenance, "
9: 1 was made k' over the realm of the 4427
10: 1 third year of Cyrus k' of Persia 4428
11: 3 And a mighty k' shall stand up, that "
5 the k' of the south shall be strong, "
6 shall come to the k' of the north "
7 the fortress of the k' of the north, "
8 more years than the k' of the north. "
9 k' of the south shall come into his "
11 the k' of the south shall be moved "
11 him, even with the k' of the north: "
13 For the k' of the north shall return, "
14 up against the k' of the south: "
15 k' of the north shall come, and cast "
25 against the k' of the south with a "
25 k' of the south shall be stirred up "
36 k' shall do according to his will; "
40 the k' of the south push at him: "
40 k' of the north shall come against "
Ho 1: 1 the son of Joash, k' of Israel. "
3: 4 shall abide many days without a k', "
5 Lord their God, and David their k'; "
5: 1 and give ye ear, O house of the k'; "
13 the Assyrian, and sent to k' Jareb: "
7: 3 the k' glad with their wickedness, "
5 In the day of our k' the princes "
8: 10 for the burden of the k' of princes. "
10: 3 We have no k', because we feared "
3 what then should a k' do to us? "
6 Assyria for a present to k' Jareb: "
7 her k' is cut off as the foam upon "
15 shall the k' of Israel utterly be cut "
11: 5 Assyrian shall be his k', because "
13: 10 I will be thy k': where is any other "
10 saidst, Give me a k' and princes? "
11 I gave thee a k' in mine anger, and "
Am 1: 1 In the days of Uzziah k' of Judah, "
1 the son of Joash k' of Israel, "
15 their k' shall go into captivity, he "
2: 1 burned the bones of the k' of Edom "
7: 10 sent to Jeroboam k' of Israel, "
Jon 3: 6 word came unto the k' of Nineveh, "
7 the decree of the k' and his nobles, "
Mic 2: 13 and their k' shall pass before them, "
4: 9 no k' in thee? is thy counsellor "
6: 5 what Balak k' of Moab consulted, "
Na 3: 18 shepherds slumber, O k' of Assyria: "
Zep 1: 1 the son of Amon, k' of Judah. "
3: 15 the k' of Israel, even the Lord, is in "
Hag 1: 1 in the second year of Darius the k', "
15 in the second year of Darius the k'. "
Zec 7: 1 pass in the fourth year of k' Darius, "
9: 5 the k' shall perish from Gaza, and "
9 behold, thy K' cometh unto thee: "
11: 6 hand, and into the hand of his k': "
14: 5 the days of Uzziah k' of Judah: "
9 Lord shall be k' over all the earth: "
16 to worship the K', the Lord of hosts, "

Zec 14:17 unto Jerusalem to worship the *K*. 4428
Mal 1:14 I am a great *K*, saith the Lord of "
M't 1: 6 And Jesse begat David the *k*; 935
6 and David the *k* begat Solomon "
2: 1 Judæa in the days of Herod the *k*, "
2 is he that is born *K* of the Jews? "
3 When Herod the *k* had heard these "
9 When they had heard the *k*, they "
5:35 for it is the city of the great *K*. "
14: 9 the *k* was sorry: nevertheless for "
18:23 of heaven likened unto a certain *k*, "
21: 5 Behold, thy *K* cometh unto thee, "
22: 2 of heaven is like unto a certain *k*, "
7 when the *k* heard thereof, he was "
11 the *k* came in to see the guests, "
13 Then said the *k* to the servants, "
25:34 Then shall the *K* say unto them "
40 the *K* shall answer and say unto "
27:11 Art thou the *K* of the Jews? "
29 him, saying, Hail, *K* of the Jews! "
37 This Is Jesus The *K* Of The Jews. "
42 If he be the *K* of Israel, let him "
M'r 6:14 And *k* Herod heard of him; (for his "
22 him, the *k* said unto the damsel, "
25 straightway with haste unto the *k*, "
26 the *k* was exceeding sorry; yet for "
27 the *k* sent an executioner, "
15: 2 him, Art thou the *K* of the Jews? "
9 release unto you the *K* of the Jews? "
12 whom ye call the *K* of the Jews? "
18 salute him, Hail, *K* of the Jews! "
26 written over, The *K* Of The Jews. "
32 Let Christ the *K* of Israel descend "
Lu 1: 5 the days of Herod, the *k* of Judæa, "
14:31 Or what *k*, going to make war "
31 against another *k*, sitteth not down "
19:38 Blessed be the *K* that cometh in "
23: 2 that he himself is Christ a *K*. "
3 Art thou the *K* of the Jews? "
37 If thou be the *K* of the Jews, save "
38 This Is The *K* Of The Jews. "
Joh 1:49 of God; thou art the *K* of Israel. "
6:15 take him by force, to make him a *k*, "
12:13 Blessed is the *K* of Israel that "
15 thy *K* cometh, sitting on an ass's "
18:33 him, Art thou the *K* of the Jews? "
37 said unto him, Art thou a *k* then? "
37 Thou sayest that I am a *k*. To this "
39 unto you the *K* of the Jews? "
19: 3 said, Hail, *K* of the Jews! and they "
12 maketh himself a *k* speaketh "
14 unto the Jews, Behold your *K*! "
15 unto them, Shall I crucify your *K*? "
15 answered, We have no *k* but Cæsar. "
19 Jesus Of Nazareth The *K* Of The "
21 Write not, The *K* of the Jews; "
21 that he said, I am *K* of the Jews. "
Ac 7:10 the sight of Pharaoh *k* of Egypt; "
18 Till another *k* arose, which knew "
12: 1 Herod the *k* stretched forth his "
13:21 And afterward they desired a *k*: "
22 unto them David to be their *k*; "
17: 7 that there is another *k*, one Jesus. "
25:13 days *k* Agrippa and Bernice came "
14 declared Paul's cause unto the *k*, "
24 Festus said, *K* Agrippa, and all "
26 specially before thee, O *k* Agrippa, "
26: 2 I think myself happy, *k* Agrippa, "
7 For which hope's sake, *k* Agrippa, "
13 At midday, O *k*, I saw in the way a "
19 O *k* Agrippa, I was not disobedient "
26 For the *k* knoweth of these things, "
27 *K* Agrippa, believest thou the "
30 the *k* rose up, and the governor, "
2Co 11:32 governor under Aretas the *k* kept "
1Ti 1:17 Now unto the *K* eternal, immortal, "
6:15 *K* of kings, and Lord of lords; "
Heb 7: 1 Melchisedec, *k* of Salem, priest "
2 interpretation *K* of righteousness, "
2 *K* of Salem, which is, *K* of peace; "
11:27 not fearing the wrath of the *k*: for "
1Pe 2:13 whether it be to the *k*, as supreme; "
17 Fear God. Honour the *k*. "
Re 9:11 they had a *k* over them, which is "
15: 3 are thy ways, thou *K* of saints. "
17:14 is Lord of lords, and *K* of kings: "
19:16 *K* Of Kings, And Lord Of Lords. "

kingdom See also KINGDOMS.
Ge 10:10 the beginning of his *k* was Babel, 4467
20: 9 on me and on my *k* a great sin? "
Ex 19: 6 ye shall be unto me a *k* of priests, "
Nu 24: 7 Agag, and his *k* shall be exalted. 4438
32:33 *k* of Sihon king of the Amorites, 4467
33 and the *k* of Og king of Bashan, "
De 3: 4 of Argob, the *k* of Og in Bashan. "
10 cities of the *k* of Og in Bashan. "
13 being the *k* of Og, gave I unto the "
17:18 sitteth upon the throne of his *k*, "
20 he may prolong his days in his *k*, "
Jos 13:12 All the *k* of Og in Bashan, which 4468
21 *k* of Sihon king of the Amorites, "
27 the *k* of Sihon king of Heshbon, "
30 all the *k* of Og king of Bashan, "
31 cities of the *k* of Og in Bashan, "
1Sa 10:16 But of the matter of the *k*, whereof 4410
25 the people the manner of the *k*, "
11:14 to Gilgal, and renew the *k* there. "
13:13 Lord have established thy *k* upon 4467
14 But now thy *k* shall not continue: "
14:47 So Saul took the *k* over Israel, 4410
15:28 The Lord hath rent the *k* of Israel 4468
18: 8 can he have more but the *k*? 4410
20:31 not be established, nor thy *k*. 4438
24:20 *k* of Israel shall be established 4467
28:17 hath rent the *k* out of thine hand, "
2Sa 3:10 the *k* from the house of Saul, "
3:28 I and my *k* are guiltless before the 4467
5:12 he had exalted his *k* for his people "
7:12 bowels, and I will establish his *k*. "
13 I will stablish the throne of his *k* "
16 and thy *k* shall be established for "
16: 3 restore me the *k* of my father. 4468
8 the *k* into the hand of Absalom 4410
1Ki 1:46 sitteth on the throne of the *k*. "
2:12 and his *k* was established greatly. 4438
15 Thou knowest that the *k* was mine, 4410
15 howbeit the *k* is turned about, "
22 ask for him the *k* also; for he is "
46 *k* was established in the hand of 4467
9: 5 the throne of thy *k* upon Israel "
10:20 was not the like made in any *k*. "
11:11 I will surely rend the *k* from thee, "
13 I will not rend away all the *k*; but "
31 I will rend the *k* out of the hand "
34 will not take the whole *k* out of his "
35 I will take the *k* out of his son's 4410
12:21 bring the *k* again to Rehoboam "
26 the *k* return to the house of David 4467
14: 8 rent the *k* away from the house "
18:10 God liveth, there is no nation or *k*, "
10 he took an oath of the *k* and "
21: 7 thou now govern the *k* of Israel? 4410
2Ki 14: 5 the *k* was confirmed in his hand, 4467
15:19 him to confirm the *k* in his hand. "
1Ch 10:14 turned the *k* unto David the son 4410
11:10 themselves with him in his *k*, 4438
12:23 to turn the *k* of Saul to him, "
14: 2 for his *k* was lifted up on high, "
16:20 from one *k* to another people; 4467
17:11 sons; and I will establish his *k*. 4438
14 mine house and in my *k* for ever: "
22:10 I will establish the throne of his *k* "
28: 5 the throne of the *k* of the Lord "
7 I will establish his *k* for ever, if "
29:11 thine is the *k*, O Lord, and thou 4467
2Ch 1: 1 David was strengthened in his *k*, 4438
2: 1 the Lord, and an house for his *k*. "
12 for the Lord, and an house for his *k*. "
7:18 will I stablish the throne of thy *k*, 4438
9:19 was not the like made in any *k*. 4467
11: 1 bring the *k* again to Rehoboam. "
17 strengthened the *k* of Judah, 4438
12: 1 Rehoboam had established the *k*, "
13: 5 gave the *k* over Israel to David 4467
8 withstand the *k* of the Lord in the "
14: 5 and the *k* was quiet before him. "
17: 5 the Lord stablished the *k* in his "
21: 3 the *k* gave he to Jehoram; because "
4 Jehoram was risen up to the *k* of "
22: 9 had no power to keep still the *k*. "
23:20 the king upon the throne of the *k*. "
25: 3 when the *k* was established to him, "
29:21 goats, for a sin offering for the *k*, "
32:15 no god of any nation or *k* was able "
33:13 again to Jerusalem into his *k*. 4438
36:20 until the reign of the *k* of Persia: "
22 proclamation throughout all his *k*, "
Ezr 1: 1 proclamation throughout all his *k*, "
Ne 9:35 have not served thee in their *k*, "
Es 1: 2 sat on the throne of his *k*, which "
4 shewed the riches of his glorious *k* "
14 and which sat the first in the *k*;) "
2: 3 in all the provinces of his *k*, that "
3: 6 the whole *k* of Ahasuerus, "
8 people in all the provinces of thy *k*; "
4:14 art come to the *k* for such a time "
5: 3 even given thee to the half of the *k*. "
6 even to the half of the *k* it shall be "
7: 2 performed, even to the half of the *k*. "
9:30 twenty and seven provinces of the *k* "
Ps 22:28 For the *k* is the Lord's: and he 4410
45: 6 sceptre of thy *k* is a right sceptre. 4438
103:19 heavens; and his *k* ruleth over all. "
105:13 from one *k* to another people; 4467
145:11 shall speak of the glory of thy *k*, 4438
12 and the glorious majesty of his *k*. "
13 Thy *k* is an everlasting *k*, and "
Ec 4:14 is born in his *k* becometh poor. "
Isa 9: 7 upon his *k*, to order it, and to 4467
17: 3 the *k* from Damascus, and the "
19: 2 city against city, and *k* against *k*. "
34:12 call the nobles thereof to the *k*, 4410
60:12 *k* that will not serve thee shall 4467
Jer 18: 7 concerning a *k*, to pluck up, and "
9 concerning a *k*, to build and to "
27: 8 nation and *k* which will not serve "
La 2: 2 hath polluted the princes and the *k* "
Eze 16:13 and thou didst prosper into a *k*. *4410
17:14 That the *k* might be base, that it 4467
29:14 and they shall be there a base *k*. "
Da 2:37 of heaven hath given thee a *k*, 4437
39 shall arise another *k* inferior to "
39 and another third *k* of brass, which "
40 fourth *k* shall be strong as iron: "
41 part of iron, the *k* shall be divided; "
42 so the *k* shall be partly strong, "
44 shall the God of heaven set up a *k*, "
44 the *k* shall not be left to other * "
4: 3 his *k* is an everlasting *k*, and his "
17 most High ruleth in the *k* of men, "
18 the wise men of my *k* are not able "
25 most High ruleth in the *k* of men, "
26 thy *k* shall be sure unto thee, after "
29 in the palace of the *k* of Babylon.* "
30 I have built for the house of the *k* * "
31 The *k* is departed from thee. "
32 most High ruleth in the *k* of men, "
34 his *k* is from generation to "
36 for the glory of my *k*, mine honour "
36 and I was established in my *k*, "
5: 7 shall be the third ruler in the *k*. "
11 There is a man in thy *k*, in whom "
Da 5:16 shalt be the third ruler in the *k*. 4437
18 Nebuchadnezzar thy father a *k*, "
21 high God ruled in the *k* of men, "
26 Mene; God hath numbered thy *k*, "
28 Peres; Thy *k* is divided, and given "
29 should be the third ruler in the *k*. "
31 And Darius the Median took the *k*, "
6: 1 pleased Darius to set over the *k* "
1 which should be over the whole *k*; "
4 against Daniel concerning the *k*; "
7 All the presidents of the *k*, the "
26 That in every dominion of my *k* "
26 his *k* that which shall not be "
7:14 him dominion, and glory, and a *k*, "
14 his *k* that which shall not be "
18 of the most High shall take the *k*, "
18 possess the *k* for ever, even for ever "
22 that the saints possessed the *k*. "
23 shall be the fourth *k* upon earth, "
24 out of this *k* are ten kings that shall "
27 And the *k* and dominion, and the "
27 greatness of the *k* under the whole* "
27 High, whose *k* is an everlasting *k*, "
8:23 And in the latter time of their *k*, 4438
10:13 But the prince of the *k* of Persia "
11: 4 stand up, his *k* shall be broken, "
4 for his *k* shall be plucked up, even "
9 of the south shall come into his *k*,* "
17 with the strength of his whole *k*, "
20 of taxes in the glory of the *k*: "
21 shall not give the honour of the *k*: "
21 and obtain the *k* by flatteries. "
Ho 1: 4 cease the *k* of the house of Israel. 4468
Am 9: 8 Lord God are upon the sinful *k*, 4467
Ob 21 and the *k* shall be the Lord's. 4410
Mic 4: 8 the *k* shall come to the daughter 4467
M't 3: 2 ye: for the *k* of heaven is at hand. 932
4:17 for the *k* of heaven is at hand. "
23 and preaching the gospel of the *k*, "
5: 3 spirit: for theirs is the *k* of heaven. "
10 sake: for theirs is the *k* of heaven. "
19 called the least in the *k* of heaven: "
19 be called great in the *k* of heaven. "
20 no case enter into the *k* of heaven. "
6:10 Thy *k* come. Thy will be done in "
13 For thine is the *k*, and the power, * "
33 seek ye first the *k* of God, and his "
7:21 shall enter into the *k* of heaven, "
8:11 Isaac, and Jacob, in the *k* of heaven: "
12 children of the *k* shall be cast out "
9:35 and preaching the gospel of the *k*, "
10: 7 saying, The *k* of heaven is at hand. "
11:11 least in the *k* of heaven is greater "
12 the *k* of heaven suffereth violence, "
12:25 *k* divided against itself is brought "
26 how shall then his *k* stand? "
28 then the *k* of God is come unto you. "
13:11 the mysteries of the *k* of heaven, "
19 any one heareth the word of the *k*, "
24 *k* of heaven is likened unto a man "
31 *k* of heaven is like to a grain of "
33 *k* of heaven is like unto leaven, "
38 good seed are the children of the *k*; "
41 shall gather out of his *k* all things "
43 as the sun in the *k* of their Father. "
44 the *k* of heaven is like unto treasure "
45 *k* of heaven is like unto a merchant "
47 the *k* of heaven is like unto a net, "
52 is instructed unto the *k* of heaven, "
16:19 thee the keys of the *k* of heaven: "
28 see the Son of man coming in his *k*. "
18: 1 is the greatest in the *k* of heaven? "
3 shall not enter into the *k* of heaven. "
4 same is greatest in the *k* of heaven. "
23 *k* of heaven likened unto a certain "
19:12 eunuchs for the *k* of heaven's sake. "
14 me; for of such is the *k* of heaven. "
23 hardly enter into the *k* of heaven. "
24 for a rich man to enter into the *k* of "
20: 1 *k* of heaven is like unto a man that "
21 and the other on the left, in thy *k*. "
21:31 harlots go into the *k* of God before "
43 *k* of God shall be taken from you, "
22: 2 The *k* of heaven is like unto a "
23:13 ye shut up the *k* of heaven against "
24: 7 against nation, and *k* against *k*: "
14 gospel of the *k* shall be preached "
25: 1 *k* of heaven be likened unto ten "
14 *k* of heaven is as a man travelling "
34 inherit the *k* prepared for you from "
26:29 it new with you in my Father's *k*. "
M'r 1:14 preaching the gospel of the *k* of God, "
15 fulfilled, and the *k* of God is at hand: "
3:24 if a *k* be divided against itself, "
24 that *k* cannot stand. "
4:11 know the mystery of the *k* of God: "
26 So is the *k* of God, as if a man "
30 Whereunto shall we liken the *k* of "
6:23 give it thee, unto the half of my *k*. "
9: 1 have seen the *k* of God come with "
47 enter into the *k* of God with one eye, "
10:14 not: for of such is the *k* of God. "
15 shall not receive the *k* of God as a "
23 have riches enter into the *k* of God! "
24 in riches to enter into the *k* of God! "
25 rich man to enter into the *k* of God. "
11:10 Blessed be the *k* of our father David, "
12:34 Thou art not far from the *k* of God. "
13: 8 against nation, and *k* against *k*: "
14:25 that I drink it new in the *k* of God "
15:43 which also waited for the *k* of God, "
Lu 1:33 of his *k* there shall be no end. "
4:43 preach the *k* of God to other cities "
6:20 ye poor: for yours is the *k* of God. "
7:28 he that is least in the *k* of God is "
8: 1 the glad tidings of the *k* of God: "

Lu 8:10 know the mysteries of the k' of God: 932
9: 2 sent them to preach the k' of God. "
11 spake unto them of the k' of God, "
27 of death, till they see the k' of God. "
60 go thou and preach the k' of God. "
62 looking back, is fit for the k' of God. "
10: 9 The k' of God is come nigh unto you. "
11 the k' of God is come nigh unto you. "
11: 2 Thy k' come. Thy will be done, as "
17 Every k' divided against itself is "
18 himself, how shall his k' stand? "
20 no doubt the k' of God is come upon "
12:31 But rather seek ye the k' of God; "
32 good pleasure to give you the k'. "
13:18 he, unto what is the k' of God like? "
20 whereunto shall I liken the k' of God? "
28 all the prophets, in the k' of God, "
29 and shall sit down in the k' of God. "
14:15 that shall eat bread in the k' of God. "
16:16 that time the k' of God is preached, "
17:20 when the k' of God should come, he "
20 The k' of God cometh not with "
21 behold, the k' of God is within you. "
18:16 not: for of such is the k' of God. "
17 shall not receive the k' of God as a "
24 have riches enter into the k' of God! "
25 rich man to enter into the k' of God. "
29 or children, for the k' of God's sake, "
19:11 they thought that the k' of God "
12 to receive for himself a k', and to "
15 was returned, having received the k', "
21:10 against nation, and k' against k': "
31 ye that the k' of God is nigh at hand. "
22:16 until it be fulfilled in the k' of God. "
18 vine, until the k' of God shall come. "
29 I appoint unto you a k', as my "
30 eat and drink at my table in my k', "
23:42 me when thou comest into thy k'. "
51 himself waited for the k' of God. "
Joh 3: 3 again, he cannot see the k' of God. "
5 he cannot enter into the k' of God. "
18:36 answered, My k' is not of this world: "
36 if my k' were of this world, then "
36 but now is my k' not from hence. "
Ac 1: 3 things pertaining to the k' of God: "
6 time restore again the k' to Israel? "
8:12 things concerning the k' of God, "
14:22 tribulation enter into the k' of God. "
19: 8 things concerning the k' of God. "
20:25 have gone, preaching the k' of God, "
28:23 and testified the k' of God, "
31 Preaching the k' of God, and "
Ro 14:17 For the k' of God is not meat and "
1Co 4:20 the k' of God is not in word, but in "
6: 9 shall not inherit the k' of God? "
10 nor..., shall inherit the k' of God. "
15:24 have delivered up the k' to God, "
50 blood cannot inherit the k' of God; "
Ga 5:21 shall not inherit the k' of God. "
Eph 5: 5 any inheritance in the k' of Christ "
Col 1:13 us into the k' of his dear Son: "
4:11 fellow-workers unto the k' of God, "
1Th 2:12 called you unto his k' and glory. "
2Th 1: 5 be counted worthy of the k' of God, "
2Ti 4: 1 dead at his appearing and his k'; "
18 preserve me unto his heavenly k': "
Heb 1: 8 righteousness is the sceptre of thy k'. "
12:28 we receiving a k' which cannot be "
Jas 2: 5 heirs of the k' which he hath "
2Pe 1:11 into the everlasting k' of our Lord "
Re 1: 9 in the k' and patience of Jesus "
12:10 strength, and the k' of our God, "
16:10 his k' was full of darkness; and "
17:12 which have received no k' as yet; "
17 give their k' unto the beast, until "

kingdoms

De 3:21 all the k' whither thou passest. 4467
28:25 removed into all the k' of the earth. "
Jos 11:10 was the head of all those k'. "
1Sa 10:18 and out of the hand of all k', "
1Ki 4:21 And Solomon reigned over all k' "
2Ki 19:15 thou alone, of all the k' of the earth; "
19 all the k' of the earth may know "
1Ch 29:30 over all the k' of the countries. "
2Ch 12: 8 service of the k' of the countries. "
17:10 fell upon all the k' of the lands "
20: 6 over all the k' of the heathen? "
29 the fear of God was on all the k' "
36:23 All the k' of the earth hath the Lord "
Ezr 1: 2 given me all the k' of the earth; "
Ne 9:22 thou gavest them k' and nations, "
Ps 46: 6 heathen raged, the k' were moved: "
68:32 Sing unto God, ye k' of the earth; "
79: 6 and upon the k' that have not called "
102:22 and the k', to serve the Lord. "
135:11 Bashan, and all the k' of Canaan: "
Isa 10:10 hand hath found the k' of the idols, "
13: 4 tumultuous noise of the k' of nations "
19 And Babylon, the glory of k', "
14:16 earth to tremble, that did shake k'; "
23:11 over the sea, he shook the k': "
17 commit fornication with all the k' "
37:16 alone, of all the k' of the earth: "
20 that all the k' of the earth may know "
47: 5 no more be called, The lady of k'. "
Jer 1:10 over the nations and over the k', "
15 the families of the k' of the north, "
10: 7 of the nations, and in all their k', * "
15: 4 be removed into all k' of the earth, "
24: 9 be removed into the k' of the earth "
25:26 another, and all the k' of the world, "
28: 8 countries, and against great k', "
29:18 be removed to all the k' of the earth, "
34: 1 and all the k' of the earth of his "
17 removed into all the k' of the earth. "
49:28 and concerning the k' of Hazor, "
Jer 51:20 and with thee will I destroy k'; 4467
27 against her the k' of Ararat, "
Eze 29:15 It shall be the basest of the k'; "
37:22 divided into two k' any more at all: "
Da 2:44 in pieces and consume all these k', 4437
7:23 which shall be diverse from all k', "
8:22 four k' shall stand up out of the 4438
Am 6: 2 be they better than these k'? 4467
Na 3: 5 nakedness, and the k' thy shame. "
Zep 3: 8 nations, that I may assemble the k', "
Hag 2:22 I will overthrow the throne of k', "
22 I will destroy the strength of the k' "
M't 4: 8 sheweth him all the k' of the world, 932
Lu 4: 5 unto him all the k' of the world in "
Heb 11:33 Who through faith subdued k', "
Re 11:15 The k' of this world are become "
15 the k' of our Lord, and of his Christ; "

kingly

Da 5:20 was deposed from his k' throne, 4437

king's

Ge 14:17 Shaveh, which is in the k' dale. 4428
39:20 where the k' prisoners were bound: "
Nu 20:17 we will go by the k' high way, we "
21:22 we will go along by the k' high way, "
1Sa 18:22 now therefore be the k' son in law. "
23 a light thing to be a k' son in law, "
25 to be avenged of the k' enemies. "
26 David well to be the k' son in law: "
27 that he might be the k' son in law. "
20:29 he cometh not unto the k' table. "
21: 8 the k' business required haste. "
22:14 David, which is the k' son in law, "
23:20 be to deliver him into the k' hand. "
26:16 And now see where the k' spear is, "
22 and said, Behold the k' spear! "
2Sa 9:11 at my table, as one of the k' sons. "
13 did eat continually at the k' table; "
11: 2 upon the roof of the k' house: "
8 Uriah departed out of the k' house, "
9 slept at the door of the k' house "
20 And if so be that the k' wrath arise, "
24 some of the k' servants be dead, "
12:30 he took their k' crown from off his* "
13: 4 Why art thou, being the k' son, * "
18 such robes were the k' daughters "
23 Absalom invited all the k' sons. "
27 and all the k' sons go with him. "
29 Then all the k' sons arose, and "
30 Absalom hath slain all the k' sons, "
32 slain all the young men the k' sons; "
33 think that all the k' sons are dead: "
35 Behold, the k' sons come: as thy "
36 the k' sons came, and lifted up "
14: 1 the k' heart was toward Absalom. "
24 house, and saw not the k' face. "
26 hundred shekels after the k' weight. "
28 Jerusalem, and saw not the k' face. "
32 therefore let me see the k' face; "
15:15 the k' servant said unto the king, "
35 thou shalt hear out of the k' house, "
16: 2 The asses be for the k' household "
18:12 mine hand against the k' son: "
18 pillar, which is in the k' dale: "
20 because the k' son is dead. "
29 When Joab sent the k' servant, "
19:18 boat to carry over the k' household, "
42 have we eaten at all of the k' cost? "
24: 4 the k' word prevailed against Joab, "
1Ki 1: 9 called all his brethren the k' sons, "
9 the men of Judah the k' servants: "
25 and hath called all the k' sons, "
28 she came into the k' presence, and "
44 him to ride upon the k' mule: "
47 k' servants came to bless our lord "
2:19 a seat to be set for the k' mother; "
4: 5 principal officer, and the k' friend: "
9: 1, 10 of the Lord, and the k' house, "
10:12 of the Lord, and for the k' house, "
28 the k' merchants received the linen "
11:14 he was of the k' seed in Edom. "
13: 6 k' hand was restored him again, "
14:26 and the treasures of the k' house; "
27 which kept the door of the k' house. "
15:18 and the treasures of the k' house, "
16:18 went into the palace of the k' house, "
18 and burnt the k' house over him "
22:12 shall deliver it into the k' hand. * "
26 of the city, and to Joash the k' son; "
2Ki 7: 9 may go and tell the k' household. "
11 they told it to the k' house within. "
9:34 bury her: for she is a k' daughter. "
10: 6 the k' sons, being seventy persons, "
7 that they took the k' sons, and slew "
8 brought the heads of the k' sons. "
11: 2 stole him from among the k' sons "
4 Lord, and shewed them the k' son. "
5 of the watch of the k' house; "
12 he brought forth the k' son, and put "
16 the horses came into the k' house: "
19 gate of the guard to the k' house. "
20 with the sword beside the k' house. "
12:10 the k' scribe and the high priest "
18 of the Lord, and in the k' house, "
13:16 put his hands upon the k' hands. "
14:14 and in the treasures of the k' house, "
15: 5 And Jotham the k' son was over the "
25 in the palace of the k' house, "
16: 8 and in the treasures of the k' house, "
15 the k' burnt sacrifice, and his meat "
18 the house, and the k' entry without, "
18:15 and in the treasures of the k' house. "
36 for the k' commandment was, "
22:12 and Asahiah a servant of the k', "
24:13 and the treasures of the k' house, "
15 the k' mother, and the k' wives, and "
2Ki 25: 4 walls, which is by the k' garden: 4428
9 house of the Lord, and the k' house, "
19 them that were in the k' presence, "
1Ch 9:18 Who hitherto waited in the k' gate "
21: 4 Nevertheless the k' word prevailed "
6 k' word was abominable to Joab. "
25: 5 Heman the k' seer in the words of "
6 according to the k' order to Asaph,* "
27:25 over the k' treasures was Azmaveth "
32 of Hachmoni was with the k' sons: "
33 Ahithophel was the k' counsellor: "
33 the Archite was the k' companion: "
34 the general of the k' army was Joab. "
29: 6 the rulers of the k' work, offered "
2Ch 1:16 the k' merchants received the linen "
7:11 house of the Lord, and the k' house: "
9:11 of the Lord, and to the k' palace, "
21 the k' ships went to Tarshish with* "
12: 9 and the treasures of the k' house; "
10 kept the entrance of the k' house. "
16: 2 of the Lord and of the k' house, "
18: 5 God will deliver it into the k' hand.* "
25 the city, and to Joash the k' son; "
19:11 of Judah, for all the k' matters: "
21:17 that was found in the k' house, "
22:11 stole him from among the k' sons "
23: 3 Behold, the k' son shall reign, as "
5 third part shall be at the k' house; "
11 Then they brought out the k' son, "
15 of the horse gate by the k' house, "
20 the high gate into the k' house, "
24: 8 at the k' commandment they made* "
11 chest was brought unto the k' office "
11 the k' scribe and the high priest's "
25:16 Art thou made of the k' counsel? "
24 and the treasures of the k' house, "
26:11 of Hananiah, one of the k' captains. "
21 his son was over the k' house, "
28: 7 Ephraim, slew Maaseiah the k' son, "
29:25 of Gad the k' seer, and Nathan the "
31: 3 He appointed also the k' portion of "
34:20 Asaiah a servant of the k', saying, "
35: 7 these were of the k' substance. "
10 according to the k' commandment. "
15 Heman, and Jeduthun the k' seer; "
Ezr 4:14 maintenance from the k' palace, *4430
14 meet for us to see the k' dishonour, "
5:17 made in the k' treasure house, "
6: 4 expences be given out of the k' house. "
8 of the k' goods, even of the tribute "
7:20 bestow it out of the k' treasure "
27 such a thing as this in the k' heart, 4428
28 before all the k' mighty princes. "
8:36 they delivered the k' commissions "
36 commissions unto the k' lieutenants, "
Ne 1:11 man. For I was the k' cupbearer.* "
2: 8 Asaph the keeper of the k' forest, "
9 river, and gave them the k' letters. "
14 of the fountain, and to the k' pool: "
18 the k' words that he had spoken "
3:15 the pool of Siloah by the k' garden, "
25 lieth out from the k' high house, * "
5: 4 borrowed money for the k' tribute, "
11:23 k' commandment concerning them,* "
24 was at the k' hand in all matters "
Es 1: 5 of the garden of the k' palace; "
12 to come at the k' commandment "
13 so was the k' manner toward all "
14 which saw the k' face, and which "
18 say this day unto all the k' princes, "
20 the k' decree, which he shall make "
22 sent letters into all the k' provinces, "
2: 2 said the k' servants that ministered "
3 Hege the k' chamberlain, keeper of "
8 when the k' commandment and his "
8 was brought also unto the k' house, "
9 to be given her, out of the k' house: "
13 of the women unto the k' house. "
14 the k' chamberlain, which kept the "
15 but what Hegai the k' chamberlain, "
19 then Mordecai sat in the k' gate. "
21 while Mordecai sat in the k' gate, "
21 two of the k' chamberlains, Bigthan "
3: 2 k' servants, that were in the k' gate, "
3 k' servants, which were in the k' gate, "
3 thou the k' commandment? "
8 neither keep they the k' laws: "
8 not for the k' profit to suffer them. "
9 to bring it into the k' treasuries. "
12 Then were the k' scribes called on "
12 commanded unto the k' lieutenants, "
12 written, and sealed with the k' ring. "
13 by posts into all the k' provinces, "
15 hastened by the k' commandment, "
4: 2 And came even before the k' gate: "
2 none might enter into the k' gate "
3 whithersoever the k' commandment "
5 one of the k' chamberlains, whom "
6 city, which was before the k' gate. "
7 promised to pay to the k' treasuries "
11 All the k' servants, and the people "
11 and the people of the k' provinces, "
13 thou shalt escape in the k' house, "
5: 1 in the inner court of the k' house, "
1 house, over against the k' house: "
9 Haman saw Mordecai in the k' gate, "
13 Mordecai...sitting at the k' gate. "
6: 2 Teresh, two of the k' chamberlains, "
3 the k' servants that ministered unto "
4 the outward court of the k' house, "
5 k' servants said unto him, Behold, "
9 of one of the k' most noble princes, "
10 the Jew, that sitteth at the k' gate: "
12 Mordecai came again to the k' gate. "
14 with him, came the k' chamberlains, "
7: 4 not countervail the k' damage. "

7: 8 the word went out of the k' mouth, 4428
10 Then was the k' wrath pacified. "
8: 5 which are in all the k' provinces: "
8 as it liketh you, in the k' name, "
8 name, and seal it with the k' ring: "
8 which is written in the k' name, "
8 name, and sealed with the k' ring, "
9 the k' scribes called at that time "
10 sealed it with the k' ring, and sent "
14 pressed on by the k' commandment. "
17 whithersoever the k' commandment "
9: 1 k' commandment and his decree "
4 Mordecai was great in the k' house, "
12 done in the rest of the k' provinces? "
16 Jews that were in the k' provinces "
Ps 45: 5 sharp in the heart of the k' enemies; "
13 k' daughter is all glorious within "
15 they shall enter into the k' palace. "
61: 6 Thou wilt prolong the k' life: and "
72: 1 thy righteousness unto the k' son. "
99: 4 k' strength also loveth judgment; "
Pr 14: 28 multitude of people is the k' honour: "
35 k' favour is toward a wise servant: "
16: 15 In the light of the k' countenance "
19: 12 The k' wrath is as the roaring of a "
21: 1 The k' heart is in the hand of the "
Ec 8: 2 thee to keep the k' commandment, "
Isa 36: 21 for the k' commandment was, "
Jer 22: 6 Lord unto the k' house of Judah; * "
26: 10 came up from the k' house unto the "
36: 12 he went down into the k' house, "
38: 7 eunuchs which was in the k' house, "
8 went forth out of the k' house, and "
39: 4 by the way of the k' garden, by the "
8 the Chaldeans burned the k' house, "
41: 10 even the k' daughters, and all the "
43: 6 and children, and the k' daughters, "
52: 7 walls, which was by the k' garden; "
13 house of the Lord, and the k' house; "
25 them that were near the k' person. "
Eze 17: 13 hath taken of the k' seed, and *4410
Da 1: 3 and of the k' seed, and of the * "
4 in them to stand in the k' palace. 4428
5 a daily provision of the k' meat, "
8 with the portion of the k' meat, "
13 eat of the portion of the k' meat: "
15 did eat the portion of the k' meat. "
2: 10 earth that can shew the k' matter: 4430
14 Arioch the captain of the k' guard, "
15 and said to Arioch the k' captain, "
23 made known unto us the k' matter. "
3: 22 the k' commandment was urgent, "
27 captains, and the k' counsellors, "
28 him, and have changed the k' word, "
4: 31 the word was in the k' mouth, "
5: 5 plaister of the wall of the k' palace: "
6 the k' countenance was changed, "
8 Then came in all the k' wise men: "
6: 12 the king concerning the k' decree; "
8: 27 rose up, and did the k' business; 4428
11: 6 the k' daughter of the south shall* "
Am 7: 1 latter growth after the k' mowings. "
13 Beth-el: for it is the k' chapel, "
13 chapel, and it is the k' court. *4467
Zep 1: 8 the princes, and the k' children, 4428
Zec 14: 10 Hananeel unto the k' winepresses. "
Ac 12: 20 Blastus the k' chamberlain their 935
20 was nourished by the k' country. 937
Heb 11: 23 afraid of the k' commandment. 935
kings See also KINGS'.
Ge 14: 5 and the k' that were with him, and 4428
9 king of Ellasar; four k' with five. "
10 the k' of Sodom and Gomorrah fled, "
17 of the k' that were with him, at the "
17: 6 thee, and k' shall come out of thee. "
16 nations; k' of people shall be of her. "
35: 11 and k' shall come out of thy loins; "
36: 31 the k' that reigned in the land of "
Nu 31: 8 they slew the k' of Midian, beside "
8 Hur, and Reba, five k' of Midian: "
De 3: 8 hand of the two k' of the Amorites "
21 God hath done unto these two k': "
4: 47 of Bashan, two k' of the Amorites, "
7: 24 deliver their k' into thine hand, "
31: 4 Sihon and to Og, k' of the Amorites, "
Jos 2: 10 unto the two k' of the Amorites, "
5: 1 all the k' of the Amorites, which "
1 and all the k' of the Canaanites, "
9: 1 all the k' which were on this side "
10 did to the two k' of the Amorites, "
10: 5 the five k' of the Amorites, the "
6 all the k' of the Amorites that dwell "
16 these five k' fled, and hid themselves "
17 The five k' are found hid in a cave "
22 bring out those five k' unto me out "
23 brought forth those five k' unto him "
24 brought out those k' unto Joshua, "
24 your feet upon the necks of these k'. "
40 and of the springs, and all their k': "
42 all these k' and their land did "
11: 2 the k' that were on the north of the "
5 all these k' were met together, "
12 And all the cities of those k', "
12 all the k' of them, did Joshua take, "
17 their k' he took, and smote them, "
18 war a long time with all those k'. "
12: 1 these are the k' of the land, which "
7 k' of the country which Joshua and "
24 one: all the k' thirty and one. "
24: 12 even the two k' of the Amorites; "
J'g 1: 7 Threescore and ten k', having their "
5: 3 Hear, O ye k'; give ear, O ye "
19 The k' came and fought, then "
19 fought the k' of Canaan in Taanach "
8: 5 Zebah and Zalmunna, k' of Midian. "
12 took the two k' of Midian, Zebah

J'g 8: 26 purple raiment that was on the k' 4428
1Sa 14: 47 Edom, and against the k' of Zobah, "
27: 6 pertaineth unto the k' of Judah "
2Sa 10: 19 k' that were servants to Hadarezer "
11: 1 the time when k' go forth to battle, "
1Ki 3: 13 there shall not be any among the k' "
4: 24 all the k' on this side the river: "
34 from all k' of the earth, which had "
10: 15 and of all the k' of Arabia, and of "
23 king Solomon exceeded all the k' "
29 and so for all the k' of the Hittites, "
29 and for the k' of Syria, did they "
14: 19 of the chronicles of the k' of Israel. "
29 of the chronicles of the k' of Judah? "
15: 7, 23 chronicles of the k' of Judah? "
31 of the chronicles of the k' of Israel? "
16: 5, 14, 20, 27 chronicles of...k' of Israel? "
33 all the k' of Israel that were before "
20: 1 were thirty and two k' with him, "
12 he and the k' in the pavilions, that "
16 in the pavilions, he and the k', "
16 thirty and two k' that helped him. "
24 Take the k' away, every man out of "
31 have heard that the k' of the house "
31 house of Israel are merciful k': "
22: 39 the chronicles of the k' of Israel? "
45 the chronicles of the k' of Judah? "
2Ki 1: 18 the chronicles of the k' of Israel? "
3: 10, 13 called these three k' together, "
21 that the k' were come up to fight "
23 k' are surely slain, and they have "
7: 6 against us the k' of the Hittites, "
6 the k' of the Egyptians, to come "
8: 18 walked in the way of the k' of Israel, "
23 the chronicles of the k' of Judah? "
10: 4 two k' stood not before him: how "
34 the chronicles of the k' of Israel? "
11: 19 And he sat on the throne of the k'. "
12: 18 k' of Judah, had dedicated, and his "
19 the chronicles of the k' of Judah? "
13: 8, 12 chronicles of the k' of Israel? "
13 in Samaria with the k' of Israel. "
14: 15 the chronicles of the k' of Israel? "
16 in Samaria with the k' of Israel; "
18 the chronicles of the k' of Judah? "
28 the chronicles of the k' of Israel? "
29 fathers, even with the k' of Israel; "
15: 6 the chronicles of the k' of Judah? "
11, 15 chronicles of the k' of Israel. "
21 the chronicles of the k' of Israel? "
26, 31 the chronicles of the k' of Israel. "
36 the chronicles of the k' of Judah? "
16: 3 walked in the way of the k' of Israel, "
19 the chronicles of the k' of Judah? "
17: 2 not as the k' of Israel that were "
8 of Israel, and of the k' of Israel, "
18: 5 him among all the k' of Judah, "
19: 11 k' of Assyria have done to all lands, "
17 k' of Assyria have destroyed the "
20: 20 the chronicles of the k' of Judah? "
21: 17, 25 chronicles of the k' of Judah? "
23: 5 k' of Judah had ordained to burn "
11 k' of Judah had given to the sun, "
12 which the k' of Judah had made, "
19 k' of Israel had made to provoke "
22 in all the days of the k' of Israel, "
22 nor of the k' of Judah; "
28 the chronicles of the k' of Judah? "
24: 5 of the chronicles of the k' of Judah? "
25: 28 k' that were with him in Babylon; "
1Ch 1: 43 k' that reigned in the land of Edom "
9: 1 book of the k' of Israel and Judah, "
16: 21 yea, he reproved k' for their sakes, "
19: 9 and the k' that were come were by "
20: 1 at the time that k' go out to battle, "
2Ch 1: 12 such as none of the k' have had that "
17 horses for all the k' of the Hittites, "
17 and for the k' of Syria, by their "
9: 14 all the k' of Arabia and governors of "
22 passed all the k' of the earth in "
23 k' of the earth sought the presence "
26 And he reigned over all the k' from "
16: 11 book of the k' of Judah and Israel. "
20: 34 in the book of the k' of Israel. "
21: 6, 13 in the way of the k' of Israel, "
20 but not in the sepulchres of the k'. "
24: 16 in the city of David among the k', "
25 him not in the sepulchres of the k'. "
27 in the story of the book of the k'. "
25: 26 book of the k' of Judah and Israel? "
26: 23 the burial which belonged to the k'; "
27: 7 book of the k' of Israel and Judah. "
28: 2 in the ways of the k' of Israel, "
16 Ahaz send unto the k' of Assyria "
23 gods of the k' of Syria help them, "
26 book of the k' of Judah and Israel. "
27 the sepulchres of the k' of Israel: "
30: 6 out of the hand of the k' of Assyria. "
32: 4 Why should the k' of Assyria come, "
32 book of the k' of Judah and Israel. "
33: 18 in the book of the k' of Israel. "
34: 11 which the k' of Judah had destroyed. "
35: 18 the k' of Israel keep such a passover "
27 book of the k' of Israel and Judah. "
36: 8 book of the k' of Israel and Judah: "
Ezr 4: 13 endamage the revenue of the k'. 4430
15 and hurtful unto k' and provinces, "
19 hath made insurrection against k', "
20 been mighty k' also over Jerusalem, "
22 damage grow to the hurt of the k'? "
6: 12 there destroy all k' and people, "
7: 12 Artaxerxes, king of k', unto Ezra 4428
9: 7 have we, our k', and our priests, "
7 into the hand of the k' of the lands, "
9 us in the sight of the k' of Persia, "
Ne 9: 24 with their k', and the people of the "

Ne 9: 32 upon us, on our k', on our princes, 4428
32 since the time of the k' of Assyria "
34 Neither have our k', our princes, "
37 the k' whom thou hast set over us "
Es 10: 2 of the chronicles of the k' of Media "
Job 3: 14 With k' and counsellors of the earth, "
12: 18 He looseth the bond of k', and "
36: 7 but with k' are they on the throne; "
Ps 2: 2 k' of the earth set themselves, and "
10 Be wise now therefore, O ye k': be "
48: 4 For, lo, the k' were assembled, they "
68: 12 K' of armies did flee apace: and she "
14 Almighty scattered k' in it, it was "
29 shall k' bring presents unto thee. "
72: 10 k' of Tarshish and of the isles shall "
10 k' of Sheba and Seba shall offer gifts. "
11 all k' shall fall down before him: "
76: 12 he is terrible to the k' of the earth. "
89: 27 higher than the k' of the earth. "
102: 15 and all the k' of the earth thy glory. "
105: 14 yea, he reproved k' for their sakes; "
30 in the chambers of their k'. "
110: 5 shall strike through k' in the day of "
119: 46 of thy testimonies also before k', "
135: 10 great nations, and slew mighty k'; "
136: 17 To him which smote great k': for "
18 And slew famous k': for his mercy "
138: 4 the k' of the earth shall praise thee, "
144: 10 is he that giveth salvation unto k': "
148: 11 K' of the earth, and all people; "
149: 8 To bind their k' with chains, and "
Pr 8: 15 By me k' reign, and princes decree "
16: 12 It is an abomination to k' to commit "
13 Righteous lips are the delight of k'; "
22: 29 business? he shall stand before k'; "
25: 2 but the honour of k' is to search out "
3 and the heart of k' is unsearchable. "
31: 3 ways to that which destroyeth k'. "
4 It is not for k', O Lemuel, it is not "
4 it is not for k' to drink wine; nor for "
Ec 2: 8 the peculiar treasure of k' and of "
Isa 1: 1 Ahaz, and Hezekiah, k' of Judah. "
7: 16 shall be forsaken of both her k'. "
10: 8 Are not my princes altogether k'? "
14: 9 thrones all the k' of the nations. "
18 All the k' of the nations, even all of "
19: 11 of the wise, the son of ancient k'? "
24: 21 the k' of the earth upon the earth. "
37: 11 heard what the k' of Assyria have "
18 the k' of Assyria have laid waste all "
41: 2 him, and made him ruler over k'? "
45: 1 I will loose the loins of k', to open "
49: 7 K' shall see and arise, princes also "
23 And k' shall be thy nursing fathers, "
52: 15 k' shall shut their mouths at him: "
60: 3 k' to the brightness of thy rising. "
10 their k' shall minister unto thee: "
11 and that their k' may be brought. "
16 and shalt suck the breast of k': "
62: 2 righteousness, and all k' thy glory: "
Jer 1: 18 whole land, against the k' of Judah, "
2: 26 they, their k', their princes, and "
8: 1 out the bones of the k' of Judah, "
13: 13 the k' that sit upon David's throne, "
17: 19 whereby the k' of Judah come in, "
20 word of the Lord, ye k' of Judah, "
25 city k' and princes sitting upon the "
19: 3 the word of the Lord, O k' of Judah, "
4 have known, nor the k' of Judah, "
13 and the houses of the k' of Judah, "
20: 5 all the treasures of the k' of Judah "
22: 4 k' sitting upon the throne of David, "
25: 14 great k' shall serve themselves of "
18 cities of Judah, and the k' thereof, "
20 and all the k' of the land of Uz, "
20 the k' of the land of the Philistines, "
22 k' of Tyrus, and all the k' of Zidon, "
22 the k' of the isles which are beyond "
24 And all the k' of Arabia, "
24 and all the k' of the mingled people "
25 k' of Zimri, and all the k' of Elam, "
25 and all the k' of the Medes, "
26 all the k' of the north, far and near, "
27: 7 great k' shall serve themselves of "
32: 32 they, their k', their princes, their "
33: 4 the houses of the k' of Judah, "
34: 5 former k' which were before thee, "
44: 9 the wickedness of the k' of Judah, "
17 fathers, our k', and our princes, "
21 fathers, your k', and your princes, "
46: 25 Egypt, with their gods, and their k'; "
50: 41 and many k' shall be raised up from "
51: 11 up the spirit of the k' of the Medes: "
28 nations with the k' of the Medes, "
52: 32 k' that were with him in Babylon, "
La 4: 12 The k' of the earth, and all the "
Eze 26: 7 king of Babylon, a king of k', "
27: 33 thou didst enrich the k' of the earth "
35 and their k' shall be sore afraid, "
28: 17 I will lay thee before k', that they "
32: 10 k' shall be horribly afraid for thee, "
29 Edom, her k', and all her princes, "
43: 7 defile, neither they, nor their k', "
7 carcases of their k' in their high "
9 the carcases of their k', far from me, "
Da 2: 21 he removeth k', and setteth up k': 4430
37 Thou, O king, art a king of k': for "
44 in the days of these k' shall the God "
47 is a God of gods, and a Lord of k', "
7: 17 beasts, which are four, are four k', "
24 kingdom are ten k' that shall arise: "
24 first, and he shall subdue three k'. "
8: 20 are the k' of Media and Persia. 4428
9: 6 which spake in thy name to our k', "
8 to our k', to our princes, and to our "
10: 13 remained there with the k' of Persia. "

Da 11: 2 stand up yet three k· in Persia; 4428
Ho 1: 1 Ahaz, and Hezekiah, k· of Judah, "
7: 7 all their k· are fallen: there is "
8: 4 They have set up k·, but not by me:"
Mic 1: 1 Ahaz, and Hezekiah, k· of Judah, "
14 shall be a lie to the k· of Israel. "
Hab 1: 10 they shall scoff at the k·, and the "
M't 10: 18 governors and k· for my sake, 935
17: 25 of whom do the k· of the earth take "
M'r 13: 9 before rulers and k· for my sake, "
Lu 10: 24 prophets and k· have desired to see "
21: 12 k· and rulers for my name's sake. "
22: 25 The k· of the Gentiles exercise "
Ac 4: 26 The k· of the earth stood up, and "
9: 15 my name before the Gentiles, and k·,"
1Co 4: 8 ye have reigned as k· without us: *
1Ti 2: 2 For k·, and for all that are in 935
6: 15 the King of k·, and Lord of lords; 936
Heb 7: 1 returning from the slaughter of k·, 935
Re 1: 5 the prince of the k· of the earth. "
6 hath made us k· and priests unto * "
5: 10 us unto our God k· and priests: * "
6: 15 the k· of the earth, and the great "
10: 11 and nations, and tongues, and k·. "
16: 12 the way of the k· of the east might "
14 go forth unto the k· of the earth "
17: 2 With whom the k· of the earth have "
10 there are seven k·: five are fallen, "
12 horns which thou sawest are ten k·, "
12 receive power as k· one hour with "
14 he is Lord of lords, and King of k·: "
18 reigneth over the k· of the earth. "
18: 3 the k· of the earth have committed "
9 the k· of the earth, who have "
19: 16 King Of K·, And Lord Of Lords. "
18 That ye may eat the flesh of k·, "
19 the beast, and the k· of the earth, "
21: 24 the k· of the earth do bring their "

kings'
Ps 45: 9 k· daughters were among thy 4428
Pr 30: 28 her hands, and is in k· palaces. "
Da 11: 27 both these k· hearts shall be to do* "
M't 11: 8 wear soft clothing are in k· houses. 935
Lu 7: 25 and live delicately, are in k· courts. 933

King's-Dale See KING'S and DALE.

King's-Pool See KING'S and POOL.

kinsfolk See also KINSFOLKS.
Job 19: 14 My k· have failed, and my familiar 7138
Lu 2: 44 they sought him among their k· 4773

kinsfolks
1Ki 16: 11 neither of his k·, nor of his 1350
2Ki 10: 11 his great men, and his k·, and his* 3045
Lu 21: 16 and brethren, and k·, and friends* 4773

kinsman See also KINSMAN'S; KINSMEN.
Nu 5: 8 the man have no k· to recompence 1350
27: 11 give his inheritance unto his k· 7607
Ru 2: 1 Naomi had a k· of her husband's, 3045
3: 9 handmaid; for thou art a near k·. 1350
12 it is true that I am thy near k·: "
12 howbeit there is a k· nearer than I. "
13 perform unto thee the part of a k·, "
13 will not do the part of a k· to thee, "
13 will I do the part of a k· to thee, "
4: 1 the k· of whom Boaz spake came "
3 he said unto the k·, Naomi, that is "
6 the k· said, I cannot redeem it for "
8 the k· said unto Boaz, Buy it for "
14 not left thee this day without a k·, "
Joh 18: 26 being his k· whose ear Peter cut 4773
Ro 16: 11 Salute Herodion my k·. Greet them "

kinsman's
Ru 3: 13 let him do the k· part: but if he 1350

kinsmen
Ru 2: 20 of kin unto us, one of our next k·. 1350
Ps 38: 11 sore; and my k· stand afar off. 7138
Lu 14: 12 neither thy k·, nor thy rich 4773
Ac 10: 24 together his k· and near friends. "
Ro 9: 3 my k· according to the flesh: "
16: 7 Andronicus and Junia, my k·, and "
21 and Jason, and Sosipater, my k·, "

kinswoman See also KINSWOMEN.
Le 18: 12 sister: she is thy father's near k·. 7607
13 for she is thy mother's near k·. "
Pr 7: 4 and call understanding thy k·: 4129

kinswomen
Le 18: 17 for they are her near k·: it is 7608

Kir (*kur*) See also KIR-HARESH.
2Ki 16: 9 the people of it captive to K·, 7024
Isa 15: 1 K· of Moab is laid waste, "
22: 6 and K· uncovered the shield. "
Am 1: 5 shall go into captivity unto K·, "
9: 7 Caphtor, and the Syrians from K·?"

Kir-haraseth (*kur-har'-a-seth*) See also KIR-HARESETH.
2Ki 3: 25 in K· left they the stones thereof; *7025

Kir-hareseth (*kur-har'-e-seth*) See also KIR-HARESH.
Isa 16: 7 foundations of K· shall ye mourn; 7025

Kir-haresh (*kur-ha'-resh*) See also KIR-HARASETH; KIR-HARESETH; KIR-HERES.
Isa 16: 11 and mine inward parts for K·. *7025

Kir-heres (*kur-he'-res*) See also KIR-HARESH.
Jer 48: 31 shall mourn for the men of K·. 7025
36 sound like pipes for the men of K·: "

Kiriathaim (*kir-e-a-thay'-im*) See also KIRTAN; KIRJATHAIM.
Ge 14: 5 and the Emims in Shaveh K·. *7741
Jer 48: 1 K· is confounded and taken: 7156
23 upon K·, and upon Beth-gamul, "
Eze 25: 9 Baal-meon, and K·, "

Kirioth (*kir'-e-oth*) See also KERIOTH.
Am 2: 2 it shall devour the palaces of K·: *7152

Kirjath (*kur'-jath*) See also KIRJATH-ARBA; KIRJATH-ARIM; KIRJATH-BAAL; KIRJATH-HUZOTH; KIRJATH-JEARIM; KIRJATH-SANNAH; KIRJATH-SEPHER.
Jos 18: 28 Jerusalem, Gibeath, and K·; *7157

Kirjathaim (*kur"-jath-a'-im*) See also KIRIATHAIM.
Nu 32: 37 Heshbon, and Elealeh, and K·, *7156
Jos 13: 19 And K·, and Sibmah, and * "
1Ch 6: 76 suburbs, and K· with her suburbs.* "

Kirjath-arba (*kur"-jath-ar'-bah*) See also HEBRON.
Ge 23: 2 And Sarah died in K·; the same *7153
Jos 14: 15 the name of Hebron before was K·;* "
15: 54 and K·, which is Hebron, and Zior;* "
20: 7 and K·, which is Hebron, in the * "
J'g 1: 10 name of Hebron before was K·:)* "
Ne 11: 25 the children of Judah dwelt at K·,* "

Kirjath-arim (*kur"-jath-a'-rim*) See also KIRJATH-JEARIM.
Ezr 2: 25 The children of K·, Chephirah, *7157

Kirjath-baal (*kur"-jath-ba'-al*) See also BAALAH; KIRJATH-JEARIM.
Jos 15: 60 K·, which is Kirjath-jearim, and *7154
18: 14 the goings out thereof were at K·,* "

Kirjath-huzoth (*kur"-jath-hu'-zoth*)
Nu 22: 39 Balak, and they came unto K·. *7155

Kirjath-jearim (*kur"-jath-je'-a-rim*) See also KIRJATH; KIRJATH-ARIM; KIRJATH-BAAL.
Jos 9: 17 Chephirah, and Beeroth, and K·. *7157
15: 9 was drawn to Baalah, which is K·:* "
60 Kirjath-baal, which is K·, and * "
18: 14 K·, a city of the children of Judah:* "
15 quarter was from the end of K·, * "
J'g 18: 12 they went up, and pitched in K·, * "
12 this day: behold, it is behind K·. * "
1Sa 6: 21 sent...to the inhabitants of K·, * "
7: 1 the men of K· came, and fetched * "
2 to pass, while the ark abode in K·,* "
1Ch 2: 50 Ephratah; Shobal the father of K·,* "
52 Shobal the father of K· had sons;* "
53 the families of K·; the Ithrites, * "
13: 5 to bring the ark of God from K·. * "
6 all Israel, to Baalah, that is, to K·,* "
2Ch 1: 4 had David brought up from K· to* "
Ne 7: 29 The men of K·, Chephirah, and * "
Jer 26: 20 Urijah the son of Shemaiah of K·,* "

Kirjath-sannah (*kur"-jath-san'-nah*) See also KIRJATH-SEPHER; SANSANNAH.
Jos 15: 49 Dannah, and K·, which is Debir, *7158

Kirjath-sepher (*kur"-jath-se'-fer*) See also DEBIR; KIRJATH-SANNAH.
Jos 15: 15 the name of Debir before was K·. *7158
16 He that smiteth K·, and taketh it,* "
J'g 1: 11 the name of Debir before was K·:* "
12 He that smiteth K·, and taketh it,* "

Kish (*kish*) See also CIS.
1Sa 9: 1 of Benjamin, whose name was K·, 7027
3 asses of K· Saul's father were lost. "
3 K· said to Saul his son, Take now "
10: 11 that is come unto the son of K·? "
21 and Saul the son of K· was taken: "
14: 51 K· was the father of Saul; and Ner "
2Sa 21: 14 in the sepulchre of K· his father: "
1Ch 8: 30 son Abdon, and Zur, and K·, and "
33 Ner begat K·, and K· begat Saul, "
9: 36 son Abdon, then Zur, and K·, and "
39 Ner begat K·; and K· begat Saul; "
12: 1 because of Saul the son of K·: "
23: 21 the sons of Mahli; Eleazar, and K·. "
22 brethren the sons of K· took them. "
24: 29 Concerning K·: the son of K· was "
26: 28 Saul the son of K·, and Abner the "
2Ch 29: 12 sons of Merari, K· the son of Abdi, "
Es 2: 5 Shimei, the son of K·, a Benjamite; "

Kishi (*kish'-i*) See also KUSHAIAH.
1Ch 6: 44 Ethan the son of K·, the son of 7029

Kishion (*kish'-e-on*) See also KEDESH; KISHON.
Jos 19: 20 And Rabbith, and K·, and Abez, 7191

Kishon (*ki'-shon*) See also KISHION; KISON.
Jos 21: 28 of Issachar, K· with her suburbs, *7191
J'g 4: 7 draw unto thee to the river K· 7028
13 of the Gentiles unto the river of K·. "
5: 21 The river of K· swept them away, "
21 that ancient river, the river K·. "
1Ki 18: 40 brought them down to the brook K·, "

Kison (*ki'-son*) See also KISHON.
Ps 83: 9 as to Jabin, at the brook of K·: *7028

kiss See also KISSED; KISSES.
Ge 27: 26 near now, and k· me, my son. 5401
31: 28 to k· my sons and my daughters? "
2Sa 20: 9 beard with the right hand to k· him. "
1Ki 19: 20 thee, k· my father and my mother, "
Ps 2: 12 K· the Son, lest he be angry, and "
Pr 24: 26 shall k· his lips that giveth a right "
Ca 1: 2 Let him k· me with the kisses of his "
8: 1 find thee without, I would k· thee; "
Ho 13: 2 the men that sacrifice k· the calves. "
M't 26: 48 Whomsoever I shall k·, that same 5368
M'r 14: 44 Whomsoever I shall k·, that same "
Lu 7: 45 Thou gavest me no k·: but this 5370
45 in hath not ceased to k· my feet. 2705
22: 47 drew near unto Jesus to k· him. 5368
48 thou the Son of man with a k·? 5370
Ro 16: 16 Salute one another with an holy k·. "
1Co 16: 20 ye one another with an holy k·. "
2Co 13: 12 Greet one another with an holy k·. "
1Th 5: 26 all the brethren with an holy k·. 5370
1Pe 5: 14 ye one another with a k· of charity. "

kissed
Ge 27: 27 And he came near, and k· him: 5401
29: 11 Jacob k· Rachel, and lifted up his "
13 him, and embraced him, and k· him, "
31: 55 and k· his sons and his daughters, "
33: 4 and fell on his neck, and k· him: "
45: 15 Moreover he k· all his brethren, "
48: 10 he k· them, and embraced them. "
50: 1 and wept upon him, and k· him. "
Ex 4: 27 in the mount of God, and k· him. "
18: 7 law, and did obeisance, and k· him; "
Ru 1: 9 Then she k· them; and they lifted up "
14 and Orpah k· her mother in law; "
1Sa 10: 1 poured it upon his head, and k· him, "
20: 41 they k· one another, and wept one "
2Sa 14: 33 the king: and the king k· Absalom. "
15: 5 his hand, and took him, and k· him. "
19: 39 the king k· Barzillai, and blessed "
1Ki 19: 18 every mouth which hath not k· him. "
Job 31: 27 or my mouth hath k· my hand: "
Ps 85: 10 righteousness and peace have k· "
Pr 7: 13 So she caught him, and k· him, and "
M't 26: 49 said, Hail, master; and k· him. 2705
M'r 14: 45 saith, Master, master; and k· him. "
Lu 7: 38 and k· his feet, and anointed them "
15: 20 and fell on his neck, and k· him. "
Ac 20: 37 and fell on Paul's neck, and k· him, "

kisses
Pr 27: 6 the k· of an enemy are deceitful. 5390
Ca 1: 2 kiss me with the k· of his mouth: "

kite
Le 11: 14 vulture, and the k· after his kind; *344
De 14: 13 the k·, and the vulture after his kind,* "

Kithlish (*kith'-lish*)
Jos 15: 40 Cabbon, and Lahmam, and K·, *3798

Kitron (*ki'-tron*) See also KATTAH.
J'g 1: 30 drive out the inhabitants of K·, 7003

Kittim (*kit'-tim*) See also CHITTIM.
Ge 10: 4 and Tarshish, K·, and Dodanim. 3794
1Ch 1: 7 and Tarshish, K·, and Dodanim. "

knead See also KNEADED; KNEADINGTROUGHS.
Ge 18: 6 of fine meal, k· it, and make cakes 3888
Jer 7: 18 and the women k· their dough, to "

kneaded
1Sa 28: 24 took flour, and k· it, and did bake 3888
2Sa 13: 8 she took flour, and k· it, and made "
Ho 7: 4 raising after he hath k· the dough,* "

kneadingtroughs
Ex 8: 3 into thine ovens, and into thy k·: 4863
12: 34 k· being bound up in their clothes "

knee See also KNEES.
Ge 41: 43 they cried before him, Bow the k·:
Isa 45: 23 That unto me every k· shall bow, 1290
M't 27: 29 they bowed the k· before him, and*
Ro 11: 4 have not bowed the k· to the image 1119
14: 11 the Lord, every k· shall bow to me, "
Ph'p 2: 10 name of Jesus every k· should bow, "

kneel See also KNEELED; KNEELING.
Ge 24: 11 he made his camels to k· down 1288
Ps 95: 6 let us k· before the Lord our maker. "

kneeled
2Ch 6: 13 k· down upon his knees before 1288
Da 6: 10 he k· upon his knees three times 1289
M'r 10: 17 came one running, and k· to him, 1120
Lu 22: 41 cast, and k· down, and prayed, 5087, 1119
Ac 7: 60 he k· down, and cried with a " "
9: 40 forth, and k· down, and prayed; " "
20: 36 he k· down, and prayed with " "
21: 5 we k· down on the shore, and* " "

kneeling
1Ki 8: 54 from k· on his knees with his 3766
M't 17: 14 a certain man, k· down to him, 1120
M'r 1: 40 beseeching him, and k· down to him, "

knees
Ge 30: 3 she shall bear upon my k·, that I 1290
48: 12 them out from between his k·, "
50: 23 were brought up upon Joseph's k·. "
De 28: 35 The Lord shall smite thee in the k·, "
J'g 7: 5 boweth down upon his k· to drink. "
6 down upon their k· to drink water. "
16: 19 made him sleep upon her k·; and "
1Ki 8: 54 kneeling on his k· with his hands "
18: 42 and put his face between his k·, "
19: 18 k· which have not bowed unto Baal, "
2Ki 1: 13 and fell on his k· before Elijah, "
4: 20 he sat on her k· till noon, and then "
2Ch 6: 13 kneeled down upon his k· before all "
Ezr 9: 5 I fell upon my k·, and spread out "
Job 3: 12 Why did the k· prevent me? or why "
4: 4 hast strengthened the feeble k·. "
Ps 109: 24 My k· are weak through fasting; "
Isa 35: 3 hands, and confirm the feeble k·. "
66: 12 sides, and be dandled upon her k·. "
Eze 7: 17 and all k· shall be weak as water. "
21: 7 and all k· shall be weak as water: "
47: 4 waters; the waters were to the k·. "
Da 5: 6 and his k· smote one against 755
6: 10 kneeled upon his k· three times a 1291
10: 10 which set me upon my k· and upon 1290
Na 2: 10 and the k· smite together, and "
M'r 15: 19 bowing their k· worshipped him. 1119
Lu 5: 8 he fell down at Jesus' k·, saying, "
Eph 3: 14 I bow my k· unto the Father of our "
Heb 12: 12 hang down, and the feeble k·; "

knew See also FOREKNEW; KNEWEST.
Ge 3: 7 and they k· that they were naked; 3045
4: 1 Adam k· Eve his wife; and she "
17 Cain k· his wife; and she conceived, "
25 Adam k· his wife again; and she "

Ge 8:11 Noah k' that the waters were abated 3045
9:24 k' what his younger son had done "
28:16 Lord is in this place; and I k' it not. "
31:32 k' not that Rachel had stolen them. "
37:33 he k' it, and said, It is my son's 5234
38: 9 Onan k' that the seed should not 3045
16 he k' not that she was his daughter "
26 son. And he k' him again no more. "
39: 6 he k' not ought he had, save the "
42: 7 saw his brethren, and he k' them, 5234
8 Joseph k' his brethren, but they k' "
23 they k' not that Joseph understood 3045
Ex 1: 8 over Egypt, which k' not Joseph. "
Nu 22:34 I k' not that thou stoodest in the "
24:16 and k' the knowledge of the most* "
De 8:16 manna, which thy fathers k' not, "
9:24 Lord from the day that I k' you. "
29:26 gods whom they k' not, and whom "
32:17 to gods whom they k' not, to new "
33: 9 brethren, nor k' his own children: "
34:10 whom the Lord k' face to face. "
J'g 2:10 which k' not the Lord, nor yet the "
3: 2 least such as before k' nothing "
11:39 had vowed: and she k' no man. † "
13:16 Manoah k' not that he was an angel "
21 k' that he was an angel of the Lord. "
14: 4 mother k' not that it was of the "
18: 3 they k' the voice of the young man 5234
19:25 they k' her, and abused her all the 3045
20:34 they k' not that evil was near them. "
1Sa 1:19 Elkanah k' Hannah his wife; and "
2:12 of Belial; they k' not the Lord. "
3:20 k' that Samuel was established to "
10:11 all that k' him beforetime saw that "
14: 3 k' not that Jonathan was gone. "
18:28 k' that the Lord was with David, "
20: 9 If I k' certainly that evil were * "
33 Jonathan k' that it was determined "
39 the lad k' not any thing: only "
39 Jonathan and David k' the matter. "
22:15 thy servant k' nothing of all this,* "
17 because they k' when he fled, and "
22 I k' it that day, when Doeg the "
23: 9 David k' that Saul secretly practised "
26:12 and no man saw it, nor k' it, neither "
17 Saul k' David's voice, and said, 5234
2Sa 3:26 well of Sirah: but David k' it not. 3045
11:16 where he k' that valiant men were. "
20 k' ye not that they would shoot the "
15:11 simplicity, and they k' not any thing. "
18:29 tumult, but I k' not what it was. "
22:44 which I k' not shall serve me. * "
1Ki 1: 4 to him: but the king k' her not. "
18: 7 and he k' him, and fell on his face, 5234
2Ki 4:39 of pottage: for they k' them not. 3045
2Ch 33:13 k' that the Lord he was God. "
Ne 2:16 the rulers k' not whither I went, "
Es 1:13 the wise men, which k' the times, 5234
13 all that k' law and judgment: "
Job 2:12 and k' him not, they lifted up their "
23: 3 I knew where I might find him! 3045
29:16 cause which I k' not I searched out. "
42: 3 wonderful for me, which I k' not. "
Ps 35:11 my charge things that I k' not. * "
15 together against me, and I k' it not; "
Pr 24:12 Behold, we k' it not; doth not he "
Isa 42:16 blind by a way that they k' not; * "
25 on fire round about, yet he k' not; "
48: 4 I k' that thou art obstinate, and 1847
7 shouldest say, Behold, I k' them. 3045
8 I k' that thou wouldest deal very "
55: 5 nations that k' not thee shall run "
Jer 1: 5 formed thee in the belly I k' thee; "
2: 8 they that handle the law k' me not: "
11:19 I k' not that they had devised "
32: 8 Then I k' that this was the word "
41: 4 slain Gedaliah, and no man k' it, "
44: 3 serve other gods, whom they k' not, "
15 the men which k' that their wives "
Eze 10:20 I k' that they were the cherubims. "
19: 7 And he k' their desolate palaces, "
Da 5:21 he k' that the most high God ruled 3046
6:10 when Daniel k' that the writing "
11:38 his fathers k' not shall he honour 3045
Ho 8: 4 have made princes, and I k' it not: "
11: 3 but they k' not that I healed them. "
Jon 1:10 the men k' that he fled from the "
4: 2 I k' that thou art a gracious God, "
Zec 7:14 all the nations whom they k' not. "
11:11 k' that it was the word of the Lord. "
M't 1:25 k' her not till she had brought 1097
7:23 profess unto them, I never k' you: "
12:15 But when Jesus k' it, he withdrew* "
25 Jesus k' their thoughts, and said *1492
17:12 already, and they k' him not, 1912
24:39 k' not until the flood came, and 1097
25:24 I k' thee that thou art an...man, "
27:18 For he k' that for envy they had 1492
M'r 1:34 to speak, because they k' him. "
6:33 them departing, and many k' him, 1921
38 when they k', they say, Five, and 1097
54 of the ship, straightway they k' him, 1921
8:17 when Jesus k' it, he saith unto *1097
12:12 k' that he had spoken the parable * "
15:10 he k' that the chief priests had "
45 when he k' it of the centurion, he* "
Lu 2:43 Joseph and his mother k' not of it. "
4:41 for they k' that he was Christ. "
6: 8 But he k' their thoughts, and said 1492
7:37 when she k' that Jesus sat at meat 1921
9:11 when they k' it, followed him: *1097
12:47 servant, which k' his lord's will, "
48 he that k' not, and did commit "
18:34 neither k' they the things which * "
23: 7 as soon as he k' that he belonged 1921
24:31 were opened, and they k' him; "
Joh 1:10 by him, and the world k' him not. 1097
31 I k' him not: but that he should 1492
33 I k' him not: but he that sent me "
2: 9 wine, and k' not whence it was: "
9 servants which drew the water k';) "
24 unto them, because he k' all men, 1097
25 of man: for he k' what was in man. "
4: 1 the Lord k' how the Pharisees had "
53 father k' that it was at the same "
5: 6 k' that he had been now a long "
6: 6 he himself k' what he would do. 1492
61 When Jesus k' in himself that his* "
64 For Jesus k' from the beginning "
11:42 I k' that thou hearest me always: "
57 that, if any man k' where he were, 1097
12: 9 the Jews therefore k' that he was* "
13: 1 Jesus k' that his hour was come *1492
11 For he k' who should betray him; "
28 k' for what intent he spake this 1097
16:19 k' that they were desirous to ask * "
18: 2 which betrayed him, k' the place: 1492
20: 9 For as yet they k' not the scripture, "
14 and k' not that it was Jesus. "
21: 4 disciples k' not that it was Jesus. "
Ac 3:10 k'...it was he which sat for alms *1921
7:18 king arose, which k' not Joseph. 1492
9:30 Which when the brethren k', they 1921
12:14 And when she k' Peter's voice, she "
13:27 because they k' him not, nor yet the 50
16: 3 k' all that his father was a Greek. 1492
19:32 k' not wherefore they were come "
34 when they k' that he was a Jew, *1921
22:29 after he k' that he was a Roman, "
26: 5 Which k' me from the beginning, *4267
27:39 it was day, they k' not the land: 1921
28: 1 k' that the island was called Melita. "
Ro 1:21 when they k' God, they glorified *1097
1Co 1:21 the world by wisdom k' not God, "
2: 8 of the princes of this world k': †‡ "
2Co 5:21 him to be sin for us, who k' no sin; "
12: 2 k' a man in Christ above fourteen *1492
3 I k' such a man, (whether in the * "
Ga 4: 8 when ye k' not God, ye did service* "
Col 1: 6 and k' the grace of God in truth: 1921
2: 1 that ye k' what great conflict I *1492
1Jo 3: 1 us not, because it k' him not. 1097
Jude 5 though ye once k' this, how that *1492
Re 19:12 a name written, that no man k', * "

knewest

De 8: 3 with manna, which thou k' not, 3045
Ru 2:11 people which thou k' not heretofore. "
Ne 9:10 for thou k' that they dealt proudly "
Ps 142: 3 within me, then thou k' my path. "
Isa 48: 8 thou heardest not; yea, thou k' not; "
Da 5:22 heart, though thou k' all this; 3046
M't 25:26 thou k' that I reap where I sowed 1492
Lu 19:22 Thou k' that I was an austere man, "
44 k' not the time of thy visitation. 1097
Joh 4:10 If thou k' the gift of God, and who 1492

knife See KNIVES; PENKNIFE.

Ge 22: 6 took the fire in his hand, and a k'; 3979
10 hand, and took the k' to slay his son. "
J'g 19:29 he took a k', and laid hold on his "
Pr 23: 2 put a k' to thy throat, if thou be a 7915
Eze 5: 1 take thee a sharp k', take thee a *2719
2 part, and smite about it with a k':* "

knit

J'g 20:11 the city, k' together as one man. 2270
1Sa 18: 1 Jonathan was k' with the soul of 7194
1Ch 12:17 mine heart shall be k' unto you: 3162
Ac 10:11 great sheet k' at the four corners, *1210
Col 2: 2 being k' together in love, and unto 4822
19 and k' together, increaseth with the "

knives

Jos 5: 2 thee sharp k', and circumcise 2719
3 him sharp k', and circumcised the "
1Ki 18:28 their manner with k' and lancets, "
Ezr 1: 9 of silver, nine and twenty k', 4252
Pr 30:14 swords, and their jaw teeth as k', 3979

knock See also KNOCKED; KNOCKETH; KNOCKING.

M't 7: 7 k', and it shall be opened unto 2925
Lu 11: 9 k', and it shall be opened unto you. "
13:25 stand without, and to k' at the door, "
Re 3:20 Behold, I stand at the door, and k': "

knocked

Ac 12:13 And as Peter k' at the door of the 2925

knocketh

Ca 5: 2 is the voice of my beloved that k', 1849
M't 7: 8 to him that k' it shall be opened. 2925
Lu 11:10 to him that k' it shall be opened. "
12:36 that when he cometh and k', they "

knocking

Ac 12:16 But Peter continued k': and when 2925

knop See also KNOPS.

Ex 25:33 a k' and a flower in one branch; 3730
33 branch, with a k' and a flower: "
35, 35, 35 k' under two branches of the "
37:19 in one branch, a k' and a flower; "
19 in another branch, a k' and a flower: "
21, 21, 21 k' under two branches of the "

knops

Ex 25:31 his k', and his flowers, shall be of 3730
34 with their k' and their flowers. "
36 k' and their branches shall be of "
37:17 his k', and his flowers, were of the "
20 almonds, his k', and his flowers: "
22 k' and their branches were of the "
1Ki 6:18 carved with k' and open flowers: 6497
7:24 about there were k' compassing it, "
24 the k' were cast in two rows, when "

know See also FOREKNOW; KNEW; KNOWEST; KNOWETH; KNOWING; KNOWN.

Ge 3: 5 God doth k' that in the day ye eat 3045
3:22 as one of us, to k' good and evil: 3045
4: 9 I k' not: Am I my brother's keeper? "
12:11 I k' that thou art a fair woman to "
15: 8 shall I k' that I shall inherit it? "
13 K' of a surety that thy seed shall "
18:19 For I k' him, that he will command* "
21 come unto me; and if not, I will k'. "
19: 5 out unto us, that we may k' them. "
20: 6 Yea, I k' that thou didst this in the "
7 k' thou that thou shalt surely die, "
22:12 for now I k' that thou fearest God, "
24:14 I k' that thou hast shewed kindness "
27: 2 old, I k' not the day of my death: "
29: 5 K' ye Laban the son of Nahor? "
5 And they said, We k' him. "
31: 6 And ye k' that with all my power I "
37:32 k' now whether it be thy son's coat 5234
42:33 shall I k' that ye are true men; 3045
34 then shall I k' that ye are no spies, "
43: 7 we certainly k' that he would say, "
44:27 k' that my wife bare me two sons: "
48:19 and said, I k' it, my son, I k' it: "
Ex 3: 7 taskmasters; for I k' their sorrows; "
4:14 I k' that he can speak well. "
5: 2 I k' not the Lord, neither will I let "
6: 7 ye shall k' that I am the Lord your "
7: 5 shall k' that I am the Lord, when I "
17 thou shalt k' that I am the Lord: "
8:10 k' that there is none like unto the "
22 end mayest k' that I am the Lord "
9:14 k' that there is none like me in all "
29 k' how that the earth is the Lord's. "
30 k' that ye will not yet fear the Lord "
10: 2 ye may k' how that I am the Lord. "
26 we k' not with what we must serve "
11: 7 may k' how that the Lord doth put "
14: 4 may k' that I am the Lord. "
18 shall k' that I am the Lord, when I "
16: 6 shall k' that the Lord hath brought "
12 ye shall k' that I am the Lord your "
18:11 I k' that the Lord is greater than all "
16 make them k' the statutes of God, "
23: 9 for ye k' the heart of a stranger, "
29:46 they shall k' that I am the Lord "
31:13 that ye may k' that I am the Lord "
33: 5 that I may k' what to do unto thee. "
12 not let me k' whom thou wilt send "
12 I k' thee by name, and thou hast "
13 that I may k' thee, that I may find "
17 in my sight, and I k' thee by name. "
36: 1 k' how to work all manner of work "
Le 23:43 That your generations may k' that "
Nu 14:31 k' the land which ye have despised. "
34 ye shall k' my breach of promise. "
16:28 ye shall k' that the Lord hath sent "
22:19 that I may k' what the Lord will say "
De 3:19 (for I k' that ye have much cattle,) "
4:35 mightest k' that the Lord he is God; "
39 K' therefore this day, and consider "
7: 9 K' therefore that the Lord thy God, "
8: 2 to k' what was in thine heart, "
3 not, neither did thy fathers k'; "
3 thee k' that man doth not live by "
11: 2 And k' ye this day: for I speak not "
13: 3 to k' whether ye love the Lord your "
18:21 How shall we k' the word which the "
22: 2 if thou k' him not, then thou shalt "
29: 6 that ye might k' that I am the Lord "
16 ye k' how we have dwelt in the land "
31:21 I k' their imagination which they "
27 I k' thy rebellion, and thy stiff neck: "
29 For I k' that after my death ye will "
Jos 2: 9 k' that the Lord hath given you the "
3: 4 k' the way by which ye must go: "
7 may k' that, as I was with Moses, "
10 k' that the living God is among you "
4:22 Then ye shall let your children k', "
24 earth might k' the hand of the Lord, "
22:22 he knoweth, and Israel he shall k'; "
23:13 K' for a certainty that the Lord "
14 k' in all your hearts and in all your "
J'g 3: 2 Israel might k', to teach them war, "
4 to k' whether they would hearken "
6:37 shall I k' that thou wilt save Israel "
17:13 k' I that the Lord will do me good, "
18: 5 k' whether our way which we go "
14 k' that there is in these houses an "
19:22 thine house, that we may k' him. "
Ru 3:11 k' that thou art a virtuous woman. "
14 up before one could k' another. *5234
18 thou k' how the matter will fall: 3045
4: 4 it, then tell me, that I may k': "
1Sa 3: 7 Samuel did not yet k' the Lord, "
6: 9 k' that it is not his hand that smote "
14:38 k' and see wherein this sin hath "
17:28 I k' thy pride, and the naughtiness "
46 may k' that there is a God in Israel. "
47 k'...the Lord saveth not with sword "
20: 3 Let not Jonathan k' this, lest he be "
30 I k' that thou hast chosen the son "
21: 2 no man k' any thing of the business "
22: 3 till I k' what God will do for me. "
23:22 k' and see his place where his haunt "
24:11 k' thou and see that there is neither "
20 I k'...that thou shalt surely be king, "
25:11 whom I k' not whence they be? "
17 k' and consider what thou wilt do; "
28: 1 K' thou assuredly, that thou shalt "
2 shalt k' what thy servant can do. "
29: 9 I k' that thou art good in my sight, "
2Sa 3:25 to k' thy going out and thy coming "
25 in, and to k' all that thou doest. "
38 K' ye not that there is a prince and "
7:21 things, to make thy servant k' them. "
14:20 k' all things that are in the earth. "
19:20 servant doth k' that I have sinned: "

2Sa 19:22 do not I *k·* that I am this day king 3045
24: 2 I may *k·* the number of the people. "
1Ki 2:37 *k·* for certain that thou shalt surely "
42 *K·* for a certain, on the day thou "
3: 7 I *k·* not how to go out or come in. "
8:38 which shall *k·* every man the plague "
43 people of the earth may *k·* thy name, "
43 that they may *k·* that this house, "
60 earth may *k·* that the Lord is God, "
17:24 I *k·* that thou art a man of God, "
18:12 shall carry thee whither I *k·* not; "
37 may *k·* that thou art the Lord God, "
20:13 thou shalt *k·* that I am the Lord. "
28 and ye shall *k·* that I am the Lord. "
22: 3 *K·* ye that Ramoth in Gilead is ours, "
2Ki 2: 3, 5 Yea, I *k·* it; hold ye your peace. "
5: 8 he shall *k·* that there is a prophet "
15 I *k·* that there is no God in all the "
7:12 They *k·* that we be hungry; "
8:12 I *k·* the evil that thou wilt do unto "
9:11 he said unto them, Ye *k·* the man, "
10:10 *K·* now that there shall fall unto "
17:26 *k·* not the manner of the God of the "
26 they *k·* not the manner of the God "
19:19 may *k·* that thou art the Lord God, "
27 I *k·* thy abode, and thy going out, "
1Ch 12:32 to *k·* what Israel ought to do; "
21: 2 of them to me, that I may *k·* it. "
28: 9 son, *k·* thou the God of thy father, "
29:17 I *k·* also, my God, that thou triest "
2Ch 2: 8 I *k·* that thy servants can skill to "
6:29 every one shall *k·* his own sore and "
33 of the earth may *k·* thy name, "
33 *k·* that this house which I have "
12: 8 that they may *k·* my service, and "
13: 5 Ought ye not to *k·* that the Lord "
20:12 neither *k·* we what to do: but our "
25:16 I *k·* that God hath determined to "
32:13 *K·* ye not what I and my fathers "
31 might *k·* all that was in his heart. "
Ezr 4:15 and *k·* that this city is a rebellious 3046
7:25 all such as *k·* the laws of thy God; "
25 teach ye them that *k·* them not. * "
Ne 4:11 They shall not *k·*, neither see, till 3045
Es 2:11 to *k·* how Esther did, and what "
4: 5 to *k·* what it was, and why it was. "
11 people of the king's provinces, do *k·*, "
Job 5:24 thou shalt *k·* that thy tabernacle "
25 shalt *k·* also that thy seed shall be "
27 hear it, and *k·* thou it for thy good. "
7:10 shall his place *k·* him any more. 5234
8: 9 but of yesterday, and *k·* nothing, 3045
9: 2 I *k·* it is so of a truth: but how "
5 the mountains, and they *k·* not: "
21 perfect, yet would I not *k·* my soul:* "
28 I *k·* that thou wilt not hold me "
10:13 heart: I *k·* that this is with thee. "
11: 6 *K·* therefore that God exacteth of "
8 than hell; what canst thou *k·*? "
13: 2 What ye *k·*, the same do I...also: 1847
2 What ye...the same do I *k·* also: 3045
18 cause; I *k·* that I shall be justified. "
23 make me to *k·* my transgression "
15: 9 What knowest thou, that we *k·* not? "
19: 6 *K·* now that God hath overthrown "
25 For I *k·* that my redeemer liveth, "
29 that ye may *k·* there is a judgment. "
21:19 rewardeth him, and he shall *k·* it. "
27 Behold, I *k·* your thoughts, and "
29 and do ye not *k·* their tokens, 5234
22:13 thou sayest, How doth God *k·*? 3045
23: 5 I would *k·* the words which he "
24: 1 they that *k·* him not see his days? 5234
13 they *k·* not the ways thereof, nor "
16 daytime: they *k·* not the light. 3045
17 if one *k·* them, they are in the 5234
30:23 I *k·* that thou wilt bring...death, 3045
31: 6 that God may *k·* mine integrity. "
32:22 I *k·* not to give flattering titles; "
34: 4 *k·* among ourselves what is good. "
36:26 God is great, and we *k·* him not, "
37: 7 man; that all men may *k·* his work. "
15 Dost thou *k·* when God disposed "
16 *k·* the balancings of the clouds, "
38:12 the dayspring to *k·* his place; "
20 that thou shouldest *k·* the paths *995
42: 2 I *k·* that thou canst do every thing, 3045
Ps 4: 3 But *k·* that the Lord hath set apart "
9:10 they that *k·* thy name will put their "
20 nations may *k·* themselves...men. "
20: 6 Now *k·* I that the Lord saveth his "
36:10 lovingkindness...them that *k·* thee; "
39: 4 Lord, make me to *k·* mine end, "
4 it is; that I may *k·* how frail I am. "
41:11 this I *k·* that thou favourest me, "
46:10 Be still, and *k·* that I am God: "
50:11 I *k·* all the fowls of the mountains: "
51: 6 thou shalt make me to *k·* wisdom. "
56: 9 back: this I *k·*; for God is for me. "
59:13 them *k·* that God ruleth in Jacob "
71:15 day; I *k·* not the numbers thereof. "
73:11 And they say, How doth God *k·*? "
16 When I thought to *k·* this, it was "
78: 6 generation to come might *k·* them, "
82: 5 They *k·* not, neither will they "
83:18 That men may *k·* that thou, whose "
87: 4 and Babylon to them that *k·* me: "
89:15 the people that *k·* the joyful sound: "
94:10 man knowledge, shall not he *k·*? * "
100: 3 *K·* ye that the Lord he is God: it 3045
101: 4 me: I will not *k·* a wicked person. "
103:16 place thereof shall *k·* it no more. 5234
109:27 they may *k·* that this is thy hand; 3045
119:75 I *k·*...that thy judgments are right, "
125 that I may *k·* thy testimonies. "
135: 5 For I *k·* that the Lord is great, "

Ps 139:23 me, O God, and *k·* my heart: 3045
23 heart: try me, and *k·* my thoughts: "
140:12 *k·* that the Lord will maintain the "
142: 4 was no man that would *k·* me: *5234
143: 8 cause me to *k·* the way wherein I 3045
Pr 1: 2 To *k·* wisdom and instruction; to "
4: 1 and attend to *k·* understanding. "
19 they *k·* not at what they stumble. "
5: 6 that thou canst not *k·* them. * "
10:32 righteous *k·* what is acceptable: "
22:21 That I might make thee *k·* the "
24:12 keepeth thy soul, doth not he *k·* it? "
25: 8 lest thou *k·* not what to do in the end "
27:23 diligent to *k·* the state of...flocks, 3045
29: 7 the wicked regardeth not to *k·* it. 1847
30:18 for me, yea, four which I *k·* not: 3045
Ec 1:17 I gave my heart to *k·* wisdom, "
17 and to *k·* madness and folly: "
3:12 I *k·* that there is no good in them, "
14 I *k·* that, whatsoever God doeth, it "
7:25 I applied mine heart to *k·*, and to "
25 to *k·* the wickedness of folly, even "
8:12 yet surely I *k·* that it shall be well "
16 I applied mine heart to *k·* wisdom, "
17 though a wise man think to *k·* it, "
9: 5 the living *k·* that they shall die: but "
5 the dead *k·* not any thing, neither "
11: 9 but *k·* thou, that for all these things "
Ca 1: 8 If thou *k·* not, O thou fairest "
Isa 1: 3 Israel doth not *k·*, my people doth "
5:19 nigh and come, that we may *k·* it! "
7:15 that he may *k·* to refuse the evil, "
16 the child shall *k·* to refuse the evil, "
9: 9 And all the people shall *k·*, even "
19:12 and let them *k·* what the Lord of "
21 and the Egyptians shall *k·* the Lord "
37:20 all the kingdoms of the earth may *k·* "
28 But I *k·* thy abode, and thy going "
41:20 That they may see, and *k·*, and "
22 them, and *k·* the latter end of them; "
23 that we may *k·* that ye are gods: "
26 the beginning, that we may *k·*? "
43:10 that ye may *k·* and believe me, "
19 spring forth; shall ye not *k·* it? "
44: 8 yea, there is no God; I *k·* not any. "
9 own witnesses; they see not, nor *k·*; "
45: 3 that thou mayest *k·* that I, the "
6 may *k·* from the rising of the sun, "
47: 8 shall I *k·* the loss of children: "
11 shalt not *k·* from whence it riseth: "
11 suddenly, which thou shalt not *k·*.* "
48: 6 things, and thou didst not *k·* them.* "
49:23 thou shalt *k·* that I am the Lord: "
26 all flesh shall *k·* that I the Lord "
50: 4 that I should *k·* how to speak a "
7 I *k·* that I shall not be ashamed. "
51: 7 unto me, ye that *k·* righteousness, "
52: 6 my people shall *k·* my name: "
6 they shall *k·* in that day that I am "
58: 2 daily, and delight to *k·* my ways, 1847
59: 8 The way of peace they *k·* not; 3045
8 goeth therein shall not *k·* peace. "
12 as for our iniquities, we *k·* them; "
60:16 and thou shalt *k·* that I the Lord "
66:18 I *k·* their works and their thoughts: "
Jer 2:19 *k·* therefore and see that it is an 3045
23 valley, *k·* what thou hast done: "
5: 1 of Jerusalem, and see now, and *k·*, "
4 for they *k·* not the way of the Lord, "
6:18 Therefore hear, ye nations, and *k·*, "
27 thou mayest *k·* and try their way. "
7: 9 after other gods whom ye *k·* not;* "
8: 7 people *k·* not the judgment of the "
9: 3 and they *k·* not me, saith the Lord. "
6 through deceit they refuse to *k·* me, "
10:23 I *k·* that the way of man is not in "
25 upon the heathen that *k·* thee not, "
11:18 me knowledge of it, and I *k·* it: * "
13:12 *k·* that every bottle shall be filled "
14:18 about into a land that they *k·* not. "
15:15 *k·* that for thy sake I have suffered "
16:13 land into a land that ye *k·* not, * "
21 I will this once cause them to *k·*, "
21 shall *k·* that my name is The Lord. "
17: 9 desperately wicked: who can *k·* it? "
22:16 was not this to *k·* me? saith the 1847
28 into a land which they *k·* not? 3045
24: 7 I will give them an heart to *k·* me, "
26:15 *k·* ye for certain, that if ye put me "
29:11 For I *k·* the thoughts that I think "
16 *k·* that thus saith the Lord of the * "
23 even I *k·*, and am a witness, saith*3045
31:34 his brother, saying, *K·* the Lord: "
36:19 and let no man *k·* where ye be. "
38:24 Let no man *k·* of these words, and "
40:14 Dost thou certainly *k·* that Baalis "
15 Nethaniah, and no man shall *k·* it: "
42:19 *k·* certainly that I have admonished "
22 *k·* certainly that ye shall die by the "
44:28 shall *k·* whose words shall stand, "
29 *k·* that my words shall surely stand "
48:17 all ye that *k·* his name, say, How is "
30 I *k·* his wrath, saith the Lord; but "
Eze 2: 5 *k·* that there hath been a prophet "
5:13 *k·* that I the Lord have spoken it "
6: 7 and ye shall *k·* that I am the Lord. "
10 they shall *k·* that I am the Lord, "
13 shall ye *k·* that I am the Lord, "
14 they shall *k·* that I am the Lord. "
7: 4 and ye shall *k·* that I am the Lord. "
9 shall *k·* I am the Lord that smiteth. "
27 they shall *k·* that I am the Lord. "
11: 5 I *k·* the things that come into your "
10 and ye shall *k·* that I am the Lord. "
12 And ye shall *k·* that I am the Lord: "
12:15 they shall *k·* that I am the Lord. "

Eze 12:16 they shall *k·* that I am the Lord. 3045
20 and ye shall *k·* that I am the Lord. "
13: 9 ye shall *k·* that I am the Lord God. "
14, 21, 23 shall *k·* that I am the Lord. "
14: 8 and ye shall *k·* that I am the Lord. "
23 *k·*...I have not done without cause "
15: 7 and ye shall *k·* that I am the Lord, "
16: 2 Jerusalem to *k·* her abominations, "
62 thou shalt *k·* that I am the Lord: "
17:12 *K·* ye not what these things mean? "
21 *k·* that I the Lord have spoken it. "
24 of the field shall *k·* that I the Lord "
20: 4 to *k·* the abominations of their "
12 *k·* that I am the Lord that sanctify "
20 *k·* that I am the Lord your God. "
26 they might *k·* that I am the Lord. "
38 and ye shall *k·* that I am the Lord. "
42, 44 ye shall *k·* that I am the Lord, "
21: 5 all flesh may *k·* that I the Lord have "
22:16 thou shalt *k·* that I am the Lord. "
22 *k·* that I the Lord have poured out "
23:49 ye shall *k·* that I am the Lord God. "
24:24 ye shall *k·* that I am the Lord God. "
27 they shall *k·* that I am the Lord. "
25: 5 and ye shall *k·* that I am the Lord. "
7 thou shalt *k·* that I am the Lord. "
11 they shall *k·* that I am the Lord. "
14 and they shall *k·* my vengeance, "
17 they shall *k·* that I am the Lord, "
26: 6 they shall *k·* that I am the Lord. "
28:19 they that *k·* thee among the people "
22 they shall *k·* that I am the Lord, "
23 they shall *k·* that I am the Lord. "
24 they shall *k·* that I am the Lord God. "
26 they shall *k·* that I am the Lord "
29: 6 all the inhabitants of Egypt shall *k·* "
9 they shall *k·* that I am the Lord: "
16 they shall *k·* that I am the Lord God. "
21 they shall *k·* that I am the Lord. "
30: 8 they shall *k·* that I am the Lord, "
19 they shall *k·* that I am the Lord. "
25 they shall *k·* that I am the Lord, "
26 they shall *k·* that I am the Lord. "
32:15 shall they *k·* that I am the Lord. "
33:29 shall they *k·* that I am the Lord, "
33 they *k·* that a prophet hath been "
34:27 and shall *k·* that I am the Lord, "
30 Thus shall they *k·* that I the Lord "
35: 4 thou shalt *k·* that I am the Lord. "
9 and ye shall *k·* that I am the Lord. "
12 thou shalt *k·* that I am the Lord, "
15 they shall *k·* that I am the Lord. "
36:11 and ye shall *k·* that I am the Lord. "
23 heathen shall *k·* that I am the Lord, "
36 *k·* that I the Lord build the ruined "
38 they shall *k·* that I am the Lord. "
37: 6 and ye shall *k·* that I am the Lord. "
13 And ye shall *k·* that I am the Lord, "
14 ye *k·* that I the Lord have spoken "
28 heathen shall *k·* that I the Lord do "
38:14 dwelleth safely, shalt thou not *k·* it? "
16 that the heathen may *k·* me, when "
23 they shall *k·* that I am the Lord. "
39: 6 they shall *k·* that I am the Lord. "
7 heathen shall *k·* that I am the Lord, "
22 Israel shall *k·* that I am the Lord "
23 heathen shall *k·* that the house of "
28 shall they *k·* that I am the Lord "
Da 2: 3 spirit was troubled to *k·* the dream. "
8 *k·* of certainty that ye would gain 3046
9 I shall *k·* that ye can shew me the "
21 to them that *k·* understanding: "
30 *k·* the thoughts of thy heart. "
4: 9 I *k·* that the spirit of the holy gods "
17 intent that the living may *k·* that "
25 till thou *k·* that the most High "
32 until thou *k·* that the most High "
5:23 which see not, nor hear, nor *k·*: "
6:15 *K·*,...that the law of the Medes and "
7:16 and made me *k·* the interpretation "
19 I would *k·* the truth of the fourth "
8:19 *k·* what shall be in the last end 3045
9:25 *K·* therefore and understand, that "
11:32 the people that do *k·* their God shall "
Ho 2: 8 she did not *k·* that I gave her corn, "
20 and thou shalt *k·* the Lord. "
5: 3 I *k·* Ephraim, and Israel is not hid "
6: 3 Then shall we *k·*, if we follow on to "
3 if we follow on to *k·* the Lord: "
8: 2 cry unto me, My God, we *k·* thee. "
9: 7 are come; Israel shall *k·* it: "
13: 4 and thou shalt *k·* no god but me: "
5 I did *k·* thee in the wilderness, in "
14: 9 prudent, and he shall *k·* them? "
Joe 2:27 ye shall *k·* that I am in the midst "
3:17 So shall ye *k·* that I am the Lord "
Am 3:10 they *k·* not to do right, saith the "
5:12 I *k·* your manifold transgressions "
Jon 1: 7 may *k·* for whose cause this evil is "
12 *k·*...for my sake this great tempest "
Mic 3: 1 Is it not for you to *k·* judgment? "
4:12 *k·* not the thoughts of the Lord, "
6: 5 *k·* the righteousness of the Lord. "
Zec 2: 9, 11 *k·*...the Lord of hosts hath sent "
4: 9 *k·* that the Lord of hosts hath sent "
6:15 *k·* that the Lord of hosts hath sent "
Mal 2: 4 *k·*...I have sent this commandment "
M't 6: 3 left hand *k·* what thy right hand 1097
7:11 *k·* how to give good gifts unto your 1492
16 Ye shall *k·* them by their fruits. 1921
20 by their fruits ye shall *k·* them. "
9: 6 *k·* that the Son of man hath power 1492
30 saying, See that no man *k·* it. 1097
13:11 *k·* the mysteries of the kingdom of "
20:22 and said, Ye *k·* not what ye ask. 1492
25 *k·* that the princes of the Gentiles "

M't 22:16 Master, we *k'* that thou art true, 1492
24:32 leaves, ye *k'* that summer is nigh: 1097
33 all these things, *k'* that it is near, "
42 for ye *k'* not what hour your Lord 1492
43 But *k'* this, that if the goodman 1097
25:12 Verily I say unto you, I *k'* you not. 1492
13 ye *k'* neither the day nor the hour "
26: 2 *k'* that after two days is the feast "
70 saying, I *k'* not what thou sayest. "
72 with an oath, I do not *k'* the man. "
74 to swear, saying, I *k'* not the man. "
28: 5 I *k'* that ye seek Jesus, which was "
M'r 1:24 *k'* thee who thou art, the Holy One "
2:10 *k'* that the Son of man hath power "
4:11 to *k'* the mystery of the kingdom *1097
13 *K'* ye not this parable? and how 1492
13 how then will ye *k'* all parables? 1097
5:43 straitly that no man should *k'* it; "
7:24 house, and would have no man *k'* it: "
9:30 would not that any man should *k'* it. "
10:38 unto them, Ye *k'* not what ye ask: 1492
42 *k'* that they which are accounted "
12:14 Master, we *k'* that thou art true, "
24 because ye *k'* not the scriptures, "
13:28 leaves, ye *k'* that summer is near: 1097
29 come to pass, *k'* that it is nigh, even "
33 for ye *k'* not when the time is. 1492
35 *k'* not when the master of the house "
14:68 he denied, saying, I *k'* not, neither "
71 I *k'* not this man of whom ye speak. "
Lu 1: 4 mightest *k'* the certainty of those 1921
18 the angel, Whereby shall I *k'* this? 1097
34 shall this be, seeing I *k'* not a man? "
4:34 I *k'* thee who thou art; the Holy 1492
5:24 *k'* that the Son of man hath power "
8:10 *k'* the mysteries of the kingdom of 1097
9:55 Ye *k'* not what manner of spirit *1492
11:13 *k'* how to give good gifts unto your "
12:39 And this *k'*, that if the goodman of 1097
13:25 you, I *k'* you not whence ye are: 1492
27 you, I *k'* you not whence ye are; "
19:15 he might *k'* how much every man 1097
20:21 *k'* that thou sayest and teachest 1492
21:20 *k'* that the desolation thereof is 1097
30 ye see and *k'* of your own selves "
31 *k'* ye that the kingdom of God is "
22:57 him, saying, Woman, I *k'* him not. 1492
60 Man, I *k'* not what thou sayest. "
23:34 them; for they *k'* not what they do. "
24:16 that they should not *k'* him. 1921
Joh 1:26 one among you, whom ye *k'* not; 1492
3: 2 we *k'* that thou art a teacher come "
11 We speak that we do *k'*, and testify "
4:22 Ye worship ye *k'* not what: "
22 we *k'* what we worship: for "
25 unto him, I *k'* that Messias cometh, "
32 have meat to eat that ye *k'* not of. "
42 *k'* that this is indeed the Christ, "
5:32 and I *k'* that the witness which he "
42 I *k'* you, that ye have not the love 1097
6:42 whose father and mother we *k'*? 1492
7:17 his will, he shall *k'* of the doctrine, 1097
26 *k'* indeed...this is the very Christ? "
27 we *k'* this man whence he is: 1492
28 both *k'* me, and ye *k'* whence I am: "
28 sent me is true, whom ye *k'* not. "
29 But I *k'* him: for I am from him, "
51 hear him, and *k'* what he doeth? 1097
8:14 I *k'* whence I came, and whither I 1492
19 Ye neither *k'* me, nor my Father: "
28 man, then shall ye *k'* that I am he, 1097
32 ye shall *k'* the truth, and the truth "
37 I *k'* that ye are Abraham's seed; 1492
52 Now we *k'* that thou hast a devil. 1492
55 have not known him; but I *k'* him: "
55 if I should say, I *k'* him not, "
55 but I *k'* him, and keep his saying. "
9:12 Where is he? He said, I *k'* not. "
20 We *k'* that this is our son, and that "
21 means he now seeth, we *k'* not; "
21 hath opened his eyes, we *k'* not: "
24 we *k'* that this man is a sinner. "
25 he be a sinner or no, I *k'* not: "
25 one thing I *k'*, that, whereas I was "
29 We *k'* that God spake unto Moses: "
29 fellow, we *k'* not from whence he is. "
30 that ye *k'* not from whence he is, "
31 we *k'* that God heareth not sinners: "
10: 4 follow him: for they *k'* his voice. "
5 they *k'* not the voice of strangers. "
14 good shepherd, and *k'* my sheep, 1097
15 me, even so *k'* I the Father: "
27 sheep hear my voice, and I *k'* them, "
38 that ye may *k'*, and believe, that "
11:22 I *k'*, that even now, whatsoever 1492
24 I *k'* that he shall rise again in the "
49 said unto them, Ye *k'* nothing at all, "
12:50 I *k'* that his commandment is life "
13: 7 now; but thou shalt *k'* hereafter. *1097
12 *K'* ye what I have done to you? "
17 If ye *k'* these things, happy are ye 1492
18 you all: I *k'* whom I have chosen: "
35 all men *k'* that ye are my disciples, 1097
14: 4 And whither I go ye *k'*, and the 1492
4 whither I go..., and the way ye *k'*.* "
5 Lord, we *k'* not whither thou goest; "
5 goest; and how can we *k'* the way? "
7 and from henceforth ye *k'* him, 1097
17 but ye *k'* him; for he dwelleth 1492
20 ye shall *k'* that I am in my Father, 1097
31 world may *k'* that I love the Father; "
15:18 *k'* that it hated me before it hated "
21 they *k'* not him that sent me. 1492
17: 3 might *k'* thee the only true God, 1097
23 may *k'* that thou hast sent me, "
18:21 behold, they *k'* what I said. 1492
Joh 19: 4 may *k'* that I find no fault in him. 1097
20: 2 *k'* not where they have laid him. 1492
13 I *k'* not where they have laid him. "
21:24 we *k'* that his testimony is true. "
Ac 1: 7 not for you to *k'* the times or the 1097
2:22 you, as ye yourselves also know: 1492
36 the house of Israel *k'* assuredly, 1097
3:16 man strong, whom ye see and *k'*: 1492
10:28 Ye *k'* how that it is an unlawful 1987
37 That word, I say, ye *k'*, which was 1492
12:11 Now I *k'* of a surety, that the Lord "
15: 7 ye *k'* how that a good while ago 1987
17:19 May we *k'* what this new doctrine, 1097
20 *k'* therefore what these things mean. "
19:15 and said, Jesus I *k'*, and Paul "
15 and Paul I *k'*; but who are ye? 1987
25 ye *k'* that by this craft we have our "
20:18 Ye *k'*, from the first day that I came "
25 I *k'* that ye all, among whom I 1492
29 I *k'* this, that after my departing "
34 ye yourselves *k'*, that these hands 1097
21:24 all may know that those things, "
34 he could not *k'* the certainty for the "
22:14 that thou shouldest *k'* his will, and "
19 they *k'* that I imprisoned and beat 1987
24 *k'* wherefore they cried so against 1921
24:10 as I *k'* that thou hast been of many 1987
22 *k'* the uttermost of your matter. *1231
26: 3 I *k'* thee to be expert in all customs* "
4 at Jerusalem, *k'* all the Jews; 2467
27 prophets? I *k'* that thou believest. 1492
28:22 we *k'* that every where it is spoken*1110
Ro 3:19 *k'* that what things soever the law 1492
6: 3 *K'* ye not, that so many of us as * 50
16 *K'* ye not, that to whom ye yield 1492
7: 1 *K'* ye not, brethren, (for I speak to* 50
1 speak to them that *k'* the law,) 1097
14 For we *k'* that the law is spiritual: 1492
18 For I *k'* that in me (that is, in my "
8:22 For we *k'* that the whole creation "
26 we *k'* not what we should pray for "
28 we *k'* that all things work together "
10:19 But I say, Did not Israel *k'*? First 1097
14:14 *k'*, and am persuaded by the Lord 1492
1Co 1:16 *k'* not whether I baptized any other. "
2: 2 not to *k'* any thing among you, save "
12 might *k'* the things that are freely "
14 neither can he *k'* them, because 1097
3:16 *K'* ye not that ye are the temple 1492
4: 4 For I *k'* nothing by myself; yet am 4892
19 and will *k'*, not the speech of them 1097
5: 6 *K'* ye not that a little leaven 1492
6: 2 ye not *k'* that the saints shall judge "
3 *K'* ye not...we shall judge angels? "
9 *K'* ye not that the unrighteous "
15 *K'* ye not that your bodies are the "
16 *k'* ye not that he which is joined to "
19 *k'* ye not...your body is the temple "
8: 1 we *k'* that we all have knowledge. "
2 nothing yet as he ought to *k'*. 1097
4 we *k'* that an idol is nothing in the 1492
9:13 ye not *k'* that they which minister "
24 *K'* ye not that they which run in a "
11: 3 I would have you *k'*, that the head "
12: 2 Ye *k'* that ye were Gentiles, carried "
13: 9 we *k'* in part, and we prophesy in 1097
12 now I *k'* in part; but then shall I "
12 shall I *k'* even as also I am known. 1921
14:11 I *k'* not the meaning of the voice, 1492
15:58 ye *k'* that your labour is not in vain "
16:15 (ye *k'* the house of Stephanas, that "
2Co 2: 4 ye might *k'* the love which I have 1097
9 I might *k'* the proof of you, whether "
5: 1 we *k'* that if our earthly house of 1492
16 *k'* we no man after the flesh: "
16 now henceforth *k'* we him no more. 1097
8: 9 ye *k'* the grace of our Lord Jesus "
9: 2 I *k'* the forwardness of your mind, 1492
13: 5 *K'* ye not your own selves, how 1921
6 *k'* that we are not reprobates. 1097
Ga 3: 7 *K'* ye therefore that they which are "
4:13 Ye *k'* how through infirmity of the 1492
Eph 1:18 *k'* what is the hope of his calling, "
3:19 And to *k'* the love of Christ, which 1097
5: 5 this ye *k'*, that no whoremonger, "
6:21 But that ye also may *k'* my affairs, 1492
22 that ye might *k'* our affairs, 1097
Ph'p 1:19 For I *k'* that this shall turn to my 1492
25 I *k'* that I shall abide and continue "
2:19 good comfort, when I *k'* your state. 1097
22 But ye *k'* the proof of him, that, as "
3:10 That I may *k'* him, and the power "
4:12 I *k'* both how to be abased, and 1492
12 abased, and I *k'* how to abound: "
15 Now ye Philippians *k'* also, that in "
Col 4: 6 ye may *k'* how ye ought to answer "
8 that he might *k'* your estate, and 1097
1Th 1: 5 ye *k'* what manner of men we were 1492
2: 1 *k'* our entrance in unto you, that it "
2 were shamefully entreated, as ye *k'*, "
5 used we flattering words, as ye *k'*, "
11 *k'* how we exhorted and comforted "
3: 3 yourselves *k'* that we are appointed "
4 even as it came to pass, and ye *k'*. "
5 forbear, I sent to *k'* your faith, 1097
4: 2 *k'* what commandments we gave 1492
4 should *k'* how to possess his vessel "
5 as the Gentiles which *k'* not God: "
5: 2 yourselves *k'* perfectly that the day "
12 *k'* them which labour among you, "
2Th 1: 8 vengeance on them that *k'* not God, "
2: 6 now ye *k'* what withholdeth that he "
3: 7 *k'* how ye ought to follow us: "
1Ti 1: 8 But we *k'* that the law is good, "
3: 5 a man *k'* not how to rule his own * "
15 *k'* how thou oughtest to behave "
1Ti 4: 3 which believe and *k'* the truth. 1921
2Ti 1:12 for I *k'* whom I have believed, 1492
3: 1 This *k'* also, that in the last days 1097
Tit 1:16 They profess that they *k'* God; 1492
Heb 8:11 his brother, saying, *K'* the Lord: 1097
11 for all shall *k'* me, from the least 1492
10:30 *k'* him that hath said, Vengeance "
12:17 For ye *k'* how that afterward, 2467
13:23 *K'* ye that our brother Timothy is 1097
Jas 2:20 wilt thou *k'*, O vain man, that faith "
4: 4 *k'* ye not that the friendship of the 1492
14 *k'* not what shall be on the morrow. 1987
5:20 him *k'*, that he which converteth 1097
1Pe 1:18 ye *k'* that ye were not redeemed *1492
2Pe 1:12 of these things, though ye *k'* them, "
3:17 seeing ye *k'* these things before, *4267
1Jo 2: 3 hereby we do *k'* that we *k'* him, 1097
4 He that saith, I *k'* him, and keepeth "
5 hereby *k'* we that we are in him. "
18 whereby we *k'* that it is the last time. "
20 the Holy One, and ye *k'* all things. 1492
21 you because ye *k'* not the truth, "
21 but because ye *k'* it, and that no lie "
29 If ye *k'* that he is righteous, "
29 ye *k'* that every one that doeth 1097
3: 2 we *k'* that, when he shall appear, 1492
5 *k'* that he was manifested to take "
14 We *k'* that we have passed from "
15 ye *k'* that no murderer hath eternal "
19 we *k'* that we are of the truth, 1097
24 hereby we *k'* that he abideth in us, "
4: 2 Hereby *k'* ye the Spirit of God: "
6 Hereby *k'* we the spirit of truth, "
13 Hereby *k'* we that we dwell in him, "
5: 2 we *k'* that we love the children of "
13 may *k'* that ye have eternal life, 1492
15 if we *k'* that he hear us, whatsoever "
15 we *k'* that we have the petitions "
18 We *k'* that whosoever is born of God "
19 we *k'* that we are of God, and the "
20 we *k'* that the Son of God is come, "
20 that we may *k'* him that is true, 1097
3Jo 12 and ye *k'* that our record is true. *1492
Jude 10 of those things which they *k'* not: "
10 but what they *k'* naturally, as *1987
Re 2: 2 I *k'* thy works, and thy labour, 1492
9 I *k'* thy works, and tribulation, "
9 I *k'* the blasphemy of them which say* "
13 I *k'* thy works, and where thou 1492
19 I *k'* thy works, and charity, and "
23 *k'* that I am he which searcheth 1097
3: 1 I *k'* thy works, that thou hast a 1492
3 shalt not *k'* what hour I will come 1097
8 I *k'* thy works: behold, I have set 1492
9 and to *k'* that I have loved thee. 1097
15 I *k'* thy works, that thou art 1492

knowest

Ge 30:26 thou *k'* my service which I have 3045
29 Thou *k'* how I have served thee, "
47: 6 and if thou *k'* any men of activity "
Ex 10: 7 *k'* thou not...Egypt is destroyed? "
32:22 thou *k'* the people, that they are set "
Nu 10:31 as thou *k'* how we are to encamp "
11:16 whom thou *k'* to be the elders of the "
20:14 *k'* all the travel that hath befallen "
De 7:15 diseases of Egypt, which thou *k'*, "
9: 2 of the Anakims, whom thou *k'*, and "
20:20 Only the trees which thou *k'* that "
28:33 a nation which thou *k'* not eat up; "
Jos 14: 6 Thou *k'* the thing that the Lord "
J'g 15:11 *K'* thou not that the Philistines "
1Sa 28: 9 thou *k'* what Saul hath done, how "
2Sa 1: 5 How *k'* thou that Saul and Jonathan "
2:26 *k'* thou not that it will be bitterness "
3:25 Thou *k'* Abner the son of Ner, that "
7:20 for thou, Lord God, *k'* thy servant. "
17: 8 thou *k'* thy father and his men, "
1Ki 1:18 my lord the king, thou *k'* it not: "
2: 5 thou *k'* also what Joab the son of "
9 *k'* what thou oughtest to do unto* "
15 Thou *k'* that the kingdom was mine, "
44 Thou *k'* all the wickedness which "
5: 3 Thou *k'* how that David my father "
6 thou *k'* that there is not among us "
8:39 to his ways, whose heart thou *k'*; "
39 *k'* the hearts of all the children of "
2Ki 2: 3, 5 *k'* thou that the Lord will take "
4: 1 thou *k'* that thy servant did fear "
1Ch 17:18 servant? for thou *k'* thy servant. "
2Ch 6:30 only *k'* the hearts of the children "
Job 10: 7 Thou *k'* that I am not wicked; 1847
15: 9 What *k'* thou, that we know not? 3045
20: 4 *K'* thou not this of old, since man "
34:33 therefore speak what thou *k'*. "
38: 5 the measures thereof, if thou *k'*? "
18 the earth? declare if thou *k'* it all. "
21 *K'* thou it, because thou wast then "
33 *K'* thou the ordinances of heaven? "
39: 1 *K'* thou the time when the wild "
2 *k'* thou the time when they bring "
Ps 40: 9 refrained my lips, O Lord, thou *k'*. "
69: 5 O God, thou *k'* my foolishness; "
139: 2 Thou *k'* my downsitting and mine "
4 lo, O Lord, thou *k'* it altogether. "
Pro 27: 1 thou *k'* not what a day may bring "
Ec 11: 2 thou *k'* not what evil shall be upon "
5 thou *k'* not what is the way of the "
5 so thou *k'* not the works of God "
6 thou *k'* not whether shall prosper, "
Isa 55: 5 shalt call a nation that thou *k'* not, "
Jer 5:15 nation whose language thou *k'* not, "
12: 3 But thou, O Lord, *k'* me: thou hast "
15:14 into a land which thou *k'* not: "
15 O Lord, thou *k'*: remember me, "
17: 4 in the land which thou *k'* not: "
16 thou *k'*: that which came out of "

Jer 18:23 thou k' all their counsel against me 3045
33: 3 mighty things, which thou k' not. "
Eze 37: 3 I answered, O Lord God, thou k'. "
Da 10:20 K'...wherefore I come unto thee? "
Zec 4: 5 me, K' thou not what these be? "
13 said, K' thou not what these be? "
M't 15:12 K' thou that the Pharisees were 1492
M'r 10:19 Thou k' the commandments, Do "
Lu 18:20 Thou k' the commandments, Do "
22:34 shalt thrice deny that thou k' me. "
Joh 1:48 unto him, Whence k' thou me? 1097
3:10 of Israel, and k' not these things?* "
13: 7 him, What I do thou k' not now; 1492
16:30 are we sure that thou k' all things, "
19:10 k' thou not that I have power to "
21:15, 16 Lord; thou k' that I love thee. "
17 unto him, Lord, thou k' all things; "
17 thou k' that I love thee. 1097
Ac 1:24 which k' the hearts of all men, 2589
25:10 no wrong, as thou very well k'. 1921
Ro 2:18 k' his will, and approvest the 1097
1Co 7:16 For what k' thou, O wife, whether 1492
16 or how k' thou, O man, whether "
2Ti 1:15 This thou k', that all they which "
18 me at Ephesus, thou k' very well. 1097
Re 3:17 and k' not that thou art wretched, 1492
7:14 And I said unto him, Sir, thou k'. "

knoweth

Ge 33:13 k' that the children are tender, 3045
Le 5: 3, 4 when he k' of it, then he shall be "
De 2: 7 he k' thy walking through this * "
34: 6 no man k' of his sepulchre unto "
Jos 22:22 gods, the Lord God of gods, he k', "
1Sa 3:13 ever for the iniquity which he k';* "
20: 3 Thy father certainly k' that I have "
23:17 and that also Saul my father k'. "
2Sa 14:22 thy servant k'...I have found grace "
17:10 Israel k' that thy father is a mighty "
1Ki 1:11 reign, and David our lord k' it not? "
Es 4:14 who k' whether thou art come to "
Job 11:11 he k' vain men: he seeth wickedness "
12: 3 who k' not such things as these? 854
9 Who k' not in all these that the 3045
14:21 come to honour, and he k' it not; "
15:23 he k' that the day of darkness is "
18:21 is the place of him that k' not God. "
23:10 he k' the way that I take: when he "
28: 7 There is a path which no fowl k', "
13 Man k' not the price thereof; "
23 thereof, and he k' the place thereof. "
34:25 Therefore he k' their works, and *5234
35:15 yet he k' it not in great extremity:*3045
Ps 1: 6 Lord k' the way of the righteous: "
37:18 The Lord k' the days of the upright: "
39: 6 and k' not who shall gather them. "
44:21 for he k' the secrets of the heart. "
74: 9 among us any that k' how long. "
90:11 Who k' the power of thine anger? "
92: 6 A brutish man k' not; neither doth "
94:11 The Lord k' the thoughts of man, "
103:14 he k' our frame; he remembereth "
104:19 seasons: the sun k' his going down. "
138: 6 lowly: but the proud he k' afar off. "
139:14 and that my soul k' right well. "
Pro 7:23 and k' not that it is for his life. "
9:13 she is simple, and k' nothing. "
18 he k' not that the dead are there; "
14:10 The heart k' his own bitterness; "
24:22 and who k' the ruin of them both? "
Ec 2:19 who k' whether he shall be a wise "
3:21 Who k' the spirit of man that "
6: 8 that k' to walk before the living? "
12 who k' what is good for man in this "
7:22 also thine own heart k' that thou "
8: 1 who k' the interpretation of a "
7 For he k' not that which shall be: "
9: 1 no man k' either love or hatred by "
12 For man also k' not his time: as the "
10:15 he k' not how to go to the city. "
Isa 1: 3 The ox k' his owner, and the ass "
29:15 Who seeth us? and who k' us? "
Jer 8: 7 the heaven k' her appointed times; "
9:24 that he understandeth and k' me, "
Da 2:22 he k' what is in the darkness, and 3046
Ho 7: 9 his strength, and he k' it not; 3045
9 and there upon him, yet he k' not. "
Joe 2:14 Who k' if he will return and repent, "
Na 1: 7 and he k' them that trust in him. "
Zep 3: 5 not; but the unjust k' no shame. "
M't 6: 8 k' what things ye have need of, 1492
32 k' that ye have need of all these "
11:27 no man k' the Son, but the Father; 1921
27 neither k' any man the Father, * "
24:36 of that day and hour k' no man, 1492
M'r 4:27 spring and grow up, he k' not how. "
13:32 that day and that hour k' no man, "
Lu 10:22 and no man k' who the Son is, 1097
12:30 k' that ye have need of all these 1492
16:15 men; but God k' your hearts: 1097
Joh 7:15 saying, How k' this man letters, 1492
27 cometh, no man k' whence he is. 1097
49 who k' not the law are cursed. "
10:15 As the Father k' me, even so know "
12:35 darkness k' not whither he goeth. 1492
14:17 it seeth him not, neither k' him: 1097
15:15 servant k' not what his lord doeth: 1492
19:35 he k' that he saith true, that ye "
Ac 15: 8 And God, which k' the hearts, bare 2589
19:35 there that k' not how that the city 1097
26:26 the king k' of these things, before 1987
Ro 8:27 k' what is the mind of the Spirit, 1492
1Co 2:11 what man k' the things of a man, "
11 the things of God k' no man, but "
3:20 Lord k' the thoughts of the wise, 1097
8: 2 man think that he k' any thing, 1492
2 he k' nothing yet as he ought to 1097
2Co 11:11 because I love you not? God k'. 1492
31 for evermore, k' that I lie not. "
12: 2, 3 of the body, I cannot tell: God k';) "
2Ti 2:19 seal, The Lord k' them that are his. 1097
Jas 4:17 to him that k' to do good, and 1492
2Pe 2: 9 Lord k' how to deliver the godly "
1Jo 2:11 k' not whither he goeth, because "
3: 1 the world k' us not, because it 1097
20 than our heart, and k' all things. "
4: 6 he that k' God heareth us; he that "
7 loveth is born of God, and k' God. "
8 He that loveth not, k' not God; for "
Re 2:17 no man k' saving he that receiveth "
12:12 he k'...he hath but a short time. *1492

knowing

Ge 3: 5 shall be as gods, k' good and evil. 3045
1Ki 2:32 my father David not k' thereof, * "
M't 9: 4 And Jesus k' their thoughts said, 1492
22:29 Ye do err, not k' the scriptures, nor "
M'r 5:30 k' in himself that virtue had gone *1921
33 k' what was done in her, came 1492
6:20 k' that he was a just man and an "
12:15 k' their hypocrisy, said unto them, "
Lu 8:53 him to scorn, k' that she was dead. "
9:33 one for Elias: not k' what he said. "
11:17 k' their thoughts, said unto them, "
Joh 13: 3 Jesus k' that the Father had given "
18: 4 k' all things that should come upon "
19:28 Jesus k' that all things were now "
21:12 art thou? k' that it was the Lord. "
Ac 2:30 k' that God had sworn with an oath "
5: 7 not k' what was done, came in. "
18:25 Lord, k' only the baptism of John. 1987
20:22 not k' the things that shall befall 1492
Ro 1:32 Who k' the judgment of God, that 1921
2: 4 not k' that the goodness of God 50
5: 3 k' that tribulation worketh 1492
6: 6 K' this, that our old man is 1097
9 K' that Christ being raised from 1492
13:11 k' the time, that now it is high time "
2Co 1: 7 k', that as ye are partakers of the "
4:14 K' that he which raised up the Lord "
5: 6 k' that, whilst we are at home in "
11 K' therefore the terror of the Lord, "
Ga 2:16 K' that a man is not justified by "
Eph 6: 8 K' that whatsoever good thing any "
9 k' that your Master...is in heaven; "
Ph'p 1:17 k' that I am set for the defence of "
Col 3:24 K' that of the Lord ye shall receive "
4: 1 k' that ye...have a Master in heaven. "
1Th 1: 4 K', brethren beloved, your election "
1Ti 1: 9 K' this, that the law is not made "
6: 4 k' nothing, but doting about 1987
2Ti 2:23 k' that they do gender strifes. 1492
3:14 k' of whom thou hast learned them; "
Tit 3:11 K' that he that is such is subverted, "
Ph'm 21 k' that thou wilt also do more than "
Heb 10:34 k' in yourselves that ye have in 1097
11: 8 went out, not k' whither he went. 1987
Jas 1: 3 K' this, that the trying of your 1097
3: 1 k' that we shall receive the greater 1492
1Pe 3: 9 k' that ye are thereunto called, * "
5: 9 k' that the same afflictions are "
2Pe 1:14 K' that shortly I must put off this "
20 K' this first, that no prophecy of 1097
3: 3 K' this first, that there shall come "

knowledge See also ACKNOWLEDGE; FOREKNOWLEDGE.

Ge 2: 9 the tree of k' of good and evil. 1847
17 the tree of the k' of good and evil. "
Ex 31: 3 and in understanding, and in k', "
35:31 in understanding, and in k', "
Le 4:23, 28 he hath sinned, come to his k';*3045
Nu 15:24 without the k' of the congregation, 5869
24:16 and knew the k' of the most High, 1847
De 1:39 had no k' between good and evil, 3045
Ru 2:10 that thou shouldest take k' of me, 5234
19 be he that did take k' of thee. "
1Sa 2: 3 the Lord is a God of k', and by 1844
23:23 take k' of all the lurking places 3045
1Ki 9:27 shipmen that had k' of the sea, "
2Ch 1:10 Give me now wisdom and k', that 4093
11 asked wisdom and k' for thyself, "
12 Wisdom and k' is granted unto "
8:18 servants that had k' of the sea; "
30:22 taught the good k' of the Lord: *7922
Ne 10:28 every one having k', and having 3045
Job 15: 2 Should a wise man utter vain k', 1847
21:14 for we desire not the k' of thy ways. "
22 Shall any teach God k'? seeing he "
33: 3 and my lips shall utter k' clearly.* "
34: 2 give ear unto me, ye that have k'. 3045
35 Job hath spoken without k', and 1847
35:16 he multiplieth words without k'. "
36: 3 I will fetch my k' from afar, 1843
4 that is perfect in k' is with thee. 1844
12 and they shall die without k'. 1847
37:16 of him which is perfect in k'? 1843
38: 2 counsel by words without k'? 1847
42: 3 he that hideth counsel without k'? "
Ps 14: 4 all the workers of iniquity no k'? 3045
19: 2 and night unto night sheweth k'. 1847
53: 4 the workers of iniquity no k'? 3045
73:11 and is there k' in the Most High? 1844
94:10 he that teacheth man k', shall not 1847
119:66 Teach me good judgment and k': "
139: 6 Such k' is too wonderful for me; "
144: 3 man, that thou takest k' of him! 3045
Pr 1: 4 the young man k' and discretion. 1847
7 the Lord is the beginning of k': "
22 their scorning, and fools hate k'? "
29 For that they hated k', and did not "
2: 3 Yea, if thou criest after k', and * 998
5 the Lord, and find the k' of God. 1847
6 out of his mouth cometh k' and "
10 and k' is pleasant unto thy soul; 1847
3:20 By his k' the depths are broken up, "
5: 2 and that thy lips may keep k'. "
8: 9 and right to them that find k'. "
10 and k' rather than choice gold, "
12 and find out k' of witty inventions. "
9:10 the k' of the holy is understanding. "
10:14 Wise men lay up k': but the mouth "
11: 9 but through k' shall the just be "
12: 1 Whoso loveth instruction loveth k': "
23 A prudent man concealeth k': "
13:16 Every prudent man dealeth with k': "
14: 6 but k' is easy unto him that "
7 perceivest not in him the lips of k'. "
18 the prudent are crowned with k'. "
15: 2 tongue of the wise useth k' aright: "
7 The lips of the wise disperse k': "
14 hath understanding seeketh k': "
17:27 He that hath k' spareth his words: "
18:15 heart of the prudent getteth k'; "
15 and the ear of the wise seeketh k'. "
19: 2 Also, that the soul be without k', "
25 and he will understand k'. "
27 causeth to err from the words of k'. "
20:15 the lips of k' are a precious jewel. "
21:11 wise is instructed, he receiveth k'. "
22:12 The eyes of the Lord preserve k', "
17 and apply thine heart unto my k'. "
20 excellent things in counsels and k', "
23:12 and thine ears to the words of k'. "
24: 4 by k' shall the chambers be filled "
5 a man of k' increaseth strength. "
14 So shall the k' of wisdom be unto *3045
28: 2 a man of understanding and k' "
30: 3 nor have the k' of the holy. 1847
Ec 1:16 great experience of wisdom and k'. "
18 increaseth k' increaseth sorrow. "
2:21 labour is in wisdom, and in k', "
26 good in his sight wisdom, and k', "
7:12 the excellency of k' is, that wisdom "
9:10 there is no work, nor device, nor k', "
12: 9 wise, he still taught the people k'; "
Isa 5:13 captivity, because they have no k': "
8: 4 the child shall have k' to cry, 3045
11: 2 the spirit of k' and of the fear of 1847
9 shall be full of the k' of the Lord, 1844
28: 9 Whom shall he teach k'? and whom "
32: 4 of the rash shall understand k', 1847
33: 6 wisdom and k' shall be the stability "
40:14 taught him k', and shewed to him "
44:19 there k' nor understanding to say, "
25 and maketh their k' foolish; "
45:20 have no k' that set up the wood 3045
47:10 thy k', it hath perverted thee; 1847
53:11 by his k' shall my righteous servant "
58: 3 our soul, and thou takest no k'? 3045
Jer 3:15 which shall feed you with k' and 1844
4:22 but to do good they have no k'. 3045
10:14 Every man is brutish in his k': 1847
11:18 the Lord hath given me k' of it, 3045
51:17 Every man is brutish by his k'; 1847
Da 1: 4 in all wisdom, and cunning in k', "
17 God gave them k' and skill in all 4093
2:21 wise, and k' to them that know 998
5:12 as an excellent spirit, and k', and "
12: 4 and fro, and k' shall be increased. 1847
Ho 4: 1 nor mercy, nor k' of God in the land. "
6 people are destroyed for lack of k': "
6 because thou hast rejected k', I will "
6: 6 k' of God more than burnt offerings. "
Hab 2:14 be filled with the k' of the glory of 3045
Mal 2: 7 the priest's lips should keep k', 1847
M't 14:35 men of that place had k' of him, *1921
Lu 1:77 give k' of salvation unto his people 1108
11:52 ye have taken away the key of k'. "
Ac 4:13 and they took k' of them, that they 1921
17:13 the Jews of Thessalonica had k' 1097
24: 8 mayest take k' of all these things, 1921
22 having more perfect k' of that way, 1492
Ro 1:28 not like to retain God in their k', 1922
2:20 hast the form of k' and of the truth 1108
3:20 for by the law is the k' of sin. 1922
10: 2 zeal of God, but not according to k'. "
11:33 both of the wisdom and k' of God! 1108
15:14 full of goodness, filled with all k', "
1Co 1: 5 him, in all utterance, and in all k'; "
8: 1 idols, we know that we all have k'. "
1 K' puffeth up, but charity edifieth. "
7 there is not in every man that k': "
10 see thee which hast k' sit at meat "
11 And through thy k' shall the weak "
12: 8 the word of k' by the same Spirit; "
13: 2 understand all mysteries, and all k'; "
8 whether there be k', it shall vanish "
14: 6 to you either by revelation, or by k'. "
15:34 for some have not the k' of God: 56
2Co 2:14 manifest the savour of his k' by us 1108
4: 6 light of the k' of the glory of God "
6: 6 pureness, by k', by longsuffering, "
8: 7 in faith, and utterance, and k', and "
10: 5 exalteth itself against the k' of God, "
11: 6 I be rude in speech, yet not in k'; "
Eph 1:17 and revelation in the k' of him: 1922
3: 4 my k' in the mystery of Christ) *4907
19 love of Christ, which passeth k', 1108
4:13 and of the k' of the Son of God, 1922
Ph'p 1: 9 abound yet more and more in k' "
3: 8 excellency of the k' of Christ Jesus 1108
Col 1: 9 be filled with the k' of his will in 1922
10 and increasing in the k' of God; "
2: 3 all the treasures of wisdom and k'. 1108
3:10 is renewed in k' after the image of 1922
1Ti 2: 4 and to come unto the k' of the truth. "
2Ti 3: 7 able to come to the k' of the truth "
Heb 10:26 have received the k' of the truth, "
Jas 3:13 and endued with k' among you? *1990

1Pe 3: 7 dwell with them according to *k*·, 1108
2Pe 1: 2 unto you through the *k*· of God, 1922
3 the *k*· of him that hath called us "
5 your faith virtue; and to virtue *k*·; 1108
6 And to *k*·, temperance; and to "
8 in the *k*· of our Lord Jesus Christ. 1922
2:20 in the *k*· of the Lord and Saviour "
3:18 in the *k*· of our Lord and Saviour 1108
known See also UNKNOWN.
Ge 19: 8 daughters which have not *k*· man; 3045
24:16 virgin, neither had any man *k*· her: "
41:21 could not be *k*· that they had eaten "
31 plenty shall not be *k*· in the land by "
45: 1 Joseph made himself *k*· unto his "
Ex 2:14 and said, Surely this thing is *k*·. "
6: 3 name Jehovah was I not *k*· to them. "
21:36 be *k*· that the ox hath used to push "
33:16 it be *k*· here that I and thy people "
Le 4:14 they have sinned against it, is *k*·, "
5: 1 whether he hath seen or *k*· of it; "
Nu 12: 6 Lord will make myself *k*· unto him "
31:17 kill every woman that hath *k*· man "
18 children, that have not *k*· a man by "
35 of women that had not *k*· man by "
De 1:13 and *k*· among your tribes, and I will "
15 wise men, and *k*·, and made them "
11: 2 your children which have not *k*·, "
28 other gods, which ye have not *k*·. "
13: 2, 6 other gods, which thou hast not *k*·, "
13 other gods, which ye have not *k*·; "
21: 1 and it be not *k*· who hath slain him: "
28:36 neither thou nor thy fathers have *k*·; "
64 neither thou nor thy fathers have *k*·, "
31:13 children, which have not *k*· any "
Jos 24:31 had *k*· all the works of the Lord, "
J'g 3: 1 had not *k*· all the wars of Canaan; "
16: 9 the fire. So his strength was not *k*·. "
21:12 young virgins, that had *k*· no man by "
Ru 3: 3 make not thyself *k*· unto the man, "
14 Let it not be *k*· that a woman came "
1Sa 6: 3 it shall be *k*· to you why his hand is "
28:15 make *k*· unto me what I shall do. "
2Sa 17:19 thereon; and the thing was not *k*·. "
1Ki 14: 2 be not *k*· to be the wife of Jeroboam; "
18:36 it be *k*· this day that thou art God "
1Ch 16: 8 make *k*· his deeds among the "
17:19 in making *k*· all these great things. "
Ezr 4:12 it *k*· unto the king, that the Jews 3046
13 Be it *k*· now unto the king, that, if "
5: 8 it *k*· unto the king, that we went "
Ne 4:15 our enemies heard that it was *k*· 3045
9:14 And madest *k*· unto them thy holy "
Es 2:22 And the thing was *k*· to Mordecai, "
Ps 9:16 The Lord is *k*· by the judgment "
18:43 a people whom I have not *k*· shall "
31: 7 thou hast *k*· my soul in adversities; "
48: 3 God is *k*· in her palaces for a refuge. "
67: 2 That thy way may be *k*· upon earth, "
69:19 Thou hast *k*· my reproach, and my* "
76: 1 In Judah is God *k*·: his name is "
77:19 waters, and thy footsteps are not *k*·. "
78: 3 Which we have heard and *k*·, and "
5 make them *k*· to their children: "
79: 6 the heathen that have not *k*· thee,* "
79:10 let him be *k*· among the heathen in "
88:12 Shall thy wonders be *k*· in the dark? "
89: 1 will I make *k*· thy faithfulness to "
91:14 high, because he hath *k*· my name. "
95:10 and they have not *k*· my ways: "
98: 2 Lord hath made *k*· his salvation: "
103: 7 He made *k*· his ways unto Moses, "
105: 1 make *k*· his deeds among the people. "
106: 8 make his mighty power to be *k*·. "
119:79 those that have *k*· thy testimonies.* "
152 *k*· of old that thou hast founded "
139: 1 thou hast searched me, and *k*· me. "
145:12 To make *k*· to the sons of men his "
147:20 judgments, they have not *k*· them. "
Pr 1:23 I will make *k*· my words unto you. "
10: 9 that perverteth his ways shall be *k*·. "
12:16 A fool's wrath is presently *k*·: but "
14:33 is in the midst of fools is made *k*·. "
20:11 Even a child is *k*· by his doings, 5234
22:19 I have made *k*· to thee this day, 3045
31:23 Her husband is *k*· in the gates, "
Ec 5: 3 a fool's voice is *k*· by multitude of* "
6: 5 not seen the sun, nor *k*· any thing: 3045
10 already, and it is *k*· that it is man: "
Isa 12: 5 things: this is *k*· in all the earth. "
19:21 the Lord shall be *k*· to Egypt, and "
38:19 children shall make *k*· thy truth. "
40:21 Have ye not *k*·? have ye not heard? "
28 Hast thou not *k*·? hast thou not "
42:16 them in paths that they have not *k*·: * "
44:18 They have not *k*· nor understood: * "
45: 4 thee, though thou hast not *k*· me. "
5 thee, though thou hast not *k*· me: "
61: 9 seed shall be *k*· among the Gentiles, "
64: 2 thy name *k*· to thine adversaries, "
66:14 hand of the Lord shall be *k*· toward "
Jer 4:22 is foolish, they have not *k*· me; * "
5: 5 they have *k*· the way of the Lord, * "
9:16 they nor their fathers have *k*·: "
19: 4 they nor their fathers have *k*·, "
28: 9 pass, then shall the prophet be *k*·, "
La 4: 8 they are not *k*· in the streets: 5234
Eze 20: 5 and made myself *k*· unto them in 3045
9 whose sight I made myself *k*· unto "
32: 9 countries which thou hast not *k*·. "
35:11 I will make myself *k*· among them, "
36:32 the Lord God, be it *k*· unto you: "
38:23 be *k*· in the eyes of many nations "
39: 7 So will I make my holy name *k*· in "
Da 2: 5, 9 not make *k*· unto me the dream, 3046
15 Arioch made the thing *k*· to Daniel. "
17 and made the thing *k*· to Hananiah, "
Da 2:23 hast made *k*· unto me now what 3046
23 thou hast now made *k*· unto us the "
25 that will make *k*· unto the king the "
26 able to make *k*· unto me the dream "
28 *k*· to the king Nebuchadnezzar "
29 *k*· to thee what shall come to pass. "
30 *k*· the interpretation to the king, "
45 God hath made *k*· to the king what "
3:18 be it *k*· unto thee, O king, that we "
4: 6, 7 *k*· unto me the interpretation "
18 make *k*· unto me the interpretation: "
26 have *k*· that the heavens do rule. "
5: 8 nor make *k*· to the king the "
15 make *k*· unto me the interpretation "
16 make *k*· to me the interpretation "
17 make *k*· to him the interpretation. "
Ho 5: 4 and they have not *k*· the Lord. *3045
9 made *k*· that which shall surely be. "
Am 3: 2 You only have I *k*· of all the "
Na 3:17 their place is not *k*· where they are. "
Hab 3: 2 in the midst of the years make *k*·; "
Zec 14: 7 day which shall be *k*· to the Lord, "
M't 10:26 and hid, that shall not be *k*·. 1097
12: 7 if ye had *k*· what this meaneth, "
16 that they should not make him *k*·: 5318
33 for the tree is *k*· by his fruit. 1097
24:43 had *k*· in what watch the thief 1492
M'r 3:12 that they should not make him *k*·. 5318
Lu 2:15 the Lord hath made *k*· unto us. 1107
17 they made *k*· abroad the saying 1232
6:44 every tree is *k*· by his own fruit. 1097
7:39 *k*· who and what manner of woman* "
8:17 shall not be *k*· and come abroad. "
12: 2 neither hid, that shall not be *k*·. "
39 had *k*· what hour the thief would 1492
19:42 Saying, If thou hadst *k*·, even thou, 1097
24:18 hast not *k*· the things which are "
35 *k*· of them in breaking of bread. "
Joh 7: 4 he himself seeketh to be *k*· openly. "
8:19 nor my Father: if ye had *k*· me, *1492
19 ye should have *k*· my Father also: * "
55 Yet ye have not *k*· him; but I 1097
10:14 know my sheep, and am *k*· of mine. * "
14: 7 *k*· me, ye should have *k*· my Father "
9 yet hast thou not *k*· me, Philip? * "
15:15 Father I have made *k*· unto you. 1107
16: 3 they have not *k*· the Father, nor 1097
17: 7 Now they have *k*· that all things * "
8 have *k*· surely that I came out from* "
25 Father, the world hath not *k*· thee: * "
25 but I have *k*· thee, and these * "
25 have *k*· that thou hast sent me. * "
18:15 that disciple was *k*· unto the high 1110
16 which was *k*· unto the high priest, "
Ac 1:19 it was *k*· unto all the dwellers at "
2:14 be this *k*· unto you, and hearken to "
28 Thou hast made *k*· to me the ways 1107
4:10 Be it *k*· unto you all, and to all 1110
7:13 Joseph was made *k*· to his brethren; 319
13 Joseph's kindred was made *k*· *5318
9:24 their laying await was *k*· of Saul. 1097
42 it was *k*· throughout all Joppa; 1110
13:38 Be it *k*· unto you therefore, men "
15:18 *K*· unto God are all his works from "
19:17 And this was *k*· to all the Jews "
22:30 he would have *k*· the certainty 1097
23:28 when I would have *k*· the cause * "
28:28 Be it *k*· therefore unto you, that 1110
Ro 1:19 that which may be *k*· of God is "
3:17 way of peace have they not *k*·: 1097
7: 7 I had not *k*· sin, but by the law: "
7 I had not *k*· lust, except the law 1492
9:22 wrath, and to make his power *k*·, 1107
23 that he might make *k*· the riches "
11:34 who hath *k*· the mind of the Lord? 1097
16:26 made *k*· to all nations for the 1107
1Co 2: 8 for had they *k*· it, they would not 1097
16 who hath *k*· the mind of the Lord, "
8: 3 love God, the same is *k*· of him. "
13:12 shall I know even as also I am *k*·. 1921
14: 7 it be *k*· what is piped or harped? 1097
9 how shall it be *k*· what is spoken? "
2Co 3: 2 our hearts, *k*· and read of all men: "
5:16 we have *k*· Christ after the flesh, "
6: 9 As unknown, and yet well *k*·; 1921
Ga 4: 9 But now, after ye have *k*· God, *1097
9 rather are *k*· of God, how turn ye "
Eph 1: 9 made *k*· unto us the mystery of his 1107
3: 3 he made *k*· unto me the mystery; "
5 not made *k*· unto the sons of men, "
10 be *k*· by the church the manifold "
6:19 make *k*· the mystery of the gospel, "
21 shall make *k*· to you all things: "
Ph'p 4: 5 moderation be *k*· unto all men 1097
6 requests be made *k*· unto God. 1107
Col 1:27 would make *k*· what is the riches "
4: 9 shall make *k*· unto you all things "
2Ti 3:10 thou hast fully *k*· my doctrine, *3877
15 thou hast *k*· the holy scriptures, 1492
4:17 the preaching might be fully *k*·, *4135
Heb 3:10 and they have not *k*· my ways. *1097
2Pe 1:16 we made *k*· unto you the power 1107
2:21 for them not to have *k*· the way 1921
21 than, after they have *k*· it, to turn * "
1Jo 2:13 *k*· him that is from the beginning. *1097
13 because ye have *k*· the Father. * "
14 *k*· him that is from the beginning. * "
3: 6 hath not seen him, neither *k*· him. * "
4:16 have *k*· and believed the love that * "
2Jo 1 also all they that have *k*· the truth; *1097
Re 2:24 have not *k*· the depths of Satan, * "
Koa (*ko'-ah*)
Eze 23:23 and Shoa, and *K*·, and all the 6970
Kohath (*ko'-hath*) See also KOHATHITES.
Ge 46:11 the sons of Levi; Gershon, *K*·, 6955
Ex 6:16 Gershon, *K*·, and Merari; 6955
18 And the sons of *K*·; Amram, and "
18 and the years of the life of *K*· were "
Nu 3:17 by their names; Gershon, and *K*·, "
19 the sons of *K*· by their families; "
27 of *K*· was the family of the "
29 The families of the sons of *K*· shall "
4: 2 sum of the sons of *K*· from among "
4 be the service of the sons of *K*· "
15 sons of *K*· shall come to bear it: "
15 are the burden of the sons of *K*· "
7: 9 unto the sons of *K*· he gave none: "
16: 1 Izhar, the son of *K*·, the son of "
26:57 of *K*·, the family of the Kohathites: "
58 Kohathites. And *K*· begat Amram. "
Jos 21: 5 the rest of the children of *K*· had "
20 the families of the children of *K*·, "
20 remained of the children of *K*·, "
26 the children of *K*· that remained. "
1Ch 6: 1 sons of Levi; Gershon, *K*·, and "
2 sons of *K*·; Amram, Izhar, and "
16 sons of Levi; Gershon, *K*·, and "
18 the sons of *K*· were, Amram, and "
22 sons of *K*·; Amminadab his son, "
38 The son of Izhar, the son of *K*·, "
61 unto the sons of *K*·, which were "
66 of the families of the sons of *K*· "
70 of the remnant of the sons of *K*·. "
15: 5 of the sons of *K*·; Uriel the chief, "
23: 6 sons of Levi, namely, Gershon, *K*·, "
12 The sons of *K*·; Amram, Izhar, "
Kohathites (*ko'-hath-ites*)
Nu 3:27 these are the families of the *K*·. 6956
30 father of the families of the *K*· "
4:18 the tribe of the families of the *K*· "
34 numbered the sons of the *K*· after "
37 numbered of the families of the *K*·, "
10:21 *K*· set forward, bearing the "
26:57 of Kohath, the family of the *K*·. "
Jos 21: 4 came out for the families of the *K*·: "
10 being of the families of the *K*·, "
1Ch 6:33 Of the sons of the *K*·: Heman a "
54 Aaron, of the families of the *K*·: "
9:32 brethren, of the sons of the *K*·, "
2Ch 20:19 Levites, of the children of the *K*·, "
29:12 Azariah, of the sons of the *K*·: "
34:12 Meshullam, of the sons of the *K*·, "
Kolaiah (*ko-la-i'-ah*)
Ne 11: 7 the son of Pedaiah, the son of *K*·, 6964
Jer 29:21 of Israel, of Ahab the son of *K*·, "
Korah (*ko'-rah*) See also CORE; KORAHITE; KORE.
Ge 36: 5 bare Jeush, and Jaalam, and *K*·. 7141
14 Esau Jeush, and Jaalam, and *K*·. "
16 Duke *K*·, duke Gatam, and duke "
18 duke Jeush, duke Jaalam, duke *K*·: "
Ex 6:21 And the sons of Izhar; *K*·, and "
24 And the sons of *K*·; Assir, and "
Nu 16: 1 Now *K*·, the son of Izhar, the son of "
5 And he spake unto *K*· and unto all "
6 censers, *K*·, and all his company; "
8 Moses said unto *K*·, Hear, I pray "
16 And Moses said unto *K*·, Be thou "
19 *K*· gathered all the congregation "
24 from about the tabernacle of *K*·, "
27 gat up from the tabernacle of *K*·, "
32 the men that appertained unto *K*·, "
40 he be not as *K*·, and as his "
49 that died about the matter of *K*·. "
26: 9 Aaron in the company of *K*·, "
10 them up together with *K*·, when "
11 the children of *K*· died not. "
27: 3 the Lord in the company of *K*·; "
1Ch 1:35 and Jeush, and Jaalam, and *K*·. "
2:43 the sons of Hebron; *K*·, and "
6:22 Amminadab his son, *K*· his son, "
37 son of Ebiasaph, the son of *K*·, "
9:19 son of Ebiasaph, the son of *K*·, "
Ps 42: *title* Maschil, for the sons of *K*·. "
44: *title* Musician for the sons of *K*·, "
45: *title* Shoshannim, for the sons of *K*·, "
46: *title* Musician for the sons of *K*·, "
47: *title* A Psalm for the sons of *K*·. "
48: *title* and Psalm for the sons of *K*·. "
49: *title* A Psalm for the sons of *K*·. "
84: *title* A Psalm for the sons of *K*·. "
85: *title* A Psalm for the sons of *K*·. "
87: *title* Psalm or Song for the sons of *K*·. "
88: *title* Song or Psalm for the sons of *K*·. "
Korahite (*ko'-ra-hite*) See also KORAHITES; KORE.
1Ch 9:31 the firstborn of Shallum the *K*·, 7145
Korahites (*ko'-ra-hites*) See also KORATHITES; KORHITES.
1Ch 9:19 the *K*·, were over the work of the 7145
Korathites (*ko'-ra-thites*) See also KORAHITES.
Nu 26:58 Mushites, the family of the *K*·. 7145
Kore (*ko'-re*) See also KORAH; KORAHITE.
1Ch 9:19 And Shallum the son of *K*·, 6981
26: 1 was Meshelemiah the son of *K*·, "
19 the porters among the sons of *K*·, *7145
2Ch 31:14 *K*· the son of Imnah the Levite, 6981
Korhites (*kor'-hites*) See also KORAHITES.
Ex 6:24 these are the families of the *K*·. *7145
1Ch 12: 6 Joezer, and Jashobeam, the *K*·, * "
26: 1 *K*· was Meshelemiah the son of * "
2Ch 20:19 and of the children of the *K*·, stood* "
Koz (*coz*) See also HAKKOZ.
Ezr 2:61 the children of *K*·, the children *6976
Ne 3: 4 the son of Urijah, the son of *K*·. * "
21 the son of *K*· another piece, from* "
7:63 of Habaiah, the children of *K*·, * "
Kushaiah (*cu-shah'-yah*) See also KISHI.
1Ch 15:17 brethren, Ethan the son of *K*·; 6984

L.

Laadah (*la'-a-dah*)
1Ch 4:21 L' the father of Mareshah, and 3935
Laadan (*la'-a-dan*) See also LIBNI.
1Ch 7:26 L' his son, Ammihud his son, *3936
23: 7 Of the Gershonites were, L', and * "
8 The sons of L'; the chief was Jehiel,*"
9 were the chief of the fathers of L'.*"
26:21 As concerning the sons of L'; the* "
21 sons of the Gershonite L', chief "
21 even of L' the Gershonite, were * "
Laban (*la'-ban*) See also LABAN'S; LIBNAH.
Ge 24:29 a brother, and his name was L': 3837
29 and L' ran out unto the man, unto "
50 L' and Bethuel answered and said, "
25:20 the sister to L' the Syrian. "
27:43 flee thou to L' my brother to Haran; "
28: 2 from thence of the daughters of L' "
5 and he went to Padan-aram unto L'. "
29: 5 them, Know ye L' the son of Nahor? "
10 Jacob saw Rachel the daughter of L' "
10 sheep of L' his mother's brother, "
10 watered the flock of L' his mother's "
13 when L' heard the tidings of Jacob "
13 And he told L' all these things. "
14 L' said to him, Surely thou art my "
15 L' said unto Jacob, Because thou "
16 L' had two daughters: the name of "
19 L' said, It is better that I give her "
21 And Jacob said unto L', Give me my "
22 L' gathered together all the men of "
24 L' gave unto his daughter Leah "
25 he said to L', What is this thou hast "
26 And L' said, It must not be so done "
29 And L' gave to Rachel his daughter "
30:25 Jacob said unto L', Send me away, "
27 And L' said unto him, I pray thee, "
34 L' said, Behold, I would it might be "
40 and all the brown in the flock of L'; "
31: 2 beheld the countenance of L', and, "
12 seen all that L' doeth unto thee. "
19 And L' went to shear his sheep: "
20 Jacob stole away unawares to L' the "
22 told L' on the third day that Jacob "
24 came to L' the Syrian in a dream "
25 Then L' overtook Jacob. Now Jacob "
25 L' with his brethren pitched in the "
26 L' said to Jacob, What hast thou "
31 Jacob answered and said to L', "
33 L' went into Jacob's tent, and into "
34 L' searched all the tent, but found "
36 was wroth, and chode with L': "
36 Jacob answered and said unto L', "
43 L' answered and said unto Jacob, "
47 And L' called it Jegar-sahadutha: "
48 And L' said, This heap is a witness "
51 L' said to Jacob, Behold this heap, "
55 L' rose up, and kissed his sons and "
55 L' departed, and returned unto his "
32: 4 have sojourned with L', and stayed "
46:18 whom L' gave to Leah his daughter; "
25 which L' gave unto Rachel his "
De 1: 1 Tophel, and L', and Hazeroth, and "
Laban's (*la'-bans*)
Ge 30:36 and Jacob fed the rest of L' flocks. 3837
40 and put them not unto L' cattle. "
42 feebler were L', and the stronger "
31: 1 heard the words of L' sons, saying, "
labour See also LABOURED; LABOURETH; LABOURING; LABOURS.
Ge 31:42 affliction and the l' of my hands, 3018
35:16 travailed, and she had hard l'. 3205
17 when she was in hard l', that the "
Ex 5: 9 the men, that they may l' therein; 6213
20: 9 Six days shalt thou l', and do all 5647
De 5:13 Six days thou shalt l', and do all "
26: 7 and our l', and our oppression: *5999
Jos 7: 3 not all the people to l' thither; *3021
24:13 you a land for which ye did not l',* "
Ne 4:22 be a guard to us, and l' on the day. 4399
5:13 from his house, and from his l', 3018
Job 9:29 be wicked, why then l' I in vain? 3021
39:11 or wilt thou leave thy l' to him? 3018
16 hers: her l' is in vain without fear; "
Ps 78:46 gave also...their l' unto the locust. "
90:10 yet is their strength l' and sorrow; 5999
104:23 forth unto his work and to his l' 5656
105:44 they inherited the l' of the people; 5999
107:12 he brought down their heart with l'; "
109:11 and let the strangers spoil his l'. 3018
127: 1 house, they l' in vain that build it: 5998
128: 2 shalt eat the l' of thine hands: 3018
144:14 our oxen may be strong to l'; *5445
Pr 10:16 l' of the righteous tendeth to life: 6468
13:11 that gathereth by l' shall increase. 3027
14:23 In all l' there is profit: but the 6089
21:25 him; for his hands refuse to l'. 6213
23: 4 L' not to be rich: cease from thine *3021
Ec 1: 3 What profit hath a man of all his l' 5999
8 All things are full of l'; man *3023
2:10 for my heart rejoiced in all my l': 5999
10 and this was my portion of all my l' "
11 the l' that I had laboured to "
18 I hated all my l' which I had taken "
19 he have rule over all my l' "
20 the l' which I took under the sun. "
21 is a man whose l' is in wisdom, and "
22 For what hath man of all his l', and "
24 make his soul enjoy good in his l'. "
3:13 and enjoy the good of all his l', it is "
4: 8 yet is there no end of all his l'; "
Ec 4: 8 For whom do I l', and bereave my 6001
9 have a good reward for their l'. 5999
5:15 shall take nothing of his l', which "
18 enjoy the good of all his l' that he "
19 his portion, and to rejoice in his l'; "
6: 7 All the l' of man is for his mouth, "
8:15 that shall abide with him of his l' "
17 though a man l' to seek it out, yet 5998
9: 9 and in thy l' which thou takest 5999
10:15 l' of the foolish wearieth every one "
Isa 22: 4 l' not to comfort me, because of the 213
45:14 The l' of Egypt, and merchandise 3018
55: 2 your l' for that which satisfieth not?" "
65:23 They shall not l' in vain, nor bring 3021
Jer 3:24 shame hath devoured the l' of our 3018
20:18 forth out of the womb to see l' and 5999
51:58 and the people shall l' in vain, and 3021
La 5: 5 we l', and have no rest. * "
Eze 23:29 and shall take away all thy l', and 3018
29:20 his l' wherewith he served against *6468
Mic 4:10 and l' to bring forth, O daughter 1518
Hab 2:13 the people shall l' in the very fire, 3021
3:17 the l' of the olive shall fail, and 4639
Hag 1:11 and upon all the l' of the hands. 3018
M't 11:28 Come unto me, all ye that l' and *2872*
Joh 4:38 that whereon ye bestowed no l': * *2872*
6:27 L' not for...meat which perisheth, *2038*
Ro 16: 6 who bestowed much l' on us. *2872*
12 and Tryphosa, who l' in the Lord. *2872*
1Co 3: 8 reward according to his own l'. *2873*
4:12 l', working with our own hands: **2872*
15:58 your l' is not in vain in the Lord. *2873*
2Co 5: 9 Wherefore we l', that, whether **5389*
Ga 4:11 have bestowed upon you l' in vain. *2872*
Eph 4:28 rather let him l', working with his "
Ph'p 1:22 the flesh, this is the fruit of my l': **2041*
2:25 my brother, and companion in l', **4904*
Col 1:29 Whereunto I also l', striving *2872*
1Th 1: 3 your work of faith, and l' of love, *2873*
2: 9 brethren, our l' and travail: "
3: 5 tempted you, and our l' be in vain. "
5:12 to know them which l' among you, *2872*
2Th 3: 8 wrought with l' and travail night *2873*
1Ti 4:10 we both l' and suffer reproach, *2872*
5:17 who l' in the word and doctrine. "
Heb 4:11 l' therefore to enter into that rest, **4704*
6:10 to forget your work and l' of love, **2873*
Re 2: 2 I know thy works, and thy l', and * "
laboured
Ne 4:21 So we l' in the work: and half of *6213
Job 20:18 which he l' for shall he restore, 3022
Ec 2:11 on the labour that I had l' to do: 5998
19 all my labour wherein I have l', "
21 to a man that hath not l' therein "
22 wherein he hath l' under the sun? *6001
5:16 hath he that hath l' for the wind? *5998
Isa 47:12 thou hast l' from thy youth; 3021
15 with whom thou hast l', even thy "
49: 4 Then I said, I have l' in vain, I have "
62: 8 thy wine, for the which thou hast l': "
Da 6:14 he l' till the going down of the sun 7712
Jon 4:10 for the which thou hast not l', 5998
Joh 4:38 other men l', and ye are entered *2872*
Ro 16:12 Persis, which l' much in the Lord. *2872*
1Co 15:10 I l' more abundantly than they all: "
Ph'p 2:16 not run in vain, neither l' in vain.* "
4: 3 which l' with me in the gospel, *4866*
Re 2: 3 and for my name's sake hast l', **2872*
labourer See also FELLOWLABOURER; LABOURERS.
Lu 10: 7 for the l' is worthy of his hire. *2040*
1Ti 5:18 And, The l' is worthy of his reward." "
labourers See also FELLOWLABOURERS.
M't 9:37 is plenteous, but the l' are few; *2040*
38 will send forth l' into his harvest. "
20: 1 morning to hire l' into his vineyard." "
2 agreed with the l' for a penny a day, "
8 Call the l', and give them their hire, "
Lu 10: 2 truly is great, but the l' are few: "
2 that he would send forth l' into his "
1Co 3: 9 For we are l' together with God: **4904*
Jas 5: 4 the hire of the l' who have reaped *2040*
laboureth
Pr 16:26 He that l'...for himself; for 6001
26 l' for himself; for his mouth 5998
Ec 3: 9 he that worketh wherein he l'? 6001
1Co 16:16 one that helpeth with us, and l'. *2872*
2Ti 2: 6 husbandman that l' must be first "
labouring
Ec 5:12 The sleep of a l' man is sweet, 5647
Ac 20:35 so l' ye ought to support the weak, *2872*
Col 4:12 l' fervently for you in prayers, * *75*
1Th 2: 9 for l' night and day, because we **2873*
labours
Ex 23:16 of harvest, the firstfruits of thy l', 4639
16 gathered in thy l' out of the field. "
De 28:33 The fruit of thy land, and all thy l', 3018
Pr 5:10 l' be in the house of a stranger; 6089
Isa 58: 3 pleasure, and exact all your l'. 6092
Jer 20: 5 of this city, and all the l' thereof, *3018
Ho 12: 8 my l' they shall find none iniquity "
Hag 2:17 hail in all the l' of your hands; *4639
Joh 4:38 and ye are entered into their l'. **2873*
2Co 6: 5 in imprisonments, in tumults, in l', "
10:15 measure, that is, of other men's l'; "
11:23 in l' more abundant, in stripes "
Re 14:13 that they may rest from their l'; "
lace
Ex 28:28 rings of the ephod with a l' of blue, 6616
37 And thou shalt put it on a blue l', "
Ex 39:21 rings of the ephod with a l' of blue, 6616
31 And they tied unto it a l' of blue, to "
Lachish (*la'-kish*)
Jos 10: 3 and unto Japhia king of L', and 3923
5, 23 king of Jarmuth, the king of L', "
31 and all Israel with him, unto L', "
32 delivered L' into the hand of Israel, "
33 king of Gezer came up to help L'; "
34 from L' Joshua passed unto Eglon, "
35 to all that he had done to L'. "
12:11 Jarmuth, one; the king of L', one; "
15:39 L', and Bozkath, and Eglon, "
2Ki 14:19 in Jerusalem: and he fled to L'; "
19 they sent after him to L', and slew "
18:14 sent to the king of Assyria to L', "
17 sent...from L' to king Hezekiah "
19: 8 heard that he was departed from L'. "
2Ch 11: 9 And Adoraim, and L', and Azekah, "
25:27 in Jerusalem; and he fled to L': "
27 they sent to L' after him, and slew "
32: 9 he himself laid siege against L', "
Ne 11:30 at L', and the fields thereof, at "
Isa 36: 2 sent...from L' to Jerusalem unto "
37: 8 heard that he was departed from L'. "
Jer 34: 7 of Judah that were left, against L', "
Mic 1:13 O thou inhabitant of L', bind the "
lack See also LACKED; LACKEST; LACKETH; LACKING.
Ge 18:28 there shall l' five of the fifty 2637
28 destroy all the city for l' of five? "
Ex 16:18 he that gathered little had no l'; 2637
De 8: 9 thou shalt not l' any thing in it; "
Job 4:11 old lion perisheth for l' of prey, 1097
38:41 God, they wander for l' of meat. "
Ps 34:10 The young lions do l', and suffer 7326
Pr 28:27 giveth unto the poor shall not l': 4270
Ec 9: 8 and let thy head l' no ointment. 2637
Ho 4: 6 are destroyed for l' of knowledge: 1097
M't 19:20 from my youth up: what l' I yet? *5302*
2Co 8:15 that had gathered little had no l'. *1641*
Ph'p 2:30 to supply your l' of service toward **5303*
1Th 4:12 that ye may have l' of nothing. **5332*
Jas 1: 5 If any of you l' wisdom, let him **3007*
lacked
De 2: 7 with thee; thou hast l' nothing. 2637
2Sa 2:30 l' of David's servants nineteen 6485
17:22 the morning light there l' not one 5737
1Ki 4:27 man in his month: they l' nothing.* "
11:22 But what hast thou l' with me, 2638
Ne 9:21 wilderness, so that they l' nothing; 2637
Lu 8: 6 away, because it l' moisture. **3361,2192*
22:35 scrip, and shoes, l' ye any thing? *5302*
Ac 4:34 was there any among them that l': *1729*
1Co 12:24 honour to that part which l': *5302*
Ph'p 4:10 also careful, but ye l' opportunity. *170*
lackest
M'r 10:21 said unto him, One thing thou l': *5302*
Lu 18:22 unto him, Yet l' thou one thing: *3007*
lacketh
Nu 31:49 and there l' not one man of us. 6485
2Sa 3:29 on the sword, or that l' bread. 2638
Pr 6:32 with a woman l' understanding: * "
12: 9 honoureth himself, and l' bread. "
2Pe 1: 9 that l' these things is blind, *3361,3918*
lacking
Le 22:13 to be l' from thy meat offering: 7673
22:23 thing superfluous or l' in his parts, 7038
J'g 21: 3 be to day one tribe l' in Israel? 6485
1Sa 30:19 And there was nothing l' to them, 5737
Jer 23: 4 neither shall they be l', saith the 6485
1Co 16:17 that which was l' on your part they *5303*
2Co 11: 9 that which was l' to me the brethren* "
1Th 3:10 that which is l' in your faith? "
lad See also LAD'S; LADS.
Ge 21:12 in thy sight because of the l', and 5288
17 And God heard the voice of the l'; "
17 God hath heard the voice of the l' "
18 Arise, lift up the l', and hold him in "
19 with water, and gave the l' drink. "
20 God was with the l'; and he grew, "
22: 5 and I and the l' will go yonder and "
12 Lay not thy hand upon the l', "
37: 2 the l' was with the sons of Bilhah, "
43: 8 Send the l' with me, and we will "
44:22 The l' cannot leave his father: for "
30 father, and the l' be not with us, "
31 he seeth that the l' is not with us, "
32 thy servant became surety for the l' "
33 thy servant abide instead of the l' "
33 let the l' go up with his brethren. "
34 father, and the l' be not with me? "
J'g 16:26 Samson said unto the l' that held "
1Sa 20:21 behold, I will send a l', saying, Go, "
21 If I expressly say unto the l', "
35 with David, and a little l' with him. "
36 he said unto his l', Run, find out "
36 And as the l' ran, he shot an arrow "
37 when the l' was come to the place "
37 Jonathan after the l', and said, "
38 Jonathan cried after the l', Make "
38 And Jonathan's l' gathered up the "
39 But the l' knew not any thing: only "
40 gave his artillery unto his l', and "
41 as soon as the l' was gone, David "
2Sa 17:18 Nevertheless a l' saw them, and told "
2Ki 4:19 And he said to a l', Carry him to his "
Joh 6: 9 There is a l' here, which hath five *3808*
ladder
Ge 28:12 behold a l' set up on the earth, 5551

lade See also LADED; LADEN; LADETH; LADING; UNLADE.
Ge 45:17 l' your beasts, and go, get you 2943
1Ki 12:11 did l' you with a heavy yoke, 6006
Lu 11:46 l' men with burdens grievous to *5412*

laded
Ge 42:26 they l' their asses with the corn, 5375
44:13 and l' every man his ass, and 6006
Ne 4:17 bare burdens, with those that l', "
Ac 28:10 l' us with such things as were **2007*

laden See also LOADEN.
Ge 45:23 ten asses l' with the good things 5375
23 ten she asses l' with corn and "
1Sa 16:20 And Jesse took an ass l' with bread,
Isa 1:4 people l' with iniquity, a seed of 3515
M't 11:28 all ye that labour and are heavy l',*5412*
2Ti 3:6 captive silly women l' with sins, *4987*

ladeth See also LOADETH.
Hab 2:6 that l' himself with thick clay! 3515

ladies
J'g 5:29 Her wise l' answered her, yea, she8282
Es 1:18 l' of Persia and Media say this day*"

lading
Ne 13:15 bringing in sheaves, and l' asses; 6006
Ac 27:10 not only of the l' and ship, but *5414*

lad's
Ge 44:30 his life is bound up in the l' life; 5288

lads
Ge 48:16 me from all evil, bless the l'; 5288

lady See also LADIES.
Isa 47:5 be called, The l' of kingdoms. ‡1404
7 thou saidst, I shall be a l' for ever:‡ "
2Jo 1 unto the elect l' and her children, *2959*
5 I beseech thee, l', not as though I "

Lael (*la'-el*)
Nu 3:24 shall be Eliasaph the son of L'. 3815

Lahad (*la'-had*)
1Ch 4:2 Jahath begat Ahumai, and L'. 3854

Lahai-roi (*la-hah'-ee-roy*) See also BEER-LAHAI-ROI.
Ge 24:62 came from the way of the well L'; *883
25:11 and Isaac dwelt by the well L'. * "

Lahmam (*lah'-mam*)
Jos 15:40 And Cabbon, and L', and Kithlish,)3903

Lahmi (*lah'-mi*) See also BETHLEHEMITE.
1Ch 20:5 the son of Jair slew L' the 3902

laid See also LAIDST; OVERLAID.
Ge 9:23 l' it upon both their shoulders, 7760
15:10 l' each piece one against another: 5414
19:16 the men l' hold upon his hand,
22:6 and l' it upon Isaac his son; 7760
9 there, and l' the wood in order,
9 l' him on the altar upon the wood. 7760
30:41 Jacob l' the rods before the eyes "
38:19 l' by her vail from her, and put on*5493
39:16 she l' up his garment by her, until3241
41:48 and l' up the food in the cities: 5414
48 every city, l' he up in the same.
48:14 and l' it upon Ephraim's head, 7896
17 l' his right hand upon the head of
Ex 2:3 she l' it in the flags by the river's 7760
5:9 more work be l' upon the men, 3515
16:24 l' up till the morning, as Moses 3241
34 Aaron l' it up before the Testimony,"
19:7 l' before their faces all these *7760
21:30 If...be l' on him a sum of money, 7896
30 his life whatsoever is l' upon him. "
24:11 of Israel he l' not his hand: also 7971
Le 8:14, 18, 22 his sons l' their hands upon 5564
Nu 16:18 l' incense thereon, and stood in 7760
17:7 Moses l' up the rods before the 3241
21:30 l' them waste even unto Nophah,
27:23 he l' his hands upon him, and 5564
De 26:6 us, and l' upon us hard bondage: 5414
29:22 which the Lord hath l' upon it; 2470
32:34 Is not this l' up in store with me, 3647
34:9 Moses had l' his hands upon him: 5564
Jos 2:6 she had l' in order upon the roof.
8 before they were l' down, she came7901
4:8 lodged, and l' them down there. 3241
7:23 and l' them out before the Lord. 3332
10:27 l' great stones in the cave's mouth,7760
J'g 9:24 blood be l' upon Abimelech their "
34 l' wait against Shechem in four
43 and l' wait in the field, and looked,
48 took it, and l' it on his shoulder, 7760
16:2 l' wait for him all night in the gate
19:29 l' hold on his concubine, and divided
Ru 3:7 uncovered his feet,...l' her down. 7901
15 of barley, and l' it on her: 7896
4:16 the child, and l' it in her bosom, "
1Sa 3:2 when Eli was l' down in his place, 7901
3 and Samuel was l' down to sleep; "
6:11 l' the ark of the Lord upon the *7760
10:25 book, and l' it up before the Lord. 3241
15:2 how he l' wait for him in the way,*7760
5 Amalek, and l' wait in the valley.
27 l' hold upon the skirt of his mantel,
19:13 took an image, and l' it in the bed,7760
21:12 David l' up these words in his "
25:18 cakes of figs, and l' them on asses. "
2Sa 13:8 Amnon's house;...he was l' down. 7901
19 her, and l' her hand on her head, 7760
18:17 and l' a very great heap of stones *5324
1Ki 3:20 slept, and l' it in her bosom, 7901
20 l' her dead child in my bosom. "
6:37 foundation of the house of the Lord l',
8:31 be l' upon him to cause him to 5375
13:29 man of God, and l' it upon the ass,3241
30 he l' his carcase in his own grave; "
15:27 and all Israel l' siege to Gibbethon.*
16:34 he l' the foundation thereof in

1Ki 17:19 and l' him upon his own bed. 7901
18:33 in pieces, and l' him on the wood, 7760
19:6 drink, and l' him down again. 7901
21:4 he l' him down upon his bed, and "
2Ki 4:21 l' him on the bed of the man of
31 and l' the staff upon the face of 7760
32 was dead, and l' upon his bed. 7901
5:23 l' them upon two of his servants; 5414
9:25 the Lord l' this burden upon him; 5375
11:16 they l' hands on her; and she *7760
12:11 they l' it out to the carpenters *3318
12 l' out for the house to repair it.
20:7 took and l' it on the boil, and he 7760
17 thy fathers have l' up in store
2Ch 6:22 an oath be l' upon him to make 5375
7:22 of Egypt, and l' hold on other gods,
16:14 l' him in the bed which was filled 7901
23:15 So they l' hands on her; and *7760
24:9 the servant of God l' upon Israel
29:23 they l' their hands upon them: 5564
31:6 their God, and l' them by heaps. 5414
32:9 he himself l' siege against Lachish,*
Ezr 3:6 foundation of the temple...was not yet l'.
10 l' the foundation of the temple of
11 foundation of...house of Lord was l'.
12 foundation of this house was l'
5:8 and timber is l' in the walls, 7760
16 l' the foundation of the house of 3052
6:1 treasures were l' up in Babylon. 5182
3 foundations thereof be strongly l';5446
Ne 3:3 build, who also l' the beams thereof,
6 they l' the beams thereof, and set
13:5 they l' the meat offerings, 5414
Es 8:7 he l' his hand upon the Jews. 7971
9:10 on the spoil l' they not their hand. "
15 on the prey they l' not their hand. "
16 they l' not their hands on the prey, "
10:1 Ahasuerus l' a tribute upon the 7760
Job 6:2 and my calamity l' in the balances5375
18:10 snare is l' for him in the ground, *
29:9 and l' their hand on their mouth. 7760
31:9 l' wait at my neighbour's door;
38:4 I l' the foundations of the earth?
5 Who hath l' the measures thereof,*7760
6 or who l' the corner stone thereof;3384
Ps 3:5 I l' me down and slept; I awaked;7901
21:5 majesty hast thou l' upon him. *7737
31:4 net that they have l' privily for 2934
19 hast l' up for them that fear thee; 6845
35:11 l' to my charge things that I knew*
49:14 Like sheep they are l' in the grave;*8371
62:9 to be l' in the balance, they are *5927
79:1 they have l' Jerusalem on heaps. 7760
7 Jacob, and l' waste his dwelling place.
88:6 Thou hast l' me in the lowest pit, 7896
89:19 l' help upon one that is mighty; 7737
102:25 thou l' the foundation of the earth:
104:5 Who l' the foundations of the earth.
105:18 with fetters: he was l' in iron: 935
119:30 judgments have I l' before me. *7737
110 wicked have l' a snare for me: 5414
139:5 before, and l' thine hand upon me.7896
141:9 snares which they have l' for me, 3369
142:3 they privily l' a snare for me. *2934
Pr 13:22 of the sinner is l' up for the just. 6845
Ca 7:13 and old, which I have l' up for thee, "
Isa 6:7 he l' it upon my mouth, and said, *5060
10:28 he hath l' up his carriages: *6485
14:8 Since thou art l' down, no feller is 7901
15:1 the night Ar of Moab is l' waste,
1 in the night Kir of Moab is l' waste,
7 that which they have l' up, shall 6486
23:1 for it is l' waste, so that there is
14 for your strength is l' waste.
18 it shall not be treasured nor l' up; 2630
37:18 Assyria have l' waste all the nations,
39:6 thy fathers have l' up in store until
42:25 him, yet he l' it not to heart. 7760
44:28 temple, Thy foundation shall be l'.
47:6 hast thou very heavily l' thy yoke.
48:13 hath l' the foundation of the earth,
51:13 and l' the foundations of the earth;
23 hast l' thy body as the ground, 7760
53:6 Lord hath l' on him the iniquity 6293
57:11 me, nor laid it to thy heart? 7760
64:11 all our pleasant things are l' waste.
Jer 4:7 and thy cities shall be l' waste, *
27:17 should this city be l' waste?
36:20 they l' up the roll in the chamber of 6485
50:24 I have l' a snare for thee, and thou
La 4:19 they l' wait for us in the wilderness.
Eze 4:5 I have l' upon thee the years of *5414
6:6 the cities shall be l' waste, and the
6 your altars may be l' waste and made
11:7 Your slain whom ye have l' in the 7760
12:20 that are inhabited shall be l' waste,
19:7 palaces, and he l' waste their cities;
26:2 be replenished, now she is l' waste:
29:12 the cities that are l' waste shall be
32:19 be thou l' with the uncircumcised.7901
27 have l' their swords under heads, 5414
29 are l' by them that were slain
32 he shall be l' in the midst of the 7901
33:29 I have l' the land most desolate *5414
35:12 They are l' desolate, they are given us
39:21 my hand that I have l' upon them.7760
40:42 also they l' the instruments 3240
Da 6:17 and l' upon the mouth of the den; 7760
Ho 11:4 jaws, and I l' meat unto them. 5186
Joe 1:7 He hath l' my vine waste, and 7760
17 clods, the garners are l' desolate,
Am 2:8 clothes l' to pledge by every altar,*
7:9 sanctuaries of Israel shall be l' waste;
Ob 7 eat thy bread have l' a wound *7760
13 have l' hands on their substance *7971
Jon 3:6 and he l' his robe from him, 5674

Mic 5:1 he hath l' siege against us: they 7760
Na 3:7 thee, and say, Nineveh is l' waste:
Hab 2:19 it is l' over with gold and silver, 8610
Hag 2:15 before a stone was l' upon a stone 7760
18 foundation of the Lord's temple was l'.
Zec 3:9 behold the stone that I have l' *5414
4:9 l' the foundation of this house;
7:14 they l' the pleasant land desolate. 7760
8:9 foundation of the house of...was l'.
Mal 1:3 l' his mountains and his heritage*7760
M't 3:10 axe is l' unto the root of the trees:‡*2749*
8:14 he saw his wife's mother l', and * *906*
14:3 Herod had l' hold on John, and bound
18:28 he l' hands on him, and took him by
19:15 he l' his hands on them, and *2007*
26:50 came they, and l' hands on Jesus, *1911*
55 the temple, and ye l' no hold on me.*
57 they that had l' hold on Jesus led him
27:60 l' it in his own new tomb, which *5087*
M'r 6:5 he l' his hands upon a few sick *2007*
17 had sent forth and l' hold upon John,
29 up his corpse, and l' it in a tomb. *5087*
56 they l' the sick in the streets, and "
7:30 and her daughter l' upon the bed. *906*
14:46 they l' their hands on him, and *1911*
51 the young men l' hold on him: and*
15:46 l' him in a sepulchre which was *2698*
47 of Joses beheld where he was l'. *5087*
16:6 behold the place where they l' him. "
Lu 1:66 them l' them up in their hearts,
2:7 clothes, and l' him in a manger; *347*
3:9 axe is l' unto the root of the trees:‡*2749*
4:40 l' his hands on every one of them, *2007*
6:48 and l' the foundation on a rock: *5087*
12:19 much goods l' up for many years; *2749*
13:13 he l' his hands on her: and *2007*
14:29 he hath l' the foundation, and is not*5087*
16:20 Lazarus, which was l' at his gate, *906*
19:20 which I have kept l' up in a napkin:*606*
22 taking up that I l' not down, and *5087*
23:26 they l' hold upon one Simon, a
26 on him they l' the cross, that he *2007*
53 l' it in a sepulchre that was hewn *5087*
53 wherein never man before was l'. **2749*
55 and how his body was l'. *5087*
24:12 the linen clothes l' by themselves,**2749*
Joh 7:30 no man l' hands on him, because *1911*
44 him; but no man l' hands on him.
8:20 temple: and no man l' hands on him;*
11:34 Where have ye l' him? They said *5087*
41 the place where the dead was l'. **2749*
13:4 supper, and l' aside his garments:**5087*
19:41 wherein was never man yet l'. "
42 There l' they Jesus therefore "
20:2 know not where they have l' him. "
13 I know not where they have l' him. "
15 tell me where thou hast l' him, and "
21:9 and fish l' thereon, and bread. *1945*
Ac 3:2 l' daily at the gate of the temple *5087*
4:3 they l' hands on them, and put *1911*
35 l' them down at the apostles' feet: *5087*
37 and l' it at the apostles' feet. "
5:2 part, and l' it at the apostles' feet. "
15 and l' them on beds and couches, "
18 l' their hands on the apostles, and *1911*
6:6 they l' their hands on them. *2007*
7:16 l' in the sepulchre that Abraham *5087*
58 witnesses l' down their clothes at *659*
8:17 Then l' they their hands on them, *2007*
9:37 they l' her in an upper chamber. *5087*
13:3 and l' their hands on them, they *2007*
29 tree, and l' him in a sepulchre. *5087*
36 was l' unto his fathers, and saw *4369*
16:23 had l' many stripes upon them, *2007*
19:6 Paul had l' his hands upon them,
20:3 And when the Jews l' wait for him,*1096*
21:27 all the people, and l' hands on him,*1911*
23:29 nothing l' to his charge worthy of *1462*
30 that the Jews l' wait for the man, *2071*
25:7 l' many and grievous complaints **5342*
16 the crime l' against him. *1462*
27 signify the crimes l' against him.
28:3 of sticks, and l' them on the fire, *2007*
8 l' his hands on him, and healed * "
Ro 16:4 my life l' down their own necks: *5294*
1Co 3:10 I have l' the foundation, and *5087*
11 can no man lay than that is l', "
9:16 for necessity is l' upon me; yea, *1945*
Col 1:5 hope which is l' up for you in *606*
2Ti 4:8 there is l' up for me a crown of "
16 it may not be l' to their charge. *3049*
Heb 1:10 hast l' the foundation of the earth;
1Jo 3:16 because he l' down his life for us: *5087*
Re 1:17 he l' his right hand upon me, *2007*
20:2 he l' hold on the dragon, that old

laidst See also LAYEDST.
Ps 66:11 thou l' affliction upon our loins. 7760

lain See also LIEN.
Nu 5:19 If no man have l' with thee, and †7901
20 some man have l' with thee †5414,7903
J'g 21:11 woman that hath l' by man. †3045,4904
Job 3:13 I have l' still and been quiet, †7901
Joh 11:17 had l' in the grave four days already.
20:12 where the body of Jesus had l'. *2749*

Laish (*la'-ish*) See also DAN; LESHEM.
J'g 18:7 men departed, and came to L'. 3919
14 went to spy out the country of L'. "
27 which he had, and came unto L'. "
29 the name of the city was L' at the "
1Sa 25:44 David's wife, to Phalti the son of L'."
2Sa 3:15 even from Phaltiel the son of L'. "
Isa 10:30 cause it to be heard unto L'. * "

lake
Lu 5:1 God, stood by the l' of Gennesaret,*3041*

Lu 5: 2 saw two ships standing by the l·: 3041
8:22 over unto the other side of the l·. "
23 down a storm of wind on the l·; "
33 down a steep place into the l·. "
Re 19:20 both were cast alive into a l· of fire "
20:10 them was cast into the l· of fire "
14 and hell were cast into the l· of fire. "
15 of life was cast into the l· of fire. "
21: 8 their part in the l· which burneth "

Lakum (*la'-kum*)
Jos 19:33 Nekeb, and Jabneel, unto L·; *3946

lama (*la'-mah*)
M't 27:46 saying, Eli, Eli, l· sabachthani? 2982
M'r 15:34 saying, Eloi, Eloi, l· sabachthani? "

lamb See also LAMBS; LAMB'S.
Ge 22: 7 where is the l· for a burnt offering? 7716
8 God will provide himself a l· for a "
Ex 12: 3 shall take to them every man a l·, "
3 of their fathers, a l· for an house: "
4 the household be too little for the l·, "
4 shall make your count for the l·. "
5 Your l· shall be without blemish, a "
21 them, Draw out and take you a l· *6629
13:13 an ass thou shalt redeem with a l·; 7716
29:39 The one l· thou shalt offer in the 3532
39 the other l· thou shalt offer at even: "
40 with the one l· a tenth deal of flour "
41 the other l· thou shalt offer at even. "
34:20 an ass thou shalt redeem with a l·: 7716
Le 3: 7 If he offer a l· for his offering, then 3775
4:32 if he bring a l· for a sin offering, 3532
35 fat of the l· is taken away from 3775
5: 6 a l· or a kid of the goats, for a sin 3776
7 he be not able to bring a l·, then he 7716
9: 3 a calf and a l·, both of the first 3532
12: 6 she shall bring a l· of the first year "
8 she be not able to bring a l·, then 7716
14:10 one ewe l· of the first year without 3535
12 priest shall take one he l·, and *3532
13 shall slay the l· in the place where* "
21 take one l· for a trespass offering * "
24 take the l· of the trespass offering, "
25 kill the l· of the trespass offering, "
17: 3 that killeth an ox, or l·, or goat, 3775
22:23 l· that hath any thing superfluous 7716
23:12 he l· without blemish of the first 3532
Nu 6:12 shall bring a l· of the first year for* "
14 one he l· of the first year without "
14 one ewe l· of the first year without 3535
7:15, 21, 27, 33, 39, 45, 51, 57, 63, 69, 75, 81 one
l· of the first year, for a burnt *3532
15: 5 offering or sacrifice, for one l·. "
11 for one ram, or for a l·, or a kid. *7716
28: 4 The one l· shalt thou offer in the 3532
4 the other l· shalt thou offer at even; "
7 fourth part of an hin for the one l·: "
8 the other l· shalt thou offer at even: "
13 oil for a meat offering unto one l·; "
14 and a fourth part of an hin unto a l·: "
21 deal shalt thou offer for every l·, "
29 A several tenth deal unto one l·, "
29: 4 one tenth deal for one l·, throughout "
10 A several tenth deal for one l·, "
15 tenth deal to each l· of the fourteen "
1Sa 7: 9 And Samuel took a sucking l·, and 2924
17:34 bear, and took a l· out of the flock: 7716
2Sa 12: 3 had nothing, save one little ewe l·, 3535
4 took the poor man's l·, and dressed "
6 And he shall restore the l· fourfold, "
Isa 11: 6 wolf also shall dwell with the l·, 3532
16: 1 Send ye the l· to the ruler of the *3733
53: 7 is brought as a l· to the slaughter, 7716
65:25 wolf and the l· shall feed together, 2924
66: 3 he that sacrificeth a l·, as if he 7716
Jer 11:19 But I was like a l· or an ox that is 3532
Eze 45:15 one l· out of the flock, out of two 7716
46:13 of a l· of the first year without 3532
15 Thus shall they prepare the l·, and "
Ho 4:16 feed them as a l· in a large place. "
Joh 1:29 and saith, Behold the L· of God, 286
36 he saith, Behold the L· of God! "
Ac 8:32 like a l· dumb before his shearer, so "
1Pe 1:19 of Christ, as of a l· without blemish "
Re 5: 6 stood a L· as it had been slain, 721
8 elders fell down before the L·, "
12 Worthy is the L· that was slain to "
13 the throne, and unto the L· for ever "
6: 1 when the L· opened one of the seals, "
16 and from the wrath of the L·: "
7: 9 before the throne, and before the L·, "
10 upon the throne, and unto the L·. "
14 them white in the blood of the L·. "
17 L· which is in the midst of the throne "
12:11 overcame him by the blood of the L·, "
13: 8 written in the book of life of the L· "
11 and he had two horns like a l·, and "
14: 1 lo, a L· stood on the mount Sion, and "
4 These are they which follow the L· "
4 firstfruits unto God and to the L·. "
10 angels, and in the presence of the L·: "
15: 3 of God, and the song of the L·, "
17:14 These shall make war with the L·, "
14 and the L· shall overcome them: "
19: 7 for the marriage of the L· is come, "
9 unto the marriage supper of the L·. "
21:14 of the twelve apostles of the L·. "
22 Lord God Almighty and the L· are "
23 it, and the L· is the light thereof. "
22: 1 of the throne of God and of the L·. "
3 throne of God and of the L· shall be "

lamb's
Re 21: 9 shew thee the bride, the L· wife. * 721
27 are written in the L· book of life. "

lambs
Ge 21:28 Abraham set seven ewe l· of the 3535
21:29 What mean these seven ewe l· which 3535
30 these seven ewe l· shalt thou take "
30:40 And Jacob did separate the l·, and 3775
Ex 29:38 two l· of the first year day by day 3532
Le 14:10 shall take two he l· without blemish, "
23:18 the bread seven l· without blemish "
19 two l· of the first year for a sacrifice "
20 before the Lord, with the two l·: "
Nu 7:17, 23, 29, 35, 41, 47, 53, 59, 65, 71, 77, 83 five
he goats, five l· of the first year: *3532
87 the l· of the first year twelve, * "
88 sixty, the l· of the first year sixty.* "
28: 3 two l· of the first year without spot* "
9 two l· of the first year without spot,* "
11 seven l· of the first year without * "
19 ram, and seven l· of the first year:* "
21 every lamb, throughout the seven l·: "
27 one ram, seven l· of the first year;* "
29 one lamb, throughout the seven l·; "
29: 2 seven l· of the first year without * "
4 one lamb, throughout the seven l·: "
8 ram, and seven l· of the first year;* "
10 one lamb, throughout the seven l·: "
13 and fourteen l· of the first year; * "
15 deal to each lamb of the fourteen l·: "
17 fourteen l· of the first year without* "
18 bullocks, for the rams, and for the l·, "
20 fourteen l· of the first year without* "
21 bullocks, for the rams, and for the l·, "
23 fourteen l· of the first year without* "
24 bullocks, for the rams, and for the l·, "
26 fourteen l· of the first year without* "
27 bullocks, for the rams, and for the l·, "
29 fourteen l· of the first year without* "
30 bullocks, for the rams, and for the l·, "
32 fourteen l· of the first year without* "
33 bullocks, for the rams, and for the l·, "
36 seven l· of the first year without * "
37 bullock, for the ram, and for the l·, "
De 32:14 with fat of l·, and rams of the breed 3733
1Sa 15: 9 and the l·, and all that was good, "
2Ki 3: 4 of Israel an hundred thousand l·, "
1Ch 29:21 thousand rams, and a thousand l·, 3532
2Ch 29:21 seven l·, and seven he goats, for a "
22 they killed also the l·, and they "
32 hundred rams, and two hundred l·: "
35: 7 the people, of the flock, l· and kids, "
Ezr 6: 9 young bullocks, and rams, and l·, 563
17 two hundred rams, four hundred l·: "
7:17 with this money bullocks, rams, l·, "
8:35 and six rams, seventy and seven l·, 3532
Ps 37:20 the Lord shall be as the fat of l·: †3733
114: 4 and the little hills like l·. *1121, 6629
6 rams; and ye little hills, like l·?* "
Pr 27:26 The l· are for thy clothing, and 3532
Isa 1:11 blood of bullocks, or of l·, or of he "
5:17 the lambs feed after their manner, "
34: 6 and with the blood of l· and goats, 3733
40:11 shall gather the l· with his arm, 2922
Jer 51:40 them down like l· to the slaughter, 3733
Eze 27:21 they occupied with thee in l·, and "
39:18 princes of the earth, of rams, of l·, "
46: 4 six l· without blemish, and a ram 3532
5 and the meat offering for the l· as he "
6 blemish, and six l·, and a ram: "
7 and for the l· according as his hand "
11 and to the l· as he is able to give, "
Am 6: 4 eat the l· out of the flock, and the 3733
Lu 10: 3 send you forth as l· among wolves. 704
Joh 21:15 He saith unto him, Feed my l·. 721

lame
Le 21:18 a blind man, or a l·, or he that hath 6455
De 15:21 as if it be l·, or blind, or have any ill "
2Sa 4: 4 had a son that was l· of his feet. 5223
4 to flee, that he fell, and became l·. 6452
5: 6 take away the blind and the l·, 6455
8 Jebusites, and the l· and the blind, "
8 the l· shall not come into the house. "
9: 3 yet a son, which is l· on his feet. 5223
13 table; and was l· on both his feet. 6455
19:26 the king; because thy servant is l·. "
Job 29:15 the blind, and feet was I to the l·. "
Pr 26: 7 The legs of the l· are not equal: so "
Isa 33:23 spoil divided; the l· take the prey. "
35: 6 shall the l· man leap as an hart, "
Jer 31: 8 and with them the blind and the l·, "
Mal 1: 8 offer the l· and sick, is it not evil? "
13 was torn, and the l·, and the sick; "
M't 11: 5 l· walk, the lepers are cleansed, 5560
15:30 with them those that were l·, blind, "
31 the l· to walk, and the blind to see: "
21:14 the l· came to him in the temple; "
Lu 7:22 l· walk, the lepers are cleansed, "
14:13 poor, the maimed, the l·, the blind: "
Ac 3: 2 man l· from his mother's womb "
11 the l· man which was healed held* "
8: 7 and that were l·, were healed. "
Heb 12:13 which is l· be turned out of the way; "

Lamech (*la'-mek*)
Ge 4:18 and Methusael begat L·. 3929
19 And L· took unto him two wives: "
23 And L· said unto his wives, Adah "
23 ye wives of L·, harken unto my "
24 truly L· seventy and sevenfold. "
5:25 and seven years, and begat L·: "
26 Methuselah lived after he begat L· "
28 L· lived an hundred eighty and two "
30 L· lived after he begat Noah five "
31 the days of L· were seven hundred "
1Ch 1: 3 Henoch, Methuselah, L·, "
Lu 3:36 Noe, which was the son of L·, 2984

lament See also LAMENTABLE; LAMENTED.
J'g 11:40 to l· the daughter of Jephthah the 8567
Isa 3:26 And her gates shall l· and mourn; 578
19: 8 cast angle into the brooks shall l·,* 56
32:12 They shall l· for the teats, for the *5594
Jer 4: 8 you with sackcloth, l· and howl: "
16: 5 neither go to l· nor bemoan them: "
6 neither shall men l· for them, nor "
22:18 They shall not l· for him, saying, "
18 they shall not l· for him, saying, "
34: 5 they will l· thee, saying, Ah lord! "
49: 3 l·, and run to and fro by the hedges; "
La 2: 8 the rampart and the wall to l·; 56
Eze 27:32 for thee, and l· over thee, saying, 6969
32:16 wherewith they shall l· her: "
16 daughters of the nations shall l· her: "
16 shall l· for her, even for Egypt, "
Joe 1: 8 L· like a virgin girded with 421
13 Gird yourselves, and l·, ye priests: 5594
Mic 2: 4 and l· with a doleful lamentation, 5091
Joh 16:20 That ye shall weep and l·, but the 2354
Re 18: 9 shall bewail her, and l· for her, *2875

lamentable
Da 6:20 cried with a l· voice unto Daniel: 6088

lamentation See also LAMENTATIONS.
Ge 50:10 with a great and very sore l·: 4553
2Sa 1:17 with this l· over Saul and over 7015
Ps 78:64 and their widows made no l·. 1058
Jer 6:26 as for an only son, most bitter l·: 4553
7:29 and take up a l· on high places; 7015
9:10 habitations of the wilderness a l·, "
20 and every one her neighbour l·. "
31:15 in Ramah, l·, and bitter weeping; 5092
48:38 There shall be l· generally upon 4553
La 2: 5 daughter of Judah mourning and l·. 592
Eze 19: 1 up a l· for the princes of Israel, 7015
14 This is a l·, and shall be for a l·. "
26:17 they shall take up a l· for thee, and "
27: 2 son of man, take up a l· for Tyrus; "
32 they shall take up a l· for thee, and "
28:12 take up a l· upon the king of Tyrus, "
32: 2 up a l· for Pharaoh king of Egypt, "
16 l· wherewith they shall lament her: "
Am 5: 1 you, even a l·, O house of Israel. "
16 such as are skilful of l· to wailing. 5092
8:10 and all your songs into l·; 7015
Mic 2: 4 and lament with a doleful l·, and 5092
M't 2:18 a voice heard, l·, and weeping, *2355
Ac 8: 2 burial, and made great l· over him. 2870

lamentations
2Ch 35:25 women spake of Josiah in their l· 7015
25 behold, they are written in the l·. "
Eze 2:10 there was written therein l·, and "

lamented
1Sa 6:19 the people l·, because the Lord had *56
7: 2 house of Israel l· after the Lord. 5091
25: 1 and l· him, and buried him in his 5594
28: 3 Israel had l· him, and buried him "
2Sa 1:17 And David l· with this lamentation 6969
3:33 the king l· over Abner, and said, "
2Ch 35:25 And Jeremiah l· for Josiah: and all "
Jer 16: 4 they shall not be l·; neither shall 5594
25:33 they shall not be l·, neither gathered, "
M't 11:17 unto you, and ye have not l·. *2875
Lu 23:27 which also bewailed and l· him. 2354

lamp See also LAMPS.
Ge 15:17 burning l· that passed between *3940
Ex 27:20 to cause the l· to burn always. 5216
1Sa 3: 3 l· of God went out in the temple the "
2Sa 22:29 For thou art my l·, O Lord: and the "
1Ki 15: 4 his God give him a l· in Jerusalem, "
Job 12: 5 as a l· despised in the thought of *3940
Ps 119:105 Thy word is a l· unto my feet, 5216
132:17 ordained a l· for mine anointed. "
Pr 6:23 For the commandment is a l·; and "
13: 9 the l· of the wicked shall be put out. "
20:20 his l· shall be put out in obscure "
Isa 62: 1 the salvation thereof as a l· that 3940
Re 8:10 heaven, burning as it were a l·, *2985

lamps
Ex 25:37 shalt make the seven l· thereof: 5216
37 they shall light the l· thereof, that "
30: 7 when he dresseth the l·, he shall "
8 when Aaron lighteth the l· at even, "
35:14 and his l·, with the oil for the light, "
37:23 And he made his seven l·, and his "
39:37 candlestick, with the l· thereof, "
37 even with the l· to be set in order, "
40: 4 candlestick, and light the l· thereof, "
25 he lighted the l· before the Lord; "
Le 24: 2 to cause the l· to burn continually.* "
4 the l· upon the pure candlestick "
Nu 4: 9 the light, and his l·, and his tongs, "
8: 2 unto him, When thou lightest the l·, "
2 the seven l· shall give light over "
3 lighted the l· thereof over against "
J'g 7:16 and l· within the pitchers. *3940
20 and held the l· in their left hands,* "
1Ki 7:49 and the l·, and the tongs of gold, 5216
1Ch 28:15 and for their l· of gold, by weight "
15 candlestick, and for the l· thereof: "
15 and also for the l· thereof, "
2Ch 4:20 the candlesticks with their l·, that "
21 flowers, and the l·, and the tongs, "
13:11 of gold with the l· thereof, to burn "
29: 7 put out the l·, and have not burned "
Job 41:19 Out of his mouth go burning l·, *3940
Eze 1:13 fire, and like the appearance of l·:* "
Da 10: 6 lightning, and his eyes as l· of fire, "
Zec 4: 2 top of it, and his seven l· thereon, 5216
2 and seven pipes to the seven l·, "
M't 25: 1 ten virgins, which took their l·, 2985
3 foolish took their l·, and took no oil "
4 took oil in their vessels with their l·. "
7 virgins arose, and trimmed their l·. "
8 of your oil; for our l· are gone out. "
Re 4: 5 seven l· of fire burning before the "

lance
Jer 50:42 shall hold the bow and the l': *3591

lancets
1Ki 18:28 their manner with knives and l', *7420

land See also ISLAND; LANDED; LANDING; LANDMARK; LANDS; OUTLANDISH.
Ge 1: 9 place, and let the dry l' appear:
10 and God called the dry l' Earth; and
2:11 compasseth the whole l' of Havilah, 776
12 the gold of that l' is good: there is "
13 compasseth the whole l' of Ethiopia. "
4:16 dwelt in the l' of Nod, on the east "
7:22 of all that was in the dry l', died. "
10:10 and Calneh, in the l' of Shinar. 776
11 Out of that l' went forth Asshur, "
11: 2 found a plain in the l' of Shinar; "
28 Terah in the l' of his nativity, "
31 Chaldees, to go into the l' of Canaan; "
12: 1 unto a l' that I will shew thee: "
5 forth to go into the l' of Canaan; "
5 into the l' of Canaan they came. "
6 Abram passed through the l' unto "
6 the Canaanite was then in the l'. "
7 said, Unto thy seed will I give this l': "
10 was a famine in the l': and Abram "
10 the famine was grievous in the l'. "
13: 6 the l' was not able to bear them, "
7 Perizzite dwelled then in the l'. "
9 Is not the whole l' before thee? "
10 like the l' of Egypt, as thou comest "
12 Abram dwelled in the l' of Canaan, "
15 For all the l' which thou seest, to "
17 walk through the l' in the length of "
15: 7 to give thee this l' to inherit it. "
13 a stranger in a l' that is not theirs, "
18 Unto thy seed have I given this l', "
16: 3 dwelt ten years in the l' of Canaan, "
17: 8 the l' wherein thou art a stranger, "
8 all the l' of Canaan, for...possession; "
19:28 toward all the l' of the plain, and "
20:15 my l' is before thee: dwell where it "
21:21 him a wife out of the l' of Egypt. "
23 l' wherein thou hast sojourned. "
32 into the l' of the Philistines. "
34 in the Philistines' l' many days. "
22: 2 and get thee into the l' of Moriah; "
23: 2 same is Hebron in the l' of Canaan: "
7 bowed himself to the people of the l', "
12 himself before the people of the l'. "
13 the audience of the people of the l', "
15 the l' is worth four hundred "
19 same is Hebron in the l' of Canaan. "
24: 5 be willing to follow me unto this l': "
5 the l' from whence thou camest? "
7 from the l' of my kindred, and "
7 Unto thy seed will I give this l'; "
37 the Canaanites, in whose l' I dwell: "
26: 1 there was a famine in the l', beside "
2 dwell in the l' which I shall tell thee "
3 Sojourn in this l', and I will be with "
12 Then Isaac sowed in that l', and "
22 and we shall be fruitful in the l'. "
27:46 which are of the daughters of the l', "
28: 4 inherit the l' wherein thou liest, to thee will I "
13 l' whereon thou liest, to thee will I "
15 will bring thee again into this l'; 127
29: 1 into the l' of the people of the east. 776
31: 3 Return unto the l' of thy fathers, "
13 now arise, get thee out from this l', "
13 return unto the land of thy kindred. "
18 Isaac his father in the l' of Canaan. "
32: 3 Esau his brother unto the l' of Seir, "
33:18 which is in the l' of Canaan, "
34: 1 out to see the daughters of the l'. "
10 us: and the l' shall be before you; "
21 let them dwell in the l', and trade "
21 for the l', behold, it is large enough "
30 among the inhabitants of the l'. "
35: 6 Luz, which is in the l' of Canaan, "
12 l' which I gave Abraham and Isaac, "
12 seed after thee will I give the l'. "
22 to pass, when Israel dwelt in the l', "
36: 5 born unto him in the l' of Canaan. "
6 which he had got in the l' of Canaan; "
7 the l' wherein they were strangers "
16 came of Eliphaz in the l' of Edom; "
17 came of Reuel in the l' of Edom; "
20 the Horite, who inhabited the l'; "
21 children of Seir in the l' of Edom. "
30 among their dukes in the l' of Seir. "
31 kings that reigned in the l' of Edom, "
34 Husham of the l' of Temani reigned "
43 in the l' of their possession: "
37: 1 Jacob dwelt in the l' wherein his "
1 was a stranger, in the l' of Canaan. "
40:15 I was stolen away out of the l' of "
41:19 I never saw in all the l' of Egypt "
29 plenty throughout all the l' of Egypt: "
30 be forgotten in the l' of Egypt; "
30 and the famine shall consume the l'; "
31 plenty shall not be known in the l' "
33 and set him over the l' of Egypt. "
34 let him appoint officers over the l', "
34 fifth part of the l' of Egypt in the "
36 that food shall be for store to the l' "
36 which shall be in the l' of Egypt; "
41 have set thee over all the l' of Egypt. "
43 him ruler over all the l' of Egypt. "
44 hand or foot in all the l' of Egypt. "
45 Joseph went out over all the l' of "
46 went throughout all the l' of Egypt. "
48 years, which were in the l' of Egypt, "
52 be fruitful in the l' of my affliction. "
53 that was in the l' of Egypt, were "
54 in all the l' of Egypt...was bread. "
Ge 41:55 all the l' of Egypt was famished, 776
56 famine waxed sore in the l' of Egypt. "
42: 5 the famine was in the l' of Canaan. "
6 Joseph was the governor over the l', "
6 that sold to all the people of the l': "
7 From the l' of Canaan to buy food. "
9, 12 nakedness of the l' ye are come. "
13 sons of one man in the l' of Canaan; "
29 their father unto the l' of Canaan, "
30 man, who is the lord of the l', spake "
32 with our father in the l' of Canaan. "
34 and ye shall traffick in the l'. "
43: 1 And the famine was sore in the l'. "
11 take of the best fruits in the l' in "
44: 8 unto thee out of the l' of Canaan: "
45: 6 hath the famine been in the l': "
8 ruler throughout all the l' of Egypt. "
10 thou shalt dwell in the l' of Goshen, "
17 go, get you unto the l' of Canaan; "
18 give you the good of the l' of Egypt, "
18 and ye shall eat the fat of the l'. "
19 you wagons out of the l' of Egypt "
20 good of all the l' of Egypt is yours. "
25 into the l' of Canaan unto Jacob "
26 governor over all the l' of Egypt. "
46: 6 they had gotten in the l' of Canaan, "
12 and Onan died in the l' of Canaan. "
20 unto Joseph in the l' of Egypt were "
28 and they came into the l' of Goshen. "
31 which were in the l' of Canaan, are "
34 ye may dwell in the l' of Goshen; "
47: 1 are come out of the l' of Canaan; "
1 behold, they are in the l' of Goshen. "
4 For to sojourn in the l' are we come; "
4 famine is sore in the l' of Canaan: "
4 servants dwell in the l' of Goshen. "
6 l' of Egypt is before thee; in the "
6 the best of the l' make thy father "
6 in the l' of Goshen let them dwell: "
11 them a possession in the l' of Egypt, "
11 best of the l', in the l' of Rameses, "
13 there was no bread in all the l'; "
13 very sore, so that the l' of Egypt "
13 and all the l' of Canaan fainted by "
14 that was found in the l' of Egypt, "
14 and in the l' of Canaan, for the corn "
15 when money failed in the l' of Egypt, "
15 and in the l' of Canaan, all the "
19 thine eyes, both we and our l'? 127
19 buy us and our l' for bread, and we "
19 and we and our l' will be servants "
19 not die, that the l' be not desolate. "
20 Joseph bought all the l' of Egypt "
20 them: so the l' became Pharaoh's. 776
22 Only the l' of the priests bought he 127
23 bought you this day and your l' for "
23 seed for you, and ye shall sow the l'. "
26 made it a law over the l' of Egypt "
26 except the l' of the priests only, "
27 And Israel dwelt in the l' of Egypt, 776
28 Jacob lived in the l' of Egypt "
48: 3 unto me at Luz in the l' of Canaan, "
4 will give this l' to thy seed after "
5 born unto thee in the l' of Egypt "
7 Rachel died by me in the l' of Canaan "
21 again unto the l' of your fathers. "
49:15 and the l' that it was pleasant; "
30 before Mamre, in the l' of Canaan, "
50: 5 which I have digged for me in the l' "
7 all the elders of the l' of Egypt, "
8 herds, they left in the l' of Goshen. "
11 And when the inhabitants of the l', "
13 carried him into the l' of Canaan, "
24 you, and bring you out of this l' "
24 the l' which he sware to Abraham, "
Ex 1: 7 and the l' was filled with them. "
10 and so get them up out of the l'. "
2:15 and dwelt in the l' of Midian: "
22 have been a stranger in a strange l'. "
3: 8 them up out of that l' unto a good l' "
8 a l' flowing with milk and honey; "
17 Egypt unto the l' of the Canaanites, "
17 a l' flowing with milk and honey. "
4: 9 river, and pour it upon the dry l': "
9 shall become blood upon the dry l'. "
20 and he returned to the l' of Egypt: 776
5: 5 the people of the l' now are many, "
12 throughout all the l' of Egypt "
6: 1 shall he drive them out of his l'. "
4 them, to give them the l' of Canaan, "
4 the l' of their pilgrimage, wherein "
8 And I will bring you in unto the l', "
11 children of Israel go out of his l'. "
13 of Israel out of the l' of Egypt. "
26 of Israel from the l' of Egypt "
28 spake unto Moses in the l' of Egypt, "
7: 2 the children of Israel out of his l'. "
3 and my wonders in the l' of Egypt. "
4 out of the l' of Egypt by great "
19 blood throughout all the l' of Egypt, "
21 throughout all the l' of Egypt. "
8: 5 to come up upon the l' of Egypt. "
6 frogs came up, and covered the l' "
7 up frogs upon the l' of Egypt. "
14 upon heaps: and the l' stank. "
16 rod, and smite the dust of the l', "
16 lice throughout all the l' of Egypt. "
17 all the dust of the l' became lice "
17 lice throughout all the l' of Egypt. "
22 sever in that day the l' of Goshen, "
24 houses, and into all the l' of Egypt: "
24 l' was corrupted by reason of...flies. "
25 ye, sacrifice to your God in the l'. "
9: 5 Lord shall do this thing in the l'. "
9 small dust in all the l' of Egypt, "
9 beast, throughout all the l' of Egypt. "
Ex 9:22 may be hail in all the l' of Egypt, 776
22 field, throughout the l' of Egypt. "
23 rained hail upon the l' of Egypt. "
24 none like it in all the l' of Egypt "
25 hail smote throughout all the l' of "
26 Only in the l' of Goshen, where the "
10:12 over the l' of Egypt for the locusts, "
12 may come upon the l' of Egypt, "
12 and eat every herb of the l', even "
13 forth his rod over the l' of Egypt, "
13 east wind upon the l' all that day, "
14 And locusts went up over all the l' "
15 earth, so that the l' was darkened; "
15 and they did eat every herb of the l', "
15 field, through all the l' of Egypt. "
21 be darkness over the l' of Egypt, "
22 thick darkness in all the l' of Egypt "
11: 3 Moses was...great in the l' of Egypt, "
5 firstborn in the l' of Egypt shall die, "
6 be a great cry throughout all the l' "
9 be multiplied in the l' of Egypt. "
10 children of Israel go out of his l'. "
12: 1 Moses and Aaron in the l' of Egypt, "
12 pass through the l' of Egypt this "
12 will smite all the firstborn in the l' "
13 you, when I smite the l' of Egypt. "
17 your armies out of the l' of Egypt: "
19 he be a stranger, or born in the l'. "
25 the l' which the Lord will give you, "
29 smote all the firstborn in the l' of "
33 send them out of the l' in haste; "
41 Lord went out from the l' of Egypt. "
42 for bringing them out from the l' of "
48 shall be as one that is born in the l': "
51 of Israel out of the l' of Egypt by "
13: 5 thee into the l' of the Canaanites, "
5 a l' flowing with milk and honey, "
11 thee into the l' of the Canaanites, "
15 all the firstborn in the l' of Egypt, "
17 the way of the l' of the Philistines, "
18 went up harnessed out of the l' of "
14: 3 Israel, They are entangled in the l', "
21 made the sea dry l', and the waters "
29 Israel walked upon dry l' in the midst
15:19 children of Israel went on dry l' in "
16: 1 after their departing out of the l' of 776
3 hand of the Lord in the l' of Egypt, "
6 brought you out from the l' of Egypt: "
32 you forth from the l' of Egypt. "
35 until they came to a l' inhabited; "
35 unto the borders of the l' of Canaan. "
18: 3 have been an alien in a strange l': "
27 he went his way into his own l'. "
19: 1 gone forth out of the l' of Egypt, "
20: 2 brought thee out of the l' of Egypt, "
12 thy days may be long upon the l' 127
22:21 were strangers in the l' of Egypt. 776
23: 9 were strangers in the l' of Egypt. "
10 six years thou shalt sow thy l', and "
19 The first of the firstfruits of thy l' *127
26 young, nor be barren, in thy l': 776
29 lest the l' become desolate, and the "
30 thou be increased, and inherit the l'. "
31 will deliver the inhabitants of the l' "
33 They shall not dwell in thy l', lest "
29:46 them forth out of the l' of Egypt, "
32: 1 brought us up out of the l' of Egypt, "
4 brought thee up out of the l' of Egypt. "
7 broughtest out of the l' of Egypt, "
8 brought thee up out of the l' of Egypt. "
11 brought forth out of the l' of Egypt "
13 all this l' that I have spoken of will "
23 brought us up out of the l' of Egypt, "
33: 1 brought up out of the l' of Egypt, "
1 the l' which I sware unto Abraham, "
3 a l' flowing with milk and honey: "
34:12 with the inhabitants of the l' "
15 with the inhabitants of the l', "
24 neither shall any man desire thy l', "
26 The first of the firstfruits of thy l' *127
Le 11:45 you up out of the l' of Egypt, 776
14:34 ye be come into the l' of Canaan, "
34 a house of the l' of your possession; "
16:22 iniquities unto a l' not inhabited: "
18: 3 After the doings of the l' of Egypt, "
3 after the doings of the l' of Canaan, "
25 And the l' is defiled: therefore I do "
25 l' itself vomiteth out her inhabitants. "
27 have the men of the l' done, which "
27 before you, and the l' is defiled;) "
28 That the l' spue not you out also, "
19: 9 when ye reap the harvest of your l', "
23 when ye shall come into the l', and "
29 whore; lest the l' fall to whoredom, "
29 and the l' become full of wickedness. "
33 stranger sojourn with thee in your l', "
34 ye were strangers in the l' of Egypt: "
36 brought you out of the l' of Egypt. "
20: 2 the people of the l' shall stone him "
4 if the people of the l' do any ways "
22 that the l', whither I bring you to "
24 unto you, Ye shall inherit their l', 127
24 l' that floweth with milk and honey: 776
22:24 make any offering thereof in your l'. "
33 brought out of the l' of Egypt, to "
23:10 When ye be come into the l' which "
22 when ye reap the harvest of your l', "
39 have gathered in the fruit of the l', "
43 brought them out of the l' of Egypt: "
24:16 as he that is born in the l', when *249
25: 2 ye come into the l' which I give 776
2 shall the l' keep a sabbath unto the "
4 shall be a sabbath of rest unto the l', "
5 for it is a year of rest unto the l'. "
6 sabbath of the l' shall be meat for "
7 and for the beast that are in thy l'. "

Le 25: 9 sound throughout all your l'. 776
10 liberty throughout all the l' unto "
18 ye shall dwell in the l' in safety. "
19 And the l' shall yield her fruit, and "
23 The l' shall not be sold for ever: "
23 for the l' is mine; for ye are "
24 And in all the l' of your possession "
24 shall grant a redemption for the l'. "
38 you forth out of the l' of Egypt, "
38 to give you the l' of Canaan, and to "
42 brought forth out of the l' of Egypt: "
45 you, which they begat in your l': "
55 brought forth out of the l' of Egypt: "
26: 1 up any image of stone in your l', "
4 and the l' shall yield her increase, "
5 the full, and dwell in your l' safely. "
6 And I will give peace in the l', and "
6 I will rid evil beasts out of the l', "
6 shall the sword go through your l'. "
13 you forth out of the l' of Egypt, "
20 your l' shall not yield her increase, "
20 neither shall the trees of the l' "
32 I will bring the l' into desolation: "
33 and your l' shall be desolate, and "
34 Then shall the l' enjoy her sabbaths, "
34 and ye be in your enemies' l'; even "
34 even then shall the l' rest, and "
38 l' of your enemies shall eat you up. "
41 them into the l' of their enemies; "
42 and I will remember the l'. "
43 The l' also shall be left of them, "
44 they be in the l' of their enemies, "
45 Brought forth out of the l' of Egypt "
27: 24 the possession of the l' did belong. "
30 And all the tithe of the l', whether "
30 whether of the seed of the l', or of "
Nu 1: 1 were come out of the l' of Egypt, "
3: 13 I smote all the firstborn in the l' "
8: 17 every firstborn in the l' of Egypt "
9: 1 were come out of the l' of Egypt, "
14 and for him that was born in the l'. "
10: 9 if ye go to war in your l' against "
30 but I will depart to mine own l', "
11: 12 l' which thou swearest unto their 127
13: 2 they may search the l' of Canaan, 776
16 which Moses sent to spy out the l'. "
17 them to spy out the l' of Canaan, "
18 see the l', what it is; and the people "
19 what the l' is that they dwell in, "
20 what the l' is, whether it be fat or "
20 and bring of the fruit of the l'. "
21 they went up, and searched the l' "
25 returned from searching of the l' "
26 and shewed them the fruit of the l'. "
27 unto the l' whither thou sentest us, "
28 people be strong that dwell in the l', "
29 The Amalekites dwell in the l' of the "
32 brought up an evil report of the l' "
32 The l', through which we have gone "
32 is a l' that eateth up the inhabitants "
14: 2 that we had died in the l' of Egypt! "
3 the Lord brought us unto this l', "
6 were of them that searched the l', "
7 The l', which we passed through to "
7 to search it, is an exceeding good l'. "
8 then he will bring us into this l', and "
8 a l' which floweth with milk and "
9 neither fear ye the people of the l'; "
14 tell it to the inhabitants of this l': "
16 able to bring this people into the l' "
23 shall not see the l' which I sware "
24 him will I bring into the l' whereinto "
30 ye shall not come into the l', "
31 they shall know the l' which ye have "
34 the days in which ye searched the l', "
36 which Moses sent to search the l', "
36 by bringing up a slander upon the l', "
37 bring up the evil report upon the l', "
38 of the men that went to search the l', "
15: 2 When ye be come into the l' of your "
18 When ye come into the l' whither I "
19 when ye eat of the bread of the l', "
30 whether he be born in the l', or a * 249
41 brought you out of the l' of Egypt, 776
16: 13 brought us up out of a l' that floweth "
14 not brought us into a l' that floweth "
18: 13 whatsoever is first ripe in the l', "
20 shalt have no inheritance in their l' "
20: 12 bring this congregation into the l' "
23 Hor, by the coast of the l' of Edom, "
24 he shall not enter into the l' which "
21: 4 Red sea, to compass the l' of Edom: "
22 Let me pass through thy l': we will "
24 and possessed his l' from Arnon unto "
26 taken all his l' out of his hand, even "
31 Israel dwelt in the l' of the Amorites. "
34 hand, and all his people, and his l'; "
35 him alive: and they possessed his l'. "
22: 5 river of the l' of the children of his "
6 that I may drive them out of the l': "
13 Get you into your l': for the Lord "
26: 4 went forth out of the l' of Egypt. "
19 Er and Onan died in the l' of Canaan. "
53 Unto these the l' shall be divided "
55 the l' shall be divided by lot: "
27: 12 see the l' which I have given unto "
32: 1 and when they saw the l' of Jazer, "
1 and the l' of Gilead, that, behold, the "
4 is a l' for cattle, and thy servants "
5 let this l' be given unto thy servants "
7 of Israel from going over into the l' "
8 from Kadesh-barnea to see the l'. "
9 and saw the l', they discouraged the "
9 that they should not go into the l' "
11 l' which I sware unto Abraham, 127
17 because of the inhabitants of the l'. 776

Nu 32: 22 the l' be subdued before the Lord: 776
22 and this l' shall be your possession "
29 the l' shall be subdued before you; "
29 ye shall give them the l' of Gilead "
30 among you in the l' of Canaan. "
32 before the Lord into the l' of Canaan, "
33 the l', with the cities thereof in the "
33: 1 went forth out of the l' of Egypt with "
37 Hor, in the edge of the l' of Edom. "
38 were come out of the l' of Egypt, "
40 in the south in the l' of Canaan, "
51 over Jordan into the l' of Canaan; "
52 inhabitants of the l' from before you, "
53 dispossess the inhabitants of the l', "
53 I have given you the l' to possess it. "
54 ye shall divide the l' by lot for an "
55 not drive out the inhabitants of the l' "
55 shall vex you in the l' wherein ye "
34: 2 When ye come into the l' of Canaan; "
2 (this is the l' that shall fall unto you "
2 even the l' of Canaan with the coasts "
12 this shall be your l' with the coasts "
13 This is the l' which ye shall inherit "
17 which shall divide the l' unto you: "
18 to divide the l' by inheritance. "
29 children of Israel in the l' of Canaan. "
35: 10 over Jordan into the l' of Canaan; "
14 shall ye give in the l' of Canaan, "
28 slayer shall return into the l' of his "
32 should come again to dwell in the l', "
33 not pollute the l' wherein ye are: "
33 ye are: for blood it defileth the l': "
33 l' cannot be cleansed of the blood "
34 Defile not therefore the l' which ye "
36: 2 to give the l' for an inheritance by "
De 1: 5 this side Jordan, in the l' of Moab, "
7 to the l' of the Canaanites, and unto "
8 Behold, I have set the l' before you: "
8 go in and possess the l' which the "
21 thy God hath set the l' before thee: "
22 they shall search us out the l', and "
25 they took of the fruit of the l' in their "
25 is a good l' which the Lord our God "
27 out of the l' of Egypt, to deliver us "
35 this evil generation see that good l', "
36 to him will I give the l' that he hath "
2: 5 I will not give you of their l', no, not "
9 I will not give thee of their l' for a "
12 as Israel did unto the l' of his "
19 not give thee of the l' of the children "
20 also was accounted a l' of giants: "
24 Sihon...king of Heshbon, and his l': "
27 Let me pass through thy l': I will go "
29 Jordan into the l' which the Lord "
31 to give Sihon and his l' before thee: "
31 that thou mayest inherit his l'. "
37 unto the l' of the children of Ammon "
3: 2 his people, and his l', into thy hand; "
8 the l' that was on this side Jordan, "
12 this l', which we possessed at that "
13 which was called the l' of giants. "
18 hath given you this l' to possess it: "
20 also possess the l' which the Lord "
25 the good l' that is beyond Jordan, "
28 cause them to inherit the l' which "
4: 1 in and possess the l' which the Lord "
5 should do so in the l' whither ye go "
14 might do them in the l' whither ye go "
21 I should not go in unto that good l', "
22 But I must die in this l', I must not "
22 go over, and possess that good l'. "
25 shall have remained long in the l', "
26 soon utterly perish from off the l' "
38 give thee their l' for an inheritance, "
46 the l' of Sihon king of the Amorites, "
47 they possessed his l', and the l' of Og "
5: 6 brought thee out of the l' of Egypt, "
15 wast a servant in the l' of Egypt, "
16 l' which the Lord thy God giveth 127
31 may do them in the l' which I give 776
33 ye may prolong your days in the l' "
6: 1 in the l' whither ye go to possess it: "
3 l' that floweth with milk and honey. "
10 thee into the l' which he sware unto "
12 thee forth out of the l' of Egypt, "
18 mayest go in and possess the good l' "
23 give us the l' which he sware unto "
7: 1 thy God shall bring thee into the l' "
13 thy womb, and the fruit of thy l', * 127
13 l' which he sware unto thy fathers "
8: 1 go in and possess the l' which the 776
7 into a good l', a l' of brooks of water, "
8 A l' of wheat, and barley, and vines, "
8 a l' of oil olive, and honey; "
9 A l' wherein thou shalt eat bread "
9 a l' whose stones are iron, and out "
10 the good l' which he hath given thee. "
14 thee forth out of the l' of Egypt, "
9: 4 brought me in to possess this l': "
5 dost thou go to possess their l': "
6 thy God giveth thee not this good l' "
7 didst depart out of the l' of Egypt, "
23 Go up and possess the l' which I "
28 Lest the l' whence thou broughtest "
28 into the l' which he promised them, "
10: 7 to Jotbath, a l' of rivers of waters. "
11 they may go in and possess the l', "
19 ye were strangers in the l' of Egypt. "
11: 3 king of Egypt, and unto all his l'; "
8 strong, and go in and possess the l', "
9 ye may prolong your days in the l', 127
9 l' that floweth with milk and honey. 776
10 For the l', whither thou goest in to "
10 is not as the l' of Egypt, from whence "
11 the l', whither ye go to possess it, "
11 is a l' of hills and valleys, and "

De 11: 12 A l' which the Lord thy God careth 776
14 the rain of your l' in his due season, "
17 and that the l' yield not her fruit; 127
17 perish quickly from off the good l' 776
21 the l' which the Lord sware unto 127
25 all the l' that ye shall tread upon, 776
29 unto the l' whither thou goest to "
30 down, in the l' of the Canaanites, "
31 to go in to possess the l' which the "
12: 1 ye shall observe to do in the l', "
10 dwell in the l' which the Lord your "
29 them, and dwellest in their l'; "
13: 5 brought you out of the l' of Egypt, "
10 brought thee out of the l' of Egypt, "
15: 4 Lord shall greatly bless thee in the l' "
7 within any of thy gates in thy l' "
11 poor shall never cease out of the l': "
11 thy poor, and to thy needy, in thy l'. "
15 wast a bondman in the l' of Egypt. "
16: 3 forth out of the l' of Egypt in haste: "
3 camest forth out of the l' of Egypt "
20 inherit the l' which the Lord thy God "
17: 14 When thou art come unto the l' "
18: 9 when thou art come into the l' "
19: 1 whose l' the Lord thy God giveth "
2 cities for thee in the midst of thy l', "
3 divide the coasts of thy l', which "
8 give thee all the l' which he promised "
10 innocent blood be not shed in thy l', "
14 which thou shalt inherit in the l' "
20: 1 thee up out of the l' of Egypt. "
21: 1 If one be found slain in the l' which 127
23 that thy l' be not defiled, which the "
23: 7 thou wast a stranger in his l'. 776
20 in the l' whither thou goest to "
24: 4 thou shalt not cause the l' to sin, "
14 strangers that are in thy l' within "
22 wast a bondman in the l' of Egypt: "
25: 15 days may be lengthened in the l' 127
19 in the l' which the Lord thy God 776
26: 1 when thou art come in unto the l' "
2 shalt bring of thy l' that the Lord "
9 place, and hath given us this l', "
9 l' that floweth with milk and honey. "
10 brought the firstfruits of the l', * 127
15 and the l' which thou hast given us, * "
15 l' that floweth with milk and honey. 776
27: 2 ye shall pass over Jordan unto the l' "
3 that thou mayest go in unto the l' "
3 l' that floweth with milk and honey; "
28: 8 bless thee in the l' which the Lord "
11 l' which the Lord sware unto thy 127
12 the rain unto thy l' in his season, 776
18 of thy body, and the fruit of thy l', 127
21 have consumed thee from off the l', "
24 the rain of thy l' powder and dust: 776
33 fruit of thy l', and all thy labours, *127
42 and fruit of thy l' shall the locust * "
51 of thy cattle, and the fruit of thy l', "
52 trustedst, throughout all thy l': 776
52 all thy gates throughout all thy l', "
63 ye shall be plucked from off the l' 127
29: 1 children of Israel in the l' of Moab, 776
2 before your eyes in the l' of Egypt "
2 all his servants, and unto all his l'; "
8 we took their l', and gave it for an "
16 how we have dwelt in the l' of Egypt; "
22 that shall come from a far l', "
22 when they see the plagues of that l', "
23 the whole l' thereof is brimstone, "
24 the Lord done thus unto this l'? "
25 them forth out of the l' of Egypt: "
27 the Lord was kindled against this l', "
28 rooted them out of their l' in anger, 127
28 and cast them into another l', 776
30: 5 thy God will bring thee into the l' "
9 thy cattle, and in the fruit of thy l', *127
16 thy God shall bless thee in the l' 776
18 not prolong your days upon the l', 127
20 thou mayest dwell in the l' which "
31: 4 Amorites, and unto the l' of them, 776
7 must go with this people unto the l' "
13 as long as ye live in the l' whither 127
16 the gods of the strangers of the l', 776
20 into the l' which I sware unto their 127
21 them into the l' which I sware. 776
23 into the l' which I sware unto them: "
32: 10 He found him in a desert l', and in "
43 will be merciful unto his l', and to 127
47 ye shall prolong your days in the l', "
49 Nebo, which is in the l' of Moab, 776
49 behold the l' of Canaan, which I "
52 thou shalt see the l' before thee; "
52 thither unto the l' which I give the "
33: 13 Blessed of the Lord be his l', for "
28 shall be upon a l' of corn and wine; "
34: 1 shewed him all the l' of Gilead, "
2 the l' of Ephraim, and Manasseh, "
2 all the l' of Judah, unto the utmost "
4 the l' which I sware unto Abraham, "
5 Lord died there in the l' of Moab, "
6 him in a valley in the l' of Moab, "
11 sent him to do in the l' of Egypt "
11 to all his servants, and to all his l', "
Jos 1: 2 unto the l' which I do give to them, "
4 all the l' of the Hittites, and unto "
6 thou divide for an inheritance the l', "
11 to go in to possess the l', which the "
13 you rest, and hath given you this l'. "
14 shall remain in the l' which Moses "
15 they also have possessed the l' "
15 return unto the l' of your possession, "
2: 1 saying, Go view the l', even Jericho. "
9 that the Lord hath given you the l', "
9 inhabitants of the l' faint because of "
14 when the Lord hath given us the l', "

Jos 2:18 we come into the l, thou shalt bind 776
24 delivered into our hands all the l; "
4:18 feet were lifted up unto the dry l, *
22 Israel came over this Jordan on dry l.
5: 6 that he would not shew them the l, 776
6 l that floweth with milk and honey. "
11 eat of the old corn of the l on the "
12 had eaten of the old corn of the l; "
12 they did eat of the fruit of the l of "
7: 9 the inhabitants of the l shall hear "
8: 1 his people, and his city, and his l: "
9:24 servant Moses to give you all the l, "
24 destroy all the inhabitants of the l "
10:42 these kings and their l did Joshua "
11: 3 under Hermon in the l of Mizpeh. "
16 So Joshua took all that l, the hills, "
16 all the l of Goshen, and the valley, "
22 none of the Anakims left in the l of "
23 Joshua took the whole l, according "
23 tribes. And the l rested from war. "
12: 1 these are the kings of the l, which "
1 possessed their l on the other side "
13: 1 yet very much l to be possessed. "
2 This is the l that yet remaineth: all "
4 all the l of the Canaanites, and "
5 And the l of the Giblites, and all "
7 divide this l for an inheritance "
25 half the l of the children of Ammon, "
14: 1 Israel inherited in the l of Canaan, "
4 no part unto the Levites in the l, "
5 Israel did, and they divided the l. "
7 Kadesh-barnea to espy out the l; "
9 l whereon thy feet have trodden "
15 And the l had rest from war. "
15:19 for thou hast given me a south l; "
17: 5 beside the l of Gilead and Bashan, "
6 Manasseh's sons had the l of Gilead. "
8 Manasseh had the l of Tappuah: "
12 Canaanites would dwell in that l. "
15 l of the Perizzites and of the giants, "
16 that dwell in the l of the valley "
18: 1 and the l was subdued before them. "
3 are ye slack to go to possess the l, "
4 they shall rise, and go through the l, "
6 describe the l into seven parts, "
8 them that went to describe the l, "
8 saying, Go and walk through the l, "
9 men went and passed through the l, "
10 there Joshua divided the l unto the "
19:49 dividing the l for inheritance by "
21: 2 them at Shiloh in the l of Canaan, "
43 the Lord gave unto Israel all the l "
22: 4 and unto the l of your possession, "
9 Shiloh, which is in the l of Canaan, "
9 l of their possession, whereof they "
10 that are in the l of Canaan, the "
11 altar over against the l of Canaan, "
13 of Manasseh, into the l of Gilead, "
15 of Manasseh, unto the l of Gilead, "
19 the l of your possession be unclean, "
19 then pass ye over unto the l of the "
32 of Gad, out of the l of Gilead, "
32 unto the l of Canaan, to the children "
33 destroy the l wherein the children "
23: 5 ye shall possess their l, as the Lord "
13 until ye perish from off the good l 127
15 destroyed you from off this good l "
16 perish quickly from off the good l 776
24: 3 him throughout all the l of Canaan, "
8 you into the l of the Amorites, "
8 hand, that ye might possess their l; "
13 you a l for which ye did not labour, "
15 the Amorites, in whose l ye dwell: "
17 our fathers out of the l of Egypt, "
18 the Amorites which dwelt in the l: "
J'g 1: 2 have delivered the l into his hand. "
15 for thou hast given me a south l; "
26 men went into the l of the Hittites, "
27 Canaanites would dwell in that l. "
32, 33 Canaanites,...inhabitants of the l: "
2: 1 have brought you unto the l which "
2 with the inhabitants of this l; "
6 his inheritance to possess the l. "
12 brought them out of the l of Egypt, "
3:11 And the l had rest forty years. "
30 And the l had rest fourscore years. "
5:31 And the l had rest forty years. "
6: 5 they entered into the l to destroy it. "
9 before you, and gave you their l; "
10 the Amorites, in whose l ye dwell; "
9:37 people down by the middle of the l, "
10: 4 day, which are in the l of Gilead. "
8 Jordan in the l of the Amorites, "
11: 3 brethren, and dwelt in the l of Tob: "
5 fetch Jephthah out of the l of Tob: "
12 come against me to fight in my l? "
13 Because Israel took away my l, "
15 Israel took not away the l of Moab, "
15 nor the l of the children of Ammon: "
17 me, I pray thee, pass through thy l: "
18 the l of Edom, and the l of Moab, "
18 by the east side of the l of Moab, "
19 thee, through thy l into my place. "
21 possessed all the l of the Amorites, "
12:15 in Pirathon in the l of Ephraim, "
18: 2 to spy out the l, and to search it; "
2 said unto them, Go, search the l: "
7 there was no magistrate in the l, "
9 for we have seen the l, and, behold, "
9 to go, and to enter to possess the l. "
10 a people secure, and to a large l: "
17 five men that went to spy out the l "
30 the day of the captivity of the l. "
19:30 Israel came up out of the l of Egypt "
20: 1 to Beer-sheba, with the l of Gilead, "
21:12 Shiloh, which is in the l of Canaan. "

J'g 21:21 Shiloh, and go to the l of Benjamin. 776
Ru 1: 1 that there was a famine in the l. "
7 way to return unto the l of Judah. "
2:11 mother, and the l of thy nativity, "
4: 3 of Moab, selleth a parcel of l, 7704
1Sa 6: 5 of your mice that mar the l; 776
5 off your gods, and from off your l. "
9: 4 passed through the l of Shalisha, "
4 passed through the l of Shalim, "
4 through the l of the Benjamites, "
5 they were come to the l of Zuph, "
16 thee a man out of the l of Benjamin, "
12: 6 your fathers up out of the l of Egypt. "
13: 3 the trumpet throughout all the l, "
7 went over Jordan to the l of Gad "
17 to Ophrah, unto the l of Shual. "
19 throughout all the l of Israel: "
14:14 as it were an half acre of l, which 7704
25 all they of the l came to a wood; * 776
29 My father hath troubled the l: "
21:11 not this David the king of the l? "
22: 5 and get thee into the l of Judah. "
23:23 if he be in the l, that I will search "
27 the Philistines have invaded the l. "
27: 1 escape into the l of the Philistines; "
8 were of old the inhabitants of the l, "
8 to Shur, even unto the l of Egypt. "
9 David smote the l, and left neither "
28: 3 and the wizards, out of the l. "
9 and the wizards, out of the l: "
29:11 return into the l of the Philistines. "
30:16 out of the l of the Philistines, "
16 and out of the l of Judah. "
31: 9 sent into the l of the Philistines "
2Sa 3:12 his behalf, saying, Whose is the l? "
5: 6 Jebusites, the inhabitants of the l: "
7:23 great things and terrible, for thy l, "
9: 7 thee all the l of Saul thy father; 7704
10 thy servants, shall till the l for him, 127
10: 2 into the l of the children of Ammon. 776
15: 4 Oh that I were made judge in the l, "
17:26 Absalom pitched in the l of Gilead. "
19: 9 he is fled out of the l for Absalom. "
29 said, Thou and Ziba divide the l. 7704
21:14 that God was intreated for the l. 776
24: 6 and to the l of Tahtim-hodshi; "
8 they had gone through all the l, "
13 of famine come unto thee in thy l? "
13 be three days' pestilence in thy l? "
25 So the Lord was intreated for the l, "
1Ki 4:10 Sochoh, and all the l of Hepher: "
19 the only officer which was in the l. "
21 river unto the l of the Philistines, "
6: 1 were come out of the l of Egypt, "
8: 9 they came out of the l of Egypt. "
21 brought them out of the l of Egypt. "
34 unto the l which thou gavest unto 127
36 give rain upon thy l, which thou 776
37 If there be in the l famine, if there "
37 besiege them in the l of their cities; "
40 all the days that they live in the l 127
46 captives unto the l of the enemy, 776
47 l whither they were carried captives, "
47 make supplication unto thee in the l "
48 in the l of their enemies, which led "
48 and pray unto thee toward their l, "
9: 7 Then will I cut off Israel out of the l 127
8 hath the Lord done thus unto this l, 776
9 their fathers out of the l of Egypt, "
11 twenty cities in the l of Galilee. "
13 And he called them the l of Cabul "
18 Tadmor in the wilderness, in the l, "
19 and in all the l of his dominion, "
21 that were left after them in the l, "
26 of the Red sea, in the l of Edom. "
10: 6 report that I heard in mine own l of "
11:18 him victuals, and gave him l. "
12:28 brought thee up out of the l of Egypt. "
14:15 root up Israel out of this good l, 127
24 there were also sodomites in the l: 776
15:12 took away the sodomites out of the l, "
20 Cinneroth, with all the l of Naphtali. "
17: 7 there had been no rain in the l. "
18: 5 said unto Obadiah, Go into the l, "
6 divided the l between them to pass "
20: 7 Israel called all the elders of the l, "
22:46 his father Asa, he took out of the l. "
2Ki 2:21 thence any more death or barren l.*
3:19 mar every good piece of l with stones.
25 on every good piece of l cast every
27 him, and returned to their own l. 776
4:38 and there was a dearth in the l; and "
5: 2 out of the l of Israel a little maid; "
4 the maid that is of the l of Israel. "
6:23 came no more into the l of Israel. "
8: 1 also come upon the l seven years. "
2 the l of the Philistines seven years. "
3 out of the l of the Philistines: and "
3, 5 king for her house and for her l. 7704
6 since the day that she left the l, 776
10:33 Jordan eastward, all the l of Gilead, "
11: 3 And Athaliah did reign over the l. "
14 all the people of the l rejoiced, and "
18 people of the l went into the house "
19 guard, and all the people of the l; "
20 all the people of the l rejoiced, and "
13:20 bands of the Moabites invaded the l "
15: 5 house, judging the people of the l. "
19 king of Assyria came against the l: "
20 back, and stayed not there in the l. "
29 all the l of Naphtali, and carried "
16:15 offering of all the people of the l, "
17: 5 came up throughout all the l, and "
7 them up out of the l of Egypt, from "
23 carried away out of their own l to 127
26 not the manner of the God of the l: 776

2Ki 17:26 not the manner of the God of the l. 776
27 them the manner of the God of the l. "
36 brought you up out of the l of Egypt "
18:25 said to me, Go up against this l, and "
32 you away to a l like your own l, "
32 a l of corn and wine, "
32 a l of bread and vineyards, "
32 a l of oil olive and of honey, "
33 of the nations delivered at all his l "
19: 7 and shall return to his own l; and "
7 him to fall by the sword in his own l. "
37 they escaped into the l of Armenia. "
21: 8 Israel move any more out of the l 127
24 people of the l slew all them that 776
24 people of the l made Josiah his son "
23:24 that were spied in the l of Judah "
30 people of the l took Jehoahaz the "
33 bands at Riblah in the l of Hamath, "
33 put the l to a tribute of an hundred "
35 but he taxed the l to give the money "
35 and the gold of the people of the l, "
24: 7 not again any more out of his l: "
14 poorest sort of the people of the l. "
15 his officers, and the mighty of the l, "
25: 3 was no bread for the people of the l. "
12 poor of the l to be vinedressers and "
19 which mustered the people of the l, "
19 threescore men of the people of the l "
21 them at Riblah in the l of Hamath. "
21 was carried away out of their l. 127
22 that remained in the l of Judah, 776
24 dwell in the l, and serve the king of "
1Ch 1:43 kings that reigned in the l of Edom "
45 Husham of the l of the Temanites "
2:22 and twenty cities in the l of Gilead. "
4:40 and the l was wide, and quiet, and "
5: 9 were multiplied in the l of Gilead. "
10 throughout all the east l of Gilead. "
11 in the l of Bashan unto Salcah: 776
23 tribe of Manasseh dwelt in the l: "
25 after the gods of the people of the l, "
6:55 gave them Hebron in the l of Judah, "
7:21 Gath that were born in that l slew, "
10: 9 and sent into the l of the Philistines "
11: 4 Jebusites...the inhabitants of the l. "
13: 2 that are left in all the l of Israel, "
16:18 Unto thee will I give the l of Canaan, "
19: 2 into the l of the children of Ammon "
3 to overthrow, and to spy out the l? "
21:12 even the pestilence, in the l, and the "
22: 2 the strangers...in the l of Israel; "
18 given the inhabitants of the l into "
18 the l is subdued before the Lord, "
28: 8 that ye may possess this good l, "
2Ch 2:17 the strangers...in the l of Israel, "
6: 5 forth my people out of the l of Egypt "
25 bring them again unto the l which 127
27 and send rain upon thy l, which 776
28 If there be dearth in the l, if there "
28 besiege them in the cities of their l; "
31 long as they live in the l which 127
36 captives unto a l far off or near; 776
37 in the l whither they are carried "
37 unto thee in the l of their captivity, "
38 their soul in the l of their captivity, "
38 captives, and pray toward their l, "
7:13 command the locusts to devour the l, "
14 their sin, and will heal their l. "
20 them up by the roots out of my l 127
21 hath the Lord done thus unto this l, 776
22 them forth out of the l of Egypt, "
8: 6 throughout all the l of his dominion. "
8 who were left after them in the l, "
17 at the sea side in the l of Edom. "
9: 5 report which I heard in mine own l "
11 such seen before in the l of Judah. "
12 turned, and went away to her own l, "
26 even unto the l of the Philistines, "
14: 1 his days the l was quiet ten years. "
6 for the l had rest, and he had no war "
7 bars, while the l is yet before us; "
15: 8 idols out of all the l of Judah and "
17: 2 and set garrisons in the l of Judah, "
19: 3 taken away the groves out of the l, "
5 he set judges in the l throughout "
20: 7 drive out the inhabitants of this l "
10 they came out of the l of Egypt, "
22:12 and Athaliah reigned over the l. "
23:13 all the people of the l rejoiced, and "
20 people, and all the people of the l, "
21 And all the people of the l rejoiced: "
26:21 house, judging the people of the l. "
30: 9 they shall come again into this l: "
25 that came out of the l of Israel, and "
32: 4 that ran through the midst of the l, "
21 with shame of face to his own l. "
31 of the wonder that was done in the l, "
33: 8 the foot of Israel from out of the l 127
25 people of the l slew all them that 776
25 people of the l made Josiah his son "
34: 7 idols throughout all the l of Israel, "
8 when he had purged the l, and the "
36: 1 people of the l took Jehoahaz the "
3 and condemned the l in an hundred "
21 the l had enjoyed her sabbaths: "
Ezr 4: 4 people of the l weakened the hands "
6:21 the filthiness of the heathen of the l, "
9:11 The l, unto which ye go to possess "
11 is an unclean l with the filthiness of "
12 be strong, and eat the good of the l, "
10: 2 strange wives of the people of the l: "
11 yourselves from the people of the l, "
Ne 4: 4 them for a prey in the l of captivity: "
5:14 be their governor in the l of Judah, "
16 this wall, neither bought we any l: 7704
9: 8 to give the l of the Canaanites, the 776

Ne 9:10 and on all the people of his *l*: 776
11 the midst of the sea on the dry *l*; "
15 they should go in to possess the *l* 776
22 so they possessed the *l* of Sihon, "
22 and the *l* of the king of Heshbon, "
22 and the *l* of Og king of Bashan. "
23 and broughtest them into the *l*, "
24 children went in and possessed the *l*," "
24 before them the inhabitants of the *l*, "
24 their kings, and the people of the *l*, "
25 they took strong cities, and a fat *l*, 127
35 large and fat *l* which thou gavest 776
36 for the *l* that thou gavest unto our "
10:30 daughters unto the people of the *l*, "
31 people of the *l* bring ware or any "
Es 8:17 of the people of the *l* became Jews; "
10: 1 Ahasuerus laid a tribute upon the *l*, "
Job 1: 1 a man in the *l* of Uz, whose name "
10 his substance is increased in the *l*. "
10:21 to the *l* of darkness and the shadow "
22 A *l* of darkness, as darkness itself; "
28:13 is it found in the *l* of the living. "
31:38 If my *l* cry against me, or that the 127
37:13 correction, or for his *l*, or for mercy. 776
39: 6 and the barren *l* his dwellings. "
42:15 the *l* were no women found so fair 776
Ps 10:16 heathen are perished out of his *l*. "
27:13 of the Lord in the *l* of the living. "
35:20 against them that are quiet in the *l*." "
37: 3 shalt thou dwell in the *l*, and verily "
29 The righteous shall inherit the *l*, "
34 he shall exalt thee to inherit the *l*: "
42: 6 remember thee from the *l* of Jordan," "
44: 3 they got not the *l* in possession by "
52: 5 root thee out of the *l* of the living. "
63: 1 for thee in a dry and thirsty *l*, where" "
66: 6 He turned the sea into dry *l*: they "
68: 6 but the rebellious dwell in a dry *l*. "
74: 8 all the synagogues of God in the *l*. 776
78:12 of their fathers, in the *l* of Egypt, in" "
80: 9 to take deep root, and it filled the *l*. "
81: 5 he went out through the *l* of Egypt:" "
10 brought thee out of the *l* of Egypt: "
85: 1 hast been favourable unto thy *l*: "
9 him; that glory may dwell in our *l*. "
12 and our *l* shall yield her increase. "
88:12 in the *l* of forgetfulness? "
95: 5 it: and his hands formed the dry *l*. "
101: 6 shall be upon the faithful of the *l*, 776
8 early destroy all the wicked of the *l*;" "
105:11 thee will I give the *l* of Canaan, "
16 he called for a famine upon the *l*: "
23 Jacob sojourned in the *l* of Ham. "
27 them, and wonders in the *l* of Ham. "
30 Their *l* brought forth frogs in "
32 for rain, and flaming fire in their *l*. "
35 did eat up all the herbs in their *l*, "
36 smote also all the firstborn in their *l*," "
106:22 Wondrous works in the *l* of Ham, "
24 they despised the pleasant *l*, they "
38 and the *l* was polluted with blood. "
107:34 A fruitful *l* into barrenness, for the "
116: 9 before the Lord in the *l* of the living." "
135:12 And gave their *l* for an heritage, an "
136:21 And gave their *l* for an heritage: for "
137: 4 sing the Lord's song in a strange *l*? 127
142: 5 my portion in the *l* of the living. 776
143: 6 thirsteth after thee, as a thirsty *l*. "
10 lead me into the *l* of uprightness. "
Pr 2:21 For the upright shall dwell in the *l*," "
12:11 that tilleth his *l* shall be satisfied 127
28: 2 For the transgression of a *l* many 776
19 that tilleth his *l* shall have plenty 127
29: 4 by judgment establisheth the *l*: 776
31:23 he sitteth among the elders of the *l*." "
Ec 10:16 Woe to thee, O *l*, when thy king is "
17 Blessed art thou, O *l*, when thy king" "
Ca 2:12 voice of the turtle is heard in our *l*;" "
Isa 1: 7 your *l*, strangers devour it in your 127
19 ye shall eat the good of the *l*: 776
2: 7 Their *l* also is full of silver and gold," "
7 their *l* is also full of horses, neither "
8 Their *l* also is full of idols; they "
5:30 look unto the *l*, behold darkness "
6:11 man, and the *l* be utterly desolate, 127
12 forsaking in the midst of the *l*. 776
7:16 the *l* that thou abhorrest shall be 127
18 the bee that is in the *l* of Assyria. 776
22 every one eat that is left in the *l*. "
24 *l* shall become briers and thorns. "
8: 8 wings shall fill the breadth of thy *l*, "
9: 1 he lightly afflicted the *l* of Zebulun, "
1 of Zebulun and the *l* of Naphtali, "
2 in the *l* of the shadow of death, "
19 the Lord of hosts is the *l* darkened, "
10:23 in the midst of all the *l*. * "
11:16 he came up out of the *l* of Egypt. "
13: 5 indignation, to destroy the whole *l*. "
9 fierce anger, to lay the *l* desolate: "
14 and flee every one into his own *l*. "
14: 1 Israel, and set them in their own *l*: 127
2 possess them in the *l* of the Lord "
20 because thou hast destroyed thy *l*, 776
21 they do not rise, nor possess the *l*,* "
25 I will break the Assyrian in my *l*, "
15: 9 and upon the remnant of the *l*. 127
16: 1 ye the lamb to the ruler of the *l* 776
4 oppressors...consumed out of the *l*. "
18: 1 Woe to the *l* shadowing with wings," "
2 whose *l* the rivers have spoiled! "
7 foot, whose *l* the rivers have spoiled," "
19:17 And the *l* of Judah shall be a terror 127
18 five cities in the *l* of Egypt speak 776
19 Lord in the midst of the *l* of Egypt, "
20 the Lord of hosts in the *l* of Egypt: "
24 even a blessing in the midst of the *l*:* "

Isa 21: 1 from the desert, from a terrible *l*. 776
14 The inhabitants of the *l* of Tema "
23: 1 from the *l* of Chittim it is revealed "
10 Pass through thy *l* as a river, O "
13 Behold the *l* of the Chaldeans; this "
24: 3 The *l* shall be utterly emptied, and* "
11 darkened, the mirth of the *l* is gone. "
13 shall be in the midst of the *l* among* "
26: 1 this song be sung in the *l* of Judah; "
10 in the *l* of uprightness will he deal "
27:13 ready to perish in the *l* of Assyria, "
13 and the outcasts in the *l* of Egypt, "
30: 6 into the *l* of trouble and anguish, "
32: 2 shadow of a great rock in a weary *l*." "
13 Upon the *l* of my people shall come 127
33:17 shall behold the *l* that is very far off. 776
34: 6 great slaughter in the *l* of Idumea. "
7 their *l* shall be soaked with blood, "
9 *l* thereof...become burning pitch. "
35: 7 and the thirsty *l* springs of water: * "
36:10 Lord against this *l*, to destroy it? 776
10 Go up against this *l*, and destroy it. "
17 a *l* like your own *l*, a *l* of corn and "
17 wine, a *l* of bread and vineyards. "
18 delivered his *l* out of the hand of the" "
20 delivered their *l* out of my hand, * "
37: 7 a rumour, and return to his own *l*; "
7 to fall by the sword in his own *l*. "
38 they escaped into the *l* of Armenia: "
38:11 even the Lord, in the *l* of the living: "
41:18 and the dry *l* springs of water. "
49:12 west: and these from the *l* of Sinim. "
19 places, and the *l* of thy destruction, "
53: 8 was cut off out of the *l* of the living: "
57:13 his trust in me shall possess the *l*. "
60:18 shall no more be heard in thy *l*, "
21 they shall inherit the *l* for ever, the "
61: 7 in their *l* they shall possess the "
62: 4 thy *l* any more be termed Desolate: "
4 Hephzi-bah, and thy *l* Beulah: for "
4 in thee, and thy *l* shall be married. "
Jer 1: 1 in Anathoth in the *l* of Benjamin: "
14 upon all the inhabitants of the *l*. "
18 brasen walls against the whole *l*, "
18 and against the people of the *l*. "
2: 2 wilderness, in a *l* that was not sown." "
6 brought us up out of the *l* of Egypt, "
6 through a *l* of deserts and of pits, "
6 through a *l* of drought, and of the "
6 a *l* that no man passed through, "
7 when ye entered, ye defiled my *l*, "
15 yelled, and they made his *l* waste: "
31 a *l* of darkness? wherefore say my "
3: 1 shall not that *l* be greatly polluted? "
2 polluted the *l* with thy whoredoms "
9 she defiled the *l*, and committed "
16 be multiplied and increased in the *l*," "
18 together out of the *l* of the north to "
18 to the *l* that I have given for an "
19 and give thee a pleasant *l*, a goodly "
4: 5 say, Blow ye the trumpet in the *l*: "
7 his place to make thy *l* desolate; "
20 the whole *l* is spoiled: suddenly are "
27 said, The whole *l* shall be desolate; "
5:19 and served strange gods in your *l*, "
19 ye serve strangers in a *l* that is not "
30 horrible thing is committed in the *l*; "
6: 8 thee desolate, a *l* not inhabited. "
12 hand upon the inhabitants of the *l*, "
7: 7 in the *l* that I gave to your fathers, "
22 brought them out of the *l* of Egypt, "
25 came forth out of the *l* of Egypt "
34 the bride: for the *l* shall be desolate." "
8:16 whole *l* trembled at the sound of "
16 have devoured the *l*, and all that is "
9:12 *l* perisheth and is burned up like a "
19 because we have forsaken the *l*, "
10:17 Gather up thy wares out of the *l*, O "
18 sling out the inhabitants of the *l* at "
11: 4 them forth out of the *l* of Egypt, "
5 a *l* flowing with milk and honey, "
7 them up out of the *l* of Egypt, "
19 cut him off from the *l* of the living. "
12: 4 How long shall the *l* mourn, and the" "
5 and if in the *l* of peace, wherein "
11 the whole *l* is made desolate, "
12 devour from the one end of the *l* "
12 even to the other end of the *l*: "
14 I will pluck them out of their *l*, 127
15 heritage, and every man to his *l*. 776
13:13 will fill all the inhabitants of this *l*, "
14: 8 thou be as a stranger in the *l*, and "
15 and famine shall not be in this *l*; "
18 go about into a *l* that they know not." "
15: 7 with a fan in the gates of the *l*; "
14 into a *l* which thou knowest not: "
16: 3 fathers that begat them in this *l*; "
6 and the small shall die in this *l*: "
13 will I cast you out of this *l*, into a "
13 into a *l* that ye know not, neither "
14 of Israel out of the *l* of Egypt; "
15 of Israel from the *l* of the north, "
15 I will bring them again into their *l* 127
18 because they have defiled my *l*, 776
17: 4 enemies in the *l* which thou knowest "
6 in a salt *l* and not inhabited. "
26 and from the *l* of Benjamin, and "
18:16 To make their *l* desolate, and a "
22:12 and shall see this *l* no more. "
27 But to the *l* whereunto they desire "
28 cast into a *l* which they know not? "
23: 7 of Israel out of the *l* of Egypt; "
8 and they shall dwell in their own *l*. 127
10 For the *l* is full of adulterers; 776
10 of swearing the *l* mourneth; "
15 profaneness gone forth into all the *l*." "

Jer 24: 5 place into the *l* of the Chaldeans for 776
6 I will bring them again to this *l*: "
8 of Jerusalem, that remain in this *l*, "
8 them that dwell in the *l* of Egypt: "
10 they be consumed from off the *l* 127
25: 5 dwell in the *l* that the Lord hath "
9 and will bring them against this *l*, 776
11 this whole *l* shall be a desolation, "
12 and the *l* of the Chaldeans, and will "
13 will bring upon that *l* all my words "
20 and all the kings of the *l* of Uz, and "
20 the kings of the *l* of the Philistines, "
38 for their *l* is desolate because of the" "
26:17 rose up certain of the elders of the *l*," "
20 against this city and against this *l* "
27: 7 until the very time of his *l* come: "
10 you, to remove you far from your *l*: 127
11 will I let remain still in their own *l*, "
30: 3 to return to the *l* that I gave to 776
10 seed from the *l* of their captivity; "
31:16 come again from the *l* of the enemy." "
23 use this speech in the *l* of Judah "
32 to bring them out of the *l* of Egypt; "
32:15 shall be possessed again in this *l*. "
20 signs and wonders in the *l* of Egypt," "
21 people Israel out of the *l* of Egypt "
22 hast given them this *l*, which thou "
22 a *l* flowing with milk and honey; "
41 I will plant them in this *l* assuredly" "
43 And fields shall be bought in this *l*, "
44 take witnesses in the *l* of Benjamin," "
33:11 cause to return the captivity of the *l*," "
13 and in the *l* of Benjamin, and in the "
15 judgment and righteousness in the *l*." "
34:13 them forth out of the *l* of Egypt, "
19 all the people of the *l*, which passed" "
35: 7 live many days in the *l* where ye 127
11 king of Babylon came up into the *l*, 776
15 dwell in the *l* which I have given 127
36:29 certainly come and destroy this *l*, 776
37: 1 made king in the *l* of Judah. "
2 nor the people of the *l*, did hearken "
7 return to Egypt into their own *l*. "
12 to go into the *l* of Benjamin, "
19 come against you, nor against this *l*?" "
39: 5 to Riblah in the *l* of Hamath, where "
10 which had nothing, in the *l* of Judah," "
40: 4 behold, all the *l* is before thee: "
6 the people that were left in the *l*. "
7 the son of Ahikam governor in the *l*," "
7 children, and of the poor of the *l*, "
9 dwell in the *l*, and serve the king of "
12 driven, and came to the *l* of Judah, "
41: 2 had made governor over the *l*. "
18 of Babylon made governor in the *l*. "
42:10 If ye will still abide in this *l*, then "
12 cause you to return to your own *l*. 127
13 ye say, We will not dwell in this *l*, 776
14 but we will go into the *l* of Egypt, "
16 overtake you there in the *l* of Egypt," "
43: 4 the Lord, to dwell in the *l* of Judah." "
5 driven, to dwell in the *l* of Judah; "
7 they came into the *l* of Egypt: for "
11 he shall smite the *l* of Egypt, and "
12 array himself with the *l* of Egypt, "
13 that is in the *l* of Egypt, "
44: 1 Jews which dwell in the *l* of Egypt, "
8 unto other gods in the *l* of Egypt, "
9 have committed in the *l* of Judah, "
12 their faces to go into the *l* of Egypt "
12 consumed and fall in the *l* of Egypt; "
13 them that dwell in the *l* of Egypt, "
14 gone into the *l* of Egypt to sojourn "
14 should return into the *l* of Judah, "
15 people that dwelt in the *l* of Egypt, "
21 princes, and the people of the *l*, "
22 therefore is your *l* a desolation, "
24 all Judah that are in the *l* of Egypt:" "
26 Judah that dwell in the *l* of Egypt; "
26 man of Judah in all the *l* of Egypt, "
27 of Judah that are in the *l* of Egypt "
28 of the *l* of Egypt into the *l* of Judah," "
28 gone into the *l* of Egypt to sojourn "
45: 4 I will pluck up, even this whole *l*. "
46:12 shame, and thy cry hath filled the *l*:* "
13 come and smite the *l* of Egypt. "
16 people, and to the *l* of our nativity, "
27 seed from the *l* of their captivity; "
47: 2 flood, and shall overflow the *l*, and "
2 the inhabitants of the *l* shall howl. "
48:24 upon all the cities of the *l* of Moab, "
33 field, and from the *l* of Moab; "
50: 1 against the *l* of the Chaldeans by "
3 which shall make her *l* desolate, "
8 forth out of the *l* of the Chaldeans, "
12 a wilderness, a dry *l*, and a desert. "
16 shall flee every one to his own *l*. 776
18 punish the king of Babylon and his *l*," "
21 Go up against the *l* of Merathaim, "
22 A sound of battle is in the *l*, and of "
25 of hosts in the *l* of the Chaldeans. "
28 and escape out of the *l* of Babylon, "
34 that he may give rest to the *l*, * "
38 up: for it is the *l* of graven images, "
45 against the *l* of the Chaldeans: "
51: 2 shall fan her, and shall empty her *l*:" "
4 shall fall in the *l* of the Chaldeans, "
5 their *l* was filled with sin against "
27 Set ye up a standard in the *l*, blow "
28 and all the *l* of his dominion. "
29 And the *l* shall tremble and sorrow: "
29 make the *l* of Babylon a desolation "
43 Her cities are a desolation, a dry *l*, "
43 a *l* wherein no man dwelleth, "
46 rumour that shall be heard in the *l*;" "
46 come a rumour, and violence in the *l*," "

landed

landing

landmark See also LANDMARKS.

landmarks

lands

2Ch32: 13 any ways able to deliver their l' out *776
17 As the gods of the nations of other l' "
Ezr 9: 1 themselves from the people of the l', "
2 mingled...with the people of those l': "
7 into the hand of the kings of the l', "
11 the filthiness of the people of the l', "
Ne 5: 3 said, We have mortgaged our l', *7704
4 and that upon our l' and vineyards.* "
5 men have our l' and vineyards. * "
11 Restore,... their l', their vineyards. * "
9: 30 into the hand of the people of the l'.776
10: 28 themselves from the people of the l' "
Ps 49: 11 call their l' after their own names. 127
66: 1 a joyful noise unto God, all ye l': *776
100: 1 joyful noise unto the Lord, all ye l'. "
105: 44 And gave them the l' of the heathen: "
106: 27 nations, and to scatter them in the l'. "
107: 3 gathered them out of the l', from "
Isa 36: 20 they among all the gods of these l',* "
37: 11 have done to all l' by destroying "
Jer 16: 15 the l' whither he had driven them: * "
27: 6 I given all these l' into the hand of "
Eze 20: 6, 15 honey, which is the glory of all l': "
39: 27 them out of their enemies' l', "
M't 19: 29 children, or l', for my name's sake, 68
M'r 10: 29 wife, or children, or l', for my sake, "
30 and mothers, and children, and l', "
Ac 4: 34 as were possessors of l' or houses 5564

lanes
Lu 14: 21 into the streets and l' of the city, 4505

language See also LANGUAGES.
Ge 11: 1 And the whole earth was of one l', 8193
6 is one, and they have all one l'; "
7 down, and there confound their l', "
9 confound the l' of all the earth: "
2Ki 18: 26 to thy servants in the Syrian l'; "
26 and talk not with us in the Jews' l' "
28 cried with a loud voice in the Jews' l', "
Ne 13: 24 and could not speak in the Jews' l', "
24 according to the l' of each people. 3956
Es 1: 22 and to every people after their l', "
22 according to the l' of every people. "
3: 12 and to every people after their l'; "
8: 9 and unto every people after their l',"
9 writing, and according to their l'. "
Ps 19: 3 There is no speech nor l', where 1697
81: 5 heard a l' that I understood not. 8193
114: 1 Jacob from a people of strange l'; 3937
Isa 19: 18 of Egypt speak the l' of Canaan, 8193
36: 11 unto thy servants in the Syrian l'; "
11 and speak not to us in the Jews' l', "
13 cried with a loud voice in the Jews' l', "
Jer 5: 15 nation whose l' thou knowest not, 3956
Eze 3: 5, 6 strange speech and of an hard l', "
Da 3: 29 That every people, nation, and l', 3961
Zep 3: 9 will I turn to the people a pure l', 8193
Ac 2: 6 heard them speak in his own l'. 1258

languages
Da 3: 4 O people, nations, and l', 3961
7 the people, the nations, and the l', "
4: 1 unto all people, nations, and l', that "
5: 19 people, nations, and l', trembled "
6: 25 unto all people, nations, and l', that "
7: 14 that all people, nations, and l', "
Zec 8: 23 hold out of all l' of the nations, 3956

languish See also LANGUISHED; LANGUISHETH; LANGUISHING.
Isa 16: 8 For the fields of Heshbon l', and 535
19: 8 spread nets upon the waters shall l'. "
24: 4 the haughty people of the earth do l'. "
Jer 14: 2 mourneth, and the gates thereof l'; "
Hos 4: 3 one that dwelleth therein shall l', "

languished
La 2: 8 wall to lament; they l' together. * 535

languisheth
Isa 24: 4 the world l' and fadeth away, the 535
7 The new wine mourneth, the vine l', "
33: 9 earth mourneth and l': Lebanon is "
Jer 15: 9 She that hath borne seven l': she "
Joe 1: 10 the new wine is dried up, the oil l'. "
12 vine is dried up, and the fig tree l'; "
Na 1: 4 rivers: Bashan l', and Carmel, "
4 and the flower of Lebanon l'. "

languishing
Ps 41: 3 strengthen him upon the bed of l':1741

lanterns
Joh 18: 3 cometh thither with l' and torches 5322

Laodicea (*la-od-i-se'-ah*) See also LAODICEANS.
Col 2: 1 have for you, and for them at L', 2993
4: 13 for you, and them that are in L', "
15 Salute the brethren which are in L',"
16 ye likewise read the epistle from L'."
1Ti *subscr.* first to Timothy was written from L' *
Re 1: 11 unto Philadelphia, and unto L'. 2993

Laodiceans (*la-od-i-se'-uns*)
Col 4: 16 read also in the church of the L'; 2994
Rev 3: 14 angel of the church of the L' write;*"

lap See also LAPPED; LAPPETH; LAPPING.
2Ki 4: 39 thereof wild gourds his l' full, and 899
Ne 5: 13 Also I shook my l', and said, So 2684
Pr 16: 33 The lot is cast into the l'; but the 2436

Lapidoth (*lap'-i-doth*)
J'g 4: 4 the wife of L', she judged Israel 3941

lapped
J'g 7: 6 And the number of them that l', 3952
7 By the three hundred men that l' "

lappeth
J'g 7: 5 Every one that l' of the water with3952
5 water with his tongue, as a dog l', "

lapwing
Le 11: 19 heron after her kind, and the l', *1744
De 14: 18 heron after her kind, and the l'. * "

large See also ENLARGE.
Ge 34: 21 behold, it is l' enough for them; 7342
Ex 3: 8 that land unto a good land and a l', "
J'g 18: 10 people secure, and to a l' land:7342,3027
2Sa 22: 20 me forth also into a l' place: 4800
Ne 4: 19 The work is great and l', and we 7342
7: 4 the city was l' and great: but*7342,3027
9: 35 in the l' and fat land which thou 7342
Ps 18: 19 me forth also into a l' place; 4800
31: 8 thou hast set my feet in a l' room. "
118: 5 me, and set me in a l' place. "
Isa 22: 18 like a ball into a l' country: 7342,3027
30: 23 shall thy cattle feed in l' pastures. 7337
33 he hath made it deep and l': "
Jer 22: 14 me a wide house and l' chambers,*7304
Eze 23: 32 of thy sister's cup deep and l': 7342
Hos 4: 16 feed them as a lamb in a l' place. 4800
M't 28: 12 gave l' money unto the soldiers, 2425
M'r 14: 15 he will shew you a l' upper room 3173
Lu 22: 12 he shall shew you a l' upper room "
Ga 6: 11 see how l' a letter I have written 4080
Re 21: 16 the length is as l' as the breadth: *5118

largeness
1Ki 4: 29 exceeding much, and l' of heart, 7341

Lasæa See LASEA.

lasciviousness
M'r 7: 22 wickedness, deceit, l', an evil eye, 766
2Co 12: 21 and l' which they have committed. "
Ga 5: 19 fornication, uncleanness, l', "
Eph 4: 19 have given themselves over unto l', "
1Pe 4: 3 when we walked in l', lusts, excess "
Jude 4 turning the grace of our God into l'. "

Lasea (*la-se'-ah*)
Ac 27: 8 nigh whereunto was the city of L'. 2996

Lasha (*la'-shah*)
Ge 10: 19 Admah, and Zeboim, even unto L'.3962

Lasharon (*lash'-ar-on*)
Jos 12: 18 Aphek, one; the king of L', one; *8289

last See also LASTED; LASTING.
Ge 49: 1 shall befall you in the l' days. * 319
19 but he shall overcome at the l' *6119
Nu 23: 10 and let my l' end be like his! 319
2Sa 19: 11 ye the l' to bring the king back 314
12 are ye the l' to bring back the king? "
23: 1 Now these be the l' words of David. "
1Ch 23: 27 For by the l' words of David the "
29: 29 acts of David the king, first and l', "
2Ch 9: 29 of the acts of Solomon, first and l', "
12: 15 the acts of Rehoboam, first and l', "
16: 11 behold, the acts of Asa, first and l', "
20: 34 acts of Jehoshaphat, first and l', "
25: 26 of the acts of Amaziah, first and l', "
26: 22 of the acts of Uzziah, first and l', "
28: 26 acts and of all his ways, first and l', "
35: 27 And his deeds, first and l', behold, "
Ezr 8: 13 And of the l' sons of Adonikam, "
Ne 8: 18 from the first day unto the l' day, "
Pr 5: 11 And thou mourn at the l', when * 319
23: 32 At the l' it biteth like a serpent, "
Isa 2: 2 it shall come to pass in the l' days,* "
41: 4 Lord, the first, and with the l'; 314
44: 6 I am the first, and I am the l'; and "
48: 12 he; I am the first, I also am the l'. "
Jer 12: 4 said, He shall not see our l' end. * 319
50: 17 and l' this Nebuchadrezzar king of 314
La 1: 9 she remembereth not her l' end; * 319
Da 4: 8 at the l' Daniel came in before me, 318
8: 3 other, and the higher came up l'. 314
19 thee know what shall be in the l' * 319
Am 9: 1 slay the l' of them with the sword: "
Mic 4: 1 in the l' days it shall come to pass,* "
M't 12: 45 l' state of that man is worse than 2078
19: 30 many that are first shall be l'; "
30 and the l' shall be first. "
20: 8 beginning from the l' unto the first."
12 These l' have wrought but one hour,"
14 I will give unto this l', even as unto"
16 So the l' shall be first, and the first l':"
21: 37 But l' of all he sent unto them his*5305
22: 27 And l' of all the woman died also. * "
26: 60 At the l' came two false witnesses,* "
27: 64 the l' error shall be worse than 2078
M'r 9: 35 be first, the same shall be l' of all, "
10: 31 are first shall be l'; and the l' first. "
12: 6 he sent him also l' unto them, "
22 seed: l' of all the woman died also. "
Lu 11: 26 l' state of that man is worse than "
12: 59 till thou hast paid the very l' mite. "
13: 30 there are l' which shall be first, "
30 there are first which shall be l'. "
20: 32 L' of all the woman died also. 5305
Joh 6: 39 raise it up again at the l' day. 2078
40, 44, 54 raise him up at the l' day. "
7: 37 In the l' day, that great day of the "
8: 9 at the eldest, even unto the l': "
11: 24 in the resurrection at the l' day. "
12: 48 same shall judge him in the l' day. "
Ac 2: 17 it shall come to pass in the l' days, "
1Co 4: 9 hath set forth us the apostles l', "
15: 8 And l' of all he was seen of me also,"
26 l' enemy that shall be destroyed is "
45 the l' Adam was made a quickening"
52 twinkling of an eye, at the l' trump: "
Ph'p 4: 10 at the l' your care of me hath *4218
2Ti 3: 1 in the l' days perilous times shall 2078
Heb 1: 2 Hath in the l' days spoken unto us *"
Jas 5: 3 treasure together for the l' days. "
1Pe 1: 5 ready to be revealed in the l' time. "
20 manifest in these l' times for you.* "
2Pe 3: 3 shall come in the l' days scoffers, 2078
1Jo 2: 18 Little children, it is the l' time: and"
18 we know that it is the l' time. "
Jude 18 should be mockers in the l' time, "
Re 1: 11 and Omega, the first and the l': * "
17 Fear not; I am the first and the l'. "
2: 8 things saith the first and the l', "
19 and the l' to be more than the first. "
15: 1 angels having the seven l' plagues; "
21: 9 vials full of the seven l' plagues, "
22: 13 and the end, the first and the l'. "

lasted
J'g 14: 17 the seven days, while their feast l':1961

lasting See also EVERLASTING.
De 33: 15 the precious things of the l' hills. *5769

latchet See also SHOELACHET.
Isa 5: 27 nor the l' of their shoes be broken: 8288
M'r 1: 7 l' of whose shoes I am not worthy 2438
Lu 3: 16 l' of whose shoes I am not worthy "
Joh 1: 27 shoe's l' I am not worthy to unloose."

late See also LAST; LATELY; LATTER.
Ps 127: 2 you to rise up early, to sit up l', 309
Mic 2: 8 of l' my people is risen up as an 865
Joh 11: 8 Jews of l' sought to stone thee; *3568

lately
Ac 18: 2 l' come from Italy, with his wife 4373

Latin (*lat'-in*)
Lu 23: 38 in letters of Greek, and L', and *4513
Joh 19: 20 in Hebrew, and Greek, and L'. "

latter
Ex 4: 8 will believe the voice of the l' sign. 314
Nu 24: 14 do to thy people in the l' days. 319
20 but his l' end shall be that he perish "
De 4: 30 even in the l' days, if thou turn to "
8: 16 thee, to do thee good at thy l' end; "
11: 14 the first rain and the l' rain, 4456
24: 3 if the l' husband hate her, and 314
3 or if the l' husband die, which took "
31: 29 evil will befall you in the l' days; 319
32: 29 they would consider their l' end! "
Ru 3: 10 shewed more kindness in the l' end 314
2Sa 2: 26 it will be bitterness in the l' end? "
Job 8: 7 thy l' end should greatly increase. 319
19: 25 stand at the l' day upon the earth:*314
29: 23 their mouth wide as for the l' rain.4456
42: 12 the Lord blessed the l' end of Job 319
Pr 16: 15 favour is as a cloud of the l' rain. 4456
19: 20 thou mayest be wise in thy l' end. 319
Isa 41: 22 and know the l' end of them; or "
47: 7 didst remember the l' end of it. "
Jer 3: 3 and there hath been no l' rain; 4456
5: 24 rain, both the former and the l', "
23: 20 in the l' days ye shall consider it 319
30: 24 in the l' days ye shall consider it. "
48: 47 the captivity of Moab in the l' days. "
49: 39 it shall come to pass in the l' days, "
Eze 38: 8 in the l' years thou shalt come into "
16 the land; it shall be in the l' days, "
Da 2: 28 what shall be in the l' days. 320
8: 23 And in the l' time of their kingdom,319
10: 14 befall thy people in the l' days: "
11: 29 not be as the former, or as the l'. 314
Ho 3: 5 and his goodness in the l' days. 319
6: 3 as the l' and former rain unto the 4456
Joe 2: 23 and the l' rain in the first month. "
Am 7: 1 the shooting up of the l' growth; 3954
1 l' growth after the king's mowings."
Hag 2: 9 The glory of this l' house shall be 314
Zec 10: 1 rain in the time of the l' rain; 4456
1Ti 4: 1 l' times some shall depart from 5305
Jas 5: 7 he receive the early and l' rain. 3797
2Pe 2: 20 l' end is worse with them than the*2078

lattice
J'g 5: 28 window, and cried through the l', 822
2Ki 1: 2 Ahaziah fell down through a l' in 7639
Ca 2: 9 shewing himself through the l'. 2762

laud
Ro 15: 11 Gentiles; and l' him, all ye people.*1867

laugh See also LAUGHED; LAUGHETH; LAUGHING.
Ge 18: 13 Wherefore did Sarah l', saying, 6711
15 And he said, Nay; but thou didst l'."
21: 6 said, God hath made me to l', 6712
6 that all that hear will l' with me. 6711
Job 5: 22 and famine thou shalt l': neither 7832
9: 23 will l' at the trial of the innocent.*3932
22: 19 and the innocent l' them to scorn. "
Ps 2: 4 sitteth in the heavens shall l': 7832
22: 7 they that see me l' me to scorn: 3932
37: 13 The Lord shall l' at him: for he 7832
52: 6 see, and fear, and shall l' at him: "
59: 8 But thou, O Lord, shalt l' at them "
80: 6 our enemies l' among themselves.3932
Pr 1: 26 I also will l' at your calamity; I 7832
29: 9 he rage or l', there is no rest. "
Ec 3: 4 A time to weep, and a time to l'; "
Lu 6: 21 ye that weep now: for ye shall l'. 1070
25 Woe unto you that l' now! for ye "

laughed
Ge 17: 17 Abraham fell upon his face, and l',6711
18: 12 Sarah l' within herself, saying, "
15 Sarah denied, saying, I l' not; for "
2Ki 19: 21 despised thee, and l' thee to scorn; 3932
2Ch 30: 10 they l' them to scorn, and mocked 7832
Ne 2: 19 heard it, they l' us to scorn, and 3932
Job 12: 4 the just upright man is l' to scorn.*7832
29: 24 If I l' on them, they believed it not; "
Isa 37: 22 despised thee, and l' thee to scorn; 3932
Eze 23: 32 be l' to scorn and had in derision; 6712
M't 9: 24 And they l' him to scorn. 2606
M r 5: 40 they l' him to scorn. But when he "
Lu 8: 53 they l' him to scorn, knowing that "

laugheth
Job41:29 he l' at the shaking of a spear. 7832
laughing
Job 8:21 Till he fill thy mouth with l', and *7814
laughter
Ps 126: 2 Then was our mouth filled with l', 7814
Pr 14:13 Even in l' the heart is sorrowful; "
Ec 2: 2 I said of l', It is mad: and of mirth, "
7: 3 Sorrow is better than l': for by the "
6 under a pot, so is the l' of the fool: "
10:19 A feast is made for l', and wine "
Jas 4: 9 let your l' be turned to mourning, *1071*
launch See also LAUNCHED.
Lu 5: 4 L' out into the deep, and let down**1877*
launched
Lu 8:22 of the lake. And they l' forth. * *321*
Ac 21: 1 were gotten from them, and had l',* "
27: 2 we l', meaning the sail by the * "
4 And when we l' from thence, we * "
laver See also LAVERS; LAVISH.
Ex 30:18 Thou shalt also make a l' of brass,3595
28 his vessels, and the l' and his foot. "
31: 9 furniture, and the l' and his foot, "
35:16 all his vessels, the l' and his foot, "
38: 8 made the l' of brass, and the foot "
39:39 all his vessels, the l' and his foot, "
40: 7 shalt set the l' between the tent "
11 shalt anoint the l' and his foot, "
30 he set the l' between the tent of "
Le 8:11 the l' and his foot, to sanctify them."
1Ki 7:30 under the l' were undersetters "
38 one l' contained forty baths: "
38 every l' was four cubits: and "
38 every one of the ten bases one l'. "
2Ki 16:17 and removed the l' from off them; "
lavers
1Ki 7:38 Then made he ten l' of brass: one 3595
40 Hiram made the l', and the shovels,"
43 ten bases, and ten l' on the bases; "
2Ch 4: 6 He made also ten l', and put five "
14 and l' made he upon the bases; "
lavish
Isa 46: 6 They l' gold out of the bag, and 2107
law See also LAWFUL; LAWGIVER; LAWLESS; LAWS.
Ge 11:31 son, and Sarai his daughter in l', 3618
19:12 son in l', and thy sons, and thy 2859
14 out, and spake unto his sons in l', "
14 that mocked unto his sons in l'. "
38:11 Judah to Tamar his daughter in l',3618
13 father in l' goeth up to Timnath 2524
16 that she was his daughter in l'.) 3618
24 thy daughter in l' hath played the "
25 forth, she sent to her father in l', 2524
47:26 Joseph made it a l' over the land *2706
Ex 3: 1 flock of Jethro his father in l', 2859
4:18 returned to Jethro his father in l', "
12:49 One l' shall be to him that is 8451
13: 9 the Lord's l' may be in thy mouth: "
16: 4 they will walk in my l', or no. "
18: 1 of Midian, Moses' father in l', 2859
2 Moses' father in l', took Zipporah, "
5 Moses' father in l', came with his "
6 I thy father in l' Jethro am come "
7 went out to meet his father in l', "
8 Moses told his father in l' all that "
12 Moses' father in l', took a burnt "
12 eat bread with Moses' father in l' "
14 Moses' father in l' saw all that he "
15 Moses said unto his father in l', "
17 Moses' father in l' said unto him, "
24 to the voice of his father in l', "
27 Moses let his father in l' depart; "
24:12 give thee tables of stone, and a l', 8451
Le 6: 9 This is the l' of the burnt offering: "
14 this is the l' of the meat offering: "
25 This is the l' of the sin offering: "
7: 1 is the l' of the trespass offering: "
7 offering: there is one l' for them: "
11 is the l' of the sacrifice of peace "
37 This is the l' of the burnt offering, "
11:46 the l' of the beasts, and of the fowl, "
12: 7 This is the l' for her that hath born "
13:59 is the l' of the plague of leprosy "
14: 2 shall be the l' of the leper in the "
32 the l' of him in whom is the plague "
54 This is the l' for all manner of "
57 is clean: this is the l' of leprosy. "
15:32 the l' of him that hath an issue, "
18:15 nakedness of thy daughter in l': 3618
20:12 a man lie with his daughter in l', "
24:22 Ye shall have one manner of l', 4941
Nu 5:29 This is the l' of jealousies, when 8451
30 shall execute upon her all this l'. "
6:13 And this is the l' of the Nazarite, "
21 This is the l' of the Nazarite who "
21 do after the l' of his separation. "
10:29 the Midianite, Moses' father in l', 2859
15:16 One l' and one manner shall be for8451
29 have one l' for him that sinneth "
19: 2 is the ordinance of the l' which the "
14 This is the l', when a man dieth in "
31:21 the ordinance of the l' which the "
De 1: 5 Moses to declare this l', saying, "
4: 8 so righteous as all this l', which "
44 And this is the l' which Moses set "
17:11 to the sentence of the l' which they "
18 write him a copy of this l' in a book "
19 keep all the words of this l' and "
27: 3 upon them all the words of this l', "
8 all the words of this l' very plainly. "
23 he that lieth with his mother in l'. 2859

De 27:26 all the words of this l' to do them. 8451
28:58 do all the words of this l' that are "
61 is not written in the book of this l', "
29:21 are written in this book of the l': "
29 we may do all the words of this l'. "
30:10 are written in this book of the l', "
31: 9 Moses wrote this l', and delivered "
11 shalt read this l' before all Israel "
12 to do all the words of this l': "
24 the words of this l' in a book, "
26 Take this book of the l', and put it "
32:46 to do, all the words of this l'. "
33: 2 right hand went a fiery l' for them.1881
4 Moses commanded us a l', even 8451
10 thy judgments, and Israel thy l': "
Jos 1: 7 observe to do according to all the l', "
8 This book of the l' shall not depart "
8:31 in the book of the l' of Moses, "
32 the stones a copy of the l' of Moses, "
34 he read all the words of the l', "
34 that is written in the book of the l'. "
22: 5 do the commandment and the l', "
23: 6 in the book of the l' of Moses, "
24:26 words in the book of the l' of God, "
J'g 1:16 Moses' father in l', went up out of 2859
4:11 of Hobab the father in l' of Moses, "
15: 6 Samson, the son in l' of the Timnite," "
19: 4 his father in l', the damsel's father, "
5 father said unto his son in l', "
7 depart, his father in l' urged him: "
9 his servant, his father in l', the "
Ru 1: 6 she arose with her daughters in l',3618
7 her two daughters in l' with her; "
8 said unto her two daughters in l', "
14 Orpah kissed her mother in l'; 2545
15 thy sister in l' is gone back unto her2994
15 return thou after thy sister in l'. "
22 the Moabitess, her daughter in l', 3618
2:11 hast done unto thy mother in l' 2545
18 her mother in l' saw what she had "
19 her mother in l' said unto her, "
19 shewed her mother in l' with whom "
20 said unto her daughter in l', 3618
22 said unto Ruth her daughter in l', "
23 and dwelt with her mother in l'. 2545
3: 1 her mother in l' said unto her, "
6 all that her mother in l' bade her. "
16 when she came to her mother in l', "
17 Go not empty unto thy mother in l'." "
4:15 thy daughter in l', which loveth 3618
1Sa 4:19 his daughter in l', Phinehas' wife, "
19 her father in l' and her husband 2524
21 because of her father in l' and her "
18:18 I should be son in l' to the king? 2859
21 Thou shalt this day be my son in l'2860
22 therefore be the king's son in l'. "
23 a light thing to be a king's son in l', "
26 David well to be the king's son in l': "
27 he might be the king's son in l'. "
22:14 which is the king's son in l', and 2859
1Ki 2: 3 as it is written in the l' of Moses, 8451
2Ki 8:27 the son in l' of the house of Ahab. 2859
10:31 to walk in the l' of the Lord God 8451
14: 6 in the book of the l' of Moses, "
17:13 according to all the l' which I "
34 or after the l' and commandment "
37 and the l', and the commandment, "
21: 8 to all the l' that my servant Moses "
22: 8 I have found the book of the l' in "
11 the words of the book of the l', "
23:24 might perform the words of the l' "
25 according to all the l' of Moses; "
1Ch 2: 4 his daughter in l' bare him Pharez 3618
16:17 the same to Jacob for a l', and *2706
40 is written in the l' of the Lord, 8451
22:12 thou mayest keep the l' of the Lord "
2Ch 6:16 heed to their way to walk in my l', "
12: 1 forsook the l' of the Lord, and all "
14: 4 to do the l' and the commandment. "
15: 3 a teaching priest, and without l'. "
17: 9 had the book of the l' of the Lord "
19:10 between l' and commandment, "
23:18 as it is written in the l' of Moses, "
25: 4 as it is written in the l' of the book "
30:16 according to the l' of Moses the "
31: 3 as it is written in the l' of the Lord. "
4 encouraged in the l' of the Lord. "
21 in the l', and in the commandments, "
33: 8 to the whole l' and the statutes "
34:14 priest found a book of the l' of the "
15 have found the book of the l' in the "
19 king had heard the words of the l', "
35:26 was written in the l' of the Lord, "
Ezr 3: 2 as it is written in the l' of Moses "
7: 6 a ready scribe in the l' of Moses, "
10 his heart to seek the l' of the Lord, "
12 a scribe of the l' of the God of 1882
14 according to the l' of thy God which "
21 the scribe of the l' of the God of "
26 will not do the l' of thy God, and "
26 the l' of the king, let judgment be "
10: 3 let it be done according to the l'. 8451
Ne 6:18 the son in l' of Shechaniah the son2859
8: 1 bring the book of the l' of Moses, 8451
2 And Ezra the priest brought the l' "
3 attentive unto the book of the l'. "
7 the people to understand the l': "
8 read in the book in the l' of God "
9 when they heard the words of the l'. "
13 to understand the words of the l'. "
14 found written in the l' which the "
18 read in the book of the l' of God. "
9: 3 read in the book of the l' of the "
26 cast thy l' behind their backs, and "
29 bring them again unto thy l': "
34 kept thy l', nor hearkened unto thy "

Ne 10:28 of the lands unto the l' of God, 8451
29 into an oath, to walk in God's l', "
34 our God, as it is written in the l': "
36 as it is written in the l', and the "
12:44 the portions of the l' for the priests "
13: 3 to pass, when they had heard the l', "
28 was son in l' to Sanballat the 2859
Es 1: 8 drinking was according to the l'; 1881
13 all that knew l' and judgment: "
15 the queen Vashti according to l', "
4:11 is one l' of his to put him to death, "
16 which is not according to the l': "
Job 22:22 I pray thee, the l' from his mouth,8451
Ps 1: 2 his delight is in the l' of the Lord; "
2 in his l' doth he meditate day and "
19: 7 The l' of the Lord is perfect, "
37:31 The l' of his God is in his heart; "
40: 8 God: yea, thy l' is within my heart. "
78: 1 Give ear, O my people, to my l': "
5 Jacob, and appointed a l' in Israel, "
10 God, and refused to walk in his l'; "
81: 4 and a l' of the God of Jacob. *4941
89:30 If his children forsake my l', and 8451
94:12 and teachest him out of thy l'; "
20 which frameth mischief by a l'? 2706
105:10 the same unto Jacob for a l', and * "
119: 1 who walk in the l' of the Lord. 8451
18 wondrous things out of thy l'. "
29 and grant me thy l' graciously. "
34 and I shall keep thy l'; yea, I shall "
44 So shall I keep thy l' continually "
51 yet have I not declined from thy l'. "
53 of the wicked that forsake thy l'. "
55 in the night, and have kept thy l'. "
61 but I have not forgotten thy l'. "
70 as grease; but I delight in thy l'. "
72 The l' of thy mouth is better unto "
77 may live: for thy l' is my delight. "
85 for me, which are not after thy l'. "
92 Unless thy l' had been my delights, "
97 O how love I thy l'! it is my "
109 hand: yet do I not forget thy l'. "
113 vain thoughts: but thy l' do I love. "
126 for they have made void thy l'. "
136 eyes, because they keep not thy l'. "
142 and thy l' is the truth. "
150 mischief: they are far from thy l'. "
153 me: for I do not forget thy l'. "
163 abhor lying: but thy l' do I love. "
165 peace have they which love thy l': "
174 O Lord; and thy l' is my delight. "
Pr 1: 8 forsake not the l' of thy mother: "
3: 1 My son, forget not my l'; but let "
4: 2 doctrine, forsake ye not my l'. "
6:20 forsake not the l' of thy mother: "
23 is a lamp; and the l' is light; "
7: 2 my l' as the apple of thine eye. "
13:14 l' of the wise is a fountain of life, "
28: 4 They that forsake the l' praise the "
4 as keep the l' contend with them. "
7 Whoso keepeth the l' is a wise son: "
9 away his ear from hearing the l', "
29:18 he that keepeth the l', happy is he. "
31: 5 Lest they drink, and forget the l', 2710
26 in her tongue is the l' of kindness. 8451
Isa 1:10 give ear unto the l' of our God, ye "
2: 3 for out of Zion shall go forth the l', "
5:24 have cast away the l' of the Lord "
8:16 seal the l' among my disciples. "
20 To the l' and to the testimony: "
30: 9 will not hear the l' of the Lord: "
42: 4 and the isles shall wait for his l'. "
21 he will magnify the l', and make it "
24 were they obedient unto his l'. "
51: 4 for a l' shall proceed from me, and "
7 the people in whose heart is my l'; "
Jer 2: 8 that handle the l' knew me not: "
6:19 unto my words, nor to my l'. "
8: 8 and the l' of the Lord is with us? "
9:13 they have forsaken my l' which I "
16:11 me, and have not kept my l'; "
18:18 for the l' shall not perish from the "
26: 4 not hearken to me, to walk in my l', "
31:33 will put my l' in their inward parts, "
32:11 according to the l' and custom, 4687
23 thy voice, neither walked in thy l';8451
44:10 they feared, nor walked in my l', "
23 of the Lord, nor walked in his l', "
La 2: 9 the l' is no more; her prophets also "
Eze 7:26 the l' shall perish from the priest, "
22:11 lewdly defiled his daughter in l'; 3618
26 Her priests have violated my l', 8451
43:12 This is the l' of the house; upon "
12 Behold, this is the l' of the house. "
Da 6: 5 him concerning the l' of his God. 1882
8, 12 l' of the Medes and Persians, "
15 the l' of the Medes and Persians is, "
9:11 Israel have transgressed thy l', 8451
11 that is written in the l' of Moses the "
13 As it is written in the l' of Moses, "
Ho 4: 6 hast forgotten the l' of thy God, "
8: 1 and trespassed against my l'. "
12 to him the great things of my l', "
Am 2: 4 have despised the l' of the Lord, "
Mic 4: 2 for the l' shall go forth of Zion, and "
7: 6 daughter in l' against her mother 3618
6 daughter...against her mother in l';2545
Hab 1: 4 Therefore the l' is slacked, and 8451
Zep 3: 4 they have done violence to the l'. "
Hag 2:11 now the priests concerning the l', "
Zec 7:12 stone, lest they should hear the l', "
Mal 2: 6 The l' of truth was in his mouth, "
7 should seek the l' at his mouth: "
8 caused many to stumble at the l'; "
9 but have been partial in the l'. "
4: 4 Remember ye the l' of Moses my "

M't 5:17 that I am come to destroy the l', 3551
18 shall in no wise pass from the l', till"
40 if any man will sue thee at the l',
7:12 for this is the l' and the prophets. 3551
10:35 daughter in l' against her mother 3565
35 daughter...against her mother in l'.3994
11:13 and the l' prophesied until John. 3551
12: 5 have ye not read in the l', how that "
22:36 the great commandment in the l'? "
40 commandments hang all the l' and "
23:23 the weightier matters of the l', "
Lu 2:22 according to the l' of Moses were "
23 it is written in the l' of the Lord, "
24 which is said in the l' of the Lord, "
27 for him after the custom of the l', "
39 according to the l' of the Lord, "
5:17 and doctors of the l' sitting by, 3547
10:26 him, What is written in the l'? 3551
12:53 mother in l' against her daughter 3994
53 mother...against her daughter in l' 3565
53 daughter in l' against her mother "
53 daughter...against her mother in l'.3994
16:16 The l' and the prophets were until 3551
17 pass, than one tittle of the l' to fail."
24:44 were written in the l' of Moses, "
Joh 1:17 For the l' was given by Moses, but "
45 found him, of whom Moses in the l', "
7:19 Did not Moses give you the l', and "
19 and yet none of you keepeth the l'? "
23 l' of Moses should not be broken; "
49 who knoweth not the l' are cursed. "
51 Doth our l' judge any man, before "
8: 5 Now Moses in the l' commanded us, "
17 It is also written in your l', that "
10:34 them, Is it not written in your l', "
12:34 have heard out of the l' that Christ "
15:25 be fulfilled that is written in their l', "
18:13 for he was father in l' to Caiaphas, 3995
31 judge him according to your l'. 3551
19: 7 a l', and by our l' he ought to die, "
Ac 5:34 named Gamaliel, a doctor of the l',3547
6:13 against this holy place, and the l': 3551
7:53 received the l' by the disposition "
13:15 after the reading of the l' and the "
39 not be justified by the l' of Moses. "
15: 5 them to keep the l' of Moses. "
24 be circumcised, and keep the l': * "
18:13 to worship God contrary to the l'. "
15 of words and names, and of your l',* "
19:38 l' is open, and there are deputies:* 60
21:20 and they are all zealous of the l': 3551
24 walkest orderly, and keepest the l'. "
28 against the people, and the l', and "
22: 3 to the perfect manner of the l' of "
12 a devout man according to the l', "
23: 3 sittest thou to judge me after the l',"
3 to be smitten contrary to the l'? 3891
29 be accused of questions of their l'.3551
24: 6 have judged according to our l'. "
14 all things which are written in the l'" "
25: 8 Neither against the l' of the Jews, "
28:23 Jesus, both out of the l' of Moses, "
Ro 2:12 as many as have sinned without l' 460
12 shall also perish without l': "
12 as many as have sinned in the l' 3551
12 shall be judged by the l'; "
13 not the hearers of the l' are just "
13 the doers of the l' shall be justified."
14 the Gentiles, which have not the l', "
14 do...the things contained in the l', "
14 having not the l', are a l' unto "
15 of the l' written in their hearts, "
17 called a Jew, and restest in the l', "
18 being instructed out of the l'; "
20 knowledge and of the truth in the l'."
23 that makest thy boast of the l', "
23 through breaking the l' dishonorest"
25 verily profiteth, if thou keep the l': "
25 but if thou be a breaker of the l', "
26 keep the righteousness of the l', "
27 which is by nature, if it fulfil the l', "
27 thee, who...dost transgress the l'? "
3:19 that what things soever the l' saith, "
19 saith to them who are under the l': "
20 by the deeds of the l' there shall no "
20 for by the l' is the knowledge of sin."
21 of God without the l' is manifested,"
21 being witnessed by the l' and the "
27 By what l'? of works? Nay: but by"
27 Nay: but by the l' of faith. "
28 by faith without the deeds of the l'. "
31 make void the l' through faith? "
31 God forbid: yea, we establish the l'."
4:13 or to his seed, through the l', but "
14 if they which are of the l' be heirs, "
15 Because the l' worketh wrath; "
15 no l' is, there is no transgression. "
16 not to that only which is of the l', "
5:13 until the l' sin was in the world: "
13 is not imputed where there is no l'. "
20 Moreover the l' entered, that the "
6:14 ye are not under the l', but under "
15 we are not under the l', but under "
7: 1 I speak to them that know the l',) "
1 the l' hath dominion over a man as "
2 is bound by the l' to her husband so"
2 is loosed from the l' of her husband."
3 be dead she is free from that l'; "
4 become dead to the l' by the body "
5 sins, which were by the l', did work "
6 now we are delivered from the l', "
7 say then, Is the l' sin? God forbid."
7 I had not known sin, but by the l': "
7 known lust, except the l' had said, "
8 For without the l' sin was dead. "
9 For I was alive without the l' once:"

Ro 7:12 Wherefore the l' is holy, and the 3551
14 For we know that the l' is spiritual: "
16 I consent unto the l' that it is good. "
21 I find then a l', that, when I would "
22 I delight in the l' of God after the "
23 I see another l' in my members, "
23 warring against the l' of my mind, "
23 me into captivity to the l' of sin "
25 mind I myself serve the l' of God, "
25 but with the flesh the l' of sin. "
8: 2 the l' of the Spirit of life in Christ "
2 me free from the l' of sin and death."
3 what the l' could not do, in that it "
4 the righteousness of the l' might be"
7 not subject to the l' of God, neither"
9: 4 and the giving of the l', and the 3548
31 after the l' of righteousness, 3551
31 attained to the l' of righteousness. "
32 as it were by the works of the l'. * "
10: 4 For Christ is the end of the l' for "
5 the righteousness which is of the l', "
13: 8 loveth another hath fulfilled the l'. "
10 love is the fulfilling of the l'. "
1Co 6: 1 go to l' before the unjust, and not 2919
6 brother goeth to l' with brother, "
7 ye go to l' one with another. *2917
7:39 wife is bound by the l' as long as *3551
9: 8 or saith not the l' the same also? "
9 For it is written in the l' of Moses, "
20 are under the l', as under the l', "
20 gain them that are under the l'; "
21 that are without l', as without l', 459
21 (being not without l' to God, "
21 but under the l' to Christ,) 1772
21 might gain them that are without l'.459
14:21 In the l' it is written, With men of 3551
34 under obedience, as also saith the l'. "
15:56 sin; and the strength of sin is the l'. "
Ga 2:16 not justified by the works of the l', "
16 and not by the works of the l': for "
16 by the works of the l' shall no flesh "
19 I through the l' am dead to the l', "
21 for if righteousness come by the l', "
3: 2 ye the Spirit by the works of the l', "
5 doeth he it by the works of the l', "
10 many as are of the works of the l' "
10 are written in the book of the l' to "
11 no man is justified by the l' in the "
12 And the l' is not of faith: but, The "
13 redeemed us from the curse of the l',"
17 the l', which was four hundred and"
18 For if the inheritance be of the l', "
19 Wherefore then serveth the l'? "
21 Is the l' then against the promises "
21 if there had been a l' given which "
21 righteousness...have been by the l'. "
23 came, we were kept under the l', "
24 the l' was our schoolmaster to bring"
4: 4 of a woman, made under the l', "
5 redeem them that were under the l', "
21 be under the l', do ye not hear the l'?"
5: 3 he is a debtor to do the whole l'. "
4 of you are justified by the l'; "
14 all the l' is fulfilled in one word, "
18 the Spirit, ye are not under the l'. "
23 against such there is no l'. "
6: 2 and so fulfil the l' of Christ. "
13 who are circumcised keep the l'; "
Eph 2:15 l' of commandments contained "
Ph'p 3: 5 as touching the l', a Pharisee; "
6 the righteousness which is in the l',"
9 righteousness, which is of the l', "
1Ti 1: 7 Desiring to be teachers of the l'; 3547
8 But we know that the l' is good, 3551
9 l' is not made for a righteous man, "
Tit 3: 9 and strivings about the l'; 3544
Heb 7: 5 of the people according to the l', 3551
11 under it the people received the l',)3549
12 necessity a change also of the l'. 3551
16 the l' of a carnal commandment, "
19 the l' made nothing perfect, but the "
28 For the l' maketh men high priests "
28 of the oath, which was since the l', "
8: 4 that offer gifts according to the l': "
9:19 to all the people according to the l',"
22 are by the l' purged with blood; "
10: 1 l' having a shadow of good things "
8 therein; which are offered by the l';"
28 He that despised Moses' l' died "
Jas 1:25 into the perfect l' of liberty, "
2: 8 If ye fulfil the royal l' according to "
9 sin, and are convinced of the l' as "
10 whosoever shall keep the whole l', "
11 art become a transgressor of the l' "
12 shall be judged by the l' of liberty. "
4:11 evil of the l', and judgeth the l': "
11 but if thou judge the l', thou art "
11 not a doer of the l', but a judge. "
1Jo 3: 4 sin transgresseth also the l': *4160,458
4 for sin is the transgression of the l'.*"

lawful See also UNLAWFUL.
Ezr 7:24 it shall not be l' to impose toll, 7990
Isa 49:24 mighty, or the l' captive delivered?6662
Eze 18: 5 and do that which is l' and right, 4941
19 have done that which is l' and right,"
21 and do that which is l' and right, he"
27 doeth that which is l' and right, he "
33:14 and do that which is l' and right; "
16 hath done that which is l' and right;"
19 and do that which is l' and right, he"
M't 12: 2 is not l' to do upon the sabbath day.1832
4 which was not l' for him to eat, "
10 Is it l' to heal on the sabbath days? "
12 l' to do well on the sabbath days. "
14: 4 It is not l' for thee to have her. "
19: 3 Is it l' for a man to put away his "
M't 20:15 Is it not l' for me to do what I will 1833
22:17 Is it l' to give tribute unto Cæsar, "
27: 6 It is not l' for to put them into the "
M'r 2:24 sabbath day that which is not l'? "
26 is not l' to eat but for the priests, "
3: 4 Is it l' to do good on the sabbath "
6:18 It is not l'...to have thy brother's "
10: 2 l' for a man to put away his wife? "
12:14 Is it l' to give tribute to Cæsar, or "
Lu 6: 2 which is not l' to do on the sabbath "
4 is not l' to eat but for the priests "
9 it l' on the sabbath days to do good,"
14: 3 Is it l' to heal on the sabbath day? "
20:22 l' for us to give tribute unto Cæsar, "
Joh 5:10 it is not l' for thee to carry thy bed."
18:31 l' for us to put any man to death: "
Ac 16:21 which are not l' for us to receive, "
19:39 be determined in a l' assembly. *1772
22:25 l' for you to scourge a man that is 1832
1Co 6:12 All things are l' unto me, but all "
12 all things are l' for me, but I will "
10:23 All things are l' for me, but all "
23 all things are l' for me, but all "
2Co 12: 4 which it is not l' for a man to utter."

lawfully
1Ti 1: 8 the law is good, if a man use it l'; 3545
2Ti 2: 5 he not crowned, except he strive l'. "

lawgiver
Ge 49:10 nor a l' from between his feet, *2710
Nu 21:18 digged it, by the direction of the l',*"
De 33:21 a portion of the l', was he seated;* "
Ps 60: 7 of mine head; Judah is my l'; * "
108: 8 of mine head; Judah is my l'; * "
Isa 33:22 the Lord is our l', the Lord is our "
Jas 4:12 There is one l', who is able to save3550

lawless
1Ti 1: 9 man, but for the l' and disobedient, 459

laws
Ge 26: 5 my statutes, and my l'. 8451
Ex 16:28 keep my commandments and my l'?"
18:16 know the statutes of God, and his l'."
20 shalt teach them ordinances and l', "
Le 26:46 the statutes and judgments and l', "
Ezr 7:25 such as know the l' of thy God; 1882
Ne 9:13 them right judgments, and true l',8451
14 them precepts, statutes, and l', * "
Es 1:19 l' of the Persians and the Medes, 1881
3: 8 their l' are diverse from all people; "
8 neither keep they the king's l': "
Ps 105:45 observe his statutes,...keep his l'. 8541
Isa 24: 5 they have transgressed the l', 8451
Eze 43:11 forms thereof, and all the l' thereof:"
44: 5 of the Lord, and all the l' thereof; "
24 they shall keep my l' and my "
Da 7:25 and think to change times and l':*1882
9:10 to walk in his l', which he set 8451
Heb 8:10 I will put my l' into their mind, 3551
10:16 I will put my l' into their hearts, "

lawyer See also LAWYERS.
M't 22:35 was a l', asked him a question, 3544
Lu 10:25 a certain l' stood up, and tempted "
Tit 3:13 Bring Zenas the l' and Apollos on "

lawyers
Lu 7:30 and l' rejected the counsel of God 3544
11:45 answered one of the l', and said "
46 he said, Woe unto you also, ye l'! "
52 Woe unto you, l'! for ye have taken"
14: 3 spake unto the l' and Pharisees. "

lay See also LAID; LAIN; LAYEDST; LAYEST; LAYETH; LAYING; LIE; OVERLAY.
Ge 19: 4 before they l' down, the men of 7901
33 went in, and l' with her father; "
33 he perceived not when she l' down, "
34 I l' yesternight with my father; "
35 the younger arose, and l' with him;"
35 he perceived not when she l' down, "
22:12 L' not thine hand upon the lad, 7971
28:11 and l' down in that place to sleep. 7901
30:16 And he l' with her that night. "
34: 2 he took her, and l' with her, and "
35:22 Reuben went and l' with Bilhah his "
37:22 l' no hand upon him; that he 7971
41:35 and l' up corn under the hand of 6651
Ex 5: 8 heretofore, ye shall l' upon them; 7760
7: 4 I may l' my hand upon Egypt, 5414
16:13 the dew l' round about the host. 7902
14 when the dew that l' was gone up, "
14 the wilderness there l' a small round* "
23 remaineth over l' up for you to 3241
33 l' it up before the Lord, to be kept "
21:22 woman's husband will l' upon him;7896
22:25 shalt thou l' upon him usury. 7760
Le 1: 7 l' the wood in order upon the fire: "
8 shall l' the parts,...in order upon "
12 the priest shall l' them in order on "
2:15 it, and l' frankincense thereon: 7760
3:2, 8, 13 he shall l' his hand upon the 5564
4: 4 shall l' his hand upon the bullock's "
15 shall l' their hands upon the head "
24, 29, 33 he shall l' his hand upon the "
6:12 l' the burnt offering in order upon "
16:21 Aaron shall l' both his hands upon5564
24:14 him l' their hands upon his head, "
Nu 8:12 Levites shall l' their hands upon "
12:11 thee, l' not the sin upon us, 7896
17: 4 shalt l' them up in the tabernacle 3241
19: 9 l' them up without the camp in a "
24: 9 He couched, he l' down as a lion, 7901
27:18 and l' thine hand upon him; 5564
De 7:15 will l' them upon all them that 5414
11:18 shall ye l' up these my words in 7760
25 your God shall l' the fear of you 5414
14:28 shalt l' it up within thy gates: 3241

De 21: 8 l' not innocent blood unto thy *5414
19 his father and his mother l' hold
22: 22 the man that l' with the woman, 7901
25 man only that l' with her shall die: "
28 and l' hold on her, and lie with her,
29 man that l' with her shall give 7901
Jos 6: 26 he shall l' the foundation thereof
8: 2 l' thee an ambush for the city *7760
15: 46 unto the sea, all that l' near Ashdod,*
J'g 4: 22 Sisera l' dead, and the nail was 5307
5: 27 feet he bowed, he fell, he l' down: 7901
6: 20 cakes, and l' them upon this rock, 3241
7: 12 children of the east l' along in the 5307
13 overturned it, that the tent l' along."
14: 17 her, because she l' sore upon him:*
16: 3 Samson l' till midnight, and arose 7901
18: 19 l' thine hand upon thy mouth, 7760
Ru 3: 4 uncover his feet, and l' thee down; 7901
8 and, behold, a woman l' at his feet. "
14 she l' at his feet until the morning: "
1Sa 2: 22 how they l' with the women that "
3: 5 again. And he went and l' down. "
9 Samuel went and l' down in his "
15 And Samuel l' until the morning, "
6: 8 the Lord, and l' it upon the cart; 5414
11: 2 l' it for a reproach upon all Israel. 7760
19: 24 l' down naked all that day and all 5307
26: 5 beheld the place where Saul l', 7901
5 Saul l' in the trench, and the people"
7 Saul l' sleeping within the trench, "
7 and the people l' round about him. "
2Sa 2: 21 and l' thee hold on one of the young
4: 5 who l' on a bed at noon. *7901
7 l' on his bed in his bedchamber, "
11: 4 in unto him, and he l' with her; "
12: 3 his own cup, and l' in his bosom, "
16 and l' all night upon the earth. "
24 went in unto her, and l' with her: "
13: 5 L' thee down on thy bed, and make "
6 Amnon l' down, and made himself "
14 than she, forced her, and l' with her. "
31 his garments, and l' on the earth; "
19: 32 while he l' at Mahanaim; for he 7871
1Ki 5: 17 to l' the foundation of the house.
7: 3 l' on forty-five pillars, fifteen in a row.*
13: 4 the altar, saying, L' hold on him.
31 l' my bones beside his bones: 3241
18: 23 cut it in pieces, and l' it on wood, 7760
23 other bullock, and l' it on wood,
19: 5 l' and slept under a juniper tree, 7901
21: 27 fasted, and l' in sackcloth, and "
2Ki 4: 11 into the chamber, and l' there. "
29 l' my staff upon the face of the 7760
34 he went up, and l' upon the child, 7901
9: 16 went to Jezreel; for Joram l' there. "
10: 8 L' ye them in two heaps at the 7760
19: 25 l' waste fenced cities into ruinous
2Ch 31: 7 l' the foundation of the heaps,
36: 21 as long as she l' desolate she kept
Ezr 8: 31 of such as l' in wait by the way. *
Ne 13: 21 do so again, I will l' hands on you. 7971
Es 2: 21 sought to l' hand on the king
3: 6 scorn to l' hands on Mordecai alone;"
4: 3 many l' in sackcloth and ashes. 3331
6: 2 who sought to l' hand on the king 7971
9: 2 to l' hand on such as sought their "
Job 9: 33 might l' his hand upon us both. 7896
17: 3 L' down now, put me in a surety *7760
21: 5 l' your hand upon your mouth. "
22: 22 and l' up his words in thine heart. "
24 Then shalt thou l' up gold as dust, 7896
29: 19 dew l' all night upon my branch. *3885
34: 23 he will not l' upon man more than *7760
40: 4 I will l' mine hand upon my mouth."
41: 8 L' thine hand upon him, remember"
Ps 4: 8 I will both l' me down in peace, 7901
7: 5 and l' mine honour in the dust. 7931
38: 12 that seek after my life l' snares
71: 10 they that l' wait for my soul take *
84: 3 where she may l' her young, 7896
104: 22 and l' them down in their dens. 7257
Pr 1: 11 with us, let us l' wait for blood,
18 they l' wait for their own blood;
3: 18 life to them that l' hold upon her:
7: 1 l' up my commandments with thee. 6845
10: 14 Wise men l' up knowledge: but the "
24: 15 L' not wait, O wicked man, against
30: 32 evil, l' thine hand upon thy mouth.
Ec 2: 3 and to l' hold on folly, till I might see
7: 2 the living will l' it to his heart. 5414
Isa 5: 6 And I will l' it waste: it shall not be
8 that l' field to field, till there be no 7126
29 shall roar, and l' hold of the prey,
11: 14 they shall l' their hand upon Edom 7971
13: 9 anger, to l' the land desolate: *
11 will l' low the haughtiness of the
22: 22 key...will I l' upon his shoulder; 5414
25: 12 walls shall he bring down, l' low, *
28: 16 l' in Zion for a foundation a stone,
17 Judgment also will I l' to the line,*7760
29: 3 l' siege against thee with a mount,
21 l' a snare for him that reproveth in
30: 32 which the Lord shall l' upon him, 5117
34: 15 great owl make her nest, and l', 4422
35: 7 where each l', shall be grass with 7258
37: 26 l' waste defenced cities into ruinous
38: 21 and l' it for a plaister upon the boil,
47: 7 didst not l'...things to thy heart, 7760
51: 16 and l' the foundations of the earth,
54: 11 will l' thy stones with fair colours, 7257
11 and l' thy foundations with sapphires.
Jer 5: 26 l' wait, as he that setteth snares; *
6: 21 will l' stumblingblocks before 5414
23 shall l' hold on bow and spear;
Eze 3: 20 I l' a stumblingblock before him, 5414
4: 1 thee a tile, and l' it before thee, "
Eze 4: 2 l' siege against it, and build a fort 5414
3 and thou shalt l' siege against it.
4 l' the iniquity of the house of 7760
8 behold, I will l' bands upon thee,
6: 5 I will l' the dead carcases of the 5414
19: 2 lioness: she l' down among lions, *7257
23: 8 for in her youth they l' with her, 7901
25: 14 will l' my vengeance upon Edom 5414
17 when I shall l' my vengeance upon "
26: 12 they shall l' thy stones and thy 7760
16 l' away their robes, and put off 5493
28: 17 I will l' thee before kings, that *5414
32: 5 will l' thy flesh upon the mountains,"
33: 28 I will l' the land most desolate, * "
35: 4 I will l' thy cities waste, and thou 7760
36: 29 it, and l' no famine upon you. 5414
34 whereas it l' desolate in the sight of *
37: 6 I will l' sinews upon you, and will 5414
42: 13 shall they l' the most holy things, 3241
14 there they shall l' their garments "
44: 19 l' them in the holy chambers, and "
Am 2: 8 they l' themselves down upon 5186
Jon 1: 5 and he l', and was fast asleep. 7901
14 and l' not upon us innocent blood: 5414
Mic 1: 7 the idols thereof will I l' desolate: 7760
7: 16 l' their hand upon their mouth, "
Zec 14: 13 they shall l' hold every one on
Mal 2: 2 and if ye will not l' it to heart, 7760
2 because ye do not l' it to heart. "
M't 6: 19 L' not up for yourselves treasures
20 l' up for yourselves treasures in
8: 20 man hath not where to l' his head. 2827
9: 18 come and l' thy hand upon her, 2007
12: 11 will he not l' hold on it, and lift it
21: 46 they sought to l' hands on him,
23: 4 and l' them on men's shoulders; 2007
28: 6 see the place where the Lord l'. 2749
M'r 1: 30 Simon's wife's mother l' sick of a 2621
2: 4 bed wherein the sick of the palsy l'."
3: 21 it, they went out to l' hold on him:
5: 23 come and l' thy hands on her, that 2007
12: 12 And they sought to l' hold on him,
15: 7 one named Barabbas, which l' bound *
16: 18 they shall l' hands on the sick, 2007
Lu 5: 18 him in, and to l' him before him. 5087
25 and took up that whereon he l', 2621
8: 42 years of age, and she l' a dying.
9: 58 man hath not where to l' his head. 2827
19: 44 shall l' thee even with the ground, *1474
20: 19 hour sought to l' hands on him; 1911
21: 12 they shall l' their hands on you,
Joh 5: 3 l' a great multitude of impotent 2621
10: 15 and I l' down my life for the sheep. 5087
17 love me, because I l' down my life "
18 from me, but I l' it down of myself."
18 I have power to l' it down, and I "
11: 38 was a cave, and a stone l' upon it. 1945
13: 37 I will l' down my life for thy sake. 5087
38 Wilt thou l' down thy life for my "
15: 13 man l' down his life for his friends. "
Ac 7: 60 l' not this sin to their charge. 2476
8: 19 that on whomsoever I l' hands, 2007
15: 28 to l' upon you no greater burden
27: 20 and no small tempest l' on us, all 1945
28: 8 father of Publius l' sick of a fever 2621
Ro 8: 33 Who shall l' any thing to the charge 1458
9: 33 I l' in Sion a stumblingstone and 5087
1Co 3: 11 other foundation can no man l' "
16: 2 every one of you l' by him in store, "
2Co 12: 14 ought not to l' up for the parents, 2343
1Ti 5: 22 L' hands suddenly on no man, 2007
6: 12 of faith, l' hold on eternal life, 1949
19 they may l' hold on eternal life. "
Heb 6: 18 to l' hold upon the hope set before us:
12: 1 let us l' aside every weight, and the 659
Jas 1: 21 Wherefore l' apart all filthiness * "
1Pe 2: 6 I l' in Sion a chief corner stone, 5087
1Jo 3: 16 we ought to l' down our lives for "

layedst See also LAIDST.
Lu 19: 21 takest up that thou l' not down, 5087

layest
Nu 11: 11 l' the burden of all this people 7760
1Sa 28: 9 then l' thou a snare for my life, to

layeth
Job 21: 19 God l' up his iniquity for his 6845
24: 12 out: yet God l' not folly to them. ††7760
41: 26 sword of him that l' at him cannot *5381
Ps 33: 7 he l' up the depth in storehouses. 5414
104: 3 Who l' the beams of his chambers 7760
Pr 2: 7 He l' up sound wisdom for the 6845
13: 16 but a fool l' open his folly. *
26: 24 lips, and l' up deceit within him; 7896
31: 19 She l' her hands to the spindle, 7971
Isa 26: 5 high; the lofty city, he l' it low;
5 he l' it low, even to the ground;
56: 2 the son of man that l' hold on it; *
57: 1 and no man l' it to heart: and 7760
Jer 9: 8 mouth, but in heart he l' his wait.
12: 11 because no man l' it to heart.
Zec 12: 1 l' the foundation of the earth, and
Lu 12: 21 he that l' up treasure for himself,
15: 5 found it, he l' it on his shoulders, 2007

laying See also OVERLAYING.
Nu 35: 20 or hurl at him by l' of wait, that *
22 him any thing without l' of wait, *
Ps 64: 5 they commune of l' snares privily 2934
M'r 7: 8 l' aside the commandment of God.* 863
Lu 11: 54 L' wait for him, and seeking to 1748
Ac 8: 18 through l' on of the apostles' hands 1936
9: 24 their l' await was known of Saul. 1917
25: 3 l' wait in the way to kill him. 4160
1Ti 4: 14 with the l' on of the hands of the 1936
6: 19 L' up in store for themselves a good 597
Heb 6: 1 not l' again the foundation of 2598
Heb 6: 2 baptisms, and of l' on of hands, 1936
1Pe 2: 1 l' aside all malice, and all guile, * 659

Lazarus (*laz'-a-rus*)
Lu 16: 20 was a certain beggar named L', 2976
23 afar off, and L' in his bosom. "
24 have mercy on me, and send L', "
25 things, and likewise L' evil things: "
Joh 11: 1 a certain man was sick, named L', "
2 her hair, whose brother L' was sick.)"
5 Martha, and her sister, and L'. "
11 unto them, Our friend L' sleepeth; "
14 unto them plainly, L' is dead. "
43 with a loud voice, L', come forth. "
12: 1 where L' was which had been dead, "
2 L' was one of them that sat at the "
9 might see L' also, whom he had "
10 they might put L' also to death; "
17 when he called L' out of his grave, "

leach See HORSELEACH.

lead See also LEADEST; LEADETH; LED.
Ge 33: 14 I will l' on softly, according as the 5095
Ex 13: 21 of a cloud, to l' them the way; 5148
15: 10 sank as l' in the mighty waters. 5777
32: 34 l' the people unto the place of 5148
Nu 27: 17 which may l' them out, and which 3318
31: 22 brass, the iron, the tin, and the l', 5777
De 4: 27 whither the Lord shall l' you. 5090
20: 9 of the armies to l' the people. *7218
28: 37 whither the Lord shall l' thee. 5090
32: 12 the Lord alone did l' him, and 5148
J'g 5: 12 and l' thy captivity captive, thou
1Sa 30: 22 that they may l' them away, and 5090
2Ch 30: 9 before them that l' them captive, *
Ne 9: 19 by day, to l' them in the way; 5148
Job 19: 24 graven with an iron pen and l' 5777
Ps 5: 8 L' me, O Lord, in thy righteousness 5148
25: 5 L' me in thy truth, and teach me: *1869
27: 11 l' me in a plain path, because of 5148
31: 3 name's sake l' me, and guide me. "
43: 3 let them l' me; let them bring me "
60: 9 city? who will l' me into Edom? * "
61: 2 l' me to the rock that is higher "
108: 10 city? who will l' me into Edom? * "
125: 5 Lord shall l' them forth with the 3212
139: 10 Even there shall thy hand l' me, 5148
24 and l' me in the way everlasting. "
143: 10 l' me into the land of uprightness. "
Pr 6: 22 When thou goest, it shall l' thee; "
8: 20 I l' in the way of righteousness, *1980
Ca 8: 2 I would l' thee, and bring thee 5090
Isa 3: 12 they which l' thee cause thee to err. 833
11: 6 and a little child shall l' them. 5090
20: 4 of Assyria l' away the Egyptians "
40: 11 shall gently l' those that are with *5095
42: 16 l' them in paths that they have not 1869
49: 10 hath mercy on them shall l' them, 5090
57: 18 I will l' him also, and restore 5148
63: 14 so didst thou l' thy people, to make 5090
Jer 6: 29 the l' is consumed of the fire; 5777
31: 9 with supplications will I l' them: 2986
32: 5 he shall l' Zedekiah to Babylon, 3212
Eze 22: 18 brass, and tin, and iron, and l', 5777
20 silver, and brass, and iron, and l', "
27: 12 silver, iron, tin, and l', they "
Na 2: 7 maids shall l' her as with the voice *5090
Zec 5: 7 there was lifted up a talent of l': 5777
8 the weight of l' upon the mouth "
M't 6: 13 And l' us not into temptation, but *1533
15: 14 if the blind l' the blind, both shall *3594
M'r 13: 11 when they shall l' you, and deliver 71
14: 44 take him, and l' him away safely. 520
Lu 6: 39 them, Can the blind l' the blind? *3594
11: 4 And l' us not into temptation; but *1533
13: 15 stall, and l' him away to watering? 520
Ac 13: 11 seeking some to l' him by the hand. 5497
1Co 9: 5 we not power to l' about a sister, 4013
1Ti 2: 2 may l' a quiet and peaceable life 1236
2Ti 3: 6 l' captive silly women laden with * 162
Heb 8: 9 to l' them out of the land of Egypt; 1806
Re 7: 17 shall l' them unto living fountains *3594

leader See also LEADERS; RINGLEADER.
1Ch 12: 27 was the l' of the Aaronites, and 5057
13: 1 and hundreds, and with every l'. "
Isa 55: 4 a l' and commander to the people. "

leaders
2Ch 32: 21 the l' and captains in the camp of 5057
Isa 9: 16 the l' of this people cause them to * 833
M't 15: 14 alone: they be blind l' of the blind. *3595

leadest
Ps 80: 1 thou that l' Joseph like a flock; 5090

leadeth
1Sa 13: 17 turned unto the way that l' to Ophrah.
Job 12: 17 He l' counsellors away spoiled, 3212
19 He l' princes away spoiled, and "
Ps 23: 2 he l' me beside the still waters. 5095
3 l' me in...paths of righteousness *5090
Pr 16: 29 l'...into the way that is not good. 3212
Isa 48: 17 which l' thee by the way that thou 1869
M't 7: 13 is the way, that l' to destruction, 520
14 narrow is the way, which l' unto life."
M'r 9: 2 l' them up into an high mountain* 399
Joh 10: 3 sheep by name, and l' them out. 1806
Ac 12: 10 the iron gate that l' unto the city; 5342
Ro 2: 4 of God l' thee to repentance? 71
Re 13: 10 He that l' into captivity shall go *4863

leaf See also LEAVED; LEAVES.
Ge 8: 11 lo, in her mouth was an olive l' 5929
Le 26: 36 the sound of a shaken l' shall chase"
Job 13: 25 thou break a l' driven to and fro? "
Ps 1: 3 his l' also shall not wither; and "
Isa 1: 30 shall be as an oak whose l' fadeth, "
34: 4 as the l' falleth off from the vine, "
64: 6 rags; and we all do fade as a l': "

Jer 8:13 on the fig tree, and the *l'* shall fade:5929
17: 8 cometh, but her *l'* shall be green; "
Eze 47:12 whose *l'* shall not fade, neither shall"
12 and the *l'* thereof for medicine. "

league
Jos 9: 6 therefore make ye a *l'* with us. *1285
7 how shall we make a *l'* with you?* "
11 therefore now make ye a *l'* with us.* "
15 them, and made a *l'* with them, * "
16 after they had made a *l'* with them,* "
J'g 2: 2 make no *l'* with the inhabitants of* "
1Sa 22: 8 made a *l'* with the son of Jesse, 3772
2Sa 3:12 Make thy *l'* with me, and, behold, 1285
13 Well; I will make a *l'* with thee: "
21 that they may make a *l'* with thee,* "
5: 3 king David made a *l'* with them in* "
1Ki 5:12 and they two made a *l'* together. "
15:19 There is a *l'* between me and thee, "
19 break thy *l'* with Baasha king of "
2Ch 16: 3 There is a *l'* between me and thee, "
3 break thy *l'* with Baasha king of "
Job 5:23 thou shalt be in *l'* with the stones "
Eze 30: 5 and the men of the land that is in *l'*. "
Da 11:23 after the *l'* made with him he shall2266

Leah (*le'-ah*) See also LEAH'S.
Ge 29:16 the name of the elder was *L'*, and 3812
17 *L'* was tender eyed; but Rachel "
23 that he took *L'* his daughter, and "
24 gave unto his daughter *L'* Zilpah "
25 in the morning, behold, it was *L'*: "
30 he loved also Rachel more than *L'*, "
31 the Lord saw that *L'* was hated, he "
32 And *L'* conceived, and bare a son, "
30: 9 *L'* saw that she had left bearing, "
11 *L'* said, A troop cometh: and she "
13 And *L'* said, Happy am I, for the "
14 brought them unto his mother *L'*. "
14 Rachel said to *L'*, Give me, I pray "
16 and *L'* went out to meet him, and "
17 God hearkened unto *L'*, and she "
18 *L'* said, God hath given me my "
19 *L'* conceived again, and bare Jacob "
20 *L'* said, God hath endued me with "
31: 4 Jacob sent and called Rachel and *L'* "
14 Rachel and *L'* answered and said "
33: 1 he divided the children unto *L'*, "
2 and *L'* and her children after, and "
7 And *L'* also with her children came "
34: 1 Dinah the daughter of *L'*, which "
35:23 The sons of *L'*; Reuben, Jacob's "
46:15 These be the sons of *L'*, which she "
18 Laban gave to *L'* his daughter, "
49:31 his wife; and there I buried *L'*. "
Ru 4:11 house like Rachel and like *L'*, "

Leah's (*le'-ahs*)
Ge 30:10 Zilpah *L'* maid bare Jacob a son. 3812
12 Zilpah *L'* maid bare Jacob a second "
31:33 into Jacob's tent, and into *L'* tent, "
33 went he out of *L'* tent, and entered "
35:26 the sons of Zilpah, *L'* handmaid; "

lean See also LEANED; LEANETH; LEANFLESHED; LEANING.
Ge 41:20 *l'* and the ill favoured kine did eat 7534
Nu 13:20 the land is, whether it be fat or *l'*, 7330
J'g 16:26 standeth, that I may *l'* upon them.8172
2Sa 13: 4 the king's son, *l'* from day to day? 1800
2Ki 18:21 on which if a man *l'*, it will go into5564
Job 8:15 He shall *l'* upon his house, but it 8172
Pro 3: 5 *l'* not unto thine...understanding. "
Isa 17: 4 fatness of his flesh shall wax *l'*. 7329
36: 6 whereon if a man *l'*, it will go into5564
Eze 34:20 fat cattle and between the *l'* cattle.7330
Mic 3:11 yet will they *l'* upon the Lord, and8172

leaned
2Sa 1: 6 behold Saul *l'* upon his spear; 8172
2Ki 7: 2 a lord on whose hand the king *l'* "
17 the lord on whose hand he *l'* to have "
Eze 29: 7 and when they *l'* upon thee, thou "
Am 5:19 house, and *l'* his hand on the wall,5564
Joh 21:20 also *l'* on his breast at supper, *377*

leaneth
2Sa 3:29 or that *l'* on a staff, or that falleth 2388
2Ki 5:18 and he *l'* on my hand, and I bow 8127

leanfleshed
Ge 41: 3 the river, ill favoured and *l'*; 1851,1320
4 ill favoured and *l'* kine did eat " "
19 poor and very ill favoured and *l'*, 7534

leaning
Ca 8: 5 wilderness, *l'* upon her beloved? 7514
Joh 13:23 there was *l'* on Jesus' bosom one * *345*
Heb 11:21 worshipped, *l'* upon the top of his staff.

leanness
Job 16: 8 and my *l'* rising up in me beareth 3585
Ps 106:15 request but sent *l'* into their soul. 7332
Isa 10:16 hosts, send among his fat ones *l'*; "
24:16 I said, My *l'*, my *l'*, woe unto me! *7334

Leannoth (*le-an'-noth*)
Ps 88: *title* Musician upon Mahalath *L'*, 6030

leap See also LEAPED; LEAPING.
Ge 31:12 the rams which *l'* upon the cattle 5927
Le 11:21 feet, to *l'* withal upon the earth; 5425
De 33:22 whelp: he shall *l'* from Bashan. *2178
Job 41:19 lamps, and sparks of fire *l'* out. 4422
Ps 68:16 Why *l'* ye, ye high hills? this is *7520
Isa 35: 6 Then shall the lame man *l'* as an 1801
Joe 2: 5 the tops of mountains shall they *l'*,7540
Zep 1: 9 all those that *l'* on the threshold. 1801
Lu 6:23 ye in that day, and *l'* for joy: *4640*

leaped
Ge 31:10 the rams which *l'* upon the cattle 5927
2Sa 22:30 by my God have I *l'* over a wall. *1801
1Ki 18:26 they *l'* upon the altar which was 6452

Ps 18:29 by my God have I *l'* over a wall. *1801
Lu 1:41 of Mary, the babe *l'* in her womb; *4640*
44 the babe *l'* in my womb for joy. "
Ac 14:10 on thy feet. And he *l'* and walked. *242*
19:16 the evil spirit was *l'* on them, and *2177*

leaping
2Sa 6:16 David *l'* and dancing before the 6339
Ca 2: 8 he cometh *l'* upon the mountains, 1801
Ac 3: 8 And he *l'* up stood, and walked, *1814*
8 walking, and *l'*, and praising God. *242*

learn See also LEARNED; LEARNING.
De 4:10 that they may *l'* to fear me all the 3925
5: 1 that ye may *l'* them, and keep, and "
14:23 mayest *l'* to fear the Lord thy God "
17:19 he may *l'* to fear the Lord his God, "
18: 9 not *l'* to do after the abominations "
31:12 that they may *l'*, and fear the Lord "
13 and *l'* to fear the Lord your God, as"
Ps 119:71 that I might *l'* thy statutes. "
73 that I may *l'* thy commandments. "
Pr 22:25 Lest thou *l'* his ways, and get a 502
Isa 1:17 *L'* to do well; seek judgment, 3925
2: 4 neither shall they *l'* war any more. "
26: 9 of the world will *l'* righteousness. "
10 yet will he not *l'* righteousness: "
29:24 that murmured shall *l'* doctrine. ‡ "
Jer 10: 2 Lord, *L'* not the way of the heathen,"
12:16 diligently *l'* the ways of my people, "
Mic 4: 3 neither shall they *l'* war any more. "
M't 9:13 go ye and *l'* what that meaneth, *3129*
11:29 my yoke upon you, and *l'* of me; "
24:32 Now *l'* a parable of the fig tree; "
M'r 13:28 Now *l'* a parable of the fig tree; "
1Co 4: 6 might *l'* in us not to think of men "
14:31 one by one, that all may *l'*, and all "
35 And if they will *l'* any thing, let "
Ga 3: 2 This only would I *l'* of you, "
1Ti 1:20 they may *l'* not to blaspheme. **3811*
2:11 Let the woman *l'* in silence with *3129*
5: 4 them *l'* first to shew piety at home, "
13 withal they *l'* to be idle, wandering "
Tit 3:14 also *l'* to maintain good works for "
Re 14: 3 no man could *l'* that song but the "

learned See also UNLEARNED.
Ge 30:27 I have *l'* by experience that the 5172
Ps 106:35 the heathen, and *l'* their works. 3925
119: 7 have *l'* thy righteous judgments. "
Pr 30: 3 I neither *l'* wisdom, nor have the "
Isa 29:11 men deliver to one that is *l'*, 3045,5612
12 delivered to him that is not *l'*, " "
12 thee: and he saith, I am not *l'*. " "
50: 4 given me the tongue of the *l'*, *3928
4 mine ear to hear as the *l'*. * "
Eze 19: 3 lion and it *l'* to catch the prey; 3925
6 young lion, and *l'* to catch the prey."
Joh 6:45 heard, and hath *l'* of the Father, *3129*
7:15 this man letters, having never *l'*? "
Ac 7:22 Moses was *l'* in all the wisdom **3811*
Ro 16:17 to the doctrine which ye have *l'*; *3129*
Eph 4:20 But ye have not so *l'* Christ; * "
Ph'p 4: 9 things, which ye have both *l'*, and "
11 for I have *l'*, in whatsoever state I "
Col 1: 7 As ye also *l'* of Epaphras our dear "
2Ti 3:14 in the things which thou hast *l'* and"
14 knowing of whom thou hast *l'* them;"
Heb 5: 8 yet *l'* he obedience by the things "

learning
Pr 1: 5 will hear, and will increase *l'*; 3948
9: 9 just man, and he will increase in *l'*. "
16:21 sweetness of the lips increaseth *l'*. "
23 his mouth, and addeth *l'* to his lips."
Da 1: 4 whom they might teach the *l'* and 5612
17 them knowledge and skill in all *l'* "
Ac 26:24 much *l'* doth make thee mad. *1121*
Ro 15: 4 aforetime were written for our *l'*. *1319*
2Ti 3: 7 Ever *l'*, and never able to come to *3129*

leasing See also LYING.
Ps 4: 2 ye love vanity, and seek after *l'*? *3577
5: 6 shalt destroy them that speak *l'*: * "

least
Ge 24:55 with us a few days, at the *l'* ten; 176
32:10 worthy of the *l'* of all the mercies, 6994
Nu 11:32 gathered *l'* gathered ten homers: 4591
J'g 3: 2 at the *l'* such as before knew 7535
6:15 I am the *l'* in my father's house. 6810
1Sa 9:21 my family the *l'* of all the families "
21: 4 kept themselves at *l'* from women.*389
2Ki 18:24 of the *l'* of my master's servants, 6996
1Ch 12:14 one of the *l'* was over an hundred, "
Isa 36: 9 of the *l'* of my master's servants, "
Jer 6:13 *l'* of them even unto the greatest "
8:10 from the *l'* even unto the greatest "
31:34 the *l'* of them unto the greatest "
42: 1 from the *l'* even unto the greatest, "
8 from the *l'* even to the greatest, "
44:12 from the *l'* even unto the greatest, "
49:20 the *l'* of the flock shall draw them*6810
50:45 the *l'* of the flock shall draw them* "
Am 9: 9 not the *l'* grain fall upon the earth. "
Jon 3: 5 of them even to the *l'* of them. 6996
M't 2: 6 the *l'* among the princes of Juda: *1646*
5:19 one of these *l'* commandments, "
19 the *l'* in the kingdom of heaven: "
11:11 is *l'* in the kingdom of heaven is **3398*
13:32 Which indeed is the *l'* of all seeds:* "
25:40 one of the *l'* of these my brethren, *1646*
45 did it not to one of the *l'* of these, "
Lu 7:28 that is *l'* in the kingdom of God **3398*
9:48 for he that is *l'* among you all, the "
12:26 not able to do that thing which is *l'*,*1646*
16:10 that is faithful in that which is *l'* * "
10 he that is unjust in the *l'* is unjust* "
19:42 even thou, at *l'* in this thy day, **2534*
Ac 5:15 that at the *l'* the shadow of Peter *2579*

Ac 8:10 heed, from the *l'* to the greatest, *3398*
1Co 6: 4 to judge who are *l'* esteemed **1848*
15: 9 I am the *l'* of the apostles, that am*1646*
Eph 3: 8 who am less than the *l'* of all saints,*1647*
Heb 8:11 me, from the *l'* to the greatest. *3398*

leather
2Ki 1: 8 with a girdle of *l'* about his loins. 5785

leathern
M't 3: 4 and a *l'* girdle about his loins; *1193*

leave See also LEAVETH; LEAVING; LEFT.
Ge 2:24 man *l'* his father and his mother, 5800
28:15 I will not *l'* thee, until I have done "
33:15 now *l'* with thee some of the folk 3322
42:33 *l'* one of your brethren here with 3241
44:22 The lad cannot *l'* his father: 5800
22 for if he should *l'* his father, his "
Ex 16:19 Let no man *l'* of it till the morning.3498
23:11 what they *l'* the beasts...shall eat. 3499
Le 7:15 not *l'* any of it until the morning. 3241
16:23 holy place, and shall *l'* them there: "
19:10 *l'* them for the poor and stranger: 5800
22:30 *l'* none of it until the morrow: 3498
23:22 thou shalt *l'* them unto the poor, 5800
Nu 9:12 *l'* none of it unto the morning, 7604
10:31 he said, *L'* us not, I pray thee; 5800
22:13 Lord refuseth to give me *l'* to go 5414
32:15 again *l'* them in the wilderness; 3241
De 28:51 shall not *l'* thee either corn, wine, 7604
54 of his children which he shall *l'*: *3498
Jos 4: 3 and *l'* them in the lodging place, *3241
J'g 9: 9 unto them, Should I *l'* my fatness,2308
13 unto them, Should I *l'* my wine, "
Ru 1:16 said, Intreat me not to *l'* thee, or 5800
2:16 *l'* them, that she may glean them, "
1Sa 9: 5 my father *l'* caring for the asses, 2308
14:36 and let us not *l'* a man of them. 7604
20: 6 asked *l'* of me that he might run
28 asked *l'* of me to go to Beth-lehem:
25:22 if I *l'* of all that pertain to him 7604
2Sa 14: 7 not *l'* to my husband neither name "
1Ki 8:57 let him not *l'* us, nor forsake us: 5800
2Ki 2: 2, 4, 6 soul liveth, I will not *l'* thee. "
4:30 as thy soul liveth, I will not *l'* thee. "
43 They shall eat, and shall *l'* thereof.3498
13: 7 he *l'* of the people to Jehoahaz *7604
1Ch 28: 8 *l'* it for an inheritance for your 5157
Ezr 9: 8 *l'* us a remnant to escape, and to 7604
12 *l'* it for an inheritance to your
Ne 5:10 I pray you, let us *l'* off this usury. 5800
6: 3 the work cease, whilst I *l'* it, 7503
10:31 we would *l'* the seventh year, *5203
13: 6 days obtained I *l'* of the king: 7592
Job 9:27 I will *l'* off my heaviness, and *5800
10: 1 *l'* my complaint upon myself; * "
39:11 or wilt thou *l'* thy labour to him? "
Ps 16:10 thou wilt not *l'* my soul in hell; "
17:14 *l'* the rest of their substance to *3241
27: 9 *l'* me not, neither forsake me, O *5203
37:33 Lord will not *l'* him in his hand, 5800
49:10 perish, and *l'* their wealth to others."
119:121 *l'* me not to mine oppressors. 3241
141: 8 trust; *l'* not my soul destitute. 6168
Pr 2:13 Who *l'* the paths of uprightness, *5800
17:14 therefore *l'* off contention, before 5203
Ec 2:18 *l'* it unto the man that shall be 3241
21 shall he *l'* it for his portion. 5414
10: 4 up against thee, *l'* not thy place; 3241
Isa 10: 3 and where will ye *l'* your glory? 5800
65:15 *l'* your name for a curse unto my 3241
Jer 9: 2 that I might *l'* my people, and go 5800
14: 9 are called by thy name; *l'* us not. 3241
17:11 shall *l'* them in the midst of his 5800
18:14 a man *l'* the snow of Lebanon
30:11 not *l'* thee altogether unpunished.
44: 7 Judah, to *l'* you none to remain; 3498
46:28 I not *l'* thee wholly unpunished.
48:28 in Moab, *l'* the cities, and dwell 5800
49: 9 they not *l'* some gleaning grapes? 7604
11 *L'* thy fatherless children, I will 5800
Eze 6: 8 Yet will I *l'* a remnant, that ye may3498
12:16 I will *l'* a few men of them from
16:39 and *l'* thee naked and bare. 3241
22:20 I will *l'* you there, and melt you. * "
23:29 and shall *l'* thee naked and bare: 5800
29: 5 *l'* thee thrown into the wilderness,‡5203
32: 4 Then will I *l'* thee upon the land, I "
39: 2 and *l'* but the sixth part of thee, *8338
Da 4:15 *l'* the stump of his roots in the 7662
23 *l'* the stump of the roots thereof in "
26 to *l'* the stump of the tree roots; "
Ho 12:14 shall he *l'* his blood upon him, 5203
Joe 2:14 and *l'* a blessing behind him; 7604
Am 5: 3 by a thousand shall *l'* an hundred, "
3 forth by an hundred shall *l'* ten, "
7 *l'* off righteousness in the earth, *3241
Ob 5 would they not *l'* some grapes? 7604
Zep 3:12 *l'* in the midst of thee an afflicted "
Mal 4: 1 *l'* them neither root nor branch. 5800
M't 5:24 *L'* there thy gift before the altar. *863*
18:12 doth he not *l'* the ninety and nine, "
19: 5 shall a man *l'* father and mother, *2641*
23:23 and not to *l'* the other undone. **863*
M'r 5:13 And forthwith Jesus gave them *l'*. *2010*
10: 7 a man *l'* his father and mother, *2641*
12:19 die, and *l'* his wife behind him, "
19 and *l'* no children, that his brother *863*
Lu 11:42 and not to *l'* the other undone. "
15: 4 doth not *l'* the ninety and nine in *2641*
19:44 shall not *l'* in thee one stone upon *863*
Joh 14:18 I will not *l'* you comfortless: I will "
27 Peace I *l'* with you, my peace I give "
16:28 I *l'* the world, and go to the Father. "
32 to his own, and shall *l'* me alone: "
19:38 of Jesus: and Pilate gave him *l'*. *2010*
Ac 2:27 thou wilt not *l'* my soul in hell. *1459*

Ac 6: 2 that we should l· the word of God,*2641
18:18 then took his l· of the brethren, 657
21: 6 had taken our l· one of another, * 782
1Co 7:13 dwell with her, let her not l· him. 863
2Co 2:13 taking my l· of them, I went from 657
Eph 5:31 a man l· his father and mother, 2641
Heb13: 5 I will never l· thee, nor forsake * 447
Rev11: 2 which is without the temple l· out, 1544

leaved
Isa 45: 1 open before him the two l· gates;*1817

leaven See also LEAVENED.
Ex 12:15 put away l· out of your houses: 7603
19 be no l· found in your houses: "
13: 7 shall there be l· seen with thee in "
34:25 the blood of my sacrifice with l·;*2557
Le 2:11 No...offering...shall be made with l·:"
11 for ye shall burn no l·, 7603
6:17 It shall not be baked with l·. I 2557
10:12 eat it without l· beside the altar: 4682
23:17 they shall be baken with l·; they 2557
Am 4: 5 sacrifice of thanksgiving with l·, * "
M't 13:33 kingdom of heaven is like unto l·. 2219
16: 6, 11 beware of the l· of the Pharisees"
12 not beware of the l· of bread, "
M'r 8:15 beware of the l· of the Pharisees, "
15 and of the l· of Herod. "
Lu 12: 1 Beware ye of the l· of the Pharisees,"
13:21 It is like l·, which a woman took "
1Co 5: 6 little l· leaveneth the whole lump? "
7 Purge out therefore the old l·, that "
8 us keep the feast, not with old l·, "
8 neither with the l· of malice and "
Ga 5: 9 little l· leaveneth the whole lump. "

leavened See also UNLEAVENED; LEAVENETH.
Ex 12:15 whosoever eateth l· bread from 2557
19 whosoever eateth that which is l·, "
20 Ye shall eat nothing l·; in all your "
34 took their dough before it was l·, "
39 forth out of Egypt, for it was not l·;"
13: 3 there shall no l· bread be eaten. "
7 shall no l· bread be seen with thee, "
23:18 blood of my sacrifice with l· bread;"
Le 7:13 shall offer for his offering l· bread "
De 16: 3 Thou shalt eat no l· bread with it; "
4 shall be no l· bread seen with thee*7603
Ho 7: 4 kneaded the dough, until it be l·. 2557
M't 13:33 of meal, till the whole was l·. 2220
Lu 13:21 of meal, till the whole was l·. "

leaveneth
1Co 5: 6 a little leaven l· the whole lump? 2220
Ga 5: 9 A little leaven l· the whole lump. "

leaves
Ge 3: 7 they sewed fig l· together, and 5929
1Ki 6:34 the two l· of the one door were 6763
34 the two l· of the other door were 7050
Isa 6:13 is in them, when they cast their l·:*
Jer 36:23 Jehudi had read three or four l·, 1817
Eze17: 9 wither in all the l· of her spring, 2964
41:24 had two l· apiece, two turning l·; 1817
24 two l· for the one door
24 and two l· for the other door. 1817
Da 4:12 The l· thereof were fair, and the 6074
14 off his branches, shake off his l·, "
21 Whose l· were fair, and the fruit "
M't 21:19 found nothing thereon, but l· only, 5444
24:32 yet tender, and putteth forth l·, "
M'r 11:13 seeing a fig tree afar off having l·, "
13 came to it, he found nothing but l·;"
13:28 yet tender, and putteth forth l·: "
Re 22: 2 l· of the trees were for the healing "

leaveth
Job 39:14 Which l· her eggs in the earth, 5800
Pr 13:22 A good man l· an inheritance to his
28: 3 like a sweeping rain which l· no food.
Zec 11:17 the idol shepherd that l· the flock! 5800
M't 4:11 Then the devil l· him, and, behold, 863
Joh 10:12 coming, and l· the sheep, and fleeth:"

leaving
M't 4:13 l· Nazareth, he came and dwelt 2641
Lu 10:30 and departed, l· him half dead. 863
Ro 1:27 l· the natural use of the woman, "
Heb 6: 1 l· the principles of the doctrine of † "
1Pe 2:21 suffered for us, l· us an example, 5277

Lebana (*leb'-a-nah*) See also LEBANAH.
Ne 7:48 The children of L·, the children 3848

Lebanah (*leb'-a-nah*) See also LEBANA.
Ezr 2:45 The children of L·, the children 3848

Lebanon (*leb'-a-non*)
De 1: 7 unto L·, unto the great river, the 3844
3:25 that goodly mountain, and L·. "
11:24 from the wilderness and L·, from "
Jos 1: 4 From the wilderness and this L· "
9: 1 of the great sea over against L·, "
11:17 unto Baal-gad in the valley of L· "
12: 7 in the valley of L· even unto the "
13: 5 the land of the Giblites, and all L·, "
6 of the hill country from L· unto "
J'g 3: 3 the Hivites that dwelt in mount L·, "
9:15 and devour the cedars of L·. "
1Ki 4:33 from the cedar tree that is in L· "
5: 6 they hew me cedar trees out of L·; "
9 shall bring them down from L· "
14 he sent them to L·, ten thousand "
14 a month they were in L·, and two "
7: 2 also the house of the forest of L·; "
9:19 to build in Jerusalem, and in L·, "
10:17 in the house of the forest of L·. "
21 of the house of the forest of L· were"
2Ki 14: 9 The thistle that was in L· sent to "
9 to the cedar that was in L·, saying, "
9 by a wild beast that was in L·, and "
19:23 of the mountains, to the sides of L·, "
2Ch 2: 8 trees, and algum trees, out of L·: 3844
8 can skill to cut timber in L·; "
16 we will cut wood out of L·, as much "
8: 6 to build in Jerusalem, and in L·, "
9:16 them in the house of the forest of L·."
20 of the house of the forest of L· were"
25:18 The thistle that was in L· sent to "
18 to the cedar that was in L·, saying, "
18 and by a wild beast that was in L·, "
Ezr 3: 7 cedar trees from L· to the sea of "
Ps 29: 5 the Lord breaketh the cedars of L·. "
6 L· and Sirion like a young unicorn. "
72:16 the fruit thereof shall shake like L·:"
92:12 he shall grow like a cedar in L·. "
104:16 cedars of L·, which he hath planted;"
Ca 3: 9 himself a chariot of the wood of L·. "
4: 8 Come with me from L·, my spouse, "
8 with me from L·: look from the top"
11 thy garments is like the smell of L·."
15 living waters, and streams from L·. "
5:15 his countenance is as L·, excellent "
7: 4 thy nose is as the tower of L· which"
Isa 2:13 upon all the cedars of L·, that are "
10:34 and L· shall fall by a mighty one. "
14: 8 at thee, and the cedars of L·, saying,"
29:17 L· shall be turned into a fruitful "
33: 9 L· is ashamed and hewn down: "
35: 2 the glory of L· shall be given unto "
37:24 the mountains, to the sides of L·; "
40:16 L· is not sufficient to burn, nor the "
60:13 The glory of L· shall come unto "
Jer 18:14 leave the snow of L· which cometh "
22: 6 Gilead unto me, and the head of L·:"
20 Go up to L·, and cry; and lift up "
23 O inhabitant of L·, that makest thy "
Eze17: 3 came unto L·, and took the highest "
27: 5 cedars from L· to make masts "
31: 3 the Assyrian was a cedar in L· with"
15 and I caused L· to mourn for him, "
16 of Eden, the choice and best of L·, "
Ho 14: 5 lily, and cast forth his roots as L·. "
6 as the olive tree, and his smell as L·."
7 thereof shall be as the wine of L·. "
Na 1: 4 and the flower of L· languisheth. "
Hab 2:17 the violence of L· shall cover thee, "
Zec 10:10 them into the land of Gilead and L·; "
11: 1 Open thy doors, O L·, that the fire "

Lebaoth (*leb'-a-oth*) See also BETH-LEBAOTH.
Jos 15:32 And L·, and Shilhim, and Ain, and3822

Lebbæus (*leb-be'-us*) See also JUDAS; THADDÆUS.
M't 10: 3 James the son of Alphæus, and L·,*3002

Lebonah (*le-bo'-nah*)
J'g 21:19 Shechem, and on the south of L·. 3829

Lecah (*le'-cah*)
1Ch 4:21 Er the father of L·, and Laadah 3922

led See also LEDDEST.
Ge 24:27 l· me to the house of my master's 5148
48 which had l· me in the right way "
Ex 3: 1 l· the flock to the backside of the 5090
13:17 l· them not through the way of the5148
18 God l· the people about, through 5437
15:13 thy mercy hast l· forth the people 5148
De 8: 2 God l· thee these forty years in the 3212
15 Who l· thee through that great and "
29: 5 l· you forty years in the wilderness:"
32:10 he l· him about, he instructed him,*5437
Jos 24: 3 l· him throughout all the land of 3212
1Ki 8:48 which l· them away captive, *
2Ki 6:19 seek. But he l· them to Samaria. 3212
1Ch 20: 1 l· forth the power of the army, and5090
2Ch 25:11 himself, and l· forth his people, "
Ps 68:18 high, thou hast l· captivity captive: "
78:14 also he l· them with a cloud, 5148
53 And he l· them on safely so that "
106: 9 so he l· them through the depths, 3212
107: 7 he l· them forth by the right way, 1869
136:16 which l· his people through the 3212
Pr 4:11 I have l· thee in right paths. 1869
Isa 9:16 that are l· of them are destroyed. 833
48:21 he l· them through the deserts: 3212
55:12 joy, and be l· forth with peace: 2986
63:12 l· them by the right hand of Moses *3212
13 That l· them through the deep, as "
Jer 2: 6 that l· us through the wilderness, "
17 God, when he l· thee by the way? "
22:12 whither they have l· him captive,
23: 8 l· the seed of the house of Israel 935
La 3: 2 He hath l· me, and brought me 5090
Eze17:12 and l· them with him to Babylon:* 935
39:28 caused them to be l· into captivity*
47: 2 and l· me about the way without 5437
Am 2:10 and l· you forty years through the 3212
7:11 Israel shall surely be l· away captive
Na 2: 7 Huzzab shall be l· away captive, *
M't 4: 1 Then was Jesus l· up of the spirit 321
26:57 had laid hold on Jesus l· him away 520
27: 2 had bound him, they l· him away, "
31 him, and l· him away to crucify him. "
M'r 8:23 hand, and l· him out of the town;*1806
14:53 And they l· Jesus away to the high 520
15:16 the soldiers l· him away into the hall,"
20 him, and l· him out to crucify him.*1806
Lu 4: 1 l· by the spirit into the wilderness, 71
29 and l· him unto the brow of the hill "
21:24 be l· away captive into all nations: 163
22:54 Then they took him, and l· him, and 71
66 and l· him into their council, 321
23: 1 of them arose, and l· him unto Pilate.*71
26 as they l· him away, they laid hold 520
32 l· with him to be put to death. 71
24:50 he l· them out as far as to Bethany, 1806
Joh 18:13 And l· him away to Annas first; for 520
28 Then l· they Jesus from Caiaphas* 71
Job 19:16 they took Jesus, and l· him away. * 520
Ac 8:32 was l· as a sheep to the slaughter; 71
9: 8 l· him by the hand, and brought 5496
21:37 Paul was to be l· into the castle, *1521
22:11 being l· by the hand of them that 5496
Ro 8:14 many as are l· by the Spirit of God, 71
1Co 12: 2 these dumb idols, even as ye were l·."
Ga 5:18 But if ye be l· of the Spirit, ye are not"
Eph 4: 8 up on high, he l· captivity captive, 162
2Ti 3: 6 with sins, l· away with divers lusts, 71
2Pe 3:17 being l· away with the error of *4879

leddest
2Sa 5: 2 wast he that l· out and broughtest3318
1Ch 11: 2 wast he that l· out and broughtest "
Ne 9:12 l· them in the day by a cloudy 5148
Ps 77:20 Thou l· thy people like a flock by "
Ac 21:38 and l· out into the wilderness four*1806

ledges
1Ki 7:28 the borders were between the l·: 7948
29 the borders that were between the l·"
29 upon the l· there was a base above:"
35 the top of the base the l· thereof *3027
36 on the plates of the l· thereof, and* "

leeks
Nu 11: 5 and the l·, and the onions, and the2682

lees
Isa 25: 6 things, a feast of wines on the l·, 8105
6 of wines on the l· well refined. "
Jer 48:11 hath settled on his l·, and hath not "
Zep 1:12 the men that are settled on their l·:"

left See also LEFTEST; LEFTHANDED.
Ge 11: 8 and they l· off to build the city. 2308
13: 9 if thou wilt take the l· hand, then 8040
9 right hand, then I will go to the l·.8041
14:15 is on the l· hand of Damascus. 8040
17:22 And he l· off talking with him, 3615
18:33 had l· communing with Abraham: "
24:27 hath not l· destitute my master of*5800
49 turn to the right hand, or to the l·.8040
29:35 his name Judah; and l· bearing. 5975
30: 9 Leah saw that she had l· bearing, "
32: 8 company which is l· shall escape. 7604
24 And Jacob was l· alone; and there3498
39: 6 l· all that he had in Joseph's hand;5800
12 he l· his garment in her hand, and "
13 she saw that he had l· his garment "
15 that he l· his garment with me, and"
18 l· his garment with me, and fled "
41:49 very much, until he l· numbering;2308
42:38 brother is dead, and he is l· alone:7604
44:12 the eldest, and l· at the youngest: 3615
20 brother is dead, and he alone is l· 3498
47:18 is not ought l· in the sight of my 7604
48:13 right hand toward Israel's l· hand,8040
13 Manasseh in his l· hand toward "
14 his l· hand upon Manasseh's head, "
50: 8 they l· in the land of Goshen. 5800
Ex 2:20 why is it that ye have l· the man? "
9:21 l· his servants and his cattle in the "
10:12 land, even all that the hail hath l·.7604
15 of the trees which the hail had l·: 3498
26 shall not an hoof be l· behind; 7604
14:22, 29 right hand, and on their l·. 8040
16:20 of them l· of it until the morning, 3498
34:25 passover be l· until the morning. 3885
Le 2:10 which is l· of the meat offering 3498
10:12 unto Ithamar, his sons that were l·,"
16 sons of Aaron which were l· alive, "
14:15 into the palm of his own l· hand: 8042
16 in the oil that is in his l· hand, "
26 into the palm of his own l· hand: "
27 some of the oil that is in his l· hand "
26:36 upon them that are l· alive of you 7604
39 they that are l· of you shall pine "
43 The land also shall be l· of them, 5800
Nu 20:17 to the right hand nor to the l·, 8040
21:35 until there was none l· him alive: 7604
22:26 to the right hand or to the l·. 8040
26:65 there was not l· a man of them, 3498
De 2:27 unto the right hand nor to the l·. 8040
34 every city, we l· none to remain: 7604
3: 3 until none was l· to him remaining."
4:27 shall be l· few in number among "
5:32 aside to the right hand or to the l·.8040
7:20 among them, until they that are l·,7604
17:11 to the right hand, nor to the l·. 8040
20 to the right hand, or to the l·: "
28:14 day, to the right hand, or to the l·, "
55 hath nothing l· him in the siege, 7604
62 And ye shall be l· few in number, "
32:36 and there is none shut up, or l·. 5800
Jos 1: 7 it to the right hand or to the l·, 8040
6:23 l· them without the camp of *3241
8:17 there was not a man l· in Ai or 7604
17 l· the city open, and pursued after 5800
10:33 until he had l· him none remaining.7604
37 he l· none remaining, according to "
39 therein; he l· none remaining: "
40 he l· none remaining, but utterly "
11: 8 until they l· them none remaining. "
11 there was not any l· to breathe: 3498
14 neither l· they any to breathe. 7604
15 l· nothing undone of all that the 5493
22 There was none of the Anakims l· 3498
19:27 goeth out to Cabul on the l· hand, 8040
22: 3 not l· your brethren these many 5800
23: 6 to the right hand or to the l·; 8040
J'g 2:21 of the nations which Joshua l· 5800
23 the Lord l· those nations, without 3241
3: 1 are the nations which the Lord l·, "
21 And Ehud put forth his l· hand, 8040
4:16 sword; and there was not a man l·.7604
6: 4 and l· no sustenance for Israel, "
7:20 held the lamps in their l· hands, 8040

J'g 8:10 l' of all the hosts of the children 3498
9: 5 youngest son of Jerubbaal was l': "
16:29 hand, and of the other with his l'. 8040
Ru 1: 3 and she was l', and her two sons. 7604
5 woman was l' of her two sons and "
18 then she l' speaking unto her. 2308
2:11 hast l' thy father and thy mother, 5800
14 did eat, and was sufficed, and l'. 3498
20 not l' off his kindness to the living5800
4:14 hath not l' thee this day without a 7673
1Sa 2:36 every one that is l' in thine house 3498
5: 4 the stump of Dagon was l' to him. 7604
6:12 aside to the right hand or to the l';8040
9:24 said, Behold that which is l'! *7604
10: 2 father hath l' the care of the asses, 5203
11:11 two of them were not l' together. 7604
17:20 and l' the sheep with a keeper, 5203
22 David l' his carriage in the hand of "
28 whom hast thou l' those few sheep "
25:34 had not been l' unto Nabal by the 3498
27: 9 l' neither man nor woman alive. *
30: 9 those that were l' behind stayed. 3498
13 my master l' me, because three 5800
2Sa 2:19 nor to the l' from following Abner. 8040
21 aside to thy right hand or to thy l', "
5:21 And there they l' their images, 5800
9: 1 any that is l' of the house of Saul, 3498
13:30 and there is not one of them l'. "
14: 7 shall quench my coal which is l', 7604
19 turn to the right hand or to the l' 8041
15:16 the king l' ten women, which were5800
16: 6 on his right hand and on his l'. 8040
21 he hath l' to keep the house; 3241
17:12 shall not be l' so much as one. *3498
20: 3 whom he had l' to keep the house, 3241
1Ki 7:21 he set up the l' pillar, and called 8042
39 five on the l' side of the house: 8040
47 And Solomon l' all the vessels 3241
49 the right side, and five on the l', 8040
9:20 all the people that were l' of the 3498
21 that were l' after them in the land, "
14:10 him that is shut up and l' in Israel,5800
15:18 gold that were l' in the treasures 3498
21 that he l' off building of Ramah, 2308
29 he l' not to Jeroboam any that 7604
16:11 he l' him not one that pisseth "
17:17 that there was no breath l' in him.3498
19: 3 Judah, and l' his servant there. 3241
10, 14 and I, even I only, am l'; and 3498
18 Yet I have l' me seven thousand *7604
20 And he l' the oxen, and ran after 5800
20:30 thousand of the men that were l'. 3498
21:21 him that is shut up and l' in Israel,5800
22:19 on his right hand and on his l'. 8040
2Ki 3:25 in Kir-haraseth l' they the stones 7604
4:44 and l' thereof, according to the 3498
7: 7 in the twilight, and l' their tents, 5800
13 remain, which are l' in the city, 7604
13 multitude of Israel that are l' in it: "
8: 6 since the day that she l' the land, 5800
9: 8 him that is shut up and l' in Israel: "
10:11 until he l' him none remaining. 7604
14 men; neither l' he any of them. "
21 was not a man l' that came not. "
11:11 to the l' corner of the temple, 8042
14:26 was not any shut up, nor any l', 5800
17:16 l' all the commandments of the * "
18 none l' but the tribe of Judah only.7604
19: 4 prayer for the remnant that are l'.4672
20:17 into Babylon: nothing shall be l', 3498
22: 2 aside to the right hand or to the l'.8040
23: 8 were on a man's l' hand at the gate "
25:11 the people that were l' in the city, 7604
12 captain of the guard l' of the poor "
22 king of Babylon had l', even over "
1Ch 6:44 sons of Merari stood on the l' hand:8040
61 were l' of the family of that tribe, *3498
12: 2 hand and the l' in hurling stones 8041
13: 2 that are l' in all the land of Israel, 7604
14:12 when they had l' their gods there, 5800
16:37 he l' there before the ark of the "
2Ch 3:17 hand, and the other on the l'; 8040
17 the name of that on the l' Boaz. 8042
4: 6 the right hand, and five on the l', 8040
7 the right hand, and five on the l'. "
8 on the right side, and five on the l'. "
8: 7 people that were l' of the Hittites, 3498
8 who were l' after them in the land, "
11:14 the Levites l' their suburbs and 5800
12: 5 also l' you in the hand of Shishak. "
16: 5 that he l' off building of Ramah, 2308
18:18 on his right hand and on his l'. 8040
21:17 that there was never a son l' him, 7604
23:10 temple to the l' side of the temple, 8042
24:18 they l' the house of the Lord God *5800
25 for they l' him in great diseases,) "
25:12 And other ten thousand l' alive did the
28:14 armed men l' the captives and the 5800
31:10 enough to eat, and have l' plenty: 3498
10 that which is l' is this great store. "
32:31 God l' him, to try him, that he 5800
34: 2 to the right hand, nor to the l'. 8040
21 that are l' in Israel and in Judah, 7604
Ne 1: 2 which were l' of the captivity, "
3 remnant that are l' of the captivity "
6: 1 there was no breach l' therein; 3498
8: 4 his l' hand, Pedaiah and Mishael, 8040
Job 20:21 There shall none of his meat be l';8300
26 it shall go ill with him that is l' in "
23: 9 On the l' hand, where he doth 8040
32:15 no more: they l' off speaking. *6275
Ps 36: 3 he hath l' off to be wise, and to do 2308
106:11 there was not one of them l'. 3498
Pr 3:16 in her l' hand riches and honour. 8040
4:27 not to the right hand nor to the l': "
29:15 a child l' to himself bringeth his 7971

Ec 10: 2 hand; but a fool's heart at his l'. 8040
Ca 2: 6 His l' hand is under my head, and "
8: 3 His l' hand should be under my "
Isa 1: 8 daughter of Zion is l' as a cottage 3498
9 the Lord of hosts had l' unto us "
4: 3 to pass, that he that is l' in Zion, 7604
7:22 every one eat that is l' in the land.3498
9:20 and he shall eat on the l' hand, 8040
10:14 as one gathereth eggs that are l', *5800
11:11, 16, his people, which shall be l', *7604
17: 6 Yet gleaning grapes shall be l' in it,"
9 they l' because of the children of *5800
18: 6 They shall be l' together unto the "
24: 6 earth are burned, and few men l'. 7604
12 In the city is l' desolation, and the "
27:10 forsaken, and l' like a wilderness:*5800
30:17 be l' as a beacon upon the top of a 3498
21 hand, and when ye turn to the l'. 8041
32:14 multitude of the city shall be l'; *5800
37: 4 prayer for the remnant that is l'. 4672
39: 6 to Babylon: nothing shall be l'. 3498
49:21 I was l' alone; these, where had 7604
54: 3 on the right hand and on the l'; 8040
Jer 12: 7 house, I have l' mine heritage; *5203
21: 7 are l' this city from the pestilence, 7604
27:18 vessels which are l' in the house 3498
31: 2 people which were l' of the sword 8300
34: 7 all the cities of Judah that were l'. 3498
38:22 women that are l' in the king of 7604
27 they l' off speaking with him; for 2790
39:10 captain of the guard l' of the poor 7604
40: 6 the people that were l' in the land. "
11 had l' a remnant of Judah, and 5414
42: 2 (for we are l' but a few of many, as7604
43: 6 captain of the guard had l' with 3240
44:18 l' off to burn incense to the queen 2308
49:25 How is the city of praise not l', the*5800
50:26 utterly: let nothing of her be l'. 7611
52:16 captain of the guard l' certain of 7604
Eze 1:10 the face of an ox on the l' side; 8040
4: 4 Lie thou also upon thy l' side, and 8042
9: 8 were slaying them, and I was l', 7604
14:22 therein shall be l' a remnant that 3498
16:46 daughters that dwell at thy l' hand:8040
21:16 on the right hand or on the l', 8041
23: 8 Neither l' she her whoredoms 5800
24:21 your daughters whom ye have l' "
31:12 have cut him off, and have l' him: 5203
12 from his shadow, and have l' him. "
36:36 heathen that are l' round about 7604
39: 3 smite thy bow out of thy l' hand, 8040
28 l' none of them any more there. *3498
41: 9 that which was l' was the place of 3240
11 were toward the place that was l', "
11 place that was l' was five cubits "
48:15 that are l' in the breadth over 3498
Da 2:44 kingdom shall not be l' to other 7662
10: 8 I was l' alone, and saw this great 7604
17 me, neither is there breath l' in me." "
12: 7 hand and his l' hand unto heaven, 8040
Ho 4:10 l' off to take heed to the Lord. 5800
9:12 them, that there shall not be a man l': "
Joe 1: 4 which the palmerworm hath l' 3499
4 that which the locust hath l' hath "
4 that which the cankerworm hath l' "
Jon 4:11 their right hand and their l' hand; 8040
Hag 2: 3 Who is l' among you that saw this 7604
Zec 4: 3 the other upon the l' side thereof. 8040
11 and upon the l' side thereof? "
12: 6 on the right hand and on the l': "
13: 8 but the third shall be l' therein. 3498
14:16 one that is l' of all the nations "
M't 4:20 they straightway l' their nets, and 863
22 they immediately l' the ship and "
6: 3 let not thy l' hand know what thy 710
8:15 her hand, and the fever l' her: 863
15:37 broken meat that was l' seven *4052
16: 4 And he l' them, and departed. 2641
20:21 the other on the l', in thy kingdom.2176
23 sit on my right hand, and on my l', "
21:17 he l' them, and went out of the 2641
22:22 and l' him, and went their way. 863
25 issue, l' his wife unto his brother: "
23:38 your house is l' unto you desolate. "
24: 2 shall not be l' here one stone upon "
40, 41 shall be taken, and the other l'. "
25:33 right hand, but the goats on the l'.2176
41 say also unto them on the l' hand, "
26:44 he l' them, and went away again, 863
27:38 right hand, and another on the l'. 2176
M'r 1: 20 and they l' their father Zebedee in 863
31 and immediately the fever l' her, "
8: 8 meat that was l' seven baskets. *4051
13 he l' them, and entering into the 863
10:28 we have l' all, and have followed "
29 There is no man that hath l' house, "
37 the other on thy l' hand, in thy 2176
40 on my l' hand is not mine to give; "
12:12 they l' him, and went their way, 863
20 took a wife, and dying l' no seed. "
21 her, and died, neither l' he any seed:*"
22 the seven had her, and l' no seed: "
13: 2 there shall not be l' one stone upon "
34 a far journey, who l' his house, "
14:52 he l' the linen cloth, and fled from 2641
15:27 right hand, and the other on his l'.2176
Lu 4:39 rebuked the fever; and it l' her: 863
5: 4 when he had l' speaking, he said 3973
28 And he l' all, rose up, and followed*2641
10:40 my sister hath l' me to serve alone? "
13:35 your house is l' unto you desolate: 863
17:34 be taken, and the other shall be l'. "
35 shall be taken, and the other l'. "
36 shall be taken, and the other l'. * "
18:28 Peter said, Lo, we have l' all, and "
29 There is no man that hath l' house, "

Lu 20:31 seven also: and they l' no children.2641
21: 6 not be l' one stone upon another, 863
23:33 right hand, and the other on the l'. 710
Joh 4: 3 He l' Judæa, and departed again 863
28 woman then l' her waterpot, and "
52 at the seventh hour the fever l' him. "
8: 9 Jesus was l' alone, and the woman2641
29 the Father hath not l' me alone; 863
Ac 2:31 his soul was not l' in hell, neither 2641
14:17 he l' not himself without witness, 863
18:19 to Ephesus, and l' them there: 2641
21: 3 we had discovered Cyprus, we l' it* "
3 it on the l' hand, and sailed into 2176
32 soldiers, they l' beating of Paul. 3973
23:32 l' the horsemen to go with him, 1439
24:27 Jews a pleasure, l' Paul bound. 2641
25:14 certain man l' in bonds by Felix: "
Ro 9:29 Lord of Sabaoth had l' us a seed, 1459
11: 3 and I am l' alone, and they seek 5275
2Co 6: 7 on the right hand and on the l', 710
1Th 3: 1 thought it good to be l' at Athens 2641
2Ti 4: 13 cloke that I l' at Troas with Carpus, 620
20 Trophimus have I l' at Miletum sick."
Tit 1: 5 For this cause l' I thee in Crete, 2641
Heb 2: 8 l' nothing that is not put under him.863
4: 1 a promise being l' us of entering 2641
Jude 6 estate, but l' their own habitation, 620
Re 2: 4 because thou hast l' thy first love.* 863
10: 2 sea, and his l' foot on the earth, 2176

leftest
Ne 9:28 therefore l' thou them in the hand 5800

left-foot See LEFT and FOOT.

left-hand See LEFT and HAND; also LEFTHANDED.

lefthanded
J'g 3:15 a Benjamite, a man l': 334,3027,3225
20:16 hundred chosen men l'; " " "

left-side See LEFT and SIDE.

leg See also LEGS.
Isa 47: 2 make bare the l', uncover the 7640

legion See also LEGIONS.
M'r 5: 9 My name is L': for we are many. 3003
15 with the devil, and had the l', "
Lu 8:30 What is thy name? And he said, L': "

legions
M't 26:53 me more than twelve l' of angels? 3003

legs
Ex 12: 9 his head with his l', and with the 3767
29:17 wash the inwards of him, and his l'."
Le 1: 9 inwards and his l' shall he wash in "
13 he shall wash the inwards and the l' "
4:11 flesh, with his head, and with his l'. "
8:21 he washed the inwards and the l' "
9:14 he did wash the inwards and the l'. "
11:21 which have l' above their feet, to "
De 28:35 thee in the knees, and in the l', 7785
1Sa 17: 6 had greaves of brass upon his l', 7272
Ps 147:10 not pleasure in the l' of a man. 7785
Pr 26: 7 The l' of the lame are not equal: so"
Ca 5:15 His l' are as pillars of marble, set "
Isa 3:20 the ornaments of the l', and the *6807
Da 2:33 His l' of iron, his feet part of iron 8243
Am 3:12 out of the mouth of the lion two l',3767
Joh 19:31 that their l' might be broken, and 4628
32 and brake the l' of the first, and of "
33 dead already, they brake not his l':"

Lehabim (*le'-ha-bim*)
Ge 10:13 Ludim, and Anamim, and L', and 3853
1Ch 1:11 begat Ludim, and Anamim, and L'."

Lehem See BETH-LEHEM; JESHUBI-LEHEM.

Lehi (*le'-hi*) See also RAMATH-LEHI.
J'g 15: 9 and spread themselves in L'. 3896
14 And when he came unto L', the "
19 which is in L' unto this day. "

leisure
M'k 6:31 they had no l' so much as to eat. 2119

Lemuel (*lem'-u-el*)
Pr 31: 1 words of king L', the prophecy 3927
4 O L', it is not for kings to drink "

lend See also LENDETH; LENT.
Ex 22:25 thou l' money to any of my people 3867
Le 25:37 l' him thy victuals for increase. *5414
De 15: 6 thou shalt l' unto many nations, 5670
8 shalt surely l' him sufficient for his"
23:19 Thou shalt not l' upon usury to 5391
20 thou mayest l' upon usury; "
20 thou shalt not l' upon usury: "
24:10 When thou dost l' thy brother any 5383
11 the man to whom thou dost l' shall "
28:12 thou shalt l' unto many nations, 3867
44 l' to thee, and thou shalt not l' to "
Lu 6:34 if ye l' to them of whom ye hope to1155
34 sinners also l' to sinners, to receive"
35 and l', hoping for nothing again; "
11: 5 him, Friend, l' me three loaves: 5531

lender
Pr 22: 7 the borrower is servant to the l'. 3867
Isa 24: 2 as with the l', so with the borrower;"

lendeth
De 15: 2 Every creditor that l' ought unto *5383
Ps 37:26 He is ever merciful, and l'; and 3867
112: 5 good man sheweth favour, and l': "
Pr 19:17 pity upon the poor l' unto the Lord;"

length
Ge 6:15 l' of the ark shall be three hundred 753
13:17 walk through the land in the l' of it "
Ex 25:10, 17 cubits and a half shall be the l' "
23 two cubits shall be the l' thereof, "
26: 2 The l' of one curtain shall be eight "
8 The l' of one curtain shall be thirty "

Ex 26:13 remaineth in the l· of the curtains 753
16 Ten cubits shall be the l· of a board, "
27:11 side in l· there shall be hangings "
18 l· of the court shall be an hundred "
28:16 a span shall be the l· thereof, and a "
30: 2 A cubit shall be the l· thereof, and a "
36: 9 The l· of one curtain was twenty "
15 The l· of one curtain was thirty "
21 The l· of a board was ten cubits, and "
37: 1 two cubits and a half was the l· of it, "
6 cubits and a half was the l· thereof, "
10 two cubits was the l· thereof, and a "
25 the l· of it was a cubit, and the "
38: 1 five cubits was the l· thereof, and "
18 and twenty cubits was the l·, and the "
39: 9 a span was the l· thereof, and a span "
De 3:11 nine cubits was the l· thereof, and "
30:20 he is thy life, and the l· of thy days: "
J'g 3:16 which had two edges, of a cubit l·; "
1Ki 6: 2 the l· thereof was threescore cubits, "
3 twenty cubits was the l· thereof, "
20 the forepart was twenty cubits in l·, "
7: 2 the l· thereof was an hundred cubits, "
6 the l· thereof was fifty cubits, and "
27 four cubits was the l· of one base, "
2Ch 3: 3 l· by cubits after the first measure "
4 l· of it was according to the breadth "
8 the l· thereof was according to the "
4: 1 of brass, twenty cubits the l· thereof, "
Job 12:12 and in l· of days understanding. "
Ps 21: 4 even l· of days for ever and ever. "
Pr 3: 2 For l· of days, and long life, and "
16 L· of days is in her right hand; and "
29:21 have him become his son at the l·.*319
Eze 31: 7 greatness, in the l· of his branches: 753
40:11 the l· of the gate, thirteen cubits. "
18 over against the l· of the gates was "
20 he measured the l· thereof, and the "
21 the l· thereof was fifty cubits, and "
25 windows: the l· was fifty cubits, "
36 the l· was fifty cubits, and the "
49 l· of the porch was twenty cubits, "
41: 2 measured the l· thereof, forty cubits: "
4 So he measured the l· thereof, "
12 and the l· thereof ninety cubits. "
15 he measured the l· of the building "
22 high, and the l· thereof two cubits; "
22 the l· thereof, and the walls thereof, "
42: 2 the l· of an hundred cubits was the "
7 the l· thereof was fifty cubits. "
8 the l· of the chambers that were in "
45: 1 the l· shall be the l· of five and "
2 for the sanctuary five hundred in l·, "
3 measure shalt thou measure the l· 753
5 the five and twenty thousand of l·, "
7 the l· shall be over against one of "
48: 8 and in l· as one of the other parts, "
9 be of five and twenty thousand in l·, "
10 north five and twenty thousand in l·, "
10 south five and twenty thousand in l·: "
13 have five and twenty thousand in l·, "
13 l· shall be five and twenty thousand, "
18 the residue in l· over against the "
Zec 2: 2 thereof, and what is the l· thereof. "
5: 2 the l· thereof is twenty cubits, and "
Ro 1:10 at l· I might have a prosperous 4218
Eph 3:18 what is the breadth, and l·, and 3372
Re 21:16 the l· is as large as the breadth: "
16 l· and the breadth and the height "

lengthen See also LENGTHENED; LENGTHENING.
1Ki 3:14 did walk then will I l· thy days. 748
Isa 54: 2 l· thy cords, and strengthen thy "

lengthened
De 25:15 that thy days may be l· in the land*748

lengthening
Da 4:27 if it may be a l· of thy tranquillity. 754

lent
Ex 12:36 l· unto them such things as they *7592
De 23:19 of any thing that is l· upon usury: 5391
1Sa 1:28 also I have l· him to the Lord; *7592
28 he liveth he shall be l· to the Lord.* "
2:20 the loan which is l· to the Lord. ‡ "
Jer 15:10 I have neither l· on usury, nor 5383
10 nor men have l· to me on usury; "

lentiles
Ge 25:34 gave Esau bread and pottage of l·; 5742
2Sa 17:28 parched corn, and beans, and l·, "
23:11 was a piece of ground full of l·: "
Eze 4: 9 and beans, and l·, and millet, and "

leopard See also LEOPARDS.
Isa 11: 6 the l· shall lie down with the kid; 5246
Jer 5: 6 a l· shall watch over their cities: "
13:23 change his skin, or the l· his spots? "
Da 7: 6 I beheld, and lo another, like a l·, 5245
Ho 13: 7 as a l· by the way will I observe 5246
Re 13: 2 which I saw was like unto a l·, 3917

leopards
Ca 4: 8 from the mountains of the l·. 5246
Hab 1: 8 horses also are swifter than the l·, "

leper See also LEPERS.
Le 13:45 And the l· in whom the plague is, 6879
14: 2 this shall be the law of the l· in "
3 plague of leprosy be healed in the l·; "
22: 4 soever of the seed of Aaron is a l·, "
Nu 5: 2 they put out of the camp every l·, "
2Sa 3:29 that hath an issue, or that is a l·, "
2Ki 5: 1 man in valour, but he was a l·. "
11 over the place, and recover the l·. "
27 he went out from his presence a l· "
15: 5 was a l· unto the day of his death, "
2Ch 26:21 Uzziah the king was a l· unto the "
21 dwelt in a several house, being a l·; "
2Ch 26:23 the kings; for they said, He is a l·: 6879
M't 8: 2 there came a l· and worshipped 3015
26: 6 in the house of Simon the l·, "
M'r 1:40 there came a l· to him, beseeching "
14: 3 in the house of Simon the l·, as he "

lepers
2Ki 7: 8 l· came to the uttermost part of 6879
M't 10: 8 sick, cleanse the l·, raise the dead, 3015
11: 5 the l· are cleansed, and the deaf "
Lu 4:27 And many l· were in Israel in the "
7:22 the l· are cleansed, the deaf hear, "
17:12 there met him ten men that were l·, "

leprosy
Le 13: 2 of his flesh like the plague of l·; 6883
3 skin of his flesh, it is a plague of l·: "
8 pronounce him unclean: it is a l·. "
9 When the plague of l· is in a man, "
11 is an old l· in the skin of his flesh, "
12 if a l· break out abroad in the skin, "
12 and the l· cover all the skin of him "
13 if the l· have covered all his flesh, "
15 the raw flesh is unclean: it is a l·. "
20 plague of l· broken out of the boil. "
25 it is a l· broken out of the burning: "
25, 27 unclean: it is the plague of l·. "
30 even a l· upon the head or beard. "
42 it is a l· sprung up in his bald head, "
43 as the l· appeareth in the skin of the "
47 garment...that the plague of l· is in, "
49 a plague of l·, and shall be shewed "
51 plague is a fretting l·; it is unclean. "
52 for it is a fretting l·; it shall be burnt "
59 This is the law of the plague of l· "
14: 3 plague of l· be healed in the leper; "
7 him that is to be cleansed from l· "
32 of him in whom is the plague of l·, "
34 I put the plague of l· in a house of "
44 it is a fretting l· in the house: it is "
54 law for all manner of plague of l·, "
55 And for the l· of a garment, and of "
57 when it is clean: this is the law of l·. "
De 24: 8 Take heed in the plague of l·, that "
2Ki 5: 3 for he would recover him of his l·. "
6 thou mayest recover him of his l·. "
7 unto me to recover a man of his l·? "
27 The l· therefore of Naaman shall "
2Ch 26:19 the l· even rose up in his forehead "
M't 8: 3 immediately his l· was cleansed. 3014
M'r 1:42 immediately the l· departed from "
Lu 5:12 certain city, behold a man full of l·: "
13 immediately the l· departed from "

leprous
Ex 4: 6 behold, his hand was l· as snow. 6879
Le 13:44 He is a l· man, he is unclean: "
Nu 12:10 Miriam became l·, white as snow: "
10 Miriam, and, behold, she was l·. "
2Ki 7: 3 were four l· men at the entering in "
2Ch 26:20 behold, he was l· in his forehead, "

Leshem (*le'-shem*) See also LAISH.
Jos 19:47 Dan went up to fight against L·, 3959
47 dwelt therein, and called L·, Dan, "

less See also BLAMELESS; BOTTOMLESS; CAUSELESS; CHILDLESS; COMFORTLESS; DOUBTLESS; ENDLESS; FAITHLESS; FATHERLESS; FAULTLESS; HARMLESS; LAWLESS; LESSER; NEVERTHELESS; SHAMELESSLY; SPEECHLESS; UNLESS.
Ex 16:17 and gathered, some more, some l·. 4591
30:15 the poor shall not give l· than half "
Nu 22:18 the Lord my God, to do l· or more. 6996
26:54 thou shalt give the l· inheritance: 4591
33:54 ye shall give the l· inheritance: "
1Sa 22:15 nothing of all this, l· or more. 6996
25:36 she told him nothing, l· or more, "
1Ki 8:27 how much l· this house that I have "
2Ch 6:18 how much l· this house which I have "
32:15 how much l· shall your God deliver "
Ezr 9:13 punished us l· than our iniquities 4295
Job 4:19 How much l· in them that dwell in* "
9:14 How much l· shall I answer him, and "
11: 6 exacteth of thee l· than thine iniquity "
25: 6 How much l· man, that is a worm? "
Pr 17: 7 a fool: much l· do lying lips a prince. "
19:10 much l· for a servant to have rule over "
Isa 40:17 are counted to him l· than nothing, 657
M'r 4:31 l· than all the seeds that be in the 3398
15:40 Mary the mother of James the l· "
1Co 12:23 which we think to be l· honourable, 820
2Co 12:15 I love you, the l· I be loved. 2276
Eph 3: 8 am l· than the least of all saints, 1647
Ph'p 2:28 and that I may be the l· sorrowful. 253
Heb 7: 7 the l· is blessed of the better. 1640

lesser
Ge 1:16 and the l· light to rule the night: 6996
Isa 7:25 and for the treading of l· cattle. *7716
Eze 43:14 and from the l· settle even to the 6996

lest
Ge 3: 3 neither shall ye touch it, l· ye die. 6435
22 l· he put forth his hand, and take "
4:15 l· any finding him should kill him. 1115
11: 4 l· we be scattered abroad upon the 6435
14:23 l· thou shouldest say, I have made 3808
19:15 l· thou be consumed in the 6435
17 mountain, l· thou be consumed. "
19 l· some evil take me, and I die. "
26: 7 l·, said he, the men of the place "
9 Because I said, L· I die for her. "
32:11 him, l· he will come and smite me, "
38: 9 l· that he should give seed to his 1115
11 L· peradventure he die also, as his 6435
23 her take it to her, l· we be shamed: "
42: 4 L· peradventure mischief befall "
44:34 l· peradventure I see the evil that "
Ge 45:11 l· thou, and thy household, and all 6435
Ex 1:10 l· they multiply, and it come to pass, "
5: 3 l· he fall upon us with pestilence, "
13:17 L· peradventure the people repent "
19:21 l· they break through unto the Lord "
22 l· the Lord break forth upon them. "
24 Lord, l· he break forth upon them. "
20:19 let not God speak with us, l· we die. "
23:29 l· the land become desolate, and the "
33 l· they make thee sin against me: "
33: 3 l· I consume thee in the way. "
34:12 l· thou make a covenant with the "
12 l· it be for a snare in the midst of "
15 L· thou make a covenant with the "
Le 10: 6 neither rend your clothes; l· ye *3808
6 l· wrath come upon all the people.* "
7 of the congregation, l· ye die: 6435
9 of the congregation, l· ye die: *3808
19:29 l· the land fall to whoredom, and "
22: 9 l· they bear sin for it, and die "
Nu 4:15 not touch any holy thing, l· they die. "
20 the holy things are covered, l· they die. "
16:26 l· ye be consumed in all their sins. 6435
34 L· the earth swallow us up also. "
18:22 congregation, l· they bear sin, and die. "
32 of the children of Israel, l· ye die. *3808
De 4: 9 l· thou forget the things which 6435
9 l· they depart from thy heart all the "
16 L· ye corrupt yourselves, and make "
19 And l· thou lift up thine eyes unto "
23 l· ye forget the covenant of the Lord "
6:12 Then beware l· thou forget the Lord, "
15 l· the anger of the Lord thy God be "
7:22 l· the beasts of the field increase "
25 unto thee, l· thou be snared therein: "
26 l· thou be a cursed thing like it: *
8:12 L· when thou hast eaten and art 6435
9:28 L· the land whence thou broughtest "
11:17 l· ye perish quickly from off the good* "
19: 6 L· the avenger of the blood pursue 6435
20: 5, 6, 7 l· he die in the battle, and "
8 l· his brethren's heart faint as well "
22: 9 l· the fruit of thy seed which thou "
24:15 l· he cry against thee unto the Lord, 3808
25: 3 l·, if he should exceed, and beat, 6435
29:18 L· there should be among you man, "
18 l· there should be among you a root "
32:27 l· their adversaries should behave "
27 and l· they should say, Our hand is "
Jos 2:16 l· the pursuers meet you; "
6:18 l· ye make yourselves accursed, "
9:20 let them live, l· wrath be upon us, 3808
24:27 unto you, l· ye deny your God. 6435
J'g 7: 2 l· Israel vaunt themselves against "
14:15 l· we burn thee and thy father's "
18:25 l· angry fellows run upon thee, and "
Ru 4: 6 l· I mar mine own inheritance: "
1Sa 9: 5 l· my father leave caring for the "
13:19 L· the Hebrews make them swords "
15: 6 l· I destroy you with them: for ye "
20: 3 know this, l· he be grieved: "
27:11 L· they should tell on us, saying, "
29: 4 l· in the battle he be an adversary 3808
31: 4 l· these uncircumcised come and 6435
2Sa 1:20 l· the daughters of the Philistines "
20 rejoice, l· the daughters of the "
12:28 l· I take the city, and it be called "
13:25 go, l· we be chargeable unto thee. 3808
14:11 any more, l· they destroy my son. "
15:14 depart, l· he overtake us suddenly, 6435
17:16 l· the king be swallowed up, and all "
20: 6 l· he get him fenced cities, and "
2Ki 2:16 l· peradventure the Spirit of the "
1Ch 10: 4 l· these uncircumcised come and "
Job 32:13 L· ye should say, We have found "
34:30 reign not, l· the people be ensnared.* "
36:18 beware l· he take thee away with ‡6435
42: 8 l· I deal with you after your folly, *1115
Ps 2:12 Kiss the Son, l· he be angry, and 6435
7: 2 L· he tear my soul like a lion, "
13: 3 eyes, l· I sleep the sleep of death; "
4 L· mine enemy say, I have prevailed "
28: 1 l·, if thou be silent to me, I become "
32: 9 l· they come near unto thee. *1077
38:16 l· otherwise they should rejoice 6435
50:22 l· I tear you in pieces, and there be "
59:11 Slay them not, l· my people forget: "
106:23 his wrath, l· he should destroy them. "
125: 3 l· the righteous put forth *4616, 3808
140: 8 device; l· they exalt themselves. "
143: 7 l· I be like unto them that go down "
Pr 5: 6 L· thou shouldest ponder the *6435
9 L· thou give thine honour unto "
10 L· strangers be filled with thy "
9: 8 not a scorner, l· he hate thee: "
20:13 not sleep, l· thou come to poverty; "
22:25 L· thou learn his ways, and get a "
24:18 L· the Lord see it, and it displease "
25: 8 l· thou know not what to do in the "
10 L· he that heareth it put thee to "
16 l· thou be filled therewith, and "
17 l· he be weary of thee, and so hate "
26: 4 folly, l· thou also be like unto him. "
5 l· he be wise in his own conceit. "
30: 6 l· he reprove thee, and thou be "
9 L· I be full, and deny thee, and say, "
10 l· he curse thee, and thou be found "
31: 5 L· they drink, and forget the law, "
Ec 7:21 l· thou hear thy servant curse 634, 3808
Isa 6:10 l· they see with their eyes, and 6435
27: 3 l· any hurt it, I will keep it night "
28:22 l· your bands be made strong: for "
36:18 Beware l· Hezekiah persuade you, "
48: 5 l· thou shouldest say, Mine idol "
7 l· thou shouldest say, Behold, I "
Jer 1:17 l· I confound thee before them. "

Jer 4: 4 *l'* my fury come forth like fire, and 6435
6: 8 *l'* my soul depart from thee; "
8 *l'* I make thee desolate, a land not "
10: 24 anger, *l'* thou bring me to nothing. "
21: 12 *l'* my fury go out like fire, and burn" "
37: 20 Jonathan the scribe, *l'* I die there. 3808
38: 19 *l'* they deliver me into their hand, 6435
51: 46 And *l'* your heart faint, and ye fear*"
Ho 2: 3 *L'* I strip her naked, and set her as "
Am 5: 6 *l'* he break out like fire in the house"
Zec 7: 12 *l'* they should hear the law, and the
Mal 4: 6 *l'* I come and smite the earth with 6435
M't 4: 6 *l'* at any time thou dash thy foot 3379
5: 25 *l'* at any time the adversary deliver "
7: 6 *l'* they trample them under their "
13: 15 *l'* at any time they should see with "
29 *l'* while ye gather up the tares, ye "
15: 32 fasting, *l'* they faint in the way. "
17: 27 *l'* we should offend them, go 2443, 3361
25: 9 *l'* there be not enough for us and *3379
26: 5 *l'* there be an uproar among 2443, 3361
27: 64 *l'* his disciples come by night, and 3379
M'r 3: 9 *l'* they should throng him. 2443, 3361
4: 12 *l'*...time they should be converted, 3379
13: 5 Take heed *l'* any man deceive you: *3361
36 *L'* coming suddenly he find you "
14: 2 *l'* there be an uproar of the people. 3379
38 *l'* ye enter into temptation. *2443, 3361
Lu 4: 11 *l'* at any time thou dash thy foot 3379
8: 12 *l'* they should believe and be *2443, 3361
12: 58 him; *l'* he hale thee to the judge, 3379
14: 8 *l'* a more honourable man than "
12 *l'* they also bid thee again, and a "
29 *L'* haply, after he hath 2443, 3361
16: 28 *l'* they also come into this " "
18: 5 *l'* by her continual coming she " "
21: 34 *l'* at any time your hearts be 3379
22: 46 *l'* ye enter into temptation. *2443, 3361
Joh 3: 20 *l'* his deeds should be reproved. " "
5: 14 *l'* a worse thing come unto thee." "
12: 35 *l'* darkness come upon you: * " "
42 *l'* they should be put out of the " "
18: 28 hall, *l'* they should be defiled;* " "
Ac 5: 26 *l'* they should have been stoned." "
39 *l'* haply ye be found even to fight 3379
13: 40 therefore, *l'* that come upon you, 3361
23: 10 fearing *l'* Paul should have been "
27: 17 fearing *l'* they should fall into the "
29 fearing *l'* we should have fallen 3381
42 *l'* any of them should swim out, 3361
28: 27 *l'* they should see with their eyes, 3379
Ro 11: 21 take heed *l'* be also spare not thee.*3381
25 *l'* ye should be wise in your 2443, 3361
15: 20 *l'* I should build upon another* " "
1Co 1: 15 *L'* any should say that I had " "
17 *l'* the cross of Christ should be " "
8: 9 heed *l'* by any means this liberty 3381
13 *l'* I make my brother to offend.*2443, 3361
9: 12 *l'* we should hinder the gospel* " "
27 *l'* that by any means, when I have 3381
10: 12 he standeth take heed *l'* he fall. 3361
2Co 2: 3 *l'*, when I came, I should have 2443, "
7 *l'* perhaps such a one should be "
11 *L'* Satan should get an 2443, 3361
4: 4 *l'* the light of the glorious *1519, 3588 "
9: 3 *l'* our boasting of you should * "
4 *L'* haply if they of Macedonia 3381
11: 3 *l'* by any means, as the serpent "
12: 6 *l'* any man should think of me 3361
7 *l'* I should be...above measure,*2443, "
7 *l'* I should be...above measure.* "
20 For I fear, *l'*, when I come, I shall 3381
20 *l'* there be debates, envyings, "
21 *l'*, when I come again, my God 3361
13: 10 *l'* being present I should use *2443, "
Ga 2: 2 *l'* by any means I should run, or 3381
4: 11 *l'* I have bestowed upon you labour"
6: 1 thyself, *l'* thou also be tempted. 3361
12 only *l'* they should suffer *2443, "
Eph 2: 9 *l'* any man should boast. * " "
Ph'p 2: 27 *l'* I should have sorrow upon* " "
Col 2: 4 *l'* any man should beguile * " "
8 Beware *l'* any man spoil you "
3: 21 *l'* they be discouraged. *2443, "
1Th 3: 5 *l'* by some means the tempter have 3381
1Ti 3: 6 *l'* being lifted up with pride 2443, 3361
7 *l'* he fall into reproach and the " "
Heb 2: 1 *l'* at any time we should let them 3379
3: 12 *l'* there be in any of you an evil "
13 *l'* any of you be hardened 2443, 3361
4: 1 fear, *l'*, a promise being left us of 3379
11 *l'* any man fall after the same*2443, 3361
11: 28 *l'* he that destroyed the " "
12: 3 *l'* ye be wearied and faint in * " "
13 *l'* that which is lame be * " "
15 *l'* any man fail of the grace of God; * "
15 *l'* any root of bitterness springing "
16 *L'* there be any fornicator, or "
Jas 5: 9 *l'* ye be condemned: behold, *2443, 3361
12 *l'* ye fall into condemnation. * " "
2Pe 3: 17 beware *l'* ye also, being led " "
Re 16: 15 *l'* he walk naked, and they see " "
let See also LETTEST; LETTETH; LETTING.
Ge 1: 3 And God said, *L'* there be light: and
6 *L'* there be a firmament in the midst
9 *L'* the waters...the heaven be gathered
11 *L'* the earth bring forth grass, the
14 *L'* there be lights in the firmament of
14 *l'* them be for signs, and for seasons,
15 *l'* them be for lights in the firmament
20 *L'* the waters bring forth abundantly
22 seas, and *l'* fowl multiply in the earth.
24 *L'* the earth bring forth the living
26 *L'* us make man in our image, after
26 *l'* them have dominion over the fish
11: 3 to, *l'* us make brick, and burn them

Ge 11: 4 Go to, *l'* us build us a city and a tower,
4 and *l'* us make us a name, lest we be
7 Go to, *l'* us go down, and there
13: 8 *L'* there be no strife, I pray thee,
14: 24 Mamre; *l'* them take their portion.
18: 4 *L'* a little water, I pray you, be fetched,
30, 32 Oh *l'* not the Lord be angry, and I
19: 8 *l'* me, I pray you, bring them out unto
20 a little one: Oh, *l'* me escape thither,
32 *l'* us make our father drink wine,
34 *l'* us make him drink wine this night
21: 12 *L'* it not be grievous in thy sight
16 *L'* me not see the death of the child.
24: 14 And *l'* it come to pass, that the damsel
14 *L'* down thy pitcher, I pray thee, 5186
14 *l'* the same be she that thou hast
17 *L'* me, I pray thee, drink a little *
18 she hasted, and *l'* down her pitcher 3381
44 *l'* the same be the woman whom the
45 unto her, *L'* me drink, I pray thee.
46 haste, and *l'* down her pitcher 3381
51 and *l'* her be thy master's son's wife,
55 *L'* the damsel abide with us a few
60 *l'* thy seed possess the gate of those
26: 28 *L'* there be now an oath betwixt us,
28 and *l'* us make a covenant with thee;
27: 29 *L'* people serve thee, and nations bow
29 *l'* thy mother's sons bow down to thee:
31 *L'* my father arise, and eat of his son's
30: 26 whom I have served thee, and *l'* me go:
31: 32 thou findest thy gods, *l'* him not live: *
35 *L'* it not displease my lord that I
44 *l'* us make a covenant, I and thou;
44 *l'* it be for a witness between me and
32: 26 *L'* me go, for the day breaketh.
26 I will not *l'* thee go, except thou
33: 12 *L'* us take our journey, and *l'* us go,
14 *L'* my lord, I pray thee, pass over
15 *L'* me now leave with thee some of
15 *l'* me find grace in the sight of my
34: 11 *L'* me find grace in your eyes, and
21 therefore *l'* them dwell in the land,
21 *l'* us take their daughters to us for
21 and *l'* us give them our daughters,
23 only *l'* us consent unto them, and they
35: 3 And *l'* us arise, and go up to Bethel;
37: 17 heard them say, *L'* us go to Dothan.
20 *l'* us slay him, and cast him into some
21 hands; and said, *L'* us not kill him.
27 and *l'* us sell him to the Ishmeelites,
27 and *l'* not our hand be upon him; for
38: 16 I pray thee, *l'* me come in unto thee;
23 *L'* her take it to her, lest we be
24 Bring her forth, and *l'* her be burnt.
41: 33 therefore *l'* Pharaoh look out a man
34 *L'* Pharaoh do this, and *l'* him appoint
35 *l'* them gather all the food of those
35 and *l'* them keep food in the cities.
42: 16 *l'* him fetch your brother, and ye shall
19 *l'* one of your brethren be bound in
43: 9 then *l'* me bear the blame forever.
44: 9 both *l'* him die, and we also will be
10 Now also *l'* it be according unto your
18 lord, *l'* thy servant, I pray thee, speak
18 *l'* not thine anger burn against thy
33 *l'* thy servant abide instead of the lad
33 and *l'* the lad go up with his brethren.
46: 30 Now *l'* me die, since I have seen thy
47: 4 *l'* thy servants dwell in the land of
6 in the land of Goshen *l'* them dwell:
25 *l'* us find grace in the sight of my
48: 16 *l'* my name be named on them, and the
16 *l'* them grow into a multitude in the
49: 21 Naphtali is a hind *l'* loose: he giveth
50: 5 Now therefore *l'* me go up, I pray thee,
Ex 1: 10 *l'* us deal wisely with them; lest they
3: 18 now *l'* us go, we beseech thee, three
19 king of Egypt will not *l'* you go, *5414
20 and after that he will *l'* you go.
4: 18 *L'* me go, I pray thee, and return unto
21 that he shall not *l'* the people go.
23 *L'* my son go, that he may serve
23 and if thou refuse to *l'* him go,
26 So he *l'* him go: then she said: A
5: 1 *L'* my people go, that they may
2 obey his voice to *l'* Israel go?
2 Lord, neither will I *l'* Israel go.
3 *l'* us go, we pray thee, three days'
4 *l'* the people from their works? *6544
7 *l'* them go and gather straw for
8 *L'* us go and sacrifice to our God.
9 *L'* there more work be laid upon the
9 and *l'* them not regard vain words.
17 *L'* us go and do sacrifice to the Lord.
6: 1 with a strong hand shall he *l'* them go,
11 he *l'* the children of Israel go out
7: 14 he refuseth to *l'* the people go.
16 *L'* my people go, that they may
8: 1 *L'* my people go, that they may
2 And if thou refuse to *l'* them go,
8 I will *l'* the people go, that they may
20 *L'* my people go, that they may
21 if thou wilt not *l'* my people go,
28 said, I will *l'* you go, that ye may
29 *l'* not Pharaoh deal deceitfully any
32 neither would he *l'* the people go.
9: 1 *L'* my people go, that they may
2 For if thou refuse to *l'* them go,
7 and he did not *l'* the people go.
8 *l'* Moses sprinkle it toward the heaven
13 *L'* my people go, that they may
17 that thou wilt not *l'* them go?
28 I will *l'* you go, and ye shall stay as
35 he *l'* the children of Israel go;
10: 3 *l'* my people go, that they may
4 if thou refuse to *l'* my people go,

Ex 10: 7 *l'* the men go, that they may serve
10 them, *L'* the Lord be so with you, *
10 I will *l'* you go, and your little ones:
20 not *l'* the children of Israel go.
24 only *l'* your flocks and your herds be
24 *l'* your little ones also go with you.
27 and he would not *l'* them go.
11: 1 afterwards he will *l'* you go hence:
1 when he shall *l'* you go, he shall
2 *l'* every man borrow of his neighbour,
10 would not *l'* the children of Israel go
12: 4 *l'* him and his neighbour next...take it*
10 shall *l'* nothing of it remain until the
48 Lord, *l'* all his males be circumcised,
48 then *l'* him come near and keep it;
13: 15 Pharaoh would hardly *l'* us go,
17 when Pharaoh had *l'* the people go,
14: 5 have *l'* Israel go from serving us?
12 *L'* us alone, that we may serve the
25 *L'* us flee from the face of Israel;
16: 19 *L'* no man leave of it till the morning.
29 *l'* no man go out of his place on the
17: 11 when he *l'* down his hand, Amalek 5117
18: 22 *l'* them judge the people at all seasons:
27 Moses *l'* his father in law depart;
19: 10 morrow, and *l'* them wash their clothes,
22 And *l'* the priests also...sanctify
24 but *l'* not the priests and people break
20: 19 *l'* not God speak with us, lest we die.
21: 8 then shall he *l'* her be redeemed:
26 *l'* him go free for his eye's sake.
27 *l'* him go free for his tooth's sake.
22: 13 pieces, then *l'* him bring it for witness,
23: 11 thou shalt *l'* it rest and lie still;
13 neither *l'* it be heard out of thy mouth
24: 14 matters to do, *l'* him come unto them.
25: 8 And *l'* them make me a sanctuary;
32: 10 Now therefore *l'* me alone, that
22 *L'* not the anger of my lord wax hot:
24 hath any gold, *l'* them break it off.
26 the Lord's side? *l'* him come unto me.
33: 12 *l'* me know whom thou wilt send
34: 3 neither *l'* any man be seen throughout
3 neither *l'* the flocks nor herds feed
9 Lord, *l'* my Lord, I pray thee, go among
35: 5 *l'* him bring it, an offering of the Lord:
36: 6 *L'* neither man nor woman make any
Le 1: 3 *l'* him offer a male without blemish: *
4: 3 then *l'* him bring for his sin, which he
10: 6 but *l'* your brethren, the whole house
14: 7 shall *l'* the living bird loose into
53 *l'* go the living bird out of the city
16: 10 to *l'* him go for a scapegoat into the *
22 *l'* go the goat in the wilderness.
26 *l'* go the goat for the scapegoat
18: 21 thou shalt not *l'* any of thy seed pass*
19: 19 not *l'* thy cattle gender with a diverse
21: 17 *l'* him not approach to offer the bread
24: 14 *l'* all that heard him lay their hands
14 and *l'* all the congregation stone him.
25: 27 Then *l'* him count the years of the sale
Nu 5: 8 *l'* the trespass be recompensed unto *
6: 5 shall *l'* the locks...of his head grow.
8: 7 them, and *l'* them shave all their flesh,
7 and *l'* them wash their clothes, and so
8 Then *l'* them take a young bullock
9: 2 *L'* the children of Israel also keep the
10: 35 and *l'* thine enemies be scattered;
35 *l'* them that hate thee flee before thee.
11: 15 and *l'* me not see my wretchedness.
31 *l'* them fall by the camp, as it were
12: 12 *L'* her not be as one dead, of whom
14 *l'* her be shut out from the camp seven
14 after that *l'* her be received in again.*
13: 30 *L'* us go up at once, and possess it;
14: 4 *L'* us make a captain, and
4 and *l'* us return into Egypt.
17 *l'* the power of my Lord be great,
16: 38 *l'* them make them broad plates for a
20: 17 *L'* us pass, I pray thee, through thy
21: 22 *L'* me pass through thy land: we will
27 *l'* the city of Sihon be built and
22: 16 *L'* nothing, I pray thee, hinder thee
23: 10 *L'* me die the death of the righteous,
10 and *l'* my last end be like his!
27: 16 *L'* the Lord...set a man over the
31: 3 *l'* them go against the Midianites, and*
32: 5 *l'* this land be given unto thy
33: 55 those which ye *l'* remain of them shall
36: 6 *L'* them marry to whom they think
De 2: 27 *L'* me pass through thy land: I will
30 Heshbon would not *l'* us pass by him:
3: 25 I pray thee, *l'* me go over, and see the
26 Lord said unto me, *L'* it suffice thee;
9: 14 *L'* me alone, that I may destroy
13: 2 *L'* us go after other gods, which thou
2 hast not known, and *l'* us serve them;
6, 13 *L'* us go and serve other gods,
15: 12 shalt *l'* him go free from thee.
13 shalt not *l'* him go away empty:
18: 16 *L'* me not hear again the voice of the
16 neither *l'* me see this great fire any
20: 3 *l'* not your hearts faint, fear not, and
5 *l'* him go and return to his house,
6 *l'* him also go and return unto his
7, 8 *l'* him go and return unto his
21: 14 shalt *l'* her go whither she will;
22: 7 shalt in any wise *l'* the dam go,
24: 1 *l'* him write her a bill of divorcement,*
25: 7 *l'* his brother's wife go up to the gate*
32: 38 *l'* them rise up and help you, and be
33: 6 *L'* Reuben live, and not die;
6 and *l'* not his men be few.
7 *l'* his hands be sufficient for him; *
8 *L'* thy Thummim and thy Urim be*
16 *l'* the blessing come upon the head of

De 33:24 L' Asher be blessed with children;*
24 l' him be acceptable to his brethren,
24 and l' him dip his foot in oil.
Jos 2:15 Then she l' them down by a cord 3381
18 which thou didst l' us down by: "
4:22 ye shall l' your children know, saying,
6: 6 l' seven priests bear seven trumpets
7 l' him that is armed pass on before the
7: 3 unto him, L' not all the people go up;
3 but l' about two or three thousand
8:22 they l' none of them remain or escape.
9:15 a league with them, to l' them live:
20 we will even l' them live, lest wrath
21 said unto them, L' them live; but
21 but l' them be hewers of wood and *
10:28 were therein; he l' none remain: *
30 therein; he l' none remain in it; *
22:23 thereon, l' the Lord himself require it;
26 L' us now prepare to build us an
24:28 So Joshua l' the people depart, *
J'g 1:25 they l' go the man and all his family.
2: 6 when Joshua had l' the people go,*
5:31 So l' all thine enemies perish, O Lord:
31 l' them that love him be as the sun
6:31 l' him be put to death whilst it is yet
31 he be a god, l' him plead for himself,
32 L' Baal plead against him, because
39 L' not thine anger be hot against me,
39 l' me prove, I pray thee, but this once
39 l' it now be dry only upon the fleece,
39 upon all the ground l' there be dew.
7: 3 l' him return and depart early
7 l' all the other people go every man
9:15 if not, l' fire come out of the bramble,
19 and l' him also rejoice in you:
20 if not, l' fire come out from Abimelech,
20 and l' fire come out from the men of
10:14 l' them deliver you in the time of your
11:17 L' me, I pray thee, pass through thy
19 L' us pass, we pray thee, through thy
37 father, L' this thing be done for me:
37 l' me alone two months, that I
12: 5 L' me go over; that the men of Gilead
13: 8 l' the man of God which thou didst
12 said, Now l' thy words come to pass.
13 I said unto the woman l' her beware.
14 neither l' her drink wine or strong
14 that I commanded her l' her observe.
15 thee, l' us detain thee, until we shall
15: 5 l' them go into the standing corn
16:30 said, L' me die with the Philistines.
18:25 L' not thy voice be heard among us,
19: 6 all night, and l' thine heart be merry.
11 and l' us turn in into this city of the
13 l' us draw near to one of these places
20 l' all thy wants lie upon me; only
25 day began to spring, they l' her go.
28 said unto her, Up, and l' us be going.
20:32 L' us flee, and draw them from the
Ru 2: 2 L' me now go to the field, and glean
7 l' me glean and gather after the
9 l' thine eyes be on the field that they
13 L' me find favour in thy sight, my
15 L' her glean even among the sheaves,
16 l' fall also some of the handfuls *
3:13 l' him do the kinsman's part: but if he
14 L' it not be known that a woman came
4:12 And l' thy house be like the house of
1Sa 1:18 L' thine handmaid find grace in thy
2: 3 l' not arrogancy come out of your
16 L' them not fail to burn the fat *
3:18 l' him do what seemeth him good.
19 did l' none of his words fall to the
4: 3 L' us fetch the ark of the covenant
5: 8 L' the ark of the God...be carried
11 and l' it go again to his own place,
6: 6 did they not l' the people go, and
9: 5 with him, Come, and l' us return;
6 now l' us go thither; peradventure he
9 Come, and l' us go to the seer: for he
10 his servant, Well said; come, l' us go.
19 to-morrow I will l' thee go, and
10: 7 And l' it be, when these signs are
11:14 Come, and l' us go to Gilgal, and
13: 3 land, saying, L' the Hebrews hear.
14: 1 and l' us go over to the Philistines'
6 and l' us go over unto the garrison of
36 L' us go down after the Philistines
36 and l' us not leave a man of them.
16:16 L' our lord now command thy
22 L' David, I pray thee, stand before
17: 8 you, and l' him come down to me.
32 L' no man's heart fail because of him;
18: 2 l' him go no more home to his
17 said, L' not mine hand be upon him,
17 l' the hand of the Philistines be upon
19: 4 L' not the king sin against his servant,
12 So Michal l' David down through 3381
17 L' me go; why should I kill thee?
20: 3 L' not Jonathan know this, lest he be
5 l' me go, that I may hide myself
11 Come, and l' us go out into the field.
16 L' the Lord even require it at the *
29 L' me go, I pray thee; for our
29 l' me get away, I pray thee, and
21: 2 L' no man know any thing of the
13 l' his spittle fall down upon his
22: 3 L' my father and my mother, I pray
15 l' not the king impute any thing unto
24:19 will he l' him go well away?
25: 8 l' the young men find favour in thine
24 my lord, upon me l' this iniquity be: *
24 l' thine handmaid, I pray thee, speak
25 L' not my lord, I pray thee, regard
26 now l' thine enemies,...be as Nabal.
27 l' it even be given unto the young
1Sa 25:41 l' thine handmaid be a servant to
26: 8 therefore l' me smite him, I pray thee,
11 and the cruse of water, and l' us go.
19 l' my lord the king hear the words of
19 against me, l' him accept an offering:
20 l' not my blood fall to the earth before
22 l' one of the young men come over
24 so l' my life be much set by in the
24 l' him deliver me out of all tribulation.
27: 5 l' them give me a place in some town
28:22 l' me set a morsel of bread before
29: 4 l' him not go down with us to
2Sa 1:21 of Gilboa, l' there be no dew,
21 neither l' there be rain upon you, nor*
2: 7 now l' your hands be strengthened,
14 L' the young men now arise, and play
14 And Joab said, L' them arise.
3:29 L' it rest on the head of Joab, and on
29 l' there not fail from the house of
5:24 l' it be, when thou hearest the sound*
7:26 And l' thy name be magnified for ever,
26 l' the house of...David be established*
29 now l' it please thee to bless the house
29 l' the house of thy servant be blessed
10:12 and l' us play the men for our people,
11:12 to-morrow I will l' thee depart.
25 Joab, L' not this thing displease thee,
13: 5 l' my sister Tamar come, and give me
6 l' Tamar my sister come, and make
24 l' the king, I beseech thee, and his
25 Nay, my son, l' us not all now go,
26 l' my brother Amnon go with us.
27 l' Amnon and all the king's sons go
32 L' not my lord suppose that they have
33 l' not my lord the king take the thing
14:11 l' the king remember the Lord thy
12 L' thine handmaid, I pray thee, speak
18 said, L' my lord the king now speak.
24 said, L' him turn to his own house,
24 and l' him not see my face.
32 therefore l' me see the king's face;
32 be any iniquity in me, l' him kill me.
15: 7 pray thee, l' me go and pay my vow,
14 at Jerusalem, Arise, and l' us flee;
26 l' him do to me as seemeth good unto
16: 9 l' me go over, I pray thee, and take
10 so l' him curse, because the Lord hath*
11 l' him alone, and l' him curse; for 3240
17: 1 L' me now choose out twelve thousand
5 and l' us hear likewise what he saith.
18:19 L' me now run, and bear the king
22 l' me, I pray thee, also run after Cushi.
23 But howsoever, said he, l' me run.*
19:19 L' not my lord impute iniquity unto
30 l' him take all, forasmuch as my lord
37 L' thy servant, I pray thee, turn back
37 l' him go over with my lord the king;
20:11 that is for David, l' him go after Joab.
21: 6 L' seven men of his sons be delivered
24:14 l' us fall now into the hand of the
14 l' me not fall into the hand of man.
17 l' thine hand, I pray thee, be against
22 L' my lord the king take and offer up
1Ki 1: 2 L' there be sought for my lord the
2 and l' her stand before the king,
2 before the king, and l' her cherish *
2 and l' her lie in thy bosom, that my
12 l' me, I pray thee, give thee counsel,
31 L' my lord king David live for ever.
34 l' Zadok the priest and...anoint him
51 L' king Solomon swear unto me to
2: 6 l' not his hoar head go down to
7 l' them be of those that eat at thy
21 L' Abishag the Shunammite be given
3:26 L' it be neither mine nor thine, but*
8:26 l' thy word, I pray thee, be verified,
57 l' him not leave us, nor forsake us:
59 And l' these my words...be nigh unto
61 L' your heart therefore be perfect
11:21 L' me depart, that I may go to
22 howbeit l' me go in any wise.
17:21 l' this child's soul come into him
18:23 L' them...give us two bullocks;
23 l' them choose one bullock for
24 that answereth by fire, l' him be God.
36 l' it be known this day that thou art
40 of Baal; l' not one of them escape.
19: 2 So l' the gods do to me, and more
20 L' me, I pray thee, kiss my father and
20:11 L' not him that girdeth on his harness
23 l' us fight against them in the plain,
31 l' us, I pray thee, put sackcloth on
32 saith, I pray thee, l' me live.
42 hast l' go out of thy hand a man
21: 7 bread, and l' thine heart be merry:
22: 8 said, L' not the king say so.
13 l' thy word, I pray thee, be like the
17 l' them return every man to his
49 L' my servants go with thy
2Ki 1:10, 12 l' fire come down from heaven,
13 l' my life, and the life...be precious in
14 l' my life now be precious in thy sight.
2: 9 l' a double portion of thy spirit be
16 l' them go, we pray thee, and seek
4:10 L' us make a little chamber, I pray
10 l' us set for him there a bed, and a
27 man of God said, L' her alone;
5: 8 l' him come now to me, and he shall
24 and he l' the men go, and they
6: 2 L' us go, we pray thee, unto
2 l' us make us a place there, where we
7: 4 l' us fall unto the host of the Syrians:
13 L' some take, I pray thee, five of the
13 consumed:) and l' us send and see.
9:15 l' none go forth nor escape out of the
17 meet them, and l' him say, Is it peace?
2Ki 10:19 all his priests; l' none be wanting:
25 and slay them; l' none come forth.
11: 8 within the ranges, l' him be slain:
15 L' her not be slain in the house of the
12: 5 L' the priests take it to them, every
5 l' them repair the breaches of the *
13:21 when the man was l' down, and *3212
14: 8 l' us look one another in the face.
17:27 and l' them go and dwell there,
27 l' him teach them the manner of the
18:29 the king, L' not Hezekiah deceive you:
30 Neither l' Hezekiah make you trust in
19:10 L' not thy God in whom thou trustest
20:10 but l' the shadow return backward
22: 5 l' them deliver it into the hand of
5 l' them give it to the doers of the
23:18 L' him alone; l' no man move his 3240
18 So they l' his bones alone, with the
1Ch 13: 2 l' us send abroad unto our
3 l' us bring again the ark of our God to
16:10 l' the heart of them rejoice that seek
31 L' the heavens be glad, and l' the
31 and l' men say among the nations, the
32 L' the sea roar, and the fulness
32 l' the fields rejoice, and all that is
17:23 l' the thing that thou...be established
24 L' it even be established, that thy
24 l' the house of David...be established*
27 l' it please thee to bless the house of*
19:13 and l' us behave ourselves valiantly
13 and l' the Lord do that which is good*
21:13 l' me fall now into the hand of the
13 but l' me not fall into the hand of man.
17 l' thine hand...O Lord my God, be on me
23 l' my lord the king do that which is
2Ch 1: 9 l' thy promise unto David my father
2:15 of, l' him send unto his servants:
6:17 God of Israel, l' thy word be verified,
40 l', I beseech thee, thine eyes be open,
40 l' thine ears be attent unto the prayer
41 l' thy priests, O Lord God, be clothed
41 and l' thy saints rejoice in goodness.
14: 7 unto Judah, L' us build these cities,
11 God; l' not man prevail against thee.
15: 7 and l' not your hands be weak:
16: 1 that he might l' none go out or *5414
5 of Ramah, and l' his work cease.
18: 7 said, L' not the king say so.
12 l' thy word therefore, I pray thee, be like
16 l' them return therefore every man
19: 7 now l' the fear of the Lord be upon
20:10 thou wouldest not l' Israel invade,
23: 6 But l' none come into the house of the
14 her, l' him be slain with the sword.
25: 7 l' not the army of Israel go with thee;
17 l' us see one another in the face.
32:15 therefore l' not Hezekiah deceive you,
36:23 his God be with him, and l' him go up.
Ezr 1: 3 l' him go up to Jerusalem, which is in
4 l' the men of his place help him with
4: 2 L' us build with you: for we seek
5:15 l' the house of God be builded in his
17 l' there be search made in the king's
17 l' the king send his pleasure to us
6: 3 L' the house be builded, the place
3 l' the foundations thereof be strongly
4 l' the expences be given out of the
5 l' the golden and...vessels...be restored
7 L' the work of this house of God alone;
7 l' the governor of the Jews...build
9 l' it be given them day by day without
11 l' timber be pulled down from his
11 set up, l' him be hanged thereon;
11 and l' his house be made a dunghill for
12 a decree; l' it be done with speed.
7:23 l' it be diligently done for the house of
26 l' judgment be executed speedily
10: 3 l' us make a covenant with our God
3 and l' it be done according to the law.
14 L' now our rulers of all the...stand,
14 l' all them which have taken...come
Ne 1: 6 L' thine ear now be attentive, and
11 l' now thine ear be attentive to the
2: 3 the king, L' the king live for ever:
7 l' letters be given me to the
17 l' us build up the wall of Jerusalem,
18 And they said, L' us rise up and build.
4: 5 l' not their sin be blotted out from
22 L' every one with his servant lodge
5:10 I pray you, l' us leave off this usury.
6: 2 Come, l' us meet together in some one
7 and l' us take counsel together.
10 L' us meet together in the house of
10 and l' us shut the doors of the temple:
7: 3 L' not the gates of Jerusalem be
3 l' them shut the doors, and bar them:
9:32 l' not all the trouble seem little before
Es 1:19 l' there go a royal commandment
19 l' it be written among the laws of the
19 l' the king give her royal estate
2: 2 L' there be fair young virgins sought
3 And l' the king appoint officers in all
3 l' their things for purification be given
4 l' the maiden which pleaseth...be queen
3: 9 l' it be written that they may be
5: 4 l' the king and Haman come this day
8 l' the king and Haman come to the
12 the queen did l' no man come in with
14 L' a gallows be made of fifty cubits
6: 5 And the king said, L' him come in.
8 L' the royal apparel be brought which
9 l' this apparel and horse be delivered
10 l' nothing fail of all that thou hast
7: 3 l' my life be given me at my
8: 5 l' it be written to reverse the letters
9:13 l' it be granted to the Jews which

Es 9:13 l' Haman's ten sons be hanged upon
Job 3: 3 l' the day perish wherein I was born,
4 L' that day be darkness;
4 l' not God regard it from above,
4 neither l' the light shine upon it.
5 L' darkness and the shadow of death
5 stain it; l' a cloud dwell upon it;
5 l' the blackness of the day terrify it.
6 that night, l' darkness seize upon it;
6 l' it not be joined unto the days of the
6 l' it not come into the number of the
7 Lo, l' that night be solitary,
7 l' no joyful voice come therein.
8 L' them curse it that curse the day,
9 L' the stars of the twilight thereof be
9 l' it look for light, but have none;
9 neither l' it see the dawning of the
6: 9 he would l' loose his hand, and cut me
10 l' him not spare; for I have not *
29 l' it not be iniquity; yea, return again,
7:16 not live alway: l' me alone; for
19 nor l' me alone till I swallow down
9:34 L' him take his rod away from me,
34 and l' not his fear terrify me:
10:20 and l' me alone, that I may take
11:14 and l' not wickedness dwell in thy
13:13 Hold your peace, l' me alone, that I
13 speak, and l' come on me what will.
21 and l' not thy dread make me afraid.
22 or l' me speak, and answer thou me.
15:31 L' not him that is deceived trust in
16:18 my blood, and l' my cry have no place.
21: 2 and l' this be your consolations.
27: 6 I hold fast, and will not l' it go:
7 L' my enemy be as the wicked, and he
30:11 have also l' loose the bridle before me.
31: 6 L' me be weighed in an even balance,
8 Then l' me sow, and l' another eat;
8 Yea, l' my offspring be rooted out.
10 Then l' my wife grind unto another,
10 and l' others bow down upon her.
22 l' mine arm fall from my shoulder
40 L' thistles grow instead of wheat, and
32:21 L' me not, I pray you, accept any
21 neither l' me give flattering titles unto
34: 4 L' us choose to us judgment:
4 l' us know among ourselves what is
34 L' men of understanding tell me,*
34 and l' a wise man hearken unto me.
40: 2 reproveth God, l' him answer it.
Ps 2: 3 L' us break their bands asunder, and
5:10 l' them fall by their own counsels;
11 l' all those that put their trust...rejoice:
11 l' them ever shout for joy, because
11 l' them...that love thy name be joyful
6:10 L' all mine enemies be ashamed and
10 l' them return and be ashamed *
7: 5 L' the enemy persecute my soul, and
5 l' him tread down my life upon the
9 l' the wickedness of the wicked come
9:19 Arise, O Lord; l' not man prevail:
19 l' the heathen be judged in thy sight.
10: 2 l' them be taken in the devices that
17: 2 L' my sentence come forth from thy
2 l' thine eyes behold the things that are
18:46 l' the God of my salvation be exalted.*
19:13 l' them not have dominion over me:
14 L' the words of my...be acceptable
20: 9 l' the king hear us when we call.
22: 8 l' him deliver him, seeing he delighted
25: 2 trust in thee: l' me not be ashamed,
2 l' not mine enemies triumph over me.
3 l' none that wait on thee be ashamed:*
3 l' them be ashamed which transgress*
20 l' me not be ashamed; for I put my
21 L' integrity and uprightness preserve
31: 1 put my trust; l' me never be ashamed:
17 L' me not be ashamed, O Lord; for I
17 upon thee: l' the wicked be ashamed,
17 and l' them be silent in the grave.
18 L' the lying lips be put to silence;
33: 8 L' all the earth fear the Lord:
8 l' all the inhabitants...stand in awe
22 L' thy mercy, O Lord, be upon us,
34: 3 me, and l' us exalt his name together.
35: 4 L' them be confounded and put to
4 l' them be turned back and brought
5 L' them be as chaff before the wind:
5 l' the angel of the Lord chase them.*
6 L' their way be dark and slippery:
6 l' the angel of the Lord persecute*
8 L' destruction come upon him at
8 l' his net that he hath hid catch
8 into that very destruction l' him fall.
19 L' not them...mine enemies rejoice
19 neither l' them wink with the eye that
24 and l' them not rejoice over me.
25 L' them not say in their hearts, Ah, so
25 l' them not say, We have swallowed
26 L' them be ashamed and brought to
26 l' them be clothed with shame and
27 L' them shout for joy, and be glad,
27 cause: yea, l' them say continually,
27 L' the Lord be magnified, which hath*
36:11 L' not the foot of pride come against
11 l' not the hand of the wicked remove
40:11 l' thylovingkindness and...preserve me,
14 L' them be ashamed and confounded
14 l' them be driven backward and put to
15 L' them be desolate for a reward of
16 L' all those that seek thee rejoice
16 l' such as love thy salvation say
43: 3 light and thy truth: l' them lead me;
3 l' them bring me unto thy holy hill,
48:11 L' mount Zion rejoice,
11 l' the daughters of Judah be glad,

Ps 55:15 L' death seize upon them,
15 and l' them go down quick into hell:
57: 5, 11 l' thy glory be above all the earth.
58: 7 L' them melt away as waters which
7 his arrows, l' them be as cut in pieces.
8 l' every one of them pass away: *
59:10 God shall l' me see my desire upon
12 l' them even be taken in their pride:
13 l' them know that God ruleth in Jacob
14 And at evening l' them return;
14 l' them make a noise like a dog, and
15 L' them wander up and down for *
66: 7 l' not the rebellious exalt themselves.
67: 3 L' the people praise thee, O God;
3 l' all the people praise thee.
4 O l' the nations be glad and sing for
5 L' the people praise thee, O God;
5 l' all the people praise thee.
68: 1 L' God arise, l' his enemies be
1 l' them also that hate him flee before
2 so l' the wicked perish at the presence
3 But l' the righteous be glad;
3 l' them rejoice before God:
3 yea, l' them exceedingly rejoice.
69: 6 L' not them that wait on...be ashamed
6 l' not those that seek...be confounded
14 out of the mire, and l' me not sink:
14 l' me be delivered from them that hate
15 L' not the waterflood overflow me,
15 neither l' the deep swallow me up,
15 l' not the pit shut her mouth upon me.
22 L' their table become a snare before
22 for their welfare, l' it become a trap.
23 L' their eyes be darkened, that they
24 l' thy wrathful anger take hold of
25 L' their habitation be desolate;
25 and l' none dwell in their tents.
27 and l' them not come into thy
28 L' them be blotted out of the book of
29 l' thy salvation, O God, set me up on
34 L' the heaven and earth praise him,
70: 2 L' them be ashamed and confounded
2 l' them be turned backward, and put
3 L' them be turned back for a reward
4 L' all those that seek thee rejoice and
4 and l' such as love thy salvation say
4 say continually, L' God be magnified.
71: 1 trust: l' me never be put to confusion.
8 L' my mouth be filled with thy praise*
13 L' them be confounded and consumed
13 l' them be covered with reproach and
72:19 l' the whole earth be filled with his
74: 8 hearts, L' us destroy them together:
21 O l' not the oppressed return ashamed:
21 l' the poor and needy praise thy name.
76:11 l' all that be round about him bring
78:28 he l' it fall in the midst of their camp,
79: 8 l' thy tender mercies speedily prevent
10 l' him be known among the heathen in
11 L' the sighing of the prisoner come
80:17 L' thy hand be upon the man of thy
83: 4 l' us cut them off from being a nation;
12 L' us take to ourselves the houses of
17 L' them be confounded and troubled
17 l' them be put to shame, and perish:
85: 8 l' them not turn again to folly.
88: 2 L' my prayer come before thee:
90:13 l' it repent thee concerning thy
16 L' thy work appear unto thy servants,
17 l' the beauty of the Lord our God be
95: 1 O come, l' us sing unto the Lord:
1 l' us make a joyful noise to the rock
2 L' us come before his presence with
6 O come, l' us worship and bow down:
6 l' us kneel before the Lord our maker.
96:11 L' the heavens rejoice, and l' the earth
11 l' the sea roar, and the fulness thereof.
12 L' the field be joyful, and all that is
97: 1 l' the earth rejoice; l' the multitude
98: 7 L' the sea roar, and the fulness
8 L' the floods clap their hands:
8 l' the hills be joyful together.
99: 1 Lord reigneth; l' the people tremble:
1 cherubims; l' the earth be moved.
3 L' them praise thy great and terrible
102: 1 O Lord, and l' my cry come unto thee.
104:35 L' the sinners be consumed out of the
35 and l' the wicked be no more. Bless
105: 3 l' the heart of them rejoice that seek
20 ruler of the people, and l' him go free.
106:48 and l' all the people say, Amen.
107: 2 L' the redeemed of the Lord say so,
22 And l' them sacrifice the sacrifices of
32 L' them exalt him also in the
109: 6 and l' Satan stand at his right hand.
7 be judged, l' him be condemned:
7 and l' his prayer become sin.
8 L' his days be few; and l' another
9 L' his children be fatherless, and his
10 L' his children be continually
10 l' them seek their bread also out of
11 L' the extortioner catch all that he
11 and l' the strangers spoil his labour.
12 L' there be none to extend mercy unto
12 neither l' there be any to favour his
13 L' his posterity be cut off; and in the
13 following l' their name be blotted out.
14 L' the iniquity of his fathers be
14 and l' not the sin of his mother be
15 L' them be before the Lord
17 loved cursing, so l' it come unto him:*
17 not in blessing, so l' it be far from him.*
18 so l' it come into his bowels like water,*
19 L' it be unto him as the garment
20 L' this be the reward of mine *
28 L' them curse, but bless thou: when

Ps 109:28 they arise, l' them be ashamed; *
28 but l' thy servant rejoice. *
29 L' mine adversaries be clothed with
29 l' them cover themselves with their
118: 2 L' Israel now say, that his mercy
3 L' the house of Aaron now say, that
4 L' them now that fear the Lord say,
119:10 O l' me not wander from thy
41 L' thy mercies come also unto me, O
76 L', I pray thee, thy merciful kindness
77 L' thy tender mercies come unto me,
78 L' the proud be ashamed; for they
79 L' those that fear thee turn unto me,
80 L' my heart be sound in thy statutes;
116 and l' me not be ashamed of my hope.
122 good: l' not the proud oppress me.
133 l' not any iniquity have dominion over
169 L' my cry come near before thee, O
170 L' my supplication come before thee:
173 L' thine hand help me; for I have
175 L' my soul live, and it shall praise
175 thee; and l' thy judgments help me.
122: 1 L' us go into the house of the Lord,
129: 5 L' them all be confounded and turned
6 L' them be as the grass upon the
130: 2 l' thine ears be attentive to the voice
7 L' Israel hope in the Lord: for with*
131: 3 L' Israel hope in the Lord from *
132: 9 L' thy priests be clothed with
9 and l' thy saints shout for joy.
137: 5 l' my right hand forget her cunning.
6 l' my tongue cleave to the roof of my
140: 9 l' the mischief of their own lips cover
10 L' burning coals fall upon them:
10 l' them be cast into the fire; into deep
11 L' not an evil speaker be established
141: 2 L' my prayer be set forth before thee
4 and l' me not eat of their dainties.
5 L' the righteous smite me; it shall be
5 l' him reprove me; it shall be an
10 L' the wicked fall into their own nets,
145:21 l' all flesh bless his holy name for ever
148: 5, 13 L' them praise the name of the Lord:
149: 2 L' Israel rejoice in him that made
2 l' the children of Zion be joyful in their
3 L' them praise his name in the dance:
3 l' them sing praises unto him with the
5 L' the saints be joyful in glory:
5 l' them sing aloud upon their beds.
6 L' the high praises of God be in their
150: 6 L' every thing that hath breath praise
Pr 1:11 Come with us, l' us lay wait for blood,
11 l' us lurk privily for the innocent
12 L' us swallow them up alive as the
14 among us; l' us all have one purse:*
3: 1 l' thine heart keep my commandments:
3 L' not mercy and truth forsake thee:
21 l' not them depart from thine eyes:
4: 4 me, L' thine heart retain my words:
13 l' her not go: keep her; for she is
21 L' them not depart from thine eyes;
25 L' thine eyes look right on, and
25 L' thine eyelids look straight before
26 and l' all thy ways be established.
5:16 L' thy fountains be dispersed abroad,
17 L' them be only thine own, and not
18 L' thy fountain be blessed: and
19 L' her be as the loving hind and *
19 l' her breasts satisfy thee at all times;
6:25 neither l' her take thee with her
7:18 l' us take our fill of love until the
18 l' us solace ourselves with loves.
25 L' not thine heart decline to her ways,
9: 4, 16 is simple, l' him turn in hither:
17:12 L' a bear robbed of her whelps meet a
19:18 l' not thy soul spare for his crying.*
23:17 L' not thine heart envy sinners: but
26 and l' thine eyes observe my ways.
24:17 l' not thine heart be glad when he
27: 2 L' another man praise thee, and not
28:17 flee to the pit; l' no man stay him.
31: 7 L' him drink, and forget his poverty,
31 l' her own works praise her in the
Ec 5: 2 l' not thine heart be hasty to utter any
2 earth: therefore l' thy words be few.
9: 8 L' thy garments be always white;
8 and l' thy head lack no ointment.
11: 8 l' him remember the days of darkness;
9 l' thy heart cheer thee in the days of
12:13 L' us hear the conclusion of the whole*
Ca 1: 2 L' him kiss me with the kisses of his
2:14 l' me see thy countenance, l' me hear
3: 4 held him, and would not l' him go,
4:16 L' my beloved come into his garden,
7:11 beloved, l' us go forth into the field;
11 l' us lodge in the villages.
12 L' us get up early to the vineyards;
12 l' us see if the vine flourish, whether
8:11 l' out the vineyards unto keepers; 5414
Isa 1:18 Come now, and l' us reason together,
2: 3 l' us go up to the mountain of the
5 l' us walk in the light of the Lord.
3: 6 and l' this ruin be under thy hand:
4: 1 only l' us be called by thy name, to
5:19 L' him make speed and hasten his
19 l' the counsel of the Holy...draw nigh
7: 6 L' us go up against Judah, and vex it,
6 l' us make a breach therein for us,
8:13 hosts himself; and l' him be your fear,
13 and l' him be your dread.
16: 4 L' mine outcasts dwell with thee,
19:12 wise men? and l' them tell thee now,
12 l' them know what the Lord of hosts
21: 6 l' him declare what he seeth.
22:13 l' us eat and drink; for to-morrow we
26:10 L' favour be shewed to the wicked, yet

Isa 27: 5 Or l' him take hold of my strength,
29: 1 ye year to year; l' them kill sacrifices.
34: 1 l' the earth hear, and all that is
36: 14 king, L' not Hezekiah deceive you:
15 Neither l' Hezekiah make you trust in
37: 10 L' not thy God, in whom...deceive thee,
38: 21 had said, L' them take a lump of figs,
41: 1 l' the people renew their strength:
1 l' them come near; then l' them speak:
1 l' us come near together to judgment.
22 L' them bring them forth, and shew us
22 l' them shew the former things, what
42: 11 L' the wilderness and the cities thereof
11 l' the inhabitants of the rock sing,
11 l' them shout from the top of the
12 L' them give glory unto the Lord,
43: 9 L' all the nations be gathered together,
9 and l' the people be assembled:
9 l' them bring forth their witnesses,
9 or l' them hear, and say, It is truth.
13 I will work, and who shall l' it? †7725
26 in remembrance: l' us plead together:
44: 7 shall come, l' them shew unto them.
11 l' them all be gathered together,
11 l' them stand up; yet they shall fear,
45: 8 l' the skies pour down righteousness:
8 l' the earth open, and l' them bring
8 l' righteousness spring up together;
9 L' the potsherd strive with the
13 he shall l' go my captives, not for
21 l' them take counsel together: who
47: 13 L' now the astrologers,...stand up,
50: 8 contend with me? l' us stand together:
8 adversary? l' him come near to me.
10 l' him trust in the name of the Lord,
54: 2 l' them stretch forth the curtains of
55: 2 l' your soul delight itself in fatness.
7 L' the wicked forsake his way, and
7 l' him return unto the Lord, and
56: 3 Neither l' the son of the...speak,
3 neither l' the eunuch say, Behold, I
57: 13 criest, l' thy companies deliver thee;
58: 6 to l' the oppressed go free, and
66: 5 L' the Lord be glorified: but he shall
Jer 2: 28 l' them arise, if they can save thee in
4: 5 and l' us go into the defenced cities.
5: 24 L' us now fear the Lord our God, that
6: 4 her; arise, and l' us go up at noon.
5 Arise, and l' us go by night,
5 and l' us destroy her palaces.
8: 14 l' us enter into the defenced cities,
14 and l' us be silent there: for the Lord
9: 18 And l' them make haste, and take up
20 and l' your ear receive the word of his
23 L' not the wise man glory in his
23 neither l' the mighty man glory in his
23 l' not the rich man glory in his riches:
24 But l' him that glorieth glory in this,
11: 19 L' us destroy the tree with the fruit
19 l' us cut him off from the land of the
20 l' me see thy vengeance on them: ‡
12: 1 l' me talk with thee of thy judgments:*
14: 17 L' mine eyes run down with tears
17 night and day, and l' them not cease:
15: 1 out of my sight, and l' them go forth.
19 l' them return unto thee; but *
17: 15 the word of the Lord? l' it come now.
18 L' them be confounded that persecute
18 but l' not me be confounded:
18 l' them be dismayed,
18 but l' not me be dismayed:
18: 18 l' us devise devices against Jeremiah;
18 and l' us smite him with the tongue,
18 l' us not give heed to any of his words.
21 l' their wives be bereaved of their
21 and l' their men be put to death;
21 l' their young men be slain by the *
22 L' a cry be heard from their houses,
23 but l' them be overthrown before thee;
20: 12 l' me see thy vengeance on them:
14 l' not the day wherein my mother bare
16 And l' that man be as the cities which
16 l' him hear the cry in the morning,
23: 28 that hath a dream, l' him tell a dream;
28 word, l' him speak my word faithfully.
27: 11 those will I l' remain still in their
18 l' them now make intercession to the
29: 8 L' not your prophets and your
31: 6 l' us go up to Zion unto the Lord our
34: 9 man should l' his manservant...go free;
10 one should l' his manservant...go free,
10 then they obeyed, and l' them go.
11 whom they had l' go free, to return,
14 l' ye go every man his brother an
14 thou shalt l' him go free from thee:
35: 11 and l' us go to Jerusalem for fear of
36: 19 and l' no man know where ye be.
37: 20 l' my supplication,...be accepted
38: 4 thee, l' this man be put to death:
6 they l' down Jeremiah with cords. 7971
11 and l' them down by cords into the "
24 L' no man know of these words, and
40: 1 captain of the guard had l' him go
5 victuals and a reward, and l' him go.
15 Mizpah secretly, saying, L' me go,
42: 2 L'...our supplication be accepted
46: 6 L' not the swift flee away, nor the
9 and l' the mighty men come forth;
16 l' us go again to our own people,
48: 2 l' us cut it off from being a nation.
49: 11 alive; and l' thy widows trust in me.
50: 5 and l' us join ourselves to the Lord*
26 her utterly: l' nothing of her be left.
27 l' them go down to the slaughter:
29 about; l' none therefore escape:
33 them fast; they refused to l' them go.

Jer 51: 3 bendeth l' the archer bend his bow,
9 l' us go every one into his own
10 l' us declare in Zion the work of the
50 l' Jerusalem come into your mind.
La 1: 22 L' all their wickedness come before
2: 18 l' tears run down like a river day
18 l' not the apple of thine eye cease.
3: 40 L' us search and try our ways, and
41 L' us lift up our heart with our hands
Eze 1: 24 stood, they l' down their wings. 7503
25 stood, and had l' down their wings. "
3: 27 God; He that heareth, l' him hear;
27 and he that forbeareth, l' him forbear:
7: 12 l' not the buyer rejoice, nor the seller
9: 5 l' not your eye spare, neither have ye
11: 3 l' us build houses: this city is the
13: 20 will l' the souls go, even the souls
21: 14 and l' the sword be doubled the third
24: 5 l' them seethe the bones of it therein.
6 piece by piece; l' no lot fall upon it.*
10 spice it well,...l' the bones be burned.
39: 7 I will not l' them pollute my holy*
43: 9 Now l' them put away their whoredom,
10 and l' them measure the pattern.
44: 6 Israel, l' it suffice you of all your
Da 1: 12 l' them give us pulse to eat, and water
13 l' our countenances be looked upon
2: 7 L' the king tell his servants the dream,
4: 14 l' the beasts get away from under it,
15 l' it be wet with the dew of heaven,
15 l' his portion be with the beasts in the
16 L' his heart be changed from man's,
16 l' a beast's heart be given unto him;
16 and l' seven times pass over him.
19 l' not the dream, or the...trouble thee.
23 l' it be wet with the dew of heaven,
23 l' his portion be with the beasts of the
27 l' my counsel be acceptable unto thee,
5: 10 ever: l' not thy thoughts trouble thee,
10 nor l' thy countenance be changed:
12 now l' Daniel be called, and he will
17 L' thy gifts be to thyself, and give thy
9: 16 l' thine anger and thy fury be turned
10: 19 said, L' my lord speak; for thou hast
Ho 2: 2 l' her therefore put away her
4: 4 Yet l' no man strive, nor reprove
15 the harlot, yet l' not Judah offend;
17 is joined to idols: l' him alone.
6: 1 and l' us return unto the Lord:
13: 2 L' the men that sacrifice kiss the
Joe 1: 3 l' your children tell their children, and
2: 1 l' all the inhabitants of the...tremble:
16 l' the bridegroom go forth of his
17 L' the priests...weep...l' them say,
3: 9 men, l' all the men of war draw near;
9 l' them come up:
10 spears: l' the weak say, I am strong.
12 L' the heathen be wakened, and come
Am 4: 1 their masters, Bring, and l' us drink.
5: 24 But l' judgment run down as waters,
Ob 1 and l' us rise up against her in battle.
Jon 1: 7 Come, and l' us cast lots, that we may
14 l' us not perish for this man's life, and
3: 7 L' neither man nor beast, herd...taste
7 l' them not feed, nor drink water:
8 But l' man and beast be covered with
8 l' them turn every one from his
Mic 1: 2 l' the Lord God be witness against
4: 2 and l' us go up to the mountain of the
11 L' her be defiled, and l' our eye look
6: 1 and l' the hills hear thy voice.
7: 14 l' them feed in Bashan and Gilead, as
Hab 2: 16 also, and l' thy foreskin be uncovered:*
20 l' all the earth keep silence before
Zep 3: 16 to Zion, L' not thine hands be slack.
Zec 3: 5 L' them set a fair mitre upon his head.
7: 10 l' none of you imagine evil against his
8: 9 L' your hands be strong, ye that hear
13 fear not, but l' your hands be strong.
17 l' none of you imagine evil in your
21 L' us go speedily to pray before the
11: 9 not feed you: that that dieth, l' it die;
9 that that is to be cut off, l' it be cut off;
9 and l' the rest eat every one the flesh
Mal 2: 15 l' none deal treacherously against the
M't 5: 31 his wife, l' him give her a writing of
37 l' your communication be, Yea,
40 thy coat, l' him have thy cloke also.
7: 4 L' me pull out the mote out of thine 863
8: 22 me; and l' the dead bury their dead.* "
10: 13 be worthy, l' your peace come upon it:
13 worthy, l' your peace return to you.
11: 15 He that hath ears to hear, l' him hear.
13: 9 Who hath ears to hear, l' him hear.
30 L' both grow together until the 863
43 Who hath ears to hear, l' him hear.
15: 4 father or mother, l' him die the death.
14 L' them alone: they be blind 863
16: 24 l' him deny himself, and take up his
17: 4 l' us make here three tabernacles;*
18: 17 l' him be unto thee as an heathen
19: 6 together, l' not man put asunder.
12 able to receive it, l' him receive it.
20: 26 you, l' him be your minister; *
27 among you, l' him be your servant:*
21: 19 L' no fruit grow on thee henceforward
33 l' it out to husbandmen, and went 1554
38 This is the heir; come, l' us kill him,
41 will l' out his vineyard unto other 1554
24: 15 (whoso readeth, l' him understand:)
16 l' them which be in Judæa flee into the
17 L' him which is on the housetop not
18 Neither l' him which is in the field
26: 39 be possible, l' this cup pass from me:
46 l' us be going: behold, he is at hand
27: 22 all say unto him, L' him be crucified.

M't 27: 23 the more, saying, L' him be crucified.
42 l' him now come down from the cross,
43 l' him deliver him now, if he will
49 The rest said, L' be, 863
49 l' us see whether Elias will come
M'r 1: 24 L' us alone; what have we to do *1439
38 L' us go into the next towns, that I
2: 4 l' down the bed wherein the sick 5465
4: 9 He that hath ears to hear, l' him hear.
23 man have ears to hear, l' him hear.
35 L' us pass over unto the other side.
7: 10 father or mother, l' him die the death:
16 man have ears to hear, l' him hear.*
27 her, L' the children first be filled: 863
8: 34 l' him deny himself, and take up his
9: 5 and l' us make three tabernacles;
10: 9 together, l' not man put asunder.
11: 6 commanded: and they l' them go. 863
12: 1 l' it out to husbandmen, and went 1554
7 This is the heir; come, l' us kill him,
13: 14 not, (l' him that readeth understand,)
14 l' them that be in Judæa flee to the
15 And l' him that is on the housetop not
16 And l' him that is in the field not turn
14: 6 And Jesus said, L' her alone; why 863
42 Rise up, l' us go; lo, he that betrayeth
15: 32 L' Christ the King of Israel descend
36 to drink, saying, L' alone; 863
36 l' us see whether Elias will come
Lu 2: 15 L' us now go even unto Bethlehem,
3: 11 l' him impart to him that hath none;
11 he that hath meat, l' him do likewise.
4: 34 Saying, L' us alone; what have *1439
5: 4 l' your nets down for a draught. 5465
5 at thy word I will l' down the net. "
19 and l' him down through the tiling 2524
6: 42 l' me pull out the mote that is in 863
8: 8 He that hath ears to hear, l' him hear.
22 L' us go over unto the other side of
9: 23 l' him deny himself, and take up his
33 l' us make three tabernacles; one for
44 L' these sayings sink down into your
60 him, L' the dead bury their dead: *863
61 l' me first go bid them farewell, *2010
12: 35 L' your loins be girded about, and
13: 8 Lord, l' it alone this year also, till I 863
14: 4 him, and healed him, and l' him go;
35 He that hath ears to hear, l' him hear.
15: 23 kill it; and l' us eat, and be merry:
16: 29 and the prophets; l' them hear them.
17: 31 l' him not come down to take it away:
31 field, l' him likewise not return back.
20: 9 and l' it forth to husbandmen, 1554
14 is the heir: come, l' us kill him,
21: 21 l' them which are in Judæa flee to
21 l' them which are in the midst...depart
21 l' not them...in the countries enter
22: 26 among you, l' him be as the younger;
36 l' him take it, and likewise his script:
36 l' him sell his garment, and buy one.
68 ye will not answer me, nor l' me go.*630
23: 22 therefore chastise him, and l' him go.*
35 l' him save himself, if he be Christ, the
Joh 7: 37 thirst, l' him come unto me and drink.
8: 7 you, l' him first cast a stone at her.
11: 7 disciples, L' us go into Judæa again.
15 nevertheless l' us go unto him.
16 L' us also go, that we may die with
44 them, Loose him, and l' him go. 863
48 If we l' him thus alone, all men will "
12: 7 said Jesus, L' her alone: against * "
26 any man serve me, l' him follow me;
14: 1 L' not your heart be troubled: ye
27 L' not your heart be troubled,
27 neither l' it be afraid.
31 even so I do. Arise, l' us go hence.
18: 8 ye seek me, l' these go their way: 863
19: 12 If thou l' this man go, thou art not *630
24 L' us not rend it, but cast lots for it,
Ac 1: 20 L' his habitation be desolate,
20 and l' no man dwell therein:
20 and his bishoprick l' another take.
2: 29 l' me freely speak unto you of the *1832
36 l' all the house of Israel know
3: 13 he was determined to l' him go. * 630
4: 17 l' us straitly threaten them, that they
21 threatened them, they l' them go,
23 And being l' go, they went to their own
5: 38 these men, and l' them alone: 1439
40 in the name of Jesus, and l' them go. 630
9: 25 l' him down by the wall in a 5465, 2524
10: 11 corners, and l' down to the earth: "
11: 5 sheet, l' down from heaven by four "
15: 33 they were l' go in peace from the * 630
36 L' us go again and visit our brethren
16: 35 serjeants, saying, L' those men go. 630
36 magistrates have sent to l' you go: "
37 l' them come themselves and fetch us
17: 9 and of the other, they l' them go. 630
19: 38 deputies: l' them implead one another.
23: 9 to him, l' us not fight against God.*
22 then l' the young man depart, 630
24: 20 Or else l' these same here say, if they
23 keep Paul, and to l' him have liberty, *
25: 5 L' them therefore,...go down with me,
27: 15 up into the wind, we l' her drive. *1929
30 had l' down the boat into the sea, *5465
32 ropes of the boat, and l' her fall off. 1439
28: 18 examined me, would have l' me go, *630
Ro 1: 13 unto you, (but was l' hitherto.) *2967
3: 4 yea, l' God be true, but every man a
8 L' us do evil, that good may come?
6: 12 L' not sin therefore reign in your
11: 9 L' their table be made a snare, and a
10 L' their eyes be darkened, that they
12: 6 l' us prophesy according to the

Ro 12: 7 ministry, l' us wait on our ministering:
8 giveth, l' him do it with simplicity;
9 L' love be without dissimulation.
13: 1 L' every soul be subject unto the
12 l' us therefore cast off the works of
12 and l' us put on the armour of light.
13 L' us walk honestly, as in the day;
14: 3 L' not him that eateth despise him
3 l' not him which eateth not judge him
5 L' every man be fully persuaded in
13 L' us not therefore judge one another
16 L' not then your good be evil spoken
19 L' us therefore follow after the things
15: 2 L' every one...please his neighbour
1Co 1:31 that glorieth, l' him glory in the Lord.
3:10 l' every man take heed how he buildeth
18 L' no man deceive himself. If any
18 l' him become a fool, that he may be
21 Therefore l' no man glory in men.
4: 1 L' a man so account of us, as of the
5: 8 Therefore l' us keep the feast, not
7: 2 l' every man have his own wife, and
2 l' every woman have her own husband.
3 L' the husband render unto the wife
9 if they cannot contain, l' them marry:
10 L' not the wife depart from her *
11 she depart, l' her remain unmarried,
11 l' not the husband put away his wife.*
12 with him, l' him not put her away.
13 to dwell with her, l' her not leave him.
15 the unbelieving depart, l' him depart.
17 hath called every one, so l' him walk.
18 l' him not become uncircumcised.
18 l' him not be circumcised.
20 L' every man abide in the same calling
24 l' every man, wherein he is...abide
36 need so require, l' him do what he will,
36 will he sinneth not: l' them marry.
10: 8 Neither l' us commit fornication, as
9 Neither l' us tempt Christ, as some of
12 l' him that...he standeth take heed
24 L' no man seek his own, but every
11: 6 be not covered, l' her also be shorn:
6 be shorn or shaven, l' her be covered.
28 But l' a man examine himself, and
28 so l' him eat of that bread, and drink
34 any man hunger, l' him eat at home;
14:13 l' him that speaketh in an...pray
26 L' all things be done unto edifying.
27 l' it be by two, or at most by three,
27 that by course; and l' one interpret.
28 l' him keep silence in the church;
28 l' him speak to himself, and to God.
29 L' the prophets speak two or three,
29 two or three, and l' the other judge.
30 sitteth by, l' the first hold his peace.
34 L' your women keep silence in the
35 l' them ask their husbands at home:
37 l' him acknowledge that the things
38 man be ignorant, l' him be ignorant.
40 L' all things be done decently and in
15:32 l' us eat and drink; for to morrow we
16: 2 l' every one of you lay by him in store,
11 L' no man therefore despise him: but
14 L' all your things be done with charity.
22 l' him be Anathema Maran-atha.
2Co 7: 1 l' us cleanse ourselves from all
9: 7 purposeth in his heart, so l' him give;
10: 7 l' him of himself think this again, that,
11 L' such an one think this, that, such
17 that glorieth, l' him glory in the Lord.
11:16 say again, L' no man think me a fool;
33 basket was I l' down by the wall. 5465
Ga 1: 8 unto you, l' him be accursed.
9 have received, l' him be accursed.
5:25 the Spirit, l' us also walk in the Spirit.
26 L' us not be desirous of vain glory,
6: 4 But l' every man prove his own work,
6 L' him that is taught...communicate
9 l' us not be weary in well doing: for
10 l' us do good unto all men, especially
17 henceforth l' no man trouble me:
Eph 4:26 l' not the sun go down upon your
28 L' him that stole steal no more: but
28 but rather l' him labour, working with
29 L' no corrupt communication proceed
31 L' all bitterness, and...be put away
5: 3 l' it not be once named among you, as
6 L' no man deceive you with vain
24 l' the wives be to their own husbands
33 l' every one of you in particular so love*
Ph'p 1:27 l' your conversation be as it becometh
2: 3 L' nothing be done through strife or*
3 mind l' each esteem other better than*
5 L' this mind be in you, which was also*
3:15 L' us therefore, as...be thus minded:
16 attained, l' us walk by the same rule,
16 l' us mind the same thing. *
4: 5 L' your moderation be known unto all
6 l' your requests be made known unto
Col 2:16 L' no man therefore judge you in
18 L' no man beguile you of your reward
3:15 l' the peace of God rule in your hearts,
16 L' the word of Christ dwell in you
4: 6 L' your speech be alway with grace,
1Th 5: 6 Therefore l' us not sleep, as do others;
6 but l' us watch and be sober.
8 But l' us, who are of the day, be sober,
2Th 2: 3 L' no man deceive you by any means:
7 only he who now letteth will l', *2722
1Ti 2:11 L' the woman learn in silence with all
3:10 And l' these also first be proved; then
10 then l' them use the office of a deacon,
12 L' the deacons be the husbands of
4:12 L' no man despise thy youth; but be
5: 4 l' them learn first to show piety at
1Ti 5: 9 L' not a widow be taken into the
16 have widows, l' them relieve them,
16 and l' not the church be charged; that
17 L' the elders that rule well be counted
6: 1 L' as many servants as are...count
2 masters, l' them not despise them,
8 raiment l' us be therewith content.*
2Ti 2:19 L' every one that nameth...depart
Tit 2:15 authority. L' no man despise thee.
3:14 l' ours also learn to maintain good
Ph'm 20 l' me have joy of thee in the Lord:
Heb 1: 6 l' all the angels of God worship him.
2: 1 at any time we should l' them slip.*
4: 1 L' us therefore fear, lest, a promise
11 L' us labour therefore to enter into
14 of God, l' us hold fast our profession.
16 L' us therefore come boldly unto the
6: 1 of Christ, l' us go on unto perfection;
10:22 L' us draw near with a true heart in
23 L' us hold fast the profession of our
24 l' us consider one another to provoke
12: 1 l' us lay aside every weight, and the
1 l' us run with patience the race that is
13 of the way; but l' it rather be healed.*
28 l' us have grace, whereby we may
13: 1 L' brotherly love continue.
5 L' your conversation be without *
13 L' us go forth therefore unto him
15 l' us offer the sacrifice of praise to God
Jas 1: 4 But l' patience have her perfect work,
5 you lack wisdom, l' him ask of God,
6 But l' him ask in faith, nothing
7 For l' not that man think that he shall
9 L' the brother of low degree rejoice
13 L' no man say when he is tempted, I
19 l' every man be swift to hear, slow to
3:13 l' him shew out of a good conversation
4: 9 l' your laughter be turned to mourning,
5:12 l' your yea be yea; and your nay, nay;
13 any among you afflicted? l' him pray.
13 Is any merry? l' him sing psalms.
14 l' him call for the elders of the church;
14 l' them pray over him, anointing him
20 L' him know, that he which converteth
1Pe 3: 3 l' it not be that outward adorning
4 But l' it be the hidden man of the
10 l' him refrain his tongue from evil,
11 L' him eschew evil, and do good,
11 l' him seek peace, and ensue it.
4:11 l' him speak as the oracles of God;*
11 l' him do it as of the ability which*
15 l' none of you suffer as a murderer,
16 as a Christian, l' him not be ashamed;
16 but l' him glorify God on this behalf.
19 l' them that suffer according to the
1Jo 2:24 L' that therefore abide in you, which
3: 7 Little children, l' no man deceive you:
18 little children, l' us not love in word,
4: 7 l' us love one another: for love is of
Re 2: 7, 11, 17, 29 l' him hear what the Spirit
3: 6, 13, 22 l' him hear what the Spirit saith
13: 9 If any man have an ear, l' him hear.
18 L' him that hath understanding count
19: 7 L' us be glad and rejoice, and give
22:11 that is unjust, l' him be unjust still:
11 he which is filthy, l' him be filthy still:
11 is righteous, l' him be righteous still:
11 and he that is holy, l' him be holy still.
17 And l' him that heareth say, Come.
17 And l' him that is athirst come.
17 l' him take the water of life freely.

letter See also LETTERS.
2Sa 11:14 David wrote a l' to Joab, and sent 5612
15 And he wrote in the l', saying, Set "
2Ki 5: 5 and I will send a l' unto the king of "
6 And he brought the l' to the king of "
6 Now when this l' is come unto thee, "
7 the king of Israel had read the l', "
10: 2 as soon as this l' cometh to you, "
6 Then he wrote a l' the second time "
7 to pass, when the l' came to them, "
19:14 And Hezekiah received the l' of the "
Ezr 4: 7 writing of the l' was written in the 5406
8 and Shimshai the scribe wrote a l' 104
11 the copy of the l' that they sent unto "
18 The l' which ye sent unto us hath 5407
23 the copy of king Artaxerxes' l' was "
5: 5 returned answer by l' concerning "
6 The copy of the l' that Tatnai, 104
7 They sent a l' unto him, wherein 6600
7:11 is the copy of the l' that the king 5406
Ne 2: 8 And a l' unto Asaph the keeper of 107
6: 5 time with an open l' in his hand; "
Es 9:26 Therefore for all the words of this l', "
29 to confirm this second l' of Purim. "
Isa 37:14 Hezekiah received the l' from the 5612
Jer 29: 1 words of the l' that Jeremiah the "
29 the priest read this l' in the ears of "
Ac 23:25 he wrote a l' after this manner: 1992
34 when the governor had read the l',*
Ro 2:27 who by the l' and circumcision 1121
29 heart, in the spirit, and not in the l'; "
7: 6 and not in the oldness of the l'. "
2Co 3: 6 not of the l', but of the spirit: "
6 the l' killeth, but the spirit giveth "
7: 8 though I made you sorry with a l', *1992
Ga 6:11 Ye see how large a l' I have *1121
2Th 2: 2 nor by word, nor by l' as from us, *1992
Heb 13:22 I have written a l' unto you in few *1989

letters
1Ki 21: 8 So she wrote l' in Ahab's name, 5612
8 and sent the l' unto the elders and "
9 And she wrote in the l', saying, "
11 as it was written in the l' which she "
2Ki 10: 1 And Jehu wrote l', and sent to "
2Ki 20:12 sent l' and a present unto Hezekiah: 5612
2Ch 30: 1 and wrote l' also to Ephraim and 107
6 the posts went with the l' from the "
32:17 He wrote also l' to rail on the Lord 5612
Ne 2: 7 let l' be given me to the governors 107
9 river, and gave them the king's l'. "
6:17 Judah sent many l' unto Tobiah, "
17 the l' of Tobiah came unto them.
19 And Tobiah sent l' to put me in fear. 107
Es 1:22 For he sent l' into all the king's 5612
3:13 the l' were sent by posts into all "
8: 5 let it be written to reverse the l' "
10 and sent l' by posts on horseback, "
9:20 sent l' unto all the Jews that were "
25 he commanded by l' that his wicked "
30 And he sent the l' unto all the Jews, "
Isa 39: 1 sent l' and a present to Hezekiah: "
Jer 29:25 thou hast sent l' in thy name unto "
Lu 23:38 written over him in l' of Greek, *1121
Joh 7:15 How knoweth this man l', having "
Ac 9: 2 And desired of him l' to Damascus 1992
15:23 And they wrote l' by them after this *
22: 5 I received l' unto the brethren, 1992
28:21 We neither received l' out of Judæa 1121
1Co 16: 3 whomsoever...approve by your l', 1992
2Co 3: 1 you, or l' of commendation from you?*
10: 9 seem as if I would terrify you by l'. 1992
10 For his l', say they, are weighty "
11 in word by l' when we are absent, "

lettest
Job 15:13 l' such words go out of thy mouth?
41: 1 with a cord which thou l' down? *8257
Lu 2:29 now l' thou thy servant depart in 630

letteth
2Ki 10:24 he that l' him go, his life shall be for
Pr 17:14 strife is as when one l' out water: 6362
2Th 2: 7 only he who now l' will let, until *2722

letting
Ex 8:29 in not l' the people go to sacrifice

Letushim (*le-tu'-shim*)
Ge 25: 3 of Dedan were Asshurim, and L'. 3912

Leummim (*le-um'-mim*)
Ge 25: 3 Asshurim, and Letushim, and L'. 3817

Levi (*le'-vi*) See also LEVITE; LEVITICAL; MATTHEW.
Ge 29:34 therefore was his name called L'. 3878
34:25 the sons of Jacob, Simeon and L', "
30 And Jacob said to Simeon and L', "
35:23 firstborn, and Simeon, and L', and "
46:11 sons of L'; Gershon, Kohath, and "
49: 5 Simeon and L' are brethren; "
Ex 1: 2 Reuben, Simeon, L', and Judah, "
2: 1 there went a man of the house of L', "
1 and took to wife a daughter of L'. "
6:16 are the names of the sons of L' "
16 life of L' were an hundred thirty "
19 Mushi: these are the families of L' *"
32:26 the sons of L' gathered themselves "
28 of L' did according to the word of "
Nu 1:49 shalt not number the tribe of L', "
3: 6 Bring the tribe of L' near, and "
15 Number the children of L' after the "
17 were the sons of L' by their names; "
4: 2 Kohath from among the sons of L', "
16: 1 the son of L', and Dathan and "
7 too much upon you, ye sons of L'. "
8 Hear, I pray you, ye sons of L': "
10 brethren the sons of L' with thee: "
17: 3 Aaron's name upon the rod of L': "
8 for the house of L' was budded, "
18: 2 thy brethren also of the tribe of L', "
21 I have given the children of L' all "
26:59 was Jochebed, the daughter of L', "
59 her mother bare to L' in Egypt: "
De 10: 8 the Lord separated the tribe of L', "
9 L' hath no part nor inheritance "
18: 1 the Levites, and all the tribe of L', "
21: 5 the sons of L' shall come near: "
27:12 Simeon, and L', and Judah, and "
31: 9 it unto the priests the sons of L', "
33: 8 of L' he said, Let thy Thummim "
Jos 13:14 of L' he gave none inheritance; "
33 L' Moses gave not any inheritance: "
21:10 who were of the children of L', had: "
1Ki 12:31 which were not of the sons of L'. "
1Ch 2: 1 Reuben, Simeon, L', and Judah, "
6: 1, 16 The sons of L'; Gershon, "
38 the son of L', the son of Israel. "
43 the son of Gershom, the son of L'. "
47 the son of Merari, the son of L'. "
9:18 the companies of the children of L'. "
12:26 Of the children of L' four thousand "
21: 6 L' and Benjamin counted he not "
23: 6 into courses among the sons of L', "
14 sons were named of the tribe of L'. "
24 These were the sons of L' after the "
24:20 rest of the sons of L' were these; "
Ezr 8:15 found there none of the sons of L'. "
18 the son of L', the son of Israel; "
Ne 10:39 the children of L' shall bring the "
12:23 sons of L', the chief of the fathers, "
Ps 135:20 Bless the Lord, O house of L': ye "
Eze 40:46 sons of Zadok among the sons of L', "
48:31 one gate of Judah, one gate of L'. "
Zec 12:13 The family of the house of L' apart, "
Mal 2: 4 that my covenant might be with L', "
8 have corrupted the covenant of L', "
3: 3 he shall purify the sons of L', and "
M'r 2:14 he saw L' the son of Alphæus 3018
Lu 3:24, 29 Matthat, which was the son of L', 3017
5:27 saw a publican, named L', sitting 3018
29 L' made him a great feast in his "
Heb 7: 5 they that are of the sons of L', 3017

Heb 7: 9 say, L' also, who receiveth tithes, 3017
Re 7: 7 Of the tribe of L' were sealed twelve "

leviathan (*le-vi'-ath-un*)
Job 41: 1 Canst thou draw out l' with an 3882
Ps 74: 14 brakest the heads of l' in pieces, "
104: 26 is that l', whom thou hast made "
Isa 27: 1 shall punish l' the piercing serpent, "
1 even l' that crooked serpent; and he "

Levite (*le'-vite*) See also LEVITES; LEVITICAL.
Ex 4: 14 Is not Aaron the L' thy brother? 3881
De 12: 12 the L' that is within your gates; "
18 and the L' that is within thy gates: "
19 forsake not the L' as long as thou "
14: 27 the L' that is within thy gates; "
29 the L', (because he hath no part "
16: 11 and the L' that is within thy gates, "
14 and the L', the stranger, and the "
18: 6 if a L' come from any of thy gates "
26: 11 the L', and the stranger that is "
12 and hast given it unto the L', "
13 also have given them unto the L', "
J'g 17: 7 the family of Judah, who was a L', "
9 I am a L' of Beth-lehem-judah, "
10 and thy victuals. So the L' went in. "
11 the L' was content to dwell with "
12 Micah consecrated the L'; and the "
13 seeing I have a L' to my priest. "
18: 3 the voice of the young man the L': "
15 the house of the young man the L', "
19: 1 there was a certain L' sojourning "
20: 4 the L', the husband of the woman "
2Ch 20: 14 a L' of the sons of Asaph, came the "
31: 12 which Cononiah the L' was ruler, "
14 And Kore the son of Imnah the L', "
Ezr 10: 15 Shabbethai the L' helped them. "
Lu 10: 32 likewise a L', when he was at the 3019
Ac 4: 36 The son of consolation,) a L', and "

Levites (*le'-vites*)
Ex 6: 25 the heads of the fathers of the L' 3881
38: 21 of Moses for the service of the L', "
Le 25: 32 Notwithstanding the cities of the L', "
32 may the L' redeem at any time. "
33 And if a man purchase of the L', "
33 for the houses of the cities of the L' "
Nu 1: 47 L' after the tribe of their fathers "
50 appoint the L' over the tabernacle "
51 forward, the L' shall take it down: "
51 to be pitched, the L' shall set it up: "
53 the L' shall pitch round about the "
53 the L' shall keep the charge of the "
2: 17 with the camp of the L' in the midst "
33 L' were not numbered among the "
3: 9 shalt give the L' unto Aaron and to "
12 I have taken the L' from among the "
12 therefore the L' shall be mine; "
20 These are the families of the L' "
32 be chief over the chief of the L', "
39 All that were numbered of the L', "
41 And thou shalt take the L' for me "
41 the cattle of the L' instead of all the "
45 the L' instead of all the firstborn "
45 the cattle of the L' instead of their "
45 the L' shall be mine: I am the Lord. "
46 Israel, which are more than the L'; "
49 them that were redeemed by the L': "
4: 18 the Kohathites from among the L': "
46 that were numbered of the L', "
7: 5 thou shalt give them unto the L', "
6 oxen, and gave them unto the L'. "
8: 6 Take the L' from among the "
9 bring the L' before the tabernacle "
10 shalt bring the L' before the Lord: "
10 shall put their hands upon the L': "
11 shall offer the L' before the Lord "
12 the L' shall lay their hands upon "
12 to make an atonement for the L'. "
13 thou shalt set the L' before Aaron, "
14 thou separate the L' from among "
14 of Israel: and the L' shall be mine. "
15 shall the L' go in to do the service "
18 taken the L' for all the firstborn "
19 have given the L' as a gift to Aaron "
20 did to the L' according unto all that "
20 Moses concerning the L', so did "
21 And the L' were purified, and they "
22 went the L' in to do their service "
22 Moses concerning the L', so did "
24 is it that belongeth unto the L': "
26 Thus shalt thou do unto the L' "
18: 6 I have taken your brethren the L' "
23 the L' shall do the service of the "
24 I have given to the L' to inherit: "
26 Thus speak unto the L', and say "
30 counted unto the L' as the increase "
26: 57 they that were numbered of the L' "
58 These are the families of the L': * "
31: 30 and give them unto the L', which "
47 and gave them unto the L', which "
35: 2 that they give unto the L' of the "
2 shall give also unto the L' suburbs "
4 which ye shall give unto the L', "
6 which ye shall give unto the L' "
7 cities which ye shall give to the L' "
8 shall give of his cities unto the L' "
De 17: 9 shalt come unto the priests the L', "
18 which is before the priests the L': "
18: 1 The priests the L', and all the tribe "
7 as all his brethren the L' do, which "
24: 8 the priests the L' shall teach you: "
27: 9 priests the L' spake unto all Israel, "
14 the L' shall speak, and say unto all "
31: 25 Moses commanded the L', which "
Jos 3: 3 the priests the L' bearing it, then "
8: 33 that side before the priests the L', "
14: 3 the L' he gave none inheritance "
Jos 14: 4 they gave no part unto the L' in 3881
18: 7 the L' have no part among you; "
21: 1 the heads of the fathers of the L' "
3 children of Israel gave unto the L' "
4 the priest, which were of the L', "
8 gave by lot unto the L' these cities "
20 L' which remained of the children "
27 of the families of the L', out of the "
34 the rest of the L', out of the tribe "
40 remaining of the families of the L', "
41 All the cities of the L' within the "
1Sa 6: 15 L' took down the ark of the Lord, "
2Sa 15: 24 also, and all the L' were with him, "
1Ki 8: 4 did the priests and the L' bring up. "
1Ch 6: 19 And these are the families of the L' "
48 brethren also the L' were appointed "
64 of Israel gave to the L' these cities "
9: 2 the priests, L', and the Nethinims. "
14 And of the L'; Shemaiah the son of "
26 For these L', the four chief porters, "
31 one of the L', who was the firstborn "
33 chief of the fathers of the L', who "
34 These chief fathers of the L' were "
13: 2 with them also to the priests and L' "
15: 2 carry the ark of God but the L':* "
4 the children of Aaron, and the L': "
11 for the L', for Uriel, Asaiah, and "
12 the chief of the fathers of the L': "
14 and the L' sanctified themselves "
15 the children of the L' bare the ark "
16 David spake to the chief of the L' "
17 the L' appointed Heman the son of "
22 chief of the L', was for song: he "
26 when God helped the L' that bare "
27 and all the L' that bare the ark, "
16: 4 he appointed certain of the L' to "
23: 2 Israel, with the priests and the L'. "
3 Now the L' were numbered from "
26 And also unto the L'; they shall no "
27 L' were numbered from twenty * "
24: 6 Nethaneel the scribe, one of the L', 3878
6 the fathers of the priests and L': 3881
30 These were the sons of the L' after "
31 the fathers of the priests and L', "
26: 17 Eastward were six L', northward "
20 And of the L', Ahijah was over the * "
27: 17 Of the L', Hashabiah the son of "
28: 13, 21 courses of the priests and the L', "
2Ch 5: 4 came; and the L' took up the ark. "
5 did the priests and the L' bring up. "
12 Also the L' which were the singers, "
7: 6 the L' also with instruments of "
8: 14 the L' to their charges, to praise "
15 of the king unto the priests and L' "
11: 13 and the L' that were in all Israel "
14 the L' left their suburbs and their "
13: 9 the sons of Aaron, and the L', "
10 the L' wait upon their business: "
17: 8 And with them he sent L', even "
8 Tobijah, and Tob-adonijah, L'; "
19: 8 did Jehoshaphat set of the L', "
11 the L' shall be officers before you. "
20: 19 And the L', of the children of the "
23: 2 gathered the L' out of all the cities "
4 of the priests and of the L', shall "
6 and they that minister of the L'; "
7 And the L' shall compass the king "
8 the L' and all Judah did according "
18 by the hand of the priests the L', "
24: 5 together the priests and the L', "
5 Howbeit the L' hastened it not. "
6 hast thou not required of the L' to "
11 king's office by the hand of the L', "
29: 4 brought in the priests and the L', "
5 And said unto them, hear me, ye L', "
12 Then the L' arose, Mahath the son "
16 And the L' took it, to carry it out "
25 he set the L' in the house of the "
26 the L' stood with the instruments "
30 commanded the L' to sing praise "
34 their brethren the L' did help them, "
34 the L' were more upright in heart "
30: 15 priests and the L' were ashamed, "
16 they received of the hand of the L'. "
17 the L' had the charge of the killing "
21 the L' and the priests praised the "
22 spake comfortably unto all the L' "
25 Judah, with the priests and the L', "
27 L' arose and blessed the people: "
31: 2 and the L' after their courses, "
2 L' for burnt offerings and for peace "
4 portion of the priests and the L', "
9 with the priests and the L' "
17 the L' from twenty years old and "
19 by genealogies among the L'. "
34: 9 which the L' that kept the doors had "
12 were Jahath and Obadiah, the L', "
12 other of the L', all that could skill "
13 of the L' there were scribes, and "
30 the priests, and the L', and all the "
35: 3 unto the L' that taught all Israel, "
5 division of the families of the L'. "
8 to the priests, and to the L': "
9 Jeiel and Jozabad, chief of the L', "
9 gave unto the L' for passover "
10 place, and the L' in their courses, "
11 their hands, and the L' flayed them. "
14 the L' prepared for themselves, "
15 brethren the L' prepared for them. "
18 and the priests, and the L', and all "
Ezr 1: 5 and the priests, and the L', with all "
2: 40 The L': the children of Jeshua "
70 and the L', and some of the people, "
3: 8 brethren the priests and the L', "
8 appointed the L', from twenty years "
9 sons and their brethren the L'. "
Ezr 3: 10 L' the sons of Asaph with cymbals, 3881
12 of the priests and L' and chief of "
6: 16 of Israel, the priests and the L', 3879
18 and the L' in their courses, for the "
20 and the L' were purified together, 3881
7: 7 the L', and the singers, and the "
13 and of his priests and L', in my 3879
24 touching any of the priests and L', "
8: 20 appointed for the service of the L', 3881
29 the chief of the priests of the L', "
30 So took the priests and the L' the "
33 Noadiah the son of Binnui, L'; "
9: 1 the priests, and the L', have not "
10: 5 chief priests, the L', and all Israel, "
23 of the L'; Jozabad, and Shimei, "
Ne 3: 17 After him repaired the L', Rehum "
7: 1 singers and the L' were appointed, "
43 The L': the children of Jeshua, "
73 So the priests, and the L', and the "
8: 7 and the L', caused the people to "
9 and the L' that taught the people, "
11 the L' stilled all the people, saying, "
13 and the L', unto Ezra the scribe, "
9: 4 upon the stairs, of the L', Jeshua, "
5 Then the L', Jeshua, and Kadmiel, "
38 princes, L', and priests, seal unto it. "
10: 9 And the L': both Jeshua the son of "
28 the priests, the L', the porters, the "
34 the lots among the priests, the L', "
37 tithes of our ground unto the L', "
37 L' might have the tithes in all the "
38 with the L', when the L' take tithes: "
38 L' shall bring up the tithe of the "
11: 3 wit, Israel, the priests, and the L', "
15 Also of the L': Shemaiah the son "
16 Jozabad, of the chief of the L', "
18 All the L' in the holy city were two "
20 Israel, of the priests, and the L', "
22 overseer also of the L' at Jerusalem "
36 of the L' were divisions in Judah, "
12: 1 priests and the L' that went up "
8 Moreover the L': Jeshua, Binnui, "
22 L' in the days of Eliashib, Joiada, "
24 And the chief of the L': Hashabiah, "
27 sought the L' out of all their places, "
30 and the L' purified themselves, "
44 of the law for the priests and L': "
44 for the priests and for the L' that "
47 sanctified holy things unto the L'; "
47 the L' sanctified them unto the "
13: 5 commanded to be given to the L', "
10 portions of the L' had not been given "
10 the L' and the singers, that did the "
13 the scribe, and of the L', Pedaiah: "
22 And I commanded the L' that they "
29 of the priesthood, and of the L', "
30 the wards of the priests and the L', "
Isa 66: 21 take of them for priests and for L', "
Jer 33: 18 shall the priests the L' want a man "
21 and with the L', the priests, my "
22 and the L' that minister unto me. "
Eze 43: 19 thou shalt give to the priests the L' "
44: 10 L' that are gone far away from me, "
15 priests the L', the sons of Zadok, "
45: 5 shall also the L', the ministers of "
48: 11 went astray, as the L' went astray. "
12 most holy by the border of the L'. "
13 the L' shall have five and twenty "
22 from the possession of the L', and "
Joh 1: 19 when the Jews sent priests and L' 3019

Levitical
Heb 7: 11 were by the L' priesthood, 3020

levy
Nu 31: 28 And l' a tribute unto the Lord of 7311
1Ki 5: 13 king Solomon raised a l' out of all 4522
13 and the l' was thirty thousand men. "
14 and Adoniram was over the l'. "
9: 15 the l' which king Solomon raised; "
21 upon those did Solomon l' a tribute 5927

lewd
Eze 16: 27 which are ashamed of thy l' way. 2154
23: 44 and unto Aholibah, the l' women. "
Ac 17: 5 certain l' fellows of the baser sort, *4190

lewdly
Eze 22: 11 hath l' defiled his daughter in law; 2154

lewdness
J'g 20: 6 committed l' and folly in Israel. 2154
Jer 11: 15 she hath wrought l' with many, 4209
13: 27 neighings, the l' of thy whoredom, 2154
Eze 16: 43 shalt not commit this l' above all "
58 Thou hast borne thy l' and thine "
22: 9 in the midst of thee they commit l'. "
23: 21 to remembrance the l' of thy youth, "
27 Thus will I make thy l' to cease "
29 both thy l' and thy whoredoms. "
35 therefore bear thou also thy l' and "
48 Thus will I cause l' to cease out of "
48 be taught not to do after your l'. "
49 shall recompense your l' upon you, "
24: 13 In thy filthiness is l': because I "
Ho 2: 10 And now will I discover her l' in 5040
6: 9 by consent: for they commit l'. 2154
Ac 18: 14 a matter of wrong or wicked l', *4467

liar See also LIARS.
Job 24: 25 not so now, who will make me a l', 3576
Pr 17: 4 l' giveth ear to a naughty tongue. 8267
19: 22 a poor man is better than a l'. 376, 3576
30: 6 thee, and thou be found a l'. "
Jer 15: 18 thou be altogether unto me as a l', *391
Joh 8: 44 for he is a l', and the father of it. 5583
55 him not, I shall be a l' like unto you: "
Ro 3: 4 let God be true, but every man a l'; "
1Jo 1: 10 have not sinned, we make him a l', "
2: 4 not his commandments, is a l', and "

1Jo 2:22 Who is a *l'* but he that denieth that 5583
4:20 and hateth his brother, he is a *l'*: "
5:10 not God hath made him a *l'*; "

liars
De 33:29 shall be found *l'* unto thee; *3584
Ps 116:11 I said in my haste, All men are *l'*.*3576
Isa 44:25 frustrateth the tokens of the *l'*, and 907
Jer 50:36 A sword is upon the *l'*; and they * "
1Ti 1:10 For *l'*, for perjured persons, and if 5583
Tit 1:12 said, The Cretians are alway *l'*, "
Re 2:2 are not, and hast found them *l'*: *5571
21:8 sorcerers, and idolaters, and all *l'*, "

liberal
Pr 11:25 The *l'* soul shall be made fat: and 1293
Isa 32:5 person shall be no more called *l'*, ‡5081
8 But the *l'* deviseth *l'* things; and "
8 and by *l'* things shall he stand. "
2Co 9:13 for your *l'* distribution unto them, *572

liberality
1Co 16:3 to bring your *l'* unto Jerusalem. *5485
2Co 8:2 abounded unto the riches of their *l'*. 572

liberally
De 15:14 furnish him *l'* out of thy flock, 6059
Jas 1:5 ask of God, that giveth to all men *l'*, 574

Libertines (*lib'-ur-tins*)
Ac 6:9 is called the synagogue of the *L'*, 3032

liberty
Le 25:10 proclaim *l'* throughout all the land 1865
Ps 119:45 And I will walk at *l'*: for I seek thy 7342
Isa 61:1 to proclaim *l'* to the captives, and 1865
Jer 34:8 to proclaim *l'* unto them; "
15 in proclaiming *l'* every man to his "
16 he had set at *l'* at their pleasure, *2670
17 in proclaiming *l'*, every one to his 1865
17 behold, I proclaim a *l'* for you, saith "
Eze 46:17 then it shall be his to the year of *l'*; "
Lu 4:18 to set at *l'* them that are bruised, 859
Ac 24:23 to keep Paul, and to let him have *l'*,*425
26:32 This man might have been set at *l'*, 630
27:3 gave him *l'* to go unto his friends *2010
Ro 8:21 glorious *l'* of the children of God. 1657
1Co 7:39 she is at *l'* to be married to whom *1658
8:9 any means this *l'* of yours become 1849
10:29 for why is my *l'* judged of another 1657
2Co 3:17 the Spirit of the Lord is, there is *l'*. "
Ga 2:4 to spy out our *l'* which we have in "
5:1 the *l'* wherewith Christ hath made * "
13 For...ye have been called unto *l'*; * "
13 only use not *l'* for an occasion to * "
Heb 13:23 our brother Timothy is set at *l'*; 630
Jas 1:25 looketh into the perfect law of *l'*, 1657
2:12 that shall be judged by the law of *l'*. "
1Pe 2:16 and not using your *l'* for a cloke of * "
2Pe 2:19 While they promise them *l'*, they "

Libnah (*lib'-nah*) See also LABAN.
Nu 33:20 Rimmon-parez, and pitched in *L'*. 3841
21 they removed from *L'*, and pitched "
Jos 10:29 unto *L'*, and fought against *L'*: "
31 And Joshua passed from *L'*, and all "
32 to all that he had done to *L'*. "
39 as he had done also to *L'*, and to "
12:15 The king of *L'*, one; the king of "
15:42 *L'*, and Ether, and Ashan, "
21:13 slayer; and *L'* with her suburbs, "
2Ki 8:22 Then *L'* revolted at the same time. "
19:8 king of Assyria warring against *L'*: "
23:31 the daughter of Jeremiah of *L'*. "
24:18 the daughter of Jeremiah of *L'*. "
1Ch 6:57 of refuge, and *L'* with her suburbs, "
2Ch 21:10 did *L'* revolt from under his hand; "
Isa 37:8 king of Assyria warring against *L'*: "
Jer 52:1 the daughter of Jeremiah of *L'*. "

Libnath See SHIHOR-LIBNATH.

Libni (*lib'-ni*) See also LAADAN; LIBNITES.
Ex 6:17 sons of Gershon; *L'*, and Shimi, 3845
Nu 3:18 Gershon by their families; *L'*, and "
1Ch 6:17 sons of Gershom; *L'*, and Shimei. "
20 Of Gershom; *L'* his son, Jahath his "
29 *L'* his son, Shimei his son, Uzza his "

Libnites (*lib'-nites*)
Nu 3:21 Gershon was the family of the *L'*, 3864
26:58 the family of the *L'*, the family of "

Libya (*lib'-e-ah*) See also LIBYANS.
Eze 30:5 Ethiopia, and *L'*, and Lydia, and *6316
38:5 Ethiopia, and *L'* with them; * "
Ac 2:10 and in the parts of *L'* about Cyrene, 3033

Libyans (*lib'-e-uns*) See also LEHABIM.
Jer 46:9 the Ethiopians and the *L'*, that *6316
Da 11:43 the *L'* and the Ethiopians shall be 3864

lice
Ex 8:16 may become *l'* throughout all the 3654
17 it became *l'* in man, and in beast; "
17 all the dust of the land became *l'* "
18 enchantments to bring forth *l'*, "
18 so there were *l'* upon man, and upon "
Ps 105:31 of flies, and *l'* in all their coasts. "

licence
Ac 21:40 when he had given him *l'*, Paul 2010
25:16 and have *l'* to answer for himself *5117

lick See also LICKED; LICKETH.
Nu 22:4 Now shall this company *l'* up all 3897
1Ki 21:19 of Naboth shall dogs *l'* thy blood, 3952
Ps 72:9 and his enemies shall *l'* the dust. 3897
Isa 49:23 and *l'* up the dust of thy feet; "
Mic 7:17 They shall *l'* the dust like a serpent, "

licked
1Ki 18:38 *l'* up the water that was in the 3897
21:19 where dogs *l'* the blood of Naboth 3952
22:38 and the dogs *l'* up his blood; "
Lu 16:21 the dogs came and *l'* his sores. 621

licketh
Nu 22:4 as the ox *l'* up the grass of the 3897

lid See also EYELIDS.
2Ki 12:9 and bored a hole in the *l'* of it, 1817

lie See also LAIN; LAY; LIED; LIEN; LIES; LIEST; LIETH; LYING.
Ge 19:32 we will *l'* with him, that we may 7901
34 go thou in, and *l'* with him, that "
30:15 he shall *l'* with thee to night for "
39:7 Joseph; and she said, *L'* with me. "
10 her, to *l'* by her, or to be with her. "
12 by his garment, saying, *L'* with me: "
14 he came in unto me to *l'* with me, "
47:30 I will *l'* with my fathers, and thou* "
Ex 21:13 if a man *l'* not in wait, but God 6658
22:16 is not betrothed, and *l'* with her, 7901
23:11 thou shalt let it rest and *l'* still; 5203
Le 6:2 and *l'* unto his neighbour in that *3584
15:18 also with whom man shall *l'* with 7901
24 And if any man *l'* with her at all, "
18:20 thou shalt not *l'* carnally with 5414,7903
22 Thou shalt not *l'* with mankind, 7901
23 Neither shalt thou *l'* with any 5414,7903
23 before a beast to *l'* down thereto: 7250
19:11 falsely, neither *l'* one to another. 8266
20:12 if a man *l'* with his daughter in law, 7901
13 If a man also *l'* with mankind, as "
15 if a man *l'* with a beast, he 5414,7903
16 any beast, and *l'* down thereto, 7250
18 if a man shall *l'* with a woman 7901
20 man shall *l'* with his uncle's wife, "
26:6 ye shall *l'* down, and none shall "
Nu 5:13 And a man *l'* with her carnally, "
10:5 camps that *l'* on the east parts 2583
6 camps that *l'* on the south side "
23:19 is not a man, that he should *l'*; 3576
24 *l'* down until he eat of the prey, 7901
De 19:11 neighbour, and *l'* in wait for him, 693
22:23 her in the city, and *l'* with her; 7901
25 the man force her, and *l'* with her: "
28 lay hold on her, and *l'* with her, "
25:2 judge shall cause him to *l'* down, 5307
28:30 and another man shall *l'* with her: 7693
29:20 written in this book shall *l'* upon 7257
Jos 8:4 ye shall *l'* in wait against the city, 693
9 they went to *l'* in ambush, and abode* "
12 *l'* in ambush between Beth-el and "
J'g 9:32 with thee, and *l'* in wait in the field: "
19:20 let all thy wants *l'* upon me; only
21:20 Go and *l'* in wait in the vineyards; "
Ru 3:4 mark the place where he shall *l'*, 7901
7 he went to *l'* down at the end of the "
13 liveth: *l'* down until the morning. "
1Sa 3:5 said, I called not; *l'* down again. "
6 called not, my son; *l'* down again. "
9 Eli said unto Samuel, Go, *l'* down: "
15:29 of Israel will not *l'* nor repent: 8266
22:8,13 me, to *l'* in wait, as at this day? "
2Sa 11:11 to drink, and to *l'* with my wife? 7901
13 at even he went out to *l'* on his bed "
12:11 he shall *l'* with thy wives in the "
13:11 her, Come *l'* with me, my sister. "
1Ki 1:2 him, and let her *l'* in thy bosom, "
2Ki 4:16 do not *l'* unto thine handmaid. 3576
Job 6:28 for it is evident unto you if I *l'*. "
7:4 When I *l'* down, I say, When shall 7901
11:19 Also thou shalt *l'* down, and none 7257
20:11 shall *l'* down with him in the dust. 7901
21:26 They shall *l'* down alike in the dust, "
27:19 The rich man shall *l'* down, but he* "
34:6 Should I *l'* against my right? my *3576
38:40 abide in the covert to *l'* in wait?
Ps 23:2 me to *l'* down in green pastures: 7257
57:4 I *l'* even among them that are set 7901
59:3 For, lo, they *l'* in wait for my soul:
62:9 and men of high degree are a *l'*: 3576
88:5 like the slain that *l'* in the grave, 7901
89:35 that I will not *l'* unto David. 3576
119:69 The proud have forged a *l'* against "
Pr 3:24 yea, thou shalt *l'* down, and thy 7901
12:6 wicked are to *l'* in wait for blood:*
14:5 A faithful witness will not *l'*: but 3576
Ec 4:11 if two *l'* together, then they have 7901
Ca 1:13 *l'* all night betwixt my breasts. *3885
Isa 11:6 leopard shall *l'* down with the kid; 7257
7 their young ones shall *l'* down "
13:21 wild beasts of the desert shall *l'* "
14:18 all of them, *l'* in glory, every one *7901
30 the needy shall *l'* down in safety: 7257
17:2 be for flocks, which shall *l'* down, "
27:10 and there shall he *l'* down, and "
33:8 The highways *l'* waste, the wayfaring
34:10 to generation it shall *l'* waste; none
43:17 they shall *l'* down together, they 7901
44:20 Is there not a *l'* in my right hand? 3576
50:11 hand; ye shall *l'* down in sorrow. 7901
51:20 they *l'* at the head of all the streets, "
63:8 people, children that will not *l'*: *8266
65:10 a place for the herds to *l'* down in, 7258
Jer 3:25 We *l'* down in our shame, and our 7901
27:10 prophesy a *l'* unto you, to remove 8267
14 for they prophesy a *l'* unto you, "
15 they prophesy a *l'* in my name; * "
16 for they prophesy a *l'* unto you, "
28:15 makest this people to trust in a *l'*. "
29:21 prophesy a *l'* unto you in my name; "
31 and he caused you to trust in a *l'*: "
33:12 causing their flocks to *l'* down. 7257
La 2:21 young and the old *l'* on the ground 7901
Eze 4:4 *L'* thou also upon thy left side, "
4 the days that thou shalt *l'* upon it "
6 *l'* again on thy right side, and thou "
9 days that thou shalt *l'* upon thy "
21:29 Whiles they divine a *l'* unto thee, *3576
31:18 *l'* in the midst of...uncircumcised 7901
Eze 32:21 they *l'* uncircumcised, slain by the 7901
27 they shall not *l'* with the mighty "
28 shalt *l'* with them that are slain "
29 shall *l'* with the uncircumcised, "
30 they *l'* uncircumcised with them "
34:14 there shall they *l'* in a good fold, 7257
15 I will cause them to *l'* down, saith "
Ho 2:18 will make them to *l'* down safely. 7901
7:6 like an oven, whiles they *l'* in wait:
Joe 1:13 *l'* all night in sackcloth,...ministers 3885
Am 6:4 That *l'* upon beds of ivory, and 7901
Mic 1:14 shall be a *l'* to the kings of Israel.* 391
2:11 in the spirit and falsehood do *l'*, 3576
7:2 men: they all *l'* in wait for blood;
Hab 2:3 the end it shall speak, and not *l'*: 3576
Zep 2:7 shall they *l'* down in the evening: 7527
14 flocks shall *l'* down in the midst of "
15 a place for beasts to *l'* down in! 4769
3:13 for they shall feed and *l'* down, 7257
Hag 1:4 houses, and this house *l'* waste? *
Zec 10:2 and the diviners have seen a *l'*, 8267
Joh 5:6 When Jesus saw him *l'*, and knew *2621
8:44 When he speaketh a *l'*, he 5579
20:6 and seeth the linen clothes *l'*, *2749
Ac 5:3 hath Satan filled thine heart to *l'* 5574
23:21 there *l'* in wait for him of them more
Ro 1:25 changed the truth of God into a *l'*, 5579
3:7 through my *l'* unto his glory; 5582
9:1 I say the truth in Christ, I *l'* not, 5574
2Co 11:31 evermore, knoweth that I *l'* not. "
Ga 1:20 you, behold, before God, I *l'* not. "
Eph 4:14 whereby they *l'* in wait to deceive;*3180
Col 3:9 *L'* not one to another, seeing that 5574
2Th 2:11 that they should believe a *l'*: 5579
1Ti 2:7 the truth in Christ, and *l'* not;) 5574
Tit 1:2 life, which God, that cannot *l'*, 893
Heb 6:18 it was impossible for God to *l'*, 5574
Jas 3:14 not, and *l'* not against the truth. "
1Jo 1:6 darkness, we *l'*, and do not the truth: "
2:21 it, and that no *l'* is of the truth. 5579
27 and is truth, and is no *l'*, and even "
Re 3:9 are Jews, and are not, but do *l'*; 5574
21:27 abomination, or maketh a *l'*: 5579
22:15 whosoever loveth and maketh a *l'*. "

lied See also BELIED.
1Ki 13:18 drink water. But he *l'* unto him. 3584
Ps 78:36 *l'* unto him with their tongues. 3576
Isa 57:11 or feared, that thou hast *l'*, and *
Ac 5:4 thou hast not *l'* unto men, but unto 5574

lien See also LAIN.
Ge 26:10 lightly have *l'* with thy wife, ‡7901
Ps 68:13 Though ye have *l'* among the pots,* "
Jer 3:2 where thou hast not been *l'* with. ‡7693

liers
Jos 8:13 *l'* in wait on the west of the city,
14 were *l'* in ambush against him
J'g 9:25 of Shechem set *l'* in wait for him in
16:12 *l'* in wait abiding in the chamber.
20:29 set *l'* in wait round about Gibeah.
33 the *l'* in wait of Israel came forth
36 they trusted unto the *l'* in wait which
37 the *l'* in wait hasted, and rushed
37 the *l'* in wait drew themselves along,
38 the men of Israel and the *l'* in wait,

lies
J'g 16:10,13 hast mocked me, and told me *l'*: 3576
Job 11:3 thy *l'* make men hold their peace? *907
13:4 But ye are forgers of *l'*, ye are all 8267
Ps 40:4 proud, nor such as turn aside to *l'*. 3576
58:3 soon as they be born, speaking *l'*. "
62:4 they delight in *l'*: they bless with "
63:11 mouth of them that speak *l'* shall be 8267
101:7 telleth *l'* shall not tarry in my sight.* "
Pr 6:19 A false witness that speaketh *l'*, 3576
14:5 lie: but a false witness will utter *l'*. "
25 but a deceitful witness speaketh *l'*. "
19:5 he that speaketh *l'* shall not escape. "
9 and he that speaketh *l'* shall perish. "
29:12 If a ruler hearken to *l'*, all his *1697,8267
30:8 far from me vanity and *l'*: " 3576
Isa 9:15 the prophet that teacheth *l'*, he is 8267
16:6 wrath: but his *l'* shall not be so. * 907
28:15 we have made *l'* our refuge, and 3576
17 shall sweep away the refuge of *l'*, "
59:3 your lips have spoken *l'*, your 8267
4 they trust in vanity, and speak *l'*; 7723
Jer 9:3 their tongue like their bow for *l'*: 8267
5 taught their tongue to speak *l'*, "
14:14 prophets prophesy *l'* in my name: "
16:19 Surely our fathers have inherited *l'*, "
20:6 to whom thou hast prophesied *l'*. * "
23:14 commit adultery, and walk in *l'*: "
25 said, that prophesy *l'* in my name, "
26 of the prophets that prophesy *l'*? "
32 cause my people to err by their *l'*, "
48:30 be so; his *l'* shall not so effect it. * 907
Eze 13:8 ye have spoken vanity, and seen *l'*, 3576
9 that see vanity, and that divine *l'*: "
19 to my people that hear your *l'*? "
22 with *l'* ye have made the heart of "
22:28 vanity, and divining *l'* unto them, "
24:12 She hath wearied herself with *l'*, *8383
Da 11:27 they shall speak *l'* at one table; 3576
Ho 7:3 and the princes with their *l'*. 3585
13 they have spoken *l'* against me. 3576
10:13 ye have eaten the fruit of *l'*: 3585
11:12 compasseth me about with *l'*, and* "
12:1 daily increaseth *l'* and desolation; 3576
Am 2:4 and their *l'* caused them to err, "
Mic 6:12 inhabitants thereof have spoken *l'*, 8267
Na 3:1 city! it is all full of *l'* and robbery; 3585
Hab 2:18 molten image, and a teacher of *l'*, 8267
Zep 3:13 shall not do iniquity, nor speak *l'*; 3576
Zec 13:3 speakest *l'* in the name of the Lord: 8267
1Ti 4:2 Speaking *l'* in hypocrisy; having 5573

liest
Ge 28:13 land whereon thou l', to thee will 7901
De 6: 7 when thou l' down, and when thou "
11:19 when thou l' down, and when thou "
Jos 7:10 l' thou thus upon thy face? *5307
Pr 3:24 When thou l' down, thou shalt not 7901

lieth
Ge 4: 7 doest not well, sin l' at the door. *7257
49:25 blessings of the deep that l' under,* "
Ex 22:19 Whosoever l' with a beast shall 7901
Le 6: 3 was lost, and l' concerning it, *3584
14:47 he that l' in the house shall wash 7901
15: 4 whereon he l' that hath the issue, "
20 every thing that she l' upon in her "
24 bed whereon he l' shall be unclean. "
26 Every bed whereon she l' all the "
33 him that l' with her that is unclean. "
19:20 whosoever l' carnally with a woman, "
20:11 man that l' with his father's wife "
13 mankind, as he l' with a woman, *4904
26:34 her sabbaths, as long as it l' desolate, "
35 As long as it l' desolate it shall rest; "
43 while she l' desolate without them: "
Nu 21:15 and l' upon the border of Moab. *8172
De 27:20 be he that l' with his father's wife; 7901
21 that l' with any manner of beast. "
22 Curse be he that l' with his sister, "
23 he that l' with his mother in law. "
Jos 15: 8 mountain that l' before the valley of "
17: 7 Michmethah, that l' before Shechem;* "
18:13 the hill that l' on the south side of the "
14 the hill that l' before Beth-horon "
16 the mountain that l' before the valley "
J'g 1:16 Judah, which l' in the south of Arad;* "
16: 5 and see wherein his great strength l', "
6 thee, wherein thy great strength l', "
15 told me wherein thy great strength l'. "
18:28 in the valley that l' by Beth-rehob. "
Ru 3: 4 when he l' down, that thou shalt 7901
2Sa 2:24 that l' before Giah by the way of the "
24: 5 city that l' in the midst of the river of* "
Ne 2: 3 of my fathers' sepulchres, l' waste, "
17 Jerusalem l' waste, and the gates "
3:25 tower which l' out from the king's*3318
26 the east, and the tower that l' out.* "
27 against the great tower that l' out,* "
Job 14:12 So man l' down, and riseth not: 7901
40:21 He l' under the shady trees, in the "
Ps 10: 9 l' in wait secretly as a lion in his * "
9 he l' in wait to catch the poor: he "
41: 8 now that he l' he shall rise up no 7901
88: 7 Thy wrath l' hard upon me, and 5564
Pr 7:12 and l' in wait at every corner.) *
23:28 She also l' in wait as for a prey, "
34 thou shall be as he that l' down in 7901
34 as he that l' upon the top of a mast. "
Eze 9: 2 gate, which l' toward the north, "
29: 3 great dragon that l' in the midst 6437
Mic 7: 5 from her that l' in thy bosom. 7901
M't 8: 6 my servant l' at home sick of the 906
M'r 5:23 daughter l' at the point of death:*2192
Ac 14: 6 unto the region that l' round about:*
27:12 l' toward the south west and north 991
Ro 12:18 as much as l' in you, live peaceably
1Jo 5:19 the whole world l' in wickedness. 2749
Re 21:16 And the city l' foursquare, and the "

lieutenants
Ezr 8:36 commissions unto the king's l', and*323
Es 3:12 had commanded unto the king's l',* "
8: 9 unto the Jews, and to the l', and * "
9: 3 rulers of the provinces, and the l', "

life See also LIFETIME; LIVES.
Ge 1:20 moving creature that hath l', 2416
30 the earth, wherein there is l', "
2: 7 into his nostrils the breath of l'; "
9 the tree of l' also in the midst of "
3:14 shalt thou eat all the days of thy l': "
17 thou eat of it all the days of thy l'; "
22 take also of the tree of l', and eat "
24 to keep the way of the tree of l'. "
6:17 flesh, wherein is the breath of l', "
7:11 the six hundredth year of Noah's l', "
15 flesh, wherein is the breath of l'. "
22 whose nostrils was the breath of l'. "
9: 4 But flesh with the l' thereof, which5315
5 brother will I require the l' of man. "
18:10 thee according to the time of l'; *2416
14 thee, according to the time of l',* "
19:17 Escape for thy l'; look not behind5315
19 shewed unto me in saving my l'; "
23: 1 were the years of the l' of Sarah. 2416
25: 7 the years of Abraham's l' which he "
17 are the years of the l' of Ishmael, "
27:46 I am weary of my l' because of the "
46 land, what good shall my l' do me? "
32:30 to face, and my l' is preserved. 5315
42:15 By the l' of Pharaoh ye shall not 2416
16 by the l' of Pharaoh surely ye are "
44:30 his l' is bound up in the lad's l'; 5315
45: 5 did send me before you to preserve l'. "
47: 9 days of the years of my l' been, 2416
9 of the years of the l' of my fathers "
48:15 the God which fed me all my l' long "
Ex 4:19 men are dead which sought thy l'. 5315
6:16 the years of the l' of Levi were an 2416
18 years of the l' of Kohath were an "
20 the years of the l' of Amram were "
21:23 then thou shalt give l' for l', 5315
30 for the ransom of his l' whatsoever "
Le 17:11 the l' of the flesh is in the blood: "
14 For it is the l' of all flesh; "
14 the blood of it is for the l' thereof: "
14 l' of all flesh is the blood thereof: "
18:18 beside the other in her l' time. 2416
Nu 35:31 for the l' of a murderer, which is 5315
De 4: 9 thy heart all the days of thy l': 2416
6: 2 thy son's son, all the days of thy l'; "
12:23 the blood: for the blood is the l'; 5315
23 mayest not eat the l' with the flesh. "
16: 3 land of Egypt all the days of thy l'. 2416
17:19 read therein all the days of his l': "
19:21 l' shall go for l', eye for eye, tooth 5315
20:19 (for the tree of the field is man's l')*
24: 6 for he taketh a man's l' to pledge. 5315
28:66 And thy l' shall hang in doubt 2416
66 shalt have none assurance of thy l': "
30:15 set before thee this day l' and good, "
19 I have set before you l' and death, "
19 therefore choose l', that both thou "
20 for he is thy l', and the length of "
32:47 thing for you; because it is your l': "
Jos 1: 5 before thee all the days of thy l': "
2:14 Our l' for yours, if ye utter not 5315
4:14 feared Moses, all the days of his l'. 2416
J'g 9:17 for you, and adventured his l' far, 5315
12: 3 I put my l' in my hands, and passed "
16:30 than they which he slew in his l'. 2416
18:25 run upon thee, and thou lose thy l', 5315
Ru 4:15 be unto thee a restorer of thy l', "
1Sa 1:11 unto the Lord all the days of his l', 2416
7:15 judged Israel all the days of his l'. "
18:18 and what is my l', or my father's "
19: 5 For he did put his l' in his hand, 5315
11 If thou save not thy l' to night, "
20: 1 thy father, that he seeketh my l'? "
22:23 he that seeketh my l' seeketh thy l': "
23:15 Saul was come out to seek his l': "
25:29 shall be bound in the bundle of l' 2416
26:24 as thy l' was much set by this day 5315
24 my l' be much set by in the eyes of "
28: 9 then layest thou a snare for my l', "
21 and I have put my l' in my hand, "
2Sa 1: 9 because my l' is yet whole in me. "
4: 8 thine enemy, which sought thy l'; "
14: 7 the l' of his brother whom he slew; "
15:21 shall be, whether in death or l', 2416
16:11 forth of my bowels, seeketh my l': 5315
18:13 falsehood against mine own l': for "
19: 5 which this day have saved thy l', "
1Ki 1:12 that thou mayest save thine own l', "
12 and the l' of thy son Solomon. "
2:23 spoken this word against his own l'. "
3:11 hast not asked for thyself long l'; 3117
11 hast asked the l' of thine enemies;5315
4:21 Solomon all the days of his l'. 2416
11:34 him prince all the days of his l' for "
15: 5 commanded...all the days of his l', "
6 and Jeroboam all the days of his l'. "
19: 2 if I make not thy l' as the l' of one 5315
3 that, he arose, and went for his l', "
4 now, O Lord, take away my l'; for "
10, 14 they seek my l', to take it away. "
20:31 peradventure he will save thy l'. "
39 then shall thy l' be for his l', or else "
42 therefore thy l' shall go for his l', "
2Ki 1:13 let my l', and the l' of these fifty "
14 my l' now be precious in thy sight. "
4:16 season, according to the time of l', *2416
17 unto her, according to the time of l'.* "
7: 7 camp as it was, and fled for their l'. 5315
8: 1 whose son he had restored to l', 2421
5 he had restored a dead body to l', "
5 whose son he had restored to l', "
5 her son, whom Elisha restored to l'. "
10:24 go, his l' shall be for the l' of him. 5315
25:29 before him all the days of his l'. 2416
30 for every day, all the days of his l'. "
2Ch 1:11 nor the l' of thine enemies, 5315
11 neither yet hast asked long l'; but3117
Ezr 6:10 and pray for the l' of the king, and2417
Ne 6:11 go into the temple to save his l'? 2425
Es 7: 3 king, let my l' be given me at my 5315
7 stood up to make request for his l' "
8:11 and to stand for their l', to destroy, "
Job 2: 4 a man hath will he give for his l'. "
6 he is in thine hand; but save his l'. "
3:20 and l' unto the bitter in soul; 2416
6:11 end, that I should prolong my l'? *5315
7: 7 O remember that my l' is wind: 2416
15 and death rather than my l'. *6106
9:21 my soul: I would despise my l'. 2416
10: 1 My soul is weary of my l'; I will "
12 hast granted me l' and favour, "
13:14 teeth, and put my l' in mine hand?5315
24:22 riseth up, and no man is sure of l'. 2416
31:39 the owners thereof to lose their l': 5315
33: 4 of the Almighty hath given me l'. 2421
18 his l' from perishing by the sword. 2416
20 So that his l' abhorreth bread, and "
22 grave, and his l' to the destroyers. "
28 the pit, and his l' shall see the light. "
36: 6 preserveth not the l' of the wicked:2421
14 and their l' is among the unclean. 2416
Ps 7: 5 tread down my l' upon the earth, "
16:11 Thou wilt shew me the path of l': "
17:14 which have their portion in this l', "
21: 4 He asked l' of thee, and thou gavest "
23: 6 follow me all the days of my l': "
26: 9 sinners, nor my l' with bloody men: "
27: 1 the Lord is the strength of my l'; "
4 of the Lord all the days of my l', "
30: 5 but a moment; in his favour is l': ‡ "
31:10 For my l' is spent with grief, and "
13 they devised to take away my l'. 5315
34:12 What man is he that desireth l', 2416
36: 9 For with thee is the fountain of l': "
38:12 They also that seek after my l' 5315
42: 8 my prayer unto the God of my l'. 2416
61: 6 wilt prolong the king's l': 3117,5921
63: 3 lovingkindness is better than l', 2416
64: 1 preserve my l' from fear of the "
66: 9 which holdeth our soul in l', and 2416
78:50 gave their l' over to the pestilence; "
88: 3 my l' draweth nigh unto the grave. "
91:16 With long l' will I satisfy him, and3117
103: 4 redeemeth thy l' from destruction;2416
128: 5 of Jerusalem all the days of thy l'. "
133: 3 the blessing, even l' for evermore. "
143: 3 he hath smitten my l' down to the "
Pr 1:19 taketh away the l' of the owners 5315
2:19 take they hold of the paths of l'. 2416
3: 2 For length of days, and long l', "
18 She is a tree of l' to them that lay "
22 So shall they be l' unto thy soul, "
4:10 the years of thy l' shall be many. "
13 not go: keep her; for she is thy l'. "
22 are l' unto those that find them, "
23 for out of it are the issues of l'. "
5: 6 shouldest ponder the path of l', "
6:23 of instruction are the way of l': "
26 will hunt for the precious l'. 5315
7:23 and knoweth not that it is for his l'. "
8:35 For whoso findeth me findeth l', 2416
9:11 years of thy l' shall be increased. "
10:11 of a righteous man is a well of l': "
16 of the righteous tendeth to l': "
17 He is in the way of l' that keepeth "
11:19 As righteousness tendeth to l': so "
30 fruit of the righteous is a tree of l'; "
12:10 man regardeth the l' of his beast: 5315
28 In the way of righteousness is l': 2416
13: 3 keepeth his mouth keepeth his l': 5315
8 ransom of a man's l' are his riches: "
12 desire cometh, it is a tree of l'. 2416
14 law of the wise is a fountain of l', "
14:27 fear of the Lord is a fountain of l', "
30 A sound heart is the l' of the flesh: "
15: 4 A wholesome tongue is a tree of l': "
24 The way of l' is above to the wise, "
31 ear that heareth the reproof of l' "
16:15 light of the king's countenance is l'; "
22 is a wellspring of l' unto him that "
18:21 Death and l' are in the power of the "
19:23 The fear of the Lord tendeth to l': "
21:21 righteousness and mercy findeth l', "
22: 4 Lord are riches, and honour, and l'. "
31:12 and not evil all the days of her l'. "
Ec 2: 3 the heaven all the days of their l'. "
17 Therefore I hated l'; because the "
3:12 to rejoice, and to do good in his l'. "
5:18 under the sun all the days of his l', "
20 much remember the days of his l'; "
6:12 what is good for man in this l', all "
12 days of his vain l' which he spendeth "
7:12 giveth l' to them that have it. 2421
15 prolongeth his l' in his wickedness.
8:15 him of his labour the days of his l', 2416
9: 9 lovest all the days of the l' of thy "
9 for that is thy portion in this l', "
Isa 15: 4 his l' shall be grievous unto him. *5315
38:12 I have cut off like a weaver my l': 2416
16 these things is the l' of my spirit: "
20 all the days of our l' in the house "
43: 4 men for thee, and people for thy l'. 5315
57:10 hast found the l' of thine hand; *2416
Jer 4:30 despise thee, they will seek thy l'. 5315
8: 3 shall be chosen rather than l' by 2416
11:21 men of Anathoth, that seek thy l', 5315
21: 7 hand of those that seek their l': "
8 I set before you the way of l', and 2416
9 his l' shall be unto him for a prey. 5315
22:25 the hand of them that seek thy l', "
34:20 the hand of them that seek their l': "
21 the hand of them that seek their l', "
38: 2 he shall have his l' for a prey, and "
16 hand of these men that seek thy l'. "
39:18 thy l' shall be for a prey unto thee: "
44:30 the hand of them that seek his l'; "
30 his enemy, and that sought his l'. "
45: 5 thy l' will I give unto thee for a prey "
49:37 and before them that seek their l': "
52:33 before him all the days of his l'. 2416
34 of his death, all the days of his l'. "
La 2:19 for the l' of thy young children, 5315
3:53 have cut off my l' in the dungeon, 2416
58 soul; thou hast redeemed my l'. "
Eze 3:18 from his wicked way, to save his l';2421
7:13 himself in the iniquity of his l'. 2416
13:22 wicked way, by promising him l':*2421
32:10 every man for his own l', in the 5315
33:15 robbed, walk in the statutes of l', 2416
Da 12: 2 awake, some to everlasting l', "
Jon 1:14 let us not perish for this man's l', 5315
2: 6 hast thou brought up my l' from 2416
4: 3 take, I beseech thee, my l' from me;5315
Mal 2: 5 My covenant was with him of l' 2416
M't 2:20 which sought the young child's l'. 5590
6:25 Take no thought for your l', what "
25 Is not the l' more than meat, and "
7:14 is the way, which leadeth unto l', 2222
10:39 He that findeth his l' shall lose it: 5590
39 he that loseth his l' for my sake "
16:25 will save his l' shall lose it: "
25 will lose his l' for my sake shall "
18: 8 better for thee to enter into l' halt 2222
9 thee to enter into l' with one eye, "
19:16 I do, that I may have eternal l'? "
17 but if thou wilt enter into l', keep "
29 and shall inherit everlasting l'. "
20:28 to give his l' a ransom for many. 5590
25:46 but the righteous into l' eternal. 2222
M'r 3: 4 or to do evil? to save l', or to kill? 5590
8:35 will save his l' shall lose it; "
35 shall lose his l' for my sake and the "
9:43 for thee to enter into l' maimed, 2222
45 better for thee to enter halt into l', "
10:17 I do that I may inherit eternal l'?

M'r 10:30 and in the world to come eternal *l*. 2222
45 to give his *l* a ransom for many. 5590
Lu 1:75 before him, all the days of our *l*. *2222
6: 9 evil? to save *l*, or to destroy it? 5590
8:14 and riches and pleasures of this *l*. 979
9:24 will save his *l* shall lose it: 5590
24 will lose his *l* for my sake, the "
10:25 shall I do to inherit eternal *l*? 2222
12:15 for a man's *l* consisteth not in the "
22 Take no thought for your *l*, what 5590
23 The *l* is more than meat, and the "
14:26 sisters, yea, and his own *l* also, "
17:33 seek to save his *l* shall lose it; "
33 shall lose his *l* shall preserve it. "
18:18 shall I do to inherit eternal *l*? 2222
30 in the world to come *l* everlasting. "
21:34 drunkenness, and cares of this *l*, 982
Joh 1: 4 In him was *l*; and the *l* was the 2222
3:15 not perish, but have eternal *l*. "
16 not perish, but have everlasting *l*. "
36 on the Son hath everlasting *l*: "
36 believeth not the Son shall not see *l*;"
4:14 springing up into everlasting *l*. "
36 gathereth fruit unto *l* eternal: "
5:24 that sent me, hath everlasting *l*, "
24 but is passed from death unto *l*. "
26 For as the Father hath *l* in himself;"
26 to the Son to have *l* in himself; "
29 good, unto the resurrection of *l*; "
39 in them ye think ye have eternal *l*: "
40 come to me, that ye might have *l*. "
6:27 which endureth unto everlasting *l*, "
33 and giveth *l* unto the world. "
35 unto them, I am the bread of *l*: "
40 on him, may have everlasting *l*: "
47 believeth on me hath everlasting *l*. "
48 I am that bread of *l*. "
51 I will give for the *l* of the world. "
53 his blood, ye have no *l* in you. "
54 drinketh my blood, hath eternal *l*; "
63 you, they are spirit, and they are *l*. "
68 thou hast the words of eternal *l*. "
8:12 but shall have the light of *l*. "
10:10 I am come that they might have *l*, "
11 giveth his *l* for the sheep. 5590
15 and I lay down my *l* for the sheep. "
17 because I lay down my *l*, that I "
28 I give unto them eternal *l*; and 2222
11:25 I am the resurrection, and the *l*: "
12:25 He that loveth his *l* shall lose it; 5590
25 hateth his *l* in this world shall "
25 shall keep it unto *l* eternal. 2222
50 his commandment is *l* everlasting: "
13:37 I will lay down my *l* for thy sake. 5590
38 thou lay down thy *l* for my sake? "
14: 6 am the way, the truth, and the *l*: 2222
15:13 man lay down his *l* for his friends. 5590
17: 2 should give eternal *l* to as many 2222
3 this is *l* eternal, that they might "
20:31 ye might have *l* through his name. "
Ac 2:28 made known to me the ways of *l*; "
3:15 And killed the Prince of *l*, whom "
5:20 the people all the words of this *l*. "
8:33 for his *l* is taken from the earth. "
11:18 Gentiles granted repentance unto *l*. "
13:46 unworthy of everlasting *l*, lo, we "
48 many as were ordained to eternal *l*. "
17:25 seeing he giveth to all *l*, and breath, "
20:10 not yourselves; for his *l* is in him. 5590
24 count I my *l* dear unto myself, "
26: 4 My manner of *l* from my youth, 981
27:22 shall be no loss of any man's *l* 5590
Ro 2: 7 honour and immortality, eternal *l*: 2222
5:10 we shall be saved by his *l*. "
17 reign in *l* by one, Jesus Christ.) "
18 upon all men unto justification of *l*. "
21 righteousness unto eternal *l* by "
6: 4 also should walk in newness of *l*. "
22 holiness, and the end everlasting *l*. "
23 but the gift of God is eternal *l* "
7:10 which was ordained to *l*, I found "
8: 2 the law of the Spirit of *l* in Christ "
6 to be spiritually minded is *l* and "
10 Spirit is *l* because of righteousness. "
38 neither death, nor *l*, nor angels, "
11: 3 am left alone, and they seek my *l*. 5590
15 of them be, but *l* from the dead? 2222
16: 4 have for my *l* laid down their own 5590
1Co 3:22 or *l*, or death, or things present, 2222
6: 3 more things that pertain to this *l*? 982
4 of things pertaining to this *l*, set "
14: 7 even things without *l* giving sound, 895
15:19 If in this *l* only we have hope in 2222
2Co 1: 8 that we despaired even of *l*: 2198
2:16 the other the savour of *l* unto *l*. 2222
3: 6 killeth, but the spirit giveth *l*. 2227
4:10, 11 the *l* also of Jesus might be 2222
12 death worketh in us, but *l* in you. "
5: 4 might be swallowed up of *l*. "
Ga 2:20 and the *l* which I now live in the flesh
3:21 given which could have given *l*. *2227
6: 8 of the Spirit reap *l* everlasting. 2222
Eph 4:18 being alienated from the *l* of God "
Ph'p 1:20 in my body, whether it be by *l*, or "
2:16 Holding forth the word of *l*; that "
30 unto death, not regarding his *l*, to 5590
4: 3 whose names are in the book of *l*. 2222
Col 3: 3 your *l* is hid with Christ in God. "
4 When Christ, who is our *l*, shall "
1Ti 1:16 believe on him to *l* everlasting. "
2: 2 lead a quiet and peaceable *l* in all 979
4: 8 promise of the *l* that now is, and 2222
6:12 lay hold on eternal *l*, whereunto "
19 that they may lay hold on eternal *l*. "
2Ti 1: 1 promise of *l* which is in Christ "
10 hath brought *l* and immortality to "

2Ti 2: 4 himself with the affairs of this *l*; 979
3:10 known my doctrine, manner of *l*, * 72
Tit 1: 2 In hope of eternal *l*, which God, 2222
3: 7 according to the hope of eternal *l*. "
Heb 7: 3 beginning of days, nor end of *l*; "
16 but after the power of an endless *l*. "
11:35 received their dead raised to *l* again:*
Jas 1:12 he shall receive the crown of *l*. 2222
4:14 For what is your *l*? It is even a "
1Pe 3: 7 heirs together of the grace of *l*; "
10 For he that will love *l*, and see good"
4: 3 time past of our *l* may suffice us * 979
2Pe 1: 3 that pertain unto *l* and godliness. 2222
1Jo 1: 1 have handled, of the Word of *l*; "
2 the *l* was manifested, and we have "
2 and shew unto you that eternal *l*, "
2:16 the pride of *l*, is not of the Father. 979
25 hath promised us, even eternal *l*. 2222
3:14 we have passed from death unto *l*, "
15 hath eternal *l* abiding in him. "
16 he laid down his *l* for us: and we 5590
5:11 God hath given to us eternal *l*, 2222
11 and this *l* is in his Son. "
12 He that hath the Son hath *l*; "
12 hath not the Son of God hath not *l*. "
13 may know that ye have eternal *l*, "
16 shall give him *l* for them that sin "
20 This is the true God, and eternal *l*. "
Jude 21 Lord Jesus Christ unto eternal *l*. "
Re 2: 7 will I give to eat of the tree of *l*, "
10 and I will give thee a crown of *l*. "
3: 5 out his name out of the book of *l*, "
8: 9 were in the sea, and had *l*, died; 5590
11:11 Spirit of *l* from God entered into 2222
13: 8 are not written in the book of *l* "
15 power to give *l* unto the image of *4151
17: 8 were not written in the book of *l* 2222
20:12 was opened, which is the book of *l*: "
15 not found written in the book of *l* "
21: 6 fountain of the water of *l* freely. "
27 written in the Lamb's book of *l*. "
22: 1 me a pure river of water of *l*, "
2 was there the tree of *l*, which bare "
14 may have right to the tree of *l*, "
17 let him take the water of *l* freely. "
19 away his part out of the book of *l*, "

lifetime
2Sa 18:18 Absalom in his *l* had taken and 2416
Lu 16:25 thou in thy *l* receivedst thy good 2222
Heb 2:15 all their *l* subject to bondage. 2198

lift See also LIFTED; LIFTEST; LIFTETH; LIFTING.
Ge 7:17 and it was *l* up above the earth. ‡7311
13:14 *L* up now thine eyes, and look 5375
14:22 I have *l* up mine hand unto the 7311
18: 2 And he *l* up his eyes and looked, ‡5375
21:16 him, and *l* up her voice, and wept. "
18 Arise, *l* up the lad, and hold him in "
31:12 *L* up now thine eyes, and see, all "
40:13 shall Pharaoh *l* up thine head, "
19 three days shall Pharaoh *l* up thy "
41:44 shall no man *l* up his hand or foot 7311
Ex 14:16 *l* thou up thy rod, and stretch out "
20:25 if thou *l* up thy tool upon it, thou 5130
Nu 6:26 The Lord *l* up his countenance 5375
16: 3 then *l* ye up yourselves above the "
23:24 and *l* up himself as a young lion: "
De 3:27 and *l* up thine eyes westward, and "
4:19 And lest thou *l* up thine eyes unto "
22: 4 help him to *l* them up again. 6965
27: 5 not *l* up any iron tool upon them. 5130
32:40 For I *l* up my hand to heaven, and 5375
Jos 8:31 which no man hath *l* up any iron: 5130
2Sa 23: 8 *l* up his spear against eight hundred,*
2Ki 19: 4 *l* up thy prayer for the remnant 5375
25:27 did *l* up the head of Jehoiachin "
1Ch 25: 5 the words of God, to *l* up the horn. 7311
Ezr 9: 6 and blush to *l* up my face to thee, "
Job 10:15 yet will I not *l* up my head. 5375
11:15 thou *l* up thy face without spot; "
22:26 and shalt *l* up thy face unto God. "
38:34 Canst thou *l* up thy voice to the 7311
Ps 4: 6 Lord, *l* thou up the light of thy 5375
7: 6 *l* up thyself because of the rage of "
10:12 O Lord; O God, *l* up thine hand: "
24: 7 *L* up your heads, O ye gates; "
7 be ye *l* up, ye everlasting doors; ‡ "
9 *L* up your heads, O ye gates; even "
9 *l* them up, ye everlasting doors; "
25: 1 thee, O Lord, do I *l* up my soul. "
28: 2 I *l* up my hands toward thy holy "
9 them also, and *l* them up for ever.* "
63: 4 I will *l* up my hands in thy name. "
74: 3 *L* up thy feet unto the perpetual 7311
75: 4 to the wicked, *L* not up the horn: "
5 *L* not up your horn on high: speak "
86: 4 thee, O Lord, do I *l* up my soul. 5375
93: 3 voice; the floods *l* up their waves. "
94: 2 *L* up thyself, thou judge of the "
110: 7 therefore shall he *l* up the head. 7311
119:48 My hands also will I *l* up unto thy 5375
121: 1 I will *l* up mine eyes unto the hills, "
123: 1 Unto thee *l* I up mine eyes, O thou "
134: 2 *L* up your hands in the sanctuary, "
143: 8 walk; for I *l* up my soul unto thee. "
Ec 4:10 fall, the one will *l* up his fellow: 6965
Isa 2: 4 nation shall not *l* up sword against 5375
5:26 he will *l* up an ensign to the nations"
10:15 itself against them that *l* it up. 7311
15 if the staff should *l* up itself, as if it "
24 shall *l* up his staff against thee, 5375
26 so shall he *l* it up after the manner "
30 *L* up thy voice, O daughter of *6670
13: 2 *L* ye up a banner upon the high 5375
24:14 They shall *l* up their voice, they "

Isa 33:10 exalted; now will I *l* up myself. 5375
37: 4 wherefore *l* up thy prayer for the "
40: 9 *l* up thy voice with strength; 7311
9 *l* it up, be not afraid; say unto the "
26 *L* up your eyes on high, and 5375
42: 2 He shall not cry, nor *l* up, nor "
11 the cities thereof *l* up their voice, "
49:18 *L* up thine eyes round about, and "
22 will *l* up mine hand to the Gentiles, "
51: 6 *L* up your eyes to the heavens, and "
52: 8 watchmen shall *l* up the voice; "
58: 1 not, *l* up thy voice like a trumpet, 7311
59:19 the Lord shall *l* up a standard *5127
60: 4 *L* up thine eyes round about, and 5375
62:10 *l* up a standard for the people. 7311
Jer 3: 2 *L* up thine eyes unto the high 5375
7:16 neither *l* up cry nor prayer for "
11:14 neither *l* up a cry or prayer for "
13:20 *L* up your eyes, and behold them "
22:20 *l* up thy voice in Bashan, and cry 5414
51:14 they shall *l* up a shout against 6030
La 2:19 *l* up thy hands toward him for the 5375
3:41 Let us *l* up our heart with our hands"
Eze 8: 5 man, *l* up thine eyes now the way "
11:22 did the cherubims *l* up their wings, "
17:14 be base, that it might not *l* itself up, "
21:22 to *l* up the voice with shouting, to 7311
23:27 thou shalt not *l* up thine eyes unto 5375
26: 8 and *l* up the buckler against thee. *6965
33:25 *l* up your eyes toward your idols, 5375
Mic 4: 3 nation shall not *l* up a sword "
Zec 1:21 so that no man did *l* up his head: "
5: 5 *L* up now thine eyes, and see what "
M't 12:11 he not lay hold on it, and *l* it out? 1458
Lu 13:11 and could in no wise *l* up herself. 352
16:23 in hell he *l* up his eyes, being in *1869
18:13 would not *l* up so much as his eyes "
21:28 then look up, and *l* up your heads; "
Joh 4:35 *L* up your eyes, and look on the "
Heb 12:12 *l* up the hands which hang down, 461
Jas 4:10 of the Lord, and he shall *l* you up. *5312

lifted See also LIFT.
Ge 13:10 Lot *l* up his eyes, and beheld all 5375
22: 4 third day Abraham *l* up his eyes, "
13 Abraham *l* up his eyes, and looked, "
24:63 and he *l* up his eyes, and saw, and, "
64 Rebekah *l* up her eyes, and when "
27:38 And Esau *l* up his voice, and wept. "
29:11 Rachel, and *l* up his voice, and wept. "
31:10 that I *l* up mine eyes, and saw in a "
33: 1 Jacob *l* up his eyes, and looked, "
5 And he *l* up his eyes, and saw the "
37:25 they *l* up their eyes and looked, "
28 and *l* up Joseph out of the pit, 5927
39:15 that I *l* up my voice and cried, 7311
18 pass, as I *l* up my voice and cried, "
40:20 he *l* up the head of the chief butler 5375
43:29 And he *l* up his eyes, and saw his "
Ex 7:20 *l* up the rod, and smote the waters 7311
14:10 children of Israel *l* up their eyes, 5375
Le 9:22 Aaron *l* up his hand toward the "
Nu 14: 1 the congregation *l* up their voice, "
20:11 Moses *l* up his hand, and with his 7311
24: 2 Balaam *l* up his eyes, and he saw 5375
De 8:14 Then thine heart be *l* up, and thou 7311
17:20 That his heart be not *l* up above "
Jos 4:18 soles of the priests' feet were *l* up 5423
5:13 that he *l* up his eyes and looked, 5375
J'g 2: 4 people *l* up their voice, and wept. "
8:28 that they *l* up their heads no more. "
9: 7 and *l* up his voice, and cried, and "
19:17 when he had *l* up his eyes, he saw "
21: 2 *l* up their voices, and wept sore; "
Ru 1: 9 and they *l* up their voice, and wept. "
14 And they *l* up their voice, and wept "
1Sa 6:13 *l* up their eyes, and saw the ark, "
11: 4 people *l* up their voices, and wept. "
24:16 And Saul *l* up his voice, and wept. "
30: 4 with him *l* up their voice and wept, "
2Sa 3:32 the king *l* up his voice, and wept at "
13:34 that kept the watch *l* up his eyes, "
36 came, and *l* up their voice and wept: "
18:24 and *l* up his eyes, and looked, and "
28 men that *l* up their hand against "
20:21 *l* up his hand against the king, "
22:49 thou also hast *l* me up on high *7311
23:18 he *l* up his spear against three 5782
1Ki 11:26 he *l* up his hand against the king. 7311
27 he *l* up his hand against the king: "
2Ki 9:32 he *l* up his face to the window, 5375
14:10 and thine heart hath *l* thee up: "
19:22 and *l* up thine eyes on high? even "
1Ch 11:11 he *l* up his spear against three 5782
14: 2 for his kingdom was *l* up on high, *5375
21:16 David *l* up his eyes, and saw the "
2Ch 5:13 when they *l* up their voice with the 7311
17: 6 heart was *l* up in the ways of the 1361
26:16 heart was *l* up to his destruction: "
32:25 unto him; for his heart was *l* up: "
Job 2:12 when they *l* up their eyes afar off, 5375
12 they *l* up their voice, and wept; "
31:21 I have *l* up my hand against the 5130
29 *l* up myself when evil found him: 5782
Ps 24: 4 hath not *l* up his soul unto vanity, 5375
27: 6 head be *l* up above mine enemies 7311
30: 1 for thou hast *l* me up, and hast *1802
41: 9 hath *l* up his heel against me. 1431
74: 5 had *l* up axes upon the thick trees. 935
83: 2 that hate thee have *l* up the head. 5375
93: 3 The floods have *l* up, O Lord, "
3 the floods have *l* up their voice: "
102:10 for thou hast *l* me up, and cast me* "
106:26 he *l* up his hand against them, "
Pr 30:13 eyes! and their eyelids are *l* up. "
Isa 2:12 and upon every one that is *l* up: "
13 of Lebanon, that are high and *l* up, "

Isa 2:14 and upon all the hills that are l' up, 5375
6: 1 upon a throne, high and l' up, and "
26:11 when thy hand is l' up, they will 7311
37:23 voice, and l' up thine eyes on high? 5375
Jer 51: 9 heaven, and is l' up even to the skies."
52:31 l' up the head of Jehoiachin king of "
Eze 1:19 when the living creatures were l' up"
19 the earth, the wheels were l' up. "
20 the wheels were l' up over against "
21 those were l' up from the earth, "
21 the wheels were l' up over against "
3:14 So the spirit l' me up, and took me "
8: 3 spirit l' me up between the earth "
5 I l' up mine eyes the way toward "
10:15 And the cherubims were l' up. *7426
16 the cherubims l' up their wings 5375
17 stood; and when they were l' up, *7311
17 these l' up themselves also: for *7426
19 the cherubims l' up their wings, 5375
11: 1 the spirit l' me up, and brought me"
18: 6 neither hath l' up his eyes to the "
12 and hath l' up his eyes to the idols, "
15 neither hath l' up his eyes to the "
20: 5 and l' up mine hand unto the seed "
5 when I l' up mine hand unto them, "
6 that I l' up mine hand unto them, "
15 Yet also I l' up my hand unto them "
23 I l' up mine hand unto them also "
28 I l' up mine hand to give it to them,"
42 I l' up mine hand to give it to your "
28: 2 Because thine heart is l' up, and 1361
5 heart is l' up because of thy riches:"
17 was l' up because of thy beauty, "
31:10 thou hast l' up thyself in height, * "
10 and his heart is l' up in his height; 7311
36: 7 I have l' up mine hand, Surely the 5375
44:12 have I l' up mine hand against them,"
47:14 the which I l' up mine hand to give "
Da 4:34 I Nebuchadnezzar l' up mine eyes 5191
5:20 when his heart was l' up, and his 7313
23 hast l' up thyself against the Lord "
7: 4 it was l' up from the earth, and 5191
8: 3 Then I l' up mine eyes, and saw, 5375
10: 5 Then I l' up mine eyes, and looked, "
11:12 multitude, his heart shall be l' up; *7311
Mic 5: 9 Thine hand shall be l' up upon thine"
Hab 2: 4 soul which is l' up is not upright *6075
3:10 voice, and l' up his hands on high. 5375
Zec 1:18 Then l' I up mine eyes, and saw, "
21 which l' up their horn over the land"
2: 1 l' up mine eyes again, and looked, "
5: 1 Then I turned, and l' up mine eyes, "
7 there was l' up a talent of lead: and "
9 Then l' I up mine eyes, and looked, 5375
9 l' up the ephah between the earth "
6: 1 And I turned, and l' up mine eyes, "
9:16 l' up as an ensign upon his land. 5264
14:10 and it shall be l' up, and inhabited 7213
M't 17: 8 when they had l' up their eyes, *1869
M'r 1:31 her by the hand, and l' her up; *1453
9:27 him by the hand, and l' him up; * "
Lu 6:20 he l' up his eyes on his disciples, 1869
11:27 of the company l' up her voice, "
17:13 they l' up their voices, and said, 142
24:50 and he l' up his hands, and blessed 1869
Joh 3:14 as Moses l' up the serpent in the 5312
14 so must the Son of man be l' up: "
6: 5 When Jesus then l' up his eyes, *1869
8: 7 l' up himself, and said unto them, 352
10 When Jesus had l' up himself, and "
28 When ye have l' up the Son of man, 5312
11:41 And Jesus l' up his eyes, and said, 142
12:32 And I, if I be l' up from the earth, 5312
34 thou, The Son of man must be l' up? "
13:18 me hath l' up his heel against me. 1869
17: 1 Jesus, and l' up his eyes to heaven, "
Ac 2:14 But Peter,...l' up his voice, and "
3: 7 by the right hand, and l' him up: *1453
4:24 l' up their voice to God with one 142
9:41 gave her his hand, and l' her up, * 450
14:11 they l' up their voices, saying in 1869
22:22 and then l' up their voices, and said, "
1Ti 3: 6 lest being l' up with pride he fall *5188
Re 10: 5 the earth l' up his hand to heaven, 142

lifter
Ps 3: 3 glory, and the l' up of mine head. 7311

liftest
Job 30:22 Thou l' me up to the wind; thou 5375
Ps 9:13 thou that l' me up from the gates 7311
18:48 thou l' me up above those that rise "
Pr 2: 3 l' up thy voice for understanding; *5414

lifteth
1Sa 2: 7 rich: he bringeth low, and l' up. 7311
8 l' up the beggar from the dunghill, "
2Ch 25:19 thine heart l' thee up to boast. 5375
Job 39:18 time she l' up herself on high, she 4754
Ps 107:25 which l' up the waves thereof. 7311
113: 7 l' the needy out of the dunghill; "
147: 6 The Lord l' up the meek: he *5749
Isa 18: 3 when he l' up an ensign on the *5375
Jer 51: 3 l' himself up in his brigandine: *5927
Na 3: 3 horseman l' up both the bright * "

lifting
1Ch 11:20 for l' up his spear against three *5782
15:16 by l' up the voice with joy. 7311
Ne 8: 6 Amen, with l' up their hands: 4607
Job 22:29 thou shalt say, There is l' up; 1466
Ps 141: 2 l' up of my hands as the evening 4864
Pr 30:32 hast done foolishly in l' up thyself, 5375
Isa 9:18 mount up like the l' up of smoke. †‡1348
33: 3 at the l' up of thyself the nations 7427
1Ti 2: 8 l' up holy hands, without wrath 1869

light See also ALIGHT; DELIGHT; ENLIGHTEN; LIGHTED; LIGHTER; LIGHTEST; LIGHTETH; LIGHTING; LIGHTS; TWILIGHT.
Ge 1: 3 Let there be l': and there was l'. 216
4 God saw the l', that it was good: "
4 divided the l' from the darkness. "
5 And God called the l' Day, and the "
15 heaven to give l' upon the earth: "
16 the greater l' to rule the day, 3974
16 and the lesser l' to rule the night: "
17 heaven to give l' upon the earth, 216
18 to divide the l' from the darkness: "
44: 3 As soon as the morning was l', the "
Ex 10:23 of Israel had l' in their dwellings. "
13:21 in a pillar of fire, to give them l'; "
14:20 but it gave l' by night to these: "
25: 6 Oil for the l', spices for anointing 3974
37 they shall l' the lamps thereof, 5927
37 they may give l' over against it. 216
27:20 thee pure oil olive beaten for the l', 3974
35: 8 oil for the l',...spices for anointing "
14 The candlestick also for the l', and "
14 and his lamps, with the oil for the l', "
28 oil for the l', and for the anointing "
39:37 vessels thereof, and the oil for l', "
40: 4 in the candlestick, and l' the lamps 5927
Le 24: 2 thee pure oil olive beaten for the l', 3974
Nu 4: 9 cover the candlestick of the l', and "
16 priest pertaineth the oil for the l', "
8: 2 the seven lamps shall give l' over 216
21: 5 our soul loatheth this l' bread. 7052
De 27:16 be he that setteth l' by his father 7034
J'g 9: 4 hired vain and l' persons, which 6348
19:26 where her lord was, till it was l'. 216
Ru 2: 3 hap was to l' on a part of the field 7136
1Sa 14:36 spoil them until the morning l', 216
18:23 Seemeth it to you a l' thing to be 7043
25:22 pertain to him by the morning l' 216
34 left unto Nabal by the morning l' "
36 less or more, until the morning l'. "
29:10 early in the morning, and have l', "
2Sa 2:18 Asahel was as l' of foot as a wild 7031
17:12 l' upon him as the dew falleth on 5117
22 by the morning l' there lacked not 216
21:17 thou quench not the l' of Israel. *5216
23: 4 shall be as the l' of the morning, 216
1Ki 7: 4, 5 l' was against l' in three ranks. 4237
11:36 l' alway before me in Jerusalem, *5216
16:31 had been a l' thing for him to walk 7043
2Ki 3:18 is but a l' thing in the sight of the "
7: 9 we tarry till the morning l', some 216
8:19 him to give him alway a l', and to *5216
20:10 It is a l' thing for the shadow to 7043
2Ch 21: 7 promised to give a l' to him and *5216
Ne 9:12 l' in the way wherein they should 216
19 of fire by night, to shew them l', "
Es 8:16 The Jews had l', and gladness, and 219
Job 3: 4 neither let the l' shine upon it. 5105
9 let it look for l', but have none; 216
16 been; as infants which never saw l'. "
20 is l' given to him that is in misery, "
23 why is l' given to a man whose way is "
10:22 and where the l' is as darkness. 3313
12:22 out to l' the shadow of death. 216
25 They grope in the dark without l', "
17:12 the l' is short because of darkness. "
18: 5 the l' of the wicked shall be put out, "
6 The l' shall be dark in his tabernacle, "
18 shall be driven from l' into darkness, "
22:28 the l' shall shine upon thy ways. "
24:13 of those that rebel against the l'; "
14 murderer rising with the l' killeth "
16 the daytime: they know not the l'. "
25: 3 upon whom doth not his l' arise? "
28:11 that is hid bringeth he forth to l'. "
29: 3 by his l' I walked through darkness; "
24 the l' of my countenance they cast "
30:26 and when I waited for l', there came "
33:28 the pit, and his life shall see the l'. "
30 enlightened with the l' of the living. "
36:30 Behold, he spreadeth his l' upon it, "
32 With clouds he covereth the l'; * "
37:15 caused the l' of his cloud to shine? * "
21 men see not the bright l' which is in "
38:15 the wicked their l' is withholden, "
19 Where is the way where l' dwelleth? "
24 By what way is the l' parted, which "
41:18 By his neesings a l' doth shine, and "
Ps 4: 6 the l' of thy countenance upon us. "
18:28 For thou wilt l' my candle: the Lord 215
27: 1 The Lord is my l' and my salvation; 216
36: 9 of life: in thy l' shall we see l'. "
37: 6 forth thy righteousness as the l', "
38:10 as for the l' of mine eyes, it also is "
43: 3 O send out thy l' and thy truth: let "
44: 3 arm, and the l' of thy countenance, "
49:19 his fathers; they shall never see l'. "
56:13 before God in the l' of the living? "
74:16 hast prepared the l' and the sun. 3974
78:14 and all the night with a l' of fire. 216
89:15 Lord, in the l' of thy countenance. "
90: 8 sins in the l' of thy countenance. 3974
97:11 L' is sown for the righteous, and 216
104: 2 coverest thyself with l' as with a "
105:39 and fire to give l' in the night. "
112: 4 Unto the upright there ariseth l' in "
118:27 the Lord, which hath shewed us l': "
119:105 my feet, and a l' unto my path. "
130 entrance of thy words giveth l'; it "
139:11 even the night shall be l' about me. "
12 darkness and the l' are both alike 219
148: 3 moon: praise him, all ye stars of l'. 216
Pr 4:18 path of the just is as the shining l', "
6:23 is a lamp; and the law is l'; "
13: 9 The l' of the righteous rejoiceth: "
15:30 l' of the eyes rejoiceth the heart: 3974

Pr 16:15 In the l' of the king's countenance 216
Ec 2:13 folly, as far as l' excelleth darkness. "
11: 7 Truly the l' is sweet, and a pleasant "
12: 2 While the sun, or the l', or the moon, "
Isa 2: 5 let us walk in the l' of the Lord. "
5:20 darkness for l', and l' for darkness; "
30 the l' is darkened in the heavens "
8:20 is because there is no l' in them. *7837
9: 2 in darkness have seen a great l': 216
2 death, upon them hath the l' shined. "
10:17 the l' of Israel shall be for a fire, "
13:10 thereof shall not give their l': "
10 moon shall not cause her l' to shine. "
30:26 Moreover the l' of the moon shall "
26 moon shall be as the l' of the sun, "
26 the l' of the sun shall be sevenfold, "
26 as the l' of seven days, in the day "
42: 6 the people, for a l' of the Gentiles; "
16 will make darkness l' before them, "
45: 7 I form the l', and create darkness: "
49: 6 It is a l' thing that thou shouldest 7043
6 give thee for a l' to the Gentiles, 216
50:10 in darkness, and hath no l'? let 5051
11 walk in the l' of your fire, and in 217
51: 4 to rest for a l' of the people. 216
58: 8 Then shall thy l' break forth as the "
10 shall thy l' rise in obscurity, and thy "
59: 9 we wait for l', but behold obscurity; "
60: 1 Arise, shine; for thy l' is come, and "
3 Gentiles shall come to thy l', and "
19 sun shall be no more thy l' by day; "
19 shall the moon give l' unto thee: "
19 shall be unto thee an everlasting l', "
20 Lord shall be thine everlasting l', "
Jer 4:23 and the heavens, and they had no l'. "
13:16 while ye look for l', he turn it into "
25:10 millstones, and the l' of the candle. "
31:35 which giveth the sun for a l' by day, "
35 and of the stars for a l' by night, "
La 3: 2 me into darkness, but not into l'. "
Eze 8:17 Is it a l' thing to the house of Judah 7043
22: 7 In thee have they set l' by father "
32: 7 and the moon shall not give her l'. 216
Da 2:22 and the l' dwelleth with him. 5094
5:11 of thy father l' and understanding "
14 and that l' and understanding and "
Ho 6: 5 thy judgments are as the l' that 216
Am 5:18 the Lord is darkness, and not l'. "
20 the Lord be darkness, and not l'? "
Mic 2: 1 when the morning is l', they practise "
7: 8 the Lord shall be a l' unto me. "
9 he will bring me forth to the l', and "
Hab 3: 4 his brightness was as the l'; he had "
11 at the l' of thine arrows they went, "
Zep 3: 4 prophets are l' and treacherous 6348
5 doth he bring his judgment to l', 216
Zec 14: 6 the l' shall not be clear, nor dark: "
7 that at evening time it shall be l'. "
M't 4:16 which sat in darkness saw great l'; 5457
16 shadow of death l' is sprung up. "
5:14 Ye are the l' of the world. A city "
15 Neither do men l' a candle, and 2545
15 giveth l' unto all that are in the *2989
16 Let your l' so shine before men, 5457
6:22 The l' of the body is the eye: if 5460
22 thy whole body shall be full of l'. 3088
23 the l' that is in thee be darkness, 5457
10:27 in darkness, that speak ye in l': "
11:30 yoke is easy, and my burden is l'. 1645
17: 2 his raiment was white as the l'. 5457
22: 5 they made l' of it, and went their 272
24:29 and the moon shall not give her l', 5338
M'r 13:24 and the moon shall not give her l', "
Lu 1:79 give l' to them that sit in darkness *2014
2:32 A l' to lighten the Gentiles, and 5457
8:16 they which enter in may see the l'. "
11:33 they which come in may see the l'. 5338
34 The l' of the body is the eye: *3088
34 thy whole body also is full of l'; 5460
35 that the l' which is in thee be not 5457
36 whole body therefore be full of l', 5460
36 dark, the whole shall be full of l', "
36 of a candle doth give thee l'. 5461
12: 3 darkness shall be heard in the l'; 5457
15: 8 doth not l' a candle, and sweep the 681
16: 8 wiser than the children of l'. 5457
Joh 1: 4 and the life was the l' of men. "
5 And the l' shineth in darkness; and "
7 witness, to bear witness of the L', "
8 He was not that L', but was sent "
8 was sent to bear witness of that L'. "
9 That was the true L', which "
3:19 that l' is come into the world, and "
19 men loved darkness rather than l', "
20 one that doeth evil hateth the l', "
20 neither cometh to the l', lest his "
21 that doeth truth cometh to the l', "
5:35 was a burning and a shining l': 3088
35 for a season to rejoice in his l'. 5457
8:12 saying, I am the l' of the world: "
12 but shall have the l' of life. "
9: 5 the world, I am the l' of the world. "
11: 9 because he seeth the l' of this world. "
10 because there is no l' in him. "
12:35 Yet a little while is the l' with you. "
35 Walk while ye have the l', lest "
36 While ye have the l', believe in the l', "
36 that ye may be the children of l'. "
46 I am come a l' into the world, that "
Ac 9: 3 round about him a l' from heaven: "
12: 7 him, and a l' shined in the prison: "
13:47 set thee to be a l' of the Gentiles, "
16:29 he called for a l', and sprang in, * "
22: 6 shone from heaven a great l' round "
9 that were with me saw indeed the l', "
11 could not see for the glory of that l', "

Ac 26:13 I saw in the way a *l* from heaven, 5457
18 to turn them from darkness to *l*, "
23 and should shew *l* unto the people, "
Ro 2:19 a *l* of them which are in darkness, "
13:12 and let us put on the armour of *l*. "
1Co 4: 5 will bring to *l* the hidden things 5461
2Co 4: 4 *l* of the glorious gospel of Christ, 5462
6 commanded the *l* to shine out of 5457
6 to give the *l* of the knowledge of 5462
17 our *l* affliction, which is but for a 1645
6:14 communion hath *l* with darkness? 5457
11:14 is transformed into an angel of *l*. "
Eph 5: 8 but now are ye *l* in the Lord: "
8 walk as children of *l*: "
13 are made manifest by the *l*: for "
13 whatsoever doth make manifest is *l*. "
14 and Christ shall give thee *l*. *2017
Col 1:12 the inheritance of the saints in *l*: 5457
1Th 5: 5 Ye are all the children of *l*, and "
1Ti 6:16 dwelling in the *l* which no man "
2Ti 1:10 brought life and immortality to *l* 5461
1Pe 2: 9 of darkness into his marvellous *l*: 5457
2Pe 1:19 as unto a *l* that shineth in a dark*3088
1Jo 1: 5 declare unto you, that God is *l*, 5457
7 if we walk in the *l*, as he is in the *l*, "
2: 8 past, and the true *l* now shineth. "
9 He that saith he is in the *l*, and "
10 loveth his brother abideth in the *l*, "
Re 7:16 neither shall the sun *l* on them, *4098
18:23 *l* of a candle shall shine no more 5457
21:11 her *l* was like unto a stone most 5458
23 it, and the Lamb is the *l* thereof. *3088
24 saved shall walk in the *l* of it: 5457
22: 5 no candle, neither *l* of the sun; "
5 for the Lord God giveth them *l*: 5461

lighted See also DELIGHTED.
Ge 24:64 she saw Isaac, she *l* off the camel. 5307
28:11 And he *l* upon a certain place, and 6293
Ex 40:25 he *l* the lamps before the Lord; as 5927
Nu 8: 3 he *l* the lamps thereof over against "
Jos 15:18 a field: and she *l* off her ass; and 6795
J'g 1:14 a field: and she *l* from off her ass; "
4:15 that Sisera *l* down off his chariot, 3381
1Sa 25:23 *l* off the ass, and fell before David "
2Ki 5:21 he *l* down from the chariot to 5307
10:15 *l* on Jehonadab the son of Rechab 4672
Isa 9: 8 Jacob, and it hath *l* upon Israel. 5307
Lu 8:16 No man, when he hath *l* a candle, 681
11:33 No man, when he hath *l* a candle, "

lighten See also ENLIGHTEN; LIGHTENED; LIGHTENETH; LIGHTNING.
1Sa 6: 5 he will *l* his hand from off you, 7043
2Sa 22:29 and the Lord will *l* my darkness. 5050
Ezr 9: 8 that our God may *l* our eyes, and 215
Ps 13: 3 *l* mine eyes, lest I sleep the sleep "
Jon 1: 5 ship into the sea, to *l* it of them. 7043
Lu 2:32 A light to *l* the Gentiles, and the * 602
Re 21:23 the glory of God did *l* it, and the 5461

lightened See also ENLIGHTENED.
Ps 34: 5 looked unto him, and were *l*: 5102
77:18 the lightnings *l* the world: the 215
Ac 27:18 the next day they *l* the ship;*1546,4160
38 they *l* the ship, and cast out the 2893
Re 18: 1 the earth was *l* with his glory. 5461

lighteneth
Pr 29:13 the Lord *l* both their eyes. 215
Lu 17:24 that *l* out of the one part under 797

lighter
1Ki 12: 4 make...which he put upon us, *l*, 7043
9 Make...father did put upon us *l*? "
10 heavy, but make thou it *l* unto us; "
2Ch 10:10 make thou it somewhat *l* for us; "
Ps 62: 9 they are altogether *l* than vanity.

lightest
Nu 8: 2 unto him, When thou *l* the lamps, 5927

lighteth
Ex 30: 8 when Aaron *l* the lamps at even, 5927
De 19: 5 and *l* upon his neighbour, that 4672
Joh 1: 9 which *l* every man that cometh 5461

lighting
Isa 30:30 shall shew the *l* down of his arm, 5183
M't 3:16 like a dove, and *l* upon him: *2064

lightly
Ge 26:10 might *l* have lien with thy wife, 4592
De 32:15 and *l* esteemed the Rock of his 5034
1Sa 2:30 despise me shall be *l* esteemed. 7043
18:23 I am a poor man, and *l* esteemed? 7034
Isa 9: 1 he *l* afflicted the land of Zebulun *7043
Jer 4:24 trembled, and all the hills moved *l*.* "
M'r 9:39 that can *l* speak evil of me. *5035

lightness
Jer 3: 9 through the *l* of her whoredom, 6963
23:32 err by their lies, and by their *l*; *6350
2Co 1:17 was thus minded, did I use *l*? *1644

lightning See also LIGHTNINGS.
2Sa 22:15 them; *l*, and discomfited them. 1300
Job 28:26 a way for the *l* of the thunder: 2385
37: 3 his *l* unto the ends of the earth. 216
38:25 or a way for the *l* of thunder; 2385
Ps 144: 6 Cast forth *l*, and scatter them: 1300
Eze 1:13 and out of the fire went forth *l*. "
14 as the appearance of a flash of *l*. 965
Da 10: 6 his face as the appearance of *l*, 1300
Zec 9:14 his arrow shall go forth as the *l*: "
M't 24 27 For as the *l* cometh out of the east, 796
28: 3 His countenance was like *l*, and "
Lu 10:18 I beheld Satan as *l* fall from heaven. "
17:24 For as the *l*, that lighteneth out of "

lightnings
Ex 19:16 that there were thunders and *l*, 1300
20:18 saw the thunderings, and the *l*, 3940
Job 38:35 Canst thou send *l*, that they may 1300
Ps 18:14 and he shot out *l*, and discomfited "
77:18 the *l* lightened the world: the earth "
97: 4 His *l* enlightened the world: the "
135: 7 he maketh *l* for the rain; he "
Jer 10:13 he maketh *l* with rain, and bringeth "
51:16 he maketh *l* with rain, and bringeth "
Na 2: 4 torches, they shall run like the *l*. "
Re 4: 5 out of the throne proceeded *l* and 796
8: 5 were voices, and thunderings, and *l*, "
11:19 and there were *l*, and voices, and "
16:18 were voices, and thunders, and *l*; "

lights See also DELIGHTS.
Ge 1:14 Let there be *l* in the firmament of 3974
15 let them be for *l* in the firmament "
16 God made two great *l*; the greater "
1Ki 6: 4 he made windows of narrow *l*. *8261
Ps 136: 7 To him that made great *l*: for his 216
Eze 32: 8 bright *l* of heaven will I make 3974
Lu 12:35 about, and your *l* burning; *3088
Ac 20: 8 there were many *l* in the upper 2985
Ph'p 2:15 whom ye shine as *l* in the world; 5458
Jas 1:17 cometh down from the Father of *l*, 5457

lign
Nu 24: 6 as the trees of *l* aloes which the Lord

lign-aloes See LIGN and ALOES.

ligure (*li'-gure*)
Ex 28:19 And the third row a *l*, an agate, *3958
39:12 the third row, a *l*, an agate, and * "

like See also ALIKE; LIKED; LIKETH; LIKING; LIKEMINDED; LIKEWISE; LIONLIKE.
Ge 13:10 *l* the land of Egypt, as thou comest
25:25 out red, all over *l* an hairy garment;
Ex 7:11 also did in *l* manner with their 3651
9:14 there is none *l* me in all the earth. 3644
24 none *l* it in all the land of Egypt * "
11: 6 none *l* it, nor shall be *l* it any more. "
15:11 Who is *l* unto thee, O Lord, among "
11 who is *l* thee, glorious in holiness, "
16:31 and it was *l* coriander seed, white;
31 the taste of it was *l* wafers made with
23:11 *l* manner thou shalt deal with thy 3651
24:17 glory of the Lord was *l* devouring fire
25:33 Three bowls made *l* unto almonds,
33 three bowls made *l* almonds in the
34 be four bowls made *l* unto almonds,
28:11 *l* the engravings of a signet, shalt
21 *l* the engravings of a signet; every
36 upon it, *l* the engravings of a signet,
30:32 shall ye make any other *l* it, after 3644
33 Whosoever compoundeth any *l* it, or "
34 of each shall there be a *l* weight:
38 shall make *l* unto that, to smell 3644
34: 1 two tables of stone *l* unto the first:
4 two tables of stone *l* unto the first;
37:19 and three bowls made *l* almonds in
20 were four bowls made *l* almonds,
39: 8 work, *l* the work of the ephod;
14 *l* the engravings of a signet, every one
30 *l* to the engravings of a signet,
Le 13: 2 his flesh *l* the plague of leprosy;*
Nu 23:10 and let my last end be *l* his! 3644
De 4:32 thing is, or hath been heard *l* it? "
7:26 lest thou be a cursed thing *l* it: "
10: 1, 3 two tables of stone *l* unto the first,
17:14 *l* as all the nations that are about me;
18: 8 They shall have *l* portions to eat,
15 thee, of thy brethren, *l* unto me; 3644
18 among their brethren, *l* unto thee, "
22: 3 In *l* manner shalt thou do with *3651
25: 7 *l* not to take his brother's wife, 2654
8 to it, and say, I *l* not to take her; "
29:23 *l* the overthrow of Sodom, and
33:17 glory is *l* the firstling of his bullock, *
17 his horns are *l* the horns of unicorns:*
26 is none *l* unto the God of Jeshurun,
29 who is *l* unto thee, O people saved 3644
34:10 prophet since in Israel *l* unto Moses,
Jos 10:14 no day *l* that before it or after it,
J'g 7:12 lay along in the valley *l* grasshoppers
11:17 in *l* manner they sent unto the 1571
13: 6 *l* the countenance of an angel of God,
16:12 them from off his arms *l* a thread.
17 become weak, and be *l* any other man.
Ru 2:13 not *l* unto one of thine handmaidens.*
4:11 into thine house *l* Rachel and *l* Leah,
12 let thy house be *l* the house of Pharez,
1Sa 2: 2 neither is there any rock *l* our God.
4: 9 Be strong, and quit yourselves *l* men,
9 quit yourselves *l* men, and fight.
8: 5 us a king to judge us *l* all the nations.
10:24 none *l* him among all the people? 3644
17: 7 his spear was *l* a weaver's beam;
19:24 before Samuel in *l* manner. *1571
21: 9 David said, There is none *l* that;
25:36 in his house, *l* the feast of a king;
26:15 and who is *l* to thee in Israel? 3644
2Sa 7: 9 *l* unto the name of the great men that
22 Lord God: for there is none *l* thee, 3644
23 earth is *l* thy people, even *l* Israel,
18:27 foremost is *l* the running of Ahimaaz
21:19 whose spear was *l* a weaver's beam.
22:34 He maketh my feet *l* hinds' feet: 7737
1Ki 3:12 there was none *l* thee before thee, 3644
12 after thee shall any arise *l* unto thee. "
13 be any among the kings *l* unto thee "
5: 6 to hew timber *l* unto the Sidonians.
7: 8 the porch, which was of the *l* work.
8 had taken to wife, *l* unto this porch.
26 was wrought *l* the brim of a cup,
33 was *l* the work of a chariot wheel:
8:23 of Israel, there is no God *l* thee, 3644
1Ki 10:20 not the *l* made in any kingdom. 3651
12:32 *l* unto the feast that is in Judah, and
16: 3 thy house *l* the house of Jeroboam
7 in being *l* the house of Jeroboam;
18:44 cloud out of the sea, *l* a man's hand.*
20:25 army, *l* the army that thou hast lost,
27 pitched before them *l* two little flocks
21:22 thine house *l* the house of Jeroboam
22 *l* the house of Baasha the son of
25 But there was none *l* unto Ahab,
22:13 thee, be *l* the word of one of them,
2Ki 3: 2 not *l* his father, and *l* his mother:
9: 9 of Ahab *l* the house of Jeroboam
9 *l* the house of Baasha the son of
20 the driving is *l* the driving of Jehu
13: 7 made them *l* the dust by threshing.
14: 3 the Lord, yet not *l* David his father:
16: 2 the Lord his God, *l* David his father.
17:14 necks, *l* to the neck of their fathers,
15 that they should not do *l* them.
18: 5 none *l* him among all the kings 3644
32 you away to a land *l* your own land,
23:25 And *l* unto him was there no king 3644
25 after him arose there any *l* him. "
25:17 *l* unto these had the second pillar
1Ch 4:27 multiply, *l* to the children of Judah.
11:23 hand was a spear *l* a weaver's beam;
12: 8 whose faces were *l* the faces of lions,
22 it was a great host, *l* the host of God.
14:11 hand *l* the breaking forth of waters:
17: 8 a name *l* the name of the great men
20 O Lord, there is none *l* thee, 3644
21 in the earth is *l* thy people Israel,
20: 5 spear staff was *l* a weaver's beam.
27:23 would increase Israel *l* to the stars of
2Ch 1: 9 a people *l* the dust of the earth in
12 there any after thee have the *l*. 3651
9:19 not the *l* made in any kingdom. "
18:12 *l* one of theirs, and speak thou good.
21: 6 of Israel, *l* as did the house of Ahab:*
13 *l* to the whoredoms of the house of
19 for him, *l* the burning of his fathers.
22: 4 sight of the Lord *l* the house of Ahab:*
28: 1 sight of the Lord, *l* David his father:
30: 7 *l* your fathers, and *l* your brethren,
33: 2 *l* unto the abominations of the *
35:18 no passover *l* to that kept in Israel 3644
Ne 6: 5 his servant unto me in *l* manner 2088
13:26 nations was there no king *l* him, 3644
Es 2:20 *l* as when she was brought up with
Job 1: 8 there is none *l* him in the earth, 3644
2: 3 there is none *l* him in the earth, "
3:24 roarings are poured out *l* the waters.
5:26 *l* as a shock of corn cometh in in his
7: 1 days also *l* the days of an hireling?
8: 2 of thy mouth be *l* a strong wind?
10:10 out as milk, and curdled me *l* cheese?
11:12 man be born *l* a wild ass's colt. *
12:25 them to stagger *l* a drunken man.
13:12 remembrances are *l* unto ashes, *4911
14: 2 forth *l* a flower, and is cut down:
9 and bring forth boughs *l* a plant. 3644
15:16 man, which drinketh iniquity *l* water?
16:14 beach, he runneth upon me *l* a giant.
19:10 mine hope hath he removed *l* a tree.
20: 7 shall perish for ever *l* his own dung:
21:11 send forth their little ones *l* a flock,
30:19 I am become *l* dust and ashes. 4911
32:19 it is ready to burst *l* new bottles?
34: 7 *l* Job, who drinketh up scorning *l*
36:22 his power: who teacheth *l* him? 3644
40: 7 Gird up thy loins now *l* a man: I will
9 Hast thou an arm *l* God?
9 thou thunder with a voice *l* him? 3644
17 He moveth his tail *l* a cedar: the "
18 of brass; his bones are *l* bars of iron.
41:18 eyes are *l* the eyelids of the morning.
31 He maketh the deep to boil *l* a pot:
31 he maketh the sea *l* a pot of ointment.
33 Upon earth there is not his *l*, who 4915
42: 8 thing which is right, *l* my servant Job.*
Ps 1: 3 And he shall be *l* a tree planted by the
4 are *l* the chaff which the wind driveth
2: 9 dash them in pieces *l* a potter's vessel.
7: 2 Lest he tear my soul *l* a lion, rending
17:12 *L* as a lion that is greedy of his 1825
18:33 He maketh my feet *l* hinds' feet, and
22:14 I am poured out *l* water, and all my
14 my heart is *l* wax; it is melted in the
15 my strength is dried up *l* a potsherd;
28: 1 I become *l* them that go down 5973
29: 6 maketh them also to skip *l* a calf; 3644
35:10 who is *l* unto thee, which deliverest "
36: 6 Thy righteousness is *l* the great
37: 2 shall soon be cut down *l* the grass,
35 spreading himself *l* a green bay tree.
39:11 his beauty to consume away *l* a moth:
44:11 Thou hast given us *l* sheep appointed
49:12 he is *l* the beasts that perish. 4911
14 *L* sheep they are laid in the grave;*
20 not, is *l* the beasts that perish. 4711
52: 2 *l* a sharp razor, working deceitfully.
8 I am *l* a green olive tree in the house
55: 6 said, Oh that I had wings *l* a dove!
58: 4 Their poison is *l* the poison of a 1823
4 they are *l* the deaf adder that 3644
8 *l* the untimely birth of a woman, that
59: 6 they make a noise *l* a dog, and go
14 let them make a noise *l* a dog, and go
64: 3 Who whet their tongue *l* a sword,
71:19 O God, who is *l* unto thee! 3644
72: 6 down *l* rain upon the mown grass:
16 fruit thereof shall shake *l* Lebanon:
73: 5 are they plagued *l* other men. 5973
77:20 Thou leddest thy people *l* a flock by
78:16 and caused waters to run down *l* rivers.

Ps 78:27 feathered fowls *l'* as the sand of the*
52 his own people to go forth *l'* sheep,
52 them in the wilderness *l'* a flock.
57 and dealt unfaithfully *l'* their fathers:
57 were turned aside *l'* a deceitful bow.
65 and *l'* a mighty man that shouteth by
69 he built his sanctuary *l'* high palaces,
69 *l'* the earth which he hath established
79: 3 Their blood have they shed *l'* water
5 ever? shall thy jealousy burn *l'* fire?
80: 1 thou that leadest Joseph *l'* a flock;
10 thereof were *l'* the goodly cedars.
82: 7 But ye shall die *l'* men,
7 and fall *l'* one of the princes.
83:11 Make their nobles *l'* Oreb, and
11 Make their nobles...*l'* Zeeb: *
13 O my God, make them *l'* a wheel; as
86: 8 the gods there is none *l'* unto thee, O
8 are there any works *l'* unto thy works.
88: 5 *l'* the slain that lie in the grave. 3644
17 came round about me daily *l'* water;
89: 8 who is a strong Lord *l'* unto thee? 3644
46 for ever? shall thy wrath burn *l'* fire?
90: 5 they are *l'* grass which groweth up.
92:10 thou exalt *l'* the horn of an unicorn:
12 shall flourish *l'* the palm tree:
12 he shall grow *l'* a cedar in Lebanon.
97: 5 hills melted *l'* wax at the presence of
102: 3 For my days are consumed *l'* smoke,
4 heart is smitten, and withered *l'* grass;
6 I am *l'* a pelican of the wilderness:1819
6 I am *l'* an owl of the desert. *
9 For I have eaten ashes *l'* bread, and
11 days are *l'* a shadow that declineth;
11 and I am withered *l'* grass.
26 them shall wax old *l'* a garment; 1819
103: 5 thy youth is renewed *l'* the eagle's.
13 *L'* as a father pitieth his children, so
104: 2 stretchest out the heavens *l'* a curtain:
107:27 fro, and stagger *l'* a drunken man,
41 and maketh him families *l'* a flock.
109:18 with cursing *l'* as with his garment,*
18 so let it come into his bowels *l'* water,
18 water, and *l'* oil into his bones.
23 gone *l'* the shadow when it declineth:
113: 5 Who is *l'* unto the Lord our God, who
114: 4 The mountains skipped *l'* rams,
4 rams, and the little hills *l'* lambs.
6 mountains, that ye skipped *l'* rams;
6 rams; and ye little hills, *l'* lambs?
115: 8 make them are *l'* unto them; 3644
118:12 They compassed me about *l'* bees;
119:83 I am become *l'* a bottle in the smoke;
176 I have gone astray *l'* a lost sheep:
126: 1 of Zion, we were *l'* them that dream.
128: 3 children *l'* olive plants round about
133: 2 It is *l'* the precious ointment upon the
135:18 that make them are *l'* unto them: 3644
140: 3 their tongues *l'* a serpent;
143: 7 lest I be *l'* unto them that go down4911
144: 4 Man is *l'* to vanity: his days are as1819
147:16 He giveth snow *l'* wool:
16 he scattereth the hoarfrost *l'* ashes.
17 He casteth forth his ice *l'* morsels:
Pr 12:18 speaketh *l'* the piercings of a sword:
17:22 merry heart doeth good *l'* a medicine:*
18:19 contentions are *l'* the bars of a castle.
20: 5 in the heart of man is *l'* deep water;
23:32 *l'* a serpent, and stingeth *l'* an adder.
25:11 A word fitly spoken is *l'* apples of gold
14 of a false gift is *l'* clouds and wind*
19 in time of trouble is *l'* a broken tooth,
28 spirit is *l'* a city that is broken down,
26: 4 lest thou also be *l'* unto him. 7737
17 is *l'* one that taketh a dog by the ears.
23 and a wicked heart are *l'* a potsherd
28: 3 is *l'* a sweeping rain which leaveth no
31:14 She is *l'* the merchants' ships; she
Ca 2: 9 My beloved is *l'* a roe or a young 1819
17 and be thou *l'* a roe or a young hart"
3: 6 of the wilderness *l'* pillars of smoke,
4: 2 Thy teeth are *l'* a flock of sheep that
3 Thy lips are *l'* a thread of scarlet, and
3 are *l'* a piece of a pomegranate
4 Thy neck is *l'* the tower of David
5 Thy two breasts are *l'* two young roes
11 garments is *l'* the smell of Lebanon.
5:13 his lips *l'* like lilies, dropping sweet*
6:12 me *l'* the chariots of Ammi-nadib.*
7: 1 joints of thy thighs are *l'* jewels, 3644
2 Thy navel is *l'* a round goblet, which
2 thy belly is *l'* an heap of wheat set
3 Thy two breasts are *l'* two young roes
4 thine eyes *l'* the fishpools in Heshbon,*
5 Thine head upon thee is *l'* Carmel,
5 and the hair of thine head *l'* purple;
7 thy stature is *l'* to a palm tree, 1819
8 and the smell of thy nose *l'* apples;
9 the roof of thy mouth *l'* the best wine
8:10 I am a wall, and my breasts *l'* towers:
14 be thou *l'* to a roe or to a young 1819
Isa 1: 9 have been *l'* unto Gomorrah. "
18 though they be red *l'* crimson, "
2: 6 and are soothsayers *l'* the Philistines,
3:18 and their round tires *l'* the moon,*
5:28 horses' hoofs shall be counted *l'* flint,
28 and their wheels like a whirlwind:
29 Their roaring shall be *l'* a lion,
29 they shall roar *l'* young lions: yea,
30 against them *l'* the roaring of the sea:
9:18 mount up *l'* the lifting up of smoke. *
10: 6 to tread them down *l'* the mire of the
13 the inhabitants *l'* a valiant man:*
16 a burning *l'* the burning of a fire.
11: 7 and the lion shall eat straw *l'* the ox.
16 *l'* as it was to Israel in the day that he

Isa 13: 4 mountains, *l'* as of a great people;1823
14:10 as we? art thou become *l'* unto us? 4911
14 clouds; I will be *l'* the most High.1819
19 of thy grave *l'* an abominable branch,
16:11 shall sound *l'* an harp for Moab,
17:12 make a noise *l'* the noise of the seas;
12 *l'* the rushing of mighty waters!
13 rush *l'* the rushing of many waters:
13 *l'* a rolling thing before the whirlwind.
18: 4 *l'* a cloud of dew in the heat of harvest.
19:16 day shall Egypt be *l'* unto women:
20: 3 *L'* as my servant Isaiah hath walked
22:18 toss thee *l'* a ball into a large country:
24:20 shall reel to and fro *l'* a drunkard,
20 and shall be removed *l'* a cottage; for
26:17 *L'* as a woman with child, that 3644
27:10 forsaken, and left *l'* a wilderness:
29: 5 thy strangers shall be *l'* small dust,
30:33 of the Lord, *l'* a stream of brimstone,
31: 4 *L'* as the lion and the young lion
33: 9 Sharon is *l'* a wilderness; and Bashan
38:12 I have cut off *l'* a weaver my life: he
14 *L'* a crane or a swallow, so did I
40:11 He shall feed his flock *l'* a shepherd:
42:13 shall stir up jealousy *l'* a man of war:
14 now will I cry *l'* a travailing woman;
46: 5 compare me, that we may be *l'*? 1819
9 I am God, and there is none *l'* me, 3644
48:19 of thy bowels *l'* the gravel thereof;
49: 2 made my mouth *l'* a sharp sword;
50: 7 therefore have I set my face *l'* a flint,
51: 3 will make her wilderness *l'* Eden,
3 her desert *l'* the garden of the Lord;
6 heavens shall vanish away *l'* smoke,
6 the earth shall wax old *l'* a garment,
6 therein shall die in *l'* manner: 3644
8 moth shall eat them up *l'* a garment,
8 and the worm shall eat them *l'* wool:
53: 6 All we *l'* sheep have gone astray;
57:20 the wicked are *l'* the troubled sea,
58: 1 lift up thy voice *l'* a trumpet, and
11 thou shalt be *l'* a watered garden,
11 *l'* a spring of water, whose waters
59:10 We grope for the wall *l'* the blind,
11 We roar all *l'* bears, and mourn sore
11 bears, and mourn sore *l'* doves:
19 the enemy shall come in *l'* a flood,*
63: 2 thy garments *l'* him that treadeth in
64: 6 our iniquities, *l'* the wind, have taken
65:25 the lion shall eat straw *l'* the bullock:
66:12 I will extend peace to her *l'* a river,
12 of the Gentiles *l'* a flowing stream:
14 your bones shall flourish *l'* an herb:
15 and with his chariots *l'* a whirlwind,
Jer 2:30 your prophets, *l'* a destroying lion.
4: 4 lest my fury come forth *l'* fire, and
5:19 *L'* as ye have forsaken me, and served
6:23 their voice roareth *l'* the sea; and
9: 3 they bend their tongues *l'* their bow
12 and is burned up *l'* a wilderness,
10: 6 as there is none *l'* unto thee, O 3644
7 there is none *l'* unto thee. "
16 The portion of Jacob is not *l'* them:
11:19 But I was *l'* a lamb or an ox that is
12: 3 them out *l'* sheep for the slaughter,
14: 6 they snuffed up the wind *l'* dragons;
17: 6 he shall be *l'* the heath in the desert,
21:12 lest my fury go out *l'* fire, and burn
23: 9 bones shake; I am *l'* a drunken man,
9 *l'* a man whom wine hath overcome,
29 Is not my word *l'* as a fire? saith 3541
29 *l'* a hammer that breaketh the rock in
24: 2 even *l'* the figs that are first ripe:
5 *L'* these good figs, so will I
25:34 and ye shall fall *l'* a pleasant vessel.
26: 6 Then will I make this house *l'* Shiloh,
9 This house shall be *l'* Shiloh, and this
18 Zion shall be plowed *l'* a field, and*
29:17 will make them *l'* vile figs, that cannot
22 make thee *l'* Zedekiah and *l'* Ahab,
30: 7 day is great, so that none is *l'* it: 3644
31:28 that *l'* as I have watched over them,
32:42 *L'* as I have brought all this great evil
36:32 besides unto them many *l'* words. 1922
38: 9 he is *l'* to die for hunger in the place
46: 8 Egypt riseth up *l'* a flood, and
8 his waters are moved *l'* the rivers;
20 Egypt is *l'* a very fair heifer, but *
21 in the midst of her *l'* fatted bullocks;
22 The voice thereof shall go *l'* a serpent;
48: 6 be *l'* the heath in the wilderness. 2421
28 be *l'* the dove that maketh her nest in
36 heart shall sound for Moab *l'* pipes,
36 heart shall sound *l'* pipes for the men
49:19 Behold, he shall come up *l'* a lion from
19 appoint over her? for who is *l'* me?3644
50:42 their voice shall roar *l'* the sea, and
42 put in array, *l'* a man to the battle,*
44 Behold, he shall come up *l'* a lion from
44 appoint over her? for who is *l'* me? 3644
51:19 The portion of Jacob is not *l'* them;
33 of Babylon is *l'* a threshingfloor,
34 he hath swallowed me up *l'* a dragon,
38 They shall roar together *l'* lions:
40 I will bring them down *l'* lambs to the
40 slaughter, *l'* rams with he goats.
55 her waves do roar *l'* great waters,
52:22 the pomegranates were *l'* unto these.
La 1: 6 princes are become *l'* harts that find
12 be any sorrow *l'* unto my sorrow,
21 and they shall be *l'* unto me. 3644
2: 3 burned against Jacob *l'* a flaming fire,
4 He hath bent his bow *l'* an enemy;
4 of Zion: he poured out his fury *l'* fire.
13 for thy breach is great *l'* the sea:
18 let tears run down *l'* a river day and

La 2:19 pour out thine heart *l'* water before
3:52 enemies chased me sore, *l'* a bird,
4: 3 *l'* the ostriches in the wilderness.
5:10 Our skin was black *l'* an oven because
Eze 1: 7 feet was *l'* the sole of a calf's foot:
7 *l'* the colour of burnished brass.
13 appearance was *l'* burning coals of fire,
13 and *l'* the appearance of lamps:
16 work was *l'* unto the colour of a beryl:
24 wings, *l'* the noise of great waters,
2: 8 rebellious *l'* that rebellious house:
5: 9 I will not do any more the *l'*. 3644
7:16 and shall be on the mountains *l'* doves
12:11 *l'* as I have done, so shall it be done
13: 4 thy prophets are *l'* the foxes in the
16:16 the *l'* things shall not come, neither
18:10 doeth the *l'* to any one of these * 251
14 considereth, and doeth not such *l'*,
19:10 Thy mother is *l'* a vine in thy blood,
20:36 *L'* as I pleaded with your fathers in
22:25 *l'* a roaring lion ravening the prey;
27 thereof are *l'* wolves ravening the prey,
23:18 *l'* as my mind was alienated from her
20 whose issue is *l'* the issue of horses.
25: 8 of Judah is *l'* unto all the heathen;
26: 4 her, and make her *l'* the top of a rock.*
14 I will make thee *l'* the top of a rock:*
19 *l'* the cities that are not inhabited;
27:32 over thee, saying, What city is *l'* Tyrus,
32 *l'* the destroyed in the midst of the
31: 2 Whom art thou *l'* in thy greatness?1819
8 the fir trees were not *l'* his boughs, "
8 God was *l'* unto him in his beauty. "
18 To whom art thou thus *l'* in glory "
32: 2 art *l'* a young lion of the nations,* "
14 cause their rivers to run *l'* oil, saith
36:35 is become *l'* the garden of Eden;
37 increase them with men *l'* a flock.
38: 9 shalt ascend and come *l'* a storm,
9 thou shalt be *l'* a cloud to cover the
40: 3 was *l'* the appearance of brass,
25 round about, *l'* those windows:
41:25 trees, *l'* as were made upon the walls;
42:11 was *l'* the appearance of the chambers
43: 2 voice was *l'* a noise of many waters:
3 visions were *l'* the vision that I saw
45:25 he do the *l'* in the feast of the seven
Da 1:19 them all was found none *l'* Daniel,
2:35 became *l'* the chaff of the summer
3:25 of the fourth is *l'* the Son of God. 1821
4:33 hairs were grown *l'* eagles' feathers,
33 and his nails *l'* birds' claws.
5:11 wisdom, *l'* the wisdom of the gods,
21 his heart was made *l'* the beasts, 5974
21 they fed him with grass *l'* oxen, and
7: 4 The first was *l'* a lion, and had eagles'
5 beast, a second, *l'* to a bear, and it 1821
6 and lo another, *l'* a leopard, which had
8 horn were eyes *l'* the eyes of man,
9 the hair of his head *l'* the pure wool:
9 his throne was *l'* the fiery flame, and*
13 one *l'* the Son of man came with the
10: 6 His body also was *l'* the beryl, and his
6 his feet *l'* in colour to polished brass,
6 his words *l'* the voice of a multitude.
18 me one *l'* the appearance of a man,
11:40 shall come against him *l'* a whirlwind,
Ho 2: 3 set her *l'* a dry land, and slay her with
4: 9 And there shall be, *l'* people, *l'* priest:
5:10 were *l'* them that remove the bound:
10 out my wrath upon them *l'* water.
6: 7 *l'* men have transgressed the covenant.
7: 6 made ready their heart *l'* an oven,
11 Ephraim also is *l'* a silly dove without
16 they are *l'* a deceitful bow: their
9:10 Israel *l'* grapes in the wilderness;
11 their glory shall fly away *l'* a bird,
11:10 he shall roar *l'* a lion: when he shall
13: 8 there will I devour them *l'* a lion:
14: 8 I am *l'* a green fir tree. From me is
Joe 1: 8 Lament *l'* a virgin girded with
2: 2 there hath not been ever the *l'*. 3644
5 *L'* the noise of chariots on the tops of
5 *l'* the noise of a flame of fire that
7 They shall run *l'* mighty men; they
7 they shall climb the wall *l'* men of war;
9 shall enter in at the windows *l'* a thief.
Am 2: 9 height was *l'* the height of the cedars,
5: 6 lest he break out *l'* fire in the house of
6: 5 instruments of musick, *l'* David;
8: 5 and it shall rise up wholly *l'* a flood;
9 nations, *l'* as corn is sifted in a sieve,
Jon 1: 4 that the ship was *l'* to be broken. 2803
Mic 1: 8 I will make a wailing *l'* the dragons,
4:10 of Zion, *l'* a woman in travail:
7:17 They shall lick the dust *l'* a serpent,
17 of their holes *l'* worms of the earth:*
18 Who is a God *l'* unto thee, that 3644
Na 1: 6 his fury is poured out *l'* fire, and the
2: 4 ways: they shall seem *l'* torches,
4 they shall run *l'* the lightnings.
8 Nineveh is of old *l'* a pool of water:
3:12 thy strong holds shall be *l'* fig trees
15 it shall eat thee up *l'* the cankerworm:
Hab 3:19 and he will make my feet *l'* hind's feet,
Zep 1:17 men, that they shall walk *l'* blind men,
2:13 a desolation, and dry *l'* a wilderness.
Zec 2: 6 *L'* as the Lord of hosts thought to do
5: 9 had wings *l'* the wings of a stork:
9:15 and they shall be filled *l'* bowls, and as
10: 7 of Ephraim shall be *l'* a mighty man,
12: 6 governors of Judah *l'* a hearth of fire
6 wood, and *l'* a torch of fire in a sheaf;
14: 5 *l'* as ye fled from before the earthquake
20 shall be *l'* the bowls before the altar.
Mal 3: 2 *l'* a refiner's fire, and *l'* a fullers' sope:

M't 3:16 Spirit of God descending *l'* a dove, 5616
6: 8 Be not ye therefore *l'* unto them: 3666
29 was not arrayed *l'* one of these. 5613
11:16 It is *l'* unto children sitting in the 3664
12:13 was restored whole, *l'* as the other.*5613
13:31 is *l'* to a grain of mustard seed, 3664
33 kingdom of heaven is *l'* unto leaven, "
44 is *l'* unto treasure hid in a field; "
45 heaven is *l'* unto a merchant man, "
47 kingdom of heaven is *l'* unto a net, "
52 *l'* unto a man that is an householder,"
20: 1 *l'* unto a man that is an householder,"
21:24 I in *l'* wise will tell you by what 2504
22: 2 of heaven is *l'* unto a certain king,*3666
39 And the second is *l'* unto it, Thou 3664
23:27 ye are *l'* unto whited sepulchres, 3945
28: 3 His countenance was *l'* lightning,*5613
M'r 1:10 and the Spirit *l'* a dove descending*5616
4:31 It is *l'* a grain of mustard seed, 3664
7: 8 many other such *l'* things ye do. *3946
13 and many such *l'* things do ye. "
12:31 And the second is *l'*, namely this, *3664
13:29 So ye in *l'* manner, when ye shall *2532
Lu 3:22 descended...bodily shape *l'* a dove *5616
6:23 in the *l'* manner did their fathers *5024
47 I will shew you to whom he is *l'*: 3664
48 He is *l'* a man which built an house,"
49 *l'* a man that without a foundation "
7:31 generation? and to what are they *l'*?"
32 They are *l'* unto children sitting in "
12:27 was not arrayed *l'* one of these. 5613
36 yourselves *l'* unto men that wait 3664
13:18 Unto what is the kingdom of God *l'*? "
19 It is *l'* a grain of mustard seed, "
21 It is *l'* leaven, which a woman took "
20:31 and in *l'* manner the seven also: *5615
Joh 1:32 descending from heaven *l'* a dove,*5616
7:46 Never man spake *l'* this man. *3779
8:55 I shall be a liar *l'* unto you: but I 3664
9: 9 is he: others said, He is *l'* him: "
Ac 1:11 shall so come in *l'* manner as ye 3779
2: 3 them cloven tongues *l'* as of fire, 5616
3:22 you of your brethren, *l'* unto me; 3945
7:37 you of your brethren, *l'* unto me; 5613
8:32 *l'* a lamb dumb before his shearer,*"
11:17 God gave them the *l'* gift as he did 2470
14:15 also are men of *l'* passions with you,3663
17:29 that the Godhead is *l'* unto gold, 3664
19:25 with the workmen of *l'* occupation,5108
Ro 1:23 image made *l'* to corruptible man,*3667
28 as they did not *l'* to retain God *1381
6: 4 *l'* as Christ was raised up from 5618
9:29 and been made *l'* unto Gomorrha. 3666
1Co 16:13 the faith, quit you *l'* men, be strong 407
Ga 5:21 revellings, and such *l'*: 3664
Ph'p 3:21 be fashioned *l'* unto his glorious *4832
1Th 2:14 have suffered *l'* things of your own 5024
1Ti 2: 9 In *l'* manner also, that women 5615
Heb 2:17 to be made *l'* unto his brethren, 3666
4:15 all points tempted *l'* as we are,2596,3665
7: 3 but made *l'* unto the Son of God; 871
Jas 1: 6 wavereth is *l'* a wave of the sea 1503
23 he is *l'* unto a man beholding his "
5:17 a man subject to *l'* passions as we 3663
1Pe 3:21 The *l'* figure whereunto even * 499
2Pe 1: 1 that have obtained *l'* precious faith 2472
1Jo 3: 2 shall appear, we shall be *l'* him; 3664
Jude 7 cities about them in *l'* manner, "
Re 1:13 candlesticks one *l'* unto the Son of "
14 and his hairs were white *l'* wool, *5616
15 his feet *l'* unto fine brass, as if 3664
2:18 his eyes *l'* unto a flame of fire, 5613
18 and his feet are *l'* fine brass; 3664
4: 3 that sat was to look upon *l'* a jasper"
3 throne, in sight *l'* unto an emerald."
6 was a sea of glass *l'* unto crystal: "
7 And the first beast was *l'* a lion, "
7 and the second beast *l'* a calf, and "
7 the fourth beast was *l'* a flying eagle."
9: 7 of the locusts were *l'* unto horses "
7 were as it were crowns *l'* gold, "
10 they had tails *l'* unto scorpions, and"
19 their tails were *l'* unto serpents, "
11: 1 was given me a reed *l'* unto a rod: "
13: 2 which I saw was *l'* unto a leopard, "
4 Who is *l'* unto the beast? who is "
11 he had two horns *l'* a lamb, and he "
14:14 cloud one sat *l'* unto the Son of man,"
16:13 I saw three unclean spirits *l'* frogs*"
18:18 What city is *l'* unto this great city! "
21 up a stone *l'* a great millstone, 5613
21:11 her light was *l'* unto a stone most 3664
11 even like a jasper stone, clear as *5613
18 was pure gold, *l'* unto clear glass. 3664

liked
1Ch 28: 4 he *l'* me to make me king over all*7521

likeminded
Ro 15: 5 to be *l'* one toward another*3588,846,5426
Ph'p 2: 2 Fulfil ye my joy, that ye be *l'*,* " "
20 For I have no man *l'*, who will 2473

liken See also LIKENED.
Isa 40:18 To whom then will ye *l'* God? or 1819
25 To whom then will ye *l'* me, or "
46: 5 To whom will ye *l'* me, and make "
La 2:13 what thing shall I *l'* to thee, O "
M't 7:24 I will *l'* him unto a wise man, *3666
11:16 whereunto shall I *l'* this generation?"
M'r 4:30 shall we *l'* the kingdom of God? "
Lu 7:31 then shall I *l'* the men of this "
13:20 shall I *l'* the kingdom of God? "

likened
Ps 89: 6 mighty can be *l'* unto the Lord? *1819
Jer 6: 2 have *l'* the daughter of Zion to a * "
M't 7:26 shall be *l'* unto a foolish man, 3666
13:24 of heaven is *l'* unto a man which "
18:23 of heaven *l'* unto a certain king, 3666
25: 1 of heaven be *l'* unto ten virgins, "

likeness
Ge 1:26 man in our image, after our *l'*: 1823
5: 1 man, in the *l'* of God made he him; "
3 begat a son in his own *l'*, after his "
Ex 20: 4 or any *l'* of any thing that is in 8544
De 4:16 figure, the *l'* of male or female, 8403
17 The *l'* of any beast that is on the "
17 the *l'* of any winged fowl that flieth "
18 The *l'* of any thing that creepeth on"
18 the *l'* of any fish that is in the "
23 image, or the *l'* of any thing, *8544
25 graven image, or the *l'* of any thing,*"
5: 8 any *l'* of any thing that is in heaven"
Ps 17:15 satisfied, when I awake, with thy *l'*.‡"
Isa 40:18 what *l'* will ye compare unto him? 1823
Eze 1: 5 came the *l'* of four living creatures."
5 they had the *l'* of a man. "
10 As for the *l'* of their faces, they four"
13 As for the *l'* of the living creatures, "
16 a beryl: and they four had one *l'*: "
22 the *l'* of the firmament upon their "
26 their heads was the *l'* of a throne, "
26 and upon the *l'* of the throne was the"
26 *l'* as the appearance of a man above"
28 of the *l'* of the glory of the Lord. "
8: 2 and lo a *l'* as the appearance of fire:"
10: 1 the appearance of the *l'* of a throne."
10 appearances, they four had one *l'*, "
21 and the *l'* of the hands of a man "
22 the *l'* of their faces was the same "
Ac 14:11 come down to us in the *l'* of men. 3666
Ro 6: 5 together in the *l'* of his death, 3667
5 be also in the *l'* of his resurrection: "
8: 3 his own Son in the *l'* of sinful flesh,3667
Ph'p 2: 7 and was made in the *l'* of men: "

liketh
De 23:16 thy gates, where it *l'* him best: ‡2896
Es 8: 8 ye also for the Jews, as it *l'* you, ‡ "
Am 4: 5 for this *l'* you, O ye children of ‡ 157

likewise See also LIKE and WISE.
Ex 22:30 *L'* shalt thou do with thine oxen, 3651
26: 4 *l'* shalt thou make in the uttermost "
27:11 *l'* for the north side in length there "
36:11 *l'* he made in the uttermost side of "
Le 7: 1 *L'* this is the law of the trespass *2063
De 9:23 *L'* when the Lord sent you from *
12:30 their gods? even so will I do *l'*. 3651
15:17 thy maidservant thou shalt do *l'*. "
22: 3 thou hast found, shalt thou do *l'*:* "
J'g 1: 3 I *l'* will go with thee into thy lot. 1571
7: 5 *l'* every one that boweth down upon
17 unto them, Look on me, and do *l'*: 3651
8: 8 Penuel, and spake unto them *l'*: *2063
9:49 people *l'* cut down every man his 1571
1Sa 14:22 *L'* all the men of Israel which had hid
19:21 and they prophesied *l'*. *1571
31: 5 was dead, he fell *l'* upon his sword, "
2Sa 1:11 *l'* all the men that were with him: "
17: 5 and let us hear *l'* what he saith. "
1Ki 11: 8 *l'* did he for all his strange wives,*3651
1Ch 10: 5 was dead, he fell *l'* on the sword, 1571
18: 8 *L'* from Tibhath, and from Chun,*
19:15 *l'* fled before Abishai his brother, 1571
23:30 praise the Lord, and *l'* at even; 3651
24:31 These *l'* cast lots over against 1571
27: 4 in his course *l'* were twenty and four*
28:16 and *l'* silver for the tables of silver:*
17 *l'* silver by weight for every bason of*
29:24 and all the sons *l'* of king David, 1571
2Ch 3:11 and the other wing was *l'* five cubits,
29:22 *l'*, when they had killed the rams,*
Ne 4:22 *L'* at the same time said I unto 1571
5:10 I, *l'*, and my brethren, and my "
Es 1:18 *L'* shall the ladies of Persia and *
4:16 I also and my maidens will fast *l'*;*3651
Job 31:38 the furrows *l'* thereof complain; *3162
37: 6 *l'* to the small rain, and to the great
Ps 49:10 *l'* the fool and the brutish person†‡
52: 5 God shall *l'* destroy thee for ever, 1571
Ec 7:22 thou thyself *l'* hast cursed others. "
Isa 30:24 The oxen *l'* and the young asses that
Jer 40:11 *L'* when all the Jews that were in 1571
Eze 13:17 *L'*, thou son of man, set thy face *
40:16 round about, and *l'* to the arches: 3651
46: 3 *L'* the people of the land shall worship*
Na 1:12 they be quiet, and *l'* many, yet 3651
M't 17:12 *L'* shall also the Son of man *3779
18:35 So *l'* shall my heavenly Father do*2532
20: 5 sixth and ninth hour, and did *l'*. 5615
10 they *l'* received every man a penny.2532
21:30 he came to the second, and said *l'*.5615
36 the first: and they did unto them *l'*.*"
22:26 *L'* the second also, and the third, *3668
24:33 So *l'* ye, when ye shall see all these*2532
25:17 *l'* he that had received two, he also*5615
26:35 thee. *L'* also said all the disciples.3668
27:41 *L'* also the chief priests mocking * "
M'r 4:16 these are they *l'* which are sown on*"
12:21 left he any seed: and the third *l'*. 5615
14:31 in any wise. *L'* also said they all.* "
15:31 *L'* also the chief priests mocking *3668
Lu 2:38 gave thanks *l'* unto the Lord, and* 437
3:11 he that hath meat, let him do *l'*. 3668
14 the soldiers *l'* demanded of him, *2532
5:33 *l'* the disciples of the Pharisees; 3668
6:31 do to you, do ye also to them *l'*. "
10:32 And *l'* a Levite, when he was at the*"
37 Jesus unto him, Go, and do thou *l'*. "
13: 3 ye repent, ye shall all *l'* perish. *5615
5 ye repent, ye shall all *l'* perish. 3668
14:33 So *l'*, whosoever he be of you that*3779
15: 7 that *l'* joy shall be in heaven over* "
10 *L'*, I say unto you, there is joy in * "
16:25 things, and *l'* Lazarus evil things:*3668
17:10 So *l'* ye, when ye shall have done *2532
28 *L'* also as it was in the days of Lot;3668
31 the field, let him *l'* not return back."
19:19 And he said *l'* to him, Be thou also*2532
21:31 So *l'* ye, when ye see these things * "
22:20 *L'* also the cup after supper, *5615
36 let him take it, and *l'* his scrip: 3668
Joh 5:19 doeth, these also doeth the Son *l'*.* "
6:11 *l'* of the fishes as much as they "
21:13 bread and giveth them, and fish *l'*. "
Ac 3:24 have *l'* foretold of these days. *2532
Ro 1:27 And *l'* also the men, leaving the 3668
6:11 *L'* reckon ye also yourselves to be*3779
8:26 *L'* the Spirit also helpeth our *5615
16: 5 *L'* greet the church that is in their*2532
1Co 7: 3 *l'* also the wife unto the husband. 3668
4 *l'* also the husband hath not power of"
22 *l'* also he that is called, being free, is"
14: 9 So *l'* ye, except ye utter by the *2532
Ga 2:13 other Jews dissembled *l'* with him; "
Col 4:16 that ye *l'* read the epistle from *2532
1Ti 3: 8 *L'* must the deacons be grave, not*5615
5:25 *L'* also the good works of some are*"
Tit 2: 3 The aged women *l'*, that they be in "
6 Young men *l'* exhort to be sober "
Heb 2:14 himself *l'* took part of the same; *3898
9:21 sprinkled [*l'*] with blood both the 3668
Jas 2:25 *L'* also was not Rahab the harlot * "
1Pe 3: 1 *L'*, ye wives, be in subjection to * "
7 *L'*, ye husbands, dwell with them * 36
4: 1 arm yourselves *l'* with the same *2532
5: 5 *L'*, ye younger, submit yourselves 3668
Jude 8 *L'* also these filthy dreamers defile*"
Re 8:12 third part of it, and the night *l'*. * "

Likhi (*lik'-hi*)
1Ch 7:19 Ahian, and Shechem, and *L'*, and 3949

liking
Job 39: 4 Their young ones are in good *l'*, 2492
Da 1:10 should he see your faces worse *l'* than

lilies
1Ki 7:26 brim of a cup, with flowers of *l'*: *7799
2Ch 4: 5 brim of a cup, with flowers of *l'*; * "
Ca 2:16 I am his: he feedeth among the *l'*. "
4: 5 are twins, which feed among the *l'*. "
5:13 his lips like *l'*, dropping sweet "
6: 2 in the gardens, and to gather *l'*. "
3 is mine: he feedeth among the *l'*. "
7: 2 an heap of wheat set about with *l'*. "
M't 6:28 Consider the *l'* of the field, how 2918
Lu 12:27 Consider the *l'* how they grow: "

lily See LILIES.
1Ki 7:19 pillars were of *l'* work in the porch,7799
22 the top of the pillars was *l'* work: "
Ca 2: 1 of Sharon, and the *l'* of the valleys. "
2 As the *l'* among thorns, so is my "
Ho 14: 5 he shall grow as the *l'*, and cast "

lily-work See LILY and WORK.

lime
Isa 33:12 shall be as the burnings of *l'*: 7875
Am 2: 1 bones of the king of Edom into *l'*: "

limit See also LIMITED; LIMITETH.
Eze 43:12 the whole *l'* thereof round about 1366

limited
Ps 78:41 and *l'* the Holy One of Israel. *8428

limiteth
Heb 4: 7 he *l'* a certain day, saying to David,*3724

line See also LINES; PLUMBLINE.
Jos 2:18 shalt bind this *l'* of scarlet thread 8615
21 bound the scarlet *l'* in the window. "
2Sa 8: 2 and measured them with a *l'*, 2256
2 and with one full *l'* to keep alive. "
1Ki 7:15 a *l'* of twelve cubits did compass 2339
23 a *l'* of thirty cubits did compass 6957
2Ki 21:13 over Jerusalem the *l'* of Samaria, "
2Ch 4: 2 a *l'* of thirty cubits did compass it "
Job 38: 5 who hath stretched the *l'* upon it? "
Ps 19: 4 Their *l'* is gone out through all the "
78:55 divided them an inheritance by *l'*, 2256
Isa 28:10, 13 *l'* upon *l'*, *l'* upon *l'*; here a 6957
17 Judgment also will I lay to the *l'*, "
34:11 out upon it the *l'* of confusion, "
17 hand hath divided it unto them by *l'*:"
44:13 he marketh it out with a *l'*; he *8279
Jer 31:39 the measuring *l'* shall yet go forth 6957
La 2: 8 he hath stretched out a *l'*, he hath "
Eze 40: 3 with a *l'* of flax in his hand, and 6616
47: 3 man that had the *l'* in his hand 6957
Am 7:17 thy land shall be divided by *l'*; 2256
Zec 1:16 a *l'* shall be stretched forth upon 6957
2: 1 with a measuring *l'* in his hand. 2256
2Co 10:16 not to boast in another man's *l'* *2583

lineage
Lu 2: 4 was of the house and *l'* of David:) *3965

linen
Ge 41:42 arrayed him in vestures of fine *l'*, 8336
Ex 25: 4 purple, and scarlet, and fine *l'*, "
26: 1 with ten curtains of fine twined *l'*. "
31 and fine twined *l'* of cunning work: "
36 and scarlet, and fine twined *l'*, "
27: 9 for the court of fine twined *l'* of an "
16 and scarlet, and fine twined *l'*, "
18 height five cubits of fine twined *l'*, "
28: 5 and purple, and scarlet, and fine *l'*. "
6 purple, of scarlet, and fine twined *l'*,"
8 and scarlet, and fine twined *l'*, "
15 and of scarlet, and of fine twined *l'*,"
39 shalt embroider the coat of fine *l'*, "
39 thou shalt make the mitre of fine *l'*,"
42 make them *l'* breeches to cover 906

Ex 35: 6, 23 purple, and scarlet, and fine *l*, 8336
25 purple, and of scarlet, and of fine *l*. "
35 in purple, in scarlet, and in fine *l*, "
36: 8 made ten curtains of fine twined *l*, "
35 and scarlet, and fine twined *l*: "
37 and scarlet, and fine twined *l*. "
38: 9 of the court were of fine twined *l*, "
16 round about were of fine twined *l*. "
18 and scarlet, and fine twined *l*: "
23 purple, and in scarlet, and fine *l*. "
39: 2 and scarlet, and fine twined *l*. "
3 and in the scarlet, and in the fine *l*," "
5 and scarlet, and fine twined *l*; "
8 and scarlet, and fine twined *l*. "
24 and purple, and scarlet, and twined *l*. "
27 made coats of fine *l* of woven work 8336
28 fine *l*, and goodly bonnets of fine *l*, "
28 and *l* breeches of fine twined 906
28 and breeches of fine twined *l*, 8336
29 And a girdle of fine twined *l*, and "
Le 6:10 priest shall put on his *l* garment, 906
10 *l* breeches shall he put upon his "
13:47 woollen garment, or a *l* garment; 6593
48 warp, or woof; of *l*, or of woollen; "
52 warp or woof, in woollen or in *l*, "
59 leprosy in a garment of woollen or *l*," "
16: 4 He shall put on the holy *l* coat, 906
4 have the *l* breeches upon his flesh, "
4 and shall be girded with a *l* girdle, "
4 with the *l* mitre shall he be attired: "
23 shall put off the *l* garments, which "
32 and shall put on the *l* clothes, even "
19:19 garment mingled of *l* and woollen*8162
De 22:11 divers sorts, as of woollen and *l* 6593
1Sa 2:18 a child, girded with a *l* ephod. 906
22:18 persons that did wear a *l* ephod. "
2Sa 6:14 David was girded with a *l* ephod. "
1Ki 10:28 brought out of Egypt, and *l* yarn:*4723
28 received the *l* yarn at a price. * "
1Ch 4:21 house of them that wrought fine *l*, 948
15:27 was clothed with a robe of fine *l*, "
27 also had upon him an ephod of *l*. 906
2Ch 1:16 brought out of Egypt, and *l* yarn:*4723
16 received the *l* yarn at a price. * "
2:14 blue, and in fine *l*, and in crimson;948
3:14 and purple, and crimson, and fine *l*," "
5:12 brethren, being arrayed in white *l*, "
Es 1: 6 hangings, fastened...cords of fine *l* "
8:15 with a garment of fine *l* and purple: "
Pr 7:16 carved works, with fine *l* of Egypt.* "
31:24 She maketh fine *l*, and selleth it; 5466
Isa 3:23 The glasses, and the fine *l*, and "
Jer 13: 1 Go and get thee a *l* girdle, and 6593
Eze 9: 2 among them was clothed with *l*, 906
3 called to the man clothed with *l*, "
11 behold, the man clothed with *l*, "
10: 2 spake unto the man clothed with *l*, "
6 commanded the man clothed with *l*," "
7 of him that was clothed with *l*: "
16:10 I girded thee about with fine *l*, 8336
13 thy raiment was of fine *l*, and silk, "
27: 7 Fine *l* with broidered work from "
16 broidered work,...fine *l*, and coral, 948
44:17 shall be clothed with *l* garments; 6593
18 have *l* bonnets upon their heads, "
18 have *l* breeches upon their loins; "
Da 10: 5 behold a certain man clothed in *l*, 906
12: 6 one said to the man clothed in *l*, "
7 And I heard the man clothed in *l*, "
M't 27:59 he wrapped it in a clean *l* cloth, *4616*
M'r 14:51 *l* cloth cast about his naked body; "
52 And he left the *l* cloth, and fled "
15:46 And he bought fine *l*, and took him" "
46 wrapped him in the *l*, and laid him" "
Lu 16:19 was clothed in purple and fine *l*, *1040*
23:53 took it down, and wrapped it in *l*, *4616*
24:12 the *l* clothes laid by themselves, *3608*
Joh 19:40 of Jesus, and wound it in *l* clothes "
20: 5 looking in, saw the *l* clothes lying; "
6 and seeth the *l* clothes lie, "
7 not lying with the *l* clothes, but "
Re 15: 6 clothed in pure and white *l*, and *3043*
18:12 pearls, and fine *l*, and purple, *1040*
16 city, that was clothed in fine *l*, *1039*
19: 8 that she should be arrayed in fine *l*, "
8 for the fine *l* is the righteousness "
14 clothed in fine *l*, white and clean. "

lines
2Sa 8: 2 even with two *l* measured he to 2256
Ps 16: 6 The *l* are fallen unto me in pleasant"

lingered See also LINGERETH.
Ge 19:16 And while he *l*, the men laid hold 4102
43:10 For except we had *l*, surely now "

lingereth See also LINGERED.
2Pe 2: 3 judgment now of a long time *l* not, *691*

lintel See also LINTELS.
Ex 12:22 strike the *l* and the two side posts4947
23 when he seeth the blood upon the *l*," "
1Ki 6:31 the *l* and side posts were a fifth 352
Am 9: 1 he said, Smite the *l* of the door, *3730

lintels
Zep 2:14 shall lodge in the upper *l* of it; 3730

Linus (*li'-nus*)
2Ti 4:21 and *L*, and Claudia, and all the *3044*

lion See also LIONESS; LIONLIKE; LION'S; LIONS.
Ge 49: 9 stooped down, he couched as a *l*, 738
9 and as an old *l*; who shall rouse *3833
Nu 23:24 people shall rise up as a great *l*, * "
24 and lift up himself as a young *l*: 738
24: 9 He couched, he lay down as a *l*, "
9 and as a great *l*: who shall stir *3833
De 33:20 he dwelleth as a *l*, and teareth * "
J'g 14: 5 a young *l* roared against him. 738
8 aside to see the carcase of the *l*: "
J'g 14: 8 and honey in the carcase of the *l*. 738
9 honey out of the carcase of the *l*. "
18 and what is stronger than a *l*? "
1Sa 17:34 and there came a *l*, and a bear, "
36 slew both the *l* and the bear: "
37 delivered me out of the paw of the *l*," "
2Sa 17:10 whose heart is as the heart of a *l*, "
23:20 slew a *l* in the midst of a pit in time" "
1Ki 13:24 *l* met him by the way, and slew him: "
24 the *l* also stood by the carcase. "
25 and the *l* standing by the carcase: "
26 Lord hath delivered him unto the *l*, "
28 and the *l* standing by the carcase: "
28 the *l* had not eaten the carcase, nor" "
20:36 from me, a *l* shall slay thee. "
36 him, a *l* found him, and slew him. "
1Ch 11:22 and slew a *l* in a pit in a snowy day. "
Job 4:10 The roaring of the *l*, and the voice "
10 the voice of the fierce *l*, and the 7826
11 old *l* perisheth for lack of prey, 3918
10:16 Thou huntest me as a fierce *l*: 7826
28: 8 it, nor the fierce *l* passed by it. "
38:39 Wilt thou hunt the prey for the *l*?*3833
Ps 7: 2 Lest he tear my soul like a *l*, 738
10: 9 in wait secretly as a *l* in his den: "
17:12 Like as a *l* that is greedy of his prey," "
12 as it were a young *l* lurking in 3715
22:13 as a ravening and a roaring *l*. 738
91:13 shalt tread upon the *l* and adder: 7826
13 the young *l* and the dragon shalt 3715
Pr 19:12 king's wrath is as the roaring of a *l*;" "
20: 2 of a king is as the roaring of a *l*: "
22:13 There is a *l* without, I shall be 738
26:13 man saith, There is a *l* in the way; "
13 a *l* is in the streets. "
28: 1 but the righteous are bold as a *l*. 3715
15 As a roaring *l*, and a ranging bear 739
30:30 A *l* which is strongest among 3918
Ec 9: 4 living dog is better than a dead *l*. 738
Isa 5:29 Their roaring shall be like a *l*, 3833
11: 6 young *l* and the fatling together; 3715
7 the *l* shall eat straw like the ox. 738
21: 8 And he cried, A *l*: My lord, I stand "
30: 6 whence come the young and old *l*,3918
31: 4 Like as the *l* and the young 738
4 the young *l* roaring on his prey, 3715
35: 9 No *l* shall be there, nor any 738
38:13 as a *l*, so will he break all my bones: "
65:25 *l* shall eat straw like the bullock: "
Jer 2:30 your prophets, like a destroying *l*. "
4: 7 The *l* is come up from his thicket, "
5: 6 a *l* out of the forest shall slay them," "
12: 8 Mine heritage is unto me as a *l* in "
25:38 hath forsaken his covert, as the *l*:3715
49:19 Behold, he shall come up like a *l* 738
50:44 Behold, he shall come up like a *l* "
La 3:10 in wait, and as a *l* in secret places. "
Eze 1:10 the face of a *l*, on the right side: "
10:14 man, and the third the face of a *l*, "
19: 3 it become a young *l*, and it 3715
5 whelps, and made him a young *l*. "
6 he became a young *l*, and learned "
22:25 like a roaring *l* ravening the prey; 738
32: 2 art like a young *l* of the nations, 3715
41:19 face of a young *l* toward the palm "
Da 7: 4 first was like a *l*, and had eagle's 738
Ho 5:14 For I will be unto Ephraim as a *l*,7826
14 a young *l* to the house of Judah: 3715
11:10 the Lord: he shall roar like a *l*: 738
13: 7 I will be unto them as a *l*: 7826
8 there will I devour them like a *l*: 3833
Joe 1: 6 whose teeth are the teeth of a *l*, 738
6 hath the cheek teeth of a great *l*. 3833
Am 3: 4 Will a *l* roar in the forest, when he 738
4 will a young *l* cry out of his den, 3715
8 The *l* hath roared, who will not 738
12 taketh out of the mouth of the *l* "
5:19 As if a man did flee from a *l*, and a "
Mic 5: 8 as a *l* among the beasts of the forest," "
8 as a young *l* among the flocks of 3715
Na 2:11 of the young lions, where the *l*, 739
11 even the old *l*, walked, and the *3833
12 The *l* did tear in pieces enough 738
2Ti 4:17 delivered out of the mouth of the *l*.*3023*
1Pe 5: 8 adversary the devil, as a roaring *l*, "
Re 4: 7 And the first beast was like a *l*, "
5: 5 behold, the *L* of the tribe of Juda, "
10: 3 loud voice, as when a *l* roareth: "
13: 2 and his mouth as the mouth of a *l*:" "

lioness See also LIONESSES.
Eze 19: 2 What is thy mother? A *l*: she lay 3833

lionesses
Na 2:12 and strangled for his *l*, and filled 3833

lionlike
2Sa 23:20 acts, he slew two *l* men of Moab:* 739
1Ch 11:22 acts; he slew two *l* men of Moab:* "

lion's
Ge 49: 9 Judah is a *l* whelp: from the prey, 738
De 33:22 of Dan he said, Dan is a *l* whelp: "
Job 4:11 the stout *l* whelps are scattered *3833
28: 8 The *l* whelps have not trodden it,*7830
Ps 22:21 Save me from the *l* mouth: for 738
Na 2:11 old lion, walked, and the *l* whelp, "

lions See also LIONS'.
2Sa 1:23 eagles, they were stronger than *l*. 738
1Ki 7:29 between the ledges were *l*, oxen, and" "
29 beneath the *l* and oxen were certain" "
36 he graved cherubims, *l*, and palm "
10:19 and two *l* stood beside the stays. "
20 twelve *l* stood there on the one side "
2Ki 17:25 the Lord sent *l* among them, which "
26 he hath sent *l* among them, and, "
1Ch 12: 8 whose faces were like the faces of *l*," "
2Ch 9:18 and two *l* standing by the stays: "
2Ch 9:19 twelve *l* stood there on the one side738
Job 4:10 teeth of the young *l*, are broken, 3715
38:39 or fill the appetite of the young *l*, "
Ps 34:10 The young *l* do lack, and suffer "
35:17 destructions, my darling from the *l*." "
57: 4 My soul is among *l*: and I lie even3833
58: 6 out the great teeth of the young *l*,3715
104:21 The young *l* roar after their prey, "
Isa 5:29 lion, they shall roar like young *l*: "
15: 9 *l* upon him that escapeth of Moab,*738
Jer 2:15 The young *l* roared upon him, and3715
50:17 the *l* have driven him away: first 738
51:38 They shall roar together like *l*: 3715
Eze 19: 2 A lioness: she lay down among *l*, 738
2 her whelps among young *l*. 3715
6 he went up and down among the *l*,738
38:13 with all the young *l* thereof, shall 3715
Da 6: 7 he shall be cast into the den of *l*. 744
12 king, shall be cast into the den of *l*?" "
16 and cast him into the den of *l*. "
19 and went in haste unto the den of *l*." "
20 able to deliver thee from the *l*? "
24 they cast them into the den of *l*, "
24 and the *l* had the mastery of them, "
27 Daniel from the power of the *l*. "
Na 2:11 Where is the dwelling of the *l*, and 738
11 the feedingplace of the young *l*, 3715
13 the sword shall devour thy young *l*: "
Zep 3: 3 princes within her are roaring *l*; 738
Zec 11: 3 a voice of the roaring of young *l*; 3715
Heb 11:33 promises, stopped the mouths of *l*,*3023*
Re 9: 8 their teeth were as the teeth of *l*, "
17 the horses were as the heads of *l*; "

lions'
Ca 4: 8 and Hermon, from the *l* dens, from738
Jer 51:38 lions: they shall yell as *l* whelps. "
Da 6:22 angel, and hath shut the *l* mouths, 744

lip See also LIPS.
Le 13:45 put a covering upon his upper *l*, 822
Ps 22: 7 they shoot out the *l*, they shake 8193
Pr 12:19 The *l* of truth shall be established "

lips
Ex 6:12 me, who am of uncircumcised *l*? 8193
30 Behold, I am of uncircumcised *l*, "
Le 5: 4 pronouncing with his *l* to do evil "
Nu 30: 6 vowed, or uttered ought out of her *l*," "
8 that which she uttered with her *l*, "
12 whatsoever proceeded out of her *l* "
De 23:23 That which is gone out of thy *l* "
1Sa 1:13 only her *l* moved, but her voice "
2Ki 19:28 in thy nose, and my bridle in thy *l*, "
Job 2:10 all this did not Job sin with his *l*. "
8:21 laughing, and thy *l* with rejoicing. "
11: 5 speak, and open his *l* against thee; "
13: 6 hearken to the pleadings of my *l*. "
15: 6 thine own *l* testify against thee. "
16: 5 the moving of my *l* should asswage" "
23:12 from the commandment of his *l*; "
27: 4 My *l* shall not speak wickedness, "
32:20 I will open my *l* and answer. "
33: 3 my *l* shall utter knowledge clearly. "
Ps 12: 2 with flattering *l* and with a double* "
3 Lord shall cut off all flattering *l*, "
4 our *l* are our own: who is lord over" "
16: 4 nor take up their names into my *l*. "
17: 1 that goeth not out of feigned *l*. "
4 by the word of thy *l* I have kept me" "
21: 2 not withholden the request of his *l*." "
31:18 Let the lying *l* be put to silence; "
34:13 evil, and thy *l* from speaking guile. "
40: 9 I have not refrained my *l*, O Lord, "
45: 2 of men: grace is poured into thy *l*: "
51:15 O Lord, open thou my *l*; and my "
59: 7 their mouth: swords are in their *l*: "
12 the words of their *l* let them even "
63: 3 than life, my *l* shall praise thee. "
5 shall praise thee with joyful *l*: "
66:14 Which my *l* have uttered, and my "
71:23 My *l* shall greatly rejoice when I "
89:34 the thing that is gone out of my *l*. "
106:33 he spake unadvisedly with his *l*. "
119:13 With my *l* have I declared all the "
171 My *l* shall utter praise, when thou "
120: 2 my soul, O Lord, from lying *l*, "
140: 3 adders' poison is under their *l*. "
9 mischief of their own *l* cover them. "
141: 3 my mouth; keep the door of my *l*. "
Pr 4:24 and perverse *l* put far from thee. "
5: 2 that thy *l* may keep knowledge. "
3 For the *l* of a strange woman drop "
7:21 with the flattering of her *l* she "
8: 6 the opening of my *l* shall be right "
7 is an abomination to my *l*. "
10:13 *l* of him that hath understanding "
18 He that hideth hatred with lying *l*, "
19 but he that refraineth his *l* is wise. "
21 The *l* of the righteous feed many: "
32 The *l* of the righteous know what "
12:13 snared by the transgression of his *l*: "
22 Lying *l* are abomination to the "
13: 3 he that openeth wide his *l* shall "
14: 3 but the *l* of the wise shall preserve "
7 not in him the *l* of knowledge. "
23 talk of the *l* tendeth only to penury. "
15: 7 *l* of the wise disperse knowledge: "
16:10 A divine sentence is in the *l* of the "
13 Righteous *l* are the delight of kings; "
21 the sweetness of the *l* increaseth "
23 mouth, and addeth learning to his *l*. "
27 in his *l* there is as a burning fire. "
30 moving his *l* he bringeth evil to "
17: 4 wicked doer giveth heed to false *l*; "
7 fool: much less do lying *l* a prince. "
28 he that shutteth his *l* is esteemed "
18: 6 A fool's *l* enter into contention, "

Pr 18: 7 and his l' are the snare of his soul. 8193
20 increase of his l' shall he be filled. "
19: 1 he that is perverse in his l', and is a "
20: 15 the l' of knowledge are a precious "
19 with him that flattereth with his l'. "
22: 11 the grace of his l' the king shall be "
18 they shall withal be fitted in thy l'. "
23: 16 when thy l' speak right things. "
24: 2 and their l' talk of mischief. "
26 Every man shall kiss his l' that "
28 cause; and deceive not with thy l'. "
26: 23 Burning l' and a wicked heart are "
24 that hateth dissembleth with his l', "
27: 2 a stranger, and not thine own l'. "
Ec 10: 12 but the l' of a fool shall swallow up "
Ca 4: 3 Thy l' are like a thread of scarlet, "
11 Thy l', O my spouse, drop as the "
5: 13 his l' like lilies, dropping sweet "
7: 9 the l' of those that are asleep to "
Isa 6: 5 because I am a man of unclean l', "
5 the midst of a people of unclean l': "
7 said, Lo, this hath touched thy l'; "
11: 4 with the breath of his l' shall he "
28: 11 with stammering l' and another "
29: 13 and with their l' do honour me, "
30: 27 his l' are full of indignation, and "
37: 29 thy nose, and my bridle in thy l', "
57: 19 I create the fruit of the l'; Peace, "
59: 3 your l' have spoken lies, your "
Jer 17: 16 which came out of my l' was right "
La 3: 62 The l' of those that rose up against "
Eze 24: 17 cover not thy l', and eat not the 8222
22 ye shall not cover your l', nor eat "
36: 3 are taken up in the l' of talkers, 8193
Da 10: 16 of the sons of men touched my l': "
Ho 14: 2 will we render the calves of our l'. "
Mic 3: 7 yea, they shall all cover their l'; 8222
Hab 3: 16 my l' quivered at the voice: 8193
Mal 2: 6 and iniquity was not found in his l': "
7 priest's l' should keep knowledge, "
M't 15: 8 and honoureth me with their l'; 5491
M'r 7: 6 people honoureth me with their l', "
Ro 3: 13 the poison of asps is under their l': "
1Co 14: 21 men of other tongues and other l' "
Heb 13: 15 the fruit of our l' giving thanks to "
1Pe 3: 10 and his l' that they speak no guile: "

liquor See also LIQUORS.
Nu 6: 3 shall he drink any l' of grapes, 4952
Ca 7: 2 round goblet, which wanteth not l': *4197

liquors
Ex 22: 29 of thy ripe fruits, and of thy l': 1831

listed
M't 17: 12 done unto him whatsoever they l'. 2309
M'r 9: 13 done unto him whatsoever they l'. "

listen
Isa 49: 1 L', O isles, unto me; and hearken, 8085

listeth
Joh 3: 8 The wind bloweth where it l', and 2309
Jas 3: 4 whithersoever...governor l'. *3730, 1014

litters
Isa 66: 20 horses, and in chariots, and in l', 6632

little See also LEAST; LESS.
Ge 18: 4 a l' water, I pray you, be fetched, 4592
19: 20 near to flee unto, and it is a l' one: 4705
20 escape thither, (is it not a l' one?) "
24: 17 drink a l' water of thy pitcher. 4592
43 a l' water of thy pitcher to drink; "
30: 30 l' which thou hadst before I came, "
34: 29 all their l' ones, and their wives 2945
35: 16 but a l' way to come to Ephrath: *3530
43: 2 them, Go again, buy us a l' food. 4592
8 we, and thou, and also our l' ones. 2945
11 a present, a l' balm, and a l' honey, 4592
44: 20 and a child of his old age, a l' one; 6996
25 Go again, and buy us a l' food. 4592
45: 19 the land of Egypt for your l' ones, 2945
46: 5 and their l' ones, and their wives, "
47: 24 and for food for your l' ones. "
48: 7 a l' way to come unto Ephrath: *3530
50: 8 only their l' ones, and their flocks, 2945
21 will nourish you, and your l' ones. "
Ex 10: 10 I will let you go, and your l' ones: "
24 let your l' ones also go with you. "
12: 4 household be too l' for the lamb, 4591
16: 18 he that gathered l' had no lack; "
23: 30 By l' and l' I will drive them out 4592
Le 11: 17 And the l' owl, and the cormorant, 3563
Nu 14: 31 But your l' ones, which ye said 2945
16: 27 their sons, and their l' children. "
31: 9 Midian captives, and their l' ones, "
17 kill every male among the l' ones, "
32: 16 our cattle, and cities for our l' ones: "
17 our l' ones shall dwell in the fenced "
24 Build you cities for your l' ones, "
26 Our l' ones, our wives, our flocks, "
De 1: 39 your l' ones, which ye said should "
2: 34 the women, and the l' ones, of every "
3: 19 your wives, and your l' ones, and "
7: 22 nations before thee by l' and l': 4592
14: 16 The l' owl, and the great owl, and 3563
20: 14 the women, and the l' ones, and 2945
28: 38 field, and shalt gather but l' in; 4592
29: 11 Your l' ones, your wives, and thy 2945
Jos 1: 14 Your wives, your l' ones, and your "
8: 35 the women, and the l' ones, and the "
19: 47 of Dan went out too l' for them: *
22: 17 Is the iniquity of Peor too l' for us, 4592
J'g 4: 19 I pray thee, a l' water to drink; "
18: 21 put the l' ones and the cattle and 2945
Ru 2: 7 that she tarried a l' in the house. 4592
1Sa 2: 19 his mother made him a l' coat, 6996
14: 29 because I tasted a l' of this honey. 4592
43 I did but taste a l' honey with the "
1Sa 15: 17 thou wast l' in thine own sight, 6996
20: 35 with David, and a l' lad with him. "
2Sa 12: 3 had nothing, save one l' ewe lamb, "
8 and if that had been too l', I would 4592
15: 22 all the l' ones that were with him. 2945
16: 1 was a l' past the top of the hill, 4592
19: 36 servant will go a l' way over Jordan *"
1Ki 3: 7 I am but a l' child: I know not how 6996
8: 64 too l' to receive the burnt offerings, "
11: 17 Egypt; Hadad being yet a l' child. "
12: 10 My l' finger shall be thicker than "
17: 10 Fetch me, I pray thee, a l' water 4592
12 in a barrel, and a l' oil in a cruse: "
13 but make me thereof a l' cake first, 6996
18: 44 ariseth a l' cloud out of the sea, * "
20: 27 them like two l' flocks of kids; 2835
2Ki 2: 23 forth l' children out of the city, ‡6996
4: 10 Let us make a l' chamber, I pray "
5: 2 out of the land of Israel a l' maid; "
14 like unto the flesh of a l' child, and 6995
19 So he departed from him a l' way. 3530
10: 18 unto them, Ahab served Baal a l'; 4592
2Ch 10: 10 My l' finger shall be thicker than 6996
20: 13 before the Lord, with their l' ones, 2945
31: 18 the genealogy of all their l' ones, "
Ezr 8: 21 way for us, and for our l' ones, and "
9: 8 now for a l' space grace hath been 4592
8 give us a l' reviving in our bondage. "
Ne 9: 32 all the trouble seem l' before thee, 4591
Es 3: 13 l' children and women, in one day, 2945
8: 11 them, both l' ones and women, "
Job 4: 12 and mine ear received a l' thereof. *8102
10: 20 alone, that I may take comfort a l', 4592
21: 11 forth their l' ones like a flock, 5759
24: 24 They are exalted for a l' while, 4592
26: 14 how l' a portion is heard of him? *8102
36: 2 Suffer me a l', and I will shew 2191
Ps 2: 12 when his wrath is kindled but a l'. *4592
8: 5 made him a l' lower than the angels, "
37: 10 For yet a l' while, and the wicked "
16 A l' that a righteous man hath is "
65: 12 the l' hills rejoice on every side. *
68: 27 There is l' Benjamin with their 6810
72: 3 and the l' hills, by righteousness. *
114: 4 like rams, and the l' hills like lambs.
6 rams; and ye l' hills, like lambs?
137: 9 dasheth thy l' ones against the 5768
Pr 6: 10 Yet a l' sleep, a l' slumber, 4592
10 a l' folding of the hands to sleep: "
10: 20 the heart of the wicked is l' worth. "
15: 16 is l' with the fear of the Lord, than "
16: 8 Better is a l' with righteousness, "
24: 33 Yet a l' sleep, a l' slumber, "
33 a l' folding of the hands to sleep: "
30: 24 four things which are l' upon the 6996
Ec 5: 12 sweet, whether he eat l' or much: 4592
9: 14 There was a l' city, and few men 6996
10: 1 so doth a l' folly him that is in 4592
Ca 2: 15 Take us the foxes, the l' foxes, 6996
3: 4 but a l' that I passed from them, 4592
8: 8 We have a l' sister, and she hath 6996
Isa 10: 25 For yet a very l' while, and the 4592
11: 6 and a l' child shall lead them. *6995
26: 20 thyself as it were for a l' moment, 4592
28: 10 line; here a l', and there a l': 2191
13 upon line; here a l', and there a l'; "
29: 17 Is it not yet a very l' while, and 4592
40: 15 up the isles as a very l' thing. 1851
54: 8 In a l' wrath I hid my face from 8241
60: 22 A l' one shall become a thousand, 6996
63: 18 have possessed it but a l' while: 4705
Jer 14: 3 sent their l' ones to the waters: 6810
48: 4 her l' ones have caused a cry to be "
51: 33 yet a l' while, and the time of her 4592
Eze 9: 6 maids, and l' children, and women: 2945
11: 16 I be to them as a l' sanctuary in 4592
16: 47 if that were a very l' thing, thou "
31: 4 out her l' rivers unto all the trees *8585
40: 7 every l' chamber was one reed *
7 between the l' chambers were five *
10 And the l' chambers of the gate *
12 space also before the l' chambers *
12 the l' chambers were six cubits on *
13 from the roof of one l' chamber to *
16 narrow windows to the l' chambers, *
21 the l' chambers thereof were three *
29, 33 the l' chambers thereof, and *
36 The l' chambers thereof, the posts *
Da 7: 8 up among them another l' horn, 2192
8: 9 one of them came forth a l' horn, 4704
11: 34 they shall be holpen with a l' help: 4592
Ho 1: 4 for yet a l' while, and I will avenge "
8: 10 shall sorrow a l' for the burden of * "
Am 6: 11 and the l' house with clefts. 6996
Mic 5: 2 thou be l' among the thousands of 6810
Hag 1: 6 have sown much, and bring in l'; 4592
9 for much, and, lo, it came to l'; "
2: 6 Yet once, it is a l' while, and I will "
Zec 1: 15 I was but a l' displeased, and they "
13: 7 turn mine hand upon the l' ones. 6819
M't 6: 30 more clothe you, O ye of l' faith? 3640
8: 26 Why are ye fearful, O ye of l' faith? "
10: 42 to drink unto one of these l' ones 3398
14: 31 O thou of l' faith, wherefore didst 3640
15: 34 they said, Seven, and a few l' fishes. *2485
16: 8 O ye of l' faith, why reason ye 3640
18: 2 Jesus called a l' child unto him, 3813
3 converted, and become as l' children, "
4 humble himself as this l' child, "
5 receive one such l' child in my "
6 shall offend one of these l' ones 3398
10 ye despise not one of these l' ones; "
14 one of these l' ones should perish. "
19: 13 brought unto him l' children, that 3813
14 Jesus said, Suffer l' children, and "
26: 39 went a l' farther, and fell on his 3397
M'k 1: 19 he had gone a l' farther thence, 3641
4: 36 were also with him other l' ships. 4142
5: 23 My l' daughter lieth at the point 2365
9: 42 shall offend one of these l' ones 3398
10: 14 Suffer the l' children to come unto 3813
15 the kingdom of God as a l' child, "
14: 35 And he went forward a l', and fell 3397
70 And a l' after, they that stood by "
Lu 5: 3 would thrust out a l' from the land. 3641
7: 47 l' is forgiven, the same loveth l'. "
12: 28 will he clothe you, O ye of l' faith? 3640
32 Fear not, l' flock; for it is your 3398
17: 2 should offend one of these l' ones. "
18: 16 Suffer l' children to come unto me, 3813
17 the kingdom of God as a l' child "
19: 3 press, because he was l' of stature. 3398
17 thou hast been faithful in a very l', 1646
22: 58 after a l' while another saw him, 1024
Joh 6: 7 every one of them may take a l'. "
7: 33 Yet a l' while am I with you, and 3398
12: 35 Yet a l' while is the light with you. "
13: 33 L' children, yet a...while I am with 5040
33 children, yet a l' while I am with 3397
14: 19 Yet a l' while, and the world seeth "
16: 16 A l' while, and ye shall not see me: "
16 a l' while, and ye shall see me: "
17 A l' while, and ye shall not see me: "
17 a l' while, and ye shall see me: "
18 What is this that he saith, A l' while? "
19 A l' while, and ye shall not see me: "
19 a l' while, and ye shall see me? "
21: 8 other disciples came in a l' ship; 4142
Ac 5: 34 to put the apostles forth a l' space; 1024
20: 12 alive, and were not a l' comforted. 3357
27: 28 when they had gone a l' further, 1024
28: 2 people shewed us no l' kindness: *5177
1Co 5: 6 not that a l' leaven leaveneth the 3398
2Co 8: 15 that had gathered l' had no lack. 3641
11: 1 could bear with me a l' in my folly: 3397
16 me, that I may boast myself a l'. "
Ga 4: 19 My l' children, of whom I travail in 5040
5: 9 A l' leaven leaveneth the whole 3398
1Ti 4: 8 For bodily exercise profiteth l': 3641
5: 23 a l' wine for thy stomach's sake "
Heb 2: 7 him a l' lower than the angels; 1024
9 made a l' lower than the angels for "
10: 37 For yet a l' while, and he that shall 3397
Jas 3: 5 Even so the tongue is a l' member, 3398
5 great a matter a l' fire kindleth! *3641
4: 14 vapour, that appeareth for a l' time, "
1Jo 2: 1 My l' children, these things write 5040
12 I write unto you, l' children, "
13 I write unto you, l' children, 3813
18 L' children, it is the last time: and "
28 And now, l' children, abide in him; 5040
3: 7 L' children, let no man deceive you: "
18 My l' children, let us not love in "
4: 4 Ye are of God, l' children, and have "
5: 21 L' children, keep yourselves from "
Re 3: 8 for thou hast a l' strength, and 3398
6: 11 they should rest yet for a l' season, "
10: 2 he had in his hand a l' book open: 974
8 take the l' book which is open in * "
9 said unto him, Give me the l' book. "
10 the l' book out of the angel's hand, "
20: 3 that he must be loosed a l' season. 3398

little-owl See LITTLE and OWL.

live See also ALIVE; LIVED; LIVES; LIVEST; LIVETH; LIVING.
Ge 3: 22 tree of life, and eat, and l' for ever: 2425
12: 13 my soul shall l' because of thee. 2421
17: 18 unto God, O that Ishmael might l' "
19: 20 not a little one?) and my soul shall l'. "
20: 7 pray for thee, and thou shalt l': "
27: 40 by thy sword shalt thou l', and shalt "
31: 32 thou findest thy gods, let him not l': "
42: 2 for us from thence; that we may l', "
18 them the third day, This do, and l'; "
43: 8 that we may l', and not die, both we, "
45: 3 am Joseph; doth my father yet l'? 2416
47: 19 and give us seed, that we may l', 2421
Ex 1: 16 if it be a daughter, then she shall l'. 2425
19: 13 it be beast or man, it shall not l': 2421
21: 35 they shall sell the l' ox, and divide 2416
22: 18 Thou shalt not suffer a witch to l'. 2421
33: 20 there shall no man see me, and l'. 2425
Le 16: 20 altar, he shall bring the l' goat: 2416
21 hands upon the head of the l' goat, "
18: 5 if a man do, he shall l' in them: 2425
25: 35 that he may l' with thee. 2416
36 that thy brother may l' with thee. "
Nu 4: 19 do unto them, that they may l', 2421
14: 21 But as truly as I l', all the earth 2416
28 As truly as I l', saith the Lord, "
21: 8 when he looketh upon it, shall l'. 2425
24: 23 who shall l' when God doeth this! 2421
De 4: 1 ye may l', and go in and possess "
10 all the days that they shall l' upon 2416
33 the fire, as thou hast heard, and l'? 2421
42 one of these cities he might l': 2425
5: 33 that ye may l', and that it may be 2421
8: 1 to do, that ye may l', and multiply, "
3 that man doth not l' by bread only, "
3 the mouth of the Lord doth man l'. "
12: 1 the days that ye l' upon the earth. 2416
16: 20 that thou mayest l', and inherit 2421
19: 4 shall flee thither, that he may l': 2425
5 flee unto one of those cities, and l': "
30: 6 all thy soul, that thou mayest l'. 2416
16 that thou mayest l' and multiply: 2421
19 that both thou and thy seed may l': "
31: 13 as long as ye l' in the land whither 2416
32: 40 to heaven, and say, I l' for ever. "
33: 6 Let Reuben l', and not die; and let 2421
Jos 6: 17 only Rahab the harlot shall l', she "

Jos 9:15 a league with them, to let them *l*: 2421
20 we will even let them *l*, lest wrath "
21 princes said unto them, Let them *l*;"
1Sa 20:14 not only while yet I *l* shew me the 2416
2Sa 1:10 not *l* after that he was fallen: 2421
12:22 to me, that the child may *l*? 2416
19:34 How long have I to *l*, that I should "
1Ki 1:31 Let my lord king David *l* for ever.2421
8:40 all the days that they *l* in the land2416
20:32 saith, I pray thee, let me *l*. And 2421
2Ki 4: 7 *l* thou and thy children of the rest."
7: 4 if they save us alive, we shall *l*; "
10:19 shall be wanting, he shall not *l*. "
18:32 honey, that ye may *l*, and not die: "
20: 1 order; for thou shalt die, and not *l*."
2Ch 6:31 so long as they *l* in the land which2416
Ne 2: 3 the king, Let the king *l* for ever: 2421
5: 2 for them, that we may eat, and *l*. "
9:29 if a man do, he shall *l* in them;) "
Es 4:11 the golden sceptre, that he may *l*: "
Job 7:16 I loathe it; I would not *l* alway: "
14:14 If a man die, shall he *l* again? "
21: 7 Wherefore do the wicked *l*, become"
27: 6 not reproach me so long as I *l*. 3117
Ps 22:26 him: your heart shall *l* for ever. 2421
49: 9 That he should still *l* for ever, "
55:23 men shall not *l* out half their days; "
63: 4 I bless thee while I *l*: I will lift 2416
69:32 your heart shall *l* that seek God. 2421
72:15 And he shall *l*, and to him shall "
104:33 sing unto the Lord as long as I *l*:2416
116: 2 will I call upon him as long as I *l*.3117
118:17 I shall not die, but *l*, and declare 2421
119:17 that I may *l*, and keep thy word. "
77 mercies come unto me,that I may *l*:"
116 unto thy word, that I may *l*: and "
144 me understanding, and I shall *l*. "
175 Let my soul *l*, and it shall praise "
146: 2 While I *l* will I praise the Lord: 2416
Pr 4: 4 keep my commandments, and *l*. 2421
7: 2 Keep my commandments, and *l*; "
9: 6 Forsake the foolish, and *l*; and go "
15:27 but he that hateth gifts shall *l*. "
Ec 6: 3 children, and *l* many years, so that"
6 Yea, though he *l* a thousand years "
9: 3 is in their heart while they *l*, and 2416
9 *L* joyfully with the wife whom "
11: 8 But if a man *l* many years, and 2421
Isa 6: 6 me, having a *l* coal in his hand, 7531
26:14 They are dead, they shall not *l*; 2421
19 Thy dead men shall *l*, together "
38: 1 for thou shalt die, and not *l*. "
16 O Lord, by these things men *l*, "
16 thou recover me, and make me to *l*."
49:18 As I *l*, saith the Lord, thou shalt 2416
55: 3 hear, and your soul shall *l*; and I 2421
Jer 21: 9 that besiege you, he shall *l*, and "
22:24 As I *l*, saith the Lord, though 2416
27:12 serve him and his people, and *l*. 2421
17 serve the king of Babylon, and *l*: "
35: 7 that ye may *l* many days in the "
38: 2 forth to the Chaldeans shall *l*; "
2 his life for a prey, and shall *l*. 2425
17 princes, then thy soul shall *l*, 2421
17 and thou shalt *l*, and thine house: "
20 unto thee, and thy soul shall *l*. "
46:18 As I *l*, saith the King, whose name 2416
La 4:20 said, Under his shadow we shall *l* 2421
Eze 3:21 he doth not sin, he shall surely *l*, "
5:11 as I *l*, saith the Lord God; Surely,2416
13:19 the souls alive that should not *l*, 2421
14:16 as I *l*, saith the Lord God, they 2416
18, 20 as I *l*, saith the Lord God, "
16: 6 when thou wast in thy blood, *L*; 2421
6 when thou wast in thy blood, *L*. "
48 As I *l*, saith the Lord God, Sodom 2416
17:16 As I *l*, saith the Lord God, surely "
19 As I *l*, surely mine oath that he "
18: 3 As I *l*, saith the Lord God, ye shall "
9 he is just, he shall surely *l*, saith 2421
13 taken increase: shall he then *l*? 2425
13 shall he then...he shall not *l*: 2421
17 of his father, he shall surely *l*. "
19 hath done them, he shall surely *l*. "
21 he shall surely *l*, he shall not die. "
22 that he hath done he shall *l*. "
23 should return from his ways, and *l*?"
24 the wicked man doeth, shall he *l*? 2425
28 he shall surely *l*, he shall not die. 2421
32 wherefore turn yourselves, and *l* ye."
20: 3 As I *l*, saith the Lord God, I will 2416
11 man do, he shall even *l* in them. 2425
13, 21 do, he shall even *l* in them; "
25 whereby they should not *l*; 2421
31 As I *l*, saith the Lord God, I will 2416
33 As I *l*, saith the Lord God, surely "
33:10 in them, how should we then *l*? 2421
11 As I *l*, saith the Lord God, I have 2416
11 wicked turn from his way and *l*: 2421
12 shall the righteous be able to *l* for "
13 righteous, that he shall surely *l*; "
15 he shall surely *l*, he shall not die. "
16 lawful and right; he shall surely *l*."
19 and right, he shall *l* thereby. "
27 As I *l*, surely they that are in the 2416
34: 8 As I *l*, saith the Lord God, surely "
35: 6, 11 as I *l*, saith the Lord God, I will"
37: 3 Son of man, can these bones *l*? 2421
5 to enter into you, and ye shall *l*: "
6 put breath in you, and ye shall *l*; "
9 upon these slain, that they may *l*. "
14 put my spirit in you, and ye shall *l*,"
47: 9 the rivers shall come, shall *l*: "
9 thing shall *l* whither the river 2425
Da 2: 4 in Syriack, O king, *l* for ever: 2418
3: 9 Nebuchadnezzar, O king, *l* for ever."

Da 5:10 spake and said, O king, *l* for ever: 2414
6: 6 unto him, King Darius, *l* for ever. "
21 unto the king, O king, *l* for ever. "
Ho 6: 2 us up, and we shall *l* in his sight. 2421
Am 5: 4 Israel, Seek ye me, and ye shall *l*: "
6 Seek the Lord, and ye shall *l*; lest "
14 good, and not evil, that ye may *l*: "
Jon 4: 3 is better for me to die than to *l*. 2416
8 It is better for me to die than to *l*. "
Hab 2: 4 but the just shall *l* by his faith. 2421
Zep 2: 9 as I *l*, saith the Lord of hosts, 2416
Zec 1: 5 the prophets, do they *l* for ever? 2421
10: 9 they shall *l* with their children, "
13: 3 say unto him, Thou shalt not *l*; "
M't 4: 4 Man shall not *l* by bread alone, *2198*
9:18 thy hand upon her, and she shall *l*. "
M'r 5:23 she may be healed; and she shall *l*."
Lu 4: 4 man shall not *l* by bread alone, but "
7:25 apparelled, and *l* delicately, are *5225*
10:28 right: this do, and thou shalt *l*. *2198*
20:38 of the living: for all *l* unto him. "
Joh 5:25 of God: and they that hear shall *l*. "
6:51 of this bread, he shall *l* for ever: "
57 hath sent me, and I *l* by the Father:"
57 eateth me, even he shall *l* by me. "
58 eateth of this bread shall *l* for ever."
11:25 though he were dead, yet shall he *l*:"
14:19 see me: because I *l*, ye shall *l* also."
Ac 7:19 to the end they might not *l*. *2225*
17:28 For in him we *l*, and move, and *2198*
22:22 for it is not fit that he should *l*. "
25:24 that he ought not to *l* any longer. "
28: 4 yet vengeance suffereth not to *l*. "
Ro 1:17 written, The just shall *l* by faith. "
6: 2 dead to sin, *l* any longer therein? "
8 that we shall also *l* with him: *4800*
8:12 not to the flesh, to *l* after the flesh.*2198*
13 For if ye *l* after the flesh, ye shall "
13 the deeds of the body, ye shall *l*. "
10: 5 doeth those things shall *l* by them."
12:18 in you, *l* peaceably with all men. **1514*
14: 8 whether we *l*, we *l* unto the Lord;*2198*
8 whether we *l* therefore, or die, we "
11 As I *l*, saith the Lord, every knee "
1Co 9:13 holy things *l* of the things of the **2068*
14 the gospel should *l* of the gospel. *2198*
2Co 4:11 For we which *l* are alway delivered "
5:15 he died for all, that they which *l* "
15 not henceforth *l* unto themselves, "
6: 9 as dying, and, behold, we *l*; as "
7: 3 our hearts to die and *l* with you. *4800*
13: 4 we shall *l* with him by the power *2198*
11 be of one mind, and *l* in peace; *1514*
Ga 2:14 the Gentiles to *l* as do the Jews? *2198*
19 the law, that I might *l* unto God. "
20 with Christ: nevertheless I *l*; ‡ "
20 the life which I now *l* in the flesh "
20 I *l* by the faith of the Son of God, "
3:11 for, The just shall *l* by faith. "
12 that doeth them shall *l* in them. "
5:25 If we *l* in the Spirit, let us also walk"
Eph 6: 3 mayest *l* long on the earth. *2071,3118*
Ph'p 1:21 For to me to *l* is Christ, and to *2198*
22 But if I *l* in the flesh, this is the "
1Th 3: 8 For now we *l*, if ye stand fast in the"
5:10 we should *l* together with him. "
2Ti 2:11 with him, we shall also *l* with him:*4800*
3:12 and all that will *l* godly in Christ *2198*
Tit 2:12 we should *l* soberly, righteously. "
Heb 10:38 Now the just shall *l* by faith: but "
12: 9 unto the Father of spirits, and *l*? "
13:18 in all things willing to *l* honestly. *390*
Jas 4:15 If the Lord will, we shall *l*, and *2198*
1Pe 2:24 sins, should *l* unto righteousness: "
4: 2 longer should *l* the rest of his time*980*
6 *l* according to God in the spirit. *2198*
2Pe 2: 6 those that after should *l* ungodly; "
18 escaped from them who *l* in error. *390*
1Jo 4: 9 that we might *l* through him. *2198*
Re 13:14 the wound by a sword, and did *l*.* "

lived See also OUTLIVED; OVERLIVED.
Ge 5: 3 Adam *l* an hundred and thirty 2421
5 And all the days that Adam *l* were2425
6 Seth *l* an hundred and five years, 2421
7 Seth *l* after he begat Enos eight "
9 Enos *l* ninety years, and begat "
10 Enos *l* after he begat Cainan eight "
12 Cainan *l* seventy years, and begat "
13 Cainan *l* after he begat Mahalaleel "
15 Mahalaleel *l* sixty and five years, "
16 Mahalaleel *l* after he begat Jared "
18 Jared *l* an hundred sixty and two "
19 Jared *l* after he begat Enoch eight "
21 Enoch *l* sixty and five years, and "
25 Methuselah *l* an hundred eighty "
26 And Methuselah *l* after he begat "
28 Lamech *l* an hundred eighty and "
30 Lamech *l* after he begat Noah five "
9:28 And Noah *l* after the flood three "
11:11 Shem *l* after he begat Arphaxad "
12 Arphaxad *l* five and thirty years, 2425
13 Arphaxad *l* after he begat Salah 2421
14 Salah *l* thirty years, and begat 2425
15 Salah *l* after he begat Eber four 2421
16 Eber *l* four and thirty years, and "
17 Eber *l* after he begat Peleg four "
18 Peleg *l* thirty years, and begat "
19 Peleg *l* after he begat Reu two "
20 Reu *l* two and thirty years, and "
21 Reu *l* after he begat Serug two "
22 Serug *l* thirty years, and begat "
23 Serug *l* after he begat Nahor two "
24 Nahor *l* nine and twenty years, and"
25 Nahor *l* after he begat Terah an "
26 Terah *l* seventy years, and begat "
25: 6 Isaac his son, while he yet *l*. 2416

Ge 25: 7 of Abraham's life which he *l*, 2425
47:28 And Jacob *l* in the land of Egypt 2421
50:22 Joseph *l* an hundred and ten years."
Nu 14:38 went to search the land, *l* still. * "
21: 9 beheld the serpent of brass, he *l*. 2425
De 5:26 of the fire, as we have, and *l*? 2421
2Sa 19: 6 I perceive, that if Absalom had *l*, 2416
1Ki 12: 6 Solomon his father while he yet *l*, "
2Ki 14:17 the son of Joash king of Judah *l* 2421
2Ch 10: 6 Solomon his father while he yet *l*,2416
25:25 the son of Joash king of Judah *l* 2421
Job 42:16 After this *l* Job an hundred and "
Ps 49:18 while he *l* he blessed his soul: 2416
Eze 37:10 breath came into them, and they *l*,2421
Lu 2:36 and had *l* with an husband seven *2198*
Ac 23: 1 I have *l* in all good conscience *4176*
26: 5 sect of our religion I *l* a Pharisee.*2198*
Col 3: 7 some time, when ye *l* in them. "
Jas 5: 5 have *l* in pleasure on the earth, *5171*
Re 18: 7 glorified herself, and *l* deliciously,*
9 and *l* deliciously with her, shall "
20: 4 they *l* and reigned with Christ a *2198*
5 rest of the dead *l* not again until *326*

lively
Ex 1:19 for they are *l*, and are delivered 2422
Ps 38:19 But mine enemies are *l*, and they 2416
Ac 7:38 the *l* oracles to give unto us: **2198*
1Pe 1: 3 begotten us again unto a *l* hope * "
2: 5 as *l* stones, are built up a spiritual*"

liver
Ex 29:13 the caul that is above the *l*, and 3516
22 the caul above the *l*, and the two "
Le 3: 4, 10, 15 the caul above the *l*, with "
4: 9 and the caul above the *l*, with the "
7: 4 the caul that is above the *l*, with "
8:16, 25 the caul above the *l*, and the "
9:10 caul above the *l* of the sin offering, "
19 kidneys, and the caul above the *l*: "
Pr 7:23 Till a dart strike through his *l*; "
La 2:11 my *l* is poured upon the earth, "
Eze 21:21 with images, he looked in the *l*. "

lives
Ge 9: 5 your blood of your *l* will I require;5315
45: 7 save your *l* by a great deliverance.2421
47:25 they said, Thou hast saved our *l*: "
Ex 1:14 their *l* bitter with hard bondage, 2416
Jos 2:13 and deliver our *l* from death. 5315
9:24 were sore afraid of our *l* because "
J'g 5:18 a people that jeoparded their *l* "
18:25 life, with the *l* of thy household. "
2Sa 1:23 lovely and pleasant in their *l*, 2416
19: 5 and the *l* of thy sons and of thy 5315
5 *l* of thy wives, and the *l* of thy "
23:17 that went in jeopardy of their *l*? "
1Ch 11:19 that have put their *l* in jeopardy? "
19 jeopardy of their *l* they brought it. "
Es 9:16 together, and stood for their *l*, "
Pr 1:18 they lurk privily for their own *l*. "
Jer 19: 7 hands of them that seek their *l*: * "
9 they that seek their *l*, shall straiten*"
46:26 hand of those that seek their *l*, "
48: 6 Flee, save your *l*, and be like the "
La 5: 9 our bread with the peril of our *l* "
Da 7:12 yet their *l* were prolonged for a 2417
Lu 9:56 is not come to destroy men's *l*, **5590*
Ac 15:26 Men that have hazarded their *l* "
27:10 lading and ship, but also of our *l*. "
1Jo 3:16 to lay down our *l* for the brethren. "
Re 12:11 loved not their *l* unto the death. * "

livest
De 12:19 as long as thou *l* upon the earth. 3117
2Sa 11:11 as thou *l*, and as thy soul liveth, 2416
Ga 2:14 *l* after the manner of Gentiles, *2198*
Re 3: 1 name that thou *l*, and art dead. "

liveth
Ge 9: 3 Every moving thing that *l* shall 2416
De 5:24 God doth talk with man, and he *l*.2425
J'g 8:19 as the Lord *l*, if ye had saved 2416
Ru 3:13 a kinsman to thee, as I the Lord *l*: "
1Sa 1:26 she said, Oh my Lord, as thy soul *l*,"
28 as long as he *l* he shall be lent to 3117
14:39 For, as the Lord *l*, which saveth 2416
45 as the Lord *l*, there shall not one "
17:55 Abner said, As thy soul *l*, O king, "
19: 6 Saul sware, As the Lord *l*, he shall "
20: 3 as the Lord *l*, and as thy soul *l*, "
21 thee, and no hurt; as the Lord *l*. "
31 long as the son of Jesse *l* upon the2425
25: 6 ye say to him that *l* in prosperity,2416
26 as the Lord *l*, and as thy soul *l*. "
34 as the Lord God of Israel *l*, which "
26:10 As the Lord *l*, the Lord shall smite "
16 As the Lord *l*, ye are worthy to die, "
28:10 saying, As the Lord *l*, there shall no "
29: 6 unto him, Surely, as the Lord *l*, "
2Sa 2:27 Joab said, As God *l*, unless thou "
4: 9 and said unto them, As the Lord *l*, "
11:11 thy soul *l*, I will not do this thing. "
12: 5 said to Nathan, As the Lord *l*, the "
14:11 As the Lord *l*, there shall not one "
19 answered and said, As thy soul *l*, "
15:21 the king, and said, As the Lord *l*, "
21 and as my lord the king *l*, surely "
22:47 The Lord *l*; and blessed be my "
1Ki 1:29 king sware, and said, As the Lord *l*,"
2:24 Now therefore, as the Lord *l*, which"
3:23 This is my son that *l*, and thy son "
17: 1 Ahab, As the Lord God of Israel *l*, "
12 she said, As the Lord thy God *l*, "
23 and Elijah said, See, thy son *l*. "
18:10 As the Lord thy God *l*, there is no "
15 Elijah said, As the Lord of hosts *l*, "
22:14 Micaiah said, As the Lord *l*, what "
2Ki 2: 2, 4, 6 the Lord *l*, and as thy soul *l*, "
3:14 Elisha said, As the Lord of hosts *l*, "

2Ki 4:30 As the Lord l', and as thy soul l', I 2416
5:16 But he said, As the Lord l', before "
20 As the Lord l', I will run after him, "
2Ch 18:13 Micaiah said, As the Lord l', even "
Job 19:25 For I know that my redeemer l', "
27: 2 As God l', who hath taken away my "
Ps 18:46 The Lord l'; and blessed be my "
89:48 What man is he that l', and shall 2421
Jer 4: 2 The Lord l', in truth, in judgment, 2416
5: 2 And though they say, The Lord l'; "
12:16 to swear by my name, The Lord l', "
16:14 shall no more be said, The Lord l', "
15 The Lord l', that brought up the "
23: 7 they shall no more say, The Lord l'," "
8 But, The Lord l', which brought up "
38:16 As the Lord l', that made us this "
44:26 of Egypt, saying, The Lord God l'. "
Eze 47: 9 pass, that every thing that l', which "
Da 4:34 and honoured him that l' for ever, "
12: 7 sware by him that l' for ever that it "
Ho 4:15 Beth-aven, nor swear, The Lord l'. "
Am 8:14 and say, Thy god, O Dan, l'; and "
14 The manner of Beer-sheba l'; even "
Joh 4:50 unto him, Go thy way; thy son l'. *2198*
51 and told him, saying, Thy son l'. "
53 Jesus said unto him, Thy son l': "
11:26 whosoever l' and believeth in me, "
Ro 6:10 but in that he l', he l' unto God. "
7: 1 over a man as long as he l'? "
2 law to her husband so long as he l';" "
3 So then if, while her husband l', she" "
14: 7 For none of us l' to himself, and no "
1Co 7:39 the law as long as her husband l'; "
2Co 13: 4 yet he l' by the power of God. For "
Ga 2:20 live; yet not I, but Christ l' in me: "
1Ti 5: 6 l' in pleasure is dead while she l'. "
Heb 7: 8 of whom it is witnessed that he l'. "
25 he ever l' to make intercession "
9:17 strength at all while the testator l'. "
1Pe 1:23 by the word of God, which l' and "
Re 1:18 I am he that l', and was dead; and,*"
4: 9 the throne, who l' for ever and ever," "
10 him that l' for ever and ever, "
5:14 him that l' for ever and ever. "
10: 6 by him that l' for ever and ever, "
15: 7 wrath of God, who l' for ever and "

living See also QUICK.
Ge 1:21 and every l' creature that moveth, 2416
24 bring forth the l' creature after his "
28 over every l' thing that moveth "
2: 7 of life; and man became a l' soul. "
19 Adam called every l' creature, "
3:20 because she was the mother of all l'. "
6:19 of every l' thing of all flesh, two of "
7: 4 and every l' substance that I have "
23 And every l' substance was destroyed "
8: 1 Noah, and every l' thing, and all 2416
17 every l' thing that is with thee, "
21 again smite any more every thing l'," "
9:10 with every l' creature that is with "
12 and every l' creature that is with you, "
15 and every l' creature of all flesh; "
16 and every l' creature of all flesh "
Le 11:10 any l' thing which is in the waters, "
46 every l' creature that moveth in the" "
14: 6 As for the l' bird, he shall take it, "
6 the l' bird in the blood of the bird "
7 the l' bird loose into the open field. "
51 and the l' bird, and dip them in the "
52 running water, and with the l' bird, "
53 shall let go the l' bird out of the city" "
20:25 any manner of l' thing that creepeth*
Nu 16:48 stood between the dead and the l'; 2416
De 5:26 hath heard the voice of the l' God "
Jos 3:10 know that the l' God is among you, "
Ru 2:20 not left off his kindness to the l' "
1Sa 17:26 defy the armies of the l' God? "
36 defied the armies of the l' God. "
2Sa 20: 3 of their death, l' in widowhood. 2424
1Ki 3:22 said, Nay; but the l' is my son, 2416
22 is thy son, and the l' is my son. "
23 is the dead, and my son is the l'. "
25 king said, Divide the l' child in two," "
26 the woman whose the l' child was "
26 said, O my lord, give her the l' child, "
27 and said, Give her the l' child, "
2Ki 19: 4 hath sent to reproach the l' God; "
16 sent him to reproach the l' God. "
Job 12:10 hand is the soul of every l' thing, "
28:13 is it found in the land of the l'. "
21 it is hid from the eyes of all l', and "
30:23 to the house appointed for all l'. "
33:30 enlightened with the light of the l'. "
Ps 27:13 of the Lord in the land of the l'. "
42: 2 thirsteth for God, for the l' God: "
52: 5 root thee out of the land of the l'. "
56:13 walk before God in the light of the l'?" "
58: 9 both l', and in his wrath. * "
69:28 be blotted out of the book of the l',* "
84: 2 my flesh crieth out for the l' God. "
116: 9 before the Lord in the land of the l'." "
142: 5 and my portion in the land of the l'." "
143: 2 sight shall no man l' be justified. "
145:16 satisfiest the desire of every l' thing." "
Ec 4: 2 than the l' which are yet alive. "
15 I considered all the l' which walk "
6: 8 that knoweth to walk before the l'? "
7: 2 and the l' will lay it to his heart. "
9: 4 For to him that is joined to all the l'" "
4 a l' dog is better than a dead lion. "
5 For the l' know that they shall die: "
Ca 4:15 of gardens, a well of l' waters, "
Isa 4: 3 written among the l' in Jerusalem: "
8:19 their God? for the l' to the dead? "
37: 4 hath sent to reproach the l' God, "
17 hath sent to reproach the l' God. "

Isa 38:11 even the Lord, in the land of the l': 2416
19 The l', the l', he shall praise thee, "
53: 8 was cut off out of the land of the l': "
Jer 2:13 me the fountain of l' waters, "
10:10 is the true God, he is the l' God, "
11:19 cut him off from the land of the l', "
17:13 the Lord, the fountain of l' waters. "
23:36 perverted the words of the l' God, "
La 3:39 Wherefore doth a l' man complain, "
Eze 1: 5 the likeness of four l' creatures. "
13 for the likeness of the l' creatures, "
13 and down among the l' creatures; "
14 the l' creatures ran and returned "
15 as I beheld the l' creatures, behold "
15 upon the earth by the l' creatures, "
19 And when the l' creatures went, the "
19 when the l' creatures were lifted up" "
20, 21 spirit of the l' creature was in "
22 upon the heads of the l' creature "
3:13 of the wings of the l' creatures that" "
10:15 This is the l' creature that I saw by" "
17 the spirit of the l' creature was in "
20 This is the l' creature that I saw "
26:20 shall set glory in the land of the l'; "
32:23 caused terror in the land of the l'. "
24 their terror in the land of the l'; "
25 was caused in the land of the l', "
26 their terror in the land of the l'. "
27 of the mighty in the land of the l'. "
32 my terror in the land of the l': "
Da 2:30 that I have more than any l', 2417
4:17 l' may know that the most High "
6:20 Daniel, servant of the l' God, is thy "
26 God of Daniel: for he is the l' God, "
Ho 1:10 them, Ye are the sons of the l' God. 2416
Zec 14: 8 that l' waters shall go out from "
M't 16:16 the Christ, the Son of the l' God. *2198*
22:32 not the God of the dead, but of the l'." "
26:63 him, I adjure thee by the l' God, "
M'r 12:27 of the dead, but the God of the l': "
44 in all that she had, even all her l'. *979*
Lu 8:43 had spent all her l' upon physicians, "
15:12 And he divided unto them his l'. "
13 his substance with riotous l'. *2198*
30 hath devoured thy l' with harlots, *979*
20:38 not a God of the dead, but of the l': *2198*
21: 4 hath cast in all the l' that she had. *979*
24: 5 seek ye the l' among the dead? *2198*
Joh 4:10 he would have given thee l' water. "
11 then hast thou that l' water? "
6:51 I am the l' bread which came down" "
57 As the l' Father hath sent me, and "
69 that Christ, the Son of the l' God. * "
7:38 belly shall flow rivers of l' water. "
Ac 14:15 from these vanities unto the l' God," "
Ro 9:26 be called the children of the l' God." "
12: 1 present your bodies a l' sacrifice, "
14: 9 be Lord both of the dead and l'. "
1Co 15:45 first man Adam was made a l' soul; "
2Co 3: 3 but with the Spirit of the l' God; "
6:16 for ye are the temple of the l' God; "
Col 2:20 why, as though l' in the world, are "
1Th 1: 9 idols to serve the l' and true God; "
1Ti 3:15 which is the church of the l' God, "
4:10 because we trust in the l' God, who "
6:17 uncertain riches, but in the l' God,* "
Tit 3: 3 pleasures, l' in malice and envy, *1236*
Heb 3:12 in departing from the l' God. *2198*
9:14 dead works to serve the l' God? "
10:20 By a new and l' way, which he hath" "
31 to fall into the hands of the l' God. "
12:22 and unto the city of the l' God, "
1Pe 2: 4 whom coming, as unto a l' stone, "
Re 7: 2 east, having the seal of the l' God: "
17 them unto l' fountains of waters: * "
16: 3 and every l' soul died in the sea. "

lizard
Le 11:30 and the chameleon, and the l', 3911

lo
Ge 8:11 l', in her mouth was an olive leaf 2009
15: 3 l', one born in my house is mine "
12 l', an horror of great darkness fell "
18: 2 l', three men stood by him: and "
10 l', Sarah thy wife shall have a son. "
19:28 l', the smoke of the country went "
29: 2 l', there were three flocks of sheep "
7 And he said, L', it is yet high day. 2005
37: 7 l', my sheaf arose, and also stood 2009
42:28 l', it is even in my sack: and their "
47:23 l', here is seed for you, and ye 1883
48:11 l', God hath shewed me also thy 2009
50: 5 made me swear, saying, L', I die: "
Ex 8:20 l', he cometh forth to the water; "
26 l',...we sacrifice the abomination 2005
19: 9 L', I come unto thee in a thick 2009
Nu 14:40 L', we be here, and will go up unto "
22:38 Balak, L', I am come unto thee: "
23: 6 l', he stood by his burnt sacrifice, "
9 l', the people shall dwell alone, 2005
24:11 l', the Lord hath kept thee back 2009
De 22:17 l', he hath given occasions of speech" "
Jos 14:10 l', I am this day fourscore and five "
J'g 7:13 l', a cake of barley bread tumbled "
13: 5 l', thou shalt conceive, and bear a "
1Sa 4:13 l', Eli sat upon a seat by the wayside" "
10: 2 l', thy father hath left the care of "
14:43 in mine hand, and, l', I must die. 2114
21:14 L', ye see the man is mad: 2009
2Sa 1: 6 and, l', the chariots and horsemen "
15:24 l' Zadok also, and all the Levites "
1Ki 1:22 l', while she yet talked with the "
51 l', he hath caught hold on the horns" "
3:12 l', I have given thee a wise and an "
1Ch 21:23 l', I give thee the oxen also for 7200
2Ch 16:11 l', they are written in the book of 2009

2Ch 25:19 L', thou hast smitten the Edomites; 2009
27: 7 l', they are written in the book of *2005
29: 9 l', our fathers have fallen by the 2009
Ne 5: 5 l', we bring into bondage our sons "
6:12 l', I perceived that God had not "
Job 3: 7 L', let that night be solitary, let no "
5:27 L' this, we have searched it, so it "
9:11 L', he goeth by me, and I see him 2005
19 speak of strength, l', he is strong: 2009
13: 1 L', mine eye hath seen all this, 2005
21:16 L', their good is not in their hand: "
26:14 L', these are parts of his ways: but "
33:29 L', all these things worketh God "
40:16 L' now, his strength is in his loins, 2009
Ps 11: 2 For, l', the wicked bend their bow, "
37:36 passed away, and, l', he was not: "
40: 7 Then said I, L', I come: in the "
9 l', I have not refrained my lips, O "
48: 4 For, l', the kings were assembled, "
52: 7 L', this is the man that made not "
55: 7 L', then would I wander far off, "
59: 3 For, l', they lie in wait for my soul: "
68:33 l', he doth send out his voice, and 2005
73:27 l', they that are far from thee shall "
83: 2 l', thine enemies make a tumult: 2009
92: 9 For, l', thine enemies, O Lord, "
9 for, l', thine enemies shall perish; "
127: 3 L', children are an heritage of the "
132: 6 L', we heard of it at Ephratah: we "
139: 4 but, l', O Lord, thou knowest it 2005
Pr 24:31 And, l', it was all grown over with 2009
Ec 1:16 L', I am come to great estate, and "
7:29 L', this only have I found, that *7200
Ca 2:11 l', the winter is past, the rain is 2009
Isa 6: 7 said, L', this hath touched thy lips;" "
25: 9 said in that day, L', this is our God;" "
36: 6 L', thou trustest in the staff of this*" "
49:12 l', these from the north and from "
50: 9 l', they all shall wax old as a *2005
Jer 1:15 l', I will call all the families of the 2009
4:23 earth, and, l', it was without form, "
24 mountains, and, l', they trembled, "
25 I beheld, and, l', there was no man, "
26 I beheld, and, l', the fruitful place "
5:15 L', I will bring a nation upon you "
8: 8 L', certainly in vain made he it; * "
9 l', they have rejected the word of "
25:29 l', I begin to bring evil on the city "
30: 3 l', the days come, saith the Lord, "
10 l', I will save thee from afar, and "
36:12 l', all the princes sat there, even "
49:15 l', I will make thee small among * "
50: 9 l', I will raise and cause to come up" "
Eze 2: 9 and, l', a roll of a book was therein; "
4:15 L', I have given thee cow's dung 7200
8: 2 l' a likeness as the appearance of 2009
17 l', they put the branch to their nose." "
13:10 l', others daubed it with...morter:* "
12 L', when the wall is fallen, shall it "
17:18 when, l', he had given his hand, * "
18:14 l', if he beget a son, that seeth all "
18 l', even he shall die in his iniquity.*" "
23:39 l', thus have they done in the midst" "
40 was sent; and, l', they came: "
30: 9 the day of Egypt: for, l', it cometh." "
21 l', it shall not be bound up to be "
33:32 l', thou art unto them as a very "
37: 2 valley; and, l', they were very dry. "
8 l', the sinews and the flesh came "
40:17 and, l', there were chambers, and a "
42: 8 and, l', before the temple were an "
Da 3:25 L', I see four men loose, walking 1888
7: 6 and l' another, like a leopard, 718
10:13 but, l', Michael, one of the chief 2009
20 l', the prince of Grecia shall come. "
Ho 9: 6 For, l', they are gone because of "
Am 4: 2 l', the days shall come upon you, "
13 l', he that formeth the mountains, "
7: 1 l', it was the latter growth after the" "
9: 9 l', I will command, and I will sift "
Hab 1: 6 l', I raise up the Chaldeans, that "
Hag 1: 9 for much, and, l', it came to little; "
Zec 2:10 l', I come, and I will dwell in the "
11: 6 l', I will deliver the men every one "
16 l', I will raise up a shepherd in the "
M't 2: 9 l', the star, which they saw in the *2400*
3:16 l', the heavens were opened unto "
17 And l' a voice from heaven, saying," "
24:23 L', here is Christ, or there; believe "
25:25 l', there thou hast that is thine. *2396*
26:47 l', Judas, one of the twelve, came, *2400*
28: 7 ye see him: l', I have told you. "
20 l', I am with you alway, even unto "
M'r 10:28 say unto him, L', we have left all, "
13:21 L', here is Christ; or, l', he is there;" "
14:42 l', he that betrayeth me is at hand.*" "
Lu 1:44 For, l', as soon as the voice of thy* "
2: 9 l', the angel of the Lord came upon*" "
9:39 And, l', a spirit taketh him, and he*" "
13:16 l', these eighteen years, be loosed "
15:29 L', these many years do I serve thee," "
17:21 shall they say, L', here! or,...there!" "
21 here! or, l' there! for, behold, * "
18:28 Peter said, L', we have left all, and "
23:15 l', nothing worthy of death is done*" "
Joh 7:26 But, l', he speaketh boldly, and *2396*
16:29 him, L', now speakest thou plainly, "
Ac 13:46 life, l', we turn to the Gentiles. *2400*
27:24 l', God hath given thee all them "
Heb 10: 7 L', I come (in the volume of the "
9 L', I come to do thy will, O God. "
Re 5: 6 l', in the midst of the throne and * "
6: 5 And I beheld, and l' a black horse;*" "
12 l', there was a great earthquake; * "
7: 9 l', a great multitude, which no man*" "
14: 1 l', a Lamb stood on the mount Sion.*"

Lo See Lo-ammi; Lo-debar; Lo-ruhamah.
loaden See also laden.
Isa 46: 1 your carriages were heavy l'; *6006
loadeth See also ladeth.
Ps 68:19 who daily l' us with benefits: *6006
loaf See also loaves.
Ex 29:23 And one l' of bread, and one cake 3603
1Ch 16: 3 to every one a l' of bread, and a "
M'r 8:14 ship with them more than one l'. 740
Lo-ammi (lo-am'-mi).
Ho 1: 9 Then said God, Call his name L': 3818
loan
1Sa 2:20 the l' which is lent to the Lord. ‡7596
loathe See also loatheth; loathsome; lothe.
Job 7:16 I l' it; I would not live alway: let 3988
loatheth See also lotheth.
Nu 21: 5 and our soul l' this light bread. 6973
Pr 27: 7 The full soul l' an honeycomb; but 947
loathsome
Nu 11:20 nostrils, and it be l' unto you: 2214
Job 7: 5 my skin is broken, and become l'.*3988
Ps 38: 7 loins are filled with a l' disease: *7033
Pr 13: 5 a wicked man is l', and cometh to 887
loaves
Le 23:17 two wave l' of two tenth deals: 3899
J'g 8: 5 l' of bread unto the people that 3603
1Sa 10: 3 another carrying three l' of bread, "
4 thee, and give thee two l' of bread; "
17:17 this parched corn, and these ten l',3899
21: 3 give me five l' of bread in mine hand,
25:18 haste, and took two hundred l', 3899
2Sa 16: 1 upon them two hundred l' of bread,
1Ki 14: 3 take with thee ten l', and cracknels,3899
2Ki 4:42 the firstfruits, twenty l' of barley,
M't 14:17 We have here but five l', and two 740
19 took the five l', and the two fishes,
19 and gave the l' to his disciples, and "
15:34 unto them, How many l' have ye? "
36 he took the seven l' and the fishes, "
16: 9 remember the five l' of the five "
10 Neither the seven l' of the four "
M'r 6:38 unto them, How many l' have ye? "
41 when he had taken the five l' and "
41 and blessed, and brake the l', and "
44 they that did eat of the l' were about"
52 not the miracle of the l': considered "
8: 5 asked them, How many l' have ye? "
6 took the seven l', and gave thanks, "
19 When I brake the five l' among five "
Lu 9:13 We have no more but five l' and two "
16 Then he took the five l' and the two "
11: 5 unto him, Friend, lend me three l'; "
Joh 6: 9 lad here, which hath five barley l', "
11 Jesus took the l'; and when he had "
13 the fragments of the five barley l', "
26 but because ye did eat of the l', and "
lock See also locked; locks; wedlock.
Ca 5: 5 myrrh, upon the handles of the l'. 4514
Eze 8: 3 and took me by a l' of mine head; 6734
locked
J'g 3:23 the parlour upon him, and l' them. 5274
24 the doors of the parlour were l', "
locks
Nu 6: 5 the l' of the hair of his head grow. 6545
J'g 16:13 weavest the seven l' of my head 4253
19 to shave off the seven l' of his head;"
Ne 3: 3, 6, 13, 14, 15 thereof, the l' thereof, *4514
Ca 4: 1 thou hast doves' eyes within thy l':*6777
3 of a pomegranate within thy l'. * "
5: 2 my l' with the drops of the night. 6977
11 his l' are bushy, and black as a "
6: 7 are thy temples within thy l'. *6777
Isa 47: 2 uncover thy l', make bare the leg,* "
Eze 44:20 nor suffer their l' to grow long; 6545
locust See also locusts.
Ex 10:19 not one l' in all the coasts of Egypt.697
Le 11:22 ye may eat; the l' after his kind,
22 and the bald l' after his kind, and 5556
De 28:38 little in; for the l' shall consume it.697
42 of thy land shall the l' consume. 6767
1Ki 8:37 pestilence, blasting, mildew, l', 697
Ps 78:46 and their labour unto the l'. "
109:23 I am tossed up and down as the l'. "
Joe 1: 4 hath left hath the l' eaten; and "
4 that which the l' hath left hath the "
2:25 you the years that the l' hath eaten, "
locusts
Ex 10: 4 will I bring the l' into thy coast: 697
12 over the land of Egypt for the l', "
13 the east wind brought the l'. "
14 the l' went up over all the land of "
14 them there were no such l' as they, "
19 westwind, which took away the l', "
2Ch 6:28 there be blasting, or mildew, l', or* "
7:13 command the l' to devour the land.*2284
Ps 105:34 He spake, and the l' came, and 697
Pr 30:27 The l' have no king, yet go they "
Isa 33: 4 as the running to and fro of l' shall 1357
Na 3:15 make thyself many as the l'. * 697
17 Thy crowned are as the l', and thy "
M't 3: 4 his meat was l' and wild honey. 200
M'r 1: 6 and he did eat l' and wild honey; "
Re 9: 3 there came out of the smoke l' upon "
7 of the l' were like unto horses "
Lod (lod) See also Lydda.
1Ch 8:12 Shamed, who built Ono, and L', 3850
Ezr 2:33 The children of L', Hadid, and Ono, "
Ne 7:37 The children of L', Hadid, and Ono, "
11:35 L', and Ono, the valley of craftsmen. "

Lo-debar (lo-de'-bar)
2Sa 9: 4, 5 Machir, the son of Ammiel, in L'.3810
17:27 Machir the son of Ammiel of L', "
lodge See also lodged; lodgest; lodgeth; lodging.
Ge 24:23 thy father's house for us to l' in? 3885
25 and provender...and room to l' in. "
Nu 22: 8 L' here this night, and I will bring "
Jos 4: 3 place, where ye shall l' this night. "
J'g 19: 9 the day groweth to an end, l' here, "
11 city of the Jebusites, and l' in it. "
13 one of these places to l' all night, "
15 to go in and to l' in Gibeah: "
20 upon me; only l' not in the street. "
20: 4 Benjamin, I and my concubine, to l'. "
Ru 1:16 and where thou lodgest, I will l': "
2Sa 17: 8 war, and will not l' with the people. "
16 L' not this night in the plains of "
Ne 4:22 Let every one with his servant l' "
13:21 unto them, Why l' ye about the wall?"
Job 24: 7 the naked to l' without clothing, * "
31:32 stranger did not l' in the street: "
Ca 7:11 the field; let us l' in the villages. "
Isa 1: 8 as a l' in a garden of cucumbers, 4412
21:13 In the forest in Arabia shall ye l', 3885
65: 4 graves, and l' in the monuments, "
Jer 4:14 How long shall thy vain thoughts l' "
Zep 2:14 bittern shall l' in the upper lintels "
M't 13:32 and l' in the branches thereof. 2681
M'r 4:32 of the air may l' under the shadow "
Lu 9:12 and country round about, and l', 2647
Ac 21:16 disciple, with whom we should l'. 3579
lodged
Ge 32:13 And he l' there that same night; 3885
21 himself l' that night in the company. "
Jos 2: 1 house, named Rahab, and l' there.*7901
3: 1 l' there before they passed over. 3885
4: 8 them unto the place where they l',4411
6:11 into the camp, and l' in the camp. 3885
8: 9 Joshua l' that night among the "
J'g 18: 2 the house of Micah, they l' there. "
19: 4 they did eat and drink, and l' there. "
7 him: therefore he l' there again. "
1Ki 19: 9 thither unto a cave, and l' there; "
1Ch 9:27 l' round about the house of God, "
Ne 13:20 sellers of all kind of ware l' without"
Isa 1:21 Judgment; righteousness l' in it; "
M't 21:17 city into Bethany; and he l' there. 835
Lu 13:19 fowls of the air l' in the branches 2681
Ac 10:18 was surnamed Peter, were l' there.*3579
23 Then called he them in, and l' them. "
32 he is l' in the house of one Simon * "
28: 7 and l' us three days courteously. "
1Ti 5:10 children, if she have l' strangers. 3580
lodgest
Ru 1:16 and where thou l', I will lodge: 3885
lodgeth
Ac 10: 6 He l' with one Simon a tanner, 3579
lodging See also lodgings.
Jos 4: 3 and leave them in the l' place, 4411
J'g 19:15 that took them into his house to l'.*3885
Isa 10:29 have taken up there l' at Geba; 4411
Jer 9: 2 I had in the wilderness a l' place "
Ac 28:23 there came many to him into his l'; 3578
Ph'm 22 But withal prepare me also a l': "
lodgings
2Ki 19:23 enter into the l' of his borders, *4411
loft
1Ki 17:19 carried him up into a l', where he*5944
loftily
Ps 73: 8 oppression: they speak l'. 4791
loftiness
Isa 2:17 the l' of man shall be bowed down,1365
Jer 48:29 his l', and his arrogancy, and his 1363
lofty
Ps 131: 1 is not haughty, nor mine eyes l': 7311
Pr 30:13 generation, O how l' are their eyes! "
Isa 2:11 l' looks of man shall be humbled, 1365
12 every one that is proud and l', *7311
5:15 eyes of the l' shall be humbled: 1364
26: 5 high; the l' city, he layeth it low; 7682
57: 7 Upon a l' and high mountain hast*1364
15 l' One that inhabiteth eternity, 5375
log
Le 14:10 mingled with oil, and one l' of oil. 3849
12 trespass offering, and the l' of oil, "
15 priest shall take some of the l' of oil, "
21 for a meat offering, and a l' of oil; "
24 trespass offering, and the l' of oil, "
loins
Ge 35:11 and kings shall come out of thy l'; 2504
37:34 and put sackcloth upon his l', 4975
46:26 which came out of his l', besides 3409
Ex 1: 5 souls that came out of the l' of Jacob "
12:11 with your l' girded, your shoes on 4975
28:42 from the l' even unto the thighs "
De 33:11 smite through the l' of them that "
2Sa 20: 8 with a sword fastened upon his l' "
1Ki 2: 5 his girdle that was about his l', "
8:19 that shall come forth out of thy l', 2504
12:10 be thicker than my father's l'. 4975
18:46 and he girded up his l', and ran "
20:31 put sackcloth on our l', and ropes "
32 So they girded sackcloth on their l',"
2Ki 1: 8 with a girdle of leather about his l'."
4:29 Gird up thy l', and take my staff in "
9: 1 Gird up thy l', and take this box of "
2Ch 6: 9 shall come forth out of thy l', 2504
10:10 be thicker than my father's l'. 4975
Job 12:18 and girdeth their l' with a girdle. "
31:20 If his l' have not blessed me, and 2504

Job 38: 3 Gird up now thy l' like a man; for 2504
40: 7 Gird up thy l' now like a man: I "
16 his strength is in his l', and his 4975
Ps 38: 7 my l' are filled with a loathsome 3689
66:11 thou laidst affliction upon our l'. 4975
69:23 make their l' continually to shake. "
Pr 31:17 She girdeth her l' with strength, "
Isa 5:27 the girdle of their l' be loosed, 2504
11: 5 righteousness...the girdle of his l',4975
20: 2 loose the sackcloth from off thy l', "
21: 3 Therefore are my l' filled with pain:"
32:11 and gird sackcloth upon your l'. 2504
45: 1 I will loose the l' of kings, to open 4975
Jer 1:17 Thou therefore gird up thy l', and "
13: 1 linen girdle, and put it upon thy l', "
2 of the Lord, and put it on my l'. "
4 thou hast got, which is upon thy l', "
11 as the girdle cleaveth to the l' of a "
30: 6 every man with his hands on his l',2504
48:37 cuttings, and upon the l' sackcloth.4975
Eze 1:27 appearance of his l' even upward, "
27 appearance of his l' even downward,"
8: 2 appearance of his l' even upward, "
2 and from his l' even upward, as the "
21: 6 of man, with the breaking of thy l'; "
23:15 Girded with girdles upon their l', "
29: 7 madest all their l' to be at a stand. "
44:18 have linen breeches upon their l'; "
47: 4 through; the waters were to the l'. "
Da 5: 6 the joints of his l' were loosed, 2783
10: 5 l' were girded with fine gold of 4975
Am 8:10 will bring up sackcloth upon all l', "
Na 2: 1 watch the way, make thy l' strong, "
10 together, and much pain is in all l', "
M't 3: 4 and a leathern girdle about his l'; 3751
M'r 1: 6 with a girdle of a skin about his l'; "
Lu 12:35 Let your l' be girded about, and "
Ac 2:30 to him, that of the fruit of his l', "
Eph 6:14 having your l' girt about with truth, "
Heb 7: 5 they come out of the l' of Abraham:"
10 For he was yet in the l' of his father,"
1Pe 1:13 gird up the l' of your mind, be sober,"
Lois (lo'-is)
2Ti 1: 5 dwelt first in thy grandmother L',3090
long See also headlong; longed; longer; longeth; longing; longsuffering; long-winged; prolong.
Ge 26: 8 when he had been there a l' time, 748
48:15 the God which fed me all my life l' 5750
Ex 10: 3 How l' wilt thou refuse to humble 4970
7 How l' shall this man be a snare 5704
16:28 How l' refuse ye to keep my "
19:13 when the trumpet soundeth l', 4900
19 the voice of the trumpet sounded l',* "
20:12 days may be l' upon the land which 748
27: 1 altar of shittim wood, five cubits l',753
9 of an hundred cubits l' for one side: "
11 be hangings of an hundred cubits l'."
Le 18:19 as l' as she is put apart for her
26:34 sabbaths, as l' as it lieth desolate,3117
35 As l' as it lieth desolate it shall rest;"
Nu 9:18 as l' as the cloud abode upon the
19 And when the cloud tarried l' upon*
14:11 How l' will this people provoke me?5704
11 how l' will it be ere they believe me,"
27 How l' shall I bear with this evil
20:15 we have dwelt in Egypt a l' time; 7227
De 1: 6 have dwelt l' enough in this mount:"
2: 3 this mountain l' enough: turn you "
4:25 shall have remained l' in the land,
12:19 as l' as thou livest upon the earth. 3117
14:24 if the way be too l' for thee, so that 7235
19: 6 overtake him, because the way is l',"
20:19 thou shalt besiege a city a l' time, 7227
28:32 longing for them all the day l': *
59 great plagues, and of l' continuance,
59 sicknesses, and of l' continuance.
31:13 as l' as ye live in the land whither 3117
33:12 shall cover him all the day l', and he
Jos 6: 5 make a l' blast with the ram's horn,4900
9:13 by reason of the very l' journey. 7230
11:18 made war a l' time with all those 7227
18: 3 How l' are ye slack to go to possess 5704
23: 1 a l' time after that the Lord had *7227
24: 7 dwelt in the wilderness a l' season. "
J'g 5:28 Why is his chariot so l' in coming? 954
1Sa 1:28 as l' as he liveth he shall be lent to 3117
7: 2 Kirjath-jearim, that...time was l'; 7235
16: 1 How l' wilt thou mourn for Saul, 5704
20:31 as l' as the son of Jesse liveth upon 3117
25:15 l' as we were conversant with them,"
8 so l' as I have been with thee unto "
2Sa 2:26 how l' shall it be then, ere thou bid 5704
3: 1 Now there was l' war between the 752
14: 2 be as a woman that had a l' time 7227
19:34 the king, How l' have I to live, *3117
1Ki 3:11 hast not asked for thyself l' life; 7227
6:17 temple before it, was forty cubits l'.
18:21 How l' halt ye between two 5704
2Ki 9:22 so l' as the whoredoms of thy
19:25 Hast thou not heard l' ago how I 7350
2Ch 1:11 neither yet hast asked l' life; but 7227
3:11 cherubims were twenty cubits l': 753
6:13 a brasen scaffold, of five cubits l', "
31 so l' as they live in the land which 3117
15: 3 for a l' season Israel hath been 7227
26: 5 as l' as he sought the Lord, God 3117
30: 5 they had not done it of a l' time *7230
36:21 as l' as she lay desolate she kept 3117
Es 5:13 so l' as I see Mordecai the Jew 6256
Job 3:21 Which l' for death, but it cometh 2442
6: 8 grant me the thing that I l' for! 8615
7:19 How l' wilt thou not depart from 4101
8: 2 How l' wilt thou speak these 5704
2 how l' shall the words of thy mouth

Job 18: 2 How l' will it be ere ye make 5704
19: 2 How l' will ye vex my soul, and "
27: 6 not reproach me so l' as I live. 3117
Ps 4: 2 how l' will ye turn my glory into 5704
2 how l' will ye love vanity, and seek
6: 3 vexed: but thou, O Lord, how l'? 5704
13: 1 How l' wilt thou forget me, O Lord?"
1 how l' wilt thou hide thy face from "
2 How l' shall I take counsel in my soul, "
2 how l' shall mine enemy be exalted "
32: 3 old through my roaring all the day l'.
35:17 Lord, how l' wilt thou look on? 5704
28 and of thy praise all the day l'.
38: 6 greatly; I go mourning all the day l'.
12 and imagine deceits all the day l'.
44: 8 In God we boast all the day l', and
22 for thy sake are we killed all the day l';
62: 3 How l' will ye imagine mischief 5704
71:24 of thy righteousness all the day l':
72: 5 as l' as the sun and moon endure, 5973
7 peace so l' as the moon endureth.*5704
17 be continued as l' as the sun: 6440
73:14 the day l' have I been plagued,
74: 9 among us any that knoweth how l'.5704
10 how l' shall the adversary reproach?"
80: 4 how l' wilt thou be angry against the"
82: 2 How l' will ye judge unjustly, and "
89:46 How l', Lord? wilt thou hide thyself"
90:13 Return, O Lord, how l'? and let it "
91:16 With l' life will I satisfy him, and 753
94: 3 Lord, how l' shall the wicked, 5704
3 how l' shall the wicked triumph? "
4 How l' shall they utter and speak* "
95:10 Forty years l' was I grieved with this
104:33 sing unto the Lord as l' as I live: 5704
116: 2 will I call upon him as l' as I live. 3117
120: 6 My soul hath l' dwelt with him 7227
129: 3 back: they made l' their furrows. 748
143: 3 as those that have been l' dead. 5769
Pr 1:22 How l', ye simple ones, will ye love5704
3: 2 l' life, and peace, shall they add * 753
6: 9 How l' wilt thou sleep, O sluggard?5704
7:19 at home, he is gone a l' journey: 7350
21:26 He coveteth greedily all the day l': but
23:17 in the fear of the Lord all the day l'.
30 They that tarry l' at the wine; they
25:15 By l' forbearing is a prince 753
Ec 12: 5 because man goeth to his l' home,5769
Isa 6:11 Then said I, Lord, how l'? And he5704
22:11 unto him that fashioned it l' ago. 7350
37:26 Hast thou not heard l' ago, how I "
42:14 I have l' time holden my peace; I 5769
65:22 elect shall l' enjoy the work of their
Jer 4:14 How l' shall...vain thoughts lodge 5704
21 How l' shall I see the standard, and "
12: 4 How l' shall the land mourn, and "
23:26 How l' shall this be in the heart of "
29:28 This captivity is l': build ye houses,752
31:22 How l' wilt thou go about, O thou 5704
47: 5 valley: how l' wilt thou cut thyself?"
6 how l' will it be ere thou be quiet? "
La 2:20 their fruit, and children of a span l'?*
5:20 for ever, and forsake us so l' time? 753
Eze 31: 5 his branches became l' because of 748
40: 5 a measuring reed of six cubits l' by
7 little chamber was one reed l', 753
29 it was fifty cubits l', and five and
30 about were five and twenty cubits l',"
33 it was fifty cubits l', and five and "
42 of a cubit and an half l', and a cubit "
47 the court, an hundred cubits l', and "
41:13 the house, an hundred cubits l'; and "
13 walls thereof, an hundred cubits l';* "
42:11 as l' as they, and as broad as they:* "
20 round about, five hundred reeds l',* "
43:16 the altar shall be twelve cubits l', "
17 the settle shall be fourteen cubits l' "
44:20 nor suffer their locks to grow l';
45: 6 and five and twenty thousand l', 753
46:22 courts joined of forty cubits l' and "
Da 8:13 l' shall be the vision concerning 5704
10: 1 but the time appointed was l': 1419
12: 6 How l' shall it be to the end of these5704
Ho 8: 5 how l' will it be ere they attain to "
13:13 should not stay l' in the place of *
Hab 1: 2 O Lord, how l' shall I cry, and thou5704
2: 6 that which is not his! how l'? "
Zec 1:12 how l' wilt thou not have mercy on "
M't 9:15 mourn, as l' as the bridegroom is 1909
11:21 repented l' ago in sackcloth and 3819
17:17 how l' shall I be with you? 2193
17 how l' shall I suffer you? bring "
23:14 for a pretence make l' prayer: *3117
25:19 After a l' time the lord of those 4183
M'r 2:19 l' as they have the bridegroom 5550
9:19 how l' shall I be with you? 2193
19 how l' shall I suffer you? bring "
21 How l' is it ago since this came 4214
12:38 which love to go in l' clothing, and
40 for a pretence make l' prayers: 3117
16: 5 side, clothed in a l' white garment;
Lu 1:21 that he tarried so l' in the temple.*
8:27 man, which had devils l' time. 2425
9:41 how l' shall I be with you, and 2193
18: 7 him, though he bear l' with them?*3114
20: 9 into a far country for a l' time. 2425
46 which desire to walk in l' robes,
47 and for a shew make l' prayers: 3117
23: 8 to see him of a l' season, 2425
Joh 5: 6 been now a l' time in that case, 4183
9: 5 As l' as I am in the world, I am the*3752
10:24 How l' dost thou make us to 2193
14: 9 Have I been so l' time with you, 5118
Ac 8:11 of l' time he had bewitched them 2425
14: 3 L' time therefore abode they "
28 they abode l' time with the *3756,3641
Ac 20: 9 as Paul was l' preaching, he *1909,4119
11 and talked a l' while, even till 2425
27:14 not l' after there arose against it 4183
21 after l' abstinence Paul stood forth "
Ro 1:11 I l' to see you, that I may impart 1971
7: 1 over a man as l' as he liveth? 5550
2 law to her husband so l' as he liveth;*
8:36 thy sake we are killed all the day l';
10:21 All day l' I have stretched forth my
1Co 7:39 as l' as her husband liveth; 5550
11:14 if a man have l' hair, it is a shame 2863
15 But if a woman have l' hair, it is a "
13: 4 Charity suffereth l', and is kind; 3114
2Co 9:14 l' after you for the exceeding grace1971
Ga 4: 1 the heir, as l' as he is a child, 5550
Eph 6: 3 thou mayest live l' on the earth. 3118
Ph'p 1: 8 how greatly I l' after you all in 1971
1Ti 3:15 But if I tarry l', that thou mayest
Heb 4: 7 in David, To day, after so l' a time;5118
Jas 5: 7 earth, and hath l' patience for it, *3114
1Pe 3: 6 daughters ye are, as l' as ye do well,*
2Pe 1:13 as l' as I am in this tabernacle, to stir
2: 3 now of a l' time lingereth not,
Re 6:10 How l', O Lord, holy and true, 2193

longed See also LONGEDST; PROLONGED.
2Sa 13:39 David l' to go forth unto Absalom:3615
23:15 And David l', and said, Oh that one 183
1Ch 11:17 And David l', and said, Oh that one "
Ps 119:40 I have l' after thy precepts: 8373
131 for I l' for thy commandments. 2968
174 I have l' for thy salvation, O Lord;8373
Ph'p 2:26 For he l' after you all, and was 1971
4: 1 brethren dearly beloved and l' for, 1973

longedst
Ge 31:30 sore l' after thy father's house, 3700

longer
Ex 2: 3 when she could not l' hide him, 5750
9:28 let you go, and ye shall stay no l'. 3254
J'g 2:14 any l' stand before their enemies. 5750
2Sa 20: 5 he tarried l' than the set time which
2Ki 6:33 should I wait for the Lord any l'? 5750
Job 11: 9 measure thereof is l' than the earth,752
Jer 44:22 So that the Lord could no l' bear, 5750
Lu 16: 2 for thou mayest be no l' steward. 2089
Ac 18:20 desired him to tarry l' time with 4119
25:24 that he ought not to live any l'. 3370
Ro 6: 2 dead to sin, live any l' therein? 2089
Ga 3:25 we are no l' under a schoolmaster. "
1Th 3: 1 we could no l' forbear, we thought3370
5 this cause, when I could no l' forbear,"
1Ti 5:23 Drink no l' water, but use a little "
1Pe 4: 2 he no l' should live the rest of his "
Re 10: 6 that there should be time no l'; 2089

longeth See also PROLONGETH.
Ge 34: 8 soul of my son Shechem l' for your2836
De 12:20 because thy soul l' to eat flesh; * 183
Ps 63: 1 my flesh l' for thee in a dry and 3642
84: 2 My soul l', yea, even fainteth for 3700

longing
De 28:32 fail with l' for them all the day long:
Ps 107: 9 he satisfieth the l' soul, and filleth 8264
119:20 My soul breaketh for the l' that it 8375

longsuffering
Ex 34: 6 merciful and gracious, l', and *750,639
Nu 14:18 Lord is l', and of great mercy, * " "
Ps 86:15 l', and plenteous in mercy and * " "
Jer 15:15 take me not away in thy l': " "
Ro 2: 4 goodness and forbearance and l'; 3115
9:22 endured with much l' the vessels "
2Co 6: 6 by l', by kindness, by the Holy "
Ga 5:22 of the Spirit is love, joy, peace, l', "
Eph 4: 2 with l', forbearing one another in "
Col 1:11 all patience and l' with joyfulness; "
3:12 humbleness of mind, meekness, l'; "
1Ti 1:16 Christ might shew forth all l', "
2Ti 3:10 of life, purpose, faith, l', charity, "
4: 2 exhort with all l' and doctrine. "
1Pe 3:20 the l' of God waited in the days of "
2Pe 3: 9 but is l' to us-ward, not willing 3114
3:15 the l' of our Lord is salvation; 3115

longwinged
Eze 17: 3 great eagle with great wings, l',*750,83

look See also LOOKED; LOOKEST; LOOKETH; LOOKING; LOOKS.
Ge 9:16 and I will l' upon it, that I may 7200
12:11 thou art a fair woman to l' upon: 4758
13:14 l' from the place where thou art 7200
15: 5 L' now toward heaven, and tell the5027
19:17 l' not behind thee, neither stay thou "
24:16 damsel was very fair to l' upon, 4758
26: 7 because she was fair to l' upon.
40: 7 Wherefore l' ye so sadly to day? 6440
41:33 l' out a man discreet and wise, 7200
42: 1 Why do ye l' one upon another? "
Ex 3: 6 for he was afraid to l' upon God. 5027
5:21 The Lord l' upon you, and judge; 7200
10:10 l' to it; for evil is before you.
25:20 their faces shall l' one to another;*
40 l' that thou make them after their *7200
39:43 And Moses did l' upon all the work,* "
Le 13: 3 the priest shall l' on the plague in "
3 and the priest shall l' on him, and "
5 And the priest shall l' on him the "
6 the priest shall l' on him again the "
21 But if the priest shall l' on it, and, "
25 Then the priest shall l' upon it: and, "
26 But if the priest shall l' on it, and, behold, "
27 And the priest shall l' upon him the "
31 priest l' on the plague of the scall, "
32 the priest shall l' on the plague: "
34 day the priest shall l' on the scall: "
36 Then the priest shall l' on him: and, "
39 Then the priest shall l': and, "
Le 13:43 Then the priest shall l' upon it: 7200
50 the priest shall l' upon the plague, "
51 And he shall l' on the plague on the "
53 if the priest shall l', and, behold, "
55 And the priest shall l' on the plague,"
56 And if the priest l', and, behold, "
14: 3 the priest shall l', and, behold, if "
37 And he shall l' on the plague, and, "
39 shall l': and, behold, if the plague "
44 Then the priest shall come and l', "
48 priest shall come in, and l' upon it, "
Nu 15:39 for a fringe, that ye may l' upon it, "
De 9:27 l' not unto the stubbornness of 6437
26:15 L' down from thy holy habitation,8259
28:32 thine eyes shall l', and fail with 7200
J'g 7:17 them, L' on me, and do likewise: "
1Sa 1:11 l' on the affliction of thine handmaid,"
16: 7 L' not on his countenance, or on 5027
12 countenance, and goodly to l' to. 7210
17:18 and l' how thy brethren fare, and 6485
2Sa 9: 8 l' upon such a dead dog as I am? 6437
11: 2 was very beautiful to l' upon. 4758
16:12 the Lord will l' on mine affliction, 7200
1Ki 18:43 Go up now, l' toward the sea. 5027
2Ki 3:14 I would not l' toward thee, nor see "
6:32 l', when the messenger cometh, 7200
9: 2 thither, l' out there Jehu the son of "
10: 3 L' even out the best and meetest of "
23 l' that there be here with you none "
14: 8 let us l' one another in the face. "
1Ch 12:17 the God of our fathers l' thereon, "
2Ch 24:22 The Lord l' upon it, and require "
Es 1:11 for she was fair to l' on. 4758
Job 3: 9 let it l' for light, but have none; 6960
6:28 therefore be content, l' upon me; 6437
20:21 shall no man l' for his goods. *2342
35: 5 L' unto the heavens, and see; and 5027
40:12 L' on every one that is proud, and 7200
Ps 5: 3 prayer unto thee, and will l' up. *6822
22:17 bones: they l' and stare upon me. 5027
25:18 L' upon mine affliction and my *7200
35:17 Lord, how long wilt thou l' on?
40:12 me, so that I am not able to l' up;
80:14 l' down from heaven, and behold 5027
84: 9 l' upon the face of thine anointed. "
85:11 righteousness shall l' down from *8259
101: 5 hath an high l' and a proud heart 5869
119:132 L'...upon me, and be merciful *6437
123: 2 eyes of servants l' unto the hand of
Pr 4:25 Let thine eyes l' right on, and let 5027
25 thine eyelids l' straight before thee.
6:17 A proud l', a lying tongue, and *5869
21: 4 An high l', and a proud heart, and "
23:31 L' not thou upon the wine when it 7200
27:23 flocks, and l' well to thy herds. 7896
Ec 12: 3 those that l' out of the windows 7200
Ca 1: 6 L' not upon me, because I am black,"
4: 8 l' from the top of Amana, from the 7789
6:13 return, that we may l' upon thee. 2372
Isa 5:30 and if one l' unto the land, behold 5027
8:17 of Jacob, and I will l' for him. 6960
21 and their God, and l' upward. *6437
22 And they shall l' unto the earth; 5027
14:16 thee shall narrowly l' upon thee, 7688
17: 7 day shall a man l' to his Maker, 8159
8 And he shall not l' to the altars, "
22: 4 L' away from me; I will weep "
8 didst l' in that day to the armour 5027
31: 1 they l' not unto the Holy One of 8159
33:20 L' upon Zion, the city of our 2372
42:18 and l', ye blind, that ye may see. 5027
45:22 L' unto me, and be ye saved, all 6437
51: 1 l' unto the rock whence ye are 5027
2 L' unto Abraham your father, and "
6 and l' upon the earth beneath: "
56:11 they all l' to their own way, every*6437
59:11 l' for judgment, but there is none;6960
63:15 L' down from heaven, and behold 5027
66: 2 but to this man will I l', even to him "
24 l' upon the carcases of the men 7200
Jer 13:16 while ye l' for light, he turn it into 6960
39:12 Take him, and l' well to him, 7760
40: 4 and I will l' well unto thee:
46: 5 are fled apace, and l' not back: 6437
47: 3 the fathers shall not l' back to their "
La 3:50 Till the Lord l' down, and behold 8259
Eze 23:15 heads, all of them princes to l' to, 4758
29:16 when they shall l' after them: 6437
43:17 his stairs shall l' toward the east.
Da 7:20 whose l' was more stout than his 2376
Ho 3: 1 of Israel, who l' to other gods, *6437
Jon 2: 4 l' again toward thy holy temple. 5027
Mic 4:11 and let our eye l' upon Zion. *2372
7: 7 Therefore I will l' unto the Lord; 6822
Na 2: 8 they cry; but none shall l' back. *6437
3: 7 all they that l' upon thee shall flee7200
Hab 1:13 evil, and canst not l' on iniquity: 5027
2:15 thou mayest l' on their nakedness! "
Zec 12:10 shall l' upon me whom they have "
M't 11: 3 come, or do we l' for another? 4328
M'k 8:25 upon his eyes, and made him l' up;*308
Lu 7:19, 20 come? or l' we for another? 4328
9:38 I beseech thee, l' upon my son: 1914
21:28 then l' up, and lift up your heads: 352
Joh 4:35 up your eyes, and l' on the fields; 2300
7:52 Search, and l': for out of *1492
19:37 shall l' on him whom they pierced.3700
Ac 3: 4 upon him with John, said, L' on us.991
12 or why l' ye so earnestly on us, as* 816
6: 3 l' ye out among you seven men of 1980
18:15 names, and of your law, l' ye to it;3700
1Co 16:11 for I l' for him with the brethren. *1551
2Co 3:13 could not stedfastly l' to the end of 816
4:18 l' not at the things which are seen,4648
10: 7 Do ye l' on things after the outward991
Ph'p 2: 4 L' not every man on his own *4648

Ph'p 3:20 whence also we l' for the Saviour,* 553
Heb 9:28 unto them that l' for him shall he* "
1Pe 1:12 things the angels desire to l' into. 3879
2Pe 3:13 l' for new heavens and a new 4328
14 seeing that ye l' for such things, "
2Jo 8 L' to yourselves, that we lose not 991
Re 4: 3 was to l' upon like a jasper and 3706
5: 3 open the book, neither to l' thereon.991
4 read the book, neither to l' thereon. "

looked
Ge 6:12 And God l' upon the earth, and, *7200
8:13 the covering of the ark, and l', and, "
16:13 here l' after him that seeth me? "
18: 2 he lift up his eyes and l', and, lo, "
16 from thence, and l' toward Sodom:8259
19:26 But his wife l' back from behind 5027
28 he l' toward Sodom and Gomorrah,8259
22:13 Abraham lifted up his eyes, and l',7200
26: 8 the Philistines l' out at a window, 8259
29: 2 he l', and behold a well in the field,7200
32 Lord hath l' upon my affliction; "
33: 1 Jacob lifted up his eyes, and l', and,"
37:25 they lifted up their eyes and l', and,"
39:23 The keeper of the prison l' not to "
40: 6 in the morning, and l' upon them,* "
Ex 2:11 brethren, and l' on their burdens: "
12 he l' this way and that way, and 6437
25 God l' upon the children of Israel,*7200
3: 2 he l', and, behold, the bush burned "
4:31 he had l' upon their affliction, * "
14:24 in the morning watch the Lord l' 8259
16:10 that they l' toward the wilderness,6437
33: 8 l' after Moses, until he was gone 5027
Nu 12:10 and Aaron l' upon Miriam, and, 6437
16:42 l' toward the tabernacle of the "
17: 9 they l', and took every man his 7200
24:20 when he l' on Amalek, he took up "
21 he l' on the Kenites, and took up "
De 9:16 And I l', and, behold, ye had sinned"
26: 7 l' on our affliction, and our labour,*"
Jos 5:13 that he lifted up his eyes and l', "
8:20 And when the men of Ai l' behind 6437
J'g 5:28 of Sisera l' out at a window, 8259
6:14 the Lord l' upon him, and said, 6437
9:43 and laid wait in the field, and l', 7200
13:19 and Manoah and his wife l' on. "
20 and Manoah and his wife l' on it, "
20:40 the Benjamites l' behind them, 6437
1Sa 6:19 had l' into the ark of the Lord, 7200
9:16 I have l' upon my people, because "
14:16 of Saul in Gibeah of Benjamin l'; "
16: 6 they were come, that he l' on Eliab,"
17:42 And when the Philistine l' about, 5027
24: 8 And when Saul l' behind him, David"
2Sa 1: 7 when he l' behind him, he saw me,6437
2:20 Then Abner l' behind him, and "
6:16 daughter l' through a window, 8259
13:34 watch lifted up his eyes, and l', 7200
18:24 wall, and lifted up his eyes, and l', "
22:42 They l', but there was none to 8159
24:20 And Araunah l', and saw the king 8259
1Ki 18:43 And he went up, and l', and said, 5027
19: 6 And he l', and, behold, there was a "
2Ki 2:24 he turned back, and l' on them, 7200
6:30 by upon the wall, and the people l', "
9:30 her head, and l' out at a window. 8259
32 l' out to him two or three eunuchs. "
11:14 And when she l', behold, the king 7200
14:11 of Judah l' one another in the face "
1Ch 21:21 Ornan, Ornan l' and saw David, 5027
2Ch 13:14 when Judah l' back, behold, the 6437
20:24 they l' unto the multitude, and, "
23:13 she l', and, behold, the king stood 7200
26:20 and all the priests, l' upon him, 6437
Ne 4:14 I l', and rose up, and said unto the "
Es 2:15 sight of all them that l' upon her. "
Job 6:19 troops of Tema l', the companies 5027
30:26 When I l' for good, then evil came6960
Ps 14: 2 Lord l' down from heaven upon 8259
34: 5 They l' unto him, and were 5027
53: 2 God l' down from heaven upon 8259
69:20 I l' for some to take pity, but there6960
102:19 he hath l' down from the height of 8259
109:25 when they l' upon me, they shaked*7200
142: 4 I l' on my right hand,and beheld, *5027
Pr 7: 6 house I l' through my casement, 8259
24:32 it well: I l' upon it, and received *7200
Ec 2:11 Then I l' on all the works that my6437
Ca 1: 6 because the sun hath l' upon me:*7805
Isa 5: 2 he l' that it should bring forth 6960
4 I l' that it should bring forth "
7 and he l' for judgment, but behold "
22:11 but ye have not l' unto the maker 5027
63: 5 I l', and there was none to help; "
64: 3 terrible things which we l' not for,6960
Jer 8:15 We l' for peace, but no good came; "
14:19 we l' for peace, and there is no "
La 2:16 this is the day that we l' for; we "
Eze 1: 4 And I l', and, behold, a whirlwind 7200
2: 9 and when I l', behold, an hand was "
8: 7 when I l', behold a hole in the wall."
10: 1 I l', and, behold, in the firmament "
9 when I l', behold the four wheels by"
11 the head l' they followed it; they 6437
16: 8 I passed by thee, and l' upon thee,7200
21:21 with images, he l' in the liver. "
40:20 court that l' toward the north, *6440
44: 4 I l', and, behold, the glory of the 7200
46:19 priests, which l' toward the north:6437
Da 1:13 let our countenances be l' upon 7200
10: 5 Then I lifted up mine eyes, and l', "
12: 5 I Daniel l', and, behold, there stood"
Ob 12 shouldest not have l' on the day * "
13 not have l' on their affliction in * "
Hag 1: 9 Ye l' for much, and, lo, it came to 6437
Zec 2: 1 lifted up mine eyes again, and l', *7200
Zec 4: 2 I have l', and behold a candlestick *7200
5: 1 and lifted up mine eyes, and l', * "
9 Then lifted I up mine eyes, and l',* "
6: 1 and lifted up mine eyes, and l', * "
M'r 3: 5 when he had l' round about on 4017
34 he l' round about on them which * "
5:32 he l' round about to see her that "
6:41 he l' up to heaven, and blessed, and*308
8:24 he l' up, and said, I see men as trees,"
33 about and l' on his disciples, *1492
9: 8 when they had l' round about, they*4017
10:23 And Jesus l' round about, and saith"
11:11 when he had l' round about upon "
14:67 warming himself, she l' upon him,1689
16: 4 And when they l', they saw that the*308
Lu 1:25 in the days wherein he l' on me, 1896
2:38 to all them that l' for redemption *4327
10:32 came and l' on him, and passed *1492
19: 5 to the place, he l' up, and saw him, 308
21: 1 he l' up, and saw the rich men "
22:56 the fire, and earnestly l' upon him, 816
61 Lord turned, and l' upon Peter. 1689
Joh 13:22 the disciples l' one on another, 991
20:11 down, and l' into the sepulchre, "
Ac 1:10 they l' stedfastly toward heaven * 816
7:55 l' up stedfastly into heaven, and "
10: 4 when he l' on him, he was afraid, * "
22:13 the same hour I l' up upon him. 308
28: 6 they l' when he should have *4328
6 but after they had l' a great while,* "
Heb11:10 l' for a city which hath foundations,1551
1Jo 1: 1 which we have l' upon, and our *2300
Re 4: 1 After this I l', and, behold, door*1492
6: 8 And I l', and behold a pale horse:* "
14: 1 I l', and, lo, a Lamb stood on the * "
14 I l', and behold a white cloud, and* "
15: 5 And after that I l', and, behold, the* "

lookest
Job 13:27 and l' narrowly unto all my paths;*8104
Hab 1:13 wherefore l' thou upon them that 5027

looketh
Le 13:12 wheresoever the priest l'; *4758,5869
Nu 21: 8 when he l' upon it, shall live. *7200
20 Pisgah, which l' toward Jeshimon.8259
23:28 of Peor, that l' toward Jeshimon. "
Jos 15: 2 from the bay that l' southward: *6437
1Sa 13:18 the border that l' to the valley of 8259
16: 7 man l' on the outward appearance,7200
7 but the Lord l' on the heart. "
Job 7: 2 an hireling l' for the reward of his6960
28:24 For he l' to the ends of the earth, 5027
33:27 He l' upon men, and if any say, *7789
Ps 33:13 The Lord l' from heaven; he 5027
14 he l' upon all the inhabitants of 7688
104:32 He l' on the earth, and it trembleth :5027
Pr 14:15 prudent man l' well to his going. 995
31:27 She l' well to the ways of her 6822
Ca 2: 9 wall, he l' forth at the windows, 7688
6:10 is she that l' forth as the morning,8259
7: 4 which l' toward Damascus. 6822
Isa 28: 4 when he that l' upon it seeth, 7200
Eze 8: 3 gate that l' toward the north; 6437
11: 1 Lord's house, which l' eastward: "
40: 6 the gate which l' toward the east, 6440
22 of the gate that l' toward the east;* "
43: 1 the gate that l' toward the east: 6437
44: 1 sanctuary which l' toward the east;"
46: 1 inner court that l' toward the east "
12 the gate that l' toward the east, "
47: 2 gate by the way that l' eastward; "
M't 5:28 l' on a woman to lust after her 991
24:50 in a day when he l' not for him, *4328
Lu 12:46 in a day when he l' not for him, * "
Jas 1:25 l' into the perfect law of liberty, 3879

looking See also LOOKINGGLASSES.
Jos 15: 7 so northward, l' toward Gilgal, 6437
1Ki 7:25 oxen, three l' toward the north, "
25 and three l' toward the west, "
25 and three l' toward the south, "
25 and three l' toward the east: "
1Ch 15:29 l' out at a window saw king David*8259
2Ch 4: 4 oxen three l' toward the north, 6437
4 and three l' toward the west, "
4 and three l' toward the south, "
4 and three l' toward the east: "
Job 37:18 strong, and as a molten l' glass? *7209
Isa 38:14 dove: mine eyes fail with l' upward:
M't 14:19 and l' up to heaven, he blessed, and308
M'r 7:34 And l' up to heaven, he sighed, and "
10:27 Jesus l' upon them saith, With men1689
15:40 were also women l' on afar off: *2334
Lu 6:10 l' round about upon them all, he *4017
9:16 l' up to heaven, he blessed them, 308
62 his hand to the plough, and l' back,991
21:26 and for l' after those things which*4329
Joh 1:36 l' upon Jesus as he walked, he *1689
20: 5 And he stooping down, and l' in, saw
Ac 6:15 l' stedfastly on him, saw his face as*816
23:21 ready, l' for a promise from thee. 4327
Tit 2:13 L' for that blessed hope, and the "
Heb10:27 a certain fearful l' for of judgment*1561
12: 2 L' unto Jesus the author and 872
15 L' diligently lest any man fail of 1983
2Pe 3:12 L' for and hasting unto the coming4328
Jude 21 l' for the mercy of our Lord Jesus 4327

looking-glass See LOOKING and GLASS; also LOOKINGGLASSES.

lookingglasses
Ex 38: 8 the l' of the women assembling, *4759

looks
Ps 18:27 but wilt bring down high l'. *5869
Isa 2:11 lofty l' of man shall be humbled, "
10:12 Assyria, and the glory of his high l'."
Eze 2: 6 words, nor be dismayed at their l',6440
3: 9 not, neither be dismayed at their l'."

loops
Ex 26: 4 make l' of blue upon the edge of 3924
5 Fifty l' shalt thou make in the one "
5 fifty l' shalt thou make in the edge "
5 the l' may take hold one of another."
10 make fifty l' on the edge of the one "
10 and fifty l' in the edge of the curtain"
11 and put the taches into the l', and "
36:11 made l' of blue on the edge of one "
12 Fifty l' made he in one curtain, and "
12 fifty l' made he in the edge of the "
12 the l' held one curtain to another. "
17 fifty l' upon the uttermost edge of "
17 fifty l' made he upon the edge of the"

loose See also LOOSED; LOOSETH; LOOSING; UNLOOSE.
Ge 49:21 Naphtali is a hind let l': he giveth 7971
Le 14: 7 the living bird l' into the open field."
De 25: and l' his shoe from off his foot, 2502
Jos 5:15 L' thy shoe from off thy foot; for *5394
Job 6: 9 that he would let l' his hand, and 5425
30:11 also let l' the bridle before me. *7971
38:31 Pleiades, or l' the bands of Orion? 6605
Ps 102:20 l' those that are appointed to death;"
Isa 20: 2 l' the sackcloth from off thy loins, "
45: 1 I will l' the loins of kings, to open "
52: 2 l' thyself from the bands of thy neck,"
58: 6 to l' the bands of wickedness, to "
Jer 40: 4 I l' thee this day from the chains "
Da 3:25 Lo, I see four men l', walking in 8271
M't 16 19 whatsoever thou shalt l' on earth 3089
18:18 whatsoever ye shall l' on earth shall"
21: 2 l' them, and bring them unto me. "
M'r 11: 2 man sat; l' him, and bring him. "
4 two ways met; and they l' him. "
Lu 13:15 on the sabbath l' his ox or his ass "
19:30 sat: l' him, and bring him thither. "
31 any man ask you, Why do ye l' him?"
33 said unto them, Why l' ye the colt? "
Joh 11:44 unto them, L' him, and let him go. "
Ac 13:25 of his feet I am not worthy to l'. * "
24:26 him of Paul, that he might l' him:* "
Re 5: 2, 5 and to l' the seven seals thereof.*"
9:14 L' the four angels which are bound "

loosed
Ex 28:28 the breastplate be not l' from the 2118
39:21 the breastplate might not be l' from"
De 25:10 house of him that hath his shoe l'.2502
J'g 15:14 his bands l' from off his hands. *4549
Job 30:11 Because he hath l' my cord, and 6605
39: 5 hath l' the bands of the wild ass? "
Ps 105:20 The king sent and l' him; even 5425
116:16 handmaid: thou hast l' my bonds. 6605
Ec 12: 6 Or ever the silver cord be l', or the7368
Isa 5:27 shall the girdle of their loins be l', 6605
33:23 Thy tacklings are l'; they could 5203
51:14 exile hasteneth that he may be l', 6605
Da 5: 6 that the joints of his loins were l', 8271
M't 16:19 loose on earth shall be l' in heaven.3089
18:18 loose on earth shall be l' in heaven. "
27 with compassion, and l' him, and * 630
M'r 7:35 and the string of his tongue was l',3089
Lu 1:64 and his tongue l', and he spake, and
13:12 thou art l' from thine infirmity. 630
16 l' from this bond on the sabbath 3089
Ac 2:24 up, having l' the pains of death:
13:13 and his company l' from Paphos, 321
16:26 and every one's bands were l'. 447
22:30 Jews, he l' him from his bands, 3089
27:21 me, and not have l' from Crete, * 321
40 l' the rudder bands, and hoised up*447
Ro 7: 2 is l' from the law of her husband.*2673
1Co 7:27 unto a wife? seek not to be l'. 3089
27 Art thou l' from a wife? seek not 3080
Re 9:15 And the four angels were l', which3089
20: 3 that he must be l' a little season. "
7 Satan shall be l' out of his prison, "

looseth
Job 12:18 He l' the bond of kings, and 6605
Ps 146: 7 hungry. The Lord l' the prisoners:5425

loosing
M'r 11: 5 unto them, What do ye, l' the colt?3089
Lu 19:33 And as they were l' the colt, the "
Ac 16:11 Therefore l' from Troas, we came* 321
27:13 l' thence, they sailed close by * 142

lop
Isa 10:33 shall l' the bough with terror: 5586

lord [or Lord] See also LORD'S [LORD'S]; LORDS.
Ge 2: 4 that the L' God made the earth ‡3068
5 L' God had not caused it to rain ‡ "
7 L' God formed man of the dust ‡ "
8 And the L' God planted a garden ‡ "
9 made the L' God to grow every ‡ "
15 the L' God took the man, and put ‡ "
16 the L' God commanded the man, ‡ "
18 L' God said, It is not good that ‡ "
19 the L' God formed every beast ‡ "
21 L' God caused a deep sleep to fall ‡ "
22 rib, which the L' God had taken ‡ "
3: 1 field which the L' God had made. ‡ "
8 heard the voice of the L' God ‡ "
8 presence of the L' God amongst ‡ "
9 L' God called unto Adam, and ‡ "
13 the L' God said unto the woman, ‡ "
14 the L' God said unto the serpent, ‡ "
21 the L' God made coats of skins, ‡ "
22 the L' God said, Behold, the man ‡ "
23 L' God sent him forth from the ‡ "
4: 1 I have gotten a man from the L'. ‡ "
3 ground an offering unto the L'. ‡ "
4 L' had respect unto Abel and to ‡ "
6 L' said unto Cain, Why art thou ‡ "

Ge 4: 9 L' said unto Cain, Where is Abel? ‡3068
13 And Cain said unto the L', My ‡ "
15 the L' said unto him, Therefore ‡ "
15 L' set a mark upon Cain, lest any‡ "
16 out from the presence of the L'. ‡ "
26 to call upon the name of the L'. ‡ "
5: 29 ground which the L' hath cursed.‡ "
6: 3 the L' said, My Spirit shall not ‡ "
6 the L' that he had made man on ‡ "
7 the L' said, I will destroy man ‡ "
8 found grace in the eyes of the L'. ‡ "
7: 1 And the L' said unto Noah, Come‡ "
5 all that the L' commanded him. ‡ "
16 him: and the L' shut him in. ‡ "
8: 20 builded an altar unto the L'; ‡ "
21 the L' smelled a sweet savour; ‡ "
21 the L' said in his heart, I will not‡ "
9: 26 Blessed be the L' God of Shem; ‡ "
10: 9 a mighty hunter before the L': ‡ "
9 the mighty hunter before the L'. ‡ "
11: 5 L' came down to see the city and ‡ "
6 the L' said, Behold, the people ‡ "
8 L' scattered them abroad from ‡ "
9 the L' did there confound the ‡ "
9 did the L' scatter them abroad ‡ "
12: 1 Now the L' had said unto Abram,‡ "
4 as the L' had spoken unto him; ‡ "
7 the L' appeared unto Abram, and‡ "
7 builded he an altar unto the L', ‡ "
8 he builded an altar unto the L', ‡ "
8 called upon the name of the L'. ‡ "
17 the L' plagued Pharaoh and his ‡ "
13: 4 called on the name of the L'. ‡ "
10 before the L' destroyed Sodom ‡ "
10 even as the garden of the L', like ‡ "
13 sinners before the L' exceedingly.‡ "
14 the L' said unto Abram, after that‡ "
18 built there an altar unto the L'. ‡ "
14: 22 lift up mine hand unto the L', ‡ "
15: 1 word of the L' came unto Abram ‡ "
2 said, L' God, what wilt thou give 136
4 the word of the L' came unto him,‡3068
6 And he believed in the L'; and he‡ "
7 L' that brought thee out of Ur of ‡ "
8 L' God, whereby shall I know that 136
18 L' made a covenant with Abram, ‡3068
16: 2 the L' hath restrained me from ‡ "
5 L' judge between me and thee ‡ "
7 the angel of the L' found her by ‡ "
9, 10, 11 angel of the L' said unto ‡ "
11 because the L' hath heard thy ‡ "
13 And she called the name of the L'‡ "
17: 1 L' appeared to Abram, and said ‡ "
18: 1 the L' appeared unto him in the ‡ "
3 My L', if now I have found favour 136
12 have pleasure, my l' being old also?113
13 And the L' said unto Abraham, ‡3068
14 Is any thing too hard for the L'? ‡ "
17 And the L' said, Shall I hide from‡ "
19 they shall keep the way of the L',‡ "
19 the L' may bring upon Abraham ‡ "
20 the L' said, Because the cry of ‡ "
22 Abraham stood yet before the L'.‡ "
26 the L' said, If I find in Sodom ‡ "
27 upon me to speak unto the L', 136
30 Oh let not the L' be angry, and I "
31 upon me to speak unto the L': "
32 Oh let not the L' be angry, and I "
33 the L' went his way, as soon as he‡3068
19: 13 great before the face of the L'; ‡ "
13 the L' hath sent us to destroy it. ‡ "
14 for the L' will destroy this city. ‡ "
16 the L' being merciful unto him: ‡ "
18 unto them, Oh, not so, my L': 113
24 L' rained upon Sodom and upon ‡3068
24 brimstone and fire from the L' ‡ "
27 where he stood before the L': ‡ "
20: 4 L', wilt thou slay also a righteous 136
18 the L' had fast closed up all the ‡3068
21: 1 L' visited Sarah as he had said, ‡ "
1 the L' did unto Sarah as he had ‡ "
33 there on the name of the L', the ‡ "
22: 11 angel of the L' called unto him ‡ "
14 mount of the L' it shall be seen. ‡ "
15 the angel of the L' called unto ‡ "
16 myself have I sworn, saith the L',‡ "
23: 6 Hear us, my l': thou art a mighty 113
11 Nay, my l', hear me: the field give "
15 My l', hearken unto me: the land is "
24: 1 L' had blessed Abraham in all ‡3068
3 I will make thee swear by the L',‡ "
7 The L' God of heaven, which took‡ "
12 O L' God of my master Abraham,‡ "
18 And she said, Drink, my l': and 113
21 wit whether the L' had made his ‡3068
26 his head, and worshipped the L'. ‡ "
27 L' God of my master Abraham, ‡ "
27 the L' led me to the house of my ‡ "
31 Come in, thou blessed of the L'; ‡ "
35 the L' hath blessed my master ‡ "
40 The L', before whom I walk, will ‡ "
42 O L' God of my master Abraham,‡ "
44 be the woman whom the L' hath ‡ "
48 my head, and worshipped the L', ‡ "
48 L' God of my master Abraham, ‡ "
50 thing proceedeth from the L': ‡ "
51 son's wife, as the L' hath spoken.‡ "
52 he worshipped the L', bowing ‡ "
56 the L' hath prospered my way; ‡ "
25: 21 And Isaac intreated the L' for his‡ "
21 the L' was intreated of him, and ‡ "
22 And she went to enquire of the L'.‡ "
23 the L' said unto her, Two nations‡ "
26: 2 the L' appeared unto him, and ‡ "
12 and the L' blessed him. ‡ "
22 the L' hath made room for us, ‡ "

Ge 26: 24 And the L' appeared unto him the ‡3068
25 called upon the name of the L', ‡ "
28 certainly that the L' was with ‡ "
29 art now the blessed of the L'. ‡ "
27: 7 bless thee before the L' before ‡ "
20 the L' thy God brought it to me. ‡ "
27 a field which the L' hath blessed:‡ "
29 be l' over thy brethren, and let 1376
37 I have made him thy l', and all his "
28: 13 behold, the L' stood above it, and‡3068
13 I am the L' God of Abraham thy ‡ "
16 Surely the L' is in this place; and‡ "
21 then shall the L' be my God: ‡ "
29: 31 the L' saw that Leah was hated, ‡ "
32 the L' hath looked upon my ‡ "
33 L' hath heard that I was hated, ‡ "
35 she said, Now will I praise the L':‡ "
30: 24 L' shall add to me another son. ‡ "
27 L' hath blessed me for thy sake. ‡ "
30 the L' hath blessed thee since my‡ "
31: 3 the L' said unto Jacob, Return ‡ "
35 Let it not displease my l' that I 113
49 The L' watch between me and ‡3068
32: 4 shall ye speak unto my l' Esau; 113
5 I have sent to tell my l', that I may "
9 the L' which saidst unto me, ‡3068
18 is a present sent unto my l' Esau: 113
33: 8 to find grace in the sight of my l'. "
13 My l' knoweth that the children are "
14 Let my l', I pray thee, pass over "
14 until I come unto my l' unto Seir. "
15 me find grace in the sight of my l'. "
38: 7 was wicked in the sight of the L';‡3068
7 and the L' slew him. ‡ "
10 which he did displeased the L': ‡ "
39: 2 the L' was with Joseph, and he ‡ "
3 saw that the L' was with him, ‡ "
3 that the L' made all that he did to‡ "
5 that the L' blessed the Egyptian's‡ "
5 blessing of the L' was upon all ‡ "
16 by her, until his l' came home. 113
21 But the L' was with Joseph, and ‡3068
23 because the L' was with him, and‡ "
23 he did, the L' made it to prosper. ‡ "
40: 1 offended their l' the king of Egypt. 113
42: 10 And they said unto him, Nay, my l', "
30 The man, who is the l' of the land, "
33 the l' of the country, said unto us, "
44: 5 not this it in which my l' drinketh, "
7 Wherefore saith my l' these words? "
16 What shall we say unto my l'? "
18 Oh my l', let thy servant, I pray "
19 My l' asked his servants, saying, "
20 And we said unto my l', We have a "
22 we said unto my l', The lad cannot "
24 we told him the words of my l'. "
33 of the lad a bondman to my l'; "
45: 8 and l' of all his house, and a ruler "
9 God hath made me l' of all Egypt: "
47: 18 We will not hide it from my l', how "
18 my l' also hath our herds of cattle;* "
18 not ought left in the sight of my l', "
25 us find grace in the sight of my l', "
49: 18 waited for thy salvation, O L'. ‡3068
Ex 3: 2 the angel of the L' appeared unto‡ "
4 L' saw that he turned aside to see,‡ "
7 the L' said, I have surely seen ‡ "
15, 16 The L' God of your fathers, ‡ "
18 The L' God of the Hebrews hath ‡ "
18 may sacrifice to the L' our God. ‡ "
4: 1 L' hath not appeared unto thee. ‡ "
2 And the L' said unto him, What is‡ "
4 the L' said unto Moses, Put forth ‡ "
5 they may believe in the L' God of‡ "
6 L' said furthermore unto him, ‡ "
10 And Moses said unto the L', ‡ "
10 O my L', I am not eloquent, 136
11 the L' said unto him, Who hath ‡3068
11 or the blind? have not I the L'? ‡ "
13 And he said, O my L', send, I pray 136
14 the anger of the L' was kindled ‡3068
19 the L' said unto Moses in Midian,‡ "
21 L' said unto Moses, When thou ‡ "
22 Thus saith the L', Israel is my ‡ "
24 the L' met him, and sought to ‡ "
27 the L' said to Aaron, Go into the ‡ "
28 told Aaron all the words of the L'‡ "
30 the L' had spoken unto Moses, ‡ "
31 heard that the L' had visited the ‡ "
5: 1 Thus saith the L' God of Israel, ‡ "
2 Pharaoh said, Who is the L', that‡ "
2 I know not the L', neither will I ‡ "
3 and sacrifice unto the L' our God;‡ "
17 us go and do sacrifice to the L'. ‡ "
21 The L' look upon you, and judge;‡ "
22 And Moses returned unto the L', ‡ "
22 L', wherefore hast thou so evil 136
6: 1 Then the L' said unto Moses, Now‡3068
2 and said unto him, I am the L': * "
6 I am the L', and I will bring you * "
7 know that I am the L' your God, * "
8 you for an heritage: I am the L'. * "
10 the L' spake unto Moses, saying, ‡ "
12 Moses spake before the L', saying,‡ "
13 L' spake unto Moses and Aaron, ‡ "
26 and Moses, to whom the L' said, ‡ "
28 L' spake unto Moses in the land ‡ "
29 the L' spake unto Moses, saying, ‡ "
29 I am the L': speak thou unto ‡ "
30 Moses said before the L', Behold, ‡ "
7: 1 And the L' said unto Moses, See, I‡ "
5 shall know that I am the L', when‡ "
6 did as the L' commanded them, ‡ "
8 the L' spake unto Moses and unto‡ "
10 did so as the L' had commanded:‡ "
13 not unto them; as the L' had said.‡ "

Ex 7: 14 the L' said unto Moses, Pharaoh's ‡3068
16 The L' God of the Hebrews hath ‡ "
17 Thus saith the L', In this thou ‡ "
17 thou shalt know that I am the L':‡ "
19 And the L' spake unto Moses, Say‡ "
20 did so, as the L' commanded; ‡ "
22 unto them; as the L' had said. ‡ "
25 that the L' had smitten the river.‡ "
8: 1 the L' spake unto Moses, Go unto‡ "
1 Thus saith the L', Let my people ‡ "
5 And the L' spake unto Moses, Say‡ "
8 Intreat the L', that he may take ‡ "
8 they may do sacrifice unto the L'.‡ "
10 is none like unto the L' our God. ‡ "
12 Moses cried unto the L' because ‡ "
13 L' did according to the word of ‡ "
15 not unto them; as the L' had said.‡ "
16 the L' said unto Moses, Say unto ‡ "
19 not unto them; as the L' had said.‡ "
20 the L' said unto Moses, Rise up ‡ "
20 Thus saith the L', Let my people ‡ "
22 I am the L' in the midst of the ‡ "
24 the L' did so; and there came a ‡ "
26 the Egyptians to the L' our God: ‡ "
27 and sacrifice to the L' our God, ‡ "
28 may sacrifice to the L' your God ‡ "
29 intreat the L' that the swarms of ‡ "
29 people go to sacrifice to the L'. ‡ "
30 Pharaoh, and intreated the L'. ‡ "
31 L' did according to the word of ‡ "
9: 1 the L' said unto Moses, Go in ‡ "
1 saith the L' God of the Hebrews, ‡ "
3 hand of the L' is upon thy cattle ‡ "
4 L' shall sever between the cattle ‡ "
5 And the L' appointed a set time, ‡ "
5 To morrow the L' shall do this ‡ "
6 And the L' did that thing on the ‡ "
8 the L' said unto Moses and unto ‡ "
12 L' hardened the heart of Pharaoh,‡ "
12 as the L' had spoken unto Moses.‡ "
13 the L' said unto Moses, Rise up ‡ "
13 saith the L' God of the Hebrews, ‡ "
20 He that feared the word of the L' ‡ "
21 regarded not the word of the L' ‡ "
22 the L' said unto Moses, Stretch ‡ "
23 and the L' sent thunder and hail,‡ "
23 the L' rained hail upon the land ‡ "
27 the L' is righteous, and I and my‡ "
28 Intreat the L' (for it is enough) ‡ "
29 abroad my hands unto the L'; ‡ "
30 ye will not yet fear the L' God. ‡ "
33 abroad his hands unto the L': ‡ "
35 as the L' had spoken by Moses. ‡ "
10: 1 And the L' said unto Moses, Go in‡ "
2 may know how that I am the L'. ‡ "
3 saith the L' God of the Hebrews, ‡ "
7 they may serve the L' their God: ‡ "
8 them, Go, serve the L' your God: ‡ "
9 we must hold a feast unto the L'. ‡ "
10 Let the L' be so with you, as I ‡ "
11 that are men, and serve the L'; ‡ "
12 the L' said unto Moses, Stretch ‡ "
13 the L' brought an east wind upon‡ "
16 sinned against the L' your God, ‡ "
17 and intreat the L' your God, that ‡ "
18 Pharaoh, and intreated the L'. ‡ "
19 L' turned a mighty strong west ‡ "
20 the L' hardened Pharaoh's heart, ‡ "
21 the L' said unto Moses, Stretch ‡ "
24 and said, Go ye, serve the L'; ‡ "
25 may sacrifice unto the L' our God.‡ "
26 we take to serve the L' our God; ‡ "
26 with what we must serve the L', ‡ "
27 the L' hardened Pharaoh's heart, ‡ "
11: 1 the L' said unto Moses, Yet will I‡ "
3 the L' gave the people favour in ‡ "
4 saith the L', About midnight will‡ "
7 L' doth put a difference between ‡ "
9 the L' said unto Moses, Pharaoh ‡ "
10 the L' hardened Pharaoh's heart,‡ "
12: 1 L' spake unto Moses and Aaron ‡ "
12 execute judgment: I am the L'. ‡ "
14 ye shall keep it a feast to the L' ‡ "
23 the L' will pass through to smite ‡ "
23 the L' will pass over the door, ‡ "
25 land which the L' will give you, ‡ "
28 did as the L' had commanded ‡ "
29 the L' smote all the firstborn in ‡ "
31 go, serve the L', as ye have said. ‡ "
36 the L' gave the people favour in ‡ "
41 all the hosts of the L' went out ‡ "
42 to be much observed unto the L' ‡ "
42 this is that night of the L' to be ‡ "
43 L' said unto Moses and Aaron, ‡ "
48 will keep the passover to the L', ‡ "
50 as the L' commanded Moses and ‡ "
51 the L' did bring the children of ‡ "
13: 1 the L' spake unto Moses, saying, ‡ "
3 L' brought you out from this ‡ "
5 when the L' shall bring thee into ‡ "
6 day shall be a feast to the L'. ‡ "
8 because of that which the L' did ‡ "
9 hath the L' brought thee out of ‡ "
11 L' shall bring thee into the land ‡ "
12 thou shalt set apart unto the L' ‡ "
14 L' brought us out from Egypt, ‡ "
15 the L' slew all the firstborn in the‡ "
15 I sacrifice to the L' all that ‡ "
16 L' brought us forth out of Egypt. ‡ "
21 L' went before them by day in a ‡ "
14: 1 And the L' spake unto Moses, ‡ "
4 may know that I am the L'. And‡ "
8 L' hardened the heart of Pharaoh‡ "
10 of Israel cried out unto the L'. ‡ "
13 and see the salvation of the L', ‡ "
14 The L' shall fight for you, and ye‡ "

Ex 14:15 the L' said unto Moses, Wherefore ‡3068
18 shall know that I am the L', when ‡ "
21 L' caused the sea to go back by a ‡ "
24 the L' looked unto the host of the ‡ "
25 L' fighteth for them against the ‡ "
26 the L' said unto Moses, Stretch ‡ "
27 L' overthrew the Egyptians in the ‡ "
30 L' saved Israel that day out of ‡ "
31 great work which the L' did upon ‡ "
31 feared the L', and believed the L', ‡ "
15: 1 of Israel this song unto the L', ‡ "
1 I will sing unto the L', for he ‡ "
2 The L' is my strength and song, ‡ "
3 L' is a man of war; the L' is his ‡ "
6 Thy right hand, O L', is become ‡ "
6 thy right hand, O L', hath dashed ‡ "
11 Who is like unto thee, O L', ‡ "
16 till thy people pass over, O L', ‡ "
17 in the place, O L', which thou ‡ "
17 Sanctuary, O L', which thy hands ‡ "
18 The L' shall reign for ever and ‡ "
19 L' brought again the waters of ‡ "
21 answered them, Sing ye to the L', ‡ "
25 And he cried unto the L'; ‡ "
25 and the L' shewed him a tree, ‡ "
26 hearken to the voice of the L' thy ‡ "
26 for I am the L' that healeth thee. ‡ "
16: 3 We had died by the hand of the L' ‡ "
4 Then said the L' unto Moses, ‡ "
6 ye shall know that the L' hath ‡ "
7 ye shall see the glory of the L'; ‡ "
7 your murmurings against the L': ‡ "
8 when the L' shall give you in the ‡ "
8 the L' heareth your murmurings ‡ "
8 against us, but against the L'. ‡ "
9 Israel, Come near before the L': ‡ "
10 of the L' appeared in the cloud. ‡ "
11 And the L' spake unto Moses, ‡ "
12 ye shall know that I am the L' ‡ "
15 bread which the L' hath given ‡ "
16 which the L' hath commanded, ‡ "
23 is that which the L' hath said, ‡ "
23 of the holy sabbath unto the L': ‡ "
25 to day is a sabbath unto the L': ‡ "
28 the L' said unto Moses, How long ‡ "
29 the L' hath given you the sabbath, ‡ "
32 thing which the L' commandeth, ‡ "
33 and lay it up before the L', to be ‡ "
34 As the L' commanded Moses, so ‡ "
17: 1 to the commandment of the L', ‡ "
2 Wherefore do ye tempt the L'? ‡ "
4 Moses cried unto the L', saying, ‡ "
5 And the L' said unto Moses, Go on ‡ "
7 and because they tempted the L', ‡ "
7 Is the L' among us, or not? ‡ "
14 the L' said unto Moses, Write ‡ "
16 Because the L' hath sworn that ‡ "
16 the L' will have war with Amalek ‡ "
18: 1 the L' hath brought Israel out of ‡ "
8 law all that the L' had done unto ‡ "
8 and how the L' delivered them. ‡ "
9 goodness which the L' had done ‡ "
10 Jethro said, Blessed be the L', ‡ "
11 the L' is greater than all gods: ‡ "
19: 3 the L' called unto him out of the ‡ "
7 words which the L' commanded ‡ "
8 the L' hath spoken we will do. ‡ "
8 words of the people unto the L'. ‡ "
9 And the L' said unto Moses, Lo, I ‡ "
9 words of the people unto the L'. ‡ "
10 the L' said unto Moses, Go unto ‡ "
11 third day the L' will come down ‡ "
18 the L' descended upon it in fire: ‡ "
20 L' came down upon mount Sinai, ‡ "
20 L' called Moses up to the top of ‡ "
21 the L' said unto Moses, Go down, ‡ "
21 they break through unto the L' ‡ "
22 also, which come near to the L', ‡ "
22 the L' break forth upon them. ‡ "
23 And Moses said unto the L', The ‡ "
24 the L' said unto him, Away, get ‡ "
24 through to come up unto the L', ‡ "
20: 2 I am the L' thy God, which have ‡ "
5 the L' thy God am a jealous God, ‡ "
7 name of the L' thy God in vain; ‡ "
7 the L' will not hold him guiltless ‡ "
10 day is the sabbath of the L' thy ‡ "
11 the L' made heaven and earth, ‡ "
11 the L' blessed the sabbath day, ‡ "
12 the land which the L' thy God ‡ "
22 the L' said unto Moses, Thus ‡ "
22:11 an oath of the L' be between ‡ "
20 any god, save unto the L' only, ‡ "
23:17 males shall appear before the L' ‡ "
19 bring into the house of the L'. ‡ "
25 ye shall serve the L' your God, ‡ "
24: 1 Come up unto the L', thou, and ‡ "
2 alone shall come near the L': ‡ "
3 the people all the words of the L', ‡ "
3 All the words which the L' hath ‡ "
4 wrote all the words of the L', ‡ "
5 offerings of oxen unto the L'. ‡ "
7 All that the L' hath said will we ‡ "
8 which the L' hath made with you ‡ "
12 the L' said unto Moses, Come up ‡ "
16 glory of the L' abode upon mount ‡ "
17 glory of the L' was like devouring ‡ "
25: 1 And the L' spake unto Moses, ‡ "
27:21 evening to morning before the L': ‡ "
28:12 bear their names before the L' ‡ "
29 before the L' continually. ‡ "
30 when he goeth in before the L': ‡ "
30 heart before the L' continually. ‡ "
35 unto the holy place before the L', ‡ "
36 of a signet, Holiness To The L'. ‡ "
38 may be accepted before the L'. ‡ "

Ex 29:11 kill the bullock before the L', ‡3068
18 it is a burnt offering unto the L': ‡ "
18 offering made by fire unto the L'. ‡ "
23 bread that is before the L': ‡ "
24 for a wave offering before the L'. ‡ "
25 for a sweet savour before the L': ‡ "
25 offering made by fire unto the L'. ‡ "
26 for a wave offering before the L': ‡ "
28 their heave offering unto the L'. ‡ "
41 offering made by fire unto the L'. ‡ "
42 of the congregation before the L': ‡ "
46 know that I am the L' their God, ‡ "
46 them: I am the L' their God. ‡ "
30: 8 a perpetual incense before the L' ‡ "
10 it is most holy unto the L'. ‡ "
11 And the L' spake unto Moses, ‡ "
12 ransom for his soul unto the L', ‡ "
13 shall be the offering of the L'. ‡ "
14 shall give an offering unto the L'. ‡ "
15 they give an offering unto the L', ‡ "
16 children of Israel before the L', ‡ "
17 And the L' spake unto Moses, ‡ "
20 offering made by fire unto the L': ‡ "
22 the L' spake unto Moses, saying, ‡ "
34 And the L' said unto Moses, Take ‡ "
37 shall be unto thee holy for the L'. ‡ "
31: 1, 12 And the L' spake unto Moses, ‡ "
13 am the L' that doth sanctify you. ‡ "
15 the sabbath of rest, holy to the L': ‡ "
17 the L' made heaven and earth, ‡ "
32: 5 To morrow is a feast to the L'. ‡ "
7 the L' said unto Moses, Go, get ‡ "
9 the L' said unto Moses, I have ‡ "
11 Moses besought the L' his God, ‡ "
11 L', Why doth thy wrath wax hot ‡ "
14 L' repented of the evil which he ‡ "
22 Let not the anger of my l' wax hot: 113
27 Thus saith the L' God of Israel, ‡3068
29 yourselves to day to the L', even ‡ "
30 and now I will go up unto the L'; ‡ "
31 Moses returned unto the L', and ‡ "
33 And the L' said unto Moses, ‡ "
35 And the L' plagued the people, ‡ "
33: 1 the L' said unto Moses, Depart, ‡ "
5 the L' had said unto Moses, Say ‡ "
7 every one which sought the L' ‡ "
9 and the L' talked with Moses.
11 L' spake unto Moses face to face, ‡3068
12 Moses said unto the L', See, thou ‡ "
17 the L' said unto Moses, I will do ‡ "
19 will proclaim the name of the L' ‡ "
21 And the L' said, Behold, there is a ‡ "
34: 1 the L' said unto Moses, Hew thee ‡ "
4 Sinai, as the L' had commanded ‡ "
5 the L' descended in the cloud, ‡ "
5 proclaimed the name of the L'. ‡ "
6 the L' passed by before him, and ‡ "
6 The L', The L' God, merciful and ‡ "
9 O L', let my L', I pray thee, go 136
10 art shall see the work of the L': ‡3068
14 for the L', whose name is Jealous, ‡ "
23 appear before the L' God, ‡ "
24 the L' thy God thrice in the year. ‡ "
26 bring unto the house of the L' thy ‡ "
27 And the L' said unto Moses, Write ‡ "
28 there with the L' forty days and ‡ "
32 that the L' hath spoken with him ‡ "
34 before the L' to speak with him, ‡ "
35: 1 These are words which the L' hath ‡ "
2 day, a sabbath of rest to the L': ‡ "
4 thing which the L' commanded, ‡ "
5 you an offering unto the L': ‡ "
5 bring it, an offering of the L'; ‡ "
10 all that the L' hath commanded; ‡ "
22 an offering of gold unto the L'. ‡ "
29 a willing offering unto the L', ‡ "
29 which the L' had commanded to ‡ "
30 See, the L' hath called by name ‡ "
36: 1 in whom the L' put wisdom and ‡ "
1 all that the L' had commanded. ‡ "
2 heart the L' had put wisdom, ‡ "
5 which the L' commanded to make. ‡ "
38:22 all that the L' commanded Moses. ‡ "
39: 1,5,7,21,26,29 L' commanded Moses. ‡ "
30 of a signet, Holiness To The L'. ‡ "
31 as the L' commanded Moses. ‡ "
32, 42 that the L' commanded Moses, ‡ "
43 done it as the L' had commanded, ‡ "
40: 1 And the L' spake unto Moses, ‡ "
16 to all that the L' commanded him, ‡ "
19, 21 as the L' commanded Moses. ‡ "
23 in order upon it before the L'; ‡ "
23 as the L' had commanded Moses. ‡ "
25 he lighted the lamps before the L'; ‡ "
25, 27, 29, 32 L' commanded Moses. ‡ "
34, 35 the glory of the L' filled the ‡ "
38 the cloud of the L' was upon the ‡ "
Le 1: 1 And the L' called unto Moses, ‡ "
2 you bring an offering unto the L', ‡ "
3 of the congregation before the L'. ‡ "
5 shall kill the bullock before the L': ‡ "
9 of a sweet savour unto the L'. ‡ "
11 the altar northward before the L': ‡ "
13 of a sweet savour unto the L'. ‡ "
14 his offering to the L' be of fowls, ‡ "
17 of a sweet savour unto the L'. ‡ "
2: 1 offer a meat offering unto the L', ‡ "
2 of a sweet savour unto the L': ‡ "
3 offerings of the L' made by fire. ‡ "
8 made of these things unto the L': ‡ "
9 of a sweet savour unto the L'. ‡ "
10 offerings of the L' made by fire. ‡ "
11 which ye shall bring unto the L', ‡ "
11 any offering of the L' made by fire. ‡ "
12 ye shall offer them unto the L': ‡ "
14 of thy firstfruits unto the L', ‡ "

Le 2:16 offering made by fire unto the L'. ‡3068
3: 1 it without blemish before the L'. ‡ "
3 offering made by fire unto the L'; ‡ "
5 of a sweet savour unto the L'. ‡ "
6 offering unto the L' be of the flock; ‡ "
7 then shall he offer it before the L'. ‡ "
9 offering made by fire unto the L'; ‡ "
11 offering made by fire unto the L'. ‡ "
12 he shall offer it before the L'. ‡ "
14 offering made by fire unto the L'; ‡ "
4: 1 And the L' spake unto Moses, ‡ "
2 of the commandments of the L' ‡ "
3 bullock without blemish unto the L' ‡ "
4 of the congregation before the L'; ‡ "
4 and kill the bullock before the L'. ‡ "
6 blood seven times before the L', ‡ "
7 of sweet incense before the L', ‡ "
13 of the commandments of the L' ‡ "
15 head of the bullock before the L': ‡ "
15 bullock shall be killed before the L'. ‡ "
17 it seven times before the L', ‡ "
18 of the altar which is before the L', ‡ "
22 of the commandments of the L' ‡ "
24 the burnt offering before the L': ‡ "
27 of the commandments of the L' ‡ "
31 for a sweet savour unto the L'; ‡ "
35 offerings made by fire unto the L': ‡ "
5: 6 his trespass offering unto the L' ‡ "
7 or two young pigeons, unto the L'; ‡ "
12 offerings made by fire unto the L': ‡ "
14 And the L' spake unto Moses, ‡ "
15 in the holy things of the L'; ‡ "
15 bring for his trespass unto the L' ‡ "
17 by the commandments of the L'; ‡ "
19 certainly trespassed against the L'. ‡ "
6: 1 And the L' spake unto Moses, ‡ "
2 commit a trespass against the L', ‡ "
6 his trespass offering unto the L', ‡ "
7 atonement for him before the L': ‡ "
8 And the L' spake unto Moses, ‡ "
14 of Aaron shall offer it before the L', ‡ "
15 the memorial of it, unto the L'. ‡ "
18 offerings of the L' made by fire: ‡ "
19 And the L' spake unto Moses, ‡ "
20 offer unto the L' in the day when ‡ "
21 for a sweet savour unto the L'. ‡ "
22 it is a statute for ever unto the L'; ‡ "
24 And the L' spake unto Moses, ‡ "
25 sin offering be killed before the L': ‡ "
7: 5 offering made by fire unto the L': ‡ "
11 which he shall offer unto the L'. ‡ "
14 for an heave offering unto the L', ‡ "
20 offerings that pertain unto the L', ‡ "
21 which pertain unto the L', ‡ "
22 And the L' spake unto Moses, ‡ "
25 offering made by fire unto the L', ‡ "
28 And the L' spake unto Moses, ‡ "
29 of his peace offerings unto the L' ‡ "
29 shall bring his oblation unto the L' ‡ "
30 offerings of the L' made by fire, ‡ "
30 for a wave offering before the L'. ‡ "
35 offerings of the L' made by fire, ‡ "
35 minister unto the L' in the priest's ‡ "
36 the L' commanded to be given ‡ "
38 L' commanded Moses in mount ‡ "
38 offer their oblations unto the L', ‡ "
8: 1 And the L' spake unto Moses, ‡ "
4 Moses did as the L' commanded ‡ "
5 the L' commanded to be done. ‡ "
9, 13, 17 the L' commanded Moses. ‡ "
21 offering made by fire unto the L'; ‡ "
21 as the L' commanded Moses. ‡ "
26 bread, that was before the L', ‡ "
27 for a wave offering before the L'. ‡ "
28 offering made by fire unto the L'. ‡ "
29 for a wave offering before the L': ‡ "
29 as the L' commanded Moses. ‡ "
34 so the L' hath commanded to do, ‡ "
35 keep the charge of the L', that ye ‡ "
36 the L' commanded by the hand of ‡ "
9: 2 and offer them before the L'. ‡ "
4 to sacrifice before the L'; ‡ "
4 to day the L' will appear unto you. ‡ "
5 drew near and stood before the L'. ‡ "
6 L' commanded that ye should do: ‡ "
6 glory of the L' shall appear unto ‡ "
7 for them; as the L' commanded. ‡ "
10 as the L' commanded Moses. ‡ "
21 for a wave offering before the L'; ‡ "
23 glory of the L' appeared unto all ‡ "
24 came a fire out from before the L', ‡ "
10: 1 offered strange fire before the L', ‡ "
2 there went out fire from the L', ‡ "
2 and they died before the L'. ‡ "
3 This is it that the L' spake, ‡ "
6 burning...the L' hath kindled. ‡ "
7 anointing oil of the L' is upon ‡ "
8 the L' spake unto Aaron, saying, ‡ "
11 statutes which the L' hath spoken ‡ "
12 offerings of the L' made by fire, ‡ "
13 sacrifices of the L' made by fire: ‡ "
15 for a wave offering before the L'; ‡ "
15 ever; as the L' hath commanded. ‡ "
17 atonement for them before the L'? ‡ "
19 their burnt offering before the L'; ‡ "
19 accepted in the sight of the L'? ‡ "
11: 1 L' spake unto Moses and to Aaron, ‡ "
44 I am the L' your God: ye shall ‡ "
45 I am the L' that bringeth you up ‡ "
12: 1 And the L' spake unto Moses, ‡ "
7 Who shall offer it before the L', ‡ "
13: 1 L' spake unto Moses and Aaron, ‡ "
14: 1 And the L' spake unto Moses, ‡ "
11 before the L', at the door of the ‡ "
12 for a wave offering before the L': ‡ "
16 finger seven times before the L': ‡ "

Le 14:18 atonement for him before the L'. ‡3068
23 of the congregation, before the L'. ‡ "
24 for a wave offering before the L': ‡ "
27 hand seven times before the L': ‡ "
29 atonement for him before the L'. ‡ "
31 that is to be cleansed before the L'. ‡ "
33 the L' spake unto Moses and unto ‡ "
15: 1 L' spake unto Moses and to Aaron, ‡ "
14 come before the L' unto the door ‡ "
15 atonement for him before the L' ‡ "
30 atonement for her before the L' ‡ "
16: 1 And the L' spake unto Moses ‡ "
1 when they offered before the L', ‡ "
2 the L' said unto Moses, Speak ‡ "
7 and present them before the L' ‡ "
8 one lot for the L', and the other ‡ "
10 be presented alive before the L', ‡ "
12 from off the altar before the L', ‡ "
13 upon the fire before the L', incense ‡ "
18 the altar that is before the L', ‡ "
30 from all your sins before the L'. ‡ "
34 did as the L' commanded Moses. ‡ "
17: 1 the L' spake unto Moses, saying, ‡ "
2 which the L' hath commanded, ‡ "
4 to offer an offering unto the L' ‡ "
4 before the tabernacle of the L'; ‡ "
5 they may bring them unto the L', ‡ "
5 for peace offerings unto the L'. ‡ "
6 the blood upon the altar of the L' ‡ "
6 for a sweet savour unto the L'. ‡ "
9 to offer it unto the L'; even ‡ "
18: 1 the L' spake unto Moses, saying, ‡ "
2 unto them, I am the L' your God. ‡ "
4 therein: I am the L' your God. ‡ "
5 he shall live in them: I am the L'. ‡ "
6 their nakedness: I am the L'. ‡ "
21 the name of thy God: I am the L'. ‡ "
30 therein: I am the L' your God. ‡ "
19: 1 the L' spake unto Moses, saying, ‡ "
2 for I the L' your God am holy. ‡ "
3 sabbaths: I am the L' your God. ‡ "
4 gods: I am the L' your God. ‡ "
5 of peace offerings unto the L', ‡ "
8 the hallowed thing of the L'; ‡ "
10 stranger: I am the L' your God. ‡ "
12 the name of thy God: I am the L'. ‡ "
14 shalt fear thy God: I am the L'. ‡ "
16 of thy neighbour: I am the L'. ‡ "
18 neighbour as thyself: I am the L'. ‡ "
21 his trespass offering unto the L', ‡ "
22 the trespass offering before the L' ‡ "
24 be holy to praise the L' withal. ‡ "
25 thereof: I am the L' your God. ‡ "
28 any marks upon you: I am the L'. ‡ "
30 my sanctuary: I am the L'. ‡ "
31 by them: I am the L' your God. ‡ "
32 and fear thy God: I am the L'. ‡ "
34 of Egypt: I am the L' your God. ‡ "
36 I am the L' your God, which ‡ "
37 and do them: I am the L'. ‡ "
20: 1 the L' spake unto Moses, saying, ‡ "
7 ye holy: for I am the L' your God. ‡ "
8 I am the L' which sanctify you. ‡ "
24 I am the L' your God, which have ‡ "
26 holy unto me: for I the L' am holy, ‡ "
21: 1 the L' said unto Moses, Speak ‡ "
6 offerings of the L' made by fire, ‡ "
8 for I the L', which sanctify you, ‡ "
12 his God is upon him: I am the L'. ‡ "
15 for I the L' do sanctify him. ‡ "
16 the L' spake unto Moses, saying, ‡ "
21 offerings of the L' made by fire: ‡ "
23 for I the L' do sanctify them. ‡ "
22: 1 the L' spake unto Moses, saying, ‡ "
2 they hallow unto me: I am the L'. ‡ "
3 of Israel hallow unto the L', ‡ "
3 from my presence: I am the L'. ‡ "
8 himself therewith: I am the L'. ‡ "
9 it: I the L' do sanctify them. ‡ "
15 which they offer unto the L'; ‡ "
16 for I the L' do sanctify them. ‡ "
17 the L' spake unto Moses, saying, ‡ "
18 they will offer unto the L' for a ‡ "
21 unto the L' to accomplish his vow, ‡ "
22 shall not offer these unto the L', ‡ "
22 them upon the altar unto the L'. ‡ "
24 unto the L' that which is bruised, ‡ "
26 the L' spake unto Moses, saying, ‡ "
27 offering made by fire unto the L'. ‡ "
29 of thanksgiving unto the L', offer ‡ "
30 it until the morrow: I am the L'. ‡ "
31 and do them: I am the L'. ‡ "
32 I am the L' which hallow you, ‡ "
33 to be your God: I am the L'. ‡ "
23: 1 the L' spake unto Moses, saying, ‡ "
2 Concerning the feasts of the L', ‡ "
3 the sabbath of the L' in all your ‡ "
4 These are the feasts of the L', ‡ "
6 of unleavened bread unto the L': ‡ "
8 offering made by fire unto the L' ‡ "
9 the L' spake unto Moses, saying, ‡ "
11 wave the sheaf before the L', ‡ "
12 for a burnt offering unto the L'. ‡ "
13 offering made by fire unto the L' ‡ "
16 a new meat offering unto the L'. ‡ "
17 they are the firstfruits unto the L'. ‡ "
18 for a burnt offering unto the L', ‡ "
18 fire, of sweet savour unto the L', ‡ "
20 for a wave offering before the L', ‡ "
20 be holy to the L' for the priest. ‡ "
22 stranger: I am the L' your God. ‡ "
23 the L' spake unto Moses, saying, ‡ "
25 offering made by fire unto the L'. ‡ "
26 the L' spake unto Moses, saying, ‡ "
27 offering made by fire unto the L'. ‡ "
28 atonement for you before the L' ‡ "

Le 23:33 the L' spake unto Moses, saying, ‡3068
34 for seven days unto the L'. ‡ "
36, 36 offering...by fire unto the L': ‡ "
37 These are the feasts of the L', ‡ "
37 offering made by fire unto the L', ‡ "
38 Beside the sabbaths of the L', ‡ "
38 offerings, which ye give unto the L'. ‡ "
39 keep a feast unto the L' seven ‡ "
40 rejoice before the L' your God ‡ "
41 keep it a feast unto the L' seven ‡ "
43 of Egypt: I am the L' your God. ‡ "
44 of Israel the feasts of the L'. ‡ "
24: 1 the L' spake unto Moses, saying, ‡ "
3 before the L' continually: morning ‡ "
4 the pure candlestick before the L' ‡ "
6 upon the pure table before the L'. ‡ "
7 offering made by fire unto the L'. ‡ "
8 shall set it in order before the L' ‡ "
9 offerings of the L' made by fire ‡ "
11 blasphemed the name of the L', *
12 mind of the L' might be shewed ‡3068
13 the L' spake unto Moses, saying, ‡ "
16 blasphemeth the name of the L', ‡ "
22 for I am the L' your God. ‡ "
23 did as the L' commanded Moses. ‡ "
25: 1 L' spake unto Moses in mount ‡ "
2 land keep a sabbath unto the L'. ‡ "
4 the land, a sabbath for the L': ‡ "
17 God: for I am the L' your God. ‡ "
38 I am the L' your God, which ‡ "
55 of Egypt: I am the L' your God. ‡ "
26: 1 unto it: for I am the L' your God. ‡ "
2 my sanctuary: I am the L'. ‡ "
13 I am the L' your God, which ‡ "
44 them: for I am the L' their God. ‡ "
45 might be their God: I am the L'. ‡ "
46 laws, which the L' made between ‡ "
27: 1 the L' spake unto Moses, saying, ‡ "
2 be for the L' by thy estimation. ‡ "
9 men bring an offering unto the L', ‡ "
9 man giveth of such unto the L' ‡ "
11 not offer a sacrifice unto the L', ‡ "
14 his house to be holy unto the L', ‡ "
16 a man shall sanctify unto the L' ‡ "
21 jubile, shall be holy unto the L', ‡ "
22 man sanctify unto the L' a field ‡ "
23 day, as a holy thing unto the L'. ‡ "
28 devote unto the L' of all that he ‡ "
28 thing is most holy unto the L'. ‡ "
30 is the Lord's: it is holy unto the L'. ‡ "
32 tenth shall be holy unto the L'. ‡ "
34 which the L' commanded Moses ‡ "
Nu 1: 1 the L' spake unto Moses in the ‡ "
19 As the L' commanded Moses, so ‡ "
48 L' had spoken unto Moses, saying, ‡ "
54 all that the L' commanded Moses, ‡ "
2: 1 the L' spake unto Moses and unto ‡ "
33 as the L' commanded Moses. ‡ "
34 all that the L' commanded Moses: ‡ "
3: 1 L' spake with Moses in mount ‡ "
4 and Abihu died before the L', ‡ "
4 offered strange fire before the L', ‡ "
5, 11 L' spake unto Moses, saying, ‡ "
13 mine shall they be: I am the L'. ‡ "
14 the L' spake unto Moses in the ‡ "
16 according to the word of the L', ‡ "
39 at the commandment of the L', ‡ "
40 the L' said unto Moses, Number ‡ "
41 the Levites for me (I am the L') ‡ "
42 as the L' commanded him, all ‡ "
44 the L' spake unto Moses, saying, ‡ "
45 shall be mine: I am the L'. ‡ "
51 according to the word of the L', ‡ "
51 as the L' commanded Moses. ‡ "
4: 1, 17 L' spake unto Moses and unto ‡ "
21 the L' spake unto Moses, saying, ‡ "
37 to the commandment of the L' ‡ "
41 to the commandment of the L'. ‡ "
45 according to the word of the L' ‡ "
49 to the commandment of the L' ‡ "
49 as the L' commanded Moses. ‡ "
5: 1 the L' spake unto Moses, saying, ‡ "
4 as the L' spake unto Moses, so ‡ "
5 the L' spake unto Moses, saying, ‡ "
6 to do a trespass against the L', ‡ "
8 be recompensed unto the L', even ‡ "
11 the L' spake unto Moses, saying, ‡ "
16 near, and set her before the L': ‡ "
18 shall set the woman before the L', ‡ "
21 L' make thee a curse and an oath ‡ "
21 L' doth make thy thigh to rot, ‡ "
25 wave the offering before the L', ‡ "
30 shall set the woman before the L', ‡ "
6: 1 the L' spake unto Moses, saying, ‡ "
2 separate themselves unto the L': ‡ "
5 separateth himself unto the L', ‡ "
6 separateth himself unto the L' ‡ "
8 separation he is holy unto the L'. ‡ "
12 consecrate unto the L' the days ‡ "
14 shall offer his offering unto the L', ‡ "
16 shall bring them before the L', ‡ "
17 of peace offerings unto the L', ‡ "
20 for a wave offering before the L': ‡ "
21 of his offering unto the L' for his ‡ "
22 the L' spake unto Moses, saying, ‡ "
24 The L' bless thee, and keep thee: ‡ "
25 L' make his face shine upon thee, ‡ "
26 L' lift up his countenance upon ‡ "
7: 3 their offering before the L', ‡ "
4 the L' spake unto Moses, saying, ‡ "
11 And the L' said unto Moses, They ‡ "
8: 1 the L' spake unto Moses, saying, ‡ "
3 as the L' commanded Moses. ‡ "
4 pattern which the L' had shewed ‡ "
5 the L' spake unto Moses, saying, ‡ "
10 bring the Levites before the L': ‡ "

Nu 8:11 offer the Levites before the L' ‡3068
11 may execute the service of the L'. ‡ "
12 for a burnt offering, unto the L', ‡ "
13 them for an offering unto the L'. ‡ "
20 all that the L' commanded Moses ‡ "
21 them as an offering before the L'; ‡ "
22 as the L' had commanded Moses ‡ "
23 the L' spake unto Moses, saying, ‡ "
9: 1 the L' spake unto Moses in the ‡ "
5 all that the L' commanded Moses, ‡ "
7 of the L' in his appointed season ‡ "
8 hear what the L' will command ‡ "
9 the L' spake unto Moses, saying, ‡ "
10 keep the passover unto the L'. ‡ "
13 of the L' in his appointed season, ‡ "
14 keep the passover unto the L'; ‡ "
18 At the commandment of the L' ‡ "
18 at the commandment of the L' ‡ "
19 Israel kept the charge of the L', ‡ "
20, 20 to the commandment of the L' ‡ "
23 At the commandment of the L' ‡ "
23 at the commandment of the L' ‡ "
23 they kept the charge of the L', ‡ "
23 at the commandment of the L' ‡ "
10: 1 the L' spake unto Moses, saying, ‡ "
9 be remembered before the L' ‡ "
10 your God: I am the L' your God. ‡ "
13 to the commandment of the L' by ‡ "
29 the place of which the L' said, ‡ "
29 L' hath spoken good concerning ‡ "
32 goodness the L' shall do unto us, ‡ "
33 departed from the mount of the L' ‡ "
33 the ark of the covenant of the L' ‡ "
34 cloud of the L' was upon them ‡ "
35 Rise up, L', and let thine enemies ‡ "
36 Return, O L', unto the many ‡ "
11: 1 complained, it displeased the L': ‡ "
1 the L' heard it; and his anger ‡ "
1 fire of the L' burnt among them, ‡ "
2 when Moses prayed unto the L', ‡ "
3 fire of the L' burnt among them. ‡ "
10 the anger of the L' was kindled ‡ "
11 Moses said unto the L', Wherefore ‡ "
16 the L' said unto Moses, Gather ‡ "
18 have wept in the ears of the L', ‡ "
18 the L' will give you flesh, and ye ‡ "
20 that ye have despised the L' ‡ "
23 the L' said unto Moses, Is the ‡ "
24 the people the words of the L', ‡ "
25 And the L' came down in a cloud, ‡ "
28 and said, My l' Moses, forbid them. 113
29 the L' would put his spirit upon ‡3068
31 went forth a wind from the L', ‡ "
33 the wrath of the L' was kindled ‡ "
33 L' smote the people with a very ‡ "
12: 2 Hath the L' indeed spoken only ‡ "
2 also by us? And the L' heard it. ‡ "
4 L' spake suddenly unto Moses, ‡ "
5 L' came down in the pillar of the ‡ "
6 I the L' will make myself known ‡ "
8 the similitude of the L' shall he ‡ "
9 the anger of the L' was kindled ‡ "
11 Aaron said unto Moses, Alas, my l', 113
13 Moses cried unto the L', saying, ‡3068
14 the L' said unto Moses, If her ‡ "
13: 1 the L' spake unto Moses, saying, ‡ "
3 by the commandment of the L' ‡ "
14: 3 wherefore hath the L' brought us ‡ "
8 If the L' delight in us, then he ‡ "
9 Only rebel not ye against the L', ‡ "
9 from them, and the L' is with us: ‡ "
10 the glory of the L' appeared in ‡ "
11 the L' said unto Moses, How long ‡ "
13 Moses said unto the L', Then the ‡ "
14 thou L' art among this people, ‡ "
14 that thou L' art seen face to face, ‡ "
16 the L' was not able to bring this ‡ "
17 let the power of my L' be great, 136
18 The L' is longsuffering, and of ‡3068
20 And the L' said, I have pardoned ‡ "
21 be filled with the glory of the L'. ‡ "
26 the L' spake unto Moses and ‡ "
28 As truly as I live, saith the L', as ‡ "
35 I the L' have said, I will surely ‡ "
37 died by the plague before the L'. ‡ "
40 place which the L' hath promised: ‡ "
41 the commandment of the L'? ‡ "
42 for the Lord is not among you; ‡ "
43 ye are turned away from the L', ‡ "
43 the L' will not be with you. ‡ "
44 the ark of the covenant of the L', ‡ "
15: 1 the L' spake unto Moses, saying, ‡ "
3 offering by fire unto the L', ‡ "
3 a sweet savour unto the L', ‡ "
4 offereth his offering unto the L' ‡ "
7 for a sweet savour unto the L'. ‡ "
8 or peace offerings unto the L': ‡ "
10, 13 of a sweet savour unto the L'. ‡ "
14 of a sweet savour unto the L'; ‡ "
15 the stranger be before the L'. ‡ "
17 the L' spake unto Moses, saying, ‡ "
19 for an heave offering unto the L'. ‡ "
21 give unto the L' a heave offering ‡ "
22 the L' hath spoken unto Moses, ‡ "
23 that the L' hath commanded you ‡ "
23 that the L' commanded Moses, ‡ "
24 for a sweet savour unto the L', ‡ "
25 sacrifice made by fire unto the L', ‡ "
25 their sin offering before the L', ‡ "
28 by ignorance before the L', to ‡ "
30 the same reproacheth the L'; ‡ "
31 hath despised the word of the L', ‡ "
35 the L' said unto Moses, The man ‡ "
36 as the L' commanded Moses. ‡ "
37 the L' spake unto Moses, saying, ‡ "
39 all the commandments of the L', ‡ "

Nu 15:41 I am the *L'* your God, which ‡3068
41 your God: I am the *L'* your God. ‡ "
16: 3 them, and the *L'* is among them: ‡ "
3 above the congregation of the *L'*? ‡ "
5 the *L'* will shew who are his, ‡ "
7 incense in them before the *L'* ‡ "
7 man whom the *L'* doth choose, ‡ "
9 service of the tabernacle of the *L'*, ‡ "
11 gathered together against the *L'*: ‡ "
15 very wroth, and said unto the *L'*, ‡ "
16 all thy company before the *L'*, ‡ "
17 bring ye before the *L'* every man ‡ "
19 the glory of the *L'* appeared unto ‡ "
20 the *L'* spake unto Moses and unto ‡ "
23 the *L'* spake unto Moses, saying, ‡ "
28 shall know that the *L'* hath sent ‡ "
29 then the *L'* hath not sent me. ‡ "
30 if the *L'* make a new thing, and ‡ "
30 these men have provoked the *L'*. ‡ "
35 there came out a fire from the *L'*, ‡ "
36 the *L'* spake to Moses, saying, ‡ "
38 they offered them before the *L'*, ‡ "
40 to offer incense before the *L'*; ‡ "
40 *L'* said to him by the hand of ‡ "
41 have killed the people of the *L'*. ‡ "
42 And the glory of the *L'* appeared. ‡ "
44 the *L'* spake unto Moses, saying, ‡ "
46 is wrath gone out from the *L'*; ‡ "
17: 1 the *L'* spake unto Moses, saying, ‡ "
7 laid up the rods before the *L'* in ‡ "
9 all the rods from before the *L'* ‡ "
10 And the *L'* said unto Moses, Bring ‡ "
11 as the *L'* commanded him, so did ‡ "
13 the tabernacle of the *L'* shall die: ‡ "
18: 1 the *L'* said unto Aaron, Thou and ‡ "
6 they are given as a gift for the *L'*, ‡ "
8 the *L'* spake unto Aaron, Behold, ‡ "
12 which they shall offer unto the *L'*, ‡ "
13 which they shall bring unto the *L'*, ‡ "
15 which they bring unto the *L'*, ‡ "
17 for a sweet savour unto the *L'*. ‡ "
19 children of Israel offer unto the *L'*, ‡ "
19 of salt for ever before the *L'* unto ‡ "
20 the *L'* spake unto Aaron, Thou ‡ "
24 as an heave offering unto the *L'*, ‡ "
25 the *L'* spake unto Moses, saying, ‡ "
26 an heave offering of it for the *L'*, ‡ "
28 an heave offering unto the *L'* of ‡ "
29 every heave offering of the *L'*, of ‡ "
19: 1 the *L'* spake unto Moses and unto ‡ "
2 which the *L'* hath commanded, ‡ "
13 defileth the tabernacle of the *L'*; ‡ "
20 defiled the sanctuary of the *L'*: ‡ "
20: 3 our brethren died before the *L'*! ‡ "
4 up the congregation of the *L'* into ‡ "
6 the glory of the *L'* appeared unto ‡ "
7 the *L'* spake unto Moses, saying, ‡ "
9 took the rod from before the *L'*, ‡ "
12 *L'* spake unto Moses and Aaron, ‡ "
13 of Israel strove with the *L'*, and ‡ "
16 And when we cried unto the *L'*, he ‡ "
23 *L'* spake unto Moses and Aaron ‡ "
27 Moses did as the *L'* commanded: ‡ "
21: 2 Israel vowed a vow unto the *L'*, ‡ "
3 the *L'* hearkened to the voice of ‡ "
6 *L'* sent fiery serpents among the ‡ "
7 we have spoken against the *L'*, ‡ "
7 pray unto the *L'*, that he take ‡ "
8 And the *L'* said unto Moses, Make ‡ "
14 in the book of the wars of the *L'*, ‡ "
16 whereof the *L'* spake unto Moses, ‡ "
34 the *L'* said unto Moses, Fear him ‡ "
22: 8 as the *L'* shall speak unto me: ‡ "
13 *L'* refuseth to give me leave to go ‡ "
18 the word of the *L'* my God, to ‡ "
19 I may know what the *L'* will say ‡ "
22 angel of the *L'* stood in the way ‡ "
23 saw the angel of the *L'* standing ‡ "
24 angel of the *L'* stood in a path of ‡ "
25 the ass saw the angel of the *L'*, ‡ "
26 angel of the *L'* went further, and ‡ "
27 the ass saw the angel of the *L'*, ‡ "
28 *L'* opened the mouth of the ass, ‡ "
31 *L'* opened the eyes of Balaam, ‡ "
31 saw the angel of the *L'* standing ‡ "
32 the angel of the *L'* said unto him, ‡ "
34 said unto the angel of the *L'*, ‡ "
35 angel of the *L'* said unto Balaam, ‡ "
23: 3 the *L'* will come to meet me: ‡ "
5 *L'* put a word in Balaam's mouth, ‡ "
8 whom the *L'* hath not defied? ‡ "
12 the *L'* hath put in my mouth? ‡ "
15 while I meet the *L'* yonder.
16 And the *L'* met Balaam, and put ‡3068
17 him, What hath the *L'* spoken? ‡ "
21 the *L'* his God is with him, and ‡ "
26 All that the *L'* speaketh, that I ‡ "
24: 1 saw that it pleased the *L'* to bless ‡ "
6 aloes which the *L'* hath planted, ‡ "
11 the *L'* hath kept thee back from ‡ "
13 the commandment of the *L'*, ‡ "
13 but what the *L'* saith, that will I ‡ "
25: 3 the anger of the *L'* was kindled ‡ "
4 the *L'* said unto Moses, Take all ‡ "
4 and hang them up before the *L'* ‡ "
4 and fierce anger of the *L'* may be ‡ "
10, 16 And the *L'* spake unto Moses, ‡ "
26: 1 the *L'* spake unto Moses and unto ‡ "
4 as the *L'* commanded Moses and ‡ "
9 when they strove against the *L'*: ‡ "
52 the *L'* spake unto Moses, saying, ‡ "
61 offered strange fire before the *L'*. ‡ "
65 For the *L'* had said of them, They ‡ "
27: 3 against the *L'* in the company of ‡ "
5 brought their cause before the *L'*, ‡ "
6 the *L'* spake unto Moses, saying, ‡ "

Nu 27:11 as the *L'* commanded Moses. ‡3068
12 the *L'* said unto Moses, Get thee ‡ "
15 Moses spake unto the *L'*, saying, ‡ "
16 Let the *L'*, the God of the spirits ‡ "
17 congregation of the *L'* be not as ‡ "
18 the *L'* said unto Moses, Take thee ‡ "
21 judgment of Urim before the *L'*: ‡ "
22 Moses did as the *L'* commanded ‡ "
23 *L'* commanded by the hand of ‡ "
28: 1 the *L'* spake unto Moses, saying, ‡ "
3 which ye shall offer unto the *L'*; ‡ "
6 sacrifice made by fire unto the *L'*. ‡ "
7 wine to be poured unto the *L'* for ‡ "
8 of a sweet savour unto the *L'*. ‡ "
11 offer a burnt offering unto the *L'*; ‡ "
13 sacrifice made by fire unto the *L'*. ‡ "
15 goats for a sin offering unto the *L'* ‡ "
16 month is the passover of the *L'*. ‡ "
19 for a burnt offering unto the *L'*; ‡ "
24 of a sweet savour unto the *L'*: ‡ "
26 a new meat offering unto the *L'*, ‡ "
27 for a sweet savour unto the *L'*; ‡ "
29: 2 for a sweet savour unto the *L'*; ‡ "
6 sacrifice made by fire unto the *L'*. ‡ "
8 offer a burnt offering unto the *L'* ‡ "
12 a feast unto the *L'* seven days: ‡ "
13 of a sweet savour unto the *L'*; ‡ "
36 of a sweet savour unto the *L'*: ‡ "
39 things ye shall do unto the *L'* in ‡ "
40 all that the *L'* commanded Moses. ‡ "
30: 1 which the *L'* hath commanded. ‡ "
2 If a man vow a vow unto the *L'*, or ‡ "
3 also vow a vow unto the *L'*, ‡ "
5 the *L'* shall forgive her, because ‡ "
8 and the *L'* shall forgive her. ‡ "
12 void; and the *L'* shall forgive her. ‡ "
16 which the *L'* commanded Moses, ‡ "
31: 1 the *L'* spake unto Moses, saying, ‡ "
3 and avenge the *L'* of Midian. ‡ "
7 as the *L'* commanded Moses; ‡ "
16 commit trespass against the *L'* ‡ "
16 among the congregation of the *L'*. ‡ "
21 the law which the *L'* commanded ‡ "
25 the *L'* spake unto Moses, saying, ‡ "
28 levy a tribute unto the *L'* of the ‡ "
29 for an heave offering of the *L'*. †‡ "
30 charge of the tabernacle of the *L'*. ‡ "
31 priest did as the *L'* commanded ‡ "
41 as the *L'* commanded Moses. ‡ "
47 charge of the tabernacle of the *L'*; ‡ "
47 as the *L'* commanded Moses. ‡ "
50 brought an oblation for the *L'*, †‡ "
50 for our souls before the *L'*. ‡ "
52 that they offered up to the *L'*, ‡ "
54 children of Israel before the *L'*. ‡ "
32: 4 the country which the *L'* smote ‡ "
7 the land which the *L'* hath given ‡ "
9 the land which the *L'* had given ‡ "
12 they have wholly followed the *L'*. ‡ "
13 done evil in the sight of the *L'*, ‡ "
14 anger of the *L'* toward Israel. ‡ "
20 go armed before the *L'* to war, ‡ "
21 armed over Jordan before the *L'*, ‡ "
22 land be subdued before the *L'*: ‡ "
22 and be guiltless before the *L'*, ‡ "
22 be your possession before the *L'*. ‡ "
23 ye have sinned against the *L'*: ‡ "
25 will do as my *l'* commandeth. 113
27 for war, before the *L'* to battle, ‡3068
27 to battle, as my *l'* saith. 113
29 armed to battle, before the *L'*, ‡3068
31 the *L'* hath said unto thy servants, ‡ "
32 will pass over armed before the *L'* ‡ "
33: 2 by the commandment of the *L'*: ‡ "
4 the *L'* had smitten among them: ‡ "
4 also the *L'* executed judgments. ‡ "
38 at the commandment of the *L'*, ‡ "
50 *L'* spake unto Moses in the plains ‡ "
34: 1 And the *L'* spake unto Moses, ‡ "
13 which the *L'* commanded to give ‡ "
16 And the *L'* spake unto Moses, ‡ "
29 the *L'* commanded to divide the ‡ "
35: 1 *L'* spake unto Moses in the plains ‡ "
9 And the *L'* spake unto Moses, ‡ "
34 I the *L'* dwell among the children ‡ "
36: 2 *L'* commanded...to give the land ‡ "
2 commanded my *l'* to give the land 113
2 my *l'* was commanded...to give the "
2 was commanded by the *L'* to give ‡3068
5 according to the word of the *L'*, ‡ "
6 thing which the *L'* doth command ‡ "
10 the *L'* commanded Moses, so did ‡ "
13 the *L'* commanded by the hand of ‡ "
De 1: 3 *L'* had given him in commandment ‡ "
6 *L'* our God spake unto us in Horeb, ‡ "
8 land which the *L'* sware unto your ‡ "
10 *L'* your God hath multiplied you, ‡ "
11 *L'* God of your fathers make you ‡ "
19 as the *L'* our God commanded us; ‡ "
20 which the *L'* our God doth give ‡ "
21 the *L'* thy God hath set the land ‡ "
21 *L'* God of thy fathers hath said ‡ "
25 which the *L'* our God doth give ‡ "
26 commandment of the *L'* your God. ‡ "
27 Because the *L'* hated us, he hath ‡ "
30 *L'* your God which goeth before ‡ "
31 how that the *L'* thy God bare thee, ‡ "
32 ye did not believe the *L'* your God, ‡ "
34 *L'* heard the voice of your words, ‡ "
36 he hath wholly followed the *L'*. ‡ "
37 the *L'* was angry with me for your ‡ "
41 We have sinned against the *L'*, ‡ "
41 that the *L'* our God commanded ‡ "
42 *L'* said unto me, Say unto them, ‡ "
43 the commandment of the *L'*, ‡ "
45 returned and went before the *L'*; ‡ "

De 1:45 the *L'* would not hearken to your ‡3068
2: 1 Red sea, as the *L'* spake unto me: ‡ "
2 the *L'* spake unto me, saying, ‡ "
7 *L'* thy God hath blessed thee in all ‡ "
7 *L'* thy God hath been with thee; ‡ "
9 the *L'* said unto me, Distress not ‡ "
12 which the *L'* gave unto them. ‡ "
14 host, as the *L'* sware unto them. ‡ "
15 hand of the *L'* was against them, ‡ "
17 the *L'* spake unto me, saying, ‡ "
21 *L'* destroyed them before them; ‡ "
29 land which the *L'* our God giveth ‡ "
30 *L'* thy God hardened his spirit, ‡ "
31 the *L'* said unto me, Behold, I ‡ "
33 *L'* our God delivered him before ‡ "
36 *L'* our God delivered all unto us: ‡ "
37 the *L'* our God forbad us. ‡ "
3: 2 *L'* said unto me, Fear him not: ‡ "
3 the *L'* our God delivered into our ‡ "
18 *L'* your God hath given you this ‡ "
20 the *L'* hath given rest unto your ‡ "
20 which the *L'* your God hath given ‡ "
21 all that the *L'* your God hath done ‡ "
21 the *L'* do unto all the kingdoms ‡ "
22 *L'* your God he shall fight for you. ‡ "
23 I besought the *L'* at that time, ‡ "
24 O *L'* God, thou hast begun to shew 136
26 *L'* was wroth with me for your ‡3068
26 the *L'* said unto me, Let it suffice ‡ "
4: 1 *L'* God of your fathers giveth ‡ "
2 commandments of the *L'* your ‡ "
3 eyes have seen what the *L'* did ‡ "
3 *L'* thy God hath destroyed them ‡ "
4 did cleave unto the *L'* your God ‡ "
5 as the *L'* my God commanded me, ‡ "
7 as the *L'* our God is in all things ‡ "
10 stoodest before the *L'* thy God in ‡ "
10 when the *L'* said unto me, Gather ‡ "
12 the *L'* spake unto you out of the ‡ "
14 *L'* commanded me at that time to ‡ "
15 the *L'* spake unto you in Horeb ‡ "
19 *L'* thy God hath divided unto all ‡ "
20 *L'* hath taken you, and brought ‡ "
21 the *L'* was angry with me for your ‡ "
21 which the *L'* thy God giveth thee ‡ "
23 forget the covenant of the *L'* your ‡ "
23 *L'* thy God hath forbidden thee. ‡ "
24 *L'* thy God is a consuming fire, ‡ "
25 evil in the sight of the *L'* thy God, ‡ "
27 *L'* shall scatter you among the ‡ "
27 whither the *L'* shall lead you. ‡ "
29 thou shalt seek the *L'* thy God, ‡ "
30 if thou turn to the *L'* thy God, ‡ "
31 the *L'* thy God is a merciful God;) ‡ "
34 *L'* your God did for you in Egypt ‡ "
35 know that the *L'* he is God; ‡ "
39 that the *L'* he is God in heaven ‡ "
40 which the *L'* thy God giveth thee, ‡ "
5: 2 *L'* our God made a covenant with ‡ "
3 *L'* made not this covenant with ‡ "
4 *L'* talked with you face to face in ‡ "
5 (I stood between the *L'* and you ‡ "
5 to shew you the word of the *L'*; ‡ "
6 am the *L'* thy God, which brought ‡ "
9 the *L'* thy God am a jealous God, ‡ "
11 name of the *L'* thy God in vain: ‡ "
11 the *L'* will not hold him guiltless ‡ "
12 *L'* thy God hath commanded thee. ‡ "
14 is the sabbath of the *L'* thy God: ‡ "
15 the *L'* thy God brought thee out ‡ "
15 *L'* thy God commanded...to keep ‡ "
16 the *L'* thy God hath commanded ‡ "
16 land which the *L'* thy God giveth ‡ "
22 *L'* spake unto all your assembly ‡ "
24 *L'* our God hath shewed us his ‡ "
25 hear the voice of the *L'* our God ‡ "
27 all that the *L'* our God shall say: ‡ "
27 all that the *L'* our God shall speak ‡ "
28 *L'* heard the voice of your words, ‡ "
28 the *L'* said unto me, I have heard ‡ "
32, 33 *L'* your God hath commanded ‡ "
6: 1 *L'* your God commanded to teach ‡ "
2 thou mightest fear the *L'* thy God, ‡ "
3 *L'* God of thy fathers...promised ‡ "
4 Israel: The *L'* our God is one *L'*: ‡ "
5 love the *L'* thy God with all thine ‡ "
10 the *L'* thy God shall have brought ‡ "
12 beware lest thou forget the *L'*, ‡ "
13 Thou shalt fear the *L'* thy God, ‡ "
15 the *L'* thy God is a jealous God ‡ "
15 anger of the *L'* thy God be kindled ‡ "
16 shall not tempt the *L'* your God, ‡ "
17 keep the commandments of the *L'* ‡ "
18 and good in the sight of the *L'*: ‡ "
18 the good land which the *L'* sware ‡ "
19 before thee, as the *L'* hath spoken. ‡ "
20 *L'* our God hath commanded you? ‡ "
21 *L'* brought us out of Egypt with ‡ "
22 *L'* shewed signs and wonders, ‡ "
24 *L'* commanded us to do all these ‡ "
24 statutes, to fear the *L'* our God, ‡ "
25 commandments before the *L'* our ‡ "
7: 1 *L'* thy God shall bring thee into ‡ "
2 the *L'* thy God shall deliver them ‡ "
4 the anger of the *L'* be kindled ‡ "
6 holy people unto the *L'* thy God: ‡ "
6 *L'* thy God hath chosen thee to be ‡ "
7 *L'* did not set his love upon you, ‡ "
8 But because the *L'* loved you, ‡ "
8 *L'* brought you out with a mighty ‡ "
9 that the *L'* thy God, he is God, ‡ "
12 *L'* thy God shall keep unto thee ‡ "
15 *L'* will take away from thee all ‡ "
16 which the *L'* thy God shall deliver ‡ "
18 the *L'* thy God did unto Pharaoh, ‡ "
19 the *L'* thy God brought thee out: ‡ "

De 7:19 so shall the L' thy God do unto all ‡3068
20 L' thy God will send the hornet ‡ "
21 for the L' thy God is among you, ‡ "
22 the L' thy God will put out those ‡ "
23 L' thy God shall deliver them unto‡ "
25 an abomination to the L' thy God.‡ "
8: 1 land which the L' sware unto your‡ "
2 way which the L' thy God led thee‡ "
3 word...out of the mouth of the L' ‡ "
5 son, so the L' thy God chasteneth‡ "
6 keep the commandments of the L'‡ "
7 L' thy God bringeth thee into a ‡ "
10 shalt bless the L' thy God for the ‡ "
11 thou forget not the L' thy God, ‡ "
14 and thou forget the L' thy God, ‡ "
18 shalt remember the L' thy God: ‡ "
19 do at all forget the L' thy God, ‡ "
20 nations which the L' destroyeth ‡ "
20 unto the voice of the L' your God.‡ "
9: 3 L' thy God is he which goeth over‡ "
3 as the L' hath said unto thee. ‡ "
4 the L' thy God hath cast them out‡ "
4 L' hath brought me in to possess ‡ "
4 the L' doth drive them out from ‡ "
5 L' thy God doth drive them out ‡ "
5 the word which the L' sware unto‡ "
6 L' thy God giveth thee not this ‡ "
7 provokedst the L' thy God to wrath‡ "
7 been rebellious against the L'. ‡ "
8 ye provoked the L' to wrath, so ‡ "
8 so that the L' was angry with you‡ "
9 covenant which the L' made with ‡ "
10 L' delivered unto me two tables of‡ "
10 L' spake with you in the mount ‡ "
11 L' gave me the two tables of stone,‡ "
12 L' said unto me, Arise, get thee ‡ "
13 the L' spake unto me, saying, I ‡ "
16 sinned against the L' your God, ‡ "
16 out of the way which the L' had ‡ "
18 I fell down before the L', as at the‡ "
18 wickedly in the sight of the L', to ‡ "
19 the L' was wroth against you to ‡ "
19 the L' hearkened unto me at that ‡ "
20 L' was very angry with Aaron to ‡ "
22 ye provoked the L' to wrath. ‡ "
23 L' sent you from Kadesh-barnea,‡ "
23 commandment of the L' your God,‡ "
24 been rebellious against the L' ‡ "
25 fell down before the L' forty days ‡ "
25 L' had said he would destroy you.‡ "
26 I prayed therefore unto the L', ‡ "
26 O L' God, destroy not thy people 136
28 the L' was not able to bring them‡3068
10: 1 that time the L' said unto me, ‡ "
4 L' spake unto you in the mount ‡ "
4 and the L' gave them unto me. ‡ "
5 they be, as the L' commanded me.‡ "
8 the L' separated the tribe of Levi,‡ "
8 the ark of the covenant of the L', ‡ "
8 before the L' to minister unto him,‡ "
9 the L' is his inheritance, ‡ "
9 as the L' thy God promised him. ‡ "
10 the L' hearkened unto me at that‡ "
10 and the L' would not destroy thee.‡ "
11 L' said unto me, Arise, take thy ‡ "
12 what doth the L' thy God require ‡ "
12 but to fear the L' thy God, to walk‡ "
12 to serve the L' thy God with all ‡ "
13 the commandments of the L', ‡ "
15 L' had a delight in thy fathers ‡ "
17 the L' your God is God of gods, ‡ "
17 L' of lords, a great God, a mighty, 113
20 Thou shalt fear the L' thy God; ‡3068
22 L' thy God hath made thee as the‡ "
11: 1 love the L' thy God, and keep his ‡ "
2 chastisement of the L' your God,‡ "
4 L' hath destroyed them unto this‡ "
7 great acts of the L' which he did. ‡ "
9 the L' sware unto your fathers ‡ "
12 land which the L' thy God careth‡ "
12 eyes of the L' thy God are always ‡ "
13 to love the L' your God, and to ‡ "
17 good land which the L' giveth you.‡ "
21 the L' sware unto your fathers ‡ "
22 to love the L' your God, to walk ‡ "
23 the L' drive out all these nations ‡ "
25 L' your God shall lay the fear of ‡ "
27, 28 obey...commandments of the L' ‡ "
29 L' thy God hath brought thee in ‡ "
31 the land which the L' your God ‡ "
12: 1 L' God of thy fathers giveth thee ‡ "
4 not do so unto the L' your God. ‡ "
5 the L' your God shall choose out ‡ "
7 shall eat before the L' your God, ‡ "
7 the L' thy God hath blessed thee. ‡ "
9 which the L' your God giveth you.‡ "
10 the land which the L' your God ‡ "
11 the L' your God shall choose to ‡ "
11 vows which ye vow unto the L': ‡ "
12 rejoice before the L' your God, ‡ "
14 place which the L' shall choose ‡ "
15 to the blessing of the L' thy God ‡ "
18 thou must eat them before the L' ‡ "
18 which the L' thy God shall choose,‡ "
18 rejoice before the L' thy God in ‡ "
20 the L' thy God shall enlarge thy ‡ "
21 which the L' thy God hath chosen‡ "
21 which the L' hath given thee, ‡ "
25 is right in the sight of the L'. ‡ "
26 place which the L' shall choose: ‡ "
27 upon the altar of the L' thy God: ‡ "
27 upon the altar of the L' thy God, ‡ "
28 and right in the sight of the L' ‡ "
29 the L' thy God shall cut off the ‡ "
31 not do so unto the L' thy God: ‡ "
31 for every abomination to the L', ‡ "

De 13: 3 for the L' your God proveth you, ‡3068
3 ye love the L' your God with all ‡ "
4 shall walk after the L' your God, ‡ "
5 to turn you away from the L' ‡ "
5 the L' thy God commanded thee ‡ "
10 to thrust thee away from the L' ‡ "
12 the L' thy God hath given thee to ‡ "
16 every whit, for the L' thy God: ‡ "
17 L' may turn from the fierceness ‡ "
18 hearken to the voice of the L' thy ‡ "
18 is right in the eyes of the L' which‡ "
14: 1 the children of the L' your God: ‡ "
2 holy people unto the L' thy God, ‡ "
2 the L' hath chosen thee to be a ‡ "
21 holy people unto the L' thy God. ‡ "
23 shalt eat before the L' thy God, ‡ "
23 to fear the L' thy God always. ‡ "
24 L' thy God shall choose to set his ‡ "
24 the L' thy God hath blessed thee:‡ "
25 which the L' thy God shall choose:‡ "
26 eat there before the L' thy God, ‡ "
29 L' thy God may bless thee in all ‡ "
15: 4 L' shall greatly bless thee in the ‡ "
4 land which the L' thy God giveth ‡ "
5 unto the voice of the L' thy God, ‡ "
6 For the L' thy God blesseth thee, ‡ "
7 land which the L' thy God giveth ‡ "
9 cry unto the L' against thee, and ‡ "
10 L' thy God shall bless thee in all ‡ "
14 the L' thy God hath blessed thee ‡ "
15 the L' thy God redeemed thee: ‡ "
18 L' thy God shall bless thee in all ‡ "
19 shalt sanctify unto the L' thy God:‡ "
20 shalt eat it before the L' thy God ‡ "
20 place which the L' shall choose, ‡ "
21 not sacrifice unto the L' thy God. ‡ "
16: 1 the passover unto the L' thy God:‡ "
1 L' thy God brought thee forth out‡ "
2 the passover unto the L' thy God,‡ "
2 place which the L' shall choose ‡ "
5 which the L' thy God giveth thee:‡ "
6 which the L' thy God shall choose‡ "
7 which the L' thy God shall choose:‡ "
8 a solemn assembly to the L' thy ‡ "
10 feast of weeks unto the L' thy God‡ "
10 shalt give unto the L' thy God, *
10 the L' thy God hath blessed thee:‡3068
11 shalt rejoice before the L' thy God,‡ "
11 which the L' thy God hath chosen‡ "
15 solemn feast unto the L' thy God ‡ "
15 place which the L' shall choose: ‡ "
15 the L' thy God shall bless thee in ‡ "
16 all thy males appear before the L'‡ "
16 not appear before the L' empty: ‡ "
17 to the blessing of the L' thy God ‡ "
18 which the L' thy God giveth thee,‡ "
20 land which the L' thy God giveth ‡ "
21 unto the altar of the L' thy God, ‡ "
22 which the L' thy God hateth. ‡ "
17: 1 not sacrifice unto the L' thy God ‡ "
1 abomination unto the L' thy God.‡ "
2 gates which the L' thy God giveth‡ "
2 wickedness in the sight of the L' ‡ "
8 which the L' thy God shall choose;‡ "
10 place which the L' shall choose ‡ "
12 to minister there before the L' thy ‡ "
14 land which the L' thy God giveth ‡ "
15 whom the L' thy God shall choose:‡ "
16 forasmuch as the L' hath said ‡ "
19 may learn to fear the L' his God, ‡ "
18: 1 offerings of the L' made by fire, ‡ "
2 the L' is their inheritance, as he ‡ "
5 L' thy God hath chosen him out ‡ "
5 to minister in the name of the L',‡ "
6 place which the L' shall choose; ‡ "
7 minister in the name of the L' his‡ "
7 which stand there before the L'. ‡ "
9 land which the L' thy God giveth ‡ "
12 are an abomination unto the L': ‡ "
12 L' thy God doth drive them out ‡ "
13 be perfect with the L' thy God. ‡ "
14 L' thy God hath not suffered thee‡ "
15 L' thy God will raise up unto thee‡ "
16 thou desiredst of the L' thy God ‡ "
16 again the voice of the L' my God,‡ "
17 L' said unto me, They have well ‡ "
21 which the L' hath not spoken? ‡ "
22 speaketh in the name of the L', ‡ "
22 which the L' hath not spoken, ‡ "
19: 1 L' thy God hath cut off the nations‡ "
1 whose land the L' thy God giveth ‡ "
2 L' thy God giveth thee to possess‡ "
3 L' thy God giveth thee to inherit, ‡ "
8 the L' thy God enlarge thy coast, ‡ "
9 this day, to love the L' thy God, ‡ "
10 land, which the L' thy God giveth‡ "
14 L' thy God giveth thee to possess ‡ "
17 shall stand before the L', before ‡ "
20: 1 for the L' thy God is with thee, ‡ "
4 L' your God is he that goeth with‡ "
13 L' thy God hath delivered it into ‡ "
14 the L' thy God hath given thee. ‡ "
16 the L' thy God doth give thee for ‡ "
17 L' thy God hath commanded thee:‡ "
18 so should ye sin against the L' ‡ "
21: 1 land which the L' thy God giveth ‡ "
5 them the L' thy God hath chosen ‡ "
5 to bless in the name of the L'; ‡ "
8 Be merciful, O L', unto thy people‡ "
9 is right in the sight of the L'. ‡ "
10 L' thy God hath delivered them ‡ "
23 the L' thy God giveth thee for an ‡ "
22: 5 do so are abominations unto the L'‡ "
23: 1 into the congregation of the L'. ‡ "
2 into the congregation of the L'; ‡ "
2 into the congregation of the L'. ‡ "

De 23: 3 into the congregation of the L'; ‡3068
3 into the congregation of the L' ‡ "
5 L' thy God would not hearken ‡ "
5 L' thy God turned the curse into ‡ "
5 because the L' thy God loved thee.‡ "
8 into the congregation of the L' ‡ "
14 L' thy God walketh in the midst ‡ "
18 into the house of the L' thy God ‡ "
18 are abomination unto the L' thy ‡ "
20 L' thy God may bless thee in all ‡ "
21 vow a vow unto the L' thy God, ‡ "
21 L' thy God will surely require it ‡ "
23 hast vowed unto the L' thy God, ‡ "
24: 4 is abomination before the L': ‡ "
4 the L' thy God giveth thee for an ‡ "
9 the L' thy God did unto Miriam ‡ "
13 unto thee before the L' thy God. ‡ "
15 he cry against thee unto the L', ‡ "
18 L' thy God redeemed thee thence:‡ "
19 L' thy God may bless thee in all ‡ "
25: 15 land which the L' thy God giveth ‡ "
16 abomination unto the L' thy God.‡ "
19 L' thy God hath given thee rest ‡ "
19 land which the L' thy God giveth ‡ "
26: 1 land which the L' thy God giveth ‡ "
2 land that the L' thy God giveth ‡ "
2 which the L' thy God shall choose‡ "
3 I profess this day unto the L' thy ‡ "
3 country which the L' swear unto ‡ "
4 before the altar of the L' thy God.‡ "
5 and say before the L' thy God, ‡ "
7 we cried unto the L' God of our ‡ "
7 L' heard our voice, and looked ‡ "
8 L' brought us forth out of Egypt ‡ "
10 which thou, O L', hast given me. ‡ "
10 shalt set it before the L' thy God, ‡ "
10 worship before the L' thy God: ‡ "
11 which the L' thy God hath given ‡ "
13 shalt say before the L' thy God, ‡ "
14 to the voice of the L' my God, ‡ "
16 the L' thy God hath commanded ‡ "
17 avouched the L' this day to be thy‡ "
18 L' hath avouched thee this day to‡ "
19 holy people unto the L' thy God, ‡ "
27: 2, 3 land which the L' thy God giveth‡ "
3 L' God of thy fathers...promised ‡ "
5 build an altar unto the L' thy God,‡ "
6 build the altar of the L' thy God ‡ "
6 offerings thereon unto the L' thy ‡ "
7 and rejoice before the L' thy God.‡ "
9 the people of the L' thy God. ‡ "
10 obey the voice of the L' thy God, ‡ "
15 an abomination unto the L', ‡ "
28: 1 unto the voice of the L' thy God, ‡ "
1 L' thy God will set thee on high ‡ "
2 unto the voice of the L' thy God. ‡ "
7 L' shall cause thine enemies that‡ "
8 L' shall command the blessing ‡ "
8 land which the L' thy God giveth ‡ "
9 L' shall establish thee an holy ‡ "
9 keep the commandments of the L'‡ "
10 art called by the name of the L'; ‡ "
11 L' shall make thee plenteous in ‡ "
11 land which the L' sware unto thy ‡ "
12 L' shall open unto thee his good ‡ "
13 the L' shall make thee the head, ‡ "
13 unto commandments of the L' thy‡ "
15 unto the voice of the L' thy God, ‡ "
20 L' shall send upon thee cursing, ‡ "
21 The L' shall make the pestilence ‡ "
22 The L' shall smite thee with a ‡ "
24 L' shall make the rain of thy land‡ "
25 L' shall cause thee to be smitten ‡ "
27 L' will smite thee with the botch ‡ "
28 L' shall smite thee with madness,‡ "
35 L' shall smite thee in the knees, ‡ "
36 L' shall bring thee, and thy king ‡ "
37 whither the L' shall lead thee. ‡ "
45 not unto the voice of the L' thy ‡ "
47 thou servedst not the L' thy God ‡ "
48 enemies which the L' shall send ‡ "
49 L' shall bring a nation against ‡ "
52 the L' thy God hath given thee. ‡ "
53 the L' thy God hath given thee, ‡ "
58 fearful name, The Lord Thy God; ‡ "
59 Then the L' will make thy plagues‡ "
61 will the L' bring upon thee, until ‡ "
62 not obey the voice of the L' thy ‡ "
63 L' rejoiced over you to do you good,‡ "
63 L' will rejoice over you to destroy‡ "
64 L' shall scatter thee among all ‡ "
65 L' shall give thee...a trembling ‡ "
68 the L' shall bring thee into Egypt‡ "
29: 1 the L' commanded Moses to make‡ "
2 seen all that the L' did before your‡ "
4 L' hath not given you an heart to ‡ "
6 know that I am the L' your God. ‡ "
10 of you before the L' your God; ‡ "
12 covenant with the L' thy God, ‡ "
12 the L' thy God maketh with thee ‡ "
15, 18 this day before the L' our God,‡ "
20 The L' will not spare him, but ‡ "
20 anger of the L' and his jealousy ‡ "
20 L' shall blot out his name from ‡ "
21 L' shall separate him unto evil ‡ "
22 sicknesses which the L' hath laid‡ "
23 the L' overthrew in his anger, ‡ "
24 the L' done thus unto the land? ‡ "
25 forsaken the covenant of the L' ‡ "
27 the anger of the L' was kindled ‡ "
28 L' rooted them out of their land ‡ "
29 belong unto the L' our God: ‡ "
30: 1 the L' thy God hath driven thee, ‡ "
2 shalt return unto the L' thy God, ‡ "
3 L' thy God will turn thy captivity,‡ "
3 L' thy God hath scattered thee. ‡ "

De 30: 4 will the L' thy God gather thee. ‡3068
5 L' thy God will bring thee into ‡ "
6 L' thy God will circumcise thine ‡ "
6 to love the L' thy God with all ‡ "
7 the L' thy God will put all these ‡ "
8 and obey the voice of the L', ‡ "
9 the L' thy God will make thee ‡ "
9 L' will again rejoice over thee ‡ "
10 unto the voice of the L' thy God, ‡ "
10 turn unto the L' thy God with all ‡ "
16 this day to love the L' thy God, ‡ "
16 L' thy God shall bless thee in the ‡ "
20 thou mayest love the L' thy God, ‡ "
20 in the land which the L' sware ‡ "
31: 2 the L' hath said unto me, Thou ‡ "
3 The L' thy God, he will go over ‡ "
3 before thee, as the L' hath said. ‡ "
4 L' shall do unto them as he did ‡ "
5 L' shall give them up before your ‡ "
6 the L' thy God, he it is that doth ‡ "
7 land which the L' hath sworn ‡ "
8 And the L', he it is that doth go ‡ "
9 the ark of the covenant of the L', ‡ "
11 is come to appear before the L' ‡ "
12 learn, and fear the L' your God, ‡ "
13 learn to fear the L' your God, as ‡ "
14 the L' said unto Moses, Behold, ‡ "
15 the L' appeared in the tabernacle ‡ "
16 the L' said unto Moses, Behold, ‡ "
25 the ark of the covenant of the L', ‡ "
26 the ark of the covenant of the L' ‡ "
27 been rebellious against the L'; ‡ "
29 will do evil in the sight of the L', ‡ "
32: 3 will publish the name of the L': ‡ "
6 Do ye thus requite the L', O ‡ "
12 So the L' alone did lead him, and ‡ "
19 when the L' saw it, he abhorred ‡ "
27 and the L' hath not done all this. ‡ "
30 and the L' hath shut them up? ‡ "
36 For the L' shall judge his people, ‡ "
48 And the L' spake unto Moses that ‡ "
33: 2 he said, The L' came from Sinai, ‡ "
7 Hear, L', the voice of Judah, and ‡ "
11 Bless, L', his substance, and ‡ "
12 The beloved of the L' shall dwell ‡ "
12 the L' shall cover him all the day *
13 Blessed of the L' be his land, for ‡3068
21 he executed the justice of the L', ‡ "
23 full with the blessing of the L', ‡ "
29 O people saved by the L', the ‡ "
34: 1 the L' shewed him all the land of ‡ "
4 And the L' said unto him, This is ‡ "
5 the servant of the L' died there ‡ "
5 according to the word of the L'. ‡ "
9 did as the L' commanded Moses. ‡ "
10 whom the L' knew face to face, ‡ "
11 which the L' sent him to do in ‡ "
Jos 1: 1 death of Moses...servant of the L', ‡ "
1 L' spake unto Joshua the son of ‡ "
9 for the L' thy God is with thee ‡ "
11 L' your God giveth you to possess ‡ "
13 servant of the L' commanded you, ‡ "
13 L' your God hath given you rest, ‡ "
15 L' have given your brethren rest, ‡ "
15 the land which the L' your God ‡ "
17 only the L' thy God be with thee, ‡ "
2: 9 the L' hath given you the land, ‡ "
10 how the L' dried up the water of ‡ "
11 for the L' your God, he is God in ‡ "
12 you, swear unto me by the L', ‡ "
14 the L' hath given us the land, ‡ "
24 L' hath delivered into our hands ‡ "
3: 3 the ark of the covenant of the L' ‡ "
5 L' will do wonders among you. ‡ "
7 And the L' said unto Joshua, ‡ "
9 hear the words of the L' your ‡ "
11 the ark of the covenant of the L' 113
13 priests that bear the ark of the L', ‡3068
13 the L' of all the earth, shall rest 113
17 the ark of the covenant of the L' ‡3068
4: 1 that the L' spake unto Joshua, ‡ "
5 Pass over before the ark of the L' ‡ "
7 the ark of the covenant of the L'; ‡ "
8 as the L' spake unto Joshua, ‡ "
10 finished that the L' commanded ‡ "
11 the ark of the L' passed over, ‡ "
13 for war passed over before the L' ‡ "
14 that day the L' magnified Joshua ‡ "
15 the L' spake unto Joshua, saying, ‡ "
18 the ark of the covenant of the L' ‡ "
23 L' your God dried up the waters ‡ "
23 L' your God did to the Red sea, ‡ "
24 might know the hand of the L'. ‡ "
24 fear the L' your God for ever. ‡ "
5: 1 the L' had dried up the waters of ‡ "
2 time the L' said unto Joshua, ‡ "
6 obeyed not the voice of the L': ‡ "
6 L' sware that he would not shew ‡ "
6 the L' sware unto their fathers ‡ "
9 the L' said unto Joshua, This ‡ "
14 as captain of the host of the L' ‡ "
14 What saith my l' unto his servant? 113
6: 2 the L' said unto Joshua, See, I ‡3068
6 horns before the ark of the L'. ‡ "
7 pass on before the ark of the L'. ‡ "
8 horns passed on before the L', ‡ "
8 the ark of the covenant of the L' ‡ "
11 So the ark of the L' compassed ‡ "
12 priests took up the ark of the L'. ‡ "
13 before the ark of the L' went on ‡ "
13 came after the ark of the L', ‡ "
16 the L' hath given you the city. ‡ "
17 and all that are therein, to the L': ‡ "
19 iron, are consecrated unto the L': ‡ "
19 come into the treasury of the L'. ‡ "
24 treasury of the house of the L'. ‡ "

Jos 6: 26 Cursed be the man before the L', ‡3068
27 So the L' was with Joshua; and ‡ "
7: 1 the anger of the L' was kindled ‡ "
6 face before the ark of the L' until ‡ "
7 And Joshua said, Alas, O L' God, 136
8 O L', what shall I say, when Israel "
10 the L' said unto Joshua, Get thee ‡3068
13 thus saith the L' God of Israel, ‡ "
14 that the tribe which the L' taketh ‡ "
14 the family which the L' shall take ‡ "
14 household which the L' shall take ‡ "
15 transgressed the covenant of the L', ‡ "
19 glory to the L' God of Israel, ‡ "
20 have sinned against the L' God ‡ "
23 and laid them out before the L'. ‡ "
25 the L' shall trouble thee this day. ‡ "
26 L' turned from the fierceness of ‡ "
8: 1 the L' said unto Joshua, Fear not, ‡ "
7 L' your God will deliver it into ‡ "
8 to the commandment of the L' ‡ "
18 the L' said unto Joshua, Stretch ‡ "
27 unto the word of the L' which he ‡ "
30 built an altar unto the L' God ‡ "
31 the servant of the L' commanded ‡ "
31 burnt offerings unto the L', ‡ "
33 the ark of the covenant of the L', ‡ "
33 servant of the L' had commanded ‡ "
9: 9 of the name of the L' thy God: ‡ "
14 counsel at the mouth of the L'. ‡ "
18, 19 sworn unto them by the L' God ‡ "
24 that the L' thy God commanded ‡ "
27 and for the altar of the L', even ‡ "
10: 8 And the L' said unto Joshua, Fear ‡ "
10 L' discomfited them before Israel, ‡ "
11 L' cast down great stones from ‡ "
12 Then spake Joshua to the L' in ‡ "
12 the L' delivered up the Amorites ‡ "
14 L' hearkened unto the voice of a ‡ "
14 man: for the L' fought for Israel. ‡ "
19 L' your God hath delivered them ‡ "
25 shall the L' do to all your enemies ‡ "
30 the L' delivered it also, and the ‡ "
32 L' delivered Lachish into the hand ‡ "
40 the L' God of Israel commanded. ‡ "
42 L' God of Israel fought for Israel. ‡ "
11: 6 the L' said unto Joshua, Be not ‡ "
8 L' delivered them into the hand ‡ "
9 did unto them as the L' bade him: ‡ "
12 the servant of the L' commanded. ‡ "
15 As the L' commanded Moses his ‡ "
15 all that the L' commanded Moses. ‡ "
20 of the L' to harden their hearts, ‡ "
20 as the L' commanded Moses. ‡ "
23 all that the L' said unto Moses; ‡ "
12: 6 Moses the servant of the L' and ‡ "
6 the servant of the L' gave it for a ‡ "
13: 1 the L' said unto him, Thou art old ‡ "
8 the servant of the L' gave them; ‡ "
14 sacrifices of the L' God of Israel ‡ "
33 the L' God of Israel was their ‡ "
14: 2 the L' commanded by the hand of ‡ "
5 As the L' commanded Moses, so ‡ "
6 thing that the L' said unto Moses ‡ "
7 servant of the L' sent me from ‡ "
8 I wholly followed the L' my God. ‡ "
9 wholly followed the L' my God. ‡ "
10 behold, the L' hath kept me alive, ‡ "
10 L' spake this word unto Moses, ‡ "
12 whereof the L' spake in that day; ‡ "
12 if so be the L' will be with me, ‡ "
12 to drive them out, as the L' said. ‡ "
14 followed the L' God of Israel. ‡ "
15: 13 to the commandment of the L' to ‡ "
17: 4 L' commanded Moses to give us ‡ "
4 to the commandment of the L' ‡ "
14 the L' hath blessed me hitherto? ‡ "
18: 3 L' God of your fathers hath given ‡ "
6 cast lots for you here before the L' ‡ "
7 the priesthood of the L' is their ‡ "
7 Moses the servant of the L' gave ‡ "
8 cast lots for you before the L' in ‡ "
10 for them in Shiloh before the L': ‡ "
19: 50 According to the word of the L' ‡ "
51 by lot in Shiloh before the L', ‡ "
20: 1 The L' also spake unto Joshua, ‡ "
21: 2 L' commanded by the hand of ‡ "
3 at the commandment of the L', ‡ "
8 L' commanded by the hand of ‡ "
43 L' gave unto Israel all the land ‡ "
44 L' gave them rest round about, ‡ "
44 the L' delivered all their enemies ‡ "
45 L' had spoken unto the house of ‡ "
22: 2 servant of the L' commanded you, ‡ "
3 of the commandment of the L' ‡ "
4 L' your God hath given rest unto ‡ "
4 the servant of the L' gave you on ‡ "
5 the servant of the L' charged you, ‡ "
5 to love the L' your God, and to ‡ "
9 the word of the L' by the hand of ‡ "
16 the whole congregation of the L', ‡ "
16 this day from following the L', ‡ "
16 rebel this day against the L'? ‡ "
17 in the congregation of the L', ‡ "
18 this day from following the L'? ‡ "
18 ye rebel to day against the L', ‡ "
19 land of the possession of the L', ‡ "
19 but rebel not against the L', nor ‡ "
19 beside the altar of the L' our God. ‡ "
22 The L' God of gods, the L' God ‡ "
22 in transgression against the L', ‡ "
23 to turn from following the L', or ‡ "
23 let the L' himself require it; ‡ "
24 What have ye to do with the L' ‡ "
25 L' hath made Jordan a border ‡ "
25 of Gad; ye have no part in the L': ‡ "
25 children cease from fearing the L'. ‡ "

Jos 22: 27 do the service of the L' before ‡3068
27 come, Ye have no part in the L'. ‡ "
28 the pattern of the altar of the L', ‡ "
29 we should rebel against the L', ‡ "
29 this day from following the L', ‡ "
29 beside the altar of the L' our God ‡ "
31 perceive that the L' is among us, ‡ "
31 this trespass against the L': ‡ "
31 of Israel out of the hand of the L'. ‡ "
34 between us that the L' is God. ‡ "
23: 1 the L' had given rest unto Israel ‡ "
3 all that the L' your God hath done ‡ "
3 the L' your God is he that hath ‡ "
5 And the L' your God, he shall ‡ "
5 L' your God hath promised unto ‡ "
8 But cleave unto the L' your God, ‡ "
9 L' hath driven out from before ‡ "
10 for the L' your God, he it is that ‡ "
11 that ye love the L' your God. ‡ "
13 L' your God will no more drive ‡ "
13 land which the L' your God hath ‡ "
14 things which the L' your God ‡ "
15 which the L' your God promised ‡ "
15 L' bring upon you all evil things, ‡ "
15 land which the L' your God hath ‡ "
16 the covenant of the L' your God, ‡ "
16 the anger of the L' be kindled ‡ "
24: 2 Thus saith the L' God of Israel, ‡ "
7 And when they cried unto the L', ‡ "
14 Now therefore fear the L', and ‡ "
14 in Egypt; and serve ye the L'. ‡ "
15 evil unto you to serve the L', ‡ "
15 my house, we will serve the L'. ‡ "
16 that we should forsake the L', to ‡ "
17 For the L' our God, he it is that ‡ "
18 L' drave out from before us all ‡ "
18 will we also serve the L'; for he ‡ "
19 people, Ye cannot serve the L': ‡ "
20 If ye forsake the L', and serve ‡ "
21 Nay; but we will serve the L'. ‡ "
22 that ye have chosen you the L', ‡ "
23 incline your heart unto the L' God ‡ "
24 The L' our God will we serve, ‡ "
26 was by the sanctuary of the L'. ‡ "
27 hath heard all the words of the L' ‡ "
29 son of Nun, the servant of the L', ‡ "
31 Israel served the L' all the days ‡ "
31 had known all the works of the L', ‡ "
J'g 1: 1 children of Israel asked the L', ‡ "
2 the L' said, Judah shall go up: ‡ "
4 the L' delivered the Canaanites ‡ "
19 And the L' was with Judah; and ‡ "
22 and the L' was with them. ‡ "
2: 1 an angel of the L' came up from ‡ "
4 the angel of the L' spake these ‡ "
5 they sacrificed there unto the L'. ‡ "
7 And the people served the L' all ‡ "
7 seen all the great works of the L', ‡ "
8 son of Nun, the servant of the L', ‡ "
10 them, which knew not the L', nor ‡ "
11 did evil in the sight of the L', ‡ "
12 they forsook the L' God of their ‡ "
12 and provoked the L' to anger. ‡ "
13 forsook the L', and served Baal ‡ "
14 anger of the L' was hot against ‡ "
15 hand of the L' was against them ‡ "
15 L' had said,...as the L' had sworn ‡ "
16 the L' raised up judges, which ‡ "
17 the commandments of the L'; ‡ "
18 the L' raised them up judges, ‡ "
18 then the L' was with the judge, ‡ "
18 repented the L' because of their ‡ "
20 anger of the L' was hot against ‡ "
22 will keep the way of the L' to ‡ "
23 Therefore the L' left those nations, ‡ "
3: 1 are the nations which the L' left, ‡ "
4 the commandments of the L', ‡ "
7 did evil in the sight of the L', ‡ "
7 and forgat the L' their God, and ‡ "
8 anger of the L' was hot against ‡ "
9 children of Israel cried unto the L', ‡ "
9 L' raised up a deliverer to the ‡ "
10 Spirit of the L' came upon him, ‡ "
10 L' delivered Chushan-rishathaim. ‡ "
12 evil again in the sight of the L': ‡ "
12 L' strengthened Eglon the king ‡ "
12 done evil in the sight of the L'. ‡ "
15 children of Israel cried unto the L', ‡ "
15 the L' raised them up a deliverer, ‡ "
25 their l' was fallen down dead on 113
28 L' hath delivered your enemies ‡3068
4: 1 did evil in the sight of the L', ‡ "
2 the L' sold them into the hand of ‡ "
3 children of Israel cried unto the L': ‡ "
6 the L' God of Israel commanded, ‡ "
9 L' shall sell Sisera into the hand ‡ "
14 the L' hath delivered Sisera into ‡ "
14 is not the L' gone out before thee? ‡ "
15 the L' discomfited Sisera, and all ‡ "
18 him, Turn in, my l', turn in to me; 113
5: 2 Praise ye the L' for the avenging ‡3068
3 I, even I, will sing unto the L'; ‡ "
3 I will sing praise to the L' God of ‡ "
4 L', when thou wentest out of Seir, ‡ "
5 mountains melted...before the L', ‡ "
5 from before the L' God of Israel. ‡ "
9 among the people. Bless ye the L'. ‡ "
11 the righteous acts of the L', ‡ "
11 people of the L' go down to the ‡ "
13 L' made me have dominion over ‡ "
23 Meroz, said the angel of the L', ‡ "
23 came not to the help of the L', ‡ "
23 help of the L' against the mighty. ‡ "
31 all thine enemies perish, O L': ‡ "
6: 1 did evil in the sight of the L': ‡ "
1 L' delivered them into the hand ‡ "

J'g 6: 6 children of Israel cried unto the *L*. ‡3068
7 children of Israel cried unto the *L*‡ "
8 *L* sent a prophet unto the children‡ "
8 Thus saith the *L* God of Israel, ‡ "
10 unto you, I am the *L* your God; ‡ "
11 there came an angel of the *L*, ‡ "
12 the angel of the *L* appeared unto ‡ "
12 The *L* is with thee, thou mighty ‡ "
13 Gideon said unto him, Oh my *L*, 113
13 if the *L* be with us, why then is ‡3068
13 the *L* bring us up from Egypt? ‡ "
13 now the *L* hath forsaken us, and ‡ "
14 the *L* looked upon him, and said,‡ "
15 Oh my *L*, wherewith shall I save 136
16 And the *L* said unto him, Surely ‡3068
21 the angel of the *L* put forth the ‡ "
21 Then the angel of the *L* departed‡ "
22 that he was an angel of the *L*, 136
22 Gideon said, Alas, O *L* God! for ‡3068
22 seen an angel of the *L* face to ‡ "
23 the *L* said unto him, Peace be ‡ "
24 build an altar there unto the *L*, ‡ "
25 that the *L* said unto him, Take ‡ "
26 build an altar unto the *L* thy God‡ "
27 did as the *L* had said unto him: ‡ "
34 Spirit of the *L* came upon Gideon,‡ "
7: 2, 4 the *L* said unto Gideon, The ‡ "
5 the *L* said unto Gideon, Every ‡ "
7 the *L* said unto Gideon, By the ‡ "
9 the *L* said unto him, Arise, get ‡ "
15 *L* hath delivered into your hand ‡ "
18 and say, The sword of the *L*, and‡ "
20 they cried, The sword of the *L*, ‡ "
22 *L* set every man's sword against ‡ "
8: 7 when the *L* hath delivered Zebah‡ "
19 as the *L* liveth, if ye had saved ‡ "
23 you: the *L* shall rule over you. ‡ "
34 of Israel remembered not the *L* ‡ "
10: 6 evil again in the sight of the *L*, ‡ "
6 Philistines, and forsook the *L*, ‡ "
7 anger of the *L* was hot against ‡ "
10 children of Israel cried unto the *L*,‡ "
11 the *L* said unto the children of ‡ "
15 children of Israel said unto the *L*,‡ "
16 among them, and served the *L*: ‡ "
11: 9 the *L* deliver them before me, ‡ "
10 The *L* be witness between us, ‡ "
11 uttered all his words before the *L*‡ "
21 *L* God of Israel delivered Sihon ‡ "
23 *L* God of Israel hath dispossessed‡ "
24 the *L* our God shall drive out ‡ "
27 the *L* the Judge be judge this day‡ "
29 the Spirit of the *L* came upon ‡ "
30 Jephthah vowed a vow unto the *L*,‡ "
32 *L* delivered them into his hands. ‡ "
35 opened my mouth unto the *L*, ‡ "
36 opened thy mouth unto the *L*, ‡ "
36 as the *L* hath taken vengeance ‡ "
12: 3 *L* delivered them into my hand: ‡ "
13: 1 evil again in the sight of the *L*; ‡ "
1 *L* delivered them into the hand ‡ "
3 angel of the *L* appeared unto ‡ "
8 Then Manoah entreated the *L*, ‡ "
8 O my *L*, let the man of God which‡ "
13 angel of the *L* said unto Manoah,‡ "
15 said unto the angel of the *L*, ‡ "
16 angel of the *L* said unto Manoah,‡ "
16 thou must offer it unto the *L*. ‡ "
16 that he was an angel of the *L*. ‡ "
17 said unto the angel of the *L*, ‡ "
18 the angel of the *L* said unto him,‡ "
19 offered it upon a rock unto the *L*:‡ "
20 the angel of the *L* ascended in ‡ "
21 the angel of the *L* did no more ‡ "
21 that he was an angel of the *L*. ‡ "
23 If the *L* were pleased to kill us, ‡ "
24 grew, and the *L* blessed him. ‡ "
25 the Spirit of the *L* began to move‡ "
14: 4 knew not that it was of the *L*, ‡ "
6 the Spirit of the *L* came mightily‡ "
19 Spirit of the *L* came upon him ‡ "
15: 14 the Spirit of the *L* came mightily‡ "
18 sore athirst, and called on the *L*, ‡ "
16: 20 wist not that the *L* was departed ‡ "
28 Samson called unto the *L*, and ‡ "
28 O *L* God, remember me, I pray 136
17: 2 said, Blessed be thou of the *L*, ‡3068
3 dedicated the silver unto the *L* ‡ "
13 I that the *L* will do me good, ‡ "
18: 6 peace: before the *L* is your way ‡ "
19: 18 now going to the house of the *L*; ‡ "
26 the man's house where her *l* was, 113
27 And her *l* rose up in the morning, "
20: 1 Gilead, unto the *L* in Mizpeh. ‡3068
18 And the *L* said, Judah shall go ‡ "
23 went up and wept before the *L* ‡ "
23 even, and asked counsel of the *L*,‡ "
23 the *L* said, Go up against him.) ‡ "
26 and sat there before the *L*, and ‡ "
26 and peace offerings before the *L*.‡ "
27 of Israel enquired of the *L*, ‡ "
28 And the *L* said, Go up; for to ‡ "
35 *L* smote Benjamin before Israel:‡ "
21: 3 O *L* God of Israel, Why is this ‡ "
5 the congregation unto the *L*? ‡ "
5 came not up to the *L* to Mizpeh, ‡ "
7 seeing we have sworn by the *L* ‡ "
8 came not up to Mizpeh to the *L*? ‡ "
15 the *L* had made a breach in the ‡ "
19 there is a feast of the *L* in Shiloh‡ "
Ru 1: 6 *L* had visited his people in giving‡ "
8 the *L* deal kindly with you, as ye‡ "
9 *L* grant you that ye may find rest,‡ "
13 the hand of the *L* is gone out ‡ "
17 the *L* do so to me, and more also,‡ "
21 *L* hath brought me home again ‡ "

Ru 1: 21 seeing the *L*...testified against ‡3068
2: 4 the reapers, The *L* be with you. ‡ "
4 answered him, The *L* bless thee. ‡ "
12 The *L* recompense thy work, ‡ "
12 reward be given thee of the *L* ‡ "
13 me find favour in thy sight, my *l*; 113
20 Blessed be he of the *L*, who hath‡3068
3: 10 Blessed be thou of the *L* my ‡ "
13 kinsman to thee, as the *L* liveth: ‡ "
4: 11 *L* make the woman that is come ‡ "
12 seed which the *L* shall give thee ‡ "
13 the *L* gave her conception, and ‡ "
14 Blessed be the *L*, which hath not‡ "
1Sa 1: 3 to sacrifice unto the *L* of hosts ‡ "
3 Phinehas, the priests of the *L*, ‡ "
5, 6 the *L* had shut up her womb. ‡ "
7 went up to the house of the *L*, ‡ "
9 by a post of the temple of the *L*. ‡ "
10 and prayed unto the *L*, and wept‡ "
11 O *L* of hosts, if thou wilt indeed ‡ "
11 give him unto the *L* all the days ‡ "
12 continued praying before the *L*, ‡ "
15 answered and said, No, my *l*, I am 113
15 poured out my soul before the *L*.‡3068
19 and worshipped before the *L*, ‡ "
19 wife; and the *L* remembered her.‡ "
20 I have asked him of the *L*. ‡ "
21 up to offer unto the *L* the yearly ‡ "
22 that he may appear before the *L*,‡ "
23 only the *L* establish his word. ‡ "
24 the house of the *L* in Shiloh: ‡ "
26 said, Oh my *l*, as thy soul liveth, 113
26 my *l*, I am the woman that stood "
26 thee here, praying unto the *L*. ‡3068
27 the *L* hath given me my petition ‡ "
28 also I have lent him to the *L*; ‡ "
28 liveth he shall be lent to the *L*. ‡ "
28 And he worshipped the *L* there. ‡ "
2: 1 said, My heart rejoiceth in the *L*,‡ "
1 mine horn is exalted in the *L*: ‡ "
2 There is none holy as the *L*: ‡ "
3 for the *L* is a God of knowledge, ‡ "
6 The *L* killeth, and maketh alive: ‡ "
7 The *L* maketh poor, and maketh ‡ "
10 adversaries of the *L* shall be ‡ "
10 the *L* shall judge the ends of the‡ "
11 the child did minister unto the *L* ‡ "
12 of Belial; they knew not the *L*. ‡ "
17 men was very great before the *L*:‡ "
17 abhorred the offering of the *L*. ‡ "
18 Samuel ministered before the *L*, ‡ "
20 *L* give thee seed of this woman ‡ "
20 the loan which is lent to the *L*. ‡ "
21 the *L* visited Hannah, so that ‡ "
21 child Samuel grew before the *L*. ‡ "
25 but if a man sin against the *L*, ‡ "
25 because the *L* would slay them. ‡ "
26 was in favour both with the *L*, ‡ "
27 Thus saith the *L*, Did I plainly ‡ "
30 the *L* God of Israel saith, I said ‡ "
30 but now the *L* saith, Be it far ‡ "
3: 1 Samuel ministered unto the *L* ‡ "
1 the word of the *L* was precious ‡ "
3 went out in the temple of the *L*, ‡ "
4 the *L* called Samuel: and he ‡ "
6 the *L* called yet again, Samuel. ‡ "
7 Samuel did not yet know the *L*, ‡ "
7 the word of the *L* yet revealed ‡ "
8 *L* called Samuel again the third ‡ "
8 perceived that the *L* had called ‡ "
9 that thou shalt say, Speak, *L*; ‡ "
10 And the *L* came, and stood, and ‡ "
11 the *L* said to Samuel, Behold, ‡ "
15 the doors of the house of the *L*. ‡ "
17 is the thing that the *L* hath said "
18 It is the *L*: let him do what ‡3068
19 grew, and the *L* was with him, ‡ "
20 to be a prophet of the *L*. ‡ "
21 the *L* appeared again in Shiloh: ‡ "
21 *L* revealed himself to Samuel ‡ "
21 in Shiloh by the word of the *L*. ‡ "
4: 3 hath the *L* smitten us to day ‡ "
3, 4, 5 ark of the covenant of the *L* ‡ "
6 that the ark of the *L* was come ‡ "
5: 3 the earth before the ark of the *L*.‡ "
4 ground before the ark of the *L*; ‡ "
6 hand of the *L* was heavy upon ‡ "
9 hand of the *L* was against the city‡ "
6: 1 ark of the *L* was in the country ‡ "
2 shall we do to the ark of the *L*? ‡ "
8 take the ark of the *L*, and lay it ‡ "
11 laid the ark of the *L* upon the cart,‡ "
14 kine a burnt offering unto the *L*.‡ "
15 Levites took...the ark of the *L*, ‡ "
15 offered...the same day unto the *L*.‡ "
17 a trespass offering unto the *L*; ‡ "
18 they set down the ark of the *L*: ‡ "
19 had looked into the ark of the *L*, ‡ "
19 *L* had smitten many of the people‡ "
20 to stand before this holy *L* God? ‡ "
21 brought again the ark of the *L*; ‡ "
7: 1 and fetched up the ark of the *L*, ‡ "
1 his son to keep the ark of the *L*. ‡ "
2 of Israel lamented after the *L*. ‡ "
3 return unto the *L* with all your ‡ "
3 prepare your hearts unto the *L*, ‡ "
4 Ashtaroth, and served the *L* only.‡ "
5 I will pray for you unto the *L*. ‡ "
6 and poured it out before the *L*, ‡ "
6 We have sinned against the *L*. ‡ "
8 Cease not to cry unto the *L* our ‡ "
9 burnt offering wholly unto the *L*:‡ "
9 and Samuel cried unto the *L* ‡ "
9 for Israel; and the *L* heard him. ‡ "
10 *L* thundered with a great thunder‡ "
12 Hitherto hath the *L* helped us. ‡ "

1Sa 7: 13 hand of the *L* was against the ‡3068
17 there he built an altar unto the *L*.‡ "
8: 6 And Samuel prayed unto the *L*. ‡ "
7 the *L* said unto Samuel, Hearken ‡ "
10 Samuel told all the words of the *L*‡ "
18 *L* will not hear you in that day. ‡ "
21 rehearsed...in the ears of the *L*. ‡ "
22 the *L* said to Samuel, Hearken ‡ "
9: 15 *L* had told Samuel in his ear a ‡ "
17 *L* said unto him, Behold the man‡ "
10: 1 because the *L* hath anointed thee‡ "
6 Spirit of the *L* will come upon ‡ "
17 together unto the *L* to Mizpeh; ‡ "
18 Thus saith the *L* God of Israel, I ‡ "
19 present yourselves before the *L* ‡ "
22 they enquired of the *L* further, ‡ "
22 *L* answered, Behold, he hath hid‡ "
24 him whom the *L* hath chosen, ‡ "
25 book, and laid it up before the *L*.‡ "
11: 7 fear of the *L* fell on the people, ‡ "
13 the *L* hath wrought salvation in ‡ "
15 made Saul king before the *L* in ‡ "
15 of peace offerings before the *L*; ‡ "
12: 3 witness against me before the *L*, ‡ "
5 The *L* is witness against you, ‡ "
6 It is the *L* that advanced Moses ‡ "
7 may reason with you before the *L*‡ "
7 of all the righteous acts of the *L*,‡ "
8 your fathers cried unto the *L*, ‡ "
8 then the *L* sent Moses and Aaron, ‡ "
9 when they forgat the *L* their God,‡ "
10 they cried unto the *L*, and said, ‡ "
10 because we have forsaken the *L*, ‡ "
11 the *L* sent Jerubbaal, and Bedan,‡ "
12 the *L* your God was your king. ‡ "
13 the *L* hath set a king over you. ‡ "
14 If ye will fear the *L*, and serve ‡ "
14 the commandment of the *L*, ‡ "
14 continue following the *L* your ‡ "
15 will not obey the voice of the *L*, ‡ "
15 the commandment of the *L*, ‡ "
15 the hand of the *L* be against you,‡ "
16 the *L* will do before your eyes. ‡ "
17 I will call unto the *L*, and he shall‡ "
17 have done in the sight of the *L*, ‡ "
18 So Samuel called unto the *L*; ‡ "
18 and the *L* sent thunder and rain ‡ "
18 greatly feared the *L* and Samuel.‡ "
19 Pray for thy servants unto the *L* ‡ "
20 not aside from following the *L*, ‡ "
20 serve the *L* with all your heart; ‡ "
22 *L* will not forsake his people for ‡ "
22 pleased the *L* to make you his ‡ "
23 that I should sin against the *L* ‡ "
24 Only fear the *L*, and serve him in‡ "
13: 12 made supplication unto the *L*: ‡ "
13 kept the commandment of the *L* ‡ "
13 *L* have established thy kingdom ‡ "
14 *L* hath sought him a man after ‡ "
14 *L*...commanded him to be captain‡ "
14 which the *L* commanded thee. ‡ "
14: 6 be that the *L* will work for us: ‡ "
6 is no restraint to the *L* to save ‡ "
10 *L* hath delivered them into our ‡ "
12 *L* hath delivered them into the ‡ "
23 So the *L* saved Israel that day: ‡ "
33 people sin against the *L*, in that ‡ "
34 sin not against the *L* in eating ‡ "
35 Saul built an altar unto the *L*: ‡ "
35 first altar that he built unto the *L*.‡ "
39 For, as the *L* liveth, which saveth‡ "
41 Saul said unto the *L* God of Israel,‡ "
45 as the *L* liveth, there shall not ‡ "
15: 1 *L* sent me to anoint thee to be ‡ "
1 the voice of the words of the *L*. ‡ "
2 saith the *L* of hosts, I remember ‡ "
10 the word of the *L* unto Samuel, ‡ "
11 and he cried unto the *L* all night.‡ "
13 him, Blessed be thou of the *L*: ‡ "
13 the commandment of the *L*. ‡ "
15 to sacrifice unto the *L* thy God; ‡ "
16 what the *L* hath said to me this ‡ "
17 *L* anointed thee king over Israel?‡ "
18 the *L* sent thee on a journey, and‡ "
19 thou not obey the voice of the *L*, ‡ "
19 didst evil in the sight of the *L*? ‡ "
20 I have obeyed the voice of the *L*,‡ "
20 gone the way which the *L* sent me,‡ "
21 to sacrifice unto the *L* thy God in‡ "
22 the *L* as great delight in burnt ‡ "
22 as in obeying the voice of the *L*? ‡ "
23 hast rejected the word of the *L*, ‡ "
24 the commandment of the *L*, ‡ "
25 with me, that I may worship the *L*.‡ "
26 hast rejected the word of the *L*, ‡ "
26 *L* hath rejected thee from being ‡ "
28 *L* hath rent the kingdom of Israel‡ "
30 that I may worship the *L* thy God.‡ "
31 Saul; and Saul worshipped the *L*.‡ "
33 hewed Agag in pieces before the *L*‡ "
35 *L* repented that he had made Saul‡ "
16: 1 the *L* said unto Samuel, How long‡ "
2 And the *L* said, Take an heifer, ‡ "
2 I am come to sacrifice to the *L*. ‡ "
4 did that which the *L* spake, ‡ "
5 am come to sacrifice unto the *L*: ‡ "
7 *L* said unto Samuel, Look not on‡ "
7 *L* seeth not as man seeth; for ‡ "
7 but the *L* looketh on the heart. ‡ "
8, 9 Neither hath the *L* chosen this.‡ "
10 The *L* hath not chosen these. ‡ "
12 the *L* said, Arise, anoint him: ‡ "
13 Spirit of the *L* came upon David ‡ "
14 Spirit of the *L* departed from Saul,‡ "
14 an evil spirit from the *L* troubled‡ "
16 our *l* now command thy servants, 113

1Sa 16: 18 person, and the L' is with him. ‡3068
17: 37 L' that delivered me out of the paw‡ "
37 Go, and the L' be with thee. ‡ "
45 in the name of the L' of hosts, ‡ "
46 This day will the L' deliver thee ‡ "
47 the L' saveth not with sword and‡ "
18: 12 because the L' was with him, and‡ "
14 ways; and the L' was with him. ‡ "
28 knew that the L' was with David,‡ "
19: 5 L' wrought a great salvation for ‡ "
6 As the L' liveth, he shall not be ‡ "
9 evil spirit from the L' was upon ‡ "
20: 3 as the L' liveth, and as thy soul ‡ "
8 into a covenant of the L' with thee.‡ "
12 unto David, O L' God of Israel, ‡ "
13 The L' do so and much more to ‡ "
13 L' be with thee, as he hath been ‡ "
14 shew me the kindness of the L', ‡ "
15 L' hath cut off...enemies of David‡ "
16 Let the L' even require it at the ‡ "
21 and no hurt; as the L' liveth. ‡ "
22 for the L' hath sent thee away. ‡ "
23 L' be between thee and me for ‡ "
42 both of us in the name of the L', ‡ "
42 The L' be between me and thee, ‡ "
21: 6 that was taken from before the L',‡ "
7 that day, detained before the L'; ‡ "
22: 10 he enquired of the L' for him, ‡ "
12 And he answered, Here I am, my l'.113
17 and slay the priests of the L'; ‡3068
17 to fall upon the priests of the L'. ‡ "
23: 2 David enquired of the L', saying, ‡ "
2 the L' said unto David, Go, and ‡ "
4 David enquired of the L' yet ‡ "
4 the L' answered him and said, ‡ "
10 O L' God of Israel, thy servant ‡ "
11 O L' God of Israel, I beseech thee,‡ "
11 the L' said, He will come down. ‡ "
12 And the L' said, They will deliver‡ "
18 made a covenant before the L': ‡ "
21 Saul said, Blessed be ye of the L';‡ "
24: 4 the day of which the L' said unto‡ "
6 L' forbid that I should do this ‡ "
6 he is the anointed of the L'. *‡ "
8 after Saul, saying, My l' the king. 113
10 the L' had delivered thee to day ‡3068
10 put forth mine hand against my l'; 113
12 L' judge between me and thee, ‡3068
12 and the L' avenge me of thee: but‡ "
15 The L' therefore be judge, and ‡ "
18 L' had delivered me into thine ‡ "
19 L' reward thee good for that thou‡ "
21 now therefore unto me by the L', ‡ "
25: 24 Upon me, my l', upon me let this 113
25 Let not my l', I pray thee, regard "
25 saw not the young men of my l', "
26 Now therefore, my l', as the "
26 as the L' liveth, and as thy soul ‡3068
26 the L' hath withholden thee from‡ "
26 they that seek evil to my l', be as 113
27 handmaid hath brought unto my l', "
27 the young men that follow my l'. "
28 handmaid: for the L' will ‡3068
28 certainly make my l' a sure house; 113
28 because my l' fighteth the battles "
28 fighteth the battles of the L', and‡3068
29 but the soul of my l' shall be bound113
29 bundle of life with the L' thy God; ‡3068
30 pass, when the L' shall have done‡ "
30 done to my l' according to all the 113
31 thee, nor offence of heart unto my l',136
31 or that my l' hath avenged himself: "
31 when the L' shall have dealt well ‡3068
31 have dealt well with my l', then 113
32 Blessed be the L' God of Israel, ‡3068
34 deed, as the L' God of Israel liveth,‡ "
38 that the L' smote Nabal, that he ‡ "
39 said, Blessed be the L', that hath ‡ "
39 L' hath returned the wickedness ‡ "
41 the feet of the servants of my l'. 113
26: 10 said furthermore, As the L' liveth,‡3068
10 the L' shall smite him; or his day‡ "
11 L' forbid that I should stretch ‡ "
12 deep sleep from the L' was fallen‡ "
15 hast thou not kept thy l' the king? 113
15 people in to destroy the king thy l'. "
16 As the L' liveth, ye are worthy to ‡3068
17 David said, It is my voice, my l', O 113
18 doth my l' thus pursue after his "
19 my l' the king hear the words of his "
19 L' have stirred thee up against ‡3068
19 men, cursed be they before the L';‡ "
19 abiding in...inheritance of the L', ‡ "
20 earth before the face of the L': ‡ "
23 The L' render to every man his ‡ "
23 L' delivered thee into my hand ‡ "
24 much set by in the eyes of the L', ‡ "
28: 6 And when Saul enquired of the L',‡ "
6 the L' answered him not, neither ‡ "
10 And Saul sware to her by the L', ‡ "
10 As the L' liveth, there shall no ‡ "
16 the L' is departed from thee, and ‡ "
17 L' hath done to him, as he spake ‡ "
17 L' hath rent the kingdom out of ‡ "
18 obeyedst not the voice of the L', ‡ "
18 the L' done this thing unto thee ‡ "
19 the L' will also deliver Israel with‡ "
19 L' also shall deliver the host of ‡ "
29: 6 Surely, as the L' liveth, thou hast‡ "
8 the enemies of my l' the king? 113
30: 6 encouraged himself in the L' his ‡3068
8 And David enquired at the Lord, ‡ "
23 that which the L' hath given us, ‡ "
26 the spoil of the enemies of the L';‡ "
2Sa 1: 10 brought them hither unto my l'. 113
12 and for the people of the L'; and ‡3068

2Sa 2: 1 that David enquired of the L', ‡3068
1 And the L' said unto him, Go up. ‡ "
5 them, Blessed be ye of the L', ‡ "
5 shewed this kindness unto your l', 113
6 L' shew kindness and truth unto ‡3068
3: 9 as the L' hath sworn to David, ‡ "
18 for the L' hath spoken of David, ‡ "
21 will gather all Israel unto my l' 113
28 guiltless before the L' for ever ‡3068
39 L' shall reward the doer of evil ‡ "
4: 8 thy life; and the L' hath avenged‡ "
8 avenged my l' the king this day of 113
9 them, As the L' liveth, who hath ‡3068
5: 2 L' said to thee, Thou shalt feed ‡ "
3 them in Hebron before the L': ‡ "
10 the L' God of hosts was with him.‡ "
12 L' had established him king over‡ "
19 David enquired of the L', saying, ‡ "
19 the L' said unto David, Go up: ‡ "
20 L' hath broken forth upon mine ‡ "
23 David enquired of the L', he said,‡ "
24 then shall the L' go out before ‡ "
25 as the L' had commanded him; ‡ "
6: 2 L' of hosts that dwelleth between‡ "
5 house of Israel played before the L'‡ "
7 anger of the L' was kindled against‡ "
8 L'...made a breach upon Uzzah: ‡ "
9 David was afraid of the L' that ‡ "
9 the ark of the L' come to me? ‡ "
10 not remove the ark of the L' unto ‡ "
11 the ark of the L' continued in the ‡ "
11 L' blessed Obed-edom, and all his‡ "
12 The L' hath blessed the house of ‡ "
13 they that bare the ark of the L' ‡ "
14 David danced before the L' with ‡ "
15 brought up the ark of the L' with ‡ "
16 ark of the L' came into the city of‡ "
16 leaping and dancing before the L'; ‡ "
17 they brought in the ark of the L', ‡ "
17 and peace offerings before the L'. ‡ "
18 in the name of the L' of hosts. ‡ "
21 unto Michal, It was before the L', ‡ "
21 me ruler over the people of the L',‡ "
21 therefore will I play before the L'.‡ "
7: 1 L' had given him rest round about‡ "
3 heart; for the L' is with thee. ‡ "
4 word of the L' came unto Nathan,‡ "
5 Thus saith the L', Shalt thou ‡ "
8 Thus saith the L' of hosts, I took ‡ "
11 L' telleth thee that he will make ‡ "
18 David in, and sat before the L', ‡ "
18 Who am I, O L' God? and what is 136
19 a small thing in thy sight, O L' God; "
19 this the manner of man, O L' God? "
20 thou, L' God, knowest thy servant. "
22 thou art great, O L' God: for ‡3068
24 thou, L', art become their God. ‡ "
25 O L' God, the word that thou hast‡ "
26 L' of hosts is the God over Israel:‡ "
27 thou, O L' of hosts, God of Israel, ‡ "
28 now, O L' God, thou art that God, 136
29 for thou, O L' God, hast spoken it: "
8: 6 L' preserved David whithersoever‡3068
11 David did dedicate unto the L', ‡ "
14 L' preserved David whithersoever‡ "
9: 11 to all that my l' the king hath 113
10: 3 Ammon said unto Hanun their l', "
12 the L' do that which seemeth him‡3068
11: 9 house with all the servants of his l',113
11 and my l' Joab, and the servants of "
11 servants of my l', are encamped in "
13 on his bed with the servants of his l', "
27 David had done displeased the L'.‡3068
12: 1 the L' sent Nathan unto David. ‡ "
5 As the L' liveth, the man that hath‡ "
7 Thus saith the L' God of Israel, I ‡ "
9 the commandment of the L', ‡ "
11 Thus saith the L', Behold, I will ‡ "
13 I have sinned against the L'. ‡ "
13 L' also hath put away thy sin; ‡ "
14 occasion to the enemies of the L' ‡ "
15 L' struck the child that Uriah's ‡ "
20 and came into the house of the L',‡ "
24 Solomon: and the L' loved him. ‡ "
25 name Jedidiah, because of the L'.*‡ "
13: 32 Let not my l' suppose that they 113
33 let not my l' the king take the thing "
14: 9 My l', O king, the iniquity be on me, "
11 let the king remember the L' thy ‡3068
11 As the L' liveth, there shall not one‡ "
12 speak one word unto my l' the king. 113
15 to speak of this thing unto my l' the "
17 The word of my l' the king shall now "
17 so is my l' the king to discern good "
17 the L' thy God will be with thee. ‡3068
18 said, Let my l' the king now speak. 113
19 As thy soul liveth, my l' the king, "
19 that my l' the king hath spoken: "
20 and my l' is wise, according to the "
22 grace in thy sight, my l', O king, "
15: 7 which I have vowed unto the L', ‡3068
8 L' shall bring me again indeed to‡ "
8 Jerusalem, then I will serve the L'.‡ "
15 my l' the king shall appoint. 113
21 king, and said, As the L' liveth, ‡3068
21 and as my l' the king liveth, surely 113
21 in what place my l' the king shall be, "
25 find favour in the eyes of the L', ‡3068
31 And David said, O L', I pray thee,‡ "
16: 4 grace in thy sight, my l', O king. 113
8 L' hath returned upon thee all ‡3068
8 L' hath delivered the kingdom into‡ "
9 this dead dog curse my l' the king? 113
10 the L' hath said unto him, Curse ‡3068
11 for the L' hath bidden him. ‡ "
12 the L' will look on mine affliction,‡ "

2Sa 16: 12 the L' will requite me good for his ‡3068
18 but whom the L', and this people,‡ "
17: 14 L'...appointed to defeat the good ‡ "
14 L' might bring evil upon Absalom.‡ "
18: 19 L' hath avenged him of his enemies.‡ "
28 Blessed be the L' thy God, which ‡ "
28 their hand against my l' the king. 113
31 Cushi said, Tidings, my l' the king: "
31 L' hath avenged thee this day of ‡3068
32 The enemies of my l' the king, and 113
19: 7 I swear by the L', if thou go not ‡3068
19 Let not my l' impute iniquity unto 113
19 my l' the king went out of Jerusalem, "
20 to go down to meet my l' the king. "
26 My l', O king, my servant deceived "
27 slandered thy servant unto my l' the "
27 my l' the king is as an angel of God: "
28 but dead men before my l' the king: "
30 my l' the king is come again in peace "
35 be yet a burden unto my l' the king? "
37 let him go over with my l' the king; "
20: 19 up the inheritance of the L'? ‡3068
21: 1 and David enquired of the L': ‡ "
1 the L' answered, It is for Saul, ‡ "
3 bless the inheritance of the L'? ‡ "
6 we will hang them up unto the L'‡ "
6 of Saul, whom the L' did choose. ‡ "
9 them in the hill before the L': ‡ "
22: 1 And David spake unto the L' the ‡ "
1 day that the L' had delivered him‡ "
2 L' is my rock, and my fortress, ‡ "
4 will call on the L', who is worthy ‡ "
7 my distress I called upon the L', ‡ "
14 The L' thundered from heaven, ‡ "
16 at the rebuking of the L', ‡ "
19 but the L' was my stay. ‡ "
21 L' rewarded me according to my ‡ "
22 I have kept the ways of the L', ‡ "
25 L' hath recompensed me according‡ "
29 For thou art my lamp, O L': ‡ "
29 the L' will lighten my darkness. ‡ "
31 the word of the L' is tried: he is ‡ "
32 For who is God, save the L'? and‡ "
42 even unto the L', but he answered‡ "
47 The L' liveth; and blessed be my ‡ "
50 I will give thanks unto thee, O L',‡ "
23: 2 The Spirit of the L' spake by me, ‡ "
10 L' wrought a great victory that ‡ "
12 the L' wrought a great victory. ‡ "
16 but poured it out unto the L'. ‡ "
17 Be it far from me, O L', that I ‡ "
24: 1 the anger of the L' was kindled ‡ "
3 L' thy God add unto the people, ‡ "
3 eyes of my l' the king may see it: 113
3 doth my l' the king delight in this "
10 David said unto the L', I have ‡3068
10 O L', take away the iniquity of ‡ "
11 word of the L' came unto...Gad, ‡ "
12 Thus saith the L', I offer thee ‡ "
14 us fall now into the hand of the L'‡ "
15 L' sent a pestilence upon Israel ‡ "
16 the L' repented him of the evil, ‡ "
16 the angel of the L' was by the ‡ "
17 David spake unto the L' when he ‡ "
18 Go up, rear an altar unto the L' ‡ "
19 went up as the L' commanded. ‡ "
21 my l' the king come to his servant? 113
21 to build an altar unto the L', ‡3068
22 Let my l' the king take and offer up113
23 king, The L' thy God accept thee.‡3068
24 offer burnt offerings unto the L' ‡ "
25 built there an altar unto the L', ‡ "
25 the L' was intreated for the land, ‡ "
1Ki 1: 2 for my l' the king a young virgin: 113
2 that my l' the king may get heat. "
11 and David our l' knoweth it not? "
13 Didst not thou, my l', O king, swear "
17 said unto him, My l', thou swarest "
17 thou swarest by the L' thy God ‡3068
18 my l' the king, thou knowest it not: 113
20 my l', O king, the eyes of all Israel "
20 on the throne of my l' the king after "
21 when my l' the king shall sleep with "
24 Nathan said, My l', O king, hast thou "
27 Is this thing done by my l' the king, "
27 on the throne of my l' the king after "
29 sware, and said, As the L' liveth, ‡3068
30 I sware unto thee by the L' God of ‡ "
31 Let my l' king David live for ever. 113
33 Take with you the servants of your l', "
36 L' God of...the king say so too. ‡3068
36 God of my l' the king say so too. 113
37 As the L' hath been with my ‡3068
37 hath been with my l' the king, 113
37 than the throne of my l' king David. "
43 l' king David hath made Solomon "
47 came to bless our l' king David, "
48 Blessed be the L' God of Israel, ‡3068
2: 3 keep the charge of the L' thy God,‡ "
4 L' may continue his word which ‡ "
8 and I sware to him by the L', ‡ "
15 brother's: for it was his from the L'.‡ "
23 Solomon sware by the L', saying, ‡ "
24 Now therefore, as the L' liveth, ‡ "
26 thou barest the ark of the L' God 136
27 from being priest unto the L'; ‡3068
27 he might fulfil the word of the L',‡ "
28 fled unto the tabernacle of the L',‡ "
29 fled unto the tabernacle of the L';‡ "
30 came to the tabernacle of the L', ‡ "
32 L' shall return his blood upon his‡ "
33 there be peace for ever from the L'.‡ "
38 as my l' the king hath said, so will 113
42 not make thee to swear by the L',‡3068
43 thou not kept the oath of the L', ‡ "
44 L' shall return thy wickedness ‡ "

1Ki 2:45 established before the L' for ever. ‡3068
3: 1 house, and the house of the L', ‡ "
2 house built unto the name of the L'.‡ "
3 Solomon loved the L', walking in ‡ "
5 the L' appeared to Solomon in a ‡ "
7 O L' my God, thou hast made thy‡ "
10 And the speech pleased the L', that136
15 the ark of the covenant of the L', ‡3068
17 O my l', I and this woman dwell 113
26 O my l', give her the living child, "
5: 3 unto the name of the L' his God ‡3068
3 the L' put them under the soles ‡ "
4 L' my God hath given me rest on ‡ "
5 unto the name of the L' my God, ‡ "
5 as the L' spake unto David my ‡ "
7 Blessed be the L' this day, which ‡ "
12 the L' gave Solomon wisdom, as ‡ "
6: 1 began to build the house of the L'.‡ "
2 king Solomon built for the L', ‡ "
11 word of the L' came to Solomon, ‡ "
19 the ark of the covenant of the L'. ‡ "
37 foundation of the house of the L' ‡ "
7: 12 inner court of the house of the L',‡ "
40 Solomon for the house of the L': ‡ "
45 Solomon for the house of the L', ‡ "
48 unto the house of the L': ‡ "
51 made for the house of the L'. ‡ "
51 treasures of the house of the L'. ‡ "
8: 1 the ark of the covenant of the L' ‡ "
4 they brought up the ark of the L',‡ "
6 the ark of the covenant of the L' ‡ "
9 when the L' made a covenant ‡ "
10 cloud filled the house of the L', ‡ "
11 glory of the L' had filled the ‡ "
11 had filled the house of the L'. ‡ "
12 The L' said that he would dwell ‡ "
15 Blessed be the L' God of Israel, ‡ "
17 the name of the L' God of Israel. ‡ "
18 L' said unto David my father, ‡ "
20 L' hath performed his word that ‡ "
20 of Israel, as the L' promised, ‡ "
20 the name of the L' God of Israel. ‡ "
21 wherein is the covenant of the L',‡ "
22 stood before the altar of the L' ‡ "
23 L' God of Israel, there is no God ‡ "
25 L' God of Israel, keep with thy ‡ "
28 O L' my God, to hearken unto ‡ "
44 pray unto the L' toward the city ‡ "
53 our fathers out of Egypt, O L' God. 136
54 and supplication unto the L', ‡3068
54 from before the altar of the L', ‡ "
56 Blessed be the L', that hath given‡ "
57 The L' our God be with us, as he ‡ "
59 made supplication before the L', ‡ "
59 be nigh unto the L' our God day ‡ "
60 may know that the L' is God, ‡ "
61 be perfect with the L' our God, ‡ "
62 offered sacrifice before the L'. ‡ "
63 which he offered unto the L', ‡ "
63 dedicated the house of the L'. ‡ "
64 was before the house of the L': ‡ "
64 altar that was before the L' was ‡ "
65 before the L' our God, seven days‡ "
66 the goodness that the L' had done‡ "
9: 1 building of the house of the L', ‡ "
2 the L' appeared to Solomon the ‡ "
3 And the L' said unto him, I have ‡ "
8 Why hath the L' done this unto ‡ "
9 they forsook the L' their God, ‡ "
9 L' brought upon them all this ‡ "
10 the house of the L', and the king's‡ "
15 for to build the house of the L', ‡ "
25 altar which he built unto the L', ‡ "
25 the altar that was before the L'. ‡ "
10: 1 concerning the name of the L', ‡ "
5 went up unto the house of the L';‡ "
9 Blessed be the L' thy God, which ‡ "
9 the L' loved Israel for ever, ‡ "
12 pillars for the house of the L', ‡ "
11: 2 concerning which the L' said ‡ "
4 not perfect with the L' his God, ‡ "
6 did evil in the sight of the L', ‡ "
6 went not fully after the L', as did‡ "
9 the L' was angry with Solomon, ‡ "
9 heart was turned from the L' God‡ "
10 not that which the L' commanded.‡ "
11 the L' said unto Solomon, ‡ "
14 L' stirred up an adversary unto ‡ "
23 which fled from his l' Hadadezer 113
31 for thus saith the L', the God of ‡3068
12: 15 for the cause was from the L', ‡ "
15 which the L' spake by Ahijah the‡ "
24 Thus saith the L', Ye shall not go‡ "
24 therefore to the word of the L', ‡ "
24 according to the word of the L'. ‡ "
27 sacrifice in the house of the L' at‡ "
27 people turn again unto their l', 113
13: 1 Judah by the word of the L' unto ‡3068
2 the altar in the word of the L', ‡ "
2 O altar, altar, thus saith the L'; ‡ "
3 sign which the L' hath spoken; ‡ "
5 had given by the word of the L'. ‡ "
6 now the face of the L' thy God, ‡ "
6 the man of God besought the L', ‡ "
9 charged me by the word of the L',‡ "
17 said to me by the word of the L', ‡ "
18 unto me by the word of the L', ‡ "
20 the word of the L' came unto the ‡ "
21 Judah, saying, Thus saith the L',‡ "
21 disobeyed the mouth of the L', ‡ "
21 which the L' thy God commanded ‡ "
22 the which the L' did say unto thee,*
26 unto the word of the L': ‡3068
26 L' hath delivered him unto the ‡ "
26 according to the word of the L', ‡ "
32 he cried by the word of the L' ‡ "

1Ki 14: 5 the L' said unto Ahijah, Behold, ‡3068
7 Thus saith the L' God of Israel, ‡ "
11 eat: for the L' hath spoken it. ‡ "
13 some good thing toward the L' ‡ "
14 L' shall raise him up a king over ‡ "
15 L' shall smite Israel, as a reed ‡ "
15 groves, provoking the L' to anger.‡ "
18 according to the word of the L', ‡ "
21 the city which the L' did choose ‡ "
22 did evil in the sight of the L', ‡ "
24 the nations which the L' cast out‡ "
26 treasures of the house of the L', ‡ "
28 went into the house of the L', ‡ "
15: 3 not perfect with the L' his God, ‡ "
4 the L' his God give him a lamp ‡ "
5, 11 was right in the eyes of the L',‡ "
14 heart was perfect with the L' all ‡ "
15 into the house of the L', silver, ‡ "
18 treasures of the house of the L', ‡ "
26 he did evil in the sight of the L', ‡ "
29 unto the saying of the L', which ‡ "
30 provoked the L' God of Israel to ‡ "
34 he did evil in the sight of the L', ‡ "
16: 1 the word of the L' came to Jehu ‡ "
7 word of the L' against Baasha, ‡ "
7 that he did in the sight of the L', ‡ "
12 according to the word of the L', ‡ "
13 provoking the L' God of Israel to ‡ "
19 doing evil in the sight of the L', ‡ "
25 wrought evil in the eyes of the L',‡ "
26 to provoke the L' God of Israel ‡ "
30 Omri did evil in the sight of the L'‡ "
33 provoke the L' God of Israel to ‡ "
34 according to the word of the L', ‡ "
17: 1 As the L' God of Israel liveth, ‡ "
2 the word of the L' came unto him, ‡ "
5 according unto the word of the L':‡ "
8 the word of the L' came unto him,‡ "
12 As the L' thy God liveth, I have ‡ "
14 thus saith the L' God of Israel, ‡ "
14 the day that the L' sendeth rain ‡ "
16 according to the word of the L', ‡ "
20 he cried unto the L', and said, ‡ "
20 O L' my God, hast thou also ‡ "
21 and cried unto the L', and said, ‡ "
21 O L' my God, I pray thee, let ‡ "
22 the L' heard the voice of Elijah; ‡ "
24 the word of the L' in thy mouth ‡ "
18: 1 the word of the L' came to Elijah ‡ "
3 Obadiah feared the L' greatly: ‡ "
4 cut off the prophets of the L', ‡ "
7 said, Art thou that my l' Elijah? 113
8 go, tell thy l', Behold, Elijah is "
10 As the L' thy God liveth, there ‡3068
10 whither my l' hath not sent to 113
11 Go, tell thy l', Behold, Elijah is "
12 Spirit of the L' shall carry thee ‡3068
12 but I thy servant fear the L' from‡ "
13 Was it not told my l' what I did 113
13 slew the prophets of the L', ‡3068
14 Go, tell thy l', Behold, Elijah is 113
15 said, As the L' of hosts liveth, ‡3068
18 the commandments of the L', ‡ "
21 if the L' be God, follow him: but ‡ "
22 only, remain a prophet of the L'; ‡ "
24 I will call on the name of the L': ‡ "
30 repaired the altar of the L' that ‡ "
31 unto whom the word of the L' ‡ "
32 an altar in the name of the L': ‡ "
36 and said, L' God of Abraham, ‡ "
37 Hear me, O L', hear me, that this‡ "
37 know that thou art the L' God, ‡ "
38 Then the fire of the L' fell, and ‡ "
39 L', he is the God; the L', he is the‡ "
46 the hand of the L' was on Elijah; ‡ "
19: 4 now, O L', take away my life; for ‡ "
7 the angel of the L' came again ‡ "
9 the word of the L' came to him, ‡ "
10 jealous for the L' God of hosts: ‡ "
11 upon the mount before the L'. ‡ "
11 the L' passed by, and a great and‡ "
11 in pieces the rocks before the L'; ‡ "
11 but the L' was not in the wind: ‡ "
11 L' was not in the earthquake: ‡ "
12 but the L' was not in the fire: ‡ "
14 jealous for the L' God of hosts: ‡ "
15 the L' said unto him, Go, return ‡ "
20: 4 Israel answered and said, My l', 113
9 Tell my l' the king, All that thou "
13 Thus saith the L', Hast thou seen‡3068
13 thou shalt know that I am the L'.‡ "
14 Thus saith the L', Even by the ‡ "
28 Thus saith the L', Because the ‡ "
28 said, The L' is God of the hills, ‡ "
28 ye shall know that I am the L'. ‡ "
35 neighbour in the word of the L', ‡ "
36 not obeyed the voice of the L', ‡ "
42 Thus saith the L', Because thou ‡ "
21: 3 said to Ahab, The L' forbid it me,‡ "
17 the word of the L' came to Elijah ‡ "
19 Thus saith the L', Hast thou ‡ "
19 Thus saith the L', In the place ‡ "
20 to work evil in the sight of the L'. ‡ "
23 And of Jezebel also spake the L', ‡ "
25 wickedness in the sight of the L', ‡ "
26 Amorites, whom the L' cast out ‡ "
28 the word of the L' came to Elijah‡ "
22: 5 thee, at the word of the L' to day. ‡ "
6 L' shall deliver it into the hand of 136
7 there not here a prophet of the L'‡3068
8 whom we may enquire of the L': ‡ "
11 Thus saith the L', With these ‡ "
12 L' shall deliver it into the king's ‡ "
14 Micaiah said, As the L' liveth, ‡ "
14 what the L' saith unto me, that ‡ "
15 L' shall deliver it into the hand of ‡ "

1Ki 22: 16 is true in the name of the L'? ‡3068
17 L' said, These have no master: ‡ "
19 thou therefore the word of the L':‡ "
19 I saw the L' sitting on his throne,‡ "
20 the L' said, Who shall persuade ‡ "
21 a spirit, and stood before the L', ‡ "
22 L' said unto him, Wherewith? ‡ "
23 L' hath put a lying spirit in the ‡ "
23 L' hath spoken evil concerning ‡ "
24 went the Spirit of the L' from me ‡ "
28 the L' hath not spoken by me. ‡ "
38 according unto the word of the L'‡ "
43 was right in the eyes of the L': ‡ "
52 he did evil in the sight of the L', ‡ "
53 and provoked to anger the L' God‡ "
2Ki 1: 3 angel of the L' said to Elijah the ‡ "
4 thus saith the L', Thou shalt not ‡ "
6 saith the L', Is it not because ‡ "
15 angel of the L' said unto Elijah, ‡ "
16 Thus saith the L', Forasmuch as ‡ "
17 according to the word of the L' ‡ "
2: 1 the L' would take up Elijah into ‡ "
2 for the L' hath sent me to Beth-el.‡ "
2 said unto him, As the L' liveth, ‡ "
3 the L' will take away thy master ‡ "
4 for the L' hath sent me to Jericho.‡ "
4 said, As the L' liveth, and as thy ‡ "
5 the L' will take away thy master ‡ "
6 for the L' hath sent me to Jordan. ‡ "
6 said, As the L' liveth, and as thy ‡ "
14 Where is the L' God of Elijah? ‡ "
16 Spirit of the L' hath taken him ‡ "
19 this city is pleasant, as my l' seeth:113
21 Thus saith the L', I have healed ‡3068
24 cursed them in the name of the L'.‡ "
3: 2 wrought evil in the sight of the L'; ‡ "
10 L' hath called these three kings ‡ "
11 there not here a prophet of the L',‡ "
11 we may enquire of the L' by him?‡ "
12 The word of the L' is with him. ‡ "
13 L' hath called these three kings ‡ "
14 As the L' of hosts liveth, before ‡ "
15 hand of the L' came upon him. ‡ "
16 saith the L', Make this valley ‡ "
17 For thus saith the L', Ye shall not‡ "
18 light thing in the sight of the L': ‡ "
4: 1 that thy servant did fear the L': ‡ "
16 said, Nay, my l', thou man of God, 113
27 the L' hath hid it from me, and ‡3068
28 said, Did I desire a son of my l'? 113
30 the child said, As the L' liveth, ‡3068
33 twain, and prayed unto the L'. ‡ "
43 thus saith the L', They shall eat, ‡ "
44 according to the word of the L'. ‡ "
5: 1 the L' had given deliverance unto‡ "
3 God my l' were with the prophet 113
4 one went in, and told his l', saying, "
11 and call on the name of the L' ‡3068
16 As the L' liveth, before whom I ‡ "
17 unto other gods, but unto the L'. ‡ "
18 thing the L' pardon thy servant, ‡ "
18 the L' pardon thy servant in this ‡ "
20 as the L' liveth, I will run after ‡ "
6: 12 servants said, None, my l', O king: 113
17 L', I pray thee, open his eyes, ‡3068
17 L' opened the eyes of the young ‡ "
18 Elisha prayed unto the L', and ‡ "
20 L', open the eyes of these men, ‡ "
20 And the L' opened their eyes, and‡ "
26 him, saying, Help, my l', O king. 113
27 said, If the L' do not help thee, ‡3068
33 said, Behold, this evil is of the L';‡ "
33 I wait for the L' any longer? ‡ "
7: 1 said, Hear ye the word of the L'; ‡ "
1 Thus saith the L', To morrow ‡ "
2 l' on whose hand the king leaned *7991
2 if the L' would make windows in ‡3068
6 L' had made the host of Syrians 136
16 according to the word of the L'. ‡3068
17 king appointed the l' on whose *7991
19 that l' answered the man of God, * "
19 if the L' should make windows in ‡3068
8: 1 the L' hath called for a famine; ‡ "
5 Gehazi said, My l', O king, this is 113
8 enquire of the L' by him, saying, ‡3068
10 L' hath shewed me that he shall ‡ "
12 Hazael said, Why weepeth my l'? 113
13 The L' hath shewed me that thou‡3068
18 he did evil in the sight of the L'. ‡ "
19 L' would not destroy Judah for ‡ "
27 and did evil in the sight of the L',‡ "
9: 3 saith the L', I have anointed ‡ "
6 Thus saith the L' God of Israel, ‡ "
6 king over the people of the L', ‡ "
7 blood of all the servants of the L',‡ "
11 came forth to the servants of his l': 113
12 Thus said the L', I have anointed ‡3068
25 the L' laid this burden upon him;‡ "
26 the blood of his sons, saith the L';‡ "
26 thee in this plat, saith the L'. ‡ "
26 according to the word of the L'. ‡ "
36 This is the word of the L', which ‡ "
10: 10 nothing of the word of the L', ‡ "
10 L' spake concerning the house of‡ "
10 L' hath done that which he spake‡ "
16 me, and see my zeal for the L'. ‡ "
17 according to the saying of the L', ‡ "
23 none of the servants of the L', ‡ "
30 the L' said unto Jehu, Because ‡ "
31 to walk in the law of the L' God ‡ "
32 the L' began to cut Israel short: ‡ "
11: 3 hid in the house of the L' six years.‡ "
4 to him into the house of the L', ‡ "
4 of them in the house of the L', ‡ "
7 the watch of the house of the L' ‡ "
10 that were in the temple of the L'. ‡ "

2Ki 11:13 people into the temple of the L'. ‡3068
15 not be slain in the house of the L'. ‡ "
17 covenant between the L' and the ‡ "
18 officers over the house of the L'. ‡ "
19 the king from the house of the L', ‡ "
12: 2 was right in the sight of the L' all ‡ "
4 brought into the house of the L', ‡ "
4 to bring into the house of the L', ‡ "
9 cometh into the house of the L': ‡ "
9 brought into the house of the L': ‡ "
10 was found in the house of the L'. ‡ "
11 oversight of the house of the L': ‡ "
11 wrought upon the house of the L', ‡ "
12 breaches of the house of the L', ‡ "
13 not made for the house of the L' ‡ "
13 brought into the house of the L': ‡ "
14 therewith the house of the L'. ‡ "
16 brought into the house of the L': ‡ "
18 treasures of the house of the L', ‡ "
13: 2 was evil in the sight of the L', ‡ "
3 anger of the L' was kindled ‡ "
4 And Jehoahaz besought the L', ‡ "
4 and the L' hearkened unto him: ‡ "
5 (And the L' gave Israel a saviour, ‡ "
11 was evil in the sight of the L'; ‡ "
23 the L' was gracious unto them, ‡ "
14: 3 was right in the sight of the L', ‡ "
6 wherein the L' commanded, ‡ "
14 were found in the house of the L', ‡ "
24 was evil in the sight of the L': ‡ "
25 according to the word of the L' God ‡ "
26 the L' saw the affliction of Israel, ‡ "
27 L' said not that he would blot out ‡ "
15: 3 was right in the sight of the L', ‡ "
5 the L' smote the king, so that he ‡ "
9 was evil in the sight of the L', ‡ "
12 the word of the L' which he spake ‡ "
18, 24, 28 evil in the sight of the L': ‡ "
34 was right in the sight of the L': ‡ "
35 higher gate of the house of the L'. ‡ "
37 L' began to send against Judah ‡ "
16: 2 was right in the sight of the L' ‡ "
3 whom the L' cast out from before ‡ "
8 was found in the house of the L', ‡ "
14 altar, which was before the L', ‡ "
14 the altar and the house of the L', ‡ "
18 he from the house of the L' for ‡ "
17: 2 was evil in the sight of the L', ‡ "
7 sinned against the L' their God, ‡ "
8 heathen, whom the L' cast out ‡ "
9 that were not right against the L' ‡ "
11 whom the L' carried away before ‡ "
11 things to provoke the L' to anger: ‡ "
12 the L' had said unto them, Ye ‡ "
13 the L' testified against Israel, ‡ "
14 that did not believe in the L' their ‡ "
15 concerning whom the L' had ‡ "
16 all the commandments of the L' ‡ "
17 to do evil in the sight of the L', ‡ "
18 the L' was very angry with Israel, ‡ "
19 not the commandments of the L' ‡ "
20 L' rejected all the seed of Israel, ‡ "
21 Israel from following the L', ‡ "
23 L' removed Israel out of his sight, ‡ "
25 there, that they feared not the L': ‡ "
25 the L' sent lions among them, ‡ "
28 how they should fear the L'. ‡ "
32 So they feared the L', and made ‡ "
33 They feared the L', and served ‡ "
34 they fear not the L', neither do ‡ "
34 and commandment which the L' ‡ "
35 the L' had made a covenant, ‡ "
36 the L', who brought you up out ‡ "
39 the L' your God ye shall fear; ‡ "
41 So these nations feared the L', ‡ "
18: 3 was right in the sight of the L', ‡ "
5 trusted in the L' God of Israel; ‡ "
6 he clave to the L', and departed ‡ "
6 which the L' commanded Moses. ‡ "
7 And the L' was with him; and he ‡ "
12 obeyed not the voice of the L' ‡ "
12 the servant of the L' commanded, ‡ "
15 was found in the house of the L', ‡ "
16 the doors of the temple of the L', ‡ "
22 me, We trust in the L' our God: ‡ "
23 give pledges to my l' the king of * 113
25 Am I now come up without the L' ‡3068
25 The L' said to me, Go up against ‡ "
30 Hezekiah make you trust in the L', ‡ "
30 The L' will surely deliver us, and ‡ "
32 saying, The L' will deliver us. ‡ "
35 L' should deliver Jerusalem out ‡ "
19: 1 and went into the house of the L'. ‡ "
4 L' thy God will hear all the words ‡ "
4 which the L' thy God hath heard: ‡ "
6 Thus saith the L', Be not afraid ‡ "
14 went up into the house of the L', ‡ "
14 and spread it before the L'. ‡ "
15 Hezekiah prayed before the L', ‡ "
15 O L' God of Israel, which dwellest ‡ "
16 L', bow down thine ear, and hear: ‡ "
16 open, L', thine eyes, and see: ‡ "
17 Of a truth, L', the kings of Assyria ‡ "
19 O L' our God, I beseech thee, save ‡ "
19 know that thou art the L' God, ‡ "
20 Thus saith the L' God of Israel, ‡ "
21 the word that the L' hath spoken ‡ "
23 thou hast reproached the L', ‡ "
31 zeal of the L' of hosts shall do ‡ "
32 thus saith the L' concerning the ‡ "
33 come into this city, saith the L'. ‡ "
35 that the angel of the L' went out, ‡ "
20: 1 Thus saith the L', Set thine house ‡ "
2 the wall, and prayed unto the L', ‡ "
3 I beseech thee, O L', remember ‡ "
4 the word of the L' came to him, ‡ "

2Ki 20: 5 Thus saith the L', the God of ‡3068
5 go up unto the house of the L'. ‡ "
8 be the sign that the L' will heal ‡ "
8 go up into the house of the L' ‡ "
9 sign shalt thou have of the L', ‡ "
9 L' will do the thing that he hath ‡ "
11 the prophet cried unto the L': ‡ "
16 Hear the word of the L'. ‡ "
17 nothing shall be left, saith the L'. ‡ "
19 Good is the word of the L' which ‡ "
21: 2 was evil in the sight of the L', ‡ "
2 L' cast out before the children of ‡ "
4 built altars in the house of the L', ‡ "
5 two courts of the house of the L'. ‡ "
6 wickedness in the sight of the L', ‡ "
7 of which the L' said to David, ‡ "
9 nations whom the L' destroyed ‡ "
10 the L' spake by his servants the ‡ "
12 thus saith the L' God of Israel, ‡ "
16 was evil in the sight of the L'. ‡ "
20 was evil in the sight of the L', ‡ "
22 forsook the L' God of his fathers, ‡ "
22 walked not in the way of the L'. ‡ "
22: 2 was right in the sight of the L', ‡ "
3 the scribe, to the house of the L', ‡ "
4 brought into the house of the L', ‡ "
5 oversight of the house of the L': ‡ "
5 which is in the house of the L', ‡ "
8 of the law in the house of the L'. ‡ "
9 oversight of the house of the L'. ‡ "
13 enquire of the L' for me, and for ‡ "
13 great is the wrath of the L' that ‡ "
15 Thus saith the L' God of Israel, ‡ "
16 Thus saith the L', Behold, I will ‡ "
18 sent you to enquire of the L', ‡ "
18 Thus saith the L' God of Israel, ‡ "
19 humbled thyself before the L', ‡ "
19 have heard thee, saith the L'. ‡ "
23: 2 went up into the house of the L', ‡ "
2 was found in the house of the L'. ‡ "
3 made a covenant before the L', ‡ "
3 to walk after the L', and to keep ‡ "
4 forth out of the temple of the L' ‡ "
6 grove from the house of the L', ‡ "
7 that were by the house of the L', ‡ "
9 came not up to the altar of the L' ‡ "
11 entering in of the house of the L', ‡ "
12 two courts of the house of the L', ‡ "
16 according to the word of the L' ‡ "
19 made to provoke the L' to anger, ‡ "
21 Keep the passover unto the L' ‡3068
23 passover was holden to the L' in ‡ "
24 found in the house of the L'. ‡ "
25 that turned to the L' with all his ‡ "
26 L' turned not from the fierceness ‡ "
27 the L' said, I will remove Judah ‡ "
32, 37 was evil in the sight of the L', ‡ "
24: 2 the L' sent against him bands of ‡ "
2 according to the word of the L', ‡ "
3 at the commandment of the L' ‡ "
4 which the L' would not pardon. ‡ "
9 was evil in the sight of the L', ‡ "
13 treasures of the house of the L', ‡ "
13 had made in the temple of the L', ‡ "
13 as the L' had said. ‡ "
19 was evil in the sight of the L', ‡ "
20 For through the anger of the L' ‡ "
25: 9 he burnt the house of the L', and ‡ "
13 that were in the house of the L', ‡ "
13 that was in the house of the L', ‡ "
16 made for the house of the L'; ‡ "
1Ch 2: 3 was evil in the sight of the L'; ‡ "
6: 15 when the L' carried away Judah ‡ "
31 of song in the house of the L', ‡ "
32 had built the house of the L' in ‡ "
9: 19 being over the host of the L', ‡ "
20 past, and the L' was with him. ‡ "
23 the gates of the house of the L', ‡ "
10: 13 he committed against the L', ‡ "
13 even against the word of the L', ‡ "
14 enquired not of the L': therefore ‡ "
11: 2 the L' thy God said unto thee, ‡ "
3 them in Hebron before the L'; ‡ "
3 the word of the L' by Samuel. ‡ "
9 for the L' of hosts was with him. ‡ "
10 word of the L' concerning Israel. ‡ "
14 and the L' saved them by a great ‡ "
18 of it, but poured it out to the L', ‡ "
12: 23 according to the word of the L'. ‡ "
13: 2 and that it be of the L' our God, ‡ "
6 up thence the ark of God the L', ‡ "
10 the anger of the L' was kindled ‡ "
11 L' had made a breach upon Uzza: ‡ "
14 And the L' blessed the house of ‡ "
14: 2 L' had confirmed him king over ‡ "
10 the L' said unto him, Go up; for ‡ "
17 L' brought the fear of him upon ‡ "
15: 2 them hath the L' chosen to carry ‡ "
3 bring up the ark of the L' unto ‡ "
12 up the ark of the L' God of Israel ‡ "
13 L' our God made a breach upon ‡ "
14 up the ark of the L' God of Israel. ‡ "
15 according to the word of the L'. ‡ "
25 the ark of the covenant of the L' ‡ "
26 the ark of the covenant of the L', ‡ "
28, 29 ark of the covenant of the L' ‡ "
16: 2 the people in the name of the L'. ‡ "
4 minister before the ark of the L', ‡ "
4 thank and praise the L' God of ‡ "
7 first this psalm to thank the L' ‡ "
8 Give thanks unto the L', call upon ‡ "
10 of them rejoice that seek the L'. ‡ "
11 Seek the L' and his strength, ‡ "
14 He is the L' our God; his ‡ "
23 Sing unto the L', all the earth; ‡ "
25 For great is the L', and greatly ‡ "

1Ch 16: 26 but the L' made the heavens. ‡3068
28 Give unto the L', ye kindreds of ‡ "
28 unto the L' glory and strength. ‡ "
29 Give unto the L' the glory due ‡ "
29 worship the L' in the beauty of ‡ "
31 the nations, The L' reigneth. ‡ "
33 sing out at the presence of the L', ‡ "
34 O give thanks unto the L'; for ‡ "
36 Blessed be the L' God of Israel ‡ "
36 said, Amen, and praised the L'. ‡ "
37 the ark of the covenant of the L' ‡ "
39 before the tabernacle of the L' ‡ "
40 offer burnt offerings unto the L' ‡ "
40 that is written in the law of the L', ‡ "
41 by name, to give thanks to the L', ‡ "
17: 1 the ark of the covenant of the L' ‡ "
4 Thus saith the L', Thou shalt not ‡ "
7 Thus saith the L' of hosts, I took ‡ "
10 the L' will build thee an house. ‡ "
16 king came and sat before the L', ‡ "
16 Who am I, O L' God, and what ‡ "
17 a man of high degree, O L' God. ‡ "
19 O L', for thy servant's sake, and ‡ "
20 O L', there is none like thee, ‡ "
22 and thou, L', becamest their God. ‡ "
23 Therefore now, L', let the thing ‡ "
24 the L' of hosts is the God of Israel, ‡ "
26 And now, L', thou art God, and ‡ "
27 for thou blessest, O L', and it shall ‡ "
18: 6 Thus the L' preserved David ‡ "
11 king David dedicated unto the L', ‡ "
13 Thus the L' preserved David ‡ "
19: 13 let the L' do that which is good in ‡ "
21: 3 L' make his people an hundred ‡ "
3 my l' the king, are they not all my 113
3 why then doth my l' require this "
9 L' spake unto Gad, David's seer, ‡3068
10 Thus saith the L', I offer thee three ‡ "
11 Thus saith the L', Choose thee ‡ "
12 three days the sword of the L', ‡ "
12 and the angel of the L' destroying ‡ "
13 fall now into the hand of the L'; ‡ "
14 L' sent pestilence upon Israel: ‡ "
15 the L' beheld, and he repented ‡ "
15 the angel of the L' stood by the ‡ "
16 and saw the angel of the L' stand ‡ "
17 hand, I pray thee, O L' my God, ‡ "
18 angel of the L' commanded Gad ‡ "
18 set up an altar unto the L' in the ‡ "
19 he spake in the name of the L'. ‡ "
22 build an altar therein unto the L': ‡ "
23 my l' the king do that which is good 113
24 take that which is thine for the L', ‡3068
26 built there an altar unto the L', ‡ "
26 offerings, and called upon the L'; ‡ "
27 And the L' commanded the angel; ‡ "
28 saw that the L' had answered him ‡ "
29 tabernacle of the L', which Moses ‡ "
30 the sword of the angel of the L'. ‡ "
22: 1 This is the house of the L' God, ‡ "
5 L' must be exceeding magnifical, ‡ "
6 to build an house for the L' God ‡ "
7 unto the name of the L' my God: ‡ "
8 the word of the L' came to me, ‡ "
11 Now, my son, the L' be with thee; ‡ "
11 build the house of the L' thy God, ‡ "
12 Only the L' give thee wisdom and ‡ "
12 keep the law of the L' thy God. ‡ "
13 which the L' charged Moses with ‡ "
14 prepared for the house of the L' ‡ "
16 be doing, and the L' be with thee. ‡ "
18 Is not the L' your God with you? ‡ "
18 the land is subdued before the L', ‡ "
19 your soul to seek the L' your God; ‡ "
19 ye the sanctuary of the L' God, ‡ "
19 the ark of the covenant of the L', ‡ "
19 to be built in the name of the L'. ‡ "
23: 4 the work of the house of the L'; ‡ "
5 four thousand praised the L' with ‡ "
13 to burn incense before the L', ‡ "
24 the service of the house of the L', ‡ "
25 L' God of Israel hath given rest ‡ "
28 the service of the house of the L', ‡ "
30 to thank and praise the L', and ‡ "
31 all burnt sacrifices unto the L' in ‡ "
31 them, continually before the L': ‡ "
32 the service of the house of the L'. ‡ "
24: 19 to come into the house of the L', ‡ "
19 L' God of Israel had commanded ‡ "
25: 3 give thanks and to praise the L'. ‡ "
6 for song in the house of the L', ‡ "
7 instructed in the songs of the L', ‡ "
26: 12 to minister in the house of the L'. ‡ "
22 treasures of the house of the L'. ‡ "
27 to maintain the house of the L'. ‡ "
30 in all the business of the L', and ‡ "
27: 23 the L' had said he would increase ‡ "
28: 2 the ark of the covenant of the L', ‡ "
4 L' God of Israel chose me before ‡ "
5 the L' hath given me many sons,) ‡ "
5 throne of the kingdom of the L' ‡ "
8 Israel the congregation of the L', ‡ "
8 all the commandments of the L' ‡ "
9 the L' searcheth all hearts, and ‡ "
10 L' hath chosen thee to build an ‡ "
12 the courts of the house of the L', ‡ "
13 the service of the house of the L', ‡ "
13 of service in the house of the L'. ‡ "
18 the ark of the covenant of the L'. ‡ "
19 L' made me understand in writing ‡ "
20 for the L' God, even my God, will ‡ "
20 the service of the house of the L'. ‡ "
29: 1 is not for man, but for the L' God. ‡ "
5 his service this day unto the L'? ‡ "
8 treasure of the house of the L', ‡ "
9 they offered willingly to the L': ‡ "

1Ch 29: 10 David blessed the L· before all ‡3068
10 be thou, L· God of Israel our father, ‡ "
11 Thine, O L·, is the greatness, and ‡ "
11 thine is the kingdom, O L·, and ‡ "
16 O L· our God, all this store that ‡ "
18 O L· God of Abraham, Isaac, and ‡ "
20 Now bless the L· your God. ‡ "
20 congregation blessed the L· God ‡ "
20 worshipped the L·, and the king. ‡ "
21 sacrificed sacrifices unto the L·, ‡ "
21 offered burnt offerings unto the L·, ‡ "
22 did eat and drink before the L· ‡ "
22 anointed him unto the L· to be ‡ "
23 sat on the throne of the L· as king ‡ "
25 And the L· magnified Solomon ‡ "
2Ch 1: 1 the L· his God was with him, and ‡ "
3 Moses the servant of the L· had ‡ "
5 before the tabernacle of the L·: ‡ "
6 to the brasen altar before the L·, ‡ "
9 Now, O L· God, let thy promise ‡ "
2: 1 an house for the name of the L·, ‡ "
4 to the name of the L· my God, ‡ "
4 solemn feasts of the L· our God. ‡ "
11 the L· hath loved his people, ‡ "
12 Blessed be the L· God of Israel, ‡ "
12 might build an house for the L·, ‡ "
14 the cunning men of my l· David thy 113
15 wine, which my l· hath spoken of, "
3: 1 began to build the house of the L· ‡3068
1 where the L· appeared unto David ‡ "
4: 16 Solomon for the house of the L· ‡3068
5: 1 the house of the L· was finished: ‡ "
2, 7 the ark of the covenant of the L· ‡ "
10 the L· made a covenant with the ‡ "
13 in praising and thanking the L·; ‡ "
13 musick, and praised the L·, saying, ‡ "
13 cloud, even the house of the L·; ‡ "
14 glory of the L· had filled the house ‡ "
6: 1 L· hath said that he would dwell ‡ "
4 Blessed be the L· God of Israel, ‡ "
7 house for the name of the L· God ‡ "
8 the L· said to David my father, ‡ "
10 The L· therefore hath performed ‡ "
10 of Israel, as the L· promised, ‡ "
10 house for the name of the L· God ‡ "
11 wherein is the covenant of the L·, ‡ "
12 he stood before the altar of the L· ‡ "
14 O L· God of Israel, there is no God ‡ "
16 O L· God of Israel, keep with thy ‡ "
17 O L· God of Israel, let thy word ‡ "
19 O L· my God, to hearken unto the ‡ "
41 arise, O L· God, into thy resting ‡ "
41 thy priests, O L· God, be clothed ‡ "
42 O L· God, turn not away the face ‡ "
7: 1 glory of the L· filled the house. ‡ "
2 not enter into the house of the L·, ‡ "
2 glory of the L· had filled the Lord's ‡ "
3 glory of the L· upon the house, ‡ "
3 and praised the L·, saying, For he ‡ "
4 offered sacrifices before the L·. ‡ "
6 instruments of musick of the L·, ‡ "
6 king had made to praise the L·, ‡ "
7 was before the house of the L·: ‡ "
10 goodness that the L· had shewed ‡ "
11 finished the house of the L·, and ‡ "
11 to make in the house of the L·, ‡ "
12 L· appeared to Solomon by night, ‡ "
21 Why hath the L· done thus unto ‡ "
22 they forsook the L· God of their ‡ "
8: 1 had built the house of the L·, and ‡ "
11 the ark of the L· hath come. ‡ "
12 unto the L· on the altar of the L·, ‡ "
16 foundation of the house of the L·, ‡ "
16 the house of the L· was perfected. ‡ "
9: 4 went up into the house of the L·; ‡ "
8 Blessed be the L· thy God, which ‡ "
8 to be king for the L· thy God: ‡ "
11 terraces to the house of the L·, ‡ "
10: 15 the L· might perform his word, ‡ "
11: 2 word of the L· came to Shemaiah ‡ "
4 Thus saith the L·, Ye shall not ‡ "
4 they obeyed the words of the L·, ‡ "
14 the priest's office unto the L·: ‡ "
16 set their hearts to seek the L· God ‡ "
16 sacrifice unto the L· God of their ‡ "
12: 1 he forsook the law of the L·, and ‡ "
2 had transgressed against the L·, ‡ "
5 saith the L·, Ye have forsaken ‡ "
6 and they said, the L· is righteous. ‡ "
7 the L· saw that they humbled ‡ "
7 word of the L· came to Shemaiah, ‡ "
9 treasures of the house of the L·, ‡ "
11 entered into the house of the L·, ‡ "
12 wrath of the L· turned from him, ‡ "
13 city which the L· had chosen out ‡ "
14 not his heart to seek the L·. ‡ "
13: 5 L· God of Israel gave the kingdom ‡ "
6 and hath rebelled against his l·. 113
8 withstand the kingdom of the L· ‡3068
9 not cast out the priests of the L·, ‡ "
10 as for us, the L· is our God, and ‡ "
10 which minister unto the L·, ‡ "
11 burn unto the L· every morning ‡ "
11 the charge of the L· our God; ‡ "
12 fight ye not against the L· God of ‡ "
14 they cried unto the L·, and the ‡ "
18 they relied upon the L· God of ‡ "
20 the L· struck him, and he died. ‡ "
14: 2 right in the eyes of the L· his God: ‡ "
4 Judah to seek the L· God of their ‡ "
6 because the L· had given him rest. ‡ "
7 we have sought the L· our God, ‡ "
11 And Asa cried unto the L· his God, ‡ "
11 L·, it is nothing with thee to help, ‡ "
11 help us, O L· our God; for we ‡ "
11 O L·, thou art our God; let not ‡ "

2Ch 14: 12 L· smote the Ethiopians before ‡3068
13 they were destroyed before the L·, ‡ "
14 fear of the L· came upon them: ‡ "
15: 2 The L· is with you, while ye be ‡ "
4 trouble did turn unto the L· God ‡ "
8 and renewed the altar of the L·, ‡ "
8 was before the porch of the L·. ‡ "
9 that the L· his God was with him. ‡ "
11 they offered unto the L· the same ‡ "
12 seek the L· God of their fathers ‡ "
13 not seek the L· God of Israel ‡ "
14 sware unto the L· with a loud ‡ "
15 L· gave them rest round about. ‡ "
16: 2 treasures of the house of the L· ‡ "
7 and not relied on the L· thy God, ‡ "
8 because thou didst rely on the L·, ‡ "
9 the eyes of the L· run to and fro ‡ "
12 his disease he sought not the L·, ‡ "
17: 3 And the L· was with Jehoshaphat, ‡ "
5 the L· stablished the kingdom in ‡ "
6 lifted up in the ways of the L·: ‡ "
9 had the book of the law of the L· ‡ "
10 the fear of the L· fell upon all the ‡ "
16 offered himself unto the L·; ‡ "
18: 4 I pray thee, at the word of the L· ‡ "
6 there not here a prophet of the L· ‡ "
7 whom we may enquire of the L·: ‡ "
10 Thus saith the L·, With these ‡ "
11 L· shall deliver it into the hand of ‡ "
13 Micaiah said, As the L· liveth, ‡ "
15 truth to me in the name of the L·? ‡ "
16 and the L· said, These have no ‡ "
18 Therefore hear the word of the L·; ‡ "
18 saw the L· sitting upon his throne, ‡ "
19 And the L· said, Who shall entice ‡ "
20 a spirit, and stood before the L·, ‡ "
20 the L· said unto him, Wherewith? ‡ "
21 And the L· said, Thou shalt entice* "
22 the L· hath put a lying spirit in ‡3068
22 L· hath spoken evil against thee. ‡ "
23 went the Spirit of the L· from me ‡ "
27 hath not the L· spoken by me. ‡ "
31 cried out, and the L· helped him; ‡ "
19: 2 and love them that hate the L·? ‡ "
2 upon thee from before the L·. ‡ "
4 back unto the L· God of their ‡ "
6 but for the L·, who is with you in ‡ "
7 the fear of the L· be upon you; ‡ "
7 no iniquity with the L· our God, ‡ "
8 for the judgment of the L·, and ‡ "
9 do in the fear of the L·, faithfully, ‡ "
10 they trespass not against the L·, ‡ "
11 over you in all matters of the L·; ‡ "
11 and the L· shall be with the good. ‡ "
20: 3 and set himself to seek the L·, ‡ "
4 together, to ask help of the L·: ‡ "
4 Judah, they came to seek the L·. ‡ "
5 in the house of the L·, before the ‡ "
6 O L· God of our fathers, art not ‡ "
13 all Judah stood before the L·, ‡ "
14 Spirit of the L· in the midst of the ‡ "
15 Thus saith the L· unto you, Be not ‡ "
17 the salvation of the L· with you, ‡ "
17 them: for the L· will be with you. ‡ "
18 before the L·, worshipping the L·. ‡ "
19 up to praise the L· God of Israel. ‡ "
20 Believe in the L· your God, so ‡ "
21 he appointed singers unto the L·, ‡ "
21 say, Praise the L·; for his mercy ‡ "
22 L· set ambushments against the ‡ "
26 for there they blessed the L·: ‡ "
27 L· had made them to rejoice over ‡ "
28 trumpets unto the house of the L·. ‡ "
29 heard that the L· fought against ‡ "
32 was right in the sight of the L·. ‡ "
37 the L· hath broken thy works. ‡ "
21: 6 was evil in the eyes of the L·. ‡ "
7 L· would not destroy the house of ‡ "
10 he had forsaken the L· God of his ‡ "
12 Thus saith the L· God of David ‡ "
14 will the L· smite thy people, and ‡ "
16 L· stirred up against Jehoram ‡ "
18 L· smote him in his bowels with ‡ "
22: 4 evil in the sight of the L· like the ‡ "
7 the L· had anointed to cut off the ‡ "
9 sought the L· with all his heart. ‡ "
23: 3 L· hath said of the sons of David. ‡ "
5 the courts of the house of the L·. ‡ "
6 come into the house of the L·, ‡ "
6 shall keep the watch of the L·. ‡ "
12 people into the house of the L·: ‡ "
14 her not in the house of the L·. ‡ "
18 the offices of the house of the L· ‡ "
18 distributed in the house of the L·, ‡ "
18 offer the burnt offerings of the L·, ‡ "
19 at the gates of the house of the L·, ‡ "
20 the king from the house of the L·: ‡ "
24: 2 was right in the sight of the L· ‡ "
4 to repair the house of the L·. ‡ "
6 of Moses the servant of the L·, ‡ "
7 things of the house of the L· did ‡ "
8 at the gate of the house of the L·. ‡ "
9 bring in to the L· the collection ‡ "
12 the service of the house of the L·, ‡ "
12 to repair the house of the L·, and ‡ "
12 brass to mend the house of the L·. ‡ "
14 vessels for the house of the L·, ‡ "
14 offerings in the house of the L· ‡ "
18 left the house of the L· God of ‡ "
19 to bring them again unto the L·; ‡ "
20 ye the commandments of the L·, ‡ "
20 because ye have forsaken the L·, ‡ "
21 in the court of the house of the L·. ‡ "
22 The L· look upon it, and require ‡ "
24 the L· delivered a very great host ‡ "
24 had forsaken the L· God of their ‡ "

2Ch 25: 2 was right in the sight of the L·, ‡3068
4 Moses, where the L· commanded, ‡ "
7 for the L· is not with Israel, to wit, ‡ "
9 L· is able to give thee much more ‡ "
15 the anger of the L· was kindled ‡ "
27 turn away from following the L· ‡ "
26: 4 was right in the sight of the L·, ‡ "
5 as long as he sought the L·, God ‡ "
16 for he transgressed against the L· ‡ "
16 into the temple of the L· to burn ‡ "
17 him fourscore priests of the L·, ‡ "
18 to burn incense unto the L·, ‡ "
18 for thine honour from the L· God. ‡ "
19 the priests in the house of the L·, ‡ "
20 because the L· had smitten him. ‡ "
21 cut off from the house of the L·: ‡ "
27: 2 was right in the sight of the L·, ‡ "
2 not into the temple of the L·. ‡ "
3 high gate of the house of the L·, ‡ "
6 prepared his ways before the L· ‡ "
28: 1 was right in the sight of the L·, ‡ "
3 heathen whom the L· had cast out ‡ "
5 L· his God delivered him into the ‡ "
6 had forsaken the L· God of their ‡ "
9 a prophet of the L· was there, ‡ "
9 L· God of your fathers was wroth ‡ "
10 sins against the L· your God? ‡ "
11 fierce wrath of the L· is upon you. ‡ "
13 offended against the L· already, ‡ "
19 L· brought Judah low because of ‡ "
19 transgressed sore against the L·. ‡ "
21 portion out of the house of the L·, ‡ "
22 trespass yet more against the L·: ‡ "
24 the doors of the house of the L·, ‡ "
25 provoked to anger the L· God of ‡ "
29: 2 was right in the sight of the L·, ‡ "
3 the doors of the house of the L·, ‡ "
5 sanctify the house of the L· God ‡ "
6 evil in the eyes of the L· our God, ‡ "
6 from the habitation of the L·, ‡ "
8 wrath of the L· was upon Judah ‡ "
10 a covenant with the L· God of ‡ "
11 the L· hath chosen you to stand ‡ "
15 the king, by the words of the L·, ‡ "
15 to cleanse the house of the L·. ‡ "
16 inner part of the house of the L·, ‡ "
16 they found in the temple of the L· ‡ "
16 the court of the house of the L·. ‡ "
17 came they to the porch of the L·: ‡ "
17 sanctified the house of the L· in ‡ "
18 cleansed all the house of the L·, ‡ "
19 they are before the altar of the L·. ‡ "
20 went up to the house of the L·. ‡ "
21 offer them on the altar of the L·. ‡ "
25 the Levites in the house of the L· ‡ "
25 was the commandment of the L· ‡ "
27 the song of the L· began also with ‡ "
30 Levites to sing praise unto the L· ‡ "
31 consecrated yourselves unto the L·, ‡ "
31 offerings into the house of the L·. ‡ "
32 for a burnt offering to the L·. ‡ "
35 house of the L· was set in order. ‡ "
30: 1 come to the house of the L· at ‡ "
1, 5 to keep the passover unto the L· ‡ "
6 turn again unto the L· God of ‡ "
7 trespassed against the L· God of ‡ "
8 but yield yourselves unto the L·, ‡ "
8 and serve the L· your God, that ‡ "
9 For if ye turn again unto the L·, ‡ "
9 for the L· your God is gracious ‡ "
12 princes, by the word of the L·. ‡ "
15 offerings into the house of the L·. ‡ "
17 to sanctify them unto the L·. ‡ "
18 The good L· pardon every one ‡ "
19 God, the L· God of his fathers, ‡ "
20 the L· hearkened to Hezekiah, ‡ "
21 priests praised the L· day by day, ‡ "
21 loud instruments unto the L·. ‡ "
22 the good knowledge of the L·: ‡ "
22 making confession to the L· God ‡ "
31: 2 in the gates of the tents of the L·. ‡ "
3 it is written in the law of the L·. ‡ "
4 encouraged in the law of the L·. ‡ "
6 consecrated unto the L· their God, ‡ "
8 blessed the L·, and his people ‡ "
10 offerings into the house of the L·, ‡ "
10 for the L· hath blessed his people; ‡ "
11 chambers in the house of the L·; ‡ "
14 distribute the oblations of the L·, ‡ "
16 entereth into the house of the L·, ‡ "
20 and truth before the L· his God. ‡ "
32: 8 with us is the L· our God to help ‡ "
11 The L· our God shall deliver us ‡ "
16 yet more against the L· God, ‡ "
17 also letters to rail on the L· God ‡ "
21 the L· sent an angel, which cut off ‡ "
22 Thus the L· saved Hezekiah and ‡ "
23 many brought gifts unto the L· to ‡ "
24 death, and prayed unto the L·: ‡ "
26 the wrath of the L· came not upon ‡ "
33: 2 was evil in the sight of the L·, ‡ "
2 heathen, whom the L· had cast out ‡ "
4 built altars in the house of the L·, ‡ "
4 the L· had said, In Jerusalem ‡ "
5 two courts of the house of the L·. ‡ "
6 much evil in the sight of the L·, ‡ "
9 whom the L· had destroyed before ‡ "
10 the L· spake to Manasseh, and to ‡ "
11 the L· brought upon them the ‡ "
12 in affliction, he besought the L· ‡ "
13 knew that the L· he was God. ‡ "
15 the idol out of the house of the L·, ‡ "
15 the mount of the house of the L·, ‡ "
16 he repaired the altar of the L·, ‡ "
16 to serve the L· God of Israel. ‡ "
17 yet unto the L· their God only. ‡ "

2Ch 33:18 the name of the L· God of Israel. ‡3068
22 was evil in the sight of the L·, ‡ "
23 humbled not himself before the L·, ‡ "
34: 2 was right in the sight of the L·, ‡ "
8 repair the house of the L· his God. ‡ "
10 oversight of the house of the L·, ‡ "
10 wrought in the house of the L·, ‡ "
14 brought into the house of the L·, ‡ "
14 found a book of the law of the L· ‡ "
15 of the law in the house of the L·. ‡ "
17 was found in the house of the L·, ‡ "
21 Go, enquire of the L· for me, and ‡ "
21 great is the wrath of the L· that ‡ "
21 have not kept the word of the L·, ‡ "
23 Thus saith the L· God of Israel, ‡ "
24 Thus saith the L·, Behold, I will ‡ "
26 who sent you to enquire of the L·, ‡ "
26 Thus saith the L· God of Israel ‡ "
27 even heard thee also, saith the L·. ‡ "
30 went up into the house of the L·, ‡ "
30 was found in the house of the L·. ‡ "
31 made a covenant before the L·, ‡ "
31 to walk after the L·, and to keep ‡ "
33 even to serve the L· their God. ‡ "
33 departed not from following the L·, ‡ "
35: 1 Josiah kept a passover unto the L· ‡ "
2 the service of the house of the L·, ‡ "
3 which were holy unto the L·, ‡ "
3 serve now the L· your God, and ‡ "
6 according to the word of the L· ‡ "
12 the people, to offer unto the L·, ‡ "
16 service of the L· was prepared the ‡ "
16 offerings upon the altar of the L·, ‡ "
26 was written in the law of the L·, ‡ "
36: 5 evil in the sight of the L· his God. ‡ "
7 the vessels of the house of the L· ‡ "
9 was evil in the sight of the L·. ‡ "
10 vessels of the house of the L·, ‡ "
12 evil in the sight of the L· his God, ‡ "
12 speaking from the mouth of the L·. ‡ "
13 his heart from turning unto the L· ‡ "
14 and polluted the house of the L· ‡ "
15 the L· God of their fathers sent to ‡ "
16 wrath of the L· arose against his ‡ "
18 treasures of the house of the L·, ‡ "
21 To fulfill the word of the L· by the ‡ "
22 the word of the L· spoken by the ‡ "
22 L· stirred up the spirit of Cyrus ‡ "
23 the L· God of heaven given me; ‡ "
23 The L· his God be with him, and ‡ "
Ezr 1: 1 word of the L· by the mouth of ‡ "
1 L· stirred up the spirit of Cyrus ‡ "
2 L· God of heaven hath given me ‡ "
3 build the house of the L· God of ‡ "
5 build the house of the L· which is ‡ "
7 the vessels of the house of the L·, ‡ "
2:68 they came to the house of the L· ‡ "
3: 3 offerings thereon unto the L·, ‡ "
5 of all the set feasts of the L· that ‡ "
5 a freewill offering unto the L·. ‡ "
6 offer burnt offerings unto the L·. ‡ "
6 foundation of the temple of the L· ‡ "
8 the work of the house of the L·. ‡ "
10 foundation of the temple of the L·, ‡ "
10 with cymbals, to praise the L·, ‡ "
11 and giving thanks unto the L·; ‡ "
11 shout, when they praised the L·, ‡ "
11 foundation of the house of the L· ‡ "
4: 1 builded the temple unto the L· ‡ "
3 build unto the L· God of Israel, ‡ "
6:21 to seek the L· God of Israel, did ‡ "
22 the L· had made them joyful, and ‡ "
7: 6 the L· God of Israel had given: ‡ "
6 hand of the L· his God upon him. ‡ "
10 heart to seek the law of the L·, ‡ "
11 of the commandments of the L·, ‡ "
27 Blessed be the L· God of our ‡ "
27 to beautify the house of the L· ‡ "
28 hand of the L· my God was upon ‡ "
8:28 them, Ye are holy unto the L·; ‡ "
28 freewill offering unto the L· God ‡ "
29 chambers of the house of the L·. ‡ "
35 was a burnt offering unto the L·. ‡ "
9: 5 spread out my hands unto the L· ‡ "
8 grace...been shewed from the L· ‡ "
15 O L· God of Israel, thou art ‡ "
10: 3 according to the counsel of my l·, 136
11 make confession unto the L· God ‡3068
Ne 1: 5 O L· God of heaven, the great and ‡ "
11 O L·, I beseech thee, let now thine 136
3: 5 their necks to the work of their L·. 113
4:14 remember the L·, which is great 136
5:13 said, Amen, and praised the L·. ‡3068
8: 1 which the L· had commanded to ‡ "
6 Ezra blessed the L·, the great God. ‡ "
6 and worshipped the L· with their ‡ "
9 This day is holy unto the L· your ‡ "
10 for this day is holy unto our L·: 113
10 the joy of the L· is your strength. ‡3068
14 law which the L· had commanded ‡ "
9: 3 book of the law of the L· their ‡ "
3 and worshipped the L· their God. ‡ "
4 with a loud voice unto the L· ‡ "
5 Stand up and bless the L· your ‡ "
6 Thou, even thou, art L· alone; ‡ "
7 Thou art the L· the God, who ‡ "
10:29 all the commandments of the L· ‡ "
29 all the commandments of...our L·, 113
34 to burn upon the altar of the L· ‡3068
35 by year, unto the house of the L·: ‡ "
Job 1: 6 present themselves before the L·, ‡ "
7 the L· said unto Satan, Whence ‡ "
7 Satan answered the L·, and said, ‡ "
8 the L· said unto Satan, Hast thou ‡ "
9 Satan answered the L·, and said, ‡ "
12 the L· said unto Satan, Behold, all ‡ "

Job 1:12 forth from the presence of the L·. ‡3068
21 L· gave, and the L· hath taken ‡ "
21 blessed be the name of the L·. ‡ "
2: 1 present themselves before the L·, ‡ "
1 to present himself before the L·. ‡ "
2 And the L· said unto Satan, From ‡ "
2 Satan answered the L·, and said, ‡ "
3 And the L· said unto Satan, Hast ‡ "
4 Satan answered the L·, and said, ‡ "
6 the L· said unto Satan, Behold, ‡ "
7 forth from the presence of the L·, ‡ "
12: 9 hand of the L· hath wrought this? ‡ "
28:28 the fear of the L·, that is wisdom; 136
38: 1 the L· answered Job out of the ‡3068
40: 1 the L· answered Job, and said, ‡ "
3 Job answered the L·, and said, ‡ "
6 Then answered the L· unto Job ‡ "
42: 1 Job answered the L·, and said, ‡ "
7 L· had spoken these words unto ‡ "
7 L· said to Eliphaz the Temanite, ‡ "
9 according as the L· commanded ‡ "
9 them: the L· also accepted Job. ‡ "
10 L· turned the captivity of Job, ‡ "
10 L· gave Job twice as much as he ‡ "
11 evil that the L· had brought upon ‡ "
12 L· blessed the latter end of Job ‡ "
Ps 1: 2 his delight is in the law of the L·; ‡ "
6 the L· knoweth the way of the ‡ "
2: 2 against the L·, and against his ‡ "
4 L· shall have them in derision. 136
7 L· hath said unto me, Thou art ‡3068
11 Serve the L· with fear, and rejoice ‡ "
3: 1 L·, how are they increased that ‡ "
3 But thou, O L·, art a shield for ‡ "
4 I cried unto the L· with my voice, ‡ "
5 awaked; for the L· sustained me. ‡ "
7 Arise, O L·; save me, O my God: ‡ "
8 Salvation belongeth unto the L·: ‡ "
4: 3 the L· hath set apart him that is ‡ "
3 the L· will hear when I call unto ‡ "
5 and put your trust in the L·. ‡ "
6 L·, lift thou up the light of thy ‡ "
8 for thou, L·, only makest me ‡ "
5: 1 Give ear to my words, O L·, ‡ "
3 thou hear in the morning, O L·; ‡ "
6 the L· will abhor the bloody and ‡ "
8 Lead me, O L·, in...righteousness ‡ "
12 thou, L·, wilt bless the righteous; ‡ "
6: 1 O L·, rebuke me not in thine ‡ "
2 Have mercy upon me, O L·; for ‡ "
2 O L·, heal me; for my bones are ‡ "
3 vexed: but thou, O L·, how long? ‡ "
4 Return, O L·, deliver my soul: oh ‡ "
8 the L· hath heard the voice of my ‡ "
9 L· hath heard my supplication; ‡ "
9 the L· will receive my prayer. ‡ "
7: *title* David, which he sang unto the L·, ‡ "
1 O L· my God, in thee do I put my ‡ "
3 O L· my God, if I have done this; ‡ "
6 Arise, O L·, in thine anger, lift up ‡ "
8 The L· shall judge the people: ‡ "
8 L·, according to my righteousness, ‡ "
17 will praise the L· according to his ‡ "
17 sing praise to the name of the L· ‡ "
8: 1 O L·...how excellent is thy name ‡ "
1 our L·, how excellent is thy name 113
9 O L·...how excellent is thy name ‡3068
9 our L·, how excellent is thy name 113
9: 1 I will praise thee, O L·, with my ‡3068
7 But the L· shall endure for ever: ‡ "
9 L· also will be a refuge for the ‡ "
10 thou, L·, hast not forsaken them ‡ "
11 Sing praises to the L·, which ‡ "
13 Have mercy upon me, O L·; ‡ "
16 The L· is known by the judgment ‡ "
19 Arise, O L·; let not man prevail: ‡ "
20 Put them in fear, O L·: that the ‡ "
10: 1 Why standest thou afar off, O L·? ‡ "
3 covetous, whom the L· abhorreth. ‡ "
12 Arise, O L·; O God, lift up thine ‡ "
16 The L· is King for ever and ever: ‡ "
17 L·, thou hast heard the desire of ‡ "
11: 1 In the L· put I my trust: how say ‡ "
4 The L· is in his holy temple, the ‡ "
5 The L· trieth the righteous: but ‡ "
7 righteous L· loveth righteousness; ‡ "
12: 1 Help, L·; for the godly man ‡ "
3 L· shall cut off all flattering lips, ‡ "
4 lips are our own: who is l· over us? 113
5 now will I arise, saith the L·; ‡3068
6 words of the L· are pure words: ‡ "
7 Thou shalt keep them, O L·, thou ‡ "
13: 1 long wilt thou forget me, O L·? ‡ "
3 and hear me, O L· my God: ‡ "
6 I will sing unto the L·, because ‡ "
14: 2 The L· looked down from heaven ‡ "
4 bread, and call not upon the L·. ‡ "
6 poor, because the L· is his refuge. ‡ "
7 L· bringeth back the captivity of ‡ "
15: 1 L·, who shall abide in thy ‡ "
4 honoureth them that fear the L·. ‡ "
16: 2 soul, thou hast said unto the L·, ‡ "
2 Thou art my L·: my goodness 136
5 The L· is the portion of mine ‡3068
7 I will bless the L·, who hath given ‡ "
8 have set the L· always before me: ‡ "
17: 1 Hear the right, O L·, attend unto ‡ "
13 Arise, O L·, disappoint him, cast ‡ "
14 men which are thy hand, O L·, ‡ "
18: *title* of David, the servant of the L·, ‡ "
title who spake unto the L· the words ‡ "
title the day that the L· delivered him ‡ "
1 I will love thee, O L·, my strength. ‡ "
2 L· is my rock, and my fortress, ‡ "
3 I will call upon the L·, who is ‡ "
6 my distress I called upon the L·, ‡ "

Ps 18:13 L· also thundered in the heavens, ‡3068
15 discovered at thy rebuke, O L·, ‡ "
18 calamity: but the L· was my stay. ‡ "
20 L· rewarded me according to my ‡ "
21 I have kept the ways of the L·, ‡ "
24 hath the L· recompensed me ‡ "
28 the L· my God will enlighten my ‡ "
30 the word of the L· is tried: ‡ "
31 For who is God save the L·? or ‡ "
41 even unto the L·, but he answered ‡ "
46 The L· liveth; and blessed be my ‡ "
49 will I give thanks unto thee, O L·, ‡ "
19: 7 The law of the L· is perfect, ‡ "
7 the testimony of the L· is sure, ‡ "
8 The statutes of the L· are right, ‡ "
8 commandment of the L· is pure, ‡ "
9 The fear of the L· is clean, ‡ "
9 the judgments of the L· are true ‡ "
14 be acceptable in thy sight, O L·, ‡ "
20: 1 L· hear thee in the day of trouble; ‡ "
5 the L· fulfil all thy petitions. ‡ "
6 I that the L· saveth his anointed; ‡ "
7 will remember the name of the L· ‡ "
9 Save, L·: let the king hear us ‡ "
21: 1 shall joy in thy strength, O L·; ‡ "
7 For the king trusteth in the L·, ‡ "
9 L· shall swallow them up in his ‡ "
13 Be thou exalted, L·, in thine own ‡ "
22: 8 trusted on the L· that he would ‡ "
19 But be not thou far from me, O L·: ‡ "
23 Ye that fear the L·, praise him; ‡ "
26 shall praise the L· that seek him: ‡ "
27 remember and turn unto the L·: ‡ "
30 it shall be accounted to the L· for a 136
23: 1 The L· is my shepherd; I shall ‡3068
6 in the house of the L· for ever. ‡ "
24: 3 shall ascend into the hill of the L·? ‡ "
5 receive the blessing from the L·, ‡ "
8 The L· strong and mighty, ‡ "
8 the L· mighty in battle. ‡ "
10 The L· of hosts, he is the King of ‡ "
25: 1 Unto thee, O L·, do I lift up my ‡ "
4 Shew me thy ways, O L·; teach ‡ "
6 Remember, O L·, thy tender ‡ "
7 me for thy goodness' sake, O L·. ‡ "
8 Good and upright is the L·: ‡ "
10 the paths of the L· are mercy and ‡ "
11 For thy name's sake, O L·, pardon ‡ "
12 man is he that feareth the L·? ‡ "
14 secret of the L· is with them that ‡ "
15 Mine eyes are ever toward the L·; ‡ "
26: 1 Judge me, O L·; for I have walked ‡ "
1 I have trusted also in the L·; ‡ "
2 Examine me, O L·, and prove me; ‡ "
6 will I compass thine altar, O L·: ‡ "
8 L·, I have loved the habitation of ‡ "
12 congregations will I bless the L·. ‡ "
27: 1 L· is my light and my salvation; ‡ "
1 the L· is the strength of my life; ‡ "
4 One thing have I desired of the L·, ‡ "
4 may dwell in the house of the L· ‡ "
4 to behold the beauty of the L·, ‡ "
6 I will sing praises unto the L·. ‡ "
7 Hear, O L·, when I cry with my ‡ "
8 thee, Thy face, L·, will I seek. ‡ "
10 me, then the L· will take me up. ‡ "
11 Teach me thy way, O L·, and lead ‡ "
13 goodness of the L· in the land of ‡ "
14 Wait on the L·: be of good ‡ "
14 thine heart: wait, I say, on the L·. ‡ "
28: 1 thee will I cry, O L· my rock; ‡ "
5 regard not the works of the L·, ‡ "
6 Blessed be the L·, because he ‡ "
7 The L· is my strength and my ‡ "
8 The L· is their strength, and he ‡ "
29: 1 Give unto the L·, O ye mighty, ‡ "
1 give unto the L· glory and ‡ "
2 Give unto the L· the glory due ‡ "
2 worship the L· in the beauty of ‡ "
3 voice of the L· is upon the waters: ‡ "
3 the L· is upon many waters. ‡ "
4 The voice of the L· is powerful; ‡ "
4 voice of the L· is full of majesty. ‡ "
5 voice of the L· breaketh the cedars; ‡ "
5 L· breaketh the cedars of Lebanon. ‡ "
7 voice of the L· divideth the flames ‡ "
8 The voice of the L· shaketh the ‡ "
8 the L· shaketh the wilderness of ‡ "
9 voice of the L· maketh the hinds ‡ "
10 The L· sitteth upon the flood; ‡ "
10 yea, the L· sitteth King for ever. ‡ "
11 The L· will give strength unto his ‡ "
11 L· will bless his people with peace. ‡ "
30: 1 I will extol thee, O L·; for thou ‡ "
2 O L· my God, I cried unto thee, ‡ "
3 O L·, thou hast brought up my soul ‡ "
4 Sing unto the L·, O ye saints of his, ‡ "
7 L·, by thy favour thou hast made ‡ "
8 I cried to thee, O L·; and unto ‡ "
8 unto the L· I made supplication. ‡ "
10 Hear, O L·, and have mercy upon ‡ "
10 upon me: L·, be thou my helper. ‡ "
12 O L· my God, I will give thanks ‡ "
31: 1 In thee, O L·, do I put my trust; ‡ "
5 redeemed me, O L· God of truth. ‡ "
6 vanities: but I trust in the L·. ‡ "
9 Have mercy upon me, O L·; for I ‡ "
14 But I trusted in thee, O L·: I said, ‡ "
17 Let me not be ashamed, O L·; for ‡ "
21 Blessed be the L·: for he hath ‡ "
23 O love the L·, all ye his saints: ‡ "
23 for the L· preserveth the faithful, ‡ "
24 heart, all ye that hope in the L·. ‡ "
32: 2 the L· imputeth not iniquity, ‡ "
5 my transgressions unto the L·; ‡ "
10 but he that trusteth in the L·, ‡ "

Ps 32:11 Be glad in the L', and rejoice, ye ‡3068
33: 1 Rejoice in the L', O ye righteous: ‡ "
2 Praise the L' with harp: sing unto‡ "
4 For the word of the L' is right; ‡ "
5 is full of the goodness of the L'. ‡ "
6 word of the L' were the heavens ‡ "
8 Let all the earth fear the L': let ‡ "
10 The L' bringeth the counsel of the‡ "
11 counsel of the L' standeth for ever,‡ "
12 is the nation whose God is the L';‡ "
13 The L' looketh from heaven; he ‡ "
18 eye of the L' is upon them that fear‡ "
20 Our soul waiteth for the L': he is‡ "
22 Let thy mercy, O L', be upon us, ‡ "
34: 1 I will bless the L' at all times: ‡ "
2 shall make her boast in the L': ‡ "
3 O magnify the L' with me, and ‡ "
4 I sought the L', and he heard me,‡ "
6 man cried, and the L' heard him, ‡ "
7 angel of the L' encampeth round ‡ "
8 taste and see that the L' is good: ‡ "
9 O fear the L', ye his saints: for ‡ "
10 that seek the L' shall not want any‡ "
11 I will teach you the fear of the L'.‡ "
15 The eyes of the L' are upon the ‡ "
16 face of the L' is against them that‡ "
17 the L' heareth, and delivereth ‡ "
18 L' is nigh unto them that are of ‡ "
19 L' delivereth him out of them all. ‡ "
22 The L' redeemeth the soul of his ‡ "
35: 1 Plead my cause, O L', with them ‡ "
5 the angel of the L' chase them. ‡ "
6 angel of the L' persecute them. ‡ "
9 my soul shall be joyful in the L': ‡ "
10 All my bones shall say, L', who is‡ "
17 L', how long wilt thou look on? 136
22 This thou hast seen, O L': keep ‡3068
22 silence: O L', be not far from me.‡ "
23 unto my cause, my God and my L'. 136
24 Judge me, O L' my God, ‡3068
27 Let the L' be magnified, which ‡ "
36: *title* of David the servant of the L'. ‡ "
5 mercy, O L', is in the heavens; ‡ "
6 O L', thou preservest man and ‡ "
37: 3 Trust in the L', and do good; so ‡ "
4 Delight thyself also in the L'; ‡ "
5 Commit thy way unto the L'; ‡ "
7 Rest in the L', and wait patiently ‡ "
9 but those that wait upon the L', ‡ "
13 the L' shall laugh at him: for he 136
17 the L' upholdeth the righteous. ‡3068
18 The L' knoweth the days of the ‡ "
20 enemies of the L' shall be as the ‡ "
23 good man are ordered by the L': ‡ "
24 L' upholdeth him with his hand. ‡ "
28 For the L' loveth judgment, and ‡ "
33 L' will not leave him in his hand, ‡ "
34 Wait on the L', and keep his way,‡ "
39 of the righteous is of the L': ‡ "
40 L' shall help them, and deliver ‡ "
38: 1 O L', rebuke me not in thy wrath:‡ "
9 L', all my desire is before thee: 136
15 For in thee, O L', do I hope: ‡3068
15 thou wilt hear, O L' my God. 136
21 Forsake me not, O L': O my God,‡3068
22 to help me, O L' my salvation. 136
39: 4 L', make me to know mine end, ‡3068
7 L', what wait I for? my hope is in 136
12 Hear my prayer, O L', and give ‡3068
40: 1 I waited patiently for the L'; and‡ "
3 and fear, and shall trust in the L'.‡ "
4 man that maketh the L' his trust,‡ "
5 Many, O L' my God, are thy ‡ "
9 have not refrained my lips, O L', ‡ "
11 tender mercies from me, O L': ‡ "
13 Be pleased, O L', to deliver me: ‡ "
13 O L', make haste to help me. ‡ "
16 continually, The L' be magnified.‡ "
17 yet the L' thinketh upon me: thou 136
41: 1 the L' will deliver him in time of ‡3068
2 The L' will preserve him, and ‡ "
3 L' will strengthen him upon the ‡ "
4 I said, L', be merciful unto me: ‡ "
10 But thou, O L', be merciful unto ‡ "
13 Blessed be the L' God of Israel ‡ "
42: 8 L' will command...lovingkindness ‡ "
44:23 Awake, why sleepest thou, O L'? 136
45:11 for he is thy L'; and worship thou 113
46: 7 The L' of hosts is with us; the ‡3068
8 Come, behold the works of the L', ‡ "
11 The L' of hosts is with us; the ‡ "
47: 2 For the L' most high is terrible; ‡ "
5 L' with the sound of a trumpet. ‡ "
48: 1 Great is the L', and greatly to be ‡ "
8 seen in the city of the L' of hosts,‡ "
50: 1 The mighty God, even the L', ‡ "
51:15 O L', open thou my lips; and my 136
54: 4 L' is with them that uphold my "
6 I will praise thy name, O L'; for ‡3068
55: 9 Destroy, O L', and divide their 136
16 God; and the L' shall save me. ‡3068
22 Cast thy burden upon the L', and‡ "
56:10 in the L' will I praise his word. ‡ "
57: 9 I will praise thee, O L', among the 136
58: 6 teeth of the young lions, O L'. ‡3068
59: 3 transgression, nor for my sin, O L'.‡ "
5 O L' God of hosts, the God of ‡ "
8 But thou, O L', shalt laugh at ‡ "
11 bring them down, O L' our shield. 136
62:12 unto thee, O L', belongeth mercy: ‡ "
64:10 righteous shall be glad in the L', ‡3068
66:18 my heart, the L' will not hear me: 136
68:11 The L' gave the word: great was "
16 the L' will dwell in it for ever. ‡3068
17 the L' is among them, as in Sinai, 136
19 Blessed be the L', who daily loadeth "

Ps 68:20 unto God the L' belong the issues 136
22 The L' said, I will bring again from "
26 even the L', from the fountain of "
32 earth; O sing praises unto the L'; "
69: 6 wait on thee, O L' God of hosts, "
13 my prayer is unto thee, O L', ‡3068
16 Hear me, O L'; for thy ‡ "
31 please the L' better than an ox ‡ "
33 For the L' heareth the poor, and ‡ "
70: 1 me; make haste to help me, O L'. ‡ "
5 O L', make no tarrying. ‡ "
71: 1 In thee, O L', do I put my trust: ‡ "
5 thou art my hope, O L' God: thou 136
16 go in the strength of the L' God: "
72:18 Blessed be the L' God, the God ‡3068
73:20 so, O L', when thou awakest, thou 136
28 I have put my trust in the L' God, "
74:18 the enemy hath reproached, O L',‡3068
75: 8 the hand of the L' there is a cup, ‡ "
76:11 and pay unto the L' your God: ‡ "
77: 2 day of my trouble I sought the L': 136
7 Will the L' cast off for ever? and "
11 remember the works of the L': ‡3050
78: 4 to come the praises of the L', ‡3068
21 the L' heard this, and was wroth: ‡ "
65 L' awaked as one out of a sleep, 136
79: 5 How long, L'? wilt thou be angry‡3068
12 they have reproached thee, O L'. 136
80: 4 O L' God of hosts, how long wilt ‡3068
19 Turn us again, O L' God of hosts,‡ "
81:10 I am the L' thy God, which brought‡ "
15 The haters of the L' should have ‡ "
83:16 they may seek thy name, O L'. ‡ "
84: 1 thy tabernacles, O L' of hosts! ‡ "
2 fainteth for the courts of the L': ‡ "
3 even thine altars, O L' of hosts, ‡ "
8 O L' God of hosts, hear my prayer:‡ "
11 the L' God is a sun and shield: ‡ "
11 the L' will give grace and glory: ‡ "
12 O L' of hosts, blessed is the man ‡ "
85: 1 L', thou hast been favourable ‡ "
7 Shew us thy mercy, O L', and ‡ "
8 hear what God the L' will speak: ‡ "
12 L' shall give that which is good; ‡ "
86: 1 Bow down thine ear, O L', hear ‡ "
3 Be merciful unto me, O L': for I 136
4 unto thee, O L', do I lift up my "
5 For thou, L', art good, and ready "
6 Give ear, O L', unto my prayer; ‡3068
8 there is none like unto thee, O L'; 136
9 and worship before thee, O L'; "
11 Teach me thy way, O L'; I will ‡3068
12 I will praise thee, O L' my God, 136
15 But thou, O L', art a God full of "
17 because thou, L', hast holpen me,‡3068
87: 2 L' loveth the gates of Zion more ‡ "
6 The L' shall count, when he ‡ "
88: 1 O L' God of my salvation, I have ‡ "
9 L', I have called daily upon thee, ‡ "
13 But unto thee have I cried, O L'; ‡ "
14 L', why castest thou off my soul? ‡ "
89: 1 I will sing of the mercies of the L'‡ "
5 shall praise thy wonders, O L': ‡ "
6 can be compared unto the L'? ‡ "
6 can be likened unto the L'? ‡ "
8 O L' God of hosts, who is a strong‡ "
8 who is a strong L' like unto thee?†‡3050
15 shall walk, O L', in the light of thy‡3068
18 For the L' is our defence; and the‡ "
46 How long, L'? wilt thou hide ‡ "
49 L', where are thy former 136
50 Remember, L', the reproach of thy "
51 enemies have reproached, O L'; ‡3068
52 Blessed be the L' for evermore. ‡ "
90: 1 L', thou hast been our dwelling 136
13 Return, O L', how long? and let it‡3068
17 let the beauty of the L' our God be‡ "
91: 2 will say of the L', He is my refuge‡ "
9 Because thou hast made the L', ‡ "
92: 1 thing to give thanks unto the L', ‡ "
4 For thou, L', hast made me glad ‡ "
5 O L', how great are thy works! ‡ "
8 But thou, L', art most high for ‡ "
9 O L', for, lo, thine enemies shall ‡ "
13 be planted in the house of the L' ‡ "
15 To shew that the L' is upright: ‡ "
93: 1 The L' reigneth, he is clothed ‡ "
1 the L' is clothed with strength, ‡ "
3 The floods have lifted up, O L', ‡ "
4 L' on high is mightier than the ‡ "
5 becometh thine house, O L', ‡ "
94: 1 O L' God, to whom vengeance ‡ "
3 L', how long shall the wicked, ‡ "
5 break in pieces thy people, O L', ‡ "
7 they say, The L' shall not see, ‡3050
11 L' knoweth the thoughts of man, ‡3068
12 man whom thou chastenest, O L',‡3050
14 the L' will not cast off his people,‡3068
17 Unless the L' had been my help, ‡ "
18 thy mercy, O L', held me up. ‡ "
22 But the L' is my defence; and my‡ "
23 the L' our God shall cut them off.‡ "
95: 1 O come, let us sing unto the L': ‡ "
3 For the L' is a great God, and a ‡ "
6 us kneel before the L' our maker.‡ "
96: 1 O sing unto the L' a new song: ‡ "
1 sing unto the L', all the earth. ‡ "
2 Sing unto the L', bless his name;‡ "
4 For the L' is great, and greatly to‡ "
5 but the L' made the heavens. ‡ "
7 Give unto the L', O ye kindreds ‡ "
7 give unto the L' glory and ‡ "
8 Give unto the L' the glory due ‡ "
9 O worship the L' in the beauty of‡ "
10 the heathen that the L' reigneth: ‡ "
13 Before the L': for he cometh, for ‡ "

Ps 97: 1 The L' reigneth; let the earth ‡3068
5 like wax at the presence of the L',‡ "
5 the presence of the L' of the whole 113
8 because of thy judgments, O L'. ‡3068
9 For thou, L', art high above all the‡ "
10 Ye that love the L', hate evil: he ‡ "
12 Rejoice in the L', ye righteous; ‡ "
98: 1 O sing unto the L' a new song; ‡ "
2 L' hath made known his salvation:‡ "
4 Make a joyful noise unto the L', ‡ "
5 Sing unto the L' with the harp; ‡ "
6 make a joyful noise before the L',‡ "
9 Before the L'; for he cometh to ‡ "
99: 1 The L' reigneth; let the people ‡ "
2 The L' is great in Zion; and he is‡ "
5 Exalt ye the L' our God, and ‡ "
6 they called upon the L', and he ‡ "
8 answeredst them, O L' our God: ‡ "
9 Exalt the L' our God, and worship‡ "
9 hill; for the L' our God is holy. ‡ "
100: 1 Make a joyful noise unto the L', ‡ "
2 Serve the L' with gladness: come‡ "
3 Know ye that the L' he is God: ‡ "
5 For the L' is good; his mercy is ‡ "
101: 1 unto thee, O L', will I sing. ‡ "
8 doers from the city of the L'. ‡ "
102: *title* out his complaint before the L'.‡ "
1 Hear my prayer, O L', and let my‡ "
12 thou, O L', shalt endure for ever;‡ "
15 shall fear the name of the L', and‡ "
16 When the L' shall build up Zion, ‡ "
18 be created shall praise the L'. ‡3050
19 from heaven did the L' behold ‡3068
21 declare the name of the L' in Zion,‡ "
22 and the kingdoms, to serve the L'.‡ "
103: 1 Bless the L', O my soul: and all ‡ "
2 Bless the L', O my soul, and forget‡ "
6 The L' executeth righteousness ‡ "
8 The L' is merciful and gracious, ‡ "
13 the L' pitieth them that fear him.‡ "
17 mercy of the L' is from everlasting‡ "
19 L' hath prepared his throne in the‡ "
20 Bless the L', ye his angels, that ‡ "
21 Bless ye the L', all ye his hosts; ‡ "
22 Bless the L', all his works in all ‡ "
22 bless the L', O my soul. ‡ "
104: 1 Bless the L', O my soul. ‡ "
1 O L' my God, thou art very great;‡ "
16 The trees of the L' are full of sap;‡ "
24 O L', how manifold are thy works!‡ "
31 The glory of the L' shall endure ‡ "
31 the L' shall rejoice in his works. ‡ "
33 I will sing unto the L' as long as ‡ "
34 be sweet: I will be glad in the L'.‡ "
35 Bless thou the L', O my soul. ‡ "
35 Praise ye the L'. ‡3050
105: 1 O give thanks unto the L'; call ‡ "
3 of them rejoice that seek the L'. ‡ "
4 Seek the L', and his strength: ‡ "
7 He is the L' our God: his ‡ "
19 came: the word of the L' tried him.‡ "
21 He made him l' of his house, and 113
45 keep his laws. Praise ye the L'. ‡3050
106: 1 Praise ye the L'. O give thanks ‡ "
1 O give thanks unto the L'; for he‡3068
2 utter the mighty acts of the L'? ‡ "
4 Remember me, O L', with the ‡ "
16 and Aaron the saint of the L'. ‡ "
25 not unto the voice of the L'. ‡ "
34 whom the L' commanded them: ‡ "
40 was the wrath of the L' kindled ‡ "
47 Save us, O L' our God, and gather‡ "
48 Blessed be the L' God of Israel ‡ "
48 say, Amen. Praise ye the L'. ‡3050
107: 1 O give thanks unto the L', for he ‡3068
2 Let the redeemed of the L' say so, ‡ "
6 cried unto the L' in their trouble, ‡ "
8 praise the L' for his goodness, ‡ "
13 cried unto the L' in their trouble,‡ "
15 praise the L' for his goodness, ‡ "
19 cry unto the L' in their trouble, ‡ "
21 praise the L' for his goodness, ‡ "
24 These see the works of the L', ‡ "
28 cry unto the L' in their trouble, ‡ "
31 praise the L' for his goodness, ‡ "
43 the lovingkindness of the L'. ‡ "
108: 3 I will praise thee, O L', among the‡ "
109:14 be remembered with the L'; ‡ "
15 them be before the L' continually,‡ "
20 of mine adversaries from the L', ‡ "
21 But do thou for me, O God the L', for136
26 Help me, O L' my God: O save ‡3068
27 hand; that thou, L', hast done it. ‡ "
30 praise the L' with my mouth; ‡ "
110: 1 The L' said...Sit thou at my right ‡ "
1 said unto my L', Sit thou at my 113
2 The L' shall send the rod of thy ‡3068
4 The L' hath sworn, and will not ‡ "
5 L' at thy right hand shall strike 136
111: 1 Praise ye the L'. I will praise ‡3050
1 will praise the L' with my whole ‡3068
2 The works of the L' are great, ‡ "
4 the L' is gracious and full of ‡ "
10 The fear of the L' is the beginning‡ "
112: 1 Praise ye the L'. Blessed is the ‡3050
1 is the man that feareth the L', ‡3068
7 heart is fixed, trusting in the L'. ‡ "
113: 1 Praise ye the L'. Praise, O ye ‡3050
1 Praise, O ye servants of the L', ‡3068
1 praise the name of the L'. ‡ "
2 Blessed be the name of the L' ‡ "
4 The L' is high above all nations, ‡ "
5 Who is like unto the L' our God, ‡ "
9 of children. Praise ye the L'. ‡3050
114: 7 thou earth, at the presence of the L',113
115: 1 Not unto us, O L', not unto us, ‡3068

Ps 115: 9 O Israel, trust thou in the *L'*: he ‡3068
10 O house of Aaron, trust in the *L'*: ‡ "
11 Ye that fear the *L'*, trust in the *L'*: ‡ "
12 The *L'* hath been mindful of us: ‡ "
13 He will bless them that fear the *L'*, ‡ "
14 *L'* shall increase you more and ‡ "
15 are blessed of the *L'* which made ‡ "
17 The dead praise not the *L'*, ‡3050
18 we will bless the *L'* from this time ‡ "
18 and for evermore. Praise the *L'*. ‡ "
116: 1 I love the *L'*, because he hath ‡3068
4 called I upon the name of the *L'*; ‡ "
4 O *L'*, I beseech thee, deliver my ‡ "
5 Gracious is the *L'*, and righteous; ‡ "
6 The *L'* preserveth the simple: ‡ "
7 the *L'* hath dealt bountifully with ‡ "
9 will walk before the *L'* in the land ‡ "
12 What shall I render unto the *L'* ‡ "
13 and call upon the name of the *L'*. ‡ "
14 I will pay my vows unto the *L'* ‡ "
15 Precious in the sight of the *L'* is ‡ "
16 O *L'*, truly I am thy servant; I am ‡ "
17 will call upon the name of the *L'*. ‡ "
18 I will pay my vows unto the *L'* ‡ "
19 O Jerusalem. Praise ye the *L'*. ‡ "
117: 1 O praise the *L'*, all ye nations: ‡ "
2 truth of the *L'* endureth for ever. ‡ "
2 for ever. Praise ye the *L'*. ‡3050
118: 1 O give thanks unto the *L'*; for he ‡3068
4 Let them now that fear the *L'* say, ‡ "
5 I called upon the *L'* in distress: ‡3050
5 the *L'* answered me, and set me in ‡ "
6 The *L'* is on my side; I will not ‡3068
7 *L'* taketh my part with them that ‡ "
8, 9 It is better to trust in the *L'* than ‡ "
10, name of the *L'* will I destroy them. ‡ "
11, 12 name of the *L'* I will destroy ‡ "
13 might fall: but the *L'* helped me. ‡ "
14 The *L'* is my strength and song, ‡3050
15 hand of the *L'* doeth valiantly. ‡3068
16 right hand of the *L'* is exalted: ‡ "
16 hand of the *L'* doeth valiantly. ‡ "
17 and declare the works of the *L'*. ‡3050
18 The *L'* hath chastened me sore: ‡ "
19 into them, and I will praise the *L'*: ‡ "
20 This gate of the *L'*, into which ‡3068
24 the day which the *L'* hath made; ‡ "
25 Save now, I beseech thee, O *L'*: ‡ "
25 O *L'*, I beseech thee, send now ‡ "
26 that cometh in the name of the *L'*: ‡ "
26 you out of the house of the *L'*. ‡ "
27 God is the *L'*, which hath shewed ‡ "
29 O give thanks unto the *L'*; for he ‡ "
119: 1 who walk in the law of the *L'*. ‡ "
12 Blessed art thou, O *L'*: teach me ‡ "
31 O *L'*, put me not to shame. ‡ "
33 Teach me, O *L'*, the way of thy ‡ "
41 mercies come also unto me, O *L'*, ‡ "
52 thy judgments of old, O *L'*; ‡ "
55 remembered thy name, O *L'*, in ‡ "
57 Thou art my portion, O *L'*: I ‡ "
64 The earth, O *L'*, is full of thy ‡ "
65 dealt well with thy servant, O *L'*, ‡ "
75 O *L'*, that thy judgments are ‡ "
89 For ever, O *L'*, thy word is settled ‡ "
107 quicken me, O *L'*, according unto ‡ "
108 offerings of my mouth, O *L'*, ‡ "
126 It is time for thee, *L'*, to work: ‡ "
137 Righteous art thou, O *L'*, and ‡ "
145 hear me, O *L'*: I will keep thy ‡ "
149 O *L'*, quicken me according to ‡ "
151 Thou art near, O *L'*; and all thy ‡ "
156 are thy tender mercies, O *L'*: ‡ "
159 quicken me, O *L'*, according to ‡ "
166 *L'*, I have hoped for thy salvation, ‡ "
169 cry come near before thee, O *L'*: ‡ "
174 longed for thy salvation, O *L'*; ‡ "
120: 1 my distress I cried unto the *L'*, ‡ "
2 Deliver my soul, O *L'*, from lying ‡ "
121: 2 My help cometh from the *L'*, ‡ "
5 The *L'* is thy keeper: the ‡ "
5 *L'* is thy shade upon thy right ‡ "
7 *L'* shall preserve thee from all ‡ "
8 *L'* shall preserve thy going out ‡ "
122: 1 us go into the house of the *L'*. ‡ "
4 tribes go up, the tribes of the *L'*, ‡3050
4 thanks unto the name of the *L'*. ‡3068
9 of the house of the *L'* our God ‡ "
123: 2 so our eyes wait upon the *L'* our ‡ "
3 Have mercy upon us, O *L'*, have ‡ "
124: 1, 2 the *L'* who was on our side, ‡ "
6 Blessed be the *L'*, who hath not ‡ "
8 Our help is in the name of the *L'*, ‡ "
125: 1 trust in the *L'* shall be as mount ‡ "
2 *L'* is round about his people from ‡ "
4 Do good, O *L'*, unto those that be ‡ "
5 *L'* shall lead them forth with the ‡ "
126: 1 *L'* turned again the captivity of ‡ "
2 *L'* hath done great things for ‡ "
3 *L'* hath done great things for us; ‡ "
4 Turn again our captivity, O *L'*, ‡ "
127: 1 Except the *L'* build the house, ‡ "
1 except the *L'* keep the city, the ‡ "
3 children are an heritage of the *L'*: ‡ "
128: 1 is every one that feareth the *L'*; ‡ "
4 be blessed that feareth the *L'*. ‡ "
5 *L'* shall bless thee out of Zion: ‡ "
129: 4 The *L'* is righteous: he hath cut ‡ "
8 blessing of the *L'* be upon you: ‡ "
8 bless you in the name of the *L'*. ‡ "
130: 1 have I cried unto thee, O *L'*. ‡ "
2 *L'*, hear my voice: let thine ears 136
3 *L'*, shouldest mark iniquities, ‡3050
3 O *L'*, who shall stand? 136
5 I wait for the *L'*, my soul doth ‡3068
6 My soul waiteth for the *L'* more 136

Ps 130: 7 Let Israel hope in the *L'*: for ‡3068
7 with the *L'* there is mercy, and ‡ "
131: 1 *L'*, my heart is not haughty, nor ‡ "
3 Let Israel hope in the *L'* from ‡ "
132: 1 *L'*, remember David, and all his ‡ "
2 How he sware unto the *L'*, and ‡ "
5 Until I find out a place for the *L'*, ‡ "
8 Arise, O *L'*, into thy rest; thou ‡ "
11 The *L'* hath sworn in truth unto ‡ "
13 For the *L'* hath chosen Zion; he ‡ "
133: 3 the *L'* commanded the blessing, ‡ "
134: 1 Behold, bless ye the *L'*, ‡ "
1 all ye servants of the *L'*, which ‡ "
1 night stand in the house of the *L'*. ‡ "
2 the sanctuary, and bless the *L'*. ‡ "
3 *L'* that made heaven and earth ‡ "
135: 1 Praise ye the *L'*. Praise ye the ‡3050
1 Praise ye the name of the *L'*; ‡3068
1 him, O ye servants of the *L'*. ‡ "
2 that stand in the house of the *L'*, ‡ "
3 Praise the *L'*; for...is good: ‡3050
3 for the *L'* is good: sing praises ‡3068
4 the *L'* hath chosen Jacob unto ‡3050
5 For I know that the *L'* is great, ‡3068
5 and that our *L'* is above all gods. 113
6 Whatsoever the *L'* pleased, that ‡3068
13 Thy name, O *L'*, endureth for ‡ "
13 thy memorial, O *L'*, throughout ‡ "
14 For the *L'* will judge his people, ‡ "
19 Bless the *L'*, O house of Israel: ‡ "
19 bless the *L'*, O house of Aaron: ‡ "
20 Bless the *L'*, O house of Levi: ‡ "
20 ye that fear the *L'*, bless the *L'*. ‡ "
21 Blessed be the *L'* out of Zion, ‡ "
21 at Jerusalem. Praise ye the *L'*. ‡3050
136: 1 O give thanks unto the *L'*; for ‡3068
3 O give thanks to the *L'* of lords: 113
137: 7 Remember, O *L'*, the children of ‡3068
138: 4 the earth shall praise thee, O *L'*, ‡ "
5 shall sing in the ways of the *L'*: ‡ "
5 for great is the glory of the *L'*. ‡ "
6 Though the *L'* be high, yet hath ‡ "
8 The *L'* will perfect that which ‡ "
8 thy mercy, O *L'*, endureth for ‡ "
139: 1 O *L'*, thou hast searched me, ‡ "
4 O *L'*, thou knowest it altogether. ‡ "
21 hate them, O *L'*, that hate thee? ‡ "
140: 1 Deliver me, O *L'*, from the evil ‡ "
4 Keep me, O *L'*, from the hands of ‡ "
6 I said unto the *L'*, Thou art my ‡ "
6 voice of my supplications, O *L'*. ‡ "
7 O God the *L'*, the strength of my 136
8 Grant not, O *L'*, the desires of ‡3068
12 *L'* will maintain the cause of the ‡ "
141: 1 *L'*, I cry unto thee: make haste ‡ "
3 watch, O *L'*, before my mouth; ‡ "
8 eyes are unto thee, O God the *L'*: 136
142: 1 cried unto the *L'* with my voice; ‡3068
1 my voice unto the *L'* did I make ‡ "
5 I cried unto thee, O *L'*: I said, ‡ "
143: 1 Hear my prayer, O *L'*, give ear to ‡ "
7 Hear me speedily, O *L'*: my spirit ‡ "
9 Deliver me, O *L'*, from mine ‡ "
11 Quicken me, O *L'*, for thy name's ‡ "
144: 1 Blessed be the *L'* my strength, ‡ "
3 *L'*, what is man, that thou takest ‡ "
5 Bow thy heavens, O *L'*, and come ‡ "
15 that people, whose God is the *L'*. ‡ "
145: 3 Great is the *L'*, and greatly to be ‡ "
8 The *L'* is gracious, and full of ‡ "
9 The *L'* is good to all: and his ‡ "
10 thy works shall praise thee, O *L'*; ‡ "
14 The *L'* upholdeth all that fall, ‡ "
17 The *L'* is righteous in all his ways, ‡ "
18 *L'* is nigh unto all them that call ‡ "
20 *L'* preserveth all them that love ‡ "
21 shall speak the praise of the *L'*: ‡ "
146: 1 Praise ye the *L'*. Praise the ‡3050
1 Praise the *L'*, O my soul. ‡3068
2 While I live will I praise the *L'*: I ‡ "
5 whose hope is in the *L'* his God: ‡ "
7 The *L'* looseth the prisoners: ‡ "
8 *L'* openeth the eyes of the blind: ‡ "
8 *L'* raiseth them that are bowed ‡ "
8 the *L'* loveth the righteous: ‡ "
9 The *L'* preserveth the strangers; ‡ "
10 The *L'* shall reign for ever, even ‡ "
10 generations. Praise ye the *L'*. ‡3050
147: 1 Praise ye the *L'*: for it is good ‡ "
2 *L'* doth build up Jerusalem: he ‡3068
5 Great is our *L'*, and of great 113
6 The *L'* lifteth up the meek: he ‡3068
7 unto the *L'* with thanksgiving; ‡ "
11 *L'* taketh pleasure in them that ‡ "
12 Praise the *L'*, O Jerusalem; ‡ "
20 known them. Praise ye the *L'*. ‡3050
148: 1 Praise ye the *L'*. Praise ye the ‡ "
1 Praise ye the *L'* from the ‡3068
5 them praise the name of the *L'*: ‡ "
7 Praise the *L'* from the earth, ye ‡ "
13 them praise the name of the *L'*: ‡ "
14 near unto him. Praise ye the *L'*. ‡3050
149: 1 Praise ye the *L'*. Sing unto the ‡ "
1 Sing unto the *L'* a new song, ‡3068
4 *L'* taketh pleasure in his people: ‡ "
9 all his saints. Praise ye the *L'*. ‡3050
150: 1 Praise ye the *L'*. Praise God in ‡ "
6 that hath breath praise the *L'*. ‡ "
6 Praise ye the *L'*. ‡ "
Pr 1: 7 fear of the *L'* is the beginning of ‡3068
29 did not choose the fear of the *L'*: ‡ "
2: 5 understand the fear of the *L'*, ‡ "
6 For the *L'* giveth wisdom: out of ‡ "
3: 5 Trust in the *L'* with all thine ‡ "
7 fear the *L'*, and depart from evil. ‡ "
9 Honour the *L'* with thy substance, ‡ "

Pr 3: 11 not the chastening of the *L'*; ‡3068
12 whom the *L'* loveth he correcteth; ‡ "
19 *L'* by wisdom hath founded the ‡ "
26 For the *L'* shall be thy confidence, ‡ "
32 froward is abomination to the *L'*: ‡ "
33 curse of the *L'* is in the house of ‡ "
5: 21 man are before the eyes of the *L'*, ‡ "
6: 16 These six things doth the *L'* hate: ‡ "
8: 13 The fear of the *L'* is to hate evil: ‡ "
22 *L'* possessed me in the beginning ‡ "
35 and shall obtain favour of the *L'*. ‡ "
9: 10 fear of the *L'* is the beginning of ‡ "
10: 3 *L'* will not suffer the soul of the ‡ "
22 The blessing of the *L'*, it maketh ‡ "
27 fear of the *L'* prolongeth days: ‡ "
29 The way of the *L'* is strength to ‡ "
11: 1 balance is abomination to the *L'*: ‡ "
20 heart are abomination to the *L'*: ‡ "
12: 2 man obtaineth favour of the *L'*: ‡ "
22 lips are abomination to the *L'*: ‡ "
14: 2 his uprightness feareth the *L'*: ‡ "
26 fear of the *L'* is strong confidence: ‡ "
27 fear of the *L'* is a fountain of life, ‡ "
15: 3 eyes of the *L'* are in every place, ‡ "
8 is an abomination to the *L'*: ‡ "
9 is an abomination unto the *L'*: ‡ "
11 and destruction are before the *L'*: ‡ "
16 little with the fear of the *L'* than ‡ "
25 *L'* will destroy the house of the ‡ "
26 are an abomination to the *L'*: ‡ "
29 The *L'* is far from the wicked: ‡ "
33 fear of the *L'* is the instruction ‡ "
16: 1 of the tongue, is from the *L'*. ‡ "
2 but the *L'* weigheth the spirits. ‡ "
3 Commit thy works unto the *L'*, ‡ "
4 The *L'* hath made all things for ‡ "
5 is an abomination to the *L'*: ‡ "
6 fear of the *L'* men depart from ‡ "
7 When a man's ways please the *L'*, ‡ "
9 but the *L'* directeth his steps. ‡ "
20 and whoso trusteth in the *L'*, ‡ "
33 disposing thereof is of the *L'*. ‡ "
17: 3 gold: but the *L'* trieth the hearts. ‡ "
15 both are abomination to the *L'*. ‡ "
18: 10 name of the *L'* is a strong tower: ‡ "
22 and obtaineth favour of the *L'*. ‡ "
19: 3 his heart fretteth against the *L'*. ‡ "
14 and a prudent wife is from the *L'*. ‡ "
17 upon the poor lendeth unto the *L'*; ‡ "
21 the counsel of the *L'*, that shall ‡ "
23 The fear of the *L'* tendeth to life: ‡ "
20: 10 are alike abomination to the *L'*. ‡ "
12 *L'* hath made even both of them. ‡ "
22 wait on the *L'*, and he shall save ‡ "
23 are an abomination unto the *L'*; ‡ "
24 Man's goings are of the *L'*; how ‡ "
27 of man is the candle of the *L'*, ‡ "
21: 1 heart is in the hand of the *L'*, ‡ "
2 but the *L'* pondereth the hearts. ‡ "
3 is more acceptable to the *L'* than ‡ "
30 nor counsel against the *L'*. ‡ "
31 of battle: but safety is of the *L'*. ‡ "
22: 2 the *L'* is the maker of them all. ‡ "
4 and the fear of the *L'* are riches, ‡ "
12 eyes of the *L'* preserve knowledge, ‡ "
14 is abhorred of the *L'* shall fall ‡ "
19 That thy trust may be in the *L'*, I ‡ "
23 For the *L'* will plead their cause, ‡ "
23: 17 fear of the *L'* all the day long. ‡ "
24: 18 Lest the *L'* see it, and it displease ‡ "
21 fear thou the *L'* and the king: ‡ "
25: 22 and the *L'* shall reward thee. ‡ "
28: 5 seek the *L'* understand all things. ‡ "
25 he that putteth his trust in the *L'* ‡ "
29: 13 the *L'* lighteneth both their eyes. ‡ "
25 whoso putteth his trust in the *L'* ‡ "
26 judgment cometh from the *L'*. ‡ "
30: 9 deny thee, and say, Who is the *L'*? ‡ "
31: 30 a woman that feareth the *L'*, she ‡ "
Isa 1: 2 for the *L'* hath spoken, I have ‡ "
4 have forsaken the *L'*, they have ‡ "
9 the *L'* of hosts had left unto us a ‡ "
10 Hear the word of the *L'*, ye ‡ "
11 sacrifices unto me? saith the *L'*: ‡ "
18 us reason together, saith the *L'*: ‡ "
20 mouth of the *L'* hath spoken it. ‡ "
24 Therefore saith the *L'*,...the 113
24 the *L'* of hosts, the mighty One ‡3068
28 they that forsake the *L'* shall be ‡ "
2: 3 go up to the mountain of the *L'*, ‡ "
3 word of the *L'* from Jerusalem. ‡ "
5 let us walk in the light of the *L'*. ‡ "
10 in the dust, for fear of the *L'*, ‡ "
11 *L'* alone shall be exalted in that ‡ "
12 *L'* of hosts shall be upon every ‡ "
17 *L'* alone shall be exalted in that ‡ "
19 of the earth, for fear of the *L'*, ‡ "
21 ragged rocks, for fear of the *L'*, ‡ "
3: 1 For, behold, the *L'*,...doth take 113
1 the *L'* of hosts, doth take away ‡3068
8 their doings are against the *L'*, ‡ "
13 The *L'* standeth up to plead, and ‡ "
14 *L'* will enter into judgment with ‡ "
15 poor? saith the *L'* God of hosts. 136
16 Moreover the *L'* saith, Because ‡3068
17 the *L'* will smite with a scab the 136
17 *L'* will discover their secret parts. ‡3068
18 the *L'* will take away the bravery 136
4: 2 branch of the *L'* be beautiful and ‡3068
4 *L'* shall have washed away the 136
5 And the *L'* will create upon every ‡3068
5: 7 vineyard of the *L'* of hosts is the ‡ "
9 In mine ears said the *L'* of hosts, ‡ "
12 regard not the work of the *L'*, ‡ "
16 the *L'* of hosts shall be exalted in ‡ "
24 cast away the law of the *L'* of ‡ "

Isa 5: 25 anger of the *L* kindled against ‡3068
6: 1 also the *L* sitting upon a throne, 136
3 Holy, holy, holy, is the *L* of ‡3068
5 seen the king, the *L* of hosts. ‡ "
8 I heard the voice of the *L*, saying, 136
11 Then said I, *L*, how long? And he "
12 *L* have removed men far away, ‡3068
7: 3 Then said the *L* unto Isaiah, Go ‡ "
7 Thus saith the *L* God, It shall not 136
10 the *L* spake again unto Ahaz, ‡3068
11 Ask thee a sign of the *L* thy God; ‡ "
12 ask, neither will I tempt the *L*. ‡ "
14 *L* himself shall give you a sign; 136
17 The *L* shall bring upon thee, and ‡3068
18 the *L* shall hiss for the fly that is ‡ "
20 day shall the *L* shave with a rasor 136
8: 1 the *L* said unto me, Take thee a ‡3068
3 Then said the *L* to me, Call his ‡ "
5 The *L* spake also unto me again, ‡ "
7 the *L* bringeth up upon them the 136
11 the *L* spake thus to me with a ‡3068
13 Sanctify the *L* of hosts himself; ‡ "
17 I will wait upon the *L*, that hideth ‡ "
18 children whom the *L* hath given ‡ "
18 wonders in Israel from the *L* of ‡ "
9: 7 zeal of the *L* of hosts will perform ‡ "
8 The *L* sent a word into Jacob, and ‡ "
11 *L* shall set up the adversaries of ‡ "
13 neither do they seek the *L* of ‡ "
14 *L* will cut off from Israel head and ‡ "
17 *L* shall have no joy in their young 136
19 the wrath of the *L* of hosts is the ‡3068
10: 12 *L* hath performed his whole work 136
16 shall the *L*,...send among his fat 113
16 the *L* of hosts, send among his fat 136
20 stay upon the *L*, the Holy One of ‡3068
23 the *L* God of hosts shall make a 136
24 thus saith the *L* God of hosts, "
26 *L* of hosts shall stir up a scourge ‡3068
33 the *L*,...shall lop the bough with 113
33 the *L* of hosts, shall lop the ‡3068
11: 2 the spirit of the *L* shall rest upon ‡ "
2 and of the fear of the *L*; ‡ "
3 quick...in the fear of the *L*: ‡ "
9 full of the knowledge of the *L*, ‡ "
11 the *L* shall set his hand again the 136
15 the *L* shall utterly destroy the ‡3068
12: 1 shalt say, O *L*, I will praise thee: ‡ "
2 *L* Jehovah is my strength and ‡3050
4 day shall ye say, Praise the *L*, ‡3068
5 Sing unto the *L*; for he hath ‡ "
13: 4 *L* of hosts mustereth the host of ‡ "
5 even the *L*, and the weapons of ‡ "
6 for the day of the *L* is at hand; ‡ "
9 Behold, the day of the *L* cometh, ‡ "
13 in the wrath of the *L* of hosts, ‡ "
14: 1 the *L* will have mercy on Jacob, ‡ "
2 them in the land of the *L* for ‡ "
3 *L* shall give thee rest from thy ‡ "
5 *L* hath broken the staff of the ‡ "
22 against them, saith the *L* of hosts, ‡ "
22 and son, and nephew, saith the *L*. ‡ "
23 destruction, saith the *L* of hosts. ‡ "
24 The *L* of hosts hath sworn, ‡ "
27 the *L* of hosts hath purposed, ‡ "
32 That the *L* hath founded Zion, ‡ "
16: 13 *L* hath spoken concerning Moab ‡ "
14 But now the *L* hath spoken, ‡ "
17: 3 of Israel, saith the *L* of hosts. ‡ "
6 saith the *L* God of Israel. ‡ "
18: 4 For so the *L* said unto me, I will ‡ "
7 be brought unto the *L* of hosts ‡ "
7 of the name of the *L* of hosts, ‡ "
19: 1 the *L* rideth upon a swift cloud, ‡ "
4 over into the hand of a cruel *l*; 113
4 shall rule over them, saith the *L*, ‡ "
4 over them, saith...the *L* of hosts. ‡3068
12 *L* of hosts hath purposed upon ‡ "
14 *L* hath mingled a perverse spirit ‡ "
16 of the hand of the *L* of hosts, ‡ "
17 of the counsel of the *L* of hosts, ‡ "
18 and swear to the *L* of hosts; ‡ "
19 shall there be an altar to the *L* ‡ "
19 at the border thereof to the *L*. ‡ "
20 for a witness unto the *L* of hosts ‡ "
20 for they shall cry unto the *L* ‡ "
21 the *L* shall be known to Egypt, ‡ "
21 the Egyptians shall know the *L* ‡ "
21 they shall vow a vow unto the *L*, ‡ "
22 And the *L* shall smite Egypt: he ‡ "
22 they shall return even to the *L*, ‡ "
25 Whom the *L* of hosts shall bless, ‡ "
20: 2 same time spake the *L* by Isaiah ‡ "
3 *L* said, Like as my servant Isaiah ‡ "
21: 6 For thus hath the *L* said unto me, 136
8 My *l*, I stand continually upon the "
10 I have heard of the *L* of hosts, ‡3068
16 For thus hath the *L* said unto me, 136
17 the *L* God of Israel hath spoken ‡3068
22: 5 perplexity by the *L* God of hosts 136
12 the *L* God of hosts call to weeping, "
14 in mine ears by the *L* of hosts, ‡3068
14 ye die, saith the *L* God of hosts. 136
15 Thus saith the *L* God of hosts, Go, "
17 the *L* will carry thee away with a ‡3068
25 In that day, saith the *L* of hosts, ‡ "
25 cut off: for the *L* hath spoken it. ‡ "
23: 9 The *L* of hosts hath purposed it, ‡ "
11 *L* hath given a commandment ‡ "
17 years, that the *L* will visit Tyre, ‡ "
18 hire shall be holiness to the *L*: ‡ "
18 for them that dwell before the *L*, ‡ "
24: 1 the *L* maketh the earth empty, ‡ "
3 for the *L* hath spoken this word. ‡ "
14 sing for the majesty of the *L*, ‡ "
15 glorify ye the *L* in the fires, even ‡ "

Isa 24: 15 the name of the *L* God of Israel ‡3068
21 *L* shall punish the host of the ‡ "
23 *L* of hosts shall reign in mount ‡ "
25: 1 O *L*, thou art my God; I will exalt ‡ "
6 *L* of hosts make unto all people ‡ "
8 *L* God will wipe away tears from 136
8 earth: for the *L* hath spoken it. ‡3068
9 this is the *L*; we have waited for ‡ "
10 shall the hand of the *L* rest, ‡ "
26: 4 Trust ye in the *L* forever: for ‡ "
4 in the *L* Jehovah is everlasting ‡3050
8 in the way of thy judgments, O *L*, ‡3068
10 not behold the majesty of the *L*. ‡ "
11 *L*, when thy hand is lifted up, they ‡ "
12 *L*, thou wilt ordain peace for us: ‡ "
13 O *L* our God, other lords beside ‡ "
15 hast increased the nation, O *L*, ‡ "
16 *L*, in trouble have they visited ‡ "
17 so have we been in thy sight, O *L*. ‡ "
21 the *L* cometh out of his place to ‡ "
27: 1 the *L* with his sore and great and ‡ "
3 I the *L* do keep it; I will water it ‡ "
12 *L* shall beat off from the channel ‡ "
13 worship the *L* in the holy mount ‡ "
28: 2 *L* hath a mighty and strong one, 136
5 *L* of hosts be for a crown of glory, ‡3068
13 the word of the *L* was unto them ‡ "
14 hear the word of the *L*, ye scornful ‡ "
16 Therefore thus saith the *L* God, 136
21 the *L* shall rise up as in mount ‡3068
22 have heard from the *L* God of hosts 136
29 cometh forth from the *L* of hosts, ‡3068
29: 6 shalt be visited of the *L* of hosts ‡ "
10 *L* hath poured out upon you the ‡ "
13 Wherefore the *L* said, Forasmuch 136
15 to hide their counsel from the *L*, ‡3068
19 shall increase their joy in the *L*, ‡ "
22 thus saith the *L*, who redeemed ‡ "
30: 1 rebellious children, saith the *L*, ‡ "
9 will not hear the law of the *L*: ‡ "
15 thus saith the *L* God, the Holy One 136
18 And therefore will the *L* wait, ‡3068
18 for the *L* is a God of judgment: ‡ "
20 *L* give you the bread of adversity, 136
26 *L* bindeth up the breach of his ‡3068
27 name of the *L* cometh from far, ‡ "
29 come into the mountain of the *L*, ‡ "
30 *L* shall cause his glorious voice ‡ "
31 through the voice of the *L* shall ‡ "
32 which the *L* shall lay upon him, ‡ "
33 the breath of the *L*, like a stream ‡ "
31: 1 One of Israel, neither seek the *L*! ‡ "
3 the *L* shall stretch out his hand, ‡ "
4 thus hath the *L* spoken unto me, ‡ "
4 the *L* of hosts come down to fight ‡ "
5 the *L* of hosts defend Jerusalem; ‡ "
9 afraid of the ensign, saith the *L*, ‡ "
32: 6 and to utter error against the *L*, ‡ "
33: 2 O *L*, be gracious unto us; we ‡ "
5 The *L* is exalted; for he dwelleth ‡ "
6 the fear of the *L* is his treasure. ‡ "
10 Now will I rise, saith the *L*; now ‡ "
21 glorious *L* will be unto us a place ‡ "
22 For the *L* is our judge, ‡ "
22 the *L* is our lawgiver, ‡ "
22 the *L* is our king; he will save us. ‡ "
34: 2 indignation of the *L* is upon all ‡ "
6 sword of the *L* is filled with blood, ‡ "
6 the *L* hath a sacrifice in Bozrah, ‡ "
16 Seek ye out of the book of the *L*, ‡ "
35: 2 they shall see the glory of the *L*, ‡ "
10 ransomed of the *L* shall return, ‡ "
36: 7 to me, We trust in the *L* our God: ‡ "
10 am I now come up without the *L* ‡ "
10 *L* said unto me, Go up against ‡ "
15 make you trust in the *L*, saying, ‡ "
15 The *L* will surely deliver us: ‡ "
18 saying, The *L* will deliver us. ‡ "
20 the *L* should deliver Jerusalem ‡ "
37: 1 and went into the house of the *L*. ‡ "
4 *L* thy God will hear the words of ‡ "
4 which the *L* thy God hath heard: ‡ "
6 Thus saith the *L*, Be not afraid ‡ "
14 went up unto the house of the *L*, ‡ "
14 and spread it before the *L*. ‡ "
15 And Hezekiah prayed unto the *L*, ‡ "
16 O *L* of hosts, God of Israel, that ‡ "
17 Incline thine ear, O *L*, and hear; ‡ "
17 open thine eyes, O *L*, and see: ‡ "
18 *L*, the kings of Assyria have laid ‡ "
20 O *L* our God, save us from his ‡ "
20 may know that thou art the *L*, ‡ "
21 Thus saith the *L* God of Israel, ‡ "
22 word which the *L* hath spoken ‡ "
24 hast thou reproached the *L*, and 136
32 zeal of the *L* of hosts shall do ‡3068
33 thus saith the *L* concerning the ‡ "
34 come into this city, saith the *L*. ‡ "
36 the angel of the *L* went forth, ‡ "
38: 1 Thus saith the *L*, Set thine house ‡ "
2 the wall, and prayed unto the *L*, ‡ "
3 Remember now, O *L*, I beseech ‡ "
4 came the word of the *L* to Isaiah, ‡ "
5 saith the *L*, the God of David ‡ "
7 be a sign unto thee from the *L*, ‡ "
7 that the *L* will do this thing that ‡ "
11 shall not see the *L*, even the *L*, ‡3050
14 O *L*, I am oppressed; undertake ‡3068
16 O *L*, by these things men live, and 136
20 The *L* was ready to save me: ‡3068
20 of our life in the house of the *L*. ‡ "
22 I shall go up to the house of the *L*? ‡ "
39: 5 Hear the word of the *L* of hosts: ‡ "
6 nothing shall be left, saith the *L*. ‡ "
8 Good is the word of the *L* which ‡ "
40: 3 Prepare ye the way of the *L*, ‡ "

Isa 40: 5 glory of the *L* shall be revealed, ‡3068
5 mouth of the *L* hath spoken it. ‡ "
7 spirit of the *L* bloweth upon it: ‡ "
10 *L* God will come with strong hand, 136
13 hath directed the Spirit of the *L*, ‡3068
27 My way is hid from the *L*, and ‡ "
28 the *L*, the Creator of the ends of ‡ "
31 that wait upon the *L* shall renew ‡ "
41: 4 I the *L*, the first, and with the ‡ "
13 I the *L* thy God will hold thy right ‡ "
14 I will help thee, saith the *L*, and ‡ "
16 and thou shalt rejoice in the *L*, ‡ "
17 I the *L* will hear them, I the God ‡ "
20 the hand of the *L* hath done this, ‡ "
21 Produce your cause, saith the *L*; ‡ "
42: 5 saith God the *L*, he that created ‡ "
6 I the *L* have called thee in ‡ "
8 I am the *L*: that is my name: ‡ "
10 Sing unto the *L* a new song, and ‡ "
12 Let them give glory unto the *L*, ‡ "
13 *L* shall go forth as a mighty man, ‡ "
21 The *L* is well pleased for his ‡ "
24 did not the *L*, he against whom ‡ "
43: 1 thus saith the *L* that created thee, ‡ "
3 I am the *L* thy God, the Holy One ‡ "
10 Ye are my witnesses, saith the *L*, ‡ "
11 I, even I, am the *L*; and beside ‡ "
12 ye are my witnesses, saith the *L*, ‡ "
14 Thus saith the *L*, your redeemer, ‡ "
15 I am the *L*, your Holy One, the ‡ "
16 Thus saith the *L*, which maketh ‡ "
44: 2 Thus saith the *L* that made thee, ‡ "
5 with his hand unto the *L*, ‡ "
6 saith the *L* the King of Israel, ‡ "
6 and his redeemer the *L* of hosts; ‡ "
23 heavens; for the *L* hath done it: ‡ "
23 for the *L* hath redeemed Jacob, ‡ "
24 saith the *L*, thy redeemer, and ‡ "
24 am the *L* that maketh all things; ‡ "
45: 1 Thus saith the *L* to his anointed, ‡ "
3 know that I, the *L*, which call ‡ "
5 I am the *L*, and there is none else, ‡ "
6 I am the *L*, and there is none else. ‡ "
7 evil: I the *L* do all these things. ‡ "
8 together; I the *L* have created it. ‡ "
11 Thus saith the *L*, the Holy One ‡ "
13 nor reward, saith the *L* of hosts. ‡ "
14 saith the *L*, The labour of Egypt, ‡ "
17 But Israel shall be saved in the *L* ‡ "
18 the *L* that created the heavens; ‡ "
18 I am the *L*; and there is none else. ‡ "
19 I the *L* speak righteousness, ‡ "
21 from that time? have not I the *L*? ‡ "
24 in the *L* have I righteousness and ‡ "
25 In the *L* shall all the seed of Israel ‡ "
47: 4 the *L* of hosts is his name, the ‡ "
48: 1 swear by the name of the *L*, and ‡ "
2 The *L* of hosts is his name. ‡ "
14 The *L* hath loved him: he will ‡ "
16 the *L* God, and his Spirit, hath 136
17 Thus saith the *L*, thy Redeemer, ‡3068
17 *L* thy God which teacheth thee ‡ "
20 The *L* hath redeemed his servant ‡ "
22 There is no peace, saith the *L*, ‡ "
49: 1 *L* hath called me from the womb; ‡ "
4 my judgment is with the *L*, and ‡ "
5 saith the *L* that formed me from ‡ "
5 be glorious in the eyes of the *L*, ‡ "
7 Thus saith the *L*, the Redeemer ‡ "
7 because of the *L* that is faithful, ‡ "
8 Thus saith the *L*, In an acceptable ‡ "
13 the *L* hath comforted his people, ‡ "
14 said, The *L* hath forsaken me, * "
14 and my *L* hath forgotten me. 136
18 saith the *L*, thou shalt surely ‡3068
22 Thus saith the *L* God, Behold, I 136
23 thou shalt know that I am the *L*: ‡3068
25 But thus saith the *L*, Even the ‡ "
26 I the *L* am thy Saviour and thy ‡ "
50: 1 saith the *L*, Where is the bill of ‡ "
4 *L* God hath given me the tongue 136
5 *L* God hath opened mine ear, and "
7 For the *L* God will help me; "
9 the *L* God will help me; who is "
10 is among you that feareth the *L*, ‡3068
10 trust in the name of the *L*, and ‡ "
51: 1 righteousness, ye that seek the *L*: ‡ "
3 For the *L* shall comfort Zion: ‡ "
3 desert like the garden of the *L*; ‡ "
9 put on strength, O arm of the *L*; ‡ "
11 redeemed of the *L* shall return, ‡ "
13 forgettest the *L* thy maker, that ‡ "
15 I am the *L* thy God, that divided ‡ "
15 The *L* of hosts is his name. ‡ "
17 drunk at the hand of the *L* the cup ‡ "
20 they are full of the fury of the *L*, ‡ "
22 Thus saith thy *L*...and thy God 113
22 Thus saith...the *L*, and thy God ‡3068
52: 3 thus saith the *L*, Ye have sold ‡ "
4 thus saith the *L* God, My people 136
5 what have I here, saith the *L*, ‡3068
5 make them to howl, saith the *L*; ‡ "
8 when the *L* shall bring again Zion, ‡ "
9 the *L* hath comforted his people, ‡ "
10 *L* hath made bare his holy arm ‡ "
11 that bear the vessels of the *L*. ‡ "
12 for the *L* will go before you; and ‡ "
53: 1 is the arm of the *L* revealed? ‡ "
6 *L* hath laid on him the iniquity ‡ "
10 it pleased the *L* to bruise him; ‡ "
10 pleasure of the *L* shall prosper in ‡ "
54: 1 of the married wife, saith the *L*. ‡ "
5 the *L* of hosts is his name; and ‡ "
6 *L* hath called thee as a woman ‡ "
8 thee, saith the *L* thy Redeemer. ‡ "
10 the *L* that hath mercy on thee. ‡ "

Isa 54:13 children shall be taught of the *L'*; ‡3068
17 heritage of the servants of the *L'*. ‡ "
17 righteousness is of me, saith the *L'*. ‡ "
55: 5 thee because of the *L'* thy God, ‡ "
6 Seek ye the *L'* while he may be ‡ "
7 and let him return unto the *L'*, ‡ "
8 your ways my ways, saith the *L'*. ‡ "
13 it shall be to the *L'* for a name, ‡ "
56: 1 saith the *L'*, Keep ye judgment, ‡ "
3 that hath joined himself to the *L'*, ‡ "
3 *L'* hath utterly separated me from ‡ "
4 saith the *L'* unto the eunuchs ‡ "
6 that join themselves to the *L'*, to ‡ "
6 love the name of the *L'*, to be his ‡ "
8 The *L'* God which gathereth the 136
57:19 to him that is near, saith the *L'*; ‡3068
58: 5 and an acceptable day to the *L'*? ‡ "
8 the glory of the *L'* shall be thy ‡ "
9 thou call, and the *L'* shall answer; ‡ "
11 the *L'* shall guide thee continually, ‡ "
13 the holy of the *L'*, honourable; ‡ "
14 thou delight thyself in the *L'*; ‡ "
14 mouth of the *L'* hath spoken it. ‡ "
59:13 and lying against the *L'*, and ‡ "
15 the *L'* saw it, and it displeased ‡ "
19 fear the name of the *L'* from the ‡ "
19 the Spirit of the *L'* shall lift up a ‡ "
20 transgression in Jacob, saith the *L'*. ‡ "
21 covenant with them, saith the *L'*; ‡ "
21 of thy seed's seed, saith the *L'*, ‡ "
60: 1 glory of the *L'* is risen upon thee. ‡ "
2 the *L'* shall arise upon thee, and ‡ "
6 shew forth the praises of the *L'*. ‡ "
9 unto the name of the *L'* thy God, ‡ "
14 shall call thee, The city of the *L'*, ‡ "
16 I the *L'* am thy Saviour and thy ‡ "
19 but the *L'* shall be unto thee an ‡ "
20 the *L'* shall be thine everlasting ‡ "
22 I the *L'* will hasten it in his time. ‡ "
61: 1 Spirit of the *L'* God is upon me; 136
1 the *L'* hath anointed me to preach ‡3068
2 the acceptable year of the *L'*, and ‡ "
3 planting of the *L'*, that he might ‡ "
6 be named the Priests of the *L'*: ‡ "
8 I the *L'* love judgment, I hate ‡ "
9 seed which the *L'* hath blessed. ‡ "
10 I will greatly rejoice in the *L'*, ‡ "
11 *L'* God will cause righteousness 136
62: 2 the mouth of the *L'* shall name. ‡3068
3 of glory in the hand of the *L'*, ‡ "
4 for the *L'* delighteth in thee, and ‡ "
6 ye that make mention of the *L'*, *‡ "
8 *L'* hath sworn by his right hand, ‡ "
9 it shall eat it, and praise the *L'*; ‡ "
11 *L'* hath proclaimed unto the end ‡ "
12 people, The redeemed of the *L'*: ‡ "
63: 7 the lovingkindnesses of the *L'*, ‡ "
7 and the praises of the *L'*, ‡ "
7 that the *L'* hath bestowed on us, ‡ "
14 Spirit of the *L'* caused him to rest: ‡ "
16 thou, O *L'*, art our father, our ‡ "
17 O *L'*, why hast thou made us to err ‡ "
64: 8 now, O *L'*, thou art our father; ‡ "
9 Be not wroth very sore, O *L'*, ‡ "
12 thyself for these things, O *L'*? ‡ "
65: 7 your fathers together, saith the *L'*, ‡ "
8 saith the *L'*, As the new wine is ‡ "
11 ye are they that forsake the *L'*, ‡ "
13 thus saith the *L'* God, Behold, my 136
15 the *L'* God shall slay thee, and "
23 the seed of the blessed of the *L'*, ‡3068
25 my holy mountain, saith the *L'*. ‡ "
66: 1 saith the *L'*, The heaven is my ‡ "
2 things have been, saith the *L'*: ‡ "
5 Hear the word of the *L'*, ye that ‡ "
5 sake, said, Let the *L'* be glorified: ‡ "
6 a voice of the *L'* that rendereth ‡ "
9 to bring forth? saith the *L'*: ‡ "
12 thus saith the *L'*, Behold, I will ‡ "
14 the hand of the *L'* shall be known ‡ "
15 behold, the *L'* will come with fire, ‡ "
16 will the *L'* plead with all flesh: ‡ "
16 the slain of the *L'* shall be many. ‡ "
17 consumed together, saith the *L'*. ‡ "
20 for an offering unto the *L'* out of ‡ "
20 mountain Jerusalem, saith the *L'*, ‡ "
20 vessel into the house of the *L'*. ‡ "
21 and for Levites, saith the *L'*. ‡ "
22 remain before me, saith the *L'*, ‡ "
23 worship before me, saith the *L'*. ‡ "
Jer 1: 2 To whom the word of the *L'* came ‡ "
4 the word of the *L'* came unto me, ‡ "
6 Ah, *L'* God! behold, I cannot speak: 136
7 But the *L'* said unto me, Say not, ‡3068
8 thee to deliver thee, saith the *L'*. ‡ "
9 the *L'* put forth his hand, and ‡ "
9 And the *L'* said unto me, Behold ‡ "
11 the word of the *L'* came unto me, ‡ "
12 Then said the *L'* unto me, Thou ‡ "
13 word of the *L'* came unto me the ‡ "
14 Then the *L'* said unto me, Out of ‡ "
15 kingdoms of the north, saith the *L'*; ‡ "
19 for I am with thee, saith the *L'*, ‡ "
2: 1 the word of the *L'* came to me, ‡ "
2 Thus saith the *L'*; I remember ‡ "
3 Israel was holiness unto the *L'*, ‡ "
3 come upon them, saith the *L'*. ‡ "
4 Hear ye the word of the *L'*, O ‡ "
5 Thus saith the *L'*, What iniquity ‡ "
6 Where is the *L'* that brought us ‡ "
8 priests said not, Where is the *L'*? ‡ "
9 yet plead with you, saith the *L'*, ‡ "
12 be ye very desolate, saith the *L'*. ‡ "
17, 19 hast forsaken the *L'* thy God, ‡ "
19 not in thee, saith the *L'* God of hosts. 136
22 marked before me, saith the *L'* God. "

Jer 2:29 against me, saith the *L'*. ‡3068
31 see ye the word of the *L'*. Have I ‡ "
37 *L'* hath rejected thy confidences, ‡ "
3: 1 return again to me, saith the *L'*. ‡ "
6 *L'* said also unto me in the days ‡ "
10 heart, but feignedly, saith the *L'*. ‡ "
11 *L'* said unto me, The backsliding ‡ "
12 backsliding Israel, saith the *L'*; ‡ "
12 I am merciful, saith the *L'*, and ‡ "
13 transgressed against the *L'* thy ‡ "
13 not obeyed my voice, saith the *L'*. ‡ "
14 backsliding children, saith the *L'*; ‡ "
16 saith the *L'*, they shall say no more, ‡ "
16 The ark of the covenant of the *L'*: ‡ "
17 call Jerusalem the throne of the *L'*; ‡ "
17 unto it, to the name of the *L'*, to ‡ "
20 me, O house of Israel, saith the *L'*. ‡ "
21 have forgotten the *L'* their God. ‡ "
22 thee; for thou art the *L'* our God. ‡ "
23 in the *L'* our God is the salvation ‡ "
25 we have sinned against the *L'* our ‡ "
25 not obeyed the voice of the *L'* our ‡ "
4: 1 wilt return, O Israel, saith the *L'*, ‡ "
2 *L'* liveth, in truth, in judgment, ‡ "
3 thus saith the *L'* to the men of ‡ "
4 Circumcise yourselves to the *L'*, ‡ "
8 anger of the *L'* is not turned back ‡ "
9 to pass at that day, saith the *L'*, ‡ "
10 *L'* God! surely thou hast greatly 136
17 rebellious against me, saith the *L'*. ‡3068
26 down at the presence of the *L'*, ‡ "
27 thus hath the *L'* said, The whole ‡ "
5: 2 though they say, The *L'* liveth; ‡ "
3 O *L'*, are not thine eyes upon the ‡ "
4 they know not the way of the *L'*, ‡ "
5 they have known the way of the *L'*, ‡ "
9 for these things? saith the *L'*: ‡ "
11 very treacherously...saith the *L'*. ‡ "
12 They have belied the *L'*, and said, ‡ "
14 thus saith the *L'* God of hosts, ‡ "
15 O house of Israel, saith the *L'*: ‡ "
18 saith the *L'*, I will not make a full ‡ "
19 Wherefore doeth the *L'* our God ‡ "
22 Fear ye not me? saith the *L'*: will ‡ "
24 Let us now fear the *L'* our God, ‡ "
29 for these things? saith the *L'*: ‡ "
6: 6 For thus hath the *L'* of hosts said, ‡ "
9 Thus saith the *L'* of hosts, They ‡ "
10 the word of the *L'* is unto them a ‡ "
11 I am full of the fury of the *L'*; ‡ "
12 inhabitants of...land, saith the *L'*. ‡ "
15 shall be cast down, saith the *L'*. ‡ "
16 Thus saith the *L'*, Stand ye in the ‡ "
21 thus saith the *L'*, Behold, I will lay ‡ "
22 Thus saith the *L'*, Behold, a people ‡ "
30 because the *L'* hath rejected them. ‡ "
7: 1 came to Jeremiah from the *L'*, ‡ "
2 Hear the word of the *L'*, all ye of ‡ "
2 at these gates to worship the *L'*. ‡ "
3 saith the *L'* of hosts, the God of ‡ "
4 The temple of the *L'*, The temple ‡ "
4 of the *L'*, The temple of the *L'*, ‡ "
11 even I have seen it, saith the *L'*. ‡ "
13 done all these works, saith the *L'*, ‡ "
19 provoke me to anger? saith the *L'*: ‡ "
20 thus saith the *L'* God; Behold, mine 136
21 the *L'* of hosts, the God of Israel; ‡3068
28 that obeyeth not the voice of the *L'* ‡ "
29 *L'* hath rejected and forsaken the ‡ "
30 done evil in my sight, saith the *L'*: ‡ "
32 saith the *L'*, that it shall no more ‡ "
8: 1 saith the *L'*, they shall bring out ‡ "
3 driven them, saith the *L'* of hosts. ‡ "
4 Thus saith the *L'*; Shall they fall, ‡ "
7 know not the judgment of the *L'*. ‡ "
8 and the law of the *L'* is with us? ‡ "
9 have rejected the word of the *L'*; ‡ "
12 shall be cast down, saith the *L'*. ‡ "
13 surely consume them, saith the *L'*: ‡ "
14 *L'* our God hath put us to silence, ‡ "
14 we have sinned against the *L'*. ‡ "
17 they shall bite you, saith the *L'*: ‡ "
19 Is not the *L'* in Zion? is not her ‡ "
9: 3 they know not me, saith the *L'*. ‡ "
6 refuse to know me, saith the *L'*. ‡ "
7 thus saith the *L'* of hosts, Behold, ‡ "
9 for these things? saith the *L'*: ‡ "
12 the mouth of the *L'* hath spoken, ‡ "
13 the *L'* saith, Because they have ‡ "
15 the *L'* of hosts, the God of Israel; ‡ "
17 saith the *L'* of hosts, Consider ‡ "
20 Yet hear the word of the *L'*, O ye ‡ "
22 Speak, Thus saith the *L'*, Even ‡ "
23 Thus saith the *L'*, Let not the wise ‡ "
24 *L'* which exercise lovingkindness ‡ "
24 these things I delight, saith the *L'*. ‡ "
25 the days come, saith the *L'*, that ‡ "
10: 1 the word which the *L'* speaketh ‡ "
2 Thus saith the *L'*, Learn not the ‡ "
6 there is none like unto thee, O *L'*; ‡ "
10 the *L'* is the true God, he is the ‡ "
16 The *L'* of hosts is his name. ‡ "
18 For thus saith the *L'*, Behold, I ‡ "
21 and have not sought the *L'*: ‡ "
23 O *L'*, I know that the way of man ‡ "
24 *L'*, correct me, but with judgment; ‡ "
11: 1 that came to Jeremiah from the *L'*, ‡ "
3 Thus saith the *L'* God of Israel; ‡ "
5 answered I, and said, So be it, O *L'*. ‡ "
6 the *L'* said unto me, Proclaim ‡ "
9 *L'* said unto me, A conspiracy ‡ "
11 thus saith the *L'*, Behold, I will ‡ "
16 The *L'* called thy name, A green ‡ "
17 For the *L'* of hosts, that planted ‡ "
18 *L'* hath given me knowledge of it, ‡ "
20 But, O *L'* of hosts, that judgest ‡ "

Jer 11:21 thus saith the *L'* of the men of ‡3068
21 prophesy not in the name of the *L'*, ‡ "
22 thus saith the *L'* of hosts, Behold, ‡ "
12: 1 Righteous art thou, O *L'*, when I ‡ "
3 But thou, O *L'*, knowest me: thou ‡ "
12 sword of the *L'* shall devour from ‡ "
13 because of the fierce anger of the *L'*. ‡ "
14 saith the *L'* against all mine evil ‡ "
16 swear by my name, The *L'* liveth; ‡ "
17 destroy that nation, saith the *L'*. ‡ "
13: 1 saith the *L'* unto me, Go and get ‡ "
2 according to the word of the *L'*, ‡ "
3 the word of the *L'* came unto me ‡ "
5 Euphrates, as the *L'* commanded ‡ "
6 the *L'* said unto me, Arise, go to ‡ "
8 the word of the *L'* came unto me, ‡ "
9 saith the *L'*, After this manner ‡ "
11 whole house of Judah, saith the *L'*; ‡ "
12 Thus saith the *L'* God of Israel, ‡ "
13 Thus saith the *L'*, Behold, I will ‡ "
14 the sons together, saith the *L'*: ‡ "
15 not proud: for the *L'* hath spoken. ‡ "
16 Give glory to the *L'* your God, ‡ "
25 measures from me, saith the *L'*; ‡ "
14: 1 The word of the *L'* that came to ‡ "
7 O *L'*, though our iniquities testify ‡ "
9 thou, O *L'*, art in the midst of us, ‡ "
10 Thus saith the *L'* unto this people, ‡ "
10 the *L'* doth not accept them; ‡ "
11 Then said the *L'* unto me, Pray ‡ "
13 Ah, *L'* God! behold, the prophets 136
14 *L'* said unto me, The prophets ‡3068
15 thus saith the *L'* concerning the ‡ "
20 We acknowledge, O *L'*, our ‡ "
22 art not thou he, O *L'* our God? ‡ "
15: 1 Then said the *L'* unto me, Though ‡ "
2 Thus saith the *L'*; Such as are for ‡ "
3 over them four kinds, saith the *L'*: ‡ "
6 hast forsaken me, saith the *L'*, ‡ "
9 before their enemies, saith the *L'*. ‡ "
11 The *L'* said, Verily it shall be well ‡ "
15 O *L'*, thou knowest: remember ‡ "
16 by thy name, O *L'* God of hosts. ‡ "
19 thus saith the *L'*, If thou return, ‡ "
20 and to deliver thee, saith the *L'*. ‡ "
16: 1 The word of the *L'* came also unto ‡ "
3 saith the *L'* concerning the sons ‡ "
5 thus saith the *L'*, Enter not into ‡ "
5 from this people, saith the *L'*, ‡ "
9 the *L'* of hosts, the God of Israel; ‡ "
10 *L'* pronounced all this great evil ‡ "
10 have committed against the *L'* our ‡ "
11 have forsaken me, saith the *L'*, ‡ "
14 the days come, saith the *L'*, that ‡ "
14, 15 The *L'* liveth, that brought up ‡ "
16 send for many fishers, saith the *L'*, ‡ "
19 *L'*, my strength, and my fortress, ‡ "
21 shall know that my name is The *L'*. ‡ "
17: 5 Thus saith the *L'*; Cursed be the ‡ "
5 whose heart departeth from the *L'*. ‡ "
7 the man that trusteth in the *L'*, ‡ "
7 and whose hope the *L'* is. ‡ "
10 I the *L'* search the heart, I try the ‡ "
13 O *L'*, the hope of Israel, all that ‡ "
13 forsaken the *L'*, the fountain of ‡ "
14 Heal me, O *L'*, and I shall be ‡ "
15 Where is the word of the *L'*? let it ‡ "
19 saith the *L'* unto me; Go and stand ‡ "
20 Hear ye the word of the *L'*, ye ‡ "
21 Thus saith the *L'*; Take heed to ‡ "
24 hearken unto me, saith the *L'*, ‡ "
26 praise, unto the house of the *L'*. ‡ "
18: 1 came to Jeremiah from the *L'*, ‡ "
5 the word of the *L'* came to me, ‡ "
6 you as this potter? saith the *L'*. ‡ "
11 saith the *L'*; Behold, I frame ‡ "
13 thus saith the *L'*; Ask ye now ‡ "
19 Give heed to me, O *L'*, and hearken ‡ "
23 *L'*, thou knowest all their counsel ‡ "
19: 1 Thus saith the *L'*, Go and get a ‡ "
3 say, Hear ye the word of the *L'*, O ‡ "
3 Thus saith the *L'* of hosts, the ‡ "
6 the days come, saith the *L'*, that ‡ "
11 them, Thus saith the *L'* of hosts; ‡ "
12 I do unto this place, saith the *L'*, ‡ "
14 the *L'* had sent him to prophesy; ‡ "
15 Thus saith the *L'* of hosts, the ‡ "
20: 1 governor in the house of the *L'*, ‡ "
2 which was by the house of the *L'*. ‡ "
3 The *L'* hath not called thy name ‡ "
4 thus saith the *L'*, Behold, I will ‡ "
7 O *L'*, thou hast deceived me, and ‡ "
8 word of the *L'* was made a reproach ‡ "
11 *L'* is with me as a mighty terrible ‡ "
12 But, O *L'* of hosts, that triest the ‡ "
13 Sing unto the *L'*, praise ye the *L'*: ‡ "
16 the cities which the *L'* overthrew, ‡ "
21: 1 came unto Jeremiah from the *L'*, ‡ "
2 Enquire, I pray thee, of the *L'* for ‡ "
2 *L'* will deal with us according to ‡ "
4 Thus saith the *L'* God of Israel; ‡ "
7 And afterward, saith the *L'*, I will ‡ "
8 Thus saith the *L'*; Behold, I set ‡ "
10 and not for good, saith the *L'*: ‡ "
11 say, Hear ye the word of the *L'*; ‡ "
12 saith the *L'*; Execute judgment ‡ "
13 and rock of the plain, saith the *L'*; ‡ "
14 fruit of your doings, saith the *L'*: ‡ "
22: 1 Thus saith the *L'*; Go down to ‡ "
2 Hear the word of the *L'*, O king ‡ "
3 Thus saith the *L'*; Execute ye ‡ "
5 I swear by myself, saith the *L'*, ‡ "
6 thus saith the *L'* unto the king's ‡ "
8 *L'* done thus unto this great city? ‡ "
9 forsaken the covenant of the *L'* ‡ "
11 saith the *L'* touching Shallum the ‡ "

Jer 22:16 not this to know me? saith the L·. ‡3068
18 saith the L· concerning Jehoiakim ‡ "
18 saying, Ah l·! or, Ah his glory! 113
24 As I live, saith the L·, though ‡3068
29 earth, hear the word of the L·. ‡ "
30 Thus saith the L·, Write ye this ‡ "
23: 1 sheep of my pasture! saith the L·. ‡ "
2 thus saith the L· God of Israel ‡ "
2 evil of your doings, saith the L·. ‡ "
4 shall they be lacking, saith the L·. ‡ "
5 the days come, saith the L·, that ‡ "
6 called, The L· Our Righteousness. ‡ "
7 the days come, saith the L·, that ‡ "
7, 8 The L· liveth, which brought up ‡ "
9 hath overcome, because of the L·, ‡ "
11 their wickedness, saith the L·. ‡ "
12 of their visitation, saith the L·. ‡ "
15 saith the L· of hosts concerning ‡ "
16 saith the L· of hosts, Hearken ‡ "
16 and not out of the mouth of the L·. ‡ "
17 The L· hath said, Ye shall have ‡ "
18 hath stood in the counsel of the L·, ‡ "
19 whirlwind of the L· is gone forth ‡ "
20 anger of the L· shall not return, ‡ "
23 Am I a God at hand, saith the L·, ‡ "
24 I shall not see him? saith the L·. ‡ "
24 heaven and earth? saith the L·. ‡ "
28 chaff to the wheat? saith the L·. ‡ "
29 word like as a fire? saith the L·; ‡ "
30, 31 the prophets, saith the L·, ‡ "
32 prophesy false dreams, saith the L·, ‡ "
32 this people at all, saith the L·. ‡ "
33 What is the burden of the L·? ‡ "
33 will even forsake you, saith the L·. ‡ "
34 The burden of the L·, I will even ‡ "
35 What hath the L· answered? ‡ "
35 and, What hath the L· spoken? ‡ "
36 burden of the L· shall ye mention ‡ "
36 God, of the L· of hosts our God. ‡ "
37 What hath the L· answered thee? ‡ "
37 and, What hath the L· spoken? ‡ "
38 ye say, The burden of the L·; ‡ "
38 therefore thus saith the L·; ‡ "
38 this word, The burden of the L·, ‡ "
38 not say, The burden of the L·; ‡ "
24: 1 The L· shewed me, and, behold, ‡ "
1 set before the temple of the L·, ‡ "
3 said the L· unto me, What seest ‡ "
4 the word of the L· came unto me, ‡ "
5 saith the L·, the God of Israel; ‡ "
7 to know me, that I am the L·: ‡ "
8 surely thus saith the L·, So will I ‡ "
25: 3 word of the L· hath come unto me, ‡ "
4 the L· hath sent unto you all his ‡ "
5 in the land that the L· hath given ‡ "
7 hearkened unto me, saith the L·; ‡ "
8 thus saith the L· of hosts; Because ‡ "
9 of the north, saith the L·, and ‡ "
12 and that nation, saith the L·, for ‡ "
15 For thus saith the L· God of Israel ‡ "
17 unto whom the L· had sent me: ‡ "
27 Thus saith the L· of hosts, the God ‡ "
28 Thus saith the L· of hosts; Ye shall ‡ "
29 of the earth, saith the L· of hosts. ‡ "
30 The L· shall roar from on high, ‡ "
31 the L· hath a controversy with the ‡ "
31 wicked to the sword, saith the L·. ‡ "
32 Thus saith the L· of hosts, Behold, ‡ "
33 slain of the L· shall be at that day ‡ "
36 the L· hath spoiled their pasture. ‡ "
37 because of the fierce anger of the L·. ‡ "
26: 1 Judah came this word from the L·, ‡ "
2 saith the L·; Stand in the court ‡ "
4 Thus saith the L·; If ye will not ‡ "
7 these words in the house of the L·. ‡ "
8 all that the L· had commanded ‡ "
9 prophesied in the name of the L·, ‡ "
9 Jeremiah in the house of the L·. ‡ "
10 house unto the house of the L·, ‡ "
12 L· sent me to prophesy against ‡ "
13 obey the voice of the L· your God; ‡ "
13 L· will repent him of the evil that ‡ "
15 for of a truth the L· hath sent me ‡ "
16 us in the name of the L· our God. ‡ "
18 saith the L· of hosts; Zion shall ‡ "
19 fear the L·, and besought the L·, ‡ "
19 L· repented him of the evil which ‡ "
20 prophesied in the name of the L·, ‡ "
27: 1 word unto Jeremiah from the L·, ‡ "
2 saith the L· to me; Make thee ‡ "
4 saith the L· of hosts, the God of ‡ "
8 nation will I punish, saith the L·, ‡ "
11 in their own land, saith the L·; ‡ "
13 as the L· hath spoken against the ‡ "
15 I have not sent them, saith the L·, ‡ "
16 Thus saith the L·; Hearken not to ‡ "
18 the word of the L· be with them, ‡ "
18 intercession to the L· of hosts, ‡ "
18 are left in the house of the L·, ‡ "
19 saith the L· of hosts concerning ‡ "
21 saith the L· of hosts, the God of ‡ "
21 remain in the house of the L·, ‡ "
22 day that I visit them, saith the L·; ‡ "
28: 1 unto me in the house of the L·, ‡ "
2 speaketh the L· of hosts, the God ‡ "
4 went into Babylon, saith the L·: ‡ "
5 that stood in the house of the L·, ‡ "
6 the L· do so: the L· perform thy ‡ "
9 that the L· hath truly sent him. ‡ "
11 Thus saith the L·; Even so will I ‡ "
12 word of the L· came unto Jeremiah ‡ "
13 saith the L·; Thou hast broken ‡ "
14 saith the L· of hosts, the God of ‡ "
15 The L· hath not sent thee; but ‡ "
16 saith the L·; Behold, I will cast ‡ "
16 taught rebellion against the L·. ‡ "

Jer 29: 4 saith the L· of hosts, the God of ‡3068
7 and pray unto the L· for it: for in ‡ "
8 saith the L· of hosts, the God of ‡ "
9 have not sent them, saith the L·. ‡ "
10 saith the L·, That after seventy ‡ "
11 I think toward you, saith the L·, ‡ "
14 will be found of you, saith the L·: ‡ "
14 I have driven you, saith the L·; ‡ "
15 The L· hath raised us up prophets ‡ "
16 that thus saith the L· of the king ‡ "
17 saith the L· of hosts; Behold, I ‡ "
19 hearkened to my words,...the L·, ‡ "
19 ye would not hear, saith the L·. ‡ "
20 Hear ye...the word of the L·, all ‡ "
21 saith the L· of hosts, the God of ‡ "
22 L· make thee like Zedekiah and ‡ "
23 and am a witness, saith the L·. ‡ "
25 Thus speaketh the L· of hosts, the ‡ "
26 L· hath made thee priest in the ‡ "
26 be officers in the house of the L·, ‡ "
30 the word of the L· unto Jeremiah, ‡ "
31 saith the L· concerning Shemaiah ‡ "
32 thus saith the L·; Behold, I will ‡ "
32 will do for my people, saith the L·; ‡ "
32 taught rebellion against the L·. ‡ "
30: 1 that came to Jeremiah from the L·, ‡ "
2 speaketh the L· God of Israel, ‡ "
3 the days come, saith the L·, that ‡ "
3 Israel and Judah, saith the L·: ‡ "
4 are the words that the L· spake ‡ "
5 thus saith the L·; We have heard ‡ "
8 saith the L· of hosts, that I will ‡ "
9 shall serve the L· their God, and ‡ "
10 O my servant Jacob, saith the L·; ‡ "
11 For I am with thee, saith the L·, ‡ "
12 thus saith the L·, Thy bruise is ‡ "
17 thee of thy wounds, saith the L·; ‡ "
18 Thus saith the L·; Behold, I will ‡ "
21 approach unto me? saith the L·. ‡ "
23 whirlwind of the L· goeth forth ‡ "
24 anger of the L· shall not return, ‡ "
31: 1 saith the L·, will I be the God of ‡ "
2 saith the L·, The people which ‡ "
3 L· hath appeared of old unto me, ‡ "
6 us go up to Zion unto the L· our ‡ "
7 saith the L·; Sing with gladness ‡ "
7 and say, O L·, save thy people, ‡ "
10 Hear the word of the L·, O ye ‡ "
11 For the L· hath redeemed Jacob, ‡ "
12 to the goodness of the L·, for ‡ "
14 with my goodness, saith the L·. ‡ "
15 saith the L·; A voice was heard ‡ "
16 saith the L·; Refrain thy voice ‡ "
16 shall be rewarded, saith the L·; ‡ "
17 is hope in thine end, saith the L·, ‡ "
18 for thou art the L· my God. ‡ "
20 mercy upon him, saith the L·. ‡ "
22 L· hath created a new thing in the ‡ "
23 saith the L· of hosts, the God of ‡ "
23 The L· bless thee, O habitation ‡ "
27 the days come, saith the L·, that ‡ "
28 build, and to plant, saith the L·. ‡ "
31 the days come, saith the L·, that ‡ "
32 husband unto them, saith the L·: ‡ "
33 After those days, saith the L·, I ‡ "
34 Know the L·: for they shall all ‡ "
34 the greatest of them, saith the L·: ‡ "
35 Thus saith the L·, which giveth ‡ "
35 The L· of hosts is his name: ‡ "
36 from before me, saith the L·, ‡ "
37 saith the L·; If heaven above can ‡ "
37 that they have done, saith the L·. ‡ "
38 the days come, saith the L·, that ‡ "
38 city shall be built to the L· from ‡ "
40 east, shall be holy unto the L·; ‡ "
32: 1 came to Jeremiah from the L· in ‡ "
3 Thus saith the L·, Behold, I will ‡ "
5 until I visit him, saith the L·: ‡ "
6 The word of the L· came unto me, ‡ "
8 according to the word of the L·, ‡ "
8 that this was the word of the L·. ‡ "
14 saith the L· of hosts, the God of ‡ "
15 For thus saith the L· of hosts, ‡ "
16 I prayed unto the L·, saying, ‡ "
17 Ah L· God! behold, thou hast made 136
18 God, The L· of hosts, is his name, ‡3068
25 thou hast said unto me, O L· God, 136
26 the word of the L· unto Jeremiah, ‡3068
27 Behold, I am the L·, the God of ‡ "
28 Therefore thus saith the L·; ‡ "
30 work of their hands, saith the L·. ‡ "
36 therefore thus saith the L·, the ‡ "
42 For thus saith the L·; Like as I ‡ "
44 captivity to return, saith the L·. ‡ "
33: 1 the word of the L· came unto ‡ "
2 saith the L· the maker thereof, ‡ "
2 the L· that formed it, to establish ‡ "
2 establish it; The L· is his name; ‡ "
4 For thus saith the L·, the God of ‡ "
10 Thus saith the L·; again there ‡ "
11 shall say, Praise the L· of hosts: ‡ "
11 for the L· is good; for his mercy ‡ "
11 of praise into the house of the L·. ‡ "
11 land, as at the first, saith the L·. ‡ "
12 Thus saith the L· of hosts; Again ‡ "
13 that telleth them, saith the L·. ‡ "
14 saith the L·, that I will perform ‡ "
16 called, The L· our righteousness. ‡ "
17 For thus saith the L·; David shall ‡ "
19 And the word of the L· came unto ‡ "
20 Thus saith the L·; If ye can break ‡ "
23 word of the L· came to Jeremiah, ‡ "
24 two families which the L· hath ‡ "
25 Thus saith the L·; If my covenant ‡ "
34: 1 came unto Jeremiah from the L·, ‡ "
2 Thus saith the L·, the God of ‡ "

Jer 34: 2 and tell him, Thus saith the L·; ‡3068
4 Yet hear the word of the L·, O ‡ "
4 Thus saith the L· of thee, Thou ‡ "
5 will lament thee, saying, Ah l·! 113
5 pronounced the word, saith the L·. ‡3068
8 came unto Jeremiah from the L·, ‡ "
12 word of the L· came to Jeremiah ‡ "
12 came to Jeremiah from the L·, ‡ "
13 Thus saith the L·, the God of ‡ "
17 thus saith the L·; Ye have not ‡ "
17 a liberty for you, saith the L·, ‡ "
22 I will command, saith the L·, and ‡ "
35: 1 came unto Jeremiah from the L·, ‡ "
2, 4 them into the house of the L·, ‡ "
12 the word of the L· unto Jeremiah, ‡ "
13 Thus saith the L· of hosts, the ‡ "
13 to my words? saith the L·. ‡ "
17 thus saith the L· God of hosts, ‡ "
18 Thus saith the L· of hosts, the ‡ "
19 thus saith the L· of hosts, the ‡ "
36: 1 came unto Jeremiah from the L·, ‡ "
4 Jeremiah all the words of the L·, ‡ "
5 go into the house of the L·: ‡ "
6 words of the L· in the ears of the ‡ "
7 their supplication before the L·, ‡ "
7 fury that the L· hath pronounced ‡ "
8 in the book the words of the L· in ‡ "
9 proclaimed a fast before the L· ‡ "
10 Jeremiah in the house of the L·, ‡ "
11 the book all the words of the L·, ‡ "
26 the prophet: but the L· hid them. ‡ "
27 word of the L· came to Jeremiah, ‡ "
29 Thus saith the L·; Thou hast ‡ "
30 saith the L· of Jehoiakim king of ‡ "
37: 2 hearken unto the words of the L·, ‡ "
3 Pray now unto the L· our God ‡ "
6 word of the L· unto the prophet ‡ "
7 Thus saith the L·, the God of ‡ "
9 Thus saith the L·; Deceive not ‡ "
17 Is there any word from the L·? ‡ "
20 I pray thee, O my l· the king: 113
38: 2 Thus saith the L·, He that ‡3068
3 Thus saith the L·, This city shall ‡ "
9 My l· the king, these men have 113
14 that is in the house of the L·: ‡3068
16 As the L· liveth, that made us this ‡ "
17 unto Zedekiah, Thus saith the L·, ‡ "
20 I beseech thee, the voice of the L·, ‡ "
21 the word that the L· hath shewed ‡ "
39: 15 the word of the L· came unto ‡ "
16 saith the L· of hosts, the God of ‡ "
17 thee in that day, saith the L·: ‡ "
18 put thy trust in me, saith the L·. ‡ "
40: 1 came to Jeremiah from the L·, ‡ "
2 L· thy God hath pronounced this ‡ "
3 Now the L· hath brought it, and ‡ "
3 ye have sinned against the L·, ‡ "
41: 5 bring them to the house of the L·. ‡ "
42: 2 pray for us unto the L· thy God, ‡ "
3 L· thy God may shew us the way ‡ "
4 I will pray unto the L· your God ‡ "
4 thing the L· shall answer you, I ‡ "
5 L· be a true and faithful witness ‡ "
5 L· thy God shall send thee to us. ‡ "
6 will obey the voice of the L· our ‡ "
6 we obey the voice of the L· our ‡ "
7 the word of the L· came unto ‡ "
9 saith the L·, the God of Israel, ‡ "
11 not afraid of him, saith the L·: ‡ "
13 neither obey the voice of the L· ‡ "
15 therefore hear the word of the L·, ‡ "
15, 18 saith the L· of hosts, the God ‡ "
19 The L· hath said concerning you, ‡ "
20 ye sent me unto the L· your God, ‡ "
20 Pray for us unto the L· our God; ‡ "
20 all that the L· our God shall say, ‡ "
21 not obeyed the voice of the L· ‡ "
43: 1 all the words of the L· their God, ‡ "
1 the L· their God had sent him ‡ "
2 L· our God hath not sent thee to ‡ "
4 obeyed not the voice of the L·, ‡ "
7 obeyed not the voice of the L·: ‡ "
8 the word of the L· unto Jeremiah ‡ "
10 saith the L· of hosts, the God of ‡ "
44: 2 saith the L· of hosts, the God of ‡ "
7 thus saith the L·, the God of hosts, ‡ "
11 saith the L· of hosts, the God of ‡ "
16 unto us in the name of the L·, ‡ "
21 did not the L· remember them, ‡ "
22 that the L· could no longer bear, ‡ "
23 ye have sinned against the L·, ‡ "
23 not obeyed the voice of the L·, ‡ "
24 Hear the word of the L·, all Judah ‡ "
25 saith the L· of hosts, the God of ‡ "
26 hear ye the word of the L·, all ‡ "
26 by my great name, saith the L·, ‡ "
26 Egypt, saying, The L· God liveth. 136
29 be a sign unto you, saith the L·, ‡3068
30 Thus saith the L·; Behold, I will ‡ "
45: 2 saith the L·, the God of Israel, ‡ "
3 L· hath added grief to my sorrow; ‡ "
4 The L· saith thus; Behold, that ‡ "
5 evil upon all flesh, saith the L·: ‡ "
46: 1 The word of the L· which came to ‡ "
5 was round about, saith the L·. ‡ "
10 is the day of the L· God of hosts, 136
10 L· God of hosts hath a sacrifice in
13 The word that the L· spake to ‡3068
15 because the L· did drive them. ‡ "
18 whose name is the L· of hosts, ‡ "
23 cut down her forest, saith the L·, ‡ "
25 The L· of hosts, the God of Israel, ‡ "
26 in the days of old, saith the L·. ‡ "
28 O Jacob my servant, saith the L·: ‡ "
47: 1 The word of the L· that came to ‡ "
2 Thus saith the L·; Behold, waters ‡ "

Jer 47: 4 the L' will spoil the Philistines. ‡3068
6 O thou sword of the L', how long ‡ "
7 seeing the L' hath given it a ‡ "
48: 1 Against Moab thus saith the L' ‡ "
8 destroyed, as the L' hath spoken.‡ "
10 he that doeth the work of the L' ‡ "
12 the days come, saith the L', that ‡ "
15 whose name is the L' of hosts. ‡ "
25 his arm is broken, saith the L'. ‡ "
26 magnified himself against the L':‡ "
30 I know his wrath, saith the L'; ‡ "
35 to cease in Moab, saith the L', ‡ "
38 is no pleasure, saith the L'. ‡ "
40 thus saith the L'; Behold, he shall‡ "
42 magnified himself against the L'.‡ "
43 inhabitant of Moab, saith the L'. ‡ "
44 of their visitation, saith the L'. ‡ "
47 in the latter days, saith the L'. ‡ "
49: 1 the Ammonites, thus saith the L';‡ "
2 saith the L', that I will cause an ‡ "
2 that were his heirs, saith the L'. ‡ "
5 a fear upon thee, saith the L' 136
6 children of Ammon, saith the L'. ‡3068
7 Concerning Edom, thus saith the L'‡ "
12 For thus saith the L'; Behold, ‡ "
13 sworn by myself, saith the L', ‡ "
14 have heard a rumour from the L',‡ "
16 down from thence, saith the L'. ‡ "
18 saith the L', no man shall abide ‡ "
20 hear the counsel of the L', that he‡ "
26 cut off in that day, saith the L' of‡ "
28 shall smite, thus saith the L'; ‡ "
30 inhabitants of Hazor, saith the L';‡ "
31 without care, saith the L', which ‡ "
32 all sides thereof, saith the L'. ‡ "
34 The word of the L' that came to ‡ "
35 Thus saith the L' of hosts, Behold,‡ "
37 even my fierce anger, saith the L';‡ "
38 and the princes, saith the L'. ‡ "
39 captivity of Elam, saith the L'. ‡ "
50: 1 word that the L' spake against ‡ "
4 saith the L', the children of Israel‡ "
4 go, and seek the L' their God. ‡ "
5 and let us join ourselves to the L'‡ "
7 they have sinned against the L', ‡ "
7 even the L', the hope of their ‡ "
10 her shall be satisfied, saith the L'.‡ "
13 Because of the wrath of the L' it ‡ "
14 she hath sinned against the L'. ‡ "
15 for it is the vengeance of the L': ‡ "
18 saith the L' of hosts, the God of ‡ "
20 saith the L', the iniquity of Israel‡ "
21 destroy after them, saith the L', ‡ "
24 thou hast striven against the L'. ‡ "
25 The L' hath opened his armoury, ‡ "
25 for this is the work of the L' God 136
28 the vengeance of the L' our God, ‡3068
29 hath been proud against the L', ‡ "
30 cut off in that day, saith the L'. ‡ "
31 most proud, saith the L' God of 136
33 Thus saith the L' of hosts; The ‡3068
34 The L' of hosts is his name: he ‡ "
35 upon the Chaldeans, saith the L', ‡ "
40 cities thereof, saith the L'; ‡ "
45 hear ye the counsel of the L', that‡ "
51: 1 Thus saith the L'; Behold, I will ‡ "
5 of his God, of the L' of hosts; ‡ "
10 The L' hath brought forth our ‡ "
10 declare in Zion the work of the L'‡ "
11 the L' hath raised up the spirit ‡ "
11 it is the vengeance of the L', ‡ "
12 L' hath both devised and done ‡ "
14 L' of hosts hath sworn by himself,‡ "
19 The L' of hosts is his name. ‡ "
24 Zion in your sight, saith the L'. ‡ "
25 destroying mountain, saith the L',‡ "
26 be desolate for ever, saith the L'.‡ "
29 every purpose of the L' shall be ‡ "
33 saith the L' of hosts, the God of ‡ "
36 thus saith the L'; Behold, I will ‡ "
39 and not awake, saith the L'. ‡ "
45 from the fierce anger of the L'. ‡ "
48 her from the north, saith the L'. ‡ "
50 remember the L' afar off, and let ‡ "
52 the days come, saith the L', that ‡ "
53 come unto her, saith the L'. ‡ "
55 the L' hath spoiled Babylon, and ‡ "
56 the L' God of recompenses shall ‡ "
57 whose name is the L' of hosts. ‡ "
58 Thus said the L' of hosts; The ‡ "
62 O L', thou hast spoken against ‡ "
52: 2 was evil in the eyes of the L', ‡ "
3 through the anger of the L' it ‡ "
13 burned the house of the L', and ‡ "
17 that were in the house of the L'. ‡ "
17 that was in the house of the L', ‡ "
20 had made in the house of the L': ‡ "
La 1: 5 the L' hath afflicted her for the ‡ "
9 O L', behold my affliction: for ‡ "
11 see, O L', and consider; for I am ‡ "
12 wherewith the L' hath afflicted ‡ "
14 the L' hath delivered me into their 136
15 L' hath trodden under foot all my "
15 the L' hath trodden the virgin, the "
17 the L' hath commanded...Jacob, ‡3068
18 The L' is righteous; for I have ‡ "
20 Behold, O L'; for I am in distress:‡ "
2: 1 hath the L' covered the daughter 136
2 The L' hath swallowed up all the "
5 The L' was as an enemy: he hath "
6 L' hath caused the solemn feasts ‡3068
7 the L' hath cast off his altar, he 136
7 a noise in the house of the L', ‡3068
8 The L' hath purposed to destroy ‡ "
9 also find no vision from the L'. ‡ "
17 L' hath done that which he had ‡ "

La 2: 18 Their heart cried unto the L', O 136
19 water before the face of the L': "
20 Behold, O L', and consider to ‡3068
20 be slain in the sanctuary of the L'? 136
3: 18 my hope is perished from the L': ‡3068
24 The L' is my portion, saith my ‡ "
25 L' is good unto them that wait ‡ "
26 wait for the salvation of the L'. ‡ "
31 For the L' will not cast off for ever:136
36 in his cause, the L' approveth not. "
37 when the L' commandeth it not? "
40 ways, and turn again to the L'. ‡3068
50 Till the L' look down, and behold ‡ "
55 I called upon thy name, O L', out ‡ "
58 O L', thou hast pleaded the causes 136
59 O L', thou hast seen my wrong: ‡3068
61 hast heard their reproach, O L', ‡ "
64 unto them a recompense, O L', ‡ "
66 from under the heavens of the L'.‡ "
4: 11 L' hath accomplished his fury; ‡ "
16 The anger of the L' hath divided ‡ "
20 nostrils, the anointed of the L', ‡ "
5: 1 Remember, O L', what is come ‡ "
19 Thou, O L', remainest for ever; ‡ "
21 Turn thou us unto thee, O L', ‡ "
Eze 1: 3 The word of the L' came expressly‡ "
3 the hand of the L' was there upon‡ "
28 likeness of the glory of the L'. ‡ "
2: 4 unto them, Thus saith the L' God. 136
3: 11 tell them, Thus saith the L' God; "
12 Blessed be the glory of the L' ‡3068
14 hand of the L' was strong upon ‡ "
16 the word of the L' came unto me, ‡ "
22 hand of the L' was there upon me;‡ "
23 the glory of the L' stood there, ‡ "
27 Thus saith the L' God; He that 136
4: 13 And the L' said, Even thus shall ‡3068
14 said I, Ah L' God! behold, my soul 136
5: 5 Thus saith the L' God; This is "
7, 8 Therefore thus saith the L' God; "
11 as I live, saith the L' God; Surely, "
13 the L' have spoken it in my zeal, ‡3068
15 rebukes. I the L' have spoken it.‡ "
17 thee. I the L' have spoken it. ‡ "
6: 1 the word of the L' came unto me, ‡ "
3 hear the word of the L' God; Thus 136
3 Thus saith the L' God to the "
7 ye shall know that I am the L'. ‡3068
10 they shall know that I am the L', ‡ "
11 Thus saith the L' God; Smite with 136
13 shall ye know that I am the L', ‡3068
14 they shall know that I am the L'.‡ "
7: 1 the word of the L' came unto me,‡ "
2 saith the L' God unto the land of 136
4 ye shall know that I am the L'. ‡3068
5 Thus saith the L' God; An evil, 136
9 that I am the L' that smiteth. ‡3068
19 in the day of the wrath of the L': ‡ "
27 they shall know that I am the L'. ‡ "
8: 1 hand of the L' God fell there upon 136
12 they say, The L' seeth us not; ‡3068
12 the L' hath forsaken the earth. ‡ "
16 at the door of the temple of the L',‡ "
16 backs toward the temple of the L',‡ "
9: 4 the L' said unto him, Go through ‡ "
8 Ah L' God! wilt thou destroy all 136
9 The L' hath forsaken the earth, ‡3068
9 the earth, and the L' seeth not. ‡ "
10: 4 the glory of the L' went up from ‡ "
18 the glory of the L' departed from ‡ "
11: 5 the Spirit of the L' fell upon me, ‡ "
5 Thus saith the L'; Thus have ye ‡ "
7 thus saith the L' God; Your slain 136
8 sword upon you, saith the L' God. "
10 ye shall know that I am the L'. ‡3068
12 ye shall know that I am the L': ‡ "
13 Ah L' God! wilt thou make a full 136
14 the word of the L' came unto me,‡3068
15 have said, Get you far from the L':‡ "
16, 17 say, Thus saith the L' God; 136
21 their own heads, saith the L' God. "
23 the glory of the L' went up from ‡3068
25 things that the L' had shewed me.‡ "
12: 1 word of the L' also came unto me,‡ "
8 came the word of the L' unto me,‡ "
10 unto them, Thus saith the L' God; 136
15 they shall know that I am the L', ‡3068
16 they shall know that I am the L'.‡ "
17 the word of the L' came to me, ‡ "
19 saith the L' God of the inhabitants 136
20 ye shall know that I am the L'. ‡3068
21 the word of the L' came unto me, ‡ "
23 Thus saith the L' God; I will make 136
25 I am the L': I will speak, and the‡3068
25 will perform it, saith the L' God. 136
26 the word of the L' came to me, ‡3068
28 saith the L' God; There shall 136
28 shall be done, saith the L' God. "
13: 1 the word of the L' came unto me,‡3068
2 Hear ye the word of the L'; ‡ "
3 Thus saith the L' God; Woe unto 136
5 in the battle in the day of the L'. ‡3068
6 The L' saith: and the L' hath not‡ "
7 whereas ye say, The L' saith it; ‡ "
8 thus saith the L' God; Because 136
8 I am against you, saith the L' God. "
9 ye shall know that I am the L' God. "
13 saith the L' God; I will even rend "
14 ye shall know that I am the L'. ‡3068
16 there is no peace, saith the L' God. 136
18 Thus saith the L' God; Woe to the "
20 Thus saith the L' God; Behold, I "
21, 23 ye shall know that I am the L'.‡3068
14: 2 the word of the L' came unto me,‡ "
4 Thus saith the L' God; Every man 136
4 L' will answer him that cometh ‡3068

Eze 14: 6 of Israel, Thus saith the L' God; 136
7 L' will answer him by myself: ‡3068
8 ye shall know that I am the L'. ‡ "
9 L' have deceived that prophet, ‡ "
11 may be their God, saith the L' God.136
12 word of the L' came again to me, ‡3068
14 righteousness, saith the L' God. 136
16, 18, 20 as I live, saith the L' God, they "
21 thus saith the L' God; How much "
23 I have done in it, saith the L' God. "
15: 1 the word of the L' came unto me,‡3068
6 thus saith the L' God; As the vine 136
7 ye shall know that I am the L', ‡3068
8 a trespass, saith the L' God. 136
16: 1 the word of the L' came unto me,‡3068
3 saith the L' God unto Jerusalem; 136
8 covenant with thee, saith the L' God, "
14 had put upon thee, saith the L' God. "
19 and thus it was, saith the L' God. "
23 woe unto thee! saith the L' God;) "
30 weak is thine heart, saith the L' God, "
35 O harlot, hear the word of the L':‡3068
36 Thus saith the L' God; Because 136
43 upon thine head, saith the L' God: "
48 saith the L' God, Sodom thy sister "
58 thine abominations, saith the L'. ‡3068
59 thus saith the L' God; I will even 136
62 thou shalt know that I am the L':‡3068
63 thou hast done, saith the L' God. 136
17: 1 the word of the L' came unto me, ‡3068
3 saith the L' God; A great eagle 136
9 saith the L' God; Shall it prosper? "
11 the word of the L' came unto me, ‡3068
16 As I live, saith the L' God, surely 136
19 Therefore thus saith the L' God; As "
21 know that I the L' have spoken it.‡3068
22 Thus saith the L' God; I will also 136
24 I the L' have brought down the ‡3068
24 L' have spoken and have done it. ‡ "
18: 1 The word of the L' came unto me‡ "
3 As I live, saith the L' God, ye shall 136
9 shall surely live, saith the L' God. "
23 wicked should die? saith the L' God:"
25 ye say, The way of the L' is not equal."
29 Israel, The way of the L' is not equal."
30 to his ways, saith the L' God. "
32 of him that dieth, saith the L' God: "
20: 1 Israel came to enquire of the L', ‡3068
2 came the word of the L' unto me,‡ "
3 saith the L' God; Are ye come to 136
3 As I live, saith the L' God, I will not "
5 Thus saith the L' God; In the day "
5 saying, I am the L' your God; ‡3068
7 of Egypt: I am the L' your God. ‡ "
12 I am the L' that sanctify them. ‡ "
19 I am the L' your God; walk in my‡ "
20 know that I am the L' your God. ‡ "
26 they might know that I am the L'.‡ "
27 saith the L' God; Yet in this your 136
30 saith the L' God; Are ye polluted "
31 As I live, saith the L' God, I will not "
33 As I live, saith the L' God, surely "
36 I plead with you, saith the L' God. "
38 ye shall know that I am the L'. ‡3068
39 saith the L' God; Go ye, serve ye 136
40 the height of Israel, saith the L' God,"
42, 44 shall know that I am the L', ‡3068
44 ye house of Israel, saith the L' God.136
45 the word of the L' came unto me,‡3068
47 the south, Hear the word of the L';‡"
47 Thus saith the L' God; Behold, I 136
48 see that I the L' have kindled it: ‡3068
49 Ah L' God! they say of me, Doth he136
21: 1 the word of the L' came unto me,‡3068
3 Thus saith the L'; Behold, I am ‡ "
5 I the L' have drawn forth my sword‡"
7 brought to pass, saith the L' God. 136
8 the word of the L' came unto me,‡3068
9 Thus saith the L'; Say, A sword, ‡ "
13 shall be no more, saith the L' God. 136
17 fury to rest: I the L' have said it.‡3068
18 word of the L' came unto me again,‡"
24 thus saith the L' God; Because ye 136
26 thus saith the L' God; Remove the "
28 thus saith the L' God concerning the"
32 for I the L' have spoken it. ‡3068
22: 1 the word of the L' came unto me, ‡ "
3 Thus saith the L' God; The city 136
12 hast forgotten me, saith the L' God. "
14 I the L' have spoken it, and will ‡3068
16 thou shalt know that I am the L'.‡ "
17 the word of the L' came unto me,‡ "
19 Therefore thus saith the L' God; 136
22 I the L' have poured out my fury ‡3068
23 the word of the L' came unto me, ‡ "
28 saying, Thus saith the L' God, 136
28 when the L' hath not spoken. ‡3068
31 upon their heads, saith the L' God. 136
23: 1 word of the L' came again unto ‡3068
22 O Aholibah, thus saith the L' God; 136
28 For thus saith the L' God; Behold, I "
32 Thus saith the L' God; Thou shalt "
34 I have spoken it, saith the L' God. "
35 Therefore thus saith the L' God; "
36 L' said moreover unto me; Son of‡3068
46 thus saith the L' God; I will bring 136
49 ye shall know that I am the L' God. "
24: 1 the word of the L' came unto me,‡3068
3 Thus saith the L' God; Set on a pot,136
6, 9 saith the L' God; Woe to the bloody"
14 I the L' have spoken it: it shall ‡3068
14 they judge thee, saith the L' God, 136
15 the word of the L' came unto me, ‡3068
20 The word of the L' came unto me,‡ "
21 Thus saith the L' God; Behold, I 136
24 ye shall know that I am the L' God. "

Eze 24:27 they shall know that I am the L. ‡3068
25: 1 word of the L. came again unto ‡ "
3 Hear the word of the L. God; 136
3 Thus saith the L. God; Because "
5 ye shall know that I am the L. ‡3068
6 For thus saith the L. God; Because136
7 thou shalt know that I am the L.‡3068
8 Thus saith the L. God; Because 136
11 they shall know that I am the L.‡3068
12 Thus saith the L. God; Because 136
13 Therefore thus saith the L. God; "
14 my vengeance, saith the L. God. "
15 Thus saith the L. God; Because "
16 Therefore thus saith the L. God; "
17 they shall know that I am the L.‡3068
26: 1 the word of the L. came unto me, ‡ "
3 Therefore thus saith the L. God; 136
5 I have spoken it, saith the L. God: "
6 they shall know that I am the L.‡3068
7 For thus saith the L. God; Behold, 136
14 for I the L. have spoken it, saith ‡3068
14 I...have spoken it, saith the L. God.136
15 Thus saith the L. God to Tyrus; "
19 thus saith the L. God; When I shall "
21 be found again, saith the L. God. "
27: 1 word of the L. came again unto ‡3068
3 Thus saith the L. God; O Tyrus, 136
28: 1 word of the L. came again unto ‡3068
2 Thus saith the L. God; Because 136
6 thus saith the L. God; Because thou"
10 I have spoken it, saith the L. God. "
11 the word of the L. came unto me, ‡3068
12 Thus saith the L. God; Thou sealest136
20 the word of the L. came unto me, ‡3068
22 Thus saith the L. God; Behold, I 136
22 they shall know that I am the L.‡3068
23 they shall know that I am the L. ‡ "
24 shall know that I am the L. God. 136
25 Thus saith the L. God; When I shall"
26 know that I am the L. their God. ‡3068
29: 1 the word of the L. came unto me, ‡ "
3 Thus saith the L. God; Behold, I 136
6 Egypt shall know that I am the L.‡3068
8 Therefore thus saith the L. God; 136
9 they shall know that I am the L.‡3068
13 thus saith the L. God; At the end 136
16 they shall know that I am the L. God."
17 the word of the L. came unto me,‡3068
19 Therefore thus saith the L. God; 136
20 wrought for me, saith the L. God. "
21 they shall know that I am the L.‡3068
30: 1 word of the L. came again unto ‡ "
2 Thus saith the L. God; Behold, I 136
3 even the day of the L. is near, ‡3068
6 Thus saith the L.; They also that‡ "
6 in it by the sword, saith the L. God.136
8 they shall know that I am the L.‡3068
10 Thus saith the L. God; I will also 136
12 strangers: I the L. have spoken it.‡3068
13 Thus saith the L. God; I will also 136
19 they shall know that I am the L.‡3068
20 the word of the L. came unto me,‡ "
22 Therefore thus saith the L. God; 136
25 they shall know that I am the L.‡3068
26 they shall know that I am the L.‡ "
31: 1 the word of the L. came unto me,‡ "
10 Therefore thus saith the L. God; 136
15 Thus saith the L. God; In the day "
18 all his multitude, saith the L. God. "
32: 1 the word of the L. came unto me,‡3068
3 saith the L. God; I will therefore 136
8 upon thy land, saith the L. God. "
11 thus saith the L. God; The sword "
14 to run like oil, saith the L. God. "
15 shall they know that I am the L.‡3068
16 all her multitude, saith the L. God.136
17 the word of the L. came unto me, ‡3068
31 by the sword, saith the L. God. 136
32 all his multitude, saith the L. God. "
33: 1 the word of the L. came unto me,‡3068
11 As I live, saith the L. God, I have 136
17 say, The way of the L. is not equal: "
20 say, The way of the L. is not equal. "
22 the hand of the L. was upon me ‡3068
23 the word of the L. came unto me, ‡ "
25 Thus saith the L. God; Ye eat with136
27 saith the L. God; As I live, surely "
29 shall they know that I am the L.‡3068
30 the word that cometh from the L.‡ "
34: 1 the word of the L. came unto me,‡ "
2 Thus saith the L. God unto the 136
7 hear the word of the L.; ‡3068
8 As I live, saith the L. God, surely 136
9 hear the word of the L.; ‡3068
10 Thus saith the L. God; Behold, I 136
11 For thus saith the L. God; Behold, "
15 them to lie down, saith the L. God. "
17 O my flock, thus saith the L. God; "
20 thus saith the L. God unto them; "
24 And I the L. will be their God, ‡3068
24 them; I the L. have spoken it. ‡ "
27 and shall know that I am the L. ‡ "
30 I the L. their God am with them, ‡ "
30 are my people, saith the L. God. 136
31 and I am your God, saith the L. God. "
35: 1 the word of the L. came unto me,‡3068
3 say unto it, Thus saith the L. God;136
4 thou shalt know that I am the L.‡3068
6 live, saith the L. God, I will prepare136
9 ye shall know that I am the L. ‡3068
10 it; whereas the L. was there: ‡ "
11 I live, saith the L. God, I will even 136
12 thou shalt know that I am the L.‡3068
14 Thus saith the L. God; When the 136
15 they shall know that I am the L.‡3068
36: 1 of Israel, hear the word of the L.:‡ "

Eze 36: 2 Thus saith the L. God; Because the136
3 Thus saith the L. God; Because they"
4 Israel, hear the word of the L. God; "
4 saith the L. God to the mountains, "
5 saith the L. God; Surely in the fire "
6 Thus saith the L. God; Behold, I "
7 thus saith the L. God; I have lifted "
11 ye shall know that I am the L. ‡3068
13 Thus saith the L. God; Because 136
14 nations any more, saith the L. God. "
15 to fall any more, saith the L. God. "
16 the word of the L. came unto me,‡3068
20 These are the people of the L., and‡"
22 Thus saith the L. God; I do not this136
23 heathen shall know...I am the L.,‡3068
23 saith the L. God, when I shall be 136
32 your sakes do I this, saith the L. "
33 Thus saith the L. God; In the day "
36 I the L. build the ruined places, ‡3068
36 I the L. have spoken it, and I will‡ "
37 saith the L. God; I will yet for this 136
38 they shall know that I am the L.‡3068
37: 1 The hand of the L. was upon me, ‡ "
1 me out in the spirit of the L., and ‡ "
3 answered, O L. God, thou knowest.136
4 bones, hear the word of the L. ‡3068
5 saith the L. God unto these bones; 136
6 ye shall know that I am the L. ‡3068
9 Thus saith the L. God; Come from 136
12 Thus saith the L. God; Behold, O my"
13 ye shall know that I am the L. ‡3068
14 know that I the L. have spoken it, "
14 it, and performed it, saith the L. 136
15 word of the L. came again unto ‡3068
19, 21 Thus saith the L. God; Behold, I 136
28 that I the L. do sanctify Israel, ‡3068
38: 1 the word of the L. came unto me, "
3 Thus saith the L. God; Behold, I 136
10 Thus saith the L. God; It shall also "
14 Thus saith the L. God; In that day "
17 Thus saith the L. God; Art thou he "
18 saith the L. God, that my fury shall "
21 all my mountains, saith the L. God: "
23 they shall know that I am the L.‡3068
39: 1 Thus saith the L. God; Behold, I 136
5 for I have spoken it, saith the L. God."
6 they shall know that I am the L.‡3068
7 heathen shall know...I am the L.,‡ "
8 and it is done, saith the L. God; 136
10 that robbed them, saith the L. God. "
13 shall be glorified, saith the L. God. "
17 son of man, thus saith the L. God; "
20 all men of war, saith the L. God. "
22 Israel shall know that I am the L.‡3068
25 Therefore thus saith the L. God; 136
28 know that I am the L. their God, ‡3068
29 house of Israel, saith the L. God. 136
40: 1 the hand of the L. was upon me, ‡3068
46 come near to the L. to minister ‡ "
41:22 is the table that is before the L. ‡ "
42:13 priests that approach unto the L. ‡ "
43: 4 glory of the L. came into the house‡ "
5 the glory of the L. filled the house.‡ "
18 Son of man, thus saith the L. God; 136
19 minister unto me, saith the L. God, "
24 shalt offer them before the L., ‡3068
24 up for a burnt offering unto the L.‡ "
27 I will accept you, saith the L. God. 136
44: 2 Then said the L. unto me; This ‡3068
2 because the L., the God of Israel, ‡ "
3 sit in it to eat bread before the L.‡ "
4 of the L. filled the house of the L.:‡ "
5 the L. said unto me, Son of man, ‡ "
5 ordinances of the house of the L.,‡ "
6 Thus saith the L. God; O ye house 136
9 Thus saith the L. God; No stranger, "
12 hand against them, saith the L. God, "
15 fat and the blood, saith the L. God: "
27 his sin offering, saith the L. God. "
45: 1 shall offer an oblation unto the L.,‡3068
4 come near to minister unto the L.:‡ "
9 saith the L. God; Let it suffice you,136
9 from my people, saith the L. God. "
15 reconciliation...saith the L. God. "
18 Thus saith the L. God; In the first "
23 prepare a burnt offering to the L.,‡3068
46: 1 Thus saith the L. God; The gate of136
3 door of this gate before the L. ‡3068
4 the prince shall offer unto the L. ‡ "
9 of the land shall come before the L.‡"
12 offerings voluntarily unto the L., ‡ "
13 a burnt offering unto the L. of a ‡ "
14 a perpetual ordinance unto the L.‡ "
16 Thus saith the L. God; If the prince136
47:13 Thus saith the L. God; This shall be"
23 his inheritance, saith the L. God. "
48: 9 that ye shall offer unto the L. ‡3068
10 sanctuary of the L. shall be in ‡ "
14 the land: for it is holy unto the L.‡ "
29 are their portions, saith the L. God.136
35 that day shall be, The L. is there. ‡3068
Da 1: 2 L. gave Jehoiakim king of Judah 136
10 I fear my l. the king, who hath 113
2:10 there is no king, l., nor ruler, that7229
47 a God of gods, and a L. of kings, 4756
4:19 My l., the dream be to them that "
24 which is come upon my l. the king: "
5:23 thyself against the L. of heaven; "
9: 2 word of the L. came to Jeremiah ‡3068
3 And I set my face unto the L. God, 136
4 I prayed unto the L. my God, ‡3068
4 O L., the great and dreadful God, 136
7 O L., righteousness belongeth unto "
8 O L., to us belongeth confusion of "
9 To the L. our God belong mercies "
10 we obeyed the voice of the L. our ‡3068

Da 9:13 not our prayer before the L. our ‡3068
14 hath the L. watched upon the evil,‡ "
14 L. our God is righteous in all his ‡ "
15 O L. our God, thou hast brought 136
16 O L., according to all thy "
19 O L., hear; O L., forgive; "
19 O L., hearken and do; defer not, "
20 my supplication before the L. my‡3068
10:16 O my l., by the vision my sorrows 113
17 of this my l. talk with this my l.? "
19 Let my l. speak; for thou hast "
12: 8 O my L., what shall be the end of "
Ho 1: 1 The word of the L. that came ‡3068
2 of the word of the L. by Hosea. ‡ "
2 the L. said to Hosea, Go, take ‡ "
2 whoredom, departing from the L.‡ "
4 L. said unto him, Call his name ‡ "
7 will save them by the L. their ‡ "
2:13 and forgat me, saith the L. ‡ "
16 saith the L., that thou shalt call ‡ "
20 and thou shalt know the L. ‡ "
21 that day, I will hear, saith the L.,‡ "
3: 1 Then said the L. unto me, Go yet, ‡ "
1 according to the love of the L. ‡ "
5 return, and seek the L. their God, ‡ "
5 shall fear the L. and his goodness‡ "
4: 1 Hear the word of the L., ye ‡ "
1 the L. hath a controversy with ‡ "
10 left off to take heed to the L. ‡ "
15 nor swear, The L. liveth. ‡ "
16 the L. will feed them as a lamb ‡ "
5: 4 and they have not known the L. ‡ "
6 with their herds to seek the L.; ‡ "
7 treacherously against the L.: ‡ "
6: 1 and let us return unto the L.: ‡ "
3 if we follow on to know the L.: ‡ "
7:10 not return to the L. their God, ‡ "
8: 1 eagle against the house of the L.,‡ "
13 but the L. accepteth them not; ‡ "
9: 4 not offer wine offerings to the L., ‡ "
4 not come into the house of the L.‡ "
5 in the day of the feast of the L.? ‡ "
14 Give them, O L.: what wilt thou ‡ "
10: 3 because we feared not the L.; ‡ "
12 for it is time to seek the L., till ‡ "
11:10 They shall walk after the L.: he ‡ "
11 them in their houses, saith the L.‡ "
12: 2 L. hath also a controversy with ‡ "
5 Even the L. God of hosts; ‡ "
5 the L. is his memorial. ‡ "
9 I that am the L. thy God from the‡ "
13 L. brought Israel out of Egypt, ‡ "
14 reproach shall his L. return unto 113
13: 4 yet I am the L. thy God from the ‡3068
15 the wind of the L. shall come up ‡ "
14: 1 return unto the L. thy God; for ‡ "
2 you words, and turn to the L.: ‡ "
9 for the ways of the L. are right, ‡ "
Joe 1: 1 word of the L. that came to Joel ‡ "
9 cut off from the house of the L.; ‡ "
14 into the house of the L. your God,‡ "
14 your God, and cry unto the L. ‡ "
15 for the day of the L. is at hand, ‡ "
19 O L., to thee will I cry: for the ‡ "
2: 1 for the day of the L. cometh, for ‡ "
11 L. shall utter his voice before his‡ "
11 for the day of the L. is great and ‡ "
12 also now, saith the L., turn ye ‡ "
13 and turn unto the L. your God: ‡ "
14 drink offering unto the L. your ‡ "
17 the ministers of the L., weep ‡ "
17 Spare thy people, O L., and give ‡ "
18 the L. be jealous for his land, ‡ "
19 L. will answer and say unto his ‡ "
21 for the L. will do great things. ‡ "
23 and rejoice in the L. your God: ‡ "
26 and praise the name of the L. ‡ "
27 and that I am the L. your God, ‡ "
31 the terrible day of the L. come. ‡ "
32 shall call on the name of the L. ‡ "
32 deliverance, as the L. hath said, ‡ "
32 remnant whom the L. shall call. ‡ "
3: 8 far off: for the L. hath spoken it.‡ "
11 mighty ones to come down, O L. ‡ "
14 day of the L. is near in the valley ‡ "
16 The L. also shall roar out of Zion,‡ "
16 L. will be the hope of his people, ‡ "
17 know that I am the L. your God ‡ "
18 come forth of the house of the L.,‡ "
21 for the L. dwelleth in Zion. ‡ "
Am 1: 2 The L. will roar from Zion, and ‡ "
3 Thus saith the L.; For three ‡ "
5 captivity unto Kir, saith the L. ‡ "
6 Thus saith the L.; For three ‡ "
8 shall perish, saith the L. God. 136
9, 11, 13 Thus saith the L.; For three‡3068
15 his princes together, saith the L.‡ "
2: 1 Thus saith the L.; For three ‡ "
3 thereof with him, saith the L. ‡ "
4 Thus saith the L.; For three ‡ "
4 have despised the law of the L., ‡ "
6 Thus saith the L.; For three ‡ "
11 children of Israel? saith the L. ‡ "
16 naked in that day, saith the L. ‡ "
3: 1 this word that the L. hath spoken‡ "
6 city, and the L. hath not done it? ‡ "
7 Surely the L. God will do nothing, 136
8 the L. God hath spoken, who can "
10 know not to do right, saith the L.,‡3068
11 Therefore thus saith the L. God; 136
12 Thus saith the L.; As the ‡3068
13 house of Jacob, saith the L. God, 136
15 shall have an end, saith the L. ‡3068
4: 2 L. God hath sworn by his holiness, 136
3 then into the palace, saith the L. ‡3068
5 of Israel, saith the L. God. 136

Am 4: 6, 8, 9, 10, 11 unto me, saith the L'. ‡3068
13 The L', The God of hosts, is his ‡ "
5: 3 For thus saith the L' God; The 136
4 the L' unto the house of Israel, ‡3068
6 Seek the L', and ye shall live: ‡ "
8 of the earth: The L' is his name: ‡ "
14 so the L', the God of hosts, shall ‡ "
15 that the L' God of hosts will be ‡ "
16 Therefore the L', the God of hosts, ‡ "
16 the L', saith thus; Wailing shall 136
17 pass through thee, saith the L'. ‡3068
18 you that desire the day of the L'! ‡ "
18 the day of the L' is darkness, and ‡ "
20 not the day of the L' be darkness, ‡ "
27 saith the L', whose name is The ‡ "
6: 8 The L' God hath sworn by himself, 136
8 saith the L' the God of hosts, I ‡3068
10 mention of the name of the L'. ‡ "
11 the L' commandeth, and he will ‡ "
14 saith the L' the God of hosts; ‡ "
7: 1 hath the L' God shewed unto me: 136
2 O L' God, forgive, I beseech thee: "
3 The L' repented for this: It shall ‡3068
3 this: It shall not be, saith the L'. ‡ "
4 hath the L' God shewed unto me: 136
4 the L' God called to contend by fire, "
5 I, O L' God, cease, I beseech thee: "
6 The L' repented for this: This ‡3068
6 also shall not be, saith the L' God. 136
7 the L' stood upon a wall made by a "
8 the L' said unto me, Amos, what ‡3068
8 Then said the L', Behold, I will set 136
15 L' took me as I followed the flock, ‡3068
15 the L' said unto me, Go, prophesy ‡ "
16 hear thou the word of the L': ‡ "
17 thus saith the L'; Thy wife shall ‡ "
8: 1 hath the L' God shewed unto me: 136
2 Then said the L' unto me, The ‡3068
3 howlings in that day, saith the L' 136
7 L' hath sworn by the excellency ‡3068
9 pass in that day, saith the L' God, 136
11 the days come, saith the L' God, "
11 of hearing the words of the L': ‡3068
12 and fro to seek the word of the L', ‡ "
9: 1 saw the L' standing upon the altar: 136
5 L' God of hosts is he that toucheth "
6 of the earth: The L' is his name. ‡3068
7 O children of Israel? saith the L'. ‡ "
8 the eyes of the L' God are upon the 136
8 the house of Jacob, saith the L'. ‡3068
12 called by my name, saith the L' ‡ "
13 the days come, saith the L', that ‡ "
15 given them, saith the L' thy God. ‡ "
Ob 1 Thus saith the L' God concerning 136
1 have heard a rumour from the L', ‡3068
4 I bring thee down, saith the L'. ‡ "
8 I not in that day, saith the L', ‡ "
15 the day of the L' is near upon all ‡ "
18 Esau; for the L' hath spoken it. ‡ "
Jon 1: 1 word of the L' came unto Jonah ‡ "
3 from the presence of the L', and ‡ "
3 from the presence of the L'. ‡ "
4 L' sent out a great wind into the ‡ "
9 I am an Hebrew; and I fear the L', ‡ "
10 fled from the presence of the L', ‡ "
14 they cried unto the L', and said, ‡ "
14 O L', we beseech thee, let us not ‡ "
14 thou, O L', hast done as it pleased ‡ "
16 the men feared the L' exceedingly, ‡ "
16 and offered a sacrifice unto the L', ‡ "
17 the L' had prepared a great fish to ‡ "
2: 1 Jonah prayed unto the L' his God ‡ "
2 of mine affliction unto the L', ‡ "
6 my life from corruption, O L' my ‡ "
7 within me I remembered the L': ‡ "
9 have vowed. Salvation is of the L'. ‡ "
10 the L' spake unto the fish, and it ‡ "
3: 1 word of the L' came unto Jonah ‡ "
3 according to the word of the L'. ‡ "
4: 2 he prayed unto the L', and said, I ‡ "
2 I pray thee, O L', was not this my ‡ "
3 O L', take, I beseech thee, my life ‡ "
4 said the L', Doest thou well to be ‡ "
6 the L' God prepared a gourd, and ‡ "
10 Then said the L', Thou hast had ‡ "
Mic 1: 1 The word of the L' that came to ‡ "
2 the L' God be witness against you, 136
2 the L' from his holy temple. "
3 L' cometh forth out of his place, ‡3068
12 evil came down from the L' unto ‡ "
2: 3 Therefore thus saith the L'; ‡ "
5 lot in the congregation of the L'. ‡ "
7 is the spirit of the L' straitened? ‡ "
13 and the L' on the head of them. ‡ "
3: 4 Then shall they cry unto the L', ‡ "
5 Thus saith the L' concerning the ‡ "
8 of power by the spirit of the L', ‡ "
11 yet will they lean upon the L', ‡ "
11 Is not the L' among us? none evil ‡ "
4: 1 house of the L' shall be established*‡ "
2 us go up to the mountain of the L', ‡ "
2 word of the L' from Jerusalem. ‡ "
4 of the L' of hosts hath spoken it. ‡ "
5 walk in the name of the L' our God ‡ "
6 In that day, saith the L', will I ‡ "
7 the L' shall reign over them in ‡ "
10 the L' shall redeem thee from the ‡ "
12 know not the thoughts of the L', ‡ "
13 consecrate their gain unto the L', ‡ "
13 unto the L' of the whole earth. 113
5: 4 and feed in the strength of the L', ‡3068
4 the majesty of the name of the L' ‡ "
7 many people as a dew from the L', ‡ "
10 to pass in that day, saith the L', ‡ "
6: 1 Hear ye now what the L' saith; ‡ "
2 the L' hath a controversy with his ‡ "

Mic 6: 5 know the righteousness of the L'. ‡3068
6 shall I come before the L', and ‡ "
7 the L' be pleased with thousands ‡ "
8 what doth the L' require of thee, ‡ "
7: 7 Therefore I will look unto the L'; ‡ "
8 the L' shall be a light unto me. ‡ "
9 will bear the indignation of the L', ‡ "
10 unto me, Where is the L' thy God? ‡ "
17 shall be afraid of the L' our God, ‡ "
Na 1: 2 is jealous, and the L' revengeth; ‡ "
2 the L' revengeth, and is furious; ‡ "
2 the L' will take vengeance on his ‡ "
3 The L' is slow to anger, and great ‡ "
3 L' hath his way in the whirlwind ‡ "
7 The L' is good, a strong hold in ‡ "
9 do ye imagine against the L'? ‡ "
11 that imagineth evil against the L', ‡ "
12 Thus saith the L'; Though they ‡ "
14 the L' hath given a commandment ‡ "
2: 2 For the L' hath turned away the ‡ "
13 against thee, saith the L' of hosts, ‡ "
3: 5 against thee, saith the L' of hosts; ‡ "
Hab 1: 2 O L', how long shall I cry, and ‡ "
12 not from everlasting, O L' my God, ‡ "
12 O L', thou hast ordained them for ‡ "
2: 2 And the L' answered me, and said, ‡ "
13 is it not of the L' of hosts that the ‡ "
14 knowledge of the glory of the L', ‡ "
20 But the L' is in his holy temple: ‡ "
3: 2 O L', I have heard thy speech, and ‡ "
2 O L', revive thy work in the midst ‡ "
8 Was the L' displeased against the ‡ "
18 Yet I will rejoice in the L', I will ‡ "
19 The L' God is my strength, and he* "
Zep 1: 1 word of the L' which came unto ‡ "
2, 3 from off the land, saith the L'. ‡ "
5 worship and that swear by the L', ‡ "
6 that are turned back from the L'; ‡ "
6 those that have not sought the L', ‡ "
7 at the presence of the L' God: 136
7 for the day of the L' is at hand: ‡3068
7 the L' hath prepared a sacrifice, ‡ "
10 to pass in that day, saith the L', ‡ "
12 The L' will not do good, neither ‡ "
14 The great day of the L' is near, it ‡ "
14 even the voice of the day of the L': ‡ "
17 they have sinned against the L': ‡ "
2: 2 fierce anger of the L' come upon ‡ "
3 Seek ye the L', all ye meek of the ‡ "
5 the word of the L' is against you; ‡ "
7 the L' their God shall visit them, ‡ "
9 saith the L' of hosts, the God of ‡ "
10 the people of the L' of hosts. ‡ "
11 The L' will be terrible unto them: ‡ "
3: 2 she trusted not in the L'; she ‡ "
5 The just L' is in the midst thereof; ‡ "
8 wait ye upon me, saith the L', ‡ "
9 all call upon the name of the L', ‡ "
12 shall trust in the name of the L'. ‡ "
15 L' hath taken away thy judgments, ‡ "
15 even the L', is in the midst of thee: ‡ "
17 L' thy God in the midst of thee is ‡ "
20 before your eyes, saith the L'. ‡ "
Hag 1: 1 the word of the L' by Haggai the ‡ "
2 speaketh the L' of hosts, saying, ‡ "
3 the word of the L' by Haggai the ‡ "
5, 7 saith the L' of hosts; Consider ‡ "
8 and I will be glorified, saith the L'. ‡ "
9 it. Why? saith the L' of hosts. ‡ "
12 obeyed the voice of the L' their ‡ "
12 as the L' their God had sent him, ‡ "
12 the people did fear before the L'. ‡ "
13 saying, I am with you, saith the L'. ‡ "
14 And the L' stirred up the spirit of ‡ "
14 did work in the house of the L' of ‡ "
2: 1 the word of the L' by the prophet ‡ "
4 strong, O Zerubbabel, saith the L'; ‡ "
4 ye people of the land, saith the L', ‡ "
4 am with you, saith the L' of hosts: ‡ "
6 For thus saith the L' of hosts; ‡ "
7 with glory, saith the L' of hosts. ‡ "
8 gold is mine, saith the L' of hosts. ‡ "
9 the former, saith the L' of hosts: ‡ "
9 I give peace, saith the L' of hosts. ‡ "
10 the word of the L' by Haggai the ‡ "
11 Thus saith the L' of hosts; Ask ‡ "
14 nation before me, saith the L'; ‡ "
15 a stone in the temple of the L': ‡ "
17 ye turned not to me, saith the L'. ‡ "
20 word of the L' came unto Haggai ‡ "
23 In that day, saith the L' of hosts, ‡ "
23 will I take thee,...saith the L', and ‡ "
23 chosen thee, saith the L' of hosts. ‡ "
Zec 1: 1 the word of the L' unto Zechariah, ‡ "
2 L' hath been sore displeased with ‡ "
3 them, Thus saith the L' of hosts; ‡ "
3 ye unto me, saith the L' of hosts, ‡ "
3 unto you, saith the L' of hosts. ‡ "
4 Thus saith the L' of hosts; Turn ‡ "
4 hearken unto me, saith the L'. ‡ "
6 Like as the L' of hosts thought ‡ "
7 the word of the L' unto Zechariah, ‡ "
9 said I, O my l', what are these? 113
10 are they whom the L' hath sent ‡3068
11 they answered the angel of the L' ‡ "
12 the angel of the L' answered and ‡ "
12 O L' of hosts, how long wilt thou ‡ "
13 L' answered the angel that talked ‡ "
14 Thus saith the L' of hosts; I am ‡ "
16 thus saith the L'; I am returned ‡ "
16 be built in it, saith the L' of hosts, ‡ "
17 Thus saith the L' of hosts; My ‡ "
17 the L' shall yet comfort Zion, and ‡ "
20 L' shewed me four carpenters. ‡ "
2: 5 For I, saith the L', will be unto ‡ "
6 land of the north, saith the L'. ‡ "

Zec 2: 6 winds of the heaven, saith the L'. ‡3068
8 thus saith the L' of hosts; After ‡ "
9 that the L' of hosts hath sent me. ‡ "
10 in the midst of thee, saith the L'. ‡ "
11 nations shall be joined to the L' ‡ "
11 that the L' of hosts hath sent me ‡ "
12 L' shall inherit Judah his portion ‡ "
13 silent, O all flesh, before the L': ‡ "
3: 1 priest...before the angel of the L', ‡ "
2 And the L' said unto Satan, ‡ "
2 The L' rebuke thee, O Satan; ‡ "
2 L' that hath chosen Jerusalem ‡ "
5 And the angel of the L' stood by. ‡ "
6 the angel of the L' protested unto ‡ "
7 Thus saith the L' of hosts; If thou ‡ "
9 the graving thereof, saith the L' ‡ "
10 In that day, saith the L' of hosts, ‡ "
4: 4 me, saying, What are these, my l'? 113
5 these be? And I said, No, my l'. "
6 word of the L' unto Zerubbabel, ‡3068
6 by my Spirit, saith the L' of hosts. ‡ "
8 the word of the L' came unto me, ‡ "
9 that the L' of hosts hath sent me ‡ "
10 they are the eyes of the L', which ‡ "
13 these be? And I said, No, my l'. 113
14 stand by the L' of the whole earth. "
5: 4 it forth, saith the L' of hosts, ‡3068
6: 4 with me, What are these, my l'? 113
5 before the L' of all the earth. "
9 the word of the L' came unto me, ‡3068
12 Thus speaketh the L' of hosts, ‡ "
12 shall build the temple of the L': ‡ "
13 shall build the temple of the L'; ‡ "
14 memorial in the temple of the L'. ‡ "
15 and build in the temple of the L', ‡ "
15 that the L' of hosts hath sent me ‡ "
15 diligently obey the voice of the L' ‡ "
7: 1 word of...L' came unto Zechariah ‡ "
2 their men, to pray before the L', ‡ "
3 were in the house of the L' of ‡ "
4 word of the L' of hosts unto me, ‡ "
7 the words which the L' hath cried ‡ "
8 word of...L' came unto Zechariah, ‡ "
9 Thus speaketh the L' of hosts, ‡ "
12 words which the L' of hosts hath ‡ "
12 came a great wrath from the L' ‡ "
13 not hear, saith the L' of hosts: ‡ "
8: 1 word of the L' of hosts came to me, ‡ "
2 Thus saith the L' of hosts; I was ‡ "
3 Thus saith the L'; I am returned ‡ "
3 the mountain of the L' of hosts ‡ "
4 Thus saith the L' of hosts; There ‡ "
6 Thus saith the L' of hosts; If it be ‡ "
6 mine eyes? saith the L' of hosts. ‡ "
7 Thus saith the L' of hosts; ‡ "
9 Thus saith the L' of hosts; Let ‡ "
9 foundation of the house of the L' ‡ "
11 former days, saith the L' of hosts. ‡ "
14 thus saith the L' of hosts; As I ‡ "
14 me to wrath, saith the L' of hosts, ‡ "
17 things that I hate, saith the L'. ‡ "
18 the word of the L' of hosts came ‡ "
19 Thus saith the L' of hosts; The ‡ "
20 saith the L' of hosts; It shall yet ‡ "
21 go speedily to pray before the L', ‡ "
21 and to seek the L' of hosts: I will ‡ "
22 shall come to seek the L' of hosts ‡ "
22 and to pray before the L'. ‡ "
23 saith the L' of hosts; In those ‡ "
9: 1 The burden of the word of the L' ‡ "
1 of Israel, shall be toward the L'. ‡ "
4 Behold, the L' will cast her out, 136
14 the L' shall be seen over them, ‡3068
14 the L' God shall blow the trumpet, 136
15 the L' of hosts shall defend them; ‡3068
16 L' their God shall save them in ‡ "
10: 1 Ask ye of the L' rain in the time ‡ "
1 the L' shall make bright clouds, ‡ "
3 L' of hosts hath visited his flock ‡ "
5 because the L' is with them, and ‡ "
6 I am the L' their God, and will ‡ "
7 their heart shall rejoice in the L'. ‡ "
12 will strengthen them in the L'; ‡ "
12 down in his name, saith the L'. ‡ "
11: 4 Thus saith the L' my God; Feed ‡ "
5 sell them say, Blessed be the L'; ‡ "
6 inhabitants of...land, saith the L': ‡ "
11 that it was the word of the L'. ‡ "
13 the L' said unto me, Cast it unto ‡ "
13 the potter in the house of the L'. ‡ "
15 the L' said unto me, Take unto ‡ "
12: 1 burden of the word of the L' for ‡ "
1 saith the L', which stretcheth ‡ "
4 In that day, saith the L', I will ‡ "
5 be my strength in the L' of hosts ‡ "
7 The L' also shall save the tents of ‡ "
8 the L' defend the inhabitants of ‡ "
8 the angel of the L' before them. ‡ "
13: 2 in that day, saith the L' of hosts, ‡ "
3 lies in the name of the L': ‡ "
7 is my fellow, saith the L' of hosts: ‡ "
8 that in all the land, saith the L', ‡ "
9 they shall say, The L' is my God. ‡ "
14: 1 Behold, the day of the L' cometh, ‡ "
3 Then shall the L' go forth, and ‡ "
5 and the L' my God shall come, ‡ "
7 which shall be known to the L', ‡ "
9 L' shall be king over all the earth: ‡ "
9 in that day shall there be one L', ‡ "
12 the L' shall smite all the people ‡ "
13 a great tumult from the L' shall ‡ "
16, 17 to worship the King, the L' of ‡ "
18 the L' will smite the heathen ‡ "
20 horses, Holiness Unto The L'; ‡ "
21 be holiness unto the L' of hosts: ‡ "
21 in the house of the L' of hosts. ‡ "

Mal 1: 1 The burden of the word of the *L*· ‡3068
2 I have loved you, saith the *L*·. ‡ "
2 Jacob's brother? saith the *L*·: ‡ "
4 thus saith the *L*· of hosts, They ‡ "
4 people against whom the *L*· hath ‡ "
5 The *L*· will be magnified from ‡ "
6 saith the *L*· of hosts unto you, ‡ "
7 The table of the *L*· is contemptible. ‡ "
8 thy person? saith the *L*· of hosts. ‡ "
9 persons? saith the *L*· of hosts. ‡ "
10 in you, saith the *L*· of hosts, ‡ "
11 the heathen, saith the *L*· of hosts. ‡ "
12 The table of the *L*· is polluted; ‡ "
13 snuffed at it, saith the *L*· of hosts; ‡ "
13 this of your hand? saith the *L*·. ‡ "
14 unto the *L*· a corrupt thing: 136
14 great King, saith the *L*· of hosts, ‡3068
2: 2 my name, saith the *L*· of hosts, ‡ "
4 with Levi, saith the *L*· of hosts. ‡ "
7 the messenger of the *L*· of hosts. ‡ "
8 of Levi, saith the *L*· of hosts. ‡ "
11 profaned the holiness of the *L*· ‡ "
12 The *L*· will cut off the man that ‡ "
12 offereth an offering unto the *L*· ‡ "
13 the altar of the *L*· with tears, ‡ "
14 the *L*· hath been witness between ‡ "
16 For the *L*·, the God of Israel, saith ‡ "
16 garment, saith the *L*· of hosts: ‡ "
17 wearied the *L*· with your words. ‡ "
17 evil is good in the sight of the *L*·, ‡ "
3: 1 and the *L*·, whom ye seek, shall 113
1 shall come, saith the *L*· of hosts. ‡3068
3 may offer unto the *L*· an offering ‡ "
4 Jerusalem be pleasant unto the *L*·, ‡ "
5 fear not me, saith the *L*· of hosts. ‡ "
6 For I am the *L*·, I change not; ‡ "
7 unto you, saith the *L*· of hosts. ‡ "
10 herewith, saith the *L*· of hosts, ‡ "
11 in the field, saith the *L*· of hosts. ‡ "
12 land, saith the *L*· of hosts. ‡ "
13 stout against me, saith the *L*·. ‡ "
14 walked mournfully before the *L*· ‡ "
16 that feared the *L*· spake often one ‡ "
16 and the *L*· hearkened, and heard ‡ "
16 him for them that feared the *L*·, ‡ "
17 they shall be mine, saith the *L*· ‡ "
4: 1 shall burn them up, saith the *L*· ‡ "
3 that I shall do this, saith the *L*· ‡ "
5 great and dreadful day of the *L*·: ‡ "
M't 1: 20 angel of the *L*· appeared unto him 2962
22 spoken of the *L*· by the prophet, "
24 angel of the *L*· had bidden him, "
2: 13 angel of the *L*· appeareth to Joseph "
15 spoken of the *L*· by the prophet, "
19 an angel of the *L*· appeareth in a "
3: 3 Prepare ye the way of the *L*·, make "
4: 7 shalt not tempt the *L*· thy God. "
10 Thou shalt worship the *L*· thy God, "
5: 33 perform unto the *L*· thine oaths: "
7: 21 every one that saith unto me, *L*·, *L*·, "
22 *L*·, *L*·, have we not prophesied in "
8: 2 *L*·, if thou wilt, thou canst make "
6 *L*·, my servant lieth at home sick "
8 said, *L*·, I am not worthy that thou "
21 *L*·, suffer me first to go and bury "
25 awoke him, saying, *L*·, save us: "
9: 28 this? They said unto him, Yea, *L*·. "
38 ye therefore the *L*· of the harvest, "
10: 24 master, nor the servant above his *l*·. "
25 master, and the servant as his *l*·. "
11: 25 O Father, *L*· of heaven and earth, "
12: 8 man is *L*· even of the sabbath day. "
13: 51 things? They say unto him, Yea, *L*·.* "
14: 28 *L*·, if it be thou, bid me come unto "
30 sink, he cried, saying, *L*·, save me. "
15: 22 Have mercy on me, O *L*·, thou son "
25 worshipped him, saying, *L*·, help me. "
27 Truth, *L*·: yet the dogs eat of the "
16: 22 him, saying, Be it far from thee, *L*·: "
17: 4 *L*·, it is good for us to be here: if "
15 *L*·, have mercy on my son: for he "
18: 21 *L*·, how oft shall my brother sin "
25 his *l*· commanded him to be sold, "
26 *L*·, have patience with me, and I "
27 *l*· of that servant was moved with "
31 told unto their *l*· all that was done. "
32 Then his *l*·, after that he had called "
34 And his *l*· was wroth, and delivered "
20: 8 the *l*· of the vineyard saith unto his "
30, 31 Have mercy on us, O *L*·, thou "
33 *L*·, that our eyes may be opened. "
21: 3 say, The *L*· hath need of them; and "
9 that cometh in the name of the *L*·; "
40 *l*· therefore of the vineyard cometh, "
22: 37 love the *L*· thy God with all thy "
43 then doth David in spirit call him *L*·, "
44 The *L*· said...Sit thou on my right "
44 unto my *L*·, Sit thou on my right "
45 If David then call him *L*·, how is he "
23: 39 that cometh in the name of the *L*·. "
24: 42 not what hour your *L*· doth come. "
45 whom his *l*· hath made ruler over "
46 his *l*· when he cometh shall find so "
48 heart, My *l*· delayeth his coming; "
50 *l*· of that servant shall come in a "
25: 11 virgins, saying, *L*·, *L*·, open to us. "
19 time the *l*· of those servants cometh, "
20 *L*·, thou deliveredst unto me five "
21 His *l*· said unto him, Well done, thou "
21 enter thou into the joy of thy *l*·. "
22 *L*·, thou deliveredst unto me two "
23 His *l*· said unto him, Well done, good "
23 enter thou into the joy of thy *l*·. "
24 *L*·, I knew thee that thou art an "
26 His *l*· answered and said unto him, "
37, 44 *L*·, when saw we thee an hungred, "

M't 26: 22 of them to say unto him, *L*·, is it I? 2962
27: 10 potter's field, as the *L*· appointed "
28: 2 the angel of the *L*· descended from "
6 Come, see the place where the *L*· lay. "
M'r 1: 3 Prepare ye the way of the *L*·, make "
2: 28 Son of man is *L*· also of the sabbath. "
5: 19 how great things the *L*· hath done "
7: 28 and said unto him, Yes, *L*·: yet the "
9: 24 *L*·, I believe; help thou mine * "
10: 51 *L*·, that I might receive my sight. *4462
11: 3 ye that the *L*· hath need of him; 2962
9 that cometh in the name of the *L*·: "
10 that cometh in the name of the *L*·:* "
12: 9 therefore the *l*· of the vineyard do? "
29 Israel; The *L*· our God is one *L*·: "
30 love the *L*· thy God with all thy "
36 The *L*· said...Sit thou on my right "
36 said to my *L*·, Sit thou on my right "
37 therefore himself calleth him *L*·; "
13: 20 the *L*· had shortened those days, "
16: 19 after the *L*· had spoken unto them, "
20 the *L*· working with them, and "
Lu 1: 6 and ordinances of the *L*· blameless. "
9 he went into the temple of the *L*·. "
11 appeared unto him an angel of the *L*· "
15 shall be great in the sight of the *L*·, "
16 shall he turn to the *L*· their God. "
17 ready a people prepared for the *L*·. "
25 Thus hath the *L*· dealt with me in "
28 highly favoured, the *L*· is with thee: "
32 the *L*· God shall give unto him the "
38 Behold the handmaid of the *L*·; be "
43 mother of my *L*· should come to me? "
45 which were told her from the *L*·. "
46 said, My soul doth magnify the *L*·, "
58 how the *L*· had shewed great mercy "
66 the hand of the *L*· was with him. "
68 Blessed be the *L*· God of Israel; for "
76 shalt go before the face of the *L*· to "
2: 9 the angel of the *L*· came upon them, "
9 glory of the *L*· shone round about "
11 a Saviour, which is Christ the *L*·. "
15 which the *L*· hath made known unto "
22 Jerusalem, to present him to the *L*·; "
23 (As it is written in the law of the *L*·, "
23 womb shall be called holy to the *L*·;) "
24 which is said in the law of the *L*·, "
29 *L*·, now lettest thou thy servant 1203
38 gave thanks likewise unto the *L*·,*2962
39 according to the law of the *L*·, they "
3: 4 Prepare ye the way of the *L*·, make "
4: 8 Thou shalt worship the *L*· thy God, "
12 shalt not tempt the *L*· thy God. "
18 Spirit of the *L*· is upon me, because "
19 preach the acceptable year of the *L*·. "
5: 8 me; for I am a sinful man, O *L*·. "
12 *L*·, if thou wilt, thou canst make me "
17 power of the *L*· was present to heal "
6: 5 Son of man is *L*· also of the sabbath. "
46 why call ye me, *L*·, *L*·, and do not "
7: 6 unto him, *L*·, trouble not thyself: "
13 And when the *L*· saw her, he had "
31 the *L*· said, Whereunto then shall* "
9: 54 *L*·, wilt thou that we command fire "
57 *L*·, I will follow thee whithersoever* "
59 *L*·, suffer me first to go and bury my "
61 also said, *L*·, I will follow thee; but "
10: 1 the *L*· appointed other seventy also, "
2 ye therefore the *L*· of the harvest, "
17 *L*·, even the devils are subject unto "
21 O Father, *L*· of heaven and earth, "
27 love the *L*· thy God with all thy "
40 said, *L*·, dost thou not care that my "
11: 1 *L*·, teach us to pray, as John also "
39 the *L*· said unto him, Now do ye "
12: 36 like unto men that wait for their *l*·, "
37 the *l*· when he cometh shall find "
41 *L*·, speakest thou this parable unto "
42 *L*· said, Who then is that faithful "
42 whom his *l*· shall make ruler over "
43 his *l*· when he cometh shall find so "
45 heart, My *l*· delayeth his coming; "
46 *l*· of that servant will come in a day "
13: 8 *L*·, let it alone this year also, till I "
15 *L*· then answered him, and said, "
23 *L*·, are there few that be saved? "
25 *L*·,...open unto us; and he shall "
25 *L*·, open unto us; and he shall * "
35 that cometh in the name of the *L*·. "
14: 21 and shewed his *l*· these things. "
22 said, *L*·, it is done as thou hast "
23 the *l*· said unto the servant, Go out "
16: 3 for my *l*· taketh away from me the "
5 How much owest thou unto my *l*·? "
8 *l*· commended the unjust steward, "
17: 5 apostles said unto the *L*·, Increase "
6 *L*· said, If ye had faith as a grain "
37 Where, *L*·? And he said unto them, "
18: 6 *L*· said, Hear what the unjust judge "
41 *L*·, that I may receive my sight. "
19: 8 Zacchæus...and said unto the *L*·; "
8 *L*·, the half of my goods I give to "
16 *L*·, thy pound hath gained ten "
18 *L*·, thy pound hath gained five "
20 *L*·, behold, here is thy pound, which "
25 unto him, *L*·, he hath ten pounds.) "
31 Because the *L*· hath need of him. "
34 they said, The *L*· hath need of him. "
38 that cometh in the name of the *L*·: "
20: 13 said the *l*· of the vineyard, What "
15 *l*· of the vineyard do unto them? "
37 calleth the *L*· the God of Abraham, "
42 The *L*· said...Sit thou on my right "
42 unto my *L*·, Sit thou on my right "
44 David therefore calleth him *L*·, "
22: 31 the *L*· said, Simon, Simon, behold,* "

Lu 22: 33 *L*·, I am ready to go with thee, 2962
38 *L*·, behold, here are two swords. "
49 *L*·, shall we smite with the sword? "
61 *L*· turned, and looked upon Peter. "
61 remembered the word of the *L*·, "
23: 42 *L*·, remember me when thou comest* "
24: 3 found not the body of the *L*· Jesus. "
34 The *L*· is risen indeed, and hath "
Joh 1: 23 Make straight the way of the *L*·, as "
4: 1 the *L*· knew how the Pharisees had "
6: 23 after that the *L*· had given thanks:) "
34 *L*·, evermore give us this bread. "
68 him, *L*·, to whom shall we go? "
8: 11 She said, No man, *L*·. And Jesus "
9: 36 Who is he, *L*·, that I might believe "
38 *L*·, I believe. And he worshipped "
11: 2 anointed the *L*· with ointment, "
3 *L*·, behold, he whom thou lovest is "
12 *L*·, if he sleep, he shall do well. "
21 Jesus, *L*·, if thou hadst been here, "
27 Yea, *L*·: I believe that thou art the "
32 *L*·, if thou hadst been here, my "
34 said unto him, *L*·, come and see. "
39 *L*·, by this time he stinketh: for he "
12: 13 that cometh in the name of the *L*·. "
38 *L*·, who hath believed our report? "
38 the arm of the *L*· been revealed? "
13: 6 him, *L*·, dost thou wash my feet? "
9 *L*·, not my feet only, but also my "
13 Ye call me Master and *L*·: and ye "
14 If I then, your *L*· and Master, have "
16 servant is not greater than his *l*·; "
25 saith unto him, *L*·, who is it? "
36 unto him, *L*·, whither goest thou? "
37 *L*·, why cannot I follow thee now? "
14: 5 *L*·, we know not whither thou goest; "
8 him, *L*·, shew us the Father, and it "
22 *L*·, how is it that thou wilt manifest "
15: 15 knoweth not what his *l*· doeth: but "
20 servant is not greater than his *l*·. "
20: 2 away the *L*· out of the sepulchre, "
13 they have taken away my *L*·, and I "
18 disciples that she had seen the *L*·, "
20 disciples glad, when they saw the *L*·. "
25 said unto him, We have seen the *L*·. "
28 said unto him, My *L*· and my God. "
21: 7 loved saith unto Peter, It is the *L*·. "
7 Peter heard that it was the *L*·, he "
12 thou? knowing that it was the *L*·. "
15, 16 *L*·; thou knowest that I love "
17 *L*·, thou knowest all things; thou "
20 *L*·, which is he that betrayeth thee? "
21 *L*·, and what shall this man do? "
Ac 1: 6 *L*·, wilt thou at this time restore "
21 time that the *L*· Jesus went in and "
24 Thou, *L*·, which knowest the hearts "
2: 20 and notable day of the *L*· come: "
21 the name of the *L*· shall be saved. "
25 the *L*· always before my face; for "
34 The *L*· said...Sit thou on my right "
34 unto my *L*·, Sit thou on my right "
36 have crucified, both *L*· and Christ. "
39 many as the *L*· our God shall call. "
47 *L*· added to the church daily such "
3: 19 come from the presence of the *L*·; "
22 prophet shall the *L*· your God raise "
4: 24 *L*·, thou art God, which hast made 1203
26 gathered together against the *L*·, 2962
29 now, *L*·, behold their threatenings: "
33 of the resurrection of the *L*· Jesus: "
5: 9 to tempt the Spirit of the *L*·? "
14 believers were...added to the *L*·, "
19 the angel of the *L*· by night opened "
7: 30 angel of the *L*· in a flame of fire in* "
31 the voice of the *L*· came unto him, "
33 Then said the *L*· to him, Put off thy "
37 prophet shall the *L*· your God raise* "
49 will ye build me? saith the *L*·: or "
59 saying, *L*· Jesus, receive my spirit. "
60 *L*·, lay not this sin to their charge. "
8: 16 in the name of the *L*· Jesus.) "
24 Pray ye to the *L*· for me, that none "
25 and preached the word of the *L*·, "
26 angel of the *L*· spake unto Philip, "
39 Spirit of the *L*· caught away Philip, "
9: 1 against the disciples of the *L*·, "
5 And he said, Who art thou, *L*·? "
5 And the *L*· said, I am Jesus whom* "
6 *L*·, what wilt thou have me to do?* "
6 *L*· said unto him, Arise, and go * "
10 said the *L*· in a vision, Ananias. "
10 And he said, Behold, I am here, *L*·. "
11 the *L*· said unto him, Arise, and go "
13 *L*·, I have heard by many of this "
15 the *L*· said unto him, Go thy way: "
17 the *L*·, even Jesus, that appeared "
27 how he had seen the *L*· in the way, "
29 boldly in the name of the *L*· Jesus, "
31 walking in the fear of the *L*·, and in "
35 saw him and turned to the *L*·. "
42 and many believed in the *L*·. "
10: 4 was afraid, and said, What is it, *L*·? "
14 Not so, *L*·; for I have never eaten "
36 by Jesus Christ: (he is *L*· of all:) "
48 be baptized in the name of the *L*·.* "
11: 8 Not so, *L*·: for nothing common or "
16 remembered I the word of the *L*·, "
17 who believed on the *L*· Jesus Christ; "
20 Grecians, preaching the *L*· Jesus. "
21 the hand of the *L*· was with them: "
21 believed, and turned unto the *L*·. "
23 they would cleave unto the *L*·. "
24 much people was added unto the *L*·. "
12: 7 the angel of the *L*· came upon him, "
11 that the *L*· hath sent his angel, and "
17 how the *L*· had brought him out of "

Ac 12:23 the angel of the L' smote him, 2962
13: 2 As they ministered to the L', and "
10 to pervert the right ways of the L'? "
11 the hand of the L' is upon thee, and "
12 astonished at the doctrine of the L'. "
47 For so hath the L' commanded us, "
48 and glorified the word of the L': * "
49 the word of the L' was published "
14: 3 they speaking boldly in the L', "
23 they commended them to the L', "
15:11 the grace of the L' Jesus Christ "
17 of men might seek after the L', "
17 saith the L', who doeth all these "
26 for the name of our L' Jesus Christ. "
35 and preaching the word of the L', "
36 have preached the word of the L', "
16:10 the L' had called us for to preach * "
14 whose heart the L' opened, that she "
15 judged me to be faithful to the L', "
31 Believe on the L' Jesus Christ, and "
32 spake unto him the word of the L', "
17:24 that he is L' of heaven and earth, "
27 That they should seek the L', if * "
18: 8 believed on the L' with all his house; "
9 spake the L' to Paul in the night by "
25 was instructed in the way of the L'; "
25 diligently the things of the L', * "
19: 5 baptized in the name of the L' Jesus. "
10 Asia heard the word of the L' Jesus, "
13 spirits the name of the L' Jesus, "
17 name of the L' Jesus was magnified. "
20:19 Serving the L' with all humility of "
21 faith toward our L' Jesus Christ. "
24 I have received of the L' Jesus, to "
35 remember the words of the L' Jesus, "
21:13 for the name of the L' Jesus. "
14 saying, The will of the L' be done. "
20 they heard it, they glorified the L', * "
22: 8 And I answered, Who art thou, L'? "
10 And I said, What shall I do, L'? "
10 And the L' said unto me, Arise, and "
16 sins, calling on the name of the L'. * "
19 L', they know that I imprisoned and "
23:11 night following the L' stood by him, "
25:26 no certain thing to write unto my l'. "
26:15 And I said, Who art thou, L'? And "
28:31 which concern the L' Jesus Christ, "
Ro 1: 3 his Son Jesus Christ our L', which* "
7 our Father, and the L' Jesus Christ. "
4: 8 to whom the L' will not impute sin. "
24 that raised up Jesus our L' from the "
5: 1 God through our L' Jesus Christ: "
11 in God through our L' Jesus Christ, "
21 eternal life by Jesus Christ our L'. "
6:11 God through Jesus Christ our L'. * "
23 life through Jesus Christ our L'. "
7:25 God through Jesus Christ our L'. "
8:39 God, which is in Christ Jesus our L'. "
9:28 a short work will the L' make upon "
29 the L' of Sabaoth had left us a seed, "
10: 9 confess with thy mouth the L' Jesus, "
12 the same L' over all is rich unto all "
13 shall call upon the name of the L' "
16 L', who hath believed our report? "
11: 3 L', they have killed thy prophets, "
34 who hath known the mind of the L'? "
12:11 fervent in spirit; serving the L'; "
19 is mine; I will repay, saith the L'. "
13:14 But put ye on the L' Jesus Christ, "
14: 6 the day, regardeth it unto the L'; "
6 day, to the L' he doth not regard it. "
6 He that eateth, eateth to the L', for "
6 eateth not, to the L' he eateth not, "
8 whether we live, we live unto the L'; "
8 whether we die, we die unto the L': "
9 be L' both of the dead and living. 2961
11 As I live, saith the L', every knee 2962
14 and am persuaded by the L' Jesus, "
15: 6 the Father of our L' Jesus Christ. "
11 again, Praise the L', all ye Gentiles; "
30 for the L' Jesus Christ's sake, and "
16: 2 That ye receive her in the L', as "
8 Greet Amplias my beloved in the L'. "
11 of Narcissus, which are in the L'. "
12 and Tryphosa, who labour in the L'. "
12 which laboured much in the L'. "
13 Salute Rufus chosen in the L', and "
18 such serve not our L' Jesus Christ, "
20 grace of our L' Jesus Christ be with "
22 this epistle, salute you in the L'. "
24 grace of our L' Jesus Christ be with* "
1Co 1: 2 the name of Jesus Christ our L', "
3 and from the L' Jesus Christ. "
7 the coming of our L' Jesus Christ: "
8 in the day of our L' Jesus Christ. "
9 of his Son Jesus Christ our L'. "
10 by the name of our L' Jesus Christ, "
31 that glorieth, let him glory in the L'. "
2: 8 not have crucified the L' of glory. "
16 who hath known the mind of the L', "
3: 5 even as the L' gave to every man? "
20 L' knoweth the thoughts of the wise, "
4: 4 but he that judgeth me is the L'. "
5 before the time, until the L' come, "
17 beloved son, and faithful in the L', "
19 come to you shortly, if the L' will, "
5: 4 In the name of our L' Jesus Christ, "
4 the power of our L' Jesus Christ. "
5 be saved in the day of the L' Jesus. "
6:11 justified in the name of the L' Jesus, "
13 not for fornication, but for the L'; "
13 and the L' for the body. "
14 God hath both raised up the L', and "
17 is joined unto the L' is one spirit. "
7:10 I command, yet not I, but the L', "
12 But to the rest speak I, not the L': "

1Co 7:17 as the L' hath called every one, as *2962
22 For he that is called in the L', being "
25 I have no commandment of the L': "
25 that hath obtained mercy of the L' "
32 for the things that belong to the L', "
32 how he may please the L': "
34 careth for the things of the L', that "
35 ye may attend upon the L' without "
39 to whom she will; only in the L'. "
8: 6 and one L' Jesus Christ, by whom "
9: 1 have I not seen Jesus Christ our L'? "
1 are not ye my work in the L'? "
2 of mine apostleship are ye in the L'. "
5 and as the brethren of the L', and "
14 Even so hath the L' ordained that "
10:21 Ye cannot drink the cup of the L', "
22 Do we provoke the L' to jealousy? "
11:11 woman without the man, in the L'. "
23 I have received of the L' that which "
23 That the L' Jesus the same night "
27 bread, and drink this cup of the L', "
27 of the body and blood of the L'. "
32 judged, we are chastened of the L', "
12: 3 no man can say that Jesus is the L', "
5 administrations, but the same L'. "
14:21 will they not hear me, saith the L'. "
37 are the commandments of the L'. "
15:31 which I have in Christ Jesus our L', "
47 second man is the L' from heaven.* "
57 victory through our L' Jesus Christ. "
58 abounding in the work of the L', "
58 your labour is not in vain in the L'. "
16: 7 a while with you, if the L' permit. "
10 for he worketh the work of the L', "
19 Priscilla salute you much in the L', "
22 man love not the L' Jesus Christ, "
23 grace of our L' Jesus Christ be with "
2Co 1: 2 and from the L' Jesus Christ. "
3 the Father of our L' Jesus Christ, "
14 are ours in the day of the L' Jesus. "
2:12 door was opened unto me of the L', "
3:16 when it shall turn to the L', the vail "
17 Now the L' is that Spirit: and where "
17 where the Spirit of the L' is, there "
18 as in a glass the glory of the L', "
18 glory even as by the Spirit of the L'. "
4: 5 ourselves, but Christ Jesus the L'; "
10 the body the dying of the L' Jesus, * "
14 he which raised up the L' Jesus "
5: 6 body, we are absent from the L': "
8 body, and to be present with the L'. "
11 Knowing...the terror of the L', we "
6:17 and be ye separate, saith the L', "
18 daughters, saith the L' Almighty. "
8: 5 gave their own selves to the L', and "
9 ye know the grace of our L' Jesus "
19 by us to the glory of the same L', "
21 not only in the sight of the L', but "
10: 8 the L' hath given us for edification, "
17 glorieth, let him glory in the L'. "
18 but whom the L' commendeth. "
11:17 I speak, I speak it not after the L', "
31 and Father of our L' Jesus Christ, "
12: 1 visions and revelations of the L'. "
8 this thing I besought the L' thrice, "
13:10 power which the L' hath given me "
14 The grace of the L' Jesus Christ, "
Ga 1: 3 and from our L' Jesus Christ, "
4: 1 a servant, though he be l' of all; "
5:10 confidence in you through the L', "
6:14 in the cross of our L' Jesus Christ, "
17 my body the marks of the L' Jesus.* "
18 grace of our L' Jesus Christ be with "
Eph 1: 2 and from the L' Jesus Christ. "
3 and Father of our L' Jesus Christ, "
15 heard of your faith in the L' Jesus, "
17 That the God of our L' Jesus Christ, "
2:21 unto an holy temple in the L': "
3:11 he purposed in Christ Jesus our L': "
14 the Father of our L' Jesus Christ,* "
4: 1 I therefore, the prisoner of the L', "
5 One L', one faith, one baptism, "
17 I say therefore, and testify in the L', "
5: 8 but now are ye light in the L': walk "
10 what is acceptable unto the L'. "
17 what the will of the L' is. "
19 melody in your heart to the L'; "
20 in the name of our L' Jesus Christ; "
22 your own husbands, as unto the L'. "
29 it, even as the L' the church: *
6: 1 obey your parents in the L': for "
4 nurture and admonition of the L'. "
7 good will doing service, as to the L', "
8 the same shall he receive of the L', "
10 my brethren, be strong in the L', "
21 and faithful minister in the L', "
23 the Father and the L' Jesus Christ. "
24 them that love our L' Jesus Christ "
Ph'p 1: 2 and from the L' Jesus Christ. "
14 And many of the brethren in the L', "
2:11 confess that Jesus Christ is L', to "
19 But I trust in the L' Jesus to send "
24 I trust in the L' that I also myself "
29 Receive him therefore in the L' with "
3: 1 my brethren, rejoice in the L'. "
8 knowledge of Christ Jesus my L': "
20 for the Saviour, the L' Jesus Christ: "
4: 1 and crown, so stand fast in the L', "
2 they be of the same mind in the L'. "
4 Rejoice in the L' alway: and again "
5 unto all men. The L' is at hand. "
10 But I rejoiced in the L' greatly, that "
23 grace of our L' Jesus Christ be with "
Col 1: 2 our Father and the L' Jesus Christ.* "
3 the Father of our L' Jesus Christ, "
10 That ye might walk worthy of the L' "

Col 2: 6 received Christ Jesus the L', so 2962
3:16 with grace in your hearts to the L'.* "
17 do all in the name of the L' Jesus, "
18 own husbands, as it is fit in the L'. "
20 for this is well pleasing unto the L'. "
23 ye do, do it heartily, as to the L', "
24 of the L' ye shall receive the reward "
24 for ye serve the L' Christ. "
4: 7 and fellowservant in the L': "
17 which thou hast received in the L', "
1Th 1: 1 Father and in the L' Jesus Christ: "
1 Father, and the L' Jesus Christ. * "
3 of hope in our L' Jesus Christ, "
6 followers of us, and of the L', "
8 you sounded out the word of the L' "
2:15 Who both killed the L' Jesus, and "
19 the presence of our L' Jesus Christ "
3: 8 we live, if ye stand fast in the L'. "
11 our Father, and our L' Jesus Christ, "
12 L' make you to increase and abound "
13 the coming of our L' Jesus Christ "
4: 1 and exhort you by the L' Jesus, "
2 we gave you by the L' Jesus. "
6 the L' is the avenger of all such, "
15 say unto you by the word of the L', "
15 remain unto the coming of the L' "
16 the L' himself shall descend from "
17 the clouds, to meet the L' in the air: "
17 and so shall we ever be with the L'. "
5: 2 day of the L' so cometh as a thief "
9 salvation by our L' Jesus Christ, "
12 you, and are over you in the L', and "
23 the coming of our L' Jesus Christ. "
27 I charge you by the L' that this "
28 grace of our L' Jesus Christ be with "
2Th 1: 1 our Father and the L' Jesus Christ: "
2 our Father and the L' Jesus Christ. "
7 the L' Jesus shall be revealed from "
8 the gospel of our L' Jesus Christ: "
9 from the presence of the L', and "
12 name of our L' Jesus Christ may be "
12 of our God and the L' Jesus Christ. "
2: 1 the coming of our L' Jesus Christ, "
8 whom the L' shall consume with the "
13 for you, brethren beloved of the L', "
14 of the glory of our L' Jesus Christ. "
16 Now our L' Jesus Christ himself, "
3: 1 the word of the L' may have free "
3 L' is faithful, who shall stablish "
4 confidence in the L' touching you, "
5 L' direct your hearts into the love "
6 in the name of our L' Jesus Christ, "
12 and exhort by our L' Jesus Christ, "
16 L' of peace himself give you peace "
16 all means. The L' be with you all. "
18 grace of our L' Jesus Christ be with "
1Ti 1: 1 our Saviour, and L' Jesus Christ, * "
2 our Father, and Jesus Christ our L'. "
12 And I thank Christ Jesus our L', "
14 the grace of our L' was exceeding "
5:21 before God, and the L' Jesus Christ,* "
6: 3 even the words of our L' Jesus, "
14 appearing of our L' Jesus Christ: "
15 the King of kings, and L' of lords; "
2Ti 1: 2 the Father and Christ Jesus our L'. "
8 ashamed of the testimony of our L', "
16 The L' give mercy unto the house of "
18 L' grant unto him that he may find "
18 find mercy of the L' in that day: "
2: 7 L' give thee understanding in all "
14 charging them before the L' that "
19 The L' knoweth them that are his. "
22 call on the L' out of a pure heart. "
24 servant of the L' must not strive; * "
3:11 out of them all the L' delivered me. "
4: 1 before God, and the L' Jesus Christ,* "
8 which the L', the righteous judge, "
14 the L' reward him according to his "
17 L' stood with me, and strengthened "
18 L' shall deliver me from every evil "
22 L' Jesus Christ be with thy spirit. "
Tit 1: 4 the L' Jesus Christ our Saviour. * "
Ph'm 3 our Father and the L' Jesus Christ. "
5 which thou hast toward the L' Jesus, "
16 both in the flesh, and in the L'? "
20 let me have joy of thee in the L': "
20 refresh my bowels in the L'. * "
25 grace of our L' Jesus Christ be with "
Heb 1:10 Thou, L', in the beginning hast "
2: 3 first began to be spoken by the L', "
7:14 that our L' sprang out of Juda; "
21 The L' sware and will not repent, "
8: 2 tabernacle, which the L' pitched, "
8 the days come, saith the L', when "
9 I regarded them not, saith the L'. "
10 Israel after those days, saith the L'; "
11 his brother, saying, Know the L': "
10:16 them after those days, saith the L', "
30 me, I will recompense, saith the L'. "
30 The L' shall judge his people. "
12: 5 not thou the chastening of the L', "
6 whom the L' loveth he chasteneth, "
14 which no man shall see the L': "
13: 6 boldly say, The L' is my helper, "
20 again from the dead our L' Jesus, "
Jas 1: 1 of God and of the L' Jesus Christ, "
7 shall receive any thing of the L'. "
12 which the L' hath promised to them "
2: 1 not the faith of our L' Jesus Christ, "
1 L' of glory, with respect of persons. "
4:10 yourselves in the sight of the L', 2962
15 that ye ought to say, If the L' will, "
5: 4 into the ears of the L' of Sabaoth. "
7 brethren unto the coming of the L'. "
8 the coming of the L' draweth nigh. "
10 have spoken in the name of the L', "

Jas 5:11 and have seen the end of the L'; 2962
11 that the L' is very pitiful, and of "
14 him with oil in the name of the L': "
15 sick, and the L' shall raise him up; "
1Pe 1: 3 and Father of our L' Jesus Christ, "
25 word of the L' endureth for ever. "
2: 3 have tasted that the L' is gracious. "
3: 6 obeyed Abraham, calling him l': "
12 For the eyes of the L' are over the "
12 the face of the L' is against them "
15 sanctify the L' God in your hearts: "
2Pe 1: 2 of God, and of Jesus our L', "
8 knowledge of our L' Jesus Christ. "
11 kingdom of our L' and Saviour "
14 L' Jesus Christ hath shewed me. "
16 and coming of our L' Jesus Christ, "
2: 1 denying the L' that bought them,*1203
9 The L' knoweth how to deliver the 2962
11 against them before the L'. "
20 knowledge of the L' and Saviour "
3: 2 the apostles of the L' and Saviour: "
8 one day is with the L' as a thousand "
9 The L' is not slack concerning his "
10 day of the L' will come as a thief "
15 that the longsuffering of our L' is "
18 knowledge of our L' and Saviour "
2Jo 3 and from the L' Jesus Christ, the * "
Jude 4 and denying the only L' God, * "
4 God, and our L' Jesus Christ. "
5 how that the L', having saved the "
9 but said, The L' rebuke thee. "
14 the L' cometh with ten thousands "
17 of the apostles of our L' Jesus "
21 for the mercy of our L' Jesus Christ "
Re 1: 8 and the ending, saith the L', which "
4: 8 Holy, holy, holy, L' God Almighty, "
11 Thou art worthy, O L', to receive "
6:10 How long, O L', holy and true, dost*1203
11: 8 where also our L' was crucified. 2962
15 are become the kingdoms of our L', "
17 thee thanks, O L' God Almighty, "
14:13 are the dead which die in the L'. "
15: 3 are thy works, L' God Almighty; "
4 Who shall not fear thee, O L', and "
16: 5 Thou art righteous, O L', which * "
7 Even so, L' God Almighty, true and "
17:14 for he is L' of lords, and King of "
18: 8 strong is the L' God which judgeth "
19: 1 and power, unto the L' our God: "
6 the L' God omnipotent reigneth. "
16 King Of Kings, And L' Of Lords. "
21:22 for the L' God Almighty and the "
22: 5 the L' God giveth them light: and "
6 the L' God of the holy prophets "
20 Amen. Even so, come, L' Jesus. "
21 grace of our L' Jesus Christ be with "

lordly
J'g 5:25 brought forth butter in a l' dish. 117

lord's [or Lord's]
Ge 40: 7 him in the ward of his l' house * 113
44: 8 we steal out of thy l' house silver "
9 and we also will be my l' bondmen. "
16 behold, we are my l' servants, both "
18 speak a word in my l' ears, and let "
Ex 9:29 know how that the earth is the L'.‡3068
12:11 it in haste: it is the L' passover. ‡ "
27 is the sacrifice of the L' passover, ‡ "
13: 9 the L' law may be in thy mouth:*‡ "
12 hast; the male shall be the L'. ‡ "
32:26 Who is on the L' side? let him ‡ "
35:21 they brought the L' offering to ‡ "
24 and brass brought the L' offering: ‡ "
Le 3:16 sweet savour: all the fat is the L'. ‡ "
16: 9 goat upon which the L' lot fell, *‡ "
23: 5 month at even is the L' passover. ‡ "
27:26 which should be the L' firstling, * "
26 it be ox, or sheep: it is the L'. ‡ "
Nu 11:23 Is the L' hand waxed short? ‡ "
29 all the L' people were prophets, ‡ "
18:28 the L' heave offering to Aaron ‡ "
31:37 the L' tribute of the sheep was ‡ "
38, 39 the L' tribute was three score ‡ "
40 the L' tribute was thirty and two ‡ "
41 which was the L' heave offering, ‡ "
32:10 L' anger was kindled the same ‡ "
13 the L' anger was kindled against ‡ "
De 10:14 of heavens is the L' thy God, *‡ "
11:17 L' wrath be kindled against you, *‡ "
15: 2 because it is called the L' release. ‡ "
32: 9 For the L' portion is his people; *‡ "
Jos 1:15 Moses the L' servant gave you ‡ "
5:15 captain of the L' host said unto ‡ "
22:19 wherein the L' tabernacle ‡ "
J'g 11:31 Ammon, shall surely be the L', ‡ "
1Sa 2: 8 the pillars of the earth are the L', ‡ "
24 make the L' people to transgress. ‡ "
14: 3 son of Eli, the L' priest in Shiloh, *‡ "
16: 6 the L' anointed is before him. ‡ "
17:47 for the battle is the L', and he will ‡ "
18:17 for me, and fight the L' battles. ‡ "
22:21 that Saul had slain the L' priests. ‡ "
24: 6 unto my master, the L' anointed, ‡ "
10 lord; for he is the L' anointed. ‡ "
26: 9 his hand against the L' anointed, ‡ "
11 hand against the L' anointed: ‡ "
16 your master, the L' anointed. ‡ "
23 hand against the L' anointed. ‡ "
2Sa 1:14 hand to destroy the L' anointed? ‡ "
16 I have slain the L' anointed. ‡ "
19:21 because he cursed the L' anointed? ‡ "
20: 6 take thou thy l' servants, and 113
21: 7 L' oath that was between them, ‡3068
1Ki 18:13 an hundred men of the L' prophets ‡ "
2Ki 11:17 that they should be the L' people; ‡ "
13:17 The arrow of the L' deliverance, ‡ "

1Ch 21: 3 are they not all my l' servants? 113
2Ch 7: 2 glory...had filled the L' house. ‡3068
23:16 that they should be the L' people. ‡ "
Ps 11: 4 the L' throne is in heaven: his *‡ "
22:28 For the kingdom is the L': and ‡ "
24: 1 earth is the L', and the fulness ‡ "
113: 3 the L' name is to be praised. ‡ "
115:16 even the heavens, are the L': *‡ "
116:19 In the courts of the L' house, in ‡ "
118:23 This is the L' doing; it is ‡ "
137: 4 How shall we sing the L' song in ‡ "
Pr 16:11 weight and balance are the L': ‡ "
Isa 2: 2 that the mountain of the L' house ‡ "
22:18 shall be the shame of thy l' house. 113
34: 8 is the day of the L' vengeance, ‡3068
40: 2 received of the L' hand double ‡ "
42:19 and blind as the L' servant? ‡ "
44: 5 One shall say, I am the L'; and ‡ "
59: 1 the L' hand is not shortened, that ‡ "
Jer 5:10 for they are not the L'. ‡ "
7: 2 Stand in the gate of the L' house, ‡ "
13:17 L' flock is carried away captive. ‡ "
19:14 stood in the court of the L' house; ‡ "
25:17 took I the cup at the L' hand, ‡ "
26: 2 Stand in the court of the L' house, ‡ "
2 come to worship in the L' house, ‡ "
10 of the new gate of the L' house. ‡ "
27:16 the vessels of the L' house shall ‡ "
28: 3 all the vessels of the L' house, ‡ "
6 again the vessels of the L' house, ‡ "
36: 6 ears of the people in the L' house ‡ "
8 words of the Lord in the L' house. ‡ "
10 of the new gate of the L' house, ‡ "
51: 6 is the time of the L' vengeance; ‡ "
7 been a golden cup in the L' hand, ‡ "
51 the sanctuaries of the L' house. ‡ "
La 2:22 day of the L' anger none escaped ‡ "
3:22 of the L' mercies that we are not ‡ "
Eze 8:14 door of the gate of the L' house ‡ "
16 the inner court of the L' house, ‡ "
10: 4 of the brightness of the L' glory. ‡ "
19 of the east gate of the L' house; ‡ "
11: 1 unto the east gate of the L' house, ‡ "
Da 9:17 that is desolate, for the L' sake. 136
Ho 9: 3 shall not dwell in the L' land; ‡3068
Joe 1: 9 priests, the L' ministers, mourn. ‡ "
Ob 21 and the kingdom shall be the L'. ‡ "
Mic 6: 2 O mountains, the L' controversy, ‡ "
9 The L' voice crieth unto the city, *‡ "
Hab 2:16 the cup of the L' right hand shall ‡ "
Zep 1: 8 pass in the day of the L' sacrifice, ‡ "
18 them in the day of the L' wrath; ‡ "
2: 2 before the day of the L' anger ‡ "
3 be hid in the day of the L' anger. ‡ "
Hag 1: 2 that the L' house should be built. ‡ "
13 spake Haggai the L' messenger ‡ "
13 in the L' message unto the people, ‡ "
2:18 the foundation of the L' temple ‡ "
Zec 14:20 pots in the L' house shall be like ‡ "
M't 21:42 this is the L' doing, and it is *2962
25:18 in the earth, and hid his l' money. "
M'r 12:11 This was the L' doing, and it is * "
Lu 2:26 before he had seen the L' Christ. "
12:47 that servant, which knew his l' will, "
16: 5 he called every one of his l' debtors "
Ro 14: 8 live therefore, or die, we are the L'. "
1Co 7:22 being a servant, is the L' freeman: "
10:21 cannot be partakers of the L' table, * "
26 the earth is the L', and the fulness "
28 earth is the L', and the fulness * "
11:20 this is not to eat the L' supper. 2960
26 do shew the L' death till he come. 2962
29 himself, not discerning the L' body. * "
Ga 1:19 none, save James the L' brother. "
1Pe 2:13 ordinance of man for the L' sake: "
Re 1:10 I was in the Spirit on the L' day, 2960

lords
Ge 19: 2 he said, Behold now, my l', turn in, 113
Nu 21:28 the l' of the high places of Arnon. 1167
De 10:17 God is God of gods, and Lord of l', 113
Jos 13: 3 five l' of the Philistines; the 5633
J'g 3: 3 five l' of the Philistines, and all the "
16: 5 l' of the Philistines came up unto "
8 l' of the Philistines brought up to "
18 called for the l' of the Philistines, "
18 l' of the Philistines came up unto "
23 the l' of the Philistines gathered "
27 l' of the Philistines were there; "
30 the house fell upon the l', and upon "
1Sa 5: 8 gathered all the l' of the Philistines "
11 together all the l' of the Philistines, "
6: 4 number of the l' of the Philistines: "
4 was on you all, and on your l'. "
12 l' of the Philistines went after them "
16 five l' of the Philistines had seen it, "
18 Philistines belonging to the five l'. "
7: 7 l' of the Philistines went up against "
29: 2 the l' of the Philistines passed on "
6 nevertheless the l' favour thee not. "
7 displease not the l' of the Philistines. "
1Ch 12:19 for the l' of the Philistines upon "
Ezr 8:25 his l', and all Israel there present, *8269
Ps 136: 3 O give thanks to the Lord of l': 113
Isa 16: 8 l' of the heathen have broken down 1167
26:13 other l' beside thee have had 113
Jer 2:31 say my people, We are l'; *7300
Eze 23:23 and rulers, great l' and renowned, *7991
Da 4:36 and my l' sought unto me; and 7261
5: 1 a great feast to a thousand of his l', "
9 in him, and his l' were astonied. "
10 of the words of the king and his l' "
23 thou, and thy l', thy wives, and thy "
6:17 and with the signet of his l'; "
M'r 6:21 birthday made a supper to his l', 3175
1Co 8: 5 there be gods many, and l' many,) 2962

1Ti 6:15 the King of kings, and Lord of l'; 2961
1Pe 5: 3 as being l' over God's heritage, *2634
Re 17:14 is Lord of l', and King of kings: 2962
19:16 King Of Kings, And Lord Of L'. "

lordship
M'r 10:42 Gentiles exercise l' over them; 2634
Lu 22:25 Gentiles exercise l' over them; 2961

Lo-ruhamah (*lo-ru-ha'-mah*)
Ho 1: 6 said unto him, Call her name L': 3819
8 Now when she had weaned L', she "

lose See also LOSETH; LOST.
J'g 18:25 and thou l' thy life, with the lives 622
1Ki 18: 5 alive, that we l' not all the beasts. 3772
Job 31:39 the owners thereof to l' their life: 5307
Pr 23: 8 vomit up, and l' thy sweet words. 7843
Ec 3: 6 A time to get, and a time to l'; a 6
M't 10:39 He that findeth his life shall l' it: 622
42 he shall in no wise l' his reward. "
16:25 will save his life shall l' it. "
25 will l' his life for my sake shall find "
26 whole world, and l' his own soul? *2210
M'r 8:35 will save his life shall l' it; 622
35 shall l' his life for my sake and "
36 whole world, and l' his own soul? *2210
9:41 unto you, he shall not l' his reward. 622
Lu 9:24 will save his life shall l' it: "
24 will l' his life for my sake, the "
25 gain the whole world, and l' himself, "
15: 4 hundred sheep, if he l' one of them, * "
8 if she l' one piece, doth not light a "
17:33 shall seek to save his life shall l' it; "
33 shall l' his life shall preserve it. "
Joh 6:39 hath given me I should l' nothing, "
12:25 He that loveth his life shall l' it; * "
2Jo 8 l' not those things which we have "

loseth
M't 10:39 l' his life for my sake shall find it. 622

loss
Ge 31:39 not unto thee; I bare the l' of it; 2398
Ex 21:19 he shall pay for the l' of his time, 7674
Isa 47: 8 shall I know the l' of children: 7921
9 in one day, the l' of children, and "
Ac 27:21 to have gained this harm and l'. 2209
22 be no l' of any man's life among 580
1Co 3:15 shall be burned, he shall suffer l': 2210
Ph'p 3: 7 me, those I counted l' for Christ. 2209
8 I count all things but l' for the "
8 I have suffered the l' of all things, 2210

lost
Ex 22: 9 or for any manner of l' thing, which 9
Lev 6: 3 Or have found that which was l', and "
4 keep, or the l' thing which he found, "
Nu 6:12 days that were before shall be l', *5307
De 22: 3 with all l' thing of thy brother's, 9
3 which he hath l', and thou hast 6
1Sa 9: 3 the asses of Kish Saul's father were l'. "
20 as for thine asses that were l' three "
1Ki 20:25 like the army that thou hast l', 5307
Ps 119:176 I have gone astray like a l' sheep; 6
Isa 49:20 have, after thou hast l' the other, *7923
21 seeing I have l' my children, and *7908
Jer 50: 6 My people hath been l' sheep: their 6
Eze 19: 5 she had waited, and her hope was l', "
34: 4 have ye sought that which was l'; "
16 I will seek that which was l', and "
37:11 bones are dried, and our hope is l': "
M't 5:13 but if the salt have l' his savour, 3471
10: 6 the l' sheep of the house of Israel. 622
15:24 the l' sheep of the house of Israel. "
18:11 is come to save that which was l'. * "
M'r 9:50 if the salt have l' his saltness, 358,1096
Lu 14:34 but if the salt have l' his savour, 3471
15: 4 and go after that which is l', until 622
6 I have found my sheep which was l'. "
9 I have found the piece which I had l'. "
24 alive again; he was l', and is found. "
32 alive again; and was l', and is found. "
19:10 to seek and to save that which was l'. "
Joh 6:12 that remain, that nothing be l'. "
17:12 and none of them is l', but the son * "
18: 9 which thou gavest me have I l' none. "
2Co 4: 3 be hid, it is hid to them that are l': * "

lot See also LOTS.
Le 16: 8 the two goats; one l' for the Lord, 1486
8 and the other l' for the scapegoat. "
9 goat upon which the Lord's l' fell, "
10 which the l' fell to be the scapegoat, "
Nu 26:55 the land shall be divided by l': "
56 According to the l' shall the "
33:54 ye shall divide the land by l' for an "
54 be in the place where his l' falleth; "
34:13 the land which ye shall inherit by l', "
36: 2 give the land for an inheritance by l' "
3 taken from the l' of our inheritance. "
De 32: 9 Jacob is the l' of his inheritance. 2256
Jos 13: 6 divide thou it by l' unto the Israelites*
14: 2 By l' was their inheritance, as the 1486
15: 1 was the l' of the tribe of...Judah "
16: 1 the l' of the children of Joseph fell "
17: 1 also a l' for the tribe of Manasseh; "
2 also a l' for the rest of the children "
14 Why hast thou given me but one l' 1486
17 thou shalt not have one l' only: "
18:11 the l' of the tribe of the children of "
18 coast of their l' came forth between "
19: 1 the second l' came forth to Simeon, "
10 third l' came up for the children of "
17 the fourth l' came out to Issachar, "
24 the fifth l' came out for the tribe of "
32 sixth l' came out to the children of "
40 seventh l' came out for the tribe "
51 for an inheritance by l' in Shiloh "
21: 4 the l' came out for the families of "

Jos 21: 4 had by l' out of the tribe of Judah, 1486
5, 6 had by l' out of the families of the "
8 Israel gave by l' unto the Levites "
10 Levi, had: for theirs was the first l'. "
20 they had cities of their l' out of the "
40 were by their l' twelve cities. "
23: 4 divided unto you by l' these nations*
J'g 1: 3 Come up with me into my l', that 1486
3 and I...will go with thee into thy l'. "
20: 9 we will go up by l' against it; "
1Sa 14: 41 Lord God of Israel, Give a perfect l'.*
1Ch 6: 54 Kohathites: for theirs was the l'. 1486
61 tribe of Manasseh, by l', ten cities. "
63 the sons of Merari were given by l', "
65 And they gave by l' out of the tribe "
16: 18 Canaan, the l' of your inheritance; 2256
24: 5 Thus were they divided by l', one 1486
7 the first l' came forth to Jehoiarib, "
25: 9 the first l' came forth for Asaph to "
26: 14 the l' eastward fell to Shelemiah. "
14 and his l' came out northward. "
16 Hosah the l' came forth westward,*
Es 3: 7 they cast Pur, that is, the l', 1486
9: 24 and had cast Pur, that is, the l', to "
Ps 16: 5 of my cup: thou maintainest my l'. "
105: 11 Canaan, the l' of your inheritance: 2256
125: 3 rest upon the l' of the righteous; 1486
Pr 1: 14 Cast in thy l' among us; let us all "
16: 33 The l' is cast into the lap; but the "
18: 18 The l' causeth contentions to cease, "
Isa 17: 14 and the l' of them that rob us. "
34: 17 And he hath cast the l' for them, "
57: 6 thy portion; they, they are thy l': "
Jer 13: 25 This is thy l', the portion of thy "
Eze 24: 6 piece by piece; let no l' fall upon it. "
45: 1 when ye shall divide by l' the land for "
47: 22 shall divide it by l' for an inheritance "
48: 29 ye shall divide by l' unto the tribes "
Da 12: 13 and stand in thy l' at the end of 1486
Jon 1: 7 cast lots, and the l' fell upon Jonah. "
Mic 2: 5 none that shall cast a cord by l' in "
Lu 1: 9 his l' was to burn incense when 2975
Ac 1: 26 and the l' fell upon Matthias; 2819
8: 21 neither part nor l' in this matter: "
13: 19 he divided their land to them by l'.*2624

Lot (*lot*) See also LOT'S.
Ge 11: 27 and Haran; and Haran begat L'. 3876
31 L' the son of Haran his son's son, "
12: 4 and L' went with him: and Abram "
5 his wife, and L' his brother's son, "
13: 1 and L' with him, into the south. "
5 L' also, which went with Abram, "
8 Abram said unto L', Let there be no "
10 L' lifted up his eyes, and beheld all "
11 Then L' chose him all the plain of "
11 of Jordan; and L' journeyed east: "
12 L' dwelled in the cities of the plain, "
14 after...L' was separated from him, "
14: 12 they took L', Abram's brother's son, "
16 also brought again his brother L', "
19: 1 and L' sat in the gate of Sodom: "
1 and L' seeing them rose up to meet "
5 they called unto L', and said unto "
6 L' went out at the door unto them, "
9 pressed sore upon the man, even L', "
10 pulled L' into the house to them, "
12 men said unto L', Hast thou here "
14 L' went...and spake unto his sons "
15 then the angels hastened L', saying, "
18 And L' said unto them, Oh, not so, "
23 earth when L' entered into Zoar. "
29 and sent L' out of the midst of the "
29 the cities in the which L' dwelt. "
30 L' went up out of Zoar, and dwelt in "
36 both the daughters of L' with child "
De 2: 9 given Ar unto the children of L' for "
19 given it unto the children of L' for "
Ps 83: 8 they have holpen the children of L'. "
Lu 17: 28 also as it was in the days of L'; 3091
29 same day that L' went out of Sodom "
2Pe 2: 7 And delivered just L', vexed with "

Lotan (*lo'-tan*) See also LOTAN'S.
Ge 36: 20 L', and Shobal, and Zibeon, and 3877
22 the children of L' were Hori and "
29 that came of the Horites; duke L', "
1Ch 1: 38 L', and Shobal, and Zibeon, and "
39 the sons of L': Hori, and Homan: "

Lotan's (*lo'-tans*)
Ge 36: 22 Hemam; and L' sister was Timna. 3877
1Ch 1: 39 Homam: and Timna was L' sister. "

lothe See also LOATHE; LOTHED; LOTHETH; LOTHING.
Ex 7: 18 Egyptians shall l' to drink of the 3811
Eze 6: 9 shall l' themselves for the evils 6962
20: 43 l' yourselves in your own sight for "
36: 31 l' yourselves in your own sight for "

lothed See also LOATHED.
Jer 14: 19 hath thy soul l' Zion? why hast 1602
Eze 16: 45 which l' their husbands and their "
Zec 11: 8 my soul l' them, and their soul *7114

lotheth See also LOATHETH.
Eze 16: 45 l' her husband and her children; 1602

lothing
Eze 16: 5 open field, to the l' of thy person, 1604

Lot's (*lots*)
Ge 13: 7 and the herdman of L' cattle: 3876
Lu 17: 32 Remember L' wife.

lots
Le 16: 8 shall cast l' upon the two goats; 1486
Jos 18: 6 cast l' for you here before the Lord "
8 here cast l' for you before the Lord "
10 Joshua cast l' for them in Shiloh "
1Sa 14: 42 Cast l' between me and Jonathan my "
1Ch 24: 31 cast l' over against their brethren 1486
25: 8 they cast l', ward against ward, as "
26: 13 they cast l', as well the small as the "
14 son, a wise counsellor, they cast l'; "
Ne 10: 34 we cast the l' among the priests, the "
11: 1 the rest of the people also cast l', to "
Ps 22: 18 them, and cast l' upon my vesture. "
Joe 3: 3 they have cast l' for my people; and "
Ob 11 gates, and cast l' upon Jerusalem, "
Jon 1: 7 Come, and let us cast l', that we "
7 So they cast l', and the lot fell upon "
Na 3: 10 they cast l' for her honourable men, "
M't 27: 35 parted his garments, casting l': 2819
35 upon my vesture did they cast l'. * "
M'r 15: 24 garments, casting l' upon them, "
Lu 23: 34 they parted his raiment, and cast l'. "
Joh 19: 24 Let us not rend it, but cast l' for it, "
24 and for my vesture they did cast l'. 2975
Ac 1: 26 they gave forth their l'; and the lot 2819

loud See also LOUDER.
Ge 39: 14 me, and I cried with a l' voice: 1419
Ex 19: 16 voice of the trumpet exceeding l'; 2389
De 27: 14 the men of Israel with a l' voice, 7311
1Sa 28: 12 Samuel, she cried with a l' voice: 1419
2Sa 15: 23 all the country wept with a l' voice, "
19: 4 and the king cried with a l' voice, "
1Ki 8: 55 congregation of Israel with a l' voice, "
2Ki 18: 28 cried with a l' voice in the Jews' "
2Ch 15: 14 sware unto the Lord with a l' voice, "
20: 19 Lord God of Israel with a l' voice "
30: 21 singing with l' instruments unto 5797
32: 18 cried with a l' voice in the Jews' 1419
Ezr 3: 12 their eyes, wept with a l' voice; "
13 the people shouted with a l' shout, "
10: 12 answered and said with a l' voice, "
Ne 9: 4 cried with a l' voice unto the Lord "
12: 42 the singers sang l', with Jezrahiah 8085
Es 4: 1 cried with a l' and a bitter cry; 1419
Ps 33: 3 song: play skilfully with a l' noise. "
98: 4 make a l' noise, and rejoice, and sing*
150: 5 Praise him upon the l' cymbals: 8085
Pr 7: 11 (She is l' and stubborn; her feet *1993
27: 14 blesseth his friend with a l' voice, 1419
Isa 36: 13 cried with a l' voice in the Jews' "
Eze 8: 18 they cry in mine ears with a l' voice, "
9: 1 also in mine ears with a l' voice, "
11: 13 my face, and cried with a l' voice, "
M't 27: 46 Jesus cried with a l' voice, saying, 3173
50 he had cried again with a l' voice, "
M'r 1: 26 torn him, and cried with a l' voice, "
5: 7 And cried with a l' voice, and said, "
15: 34 Jesus cried with a l' voice, saying, "
37 And Jesus cried with a l' voice, and "
Lu 1: 42 she spake out with a l' voice, and "
4: 33 devil, and cried out with a l' voice, "
8: 28 and with a l' voice said, What have "
17: 15 and with a l' voice glorified God, "
19: 37 and praise God with a l' voice for "
23: 23 they were instant with l' voices, "
46 Jesus had cried with a l' voice, "
Joh 11: 43 he cried with a l' voice, Lazarus, "
Ac 7: 57 Then they cried out with a l' voice, "
60 and cried with a l' voice, Lord, lay "
8: 7 unclean spirits, crying with l' voice, "
14: 10 Said with a l' voice, Stand upright "
16: 28 Paul cried with a l' voice, saying, "
26: 24 Festus said with a l' voice, Paul, "
Re 5: 2 angel proclaiming with a l' voice,* "
12 Saying with a l' voice, Worthy is * "
6: 10 they cried with a l' voice, saying, * "
7: 2 with a l' voice to the four angels, * "
10 and cried with a l' voice, saying, * "
8: 13 saying with a l' voice, Woe, woe, * "
10: 3 cried with a l' voice, as when a lion* "
12: 10 I heard a l' voice saying in heaven,* "
14: 7 Saying with a l' voice, Fear God, * "
9 saying with a l' voice, If any man* "
15 crying with a l' voice to him that * "
18 cried with a l' voice to him that had* "
19: 17 he cried with a l' voice, saying to all "

louder
Ex 19: 19 sounded long, and waxed l' and l', 3966

love See also LOVED; LOVE'S; LOVES; LOVEST; LOVETH; LOVING.
Ge 27: 4 make me savoury meat, such as I l', 157
29: 20 few days, for the l' he had to her. 160
32 therefore my husband will l' me. 157
Ex 20: 6 unto thousands of them that l' me, "
21: 5 I l' my master, my wife, and my "
Le 19: 18 but thou shalt l' thy neighbour as "
34 and thou shalt l' him as thyself; for "
De 5: 10 unto thousands of them that l' me "
6: 5 thou shalt l' the Lord thy God with "
7: 7 Lord did not set his l' upon you, 2836
9 mercy with them that l' him and 157
13 he will l' thee, and bless thee, and "
10: 12 walk in all his ways, and to l' him, "
15 a delight in thy fathers to l' them, "
19 L' ye therefore the stranger: for ye "
11: 1 Therefore thou shalt l' the Lord thy "
13 you this day, to l' the Lord your God, "
22 to l' the Lord your God, to walk in "
13: 3 whether ye l' the Lord your God "
19: 9 to l' the Lord thy God, and to walk "
30: 6 to l' the Lord thy God with all thine "
16 thee this day to l' the Lord thy God, "
20 thou mayest l' the Lord thy God, "
Jos 22: 5 to l' the Lord your God, and to walk "
23: 11 selves, that ye l' the Lord your God. "
J'g 5: 31 let them that l' him be as the sun "
16: 15 How canst thou say, I l' thee, when "
1Sa 18: 22 in thee, and all his servants l' thee: "
2Sa 1: 26 me: thy l' to me was wonderful. 160
26 wonderful, passing the l' of women. 160
13: 4 Amnon said unto him, I l' Tamar, 157
15 greater than the l' wherewith he had 160
1Ki 11: 2 Solomon clave unto these in l'. "
2Ch 19: 2 and l' them that hate the Lord? 157
Ne 1: 5 and mercy for them that l' him and "
Ps 4: 2 how long will ye l' vanity, and seek "
5: 11 let them also that l' thy name be "
18: 1 I will l' thee, O Lord, my strength. 7355
31: 23 O l' the Lord, all ye his saints: for 157
40: 16 let such as l' thy salvation say "
69: 36 they that l' his name shall dwell "
70: 4 and let such as l' thy salvation say "
91: 14 Because he hath set his l' upon me, 2836
97: 10 Ye that l' the Lord, hate evil: he 157
109: 4 For my l' they are my adversaries: 160
5 evil for good, and hatred for my l'. "
116: 1 I l' the Lord, because he hath heard 157
119: 97 O how l' I thy law! it is my "
113 vain thoughts: but thy law do I l'. "
119 dross: therefore I l' thy testimonies. "
127 Therefore I l' thy commandments "
132 to do unto those that l' thy name. "
159 Consider how I l' thy precepts: "
163 and abhor lying: but thy law do I l'. "
165 peace have they which l' thy law: "
167 and I l' them exceedingly. "
122: 6 they shall prosper that l' thee. "
145: 20 Lord preserveth all them that l' him: "
Pr 1: 22 ye simple ones, will ye l' simplicity? "
4: 6 thee: l' her, and she shall keep thee. "
5: 19 thou ravished always with her l'. 160
7: 18 let us take our fill of l' until the 1730
8: 17 I l' them that l' me; and those that 157
21 cause those that l' me to inherit "
36 soul: all they that hate me l' death. "
9: 8 a wise man, and he will l' thee. "
10: 12 up strifes: but l' covereth all sins. 160
15: 17 is a dinner of herbs where l' is, than "
16: 13 and they l' him that speaketh right. 157
17: 9 covereth a transgression seeketh l'; 160
18: 21 and they that l' it shall eat the fruit 157
20: 13 L' not sleep, lest thou come to "
27: 5 rebuke is better than secret l'. 160
Ec 3: 8 A time to l', and a time to hate; a 157
9: 1 man knoweth either l' or hatred by 160
6 Also their l', and their hatred, and "
Ca 1: 2 for thy l' is better than wine. 1730
3 therefore do the virgins l' thee. 157
4 remember thy l' more than wine: 1730
4 than wine: the upright l' thee. 157
9 I have compared thee, O my l', to 7474
15 Behold, thou art fair, my l'; behold, "
2: 2 so is my l' among the daughters. "
4 and his banner over me was l'. 160
5 me with apples: for I am sick of l'. "
7 up, nor awake my l', till he please. "
10 Rise up, my l', my fair one, and 7474
13 Arise, my l', my fair one, and come "
3: 5 up, nor awake my l', till he please. 160
10 midst thereof being paved with l', "
4: 1 Behold, thou art fair, my l'; 7474
7 Thou art all fair, my l'; there is no "
10 How fair is thy l', my sister, my 1730
10 how much better is thy l' than wine! "
5: 2 to me, that my sister, my l', my dove, 7474
8 that ye tell him, I am sick of l'. 160
6: 4 Thou art beautiful, O my l', as 7474
7: 6 and how pleasant art thou, O l', for 160
8: 4 that ye stir not up, nor awake my l', "
6 for l' is strong as death; jealousy "
7 Many waters cannot quench l', "
7 all the substance of his house for l', "
Isa 38: 17 but thou hast in l' to my soul 2836
56: 6 to l' the name of the Lord, to be 157
61: 8 For I the Lord l' judgment, I hate "
63: 9 in his l' and in his pity he redeemed 160
66: 10 be glad with her, all ye that l' her: 157
Jer 2: 2 the l' of thine espousals, when thou 160
33 trimmest thou thy way to seek l'? "
5: 31 and my people l' to have it so: and 157
31: 3 loved thee with an everlasting l': 160
Eze 16: 8 behold, thy time was the time of l'; 1730
23: 11 more corrupt in her inordinate l' *5691
17 came to her into the bed of l', and 1730
33: 31 their mouth they shew much l', 5690
Da 1: 9 Daniel into favour and tender l' *
9: 4 and mercy to them that l' him, 157
Ho 3: 1 l' a woman beloved of her friend, "
1 according to the l' of the Lord * 160
1 other gods, and l' flagons of wine. 157
4: 18 her rulers with shame do l', Give "
9: 15 mine house, I will l' them no more: 160
11: 4 cords of a man, with bands of l': "
14: 4 backsliding, I will l' them freely: 157
Am 5: 15 Hate the evil, and l' the good, and "
Mic 3: 2 Who hate the good, and l' the evil; "
6: 8 but to do justly, and to l' mercy, 160
Zep 3: 17 he will rest in his l', he will joy over "
Zec 8: 17 l' no false oath: for all these are 157
19 therefore l' the truth and peace. "
M't 5: 43 Thou shalt l' thy neighbour, and hate 25
44 But I say unto you, L' your enemies, "
46 For if ye l' them which l' you, what "
6: 5 for they l' to pray standing in the 5368
24 he will hate the one, and l' the other; 25
19: 19 shalt l' thy neighbour as thyself. "
22: 37 Thou shalt l' the Lord thy God with "
39 shalt l' thy neighbour as thyself. "
23: 6 l' the uppermost rooms at feasts, 5368
24: 12 the l' of many shall wax cold. 26
M'r 12: 30 thou shalt l' the Lord thy God with 25
31 shalt l' thy neighbour as thyself. "
33 to l' him with all the heart, and with "
33 and to l' his neighbour as himself, "
38 the scribes, which l' to go in long *2309

M'r 12:38 l' salutations in the marketplaces.*
Lu 6:27 L' your enemies, do good to them 25
32 For if ye l' them which l' you, what "
32 for sinners also l' those that l' them. "
35 But l' ye your enemies, and do good, "
7:42 which of them will l' him most? "
10:27 Thou shalt l' the Lord thy God with "
11:42 pass over judgment and the l' of God:26
43 for ye l' the uppermost seats in the 25
16:13 he will hate the one, and l' the other;"
20:46 and l' greetings in the markets, 5368
Joh 5:42 that ye have not the l' of God in you. 26
8:42 were your Father, ye would l' me: 25
10:17 Therefore doth my Father l' me, "
13:34 give unto you, That ye l' one another;"
34 loved you, that ye also l' one another."
35 disciples, if ye have l' one to another.26
14:15 If ye l' me, keep my commandments.25
21 and I will l' him, and will manifest "
23 a man l' me, he will keep my words: "
23 my Father will l' him, and we will "
31 may know that I l' the Father; and "
15:9 I loved you: continue ye in my l'. 26
10 ye shall abide in my l'; even as I "
10 commandments, and abide in his l'. "
12 That ye l' one another, as I have 25
13 Greater l' hath no man than this, 26
17 command you, that ye l' one another.25
19 world, the world would l' his own: 5368
17:26 l' wherewith thou hast loved me 26
21:15, 16, 17 thou knowest that I l' thee. 5368
Ro 5:5 because the l' of God is shed abroad 26
8 God commendeth his l' toward us, "
8:28 together for good to them that l' God,25
35 separate us from the l' of Christ? 26
39 able to separate us from the l' of God,"
12:9 Let l' be without dissimulation. "
10 one to another with brotherly l'; 5360
13:8 any thing, but to l' one another: 25
9 Thou shalt l' thy neighbour as "
10 L' worketh no ill to his neighbour: 26
10 therefore l' is the fulfilling of the law."
15:30 sake, and for the l' of the Spirit, "
1Co 2:9 hath prepared for them that l' him. 25
4:21 come unto you with a rod, or in l'; 26
8:3 if any man l' God, the same is known*25
16:22 If any man l' not the Lord Jesus *5368
24 My l' be with you all in Christ Jesus.26
2Co 2:4 ye might know the l' which I have "
8 would confirm your l' toward him. "
5:14 For the l' of Christ constraineth us; "
6:6 by the Holy Ghost, by l' unfeigned, "
8:7 in all diligence, and in your l' to us. "
8 and to prove the sincerity of your l'. "
24 the churches, the proof of your l', "
11:11 because I l' you not? God knoweth. 25
12:15 though the more abundantly I l' you,"
13:11 God of l' and peace shall be with you.26
14 the l' of God, and the communion "
Ga 5:6 but faith which worketh by l'. "
13 flesh, but by l' serve one another. "
14 shalt l' thy neighbour as thyself. 25
22 the fruit of the Spirit is l', joy, peace,26
Eph 1:4 and without blame before him in l': "
15 Jesus, and l' unto all the saints. †
2:4 great l' wherewith he loved us, "
3:17 ye, being rooted and grounded in l', "
19 And to know the l' of Christ, which "
4:2 forbearing one another in l'; "
15 speaking the truth in l', may grow "
16 body unto the edifying of itself in l'. "
5:2 And walk in l', as Christ also hath "
25 Husbands, l' your wives, even as 25
28 So ought men to l' their wives as "
33 so l' his wife even as himself; and "
6:23 be to the brethren, and l' with faith, 26
24 with all them that l' our Lord Jesus 25
Ph'p 1:9 your l' may abound yet more and 26
17 the other of l', knowing that I am * "
2:1 in Christ, if any comfort of l', if any "
2 be likeminded, having the same l', "
Col 1:4 and of the l' which ye have to all the"
8 Who also declared unto us your l' in "
2:2 comforted, being knit together in l', "
3:19 Husbands, l' your wives, and be not 25
1Th 1:3 your work of faith, and labour of l', 26
3:12 abound in l' one toward another, "
4:9 as touching brotherly l' ye need 5360
9 are taught of God to l' one another. 25
5:8 on the breastplate of faith and l'. 26
13 highly in l' for their work's sake. "
2Th 2:10 they received not the l' of the truth, "
3:5 direct your hearts into the l' of God, "
1Ti 1:14 faith and l' which is in Christ Jesus. "
6:10 l' of money is the root of all evil: 5365
11 faith, l', patience, meekness. 26
2Ti 1:7 and of l', and of a sound mind. "
13 faith and l' which is in Christ Jesus. "
4:8 all them also that l' his appearing. 25
Tit 2:4 to be sober, to l' their husbands, 5362
4 to be sober,...to l' their children, 5388
3:4 that the kindness and l' of God 5363
15 Greet them that l' us in the faith. 5368
Ph'm 5 Hearing of thy l' and faith, which 26
7 great joy and consolation in thy l', "
Heb 6:10 to forget your work and labour of l', "
10:24 to provoke unto l' and to good works:"
13:1 Let brotherly l' continue. 5360
Jas 1:12 hath promised to them that l' him. 25
2:5 hath promised to them that l' him? "
8 shalt l' thy neighbour as thyself. "
1Pe 1:8 Whom having not seen, ye l'; in "
22 unto unfeigned l' of the brethren, 5360
22 ye l' one another with a pure heart 25
2:17 L' the brotherhood. Fear God. "
3:8 one to another, l' as brethren, be 5361
1Pe 3:10 For he that will l' life, and see good 25
1Jo 2:5 him verily is the l' of God perfected: 26
15 L' not the world, neither the things 25
15 If any man l' the world, "
15 the l' of the Father is not in him. 26
3:1 what manner of l' the Father hath "
11 that we should l' one another. 25
14 unto life, because we l' the brethren."
16 Hereby perceive we the l' of God, 26
17 how dwelleth the l' of God in him? "
18 little children, let us not l' in word, 25
23 Son Jesus Christ, and l' one another,"
4:7 Beloved, let us l' one another: "
7 for l' is of God; and every one that 26
8 not knoweth not God; for God is l'. "
9 manifested the l' of God toward us, "
10 Herein is l', not that we loved God, "
11 us, we ought also to l' one another. 25
12 If we l' one another, God dwelleth in26
12 in us, and his l' is perfected in us. 26
16 believed the l' that God hath to us. 26
16 God is l'; and he that dwelleth in "
16 that dwelleth in l' dwelleth in God, "
17 Herein is our l' made perfect, that "
18 There is no fear in l'; but perfect "
18 but perfect l' casteth out fear: "
18 that feareth is not made perfect in l'."
19 We l' him, because he first loved us. 25
20 If a man say, I l' God, and hateth "
20 how can he l' God whom he hath not "
21 who loveth God l' his brother also. "
5:2 know that we l' the children of God, "
2 when we l' God, and keep his "
3 this is the l' of God, that we keep 26
2Jo 1 her children, whom I l' in the truth;25
3 the Son of the Father, in truth and l'.26
5 beginning, that we l' one another. 25
6 And this is l', that we walk after his 26
3Jo 1 unto...Gaius, whom I l' in the truth. 25
Jude 2 Mercy unto you, and peace, and l'. 26
21 Keep yourselves in the l' of God, "
Re 2:4 because thou hast left thy first l'. "
3:19 As many as I l', I rebuke and 5368

loved See also BELOVED; LOVEDST.
Ge 24:67 she became his wife; and he l' her:157
25:28 And Isaac l' Esau, because he did "
28 his venison: but Rebekah l' Jacob. "
27:14 savoury meat, such as his father l'. "
29:18 Jacob l' Rachel; and said, I will "
30 he l' also Rachel more than Leah, "
34:3 he l' the damsel, and spake kindly "
37:3 Now Israel l' Joseph more than all "
4 saw that their father l' him more "
De 4:37 because he l' thy fathers, therefore "
7:8 But because the Lord l' you, and * 160
23:5 because the Lord thy God l' thee. 157
33:3 Yea, he l' the people; all his *2245
J'g 16:4 l' a woman in the valley of Sorek, 157
1Sa 1:5 he l' Hannah: but the Lord had "
16:21 before him: and he l' him greatly: "
18:1 and Jonathan l' him as his own soul."
3 because he l' him as his own soul. 160
16 But all Israel and Judah l' David, 157
20 Michal Saul's daughter l' David: "
28 that Michal Saul's daughter l' him. "
20:17 to swear again, because he l' him: *160
17 for he l' him as he...his own soul. 157
17 for he...him as he l' his own soul. 160
2Sa 12:24 name Solomon: and the Lord l' him.157
13:1 and Amnon the son of David l' her. "
15 the love wherewith he had l' her. "
1Ki 3:3 And Solomon l' the Lord, walking "
10:9 because the Lord l' Israel for ever, 160
11:1 Solomon l' many strange women, 157
2Ch 2:11 Because the Lord hath l' his people,*160
9:8 thy God: because thy God l' Israel, "
11:21 And Rehoboam l' Maachah the 157
26:10 and in Carmel: for he l' husbandry. "
Es 2:17 And the king l' Esther above all the "
Job 19:19 they whom I l' are turned against "
Ps 26:8 Lord, I have l' the habitation of thy*"
47:4 the excellency of Jacob whom he l'. "
78:68 Judah, the mount Zion which he l'. "
109:17 As he l' cursing, so let it come unto "
119:47 thy commandments, which I have l'. "
48 thy commandments, which I have l'; "
Isa 43:4 been honourable, and I have l' thee: "
48:14 The Lord hath l' him: he will do his "
Jer 2:25 I have l' strangers, and after them "
8:2 host of heaven, whom they have l', "
14:10 Thus have they l' to wander, they "
31:3 I have l' thee with an everlasting "
Eze 16:37 all them that thou hast l', with all "
Ho 9:1 l' a reward upon every cornfloor. "
10 were according as they l'. "
11:1 Israel was a child, then I l' him, and"
Mal 1:2 I have l' you, saith the Lord. "
2 Yet ye say, Wherein hast thou l' us?"
2 saith the Lord: yet I l' Jacob, "
2:11 the holiness of the Lord which he l',*"
M'r 10:21 Jesus beholding him l' him, and said25
Lu 7:47 many, are forgiven; for she l' much: "
Joh 3:16 For God so l' the world, that he "
19 men l' darkness rather than light, "
11:5 Now Jesus l' Martha, and her sister, "
36 the Jews, Behold how he l' him! 5368
12:43 they l' the praise of men more than 25
13:1 having l' his own which were in the "
1 the world, he l' them unto the end. "
23 one of his disciples, whom Jesus l'. "
34 as I have l' you, that ye also love one"
14:21 loveth me shall be l' of my Father, "
28 If ye l' me, ye would rejoice, because"
15:9 As the Father hath l' me, so have I "
9 me, so have I l' you: continue ye in "
12 ye love one another, as I have l' you."
Joh 16:27 because ye have l' me, and have 5368
17:23 and hast l' them, as thou hast l' me.*25
26 the love wherewith thou hast l' me*"
19:26 the disciple standing by, whom he l',"
20:2 the other disciple, whom Jesus l', 5368
21:7 that disciple whom Jesus l' saith 25
20 the disciple whom Jesus l' following;"
Ro 8:37 conquerors through him that l' us. "
9:13 As it is written, Jacob have I l', but "
2Co 12:15 abundantly I love you, the less I be l'."
Ga 2:20 faith of the Son of God, who l' me, "
Eph 2:4 his great love wherewith he l' us, "
5:2 in love, as Christ also hath l' us, 26
25 even as Christ also l' the church, 25
2Th 2:16 even our Father, which hath l' us, "
2Ti 4:10 me, having l' this present world, "
Heb 1:9 hast l' righteousness, and hated "
2Pe 2:15 who l' the wages of unrighteousness;"
1Jo 4:10 Herein is love, not that we l' God, "
10 but that he l' us, and sent his Son to "
11 Beloved, if God so l' us, we ought "
19 We love him, because he first l' us. "
Re 1:5 Unto him that l' us, and washed us* "
3:9 feet, and to know that I have l' thee. "
12:11 they l' not their lives unto the death."

lovedst
Isa 57:8 l' their bed where thou sawest it. 157
Joh 17:24 l' me before the foundation of the 25

lovely
2Sa 1:23 and Jonathan were l' and pleasant 157
Ca 5:16 sweet: yea, he is altogether l'. 4261
Eze 33:32 art unto them as a very l' song of 5690
Ph'p 4:8 are pure, whatsoever things are l',4375

lover See also LOVERS.
1Ki 5:1 for Hiram was ever a l' of David. 157
Ps 88:18 L' and friend hast thou put far from "
Tit 1:8 But a l' of hospitality,...of good *5382
8 a l' of good men, sober, just, holy, 5358

lovers
Ps 38:11 My l' and my friends stand aloof 157
Jer 3:1 played the harlot with many l'; 7453
4:30 thy l' will despise thee, they will 5689
22:20 for all thy l' are destroyed. 157
22 and thy l' shall go into captivity: "
30:14 All thy l' have forgotten thee; they "
La 1:2 among all her l' she hath none to "
19 I called for my l', but they deceived "
Eze 16:33 but thou givest thy gifts to all thy l'."
36 through thy whoredoms with thy l', "
37 therefore I will gather all thy l', "
23:5 doted on her l', on the Assyrians "
9 delivered her into the hand of her l', "
22 I will raise up thy l' against thee, "
Ho 2:5 I will go after my l', that give me my"
7 she shall follow after her l', but she "
10 her lewdness in the sight of her l', "
12 rewards that my l' have given me: "
13 she went after her l', and forgat me, "
8:9 by himself: Ephraim hath hired l'.158
2Ti 3:2 men shall be l' of their own selves,5367
4 highminded, l' of pleasures more 5369
4 of pleasures more than l' of God; 5377

love's
Ph'm 9 for l' sake I rather beseech thee, 26

loves
Ps 45:title of Korah, Maschil, A Song of l'. 3039
Pr 7:18 let us solace ourselves with l'. 159
Ca 7:12 forth: there will I give thee my l'.*1730

lovest
Ge 22:2 thine only son Isaac, whom thou l',157
J'g 14:16 dost but hate me, and l' me not: "
2Sa 19:6 In that thou l' thine enemies, and "
Ps 45:7 Thou l' righteousness, and hatest * "
52:3 Thou l' evil more than good; and "
4 Thou l' all devouring words, O thou "
Ec 9:9 joyfully with the wife whom thou l' "
Joh 11:3 behold, he whom thou l' is sick. 5368
21:15 Jonas, l' thou me more than these? 25
16 Simon, son of Jonas, l' thou me? "
17 Simon, son of Jonas, l' thou me? 5368
17 him the third time, L' thou me? "

loveth
Ge 27:9 meat for thy father, such as he l': 157
44:20 of his mother, and his father l' him. "
De 10:18 l' the stranger, in giving him food "
15:16 because he l' thee and thine house, "
Ru 4:15 thy daughter in law, which l' thee, "
Ps 11:5 him that l' violence his soul hateth. "
7 the righteous Lord l' righteousness;"
33:5 He l' righteousness and judgment: "
34:12 that desireth life, and l' many days, "
37:28 the Lord l' judgment, and forsaketh "
87:2 The Lord l' the gates of Zion more "
99:4 king's strength also l' judgment; "
119:140 pure: therefore thy servant l' it. "
146:8 down: the Lord l' the righteous: "
Pr 3:12 for whom the Lord l' he correcteth; "
12:1 Whoso l' instruction l' knowledge: "
13:24 that l' him chasteneth him betimes. "
15:9 but he l' him that followeth after "
12 A scorner l' not one that reproveth "
17:17 friend l' at all times, and a brother "
19 He l' transgression that l' strife: "
19:8 that getteth wisdom l' his own soul: "
21:17 that l' pleasure shall be a poor man:"
17 that l' wine and oil shall not be rich."
22:11 He that l' pureness of heart, for the "
29:3 Whoso l' wisdom rejoiceth his "
Ec 5:10 that l' silver shall not be satisfied "
10 he that l' abundance with increase: "
Ca 1:7 Tell me, O thou whom my soul l', "
3:1 bed I sought him whom my soul l': "
2 I will seek him whom my soul l': "
3 I said, Saw ye him whom my soul l'?"
4 but I found him whom my soul l': "

Isa 1:23 every one *l·* gifts, and followeth 157
Ho 10:11 taught, and *l·* to tread out the corn; "
12: 7 are in his hand: he *l·* to oppress. "
M't 10:37 *l·* father or mother more than me *5368*
37 *l·* son or daughter more than me "
Lu 7: 5 he *l·* our nation, and he hath built *25*
47 little is forgiven, the same *l·* little. "
Joh 3:35 Father *l·* the Son, and hath given "
5:20 Father *l·* the Son, and sheweth *5368*
12:25 He that *l·* his life shall lose it; and "
14:21 keepeth them, he it is that *l·* me: *25*
21 *l·* me shall be loved by my Father, "
24 *l·* me not keepeth not my sayings: "
16:27 the Father himself *l·* you, because *5368*
Ro 13: 8 that *l·* another hath fulfilled the law.*25*
2Co 9: 7 necessity: for God *l·* a cheerful giver."
Eph 5:28 bodies. He that *l·* his wife *l·* himself."
Heb12: 6 For whom the Lord *l·* he chasteneth, "
1Jo 2:10 *l·* his brother abideth in the light, "
3:10 neither he that *l·* not his brother. "
14 *l·* not his brother abideth in death. "
4: 7 and every one that *l·* is born of God, "
8 He that *l·* not knoweth not God; for "
20 *l·* not his brother whom he hath seen, "
21 he who *l·* God love his brother also. "
5: 1 and every one that *l·* him that begat "
1 *l·* him also that is begotten of him. "
3Jo 9 *l·* to have the preeminence among *5383*
Re 22:15 and whosoever *l·* and maketh a lie.*5368*

loving See also LOVINGKINDNESS.
Pr 5:19 be as the *l·* hind and pleasant roe; 158
22: 1 *l·* favour rather than silver and 2896
Isa 56:10 sleeping, lying down, *l·* to slumber.157

lovingkindness See also LOVINGKINDNESSES.
Ps 17: 7 Shew thy marvellous *l·*, O thou 2617
26: 3 For thy *l·* is before mine eyes: and "
36: 7 How excellent is thy *l·*, O God! "
10 continue thy *l·* unto them that know"
40:10 I have not concealed thy *l·* and thy "
11 let thy *l·* and thy truth continually "
42: 8 Yet the Lord will command his *l·* "
48: 9 We have thought of thy *l·*, O God, "
51: 1 upon me, O God, according to thy *l·*: "
63: 3 Because thy *l·* is better than life, "
69:16 Hear me, O Lord; for thy *l·* is good;"
88:11 Shall thy *l·* be declared in the grave?"
89:33 my *l·* will I not utterly take from "
92: 2 To shew forth thy *l·* in the morning,"
103: 4 crowneth thee with *l·* and tender "
107:43 shall understand the *l·* of the Lord.† "
119:88 Quicken me after thy *l·*; so shall I "
149 my voice according unto thy *l·*: "
159 me, O Lord, according to thy *l·*. "
138: 2 name for thy *l·* and for thy truth: "
143: 8 me to hear thy *l·* in the morning; "
Jer 9:24 I am the Lord which exercise *l·*, "
16: 5 saith the Lord, even *l·* and mercies."
31: 3 therefore with *l·* have I drawn thee."
32:18 Thou shewest *l·* unto thousands, † "
Ho 2:19 judgment, and in *l·*, and in mercies."

lovingkindnesses
Ps 25: 6 thy tender mercies and thy *l·*; 2617
89:49 Lord, where are thy former *l·*, † "
Isa 63: 7 I will mention the *l·* of the Lord, "
7 according to the multitude of his *l·*."

low See also LOWER; LOWEST; LOWETH; LOWING.
De 28:43 and thou shalt come down very *l·*.*4295
J'g 11:35 thou hast brought me very *l·*, and 3766
1Sa 2: 7 rich: he bringeth *l·*, and lifteth up.8213
1Ch 27:28 trees that were in the *l·* plains 8219
2Ch 9:27 trees that are in the *l·* plains in "
26:10 much cattle, both in the *l·* country, "
28:18 invaded the cities of the *l·* country, "
19 the Lord brought Judah *l·* because3665
Job 5:11 To set up on high those that be *l·*;8217
14:21 and they are brought *l·*, but he 6819
24:24 but are gone and brought *l·*; they 4355
40:12 that is proud, and bring him *l·*: 3665
Ps 49: 2 Both *l·* and high, rich and poor, 120
62: 9 Surely men of *l·* degree are vanity, "
79: 8 us: for we are brought very *l·*. 1809
106:43 were brought *l·* for their iniquity. 4355
107:39 they are minished and brought *l·* *7817
116: 6 I was brought *l·*, and he helped me.1809
136:23 remembered us in our *l·* estate: 8213
142: 6 my cry; for I am brought very *l·*: 1809
Pr 29:23 A man's pride shall bring him *l·*: 8213
Ec 10: 6 dignity, and the rich sit in *l·* place.8216
12: 4 the sound of the grinding is *l·*, and8217
4 of musick shall be brought *l·*. 7817
Isa 2:12 up; and he shall be brought *l·*: 8213
17 haughtiness of men shall be made *l·*:"
13:11 will lay *l·* the haughtiness of the "
25: 5 terrible ones shall be brought *l·*. 6030
12 lay *l·*, and bring to the ground, 8213
26: 5 high; the lofty city, he layeth it *l·*; "
5 he layeth it *l·*, even to the ground; "
29: 4 speech shall be *l·* out of the dust, 7817
32:19 the forest; and the city shall be *l·* 8213
19 and the city shall be...in a *l·* place.*8219
40: 4 mountain and hill shall be made *l·*:8213
La 3:55 O Lord, out of the *l·* dungeon. *8482
Eze 17: 6 a spreading vine of *l·* stature, 8217
24 have exalted the *l·* tree, have dried "
21:26 exalt him that is *l·*, and abase him "
26:20 thee in the *l·* parts of the earth, *8482
Lu 1:48 hath regarded the *l·* estate of his *5014*
52 and exalted them of *l·* degree. *5011*
3: 5 and hill shall be brought *l·*; *5013*
Ro 12:16 but condescend to men of *l·* estate.**5011*
Jas 1: 9 brother of *l·* degree rejoice in that "
10 the rich, in that he is made *l·*: *5014*

lower See also LOWRING.
Ge 6:16 with *l·*, second, and third stories 8482
Le 13:20 it be in sight *l·* than the skin, and 8217
21 if it be not *l·* than the skin, but be "
26 and it be no *l·* than the other skin, "
14:37 which in sight are *l·* than the wall; "
Ne 4:13 set I in the *l·* places behind the *8482
Ps 8: 5 him a little *l·* than the angels, 2637
63: 9 go into the *l·* parts of the earth. 8482
Pr 25: 7 *l·* in the presence of the prince 8213
Isa 22: 9 together the waters of the *l·* pool. 8481
44:23 shout, ye *l·* parts of the earth: 8482
Eze 40:18 of the gates was the *l·* pavement. 8481
19 from the forefront of the *l·* gate "
42: 5 were higher than these, than the *l·*, "
43:14 the ground even to the *l·* settle "
Eph 4: 9 descended first into the *l·* parts *2737*
Heb 2: 7 madest him a little *l·* than...angels;*1642*
9 was made a little *l·* than the angels"

lowering See LOWRING.

lowest
De 32:22 and shall burn unto the *l·* hell, ‡8482
1Ki 12:31 priests of the *l·* of the people, *7098
13:33 again of the *l·* of the people priests*"
2Ki 17:32 of the *l·* of them priests of the high*"
Ps 86:13 delivered my soul from the *l·* hell.‡8482
88: 6 Thou hast laid me in the *l·* pit, in "
139:15 wrought in the lowest parts of the "
Eze 41: 7 increased from the *l·* chamber to 8481
42: 6 was straitened more than the *l·* "
Lu 14: 9 with shame to take the *l·* room. *2078*
10 go and sit down in the *l·* room; "

loweth
Job 6: 5 grass? or *l·* the ox over his fodder?1600

lowing
1Sa 6:12 *l·* as they went, and turned not 1600
15:14 the *l·* of the oxen which I hear? 6963

lowliness
Eph 4: 2 With all *l·* and meekness, with *5012*
Ph'p 2: 3 in *l·* of mind let each esteem other "

lowly
Ps 138: 6 yet hath he respect unto the *l·*: 8217
Pr 3:34 but he giveth grace unto the *l·*. 6041
11: 2 shame: but with the *l·* is wisdom. 6800
16:19 be of an humble spirit with the *l·*,*6041
Zec 9: 9 *l·*, and riding upon an ass, and upon"
M't 11:29 me; for I am meek and *l·* in heart:*5011*

lowring
M't 16: 3 to-day: for the sky is red and *l·*. *4768*

Lubim (*lu'-bim*) See also LUBIMS.
Na 3: 9 Put and *L·* were thy helpers. 3864

Lubims (*lu'-bims*) See also LEHABIM; LUBIM.
2Ch 12: 3 the *L·*, the Sukkiims, and the *3864
16: 8 Ethiopians and the *L·* a huge host,*"

Lucas (*lu'-cas*) See also LUKE.
2Co *subscr.* of Macedonia, by Titus and *L·*. **3065*
Ph'm 24 Demas, *L·*, my fellowlabourers. * "

Lucifer (*lu'-sif-ur*)
Isa 14:12 O *L·*, son of the morning! how *1966

Lucius (*lu'-she-us*)
Ac 13: 1 and *L·* of Cyrene, and Manaen, *3066*
Ro 16:21 Timotheus my workfellow, and *L·*, "

lucre See also LUCRE'S.
1Sa 8: 3 but turned aside after *l·*, and took 1215
1Ti 3: 3 no striker, not greedy of filthy *l·*; * *866*
8 much wine, not greedy of filthy *l·*; *146*
Tit 1: 7 no striker, not given to filthy *l·*; "
1Pe 5: 2 not for filthy *l·*, but of a ready *147*

lucre's
Tit 1:11 they ought not, for filthy *l·* sake. *2771*

Lud (*lud*) See also LUDIM; LYDIA.
Ge 10:22 Asshur, and Arphaxad, and *L·*, 3865
1Ch 1:17 and *L·*, and Aram, and Uz, and "
Isa 66:19 Pul, and *L·*, that draw the bow, "
Eze 27:10 They of Persia and of *L·* and of "

Ludim (*lu'-dim*) See also LUD.
Ge 10:13 Mizraim begat *L·*, and Anamim, 3866
1Ch 1:11 Mizraim begat *L·*, and Anamim, "

Luhith (*lu'-hith*)
Isa 15: 5 mounting up of *L·* with weeping 3872
Jer 48: 5 going up of *L·* continual weeping "

Luke (*luke*) See also LUCAS.
Col 4:14 *L·*, the beloved physician, and *3065*
2Ti 4:11 Only *L·* is with me. Take Mark, "

lukewarm
Re 3:16 So then because thou art *l·*, and *5513*

lump
2Ki 20: 7 And Isaiah said, Take a *l·* of figs.*1690
Isa 38:21 had said, Let them take a *l·* of figs,*"
Ro 9:21 same *l·* to make one vessel unto *5445*
11:16 firstfruit be holy, the *l·* is also holy: "
1Co 5: 6 little leaven leaveneth the whole *l·*?"
7 old leaven, that ye may be a new *l·*, "
Ga 5: 9 little leaven leaveneth the whole *l·*. "

lunatick
M't 4:24 and those which were *l·*, and those*4583*
17:15 son: for he is *l·*, and sore vexed: * "

lure See ALLURE.

lurk See also LURKING.
Pr 1:11 let us *l·* privily for the innocent 6845
18 they *l·* privily for their own lives. "

lurking
1Sa 23:23 take knowledge of all the *l·* places4224
Ps 10: 8 in the *l·* places of the villages: 3993
17:12 a young lion *l·* in secret places. 3427

lurking-places See LURKING and PLACES.

lust See also LUSTED; LUSTETH; LUSTING; LUSTS.
Ex 15: 9 my *l·* shall be satisfied upon them;‡5315
Ps 78:18 heart by asking meat for their *l·*. "
30 were not estranged from their *l·*. 8378
81:12 them up unto their own hearts' *l·*:*8307
Pr 6:25 *L·* not after her beauty in thine 2530
M't 5:28 looketh on a woman to *l·* after her *1937*
Ro 1:27 burned in their *l·* one toward *3715*
7: 7 for I had not known *l·*, except the**1939*
1Co 10: 6 should not *l·* after evil things, *1511,1938*
Ga 5:16 shall not fulfil the *l·* of the flesh. *1939*
1Th 4: 5 Not in the *l·* of concupiscence, **3806*
Jas 1:14 he is drawn away of his own *l·*, *1939*
15 Then when *l·* hath conceived, it "
4: 2 Ye *l·*, and have not: ye kill, and *1937*
2Pe 1: 4 that is in the world through *l·*. *1939*
2:10 the flesh in the *l·* of uncleanness, "
1Jo 2:16 *l·* of the flesh, and the *l·* of the eyes,"
17 passeth away, and the *l·* thereof: "

lusted
Nu 11:34 there they buried the people that *l·*.183
Ps 106:14 But *l·* exceedingly in the wilderness,"
1Co 10: 6 after evil things, as they also *l·*. *1937*
Re 18:14 the fruits that thy soul *l·* after are "

lusteth
De 12:15 eat...whatsoever thy soul *l·* after, * 183
20 flesh, whatsoever thy soul *l·* after.* "
21 gates whatsoever thy soul *l·* after.* "
14:26 for whatsoever thy soul *l·* after, * "
Ga 5:17 For the flesh *l·* against the Spirit, *1937*
Jas 4: 5 that dwelleth in us *l·* to envy? **1971*

lusting
Nu 11: 4 that was among them fell a *l·*: 8378

lusts
M'r 4:19 the *l·* of other things entering in, *1939*
Joh 8:44 and the *l·* of your father ye will do: "
Ro 1:24 through the *l·* of their own hearts, to"
6:12 ye should obey it in the *l·* thereof. "
13:14 for the flesh, to fulfil the *l·* thereof. "
Ga 5:24 the flesh with the affections and *l·*. "
Eph 2: 3 in times past in the *l·* of our flesh, "
4:22 corrupt according to the deceitful *l·*;"
1Ti 6: 9 and into many foolish and hurtful *l·*,"
2Ti 2:22 Flee also youthful *l·*: but follow "
3: 6 with sins, led away with divers *l·*, "
4: 3 after their own *l·* shall they heap "
Tit 2:12 denying ungodliness and worldly *l·*,"
3: 3 serving divers *l·* and pleasures, "
Jas 4: 1 your *l·* that war in your members?**2237*
3 ye may consume it upon your *l·*. * "
1Pe 1:14 to the former *l·* in your ignorance: *1939*
2:11 abstain from fleshly *l·*, which war "
4: 2 time in the flesh to the *l·* of men, "
3 walked in lasciviousness, *l·*, excess "
2Pe 2:18 allure through the *l·* of the flesh, "
3: 3 scoffers, walking after their own *l·*, "
Jude 16 walking after their own *l·*; "
18 walk after their own ungodly *l·*. "

lusty
J'g 3:29 men, all *l·*, and all men of valour; 8082

Luz (*luz*) See also BETH-EL.
Ge 28:19 the name of that city was called *L·* 3870
35: 6 So Jacob came to *L·*, which is in the"
48: 3 Almighty appeared unto me at *L·* "
Jos 16: 2 And goeth out from Beth-el to *L·*, "
18:13 thence toward *L·*, to the side of *L·*, "
J'g 1:23 the name of the city before was *L·*.)"
26 and called the name thereof *L·*: "

Lycaonia (*li-ca-o'-ne-ah*)
Ac 14: 6 Lystra and Derbe, cities of *L·*, and *3071*
11 voices, saying in the speech of *L·*, "

Lycia (*lish'-e-ah*)
Ac 27: 5 we came to Myra, a city of *L·*. *3073*

Lydda (*lid'-dah*) See also LOD.
Ac 9:32 to the saints which dwelt at *L·*. *3069*
35 And all that dwelt at *L·* and Saron "
38 forasmuch as *L·* was nigh to Joppa,"

Lydia (*lid'-e-ah*) See also LUDIM; LYDIANS.
Eze 30: 5 Ethiopia, and Libya, and *L·*, and *3865*
Ac 16:14 And a certain woman named *L·*, *3070*
40 and entered into the house of *L·*: "

Lydians (*lid'-e-uns*) See also LUDIMS.
Jer 46: 9 *L·*, that handle and bend the bow.*3866

lying See also LEASING.
Ge 29: 2 were three flocks of sheep *l·* by it; 7257
34: 7 Israel in *l·* with Jacob's daughter;7901
Ex 23: 5 hateth thee *l·* under his burden, 7257
Nu 31:17 hath known man by *l·* with him. 4904
18 not known a man by *l·* with him, "
35 not known a man by *l·* with him. "
De 21: 1 *l·* in the field, and it be not known 5307
22:22 a man be found *l·* with a woman 7901
J'g 9:35 were with him, from *l·* in wait. *
16: 9 Now there were men *l·* in wait, *
21:12 known no man by *l·* with any male:4904
1Ki 22:22 be a *l·* spirit in the mouth of all his 8267
23 Lord hath put a *l·* spirit in the mouth"
2Ch 18:21 be a *l·* spirit in the mouth of all his "
22 Lord hath put a *l·* spirit in the mouth"
Ps 31: 6 them that regard *l·* vanities: 7723
18 Let the *l·* lips be put to silence; 8267
52: 3 and *l·* rather than...righteousness. "
59:12 and for cursing and *l·*, which they 3585
109: 2 against me with a *l·* tongue. 8267
119:29 Remove from me the way of *l·*: * "
163 I hate and abhor *l·*: but thy law * "
120: 2 Deliver my soul, O Lord, from *l·* lips,"
139: 3 Thou compassest...my *l·* down, 7252
Pr 6:17 proud look, a *l·* tongue, and hands8267
10:18 He that hideth hatred with *l·* lips, "
12:19 but a *l·* tongue is but for a moment."
22 *L·* lips are abomination to the Lord:"
13: 5 A righteous man hateth *l·*: but1697,"

Pr 17: 7 fool: much less do l· lips a prince.8267
21: 6 getting of treasures by a l· tongue "
26:28 A l· tongue hateth those that are "
Isa 30: 9 is a rebellious people, l· children, 3586
32: 7 to destroy the poor with l· words, 8267
56:10 l· down, loving to slumber. 7901
59:13 and l· against the Lord, and *3584
Jer 7: 4 Trust ye not in l· words, saying, 8267
8 ye trust in l· words, that cannot "
29:23 have spoken l· words in my name,* "
La 3:10 He was unto me as a bear l· in wait,
Eze 13: 6 have seen vanity and l· divination,3577
7 have ye not spoken a l· divination, "
19 by your l· to my people that hear 3576

Da 2: 9 prepared l· and corrupt words to 3538
Ho 4: 2 By swearing, and l·, and killing, *3584
Jon 2: 8 that observe l· vanities forsake 7723
M't 9: 2 a man sick of the palsy, l· on a bed: 906
M'r 5:40 entereth in where...damsel was l·. * 345
Lu 2:12 swaddling clothes, l· in a manger.2749
16 Joseph, and the babe l· in a manger."
Joh 13:25 He then l· on Jesus' breast saith *1968
20: 5 looking in, saw the linen clothes l·;2749
7 not l· with the linen clothes, but "
Ac 20:19 me by the l· in wait of the Jews: *
23:16 sister's son heard of their l· in wait,
Eph 4:25 Wherefore putting away l·, speak *5579
2Th 2: 9 all power and signs and l· wonders, "

Lysanias (li-sa'-ne-as)
Lu 3: 1 and L· the tetrarch of Abilene, 3078
Lysias (lis'-e-as)
Ac 23:26 Claudius L· unto...Felix sendeth 3079
24: 7 the chief captain L· came upon us,*"
22 L· the chief captain shall come "
Lystra (lis'-trah)
Ac 14: 6 fled unto L· and Derbe, cities of 3082
8 And there sat a certain man at L·. "
21 they returned again to L·, and to "
16: 1 Then came he to Derbe and L·: "
2 by the brethren that were at L· and"
2Ti 3:11 me at Antioch, at Iconium, at L·; "

M.

Maacah (ma'-a-kah) See also MAACHAH.
2Sa 3: 3 son of M· the daughter of Talmai 4601
10: 6 and of king M· a thousand men, "
8 and M·, were by themselves in "
Maachah (ma'-a-kah) See also BETH-MAACHAH; MAACAH; MAACHATHITE; SYRIA-MAACHAH.
Ge 22:24 and Gaham, and Thahash, and M·.*4601
1Ki 2:39 Achish son of M· king of Gath. * "
15: 2, 10 his mother's name was M·, the* "
13 And also M· his mother, even her* "
1Ch 2:48 M·, Caleb's concubine, bare * "
3: 2 son of M· the daughter of Talmai* "
7:15 whose sister's name was M·,) * "
16 M· the wife of Machir bare a son,* "
8:29 whose wife's name was M·: * "
9:35 Jehiel, whose wife's name was M·:* "
11:43 Hanan the son of M·, and * "
19: 7 and the king of M· and his people;* "
27:16 Shephatiah the son of M·: * "
2Ch 11:20 took M· the daughter of Absalom;* "
21 Rehoboam loved M· the daughter* "
22 Abijah the son of M· the chief, * "
15:16 concerning M· the mother of Asa * "
Maachathi (ma-ak'-a-thi) See also MAACHATHITE.
De 3:14 the coasts of Geshuri and M·; *4602
Maachathite (ma-ak'-a-thite) See also MAACHATHI; MAACHATHITES.
2Sa 23:34 son of Ahasbai, the son of the M·,*4602
2Ki 25:23 Jaazaniah the son of a M·, they * "
1Ch 4:19 Garmite, and Eshtemoa the M·. * "
Jer 40: 8 and Jezaniah the son of a M·, * "
Maachathites (ma-ak'-a-thites)
Jos 12: 5 of the Geshurites and the M·, *4602
13:11 border of the Geshurites and M·, * "
13 not the Geshurites, nor the M·: * "
13 M· dwell among the Israelites * "
Maadai (ma'-a-dahee)
Ezr 10:34 of Bani; M·, Amram, and Uel, 4572
Maadiah (ma-a-di'-ah) See also MOADIAH.
Ne 12: 5 Miamin, M·, Bilgah, 4573
Maai (ma'-ahee)
Ne 12:36 Milalai, Gilalai, M·, Nethaneel, 4597
Maaleh-acrabbim (ma"-a-leh-ac-rab'-bim) See also AKRABBIM.
Jos 15: 3 went out to the south side to M·,*4610
Maarath (ma'-a-rath)
Jos 15:59 And M·, and Beth-anoth, and 4638
Maaseiah (ma-a-si'-ah)
1Ch 15:18 Eliab, and Benaiah, and M·, and 4641
20 M·, and Benaiah, with psalteries "
2Ch 23: 1 Obed, and M· the son of Adaiah, "
26:11 Jeiel the scribe and M· the ruler, "
28: 7 a mighty man of Ephraim, slew M· "
34: 8 and M· the governor of the city, "
Ezr 10:18 M·, and Eliezer, and Jarib, and "
21 And of the sons of Harim; M·, and "
22 the sons of Pashur; Elioenai, M·, "
30 Chelal, Benaiah, M·, Mattaniah, "
Ne 3:23 repaired Azariah the son of M· the "
8: 4 and M·, on his right hand; and "
7 Hodijah, M·, Kelita, Azariah, "
10:25 Rehum, Hashabnah, M·, "
11: 5 And M· the son of Baruch, the son "
7 the son of M·, the son of Ithiel, the "
12:41 the priests; Eliakim, M·, Miniamin,"
42 M·, and Shemaiah, and Eleazar, "
Jer 21: 1 Zephaniah the son of M· the priest,"
29:21 Zedekiah the son of M·, which "
25 to Zephaniah the son of M· the "
32:12 the son of M·, in the sight of 4271
35: 4 was above the chamber of M· 4641
37: 3 Zephaniah the son of M· the "
51:59 the son of M·, when he went with 4271
Maasiai (ma-a'-see-ahee)
1Ch 9:12 and M· the son of Adiel, the son *4640
Maath (ma'-ath)
Lu 3:26 Which was the son of M·, which was3092
Maaz (ma'-az)
1Ch 2:27 firstborn of Jerahmeel were, M·, 4619
Maaziah (ma-a-zi'-ah)
1Ch 24:18 the four and twentieth to M·. 4590
Ne 10: 8 M·, Bilgai, Shemaiah: these were "
Macedonia (mas-e-do'-nee-ah) See also MACEDONIAN.
Ac 16: 9 stood a man of M·, and prayed 3110
9 Come over into M·, and help us. 3109
10 we endeavoured to go into M·, "
12 is the chief city of that part of M·, "
18: 5 and Timotheus were come from M·,"

Ac 19:21 when he had passed through M· and3109
22 he sent into M· two of them that "
29 men of M·, Paul's companions in 3110
20: 1 and departed for to go into M·. 3109
3 he purposed to return through M·."
Ro 15:26 it hath pleased them of M· and "
1Co 16: 5 when I shall pass through M·: "
5 for I do pass through M·. "
2Co 1:16 to pass by you into M·, and to "
16 come again out of M· unto you, "
2:13 them, I went from thence into M·. "
7: 5 when we were come into M·, our "
8: 1 bestowed on the churches of M·; "
9: 2 I boast of you to them of M·, that 3110
4 Lest haply if they of M· come with "
11: 9 the brethren which came from M· 3109
subscr. from Philippi, a city of M·, * "
Ph'p 4:15 when I departed from M·, no "
1Th 1: 7 ensamples to all that believe in M· "
8 word of the Lord not only in M· "
4:10 the brethren which are in all M·: "
1Ti 1: 3 at Ephesus, when I went into M·, "
Tit subscr. Cretians, from Nicopolis of M·.* "
Macedonian (mas-e-do'-nee-an)
Ac 27: 2 Aristarchus,...being with a M· of 3110
Machbanai (mak'-ba-nahee)
1Ch 12:13 the tenth, M· the eleventh. *4344
Machbenah (mak'-be-nah)
1Ch 2:49 Sheva the father of M·, and the *4343
Machi (ma'-ki)
Nu 13:15 tribe of Gad, Geuel the son of M·. 4352
Machir (ma'-kur) See also MACHIRITE.
Ge 50:23 also of M· the son of Manasseh 4353
Nu 26:29 of M·, the family of the Machirites:"
29 M· begat Gilead: of Gilead come "
27: 1 son of M·, the son of Manasseh, "
32:39 children of M· the son of Manasseh "
40 unto M· the son of Manasseh, "
36: 1 children of Gilead, the son of M·, "
De 3:15 And I gave Gilead unto M·. "
Jos 13:31 pertaining unto the children of M· "
31 to the one half of the children of M·"
17: 1 for M· the firstborn of Manasseh, "
3 son of M·, the son of Manasseh, "
J'g 5:14 out of M· came down governors, "
2Sa 9: 4 he is in the house of M·, the son of "
5 fetched him out of the house of M·, "
17:27 M· the son of Ammiel of Lo-debar, "
1Ch 2:21 went in to the daughter of M· the "
23 these belonged to the sons of M· "
7:14 concubine the Aramitess bare M· "
15 And M· took to wife the sister of "
16 the wife of M· bare a son, and "
17 son of M·, the son of Manasseh. "
Machirites (ma'-kur-ites)
Nu 26:29 of Machir, the family of the M·: 4354
Machnadebai (mak-nad'-e-bahee)
Ezr 10:40 M·, Shashai, Sharai, 4367
Machpelah (mak-pe'-lah)
Ge 23: 9 he may give me the cave of M·, 4375
17 field of Ephron, which was in M·, "
19 wife in the cave of the field of M· "
25: 9 buried him in the cave of M·, in "
49:30 In the cave that is in the field of M·,"
50:13 him in the cave of the field of M·, "
mad
De 28:34 be m· for the sight of thine eyes 7696
1Sa 21:13 feigned himself m· in their hands, 1984
14 servants, Lo, ye see the man is m·:7696
15 Have I need of m· men, that ye "
15 to play the m· man in my presence?"
2Ki 9:11 came this m· fellow to thee? And "
Ps 102: 8 m· against me are sworn against 1984
Pr 26:18 a m· man who casteth firebrands, 3856
Ec 2: 2 I said of laughter, It is m·: and of 1984
7: 7 oppression maketh a wise man m·;*"
Isa 44:25 the liars, and maketh diviners m·; "
Jer 25:16 drink, and be moved, and be m·, "
29:26 every man that is m·, and maketh 7696
50:38 and they are m· upon their idols. 1984
51: 7 wine; therefore the nations are m·. "
Hos 9: 7 is a fool, the spiritual man is m·, 7696
Joh 10:20 said, He hath a devil, and is m·; 3105
Ac 12:15 they said unto her, Thou art m·. "
26:11 exceedingly m· against them, 1693
24 learning doth make thee m·. 1519,3130
25 I am not m·, most noble Festus; 3105
1Co 14:23 will they not say that ye are m·? "
Madai (ma'-dahee) See also MEDE; MEDIA.
Ge 10: 2 Magog, and M·, and Javan, and 4074
1Ch 1: 5 Magog, and M·, and Javan, and "

made See also MADEST.
Ge 1: 7 And God m· the firmament, and 6213
16 God made two great lights; the "
16 to rule the night: he m· the stars also."
25 And God m· the beast of the earth 6213
31 God saw every thing that he had m·,"
2: 2 ended his work which he had m·; "
2 from all his work which he had m·. "
3 work which God created and m·. "
4 the Lord God m· the earth and the "
9 of the ground m· the Lord God to grow
22 taken from man, m· he a woman, 1129
3: 1 beast...which the Lord God had m·.6213
7 together, and m· themselves aprons."
5: 1 in the likeness of God m· he him; "
6: 6 the Lord that he had m· man on "
7 repenteth me that I have m· them. "
7: 4 living substance that I have m· will"
8: 1 God m· a wind to pass over the earth,
6 window of the ark which he...m·: 6213
9: 6 for in the image of God m· he man. "
13: 4 which he had m· there at the first: "
14: 2 m· war with Bera king of Sodom, "
23 shouldest say, I have m· Abram rich: "
15:18 Lord m· a covenant with Abram, 3772
17: 5 of many nations have I m· thee. 5414
19: 3 he m· them a feast, and did bake 6213
33, 35 they m· their father drink wine
21: 6 God hath m· me to laugh, so that all
8 and Abraham m· a great feast the 6213
27 and both of them m· a covenant. 3772
32 they m· a covenant at Beer-sheba: "
23:17 borders round about, were m· sure
20 cave that is therein, were m· sure
24:11 And he m· his camels to kneel down
21 had m· his journey prosperous 6743
37 And my master m· me swear, saying,
46 And she m· haste, and let down
46 and she m· the camels drink also.
26:22 now the Lord hath m· room for us,
30 And he m· them a feast, and they 6213
27:14 and his mother m· savoury meat, "
30 had m· an end of blessing Jacob,
31 And he also had m· savoury meat,6213
37 I have m· him thy lord, and all his 7760
29:22 men of the place, and m· a feast. 6213
30:37 m· the white appear which was in the
31:46 they took stones, and m· an heap: 6213
33:17 house, and m· booths for his cattle: "
37: 3 he m· him a coat of many colours. "
7 and m· obeisance to my sheaf.
9 and the eleven stars m· obeisance
39: 3 the Lord m· all that he did to prosper
4 he m· him overseer over his house,
5 had m· him overseer in his house,
23 he did, the Lord m· it to prosper.
40:20 m· a feast unto all his servants: 6213
41:43 he m· him to ride in the second chariot
43 he m· him ruler over all the land *5414
51 said he, hath m· me forget all my toil,
42: 7 but m· himself strange unto them,
43:25 they m· ready the present against
28 their heads, and m· obeisance.
30 Joseph m· haste; for his bowels
45: 1 Joseph m· himself known unto his
8 hath m· me a father to Pharaoh, 7760
9 God hath m· me lord of all Egypt: "
46:29 And Joseph m· ready his chariot,
47:26 Joseph m· it a law over the land 7760
49:24 arms of his hands were m· strong
33 had m· an end of commanding his
50: 5 My father m· me swear, saying, Lo, I
6 according as he m· thee swear.
10 he m· a mourning for his father 6213
Ex 1:13 m· the children of Israel to serve
14 and they m· their lives bitter with
14 service, wherein they m· them serve,
21 God, that he m· them houses. 6213
2:14 Who m· thee a prince and a judge 7760
4:11 him, Who hath m· man's mouth? "
5:21 ye have m· our savour to be abhorred
7: 1 I have m· thee a god to Pharaoh: 5414
9:20 m· his servants and his cattle flee into
14: 6 he m· ready his chariot, and took
21 and m· the sea dry land, and the 7760
15:17 thou hast m· for thee to dwell in; 6466
25 waters, the waters were m· sweet:
25 he m· for them a statute and an 7760
16:31 of it was like wafers m· with honey.
18:25 m· them heads over the people, 5414
20:11 the Lord m· heaven and earth, 6213
24: 8 which the Lord hath m· with you 3772
25:31 work shall the candlestick be m·: 6213
33 Three bowls m· like unto almonds,
33 and three bowls m· like almonds in
34 be four bowls m· like unto almonds,

Ex 26:31 with cherubims shall it be m': 6213
29:18, 25 offering m' by fire unto the Lord.
33 wherewith the atonement was m',
36 thou hast m' an atonement for it, *
41 an offering m' by fire unto the Lord.
30:20 offering m' by fire unto the Lord:
31:17 the Lord m' heaven and earth, 6213
18 had m' an end of communing with
32: 4 after he had m' it a molten calf: 6213
5 Aaron m' proclamation, and said,
8 they have m' them a molten calf, 6213
20 he took the calf which they had m', "
20 m' the children of Israel drink of it.
25 Aaron had m' them naked unto *
31 and have m' them gods of gold. 6213
35 they m' the calf, which Aaron m'. "
34: 8 And Moses m' haste, and bowed his
27 I have m' a covenant with thee and 3772
35:21 every one whom his spirit m' willing,
29 whose heart m' them willing to bring
29 to be m' by the hand of Moses. 6213
36: 4 man from his work which they m';*"
8 m' ten curtains of fine twined linen, "
8 of cunning work m' he them. "
11 And he m' loops of blue on the edge "
11 he m' in the uttermost side of "
12 Fifty loops m' he in one curtain, "
12 fifty loops m' he in the edge of the "
13 And he m' fifty taches of gold, and "
14 And he m' curtains of goats' hair "
14 eleven curtains he m' them. "
17 he m' fifty loops upon the uttermost "
17 and fifty loops m' he upon the edge "
18 he m' fifty taches of brass to couple "
19 And he m' a covering for the tent of "
20 he m' boards for the tabernacle of "
23 he m' boards for the tabernacle; "
24 forty sockets of silver he m' under "
25 north corner, he m' twenty boards, "
27 westward he m' six boards. "
28 two boards m' he for the corners of "
31 And he m' bars of shittim wood; "
33 m' the middle bar to shoot through "
34 m' their rings of gold to be places "
35 he m' a vail of blue, and purple, "
35 cherubims m' he it of cunning work. "
36 m' thereunto four pillars of shittim "
37 m' an hanging for the tabernacle "
37: 1 Bezaleel m' the ark of shittim "
2 and m' a crown of gold to it round "
4 And he m' staves of shittim wood, "
6 he m' the mercy seat of pure gold: "
7 And he m' two cherubims of gold, "
7 beaten out of one piece m' he them, "
8 mercy seat m' he the cherubims "
10 And he m' the table of shittim wood: "
11 and m' thereunto a crown of gold "
12 Also he m' thereunto a border of an "
12 m' a crown of gold for the border "
15 he m' the staves of shittim wood, "
16 m' the vessels which were upon the "
17 he m' the candlestick of pure gold: "
17 beaten work m' he the candlestick; "
19 m' after the fashion of almonds in "
19 and three bowls m' like almonds in "
20 were four bowls m' like almonds, "
23 he m' his seven lamps, and his 6213
24 Of a talent of pure gold m' he it, "
25 he m' the incense altar of shittim "
26 he m' unto it a crown of gold round "
27 he m' two rings of gold for it under "
28 m' the staves of shittim wood, and "
29 he m' the holy anointing oil, and "
38: 1 he m' the altar of burnt offering of "
2 he m' the horns thereof on the four "
3 m' all the vessels of the altar, the "
3 the vessels thereof m' he of brass. "
4 he m' for the altar a brasen grate of "
6 m' the staves of shittim wood, and "
7 he m' the altar hollow with boards. "
8 And he m' the laver of brass, and "
9 And he m' the court: on the south "
22 m' all that the Lord commanded "
28 shekels he m' hooks for the pillars, "
30 he m' the sockets to the door of the "
39: 1 m' cloths of service, to do service "
1 m' the holy garments for Aaron; "
2 he m' the ephod of gold, blue, and "
4 They m' shoulderpieces for it, to "
8 m' the breastplate of cunning work, "
9 they m' the breastplate double: a "
15 m' upon the breastplate chains at "
16 they m' two ouches of gold, and "
19 And they m' two rings of gold, and "
20 And they m' two other golden rings, "
22 m' the robe of the ephod of woven "
24 they m' upon the hems of the robe "
25 And they m' bells of pure gold, and "
27 m' coats of fine linen of woven work "
30 m' the plate of the holy crown of "
42 children of Israel m' all the work.* "
Le 1: 9, 13, 17 an offering m' by fire, of a sweet
2: 2 to be an offering m' by fire, of a sweet
3 of the offerings of the Lord m' by fire.
7 it shall be m' of fine flour with oil. 6213
8 offering that is m' of these things "
9 it is an offering m' by fire, of a sweet
10 of the offerings of the Lord m' by fire.
11 the Lord, shall be m' with leaven: 6213
11 in any offering of the Lord m' by fire.
16 is an offering m' by fire unto the Lord.
3: 3 an offering m' by fire unto the Lord;
5 it is an offering m' by fire, of a sweet
9 an offering m' by fire unto the Lord;
11 it is the food of the offering m' by fire
14 an offering m' by fire unto the Lord;

Le 3:16 it is the food of the offering m' by fire
4:35 the offerings m' by fire unto the Lord:
5:12 the offerings m' by fire unto the Lord:
6:17 portion of my offerings m' by fire;
18 the offerings of the Lord m' by fire:
21 In a pan it shall be m' with oil; 6213
7: 5 an offering m' by fire unto the Lord:
25 an offering m' by fire unto the Lord,
30, 35 offerings of the Lord m' by fire,
8:21 an offering m' by fire unto the Lord;
28 is an offering m' by fire unto the Lord.
10:12 of the offerings of the Lord m' by fire,
13 of the sacrifices of the Lord m' by fire:
15 with the offerings m' by fire of the fat,
13:48 a skin, or in any thing m' of skin; 4399
51 or in any work that is m' of skin;*6213
14:11 the man that is to be m' clean, *
36 in the house be not m' unclean:
16:17 have m' an atonement for himself,
20 he hath m' an end of reconciling
21: 6 the offerings of the Lord m' by fire,
21 the offerings of the Lord m' by fire:
22: 5 whereby he may be m' unclean,
27 an offering m' by fire unto the Lord.
23: 8, 13 offering m' by fire unto the Lord
18 even an offering m' by fire, of sweet
25, 27 offering m' by fire unto the Lord.
36, 36 offering m' by fire unto the Lord:
37 an offering m' by fire unto the Lord,
43 I m' the children of Israel to dwell
24: 7 an offering m' by fire unto the Lord.
9 Lord m' by fire by a perpetual statute.
26:13 of your yoke, and m' you go upright.
46 which the Lord m' between him 5414
Nu 4:15 have m' an end of covering the
26 service, and all that is m' for them:*6213
5: 8 an atonement shall be m' for him.
27 he hath m' her to drink the water,
6: 4 nothing that is m' of the vine tree,6213
8: 4 Moses, so he m' the candlestick. "
21 Aaron m' an atonement for them
11: 8 baked it in pans, and m' cakes of 6213
14:36 m' all the congregation to murmur
15:10, 13, 14 an offering m' by fire, of a
25 a sacrifice m' by fire unto the Lord,
16:31 as he had m' an end of speaking *
39 they were m' broad plates for a
47 m' an atonement for the people.
18:17 an offering m' by fire, for a sweet
20: 5 ye m' us to come up out of Egypt,
21: 9 Moses m' a serpent of brass, and 6213
25:13 m' an atonement for the children
28: 2 my bread for my sacrifices m' by fire,
3 This is the offering m' by fire which
6 a sacrifice m' by fire unto the Lord.
8 a sacrifice m' by fire, of a sweet savour
13 a sacrifice m' by fire unto the Lord.
19 ye shall offer a sacrifice m' by fire for
24 meat of the sacrifice m' by fire, of a
29: 6 a sacrifice m' by fire unto the Lord.
13, 36 offering, a sacrifice m' by fire,
30:12 hath utterly m' them void on the day
12 her husband hath m' them void; and
31:20 and all that is m' of skins, and all 3627
20 goats' hair, and all things m' of wood.
32:13 m' them wander in the wilderness
De 1:15 and m' them heads over you, 5414
2:30 and m' his heart obstinate, that he
4:23 covenant...which he m' with you,
36 heaven he m' thee to hear his voice,
5: 2 our God m' a covenant with us in 3772
3 The Lord m' not this covenant with "
9: 9 covenant which the Lord m' with "
12 have m' them a molten image. 6213
16 had m' you a molten calf: ye had "
21 the calf which ye had m', and burnt "
10: 3 I m' an ark of shittim wood, and "
5 tables in the ark which I had m'; "
22 thy God hath m' thee as the stars 7760
11: 4 m' the water of the Red sea to overflow
18: 1 of the offerings of the Lord m' by fire,
20: 9 officers have m' an end of speaking
26:12 m' an end of tithing all the tithes
19 all nations which he hath m', 6213
29: 1 covenant which he m' with them 3772
25 he m' with them when he brought "
31:16 my covenant which I have m' with "
24 Moses had m' an end of writing
32: 6 not m' thee, and established thee 6213
13 m' him ride on the high places of the
13 m' him to suck honey out of the rock,
15 he forsook God which m' him, 6213
45 Moses m' an end of speaking all
Jos 2:17 oath which thou hast m' us swear.
20 oath which thou hast m' us to swear.
5: 3 And Joshua m' him sharp knives, 6213
8:15 all Israel m' as if they were beaten
24 Israel had m' an end of slaying
28 Ai, and m' it an heap for ever, 7760
9: 4 m' as if they had been ambassadors,
15 And Joshua m' peace with them, 6213
15 and m' a league with them, to let "
16 they had m' a league with them, 3772
27 Joshua m' them that day hewers 5414
10: 1 Gibeon had m' peace with Israel,
4 it hath m' peace with Joshua and
5 before Gibeon; and m' war against it.
20 Israel had m' an end of slaying
11:18 Joshua m' war a long time with 6213
19 not a city that m' peace with the
13:14 sacrifices...of Israel m' by fire
14: 8 me m' the heart of the people melt:
19:49 had m' an end of dividing the land
51 m' an end of dividing the country.
22:25 hath m' Jordan a border between 5414
28 of the Lord, which our fathers m', 6213

Jos 24:25 m' a covenant with the people that 3772
J'g 2: 1 m' you to go up out of Egypt, and have
3:16 m' him a dagger which had two 6213
18 had m' an end to offer the present, *
5:13 he m' him that remaineth have *
13 Lord m' me have dominion over the *
6: 2 of Israel m' them the dens which 6213
19 went in, and m' ready a kid, and "
8:27 Gideon m' an ephod thereof, and "
33 and m' Baal-berith their god. 7760
9: 6 and went, and m' Abimelech king,
16 in that ye have m' Abimelech king,
18 and have m' Abimelech, the son...king
27 and m' merry, and went into the *6213
11: 4 of Ammon m' war against Israel.
5 of Ammon m' war against Israel,
11 people m' him head and captain 7760
13:10 the woman m' haste, and ran, and
15 shall have m' ready a kid for thee.*6213
14:10 and Samson m' there a feast; for "
15:17 he had m' an end of speaking,
16:19 And she m' him sleep upon her knees;
25 prison house; and he m' them sport:
27 that beheld while Samson m' sport.
17: 4 who m' thereof a graven image 6213
5 and m' an ephod, and teraphim, "
18:24 taken away my gods which I m', "
27 took the things which Micah had m', "
31 Micah's graven image, which he m', "
21: 5 had m' a great oath concerning him
15 Lord had m' a breach in the tribes 6213
1Sa 2:19 his mother m' him a little coat, "
28 father all the offerings m' by fire
3:13 his sons m' themselves vile, and *
4:18 when he m' mention of the ark of God,
8: 1 he m' his sons judges over Israel. 7760
9:22 m' them sit in the chiefest place 5414
10:13 he had m' an end of prophesying,
11:15 they m' Saul king before the Lord
12: 1 me, and have m' a king over you.
8 Egypt, and m' them dwell in this place.
13:10 as he had m' an end of offering
12 I have not m' supplication unto
14:14 and his armourbearer m', was 5221
15:17 wast thou not m' the head of the
33 sword hath m' women childless,
35 he had m' Saul king over Israel.
16: 8 and m' him pass before Samuel.
9 Then Jesse m' Shammah to pass by.
10 Jesse m' seven of his sons to pass
18: 1 he had m' an end of speaking unto
3 and David m' a covenant, because 3772
13 and m' him his captain over a 7760
20:16 So Jonathan m' a covenant with 3772
22: 8 m' a league with the son of Jesse,* "
23:18 two m' a covenant before the Lord: "
26 David m' haste to get away for
24:16 David had m' an end of speaking
25:18 Abigail m' haste, and took two
27:10 said, Whither have ye m' a road to day?
12 m' his people Israel utterly to abhor
30:11 eat; and they m' him drink water;*
14 We m' an invasion upon the south
21 whom they had m' also to abide at the
25 he m' it a statute and an ordinance 7760
2Sa 2: 9 m' him king over Gilead, and over
3: 6 Abner m' himself strong for the
20 David m' Abner and the men that 6213
4: 4 she m' haste to flee, that he fell,
5: 3 king David m' a league with them 3772
6: 5 manner of instruments m' of fir wood,
8 Lord had m' a breach upon Uzzah: 6555
18 David had m' an end of offering
7: 9 have m' thee a great name, like *6213
10:19 they m' peace with Israel, and
11:13 before him; and he m' him drunk:
19 thou hast m' an end of telling
12:31 m' them pass through the brickkiln:
13: 6 lay down, and m' himself sick: *
8 and m' cakes in his sight, and did 3835
10 took the cakes which she had m', 6213
36 as he had m' an end of speaking,
14:15 the people have m' me afraid:
15: 4 that I were m' judge in the land, 7760
17:25 Absalom m' Amasa captain of the "
22: 5 of ungodly men m' me afraid; "
12 he m' darkness pavilions round 7896
36 thy gentleness hath m' me great.
23: 5 he hath m' with me an everlasting 7760
1Ki 1:41 as they had m' an end of eating.
43 king David hath m' Solomon king.
2:24 who hath m' me an house, as he 6213
3: 1 Solomon m' affinity with Pharaoh king
1 had m' an end of building his own
7 hast m' thy servant king instead of
15 and m' a feast to all his servants. 6213
4: 7 his month in a year m' provision.*
5:12 and they two m' a league together. 3772
6: 4 he m' windows of narrow lights. 6213
5 and he m' chambers round about: "
6 house he m' narrowed rests round*5414
7 of stone m' ready before it was
21 m' a partition by the chains of gold*
23 the oracle he m' two cherubims 6213
31 the oracle he m' doors of olive tree: "
33 m' he for the door of the temple "
7: 6 And he m' a porch of pillars; the "
7 m' a porch for the throne where he "
8 m' also an house for Pharaoh's "
16 m' two chapiters of molten brass, "
18 And he m' the pillars, and two rows "
23 he m' a molten sea, ten cubits from "
27 m' ten bases of brass; four cubits "
29 certain additions m' of thin work.* "
37 this manner he m' the ten bases: "
38 m' he ten lavers of brass: one laver "

1Ki 7:40 And Hiram m· the lavers, and the 6213
40 m· an end of doing all the work "
40 m· king Solomon for the house * "
45 Hiram m· to king Solomon for the "
48 And Solomon m· all the vessels that "
51 work that king Solomon m· for the* "
8: 9 the Lord m· a covenant with the 3772
21 Lord, which he m· with our fathers, "
38 supplication soever be m· by any man,
54 Solomon had m· an end of praying
59 have m· supplication before the Lord,
9: 3 supplication, that thou hast m· before
26 king Solomon m· a navy of ships 6213
10: 9 therefore m· he thee king, to do 7760
12 king m· of the almug trees pillars 6213
16 m· two hundred targets of beaten "
17 he m· three hundred shields of beaten
18 king m· a great throne of ivory, 6213
20 was not the like m· in any kingdom. "
27 king m· silver to be in Jerusalem 5414
27 cedars m· he to be as the sycomore "
11:28 m· him ruler over all the charge of*
12: 4 Thy father m· our yoke grievous: now
10 Thy father m· our yoke heavy, but
14 My father m· your yoke heavy, and I
18 m· speed to get him up to his chariot,
20 and m· him king over all Israel:
28 counsel, and m· two calves of gold, 6213
31 And he m· an house of high places, "
31 m· priests of the lowest of...people, "
32 unto the calves that he had m·: "
32 of the high places which he had m·. "
33 upon the altar which he had m· in "
13:33 m· again of the lowest of the people "
14: 7 and m· thee prince over my people 5414
15 because they have m· their groves, 6213
16 who did sin, and who m· Israel to sin.
26 shields...which Solomon had m·. 6213
27 m· in their stead brasen shields, "
15:12 all the idols that his fathers had m·. "
13 she had m· an idol in a grove; "
22 Then king Asa m· a proclamation
26 his sin wherewith he m· Israel to sin.
30 sinned, and which he m· Israel to sin,
34 his sin wherewith he m· Israel to sin,
16: 2 and m· thee prince over my people 5414
2 hast m· my people Israel to sin, to
13 and by which they m· Israel to sin,
16 all Israel m· Omri...king
26 his sin wherewith he m· Israel to sin.
33 Ahab m· a grove; and Ahab did 6213
18:26 upon the altar which was m·. "
32 he m· a trench about the altar, as "
20:34 as my father m· in Samaria. Then 7760
34 So he m· a covenant with him, and 3772
21:22 me to anger, and m· Israel to sin.
22:11 son of Chenaanah m· him horns of 6213
39 the ivory house which he m·, and *1129
44 Jehoshaphat m· peace with the
48 m· ships of Tarshish to go to 6235
52 the son of Nebat, who m· Israel to sin:
2Ki 3: 2 of Baal that his father had m·. 6213
3 son of Nebat, which m· Israel to sin;
7: 6 had m· the host of the Syrians to hear
8:20 and m· a king over themselves.
9:21 And his chariot was m· ready.
10:16 So they m· him ride in his chariot.
25 as he had m· an end of offering the
27 m· it a draught house unto this 7760
29 the son of Nebat, who m· Israel to sin,
31 of Jeroboam, which m· Israel to sin.
11: 4 and m· a covenant with them, and 3772
12 they m· him king, and anointed
17 Jehoiada m· a covenant between 3772
12:13 not m· for the house of the Lord 6213
20 servants arose, and m· a conspiracy,
13: 2 son of Nebat, which m· Israel to sin;
6 house of Jeroboam, who m· Israel sin,
7 and had m· them like the dust by 7760
11 the son of Nebat, who m· Israel sin:
14:19 they m· a conspiracy against him
21 m· him king instead of his father
24 the son of Nebat, who m· Israel to sin.
15: 9 the son of Nebat, who m· Israel to sin.
15 and his conspiracy which he m·, 7194
18, 24, 28 Nebat, who m· Israel to sin.
30 the son of Elah m· a conspiracy
16: 3 m· his son to pass through the fire,
11 the priest m· it against king Ahaz* 6213
17: 8 kings of Israel, which they had m·. "
15 his covenant that he m· with their 3772
16 m· them molten images, even two 6213
16 and m· a grove, and worshipped all "
19 statutes of Israel which they m·. "
21 and they m· Jeroboam...king:
21 the Lord, and m· them sin a great sin.
29 every nation m· gods of their own, 6213
29 which the Samaritans had m·, "
30 men of Babylon m· Succoth-benoth, "
30 and the men of Cuth m· Nergal, "
30 and the men of Hamath m· Ashima, "
31 the Avites m· Nibhaz and Tartak, "
32 m· unto themselves of the lowest of "
35 whom the Lord had m· a covenant, 3772
38 covenant that I have m· with you "
18: 4 brasen serpent that Moses had m·: 6213
19:15 thou hast m· heaven and earth. "
20:20 how he m· a pool, and a conduit, "
21: 3 up altars for Baal, and m· a grove, "
6 he m· his son pass through the fire,
7 grove that he had m· in the house, 6213
11 m· Judah also to sin with his idols:
16 his sin wherewith he m· Judah to sin,
24 of the land m· Josiah his son king
22: 7 no reckoning m· with them of the
23: 3 and m· a covenant before the Lord, 3772

2Ki 23: 4 all the vessels that were m· for Baal,
12 which the kings of Judah had m·, 6213
12 altars which Manasseh had m· in "
15 the son of Nebat, who m· Israel to sin,
15 which Jeroboam the son...had m·, 6213
19 Israel had m· to provoke the Lord "
30 m· him king in his father's stead.
34 m· Eliakim the son of Josiah king
24:13 had m· in the temple of the Lord, 6213
17 m· Mattaniah his father's brother king
25:16 Solomon had m· for the house of 6213
22 over them he m· Gedaliah...ruler.
23 Babylon had m· Gedaliah governor,
1Ch 5:10, 19 they m· war with the Hagarites, 6213
9:30 of the priests m· the ointment of *7543
31 things that were m· in the pans. *4639
11: 3 David m· a covenant with them in 3772
12:18 and m· them captains of the band. 5414
13:11 Lord had m· a breach upon Uzza:*
15: 1 David m· him houses in the city of 6213
13 Lord our God m· a breach upon us,
16: 2 David had m· an end of offering
5 Asaph m· a sound with cymbals; *
16 which he m· with Abraham, and 3772
26 but the Lord m· the heavens. 6213
17: 8 m· thee a name like the name of * "
18: 8 Solomon m· the brasen sea, and "
19: 6 had m· themselves odious to David,
19 they m· peace with David, and
21:29 which Moses m· in the wilderness, 6213
22: 8 abundantly, and hast m· great wars: "
23: 1 he m· Solomon his son king over
5 with the instruments which I m·, 6213
26:10 yet his father m· him the chief;) 7760
32 whom king David m· rulers over the
28:19 the Lord m· me understand in writing
29: 2 the gold for things to be m· of gold,*
5 manner of work to be m· by the hands
19 for the which I have m· provision.
22 they m· Solomon the son of David king
2Ch 1: 3 the servant of the Lord had m· in 6213
5 brasen altar, that Bezaleel...had m·, "
8 hast m· me to reign in his stead.
9 thou hast m· me king over a people
11 over whom I have m· thee king:
15 And the king m· silver and gold at 5414
15 cedar trees m· he as the sycomore "
2:11 he hath m· thee king over them. "
12 Israel, that m· heaven and earth, 6213
3: 8 And he m· the most holy house, the "
10 he m· two cherubims of image work, "
14 he m· the vail of blue, and purple, "
15 he m· before the house two pillars "
16 And he m· chains, as in the oracle, "
16 and m· an hundred pomegranates, "
4: 1 Moreover he m· an altar of brass, "
2 he m· a molten sea of ten cubits "
6 He m· also ten lavers, and put five "
7 And he m· ten candlesticks of gold "
8 He m· also ten tables, and placed "
8 he m· an hundred basons of gold. "
9 he m· the court of the priests, and "
11 Huram m· the pots, and the shovels, "
14 He m· also bases, and lavers m· he "
18 Thus Solomon m· all these vessels "
19 And Solomon m· all the vessels that "
21 lamps, and the tongs, m· he of gold,*
5: 1 all the work that Solomon m· for *6213
10 when the Lord m· a covenant with 3772
6:11 that he m· with the children of
13 Solomon had m· a brasen scaffold, 6213
29 supplication soever shall be m· of any
40 the prayer that is m· in this place.
7: 1 Solomon had m· an end of praying,
6 the king had m· to praise the Lord, 6213
7 brasen altar which Solomon had m· "
9 day they m· a solemn assembly: * "
15 the prayer that is m· in this place.
9: 8 therefore m· he thee king over 5414
11 king m· of the algum trees terraces 6213
15 Solomon m· two hundred targets "
16 hundred shields m· he of beaten gold:
17 king m· a great throne of ivory, 6213
19 not the like m· in any kingdom. "
27 the king m· silver in Jerusalem as 5414
27 cedar trees m· he as the sycomore "
10: 4 Thy father m· our yoke grievous:
10 Thy father m· our yoke heavy, but
14 My father m· your yoke heavy, but
18 Rehoboam m· speed to get him up to
11:12 and m· them exceeding strong,
15 for the calves which he had m·. 6213
17 m· Rehoboam...son of Solomon strong
22 m· Abijah the son...to be ruler among*
12: 9 of gold which Solomon had m·. 6213
10 king Rehoboam m· shields of brass, "
13: 8 which Jeroboam m· you for gods. "
9 m· you priests after the manner of "
15:16 she had m· an idol in a grove: and "
16:14 m· for himself in the city of David, *3738
14 m· a very great burning for him.
17:10 they m· no war against Jehoshaphat.
18:10 Chenaanah had m· him horns of 6213
20:23 had m· an end of the inhabitants
27 m· them to rejoice over their enemies.
36 they m· the ships in Ezion-gaber. 6213
21: 7 covenant...he had m· with David, 3772
8 Judah, and m· themselves a king.
11 m· high places in the mountains of 6213
13 hast m· Judah and the inhabitants of
19 his people m· no burning for him, 6213
22: 1 m· Ahaziah his youngest son king
23: 3 congregation m· a covenant with 3772
11 the testimony, and m· him king.
16 Jehoiada m· a covenant between 3772
24: 8 commandment they m· a chest, 6213

2Ch 24: 9 m· a proclamation through Judah 5414
10 the chest, until they had m· an end.
14 were m· vessels for the house of 6213
17 and m· obeisance to the king.
25: 5 m· them captains over thousands,*
16 Art thou m· of the king's counsel? 5414
27 they m· a conspiracy against him
26: 1 and m· him king in the room of his
5 the Lord, God m· him to prosper.
13 that m· war with mighty power, to 6213
15 And he m· in Jerusalem engines, "
28: 2 m· also molten images for Baalim. "
19 for he m· Judah naked, and *
24 he m· him altars in every corner 6213
25 he m· high places to burn incense "
29:17 of the first month they m· an end.
24 they m· reconciliation with their
24 offering should be m· for all Israel.
29 they had m· an end of offering,
32: 5 m· darts and shields in abundance. 6213
27 he m· himself treasuries for silver,* "
33: 3 up altars for Baalim, and m· groves, "
7 the idol which he had m·, in the "
9 Manasseh m· Judah and the...to err,
22 which Manasseh his father had m·, 6213
25 the land m· Josiah his son king
34: 4 brake in pieces, and m· dust of them,
31 and m· a covenant before the Lord, 3772
33 m· all that were...in Israel to serve,
35:14 they m· ready for themselves, and*
25 m· them an ordinance in Israel: 5414
36: 1 m· him king in his father's stead
4 Egypt m· Eliakim his brother king
10 m· Zedekiah his brother king over
13 who had m· him swear by God:
22 m· a proclamation throughout all his
Ezr 1: 1 m· a proclamation throughout all his
4:15 search may be m· in the book of
19 and search hath been m·, and it is
19 hath m· insurrection against kings,
19 and sedition have been m· therein. 5648
23 and m· them to cease by force and
5:13 Cyrus m· a decree to build this 7761
14 whom he had m· governor;
17 be search m· in the king's treasure
17 decree was m· of Cyrus the king to 7761
6: 1 Darius the king m· a decree, and "
1 search was m· in the house of the
3 same Cyrus the king m· a decree 7761
11 have m· a decree, that whosoever "
11 let his house be m· a dunghill for 5648
12 I Darius have m· a decree; let it 7761
22 for the Lord had m· them joyful,
10: 5 m· the chief priests, the Levites...swear
7 m· proclamation throughout Judah
17 m· an end with all the men that
Ne 3:16 to the pool that was m·, and unto 6213
4: 7 walls of Jerusalem were m· up, *5927,752
9 Nevertheless we m· our prayer
6: 9 For they all m· us afraid, saying,
8: 4 pulpit of wood, which they had m· 6213
16 them, and m· themselves booths, "
17 m· booths, and sat under the booths: "
9: 6 thou hast m· heaven, the heaven of "
18 they had m· them a molten calf, "
10:32 Also we m· ordinances for us, to 5975
12:43 God had m· them rejoice with great joy:
13:13 I m· treasurers over the treasuries,
25 their hair, and m· them swear by God,
26 God m· him king over all Israel: 5414
Es 1: 3 he m· a feast unto all his princes 6213
5 king m· a feast unto all the people "
9 Vashti the queen m· a feast for the "
2:17 m· her queen instead of Vashti.
18 Then the king m· a great feast 6213
18 he m· a release to the provinces, "
23 inquisition was m· of the matter,
5:14 Let a gallows be m· of fifty cubits 6213
14 and he caused the gallows to be m·. "
7: 9 which Haman had m· for Mordecai, "
9:17, 18 and m· it a day of feasting and "
19 m· the fourteenth day of the month* "
Job 1:10 not thou m· an hedge about him,
17 The Chaldeans m· out three bands, 7760
2:11 had m· an appointment together
4:14 which m· all my bones to shake.
7: 3 am I m· to possess months of vanity,
10: 8 Thine hands have m· me and *6087
9 that thou hast m· me as the clay; *6213
15: 7 or wast thou m· before the hills? *2342
16: 7 But now he hath m· me weary:
7 hast m· desolate all my company.
17: 6 m· me also a byword of the people; 3322
13 have m· my bed in the darkness. *7502
28:18 No mention shall be m· of coral, or of
26 When he m· a decree for the rain, 6213
31: 1 I m· a covenant with mine eyes; 3772
15 m· me in the womb make him? 6213
24 If I have m· gold my hope, or have 7760
33: 4 The Spirit of God hath m· me, and 6213
38: 9 m· the cloud the garment thereof, 7760
39: 6 house I have m· the wilderness, "
40:15 behemoth, which I m· with thee; 6213
19 m· him can make his sword to "
41:33 not his like, who is m· without fear. "
Ps 7:12 hath bent his bow, and m· it ready.
15 He m· a pit, and digged it, and 3738
15 fallen into the ditch which he m·. 6466
8: 5 thou hast m· him a little lower
9:15 sunk down in the pit that they m·: 6213
18: 4 of ungodly men m· me afraid.
11 He m· darkness his secret place; 7896
35 thy gentleness hath m· me great.
43 m· me the head of the heathen: 7760
21: 6 m· him most blessed for ever: *7896
6 thou hast m· him exceeding glad*

Ps 30: 1 hast not m' my foes to rejoice over me.
7 m' my mountain to stand strong:
8 unto the Lord I m' supplication and
33: 6 of the Lord were the heavens m'; 6213
39: 5 m' my days as an handbreadth; 5414
45: 1 things which I have m' touching 4639
8 whereby they have m' thee glad.
46: 8 he hath m' in the earth. 7760
49: 16 thou afraid when one is m' rich,
50: 5 that have m' a covenant with me 3772
52: 7 man that m' not God his strength; 7760
60: 2 Thou hast m' the earth to tremble;
3 hast m' us to drink the wine of
69: 11 I m' sackcloth also my garment; 5414
72: 15 prayer also shall be m' for him *
74: 17 thou hast m' summer and winter. 3335
77: 6 and my spirit m' diligent search.
78: 13 m' the waters to stand as an heap.
50 He m' a way to his anger; he
52 m' his own people to go forth like*
55 m' the tribes of Israel to dwell in their
64 their widows m' no lamentation.
86: 9 nations whom thou hast m' shall 6213
88: 8 hast m' me an abomination unto 7896
89: 3 m' a covenant with my chosen, 3772
39 Thou hast m' void the covenant of thy*
42 thou hast m' all his enemies to rejoice.
43 hast not m' him to stand in the battle.
44 Thou hast m' his glory to cease, and
47 hast thou m' all men in vain? *
91: 9 m' the Lord, which is my refuge, 7760
92: 4 m' me glad through thy work:
95: 5 The sea is his, and he m' it: and 6213
96: 5 idols: but the Lord m' the heavens. "
98: 2 Lord hath m' known his salvation:
100: 3 he is God: it is he that hath m' us, 6213
103: 7 He m' known his ways unto Moses,
104: 24 in wisdom hast thou m' them all: 6213
26 thou hast m' to play therein. *3335
105: 9 covenant he m' with Abraham, 3772
21 He m' him lord of his house, and 7760
24 and m' them stronger than their
28 He sent darkness, and m' it dark;
106: 19 They m' a calf in Horeb, and 6213
46 He m' them also to be pitied of all 5414
111: 4 He hath m' his wonderful works 6213
115: 15 Lord which m' heaven and earth. "
118: 24 the day which the Lord hath m'; "
119: 60 I m' haste, and delayed not to
73 Thy hands have m' me and 6213
98 hast m' me wiser than mine enemies:*
126 work; for they have m' void thy law.
121: 2 Lord, which m' heaven and earth. 6213
124: 8 Lord, who m' heaven and earth. "
129: 3 back: they m' long their furrows.
134: 3 Lord that m' heaven and earth 6213
136: 5 that by wisdom m' the heavens: "
7 To him that m' great lights: for "
14 m' Israel to pass through the midst of
139: 14 for I am fearfully and wonderfully m':
15 when I was m' in secret, and 6213
143: 3 he hath m' me to dwell in darkness,
146: 6 Which m' heaven, and earth, the 6213
148: 6 m' a decree which shall not pass. 5414
149: 2 Israel rejoice in him that m' him: 6213
Pr 8: 26 as yet he had not m' the earth, nor "
11: 25 The liberal soul shall be m' fat:
13: 4 soul of the diligent shall be m' fat.
14: 33 is in the midst of fools is m' known.
15: 19 way of the righteous is m' plain.
16: 4 hath m' all things for himself: 6466
20: 9 can say, I have m' my heart clean,
12 Lord hath m' even both of them. 6213
21: 11 is punished, the simple is m' wise:
22: 19 I have m' known to thee this day, even
28: 25 trust in the Lord shall be m' fat.
Ec 1: 15 is crooked cannot be m' straight:
2: 4 I m' me great works; I builded me
5 I m' me gardens and orchards, 6213
6 I m' me pools of water, to water "
3: 11 He hath m' every thing beautiful in"
7: 3 countenance the heart is m' better.
13 which he hath m' crooked?
29 that God hath m' man upright; 6213
10: 19 A feast is m' for laughter, and wine "
Ca 1: 6 m' me the keeper of the vineyards; 7760
3: 9 Solomon m' himself a chariot of 6213
10 He m' the pillars thereof of silver, "
6: 12 my soul m' me like the chariots of*7760
Isa 2: 8 which their own fingers have m': 6213
17 haughtiness...shall be m' low: *
20 they m' each one for himself to
5: 2 and also m' a winepress therein: *2672
14: 3 wherein thou wast m' to serve,
16 man that m' the earth to tremble,
17 That m' the world as a wilderness, 7760
16: 10 m' their vintage shouting to cease.
17: 4 the glory of Jacob shall be m' thin,
8 that which his fingers have m', 6213
21: 2 sighing thereof have I m' to cease.
22: 11 m' also a ditch between the two 6213
25: 2 thou hast m' of a city an heap; 7760
26: 14 and m' all their memory to perish.
27: 11 that m' them will not have mercy 6213
28: 15 have m' a covenant with death, 3772
15 for we have m' lies our refuge, 7760
22 lest your bands be m' strong:
25 hath m' plain the face thereof, ‡
29: 16 of him that m' it, He m' me not? 6213
30: 33 he hath m' it deep and large:
31: 7 idols of God, own hands have m' 6213
34: 6 it is m' fat with fatness, and with
7 and their dust m' fat with fatness.
37: 16 thou hast m' heaven and earth. 6213
40: 4 mountain and hill shall be m' low:
4 the crooked shall be m' straight, and

Isa 41: 2 him, and m' him rule over kings?*
43: 7 formed him; yea, I have m' him. 6213
24 hast m' me to serve with thy sins, ‡
44: 2 Thus saith the Lord that m' thee, 6213
45: 12 have m' the earth, and created man"
18 that formed the earth and m' it; he "
46: 4 I have m', and I will bear; even I "
49: 1 hath he m' mention of my name.
2 m' my mouth like a sharp sword; 7760
2 hid me, and m' me a polished shaft;"
17 that m' thee waste shall go forth of
51: 10 hath m' the depths of the sea a way 7760
12 man which shall be m' as grass; 5414
52: 10 Lord hath m' bare his holy arm
53: 9 he m' his grave with the wicked, 5414
12 many, and m' intercession for the
57: 8 and m' thee a covenant with them; 3772
16 me, and the souls which I have m'. 6213
59: 8 they have m' them crooked paths:
63: 17 hast thou m' us to err from thy ways, *
66: 2 those things hath mine hand m', 6213
8 the earth be m' to bring forth in one*
Jer 1: 18 I have m' thee this day a defenced 5414
2: 7 m' mine heritage an abomination. 7760
15 yelled, and they m' his land waste: 7896
28 thy gods that thou hast m' thee? 6213
5: 3 m' their faces harder than a rock;
8: 8 Lo, certainly in vain m' he it; *6213
10: 11 gods that have not m' the heavens 5648
12 He hath m' the earth by his power, 6213
25 have m' his habitation desolate. *
11: 10 broken my covenant which I m' 3772
12: 10 they have m' my pleasant portion 5414
11 They have m' it desolate, and being 7760
11 the whole land is m' desolate,
13: 22 discovered, and thy heels m' bare. *
27 Jerusalem! wilt thou not be m' clean?
14: 22 for thou hast m' all these things. 6213
17: 23 but m' their neck stiff, that they might
18: 4 the vessel that he m' of clay was 6213
4 so he m' it again another vessel, as "
19: 11 that cannot be m' whole again: 7495
20: 8 word of the Lord was m' a reproach 1961
25: 17 and m' all the nations to drink,
26: 8 Jeremiah had m' an end of speaking
27: 5 I have m' the earth, the man and 6213
29: 26 The Lord hath m' thee priest in 5414
31: 32 according to the covenant that I m' 3772
32: 17 hast m' the heaven and the earth 6213
20 and hast m' thee a name, as at this*"
34: 8 king Zedekiah had m' a covenant 3772
13 I m' a covenant with your fathers "
15 ye had m' a covenant before me in "
18 covenant which they had m' before "
36: 25 Gemariah had m' intercession to
37: 1 m' king in the land of Judah.
15 for they had m' that the prison. 6213
38: 16 the Lord liveth, that m' us this soul, "
40: 5 king of Babylon hath m' governor
7 had m' Gedaliah...governor in
41: 2 king of Babylon had m' governor
9 which Asa the king had m' for fear 6213
18 the king of Babylon m' governor
43: 1 Jeremiah had m' an end of speaking
46: 10 and m' drunk with their blood: *
16 He m' many to fall, yea, one fell
49: 10 But I have m' Esau bare, I have
51: 7 that m' all the earth drunken:
15 He hath m' the earth by his power, 6213
34 he hath m' me an empty vessel, he 3322
63 thou hast m' an end of reading this
52: 20 Solomon had m' in the house of 6213
La 1: 13 he hath m' me desolate and faint 5414
14 he hath m' my strength to fall, the
2: 7 m' a noise in the house of the Lord, 5414
8 m' the rampart and the wall to lament;
3: 4 flesh and my skin hath he m' old;
7 out: he hath m' my chain heavy.
9 he hath m' my paths crooked.
11 in pieces: he hath m' me desolate. 7760
15 m' me drunken with wormwood. *
45 Thou hast m' us as the offscouring 7760
Eze 3: 8 I have m' thy face strong against 5414
9 than flint have I m' thy forehead: "
17 m' thee a watchman unto the house "
6: 6 may be laid waste and m' desolate,
7: 20 m'...images of their abominations 6213
13: 5 m' up the hedge for the house ‡1443
6 have m' others to hope that they
22 m' the heart of the righteous sad, *
22 sad, whom I have not m' sad; and
16: 24 hast m' thee an high place in every 6213
25 hast m' thy beauty to be abhorred, and
17: 13 and m' a covenant with him, and 3772
16 king dwelleth that m' him king,
24 and have m' the dry tree to flourish:
19: 5 whelps, and m' him a young lion. 7760
20: 5 and m' myself known unto them in the
9 sight I m' myself known unto them,
28 also they m' their sweet savour, 7760
21: 15 it is m' bright, it is wrapped up for the
21 m' his arrows bright, he consulted*
24 m' your iniquity to be remembered,
22: 4 thine idols which thou hast m'; 6213
4 have I m' thee a reproach unto the 5414
13 dishonest gain which thou hast m', 6213
25 have m' her many widows in the midst
26: 10 into a city wherein is m' a breach.
15 slaughter is m' in the midst of thee?
27: 5 m' all thy ship boards of fir trees 1129
6 Bashan have they m' thine oars; 6213
6 have m' thy benches of ivory,
11 they have m' thy beauty perfect. * "
24 bound with cords, and m' of cedar,
25 replenished, and m' very glorious
29: 3 own, and I have m' it for myself. 6213

Eze 29: 9 The river is mine, and I have m' it. 6213
18 every head was m' bald, and every
31: 4 The waters m' him great, the deep*
6 heaven m' their nests in his boughs,
9 m' him fair by the multitude of his
16 I m' the nations to shake at the
36: 3 they have m' you desolate, and
39: 26 land, and none m' them afraid. *
40: 14 m' also posts of threescore cubits, 6213
17 a pavement m' for the court round "
41: 18 it was m' with cherubims and palm "
19 was m' through all the house round "
20 were cherubims and palm trees m', "
25 there were m' on them, on the doors "
25 like as were m' upon the walls; "
42: 15 he had m' an end of measuring
43: 23 thou hast m' an end of cleansing it,
46: 23 it was m' with boiling places under 6213
Da 2: 5 houses shall be m' a dunghill. 7761
15 Arioch m' the thing known to Daniel.
17 m' the thing known to Hananiah,
23 hast m' known unto me now what we
23 hast now m' known unto us the king's
38 and hath m' thee ruler over them all.
45 God hath m' known to the king what
48 the king m' Daniel a great man, 7236
48 m' him ruler over the whole province
3: 1 the king m' an image of gold, 5648
10 Thou, O king, hast m' a decree, 7761
15 the image which I have m'; 5648
29 houses shall be m' a dunghill: 7739
4: 5 saw a dream which m' me afraid,
6 Therefore m' I a decree to bring 7761
5: 1 the king m' a great feast to a 5648
11 father, m' master of the magicians,
21 his heart was m' like the beasts, 7737
29 and m' a proclamation concerning
7: 4 m' stand upon the feet as a man,
16 m' me know the interpretation of
21 same horn m' war with the saints, 5648
9: 1 was m' king over the realm of the
4 my God, and m' my confession,
13 yet m' we not our prayer before *
11: 23 after the league m' with him he shall
12: 10 shall be purified, and m' white, *
Ho 5: 9 m' known that which shall surely
7: 5 the princes have m' him sick with
6 they have m' ready their heart like
8: 4 they have m' princes, and I knew
4 gold have they m' them idols, 6213
6 the workman m' it; therefore it is "
11 Ephraim hath m' many altars to sin, *
10: 1 land they have m' goodly images.
12: 4 and m' supplication unto him:
13: 2 m' them molten images of their 6213
Joe 1: 7 he hath m' it clean bare, and cast
7 the branches thereof are m' white.
18 the flocks of sheep are m' desolate.
Am 4: 10 m' the stink of your camp to come
5: 26 god, which ye m' to yourselves. 6213
7: 2 had m' an end of eating the grass
7 stood upon a wall m' by a plumbline,
Ob 2 m' thee small among the heathen: 5414
Jon 1: 9 hath m' the sea and the dry land. 6213
16 unto the Lord, and m' vows.
4: 5 city, and there m' him a booth, 6213
6 and m' it to come up over Jonah,
Na 2: 3 shield of his mighty men is m' red,
11 whelp, and none m' them afraid?
Hab 2: 17 of beasts, which m' them afraid,
3: 9 Thy bow was m' quite naked,
Zep 3: 6 I m' their streets waste, that none
Zec 7: 12 m' their hearts as an adamant 7760
9: 13 m' thee as the sword of a mighty "
10: 3 m' them as his goodly horse in the* "
11: 10 covenant which I had m' with all 3772
Mal 2: 9 have I also m' you contemptible 5414
M't 4: 3 that these stones be m' bread. *1096
9: 16 garment, and the rent is m' worse.
22 thy faith hath m' thee whole. 4982
22 the woman was m' whole from that "
11: 1 had m' an end of commanding his 5055
14: 36 touched were m' perfectly whole. 1295
15: 6 m' the commandment...none effect 208
28 her daughter was m' whole from *2390
18: 25 that he had, and payment to be m'. 591
19: 4 read, that he which m' them at the 4160
4 beginning m' them male and female, "
12 which were m' eunuchs of men: 2134
12 have m' themselves eunuchs for the "
20: 12 thou hast m' them equal unto us, 4160
21: 13 but ye have m' it a den of thieves. "
22: 2 which m' a marriage for his son, "
5 they m' light of it, and went their 272
23: 15 when he is m', ye make him *1096
24: 45 his lord hath m' ruler over his 2525
25: 6 at midnight there was a cry m', 1096
16 and m' them other five talents. 4160
26: 19 and they m' ready the passover. 2090
27: 24 but that rather a tumult was m', *1096
64 sepulchre be m' sure until the third 805
66 they went, and m' the sepulchre sure, "
M'r 2: 21 the old, and the rent is m' worse. 1096
27 The sabbath was m' for man, and "
5: 34 thy faith hath m' thee whole; go 4982
6: 21 birthday m' a supper to his lords, 4160
56 as touched him were m' whole. 4982
8: 25 upon his eyes, and m' him look up: *4160
10: 6 God m' them male and female. "
52 way; thy faith hath m' thee whole. 4982
11: 17 but ye have m' it a den of thieves. 4160
14: 4 was this waste of the ointment m'? 1096
16 and they m' ready the passover. 2090
58 this temple that is m' with hands, 5499
58 build another m' without hands. 886
15: 7 that had m' insurrection with him, 4955

Lu 1:62 they *m'* signs to his father, how *1770*
2: 2 taxing was first *m'* when Cyrenius *1096*
15 the Lord hath *m'* known unto us. *1107*
17 they *m'* known abroad the saying *1232*
3: 5 the crooked shall be *m'* straight, **1519*
5 the rough ways shall be *m'* smooth;*"
4: 3 this stone that it be *m'* bread. **1096*
5:29 Levi *m'* him a great feast in his *4160*
8:17 that shall not be *m'* manifest; *1096*
48 thy faith hath *m'* thee whole; go *4982*
50 believe only, she shall be *m'* whole. "
9:15 did so, and *m'* them all sit down. *347*
11:40 he that *m'* that which is without *4160*
12:14 *m'* me a judge or a divider over *2525*
13:13 immediately she was *m'* straight, *461*
14:12 and a recompense be *m'* thee. *1096*
16 A certain man *m'* a great supper, *4160*
17:19 way: thy faith hath *m'* thee whole.*4982*
19: 6 and he *m'* haste, and came down, *4692*
46 but ye have *m'* it a den of thieves. *4160*
22:13 and they *m'* ready the passover. *2090*
23:12 Pilate and Herod were *m'* friends **1096*
19 a certain sedition *m'* in the city, "
24:22 of our company *m'* us astonished,**1839*
28 *m'* as though he would have gone *4364*
Joh 1: 3 All things were *m'* by him; and *1096*
3 was not anything *m'* that was *m'*. "
10 the world was *m'* by him, and the "
14 the Word was *m'* flesh, and dwelt * "
2: 9 tasted the water that was *m'* wine,*"
15 had *m'* a scourge of small cords, *4160*
3:21 that his deeds may be *m'* manifest,*5319*
4: 1 that Jesus *m'* and baptized more **4160*
46 Galilee, where he *m'* the water wine."
5: 4 water stepped in was *m'* whole of *1096*
6 unto him, Wilt thou be *m'* whole? "
9 immediately the man was *m'* whole,"
11 He that *m'* me whole, the same *4160*
14 him, Behold, thou art *m'* whole: *1096*
15 Jesus, which had *m'* him whole. *4160*
7:23 I have *m'* a man every whit whole "
8:33 sayest thou, Ye shall be *m'* free? *1096*
9: 3 of God should be *m'* manifest in him.
6 and *m'* clay of the spittle, and he *4160*
11 man that is called Jesus *m'* clay, "
14 sabbath day when Jesus *m'* the clay,"
39 they which see might be *m'* blind.**1096*
12: 2 There they *m'* him a supper; and *4160*
15:15 Father I have *m'* known unto you.*1107*
17:23 that they may be *m'* perfect in one;**5048*
18:18 had *m'* a fire of coals, for it was *4160*
19: 7 he *m'* himself the Son of God. "
23 his garments, and *m'* four parts, "
Ac 1: 1 The former treatise have I *m'*, O "
2:28 *m'* known to me the ways of life; *1107*
36 hath *m'* that same Jesus...Lord *4160*
3:12 we had *m'* this man to walk? "
16 name hath *m'* this man strong, *4732*
25 which God *m'* with our fathers, *1303*
4: 9 by what means he is *m'* whole; *4982*
24 which hast *m'* heaven, and earth, **4160*
35 distribution was *m'* unto every man *1239*
7:10 he *m'* him governor over Egypt *2525*
13 Joseph was *m'* known to his *319*
13 Joseph's kindred was *m'* known **1096*
27 Who *m'* thee a ruler and a judge *2525*
35 Who *m'* thee a ruler and a judge? "
41 they *m'* a calf in those days, and *3447*
43 which ye *m'* to worship them: *4160*
48 not in temples *m'* with hands; as *5499*
50 not my hand *m'* all these things? *4160*
8: 2 *m'* great lamentation over him. "
9:39 and garments which Dorcas *m'*, "
10:10 they *m'* ready, he fell into a trance, *3903*
17 had *m'* enquiry for Simon's house, *1239*
12: 5 prayer was *m'* without ceasing of *1096*
20 *m'* Blastus the king's...their friend.*3982*
21 and *m'* an oration unto them. *1215*
13:32 which was *m'* unto the fathers, *1096*
14: 2 and *m'* their minds evil affected *2559*
5 an assault *m'* both of the Gentiles, *1096*
15 God, which *m'* heaven, and earth, *4160*
15: 7 ago God *m'* choice among us, *1586*
16:13 where prayer was wont to be *m'*; **1511*
24 and *m'* their feet fast in the stocks. *805*
17:24 *m'* the world and all things therein.*4160*
24 not in temples *m'* with hands; *5499*
26 *m'* of one blood all nations of men *4160*
18:12 Jews *m'* insurrection with one **2721*
19:24 which *m'* silver shrines for Diana, *4160*
26 no gods, which are *m'* with hands: *1096*
33 have *m'* his defence unto the people.*626*
20:28 Holy Ghost hath *m'* you overseers.*5087*
21:40 when there was *m'* a great silence,*1096*
22: 6 as I *m'* my journey, and was come *4198*
23:13 forty which had *m'* this conspiracy.*4160*
26: 6 the hope of the promise *m'* of God *1096*
27:40 to the wind, and *m'* toward shore. *2722*
Ro 1: 3 which was *m'* of the seed of David**1096*
20 by the things that are *m'*, even *4161*
23 an image *m'* like to corruptible man, *
2:25 circumcision...*m'* uncircumcision.**1096*
4:14 of the law be heirs, faith is *m'* void,*2758*
14 and the promise *m'* of none effect: *2673*
17 *m'* thee a father of many nations,) *5087*
5:19 disobedience...were *m'* sinners, *2525*
19 of one shall many be *m'* righteous. "
6:18 Being then *m'* free from sin, ye *1659*
22 But now being *m'* free from sin, "
7:13 which is good *m'* death unto me? **1096*
8: 2 hath *m'* me free from the law of *1659*
20 creature was *m'* subject to vanity,**5293*
9:20 it, Why hast thou *m'* me thus? **4160*
29 and been *m'* like unto Gomorrha. *3666*
10:10 confession is *m'* unto salvation. *3670*
20 I was *m'* manifest unto them that**1096*

Ro 11: 9 Let their table be *m'* a snare, and a *1096*
14:21 or is offended, or is *m'* weak. ** 770*
15: 8 the promises *m'* unto the fathers:*
27 Gentiles have been *m'* partakers *2841*
16:26 now is *m'* manifest, and by the **5319*
26 *m'* known to all nations for the *1107*
1Co 1:17 Christ should be *m'* of none effect. *2758*
20 not God *m'* foolish the wisdom of *3471*
30 who of God is *m'* unto us wisdom, *1096*
3:13 man's work shall be *m'* manifest: "
4: 9 are *m'* a spectacle unto the world, "
13 we are *m'* as the filth of the world, "
7:21 if thou mayest be *m'* free, use it * "
9:19 have I *m'* myself servant unto all,**1402*
22 I am *m'* all things to all men, that**1096*
11:19 may be *m'* manifest among you. "
12:13 been all *m'* to drink into one Spirit.*4222*
14:25 secrets of his heart *m'* manifest; *1096*
15:22 so in Christ shall all be *m'* alive. *2227*
45 man Adam was *m'* a living soul; **1096*
45 Adam was *m'* a quickening spirit.*
2Co 2: 2 the same which is *m'* sorry by me?*3076*
3: 6 Who also hath *m'* us able ministers*2427*
10 was *m'* glorious had no glory in *1392*
4:10 might be *m'* manifest in our body.**5319*
11 be *m'* manifest in our mortal flesh.*"
5: 1 God, an house not *m'* with hands, *886*
11 but we are *m'* manifest unto God; *5319*
11 *m'* manifest in your consciences. "
21 For he hath *m'* him to be sin for us,*4160*
21 be *m'* the righteousness of God in**1096*
7: 8 though I *m'* you sorry with a letter,*3076*
8 the same epistle hath *m'* you sorry, "
9 I rejoice, not that ye were *m'* sorry, "
9 were *m'* sorry after a godly manner, "
14 boasting, which I *m'* before Titus, is
10:16 of things *m'* ready to our hand. **2092*
11: 6 have been thoroughly *m'* manifest *5319*
12: 9 strength is *m'* perfect in weakness.*5048*
Ga 3: 3 are ye now *m'* perfect by the flesh?**2005*
13 the law, being *m'* a curse for us: **1096*
16 his seed were the promises *m'*. **4483*
19 come to whom the promise was *m'*;*1861*
4: 4 *m'* of a woman, *m'* under the law, **1096*
5: 1 wherewith Christ hath *m'* us free,**1659*
Eph 1: 6 *m'* us accepted in the beloved: **5487*
9 Having *m'* known unto us the *1107*
2: 6 and *m'* us sit together in heavenly *4776*
11 Circumcision in...flesh *m'* by hands;*5499*
13 are *m'* nigh by the blood of Christ. *1096*
14 our peace, who hath *m'* both one, *4160*
3: 3 *m'* known unto me the mystery; *1107*
5 was not *m'* known unto the sons of "
7 Whereof I was *m'* a minister, **1096*
5:13 reproved are *m'* manifest by...light:*5319*
Ph'p 2: 7 But *m'* himself of no reputation, **1096*
7 and was *m'* in the likeness of men: "
3:10 *m'* conformable unto his death; **4833*
4: 6 requests be *m'* known unto God. *1107*
Col 1:12 hath *m'* us meet to be partakers of*2427*
20 having *m'* peace through the blood*1517*
23 whereof I Paul am *m'* a minister; *1096*
25 Whereof I am *m'* a minister, "
26 now is *m'* manifest to his saints: **5319*
2:11 circumcision *m'* without hands, *1096*
15 he *m'* a shew of them openly, *1165*
1Ti 1: 9 law is not *m'* for a righteous man, *2749*
19 faith have *m'* shipwreck: *3489*
2: 1 giving of thanks, be *m'* for all men;*4160*
2Ti 1:10 now *m'* manifest by the appearing *5319*
Tit 3: 7 *m'* heirs according to the hope of *1096*
Heb 1: 2 by whom also he *m'* the worlds; **4160*
4 Being *m'* so much better than the**1096*
2: 9 *m'* a little lower than the angels *1642*
17 to be *m'* like unto his brethren, *3666*
3:14 For we are *m'* partakers of Christ,**1096*
5: 5 not himself to be *m'* an high priest;"
9 And being *m'* perfect, he became *5048*
6: 4 and were *m'* partakers of the Holy*1096*
13 when God *m'* promise to Abraham,*1861*
20 Jesus, *m'* an high priest for ever **1096*
7: 3 but *m'* like unto the Son of God; *871*
12 is *m'* of necessity a change also of *1096*
16 Who is *m'*, not after the law of a "
19 For the law *m'* nothing perfect, but*5048*
20 not without an oath he was *m'* priest:*
21 priests were *m'* without an oath; *1096*
22 was Jesus *m'* a surety of a better * "
26 and *m'* higher than the heavens; "
8: 9 the covenant that I *m'* with their *4160*
13 covenant, he hath *m'* the first old. *3822*
9: 2 For there was a tabernacle *m'*; **2680*
8 holiest...was not yet *m'* manifest, *5319*
11 tabernacle, not *m'* with hands, *5499*
24 into the holy places *m'* with hands, "
10: 3 is a remembrance again *m'* of sins
13 till his enemies be *m'* his footstool.*5087*
33 whilst ye were *m'* a gazingstock *2301*
11: 3 not *m'* of things which do appear. *1096*
22 *m'* mention of the departing of the *3421*
34 out of weakness were *m'* strong, *1743*
40 without us should not be *m'* perfect.*5048*
12:23 to the spirits of just men *m'* perfect,"
27 shaken, as of things that are *m'*, *4160*
Jas 1:10 But the rich, in that he is *m'* low: *5014*
2:22 and by works was faith *m'* perfect?*5048*
3: 9 are *m'* after the similitude of God. *1096*
1Pe 2: 7 same is *m'* the head of the corner, "
3:22 powers being *m'* subject unto him.*5293*
2Pe 1:16 we *m'* known unto you the power *1107*
2:12 *m'* to be taken and destroyed, **1080*
1Jo 2:19 that they might be *m'* manifest that*5319*
4:17 Herein is our love *m'* perfect, that *5048*
18 that feareth is not *m'* perfect in love."
5:10 not God hath *m'* him a liar; *4160*
Re 1: 6 *m'* us kings and priests unto God "

Re 5:10 hast *m'* us unto our God kings and**4160*
7:14 and *m'* them white in the blood of *3021*
8:11 because they were *m'* bitter. *4087*
14: 7 worship him that *m'* heaven, and *4160*
8 she *m'* all nations drink of the wine*4222*
15: 4 for thy judgments are *m'* manifest.*5319*
17: 2 have been *m'* drunk with the wine *3182*
18:15 things, which were *m'* rich by her, *4147*
19 were *m'* rich all that had ships in "
19 for in one hour is she *m'* desolate. *2049*
19: 7 his wife hath *m'* herself ready. *2090*

madest
Ne 9: 8 *m'* a covenant with him to give 3772
14 And *m'* known unto them thy holy 3045
Ps 8: 6 Thou *m'* him to have dominion over
80:15 that thou *m'* strong for thyself.
17 whom thou *m'* strong for thyself.
Eze 16:17 *m'* to thyself images of men, and 6213
29: 7 *m'* all their loins to be at a stand.
Jon 4:10 not laboured, neither *m'* it grow;
Ac 21:38 before these days *m'* an uproar, * *387*
Heb 2: 7 *m'* him a little lower than the *1642*

Madian (*ma'-de-an*) See also MIDIAN.
Ac 7:29 was a stranger in the land of *M'*, **3099*

madman See MAD and MAN.

Madmannah (*mad-man'-nah*)
Jos 15:31 Ziklag, and *M'*, and Sansannah, 4089
1Ch 2:49 bare also Shaaph the father of *M'*. "

Madmen (*mad'-men*) See also MADMENAH.
Jer 48: 2 thou shalt be cut down, O *M'*; 4086

Madmenah (*mad-me'-nah*) See also MADMEN.
Isa 10:31 *M'* is removed; the inhabitants of 4088

madness
De 28:28 The Lord shall smite thee with *m'*,7697
Ec 1:17 wisdom, and to know *m'* and folly:1947
2:12 behold wisdom, and *m'*, and folly: "
7:25 of folly, even of foolishness and *m'*:"
9: 3 *m'* is in their heart while they live, "
10:13 end of his talk is mischievous *m'*. 1948
Zec 12: 4 and his rider with *m'*: 7697
Lu 6:11 And they were filled with *m'*; and *454*
2Pe 2:16 voice forbad the *m'* of the prophet.*3913*

Madon (*ma'-don*)
Jos 11: 1 that he sent to Jobab king of *M'*, 4068
12:19 The king of *M'*, one; the king of "

Mag See RAB-MAG.

Magbish (*mag'-bish*)
Ezr 2:30 The children of *M'*, an hundred 4019

Magdala (*mag'-da-lah*) See also MAGDALENE.
M't 15:39 and came into the coasts of *M'*. **3093*

Magdalene (*mag'-da-leen*)
M't 27:56 Among which was Mary *M'*, and *3094*
61 there was Mary *M'*, and the other "
28: 1 came Mary *M'* and the other Mary "
M'r 15:40 among whom was Mary *M'*, and "
47 Mary *M'* and Mary the mother of "
16: 1 Mary *M'*, and Mary the mother of "
9 week, he appeared first to Mary *M'*."
Lu 8: 2 Mary called *M'*, out of whom went "
24:10 It was Mary *M'*, and Joanna, and "
Joh 19:25 the wife of Cleophas, and Mary *M'*. "
20: 1 day of the week cometh Mary *M'* "
18 Mary *M'* came and told...disciples "

Magdiel (*mag'-de-el*)
Ge 36:43 Duke *M'*, duke Iram: these be 4025
1Ch 1:54 Duke *M'*, duke Iram. These are "

magician See also MAGICIANS.
Da 2:10 that asked such things at any *m'*. 2749

magicians
Ge 41: 8 and called for all the *m'* of Egypt, 2748
24 I told this unto the *m'*; but there "
Ex 7:11 now the *m'* of Egypt, they also did "
22 the *m'* of Egypt did so with their "
8: 7 *m'* did so with their enchantments, "
18 *m'* did so with their enchantments "
19 Then the *m'* said unto Pharaoh, "
9:11 *m'* could not stand before Moses "
11 the boil was upon the *m'*, and upon "
Da 1:20 ten times better than all the *m'* and"
2: 2 the king commanded to call the *m'*,"
27 wise men, the astrologers, the *m'*, 2749
4: 7 came in the *m'*, the astrologers, "
9 O Belteshazzar, master of the *m'*, "
5:11 thy father, made master of the *m'*, "

magistrate See also MAGISTRATES.
J'g 18: 7 there was no *m'* in the land, *3423,6114
Lu 12:58 with thine adversary to the *m'*, *758*

magistrates
Ezr 7:25 set *m'* and judges, which may 8200
Lu 12:11 unto the synagogues, and unto *m'*,**746*
Ac 16:20 brought them to the *m'*, saying, *4755*
22 and the *m'* rent off their clothes, "
35 the *m'* sent the serjeants, saying, "
36 The *m'* have sent to let you go: "
38 told these words unto the *m'*: "
Tit 3: 1 to obey *m'*, to be ready to every **3980*

magnifical
1Ch 22: 5 the Lord must be exceeding *m'*, 1431

magnificence
Ac 19:27 and her *m'* should be destroyed, *3168*

magnified
Ge 19:19 and thou hast *m'* thy mercy, 1431
Jos 4:14 *m'* Joshua in the sight of all Israel;"
2Sa 7:26 And let thy name be *m'* for ever, "
1Ch 17:24 that thy name may be *m'* for ever, "
29:25 the Lord *m'* Solomon exceedingly "
2Ch 1: 1 with him, and *m'* him exceedingly. "

2Ch 32:23 was m· in the sight of all nations *5375
Ps 35:27 Let the Lord be m·, which hath 1431
40:16 say continually, The Lord be m·. "
70: 4 say continually, Let God be m·. "
138: 2 m· thy word above all thy name. "
Jer 48:26 for he m· himself against the Lord: "
42 hath m· himself against the Lord. "
La 1: 9 for the enemy hath m· himself. "
Da 8:11 he m· himself even to the prince "
Zep 2: 8 m· themselves against their border. "
10 m· themselves against the people "
Mal 1: 5 Lord will be m· from the border of "
Ac 5:13 to them: but the people m· them. 3170
19:17 the name of the Lord Jesus was m·. "
Ph'p 1:20 also Christ shall be m· in my body, "

magnify See also MAGNIFIED.
Jos 3: 7 begin to m· thee in the sight of all 1431
Job 7:17 man, that thou shouldest m· him? "
19: 5 ye will m· yourselves against me, "
36:24 Remember that thou m· his work, 7679
Ps 34: 3 O m· the Lord with me, and let us 1431
35:26 that m· themselves against me. "
38:16 they m· themselves against me. "
55:12 me that did m· himself against me; "
69:30 and will m· him with thanksgiving. "
Isa 10:15 the saw m· itself against him that "
42:21 he will m· the law, and make it "
Eze 38:23 Thus will I m· myself, and sanctify "
Da 8:25 he shall m· himself in his heart, "
11:36 and m· himself above every god, "
37 for he shall m· himself above all. "
Zec 12: 7 not m· themselves against Judah.* "
Lu 1:46 said, My soul doth m· the Lord, 3170
Ac 10:46 speak with tongues, and m· God. "
Ro 11:13 of the Gentiles, I m· mine office: *1392

Magog (*ma'-gog*)
Ge 10: 2 sons of Japheth; Gomer, and M·, 4031
1Ch 1: 5 sons of Japheth; Gomer, and M·, "
Eze 38: 2 face against Gog, the land of M·, "
39: 6 I will send a fire on M·, and among "
Re 20: 8 quarters of the earth, Gog and M·, 3098

Magor-missabib (*ma''-gor-mis'-sa-bib*)
Jer 20: 3 called thy name Pashur, but M·. 4036

Magpiash (*mag'-pe-ash*)
Ne 10:20 M·, Meshullam, Hezir, 4047

Mahalah (*ma'-ha-lah*) See also MAHLAH.
1Ch 7:18 bare Ishod, and Abiezer, and M·.*4244

Mahalaleel (*ma-hal'-a-le-el*) See also MALELEEL.
Ge 5:12 lived seventy years, and begat M·:*4111
13 Cainan lived after he begat M· * "
15 And M· lived sixty and five years,* "
16 M· lived after he begat Jared eight* "
17 And all the days of M· were eight* "
1Ch 1: 2 Kenan, M·, Jered, "
Ne 11: 4 son of M·, of the children of Perez;* "

Mahalath (*ma'-ha-lath*) See also BASHEMATH.
Ge 28: 9 had M· the daughter of Ishmael 4258
2Ch 11:18 Rehoboam took him M· the "
Ps 53: *title* To the chief Musician upon M·. 4257
88: *title* to the chief Musician upon M· "

Mahali (*ma'-ha-li*) See also MAHLI.
Ex 6:19 sons of Merari; M· and Mushi: *4249

Mahanaim (*ma-ha-na'-im*)
Ge 32: 2 called the name of that place M·. 4266
Jos 13:26 from M· unto the border of Debir; "
30 And their coast was from M·, all "
21:38 slayer; and M· with her suburbs, "
2Sa 2: 8 Saul, and brought him over to M·; "
12 Saul, went out from M· to Gibeon. "
29 all Bithron, and they came to M·. "
17:24 Then David came to M·. And "
27 pass, when David was come to M·, "
19:32 of sustenance while he lay at M·; "
1Ki 2: 8 in the day when I went to M·: "
4:14 Ahinadab the son of Iddo had M·: "
1Ch 6:80 suburbs, and M· with her suburbs, "

Mahaneh-dan (*ma'-ha-neh-dan*)
J'g 18:12 they called that place M· unto 4265

Maharai (*ma'-ha-rahee*)
2Sa 23:28 the Ahohite, M· the Netophathite,4121
1Ch 11:30 M· the Netophathite, Heled the son "
27:13 captain for the tenth month was M· "

Mahath (*ma'-hath*) See also AHIMOTH.
1Ch 6:35 the son of M·, the son of Amasai, 4287
2Ch 29:12 arose, M· the son of Amasai, "
31:13 M·, and Benaiah, were overseers "

Mahavite (*ma'-ha-vite*)
1Ch 11:46 Eliel the M·, and Jeribai, and 4233

Mahazioth (*ma-ha'-ze-oth*)
1Ch 25: 4 Mallothi, Hothir, and M·: 4238
30 three and twentieth to M·, he, his "

Maher-shalal-hash-baz (*ma''-her-sha''-lal-hash'-baz*)
Isa 8: 1 with a man's pen concerning M·. 4122
3 the Lord to me, Call his name M·. "

Mahlah (*mah'-lah*) See also MAHALAH.
Nu 26:33 daughters of Zelophehad were M·,4244
27: 1 M·, Noah, and Hoglah, and Milcah, "
36:11 For M·, Tirzah, and Hoglah, and "
Jos 17: 3 the names of his daughters, M·, "

Mahli (*mah'-li*) See also MAHALI; MAHLITES.
Nu 3:20 of Merari by their families; M·. 4249
1Ch 6:19 sons of Merari; M·, and Mushi. "
29 sons of Merari; M·; Libni his son, "
47 The son of M·, the son of Mushi, "
23:21 sons of Merari; M·, and Mushi. "
23 sons of Mushi; M·, and Eder, and "
24:26 sons of Merari were M· and Mushi: "
1Ch 24:28 Of M· came Eleazar, who had no 4249
30 sons also of Mushi; M·, and Eder, "
Ezr 8:18 understanding, of the sons of M·, "

Mahlites (*mah'-lites*)
Nu 3:33 Merari was the family of the M·, 4250
26:58 the family of the M·, the family of "

Mahlon (*mah'-lon*) See also MAHLON'S.
Ru 1: 2 of his two sons M· and Chilion, 4248
5 M· and Chilion died also both of "
4:10 Ruth the Moabitess, the wife of M·, "

Mahlon's (*mah'-lons*)
Ru 4: 9 and all that was Chilion's and M·, 4248

Mahol (*ma'-hol*)
1Ki 4:31 and Darda, the sons of M·: 4235

maid See also BONDMAID; HANDMAID; MAIDEN; MAID'S; MAIDS; MAIDSERVANT.
Ge 16: 2 I pray thee, go in unto my m·; it *8198
3 took Hagar her m· the Egyptian, * "
5 I have given my m· into thy bosom;* "
6 Behold, thy m· is in thy hand; do "
8 Sarai's m·, Whence camest thou? * "
29:24 Zilpah his m· for an handmaid. * "
29 Bilhah his handmaid to be her m·.* "
30: 3 Behold my m· Bilhah, go in unto 519
7 Rachel's m· conceived again, and *8198
9 she took Zilpah her m·, and gave * "
10 Zilpah Leah's m· bare Jacob a son.* "
12 Leah's m· bare Jacob a second son.* "
Ex 2: 5 flags, she sent her m· to fetch it. * 519
8 the m· went and called the child's 5959
21:20 a man smite his servant, or his m·, 519
26 or the eye of his m·, that it perish; "
22:16 if a man entice a m· that is not *1330
Le 12: 5 if she bear a m· child, then she 5347
25: 6 and for thy servant, and for thy m·,519
De 22:14 came to her, I found her not a m·:*1331
17 I found not thy daughter a m·; * "
2Ki 5: 2 of the land of Israel a little m·; 5291
4 Thus and thus said the m· that is of "
Es 2: 7 and the m· was fair and beautiful;* "
Job 31: 1 then should I think upon a m·? 1330
Pr 30:19 and the way of a man with a m·. 5959
Isa 24: 2 master; as with the m·, so with her8198
Jer 2:32 Can a m· forget her ornaments, or 1330
51:22 pieces the young man and the m·; "
Am 2: 7 father will go in unto the same m·,5291
M't 9:24 the m· is not dead, but sleepeth. *2877
25 her by the hand, and the m· arose.* "
26:71 into the porch, another m· saw him, "
M'r 14:69 a m· saw him again, and began to 3814
Lu 8:54 hand, and called, saying, M·, arise.*3816
22:56 a certain m· beheld him as he sat 3814

maiden See also HANDMAIDEN; MAIDENS.
Ge 30:18 have given my m· to my husband:*8198
J'g 19:24 Behold, here is my daughter a m·,1330
2Ch 36:17 compassion upon young man or m·, "
Es 2: 4 let the m· which pleaseth the king5291
9 m· pleased him, and she obtained "
13 thus came every m· unto the king; "
Ps 123: 2 eyes of a m· unto the hand of her 8198
Lu 8:51 father and the mother of the m·. 3816

maidens See also HANDMAIDENS.
Ex 2: 5 her m· walked along by the river's5291
Ru 2: 8 but abide here fast by my m·: "
22 that thou go out with his m·, that "
23 So she kept fast by the m· of Boaz "
3: 2 kindred, with those m· thou wast? "
1Sa 9:11 found young m· going out to draw "
Es 2: 8 many m· were gathered together "
9 as belonged to her, and seven m·, "
4:16 I also and my m· will fast likewise; "
Job 41: 5 or wilt thou bind him for thy m·? "
Ps 78:63 m· were not given to marriage. 1330
148:12 Both young men, and m·; old men, "
Pr 9: 3 She hath sent forth her m·: she 5291
27:27 and for the maintenance for thy m·. "
31:15 household, and a portion to her m·. "
Ec 2: 7 I got me servants and m·, and had8198
Eze 44:22 they shall take m· of the seed of *1330
Lu 12:45 to beat the menservants and m·, *3814

maid-child See MAID and CHILD.

maid's
Es 2:12 when every m· turn was come to *5291

maids See also BONDMAIDS.
Ezr 2:65 Beside their servants and their m·,* 519
Es 2: 9 he preferred her and her m· unto *5291
4: 4 So Esther's m· and...chamberlains* "
Job 19:15 my m·, count me for a stranger: 519
La 5:11 and the m· in the cities of Judah. *1330
Eze 9: 6 utterly old and young, both m·, and* "
Na 2: 7 her m· shall lead her as with the * 519
Zec 9:17 cheerful, and new wine the m·. 1330
M'r 14:66 one of the m· of the high priest: 3814

maidservant See also MAIDSERVANT'S; MAIDSERVANTS.
Ex 11: 5 unto the firstborn of the m· that is 8198
20:10 thy manservant, nor thy m·, nor thy519
17 his manservant, nor his m·, nor his "
21: 7 a man sell his daughter to be a m·, "
32 ox shall push a manservant or a m·; "
De 5:14 nor thy manservant, nor thy m·, nor "
14 and thy m· may rest as well as thou. "
21 or his manservant, or his m·, his ox, "
12:18 thy manservant, and thy m·, and the "
15:17 unto thy m· thou shalt do likewise. "
16:11, 14 thy manservant, and thy m·, and "
J'g 9:18 made Abimelech, the son of his m·, "
Job 31:13 cause of my manservant or of my m·, "
Jer 34: 9 manservant, and every man his m·,8198
10 manservant, and every one his m·, "

maidservant's
Ex 21:27 manservant's tooth, or his m· tooth;519

maidservants See also MAIDSERVANTS'.
Ge 12:16 asses, and menservants, and m·, 8198
20:17 Abimelech, and his wife, and his m·;519
24:35 menservants, and m·, and camels,8198
30:43 cattle, and m·, and menservants, "
De 12:12 menservants, and your m·, and the 519
1Sa 8:16 menservants, and your m·, and 8198
2Sa 6:22 of the m· which thou hast spoken* 519
2Ki 5:26 oxen, and menservants, and m·? 8198
Ne 7:67 their manservants and their m·, of 519

maidservants'
Ge 31:33 tent, and into the two m· tents; 519

mail
1Sa 17: 5 he was armed with a coat of m·; 7193
38 also he armed him with a coat of m·.

maimed
Le 22:22 Blind, or broken, or m·, or having 2782
M't 15:30 that were lame, blind, dumb, m·, 2948
31 dumb to speak, the m· to be whole, "
18: 8 thee to enter into life halt or m·, * "
M'r 9:43 better for thee to enter into life m·, "
Lu 14:13 a feast, call the poor, the m·, the 376
21 bring in hither the poor, and the m·, "

mainsail
Ac 27:40 and hoised up the m· to the wind,* 736

maintain See also MAINTAINED; MAINTAINEST.
1Ki 8:45 supplication, and m· their cause. 6213
49 dwelling place, and m· their cause, "
59 that he m· the cause of his servant, "
1Ch 26:27 to m· the house of the Lord. *2388
2Ch 6:35 supplication, and m· their cause. 6213
39 supplications, and m· their cause, "
Job 13:15 I will m· mine own ways before 3198
Ps 140:12 will m· the cause of the afflicted, 6213
Tit 3: 8 might be careful to m· good works.4291
14 let ours also learn to m· good works "

maintained
Ps 9: 4 hast m· my right and my cause; 6213

maintainest
Ps 16: 5 and of my cup: thou m· my lot. 8551

maintenance
Ezr 4:14 have m· from the king's palace, *4415
Pr 27:27 and for the m· for thy maidens. 2416

majesty
1Ch 29:11 glory, and the victory, and the m·:1935
25 bestowed upon him such royal m· "
Es 1: 4 and the honour of his excellent m·1420
Job 37:22 the north: with God is terrible m·.1935
40:10 Deck thyself now with m· and *1347
Ps 21: 5 honour and m· hast thou laid upon1926
29: 4 the voice of the Lord is full of m·. "
45: 3 mighty, with thy glory and thy m·. "
4 And in thy m· ride prosperously "
93: 1 reigneth, he is clothed with m·; 1348
96: 6 Honour and m· are before him: 1926
104: 1 thou art clothed with honour and m·. "
145: 5 of the glorious honour of thy m·, *1935
12 the glorious m· of his kingdom. 1926
Isa 2:10 Lord, and for the glory of his m·. 1347
19, 21 Lord, and for the glory of his m·, "
24:14 shall sing for the m· of the Lord, "
26:10 will not behold the m· of the Lord.1348
Eze 7:20 of his ornament, he set it in m·: 1347
Da 4:30 and for the honour of my m·? 1923
36 excellent m· was added unto me. *7238
5:18 and m·, and glory, and honour: * "
19 And for the m· that he gave him, * "
Mic 5: 4 in the m· of the name of the Lord 1347
Heb 1: 3 the right hand of the M· on high; 3172
8: 1 throne of the M· in the heavens; "
2Pe 1:16 but were eyewitnesses of his m·. 3168
Jude 25 be glory and m·, dominion and 3172

Makaz (*ma'-kaz*)
1Ki 4: 9 The son of Dekar, in M·, and in 4739

make See also MADE; MAKEST; MAKETH; MAKING.
Ge 1:26 said, Let us m· man in our image, 6213
2:18 I will m· him an help meet for him. "
3: 6 a tree to be desired to m· one wise,
21 did the Lord m· coats of skins, *6213
6:14 M· thee an ark of gopher wood; "
14 rooms shalt thou m· in the ark, and "
15 fashion which thou shalt m· it of: "
16 window shalt thou m· to the ark, "
16 and third stories shalt thou m· it. "
9:12 covenant which I m· between me 5414
11: 3 let us m· brick, and burn them
4 and let us m· us a name, lest we be6213
12: 2 And I will m· of thee a great nation, "
2 bless thee, and m· thy name great; "
13:16 I will m· thy seed as the dust of 7760
17: 2 will m· my covenant between me 5414
6 I will m· thee exceeding fruitful,
6 and I will m· nations of thee, and 5414
20 him, and will m· him fruitful, and will
20 and I will m· him a great nation. 5414
18: 6 M· ready quickly three measures of
6 it, and m· cakes upon the hearth. 6213
19:32 let us m· our father drink wine,
34 let us m· him drink wine this night
21:13 the bondwoman will I m· a nation,7760
18 for I will m· him a great nation. "
24: 3 And I will m· thee swear by the Lord,
26: 4 I will m· thy seed to multiply as *
28 let us m· a covenant with thee; 3772
27: 4 m· me savoury meat, such as I 6213
7 venison, and m· me savoury meat, "
9 I will m· them savoury meat for thy "
28: 3 bless thee, and m· thee fruitful,
31:44 come thou, let us m· a covenant, 3772
32:12 m· thy seed as the sand of the sea,7760
34: 9 m· ye marriages with us, and give
30 have troubled me to m· me to stink

Ge 35: 1 and *m'* there an altar unto God, 6213
3 I will *m'* there an altar unto God, "
40: 14 and *m'* mention of me unto Pharaoh,
43: 16 men home, and slay, and *m'* ready;
46: 3 there *m'* of thee a great nation: 6213
47: 6 *m'* thy father and brethren to dwell;
6 *m'* them rulers over my cattle. 7760
48: 4 me, Behold, I will *m'* thee fruitful,
4 *m'* of thee a multitude of people; 5414
20 God *m'* thee as Ephraim and as 6213
Ex 5: 5 ye *m'* them rest from their burdens.*
7 give the people straw to *m'* brick,
8 which they did *m'* heretofore, 6213
16 and they say to us, *M'* brick: and, "
12: 4 shall *m'* your count for the lamb.
18: 16 *m'* them know the statutes of God.5414
20: 4 *m'* unto thee any graven image, 6213
23 shall not *m'* with me gods of silver, "
23 shall ye *m'* unto you gods of gold. "
24 An altar of earth thou shalt *m'* "
25 thou wilt *m'* me an altar of stone, "
21: 34 owner of the pit shall *m'* it good,
22: 3 for he should *m'* full restitution;
5 vineyard, shall he *m'* restitution.
6 the fire shall surely *m'* restitution.
11 thereof, and he shall not *m'* it good.
12 shall *m'* restitution unto the owner
13 he shall not *m'* good that which
14 with it, he shall surely *m'* it good.
15 be with it, he shall not *m'* it good:
23: 13 *m'* no mention of the name of other
27 I will *m'* all thine enemies turn 5414
32 Thou shalt *m'* no covenant with 3772
33 land, lest they *m'* thee sin against me:
25: 8 And let them *m'* me a sanctuary; 6213
9 thereof, even so shall ye *m'* it. "
10 shall *m'* an ark of shittim wood: "
11 and shalt *m'* upon it a crown of gold*"
13 shalt *m'* staves of shittim wood, "
17 shalt *m'* a mercy seat of pure gold: "
18 thou shalt *m'* two cherubims of gold, "
18 of beaten work shalt thou *m'* them, "
19 And *m'* one cherub on the one end, "
19 ye *m'* the cherubims on the two ends"
23 also *m'* a table of shittim wood: "
24 *m'* thereto a crown of gold round "
25 thou shalt *m'* unto it a border of an "
25 thou shalt *m'* a golden crown to "
26 shalt *m'* for it four rings of gold, "
28 shalt *m'* the staves of shittim wood, "
29 thou shalt *m'* the dishes thereof, "
29 of pure gold shalt thou *m'* them. "
31 shalt *m'* a candlestick of pure gold: "
37 shalt *m'* the seven lamps thereof: "
39 a talent of pure gold shall he *m'* it,*"
40 thou *m'* them after their pattern, "
26: 1 thou shalt *m'* the tabernacle with "
1 of cunning work shalt thou *m'* them."
4 thou shalt *m'* loops of blue upon the"
4 shalt thou *m'* in the uttermost edge"
5 Fifty loops shalt thou *m'* in the one "
5 and fifty loops shalt thou *m'* in the "
6 thou shalt *m'* fifty taches of gold, "
7 thou shalt *m'* curtains of goats' hair"
7 eleven curtains shalt thou *m'*. "
10 thou shalt *m'* fifty loops on the edge"
11 thou shalt *m'* fifty taches of brass, "
14 shalt *m'* a covering for the tent of "
15 shalt *m'* boards for the tabernacle, "
17 thou *m'* for all the boards of the "
18 *m'* the boards for the tabernacle, "
19 thou shalt *m'* forty sockets of silver"
22 westward thou shalt *m'* six boards. "
23 two boards shalt thou *m'* for the "
26 thou shalt *m'* bars of shittim wood; "
29 *m'* their rings of gold for places for "
31 And thou shalt *m'* a vail of blue, "
36 And thou shalt *m'* an hanging for "
37 *m'* for the hanging five pillars "
27: 1 shalt *m'* an altar of shittim wood, "
2 thou shalt *m'* the horns of it upon "
3 *m'* his pans to receive his ashes, "
3 vessels...thou shalt *m'* of brass. "
4 shalt *m'* for it a grate of network of "
4 shalt thou *m'* four brasen rings in "
6 thou shalt *m'* staves for the altar, "
8 Hollow with boards shalt thou *m'* it: "
8 in the mount, so shall they *m'* it. "
9 shalt *m'* the court of the tabernacle: "
28: 2 shalt *m'* holy garments for Aaron "
3 they may *m'* Aaron's garments to "
4 the garments which they shall *m'*; "
4 shall *m'* holy garments for Aaron "
6 they shall *m'* the ephod of gold, "
11 *m'* them to be set in ouches of gold. "
13 And thou shalt *m'* ouches of gold; "
14 wreathen work shalt thou *m'* them, "
15 *m'* the breastplate of judgment "
15 work of the ephod thou shalt *m'* it; "
15 fine twined linen, shalt thou *m'* it. "
22 *m'* upon the breastplate chains at "
23 *m'* upon the breastplate two rings "
26 And thou shalt *m'* two rings of gold, "
27 other rings of gold thou shalt *m'*, "
31 *m'* the robe of the ephod all of blue. "
33 shalt *m'* pomegranates of blue, and "
36 thou shalt *m'* a plate of pure gold, "
39 shalt *m'* the mitre of fine linen, and "
39 shalt *m'* the girdle of needlework. "
40 Aaron's sons thou shalt *m'* coats, "
40 *m'* for them girdles, and bonnets "
40 and bonnets shalt thou *m'* for them, "
42 *m'* them linen breeches to cover "
29: 2 wheaten flour shalt thou *m'* them. "
37 *m'* an atonement for the altar, and
30: 1 *m'* an altar to burn incense upon: 6213
Ex 30: 1 of shittim wood shalt thou *m'* it. 6213
3 *m'* unto it a crown of gold round "
4 two golden rings shalt thou *m'* to it "
4 the two sides of it shalt thou *m'* it; "
5 shalt *m'* the staves of shittim wood, "
10 Aaron shall *m'* an atonement upon
10 in the year shall he *m'* atonement
15, 16 to *m'* an atonement for your souls.
18 shalt also *m'* a laver of brass, and 6213
25 shalt *m'* it an oil of holy ointment, "
32 neither shall ye *m'* any other like it, "
35 And thou shalt *m'* it a perfume, a "
37 the perfume which thou shalt *m'*, "
37 not *m'* to yourselves according to "
38 Whosoever shall *m'* like unto that, "
31: 6 *m'* all that I have commanded thee; "
32: 1 *m'* us gods, which shall go before "
10 and I will *m'* of thee a great nation."
23 *M'* us gods, which shall go before "
30 shall *m'* an atonement for your sin.
33: 19 *m'* all my goodness pass before thee,
34: 10 Behold, I *m'* a covenant: before 3772
12, 15 *m'* a covenant with...inhabitants "
16 *m'* thy sons go a whoring after their
17 Thou shalt *m'* thee no molten gods.6213
35: 10 and *m'* all that the Lord hath "
33 to *m'* any manner of cunning work.*"
36: 3 of the sanctuary, to *m'* it withal. "
5 which the Lord commanded to *m'*. "
6 man nor woman *m'* any more work "
7 sufficient for all the work to *m'* it, "
22 did he *m'* for all the boards of the "
Le 1: 4 for him to *m'* atonement for him.
4: 20, 26, 31, 35 priest shall *m'* an atonement
5: 6, 10, 13 priest shall *m'* an atonement
16 he shall *m'* amends for the harm
16, 18 priest shall *m'* an atonement for
6: 7 the priest shall *m'* an atonement for
8: 15 it, to *m'* reconciliation upon it.
34 to do, to *m'* an atonement for you.
9: 7 and *m'* an atonement for thyself,
7 and *m'* an atonement for them; as
10: 17 *m'* atonement for them before the
11: 43 not *m'* yourselves abominable
43 ye *m'* yourselves unclean with
47 *m'* a difference between the unclean
12: 7 and *m'* an atonement for her; and
8 priest shall *m'* an atonement for
14: 18 priest shall *m'* an atonement for him
19 *m'* an atonement for him that is to
20 priest shall *m'* an atonement for him,
21 waved, to *m'* an atonement for him,
29 to *m'* an atonement for him before
31 priest shall *m'* an atonement for
53 and *m'* an atonement for the house:
15: 15, 30 priest shall *m'* an atonement for
16: 6 *m'* an atonement for himself, and for
10 to *m'* an atonement with him, and
11 shall *m'* an atonement for himself,
16 shall *m'* an atonement for the holy
17 in to *m'* an atonement in the holy
18 Lord, and *m'* an atonement for it;
24 *m'* an atonement for himself, and for
27 to *m'* atonement in the holy place,
30 the priest *m'* an atonement for you,
32 shall *m'* the atonement, and shall
33 shall *m'* an atonement for the holy
33 he shall *m'* an atonement for the
33 *m'* an atonement for the priests,
34 *m'* an atonement for the children of
17: 11 to *m'* an atonement for your souls:
19: 4 nor *m'* to yourselves molten gods: 6213
22 priest shall *m'* an atonement for him
28 not *m'* any cuttings in your flesh 5414
20: 25 *m'* your souls abominable by beast,
21: 5 not *m'* baldness upon their head,
5 nor *m'* any cuttings in their flesh.
22: 22 nor *m'* an offering by fire of them 5414
24 shall ye *m'* any offering thereof in*6213
23: 22 shalt not *m'* clean riddance of the*
28 to *m'* an atonement for you before
24: 18 killeth a beast shall *m'* it good;
25: 9 ye *m'* the trumpet sound throughout*
26: 1 shall *m'* you no idols nor graven 6213
6 and none shall *m'* you afraid:
9 unto you, and *m'* you fruitful, and
19 and I will *m'* your heaven as iron, 5414
22 cattle, and *m'* you few in number;
31 And I will *m'* your cities waste, 5414
27: 2 When a man shall *m'* a singular vow.*
Nu 5: 21 The Lord *m'* thee a curse and an 5414
21 the Lord doth *m'* thy thigh to rot,
22 thy bowels, to *m'* thy belly to swell,
6: 7 shall not *m'* himself unclean for
11 and *m'* an atonement for him, for
25 the Lord *m'* his face shine upon thee,
8: 7 and so *m'* themselves clean. *
12 *m'* an atonement for the Levites.
19 to *m'* an atonement for the children
10: 2 *M'* thee two trumpets of silver; of 6213
2 a whole piece shalt thou *m'* them: "
12: 6 I the Lord will *m'* myself known
14: 4 Let us *m'* a captain, and let us 5414
12 will *m'* of thee a greater nation 6213
30 which I sware to *m'* you dwell therein,
15: 3 will *m'* an offering by fire unto the6213
3 to *m'* a sweet savour unto the Lord, "
25, 28 priest shall *m'* an atonement for
28 Lord, to *m'* an atonement for him;
38 *m'* them fringes in the borders 6213
16: 13 *m'* thyself altogether a prince over
30 But if the Lord *m'* a new thing, 1254
38 *m'* them broad plates for a covering*
46 and *m'* an atonement for them;
17: 5 and I will *m'* to cease from me the
21: 8 *M'* thee a fiery serpent, and set it 6213
Nu 23: 19 spoken, and shall he not *m'* it good?
28: 22, 30 to *m'* an atonement for you.
29: 5 to *m'* an atonement for you:
30: 8 shall *m'* her vow which she vowed,
13 it, or her husband may *m'* it void.
15 shall any ways *m'* them void after that
31: 23 ye shall *m'* it go through the fire, 5674
23 ye shall *m'* go through the water. "
50 to *m'* an atonement for our souls
De 1: 11 *m'* you a thousand times so many more
13 and I will *m'* them rulers over you.7760
4: 10 and I will *m'* them hear my words,
16, 23, 25 and *m'* you a graven image,6213
5: 8 shalt not *m'* thee any graven image, "
7: 2 shalt *m'* no covenant with them, 3772
3 thou *m'* marriages with them;
8: 3 might *m'* thee know that man doth not
9: 14 I will *m'* of thee a nation mightier 6213
10: 1 mount, and *m'* thee an ark of wood. "
13: 14 enquire, and *m'* search, and ask
14: 1 nor *m'* any baldness between your7760
15: 1 years thou shalt *m'* a release. 6213
16: 18 and officers shalt thou *m'* thee in 5414
21 thy God, which thou shalt *m'* thee. 6213
19: 18 shall *m'* diligent inquisition: and,
20: 9 they shall *m'* captains of the armies*
11 if it *m'* thee answer of peace, and open
12 if it will *m'* no peace with thee, but will
21: 14 shalt not *m'* merchandise of her, *6014
16 *m'* the son of the beloved firstborn
22: 8 shalt *m'* a battlement for thy roof, 6213
12 Thou shalt *m'* thee fringes upon the "
26: 19 to *m'* thee high above all nations "
28: 11 the Lord shall *m'* thee plenteous
13 the Lord shall *m'* thee the head, 5414
21 *m'* the pestilence cleave unto thee,
24 The Lord shall *m'* the rain of thy 5414
59 Then the Lord will *m'* thy plagues 6381
29: 1 the Lord commanded Moses to *m'* 3772
14 I *m'* this covenant and this oath; "
30: 9 thy God will *m'* thee plenteous in
32: 26 *m'* the remembrance of them to cease
35 that shall come upon them *m'* haste.
39 I kill, and I *m'* alive; I wound, and
42 *m'* mine arrows drunk with blood,
Jos 1: 8 thou shalt *m'* thy way prosperous,
5: 2 Joshua, *M'* thee sharp knives, and6213
6: 5 when they *m'* a long blast with the
10 shall not shout, nor *m'* any noise *
18 ye *m'* yourselves accursed, when *
18 and *m'* the camp of Israel a curse.7760
7: 3 and *m'* not all the people to labour
19 and *m'* confession unto him; and 5414
9: 6 therefore *m'* ye a league with us. 3772
7 how shall we *m'* a league with you? "
11 now *m'* ye a league with us. "
22: 25 *m'* our children cease from fearing
23: 7 neither *m'* mention of the name of their
12 and shall *m'* marriages with them.
J'g 2: 2 *m'* no league with the inhabitants 3772
9: 48 *m'* haste, and do as I have done.
16: 25 for Samson, that he may *m'* us sport.
17: 3 *m'* a graven image and a molten 6213
20: 38 should *m'* a great flame with smoke
Ru 3: 3 but *m'* not thyself known unto the
4: 11 Lord *m'* the woman...like Rachel 5414
1Sa 1: 6 her sore, for to *m'* her fret, because
2: 8 to *m'* them inherit the throne of
24 *m'* the Lord's people to transgress.
29 *m'* yourselves fat with the chiefest
3: 12 when I begin, I will also *m'* an end.*
6: 5 shall *m'* images of your emerods, 6213
7 Now therefore *m'* a new cart, and * "
8: 5 *m'* us a king to judge us like all 7760
12 and to *m'* his instruments of war, 6213
22 their voice, and *m'* them a king.
9: 12 *m'* haste now, for he came to day
11: 1 *M'* a covenant with us, and we 3772
2 will I *m'* a covenant with you,
12: 22 the Lord to *m'* you his people. 6213
13: 19 Lest the Hebrews *m'* them swords "
17: 25 *m'* his father's house free in Israel. "
18: 25 Saul thought to *m'* David fall by
20: 38 cried after the lad, *M'* speed, haste,
22: 7 *m'* you all captains of thousands, 7760
25: 28 certainly *m'* my lord a sure house;6213
28: 2 I *m'* thee keeper of mine head for 7760
15 the Philistines *m'* war against me,
15 *m'* known unto me what I shall do.
29: 4 *M'* this fellow return, that he may
2Sa 3: 12 also, *M'* thy league with me, and, 3772
13 Well; I will *m'* a league with thee: "
21 they may *m'* a league with thee, "
7: 11 thee that he will *m'* thee an house.6213
21 to *m'* thy servant know them.
23 to himself, and to *m'* him a name, 7760
11: 25 *m'* thy battle more strong against
13: 5 on thy bed, and *m'* thyself sick: *
6 and *m'* me a couple of cakes in my3823
15: 14 *m'* speed to depart, lest he overtake us
20 *m'* thee go up and down with us?
17: 2 handed, and will *m'* him afraid:
21: 3 shall I *m'* the atonement, that
23: 5 although he *m'* it not to grow. *
1Ki 1: 37 *m'* his throne greater than the throne
47 *m'* the name of Solomon better than
47 *m'* his throne greater than thy throne.
2: 42 I not *m'* thee to swear by the Lord,
8: 29 prayer which thy servant shall *m'**
33, 47 and *m'* supplication unto thee
9: 22 did Solomon *m'* no bondmen: but 5414
11: 34 I will *m'* him prince all the days
12: 1 come to Shechem to *m'* him king.
4 *m'* thou the grievous service of
9 *M'* the yoke which thy father...lighten?
10 but *m'* thou it lighter unto us;

1Ki 16: 3 m· thy house like the house of 5414
19 which he did, to m· Israel to sin.
21 the son of Ginath, to m· him king;
17:13 m· me thereof a little cake first. 6213
13 after m· for thee and for thy son. "
19: 2 m· not thy life as the life of one of 7760
20:34 m· streets for thee in Damascus,
21:22 m· thine house like the house of 5414
2Ki 3:16 M· this valley full of ditches. 6213
4:10 Let us m· a little chamber, I pray "
5: 7 Am I God, to kill and to m· alive,
6: 2 let us m· us a place there, where 6213
7: 2 Lord would m· windows in heaven, "
19 Lord should m· windows in heaven, "
9: 2 and m· him arise up from among his
9 And I will m· the house of Ahab 5414
21 And Joram said, M· ready. And his
10: 5 bid us; we will not m· any king:
18:30 let Hezekiah m· you trust in the Lord,
31 M· an agreement with me by a 6213
21: 8 will I m· the feet of Israel move
23:10 might m· his son...pass through the
1Ch 6:49 and to m· an atonement for Israel,
11:10 with all Israel, to m· him king,
12:31 name, to come and m· David king.
38 to m· David king over all Israel:
38 were of one heart to m· David king.
16: 8 name, m· known his deeds among
42 for those that should m· a sound,*
17:21 to m· thee a name of greatness 7760
22 didst thou m· thine own people 5414
21: 3 Lord m· his people an hundred...more
22: 5 will therefore now m· preparation
28: 4 me to m· me king over all Israel:
29:12 and in thine hand it is to m· great,
2Ch 4:11 work that he was to m· for king *6213
16 his father m· to king Solomon for "
5:13 to m· one sound to be heard in
6:21 supplication...they shall m· toward*
22 be laid upon him to m· him swear,*
24 pray and m· supplication before
7:11 came into Solomon's heart to m· 6213
20 and will m· it to be a proverb and 5414
8: 8 did Solomon m· to pay tribute *
9 m· no servants for his work; but 5414
10: 1 all Israel come to m· him king.
10 m· thou it somewhat lighter for us;
11:22 for he thought to m· him king.
14: 7 m· about them walls, and towers,
20:36 joined himself with him to m· ships 6213
25: 8 shall m· thee fall before the enemy:*
29:10 m· a covenant with the Lord God 3772
24 to m· an atonement for all Israel:
30: 5 m· proclamation throughout all Israel,
35:21 God commanded me to m· haste:
Ezr 5: 3 house, and to m· up this wall? *3635
4 of the men that m· this building? 1124
9 house, and to m· up these walls? 3635
6: 8 I m· a decree what ye shall do to 7761
7:13 I m· a decree, that all they of the "
21 do m· a decree to all the treasurers "
10: 3 let us m· a covenant with our God 3772
11 m· confession unto the Lord God 5414
Ne 2: 4 me, For what dost thou m· request?
8 timber to m· beams for the gates
4: 2 will they m· an end in a day? will
8:12 portions, and to m· great mirth, 6213
15 of thick trees, to m· booths, as it "
9:38 of all this we m· a sure covenant, 3772
10:33 to m· an atonement for Israel,
Es 1:20 king's decree which he shall m· 6213
4: 8 to m· supplication unto him, and
8 to m· request before him for her
5: 5 said, Cause Haman to m· haste,
6:10 M· haste, and take the apparel and
7: 7 Haman stood up to m· request for his
9:22 should m· them days of feasting 6213
Job 5:18 and his hands m· whole.
8: 5 and m· thy supplication to the
6 m· the habitation of thy...prosperous.
9:15 I would m· supplication to my judge.
30 and m· my hands never so clean;
11: 3 thy lies m· men hold their peace?
3 shall no man m· thee ashamed?
19 and none shall m· thee afraid;
19 yea, many shall m· suit unto thee.
13:11 not his excellency m· you afraid?
21 and let not thy dread m· me afraid.
23 m· me to know my transgression
15:24 and anguish shall m· him afraid;
18: 2 it be ere ye m· an end of words? *7760
11 Terrors shall m· him afraid on
19: 3 ye m· yourselves strange to me. *
20: 2 to answer, and for this I m· haste.*
22:27 shalt m· thy prayer unto him, and
24:11 Which m· oil within their walls,
25 not so now, who will m· me a liar,*7760
25 and m· my speech nothing worth?
28:25 To m· the weight for the winds: 6213
31:15 made me in the womb m· him?
33: 7 my terror shall not m· thee afraid,
34:29 who then can m· trouble? and *
35: 9 they m· the oppressed to cry: *
39:20 m· him afraid as a grasshopper? *
27 and m· her nest on high?
40:19 can m· his sword to approach unto
41: 3 Will he m· many supplications
4 Will he m· a covenant with thee? 3772
Ps 5: 8 m· thy way straight before my face.
6: 6 all the night m· I my bed to swim;
11: 2 they m· ready their arrow upon
21: 9 shalt m· them as a fiery oven in 7896
12 shalt thou m· them turn their back,
12 thou shalt m· ready thine arrows
22: 9 didst m· me hope when I was upon
31:16 M· thy face to shine upon thy

Ps 34: 2 shall m· her boast in the Lord:
36: 8 shalt m· them drink of the river of
38:22 M· haste to help me, O Lord my
39: 4 Lord, m· me to know mine end,
8 m· me not the reproach of the 7760
40:13 me: O Lord, m· haste to help me.
17 deliverer; m· no tarrying, O my God.
41: 3 wilt m· all his bed in his sickness.*2015
45:16 mayest m· princes in all the earth.
17 m· thy name to be remembered in all
46: 4 shall m· glad the city of God,
51: 6 thou shalt m· me to know wisdom.
8 M· me to hear joy and gladness;
55: 2 in my complaint, and m· a noise; *
57: 1 of thy wings will I m· my refuge, *
59: 6 they m· a noise like a dog, and go
14 them m· a noise like a dog, and go
64: 8 shall m· their own tongue to fall *
66: 1 M· a joyful noise unto God, all ye
2 his name: m· his praise glorious. 7760
8 m· the voice of his praise to be heard:
69:23 m· their loins continually to shake.
70: 1 M· haste, O God, to deliver me;
1 m· haste to help me, O Lord.
5 needy: m· haste unto me, O God:
5 my deliverer; O Lord, m· no tarrying.
71:12 O my God, m· haste for my help.
16 will m· mention of thy righteousness,
78: 5 m· them known to their children:
81: 1 m· a joyful noise unto the God of
83: 2 For, lo, thine enemies m· a tumult:
11 M· their nobles like Oreb, and like7896
13 O my God, m· them like a wheel; as"
15 and m· them afraid with thy storm.*
84: 6 the valley of Baca m· it a well; 6213
87: 4 will m· mention of Rahab and Babylon
89: 1 will I m· known thy faithfulness to all
27 I will m· him my firstborn, higher 5414
29 His seed also will I m· to endure 7760
90:15 M· us glad according to the days
95: 1 us m· a joyful noise to the rock of
2 and m· a joyful noise unto him with
98: 4 M· a joyful noise unto the Lord, all
4 m· a loud noise, and rejoice, and *
6 m· a joyful noise before the Lord,
100: 1 M· a joyful noise unto the Lord, all
104:15 oil to m· his face to shine, and bread
17 Where the birds m· their nests: as
105: 1 m· known his deeds among the people.
106: 8 m· his mighty power to be known.
110: 1 I m· thine enemies thy footstool. 7896
115: 8 that m· them are like unto them; 6213
119:27 M· me to understand the way of thy
35 M· me to go in the path of thy
135 M· thy face to shine upon thy servant;
135:18 They that m· them are like unto 6213
139: 8 if I m· my bed in hell, behold, thou3331
141: 1 cry unto thee: m· haste unto me;
142: 1 the Lord did I m· my supplication.
145:12 To m· known to the sons of men his
Pr 1:16 evil, and m· haste to shed blood.
23 I will m· known my words unto you.
6: 3 thyself, and m· sure thy friend. *
14: 9 Fools m· a mock at sin: but
20:18 and with good advice m· war. 6213
25 holy, and after vows to m· enquiry.
22:21 might m· thee know the certainty
24 M· no friendship with an angry
23: 5 certainly m· themselves wings; 6213
24: 6 wise counsel thou shalt m· thy war:
27 and m· it fit for thyself in the field;
27:11 be wise, and m· my heart glad,
30:26 m· they their houses in the rocks;7760
Ec 2:24 and that he should m· his soul enjoy
7:13 who can m· that straight, which
16 much; neither m· thyself over wise:
Ca 1:11 We will m· thee borders of gold 6213
8:14 M· haste, my beloved, and be thou
Isa 1:15 when ye m· many prayers, I will not
16 Wash you, m· you clean; put away
3: 7 m· me not a ruler of the people. 7760
5:19 Let him m· speed, and hasten his work,
6:10 M· the heart of this people fat,
10 m· their ears heavy, and shut their
7: 6 let us m· a breach therein for us,
10:23 of hosts shall m· a consumption, 6213
11: 3 m· him of quick understanding in*
15 and m· men go over dryshod. *
12: 4 m· mention that his name is exalted.
13:12 m· a man more precious than fine
20 the shepherds m· their fold there.
14:23 m· it a possession for the bittern, 7760
16: 3 m· thy shadow as the night in the 7896
17: 2 and none shall m· them afraid.
11 day shalt thou m· thy plant to grow,*
11 shalt thou m· thy seed to flourish:*
12 m· a noise like the noise of the seas;*
12 m· a rushing like the rushing of *
19:10 that m· sluices and ponds for fish.*6213
23:16 m· sweet melody, sing many songs,
25: 6 m· unto all people a feast of fat 6213
26:13 only will we m· mention of thy name.
27: 5 that he may m· peace with me; 6213
5 and he shall m· peace with me. "
28: 9 shall he m· to understand doctrine?
16 that believeth shall not m· haste.
29:21 That m· a man an offender for a word,
32: 6 m· empty the soul of the hungry,
11 strip you, and m· you bare, and
33: 1 m· an end to deal treacherously. *
34:15 shall the great owl m· her nest,
36:15 let Hezekiah m· you trust in the Lord,
16 M· an agreement with me by a 6213
37: 9 He is come forth to m· war with thee.*
38:12, 13 wilt thou m· an end of me.
16 thou recover me, and m· me to live.

Isa 38:19 the children shall m· known thy truth.
40: 3 m·...in the desert a highway for ‡
41:15 I will m·...a new sharp threshing 7760
15 and shalt m· the hills as chaff. "
18 m· the wilderness a pool of water, ‡"
42:15 I will m· waste mountains and hills,‡"
15 and I will m· the rivers islands, and"
16 will m· darkness light before them, "
21 the law, and m· it honourable.
43:19 even m· a way in the wilderness, 7760
44: 9 They that m· a graven image are *3335
19 shall I m· the residue thereof an 6213
45: 2 m· the crooked places straight:
7 I m· peace, and create evil: I the 6213
14 they shall m· supplication unto thee,
46: 5 will ye liken me, and m· me equal,
47: 2 m· bare the leg, uncover the thigh,*
48: 1 and m· mention of the God of Israel,
15 he shall m· his way prosperous.
49:11 I will m· all my mountains a way, 7760
17 Thy children shall m· haste: thy
50: 2 sea, I m· the rivers a wilderness: 7760
3 and I m· sackcloth their covering. "
51: 3 will m· her wilderness like Eden,* "
4 m· my judgment to rest for a light of*
52: 5 rule over them m· them to howl, *
53:10 thou shalt m· his soul an offering 7760
54: 3 m· the desolate cities to be inhabited.
12 I will m· thy windows of agates, 7760
55: 3 I will m· an everlasting covenant 3772
56: 7 m· them joyful in my house of
57: 4 against whom m· ye a wide mouth,
58: 4 m· your voice to be heard on high.
11 in drought, and m· fat thy bones:
59: 7 m· haste to shed innocent blood:
60:13 m· the place of my feet glorious. 7760
15 will m· thee an eternal excellency, "
17 I will also m· thy officers peace,
61: 8 I will m· an everlasting covenant 3772
62: 6 ye that m· mention of the Lord, keep*
7 till he m· Jerusalem a praise in 7760
63: 6 and m· them drunk in my fury, and
12 m· himself an everlasting name? 6213
14 to m· thyself a glorious name. "
64: 2 to m· thy name known to thine
66:22 and the new earth, which I will m·,6213
Jer 4: 7 his place to m· thy land desolate; 7760
16 M· ye mention to the nations; behold,
27 yet will I not m· a full end. 6213
30 in vain shalt thou m· thyself fair;
5:10 and destroy; but m· not a full end:6213
14 m· my words in thy mouth fire, 5414
18 I will not m· a full end with you. 6213
6: 8 lest I m· thee desolate, a land not 7760
26 m· thee mourning, as for an only 6213
7:16 neither m· intercession to me: for
18 dough, to m· cakes to the queen 6213
9:11 And I will m· Jerusalem heaps, 5414
11 will m· the cities of Judah desolate, "
18 let them m· haste, and take up a
10:22 to m· the cities of Judah desolate, 7760
13:16 of death, and m· it gross darkness. 7896
15:14 I will m· thee to pass with thine
20 And I will m· thee unto this people5414
16: 6 nor m· themselves bald for them:
20 Shall a man m· gods unto himself, 6213
18: 4 seemed good to the potter to m· it. "
11 m· your ways and your doings good.
16 To m· their land desolate, and a 7760
19: 7 I will m· void the counsel of Judah
8 And I will m· this city desolate,
12 and even m· this city as Tophet: *5414
20: 4 I will m· thee a terror to thyself,
9 I will not m· mention of him, nor
22: 6 surely I will m· thee a wilderness, 7896
23:15 and m· them drink the water of gall:
16 prophesy unto you; they m· you vain:
25: 9 and m· them an astonishment, and7760
12 and will m· it perpetual desolations."
18 thereof, to m· them a desolation, 5414
26: 6 will I m· this house like Shiloh, "
6 and will m· this city a curse to all "
27: 2 M· thee bonds and yokes, and put6213
18 now m· intercession to the Lord of
28:13 shalt m· for them yokes of iron. 6213
29:17 and will m· them like vile figs, that5414
22 The Lord m· thee like Zedekiah 7760
30:10 and none shall m· him afraid.
11 I m· a full end of all nations 6213
11 yet will I not m· a full end of thee:
19 the voice of them that m· merry:
31: 4 the dances of them that m· merry.
13 m· them rejoice from their sorrow.
21 waymarks, m· thee high heaps: 7760
31 m· a new covenant with the house 3772
33 the covenant that I will m· with the "
32:40 I will m· an everlasting covenant "
34:17 I will m· you to be removed into all5414
22 and I will m· the cities of Judah a "
44:19 we m· her cakes to worship her, 6213
46:27 ease, and none shall m· him afraid.
28 will m· a full end of all the nations6213
28 I will not m· a full end of thee, but "
48:26 M· ye him drunken; for he
49:15 m· thee small among the heathen,*5414
16 m· thy nest as high as the eagle,
19 will...m· him run away from her:
20 shall m· their habitations desolate
50: 3 which shall m· her land desolate, 7896
44 will m· them...run away from her:
45 shall m· their habitation desolate
51:11 M· bright the arrows; gather the
12 m· the watch strong, set up the
25 will m· thee a burnt mountain. 5414
29 m· the land of Babylon a desolation7760
36 her sea, and m· her springs dry.

Jer 51:39 In their heat I will m' their feasts, 7896
39 and I will m' them drunken, that
57 And I will m' drunk her princes,
La 4:21 and shalt m' thyself naked.
Eze 3:26 m' thy tongue cleave to the roof
4: 9 vessel, and m' thee bread thereof, 6213
5:14 Moreover I will m' thee waste, 5414
6:14 them, and m' the land desolate, "
7:14 the trumpet, even to m' all ready;
23 M' a chain: for the land is full of 6213
24 m' the pomp of the strong to cease;
11:13 m' a full end of the remnant of 6213
12:23 I will m' this proverb to cease, and
13:18 and m' kerchiefs upon the head of 6213
20 hunt the souls to m' them fly,
20 souls that ye hunt to m' them fly.
14: 8 will m' him a sign and a proverb, 8074
15: 8 And I will m' the land desolate, 5414
16:42 I m' my fury toward thee to rest, *
17:17 company m' for him in the war, 6213
18:31 and m' you a new heart and a new "
20:17 neither did I m' an end of them in "
26 that I might m' them desolate, to
31 ye m' your sons to pass through the
21:10 sharpened to m' a sore slaughter;
10 glitter: should we then m' mirth?
22:30 them, that should m' up the hedge,‡1443
23:27 will I m' thy lewdness to cease
24: 5 bones under it, and m' it boil well,
9 will even m' the pile for fire great.
17 cry, m' no mourning for the dead, 6213
25: 4 and m' their dwellings in thee: 5414
5 m' Rabbah a stable for camels, "
13 I will m' it desolate from Teman; "
26: 4 and m' her like the top of a rock. "
8 and he shall m' a fort against thee, "
12 they shall m' a spoil of thy riches, "
12 m' a prey of thy merchandise: and
14 I will m' thee like the top of a rock: "
19 shall m' thee a desolate city, like 5414
21 I will m' thee a terror, and thou "
27: 5 cedars from Lebanon to m' masts 6213
31 shall m' themselves utterly bald
29:10 m' the land of Egypt utterly waste5414
12 will m' the land of Egypt desolate "
30: 9 m' the careless Ethiopians afraid,
10 m' the multitude of Egypt to cease
12 And I will m' the rivers dry, and
12 and I will m' the land waste, and all
14 And I will m' Pathros desolate,
21 to m' it strong to hold the sword.
32: 7 and m' the stars thereof dark; I
8 heaven will I m' dark over thee,
10 m' many people amazed at thee,
14 Then will I m' their waters deep,
15 shall m' the land of Egypt desolate,5414
34:25 m' with them a covenant of peace,3772
26 will m' them and the places round5414
28 and none shall m' them afraid.
35: 3 and I will m' thee most desolate. 5414
7 will I m' mount Seir most desolate, "
9 will m' thee perpetual desolations, "
14 rejoiceth, I will m' thee desolate. 6213
37:19 of Judah, and m' them one stick, "
22 will m' them one nation in the land "
26 I will m' a covenant of peace with 3772
39: 7 So will I m' my holy name known
42:20 to m' a separation between the
43:18 in the day when they shall m' it, 6213
27 the priests shall m' your burnt "
44:14 I will m' them keepers of the charge
45:15 to m' reconciliation for them,
17 to m' reconciliation for the house of
Da 1:10 shall ye m' me endanger my head*
2: 5, 9 m' known unto me the dream,
25 will m' known unto the king the
26 able to m' known unto me the dream
30 shall m' known the interpretation*
3:29 Therefore I m' a decree, that 7761
4: 6 might m' known...the interpretation
7 not m' known...the interpretation
18 m' known unto me the interpretation:
25, 32 shall m' thee to eat grass as oxen,
5: 8 nor m' known to the king the
15 m' known unto me the interpretation
16 thou canst m' interpretations, and*
16 m' known to me the interpretation
17 m' known to him the interpretation.
6: 7 statute, and to m' a firm decree,
26 I m' a decree, That in every 7761
8:16 m' this man to understand the vision.
19 m' thee know what shall be in the last
9:24 and to m' an end of sins, and to
24 to m' reconciliation for iniquity,
27 he shall m' it desolate, even until*
10:14 m' thee understand what shall befall
11: 6 of the north to m' an agreement: 6213
35 to purge, and to m' them white,
44 and utterly to m' away many.
Ho 2: 3 and m' her as a wilderness, and 7760
6 and m' a wall, that she shall not 1443
12 and I will m' them a forest, and 7760
18 day will I m' a covenant for them 3772
18 and will m' them to lie down safely.
5: 2 are profound to m' slaughter, *
7: 3 They m' the king glad with their
10:11 I will m' Ephraim to ride; Judah shall*
11: 8 how shall I m' thee as Admah? 5414
12: 1 m' a covenant with the Assyrians, 3772
9 yet m' thee to dwell in tabernacles,
Joe 2:19 no more m' you a reproach among5414
Am 6:10 m' mention of the name of the Lord.
8: 4 even to m' the poor of the land to fail,*
10 I will m' it as the mourning of an 7760
9:14 they shall also m' gardens, and 6213
Mic 1: 6 I will m' Samaria as an heap of 7760

Mic 1: 8 will m' a wailing like the dragons,6213
16 M' thee bald, and poll thee for thy
2:12 they shall m' great noise by reason
3: 5 the prophets that m' my people err,
4: 4 none shall m' them afraid: for the
7 will m' her that halted a remnant,7760
13 Zion: for I will m' thine horn iron, "
13 I will m' thy hoofs brass: and thou "
6:13 also will I m' thee sick in smiting*
16 that I should m' thee a desolation, 5414
Na 1: 8 will m' an utter end of the place 6213
9 he will m' an utter end: affliction
14 I will m' thy grave; for thou art 7760
2: 1 m' thy loins strong, fortify thy
5 shall m' haste to the wall thereof,
3: 6 filth upon thee, and m' thee vile,
14 morter, m' strong the brickkiln.
15 m' thyself many as the cankerworm,
15 m' thyself many as the locusts.
Hab 2: 2 and m' it plain upon the tables,
18 trusteth therein, to m' dumb idols?6213
3: 2 in the midst of the years m' known;
19 he will m' my feet like hinds' feet,*7760
19 he will m' me to walk upon mine high
Zep 1:18 he shall m' even a speedy riddance6213
2:13 will m' Nineveh a desolation, and 7760
3:13 and none shall m' them afraid.
20 I will m' you a name and a praise 5414
Hag 2:23 will m' thee as a signet: for I have7760
Zec 6:11 silver and gold, and m' crowns, 6213
9:15 and m' a noise as through wine;
17 shall m' the young men cheerful,
10: 1 Lord shall m' bright clouds, and *6213
12: 2 m' Jerusalem a cup of trembling 7760
3 m' Jerusalem a burdensome stone "
6 m' the governors of Judah like an "
Mal 2:15 And did not he m' one? Yet had he6213
3:17 that day when I m' up my jewels; "
M't 1:19 to m' her a publick example, was 3856
3: 3 of the Lord, m' his paths straight. 4160
4:19 and I will m' you fishers of men. "
5:36 canst not m' one hair white or black."
8: 2 thou wilt, thou canst m' me clean. 2511
12:16 they should not m' him known: 4160
33 Either m' the tree good, and his "
33 or else m' the tree corrupt, and his "
17: 4 let us m' here three tabernacles; "
22:44 I m' thine enemies thy footstool? *5087
23: 5 they m' broad their phylacteries, 4115
14 and for a pretence m' long prayer:*4336
15 sea and land to m' one proselyte, 4160
15 m' him twofold more the child of "
25 m' clean the outside of the cup and*2511
24:47 m' him ruler over all his goods. *2525
25:21, 23 m' thee ruler over many things:*"
27:65 your way, m' it as sure as ye can. 805
M'r 1: 3 of the Lord, m' his paths straight. 4160
17 m' you to become fishers of men. "
40 thou wilt, thou canst m' me clean. 2511
3:12 they should not m' him known. 4160
5:39 Why m' ye this ado, and weep? the2350
6:39 m' all sit down by companies upon* 347
9: 5 let us m' three tabernacles; one 4160
12:36 I m' thine enemies thy footstool. 5087
40 for a pretence m' long prayers: 4336
42 in two mites, which m' a farthing. 1510
14:15 prepared: there m' ready for us. 2090
Lu 1:17 m' ready a people prepared for the "
3: 4 of the Lord, m' his paths straight. 4160
5:12 thou wilt, thou canst m' me clean. 2511
33 of John fast often, and m' prayers,4160
34 m' the children of the bridechamber"
9:14 M' them sit down by fifties in a 2625
33 let us m' three tabernacles; one 4160
52 Samaritans, to m' ready for him. 2090
11:39 ye Pharisees m' clean the outside*2511
40 m' that which is within also? 4160
12:37 and m' them to sit down to meat, 347
42 whom his lord shall m' ruler over*2525
44 that he will m' him ruler over all * "
14:18 one consent began to m' excuse. 3868
31 to m' war against another king, *4820
15:19 m' me as one of thy hired servants.4160
29 I might m' merry with my friends:2165
32 was meet that we should m' merry, "
16: 9 M' to yourself friends of the 4160
17: 8 M' ready wherewith I may sup, 2090
19: 5 Zacchæus, m' haste, and come 4692
20:43 I m' thine enemies thy footstool. 5087
47 and for a shew m' long prayers: 4336
22:12 room furnished: there m' ready. 2090
Joh 1:23 M' straight the way of the Lord, 2116
2:16 m' not my Father's house an house4160
6:10 Jesus said, M' the men sit down. "
15 take him by force, to m' him a king,"
8:32 and the truth shall m' you free, 1659
36 the Son therefore shall m' you free, "
10:24 long dost thou m' us to doubt? * 142
14:23 him, and m' our abode with him. 4160
Ac 2:28 shalt m' me full of joy with thy 4137
35 Until I m' thy foes thy footstool. 5087
7:40 Aaron, M' us gods to go before us:4160
44 m' it according to the fashion "
9:34 thee whole: arise, and m' thy bed. 4766
22: 1 my defence which I m' now unto you.
18 M' haste, and get thee quickly out4692
23:23 M' ready two hundred soldiers to 2090
26:16 m' thee a minister and a witness *4400
24 much learning doth m' thee mad. *4062
Ro 1: 9 m' mention of you always in my 4160
3: 3 m' the faith of God without effect? 2673
31 then m' void the law through faith?"
9:21 to m' one vessel unto honour, 4160
22 wrath, and to m' his power known,1107
23 m' known the riches of his glory "
28 short work will the Lord m' upon *4160

Ro 13:14 and m' not provision for the flesh, 4160
14: 4 for God is able to m' him stand. 2476
19 the things which m' for peace, 3753
15:18 m' the Gentiles obedient, by word*1519
26 to m' a certain contribution for the4160
1Co 4: 5 will m' manifest the counsels of the5319
6:15 m' them the members of an harlot? 4160
8:13 if meat m' my brother to offend, †‡4624
13 lest I m' my brother to offend. ‡ "
9:15 man should m' my glorying void. 2758
18 m' the gospel of Christ without 5087
10:13 temptation...m' a way to escape, 4160
2Co 2: 2 For if I m' you sorry, who is he 3076
9: 5 m' up beforehand your bounty, 4294
8 God is able to m' all grace abound4052
10:12 dare not m' ourselves of the number,*
12:17 Did I m' a gain of you by any of *4122
18 Did Titus m' a gain of you? walked*"
Ga 2:18 I m' myself a transgressor. *4921
3:17 m' the promise of none effect. 2673
6:12 to m' a fair shew in the flesh, 2146
Eph 2:15 to m' in himself of twain one new *2936
3: 9 to m' all men see...the fellowship 5461
6:19 to m' known the mystery of the 1107
21 shall m' known to you all things: "
Col 1:27 m' known what is the riches of the "
4: 4 That I may m' it manifest, as I 5319
9 m' known unto you all things 1107
1Th 3:12 m' you to increase and abound in 4121
2Th 3: 9 to m' ourselves an ensample unto 1325
2Ti 3:15 able to m' thee wise unto salvation4679
4: 5 m' full proof of thy ministry. *4135
Heb 1:13 I m' thine enemies thy footstool? 5087
2:10 m' the captain of...salvation perfect5055
17 to m' reconciliation for the sins of 2433
7:25 he ever liveth to m' intercession 1793
8: 5 he was about to m' the tabernacle:2005
5 thou m' all things according to the4160
8 m' a new covenant with the house4931
10 this is the covenant that I will m' 1303
9: 9 m' him that did the service perfect,5055
10: 1 m' the comers thereunto perfect. "
16 This is the covenant that I will m' 1303
12:13 m' straight paths for your feet, 4160
13:21 M' you perfect in every good work 2675
Jas 3:18 in peace of them that m' peace. 4160
1Pe 5:10 m'...perfect, stablish, strengthen, *2675
2Pe 1: 8 they m' you that ye shall neither 2525
10 m' your calling and election sure: 4160
2: 3 words m' merchandise of you: 1710
1Jo 1:10 have not sinned, we m' him a liar, 4160
Re 3: 9 I will m' them of the synagogue *1325
9 will m' them to come and worship 4160
12 will I m' a pillar in the temple of "
10: 9 and it shall m' thy belly bitter, 4087
11: 7 pit shall m' war against them, 4160
10 rejoice over them, and m' merry, 2165
12:17 went to m' war with the remnant 4160
13: 4 who is able to m' war with him? *4170
7 to m' war with the saints, and to 4160
14 should m' an image to the beast, "
17:14 These shall m' war with the Lamb,*4170
16 shall m' her desolate and naked, 4160
19:11 he doth judge and m' war. 4170
19 to m' war against him that sat on 4160
21: 5 said, Behold, I m' all things new. "

maker See also MAKERS.
Job 4:17 a man be more pure than his m'? 6213
32:22 my m' would soon take me away. "
35:10 Where is God my m', who giveth "
36: 3 ascribe righteousness to my M'. 6466
Ps 95: 6 us kneel before the Lord our M'. 6213
Pr 14:31 the poor reproacheth his M': "
17: 5 the poor reproacheth his M': "
22: 2 the Lord is the m' of them all. "
Isa 1:31 tow, and the m' of it as a spark, *6467
17: 7 day shall a man look to his M', 6213
22:11 not looked unto the m' thereof, * "
45: 9 him that striveth with his M'! 3335
11 the Holy One of Israel, and his M', "
51:13 And forgettest the Lord thy m', 6213
54: 5 For thy M' is thine husband; The "
Jer 33: 2 Thus saith the Lord the m' thereof,*"
Hos 8:14 For Israel hath forgotten his M', "
Hab 2:18 the m' thereof hath graven it; 3335
18 the m' of his work trusteth therein,"
Heb 11:10 whose builder and m' is God. 1217

makers See also PEACEMAKERS; TENTMAKERS.
Isa 45:16 together that are m' of idols. 2796

makest
J'g 18: 3 and what m' thou in this place? *6213
Job 13:26 m' me to possess the iniquities of
22: 3 him, that thou m' thy ways perfect?
Ps 4: 8 Lord, only m' me dwell in safety.
39:11 m' his beauty to consume away
44:10 Thou m' us to turn back from the
13 Thou m' us a reproach to our 6213
14 Thou m' us a byword among the "
65: 8 thou m' the outgoings of...to rejoice
10 thou m' it soft with showers:
80: 6 Thou m' us a strife unto our 7760
104:20 Thou m' darkness, and it is night:7896
144: 3 man, that thou m' account of him!
Ca 1: 7 thou m' thy flock to rest at noon:
Isa 45: 9 that fashioned it, What m' thou? 6213
Jer 22:23 that m' thy nest in the cedars,
28:15 thou m' this people to trust in a lie.
Eze 16:31 and m' thine high place in every 6213
Hab 1:14 And m' men as the fishes of the sea,"
2:15 to him, and m' him drunken also,
Lu 14:12 When thou m' a dinner or a supper,4160
13 when thou m' a feast, call the poor, "
Joh 8:53 are dead: whom m' thou thyself? "
10:33 thou, being a man, m' thyself God. "

Ro 2:17 the law, and m' thy boast of God, *2744
23 Thou that m' thy boast of the law," "
maketh
Ex 4:11 who m' the dumb, or deaf, or the 7760
Le 7: 7 the priest that m' atonement
14:11 the priest that m' him clean shall*
17:11 blood that m' an atonement for the
De 18:10 m' his son or his daughter to pass
20:20 the city that m' war with thee, 6213
21:16 m' his sons to inherit that which *
24: 7 and m' merchandise of him, or *
27:15 man that m' any graven or 6213
18 be he that m' the blind to wander out
29:12 the Lord thy God m' with thee this3772
1Sa 2: 6 The Lord killeth, and m' alive:
7 The Lord m' poor, and m' rich:
2Sa 22:33 power: and he m' my way perfect.*
34 He m' my feet like hinds' feet: and7737
Job 5:18 For he m' sore, and bindeth up: he
9: 9 Which m' Arcturus, Orion, and 6213
12:17 spoiled, and m' the judges fools.
25 m' them to stagger like a drunken
15:47 m' collops of fat on his flanks. ††6213
23:16 For God m' my heart soft, and the*
25: 2 he m' peace in his high places. 6213
27:18 and as a booth that the keeper m'. "
35:11 and m' us wiser than the fowls of
36:27 he m' small the drops of water: *
41:31 He m' the deep to boil like a pot: he
31 m' the sea like a pot of ointment. 7760
32 He m' a path to shine after him; one
Ps 9:12 When he m' inquisition for blood,
18:32 strength, and m' my way perfect. 5414
33 He m' my feet like hinds' feet, and7737
23: 2 He m' me to lie down in green
29: 6 He m' them also to skip like a calf;
9 voice of the Lord m' the hinds to calve,
33:10 m' the devices of the people of none
40: 4 man that m' the Lord his trust, 7760
46: 9 He m' wars to cease unto the end
104: 3 who m' the clouds his chariot: 7760
4 Who m' his angels spirits; his 6213
15 wine that m' glad the heart of
107:29 He m' the storm a calm, so that
36 there he m' the hungry to dwell,
41 and m' him families like a flock. 7760
113: 9 He m' the barren woman to keep
135: 7 he m' lightnings for the rain; 6213
147: 8 who m' grass to grow upon the
14 He m' peace in thy borders, and 7760
Pr 10: 1 A wise son m' a glad father: but a
4 the hand of the diligent m' rich.
22 The blessing of the Lord, it m' rich,
12: 4 she that m' ashamed is as rottenness
25 in the heart of man m' it stoop:
25 but a good word m' it glad.
13: 7 There is that m' himself rich, yet
7 there is that m' himself poor, yet
12 Hope deferred m' the heart sick:
15:13 A merry heart m' a cheerful
20 A wise son m' a glad father: but a
30 a good report m' the bones fat. *
16: 7 he m' even his enemies to be at peace
18:16 A man's gift m' room for him, and
19: 4 Wealth m' many friends; but the*
28:20 he that m' haste to be rich shall not
31:22 She m' herself coverings of 6213
24 She m' fine linen, and selleth it; "
Ec 3:11 can find out the work that God m'* "
7: 7 oppression m' a wise man mad;
8: 1 man's wisdom m' his face to shine,
10:19 made for laughter, and wine m' merry:
11: 5 not the works of God who m' all. *6213
Isa 19:17 every one that m' mention thereof *
24: 1 the Lord m' the earth empty,
1 and m' it waste, and turneth it upside
27: 9 he m' all the stones of the altar 7760
40:23 he m' the judges of the earth as 6213
43:16 Lord, which m' a way in the sea, 5414
44:13 m' it after the figure of a man, *6213
15 he m' a god, and worshippeth it; 6466
15 he m' it a graven image, and 6213
17 the residue thereof he m' a god, "
24 I am the Lord that m' all things; "
25 of the liars, and m' diviners mad;
25 and m' their knowledge foolish;
46: 6 a goldsmith; and he m' it a god: 6213
55:10 m' it bring forth and bud, that it
59:15 departeth from evil m' himself a prey:
Jer 4:19 my heart m' a noise in me; *
10:13 he m' lightnings with rain, and 6213
17: 5 trusteth in man, and m' flesh his arm,
21: 2 king of Babylon m' war against us;
29:26 that is mad, and m' himself a prophet,
27 which m' himself a prophet to you?
48:28 dove that m' her nest in the sides
51:16 he m' lightnings with rain, and 6213
Eze 22: 3 m' idols against herself to defile "
Da 2:28 and m' known to the king *
29 m' known to thee what shall come*
6:13 m' his petition three times a day.
11:31 the abomination that m' desolate.
12:11 the abomination that m' desolate set
Am 4:13 that m' the morning darkness, 6213
5: 8 that m' the seven stars and Orion,
8 and m' the day dark with night:
Na 1: 4 He rebuketh the sea, and m' it dry,
M't 5:45 for he m' his sun to rise on the evil 393
M'k 7:37 he m' both the deaf to hear, and 4160
Lu 5:36 then both the new m' a rent, and *4977
Joh 19:12 whosoever m' himself a king 4160
Ac 9:34 Jesus Christ m' thee whole: *2390
Ro 5: 5 hope m' not ashamed; because *2617
8:26 Spirit itself m' intercession for us 5241
27 he m' intercession for the saints 1793
34 who also m' intercession for us. "
Ro 11: 2 he m' intercession to God against*1793
1Co 4: 7 For who m' thee to differ from 1252
2Co 2: 2 who is he then that m' me glad, 2165
14 and m' manifest the savour of his 5319
Ga 2: 6 they were, it m' no matter to me: 1308
Eph 4:16 m' increase of the body unto the 4160
Heb 1: 7 Who m' his angels spirits, and his "
7:28 law m' men high priests which *2525
28 m' the Son, who is consecrated for* "
Re 13:13 he m' fire come down from heaven*4160
21:27 worketh abomination, or m' a lie:
22:15 and whosoever loveth and m' a lie. 4160
Makheloth (*mak'-he-loth*)
Nu 33:25 from Haradah, and pitched in M'. 4721
26 And they removed from M', and "
making
Ex 5:14 not fulfilled your task in m' brick
De 20:19 time, in m' war against it to take it,
J'g 19:22 they were m' their hearts merry,
1Ki 4:20 and drinking, and m' merry.
1Ch 15:28 m' a noise with psalteries and *
17:19 m' known all these great things. *
2Ch 30:22 m' confession to the Lord God of
Ps 19: 7 Lord is sure, m' wise the simple.
Ec 12:12 m' many books there is no end; 6213
Isa 3:16 and m' a tinkling with their feet:
Jer 20:15 born unto thee; m' him very glad.
Eze 27:16 multitude of the wares of thy m': *4639
18 multitude of the wares of thy m', * "
Da 6:11 and m' supplication before his God.
Ho 10: 4 swearing falsely in m' a covenant:3772
Am 8: 5 m' the ephah small, and the shekel
Mic 6:13 in m' thee desolate because of thy*
M't 9:23 and the people m' a noise, 2350
M'k 7:13 M' the word of God of none effect 208
Joh 5:18 Father, m' himself equal with God. 4160
Ro 1:10 M' request, if by any means now 1189
2Co 6:10 as poor, yet m' many rich; as 4148
Eph 1:16 m' mention of you in my prayers; 4160
2:15 twain one new man, so m' peace; "
5:19 and m' melody in your heart to the5567
Ph'p 1: 4 for you all m' request with joy, 4160
1Th 1: 2 m' mention of you in our prayers; "
Ph'm 4 m' mention of thee always in my "
2Pe 2: 6 m' them an ensample unto those * "
Jude 22 have compassion, m' a difference:*1252
Makkedah (*mak'-ke-dah*)
Jos 10:10 them to Azekah, and unto M'. 4719
16 and hid themselves in a cave at M'. "
17 kings are found hid in a cave at M'. "
21 the camp to Joshua at M' in peace: "
28 And that day Joshua took M', and "
28 he did to the king of M' as he did "
29 Then Joshua passed from M', and "
12:16 The king of M', one; the king of "
15:41 Beth-dagon, and Naamah, and M'; "
Maktesh (*mak'-tesh*)
Zep 1:11 Howl, ye inhabitants of M', for all4389
Malachi (*mal'-a-ki*)
Mal 1: 1 word of the Lord to Israel by M'. 4401
Malcham (*mal'-kam*) See also MILCOM.
1Ch 8: 9 and Zibia, and Mesha, and M', *4445
Zep 1: 5 the Lord, and that swear by M'; * "
Malchiah (*mal-ki'-ah*) See also MALCHIJAH; MELCHIAH.
1Ch 6:40 son of Baaseiah, the son of M', *4441
Ezr 10:25 and Jeziah, and M', and Miamin,* "
31 Eliezer, Ishijah, M', Shemaiah, * "
Ne 3:14 the dung gate repaired M' the son* "
31 him repaired M' the goldsmith's * "
8: 4 Pedaiah, and Mishael, and M', * "
11:12 the son of Pashur, the son of M', * "
Jer 38: 1 and Pashur the son of M', heard "
6 and cast him into the dungeon of M' "
Malchiel (*mal'-ke-el*) See also MALCHIELITES.
Ge 46:17 sons of Beriah; Heber, and M'. 4439
Nu 26:45 M', the family of the Malchielites. "
1Ch 7:31 sons of Beriah; Heber, and M'. "
Malchielites (*mal'-ke-el-ites*)
Nu 26:45 Malchiel, the family of the M'. 4440
Malchijah (*mal-ki'-jah*) See also MALCHIAH.
1Ch 9:12 the son of Pashur, the son of M', 4441
24: 9 The fifth to M', the sixth to "
Ezr 10:25 and Eleazar, and M', and Benaiah. "
Ne 3:11 M' the son of Harim, and Hashub "
10: 3 Pashur, Amariah, M', "
12:42 Jehohanan, and M', and Elam, and "
Malchiram (*mal'-ki-ram*)
1Ch 3:18 M' also, and Pedaiah, and 4443
Malchi-shua (*mal''-ki-shu'-ah*) See also MELCHI-SHUA.
1Ch 8:33 Saul begat Jonathan, and M', 4444
9:39 Saul begat Jonathan, and M', "
10: 2 and Abinadab, and M', the sons of "
Malchus (*mal'-kus*)
Joh 18:10 ear. The servant's name was M'. 3124
male See also MALES.
Ge 1:27 m' and female created he them. 2145
5: 2 M' and female created he them; "
6:19 thee; they shall be m' and female. "
7: 2 by sevens, the m' and his female: 376
2 clean by two, the m' and his female. "
3 by sevens, the m' and the female; 2145
9 into the ark, the m' and the female, "
16 went in m' and female of all flesh. "
17:23 every m' among the men of "
34:15 every m' of you be circumcised; "
22 every m' among us be circumcised, "
24 and every m was circumcised, all "
Ex 12: 5 blemish, a m' of the first year: "
Ex 34:19 whether ox or sheep, that is m'. 2142
Le 1: 3 him offer a m' without blemish: 2145
10 shall bring it a m' without blemish. "
3: 1 whether it be a m' or a female, he "
6 Lord be of the flock; m' or female, "
4:23 the goats, a m' without blemish: "
7: 6 Every m' among the priests shall "
12: 7 her that hath born a m' or a female. "
22:19 own will a m' without blemish, "
27: 3 of the m' from twenty years old "
5 shall be of the m' twenty shekels, "
6 be of the m' five shekels of silver, "
7 if it be a m', then thy estimation "
Nu 1: 2 names, every m' by their polls; "
20, 22 every m' from twenty years old "
3:15 every m' from a month old and "
5: 3 Both m' and female shall be put "
18:10 every m' shall eat it: it shall be "
31:17 kill every m' among the little ones, "
De 4:16 figure, the likeness of m' or female, "
7:14 be m' or female barren among you,
20:13 shalt smite every m' thereof with 2138
Jos 17: 2 m' children of Manasseh the son 2145
J'g 21:11 Ye shall utterly destroy every m', "
12 no man by lying with any m': * "
1Ki 11:15 he had smitten every m' in Edom; "
16 he had cut off every m' in Edom:) "
Mal 1:14 which hath in his flock a m', and "
M't 19: 4 made them m' and female, 730
M'r 10: 6 God made them m' and female. "
Lu 2:23 Every m' that openeth the womb "
Ga 3:28 free, there is neither m' nor female: "
malefactor See also MALEFACTORS.
Joh 18:30 If he were not a m', we would not*2555
malefactors
Lu 23:32 m', led with him to be put to death. 2557
33 they crucified him, and the m', "
39 one of the m' which were hanged "
Maleleel (*mal'-e-le-el*) See also MAHALALEEL.
Lu 3:37 which was the son of M', which *3121
males
Ge 34:25 the city boldly, and slew all the m'. 2145
Ex 12:48 let all his m' be circumcised, and "
13:12 hast; the m' shall be the Lord's. "
15 that openeth the matrix, being m'; "
23:17 all thy m' shall appear before the 2138
Le 6:18 All the m' among the children of *2145
29 the m' among the priests shall eat* "
Nu 3:22 to the number of all the m', from a "
28 In the number of all the m', from a "
34 to the number of all the m', from a "
39 m' from a month old and upward, "
40 Number all the firstborn of the m' "
43 the firstborn m' by the number of "
26:62 m' from a month old and upward:* "
31: 7 Moses; and they slew all the m'. * "
De 15:19 firstling m' that come of thy herd "
16:16 all thy m' appear before the Lord 2138
Jos 5: 4 came out of Egypt, that were m', 2145
2Ch 31:16 Beside their genealogy of m', from "
19 to give portions to all the m' among "
Ezr 8: 3 reckoned by genealogy of the m' an "
4 and with him two hundred m'. "
5 and with him three hundred m'. "
6 of Jonathan, and with him fifty m'. "
7 Athaliah, and with him seventy m'. "
8 Michael, and with him fourscore m'. "
9 him two hundred and eighteen m'. "
10 him an hundred and threescore m'. "
11 and with him twenty and eight m'. "
12 with him an hundred and ten m'. "
13 and with him threescore m'. "
14 Zabbud, and with him seventy m'. "
malice
1Co 5: 8 the leaven of m' and wickedness; 2549
14:20 howbeit in m' be ye children, but in "
Eph 4:31 be put away from you, with all m': "
Col 3: 8 anger, wrath, m', blasphemy, "
Tit 3: 3 living in m' and envy, hateful, and "
1Pe 2: 1 laying aside all m', and all guile, * "
malicious
3Jo 10 prating against us with m' words:*4190
maliciousness
Ro 1:29 wickedness, covetousness, m'; 2549
1Pe 2:16 using your liberty for a cloke of m',* "
malignity
Ro 1:29 envy, murder, debate, deceit, m'; 2550
Mallothi (*mal'-lo-thi*)
1Ch 25: 4 Romamti-ezer, Joshbekashah, M', 4413
26 The nineteenth to M', he, his sons, "
mallows
Job 30: 4 Who cut up m' by the bushes, *4408
Malluch (*mal'-luk*) See also MELICU.
1Ch 6:44 the son of Abdi, the son of M', 4409
Ezr 10:29 the sons of Bani; Meshullam, M', "
32 Benjamin, M', and Shemariah. "
Ne 10: 4 Hattush, Shebaniah, M', "
27 M', Harim, Baanah. "
12: 2 Amariah, M', Hattush, "
mammon (*mam'-mon*)
M't 6:24 Ye cannot serve God and m'. 3126
Lu 16: 9 friends of the m' of unrighteousness; "
11 been faithful in the unrighteous m', "
13 other. Ye cannot serve God and m'. "
Mamre (*mam'-re*)
Ge 13:18 came and dwelt in the plain of M', 4471
14:13 in the plain of M' the Amorite, "
24 with me, Aner, Eshcol, and M'; "
18: 1 unto him in the plains of M': "
23:17 Machpelah, which was before M', "
19 of the field of Machpelah before M': "

Ge 25: 9 the Hittite, which is before *M*·; 4471
35: 27 came unto Isaac his father unto *M*·, "
49: 30 Machpelah, which is before *M*·, "
50: 13 of Ephron the Hittite, before *M*·. "

man See also BONDMAN; CRAFTSMAN; DAYSMAN; FREEMAN; HARVESTMAN; HERDMAN; HORSEMAN; HUSBANDMAN; KINSMAN; MAN'S; MANSERVANT; MANSLAYER; MANKIND; MEN; NOBLEMAN; PLOWMAN; SPOKESMAN; WATCHMAN; WOMAN; WORKMAN.

Ge 1: 26 said, Let us make *m*· in our image, 120
27 So God created *m*· in his own image, "
2: 5 there was not a *m*· to till the ground. "
7 Lord God formed *m*· of the dust of "
7 of life; and *m*· became a living soul. "
8 he put the *m*· whom he had formed. "
15 the Lord God took the *m*·, and put "
16 the Lord God commanded the *m*·, "
18 good that the *m*· should be alone; "
22 the Lord God had taken from *m*·, "
22 woman, and brought her unto the *m*·. "
23 because she was taken out of *M*·. 376
24 shall a *m*· leave his father and his "
25 both naked, the *m*· and his wife, 120
3: 12 the *m*· said, The woman whom thou "
22 *m*· is become as one of us, to know "
24 So he drove out the *m*·; and he "
4: 1 I have gotten a *m*· from the Lord. 376
23 I have slain a *m*· to my wounding, "
23 and a young *m*· to my hurt. "
5: 1 In the day that God created *m*·, in 120
6: 3 shall not always strive with *m*·, "
5 that the wickedness of *m*· was great, "
6 repented the Lord...he had made *m*· "
7 will destroy *m*· whom I have created "
7 both *m*·, and beast, and the creeping "
9 Noah was a just *m*· and perfect in 376
7: 21 upon the earth, and every *m*·: 120
23 both *m*·, and cattle, and the creeping "
9: 5 I require it, and at the hand of *m*·; "
5 brother will I require the life of *m*·. "
6 blood, by *m*· shall his blood be shed: "
6 for in the image of God made he *m*·. "
13: 16 if a *m*· can number the dust of the 376
16: 12 And he will be a wild *m*·; his hand*120
12 his hand will be against every *m*·, and "
17: 10 Every *m*· child among you shall *2145
12 every *m*· child in your generations,* "
14 the uncircumcised *m*· child whose* "
18: 7 good, and gave it unto a young *m*·;* "
19: 8 which have not known *m*·; 376
9 And they pressed sore upon the *m*·, "
31 not a *m*· in the earth to come in unto "
20: 7 therefore restore the *m*· his wife; * "
24: 16 neither had any *m*· known her: "
21 *m*· wondering at her held his peace, "
22 the *m*· took a golden earring of half "
26 And the *m*· bowed down his head, "
29 and Laban ran out unto the *m*·, unto "
30 saying, Thus spake the *m*· unto me; "
30 that he came unto the *m*·; and, "
32 And the *m*· came into the house: "
58 unto her, Wilt thou go with this *m*·? "
61 the camels, and followed the *m*·: "
65 *m*· is this that walketh in the field "
25: 8 old age, an old *m*·, and full of years; "
27 a cunning hunter, a *m*· of the field; 376
27 and Jacob was a plain *m*·, dwelling "
26: 11 He that toucheth this *m*· or his wife "
13 *m*· waxed great, and went forward, "
27: 11 is a hairy *m*·, and I am a smooth *m*·: "
29: 19 that I should give her to another *m*·: "
30: 43 And the *m*· increased exceedingly, "
31: 50 my daughters, no *m*· is with us; "
32: 24 there wrestled a *m*· with him until "
34: 19 the young *m*· deferred not to do the "
25 brethren, took each *m*· his sword, 376
37: 15 And a certain *m*· found him, and, "
15 and the *m*· asked him, saying, What "
17 And the *m*· said, They are departed "
38: 25 By the *m*·, whose these are, am I "
39: 2 Joseph, and he was a prosperous *m*·; "
40: 5 them, each *m*· his dream in one night, "
5 *m*· according to the interpretation "
41: 11 *m*· according to the interpretation "
12 there was there with us a young *m*·, "
12 each *m*· according to his dream he "
33 look out a *m*· discreet and wise, "
38 a *m*· in whom the Spirit of God is? "
44 shall no *m*· lift up his hand or foot in "
42: 13 twelve brethren, the sons of one *m*· "
30 The *m*·, who is the lord of the land, "
33 the *m*·, the lord of the country, said "
43: 3 The *m*· did solemnly protest unto us, "
5 the *m*· said unto us, Ye shall not see "
6 as to tell the *m*· whether ye had yet a "
7 *m*· asked us straitly of our state, "
11 carry down the *m*· a present, a little "
13 and arise, go again unto the *m*·: "
14 God...give you mercy before the *m*·, "
17 And the *m*· did as Joseph bade; "
17, 24 *m*· brought the men into Joseph's "
27 well, the old *m*· of whom ye spake? "
44: 11 took down every *m*· his sack to the 376
11 and opened every *m*· his sack. "
13 clothes, and laded every *m*· his ass, "
15 such a *m*· as I can certainly divine? "
17 but the *m*· in whose hand the cup is "
20 We have a father, an old *m*·, and a "
45: 1 Cause every *m*· to go out from me. "
1 there stood no *m*· with him, while "
22 he gave each *m*· changes of raiment; "
47: 20 Egyptians sold every *m*· his field, "
49: 6 for in their anger they slew a *m*·, "
Ex 1: 1 every *m*· and his household came "
2: 1 there went a *m*· of the house of Levi, "

Ex 2: 12 when he saw that there was no *m*·, 376
20 why is it that ye have left the *m*·? "
21 was content to dwell with the *m*·: "
7: 12 For they cast down every *m*· his rod, "
8: 17 it became lice in *m*·, and in beast; 120
18 were lice upon *m*·, and upon beast. "
9: 9, 10 forth with blains upon *m*·, and "
19 for upon every *m*· and beast which "
22 hail in all the land of Egypt, upon *m*·, "
25 was in the field, both *m*· and beast; "
10: 7 long shall this *m*· be a snare unto us? "
11: 2 every *m*· borrow of his neighbour, 376
3 *m*· Moses was very great in the land "
7 a dog move his tongue, against *m*· or "
12: 3 shall take to them every *m*· a lamb, "
4 *m*· according to his eating shall * "
12 firstborn...both *m*· and beast; 120
16 save that which every *m*· must eat. 5315
13: 2 both of *m*· and of beast: it is mine. 120
13 firstborn of *m*· among thy children "
15 of Egypt, both the firstborn of *m*·, "
15: 3 The Lord is a *m*· of war: the Lord 376
16: 16 it every *m*· according to his eating, "
16 an omer for every *m*·, according *1538
16 take ye every *m*· for them which are 376
18 every *m*· according to his eating. "
19 no *m*· leave of it till the morning. "
21 every *m*· according to his eating: "
22 much bread, two omers for one *m*·:* "
29 *m*· in his place, let no *m*· go out of 376
19: 13 whether it be beast or *m*·, it shall "
21: 7 And if a *m*· sell his daughter to be a "
12 He that smiteth a *m*·, so that he die, "
13 And if a *m*· lie not in wait, but God "
14 a *m*· come presumptuously upon his 376
16 he that stealeth a *m*·, and selleth "
20 And if a *m*· smite his servant, or his "
26 if a *m*· smite the eye of his servant, "
28 If an ox gore a *m*· or a woman, that "
29 that he hath killed a *m*· or a woman; "
33 And if a *m*· shall open a pit, or if "
33 a *m*· shall dig a pit, and not cover it, "
22: 1 If a *m*· shall steal an ox, or a sheep, "
5 If a *m*· shall cause a field or "
7 If a *m*·...deliver unto his neighbour "
10 If a *m*· deliver unto his neighbour "
10 hurt, or driven away, no *m*· seeing it: "
14 And if a *m*· borrow ought of his 376
16 And if a *m*· entice a maid that is not "
23: 3 shalt thou countenance a poor *m*· in "
24: 14 if any *m*· have any matters to do, *1167
25: 2 of every *m*· that giveth it willingly 376
30: 12 give every *m*· a ransom for his soul "
32: 1, 23 the *m*· that brought us up out of "
27 Put every *m*· his sword by his side, "
27 camp, and slay every *m*· his brother, "
27 and every *m*· his companion, "
27 and every *m*· his neighbour. "
29 every *m*· upon his son, and upon his "
33: 4 no *m*· did put on him his ornaments. "
8 stood every *m*· at his tent door, and "
10 worshipped, every *m*· in his tent door. "
11 as a *m*· speaketh unto his friend. "
11 the son of Nun, a young *m*·, departed "
20 face: for there shall no *m*· see me, 120
34: 3 And no *m*· shall come up with thee, 376
3 neither let...*m*· be seen throughout "
24 neither shall any *m*· desire thy land, "
35: 22 every *m*· that offered offered an "
23, 24 every *m*·, with whom was found "
29 every *m*· and woman, whose heart "
36: 1 every wise hearted *m*·, in whom the "
2 and every wise hearted *m*·, in whose "
4 came every *m*· from his work which "
6 Let neither *m*· nor woman make any "
8 every wise hearted *m*· among them "
38: 26 A bekah for every *m*·, that is, half *1538
Le 1: 2 *m*· of you bring an offering unto 120
5: 3 Or if he touch the uncleanness of *m*·, "
3 be that a *m*· shall be defiled withal, * "
4 a *m*· shall pronounce with an oath, 120
6: 3 of all these that a *m*· doeth, sinning "
7: 21 as the uncleanness of *m*·, or any "
12: 2 conceived seed,...born a *m*· child: 2145
13: 2 a *m*· shall have in the skin of his 120
9 the plague of leprosy is in a *m*·, then "
29 If a *m*· or woman have a plague 376
38 If a *m*· also or a woman have in the "
40 *m*· whose hair is fallen off his head, "
44 He is a leprous *m*·, he is unclean: "
14: 11 present the *m*· that is to be clean, "
15: 2 When any *m*· hath a running issue "
18 The woman also with whom *m*· shall "
24 if any *m*· lie with her at all, and her "
33 of the *m*·, and of the woman, and 2145
16: 17 shall be no *m*· in the tabernacle of 120
21 away by the hand of a fit *m*· in the 376
17: 3 What *m*· soever there be of the house "
4 shall be imputed unto that *m*·; he "
4 that *m*· shall be cut off from among "
8 Whatsoever *m*· there be of the house "
9 even that *m*· shall be cut off from "
10 whatsoever *m*· there be of the house "
13 And whatsoever *m*· there be of the "
18: 5 which if a *m*· do, he shall live in 120
19: 3 Ye shall fear every *m*· his mother, 376
32 honour the face of the old *m*·, and "
20: 3 I will set my face against that *m*·, 376
4 ways hide their eyes from the *m*·, "
5 I will set my face against that *m*·, "
10 *m*· that committeth adultery with "
11 *m*· that lieth with his father's wife "
12 if a *m*· lie with his daughter in law, "
13 If a *m*· also lie with mankind, as he "
14 if a *m*· take a wife and her mother, "
15 And if a *m*· lie with a beast, he shall "

Le 20: 17 And if a *m*· shall take his sister, his 376
18 if a *m*· shall lie with a woman having "
20 if a *m*· shall lie with his uncle's wife, "
21 if a *m*· shall take his brother's wife, "
27 A *m*· also or woman that hath a "
21: 4 being a chief *m*· among his people, 1167
18 *m*· he be that hath a blemish, he 376
18 a blind *m*·, or a lame, or he that hath "
19 Or a *m*· that is brokenfooted, or "
21 No *m*· that hath a blemish of the "
22: 4 What *m*· soever of the seed of Aaron "
4 or a *m*· whose seed goeth from him; "
5 or a *m*· of whom he may take 120
14 And if a *m*· eat of the holy thing 376
24: 10 a *m*· of Israel strove together in the "
17 And he that killeth any *m*· shall 5315, 120
19 *m*· cause a blemish in his 376
20 he hath caused a blemish in a *m*·, 120
21 he that killeth a *m*·, he shall be put "
25: 10 return every *m*· unto his possession, 376
10 return every *m*· unto his family: "
13 return every *m*· unto his possession. "
26 And if the *m*· have none to redeem it, "
27 restore the overplus unto the *m*· to "
29 And if a *m*· sell a dwelling house in a "
33 And if a *m*· purchase of the Levites, * "
27: 2 a *m*· shall make a singular vow, the 376
9 all that any *m*· giveth of such unto "
14 when a *m*· shall sanctify his house 376
16 if a *m*· shall sanctify unto the Lord "
20 he have sold the field to another *m*·, "
22 And if a *m*· sanctify unto the Lord a* "
26 firstling, no *m*· shall sanctify it; 376
28 that *m*· shall devote unto the Lord "
28 that he hath, both of *m*· and beast, 120
31 *m*· will at all redeem ought of his 376
Nu 1: 4 there shall be a *m*· of every tribe; "
52 tents, every *m*· by his own camp, "
52 and every *m*· by his own standard, "
2: 2 Every *m*· of the children of Israel "
17 *m*· in his place by their standards. "
3: 13 in Israel, both *m*· and beast: 120
5: 6 *m*· or woman shall commit any sin 376
8 But if the *m*· have no kinsman to "
10 whatsoever any *m*· giveth the priest, "
13 a *m*· lie with her carnally, and it be "
15 the *m*· bring his wife unto the priest, "
19 If no *m*· have lain with thee, and if "
20 some *m*· have lain with thee beside "
31 the *m*· be guiltless from iniquity, "
6: 2 either *m*· or woman shall separate "
9 if any *m*· die very suddenly by him, "
7: 5 every *m*· according to his service. 376
8: 17 Israel are mine, both *m*· and beast: 120
9: 6 defiled by the dead body of a *m*·, "
7 are defiled by the dead body of a *m*·: "
10 if any *m*· of you or of your posterity 376
13 But the *m*· that is clean, and is not "
13 season, that *m*· shall bear his sin. "
11: 10 every *m*· in the door of his tent: "
27 there ran a young *m*·, and told Moses, "
12: 3 the *m*· Moses was very meek, above 376
13: 2 of their fathers shall ye send a *m*·, "
14: 15 shalt kill all this people as one *m*·, "
15: 32 a *m*· that gathered sticks upon the * "
35 The *m*· shall be surely put to death: "
16: 7 the *m*· whom the Lord doth choose, "
17 take every *m*· his censer, and put "
17 before the Lord every *m*· his censer, "
18 they took every *m*· his censer, and "
22 shall one *m*· sin, and wilt thou be "
17: 9 looked, and took every *m*· his rod. "
18: 15 firstborn of *m*· shalt thou surely 120
19: 9 a *m*· that is clean shall gather up the 376
11 the dead body of any *m*· shall be 120
13 dead body of any *m*· that is dead, "
14 the law, when a *m*· dieth in a tent: "
16 or a dead body, or a bone of a *m*·, "
20 But the *m*· that shall be unclean, 376
21: 9 if a serpent had bitten any *m*·, "
23: 19 God is not a *m*·, that he should lie; "
19 neither the son of *m*·, that he should 120
24: 3, 15 the *m*· whose eyes are open hath 1397
25: 8 he went after the *m*· of Israel into 376
8 the *m*· of Israel, and the woman "
26: 64 there was not a *m*· of them whom "
65 there was not left a *m*· of them, save "
27: 8 If a *m*· die, and have no son, then ye "
16 flesh, set a *m*· over the congregation, "
18 a *m*· in whom is the spirit, and lay "
30: 2 If a *m*· vow a vow unto the Lord, or "
16 Moses, between a *m*· and his wife, "
31: 17 hath known *m*· by lying with 376, 2145
18 not known a *m*· by lying with him, "
26 was taken, both of *m*· and of beast, 120
35 not known *m*· by lying with him. 2145
47 both of *m*· and of beast, and gave 120
49 and there lacketh not one *m*· of us. 376
50 what every *m*· hath gotten, of jewels "
53 taken spoil, every *m*· for himself.) "
32: 18 inherited every *m*· his inheritance. "
27 pass over, every *m*· armed for war, "
29 every *m*· armed to battle, before the "
35: 23 any stone, wherewith a *m*· may die, "
36: 8 enjoy every *m*· the inheritance of his 376
De 1: 16 between every *m*· and his brother, "
17 shall not be afraid of the face of *m*·; "
31 as a *m*· doth bear his son, in all the "
41 had girded on every *m*· his weapons "
3: 11 breadth of it, after the cubit of a *m*·. "
20 return every *m*· unto his possession, "
4: 32 the day that God created *m*· upon 120
5: 24 that God doth talk with *m*·, and he "
7: 24 shall no *m*· be able to stand before 376
8: 3 *m*· doth not live by bread only, but 120
3 the mouth of the Lord doth *m*· live. "

De 8: 5 as a m' chasteneth his son, so the 376
11: 25 shall no m' be able to stand before "
12: 8 every m' whatsoever is right in his "
15: 7 If there be among you a poor m' "
12 if thy brother, an Hebrew m', or an "
16: 17 Every m' shall give as he is able, 376
17: 2 m' or woman, that hath wrought "
5 bring forth that m' or that woman, "
5 even that m' or that woman, and "
12 the m' that will do presumptuously, "
12 the judge, even that m' shall die: "
19: 5 As when a m' goeth into the wood with "
11 But if any m' hate his neighbour, 376
15 rise up against a m' for any iniquity, "
16 false witness rise up against any m' "
20: 5 What m' is there that hath built a "
5 battle, and another m' dedicate it. "
6 what m' is he that hath planted a "
6 the battle, and another m' eat of it. "
7 what m' is there that hath betrothed "
7 the battle, and another m' take her. "
8 What m' is there that is fearful and "
21: 3 city which is next unto the slain m', "
6 city, that are next unto the slain m', "
15 If a m' have two wives, one beloved, 376
18 m' have a stubborn and rebellious "
22 If a m' have committed a sin worthy "
22: 5 that which pertaineth unto a m', 1397
5 a m' put on a woman's garment: "
8 house, if any m' fall from thence. "
13 If any m' take a wife, and go in unto 376
16 my daughter unto this m' to wife, "
18 shall take that m' and chastise him; "
22 If a m' be found lying with a woman "
22 the m' that lay with the woman, and "
23 m' find her in the city, and lie with "
24 the m', because he hath humbled his "
25 a m' find a betrothed damsel in the "
25 the m' force her, and lie with her: "
25 m' only that lay with her shall die: "
26 a m' riseth against his neighbour, "
28 a m' find a damsel that is a virgin, "
29 m' that lay with her shall give unto "
30 A m' shall not take his father's wife, "
23: 10 among you any m', that is not clean "
24: 1 a m' hath taken a wife, and married "
5 When a m' hath taken a new wife, "
6 No m' shall take the nether or the "
7 If a m' be found stealing any of his 376
11 m' to whom thou dost lend shall "
12 And if the m' be poor, thou shalt not "
16 every m' shall be put to death for his "
25: 2 the wicked m' be worthy to be beaten, "
7 m' like not to take his brother's wife, 376
9 be done unto that m' that will not "
27: 15 Cursed be the m' that maketh any "
28: 26 earth, and no m' shall fray them away. *
29 evermore, and no m' shall save thee. *
30 and another m' shall lie with her: 376
54 the m' that is tender among you, "
68 bondwomen, and no m' shall buy you. "
29: 18 Lest there should be among you m', 376
20 shall smoke against that m', and "
25 destroy both the young m' and the "
32: 25 also with the m' of gray hairs. 376
33: 1 m' of God blessed the children of "
34: 6 but no m' knoweth of his sepulchre "
Jos 1: 5 shall not any m' be able to stand "
2: 11 remain any more courage in any m', "
3: 12 of Israel, out of every tribe a m'. "
4: 2 the people, out of every tribe a m': "
4 of Israel, out of every tribe a m': "
5 take ye up every m' of you a stone "
5: 13 stood a m' over against him with a "
6: 5 up every m' straight before him. "
20 every m' straight before him, and "
21 was in the city, both m' and woman, "
26 Cursed be the m' before the Lord, "
7: 14 shall take shall come m' by m'. 1397
17 family of the Zarhites m' by m'; "
18 he brought his household m' by m'; "
8: 17 And there was not a m' left in Ai or 376
31 which no m' hath lifted up any iron: "
10: 8 there shall not a m' of them stand 376
14 hearkened unto the voice of a m': "
11: 14 every m' they smote with the edge 120
14: 6 Lord said unto Moses the m' of God 376
15 was a great m' among the Anakims. 120
17: 1 he was a m' of war, therefore he 376
21: 44 stood not a m' of all their enemies "
22: 20 and that m' perished not alone in "
23: 9 no m' hath been able to stand before "
10 One m' of you...chase a thousand: "
24: 28 every m' unto his inheritance. "
J'g 1: 24 spies saw a m' come forth out of the "
25 they let go the m' and all his family. "
26 And the m' went into the land of the "
2: 6 went every m' unto his inheritance "
3: 15 Gera, a Benjamite, a m' lefthanded: "
17 Moab: and Eglon was a very fat m'. "
28 and suffered not a m' to pass over. "
29 valour; and there escaped not a m'. "
4: 16 sword; and there was not a m' left. "
20 when any m' doth come and enquire 376
20 say, Is there any m' here? that thou "
22 I will shew thee the m' whom thou "
5: 30 to every m' a damsel or two; to 1397
6: 12 is with thee, thou mighty m' of valour. "
16 smite the Midianites as one m'. 376
7: 7 people go every m' unto his place. "
8 rest of Israel every m' unto his tent, "
13 was a m' that told a dream unto his "
14 the son of Joash, a m' of Israel: "
21 stood every m' in his place round "
8: 14 a young m' of the men of Succoth, "
21 for as the m' is, so is his strength. 376

J'g 8: 24 give me every m' the earrings of his 376
25 cast therein every m' the earrings "
9: 9 by me they honour God and m', "
13 my wine, which cheereth God and m', "
49 cut down every m' his bough, and "
54 unto the young m' his armourbearer, "
54 And his young m' thrust him through, "
55 departed every m' unto his place. 376
10: 1 the son of Dodo, a m' of Issachar; "
18 What m' is he that will begin to "
11: 1 Gileadite was a mighty m' of valour, "
39 had vowed: and she knew no m'. 376
13: 2 there was a certain m' of Zorah, of "
6 saying, A m' of God came unto me, "
8 the m' of God which thou didst send "
10 the m' hath appeared unto me, that "
11 came to the m', and said unto him, "
11 Art thou the m' that spakest unto "
16: 7, 11 be weak, and be as another m'. 120
17 weak, and be like any other m'. "
19 she called for a m', and she caused 376
17: 1 there was a m' of mount Ephraim, "
5 the m' Micah had an house of gods, "
6 every m' did that which was right "
7 a young m' out of Beth-lehem-judah "
8 And the m' departed out of the city 376
11 was content to dwell with the m'; "
11 the young m' was unto him as one of "
12 and the young m' became his priest, "
18: 3 they knew the voice of the young m' "
7 and had no business with any m'. 120
15 came to the house of the young m' "
19 a priest unto the house of one m', 376
28 they had no business with any m'; 120
19: 6 damsel's father...said unto the m', 376
7, 9 when the m' rose up to depart, "
10 the m' would not tarry that night, "
15 no m' that took them into his house "
16 there came an old m' from his work "
17 saw a wayfaring m' in the street of "
17 and the old m' said, Whither goest "
18 is no m' that receiveth me to house. "
19 for the young m' which is with thy "
20 And the old m' said, Peace be with 376
22 the master of the house, the old m', "
22 the m' that came into thine house, "
23 And the m', the master of the house, "
23 this m' is come into mine house, "
24 unto this m' do not so vile a thing. "
25 so the m' took his concubine, and "
28 the m' took her up upon an ass, * "
28 the m' rose up, and gat him unto his "
20: 1 was gathered together as one m', "
8 And all the people arose as one m', "
11 the city, knit together as one m'. "
21: 11 every woman that hath lain by m'. 2145
12 had known no m' by lying with any 376
21 catch you every m' his wife of the "
22 not to each m' his wife in the war: "
24 every m' to his tribe and to his "
24 thence every m' to his inheritance. "
25 every m' did that which was right in "
Ru 1: 1 a certain m' of Beth-lehem-judah "
2 the name of the m' was Elimelech, "
2: 1 husband's, a mighty m' of wealth, "
20 The m' is near of kin unto us, one of "
3: 3 make not thyself known unto the m', "
8 that the m' was afraid, and turned "
16 told her all that the m' had done to "
18 for the m' will not be in rest, until "
4: 7 a m' plucked off his shoe, and gave "
1Sa 1: 1 Now there was a certain m' of "
3 And this m' went up out of his city "
11 unto thine handmaid a m' child, 582
21 the m' Elkanah, and all his house, 376
2: 9 for by strength shall no m' prevail. "
13 when any m' offered sacrifice, the "
15 said to the m' that sacrificed, Give "
16 if any m' said unto him, Let them "
25 If one m' sin against another, the "
25 but if a m' sin against the Lord, who "
27 there came a m' of God unto Eli, "
31 shall not be an old m' in thine house. "
32 not be an old m' in thine house for "
33 And the m' of thine, whom I shall 376
4: 10 and they fled every m' into his tent: "
12 ran a m' of Benjamin out of the army, "
13 when the m' came into the city, and "
14 And the m' came in hastily, and told "
16 the m' said unto Eli, I am he that "
18 for he was an old m', and heavy. "
8: 22 Israel, Go ye every m' unto his city. "
9: 1 Now there was a m' of Benjamin, "
1 a Benjamite, a mighty m' of power. "
2 was Saul, a choice young m', and a "
6 there is in this city a m' of God, 376
6 he is an honourable m'; all that he "
7 if we go, what shall we bring the m'? "
7 a present to bring to the m' of God: "
8 that will I give to the m' of God, to "
9 when a m' went to enquire of God, "
10 the city where the m' of God was. "
16 I will send thee a m' out of the land "
17 the m' whom I spake to thee of! "
10: 6 and shalt be turned into another m'. "
22 if the m' should yet come thither. "
25 people away, every m' to his house. "
27 said, How shall this m' save us? "
11: 3 if there be no m' to save us, we will *
13 shall not be a m' put to death this 376
13: 2 people he sent every m' to his tent. "
14 sought him a m' after his own heart, "
20 to sharpen every m' his share, and "
14: 1 the son of Saul said unto the young m' "
6 Jonathan said to the young m' that "
24 Cursed be the m' that eateth any 376

1Sa 14: 26 but no m' put his hand to his mouth: "
28 Cursed be the m' that eateth any 376
34 m' his ox, and every m' his sheep, "
34 brought every m' his ox with him "
36 and let us not leave a m' of them. "
39 was not a m' among all the people "
52 and when Saul saw any strong m', 376
52 or any valiant m', he took him 1121
15: 3 slay both m' and woman, infant and 376
29 for he is not a m', that he should 120
16: 7 for the Lord seeth not as m' seeth; "
7 for m' looketh on the outward "
16 to seek out a m', who is a cunning 376
17 Provide me now a m' that can play "
18 in playing, and a mighty valiant m', "
18 and a m' of war, and prudent in 376
17: 8 choose you a m' for you, and let him "
10 give me a m', that we may fight "
12 the m' went among men for an old "
12 went among men for an old m' in the "
24 when they saw the m', fled from him, 376
25 ye seen this m' that is come up? "
25 the m' who killeth him, the king "
26 be done to the m' that killeth this "
27 be done to the m' that killeth him. "
33 and he a m' of war from his youth. "
41 m' that bare the shield went before "
58 Whose son art thou, thou young m'? "
18: 23 am a poor m', and lightly esteemed? 376
20: 22 if I say thus unto the young m', *5958
21: 1 thou alone, and no m' with thee? 376
2 Let no m' know any thing of the "
7 a certain m' of the servants of Saul "
14 Lo, ye see the m' is mad: wherefore "
15 this fellow to play the mad m' in my "
24: 19 if a m' find his enemy, will he let 376
25: 2 And there was a m' in Maon, whose "
2 and the m' was very great, and he "
3 Now the name of the m' was Nabal; "
3 the m' was churlish and evil in his "
10 away every m' from his master. "
13 men, Gird ye on every m' his sword. "
13 they girded on every m' his sword; "
17 Belial, that a m' cannot speak to him. *
25 pray thee, regard this m' of Belial, 376
29 Yet a m' is risen to pursue thee, 120
26: 12 they gat them away, and no m' saw it, "
15 Abner, Art not thou a valiant m'? 376
23 The Lord render to every m' his "
27: 3 every m' with his household, even "
9 and left neither m' nor woman alive, "
11 saved neither m' nor woman alive, "
28: 14 An old m' cometh up; and he is "
30: 6 every m' for his sons and for his "
13 I am a young m' of Egypt, servant "
17 there escaped not a m' of them, 376
22 save to every m' his wife and his "
2Sa 1: 2 a m' came out of the camp from Saul "
5 said unto the young m' that told him, "
6 the young m' that told him said, As I "
13 said unto the young m' that told him, "
2: 3 up, every m' with his household: 376
3: 34 as a m' falleth before wicked men. 1121
38 a great m' fallen this day in Israel? "
7: 19 is this the manner of m', O Lord * 120
12: 2 rich m' had exceeding many flocks "
3 But the poor m' had nothing, save one "
4 came a traveller unto the rich m', 376
4 to dress for the wayfaring m' that "
4 dressed it for the m' that was come 376
5 was greatly kindled against the m'; "
5 m' that hath done this thing shall "
7 said to David, Thou art the m'. "
13: 3 and Jonadab was a very subtil m'. "
9 they went out every m' from him. "
29 every m' gat him up upon his mule. "
34 And the young m' that kept the watch "
14: 16 out of the hand of the m' that would 376
21 bring the young m' Absalom again. "
15: 2 any m' that had a controversy came 376
3 is no m' deputed of the king to hear "
4 every m' which hath any suit or 376
5 that when any m' came nigh to him "
30 with him covered every m' his head, "
16: 5 thence came out a m' of the family "
7 thou bloody m', and thou m' of Belial: "
8 because thou art a bloody m'. "
23 as if a m' had enquired at the oracle "
17: 3 the m' whom thou seekest is as if all "
8 thy father is a m' of war, and will "
10 that thy father is a mighty m', and "
18: 5 gently for my sake with the young m', "
10 a certain m' saw it, and told Joab, 376
11 Joab said unto the m' that told him, "
12 And the m' said unto Joab, Though I "
12 none touch the young m' Absalom. "
24 and behold a m' running alone. 376
26 watchman saw another m' running: "
26 Behold another m' running alone. "
27 He is a good m', and cometh with "
29 said, Is the young m' Absalom safe? "
32 Cushi, Is the young m' Absalom safe? "
32 do thee hurt, be as that young m' is. "
19: 8 Israel had fled every m' to his tent. 376
14 Judah, even as the heart of one m'; "
22 any m' be put to death this day in "
32 Barzillai was a very aged m', even "
32 for he was a very great m'. 376
20: 1 happened to be there a m' of Belial, "
1 every m' to his tents, O Israel. "
2 So every m' of Israel went up from *
12 when the m' saw that all the people "
21 a m' of mount Ephraim, Sheba the "
22 from the city, every m' to his tent. "
21: 4 for us shalt thou kill any m' in Israel. "
5 The m' that consumed us, and that "

2Sa 21: 20 was a *m'* of great stature, that had 376
22: 26 upright *m'* thou wilt shew thyself
49 delivered me from the violent *m'*. 376
23: 1 the *m'* who was raised up on high,1397
7 *m'* that shall touch them must be 376
20 the son of a valiant *m'*, of Kabzeel, "
21 he slew an Egyptian, a goodly *m'*: "
24: 14 let me not fall into the hand of *m'*. 120
1Ki 1: 6 and he also was a very goodly *m'*;
42 thou art a valiant *m'*, and bringest 376
49 rose up, and went every *m'* his way. "
52 he will shew himself a worthy *m'*, 1121
2: 2 therefore, and shew thyself a *m'*; 376
4 a *m'* on the throne of Israel.
9 for thou art a wise *m'*, and knowest "
4: 7 each *m'* his month in a year made
25 every *m'* under his vine and under 376
27 table, every *m'* in his month: "
28 every *m'* according to his charge. "
7: 14 and his father was a *m'* of Tyre, a "
8: 25 shall not fail thee a *m'* in my sight "
31 *m'* trespass against his neighbour, "
38 supplication...be made by any *m'*, 120
38 shall know every *m'* the plague of 376
39 give to every *m'* according to his "
46 (for there is no *m'* that sinneth not,)120
9: 5 not fail thee a *m'* upon the throne 376
10: 25 they brought every *m'* his present, "
11: 28 And the *m'* Jeroboam was a mighty "
28 Jeroboam was a mighty *m'* of valour.
28 young *m'* that he was industrious,
12: 22 came unto Shemaiah the *m'* of God, 376
24 return every *m'* to his house; for "
13: 1 there came a *m'* of God out of Judah "
4 heard the saying of the *m'* of God, "
5 sign which the *m'* of God had given "
6 said unto the *m'* of God, Intreat "
6 the *m'* of God besought the Lord, "
7 the king said unto the *m'* of God, "
8 the *m'* of God said unto the king, "
11 works that the *m'* of God had done "
12 seen what way the *m'* of God went, "
14 went after the *m'* of God, and found "
14 Art thou the *m'* of God that camest "
21 cried unto the *m'* of God that came "
26 he said, It is the *m'* of God, who was "
29 took up the carcase of the *m'* of God,"
31 wherein the *m'* of God is buried; "
14: 10 as a *m'* taketh away dung, till it be all
17: 18 to do with thee, O thou *m'* of God? 376
24 I know that thou art a *m'* of God,
20: 7 and see how this *m'* seeketh mischief:
20 And they slew every one his *m'*: 376
24 every *m'* out of his place, and put "
28 there came a *m'* of God, and spake "
35 *m'* of the sons of the prophets said "
35 And the *m'* refused to smite him. "
37 Then he found another *m'*, and said,"
37 the *m'* smote him, so that in smiting"
39 and, behold, a *m'* turned aside, "
39 and brought a *m'* unto me, and said,"
39 Keep this *m'*: if by any means he be"
42 hand a *m'* whom I appointed to utter"
22: 8 There is yet one *m'*, Micaiah the son "
17 them return every *m'* to his house in"
34 certain *m'* drew a bow at a venture, "
36 Every *m'* to his city, and every *m'* to "
2Ki 1: 6 came a *m'* up to meet us, and said "
7 What manner of *m'* was he which "
8 He was an hairy *m'*, and girt with "
9 Thou *m'* of God, the king hath said, "
10 If I be a *m'* of God, then let fire come"
11 O *m'* of God, thus hath the king said,"
12 I be a *m'* of God, let fire come down "
13 O *m'* of God, I pray thee, let my life, "
3: 25 of land cast every *m'* his stone,
4: 7 she came and told the *m'* of God.
9 that this is an holy *m'* of God,
16 Nay, my lord, thou *m'* of God, do not "
21 laid him on the bed of the *m'* of God,"
22 that I may run to the *m'* of God,
25 came unto the *m'* of God to mount "
25 when the *m'* of God saw her afar off, "
27 when she came to the *m'* of God to "
27 the *m'* of God said, Let her alone; "
29 if thou meet any *m'*, salute him not; "
40 O thou *m'* of God, there is death in "
42 came a *m'* from Baal-shalisha, "
42 and brought the *m'* of God bread of "
5: 1 was a great *m'* with his master, "
1 he was also a mighty *m'* in valour, "
7 that this *m'* doth send unto me to "
7 me to recover a *m'* of his leprosy? 376
8 Elisha the *m'* of God had heard that "
14 to the saying of the *m'* of God: "
15 he returned to the *m'* of God, he and "
20 the servant of Elisha the *m'* of God, "
26 *m'* turned again from his chariot "
6: 2 take thence every *m'* a beam, and "
6 the *m'* of God said, Where fell it? "
9 the *m'* of God sent unto the king of "
10 which the *m'* of God told him and "
15 servant of the *m'* of God was risen "
17 opened the eyes of the young *m'*; "
19 bring you to the *m'* whom ye seek. 376
32 the king sent a *m'* from before him: "
7: 2 king leaned answered the *m'* of God,"
5 Syria, behold, there was no *m'* there."
10 and, behold, there was no *m'* there, "
10 neither voice of *m'*, but horses tied,120
17 he died, as the *m'* of God had said, 376
18 as the *m'* of God had spoken to the "
19 that lord answered the *m'* of God, "
8: 2 after the saying of the *m'* of God: "
4 Gehazi the servant of the *m'* of God, "
7 saying, The *m'* of God is come hither."

2Ki 8: 8 meet the *m'* of God, and enquire of 376
11 ashamed: and the *m'* of God wept. "
9: 4 So the young *m'*, even the young *m'*
11 said unto them, Ye know the *m'*, 376
13 took every *m'* his garment, and put "
10: 21 was not a *m'* left that came not. "
11: 8 every *m'* with his weapons in his "
9 and they took every *m'* his men that "
11 every *m'* with his weapons in his "
12: 4 the money that every *m'* is set at, 5315
5 every *m'* of his acquaintance: 376
13: 19 the *m'* of God was wroth with him, "
21 to pass, as they were burying a *m'*, "
21 they cast the *m'* into the sepulchre of"
21 and when the *m'* was let down, and "
14: 6 every *m'* shall be put to death for "
12 and they fled every *m'* to their tents. "
15: 20 of each *m'* fifty shekels of silver, "
18: 21 on which if a *m'* lean, it will go into "
31 eat ye every *m'* of his own vine, and*"
21: 13 wipe Jerusalem as a *m'* wipeth a dish,
22: 15 Tell the *m'* that sent you to me, 376
23: 10 that no *m'* might make his son or "
16 which the *m'* of God proclaimed, "
17 It is the sepulchre of the *m'* of God, "
18 alone; let no *m'* move his bones. "
1Ch 11: 22 the son of a valiant *m'* of Habzeel, "
23 Egyptian, a *m'* of great stature, five "
12: 4 a mighty *m'* among the thirty, and
28 Zadok, a young *m'* mighty of valour,
16: 3 both *m'* and woman, to every one a 376
21 He suffered no *m'* to do them wrong:"
43 departed every *m'* to his house: "
17: 17 to the estate of a *m'* of high degree,120
20: 6 where was a *m'* of great stature, 376
21: 13 let me not fall into the hand of *m'*. 120
22: 9 to thee, who shall be a *m'* of rest; 376
23: 3 number by their polls, *m'* by *m'*, 1397
14 concerning Moses the *m'* of God. 376
27: 32 counsellor, a wise *m'*, and a scribe: "
28: 3 because thou hast been a *m'* of war, "
21 workmanship every willing skilful *m'*,
29: 1 for the palace is not for *m'*, but for 120
2Ch 2: 7 Send...a *m'* cunning to work in gold,376
13 And now I have sent a cunning *m'*, "
14 his father was a *m'* of Tyre, skilful "
6: 5 chose I any *m'* to be ruler over my "
16 not fail thee a *m'* in my sight to sit "
22 If a *m'* sin against his neighbour, "
29 soever shall be made of any *m'*, 120
30 *m'* according unto all his ways, "
36 there is no *m'* which sinneth not,) "
7: 18 shall not fail thee a *m'* to be ruler 376
8: 14 David the *m'* of God commanded. "
9: 24 they brought every *m'* his present, "
10: 16 every *m'* to your tents, O Israel: and"
11: 2 came to Shemaiah the *m'* of God, "
4 return every *m'* to his house: for "
14: 11 let not *m'* prevail against thee. 582
15: 13 or great, whether *m'* or woman. 376
17: 17 Eliada a mighty *m'* of valour, and
18: 7 There is yet one *m'*, by whom we 376
16 every *m'* to his house in peace. "
33 certain *m'* drew a bow at a venture, "
33 therefore he said to his chariot *m'*,*
19: 6 for ye judge not for *m'*, but for the 120
20: 27 every *m'* of Judah and Jerusalem, 376
23: 7 every *m'* with his weapons in his "
8 took every *m'* his men that were to "
10 every *m'* having his weapon in his "
25: 4 every *m'* shall die for his own sin. "
7 But there came a *m'* of God to him, "
9 Amaziah said to the *m'* of God, But "
9 the *m'* of God answered, The Lord is "
22 and they fled every *m'* to his tent. "
28: 7 And Zichri, a mighty *m'* of Ephraim,
30: 16 to the law of Moses the *m'* of God: 376
31: 1 returned, every *m'* to his possession,"
2 every *m'* according to his service, "
32: 19 were the work of the hands of *m'*. *120
34: 23 Tell ye the *m'* that sent you to me, 376
36: 17 no compassion upon young *m'* or "
17 or maiden, old *m'*, or him that stooped
Ezr 3: 1 together as one *m'* to Jerusalem. 376
2 in the law of Moses the *m'* of God. "
8: 18 brought us a *m'* of understanding, "
Ne 1: 11 him mercy in the sight of this *m'*. "
2: 10 was come a *m'* to seek the welfare 120
12 told I any *m'* what my Lord had put "
5: 13 shake out every *m'* from his house, 376
6: 11 I said, Should such a *m'* as I flee? "
7: 2 for he was a faithful *m'*, and feared "
8: 1 themselves together as one *m'* into "
9: 29 (which if a *m'* do, he shall live in 120
12: 24 of David the *m'* of God, ward over 376
36 instruments of David the *m'* of God,"
Es 1: 22 every *m'* should bear rule in his own"
4: 11 whether *m'* or woman, shall come "
5: 12 did let no *m'* come in with the king "
6: 6, 7 the *m'* whom the king delighteth 376
9 they may array the *m'* withal whom "
9 Thus shall it be done to the *m'* "
11 Thus shall it be done unto the *m'* "
8: 8 the king's ring, may no *m'* reverse. "
9: 2 no *m'* could withstand them; for 376
4 this *m'* Mordecai waxed greater and"
Job 1: 1 was a *m'* in the land of Uz, whose "
1 and that *m'* was perfect and upright,"
3 this *m'* was the greatest of all the "
8 a perfect and an upright *m'*, one "
2: 3 perfect and an upright *m'*, one that "
4 all that a *m'* hath will he give for his"
3: 3 said, There is a *m'* child conceived.1397
23 given to a *m'* whose way is hid, "
4: 17 Shall mortal *m'* be more just than 582
17 shall a *m'* be more pure than his 1396

Job 5: 2 For wrath killeth the foolish *m'*, and
7 Yet *m'* is born unto trouble, as the 120
17 Behold, happy is the *m'* whom God 582
7: 1 appointed time to *m'* upon earth? "
17 What is *m'*, that thou shouldest "
8: 20 God will not cast away a perfect *m'*,
9: 2 how should *m'* be just with God? 582
32 For he is not a *m'*, as I am, that I 376
10: 4 of flesh? or seest thou as *m'* seeth? 582
5 Are thy days as the days of *m'*? "
11: 2 should a *m'* full of talk be justified?376
3 shall no *m'* make thee ashamed?
12 For vain *m'* would be wise, though 376
12 *m'* be born like a wild ass's colt. 120
12: 4 just upright *m'* is laughed to scorn.
14 he shutteth up a *m'*, and there can 376
25 them to stagger like a drunken *m'*.
13: 9 or as one *m'* mocketh another, do 582
14: 1 *M'* that is born of a woman is of 120
10 But *m'* dieth, and wasteth away: 1397
10 *m'* giveth up the ghost, and where 120
12 So *m'* lieth down, and riseth not: 376
14 If a *m'* die, shall he live again? all1397
19 and thou destroyest the hope of *m'*.582
15: 2 a wise *m'* utter vain knowledge,
7 thou the first *m'* that was born? or 120
14 What is *m'*, that he should be 582
16 more abominable and filthy is *m'*, *376
20 The wicked *m'* travaileth with pain
28 houses which no *m'* inhabiteth, which
16: 21 one might plead for a *m'* with God,1397
21 as a *m'* pleadeth for his neighbour! 120
17: 10 I cannot find one wise *m'* among you.
20: 4 old, since *m'* was placed upon earth,120
21 shall no *m'* look for his goods. *
29 the portion of a wicked *m'* from God,120
21: 4 As for me, is my complaint to *m'*? "
33 every *m'* shall draw after him, as* "
22: 2 Can a *m'* be profitable unto God, 1397
8 But as for the mighty *m'*, he had 376
8 and the honourable *m'* dwelt in it.
24: 22 he riseth up, and no *m'* is sure of life.
25: 4 then can *m'* be justified with God? 582
6 How much less *m'*, that is a worm? "
6 the son of *m'*, which is a worm? 120
27: 13 the portion of a wicked *m'* with God,"
19 The rich *m'* shall lie down, but he*
28: 13 *M'* knoweth not the price thereof; 582
28 unto *m'* he said, Behold, the fear of 120
32: 8 But there is a spirit in *m'*: and the 582
13 God thrusteth him down, not *m'*. 376
21 let me give flattering titles unto *m'*.120
33: 12 thee, that God is greater than *m'*. 582
14 yea twice, yet *m'* perceiveth it not.
17 may withdraw *m'* from his purpose,120
17 purpose, and hide pride from *m'*. 1397
23 to shew unto *m'* his uprightness: 120
26 render unto *m'* his righteousness. 582
29 worketh God oftentimes with *m'*, 1397
34: 7 What *m'* is like Job, who drinketh "
9 It profiteth a *m'* nothing that he "
11 work of a *m'* shall he render unto 120
11 cause every *m'* to find according 376
14 If he set his heart upon *m'*, if he
15 and *m'* shall turn again unto dust. 120
21 his eyes are upon the ways of *m'*, 376
23 not lay upon *m'* more than right; "
29 a nation, or against a *m'* only: 120
34 let a wise *m'* hearken unto me. 1397
35: 8 Thy wickedness may hurt a *m'* as 376
8 may profit the son of *m'*. 120
36: 25 Every *m'* may see it; * "
25 *m'* may behold it afar off. 582
28 clouds do drop and distil upon *m'* 120
37: 7 He sealeth up the hand of every *m'*; "
20 if a *m'* speak, surely he shall be 376
38: 3 Gird up now thy loins like a *m'*; 1397
26 rain on the earth, where no *m'* is; 376
26 wilderness, wherein there is no *m'*;120
40: 7 Gird up thy loins now like a *m'*: 1397
42: 11 every *m'* also gave him a piece of 376
Ps 1: 1 Blessed is the *m'* that walketh not "
5: 6 abhor the bloody and deceitful *m'*. "
8: 4 What is *m'*, that thou art mindful 582
4 son of *m'*, that thou visitest him? 120
9: 19 Arise, O Lord; let not *m'* prevail: 582
10: 15 arm of the wicked and the evil *m'*:
18 *m'* of the earth...no more oppress. 582
18: 25 with an upright *m'* thou wilt shew1397
48 delivered me from the violent *m'*. 376
19: 5 rejoiceth as a strong *m'* to run a race.
22: 6 But I am a worm, and no *m'*; a 376
25: 12 What *m'* is he that feareth the Lord?"
31: 12 forgotten as a dead *m'* out of mind:
20 thy presence from the pride of *m'*: 376
32: 2 Blessed is the *m'* unto whom the 120
33: 16 mighty *m'* is not delivered by much
34: 6 poor *m'* cried, and the Lord heard
8 blessed is the *m'* that trusteth in 1397
12 What *m'* is he that desireth life,
36: 6 Lord, thou preservest *m'* and beast.120
37: 7 *m'* who bringeth wicked devices to 376
16 little that a righteous *m'* hath is better*
23 steps of a good *m'* are ordered by *1397
37 Mark the perfect *m'*, and behold the
37 for the end of that *m'* is peace. 376
38: 13 But I, as a deaf *m'*, heard not; and I
13 I was as a dumb *m'* that openeth not
14 I was as a *m'* that heareth not, and 376
39: 5 *m'* at his best state is altogether 120
6 every *m'* walketh in a vain shew: 376
11 rebukes dost correct *m'* for iniquity, "
11 a moth: surely every *m'* is vanity. 120
40: 4 Blessed is that *m'* that maketh the1397
43: 1 from the deceitful and unjust *m'*. 376
49: 12 *m'* being in honour abideth not: 120

Ps 49:20 M· that is in honour, and 120
52: 1 thyself in mischief, O mighty m·? "
7 this is the m· that made not God 1397
55:13 But it was thou, a m· mine equal, 582
56: 1 God: for m· would swallow me up; "
11 I will not be afraid what m· can do 120
58:11 So that a m· shall say, Verily there* "
60:11 trouble: for vain is the help of m·. "
62: 3 ye imagine mischief against a m·? 376
12 to every m· according to his work. "
65: 4 Blessed is the m· whom thou choosest, "
71: 4 hand of the unrighteous and cruel m·. "
74: 5 A m· was famous according as he had* "
22 the foolish m· reproacheth thee daily. "
76:10 the wrath of m· shall praise thee: 120
78:25 M· did eat angels' food: he sent 376
65 and like a mighty m· that shouteth "
80:17 be upon the m· of thy right hand, 376
17 the son of m· whom thou madest 120
84: 5 Blessed is the m· whose strength is "
12 blessed is the m· that trusteth in "
87: 4 Ethiopia; this m· was born there. *
5 This and that m· was born in her: *376
6 people, that this m· was born there.* "
88: 4 am as a m· that hath no strength: 1397
89:48 What m· is he that liveth, and shall "
90: *title* A Prayer of Moses the m· of God. 376
3 Thou turnest m· to destruction; 582
92: 6 A brutish m· knoweth not; neither 376
94:10 he that teacheth m· knowledge, 120
11 Lord knoweth the thoughts of m·, "
12 is the m· whom thou chastenest, 1397
103:15 As for m·, his days are as grass: 582
104:14 and herb for the service of m·: 120
15 that maketh glad the heart of m·, 582
23 M· goeth forth unto his work and 120
105:14 He suffered no m· to do them wrong:"
17 He sent a m· before them, even 376
107:27 fro, and stagger like a drunken m·, "
108:12 trouble: for vain is the help of m·. 120
109: 6 Set thou a wicked m· over him: and "
16 persecuted the poor and needy m·, 376
112: 1 Blessed is the m· that feareth the "
5 A good m· sheweth favour, and "
118: 6 not fear: what can m· do unto me? 120
8 Lord than to put confidence in m·. "
119: 9 shall a young m· cleanse his way? "
134 me from the oppression of m·: 120
127: 4 are in the hand of a mighty m·; "
5 Happy is the m· that hath his 1397
128: 4 shall the m· be blessed that feareth "
135: 8 of Egypt, both of m· and beast. 120
140: 1 me, O Lord, from the evil m·: "
1, 4 preserve me from the violent m·;376
11 evil shall hunt the violent m· to "
142: 4 there was no m· that would know me: "
4 failed me; no m· cared for my soul. "
143: 2 sight shall no m· living be justified. "
144: 3 is m·, that thou takest knowledge 120
3 or the son of m·, that thou makest 582
4 M· is like to vanity: his days are 120
146: 3 son of m·, in whom there is no help. "
147:10 not pleasure in the legs of a m·. 376
Pr 1: 4 to the young m· knowledge and "
5 wise m· will hear, and will increase "
5 m· of understanding shall attain "
24 out my hand, and no m· regarded; "
2:12 thee from the way of the evil m·, *
12 m· that speaketh froward things;* 376
3: 4 favour...in the sight of God and m·. 120
13 Happy is the m· that findeth wisdom,"
13 the m· that getteth understanding. "
30 Strive not with a m· without cause, "
5:21 ways of m· are before the eyes of 376
6:11 and thy want as an armed m·. "
12 A naughty person, a wicked m·, "
26 a m· is brought to a piece of bread: "
27 Can a m· take fire in his bosom, 376
34 For jealousy is the rage of a m·: 1397
7: 7 a young m· void of understanding, "
8: 4 and my voice is to the sons of m·.* 120
34 Blessed is the m· that heareth me, "
9: 7 he that rebuketh a wicked m· getteth "
8 rebuke a wise m·, and he will love "
9 Give instruction to a wise m·, and he "
9 teach a just m·, and he will increase "
10:11 mouth of a righteous m· is a well of*
23 m· of understanding hath wisdom. 376
11: 7 When a wicked m· dieth, his 120
12 m· of understanding holdeth his 376
17 merciful m· doeth good to his own "
12: 2 A good m· obtaineth favour of the "
2 but a m· of wicked devices will he 376
3 A m· shall not be established by 120
8 m· shall be commended according 376
10 A righteous m· regardeth the life of "
14 A m· shall be satisfied with good 376
16 but a prudent m· covereth shame. "
23 prudent m· concealeth knowledge: 120
25 Heaviness in the heart of m· 376
27 slothful m· roasteth not that which he "
27 the substance of a diligent m· is * 120
13: 2 m· shall eat good by the fruit of 376
5 A righteous m· hateth lying: but a "
5 but a wicked m· is loathsome, and "
16 prudent m· dealeth with knowledge: "
22 A good m· leaveth an inheritance to "
14: 7 from the presence of a foolish m·, 376
12 way which seemeth right unto a m·, "
14 a good m· shall be satisfied from "
15 prudent m· looketh well to his going. "
16 A wise m· feareth, and departeth "
17 a m· of wicked devices is hated. 376
15:18 A wrathful m· stirreth up strife: but"
19 way of the slothful m· is as an hedge "
20 a foolish m· despiseth his mother. 120

Pr 15:21 but a m· of understanding walketh 376
23 A m· hath joy by the answer of his "
16: 1 The preparations of the heart in m·,120
2 ways of a m· are clean in his own 376
14 death: but a wise m· will pacify it. "
25 way that seemeth right unto a m·, "
27 An ungodly m· diggeth up evil: and "
28 A froward m· soweth strife: and a "
29 A violent m· enticeth his neighbour, "
17:10 a wise m· than an hundred stripes*
11 An evil m· seeketh only rebellion:
12 robbed of her whelps meet a m·. 376
18 A m· void of understanding striketh120
23 A wicked m· taketh a gift out of the
27 and a m· of understanding is of an 376
28 shutteth his lips is esteemed a m· of*
18: 1 Through desire a m·, having *
12 the heart of m· is haughty, and 376
14 The spirit of a m· will sustain his "
24 A m· that hath friends must shew * "
19: 3 The foolishness of m· perverteth 120
6 and every m· is a friend to him that
11 The discretion of a m· deferreth his120
19 A m· of great wrath shall suffer
22 The desire of a m· is his kindness: 120
22 and a poor m· is better than a liar.
24 A slothful m· hideth his hand in his
20: 3 honour for a m· to cease from strife:376
5 in the heart of m· is like deep water;"
5 a m· of understanding will draw it "
6 but a faithful m· who can find? "
7 The just m· walketh in his integrity:
17 Bread of deceit is sweet to a m·; 376
24 how can a m· then understand his 120
25 is a snare to the m· who devoureth "
27 spirit of m· is the candle of the Lord,"
21: 2 way of a m· is right in his own 376
8 way of m· is froward and strange:* "
12 The righteous m· wisely considereth
16 The m· that wandereth out of the 120
17 loveth pleasure shall be a poor m·: 376
20 but a foolish m· spendeth it up. 120
22 A wise m· scaleth the city of the
28 but the m· that heareth speaketh 376
29 A wicked m· hardeneth his face:
22: 3 A prudent m· foreseeth the evil, and
13 The slothful m· saith, There is a lion*
24 no friendship with an angry m·; 1167
24 with a furious m· thou shalt not go:376
29 thou a m· diligent in his business?
23: 2 if thou be a m· given to appetite. 1167
21 drowsiness shall clothe a m· with rags.
24: 5 A wise m· is strong; yea, 1397
5 yea, a m· of knowledge increaseth 376
12 to every m· according to his works?120
16 For a just m· falleth seven times, and
20 shall be no reward to the evil m·;
26 Every m· shall kiss his lips that *
29 to the m· according to his work. 376
30 of the m· void of understanding; 120
34 and thy want as an armed m·. 376
25:18 A m· that beareth false witness
19 Confidence in an unfaithful m· in
26 A righteous m· falleth down before
26:12 thou a m· wise in his own conceit? 376
13 The slothful m· saith, There is a lion*
18 As a mad m· who casteth firebrands,
19 m· that deceiveth his neighbour, 376
21 is a contentious m· to kindle strife. "
27: 2 Let another m· praise thee, and not
8 m· that wandereth from his place. 376
12 A prudent m· foreseeth the evil, and
17 so a m· sharpeneth the countenance376
19 to face, so the heart of m· to m·. 120
20 the eyes of m· are never satisfied. "
21 for gold; so is a m· to his praise. 376
28: 1 The wicked flee when no m· pursueth:
2 but by a m· of understanding and* 120
3 poor m· that oppresseth the poor 1397
11 rich m· is wise in his own conceit; 376
12 the wicked rise, a m· is hidden. * 120
14 Happy is the m· that feareth alway: "
17 m· that doeth violence to the blood "
20 A faithful m· shall abound with 376
21 of bread that m· will transgress. 1397
23 He that rebuketh a m· afterwards 120
29: 5 m· that flattereth his neighbour 1397
6 transgression of an evil m· there 376
9 m· contendeth with a foolish m·, "
11 wise m· keepeth it in till afterwards.
13 The poor and the deceitful m· meet376
20 a m· that is hasty in his words? "
22 An angry m· stirreth up strife, and "
22 and a furious m· aboundeth in 1167
25 fear of m· bringeth a snare: but 120
27 An unjust m· is an abomination to 376
30: 1 the m· spake unto Ithiel, even 1397
2 I am more brutish than any m·, 376
2 have not the understanding of a m·.120
19 and the way of a m· with a maid. 1397
Ec 1: 3 What profit hath a m· of all his 120
8 full of labour; m· cannot utter it: "
13 God given to the sons of m· to be * 120
2:12 what can the m· do that cometh "
16 And how dieth the wise m·? as the "
18 I should leave it unto the m· that 120
19 he shall be a wise m· or a fool? yet "
21 is a m· whose labour is in wisdom, "
21 yet to a m· that hath not laboured "
22 For what hath m· of all his labour, "
24 There is nothing better for a m·, "
26 to a m· that is good in his sight "
3:11 no m· can find out the work that God"
12 but for a m· to rejoice, and to do good*
13 that every m· should eat and drink,120
19 so that a m· hath no preeminence "

Ec 3:21 Who knoweth the spirit of m· 1121,120
22 a m· should rejoice in his own works;"
4: 4 a m· is envied of his neighbour. 376
5:12 The sleep of a labouring m· is sweet,
19 m· also to whom God hath given 120
6: 2 m· to whom God hath given riches, 376
3 If a m· beget an hundred children, "
7 labour of m· is for his mouth, and 120
10 already, and it is known that it is m·:"
11 vanity, what is m· the better? "
12 what is good for m· in this life, all "
12 who can tell a m· what shall be after "
7: 5 for a m· to hear the song of fools. 376
7 oppression maketh a wise m· mad;
14 m· should find nothing after him. 120
15 there is a just m· that perisheth in
15 wicked m· that prolongeth his life in
20 there is not a just m· upon earth, 120
28 one m· among a thousand have I "
29 that God hath made m· upright; but "
8: 6 the misery of m· is great upon him. "
8 is no m· that hath power over the "
9 m· ruleth over another to his hurt. "
15 a m· hath no better thing under the "
17 a m· cannot find out the work that "
17 though a m· labour to seek it out, "
17 a wise m· think to know it, yet shall
9: 1 m· knoweth either love or hatred 120
12 For m· also knoweth not his time: "
15 was found in it a poor wise m·, 376
15 yet no m· remembered that same 120
15 remembered that same poor m·. 376
10:14 a m· cannot tell what shall be; 120
11: 8 But if a m· live many years, and "
9 Rejoice, O young m·, in thy youth; and
12: 5 because m· goeth to his long home, 120
13 for this is the whole duty of m·. "
Ca 3: 8 every m· hath his sword upon his 376
8: 7 if a m· would give all the substance "
Isa 2: 9 And the mean m· boweth down, 1201
9 and the great m· humbleth himself:376
11 lofty looks of m· shall be humbled, 120
17 loftiness of m· shall be bowed down, "
20 In that day a m· shall cast his idols "
22 Cease ye from m·, whose breath is "
3: 2 The mighty m·, and the...of war,
2 The mighty..., and the m· of war, 376
3 the honourable m·, and the counsellor,
6 a m· shall take hold of his brother 376
4: 1 women shall take hold of one m·,
5:15 the mean m· shall be brought down,120
15 the mighty m· shall be humbled, 376
6: 5 because I am a m· of unclean lips,
11 and the houses without m·, and the 120
7:21 a m· shall nourish a young cow, 376
9:19 fire: no m· shall spare his brother. "
20 eat every m· the flesh of his own "
10:13 down the inhabitants like a valiant m·:
13:12 I will make a m· more precious 582
12 even a m· than the golden wedge of 120
14 and as a sheep that no m· taketh up:
14 every m· turn to his own people, 376
14:16 m· that made the earth to tremble,
17: 7 day shall a m· look to his Maker, 120
19:14 drunken m· staggereth in his vomit.
24:10 is shut up, that no m· may come in. 935
29: 8 be as when an hungry m· dreameth,
8 or as when a thirsty m· dreameth, and,
21 make a m· an offender for a word, 120
31: 7 every m· shall cast away his idols 376
8 with the sword, not of a mighty m·; "
8 the sword, not of a mean m·, shall *120
32: 2 a m· shall be as an hiding place 376
33: 8 lie waste, the wayfaring m· ceaseth:
8 the cities, he regardeth no m·. 582
35: 6 shall the lame m· leap as an hart, and
36: 6 whereon if a m· lean, it will go into376
38:11 I shall behold m· no more with the 120
41: 2 Who raised up the righteous m· from*
28 For I beheld, and there was no m·; 376
42:13 Lord shall go forth as a mighty m·, "
13 stir up jealousy like a m· of war: "
44:13 maketh it after the figure of a m·,
13 according to the beauty of a m·; 120
15 Then shall it be for a m· to burn: for "
45:12 the earth, and created m· upon it: "
46:11 the m· that executeth my counsel 376
47: 3 and I will not meet thee as a m·. 120
49: 7 One, to him whom m· despiseth, 5315
50: 2 when I came, was there no m·? 376
51:12 be afraid of a m· that shall die, 582
12 son of m· which shall be made as 120
52:14 was so marred more than any m·, 376
53: 3 a m· of sorrows, and acquainted with"
55: 7 the unrighteous m· his thoughts:
56: 2 Blessed is the m· that doeth this, 582
2 the son of m· that layeth hold on it;120
57: 1 and no m· layeth it to heart: 376
58: 5 a day for a m· to afflict his soul? 120
59:16 he saw that there was no m·, and 376
60:15 hated, so that no m· went through thee,
62: 5 For as a young m· marrieth a virgin,
65:20 an old m· that hath not filled his days:
66: 2 but to this m· will I look, even to him
3 killeth an ox is as if he slew a m·; 376
7 she was delivered of a m· child. 2145
Jer 2: 6 a land that no m· passed through, *376
6 through, and where no m· dwelt? 120
3: 1 If a m· put away his wife, and she 376
4:25 I beheld, and, lo, there was no m·, 120
29 and not a m· dwell therein. 376
5: 1 if ye can find a m·, if there be any "
7: 5 between a m· and his neighbour; "
20 this place, upon m·, and upon beast,120
8: 6 no m· repented...of his wickedness,376
9:12 is the wise m·, that may understand "

Jer 9:23 not the wise *m'* glory in his wisdom,
23 let the mighty *m'* glory in his might,
23 let not the rich *m'* glory in his riches:
10:14 *m'* is brutish in his knowledge: 120
23 that the way of *m'* is not in himself: "
23 it is not in *m'* that walketh to direct
11: 3 Cursed be the *m'* that obeyeth not 376
12:11 because no *m'* layeth it to heart. "
15 them again, every *m'* to his heritage, "
15 heritage, and every *m'* to his land. "
13:11 girdle cleaveth to the loins of a *m'*, "
14: 8 as a wayfaring *m'* that turneth aside
9 shouldest thou be as a *m'* astonied, 376
9 as a mighty *m'* that cannot save? "
15:10 hast borne me a *m'* of strife and a "
10 *m'* of contention to the whole earth! "
16:20 Shall a *m'* make gods unto himself, 120
17: 5 Cursed be the *m'* that trusteth in 1397
5 that trusteth in *m'*, and maketh 120
7 is the *m'* that trusteth in the Lord, 1397
10 to give every *m'* according to his 376
18:14 Will a *m'* leave the snow of Lebanon*
20:15 the *m'* who brought tidings to my 376
15 A *m'* child is born unto thee; 2145
16 let that *m'* be as the cities which 376
21: 6 of this city, both *m'* and beast: 120
22: 8 shall say every *m'* to his neighbour, 376
28 Is this *m'* Coniah a despised broken "
30 the Lord, Write ye this *m'* childless, "
30 a *m'* that shall not prosper in his 1397
30 for no *m'* of his seed shall prosper, 376
23: 9 I am like a drunken *m'*, and like "
9 a *m'* whom wine hath overcome, 1397
27 they tell every *m'* to his neighbour, 376
34 even punish that *m'* and his house. "
26: 3 turn every *m'* from his evil way, that "
11 This *m'* is worthy to die; for he hath "
16 This *m'* is not worthy to die: for he "
20 there was also a *m'* that prophesied "
27: 5 the earth, the *m'* and the beast that 120
29:26 every *m'* that is mad, and maketh 376
32 shall not have a *m'* to dwell among "
30: 6 see whether a *m'* doth travail with 2145
6 *m'* with his hands on his loins, 1397
17 is Zion, whom no *m'* seeketh after.
31:22 A woman shall compass a *m'*. 1397
27 with the seed of *m'*, and with the 120
30 every *m'* that eateth the sour grape, "
34 shall teach no more every *m'* his 376
34 neighbour, and every *m'* his brother," "
32:43 It is desolate without *m'* or beast; 120
33:10 be desolate without *m'* and without "
10 desolate, without *m'*, and without "
12 is desolate without *m'* and without "
17 David shall never want a *m'* to sit 376
18 Levites want a *m'* before me to offer "
34: 9 every *m'* should let his manservant, "
9 and every *m'* his maidservant, being "
14 years let ye go every *m'* his brother "
15 liberty every *m'* to his neighbour; "
16 and caused every *m'* his servant, "
16 and every *m'* his handmaid, whom "
17 and every *m'* to his neighbour: "
35: 4 son of Igdaliah, a *m'* of God, which "
15 ye now every *m'* from his evil way, "
19 not want a *m'* to stand before me "
36: 3 return every *m'* from his evil way; "
19 and let no *m'* know where ye be. "
29 to cease from thence *m'* and beast? 120
37:10 they rise up every *m'* in his tent, 376
38: 4 thee, let this *m'* be put to death: "
4 this *m'* seeketh not the welfare of "
24 Let no *m'* know of these words, and "
40:15 Nethaniah, and no *m'* shall know it: "
41: 4 slain Gedaliah, and no *m'* knew it, "
44: 2 and no *m'* dwelleth therein, "
7 to cut off from you *m'* and woman, 376
26 be named in the mouth of any *m'* of "
46: 6 flee away, nor the mighty *m'* escape; "
12 the mighty *m'* hath stumbled against "
49: 5 and ye shall be driven out every *m'* 376
18 the Lord, no *m'* shall abide there, "
18 neither shall a son of *m'* dwell in it. 120
19 who is a chosen *m'*, that I may appoint*
33 ever: there shall no *m'* abide there, 376
33 nor any son of *m'* dwell in it. 120
50: 3 they shall depart, both *m'* and beast. "
9 shall be as of a mighty expert *m'*;
40 Lord; so shall no *m'* abide there, 376
40 shall any son of *m'* dwell therein. 120
42 put in array, like a *m'* to the battle, 376
44 who is a chosen *m'*, that I may appoint*
51: 6 and deliver every *m'* his soul: 376
17 *m'* is brutish by his knowledge; 120
22 I break in pieces *m'* and woman; 376
22 in pieces the young *m'* and the maid;
43 a land wherein no *m'* dwelleth, 376
43 doth any son of *m'* pass thereby. 120
45 deliver ye every *m'* his soul from 376
62 remain in it, neither *m'* nor beast, 120
La 3: 1 am the *m'* that hath seen affliction 1397
26 It is good that a *m'* should both hope
27 good for a *m'* that he bear the yoke 1397
35 turn aside the right of a *m'* before "
36 subvert a *m'* in his cause, the Lord 120
39 doth a living *m'* complain, a "
39 *m'* for the punishment of his sins? 1397
4: 4 and no *m'* breaketh it unto them.
Eze 1: 5 they had the likeness of a *m'*. 120
8 hands of a *m'* under their wings "
10 faces, they four had the face of a *m'*, "
26 appearance of a *m'* above upon it. "
2: 1 Son of *m'*, stand upon thy feet, and "
3 Son of *m'*, I send thee to the children "
6 son of *m'*, be not afraid of them, "
8 son of *m'*, hear what I say unto thee; "

Eze 3: 1 Son of *m'*, eat that thou findest; 120
3 Son of *m'*, cause thy belly to eat, "
4 Son of *m'*, go, get thee unto the house "
10 Son of *m'*, all my words that I shall "
17 Son of *m'*, I have made thee a "
18 wicked *m'* shall die in his iniquity; "
20 When a righteous *m'* doth turn from "
21 if thou warn the righteous *m'*, that the "
25 O son of *m'*, behold, they shall put 120
4: 1 son of *m'*, take thee a tile, and lay it "
12 it with dung that cometh out of *m'*, "
16 Son of *m'*, behold, I will break the "
5: 1 son of *m'*, take thee a sharp knife, "
6: 2 Son of *m'*, set thy face toward the "
7: 2 thou son of *m'*, thus saith the Lord "
8: 5 Son of *m'*, lift up thine eyes now the "
6 Son of *m'*, seest thou what they do? "
8 Son of *m'*, dig now in the wall: and "
11 every *m'* his censer in his hand; 376
12 Son of *m'*, hast thou seen what the 120
12 every *m'* in the chambers of his 376
15, 17 thou seen this, O son of *m'*? 120
9: 1 *m'* with his destroying weapon in 376
2 every *m'* a slaughter weapon in his "
2 and one *m'* among them was clothed "
3 called to the *m'* clothed with linen, "
6 come not near any *m'* upon whom "
11 behold, the *m'* clothed with linen, "
10: 2 spake unto the *m'* clothed with linen, "
3 of the house, when the *m'* went in; "
6 had commanded the *m'* clothed with "
14 second face was the face of a *m'*, 120
21 the likeness of the hands of a *m'* "
11: 2 Then said he unto me, Son of *m'*, "
4 against them, prophesy, O son of *m'*. "
15 Son of *m'*, thy brethren, even thy "
12: 2 Son of *m'*, thou dwellest in the midst "
3 thou son of *m'*, prepare thee stuff "
9 Son of *m'*, hath not the house of "
18 Son of *m'*, eat...bread with quaking, "
22 Son of *m'*, what is that proverb that "
27 Son of *m'*, behold, they of the house "
13: 2 Son of *m'*, prophesy against the "
17 thou son of *m'*, set thy face against "
14: 3 Son of *m'*, these men have set up "
4 Every *m'* of the house of Israel 376
8 I will set my face against that *m'*, "
13 Son of *m'*, when the land sinneth 120
13 will cut off *m'* and beast from it: "
15 no *m'* may pass through because of "
17 that I cut off *m'* and beast from it: 120
19 to cut off from it *m'* and beast: "
21 to cut off from it *m'* and beast? "
15: 2 Son of *m'*, What is the vine tree "
16: 2 Son of *m'*, cause Jerusalem to know "
17: 2 Son of *m'*, put forth a riddle, and "
18: 5 But if a *m'* be just, and do that 376
8 true judgment between *m'* and *m'*, "
24 abominations that the wicked *m'* doeth, "
26 a righteous *m'* turneth away from his "
27 when the wicked *m'* turneth away from "
20: 3 Son of *m'*, speak unto the elders of 120
4 Wilt thou judge them, son of *m'*, "
7 ye away every *m'* the abominations 376
8 did not every *m'* cast away the "
11, 13, 21 which if a *m'* do, he shall even 120
27 son of *m'*, speak unto the house of "
46 Son of *m'*, set thy face toward the "
21: 2 Son of *m'*, set thy face toward "
6 Sigh therefore, thou son of *m'*, with "
9 Son of *m'*, prophesy, and say, Thus "
12 Cry and howl, son of *m'*: for it shall "
14 Thou therefore, son of *m'*, prophesy, "
19 thou son of *m'*, appoint thee two "
28 And thou, son of *m'*, prophesy and "
22: 2 Now, thou son of *m'*, wilt thou judge, "
18 Son of *m'*, the house of Israel is to "
24 Son of *m'*, say unto her, Thou art "
30 I sought for a *m'* among them, that 376
23: 2 Son of *m'*, there were two women, 120
36 Son of *m'*, wilt thou judge Aholah "
24: 2 Son of *m'*, write thee the name of "
16 Son of *m'*, behold, I take away from "
25 thou son of *m'*, shall it not be in the "
25: 2 Son of *m'*, set thy face against the "
13 will cut off *m'* and beast from it; "
26: 2 Son of *m'*, because that Tyrus hath "
27: 2 son of *m'*, take up a lamentation "
28: 2 Son of *m'*, say unto the prince of "
2 yet thou art a *m'*, and not God, "
9 thou shalt be a *m'*, and no God, in "
12 Son of *m'*, take up a lamentation "
21 Son of *m'*, set thy face against "
29: 2 Son of *m'*, set thy face against "
8 and cut off *m'* and beast out of thee. "
11 No foot of *m'* shall pass through it, "
18 Son of *m'*, Nebuchadrezzar king of "
30: 2 Son of *m'*, prophesy and say, Thus "
21 Son of *m'*, I have broken the arm of "
24 groanings of a deadly wounded *m'*.
31: 2 Son of *m'*, speak unto Pharaoh king 120
32: 2 Son of *m'*, take up a lamentation "
10 every *m'* for his own life, in the day 376
13 shall the foot of *m'* trouble them 120
18 Son of *m'*, wail for the multitude of "
33: 2 Son of *m'*, speak to the children of "
2 the land take a *m'* of their coasts, 376
7 O Son of *m'*, I have set thee a 120
8 O wicked *m'*, thou shalt surely die; "
8 wicked *m'* shall die in his iniquity; "
10 O thou son of *m'*, speak unto the 120
12 thou son of *m'*, say unto the children "
24 Son of *m'*, they that inhabit those "
30 thou son of *m'*, the children of thy "
34: 2 Son of *m'*, prophesy against the "
35: 2 Son of *m'*, set thy face against "

Eze 36: 1 thou son of *m'*, prophesy unto the 120
11 multiply upon you *m'* and beast; "
17 Son of *m'*, when the house of Israel "
37: 3 Son of *m'*, can these bones live? "
9 prophesy, son of *m'*, and say to the "
11 Son of *m'*, these bones are the whole "
16 thou son of *m'*, take thee one stick, "
38: 2 Son of *m'*, set thy face against Gog, "
14 son of *m'*, prophesy and say unto "
39: 1 thou son of *m'*, prophesy against "
17 thou son of *m'*, thus saith the Lord "
40: 3 there was a *m'*, whose appearance 376
4 And the *m'* said unto me, "
4 Son of *m'*, behold with thine eyes, 120
41:19 the face of a *m'* was toward the palm "
43: 6 the house; and the *m'* stood by me. 376
7 Son of *m'*, the place of my throne, 120
10 Thou son of *m'*, shew the house to "
18 Son of *m'*, thus saith the Lord God; "
44: 2 and no *m'* shall enter in by it; 376
5 Son of *m'*, mark well, and behold 120
46:18 every *m'* from his possession. 376
47: 3 when the *m'* that had the line in his "
6 me, Son of *m'*, hast thou seen this? 120
20 till a *m'* come over against Hamath.*
Da 2:10 There is not a *m'* upon the earth 606
25 I have found a *m'* of the captives 1400
48 the king made Daniel a great *m'*, *
3:10 every *m'* that shall hear the sound 606
5:11 There is a *m'* in thy kingdom, in 1400
6: 7 ask a petition of any God or *m'* for 606
12 every *m'* that shall ask a petition "
12 a petition of any God or *m'* within "
7: 4 made stand upon the feet as a *m'*, "
8 horn were eyes like the eyes of *m'*, "
13 one like the Son of *m'* came with the "
8:15 me as the appearance of a *m'*. 1397
16 make this *m'* to understand the vision.
17 Understand, O Son of *m'*: for at the 120
9:21 even the *m'* Gabriel, whom I had 376
10: 5 a certain *m'* clothed in linen, whose "
11 me, O Daniel, a *m'* greatly beloved, "
18 one like the appearance of a *m'*, 120
19 O *m'* greatly beloved, fear not: 376
12: 6 one said to the *m'* clothed in linen, "
7 And I heard the *m'* clothed in linen, "
Ho 3: 3 thou shalt not be for another *m'*: * "
4: 4 Yet let no *m'* strive, nor reprove "
6: 9 as troops of robbers wait for a *m'*, "
9: 7 is a fool, the spiritual *m'* is mad, "
12 that there shall not be a *m'* left: 120
11: 4 I drew them with cords of a *m'*, "
9 for I am God, and not *m'*; the Holy 376
Am 2: 7 and a *m'* and his father will go in "
4:13 unto *m'* what is his thought, that 120
5:19 As if a *m'* did flee from a lion, and 376
Jon 1: 5 and cried every *m'* unto his god, and "
3: 7 Let neither *m'* nor beast, herd nor 120
8 But let *m'* and beast be covered "
Mic 2: 2 they oppress a *m'* and his house, 1397
2 house, even a *m'* and his heritage. 376
11 If a *m'* walking in the spirit and "
4: 4 shall sit every *m'* under his vine and "
5: 5 this *m'* shall be the peace, when the
7 the grass, that tarrieth not for *m'*, 376
6: 8 shewed thee, O *m'*, what is good; 120
9 the *m'* of wisdom shall see thy name:
7: 2 The good *m'* is perished out of the
2 they hunt every *m'* his brother 376
3 and the great *m'* he uttereth his
Na 3:18 mountains, and no *m'* gathereth them.*
Hab 1:13 the wicked devoureth the *m'* that is
2: 5 he is a proud *m'*, neither keepeth 1397
Zep 1: 3 I will consume *m'* and beast; I 120
3 I will cut off *m'* from off the land, "
14 the mighty *m'* shall cry there bitterly.
3: 6 destroyed, so that there is no *m'*, 376
Hag 1: 9 ye run every *m'* unto his own house. "
Zec 1: 8 a *m'* riding upon a red horse, and "
10 the *m'* that stood among the myrtle "
21 so that no *m'* did lift up his head: "
2: 1 behold a *m'* with a measuring line "
4 Run, speak to this young *m'*, saying,
3:10 shall ye call every *m'* his neighbour
4: 1 as a *m'* that is wakened out of his 376
6:12 the *m'* whose name is The Branch; "
7: 9 compassions every *m'* to his brother: "
14 no *m'* passed through nor returned:
8: 4 every *m'* with his staff in his hand 376
10 days there was no hire for *m'*, nor 120
16 Speak ye every *m'* the truth to his 376
9: 1 the eyes of *m'*, as of all the tribes 120
13 thee as the sword of a mighty *m'*.
10: 7 of Ephraim shall be like a mighty *m'*,
12: 1 and formeth the spirit of *m'* within 120
13: 5 for *m'* taught me to keep cattle * "
7 against the *m'* that is my fellow, 1397
Mal 2:10 deal treacherously every *m'* against 376
12 will cut off the *m'* that doeth this, "
3: 8 Will a *m'* rob God? Yet ye have 120
17 as a *m'* spareth his own son that 376
M't 1:19 her husband, being a just *m'*, and
4: 4 *M'* shall not live by bread alone, *444*
5:40 And if any *m'* will sue thee at the law,
6:24 No *m'* can serve two masters: for *3762*
7: 9 what *m'* is there of you, whom if *444*
24 I will liken him unto a wise *m'*, *435*
26 shall be likened unto a foolish *m'*, "
8: 4 See thou tell no *m'*; but go thy *3367*
9 For I am a *m'* under authority, *444*
9 I say to this *m'*, Go, and he goeth; and
20 the Son of *m'* hath not where to lay *444*
27 What manner of *m'* is this, that even
28 that no *m'* might pass by that way. *5100*
9: 2 brought to him a *m'* sick of the palsy,
3 themselves, This *m'* blasphemeth.

M't 9: 6 know that the Son of m' hath power 444
9 he saw a m', named Matthew, sitting "
16 No m' putteth a piece of new cloth 3762
30 saying, See that no m' know it. 3367
32 they brought to him a dumb m' 444
10: 23 of Israel, till the Son of m' be come. "
35 I am come to set a m' at variance "
41 he that receiveth a righteous m' in
41 in the name of a righteous m' shall
11: 8 see? A m' clothed in soft raiment? 444
19 The Son of m' came eating and "
19 Behold a m' gluttonous, and a "
27 no m' knoweth the Son, but the *3762
27 neither knoweth any m' the Father,*
12: 8 the Son of m' is Lord even of the 444
10 there was a m' which had his hand "
11 What m' shall there be among you, "
12 then is a m' better than a sheep? "
13 to the m', Stretch forth thine hand. "
19 shall any m' hear his voice in the
29 except he first bind the strong m'?
32 a word against the Son of m', 444
35 A good m' out of the good treasure "
35 an evil m' out of the evil treasure "
40 so shall the Son of m' be three days "
43 unclean spirit is gone out of a m', "
45 last state of that m' is worse than "
13: 24 of heaven is likened unto a m' which "
31 of mustard seed, which a m' took, "
37 the good seed is the Son of m'; "
41 The Son of m' shall send forth his "
44 the which when a m' hath found, he "
45 of heaven is like unto a merchant m', "
52 unto a m' that is an householder, "
54 Whence hath this m' this wisdom,
56 then hath this m' all these things?
15: 11 goeth into the mouth defileth a m'; 444
11 out of the mouth, this defileth a m'. "
18 the heart; and they defile the m'. "
20 are the things which defile a m': "
20 unwashen hands defileth not a m'. "
16: 13 do men say that I the Son of m' am? "
20 tell no m' that he was Jesus the 3367
24 If any m' will come after me, let him
26 For what is a m' profited, if he shall 444
26 a m' give in exchange for his soul? "
27 Son of m' shall come in the glory of
27 shall reward every m' according to his
28 till they see the Son of m' coming 444
17: 8 they saw no m', save Jesus only. *3762
9 saying, Tell the vision to no m', 3367
9 until the Son of m' be risen again 444
12 shall also the Son of m' suffer of "
14 came to him a certain m', kneeling "
22 The Son of m' shall be betrayed into "
18: 7 woe to that m' by whom the offence "
11 For the Son of m' is come to save * "
12 if a m' have an hundred sheep, and "
17 let him be unto thee as an heathen m'*
19: 3 lawful for a m' to put away his wife 444
5 this cause shall a m' leave father "
6 together, let not m' put asunder. "
10 case of the m' be so with his wife. "
20 The young m' saith unto him, All 3495
22 the young m' heard that saying, "
23 a rich m' shall hardly enter into the
24 than for a rich m' to enter into the
28 when the Son of m' shall sit in the 444
20: 1 unto a m' that is an householder, "
7 him, Because no m' hath hired us. 3762
9 hour, they received every m' a penny.
10 likewise received every m' a penny.
18 Son of m' shall be betrayed unto 444
28 Even as the Son of m' came not to "
21: 3 And if any m' say ought unto you,*
28 A certain m' had two sons; and he 444
22: 11 a m' which had not on a wedding "
16 neither carest thou for any m': for *3762
24 If a m' die, having no children, his 5100
46 no m' was able to answer him a *3762
46 neither durst any m' from that day
23: 9 And call no m' your father upon the
24: 4 Take heed that no m' deceive you. 5100
23 Then if any m' shall say unto you,
27 also the coming of the Son of m' be. 444
30 the sign of the Son of m' in heaven: "
30 see the Son of m' coming in the clouds "
36 that day and hour knoweth no m',*3762
37, 39 the coming of the Son of m' be. 444
44 ye think not the Son of m' cometh. "
25: 13 hour wherein the Son of m' cometh.* "
14 as a m' travelling into a far country, "
15 every m' according to his...ability;*
24 knew thee that thou art an hard m', 444
31 Son of m' shall come in his glory, "
26: 2 and the Son of m' is betrayed to be "
18 Go into the city to such a m', and say
24 Son of m' goeth as it is written of 444
24 but woe unto that m' by whom the "
24 by whom the Son of m' is betrayed! "
24 been good for that m' if he had not "
45 Son of m' is betrayed into the hands "
64 ye see the Son of m' sitting on the "
72 with an oath, I do not know the m'. "
74 to swear, saying, I know not the m'. "
27: 19 thou nothing to do with that just m': "
32 they found a m' of Cyrene, Simon 444
47 that, said, This m' calleth for Elias.
57 there came a rich m' of Arimathæa, 444
M'r 1: 23 a m' with an unclean spirit; and "
44 See thou say nothing to any m': 3367
2: 7 doth this m' thus speak blasphemies?
10 know that the Son of m' hath power 444
21 No m' also seweth a piece of new 3762
22 no m' putteth new wine into old "
27 The sabbath was made for m', 444

M'r 2: 27 and not m' for the sabbath. 444
28 the Son of m' is Lord also of the "
3: 1 was a m' there which had a withered "
3 the m' which had the withered hand, "
5 unto the m', Stretch forth thine hand. "
27 No m' can enter into a strong *3762
27 he will first bind the strong m'; 2478
4: 23 If any m' have ears to hear, let him
26 as if a m' should cast seed into the 444
41 What manner of m' is this, that even*
5: 2 tombs a m' with an unclean spirit, 444
3 no m' could bind him, no, not with 3762
4 neither could any m' tame him.
8 Come out of the m', thou unclean 444
37 he suffered no m' to follow him, 3762
43 that no m' should know it; and 3367
6: 2 whence hath this m' these things?
20 knowing that he was a just m' and 435
7: 11 If a m' shall say to his father or 444
15 There is nothing from without a m', "
15 those are they that defile the m'. "
16 If any m' have ears to hear, let him*
18 from without entereth into the m', 444
20 out of the m', that defileth the m'. "
23 come from within, and defile the m'. "
24 and would have no m' know it: 3762
36 them that they should tell no m': 3367
8: 4 can a m' satisfy these men with *5100
22 and they bring a blind m' unto him,
23 And he took the blind m' by the hand,
25 restored, and saw every m' clearly.*
30 that they should tell no m' of him. 3367
31 Son of m' must suffer many things, 444
36 For what shall it profit a m', if he "
37 a m' give in exchange for his soul? "
38 also shall the Son of m' be ashamed, "
9: 8 saw no m' any more, save Jesus *3762
9 them that they should tell no m' 3367
9 till the Son of m' were risen from 444
12 how it is written of the Son of m', "
30 not that any m' should know it.
31 The Son of m' is delivered into the 444
35 If any m' desire to be first, the same
39 is no m' which shall do a miracle 3762
10: 2 lawful for a m' to put away his wife? 435
7 cause shall a m' leave his father and 444
9 together, let not m' put asunder. "
25 for a rich m' to enter into the kingdom
29 is no m' that hath left house, or 3762
33 Son of m' shall be delivered unto 444
45 For even the Son of m' came not to "
49 And they call the blind m', saying
51 The blind m' said unto him, Lord,
11: 2 a colt tied, whereon never m' sat; 444
3 if any m' say unto you, Why do ye*
14 No m' eat fruit of thee hereafter 3367
16 any m' should carry any vessel
12: 1 A certain m' planted a vineyard, 444
14 thou art true, and carest for no m':* "
34 no m' after that durst ask him any 3762
13: 5 Take heed lest any m' deceive you:
21 then if any m' shall say to you, Lo,
26 shall they see the Son of m' coming 444
32 day and that hour knoweth no m',*3762
34 For the Son of m' is as a...taking a*
34 is as a m' taking a far journey, 444
34 servants, and to every m' his work,*
14: 13 meet you a m' bearing a pitcher 444
21 The Son of m' indeed goeth, as it is "
21 woe to that m' by whom the Son of "
21 by whom the Son of m' is betrayed! "
21 were it for that m' if he had never "
41 Son of m' is betrayed into the hands "
51 followed him a certain young m', 3495
62 ye shall see the Son of m' sitting on 444
71 know not this m' of whom ye speak. "
15: 24 upon them, what every m' should take.*
39 Truly this m' was the Son of God. 444
16: 5 they saw a young m' sitting on the 3495
8 said they any thing to any m'; *3762
Lu 1: 18 for I am an old m', and my wife well
27 to a m' whose name was Joseph, 435
34 shall this be, seeing I know not a m'? "
2: 25 there was a m' in Jerusalem, whose 444
25 the same m' was just and devout, "
52 and in favour with God and m'. * "
3: 14 Do violence to no m', neither 3367
4: 4 m' shall not live by bread alone, 444
33 in the synagogue there was a m', "
5: 8 me; for I am a sinful m', O Lord. 435
12 city; behold a m' full of leprosy: "
14 And he charged him to tell no m': 3367
18 brought in a bed a m' which was 444
20 him, M', thy sins are forgiven thee. "
24 Son of m' hath power upon earth to "
36 No m' putteth a piece of a new 3762
37 no m' putteth new wine into old "
39 No m' also having drunk old wine "
6: 5 the Son of m' is Lord also of the 444
6 a m' whose right hand was withered. "
8 the m' which had the withered hand, "
10 he said unto the m', Stretch forth*
30 Give to every m' that asketh of thee;*
45 good m' out of the good treasure 444
45 an evil m' out of the evil treasure of "
48 He is like a m' which built an house, "
49 like a m' that without a foundation "
7: 8 I also am a m' set under authority, "
12 there was a dead m' carried out, *
14 Young m', I say unto thee, Arise. 3495
25 see? A m' clothed in soft raiment? 444
34 The Son of m' is come eating and "
34 Behold a gluttonous m', and a "
39 This m', if he were a prophet, would
8: 16 No m', when he hath lighted a 3762
25 What manner of m' is this! for he*

Lu 8: 27 a certain m', which had devils long 435
29 unclean spirit to come out of the m' 444
33 Then went the devils out of the m', "
35 found the m', out of whom the devils "
38 the m' out of whom the devils were 435
41 there came a m' named Jairus, "
51 he suffered no m' to go in, save 3762
56 should tell no m' what was done. 3367
9: 21 commanded them to tell no m' that "
22 The Son of m' must suffer many 444
23 If any m' will come after me, let him
25 For what is a m' advantaged, if he 444
26 him shall the Son of m' be ashamed, "
36 and told no m' in those days any of 3762
38 a m' of the company cried out, 435
44 for the Son of m' shall be delivered 444
56 Son of m' is not come to destroy * "
57 a certain m' said unto him, Lord,
58 Son of m' hath not where to lay his 444
62 No m', having put his hand to the 3762
10: 4 and salute no m' by the way. 3367
22 no m' knoweth who the Son is, *3762
30 m' went down from Jerusalem to 444
11: 21 a strong m' armed keepeth his
24 unclean spirit is gone out of a m', 444
26 last state of that m' is worse than "
30 Son of the m' be to this generation. "
33 No m', when he hath lighted a 3762
12: 8 him shall the Son of m' also confess 444
10 speak a word against the Son of m', "
14 unto him, M', who made me a judge "
16 ground of a certain rich m' brought "
40 Son of m' cometh at an hour when "
13: 6 A certain m' had a fig tree planted in
19 of mustard seed, which a m' took, 444
14: 2 a certain m' before him which had "
8 art bidden of any m' to a wedding,
8 lest a more honourable m' than thou
9 and say to thee, Give this m' place;
16 certain m' made a great supper, and 444
26 If any m' come to me, and hate not his
30 This m' began to build, and was 444
15: 2 This m' receiveth sinners, and eateth "
4 What m' of you, having an hundred 444
11 he said, A certain m' had two sons: "
16 did eat: and no m' gave unto him. 3762
16: 1 There was a certain rich m', which 444
16 preached, and every m' presseth into
19 There was a certain rich m', which 444
22 the rich m' also died, and was buried;
17: 22 one of the days of the Son of m', 444
24 so shall also the Son of m' be in his "
26 be also in the days of the Son of m'. "
30 day when the Son of m' is revealed. "
18: 2 feared not God, neither regarded m': "
4 I fear not God, nor regard m';
8 when the Son of m' cometh, shall he "
14 this m' went down to his house justified
25 a rich m' to enter into the kingdom
29 is no m' that hath left house, or 3762
31 prophets concerning the Son of m' 444
35 blind m' sat by the wayside begging:
19: 2 was a m' named Zacchæus, which 435
7 be guest with a m' that is a sinner. "
8 have taken any thing from any m'
10 the Son of m' is come to seek and 444
14 will not have this m' to reign over us.
15 how much every m' had gained by*
21 because thou art an austere m': 444
22 knewest that I was an austere m', "
30 colt tied, whereon yet never m' sat: "
31 if any m' ask you, Why do ye loose*
20: 9 A certain m' planted a vineyard, 444
21: 27 see the Son of m' coming in a cloud "
36 and to stand before the Son of m'. "
22: 10 a m' meet you, bearing a pitcher "
22 And truly the Son of m' goeth, as it "
22 that m' by whom he is betrayed! "
48 betrayest thou the Son of m' with a "
56 and said, This m' was also with him.
58 And Peter said, M', I am not. 444
60 M', I know not what thou sayest. "
69 Hereafter shall the Son of m' sit on "
23: 4 the people, I find no fault in this m'. "
6 whether the m' were a Galilæan. "
14 Ye have brought this m' unto me, as "
14 I,...have found no fault in this m' "
18 Away with this m', and release unto
41 but this m' hath done nothing amiss.
47 Certainly this was a righteous m'. 444
50 there was a m' named Joseph, a 435
50 and he was a good m', and a just: "
52 This m' went unto Pilate, and begged
53 wherein never m' before was laid. 3762
24: 7 The Son of m' must be delivered 444
Joh 1: 6 There was a m' sent from God, whose "
9 lighteth every m' that cometh into "
13 nor of the will of m', but of God. 435
18 No m' hath seen God at any time; 3762
30 me cometh a m' which is preferred 435
51 and descending upon the Son of m'. 444
2: 10 Every m' at the beginning doth set "
25 not that any should testify of m': "
25 for he knew what was in m'. "
3: 1 There was a m' of the Pharisees, "
2 for no m' can do these miracles 3762
3 Except a m' be born again, he 5100
4 How can a m' be born when he is 444
5 Except a m' be born of water and 5100
13 no m' hath ascended up to heaven, 3762
13 the Son of m' which is in heaven. 444
14 so must the Son of m' be lifted up: "
27 A m' can receive nothing, except it "
32 and no m' receiveth his testimony. 3762
4: 27 no m' said, What seekest thou? or, "
29 Come, see a m', which told me all 444

Joh 4:33 any m' brought him ought to eat?
50 the m' believed the word that Jesus 444
5: 5 certain m' was there, which had an "
7 The impotent m' answered him, Sir, "
7 I have no m', when the water is 444
9 immediately the m' was made whole, "
12 What m' is that which said unto "
15 m' departed, and told the Jews that "
22 the Father judgeth no m', but hath 3762
27 also, because he is the Son of m'. 444
34 But I receive not testimony from m': "
6:27 the Son of m' shall give unto you: "
44 No m' can come to me, except the 3762
45 Every m' therefore that hath heard,*
46 that any m' hath seen the Father, "
50 a m' may eat thereof, and not die. 5100
51 if any m' eat of this bread, he shall "
52 can this m' give us his flesh to eat?
53 ye eat the flesh of the Son of m', 444
62 if ye shall see the Son of m' ascend "
65 no m' can come unto me, except 3762
7: 4 is no m' that doeth any thing in "
12 some said, He is a good m': others
13 no m' spake openly of him for fear 3762
15 How knoweth this m' letters, having
17 If any m' will do his will, he shall
22 on the sabbath day circumcise a m'. 444
23 If a m' on the sabbath day receive "
23 made a m' every whit whole on the "
27 we know this m' whence he is: but
27 no m' knoweth whence he is. *3762
30 him: but no m' laid hands on him, "
31 than these which this m' hath done?
37 If any m' thirst, let him come unto
44 him; but no m' laid hands on him. 3762
46 answered, Never m' spake like this 444
46 Never...spake like this m'. * "
51 Doth our law judge any m', before "
53 And every m' went unto his own house.
8:10 hath no m' condemned thee? 3762
11 She said, No m', Lord. And Jesus "
15 judge after the flesh; I judge no m'. "
20 and no m' laid hands on him; for "
28 ye have lifted up the Son of m', 444
33 and were never in bondage to any m': "
40 a m' that hath told you the truth, 444
51, 52 If a m' keep my saying, he shall 5100
9: 1 he saw a m' which was blind from 444
2 who did sin, this m', or his parents,
3 hath this m' sinned, nor his parents:
4 cometh, when no m' can work. 3762
6 he anointed the eyes of the blind m' *
11 A m' that is called Jesus made clay, 444
16 This m' is not of God, because he "
16 said, How can a m' that is a sinner "
17 say unto the blind m' again, What
22 if any m' did confess that he was
24 called they the m' that was blind, 444
24 we know that this m' is a sinner. "
30 m' answered and said unto them, "
31 but if any m' be a worshipper of God,
32 that any m' opened the eyes of one
33 If this m' were not of God, he could do
10: 9 by me if any m' enter in, he shall be
18 No m' taketh it from me, but I lay *3762
28 any m' pluck them out of my hand.*
29 no m' is able to pluck them out of *3762
33 being a m', makest thyself God. 444
41 that John spake of this m' were true.
11: 1 a certain m' was sick, named Lazarus,
9 If any m' walk in the day, he stumbleth
10 But if a m' walk in the night, he 5100
37 Could not this m', which opened the
37 even this m' should not have died?
47 for this m' doeth many miracles. 444
50 one m' should die for the people, "
57 if any m' knew where he were, he
12:23 the Son of m' should be glorified. 444
26 If any m' serve me, let him follow
26 if any m' serve me, him will my
34 The Son of m' must be lifted up? 444
34 who is this Son of m'? "
47 And if any m' hear my words, and
13:28 no m' at the table knew for what 3762
31 said, Now is the Son of m' glorified, 444
14: 6 no m' cometh unto the Father, but *3762
23 If a m' love me, he will keep my 5100
15: 6 If a m' abide not in me, he is cast "
13 Greater love hath no m' than this, 3762
13 that a m' lay down his life for his 5100
24 the works which none other m' did,*
16:21 joy that a m' is born into the world. 444
22 your joy no m' taketh from you. *3762
30 not that any m' should ask thee:
32 shall be scattered, every m' to his own,
18:14 one m' should die for the people. 444
29 accusation bring ye against this m'? "
31 lawful for us to put any m' to death: 3762
19: 5 saith unto them, Behold the m'! 444
41 wherein was never m' yet laid. 3762
21:21 Jesus, Lord, and what shall this m' do?
Ac 1:18 this m' purchased a field with the
20 desolate, and let no m' dwell therein:
2: 6 m' heard them speak in his own 1520
8 we every m' in our own tongue,
22 a m' approved of God among you 435
45 to all men, as every m' had need.
3: 2 m' lame from his mother's womb 435
11 lame m' which was healed held Peter*
12 holiness we had made this m' to walk?*
16 his name hath made this m' strong,
4: 9 good deed done to the impotent m', 444
10 doth this m' stand here before you
14 the m' which was healed standing 444
17 henceforth to no m' in this name. "
22 the m' was above forty years old, "

Ac 4:35 every m' according as he had need.*
5: 1 a certain m' named Ananias, with 435
13 durst no m' join himself to them: 3762
23 had opened, we found no m' within."
37 After this m' rose up Judas of Galilee
6: 5 a m' full of faith and of the Holy 435
13 said, This m' ceaseth not to speak 444
7:56 Son of m' standing on the right hand "
8: 9 was a certain m', called Simon, 435
10 This m' is the great power of God.
27 behold, a m' of Ethiopia, an eunuch 435
31 I, except some m' should guide me?*
34 this? of himself, or of some other m'?*
9: 7 hearing a voice, but seeing no m'. 3367
8 eyes were opened, he saw no m': *3762
12 in a vision a m' named Ananias 435
13 heard by many of this m', how much "
33 he found a certain m' named Æneas, 444
10: 1 m' in Cæsarea called Cornelius, 435
2 A devout m', and one that feared God
22 just m', and one that feareth God, 435
26 Stand up; I myself also am a m'. 444
28 a m' that is a Jew to keep company, 435
28 should not call any m' common or 444
30 a m' stood before me in bright 435
47 Can any m' forbid water, that 5100
11:24 he was a good m', and full of the 435
29 every m' according to his ability, 1538
12:22 the voice of a god, and not of a m'. 444
13: 7 Sergius Paulus, a prudent m'; who 435
21 of Cis, a m' of the tribe of Benjamin, "
22 of Jesse, a m' after mine own heart, "
38 through this m' is preached unto you
41 though a m' declare it unto you. *5100
14: 8 there sat a certain m' at Lystra, 435
16: 9 There stood a m' of Macedonia, and "
17:31 by that m' whom he hath ordained; "
18:10 and no m' shall set on thee to hurt 3762
24 an eloquent m', and mighty in the 435
25 This m' was instructed in the way of
19:16 the m' in whom the evil spirit was 444
24 For a certain m' named Demetrius,
35 what m' is there that knoweth not 444
38 have a matter against any m', the law
20: 9 sat in a window a certain young m' 3494
12 And they brought the young m' alive.*
21: 9 And the same m' had four daughters,
11 bind the m' that owneth this girdle, 435
28 This is the m', that teacheth all men 444
39 I am a m' which am a Jew of Tarsus,* "
22: 3 I am verily a m' which am a Jew, * 435
12 a devout m' according to the law, "
25 to scourge a m' that is a Roman, 444
26 thou doest: for this m' is a Roman. "
23: 9 saying, We find no evil in this m': "
17 Bring this young m' unto the chief 3494
18 to bring this young m' unto thee, "
22 captain...let the young m' depart, "
22 tell no m' that thou hast shewed 3367
27 This m' was taken of the Jews, and 435
30 that the Jews laid wait for the m', "
24: 5 have found this m' a pestilent fellow, "
12 the temple disputing with any m',
25: 5 down with me, and accuse this m', 435
11 no m' may deliver me unto them. 3762
14 a certain m' left in bonds by Felix: 435
16 the Romans to deliver any m' to die, 444
17 commanded the m' to be brought 435
22 I would also hear the m' myself. 444
24 ye see this m', about whom all the
26:31 This m' doeth nothing worthy of 444
32 This m' might have been set at "
28: 4 No doubt this m' is a murderer, "
7 possessions of the chief m' of the island,
31 all confidence, no m' forbidding him.*
Ro 1:23 image made like to corruptible m', 444
2: 1 inexcusable, O m', whosoever thou "
3 And thinkest thou this, O m', that "
6 to every m' according to his deeds:
9 every soul of m' that doeth evil, 444
10 to every m' that worketh good, 3956
21 that preachest a m' should not steal,
22 that sayest a m' should not commit
3: 4 let God be true, but every m' a liar; 444
5 taketh vengeance? (I speak as a m')* "
28 a m' is justified by faith without the "
4: 6 describeth the blessedness of the m', "
8 Blessed is the m' to whom the Lord 435
5: 7 for a righteous m' will one die:
7 good m' some would even dare to die.
12 as by one m' sin entered into the 444
15 gift by grace, which is by one m',
6: 6 our old m' is crucified with him, 444
7: 1 law hath dominion over a m' as long "
3 liveth, she be married to another m', 435
3 though she be married to another m'. "
22 the law of God after the inward m': 444
24 O wretched m' that I am! who shall "
8: 9 if any m' have not the Spirit of Christ,
24 for what a m' seeth, why doth he *5100
9:20 O m', who art thou that repliest 444
10: 5 the m' which doeth those things "
10 For with the heart m' believeth unto
12: 3 to every m' that is among you, not to
3 dealt to every m' the measure of
17 Recompense to no m' evil for evil. 3367
13: 8 Owe no m' any thing, but to love "
14: 5 One m' esteemeth one day above
5 Let every m' be fully persuaded in
7 himself, and no m' dieth to himself. *3762
13 that no m' put a stumblingblock
20 for that m' who eateth with offence 444
1Co 2: 9 have entered into the heart of m', "
11 For what m' knoweth the things * "
11 knoweth the things of a m', save "
11 the spirit of m' which is in him? "

1Co 2:11 the things of God knoweth no m', *3762
14 natural m' receiveth not the things 444
15 yet he himself is judged of no m'. 3762
3: 5 as the Lord gave to every m'? *
8 and every m' shall receive his own*
10 every m' take heed how he buildeth
11 can no m' lay than that is laid, 3762
12 if any m' build upon this foundation
17 If any m' defile the temple of God,
18 Let no m' deceive himself. 3367
18 any m' among you seemeth to be wise
21 Therefore let no m' glory in men. *3367
4: 1 Let a m' so account of us, as of the 444
2 that a m' be found faithful. 5100
5 shall every m' have praise of God.
5:11 if any m' that is called a brother be
6: 5 that there is not a wise m' among you?
18 Every sin that a m' doeth is without 444
7: 1 good for a m' not to touch a woman. "
2 let every m' have his own wife, and
7 But every m' hath his proper gift
16 how knowest thou, O m', whether * 435
17 God hath distributed to every m',
18 any m' called being circumcised?
20 every m' abide in the same calling
24 let every m', wherein he is called,
26 say, that it is good for a m' so to be. 444
36 But if any m' think that he behaveth
8: 2 if any m' think that he knoweth any
3 But if any m' love God, the same is
7 not in every m' that knowledge: *3956
10 For if any m' see thee which hast
9: 8 Say I these things as a m'? or saith* 444
15 any m' should make my glorying
25 And every m' that striveth for the
10:13 you but such as is common to m': 442
24 Let no m' seek his own, 3367
24 but every m' another's wealth. *
28 But if any m' say unto you, This
11: 3 that the head of every m' is Christ; 435
3 the head of the woman is the m'; "
4 Every m' praying or prophesying, "
7 a m' indeed ought not to cover his "
7 the woman is the glory of the m'. "
8 For the m' is not of the woman; "
8 woman; but the woman of the m'. "
9 was the m' created for the woman; "
9 woman; but the woman for the m'. "
11 neither is the m' without the woman, "
11 neither the woman without the m', "
12 For as the woman is of the m', even "
12 so is the m' also by the woman; "
14 if a m' have long hair, it is a shame "
16 if any m' seem to be contentious, we
28 But let a m' examine himself, and 444
34 if any m' hunger, let him eat at home;
12: 3 no m' speaking by the Spirit of God 3762
3 that no m' can say that Jesus is the "
7 given to every m' to profit withal. *1538
11 dividing to every m' severally as he* "
13:11 when I became a m', I put away 435
14: 2 for no m' understandeth him; 3762
27 any m' speak in an unknown tongue,
37 any m' think himself to be a prophet,
38 But if any m' be ignorant, let him be
15:21 For since by m' came death, 444
21 by m' came also the resurrection of "
23 But every m' in his own order: *
35 some m' will say, How are the dead*
45 first m' Adam was made a living 444
47 The first m' is of the earth, earthy: "
47 second m' is the Lord from heaven. "
16:11 Let no m' therefore despise him: 5100
22 If any m' love not the Lord Jesus
2Co 2: 6 Sufficient to such a m' is this
4:16 but though our outward m' perish, 444
16 the inward m' is renewed day by day.
5:16 know we no m' after the flesh: 3762
17 Therefore if any m' be in Christ, he is
7: 2 us; we have wronged no m', 3762
2 we have corrupted no m', "
2 we have defrauded no m'. "
8:12 is...according to that a m' hath, 5100
20 that no m' should blame us in this "
9: 7 Every m' according as he purposeth
10: 7 If any m' trust to himself that he is
11: 9 I was chargeable to no m': for 3762
10 no m' shall stop me of this boasting
16 again, let no m' think me a fool; if 5100
20 if a m' bring you into bondage, "
20 if a m' devour you, if a m' take of * "
20 a m' exalt himself, if a m' smite * "
12: 2 I knew a m' in Christ above 444
3 I knew such a m', (whether in the "
4 it is not lawful for a m' to utter. "
6 any m' should think of me above
Ga 1: 1 men, neither by m', but by Jesus 444
9 any m' preach any other gospel unto
11 was preached of me is not after m'. 444
12 I neither received it of m', neither "
2:16 knowing that a m' is not justified by "
3:11 no m' is justified by the law in the 3762
12 m' that doeth them shall live in * 444
15 no m' disannulleth, or addeth *3762
5: 3 I testify again to every m' that is 444
6: 1 if a m' be overtaken in a fault, ye
3 For if a m' think himself to be 5100
4 let every m' prove his own work,
5 every m' shall bear his own burden.
7 whatsoever a m' soweth, that shall 444
17 henceforth let no m' trouble me: 3367
Eph 2: 9 works, lest any m' should boast.
15 in himself of twain one new m', 444
3:16 might by his Spirit in the inner m'; "
4:13 the Son of God, unto a perfect m', 435
22 former conversation the old m', 444

Eph 4:24 that ye put on the new m', which 444
25 every m' truth with his neighbour:*
5: 6 Let no m' deceive you with vain 3367
29 For no m' ever yet hated his own 3762
31 cause shall a m' leave his father 444
6: 8 whatsoever good thing any m' doeth,
Ph'p 2: 4 Look not every m' on his own *
4 but every m' also on the things of*
8 being found in fashion as a man, 444
20 I have no m' likeminded, who will 3762
3: 4 If any other m' thinketh that he hath
Col 1:28 we preach, warning every m', and 444
28 teaching every m' in all wisdom; "
28 we may present every m' perfect in "
2: 4 lest any m' should beguile you *
8 Beware lest any m' spoil you *
16 Let no m' therefore judge you in 5100
18 Let no m' beguile you of your 3367
3: 9 put off the old m' with his deeds; 444
10 And have put on the new m', which is
13 any m' have a quarrel against any:
4: 6 how ye ought to answer every m'.*1520
1Th 3: 3 no m' should be moved by these 3367
4: 6 That no m' go beyond and defraud his
8 despiseth not m', but God, who 444
5:15 none render evil for evil unto any m';*
2Th 2: 3 Let no m' deceive you by any 5100
3 that m' of sin be revealed, the son 444
3:14 if any m' obey not our word by this
14 note that m', and have no company
1Ti 1: 8 is good, if a m' use it lawfully; 5100
9 the law is not made for a righteous m',
2: 5 God and men, the m' Christ Jesus; 444
12 nor to usurp authority over the m', 435
3: 1 a m' desire the office of a bishop, 5100
5 if a m' know not how to rule his
4:12 no m' despise thy youth; but be 3367
5: 9 having been the wife of one m', 435
16 If any m' or woman that believeth*
22 Lay hands suddenly on no m', 3367
6: 3 If any m' teach otherwise, and
11 O m' of God, flee these things; and 444
16 the light which no m' can approach*
16 whom no m' hath seen, nor can see:444
2Ti 2: 4 No m' that warreth entangleth 3762
5 if a m' also strive for masteries, 5100
21 If a m' therefore purge himself "
3:17 That the m' of God may be perfect,444
4:16 first answer no m' stood with me,*3762
Tit 2:15 authority. Let no m' despise thee.3367
3: 2 To speak evil of no m', to be no "
4 God our Saviour toward m' appeared,
10 A m' that is an heretick, after the 444
Heb 2: 6 What is m', that thou art mindful "
6 son of m', that thou visitest him? "
9 God should taste death for every m'.
3: 3 this m' was counted worthy of more*
4 every house is builded by some m';*
4:11 lest any m' fall after the same example
5: 4 And no m' taketh this honour unto5100
7: 4 consider how great this m' was,
13 no m' gave attendance at the altar.3762
24 But this m', because he continueth*
8: 2 which the Lord pitched, and not m'.444
3 this m' have somewhat also to offer.*
11 shall not teach every m' his neighbour,
11 and every m' his brother, saying,
10:12 this m', after he had offered one *
38 but if any m' draw back, my soul *
12:14 which no m' shall see the Lord: 3762
15 any m' fail of the grace of God;
13: 6 not fear what m' shall do unto me. 444
Jas 1: 7 that m' think that he shall receive "
8 double minded m' is unstable in 435
11 the rich m' fade away in his ways.
12 Blessed is the m' that endureth 435
13 no m' say when he is tempted, 3367
13 evil, neither tempteth he any m': 3762
14 every m' is tempted, when he is
19 let every m' be swift to hear, slow 444
20 For the wrath of m' worketh not the435
23 unto a m' beholding his natural face"
24 forgetteth what manner of m' he was.
25 this m' shall be blessed in his deed.
26 any m' among you seem to be religious,
2: 2 assembly a m' with a gold ring, 435
2 come in also a poor m' in vile raiment;
14 though a m' say he hath faith, and5100
18 a m' may say, Thou hast faith, and "
20 O vain m', that faith without works 444
24 how that by works a m' is justified,
3: 2 any m' offend not in word, the same*
2 the same is a perfect m', and able 435
8 the tongue can no m' tame; it is an444
13 Who is a wise m' and endued with*
5:16 fervent prayer of a righteous m'
17 m' subject to like passions as we 444
1Pe 1:24 glory of m' as the flower of grass.*
2:13 ordinance of m' for the Lord's sake:442
19 if a m' for conscience toward God 5100
3: 4 it be the hidden m' of the heart, 444
15 answer to every m' that asketh
4:10 As every m' hath received the gift,*
11 If any m' speak, let him speak as the
11 if any m' minister, let him do it as of
16 if any m' suffer as a Christian, let him
2Pe 1:21 not in old time by the will of m': 444
2: 8 that righteous m' dwelling among
19 of whom a m' is overcome, of the 5100
1Jo 2: 1 if any m' sin, we have an advocate
15 If any m' love the world, the love
27 ye need not that any m' teach you:
3: 3 And every m' that hath this hope
7 children, let no m' deceive you: 3367
4:12 No m' hath seen God at any time. 3762
20 If any m' say, I love God, and

1Jo 5:16 If any m' see his brother sin a sin
Re 1:13 one like unto the Son of m', clothed 444
2:17 which no m' knoweth saving he *3762
3: 7 that openeth, and no m' shutteth;* "
7 and shutteth, and no m' openeth;* "
8 open door, and no m' can shut it: * "
11 hast, that no m' take thy crown. *3367
20 if any m' hear my voice, and open
4: 7 the third beast had a face as a m', 444
5: 3 And no m' in heaven, nor in earth,*3762
4 no m' was found worthy to open * "
6:15 every bondman, and every free m',
7: 9 multitude,...no m' could number, 3762
9: 5 a scorpion, when he striketh a m'. 444
11: 5 And if any m' will hurt them, fire
5 and if any m' will hurt them, he must
12: 5 And she brought forth a m' child, 730
13 which brought forth the m' child. "
13: 9 If any m' have an ear, let him hear.
17 And that no m' might buy or sell, 5100
18 for it is the number of a m'; and 444
14: 3 no m' could learn that song but 3762
9 If any m' worship the beast and his
14 cloud one sat like unto the Son of m',444
15: 8 no m' was able to enter into the *3762
16: 3 it became as the blood of a dead m':
18:11 no m' buyeth their merchandise 3762
19:12 a name written, that no m' knew, * "
20:13 every m' according to their works.
21:17 according to the measure of a m', 444
22:12 every m' according as his work
18 every m' that heareth the words 3956
18 If any m' shall add unto these
19 if any m' shall take away from the

Manaen (*man'-a-en*)
Ac 13: 1 and Lucius of Cyrene, and M', 3127

Manahath (*man'-a-hath*)
Ge 36:23 Alvan, and M', and Ebal, Shepho, 4506
1Ch 1:40 Alian, and M', and Ebal, Shephi, "
8: 6 and they removed them to M':

Manahethites (*man'-a-heth-ites*)
1Ch 2:52 sons; Haroeh, and half of the M'.*2679
54 and half of the M', the Zorites. 2680

Manasseh (*ma-nas'-seh*) See also MANASSEH'S; MANASSES; MANASSITES.
Ge 41:51 the name of the firstborn M': 4519
46:20 Egypt were born M' and Ephraim, "
48: 1 him his two sons, M' and Ephraim."
5 now thy two sons, Ephraim and M'," "
13 M' in his left hand toward Israel's "
14 wittingly; for M' was the firstborn." "
20 make thee as Ephraim and as M': "
20 and he set Ephraim before M'. "
50:23 also of Machir the son of M' were "
Nu 1:10 the son of Ammihud: of M'; "
34 Of the children of M', by their "
35 even of the tribe of M', were thirty "
2:20 by him shall be the tribe of M': "
20 the captain of the children of M' "
7:54 prince of the children of M': "
10:23 of the tribe of the children of M' "
13:11 Joseph, namely, of the tribe of M', "
26:28 after their families were M' and "
29 Of the sons of M': of Machir, the "
34 These are the families of M', and "
27: 1 son of M', of the families of M' "
32:33 unto half the tribe of M' the son "
39 children of Machir the son of M' "
40 Gilead unto Machir the son of M'; "
41 Jair the son of M' went and took "
34:14 the tribe of M' have received their "
23 for the tribe of the children of M', "
36: 1 the son of M', of the families of the "
12 into the families of the sons of M' "
De 3:13 gave I unto the half tribe of M'; "
14 Jair the son of M' took all the "
29: 8 Gadites, and to the half tribe of M'.4520
33:17 and they are the thousands of M'. 4519
34: 2 and the land of Ephraim, and M', "
Jos 1:12 and to the half the tribe of M', spake "
4:12 half the tribe of M', passed over "
12: 6 Gadites, and the half tribe of M'. "
13: 7 tribes, and the half tribe of M', "
29 unto the half tribe of M': and this "
29 the half tribe of the children of M' "
31 children of Machir the son of M', "
14: 4 of Joseph were two tribes, M' and "
16: 4 M' and Ephraim, took their "
9 inheritance of the children of M', "
17: 1 was also a lot for the tribe of M'; "
1 for Machir the firstborn of M', the "
2 for the rest of the children of M' "
2 these were the male children of M' "
3 the son of M', had no sons, but "
5 And there fell ten portions to M', "
6 Because the daughters of M' had an "
7 the coast of M' was from Asher "
8 Now M' had the land of Tappuah: "
8 but Tappuah on the border of M' "
9 are among the cities of M': the "
9 coast of M' also was on the north "
11 M' had in Issachar and in Asher "
12 children of M' could not drive out "
17 and to M', saying, Thou art a great "
18: 7 half the tribe of M', have received "
20: 8 in Bashan out of the tribe of M'. "
21: 5 Dan, and out of the half tribe of M', "
6 of the half tribe of M' in Bashan, "
25 And out of the half tribe of M', "
27 out of the other half tribe of M' "
22: 1 Gadites, and the half tribe of M', "
7 to the one half of the tribe of M' "
9, 10, 11 Gad and the half tribe of M' "
13, 15 Gad, and to the half tribe of M'. "

Jos 22:21 of Gad and the half tribe of M' 4519
30 Gad and the children of M' spake, "
31 of Gad, and to the children of M', "
J'g 1:27 did M' drive out the inhabitants "
6:15 my family is poor in M', and I am "
35 messengers throughout all M'; "
7:23 out of Asher, and out of all M', "
11:29 he passed over Gilead, and M', and "
18:30 the son of Gershom, the son of M', "
1Ki 4:13 the towns of Jair the son of M', "
2Ki 20:21 and M' his son reigned in his stead." "
21: 1 M' was twelve years old when he "
9 M' seduced them to do more evil "
11 M' king of Judah had done these "
16 M' shed innocent blood very much, "
17 the rest of the acts of M', and all "
18 M' slept with his fathers, and was "
20 of the Lord, as his father M' did. "
23:12 the altars which M' had made in "
26 provocations that M' had provoked" "
24: 3 for the sins of M', according to all "
1Ch 3:13 son, Hezekiah his son, M' his son, "
5:18 Gadites, and half the tribe of M', "
23 the children of the half tribe of M' "
26 Gadites, and the half tribe of M', "
6:61 out of the half tribe of M', by lot, "
62 out of the tribe of M' in Bashan, "
70 And out of the half tribe of M'; "
71 the family of the half tribe of M', "
7:14 The sons of M'; Ashriel, whom she" "
17 Gilead, son of Machir, the son of M'." "
29 the borders of the children of M', "
9: 3 the children of Ephraim, and M'; "
12:19 And there fell some of M' to David, "
20 there fell to him of M', Adnah, and "
20 of the thousands that were of M'. "
31 of the half tribe of M' eighteen "
37 and of the half tribe of M', with all "
26:32 and the half tribe of M', for every*4520
27:20 the half tribe of M', Joel the son of4519
21 Of the half tribe of M' in Gilead, "
2Ch 15: 9 with them out of Ephraim and M', "
30: 1 letters also to Ephraim and M', "
10 the country of Ephraim and M' "
11 and M' and of Zebulun humbled "
18 even many of Ephraim and M', "
31: 1 in Ephraim also and M', until they "
32:33 M' his son reigned in his stead. "
33: 1 M' was twelve years old when he "
9 So M' made Judah and the "
10 the Lord spake to M', and to his "
11 which took M' among the thorns, "
13 M' knew that the Lord he was God." "
18 the rest of the acts of M', and his "
20 So M' slept with his fathers, and "
22 of the Lord, as did M' his father: "
22 images which M' his father had "
23 as M' his father had humbled "
34: 6 And so did he in the cities of M', "
9 had gathered of the hand of M' and" "
Ezr 10:30 Bezaleel, and Binnui, and M'. "
33 Eliphelet, Jeremai, M', and Shimei." "
Ps 60: 7 Gilead is mine, and M' is mine; "
80: 2 and M' stir up thy strength, and "
108: 8 Gilead is mine; M' is mine; "
Isa 9:21 M', Ephraim; and Ephraim, M': "
Jer 15: 4 of M' the son of Hezekiah king of "
Eze 48: 4 unto the west side, a portion for M'." "
5 by the border of M', from the east "

Manasseh's (*ma-nas'-sez*)
Ge 48:14 and his left hand upon M' head. 4519
17 Ephraim's head unto M' head. "
Jos 17: 6 the rest of M' sons had the lands* "
10 northward it was M', and the sea "

Manasses (*ma-nas'-seez*) See also MANASSEH.
M't 1:10 And Ezekias begat M'; and *3128
10 M' begat Amon; and Amon begat* "
Re 7: 6 the tribe of M' were sealed twelve* "

Manassites (*ma-nas'-sites*)
De 4:43 and Golan in Bashan, of the M'. 4520
J'g 12: 4 Ephraimites, and among the M'. *4519
2Ki 10:33 and the Reubenites, and the M', 4520

mandrakes
Ge 30:14 found m' in the field, and brought 1736
14 Give me, I pray thee, of thy son's m'. "
15 thou take away my son's m' also? "
15 with thee to night for thy son's m'. "
16 have hired thee with my son's m'. "
Ca 7:13 The m' give a smell, and our gates "

maneh (*ma'-neh*)
Eze 45:12 fifteen shekels, shall be your m'. 4488

manger
Lu 2: 7 clothes, and laid him in a m'; 5336
12 in swaddling clothes, lying in a m'. "
16 and the babe lying in the m'. "

manifest See also MANIFESTED.
Ec 3:18 that God might m' them, and that*1305
Lu 8:17 secret, that shall not be made m'; 5318
Joh 1:31 he should be made m' to Israel, 5319
3:21 that his deeds may be made m', "
9: 3 works of God should be made m'. "
14:21 him, and will m' myself to him. 1718
22 that thou wilt m' thyself unto us, "
Ac 4:16 is m' to all them that dwell in 5319
Ro 1:19 be known of God is m' in them; "
10:20 I was made m' unto them that 1717
16:26 But now is made m', and by the *5319
1Co 3:13 man's work shall be made m': for 5318
4: 5 make m' the counsels of the hearts:5319
11:19 may be made m' among you. 5318
14:25 the secrets of his heart made m'; "
15:27 him, it is m' that he is excepted, *1212
2Co 2:14 and maketh m' the savour of his 5319
4:10 of Jesus...be made m' in our body.* "

2Co 4:11 of Jesus might be made m' in our *5319
5:11 but we are made m' unto God; and "
11 I trust also are made m' in your "
11: 6 we have been thoroughly made m' "
Ga 5:19 Now the works of the flesh are m', 5318
Eph 5:13 reproved are made m' by the light:5319
13 whatsoever doth make m' is light. "
Ph'p 1:13 my bonds in Christ are m' in all 5318
Col 1:26 but now is made m' to his saints: *5319
4: 4 I may make it m', as I ought to "
2Th 1: 5 a m' token of the righteous judgment
1Ti 3:16 God was m' in the flesh, justified *5319
5:25 the good works of some are m' *4271
2Ti 1:10 is now made m' by the appearing *5319
3: 9 folly shall be m' unto all men, as *1552
Heb 4:13 creature that is not m' in his sight: 852
9: 8 holiest of all was not yet made m', 5319
1Pe 1:20 was m' in these last times for you,* "
1Jo 2:19 they might be made m' that they "
3:10 In this the children of God are m', 5318
Re 15: 4 for thy judgments are made m'. 5319

manifestation
Ro 8:19 for the m' of the sons of God. * 602
1Co 12: 7 But the m' of the Spirit is given to 5321
2Co 4: 2 by m' of the truth commending "

manifested
M'k 4:22 nothing hid, which shall not be m';5319
Joh 2:11 of Galilee, and m' forth his glory; "
17: 6 I have m' thy name unto the men "
Ro 3:21 of God without the law is m', being "
Tit 1: 3 But hath in due times m' his word "
1Jo 1: 2 the life was m', and we have seen "
2 the Father, and was m' unto us;) "
3: 5 that he was m' to take away our "
8 purpose the Son of God was m', "
4: 9 In this was m' the love of God "

manifestly
2Co 3: 3 m' declared to be the epistle of *5319

manifold
Ne 9:19 thou in thy m' mercies forsookest 7227
27 according to thy m' mercies thou "
Ps 104:24 O Lord, how m' are thy works! in 7231
Am 5:12 I know your m' transgressions 7227
Lu 18:30 Who shall not receive m' more in 4179
Eph 3:10 the church the m' wisdom of God, 4182
1Pe 1: 6 through m' temptations: 4164
4:10 stewards of the m' grace of God.

mankind See also WOMANKIND.
Le 18:22 Thou shalt not lie with m', as with2145
20:13 If a man also lie with m', as he
Job 12:10 thing, and the breath of all m',1320,376
1Co 6: 9 nor abusers of themselves with m',*733
1Ti 1:10 them that defile themselves with m',*"
Jas 3: 7 and hath been tamed of m': 5449,442

manna (man'-nah)
Ex 16:15 it, said one to another, It is m': *4478
31 Israel called the name thereof M': "
33 and put an omer full of m' therein, "
35 children of Israel did eat m' forty "
35 they did eat m', until they came "
Nu 11: 6 is nothing at all, besides this m', "
7 And the m' was as coriander seed, "
9 in the night, the m' fell upon it. "
De 8: 3 and fed thee with m', which thou "
16 fed thee in the wilderness with m', "
Jos 5:12 And the m' ceased on the morrow "
12 the children of Israel m' any more;"
Ne 9:20 withheldest not thy m' from their "
Ps 78:24 rained down m' upon them to eat, "
Joh 6:31 Our fathers did eat m' in the 3131
49 Your fathers did eat m' in the "
58 not as your fathers did eat m', and* "
Heb 9: 4 was the golden pot that had m', "
Re 2:17 will I give to eat of the hidden m', "

manner See also MANNERS.
Ge 18:11 with Sarah after the m' of women. 734
25 far from thee to do after this m', 1697
19:31 us after the m' of all the earth: 1870
25:23 two m' of people shall be separated*
32:19 this m' shall ye speak unto Esau, 1697
39:19 After this m' did thy servant to me;"
40:13 the former m' when thou wast his 4941
17 of all m' of bakemeats for Pharaoh;
45:23 to his father he sent after this m';
Ex 1:14 and in all m' of service in the field:
7:11 like m' with their enchantments. 3651
12:16 no m' of work shall be done in them,
21: 9 with her after the m' of daughters.4941
22: 9 For all m' of trespass, whether it 1697
9 or for any m' of lost thing, which
23:11 In like m' thou shalt deal with thy 3651
31: 3 and in all m' of workmanship,
5 to work in all m' of workmanship.
35:29 willing to bring for all m' of work,
31 in all m' of workmanship; and
33 to make any m' of cunning work.
35 all m' of work, of the engraver, 3605
36: 1 all m' of work for the service of the*
Le 5:10 offering, according to the m': *4941
7:23 Ye shall eat no m' of fat, of ox, or of*
26 Moreover ye shall eat no m' of blood,
27 soul it be that eateth any m' of blood,*
9:16 and offered it according to the m'.*4941
11:27 among all m' of beasts that go on all*
44 with any m' of creeping thing
14:54 law for all m' of plague of leprosy,
17:10 you, that eateth any m' of blood;
14 shall eat the blood of no m' of flesh:
19:23 have planted all m' of trees for food,
20:25 any m' of living thing that creepeth*
23:31 Ye shall do no m' of work: it shall be
24:22 Ye shall have one m' of law, as 4941
Nu 5:13 her, neither she be taken with the m';*
9:14 and according to the m' thereof, *4941
15:13 shall do these things after this m', 3541
16 One law and one m' shall be for *4941
24 drink offering, according to the m',*"
28:18 ye shall do no m' of servile work *
24 After this m' ye shall offer daily,
29: 6 offerings, according unto their m',*4941
18, 21, 24, 27, 30, 33, 37 according to their
number, after the m': *4941
31:30 and of the flocks, of all m' of beasts,*
De 4:15 ye saw no m' of similitude on the day
15: 2 And this is the m' of the release: 1697
22: 3 like m' shalt thou do with his ass;*3651
27:21 be he that lieth with any m' of beast.
Jos 6:15 after the same m' seven times: 4941
J'g 8:18 m' of men were they whom ye slew at
11:17 in like m' they sent unto the king of
18: 7 after the m' of the Zidonians, 4941
Ru 4: 7 this was the m' in former time in *
1Sa 8: 9, 11 m' of the king that shall reign 4941
10:25 the people the m' of the kingdom, "
17:27 people answered him after this m',1697
30 and spake after the same m': and "
30 him again after the former m'. "
18:24 saying, On this m' spake David. "
19:24 before Samuel in like m', and *1571
21: 5 the bread is in a m' common, yea,*1870
27:11 so will be his m' all the while he 3541
2Sa 6: 5 m' of instruments made of fir wood,
7:19 And is this the m' of man, O Lord 8452
14: 3 and speak on this m' unto him. 1697
15: 6 And on this m' did Absalom to all "
17: 6 hath spoken after this m': shall "
1Ki 7:28 the work of the bases was on this m':
37 After this m' he made the ten bases:
18:28 cut themselves after their m' with 4941
22:20 And one said on this m', and 3541
20 and another said on that m'.
2Ki 1: 7 What m' of man was he which 4941
11:14 stood by a pillar, as the m' was, "
17:26 not the m' of the God of the land: "
26 not the m' of the God of the land. "
27 them the m' of the God of the land. "
33 after the m' of the nations whom "
40 but they did after their former m'. "
1Ch 6:48 appointed unto all m' of service of*
12:37 with all m' of instruments of war for
18:10 all m' of vessels of gold and silver and
22:15 and timber, and all m' of cunning men*
15 cunning men for every m' of work.
23:29 and for all m' of measure and size;
24:19 of the Lord, according to their m',*4941
28:14 for all instruments of all m' of service;*
21 with thee for all m' of workmanship
21 skilful man, for any m' of service:
29: 2 and all m' of precious stones, and
5 m' of work to be made by the hands
2Ch 2:14 also to grave any m' of graving, and
4:20 should burn after the m' before *4941
13: 9 priests after the m' of the nations of
18:19 one spake saying after this m', 3541
19 and another saying after that m'.
30:16 stood in their place after their m',*4941
32:27 and for all m' of pleasant jewels;
28 stalls for all m' of beasts, and cotes
34:13 wrought the work in any m' of service:
Ezr 5: 4 Then said we unto them after this m',
Ne 6: 4 answered them after the same m'.1697
5 unto me in like m' the fifth time "
8:18 assembly, according unto the m',*4941
10:37 the fruit of all m' of trees, of wine and
13:15 grapes, and figs, and all m' of burdens,
16 brought fish, and all m' of ware, and
Es 1:13 king's m' toward all that knew law1697
2:12 according to the m' of the women,*1881
Ps 107:18 Their soul abhorreth all m' of meat;
144:13 be full, affording all m' of store: 2177
Ca 7:13 our gates are all m' of pleasant fruits,
Isa 5:17 the lambs feed after their m', *1699
10:24 against thee, after the m' of Egypt.1870
26 he lift it up after the m' of Egypt. "
51: 6 dwell therein shall die in like m': 3654
Jer 13: 9 After this m' will I mar the pride 3541
22:21 hath been thy m' from thy youth, 1870
30:18 shall remain after the m' thereof. 4941
Eze 20:30 after the m' of your fathers? 1870
23:15 after the m' of the Babylonians of*1823
45 them after the m' of adulteresses,*4941
45 the m' of women that shed blood;* "
Da 6:23 no m' of hurt was found upon him,
Am 4:10 pestilence after the m' of Egypt: 1870
8:14 The m' of Beer-sheba liveth; even* "
M't 4:23 and healing all m' of sickness and
23 all m' of disease among the people.
5:11 shall say all m' of evil against you
6: 9 After this m' therefore pray ye: 3779
8:27 What m' of man is this, that even 4217
10: 1 and to heal all m' of sickness and
1 of sickness and all m' of disease.
12:31 All m' of sin and blasphemy shall *
M'r 4:41 What m' of man is this, that * 686
13: 1 Master, see what m' of stones and 4217
29 So ye in like m', when ye shall see*3779
Lu 1:29 what m' of salutation this should 4217
66 What m' of child shall this be! * 686
6:23 in the like m' did their fathers
7:39 who and what m' of woman this is4217
8:25 What m' of man is this! for he * 686
9:55 not what m' of spirit ye are of. *3634
11:42 mint and rue and all m' of herbs, *
20:31 and in like m' the seven also: and 5615
24:17 What m' of communications are *
Joh 2: 6 the m' of the purifying of the Jews,
7:36 What m' of saying is this that he said,*
19:40 as the m' of the Jews is to bury. *1485
Ac 1:11 like m' as ye have seen him go 5158
10:12 were all m' of fourfooted beasts of 1485
15: 1 circumcised after the m' of Moses,*1485
23 letters by them after this m': *3592
17: 2 And Paul, as his m' was, went *1486
20:18 after what m' I have been with you4458
22: 3 to the perfect m' of the law of the 195
23:25 And he wrote a letter after this m':*5179
25:16 It is not the m' of the Romans to *1485
20 doubted of such m' of questions, 4012
26: 4 My m' of life from my youth, which 981
Ro 6:19 I speak after the m' of men because442
7: 8 in me all m' of concupiscence.
1Co 7: 7 one after this m', and another 3779
11:25 the same m' also he took the cup, 5615
15:32 If after the m' of men I have fought
2Co 7: 9 ye were made sorry after a godly m',*
Ga 2:14 livest after the m' of Gentiles, *1483
3:15 I speak after the m' of men;
1Th 1: 5 ye know what m' of men we were 3634
9 what m' of entering in we had 3697
1Ti 2: 9 In like m' also, that women adorn
2Ti 3:10 known my doctrine, m' of life, * 72
Heb10:25 together, as the m' of some is; *1485
Jas 1:24 forgetteth what m' of man he was. 3697
1Pe 1:11 what m' of time the Spirit of 4169
15 ye holy in all m' of conversation;
3: 5 For after this m' in the old time 3779
2Pe 3:11 what m' of persons ought ye to be 4217
1Jo 3: 1 what m' of love the Father hath "
Jude 7 cities about them in like m', 5158
Re 11: 5 them, he must in this m' be killed.3779
18:12 wood, and all m' vessels of ivory, *
12 and all m' vessels of most precious*
21:19 with all m' of precious stones.
22: 2 of life, which bare twelve m' of fruits,

manners
Le 20:23 not walk in the m' of the nation, *2708
2Ki 17:34 day they do after the former m': ‡4941
Eze 11:12 done after the m' of the heathen *
Ac 13:18 he their m' in the wilderness. ‡5159
1Co 15:33 communications corrupt good m'.‡2239
Heb 1: 1 and in divers m' spake in time past4187

Manoah (ma-no'-ah)
J'g 13: 2 the Danites, whose name was M';4495
8 Then M' intreated the Lord, and "
9 God hearkened to the voice of M'; "
9 M' her husband was not with her. "
11 M' arose, and went after his wife, "
12 M' said, Now let thy words come to "
13 the angel of the Lord said unto M', "
15 M' said unto the angel of the Lord, "
16 the angel of the Lord said unto M', "
16 M' knew not that he was an angel "
17 M' said unto the angel of the Lord, "
19 M' took a kid with a meat offering, "
19 and M' and his wife looked on. "
20 M' and his wife looked on it, and "
21 the Lord did no more appear to M' "
21 Then M' knew that he was an angel"
22 And M' said unto his wife, We shall"
16:31 the buryingplace of M' his father. "

man's See also WOMAN'S.
Ge 8:21 the ground any more for m' sake; 120
21 the imagination of m' heart is evil "
9: 5 at the hand of every m' brother will "
6 Whoso sheddeth m' blood, by man "
20: 3 hast taken; for she is a m' wife. 1167
42:11 We are all one m' sons; we are true376
25 to restore every m' money into his "
35 every m' bundle of money was in his "
43:21 every m' money was in the mouth of "
44: 1 every m' money in his sack's mouth."
26 we may not see the m' face, except "
Ex 4:11 him, Who hath made m' mouth? 120
12:44 But every m' servant that is bought376
21:35 if one m' ox hurt another's, that he "
22: 5 and shall feed in another m' field; 312
7 and it be stolen out of the m' house;376
30:32 Upon m' flesh shall it not be * 120
Le 7: 8 that offereth any m' burnt offering, 376
15:16 if any m' seed of copulation go out "
20:10 adultery with another m' wife, "
Nu 5:10 every m' hallowed things shall be "
12 If any m' wife go aside, and commit "
17: 2 write...every m' name upon his rod. "
5 the m' rod, whom I shall choose, * "
33:54 every m' inheritance shall be in the*
De 20:19 (for the tree of the field is m' life) * 120
24: 2 she may go and be another m' wife.376
6 for he taketh a m' life to pledge.
J'g 7:16 he put a trumpet in every m' hand,*
22 every m' sword against his fellow, 376
19:26 down at the door of the m' house "
Ru 2:19 The m' name with whom I wrought "
1Sa 12: 4 thou taken ought of any m' hand. "
14:20 every m' sword...against his fellow "
17:32 Let no m' heart fail because of him;120
2Sa 12: 4 took the poor m' lamb, and dressed376
17:18 came to a m' house in Bahurim, * "
25 which Amasa was a m' son, whose* "
1Ki 18:44 cloud out of the sea, like a m' hand. "
2Ki 12: 4 money that cometh into any m' heart"
23: 8 which were on a m' left hand at the "
25: 9 great m' house burnt he with fire.*
Es 1: 8 do according to every m' pleasure. 376
Job10: 5 of man? are thy years as m' days, 1397
32:21 I pray you, accept any m' person. 376
Ps 104:15 which strengtheneth m' heart. 582
Pr 10:15 The rich m' wealth is his strong city:
12:14 recompence of a m' hands shall be 120
13: 8 ransom of a m' life are his riches: 376
16: 7 When a m' ways please the Lord, he "
9 A m' heart deviseth his way: but 120
18: 4 words of a m' mouth are as deep 376
11 The rich m' wealth is his strong city,
16 A m' gift maketh room for him, and120

Pr 18:20 A m' belly shall be satisfied with 376
19:21 are many devices in a m' heart; "
20:24 M' goings are of the Lord; how 1397
27: 9 so doth the sweetness of a m' friend
29:23 A m' pride shall bring him low: but120
26 m' judgment cometh from the Lord.376
Ec 2:14 The wise m' eyes are in his head; but
8: 1 a m' wisdom maketh his face to 120
5 wise m' heart discerneth both time
9:16 the poor m' wisdom is despised, and
10: 2 A wise m' heart is at his right hand;
12 The words of a wise m' mouth are
Isa 8: 1 roll, and write in it with a m' pen * 582
13: 7 faint, and every m' heart shall melt:*"
Jer 3: 1 from him, and become another m', 376
23:36 every m' word shall be his burden; "
Eze 4:15 given thee cow's dung for m' dung, 120
10: 8 form of a m' hand under their wings."
38:21 every m' sword shall be against his 376
39:15 when any seeth a m' bone, then 120
40: 5 in the m' hand a measuring reed of
Da 4:16 Let his heart be changed from m', 606
5: 5 hour came forth fingers of a m' hand,"
7: 4 man, and a m' heart was given to it. "
8:16 heard a m' voice between the banks120
Am 6:10 And a m' uncle shall take him up, and
Jon 1:14 let us not perish for this m' life, 376
Mic 7: 6 a m' enemies are the men of his own"
M't 10:36 a m' foes shall be they of his own 444
41 shall receive a righteous m' reward.
12:29 can one enter into a strong m' house,*
M'r 3:27 man can enter into a strong m' house,
12:19 If a m' brother die, and leave his 5100
Lu 6:22 as evil, for the Son of m' sake. 444
12:15 for a m' life consisteth not in the 5100
16:12 in that which is another m', who * 245
21 which fell from the rich m' table:
20:28 If any m' brother die, having a 5100
Joh 18:17 thou also one of this m' disciples? 444
Ac 5:28 to bring this m' blood upon us.
7:58 their clothes at a young m' feet, 3494
11:12 and we entered into the m' house: 435
13:23 Of this m' seed hath God according
17:29 stone, graven by art and m' device.*444
18: 7 and entered into a certain m' house,*
20:33 I have coveted no m' silver, or 3762
27:22 be no loss of any m' life among you,*
Ro 5:17 For if by one m' offence death reigned*
19 by one m' disobedience many were 444
14: 4 that judgest another m' servant? * 245
15:20 build upon another m' foundation:
1Co 2: 4 with enticing words of m' wisdom,*442
13 words which m' wisdom teacheth,
3:13 Every m' work...be made manifest:
13 fire shall try every m' work of what
14 If any m' work abide which he hath
15 If any m' work shall be burned, he
4: 3 judged of you, or of m' judgment: 442
10:29 judged of another m' conscience? *
2Co 4: 2 every m' conscience in the sight of 444
10:16 boast in another m' line of things * 245
Ga 2: 6 me: God accepteth no m' person:) 444
3:15 Though it be but a m' covenant, yet "
2Th 3: 8 we eat any m' bread for nought;
Jas 1:26 his own heart, this m' religion is vain.
1Pe 1:17 according to every m' work,
2Pe 2:16 dumb ass speaking with m' voice 444

manservant See also MANSERVANT'S; MANSERVANTS.
Ex 20:10 thy son, nor thy daughter, thy m',5650
17 thy neighbour's wife, nor his m', "
21:32 If the ox shall push a m' or a) "
De 5:14 son, nor thy daughter, nor thy m', "
14 that thy m' and thy maidservant "
21 house, his field, or his m', or his "
12:18 son, and thy daughter, and thy m', "
16:11, 14 and thy daughter, and thy m', "
Job 31:13 If I did despise the cause of my m', "
Jer 34: 9 That every man should let his m', "
10 that every one should let his m', "

manservant's
Ex 21:27 And if he smite out his m' tooth, 5650

manservants
Ne 7:67 Besides their m' and their 5650

mansions
Joh 14: 2 my Father's house are many m': 3438

manslayer See also MANSLAYERS.
Nu 35: 6 which ye shall appoint for the m', 7523
12 that the m' die not, until he stand "

manslayers
1Ti 1: 9 and murderers of mothers, for m', 409

mantle See also MANTLES.
J'g 4:18 tent, she covered him with a m'. *8063
1Sa 15:27 hold upon the skirt of his m', and*4598
28:14 up; and he is covered with a m'. "
1Ki 19:13 that he wrapped his face in his m', 155
19 by him, and cast his m' upon him. "
2Ki 2: 8 Elijah took his m', and wrapped it "
13 He took up also the m' of Elijah that"
14 took the m' of Elijah that fell from "
Ezr 9: 3 I rent my garment and my m', ‡4598
5 rent my garment and my m', I ‡ "
Job 1:20 Then Job arose, and rent his m', ‡ "
2:12 they rent every one his m', and ‡ "
Ps 109:29 their own confusion, as with a m'.‡ "

mantles
Isa 3:22 suits of apparel, and the m', and 4595

many See also MANIFOLD.
Ge 17: 4 shalt be a father of m' nations. *1995
5 father of m' nations have I made * "
21:34 in the Philistines' land m' days. 7227
37: 3 and he made him a coat of m' colours.
Ge 37:23 his coat of m' colours that was on him;
32 And they sent the coat of m' colours,
34 and mourned for his son m' days. 7227
Ex 5: 5 the people of the land now are m', "
19:21 to gaze, and m' of them perish. "
23: 2 decline after m' to wrest judgment:* "
35:22 as m' as were willing hearted, and
Le 15:25 issue of her blood m' days out of 7227
25:51 If there be yet m' years behind, "
Nu 9:19 long upon the tabernacle m' days, "
10:36 unto the m' thousands of Israel. 7233
13:18 they be strong or weak, few or m';7227
22: 3 the people, because they were m': "
24: 7 his seed shall be in m' waters, and "
26:54 To m' thou shalt give the more * "
56 be divided between m' and few. * "
35: 8 that have m' ye shall give
8 that have... ye shall give m': 7235
De 1:11 thousand times as m' more as ye are,
46 So ye abode in Kadesh m' days. 7227
2: 1 we compassed mount Seir m' days. "
10, 21 and m', and tall, as the Anakims;"
3: 5 beside unwalled towns a great m'. "
7: 1 cast out m' nations before thee, the"
15: 6 thou shalt lend unto m' nations, "
6 thou shalt reign over m' nations, "
25: 3 him above these with m' stripes, "
28:12 thou shalt lend unto m' nations, "
31:17 m' evils and troubles shall befall "
21 when m' evils and troubles are "
32: 7 consider the years of m' generations:
Jos 11: 4 with horses and chariots very m'. 7227
22: 3 left your brethren these m' days "
J'g 3: 1 even as m' of Israel as had not known
7: 2 are with thee are too m' for me to 7227
4 The people are yet too m'; bring "
8:30 begotten: for he had m' wives. "
9:40 m' were overthrown and wounded.*"
16:24 our country, which slew m' of us. 7235
1Sa 2: 5 hath m' children is waxed feeble. 7227
6:19 Lord had smitten m' of the people*
14: 6 the Lord to save by m' or by few. 7227
25:10 be m' servants now a days that 7231
2Sa 1: 4 m' of the people also are fallen 7235
2:23 as m' as came to the place where
12: 2 exceeding m' flocks and herds: 7235
22:17 me; he drew me out of m' waters; 7227
23:20 who had done m' acts, he slew two*"
24: 3 the people, how m' soever they be,
1Ki 2:38 dwelt in Jerusalem m' days. 7227
4:20 Judah and Israel were m', as the "
7:47 because they were exceeding m': 7230
11: 1 Solomon loved m' strange women,7227
17:15 he, and her house, did eat m' days.
18: 1 it came to pass after m' days, that 7227
25 for ye are m'; and call on the name "
22:16 How m' times shall I adjure thee that
2Ki 9:22 Jezebel and...witchcrafts are so m'?7227
1Ch 4:27 his brethren had not m' children, "
5:22 there fell down m' slain, because "
7: 4 for they had m' wives and sons. 7235
22 Ephraim...mourned m' days, and 7227
8:40 had m' sons, and sons' sons, an 7235
11:22 Kabzeel, who had done m' acts; *7227
21: 3 an hundred times so m' more as they
23:11 and Beriah had not m' sons; 7235
17 the sons of Rehabiah were very m'. "
28: 5 the Lord hath given me m' sons,) 7227
2Ch 11:23 And he desired m' wives. 1995
14:11 whether with m', or with them *7227
16: 8 very m' chariots and horsemen? 7235
18:15 How m' times shall I adjure thee that
26:10 the desert, and digged m' wells: 7227
29:31 and as m' as were of a free heart
30:17 m' in the congregation that were 7227
18 m' of Ephraim, and Manasseh, and "
32:23 m' brought gifts unto the Lord to "
Ezr 3:12 But m' of the priests and Levites "
12 voice; and m' shouted aloud for joy: "
5:11 was builded these m' years ago, 7690
10:13 But the people are m', and it is a 7227
13 we are m' that have transgressed *7235
Ne 5: 2 sons, and our daughters, are m': 7227
6:17 the nobles of Judah sent m' letters 7235
18 there were m' in Judah sworn unto 7227
7: 2 man, and feared God above m'. "
9:28 m' times didst thou deliver them "
30 m' years didst thou forbear them, "
13:26 among m' nations was there no "
Es 1: 4 of his excellent majesty m' days, "
2: 8 when m' maidens were gathered "
4: 3 and m' lay in sackcloth and ashes. "
8:17 m' of the people of the land became"
Job 4: 3 Behold, thou hast instructed m', "
11:19 yea, m' shall make suit unto thee. "
13:23 How m' are mine iniquities and sins?
16: 2 I have heard m' such things: 7227
23:14 and m' such things are with him.
41: 3 Will he make m' supplications 7235
Ps 3: 1 m' are they that rise up against 7227
2 M' there be which say of my soul, "
4: 6 m' that say, Who will show us any "
18:16 me, he drew me out of m' waters. "
22:12 M' bulls have compassed me: "
25:19 mine enemies; for they are m'; 7231
29: 3 the Lord is upon m' waters. 7227
31:13 I have heard the slander of m': "
32:10 M' sorrows shall be to the wicked: "
34:12 loveth m' days, that he may see good?
19 M' are the afflictions of the 7227
37:16 better than the riches of m' wicked."
40: 3 m' shall see it, and fear, and shall "
5 M', O Lord my God, are thy "
55:18 me: for there were m' with me. "
56: 2 they be m' that fight against me, "
61: 6 life: and his years as m' generations.
Ps 71: 7 I am as a wonder unto m'; but 7227
78:38 yea, m' a time turned he his anger7235
93: 4 than the noise of m' waters, yea, 7227
106:43 M' times did he deliver them; but "
110: 6 wound the heads over m' countries."
119:84 How m' are the days of thy servant?
157 M' are my persecutors and mine 7227
129: 1, 2 M' a time have they afflicted me "
Pr 4:10 the years of thy life shall be m'. 7235
6:35 though thou givest m' gifts.
7:26 she hath cast down m' wounded: 7227
26 m' strong men have been slain by *3605
10:21 The lips of the righteous feed m': 7227
14:20 but the rich hath m' friends.
19: 4 Wealth maketh m' friends; but the "
6 M' will intreat the favour of the "
21 are m' devices in a man's heart; "
28: 2 of a land m' are the princes thereof:"
27 his eyes shall have m' a curse. "
29:26 M' seek the ruler's favour; but "
31:29 M' daughters have done virtuously."
Ec 5: 7 multitude of dreams and m' words7230
6: 3 and live m' years, so that the 7227
3 so that the days of his years be m', "
11 be m' things that increase vanity, 7235
7:29 have sought out m' inventions. 7227
11: 1 thou shalt find it after m' days. 7230
8 But if a man live m' years, and 7235
8 of darkness; for they shall be m'. "
12: 9 out, and set in order m' proverbs. "
12 of making m' books there is no end;"
Ca 8: 7 M' waters cannot quench love, 7227
Isa 1:15 when ye make m' prayers, I will 7235
2: 3 And m' people shall go and say, 7227
4 and shall rebuke m' people: and "
5: 9 truth m' houses shall be desolate, "
8: 7 waters of the river, strong and m', "
15 And m' among them shall stumble, "
17:12 Woe to the multitude of m' people, "
13 rush like the rushing of m' waters: "
22: 9 the city of David, that they are m':7231
23:16 sweet melody, sing m' songs, 7235
24:22 after m' days...they be visited. 7230
31: 1 in chariots, because they are m'; 7227
32:10 M' days and years shall ye be troubled,*
42:20 Seeing m' things, but thou 7227
52:14 As m' were astonied at thee; his "
15 So shall he sprinkle m' nations; "
53:11 my righteous servant justify m'; "
12 and he bare the sin of m', and made"
58:12 up the foundations of m' generations;
60:15 excellency, a joy of m' generations.
66:16 the slain of the Lord shall be m'. 7231
Jer 3: 1 played the harlot with m' lovers; 7227
5: 6 their transgressions are m', and 7231
11:15 hath wrought lewdness with m', 7227
12:10 M' pastors have destroyed my "
13: 6 And it came to pass after m' days, "
14: 7 for our backslidings are m'; we 7231
16:16 I will send for m' fishers, saith 7227
16 after will I send for m' hunters, "
20:10 For I heard the defaming of m', "
22: 8 m' nations shall pass by this city, "
25:14 m' nations and great kings shall "
27: 7 m' nations and great kings shall "
28: 8 both against m' countries, and "
32:14 that they may continue m' days. "
35: 7 that ye may live m' days in the land"
36:32 besides unto them m' like words. "
37:16 had remained there m' days; "
42: 2 (for we are left but a few of m', as 7235
46:11 vain shalt thou use m' medicines; "
16 He made m' to fall, yea, one fell "
50:41 m' kings shall be raised up from 7227
51:13 thou that dwellest upon m' waters, "
La 1:22 for my sighs are m', and my heart "
Eze 3: 6 Not to m' people of a strange speech"
12:27 he seeth is for m' days to come, "
16:41 upon thee in the sight of m' women: "
17: 7 with great wings and m' feathers: "
9 m' people to pluck it up by the roots*"
17 building forts, to cut off m' persons: "
19:10 of branches by reason of m' waters."
22:25 they have made her m' widows 7235
26: 3 m' nations to come up against 7227
27: 3 merchant of the people for m' isles, "
15 m' isles were the merchandise of "
33 of the seas, thou filledst m' people; "
32: 3 thee with a company of m' people; "
9 also vex the hearts of m' people, "
10 make m' people amazed at thee, "
33:24 but we are m'; the land is given us "
37: 2 were very m' in the open valley; "
38: 6 bands: and m' people with thee. "
8 After m' days thou shalt be visited:"
8 and is gathered out of m' people, "
9 thy bands, and m' people with thee."
15 thou, and m' people with thee, all "
17 prophesied in those days m' years "
22 the m' people that are with him, 7227
23 be known in the eyes of m' nations,"
39:27 in them in the sight of m' nations; "
43: 2 voice was like a noise of m' waters: "
47: 7 very m' trees on the one side and "
10 fish of the great sea, exceeding m'. "
Da 2:48 and gave him m' great gifts, and 7690
8:25 and by peace shall destroy m': 7227
26 vision; for it shall be for m' days. "
9:27 shall confirm the covenant with m' "
10:14 days: for yet the vision is for m' days.
11:12 he shall cast down m' ten thousands:*
14 there shall m' stand up against 7227
18 unto the isles, and shall take m': "
26 and m' shall fall down slain. "
33 among the people shall instruct m':"
33 by captivity, and by spoil, m' days.

Da 11: 34 but m' shall cleave to them with 7227
39 shall cause them to rule over m', "
40 with horsemen, and with m' ships; "
41 m' countries shall be overthrown: "
44 and utterly to make away m'. "
12: 2 m' of them that sleep in the dust "
3 they that turn m' to righteousness "
4 of the end: m' shall run to and fro, "
10 M' shall be purified, and made "
Ho 3: 3 Thou shalt abide for me m' days; "
4 Israel shall abide m' days without "
8: 11 Ephraim hath made m' altars to *7235
Joe 2: 2 it, even to the years of m' generations.
Am 8: 3 be m' dead bodies in every place; 7227
Mic 4: 2 m' nations shall come, and say, "
3 he shall judge among m' people, "
11 Now also m' nations are gathered "
13 thou shalt beat in pieces m' people: "
5: 7 shall be in the midst of m' people "
8 Gentiles in the midst of m' people "
Na 1: 12 they be quiet, and likewise m', "
3: 15 thyself m' as the cankerworm, 3513
15 make thyself m' as the locusts. "
Hab 2: 8 thou hast spoiled m' nations, all 7227
10 thy house by cutting off m' people, "
Zec 2: 11 m' nations shall be joined to the "
7: 3 as I have done these so m' years? "
8: 20 and the inhabitants of m' cities: 7227
22 m' people and strong nations shall "
Mal 2: 6 did turn m' away from iniquity. "
8 caused m' to stumble at the law; "
M't 3: 7 when he saw m' of the Pharisees 4183
7: 13 m' there be which go in thereat: "
22 M' will say to me in that day, Lord, "
22 thy name done m' wonderful works? "
8: 11 m' shall come from the east and "
16 m' that were possessed with devils: "
30 them an herd of m' swine feeding. "
9: 10 m' publicans and sinners came and "
10: 31 of more value than m' sparrows. "
13: 3 he spake m' things...in parables, "
17 m' prophets and righteous men "
58 he did not m' mighty works there "
14: 36 m' as touched were made perfectly 3745
15: 30 dumb, maimed, and m' others, 4183
34 them, How m' loaves have ye? 4214
16: 9, 10 and how m' baskets ye took up? "
21 suffer m' things of the elders and 4183
19: 30 m' that are first shall be last; and "
20: 16 for m' be called, but few chosen. * "
28 and to give his life a ransom for m'. "
22: 9 as m' as ye shall find, bid to the 3745
10 together all as m' as they found, "
14 m' are called, but few are chosen. 4183
24: 5 m' shall come in my name, saying, "
5 I am Christ; and shall deceive m'. "
10 then shall m' be offended, and shall "
11 And m' false prophets shall rise, "
11 shall rise, and shall deceive m'. "
12 the love of m' shall wax cold. "
25: 21, 23 make thee ruler over m' things: "
26: 28 shed for m' for the remission of sins. "
60 though m' false witnesses came, "
27: 13 not how m' things they witness 4214
19 I have suffered m' things this day 4183
52 m' bodies of the saints which slept "
53 holy city, and appeared unto m'. "
55 m' women were there beholding "
M'r 1: 34 healed m' that were sick of divers "
34 and cast out m' devils; and suffered "
2: 2 m' were gathered together, "
15 m' publicans and sinners sat also "
15 for there were m', and they followed "
3: 10 For he had healed m'; insomuch "
10 to touch him, as m' as had plagues. 3745
4: 2 he taught...m' things by parables, 4183
33 with m' such parables spake he the "
5: 9 My name is Legion: for we are m'. "
26 suffered m' things of m' physicians, "
6: 2 m' hearing him were astonished, "
13 And they cast out m' devils, and "
13 anointed with oil m' that were sick, "
20 he did m' things, and heard him * "
31 there were m' coming and going, "
33 m' knew him, and ran afoot thither "
34 he began to teach them m' things. "
38 them, How m' loaves have ye? 4214
56 as m' as touched him were made 3745
7: 4 m' other things there be, which 4183
8 and m' other such like things ye do.* "
13 and m' such like things do ye. "
8: 5 them, How m' loaves have ye? 4214
19, 20 how m' baskets full of fragments "
31 Son of man must suffer m' things, 4183
9: 12 that he must suffer m' things, and "
26 insomuch that m' said, He is dead.* "
10: 31 But m' that are first shall be last; "
45 and to give his life a ransom for m'. "
48 And m' charged him that he should "
11: 8 m' spread their garments in the "
12: 5 and him they killed, and m' others; "
41 and m' that were rich cast in much. "
13: 6 m' shall come in my name, saying, "
6 I am Christ; and shall deceive m'. "
14: 24 testament, which is shed for m'. "
56 m' bare false witness against him, "
15: 3 priests accused him of m' things: "
4 m' things they witness against 4214
41 m' other women which came up 4183
Lu 1: 1 as m' have taken in hand to set "
14 and m' shall rejoice at his birth. "
16 m' of the children of Israel shall he "
2: 34 and rising again of m' in Israel; "
35 the thoughts of m' hearts may be "
3: 18 m' other things in his exhortation "
4: 25 m' widows were in Israel in the "
Lu 4: 27 And m' lepers were in Israel in the 4183
41 devils also came out of m', crying "
7: 11 m' of his disciples went with him, *2425
21 cured m' of their infirmities and 4183
21 m' that were blind he gave sight. "
47 thee, Her sins, which are m', are "
8: 3 m' others, which ministered unto "
30 m' devils were entered into him. "
32 there an herd of m' swine feeding 2425
9: 22 Son of man must suffer m' things, 4183
10: 24 m' prophets and kings have desired "
41 and troubled about m' things: "
11: 8 and give him as m' as he needeth. 3745
53 provoke him to speak of m' things: 4119
12: 7 of more value than m' sparrows. 4183
19 much goods laid up for m' years; "
47 shall be beaten with m' stripes. "
13: 24 m', I say unto you, will seek to enter "
14: 16 made a great supper, and bade m': "
15: 13 not m' days after the younger son "
17 m' hired servants of my father's 4214
29 Lo, these m' years do I serve thee, 5118
17: 25 first must he suffer m' things, and 4183
21: 8 m' shall come in my name, saying, "
22: 65 And m' other things blasphemously "
23: 8 he had heard m' things of him; * "
9 questioned with him in m' words; 2425
Joh 1: 12 But as m' as received him, to them 3745
2: 12 they continued there not m' days. 4183
23 m' believed in his name, when they "
4: 39 m' of the Samaritans of that city "
41 m' more believed because of his "
6: 9 but what are they among so m'? 5118
60 M' therefore of his disciples, when 4183
66 time m' of his disciples went back, "
7: 31 m' of the people believed on him, "
40 M' of the people therefore, when * "
8: 26 m' things to say and to judge of "
30 these words, m' believed on him. "
10: 20 m' of them said, He hath a devil, "
32 M' good works have I shewed you "
41 m' resorted unto him, and said, "
42 And m' believed on him there. "
11: 19 m' of the Jews came to Martha and "
45 m' of the Jews which came to Mary, "
47 for this man doeth m' miracles. "
55 m' went out of the country up to "
12: 11 of him m' of the Jews went away, "
37 done so m' miracles before them, 5118
42 rulers also m' believed on him; 4183
14: 2 Father's house are m' mansions: "
16: 12 I have yet m' things to say unto you, "
17: 2 give eternal life to as m' as thou hast *
19: 20 This title then read m' of the Jews: 4183
20: 30 m' other signs truly did Jesus in "
21: 11 for all there were so m', yet was 5118
25 And there are also m' other things 4183
Ac 1: 3 his passion by m' infallible proofs, "
5 the Holy Ghost not m' days hence. "
2: 39 as m' as the Lord our God shall call. 3745
40 with m' other words did he testify 4119
43 m' wonders and signs were done 4183
3: 24 as m' as have spoken, have likewise 3745
4: 4 m' of them which heard the word 4183
6 as m' as were of the kindred of the 3745
34 for as m' as were possessors of lands "
5: 11 upon as m' as heard these things.* "
12 m' signs and wonders wrought 4183
36 m' as obeyed him, were scattered, 3745
37 as m' as obeyed him, were dispersed. "
8: 7 came out of m' that were possessed 4183
7 and m' taken with palsies, and that "
25 in m' villages of the Samaritans. "
9: 13 I have heard by m' of this man, "
23 after that m' days were fulfilled, 2425
42 and m' believed in the Lord. 4183
43 tarried m' days in Joppa with one 2425
10: 27 found m' that were come together. 4183
45 as m' as came with Peter, 3745
12: 12 m' were gathered together praying. 2425
13: 31 And he was seen m' days of them 4119
43 m' of the Jews and religious 4183
48 as m' as were ordained to eternal 3745
14: 21 to that city, and had taught m', 2425
15: 32 the brethren with m' words, and 4183
35 of the Lord, with m' others also. "
16: 18 And this did she m' days. But Paul, "
23 they had laid m' stripes upon them, "
17: 12 Therefore m' of them believed; "
18: 8 and m' of the Corinthians hearing "
19: 18 And m' that believed came, and "
19 M' of them...which used curious *2425
20: 8 were m' lights in the upper chamber, "
19 with m' tears, and temptations, *4183
21: 10 as we tarried there m' days, there ‡4119
20 how m' thousands of Jews there 4214
24: 10 thou hast been of m' years a judge 4183
17 after m' years I came to bring ‡4119
25: 7 laid m' and grievous complaints 4183
14 when they had been there m' days, 4119
26: 9 do m' things contrary to the name 4183
10 and m' of the saints did I shut up "
27: 7 when we had sailed slowly m' days, 2425
20 nor stars in m' days appeared, 4119
28: 10 honoured us with m' honours; 4183
23 came m' to him into his lodging; *4119
Ro 2: 12 as m' as have sinned without law 3745
12 as m' as have sinned in the law "
4: 17 made thee a father of m' nations,) 4183
18 become the father of m' nations, "
5: 15 the offence of one m' be dead, "
15 Christ, hath abounded unto m'. "
16 is of m' offences unto justification. "
19 disobedience m' were made sinners, "
19 of one shall m' be made righteous. "
6: 3 as m' of us as were baptized into *3745
Ro 8: 14 as m' as are led by the Spirit of God, 3745
29 the firstborn among m' brethren. 4183
12: 4 we have m' members in one body, "
5 So we, being m', are one body in "
15: 23 these m' years to come unto you; "
16: 2 for she hath been a succourer of m', "
1Co 1: 26 that not m' wise men after the flesh, "
26 not m' mighty, not m' noble, are "
4: 15 Christ, yet have ye not m' fathers: "
8: 5 (as there be gods m', and lords m',) "
10: 5 with m' of them God was not well *4119
17 we being m' are one bread, and 4183
33 own profit, but the profit of m', "
11: 30 For this cause m' are weak and "
30 sickly among you, and m' sleep. *2425
12: 12 body is one, and hath m' members, 4183
12 members of that one body, being m', "
14 the body is not one member, but m'. "
20 But now are they m' members, yet "
14: 10 so m' kinds of voices in the world, 5118
16: 9 me, and there are m' adversaries. 4183
2Co 1: 11 upon us by the means of m' persons "
11 thanks may be given by m' on our "
2: 4 I wrote unto you with m' tears; "
6 which was inflicted of m'. 4119
17 we are not as m', which corrupt 4183
4: 15 through the thanksgiving of m' 4119
6: 10 as poor, yet making m' rich; as 4183
8: 22 proved diligent in m' things, but "
9: 2 your zeal hath provoked very m'. 4119
12 by m' thanksgivings unto God; 4183
11: 18 Seeing that m' glory after the flesh, "
12: 21 shall bewail m' which have sinned "
Ga 1: 14 Jews' religion above m' my equals "
3: 4 ye suffered so m' things in vain? 5118
10 as m' as are of the works of the law 3745
16 saith not, And to seeds, as of m'; 4183
27 as m' of you as have been baptized 3745
4: 27 desolate hath m' more children *4183
6: 12 As m' as desire to make a fair shew 3745
16 as m' as walk according to this rule, "
Ph'p 1: 14 m' of the brethren in the Lord, *4119
3: 15 us therefore, as m' as be perfect, 3745
18 (For m' walk, of whom I have told 4183
Col 2: 1 as m' as have not seen my face in 3745
1Ti 6: 1 Let as m' servants as are under the "
9 into m' foolish and hurtful lusts, 4183
10 pierced...through with m' sorrows. "
12 good profession before m' witnesses. "
2Ti 1: 18 in how m' things he ministered 3745
2: 2 heard of me among m' witnesses, 4183
Tit 1: 10 there are m' unruly and vain talkers "
He 2: 10 in bringing m' sons unto glory, to "
5: 11 Of whom we have m' things to say, "
7: 23 And they truly were m' priests, 4119
9: 28 once offered to bear the sins of m'; 4183
11: 12 so m' as the stars of the sky in
12: 15 you, and thereby m' be defiled; 4183
Jas 3: 1 My brethren, be not m' masters, "
2 For in m' things we offend all. If "
2Pe 2: 2 And m' shall follow their pernicious "
1Jo 2: 18 even now are there m' antichrists; "
4: 1 m' false prophets are gone out into "
2Jo 7 For m' deceivers are entered into "
12 Having m' things to write unto you, "
3Jo 13 I had m' things to write, but I will "
Re 1: 15 his voice as the sound of m' waters. "
2: 24 as m' as have not this doctrine, and 3745
3: 19 As m' as I love, I rebuke and chasten: "
5: 11 and I heard the voice of m' angels 4183
8: 11 and m' men died of the waters, "
9: 9 of m' horses running to battle. "
10: 11 prophesy again before m' peoples, "
13: 15 as m' as would not worship the 3745
14: 2 heaven, as the voice of m' waters, 4183
17: 1 whore that sitteth upon m' waters: "
18: 17 sailors, and as m' as trade by sea, 3745
19: 6 and as the voice of m' waters, and 4183
12 and on his head were m' crowns; "

Maoch (*ma'-ok*)
1Sa 27: 2 the son of M', king of Gath. 4582

Maon (*ma'-on*) See also MAONITES.
Jos 15: 55 M', Carmel, and Ziph, and Juttah, 4584
1Sa 23: 24 men were in the wilderness of M', "
25 and abode in the wilderness of M'. "
25 after David in the wilderness of M'. "
25: 2 And there was a man in M', whose "
1Ch 2: 45 And the son of Shammai was M': "
45 and M' was the father of Beth-zur. "

Maonites (*ma'-on-ites*) See also MEHUNIM.
J'g 10: 12 and the M', did oppress you; 4584

mar See also MARRED.
Le 19: 27 thou m' the corners of thy beard. 7843
Ru 4: 6 lest I m' mine own inheritance: "
1Sa 6: 5 of your mice that m' the land; "
2Ki 3: 19 and m' every good piece of land 3510
Job 30: 13 They m' my path, they set forward 5420
Jer 13: 9 will I m' the pride of Judah, and 7843

Mara (*ma'-rah*)
Ru 1: 20 Call me not Naomi, call me M': 4755

Marah (*ma'-rah*)
Ex 15: 23 when they came to M', they could 4785
23 could not drink of the waters of M', "
23 the name of it was called M'. "
Nu 33: 8 of Etham, and pitched in M'. "
9 they removed from M', and came "

Maralah (*mar'-a-lah*)
Jos 19: 11 went up toward the sea, and M', 4831

Maran-atha (*mar-an-a'-thah*)
1Co 16: 22 Christ, let him be Anathema M'. 3134

marble
1Ch 29: 2 and m' stones in abundance. 7898
Es 1: 6 to silver rings and pillars of m': 8336

Es 1: 6 and blue, and white, and black, *m*. 8336
Ca 5: 15 His legs are as pillars of *m*, set "
Re 18: 12 and of brass, and iron, and *m*, 8139

Marcaboth See BETH-MARCABOTH.

march See also MARCHED; MARCHEDST.
Ps 68: 7 didst *m* through the wilderness; 6805
Jer 46: 22 for they shall *m* with an army, 3212
Joe 2: 7 they shall *m* every one on his ways, "
Hab 1: 6 shall *m* through the breadth of 1980
3: 12 Thou didst *m* through the land in 6805

marched See also MARCHEDST.
Ex 14: 10 the Egyptians *m* after them; 5265

marchedst
J'g 5: 4 thou *m* out of the field of Edom, 6805

Marcus (*mar'-cus*) See also MARK.
Col 4: 10 and *M*, sister's son to Barnabas, *3138
Ph'm 24 *M*, Aristarchus, Demas, Lucas, * "
1Pe 5: 13 you; and so doth *M* my son. * "

Mareshah (*mar'-e-shah*)
Jos 15: 44 And Keilah, and Achzib, and *M*; 4762
1Ch 2: 42 sons of *M* the father of Hebron. "
4: 21 and Laadah the father of *M*, and "
2Ch 11: 8 And Gath, and *M*, and Ziph, "
14: 9 chariots; and came unto *M*. "
10 in the valley of Zephathah at *M*. "
20: 37 Eliezer the son of Dodavah of *M* "
Mic 1: 15 heir unto thee, O inhabitant of *M*: "

mariners
Eze 27: 8 of Zidon and Arvad were thy *m*: *7751
9 the ships of the sea with their *m* 4419
27 thy *m*, and thy pilots, thy calkers, "
29 the *m*, and all the pilots of the sea, "
Jon 1: 5 Then the *m* were afraid, and cried "

marishes
Eze 47: 11 *m* thereof shall not be healed; 1360

mark See also LANDMARK; MARKED; MARKEST; MARKETH; MARKS.
Ge 4: 15 the Lord set a *m* upon Cain, lest * 226
Ru 3: 4 *m* the place where he shall lie, 3045
1Sa 20: 20 thereof, as though I shot at a *m*. 4307
2Sa 13: 28 *M* ye now when Amnon's heart 7200
1Ki 20: 7 *M*, I pray you, and see how this 3045
22 and *m*, and see what thou doest: "
Job 7: 20 thou set me as a *m* against thee, 4645
16: 12 pieces, and set me up for his *m*. 4307
18: 2 *m*, and afterwards we will speak.* 995
21: 5 *M* me, and be astonished, and lay 6437
33: 31 *M* well, O Job, hearken unto me: 7181
39: 1 thou *m* when the hinds do calve? 8104
Ps 37: 37 *M* the perfect man, and behold "
48: 13 *M* ye well her bulwarks, consider 7896
56: 6 they *m* my steps, when they wait 8104
130: 3 thou, Lord, shouldest *m* iniquities, "
La 3: 12 and set me as a *m* for the arrow. 4307
Eze 9: 4 *m* upon the foreheads of the men 8420
6 any man upon whom is the *m*; "
44: 5 Son of man, *m* well, and behold 7760
5 *m* well the entering in of the "
Ro 16: 17 *m* them which cause divisions and 4648
Ph'p 3: 14 press toward the *m* for the prize 4649
17 *m* them which walk so as ye have 4648
Re 13: 16 to receive a *m* in their right hand, 5480
17 save he that had the *m*, or the "
14: 9 and receive his *m* in his forehead, "
11 receiveth the *m* of his name. "
15: 2 over his image, and over his *m*, * "
16: 2 upon the men which had the *m* of "
19: 20 had received the *m* of the beast, "
20: 4 had received his *m* upon their "

Mark See also MARCUS.
Ac 12: 12 of John, whose surname was *M*; 3138
25 John, whose surname was *M*. "
15: 37 John, whose surname was *M*. "
39 and so Barnabas took *M*, and "
2Ti 4: 11 Take *M*, and bring him with thee: "

marked
1Sa 1: 12 the Lord, and Eli *m* her mouth. 8104
Job 22: 15 Hast thou *m* the old way which * "
24: 16 *m* for themselves in the daytime: *2856
Jer 2: 22 yet thine iniquity is *m* before me, 3799
23: 18 who hath *m* his word, and heard 7181
Lu 14: 7 when he *m* how they chose out 1907

markest
Job 10: 14 If I sin, then thou *m* me, and 8104

market See also MARKETPLACE; MARKETS.
Eze 27: 13 and vessels of brass in thy *m*. *4627
17 they traded in thy *m* wheat of * "
19 and calamus, were in thy *m*. * "
25 Tarshish did sing of thee in thy *m*: * "
M'r 7: 4 And when they come from the *m*, * 58
Joh 5: 2 at Jerusalem by the sheep *m* a pool, *
Ac 17: 17 in the *m* daily with them that met * 58

marketh
Job 33: 11 in the stocks, he *m* all my paths. 8104
Isa 44: 13 *m* it out with a line; he fitteth it 8388
13 *m* it out with the compass, and "

marketplace
M't 20: 3 saw others standing idle in the *m*, 58
Lu 7: 32 like unto children sitting in the *m*, "
Ac 16: 19 them into the *m* unto the rulers, "

marketplaces
M'r 12: 38 and love salutations in the *m*, 58

markets
M't 11: 16 like unto children sitting in the *m*, * 58
23: 7 greetings in the *m*, and to be called* "
Lu 11: 43 synagogues, and greetings in the *m*. * "
20: 46 robes, and love greetings in the *m*, * "

marks See also WAYMARKS.
Le 19: 28 dead, nor print any *m* upon you: 7085
Ga 6: 17 my body the *m* of the Lord Jesus. 4742

Maroth (*ma'-roth*)
Mic 1: 12 inhabitant of *M* waited carefully 4796

marred
Isa 52: 14 his visage was so *m* more than 4893
Jer 13: 7 the girdle was *m*, it was profitable 7843
18: 4 vessel that he made of clay was *m* "
Na 2: 2 out, and *m* their vine branches. "
M'r 2: 22 spilled, and the bottles will be *m*: * 622

marriage See also MARRIAGES.
Ex 21: 10 her raiment, and her duty of *m*, 5772
Ps 78: 63 maidens were not given to *m*. 1984
M't 22: 2 king which made a *m* for his son, 1062
4 are ready: come unto the *m*. "
9 many as ye shall find, bid to the *m*. "
30 neither marry, nor are given in *m*, 1548
24: 38 marrying and giving in *m*, until 1547
25: 10 ready went in with him to the *m*: 1062
M'r 12: 25 neither marry, nor are given in *m*; 1061
Lu 17: 27 they were given in *m*, until the 1548
20: 34 world marry, and are given in *m*: "
35 neither marry, nor are given in *m*: "
Jo 2: 1 there was a *m* in Cana of Galilee; 1062
2 called, and his disciples, to the *m*. "
1Co 7: 38 that giveth her in *m* doeth well; 1547
38 giveth her not in *m* doeth better. "
Heb 13: 4 *M* is honourable in all, and the 1062
Re 19: 7 for the *m* of the Lamb is come, "
9 unto the *m* supper of the Lamb. "

marriages
Ge 34: 9 make ye *m* with us, and give your 2859
De 7: 3 Neither shalt thou make *m* with "
Jos 23: 12 shall make *m* with them, and go "

married See also UNMARRIED.
Ge 19: 14 in law, which *m* his daughters, 3947
Ex 21: 3 if he were *m*, then his wife 1166, 802
Le 22: 12 If the priest's daughter also be *m* "
Nu 12: 1 of the...woman whom he had *m*: 3947
1 he had *m* an Ethiopian woman. "
36: 3 And if they be *m* to any of the sons 802
11 *m* unto their father's brother's sons: "
12 were *m* into the families of the sons "
De 22: 22 with a woman *m* to an husband. 1166
24: 1 hath taken a wife, and *m* her, "
1Ch 2: 21 he *m* when he was threescore *3947
2Ch 13: 21 mighty, and *m* fourteen wives, *5375
Ne 13: 23 that had *m* wives of Ashdod, 3427
Pr 30: 23 odious woman when she is *m*; 1166
Isa 54: 1 than the children of the *m* wife, "
62: 4 in thee, and thy land shall be *m*. "
Jer 3: 14 the Lord; for I am *m* unto you: * "
Mal 2: 11 *m* the daughter of a strange god. "
M't 22: 25 the first, when he had *m* a wife, 1060
M'r 6: 17 Philip's wife: for he had *m* her. "
10: 12 husband, and be *m* to another, * "
Lu 14: 20 another said, I have *m* a wife, "
17: 27 did eat, they drank, they *m* wives, "
Ro 7: 3 liveth, she be *m* to another man, *1096
3 though she be *m* to another man. * "
4 that ye should be *m* to another, * "
1Co 7: 10 unto the *m* I command, yet not I, 1060
33 he that is *m* careth for the things "
34 she that is *m* careth for the things "
39 liberty to be *m* to whom she will; "

marrieth
Isa 62: 5 For as a young man *m* a virgin, 1166
M't 19: 9 whoso *m* her which is put away 1060
Lu 16: 18 away his wife, and *m* another, "
18 whosoever *m* her that is put away "

marrow
Job 21: 24 his bones are moistened with *m*. 4221
Ps 63: 5 satisfied as with *m* and fatness; 2459
Pr 3: 8 to thy navel, and *m* to thy bones. 8250
Isa 25: 6 of fat things full of *m*, of wines 4229
Heb 4: 12 spirit, and of the joints and *m*, 3452

marry See also MARRIED; MARRIETH; MARRYING.
Ge 38: 8 thy brother's wife, and *m* her, *2992
Nu 36: 6 them *m* to whom they think best; 802
6 tribe of their father shall they *m*. "
De 25: 5 not *m* without unto a stranger: 1961, 376
Isa 62: 5 virgin, so shall thy sons *m* thee: 1166
M't 5: 32 shall *m* her that is divorced 1060
19: 9 *m* another, committeth adultery: "
10 with his wife, it is not good to *m*. "
22: 24 his brother shall *m* his wife, and 1918
30 in the resurrection they neither *m*, 1060
M'r 10: 11 put away his wife, and *m* another, "
12: 25 they neither *m*, nor are given in "
Lu 20: 34 The children of this world *m*, and "
35 the dead, neither *m*, nor are given "
1Co 7: 9 they cannot contain, let them *m*: "
9 for it is better to *m* than to burn. "
28 if thou *m*, thou hast not sinned; "
28 if a virgin *m*, she hath not sinned. "
36 will, he sinneth not: let them *m*. "
1Ti 4: 3 Forbidding to *m*, and commanding "
5: 11 wanton against Christ, they will *m*; "
14 that the younger women *m*, bear "

marrying
Ne 13: 27 our God in *m* strange wives? 3427
M't 24: 38 *m* and giving in marriage, until 1060

Mars' (*marz*)
Ac 17: 22 Paul stood in the midst of *M* hill, *697

Marsena (*mar'-se-nah*)
Es 1: 14 *M*, and Memucan, the seven 4826

marshes See MARISHES.

Mars'-Hill See MARS' and HILL; also AREOPAGUS.

mart
Isa 23: 3 and she is a *m* of nations. 5505

Martha (*mar'-thah*)
Lu 10: 38 and a certain woman named *M* 3136
40 But *M* was cumbered about much 3136
41 *M*, *M*, thou art careful and "
Joh 11: 1 the town of Mary and her sister *M*. "
5 Jesus loved *M*, and her sister, "
19 the Jews came to *M* and Mary, to "
20 Then *M*, as soon as she heard that "
21 Then said *M* unto Jesus, Lord, if "
24 *M* saith unto him, I know that he "
30 in that place where *M* met him. "
39 *M*, the sister of him that was dead, "
12: 2 made him a supper; and *M* served: "

martyr See also MARTYRS.
Ac 22: 20 blood of thy *m* Stephen was shed, *3144
Re 2: 13 Antipas was my faithful *m*, who * "

martyrs
Re 17: 6 with the blood of the *m* of Jesus: 3144

marvel See also MARVELLED; MARVELS.
Ec 5: 8 in a province, *m* not at the matter: 8539
M'r 5: 20 done for him: and all men did *m*. 2296
Joh 3: 7 *M* not that I said unto thee, Ye "
5: 20 works than these, that ye may *m*. "
28 *M* not at this: for the hour is "
7: 21 have done one work, and ye all *m*. "
Ac 3: 12 men of Israel, why *m* ye at this? "
2Co 11: 14 And no *m*; for Satan himself is 2298
Ga 1: 6 I *m* that ye are so soon removed 2296
1Jo 3: 13 *M* not, my brethren, if the world "
Re 17: 7 unto me, Wherefore didst thou *m*? * "

marvelled
Ge 43: 33 and the men *m* one at another. 8539
Ps 48: 5 They saw it, and so they *m*; they* "
M't 8: 10 When Jesus heard it, he *m*, and 2296
27 the men *m*, saying, What manner "
9: 8 when the multitudes saw it, they *m*, * "
33 the multitudes *m*, saying, It was "
21: 20 when the disciples saw it, they *m*, "
22: 22 had heard these words, they *m*, "
27: 14 that the governor *m* greatly. * "
M'r 6: 6 he *m* because of their unbelief. "
12: 17 are God's. And they *m* at him. "
15: 5 answered nothing; so that Pilate *m*. "
44 Pilate *m* if he were already dead: "
Lu 1: 21 and *m* that he tarried so long in the "
63 name is John. And they *m* all. "
2: 33 And Joseph and his mother *m* at* "
7: 9 heard these things, he *m* at him, "
11: 38 he *m* that he had not first washed "
20: 26 and they *m* at his answer, and held "
Joh 4: 27 *m* that he talked with the woman: "
7: 15 the Jews *m*, saying, How knoweth "
Ac 2: 7 they were all amazed and *m*, "
4: 13 and ignorant men, they *m*; and "

marvellous
1Ch 16: 12 Remember his *m* works that he 6381
24 his *m* works among all nations. "
Job 5: 9 *m* things without number: "
10: 16 thou shewest thyself *m* upon me. "
Ps 9: 1 I will shew forth all thy *m* works. "
17: 7 Shew thy *m* lovingkindness, O 6395
31: 21 hath shewed me his *m* kindness 6381
78: 12 *M* things did he in the sight of 6382
98: 1 for he hath done *m* things: his 6381
105: 5 Remember his *m* works that he "
118: 23 Lord's doing; it is *m* in our eyes. "
139: 14 *m* are thy works; and that my soul * "
Isa 29: 14 I will proceed to do a *m* work "
14 even a *m* work and a wonder: "
Da 11: 36 speak *m* things against the God of "
Mic 7: 15 will I shew unto him *m* things. "
Zec 8: 6 it be *m* in the eyes of the remnant "
6 should it also be *m* in mine eyes? "
M't 21: 42 doing, and it is *m* in our eyes? 2298
M'r 12: 11 doing, and it is *m* in our eyes? "
Joh 9: 30 Why herein is a *m* thing, that ye * "
1Pe 2: 9 out of darkness into his *m* light: "
Re 15: 1 sign in heaven, great and *m*, seven "
3 Great and *m* are thy works, Lord "

marvellously
2Ch 26: 15 for he was *m* helped, till he was 6381
Job 37: 5 God thundereth *m* with his voice; "
Hab 1: 5 and regard, and wonder *m*: 8539

marvels
Ex 34: 10 before all thy people I will do *m*, 6381

Mary (*ma'-ry*) See also MIRIAM.
M't 1: 16 begat Joseph the husband of *M*, 3137
18 mother *M* was espoused to Joseph, "
20 fear not to take unto thee *M* thy "
2: 11 young child with *M* his mother, "
13: 55 son? is not his mother called *M*? "
27: 56 Among which was *M* Magdalene, "
56 *M* the mother of James and Joses, "
61 And there was *M* Magdalene, and "
61 the other *M*, sitting over against "
28: 1 came *M* Magdalene and the other "
1 the other *M* to see the sepulchre. "
M'r 6: 3 this the carpenter, the son of *M*, "
15: 40 among whom was *M* Magdalene, "
40 *M* the mother of James the less "
47 *M* Magdalene and...the mother of "
47 and *M* the mother of Joses beheld "
16: 1 sabbath was past, *M* Magdalene, "
1 and *M* the mother of James, and "
9 he appeared first to *M* Magdalene, "
Lu 1: 27 and the virgin's name was *M*. "
30 angel said unto her, Fear not, *M*: "
34 Then said *M* unto the angel, How "
38 And *M* said, Behold the handmaid "
39 *M* arose in those days, and went "
41 heard the salutation of *M*, the "
46 And *M* said, My soul doth magnify "
56 And *M* abode with her about three "
2: 5 be taxed with *M* his espoused wife, "

Lu 2:16 haste, and found *M*', and Joseph, 3137
19 But *M*' kept all these things, and "
34 said unto *M*' his mother, Behold, "
8: 2 *M*' called Magdalene, out of whom "
10:39 And she had a sister called *M*', "
42 and *M*' hath chosen that good part, "
24:10 It was *M*' Magdalene, and Joanna, "
10 *M*' the mother of James, and other "
Joh 11: 1 town of *M*' and her sister Martha. "
2 that *M*' which anointed the Lord "
19 the Jews came to Martha and *M*', "
20 him: but *M*' sat still in the house. "
28 and called *M*' her sister secretly, "
31 when they saw *M*', that she rose up "
32 *M*' was come where Jesus was, "
45 of the Jews which came to *M*', and "
12: 3 Then took *M*' a pound of ointment "
19:25 *M*' the wife of Cleophas, and "
25 wife of Cleophas, and *M*' Magdalene. "
20: 1 week cometh *M*' Magdalene early, "
11 *M*' stood without at the sepulchre "
16 Jesus saith unto her, *M*'. She "
18 *M*' Magdalene came and told the "
Ac 1:14 and *M*' the mother of Jesus, and "
12:12 house of *M*' the mother of John, "
Ro 16: 6 Greet *M*', who bestowed much "

Maschil (*mas'-kil*)
Ps 32: *title* A Psalm of David, *M*'. 4905
42: *title* To the chief Musician, *M*', for the "
44: *title* for the sons of Korah, *M*'. "
45: *title* for the sons of Korah, *M*', A Song "
52: *title* To the chief Musician, *M*', A "
53: *title* Musician upon Mahalath, *M*', A "
54: *title* chief Musician on Neginoth, *M*', "
55: *title* chief Musician on Neginoth, *M*', "
74: *title* *M*' of Asaph. "
78: *title* *M*' of Asaph. "
88: *title* *M*' of Heman the Ezrahite. "
89: *title* *M*' of Ethan the Ezrahite. "
142: *title* *M*' of David; A Prayer when he "

Mash (*mash*)
Ge 10:23 Uz, and Hul, and Gether, and *M*'. 4851

Mashal (*ma'-shal*)
1Ch 6:74 *M*' with her suburbs, and Abdon 4913

masons
2Sa 5:11 trees, and carpenters, and *m*': 2796,68
2Ki 12:12 And to *m*', and hewers of stone, 1443
22: 6 carpenters, and builders, and *m*', "
1Ch 14: 1 with *m*' and carpenters, to 2796,7023
22: 2 he set *m*' to hew wrought stones 2672
2Ch 24:12 hired *m*' and carpenters to repair "
Ezr 3: 7 They gave money also unto the *m*', "

Masrekah (*mas'-re-kah*)
Ge 36:36 Samlah of *M*' reigned in his stead. 4957
1Ch 1:47 Samlah of *M*' reigned in his stead. "

Massa (*mas'-sah*)
Ge 25:14 And Mishma, and Dumah, and *M*', 4854
1Ch 1:30 Dumah, *M*', Hadad, and Tema, "

Massah (*mas'-sah*) See also MERIBAH.
Ex 17: 7 called the name of the place *M*', 4532
De 6:16 your God, as ye tempted him in *M*'. "
9:22 at *M*', and at Kibroth-hattaavah, "
33: 8 whom thou didst prove at *M*', and "

mast See also MASTS.
Pr 23:34 he that lieth upon the top of a *m*'. 2260
Isa 33:23 not well strengthen their *m*', 8650

master See also MASTERBUILDER; MASTER'S; MASTERS; MISTRESS; SCHOOLMASTERS; SHEEPMASTER; SHIPMASTER; TASKMASTERS.
Ge 24: 9 under the thigh of Abraham his *m*', 113
10 ten camels of the camels of his *m*', "
10 goods of his *m*' were in his hand: * "
12 said, O Lord God of my *m*' Abraham, "
12 shew kindness unto my *m*' Abraham. "
14 hast shewed kindness unto my *m*'. "
27 be the Lord God of my *m*' Abraham, "
27 hath not left destitute my *m*' of his "
35 Lord hath blessed my *m*' greatly; "
36 bare a son to my *m*' when she was "
37 my *m*' made me swear, saying, Thou "
39 I said unto my *m*', Peradventure "
42 O Lord God of my *m*' Abraham, if "
48 the Lord God of my *m*' Abraham, "
49 deal kindly and truly with my *m*', "
54 he said, Send me away unto my *m*'. "
56 me away that I may go to my *m*'. "
65 the servant had said, It is my *m*': "
39: 2 in the house of his *m*' the Egyptian. "
3 And his *m*' saw that the Lord was "
8 my *m*' wotteth not what is with me "
19 his *m*' heard the words of his wife, "
20 And Joseph's *m*' took him, and put "
Ex 21: 4 If his *m*' have given him a wife, and "
5 say, I love my *m*', my wife, and my "
6 *m*' shall bring him unto the judges; "
6 his *m*' shall bore his ear through "
8 If she please not her *m*', who hath "
32 give unto their *m*' thirty shekels of "
22: 8 *m*' of the house shall be brought 1167
De 23:15 not deliver unto his *m*' the servant 113
15 is escaped from his *m*' unto thee: "
J'g 19:11 the servant said unto his *m*', Come, "
12 And his *m*' said unto him, We will "
22 and spake to the *m*' of the house, 1167
23 the *m*' of the house, went out unto "
1Sa 20:38 up the arrows, and came to his *m*'. 113
24: 6 I should do this thing unto my *m*', * "
25:10 break away every man from his *m*'. "
14 of the wilderness to salute our *m*'; "
17 evil is determined against our *m*', "
26:16 ye have not kept your *m*', the Lord's* "
29: 4 he reconcile himself unto his *m*'? * "
30:13 my *m*' left me, because three days "
1Sa 30:15 deliver me into the hands of my *m*', 113
2Sa 2: 7 your *m*' Saul is dead, and also the * "
1Ki 22:17 the Lord said, These have no *m*': "
2Ki 2: 3, 5 that the Lord will take away thy *m*' "
16 go, we pray thee, and seek thy *m*': "
5: 1 was a great man with his *m*', and "
18 when my *m*' goeth into the house of "
20 my *m*' hath spared Naaman this "
22 well. My *m*' hath sent me, saying, "
25 he went in, and stood before his *m*'. "
6: 5 said, Alas, *m*'! for it was borrowed. "
15 him, Alas, my *m*'! how shall we do? "
22 eat and drink, and go to their *m*'. "
23 away, and they went to their *m*'. "
8:14 from Elisha, and came to his *m*'; "
9: 7 smite the house of Ahab thy *m*', "
31 Had Zimri peace, who slew his *m*'?* "
10: 9 I conspired against my *m*', and slew "
18:27 Hath my *m*' sent me to thy *m*', and "
19: 4 the king of Assyria his *m*' hath sent "
6 them, Thus shall ye say to your *m*', "
1Ch 12:19 He will fall to his *m*' Saul to the "
15:27 and Chenaniah the *m*' of the song 8269
2Ch 18:16 These have no *m*'; let them return 113
Job 3:19 and the servant is free from his *m*'. "
Pr 27:18 he that waiteth on his *m*' shall be "
30:10 Accuse not a servant unto his *m*', "
Isa 24: 2 as with the servant, so with his *m*'; "
36: 8 thee, to my *m*' the king of Assyria, "
12 Hath my *m*' sent me to thy *m*' and to "
37: 4 the king of Assyria his *m*' hath sent "
6 Thus shall ye say unto your *m*', "
Da 1: 3 Ashpenaz the *m*' of his eunuchs, 7227
4: 9 Belteshazzar, *m*' of the magicians, 729
5:11 father, made *m*' of the magicians, "
Mal 1: 6 his father, and a servant his *m*': 113
6 and if I be a *m*', where is my fear? "
2:12 doeth this, the *m*' and the scholar, *5782
M't 8:19 unto him, *M*', I will follow thee 1320
9:11 Why eateth your *M*' with publicans "
10:24 The disciple is not above his *m*', "
25 for the disciple that he be as his *m*', "
25 they have called the *m*' of the house "
12:38 *M*', we would see a sign from thee. "
17:24 said, Doth not your *m*' pay tribute? "
19:16 Good *M*', what good thing shall I "
22:16 *M*', we know that thou art true, "
24 *M*', Moses said, If a man die, "
36 *M*', which is...great commandment "
23: 8 for one is your *M*', even Christ; *2519
10 for one is your *M*', even Christ. "
26:18 The *M*' saith, My time is at hand; 1320
25 answered and said, *M*', is it I? *4461
49 and said, Hail, *m*'; and kissed him.* "
M'r 4:38 him, *M*', carest thou not that we 1320
5:35 troublest thou the *M*' any further? "
9: 5 *M*', it is good for us to be here: *4461
17 *M*', I have brought unto thee my 1320
38 *M*', we saw one casting out devils "
10:17 Good *M*', what shall I do that I "
20 *M*', all these have I observed from "
35 *M*', we would that thou shouldest "
11:21 *M*', behold, the fig tree which thou *4461
12:14 *M*', we know that thou art true, 1320
19 *M*', Moses wrote unto us, If a man's "
32 Well, *M*', thou hast said the truth: "
13: 1 *M*', see what manner of stones and "
35 when the *m*' of the house cometh, *2962
14:14 to the goodman...The *M*' saith, 1320
45 saith, *M*', *m*'; and kissed him. *4461
Lu 3:12 unto him, *M*', what shall we do? 1320
5: 5 *M*', we have toiled all the night, 1988
6:40 The disciple is not above his *m*': 1320
40 that is perfect shall be as his *m*'. "
7:40 thee. And he saith, *M*', say on. "
8:24 him, saying, *M*', *m*', we perish. 1988
45 *M*', the multitude throng thee and "
49 is dead; trouble not the *M*'. 1320
9:33 *M*', it is good for us to be here: 1988
38 *M*', I beseech thee, look upon my 1320
49 *M*', we saw one casting out devils 1988
10:25 *M*', what shall I do to inherit 1320
11:45 *M*', thus saying thou reproachest "
12:13 *M*', speak to my brother, that he "
13:25 When once the *m*' of the house is 3617
14:21 *m*' of the house being angry said "
17:13 said, Jesus, *M*', have mercy on us. 1988
18:18 Good *M*', what shall I do to inherit 1320
19:39 unto him, *M*', rebuke thy disciples. "
20:21 *M*', we know that thou sayest and "
28 *M*', Moses wrote unto us, If any "
39 said, *M*', thou hast well said. "
21: 7 *M*', but when shall these things be? "
22:11 The *M*' saith unto thee, Where is "
Joh 1:38 is to say, being interpreted, *M*',) "
3:10 Art thou a *m*' of Israel, and knowest* "
4:31 prayed him, saying, *M*', eat. *4461
8: 4 *M*', this woman was taken in 1320
9: 2 *M*', who did sin, this man, or his *4461
11: 8 *M*', the Jews of late sought to stone* "
28 The *M*' is come, and calleth for 1320
13:13 Ye call me *M*' and Lord: and ye "
14 If I then, your Lord and *M*', have "
20:16 him, Rabboni; which is to say, *M*'. "
Ac 27:11 the *m*' and the owner of the ship, 2942
Ro 14: 4 to his own *m*' he standeth or *2962
Eph 6: 9 that your *M*' also is in heaven; "
Col 4: 1 that ye also have a *M*' in heaven. "

masterbuilder
1Co 3:10 is given unto me, as a wise *m*', 753

master's
Ge 24:27 me to the house of my *m*' brethren. 113
36 And Sarah my *m*' wife bare a son to "
44 hath appointed out for my *m*' son. "
48 to take my *m*' brother's daughter "
Ge 24:51 and let her be thy *m*' son's wife, as 113
39: 7 *m*' wife cast her eyes upon Joseph; "
8 said unto his *m*' wife, Behold, my "
Ex 21: 4 and her children shall be her *m*', "
1Sa 29:10 thy *m*' servants that are come with* "
2Sa 9: 9 have given unto thy *m*' son all that "
10 that thy *m*' son may have food to "
10 thy *m*' son shall eat bread alway "
12: 8 I gave thee thy *m*' house, and thy "
8 thy *m*' wives into thy bosom, and "
16: 3 said, And where is thy *m*' son? "
2Ki 6:32 the sound of his *m*' feet behind him? "
10: 2 seeing your *m*' sons are with you, "
3 best and meetest of your *m*' sons, "
3 throne, and fight for your *m*' house. "
6 the heads of the men your *m*' sons, "
18:24 of the least of my *m*' servants, "
Isa 1: 3 his owner, and the ass his *m*' crib: 1167
36: 9 of the least of my *m*' servants, and 113
2Ti 2:21 and meet for the *m*' use, and 1203

masters See also MASTERS'; TASKMASTERS.
Ps 123: 2 look unto the hand of their *m*', 113
Pr 25:13 for he refresheth the soul of his *m*'. "
Ec 12:11 fastened by the *m*' of assemblies, 1167
Jer 27: 4 command them to say unto their *m*', 113
4 Thus shall ye say unto your *m*'; "
Am 4: 1 which say to their *m*', Bring, and * "
M't 6:24 No man can serve two *m*': for 2962
23:10 Neither be ye called *m*': for one is 2519
Lu 16:13 No servant can serve two *m*': for 2962
Ac 16:16 which brought her *m*' much gain "
19 when her *m*' saw that the hope of "
Eph 6: 5 obedient to them that are your *m*' "
9 ye *m*', do the same things unto "
Col 3:22 Servants, obey in all things your *m*' "
4: 1 *M*', give unto your servants that "
1Ti 6: 1 their own *m*' worthy of all honour, 1203
2 And they that have believing *m*', "
Tit 2: 9 to be obedient unto their own *m*', "
Jas 3: 1 My brethren, be not many *m*', *1320
1Pe 2:18 subject to your *m*' with all fear; 1203

masters'
Zep 1: 9 fill their *m*' houses with violence 113
M't 15:27 which fall from their *m*' table. 2962

masteries
2Ti 2: 5 And if a man also strive for *m*', yet

mastery See also MASTERIES.
Ex 32:18 voice of them that shout for *m*', 1369
Da 6:24 and the lions had the *m*' of them, 6981
1Co 9:25 every man that striveth for the *m*' *

masts
Eze 27: 5 cedars from Lebanon to make *m*' 8650

mate
Isa 34:15 gathered, every one with her *m*'. 7468
16 shall fail, none shall want her *m*': "

Mathusala (*ma-thu'-sa-lah*) See also METHUSALAH.
Lu 3:37 Which was the son of *M*', which *3103

Matred (*ma'-tred*)
Ge 36:39 Mehetabel, the daughter of *M*', 4308
1Ch 1:50 Mehetabel, the daughter of *M*', "

Matri (*ma'-tri*)
1Sa 10:21 the family of *M*' was taken, and *4309

matrix
Ex 13:12 the Lord all that openeth the *m*', *7358
15 to the Lord all that openeth the *m*', * "
34:19 All that openeth the *m*' is mine; * "
Nu 3:12 the firstborn that openeth the *m*' * "
18:15 that openeth the *m*' in all flesh, * "

Mattan (*mat'-tan*)
2Ki 11:18 slew *M*' the priest of Baal before 4977
2Ch 23:17 slew *M*' the priest of Baal before "
Jer 38: 1 Then Shephatiah the son of *M*', "

Mattanah (*mat'-ta-nah*)
Nu 21:18 the wilderness they went to *M*': 4980
19 And from *M*' to Nahaliel: and from "

Mattaniah (*mat-ta-ni'-ah*) See also ZEDEKIAH.
2Ki 24:17 made *M*' his father's brother king 4983
1Ch 9:15 and *M*' the son of Micah, the son of "
25: 4 the sons of Heman; Bukkiah, *M*', "
16 The ninth to *M*', he, his sons, and "
2Ch 20:14 the son of *M*', a Levite of the sons "
29:13 sons of Asaph; Zechariah, and *M*': "
Ezr 10:26 sons of Elam; *M*', Zechariah, "
27 of Zattu; Elioenai, Eliashib, *M*', "
30 *M*', Bezaleel, and Binnui, and "
37 *M*', Mattenai, and Jaasau, "
Ne 11:17 *M*' the son of Micha, the son of "
22 son of Hashabiah, the son of *M*', "
12: 8 Judah, and *M*', which was over the "
25 *M*', and Bakbukiah, Obadiah, "
35 the son of *M*', the son of Michaiah, "
13:13 the son of Zaccur, the son of *M*': "

Mattatha (*mat'-ta-thah*) See also MATTATHAH.
Lu 3:31 which was the son of *M*', which 3160

Mattathah (*mat'-ta-thah*) See also MATTATHA.
Ezr 10:33 Mattenai, *M*', Zabad, Eliphelet, 4992

Mattathias (*mat-ta-thi'-as*) See also MATTITHIAH.
Lu 3:25 Which was the son of *M*', which 3161
26 of Maath, which was the son of *M*', "

Mattenai (*mat'-te-nahee*)
Ezr 10:33 sons of Hashum; *M*', Mattathah, 4982
37 Mattaniah, *M*', and Jaasau, "
Ne 12:19 And of Joiarib, *M*'; of Jedaiah, "

matter See also MATTERS.
Ge 24: 9 sware to him concerning that *m*'. 1697
30:15 Is it a small *m*' that thou hast taken
16 When they have a *m*', they come 1697

Ex 18: 22 every great *m·* they shall bring 1697
22 but every small *m·* they shall judge: "
26 but every small *m·* they judged "
23: 7 Keep thee far from a false *m·*; and "
Nu 16: 49 that died about the *m·* of Korah. "
25: 18 in the *m·* of Peor, and in the *m·* of "
31: 16 against the Lord in the *m·* of Peor, "
De 3: 26 speak no more unto me of this *m·*. "
17: 8 If there arise a *m·* too hard for thee "
19: 15 shall the *m·* be established. "
22: 26 and slayeth him, even so is this *m·*: "
Ru 3: 18 thou know how the *m·* will fall: "
1Sa 10: 16 But of the *m·* of the kingdom, "
20: 23 as touching the *m·* which thou and "
39 Jonathan and David knew the *m·*. "
30: 24 will hearken unto you in this *m·*? "
2Sa 1: 4 said unto him, How went the *m·*? "
18: 13 there is no *m·* hid from the king, "
19: 42 then be ye angry for this *m·*? "
20: 18 at Abel: and so they ended the *m·*. "
21 The *m·* is not so: but a man of 1697
1Ki 8: 59 all times, as the *m·* shall require: * "
15: 5 only in the *m·* of Uriah the Hittite. "
1Ch 26: 32 for every *m·* pertaining to God, and "
27: 1 the king in any *m·* of the courses, "
2Ch 8: 15 and Levites concerning any *m·*, or "
24: 5 year, and see that ye hasten the *m·*. "
Ezr 5: 5 to cease, till the *m·* came to Darius: 2941
5 answer by letter concerning this *m·*.*
17 pleasure to us concerning this *m·*. 1836
10: 4 for this *m·* belongeth unto thee: 1697
9 trembling because of this *m·*, and "
14 fierce wrath of our God for this *m·* "
15 Tikvah were employed about this *m·*:
16 tenth month to examine the *m·*. 1697
Ne 6: 13 they might have *m·* for an evil report, "
Es 2: 23 inquisition was made of the *m·*, 1697
9: 26 they had seen concerning this *m·*, 3602
Job 19: 28 the root of the *m·* is found in me? 1697
32: 18 I am full of *m·*, the spirit within *4405
Ps 45: 1 My heart is inditing a good *m·*: 1697
64: 5 encourage themselves in an evil *m·*:*"
Pr 11: 13 a faithful spirit concealeth the *m·*. "
16: 20 He that handleth a *m·* wisely shall* "
17: 9 he that repeateth a *m·* separateth "
18: 13 answereth a *m·* before he heareth* "
25: 2 of kings is to search out a *m·*. "
Ec 5: 8 a province, marvel not at the *m·*: 2659
10: 20 hath wings shall tell the *m·*. 1697
12: 13 the conclusion of the whole *m·*: "
Jer 38: 27 him; for the *m·* was not perceived. "
Eze 9: 11 by his side, reported the *m·*, saying, "
16: 20 this of thy whoredoms a small *m·*,
Da 1: 14 he consented to them in this *m·*, 1697
2: 10 earth that can shew the king's *m·*: 4406
23 made known unto us the king's *m·*. "
3: 16 careful to answer thee in this *m·*. 6600
4: 17 This *m·* is by the decree of the * "
7: 28 Hitherto is the end of the *m·*. 4406
28 me: but I kept the *m·* in my heart. "
9: 23 understand the *m·*, and consider 1697
M'r 1: 45 much, and to blaze abroad the *m·*, *3056*
10: 10 asked him again of the same *m·*.
Ac 8: 21 neither part nor lot in this *m·*: *3056*
11: 4 rehearsed the *m·* from the beginning,
15: 6 together for to consider of this *m·*. *3056*
17: 32 We will hear thee again of this *m·*.*
18: 14 a *m·* of wrong or wicked lewdness,
19: 38 him, have a *m·* against any man, *3056*
24: 22 know the uttermost of your *m·*. *2596*
1Co 6: 1 you, having a *m·* against another, *4229*
2Co 7: 11 yourselves to be clear in this *m·*.
9: 5 might be ready, as a *m·* of bounty,
Gal 2: 6 they were, it maketh no *m·* to me: *1308*
1Th 4: 6 and defraud his brother in any *m·*: *4229*
Jas 3: 5 great a *m·* a little fire kindleth! *5208*

matters
Ex 24: 14 if any man have any *m·* to do, let *1697
De 17: 8 *m·* of controversy within thy gates: "
1Sa 16: 18 a man of war, and prudent in *m·*, * "
2Sa 11: 19 an end of telling the *m·* of the war* "
15: 3 See, thy *m·* are good and right; "
19: 29 speakest thou any more of thy *m·*? "
2Ch 19: 11 is over you in all *m·* of the Lord; "
11 house of Judah, for all the king's *m·*: "
Ne 11: 24 in all *m·* concerning the people. "
Es 3: 4 whether Mordecai's *m·* would stand: "
9: 31 the *m·* of the fastings and their cry.*"
32 confirmed these *m·* of Purim; "
Job 33: 13 giveth not account of any of his *m·*. "
Ps 35: 20 devise deceitful *m·* against them * "
131: 1 do I exercise myself in great *m·*, 1419
Da 1: 20 *m·* of wisdom and understanding,*1697
7: 1 dream, and told the sum of the *m·*. 4406
M't 23: 23 omitted the weightier *m·* of the law,
Ac 18: 15 to it; for I will be no judge of such *m·*.
19: 39 enquire any thing concerning other *m·*,
25: 20 and there be judged of these *m·*.
1Co 6: 2 ye unworthy to judge the smallest *m·*?
1Pe 4: 15 or as a busybody in other men's *m·*.

Matthan (*mat'-than*)
M't 1: 15 Eleazar begat *M·*; and *M·* begat *3157*

Matthat (*mat'-that*)
Lu 3: 24 Which was the son of *M·*, which *3158*
29 which was the son of *M·*, which

Matthew (*math'-ew*) See also LEVI.
M't 9: 9 he saw a man, named *M·*, sitting *3156*
10: 3 Thomas, and *M·* the publican; "
M'r 3: 18 Bartholomew, and *M·*, and Thomas, "
Lu 6: 15 *M·* and Thomas, James the son of "
Ac 1: 13 Thomas, Bartholomew, and *M·*. "

Matthias (*mat'-thias*)
Ac 1: 23 was surnamed Justus, and *M·*. *3159*
26 their lots; and the lot fell upon *M·*: "

Mattithiah (*mat-tith-i'-ah*) See also MATTATHIAS.
1Ch 9: 31 *M·*, one of the Levites, who was 4993
15: 18 And *M·*, and Elipheleh, and "
21 and *M·*, and Elipheleh, and Mikneiah, "
16: 5 Shemiramoth, and Jehiel, and *M·*, "
25: 3 Jeshaiah, Hashabiah, and *M·*, "
21 fourteenth to *M·*, he, his sons, and "
Ezr 10: 43 Jeiel, *M·*, Zabad, Zebina, Jadau, "
Ne 8: 4 and beside him stood *M·*, and "

mattock See also MATTOCKS.
1Sa 13: 20 coulter, and his axe, and his *m·*. 4281
Isa 7: 25 that shall be digged with the *m·*, 4576

mattocks
1Sa 13: 21 they had a file for the *m·*, and for 4281
2Ch 34: 6 with their *m·* round about. *2719

maul
Pr 25: 18 against his neighbour is a *m·*, and 4650

maw
De 18: 3 and the two cheeks, and the *m·*. 6896

may See also MAYEST; MIGHT.
Ge 1: 20 fowl that *m·* fly above the earth in the*
3: 2 We *m·* eat of the fruit of the trees of
8: 17 they *m·* breed abundantly in the earth,
9: 16 that I *m·* remember the everlasting
11: 4 whose top *m·* reach unto heaven;
7 that they *m·* not understand one
12: 13 it *m·* be well with me for thy sake;
16: 2 it *m·* be that I...obtain children by 194
2 be that I *m·* obtain children by her*
18: 19 the Lord *m·* bring upon Abraham
19: 5 out unto us, that we *m·* know them.
32, 34 we *m·* preserve seed of our father.
21: 30 that they *m·* be a witness unto me,
23: 4 I *m·* bury my dead out of my sight.
9 That he *m·* give me the cave of
24: 14 pitcher, I pray thee, that I *m·* drink;
49 that I *m·* turn to the right hand, or to
56 me away that I *m·* go to my master.
27: 4 and bring it to me, that I *m·* eat;
4 my soul *m·* bless thee before I die.
7 make me savoury meat, that I *m·* eat,
10 bring it to thy father, that he *m·* eat,
10 that he *m·* bless thee before his death.
19 my venison, that thy soul *m·* bless me.
21 I pray thee, that I *m·* feel thee, my
25 venison, that my soul *m·* bless thee.
31 venison, that thy soul *m·* bless me.
29: 21 are fulfilled, that I *m·* go in unto her.
30: 3 that I *m·* also have children by her.
25 that I *m·* go unto mine own place,
31: 37 that they *m·* judge betwixt us both.
32: 5 that I *m·* find grace in thy sight.
42: 2 thence; that we *m·* live, and not die.
16 that your words *m·* be proved,
43: 8 that we *m·* live, and not die, both we,
14 he *m·* send away your other brother,
18 that he *m·* seek occasion against us,
44: 21 that I *m·* set mine eyes upon him.
26 for we *m·* not see the man's face, 3201
46: 34 that ye *m·* dwell in the land of Goshen;
47: 19 us seed, that we *m·* live, and not die,
49: 1 I *m·* tell you that which shall befall
Ex 2: 7 that she *m·* nurse the child for thee?
20 man? call him, that he *m·* eat bread.
3: 18 we *m·* sacrifice to the Lord our God.
4: 5 they *m·* believe that the Lord God
23 Let my son go, that he *m·* serve me:
5: 1 people go, that they *m·* hold a feast
9 men, that they *m·* labour therein;
7: 4 that I *m·* lay my hand upon Egypt,
16 they *m·* serve me in the wilderness:
19 water, that they *m·* become blood;
19 there *m·* be blood throughout all the*
8: 1 my people go, that they *m·* serve me.
8 that he *m·* take away the frogs from*
8 they *m·* do sacrifice unto the Lord.
9 they *m·* remain in the river only?*
16 that it *m·* become lice throughout all
20 my people go, that they *m·* serve me.
28 that ye *m·* sacrifice to the Lord your
29 the swarms of flies *m·* depart from
9: 1, 13 people go, that they *m·* serve me.
15 that I *m·* smite thee and thy people*
16 my name *m·* be declared throughout
22 *m·* be hail in all the land of Egypt,
10: 2 ye *m·* know how that I am the Lord.
3 my people go, that they *m·* serve me.
7 men go, that they *m·* serve the Lord
12 *m·* come up upon the land of Egypt,
17 he *m·* take away from me this death
21 *m·* be darkness over the land of Egypt,
21 Egypt, even darkness which *m·* be felt.
25 *m·* sacrifice unto the Lord our God.
11: 7 ye *m·* know how that the Lord doth
9 my wonders *m·* be multiplied in the
12: 16 must eat, that only *m·* be done of you.
13: 9 the Lord's law *m·* be in thy mouth:
14: 4 *m·* know that I am the Lord.
12 that we *m·* serve the Egyptians?
26 the waters *m·* come again upon the
16: 4 that I may prove them, whether they
32 *m·* see the bread wherewith I have fed
17: 2 said, Give us water that we *m·* drink.
6 out of it, that the people *m·* drink.
19: 9 people *m·* hear when I speak with
20: 12 thy days *m·* be long upon the land
20 that his fear *m·* be before your faces,
21: 14 him from mine altar, that he *m·* die.
23: 11 that the poor of thy people *m·* eat:
12 that thine ox and thine ass *m·* rest, and
12 that thy stranger, *m·* be refreshed.
25: 8 that I *m·* dwell among them.
14 that the ark *m·* be borne with them.*
28 that the table *m·* be borne with them.

Ex 25: 37 that they *m·* give light over against it.*
26: 5 loops *m·* take hold one of another.*
11 the tent together, that it *m·* be one.
27: 5 net *m·* be even to the midst of the
28: 1 *m·* minister unto me in the priest's
3 they *m·* make Aaron's garments to*
3, 4 *m·* minister unto me in the priest's
28 it *m·* be above the curious girdle of
37 blue lace, that it *m·* be upon the mitre;*
38 Aaron *m·* bear the iniquity of the holy*
38 they *m·* be accepted before the Lord.
41 *m·* minister unto me in the priest's
29: 46 Egypt, that I *m·* dwell among them:
30: 16 *m·* be a memorial unto the children
29 them, that they *m·* be most holy:
30 *m·* minister unto me in the priest's
31: 13 *m·* know that I am the Lord that doth
15 Six days *m·* work be done; but in the*
32: 10 my wrath *m·* wax hot against them,
10 and that I *m·* consume them: and I
29 *m·* bestow upon you a blessing this
33: 5 that I *m·* know what to do unto thee.
13 now thy way, that I *m·* know thee,
13 that I *m·* find grace in thy sight:
35: 34 put in his heart that he *m·* teach,
40: 13, 15 *m·* minister unto me in the
Le 7: 24 beasts, *m·* be used in any other use:
30 *m·* be waved for a wave offering
10: 10 *m·* put difference between holy and
11 *m·* teach the children of Israel all the
11: 21 *m·* ye eat of every flying creeping
22 Even these of them ye *m·* eat; the
34 Of all meat which *m·* be eaten, that on
34 all drink that *m·* be drunk in every
47 between the beast that *m·* be eaten
47 and the beast that *m·* not be eaten.
14: 8 himself in water, that he *m·* be clean:*
16: 13 the incense *m·* cover the mercy seat
30 *m·* be clean from all your sins before*
17: 5 of Israel *m·* bring their sacrifices,
5 they *m·* bring them unto the Lord,
19: 25 *m·* yield unto you the increase thereof:
21: 3 no husband; for her *m·* he be defiled.
22: 5 whereby he *m·* be made unclean,
5 man of whom he *m·* take uncleanness,
12 *m·* not eat of an offering of the holy*
23: 21 it *m·* be a holy convocation unto you:*
43 That your generations *m·* know that I
24: 7 it *m·* be on the bread for a memorial,
25: 27 that he *m·* return unto his possession.*
29 then he *m·* redeem it within a whole
29 within a full year *m·* he redeem it.*
31 they *m·* be redeemed, and they shall
32 *m·* the Levites redeem at any time.
34 suburbs of their cities *m·* not be sold;
35 a sojourner; that he *m·* live with thee.*
36 that thy brother *m·* live with thee.
48 that he is sold he *m·* be redeemed
48 one of his brethren *m·* redeem him:
49 or his uncle's son, *m·* redeem him,
49 him of his family *m·* redeem him;
49 if he be able, he *m·* redeem himself.
Nu 3: 6 priest, that they *m·* minister unto him.
4: 19 thus do unto them, that they *m·* live,
6: 20 after that the Nazarite *m·* drink wine.
7: 5 they *m·* be to do the service of the
8: 11 that they *m·* execute the service of the
9: 7 that we *m·* not offer an offering of the
10: 10 *m·* be to you for a memorial before*
11: 13 saying, Give us flesh, that we *m·* eat.
16 that they *m·* stand there with thee.
21 flesh, that they *m·* eat a whole month.
13: 2 they *m·* search the land of Canaan,
15: 39 that ye *m·* look upon it, and remember
40 That ye *m·* remember, and do all my
16: 21, 45 I *m·* consume them in a moment.
18: 2 thee, that they *m·* be joined unto thee,
19: 3 he *m·* bring her forth without the*
22: 6 shall prevail, that we *m·* smite them,
6 that I *m·* drive them out of the land:
19 I *m·* know what the Lord will say unto
25: 4 Lord *m·* be turned away from Israel.
27: 17 Which *m·* go out before them, and
17 which *m·* go in before them, and
17 and which *m·* lead them out, and
17 which *m·* bring them in; that the
30: 13 the soul, her husband *m·* establish it,
13 it, or her husband *m·* make it void.
31: 23 Every thing that *m·* abide the fire, ye
32: 32 on this side Jordan *m·* be ours. *
35: 6 manslayer, that he *m·* flee thither:*
11 that the slayer *m·* flee thither, which
15 killeth any person unawares *m·* flee
17 a stone, wherewith he *m·* die, and
18 weapon of wood, wherewith he *m·* die,
23 any stone, wherewith a man *m·* die,
36: 8 *m·* enjoy every man the inheritance
De 2: 6 of them for money, that ye *m·* eat;
6 of them for money, that ye *m·* drink.
28 sell me meat for money, that I *m·* eat;
28 me water for money, that I *m·* drink:
4: 1 you, for to do them, that ye *m·* live,
2 ye *m·* keep the commandments of the
10 they *m·* learn to fear me all the days
10 and that they *m·* teach their children.
40 this day, that it *m·* go well with thee,
5: 1 *m·* learn them, and keep, and do them.
14 maidservant *m·* rest as well as thou.
16 that thy days *m·* be prolonged,
16 and that it *m·* go well with thee,
31 shall teach them, that they *m·* do them
33 hath commanded you, that ye *m·* live,
33 that it *m·* be well with you, and that
33 ye *m·* prolong your days in the land
6: 2 and that thy days *m·* be prolonged.
3 to do it; that it *m·* be well with thee,

De 6: 3 that ye m' increase mightily, as the
18 that it m' be well with thee, and that
7: 4 me, that they m' serve other gods:
8: 1 shall ye observe to do, that ye m' live,
18 m' establish his covenant which he
9: 5 and that he m' perform the word
14 that I m' destroy them, and blot out
10: 11 they m' go in and possess the land,*
11: 8 that ye m' be strong, and go in and
9 ye m' prolong your days in the land,
18 m' be as frontlets between your eyes.*
21 That your days m' be multiplied,
12: 15 unclean and the clean m' eat thereof,
25, 28 that it m' go well with thee, and
13: 17 Lord m' turn from the fierceness of
14: 10 hath not fins and scales ye m' not eat;*
20 But of all clean fowls ye m' eat.
21 that is in thy gates, that he m' eat it;
17: 19 he m' learn to fear the Lord his God,
20 m' prolong his days in his kingdom,
19: 3 parts, that every slayer m' flee thither.
4 shall flee thither, that he m' live: *
12 of the avenger of blood, that he m' die.
13 Israel, that it m' go well with thee.
21: 16 m' not make the son of the beloved 3201
22: 7 that it m' be well with thee, and that
19, 29 he m' not put her away all his 3201
23: 20 that the Lord thy God m' bless thee
24: 2 she m' go and be another man's wife.
4 m' not take her again to be his 3201
13 that he m' sleep in his own raiment,
19 that the Lord thy God m' bless thee in
25: 1 that the judges m' judge them; *
3 Forty stripes he m' give him, and not
15 thy days m' be lengthened in the land
26: 12 they m' eat within thy gates, and be
29: 9 that ye m' prosper in all that ye do.
13 he m' establish thee to day for a people
13 and that he m' be unto thee a God, as
29 we m' do all the words of this law.
30: 12, 13 us, that we m' hear it, and do it?
19 that both thou and thy seed m' live:*
31: 5 that ye m' do unto them according*
12 within thy gates, that they m' hear,
12 and that they m' learn, and fear the
13 have not known any thing, m' hear,
14 that I m' give him a charge.
19 that this song m' be a witness for me
26 it m' be there for a witness against
28 m' speak these words in their ears,
Jos 2: 16 and afterward m' ye go your way.
3: 4 that ye m' know the way by which ye
7 that they m' know that, as I was with
4: 6 That this m' be a sign among you,
9: 19 therefore we m' not touch them. 3201
10: 4 and help me, that we m' smite Gibeon:*
18: 6 that I m' cast lots for you here before*
8 that I m' here cast lots for you before*
20: 3 and unwittingly m' flee thither:
4 a place, that he m' dwell among them.
22: 27 But that it m' be a witness between us,*
27 children m' not say to our children
28 we m' say again, Behold the pattern*
J'g 1: 3 my lot, that we m' fight against the
2: 22 That through them I m' prove Israel,
6: 30 Bring out thy son, that he m' die:
9: 7 that God m' hearken unto you.
11: 6 m' fight with the children of Ammon.
37 that I m' go up and down upon the
13: 14 m' not eat of any thing that cometh
17 come to pass we m' do thee honour?
14: 13 Put forth thy riddle, that we m' hear it.
15 that he m' declare unto us the riddle,
15: 12 m' deliver thee into the hand of the
16: 5 means we m' prevail against him,
5 that we m' bind him to afflict him:
25 for Samson, that he m' make us sport.
26 Suffer me that I m' feel the pillars
26 standeth, that I m' lean upon them.
28 that I m' be at once avenged of the
17: 9 go to sojourn where I m' find a place.
18: 5 m' know whether our way which we
9 Arise, that we m' go up against them:*
19: 9 here, that thine heart m' be merry;
22 thine house, that we m' know him.
20: 10 for the people, that they m' do,
13 that we m' put them to death, and put
21: 18 we m' not give them wives of our 3201
Ru 1: 9 Lord grant you that ye m' find rest,
11 womb, that they m' be your husbands?
2: 16 leave them, that she m' glean them,*
3: 1 for thee, that it m' be well with thee?
4: 4 it, then tell me, that I m' know:
14 that his name m' be famous in Israel.*
1Sa 1: 22 that he m' appear before the Lord,
2: 36 offices, that I m' eat a piece of bread.
4: 3 it m' save us out of the hand of our
6: 8 and send it away, that it m' go.
20 and that our king m' judge us, and
8: 20 we also m' be like all the nations;
9: 16 he m' save my people out of the hand*
26 saying, Up, that I m' send thee away.
27 that I m' shew thee the word of God.
11: 2 that I m' thrust out all your right eyes,*
3 that we m' send messengers unto all
12 men, that we m' put them to death.
12: 7 m' reason with you before the Lord
17 that ye m' perceive and see that your*
14: 6 it m' be that the Lord will work for us:
24 that I m' be avenged on mine enemies.*
15: 25 with me, that I m' worship the Lord.
30 that I m' worship the Lord thy God.
17: 10 me a man, that we m' fight together.
46 earth m' know that there is a God in
18: 21 him her, that she m' be a snare to him,
21 of the Philistines m' be against him.

1Sa 19: 15 to me in the bed, that I m' slay him.
20: 5 that I m' hide myself in the field unto
27: 5 in the country, that I m' dwell there:
28: 7 I m' go to her, and enquire of her.
29: 4 that he m' go again to his place which
8 I m' not go fight against the enemies
30: 22 m' lead them away, and depart.
2Sa 3: 21 that they m' make a league with thee,
7: 10 they m' dwell in a place of their own,
29 it m' continue for ever before thee:
9: 1 that I m' shew him kindness for
3 m' shew the kindness of God unto him?
10 thy master's son m' have food to eat:
11: 15 him, that he m' be smitten, and die.
12: 22 to me, that the children m' live?
13: 5 the meat in my sight, that I m' see it,
6 in my sight, that I m' eat at her hand.
10 chamber, that I m' eat of thine hand.
14: 7 m' kill him, for the life of his brother
15 m' be that the king will perform the
32 that I m' send thee to the king, to say,
15: 20 seeing I go whither I m', return thou,
16: 2 as be faint in the wilderness m' drink.
4 thee that I m' find grace in thy sight,*
11 more now m' this Benjamite do it?
12 It m' be that the Lord will look on
19: 26 me an ass, that I m' ride thereon,
37 again, that I m' die in mine own city,
20: 16 near hither, that I m' speak with thee.
21: 3 ye m' bless the inheritance of the
24: 2 m' know the number of the people.
3 the eyes of my lord the king m' see it:
12 one of them, that I m' do it unto thee.
21 plague m' be stayed from the people.
1Ki 1: 2 that my lord the king m' get heat.
35 that he m' come and sit upon my*
2: 4 That the Lord m' continue his word
3: 9 I m' discern between good and bad:
8: 29 That thine eyes m' be open toward
40 they m' fear thee all the days that
43 people of the earth m' know thy name,
43 that they m' know that this house,
50 they m' have compassion on them:
52 eyes m' be open unto the supplication
58 he m' incline our hearts unto him,
60 earth m' know that the Lord is God,
11: 21 that I m' go to mine own country.
36 David my servant m' have a light
12: 6 advise that I m' answer this people?*
9 give ye that we m' answer this people,
13: 6 my hand m' be restored me again.
16 I m' not return with thee, nor go 3201
18 that he m' eat bread and drink water.
15: 19 of Israel, that he m' depart from me.
17: 10 water in a vessel, that I m' drink.
12 that I m' go in and dress it for me
12 and my son, that we m' eat it, and die.
18: 5 we m' find grass to save the horses
37 people m' know that thou art the Lord
20: 9 will do: but this thing I m' not do. 3201
21: 2 that I m' have it for a garden of herbs,
10 out, and stone him, that he m' die.*
22: 8 by whom we m' enquire of the Lord:
20 m' go up and fall at Ramoth-gilead?
2Ki 3: 11 we m' enquire of the Lord by him?
17 ye m' drink, both ye, and your cattle,*
4: 22 I m' run to the man of God, and come
41 out for the people, that they m' eat.
42 Give unto the people, that they m' eat.
43 Give the people, that they m' eat:
5: 12 m' I not wash in them, and be clean?
6: 2 us a place there, where we m' dwell.
13 he is, that I m' send and fetch him.
17 thee, open his eyes, that he m' see.
20 eyes of these men, that they m' see.
22 they m' eat and drink, and go to their
28 thy son, that we m' eat him to day,
29 Give thy son, that we m' eat him: and
7: 9 m' go and tell the king's household.*
9: 7 m' avenge the blood of my servants
18: 27 that they m' eat their own dung, and*
32 of honey, that ye m' live, and not die:
19: 4 It m' be the Lord thy God will hear 194
19 earth m' know that thou art the Lord
22: 4 that he m' sum the silver which is
1Ch 4: 10 from evil, that it m' not grieve me!*
13: 2 they m' gather themselves unto us:
15: 12 ye m' bring up the ark of the Lord God
16: 35 we m' give thanks to thy holy name,*
17: 24 thy name m' be magnified for ever,*
27 that it m' be before thee for ever:
21: 2 of them to me, that I m' know it.
10 one of them, that I m' do it unto thee.
22 that I m' build an altar therein unto
22 plague m' be stayed from the people.
23: 25 they m' dwell in Jerusalem for ever:*
28: 8 that ye m' possess this good land, and
2Ch 1: 10 I m' go out and come in before this
6: 20 That thine eyes m' be open upon this
31 That they m' fear thee, to walk in thy
33 people of the earth m' know thy name,
33 m' know that this house which I have
7: 16 that my name m' be there for ever:
10: 9 we m' return answer to this people,
12: 8 that they m' know my service, and the
13: 9 the same m' be a priest of them that
16: 3 of Israel, that he m' depart from me.
18: 7 by whom we m' enquire of the Lord:
19 m' go up and fall at Ramoth-gilead?
28: 23 to them, that they m' help me.
29: 10 fierce wrath m' turn away from us.
30: 8 of his wrath m' turn away from you.
35: 6 m' do according to the word of the*
Ezr 4: 15 search m' be made in the book of the
6: 10 m' offer sacrifices of sweet savours
7: 25 which m' judge all the people that are

Ezr 9: 8 our God m' lighten our eyes, and give
12 that ye m' be strong, and eat the good
Ne 2: 5 fathers' sepulchres, that I m' build it.
7 they m' convey me over till I come
8 he m' give me timber to make beams
4: 22 in the night they m' be a guard to us,
5: 2 take up corn for them, that we m' eat,
Es 2: 3 they m' gather together all the fair
3: 9 be written that they m' be destroyed:*
4: 11 the golden sceptre, that he m' live:
5: 5 that he m' do as Esther hath said.
14 that Mordecai m' be hanged thereon:
6: 9 they m' array the man withal whom
8: 8 the king's ring, m' no man reverse.
Job 1: 5 It m' be that my sons have sinned, 194
5: 11 which mourn m' be exalted to safety.*
6: 8 I m' have my request; and that God*
10: 20 alone, that I m' take comfort a little,
13: 13 peace, let me alone, that I m' speak,
14: 6 Turn from him, that he m' rest, till he
19: 29 that ye m' know there is a judgment.
21: 3 Suffer me that I m' speak; and after*
22: 2 he that is wise m' be profitable unto*
27: 17 He m' prepare it, but the just shall
31: 6 that God m' know mine integrity.
32: 20 I will speak, that I m' be refreshed:
33: 17 m' withdraw man from his purpose,
34: 22 the workers of iniquity m' hide
36 is that Job m' be tried unto the end*
35: 8 wickedness m' hurt a man as thou
8 righteousness m' profit the son of
36: 25 Every man m' see it; *
25 man m' behold it afar off. *
37: 7 man; that all men m' know his work.
12 m' do whatsoever he commandeth
38: 34 abundance of waters m' cover thee?
35 that they m' go, and say unto thee,
39: 15 that the foot m' crush them, or
15 that the wild beast m' break them.
Ps 9: 14 That I m' shew forth all thy praise in
20 m' know themselves to be but men.*
10: 10 the poor m' fall by his strong ones.*
18 man of the earth m' no more oppress.
11: 2 they m' privily shoot at the upright in
22: 17 I m' tell all my bones: they look and
26: 7 That I m' publish with the voice of
27: 4 I m' dwell in the house of the Lord
30: 5 weeping m' endure for a night, but joy
12 that my glory m' sing praise to thee,
34: 12 loveth many days, that he m' see good?
39: 4 it is; that I m' know how frail I am.*
13 that I m' recover strength, before I go
41: 10 raise me up, that I m' requite them.
48: 13 that ye m' tell it to the generation
50: 4 the earth, that he m' judge his people.
51: 8 bones...thou hast broken m' rejoice.
56: 13 I m' walk before God in the light of
58: 8 woman, that they m' not see the sun.*
59: 13 consume them, that they m' not be:*
60: 4 m' be displayed because of the truth.
5 That thy beloved m' be delivered;
61: 7 and truth, which m' preserve him.
8 that I m' daily perform my vows.
64: 4 they m' shoot in secret at the perfect:
65: 4 thee, that he m' dwell in thy courts:
67: 2 That thy way m' be known upon earth,
68: 23 thy foot m' be dipped in the blood*
69: 35 that they m' dwell there, and have it*
71: 3 whereunto I m' continually resort:
73: 28 God, that I m' declare all thy works.
76: 7 and who m' stand in thy sight when
83: 4 the name of Israel m' be no more in
16 that they m' seek thy name, O Lord.
18 That men m' know that thou, whose
84: 3 nest...where she m' lay her young,
85: 6 that thy people m' rejoice in thee?
9 him; that glory m' dwell in our land.
86: 17 that they which hate me m' see it, and
90: 12 we m' apply our hearts unto wisdom.
14 we m' rejoice and be glad all our days.
101: 6 the land, that they m' dwell with me:
8 I m' cut off all wicked doers from the*
104: 9 set a bound that they m' not pass over;
14 m' bring forth food out of the earth;
106: 5 That I m' see the good of thy chosen,
5 that I m' rejoice in the gladness of thy
5 that I m' glory with thine inheritance.
107: 36 they m' prepare a city for habitation;
37 which m' yield fruits of increase. *
108: 6 That thy beloved m' be delivered:
109: 15 he m' cut off the memory of them from
27 they m' know that this is thy hand;
111: 6 he m' give them the heritage of the*
113: 8 he m' set him with princes, even with
119: 17 that I m' live, and keep thy word.
18 I m' behold wondrous things out of
73 that I m' learn thy commandments.
77 mercies come unto me, that I m' live:
116 according unto thy word, that I m' live:
125 that I m' know thy testimonies.
124: 1 was on our side, now m' Israel say;*
129: 1 me from my youth, m' Israel now say:*
142: 7 of prison, that I m' praise thy name:
144: 12 our sons m' be as plants grown up in*
12 our daughters m' be as corner stones,*
13 That our garners m' be full, affording*
13 our sheep m' bring forth thousands*
14 That our oxen m' be strong to labour;*
Pr 5: 2 and that thy lips m' keep knowledge.
7: 5 m' keep thee from the strange woman,
8: 11 all things that m' be desired are not to
21 I m' cause those that love me to inherit
15: 24 that he m' depart from hell beneath.
18: 2 but that his heart m' discover itself.
20: 21 An inheritance m' be gotten hastily at
22: 19 That thy trust m' be in the Lord, I
27: 1 knowest not what a day m' bring forth.

Pr 27:11 I m' answer him that reproacheth me.
Ec 1:10 there any thing whereof it m' be said.*
2:26 m' give to him that is good before God.
5:15 which he m' carry away in his hand.
6:10 neither m' he contend with him *3201
8: 4 and who m' say unto him, What doest
Ca 4:16 that the spices thereof m' flow out.
6: 1 aside? that we m' seek him with thee.
13 return, that we m' look upon thee.
Isa 5: 8 m' be placed alone in the midst of the*
11 that they m' follow strong drink;
19 hasten his work, that we m' see it:
19 nigh and come, that we m' know it!
7:15 he m' know to refuse the evil, and*
10: 2 people, that widows m' be their prey,
2 and that they m' rob the fatherless!
19 be few, that a child m' write them.
13: 2 they m' go into the gates of the nobles.
19:15 the head or tail, branch or rush, m' do.
24:10 is shut up, that no man m' come in.
26: 2 which keepeth the truth m' enter in.
27: 5 that he m' make peace with me;
28:12 ye m' cause the weary to rest; *
21 that he m' do his work, his strange
30: 1 my spirit, that they m' add sin to sin:
8 it m' be for the time to come for ever
18 wait, that he m' be gracious unto you,
18 that he m' have mercy upon you:
36:12 wall, that they m' eat their own dung,*
37: 4 It m' be the Lord thy God will hear the
20 all the kingdoms of the earth m' know
41:20 they m' see, and know, and consider,
22 that we m' consider them, and know
23 that we m' know that ye are gods:
23 that we m' be dismayed, and behold it
26 from the beginning, that we m' know?
26 that we m' say, He is righteous?
42:18 and look, ye blind, that ye m' see.
43: 9 witnesses, that they m' be justified:
10 that ye m' know and believe me, and
44: 9 nor know; that they m' be ashamed.
13 a man; that it m' remain in the house.*
45: 6 m' know from the rising of the sun,
46: 5 and compare me, that we m' be like?
49:15 yea, they m' forget, yet will I not forget
20 me: give place to me that I m' dwell.
51:14 exile hasteneth that he m' be loosed.*
16 that I m' plant the heavens, and lay
23 soul, Bow down, that we m' go over:
55: 6 Seek ye the Lord while he m' be found,
10 bud, that it m' give seed to the sower,*
60:11 that men m' bring unto thee the forces
11 and that their kings m' be brought.*
21 of my hands, that I m' be glorified.
64: 2 nations m' tremble at thy presence!
65: 8 sakes, that I m' not destroy them all.
66:11 That ye m' suck, and be satisfied with
11 that ye m' milk out, and be delighted
Jer 6:10 and give warning, that they m' hear?
7:18 that they m' provoke me to anger.
23 you, that it m' be well unto you.
9:12 wise man, that m' understand this?
12 hath spoken, that he m' declare it,
17 mourning women, that they m' come;
17 cunning women, that they m' come:
18 that our eyes m' run down with tears,
10:18 distress them, that they m' find it so.
11: 5 I m' perform the oath which I have
19 his name m' be no more remembered.
13:23 then m' ye also do good, that are 3201
26 thy face, that thy shame m' appear.*
16:12 that they m' not hearken unto me:*
21: 2 works, that he m' go up from us.
26: 3 that I m' repent me of the evil, which
28:14 they m' serve Nebuchadnezzar king
29: 6 that they m' bear sons and daughters;
6 that ye m' be increased there, and not*
32:14 that they m' continue many days.
39 one way, that they m' fear me for ever,
33:21 Then m' also my covenant be broken
35: 7 that ye m' live many days in the land
36: 3 It m' be that the house of Judah will
3 they m' return every man from his evil
3 I m' forgive their iniquity and their
7 It m' be they will present their
42: 3 the Lord thy God m' shew us the way
3 shew us the way wherein we m' walk,*
3 walk, and the thing that we m' do.*
6 that it m' be well with us, when we
12 that he m' have mercy upon you, and
44:29 ye m' know that my words shall surely
48: 9 Moab, that it m' flee and get away:
49:19 man, that I m' appoint over her? *
50:34 that he m' give rest to the land, and
44 man that I m' appoint over her?
51: 8 for her pain, if so be she m' be healed.
39 that they m' rejoice, and sleep a
La 2:13 that I m' comfort thee, O virgin
3:29 in the dust; if so be there m' be hope.
Eze 4:17 That they m' want bread and water,
6: 6 that your altars m' be laid waste and
6 and your idols m' be broken and cease,
6 and your images m' be cut down,
6 and your works m' be abolished.
8 ye m' have some that shall escape the*
11:20 That they m' walk in my statutes, and
12: 3 it m' be they will consider, though
16 they m' declare all their abominations
19 that her land m' be desolate from all
14: 5 I m' take the house of Israel in their
11 That the house of Israel m' go no more
11 but that they m' be my people, and I
11 I m' be their God, saith the Lord God.
15 no man m' pass through because of
16:33 they m' come unto thee on every side
37 that they m' see all thy nakedness.
Eze 20:20 m' know that I am the Lord your God.
21: 5 all flesh m' know that I the Lord*
10 it is furbished that it m' glitter:
11 to be furbished, that it m' be handled:
15 that their heart m' faint, and their
19 sword of the king of Babylon m' come:
20 that the sword m' come to Rabbath*
23 the iniquity, that they m' be taken.
22: 3 midst of it, that her time m' come,
23:48 all women m' be taught not to do after
24:11 the brass of it m' be hot, and m' burn,
11 the filthiness of it m' be molten in it,
11 it, that the scum of it m' be consumed.
25:10 the Ammonites m' not be remembered
28:17 before kings, that they m' behold thee.
37: 9 upon these slain, that they m' live.
38:16 that the heathen m' know me, when I
39:12 of them, that they m' cleanse the land.
17 that ye m' eat flesh, and drink blood.
43:10 they m' be ashamed of their iniquities:
11 they m' keep the whole form thereof,*
44:25 no husband, they m' defile themselves.
30 m' cause the blessing to rest in thine*
45:11 the bath m' contain the tenth part of
Da 4:17 the living m' know that the Most High
27 m' be a lengthening of thy tranquillity.
6:15 the king establisheth m' be changed.
Ho 8: 4 them idols, that they m' be cut off.
13:10 that m' save thee in all thy cities?
Am 5:14 good, and not evil, that ye m' live:
15 it m' be that the Lord God of hosts
6:10 we m' not make mention of the name
8: 5 moon be gone, that we m' sell corn?
5 that we m' set forth wheat, making
6 That we m' buy the poor for silver,
9: 1 of the door, that the posts m' shake:
12 they m' possess the remnant of Edom,
Ob 9 of Esau m' be cut off by slaughter.
Jon 1: 7 m' know for whose cause this evil is
11 thee, that the sea m' be calm unto us?
Mic 6: 5 ye m' know the righteousness of the
7: 3 m' do evil with both hands earnestly,
Hab 2: 2 tables, that he m' run that readeth it.
9 house, that he m' set his rest on high,
9 m' be delivered from the power of evil!
Zep 2: 3 it m' be ye shall be hid in the day of 194
3: 8 that I m' assemble the kingdoms, to
9 m' all call upon the name of the Lord,
Zec 11: 1 that the fire m' devour thy cedars.
Mal 3: 2 who m' abide the day of his coming?
3 m' offer unto the Lord an offering*
10 that there m' be meat in mine house,
M't 2: 8 that I m' come and worship him also.
5:16 that they m' see your good works, and
45 ye m' be the children of your Father
6: 2 that they m' have glory of men.
4 That thine alms m' be in secret: and
5 streets, that they m' be seen of men.
16 that they m' appear unto men to fast.
9: 6 that ye m' know that the Son of man
21 If I m' but touch his garment, I shall*
14:15 away, that they m' go into the villages,
18:16 witnesses every word m' be established.
19:16 shall I do, that I m' have eternal life?
20:21 Grant that these my two sons m' sit,
33 him, Lord, that our eyes m' be opened.
23:26 the outside of them m' be clean also.
35 you m' come all the righteous blood
26:42 if this cup m' not pass away from *1410
M'r 1:38 next towns, that I m' preach there also:
2:10 that ye m' know that the Son of man
4:12 That seeing they m' see, and not
12 and hearing they m' hear, and not
32 fowls of the air m' lodge under the*1410
5:12 the swine, that we m' enter into them.
23 hands on her, that she m' be healed;
28 If I m' touch but his clothes, I shall*
6:36 m' go into the country round about,
7: 9 that ye m' keep your own tradition.
10:17 shall I do that I m' inherit eternal life?
37 Grant unto us that we m' sit, one on
11:25 also which is in heaven m' forgive you
12:15 me? bring me a penny, that I m' see it.
14: 7 ye will ye m' do them good: but *1410
15:32 the cross, that we m' see and believe.
Lu 2:35 thoughts of many hearts m' be revealed.
5:24 that ye m' know that the Son of man
8:16 they which enter in m' see the light.
9:12 they m' go into the towns and country
11:33 they which come in m' see the light.
50 m' be required of this generation.
12:36 they m' open unto him immediately.*
14:10 he m' say unto thee, Friend, go up
23 to come in, that my house m' be filled.
16: 4 they m' receive me into their houses.
9 they m' receive you into everlasting
24 he m' dip the tip of his finger in water,
28 that he m' testify unto them, lest they
17: 8 Make ready wherewith I m' sup, and
18:41 said, Lord, that I m' receive my sight.
20:13 it m' be they will reverence him 2481
14 him, that the inheritance m' be ours.
21:22 which are written m' be fulfilled.
36 ye m' be accounted worthy to escape
22: 8 prepare us the passover, that we m' eat.
30 That ye m' eat and drink at my table
31 you, that he m' sift you as wheat:
Joh 1:22 that we m' give an answer to them
3:21 that his deeds m' be made manifest,
4:36 he that reapeth m' rejoice together.
5:20 works than these, that ye m' marvel.
6: 5 shall we buy bread, that these m' eat?
7 that every one of them m' take a little.
30 shewest thou then, that we m' see,
40 on him, m' have everlasting life: and*
50 that a man m' eat thereof, and not die.
Joh 7: 3 that thy disciples also m' see the works
10:38 that ye m' know, and believe, that the
11:11 I go, that I m' awake him out of sleep.
15 there, to the intent that ye m' believe;
16 us also go, that we m' die with him.
42 they m' believe that thou hast sent me.
12:36 that ye m' be the children of light.
13:18 but that the scripture m' be fulfilled.
19 to pass, ye m' believe that I am he.
14: 3 that where I am, there ye m' be also.
13 the Father m' be glorified in the Son.
16 that he m' abide with you for ever;
31 world m' know that I love the Father;
15: 2 it, that it m' bring forth more fruit.
16 Father in my name, he m' give it you.
16: 4 ye m' remember that I told you of
24 shall receive, that your joy m' be full.
17: 1 Son, that thy Son also m' glorify thee:
11 me, that they m' be one, as we are.
21 That they all m' be one; as thou,
21 in thee, that they also m' be one in us:
21 that the world m' believe that thou
22 that they m' be one, even as we are
23 that they m' be made perfect in one;
23 that the world m' know that thou hast
24 that they m' behold my glory, which
26 thou hast loved me m' be in them,
19: 4 that ye m' know I find no fault in him.
Ac 1:25 That they m' take part of this ministry*
3:19 that your sins m' be blotted out, when
4:29 all boldness they m' speak thy word.*
30 signs and wonders m' be done by the
6: 3 wisdom, whom we m' appoint over
8:19 hands, he m' receive the Holy Ghost.
20 the gift of God m' be purchased with*
22 thought of thine heart m' be forgiven*
17:19 M' we know what this new doctrine, 1410
19:40 whereby we m' give an account of* "
21:24 them, that they m' shave their heads:
24 and all m' know that those things,*
37 captain, M' I speak unto thee? 1832
23:24 them beasts, that they m' set Paul on,*
25:11 no man m' deliver me unto them. *1410
26:18 that they m' receive forgiveness of
Ro 1:11 I m' impart to you some spiritual gift,
11 gift, to the end ye m' be established;
12 that I m' be comforted together with
19 that which m' be known of God is
3: 8 Let us do evil, that good m' come?
19 that every mouth m' be stopped, and
19 world m' become guilty before God.
6: 1 continue in sin, that grace m' abound?
8:17 that we m' be also glorified together.
11:10 be darkened, that they m' not see,
14 any means I m' provoke to emulation
31 your mercy they also m' obtain mercy.
12: 2 that ye m' prove what is that good, and
14: 2 believeth that he m' eat all things:*
19 wherewith one m' edify another.
15: 6 ye m' with one mind and one mouth
13 m' abound in hope, through the power
17 I m' glory through Jesus Christ in*
31 That I m' be delivered from them that
31 I have for Jerusalem m' be accepted
32 That I m' come unto you with joy by
32 of God, and m' with you be refreshed.*
1Co 1: 8 m' be blameless in the day of our Lord*
2:16 of the Lord, that he m' instruct him?*
3:18 him become a fool, that he m' be wise.
5: 5 the spirit m' be saved in the day of the
7 old leaven, that ye m' be a new lump,
7: 5 that ye m' give yourselves to fasting
32 the Lord, how he m' please the Lord:
33 the world, how he m' please his wife.
34 that she m' be holy both in body and
34 world, how she m' please her husband.
35 not that I m' cast a snare upon you,
35 and that ye m' attend upon the Lord
9:18 I m' make the gospel of Christ without
24 the prize? So run, that ye m' obtain.
10:13 to escape, that ye m' be able to bear it.
33 profit of many, that they m' be saved.
11:19 m' be made manifest among you.
14: 1 gifts, but rather that ye m' prophesy.
5 that the church m' receive edifying.
10 There are, it m' be, so many kinds of
12 seek that ye m' excel to the edifying
13 tongue pray that he m' interpret.
31 For ye m' all prophesy one by one,*1410
31 all m' learn, and all m' be comforted.
15:28 under him, that God m' be all in all.
37 it m' chance of wheat, or of some
16: 6 And it m' be that I will abide, yea, and
6 that ye m' bring me on my journey
10 that he m' be with you without fear:*
11 in peace, that he m' come unto me:
2Co 1: 4 that we m' be able to comfort them
11 thanks m' be given by many on our
2: 5 part: that I m' not overcharge you all.*
4: 7 excellency of the power m' be of God,
5: 9 or absent, we m' be accepted of him.*
10 that every one m' receive the things
12 that ye m' have somewhat to answer
8:11 so there m' be a performance also out
14 your abundance m' be a supply for*
14 their abundance also m' be a supply
14 want: that there m' be equality:
9: 3 that, as I said, ye m' be ready:
8 things, m' abound to every good work:
10: 2 I m' not be bold when I am present
9 I m' not seem as if I would terrify you
11: 2 I m' present you as a chaste virgin to*
12 I m' cut off occasion from them which
12 glory, they m' be found even as we.
16 me, that I m' boast myself a little.
12: 9 the power of Christ m' rest upon me.

Ga 6:13 that they *m·* glory in your flesh.
Eph 1:17 *m·* give unto you the spirit of wisdom
18 *m·* know what is the hope of his calling,
3: 4 ye *m·* understand my knowledge *1410*
17 Christ *m·* dwell in your hearts by faith;
18 *M·* be able to comprehend with all
4:15 *m·* grow up into him in all things,
28 that he *m·* have to give to him that
29 it *m·* minister grace unto the hearers.
6: 3 That it *m·* be well with thee, and thou
11 *m·* be able to stand against the wiles
13 ye *m·* be able to withstand in the evil
19 that utterance *m·* be given unto me,
19 that I *m·* open my mouth boldly, to*
20 that therein I *m·* speak boldly, as I
21 But that ye also *m·* know my affairs,
Ph'p 1: 9 love *m·* abound yet more and more
10 *m·* approve things that are excellent;
10 ye *m·* be sincere and without offence
26 your rejoicing *m·* be more abundant in
27 I *m·* hear of your affairs, that ye
2:15 ye *m·* be blameless and harmless, the
16 that I *m·* rejoice in the day of Christ,
19 I also *m·* be of good comfort, when I
28 when ye see him again, ye *m·* rejoice,
28 and that I *m·* be the less sorrowful.
3: 8 them but dung, that I *m·* win Christ,
10 That I *m·* know him, and the power of
12 I *m·* apprehend that for which also I
21 that it *m·* be fashioned like unto his
4:17 fruit that *m·* abound to your account.*
Col 1:28 we *m·* present every man perfect in
4: 4 I *m·* make it manifest, as I ought to
6 ye *m·* know how ye ought to answer
12 that ye *m·* stand perfect and complete
1Th 3:13 To the end he *m·* stablish your hearts
4:12 ye *m·* walk honestly toward them that
12 and that ye *m·* have lack of nothing.
2Th 1: 5 that ye *m·* be counted worthy of the
12 our Lord Jesus Christ *m·* be glorified
3: 1 word of the Lord *m·* have free course,
2 we *m·* be delivered from unreasonable
14 with him, that he *m·* be ashamed.
1Ti 1:20 that they *m·* learn not to blaspheme.*
2: 2 we *m·* lead a quiet and peaceable life
4:15 that thy profiting *m·* appear to all.
5: 7 in charge, that they *m·* be blameless.
16 it *m·* relieve them that are widows
20 before all, that others also *m·* fear.
6:19 that they *m·* lay hold on eternal life.
2Ti 1: 4 thy tears, that I *m·* be filled with joy;
18 grant unto him that he *m·* find mercy*
2: 4 he *m·* please him who hath chosen
10 *m·* also obtain the salvation which is
26 And that they *m·* recover themselves
3:17 That the man of God *m·* be perfect,
4:16 that it *m·* not be laid to their charge.
Tit 1: 9 that he *m·* be able by sound doctrine
13 that they *m·* be sound in the faith;
2: 4 they *m·* teach the young women to be
8 is of the contrary part *m·* be ashamed,
10 they *m·* adorn the doctrine of God our
Ph'm 6 of thy faith *m·* become effectual by
Heb 4:16 we *m·* obtain mercy, and find grace
5: 1 he *m·* offer both gifts and sacrifices for
7: 9 And as I *m·* so say, Levi also, who*
10: 9 first, that he *m·* establish the second.
12:27 which cannot be shaken *m·* remain.
28 whereby we *m·* serve God acceptably
13: 6 So that we *m·* boldly say, The Lord is*
17 that they *m·* do it with joy, and not
19 I *m·* be restored to you the sooner.
Jas 1: 4 ye *m·* be perfect and entire, wanting
2:18 Yea, a man *m·* say, Thou hast faith,*
3: 3 horses' mouths, that they *m·* obey us;
4: 3 ye *m·* consume it upon your lusts.
5:16 one for another, that ye *m·* be healed.
1Pe 2: 2 of the word, that ye *m·* grow thereby:
12 they *m·* by your good works, which
15 with well doing ye *m·* put to silence*
3: 1 they also *m·* without the word be won
16 *m·* be ashamed that falsely accuse
4: 3 *m·* suffice us to have wrought the will
11 that God in all things *m·* be glorified
13 ye *m·* be glad also with exceeding
5: 6 God, that he *m·* exalt you in due time:
8 about, seeking whom he *m·* devour:
2Pe 1:15 that ye *m·* be able after my decease
3: 2 That ye *m·* be mindful of the words*
14 be diligent that ye *m·* be found of him
1Jo 1: 3 ye also *m·* have fellowship with us:
4 we unto you, that your joy *m·* be full.
2:28 we *m·* have confidence, and not be
4:17 that we *m·* have boldness in the day of
5:13 ye *m·* know that ye have eternal life,
13 ye *m·* believe on the name of the Son*
20 that we *m·* know him that is true;*
2Jo 1:12 face to face, that our joy *m·* be full.
Re 2:10 of you into prison, that ye *m·* be tried;
14:13 that they *m·* rest from their labours;
19:18 That ye *m·* eat the flesh of kings, and
22:14 they *m·* have right to the tree of life,
14 *m·* enter in through the gates into the

mayest
Ge 2:16 tree of the garden thou *m·* freely eat:
23: 6 but that thou *m·* bury thy dead.
28: 3 that thou *m·* be a multitude of people;
4 thou *m·* inherit the land wherein thou
38:16 me, that thou *m·* come in unto me?
Ex 3:10 that thou *m·* bring forth my people
8:10 *m·* know that there is none like unto
22 thou *m·* know that I am the Lord in
9:14 *m·* know that there is none like me
29 *m·* know...that the earth is the Lord's.
10: 2 thou *m·* tell in the ears of thy son, and
18:19 thou *m·* bring the causes unto God:*
Ex 24:12 written; that thou *m·* teach them.
26:33 *m·* bring in thither within the vail*
Le 22:23 *m·* thou offer for a free will offering;
Nu 10: 2 thou *m·* use them for the calling of*
31 and thou *m·* be to us instead of eyes.*
23:13 place, from whence thou *m·* see them:
27 thou *m·* curse me them from thence.
De 2:31 possess, that thou *m·* inherit his land.
4:40 that thou *m·* prolong thy days upon
6:18 *m·* go in and possess the good land
7:22 thou *m·* not consume them at once. 3201
8: 9 out of whose hills thou *m·* dig brass.
11:14 thou *m·* gather in thy corn, and thy
15 cattle, that thou *m·* eat and be full.*
12:15 thou *m·* kill and eat flesh in all thy
17 Thou *m·* not eat within thy gates 3201
20 thou *m·* eat flesh, whatsoever thy soul
23 thou *m·* not eat the life with the flesh.*
14:21 eat it; or thou *m·* sell it unto an alien:
23 thou *m·* learn to fear the Lord thy God
15: 3 Of a foreigner thou *m·* exact it again:
16: 3 thou *m·* remember the day when thou
5 Thou *m·* not sacrifice the passover 3201
20 that thou *m·* live, and inherit the land
17:15 *m·* not set a stranger over thee, 3021
20:19 for thou *m·* eat of them, and thou shalt
22: 3 likewise: thou *m·* not hide thyself. 3201
7 and that thou *m·* prolong thy days.
23:20 a stranger thou *m·* lend upon usury:
24 *m·* eat grapes thy fill at thine own
25 *m·* pluck the ears with thine hand;
26:19 that thou *m·* be an holy people unto the
27: 3 thou *m·* go in unto the land which
28:58 *m·* fear this glorious and fearful name,
30: 6 with all thy soul, that thou *m·* live.
14 and in thy heart, that thou *m·* do it.
16 that thou *m·* live and multiply: and
20 That thou *m·* love the Lord thy God,*
20 and that thou *m·* obey his voice, and*
20 and that thou *m·* cleave unto him:*
20 thou *m·* dwell in the land which the
Jos 1: 7 thou *m·* observe to do according to all*
7 *m·* prosper wheresoever thou goest.
8 *m·* observe to do according to all that
J'g 9:33 *m·* thou do to them as thou shalt find
11: 8 that thou *m·* go with us, and fight
19: 9 on your way, that thou *m·* go home.
1Sa 20:13 thee away, that thou *m·* go in peace:
24: 4 *m·* do to him as it shall seem good*
28:15 *m·* make known unto me what I shall
22 *m·* have strength, when thou goest on
2Sa 3:21 *m·* reign over all that thine heart
15:34 *m·* thou for me defeat the counsel of
22:28 that thou *m·* bring them down.
1Ki 1:12 thou *m·* save thine own life, and the
2: 3 *m·* prosper in all that thou doest, and
31 thou *m·* take away the innocent blood,
8:29 *m·* hearken unto the prayer which thy*
2Ki 5: 6 thou *m·* recover him of his leprosy.
8:10 unto him, Thou *m·* certainly recover:
1Ch 22:12 *m·* keep the law of the Lord thy God.
14 I prepared; and thou *m·* add thereto.
2Ch 1:11 thyself, that thou *m·* judge my people,
18:33 that thou *m·* carry me out of the host;*
Ezr 7:17 thou *m·* buy speedily with this money*
Ne 1: 6 that thou *m·* hear the prayer of thy
6: 6 that thou *m·* be their king, according*
Job 40: 8 me, that thou *m·* be righteous?
Ps 32: 6 thee in a time when thou *m·* be found:
45:16 thou *m·* make princes in all the earth.*
94:13 That thou *m·* give him rest from the
104:27 thou *m·* give them their meat in due
130: 4 with thee, that thou *m·* be feared.
Pr 2:20 thou *m·* walk in the way of good men,
5: 2 That thou *m·* regard discretion, and
19:20 that thou *m·* be wise in thy latter end.
Isa 23:16 songs, that thou *m·* be remembered.
43:26 declare thou, that thou *m·* be justified.
45: 3 that thou *m·* know that I, the Lord,
47:12 able to profit, if so be thou *m·* prevail.
49: 6 thou *m·* be my salvation unto the end
9 That thou *m·* say to the prisoners, Go*
Jer 4:14 wickedness, that thou *m·* be saved.
6:27 that thou *m·* know and try their way.
30:13 thy cause, that thou *m·* be bound up:
Eze 16:54 That thou *m·* bear thine own shame,
54 *m·* be confounded in all that thou hast
63 That thou *m·* remember, and be
Hab 2:15 that thou *m·* look on their nakedness!
M'r 14:12 prepare that thou *m·* eat the passover?
Lu 12:58 that thou *m·* be delivered from him;*
16: 2 for thou *m·* be no longer steward. *1410*
Ac 8:37 with all thine heart, thou *m·*. *1832*
24: 8 *m·* take knowledge of all these things,*
11 Because that thou *m·* understand,*
1Co 7:21 but if thou *m·* be made free, use *1410*
Eph 6: 3 and thou *m·* live long on the earth.
1Ti 3:15 that thou *m·* know how thou oughtest
3Jo 2 that thou *m·* prosper and be in health,
Re 3:18 tried in the fire, that thou *m·* be rich;
18 that thou *m·* be clothed, and that the
18 eyes with eyesalve, that thou *m·* see.

maze See AMAZE.

Mazzaroth (*maz'-za-roth*)
Job 38:32 thou bring forth *M·* in his season? 4216

me See in the APPENDIX.

meadow See also MEADOWS.
Ge 41: 2 fatfleshed; and they fed in a *m·*. * 260
18 well favoured; and they fed in a *m·*.* "

meadows
J'g 20:33 even out of the *m·* of Gibeah. *4629

Meah (*me'-ah*)
Ne 3: 1 the tower of *M·* they sanctified it,*3968
12:39 the tower of *M·*, even unto the * "

meal See also MEALTIME.
Ge 18: 6 three measures of fine *m·*, 7058,5560
Nu 5:15 part of an ephah of barley *m·*; 7058
1Ki 4:22 and threescore measures of *m·*, "
17:12 but an handful of *m·* in a barrel, "
14 barrel of *m·* shall not waste, neither"
16 the barrel of *m·* wasted not, neither"
2Ki 4:41 But he said, Then bring *m·*. And "
1Ch 12:40 meat, *m·*, cakes of figs, and bunches "
Isa 47: 2 Take the millstones, and grind *m·*: "
Ho 8: 7 stalk: the bud shall yield no *m·*: "
M't 13:33 and hid in three measures of *m·*, *224*
Lu 13:21 and hid in three measures of *m·*, "

mealtime
Ru 2:14 her, At *m·* come thou hither, 6256,400

mean See also MEANEST; MEANETH; MEANING; MEANS; MEANT.
Ex 12:26 unto you, What *m·* ye by this service?
De 6:20 What *m·* the testimonies, and the
Jos 4: 6 saying, What *m·* ye by these stones?
21 to come, saying, What *m·* these stones?
1Ki 18:45 came to pass in the *m·* while,*5704,3541
Pr 22:29 he shall not stand before *m·* men. 2823
Isa 2: 9 the *m·* man boweth down, and the 120
3:15 *m·* ye that ye beat my people to pieces,
5:15 the *m·* man shall be brought down, 120
31: 8 the sword, not of a *m·* man, shall * "
Eze 17:12 Know ye not what these things *m·*?
18: 2 What *m·* ye, that ye use this proverb
M'r 9:10 rising from the dead should *m·*. *2076*
Lu 12: 1 In the *m·* time, when there were
Joh 4:31 the *m·* while his disciples prayed *3342*
Ac 10:17 vision...he had seen should *m·*. *1498*
17:20 know...what these things *m·*. *2309,1511*
21:13 What *m·* ye to weep and to break *4160*
39 in Cilicia, a citizen of no *m·* city: *767*
Ro 2:15 thoughts the *m·* while accusing *3342*
2Co 8:13 I *m·* not that other men be eased, and*

meanest
Ge 33: 8 What *m·* thou by all this drove which
2Sa 16: 2 unto Ziba, What *m·* thou by these?
Eze 37:18 not shew us what thou *m·* by these?
Jon 1: 6 unto him, What *m·* thou, O sleeper?

meaneth
De 29:24 what *m·* the heat of this great anger?
1Sa 4: 6 What *m·* the noise of this great shout
14 What *m·* the noise of this tumult?
15:14 *m·* then this bleating of the sheep
Isa 10: 7 Howbeit he *m·* not so, neither 1819
M't 9:13 But go ye and learn what that *m·*, *2076*
12: 7 But if ye had known what this *m·*, "
Ac 2:12 one to another, What *m·* this? *2309,1511*

meaning
Da 8:15 the vision, and sought for the *m·*, * 998
Ac 27: 2 *m·* to sail by the coasts of Asia; *3195*
1Co 14:11 if I know not the *m·* of the voice, *1411*

means
Ex 34: 7 that will by no *m·* clear the guilty;
Nu 14:18 and by no *m·* clearing the guilty,
J'g 5:22 broken by *m·* of the pransings, the*
16: 5 by what *m·* we may prevail against
2Sa 14:14 yet doth he devise *m·*, that his 4284
1Ki 10:29 they bring them out by their *m·*. 3027
20:39 if by any *m·* he be missing, then shall
2Ch 1:17 for the kings of Syria, by their *m·*. 3027
Ezr 4:16 by this *m·* thou shalt have no 6903
Ps 49: 7 can by any *m·* redeem his brother,
Pr 6:26 For by *m·* of a whorish woman a *1157
Jer 5:31 the priests bear rule by their *m·*; 3027
Mal 1: 9 this hath been by your *m·*: will he "
M't 5:26 Thou shalt by no *m·* come out *3361*
Lu 5:18 and they sought *m·* to bring him in,*
8:36 by what *m·* he that was possessed**4459*
10:19 nothing shall by any *m·* hurt you.**3364*
Joh 9:21 But by what *m·* he now seeth, we **4459*
Ac 4: 9 by what *m·* he is made whole;
18:21 I must by all *m·* keep this feast *3843*
27:12 if by any *m·* they might attain to *4458*
Ro 1:10 if by any *m·* now at length I might "
11:14 If by any *m·* I may provoke to "
1Co 8: 9 heed lest by any *m·* this liberty of "
9:22 that I might by all *m·* save some. *3843*
27 lest that by any *m·*, when I have *4458*
2Co 1:11 upon us by the *m·* of many persons
11: 3 lest by any *m·*, as the serpent *4458*
Ga 2: 2 lest by any *m·* I should run, or had "
Ph'p 3:11 If by any *m·* I might attain unto "
1Th 3: 5 lest by some *m·* the tempter have "
2Th 2: 3 no man deceive you by any *m·*: **5158*
3:16 give you peace always by all *m·*. * "
Heb 9:15 testament, that by *m·* of death, **1096*
Re 13:14 by the *m·* of those miracles which he*

meant
Ge 50:20 God *m·* it unto good, to bring to 2803
Lu 15:26 and asked what these things *m·*. *1498*
18:36 pass by, he asked what it *m·*. "

meanwhile See MEAN and WHILE.

Mearah (*me'-a-rah*)
Jos 13: 4 *M·* that is beside the Sidonians, 4632

measure See also MEASURED; MEASURES; MEASURING.
Ex 26: 2 the curtains shall have one *m·*. 4060
8 curtains shall be all of one *m·*. "
Le 19:35 in meteyard, in weight, or in *m·*. 4884
Nu 35: 5 ye shall *m·* from without the city 4058
De 21: 2 they shall *m·* unto the cities which "
25:15 and just *m·* shalt thou have: that 374
Jos 3: 4 about two thousand cubits by *m·*: 4060
1Ki 6:25 were of one *m·* and one size. "
7:37 one casting, one *m·*, and one size. "

2Ki 7: 1 shall a m· of fine flour be sold for 5429
16 So a m· of fine flour was sold for a "
18 a m· of fine flour for a shekel, shall "
1Ch 23: 29 and for all manner of m· and size; 4884
2Ch 3: 3 first m· was threescore cubits, 4060
Job 11: 9 The m· thereof is longer than the 4055
28: 25 he weigheth the waters by m·. 4060
Ps 39: 4 and the m· of my days, what it is; "
80: 5 them tears to drink in great m·. 7991
Isa 5: 14 opened her mouth without m·: 2706
27: 8 In m·, when it shooteth forth, 5432
40: 12 the dust of the earth in a m·, and 7991
65: 7 I m· their former work into their 4058
Jer 30: 11 but I will correct thee in m·, and †4941
46: 28 end of thee, but correct thee in m·;† "
51: 13 and the m· of thy covetousness. 520
Eze 4: 11 Thou shalt drink also water by m·, 4884
16 and they shall drink water by m·, "
40: 10 side; they three were of one m·: 4060
10 the posts had one m· on this side "
21 were after the m· of the first gate: "
22 were after the m· of the gate that "
41: 17 about within and without, by m·. "
43: 10 and let them m· the pattern. 4058
45: 3 of this m· shalt thou...the length 4060
3 of this...shalt thou m· the length 4058
11 and the bath shall be of one m·, 8506
11 the m· thereof shall be after the 4971
46: 22 these four corners were of one m·. 4060
47: 18 east side ye shall m· from Hauran, 4058
Mic 6: 10 the scant m· that is abominable? 374
Zec 2: 2 To m· Jerusalem, to see what is 4058
M't 7: 2 and with what m· ye mete, it shall 3358
23: 32 Fill ye up then the m· of your "
M'r 4: 24 With what m· ye mete, it shall be "
6: 51 in themselves beyond m·, and *4053
7: 37 And were beyond m· astonished, 5249
10: 26 they were astonished out of m·, *4057
Lu 6: 38 good m·, pressed down, and 3358
38 For with the same m· that ye mete "
Joh 3: 34 not the Spirit by m· unto him. "
Ro 12: 3 dealt to every man the m· of faith. "
2Co 1: 8 we were pressed out of m·, *5236
10: 13 not boast of things without our m·, 280
13 but according to the m· of the rule 3358
13 to us, a m· to reach even unto you. "
14 stretch not ourselves beyond our m·,
15 boasting of things without our m·, 280
11: 23 in stripes above m·, in prisons 5234
12: 7 lest I should be exalted above m· *
7 lest I should be exalted above m·. *
Ga 1: 13 beyond m· I persecuted the 5236
Eph 4: 7 to the m· of the gift of Christ. 3358
13 the m· of the stature of the fulness "
16 working in the m· of every part, "
Re 6: 6 A m· of wheat for a penny, and 5518
11: 1 Rise, and m· the temple of God, 3354
2 temple leave out, and m· it not; "
21: 15 had a golden reed to m· the city, "
17 according to the m· of a man, that 3358

measured

Ru 3: 15 it, he m· six measures of barley, 4058
2Sa 8: 2 Moab, and m· them with a line, "
2 even with two lines m· he to put to "
Isa 40: 12 hath m· the waters in the hollow "
Jer 31: 37 If heaven above can be m·, and the "
33: 22 neither the sand of the sea m·: "
Eze 40: 5 he m· the breadth of the building, "
6 and m· the threshold of the gate, "
8 He m· also the porch of the gate "
9 Then m· he the porch of the gate, "
11 And he m· the breadth of the entry "
13 He m· then the gate from the roof "
19 Then he m· the breadth from the "
20 he m· the length thereof, and the "
23 m· from gate to gate an hundred "
24 and he m· the posts thereof and the "
27 and he m· from gate to gate toward "
28 and he m· the south gate according "
32 and he m· the gate according to "
35 gate, and m· it according to these "
47 So he m· the court, an hundred "
48 and m· each post of the porch, five "
41: 1 and m· the posts, six cubits broad "
2 and he m· the length thereof, forty "
3 inward, and m· the post of the door, "
4 So he m· the length thereof, twenty "
5 After he m· the wall of the house, "
13 So he m· the house, an hundred "
15 And he m· the length of the building "
42: 15 the east, and m· it round about. "
16 He m· the east side with the "
17 He m· the north side, five hundred "
18 He m· the south side, five hundred "
19 and m· five hundred reeds with the "
20 He m· it by the four sides: it had a "
47: 3 eastward he m· a thousand cubits, "
4, 4 Again he m· a thousand, and "
5 Afterward he m· a thousand; and "
Ho 1: 10 which cannot be m· nor numbered; "
Hab 3: 6 He stood, and m· the earth: he 4128
M't 7: 2 mete, it shall be m· to you again. 488
M'r 4: 24 ye mete, it shall be m· to you: 3354
Lu 6: 38 withal it shall be m· to you again. 488
Re 21: 16 and he m· the city with the reed, 3354
17 he m· the wall thereof, an hundred "

measures

Ge 18: 6 quickly three m· of fine meal, 5429
De 25: 14 not have in thine house divers m·, 374
Ru 3: 15 he measured six m· of barley, and
17 These six m· of barley gave he me;
1Sa 25: 18 five m· of parched corn, and an 5429
1Ki 4: 22 one day was thirty m· of fine flour, 3734
22 flour, and threescore m· of meal, "
5: 11 Hiram twenty thousand m· of wheat "

1Ki 5: 11 and twenty m· of pure oil: 3734
7: 9 to the m· of hewed stones, *4060
11 after the m· of hewed stones, and* "
18: 32 as would contain two m· of seed. 5429
2Ki 7: 1, 16 and two m· of barley for a shekel, "
18 Two m· of barley for a shekel, and "
2Ch 2: 10 thousand m· of beaten wheat, and 3734
10 twenty thousand m· of barley, and "
27: 5 ten thousand m· of wheat, and ten "
Ezr 7: 22 and to an hundred m· of wheat, and "
Job 38: 5 Who hath laid the m· thereof, if 4461
Pr 20: 10 Divers weights, and divers m·, 374
Jer 13: 25 the portion of thy m· from me, *4055
Eze 40: 24 thereof according to these m·. 4060
28 south gate according to these m·; "
29 thereof, according to these m·: "
32 the gate according to these m·. "
33 thereof, were according to these m·: "
35 measured it according to these m·; "
43: 13 these are the m· of the altar after "
48: 16 And these shall be the m· thereof; "
30 four thousand and five hundred m·:* "
33 four thousand and five hundred m·:* "
35 round about eighteen thousand m·:*
Hag 2: 16 one came to an heap of twenty m·,
M't 13: 33 took, and hid in three m· of meal, 4568
Lu 13: 21 took and hid in three m· of meal, "
16: 6 And he said, An hundred m· of oil. 943
7 he said, An hundred m· of wheat. 2884
Re 6: 6 three m· of barley for a penny; 5518

measuring

Jer 31: 39 the m· line shall yet go forth over 4060
Eze 40: 3 of flax in his hand, and a m· reed; "
5 in the man's hand a m· reed of six "
42: 15 made an end of m· the inner house, "
16 the east side with the m· reed, "
16, 17 with the m· reed round about. "
18 hundred reeds, with the m· reed. "
19 hundred reeds with the m· reed. "
Zec 2: 1 a man with a m· line in his hand. "
2Co 10: 12 they m· themselves by themselves, 3354

measuring-line See MEASURING and LINE.

meat See also MEATS.

Ge 1: 29 seed; to you it shall be for m·. ‡ 402
30 have given every green herb for m·: ‡ "
9: 3 that liveth shall be m· for you; "
27: 4 make me savoury m·, such as I ‡
7 make me savoury m·, that I may ‡
9 make them savoury m· for thy ‡
14 and his mother made savoury m·, ‡
17 she gave the savoury m· and the ‡
31 And he also had made savoury m·, ‡
45: 23 laden with corn and bread and m· *4202
Ex 29: 41 to the m· offering of the morning,*
30: 9 nor burnt sacrifice, nor m· offering;*
40: 29 burnt offering and the m· offering;*
Le 2: 1 when any will offer a m· offering *
3 remnant of the m· offering shall be*
4 bring an oblation of a m· offering *
5 And if thy oblation be a m· offering*
6 oil thereon: it is a m· offering. *
7 And if thy oblation be a m· offering*
8 thou shalt bring the m· offering *
9 shall take from the m· offering *
10 that which is left of the m· offering*
11 No m· offering, which ye shall bring*
13 every oblation of thy m· offering *
13 to be lacking from thy m· offering:*
14 offer a m· offering of thy firstfruits*
14 thou shalt offer for the m· offering*
15 thereon: it is a m· offering. *
5: 13 be the priest's, as a m· offering. *
6: 14 this is the law of the m· offering: *
15 of the flour of the m· offering, *
15 which is upon the m· offering, *
20 flour for a m· offering perpetual, *
21 the baken pieces of the m· offering*
23 every m· offering for the priest *
7: 9 And all the m· offering that is baken*
10 every m· offering, mingled with oil,*
37 burnt offering, of the m· offering, *
9: 4 and a m· offering mingled with oil:*
17 he brought the m· offering, and took*
10: 12 Take the m· offering that remaineth*
11: 34 Of all m· which may be eaten, that* 400
14: 10 deals of fine flour for a m· offering,*
20 and the m· offering upon the altar:*
21 mingled with oil for a m· offering,*
31 offering, with the m· offering: *
22: 11 house: they shall eat of his m·. *3899
13 she shall eat of her father's m·: * "
23: 13 the m· offering thereof shall be *
16 shall offer a new m· offering unto *
18 the Lord, with their m· offering, *
37 a burnt offering, and a m· offering,*
25: 6 of the land shall be m· for you; * 402
7 all the increase thereof be m·. * 398
Nu 4: 16 and the daily m· offering, *
6: 15 and their m· offering, and their *
17 shall offer also his m· offering, *
7: 13, 19, 25, 31, 37, 43, 49, 55, 61, 67, 73, 79 flour
mingled with oil for a m· offering:*
87 twelve, with their m· offering: *
8: 8 young bullock with his m· offering,*
15: 4 bring a m· offering of a tenth deal*
6 shalt prepare for a m· offering *
9 a m· offering of three tenth deals of*
24 with his m· offering, and his drink*
18: 9 every m· offering of theirs, and *
28: 5 ephah of flour for a m· offering, *
8 as the m· offering of the morning,*
9, 12, 12 of flour for a m· offering, *
13 mingled with oil for a m· offering*
20 their m· offering shall be of flour *

Nu 28: 24 m· of the sacrifice made by fire, *3899
26 when ye bring a new m· offering *
28 m· offering of flour mingled with *
31 offering, and his m· offering, *
29: 3 their m· offering shall be of flour *
6 his m· offering, and the daily burnt*
6 and his m· offering, and their drink*
9 their m· offerings shall be of flour*
11 and the m· offering of it, and their*
14 their m· offering shall be of flour *
16 his m· offering, and his drink *
18 their m· offering and their drink *
19 the m· offering thereof, and their *
21 their m· offering and their drink *
22 burnt offering, and his m· offering,*
24 Their m· offering and their drink *
25 burnt offering, his m· offering, and*
27 their m· offering and their drink *
28 and his m· offering, and his drink*
30 their m· offering and their drink *
31 his m· offering, and his drink *
33 their m· offering and their drink *
34 his m· offering, and his drink *
37 Their m· offering and their drink *
38 and his m· offering, and his drink*
39 for your m· offerings, and for your*
De 2: 6 Ye shall buy m· of them for money, *400
28 Thou shalt sell me m· for money, * "
20: 20 that they be not trees for m·, thou‡3978
28: 26 thy carcase shall be m· unto all "
Jos 22: 23 burnt offering or m· offering, *
29 burnt offerings, for m· offerings, or*
J'g 1: 7 off, gathered their m· under my table: ‡
13: 19 took a kid with a m· offering, and*
23 and a m· offering at our hands, *
14: 14 Out of the eater came forth m·, ‡3978
1Sa 20: 5 not fail to sit with the king at m·: 398
24 the king sat him down to eat m·. 3899
27 cometh not the son of Jesse to m·, "
34 did eat no m· the second day of the‡ "
2Sa 3: 35 to eat m· while it was yet day, * "
11: 8 him a mess of m· from the king, ‡
12: 3 it did eat of his own m·, and drank‡6595
13: 5 Tamar come, and give me m·, *3899
5 dress the m· in my sight, that I *1279
7 Amnon's house, and dress him m·.* "
10 Bring the m· into the chamber, * "
1Ki 8: 64, 64 offerings, and m· offerings, *
10: 5 the m· of his table, and the sitting‡3978
19: 8 the strength of that m· forty days ‡ 396
2Ki 3: 20 when the m· offering was offered, *
16: 13 burnt offering, and his m· offering,*
15 evening m· offering, and the king's*
15 and his m· offering, with the burnt*
15 their m· offering, and their drink *
1Ch 12: 40 on oxen, and m·, meal, cakes of *3978
21: 23 and the wheat for the m· offering;*
23: 29 fine flour for m· offering, and for *
2Ch 7: 7 and the m· offerings, and the fat. *
9: 4 And the m· of his table, and the ‡3978
Ezr 3: 7 and m·, and drink, and oil, unto ‡ "
7: 17 their m· offerings and their drink*
Ne 10: 33 for the continual m· offering, and*
13: 5 aforetime they laid the m· offerings,*
9 m· offering and the frankincense,*
Job 6: 7 to touch are as my sorrowful m·. ‡3899
12: 11 words? and the mouth taste his m·? ‡400
20: 14 his m· in his bowels is turned, it ‡3899
21 There shall none of his m· be left; *400
30: 4 and juniper roots for their m·. ‡3899
33: 20 bread, and his soul dainty m·. ‡3978
34: 3 words, as the mouth tasteth m·. ‡ 398
36: 31 people; he giveth m· in abundance. ‡400
38: 41 God, they wander for lack of m·. ‡ "
Ps 42: 3 My tears have been my m· day ‡3899
44: 11 us like sheep appointed for m·; ‡3978
59: 15 them wander up and down for m·, ‡ 398
69: 21 They gave me also gall for my m·; ‡1267
74: 14 gavest him to be m· to the people ‡3978
78: 18 heart by asking m· for their lust. ‡ 400
25 food: he sent them m· to the full. ‡6720
30 their m· was yet in their mouths, ‡ 400
79: 2 servants have they given to be m· ‡3978
104: 21 prey, and seek their m· from God. ‡ 400
27 give them their m· in due season. ‡ "
107: 18 soul abhorreth all manner of m·; ‡ "
111: 5 hath given m· unto them that fear‡2964
145: 15 givest them their m· in due season. ‡400
Pr 6: 8 Provideth her m· in the summer, ‡3899
23: 3 dainties: for they are deceitful m·. ‡ "
30: 22 and a fool when he is filled with m·; ‡ "
25 prepare their m· in the summer; ‡ "
31: 15 giveth m· to her household, and a ‡2964
Isa 57: 6 thou hast offered a m· offering. *
62: 8 no more give thy corn to be m· ‡3978
65: 25 dust shall be the serpent's m·. ‡3899
Jer 7: 33 carcases of this people shall be m· 3978
16: 4 carcases shall be m· for the fowls "
17: 26 and m· offerings, and incense, and*
19: 7 will I give to be m· for the fowls 3978
33: 18 to kindle m· offerings, and to do *
34: 20 dead bodies shall be for m· unto 3978
La 1: 11 given their pleasant things for m· ‡ 400
19 they sought their m· to relieve ‡ "
4: 10 were their m· in the destruction ‡1262
Eze 4: 10 thy m· which thou shalt eat shall ‡3978
16: 19 My m· also which I gave thee, *3899
29: 5 given thee for m· to the beasts of ‡ 402
34: 5 became m· to all the beasts of the‡ "
8 flock became m· to every beast of ‡ "
10 that they may not be m· for them. ‡ "
42: 13 holy things, and the m· offering, *
44: 29 They shall eat the m· offering, and*
45: 15 for a m· offering, and for a burnt *
17 burnt offerings, and m· offerings, *
17 and the m· offering, and the burnt*

Eze 45: 24 he shall prepare a m· offering of an*
25 according to the m· offering, and *
46: 5 m· offering shall be an ephah for *
5 the m· offering for the lambs as he*
7 he shall prepare a m· offering, an*
11 the m· offering shall be an ephah *
14 shalt prepare a m· offering for it *
14 a m· offering continually by a *
15 the m· offering, and the oil, every *
20 they shall bake the m· offering; *
47: 12 shall grow all trees for m·, whose ‡3978
12 the fruit thereof shall be for m·, ‡ "
Da 1: 5 a daily provision of the king's m·,‡6598
8 with the portion of the king's m·, ‡ "
10 hath appointed your m· and your ‡3978
13 eat of the portion of the king's m·: ‡6598
15 eat the portion of the king's m·. ‡ "
16 took away the portion of their m·,‡ "
4: 12 much, and in it was m· for all: ‡4203
21 much, and in it was m· for all; ‡ "
11: 26 feed of the portion of his m· shall ‡6598
Ho 11: 4 their jaws, and I laid m· unto them.‡398
Joel 1: 9 The m· offering and the drink *
13 for the m· offering and the drink *
16 Is not the m· cut off before our ‡ 400
2: 14 a m· offering and a drink offering *
Am 5: 22 offerings and your m· offerings, *
Hab 1: 16 is fat, and their m· plenteous. ‡3978
3: 17 and the fields shall yield no m·; ‡ 400
Hag 2: 12 pottage, or wine, or oil, or any m·,‡3978
Mal 1: 12 even his m·, is contemptible. ‡ 400
3: 10 there may be m· in mine house, ‡2964
M't 3: 4 his m· was locusts and wild honey.*5160
6: 25 Is not the life more than m·, and * "
9: 10 as Jesus sat at m· in the house,
10: 10 the workman is worthy of his m·. *5160
14: 9 and them which sat with him at m·,
15: 37 broken m· that was left seven baskets*
24: 45 to give them m· in due season? *5160
25: 35 an hungred, and ye gave me m·: 5315
42 hungred, and ye gave me no m·: "
26: 7 poured it on his head, as he sat at m·.
M'r 2: 15 as Jesus sat at m· in his house,
8: 8 broken m· that was left seven baskets.*
14: 3 as he sat at m·, there came a woman
16: 14 unto the eleven as they sat at m·,
Lu 3: 11 and he that hath m·, let him do *1033
7: 36 Pharisee's house, and sat down to m·.
37 sat at m· in the Pharisee's house,
49 they that sat at m· with him began to
8: 55 and he commanded to give her m·.*5315
9: 13 go and buy m· for all this people. *1033
11: 37 and he went in, and sat down to m·.
12: 23 The life is more than m·, and the *5160
37 and make them to sit down to m·,
42 their portion of m· in due season?*4620
14: 10 of them that sit at m· with thee.
15 them that sat at m· with him heard
17: 7 from the field, Go and sit down to m·?
22: 27 is greater, he that sitteth at m·, or
27 serveth? is not he that sitteth at m·?
24: 30 as he sat at m· with them, he took
41 unto them, Have ye here any m·? *1034
Joh 4: 8 away unto the city to buy m·.) *5160
32 have m· to eat that ye know not of.1035
34 My m· is to do the will of him that 1033
6: 27 not for the m· which perisheth, 1035
27 m· which endureth unto everlasting "
55 For my flesh is m· indeed, and my "
21: 5 them, Children, have ye any m·? *4371
Ac 2: 46 did eat their m· with gladness and*5160
9: 19 received m·, he was strengthened.* "
16: 34 set m· before them, and rejoiced, 5132
27: 33 besought them all to take m·, *5160
34 I pray you to take some m·: for * "
36 cheer, and they also took some m·.* "
Ro 14: 15 brother be grieved with thy m·, 1033
15 Destroy not him with thy m·, for "
17 the kingdom of God is not m· and*1035
20 m· destroy not the work of God. *1033
1Co 3: 2 fed you with milk, and not with m·: "
8: 8 But m· commendeth us not to God: "
10 sit at m· in the idol's temple,
13 if m· make my brother to offend, 1033
10: 3 did all eat the same spiritual m·; "
Col 2: 16 no man therefore judge you in m·, 1035
Heb 5: 12 of milk, and not of strong m·. *5160
14 strong m· belongeth to them that* "
12: 16 morsel of m· sold his birthright. 1035

meat-offering See MEAT and OFFERING.

meats See also BAKEMEATS.
Pr 23: 6 neither desire thou his dainty m·:*
M'r 7: 19 into the draught, purging all m·? 1033
Ac 15: 29 abstain from m· offered to idols, *
1Co 6: 13 M· for the belly, and the belly for 1033
13 and the belly for m·: but God shall "
1Ti 4: 3 commanding to abstain from m·, "
Heb 9: 10 Which stood only in m· and drinks, "
13: 9 not with m·, which have not "

Mebunnai (*me-bun'-nahee*) See also SIBBECHAI.
2Sa 23: 27 Anethothite, M· the Hushathite, 4012

Mecherathite (*me-ker'-ath-ite*)
1Ch 11: 36 Hepher the M·, Ahijah the 4382

Medad (*me'-dad*)
Nu 11: 26 and the name of the other M·: 4312
27 Eldad and M· do prophesy in the "

Medan (*me'-dan*)
Ge 25: 2 Zimran, and Jokshan, and M·, 4091
1Ch 1: 32 M·, and Midian, and Ishbak, and "

meddle See also INTERMEDDLE; MEDDLED; MEDDLETH; MEDDLING.
De 2: 5 M· not with them; for I will not *1624
19 them not, nor m· with them: * "
2Ki 14: 10 why shouldest thou m· to thy hurt, "
2Ch 25: 19 shouldest thou m· to thine hurt, 1624
Pr 20: 19 m· not with him that flattereth 6148
24: 21 m· not with them that are given to "

meddled
Pr 17: 14 contention, before it be m· with. *1566

meddleth See also INTERMEDDLETH.
Pr 26: 17 m· with strife belonging not to *5674

meddling
2Ch 35: 21 forbear thee from m· with God, who
Pr 20: 3 strife: but every fool will be m·. *1566

Mede (*meed*) See also MEDES; MEDIAN.
Da 11: 1 in the first year of Darius the M·, 4075

Medeba (*med'-e-bah*)
Nu 21: 30 Nophah, which reacheth unto M·. 4311
Jos 13: 9 and all the plain of M· unto Dibon; "
16 the river, and all the plain by M·; "
1Ch 19: 7 who came and pitched before M·. "
Isa 15: 2 shall howl over Nebo, and over M·: "

Medes (*meeds*)
2Ki 17: 6 Gozan, and in the cities of the M·. 4074
18: 11 Gozan, and in the cities of the M·: "
Ezr 6: 2 that is in the province of the M·, * "
Es 1: 19 laws of the Persians and the M·, "
Isa 13: 17 I will stir up the M· against them, "
Jer 25: 25 Elam, and all the kings of the M·, "
51: 11 up the spirit of the kings of the M·: "
28 nations with the kings of the M·, "
Da 5: 28 is divided, and given to the M· and 4076
6: 8, 12 according to the law of the M· "
15 O king, that the law of the M· and "
9: 1 Ahasuerus, of the seed of the M·, 4074
Ac 2: 9 Parthians, and M·, and Elamites, 3370

Media (*me'-de-ah*) See also MADAI; MEDE; MEDIAN.
Es 1: 3 power of Persia and M·, the nobles 4074
14 the seven princes of Persia and M·, "
18 shall the ladies of Persia and M· "
10: 2 of the chronicles of the kings of M· "
Isa 21: 2 Go up, O Elam: besiege, O M·; all "
Da 8: 20 two horns are the kings of M· and "

Median (*me'-de-an*) See also MEDE.
Da 5: 31 Darius the M· took the kingdom, *4077

mediator
Ga 3: 19 by angels in the hand of a m·. 3316
20 a m· is not...of one, but God is one. "
20 is not a m· of one, but God is one.
1Ti 2: 5 and one m· between God and men, 3316
Heb 8: 6 he is the m· of a better covenant, "
9: 15 he is the m· of the new testament, "
12: 24 Jesus the m· of the new covenant, "

medicine See also MEDICINES.
Pr 17: 22 merry heart doeth good like a m·: 1456
Eze 47: 12 meat, and the leaf thereof for m·. *8644

medicines
Jer 30: 13 up: thou hast no healing m·. 7499
46: 11 in vain shalt thou use many m·; "

meditate See also PREMEDITATE.
Ge 24: 63 went out to m· in the field at the
Jos 1: 8 shalt m· therein day and night, 1897
Ps 1: 2 his law doth he m· day and night. "
63: 6 m· on thee in the night watches. "
77: 12 I will m· also of all thy work, and "
119: 15 I will m· in thy precepts, and have 7878
23 thy servant did m· in thy statutes. "
48 loved; and I will m· in thy statutes. "
78 cause: but I will m· in thy precepts. "
148 that I might m· in thy word. "
143: 5 I m· on all thy works; I muse on 1897
Isa 33: 18 Thine heart shall m· terror. Where* "
Lu 21: 14 not to m· before what ye shall 4304
1Ti 4: 15 M· upon these things; give thyself*3191

meditation
Ps 5: 1 words, O Lord, consider my m·. 1901
19: 14 the m· of my heart, be acceptable 1902
49: 3 m· of my heart...be understanding. 1900
104: 34 My m· of him shall be sweet: I will 7879
119: 97 I thy law! it is my m· all the day. 7881
99 for thy testimonies are my m·. "

meek
Nu 12: 3 man Moses was very m·, above all 6035
Ps 22: 26 The m· shall eat and be satisfied: "
25: 9 The m· will he guide in judgment: "
9 and the m· will he teach his way. "
37: 11 But the m· shall inherit the earth; "
76: 9 to save all the m· of the earth. "
147: 6 The Lord lifteth up the m·: he "
149: 4 will beautify the m· with salvation. "
Isa 11: 4 with equity for the m· of the earth: "
29: 19 The m· also shall increase their joy "
61: 1 preach good tidings unto the m·; "
Am 2: 7 and turn aside the way of the m·: "
Zep 2: 3 ye the Lord, all ye m· of the earth, "
M't 5: 5 Blessed are the m·: for they shall 4239
11: 29 for I am m· and lowly in heart: 4235
21: 5 thee, m·, and sitting upon an ass, 4239
1Pe 3: 4 ornament of a m· and quiet spirit, "

meekness
Ps 45: 4 truth and m· and righteousness; 6037
Zep 2: 3 seek righteousness, seek m·: it 6038
1Co 4: 21 or in love, and in the spirit of m·? ‡4236
2Co 10: 1 by the m· and gentleness of Christ, "
Ga 5: 23 M·, temperance: against such "
6: 1 such an one in the spirit of m·; "
Eph 4: 2 With all lowliness and m·, with "
Col 3: 12 of mind, m·, longsuffering; "
1Ti 6: 11 godliness, faith, love, patience, m·. "
2Ti 2: 25 In m· instructing those that oppose "
Tit 3: 2 gentle, shewing all m· unto all men. "
Jas 1: 21 and receive with m· the engrafted 4240
3: 13 his works with m· of wisdom. "
1Pe 3: 15 that is in you with m· and fear: "

meet See also MEETEST; MEETETH; MEETING; MET.
Ge 2: 18 will make him an help m· for him. 5828
20 was not found an help m· for him. "
14: 17 king of Sodom went out to m· him, 7125
18: 2 he ran to m· them from the tent "
19: 1 seeing them rose up to m· them; "
24: 17 servant ran to m· her, and said, Let "
65 that walketh in the field to m· us? "
29: 13 he ran to m· him, and embraced "
30: 16 Leah went out to m· him, and said, "
32: 6 and also he cometh to m· thee, and "
33: 4 Esau ran to m· him, and embraced "
46: 29 went up to m· Israel his father, to "
Ex 4: 14 behold, he cometh forth to m· thee: "
27 Go into the wilderness to m· Moses. "
8: 26 Moses said, It is not m· so to do; 3559
18: 7 went out to m· his father in law, 7125
19: 17 out of the camp to m· with God; "
23: 4 If thou m· thine enemy's ox or his 6293
25: 22 there I will m· with thee, and I 3259
29: 42 where I will m· you, to speak there "
43 I will m· with the children of Israel, "
30: 6 testimony, where I will m·...thee: "
36 where I will m· with thee: it "
Nu 17: 4 testimony, where I will m· with you. "
22: 36 he went out to m· him unto a city 7125
23: 3 the Lord will come to m· me: and "
15 while I m· the Lord yonder. 7136
31: 13 to m· them without the camp. 7125
De 3: 18 Israel, all that are m· for the war.*1121
Jos 2: 16 lest the pursuers m· you; and *6293
9: 11 and go to m· them, and say unto 7125
J'g 4: 18 Jael went out to m· Sisera, and said "
22 Jael came out to m· him, and said "
5: 30 m· for the necks of them that take the*
6: 35 and they came up to m· them. 7125
11: 31 of the doors of my house to m· me, "
34 came out to m· him with timbrels "
19: 3 saw him, he rejoiced to m· him. "
Ru 2: 22 that they m· thee not in any other 6293
1Sa 10: 3 and there shall m· thee three men 4672
5 that thou shalt m· a company of 6293
13: 10 Saul went out to m· him, that he 7125
15: 12 Samuel rose early to m· Saul in the "
17: 48 drew nigh to m· David, that David "
48 the army to m· the Philistine. "
18: 6 to m· king Saul, with tabrets, with "
25: 32 which sent thee this day to m· me: "
34 hadst hasted and come to m· me, "
30: 21 they went forth to m· David, and to "
21 m· the people that were with him: "
2Sa 6: 20 of Saul came out to m· David, "
10: 5 he sent to m· them, because the "
15: 32 the Archite came to m· him with his "
19: 15 came to Gilgal, to go to m· the king, "
16 the men of Judah to m· king David. "
20 to go down to m· my lord the king. "
24 of Saul came down to m· the king, "
25 come to Jerusalem to m· the king, "
1Ki 2: 8 he came down to m· me at Jordan, "
19 And the king rose up to m· her, and "
18: 16 Obadiah went to m· Ahab, and told "
16 him: and Ahab went to m· Elijah. "
21: 18 go down to m· Ahab king of Israel, "
2Ki 1: 3 go up to m· the messengers of the "
6 There came a man up to m· us, and "
7 was he which came up to m· you, "
2: 15 they came to m· him, and bowed "
4: 26 Run now, I pray thee, to m· her, "
29 if thou m· any man, salute him not;4672
31 he went again to m· him, and told 7125
5: 21 down from the chariot to m· him, "
26 again from his chariot to m· thee? "
8: 8 hand, and go, m· the man of God, "
9 Hazael went to m· him, and took a "
9: 17 send to m· them, and let him say, Is "
18 went one on horseback to m· him, "
10: 15 son of Rechab coming to m· him: "
16: 10 to Damascus to m· Tiglath-pileser "
1Ch 12: 17 And David went out to m· them, 6440
19: 5 he sent to m· them: for the men 7125
2Ch 15: 2 he went out to m· Asa, and said 6440
19: 2 Hanani the seer went out to m· him, "
Ezr 4: 14 was not m· for us to see the king's 749
Ne 6: 2 let us m· together in some one of 3259
10 us m· together in the house of God, "
Es 2: 9 which were m· to be given her, 7200
Job 5: 14 They m· with darkness in the 6298
34: 31 it is m· to be said unto God, I have*
39: 21 he goeth on to m· the armed men. 7125
Pr 7: 15 came I forth to m· thee, diligently "
11: 24 that withholdeth more than is m·, 3476
17: 12 robbed of her whelps m· a man, 6298
22: 2 The rich and poor m· together: the "
29: 13 and the deceitful man m· together: "
Isa 7: 3 Isaiah, Go forth now to m· Ahaz, 7125
14: 9 is moved for thee to m· thee at thy "
34: 14 beasts of the desert shall also m· 6298
47: 3 and I will not m· thee as a man. *6293
Jer 26: 14 as seemeth good and m· unto you.*3477
27: 5 unto whom it seemed m· unto me.*3474
41: 6 forth from Mizpah to m· them, 7125
51: 31 One post shall run to m· another, "
31 and one messenger to m· another, "
Eze 15: 4 burned. Is it m· for any work? *6743
5 was whole, it was m· for no work: 6213
5 less shall it be m· yet for any work, "
Ho 13: 8 I will m· them as a bear that is 6298
Am 4: 12 prepare to m· thy God, O Israel. 7125
Zec 2: 3 another angel went out to m· him, "
M't 3: 8 therefore fruits m· for repentance:*514
8: 34 city came out to m· Jesus: 4877
15: 26 not m· to take the children's bread, 2570
25: 1 forth to m· the bridegroom. 529
6 cometh; go ye out to m· him. "

M'r 7:27 not *m'* to take the children's bread, *2570*
14:13 *m'* you a man bearing a pitcher of *528*
Lu 14:31 to *m'* him that cometh against him "
15:32 *m'* that we should make merry, *1163*
22:10 a man *m'* you, bearing a pitcher *4876*
Joh 12:13 and went forth to *m'* him, 5222
Ac 26:20 and do works *m'* for repentance. * *514*
28:15 to *m'* us as far as Appii forum, *529*
Ro 1:27 that recompence...which was *m'*. **1163*
1Co 15:9 am not *m'* to be called an apostle, *2425*
16:4 if it be *m'* that I go also, they shall *514*
Ph'p 1:7 is *m'* for me to think this of you **1342*
Col 1:12 hath made us *m'* to be partakers *2427*
1Th 4:17 to *m'* the Lord in the air: *529*
2Th 1:3 always for you, brethren, as it is *m'*, *514*
2Ti 2:21 and *m'* for the master's use, and *2173*
Heb 6:7 forth herbs *m'* for them by whom *2111*
2Pe 1:13 I think it *m'*, as long as I am in **1342*

meetest
2Ki 10:3 the best and *m'* of your master's 3477
Isa 64:5 Thou *m'* him that rejoiceth and 6293

meeteth
Ge 32:17 When Esau my brother *m'* thee, 6298
Nu 35:19 when he *m'* him, he shall slay him. 6293
21 slay the murderer, when he *m'* him."

meeting
1Sa 21:1 was afraid at the *m'* of David, *7125
Isa 1:13 it is inquity, even the solemn *m'*. 6116

Megiddo (*me-ghid'-do*) See also MEGIDDON.
Jos 12:21 one; the king of *M'*, one; 4023
17:11 inhabitants of *M'* and her towns, "
J'g 1:27 inhabitants of *M'* and her towns: "
5:19 in Taanach by the waters of *M'*; "
1Ki 4:12 to him pertained Taanach and *M'*, "
9:15 and Hazor, and *M'*, and Gezer. "
2Ki 9:27 And he fled to *M'*, and died there. "
23:29 slew him at *M'*, when he had seen "
30 him in a chariot dead from *M'*, "
1Ch 7:29 *M'* and her towns, Dor and her "
2Ch 35:22 came to fight in the valley of *M'*. "

Megiddon (*me-ghid'-don*) See also ARMAGEDDON; MEGIDDO.
Zec 12:11 mourning...in the valley of *M'*. 4023

Mehetabeel (*me-het'-a-be-el*) See also MEHETABEL.
Ne 6:10 son of Delaiah the son of *M'*, *4105

Mehetabel (*me-het'-a-bel*) See also MEHETABEEL
Ge 36:39 wife's name was *M'*, the daughter 4105
1Ch 1:50 wife's name was *M'*, the daughter "

Mehida (*me-hi'-dah*)
Ezr 2:52 of Bazluth, the children of *M'*, 4240
Neh 7:54 of Bazlith, the children of *M'*, "

Mehir (*me'-hur*)
1Ch 4:11 the brother of Shuah begat *M'*, 4243

Meholah See ABEL-BETH-MEHOLAH; MEHOLATHITE.

Meholathite (*me-ho'-lath-ite*)
1Sa 18:19 given unto Adriel the *M'* to wife. 4259
2Sa 21:8 Adriel the son of Barzillai the *M'*: "

Mehujael (*me-hu'-ja-el*)
Ge 4:18 and Irad begat *M'*: and *M'* begat 4232

Mehuman (*me-hu'-man*)
Es 1:10 with wine, he commanded *M'*, 4104

Mehunim (*me-hu'-nim*) See also MAONITE; MEHUNIMS; MEUNIM.
Ezr 2:50 of Asnah, the children of *M'*, *4586

Mehunims (*me-hu'-nims*) See also MEHUNIM.
2Ch 26:7 dwelt in Gur-baal, and the *M'*. *4586

Me-jarkon (*me-jar'-kon*)
Jos 19:46 *M'*, and Rakkon, with the border 4313

Mekonah (*me-ko'-nah*)
Ne 11:28 and at *M'*, and in the villages *4368

Melatiah (*mel-a-ti'-ah*)
Ne 3:7 them repaired *M'* the Gibeonite, 4424

Melchi (*mel'-ki*) See also MELCHI-SHUA; MELCHIZEDEK.
Lu 3:24 which was the son of *M'*, which *3197*
28 Which was the son of *M'*, which

Melchiah (*mel-ki'-ah*) See also MALCHIAH.
Jer 21:1 unto him Pasnur the son of *M'*, *4441

Melchisedec (*mel-kis'-e-dek*) See also MELCHIZEDEK.
Heb 5:6 for ever after the order of *M'*. **3198*
10 high priest after the order of *M'*.* "
6:20 for ever after the order of *M'*. "
7:1 For this *M'*, king of Salem, priest* "
10 of his father, when *M'* met him. * "
11 should rise after the order of *M'*, * "
15 for that after the similitude of *M'** "
17 for ever after the order of *M'*. * "
21 for ever after the order of *M'*:) * "

Melchi-shua (*mel'-ki-shu'-ah*) See also MALCHISHUA.
1Sa 14:49 Jonathan, and Ishui, and *M'*: *4444
31:2 Jonathan, and Abinadab, and *M'*,* "

Melchizedek (*mel-kiz'-e-dek*) See also MELCHISEDEC.
Ge 14:18 *M'* king of Salem brought forth 4442
Ps 110:4 for ever after the order of *M'*. "

Melea (*mel'-e-ah*)
Lu 3:31 Which was the son of *M* which *3190*

Melech (*me'-lek*) See also EBED-MELECH; HAMMELECH; NATHAN-MELECH; REGEM-MELECH.
1Ch 8:35 of Micah were, Pithon, and *M'*, 4429
9:41 sons of Micah were, Pithon, and *M'*."

Melicu (*mel'-i-cu*) See also MALLUCH.
Ne 12:14 Of *M'*, Jonathan; of Shebaniah, *4409

Melita (*mel'-i-tah*)
Ac 28:1 that the island was called *M'*. *3194*

melody
Isa 23:16 make sweet *m'*, sing many songs, 5059
51:3 thanksgiving, and the voice of *m'*. 2172
Am 5:23 I will not hear the *m'* of thy viols. "
Eph 5:19 making *m'* in your heart to the *5567*

melons
Nu 11:5 the *m'*, and the leeks, and the onions, 20

melt See also MELTED; MELTETH; MELTING; MOLTEN.
Ex 15:15 inhabitants of Caanan shall *m'* *4127
Jos 2:11 these things, our hearts did *m'*, 4549
14:8 made the heart of the people *m'*: 4529
2Sa 17:10 heart of a lion, shall utterly *m'*: 4549
Ps 58:7 Let them *m'* away as waters which 3988
112:10 gnash with his teeth, and *m'* away: 4549
Isa 13:7 and every man's heart shall *m'*: "
19:1 heart of Egypt shall *m'* in the midst"
Jer 9:7 I will *m'* them, and try them; 6884
Eze 21:7 every heart shall *m'*, and all hands 4549
22:20 to blow the fire upon it, to *m'* it; 5413
20 I will leave you there, and *m'* you. "
Am 9:5 toucheth the land, and it shall *m'*, *4127
13 wine, and all the hills shall *m'*. "
Na 1:5 the hills *m'*, and the earth is burned"
2Pe 3:10 elements shall *m'* with fervent **3089*
12 elements shall *m'* with fervent *5080*

melted See also MOLTEN.
Ex 16:21 when the sun waxed hot, it *m'*. 4549
Jos 5:1 that their heart *m'*, neither was "
7:5 the hearts of the people *m'*, and "
J'g 5:5 The mountains *m'* from before *5140
1Sa 14:16 the multitude *m'* away, and they 4127
Ps 22:14 is *m'* in the midst of my bowels. 4549
46:6 he uttered his voice, the earth *m'*. 4127
97:5 hills *m'* like wax at the presence 4549
107:26 their soul is *m'* because of trouble. *4127
Isa 34:3 mountains...*m'* with their blood. 4549
Eze 22:21 and ye shall be *m'* in the midst 5413
22 As silver is *m'* in the midst of the 2046
22 so shall ye be *m'* in the midst 5413

melteth
Ps 58:8 As a snail which *m'*, let every one 8557
68:2 as wax *m'* before the fire, so let 4549
119:28 My soul *m'* for heaviness: 1811
147:18 out this word, and *m'* them: he 4529
Isa 40:19 The workman *m'* a graven image, *5258
Jer 6:29 the founder *m'* in vain: for the *6884
Na 2:10 and the heart *m'*, and the knees 4549

melting
Isa 64:2 As when the *m'* fire burneth, the *2003

Melzar (*mel'-zar*)
Da 1:11 Then said Daniel to *M'*, whom *4453
16 *M'* took away the portion of their* "

member See also MEMBERS.
De 23:1 or hath his privy *m'* cut off, shall not
1Co 12:14 For the body is not one *m'*, but *3196*
19 And if they were all one *m'*, where "
26 And whether one *m'* suffer, all the "
26 or one *m'* be honoured, all the "
Jas 3:5 Even so the tongue is a little *m'*, "

members
Job 17:7 and all my *m'* are as a shadow. 3338
Ps 139:16 in thy book all my *m'* were written,
M't 5:29, 30 one of thy *m'* should perish, *3196*
Ro 6:13 Neither yield ye your *m'* as "
13 and your *m'* as instruments of "
19 as ye have yielded your *m'* servants "
19 so now yield your *m'* servants to "
7:5 did work in our *m'* to bring forth "
23 But I see another law in my *m'*, "
23 to the law of sin which is in my *m'*. "
12:4 as we have many *m'* in one body, "
4 all *m'* have not the same office: "
5 and every one *m'* one of another. "
1Co 6:15 your bodies are the *m'* of Christ? "
15 shall I then take the *m'* of Christ, "
15 and make them the *m'* of a harlot? "
12:12 the body is one, and hath many *m'*, "
12 and all the *m'* of that one body, "
18 now hath God set the *m'* every one "
20 But now are they many *m'*, yet but "
22 much more those *m'* of the body, "
23 And those *m'* of the body, which we*
25 that the *m'* should have the same *3196*
26 suffer, all the *m'* suffer with it; "
26 honoured, all the *m'* rejoice with it. "
27 body of Christ, and *m'* in particular. "
Eph 4:25 for we are *m'* one of another. "
5:30 For we are *m'* of his body, of his "
Col 3:5 Mortify therefore your *m'* which "
Jas 3:6 so is the tongue among our *m'*, that"
4:1 of your lusts that war in your *m'*? "

memorial
Ex 3:15 is my *m'* unto all generations. 2143
12:14 day shall be unto you for a *m'*; 2146
13:9 and for a *m'* between thine eyes, "
17:14 Write this for a *m'* in a book, and "
28:12 the ephod for stones of *m'* unto the "
12 upon his two shoulders for a *m'*. "
29 for a *m'* before the Lord continually."
30:16 it may be a *m'* unto the children "
39:7 stones for a *m'* to the children of "
Le 2:2 the priest shall burn the *m'* of it 234
9 from the meat offering a *m'* thereof, "
16 the priest shall burn the *m'* of it, "
5:12 even a *m'* thereof, and burn it on the"
6:15 even the *m'* of it, unto the Lord. "
Le 23:24 a *m'* of blowing of trumpets, an 2146
24:7 it may be on the bread for a *m'*, 234
Nu 5:15 an offering of *m'*, bringing iniquity 2146
18 put the offering of *m'* in her hands, "
26 the *m'* thereof, and burn it upon 234
10:10 that they may be to you for a *m'* 2146
16:40 be a *m'* unto the children of Israel, "
31:54 for a *m'* for the children of Israel "
Jos 4:7 these stones shall be for a *m'* unto "
Ne 2:20 nor right, nor *m'*, in Jerusalem. "
Es 9:28 the *m'* of them perish from their 2143
Ps 9:6 their *m'* is perished with them. "
135:13 and thy *m'*, O Lord, throughout all "
Ho 12:5 God of hosts; the Lord is his *m'*. "
Zec 6:14 for a *m'* in the temple of the Lord. 2146
M't 26:13 hath done, be told for a *m'* of her. *3422*
M'r 14:9 shall be spoken of for a *m'* of her. "
Ac 10:4 thine alms are come up for a *m'* "

memory
Ps 109:15 cut off the *m'* of them from the 2143
145:7 utter the *m'* of thy great goodness, "
Pr 10:7 The *m'* of the just is blessed: but "
Ec 9:5 for the *m'* of them is forgotten. "
Isa 26:14 and made all their *m'* to perish. "
1Co 15:2 if ye keep in *m'* what I preached unto*

Memphis (*mem'-fis*) See also NOPH.
Ho 9:6 them up, *M'* shall bury them: 4644

Memucan (*mem-u'-can*)
Es 1:14 Meres, Mersena, and *M'*, the 4462
16 *M'* answered before the king and "
21 did according to the word of *M'*: "

men See also BONDMEN; BOWMEN; CHAPMEN; COUNTRYMEN; CRAFTSMEN; FISHERMEN; FOOTMEN; HERDMEN; HORSEMEN; HUSBANDMEN; KINSMEN; MENCHILDREN; MENPLEASERS; MEN'S; MENSERVANTS; MENSTEALERS; MERCHANTMEN; PLOWMEN; SHIPMEN; SPEARMEN; WATCHMEN, WORKMEN; WOMEN.
Ge 6:1 *m'* began to multiply on the face 120
2 daughters of *m'* that they were fair; "
4 came in unto the daughters of *m'*, "
4 the same became mighty *m'* which "
4 which were of old, *m'* of renown. 582
11:5 which the children of *m'* builded. 120
12:20 commanded his *m'* concerning 582
13:13 the *m'* of Sodom were wicked and "
14:24 that which the young *m'* have eaten, "
24 of the *m'* which went with me, by 582
17:23 male among the *m'* of Abraham's "
27 all the *m'* of his house, born in the "
18:2 and, lo, three *m'* stood by him: "
16 the *m'* rose up from thence, and "
22 *m'* turned their faces from thence, "
19:4 the *m'* of the city, even the *m'* of "
5 Where are the *m'* which came in to "
8 only unto these *m'* do nothing; for "
10 But the *m'* put forth their hand, and "
11 smote the *m'* that were at the door "
12 the *m'* said unto Lot, Hast thou here "
16 the *m'* laid hold upon his hand, and "
20:8 ears: and the *m'* were sore afraid. "
22:3 took two of his young *m'* with him,
5 And Abraham said unto his young *m'*,
19 Abraham returned unto his young *m'*,
24:13 the daughters of the *m'* of the city 582
54 he and the *m'* that were with him, "
59 and Abraham's servant, and his *m'*. "
26:7 the *m'* of the place asked him of his "
7 the *m'* of the place should kill me "
29:22 together all the *m'* of the place, "
32:6 and four hundred *m'* with him. 376
28 thou power with God and with *m'*, 582
33:1 and with him four hundred *m'*. 376
13 if *m'* should overdrive them one day,*
34:7 the *m'* were grieved, and they were 582
20 communed with the *m'* of their city, "
21 These *m'* are peaceable with us; "
22 Only herein will the *m'* consent unto "
38:21 Then he asked the *m'* of that place, "
22 also the *m'* of the place said, that "
39:11 none of the *m'* of the house there "
14 she called unto the *m'* of her house, "
41:8 of Egypt, and all the wise *m'* thereof: "
42:11 we are true *m'*; thy servants are no "
19 If ye be true *m'*, let one of your "
31 him, We are true *m'*; we are no spies: "
33 shall I know that ye are true *m'*; "
34 are no spies, but that ye are true *m'*: "
43:15 *m'* took that present, and they took 582
16 Bring these *m'* home, and slay, and "
16 these *m'* shall dine with me at noon. "
17 brought the *m'* into Joseph's house. "
18 the *m'* were afraid, because they "
24 brought the *m'* into Joseph's house, "
33 and the *m'* marvelled one at another. "
44:3 *m'* were sent away, they and their "
4 his steward, Up, follow after the *m'*; "
46:32 And the *m'* are shepherds, for their "
47:2 some of his brethren, even five *m'*, "
6 any *m'* of activity among them, "
Ex 1:17 them, but saved the *m'* children alive. "
18 and have saved the *m'* children alive? "
2:13 two *m'* of the Hebrews strove 582
4:19 *m'* are dead which sought thy life. "
5:9 more work be laid upon the *m'*, "
7:11 Pharaoh also called the wise *m'* and "
10:7 let the *m'* go, that they may serve 582
11 go now ye that are *m'*, and serve 1397
12:33 haste; for they said, We be all dead *m'*. "
37 thousand on foot that were *m'*, 1397
15:15 the mighty *m'* of Moab, trembling "
17:9 said unto Joshua, Choose us out *m'*, 582
18:21 the people able *m'*, such as fear God, "
21 *m'* of truth, hating covetousness;

Ex 18:25 chose able *m'* out of all Israel, and 582
21:18 if *m'* strive together, and one smite "
22 If *m'* strive, and hurt a woman with "
22:31 And ye shall be holy *m'* unto me:
24: 5 sent young *m'* of the children of Israel,
32:28 that day about three thousand *m'*. 376
35:22 they came, both *m'* and women, as 582
36: 4 And all the wise *m'*, that wrought all
38:26 thousand and five hundred and fifty *m'*.
Le 7:25 *m'* offer an offering made by fire
18:27 have the *m'* of the land done, which582
27: 9 *m'* bring an offering unto the Lord,
29 which shall be devoted of *m'*, shall 120
Nu 1: 5 these are the names of the *m'* that 582
17 And Moses and Aaron took these *m'* "
44 princes of Israel, being twelve *m'*: 376
5: 6 commit any sin that *m'* commit, to 120
9: 6 there were certain *m'*, who were 582
7 And those *m'* said unto him, We are "
11:16 Gather unto me seventy *m'* of the 376
24 and gathered the seventy *m'* of the "
26 remained two of the *m'* in the camp,582
28 servant of Moses, one of his young *m'*,
12: 3 above all the *m'* which were upon 120
13: 2 Send thou *m'*, that they may search582
3 all those *m'* were heads of the "
16 names of the *m'* which Moses sent "
21 unto Rehob, as *m'* come to Hamath.*
31 the *m'* that went up with him said, 582
32 saw in it are *m'* of a great stature. "
14:22 those *m'* which have seen my glory, "
36 the *m'*, which Moses sent to search "
37 those *m'* that did bring up the evil "
38 the *m'* that went to search the land, "
16: 1 of Peleth, sons of Reuben, took *m'*:
2 in the congregation, *m'* of renown: 582
14 thou put out the eyes of these *m'* ? "
26 from the tents of these wicked *m'*, "
29 If these *m'* die the common death
29 die the common death of all *m'*, 120
29 visited after the visitation of all *m'*; "
30 these *m'* have provoked the Lord. 582
32 the *m'* that appertained unto Korah,120
35 the two hundred and fifty *m'* 376
18:15 be of *m'* or beasts, shall be thine: * 120
22: 9 said, What *m'* are these with thee? 582
20 If the *m'* come to call thee, rise up, "
35 said unto Balaam, Go with the *m'*: "
25: 5 Slay ye every one his *m'* that were "
26:10 devoured two hundred and fifty *m'*:376
31:11 the prey, both of *m'* and of beasts.* 120
21 the priest said unto the *m'* of war 582
28 *m'* of war which went out to battle: "
42 divided from the *m'* that warred, "
49 have taken the sum of the *m'* of war"
53 the *m'* of war had taken spoil, every "
32:11 Surely none of the *m'* that came up "
14 an increase of sinful *m'*, to augment"
34:17 names of the *m'* which shall divide "
19 And the names of the *m'* are these: "
De 1:13 you wise *m'*, and understanding, "
15 the chief of your tribes, wise *m'*, and"
22 We will send *m'* before us, and they "
23 and I took twelve *m'* of you, one of "
35 shall not one of these *m'* of this evil "
2:14 all the generation of the *m'* of war "
16 *m'* of war were consumed and dead "
34 utterly destroyed the *m'*, and the *4962
3: 6 utterly destroying the *m'*, women,* "
4: 3 all the *m'* that followed Baal-peor, 376
13:13 Certain *m'*, the children of Belial, * 582
19:17 Then both the *m'*, between whom "
21:21 all the *m'* of his city shall stone him "
22:21 *m'* of her city shall stone her with "
25: 1 there be a controversy between *m'*, "
11 When *m'* strive together one with "
27:14 say unto all the *m'* of Israel with a 376
29:10 officers, with all the *m'* of Israel, "
25 Then *m'* shall say, Because they have
31:12 Gather the people together, *m'*, and582
32:26 of them to cease from among *m'*: "
33: 6 not die; and let not his *m'* be few. 4962
Jos 1:14 all the mighty *m'* of valour, and help
2: 1 sent out of Shittim two *m'* to spy 582
2 came *m'* in hither to night of the "
3 Bring forth the *m'* that are come to "
4 the woman took the two *m'*, and hid "
4 There came *m'* unto me, but I wist "
5 it was dark, that the *m'* went out: "
5 whither the *m'* went I wot not: "
7 the *m'* pursued after them the way "
9 she said unto the *m'*, I know that "
14 *m'* answered her, Our life for yours, "
17 And the *m'* said unto her, We will be"
23 the two *m'* returned, and descended "
3:12 take you twelve *m'* out of the tribes376
4: 2 twelve *m'* out of the people, out of 582
4 Joshua called the twelve *m'*, whom 376
5: 4 even all the *m'* of war, died in the 582
6 all the people that were *m'* of war, "
6: 2 thereof, and the mighty *m'* of valour.
3 compass the city, all ye *m'* of war, 582
9 the armed *m'* went before the priests
13 and the armed *m'* went before them;
22 Joshua had said unto the two *m'* 582
23 the young *m'* that were spies went in,
7: 2 Joshua sent *m'* from Jericho to Ai, 582
2 And the *m'* went up and viewed Ai. "
3 two or three thousand *m'* go up 376
4 people about three thousand *m'*: "
4 and they fled before the *m'* of Ai. 582
5 the *m'* of Ai smote of them about "
5 of them about thirty and six *m'*: 376
8: 3 chose out thirty thousand mighty *m'*"
12 he took about five thousand *m'*, and "
14 the *m'* of the city went out against 582

Jos 8:20 the *m'* of Ai looked behind them, 582
21 turned again, and slew the *m'* of Ai. "
25 that day, both of *m'* and women, 376
25 thousand, even all the *m'* of Ai. 582
9: 6 unto him, and to the *m'* of Israel, 376
7 And the *m'* of Israel said unto the "
14 the *m'* took of their victuals, and 582
10: 2 and all the *m'* thereof were mighty. "
6 the *m'* of Gibeon sent unto Joshua "
7 him, and all the mighty *m'* of valour,
18 and set *m'* by it for to keep them: 582
24 called for all the *m'* of Israel, and 376
24 said unto the captains of the *m'* of war
18: 4 from among you three *m'* for each 582
8 the *m'* arose, and went away: and "
9 the *m'* went and passed through the "
24:11 *m'* of Jericho fought against you, 1167
J'g 1: 4 of them in Bezek ten thousand *m'*. 376
3:29 at that time about ten thousand *m'*, "
29 all lusty, and all *m'* of valour; and* "
31 of the Philistines six hundred *m'* "
4: 6 take with thee ten thousand *m'* of "
10 up with ten thousand *m'* at his feet: "
14 and ten thousand *m'* after him. "
6:27 Gideon took ten *m'* of his servants, 582
27 household, and the *m'* of the city, "
28 the *m'* of the city arose early in the "
30 the *m'* of the city said unto Joash, "
7: 6 mouth, were three hundred *m'*: 376
7 By the three hundred *m'* that lapped"
8 retained those three hundred *m'*: "
11 of the armed *m'* that were in the host.
16 the three hundred *m'* into three 376
19 the hundred *m'* that were with him, "
23 the *m'* of Israel gathered themselves"
24 *m'* of Ephraim gathered themselves "
8: 1 the *m'* of Ephraim said unto him, "
4 three hundred *m'* that were with "
5 And he said unto the *m'* of Succoth,582
8 and the *m'* of Penuel answered him "
8 *m'* of Succoth had answered him. "
9 he spake also unto the *m'* of Penuel,"
10 with them, about fifteen thousand *m'*,
10 thousand *m'* that drew sword. 376
14 a young man of the *m'* of Succoth, 582
14 even threescore and seventeen *m'*. 376
15 he came unto the *m'* of Succoth, 582
15 bread unto thy *m'* that are weary? "
16 them he taught the *m'* of Succoth. "
17 Penuel, and slew the *m'* of the city. "
18 What manner of *m'* were they whom"
22 the *m'* of Israel said unto Gideon, 376
9: 2 the ears of all the *m'* of Shechem, 1167
3 in the ears of all the *m'* of Shechem"
6 *m'* of Shechem gathered together, "
7 unto me, ye *m'* of Shechem, that "
18 king over the *m'* of Shechem, "
20 devour the *m'* of Shechem, and the "
20 come out from the *m'* of Shechem, "
23 Abimelech and the *m'* of Shechem; "
23 *m'* of Shechem dealt treacherously "
24 and upon the *m'* of Shechem, which"
25 the *m'* of Shechem set liers in wait "
26 *m'* of Shechem put their confidence"
28 *m'* of Hamor...father of Shechem: 582
36 of the mountains as if they were *m'*. "
39 went out before the *m'* of Shechem,1167
46, 47 the *m'* of the tower of Shechem "
49 the *m'* of the tower of Shechem died582
49 about a thousand *m'* and women. 376
51 thither fled all the *m'* and women, 582
54 that *m'* say not of me, A woman slew
55 the *m'* of Israel saw that Abimelech376
57 evil of the *m'* of Shechem did God 582
11: 3 were gathered vain *m'* to Jephthah,*"
12: 1 *m'* of Ephraim gathered themselves376
4 together all the *m'* of Gilead, 582
4 the *m'* of Gilead smote Ephraim, "
5 the *m'* of Gilead said unto him, Art "
14:10 feast; for so used the young *m'* to do.
18 the *m'* of the city said unto him on 582
19 slew thirty *m'* of them, and took 376
15:10 And the *m'* of Judah said, Why are "
11 three thousand *m'* of Judah went to "
15 and slew a thousand *m'* therewith. "
16 of an ass have I slain a thousand *m'*."
16: 9 there were *m'* lying in wait, abiding*
27 house was full of *m'* and women; 582
27 three thousand *m'* and women, 376
18: 2 five *m'* from their coasts, 582,1121
2 *m'* of valour, from Zorah, and "
7 the five *m'* departed, and came to 582
11 six hundred *m'* appointed with 376
14 Then answered the five *m'* that 582
16 the six hundred *m'* appointed with 376
17 the five *m'* that went to spy out the582
17 with the six hundred *m'* that were 376
22 the *m'* that were in the houses near582
19:16 the *m'* of the place were Benjamites."
22 *m'* of the city, certain sons of Belial, "
25 the *m'* would not hearken to him: so"
20: 5 the *m'* of Gibeah rose against me, 1167
10 we will take ten *m'* of an hundred 582
11 all the *m'* of Israel were gathered 376
12 Israel sent *m'* through all the tribe 582
13 Now therefore deliver us the *m'*, the "
15 six thousand *m'* that drew sword, 376
15 numbered seven hundred chosen *m'*."
16 seven hundred chosen *m'* lefthanded;"
17 *m'* of Israel, beside Benjamin, were "
17 four hundred thousand *m'* that drew"
17 sword: all these were *m'* of war. "
20 the *m'* of Israel went out to battle "
20 *m'* of Israel put themselves in array "
21 day twenty and two thousand *m'*. "
22 people the *m'* of Israel encouraged "

J'g 20:25 again eighteen thousand *m'*; all 376
31 in the field, about thirty *m'* of Israel."
33 all the *m'* of Israel rose up out of "
34 thousand chosen *m'* out of all Israel, "
35 five thousand and an hundred *m'*: "
36 for the *m'* of Israel gave place to the"
38 sign between the *m'* of Israel and "
39 the *m'* of Israel retired in the battle, "
39 to smite and kill of the *m'* of Israel "
41 when the *m'* of Israel turned again, "
41 the *m'* of Benjamin were amazed: "
42 their backs before the *m'* of Israel "
44 fell...eighteen thousand *m'*; "
44 all these were *m'* of valour. 582
45 in the highways five thousand *m'*; 376
45 and slew two thousand *m'* of them. "
46 thousand *m'* that drew the sword; "
46 all these were *m'* of valour. 582
47 six hundred *m'* turned and fled to 376
48 the *m'* of Israel turned again upon "
48 as well the *m'* of every city, as the*4974
21: 1 *m'* of Israel had sworn in Mizpeh, 376
10 sent thither twelve thousand *m'* of "
Ru 2: 9 have I not charged the young *m'* that
9 that which the young *m'* have drawn.
15 Boaz commanded his young *m'*,
21 Thou shalt keep fast by my young *m'*,
3:10 as thou followedst not young *m'*,
4: 2 took ten *m'* of the elders of the city,582
1Sa 2: 4 The bows of the mighty *m'* are broken,
17 the sin of the young *m'* was very great
17 for *m'* abhorred the offering of the 582
26 both with the Lord, and also with *m'*."
4: 2 in the field about four thousand *m'*.376
9 strong, and quit yourselves like *m'*,582
9 quit yourselves like *m'*, and fight. "
5: 7 the *m'* of Ashdod saw that it was so, "
9 smote the *m'* of the city, both small "
12 *m'* that died not were smitten with "
6:10 the *m'* did so; and took two milch "
15 *m'* of Beth-shemesh offered burnt "
19 he smote the *m'* of Beth-shemesh, 376
19 thousand and threescore and ten *m'*: "
20 the *m'* of Beth-shemesh said, Who 582
7: 1 And the *m'* of Kirjath-jearim came, "
11 the *m'* of Israel went out of Mizpeh, "
8:16 your goodliest young *m'*, and your
22 Samuel said unto the *m'* of Israel, 582
10: 2 find two *m'* by Rachel's sepulchre "
3 there shall meet thee three *m'* going"
26 there went with him a band of *m'*,*
11: 1 the *m'* of Jabesh said unto Nahash,582
5 him the tidings of the *m'* of Jabesh. "
8 the *m'* of Judah thirty thousand. 376
9 say unto the *m'* of Jabesh-gilead, 582
9 and shewed it to the *m'* of Jabesh; 582
10 Therefore the *m'* of Jabesh said, "
12 bring the *m'*, that we may put them "
15 Saul and all the *m'* of Israel rejoiced"
13: 2 Saul chose him three thousand *m'* of
6 When the *m'* of Israel saw that they376
15 with him, about six hundred *m'*; "
14: 2 with him were about six hundred *m'*:"
8 we will pass over unto these *m'*, 582
12 the *m'* of the garrison answered "
14 slaughter,...was about twenty *m'*, 376
22 all the *m'* of Israel which had hid "
24 the *m'* of Israel were distressed that"
15: 4 and ten thousand *m'* of Judah. "
17: 2 And Saul and the *m'* of Israel were "
12 man went among *m'* for an old man582
19 and they, and all the *m'* of Israel, 376
24 all the *m'* of Israel, when they saw "
25 the *m'* of Israel said, Have ye seen "
26 David spake to the *m'* that stood 582
28 heard when he spake unto the *m'*; "
52 the *m'* of Israel and of Judah arose, "
18: 5 and Saul set him over the *m'* of war, "
27 arose and went, he and his *m'*, and "
27 of the Philistines two hundred *m'*; 376
21: 4 if the young *m'* have kept themselves
5 the vessels of the young *m'* are holy,
15 Have I need of mad *m'*, that ye have
22: 2 with him about four hundred *m'*. 376
6 and the *m'* that were with him, 582
19 both *m'* and women, children and 376
23: 3 David's *m'* said unto him, Behold, 582
5 So David and his *m'* went to Keilah, "
8 Keilah, to besiege David and his *m'*."
11 Will the *m'* of Keilah deliver me up1167
12 Will the *m'* of Keilah deliver me and"
12 and my *m'* into the hand of Saul? 582
13 David and his *m'*, which were about "
24 and his *m'* were in the wilderness "
25 also and his *m'* went to seek him. "
26 his *m'* on that side of the mountain: "
26 for Saul and his *m'* compassed David"
26 compassed David and his *m'* round "
24: 2 Saul took three thousand chosen *m'*376
2 and went to seek David and his *m'* 582
3 David and his *m'* remained in the "
4 And the *m'* of David said unto him, "
6 he said unto his *m'*, The Lord forbid"
22 David and his *m'* gat them up unto "
25: 5 And David sent out ten young *m'*, and
5 David said unto the young *m'*, Get you
8 Ask thy young *m'*, and they will shew
8 let the young *m'* find favour in thine
9 when David's young *m'* came, they
11 give it unto *m'*, whom I know not 582
12 So David's young *m'* turned their way,
13 David said unto his *m'*, Gird ye on 582
13 after David about four hundred *m'*;376
14 But one of the young *m'* told Abigail,
15 But the *m'* were very good unto us, 582
20 David and his *m'* came down against"

1Sa 25: 25 thine handmaid saw not the young *m'*
27 unto the young *m'* that follow my lord.
26: 2 three thousand chosen *m'* of Israel 376
19 if they be the children of *m'*, cursed 120
22 and let one of the young *m'* come over
27: 2 passed over with the six hundred *m'* 376
3 with Achish at Gath, he and his *m'*, 582
8 And David and his *m'* went up, and "
28: 1 with me to battle, thou and thy *m'*. "
8 he went, and two *m'* with him, and "
29: 2 David and his *m'* passed on in the "
4 it not be with the heads of these *m'*? "
11 So David and his *m'* rose up early "
30: 1 David and his *m'* were come to Ziklag "
3 David and his *m'* came to the city, "
9 six hundred *m'* that were with him, 376
10 pursued, he and four hundred *m'*: "
17 save four hundred young *m'*, which "
21 David came to the two hundred *m'*, 582
22 Then answered all the wicked *m'* 376
22 all the wicked *m'* and...of Belial,
31 and his *m'* were wont to haunt. 582
31: 1 the *m'* of Israel fled from before the "
6 his armourbearer, and all his *m'*, "
7 the *m'* of Israel...on the other side "
7 saw that the *m'* of Israel fled, and "
12 All the valiant *m'* arose, and went 376
2Sa 1: 11 all the *m'* that were with him: 582
15 And David called one of the young *m'*,
2: 3 *m'* that were with him did David 582
4 And the *m'* of Judah came, and there "
4 *m'* of Jabesh-gilead were they that "
5 sent...unto the *m'* of Jabesh-gilead, "
14 Let the young *m'* now arise, and play
17 was beaten, and the *m'* of Israel, 582
21 lay thee hold on one of the young *m'*,
29 Abner and his *m'* walked all that 582
30 of David's servants nineteen *m'* 376
31 of Benjamin, and of Abner's *m'*, 582
31 hundred and threescore *m'* died. 376
32 Joab and his *m'* went all night, and 582
3: 20 to Hebron, and twenty *m'* with him. "
20 the *m'* that were with him a feast. "
34 as a man falleth before wicked *m'*,* 1121
39 these *m'* the sons of Zeruiah be too 582
4: 2 son had two *m'* that were captains "
11 wicked *m'* have slain a righteous "
12 David commanded his young *m'*, and
5: 6 king and his *m'* went to Jerusalem 582
21 and David and his *m'* burned them. "
6: 1 together all the chosen *m'* of Israel,
19 Israel, as well to the women as *m'*, 376
7: 9 like unto the name of the great *m'* *
14 chasten him with the rod of *m'*, 582
14 the stripes of the children of *m'*: 120
8: 5 two and twenty thousand *m'*. 376
13 of salt, being eighteen thousand *m'*.
10: 5 the *m'* were greatly ashamed: 582
6 and of king Maacah a thousand *m'*, 376
6 and of Ish-tob twelve thousand *m'*. "
7 and all the host of the mighty *m'*.
9 chose of all the choice *m'* of Israel, and
12 let us play the *m'* for our people, ‡2388
18 David slew the *m'* of seven hundred
11: 16 where he knew...valiant *m'* were. 582
17 the *m'* of the city went out, and "
23 Surely the *m'* prevailed against us, "
12: 1 There were two *m'* in one city; the "
13: 9 said, Have out all *m'* from me. 376
32 slain all the young *m'* the king's sons;
15: 1 and fifty *m'* to run before him. 376
6 stole the hearts of the *m'* of Israel. 582
11 with Absalom went two hundred *m'* 376
13 hearts of the *m'* of Israel are after "
18 six hundred *m'* which came after "
22 Gittite passed over, and all his *m'*, 582
16: 2 summer fruit for the young *m'* to eat;
6 all the mighty *m'* were on his right
13 David and his *m'* went by the way, 582
15 the *m'* of Israel, came to Jerusalem, 376
18 this people, and all the *m'* of Israel, "
17: 1 now choose out twelve thousand *m'*, "
8 knowest thy father and his *m'*, 582
8 that they be mighty *m'*, and they be
10 which be with him are valiant *m'*. 1121
12 and of all the *m'* that are with him 582
14 Absalom and all the *m'* of Israel 376
24 he and all the *m'* of Israel with him. "
18: 7 that day of twenty thousand *m'*.
15 young *m'* that bare Joab's armour
28 which hath delivered up the *m'* 582
19: 14 the heart of all the *m'* of Judah, 376
16 came down with the *m'* of Judah "
17 were a thousand *m'* of Benjamin "
28 father's house were but dead *m'* 582
41 all the *m'* of Israel came to the 376
41 our brethren the *m'* of Judah stolen "
41 David's *m'* with him, over Jordan? 582
42 the *m'* of Judah answered the *m'* of 376
43 the *m'* of Israel answered the *m'* of "
43 the words of the *m'* of Judah were "
43 than the words of the *m'* of Israel. "
20: 2 *m'* of Judah clave unto their king, "
4 Assemble me the *m'* of Judah within "
5 went to assemble the *m'* of Judah:
7 went out after him Joab's *m'*, and 582
7 the Pelethites, and all the mighty *m'*:
11 and one of Joab's *m'* stood by him, 376
21: 6 seven *m'* of his sons be delivered 582
12 son from the *m'* of Jabesh-gilead, 1167
17 the *m'* of David sware unto him, 582
22: 5 floods of ungodly *m'* made me afraid;*
23: 3 that ruleth over *m'* must be just, 120
8 the names of the mighty *m'* whom
9 of the three mighty *m'* with David,
9 the *m'* of Israel were gone away: 376

2Sa 23: 16 three mighty *m'* brake through the
17 the blood of the *m'* that went in 582
17 things did these three mighty *m'*.
20 acts, he slew two lionlike *m'* of Moab:*
22 the name among three mighty *m'*.
24: 9 valiant *m'* that draw the sword; 376
9 the *m'* of Judah were five hundred "
9 were five hundred thousand *m'*. "
15 to Beer-sheba seventy thousand *m'*. "
1Ki 1: 5 and fifty *m'* to run before him. "
8 mighty *m'* which belonged to David,
9 *m'* of Judah the king's servants: 582
10 and the mighty *m'*, and Solomon his
2: 32 two *m'* more righteous and better 582
4: 31 For he was wiser than all *m'*; than 120
5: 13 the levy was thirty thousand *m'*. 376
8: 2 *m'* of Israel assembled themselves "
39 the hearts of all the children of *m'*;) 120
9: 22 but they were *m'* of war, and his 582
10: 8 Happy are thy *m'*, happy are these "
11: 18 took *m'* with them out of Paran, "
24 And he gathered *m'* unto him, and "
12: 6 Rehoboam consulted with the old *m'*,
8 he forsook the counsel of the old *m'*,
8 and consulted with the young *m'* that
10 the young *m'* that were grown up with
14 after the counsel of the young *m'*,
21 and fourscore thousand chosen *m'*,
13: 25 *m'* passed by, and saw the carcase 582
18: 13 hundred *m'* of the Lord's prophets 376
22 are four hundred and fifty *m'*. "
20: 14 by the young *m'* of the princes of the
15 he numbered the young *m'* of the
17 the young *m'* of the princes of the
17 There are *m'* come out of Samaria. 582
19 So these young *m'* of the princes of
30 and seven thousand of the *m'* that 376
33 Now the *m'* did diligently observe 582
21: 10 And set two *m'*, sons of Belial, before‡ "
11 the *m'* of his city, even the elders "
13 there came in two *m'*, children of ‡ "
13 the *m'* of Belial witnessed against‡ "
22: 6 together, about four hundred *m'*, 376
2Ki 2: 7 fifty *m'* of the sons of the prophets
16 thy servants fifty strong *m'*; 582,1121
17 They sent therefore fifty *m'*; and 376
19 the *m'* of the city said unto Elisha, 582
3: 26 him seven hundred *m'* that drew 376
4: 22 me, I pray thee, one of the young *m'*,*
40 they poured out for the *m'* to eat. 582
43 I set this before an hundred *m'*? 376
5: 22 two young *m'* of the sons of the
24 he let the *m'* go, and they departed. 582
6: 20 open the eyes of these *m'*, that they
7: 3 there were four leprous *m'* at the 582
8: 12 and their young *m'* wilt thou slay
10: 6 heads of the *m'* your master's sons, 582
6 were with the great *m'* of the city,
11 all his great *m'*, and his kinsfolks, and
14 house, even two and forty *m'*; 376
24 appointed fourscore *m'* without, "
24 any of the *m'* whom I have brought 582
11: 9 and they took every man his *m'* that "
12: 15 they reckoned not with the *m'*, into "
13: 21 that, behold, they spied a band of *m'*;* "
15: 20 of all the mighty *m'* of wealth, of each
25 with him fifty *m'* of the Gileadites: 376
17: 24 of Assyria brought *m'* from Babylon,
30 And the *m'* of Babylon made 582
30 the *m'* of Cuth made Nergal, and the "
30 the *m'* of Hamath made Ashima, "
18: 27 me to the *m'* which sit on the wall, "
20: 14 said unto him, What said these *m'*? "
23: 2 and all the *m'* of Judah and all the 376
14 their places with the bones of *m'*. 120
17 the *m'* of the city told him, It is the 582
24: 14 all the mighty *m'* of valour, even ten
16 And all the *m'* of might, even seven 582
25: 4 all the *m'* of war fled by night by the "
19 that was set over the *m'* of war, and "
19 and five *m'* of them that were in the "
19 threescore *m'* of the people of the 376
23 they and their *m'*, heard that the 582
23 of a Maachathite, they and their *m'*. "
24 and to their *m'*, and said unto them, "
25 royal, came, and ten *m'* with him. "
1Ch 4: 12 These are the *m'* of Rechah. "
22 the *m'* of Chozeba, and Joash, and "
42 the sons of Simeon, five hundred *m'*, "
5: 18 the tribe of Manasseh, of valiant *m'*,
18 *m'* able to bear buckler and sword, 582
21 of *m'* an hundred thousand. 5315,120
24 and Jahdiel, mighty *m'* of valour, 582
24 famous *m'*, and heads of the house "
7: 2 were valiant *m'* of might in their
3 Joel, Ishiah, five: all of them chief *m'*.
4 for war, six and thirty thousand *m'*:*
5 of Issachar were valiant *m'* of might,
7, 9 fathers, mighty *m'* of valour;
11 their fathers, mighty *m'* of valour,
21 whom the *m'* of Gath that were born 582
40 choice and mighty *m'* of valour,
40 was twenty and six thousand *m'*. 582
8: 28 fathers, by their generations, chief *m'*.
40 of Ulam were mighty *m'* of valour, 582
9: 9 these *m'* were chief of the fathers
13 very able *m'* for the work of the 1368
10: 1 the *m'* of Israel fled from before the 376
7 *m'* of Israel that were in the valley "
12 They arose, all the valiant *m'*, and "
11: 10 of the mighty *m'* whom David had,
11 of the mighty *m'* whom David had;
19 shall I drink the blood of these *m'* 582
26 the valiant *m'* of the armies were,
12: 1 and they were among the mighty *m'*,
8 to the wilderness *m'* of might, 582

1Ch 12: 8 and *m'* of war fit for the battle,
21 for they were all mighty *m'* of valour,
25 mighty *m'* of valour for the war,
30 mighty *m'* of valour, famous
38 All these *m'* of war, that could keep 582
16: 31 and let *m'* say among the nations,*
17: 8 like the name of the great *m'* that are*
18: 5 two and twenty thousand *m'*. 376
19: 5 told David how the *m'* were served. 582
5 for the *m'* were greatly ashamed. "
8 and all the host of the mighty *m'*.
18 seven thousand *m'* which fought in
21: 5 thousand *m'* that drew sword: and 376
5 ten thousand *m'* that drew sword. "
14 fell of Israel seventy thousand *m'*. "
22: 15 all manner of cunning *m'* for every
24: 4 there were more chief *m'* found of 1397
4 of Eleazar there were sixteen chief *m'*.*
26: 6 for they were mighty *m'* of valour.
7 whose brethren were strong *m'*, 1121
8 able *m'* for strength for the service, 376
9 had sons and brethren, strong *m'*, 1121
12 porters, even among the chief *m'*, 1397
30 and his brethren, *m'* of valour, 1121
31 among them mighty *m'* of valour at
32 And his brethren, *m'* of valour, 1121
28: 1 the officers, and with the mighty *m'*,
1 and with all the valiant *m'*, unto
29: 24 all the princes, and the mighty *m'*,
2Ch 2: 2 ten thousand *m'* to bear burdens, 376
7 cunning *m'* that are with me in Judah
14 be put to him, with thy cunning *m'*,
14 with the cunning *m'* of my lord David
5: 3 *m'* of Israel assembled themselves 376
6: 18 God in very deed dwell with *m'* on 120
30 the hearts of the children of *m'*:) "
8: 9 but they were *m'* of war, and chief 582
9: 7 Happy are thy *m'*, and happy are "
10: 6 Rehoboam took counsel with the old *m'*
8 the counsel which the old *m'* gave him,
8 and took counsel with the young *m'*
10 young *m'* that were brought up with
13 forsook the counsel of the old *m'*,
14 them after the advice of the young *m'*,
11: 1 chosen *m'*, which were warriors, to
13: 3 with an army of valiant *m'* of war,
3 four hundred thousand chosen *m'*: 376
3 eight hundred thousand chosen *m'*, "
3 being mighty *m'* of valour.
7 are gathered unto him vain *m'*, the 582
15 Then the *m'* of Judah gave a shout: 376
15 and as the *m'* of Judah shouted, it "
17 five hundred thousand chosen *m'*. "
14: 8 And Asa had an army of *m'* that bare*
8 all these were mighty *m'* of valour.
17: 13 and the *m'* of war, mighty...of 582
13 mighty *m'* of valour were in Jerusalem.
14 mighty *m'* of valour three hundred
16 thousand mighty *m'* of valour.
17 him armed *m'* with bow and shield*
18: 5 of prophets four hundred *m'*, and 376
23: 8 and took every man his *m'* that 582
24: 24 came with a small company of *m'*, "
25: 5 three hundred thousand choice *m'*,
6 thousand mighty *m'* of valour out of
26: 11 Uzziah had an host of fighting *m'*,
12 the fathers of the mighty *m'* of valour
15 engines, invented by cunning *m'*, to be
17 of the Lord, that were valiant *m'*: 1121
28: 6 one day, which were all valiant *m'*; "
14 So the armed *m'* left the captives and
15 *m'* which were expressed by name 582
31: 19 the *m'* that were expressed by name, "
32: 3 and his mighty *m'* to stop the waters
21 cut off all the mighty *m'* of valour,
34: 12 And the *m'* did the work faithfully: 582
30 the Lord, and all the *m'* of Judah, 376
35: 25 all the singing *m'* and the singing
36: 17 slew their young *m'* with the sword
Ezr 1: 4 *m'* of his place help him with silver, 582
2: 2 of the *m'* of the people of Israel: "
22 The *m'* of Netophah, fifty and six. "
23 The *m'* of Anathoth, an hundred "
27 The *m'* of Michmas, an hundred "
28 *m'* of Beth-el and Ai, two hundred "
3: 12 of the fathers, who were ancient *m'*,
4: 11 the *m'* on this side of the river, 606
21 to cause these *m'* to cease, and 1400
5: 4 the names of the *m'* that make this "
10 names of the *m'* that were the chief "
6: 8 expences be given unto these *m'*, "
8: 16 and for Meshullam, chief *m'*; also "
10: 1 very great congregation of *m'* and 582
9 all the *m'* of Judah and Benjamin "
17 the *m'* that had taken strange wives "
Neh 1: 2 came, he and certain *m'* of Judah; "
2: 12 night, I and some few *m'* with me; "
3: 2 unto him builded the *m'* of Jericho. "
7 the *m'* of Gibeon, and of Mizpah, "
22 the priests, the *m'* of the plain. "
4: 23 servants, nor the *m'* of the guard "
5: 5 for other *m'* have our lands and "
7: 7 *m'* of the people of Israel was this; "
26 The *m'* of Beth-lehem and Netophah, "
27 The *m'* of Anathoth, an hundred "
28 The *m'* of Beth-azmaveth, forty and "
29 *m'* of Kirjath-jearim, Chephirah, "
30 *m'* of Ramah and Gaba, six "
31 The *m'* of Michmas, an hundred and "
32 *m'* of Beth-el and Ai, an hundred "
33 The *m'* of the other Nebo, fifty and "
67 forty and five singing *m'* and singing
8: 2 congregation both of *m'* and women, 376
3 before the *m'* and the women, and 582
11: 2 And the people blessed all the *m'*, "
6 threescore and eight valiant *m'*. "

Neh 11:14 their brethren, mighty m' of valour,
14 the son of one of the great m'. *
Es 1:13 Then the king said to the wise m',
6:13 said his wise m' and Zeresh his wife
9: 6 slew and destroyed five hundred m'.376
12 and destroyed five hundred m' in "
15 slew three hundred m' at Shushan; "
Job 1: 3 greatest of all the m' of the east. *1121
19 it fell upon the young m', and they are
4:13 night, when deep sleep falleth on m',582
7:20 unto thee, O thou preserver of m'? 120
11: 3 thy lies make m' hold their peace? 4962
11 For he knoweth vain m': he seeth "
15:10 the grayheaded and very aged m',
18 Which wise m' have told from their
17: 8 Upright m' shall be astonied at this,
22:15 which wicked m' have trodden? 4962
29 When m' are cast down, then thou*
24:12 M' groan from out of the city, and4962
27:23 M' shall clap their hands at him, and
28: 4 up, they are gone away from m'. 582
29: 8 The young m' saw me, and hid
21 Unto me m' gave ear, and waited,
30: 5 were driven forth from among m',
8 of fools, yea, children of base m':
31:31 the m' of my tabernacle said not, 4962
32: 1 So these three m' ceased to answer 582
5 in the mouth of these three m', "
9 Great m' are not always wise: neither*
33:15 when deep sleep falleth upon m', 582
16 Then he openeth the ears of m', and "
27 He looketh upon m', and if any say, "
34: 2 Hear my words, O ye wise m'; and
8 and walketh with wicked m'. 582
10 unto me, ye m' of understanding: "
24 He shall break in pieces mighty m'
26 He striketh them as wicked m' in the
34 Let m' of understanding tell me, 582
36 of his answers for wicked m'.
35:12 because of the pride of evil m'.
36:24 magnify his work, which m' behold.582
37: 7 that all m' may know his work. "
21 And now m' see not the bright light
24 M' do therefore fear him: he 582
39:21 he goeth on to meet the armed m'.
Ps 4: 2 O ye sons of m', how long will ye 376
9:20 may know themselves to be but m'.582
11: 4 his eyelids try, the children of m'. 120
12: 1 fail from among the children of m'. "
8 when the vilest m' are exalted.1121, "
14: 2 from heaven upon the children of m', "
17: 4 Concerning the works of m', by the "
14 From m' which are thy hand, O 4962
14 from m' of the world, which have "
18: 4 floods of ungodly m' made me afraid.*
21:10 seed from among the children of m'.120
22: 6 a reproach of m', and despised of "
26: 9 sinners, nor my life with bloody m':582
31:19 trust in thee before the sons of m'! 120
33:13 he beholdeth all the sons of m'. "
36: 7 children of m' put their trust under "
45: 2 art fairer than the children of m': "
49:10 For he seeth that wise m' die, likewise
18 and m' will praise thee, when thou
53: 2 from heaven upon the children of m',120
55:23 deceitful m' shall not live out half 582
57: 4 are set on fire, even the sons of m', 120
58: 1 ye judge uprightly, O ye sons of m'? "
59: 2 and save me from bloody m'. 582
62: 9 m' of low degree are vanity, 1121,120
9 m' of high degree are a lie: to be" 376
64: 9 all m' shall fear, and shall declare 120
66: 5 his doing toward the children of m'. "
12 caused m' to ride over our heads; 582
68:18 thou hast received gifts for m'; yea,120
72:17 sun: and m' shall be blessed in him:
73: 5 They are not in trouble as other m';582
5 are they plagued like other m'. 120
76: 5 m' of might have found their hands.582
78:31 smote down the chosen m' of Israel.
60 the tent which he placed among m';120
63 The fire consumed their young m';
82: 7 But ye shall die like m', and fall like120
83:18 That m' may know that thou, whose*
86:14 violent m' have sought after my soul;
89:47 hast thou made all m' in vain? 1121,120
90: 3 and sayest, Return, ye children of m'. "
105:12 they were but a few m' in number;4962
107: 8 Oh that m' would praise the Lord for
8 works to the children of m'! 120
15 Oh that m' would praise the Lord for
15 works to the children of m'! 120
21 Oh that m' would praise the Lord for
21 works to the children of m'! 120
31 Oh that m' would praise the Lord for
31 works to the children of m'! 120
115:16 hath he given to the children of m'. "
116:11 I said in my haste, All m' are liars. "
124: 2 side, when m' rose up against us: "
139:19 from me therefore, ye bloody m'. 582
141: 4 works with m' that work iniquity: 376
145: 6 m' shall speak of the might of thy
12 To make known to the sons of m' 120
148:12 Both young m', and maidens;
12 and maidens; old m', and children:
Pr 2:20 mayest walk in the way of good m',
4:14 and go not in the way of evil m'.
6:30 M' do not despise a thief, if he steal to
8: 4 Unto you, O m', I call; and my 376
31 delights were with the sons of m'. 120
10:14 Wise m' lay up knowledge: but the
11: 7 and the hope of unjust m' perisheth.*
16 honour: and strong m' retain riches.
12:12 The wicked desireth the net of evil m':
13:20 walketh with wise m' shall be wise:
15:11 the hearts of the children of m'? 120

Pr 16: 6 fear of the Lord m' depart from evil.
17: 6 children are the crown of old m';
18:16 and bringeth him before great m'.
20: 6 Most m' will proclaim every one 120
29 glory of young m' is their strength:
29 the beauty of old m' is the gray head.
22:29 he shall not stand before mean m'.
23:28 the transgressors among m'. 120
24: 1 not thou envious against evil m', 582
9 scorner is an abomination to m'. 120
19 Fret not thyself because of evil m',*
25: 1 the m' of Hezekiah king of Judah 582
6 and stand not in the place of great m':
27 for m' to search their own glory is not
26:16 seven m' that can render a reason.
28: 5 Evil m' understand not judgment: 582
7 that is a companion of riotous m'
12 When righteous m' do rejoice, there is*
28 wicked rise, m' hide themselves: 120
29: 8 Scornful m' bring a city into a 582
8 snare: but wise m' turn away wrath.
30:14 and the needy from among m'. 120
Ec 2: 3 was that good for the sons of m', "
8 me m' singers and women singers,
8 and the delights of the sons of m', 120
3:10 God hath given to the sons of m' "
18 the estate of the sons of m', that God"
19 that which befalleth the sons of m' "
6: 1 sun, and it is common among m': "
7: 2 for that is the end of all m'; and the"
19 ten mighty m' which are in the city.*
8:11 heart of the sons of m' is fully set 120
14 that there be just m', unto whom it
14 again, there be wicked m', to whom it
9: 3 heart of the sons of m' is full of evil,120
11 nor yet riches to m' of understanding,
11 nor yet favour to m' of skill; but time
12 so are the sons of m' snared in an 120
14 a little city, and few m' within it; 582
17 words of wise m' are heard in quiet*
12: 3 strong m' shall bow themselves, 582
Ca 3: 7 threescore valiant m' are about it,
4: 4 bucklers, all shields of mighty m'.
Isa 2:11 haughtiness of m' shall be bowed 582
17 haughtiness of m' shall be made low:"
3:25 Thy m' shall fall by the sword, and4962
5: 3 and m' of Judah, judge, I pray you,376
7 the m' of Judah his pleasant plant: "
13 their honourable m' are famished,4962
22 and m' of strength to mingle strong582
6:12 Lord have removed m' far away, 120
7:13 a small thing for you to weary m', 582
24 and with bows shall m' come thither;*
9: 3 m' rejoice when they divide the spoil.
17 shall have no joy in their young m',
11:15 streams, and make m' go over dryshod.
13:18 shall dash the young m' to pieces;
19:12 where are thy wise m'? and let them
21: 9 here cometh a chariot of m', with 376
17 mighty m' of the children of Kedar,
22: 2 slain m' are not slain with the sword,*
6 with chariots of m' and horsemen, 120
23: 4 neither do I nourish up young m', nor
24: 6 earth are burned, and few m' left. 582
26:19 Thy dead m' shall live, together with*
28:14 word of the Lord, ye scornful m', 582
29:11 which m' deliver to one that is learned,
13 me is taught by the precept of m': 582
14 wisdom of their wise m' shall perish,
14 the understanding of their prudent m'
19 the poor among m' shall rejoice in 120
31: 3 the Egyptians are m', and not God; "
8 and his young m' shall be discomfited.
36:12 me to the m' that sit upon the wall, 582
38:16 O Lord, by these things m' live, and in
39: 3 What said these m'? and from 582
40:30 and the young m' shall utterly fall:
41: 9 called thee from the chief m' thereof,*
14 worm Jacob, and ye m' of Israel; 4962
43: 4 therefore will I give m' for thee, 120
44:11 and the workmen, they are of m': let"
25 that turneth wise m' backward, and
45:14 and of the Sabeans, m' of stature, 582
24 even to him shall m' come; and all that
46: 8 this, and shew yourselves m': 376
51: 7 fear ye not the reproach of m', 582
52:14 his form more than the sons of m': 120
53: 3 He is despised and rejected of m'; 376
57: 1 merciful m' are taken away, none 582
59:10 we are in desolate places as dead m'.
60:11 that m' may bring unto thee the forces
61: 6 m' shall call you the Ministers of our
64: 4 m' have not heard, nor perceived by
66:24 look upon the carcases of the m' 582
Jer 4: 3 saith the Lord to the m' of Judah 376
4 ye m' of Judah and inhabitants of "
5: 5 I will get me unto the great m', and
16 sepulchre, they are all mighty m'.
26 my people are found wicked m': they
26 they set a trap, they catch m'. 582
6:11 and upon the assembly of young m'
23 set in array as m' for war against* 376
30 Reprobate silver shall m' call them,
8: 9 The wise m' are ashamed, they are
9: 2 a lodging place of wayfaring m'; that
2 an assembly of treacherous m'.
10 can m' hear the voice of the cattle;
21 and the young m' from the streets.
22 Even the carcases of m' shall fall 120
10: 7 among all the wise m' of the nations,
9 they are all the work of cunning m'.
11: 2 speak unto the m' of Judah, and 376
9 is found among the m' of Judah, "
21 the Lord of the m' of Anathoth, 582
22 the young m' shall die by the sword;
23 bring evil upon the m' of Anathoth,582

Jer 15: 8 against the mother of the young m' a
10 nor m' have lent to me on usury; yet
16: 6 neither shall m' lament for them, nor
7 shall m' tear themselves for them in
7 m' give them the cup of consolation
17:25 m' of Judah, and the inabitants of 376
18:11 speak to the m' of Judah, and to "
21 and let their m' be put to death; 582
21 young m' be slain by the sword in
19:10 sight of the m' that go with thee, 582
26:21 the king, with all his mighty m',
22 the king sent m' into Egypt, 582
22 and certain m' with him into Egypt."
31:13 both young m' and old together:
32:19 upon all the ways of the sons of m':120
20 and in Israel, and among other m'; "
32 prophets, and the m' of Judah, and 376
44 M' shall buy fields for money, and
33: 5 them with the dead bodies of m', 120
34:18 give the m' that have transgressed 582
35:13 Go and tell the m' of Judah and 376
36:31 and upon the m' of Judah, all the "
37:10 there remained but wounded m' 582
38: 4 weakeneth the hands of the m' of "
9 m' have done evil in all that they "
10 from hence thirty m' with thee, and "
11 Ebed-melech took the m' with him, "
16 give thee into the hand of these m' "
39: 4 saw them, and all the m' of war, "
17 not be given into the hand of the m' "
40: 7 and their m', heard that the king "
7 had committed unto him m', and "
8 a Maachathite, they and their m'. "
9 sware unto them and to their m', "
41: 1 of the king, even ten m' with him, "
2 and the ten m' that were with him, "
3 were found there, and the m' of war."
5 from Samaria, even fourscore m', 376
7 he, and the m' that were with him. 582
8 ten m' were found among them that"
9 cast all the dead bodies of the m', "
12 Then they took all the m', and went "
15 from Johanan with eight m', and "
16 even mighty m' of war, and the "
42:17 shall it be with all the m' that set "
43: 2 Johanan...and all the proud m', "
6 Even m', and women, and the 1397
9 in the sight of the m' of Judah; 582
44:15 Then all the m' which knew that "
19 offerings unto her, without our m'?*"
20 to the m', and to the women, and 1397
27 all the m' of Judah that are in the 376
46: 9 and let the mighty m' come forth;
15 Why are thy valiant m' swept away?*
21 Also her hired m' are in the midst of
47: 2 then the m' shall cry, and all the 120
48:14 mighty and strong m' for the war? 582
15 his chosen young m' are gone down to
31 mourn for the m' of Kir-heres. 582
36 like pipes for the m' of Kir-heres: "
49:15 heathen, and despised among m'. 120
22 the heart of the mighty m' of Edom be
26 her young m' shall fall in her streets,
26 all the m' of war shall be cut off 582
28 and spoil the m' of the east. *1121
50:30 shall her young m' fall in her streets,
30 all her m' of war shall be cut off in 582
35 her princes, and upon her wise m'.
36 a sword is upon her mighty m'; and
51: 3 spare ye not her young m'; destroy ye
14 Surely I will fill thee with m', as 120
30 mighty m' of Babylon have forborn
32 and the m' of war are affrighted. 582
56 her mighty m' are taken, every one
57 drunk her princes, and her wise m',
57 and her rulers, and her mighty m':
52: 7 all the m' of war fled, and went 582
13 all houses of the great m', burned he
25 had the charge of the m' of war; 582
25 and seven m' of them that were near"
25 m' of the people of the land, that 376
La 1:15 trodden under foot all my mighty m'
15 against me to crush my young m':
18 my young m' are gone into captivity.
2:15 the city that m' call The perfection
21 my young m' are fallen by the sword;
3:33 nor grieve the children of m'. 376
4:14 wandered as blind m' in the streets,
14 m' could not touch their garments.
5:13 They took the young m' to grind, and
14 gate, the young m' from their musick.
Eze 6: 4 cast down your slain m' before your
13 slain m' shall be among their idols
8:11 there stood before them seventy m' 376
16 about five and twenty m', with their"
9: 2 six m' came from the way of the 582
4 mark upon the foreheads of the m' "
6 they began at the ancient m' which "
11: 1 door of the gate five and twenty m';376
2 are the m' that devise mischief, 582
15 thy brethren, the m' of thy kindred, "
12:16 a few m' of them from the sword, "
14: 3 these m' have set up their idols in "
14 these three m', Noah, Daniel, and "
16, 18 these three m' were in it, as I "
15: 3 will m' take a pin of it to hang any
16:17 madest to thyself images of m', 2145
19: 3 to catch the prey; it devoured m'. 120
6 to catch the prey, and devoured m'. "
21:14 is the sword of the great m' that are*
31 thee into the hand of brutish m', 582
22: 9 In thee are m' that carry tales to "
23: 6 rulers, all of them desirable young m',
7 were the chosen m' of Assyria, 1121
12 horses, all of them desirable young m'.
14 she saw m' pourtrayed upon the 582

Eze 23:23 all of them desirable young *m'*,
40 have sent for *m'* to come from far, 582
42 and with the *m'* of the common sort "
45 the righteous *m'*, they shall judge "
24:17 thy lips, and eat not the bread of *m'*. "
22 your lips, nor eat the bread of *m'*. "
25: 4 deliver thee to the *m'* of the east 1121
10 *m'* of the east with the Ammonites,*"
26:10 as *m'* enter into a city wherein is made
17 that wast inhabited of seafaring *m'*,
27: 8 thy wise *m'*, O Tyrus, that were in
9 the wise *m'* thereof were in thee thy
10 were in thine army, thy *m'* of war: 582
11 The *m'* of Arvad with thine army 1121
13 they traded the persons of *m'* and 120
15 *m'* of Dedan were thy merchants; 1121
27 all thy *m'* of war, that are in thee, 582
30: 5 *m'* of the land that is in league, *1121
17 The young *m'* of Aven...shall fall
31:14 in the midst of the children of *m'*, 120
34:31 the flock of my pasture, are *m'*, and "
35: 8 fill his mountains with his slain *m'*:*
36:10 And I will multiply *m'* upon you, 120
12 I will cause *m'* to walk upon you, "
12 more henceforth bereave them of *m'*.*
13 Thou land devourest up *m'*, and 120
14 thou shalt devour *m'* no more, "
15 Neither will I cause *m'* to hear in thee*
37 increase them with *m'* like a flock. 120
38 cities be filled with flocks of *m'*: "
38:20 all the *m'* that are upon the face of "
39:14 they shall sever out *m'* of continual 582
20 horses and chariots, with mighty *m'*,
20 and with all *m'* of war, saith the 376
47:15 way of Hethlon, as *m'* go to Zedad;*
Da 2:12 to destroy all the wise *m'* of Babylon.
13 forth that the wise *m'* should be slain;
14 forth to slay the wise *m'* of Babylon:
18 with the rest of the wise *m'* of Babylon.
24 to destroy the wise *m'* of Babylon: he
24 Destroy not the wise *m'* of Babylon:
27 hath demanded cannot the wise *m'*,
38 the children of *m'* dwell, the 606
43 themselves with the seed of *m'*: "
48 over all the wise *m'* of Babylon.
3:12 these *m'*, O king, have not 1400
13 brought these *m'* before the king. "
20 commanded the most mighty *m'* "
21 these *m'* were bound in their coats, "
22 the fire slew those *m'* that took up "
23 these three *m'*, Shadrach, Meshach, "
24 Did not we cast three *m'* bound "
25 Lo, I see four *m'* loose, walking in "
27 saw these *m'*, upon whose bodies "
4: 6 to bring in all the wise *m'* of Babylon
17 High ruleth in the kingdom of *m'*, 606
17 setteth up over it the basest of *m'*. "
18 wise *m'* of my kingdom are not able
25 they shall drive thee from *m'*, and 606
25 High ruleth in the kingdom of *m'*, "
32 they shall drive thee from *m'*, and "
32 High ruleth in the kingdom of *m'*, "
33 he was driven from *m'*, and did eat "
5: 7 and said to the wise *m'* of Babylon,
8 Then came in all the king's wise *m'*:
15 And now the wise *m'*, the astrologers,
21 he was driven from the sons of *m'*; 606
21 God ruled in the kingdom of *m'*, "
6: 5 Then said these *m'*, We shall not 1400
11 Then these *m'* assembled, and found "
15 Then these *m'* assembled unto the "
24 *m'* which had accused Daniel, "
26 *m'* tremble and fear before the God of
9: 7 *m'* of Judah, and to the inhabitants 376
10: 7 *m'* that were with me saw not the 582
16 like the similitude of the sons of *m'* 120
Ho 6: 7 But they like *m'* have transgressed* "
10:13 in the multitude of thy mighty *m'*.
13: 2 *m'* that sacrifice kiss the calves. 120
Joe 1: 2 Hear this, ye old *m'*, and give ear, all
12 withered away from the sons of *m'*. 120
2: 7 shall run like mighty *m'*; they shall
7 shall climb the wall like *m'* of war; 582
28 your old *m'* shall dream dreams,
28 your young *m'* shall see visions:
3: 9 war, wake up the mighty *m'*, let 582
9 let all the *m'* of war draw near; let "
Am 2:11 and of your young *m'* for Nazarites.
4:10 your young *m'* have I slain with the
6: 9 there remain ten *m'* in one house, 582
8:13 virgins and young *m'* faint for thirst.
Ob 7 *m'* of thy confederacy have brought 582
7 the *m'* that were at peace with thee "
8 even destroy the wise *m'* out of Edom,
9 And thy mighty *m'*, O Teman, shall be
Jon 1:10 were the *m'* exceedingly afraid, 582
10 For the *m'* knew that he fled from "
13 Nevertheless the *m'* rowed hard to "
16 the *m'* feared the Lord exceedingly, "
Mic 2: 8 by securely as *m'* averse from war.
12 by reason of the multitude of *m'*. 120
5: 5 shepherds, and eight principal *m'*.
7 man, nor waiteth for the sons of *m'*.
6:12 rich *m'* thereof are full of violence,
7: 2 there is none upright among *m'*: 120
6 enemies are...*m'* of his own house. 582
Na 2: 3 shield of his mighty *m'* is made red,
3 red, the valiant *m'* are in scarlet: 582
3:10 they cast lots for her honourable *m'*,
10 all her great *m'* were bound in chains.
Hab 1:14 makest *m'* as the fishes of the sea, 120
Zep 1:12 punish the *m'* that are settled on 582
17 I will bring distress upon *m'*, that 120
17 that they shall walk like blind *m'*,
2:11 and *m'* shall worship him, every
Hag 1:11 and upon *m'*, and upon cattle, and 120

Zec 2: 4 for the multitude of *m'* and cattle 120
3: 8 for they are *m'* wondered at: for, 582
7: 2 their *m'*, to pray before the Lord,
7 when *m'* inhabited the south and the*
8: 4 There shall yet old *m'* and old women
10 I set all *m'* every one against his 120
23 that ten *m'* shall take hold out of 582
9:17 shall make the young *m'* cheerful,
10: 5 And they shall be as mighty *m'*, which
11: 6 I will deliver the *m'* every one into 120
14:11 And *m'* shall dwell in it, and there
M't 2: 1 there came wise *m'* from the east to
7 he had privily called the wise *m'*,
16 saw that he was mocked of the wise *m'*,
16 had diligently enquired of the wise *m'*.
4:19 and I will make you fishers of *m'*. 444
5:11 are ye, when *m'* shall revile you,
13 and to be trodden under foot of *m'*. 444
15 Neither do *m'* light a candle, and put
16 Let your light so shine before *m'*, 444
19 and shall teach *m'* so, he shall be "
6: 1 that ye do not your alms before *m'*, "
2 that they may have glory of *m'*. "
5 streets, that they may be seen of *m'*. "
14 For if ye forgive *m'* their trespasses, "
15 if ye forgive not *m'* their trespasses, "
16 they may appear unto *m'* to fast. "
18 thou appear not unto *m'* to fast, but "
7:12 ye would that *m'* should do to you, "
16 Do *m'* gather grapes of thorns, or figs
8:27 the *m'* marvelled, saying, What 444
9: 8 had given such power unto *m'*. "
17 Neither do *m'* put new wine into old
27 two blind *m'* followed him, crying, and
28 the house, the blind *m'* came to him:
10:17 beware of *m'*: for they will deliver 444
22 be hated of all *m'* for my name's
32 shall confess me before *m'*, him 444
33 whosoever shall deny me before *m'*, "
12:31 blasphemy shall be forgiven unto *m'*: "
31 Ghost shall not be forgiven unto *m'*.*"
36 every idle word that *m'* shall speak, "
41 The *m'* of Nineveh shall rise in 435
13:17 righteous *m'* have desired to see those
25 while *m'* slept, his enemy came and 444
14:21 eaten were about five thousand *m'*, 435
35 the *m'* of that place had knowledge "
15: 9 doctrines the commandments of *m'*. 444
38 that did eat were four thousand *m'*, 435
16:13 Whom do *m'* say that I the Son of 444
23 be of God, but those that be of *m'*. "
17:22 be betrayed into the hands of *m'*: "
19:11 All *m'* cannot receive this saying, save
12 which were made eunuchs of *m'*: 444
26 With *m'* this is impossible; but with "
20:30 two blind *m'* sitting by the way side,
21:25 was it? from heaven, or of *m'*? 444
26 if we shall say, Of *m'*; we fear the "
22:16 thou regardest not the person of *m'*. "
23: 5 works they do for to be seen of *m'*: "
7 and to be called of *m'*, Rabbi, Rabbi. "
13 the kingdom of heaven against *m'*: "
28 appear righteous unto *m'*, but "
34 send unto you prophets, and wise *m'*,
26:33 Though all *m'* shall be offended *
28: 4 did shake, and became as dead *m'*.
M'r 1:17 make you to become fishers of *m'*. 444
37 said unto him, All *m'* seek for thee.*
3:28 be forgiven unto the sons of *m'*, 444
5:20 done for him: and all *m'* did marvel.
6:12 and preached that *m'* should repent.
44 loaves were about five thousand *m'*. 435
7: 7 doctrines the commandments of *m'*. 444
8 ye hold the tradition of *m'*, as the "
21 out of the heart of *m'*, proceed evil "
8: 4 man satisfy these *m'* with bread here
24 and said, I see *m'* as trees, walking. 444
27 them, Whom do *m'* say that I am? "
33 of God, but the things that be of *m'*. "
9:31 is delivered into the hands of *m'*, "
10:27 With *m'* it is impossible, but not with "
11:30 John, was it from heaven, or of *m'*? "
32 if we shall say, Of *m'*; they feared "
32 for all *m'* counted John, that he was a*
12:14 regardest not the person of *m'*, but 444
13:13 be hated of all *m'* for my name's sake:
14:51 and the young *m'* laid hold on him:*3495
Lu 1:25 take away my reproach among *m'*. 444
2:14 on earth peace, good will toward *m'*. "
3:15 all *m'* mused in their hearts of John,
5:10 from henceforth thou shalt catch *m'*. 444
18 *m'* brought in a bed a man which 435
6:22 are ye, when *m'* shall hate you, and 444
26 when all *m'* shall speak well of you! "
31 ye would that *m'* should do to you, "
38 over, shall *m'* give into your bosom.*
44 For of thorns *m'* do not gather figs,
7:20 When the *m'* were come unto him, 435
31 I liken the *m'* of this generation? 444
9:14 they were about five thousand *m'*. 435
30 behold, there talked with him two *m'*, "
32 and the two *m'* that stood with him.
44 be delivered into the hands of *m'*. 444
11:31 with the *m'* of this generation, and 435
32 *m'* of Nineve shall rise up in the "
44 the *m'* that walk over them are not 444
46 ye lade *m'* with burdens grievous to "
12: 8 shall confess me before *m'*, him shall "
9 he that denieth me before *m'* shall "
36 like unto *m'* that wait for their lord,
48 to whom *m'* have committed much,*
13: 4 that they were sinners above all *m'* 444
14 six days in which *m'* ought to work:
14:24 none of those *m'* which were bidden 435
35 yet for the dunghill; but *m'* cast it out.
16:15 which justify yourselves before *m'*; 444

Lu 16:15 esteemed among *m'* is abomination 444
17:12 met him ten *m'* that were lepers, 435
34 there shall be two *m'* in one bed;
36 Two *m'* shall be in the field; the one*
18: 1 that *m'* ought always to pray, and not*
10 Two *m'* went up into the temple to 444
11 thee, that I am not as other *m'* are, "
27 impossible with *m'* are possible with "
20: 4 John, was it from heaven, or of *m'*? "
6 if we say, Of *m'*; all the people will "
20 which should feign themselves just *m'*,*
21: 1 rich *m'* casting their gifts into the
17 be hated of all *m'* for my name's sake.
22:63 the *m'* that held Jesus mocked him, 435
23:11 his *m'* of war set him at nought, *4753
24: 4 two *m'* stood by them in shining 435
7 delivered into the hands of sinful *m'*, 444
Joh 1: 4 and the life was the light of *m'*. "
7 that all *m'* through him might believe.*
2:10 and when *m'* have well drunk, then
24 unto them, because he knew all *m'*,
3:19 *m'* loved darkness rather than light, 444
26 baptizeth, and all *m'* come to him.
4:20 the place where *m'* ought to worship.
28 into the city, and saith to the *m'*, 444
38 other *m'* laboured, and ye are *
5:23 That all *m'* should honour the Son,*
41 I receive not honour from *m'*. 444
6:10 Jesus said, Make the *m'* sit down.* "
10 the *m'* sat down, in number about 435
14 Then those *m'*, when they had seen* 444
8:17 that the testimony of two *m'* is true. "
11:48 thus alone, all *m'* will believe on him:
12:32 the earth, will draw all *m'* unto me.
43 For they loved the praise of *m'* more 444
13:35 this shall all *m'* know that ye are my
15: 6 *m'* gather them, and cast them into the*
17: 6 manifested thy name unto the *m'* 444
18: 3 having received a band of *m'* and*
Ac 1:10 two *m'* stood by them in white 435
11 *m'* of Galilee, why stand ye gazing "
16 *M'* and brethren, this scripture "
21 these *m'* which have companied with
24 which knowest the hearts of all *m'*,
2: 5 Jews, devout *m'*, out of every nation 435
13 said, These *m'* are full of new wine.
14 Ye *m'* of Judæa, and all ye that 435
17 your young *m'* shall see visions, 3495
17 and your old *m'* shall dream dreams:
22 Ye *m'* of Israel, hear these words; 435
29 *M'* and brethren, let me freely *
37 *M'* and brethren, what shall we do?* "
45 parted them to all *m'*, as every man*
3:12 Ye *m'* of Israel, why marvel ye at 435
4: 4 the number of the *m'* was about five "
12 under heaven given among *m'*, 444
13 they were unlearned and ignorant *m'*, "
16 What shall we do to these *m'*? for
21 all *m'* glorified God for that which was
5: 4 thou hast not lied unto *m'*, but unto 444
6 the young *m'* arose, wound him up,
10 the young *m'* came in, and found 3495
14 multitudes both of *m'* and women.) 435
25 the *m'* whom ye put in prison are
29 ought to obey God rather than *m'*. 444
35 *m'* of Israel, take heed to yourselves 435
35 intend to do as touching these *m'*. 444
36 to whom a number of *m'*, about 435
38 Refrain from these *m'*, and let them 444
38 if this counsel or this work be of *m'*, "
6: 3 among you seven *m'* of honest 435
11 Then they suborned *m'*, which said, "
7: 2 *M'*, brethren, and fathers, hearken;* "
8: 2 *m'* carried Stephen to his burial, and "
3 *m'* and women committed them to "
12 were baptized, both *m'* and women. "
9: 2 whether they were *m'* or women, he "
7 the *m'* which journeyed with him "
38 there, they sent unto him two *m'*, "
10: 5 send *m'* to Joppa, and call for one "
17 *m'* which were sent from Cornelius "
19 unto him, Behold, three *m'* seek thee. "
21 went down to the *m'* which were sent "
11: 3 wentest in to *m'* uncircumcised, and "
11 there were three *m'* already come "
13 Send *m'* to Joppa, and call for *
20 them were *m'* of Cyprus and Cyrene, "
13:15 Ye *m'* and brethren, if ye have any* "
16 *M'* of Israel, and ye that fear God, "
26 *M'* and brethren, children of the * "
38 unto you therefore, *m'* and brethren,* "
50 women, and the chief *m'* of the city,
14:11 down to us in the likeness of *m'*. 444
15 We also are *m'* of like passions with "
15: 1 certain *m'* which came...from Judæa
7 *M'* and brethren, ye know how 435
13 *M'* and brethren, hearken unto me:* "
17 the residue of *m'* might seek after 444
22 send chosen *m'* of their...company 435
22 Silas, chief *m'* among the brethren: "
25 to send chosen *m'* unto you with our "
26 *M'* that have hazarded their lives 444
16:17 *m'* are the servants of the most high "
20 saying, These *m'*, being Jews, do "
35 serjeants, saying, Let those *m'* go. "
17:12 were Greeks, and of *m'*, not a few. 435
22 Ye *m'* of Athens, I perceive that in "
26 made of one blood all nations of *m'* 444
30 all *m'* every where to repent:
31 he hath given assurance unto all *m'*,
34 Howbeit certain *m'* clave unto him, 435
18:13 persuadeth *m'* to worship God 444
19: 7 And all the *m'* were about twelve. 435
19 and burned them before all *m'*: *
29 and Aristarchus, *m'* of Macedonia,
35 Ye *m'* of Ephesus, what man is there 435

Ac 19:37 ye have brought hither these m'. 435
20:26 I am pure from the blood of all m'.
30 of your own selves shall m' arise, 435
21:23 We have four m' which have a vow "
26 Then Paul took the m', and the next "
28 Crying out, M' of Israel, help: This "
28 man, that teacheth all m' every where
38 thousand m' that were murderers? 435
22: 1 M', brethren, and fathers, hear ye* "
4 into prisons both m' and women. "
15 thou shalt be his witness unto all m' 444
23: 1 M' and brethren, I have lived in * 435
6 M' and brethren, I am a Pharisee,* "
21 for him of them more than forty m', "
24:16 offence toward God, and toward m'. 444
25:23 and principal m' of the city, 435
24 all m' which are here present with "
28:17 M' and brethren, though I have * "
Ro 1:18 unrighteousness of m', who hold 444
27 also the m', leaving the natural use 730
27 m' with m' working that which is "
2:16 God shall judge the secrets of m' 444
29 whose praise is not of m', but of "
5:12 so death passed upon all m', for "
18 judgment came upon all m' to "
18 the free gift came upon all m' unto "
6:19 I speak after the manner of m' 442
11: 4 reserved...seven thousand m', 435
12:16 but condescend to m' of low estate.*
17 things honest in the sight of all m'. 444
18 in you, live peaceably with all m'. "
14:18 to God, and approved of m'. "
16:19 obedience is come abroad unto all m'.
1Co 1:25 foolishness of God is wiser than m', 444
25 weakness of God is stronger than m'."
26 that not many wise m' after the flesh,*
2: 5 not stand in the wisdom of m', but 444
3: 3 are ye not carnal, and walk as m'? "
21 Therefore let no man glory in m': "
4: 6 not to think of m' above that which is*
9 the world, and to angels, and to m'. 444
7: 7 that all m' were even as I myself. "
23 price; be not ye the servants of m'. "
9:19 For though I be free from all m', yet
22 I am made all things to all m', that I
10:15 I speak as to wise m'; judge ye what I
33 Even as I please all m' in all things,
13: 1 the tongues of m' and of angels, 444
14: 2 speaketh not unto m', but unto God: "
3 speaketh unto m' to edification, and "
20 but in understanding be m'. 5046
21 With m' of other tongues and other
15:19 we are of all m' most miserable. 444
32 after the manner of m' I have fought"
39 but there is one kind of flesh of m', "
16:13 faith, quit you like m', be strong. 407
2Co 3: 2 hearts, known and read of all m': 444
5:11 terror of the Lord, we persuade m'; "
8:13 mean not that other m' be eased, and*
21 Lord, but also in the sight of m'. 444
9:13 unto them, and unto all m'; *
Ga 1: 1 apostle, (not of m', neither by man, 444
10 For do I now persuade m', or God? "
10 or do I seek to please m'? for if I yet "
10 if I yet pleased m', I should not be "
3:15 I speak after the manner of m'; "
6:10 let us do good unto all m', especially
Eph 3: 5 made known unto the sons of m', 444
9 make all m' see what is the fellowship
4: 8 captive, and gave gifts unto m'. 444
14 by the sleight of m', and cunning "
5:28 So ought m' to love their wives as * 435
6: 7 as to the Lord, and not to m': 444
Ph'p 2: 7 and was made in the likeness of m': "
4: 5 moderation be known unto all m'. "
Col 2: 8 vain deceit, after the tradition of m', "
22 commandments and doctrines of m'? "
3:23 as to the Lord, and not unto m'; "
1Th 1: 5 what manner of m' we were among "
2: 4 not as pleasing m', but God, which 444
6 Nor of m' sought we glory, neither "
13 ye received it not as the word of m', "
15 not God, and are contrary to all m': "
5:14 the weak, be patient toward all m'.* "
15 both among yourselves, and to all m'.*
2Th 3: 2 from unreasonable and wicked m': 444
2 for all m' have not faith. *
1Ti 2: 1 of thanks, be made for all m'; 444
4 Who will have all m' to be saved, "
5 one mediator between God and m', "
8 I will...that m' pray every where, 435
4:10 God, who is the Saviour of all m', 444
5:24 and some m' they follow after. "
6: 5 disputings of m' of corrupt minds, "
9 which drown m' in destruction and "
2Ti 2: 2 the same commit thou to faithful m', "
24 be gentle unto all m', apt to teach,*
3: 2 For m' shall be lovers of their own 444
8 m' of corrupt minds, reprobate "
9 folly shall be manifest unto all m', "
13 But evil m' and seducers shall wax 444
4:16 stood with me, but all m' forsook me:*
Tit 1: 8 of hospitality, a lover of good m', *
14 fables, and commandments of m', 444
2: 2 That the aged m' be sober, grave,
6 Young m' likewise exhort to be sober
11 salvation hath appeared to all m', 444
3: 2 shewing all meekness unto all m'. "
8 are good and profitable unto m'. "
Heb 5: 1 high priest taken from among m' is "
1 for m' in things pertaining to God, "
6:16 For m' verily swear by the greater: "
7: 8 And here m' that die receive tithes; "
28 For the law maketh m' high priests "
9:17 is of force after m' are dead: *
27 it is appointed unto m' once to die, 444
Heb12:14 Follow peace with all m', and holiness,
Jas 2: 6 Do not rich m' oppress you, and draw*
3: 9 Therewith curse we m', which are 444
5: 1 Go to now, ye rich m', weep and howl *
1Pe 2: 4 disallowed indeed of m', but chosen 444
15 silence the ignorance of foolish m': "
17 Honour all m'. Love the brotherhood.*
4: 2 time in the flesh to the lusts of m', 444
6 judged according to m' in the flesh, "
2Pe 1:21 holy m' of God spake as they were "
3: 7 and perdition of ungodly m'. "
9 promise, as some m' count slackness;*
1Jo 2:13 I write unto you, young m', 3495
14 I have written unto you, young m', "
5: 9 If we receive the witness of m', 444
3Jo 12 Demetrius hath good report of all m', "
Jude 4 are certain m' crept in unawares, 444
4 ungodly m', turning the grace of "
Re 6:15 the great m', and the rich m', and the*
15 the chief captains, and the mighty m',*
8:11 and many m' died of the waters, 444
9: 4 m' which have not the seal of God "
6 in those days shall m' seek death, "
7 their faces were as the faces of m'.* "
10 power was to hurt m' five months. "
15 year, for to slay the third part of m'. "
18 three was the third part of m' killed, "
20 rest of the m' which were not killed* "
11:13 were slain of m' seven thousand: * "
13:13 on the earth in the sight of m', "
14: 4 These were redeemed from among m', "
16: 2 grievous sore upon the m' which had "
8 unto him to scorch m' with fire. "
9 m' were scorched with great heat, "
18 not since m' were upon the earth, "
21 there fell upon m' a great hail out of "
21 m' blasphemed God because of the "
18:13 chariots, and slaves, and souls of m'. "
23 were the great m' of the earth; *
19:18 the flesh of mighty m', and the flesh of
18 the flesh of all m', both free and bond,
21: 3 the tabernacle of God is with m', 444

Menahem (*men'-a-hem*)
2Ki 15:14 M' the son of Gadi went up from 4505
16 M' smote Tiphsah, and all that "
17 began M' the son of Gadi to reign "
19 M' gave Pul a thousand talents of "
20 M' exacted the money of Israel, "
21 the rest of the acts of M', and all "
22 And M' slept with his father; and "
23 the son of M' began to reign over "

Menan (*me'-nan*)
Lu 3:31 which was the son of M', which *3104

menchildren See also MEN and CHILDREN.
Ex 34:23 the year shall all your m' appear *2138

mend See also AMEND; MENDING.
2Ch 24:12 brass to m' the house of the Lord.*2388

mending
M't 4:21 with...their father, m' their nets; 2675
M'r 1:19 also were in the ship m' their nets. "

Mene (*me'-ne*)
Da 5:25 written, M', M', Tekel, Upharsin. 4484
26 M'; God hath numbered thy "

menpleasers
Eph 6: 6 Not with eyeservice, as m'; but as 441
Col 3:22 not with eyeservice, as m'; but in "

men's
Ge 24:32 and the m' feet that were with him. 582
44: 1 Fill the m' sacks with food, as much "
De 4:28 serve gods, the work of m' hands, 120
1Sa 24: 9 Wherefore hearest thou m' words,
1Ki 12:13 forsook the old m' counsel that they*
13: 2 m' bones shall be burnt upon thee. 120
2Ki 19:18 no gods, but the work of m' hands, "
23:20 and burned m' bones upon them, "
Ps 115: 4 and gold, the work of m' hands. "
135:15 and gold, the work of m' hands. "
Isa 37:19 no gods, but the work of m' hands. "
Jer 48:41 the mighty m' hearts in Moab at that*
Hab 2: 8, 17 because of m' blood, and for the120
M't 23: 4 and lay them on m' shoulders; but 444
27 but are within full of dead m' bones,
Lu 9:56 is not come to destroy m' lives, * 444
21:26 M' hearts failing them for fear, and*"
Ac 17:25 Neither is worshiped with m' hands, "
2Co 10:15 measure, that is, of other m' labours;
1Ti 5:22 neither be partaker of other m' sins:
24 Some m' sins are open beforehand,
1Pe 4:15 or as a busy body in other m' matters.
Jude 16 having m' persons in admiration *4283

menservants
Ge 12:16 and oxen, and he asses, and m', 5650
20:14 took sheep, and oxen, and m', and "
24:35 herds, and silver, and gold, and m', "
30:43 cattle, and maidservants, and m', "
32: 5 oxen, and asses, flocks, and m', and "
Ex 21: 7 she shall not go out as the m' do. "
De 12:12 your m', and your maidservants, "
1Sa 8:16 he will take your m', and your "
2Ki 5:26 and sheep, and oxen, and m', and "
Lu 12:45 shall begin to beat the m' and 3816

menstealers
1Ti 1:10 with mankind, for m', for liars, 405

menstruous
Isa 30:22 cast them away as a m' cloth; *1739
La 1:17 Jerusalem is as a m' woman *5079
Eze 18: 6 hath come near to a m' woman, * "

mention See also MENTIONED.
Ge 40:14 and make m' of me unto Pharaoh, 2142
Ex 23:13 make no m' of the name of other "
Jos 23: 7 make m' of the name of their gods, "
1Sa 4:18 when he made m' of the ark of God, 2142
Job 28:18 No m' shall be made of coral, or of "
Ps 71:16 will make m' of thy righteousness, "
87: 4 make m' of Rahab and Babylon to "
Isa 12: 4 make m' that his name is exalted. "
19:17 every one that maketh m' thereof "
26:13 only will we make m' of thy name. "
48: 1 and make m' of the God of Israel, "
49: 1 hath he made m' of my name. "
62: 6 ye that make m' of the Lord, keep* "
63: 7 m' the lovingkindness of the Lord, "
Jer 4:16 Make ye m' to the nations; behold, "
20: 9 I said, I will not make m' of him, "
23:36 burden of the Lord shall ye m' no "
Am 6:10 make m' of the name of the Lord. "
Ro 1: 9 m' of you always in my prayers; 3417
Eph 1:16 making m' of you in my prayers; "
1Th 1: 2 making m' of you in our prayers; "
Ph'm 4 m' of thee always in my prayers, "
Heb11:22 died, made m' of the departing of 3421

mentioned
Jos 21: 9 these cities which are here m' by 7121
1Ch 4:38 m' by their names were princes 935
2Ch 20:34 who is m' in the book of the kings*5927
Eze 16:56 For thy sister Sodom was not m' 8052
18:22 they shall not be m' unto him: *2142
24 that he hath done shall not be m':* "
33:16 hath committed shall be m' unto * "

Meon See BAAL-MEON; BETH-MEON.

Meonenim (*me-on'-e-nim*)
J'g 9:37 come along by the plain of M'. 6049

Meonothai (*me-on'-o-thahee*)
1Ch 4:14 M' begat Ophrah: and Seraiah 4587

Mephaath (*mef'-a-ath*)
Jos 13:18 Jahaza, and Kedemoth, and M', 4158
21:37 M' with her suburbs; four cities. "
1Ch 6:79 suburbs, and M' with her suburbs: "
Jer 48:21 and upon Jahazah, and upon M', "

Mephibosheth (*me-fib'-o-sheth*) See also MERIB-BAAL.
2Sa 4: 4 lame. And his name was M'. 4648
9: 6 Now when M', the son of Jonathan, "
6 And David said, M'. And he "
10 M' thy master's son shall eat bread "
11 As for M', said the king, he shall "
12 M' had a young son, whose name "
12 of Ziba were servants unto M'. "
13 So M' dwelt in Jerusalem: for he "
16: 1 Ziba the servant of M' met him, "
4 are all that pertained unto M'. "
19:24 M' the son of Saul came down to "
25 wentest not thou with me, M'? "
30 M' said unto the king, Yea, let him "
21: 7 But the king spared M', the son of "
8 bare unto Saul, Armoni and M'; "

Merab (*me'-rab*)
1Sa 14:49 the name of the firstborn M', and 4764
18:17 Behold my elder daughter M', her "
19 pass at the time when M' Saul's "

Meraiah (*mer-a-i'-ah*)
Ne 12:12 of the fathers: of Seraiah, M'; of 4811

Meraioth (*me-rah'-yoth*) See also MEREMOTH.
1Ch 6: 6 Zerahiah, and Zerahiah begat M', 4812
7 M' begat Amariah, and Amariah "
52 M' his son, Amariah his son, "
9:11 the son of M', the son of Ahitub, "
Ezr 7: 3 the son of Azariah, the son of M', "
Ne 11:11 the son of Zadok, the son of M', the "
12:15 Of Harim, Adna; of M', Helkai; "

Merari (*me-ra'-ri*) See also MERARITES.
Ge 46:11 Levi; Gershon, Kohath, and M'. 4847
Ex 6:16 Gershon, and Kohath, and M': "
19 the sons of M'; Mahali and Mushi: "
Nu 3:17 Gershon, and Kohath, and M'. "
20 the sons of M' by their families; "
33 M' was the family of the Mahlites, "
33 these are the families of M'. "
35 of the families of M' was Zuriel the "
36 custody and charge of the sons of M' "
4:29 the sons of M', thou shalt number "
33, 42, 45 the families of the sons of M', "
7: 8 oxen he gave unto the sons of M', "
10:17 sons of M' set forward, bearing the "
26:57 of M', the family of the Merarites. "
Jos 21: 7 The children of M' by their families "
34 the families of the children of M', "
40 all the cities for the children of M' "
1Ch 6: 1 of Levi; Gershon, Kohath, and M'. "
16 of Levi; Gershom, Kohath, and M'. "
19 The sons of M'; Mahli, and Mushi. "
29 The sons of M'; Mahli; Libni his "
44 sons of M' stood on the left hand: "
47 the son of Mushi, the son of M', "
63 Unto the sons of M' were given by "
77 Unto the rest of the children of M' "
9:14 of Hashabiah, of the sons of M'; "
15: 6 Of the sons of M'; Asaiah the chief, "
17 of the sons of M' their brethren, "
23: 6 namely, Gershon, Kohath, and M'. "
21 The sons of M'; Mahli, and Mushi. "
24:26 sons of M' were Mahli and Mushi: "
27 The sons of M' by Jaaziah; Beno, "
26:10 Hosah, of the children of M', had "
19 Kore, and among the sons of M'. "
2Ch 29:12 and of the sons of M'; Kish the son "
34:12 the Levites, of the sons of M', "
Ezr 8:19 him Jeshaiah of the sons of M', "

Merarites (*me-ra'-rites*)
Nu 26:57 of Merari, the family of the M'. 4848

Merathaim (*mer-a-tha'-im*)
Jer 50:21 Go up against the land of M', 4850

merchandise
De 21:14 thou shalt not make m' of her, *6014
24: 7 maketh m' of him, or selleth him;* "
Pr 3:14 For the m' of it is better than the 5504
14 is better than the m' of silver, 5505
31:18 perceiveth that her m' is good: 5504
Isa 23:18 m' and her hire shall be holiness "
18 her m' shall be for them that dwell "
45:14 m' of Ethiopia and of the Sabeans.5505
Eze 26:12 riches, and make a prey of thy m': 7404
27: 9 were in thee to occupy thy m'. 4627
15 isles were the m' of thine hand: *5506
24 and made of cedar, among thy m'.4819
27 and thy fairs, thy m', thy mariners,4627
27 calkers, and the occupiers of thy m'."
33 multitude of thy riches and of thy m'."
34 thy m' and all thy company in the "
28:16 By the multitude of thy m' they *7404
M't 22: 5 one to his farm, another to his m': 1711
Joh 2:16 my Father's house an house of m'.1712
2Pe 2: 3 with feigned words make m' of you:
Re 18:11 no man buyeth their m' any more: 1117
12 m' of gold, and silver, and precious "

merchant See also MERCHANTMEN; MERCHANTS.
Ge 23:16 silver, current money with the m'.
Pr 31:24 delivereth girdles unto the m'. 5503
Ca 3: 6 with all powders of the m'? 7402
Isa 23:11 against the m' city, to destroy *3667
Eze 27: 3 a m' of the people for many isles, 7402
12 Tarshish was thy m' by reason of 5503
16 Syria was thy m' by reason of the "
18 Damascus was thy m' in the "
20 Dedan was thy m' in precious *7402
Ho 12: 7 He is a m', the balances of deceit*3667
Zep 1:11 for all the m' people are cut down;*"
M't 13:45 of heaven is like unto a m' man, 1713

merchantmen See also MERCHANT and MEN.
Ge 37:28 there passed by Midianites m'; 5503
1Ki 10:15 Besides that he had of the m', *8446

merchants See also MERCHANTS'.
1Ki 10:15 and of the traffick of the spice m', 7402
28 king's m' received the linen yarn 5503
2Ch 1:16 king's m' received the linen yarn at"
9:14 which chapmen and m' brought. "
Ne 3:31 of the Nethinims, and of the m', 7402
32 repaired the goldsmiths and the m'."
13:20 m' and sellers of all kind of ware "
Job 41: 6 shall they part him among the m'?3669
Isa 23: 2 the m' of Zidon, that pass over 5503
8 crowning city, whose m' are princes,"
47:15 thou hast laboured, even thy m', * "
Eze 17: 4 traffick; he set it in a city of m'. 7402
27:13 and Mesech, they were thy m': * "
15 The men of Dedan were thy m'; * "
17 land of Israel, they were thy m': * "
21 goats: in these were they thy m'. 5503
22 The m' of Sheba and Raamah, *7402
22 they were thy m': they occupied in*"
23 Canneh, and Eden, the m' of Sheba,*"
23 Asshur, and Chilmad, were thy m'.*"
24 were thy m' in all sorts of things, * "
36 m' among the people shall hiss at 5503
38:13 and Dedan, and the m' of Tarshish,"
Na 3:16 multiplied thy m' above the stars 7402
Re 18: 3 the m' of the earth are waxed rich 1713
11 the m' of the earth shall weep and "
15 The m' of these things, which were "
23 m' were the great men of the earth;"

merchants'
Pr 31:14 She is like the m' ships; she *5503

mercies See also MERCIES'.
Ge 32:10 worthy of the least of all the m', ‡2617
2Sa 24:14 of the Lord, for his m' are great: 7356
1Ch 21:13 the Lord; for very great are his m':"
2Ch 6:42 remember the m' of David thy ‡2617
Ne 9:19 thou in thy manifold m' forsookest7356
27 according to thy manifold m' thou "
28 deliver them according to thy m'; "
Ps 25: 6 O Lord, thy tender m' and thy "
40:11 not thou thy tender m' from me, "
51: 1 unto the multitude of thy tender m'"
69:16 to the multitude of thy tender m'. "
77: 9 he in anger shut up his tender m'? "
79: 8 let thy tender m' speedily prevent "
89: 1 I will sing of the m' of the Lord ‡2617
103: 4 lovingkindness and tender m'; 7356
106: 7 not the multitude of thy m'; ‡2617
45 according to the multitude of his m'.‡"
119:41 thy m' come also unto me, O Lord,‡ "
77 Let thy tender m' come unto me, 7356
156 Great are thy tender m', O Lord: "
145: 9 his tender m' are over all his works."
Pr 12:10 tender m' of the wicked are cruel. "
Isa 54: 7 with great m' will I gather thee. "
55: 3 you, even the sure m' of David. ‡2617
63: 7 on them according to his m', and 7356
15 of thy bowels and of thy m' toward* "
Jer 16: 5 Lord, even lovingkindness and m'. "
42:12 I will shew m' unto you, that ye may*"
La 3:22 It is of the Lord's m' that we are ‡2617
32 according...the multitude of his m'.‡"
Da 2:18 they would desire m' of the God 7359
9: 9 To the Lord our God belong m' 7356
18 righteousnesses,...for thy great m'. "
Ho 2:19 and in lovingkindness, and in m'. "
Zec 1:16 I am returned to Jerusalem with m':"
Ac 13:34 will give you the sure m' of David.*3741
Ro 12: 1 by the m' of God, that ye present 3628
2Co 1: 3 the Father of m', and the God of all "
Ph'p 2: 1 of the Spirit, if any bowels and m',* "
Col 3:12 bowels of m', kindness, humbleness*"

mercies'
Ne 9:31 Nevertheless for thy great m' sake*7356
Ps 6: 4 soul: oh save me for thy m' sake.*2617
31:16 servant: save me for thy m' sake.*2617
44:26 help, and redeem us for thy m' sake.*"

merciful
Ge 19:16 the Lord being m' unto him: and 2551
Ex 34: 6 The Lord God, m' and gracious, *7349
De 4:31 (For the Lord thy God is a m' God;) "
21: 8 Be m', O Lord, unto thy people 3722
32:43 and will be m' unto his land, and * "
2Sa 22:26 With the m' thou wilt shew thyself2623
26 wilt shew thyself m', and with the 2616
1Ki 20:31 the house of Israel are m' kings: ‡2617
2Ch 30: 9 Lord your God is gracious and m'.7349
Ne 9:17 ready to pardon, gracious and m',* "
31 for thou art a gracious and m' God. "
Ps 18:25 With the m' thou wilt shew thyself2623
25 shew thyself m'; with an upright 2616
26:11 redeem me, and be m' unto me. 2603
37:26 He is ever m', and lendeth; and his*"
41: 4 Lord, be m' unto me: heal my soul;*"
10 But thou, O Lord, be m' unto me, * "
56: 1 Be m' unto me, O God: for man "
57: 1 Be m' unto me, O God, be m' unto "
59: 5 be not m' to...wicked transgressors."
67: 1 God be m' unto us, and bless us; "
86: 3 Be m' unto me, O Lord: for I cry "
103: 8 the Lord is m' and gracious, slow*7349
116: 5 and righteous; yea, our God is m'. "
117: 2 his m' kindness is great toward †‡2617
119:58 be m' unto me according to thy 2603
76 m' kindness be for my comfort, *2617
132 be m' unto me, as thou usest to do*2603
Pr 11:17 The m' man doeth good to his own‡2617
Isa 57: 1 and m' men are taken away, none‡ "
Jer 3:12 for I am m', saith the Lord, and 2623
Joe 2:13 for he is gracious and m', slow to *7349
Jon 4: 2 art a gracious God, and m', slow to*"
M't 5: 7 Blessed are the m': for they shall 1655
Lu 6:36 m', as your Father also is m'. 3629
18:13 saying, God be m' to me a sinner. 2433
Heb 2:17 be a m' and faithful high priest 1655
8:12 be m' to their unrighteousness, 2436

Mercurius (*mer-cu'-re-us*)
Ac 14:12 Barnabas, Jupiter; and Paul, M'. *2060

mercy See also MERCIES; MERCIFUL; MERCYSEAT.
Ge 19:19 and thou hast magnified thy m', ‡2617
24:27 left destitute my master of his m' ‡ "
39:21 with Joseph, and shewed him m',* "
43:14 Almighty give you m' before the 7356
Ex 15:13 Thou in thy m' hast led forth the ‡2617
20: 6 shewing m' unto thousands of them‡"
25:17 shalt make a m' seat of pure gold: 3727
18 them, in the two ends of the m' seat."
19 of the m' seat shall ye make the "
20 covering...m' seat with their wings, "
20 toward the m' seat shall the faces of"
21 put the m' seat above upon the ark;"
22 with thee from above the m' seat, "
26:34 put the m' seat upon the ark of the "
30: 6 m' seat that is over the testimony, "
31: 7 the m' seat that is thereupon, and "
33:19 shew m' on whom I will shew m'. 7355
34: 7 Keeping m' for thousands, ‡2617
35:12 staves thereof, with the m' seat, 3727
37: 6 he made the m' seat of pure gold: "
7 on the two ends of the m' seat; "
8 out of the m' seat made he the "
9 with their wings over the m' seat, "
9 to the m' seatward were the faces "
39:35 the staves thereof, and the m' seat, "
40:20 put the m' seat above upon the ark: "
Le 16: 2 within the vail before the m' seat, "
2 appear in the cloud upon the m' seat."
13 the incense may cover the m' seat "
14 finger upon the m' seat eastward; "
14 before the m' seat shall he sprinkle "
15 and sprinkle it upon the m' seat, "
15 and before the m' seat: "
Nu 7:89 unto him from off the m' seat that "
14:18 is longsuffering, and of great m', ‡2617
19 unto the greatness of thy m', and ‡ "
De 5:10 shewing m' unto thousands of them‡"
7: 2 with them, nor shew m' unto them:2603
9 covenant and m' with them that ‡2617
12 and the m' which he sware unto ‡ "
13:17 of his anger, and shew thee m', 7356
J'g 1:24 city, and we will shew thee m'. *2617
2Sa 7:15 But my m' shall not depart away ‡ "
15:20 m' and truth be with thee. ‡ "
22:51 sheweth m' to his anointed, unto * "
1Ki 3: 6 servant David my father great m',* "
8:23 covenant and m' with thy servants‡ "
1Ch 16:34 good; for his m' endureth for ever.‡"
41 because his m' endureth for ever;‡ "
17:13 not take my m' away from him, as‡ "
28:11 and of the place of the m' seat. 3727
2Ch 1: 8 hast shewed great m' unto David *2617
5:13 good; for his m' endureth for ever:‡"
6:14 shewest m' unto thy servants, that‡ "
7: 3 good; for his m' endureth for ever; "
6 because his m' endureth for ever,‡ "
20:21 Lord; for his m' endureth for ever.‡"
Ezr 3:11 his m' endureth for ever toward ‡ "
7:28 hath extended m' unto me before‡ "
9: 9 hath extended m' unto us in the ‡ "
Ne 1: 5 keepeth covenant and m' for them‡ "
11 and grant him m' in the sight of 7356
9:32 who keepest covenant and m', let‡2617
13:22 to the greatness of thy m'. ‡ "
Job 37:13 or for his land, or for m'. ‡ "
Ps 4: 1 have m' upon me, and hear my 2603
5: 7 house in the multitude of thy m':*2617
6: 2 Have m' upon me, O Lord; for I 2603
9:13 Have m' upon me, O Lord; consider"
13: 5 But I have trusted in thy m'; my ‡2617
18:50 and sheweth m' to his anointed, to* "
Ps 21: 7 through the m' of the most High *2617
23: 6 goodness and m' shall follow me ‡ "
25: 7 according to thy m' remember thou*"
10 paths of the Lord are m' and truth*"
16 unto me, and have m' upon me; 2603
27: 7 have m' also upon me, and answer "
30:10 O Lord, and have m' upon me: "
31: 7 will be glad and rejoice in thy m':‡2617
9 Have m' upon me, O Lord, for I am2603
32:10 Lord, m' shall compass him about.‡2617
33:18 upon them that hope in his m'; ‡ "
22 Let thy m', O Lord, be upon us, ‡ "
36: 5 Thy m', O Lord, is in the heavens;* "
37:21 but the righteous sheweth m', *2603
51: 1 Have m' upon me, O God, according"
52: 8 I trust in the m' of God for ever ‡2617
57: 3 God shall send forth his m' and his‡"
10 thy m' is great unto the heavens, ‡ "
59:10 The God of my m' shall prevent ‡ "
16 I will sing aloud of thy m' in the ‡ "
17 my defence, and the God of my m'.‡"
61: 7 O prepare m' and truth, which may*"
62:12 unto thee, O Lord, belongeth m': ‡ "
66:20 my prayer, nor his m' from me. ‡ "
69:13 in the multitude of thy m' hear me,‡"
77: 8 Is his m' clean gone for ever? doth‡ "
85: 7 Shew us thy m', O Lord, and grant‡ "
10 M' and truth are met together; ‡ "
86: 5 plenteous in m' unto all them that‡ "
13 For great is thy m' toward me: and‡"
15 and plenteous in m' and truth. ‡ "
16 unto me, and have m' upon me; 2603
89: 2 said, M' shall be built up for ever:‡2617
14 m' and truth shall go before thy ‡ "
24 and my m' shall be with him: and‡ "
28 My m' will I keep for him for ‡ "
90:14 O satisfy us early with thy m'; that‡"
94:18 thy m', O Lord, held me up. ‡ "
98: 3 He hath remembered his m' and ‡ "
100: 5 is good; his m' is everlasting; ‡ "
101: 1 I will sing of m' and judgment: unto‡"
102:13 arise, and have m' upon Zion: for 7355
103: 8 to anger, and plenteous in m'. ‡2617
11 great is his m' toward them that ‡ "
17 But the m' of the Lord is from ‡ "
106: 1 good: for his m' endureth for ever.‡"
107: 1 good: for his m' endureth for ever.‡"
108: 4 thy m' is great above the heavens:‡ "
109:12 be none to extend m' unto him: ‡ "
16 he remembered not to shew m', ‡ "
21 because thy m' is good, deliver thou‡"
26 O save me according to thy m': ‡ "
115: 1 for thy m', and for thy truth's sake.‡"
118: 1 because his m' endureth for ever. ‡ "
2, 3, 4 that his m' endureth for ever.‡ "
29 good: for his m' endureth for ever.‡"
119:64 The earth, O Lord, is full of thy m':‡"
124 thy servant according unto thy m',‡ "
123: 2 God, until that he have m' upon us.2603
3 Have m' upon us, O Lord, have m' "
130: 7 for with the Lord there is m', and ‡2617
136: 1, 2, 3, 4, 5, 6 his m' endureth for ever.‡"
7, 8 for his m' endureth for ever: ‡ "
9 for his m' endureth for ever. ‡ "
10, 11 for his m' endureth for ever: ‡ "
12 arm: for his m' endureth for ever.‡ "
13, 14 for his m' endureth for ever: ‡ "
15, 16 for his m' endureth for ever. ‡ "
17, 18, 19, 20, 21 for his m' endureth for‡"
22 for his m' endureth for ever. ‡ "
23 for his m' endureth for ever: ‡ "
24, 25, 26 for his m' endureth for ever.‡ "
138: 8 thy m', O Lord, endureth for ever:‡ "
143:12 And of thy m' cut off mine enemies,*"
145: 8 slow to anger, and of great m'. ‡ "
147:11 him, in those that hope in his m'. ‡ "
Pr 3: 3 Let not m' and truth forsake thee:‡ "
14:21 but he that hath m' on the poor, *2603
22 m' and truth shall be to them that‡2617
31 honoureth him hath m' on the 2603
16: 6 m' and truth iniquity is purged: ‡2617
20:28 M' and truth preserve the king: ‡ "
28 and his throne is upholden by m'.‡ "
21:21 righteousness and m' findeth life, "
28:13 and forsaketh them shall have m'. 7355
Isa 9:17 shall have m' on their fatherless * "
14: 1 the Lord will have m' on Jacob, "
16: 5 And in m' shall the throne be *2617
27:11 them will not have m' on them, *7355
30:18 that he may have m' upon you: "
47: 6 thou didst shew them no m'; upon7356
49:10 he that hath m' on them shall lead7355
13 and will have m' upon his afflicted.*"
54: 8 kindness will I have m' on thee, "
10 saith the Lord that hath m' on thee."
55: 7 and he will have m' upon him; and "
60:10 in my favour have I had m' on thee."
Jer 6:23 they are cruel, and have no m'; "
13:14 not pity, nor spare, nor have m', * "
21: 7 neither have pity, nor have m'. "
30:18 and have m' on his dwellingplaces;*"
31:20 I will surely have m' upon him, "
33:11 for his m' endureth for ever: and ‡2617
26 to return, and have m' on them. 7355
42:12 that he may have m' upon you, and "
50:42 are cruel, and will not shew m': "
Eze 39:25 and have m' upon the whole house "
Da 4:27 by shewing m' to the poor; if it 2604
9: 4 and m' to them that love him, ‡2617
Ho 1: 6 no more have m' upon the house 7355
7 have m' upon the house of Judah, "
2: 4 will not have m' upon her children; "
23 earth; and I will have m' upon her "
23 upon her that had not obtained m'; "
4: 1 because there is no truth, nor m',‡2617
6: 6 For I desired m', and not sacrifice;‡"

Ho 10:12 in righteousness, reap in m'; break‡2617
12: 6 keep m' and judgment, and wait ‡ "
14: 3 in thee the fatherless findeth m'. 7355
Jon 2: 8 vanities forsake their own m'. ‡2617
Mic 6: 8 but to do justly, and to love m', ‡ "
7:18 ever, because he delighteth in m'.‡ "
20 the m' to Abraham, which thou ‡ "
Hab 3: 2 known; in wrath remember m'. 7355
Zec 1:12 thou not have m' on Jerusalem and "
7: 9 and shew m' and compassions ‡2617
10: 6 for I have m' upon them: and they7355
M't 5: 7 merciful: for they shall obtain m'. 1653
9:13 I will have m', and not sacrifice: 1656
27 Thou son of David, have m' on us. 1653
12: 7 I will have m', and not sacrifice, 1656
15:22 Have m' on me, O Lord, thou son 1653
17:15 Lord, have m' on my son: for he is "
20:30, 31 Have m' on us, O Lord, thou son "
23:23 the law, judgment, m', and faith: 1656
M'r 10:47, 48 son of David, have m' on me. 1653
Lu 1:50 his m' is on them that fear him 1656
54 Israel, in remembrance of his m'; "
58 Lord had shewed great m' upon her; "
72 To perform the m' promised to our "
78 Through the tender m' of our God; "
10:37 he said, He that shewed m' on him. "
16:24 Father Abraham, have m' on me, 1653
17:13 said, Jesus, Master, have m' on us. "
18:38, 39 thou son of David, have m' on me. "
Ro 9:15 have m' on whom I will have m', "
16 but of God that sheweth m'. "
18 Therefore hath he m' on whom he "
18 on whom he will have m', and on *
23 of his glory on the vessels of m', 1656
11:30 yet have now obtained m' through 1653
31 that through your m' they also 1656
31 they also may obtain m'. 1653
32 that he might have m' upon all. "
12: 8 that sheweth m', with cheerfulness. "
15: 9 might glorify God for his m'; 1656
1Co 7:25 that hath obtained m' of the Lord 1653
2Co 4: 1 as we have received m', we faint not; "
Ga 6:16 rule, peace be on them, and m', 1656
Eph 2: 4 But God, who is rich in m', for his "
Ph'p 2:27 but God had m' on him; and not on 1653
1Ti 1: 2 Grace, m', and peace, from God 1656
13 but I obtained m', because I did it 1653
16 for this cause I obtained m', that "
2Ti 1: 2 Grace, m', and peace, from God 1656
16 The Lord give m' unto the house "
18 that he may find m' of the Lord in "
Tit 1: 4 Grace, m', and peace, from God * "
3: 5 but according to his m' he saved us, "
Heb 4:16 that we may obtain m', and find "
10:28 Moses' law died without m' under*3628
Jas 2:13 he shall have judgment without m', 448
13 that hath shewed no m'; 1656
13 and m' rejoiceth against judgment. "
3:17 full of m' and good fruits, without "
5:11 is very pitiful, and of tender m'. *3629
1Pe 1: 3 according to his abundant m' hath1656
2:10 of God: which had not obtained m',1653
10 but now have obtained m'. "
2Jo 3 Grace be with you, m', and peace, 1656
Jude 2 M' unto you, and peace, and love, "
21 for the m' of our Lord Jesus Christ "

mercyseat See also MERCY and SEAT.
Heb 9: 5 of glory shadowing the m'; 2435

Mered (me'-red)
1Ch 4:17 sons of Ezra were, Jether, and M',4778
18 daughter of Pharaoh, which M' took. "

Meremoth (mer'-e-moth) See also MERAIOTH.
Ezr 8:33 by the hand of M' the son of Uriah4822
10:36 Vaniah, M', Eliashib, "
Ne 3: 4 them repaired M' the son of Urijah, "
21 him repaired M' the son of Urijah "
10: 5 Harim, M', Obadiah, "
12: 3 Shechaniah, Rehum, M', "

Meres (me'-res)
Es 1:14 M', Marsena, and Memucan, 4825

Meribah (mer'-i-bah) See also MASSAH; MERIBAH-KADESH.
Ex 17: 7 name of the place Massah, and M',4809
Nu 20:13 This is the water of M'; because "
24 against my word at the water of M'. "
27:14 that is the water of M' in Kadesh "
De 33: 8 didst strive at the waters of M'; "
Ps 81: 7 I proved thee at the waters of M'. "

Meribah-Kadesh (mer''-i-bah-ka'-desh)
De 32:51 of Israel at the waters of M',*4809, 6946

Merib-baal (me-rib'-ba-al) See also MEPHIBOSHETH.
1Ch 8:34 And the son of Jonathan was M'; 4807
34 and M' begat Micah. "
9:40 And the son of Jonathan was M': "
40 and M' begat Micah. 4810

Merodach (mer'-o-dak) See also BERODACH; EVIL-MERODACH; MERODACH-BALADAN.
Jer 50: 2 M' is broken in pieces; 4781

Merodach-baladan (mer''-o-dak-bal'-a-dan) See also BERODACH-BALADAN.
Isa 39: 1 that time M', the son of Baladan, 4757

Merom (me'-rom)
Jos 11: 5 together at the waters of M', 4792
7 against them by the waters of M' "

Meron See SHIMRON-MERON; MERONOTHITE.

Meronothite (me-ron'-o-thite)
1Ch 27:30 the asses was Jehdeiah the M': 4824
Ne 3: 7 the Gibeonite, and Jadon the M', "

Meroz (me'-roz)
J'g 5:23 Curse ye M', said the angel of the 4789

merrily
Es 5:14 then go thou in m' with the king 8056

merry See also MERRYHEARTED.
Ge 43:34 they drank, and were m' with him. 7937
J'g 9:27 trode the grapes, and made m', *1974
16:25 pass, when their hearts were m', 2896
19: 6 all night, and let thine heart be m'. 3190
9 here, that thine heart may be m'; "
22 they were making their hearts m', "
Ru 3: 7 and drunk, and his heart was m', "
1Sa 25:36 Nabal's heart was m' within him, 2896
2Sa 13:28 Amnon's heart is m' with wine, "
1Ki 4:20 and drinking, and making m'. 8056
21: 7 bread, and let thine heart be m': 3190
2Ch 7:10 their tents, glad and m' in heart 2896
Es 1:10 when the heart of the king was m' "
Pr 15:13 A m' heart maketh a cheerful 8056
15 but he that is of a m' heart hath a*2896
17:22 A m' heart doeth good like a 8056
Ec 8:15 to eat, and to drink, and to be m': 8055
9: 7 drink thy wine with a m' heart; 2896
10:19 for laughter, and wine maketh m':8055
Jer 30:19 the voice of them that make m': 7832
31: 4 in the dances of them that make m'. "
Lu 12:19 thine ease, eat, drink, and be m'. 2165
15:23 and kill it; and let us eat, and be m': "
24 is found. And they began to be m'. "
29 I might make m' with my friends: "
32 was meet that we should make m', "
Jas 5:13 Is any m'? let him sing psalms. *2114
Re 11:10 rejoice over them, and make m', 2165

merryhearted
Isa 24: 7 languisheth, all the m' do sigh. 8056, 3820

Mesech (me'-sek) See also MESHECH.
Ps 120: 5 Woe is me, that I sojourn in M', *4902

Mesha (me'-shah)
Ge 10:30 And their dwelling was from M', 4331
2Ki 3: 4 M'...of Moab was a sheepmaster, 4337
1Ch 2:42 M' his firstborn, which was the 4338
8: 9 and Zibia, and M', and Malcham, 4331

Meshach (me'-shak)
Da 1: 7 Shadrach; and to Mishael, of M'; 4335
2:49 set Shadrach, M', and Abed-nego, 4336
3:12 Shadrach, M', and Abed-nego; "
13 bring Shadrach, M', and Abed-nego. "
14 O Shadrach, M', and Abed-nego, "
16 Shadrach, M', and Abed-nego, "
19 was changed against Shadrach, M'," "
20 bind Shadrach, M', and Abed-nego, "
22 men that took up Shadrach, M', "
23 Shadrach, M', and Abed-nego, fell "
26 spake, and said, Shadrach, M', and "
26 Shadrach, M', and Abed-nego, "
28 be the God of Shadrach, M', and "
29 against the God of Shadrach, M', "
30 the king promoted Shadrach, M', "

Meshech (me'-shek) See also MESECH.
Ge 10: 2 and Tubal, and M', and Tiras. 4902
1Ch 1: 5 and Tubal, and M', and Tiras. "
17 Uz, and Hul, and Gether, and M'. "
Eze 27:13 and M', they were thy merchants: "
32:26 There is M', Tubal, and all her "
38: 2 the chief prince of M' and Tubal, "
3 the chief prince of M' and Tubal: "
39: 1 the chief prince of M' and Tubal: "

Meshelemiah (me-shel-e-mi'-ah) See also MESHULLAM; SHELEMIAH; SHALLUM.
1Ch 9:21 the son of M' was porter of the 4920
26: 1 Korhites was M' the son of Kore, "
2 the sons of M' were, Zechariah the "
9 M' had sons and brethren, strong "

Meshezabeel (me-shez'-a-be-el)
Ne 3: 4 son of Berechiah, the son of M'. *4898
10:21 M', Zadok, Juddua, * "
11:24 And Pethahiah the son of M', of * "

Meshillemith (me-shil'-le-mith) See also MESHILLEMOTH.
1Ch 9:12 son of Meshullam, the son of M', 4921

Meshillemoth (me-shil'-le-moth) See also MESHILLEMITH.
2Ch 28:12 Berechiah the son of M', and 4919
Ne 11:13 the son of Ahasai, the son of M', "

Meshobab (me-sho'-bab)
1Ch 4:34 And M', and Jamlech, and Joshah4877

Meshullam (me-shul'-lam) See also MESHELLEMIAH.
2Ki 22: 3 son of M', the scribe, to the house4918
1Ch 3:19 M', and Hananiah, and Shelomith "
5:13 and M', and Sheba, and Jorai, and "
8:17 And Zebadiah, and M', and Hezeki, "
9: 7 Sallu the son of M', the son of "
8 M' the son of Shephathiah, the son "
11 the son of Hilkiah, the son of M', "
12 son of M', the son of Meshillemith, "
2Ch 34:12 M', of the sons of the Kohathites, "
Ezr 8:16 and for Zechariah, and for M', chief "
10:15 and M' and Shabbethai the Levite "
29 of the sons of Bani; M', Malluch, "
Ne 3: 4 And next unto them repaired M' "
6 and M' the son of Besodeiah; they "
30 repaired M' the son of Berechiah "
6:18 had taken the daughter of M' the "
8: 4 Hashbadana, Zechariah, and M'. "
10: 7 M', Abijah, Mijamin, "
20 Magpiash, M', Hezir, "
11: 7 Sallu the son of M', the son of Joed, "
11 the son of Hilkiah, the son of M', "
12:13 Of Ezra, M'; of Amariah, "
16 Iddo, Zechariah; of Ginnethon, M'; "
25 and Bakbukiah, Obadiah, M', "
33 And Azariah, Ezra, and M', "

Meshullemeth (me-shul'-le-meth)
2Ki 21:19 And his mother's name was M'. 4922

Mesobaite (me-so'-ba-ite)
1Ch 11:47 Eliel, and Obed, and Jasiel the M'.*4677

Mesopotamia (mes-o-po-ta'-me-ah) See also ARAM and NAHARAIM.
Ge 24:10 and he arose, and went to M', unto 763
De 23: 4 the son of Beor of Pethor of M', "
J'g 3: 8 of Chushan-rishathaim king of M': "
10 Chushan-rishathaim king of M' "
1Ch 19: 6 chariots and horsemen out of M', "
Ac 2: 9 the dwellers in M', and in Judæa, 3318
7: 2 father Abraham, when he was in M', "

mess See also MESSES.
Ge 43:34 Benjamin's m' was five times so 4864
2Sa 11: 8 there followed him a m' of meat "

message
J'g 3:20 I have a m' from God unto thee. 1697
1Ki 20:12 when Ben-hadad heard this m', as "
Pr 26: 6 He that sendeth a m' by the hand "
Hag 1:13 in the Lord's m' unto the people, 4400
Lu 19:14 him, and sent a m' after him, *4242
1Jo 1: 5 is the m' which we have heard of 1860
3:11 is the m' that ye heard from the 31

messenger See also MESSENGERS.
Ge 50:16 And they sent a m' unto Joseph, *6680
1Sa 4:17 the m' answered and said, Israel *1319
23:27 But there came a m' unto Saul, 4397
2Sa 11:19 And charged the m', saying, When "
22 So the m' went, and came and "
23 the m' said unto David, Surely the "
25 David said unto the m', Thus shalt "
15:13 there came a m' to David, saying, 5046
1Ki 19: 2 Jezebel sent a m' unto Elijah, 4397
22:13 And the m' that was gone to call "
2Ki 5:10 Elisha sent a m' unto him, saying, "
6:32 ere the m' came to him, he said to "
32 when the m' cometh, shut the door, "
33 the m' came down unto him: and "
9:18 The m' came to them, but he "
10: 8 And there came a m', and told him, "
2Ch 18:12 the m' that went to call Micaiah "
Job 1:14 And there came a m' unto Job, and "
33:23 If there be a m' with him, an * "
Pr 13:17 A wicked m' falleth into mischief: "
17:11 a cruel m' shall be sent against "
25:13 is a faithful m' to them that send 6735
Isa 42:19 or deaf, as my m' that I sent? 4397
Jer 51:31 and one m' to meet another, to 5046
Eze 23:40 unto whom a m' was sent; and, 4397
Hag 1:13 spake Haggai the Lord's m' in the "
Mal 2: 7 he is the m' of the Lord of hosts. "
3: 1 I will send my m', and he shall "
1 even the m' of the covenant, whom "
M't 11:10 I send my m' before thy face, which 32
M'r 1: 2 I send my m' before thy face, which "
Lu 7:27 I send my m' before thy face, which "
2Co 12: 7 the m' of Satan to buffet me, lest I "
Ph'p 2:25 your m', and he that ministered 652

messengers
Ge 32: 3 Jacob sent m' before him to Esau 4397
6 the m' returned to Jacob, saying, "
Nu 20:14 And Moses sent m' from Kadesh "
21:21 Israel sent m' unto Sihon king of "
22: 5 He sent m' therefore unto Balaam "
24:12 Spake I not also to thy m' which "
De 2:26 And I sent m' out of the wilderness "
Jos 6:17 because he hid the m' that we sent. "
25 she hid the m', which Joshua sent "
7:22 So Joshua sent m', and they ran "
J'g 6:35 sent m' throughout all Manasseh; "
35 he sent m' unto Asher, and unto "
7:24 And Gideon sent m' throughout all "
9:31 he sent m' unto Abimelech privily, "
11:12 Jephthah sent m' unto the king "
13 answered unto the m' of Jephthah, "
14 Jephthah sent m' again unto the "
17 Israel sent m' unto the king of "
19 Israel sent m' unto Sihon king of "
1Sa 6:21 And they sent m' to the inhabitants "
11: 3 may send m' unto all the coasts of "
4 Then came the m' to Gibeah of "
7 coasts of Israel by the hands of m', "
9 they said unto the m' that came "
9 m' came and shewed it to the men "
16:19 Wherefore Saul sent m' unto Jesse, "
19:11 also sent m' unto David's house, "
14 when Saul sent m' to take David, "
15 Saul sent the m' again to see David, "
16 when the m' were come in, behold, "
20 And Saul sent m' to take David: "
20 Spirit of God was upon the m' of "
21 it was told Saul, he sent other m', "
21 Saul sent m' again the third time, "
25:14 David sent m' out of the wilderness "
42 and she went after the m' of David, "
2Sa 2: 5 And David sent m' unto the men "
3:12 And Abner sent m' to David on his "
14 And David sent m' to Ish-bosheth "
26 he sent m' after Abner, which "
5:11 king of Tyre sent m' to David, "
11: 4 And David sent m', and took her; "
12:27 Joab sent m' to David, and said, "
1Ki 20: 2 he sent m' to Ahab king of Israel "
5 And the m' came again, and said, "
9 he said unto the m' of Ben-hadad, "
9 the m' departed, and brought him "
2Ki 1: 2 he sent m' and said unto them, Go, "
3 meet the m' of the king of Samaria, "
5 when the m' turned back unto him, "
16 as thou hast sent m' to enquire of "
7:15 the m' returned, and told the king. "
14: 8 Then Amaziah sent m' to Jehoash, "
16: 7 So Ahaz sent m' to Tiglath-pileser "

2Ki 17: 4 he had sent m· to So king of Egypt, 4397
19: 9 he sent m· again unto Hezekiah, "
14 the letter of the hand of the m·, and "
23 By thy m· thou hast reproached the "
1Ch 14: 1 king of Tyre sent m· to David, "
19: 2 And David sent m· to comfort him "
16 worse before Israel, they sent m·, "
2Ch 36: 15 their father sent to them by his m·, "
16 But they mocked the m· of God, and "
Ne 6: 3 I sent m· unto them, saying, I am "
Pr 16: 14 wrath of a king is as m· of death: "
Isa 14: 32 then answer the m· of the nation? "
18: 2 saying, Go, ye swift m·, to a nation "
37: 9 he heard it, he sent m· to Hezekiah, "
14 the letter from the hand of the m·, "
44: 26 performeth the counsel of his m·; "
57: 9 didst send thy m· far off, and didst *6735
Jer 27: 3 by the hand of the m· which come 4397
Eze 23: 16 and sent m· unto them into Chaldea. "
30: 9 that day shall m· go forth from me "
Na 2: 13 the voice of thy m· shall no more be "
Lu 7: 24 when the m· of John were departed, *32*
9: 52 And sent m· before his face: and "
2Co 8: 23 they are the m· of the churches, *652*
Jas 2: 25 she had received the m·, and had *32*

messes
Ge 43: 34 sent m· unto them from before 4864

Messiah (*mes-si'-ah*) See also MESSIAS.
Da 9: 25 and build Jerusalem unto the M· *4899
26 and two weeks shall M· be cut off,* "

Messias (*mes-si'-as*) See also MESSIAH.
Joh 1: 41 unto him, We have found the M·, **3323*
4: 25 I know that M· cometh, which is* "

met
Ge 32: 1 and the angels of God m· him. 6293
33: 8 thou by all this drove which I m·? 6298
Ex 3: 18 of the Hebrews hath m· with us: 7136
4: 24 that the Lord m· him, and sought 6298
27 and m· him in the mount of God, "
5: 3 of the Hebrews hath m· with us: 7122
20 And they m· Moses and Aaron, 6293
Nu 23: 4 And God m· Balaam: and he said 7136
16 Lord m· Balaam, and put a word "
De 23: 4 they m· you not with bread and 6923
25: 18 How he m· thee by the way, and 7136
Jos 11: 5 all these kings were m· together, 3259
17: 10 m· together in Asher on the north, *6293
1Sa 10: 10 a company of prophets m· him; 7125
25: 20 against her; and she m· them. 6298
2Sa 2: 13 m· together by the pool of Gibeon: "
16: 1 servant of Mephibosheth m· him, 7135
18: 9 Absalom m· the servants of David. *7122
1Ki 13: 24 a lion m· him by the way, and slew 4672
18: 7 in the way, behold, Elijah m· him: 7125
2Ki 9: 21 m· him in the portion of Naboth *4672
10: 13 m· with the brethren of Ahaziah "
Ne 13: 2 m· not the children of Israel with 6923
Ps 85: 10 Mercy and truth are m· together 6298
Pr 7: 10 m· him a woman with the attire 7125
Jer 41: 6 as he m· them, he said unto them, 6298
Am 5: 19 flee from a lion, and a bear m· him; 6293
M't 8: 28 m· him two possessed with devils, *5221*
28: 9 Jesus m· them, saying, All hail. *528*
M'r 5: 2 there m· him out of the tombs a man "
11: 4 in a place where two ways m·; * *296*
Lu 8: 27 m· him out of the city a certain *5221*
9: 37 from the hill, much people m· him. *4876*
17: 12 m· him ten men that were lepers, *528*
Joh 4: 51 his servants m· him, and told him, "
11: 20 was coming, went and m· him: *5221*
30 in that place where Martha m· him. "
12: 18 this cause the people also m· him, "
Ac 10: 25 was coming in, Cornelius m· him, *4876*
16: 16 with a spirit of divination m· us, *528*
17: 17 daily with them that m· with him. *3909*
20: 14 when he m· with us at Assos, we *4820*
27: 41 falling into a place where two seas m·, "
Heb 7: 1 who m· Abraham returning from *4876*
10 father, when Melchisedec m· him. "

mete See also METED; METEYARD.
Ex 16: 18 when they did m· it with an omer, 4058
Ps 60: 6 and m· out the valley of Succoth. "
108: 7 and m· out the valley of Succoth. "
M't 7: 2 with what measure ye m·, it shall *3354*
M'r 4: 24 with what measure ye m·, it shall "
Lu 6: 38 with the same measure that ye m· "

meted
Isa 18: 2 a nation m· out and trodden down, *6978
7 a nation m· out and trodden under* "
40: 12 and m· out heaven with the span, 8505

meteyard
Le 19: 35 in m·, in weight, or in measure. 4060

Metheg-ammah (*me''-theg-am'-mah*)
2Sa 8: 1 David took M· out of the hand of *4965

Methoar See REMMON-METHOAR.

Methusael (*me-thu'-sa-el*)
Ge 4: 18 Mehujael begat M·: and M· begat *4967

Methuselah (*me-thu'-se-lah*) See also MATHUSALA.
Ge 5: 21 and five years, and begat M·: 4968
22 walked with God after he begat M· "
25 M· lived an hundred eighty and "
26 M· lived after he begat Lamech "
27 the days of M· were nine hundred "
1Ch 1: 3 Henoch, M·, Lamech,

Meunim (*me-u'-nim*) See also MEHUNIM.
Ne 7: 52 the children of M·, the children 4586

Mezahab (*mez'-a-hab*)
Ge 36: 39 of Matred, the daughter of M·. 4314
1Ch 1: 50 of Matred, the daughter of M·. "

Miamin (*mi'-a-min*) See also MIJAMIN; MINIAMIN.
Ezr 10: 25 Malchiah, and M·, and Eleazar, *4326
Ne 12: 5 M·, Maadiah, Bilgah, * "

Mibhar (*mib'-har*)
1Ch 11: 38 Nathan, M· the son of Haggeri, *4006

Mibsam (*mib'-sam*)
Ge 25: 13 and Kedar, and Adbeel, and M·, 4017
1Ch 1: 29 then Kedar, and Adbeel, and M·, "
4: 25 Shallum his son, M· his son, "

Mibzar (*mib'-zar*)
Ge 36: 42 Kenaz, duke Teman, duke M·, 4014
1Ch 1: 53 Kenaz, duke Teman, duke M·, "

Micah (*mi'-cah*) See also MICAIAH; MICAH'S; MICHAH.
J'g 17: 1 Ephraim, whose name was M·. 4319
4 and they were in the house of M·. "
5 the man M· had an house of gods, 4318
8 mount Ephraim to the house of M·, "
9 M· said unto him, Whence comest 4319
10 M· said unto him, Dwell with me, "
11 M· consecrated the Levite; and 4318
12 priest, and was in the house of M·. "
13 said M·, Now know I that the Lord "
18: 2 mount Ephraim, to the house of M·, "
3 they were by the house of M·, they "
4 Thus and thus dealeth M· with me, "
13 and come unto the house of M·. "
15 even unto the house of M·, and "
22 a good way from the house of M·, "
23 said unto M·, What aileth thee, "
26 when M· saw that they were too "
27 the things which M· had made, "
1Ch 5: 5 M· his son, Reaia his son, Baal his "
8: 34 and Merib-baal begat M·. "
35 the sons of M· were, Pithon, and "
9: 15 Mattaniah the son of M·, the son *4316
40 and Merib-baal begat M·. 4318
41 the sons of M· were, Pithon, and "
23: 20 Of the sons of Uzziel; M· the first, "
2Ch 34: 20 Abdon the son of M·, and Shaphan "
Jer 26: 18 M· the Morashite prophesied in †4320
Mic 1: 1 word of the Lord that came to M· 4318

Micah's (*mi'-cahs*)
J'g 18: 18 And these went into M· house, and 4318
22 in the houses near to M· house "
31 they set them up M· graven image, "

Micaiah (*mi-ka-i'-ah*) See also MICHA; MICHAIAH.
1Ki 22: 8 yet one man, M· the son of Imlah, 4321
9 said, Hasten hither M· the son of "
13 messenger that was gone to call M· "
14 M· said, As the Lord liveth, what "
15 unto him M·, shall we go against "
24 and smote M· on the cheek, and "
25 M· said, Behold, thou shalt see in "
26 Take M·, and carry him back unto "
28 And M· said, If thou return at all in "
2Ch 18: 7 the same is M· the son of Imla. "
8 Fetch quickly M· the son of Imla. 4319
12 the messenger that went to call M· 4321
13 M· said, As the Lord liveth, even "
14 king said unto him, M·, shall we 4318
23 and smote M· upon the cheek, and 4321
24 M· said, Behold, thou shalt see on "
25 Take ye M·, and carry him back to "
27 M· said, If thou certainly return in "

mice
1Sa 6: 4 and five golden m·, according to the 5909
5 images of your m· that mar the "
11 the coffer with the m· of gold and "
18 the golden m·, according to the "

Micha (*mi'-cah*) See also MICAH; MICAIAH.
2Sa 9: 12 young son, whose name was M·. *4316
Ne 10: 11 M·, Rehob, Hashabiah, "
11: 17 And Mattaniah the son of M·, the* "
22 son of Mattaniah, the son of M·. * "

Michael (*mi'-ka-el*)
Nu 13: 13 of Asher, Sethur the son of M·. 4317
1Ch 5: 13 house of their fathers were, M·, "
14 the son of M·, the son of Jeshishai, "
6: 40 son of M·, the son of Baaseiah, the "
7: 3 M·, and Obadiah, and Joel, Ishiah, "
8: 16 M·, and Ispah, and Joha, the sons "
12: 20 M·, and Jozabad, and Elihu, and "
27: 18 of Issachar, Omri the son of M·: "
2Ch 21: 2 Zechariah, and Azariah, and M·, "
Ezr 8: 8 Zebadiah the son of M·, and with "
Da 10: 13 M·, one of the chief princes, came "
21 in these things, but M· your prince. "
12: 1 at that time shall M· stand up, "
Jude 9 Yet M· the archangel, when *3413*
Re 12: 7 M· and his angels fought against "

Michah (*mi'-cah*) See also MICAH; MICHAIAH.
1Ch 24: 24 Of the sons of Uzziel; M·: of the 4318
of the sons of M·; Shamir. "
25 The brother of M· was Isshiah: of "

Michaiah (*mi-ka-i'-ah*) See also MICAH; MICAIAH.
2Ki 22: 12 and Achbor the son of M·, and *4320
2Ch 13: 2 His mother's name also was M· *4322
17: 7 and to M·, to teach in the cities of* "
Ne 12: 35 the son of M·, the son of Zaccur, *4320
41 Eliakim, Maaseiah, Miniamin, M·,* "
Jer 36: 11 When M· the son of Gemariah, *4321
13 M· declared unto them all the "

Michal (*mi'-kal*) See also EGLAH.
1Sa 14: 49 and the name of the younger M·: 4324
18: 20 M· Saul's daughter loved David: "
27 Saul gave him M· his daughter to "
28 that M· Saul's daughter loved him. 4324
19: 11 M· David's wife told him, saying, "
12 So M· let David down through a "
13 M· took an image, and laid it in "
17 Saul said unto M·, Why hast thou "
17 M· answered Saul, He said unto "
25: 44 Saul had given M· his daughter, "
2Sa 3: 13 first bring M· Saul's daughter, "
14 Deliver me my wife M·, which I "
6: 16 M· Saul's daughter looked through "
20 M· the daughter of Saul came out "
21 David said unto M·, It was before "
23 M· the daughter of Saul had no "
21: 8 sons of M· the daughter of Saul, "
1Ch 15: 29 M· the daughter of Saul looking "

Michmas (*mik'-mas*) See also MICHMASH.
Ezr 2: 27 The men of M·, an hundred 4363
Ne 7: 31 The men of M·, an hundred "

Michmash (*mik'-mash*) See also MICHMAS.
1Sa 13: 2 thousand were with Saul in M· 4363
5 they came up, and pitched in M·, "
11 themselves together at M·; "
16 the Philistines encamped in M·. "
23 went out to the passage of M·. "
14: 5 situate northward over against M·. "
31 the Philistines that day from M· "
Ne 11: 31 Benjamin from Geba dwelt at M·, "
Isa 10: 28 at M· he had laid up his carriages: "

Michmethah (*mik'-me-thah*)
Jos 16: 6 went out toward the sea to M· 4366
17: 7 Manasseh was from Asher to M·, "

Michri (*mik'-ri*)
1Ch 9: 8 the son of Uzzi, the son of M·, 4381

Michtam (*mik'-tam*)
Ps 16: *title* M· of David. 4387
56: *title* M· of David, when the Philistines "
57: *title* M· of David, when he fled from "
58: *title* Al-taschith, M· of David. "
59: *title* M· of David; when Saul sent, "
60: *title* M· of David, to teach; when he "

midday
1Ki 18: 29 came to pass, when m· was past, 6672
Ne 8: 3 from the morning until m·, 4276,3117
Ac 26: 13 At m·, O king, I saw in the *2250,3319*

Middin (*mid'-din*)
Jos 15: 61 the wilderness, Beth-arabah, M·, 4081

middle See also MIDDLEMOST; MIDST.
Ex 26: 28 m· bar in the midst of the boards 8432
36: 33 And he made the m· bar to shoot 8484
Jos 12: 2 from the m· of the river, and from 8432
J'g 7: 19 in the beginning of the m· watch; 8484
9: 37 people down by the m· of the land, 2872
16: 29 took hold of the two m· pillars 8432
1Sa 25: 29 out, as out of the m· of a sling. * "
2Sa 10: 4 cut off their garments in the m·, 2677
1Ki 6: 6 and the m· was six cubits broad, 8484
8 door for the m· chamber was in the "
8 winding stairs into the m· chamber, "
8 and out of the m· into the third. "
8: 64 the king hallow the m· of the court 8432
2Ki 20: 4 was gone out into the m· court, 8484
2Ch 7: 7 hallowed the m· of the court that "
Jer 39: 3 came in, and sat in the m· gate, "
Eze 1: 16 were a wheel in the m· of a wheel. *8432
Eph 2: 14 hath broken down the m· wall of *3320*

middlemost
Eze 42: 5 and than the m· of the building. 8484
6 lowest and the m· from the ground. "

Midian (*mid'-e-an*) See also MADIAN; MIDIANITE.
Ge 25: 2 and Medan, and M·, and Ishbak, 4080
4 sons of M·; Ephah, and Epher, and "
36: 35 who smote M· in the field of Moab, "
Ex 2: 15 and dwelt in the land of M·: and "
16 priest of M· had seven daughters: "
3: 1 his father in law, the priest of M·: "
4: 19 the Lord said unto Moses in M·, Go, "
18: 1 When Jethro, the priest of M·, "
Nu 22: 4 Moab said unto the elders of M·, "
7 and the elders of M· departed with "
25: 15 people, and of a chief house in M·. "
18 the daughter of a prince of M·, "
31: 3 and avenge the Lord of M·. "
8 they slew the kings of M·, beside "
8 Hur, and Reba, five kings of M·: "
9 took all the women of M· captives, "
Jos 13: 21 Moses smote with the princes of M·, "
J'g 6: 1 delivered them into the hand of M· "
2 the hand of M· prevailed against "
7: 8 host of M· was beneath him in the "
13 bread tumbled into the host of M·, "
14 his hand hath God delivered M·, "
15 into your hand the host of M·. "
25 and pursued M·, and brought the "
8: 3 into your hands the princes of M·, "
5 Zebah and Zalmunna, kings of M·. "
12 them, and took the two kings of M·, "
22 delivered us from the hand of M·. "
26 that was on the kings of M·, and "
28 M· subdued before the children of "
9: 17 you out of the hand of M·: "
1Ki 11: 18 they arose out of M·, and came to "
1Ch 1: 32 and Medan, and M·, and Ishbak, "
33 the sons of M·; Ephah, and Epher, "
46 smote M· in the field of Moab, "
Isa 9: 4 his oppressor, as in the days of M·. "
10: 26 to the slaughter of M· at the rock "
60: 6 the dromedaries of M· and Ephah; "
Hab 3: 7 the curtains of the land of M· did "

Midianite (*mid'-e-an-ite*) See also MIDIANITES; MIDIANITISH.
Nu 10: 29 Hobab, the son of Raguel the M·. 4084

Midianites (*mid'-e-an-ites*) See also KENITES.
Ge 37:28 there passed by M' merchantmen;4084
36 the M' sold him into Egypt unto 4092
Nu 25:17 Vex the M', and smite them: 4084
31: 2 the children of Israel of the M': "
3 and let them go against the M', *4080
7 And they warred against the M', * "
J'g 6: 2 because of the M' the children of* "
3 had sown, that the M' came up, "
6 impoverished because of the M'; * "
7 unto the Lord because of the M', * "
11 winepress, to hide it from the M'. "
13 us into the hands of the M'. * "
14 Israel from the hand of the M': * "
16 thou shall smite the M' as one man." "
33 Then all the M' and the Amalekites" "
7: 1 host of the M' were on the north * "
2 me to give the M' into their hands, "
7 deliver the M' into thine hand: "
12 And the M' and the Amalekites and" "
23 Manasseh,...pursued after the M'.* "
24 saying, Come down against the M',*" "
25 they took two princes of the M', * "
8: 1 thou wentest to fight with the M'?* "
Ps 83: 9 Do unto them as unto the M'; as* "

Midianitish (*mid''-e-an-i'-tish*)
Nu 25: 6 a M' woman in the sight of Moses,4084
14 that was slain with the M' woman, "
15 the name of the M' woman that "

midnight
Ex 11: 4 About m' will I go out into 2676,3915
12:29 at m' the Lord smote all the 2677, "
J'g 16: 3 lay till m', and arose at m', "
Ru 3: 8 it came to pass at m', that the "
1Ki 3:20 she arose at m', and took my 8432, "
Job 34:20 people shall be troubled at m',2676, "
Ps 119:62 At m' I will rise to give thanks "
M't 25: 6 at m' there was a cry made, 3319,3571
M'r 13:35 or at m', or at the cockcrowing, or 3317
Lu 11: 5 and shall go unto him at m', and "
Ac 16:25 at m' Paul and Silas prayed, and "
20: 7 and continued his speech until m'. "
27:27 about m' the shipmen deemed3319,3571

midst See also MIDDLE.
Ge 1: 6 firmament in the m' of the waters, 8432
2: 9 tree of life...in the m' of the garden," "
3: 3 which is in the m' of the garden, "
15:10 and divided them in the m', and laid" "
19:29 Lot out of the m' of the overthrow, "
48:16 multitude in the m' of the earth. 7130
Ex 3: 2 of fire out of the m' of a bush: 8432
4 unto him out of the m' of the bush, "
20 which I will do in the m' thereof: 7130
8:22 am the Lord in the m' of the earth. "
11: 4 will I go out into the m' of Egypt: 8432
14:16 ground through the m' of the sea. "
22 of Israel went into the m' of the sea "
23 in after them to the m' of the sea, "
27 the Egyptians in the m' of the sea. "
29 upon dry land in the m' of the sea; "
15:19 on dry land in the m' of the sea. "
23:25 sickness away from the m' of thee.7130
24:16 Moses out of the m' of the cloud. 8432
18 Moses went into the m' of the cloud," "
26:28 middle bar in the m' of the boards "
27: 5 may be even to the m' of the altar.*2677
28:32 in the top of it, in the m' thereof: 8432
33: 3 I will not go up in the m' of thee; 7130
5 I will come up into the m' of thee "
34:12 it be for a snare in the m' of thee: "
38: 4 thereof beneath unto the m' of it. 2677
39:23 was an hole in the m' of the robe, 8432
Le 16:16 them in the m' of their uncleanness. "
Nu 2:17 the Levites in the m' of the camp: "
5: 3 camps, in the m' whereof I dwell. "
16:47 ran into the m' of the congregation;" "
19: 6 into the m' of the burning of the "
33: 8 passed through the m' of the sea "
35: 5 and the city shall be in the m': this "
De 4:11 with fire unto the m' of heaven, *3820
12 unto you out of the m' of the fire: 8432
15 in Horeb out of the m' of the fire: "
33 speaking out of the m' of the fire, "
34 from the m' of another nation, by 7130
36 his words out of the m' of the fire.8432
5: 4, 22 mount out of the m' of the fire, "
23 voice out of the m' of the darkness, "
24 his voice out of the m' of the fire: "
26 speaking out of the m' of the fire, "
9:10 out of the m' of the fire in the day "
10: 4 out of the m' of the fire in the day "
11: 3 did in the m' of Egypt unto Pharaoh "
6 possession, in the m' of all Israel: 7130
13: 5 the evil away from the m' of thee. "
16 spoil of it into the m' of the street 8432
17:20 his children, in the m' of Israel. 7130
18:15 thee a Prophet from the m' of thee, "
19: 2 for thee in the m' of thy land, 8432
23:14 walketh in the m' of thy camp, 7130
32:51 in the m' of the children of Israel. 8432
Jos 3:17 on dry ground in the m' of Jordan, "
4: 3 you hence out of the m' of Jordan, "
5 your God into the m' of Jordan, "
8 stones out of the m' of Jordan, as "
9 twelve stones in the m' of Jordan, "
10 the ark stood in the m' of Jordan, "
18 come up out of the m' of Jordan, "
7:13 accursed thing in the m' of thee, 7130
21 in the earth in the m' of my tent, 8432
23 took them out of the m' of the tent, "
8:13 that night into the m' of the valley. "
22 so they were in the m' of Israel, "
10:13 sun stood still in the m' of heaven,2677
13: 9, 16 city that is in the m' of the river, *8432
J'g 15: 4 put a firebrand in the m' between "
J'g 18:20 and went in the m' of the people. 7130
20:42 they destroyed in the m' of them. 8432
1Sa 11:11 they came into the m' of the host "
16:13 him in the m' of his brethren: and7130
18:10 prophesied in the m' of the house: 8432
2Sa 1:25 mighty fallen in the m' of the battle!" "
4: 6 thither into the m' of the house, "
6:17 in the m' of the tabernacle that "
18:14 was yet alive in the m' of the oak. 3820
20:12 in blood in the m' of the highway. 8432
23:12 he stood in the m' of the ground, "
20 slew a lion in the m' of a pit in time "
24: 5 city that lieth in the m' of the river*" "
1Ki 3: 8 thy servant is in the m' of thy people" "
6:27 one another in the m' of the house. "
8:51 from the m' of the furnace of iron: "
20:39 went out into the m' of the battle; 7130
22:35 wound into the m' of the chariot. *2436
2Ki 6:20 they were in the m' of Samaria. 8432
1Ch 11:14 themselves in the m' of that parcel, "
16: 1 and set it in the m' of the tent that "
19: 4 their garments in the m' hard by *2677
2Ch 6:13 had set it in the m' of the court: 8432
20:14 Lord in the m' of the congregation; "
32: 4 that ran through the m' of the land," "
Ne 4:11 till we come in the m' among them, "
9:11 through the m' of the sea on dry "
Es 4: 1 and went out into the m' of the city," "
Job 21:21 of his months is cut off in the m'?†2686
Ps 22:14 is melted in the m' of my bowels. 8432
22 in the m' of the congregation will I "
46: 2 be carried into the m' of the sea; *3820
5 God is in the m' of her; she shall 7130
48: 9 O God, in the m' of thy temple. "
55:10 also and sorrow are in the m' of it. "
11 Wickedness is in the m' thereof: "
57: 6 into the m' whereof they are fallen8432
74: 4 roar in the m' of thy congregation;7130
12 salvation in the m' of the earth. "
78:28 he let it fall in the m' of their camp," "
102:24 me not away in the m' of my days:2677
110: 2 thou in the m' of thine enemies. 7130
116:19 Lord's house, in the m' of thee, O 8432
135: 9 and wonders in the m' of thee, "
136:14 Israel to pass through the m' of it: "
137: 2 upon the willows in the m' thereof. "
138: 7 Though I walk in the m' of trouble,7130
Pro 4:21 keep them in the m' of thine heart.8432
5:14 all evil in the m' of the congregation" "
8:20 in the m' of the paths of judgment: "
14:33 that which is in the m' of fools is *7130
23:34 he lieth down in the m' of the sea, 3820
30:19 way of a ship in the m' of the sea; "
Ca 3:10 m' thereof being paved with love, 8432
Isa 4: 4 the blood of Jerusalem from the m'7130
5: 2 and built a tower in the m' of it, 8432
8 be...alone in the m' of the earth! 7130
25 were torn in the m' of the streets. "
6: 5 I dwell in the m' of a people of 8432
12 forsaking in the m' of the land. 7130
7: 6 and set a king in the m' of it, even 8432
10:23 even...in the m' of all the land. 7130
12: 6 Holy One of Israel in the m' of thee." "
16: 3 night in the m' of the noonday; 8432
19: 1 of Egypt shall melt in the m' of it. 7130
3 Egypt shall fail in the m' thereof; "
14 a perverse spirit in the m' thereof: "
19 Lord in the m' of the land of Egypt,8432
24 a blessing in the m' of the land: 7130
24:13 it shall be in the m' of the land "
18 cometh up out of the m' of the pit 8432
25:11 forth his hand in the m' of them, 7130
29:23 of mine hands, in the m' of him, "
30:28 shall reach to the m' of the neck, *2673
41:18 fountains in the m' of the valleys: 8432
52:11 go ye out of the m' of her; be ye "
58: 9 thou take away from the m' of thee "
66:17 gardens behind one tree in the m', "
Jer 6: 1 flee out of the m' of Jerusalem, 7130
6 wholly oppression in the m' of her. "
9: 6 habitation is in the m' of deceit; 8432
12:16 they be built in the m' of my people." "
14: 9 thou, O Lord, art in the m' of us, 7130
17:11 leave them in the m' of his days, 2677
21: 4 them into the m' of this city. 8432
29: 8 that be in the m' of you, deceive 7130
30:21 shall proceed from the m' of them; "
37:12 thence in the m' of the people, 8432
41: 7 they came into the m' of the city, "
7 and cast them into the m' of the pit, "
46:21 her hired men are in the m' of her 7130
48:45 flame from the m' of Sihon, and shall "
50: 8 Remove out of the m' of Babylon, 8432
37 people that are in the m' of her; "
51: 1 them that dwell in the m' of them*3820
6 Flee out of the m' of Babylon, and 8432
45 people, go ye out of the m' of her, "
47 her slain shall fall in the m' of her. "
63 cast it into the m' of Euphrates: "
52:25 that were found in the m' of the city." "
La 1:15 my mighty men in the m' of me: 7130
3:45 and refuse in the m' of the people. "
4:13 blood of the just in the m' of her, "
Eze 1: 4 and out of the m' thereof as the 8432
4 of amber, out of the m' of the fire. "
5 Also out of the m' thereof came the "
5: 2 fire a third part in the m' of the city," "
4 and cast them into the m' of the fire," "
5 I have set it in the m' of the nations" "
8 judgments in the m' of thee in the "
10 shall eat the sons in the m' of thee," "
12 they be consumed in the m' of thee:" "
6: 7 the slain shall fall in the m' of you, "
7: 4 abominations shall be in the m' of "
9 abominations that are in the m' of "
8:11 in the m' of them stood Jaazaniah "
Eze 9: 4 him, Go through the m' of the city, 8432
4 through the m' of Jerusalem, and "
4 that be done in the m' thereof. "
10:10 wheel had been in the m' of a wheel." "
11: 7 whom ye have laid in the m' of it, "
7 bring you forth out of the m' of it. "
9 will bring you out of the m' thereof," "
11 ye be the flesh in the m' thereof; "
23 went up from the m' of the city, "
12: 2 in the m' of a rebellious house, "
13:14 be consumed in the m' thereof: "
14: 8 him off from the m' of my people; "
9 from the m' of my people Israel. "
15: 4 ends of it, and the m' of it is burned." "
16:53 of thy captives in the m' of them: "
17:16 in the m' of Babylon he shall die. "
20: 8 them in the m' of the land of Egypt." "
21:32 blood shall be in the m' of the land;" "
22: 3 city sheddeth blood in the m' of it, "
7 in the m' of thee have they dealt by "
9 m' of thee they commit lewdness. "
13 which hath been in the m' of thee. "
18 and lead, in the m' of the furnace; "
19 gather you into the m' of Jerusalem "
20 and tin, into the m' of the furnace, "
21 ye shall be melted in the m' thereof. "
22 is melted in the m' of the furnace, "
22 shall ye be melted in the m' thereof;" "
25 of her prophets in the m' thereof, "
25 her many widows in the m' thereof." "
27 Her princes in the m' thereof are 7130
23:39 they done in the m' of mine house.8432
24: 7 For her blood is in the m' of her; "
26: 5 of nets in the m' of the sea: "
12 and thy dust in the m' of the water." "
15 slaughter is made in the m' of thee?" "
27: 4 borders are in the m' of the seas, *3820
25 very glorious in the m' of the seas.*" "
26 broken thee in the m' of the seas. * "
27 company which is in the m' of thee8432
27 shall fall into the m' of the seas *3820
32 the destroyed in the m' of the sea? 8432
34 company in the m' of thee shall fall." "
28: 2 seat of God, in the m' of the seas; 3820
8 that are slain in the m' of the seas.*" "
14 in the m' of the stones of fire. 8432
16 filled the m' of thee with violence, "
16 from the m' of the stones of fire. "
18 forth a fire from the m' of thee, "
22 I will be glorified in the m' of thee: "
23 shall be judged in the m' of her by "
29: 3 that lieth in the m' of his rivers, "
4 thee up out of the m' of thy rivers, "
12 the m' of the countries are desolate, "
21 of the mouth in the m' of them; "
30: 7 the m' of the countries are desolate," "
7 the m' of the cities that are wasted." "
31:14 in the m' of the children of men, "
17 shadow in the m' of the heathen. "
18 lie in the m' of the uncircumcised "
32:20 fall in the m' of them that are slain "
21 speak to him out of the m' of hell "
25 set her a bed in the m' of the slain "
25 put in the m' of them that be slain. "
28 in the m' of the uncircumcised, "
32 laid in the m' of the uncircumcised" "
36:23 ye have profaned in the m' of them;" "
37: 1 set me down in the m' of the valley "
26 set my sanctuary in the m' of them "
28 sanctuary shall be in the m' of them" "
38:12 that dwell in the m' of the land. *2872
39: 7 in the m' of my people Israel; 8432
41: 7 chamber to the highest by the m'.*8484
43: 7 in the m' of the children of Israel 8432
9 and I will dwell in the m' of them "
46:10 And the prince in the m' of them, "
48: 8 sanctuary shall be in the m' of it. "
10 the Lord shall be in the m' thereof. "
15 the city shall be in the m' thereof. "
21 the house shall be in the m' thereof." "
22 the m' of that which is the prince's, "
Da 3: 6, 11 m' of a burning fiery furnace. 1459
15 the m' of a burning fiery furnace; "
21, 23 m' of the burning fiery furnace. "
24 men bound into the m' of the fire? "
25 loose, walking in the m' of the fire, "
26 came forth of the m' of the fire. "
4:10 behold a tree in the m' of the earth, "
7:15 in my spirit in the m' of my body, "
9:27 m' of the week he shall cause the †2677
Ho 5: 4 of whoredoms is in the m' of them,*7130
11: 9 man; the Holy One in the m' of thee:" "
Joe 2:27 know that I am in the m' of Israel, "
Am 2: 3 off the judge from the m' thereof, "
3: 9 great tumults in the m' thereof, * "
9 the oppressed in the m' thereof. 8432
6: 4 the calves out of the m' of the stall; "
7: 8 plumbline in the m' of my people 7130
10 in the m' of the house of Israel: "
Jon 2: 3 the deep, in the m' of the seas; *3824
Mic 2:12 as the flock in the m' of their fold: 8432
5: 7 in the m' of many people as a dew 7130
8 in the m' of many people as a lion "
10 off thy horses out of the m' of thee," "
13 images out of the m' of thee; "
14 up thy groves out of the m' of thee:" "
6:14 down shall be in the m' of thee; "
7:14 in the wood, in the m' of Carmel: 8432
Na 3:13 people in the m' of thee are women:7130
Hab 2:19 is no breath at all in the m' of it. "
3: 2 thy work in the m' of the years, "
2 in the m' of the years make known;" "
Zep 2:14 shall lie down in the m' of her. 8432
3: 5 The just Lord is in the m' thereof;7130
11 will take away out of the m' of thee" "
12 leave in the m' of thee an afflicted "

Zep 3: 15 even the Lord, is in the *m'* of thee: 7130
17 thy God in the *m'* of thee is mighty; "
Zec 2: 5 will be the glory in the *m'* of her. 8432
10, 11 and I will dwell in the *m'* of thee, "
5: 4 shall remain in the *m'* of his house, "
7 that sitteth in the *m'* of the ephah. "
8 he cast it into the *m'* of the ephah; "
8: 3 will dwell in the *m'* of Jerusalem: "
8 shall dwell in the *m'* of Jerusalem; "
14: 1 shall be divided in the *m'* of thee. 7130
4 shall cleave in the *m'* thereof 2677
M't 10: 16 forth as sheep in the *m'* of wolves: *3319*
14: 24 ship was now in the *m'* of the sea, "
18: 2 him, and set him in the *m'* of them, "
20 name, there am I in the *m'* of them. "
M'r 6: 47 the ship was in the *m'* of the sea, "
7: 31 the *m'* of the coasts of Decapolis. "
9: 36 child, and set him in the *m'* of them: "
14: 60 the high priest stood up in the *m'*, "
Lu 2: 46 sitting in the *m'* of the doctors, "
4: 30 he passing through the *m'* of them "
35 the devil had thrown him in the *m'*, "
5: 19 his couch into the *m'* before Jesus. "
6: 8 Rise up, and stand forth in the *m'*. "
17: 11 passed through the *m'* of Samaria‡ "
21: 21 which are in the *m'* of it depart out; "
22: 55 kindled a fire in the *m'* of the hall, "
23: 45 of the temple was rent in the *m'*. "
24: 36 Jesus...stood in the *m'* of them, "
Joh 7: 14 the *m'* of the feast Jesus went up *3322*
8: 3 when they had set her in the *m'*, *3319*
9 and the woman standing in the *m'*. "
59 going through the *m'* of them, and* "
19: 18 either side one, and Jesus in the *m'*. "
20: 19 came Jesus and stood in the *m'*, "
26 stood in the *m'*, and said, Peace be "
Ac 1: 15 stood up in the *m'* of the disciples, "
18 he burst asunder in the *m'*, and all "
2: 22 God did by him in the *m'* of you, "
4: 7 when they had set them in the *m'*, "
17: 22 Paul stood in the *m'* of Mars' hill, "
27: 21 Paul stood forth in the *m'* of them, "
Ph'p 2: 15 in the *m'* of a crooked and perverse" "
Heb 2: 12 *m'* of the church will I sing praise "
Re 1: 13 in the *m'* of the seven candlesticks "
2: 1 *m'* of the seven golden candlesticks; "
7 is in the *m'* of the paradise of God.* "
4: 6 in the *m'* of the throne, and round "
5: 6 in the *m'* of the throne and of the "
6 in the *m'* of the elders, stood a Lamb "
6: 6 a voice in the *m'* of the four beasts "
7: 17 which is in the *m'* of the throne "
8: 13 flying through the *m'* of heaven, **3321*
14: 6 angel fly in the *m'* of heaven, * "
19: 17 fowls that fly in the *m'* of heaven, * "
22: 2 In the *m'* of the street of it, and on *3319*

midwife See also MIDWIVES.
Ge 35: 17 labour, that the *m'* said unto her, 3205
38: 28 *m'* took and bound upon his hand a "
Ex 1: 16 When ye do the office of a *m'* to the "

midwives
Ex 1: 15 of Egypt spake to the Hebrew *m'*, 3205
17 the *m'* feared God, and did not as "
18 the king of Egypt called for the *m'*, "
19 the *m'* said unto Pharaoh, Because "
19 ere the *m'* come in unto them. * "
20 God dealt well with the *m'*: and the "
21 to pass because the *m'* feared God, "

Migdal-el (*mig'-dal-el*)
Jos 19: 38 And Iron, and *M'*, Horem, and 4027

Migdal-gad (*mig'-dal-gad*)
Jos 15: 37 Zenan, and Hadashah, and *M'*, 4028

Migdol (*mig'-dol*)
Ex 14: 2 between *M'* and the sea, over 4024
Nu 33: 7 and they pitched before *M'*. "
Jer 44: 1 land of Egypt, which dwelt at *M'*, "
46: 14 ye in Egypt, and publish in *M'*, and" "

might See also MIGHTEST.
Ge 12: 19 so I *m'* have taken her to me to wife:*
13: 6 them, that they *m'* dwell together:
17: 18 O that Ishmael *m'* live before thee!
26: 10 *m'* lightly have lien with thy wife,
30: 34 would it *m'* be according to thy word.
41 that they *m'* conceive among the rods.
31: 27 I *m'* have sent thee away with mirth,
36: 7 than that they *m'* dwell together; *
37: 22 that he *m'* rid him out of their hands,
43: 32 Egyptians *m'* not eat bread with 3201
49: 3 thou art my firstborn, my *m'*, and 3581
Ex 10: 1 I *m'* shew these my signs before him:
12: 33 *m'* send them out of the land in haste;*
36: 18 the tent together, that it *m'* be one.
39: 21 *m'* be above the curious girdle of the
21 that the breastplate *m'* not be loosed
Le 24: 12 mind of the Lord *m'* be shewed them.
26: 45 the heathen, that I *m'* be their God:
Nu 4: 37, 41 that *m'* do service in the tabernacle*
14: 13 broughtest up this people in thy *m'* 3581
22: 41 *m'* see the utmost part of the people.*
De 2: 30 that he *m'* deliver him into thy hand,
3: 24 works, and according to thy *m'*? *1369
4: 14 *m'* do them in the land whither ye go
36 his voice, that he *m'* instruct thee:
42 That the slayer *m'* flee thither, which
42 unto one of these cities he *m'* live:
5: 29 that it *m'* be well with them, and with
6: 1 *m'* do them in the land whither ye go
5 all thy soul, and with all thy *m'* 3966
23 that he *m'* bring us in, to give us the
24 that he *m'* preserve us alive, as it is at
8: 3 he *m'* make thee know that man doth
16 *m'* humble thee, and that he *m'* prove
17 the *m'* of mine hand hath gotten 6108
28: 32 there shall be no *m'* in thine hand.* 410

De 29: 6 ye *m'* know that I am the Lord your
32: 13 he *m'* eat the increase of the fields;*
Jos 4: 24 people of the earth *m'* know the hand*
24 ye *m'* fear the Lord your God for ever.*
11: 20 that he *m'* destroy them utterly, and
20 and that they *m'* have no favour,
20 but that he *m'* destroy them, as the
20: 9 killeth any person at unawares *m'* flee
22: 16 ye *m'* rebel this day against the Lord?*
24 your children *m'* speak unto our
27 that we *m'* do the service of the Lord*
24: 8 hand, that ye *m'* possess their land;*
J'g 3: 2 of Israel *m'* know, to teach them war,
5: 31 sun when he goeth forth in his *m'*. 1369
6: 14 Go in this thy *m'*, and thou shalt 3581
9: 24 ten sons of Jerubbaal *m'* come, and
16: 30 he bowed himself with all his *m'*; 3581
18: 7 *m'* put them to shame in any thing;
Ru 1: 6 *m'* return from the country of Moab:
1Sa 4: 4 they *m'* bring from thence the ark of*
13: 10 to meet him, that he *m'* salute him.
14: 14 of land, which a yoke of oxen *m'* plow.*
18: 27 that he *m'* be the king's son in law.
20: 6 of me that he *m'* run to Beth-lehem
2Sa 6: 14 before the Lord with all his *m'*; 5797
10: 10 that he *m'* put them in array against*
15: 4 any suit or cause *m'* come unto me,
17: 14 the Lord *m'* bring evil upon Absalom.
17 they *m'* not be seen to come into 3201
22: 41 that I *m'* destroy them that hate me.
1Ki 2: 27 that he *m'* fulfil the word of the Lord,
7: 7 for the throne where he *m'* judge,
8: 1 that they *m'* bring up the ark of the*
16 an house, that my name *m'* be therein;
12: 15 that he *m'* perform his saying, which
15: 17 that he *m'* not suffer any to go out or
23 all the acts of Asa, and all his *m'*, 1369
16: 5 what he did, and his *m'*, are they "
27 he did, and his *m'* that he shewed, "
19: 4 requested for himself that he *m'* die;
22: 7 besides, that we *m'* enquire of him?
45 and his *m'* that he shewed, and 1369
2Ki 7: 2 windows in heaven, *m'* this thing be?
19 in heaven, *m'* such a thing be?
10: 19 he *m'* destroy the worshippers of Baal.
34 and all that he did, and all his *m'*, 1369
13: 8 and all that he did, and his *m'*, are "
12 and all that he did, and his *m'* "
14: 15 Jehoash which he did, and his *m'*, "
28 and all that he did, and his *m'*, how "
15: 19 his hand *m'* be with him to confirm
20: 20 acts of Hezekiah, and all his *m'*, 1369
22: 17 that they *m'* provoke me to anger with
23: 10 man *m'* make his son or his daughter
24 he *m'* perform the words of the law
25 all his soul, and with all his *m'*, 3966
33 that he *m'* not reign in Jerusalem;
24: 16 And all the men of *m'*, even seven 2428
1Ch 4: 10 that thine hand *m'* be with me, and
7: 2 men of *m'* in the generations; 2428
5 Issachar were valiant men of *m'*, * "
12: 8 hold to the wilderness men of *m'*, * "
13: 8 before God with all their *m'*, and 5797
29: 2 prepared with all my *m'* for the 3581
12 and in thine hand is power and *m'*; 1369
30 With all his reign and his *m'*, and "
2Ch 2: 12 that *m'* build an house for the Lord,*
6: 5 an house in, that my name *m'* be there;
6 Jerusalem, that my name *m'* be there;
10: 15 that the Lord *m'* perform his word,
11: 1 he *m'* bring the kingdom again to*
16: 1 he *m'* let none go out or come in to
18: 6 besides, that we *m'* enquire of him?
20: 6 hand is there not power and *m'*, 1369
12 no *m'* against this great company 3581
25: 20 *m'* deliver them into the hand of their
31: 4 *m'* be encouraged in the law of the
32: 18 them; that they *m'* take the city.
31 he *m'* know all that was in his heart.
34: 25 they *m'* provoke me to anger with all
35: 12 they *m'* give according to the divisions
15 they *m'* not depart from their service;*
22 he *m'* fight with him, and hearkened
36: 22 of Jeremiah *m'* be accomplished,
Ezr 1: 1 mouth of Jeremiah *m'* be fulfilled,
5: 10 *m'* write the names of the men that
8: 21 we *m'* afflict ourselves before our God,
Ne 5: 3 that we *m'* buy corn, because of the*
11 *m'* exact of them money and corn:*
6: 13 *m'* have matter for an evil report,
13 evil report, that they *m'* reproach me.
7: 5 they *m'* be reckoned by genealogy.
9: 24 they *m'* do with them as they would.
10: 37 the same Levites *m'* have the tithes*
Es 4: 2 for none *m'* enter into the king's gate
10: 2 the acts of his power and of his *m'*, 1369
Job 6: 8 that I *m'* have my request; and that
9: 33 us, that *m'* lay his hand upon us both.
16: 21 that one *m'* plead for a man with God,*
23: 3 Oh that I knew where I *m'* find him!
3 that I *m'* come even to his seat!
7 the righteous *m'* dispute with him;
30: 2 whereto *m'* the strength of their *
38: 13 *m'* take hold of the ends of the earth,
13 that the wicked *m'* be shaken out of it?*
Ps 18: 40 that I *m'* destroy them that hate me.
68: 18 the Lord God *m'* dwell among them.
76: 5 none of the men of *m'* have found 2428
78: 6 the generation to come *m'* know them,
7 That they *m'* set their hope in God,
8 *m'* not be as their fathers, a stubborn
105: 45 That they *m'* observe his statutes, and
106: 8 he *m'* make his mighty power to be
107: 7 that they *m'* go to a city of habitation.
109: 16 he *m'* even slay the broken in heart.*
118: 13 hast thrust sore at me that I *m'* fall;

Ps 119: 11 heart, that I *m'* not sin against thee.
71 afflicted; that I *m'* learn thy statutes.
101 evil way, that I *m'* keep thy word.
148 that I *m'* meditate in thy word.
145: 6 speak of the *m'* of thy terrible acts: 5807
Pr 22: 21 I *m'* make thee know the certainty*
Ec 2: 3 I *m'* see what was that good for the
3: 18 of men, that God *m'* manifest them,*
18 they *m'* see that they themselves are*
9: 10 findeth to do, do it with thy *m'*; 3581
Isa 11: 2 the spirit of counsel and *m'*, the 1369
28: 13 that they *m'* go, and fall backward,*
33: 13 that are near, acknowledge my *m'*. 1369
40: 26 names by the greatness of his *m'*, 202
29 have no *m'* he increaseth strength. "
61: 3 *m'* be called trees of righteousness,
3 of the Lord, that he *m'* be glorified.
64: 1 *m'* flow down at thy presence,
Jer 9: 1 I *m'* weep day and night for the slain
2 I *m'* leave my people, and go from
23 let the mighty man glory in his *m'*, 1369
10: 6 great, and thy name is great in *m'*. "
13: 11 that they *m'* be unto me for a people,
16: 21 to know mine hand and my *m'*; 1369
17: 23 their neck stiff, that they *m'* not hear,
19: 15 necks, that they *m'* not hear my words.
20: 17 my mother *m'* have been my grave,*
25: 7 ye *m'* provoke me to anger with the
26: 19 *m'* we procure great evil against our*
27: 15 in my name; that I *m'* drive you out,
15 that ye *m'* perish, ye, and the prophets
43: 3 that they *m'* put us to death, and carry
44: 8 that ye *m'* cut yourselves off, and that*
8 that ye *m'* be a curse and a reproach*
49: 35 bow of Elam, the chief of their *m'*. 1369
51: 30 their *m'* hath failed; they became "
Eze 17: 7 that he *m'* water it by the furrows of
8 that it *m'* bring forth branches, and
8 branches, and that it *m'* bear fruit,
8 bear fruit, that it *m'* be a goodly vine.
14 That the kingdom *m'* be base, that
14 that it *m'* not lift itself up, but that
14 by keeping of his covenant it *m'* stand.
15 they *m'* give him horses and much
20: 12 that they *m'* know that I am the Lord
26 that I *m'* make them desolate, to the
26 that they *m'* know that I am the Lord.
24: 8 That it *m'* cause fury to come up to
32: 29 with their *m'* are laid by them that 1369
30 terror they are ashamed of their *m'*; "
36: 3 ye *m'* be a possession unto the residue
40: 4 intent that I *m'* shew them unto thee
41: 6 that they *m'* have hold, but they had
Da 1: 4 whom they *m'* teach the learning and*
5 thereof they *m'* stand before the king.
8 eunuchs that he *m'* not defile himself.
2: 20 ever: for wisdom and *m'* are his: 1370
23 who hast given me wisdom and *m'*, "
3: 28 *m'* not serve nor worship any god,
4: 6 that they *m'* make known unto me the
30 kingdom by the *m'* of my power, 8632
5: 2 and his concubines, *m'* drink therein.
6: 2 princes *m'* give accounts unto them,
17 that the purpose *m'* not be changed
8: 4 so that no beasts *m'* stand before him,
9: 11 that they *m'* not obey thy voice; *
13 that we *m'* turn from our iniquities,*
Joe 3: 3 sold a girl for wine, that they *m'* drink.
6 ye *m'* remove them far from their
Am 1: 13 that they *m'* enlarge their border:
Jon 4: 5 *m'* see what would become of the city.
6 that it *m'* be a shadow over his head,
Mic 3: 8 of judgment, and of *m'*, to declare 1369
7: 16 and be confounded at all their *m'*: "
Hab 3: 16 that I *m'* rest in the day of trouble:
Zec 4: 6 Not by *m'*, nor by power, but by 2428
6: 7 to go that they *m'* walk to and fro
8: 9 was laid, that the temple *m'* be built.
11: 10 *m'* break my covenant which I had
14 I *m'* break the brotherhood between
Mal 2: 4 that my covenant *m'* be with Levi,
15 one? That he *m'* seek a godly seed.*
M't 1: 22 it *m'* be fulfilled which was spoken
2: 15, 23 it *m'* be fulfilled which was spoken
4: 14 it *m'* be fulfilled which was spoken
8: 17 it *m'* be fulfilled which was spoken
28 that no man *m'* pass by that way. **2480*
12: 10 days? that they *m'* accuse him.
14 him, how they *m'* destroy him.
17 it *m'* be fulfilled which was spoken
13: 35 it *m'* be fulfilled which was spoken
14: 36 they *m'* only touch the hem of his
21: 4 it *m'* be fulfilled which was spoken by
32 not afterward, that ye *m'* believe him.
34 that they *m'* receive the fruits of it.*
22: 15 how they *m'* entangle him in his talk.
26: 4 that they *m'* take Jesus by subtilty,
9 this ointment *m'* have been sold for *1410*
56 of the prophets *m'* be fulfilled.
27: 35 it *m'* be fulfilled which was spoken by*
M'r 3: 2 day; that they *m'* accuse him.
6 against him, how they *m'* destroy him.
14 that he *m'* send them forth to preach,
5: 18 prayed him that he *m'* be with him.
6: 56 they *m'* touch if it were but the border
10: 51 him, Lord, that I *m'* receive my sight.*
11: 13 if haply he *m'* find any thing thereon:
18 and sought how they *m'* destroy him:
12: 2 he *m'* receive from the husbandmen
14: 1 scribes sought how they *m'* take him
5 For it *m'* have been sold for more *1410*
11 how he *m'* conveniently betray him.
35 possible, the hour *m'* pass from him.
16: 1 that they *m'* come and anoint him.
Lu 1: 74 enemies *m'* serve him without fear,*
4: 29 that they *m'* cast him down headlong.

Lu 5:19 by what way they m' bring him in
6: 7 m' find an accusation against him.
11 another what they m' do to Jesus.
8: 9 saying, What m' this parable be?
10 parables; that seeing they m' not see,*
10 and hearing they m' not understand.*
38 besought him that he m' be with him:
11:54 of his mouth, that they m' accuse him.*
15:29 that I m' make merry with my friends:
17: 6 ye m' say unto this sycamine tree, *
19:15 m' know how much every man had
23 I m' have required mine own with*
48 And could not find what they m' do:
20:20 that they m' take hold of his words,
20 m' deliver him unto the power and*
22: 2 scribes sought how they m' kill him;
4 how he m' betray him unto them.
23:23 requiring that he m' be crucified.
26 cross, that he m' bear it after Jesus.*
24:45 they m' understand the scriptures,
Joh 1: 7 that all men through him m' believe.
3:17 the world through him m' be saved.*
5:34 things I say, that ye m' be saved.*
40 not come to me, that ye m' have life.*
6:28 that we m' work the works of God?*
8: 6 him, that they m' have to accuse him.
9:36 is he, Lord, that I m' believe on him?*
39 world, that they which see not m' see;*
39 that they which see m' be made blind.*
10:10 I am come that they m' have life,*
10 that they m' have it more abundantly.*
17 down my life, that I m' take it again.*
11: 4 that the Son of God m' be glorified*
57 should shew it, that they m' take him.
12: 9 that they m' see Lazarus also, whom
10 they m' put Lazarus also to death;
38 of Esaias the prophet m' be fulfilled,
14:29 when it is come to pass, ye m' believe.*
15:11 you, that my joy m' remain in you, *
11 in you, and that your joy m' be full.*
25 that the word m' be fulfilled that is*
16:33 unto you, that in me ye m' have peace.*
17: 3 they m' know thee the only true God, *
12 that the scripture m' be fulfilled.
13 that they m' have my joy fulfilled in*
19 that they also m' be sanctified *
18: 9 That the saying m' be fulfilled, which
28 but that they m' eat the passover.
32 the saying of Jesus m' be fulfilled,
19:24, 38 that the scripture m' be fulfilled,
31 Pilate that their legs m' be broken,
31 and that they m' be taken away.
35 that he saith true, that ye m' believe.*
38 he m' take away the body of Jesus:
20:31 ye m' believe that Jesus is the Christ,*
31 ye m' have life through his name.*
Ac 1:25 fell, that he m' go to his own place.
4:21 nothing how they m' punish them,
5:15 Peter passing by m' overshadow some
7:19 children, to the end they m' not live.
8:15 that they m' receive the Holy Ghost:
9: 2 m' bring them bound unto Jerusalem.
12 on him, that he m' receive his sight.
21 that he m' bring them bound unto
13:42 that these words m' be preached to
15:17 residue of men m' seek after the Lord.*
17:27 if haply they m' feel after him, and
20:24 so that I m' finish my course with joy,*
22:24 that he m' know wherefore they cried
24:26 him of Paul, that he m' loose him:*
25:21 be kept till I m' send him to Cæsar.*
26 had, I m' have somewhat to write.*
26:32 man m' have been set at liberty, if 1410
27:12 means they m' attain to Phenice, * "
Ro 1:10 length I m' have a prosperous journey*
13 I m' have some fruit among you also,
3:26 that he m' be just, and the justifier of
4:11 that he m' be the father of all them
11 righteousness m' be imputed unto
16 it is of faith, that it m' be by grace;*
16 the promise m' be sure to all the seed;*
18 m' become the father of many nations,
5:20 entered, that the offence m' abound.
21 m' grace reign through righteousness
6: 6 that the body of sin m' be destroyed,
7:13 But sin, that it m' appear sin, working
13 that sin...m' become exceeding sinful.
8: 4 the law m' be fulfilled in us, who walk
29 he m' be the firstborn among many
9:11 of God according to election m' stand,
17 up, that I m' shew my power in thee,
17 my name m' be declared throughout
23 that he m' make known the riches of
10: 1 for Israel is, that they m' be saved.*
11:14 my flesh, and m' save some of them.*
19 broken off, that I m' be graffed in.
32 that he m' have mercy upon all.
14: 9 that he m' be Lord both of the dead
15: 4 comfort of the scriptures m' have hope.
9 Gentiles m' glorify God for his mercy;
16 up of the Gentiles m' be acceptable,
1Co 2:12 that we m' know the things that are
4: 6 ye m' learn in us not to think of men
8 reign, that we also m' reign with you.
5: 2 hath done this deed m' be taken away
9:19 unto all, that I m' gain the more.
20 as a Jew, that I m' gain the Jews;
20 I m' gain them that are under the
21 I m' gain them that are without law.
22 I as weak, that I m' gain the weak:
22 that I m' by all means save some.*
23 that I m' be partaker thereof with you.*
14:19 by my voice I m' teach others also,
2Co 1:15 that ye m' have a second benefit;
2: 4 that ye m' know the love which I have
9 that I m' know the proof of you,
2Co 4:10, 11 also of Jesus m' be made manifest*
15 grace m' through the thanksgiving of*
5: 4 mortality m' be swallowed up of life.*
21 m' be made the righteousness of God
7: 9 ye m' receive damage by us in nothing.
12 in the sight of God m' appear unto you.
8: 9 that ye through his poverty m' be rich.
9: 5 that the same m' be ready, as a matter
11: 4 not accepted, ye m' well bear with him.*
7 abasing myself that ye m' be exalted,
12: 8 Lord thrice, that it m' depart from me.
Ga 1: 4 he m' deliver us from this present evil
16 I m' preach him among the heathen;
2: 4 that they m' bring us into bondage:
5 truth of the gospel m' continue with
16 m' be justified by the faith of Christ,
19 to the law, that I m' live unto God.
3:14 blessing of Abraham m' come on the
14 we m' receive the promise of the Spirit
22 m' be given to them that believe.
24 Christ, that we m' be justified by faith.
4: 5 we m' receive the adoption of sons.
17 exclude you, that ye m' affect them.*
Eph 1:10 he m' gather together in one all things*
21 principality, and power, and m', *1411
2: 7 he m' shew the exceeding riches of
16 m' reconcile both unto God in one
3:10 places m' be known by the church
16 to be strengthened with m' by his *1411
19 m' be filled with all the fulness of *
4:10 all heavens, that he m' fill all things,)
5:26 he m' sanctify and cleanse it with the
27 he m' present it to himself a glorious
6:10 Lord, and in the power of his m'. 2479
22 purpose, that ye m' know our affairs,*
22 and that he m' comfort your hearts.*
Ph'p 3: 4 I m' also have confidence in the flesh.
4 hath whereof he m' trust in the flesh,*
11 I m' attain unto the resurrection of*
Col 1: 9 m' be filled with the knowledge of his*
10 That ye m' walk worthy of the Lord*
11 Strengthened with all m', *1411
18 all things he m' have the preeminence.
2: 2 their hearts m' be comforted, being*
4: 8 he m' know your estate, and comfort*
1Th 2: 6 we m' have been burdensome, as 1410
16 to the Gentiles that they m' be saved,*
3:10 exceedingly that we m' see your face,*
10 m' perfect that which is lacking in*
2Th 2: 6 that he m' be revealed in his time.*
10 of the truth, that they m' be saved.
12 all m' be damned who believed not
3: 8 m' not be chargeable to any of you:
1Ti 1:16 Christ m' shew forth all longsuffering,
2Ti 4:17 me the preaching m' be fully known,
17 and that all the Gentiles m' hear:
Tit 2:14 m' redeem us from all iniquity, and
3: 8 God m' be careful to maintain good*
Ph'm 13 stead he m' have ministered unto me
Heb 2:14 through death he m' destroy him that
17 he m' be a merciful and faithful high
6:18 we m' have a strong consolation, who*
9:15 are called m' receive the promise of*
10:36 of God, ye m' receive the promise.*
11:15 they m' have had an opportunity to*
35 they m' obtain a better resurrection:
12:10 that we m' be partakers of his holiness.*
18 unto the mount that m' be touched,
13:12 he m' sanctify the people with his own
Jas 5:17 prayed earnestly that it m' not rain:
1Pe 1: 7 m' be found unto praise and honour
21 your faith and hope m' be in God.
3:18 unjust, that he m' bring us to God,
4: 6 that they m' be judged according to
2Pe 1: 4 m' be partaker of the divine nature *
2:11 which are greater in power and m',1411
1Jo 2:19 they m' be made manifest that they
3: 8 he m' destroy the works of the devil.
4: 9 world, that we m' live through him.
3Jo 8 we m' be fellowhelpers to the truth.*
Re 7:12 power, and m', be unto our God 2479
12:14 that she m' fly into the wilderness,
15 he m' cause her to be carried away
13:17 that no man m' buy or sell, save *1410
16:12 the kings of the east m' be prepared.

mightest
De 4:35 thou m' know that the Lord he is God;
6: 2 That thou m' fear the Lord thy God,
J'g 16: 6 thou m' be bound to afflict thee.
10 thee, wherewith thou m' be bound.
13 tell me wherewith thou m' be bound.
1Sa 17:28 come down that thou m' see the battle.
Ne 9:29 that thou m' bring them again unto
Ps 8: 2 that thou m' still the enemy and the
51: 4 m' be justified when thou speakest,*
Pr 22:21 thou m' answer the words of truth*
Da 2:30 that thou m' know the thoughts of*
M't 15: 5 whatsoever thou m' be profited by me;
M'r 7:11 whatsoever thou m' be profited by me;
Lu 1: 4 thou m' know the certainty of those
Ac 9:17 that thou m' receive thy sight, and
Ro 3: 4 thou m' be justified in thy sayings,
4 m' overcome when thou art judged.
1Ti 1: 3 thou m' charge some that they teach
18 thou by them m' war a good warfare;

mightier
Ge 26:16 for thou are much m' than we. 6105
Ex 1: 9 of Israel are more and m' than we:6099
Nu 14:12 a greater nation and m' than they. "
De 4:38 thee greater and m' than thou art, "
7: 1 nations greater and m' than thou; "
9: 1 greater and m' than thyself, cities "
14 a nation m' and greater than they. "
11:23 nations and m' than yourselves. "
Ps 93: 4 Lord on high is m' than the noise* 117
Ec 6:10 with him that is m' than he. 8623
M't 3:11 that cometh after me is m' than I, 2478
M'r 1: 7 cometh one m' than I after me, "
Lu 3:16 one m' than I cometh, the lachet of "

mighties
1Ch 11:12 who was one of the three m'. 1368
24 had the name among the three m'.* "

mightiest
1Ch 11:19 These things did these three m'. *1368

mightily
De 6: 3 that ye may increase m', as the 3966
J'g 4: 3 twenty years he m' oppressed the 2393
14: 6 Spirit of the Lord came m' upon him,
15:14 Spirit of the Lord came m' upon him,
Jer 25:30 he shall m' roar upon his habitation;
Jon 3: 8 sackcloth, and cry m' unto God: 2393
Na 2: 1 loins strong, fortify thy power m'.3966
Ac 18:28 For he m' convinced the Jews, and*2159
19:20 m' grew the word of God and 2596,2904
Col 1:29 which worketh in me m'. 1722,1411
Re 18: 2 cried m' with a strong voice, * " 2479

mighty See also ALMIGHTY; MIGHTIER; MIGHTIES; MIGHTIEST.
Ge 6: 4 the same became m' men which 1368
10: 8 began to be a m' one in the earth. "
9 was a m' hunter before the Lord: "
9 the m' hunter before the Lord. "
18:18 become a great and m' nation, 6099
23: 6 thou art a m' prince among us: ‡ 430
49:24 strong by the hands of the m' God 46
Ex 1: 7 and waxed exceeding m'; and the 6105
20 multiplied, and waxed very m'.
3:19 let you go, no, not by a m' hand. 2389
9:28 be no more m' thunderings and hail;430
10:19 turned a m' strong west wind, *3966
15:10 they sank as lead in the m' waters. 117
15 the m' men of Moab, trembling 352
32:11 great power, and with a m' hand? 2389
Le 19:15 nor honour the person of the m': 1419
Nu 22: 6 people; for they are too m' for me:6099
De 3:24 thy greatness, and thy m' hand: *2389
4:34 and by war, and by a m' hand, "
37 in his sight with his m' power out*1419
5:15 out thence through a m' hand, and2389
6:21 us out of Egypt with a m' hand: "
7: 8 brought you out with a m' hand, "
19 m' hand, and the stretched out arm, "
21 among you, a m' God and terrible.*1419
23 destroy them with a m' destruction.*"
9:26 forth out of Egypt with a m' hand.2389
29 broughtest out by thy m' power *1419
10:17 a great God, a m', and a terrible, 1368
11: 2 God, his greatness, his m' hand, 2389
26: 5 nation, great, m', and populous: 6099
8 forth out of Egypt with a m' hand,2389
34:12 in all that m' hand, and in all the "
Jos 1:14 armed, all the m' men of valour, 1368
4:24 the hand of the Lord, that it is m':2389
6: 2 thereof, and the m' men of valour.1368
8: 3 thirty thousand m' men of valour, "
10: 2 and all the men thereof were m'. "
7 him, and all the m' men of valour. "
J'g 5:13 me have dominion over the m'. "
22 the pransings of their m' ones. * 47
23 help of the Lord against the m'. 1368
6:12 with thee, thou m' man of valour. "
11: 1 Gileadite was a m' man of valour, "
Ru 2: 1 a m' man of wealth, of the family of "
1Sa 2: 4 bows of the m' men are broken, "
4: 8 out of the hand of these m' Gods? 117
9: 1 a Benjamite, a m' man of power. 1368
16:18 in playing, and a m' valiant man, "
2Sa 1:19 high places: how are the m' fallen! "
21 shield of the m' is vilely cast away, "
22 from the fat of the m', the bow of "
25 How are the m' fallen in the midst "
27 How are the m' fallen, and the "
10: 7 and all the host of the m' men. "
16: 6 the m' men were on his right hand "
17: 8 that they be m' men, and they be "
10 knoweth that thy father is a m' man,"
20: 7 the Pelethites, and all the m' men: "
23: 8 be the names of the m' men whom "
9 one of the three m' men with David, "
16 the three m' men brake through the"
17 things did these three m' men. "
22 had the name among three m' men."
1Ki 1: 8 m' men which belonged to David, "
10 and the m' men, and Solomon his "
11:28 Jeroboam was a m' man of valour: "
2Ki 5: 1 he was also a m' man in valour, but"
15:20 even of all the m' men of wealth, of "
24:14 and all the m' men of valour, even "
15 the m' of the land, those carried he*193
1Ch 1:10 he began to be m' upon the earth. 1368
5:24 m' men of valour, famous men, and"
7: 7 their fathers, m' men of valour; "
9, 11 their fathers, m' men of valour, "
40 choice and m' men of valour, chief "
8:40 of Ulam were m' men of valour, "
11:10 of the m' men whom David had, "
11 of the m' men whom David had; "
12: 1 were among the m' men, helpers of "
4 a m' man among the thirty, and "
21 for they were all m' men of valour, "
25 m' men of valour for the war, seven"
28 Zadok, a young man m' of valour, "
30 eight hundred, m' men of valour, "
19: 8 and all the host of the m' men. "
26: 6 for they were m' men of valour. "
31 them m' men of valour at Jazer of "
27: 6 who was m' among the thirty, and "
28: 1 the officers, and with the m' men, "
29:24 all the princes, and the m' men, and"

2Ch 6:32 thy m' hand, and thy stretched out2389
13: 3 men, being m' men of valour. 1368
21 But Abijah waxed m', and married2388
14: 8 all these were m' men of valour. 1368
17:13 m' men of valour, were in Jerusalem."
14 m' men of valour three hundred "
16 hundred thousand m' men of valour."
17 Eliada a m' man of valour, and with"
25: 6 m' men of valour out of Israel for "
26:12 the fathers of the m' men of valour "
13 that made war with m' power, to 2428
27: 6 So Jotham became m', because he 2388
28: 7 And Zichri, a m' man of Ephraim, 1368
32: 3 and his m' men to stop the waters "
21 cut off all the m' men of valour, and"
Ezr 4:20 been m' kings also over Jerusalem,8624
7:28 before all the king's m' princes. 1368
Ne 3:16 and unto the house of the m'. "
9:11 as a stone into the m' waters. 5794
32 our God, the great, the m', and the1368
11:14 their brethren, m' men of valour, "
Job 5:15 and from the hand of the m'. 2389
6:23 me from the hand of the m'? *6184
9: 4 wise in heart, and m' in strength: 533
12:19 spoiled, and overthroweth the m'. 386
21 weakeneth the strength of the m'.* 650
21: 7 become old, yea, are m' in power? 1396
22: 8 But as for the m' man, he had the 2220
24:22 draweth also the m' with his power: 47
34:20 the m' shall be taken away without "
24 break in pieces m' men without 3524
35: 9 out by reason of the arm of the m'.7227
36: 5 God is m', and despiseth not any: 3524
5 he is m' in strength and wisdom. "
41:25 up himself, the m' are afraid: by 410
Ps 24: 8 strong and m', the Lord m' in battle1368
29: 1 Give unto the Lord, O ye m', 1121,410
33:16 a m' man is not delivered by much 1368
45: 3 sword upon thy thigh, O most m', "
50: 1 The m' God, even the Lord, hath † 410
52: 1 thou thyself in mischief, O m' man?1368
59: 3 the m' are gathered against me; 5794
68:33 out his voice, and that a m' voice. 5797
69: 4 mine enemies wrongfully, are m': 6105
74:15 the flood: thou driedst up m' rivers.386
78:65 m' man that shouteth by reason of1368
82: 1 in the congregation of the m'; he* 410
89: 6 who among the sons of the m' can "
13 Thou hast a m' arm: strong is thy1369
19 have laid help upon one that is m';1368
50 the reproach of all the m' people; 7227
93: 4 yea, than the m' waves of the sea. 117
106: 2 can utter the m' acts of the Lord? 1369
8 make his m' power to be known. "
112: 2 His seed shall be m' upon earth: 1368
120: 4 Sharp arrows of the m', with coals "
127: 4 arrows are in the hand of a m' man;"
132: 2 vowed unto the m' God of Jacob; 46
5 habitation for the m' God of Jacob. "
135:10 great nations, and slew m' kings; 6099
145: 4 and shall declare thy m' acts. 1369
12 to the sons of men his m' acts, "
150: 2 Praise him for his m' acts: praise "
Pr 16:32 to anger is better than the m'; 1368
18:18 cease, and parteth between the m'.6099
21:22 man scaleth the city of the m', and1368
23:11 For their redeemer is m'; he shall*2389
Ec 7:19 more than ten m' men which are 7989
Ca 4: 4 bucklers, all shields of m' men. 1368
Isa 1:24 Lord of hosts, the m' One of Israel. 46
3: 2 The m' man, and the man of war, 1368
25 the sword, and thy m' in the war. 1369
5:15 and the m' man shall be humbled,* 376
22 them that are m' to drink wine, 1368
9: 6 Wonderful, Counsellor, The m' God, "
10:21 remnant of Jacob, unto the m' God. "
34 and Lebanon shall fall by a m' one. 117
11:15 with his m' wind shall he shake *5868
13: 3 called my m' ones for mine anger, 1368
17:12 like the rushing of m' waters! 3524
21:17 m' men of the children of Kedar, 1368
22:17 thee away with a m' captivity, *1397
28: 2 Lord hath a m' and strong one, 2389
2 as a flood of m' waters overflowing,3524
30:29 the Lord, to the m' One of Israel. *6697
31: 8 with the sword, not of a m' man;* 376
42:13 Lord shall go forth as a m' man, 1368
43:16 sea, and a path in the m' waters; 5794
49:24 the prey be taken from the m', or 1368
25 the captives of the m' shall be taken"
26 thy Redeemer, the m' One of Jacob. 46
60:16 thy Redeemer, the m' One of Jacob. "
63: 1 speak in righteousness, m' to save.7227
Jer 5:15 it is a m' nation, it is an ancient 386
16 sepulchre, they are all m' men. 1368
9:23 let the m man glory in his might, "
14: 9 as a m' man that cannot save? "
20:11 Lord is with me as a m' terrible one:"
26:21 the king, with all his m' men, and all "
32:18 the Great, the M' God, the Lord "
19 Great in counsel, and m' in work: 7227
33: 3 shew thee great and m' things, *1219
41:16 m' men of war, and the women, *1397
46: 5 their m' ones are beaten down, 1368
6 flee away, nor the m' man escape; "
9 and let the m' men come forth; the "
12 m' man...stumbled against the m', "
48:14 are m' and strong men for the war?"
41 the m' men's hearts in Moab at that"
49:22 heart of the m' men of Edom be as "
50: 9 shall be as of a m' expert man; "
36 a sword is upon her m' men; and "
51:30 The m' men of Babylon have forborn"
56 Babylon, and her m' men are taken,"
57 and her rulers, and her m' men: "
La 1:15 trodden under foot all my m' men 47

Eze 17:13 hath also taken the m' of the land: 352
17 shall Pharaoh with his m' army 1419
20:33, 34 with a m' hand, and with a 2389
31:11 hand of the m' one of the heathen; 410
32:12 By the swords of the m' will I cause1368
21 strong among the m' shall speak "
27 not lie with the m' that are fallen "
27 terror of the m' in the land of the "
38:15 a great company, and a m' army: 7227
39:18 Ye shall eat the flesh of the m', 1368
20 with m' men, and with all men of "
Da 3:20 he commanded the most m' men 1401
4: 3 and how m' are his wonders! 8624
8:24 And his power shall be m', but not6105
24 the m' and the holy people. 6099
9:15 the land of Egypt with a m' hand, 2389
11: 3 And a m' king shall stand up, that1368
25 with a very great and m' army; 6099
Ho 10:13 in the multitude of thy m' men. 1368
Joe 2: 7 They shall run like m' men; they "
3: 9 Prepare war, wake up the m' men, "
11 thy m' ones to come down, O Lord. "
Am 2:14 neither shall the m' deliver himself:"
16 he that is courageous among the m'"
5:12 transgressions and your m' sins: 6099
24 and righteousness as a m' stream. 386
Ob 9 thy m' men, O Teman, shall be 1368
Jon 1: 4 there was a m' tempest in the sea. 1419
Na 2: 3 shield of his m' men is made red, 1368
Hab 1:12 O m' God, thou hast established *6697
Zep 1:14 m' man shall cry there bitterly. 1368
3:17 thy God in the midst of thee is m'; "
Zec 9:13 made thee as the sword of a m' man."
10: 5 And they shall be as m' men, which "
7 of Ephraim shall be like a m' man, "
11: 2 because the m' are spoiled: howl, * 117
M't 11:20 most of his m' works were done, 1411
21 if the m' works, which were done "
23 if the m' works, which have been "
13:54 this wisdom, and these m' works? "
58 he did not many m' works there "
14: 2 m' works do shew forth themselves*"
M'r 6: 2 such m' works are wrought by his "
5 he could there do no m' work, save "
14 m' works do shew forth themselves*"
Lu 1:49 he that is m' hath done to me great1415
52 put down the m' from their seats,*1413
9:43 all amazed at the m' power of God.*3168
10:13 if the m' works had been done in 1411
15:14 arose a m' famine in that land; 2478
19:37 the m' works that they had seen; 1411
24:19 was a prophet m' in deed and word1415
Ac 2: 2 heaven as of a rushing m' wind, 972
7:22 and was m' in words and in deeds. 1415
18:24 man, and m' in the scriptures, "
Ro 15:19 Through m' signs and wonders, *1411
1Co 1:26 not many m', not many noble, are 1415
27 confound the things which are m';*2478
2Co 10: 4 but m' through God to the pulling 1415
12:12 signs, and wonders, and m' deeds. 1411
13: 3 is not weak, but is m' in you. *1414
Ga 2: 8 m' in me toward the Gentiles:) *1754
Eph 1:19 to the working of his m' power, *2479
2Th 1: 7 from heaven with his m' angels, *1411
1Pe 5: 6 under the m' hand of God, that he 2900
Re 6:13 when she is shaken of a m' wind. *3173
15 chief captains, and the m' men, *1415
10: 1 saw another m' angel come down *2478
16:18 so m' an earthquake, and so great.*5082
18:10 great city Babylon, that m' city! *2478
21 a m' angel took up a stone like a * "
19: 6 and as the voice of m' thunderings, "
18 captains, and the flesh of m' men, "

Migron (mi'-gron)
1Sa 14: 2 pomegranate tree which is in M': 4051
Isa 10:28 come to Aiath, he is passed to M': "

Mijamin (mij'-a-min) See also MIAMIN.
1Ch 24: 9 fifth to Malchijah, the sixth to M', 4326
Ne 10: 7 Meshullam, Abijah, M', "

Mikloth (mik'-loth)
1Ch 8:32 And M' begat Shimeah. And 4732
9:37 and Ahio, and Zechariah, and M'. "
38 And M' begat Shimeam. And they "
27: 4 his course was M' also the ruler: "

Mikneiah (mik-ne-i'-ah)
1Ch 15:18, 21 M', and Obed-edom, and Jeiel,4737

Milalai (mil'-a-lahee)
Ne 12:36 and Azarael, M', Gilalai, Maai, 4450

Milcah (mil'-cah)
Ge 11:29 and the name of Nahor's wife, M', 4435
29 the father of M', and the father of "
22:20 M', she hath also borne children "
23 these eight M' did bear to Nahor, "
24:15 who was born to Bethuel, son of M', "
24 daughter of Bethuel the son of M', "
47 son, whom M' bare unto him: "
Nu 26:33 and Noah, Hoglah, M', and Tirzah. "
27: 1 and Hoglah, and M', and Tirzah. "
36:11 Tirzah, and Hoglah, and M', and "
Jos 17: 3 and Noah, Hoglah, M', and Tirzah. "

milch See also MILK.
Ge 32:15 Thirty m' camels with their colts, 3243
1Sa 6: 7 new cart, and take two m' kine, 5763
10 took two m' kine, and tied them to "

Milcom (mil'-com) See also MALCHAM; MOLECH.
1Ki 11: 5 after M' the abomination of the 4445
33 and M' the god of the children of "
2Ki 23:13 M' the abomination of the children "

mildew
De 28:22 and with blasting, and with m'; 3420
1Ki 8:37 if there be pestilence, blasting, m', "
2Ch 6:28 pestilence, if there be blasting, or m', "

Am 4: 9 smitten you with blasting and m': 3420
Hag 2:17 smote you with blasting and with m' "

mile
M't 5:41 shall compel thee to go a m', go 3400

Miletum (mi-le'-tum) See also MILETUS.
2Ti 4:20 Trophimus have I left at M' sick. *3399

Miletus (mi-le'-tus) See also MILETUM.
Ac 20:15 and the next day we came to M'. 3399
17 from M' he sent to Ephesus, and "

milk See also MILCH.
Ge 18: 8 he took butter, and m', and the 2461
49:12 wine, and his teeth white with m'. "
Ex 3: 8 a land flowing with m' and honey; "
17 a land flowing with m' and honey. "
13: 5 a land flowing with m' and honey, "
23:19 not seethe a kid in his mother's m'. "
33: 3 a land flowing with m' and honey: "
34:26 not seethe a kid in his mother's m'. "
Le 20:24 that floweth with m' and honey: "
Nu 13:27 it floweth with m' and honey; and "
14: 8 which floweth with m' and honey. "
16:13, 14 that floweth with m' and honey, "
De 6: 3 that floweth with m' and honey. "
11: 9 that floweth with m' and honey. "
14:21 not seethe a kid in his mother's m'. "
26: 9, 15 that floweth with m' and honey. "
27: 3 that floweth with m' and honey; "
31:20 that floweth with m' and honey; "
32:14 Butter of kine, and m' of sheep, "
Jos 5: 6 that floweth with m' and honey. "
J'g 4:19 she opened a bottle of m', and gave "
5:25 asked water, and she gave him m'; "
Job 10:10 thou not poured me out as m', and "
21:24 His breasts are full of m', and his "
Pr 27:27 have goats' m' enough for thy food, "
30:33 the churning of m' bringeth forth "
Ca 4:11 honey and m' are under thy tongue; "
5: 1 I have drunk my wine with my m': "
12 rivers of waters, washed with m', "
Isa 7:22 abundance of m' that they shall "
28: 9 them that are weaned from the m', "
55: 1 buy wine and m' without money "
60:16 also suck the m' of the Gentiles, "
66:11 that ye may m' out, and be 4711
Jer 11: 5 a land flowing with m' and honey, 2461
32:22 a land flowing with m' and honey; "
La 4: 7 than snow, they were whiter than m', "
Eze 20: 6, 15 flowing with m' and honey, "
25: 4 fruit, and they shall drink thy m'. "
Joe 3:18 and the hills shall flow with m', and "
1Co 3: 2 I have fed you with m', and not 1051
9: 7 eateth not of the m' of the flock? "
Heb 5:12 become such as have need of m', "
13 every one that useth m' is unskilful "
1Pe 2: 2 desire the sincere m' of the word, "

mill See also MILLS; MILLSTONE.
Ex 11: 5 maidservant that is behind the m';7347
M't 24:41 shall be grinding at the m'; the 3459

millet
Eze 4: 9 and lentiles, and m', and fitches, 1764

millions
Ge 24:60 the mother of thousands of m', *7233

Millo (mil'-lo)
J'g 9: 6 together, and all the house of M', 4407
20 of Shechem, and the house of M'; "
20 and from the house of M', and "
2Sa 5: 9 David built round about from M' "
1Ki 9:15 and M', and the wall of Jerusalem, "
24 built for her: then did he build M'. "
11:27 Solomon built M', and repaired "
2Ki 12:20 and slew Joash in the house of M', "
1Ch 11: 8 about, even from M' round about: "
2Ch 32: 5 repaired M' in the city of David, "

mills
Nu 11: 8 and ground it in m', or beat it in a 7347

millstone See also MILLSTONES.
De 24: 6 nether or the upper m' to pledge: 7347
J'g 9:53 of a m' upon Abimelech's head, 7393
2Sa 11:21 woman cast a piece of a m' upon him"
Job 41:24 as hard as a piece of the nether m'. "
M't 18: 6 a m' were hanged about his 3458,3684
M'r 9:42 a m' were hanged about his 3037,3457
Lu 17: 2 a m' were hanged about his 3458,3684
Re 18:21 took up a stone like a great m', 3458
22 the sound of a m' shall be heard no "

millstones
Isa 47: 2 Take the m', and grind meal: 7347
Jer 25:10 sound of the m', and the light of "

mincing
Isa 3:16 walking and m' as they go, and 2952

mind See also MINDED; MINDFUL; MINDING; MINDS.
Ge 23: 8 if it be your m' that I should bury 5315
26:35 were a grief of m' unto Isaac and 7307
Le 24:12 m' of the Lord might be shewed *6310
Nu 16:28 not done them of mine own m'. 3820
24:13 either good or bad of mine own m'; "
De 18: 6 come with all the desire of his m' *5315
28:65 failing of eyes, and sorrow of m': * "
30: 1 thou shalt call them to m' among 3824
1Sa 2:35 is in mine heart and in my m': 5315
9:20 days ago, set not thy m' on them; 3820
1Ch 22: 7 was in my m' to build an house *3824
28: 9 heart and with a willing m': for 5315
Ne 4: 6 for the people had a m' to work. 3820
Job 23:13 he is in one m', and who can turn him?
34:33 Should it be according to thy m'? 5973
Ps 31:12 forgotten as a dead man out of m':3820
Pr 21:27 he bringeth it with a wicked m'? "
29:11 A fool uttereth all his m': but a *7307

Isa 26: 3 peace, whose m· is stayed on thee: 3336
46: 8 men: bring it again to m·, O ye 3820
65: 17 be remembered, nor come into m·. "
Jer 3: 16 Lord: neither shall it come to m·: "
15: 1 yet my m· could not be toward this 5315
19: 5 it, neither came it into my m·: 3820
32: 35 neither came it into my m·, that "
44: 21 them, and came it not into his m·? "
51: 50 let Jerusalem come into your m·. 3824
La 3: 21 This I recall to my m·, therefore 3820
Eze 11: 5 the things that come into your m·, 7307
20: 32 that which cometh into your m· "
23: 17 her m· was alienated from them. *5315
18 then my m· was alienated from her. *"
18 m· was alienated from her sister. * "
22 from whom thy m· is alienated, and *"
28 from whom thy m· is alienated: * "
38: 10 shall things come into thy m·, 3824
Da 2: 29 came into thy m· upon thy bed,
5: 20 up, and his m· hardened in pride, 7307
Hab 1: 11 Then shall his m· change, and he * "
M't 22: 37 all thy soul, and with all thy m·. 1271
M'r 5: 15 and clothed, and in his right m·: 4993
12: 30 all thy soul, and with all thy m·, 1271
14: 72 Peter called to m· the word that 363
Lu 1: 29 and cast in her m· what manner of
8: 35 Jesus, clothed, and in his right m·: 4993
10: 27 thy strength, and with all thy m·; 1271
12: 29 neither be ye of doubtful m·.
Ac 17: 11 the word with all readiness of m·, 4288
20: 19 the Lord with all humility of m·,
Ro 1: 28 gave them over to a reprobate m·, 3563
7: 23 warring against the law of my m·, "
25 then with the m· I myself serve the "
8: 5 flesh do m· the things of the flesh: 5426
7 carnal m· is enmity against God: 5427
27 knoweth what is the m· of the Spirit, "
11: 34 hath known the m· of the Lord? 3563
12: 2 by the renewing of your m·, that "
16 the same m· one toward another. 5426
16 M· not high things, but condescend "
14: 5 be fully persuaded in his own m·. 3563
15: 6 may with one m· and one mouth *3661
15 as putting you in m·, because of *1878
1Co 1: 10 joined together in the same m· 3563
2: 16 who hath known the m· of the Lord, "
16 him? But we have the m· of Christ. "
2Co 7: 7 mourning, your fervent m· toward me;*
8: 12 if there be first a willing m·, it is *4288
19 and declaration of your ready m·: * "
9: 2 I know the forwardness of your m·, "
13: 11 be of one m·, live in peace; and 5426
Eph 2: 3 desires of the flesh and of the m·; 1271
4: 17 walk, in the vanity of the m·, 3563
23 renewed in the spirit of your m·; "
Ph'p 1: 27 with one m· striving together for *5590
2: 2 being of one accord, of one m·. 5426
3 in lowliness of m· let each esteem 5012
5 Let this m· be in you, which was 5426
3: 16 rule, let us m· the same thing. * "
19 shame, who m· earthly things.) "
4: 2 they be of the same m· in the Lord. "
Col 1: 21 enemies in your m· by wicked 1271
2: 18 vainly puffed up by his fleshly m·, 3563
3: 12 humbleness of m·, meekness, *
2Th 2: 2 That ye be not soon shaken in m·, 3563
2Ti 1: 7 and of love, and of sound m·. *4995
Tit 1: 15 their m· and conscience is defiled. 3563
3: 1 Put them in m· to be subject to 5279
Ph'm 14 But without thy m· would I do 1106
Heb 8: 10 I will put my laws into their m·, 1271
1Pe 1: 13 gird up the loins of your m·, be "
3: 8 be ye all of one m·, having *3675
4: 1 likewise with the same m·: for 1771
5: 2 for filthy lucre, but of a ready m·; 4290
Re 17: 9 here is the m· which hath wisdom. 3563
13 These have one m·, and shall give 1106

minded See also FEEBLEMINDED; HIGHMINDED; LIKEMINDED
Ru 1: 18 she was steadfastly m· to go with her.
2Ch 24: 4 was m· to repair the house 5973, 3820
Ezr 7: 13 are m· of their own freewill to go up
M't 1: 19 was m· to put her away privily. 1014
Ac 27: 39 shore, into the which they were m·, * "
Ro 8: 6 to be carnally m· is death; *5427
6 spiritually m· is life and peace. * "
2Co 1: 15 I was m· to come unto you before, 1014
17 When I therefore was thus m·, did 1011
Gal 5: 10 that ye will be none otherwise m·: 5426
Ph'p 3: 15 as many as be perfect, be thus m·: "
15 if in any thing ye be otherwise m·, "
Ti 2: 6 likewise exhort to be sober m·. 4993
Jas 1: 8 A double m· man is unstable in all 1374
4: 8 purify your hearts, ye double m·.

mindful See also UNMINDFUL.
1Ch 16: 15 Be ye m· always of his covenant; *2142
Ne 9: 17 neither were m· of thy wonders that "
Ps 8: 4 is man, that thou art m· of him? "
111: 5 he will ever be m· of his covenant. "
115: 12 The Lord hath been m· of us: he "
Isa 17: 10 hast not been m· of the rock of thy "
2Ti 1: 4 being m· of thy tears, that I may *3403
Heb 2: 6 is man, that thou art m· of him? "
11: 15 they had been m· of that country 3421
2Pe 3: 2 That ye may be m· of the words *3403

minding
Ac 20: 13 appointed, m· himself to go afoot. *3195

minds
J'g 19: 30 of it, take advice, and speak your m·. *
2Sa 17: 8 they be chafed in their m·, as a 5315
2Ki 9: 15 If it be your m·, then let none go * "
Eze 24: 25 whereupon they set their m·, their * "
36: 5 all their heart, with despiteful m·, * "
Ac 14: 2 made their m· evil affected against *5590
28: 6 changed their m·, and said that he
2Co 3: 14 But their m· were blinded: for until 3540
4: 4 hath blinded the m· of them which "
11: 3 so your m· should be corrupted "
Ph'p 4: 7 keep your hearts and m· through * "
1Ti 6: 5 disputings of men of corrupt m·, *3563
2Ti 3: 8 men of corrupt m·, reprobate * "
Heb 10: 16 and in their m· will I write them; *1271
12: 3 be wearied and faint in your m·. *5590
2Pe 3: 1 I stir up your pure m· by way of *1271

mine See also MY.
Ge 14: 22 I have lifted up m· hand unto the
15: 3 lo, one born in my house is m· heir.
24: 33 not eat, until I have told m· errand.
45 I had done speaking in m· heart, ‡
30: 25 that I may go unto m· own place,
30 shall I provide for m· own house also?
31: 10 that I lifted up m· eyes, and saw in a
40 and my sleep departed from m· eyes.
42 God hath seen m· affliction and the
43 cattle, and all that thou seest is m·:
41: 13 me he restored unto m· office, and
44: 21 me, that I may set m· eyes upon him.
48: 5 came unto thee into Egypt, are m·;
5 Reuben and Simeon, they shall be m·.
Ex 7: 4 bring forth m· armies, and my people*
5 I stretch forth m· hand upon Egypt, ‡
17 with the rod that is in m· hand upon‡
13: 2 both of man and of beast: it is m·.
17: 9 hill with the rod of God in m· hand. ‡
18: 4 of my father, said he, was m· help, ‡
19: 5 all people: for all the earth is m·:
20: 26 shalt thou go up by steps unto m· altar,
21: 14 shalt take him from m· altar, that he
23: 23 For m· Angel shall go before thee, and
32: 34 behold, m· Angel shall go before thee:
33: 23 And I will take away m· hand, and ‡
34: 19 All that open the matrix is m·; and
Le 18: 4 keep m· ordinances, to walk therein:*
30 Therefore shall ye keep m· ordinance,*
20: 26 other people, that ye should be m·.
22: 9 shall therefore keep m· ordinance, *
25: 23 be sold for ever: for the land is m·;
Nu 3: 12 therefore the Levites shall be m·;
13 Because all the first born are m·;
13 m· shall they be: I am the Lord.
45 and the Levites shall be m·: I am the
8: 14 of Israel: and the Levites shall be m·.
10: 30 but I will depart to m· own land, and
12: 7 not so, who is faithful in all m· house. ‡
14: 28 as ye have spoken in m· ears, so will I
16: 28 I have not done them of m· own mind.
18: 8 thee the charge of m· heave offerings‡
22: 29 would there were a sword in m· hand, ‡
23: 11 I took thee to curse m· enemies, and
24: 10 I called thee to curse m· enemies, and,
13 do either good or bad of m· own mind;
De 8: 17 My power and the might of m· hand ‡
10: 3 having the two tables in m· hand. ‡
26: 13 the hallowed things out of m· house, ‡
29: 19 I walk in the imagination of m· heart, ‡
32: 22 For a fire is kindled in m· anger, and
23 I will spend m· arrows upon them.
41 and m· hand take hold on judgment; ‡
41 will render vengeance to m· enemies,
42 make m· arrows drunk with blood,
Jos 14: 7 him word again as it was in m· heart. ‡
J'g 6: 36 If thou wilt save Israel by m· hand, as‡
37 that thou wilt save Israel by m· hand, ‡
7: 2 saying, M· own hand hath saved me. ‡
8: 7 Zebah and Zalmunna unto m· hand, ‡
11: 30 the children of Ammon into m· hands, ‡
16: 17 hath not come a rasor upon m· head; ‡
17: 2 and spakest of also in m· ears, behold,
19: 23 that this man is come into m· house, ‡
Ru 4: 6 myself, lest I mar m· own inheritance:
1Sa 2: 1 Lord, m· horn is exalted in the Lord: ‡
1 mouth is enlarged over m· enemies;
28 be my priest, to offer upon m· altar,
29 ye at my sacrifice and at m· offering,
33 whom I shall not cut off from m· altar,
35 according to that which is in m· heart‡
35 shall walk before m· anointed for ever.
12: 3 I received any bribe to blind m· eyes
14: 24 that I may be avenged on m· enemies.
29 how m· eyes have been enlightened,
43 end of the rod that was in m· hand, ‡
15: 14 this bleating of the sheep in m· ears,
17: 46 the Lord deliver thee into m· hand; ‡
18: 17 said, Let not m· hand be upon him, ‡
19: 17 me so, and sent away m· enemy,
20: 1 what is m· iniquity? and what is my
21: 3 give me five loaves of bread in m· hand, ‡
4 is no common bread under m· hand, ‡
23: 7 have delivered him into m· hand; ‡
24: 6 to stretch forth m· hand against him, ‡
10 delivered thee to day into m· hand‡
10 me kill thee: but m· eye spared thee;
10 not put forth m· hand against my ‡
11 evil nor transgression in m· hand, ‡
12, 13 but m· hand shall not be upon thee, ‡
25: 33 avenging myself with m· own hand.
26: 11 m· hand against the Lord's anointed: ‡
18 I done? or what evil is in m· hand? ‡
23 m· hand against the Lord's anointed.
24 was much set by this day in m· eyes,
28: 2 make thee keeper of m· head for ever. ‡
2Sa 5: 19 wilt thou deliver them into m· hand? ‡
20 hath broken forth upon m· enemies
6: 22 and will be base in m· own sight:
11: 11 shall I then go into m· house, to eat‡
14: 5 woman, and m· husband is dead. ‡
30 See, Joab's field is near m·, and he 3027
16: 12 the Lord will look on m· affliction, *
18: 12 thousand shekels of silver in m· hand, ‡
12 would I not put forth m· hand against‡
2Sa 18: 13 wrought falsehood against m· own life: *
19: 37 that I may die in m· own city, and be
22: 4 so shall I be saved from m· enemies.
24 and have kept myself from m· iniquity.
35 a bow of steel is broken by m· arms.
38 I have pursued m· enemies, and
41 also given me the necks of m· enemies,
49 bringeth me forth from m· enemies:
1Ki 1: 33 my son to ride upon m· own mule,
48 throne this day, m· eyes even seeing it.
2: 22 for he is m· elder brother; even for
3: 26 Let it be neither m· nor thine, but
9: 3 m· eyes and m· [‡] heart shall be there
10: 6 report that I heard in m· own land of
7 until I came, and m· eyes had seen it.
11: 21 that I may go to m· own country.
33 to do that which is right in m· eyes,
14: 8 that only which was right in m· eyes.
20: 3 Thy silver and thy gold is m·; thy
3 children, even the goodliest, are m·.
21: 20 Hast thou found me, O m· enemy?
2Ki 4: 13 I dwell among m· own people.
5: 26 Went not m· heart with thee, when‡
6: 32 hath sent to take away m· head? ‡
10: 6 If ye be m·, and if ye will hearken unto*
30 that which is right in m· eyes, and
30 according to all that was in m· heart, ‡
18: 34 delivered Samaria out of m· hand? *
35 delivered their country out of m· hand, *
35 deliver Jerusalem out of m· hand? *
19: 28 thy tumult is come up into m· ears,
34 for m· own sake, and for my servant
20: 6 will defend this city for m· own sake,
15 All the things that are in m· house‡
21: 14 forsake the remnant of m· inheritance,
1Ch 12: 17 me, m· heart shall be knit unto you: ‡
17 ye be come to betray me to m· enemies,
17 seeing there is no wrong in m· hands, ‡
14: 10 wilt thou deliver them into m· hand? ‡
11 in upon m· enemies by m· hand like‡
16: 22 Touch not m· anointed, and do my
17: 14 I will settle him in m· house and in‡
16 and what is m· house, that thou hast*
22: 18 inhabitants of the land into m· hand; ‡
28: 2 I had in m· heart to build an house of ‡
29: 3 I have of m· own proper good, of gold
17 in the uprightness of m· heart I have‡
2Ch 7: 15 Now m· eyes shall be open, and
15 m· ears attent unto the prayer that is
16 m· eyes and...heart shall be there
16 eyes and m· heart shall be there ‡
9: 5 report which I heard in m· own land
6 until I came, and m· eyes had seen it:
29: 10 it is in m· heart to make a covenant‡
32: 13 to deliver their lands out of m· hand? ‡
14 deliver his people out of m· hand, ‡
14 be able to deliver you out of m· hand? ‡
15 to deliver his people out of m· hand, ‡
15 your God deliver you out of m· hand? ‡
17 delivered their people out of m· hand, ‡
17 deliver his people out of m· hand. ‡
Job 3: 10 womb, nor hid sorrow from m· eyes.
4: 12 and m· ear received a little thereof.
16 an image was before m· eyes, there
6: 11 and what is m· end, that I should
7: 7 wind: m· eye shall no more see good.
21 and take away m· iniquity? for now
9: 20 m· own mouth shall condemn me:
31 and m· own clothes shall abhor me.
10: 6 That thou enquirest after m· iniquity,
14 wilt not acquit me from m· iniquity.
15 therefore see thou m· affliction;
13: 1 Lo, m· eye hath seen all this,
1 m· ear hath heard and understood it.
14 my teeth, and put my life in m· hand? ‡
15 I will maintain m· own ways before*
23 How many are m· iniquities and sins?
14: 17 a bag, and thou sewest up m· iniquity.
16: 4 against you, and shake m· head at you. ‡
9 m· enemy sharpeneth his eyes upon
17 Not for any injustice in m· hands: also‡
20 but m· eye poureth out tears unto God.
17: 2 and doth not m· eye continue in their
7 M· eye also is dim by reason of
13 If I wait, the grave is m· house: I ‡
19: 4 erred, m· error remaineth with myself.
10 m· hope hath he removed like a tree.
13 m· acquaintance are verily estranged
15 They that dwell in m· house, and my‡
17 for the children's sake of m· own body. †
27 m· eyes shall behold, and not another;
27: 5 till I die I will not remove m· integrity
7 Let m· enemy be as the wicked, and
31: 1 I made a covenant with m· eyes; why
6 that God may know m· integrity.
7 and m· heart walked after m· eyes,
7 if any blot hath cleaved to m· hands; ‡
9 If m· heart have been deceived by a‡
12 and would root out all m· increase.
22 Then let m· arm fall from my shoulder*
22 and m· arm be broken from the bone.
25 because m· hand hath gotten much; ‡
33 by hiding m· iniquity in my bosom:
35 that m· adversary had written a book.
32: 6 and durst not shew you m· opinion.
10 to me; I also will shew m· opinion.
17 my part; I also will shew m· opinion.
33: 8 thou hast spoken in m· hearing, and‡
40: 4 I will lay m· hand upon my mouth. ‡
41: 11 is under the whole heaven is m·.
42: 5 of the ear: but now m· eye seeth thee.
Ps 3: 3 my glory, and the lifter up of m· head. ‡
7 for thou hast smitten all m· enemies
5: 8 righteousness because of m· enemies;
6: 7 M· eye is consumed because of grief;
7 waxeth old because of all m· enemies.

Ps 6:10 Let all m' enemies be ashamed and
7: 4 him that without cause is m' enemy:
5 earth, and lay m' honour in the dust.*
6 because of the rage of m' enemies:
8 according to m' integrity that is in me.
9: 3 When m' enemies are turned back,
13: 2 how long shall m' enemy be exalted
3 lighten m' eyes, lest I sleep the sleep
4 Lest m' enemy say, I have prevailed
16: 5 Lord is the portion of m' inheritance
17: 3 Thou hast proved m' heart; thou hast‡
18: 3 so shall I be saved from m' enemies.
23 and I kept myself from m' iniquity.
34 a bow of steel is broken by m' arms.
37 I have pursued m' enemies, and
40 given me the necks of m' enemies;
48 He delivereth me from m' enemies:
23: 5 me in the presence of m' enemies:
25: 2 let not m' enemies triumph over me.
11 O Lord, pardon m' iniquity; for it is
15 M' eyes are ever toward the Lord; for
18 Look upon m' affliction and my pain;
19 Consider m' enemies; for they are
26: 1 for I have walked in m' integrity: I
3 thy lovingkindness is before m' eyes:
6 I will wash m' hands in innocency: so‡
11 as for me, I will walk in m' integrity:
27: 2 even m' enemies and my foes, came
6 now shall m' head be lifted up above‡
6 above m' enemies round about me:
11 in a plain path, because of m' enemies.
12 not over unto the will of m' enemies:
31: 9 m' eye is consumed with grief, yea,
10 faileth because of m' iniquity, and my
11 was a reproach among all m' enemies,
11 and a fear to m' acquaintance:
15 me from the hand of m' enemies, and
32: 5 thee, and m' iniquity have I not hid.
8 go: I will guide thee with m' eye.
35: 2 and buckler, and stand up for m' help.‡
13 prayer returned into m' own bosom.
15 But in m' adversity they rejoiced, and†
19 m' enemies wrongfully rejoice over
26 together that rejoice at m' hurt:‡
38: 4 For m' iniquities are gone over m' head:‡
10 as for the light of m' eyes, it also is
18 For I will declare m' iniquity; I will
19 But m' enemies are lively, and they
20 evil for good are m' adversaries;*
39: 4 Lord, make me to know m' end, and
5 and m' age is as nothing before thee:
40: 6 desire; m' ears hast thou opened:
12 m' iniquities have taken hold upon me,
12 are more than the hairs of m' head:‡
41: 5 M' enemies speak evil of me, When
9 m' own familiar friend, in whom I
11 m' enemy doth not triumph over me.
12 thou upholdest me in m' integrity, and
42: 10 my bones, m' enemies reproach me;
49: 4 I will incline m' ear to a parable: I
50: 10 For every beast of the forest is m',
11 the wild beasts of the field are m'. 5978
12 for the world is m', and the fulness
51: 2 Wash me throughly from m' iniquity,
9 my sins, and blot out all m' iniquities.
54: 4 Behold, God is m' helper: the Lord is‡
5 He shall reward evil unto m' enemies:
7 m' eye hath seen his desire upon m'
55: 13 But it was thou, a man m' equal, my
13 my guide, and m' acquaintance.*
56: 2 M' enemies would daily swallow me
9 thee, then shall m' enemies turn back:
59: 1 Deliver me from m' enemies, O my
10 me see my desire upon m' enemies.
60: 7 Gilead is m', and Manasseh is m';
7 also is the strength of m' head; ‡
69: 3 m' eyes fail while I wait for my God.
4 are more than the hairs of m' head:‡
4 me, being m' enemies wrongfully,
18 it: deliver me because of m' enemies.
19 m' adversaries are all before thee.
71: 10 For m' enemies speak against me;
77: 4 Thou holdest m' eyes waking: I am
6 I commune with m' own heart: and
88: 8 Thou hast put away m' acquaintance
9 M' eye mourneth by reason of
18 and m' acquaintance into darkness.
89: 21 m' arm also shall strengthen him.
92: 11 M' eye also shall see my desire on
11 shall see my desire on m' enemies,
11 and m' ears shall hear my desire of
101: 3 set no wicked thing before m' eyes:
6 M' eyes shall be upon the faithful of
102: 8 M' enemies reproach me all the day;
105: 15 Touch not m' anointed, and do my
108: 8 Gilead is m'; Manasseh is m';
8 also is the strength of m' head;‡
109: 20 this be the reward of m' adversaries
29 Let m' adversaries be clothed with
116: 8 soul from death, m' eyes from tears,
119: 11 Thy word have I hid in m' heart, that‡
18 Open thou m' eyes, that I may behold
37 Turn away m' eyes from beholding
82 M' eyes fail for thy word, saying,
92 then have perished in m' affliction.
98 made me wiser than m' enemies: for
112 I have inclined m' heart to perform ‡
121 justice: leave me not to m' oppressors.
123 M' eyes fail for thy salvation, and for
136 Rivers of waters run down m' eyes,
139 m' enemies have forgotten thy words.
148 M' eyes prevent the night watches,
153 Consider m' affliction, and deliver me:
157 are my persecutors and m' enemies;
121: 1 I will lift up m' eyes unto the hills,
123: 1 Unto thee lift I up m' eyes, O thou that

Ps 131: 1 heart is not haughty, nor m' eyes lofty:
132: 4 I will not give sleep to m' eyes,
4 or slumber to m' eyelids,
17 have ordained a lamp for m' anointed.
139: 2 my downsitting and m' uprising,
22 hatred: I count them m' enemies.
141: 8 But m' eyes are unto thee, O God the
143: 9 Deliver me, O Lord, from m' enemies:
12 And of thy mercy cut off m' enemies,
Pr 5: 13 inclined m' ear to them that instructed
23: 15 my heart shall rejoice, even m'. 589
Ec 1: 16 I communed with m' own heart,
2: 1 I said in m' heart, Go to now, I will‡
3 in m' heart to give myself unto wine,‡
3 acquainting m' heart with wisdom;‡
10 whatsoever m' eyes desired I kept not
3: 17 I said in m' heart, God shall judge the‡
18 I said in m' heart concerning the‡
7: 25 I applied m' heart to know, and to*
8: 16 I applied m' heart to know wisdom,‡
Ca 1: 6 but m' own vineyard have I not kept.
2: 16 My beloved is m', and I am his: he
6: 3 my beloved's, and my beloved is m':
8: 12 My vineyard, which is m', is before
Isa 1: 15 hands, I will hide m' eyes from you:
16 of your doings from before m' eyes;
24 Ah, I will ease me of m' adversaries,
24 and avenge me of m' enemies:
5: 9 In m' ears said the Lord of hosts, Of a
6: 5 m' eyes have seen the King, the Lord
10: 5 O Assyrian, the rod of m' anger, and
5 staff in their hand is m' indignation.
25 and m' anger in their destruction.
13: 3 called my mighty ones for m' anger,
16: 4 Let m' outcasts dwell with thee,
11 and m' inward parts for Kir-haresh.
19: 25 my hands, and Israel m' inheritance.
22: 14 it was revealed in m' ears by the Lord
29: 23 his children, the work of m' hands,‡
37: 29 and thy tumult, is come into m' ears,
35 this city to save it for m' own sake,
38: 12 M' age is departed, and is removed* O
14 m' eyes fail with looking upward: O
39: 4 All that is in m' house have they seen:‡
42: 1 m' elect, in whom my soul delighteth;*
43: 1 called thee by thy name; thou art m'.
25 thy transgressions for m' own sake,
45: 4 my servant's sake, and Israel m' elect,*
47: 6 I have polluted m' inheritance, and
48: 5 say, M' idol hath done them; and my
9 my name's sake will I defer m' anger,
11 For m' own sake, even for m' own sake,
13 M' hand also hath laid the foundation‡
49: 22 I will lift up m' hand to the Gentiles,‡
50: 4 he wakeneth m' ear to hear as the
5 The Lord God hath opened m' ear,
8 who is m' adversary? let him come
11 This shall ye have of m' hand; ye‡
51: 5 and m' arms shall judge the people;
5 me, and on m' arm shall they trust.
16 covered thee in the shadow of m' hand,‡
56: 5 unto them will I give in m' house and‡
7 shall be accepted upon m' altar;
7 m' house shall be called an house of‡
60: 7 come up with acceptance on m' altar,
63: 3 for I will tread them in m' anger, and
4 the day of vengeance is in m' heart, ‡
5 m' own arm brought salvation unto
6 tread down the people in m' anger,
65: 9 and m' elect shall inherit it, and my*
12 but did evil before m' eyes, and did
16 and because they are hid from m' eyes.
22 m' elect shall long enjoy the work of*
66: 2 all those things hath m' hand made, ‡
4 but they did evil before m' eyes, and
Jer 2: 7 and made m' heritage an abomination.‡
3: 12 not cause m' anger to fall upon you: ‡
15 give you pastors according to m' heart,‡
7: 20 m' anger and my fury shall be poured
9: 1 and m' eyes a fountain of tears, that I
11: 15 hath my beloved to do in m' house, ‡
12: 3 me, and tried m' heart toward thee: ‡
7 I have forsaken m' house, I have left‡
7 I have left m' heritage; I have given‡
8 M' heritage is unto me as a lion in the‡
9 M' heritage is unto me as a speckled‡
14 Lord against all m' evil neighbours,
13: 17 and m' eye shall weep sore, and run
14: 17 Let m' eyes run down with tears night
15: 14 for a fire is kindled in m' anger, which
16 me the joy and rejoicing of m' heart: ‡
16: 17 For m' eyes are upon all their ways:
17 is their iniquity hid from m' eyes.
18 they have filled m' inheritance with*
21 them to know m' hand and my might;‡
17: 4 for ye have kindled a fire in m' anger,
18: 6 potter's hand, so are ye in m' hand, O‡
20: 9 his word was in m' heart as a burning‡
23: 9 M' heart within me is broken because‡
24: 6 I will set m' eyes upon them for good,
32: 8 Hanameel m' uncle's son came to me
12 the sight of Hanameel m' uncle's son,
31 been to me a provocation of m' anger
37 I have driven them in m' anger, and
33: 5 whom I have slain in m' anger and in
42: 18 As m' anger and my fury hath been
44: 6 my fury and m' anger was poured
28 words shall stand, m', or theirs,
48: 31 m' heart shall mourn for the men of*
36 m' heart shall sound for Moab like ‡
36 and m' heart shall sound like pipes for‡
50: 11 O ye destroyers of m' heritage, ‡
51: 25 I will stretch out m' hand upon thee, ‡
La 1: 16 m' eye, m' eye runneth down with
19 and m' elders gave up the ghost in
20 m' heart is turned within me; for I‡

La 1: 21 m' enemies have heard of my trouble,
2: 11 M' eyes do fail with tears, my bowels
22 brought up hath m' enemy consumed.
3: 19 Remembering m' affliction and my
48 M' eye runneth down with rivers of
49 M' eye trickleth down, and ceaseth
51 M' eye affecteth m' heart because of
52 M' enemies chased me sore, like a
54 Waters flowed over m' head; then I‡
Eze 5: 11 neither shall m' eye spare, neither will
13 Thus shall m' anger be accomplished,
7: 3 I will send m' anger upon thee, and
4 m' eye shall not spare thee, neither
8 and accomplish m' anger upon thee:
9 And m' eye shall not spare, neither
8: 1 as I sat in m' house, and the elders of‡
3 and took me by a lock of m' head; ‡
5 up m' eyes the way toward the north,
18 m' eye shall not spare, neither will I
18 they cry in m' ears with a loud voice,
9: 1 He cried also in m' ears with a loud
5 to the others he said in m' hearing, ‡
10 m' eye shall not spare, neither will I
11: 20 and keep m' ordinances, and do them:
12: 7 digged through the wall with m' hand;‡
13: 9 m' hand shall be upon the prophets
13 be an overflowing shower in m' anger,
14: 13 then will I stretch out m' hand upon it,‡
16: 8 the Lord God, and thou becamest m'.
18 hast set m' oil and m' incense before
17: 19 surely m' oath that he hath despised,
18: 4 Behold, all souls are m'; as the soul
4 so also the soul of the son is m':
20: 5 lifted up m' hand unto the seed of the‡
5 when I lifted up m' hand unto them, ‡
6 that I lifted up m' hand unto them, ‡
17 m' eye spared them from destroying
22 Nevertheless I withdrew m' hand, ‡
23 I lifted up m' hand unto them also in‡
28 I lifted up m' hand to give it to them, ‡
40 For in m' holy mountain, in the ‡
42 I lifted up m' hand to give it to your‡
21: 17 I will also smite m' hands together, ‡
31 I will pour out m' indignation upon
22: 8 Thou hast despised m' holy things, ‡
13 smitten m' hand at thy dishonest‡
20 so will I gather you in m' anger and
26 and have profaned m' holy things: ‡
31 I poured out m' indignation upon
23: 4 and they were m', and they bare sons
5 played the harlot when she was m';
39 they done in the midst of m' house.‡
41 thou hast set m' incense and m' oil.
25: 7 I will stretch out m' hand upon thee,‡
13 also stretch out m' hand upon Edom, ‡
14 shall do in Edom according to m' anger
16 out m' hand upon the Philistines,‡
29: 3 My river is m' own, and I have made it
9 The river is m', and I have made it.
35: 3 I will stretch out m' hand against thee,‡
10 and these two countries shall be m',
36: 7 I have lifted up m' hand, Surely the ‡
21 But I had pity for m' holy name, which‡
22 but for m' holy name's sake, which ye‡
37: 19 and they shall be one in m' hand.‡
43: 8 I have consumed them in m' anger.
44: 8 not kept the charge of m' holy things:‡
12 have I lifted up m' hand against them,‡
24 and my statutes in all m' assemblies;*
47: 14 I lifted up m' hand to give it unto your‡
Da 4: 4 I Nebuchadnezzar was...in m' house,‡
10 the visions of m' head in my bed;‡
34 lifted up m' eyes unto heaven, and
34 m' understanding returned unto me,
36 m' honour and brightness returned*
8: 3 Then I lifted up m' eyes, and saw, and
10: 5 Then I lifted up m' eyes, and looked,
Ho 2: 5 wool and my flax, m' oil and my drink,
10 none shall deliver her out of m' hand.‡
8: 5 m' anger is kindled against them:
13 flesh for the sacrifices of m' offerings,
9: 15 I will drive them out of m' house,‡
11: 8 m' heart is turned within me, my‡
9 not execute the fierceness of m' anger.
13: 11 I gave thee a king in m' anger, and
14 repentance shall be hid from m' eyes.
14: 4 for m' anger is turned away from him
Am 1: 8 I will turn m' hand against Ekron:‡
9: 2 hell, thence shall m' hand take them;‡
4 I will set m' eyes upon them for evil,
Jon 2: 2 I cried by reason of m' affliction unto
Mic 7: 8 Rejoice not against me, O m' enemy:
10 Then she that is m' enemy shall see it,
10 m' eyes shall behold her: now shall
Hab 1: 12 O Lord my God, m' Holy One? we shall‡
3: 19 make me to walk upon m' high places.‡
Zep 1: 4 also stretch out m' hand upon Judah,‡
3: 8 pour upon them m' indignation, even
10 my dispersed, shall bring m' offering.
Hag 1: 9 Because of m' house that is waste, and‡
2: 8 The silver is m', and the gold is m',
Zec 1: 18 Then lifted I up m' eyes, and saw, and
2: 1 I lifted up m' eyes again, and looked,
9 I will shake m' hand upon them, and‡
5: 1 and lifted up m' eyes, and looked, and
9 Then lifted I up m' eyes, and looked,
6: 1 and lifted up m' eyes, and looked, and
8: 6 it also be marvellous in m' eyes?
9: 8 I will encamp about m' house because‡
8 for now have I seen with m' eyes.
10: 3 M' anger was kindled against the
11: 14 I cut asunder m' other staff, even
12: 4 open m' eyes upon the house of Judah,
13: 7 will turn m' hand upon the little ones.‡
Mal 1: 6 I be a father, where is m' honour?‡
7 Ye offer polluted bread upon m' altar;

Mal 1:10 ye kindle fire on *m'* altar for nought.
3: 7 are gone away from *m'* ordinances,
10 that there may be meat in *m'* house,‡
17 shall be *m'*, saith the Lord of hosts,
M't 7:24, 26 heareth these sayings of *m'*, 3450
20:15 me to do what I will with *m'* own? 1699
23 not *m'* to give, but it shall be given "
25:27 have received *m'* own with usury."
M'r 9:24 I believe; help thou *m'* unbelief. 3450
10:40 and on my left hand is not *m'* to give;
Lu 1:44 thy salutation sounded in *m'* ears,3450
2:30 *m'* eyes have seen thy salvation. "
9:38 my son: for he is *m'* only child. 3427
11: 6 friend of *m'* in his journey is come 3450
18: 3 saying, Avenge me of *m'* adversary."
19:23 have required *m'* own with usury?* 846
27 those *m'* enemies, which would 3450
Joh 2: 4 with thee? *m'* hour is not yet come."
5:30 I can of *m'* own self do nothing; *1683
30 I seek not *m'* own will, but the will1699
6:38 not to do *m'* own will, but the will of"
7:16 My doctrine is not *m'*, but his that "
8:50 I seek not *m'* own glory: there is 3450
9:11 made clay, and anointed *m'* eyes, "
15 He put clay upon *m'* eyes, and I "
30 is, and yet he hath opened *m'* eyes. "
10:14 my sheep, and am known of *m'*. 1699
14:24 word which ye hear is not *m'*, but "
16:14 for he shall receive of *m'*, and shall "
15 things that the Father hath are *m'*; "
15 that he shall take of *m'*, and shall "
17:10 And all *m'* are thine, and thine, *m'*; "
Ac 11: 6 which when I had fastened *m'* eyes, "
13:22 a man after *m'* own heart, which *3450
21:13 ye to weep and to break *m'* heart?* "
26: 4 at the first among *m'* own nation "
Ro 11:13 of the Gentiles, I magnify *m'* office:*"
12:19 Vengeance is *m'*; I will repay,saith*1698
16:13 the Lord, and his mother and *m'*. 1700
23 Gaius *m'* host, and of the whole *3450
1Co 1:15 I had baptized in *m'* own name. *1699
4: 3 yea, I judge not *m'* own self. 1683
9: 2 for the seal of *m'* apostleship are 1699
3 *M'* answer to them that do examine*"
10:33 not seeking *m'* own profit, but the 1683
16:21 of me Paul with *m'* own hand. 1699
2Co 11:26 in perils by *m'* own countrymen, in*
30 which concern *m'* infirmities. *3450
12: 5 will not glory, but in *m'* infirmities."
Ga 1:14 many my equals in *m'* own nation, "
6:11 unto you with *m'* own hand. 1699
Ph'p 1: 4 in every prayer of *m'* for you all 3450
3: 9 not having *m'* own righteousness, 1699
2Th 3:17 of Paul with *m'* own hand, which "
Tit 1: 4 *m'* own son after the common faith:*
Ph'm 12 him, that is, *m'* own bowels: *1699
18 thee ought, put that on *m'* account;"
19 Paul have written it with *m'* own hand,
Re 22:16 sent *m'* angel to testify unto you 3450

mingle See also MINGLED.
Isa 5:22 of strength to *m'* strong drink: 4537
Da 2:43 *m'* themselves with the seed of 6151

mingled
Ex 9:24 was hail, and fire *m'* with the hail,3947
29:40 of flour *m'* with the fourth part of 1101
Le 2: 4 cakes of fine flour *m'* with oil, or "
5 fine flour unleavened, *m'* with oil. "
7:10 every meat offering, *m'* with oil, "
12 unleavened cakes *m'* with oil, and "
12 and cakes *m'* with oil, of fine flour, "
9: 4 and a meat offering *m'* with oil: for"
14:10 flour for a meat offering *m'* with oil."
21 flour *m'* with oil for a meat offering,"
19:19 not sow thy field with *m'* seed: *3610
19 a garment *m'* of linen and woollen "
23:13 tenth deals of fine flour *m'* with oil,1101
Nu 6:15 cakes of fine flour *m'* with oil, and "
7:13, 19, 25, 31, 37, 43, 49, 55, 61, 67, 73,
79 full of fine flour *m'* with oil for a "
8: 8 even fine flour *m'* with oil, and "
15: 4 *m'* with the fourth part of an hin of "
6 *m'* with the third part of an hin of "
9 of flour *m'* with half a hin of oil. "
28: 5 *m'* with the fourth part of an hin of "
9, 12, 12 a meat offering, *m'* with oil, "
13 tenth deal of flour *m'* with oil for a "
20 offering shall be of flour *m'* with oil:"
28 meat offering of flour *m'* with oil, "
29: 3 offering shall be of flour *m'* with oil,"
9, 14 shall be of flour *m'* with oil, "
Ezr 9: 2 the holy seed have *m'* themselves 6148
Ps 102: 9 and *m'* my drink with weeping, 4537
106:35 were *m'* among the heathen, and 6148
Pr 9: 2 she hath *m'* her wine; she hath 4537
5 drink the wine which I have *m'*. "
Isa 19:14 The Lord hath *m'* a perverse spirit "
Jer 25:20 And all the *m'* people, and all the 6154
24 all the kings of the *m'* people that "
50:37 upon all the *m'* people that are in the"
Ezr 30: 5 all the *m'* people, and Chub, and "
M't 27:34 him vinegar to drink *m'* with gall:3396
M'r 15:23 him to drink wine *m'* with myrrh:
Lu 13: 1 Pilate had *m'* with their sacrifices.3396
Re 8: 7 followed hail and fire *m'* with blood,"
15: 2 it were a sea of glass *m'* with fire: "

Miniamin (*min'-e-a-min*) See also MIAMIN.
2Ch 31:15 were Eden, and *M'*, and Jeshua, 4509
Ne 12:17 Of Abijah, Zichri; of *M'*,...Moadiah,"
41 the priests; Eliakim, Maaseiah, *M'*,"

minish See also DIMINISH; MINISHED.
Ex 5:19 not *m'* ought from your bricks of ‡1639

minished See also DIMINISHED.
Ps 107:39 they are *m'* and brought low ‡4591

minister See also ADMINISTER; MINISTERED; MINISTERETH; MINISTERING; MINISTERS.
Ex 24:13 rose up, and his *m'* Joshua: and 8334
28: 1 may *m'* unto me in the priest's office,
3, 4 *m'* unto me in the priest's office.
35 And it shall be upon Aaron to *m'*: 8334
41 may *m'* unto me in the priest's office.
43 the altar to *m'* in the holy place; 8334
29: 1 to *m'* unto me in the priest's office:
30 cometh...to *m'* in the holy place. 8334
44 sons, to *m'* to me in the priest's office.
30:20 they come near to the altar to *m'*, 8334
30 may *m'* unto me in the priest's office.
31:10 his sons, to *m'* in the priest's office,
35:19 sons, to *m'* in the priest's office. 8334
39:26 about the hem of the robe to *m'* in; "
41 to *m'* in the priest's office. "
40:13 may *m'* unto me in the priest's office.
15 may *m'* unto me in the priest's office:
Le 7:35 to *m'* unto the Lord in the priest's
16:32 consecrate to *m'* in the priest's office*
Nu 1:50 and they shall *m'* unto it, and shall8334
3: 3 consecrated to *m'* in the priest's office.
6 priest, that they may *m'* unto him.8334
31 the sanctuary wherewith they *m'*, "
4: 9 thereof, wherewith they *m'* unto it: "
12 wherewith they *m'* in the sanctuary,"
14 wherewith they *m'* about it, even "
8:26 But shall *m'* with their brethren in "
16: 9 the congregation to *m'* unto them? "
18: 2 joined unto thee, and *m'* unto thee:"
2 thou and thy sons with thee shall *m'**
De 10: 8 before the Lord to *m'* unto him, 8334
17:12 that standeth to *m'* there before the"
18: 5 stand to *m'* in the name of the Lord,"
7 he shall *m'* in the name of the Lord "
21: 5 God hath chosen to *m'* unto him, "
Jos 1: 1 Joshua the son of Nun, Moses' *m'*, "
1Sa 2:11 And the child did *m'* unto the Lord "
1Ki 8:11 the priests could not stand to *m'* "
1Ch 15: 2 of God, and to *m'* unto him for ever."
16: 4 Levites to *m'* before the ark of the "
37 to *m'* before ark continually, as "
23:13 before the Lord, to *m'* unto him, and"
26:12 to *m'* in the house of the Lord. "
2Ch 5:14 the priests could not stand to *m'* by "
8:14 to praise and *m'* before the priests, "
13:10 the priests, which *m'* unto the Lord,*"
23: 6 and they that *m'* of the Levites; "
24:14 even vessels to *m'*, and to offer 8335
29:11 ye should *m'* unto him, and burn *8334
31: 2 to *m'*, and to give thanks, and to "
Ne 10:36 that *m'* in the house of our God: "
39 priests that *m'*, and the porters, "
Ps 9: 8 shall *m'* judgment to the people in 1777
Isa 60: 7 rams of Nebaioth...*m'* unto thee: 8334
10 and their kings shall *m'* unto thee: "
Jer 33:22 and the Levites that *m'* unto me. "
Eze 40:46 near to the Lord to *m'* unto him. "
42:14 lay their garments wherein they *m'*;"
43:19 approach unto me, to *m'* unto me, "
44:11 stand before them to *m'* unto them. "
15 come near to me to *m'* unto me, "
16 near to my table, to *m'* unto me, "
17 *m'* in the gates of the inner court, "
27 inner court, to *m'* in the sanctuary, "
45: 4 shall come near to *m'* unto the Lord: "
M't 20:26 among you, let him be your *m'*; 1249
28 to be ministered unto, but to *m'*, 1247
25:44 prison, and did not *m'* unto thee? "
M'r 10:43 among you, shall be your *m'*: 1249
45 to be ministered unto, but to *m'*, 1247
Lu 4:20 he gave it again to the *m'*, and sat*5257
Ac 13: 5 and they had also John to their *m'*.*"
24:23 none...to *m'* or come unto him. 5256
26:16 to make thee a *m'* and a witness 5257
Ro 13: 4 is the *m'* of God to thee for good. 1249
4 he is the *m'* of God, a revenger to "
15: 8 a *m'* of the circumcision for the "
16 I should be the *m'* of Jesus Christ 3011
25 Jerusalem to *m'* unto the saints. *1247
27 to *m'* unto them in carnal things. 3008
1Co 9:13 they which *m'* about holy things 2038
2Co 9:10 sower both *m'* bread for your food,*5524
Ga 2:17 is therefore Christ the *m'* of sin? 1249
Eph 3: 7 Whereof I was made a *m'*, according"
4:29 it may *m'* grace unto the hearers.*1325
6:21 a beloved brother and faithful *m'* 1249
Col 1: 7 is for you a faithful *m'* of Christ; "
23 whereof I Paul am made a *m'*; "
25 Whereof I am made a *m'*, according"
4: 7 a faithful *m'* and fellowservant in "
1Th 3: 2 our brother, and *m'* of God, and our"
1Ti 1: 4 *m'* questions, rather than godly 3930
4: 6 shalt be a good *m'* of Jesus Christ,1249
Heb 1:14 sent forth to *m'* for them who shall1248
6:10 ministered to the saints, and do *m'*.1247
8: 2 A *m'* of the sanctuary, and of the 3011
1Pe 1:12 but unto us they did *m'* the things,1247
4:10 even so *m'* the same one to another,*"
11 if any man *m'*, let him do it as of * "

ministered
Nu 3: 4 Ithamar *m'* in the priest's office
De 10: 6 his son *m'* in the priest's office in
1Sa 2:18 Samuel *m'* before the Lord, being 8334
3: 1 the child Samuel *m'* unto the Lord "
2Sa 13:17 called his servant that *m'* unto him,"
1Ki 1: 4 cherished the king, and *m'* to him: "
15 the Shunammite *m'* unto the king. "
19:21 went after Elijah, and *m'* unto him. "
2Ki 25:14 vessels of brass wherewith they *m'*, "
1Ch 6:32 *m'* before the dwelling place of the "
28: 1 companies that *m'* to the king by "
2Ch 22: 8 of Ahaziah, that *m'* to Ahaziah, he "
Es 2: 2 king's servants that *m'* unto him, "
6: 3 king's servants that *m'* unto him. "

Jer 52:18 vessels of brass wherewith they *m'*,8334
Eze 44:12 they *m'* unto them before their idols,"
19 their garments wherein they *m'*, * "
Da 7:10 thousand thousands *m'* unto him, 8120
M't 4:11 angels came and *m'* unto him. 1247
8:15 and she arose, and *m'* unto them. "
20:28 Son of man came not to be *m'* unto, "
M'r 1:13 beasts; and the angels *m'* unto him."
31 left her, and she *m'* unto them. "
10:45 Son of man came not to be *m'* unto,"
15:41 followed him, and *m'* unto him;) "
Lu 4:39 she arose and *m'* unto them. "
8: 3 *m'* unto him of their substance. "
Ac 13: 2 As they *m'* to the Lord, and fasted,3008
19:22 two of them that *m'* unto him, 1247
20:34 hands have *m'* unto my necessities,5256
2Co 3: 3 to be the epistle of Christ *m'* by us,1247
Phil 2:25 and he that *m'* to my wants. *3011
Col 2:19 and bands having nourishment *m'*,*2023
2Ti 1:18 things he *m'* unto me at Ephesus, 1247
Ph'm 13 might have *m'* unto me in the bonds"
Heb 6:10 *m'* to the saints, and do minister. "
2Pe 1:11 an entrance shall be *m'* unto you *2023

ministereth
2Co 9:10 Now he that *m'* seed to the sower *2023
Ga 3: 5 therefore that *m'* to you the Spirit,*"

ministering
1Ch 9:28 had the charge of the *m'* vessels, *5656
Eze 44:11 of the house, and *m'* to the house:8334
M't 27:55 Jesus from Galilee, *m'* unto him: 1247
Ro 12: 7 Or ministry, let us wait on our *m'*:*1248
15:16 the Gentiles, *m'* the gospel of God, 2418
2Co 8: 4 fellowship of the *m'* to the saints. 1248
9: 1 as touching the *m'* to the saints, "
Heb 1:14 Are they not all *m'* spirits, sent 3010
10:11 every priest standeth daily *m'* and 3008

ministers
1Ki 10: 5 attendance of his *m'*, and their 8334
2Ch 9: 4 attendance of his *m'*, and their "
Ezr 7:24 or *m'* of this house of God, *6399
8:17 that they should bring unto us *m'* 8334
Ps 103:21 ye *m'* of his, that do his pleasure. "
104: 4 angels spirits; his *m'* a flaming fire:"
Isa 61: 6 shall call you the *M'* of our God: "
Jer 33:21 with the Levites the priests, my *m'*."
Eze 44:11 they shall be *m'* in my sanctuary, "
45: 4 the priests the *m'* of the sanctuary, "
5 the Levites, the *m'* of the house, "
46:24 with the *m'* of the house shall boil "
Joe 1: 9 the priests, the Lord's *m'*, mourn. "
13 howl, ye *m'* of the altar: come, lie "
13 night in sackcloth, ye *m'* of my God:"
2:17 Let the priests, the *m'* of the Lord, "
Lu 1: 2 eyewitnesses, and *m'* of the word; 5257
Ro 13: 6 for they are God's *m'*, attending 3011
1Co 3: 5 *m'* by whom ye believed, even as 1249
4: 1 account of us, as of...*m'* of Christ, 5257
2Co 3: 6 hath made us able *m'* of the new 1249
6: 4 approving ourselves as...*m'* of God, "
11:15 thing if his *m'* also be transformed "
15 as the *m'* of righteousness; whose "
23 Are they *m'* of Christ? (I speak as a "
Heb 1: 7 spirits, and his *m'* a flame of fire. 3011

ministration
Lu 1:23 days of his *m'* were accomplished, 3009
Ac 6: 1 were neglected in the daily *m'*. 1248
2Co 3: 7 But if the *m'* of death, written and "
8 *m'* of the spirit be rather glorious? "
9 if the *m'* of condemnation be glory, "
9 *m'* of righteousness exceed in glory."
9:13 Whiles by the experiment of this *m'*"

ministry
Nu 4:12 take all the instruments of *m'*, 8335
47 came to do the service of the *m'*, *5656
2Ch 7: 6 when David praised by their *m'*; 3027
Ho 12:10 by the *m'* of the prophets.
Ac 1:17 and had obtained part of this *m'*. 1248
25 That he may take part of this *m'* "
6: 4 prayer, and to the *m'* of the word. "
12:25 when they had fulfilled their *m'*, * "
20:24 and the *m'*, which I have received "
21:19 among the Gentiles by his *m'*. "
Ro 12: 7 Or *m'*, let us wait on...ministering; "
1Co 16:15 addicted...to the *m'* of the saints,)* "
2Co 4: 1 Therefore seeing we have this *m'*, "
5:18 given to us the *m'* of reconciliation;"
6: 3 thing, that the *m'* be not blamed:* "
Eph 4:12 for the work of the *m'*, for the "
Col 4:17 Take heed to the *m'* which thou hast"
1Ti 1:12 faithful, putting me into the *m'*; * "
2Ti 4: 5 evangelist, make full proof of thy *m'*."
11 for he is profitable to me for the *m'*.*"
Heb 8: 6 he obtained a more excellent *m'*, 3009
9:21 and all the vessels of the *m'*. "

Minni (*min'-ni*)
Jer 51:27 the kingdoms of Ararat, *M'*, and 4508

Minnith (*min'-nith*)
J'g 11:33 Aroer, even till thou come to *M'*, 4511
Eze 27:17 traded in thy market wheat of *M'*, "

minstrel See also MINSTRELS.
2Ki 3:15 But now bring me a *m'*. And it 5059
15 came to pass, when the *m'* played, "

minstrels
M't 9:23 *m'* and the people making a noise,*834

mint
M't 23:23 ye pay the tithe of *m'* and anise 2238
Lu 11:42 ye tithe *m'* and rue and all manner "

Miphkad (*mif'-kad*)
Ne 3:31 over against the gate *M'*, *4663

miracle See also MIRACLES.
Ex 7: 9 you, saying, Shew a *m'* for you: *4159
M'r 6:52 considered not the *m'* of the loaves:*
9:39 which shall do a *m'* in my name, *1411*
Lu 23: 8 hoped to have seen some *m'* done *4592*
Joh 4:54 again the second *m'* that Jesus did,*"
6:14 they had seen the *m'* that Jesus did,*"
10:41 him, and said, John did no *m'*: * "
12:18 heard that he had done this *m'*. * "
Ac 4:16 notable *m'* hath been done by them"
22 this *m'* of healing was shewed. "

miracles
Nu 14:22 and my *m'*, which I did in Egypt * 226
De 11: 3 his *m'*, and his acts, which he did* "
29: 3 the signs, and those great *m'*: *4159
J'g 6:13 and where be all his *m'* which our*6381
Joh 2:11 beginning of *m'* did Jesus in Cana*4592
23 they saw the *m'* which he did. * "
3: 2 can do these *m'* that thou doest, * "
6: 2 because they saw his *m'* which he* "
26 seek me, not because ye saw the *m'*,*"
7:31 will he do more *m'* than these * "
9:16 man that is a sinner do such *m'*?* "
11:47 we? for this man doeth many *m'*. * "
12:37 though he had done so many *m'* * "
Ac 2:22 approved of God among you by *m'**1411*
6: 8 did great wonders and *m'* among *4592*
8: 6 and seeing the *m'* which he did. * "
13 the *m'* and signs which were done.*1411*
15:12 *m'* and wonders God had wrought*4592*
19:11 special *m'* by the hands of Paul: *1411*
1Co 12:10 To another the working of *m'*; to "
28 after that *m'*, then gifts of healings," "
29 all teachers? are all workers of *m'*? "
Ga 3: 5 worketh *m'* among you, doeth he it "
Heb 2: 4 and wonders, and with divers *m'*,* "
Re 13:14 those *m'* which he had power to do*4592*
16:14 the spirits of devils, working *m'*, * "
19:20 the false prophet that wrought *m'** "

mire
2Sa 22:43 them as the *m'* of the street, and 2916
Job 8:11 Can the rush grow up without *m'*?1207
30:19 He hath cast me into the *m'*, and 2563
41:30 sharp pointed things upon the *m'*.2916
Ps 69: 2 I sink in deep *m'*, where there is 3121
14 Deliver me out of the *m'*, and let 2916
Isa 10: 6 down like the *m'* of the streets. 2563
57:20 whose waters cast up *m'* and dirt. 7516
Jer 38: 6 there was no water, but *m'*: 2916
6 so Jeremiah sunk in the *m'*. "
22 thy feet are sunk in the *m'*, and 1206
Mic 7:10 down as the *m'* of the streets. 2916
Zec 9: 3 fine gold as the *m'* of the streets. "
10: 5 enemies in the *m'* of the streets in "
2Pe 2:22 washed to her wallowing in the *m'*.*1004*

Miriam (*mir'-e-am*) See also MARY.
Ex 15:20 *M'* the prophetess, the sister of 4813
21 *M'* answered them, Sing ye to the "
Nu 12: 1 *M'* and Aaron spake against Moses" "
4 unto *M'*, Come out ye three unto "
5 and called Aaron and *M'*: and they" "
10 *M'* became leprous, white as snow: "
10 Aaron looked upon *M'*, and, behold," "
15 *M'* was shut out from the camp "
15 not till *M'* was brought in again. "
20: 1 and *M'* died there, and was buried "
26:59 and Moses, and *M'* their sister. "
De 24: 9 what the Lord thy God did unto *M'* "
1Ch 4:17 and she bare *M'*, and Shammai, "
6: 3 Aaron, and Moses, and *M'*. The "
Mic 6: 4 before thee Moses, Aaron, and *M'*. "

Mirma (*mur'-mah*)
1Ch 8:10 And Jeuz, and Shachia, and *M'*. *4821

mirth
Ge 31:27 have sent thee away with *m'*, and 8057
Ne 8:12 portions, and to make great *m'*, "
Ps 137: 3 that wasted us required of us *m'*, "
Pr 14:13 and the end of that *m'* is heaviness. "
Ec 2: 1 to now, I will prove thee with *m'*, "
2 is mad: and of *m'*, What doeth it? "
7: 4 heart of fools is in the house of *m'*. "
8:15 Then I commended *m'*, because a "
Isa 24: 8 The *m'* of tabrets ceaseth, the 4885
11 the *m'* of the land is gone. "
Jer 7:34 the voice of *m'*, and the voice of 8342
16: 9 and in your days, the voice of *m'*, "
25:10 will take from them the voice of *m'*," "
Eze 21:10 glitter: should we then make *m'*? 7797
Ho 2:11 will also cause all her *m'* to cease, 4885

miry
Ps 40: 2 an horrible pit, out of the *m'* clay, 3121
Eze 47:11 But the *m'* places thereof and the 1207
Da 2:41 the iron mixed with *m'* clay. 2917
43 sawest iron mixed with *m'* clay, "

miscarrying
Ho 9:14 give them a *m'* womb and dry 7921

mischief See also MISCHIEFS.
Ge 42: 4 Lest peradventure *m'* befall him. 611
38 if *m'* befall him by the way in the "
44:29 this also from me, and *m'* befall him," "
Ex 21:22 from her, and yet no *m'* follow: "
23 if any *m'* follow, then thou shalt "
32:12 For *m'* did he bring them out, to *7451
22 the people, that they are set on *m'*.*"
1Sa 23: 9 secretly practised *m'* against him; "
2Sa 16: 8 thou art taken in thy *m'*, because "
1Ki 11:25 beside the *m'* that Hadad did: and "
20: 7 and see how this man seeketh *m'*: "
2Ki 7: 9 light, some *m'* will come upon us:*5771
Ne 6: 2 But they thought to do me *m'* 7451
Es 8: 3 tears to put away the *m'* of Haman "
Job 15:35 They conceive *m'*, and bring forth 5999
Ps 7:14 iniquity, and hath conceived *m'*, 5999
16 His *m'* shall return upon his own "
10: 7 under his tongue is *m'* and vanity. "
14 for thou beholdest *m'* and spite, to "
26:10 In whose hands is *m'*, and their 2154
28: 3 but *m'* is in their hearts. 7451
36: 4 He deviseth *m'* upon his bed; he * 205
52: 1 Why boastest thou thyself in *m'*, 7451
55:10 *m'* also and sorrow are in the midst 205
62: 3 will ye imagine *m'* against a man?* "
94:20 thee, which frameth *m'* by a law? 5999
119:150 draw nigh that follow after *m'*: *2154
140: 9 *m'* of their own lips cover them. 5999
Pr 4:16 not, except they have done *m'*; 7489
6:14 he deviseth *m'* continually; he *7451
18 feet that be swift in running to *m'*, "
10:23 It is as sport to a fool to do *m'*: *2154
11:27 he that seeketh *m'*, it shall come 7451
12:21 the wicked shall be filled with *m'*.* "
13:17 wicked messenger falleth into *m'*:* "
17:20 a perverse tongue falleth into *m'*. "
24: 2 and their lips talk of *m'*. 5999
16 but the wicked shall fall into *m'*. *7451
28:14 his heart shall fall into *m'*. "
Isa 47:11 *m'* shall fall upon thee; thou shalt1943
59: 4 they conceive *m'*, and bring forth 5999
Eze 7:26 *M'* shall come upon *m'*, and 1943
11: 2 these are the men that devise *m'*,* 205
Da 11:27 king's hearts shall be to do *m'*, 4827
Ho 7:15 do they imagine *m'* against me. 7451
Ac 13:10 O full of all subtilty and all *m'*, *4468*

mischiefs
De 32:23 I will heap *m'* upon them; I will 7451
Ps 52: 2 Thy tongue deviseth *m'*; like a *1942
140: 2 Which imagine *m'* in their hearts;7451

mischievous
Ps 21:11 they imagined a *m'* device, which*4209
38:12 that seek my hurt speak *m'* things,1942
Pr 24: 8 evil shall be called a *m'* person. 4209
Ec 10:13 the end of his talk is *m'* madness. 7451
Mic 7: 3 man, he uttereth his *m'* desire: *1942

miserable
Job 16: 2 things: *m'* comforters are ye all. 5999
1Co 15:19 Christ, we are of all men most *m'*.*1652*
Re 3:17 that thou art wretched, and *m'*, "

miserably
M't 21:41 will *m'* destroy those wicked men, *2560*

miseries
La 1: 7 days of her affliction and of her *m'*4788
Jas 5: 1 weep and howl for your *m'* that *5004*

misery See also MISERABLE; MISERIES.
J'g 10:16 was grieved for the *m'* of Israel. 5999
Job 3:20 is light given to him that is in *m'*, 6001
11:16 Because thou shalt forget thy *m'*, 5999
Pr 31: 7 and remember his *m'* no more. "
Ec 8: 6 the *m'* of man is great upon him. 7451
La 3:19 mine affliction and my *m'*, the 4788
Ro 3:16 and *m'* are in their ways: *5004*

Misgab (*mis'-gab*)
Jer 48: 1 *M'* is confounded and dismayed. 4869

Mishael (*mish'-a-el*) See also MISHAL.
Ex 6:22 And the sons of Uzziel; *M'*, and 4332
Lev 10: 4 Moses called *M'* and Elzaphan, "
Ne 8: 4 on his left hand, Pedaiah, and *M'*, "
Da 1: 6 of Judah, Daniel, Hananiah, *M'*, "
7 and to *M'*, of Meshach; and to "
11 had set over Daniel, Hananiah, *M'*, "
19 none like Daniel, Hananiah, *M'*, "
2:17 the thing known to Hananiah, *M'*, "

Mishal (*mi'-shal*) See also MISHEAL.
Jos 21:30 of Asher, *M'* with her suburbs, 4861

Misham (*mi'-sham*)
1Ch 8:12 and *M'*, and Shamed, who built 4936

Misheal (*mish'-e-al*)
Jos 19:26 Alammelech, and Amad, and *M'*;*4861

Mishma (*mish'-mah*)
Ge 25:14 And *M'*, and Dumah, and Massa, 4927
1Ch 1:30 *M'*, and Dumah, Massa, Hadad, "
4:25 son, Mibsam his son, *M'* his son. "
26 And the sons of *M'*; Hamuel his "

Mishmannah (*mish-man'-nah*)
1Ch 12:10 *M'* the fourth, Jeremiah the fifth, 4925

Mishpat See EN-MISHPAT.

Mishraites (*mish'-ra-ites*)
1Ch 2:53 and the Shumathites, and the *M'*;4954

Mispereth (*mis-pe'-reth*) See also MIZPAR.
Ne 7: 7 Bilshan, *M'*, Bigvai, Nehum, 4559

Misrephoth-maim (*mis''-re-foth-mah'-yim*) See also ZAREPHATH.
Jos 11: 8 unto great Zidon, and unto *M'*. 4956
13: 6 country from Lebanon unto *M'*, "

miss See also AMISS; MISSED; MISSING; MISCARRYING; MISUSED.
J'g 20:16 at an hair breadth, and not *m'*. 2398
1Sa 20: 6 If thy father at all *m'* me, then 6485

missed
1Sa 20:18 and thou shalt be *m'*, because thy 6485
25:15 not hurt, neither *m'* we any thing, "
21 nothing was *m'* of all that pertained" "

missing
1Sa 25: 7 neither was there ought *m'* unto 6485
1Ki 20:39 if by any means he be *m'*, then shall" "

mist
Ge 2: 6 there went up a *m'* from the earth, 108
Ac 13:11 fell on him a *m'* and a darkness; *887*
2Pe 2:17 the *m'* of darkness is reserved for*2217*

mistress
Ge 16: 4 her *m'* was despised in her eyes. 1404
8 flee from the face of my *m'* Sarai. "
9 said unto her, Return to thy *m'*, "
1Ki 17:17 the *m'* of the house, fell sick; and 1172
2Ki 5: 3 And she said unto her *m'*, Would 1404
Ps 123: 2 maiden unto the hand of her *m'*; "
Pr 30:23 handmaid that is heir to her *m'*. "
Isa 24: 2 as with the maid, so with her *m'*; "
Na 3: 4 the *m'* of witchcrafts, that selleth 1172

misused
2Ch 36:16 and *m'* his prophets, until the *8591

mite See also MITES.
Lu 12:59 till thou hast paid the very last *m'*. *3016*

mites
M'r 12:42 and she threw in two *m'*, which *3016*
Lu 21: 2 widow casting in thither two *m'*. "

Mithcah (*mith'-cah*)
Nu 33:28 from Tarah, and pitched in *M'*. *4989
29 they went from *M'*, and pitched in* "

Mithnite (*mith'-nite*)
1Ch 11:43 Maachah, and Joshaphat the *M'*. 4981

Mithredath (*mith'-re-dath*)
Ezr 1: 8 by the hand of *M'* the treasurer, 4990
4: 7 Artaxerxes wrote Bishlam, *M'*, "

mitre
Ex 28: 4 broidered coat, a *m'*, and a girdle:4701
37 lace, that it may be upon the *m'*; "
37 the forefront of the *m'* it shall be. "
39 shalt make the *m'* of fine linen, and" "
29: 6 shalt put the *m'* upon his head, and" "
6 put the holy crown upon the *m'*. "
39:28 And a *m'* of fine linen, and goodly "
31 to fasten it on high upon the *m'*; "
Le 8: 9 And he put the *m'* upon his head; "
9 also upon the *m'*, even upon his "
16: 4 and with the linen *m'* shall he be "
Zec 3: 5 them set a fair *m'* upon his head. 6797
5 So they set a fair *m'* upon his head, "

Mitylene (*mit-i-le'-ne*)
Ac 20:14 we took him in, and came to *M'*. *3412*

mixed See also MIXT.
Ex 12:38 a *m'* multitude went up also with 6154
Ne 13: 3 from Israel all the *m'* multitude. "
Pr 23:30 wine; they that go to seek *m'* wine.4469
Isa 1:22 dross, thy wine *m'* with water: 4107
Da 2:41 sawest the iron *m'* with miry clay.6151
43 thou sawest iron *m'* with miry clay," "
43 even as iron is not *m'* with clay. * "
Ho 7: 8 he hath *m'* himself among the *1101
Heb 4: 2 not being *m'* with faith in them **4786*

mixt See also MIXED
Nu 11: 4 the *m'* multitude that was among them*

mixture
Ps 75: 8 the wine is red; it is full of *m'*; 4538
Joh 19:39 brought a *m'* of myrrh and aloes, *3395*
Re 14:10 is poured out without *m'* into the * *194*

Mizar (*mi'-zar*)
Ps 42: 6 the Hermonites, from the hill *M'*. 4706

Mizpah (*miz'-pah*) See also MIZPEH.
Ge 31:49 *M'*; for he said, The Lord watch 4709
1Ki 15:22 them Geba of Benjamin, and *M'*. "
2Ki 25:23 there came to Gedaliah to *M'*, even" "
25 Chaldees that were with him at *M'*." "
2Ch 16: 6 he built therewith Geba and *M'*. "
Ne 3: 7 and of *M'*, unto the throne of the "
15 Col-hozeh, the ruler of part of *M'*; "
19 the son of Jeshua, the ruler of *M'*, "
Jer 40: 6 Gedaliah the son of Ahikam to *M'*;4708
8 they came to Gedaliah to *M'*, even "
10 for me, behold, I will dwell at *M'*, "
12 land of Judah, to Gedaliah, unto *M'*," "
13 the fields, came to Gedaliah to *M'*, "
15 spake to Gedaliah in *M'* secretly, 4709
41: 1 Gedaliah the son of Ahikam to *M'*; "
1 they did eat bread together in *M'*. "
3 at *M'*, and the Chaldeans that were" "
6 went forth from *M'* to meet them, "
10 of the people that were in *M'*, "
10 all the people that remained in *M'*, "
14 had carried away captive from *M'* "
16 from *M'*, after that he had slain "
Ho 5: 1 ye have been a snare on *M'*, "

Mizpar (*miz'-par*) See also MISPERETH.
Ezr 2: 2 Bilshan, *M'*, Bigvai, Rehum, 4558

Mizpeh (*miz'-peh*) See also MIZPAH; RAMATH-MIZPEH.
Jos 11: 3 under Hermon in the land of *M'*. *4709
8 unto the valley of *M'* eastward; 4708
15:38 And Dilean, and *M'*, and Joktheel, "
18:26 *M'*, and Chephirah, and Mozah, "
J'g 10:17 together, and encamped in *M'*. *4709
11:11 all his words before the Lord in *M'*.*"
29 and passed over *M'* of Gilead, and 4708
29 from *M'* of Gilead he passed over "
34 came to *M'* unto his house, and *4709
20: 1 land of Gilead, unto the Lord in *M'*.* "
3 of Israel were gone up to *M'*.) "
21: 1 the men of Israel had sworn in *M'*,*"
5 came not up to the Lord to *M'*, "
8 of Israel that came not up to *M'* to*"
1Sa 7: 5 said, Gather all Israel to *M'*, and *4708
6 they gathered together to *M'*, *4709
6 Samuel judged...of Israel in *M'*. *4708
7 were gathered together to *M'*, "
11 the men of Israel went out of *M'*,*4709
12 and set it between *M'* and Shen, * "
16 to Beth-el, and Gilgal, and *M'*,and* "
10:17 together unto the Lord to *M'*; * "
22: 3 David went thence to *M'* of Moab:4708

Mizraim (*miz'-ra-im*) See also ABEL-MIZRAIM; EGYPT.
Ge 10: 6 sons of Ham; Cush, and *M'*, and 4714
13 And *M'* begat Ludim, and Anamim,"
1Ch 1: 8 The sons of Ham; Cush, and *M'*, "
11 And *M'* begat Ludim, and Anamim,"

Mizzah (*miz'-zah*)
Ge 36: 13 and Zerah, Shammah, and *M'*: 4199
17 Zerah, duke Shammah, duke *M'*: "
1Ch 1: 37 Nahath, Zerah, Shammah, and *M'*. "

Mnason (*na'-son*)
Ac 21: 16 with them one *M'* of Cyprus, an *3416*

Moab (*mo'-ab*) See also MOABITE; PAHATH-MOAB.
Ge 19: 37 a son, and called his name *M'*: 4124
36: 35 who smote Midian in the field of *M'*, "
Ex 15: 15 the mighty men of *M'*, trembling "
Nu 21: 11 the wilderness which is before *M'*, "
13 for Arnon is the border of *M'*, "
13 between *M'* and the Amorites. "
15 Ar, and lieth upon the border of *M'*. "
20 in the country of *M'*, to the top of "
26 against the former king of *M'*, and "
28 it hath consumed Ar of *M'*, and the "
29 Woe to thee, *M'*! thou art undone, "
22: 1 pitched in the plains of *M'* on this "
3 *M'* was sore afraid of the people, "
3 *M'* was distressed because of the "
4 *M'* said unto the elders of Midian, "
7 the elders of *M'* and the elders of "
8 princes of *M'* abode with Balaam. "
10 king of *M'*, hath sent unto me, "
14 the princes of *M'* rose up, and they "
21 and went with the princes of *M'*. "
36 out to meet him unto a city of *M'*, "
23: 6 he, and all the princes of *M'*. "
7 king of *M'* hath brought me from "
17 and the princes of *M'* with him. "
24: 17 and shall smite the corners of *M'*, "
25: 1 whoredom with the daughters of *M'*. "
26: 3 spake with them in the plains of *M'* "
63 children of Israel in the plains of *M'* "
31: 12 unto the camp at the plains of *M'*, "
33: 44 in Ije-abarim, in the border of *M'*. "
48 and pitched in the plains of *M'* by "
49 Abel-shittim in the plains of *M'*. "
50 spake unto Moses in...plains of *M'**"
35: 1 spake unto Moses in the plains of *M'*"
36: 13 children of Israel in the plains of *M'*"
De 1: 5 this side Jordan, in the land of *M'*, "
2: 8 by the way of the wilderness of *M'*. "
18 over through Ar, the coast of *M'*, "
29: 1 children of Israel in the land of *M'*, "
32: 49 which is in the land of *M'*, that is "
34: 1 went up from the plains of *M'* unto "
5 Lord died there in the land of *M'*, "
6 him in a valley in the land of *M'*, "
8 wept for Moses in the plains of *M'* "
Jos 13: 32 for inheritance in the plains of *M'*, "
24: 9 the son of Zippor, king of *M'*, arose "
J'g 3: 12 strengthened Eglon the king of *M'* "
14 Israel served Eglon the king of *M'* "
15 present unto Eglon king of *M'*. "
17 the present unto Eglon king of *M'*: "
28 took the fords of Jordan toward *M'*,*"
29 slew of *M'* at that time about ten "
30 *M'* was subdued that day under "
10: 6 gods of Zidon, and the gods of *M'*, "
11: 15 Israel took not away the land of *M'*, "
17 they sent unto the king of *M'*: but "
18 land of Edom, and the land of *M'*, "
18 by the east side of the land of *M'*, "
18 came not within the border of *M'*: "
18 for Arnon was the border of *M'*. "
25 the son of Zippor, king of *M'*? "
Ru 1: 1 to sojourn in the country of *M'*, he,"
2 they came into the country of *M'*, "
4 them wives of the women of *M'*; 4125
6 return from the country of *M'*: 4124
6 had heard in the country of *M'* how"
22 returned out of the country of *M'*: "
2: 6 Naomi out of the country of *M'*: "
4: 3 come again out of the country of *M'*, "
1Sa 12: 9 and into the hand of the king of *M'*, "
14: 47 enemies on every side, against *M'*, "
22: 3 David went thence to Mizpeh of *M'*: "
3 and he said unto the king of *M'*, "
4 brought them before the king of *M'*: "
2Sa 8: 2 he smote *M'*, and measured them "
12 and of *M'*, and of the children of "
23: 20 he slew two lionlike men of *M'*: he "
1Ki 11: 7 for Chemosh, the abomination of *M'*, "
2Ki 1: 1 *M'* rebelled against Israel after the"
3: 4 king of *M'* was a sheepmaster, and "
5 the king of *M'* rebelled against the "
7 king of *M'* hath rebelled against "
7 go with me against *M'* to battle? "
10 to deliver them into the hand of *M'*! "
13 to deliver them into the hand of *M'*. "
23 now therefore, *M'*, to the spoil. "
26 king of *M'* saw that the battle "
1Ch 1: 46 smote Midian in the field of *M'*, "
4: 22 who had the dominion in *M'*, and "
8: 8 begat children in the country of *M'*, "
11: 22 he slew two lionlike men of *M'*: "
18: 2 And he smote *M'*; and the Moabites "
11 from *M'*, and from the children of "
2Ch 20: 1 that the children of *M'*, and the "
10 the children of Ammon and *M'* and"
22 against the children of Ammon, *M'*, "
23 children of Ammon and *M'* stood up"
Ne 13: 23 of Ashdod, of Ammon, and of *M'*: 4125
Ps 60: 8 *M'* is my washpot; over Edom will 4124
83: 6 of *M'*, and the Hagarenes; "
108: 9 *M'* is my washpot; over Edom will "
Isa 11: 14 lay their hand upon Edom and *M'*; 4124
15: 1 The burden of *M'*. Because in the "
1 in the night Ar of *M'* is laid waste, "
1 in the night Kir of *M'* is laid waste,"
2 *M'* shall howl over Nebo, and over "
4 armed soldiers of *M'* shall cry out; "
5 My heart shall cry out for *M'*; his "
8 round about the borders of *M'*; "
9 lions upon him that escapeth of *M'*, "
16: 2 the daughters of *M'* shall be at the "
4 mine outcasts dwell with thee, *M'*; "
6 We have heard of the pride of *M'*; "
7 Therefore shall *M'* howl for *M'*, "
11 shall sound like an harp for *M'*, and"
12 that *M'* is weary on the high place,"
13 Lord hath spoken concerning *M'* "
14 the glory of *M'* shall be contemned,"
25: 10 *M'* shall be trodden down under "
Jer 9: 26 *M'*, and all that are in the utmost "
25: 21 and *M'*, and the children of Ammon,"
27: 3 of Edom, and to the king of *M'*, "
40: 11 when all the Jews that were in *M'*, "
48: 1 Against *M'* thus saith the Lord of "
2 There shall be no more praise of *M'*: "
4 *M'* is destroyed; her little ones "
9 Give wings unto *M'*, that it may "
11 *M'*...been at ease from his youth, "
13 *M'* shall be ashamed of Chemosh, "
15 *M'* is spoiled, and gone up out of "
16 The calamity of *M'* is near to come,"
18 the spoiler of *M'* shall come upon "
20 *M'* is confounded; for it is broken "
20 ye it in Arnon, that *M'* is spoiled, "
24 upon all the cities of the land of *M'*, "
25 The horn of *M'* is cut off, and his "
26 *M'* also shall wallow in his vomit, "
28 O ye that dwell in *M'*, leave the "
29 We have heard the pride of *M'*, (he "
31 Therefore will I howl for *M'*, and I "
31 and I will cry out for all *M'*; mine "
33 field, and from the land of *M'*; "
35 I will cause to cease in *M'*, saith "
36 heart shall sound for *M'* like pipes,"
38 upon all the housetops of *M'*, and in"
38 for I have broken *M'* like a vessel "
39 *M'* turned the back with shame! "
39 *M'* be a derision and a dismaying "
40 and shall spread his wings over *M'*. "
41 mighty men's hearts in *M'* at that "
42 *M'* shall be destroyed from being "
43 be upon thee, O inhabitant of *M'*, "
44 I will bring upon it, even upon *M'*, "
45 and shall devour the corner of *M'*, "
46 Woe be unto thee, O *M'*! the people"
47 I bring again the captivity of *M'* "
47 Thus far is the judgment of *M'*. "
Eze 25: 8 Because that *M'* and Seir do say, "
9 open the side of *M'* from the cities, "
11 I will execute judgments upon *M'*; "
Da 11: 41 even Edom, and *M'*, and the chief "
Am 2: 1 For three transgressions of *M'*, "
2 But I will send a fire upon *M'*, and "
2 and *M'* shall die with tumult, with "
Mic 6: 5 what Balak king of *M'* consulted, "
Zep 2: 8 I have heard the reproach of *M'*, "
9 Surely *M'* shall be as Sodom, and "

Moabite (*mo'-ab-ite*) See also MOABITES; MOABITESS; MOABITISH.
De 23: 3 Ammonite or *M'* shall not enter 4125
1Ch 11: 46 sons of Elnaam, and Ithmah the *M'*,"
Ne 13: 1 and the *M'* shall not come into the "

Moabites (*mo'-ab-ites*)
Ge 19: 37 the same is the father of the *M'* 4124
Nu 22: 4 son of Zippor was king of the *M'* * "
De 2: 9 Distress not the *M'*, neither * "
11 but the *M'* call them Emims. 4125
29 *M'* which dwell in Ar, did unto me;)"
J'g 3: 28 delivered your enemies the *M'* into 4124
2Sa 8: 2 so the *M'* became David's servants,"
1Ki 11: 1 of Pharaoh, women of the *M'*, 4125
33 Chemosh the god of the *M'*, and *4124
2Ki 3: 18 deliver the *M'* also into your hand."
21 *M'* heard that the kings were come"
22 the *M'* saw the water on the other "
24 rose up and smote the *M'*, so that "
24 they went forward smiting the *M'*, "
13: 20 bands of the *M'* invaded the land "
23: 13 Chemosh the abomination of...*M'*,*"
24: 2 the Syrians, and bands of the *M'*, "
1Ch 18: 2 the *M'* became David's servants, "
Ezr 9: 1 the *M'*, the Egyptians, and the "

Moabitess (*mo'-ab-i-tess*)
Ru 1: 22 and Ruth the *M'*, her daughter in 4125
2: 2 And Ruth the *M'* said unto Naomi, "
21 Ruth the *M'* said, He said unto me "
4: 5 must buy it also of Ruth the *M'*, "
10 Moreover Ruth the *M'*, the wife of "
2Ch 24: 26 the son of Shimrith a *M'*. "

Moabitish (*mo'-ab-i-tish*)
Ru 2: 6 It is the *M'* damsel that came back 4125

Moadiah (*mo-ad-i'-ah*) See also MAADIAH.
Ne 12: 17 Zichri; of Miniamin, of *M'*, Piltai; 4153

moan See BEMOAN.

mock See also MOCKED; MOCKEST; MOCKETH; MOCKING.
Ge 39: 14 in an Hebrew unto us to *m'* us; 6711
17 unto us, came in unto me to *m'* me:"
Job 13: 9 mocketh another, do ye so *m'* him?*2048
21: 3 after that I have spoken, *m'* on. 3932
Pr 1: 26 I will *m'* when your fear cometh; "
14: 9 Fools make a *m'* at sin: but among 3887
Jer 38: 19 into their hand, and they *m'* me. 5953
La 1: 7 her, and did *m'* at her sabbaths. 7832
Eze 22: 5 be far from thee, shall *m'* thee, 7046
M't 20: 19 deliver him to the Gentiles to *m'*, *1702*
M'r 10: 34 they shall *m'* him, and shall scourge"
Lu 14: 29 all that behold it begin to *m'* him, "

mocked
Ge 19: 14 one that *m'* unto his sons in law. 6711
Nu 22: 29 the ass, Because thou hast *m'* me: 5953
J'g 16: 10, 13 hast *m'* me, and told me lies: 2048
15 thou hast *m'* me these three times, "
1Ki 18: 27 pass at noon, that Elijah *m'* them, "
2Ki 2: 23 children out of the city, and *m'* him, 7046
2Ch 30: 10 them to scorn, and *m'* them. 3932
36: 16 But they *m'* the messengers of God. 3931
Ne 4: 1 great indignation, and *m'* the Jews. 3932
Job 12: 4 I am as one *m'* of his neighbour, *7832
M't 2: 16 that he was *m'* of the wise men, *1702*
27: 29 the knee before him, and *m'* him, "
31 after that they had *m'* him, they "
M'r 15: 20 And when they had *m'* him, they "
Lu 18: 32 shall be *m'*, and spitefully entreated,"
22: 63 and the men that held Jesus *m'* him,"
23: 11 war set him at nought, and *m'* him, "
36 the soldiers also *m'* him, coming "
Ac 17: 32 resurrection of the dead, some *m'*: *5512*
Ga 6: 7 Be not deceived; God is not *m'*: for *3456*

mocker See also MOCKERS.
Pr 20: 1 Wine is a *m'*, strong drink is 3887

mockers
Job 17: 2 Are there not *m'* with me? and 2049
Ps 35: 16 With hypocritical *m'* in feasts, they 3934
Isa 28: 22 therefore be ye not *m'*, lest your *3887
Jer 15: 17 sat not in the assembly of the *m'*, *7832
Jude 18 there should be *m'* in the last time, *1703*

mockest
Job 11: 3 when thou *m'*, shall no man make 3932

mocketh
Job 13: 9 or as one man *m'* another, do ye so *2048
39: 22 He *m'* at fear, and is not affrighted; 7832
Pr 17: 5 Whoso *m'* the poor reproacheth 3932
30: 17 The eye that *m'* at his father, and "
Jer 20: 7 in derision daily, every one *m'* me. "

mocking See also MOCKINGS.
Ge 21: 9 she had born unto Abraham, *m'*. 6711
Eze 22: 4 heathen, and a *m'* to all countries. 7048
M't 27: 41 Likewise also the chief priests *m'* *1702*
M'r 15: 31 Likewise also the chief priests *m'* "
Ac 2: 13 Others *m'* said, These men are full *5512*

mockings
Heb 11: 36 trial of cruel *m'* and scourgings, *1701*

moderately
Joe 2: 23 given you the former rain *m'*, *6666

moderation
Ph'p 4: 5 Let your *m'* be known unto all **1933*

modest
1Ti 2: 9 adorn themselves in *m'* apparel, *2887*

moist
Nu 6: 3 nor eat *m'* grapes, or dried. *3892

moistened
Job 21: 24 his bones are *m'* with marrow. 8248

moisture
Ps 32: 4 my *m'* is turned into the drought of 3955
Lu 8: 6 it withered...because it lacked *m'*. *2429*

Moladah (*mo-la'-dah*)
Jos 15: 26 Amam, and Shema, and *M'*, 4137
19: 2 Beer-sheba, and Sheba, and *M'*, "
1Ch 4: 28 they dwelt at Beer-sheba, and *M'*, "
Ne 11: 26 And at Jeshua, and at *M'*, and at "

mole See also MOLES.
Le 11: 30 lizard, and the snail, and the *m'*. *8580

Molech (*mo'-lek*) See also MALCHAM; MOLOCH.
Le 18: 21 seed pass through the fire to *M'*, 4432
20: 2 that giveth any of his seed unto *M'*; "
3 he hath given of his seed unto *M'*, "
4 when he giveth of his seed unto *M'*,"
5 to commit whoredom with *M'*, from "
1Ki 11: 7 is before Jerusalem, and for *M'*, "
2Ki 23: 10 to pass through the fire to *M'*. "
Jer 32: 35 to pass through the fire unto *M'*; "

moles
Isa 2: 20 worship, to the *m'* and to the bats; 2661

Molid (*mo'-lid*)
1Ch 2: 29 and she bare him Ahban, and *M'*. 4140

mollified
Isa 1: 6 up, neither *m'* with ointment. 7401

Moloch (*mo'-loch*) See also MILCHOM; MOLECH.
Am 5: 26 borne the tabernacle of your *M'* *4432
Ac 7: 43 ye took up the tabernacle of *M'*, *3434*

molten See also MELTED.
Ex 32: 4 after he had made it a *m'* calf: 4541
8 they have made them a *m'* calf, and"
34: 17 Thou shalt make thee no *m'* gods. "
Le 19: 4 nor make to yourselves *m'* gods: I "
Nu 33: 52 and destroy all their *m'* images, and"
De 9: 12 they have made them a *m'* image. "
16 God, and had made you a *m'* calf: "
27: 15 maketh any graven or *m'* image, an"
J'g 17: 3, 4 a graven image and a *m'* image: "
18: 14 a graven image, and a *m'* image? "
17 the teraphim, and the *m'* image: "
18 the teraphim, and the *m'* image. "
1Ki 7: 16 made two chapiters of *m'* brass, 3332
23 he made a *m'* sea, ten cubits from "
30 the laver were undersetters *m'*, at "
33 and their spokes, were all *m'*. "
14: 9 thee other gods, and *m'* images, 4541
2Ki 17: 16 made them *m'* images, even two "

2Ch 4: 2 made a *m'* sea of ten cubits from 3332
28: 2 made also *m'* images for Baalim. 4541
34: 3 carved images, and the *m'* images, "
4 carved images, and the *m'* images, "
Ne 9:18 they had made them a *m'* calf, "
Job 28: 2 and brass is *m'* out of the stone. 6694
37:18 strong, and as a *m'* looking glass ?3332
Ps 106:19 and worshipped the *m'* image. 4541
Isa 30:22 ornament of thy *m'* images of gold: "
41:29 *m'* images are wind and confusion.5262
42:17 say to the *m'* images, Ye are our 4541
44:10 god, or *m'* a graven image that is 5258
48: 5 my *m'* image, hath commanded 5262
Jer 10:14 for his *m'* image is falsehood, and "
51:17 for his *m'* image is falsehood, and "
Eze 24:11 the filthiness of it may be *m'* in it, 5413
Ho 13: 2 them *m'* images of their silver, 4541
Mic 1: 4 mountains shall be *m'* under him,†4549
Na 1:14 graven image and the *m'* image: 4541
Hab 2:18 the *m'* image, and a teacher of lies, "

moment
Ex 33: 5 up into the midst of thee in a *m'*. 7281
Nu 16:21 that I may consume them in a *m'*. "
45 I may consume them as in a *m'*. "
Job 7:18 morning, and try him every *m'*? "
20: 5 joy of the hypocrite but for a *m'*? "
21:13 and in a *m'* go down to the grave. "
34:20 In a *m'* shall they die, and the "
Ps 30: 5 For his anger endureth but a *m'*; "
73:19 brought into desolation, as in a *m'*! "
Pr 12:19 but a lying tongue is but for a *m'*. "
Isa 26:20 thyself as it were for a little *m'*, "
27: 3 I will water it every *m'*: lest any "
47: 9 things shall come to thee in a *m'* in "
54: 7 a small *m'* have I forsaken thee; "
8 I hid my face from thee for a *m'*; "
Jer 4:20 spoiled, and my curtains in a *m'*. "
La 4: 6 that was overthrown as in a *m'*, and "
Eze 26:16 and shall tremble at every *m'*, and "
32:10 shall tremble at every *m'*, and they "
Lu 4: 5 kingdoms of the world in a *m'* of *4743*
1Co 15:52 In a *m'*, in the twinkling of an eye, *823*
2Co 4:17 affliction, which is but for a *m'*, *3901*

money See also MONEYCHANGERS.
Ge 17:12 or bought with *m'* of any stranger,3701
13 he that is bought with thy *m'*, must "
23 all that were bought with his *m'*, "
27 and bought with *m'* of the stranger, "
23: 9 for as much *m'* as it is worth he * "
13 I will give thee *m'* for the field; * "
31:15 hath quite devoured also our *m'*. "
33:19 for an hundred pieces of *m'*. 7192
42:25 to restore every man's *m'* into his 3701
27 he espied his *m'*; for, behold, it was "
28 My *m'* is restored; and, lo, it is "
35 man's bundle of *m'* was in his sack: "
35 their father saw the bundles of *m'*, "
43:12 And take double *m'* in your hand; "
12 the *m'* that was brought again in "
15 they took double *m'* in their hand, "
18 *m'* that was returned in our sacks "
21 *m'* was in the mouth of his sack, "
21 of his sack, our *m'* in full weight: "
22 other *m'* have we brought down in "
22 tell who put our *m'* in our sacks. "
23 in your sacks: I had your *m'*. "
44: 1 every man's *m'* in his sack's mouth. "
2 of the youngest, and his corn *m'*. "
8 Behold, the *m'*, which we found in "
47:14 Joseph gathered up all the *m'* that "
14 Joseph brought...*m'* into Pharaoh's "
15 when *m'* failed in the land of Egypt, "
15 in thy presence? for the *m'* faileth. "
16 give you for your cattle, if *m'* fail. "
18 my lord, how that our *m'* is spent; "
Ex 12:44 man's servant that is bought for *m'*, "
21:11 shall she go out free without *m'*. "
21 not be punished: for he is his *m'*. "
30 If there be laid on him a sum of *m'*,*
34 give *m'* unto the owner of them; 3701
35 the live ox, and divide the *m'* of it;* "
22: 7 deliver unto his neighbour *m'* or "
17 pay *m'* according to the dowry of "
25 If thou lend *m'* to any of my people "
30:16 thou shalt take the atonement *m'* "
Le 22:11 priest buy any soul with his *m'*, "
25:37 not give him thy *m'* upon usury, "
51 out of the *m'* that he was bought "
27:15 fifth part of the *m'* of thy estimation "
18 priest shall reckon unto him the *m'* "
19 fifth part of the *m'* of thy estimation "
Nu 3:48 thou shalt give the *m'*, wherewith "
49 Moses took the redemption *m'* of "
50 children of Israel took he the *m'*; "
51 And Moses gave the *m'* of them that "
18:16 for the *m'* of five shekels, after the "
De 2: 6 Ye shall buy meat of them for *m'*, "
6 shall also buy water of them for *m'*, "
28 Thou shalt sell me meat for *m'*, "
28 give me water for *m'*, that I may "
14:25 Then shalt thou turn it into *m'*, "
25 and bind up the *m'* in thine hand, "
26 And thou shalt bestow that *m'* for "
21:14 thou shalt not sell her at all for *m'*, "
23:19 usury of *m'*, usury of victuals, usury "
J'g 5:19 Megiddo; they took no gain of *m'*. "
16:18 her, and brought *m'* in their hand. "
17: 4 he restored the *m'* unto his mother; "
1Ki 21: 2 will give thee the worth of it in *m'*. "
6 him, Give me thy vineyard for *m'*; "
15 he refused to give thee for *m'*: for "
2Ki 5:26 Is it a time to receive *m'*, and to "
12: 4 All the *m'* of the dedicated things "
4 the *m'* of every one that passeth the "
4 the *m'* that every man is set at, and "

2Ki 12: 4 the *m'* that cometh into any man's 3701
7 no more *m'* of your acquaintance, "
8 receive no more *m'* of the people, "
9 the *m'* that was brought into the "
10 there was much *m'* in the chest, "
10 the *m'* that was found in the house "
11 And they gave the *m'*, being told, "
13 *m'* that was brought into the house "
15 the *m'* to be bestowed on workmen: "
16 The trespass *m'* and sin *m'* was not "
15:20 Menahem exacted the *m'* of Israel, "
22: 7 made with them of the *m'* that "
9 Thy servants have gathered the *m'* "
23:35 but he taxed the land to give the *m'* "
2Ch 24: 5 of all Israel *m'* to repair the house "
11 they saw that there was much *m'*, "
11 and gathered *m'* in abundance. "
14 brought the rest of the *m'* before "
34: 9 delivered the *m'* that was brought "
14 when they brought out the *m'* that "
17 they have gathered together the *m'* "
Ezr 3: 7 They gave *m'* also unto the masons, "
7:17 mayest buy speedily with this *m'* 3702
Ne 5: 4 have borrowed *m'* for the king's 3701
10 might exact of them *m'* and corn: "
11 also the hundredth part of the *m'*, "
Es 4: 7 the *m'* that Haman had promised "
Job 31:39 eaten the fruits thereof without *m'*, "
42:11 man also gave him a piece of *m'*. 7192
Ps 15: 5 putteth not out his *m'* to usury, 3701
Pro 7:20 hath taken a bag of *m'* with him, "
Ec 7:12 is a defence, and *m'* is a defence: "
10:19 merry: but *m'* answereth all things. "
Isa 43:24 bought me no sweet cane with *m'*, "
52: 3 ye shall be redeemed without *m'*. "
55: 1 the waters, and he that hath no *m'*; "
1 milk without *m'* and without price. "
2 do ye spend *m'* for that which is not "
Jer 32: 9 weighed him the *m'*, even seventeen "
10 weighed him the *m'* in the balances. "
25 Buy thee the field for *m'*, and take "
44 Men shall buy fields for *m'*, and "
La 5: 4 We have drunken our water for *m'*; "
Mic 3:11 the prophets thereof divine for *m'*: "
M't 17:24 that received tribute *m'* came to * "
27 thou shalt find a piece of *m'*: that *4715*
22:19 Shew me the tribute *m'*. And they *3546*
25:18 in the earth, and hid his lord's *m'*. *694*
27 have put my *m'* to the exchangers, "
28:12 they gave large *m'* unto the soldiers, "
15 So they took the *m'*, and did as they "
M'r 6: 8 no bread, no *m'* in their purse: *5475*
12:41 the people cast *m'* into the treasury: "
14:11 glad, and promised to give him *m'*. *694*
Lu 9: 3 nor scrip, neither bread, neither *m'*; "
19:15 to whom he had given the *m'*, that "
23 not thou my *m'* into the bank, that "
22: 5 glad, and covenanted to give him *m'*. "
Joh 2:14 and the changers of *m'* sitting: *2773*
15 poured out the changers' *m'*, and *2772*
Ac 4:37 land, sold it, and brought the *m'*, *5536*
7:16 Abraham bought for a sum of *m'* of *694*
8:18 was given, he offered them *m'*, *5536*
20 Thy *m'* perish with thee, because * *694*
20 of God may be purchased with *m'*. *5536*
24:26 hoped also that *m'* should have "
1Ti 6:10 the love of *m'* is the root of all evil: *5365*

moneychangers
M't 21:12 and overthrew the tables of the *m'*, *2855*
M'r 11:15 and overthrew the tables of the *m'*, "

monsters
La 4: 3 the sea *m'* draw out the breast, *8577

month See also MONTHS.
Ge 7:11 *m'*, the seventeenth day of the *m'*, 2320
8: 4 the ark rested in the seventh *m'*, "
4 the seventeenth day of the *m'*, upon "
5 continually until the tenth *m'*: "
5 in the tenth *m'*, on the first day of the "
5 on the first day of the *m'*, were the 2320
13 first year, in the first *m'*, the first "
13 the first day of the *m'*, the waters 2320
14 And in the second *m'*, on the seven "
14 seven and twentieth day of the *m'*, "
29:14 abode with him the space of a *m'*. "
Ex 12: 2 This *m'* shall be unto you the "
2 be the first *m'* of the year to you. "
3 the tenth day of this *m'* they shall "
6 the fourteenth day of the same *m'*: "
18 In the first *m'*, on the fourteenth day "
18 fourteenth day of the *m'* at even, 2320
18 one and twentieth day of the *m'* at "
13: 4 This day came ye out in the *m'* Abib. "
5 shalt keep this service in this *m'*. "
16: 1 on the fifteenth day of the second *m'* "
19: 1 In the third *m'*, when the children "
23:15 the time appointed of the *m'* Abib; "
34:18 thee, in the time of the *m'* Abib: "
18 the *m'* Abib thou camest out from "
40: 2 first day of the first *m'* shalt thou "
17 in the first *m'* in the second year, "
17 on the first day of the *m'*, that the "
Lev 16:29 seventh *m'*, on...tenth day of the *m'*, "
23: 5 the fourteenth day of the first *m'* at "
6 on the fifteenth day of the same *m'* "
24 seventh *m'*, in...first day of the *m'*, "
27 tenth day of this seventh *m'* there "
32 in the ninth day of the *m'* at even, "
34 The fifteenth day of this seventh *m'* "
39 the fifteenth day of the seventh *m'*, "
41 shall celebrate it in the seventh *m'*. "
25: 9 on the tenth day of the seventh *m'*, "
27: 6 from a *m'* old even unto five years "
Nu 1: 1, 18 on the first day of the second *m'*, "
3:15 every male from a *m'* old and "

Nu 3:22, 28, 34, 39 from a *m'* old and upward2320
40 children of Israel from a *m'* old and "
43 names, from a *m'* old and upward, "
9: 1 in the first *m'* of the second year "
3 In the fourteenth day of this *m'*, at "
5 on the fourteenth day of the first *m'* "
11 The fourteenth day of the second *m'* "
22 or a *m'*, or a year, that the cloud "
10:11 the twentieth day of the second *m'*, "
11:20 even a whole *m'*, until it come out "
21 flesh, that they may eat a whole *m'*. "
18:16 from a *m'* old shalt thou redeem, "
20: 1 the desert of Zin in the first *m'*: "
26:62 males from a *m'* old and upward: "
28:14 is the burnt offering of every *m'* "
16 the fourteenth day of the first *m'* "
17 in the fifteenth day of this *m'* is the "
29: 1 And in the seventh *m'*, on the first "
1 first day of the *m'*, ye shall have an "
6 Beside the burnt offering of the *m'*,* "
7 on the tenth day of this seventh *m'* "
12 the fifteenth day of the seventh *m'* "
33: 3 from Rameses in the first *m'*, "
3 on the fifteenth day of the first *m'*; "
38 in the first day of the fifth *m'*. "
De 1: 3 eleventh *m'*, on...first day of the *m'*, "
16: 1 Observe the *m'* of Abib, and keep "
1 for in the *m'* of Abib the Lord thy "
21:13 her father and her mother a full *m'*: 3391
Jos 4:19 on the tenth day of the first *m'*, 2320
5:10 on the fourteenth day of the *m'* at "
1Sa 20:27 was the second day of the *m'*, that* "
34 no meat the second day of the *m'*: "
1Ki 4: 7 each man his *m'* in a year made "
27 table, every man in his *m'*: they "
5:14 ten thousand a *m'* by courses: "
14 a *m'* they were in Lebanon, and two "
6: 1 the *m'* Zif, which is the second *m'*, "
37 of the Lord laid, in the *m'* Zif: 3391
38 in the eleventh year, in the *m'* Bul, "
38 Bul, which is the eighth *m'*, 2320
8: 2 at the feast of the *m'* Ethanim, 3391
2 Ethanim, which is the seventh *m'*. 2320
12:32 ordained a feast in the eighth *m'*, "
32 on the fifteenth day of the *m'*, like "
33 the fifteenth day of the eighth *m'*, "
33 even in the *m'* which he had devised "
2Ki 15:13 he reigned a full *m'* in Samaria. 3391
25: 1 tenth *m'*, in...tenth day of the *m'*, 2320
3 on the ninth day of the fourth *m'* "
8 fifth *m'*, on...seventh day of the *m'*, "
25 it came to pass in the seventh *m'*, "
27 king of Judah, in the twelfth *m'*, "
27 seven and twentieth day of the *m'*, "
1Ch 12:15 went over Jordan in the first *m'*, "
27: 1 came in and went out *m'* by *m'* "
2 for the first *m'* was Jashobeam the "
3 captains of the host for the first *m'*. "
4 course of the second *m'* was Dodai "
5 host for the third *m'* was Benaiah "
7 for the fourth *m'* was Asahel the "
8 for the fifth *m'* was Shamhuth the "
9 captain for the sixth *m'* was Ira the "
10 for the seventh *m'* was Helez the "
11 for the eighth *m'* was Sibbecai the "
12 captain for the ninth *m'* was Abiezer "
13 for the tenth *m'* was Maharai the "
14 for the eleventh *m'* was Benaiah "
15 for the twelfth *m'* was Heldai the "
2Ch 3: 2 in the second day of the second *m'*, "
5: 3 feast which was in the seventh *m'*. "
7:10 and twentieth day of the seventh *m'* "
15:10 at Jerusalem in the third *m'*, in "
29: 3 year of his reign, in the first *m'*, "
17 first day of the first *m'* to sanctify, "
17 on the eighth day of the *m'* came "
17 sixteenth day of the first *m'* they "
30: 2 keep the passover in the second *m'*. "
13 unleavened bread in the second *m'*, "
15 fourteenth day of the second *m'*: "
31: 7 the third *m'* they began to lay the "
7 finished them in the seventh *m'*. "
35: 1 the fourteenth day of the first *m'*. "
Ezr 3: 1 when the seventh *m'* was come, and "
6 first day of the seventh *m'* began "
8 second *m'*, began Zerubbabel the "
6:15 on the third day of the *m'* Adar, 3393
19 the fourteenth day of the first *m'*. 2320
7: 8 came to Jerusalem in the fifth *m'*, "
9 first day of the first *m'* began he to "
9 first day of the fifth *m'* came he to "
8:31 on the twelfth day of the first *m'*, "
10: 9 the ninth *m'*, on the twentieth day "
9 twentieth day of the *m'*; and all the "
16 down in the first day of the tenth *m'* "
17 wives by the first day of the first *m'*. "
Ne 1: 1 it came to pass in the *m'* Chisleu, in "
2: 1 it came to pass in the *m'* Nisan, in "
6:15 twenty and fifth day of the *m'* Elul, "
7:73 and when the seventh *m'* came, the 2320
8: 2 upon the first day of the seventh *m'*. "
14 in the feast of the seventh *m'*: "
9: 1 twenty and fourth day of this *m'* "
Es 2:16 tenth *m'*, which is the *m'* Tebeth, "
3: 7 the first *m'*, that is, the *m'* Nisan, "
7 from day to day, and from *m'* to *m'*, "
7 to the twelfth *m'*, that is,...Adar. "
7 the twelfth...that is, the *m'* Adar. 2320
12 the thirteenth day of the first *m'*, "
13 twelfth *m'*, which is the *m'* Adar, "
8: 9 the third *m'*, that is, the *m'* Sivan, "
12 twelfth *m'*, which is the *m'* Adar. "
9: 1 the twelfth *m'*, that is, the *m'* Adar, "
15 fourteenth day also of the *m'* Adar, "
17 the thirteenth day of the *m'* Adar; "
19 fourteenth day of the *m'* Adar a day "

Es 9:21 the fourteenth day of the *m'* Adar, 2320
22 the *m'* which was turned unto them "
Jer 1: 3 Jerusalem captive in the fifth *m'*. "
2:24 in her *m'* they shall find her. "
28: 1 the fourth year, and in the fifth *m'*, "
17 the same year in the seventh *m'*. "
36: 9 the ninth *m'*, that they proclaimed a "
22 in the winterhouse in the ninth *m'*: "
39: 1 the tenth *m'*, came Nebuchadrezzar "
2 fourth *m'*, the ninth day of the *m'*, "
41: 1 it came to pass in the seventh *m'*, "
52: 4 tenth *m'*, in the tenth day of the *m'*, "
6 fourth *m'*,...the ninth day of the *m'*, "
12 fifth *m'*, in the tenth day of the *m'*, "
31 in the twelfth *m'*, in the five and "
31 five and twentieth day of the *m'*, "
Eze 1: 1 in the thirtieth year, the fourth *m'*,
1 in the fifth day of the *m'*, as I was 2320
2 In the fifth day of the *m'*, which "
8: 1 in the sixth year, in the sixth *m'*,
1 in the fifth day of the *m'*, as I sat 2320
20: 1 in the seventh year, in the fifth *m'*,
1 tenth day of the *m'*, that certain 2320
24: 1 in the ninth year, in the tenth *m'*,
1 in the tenth day of the *m'*, the word "
26: 1 eleventh year,...first day of the *m'*, "
29: 1 In the tenth year, in the tenth *m'*,
1 in the twelfth day of the *m'*, 2320
17 and twentieth year, in the first *m'*,
17 in the first day of the *m'*, the word 2320
30:20 in the eleventh year, in the first *m'*, "
20 in the seventh day of the *m'*, that "
31: 1 the eleventh year, in the third *m'*,
1 in the first day of the *m'*, that the 2320
32: 1 the twelfth year, in the twelfth *m'*,
1 in the first day of the *m'*, that the "
17 year, in the fifteenth day of the *m'*, "
33:21 of our captivity, in the tenth *m'*,
21 in the fifth day of the *m'*, that one 2320
40: 1 the year, in the tenth day of the *m'*, "
45:18 saith the Lord God; in the first *m'*,
18 in the first day of the *m'*, thou shalt 2320
20 shalt do the seventh day of the *m'* "
21 In the first *m'*, in the fourteenth
21 in the fourteenth day of the *m'*, ye 2320
25 In the seventh *m'*, in the fifteenth
25 in the fifteenth day of the *m'*, shall 2320
Da 10: 4 and twentieth day of the first *m'*, "
Ho 5: 7 now shall a *m'* devour them with * "
Joe 2:23 and the latter rain in the first *m'*. "
Hag 1: 1 sixth *m'*, in the first day of the *m'*, 2320
15 and twentieth day of the sixth *m'*, "
2: 1 In the seventh *m'*, in the one and
1 twentieth day of the *m'*, came the 2320
10, 18 and twentieth day of the ninth *m'*,
20 four and twentieth day of the *m'*, 2320
Zec 1: 1 In the eighth *m'*, in the second year "
7 twentieth day of the eleventh *m'*, "
7 which is the *m'* Sebat, in the second "
7: 1 in the fourth day of the ninth *m'*, "
3 Should I weep in the fifth *m'*, "
5 in the fifth and seventh *m'*, even "
8:19 The fast of the fourth *m'*, and the fast "
11: 8 shepherds also I cut off in one *m'*; 3391
Lu 1:26 in the sixth *m'* the angel Gabriel 3376
36 this is the sixth *m'* with her, who "
Re 9:15 and a day, and a *m'*, and a year, for "
22: 2 and yielded her fruit every *m'*: "

monthly
Isa 47:13 the *m'* prognosticators, stand up, 2320

months
Ge 38:24 came to pass about three *m'* after, 2320
Ex 2: 2 child, she hid him three *m'*. 3391
12: 2 be unto you the beginning of *m'*: 2320
Nu 10:10 the beginnings of your *m'*, ye shall "
28:11 the beginnings of your *m'* ye shall "
14 throughout the *m'* of the year. "
J'g 11:37 let me alone two *m'*, that I may go "
38 And he sent her away for two *m'*: "
39 it came to pass at the end of two *m'*, "
19: 2 and was there four whole *m'*. "
20:47 abode in the rock Rimmon four *m'*. "
1Sa 6: 1 country of the Philistines seven *m'*. "
27: 7 was a full year and four *m'*. "
2Sa 2:11 Judah was seven years and six *m'*. "
5: 5 Judah seven years and six *m'*. "
6:11 of Obed-edom the Gittite three *m'*: "
24: 8 to Jerusalem at the end of nine *m'* "
13 flee three *m'* before thine enemies, "
1Ki 5:14 in Lebanon, and two *m'* at home: "
11:16 (For six *m'* did Joab remain there "
2Ki 15: 8 reign over Israel in Samaria six *m'*. "
23:31 he reigned three *m'* in Jerusalem. "
24: 8 he reigned in Jerusalem three *m'*. "
1Ch 3: 4 he reigned seven years and six *m'*: "
13:14 Obed-edom in his house three *m'*. "
21:12 three *m'* to be destroyed before thy "
27: 1 throughout all the *m'* of the year, "
2Ch 36: 2 he reigned three *m'* in Jerusalem. "
9 he reigned three *m'* and ten days "
Es 2:12 after that she had been twelve *m'*, "
12 to wit, six *m'* with oil of myrrh, and "
12 six *m'* with sweet odours, and with "
Job 3: 6 come into the number of the *m'*. 3391
7: 3 am I made to possess *m'* of vanity, "
14: 5 number of his *m'* are with thee, 2320
21:21 the number of his *m'* is cut off in "
29: 2 Oh that I were as in *m'* past, as in 3391
39: 2 Canst thou number the *m'* that they "
Eze 39:12 seven *m'* shall the house of Israel 2320
14 after the end of seven *m'* shall they "
47:12 forth new fruit according to his *m'*, * "
Da 4:29 At the end of twelve *m'* he walked 3393
Am 4: 7 were yet three *m'* to the harvest: 2320
Lu 1:24 conceived, and hid herself five *m'*, 3376
1:56 abode with her about three *m'*, 3376
4:25 was shut up three years and six *m'*, "
Joh 4:35 Say not ye, There are yet four *m'*, 5072
Ac 7:20 up in his father's house three *m'*: 3376
18:11 he continued a year and six *m'*, "
19: 8 boldly for the space of three *m'*, "
20: 3 there abode three *m'*. And when "
28:11 after three *m'* we departed in a ship "
Ga 4:10 Ye observe days, and *m'*, and times, "
Heb 11:23 was hid three *m'* of his parents, 5150
Jas 5:17 space of three years and six *m'*. 3376
Re 9: 5 they should be tormented five *m'*: "
10 power was to hurt men five *m'*. "
11: 2 tread under foot forty and two *m'*. "
13: 5 him to continue forty and two *m'*. "

monuments
Isa 65: 4 the graves, and lodge in the *m'*, *5341

moon See also MOONS.
Ge 37: 9 sun...the *m'* and the eleven stars 3394
De 4:19 the sun, and the *m'*, and the stars, "
17: 3 either the sun, or *m'*, or any of the "
33:14 things put forth by the *m'*, *3391
Jos 10:12 thou, *M'*, in the valley of Ajalon. 3394
13 sun stood still, and the *m'* stayed, "
1Sa 20: 5 Behold, to morrow is the new *m'*, 2320
18 To morrow is the new *m'*: and thou "
24 and when the new *m'* was come, "
2Ki 4:23 it is neither new *m'*, nor sabbath. "
23: 5 to the sun, and to the *m'*, and to 3394
Job 25: 5 even to the *m'*, and it shineth not; "
31:26 or the *m'* walking in brightness; "
Ps 8: 3 *m'* and the stars, which thou hast "
72: 5 as long as the sun and *m'* endure, "
7 of peace so long as the *m'* endureth. "
81: 3 Blow up the trumpet in the new *m'*, 2320
89:37 be established for ever as the *m'*, 3394
104:19 He appointed the *m'* for seasons: "
121: 6 thee by day, nor the *m'* by night. "
136: 9 The *m'* and stars to rule by night: "
148: 3 Praise ye him, sun and *m'*: praise "
Ec 12: 2 *m'*, or the stars, be not darkened, "
Ca 6:10 fair as the *m'*, clear as the sun, 3842
Isa 3:18 and their round tires like the *m'*,
13:10 the *m'* shall not cause her light to 3394
24:23 Then the *m'* shall be confounded, 3842
30:26 light of the *m'* shall be as the light "
60:19 shall the *m'* give light unto thee: 3394
20 neither shall thy *m'* withdraw 3391
66:23 that from one new *m'* to another, 2320
Jer 8: 2 before the sun, and the *m'*, and all 3394
31:35 ordinances of the *m'* and of the stars "
Eze 32: 7 and the *m'* shall not give her light. "
46: 1, 6 in the day of the new *m'* it shall 2320
Joe 2:10 the sun and the *m'* shall be dark, 3394
31 darkness, and the *m'* into blood, "
3:15 sun and the *m'* shall be darkened, "
Am 8: 5 When will the new *m'* be gone, 2320
Hab 3:11 The sun and *m'* stood still in their 3394
M't 24:29 and the *m'* shall not give her light, 4582
M'r 13:24 and the *m'* shall not give her light, "
Lu 21:25 be signs in the sun, and in the *m'*, "
Ac 2:20 darkness, and the *m'* into blood, "
1Co 15:41 sun, and another glory of the *m'*, "
Col 2:16 or of the new *m'*, or of the sabbath 3561
Re 6:12 hair, and the *m'* became as blood; 4582
8:12 and the third part of the *m'*, and the "
12: 1 the sun, and the *m'* under her feet, "
21:23 need of the sun, neither of the *m'*, "

moons
1Ch 23:31 the new *m'*, and on the set feasts, 2320
2Ch 2: 4 on the new *m'*, and on the solemn "
8:13 on the new *m'*, and on the solemn "
31: 3 the new *m'*, and for the set feasts, "
Ezr 3: 5 both of the new *m'*, and of all the set "
Ne 10:33 of the sabbaths, of the new *m'*, for "
Isa 1:13 the new *m'* and sabbaths, the * "
14 new *m'* and your appointed feasts "
Eze 45:17 in the feasts, and in the new *m'*, "
46: 3 in the sabbaths and in the new *m'*. "
Ho 2:11 her feast days, her new *m'*, and her "

Morasthite (*mo'-ras-thite*)
Jer 26:18 Micah the *M'* prophesied in the *4183
Mic 1: 1 Lord that came to Micah the *M'* * "

Mordecai (*mor'-de-cahee*) See also MORDECAI'S.
Ezr 2: 2 Nehemiah, Seraiah, Reelaiah, *M'*, 4782
Ne 7: 7 Nahamani, *M'*, Bilshan, Mispereth, "
Es 2: 5 a certain Jew, whose name was *M'*, "
7 whom *M'*,...took for his own "
10 *M'* had charged her that she should "
11 *M'* walked every day before the "
15 daughter of Abihail the uncle of *M'*, "
19 then *M'* sat in the king's gate. "
20 her people; as *M'* had charged her: "
20 Esther did the commandment of *M'*, "
21 while *M'* sat in the king's gate, "
22 And the thing was known to *M'*, "
3: 2 But *M'* bowed not, nor did him "
3 said unto *M'*, Why transgressest "
5 Haman saw that *M'* bowed not, "
6 scorn to lay hands on *M'* alone; "
6 had shewed him the people of *M'*: "
6 Ahasuerus, even the people of *M'*. "
4: 1 *M'* perceived all that was done, "
1 *M'* rent his clothes, and put on "
4 and she sent raiment to clothe *M'*, "
5 gave him a commandment to *M'*, "
6 Hatach went forth to *M'* unto the "
7 *M'* told him of all that had happened "
9 and told Esther the words of *M'*. "
10 gave him commandment unto *M'*; "
12 And they told to *M'* Esther's words. "
13 *M'* commanded to answer Esther, "
15 bade them return *M'* this answer, "
17 *M'* went his way, and did according "
Es 5: 9 Haman saw *M'* in the king's gate, 4782
9 was full of indignation against *M'*. "
13 so long as I see *M'* the Jew sitting "
14 that *M'* may be hanged thereon: "
6: 2 that *M'* had told of Bigthana and "
3 and dignity hath been done to *M'* "
4 the king to hang *M'* on the gallows "
10 and do even so to *M'* the Jew, that "
11 arrayed *M'*, and brought him on "
12 *M'* came again to the king's gate. "
13 If *M'* be of the seed of the Jews, "
7: 9 which Haman had made for *M'*, "
10 that he had prepared for *M'*. Then "
8: 1 And *M'* came before the king; for "
2 from Haman, and gave it unto *M'*. "
2 Esther set *M'* over the house of "
7 unto Esther...and to *M'* the Jew, "
9 that *M'* commanded unto the Jews, "
15 *M'* went out from the presence of "
9: 3 the fear of *M'* fell upon them. "
4 *M'* was great in the king's house, "
4 man *M'* waxed greater and greater. "
20 *M'* wrote these things, and sent "
23 and as *M'* had written unto them; "
29 and *M'* the Jew, wrote with all "
31 *M'* the Jew and Esther the queen "
10: 2 declaration of the greatness of *M'*, "
3 For *M'* the Jew was next unto king "

Mordecai's (*mor'-de-cahees*)
Es 2:22 the king thereof in *M'* name. 4782
3: 4 whether *M'* matters would stand: "

more See also EVERMORE; FURTHERMORE; MOREOVER.
Ge 3: 1 Now the serpent was *m'* subtil than
8:12 returned not...unto him any *m'*. 5750
21 curse the ground any *m'* for man's "
21 smite any *m'* everything living, as "
9:11 shall all flesh be cut off any *m'* by "
11 shall there any *m'* be a flood to "
15 waters shall no *m'* become a flood "
17: 5 thy name any *m'* be called Abram, "
29:30 he loved also Rachel *m'* than Leah,
32:28 name shall be called no *m'* Jacob, 5750
34:19 *m'* honourable than all the house 3513
35:10 shall not be called any *m'* Jacob, 5750
36: 7 For their riches were *m'* than that *7227
37: 3 loved Joseph *m'* than all his children,
4 loved him *m'* than all his brethren,
5 and they hated him yet the *m'*. 3254
8 they hated him yet the *m'* for his "
9 I have dreamed a dream *m'*; and, 5750
38:26 She hath been *m'* righteous than I;
26 And he knew her again no *m'*. 5750
44:23 you, ye shall see my face no *m'*. 3254
Ex 1: 9 of Israel are *m'* and mightier than 7227
12 But the *m'* they afflicted them, 3651
12 the *m'* they multiplied and grew. "
5: 7 shall no *m'* give the people straw 3254
9 there *m'* work be laid upon the men, *
8:29 Pharaoh deal deceitfully any *m'* 3254
9:28 be no *m'* mighty thunderings and
29 neither shall there be any *m'* hail; 5750
34 he sinned yet *m'*, and hardened 3254
10:28 heed to thyself, see my face no *m'*; "
29 I will see thy face again no *m'*. 5750
11: 1 I bring one plague *m'* upon Pharaoh,
6 like it, nor shall be like it any *m'*. 3254
14:13 see them again no *m'* for ever. 5750
16:17 and gathered, some *m'*, some less. 7227
30:15 The rich shall not give *m'*, and 7235
36: 5 people bring much *m'* than enough "
6 man nor woman make any *m'* work 5750
Le 6: 5 and shall add the fifth part *m'* 3254
11:42 hath *m'* feet among all creeping *7235
13: 5 shall shut him up seven days *m'*: 8145
33 that hath the scall seven days *m'*: "
54 he shall shut it up seven days *m'*: "
17: 7 shall no *m'* offer their sacrifices 5750
26:18 will punish you seven times *m'* for 3254
21 bring seven times *m'* plagues upon "
27:20 it shall not be redeemed any *m'*. 5750
Nu 3:46 which are *m'* than the Levites; *5736
8:25 thereof, and shall serve no *m'*: 5750
18: 5 no wrath any *m'* upon the children "
22:15 Balak sent yet again princes, *m'*, 7227
15 princes...*m'* honourable than they.
18 the Lord my God, to do less or *m'*. 1490
19 the Lord will say unto me *m'*. 3254
26:54 thou shalt give the *m'* inheritance, 7235
33:54 and to the *m'* ye shall give the 7227
54 ye shall give the *m'* inheritance, 7235
De 1:11 thousand times so many *m'* as ye 3254
3:26 speak no *m'* unto me of this 5750
5:22 great voice: and he added no *m'*. 3254
25 voice of the Lord our God any *m'*, "
7: 7 ye were *m'* in number than any 7230
17 These nations are *m'* than I; how 7227
10:16 heart, and be no *m'* stiffnecked. 5750
13:11 do no *m'* any such wickedness as 3254
17:13 and do no *m'* presumptuously. 5750
16 henceforth return no *m'* that way. "
18:16 let me see this great fire any *m'*, "
19: 9 thou add three cities *m'* for thee, "
20 commit no *m'* any such evil among "
20: 1 and a people *m'* than thou, be not 7227
28:68 Thou shalt see it no *m'* again: 5750
31: 2 I can no *m'* go out and come in: "
27 and how much *m'* after my death?
Jos 2:11 neither did there remain any *m'* 5750
5: 1 was there spirit in them any *m'*, "
12 children of Israel manna any *m'*; "
7:12 neither will I be with you any *m'*, 3254
10:11 they were *m'* which died with 7227
23:13 will no *m'* drive out any of these 3254
J'g 2:19 themselves *m'* than their fathers,
8:28 they lifted up their heads no *m'*. 3254

J'g 10:13 wherefore I will deliver you no m'. 3254
13:21 angel of the Lord did no m' appear "
15: 3 shall I be m' blameless than the
16:30 which he slew at his death were m' 7227
18:24 gone away: and what have I m'? 5750
Ru 1:11 are there yet any m' sons in my womb,*
17 the Lord do so to me, and m' also, 3254
3:10 thou hast shewed m' kindness in the
1Sa 1:18 her countenance was no m' sad. 5750
2: 3 Talk no m' so exceeding proudly; 7235
3:17 God do so to thee, and m' also, 3254
7:13 came no m' into the coast of 3254,5750
14:30 How much m', if haply the people 637
44 answered, God do so and m' also: 3254
15:35 And Samuel came no m' to see Saul"
18: 2 go no m' home to his father's house.
8 can he have m' but the kingdom? 5750
29 was yet the m' afraid of David; 3254
30 that David behaved himself m' wisely
20:13 do so and much m' to Jonathan: 3254
22:15 knew nothing of all this, less or m'.1490
23: 3 much m' then if we come to Keilah
24:17 Thou art m' righteous than I: for thou
25:22 m' also do God unto the enemies 3254
36 she told him nothing, less or m'. 1490
26:21 for I will no m' do thee harm. 5750
27: 1 to seek me any m' in any coast of "
4 he sought no m' again for him. 3254
28:15 and answereth me no m', neither by
30: 4 until they had no m' power to weep.
2Sa 2:28 and pursued after Israel no m', 5750
28 neither fought they any m'. 3254,
3: 9 So do God to Abner, and m' also, 3254
35 So do God to me, and m' also, if I "
4:11 How much m', when wicked men
5:13 David took him m' concubines 5750
6:22 And I will yet be m' vile than thus,
7:10 place of their own, and move no m';5750
10 of wickedness afflict them any m',3254
20 what can David say m' unto thee? 5750
10:19 help the children of Ammon any m'."
11:25 thy battle m' strong against the city,
14:10 shall not touch thee any m'. 3254,5750
11 revengers of blood to destroy...m',7235
16:11 much m' now may this Benjamite do it?
18: 8 and the wood devoured m' people 7235
19:13 God do so to me, and m' also, if 3254
28 I yet to cry any m' unto the king? 5750
29 Why speakest thou any m' of thy "
35 I hear any m' the voice of singing "
43 have also m' right in David than ye:
20: 6 do us m' harm than did Absalom:
21:17 Thou shalt go no m' out with us 5750
23:23 He was m' honourable than the thirty,
1Ki 2:23 God do so to me, and m' also, if 3254
32 who fell upon two men m' righteous
10: 5 there was no m' spirit in her. 5750
10 no m' such abundance of spices "
16:33 Ahab did m' to provoke the Lord 3254
19: 2 let the gods do to me, and m' also, "
20:10 gods do so unto me, and m' also, if "
2Ki 2:12 And he saw him no m': and he 5750
21 thence any m' death or barren land."
4: 6 unto her, There is not a vessel m'. "
6:16 they that be with us are m' than 7227
23 came no m' into the...of Israel.3254,5750
31 God do so and m' also to me, if the3254
9:35 they found no m' of her than the3588,518
12: 7 now therefore receive no m' money of
8 consented to receive no m' money of
21: 8 make the feet of Israel move any m'3254
9 seduced them to do m' evil than did
24: 7 Egypt came not again any m' out 5750
1Ch 4: 9 And Jabez was m' honourable than
11:21 he was m' honourable than the two;
14: 3 David took m' wives at Jerusalem:5750
3 David begat m' sons and daughters."
17: 9 place, and shall be moved no m'; "
9 of wickedness waste them any m',3254
18 can David speak m' to thee 3254,5750
19:19 help the children of Ammon any m'."
21: 3 hundred times so many m' as they3254
23:26 they shall no m' carry the tabernacle,
24: 4 there were m' chief men found of 7227
2Ch 9: 4 there was no m' spirit in her. 5750
10:11 you, I will put m' to your yoke: *3254
15:19 there was no m' war unto the five and
20:25 m' than they could carry away:
25: 9 is able to give thee much m' than 7235
28:13 ye intend to add m' to our sins *
22 trespass yet m' against the Lord: 3254
29:34 the Levites were m' upright in heart
32: 7 there be m' with us than with him:*7227
16 spake yet m' against the Lord God,
33: 8 will I any m' remove the foot of Israel
23 himself; but Amon trespassed m' 7235
23 but Amon trespassed...and m'.
Ezr 7:20 whatsoever m' shall be needful 7608
Ne 2:17 that we be no m' a reproach. 5750
13:18 yet ye bring m' wrath upon Israel 3254
21 forth came they no m' on the sabbath.
Es 1:19 Vashti come no m' before king
2:14 she came in unto the king no m', 5750
17 in his sight m' than all the virgins;
4:13 the king's house, m' than all the Jews.
6: 6 to do honour m' than to myself? 3148
Job 3:21 dig for it m' than for hid treasures;
4:17 mortal man be m' just than God?
17 a man be m' pure than his maker?
7: 7 mine eye shall no m' see good. 7725
8 that hath seen me shall see me no m':
9 down to the grave shall come up no m'.
10 shall return no m' to his house, 5750
10 shall his place know him any m'. "
14:12 till the heavens be no m', they shall
15:16 m' abominable and filthy is man, *

Job 20: 9 saw him shall see him no m'; 3254
9 shall his place any m' behold him.5750
23:12 his mouth m' than my necessary food.
24:20 he shall be no m' remembered; 5750
32:15 were amazed, they answered no m':"
16 stood still, and answered no m';)
34:19 regardeth...rich m' than the poor? 6440
23 not lay upon man m' than right; *5750
31 chastisement, I will not offend any m'.
32 have done iniquity, I will do no m'.
35: 2 My righteousness is m' than God's?3254
11 Who teacheth us m' than the beasts of
41: 8 remember the battle, do no m'. 3254
42:12 end of Job m' than his beginning:
Ps 4: 7 m' than in the time that their corn and
10:18 the earth may no m' oppress. 3254,5750
19:10 M' to be desired are they than gold,
39:13 before I go hence, and be no m'.
40: 5 are m' than can be numbered. 6105
12 are m' than the hairs of mine head:"
41: 8 he lieth he shall rise up no m'. 3254
52: 3 Thou lovest evil m' than good; and
69: 4 m' than the hairs of mine head: 7231
71:14 and will yet praise thee m' and m'.3254
73: 7 have m' than heart could wish. 5674
74: 9 there is no m' any prophet: 5750
76: 4 Thou art m' glorious and excellent*
77: 7 will he be favourable no m'? 3254,5750
78:17 they sinned yet m' against him by* "
83: 4 may be no m' in remembrance. "
87: 2 m' than all the dwellings of Jacob.
88: 5 whom thou rememberest no m': 5750
103:16 place thereof shall know it no m'. "
104:35 earth, and let the wicked be no m'. "
115:14 Lord shall increase you m' and m'.
119:99 m' understanding than all my teachers:
100 I understand m' than the ancients,
130: 6 m' than they that watch for...morning:
6 m' than they that watch for...morning.
139:18 are m' in number than the sand: 7235
Pr 3:15 She is m' precious than rubies: and
4:18 that shineth m' and m' unto the 1980
10:25 passeth, so is the wicked no m':
11:24 is that withholdeth m' than is meet,
31 much m' the wicked and the sinner.
12:26 is m' excellent than his neighbour:*
15:11 how much m' then the hearts of the
17:10 A reproof entereth m' into a wise man*
19: 7 how much m' do his friends go far
21: 3 justice and judgment is m' acceptable
27 how much m', when he bringeth it
26:12 there is m' hope of a fool than of him.
28:23 rebuketh a man...shall find m' favour
29:20 there is m' hope of a fool than of him.
30: 2 Surely I am m' brutish than any man,
31: 7 and remember his misery no m'. 5750
Ec 1:16 and have gotten m' wisdom than all*
2: 9 and increased m' than all that were
15 me; and why was I then m' wise? 3148
16 of the wise m' than of the fool *5973
25 can hasten hereunto, m' than I? 2351
4: 2 m' than the living which are yet 4480
13 who will no m' be admonished. 5750
5: 1 and be m' ready to hear, than to *7138
6: 5 this hath m' rest than the other. *
8 hath the wise m' than the fool? 3148
7:19 m' than ten mighty men which are
26 I find m' bitter than death the woman,
9: 5 neither have they any m' a reward ;5750
6 neither have they any m' a portion "
17 m' than the cry of him that ruleth
10:10 edge, then must he put to m' strength:
Ca 1: 4 will remember thy love m' than wine:
5: 9, 9 thy beloved m' than another beloved,
Isa 1: 5 Why should ye be stricken any m'?*5750
5 ye will revolt m' [3254] and m': the
13 Bring no m' vain oblations; incense"
2: 4 shall they learn war any m'. 5750
5: 4 have been done m' to my vineyard, "
9: 1 did m' grievously afflict her by the*
10:20 shall no m' again stay upon him 5750
13:12 make a man m' precious than fine gold;
15: 9 for I will bring m' upon Dimon, 3254
19: 7 wither, be driven away, and be no m'.
23:10 Tarshish: there is no m' strength.5750
12 Thou shalt no m' rejoice, O thou3254, "
26:21 and shall no m' cover her slain.
30:19 thou shalt weep no m': he will be 1058
20 be removed into a corner any m', 5750
32: 5 shall be no m' called liberal, nor "
38:11 I shall behold man no m' with the
47: 1 thou shalt no m' be called tender 3254
5 thou shalt no m' be called, The lady"
51:22 thou shalt no m' drink it again: "
52: 1 shall no m' come into thee 3254,5750
14 was so marred m' than any man,
14 and his form m' than the sons of men:
54: 1 m' are the children of the desolate7227
4 reproach of...widowhood any m'. 5750
9 should no m' go over the earth; "
56:12 this day, and much m' abundant.*3499
60:18 Violence shall no m' be heard in 5750
19 sun shall be no m' thy light by day;"
20 Thy sun shall no m' go down; "
62: 4 shalt no m' be termed Forsaken; "
4 land any m' be termed Desolate: "
8 will no m' give thy corn to be meat "
65:19 weeping shall be no m' heard in her,"
20 be no m' thence an infant of days, "
Jer 2:31 we will come no m' unto thee?
3:11 herself m' than treacherous Judah.
16 they shall say no m', The ark of 5750
16 neither shall that be done any m'. "
17 walk any m' after the imagination "
7:32 it shall no m' be called Tophet, nor "
10:20 to stretch forth my tent any m',

Jer 11:19 name may be no m' remembered. 5750
16:14 that it shall no m' be said, The "
19: 6 that this place shall no m' be called "
20: 9 him, nor speak any m' in his name. "
22:10 he shall return no m', nor see his "
11 He shall not return thither any m': "
12 and shall see this land no m'. "
30 David, and ruling any m' in Judah. "
23: 4 and they shall fear no m', nor be "
7 that they shall no m' say, The Lord "
36 the Lord shall ye mention no m': "
25:27 and spue, and fall, and rise no m',
30: 8 no m' serve themselves of him. 5750
31:12 shall not sorrow any m' at all. 3254
29 In those days they shall say no m',5750
34 they shall teach no m' every man "
34 I will remember their sin no m'. "
40 nor thrown down any m' for ever. "
33:24 be no m' a nation before them. "
34:10 serve themselves of them any m', "
38: 9 for there is no m' bread in the city. "
42:18 and ye shall see this place no m'. "
44:26 my name shall no m' be named in "
46:23 they are m' than the grasshoppers,7231
48: 2 shall be no m' praise of Moab: 5750
49: 7 Is wisdom no m' in Teman? is "
50:39 and it shall be no m' inhabited for "
51:44 not flow together any m' unto him: "
La 2: 9 the law is no m'; her prophets also*
4: 7 they were m' ruddy in body than
15 They shall no m' sojourn there. 3254
16 them; he will no m' regard them: "
22 he will no m' carry thee away into "
Eze 5: 6 my judgments into wickedness m' 4480
6 my statutes m' than the countries
7 Because ye multiplied m' than the "
9 I will not do any m' the like, 5750
6:14 m' desolate than the wilderness *
12:23 shall no m' use it as a proverb in 5750
24 shall be no m' any vain vision nor "
25 it shall be no m' prolonged: for in "
28 of my words be prolonged any m', "
13:15 the wall is no m', neither they that
21 shall be no m' in your hand to be 5750
23 shall see no m' vanity, nor divine "
14:11 may go no m' astray from me, "
11 polluted any m' with all their "
21 How much m' when I send my four "
15: 2 is the vine tree m' than any tree, or
16:41 also shalt give no hire any m'. 5750
42 be quiet, and will be no m' angry. "
47 thou wast corrupted m' than they in
51 thine abominations m' than they,
52 committed m' abominable than
52 they are m' righteous than thou: yea,
63 and never open thy mouth any m' 5750
18: 3 not have occasion any m' to use this"
19: 9 that his voice should no m' be heard"
20:39 pollute ye my holy name no m' with"
21: 5 sheath: it shall not return any m'. "
13 it shall be no m', saith the Lord God.
27 and it shall be no m', until he come
32 thou shalt be no m' remembered: for
23:11 was m' corrupt in her inordinate love
11 m' than her sister in her whoredoms.
27 nor remember Egypt any m'. 5750
24:13 purged from thy filthiness any m', "
27 shalt speak, and be no m' dumb: "
26:13 of thy harps shall be no m' heard. "
14 thou shalt be built no m': for I the "
21 thee a terror, and thou shalt be no m':
27:36 terror, and never shalt be any m'.
28:19 and never shalt thou be any m'.
24 shall be no m' a pricking brier 5750
29:15 itself any m' above the nations:
15 that they shall no m' rule over the
16 shall be no m' the confidence of 5750
30:13 shall be no m' a prince of the land "
32:13 foot of man trouble them any m', "
33:22 opened, and I was no m' dumb. "
34:10 shepherds feed themselves any m'; "
22 they shall no m' be a prey; and I "
28 they shall no m' be a prey to the "
29 they shall no m' be consumed with "
29 the shame of the heathen any m'. "
36:12 shalt no m' henceforth bereave "
14 thou shalt devour men no m', "
14 neither bereave thy nations any m', "
15 the shame of the heathen any m', "
15 the reproach of the people any m', "
15 cause thy nations to fall any m', "
30 ye shall receive no m' reproach of "
37:22 they shall be no m' two nations, "
22 into two kingdoms any m' at all. "
23 defile themselves any m' with their "
39: 7 them pollute my holy name any m': "
28 left none of them any m' there. "
29 I hide my face any m' from them: "
42: 6 was straitened m' than the lowest
43: 7 the house of Israel no m' defile, 5750
45: 8 shall no m' oppress my people; "
Da 2:30 that I have m' than any living, 4481
3:19 seven times m' than it was wont 5922
7:20 whose look was m' stout than his 5750
11: 8 continue m' years than the king of*
Ho 1: 6 I will no m' have mercy upon the 5750
2:16 and shalt call me no m' Baali. "
17 they shall no m' be remembered "
6: 6 of God m' than burnt offerings,
9:15 house, I will love them no m': 3254
13: 2 And now they sin m' [3254] and m', and
14: 3 will we say any m' to the work of 5750
8 have I to do any m' with idols? "
Joe 2: 2 neither shall be any m' after it, 3254
19 I will no m' make you a reproach 5750
3:17 strangers pass through her any m'. "

Am 5: 2 is fallen; she shall no *m'* rise: 5750
7: 8 will not again pass by them any *m'*: "
13 prophesy not...any *m'* at Beth-el: "
8: 2 will not again pass by them any *m'*. "
9:15 they shall no *m'* be pulled up out "
Jon 4:11 wherein are *m'* than sixscore 7227
Mic 4: 3 shall they learn war any *m'*. 5750
5:12 thou shalt have no *m'* soothsayers:
13 shalt no *m'* worship the work of 5750
Na 1:12 thee, I will afflict thee no *m'*. "
14 that no *m'* of thy name be sown: "
15 the wicked shall no *m'* pass 3254, "
2:13 messengers shall no *m'* be heard. "
Hab 1: 8 are *m'* fierce than the evening wolves:
13 the man that is *m'* righteous than he?
Zep 3:11 thou shalt no *m'* be haughty 3254,5750
15 thee: thou shalt not see evil any *m'*. "
Zec 9: 8 shall pass through them any *m'*: "
11: 6 For I will no *m'* pity the inhabitants "
13: 2 they shall no *m'* be remembered: "
14:11 shall be no *m'* utter destruction; "
21 shall be no *m'* the Canaanite in the "
Mal 2:13 regardeth not the offering any *m'*, "
M't 5:37 is *m'* than these cometh of evil. 4053
47 only, what do ye *m'* than others? "
6:25 Is not the life *m'* than meat, and 4119
30 shall he not much *m'* clothe you, 3123
7:11 how much *m'* shall your Father "
10:15 It shall be *m'* tolerable for the land 414
25 how much *m'* shall they call them 3123
31 are of *m'* value than many sparrows. 1308
37 father or mother *m'* than me is 5228
37 loveth son or daughter *m'* than me "
11: 9 unto you, and *m'* than a prophet. 4055
22 be *m'* tolerable for Tyre and Sidon 414
24 it shall be *m'* tolerable for the land "
12:45 seven other spirits *m'* wicked than
13:12 and he shall have *m'* abundance: *
18:13 he rejoiceth *m'* of that sheep, than 3123
16 take with thee one or two *m'*, that 2089
19: 6 they are no *m'* twain, but one flesh 3765
20:10 they should have received *m'*; and 4119
31 but they cried the *m'*, saying, 3185
21:36 other servants *m'* than the first: 4119
22:46 forth ask him any *m'* questions. 3765
23:15 make him twofold *m'* the child of hell
25:20 gained besides them five talents *m'*. *243
26:53 give me *m'* than twelve legions 4119
27:23 But they cried out the *m'*, saying, *4057
Mr 1:45 Jesus could no *m'* openly enter 3370
4:24 you that hear shall *m'* be given. 4369
6:11 It shall be *m'* tolerable for Sodom* 414
7:12 suffer him no *m'* to do ought for *3765
36 but the *m'* he charged them, so 3745
36 much the *m'* a great deal they 3123
8:14 ship with them *m'* than one loaf. 1508
9: 8 they saw no man any *m'*, save Jesus 3765
25 out of him, and enter no *m'* into 3370
10: 8 they are no *m'* twain, but one flesh. 3765
48 he cried the *m'* a great deal, Thou 3123
12:33 *m'* than all whole burnt offerings 4119
43 this poor widow hath cast *m'* in, "
14: 5 sold for *m'* than three hundred *1883
25 drink no *m'* of the fruit of the vine, 3765
31 But he spake the *m'* vehemently, *3123
15:14 cried out...*m'* exceedingly, Crucify* 4056
Lu 3:13 Exact no *m'* than that which is 4119
5:15 But so much the *m'* went there a 3123
7:26 you, and much *m'* than a prophet. 4055
9:13 We have no *m'* but five loaves and 4119
10:12 it shall be *m'* tolerable in that day 414
14 it shall be *m'* tolerable for Tyre and "
35 whatsoever thou spendest *m'*, when 4325
11:13 how much *m'* shall your heavenly 3123
26 seven other spirits *m'* wicked than
12: 4 that have no *m'* that they can do. 4055
7 of *m'* value than many sparrows. 1308
23 The life is *m'* than meat, 4119
23 and the body is *m'* than raiment. *
24 how much *m'* are ye better than 3123
28 how much *m'* will he clothe you, "
48 much, of him they will ask the *m'*. 4055
14: 8 lest a *m'* honourable man than thou
15: 7 *m'* than over ninety and nine just
19, 21 am no *m'* worthy to be called 3765
18:30 receive manifold *m'* in this present 4179
39 cried so much the *m'*, Thou Son 3123
20:36 Neither can they die any *m'*: for 2089
21: 3 poor widow hath cast in *m'* than 4119
22:16 I will not any *m'* eat thereof, until *3765
44 an agony he prayed *m'* earnestly: 1617
23: 5 they were the *m'* fierce, saying, He 2001
Joh 4: 1 made and baptized *m'* disciples 4119
41 many *m'* believed because of his "
5:14 sin no *m'*, lest a worse thing come 3370
18 Jews sought the *m'* to kill him, 3123
6:66 back, and walked no *m'* with him. 3765
7:31 will he do *m'* miracles than these 4119
8:11 I condemn thee: go, and sin no *m'*. 2001
10:10 that they might have it *m'* abundantly.*
11:54 Jesus...walked no *m'* openly 2089
12:43 praise of men *m'* than the praise 3123
14:19 and the world seeth me no *m'*; 2089
15: 2 that it may bring forth *m'* fruit. 4119
4 *m'* can ye, except ye abide in me *3761
16:10 my Father, and ye see me no *m'*; 2089
21 remembereth no *m'* the anguish, "
25 I shall no *m'* speak unto you in "
17:11 now I am no *m'* in the world, but "
19: 8 that saying, he was the *m'* afraid; 3123
21:15 lovest thou me *m'* than these? 4119
Ac 4:19 unto you *m'* than unto God, judge 3123
5:14 were the *m'* added to the Lord,
8:39 that the eunuch saw him no *m'*: 3765
9:22 Saul increased the *m'* in strength, 3123
13:34 now no *m'* to return to corruption, 2001
Ac 17:11 *m'* noble than those in Thessalonica,
18:26 him the way of God *m'* perfectly. 197
19:32 *m'* part knew not wherefore they 4119
20:25 of God, shall see my face no *m'*. 3765
35 *m'* blessed to give than to receive. 3123
38 that they should see his face no *m'*. 3765
22: 2 to them, they kept the *m'* silence: 3123
23:13 *m'* than forty which had made 4119
15 something *m'* perfectly concerning 197
20 somewhat of him *m'* perfectly. "
21 for him of them *m'* than forty men, 4119
24:10 *m'* cheerfully answer for myself: *2115
22 *m'* perfect knowledge of that way, 197
25: 6 among them *m'* than ten days, 4119
27:11 *m'* than those things which were 3123
12 *m'* part advised to depart thence 4119
Ro 1:25 the creature *m'* than the Creator, *3844
2:18 the things that are *m'* excellent, *
3: 7 if the truth of God hath *m'* abounded *
5: 9 Much *m'* then, being now justified 3123
10 much *m'*, being reconciled, we shall "
15 much *m'* the grace of God, and the "
17 *m'* they which receive abundance "
20 abounded, grace did much *m'* abound:
6: 9 raised from the dead dieth no *m'*; 2089
9 death hath no *m'* dominion over 3765
7:17 Now then it is no *m'* I that do it, 2089
20 it is no *m'* I that do it, but sin that "
8:37 *m'* than conquerors through him 5245
11: 6 by grace, then is it no *m'* of works: 2089
6 otherwise grace is no *m'* grace. "
6 of works, then is it no *m'* grace: * "
6 otherwise work is no *m'* work. * "
12 how much *m'* their fulness? 3123
24 how much *m'* shall these, which be "
12: 3 *m'* highly than he ought to think; 3844
14:13 therefore judge one another any *m'*: 2001
15:15 I have written the *m'* boldly unto 5112
23 having no *m'* place in these parts, 2001
1Co 6: 3 how much *m'* things that pertain to 1065
9:19 unto all, that I might gain the *m'*. 4119
12:22 much *m'* those members of the *3123
23 we bestow *m'* abundant honour; 4055
24 having given *m'* abundant honour to "
31 unto you a *m'* excellent way. ‡2596,5236
14:18 speak with tongues *m'* than ye all: 3123
15:10 laboured *m'* abundantly than they 4055
2Co 1:12 and *m'* abundantly to you-ward. 4056
2: 4 the love which I have *m'* abundantly "
3: 9 much *m'* doth the ministration of *3123
11 much *m'* that which remaineth is "
4:17 for us a far *m'* exceeding and 1519,5236
5:16 henceforth know we him no *m'*. 2089
7: 7 me; so that I rejoiced the *m'*. 3123
13 and exceedingly the *m'* joyed we "
15 his inward affection is *m'* abundant 4056
8:17 but being *m'* forward, of his own *4707
22 but now much *m'* diligent, upon the "
10: 8 somewhat *m'* of our authority, *4055
11:23 ministers of Christ?...I am *m'*; 5228
23 in labors *m'* abundant, in stripes 4056
23 in prisons *m'* frequent, in deaths "
12:15 the *m'* abundantly I love you, the "
Ga 1:14 being *m'* exceedingly zealous of the "
3:18 of the law, it is no *m'* of promise: 2089
4: 7 thou art no *m'* a servant, but a son;* "
27 the desolate hath many *m'* children 3123
Eph 2:19 are no *m'* strangers and foreigners, 3765
4:14 we henceforth be no *m'* children, *2001
28 Let him that stole steal no *m'*: but "
Ph'p 1: 9 love may abound yet *m'* and *m'* in 3123
14 are much *m'* bold to speak the 4056
24 to abide in the flesh is *m'* needful for 316
26 your rejoicing may be *m'* abundant
2:12 but now much *m'* in my absence, 3123
3: 4 he might trust in the flesh, I *m'*: "
1Th 2:17 endeavoured the *m'* abundantly to 4056
4: 1 so ye would abound *m'* and *m'*. 3123
10 that ye increase *m'* and *m'*; "
2Ti 2:16 will increase unto *m'* ungodliness.*4119
3: 4 pleasures *m'* than lovers of God; *3123
Ph'm 16 me, but how much *m'* unto thee, * "
21 thou wilt also do *m'* than I say. *5228
Heb 1: 4 obtained a *m'* excellent name than
2: 1 ought to give the *m'* earnest heed 4056
3: 3 worthy of *m'* glory than Moses, 4119
3 the house hath *m'* honour than the "
6:17 willing *m'* abundantly to shew unto 4054
7:15 it is yet far *m'* evident: for that 4055
8: 6 obtained a *m'* excellent ministry,
12 iniquities will I remember no *m'*. 2089
9:11 a greater and *m'* perfect tabernacle,
14 How much *m'* shall the blood of 3123
10: 2 have had no *m'* conscience of sins. 2089
17 iniquities will I remember no *m'*. "
18 is, there is no *m'* offering for sin. "
25 so much the *m'*, as ye see the day 3123
26 remaineth no *m'* sacrifice for sins, 2089
11: 4 unto God a *m'* excellent sacrifice
32 what shall I *m'* say? for the time 2089
12:19 not be spoken to them any *m'*: 4369
25 much *m'* shall not we escape, if 3123
26 once *m'* I shake not the earth only, 2089
27 And this word, Yet once *m'*, signifieth
Jas 4: 6 But he giveth *m'* grace. Wherefore 3187
1Pe 1: 7 being much *m'* precious than of gold
2Pe 1:19 have also a *m'* sure word of prophecy;
Re 2:19 and the last to be *m'* than the first. 4119
3:12 God, and he shall go no *m'* out: 2089
7:16 hunger no *m'*, neither thirst any *m'*; "
9:12 there come two woes *m'* hereafter.* "
12: 8 their place found any *m'* in heaven. "
18:11 buyeth their merchandise any *m'*: 3765
14 and thou shalt find them no *m'* at all. "
21 and shall be found no *m'* at all. 2089
22 shall be heard no *m'* at all in thee; "
Re 18:22 be, shall be found any *m'* in thee; 2089
22 shall be heard no *m'* at all in thee; "
23 of a candle shall shine no *m'* at all "
23 shall be heard no *m'* at all in thee: "
20: 3 should deceive the nations no *m'*, "
21: 1 away; and there was no *m'* sea. "
4 there shall be no *m'* death, neither "
4 neither shall there be any *m'* pain: "
22: 3 there shall be no *m'* curse: but "

Moreh (*mo'-reh*)
Ge 12: 6 of Sichem, unto the plain of *M'*. 4176
De 11:30 Gilgal, beside the plains of *M'*? "
J'g 7: 1 by the hill of *M'*, in the valley. "

moreover
Ge 32:20 say ye *m'*, Behold, thy servant 1571
45:15 *M'* he kissed all his brethren, and*
47: 4 They said *m'* unto Pharaoh, For to*
48:22 *M'* I have given to thee one portion
Ex 3:15 God said *m'* unto Moses, Thus 5750
18:21 *M'* thou shalt provide out of all the
26: 1 *M'* thou shalt make the tabernacle
30:22 *M'* the Lord spake unto Moses, saying,
Le 7:21 *M'* the soul that shall touch any *
26 *M'* ye shall eat no manner of blood,*
14:46 *M'* he that goeth into the house all
18:20 *M'* thou shalt not lie carnally with thy*
25:45 *M'* of the children of the strangers 1571
Nu 13:28 and *m'* we saw the children of Anak*
16:14 *M'* thou hast not brought us into a 637
33:56 *M'* it shall come to pass, that I *
35:31 *M'* ye shall take no satisfaction for
De 1:28 *m'* we have seen the sons of the 1571
39 *M'* your little ones, which ye said
7:20 *M'* the Lord thy God will send the 1571
28:45 *M'* all these curses shall come upon*
60 *M'* he will bring upon thee all the*
J'g 10: 9 *M'* the children of Ammon passed*
Ru 4:10 *M'* Ruth the Moabitess, the wife of 1571
1Sa 2:19 *M'* his mother made him a little
12:23 *M'* as for me, God forbid that I 1571
14:21 *M'* the Hebrews that were with the*
17:37 David said *m'*, The Lord that *
20: 3 And David sware *m'*, and said, Thy 5750
24:11 *M'*, my father, see, yea, see the skirt
28:19 *M'* the Lord will also deliver 1571
2Sa 7:10 *M'* I will appoint a place for my people*
12: 8 *m'* have given unto thee such and *3254
15: 4 Absalom said *m'*, Oh that I were made
17: 1 *M'* Ahithophel said unto Absalom,
13 *M'*, if he be gotten into a city, then 518
21:15 *M'* the Philistines had yet war again*
1Ki 2: 5 *M'* thou knowest also what Joab 1571
14 He said *m'*, I have somewhat to say
44 The king said *m'* to Shimei, Thou
8:41 *M'* concerning a stranger, that is 1571
10:18 *M'* the king made a great throne of
14:14 *M'* the Lord shall raise him up a king
2Ki 12:15 *M'* they reckoned not with the men,
21:16 *M'* Manasseh shed innocent blood 1571
23:15 *M'* the altar that was at Beth-el, "
24 *M'* the workers with familiar "
1Ch 11: 2 *m'* in time past, even when Saul "
12:40 *M'* they that were nigh them, even "
17:10 *M'* I will subdue all thine enemies.*
18:12 *M'* Abishai the son of Zeruiah slew
22:15 *M'* there are workmen with thee in
23: 5 *M'* four thousand were porters; and*
25: 1 *M'* David and the captains of the host
26: 4 *M'* the sons of Obed-edom were, *
28: 7 *M'* I will establish his kingdom *
29: 3 *M'*, because I have set my 5750
2Ch 1: 5 *M'* the brasen altar, that Bezaleel
2:12 Huram said *m'*, Blessed be the Lord
4: 1 *M'* he made an altar of brass, twenty
20 *M'* the candlesticks with their lamps,*
6:32 *M'* concerning the stranger, which 1571
7: 7 *M'* Solomon hallowed the middle of
9:17 *M'* the king made a great throne of
17: 6 *m'* he took away the high places *5750
19: 8 *M'* in Jerusalem did Jehoshaphat 1571
21:11 *M'* he made high places in the "
16 *M'* the Lord stirred up against *
23: 9 *M'* Jehoiada the priest delivered to
25: 5 *M'* Amaziah gathered Judah
26: 9 *M'* Uzziah built towers in Jerusalem
11 *M'* Uzziah had an host of fighting
27: 4 *M'* he built cities in the mountains
28: 3 *M'* he burnt incense in the valley
29:19 *M'* all the vessels, which king Ahaz
30 *M'* Hezekiah the king and the princes
31: 4 *M'* he commanded the people that
32:29 *M'* he provided him cities, and
35: 1 *M'* Josiah kept a passover unto the
36:14 *M'* all the chief of the priests, and 1571
Ezr 6: 8 *M'* I make a decree what ye shall do
10:25 *M'* of Israel: of the sons of Parosh;*
Ne 2: 7 *M'* I said unto the king, If it please
3: 6 *M'* the old gate repaired Jehoiada*
26 *M'* the Nethinims dwelt in Ophel, *
5:14 *M'* from the time that I was 1571
17 *M'* there were at my table an hundred
6:17 *M'* in those days the nobles of 1571
9:12 *M'* thou leddest them in the day by
22 *M'* thou gavest them kingdoms and
11:19 *M'* the porters, Akkub, Talmon, and
Es 5:12 Haman said *m'*, Yea, Esther the 637
Job 27: 1 *M'* Job continued his parable, and*
29: 1 *M'* Job continued his parable, and*
35: 1 Elihu spake *m'*, and said,
40: 1 *M'* the Lord answered Job, and said,
Ps 19:11 *M'* by them is...servant warned: 1571
78:66 *M'* he refused the tabernacle of
105:16 *M'* he called for a famine upon the*
Ec 3:16 *m'* I saw under the sun the place 5750
5: 9 *M'* the profit of the earth is for all:

Ec 6: 5 *M*· he hath not seen the sun, nor 1571
12: 9 *m*·, because the preacher was *3148
Isa 3:16 *M*· the Lord saith, Because the
7:10 *M*· the Lord spake again unto Ahaz,*
19: 9 *M*· they that work in fine flax, and
29: 5 *M*· the multitude of thy strangers*
30:26 *M*· the light of the moon shall be as
39: 8 He said *m*·, For there shall be peace
Jer 1:11 *M*· the word of the Lord came unto
2: 1 *M*· the word of the Lord came to me,*
8: 4 *M*· thou shalt say unto them, Thus
20: 5 *M*· I will deliver all the strength of
25:10 *M*· I will take from them the voice of
33: 1 *M*· the word of the Lord came unto
23 *M*· the word of the Lord came to*
37:18 *M*· Jeremiah said unto king Zedekiah,
39: 7 *M*· he put out Zedekiah's eyes, and
40:13 *M*· Johanan the son of Kareah, and
44:24 *M*· Jeremiah said unto all the people,
48:35 *M*· I will cause to cease in Moab,
Eze 3: 1 *M*· he said unto me, Son of man, eat*
10 *M*· he said unto me, Son of man, all
4: 3 *M*· take thou unto thee an iron pan,*
16 *M*· he said unto me, Son of man,
5:14 *M*· I will make thee waste, and a
7: 1 *M*· the word of the Lord came unto
11: 1 *M*· the spirit lifted me up, and
12:17 *M*· the word of the Lord came to me,
16:20 *M*· thou hast taken thy sons and thy
29 hast *m*· multiplied thy fornication
17:11 *M*· the word of the Lord came unto
19: 1 *M*· take thou up a lamentation for
20:12 *M*· also I gave them my sabbaths,1571
45 *M*· the word of the Lord came unto*
22: 1 *M*· the word of the Lord came unto
23:36 The Lord said *m*· unto me; Son of
38 *M*· this they have done unto me: 5750
28:11 *M*· the word of the Lord came unto
36:16 *M*· the word of the Lord came unto
37:16 *M*·, thou son of man, take thee one*
26 *M*· I will make a covenant of peace
45: 1 *M*·, when ye shall divide by lot the
46:18 *M*· the prince shall not take of the
48:22 *M*· from the possession of the Levites,
Zec 4: 8 *M*· the word of the Lord came unto
5: 6 He said *m*·, This is their resemblance
M't 6:16 *M*· when ye fast, be not, as the *1161*
18:15 *M*· if thy brother shall trespass * "
Lu 16:21 *m*· the dogs came and licked **235,2532*
Ac 2:26 *m*· also my flesh shall rest in hope:*2089*
11:12 *M*· these...brethren accompanied**1161*
19:26 *M*· ye see and hear, that not alone**2532*
Ro 5:20 *M*· the law entered, that...offence**1161*
8:30 *M*· whom he did predestinate, them*"
1Co 4: 2 *M*·...required...stewards, *3739,1161,3063*
10: 1 *M*·, brethren, I would not that ye**1161*
15: 1 *M*·, brethren, I declare unto you * "
2Co 1:23 *M*· I call God for a record upon my*"
8: 1 *M*·, brethren, we do you to wit of "
1Ti 3: 7 *M*· he must have a good report of "
Heb 9:21 *M*· he sprinkled with blood "
11:36 *m*· of bonds and imprisonments: "
2Pe 1:15 *M*· I will endeavour that ye **1161,2532*

Moresheth-gath (*mor'-e-sheth-gath*) See also MORASTHITE.
Mic 1:14 shalt thou give presents to *M*·: 4182

Moriah (*mo-ri'-ah*)
Ge 22: 2 and get thee into the land of *M*·: 4179
2Ch 3: 1 Lord at Jerusalem in mount *M*·, "

morning
Ge 1: 5 evening and the *m*· were the first 1242
8 evening and the *m*· were the second"
13 evening and the *m*· were the third "
19 evening and the *m*· were the fourth"
23 evening and the *m*· were the fifth "
31 evening and the *m*· were the sixth "
19:15 And when the *m*· arose, then the 7837
27 Abraham gat up early in the *m*· 1242
20: 8 Abimelech rose early in the *m*·, "
21:14 Abraham rose up early in the *m*·, "
22: 3 Abraham rose up early in the *m*·, "
24:54 they rose up in the *m*·, and he said, "
26:31 they rose up betimes in the *m*·, "
28:18 Jacob rose up early in the *m*·, and "
29:25 that in the *m*·, behold, it was Leah: "
31:55 early in the *m*· Laban rose up, and "
40: 6 Joseph came in unto them in the *m*·, "
41: 8 it came to pass in the *m*· that his "
44: 3 soon as the *m*· was light, the men "
49:27 in the *m*· he shall devour the prey, "
Ex 7:15 Get thee unto Pharaoh in the *m*·; "
8:20 Rise up early in the *m*·, and stand "
9:13 Rise up early in the *m*·, and stand "
10:13 and when it was *m*·, the east wind "
12:10 nothing of it remain until the *m*·; "
10 which remaineth of it until the *m*· "
22 the door of his house until the *m*·. "
14:24 *m*· watch the Lord looked unto the "
27 his strength when the *m*· appeared;"
16: 7 And in the *m*·, then ye shall see the "
8 and in the *m*· bread to the full; for "
12 and in the *m*· ye shall be filled with "
13 in the *m*· the dew lay round about "
19 Let no man leave of it till the *m*·. "
20 some of them left of it until the *m*·. "
21 they gathered it every *m*·, every "
23 up for you to be kept until the *m*·. "
24 they laid it up till the *m*·, as Moses "
18:13 from the *m*· unto the evening. "
14 stand by thee from *m*· unto even? "
19:16 to pass on the third day in the *m*·, "
23:18 of my sacrifice remain until the *m*·. "
24: 4 and rose up early in the *m*·, and "
27:21 from evening to *m*· before the Lord:"
29:34 remain unto the *m*·, then thou shalt"

Ex 29:39 one lamb thou shalt offer in the *m*·;1242
41 to the meat offering of the *m*·, and "
30: 7 thereon sweet incense every *m*·: "
34: 2 be ready in the *m*·, and come up in "
2 and come up in the *m*· unto mount "
4 and Moses rose up early in the *m*·, "
25 of the passover be left unto the *m*·. "
36: 3 unto him free offerings every *m*·. "
Le 6: 9 upon the altar all night unto the *m*·,"
12 shall burn wood on it every *m*·, and"
20 perpetual, half of it in the *m*·, and "
7:15 shall not leave any of it until the *m*·."
9:17 beside the burnt sacrifice of the *m*·."
19:13 with thee all night until the *m*·. "
24: 3 it from the evening unto the *m*· "
Nu 9:12 shall leave none of it unto the *m*·, "
15 the appearance of fire, until the *m*·. "
21 cloud abode from even unto the *m*·, "
21 the cloud was taken up in the *m*·, "
14:40 they rose up early in the *m*·, and "
22:13, 21 Balaam rose up in the *m*·, and "
28: 4 one lamb shalt thou offer in the *m*·, "
8 as the meat offering of the *m*·, and "
23 beside the burnt offering in the *m*·, "
De 16: 4 even, remain all night until the *m*·. "
7 thou shalt turn in the *m*·, and go "
28:67 In the *m*· thou shalt say, Would God"
67 shalt say, Would God it were *m*·! "
Jos 3: 1 Joshua rose early in the *m*·; and "
6:12 Joshua rose early in the *m*·, and "
7:14 In the *m*· therefore ye shall be "
16 So Joshua rose up early in the *m*·, "
8:10 And Joshua rose up early in the *m*·,"
J'g 6:28 of the city arose early in the *m*·, "
31 be put to death whilst it is yet *m*·: "
9:33 it shall be, that in the *m*·, as soon "
16: 2 In the *m*·, when it is day, we shall "
19: 5 when they arose early in the *m*·, "
8 And he arose early in the *m*· on the "
25 abused her all...night until the *m*·: "
27 And her lord rose up in the *m*·, and "
20:19 children of Israel rose up in the *m*·, "
Ru 2: 7 even from the *m*· until now, that "
3:13 it shall be in the *m*·, that if he will "
13 Lord liveth: lie down until the *m*·. "
14 And she lay at his feet until the *m*·:"
1Sa 1:19 they rose up in the *m*· early, and "
3:15 And Samuel lay until the *m*·, and "
5: 4 they arose early on the morrow *m*·, "
11:11 midst of the host in the *m*· watch, "
14:36 and spoil them until the *m*· light, "
15:12 rose early to meet Saul in the *m*·, "
17:16 drew near *m*· and evening, and 7925
20 David rose up early in the *m*·, and1242
19: 2 take heed to thyself until the *m*·, "
11 him, and to slay him in the *m*·: "
20:35 And it came to pass in the *m*·, that "
25:22 that pertain to him by the *m*· light "
34 been left unto Nabal by the *m*· light"
36 less or more, until the *m*· light. "
37 it came to pass in the *m*·, when the "
29:10 now rise up early in the *m*· with "
10 as soon as ye be up early in the *m*·, "
11 rose up early to depart in the *m*·, "
2Sa 2:27 then in the *m*· the people had gone "
11:14 And it came to pass in the *m*·, that "
17:22 by the *m*· light there lacked not one"
23: 4 he shall be as the light of the *m*·, "
4 riseth, even a *m*· without clouds; "
24:11 For when David was up in the *m*·, "
15 upon Israel from the *m*· even to the"
1Ki 3:21 I rose in the *m*· to give my child "
21 when I had considered it in the *m*·, "
17: 6 him bread and flesh in the *m*·, and "
18:26 of Baal from *m*· even until noon, "
2Ki 3:20 it came to pass in the *m*·, when the "
22 they rose up early in the *m*·, and the"
7: 9 if we tarry till the *m*· light, some "
10: 8 entering in of the gate until the *m*·, "
9 it came to pass in the *m*·, that he "
16:15 altar burn the *m*· burnt offering, "
19:35 and when they arose early in the *m*·,"
1Ch 9:27 and the opening thereof every *m*· "
16:40 offering continually *m*· and evening,"
23:30 every *m*· to thank and praise the "
2Ch 2: 4 the burnt offerings *m*· and evening, "
13:11 every *m*· and every evening burnt "
20:20 they rose early in the *m*·, and went "
31: 3 the *m*· and evening burnt offerings, "
Ezr 3: 3 burnt offerings *m*· and evening. "
Neh 4:21 the rising of the *m*· till the stars 7837
8: 3 water gate from the *m*· until midday,216
Job 1: 5 and rose up early in the *m*·, and 1242
4:20 are destroyed from *m*· to evening: "
7:18 thou shouldest visit him every *m*·, "
21 thou shalt seek me in the *m*·, but*7836
11:17 shine forth, thou shalt be as the *m*·.1242
24:17 For the *m*· is to them even as the "
38: 7 When the *m*· stars sang together, "
12 Hast thou commanded the *m*· since"
41:18 eyes are like the eyelids of the *m*·. 7837
Ps 5: 3 voice shalt thou hear in the *m*·, 1242
3 in the *m*· will I direct my prayer "
30: 5 a night, but joy cometh in the *m*·. "
49:14 have dominion over them in the *m*·; "
55:17 and *m*·, and at noon, will I pray, "
59:16 sing aloud of thy mercy in the *m*·: "
65: 8 of the *m*· and evening to rejoice. "
73:14 plagued, and chastened every *m*·. "
88:13 in the *m*· shall my prayer prevent "
90: 5 in the *m*· they are like grass which "
6 In the *m*· it flourisheth, and groweth"
92: 2 forth thy lovingkindness in the *m*·, "
110: 3 holiness from the womb of the *m*·:4891
119:147 prevented the dawning of the *m*·, and
130: 6 than they that watch for the *m*·: 1242

Ps 130: 6 than they that watch for the *m*·. 1242
139: 9 If I take the wings of the *m*·, and 7837
143: 8 hear thy lovingkindness in the *m*·;1242
Pr 7:18 us take our fill of love until the *m*·: "
27:14 rising early in the *m*·, it shall be "
Ec 10:16 and thy princes eat in the *m*·! "
11: 6 In the *m*· sow thy seed, and in the "
Ca 6:10 is she that looketh forth as the *m*·,7837
Isa 5:11 them that rise up early in the *m*·, 1242
14:12 heaven, O Lucifer, son of the *m*·! 7837
17:11 in the *m*· shalt thou make thy seed 1242
14 and before the *m*· he is not. "
21:12 The *m*· cometh, and also the night: "
28:19 for *m*· by *m*· shall it pass over, by "
33: 2 be thou their arm every *m*·, our "
37:36 when they arose early in the *m*·, "
38:13 I reckoned till *m*·, that, as a lion, so"
50: 4 he wakeneth *m*· by *m*·, he wakeneth"
58: 8 thy light break forth as the *m*·, 7837
Jer 5: 8 They were as fed horses in the *m*·:7904
20:16 and let him hear the cry in the *m*·,1242
21:12 Execute judgment in the *m*·, and "
La 3:23 They are new every *m*·: great is thy"
Eze 7: 7 The *m*· is come unto thee, O thou*6843
10 the *m*· is gone forth; the rod hath* "
12: 8 the *m*· came the word of the Lord 1242
24:18 I spake unto the people in the *m*·: "
18 I did in the *m*· as I was commanded."
33:22 until he came to me in the *m*·; "
46:13 thou shalt prepare it every *m*·. "
14 a meat offering for it every *m*·, "
15 every *m*· for a continual...offering. "
Da 6:19 king arose very early in the *m*·, 5053
8:26 vision of the evening and the *m*· *1242
Ho 6: 3 going forth is prepared as the *m*·;7837
4 your goodness is as a *m*· cloud, 1242
7: 6 the *m*· it burneth as a flaming fire. "
10:15 in a *m*· shall the king of Israel *7837
13: 3 they shall be as the *m*· cloud, and 1242
Joe 2: 2 *m*· spread upon the mountains: *7837
Am 4: 4 bring your sacrifices every *m*·, 1242
13 that maketh the *m*· darkness, and 7837
5: 8 the shadow of death into the *m*·, 1242
Jon 4: 7 when the *m*· rose the next day, 7837
Mic 2: 1 when the *m*· is light, they practise1242
Zep 3: 5 every *m*· doth he bring his judgment"
M't 16: 3 in the *m*·, It will be foul weather *4404*
20: 1 out early in the *m*· to hire labourers
21:18 Now in the *m*· as he returned into *4405*
27: 1 When the *m*· was come, all the chief"
M'r 1:35 in the *m*·, rising up a great while *4404*
11:20 And in the *m*·, as they passed by, "
13:35 or at the cockcrowing, or in the *m*·:"
15: 1 in the *m*· the chief priests held "
16: 2 very early in the *m*·, the first day *
Lu 21:38 all the people came early in the *m*·
24: 1 very early in the *m*·, they came unto*
Joh 8: 2 early in the *m*· he came again into "
21: 4 But when the *m*· was now come, **4405*
Ac 5:21 into the temple early in the *m*·, *
28:23 the prophets, from *m*· till evening. *4404*
Re 2:28 And I will give him the *m*· star. *4407*
22:16 David, and the bright and *m*· star. *3720*

morning-cloud See MORNING and CLOUD.
morning-light See MORNING and LIGHT.
morning-star See MORNING and STAR.
morning-watch See MORNING and WATCH.

morrow
Ge 19:34 it came to pass on the *m*·, that the 4283
Ex 8:10 And he said, To *m*·. And he said, 4279
23 thy people: to *m*· shall this sign be. "
29 servants, and from his people, to *m*·:"
9: 5 To *m*· the Lord shall do this thing "
6 the Lord did that thing on the *m*·, 4283
18 to *m*· about this time I will cause 4279
10: 4 to *m*· will I bring the locusts into "
16:23 To *m*· is the rest of the holy sabbath "
17: 9 to *m*· I will stand on the top of the "
18:13 pass on the *m*·, that Moses sat to 4283
19:10 sanctify them to day and to *m*·, 4279
32: 5 said, To *m*· is a feast to the Lord. "
6 And they rose up early on the *m*·, 4283
30 to pass on the *m*·, that Moses said "
Le 7:16 on the *m*· also the remainder of it "
19: 6 same day ye offer it, and on the *m*·: "
22:30 shall leave none of it until the *m*·:*1242
23:11 on the *m*· after the sabbath the 4283
15 you from the *m*· after the sabbath, "
16 Even unto the *m*· after the seventh "
Nu 11:18 Sanctify yourselves against to *m*·, 4279
14:25 To *m*· turn you, and get you into "
16: 5 to *m*· the Lord will shew who are *1242
7 in them before the Lord to *m*·: 4279
16 thou, and they, and Aaron, to *m*·: "
41 But on the *m*· all the congregation4283
17: 8 that on the *m*· Moses went into the "
22:41 to pass on the *m*·, that Balak *1242
33: 3 on the *m*· after the passover the 4283
Jos 3: 5 for to *m*· the Lord will do wonders4279
5:11 land on the *m*· after the passover, 4283
12 the manna ceased on the *m*· after "
7:13 Sanctify yourselves against to *m*·:4279
11: 6 to *m*· about this time will I deliver "
22:18 the Lord, that to *m*· he will be wroth "
J'g 6:38 for he rose up early on the *m*·, and 4283
9:42 to pass on the *m*·, that the people "
19: 9 to *m*· get you early on your way, 4279
20:28 to *m*· I will deliver them into "
21: 4 to pass on the *m*·, that the people "
1Sa 5: 3 of Ashdod arose early on the *m*·, 4283
4 they arose early on the *m*· morning, "
9:16 To *m*· about this time I will send 4279
19 to *m*· I will let thee go, and will *1242
11: 9 To *m*·, by that time the sun be hot.4279

1Sa 11:10 To *m'* we will come out unto you, 4279
11 it was so on the *m'*, that Saul put 4283
18:10 to pass on the *m'*, that the evil "
19:11 to night, to *m'* thou shalt be slain. 4279
20: 5 to *m'* is the new moon, and I should "
12 sounded my father about to *m'* any "
18 to David, To *m'* is the new moon: "
27 came to pass on the *m'*, which was 4283
28:19 to *m'* shalt thou and thy sons be 4279
31: 8 on the *m'*, when the Philistines 4283
2Sa 11:12 and to *m'* I will let thee depart. 4279
12 in Jerusalem that day, and the *m'*. 4283
1Ki 19: 2 of them by to *m'* about this time. 4279
20: 6 send my servants unto thee to *m'* "
2Ki 6:28 day, and we will eat my son to *m'*. "
7: 1 To *m'* about this time...a measure "
18 be to *m'* about this time in the gate "
8:15 it came to pass on the *m'*, that he 4283
10: 6 me to Jezreel by to *m'* this time. 4279
1Ch 10: 8 on the *m'*, when the Philistines 4283
29:21 on the *m'* after that day, even a "
2Ch 20:16 To *m'* go ye down against them: 4279
17 to *m'* go out against them: for the "
Es 2:14 on the *m'* she returned into the 1242
5: 8 will do to *m'* as the king hath said. 4279
12 and to *m'* am I invited unto her also "
14 to *m'* speak thou unto the king *1242
9:13 to do to *m'* also according unto 4279
Pr 3:28 come again, and to *m'* I will give; "
27: 1 Boast not thyself of to *m'*; for thou "
Isa 22:13 and drink; for to *m'* we shall die. "
56:12 to *m'* shall be as this day, and much "
Jer 20: 3 to pass on the *m'*, that Pashur 4283
Zep 3: 3 they gnaw not the bones till the *m'*. 1242
M't 6:30 is, and to *m'* is cast into the oven, *839*
34 therefore no thought for the *m'*: "
34 for the *m'* shall take thought for the "
M'r 11:12 on the *m'*, when they were come *1887*
Lu 10:35 And on the *m'* when he departed, *839*
12:28 field, and to *m'* is cast into the oven; "
13:32 and I do cures to day and to *m'*, "
33 and to *m'*, and the day following: "
Ac 4: 5 to pass on the *m'*, that their rulers, "
10: 9 On the *m'*, as they went on their *1887*
23 And on the *m'* Peter went away with "
24 And the *m'* after they entered into "
20: 7 them, ready to depart on the *m'*; "
22:30 On the *m'*, because he would have "
23:15 he bring him down unto you to *m'*, *839*
20 down Paul to *m'* into the council, "
32 On the *m'* they left the horsemen *1887*
25:17 on the *m'* I sat on the judgment *1836*
22 To *m'*, said he, thou shalt hear him. *839*
23 And on the *m'*, when Agrippa was *1887*
1Co 15:32 us eat and drink; for to *m'* we die. *839*
Jas 4:13 To day or to *m'* we will go into such "
14 ye know not what shall be on the *m'*. "

morsel See also MORSELS.
Ge 18: 5 And I will fetch a *m'* of bread, and 6595
J'g 19: 5 thine heart with a *m'* of bread, and "
Ru 2:14 bread, and dip thy *m'* in the vinegar. "
1Sa 2:36 piece of silver and a *m'* of bread, *3603
28:22 let me set a *m'* of bread before 6595
1Ki 17:11 Bring me, I pray thee, a *m'* of bread "
Job 31:17 Or have eaten my *m'* myself alone, "
Pr 17: 1 Better is a dry *m'*, and quietness "
23: 8 The *m'* which thou hast eaten shalt "
Heb 12:16 one *m'* of meat sold his birthright. *1035*

morsels
Ps 147:17 He casteth forth his ice like *m'*: 6595

mortal See also IMMORTAL.
Job 4:17 *m'* man be more just than God? 582
Ro 6:12 therefore reign in your *m'* body, *2349*
8:11 also quicken your *m'* bodies by his "
1Co 15:53 this *m'* must put on immortality. "
54 *m'* shall have put on immortality, "
2Co 4:11 be made manifest in our *m'* flesh. "

mortality See also IMMORTALITY.
2Co 5: 4 *m'* might be swallowed up of life. **2349*

mortally
De 19:11 and smite him *m'* that he die, and 5315

mortar See also MORTER.
Nu 11: 8 or beat it in a *m'*, and baked it in *4085
Pr 27:22 thou shouldest bray a fool in a *m'* 4388

morter See also MORTAR.
Ge 11: 3 stone, and slime had they for *m'*. *2563
Ex 1:14 hard bondage, in *m'*, and in brick,* "
Le 14:42 and he shall take other *m'*, and *6083
45 and all the *m'* of the house; * "
Isa 41:25 come upon princes as upon *m'*, *2563
Eze 13:10 others daubed it with untempered *m'*:*
11 which daub it with untempered *m'*,*
14 ye have daubed with untempered *m'*,*
15 have daubed it with untempered *m'*,*
22:28 daubed them with untempered *m'*,*
Na 3:14 go into clay, and tread the *m'*, *2563

mortgaged
Ne 5: 3 We have *m'* our lands, vineyards, *6148

mortify
Ro 8:13 the Spirit do *m'* the deeds of the ‡*2289*
Col 3: 5 *M'* therefore your members which *3499*

Mosera (*mo-se'-rah*) See also MOSEROTH.
De 10: 6 of the children of Jaakan to *M'*: *4149

Moseroth (*mo-se'-roth*) See also MOSERA.
Nu 33:30 Hashmonah,...encamped at *M'*. 4149
31 they departed from *M'*, and pitched "

Moses (*mo'-zez*) See also MOSES'.
Ex 2:10 she called his name *M'*: and she 4872
11 in those days, when *M'* was grown, "
14 *M'* feared, and said, Surely this "
15 this thing, he sought to slay *M'*. "
15 *M'* fled from the face of Pharaoh, "

Ex 2:17 *M'* stood up and helped them, and 4872
21 *M'* was content to dwell with the "
21 he gave *M'* Zipporah his daughter. "
3: 1 Now *M'* kept the flock of Jethro his "
3 *M'* said, I will now turn aside, and "
4 midst of the bush, and said, *M'*, *M'*. "
6 *M'* hid his face; for he was afraid to "
11 *M'* said unto God, Who am I, that I "
13 *M'* said unto God, Behold, when I "
14 God said unto *M'*, I Am That I Am: "
15 God said moreover unto *M'*, Thus "
4: 1 And *M'* answered and said, But, "
3 serpent; and *M'* fled from before it. "
4 Lord said unto *M'*, Put forth thine "
10 *M'* said unto the Lord, O my Lord, "
14 the Lord was kindled against *M'*, "
18 *M'* went and returned to Jethro his "
18 And Jethro said to *M'*, Go in peace. "
19 Lord said unto *M'* in Midian, Go, "
20 *M'* took his wife and his sons, and "
20 *M'* took the rod of God in his hand. "
21 the Lord said unto *M'*, When thou "
27 Go into the wilderness to meet *M'*. "
28 *M'* told Aaron all the words of the "
29 *M'* and Aaron went and gathered "
30 the Lord had spoken unto *M'*, and "
5: 1 afterward *M'* and Aaron went in, "
4 *M'* and Aaron, let the people from "
20 they met *M'* and Aaron, who stood "
22 *M'* returned unto the Lord, and "
6: 1 the Lord said unto *M'*, Now shalt "
2 God spake unto *M'*, and said unto "
9 *M'* spake so unto the children of "
9 they hearkened not unto *M'* for "
10 the Lord spake unto *M'*, saying, "
12 *M'* spake unto the Lord, saying, "
13 the Lord spake unto *M'* and unto "
20 and she bare him Aaron and *M'*: "
26 These are that Aaron and *M'*, to "
27 these are that *M'* and Aaron. "
28 the Lord spake unto *M'* in the land "
29 the Lord spake unto *M'*, saying, I "
30 *M'* said before the Lord, Behold, I "
7: 1 The Lord said unto *M'*, See, I have "
6 And *M'* and Aaron did as the Lord "
7 *M'* was fourscore years old, and "
8 the Lord spake unto *M'* and unto "
10 *M'*...Aaron went in unto Pharaoh, "
14 Lord said unto *M'*, Pharaoh's heart "
19 the Lord spake unto *M'*, Say unto "
20 *M'* and Aaron did so, as the Lord "
8: 1 the Lord spake unto *M'*, Go unto "
5 the Lord spake unto *M'*, Say unto "
8 Pharaoh called for *M'* and Aaron, "
9 *M'* said unto Pharaoh, Glory over "
12 And *M'* and Aaron went out from "
12 *M'* cried unto the Lord because of "
13 did according to the word of *M'*; "
16 Lord said unto *M'*, Say unto Aaron, "
20 Lord said unto *M'*, Rise up early "
25 called for *M'* and for Aaron, and "
26 *M'* said, It is not meet so to do; for "
29 And *M'* said, Behold, I go out from "
30 *M'* went out from Pharaoh, and "
31 did according to the word of *M'*; "
9: 1 the Lord said unto *M'*, Go in unto "
8 Lord said unto *M'* and unto Aaron, "
8 *M'* sprinkle it toward the heaven "
10 *M'* sprinkled it up toward heaven; "
11 could not stand before *M'* because "
12 as the Lord had spoken unto *M'*. "
13 Lord said unto *M'*, Rise up early "
22 Lord said unto *M'*, Stretch forth "
23 *M'* stretched forth his rod toward "
27 sent, and called for *M'* and Aaron, "
29 *M'* said unto him, As soon as I am "
33 And *M'* went out of the city from "
35 go; as the Lord had spoken by *M'*. "
10: 1 the Lord said unto *M'*, Go in unto "
3 And *M'* and Aaron came in unto "
8 *M'* and Aaron were brought again "
9 *M'* said, We will go with our young "
12 the Lord said unto *M'*, Stretch out "
13 *M'* stretched forth his rod over the "
16 Pharaoh called for *M'* and Aaron "
21 Lord said unto *M'*, Stretch out "
22 *M'* stretched forth his hand toward "
24 Pharaoh called unto *M'*, and said, "
25 *M'* said, Thou must give us also "
29 *M'* said, Thou hast spoken well, I "
11: 1 Lord said unto *M'*, Yet will I bring "
3 *M'* was very great in the land of "
4 And *M'* said, Thus saith the Lord, "
9 Lord said unto *M'*, Pharaoh shall "
10 *M'* and Aaron did all these wonders "
12: 1 unto *M'* and Aaron in the land of "
21 *M'* called for all the elders of Israel, "
28 Lord had commanded *M'*...Aaron, "
31 called for *M'* and Aaron by night, "
35 did according to the word of *M'*; "
43 the Lord said unto *M'* and Aaron, "
50 Lord commanded *M'* and Aaron, "
13: 1 the Lord spake unto *M'*, saying, "
3 *M'* said unto the people, Remember "
19 *M'* took the bones of Joseph with "
14: 1 the Lord spake unto *M'*, saying, "
11 they said unto *M'*, Because there "
13 *M'* said unto the people, Fear ye "
15 the Lord said unto *M'*, Wherefore "
21 *M'* stretched out his hand over the "
26 unto *M'*, Stretch out thine hand "
27 *M'* stretched forth his hand over "
31 the Lord, and his servant *M'*. "
15: 1 Then sang *M'* and the children of "
22 *M'* brought Israel from the Red "
24 the people murmured against *M'*, "

Ex 16: 2 murmured against *M'* and Aaron 4872
4 unto *M'*, Behold, I will rain bread "
6 *M'* and Aaron said unto all the "
8 *M'* said, This shall be, when the "
9 *M'* spake unto Aaron, Say unto all "
11 the Lord spake unto *M'*, saying, "
15 And *M'* said unto them, This is the "
19 *M'* said, Let no man leave of it till "
20 they hearkened not unto *M'*; but "
20 and *M'* was wroth with them. "
22 the congregation came and told *M'*. "
24 it up till the morning, as *M'* bade: "
25 And *M'* said, Eat that to day; for "
28 the Lord said unto *M'*, How long "
32 *M'* said, This is the thing which "
33 *M'* said unto Aaron, Take a pot, "
34 As the Lord commanded *M'*, so "
17: 2 the people did chide with *M'*, and "
2 *M'* said unto them, Why chide ye "
3 people murmured against *M'*, and "
4 *M'* cried unto the Lord, saying, "
5 Lord said unto *M'*, Go on before "
6 *M'* did so in the sight of the elders "
9 *M'* said unto Joshua, Choose us "
10 Joshua did as *M'* had said to him, "
10 *M'*, Aaron, and Hur went up to the "
11 when *M'* held up his hand, that "
14 the Lord said unto *M'*, Write this "
15 *M'* built an altar, and called the "
18: 1 of all that God had done for *M'*, "
5 wife unto *M'* in the wilderness, "
6 he said unto *M'*, I thy father in law "
7 *M'* went out to meet his father in "
8 *M'* told his father in law all that "
13 that *M'* sat to judge the people: "
13 stood by *M'* from the morning unto "
15 And *M'* said unto his father in law, "
24 *M'* hearkened to the voice of his "
25 *M'* chose able men out of all Israel, "
26 hard causes they brought unto *M'*, "
27 *M'* let his father in law depart; "
19: 3 And *M'* went up unto God, and the "
7 *M'* came and called for the elders "
8 And *M'* returned the words of the "
9 the Lord said unto *M'*, Lo, I come "
9 *M'* told the words of the people "
10 Lord said unto *M'*, Go unto the "
14 And *M'* went down from the mount "
17 *M'* brought forth the people out of "
19 *M'* spake, and God answered him "
20 Lord called *M'* up to the top of the "
20 top of the mount; and *M'* went up. "
21 the Lord said unto *M'*, Go down, "
23 *M'* said unto the Lord, The people "
25 *M'* went down unto the people, and "
20:19 said unto *M'*, Speak thou with us, "
20 *M'* said unto the people, Fear not: "
21 and *M'* drew near unto the thick "
22 the Lord said unto *M'*, Thus thou "
24: 1 unto *M'*, Come up unto the Lord, "
2 *M'* alone shall come near the Lord: "
3 *M'* came and told the people all "
4 *M'* wrote all the words of the Lord, "
6 *M'* took half of the blood, and put "
8 *M'* took the blood, and sprinkled it "
9 Then went up *M'*, and Aaron, and "
12 Lord said unto *M'*, Come up to me "
13 And *M'* rose up, and his minister "
13 *M'* went up into the mount of God. "
15 *M'* went up into the mount, and a "
16 he called unto *M'* out of the midst "
18 *M'* went into the midst of the cloud, "
18 *M'* was in the mount forty days "
25: 1 the Lord spake unto *M'*, saying, "
30:11, 17 the Lord spake unto *M'*, saying, "
22 the Lord spake unto *M'*, saying, "
34 the Lord said unto *M'*, Take unto "
31: 1, 12 the Lord spake unto *M'*, saying, "
18 And he gave unto *M'*, when he had "
32: 1 the people saw that *M'* delayed to "
1 for as for this *M'*, the man that "
7 Lord said unto *M'*, Go, get thee "
9 the Lord said unto *M'*, I have seen "
11 *M'* besought the Lord his God, and "
17 as they shouted, he said unto *M'*, "
21 And *M'* said unto Aaron, What did "
23 for as for this *M'*, the man that "
25 when *M'* saw that the people were "
26 *M'* stood in the gate of the camp, "
28 did according to the word of *M'*: "
29 *M'* had said, Consecrate yourselves "
30 *M'* said unto the people, Ye have "
31 *M'* returned unto the Lord, and "
33 the Lord said unto *M'*, Whosoever "
33: 1 Lord said unto *M'*, Depart, and go "
5 Lord had said unto *M'*, Say unto "
7 And *M'* took the tabernacle, and "
8 *M'* went out unto the tabernacle, "
8 his tent door, and looked after *M'*, "
9 *M'* entered into the tabernacle, the "
9 and the Lord talked with *M'*. "
11 Lord spake unto *M'* face to face, "
12 *M'* said unto the Lord, See, thou "
17 Lord said unto *M'*, I will do this "
34: 1 Lord said unto *M'*, Hew thee two "
4 *M'* rose up early in the morning, "
8 *M'* made haste, and bowed his "
27 the Lord said unto *M'*, Write thou "
29 *M'* came down from mount Sinai "
29 *M'* wist not that the skin of his face "
30 all the children of Israel saw *M'*, "
31 *M'* called unto them; and Aaron "
31 him: and *M'* talked with them. "
33 *M'* had done speaking with them, "
34 when *M'* went in before the Lord "
35 of Israel saw the face of *M'*, that "

Ex 34: 35 M· put the vail upon his face again. 4872
35: 1 M· gathered all the congregation "
4 M· spake unto all the congregation "
20 departed from the presence of M·. "
29 to be made by the hand of M·. "
30 M· said unto the children of Israel, "
36: 2 M· called Bezaleel and Aholiab, "
3 they received of M· all the offering, "
5 they spake unto M·, saying, The "
6 M· gave commandment, and they "
38: 21 to the commandment of M·, for "
22 all that the Lord commanded M·. "
39: 1, 5, 7, 21, 26, 29, 31 as the Lord commanded M·. "
32 all that the Lord commanded M·, "
33 brought the tabernacle unto M·, "
42 all that the Lord commanded M·, "
43 M· did look upon all the work, and, "
43 they done it: and M· blessed them. "
40: 1 the Lord spake unto M·, saying, "
16 Thus did M·: according to all that "
18 M· reared up the tabernacle, and "
19 it; as the Lord commanded M·. "
21 as the Lord commanded M·. "
23 as the Lord had commanded M·. "
25, 27, 29 the Lord commanded M·. "
31 M· and Aaron and his sons washed "
32 as the Lord commanded M·. "
33 gate. So M· finished the work. "
35 M· was not able to enter into the "
Le 1: 1 the Lord called unto M·, and spake "
4: 1 the Lord spake unto M·, saying, "
5: 14 the Lord spake unto M·, saying, "
6: 1, 8, 19, 24 the Lord spake unto M·, "
7: 22, 28 the Lord spake unto M·, saying, "
38 Which the Lord commanded M· in "
8: 1 the Lord spake unto M·, saying, "
4 M· did as the Lord commanded "
5 M· said unto the congregation, "
6 M· brought Aaron and his sons, "
9 as the Lord commanded M·. "
10 And M· took the anointing oil, and "
13 M· brought Aaron's sons, and put "
13 them; as the Lord commanded M·. "
15 M· took the blood, and put it upon "
16 and M· burned it upon the altar. "
17 camp; as the Lord commanded M·. "
19 and M· sprinkled the blood upon the "
20 M· burnt the head, and the pieces, "
21 M· burnt the whole ram upon the "
21 Lord; as the Lord commanded M·. "
23 M· took of the blood of it, and put "
24 M· put of the blood upon the tip of "
24 and M· sprinkled the blood upon the "
28 M· took them from off their hands, "
29 M· took the breast, and waved it "
29 part; as the Lord commanded M·. "
30 M· took of the anointing oil, and of "
31 M· said unto Aaron and to his sons, "
36 Lord commanded by the hand of M·. "
9: 1 that M· called Aaron and his sons, "
5 brought that which M· commanded "
6 M· said, This is the thing which the "
7 M· said unto Aaron, Go unto the "
10 altar; as the Lord commanded M·. "
21 before the Lord; as M· commanded. "
23 And M· and Aaron went into the "
10: 3 M· said unto Aaron, This is it that "
4 M· called Mishael and Elzaphan, "
5 out of the camp; as M· had said. "
6 And M· said unto Aaron, and unto "
7 did according to the word of M·. "
11 unto them by the hand of M·. "
12 And M· spake unto Aaron, and unto "
16 M· diligently sought the goat of the "
19 Aaron said unto M·, Behold, this "
20 And when M· heard that, he was "
11: 1 Lord spake unto M· and to Aaron, "
12: 1 the Lord spake unto M·, saying, "
13: 1 the Lord spake unto M· and Aaron, "
14: 1 the Lord spake unto M·, saying, "
33 the Lord spake unto M· and unto "
15: 1 Lord spake unto M· and to Aaron, "
16: 1 Lord spake unto M· after the death "
2 And the Lord said unto M·, Speak "
34 did as the Lord commanded M·. "
17: 1 the Lord spake unto M·, saying, "
18: 1 the Lord spake unto M·, saying, "
19: 1 the Lord spake unto M·, saying, "
20: 1 the Lord spake unto M·, saying, "
21: 1 And the Lord said unto M·, Speak "
16 the Lord spake unto M·, saying, "
24 M· told it unto Aaron, and to his "
22: 1, 17, 26 Lord spake unto M·, saying, "
23: 1, 9, 23, 26, 33 spake unto M·, saying, "
44 M· declared unto the children of "
24: 1 the Lord spake unto M·, saying, "
11 they brought him unto M·: (and his "
13 the Lord spake unto M·, saying, "
23 And M· spake unto the children of "
23 did as the Lord commanded M·. "
25: 1 Lord spake unto M· in mount Sinai, "
26: 46 in mount Sinai by the hand of M·. "
27: 1 the Lord spake unto M·, saying, "
34 which the Lord commanded M· for "
Nu 1: 1 And the Lord spake unto M· in the "
17 And M· and Aaron took these men "
19 As the Lord commanded M·, so he "
44 which M· and Aaron numbered, "
48 For the Lord had spoken unto M·, "
54 all that the Lord commanded M·, "
2: 1 the Lord spake unto M· and unto "
33 Israel; as the Lord commanded M·. "
34 all that the Lord commanded M·: "
3: 1 the generations of Aaron and M· "
5, 11 the Lord spake unto M·, saying, "

Nu 3: 14 And the Lord spake unto M· in the 4872
16 M· numbered them according to "
38 congregation eastward, shall be M·, "
39 which M· and Aaron numbered at "
40 the Lord said unto M·, Number all "
42 And M· numbered, as the Lord "
44 the Lord spake unto M·, saying, "
49 M· took the redemption money of "
51 M· gave the money of them that "
51 Lord, as the Lord commanded M·. "
4: 1, 17 Lord spake unto M· and unto "
21 the Lord spake unto M·, saying, "
34 M· and Aaron and the chief of the "
37 which M· and Aaron did number "
37 of the Lord by the hand of M·. "
41 whom M· and Aaron did number "
45 whom M· and Aaron numbered "
45 word of the Lord by the hand of M·. "
46 whom M· and Aaron and the chief "
49 were numbered by the hand of M·, "
49 him, as the Lord commanded M·. "
5: 1 the Lord spake unto M·, saying, "
4 as the Lord spake unto M·, so did "
11 the Lord spake unto M·, saying, "
6: 1, 22 the Lord spake unto M·, saying, "
7: 1 M· had fully set up the tabernacle, "
4 the Lord spake unto M·, saying, "
6 M· took the wagons and the oxen, "
11 the Lord said unto M·, They shall "
89 M· was gone into the tabernacle of "
8: 1 the Lord spake unto M·, saying, "
3 as the Lord commanded M·. "
4 which the Lord had shewed M·, so "
5 the Lord spake unto M·, saying, "
20 And M·, and Aaron, and all the "
20 Lord commanded M· concerning "
22 had commanded M· concerning the "
23 the Lord spake unto M·, saying, "
9: 1 And the Lord spake unto M· in the "
4 And M· spake unto the children of "
5 all that the Lord commanded M·, "
6 came before M· and before Aaron "
8 M· said unto them, Stand still, and "
9 the Lord spake unto M·, saying, "
23 of the Lord by the hand of M·. "
10: 1 the Lord spake unto M·, saying, "
13 of the Lord by the hand of M·. "
29 And M· said unto Hobab, the son of "
35 that M· said, Rise up, Lord, and let "
11: 2 And the people cried unto M·; and "
2 M· prayed unto the Lord, the fire "
10 Then M· heard the people weep "
10 greatly; M· also was displeased. "
11 M· said unto the Lord, Wherefore "
16 the Lord said unto M·, Gather unto "
21 M· said, The people, among whom "
23 said unto M·, Is the Lord's hand "
24 M· went out, and told the people the "
27 ran a young man, and told M·, and "
28 the son of Nun, the servant of M·, "
28 answered and said, My lord M·, "
29 M· said unto him, Enviest thou for "
30 M· gat him into the camp, he and "
12: 1 Aaron spake against M· because of "
2 Lord indeed spoken only by M·? "
3 the man M· was very meek, above "
4 the Lord spake suddenly unto M·, "
7 My servant M· is not so, who is "
8 to speak against my servant M·? "
11 And Aaron said unto M·, Alas, my "
13 M· cried unto the Lord, saying, "
14 And the Lord said unto M·, If her "
13: 1 the Lord spake unto M·, saying, "
3 M· by the commandment of the "
16 which M· sent to spy out the land. "
16 M· called Oshea the son of Nun "
17 M· sent them to spy out the land "
26 And they went and came to M·, and "
30 Caleb stilled the people before M·, "
14: 2 Israel murmured against M· and "
5 M· and Aaron fell on their faces "
11 the Lord said unto M·, How long "
13 And M· said unto the Lord, Then "
26 the Lord spake unto M· and unto "
36 the men, which M· sent to search "
39 M· told these sayings unto all the "
41 And M· said, Wherefore now do ye "
44 M·, departed not out of the camp. "
15: 1, 17 the Lord spake unto M·, saying, "
22 the Lord hath spoken unto M·, "
23 commanded you by the hand of M·, "
23 day that the Lord commanded M·,* "
33 brought him unto M· and Aaron, 4872
35 the Lord said unto M·, The man "
36 died; as the Lord commanded M·. "
37 the Lord spake unto M·, saying, "
16: 2 And they rose up before M·, with "
3 themselves together against M· and "
4 when M· heard it, he fell upon his "
8 M· said unto Korah, Hear, I pray "
12 And M· sent to call Dathan and "
15 M· was very wroth, and said unto "
16 M· said unto Korah, Be thou and "
18 of the congregation with M· and "
20 the Lord spake unto M· and unto "
23 the Lord spake unto M·, saying, "
25 M· rose up and went unto Dathan "
28 M· said, Hereby ye shall know that "
36 the Lord spake unto M·, saying, "
40 Lord said to him by the hand of M·. "
41 murmured against M· and against "
42 gathered against M· and against "
43 And M· and Aaron came before the "
44 the Lord spake unto M·, saying, "
46 M· said unto Aaron, Take a censer, "
47 Aaron took as M· commanded, and "

Nu 16: 50 returned unto M· unto the door of 4872
17: 1 the Lord spake unto M·, saying, "
6 And M· spake unto the children of "
7 M· laid up the rods before the Lord "
8 M· went into the tabernacle of "
9 M· brought out all the rods from "
10 Lord said unto M·, Bring Aaron's "
11 M· did so: as the Lord commanded "
12 children of Israel spake unto M·, "
18: 25 the Lord spake unto M·, saying, "
19: 1 the Lord spake unto M· and unto "
20: 2 together against M· and against "
3 And the people chode with M·, and "
6 And M· and Aaron went from the "
7 the Lord spake unto M·, saying, "
9 M· took the rod from before the "
10 And M· and Aaron gathered the "
11 M· lifted up his hand, and with his "
12 the Lord spake unto M· and Aaron, "
14 M· sent messengers from Kadesh "
23 spake unto M· and Aaron in mount "
27 M· did as the Lord commanded: "
28 M· stripped Aaron of his garments, "
28 M· and Eleazar came down from "
21: 5 spake against God, and against M·, "
7 Therefore the people came to M·, "
7 And M· prayed for the people. "
8 the Lord said unto M·, Make thee "
9 M· made a serpent of brass, and "
16 whereof the Lord spake unto M·, "
32 M· sent to spy out Jaazer, and they "
34 Lord said unto M·, Fear him not: "
25: 4 the Lord said unto M·, Take all the "
5 M· said unto the judges of Israel, "
6 woman in the sight of M·, and in "
10, 16 the Lord spake unto M·, saying, "
26: 1 the Lord spake unto M· and unto "
3 M· and Eleazar the priest spake "
4 as the Lord commanded M· and the "
9 who strove against M· and against "
52 the Lord spake unto M·, saying, "
59 bare unto Amram Aaron and M·, "
63 they that were numbered by M· and "
64 was not a man of them whom M· "
27: 2 they stood before M·, and before "
5 M· brought their cause before the "
6 the Lord spake unto M·, saying, "
11 as the Lord commanded M·. "
12 said unto M·, Get thee up into this "
15 M· spake unto the Lord, saying, "
18 the Lord said unto M·, Take thee "
22 M· did as the Lord commanded him: "
23 commanded by the hand of M·. "
28: 1 the Lord spake unto M·, saying, "
29: 40 And M· told the children of Israel "
40 all that the Lord commanded M·. "
30: 1 And M· spake unto the heads of the "
16 which the Lord commanded M·, "
31: 1 the Lord spake unto M·, saying, "
3 M· spake unto the people, saying, "
6 And M· sent them to the war, a "
7 as the Lord commanded M·; and "
12 the prey, and the spoil, unto M·, "
13 M·, and Eleazar the priest, and all "
14 M· was wroth with the officers of "
15 M· said unto them, Have ye saved "
21 which the Lord commanded M·; "
25 the Lord spake unto M·, saying, "
31 M· and Eleazar the priest did as the "
31 did as the Lord commanded M·. "
41 M· gave the tribute, which was the "
41 priest, as the Lord commanded M·. "
42 which M· divided from the men that "
47 M· took one portion of fifty, both of "
47 Lord; as the Lord commanded M·. "
48 of hundreds, came near unto M·: "
49 they said unto M·, Thy servants "
51, 54 M· and Eleazar the priest took "
32: 2 Reuben came and spake unto M·, "
6 M· said unto the children of Gad "
20 M· said unto them, If ye will do "
25 children of Reuben spake unto M·, "
28 M· commanded Eleazar the priest, "
29 M· said unto them, If the children "
33 M· gave unto them, even to the "
40 M· gave Gilead unto Machir the son "
33: 1 their armies under the hand of M· "
2 And M· wrote their goings out "
50 Lord spake unto M· in the plains of "
34: 1 the Lord spake unto M·, saying, "
13 And M· commanded the children of "
16 the Lord spake unto M·, saying, "
35: 1 Lord spake unto M· in the plains of "
9 the Lord spake unto M·, saying, "
36: 1 came near, and spake before M·, "
5 And M· commanded the children of "
10 Even as the Lord commanded M·, "
13 commanded by the hand of M· unto "
De 1: 1 which M· spake unto all Israel on "
3 that M· spake unto the children "
5 Moab, began M· to declare this law, "
4: 41 M· severed three cities on this side "
44 M· set before the children of Israel: "
45 which M· spake unto the children "
46 M· and the children of Israel smote, "
5: 1 M· called all Israel, and said unto "
27: 1 And M· with the elders of Israel "
9 And M· and the priests the Levites "
11 M· charged the people the same "
29: 1 which the Lord commanded M· to "
2 M· called unto all Israel, and said "
31: 1 And M· went and spake these words "
7 M· called unto Joshua, and said "
9 M· wrote this law, and delivered it "
10 And M· commanded them, saying, "
14 the Lord said unto M·, Behold, thy "

De 31:14 And M' and Joshua went, and 4872
16 the Lord said unto M', Behold, thou "
22 M' therefore wrote this song the "
24 M' had made an end of writing the "
25 That M' commanded the Levites, "
30 And M' spake in the ears of all the "
32:44 M' came and spake all the words of "
45 M' made an end of speaking all "
48 And the Lord spake unto M' that "
33: 1 M' the man of God blessed the "
4 M' commanded us a law, even the "
34: 1 And M' went up from the plains of "
5 So M' the servant of the Lord died "
7 M' was an hundred and twenty "
8 the children of Israel wept for M' "
8 and mourning for M' were ended. "
9 M' had laid his hands upon him: "
9 and did as the Lord commanded M'. "
10 prophet since in Israel like unto M', "
12 terror which M' shewed in the "
Jos 1: 1 after the death of M' the servant of "
2 M' my servant is dead; now "
3 given unto you, as I said unto M'. "
5 as I was with M', so I will be with "
7 which M' my servant commanded "
13 Remember the word which M' the "
14 in the land which M' gave you on "
15 which M' the Lord's servant gave "
17 we hearkened unto M' in all things, "
17 be with thee, as he was with M'. "
3: 7 as I was with M', so I will be with "
4:10 to all that M' commanded Joshua: "
12 of Israel, as M' spake unto them: "
14 they feared him, as they feared M', "
8:31 As M' the servant of the Lord "
31 written in the book of the law of M', "
32 the stones a copy of the law of M', "
33 as M' the servant of the Lord had "
35 a word of all that M' commanded, "
9:24 commanded his servant M' to give "
11:12 as M' the servant of the Lord "
15 As the Lord commanded M' his "
15 so did M' command Joshua, and so "
15 of all that the Lord commanded M'. "
20 them, as the Lord commanded M'. "
23 to all that the Lord said unto M'; "
12: 6 did M' the servant of the Lord and "
6 M' the servant of the Lord gave it "
13: 8 inheritance, which M' gave them, "
8 as M' the servant of the Lord gave "
12 for these did M' smite, and cast "
15 And M' gave unto the tribe of the "
21 whom M' smote with the princes of "
24 M' gave inheritance unto the tribe "
29 M' gave inheritance unto the half "
32 countries which M' did distribute "
33 Levi M' gave not any inheritance: "
14: 2 commanded by the hand of M', for "
3 M' had given the inheritance of two "
5 As the Lord commanded M', so "
6 the thing that the Lord said unto M' "
7 M' the servant of the Lord sent me "
9 And M' sware on that day, saying, "
10 the Lord spake this word unto M', "
11 I was in the day that M' sent me: "
17: 4 Lord commanded M' to give us an "
18: 7 M' the servant of the Lord gave "
20: 2 spake unto you by the hand of M': "
21: 2 commanded by the hand of M' to "
8 commanded by the hand of M'. "
22: 2 all that M' the servant of the Lord "
4 M' the servant of the Lord gave "
5 M' the servant of the Lord charged "
7 M' had given possession in Bashan: "
9 word of the Lord by the hand of M'. "
23: 6 written in the book of the law of M', "
24: 5 I sent M' also and Aaron, and I "
J'g 1:20 Hebron unto Caleb, as M' said: "
3: 4 their fathers by the hand of M'. "
4:11 of Hobab the father in law of M', "
1Sa 12: 6 Lord that advanced M' and Aaron, "
8 then the Lord sent M' and Aaron, "
1Ki 2: 3 as it is written in the law of M', "
8: 9 stone, which M' put there at Horeb, "
53 as thou spakest by the hand of M' "
56 he promised by the hand of M' his "
2Ki 14: 6 in the book of the law of M', "
18: 4 brasen serpent that M' had made: "
6 which the Lord commanded M'. "
12 that M' the servant of the Lord "
21: 8 that my servant M' commanded "
23:25 according to all the law of M'; "
1Ch 6: 3 children of Amram; Aaron, and M', "
49 to all that M' the servant of God "
15:15 as M' commanded according to "
21:29 which M' made in the wilderness, "
22:13 which the Lord charged M' with "
23:13 sons of Amram; Aaron and M': "
14 concerning M' the man of God, "
15 The sons of M' were, Gershom, and "
26:24 the son of Gershom, the son of M', "
2Ch 1: 3 M'...servant of the Lord had made "
5:10 two tables which M' put therein "
8:13 to the commandment of M', "
23:18 as it is written in the law of M', "
24: 6 commandment of M' the servant of "
9 that M' the servant of God laid upon "
25: 4 written in the law in the book of M', "
30:16 to the law of M' the man of God: "
33: 8 the ordinances by the hand of M'. "
34:14 of the law of the Lord given by M'. "
35: 6 word of the Lord by the hand of M'. "
12 as it is written in the book of M'. "
Ezr 3: 2 in the law of M' the man of God. "
6:18 as it is written in the book of M'. 4873
7: 6 a ready scribe in the law of M', 4872

Ne 1: 7 thou commandest thy servant M'. 4872
8 thou commandest thy servant M', "
8: 1 to bring the book of the law of M', "
14 the Lord had commanded by M', "
9:14 by the hand of M' thy servant: "
10:29 was given by M' the servant of God, "
13: 1 that day they read in the book of M' "
Ps 77:20 flock by the hand of M' and Aaron. "
90: title A Prayer of M' the man of God. "
99: 6 M' and Aaron among his priests, "
103: 7 He made known his ways unto M', "
105:26 He sent M' his servant; and Aaron "
106:16 They envied M' also in the camp, "
23 had not M' his chosen stood before "
32 it went ill with M' for their sakes: "
Isa 63:11 the days of old, M', and his people, "
12 led them by the right hand of M' "
Jer 15: 1 M' and Samuel stood before me, "
Da 9:11 in the law of M' the servant of God, "
13 As it is written in the law of M', "
Mic 6: 4 I sent before thee M', Aaron, and "
Mal 4: 4 ye the law of M' my servant, which "
M't 8: 4 offer the gift that M' commanded, 3475
17: 3 appeared unto them M' and Elias "
4 one for thee, and one for M', and "
19: 7 Why did M' then command to give "
8 M' because of the hardness of your "
22:24 M' said, If a man die, having no "
M'r 1:44 those things which M' commanded, "
7:10 M' said, Honour thy father and thy "
9: 4 appeared unto them Elias with M': "
5 one for thee, and one for M', and "
10: 3 them, What did M' command you? "
4 M' suffered...a bill of divorcement, "
12:19 M' wrote...If a man's brother die, "
26 have ye not read in the book of M', "
Lu 2:22 the law of M' were accomplished, "
5:14 according as M' commanded, for a "
9:30 two men, which were M' and Elias: "
33 one for thee, and one for M', and "
16:29 They have M' and the prophets; "
31 they hear not M' and the prophets, "
20:28 M' wrote...If any man's brother die, "
37 even M' shewed at the bush, when "
24:27 And beginning at M' and all the "
44 which were written in the law of M', "
Joh 1:17 For the law was given by M', but "
45 found him, of whom M' in the law, "
3:14 as M' lifted up the serpent in the "
5:45 you, even M', in whom ye trust. "
46 For had ye believed M', ye would "
6:32 M' gave you not that bread from "
7:19 Did not M' give you the law, and "
22 M'...gave unto you circumcision; "
22 (not because it is of M', but of the "
23 the law of M' should not be broken; "
8: 5 M' in the law commanded us, that "
9:29 We know that God spake unto M': "
Ac 3:22 For M' truly said unto the fathers, "
6:11 blasphemous words against M', "
14 the customs which M' delivered us. "
7:20 In which time M' was born, and "
22 M' was learned in all the wisdom "
29 Then fled M' at this saying, and "
31 When M' saw it, he wondered at "
32 Then M' trembled, and durst not "
35 This M' whom they refused, saying, "
37 This is that M', which said unto the "
40 for as for this M', which brought us "
44 had appointed, speaking unto M', "
13:39 not be justified by the law of M'. "
15: 1 circumcised after the manner of M', "
5 command...to keep the law of M'. "
21 M' of old time hath in every city "
21:21 among the Gentiles to forsake M', "
26:22 the prophets and M' did say should "
28:23 both out of the law of M', and out "
Ro 5:14 death reigned from Adam to M', "
9:15 he saith to M', I will have mercy "
10: 5 M' describeth the righteousness "
19 First M' saith, I will provoke you "
1Co 9: 9 For it is written in the law of M', "
10: 2 all baptized unto M' in the cloud "
2Co 3: 7 not stedfastly behold the face of M' "
13 not as M', which put a vail over his "
15 unto this day, when M' is read, "
2Ti 3: 8 Jannes and Jambres withstood M', "
Heb 3: 2 as also M' was faithful in all his "
3 worthy of more glory than M', "
5 And M' verily was faithful in all his "
16 all that came out of Egypt by M'. "
7:14 of which tribe M' spake nothing "
8: 5 as M' was admonished of God when "
9:19 when M' had spoken every precept "
11:23 By faith M', when he was born, was "
24 By faith M', when he was come to "
12:21 that M' said, I exceedingly fear and "
Jude 9 he disputed about the body of M', "
Re 15: 3 sing the song of M' the servant of "

Moses' (mo'-zez)
Ex 17:12 M' hands were heavy; and they 4872
18: 1 priest of Midian, M' father in law, "
2 Then Jethro, M' father in law, took "
2 took Zipporah, M' wife, after he "
5 M' father in law, came with his "
12 M' father in law, took a burnt "
12 to eat bread with M' father in law "
14 M' father in law saw all that he did "
17 And M' father in law said unto him, "
32:19 M' anger waxed hot, and he cast "
34:29 two tables of testimony in M' hand, "
35 that the skin of M' face shone: and "
Le 8:29 ram of consecration it was M' part; "
Nu 10:29 the Midianite, M' father in law, "
Jos 1: 1 Joshua the son of Nun, M' minister, "
J'g 1:16 of the Kenite, M' father in law, "
M't 23: 2 and the Pharisees sit in M' seat: 3475
Joh 9:28 disciple; but we are M' disciples.* "
Heb 10:28 that despised M' law died without "

most See also ALMOST; FOREMOST; HINDERMOST; HINDMOST; INNERMOST; MIDDLEMOST; NETHERMOST; OUTMOST; UTMOST; UTTERMOST.
Ge 14:18 was the priest of the m' high God. 5945
19 be Abram of the m' high God, "
20 blessed be the m' high God, which "
22 unto the Lord, the m' high God, "
Ex 26:33 the holy place and the m' holy. 6944
34 the testimony in the m' holy place. "
29:37 and it shall be an altar m' holy: "
30:10 it is m' holy unto the Lord. "
29 them, that they may be m' holy: "
36 thee: it shall be unto you m' holy. "
40:10 and it shall be an altar m' holy. "
Le 2: 3, 10 a thing m' holy of the offerings "
6:17 it is m' holy, as is the sin offering, "
25 killed before the Lord: it is m' holy. "
29 shall eat thereof: it is m' holy. "
7: 1 the trespass offering: it is m' holy. "
6 eaten in the holy place: it is m' holy. "
10:12 beside the altar: for it is m' holy. "
17 the holy place, seeing it is m' holy, "
14:13 the trespass offering: it is m' holy: "
21:22 both of the m' holy, and of the holy. "
24: 9 is m' holy unto him of the offerings "
27:28 every devoted thing is m' holy unto "
Nu 4: 4 about the m' holy things: "
19 approach unto the m' holy things: "
18: 9 shall be thine of the m' holy things, "
9 be m' holy for thee and thy sons. "
10 In the m' holy place shalt thou eat "
24:16 knew the knowledge of the m' High, "
De 32: 8 When the m' High divided to the "
2Sa 22:14 and the m' High uttered his voice. "
23:19 Was he not m' honourable of three?
1Ki 6:16 oracle, even for the m' holy place. 6944
7:50 the inner house, the m' holy place, "
8: 6 of the house, to the m' holy place, "
1Ch 6:49 all the work of the place m' holy, "
23:13 should sanctify the m' holy things, "
2Ch 3: 8 And he made the m' holy house, "
10 in the m' holy house he made two "
4:22 doors thereof for the m' holy place, "
5: 7 into the m' holy place, even under "
31:14 the Lord, and the m' holy things. "
Ne 7:65 should not eat of the m' holy things, "
Es 6: 9 one of the king's m' noble princes, 6579
Job 34:17 thou condemn him that is m' just?*3524
Ps 7:17 to the name of the Lord m' high. 5945
9: 2 to thy name, O thou m' High. "
21: 6 hast made him m' blessed for ever: "
7 the mercy of the m' High he shall 5945
45: 3 sword upon thy thigh, O m' mighty,*
46: 4 of the tabernacles of the m' High. 5945
47: 2 For the Lord m' high is terrible; he "
50:14 pay thy vows unto the m' High: "
56: 2 against me, O thou m' High. *4791
57: 2 I will cry unto God m' high; unto 5945
73:11 there knowledge in the m' High? "
77:10 of the right hand of the m' High. "
78:17 by provoking the m' High in the "
56 and provoked the m' high God, and "
83:18 art the m' High over all the earth. "
91: 1 in the secret place of the m' High "
9 even the m' High, thy habitation; "
92: 1 praises unto thy name, O m' High: "
8 thou, Lord, art m' high for evermore.*
107:11 the counsel of the m' High: 5945
Pr 20: 6 M' men will proclaim every one 7230
Ca 5:11 His head is as the m' fine gold, 3800
16 His mouth is m' sweet: yea, he is
8: 6 which hath a m' vehement flame.*
Isa 14:14 clouds; I will be like the m' High. 5945
26: 7 m' upright, dost weigh the path of the*
Jer 6:26 an only son, m' bitter lamentation:
50:31 I am against thee, O thou m' proud,*
32 the m' proud shall stumble and fall,*
La 3:35 man before the face of the m' High, 5945
38 Out of the mouth of the m' High "
4: 1 how is the m' fine gold changed! 2896
Eze 2: 7 forbear: for they are m' rebellious.
23:12 and rulers clothed m' gorgeously.
33:28 For I will lay the land m' desolate,*
29 when I have laid the land m' desolate*
35: 3 and I will make thee m' desolate.*
7 I make mount Seir m' desolate, 8077
41: 4 unto me, This is the m' holy place. 6944
42:13 Lord shall eat the m' holy things: "
13 shall they lay the m' holy things, "
43:12 round about shall be m' holy. "
44:13 holy things, in the m' holy place: "
45: 3 sanctuary and the m' holy place. "
48:12 be unto them a thing m' holy "
Da 3:20 commanded the m' mighty men* 2429
26 ye servants of the m' high God, 5943
4:17 may know that the m' High ruleth "
24 this is the decree of the m' High, "
25, 32 know that the m' High ruleth in "
34 and I blessed the m' High, and I "
5:18 m' high God gave Nebuchadnezzar "
21 knew that the m' high God ruled "
7:18 saints of the m' High shall take 5946
22 given to the saints of the m' High; "
25 great words against the m' High, 5943
25 wear out the saints of the m' High, 5946
27 of the saints of the m' High, whose 5945
9:24 and to anoint the m' Holy. 6944
11:15 mount, and take the m' fenced cities:*
39 he do in the m' strong holds with *4581
Ho 7:16 return, but not to the m' High: *5920
11: 7 they called them to the m' High, * "
12:14 provoked him to anger m' bitterly: 8563
Mic 7: 4 the m' upright is sharper than a thorn

M't 11: 20 m· of his mighty works were done, 4118
M'r 5: 7 thou Son of the m· high God? I 5310
Lu 1: 1 are m· surely believed among us, *
3 in order, m· excellent Theophilus, 2903
7: 42 which of them will love him m·? 4119
43 that he, to whom he forgave m·. "
8: 28 Jesus, thou Son of God m· high? 5310
Ac 7: 48 m· High dwelleth not in temples "
16: 17 the servants of the m· high God, "
20: 38 Sorrowing m· of all for the words 3122
23: 26 unto the m· excellent governor 2903
24: 3 and in all places, m· noble Felix, "
26: 5 that after the m· straitest sect of our
25 I am not mad, m· noble Festus; 2903
1Co 14: 27 let it be by two, or at the m· by three, 4119
15: 19 we are of all men m· miserable.
2Co 12: 9 M· gladly therefore will I rather 2236
Heb 7: 1 Salem, priest of the m· high God, 5310
Jude 20 yourselves on your m· holy faith, 40
Re 18: 12 manner vessels of m· precious wood,
21: 11 was like unto a stone m· precious,

Most-High See MOST and HIGH.

Most-Holy See MOST and HOLY.

mote
M't 7: 3 the m· that is in thy brother's eye, 2595
4 me pull out the m· out of thine eye; "
5 out the m· out of thy brother's eye. "
Lu 6: 41 the m· that is in thy brother's eye, "
42 pull out the m· that is in thine eye, "
42 the m· that is in thy brother's eye. "

moth See also MOTHEATEN.
Job 4: 19 which are crushed before the m·? 6211
13: 28 as a garment that is m· eaten. "
27: 18 He buildeth his house as a m·, and "
Ps 39: 11 beauty to consume away like a m·: "
Isa 50: 9 garment; the m· shall eat them up. "
51: 8 For the m· shall eat them up like a "
Ho 5: 12 will I be unto Ephraim as a m·, "
M't 6: 19 where m· and rust doth corrupt, 4597
20 where neither m· nor rust doth "
Lu 12: 33 approacheth, neither m· corrupteth. "

motheaten See also MOTH and EATEN.
Jas 5: 2 and your garments are m·. 4598

mother See also GRANDMOTHER; MOTHERS'; MOTHERS.
Ge 2: 24 a man leave his father and his m·, 517
3: 20 because she was the m· of all living. "
17: 16 and she shall be a m· of nations; "
20: 12 but not the daughter of my m·; and 517
21: 21 his m· took him a wife out of the "
24: 53 and to her m· precious things. "
55 her m· said, Let the damsel abide "
60 be thou the m· of thousands of "
67 her into his m· Sarah's tent, and 517
27: 11 And Jacob said to Rebekah his m·, "
13 his m· said unto him, Upon me be "
14 and brought them to his m·: and "
14 and his m· made savoury meat, such "
28: 5 of Rebekah, Jacob's and Esau's m·. "
7 Jacob obeyed his father and his m·, "
30: 14 and brought them unto his m· Leah. "
32: 11 me, and the m· with the children. "
37: 10 I and thy m· and thy brethren indeed "
44: 20 he alone is left of his m·, and his "
Ex 2: 8 maid went and called the child's m·. "
20: 12 Honour thy father and thy m·: that "
21: 15 that smiteth his father, or his m·, "
17 he that curseth his father, or his m·, "
Le 18: 7 father, or the nakedness of thy m·, "
7 she is thy m·; thou shalt not "
9 of thy father, or daughter of thy m·, "
19: 3 Ye shall fear every man his m·, and "
20: 9 that curseth his father or his m· "
9 he hath cursed his father or his m·; "
14 If a man take a wife and her m·, it is "
21: 2 for his m·, and for his father, and for "
11 himself for his father, or for his m·; "
Nu 6: 7 unclean for his father, or for his m·, "
26: 59 whom her m· bare to Levi in Egypt: *
De 5: 16 Honour thy father and thy m·, as 517
13: 6 the son of thy m·, or thy son, or thy "
21: 13 bewail her father and her m· a full "
18 of his father, or the voice of his m·, "
19 father and his m· lay hold on him, "
22: 15 father of the damsel, and her m·, "
27: 16 setteth light by his father or his m·. "
22 father, or the daughter of his m·. "
23 he that lieth with his m· in law. 2859
33: 9 said unto his father and to his m·, 517
Jos 2: 13 save alive my father, and my m·, "
18 shalt bring thy father, and thy m·, "
6: 23 and her father, and her m·, and her "
J'g 5: 7 arose, that I arose a m· in Israel. "
28 The m· of Sisera looked out at a "
8: 19 brethren, even the sons of my m·: "
14: 2 up, and told his father and his m·, "
3 Then his father and his m· said unto "
4 But his father and his m· knew not "
5 his father and his m·, to Timnath, "
6 he told not...his m· what he had done. "
9 came to his father and m·, and he "
16 have not told it my father nor my m·, "
17: 2 he said unto his m·, The eleven "
2 his m· said, Blessed be thou of the "
3 hundred shekels of silver to his m·, "
3 his m· said, I had wholly dedicated "
4 he restored the money unto his m·; "
4 his m· took two hundred shekels of "
Ru 1: 14 and Orpah kissed her m· in law; 2545
2: 11 hast done unto thy m· in law since "
11 hast left thy father and thy m·, 517
18 her m· in law saw what she had 2545
19 And her m· in law said unto her, "
19 And she shewed her m· in law with "
2: 23 and dwelt with her m· in law. 2545
3: 1 Naomi her m· in law said unto her, "
6 to all that her m· in law bade her. "
16 when she came to her m· in law, "
17 Go not empty unto thy m· in law. "
1Sa 2: 19 his m· made him a little coat, and 517
15: 33 so shall thy m· be childless among "
22: 3 Let my father and my m·, I pray "
2Sa 17: 25 sister to Zeruiah Joab's m·. "
19: 37 grave of my father and of my m·. "
20: 19 to destroy a city and a m· in Israel: "
1Ki 1: 6 and his m· bare him after Absalom. *
11 unto Bath-sheba the m· of Solomon, 517
2: 13 to Bath-sheba the m· of Solomon. "
19 a seat to be set for the king's m·; "
20 king said unto her, Ask on, my m·: "
22 answered and said unto his m·, "
3: 27 no wise slay it: she is the m· thereof. "
15: 13 And also Maachah his m·, even her "
17: 23 and delivered him unto his m·: "
19: 20 pray thee, kiss my father and my m·, "
22: 52 his father, and in the way of his m·, "
2Ki 3: 2 not like his father, and like his m·: "
13 and to the prophets of thy m·. And "
4: 19 said to a lad, Carry him to his m·. "
20 and brought him to his m·, he sat "
30 And the m· of the child said, As the "
9: 22 thy m· Jezebel and her witchcrafts "
11: 1 Athaliah the m· of Ahaziah saw "
24: 12 his m·, and his servants, and his "
15 and the king's m·, and the king's "
1Ch 2: 26 Atarah, she was the m· of Onam. "
4: 9 and his m· called his name Jabez, "
2Ch 15: 16 Maachah the m· of Asa the king, he "
22: 3 for his m· was his counsellor to do "
10 Athaliah the m· of Ahaziah saw that "
Es 2: 7 she had neither father nor m·, and "
7 when her father and m· were dead, "
Job 17: 14 Thou art my m·, and my sister. "
Ps 27: 10 my father and my m· forsake me, "
35: 14 as one that mourneth for his m·. "
51: 5 and in sin did my m· conceive me. "
109: 14 not the sin of his m· be blotted out. "
113: 9 and to be a joyful m· of children. "
131: 2 as a child that is weaned of his m·: "
Pr 1: 8 and forsake not the law of thy m·: "
4: 3 only beloved in the sight of my m·. "
6: 20 and forsake not the law of thy m·: "
10: 1 foolish son is the heaviness of his m·. "
15: 20 but a foolish man despiseth his m·. "
19: 26 chaseth away his m·, is a son that "
20: 20 Whoso curseth his father or his m·, "
23: 22 despise not thy m· when she is old. "
25 Thy father and thy m· shall be glad, "
28: 24 Whoso robbeth his father or his m·, "
29: 15 to himself bringeth his m· to shame. "
30: 11 father, and doth not bless their m·. "
17 despiseth to obey his m·, the ravens "
31: 1 prophecy that his m· taught him. "
Ca 3: 11 wherewith his m· crowned him in "
6: 9 she is the only one of her m·, she is "
8: 1 that sucked the breasts of my m·! "
5 there thy m· brought thee forth: "
Isa 8: 4 to cry, My father, and my m·, the "
49: 1 from the bowels of my m· hath he "
50: 1 transgressions is your m· put away. "
66: 13 As one whom his m· comforteth, so "
Jer 15: 8 against the m· of the young men a "
10 Woe is me, my m·, that thou hast "
16: 7 for their father or for their m·. "
20: 14 not the day wherein my m· bare me "
17 my m· might have been my grave, "
22: 26 thee out, and thy m· that bare thee, "
50: 12 Your m· shall be sore confounded; "
Eze 16: 3 an Amorite, and thy m· an Hittite. "
44 As is the m·, so is her daughter. "
45 your m· was an Hittite, and your "
19: 2 And say, What is thy m·? A lioness: "
10 Thy m· is like a vine in thy blood, "
22: 7 they set light by father and m·: in "
23: 2 women, the daughters of one m·: "
44: 25 but for father, or for m·, or for son, "
Ho 2: 2 Plead with your m·, plead: for she "
5 For their m· hath played the harlot: "
4: 5 the night, and I will destroy thy m·. "
10: 14 m· was dashed in pieces upon her "
Mic 7: 6 daughter riseth up against her m·, "
6 in law against her m· in law; 2545
Zec 13: 3, 3 father and his m· that begat him 517
M't 1: 18 as his m· Mary was espoused to 3384
2: 11 the young child with Mary his m·, "
13 take the young child and his m·, "
14 took the young child and his m· by "
20 take the young child and his m·, "
21 took the young child and his m·, "
8: 14 he saw his wife's m· laid, and sick 3994
10: 35 and the daughter against her m·, 3384
35 in law against her m· in law. 3994
37 that loveth father or m· more than 3384
12: 46 his m· and his brethren stood "
47 thy m· and thy brethren stand "
48 Who is my m·? and who are my "
49 behold my m· and my brethren! "
50 is my brother, and sister, and m·. "
13: 55 son? is not his m· called Mary? "
14: 8 being before instructed of her m·, "
11 and she brought it to her m·. "
15: 4 saying, Honour thy father and m·: "
4 that curseth father or m·, let him "
5 shall say to his father or his m·, "
6 honour not his father or his m·, *
19: 5 shall a man leave father and m·, "
19 Honour thy father and thy m·: and, "
29 father, or m·, or wife, or children, "
20: 20 to him the m· of Zebedee's children "
27: 56 Mary the m· of James and Joses, "
M't 27: 56 and the m· of Zebedee's children. 3384
M'r 1: 30 But Simon's wife's m· lay sick of a 3994
3: 31 then his brethren and his m·, 3384
32 thy m· and thy brethren without "
33 Who is my m·, or my brethren? "
34 Behold my m· and my brethren! "
35 my brother, and my sister, and m·. "
5: 40 father and the m· of the damsel, "
6: 24 said unto her m·, What shall I ask? "
28 and the damsel gave it to her m·. "
7: 10 Honour thy father and thy m·; "
10 Whoso curseth father or m·, let him "
11 man shall say to his father or m·, "
12 do ought for his father or his m·; "
10: 7 shall a man leave his father and m·, "
19 not, Honour thy father and m·. "
29 or sisters, or father, or m·, or wife, "
15: 40 Mary the m· of James the less and "
47 Mary the m· of Joses beheld where he
16: 1 Mary the m· of James, and Salome
Lu 1: 43 the m· of my Lord should come to 3384
60 his m· answered and said, Not so; "
2: 33 Joseph and his m· marvelled at "
34 and said unto Mary his m·, Behold, "
43 Joseph and his m· knew not of it. *
48 and his m· said unto him, Son, why "
51 his m· kept all these sayings in her "
4: 38 Simon's wife's m· was taken with 3994
7: 12 the only son of his m·, and she 3384
15 and he delivered him to his m·. "
8: 19 Then came to him his m· and his "
20 Thy m· and thy brethren stand "
21 My m· and my brethren are these "
51 father and the m· of the maiden. "
12: 53 the m· against the daughter, and "
53 and the daughter against the m·; "
53 m· in law against the daughter 3994
53 in law against the m· in law. "
14: 26 hate not his father, and m·, and 3384
18: 20 Honour thy father and thy m·. "
24: 10 Joanna, and Mary the m· of James, "
Joh 2: 1 and the m· of Jesus was there: 3384
3 m· of Jesus saith unto him, They "
5 His m· saith unto the servants, "
12 and his m·, and his brethren, and "
6: 42 whose father and m· we know? how "
19: 25 stood by the cross of Jesus his m·, "
26 When Jesus therefore saw his m·, "
26 he saith unto his m·, Woman, "
27 he to the disciple, Behold thy m·! "
Ac 1: 14 and Mary the m· of Jesus, and with "
12: 12 the house of Mary the m· of John, "
Ro 16: 13 in the Lord, and his m· and mine. "
Ga 4: 26 is free, which is the m· of us all. "
Eph 5: 31 shall a man leave his father and m· "
6: 2 Honour thy father and m·; which "
2Ti 1: 5 Lois, and thy m· Eunice; and I "
Heb 7: 3 Without father, without m·, without 282
Re 17: 5 Great, The M· Of Harlots And 3384

mother-in-law See MOTHER and LAW.

mother's
Ge 24: 28 told them of her m· house these 517
67 was comforted after his m· death. "
27: 29 let thy m· sons bow down to thee: "
28: 2 the house of Bethuel thy m· father; "
2 daughters of Laban thy m· brother. "
29: 10 daughter of Laban his m· brother, "
10 the sheep of Laban his m· brother, "
10 the flock of Laban his m· brother. "
43: 29 his brother Benjamin, his m· son, "
Ex 23: 19 shalt not seethe a kid in his m· milk. "
34: 26 shalt not seethe a kid in his m· milk. "
Le 18: 13 the nakedness of thy m· sister: "
13 for she is thy m· near kinswoman. "
20: 17 or his m· daughter, and see her "
19 the nakedness of thy m· sister, nor "
24: 11 (and his m· name was Shelomith, "
Nu 12: 12 he cometh out of his m· womb. "
De 14: 21 shalt not seethe a kid in his m· milk. "
J'g 9: 1 to Shechem unto his m· brethren, "
1 family of the house of his m· father, "
3 his m· brethren spake of him in the "
16: 17 unto God from my m· womb: if I "
Ru 1: 8 Go, return each to her m· house: "
1Sa 20: 30 the confusion of thy m· nakedness? "
1Ki 11: 26 whose m· name was Zeruah, a "
14: 21, 31 And his m· name was Naamah "
15: 2, 10 And his m· name was Maachah, "
22: 42 And his m· name was Azubah the "
2Ki 8: 26 And his m· name was Athaliah, the "
12: 1 m· name was Zibiah of Beer-sheba. "
14: 2 And his m· name was Jehoaddan of "
15: 2 And his m· name was Jecholiah of "
33 And his m· name was Jerusha, the "
18: 2 m· name also was Abi, the daughter "
21: 1 And his m· name was Hephzi-bah. "
19 his m· name was Meshullemeth, "
22: 1 And his m· name was Jedidah, the "
23: 31 And his m· name was Hamutal, the "
36 And his m· name was Zebudah, the "
24: 8 And his m· name was Nehushta, the "
18 And his m· name was Hamutal, the "
2Ch 12: 13 And his m· name was Naamah an "
13: 2 His m· name also was Michaiah the "
20: 31 And his m· name was Azubah the "
22: 2 His m· name also was Athaliah the "
24: 1 His m· name also was Zibiah of "
25: 1 And his m· name was Jehoaddan of "
26: 3 His m· name also was Jecoliah of "
27: 1 His m· name also was Jerushah, the "
29: 1 And his m· name was Abijah, the "
Job 1: 21 Naked came I out of my m· womb, "
3: 10 shut not up the doors of my m· womb, "
31: 18 guided her from my m· womb;) 517
Ps 22: 9 when I was upon my m· breasts. "

Ps 22:10 thou art my God from my m' belly. *517
50:20 thou slanderest thine own m' son. "
69: 8 and an alien unto my m' children. "
71: 6 that took me out of my m' bowels: "
139:13 hast covered me in my m' womb. "
Ec 5:15 As he came forth of his m' womb, "
Ca 1: 6 my m' children were angry with me; "
3: 4 had brought him into my m' house, "
8: 2 and bring thee into my m' house, "
Isa 50: 1 is the bill of your m' divorcement, "
Jer 52: 1 And his m' name was Hamutal the "
Eze 16:45 Thou art thy m' daughter, that "
M't 19:12 were so born from their m' womb: 3384
Lu 1:15 Ghost, even from his m' womb. "
Joh 3: 4 the second time into his m' womb, "
19:25 And his m' sister, Mary the wife of "
Ac 3: 2 man lame from his m' womb was "
14: 8 being a cripple from his m' womb, "
Ga 1:15 separated me from my m' womb, "

mothers See also MOTHERS'.
Isa 49:23 and their queens thy nursing m': "
Jer 16: 3 concerning their m' that bare them, 517
La 2:12 They say to their m', Where is corn "
5: 3 fatherless, our m' are as widows. "
M'r 10:30 and sisters, and m', and children, 3384
1Ti 1: 9 of fathers and murderers of m', 3389
5: 2 The elder women as m'; the 3384

mothers'
La 2:12 poured out into their m' bosom. 517

motions
Ro 7: 5 the m' of sin, which were by the *3804

mouldy
Jos 9: 5 their provision was dry and m'. 5350
12 now, behold, it is dry, and it is m': "

mount See also MOUNTAIN; MOUNTED; MOUNTING; MOUNTS.
Ge 10:30 unto Sephar a m' of the east. *2022
14: 6 And the Horites in their m' Seir, 2042
22:14 in the m' of the Lord it shall be 2022
31:21 set his face toward the m' Gilead. * "
23 they overtook him in the m' Gilead.* "
25 had pitched his tent in the m': * "
25 Laban...pitched in the m' of Gilead.* "
54 Jacob offered sacrifice upon the m',* "
54 and tarried all night in the m'. * "
36: 8 Thus dwelt Esau in m' Seir: Esau "
9 father of the Edomites in m' Seir: "
Ex 4:27 went, and met him in the m' of God, "
18: 5 he encamped at the m' of God: "
19: 2 there Israel camped before the m'. "
11 sight of all the people upon m' Sinai. "
12 that ye go not up into the m', or "
12 whosoever toucheth the m' shall be "
13 long, they shall come up to the m'. "
14 Moses went down from the m' unto "
16 and a thick cloud upon the m', and "
17 stood at the nether part of the m'. "
18 m' Sinai was altogether on a smoke, "
18 and the whole m' quaked greatly. "
20 the Lord came down upon m' Sinai, "
20 on the top of the m': and the Lord "
20 called Moses up to the top of the m'; "
23 people cannot come up to m' Sinai: "
23 us, saying, Set bounds about the m', "
24:12 Moses, Come up to me into the m', "
13 Moses went up into the m' of God. "
15 And Moses went up into the m', "
15 and a cloud covered the m'. "
16 of the Lord abode upon m' Sinai, "
17 devouring fire on the top of the m' "
18 cloud, and gat him up into the m': "
18 Moses was in the m' forty days and "
25:40 which was shewed thee in the m'. "
26:30 which was shewed thee in the m'. "
27: 8 as it was shewed thee in the m', so "
31:18 communing with him upon m' Sinai, "
32: 1 delayed to come down out of the m', "
15 turned, and went down from the m', "
19 and brake them beneath the m'. "
33: 6 of their ornaments by the m' Horeb. "
34: 2 up in the morning unto m' Sinai, "
2 there to me in the top of the m'. "
3 man be seen throughout all the m'; "
3 flocks nor herds feed before that m'. "
4 and went up unto m' Sinai, as "
29 Moses came down from m' Sinai "
29 when he came down from the m', "
32 had spoken with him in m' Sinai. "
Le 7:38 Lord commanded Moses in m' Sinai, "
25: 1 Lord spake unto Moses in m' Sinai, "
26:46 in m' Sinai by the hand of Moses. "
27:34 for the children of Israel in m' Sinai. "
Nu 3: 1 Lord spake with Moses in m' Sinai. "
10:33 departed from the m' of the Lord "
20:22 Kadesh, and came unto m' Hor. "
23 unto Moses and Aaron in m' Hor, "
25 and bring them up unto m' Hor: "
27 and they went up into m' Hor in the "
28 died there in the top of the m': "
28 Eleazar came down from the m'. "
21: 4 they journeyed from m' Hor by the "
27:12 Get thee up into this m' Abarim, * "
28: 6 ordained in m' Sinai for a sweet "
33:23 and pitched in m' Shapher. "
24 And they removed from m' Shapher, "
37 Kadesh, and pitched in m' Hor, "
38 the priest went up into m' Hor at "
39 years old when he died in m' Hor. "
41 they departed from m' Hor, and "
34: 7 ye shall point out for you m' Hor: "
8 From m' Hor ye shall point out "
De 1: 2 from Horeb by the way of m' Seir "
6 have dwelt long enough in this m':* "
7 go to the m' of the Amorites, and * "
De 2: 1 we compassed m' Seir many days. 2022
5 I have given m' Seir unto Esau for "
3: 8 the river of Arnon unto m' Hermon; "
12 the river Arnon, and half m' Gilead,* "
4:48 unto m' Sion, which is Hermon, "
5: 4 with you face to face in the m' out "
5 fire, and went not up into the m';) "
22 unto all your assembly in the m' "
9: 9 When I was gone up into the m' to "
9 I abode in the m' forty days and "
10 the Lord spake with you in the m' "
15 turned and came down from the m', "
15 and the m' burned with fire: and "
21 brook that descended out of the m'. "
10: 1 and come up unto me into the m', "
3 the first, and went up into the m', "
4 the Lord spake unto you in the m' "
5 came down from the m', and put "
10 I stayed in the m', according to the "
11:29 put the blessing upon m' Gerizim, "
29 and the curse upon m' Ebal. "
27: 4 in m' Ebal, and thou shalt plaister "
12 stand upon m' Gerizim to bless the "
13 shall stand upon m' Ebal to curse; "
32:49 unto m' Nebo, which is in the land "
50 die in the m' whither thou goest up, "
50 Aaron thy brother died in m' Hor, "
33: 2 he shined forth from m' Paran, and "
Jos 8:30 the Lord God of Israel in m' Ebal, "
33 of them over against m' Gerizim, "
33 half of them over against m' Ebal; "
11:17 from the m' Halak, that goeth up "
17 of Lebanon under m' Hermon: "
12: 1 the river Arnon unto m' Hermon, "
5 And reigned in m' Hermon, and in "
7 Lebanon even unto the m' Halak, "
13: 5 from Baal-gad under m' Hermon "
11 all m' Hermon, and all Bashan unto "
19 Zareth-Shahar in...m' of the valley, "
15: 9 went out to the cities of m' Ephron; "
10 from Baalah westward unto m' Seir, "
10 along unto the side of m' Jearim, "
11 And passed along to m' Baalah, and "
16: 1 Jericho throughout m' Beth-el, * "
17:15 if m' Ephraim be too narrow for * "
19:50 Timnath-serah in m' Ephraim: * "
20: 7 Kedesh in Galilee in m' Naphtali, * "
7 and Shechem in m' Ephraim, and* "
21:21 with her suburbs in m' Ephraim, * "
24: 4 I gave unto Esau m' Seir, to possess "
30 which is in m' Ephraim, on the * "
33 was given him in m' Ephraim. * "
J'g 1:35 Amorites would dwell in m' Heres "
2: 9 in the m' of Ephraim, on the north* "
3: 3 Hivites that dwell in m' Lebanon, "
3 from m' Baal-hermon unto the "
27 went down with him from the m',* "
4: 5 Ramah and Beth-el in m' Ephraim:* "
6 Go and draw toward m' Tabor, and "
12 Abinoam was gone up to m' Tabor. "
14 Barak went down from m' Tabor, "
7: 3 and depart early from m' Gilead. "
24 throughout all m' Ephraim, saying,* "
9: 7 and stood in the top of m' Gerizim, "
48 gat him up to m' Zalmon, he and "
10: 1 he dwelt in Shamir in m' Ephraim.* "
12:15 in the m' of the Amalekites. * "
17: 1 there was a man of m' Ephraim, * "
8 and he came to m' Ephraim to the* "
18: 2 when they came to m' Ephraim, to* "
13 passed thence unto m' Ephraim, * "
19: 1 on the side of m' Ephraim, who * "
16 which was also of m' Ephraim; * "
18 toward the side of m' Ephraim; * "
1Sa 1: 1 of m' Ephraim, and his name was* "
9: 4 he passed through m' Ephraim, * "
13: 2 in Michmash and in m' Beth-el, and "
14:22 had hid themselves in m' Ephraim,* "
31: 1 and fell down slain in m' Gilboa. "
8 his three sons fallen in m' Gilboa. "
2Sa 1: 6 by chance upon m' Gilboa, behold, "
15:30 went up by the ascent of m' Olivet, "
32 David was come to the top of the m',* "
20:21 but a man of m' Ephraim, Sheba *2022
1Ki 4: 8 The son of Hur, in m' Ephraim: * "
12:25 built Shechem in m' Ephraim, and* "
18:19 to me all Israel unto m' Carmel, "
20 prophets together unto m' Carmel. "
19: 8 nights unto Horeb the m' of God. "
11 stand upon the m' before the Lord. "
2Ki 2:25 he went from thence to m' Carmel, "
4:25 unto the man of God to m' Carmel. "
5:22 from m' Ephraim two young men* "
19:31 and they that escape out of m' Zion: "
23:13 right hand of the m' of corruption, "
16 sepulchres...were there in the m', "
1Ch 4:42 five hundred men, went to m' Seir, "
5:23 and Senir, and unto m' Hermon. "
6:67 Shechem in m' Ephraim with her* "
10: 1 and fell down slain in m' Gilboa. "
8 and his sons fallen in m' Gilboa. "
2Ch 3: 1 the Lord at Jerusalem in m' Moriah, "
13: 4 Abijah stood up upon m' Zemaraim, "
4 which is in m' Ephraim, and said,* "
15: 8 he had taken from m' Ephraim, * "
19: 4 from Beer-sheba to m' Ephraim, * "
20:10 of Ammon and Moab and m' Seir, "
22 of Ammon, Moab, and m' Seir, "
23 against the inhabitants of m' Seir, "
33:15 altars that he had built in the m' of "
Ne 8:15 Go forth unto the m', and fetch "
9:13 camest down also upon m' Sinai, "
Job 20: 6 excellency m' up to the heavens, 5927
39:27 the eagle m' up at thy command, 1361
Ps 48: 2 joy of the whole earth, is m' Zion, 2022
11 m' Zion rejoice, let the daughters "
Ps 74: 2 m' Zion, wherein thou hast dwelt. 2022
78:68 Judah, the m' Zion which he loved. "
107:26 They m' up to the heaven, they go 5927
125: 1 in the Lord shall be as m' Zion, 2022
Ca 4: 1 goats, that appear from m' Gilead. "
Isa 4: 5 every dwelling place of m' Zion, "
8:18 of hosts, which dwelleth in m' Zion. "
9:18 m' up like the lifting up of smoke.* 55
10:12 his whole work upon m' Zion and 2022
32 the m' of the daughter of Zion, "
14:13 upon the m' of the congregation, "
16: 1 unto the m' of the daughter of Zion. "
18: 7 of the Lord of hosts, the m' Zion. "
24:23 Lord of hosts shall reign in m' Zion, "
27:13 Lord in the holy m' at Jerusalem. "
28:21 shall rise up as in m' Perazim, he "
29: 3 lay siege against thee with a m', *4674
8 be, that fight against m' Zion. 2022
31: 4 come down to fight for m' Zion, and "
37:32 they that escape out of m' Zion: "
40:31 shall m' up with wings as eagles; 5927
Jer 4:15 affliction from m' Ephraim. *2022
6: 6 and cast a m' against Jerusalem: ‡5550
31: 6 upon the m' Ephraim shall cry, *2022
50:19 upon m' Ephraim and Gilead. * "
51:53 Babylon should m' up to heaven, 5927
Eze 4: 2 against it, and cast a m' against it: 5550
10:16 wings to m' up from the earth, the 7311
21:22 to cast a m', and to build a fort. †‡5550
26: 8 cast a m' against thee, and lift up‡ "
35: 2 man, set thy face against m' Seir, 2022
3 Behold, O m' Seir, I am against "
7 will I make m' Seir most desolate, "
15 thou shalt be desolate, O m' Seir, "
Da 11:15 north shall come, and cast up a m',*5550
Joe 2:32 in m' Zion and in Jerusalem shall 2022
Ob 8 understanding out of the m' of "
9 every one of the m' of Esau may be "
17 upon m' Zion shall be deliverance, "
19 south shall possess the m' of Esau; "
21 saviours shall come up on m' Zion "
21 to judge the m' of Esau; and the "
Mic 4: 7 shall reign over them in m' Zion "
Hab 3: 3 and the Holy One from m' Paran. "
Zec 14: 4 in that day upon the m' of Olives, "
4 the m' of Olives shall cleave in the "
M't 21: 1 Bethphage, unto the m' of Olives, 3735
24: 3 as he sat upon the m' of Olives, the "
26:30 they went out into the m' of Olives. "
M'r 11: 1 and Bethany, at the m' of Olives, "
13: 3 And as he sat upon the m' of Olives "
14:26 they went out into the m' of Olives. "
Lu 19:29 Bethany, at the m' called...Olives, "
29 at...the m' of Olives, he sent two ‡
37 at the descent of the m' of Olives, 3735
21:37 he went out, and abode in the m' "
37 out, and abode in...the m' of Olives.‡
22:39 as he was wont, to the m' of Olives; 3735
Joh 8: 1 Jesus went unto the m' of Olives. "
Ac 1:12 from the m' called Olivet, which is "
7:30 to him in the wilderness of m' Sina "
38 which spake to him in the m' Sina, "
Ga 4:24 the one from the m' Sinai, which "
25 For this Agar is m' Sinai in Arabia, "
Heb 8: 5 the pattern shewed to thee in the m'. "
12:18 unto the m' that might be touched, "
22 ye are come unto m' Sion, and unto "
2Pe 1:18 we were with him in the holy m'. "
Re 14: 1 lo, a Lamb stood on the m' Sion, "

mountain See also MOUNTAINS.
Ge 12: 8 unto a m' on the east of Beth-el, 2022
14:10 they that remained fled to the m'. "
19:17 escape to the m', lest thou be "
19 I cannot escape to the m', lest some "
30 and dwelt in the m', and his two "
Ex 3: 1 and came to the m' of God, even to "
12 ye shall serve God upon this m'. "
15:17 in the m' of thine inheritance, in "
19: 3 Lord called unto him out of the m', "
20:18 of the trumpet, and the m' smoking: "
Nu 13:17 southward, and go up into the m': * "
14:40 gat them up into the top of the m', "
De 1:19 the way of the m' of the Amorites,* "
20 come unto the m' of the Amorites,* "
24 turned and went up into the m', "
44 Amorites, which dwelt in that m', "
2: 3 Ye have compassed this m' long "
3:25 that goodly m', and Lebanon. "
4:11 came near and stood under the m'; "
11 and the m' burned with fire unto the "
5:23 (for the m' did burn with fire,) that "
32:49 Get thee up into this m' Abarim, "
33:19 shall call the people unto the m'; "
34: 1 plains of Moab unto the m' of Nebo,* "
Jos 2:16 Get you to the m', lest the pursuers "
22 came unto the m', and abode there "
23 descended from the m', and passed "
11:16 and the plain, and the m' of Israel,* "
14:12 therefore give me this m', whereof "
15: 8 border went up to the top of the m' "
17:18 But the m' shall be thine; for it is* "
18:16 came down to the end of the m' "
20: 7 which is Hebron, in the m' of Judah.* "
J'g 1: 9 Canaanites, that dwelt in the m', * "
19 drave out the inhabitants of the m';* "
34 the children of Dan into the m': * "
3:27 a trumpet in the m' of Ephraim, * "
1Sa 17: 3 the Philistines stood on a m' on the "
3 Israel stood on a m' on the other "
23:14 remained in a m' in the wilderness* "
26 Saul went on this side of the m', "
26 and his men on that side of the m': "
2Ki 2:16 cast him upon some m', or into "
6:17 behold, the m' was full of horses "
2Ch 2: 2 thousand to hew in the m', and * "
18 thousand to be hewers in the m'. * "

Job 14:18 the *m'* falling cometh to nought, 2022
Ps 11: 1 my soul, Flee as a bird to your *m'*? "
30: 7 hast made my *m'* to stand strong: 2042
48: 1 our God, in the *m'* of his holiness. 2022
78:54 to this *m'*, which his right hand had "
Ca 4: 6 I will get me to the *m'* of myrrh, "
Isa 2: 2 the *m'* of the Lord's house shall be "
3 let us go up to the *m'* of the Lord, "
11: 9 hurt nor destroy in all my holy *m'*: "
13: 2 ye up a banner upon the high *m'*, "
25: 6 in this *m'* shall the Lord of hosts "
7 he will destroy in this *m'* the face "
10 For in this *m'* shall the hand of the "
30:17 as a beacon upon the top of a *m'*, "
25 there shall be upon every high *m'*, "
29 to come into the *m'* of the Lord, "
40: 4 and every *m'* and hill shall be made "
9 get thee up into the high *m'*: O "
56: 7 them will I bring to my holy *m'*, "
57: 7 Upon a lofty and high *m'* hast thou "
13 land, and shall inherit my holy *m'*; "
65:11 that forget my holy *m'*, that "
25 hurt nor destroy in all my holy *m'*, "
66:20 beasts, to my holy *m'* Jerusalem, "
Jer 3: 6 she is gone up upon every high *m'* "
16:16 they shall hunt them from every *m'*, "
17: 3 O my *m'* in the field, I will give thy 2042
26:18 the *m'* of the house as the high 2022
31:23 of justice, and *m'* of holiness. "
50: 6 they have gone from *m'* to hill, they "
51:25 I am against thee, O destroying *m'*, "
25 and will make thee a burnt *m'*. "
La 5:18 Because of the *m'* of Zion, which "
Eze 11:23 stood upon the *m'* which is on the "
17:22 will plant it upon an high *m'* and "
23 In the *m'* of the height of Israel "
20:40 For in mine holy *m'* in the "
40 in the *m'* of the height of Israel, "
28:14 thou wast upon the holy *m'* of God; "
16 as profane out of the *m'* of God: "
40: 2 and set me upon a very high *m'*, "
43:12 Upon the top of the *m'* the whole "
Da 2:35 the image became a great *m'*, 2906
45 cut out of the *m'* without hands, "
9:16 thy city Jerusalem, thy holy *m'*: 2022
20 my God for the holy *m'* of my God; "
11:45 the seas in the glorious holy *m'*; "
Joe 2: 1 and sound an alarm in my holy *m'*: "
3:17 God dwelling in Zion, my holy *m'*: "
Am 4: 1 that are in the *m'* of Samaria, "
6: 1 and trust in the *m'* of Samaria, "
Ob 16 as ye have drunk upon my holy *m'*, "
Mic 3:12 and the *m'* of the house as the high "
4: 1 that the *m'* of the house of the Lord "
2 let us go up to the *m'* of the Lord, "
7:12 from sea to sea, and from *m'* to *m'*. "
Zep 3:11 be haughty because of my holy *m'*. "
Hag 1: 8 Go up to the *m'*, and bring wood, "
Zec 4: 7 Who art thou, O great *m'*? before "
8: 3 *m'* of the Lord of hosts the holy *m'*. "
14: 4 half of the *m'* shall remove toward "
M't 4: 8 up into an exceeding high *m'*, 3735
5: 1 multitudes, he went up into a *m'*: "
8: 1 he was come down from the *m'*, "
14:23 went up into a *m'* apart to pray: "
15:29 went up into a *m'*, and sat down "
17: 1 them up into an high *m'* apart, "
9 as they came down from the *m'*, "
20 ye shall say unto this *m'*, Remove "
21:21 but also if ye shall say unto this *m'*, "
28:16 Galilee, into a *m'* where Jesus had "
M'r 3:13 And he goeth up into a *m'*, and "
6:46 he departed into a *m'* to pray. "
9: 2 leadeth them up into an high *m'* "
9 as they came down from the *m'*, he "
11:23 whosoever shall say unto this *m'*, "
Lu 3: 5 every *m'* and hill shall be brought "
4: 5 taking him up into an high *m'*, * "
6:12 that he went out into a *m'* to pray, "
8:32 of many swine feeding on the *m'*: "
9:28 and went up into a *m'* to pray. "
Joh 4:20 Our fathers worshipped in this *m'*; "
21 when ye shall neither in this *m'*, "
6: 3 And Jesus went up into a *m'*, and "
15 again into a *m'* himself alone. "
Heb12:20 if so much as a beast touch the *m'*, "
Re 6:14 every *m'* and island were moved "
8: 8 as it were a great *m'* burning with "
21:10 in the spirit to a great and high *m'*, "

mountains
Ge 7:20 prevail; and the *m'* were covered. 2022
8: 4 the month, upon the *m'* of Ararat. "
5 month, were the tops of the *m'* seen. "
22: 2 burnt offering upon one of the *m'* "
Ex 32:12 them out, to slay them in the *m'*, "
Nu 13:29 and the Amorites, dwell in the *m'*: "
23: 7 Aram, out of the *m'* of the east, 2042
33:47 and pitched in the *m'* of Abarim, 2022
48 departed from the *m'* of Abarim, "
De 2:37 nor unto the cities in the *m'*, nor* "
12: 2 their gods, upon the high *m'*, and "
32:22 on fire the foundations of the *m'*. "
33:15 the chief things of the ancient *m'*, 2042
Jos 10: 6 the Amorites that dwell in the *m'* *2022
11: 2 that were on the north of the *m'*, * "
3 and the Jebusite in the *m'*, and to* "
21 cut off the Anakims from the *m'*, * "
21 and from all the *m'* of Judah, and* "
21 and from all the *m'* of Israel: * "
12: 8 In the *m'*, and in the valleys, and * "
15:48 And in the *m'*, Shamir, and Jattir,* "
18:12 went up through the *m'* westward;* "
J'g 5: 5 *m'* melted from before the Lord, "
6: 2 them the dens which are in the *m'*, "
9:25 in wait for him in the top of the *m'*, "
36 people down from the top of the *m'*. "
J'g 9:36 Thou seest the shadow of the *m'* as 2022
11:37 may go up and down upon the *m'*, "
38 bewailed her virginity upon the *m'*. "
1Sa 26:20 doth hunt a partridge in the *m'*. "
2Sa 1:21 Ye *m'* of Gilboa, let there be no "
1Ki 5:15 thousand hewers in the *m'*; "
19:11 great and strong wind rent the *m'*, "
2Ki 19:23 come up to the height of the *m'*, to "
1Ch 12: 8 as swift as the roes upon the *m'*; "
2Ch 18:16 all Israel scattered upon the *m'*, "
21:11 high places in the *m'* of Judah, "
26:10 and vine dressers in the *m'*, and in "
27: 4 he built cities in the *m'* of Judah, * "
Job 9: 5 Which removeth the *m'*, and they "
24: 8 are wet with the showers of the *m'*, "
28: 9 he overturneth the *m'* by the roots. "
39: 8 The range of the *m'* is his pastures, "
40:20 Surely the *m'* bring him forth food, "
Ps 36: 6 righteousness is like the great *m'*; 2042
46: 2 the *m'* be carried into the midst 2022
3 *m'* shake with the swelling thereof. "
50:11 I know all the fowls of the *m'*: and "
65: 6 by his strength setteth fast the *m'*; "
72: 3 The *m'* shall bring peace to the "
16 in the earth upon the top of the *m'*; "
76: 4 and excellent than the *m'* of prey. 2042
83:14 as the flame setteth the *m'* on fire; 2022
87: 1 His foundation is in the holy *m'*. 2042
90: 2 Before the *m'* were brought forth, 2022
104: 6 the waters stood above the *m'*. "
8 They go up by the *m'*; they go down "
114: 4 The *m'* skipped like rams, and the "
6 Ye *m'*, that ye skipped like rams; "
125: 2 the *m'* are round about Jerusalem, "
133: 3 descended upon the *m'* of Zion: 2042
144: 5 touch the *m'*, and they shall 2022
147: 8 maketh grass to grow upon the *m'*. "
148: 9 *M'*, and all hills; fruitful trees, and "
Pr 8:25 Before the *m'* were settled, before "
27:25 and herbs of the *m'* are gathered. "
Ca 2: 8 he cometh leaping upon the *m'*, "
17 young hart upon the *m'* of Bether. "
4: 8 dens, from the *m'* of the leopards. 2042
8:14 young hart upon the *m'* of spices. 2022
Isa 2: 2 established in the top of the *m'*, "
14 upon all the high *m'*, and upon all "
13: 4 noise of a multitude in the *m'*, like "
14:25 upon my *m'* tread him under foot: "
17:13 shall be chased as the chaff of the *m'* "
18: 3 he lifteth up an ensign on the *m'*; "
6 together unto the fowls of the *m'*, "
22: 5 the walls, and of crying to the *m'*. "
34: 3 the *m'* shall be melted with their "
37:24 I come up to the height of the *m'*, "
40:12 weighed the *m'* in scales, and the "
41:15 thou shalt thresh the *m'*, and beat "
42:11 them shout from the top of the *m'*. "
15 I will make waste *m'* and hills, and "
44:23 break forth into singing, ye *m'*, O "
49:11 I will make all my *m'* a way, and "
13 break forth into singing, O *m'*: for "
52: 7 How beautiful upon the *m'* are the "
54:10 For the *m'* shall depart, and the "
55:12 the *m'* and the hills shall break "
64: 1 that the *m'* might flow down at thy "
3 the *m'* flowed down at thy presence. "
65: 7 have burned incense upon the *m'*, "
9 out of Judah an inheritor of my *m'*: "
Jer 3:23 hills, and from the multitude of *m'*: "
4:24 I beheld the *m'*, and, lo, they "
9:10 For the *m'* will I take up a weeping "
13:16 your feet stumble upon the dark *m'*, "
17:26 and from the *m'*, and from the "
31: 5 vines upon the *m'* of Samaria: "
32:44 Judah, and in the cities of the *m'*,* "
33:13 In the cities of the *m'*, in the cities* "
46:18 Surely as Tabor is among the *m'*, "
50: 6 have turned them away on the *m'*: "
La 4:19 they pursued us upon the *m'*, they "
Eze 6: 2 thy face toward the *m'* of Israel, "
3 Ye *m'* of Israel, hear the word of "
3 Thus saith the Lord God to the *m'*, "
13 in all the tops of the *m'*, and under "
7: 7 not the sounding again of the *m'*. "
16 and shall be on the *m'* like doves "
18: 6 And hath not eaten upon the *m'*, "
11 but even hath eaten upon the *m'*, "
15 That hath not eaten upon the *m'*, "
19: 9 be heard upon the *m'* of Israel. "
22: 9 and in thee they eat upon the *m'*: "
31:12 upon the *m'* and in all the valleys "
32: 5 I will lay thy flesh upon the *m'*, "
6 thou swimmest, even to the *m'*; "
33:28 the *m'* of Israel shall be desolate, "
34: 6 sheep wandered through all the *m'*, "
13 feed them upon the *m'* of Israel "
14 upon the high *m'* of Israel shall "
14 they feed upon the *m'* of Israel. "
35: 8 I will fill his *m'* with his slain men: "
12 spoken against the *m'* of Israel, "
36: 1 prophesy unto the *m'* of Israel, and "
1, 4 Ye *m'* of Israel, hear the word "
4 Thus saith the Lord God to the *m'*, "
6 say unto the *m'*, and to the hills, "
8 O *m'* of Israel, ye shall shoot forth "
37:22 in the land upon the *m'* of Israel; "
38: 8 people, against the *m'* of Israel, "
20 and the *m'* shall be thrown down, "
21 against him throughout all my *m'*, "
39: 2 bring thee upon the *m'* of Israel: "
4 shalt fall upon the *m'* of Israel, "
17 sacrifice upon the *m'* of Israel, that "
Ho 4:13 sacrifice upon the tops of the *m'*, "
10: 8 they shall say to the *m'*, Cover us; "
Joe 2: 2 the morning spread upon the *m'*: "
5 noise of chariots on the tops of *m'* "
Joe 3:18 the *m'* shall drop down new wine, 2022
Am 3: 9 yourselves upon the *m'* of Samaria, "
4:13 For, lo, he that formeth the *m'*, and "
9:13 and the *m'* shall drop sweet wine, "
Jon 2: 6 went down to the bottoms of the *m'*; "
Mic 1: 4 the *m'* shall be molten under him, "
4: 1 be established in the top of the *m'*, "
6: 1 Arise, contend thou before the *m'*, "
2 Hear ye, O *m'*, the Lord's "
Na 1: 5 The *m'* quake at him, and the hills "
15 Behold upon the *m'* the feet of him "
3:18 thy people is scattered upon the *m'*, "
Hab 3: 6 the everlasting *m'* were scattered, 2042
10 *m'* saw thee, and they trembled: 2022
Hag 1:11 upon the land, and upon the *m'*, "
Zec 6: 1 chariots out from between two *m'*; "
1 and the *m'* were *m'* of brass. "
14: 5 ye shall flee to the valley of the *m'*; "
5 for the valley of the *m'* shall reach "
Mal 1: 3 laid his *m'* and his heritage waste "
M't 18:12 goeth into the *m'*, and seeketh 3735
24:16 which be in Judæa flee into the *m'*: "
M'r 5: 5 night and day, he was in the *m'*, "
11 there nigh unto the *m'* a great herd* "
13:14 them that be in Judæa flee to the *m'*: "
Lu 21:21 which are in Judæa flee to the *m'*; "
23:30 begin to say to the *m'*, Fall on us; "
1Co 13: 2 faith, so that I could remove *m'*, "
Heb11:38 wandered in deserts, and in *m'*, "
Re 6:15 dens and in the rocks of the *m'*; "
16 said to the *m'* and rocks, Fall on us, "
16:20 away, and the *m'* were not found. "
17: 9 The seven heads are seven *m'*, on "

mounted
Eze 10:19 *m'* up from the earth in my sight: 7426

mounting
Isa 15: 5 for by the *m'* up of Luhith with 4608

mounts
Jer 32:24 the *m'*, they are come unto the ‡5550
33: 4 which are thrown down by the *m'*,‡ "
Eze 17:17 by casting up *m'*, and building ‡ "

mourn See also MOURNED; MOURNETH; MOURNFULLY; MOURNING.
Ge 23: 2 Abraham came to *m'* for Sarah, 5594
1Sa 16: 1 How long wilt thou *m'* for Saul, 56
2Sa 3:31 sackcloth, and *m'* before Abner. 5594
1Ki 13:29 to the city, to *m'* and to bury him. "
14:13 And all Israel shall *m'* for him, and "
Ne 8: 9 Lord your God; *m'* not, nor weep. 56
Job 2:11 together to come to *m'* with him *5110
5:11 those which *m'* may be exalted 6937
14:22 and his soul within him shall *m'*. * 56
Ps 55: 2 I *m'* in my complaint, and make a*7300
Pr 5:11 And thou *m'* at the last, when they5098
29: 2 wicked beareth rule, the people *m'*.* 584
Ec 3: 4 a time to *m'*, and a time to dance; 5594
Isa 3:26 her gates shall lament and *m'*; and 56
16: 7 of Kir-hareseth shall ye *m'*; 1897
19: 8 The fishers also shall *m'*, and all * 578
38:14 I did *m'* as a dove: mine eyes fail ‡1897
59:11 like bears, and *m'* sore like doves:‡ "
61: 2 of our God; to comfort all that *m'*; 57
3 To appoint unto them that *m'* in "
66:10 joy with her, all ye that *m'* for her: 56
Jer 4:28 For this shall the earth *m'*, and the "
12: 4 How long shall the land *m'*, and the "
48:31 shall *m'* for the men of Kir-heres. 1897
La 1: 4 The ways of Zion do *m'*, because 57
Eze 7:12 the buyer rejoice, nor the seller *m'*: 56
27 The king shall *m'*, and the prince "
24:16 neither shalt thou *m'* nor weep, 5594
23 ye shall not *m'* nor weep; but ye "
23 and *m'* one toward another. *5098
31:15 I caused Lebanon to *m'* for him, 6937
Ho 4: 3 Therefore shall the land *m'*, and 56
10: 5 the people thereof shall *m'* over it, "
Joe 1: 9 the priests, the Lord's ministers, *m'*. "
Am 1: 2 habitations of the shepherds shall *m'*, "
8: 8 every one *m'* that dwelleth therein? "
9: 5 and all that dwell therein shall *m'*: "
Zec 12:10 and they shall *m'* for him, as one 5594
12 land shall *m'*, every family apart; "
M't 5: 4 Blessed are they that *m'*: for they 3996
9:15 children of the bridechamber *m'*, "
24:30 shall all the tribes of the earth *m'*, 2875
Lu 6:25 now! for ye shall *m'* and weep. 3996
Jas 4: 9 Be afflicted, and *m'*, and weep: let "
Re 18:11 earth shall weep and *m'* over her; "

mourned
Ge 37:34 loins, and *m'* for his son many days. 56
50: 3 Egyptians *m'* for him threescore *1058
10 there they *m'* with a great and *5594
Ex 33: 4 heard these evil tidings, they *m'*: 56
Nu 14:39 of Israel: and the people *m'* greatly. "
20:29 they *m'* for Aaron thirty days, *1058
1Sa 15:35 nevertheless Samuel *m'* for Saul: 56
2Sa 1:12 And they *m'*, and wept, and fasted5594
11:26 was dead, she *m'* for her husband.* 56
13:37 And David *m'* for his son every day. 56
14: 2 that had a long time *m'* for the dead: "
1Ki 13:30 and they *m'* over him, saying, 5594
14:18 and all Israel *m'* for him, according "
1Ch 7:22 Ephraim their father *m'* many days, 56
2Ch 35:24 Judah and Jerusalem *m'* for Josiah. "
Ezr 10: 6 he *m'* because of the transgression of "
Ne 1: 4 I...wept, and *m'* certain days, and "
Zec 7: 5 When ye fasted and *m'* in the 5594
M't 11:17 we have *m'* unto you, and ye have *2354
M'r 16:10 with him, as they *m'* and wept. 3996
Lu 7:32 we have *m'* to you, and ye have *2354
1Co 5: 2 and have not rather *m'*, that he *3996

mourner See also MOURNERS.
2Sa 14: 2 I pray thee, feign thyself to be a *m'*, 56

mourners
Job 29:25 army, as one that comforteth the *m'*.57
Ec 12: 5 and the *m'* go about the streets: 5594
Isa 57:18 comforts unto him and to his *m'*. 57
Hos 9: 4 be unto them as the bread of *m'*; 205

mourneth
2Sa 19: 1 king weepeth and *m'* for Absalom. 56
Ps 35:14 as one that *m'* for his mother. * 57
88: 9 Mine eye *m'* by reason of *1669
Isa 24: 4 The earth *m'* and fadeth away, the 56
7 new wine *m'*, the vine languisheth, "
33: 9 The earth *m'* and languisheth: "
Jer 12:11 and being desolate it *m'* unto me; "
14: 2 Judah *m'*, and the gates thereof "
23:10 for because of swearing the land *m'*;"
Joe 1:10 The field is wasted, the land *m'*; for "
Zec 12:10 for him, as one *m'* for his only son,5594

mournfully
Mal 3:14 that we have walked *m'* before the6941

mourning
Ge 27:41 The days of *m'* for my father are at 60
37:35 down into the grave unto my son *m'*.57
50: 4 when the days of his *m'* were past,*1086
10 made a *m'* for his father seven days.60
11 saw the *m'* in the floor of Atad, they "
11 is a grievous *m'* to the Egyptians: "
De 26:14 I have not eaten thereof in my *m'*, 205
34: 8 and *m'* for Moses were ended. 60
2Sa 11:27 when the *m'* was past, David sent "
14: 2 put on now *m'* apparel, and anoint "
19: 2 that day was turned into *m'* unto all "
Es 4: 3 great *m'* among the Jews,...fasting, "
6:12 Haman hasted to his house *m'*, and 57
9:22 to joy, and from *m'* into a good day: 60
Job 3: 8 who are ready to raise up their *m'*.*3882
30:28 I went *m'* without the sun: I stood6937
31 My harp also is turned to *m'*, and my60
Ps 30:11 turned for me my *m'* into dancing:4553
38: 6 greatly; I go *m'* all the day long. 6937
42: 9 go I *m'* because of the oppression "
43: 2 go I *m'* because of the oppression "
Ec 7: 2 better to go to the house of *m'*, than 60
4 of the wise is in the house of *m'*; "
Isa 22:12 hosts call to weeping, and to *m'*, 4553
51:11 and sorrow and *m'* shall flee away.*585
60:20 the days of thy *m'* shall be ended. 60
61: 3 beauty for ashes, the oil of joy for *m'*,"
Jer 6:26 make thee *m'*, as for an only son, "
9:17 call for the *m'* women, that they 6969
16: 5 not into the house of *m'*, neither 4798
7 men tear themselves for them in *m'*,60
31:13 I will turn their *m'* into joy, and will "
La 2: 5 in the daughter of Judah *m'* and 8386
5:15 ceased; our dance is turned into *m'*.60
Eze 2:10 lamentations, and *m'*, and woe. 1899
7:16 all of them *m'*, every one for his 1993
24:17 to cry, make no *m'* for the dead, 60
31:15 down to the grave I caused a *m'*: 56
Da 10: 2 I Daniel was *m'* three full weeks. "
Joe 2:12 and with weeping, and with *m'*: 4553
Am 5:16 shall call the husbandman to *m'*, 60
8:10 And I will turn your feasts into *m'*, "
10 will make it as the *m'* of an only son,"
Mic 1: 8 like the dragons, and *m'* as the owls."
11 not forth in the *m'* of Beth-ezel; *4553
Zec 12:11 there be a great *m'* in Jerusalem, "
11 as the *m'* of Hadadrimmon in the "
M't 2:18 and great *m'*, Rachel weeping for 3602
2Co 7: 7 your *m'*, your fervent mind toward "
Jas 4: 9 laughter be turned to *m'*, and your3997
Re 18: 8 day, death, and *m'*, and famine; "

mouse See also MICE.
Le 11:29 the weasel, and the *m'*, and the 5909
Isa 66:17 and the *m'*, shall be consumed "

mouth See also MOUTHS.
Ge 4:11 hath opened her *m'* to receive thy 6310
8:11 in her *m'* was an olive leaf pluckt "
24:57 the damsel, and enquire at her *m'*. "
29: 2 great stone was upon the well's *m'*. "
3 rolled the stone from the well's *m'*, "
3 the stone again upon the well's *m'* "
8 roll the stone from the well's *m'*; "
10 rolled the stone from the well's *m'*, "
42:27 for, behold, it was in his sack's *m'*. "
43:12 again in the *m'* of your sacks, carry "
21 money was in the *m'* of his sack, "
44: 1 every man's money in his sack's *m'*."
2 in the sack's *m'* of the youngest, "
45:12 it is my *m'* that speaketh unto you. "
Ex 4:11 him, Who hath made man's *m'*? or "
12 and I will be with thy *m'*, and teach"
15 unto him, and put words in his *m'*: "
15 will be with thy *m'*, and with his *m'*,"
16 he shall be to thee instead of a *m'*, "
13: 9 the Lord's law may be in thy *m'*: "
23:13 neither let it be heard out of thy *m'*."
Nu 12: 8 With him will I speak *m'* to *m'*, even "
16:30 thing, and the earth open her *m'*, "
32 earth opened her *m'*, and swallowed"
22:28 the Lord opened the *m'* of the ass, "
38 the word that God putteth in my *m'*,"
23: 5 the Lord put a word in Balaam's *m'*,"
12 which the Lord hath put in my *m'*? "
16 Balaam, and put a word in his *m'*, "
26:10 earth opened her *m'*, and swallowed"
30: 2 to all that proceedeth out of his *m'*. "
32:24 hath proceeded out of your *m'*. "
35:30 put to death by the *m'* of witnesses:"
De 8: 3 of the *m'* of the Lord doth man live."
11: 6 earth opened her *m'*, and swallowed"
17: 6 At the *m'* of two witnesses, or three "
6 at the *m'* of one witness he shall not"
18:18 and will put my words in his *m'*; "
De 19:15 sinneth: at the *m'* of two witnesses, 6310
15 or at the *m'* of three witnesses, shall"
23:23 thou hast promised with thy *m'*. "
30:14 is very nigh unto thee, in thy *m'*, "
32: 1 hear, O earth, the words of my *m'*. "
Jos 1: 8 law shall not depart out of thy *m'*; "
6:10 any word proceed out of your *m'*, "
9:14 not counsel at the *m'* of the Lord. "
10:18 stones upon the *m'* of the cave, and "
22 Open the *m'* of the cave, and bring "
27 laid great stones in the cave's *m'*, "
J'g 7: 6 putting their hand to their *m'*, were"
9:38 Where is now thy *m'*, wherewith "
11:35 I have opened my *m'* unto the Lord,"
36 hast opened thy *m'* unto the Lord, "
36 hath proceeded out of thy *m'*; "
18:19 lay thine hand upon thy *m'*, and go "
1Sa 1:12 the Lord, that Eli marked her *m'*. "
2: 1 my *m'* is enlarged over mine "
3 not arrogancy come out of your *m'*:"
14:26 but no man put his hand to his *m'*: "
27 honeycomb,...put his hand to his *m'*; "
17:35 him, and delivered it out of his *m'*: "
2Sa 1:16 thy *m'* hath testified against thee, "
14: 3 So Joab put the words in her *m'*. "
19 words in the *m'* of thine handmaid:"
17:19 spread a covering over the well's *m'*,"
18:25 be alone, there is tidings in his *m'*. "
22: 9 and fire out of his *m'* devoured: "
1Ki 7:31 And the *m'* of it within the chapiter"
31 but the *m'* thereof was round after "
31 also upon the *m'* of it were gravings"
8:15 spake with his *m'* unto David my "
24 thou spakest also with thy *m'*, and "
13:21 hast disobeyed the *m'* of the Lord, "
17:24 word of the Lord in thy *m'* is truth. "
19:18 every *m'* which hath not kissed him."
22:13 good unto the king with one *m'*: "
22 spirit in the *m'* of all his prophets. "
23 in the *m'* of all these thy prophets, "
2Ki 4:34 child, and put his *m'* upon his *m'*, "
1Ch 16:12 and the judgments of his *m'*; "
2Ch 6: 4 he spake with his *m'* to my father "
15 and spakest with thy *m'*, and hast "
18:21 spirit in the *m'* of all his prophets. "
22 in the *m'* of these thy prophets, and "
35:22 words of Necho from the *m'* of God, "
36:12 speaking from the *m'* of the Lord. "
21 of the Lord by the *m'* of Jeremiah, "
22 Lord spoken by the *m'* of Jeremiah "
Ezr 1: 1 of the Lord by the *m'* of Jeremiah "
Ne 9:20 not thy manna from their *m'*, and "
Es 7: 8 word went out of the king's *m'*, they"
Job 3: 1 After this opened Job his *m'*, and "
5:15 from their *m'*, and from the hand of"
16 hope, and iniquity stoppeth her *m'*. "
7:11 Therefore I will not refrain my *m'*; "
8: 2 the words of thy *m'* be like a strong"
21 Till he fill thy *m'* with laughing, "
9:20 mine own *m'* shall condemn me: "
12:11 words? and the *m'* taste his meat?*2441
15: 5 For thy *m'* uttereth thine iniquity, 6310
6 Thine own *m'* condemneth thee, "
13 lettest such words go out of thy *m'*?"
30 by the breath of his *m'* shall he go "
16: 5 would strengthen you with my *m'*, "
10 have gaped upon me with their *m'*; "
19:16 I intreated him with my *m'*. "
20:12 wickedness be sweet in his *m'*, "
13 not; but keep it still within his *m'*:2441
21: 5 and lay your hand upon your *m'*. 6310
22:22 I pray thee, the law from his *m'*, "
23: 4 and fill my *m'* with arguments. "
12 have esteemed the words of his *m'* "
29: 9 and laid their hand on their *m'*. "
10 cleaved to the roof of their *m'*. 2441
23 they opened their *m'* wide as for 6310
31:27 or my *m'* hath kissed my hand: "
30 have I suffered my *m'* to sin by 2441
32: 5 no answer in the *m'* of these three 6310
33: 2 Behold, now I have opened my *m'*, "
2 my tongue hath spoken in my *m'*. 2441
34: 3 trieth words, as the *m'* tasteth meat.*"
35:16 doth Job open his *m'* in vain; 6310
37: 2 the sound that goeth out of his *m'*. "
40: 4 I will lay mine hand upon my *m'*. "
23 he can draw up Jordan into his *m'*. "
41:19 Out of his *m'* go burning lamps, "
21 and a flame goeth out of his *m'*. "
Ps 5: 9 there is no faithfulness in their *m'*; "
8: 2 Out of...*m'* of babes and sucklings "
10: 7 His *m'* is full of cursing and deceit "
17: 3 that my *m'* shall not transgress. "
10 with their *m'* they speak proudly. "
18: 8 and fire out of his *m'* devoured: "
19:14 Let the words of my *m'*, and the "
22:21 Save me from the lion's *m'*: for "
32: 9 whose *m'* must be held in with bit*5716
33: 6 of them by the breath of his *m'*. 6310
34: 1 shall continually be in my *m'*. "
35:21 they opened their *m'* wide against "
36: 3 The words of his *m'* are iniquity "
37:30 The *m'* of the righteous speaketh "
38:13 dumb man that openeth not his *m'*. "
14 and in whose *m'* are no reproofs. "
39: 1 I will keep my *m'* with a bridle, "
9 I was dumb, I opened not my *m'*; "
40: 3 he hath put a new song in my *m'*, "
49: 3 My *m'* shall speak of wisdom; and "
50:16 that...take my covenant in thy *m'*? "
19 Thou givest thy *m'* to evil, and thy "
51:15 my *m'* shall shew forth thy praise. "
54: 2 give ear to the words of my *m'*. "
55:21 The words of his *m'* were smoother "
58: 6 Break their teeth, O God, in their *m'*:"
59: 7 they belch out with their *m'*: "
Ps 59:12 the sin of their *m'* and the words 6310
62: 4 they bless with their *m'*, but they "
63: 5 my *m'* shall praise thee with joyful "
11 the *m'* of them that speak lies shall "
66:14 and my *m'* hath spoken, when I was"
17 I cried unto him with my *m'*, and "
69:15 not the pit shut her *m'* upon me. "
71: 8 Let my *m'* be filled with thy praise "
15 My *m'* shall shew forth thy "
73: 9 set their *m'* against the heavens, "
78: 1 your ears to the words of my *m'*. "
2 I will open my *m'* in a parable: I "
36 they did flatter him with their *m'*, "
81:10 open thy *m'* wide, and I will fill it. "
89: 1 with my *m'* will I make known thy "
103: 5 satisfieth thy *m'* with good things;*5716
105: 5 and the judgments of his *m'*; 6310
107:42 and all iniquity shall stop her *m'*. "
109: 2 For the *m'* of the wicked and the "
2 the *m'* of the deceitful are opened "
30 greatly praise the Lord with my *m'*;"
119:13 all the judgments of thy *m'*. "
43 word of truth utterly out of my *m'*; "
72 The law of thy *m'* is better unto me"
88 shall I keep the testimony of thy *m'*."
103 yea, sweeter than honey to my *m'*! "
108 the freewill offerings of my *m'*, O "
131 I opened my *m'*, and panted: for I "
126: 2 was our *m'* filled with laughter, "
137: 6 tongue cleave to the roof of my *m'*;2441
138: 4 they hear the words of thy *m'*. 6310
141: 3 Set a watch, O Lord, before my *m'*; "
7 are scattered at the grave's *m'*, "
144: 8 Whose *m'* speaketh vanity, and "
11 whose *m'* speaketh vanity, and "
145:21 My *m'* shall speak the praise of the "
149: 6 high praises of God be in their *m'*, 1627
Pr 2: 6 out of his *m'* cometh knowledge 6310
4: 5 decline from the words of my *m'*. "
24 put away from thee a froward *m'*, "
5: 3 and her *m'* is smoother than oil: 2441
7 not from the words of my *m'*. 6310
6: 2 snared with the words of thy *m'*, "
2 art taken with the words of thy *m'*. "
12 man, walketh with a froward *m'*. "
7:24 and attend to the words of my *m'*. "
8: 7 For my *m'* shall speak truth; and 2441
8 All the words of my *m'* are in 6310
13 way, and the froward *m'*, do I hate. "
10: 6 covereth the *m'* of the wicked. "
11 The *m'* of a righteous man is a well"
11 covereth the *m'* of the wicked. "
14 but the *m'* of the foolish is near "
31 The *m'* of the just bringeth forth "
32 but the *m'* of the wicked speaketh "
11: 9 An hypocrite with his *m'* destroyeth"
11 overthrown by the *m'* of the wicked."
12: 6 the *m'* of the upright shall deliver "
14 with good by the fruit of his *m'*. "
13: 2 shall eat good by the fruit of his *m'*: "
3 He that keepeth his *m'* keepeth his "
14: 3 In the *m'* of the foolish is a rod of "
15: 2 but the *m'* of fools poureth out "
14 but the *m'* of fools feedeth on "
23 hath joy by the answer of his *m'*: "
28 the *m'* of the wicked poureth out "
16:10 king: his *m'* transgresseth not in "
23 heart of the wise teacheth his *m'*, "
26 for his *m'* craveth it of him. "
18: 4 The words of a man's *m'* are as "
6 and his *m'* calleth for strokes. "
7 A fool's *m'* is his destruction, and "
20 satisfied with the fruit of his *m'*; "
19:24 much as bring it to his *m'* again. "
28 and the *m'* of the wicked devoureth"
20:17 his *m'* shall be filled with gravel. "
21:23 Whoso keepeth his *m'* and his "
22:14 The *m'* of strange women is a deep "
24: 7 he openeth not his *m'* in the gate. "
26: 7, 9 so is a parable in the *m'* of fools. "
15 him to bring it again to his *m'*. "
28 and a flattering *m'* worketh ruin. "
27: 2 praise thee, and not thine own *m'*; "
30:20 she eateth, and wipeth her *m'*, and "
32 evil, lay thine hand upon thy *m'*. "
31: 8 Open thy *m'* for the dumb in the "
9 Open thy *m'*, judge righteously, "
26 She openeth her *m'* with wisdom; "
Ec 5: 2 Be not rash with thy *m'*, and let not"
6 Suffer not thy *m'* to cause thy flesh "
6: 7 All the labour of man is for his *m'*, "
10:12 The words of a wise man's *m'* are "
13 beginning of the words of his *m'* "
Ca 1: 2 kiss me with the kisses of his *m'*: "
5:16 His *m'* is most sweet: yea, he is 2441
7: 9 And the roof of thy *m'* like the best "
Isa 1:20 the *m'* of the Lord hath spoken it. 6310
5:14 opened her *m'* without measure: "
6: 7 he laid it upon my *m'*, and said, Lo, "
9:12 shall devour Israel with open *m'*. "
17 and every *m'* speaketh folly. For "
10:14 wing, or opened the *m'*, or peeped. "
11: 4 the earth with the rod of his *m'*, "
19: 7 by the *m'* of the brooks, and every* "
29:13 people draw near me with their *m'*, "
30: 2 and have not asked at my *m'*; to "
34:16 for my *m'* it hath commanded, and "
40: 5 the *m'* of the Lord hath spoken it. "
45:23 the word is gone out of my *m'* in "
48: 3 and they went forth out of my *m'*, "
49: 2 made my *m'* like a sharp sword; "
51:16 I have put my words in thy *m'*, "
53: 7 afflicted, yet he opened not his *m'*: "
7 is dumb, so he openeth not his *m'*. "
9 neither was any deceit in his *m'*. "
55:11 be that goeth forth out of my *m'*: "

Isa 57: 4 against whom make ye a wide m', 6310
58:14 the m' of the Lord hath spoken it. "
59:21 words, which I have put in thy m', "
21 shall not depart out of thy m', nor "
21 nor out of the m' of thy seed, nor "
21 nor out of the m' of thy seed's seed, "
62: 2 the m' of the Lord shall name. "
Jer 1: 9 forth his hand, and touched my m'. "
9 I have put my words in thy m'. "
5:14 I will make my words in thy m' fire, "
7:28 and is cut off from their m'. "
9: 8 to his neighbour with his m', but "
12 the m' of the Lord hath spoken, "
20 your ear receive the word of his m', "
12: 2 thou art near in their m', and far "
15:19 the vile, thou shalt be as my m': "
23:16 and not out of the m' of the Lord. "
32: 4 and shall speak with him m' to m', "
34: 3 he shall speak with thee m' to m', "
36: 4 wrote from the m' of Jeremiah all "
6 thou hast written from my m', the "
17 write all these words at his m'? "
18 these words unto me with his m', "
27 wrote at the m' of Jeremiah, "
32 therein from the m' of Jeremiah "
44:17 thing goeth forth out of our own m', "
26 be named in the m' of any man of "
45: 1 in a book at the m' of Jeremiah, "
48:28 nest in the sides of the hole's m'. "
51:44 bring forth out of his m' that which "
La 2:16 have opened their m' against thee: "
3:29 He putteth his m' in the dust; if so "
38 Out of the m' of the most High "
4: 4 cleaveth to the roof of his m' for 2441
Eze 2: 8 open thy m', and eat that I give 6310
3: 2 So I opened my m', and he caused "
3 and it was in my m' as honey for "
17 hear the word at my m', and give "
26 tongue cleave to the roof of thy m',2441
27 I will open thy m', and thou shalt 6310
4:14 there abominable flesh into my m'. "
16:56 was not mentioned by thy m' in "
63 and never open thy m' any more "
21:22 open the m' in the slaughter, to lift "
24:27 thy m' be opened to him which is "
29:21 the opening of the m' in the midst "
33: 7 thou shalt hear the word at my m', "
22 had opened my m', until he came "
22 my m' was opened, and I was no "
31 with their m' they shew much love, "
34:10 will deliver my flock from their m', "
35:13 Thus with your m' ye have boasted "
Da 3:26 near to the m' of the burning fiery8651
4:31 the word was in the king's m', 6433
6:17 and laid upon the m' of the den; "
7: 5 and it had three ribs in the m' of it "
8 and a m' speaking great things. "
20 a m' that spake very great things. "
10: 3 came flesh nor wine in my m', 6310
16 then I opened my m', and spake, "
Ho 2:17 the names of Baalim out of her m', "
6: 5 slain them by the words of my m': "
8: 1 Set the trumpet to thy m'. He 2441
Joe 1: 5 for it is cut off from your m'. 6310
Am 3:12 out of the m' of the lion two legs, "
Mic 4: 4 m' of the Lord of hosts hath spoken. "
6:12 tongue is deceitful in their m'. "
7: 5 keep the doors of thy m' from her "
16 shall lay their hand upon their m', "
Na 3:12 even fall into the m' of the eater. "
Zep 3:13 tongue be found in their m': for "
Zec 5: 8 weight of lead upon the m' thereof. "
8: 9 words by the m' of the prophets, "
9: 7 take away his blood out of his m', "
14:12 shall consume away in their m'. "
Mal 2: 6 The law of truth was in his m', and "
7 they should seek the law at his m': "
M't 4: 4 proceedeth out of the m' of God. *4750*
5: 2 he opened his m', and taught them, "
12:34 of the heart the m' speaketh. "
13:35 I will open my m' in parables; I will "
15: 8 draweth nigh unto me with their m',* "
11 which goeth into the m' defileth a "
11 but that which cometh out of the m', "
17 entereth in at the m' goeth into the "
18 which proceed out of the m' come "
17:27 and when thou hast opened his m', "
18:16 in the m' of two or three witnesses "
21:16 Out of the m' of babes and sucklings "
Lu 1:64 his m' was opened immediately, and "
70 spake by the m' of his holy prophets, "
4:22 which proceeded out of his m'. And "
6:45 of the heart his m' speaketh. "
11:54 to catch something out of his m', "
19:22 of thine own m' will I judge thee, "
21:15 I will give you a m' and wisdom, "
22:71 ourselves have heard of his own m'. "
Joh 19:29 upon hyssop, and put it to his m'. "
Ac 1:16 the Holy Ghost by the m' of David "
3:18 by the m' of all his prophets, that "
21 by the m' of all his holy prophets "
4:25 by the m' of thy servant David hast "
8:32 shearer, so opened he not his m': "
35 Philip opened his m', and began at "
10:34 Then Peter opened his m', and said, "
11: 8 hath at any time entered into my m'. "
15: 7 the Gentiles by my m' should hear "
27 tell you the same things by m'. *3056*
18:14 was now about to open his m', *4750*
22:14 shouldest hear the voice of his m'. "
23: 2 by him to smite him on the m'. "
Ro 3:14 Whose m' is full of cursing and "
19 that every m' may be stopped, and "
10: 8 word is nigh thee, even in thy m', "
9 confess with thy m' the Lord Jesus, "
10 and with the m' confession is made "
Ro 15: 6 one mind and one m' glorify God, *4750*
1Co 9: 9 shalt not muzzle the m' of the ox *
2Co 6:11 our m' is open unto you, our *4750*
13: 1 In the m' of two or three witnesses "
Eph 4:29 proceed out of your m', but that "
6:19 that I may open my m' boldly, to "
Col 3: 8 communication out of your m'. "
2Th 2: 8 consume with the spirit of his m', "
2Ti 4:17 delivered out of the m' of the lion. "
Jas 3:10 of the same m' proceedeth blessing "
1Pe 2:22 neither was guile found in his m': "
Jude 16 m' speaketh great swelling words, "
Re 1:16 and out of his m' went a sharp "
2:16 them with the sword of my m'. "
3:16 hot, I will spue thee out of my m'. "
9:19 For their power is in their m', and "
10: 9 shall be in thy m' sweet as honey. "
10 it was in my m' sweet as honey: "
11: 5 fire proceedeth out of their m', and "
12:15 cast out of his m' water as a flood "
16 earth opened her m', and swallowed "
16 which the dragon cast out of his m'. "
13: 2 and his m' as the m' of a lion: and "
5 him a m' speaking great things and "
6 And he opened his m' in blasphemy "
14: 5 And in their m' was found no guile: "
16:13 come out of the m' of the dragon, "
13 and out of the m' of the beast, "
13 out of the m' of the false prophet. "
19:15 out of his m' goeth a sharp sword. "
21 sword proceeded out of his m': "

mouths
Ge 44: 8 which we found in our sacks' m', 6310
De 31:19 put it in their m', that this song "
21 out of the m' of their seed: for I "
Ps 22:13 They gaped upon me with their m',* "
78:30 their meat was yet in their m', "
115: 5 They have m', but they speak not: "
135:16 They have m', but they speak not; "
17 is there any breath in their m'. "
Isa 52:15 the kings shall shut their m' at him: "
Jer 44:25 have both spoken with your m', and "
La 3:46 our enemies have opened their m' "
Da 6:22 angel, and hath shut the lions' m', 6433
Mic 3: 5 he that putteth not into their m', 6310
Tit 1:11 Whose m' must be stopped, who *1993*
Heb11:33 promises, stopped the m' of lions, *4750*
Jas 3: 3 we put bits in the horses' m', that "
Re 9:17 and out of their m' issued fire and "
18 which issued out of their m'. "

move See also MOVEABLE; MOVED; MOVETH; MOVING; REMOVE.
Ex 11: 7 shall not a dog m' his tongue, 2782
Le 11:10 of all that m' in the waters, and of 8318
De 23:25 thou shalt not m' a sickle unto thy5130
32:21 I will m' them to jealousy with those "
J'g 13:25 Spirit of the Lord began to m' him6470
2Sa 7:10 of their own, and m' no more; *7264
2Ki 21: 8 will I make the feet of Israel m' *5110
23:18 alone; let no man m' his bones. 5128
Jer 10: 4 and with hammers, that it m' not. 6328
Mic 7:17 they shall m' out of their holes *7264
M't 23: 4 will not m' them with one of their *2795*
Ac 17:28 in him we live, and m', and have "
20:24 none of these things m' me, *3056, 4160*

moveable See also UNMOVEABLE.
Pr 5: 6 her ways are m', that thou canst *5128

moved See also MOVEDST; REMOVED.
Ge 1: 2 the Spirit of God m' upon the face 7363
7:21 And all flesh died that m' upon the7430
De 32:21 They have m' me to jealousy with that
Jos 10:21 none m' his tongue against any of 2782
15:18 she m' him to ask of her father a 5496
J'g 1:14 she m' him to ask of her father a "
Ru 1:19 all the city was m' about them, 1949
1Sa 1:13 only her lips m', but her voice was5128
2Sa 18:33 the king was much m', and went 7264
22: 8 the foundations of heaven m' and "
24: 1 he m' David against them to say, 5496
1Ch 16:30 shall be stable, that it be not m'. 4131
17: 9 place, and shall be m' no more; 7264
2Ch 18:31 God m' them to depart from him. 5496
Ezr 4:15 they have m' sedition within the 5648
Es 5: 9 he stood not up, nor m' for him, 2111
Job 37: 1 my heart...is m' out of his place. 5425
41:23 in themselves; they cannot be m'. 4131
Ps 10: 6 said in his heart, I shall not be m': "
13: 4 trouble me rejoice when I am m'. "
15: 5 doeth these things shall never be m'. "
16: 8 at my right hand, I shall not be m'. "
18: 7 foundations also of the hills m' ‡7264
21: 7 the most High he shall not be m'. 4131
30: 6 I said, I shall never be m'. "
46: 5 she shall not be m': God shall help "
6 raged, the kingdoms were m': he "
55:22 never suffer the righteous to be m'. "
62: 2 defence; I shall not be greatly m'. "
6 he is my defence; I shall not be m'. "
66: 9 and suffereth not our feet to be m'.4132
68: 8 Sinai itself was m' at the presence of*
78:58 m' him to jealousy with their graven
93: 1 is stablished, that it cannot be m'. 4131
96:10 established that it shall not be m': "
99: 1 cherubims; let the earth be m'. 5120
112: 6 Surely he shall not be m' for ever: 4131
121: 3 He will not suffer thy foot to be m':4132
Pr 12: 3 of the righteous shall not be m'. 4131
Ca 5: 4 and my bowels were m' for him. 1993
Isa 6: 4 posts of the door m' at the voice 5128
7: 2 his heart was m', and the heart of "
2 the trees of the wood are m' with "
10:14 there was none that m' the wing, 5074
14: 9 Hell from beneath is m' for thee 7264
19: 1 the idols of Egypt shall be m' at 5128
24:19 the earth is m' exceedingly. 4132
Isa 40:20 graven image, that shall not be m'.4131
41: 7 with nails, that it should not be m'. "
Jer 4:24 and all the hills m' lightly. 7043
25:16 And they shall drink, and be m', *1607
46: 7 whose waters are m' as the rivers?* "
8 his waters are m' like the rivers; * "
49:21 The earth is m' at the noise of *7493
50:46 taking of Babylon the earth is m',* "
Da 8: 7 he was m' with choler against him,
11:11 of the south shall be m' with choler,
M't 9:36 was m' with compassion on them, *4697*
14:14 m' with compassion toward them,* "
18:27 servant was m' with compassion, "
20:24 were m' with indignation against *23*
21:10 all the city was m', saying, Who is**4579*
M'r 1:41 Jesus, m' with compassion, put *4697*
6:34 and was m' with compassion toward* "
15:11 But the chief priests m' the people,**383*
Ac 2:25 hand, that I should not be m': *4531*
7: 9 the patriarchs, m' with envy, sold *2206*
17: 5 Jews which believed not, m' with "
21:30 And all the city was m', and the *2795*
Col 1:23 and be not m' away from the hope *3334*
1Th 3: 3 no man should be m' by these *4525*
Heb11: 7 By faith Noah,...m' with fear, *2125*
12:28 a kingdom which cannot be m', * *761*
2Pe 1:21 they were m' by the Holy Ghost. *5342*
Re 6:14 every mountain and island were m'*2795*

movedst
Job 2: 3 thou m' me against him, to destroy5496

mover
Ac 24: 5 and a m' of sedition among all the*2795*

moveth See also REMOVETH.
Ge 1:21 and every living creature that m', 7430
28 over every living thing that m' upon "
9: 2 upon all that m' upon the earth, and* "
Le 11:46 living creature that m' in the waters, "
Job 40:17 He m' his tail like a cedar: the 2654
Ps 69:34 seas,...every thing that m' therein.7430
Pr 23:31 the cup, when it m' itself aright. *1980
Eze 47: 9 every thing that liveth, which m',*8317

moving See also REMOVING.
Ge 1:20 the m' creature that hath life, 8318
9: 3 Every m' thing that liveth shall be7430
Job 16: 5 the m' of my lips should asswage *5205
Pr 16:30 m' his lips he bringeth evil to 7169
Joh 5: 3 waiting for the m' of the water. **2796*

mower
Ps 129: 7 the m' filleth not his hand: nor *7114

mowings
Am 7: 1 latter growth after the king's m'. 1488

mown
Ps 72: 6 down like rain upon the m' grass: 1488

Moza (*mo'-zah*)
1Ch 2:46 concubine, bare Haran, and M', 4162
8:36 and Zimri; and Zimri begat M', "
37 M' begat Binea: Rapha was his "
9:42 and Zimri; and Zimri begat M'; "
43 And M' begat Binea; and Rephaiah "

Mozah (*mo'-zah*)
Jos 18:26 Mizpeh, and Chephirah, and M', 4681

much See also INASMUCH; FORASMUCH; FORSOMUCH.
Ge 26:16 for thou art m' mightier than we. 3966
30:43 had m' cattle, and maidservants, 3966,7235
34:12 Ask me never so m' dowry "
41:49 corn as the sand of the sea, very m', "
43:34 mess was five times so m' as any of "
44: 1 with food, as m' as they can carry, 834
50:20 this day, to save m' people alive. 7227
Ex 12:38 and herds, even very m' cattle. 3515
42 a night to be m' observed unto the
14:28 remained not so m' as one of them.5704
16: 5 be twice as m' as they gather daily.834
18 gathered m' had nothing over, and7235
22 day they gathered twice as m' bread, "
30:23 of sweet cinnamon half so m', even4276
36: 5 The people bring m' more than 7235
7 the work to make it, and too m'. 3498
Le 7:10 of Aaron have, one as m' as another.*
13: 7 But if the scab spread m' abroad *6581
22 if it spread m' abroad in the skin,* "
27 it be spread m' abroad in the skin,* "
37 if the scall spread m' in the skin * "
14:21 if he be poor, and cannot get so m'; "
Nu 16: 3 Ye take too m' upon you, seeing 7227
7 Ye take too m' upon you, ye sons of "
20:20 out against him with m' people. 3515
21: 4 of the people was m' discouraged 7114
6 and m' people of Israel died. 7227
De 2: 5 land,...not so m' as a foot breadth; 5704
3:19 (for I know that ye have m' cattle,)7227
28:38 carry m' seed out into the field, "
Jos 11: 4 m' people, even as the sand that is "
13: 1 yet very m' land to be possessed. 7235
19: 9 of Judah was too m' for them: 7227
22: 8 with m' riches unto your tents, and "
8 with very m' cattle, with silver, and "
8 iron, and with very m' raiment: 7235
Ru 1:13 it grieveth me m' for your sakes 3966
1Sa 2:16 then take as m' as thy soul desireth, *
14:30 How m' more, if haply the people 637
30 m' greater slaughter among the "
18:30 so that his name was m' set by. 3966
19: 2 Saul's son delighted m' in David: "
20:13 do so and m' more to Jonathan: *3254
23: 3 how m' more then if we come to 637
26:24 as thy life was m' set by this day 1431
24 so let my life be m' set by in the "
2Sa 4:11 How m' more, when wicked men 637
8: 8 David took exceeding m' brass. 7235

2Sa 13:34 there came m' people by the way 7227
14:25 to be so m' praised as Absalom for 3966
16:11 m' more now may this Benjamite 637
17:12 there shall not be left so m' as one. 1571
18:33 the king was m' moved, and went up
1Ki 4:29 and understanding exceeding m', 7235
8:27 how m' less this house that I have 637
10: 2 very m' gold, and precious stones: 7227
12:28 It is too m' for you to go up to
2Ki 5:13 how m' rather then, when he 637,3588
10:18 little; but Jehu shall serve him m'. 7235
12:10 there was m' money in the chest, 7225
21: 6 he wrought m' wickedness in the 7235
16 shed innocent blood very m', till he "
1Ch 18: 8 brought David very m' brass, 7227
20: 2 brought also exceeding m' spoil 7235
22: 4 brought m' cedar wood to David. *7230
8 thou hast shed m' blood upon the 7227
2Ch 2:16 Lebanon, as m' as thou shalt need: 3605
6:18 how m' less this house which I have 637
14:13 they carried away very m' spoil. 7235
14 was exceeding m' spoil in them. "
17:13 m' business in the cities of Judah: *7227
20:25 gathering of the spoil, it was so m'. "
24:11 they saw that there was m' money, "
25: 9 Lord is able to give thee m' more 7235
13 of them, and took m' spoil. 7227
26:10 he had m' cattle, both in the low "
27: 3 on the wall of Ophel he built m'. 7230
5 So m'...the children of Ammon pay 1931
28: 8 took also away m' spoil from them. 7227
30:13 assembled at Jerusalem m' people "
32: 4 was gathered m' people together, "
4 Assyria come, and find m' water? "
15 how m' less shall your God 637,3588
27 Hezekiah had exceeding m' riches 7235
29 had given him substance very m'. 7227
33: 6 wrought m' evil in the sight of the 7235
36:14 transgressed very m' after all the *7227
Ezr 10:13 it is a time of m' rain, and we are
Ne 4:10 decayed, and there is m' rubbish; 7235
6:16 m' cast down in their own eyes: 3966
9:37 it yieldeth m' increase unto the 7235
Es 1:18 shall there arise too m' contempt 1767
Job 4:19 How m' less in them that dwell in 637
9:14 How m' less shall I answer him, 637,3588
15:10 men, m' elder than thy father. 3524
25: 6 How m' less man, that is a worm? 637
31:25 because mine hand had gotten m'; 3524
34:19 How m' less to him that accepteth not
42:10 gave Job twice as m' as he...before. 634
Ps 19:10 than gold, yea, than m' fine gold: 7227
33:16 is not delivered by m' strength. *7230
35:18 will praise thee among m' people. 6079
119:14 thy testimonies, as m' as in all riches.
107 I am afflicted very m': quicken 3966
Pr 7:21 With...m' fair speech she caused 7230
11:31 m' more the wicked and the sinner. 637
13:23 M' food is in the tillage of the 7230
14: 4 m' increase is by the strength of "
15: 6 of the righteous is m' treasure: 7227
11 how m' more then the hearts of the 637
16:16 How m' better is it to get wisdom than
17: 7 fool: m' less do lying lips a prince. 637
19: 7 how m' more do his friends go far "
10 m' less for a servant to have rule "
24 not so m' as bring it to his mouth 1571
21:27 how m' more, when he bringeth it 637
25:16 eat so m' as is sufficient for thee, 1767
27 It is not good to eat m' honey: 7235
Ec 1:18 in m' wisdom is m' grief: and he 7230
5:12 sweet, whether he eat little or m': 7235
17 he hath m' sorrow and wrath with* "
20 he shall not m' remember the days "
7:16 Be not righteous over m'; neither "
17 Be not over m' wicked, neither be "
9:18 but one sinner destroyeth m' good. "
10:18 By m' slothfulness the building *
12:12 and m' study is a weariness of the 7235
Ca 4:10 how m' better is thy love than wine!
Isa 21: 7 hearkened diligently with m' heed: 7227
30:33 pile thereof is fire and m' wood; 7235
56:12 this day, and m' more abundant. *3966
Jer 2:22 with nitre, and take thee m' sope, 7235
36 Why gaddest thou about so m' to 3966
40:12 wine and summer fruits very m'. 7335
Eze 14:21 How m' more when I send my four 637
17:15 give him horses and m' people. 7227
22: 5 which art infamous and m' vexed.* "
23:32 had in derision; it containeth m'. 4767
26: 7 and companies, and m' people. 7227
33:31 their mouth they shew m' love,
Da 4:12, 21 fair, and the fruit thereof m', 7690
7: 5 thus unto it, Arise, devour m' flesh. "
28 my cogitations m' troubled me, and "
11:13 with a great army and with m' riches.
Joe 2: 6 the people shall be m' pained: *
Jon 4:11 their left hand; and also m' cattle? 7227
Na 2:10 and m' pain is in all loins, *2479
Hag 1: 6 Ye have sown m', and bring in 7235
9 Ye looked for m', and lo, it came to "
Mal 3:13 have we spoken so m' against thee?*
M't 6: 7 be heard for their m' speaking. 4180
26 Are ye not m' better than they? 3123
30 shall he not m' more clothe you, O 4183
7:11 how m' more shall your Father 4214
10:25 how m' more shall they call them "
12:12 How m' then is a man better than a "
13: 5 where they had not m' earth: and 4183
15:33 so m' bread in the wilderness, as *5118
26: 9 might have been sold for m', and 4183
M'r 1:45 out, and began to publish it m', "
2: 2 no, not so m' as about the door: *3366
3:20 they could not so m' as eat bread. 3383
4: 5 ground, where it had not m' earth; 4183
5:10 he besought him m' that he would "
M'r 5:21 side, m' people gathered unto him: *4183
24 and m' people followed him, and * "
6:31 they had no leisure so m' as to eat.
34 when he came out, saw m' people, *4183
7:36 so m' the more a great deal they 3123
10:14 Jesus saw it, he was m' displeased, * 23
41 they began to be m' displeased with* "
12:41 and many that were rich cast in m'. 4183
Lu 5:15 so m' the more went there a fame 3123
6: 3 Have ye not read so m' as this, *3761
34 to sinners, to receive as m' again. 2470
7:11 went with him, and m' people. *4183
12 m' people of the city was with her. 2425
26 you, and m' more than a prophet. 4055
47 are forgiven; for she loved m': 4183
8: 4 m' people were gathered together,* "
9:37 from the hill, m' people met him. * "
10:40 was cumbered about m' serving, "
11:13 how m' more shall your heavenly 4214
12:19 m' goods laid up for many years; 4183
24 how m' more are ye better than 4214
28 m' more will he clothe you, O ye of "
48 unto whomsoever m' is given, of 4183
48 given, of him shall be m' required: "
48 to whom men have committed m', "
16: 5 How m' owest thou unto my lord? 4214
7 another, And how m' owest thou? "
10 is least is faithful also in m': 4183
10 in the least is unjust also in m'. "
18:13 not lift up so m' as his eyes unto 3761
39 but he cried so m' the more, Thou* 4183
19:15 how m' every man had gained by
24: 4 were m' perplexed thereabout, *1280
Joh 3:23 because there was m' water there: 4183
6:10 there was m' grass in the place. "
11 of the fishes as m' as they would. 3745
7:12 m' murmuring among the people 4183
12: 9 M' people of the Jews therefore * "
12 m' people that were come to the * "
24 if it die, it bringeth forth m' fruit. "
14:30 I will not talk m' with you: for the "
15: 5 the same bringeth forth m' fruit: "
8 glorified, that ye bear m' fruit; "
Ac 5: 8 whether ye sold the land for so m'? 5118
8 And she said, Yea, for so m'. "
37 drew away m' people after him: *2425
7: 5 it, no, not so m' as to set his foot on:
9:13 how m' evil he hath done to thy 3745
10: 2 which gave m' alms to the people, 4183
11:24 and m' people was added unto the 2425
26 the church, and taught m' people. "
14:22 through m' tribulation enter into *4183
15: 7 when there had been m' disputing, "
16:16 brought her masters m' gain by "
18:10 for I have m' people in this city. "
27 helped them m' which had believed "
19: 2 have not so m' as heard whether 3761
26 and turned away m' people, saying 2425
20: 2 had given them m' exhortation, he 4183
26:24 m' learning doth make thee mad. "
27: 9 Now when m' time was spent, and 2425
10 will be with hurt and m' damage, 4183
16 had m' work to come by the boat: *3433
Ro 1:15 So, as m' as in me is, I am ready 3588
3: 2 M' every way: chiefly, because 4183
5: 9 M' more then, being now justified "
10 m' more, being reconciled, we shall "
15 m' more the grace of God, and the "
17 m' more they which receive...grace "
20 grace did m' more abound: *5248
9:22 endured with m' longsuffering the 4183
11:12 how m' more their fulness? 4124
24 how m' more shall these, which be "
12:18 as m' as lieth in you, live peaceably 3588
15:22 I have been m' hindered from *5248
16: 6 who bestowed m' labour on us. 4183
12 which laboured m' in the Lord. "
1Co 2: 3 and in fear, and in m' trembling. "
5: 1 fornication as is not so m' as *3761
6: 3 m' more things that pertain to this 3386
12:22 m' more those members of the 4183
16:19 Priscilla salute you m' in the Lord. "
2Co 2: 4 out of m' affliction and anguish of "
3: 9 m' more doth the ministration of "
11 m' more that which remaineth is "
6: 4 in m' patience, in afflictions, in "
8: 4 Praying us with m' intreaty that "
15 had gathered m' had nothing over; "
22 things, but now m' more diligent, "
Ph'p 1:14 m' more bold to speak the word *4056
2:12 but now m' more in my absence, 4183
1Th 1: 5 Holy Ghost, and in m' assurance; "
6 received the word in m' affliction, "
2: 2 gospel of God with m' contention. "
1Ti 3: 8 not given to m' wine, not greedy of "
2Ti 4:14 the coppersmith did me m' evil: "
Tit 2: 3 false accusers, not given to m' wine, "
Ph'm 8 though I might be m' bold in Christ* "
16 how m' more unto thee, both in the 4214
Heb 1: 4 made so m' better than the angels, 5118
7:22 By so m' was Jesus made a surety "
8: 6 by how m' also he is the mediator 3745
9:14 How m' more shall the blood of 4214
10:25 so m' the more, as ye see the day 5118
29 how m' sorer punishment, suppose 4214
12: 9 we not m' rather be in subjection 4183
20 if so m' as a beast touch the *2579
25 m' more shall not we escape, if we 4183
Jas 5:16 of a righteous man availeth m'. "
1Pe 1: 7 being m' more precious than of gold* "
2Pe 2:18 the flesh, through m' wantonness,* "
Re 5: 4 I wept m', because no man was 4183
8: 3 was given unto him m' incense, "
18: 7 How m' she hath glorified herself, 3745
7 so m' torment and sorrow give her: 5118
19: 1 I heard a great voice of m' people* 4183

mufflers
Isa 3:19 and the bracelets, and the m', 7479

mulberry
2Sa 5:23 them over against the m' trees. 1057
24 a going in the tops of the m' trees, "
1Ch 14:14 them over against the m' trees. "
15 of going in the tops of the m' trees, "

mulberry-trees See MULBERRY and TREES.

mule See also MULES.
2Sa 13:29 every man gat him up upon his m', 6505
18: 9 And Absalom rode upon a m', and "
9 the m' went under the thick boughs "
9 m' that was under him went away. "
1Ki 1:33 my son to ride upon mine own m', 6506
38 to ride upon king David's m', "
44 him to ride upon the king's m': "
Ps 32: 9 ye not as the horse, or as the m', 6505
Zec 14:15 the plague of the horse, of the m', "

mules See also MULES'.
Ge 36:24 found the m' in the wilderness, *3222
1Ki 10:25 armour, and spices, horses, and m', 6505
18: 5 to save the horses and the m' alive, "
1Ch 12:40 on asses, and on camels, and on m', "
2Ch 9:24 harness, and spices, horses, and m', "
Ezr 2:66 their m', two hundred forty and "
Ne 7:68 their m', two hundred forty and "
Es 8:10 on horseback, and riders on m', *7409
14 posts that rode upon m' and camels* "
Isa 66:20 and in litters, and upon m', and 6505
Eze 27:14 with horses and horsemen and m'. "

mules'
2Ki 5:17 servant two m' burden of earth? 6505

multiplied See also MULTIPLIEDST.
Ge 47:27 and grew, and m' exceedingly. 7235
Ex 1: 7 m', and waxed exceeding mighty; "
12 them, the more they m' and grew. "
20 people m', and waxed very mighty. "
11: 9 my wonders may be m' in the land "
De 1:10 The Lord your God hath m' you, "
8:13 and thy silver and thy gold is m', "
13 and all that thou hast is m'; "
11:21 That your days may be m', and the "
Jos 24: 3 m' his seed, and gave him Isaac. "
1Ch 5: 9 their cattle were m' in the land of "
Job 27:14 If his children be m', it is for the "
35: 6 or if thy transgressions be m', 7231
Ps 16: 4 Their sorrows shall be m' that 7235
38:19 that hate me wrongfully are m'. 7231
107:38 also, so that they are m' greatly; 7235
Pr 9:11 For by me thy days shall be m', "
29:16 When the wicked are m', * "
Isa 9: 3 Thou hast m' the nation, and not "
59:12 our transgressions are m' before 7231
Jer 3:16 when ye be m' and increased in 7235
Eze 5: 7 ye m' more than the nations that *1995
11: 6 Ye have m' your slain in this city, 7235
16:25 passed by, and m' thy whoredoms. "
29 hast moreover m' thy fornication "
51 thou hast m' thine abominations "
21:15 may faint, and their ruins be m': "
23:19 she m' her whoredoms, in calling "
31: 5 boughs were m', and his branches "
35:13 have m' your words against me: 6280
Da 4: 1 the earth; Peace be m' unto you. 7680
6:25 the earth; Peace be m' unto you. "
Ho 2: 8 and oil, and m' her silver and gold, 7235
8:14 and Judah hath m' fenced cities: "
12:10 m' visions, and used similitudes, "
Na 3:16 m' thy merchants above the stars "
Ac 6: 1 number of the disciples was m', *4129
7 of the disciples m' in Jerusalem "
7:17 the people grew and m' in Egypt, "
9:31 comfort of the Holy Ghost, were m'. "
12:24 But the word of God grew and m'. "
1Pe 1: 2 Grace unto you, and peace, be m'. "
2Pe 1: 2 Grace and peace be m' unto you "
Jude 2 unto you, and peace, and love, be m'. "

multipliedst
Ne 9:23 children also m' thou as stars 7235

multiplieth
Job 9:17 and m' my wounds without cause. 7235
34:37 us, and m' his words against God. "
35:16 he m' words without knowledge. 3527

multiply See also MULTIPLIED; MULTIPLIETH; MULTIPLYING.
Ge 1:22 Be fruitful, and m', and fill the 7235
22 seas, and let fowl m' in the earth. "
28 Be fruitful, and m', and replenish "
3:16 I will greatly m' thy sorrow and thy "
6: 1 men began to m' on the face of the 7231
8:17 be fruitful, and m' upon the earth. 7235
9: 1 Be fruitful, and m', and replenish "
7 be ye fruitful, and m'; bring forth "
7 in the earth, and m' therein. "
16:10 I will m' thy seed exceedingly, that "
17: 2 thee, and will m' thee exceedingly. "
20 and will m' him exceedingly; "
22:17 I will m' thy seed as the stars of the "
26: 4 make thy seed to m' as the stars of "
24 and m' thy seed for my servant "
28: 3 and make thee fruitful, and m' thee, "
35:11 be fruitful and m'; a nation and a "
48: 4 will make thee fruitful, and m' thee, "
Ex 1:10 lest they m', and it come to pass, "
7: 3 m' my signs and my wonders in the "
23:29 beast of the field m' against thee. 7227
32:13 I will m' your seed as the stars of 7235
Le 26: 9 and make you fruitful, and m' you, "
De 7:13 thee, and bless thee, and m' thee: "
8: 1 that ye may live, and m', and go in "
13 when thy herds and thy flocks m', "

De 13:17 compassion upon thee, and *m'* thee, 7235
17:16 he shall not *m'* horses to himself, "
16 to the end that he should *m'* horses: "
17 Neither shall he *m'* wives to himself, "
17 *m'* to himself silver and gold. "
28:63 you to do you good, and to *m'* you; "
30: 5 good, and *m'* thee above thy fathers. "
16 that thou mayest live and *m'*: "
1Ch 4:27 neither did all their family *m'*, like "
Job 29:18 and I shall *m'* my days as the sand. "
Jer 30:19 I will *m'* them, and they shall not "
33:22 so will I *m'* the seed of David my "
Eze 16: 7 I have caused thee to *m'* as the bud 7233
36:10 And I will *m'* men upon you, all 7235
11 I will *m'* upon you man and beast; "
30 And I will *m'* the fruit of the tree, "
37:26 and I will place them, and *m'* them, "
Am 4: 4 at Gilgal *m'* transgression; and "
2Co 9:10 *m'* your seed sown, and increase 4129
Heb 6:14 and multiplying I will *m'* thee. "

multiplying
Ge 22:17 in *m'* I will multiply thy seed as 7235
Heb 6:14 thee, and *m'* I will multiply thee. 4129

multitude See also MULTITUDES.
Ge 16:10 it shall not be numbered for *m'*. 7230
28: 3 thou mayest be a *m'* of people; *6951
30:30 and it is now increased unto a *m'*; 7230
32:12 which cannot be numbered for *m'*. "
48: 4 I will make of thee a *m'* of people; *6951
16 let them grow into a *m'* in the midst 7230
19 seed shall become a *m'* of nations. 4393
Ex 12:38 mixed *m'* went up also with them; 7227
23: 2 shalt not follow a *m'* to do evil; "
Le 25:16 According to the *m'* of years thou 7230
Nu 11: 4 the mixt *m'* that was among them 628
32: 1 Gad had a very great *m'* of cattle: 7227
De 1:10 day as the stars of heaven for *m'*. 7230
10:22 thee as the stars of heaven for *m'*. "
28:62 were as the stars of heaven for *m'*: "
Jos 11: 4 that is upon the sea shore in *m'*, "
J'g 4: 7 army, with his chariots and his *m'*; 1995
6: 5 they came as grasshoppers for *m'*; 7230
7:12 valley like grasshoppers for *m'*; "
12 as the sand by the sea side for *m'*. "
1Sa 13: 5 sand which is on the sea shore in *m'*: "
14:16 and, behold, the *m'* melted away, 1995
2Sa 6:19 even among the whole *m'* of Israel, "
17:11 the sand that is by the sea for *m'*; 7230
1Ki 3: 8 be numbered nor counted for *m'*. "
4:20 the sand which is by the sea in *m'*, "
8: 5 not be told nor numbered for *m'*. "
20:13 Hast thou seen all this great *m'*? 1995
28 deliver all this great *m'* into thine "
2Ki 7:13 they are as all the *m'* of Israel that 1995
13 even as all the *m'* of the Israelites "
19:23 With the *m'* of my chariots I am 7393
25:11 with the remnant of the *m'*, did 1995
2Ch 1: 9 like the dust of the earth in *m'*. 7227
5: 6 not be told nor numbered for *m'*. 7230
13: 8 and ye be a great *m'*, and there are 1995
14:11 in thy name we go against this *m'*. "
20: 2 cometh a great *m'* against thee "
15 dismayed by reason of this great *m'*; "
24 wilderness, they looked unto the *m'*, "
28: 5 and carried away a great *m'* of them "
30:18 For a *m'* of the people, even many 4768
32: 7 nor for all the *m'* that is with him: 1995
Ne 13: 3 from Israel all the mixed *m'*. 6154
Es 5:11 riches, and the *m'* of his children, 7230
10: 3 accepted of the *m'* of his brethren, "
Job 11: 2 not the *m'* of words be answered? "
31:34 Did I fear a great *m'*, or did the 1995
32: 7 *m'* of years should teach wisdom. 7230
33:19 *m'* of his bones with strong pain: *7379
35: 9 By reason of the *m'* of the oppressions 7230
39: 7 He scorneth the *m'* of the city, *1995
Ps 5: 7 thy house in the *m'* of thy mercy: ‡7230
10 in the *m'* of their transgressions; "
33:16 no king saved by the *m'* of an host: "
42: 4 for I had gone with the *m'*, I went *5519
4 praise, with a *m'* that kept holyday. 1995
49: 6 in the *m'* of their riches; 7230
51: 1 unto the *m'* of thy tender mercies "
68:30 of spearmen, the *m'* of the bulls, 5712
69:13 in the *m'* of thy mercy hear me, ‡7230
16 to the *m'* of thy tender mercies: "
74:19 unto the *m'* of the wicked: forget 2416
94:19 In the *m'* of my thoughts within 7230
97: 1 let the *m'* of isles be glad thereof. 7227
106: 7 not the *m'* of thy mercies; but 7230
45 according to the *m'* of his mercies. "
109:30 I will praise him among the *m'*. 7227
Pr 10:19 In the *m'* of words there wanteth 7230
11:14 in the *m'* of counsellors there is "
14:28 In the *m'* of people is the king's "
15:22 in the *m'* of counsellors they are "
20:15 There is gold, and a *m'* of rubies: "
24: 6 in *m'* of counsellors there is safety. "
Ec 5: 3 cometh through the *m'* of business; "
3 a fool's voice is known by *m'* of "
7 For in the *m'* of dreams and many "
Isa 1:11 the *m'* of your sacrifices unto me? "
5:13 and their *m'* dried up with thirst. 1995
14 their glory, and their *m'*, and their "
13: 4 The noise of a *m'* in the mountains, "
16:14 contemned, with all that great *m'*; "
17:12 Woe to the *m'* of many people, "
29: 5 Moreover the *m'* of thy strangers "
5 the *m'* of the terrible ones shall be "
7 the *m'* of all the nations that fight "
8 So shall the *m'* of all the nations be, "
31: 4 a *m'* of shepherds is called forth 4393
32:14 the *m'* of the city shall be left; the 1995
37:24 By the *m'* of my chariots am I 7230
47: 9 and for the *m'* of thy sorceries, "

Isa 47:12 and with the *m'* of thy sorceries, 7230
13 wearied in the *m'* of thy counsels. "
60: 6 The *m'* of camels shall cover thee, 8229
63: 7 and according to the *m'* of his *7230
Jer 3:23 and from the *m'* of mountains: *1995
10:13 is a *m'* of waters in the heavens, * "
12: 6 they have called a *m'* after thee: *4392
30:14 one, for the *m'* of thine iniquity; *7230
15 for the *m'* of thine iniquity: * "
44:15 a great *m'*, even all the people *6951
46:25 I will punish the *m'* of No, and * 582
49:32 and the *m'* of their cattle a spoil: 527
51:16 is a *m'* of waters in the heavens; * "
42 covered with the *m'* of the waves "
52:15 of Babylon, and the rest of the *m'*. "
La 1: 5 for the *m'* of her transgressions: 7230
3:32 according to the *m'* of his mercies. "
Eze 7:11 shall remain, nor of their *m'*, nor 1995
12 wrath is upon all the *m'* thereof. "
13 is touching the whole *m'* thereof, "
14 wrath is upon all the *m'* thereof. "
14: 4 according to the *m'* of his idols; 7230
19:11 height with the *m'* of her branches. "
23:42 a voice of a *m'* being at ease was 1995
27:12 of the *m'* of all kind of riches; 7230
16 by reason of the *m'* of the wares "
18 thy merchant in the *m'* of the wares "
18 making, for the *m'* of all riches; "
33 the earth with the *m'* of thy riches "
28:16 By the *m'* of thy merchandise they‡ "
18 by the *m'* of thine iniquities, by "
29:19 he shall take her *m'*, and take her 1995
30: 4 and they shall take away her *m'*, "
10 make the *m'* of Egypt to cease by "
15 and I will cut off the *m'* of No. "
31: 2 king of Egypt, and to his *m'*; Whom "
5 long because of the *m'* of waters, *7227
9 him fair by the *m'* of his branches: 7230
18 This is Pharaoh and all his *m'*, 1995
32:12 mighty will I cause thy *m'* to fall, "
12 all the *m'* thereof shall be destroyed. "
16 even for Egypt, and for all her *m'*, "
18 of man, wail for the *m'* of Egypt, "
24 There is Elam and all her *m'* round "
25 midst of the slain with all her *m'*: "
26 is Meshech, Tubal, and all her *m'*: "
31 shall be comforted over all his *m'*, "
32 even Pharaoh and all his *m'*, saith "
39:11 shall they bury Gog and all his *m'*: "
47: 9 there shall be a very great *m'* of fish, "
Da 10: 6 of his words like the voice of a *m'*. 1995
11:10 shall assemble a *m'* of great forces: "
11 and he shall set forth a great *m'*; "
11 the *m'* shall be given into his hand. "
12 when he hath taken away the *m'*, "
13 shall set forth a *m'* greater than "
Hos 9: 7 mad, for the *m'* of thine iniquity, ‡7230
10: 1 according to the *m'* of his fruit he‡ "
13 way, in the *m'* of thy mighty men. "
Mic 2:12 noise by reason of the *m'* of men. "
Na 3: 3 and there is a *m'* of slain, and a 7230
4 Because of the *m'* of the whoredoms "
Zec 2: 4 the *m'* of m n and cattle therein: "
M't 13: 2 the whole *m'* stood on the shore. 3793
34 things spake Jesus unto the *m'* in "
36 Then Jesus sent the *m'* away, and* "
14: 5 put him to death, he feared the *m'*, "
14 went forth, and saw a great *m'*, "
15 send the *m'* away, that they may * "
19 he commanded the *m'* to sit down* "
19 disciples, and...disciples to the *m'*.* "
15:10 And he called the *m'*, and said unto "
31 Insomuch that the *m'* wondered, "
32 said, I have compassion on the *m'*, "
33 wilderness, as to fill so great a *m'*? "
35 he commanded the *m'* to sit down "
36 disciples, and...disciples to the *m'*.* "
39 And he sent away the *m'*, and took* "
17:14 And when they were come to the *m'*, "
20:29 Jericho, a great *m'* followed him. "
31 And the *m'* rebuked them, because "
21: 8 And a very great *m'* spread their "
11 And the *m'* said, This is Jesus the* "
46 hands on him, they feared the *m'*.* "
22:33 And when the *m'* heard this, they* "
23: 1 Then spake Jesus to the *m'*, and to* "
26:47 with him a great *m'* with swords "
27:20 *m'* that they should ask Barabbas,* "
24 washed his hands before the *m'*, "
M'r 2:13 and all the *m'* resorted unto him, "
3: 7 a great *m'* from Galilee followed 4128
8 a great *m'*, when they had heard "
9 wait on him because of the *m'*, *3793
20 And the *m'* cometh together again, "
32 And the *m'* sat about him, and they "
4: 1 was gathered unto him a great *m'*, "
1 and the whole *m'* was by the sea on "
36 when they had sent away the *m'*, "
5:31 Thou seest the *m'* thronging thee, "
7:33 And he took him aside from the *m'*, "
8: 1 those days the *m'* being very great, "
2 I have compassion on the *m'*, "
9:14 he saw a great *m'* about them, and "
17 one of the *m'* answered and said, "
14:43 with him a great *m'* with swords "
15: 8 the *m'* crying aloud began to desire "
Lu 1:10 *m'* of the people were praying 4128
2:13 a *m'* of the heavenly host praising "
3: 7 *m'* that came forth to be baptized *3793
5: 6 they inclosed a great *m'* of fishes: 4128
19 bring him in because of the *m'*, 3793
6:17 and a great *m'* of people out of all *4128
19 the whole *m'* sought to touch him: 3793
8:37 Then the whole *m'* of the country *4128
45 the *m'* throng thee and press thee, *3793
9:12 Send the *m'* away, that they may "

Lu 9:16 the disciples to set before the *m'*. 3793
12: 1 an innumerable *m'* of people, 3461
18:36 hearing the *m'* pass by, he asked 3793
19:37 whole *m'* of the disciples began to 4128
39 the Pharisees from among the *m'* 3793
22: 6 unto them in the absence of the *m'*. "
47 while he yet spake, behold a *m'*, "
23: 1 And the whole *m'* of them arose, *4128
Joh 5: 3 lay a great *m'* of impotent folk, "
13 away, a *m'* being in that place. 3793
6: 2 a great *m'* followed him, because "
21: 6 able to draw it for the *m'* of fishes. 4128
Ac 2: 6 abroad, the *m'* came together, and "
4:32 the *m'* of them that believed were "
5:16 came also a *m'* out of the cities "
6: 2 called the *m'* of the disciples unto "
5 the saying pleased the whole *m'*: "
14: 1 that a great *m'* both of the Jews "
4 But the *m'* of the city was divided: "
15:12 Then all the *m'* kept silence, and "
30 they had gathered the *m'* together, "
16:22 *m'* rose up together against them: 3793
17: 4 of the devout Greeks a great *m'*, 4128
19: 9 spake evil of that way before the *m'*, "
33 they drew Alexander out of the *m'*, 3793
21:22 the *m'* must needs come together: *4128
34 thing, some another, among...*m'*: *3793
36 the *m'* of the people followed after, 4128
23: 7 Sadducees: and the *m'* was divided. "
24:18 neither with *m'*, nor with tumult. *3793
25:24 about whom all the *m'* of the Jews 4128
Heb 11:12 many as the stars of the sky in *m'*, "
Jas 5:20 death, and shall hide a *m'* of sins. "
1Pe 4: 8 for charity shall cover a *m'* of sins. "
Re 7: 9 a great *m'*, which no man could 3793
19: 6 as it were the voice of a great *m'*, "

multitudes
Eze 32:20 the sword: draw her and all her *m'*. 1995
Joe 3:14 *M'*, *m'* in the valley of decision: "
M't 4:25 followed him great *m'* of people 3793
5: 1 And seeing the *m'*, he went up into "
8: 1 mountain, great *m'* followed him. "
18 Jesus saw great *m'* about him, "
9: 8 But when the *m'* saw it, they "
33 and the *m'* marvelled, saying, It "
36 But when he saw the *m'*, he was "
11: 7 Jesus began to say unto the *m'* "
12:15 and great *m'* followed him, and he* "
13: 2 great *m'* were gathered together "
14:22 side, while he sent the *m'* away: "
23 when he had sent the *m'* away, he "
15:30 great *m'* came unto him, having "
19: 2 And great *m'* followed him; and he "
21: 9 And the *m'* that went before, and "
26:55 same hour said Jesus to the *m'*, "
Lu 5:15 great *m'* came together to hear, "
14:25 there went great *m'* with him: and "
Ac 5:14 Lord, *m'* both of men and women.) 4128
13:45 when the Jews saw the *m'*, they 3793
Re 17:15 are peoples, and *m'*, and nations, "

munition See also MUNITIONS.
Isa 29: 7 that fight against her and her *m'*, *4685
Na 2: 1 keep the *m'*, watch the way, make‡4694

munitions
Isa 33:16 defence shall be the *m'* of rocks: 4679

Muppim (*mup'-pim*) See also SHUPPIM.
Ge 46:21 and Rosh, *M'*, and Huppim, and 4649

murder See also MURDERS.
Ps 10: 8 places doth he *m'* the innocent: 2026
94: 6 stranger, and *m'* the fatherless. 7523
Jer 7: 9 Will ye steal, *m'*, and commit "
Ho 6: 9 company of priests *m'* in the way "
M't 19:18 Jesus said, Thou shalt do no *m'*, *5407
M'r 15: 7 committed *m'* in the insurrection. 5408
Lu 23:19 and for *m'*, was cast into prison.) "
25 and *m'* was cast into prison, whom "
Ro 1:29 full of envy, *m'*, debate, deceit, "

murderer See also MURDERERS.
Nu 35:16 of iron, so that he die, he is a *m'*: *7523
16 the *m'* shall surely be put to death.* "
17 he may die, and he die, he is a *m'*: * "
17 the *m'* shall surely be put to death.* "
18 he may die, and he die, he is a *m'*: * "
18 the *m'* shall surely be put to death.* "
19 of blood himself shall slay the *m'*: * "
21 for he is a *m'*: the revenger of blood* "
21 shall slay the *m'*, when he meeteth* "
30 the *m'* shall be put to death by the* "
31 no satisfaction for the life of a *m'*,* "
2Ki 6:32 this son of a *m'* hath sent to take "
Job 24:14 *m'* rising with the light killeth the "
Ho 9:13 bring forth his children to the *m'*. *2026
Joh 8:44 He was a *m'* from the beginning, 443
Ac 3:14 desired a *m'* to be granted unto 5406
28: 4 No doubt this man is a *m'*, whom, "
1Pe 4:15 let none of you suffer as a *m'*, or as "
1Jo 3:15 hateth his brother is a *m'*: and ye 443
15 know that no *m'* hath eternal life "

murderers
2Ki 14: 6 children of the *m'* he slew not: 5221
Isa 1:21 lodged in it; but now *m'*. 7523
Jer 4:31 my soul is wearied because of *m'*. 2026
M't 22: 7 armies, and destroyed those *m'*, 5406
Ac 7:52 been now the betrayers and *m'*: "
21:38 four thousand men that were *m'*? *4607
1Ti 1: 9 and profane, for *m'* of fathers 3964
9 and *m'* of mothers, for manslayers, 3389
Re 21: 8 and the abominable, and *m'*, and 5406
22:15 and whoremongers, and *m'*, and "

murders
M't 15:19 heart proceed evil thoughts, *m'*, 5408
M'r 7:21 adulteries, fornications, *m'*, "

Ga 5:21 Envyings, *m*', drunkenness, *5408
Re 9:21 Neither repented they of their *m*', "

murmur See also MURMURED; MURMURING.
Ex 16: 7 are we, that ye *m*' against us? 3885
8 which ye *m*' against him: and "
Nu 14:27 congregation which *m*' against me?"
27 Israel, which they *m*' against me. "
36 congregation to *m*' against him, "
16:11 is Aaron, that ye *m*' against him? "
17: 5 whereby they *m*' against you. "
Joh 6:43 them, *M*' not among yourselves. 1111
1Co 10:10 Neither *m*' ye, as some of them also"

murmured
Ex 15:24 And the people *m*' against Moses, 3885
16: 2 children of Israel *m*' against Moses "
17: 3 and the people *m*' against Moses, "
Nu 14: 2 children of Israel *m*' against Moses "
29 upward, which have *m*' against me, "
16:41 children of Israel *m*' against Moses "
De 1:27 And ye *m*' in your tents, and said, 7279
Jos 9:18 And all...*m*' against the princes. 3885
Ps 106:25 But *m*' in their tents, and 7279
Isa 29:24 they that *m*' shall learn doctrine. "
M't 20:11 they *m*' against the goodman of 1111
M'r 14: 5 poor. And they *m*' against her. 1690
Lu 5:30 Pharisees *m*' against his disciples, 1111
15: 2 And the Pharisees and scribes *m*', 1234
19: 7 And when they saw it, they all *m*', "
Joh 6:41 The Jews then *m*' at him, because 1111
61 himself that his disciples *m*' at it, "
7:32 that the people *m*' such things * "
1Co 10:10 as some of them also *m*', and were "

murmurers
Jude 16 These are *m*', complainers, 1113

murmuring See also MURMURINGS.
Joh 7:12 was much *m*' among the people 1112
Ac 6: 1 there arose a *m*' of the Grecians "

murmurings
Ex 16: 7 heareth your *m*' against the Lord: 8519
8 for that the Lord heareth your *m*' "
8 your *m*' are not against us, but "
9 Lord: for he hath heard your *m*'. "
12 have heard the *m*' of the children of"
Nu 14:27 have heard the *m*' of the children of"
17: 5 me the *m*' of the children of Israel, "
10 quite take away their *m*' from me, "
Ph'p 2:14 Do all things without *m*' and 1112

murrain
Ex 9: 3 there shall be a very grievous *m*'. 1698

muse See also MUSED; MUSING.
Ps 143: 5 I *m*' on the work of thy hands. 7878

mused
Lu 3:15 all men *m*' in their hearts of John,*1260

Mushi (*mu'-shi*) See also MUSHITES.
Ex 6:19 sons of Merari; Mahali and *M*': 4187
Nu 3:20 by their families; Mahli, and *M*'. "
1Ch 6:19 The sons of Merari; Mahli, and *M*'. "
47 the son of *M*', the son of Merari, "
23:21 sons of Merari; Mahli, and *M*'. "
23 sons of *M*'; Mahli, and Eder, and "
24:26 sons of Merari were Mahli and *M*': "
30 sons also of *M*'; Mahli, and Eder, "

Mushites (*mu'-shites*)
Nu 3:33 and the family of the *M*': these 4188
26:58 family of the *M*', the family of the "

music See MUSICK.

musical
1Ch 16:42 and with *m*' instruments of God. *7892
Ne 12:36 with the *m*' instruments of David "
Ec 2: 8 as *m*' instruments, and that of all†7705

musician See also MUSICIANS.
Ps 4: *title* To the chief *M*' on Neginoth, 5329
5: *title* To the chief *M*' upon Nehiloth, "
6: *title* To the chief *M*' upon Neginoth "
8: *title* To the chief *M*' upon Gittith, "
9: *title* To the chief *M*' upon Muth-labben,"
11: *title* To the chief *M*', A Psalm of "
12: *title* To the chief *M*' upon Sheminith, "
13: *title* To the chief *M*', A Psalm of "
14: *title* To the chief *M*', A Psalm of "
18: *title* To the chief *M*', A Psalm of "
19: *title* To the chief *M*', A Psalm of "
20: *title* To the chief *M*', A Psalm of "
21: *title* To the chief *M*', A Psalm of "
22: *title* To the chief *M*' upon Aijeleth "
31: *title* To the chief *M*', A Psalm of "
36: *title* To the chief *M*', A Psalm of "
39: *title* To the chief *M*', even to "
40: *title* To the chief *M*', A Psalm of "
41: *title* To the chief *M*', A Psalm of "
42: *title* To the chief *M*', Maschil, for "
44: *title* To the chief *M*' for the sons of "
45: *title* To the chief *M*' upon Shoshannim,"
46: *title* To the chief *M*' for the sons of "
47: *title* To the chief *M*', A Psalm for "
49: *title* To the chief *M*', A Psalm for "
51: *title* To the chief *M*', A Psalm of "
52: *title* To the chief *M*', Maschil, A "
53: *title* To the chief *M*' upon Mahalath, "
54: *title* To the chief *M*' on Neginoth, "
55: *title* To the chief *M*' on Neginoth, "
56: *title* To the chief *M*' upon Jonath-... "
57: *title* To the chief *M*', Al-taschith, "
58: *title* To the chief *M*', Al-taschith, "
59: *title* To the chief *M*', Al-taschith, "
60: *title* To the chief *M*' upon Shushan-... "
61: *title* To the chief *M*' upon Neginah, "
62: *title* To the chief *M*', to Jeduthun, "
64: *title* To the chief *M*', A Psalm of "
65: *title* To the chief *M*', A Psalm and "
66: *title* To the chief *M*', A Song or "
Ps 67: *title* To the chief *M*' on Neginoth. 5329
68: *title* To the chief *M*', a Psalm or "
69: *title* To the chief *M*' upon Shoshannim,"
70: *title* To the chief *M*', A Psalm of "
75: *title* To the chief *M*', Al-taschith, "
76: *title* To the chief *M*' on Neginoth, "
77: *title* To the chief *M*', to Jeduthun, "
80: *title* To...chief *M*' upon Shoshannim-..."
81: *title* To the chief *M*' upon Gittith, "
84: *title* To the chief *M*' upon Gittith, "
85: *title* To the chief *M*', A Psalm for "
88: *title* to the chief *M*' upon Mahalath "
109: *title* To the chief *M*', A Psalm of "
139: *title* To the chief *M*', A Psalm of "
140: *title* To the chief *M*', A Psalm of "

musicians
Re 18:22 of harpers, and *m*', and of pipers,*3451

musick
1Sa 18: 6 with joy, and with instruments of *m*'.
1Ch 15:16 singers with instruments of *m*', 7892
2Ch 5:13 cymbals and instruments of *m*', "
7: 6 instruments of *m*' of the Lord, "
23:13 the singers with instruments of *m*'."
34:12 could skill of instruments of *m*'. "
Ec 12: 4 all the daughters of *m*' shall be "
La 3:63 their rising up; I am their *m*'. *4485
5:14 gate, the young men from their *m*'.5058
Da 3: 5 dulcimer, and all kinds of *m*', ye 2170
7 psaltery, and all kinds of *m*', all "
10, 15 dulcimer, and all kinds of *m*', "
6:18 neither were instruments of *m*' "
Am 6: 5 to themselves instruments of *m*', 7892
Lu 15:25 house, he heard *m*' and dancing. 4858

musing
Ps 39: 3 while I was *m*' the fire burned: 1901

must
Ge 29:26 Laban said, It *m*' not be so done in*
30:16 Thou *m*' come in unto me; for surely
43:11 If it *m*' be so now, do this; take of the*
47:29 the time drew nigh that Israel *m*' die:
Ex 10: 9 for we *m*' hold a feast unto the Lord.
25 Thou *m*' give us also sacrifices and
26 thereof *m*' we take to serve the Lord
26 not with what we *m*' serve the Lord,
12:16 save that which every man *m*' eat,
18:20 *m*' walk, and the work that they *m*' do.
Le 11:32 it *m*' be put into water, and it shall be
23: 6 days ye *m*' eat unleavened bread. *
Nu 6:21 so he *m*' do after the law of his
20:10 *m*' we fetch you water out of this *
23:12 *M*' I not take heed to speak that
26 that the Lord speaketh, that I *m*' do?
De 1:22 again by what way we *m*' go up,
4:22 But I *m*' die in this land,
22 I *m*' not go over Jordan: but ye
12:18 *m*' eat them before the Lord thy God*
31: 7 thou *m*' go with this people unto the*
14 thy days approach that thou *m*' die:
Jos 3: 4 know the way by which ye *m*' go:
22:18 that ye *m*' turn away this day from
J'g 13:16 thou *m*' offer it unto the Lord.
21:17 There *m*' be an inheritance for them
Ru 4: 5 thou *m*' buy it also of Ruth the
1Sa 14:43 was in mine hand, and, lo, I *m*' die.
2Sa 14:14 we *m*' needs die, and are as water
23: 3 that ruleth over men *m*' be just, *
7 touch them *m*' be fenced with iron
1Ki 18:27 he sleepeth, and *m*' be awaked.
1Ch 22: 5 Lord *m*' be exceedingly magnifical,
Ps 32: 9 mouth *m*' be held in with bit and
Pr 18:24 hath friends *m*' shew himself friendly:*
19:19 deliver him, yet thou *m*' do it again.
Ec 10:10 edge, then *m*' he put to more strength:
Ca 8:12 O Solomon, *m*' have a thousand, and*
Jer 10: 5 they *m*' needs be borne, because thy
19 Truly this is a grief, and I *m*' bear it.
Eze 34:18 but ye *m*' tread down with your feet
18 ye *m*' foul the residue with your feet?
M't 16:21 that he *m*' go unto Jerusalem, 1163
17:10 scribes that Elias *m*' first come? "
18: 7 it *m*' needs be that offences come; 318
24: 6 all these things *m*' come to pass, 1163
26:54 be fulfilled, that thus it *m*' be? "
M'r 2:22 new wine *m*' be put into new bottles.*
8:31 Son of man *m*' suffer many things,1163
9:11 the scribes that Elias *m*' first come?"
12 man, that he *m*' suffer many things, "
13: 7 for such things *m*' needs be; but 1163
10 the gospel *m*' first be published "
14:49 but the scriptures *m*' be fulfilled. *2443
Lu 2:49 that I *m*' be about my Father's 1163
4:43 I *m*' preach the kingdom of God to "
5:38 new wine *m*' be put into new bottles;
9:22 Son of man *m*' suffer many things,1163
13:33 Nevertheless I *m*' walk to-day, and "
14:18 and I *m*' needs go and see it: 2192
17:25 first *m*' he suffer many things, and1163
19: 5 for to day I *m*' abide at thy house. "
21: 9 these things *m*' first come to pass; "
22: 7 when the passover *m*' be killed. "
37 *m*' yet be accomplished in me, "
23:17 (he *m*' release one unto them at *
24: 7 Son of man *m*' be delivered into 1163
44 that all things *m*' be fulfilled, which"
Joh 3: 7 unto thee, Ye *m*' be born again. "
14 so *m*' the Son of man be lifted up: "
30 He *m*' increase, but I *m*' decrease. "
30 He...increase, but I...decrease. "
4: 4 he *m*' needs go through Samaria. "
24 *m*' worship him in spirit and in 1163
9: 4 I *m*' work the works of him that "
10:16 them also I *m*' bring, and they "
12:34 The Son of man *m*' be lifted up? "
Joh 20: 9 he *m*' rise again from the dead. 1163
Ac 1:16 *m*' needs have been fulfilled, "
22 *m*' one be ordained to be a witness "
3:21 Whom the heaven *m*' receive until "
4:12 men, whereby we *m*' be saved. "
9: 6 shall be told thee what thou *m*' do. "
16 he *m*' suffer for my name's sake. "
14:22 *m*' through much tribulation enter*"
15:24 souls, saying, Ye *m*' be circumcised,*
16:30 Sirs, what *m*' I do to be saved? 1163
17: 3 Christ *m*' needs have suffered, * "
18:21 I *m*' by all means keep this feast * "
19:21 been there, I *m*' also see Rome. "
21:22 the multitude *m*' needs come * "
23:11 so *m*' thou bear witness also at "
27:24 thou *m*' be brought before Cæsar: "
26 *m*' be cast upon a certain island. "
Ro 13: 5 ye *m*' needs be subject, not only "
1Co 5:10 for then *m*' ye needs go out of the 3784
11:19 there *m*' be also heresies among 1163
15:25 For he *m*' reign, till he hath put all "
53 corruptible *m*' put on incorruption,"
53 this mortal *m*' put on immortality. "
2Co 5:10 For we *m*' all appear before the 1163
11:30 If I *m*' needs glory, I will glory of "
1Ti 3: 2 A bishop then *m*' be blameless, the "
7 Moreover he *m*' have a good report"
8 Likewise *m*' the deacons be grave, not
11 Even so *m*' their wives be grave, not
2Ti 2: 6 laboureth *m*' be first partaker of 1163
24 servant of the Lord *m*' not strive; "
Tit 1: 7 For a bishop *m*' be blameless, as "
11 Whose mouths *m*' be stopped, who "
Heb 4: 6 remaineth that some *m*' enter therein,*
9:16 there *m*' also of necessity be the
26 For then *m*' he often have suffered 1163
11: 6 he that cometh to God *m*' believe "
13:17 as they that *m*' give account, that *
1Pe 4:17 judgment *m*' begin at the house of*
2Pe 1:14 shortly I *m*' put off this my tabernacle,*
Re 1: 1 which *m*' shortly come to pass; 1163
4: 1 thee things which *m*' be hereafter. "
10:11 Thou *m*' prophesy again before "
11: 5 he *m*' in this manner be killed. "
13:10 sword *m*' be killed with the sword. "
17:10 he *m*' continue a short space. "
20: 3 after that he *m*' be loosed a little "
22: 6 things which *m*' shortly be done. "

mustard
M't 13:31 heaven is like a grain of *m*' seed, 4615
17:20 ye have faith as a grain of *m*' seed, "
M'r 4:31 It is like a grain of *m*' seed, which "
Lu 13:19 It is like a grain of *m*' seed, which "
17: 6 ye had faith as a grain of *m*' seed, "

mustard-seed See MUSTARD and SEED.

mustered
2Ki 25:19 which *m*' the people of the land, 6633
Jer 52:25 host, who *m*' the people of the land;"

mustereth
Isa 13: 4 the Lord of hosts *m*' the host of 6485

mutability See IMMUTABILITY.

mutable See IMMUTABLE.

Muth-labben (*muth-lab'-ben*)
Ps 9: *title* To the chief Musician upon *M*', 4192

mutter See also MUTTERED.
Isa 8:19 wizards that peep, and that *m*': 1897

muttered
Isa 59: 3 your tongue hath *m*' perverseness.*1897

mutual
Ro 1:12 *m*' faith both of you and me. *1722,240

muzzle
De 25: 4 not *m*' the ox when he treadeth 2629
1Co 9: 9 not *m*' the mouth of the ox that 5392
1Ti 5:18 not *m*' the ox that treadeth out "

my See in the APPENDIX; also MINE; MYSELF.

Myra (*mi'-rah*)
Ac 27: 5 we came to *M*', a city of Lycia. 3460

myrrh
Ge 37:25 bearing spicery and balm and *m*', 3910
43:11 spices, and *m*', nuts, and almonds: "
Ex 30:23 of pure *m*' five hundred shekels, 4753
Es 2:12 six months with oil of *m*', and six "
Ps 45: 8 thy garments smell of *m*', and aloes,"
Pr 7:17 I have perfumed my bed with *m*', "
Ca 1:13 A bundle of *m*' is my wellbeloved "
3: 6 of smoke, perfumed with *m*' and "
4: 6 will get me to the mountain of *m*', "
14 *m*' and aloes, with all the chief "
5: 1 gathered my *m*' with my spice; I "
5 my hands dropped with *m*', and my"
5 my fingers with sweet smelling *m*',"
13 lilies, dropping sweet smelling *m*'. "
M't 2:11 gold, and frankincense, and *m*'. 4666
M'r 15:23 to drink wine mingled with *m*': 4669
Joh 19:39 a mixture of *m*' and aloes, about 4666

myrtle
Ne 8:15 *m*' branches, and palm branches, 1918
Isa 41:19 the shittah tree, and the *m*', and "
55:13 brier shall come up the *m*' tree: "
Zec 1: 8 he stood among the *m*' trees that "
10 man that stood among the *m*' trees"
11 that stood among the *m*' trees, and "

myrtle-tree See MYRTLE and TREE.

myself
Ge 3:10 because I was naked; and I hid *m*'.
22:16 By *m*' have I sworn, saith the Lord,
Ex 19: 4 wings, and brought you unto *m*'.
Nu 8:17 land of Egypt I sanctified them for *m*.
12: 6 I the Lord will make *m*' known unto
De 1: 9 I am not able to bear you *m*' alone:

De 1:12 How can I m· alone bear your
10: 5 I turned m· and came down from the*
J'g 16:20 at other times before, and shake m·.
Ru 4: 6 I cannot redeem it for m·, lest I mar
1Sa 13:12 I forced m· therefore, and offered a
20: 5 that I may hide m· in the field unto
25:33 avenging m· with mine own hand.
2Sa 18: 2 surely go forth with you m· also. 589
22:24 and have kept m· from mine iniquity.
1Ki 18:15 I will surely show m· unto him to-day.
22:30 I will disguise m·, and enter into the
2Ki 5:18 and I bow m· in the house of Rimmon:
18 when I bow down m· in the house of
2Ch 7:12 place to m· for a house of sacrifice.
18:29 I will disguise m·, and will go to the
Es 5:12 banquet that she had prepared but m·.
6: 6 delight to do honour more than to m·?
Job 6:10 I would harden m· in sorrow: let him*
7:20 thee, so that I am a burden to m·?
9:20 If I justify m·, mine own mouth shall*
27 off my heaviness, and comfort m·:*
30 If I wash m· with snow water, and
10: 1 I will leave my complaint upon m·;*
13:20 then will I not hide m· from thee.
19: 4 erred, mine error remaineth with m·.
27 Whom I shall see for m·, and mine†
31:17 have eaten my morsel m· alone, and*
29 or lifted up m· when evil found him:
42: 6 I abhor m·, and repent in dust and
Ps 18:23 and I kept m· from mine iniquity.
35:14 I behaved m· as though he had been
55:12 then I would have hid m· from him:
57: 8 and harp: I m· will awake early.
101: 2 behave m· wisely in a perfect way.
108: 2 and harp: I m· will awake early.
109: 4 adversaries: but I give m· unto prayer.
119:16 I will delight m· in thy statutes: I will
47 will delight m· in thy commandments,
52 old, O Lord; and I have comforted m·.
131: 1 do I exercise m· in great matters,
2 I have behaved and quieted m·, *5315
Ec 2: 3 in mine heart to give m· unto wine,*
12 I turned m· to behold wisdom, and
14 I m· perceived also that one event* 589
19 I have shewed m· wise under the sun.*
Isa 33:10 I be exalted; now will I lift up m·.
42:14 I have been still, and refrained m·:
43:21 This people have I formed for m·; they

Isa 44:24 spreadeth abroad the earth by m·;*
45:23 I have sworn by m·, the word is gone
Jer 8:18 I would comfort m· against sorrow,
21: 5 I m· will fight against you with an 589
22: 5 words, I swear by m·, saith the Lord,
49:13 I have sworn by m·, saith the Lord,
Eze 14: 7 I the Lord will answer him by m·:
20: 5 made m· known unto them in the land
9 sight I made m· known unto them,
29: 3 mine own, and I have made it for m·.
35:11 I will make m· known among them,
38:23 will I magnify m·, and sanctify m·;
Da 10: 3 neither did I anoint m· at all, till
Mic 6: 6 and bow m· before the high God?
Hab 3:16 I trembled in m·, that I might rest*
Zec 7: 3 separating m·, as I have done these
Lu 7: 7 I m· worthy to come unto thee: 1683
24:39 my hands and my feet, that it is I m·:
Joh 5:31 If I bear witness of m·, my witness 1683
7:17 be of God, or whether I speak of m·. "
28 I am not come of m·, but he that "
8:14 Though I bear record of m·, yet my "
18 I am one that bear witness of m·, "
28 am he, and that I do nothing of m·; "
42 neither came I of m·, but he sent "
54 If I honour m·, my honour is "
10:18 it from me, but I lay it down of m·. "
12:49 For I have not spoken of m·; but "
14: 3 again, and receive you unto m·; "
10 speak unto you I speak not of m·: "
21 him, and will manifest m· to him. "
17:19 for their sakes I sanctify m·, that "
Ac 10:26 saying, Stand up; I m· also am a man.
20:24 count I my life dear unto m·, so 1683
24:10 the more cheerfully answer for m·:* "
16 And herein do I exercise m·, to have
25:22 Festus, I would also hear the man m·.
26: 2 I think m· happy, king Agrippa, 1683
2 I shall answer for m· this day before*
9 I verily thought with m·, that I 1683
Ro 7:25 the mind I m· serve the law of God;
9: 3 could wish that m· were accursed 846
11: 4 reserved to m· seven thousand 1683
15:14 I m· also am persuaded of you, my
16: 2 succourer of many, and of m· also.* 846
1Co 4: 4 For I know nothing by m·; yet am 1683
6 I have in a figure transferred to m· "
7: 7 that all men were even as I m·.

1Co 9:19 I made m· servant unto all, that I 1683
27 to others, I m· should be a castaway.
2Co 2: 1 But I determined this with m·, 1683
10: 1 Now I Paul m· beseech you by the
11: 7 an offence in abasing m· that ye 1683
9 kept m· from being burdensome "
9 unto you, and so will I keep m·. "
16 me, that I may boast m· a little. *
12: 5 of m· I will not glory, but in mine*1683
13 it be that I m· was not burdensome
Ga 2:18 I make m· a transgressor. 1683
Ph'p 2:24 that I also m· shall come shortly.
3:13 I count not m· to have apprehended:
Ph'm 17 a partner, receive him as m·. 1691

Mysia (*miz'-ye-ah*)
Ac 16: 7 After they were come to M·, they 3463
8 passing by M· came down to Troas. "

mysteries
M't 13:11 the m· of the kingdom of heaven, 3466
Lu 8:10 the m· of the kingdom of God: "
1Co 4: 1 and stewards of the m· of God. "
13: 2 and understand all m·, and all "
14: 2 in the spirit he speaketh m·. "

mystery See also MYSTERIES.
M'k 4:11 the m· of the kingdom of God: 3466
Ro 11:25 ye should be ignorant of this m·, "
16:25 to the revelation of the m·, which "
1Co 2: 7 speak the wisdom of God in a m·, "
15:51 I shew you a m·; We shall not all "
Eph 1: 9 known unto us the m· of his will, "
3: 3 he made known unto me the m·; "
4 my knowledge in the m· of Christ) "
9 what is the fellowship of the m·, "
5:32 This is a great m·: but I speak "
6:19 make known the m· of the gospel, "
Col 1:26 even the m· which hath been hid "
27 glory of this m· among the Gentiles; "
2: 2 acknowledgment of the m· of God, "
4: 3 to speak the m· of Christ, for which "
2Th 2: 7 m· of iniquity doth already work: "
1Ti 3: 9 Holding the m· of the faith in a "
16 great is the m· of godliness: "
Re 1:20 The m· of the seven stars which "
10: 7 the m· of God should be finished, "
17: 5 written, M·, Babylon The Great, "
7 will tell thee the m· of the woman, "

N.

Naam (*na'-am*)
1Ch 4:15 of Jephunneh; Iru, Elah, and N·: 5277

Naamah (*na'-a-mah*) See also NAAMATHITE.
Ge 4:22 the sister of Tubal-cain was N·. 5279
Jos 15:41 Gederoth, Beth-dagon, and N·, "
1Ki 14:21, 31 And his mother's name was N· "
2Ch 12:13 And his mother's name was N· an "

Naaman (*na'-a-man*) See also NAAMAN'S; NAAMITES.
Ge 46:21 N·, Ehi, and Rosh, Muppim, and 5283
Nu 26:40 the sons of Bela were Ard and N·: "
40 Ardites: and of N·, the family of "
2Ki 5: 1 Now N·, captain of the host of the "
6 sent N· my servant to thee, that "
9 So N· came with his horses and "
11 But N· was wroth, and went away, "
17 And N· said, Shall there not then, "
20 master hath spared N· this Syrian, "
21 So Gehazi followed after N·. And "
21 when N· saw him running after "
23 And N· said, Be content, take two "
27 leprosy therefore of N· shall cleave "
1Ch 8: 4 And Abishua, and N·, and Ahoah, "
7 And N·, and Ahiah, and Gera, he "
Lu 4:27 cleansed, saving N· the Syrian. 3497

Naaman's (*na'-a-mans*)
2Ki 5: 2 maid; and she waited on N· wife. 5283

Naamathite (*na'-a-math-ite*)
Job 2:11 the Shuhite, and Zophar the N·: 5284
11: 1 Then answered Zophar the N·, "
20: 1 Then answered Zophar the N·, "
42: 9 Shuhite and Zophar the N· went, "

Naamites (*na'-a-mites*)
Nu 26:40 of Naaman, the family of the N·. 5280

Naarah (*na'-a-rah*) See also NAARAN; NAARATH.
1Ch 4: 5 had two wives, Helah and N·. 5292
6 And N· bare him Ahuzam, and "
6 These were the sons of N·. "

Naarai (*na'-a-rahee*) See also PAARAI.
1Ch 11:37 Carmelite, N· the son of Ezbai, 5293

Naaran (*na'-a-ran*) See also NAARATH.
1Ch 7:28 eastward N·, and westward Gezer, 5295

Naarath (*na'-a-rath*) See also NAARAH; NAARAN.
Jos 16: 7 and to N·, and came to Jericho, *5292

Naashon (*na'-a-shon*) See also NAHSHON.
Ex 6:23 Amminadab, sister of N·, to wife;*5177

Naasson (*na'-as-son*) See also NAASHON.
M't 1: 4 Aminadab begat N·; and N· *3476
Lu 3:32 Salmon, which was the son of N·,* "

Nabal (*na'-bal*) See also NABAL'S.
1Sa 25: 3 Now the name of the man was N·; 5037
4 that N· did shear his sheep. "
5 and go to N·, and greet him in my "
9 they spake to N· according to all "
10 N· answered David's servants, and "
19 But she told not her husband N·. "
25 regard this man of Belial, even N·: "

1Sa 25:25 N· is his name, and folly is with 5037
26 that seek evil to my lord, be as N·. "
34 there had not been left unto N· by "
36 Abigail came to N·; and, behold, "
37 when the wine was gone out of N·, "
38 the Lord smote N·, that he died. "
39 David heard that N· was dead, "
39 my reproach from the hand of N·, "
39 the wickedness of N· upon his own "
30: 5 the wife of N· the Carmelite. "
2Sa 3: 3 the wife of N· the Carmelite; "

Nabal's (*na'-balz*)
1Sa 25:14 young men told Abigail, N· wife, 5037
36 N· heart was merry within him, "
27: 3 Abigail the Carmelitess, N· wife, "
2Sa 2: 2 Abigail N· wife the Carmelite. * "

Nabas See BARNABAS.

Naboth (*na'-both*)
1Ki 21: 1 N· the Jezreelite had a vineyard, 5022
2 Ahab spake unto N·, saying, Give "
3 N· said to Ahab, The Lord forbid it "
4 which N· the Jezreelite had spoken "
6 I spake unto N· the Jezreelite, and "
7 the vineyard of N· the Jezreelite. "
8 were in his city, dwelling with N·. "
9 set N· on high among the people: "
12 set N· on high among the people. "
13 against him, even against N·, in "
13 N· did blaspheme God and the "
14 saying, N· is stoned, and is dead. "
15 Jezebel heard that N· was stoned, "
15 possession of the vineyard of N· the "
15 for N· is not alive, but dead. "
16 when Ahab heard that N· was dead, "
16 to go down to the vineyard of N· "
18 he is in the vineyard of N·, whither "
19 where dogs licked the blood of N· "
2Ki 9:21 in the portion of N· the Jezreelite. "
25 in the portion of the field of N· the "
26 seen yesterday the blood of N·, "

Nachon's (*na'-kons*) See also CHIDON.
2Sa 6: 6 they came to N· threshingfloor, *5225

Nachor (*na'-kor*) See also NAHOR.
Jos 24: 2 Abraham, and the father of N·: *5152
Lu 3:34 Thara, which was the son of N·, *3493

Nadab (*na'-dab*)
Ex 6:23 to wife; and she bare him N·, and 5070
24: 1 the Lord, thou, and Aaron, N·, and "
9 went up Moses, and Aaron, N·, and "
28: 1 office, even Aaron, N· and Abihu, "
Le 10: 1 N· and Abihu, the sons of Aaron, "
Nu 3: 2 the names of the sons of Aaron; N· "
4 N· and Abihu died before the Lord, "
26:60 And unto Aaron was born N·, and "
61 And N· and Abihu died, when they "
1Ki 14:20 N· his son reigned in his stead. "
15:25 N· the son of Jeroboam began to "
27 for N· and all Israel laid siege to "
31 the rest of the acts of N·, and all "

1Ch 2:28 sons of Shammai; N·, and Abishur. 5070
30 sons of N·; Seled, and Appaim: "
6: 3 sons also of Aaron; N·, and Abihu, "
8:30 Zur, and Kish, and Baal, and N·, "
9:36 Kish, and Baal, and Ner, and N·, "
24: 1 The sons of Aaron; N·, and Abihu, "
2 N· and Abihu died before their "

Nadib See AMMI-NADIB.

Naggæ See NAGGE.

Nagge (*nag'-e*) See also NEARIAH.
Lu 3:25 of Esli, which was the son of N·, *3477

Nahalal (*na'-ha-lal*) See also NAHALLAL; NAHALOL.
Jos 21:35 N· with her suburbs; four cities. 5096

Nahaliel (*na-ha'-le-el*)
Nu 21:19 And from Mattanah to N·: 5160
19 and from N· to Bamoth:

Nahallal (*na'-hal-el*) See also NAHALAL.
Jos 19:15 Kattath, and N·, and Shimron, *5096

Nahalol (*na'-ha-lol*) See also NAHALAL.
J'g 1:30 Kitron, nor the inhabitants of N·; 5096

Naham (*na'-ham*) See also ISHBAH.
1Ch 4:19 the sister of N·, the father of 5163

Nahamani (*na-ham'-a-ni*)
Ne 7: 7 Azariah, Raamiah, N·, Mordecai, 5167

Naharai (*na'-ha-rahee*) See also NAHARI.
1Ch 11:39 the Ammonite, N· the Berothite, 5171

Naharaim See ARAM-NAHARAIM.

Nahari (*na'-ha-ri*) See also NAHARAI.
2Sa 23:37 N· the Beerothite, armourbearer*5171

Nahash (*na'-hash*) See also IR-NAHASH.
1Sa 11: 1 Then N· the Ammonite came up, 5176
1 the men of Jabesh said unto N·, "
2 N· the Ammonite answered them, "
12:12 that N· the king of the children of "
2Sa 10: 2 kindness unto Hanun the son of N·, "
17:25 in to Abigail the daughter of N·, "
27 that Shobi the son of N· of Rabbah "
1Ch 19: 1 that N· the king of the children of "
2 kindness unto Hanun the son of N·. "

Nahath (*na'-hath*) See also TOHU.
Ge 36:13 the sons of Reuel; N·, and Zerah, 5184
17 duke N·, duke Zerah, duke "
1Ch 1:37 N·, Zerah, Shammah, and Mizzah. "
6:26 Zophai his son, and N· his son, "
2Ch 31:13 and Azaziah, and N·, and Asahel, "

Nahbi (*nah'-bi*)
Nu 13:14 of Naphtali, N· the son of Vophsi. 5147

Nahor (*na'-hor*) See also NACHOR; NAHOR'S.
Ge 11:22 lived thirty years, and begat N·: 5152
23 Serug lived after he begat N· two "
24 N· lived nine and twenty years, "
25 N· lived after he begat Terah an "
26 and begat Abram, N·, and Haran. "
27 begat Abram, N·, and Haran: and "

Ge 11:29 Abram and *N'* took them wives: 5152
22:20 born children unto thy brother *N'*; "
23 these eight Milcah did bear to *N'*. "
24:10 Mesopotamia, unto the city of *N'*. "
15 the wife of *N'*, Abraham's brother, "
24 of Milcah, which she bare unto *N'*. "
29: 5 Know ye Laban the son of *N'*? "
31:53 God of *N'*, the God of their father, "
1Ch 1:26 Serug, *N'*, Terah, "

Nahor's (*na'-hors*)
Ge 11:29 and the name of *N'* wife, Milcah, 5152
24:47 The daughter of Bethuel, *N'* son, "

Nahshon (*nah'-shon*) See also NAASHON; NAASSON.
Nu 1: 7 *N'* the son of Amminadab. 5177
2: 3 *N'* the son of Amminadab shall be "
7:12 his offering the first day was *N'* "
17 of *N'* the son of Amminadab. "
10:14 was *N'* the son of Amminadab. "
Ru 4:20 begat *N'*, and *N'* begat Salmon, "
1Ch 2:10 and Amminadab begat *N'*, prince "
11 *N'* begat Salma, and Salma begat "

Nahum (*na'-hum*) See also NAUM.
Na 1: 1 the vision of *N'* the Elkoshite. 5151

nail See also NAILING; NAILS.
J'g 4:21 Heber's wife took a *n'* of the tent,*3489
21 and smote the *n'* into his temples,* "
22 dead, and the *n'* was in his temples.* "
5:26 She put her hand to the *n'*, and her‡ "
Ezr 9: 8 to give us a *n'* in his holy place, "
Isa 22:23 fasten him as a *n'* in a sure place; "
25 *n'* that is fastened in the sure place "
Zec 10: 4 out of him the *n'*, out of him the "

nailing
Col 2:14 out of the way, *n'* it to his cross: 4338

nails
De 21:12 shave her head, and pare her *n'*; 6856
1Ch 22: 3 iron in abundance for the *n'* for 4548
2Ch 3: 9 weight of the *n'* was fifty shekels "
Ec 12:11 as *n'* fastened by the masters of 4930
Isa 41: 7 and he fastened it with *n'*, that it 4548
Jer 10: 4 it with *n'* and with hammers, that "
Da 4:33 and his *n'* like birds' claws. 2953
7:19 were of iron, and his *n'* of brass; "
Joh 20:25 in his hands the print of the *n'*, 2247
25 my finger into the print of the *n'*, "

Nain (*nane*)
Lu 7:11 that he went into a city called *N'*; 3484

Naioth (*nah'-yoth*)
1Sa 19:18 Samuel went and dwelt in *N'*. 5121
19 Behold, David is at *N'* in Ramah. "
22 Behold, they be at *N'* in Ramah. "
23 he went thither to *N'* in Ramah: "
23 until he came to *N'* in Ramah. "
20: 1 David fled from *N'* in Ramah, and "

naked
Ge 2:25 they were both *n'*, the man and 6174
3: 7 knew that they were *n'*; and they 5903
10 I was afraid, because I was *n'*; "
11 Who told thee that thou wast *n'*? "
Ex 32:25 saw that the people were *n'*, *6544
25 had made them *n'* unto their shame* "
1Sa 19:24 lay down *n'* all that day and all 6174
2Ch 28:15 all that were *n'* among them, and 4636
19 Israel; for he made Judah *n'*, *6544
Job 1:21 *N'* came I out of my mother's 6174
21 and *n'* shall I return thither: the "
22: 6 stripped the *n'* of their clothing. "
24: 7 the *n'* to lodge without clothing, "
10 him to go *n'* without clothing, and "
26: 6 Hell is *n'* before him, and "
Ec 5:15 *n'* shall he return to go as he came, "
Isa 20: 2 he did so, walking *n'* and barefoot. "
3 servant Isaiah hath walked *n'* and "
4 young and old, *n'*, and barefoot, "
58: 7 when thou seest the *n'*, that thou "
La 4:21 and shalt make thyself *n'*. 6168
Eze 16: 7 whereas thou wast *n'* and bare. 5903
22 youth, when thou wast *n'* and bare, "
39 jewels, and leave thee *n'* and bare. "
18: 7 hath covered the *n'* with a garment; "
16 hath covered the *n'* with a garment, "
23:29 and shall leave thee *n'* and bare: "
Ho 2: 3 Lest I strip her *n'*, and set her as 6174
Am 2:16 the mighty shall flee away *n'* in "
Mic 1: 8 howl, I will go stripped and *n'*: "
11 of Saphir, having thy shame *n'*: *6181
Hab 3: 9 Thy bow was made quite *n'*. *5783
M't 25:36 *N'*, and ye clothed me: I was sick 1131
38 thee in? or *n'*, and clothed thee? "
43 *n'*, and ye clothed me not: sick, "
44 or *n'*, or sick, or in prison, and did "
M'r 14:51 linen cloth cast about his *n'* body; "
52 linen cloth, and fled from them *n'*. "
Joh 21: 7 coat unto him, (for he was *n'*,) and "
Ac 19:16 out of that house *n'* and wounded. "
1Co 4:11 hunger, and thirst, and are *n'*, 1130
2Co 5: 3 clothed we shall not be found *n'*. 1131
Heb 4:13 all things are *n'* and opened unto "
Jas 2:15 If a brother or sister be *n'*, and "
Re 3:17 and poor, and blind, and *n'*: "
16:15 lest he walk *n'*, and they see his "
17:16 and shall make her desolate and *n'*. "

nakedness
Ge 9:22 Canaan, saw the *n'* of his father, 6172
23 and covered the *n'* of their father; "
23 and they saw not their father's *n'*. "
42: 9, 12 to see the *n'* of the land ye are "
Ex 20:26 thy *n'* be not discovered thereon. "
28:42 them linen breeches to cover their *n'*; "
Le 18: 6 of kin to him, to uncover their *n'*: "
7 *n'* of thy father, or the *n'* of thy "

Le 18: 7 thou shalt not uncover her *n'*. 6172
8 The *n'* of thy father's wife shalt "
8 not uncover: it is thy father's *n'*. "
9 The *n'* of thy sister, the daughter "
9 their *n'* thou shalt not uncover. "
10 The *n'* of thy son's daughter, or of "
10 their *n'* thou shalt not uncover: "
10 uncover: for theirs is thine own *n'*. "
11 *n'* of thy father's wife's daughter, "
11 sister, thou shalt not uncover her *n'*. "
12 uncover the *n'* of thy father's sister: "
13 the *n'* of thy mother's sister: "
14 the *n'* of thy father's brother, "
15 the *n'* of thy daughter in law: "
15 wife; thou shalt not uncover her *n'*. "
16 uncover the *n'* of thy brother's wife: "
16 brother's wife: it is thy brother's *n'*. "
17 not uncover the *n'* of a woman and "
17 daughter, to uncover her *n'*; for "
18 vex her, to uncover her *n'*, besides "
19 unto a woman to uncover her *n'*, "
20:11 uncovered his father's *n'*: both of "
17 and see her *n'*, and she see his *n'*; "
17 he hath uncovered his sister's *n'*; "
18 sickness and shall uncover her *n'*; "
19 th *n'* of thy mother's sister, nor "
20 he hath uncovered his uncle's *n'*: "
21 he hath uncovered his brother's *n'*; "
De 28:48 hunger, and in thirst, and in *n'*, 5903
1Sa 20:30 the confusion of thy mother's *n'*? 6172
Isa 47: 3 Thy *n'* shall be uncovered, yea, thy "
La 1: 8 because they have seen her *n'*: yea, "
Eze 16: 8 skirt over thee, and covered thy *n'*: "
36 and thy *n'* discovered through thy "
37 and will discover thy *n'* unto them, "
37 them, that they may see all thy *n'*. "
22:10 they discovered their father's *n'*: "
23:10 These discovered her *n'*: they took "
18 discovered her *n'*: then my mind "
29 the *n'* of thy whoredoms shall be "
Ho 2: 9 and my flax given to cover her *n'*. "
Na 3: 5 and I will shew the nations thy *n'*,4626
Hab 2:15 that thou mayest look on their *n'*! 4589
Ro 8:35 famine, or *n'*, or peril, or sword? 1132
2Co 11:27 in fastings often, in cold and *n'*. "
Re 3:18 the shame of thy *n'* do not appear; "

name See also NAMED; NAME'S; NAMES; NAMETH; SURNAME.
Ge 2:11 *n'* of the first is Pison: that is it 8034
13 the *n'* of the second river is Gihon: "
14 the *n'* of the third river is Hiddekel: "
19 creature, that was the *n'* thereof. "
3:20 And Adam called his wife's *n'* Eve; "
4:17 *n'* of the city, after the *n'* of his son, "
19 wives: the *n'* of the one was Adah, "
19 Adah, and the *n'* of the other Zillah. "
21 his brother's *n'* was Jubal: he was "
25 bare a son, and called his *n'* Seth: "
26 a son; and he called his *n'* Enos: "
26 men to call upon the *n'* of the Lord. "
5: 2 and called their *n'* Adam, in the "
3 his image; and called his *n'* Seth: "
29 And he called his *n'* Noah, saying, "
10:25 two sons: the *n'* of one was Peleg; "
25 and his brother's *n'* was Joktan. "
11: 4 and let us make us a *n'*, lest we be "
9 is the *n'* of it called Babel; because "
29 the *n'* of Abram's wife was Sarai; "
29 the *n'* of Nahor's wife, Milcah, the "
12: 2 bless thee, and make thy *n'* great; "
8 and called upon the *n'* of the Lord. "
13: 4 Abram called on the *n'* of the Lord. "
16: 1 an Egyptian, whose *n'* was Hagar. "
11 son, and shalt call his *n'* Ishmael; "
13 she called the *n'* of the Lord that "
15 Abram called his son's *n'*, which "
17: 5 thy *n'* any more be called Abram, "
5 but thy *n'* shall be Abraham; "
15 thou shalt not call her *n'* Sarai, "
15 Sarai, but Sarah shall her *n'* be. "
19 and thou shalt call his *n'* Isaac: "
19:22 the *n'* of the city was called Zoar. "
37 bare a son, and called his *n'* Moab: "
38 a son, and called his *n'* Ben-ammi: "
21: 3 Abraham called the *n'* of his son "
33 called there on the *n'* of the Lord, "
22:14 the *n'* of that place Jehovah-jireh: "
24 concubine, whose *n'* was Reumah, "
24:29 a brother, and his *n'* was Laban: "
25: 1 a wife, and her *n'* was Keturah. "
25 and they called his *n'* Esau. "
26 his *n'* was called Jacob: and Isaac "
30 therefore was his *n'* called Edom. "
26:20 he called the *n'* of the well Esek; "
21 and he called the *n'* of it Sitnah. "
22 he called the *n'* of it Rehoboth; and "
25 called upon the *n'* of the Lord, and "
33 the *n'* of the city is Beer-sheba "
28:19 called the *n'* of that place Beth-el: "
19 *n'* of that city was called Luz at the "
29:16 the *n'* of the elder was Leah, and "
16 the *n'* of the younger was Rachel. "
32 a son, and she called his *n'* Reuben: "
33 also: and she called his *n'* Simeon. "
34 therefore was his *n'* called Levi. "
35 she called his *n'* Judah; and left "
30: 6 son: therefore called she his *n'* Dan. "
8 and she called his *n'* Naphtali. "
11 cometh: and she called his *n'* Gad. "
13 blessed: and she called his *n'* Asher. "
18 and she called his *n'* Issachar. "
20 sons: and she called his *n'* Zebulun. "
21 daughter, and called her *n'* Dinah. "
24 she called his *n'* Joseph; and said, "
31:48 was the *n'* of it called Galeed; "
32: 2 the *n'* of that place Mahanaim. "

Ge 32:27 What is thy *n'*? And he said, Jacob. 8034
28 *n'* shall be called no more Jacob, "
29 said, Tell me, I pray thee, thy *n'*. "
29 it that thou dost ask after my *n'*? "
30 called the *n'* of the place Peniel: "
33:17 *n'* of the place is called Succoth. "
35: 8 the *n'* of it was called Allon-bachuth. "
10 said unto him, Thy *n'* is Jacob: "
10 thy *n'* shall not be called any more "
10 Jacob, but Israel shall be thy *n'*: "
10 and he called his *n'* Israel. "
15 And Jacob called the *n'* of the place "
18 she called his *n'* Ben-oni: but his "
36:32 the *n'* of his city was Dinhabah. "
35 and the *n'* of his city was Avith. "
39 stead: and the *n'* of his city was Pau; "
39 and his wife's *n'* was Mehetabel, the "
38: 1 Adullamite, whose *n'* was Hirah. "
2 Canaanite, whose *n'* was Shuah; "
3 bare a son; and he called his *n'* Er. "
4 a son; and she called his *n'* Onan. "
5 bare a son; and called his *n'* Shelah: "
6 his firstborn, whose *n'* was Tamar. "
29 therefore his *n'* was called Pharez. "
30 hand: and his *n'* was called Zarah. "
41:45 And Pharaoh called Joseph's *n'* "
51 Joseph called the *n'* of the firstborn "
52 *n'* of the second called he Ephraim: "
48: 6 called after the *n'* of their brethren "
16 and let my *n'* be named on them, "
16 the *n'* of my fathers Abraham and "
50:11 the *n'* of it was called Abel-mizraim, "
Ex 1:15 which the *n'* of the one was Shiphrah, "
15 and the *n'* of the other Puah: "
2:10 son. And she called his *n'* Moses: "
22 son, and he called his *n'* Gershom: "
3:13 shall say to me, What is his *n'*? "
15 this is my *n'* for ever, and this is "
5:23 I came to Pharaoh to speak in thy *n'*, "
6: 3 Jacob, by the *n'* of God Almighty,* "
3 by my *n'* Jehovah was I not known 8034
9:16 and that my *n'* may be declared "
15: 3 is a man of war: the Lord is his *n'*. "
23 the *n'* of it was called Marah. "
16:31 Israel called the *n'* thereof Manna: "
17: 7 called the *n'* of the place Massah, "
15 called the *n'* of it Jehovah-nissi: "
18: 3 the *n'* of the one was Gershom; for "
4 And the *n'* of the other was Eliezer; "
20: 7 the *n'* of the Lord thy God in vain; "
7 guiltless that taketh his *n'* in vain. "
24 in all places where I record my *n'* I "
23:13 no mention of the *n'* of other gods, "
21 transgressions: for my *n'* is in him. "
28:21 every one with his *n'* shall they be "
31: 2 called by *n'* Bezaleel the son of Uri, "
33:12 I know thee by *n'*, and thou hast "
17 in my sight, and I know thee by *n'*. "
19 proclaim the *n'* of the Lord before "
34: 5 and proclaimed the *n'* of the Lord. "
14 the Lord, whose *n'* is Jealous, is a "
35:30 the Lord hath called by *n'* Bezaleel "
39:14 of a signet, every one with his *n'*, "
Le 18:21 shalt thou profane the *n'* of thy God: "
19:12 ye shall not swear by my *n'* falsely, "
12 shalt thou profane the *n'* of thy God: "
20: 3 and to profane my holy *n'*. "
21: 6 and not profane the *n'* of their God: "
22: 2 that they profane not my holy *n'* in "
32 Neither shall ye profane my holy *n'*; "
24:11 son blasphemed the *n'* of the Lord, "
11 his mother's *n'* was Shelomith, the "
16 that blasphemeth the *n'* of the Lord, "
16 he blasphemeth the *n'* of the Lord, "
Nu 4:32 *n'* ye shall reckon the instruments "
6:27 shall put my *n'* upon the children of "
11: 3 called the *n'* of the place Taberah: "
26 camp, the *n'* of the one was Eldad, "
26 and the *n'* of the other Medad: "
34 *n'* of that place Kibroth-hattaavah: "
17: 2 thou every man's *n'* upon his rod. "
3 Aaron's *n'* upon the rod of Levi: "
21: 3 called the *n'* of the place Hormah. "
25:14 the *n'* of the Israelite that was slain, "
15 And the *n'* of the Midianitish woman "
26:46 the *n'* of the daughter of Asher was "
59 *n'* of Amram's wife was Jochebed, "
27: 4 the *n'* of our father be done away "
32:42 and called it Nobah, after his own *n'*. "
De 3:14 and called them after his own *n'*, "
5:11 the *n'* of the Lord thy God in vain: "
11 guiltless that taketh his *n'* in vain. "
6:13 serve him, and shalt swear by his *n'*. "
7:24 destroy their *n'* from under heaven: "
9:14 blot out their *n'* from under heaven: "
10: 8 and to bless in his *n'*, unto this day. "
20 thou cleave, and swear by his *n'*. "
12: 5 of all your tribes to put his *n'* there, "
11 to cause his *n'* to dwell there; "
21 God hath chosen to put his *n'* there "
14:23 he shall choose to place his *n'* there, "
24 God shall choose to set his *n'* there, "
16: 2 shall choose to place his *n'* there. "
6 God shall choose to place his *n'* in, "
11 hath chosen to place his *n'* there. "
18: 5 to minister in the *n'* of the Lord, "
7 shall minister in the *n'* of the Lord "
19 words which he shall speak in my *n'*, "
20 presume to speak a word in my *n'*, "
20 shall speak in the *n'* of other gods, "
22 speaketh in the *n'* of the Lord, if "
21: 5 and to bless in the *n'* of the Lord; "
22:14 bring up an evil *n'* upon her, and "
19 hath brought up an evil *n'* upon a "
25: 6 shall succeed in the *n'* of his brother "
6 that his *n'* be not put out of Israel. "

De 25: 7 up unto his brother a *n'* in Israel, 8034
10 And his *n'* shall be called in Israel, "
26: 2 shall choose to place his *n'* there. "
19 in praise, and in *n'*, and in honour; "
28: 10 thou art called by the *n'* of the Lord; "
58 fear this glorious and fearful *n'*, "
29: 20 blot out his *n'* from under heaven. "
32: 3 I will publish the *n'* of the Lord: "
Jos 5: 9 the *n'* of the place is called Gilgal "
7: 9 and cut off our *n'* from the earth: "
9 what wilt thou do unto thy great *n'*? "
26 the *n'* of that place was called, The "
9: 9 of the *n'* of the Lord thy God: for "
14: 15 And the *n'* of Hebron before was "
15: 15 and the *n'* of Debir before was "
19: 47 Dan, after the *n'* of Dan their father. "
21: 9 which are here mentioned by *n'*, "
23: 7 make mention of the *n'* of their gods, "
J'g 1: 10 (now the *n'* of Hebron before was "
11 and the *n'* of Debir before was "
17 the *n'* of the city was called Hormah. "
23 the *n'* of the city before was Luz.) "
26 city, and called the *n'* thereof Luz: "
26 which is the *n'* thereof unto this day. "
2: 5 called the *n'* of that place Bochim: "
8: 31 son, whose *n'* he called Abimelech. "
13: 2 the Danites, whose *n'* was Manoah; "
6 he was, neither told he me his *n'*: "
17 What is thy *n'*, that when thy sayings "
18 Why askest thou thus after my *n'*, "
24 a son, and called his *n'* Samson: "
15: 19 wherefore he called the *n'* thereof "
16: 4 of Sorek, whose *n'* was Delilah. "
17: 1 Ephraim, whose *n'* was Micah. "
18: 29 they called the *n'* of the city Dan, "
29 after the *n'* of Dan their father, who "
29 howbeit the *n'* of the city was Laish "
Ru 1: 2 the *n'* of the man was Elimelech, "
2 and the *n'* of his wife Naomi, and "
2 the *n'* of his two sons Mahlon and "
4 Moab; the *n'* of the one was Orpah, "
4 and the *n'* of the other Ruth: and "
2: 1 of Elimelech; and his *n'* was Boaz. "
19 The man's *n'* with whom I wrought "
4: 5, 10 to raise up the *n'* of the dead upon "
10 the *n'* of the dead be not cut off from "
14 that his *n'* may be famous in Israel. "
17 women her neighbours gave it a *n'*, "
17 Naomi; and they called his *n'* Obed: "
1Sa 1: 1 and his *n'* was Elkanah, the son of "
2 the *n'* of the one was Hannah, and "
2 and the *n'* of the other Peninnah: "
20 bare a son, and called his *n'* Samuel, "
7: 12 and called the *n'* of it Eben-ezer, "
8: 2 Now the *n'* of his firstborn was Joel; "
2 and the *n'* of his second, Abiah: "
9: 1 whose *n'* was Kish, the son of Abiel, "
2 he had a son, whose *n'* was Saul, a "
14: 4 and the *n'* of the one was Bozez, "
4 and the *n'* of the other Seneh. "
49 these; the *n'* of the firstborn Merab, "
49 and the *n'* of the younger Michal: "
50 the *n'* of Saul's wife was Ahinoam, "
50 the *n'* of the captain of his host was "
16: 3 unto me him whom I *n'* unto thee. 559
17: 12 whose *n'* was Jesse; and he had 8034
23 the Philistine of Gath, Goliath by *n'*, "
45 to thee in the *n'* of the Lord of hosts, "
18: 30 Saul; so that his *n'* was much set by. "
20: 42 both of us in the *n'* of the Lord, "
21: 7 and his *n'* was Doeg, an Edomite, "
24: 21 wilt not destroy my *n'* out of my "
25: 3 Now the *n'* of the man was Nabal; "
3 and the *n'* of his wife Abigail: and "
5 go to Nabal, and greet him in my *n'*: "
9 to all those words in the *n'* of David, "
25 even Nabal: for as his *n'* is, so is he; "
25 Nabal is his *n'*, and folly is with him: "
28: 8 him up, whom I shall *n'* unto thee. 559
2Sa 3: 7 a concubine, whose *n'* was Rizpah, 8034
4: 2 the *n'* of the one was Baanah, and "
2 and the *n'* of the other Rechab, the "
4 lame. And his *n'* was Mephibosheth. "
5: 20 the *n'* of that place Baal-perazim. "
6: 2 *n'* is called by the *n'* of the Lord of "
18 the people in the *n'* of the Lord of "
7: 9 and have made thee a great *n'*, "
9 like unto the *n'* of the great men "
13 He shall build an house for my *n'*, "
23 to make him a *n'*, and to do for you "
26 thy *n'* be magnified for ever, saying, "
8: 13 And David gat him a *n'* when he "
9: 2 Saul a servant whose *n'* was Ziba. "
12 a young son, whose *n'* was Micha. "
12: 24 a son, and he called his *n'* Solomon: "
25 and he called his *n'* Jedidiah, "
28 the city, and it be called after my *n'*. "
13: 1 a fair sister, whose *n'* was Tamar; "
3 had a friend, whose *n'* was Jonadab, "
14: 7 not leave to my husband neither *n'* "
27 one daughter, whose *n'* was Tamar: "
16: 5 whose *n'* was Shimei, the son of Gera: "
17: 25 whose *n'* was Ithra an Israelite, "
18: 18 I have no son to keep my *n'* in "
18 he called the pillar after his own *n'*: "
20: 1 man of Belial, whose *n'* was Sheba, "
21 Sheba the son of Bichri by *n'*, hath "
22: 50 and I will sing praises unto thy *n'*. "
23: 18 them, and had the *n'* among three. "
22 had the *n'* among three mighty men. "
1Ki 1: 47 God make the *n'* of Solomon better "
47 of Solomon better than thy *n'*, and "
3: 2 house built unto the *n'* of the Lord, "
5: 3 house unto the *n'* of the Lord his "
5 house unto the *n'* of the Lord my "
5 he shall build an house unto my *n'*. "
1Ki 7: 21 and called the *n'* thereof Jachin: 8034
21 pillar, and called the *n'* thereof Boaz. "
8: 16 house, that my *n'* might be therein; "
17 an house for the *n'* of the Lord God "
18 heart to build an house unto my *n'*, "
19 he shall build the house unto my *n'*. "
20 an house for the *n'* of the Lord God "
29 thou hast said, My *n'* shall be there: "
33 thee, and confess thy *n'*, and pray, "
35 confess thy *n'*, and turn from their "
42 (For they shall hear of thy great *n'*, "
43 people of the earth may know thy *n'*, "
43 I have builded, is called by thy *n'*. "
44 house that I have built for thy *n'*: "
48 house which I have built for thy *n'*: "
9: 3 built, to put my *n'* there for ever; "
7 which I have hallowed for my *n'*, "
10: 1 concerning the *n'* of the Lord, she "
11: 26 whose mother's *n'* was Zeruah, a "
36 have chosen me to put my *n'* there. "
13: 2 the house of David, Josiah by *n'*; "
14: 21 tribes of Israel, to put his *n'* there. "
21, 31 his mother's *n'* was Naamah an "
15: 2, 10 his mother's *n'* was Maachah, the "
16: 24 the *n'* of the city which he built, "
24 after the *n'* of Shemer, owner of the "
18: 24 And call ye on the *n'* of your gods, "
24 and I will call on the *n'* of the Lord: "
25 call on the *n'* of your gods, but put "
26 and called on the *n'* of Baal from "
31 came, saying, Israel shall be thy *n'*: "
32 built an altar in the *n'* of the Lord: "
21: 8 So she wrote letters in Ahab's *n'*, "
22: 16 which is true in the *n'* of the Lord? "
42 And his mother's *n'* was Azubah "
2Ki 2: 24 cursed them in the *n'* of the Lord. "
5: 11 call on the *n'* of the Lord his God, "
8: 26 And his mother's *n'* was Athaliah, "
12: 1 And his mother's *n'* was Zibiah of "
14: 2 his mother's *n'* was Jehoaddan of "
7 called the *n'* of it Joktheel unto this "
27 he would blot out the *n'* of Israel "
15: 2 his mother's *n'* was Jecholiah of "
33 And his mother's *n'* was Jerusha, "
18: 2 His mother's *n'* also was Abi, the "
21: 1 his mother's *n'* was Hephzi-bah. "
4 said, In Jerusalem will I put my *n'*. "
7 of Israel, will I put my *n'* for ever: "
19 his mother's *n'* was Meshullemeth, "
22: 1 And his mother's *n'* was Jedidah, "
23: 27 which I said, My *n'* shall be there. "
31 And his mother's *n'* was Hamutal, "
34 and turned his *n'* to Jehoiakim, and "
36 And his mother's *n'* was Zebudah, "
24: 8 And his mother's *n'* was Nehushta, "
17 and changed his *n'* to Zedekiah. "
18 And his mother's *n'* was Hamutal, "
1Ch 1: 19 sons: the *n'* of the one was Peleg; "
19 and his brother's *n'* was Joktan. "
43 and the *n'* of his city was Dinhabah. "
46 and the *n'* of his city was Avith. "
50 and the *n'* of his city was Pai; "
50 and his wife's *n'* was Mehetabel, "
2: 26 wife, whose *n'* was Atarah; she was "
29 the *n'* of the wife of Abishur was "
34 an Egyptian, whose *n'* was Jarha. "
4: 3 *n'* of their sister was Hazelelponi: "
9 and his mother called his *n'* Jabez, "
41 these written by *n'* came in the days "
7: 15 whose sister's *n'* was Maachah;) "
15 the *n'* of the second...Zelophehad: "
16 son, and she called his *n'* Peresh; "
16 the *n'* of his brother was Sheresh; "
23 he called his *n'* Beriah, because it "
8: 29 whose wife's *n'* was Maachah: "
9: 35 whose wife's *n'* was Maachah: "
11: 20 them, and had a *n'* among the three. "
24 the *n'* among the three mighties. "
12: 31 which were expressed by *n'*, to "
13: 6 cherubims, whose *n'* is called on it. "
14: 11 the *n'* of that place Baal-perazim. "
16: 2 the people in the *n'* of the Lord. "
8 call upon his *n'*, make known his "
10 Glory ye in his holy *n'*: let the heart "
29 the Lord the glory due unto his *n'*: "
35 we may give thanks to thy holy *n'*, "
41 who were expressed by *n'*, to give "
17: 8 thee a *n'* like the *n'* of the great men "
21 to make thee a *n'* of greatness and "
24 thy *n'* may be magnified for ever, "
21: 19 he spake in the *n'* of the Lord. "
22: 7 unto the *n'* of the Lord my God: "
8 shalt not build an house unto my *n'*, "
9 for his *n'* shall be Solomon, and I "
10 He shall build an house for my *n'*; "
19 is to be built to the *n'* of the Lord. "
23: 13 him, and to bless in his *n'* for ever. "
28: 3 shalt not build an house for my *n'*, "
29: 13 thee, and praise thy glorious *n'*. "
16 build thee an house for thine holy *n'* "
2Ch 2: 1 an house for the *n'* of the Lord, "
4 build an house to the *n'* of the Lord "
3: 17 *n'* of that on the right hand Jachin, "
17 and the *n'* of that on the left Boaz. "
6: 5 house in, that my *n'* might be there; "
6 Jerusalem,...my *n'* might be there; "
7 an house for the *n'* of the Lord God "
8 heart to build an house for my *n'*, "
9 he shall build the house for my *n'*. "
10 the house for the *n'* of the Lord God "
20 that thou wouldest put thy *n'* there; "
24 and shall return and confess thy *n'*, "
26 and confess thy *n'*, and turn from "
33 people of the earth may know thy *n'*, "
33 I have built is called by thy *n'*. "
34 house which I have built for thy *n'*; "
2Ch 6: 38 house which I have built for thy *n'*: 8034
7: 14 people, which are called by my *n'*, "
16 that my *n'* may be there for ever: "
20 which I have sanctified for my *n'*, "
12: 13 tribes of Israel, to put his *n'* there. "
13 And his mother's *n'* was Naamah "
13: 2 His mother's *n'* also was Michaiah "
14: 11 and in thy *n'* we go against this "
18: 15 truth to me in the *n'* of the Lord? "
20: 8 thee a sanctuary therein for thy *n'*, "
9 presence, (for thy *n'* is in this house,) "
26 the *n'* of the same place was called, "
31 And his mother's *n'* was Azubah "
22: 2 His mother's *n'* also was Athaliah "
24: 1 His mother's *n'* also was Zibiah of "
25: 1 And his mother's *n'* was Jehoaddan "
26: 3 His mother's *n'* also was Jecoliah of "
8 his *n'* spread abroad even to the "
15 And his *n'* spread far abroad; for "
27: 1 His mother's *n'* also was Jerushah, "
28: 9 Lord was there, whose *n'* was Oded: "
15 which were expressed by *n'* rose up, "
29: 1 And his mother's *n'* was Abijah, "
31: 19 the men that were expressed by *n'*, "
33: 4 Jerusalem shall my *n'* be for ever. "
7 of Israel, will I put my *n'* for ever: "
18 spake to him in the *n'* of the Lord "
36: 4 and turned his *n'* to Jehoiakim. "
Ezr 2: 61 Gileadite,...was called after their *n'*: "
5: 1 in the *n'* of the God of Israel, even 8036
14 one, whose *n'* was Sheshbazzar, "
6: 12 hath caused his *n'* to dwell there "
8: 20 all of them were expressed by *n'*. 8034
Ne 1: 9 I have chosen to set my *n'* there. "
11 servants, who desire to fear thy *n'*: "
7: 63 to wife, and was called after their *n'*. "
9: 5 and blessed be thy glorious *n'*, "
7 and gavest him the *n'* of Abraham; "
10 So didst thou get thee a *n'*, as it is "
Es 2: 5 whose *n'* was Mordecai, the son of "
14 her, and that she were called by *n'*. "
22 the king thereof in Mordecai's *n'*. "
3: 12 in the *n'* of king Ahasuerus was it "
8: 8 as it liketh you, in the king's *n'*, "
8 which is written in the king's *n'*, "
10 he wrote in the king Ahasuerus' *n'*, "
9: 26 days Purim after the *n'* of Pur. "
Job 1: 1 whose *n'* was Job; and that man "
21 away; blessed be the *n'* of the Lord. "
18: 17 he shall have no *n'* in the street. "
42: 14 called the *n'* of the first, Jemima; "
14 and the *n'* of the second, Kezia; "
14 the *n'* of the third, Keren-happuch. "
Ps 5: 11 them also that love thy *n'* be joyful "
7: 17 will sing praise to the *n'* of the Lord "
8: 1, 9 excellent is thy *n'* in all the earth! "
9: 2 I will sing praise to thy *n'*, O thou "
5 thou hast put out their *n'* for ever "
10 they that know thy *n'* will put their "
18: 49 and sing praises unto thy *n'*. "
20: 1 *n'* of the God of Jacob defend thee; "
5 in the *n'* of our God we will set up "
7 we will remember the *n'* of the Lord "
22: 22 declare thy *n'* unto my brethren: "
29: 2 the Lord the glory due unto his *n'*; "
33: 21 we have trusted in his holy *n'*. "
34: 3 me, and let us exalt his *n'* together. "
41: 5 When shall he die, and his *n'* perish? "
44: 5 through thy *n'* will we tread them "
8 day long, and praise thy *n'* for ever. "
20 we have forgotten the *n'* of our God, "
45: 17 will make thy *n'* to be remembered "
48: 10 According to thy *n'*, O God, so is "
52: 9 I will wait on thy *n'*; for it is good "
54: 1 Save me, O God, by thy *n'*, and "
6 I will praise thy *n'*, O Lord; for it is "
61: 5 heritage of those that fear thy *n'*. "
8 I sing praise unto thy *n'* for ever, "
63: 4 I will lift up my hands in thy *n'*. "
66: 2 Sing forth the honour of his *n'*: "
4 unto thee; they shall sing to thy *n'*. "
68: 4 unto God, sing praises to his *n'*: "
4 upon the heavens by his *n'* Jah, "
69: 30 will praise the *n'* of God with a song, "
36 that love his *n'* shall dwell therein. "
72: 17 His *n'* shall endure for ever: "
17 his *n'* shall be continued as long as "
19 blessed be his glorious *n'* for ever: "
74: 7 the dwelling place of thy *n'* to the "
10 enemy blaspheme thy *n'* for ever? "
18 people have blasphemed thy *n'*. "
21 let the poor and needy praise thy *n'*. "
75: 1 thy *n'* is near thy wondrous works "
76: 1 God known: his *n'* is great in Israel. "
79: 6 that have not called upon thy *n'*. "
9 salvation, for the glory of thy *n'*: "
80: 18 us, and we will call upon thy *n'*. "
83: 4 that the *n'* of Israel be no more in "
16 shame; that they may seek thy *n'*, "
18 thou, whose *n'* alone is Jehovah, "
86: 9 O Lord; and shall glorify thy *n'*. "
11 truth: unite my heart to fear thy *n'*. "
12 I will glorify thy *n'* for evermore. "
89: 12 and Hermon shall rejoice in thy *n'*. "
16 In thy *n'* shall they rejoice all the "
24 in my *n'* shall his horn be exalted. "
91: 14 high, because he hath known my *n'*. "
92: 1 to sing praises unto thy *n'*, O most "
96: 2 Sing unto the Lord, bless his *n'*; "
8 the Lord the glory due unto his *n'*: "
99: 3 praise thy great and terrible *n'*; "
6 among them that call upon his *n'*; "
100: 4 thankful unto him, and bless his *n'*. "
102: 15 shall fear the *n'* of the Lord, and "
21 declare the *n'* of the Lord in Zion, "
103: 1 that is within me, bless his holy *n'*. "

Ps 105: 1 call upon his n·: make known his 8034
3 Glory ye in his holy n·: let the "
106:47 to give thanks unto thy holy n·, and "
109:13 following let their n· be blotted out. "
111: 9 ever: holy and reverend is his n·. "
113: 1 Lord, praise the n· of the Lord. "
2 Blessed be the n· of the Lord from "
3 same the Lord's n· is to be praised. "
115: 1 but unto thy n· give glory, for thy "
116: 4 called I upon the n· of the Lord; "
13 and call upon the n· of the Lord. "
17 and will call upon the n· of the Lord. "
118:10 in the n· of the Lord will I destroy "
11, 12 the n· of the Lord I will destroy "
26 that cometh in the n· of the Lord: "
119:55 I have remembered thy n·, O Lord, "
132 to do unto those that love thy n·. "
122: 4 give thanks unto the n· of the Lord. "
124: 8 Our help is in the n· of the Lord, "
129: 8 we bless you in the n· of the Lord. "
135: 1 Praise ye the n· of the Lord; praise "
3 sing praises unto his n·; for it is "
13 Thy n·, O Lord, endureth for ever; "
138: 2 praise thy n· for thy lovingkindness "
2 magnified thy word above all thy n·. "
139:20 and thine enemies take thy n· in vain. "
140:13 shall give thanks unto thy n·: 8034
142: 7 of prison, that I may praise thy n·: "
145: 1 I will bless thy n· for ever and ever. "
2 and I will praise thy n· for ever and "
21 let all flesh bless his holy n· for ever "
148: 5, 13 them praise the n· of the Lord: "
13 for his n· alone is excellent; his "
149: 3 Let them praise his n· in the dance: "
Pr 10: 7 but the n· of the wicked shall rot. "
18:10 n· of the Lord is a strong tower: "
21:24 Proud and haughty scorner is his n·, "
22: 1 A good n· is rather to be chosen "
30: 4 is his n·, and what is his son's n·, "
9 and take the n· of my God in vain. "
Ec 6: 4 and his n· shall be covered with "
7: 1 A good n· is better than precious "
Ca 1: 3 thy n· is as ointment poured forth, "
Isa 4: 1 only let us be called by thy n·, to "
7:14 son, and shall call his n· Immanuel. "
8: 3 Call his n· Maher-shalal-hash-baz. "
9: 6 his n· shall be called Wonderful, "
12: 4 Praise the Lord, call upon his n·, "
4 mention that his n· is exalted. "
14:22 cut off from Babylon the n·, and "
18: 7 to the place of the n· of the Lord "
24:15 even the n· of the Lord God of "
25: 1 I will exalt thee, I will praise thy n·; "
26: 8 the desire of our soul is to thy n·, "
13 will we make mention of thy n·. "
29:23 of him, they shall sanctify my n·, "
30:27 the n· of the Lord cometh from far, "
41:25 the sun shall he call upon my n·: "
42: 8 I am the Lord: that is my n·: and "
43: 1 thee, I have called thee by thy n·; "
7 every one that is called by my n·: "
44: 5 shall call himself by the n· of Jacob; "
5 himself by the n· of Israel. "
45: 3 the Lord, which call thee by thy n·, "
4 I have even called thee by thy n·: "
47: 4 the Lord of hosts is his n·, the "
48: 1 are called by the n· of Israel, and "
1 which swear by the n· of the Lord, "
2 Israel; The Lord of hosts is his n·. "
11 for how should my n· be polluted? and "
19 his n· should not have been cut off 8034
49: 1 hath he made mention of my n·. "
50:10 let him trust in the n· of the Lord, "
51:15 roared: The Lord of hosts is his n·. "
52: 5 and my n· continually every day is "
6 my people shall know my n·: "
54: 5 the Lord of hosts is his n·; and thy "
55:13 and it shall be to the Lord for a n·, "
56: 5 and a n· better than of sons and of "
5 I will give them an everlasting n·, "
6 him, and to love the n· of the Lord, "
57:15 eternity, whose n· is Holy; I dwell "
59:19 shall they fear the n· of the Lord "
60: 9 unto the n· of the Lord thy God, "
62: 2 thou shalt be called by a new n·, "
2 the mouth of the Lord shall n·. "
63:12 to make himself an everlasting n·? "
14 to make thyself a glorious n·. "
16 redeemer; thy n· is from everlasting. "
19 they were not called by thy n·. "
64: 2 thy n· known to thine adversaries, "
7 is none that calleth upon thy n·, "
65: 1 nation that was not called by my n·. "
15 leave your n· for a curse unto my "
15 and call his servants by another n·: "
66:22 shall your seed and your n· remain. "
Jer 3:17 unto it, to the n· of the Lord, to "
7:10, 11 house, which is called by my n·, "
12 where I set my n· at the first, and "
14 house, which is called by my n·, "
30 the house which is called by my n·, "
10: 6 great, and thy n· is great in might. "
16 The Lord of hosts is his n·. "
25 the families that call not on thy n·: "
11:16 The Lord called thy n·, A green "
19 his n· may be no more remembered. "
21 Prophesy not in the n· of the Lord, "
12:16 of my people, to swear by my n·, "
13:11 unto me for a people, and for a n·, "
14: 9 and we are called by thy n·; leave "
14 prophets prophesy lies in my n·: "
15 prophets that prophesy in my n·, "
15:16 for I am called by thy n·, O Lord "
16:21 shall know that my n· is The Lord. "
20: 3 Lord hath not called thy n· Pashur, "
9 him, nor speak any more in his n·. "

Jer 23: 6 his n· whereby he shall be called, 8034
25 that prophesy lies in my n·, saying, "
27 to forget my n· by their dreams "
27 have forgotten my n· for Baal. "
25:29 the city which is called by my n·, "
26: 9 prophesied in the n· of the Lord, "
16 spoken to us in the n· of the Lord "
20 prophesied in the n· of the Lord, "
27:15 yet they prophesy a lie in my n·; "
29: 9 prophesy falsely unto you in my n·: "
21 prophesy a lie unto you in my n·; "
23 have spoken lying words in my n·, "
25 hast sent letters in thy n· unto all "
31:35 roar; The Lord of hosts is his n·: "
32:18 God, The Lord of hosts, is his n·, "
20 and hast made thee a n·, as at this "
34 the house which is called by my n·, "
33: 2 to establish it; the Lord is his n·; "
9 it shall be to me a n· of joy, a praise "
16 is the n· wherewith she shall be called, "
34:15 house which is called by my n·: 8034
16 But ye turned and polluted my n·, "
37:13 was there, whose n· was Irijah, "
44:16 unto us in the n· of the Lord, we "
26 I have sworn by my great n·, saith "
26 that my n· shall no more be named "
46:18 King, whose n· is the Lord of hosts, "
48:15 King, whose n· is the Lord of hosts, "
17 all ye that know his n·, say, How is "
50:34 strong; the Lord of hosts is his n·: "
51:19 the Lord of hosts is his n·. "
57 King, whose n· is the Lord of hosts. "
52: 1 his mother's n· was Hamutal the "
La 3:55 I called upon thy n·, O Lord, out of "
Eze 20:29 And the n· thereof is called Bamah "
39 but pollute ye my holy n· no more "
24: 2 man, write thee the n· of the day, "
36:20 they went, they profaned my holy n·, "
21 But I had pity for mine holy n·, "
23 I will sanctify my great n·, which "
39: 7 So will I make my holy n· known in "
7 them pollute my holy n· any more: "
16 n· of the city shall be Hamonah. "
25 and will be jealous for my holy n·; "
43: 7 my holy n·, shall the house of Israel "
8 even defiled my holy n· by their "
48:35 n· of the city from that day shall be "
Da 1: 7 unto Daniel the n· of Belteshazzar: "
2:20 Blessed be the n· of God for ever 8036
26 Daniel, whose n· was Belteshazzar, "
4: 8 me, whose n· was Belteshazzar, "
8 according to the n· of my god, and "
19 Daniel, whose n· was Belteshazzar, "
9: 6 spake in thy n· to our kings, our 8034
18 the city which is called by thy n·: "
19 and thy people are called by thy n·. "
10: 1 whose n· was called Belteshazzar; "
Ho 1: 4 said unto him, Call his n· Jezreel; "
6 unto him, Call her n· Lo-ruhamah: "
9 said God, Call his n· Lo-ammi: "
2:17 more be remembered by their n·. "
Joe 2:26 praise the n· of the Lord your God, "
32 shall call on the n· of the Lord shall "
Am 2: 7 same maid, to profane my holy n·: "
4:13 Lord, The God of hosts, is his n·. "
5: 8 of the earth: The Lord is his n·: "
27 Lord, whose n· is the God of hosts. "
6:10 make mention of the n· of the Lord. "
9: 6 of the earth: The Lord is his n·. "
12 heathen, which are called by my n·, "
Mic 4: 5 walk every one in the n· of his god, "
5 we will walk in the n· of the Lord "
5: 4 in the majesty of the n· of the Lord "
6: 9 the man of wisdom shall see thy n·: "
Na 1:14 that no more of thy n· be sown: out "
Zep 1: 4 the n· of the Chemarims with the "
3: 9 all call upon the n· of the Lord, "
12 shall trust in the n· of the Lord. "
20 I will make you a n· and a praise "
Zec 5: 4 him that sweareth falsely by my n·: "
6:12 the man whose n· is The Branch; "
10:12 shall walk up and down in his n·, "
13: 3 speakest lies in the n· of the Lord: "
9 they shall call on my n·, and I will "
14: 9 there be one Lord, and his n· one. "
Mal 1: 6 you, O priests, that despise my n·. "
6 Wherein have we despised thy n·? "
11 same my n· shall be great among "
11 incense shall be offered unto my n·, "
11 for my n· shall be great among the "
14 and my n· is dreadful among the "
2: 2 to heart, to give glory unto my n·, "
5 me, and was afraid before my n·. "
3:16 Lord, and that thought upon his n·. "
4: 2 But unto you that fear my n· shall "
M't 1:21 and thou shalt call his n· Jesus: 3686
23 they shall call his n· Emmanuel, "
25 son: and he called his n· Jesus. "
6: 9 art in heaven, Hallowed be thy n·. "
7:22 have we not prophesied in thy n·? "
22 and in thy n· have cast out devils? "
22 and in thy n· done many wonderful "
10:41 a prophet in the n· of a prophet "
41 man in the n· of a righteous man "
42 water only in the n· of a disciple, "
12:21 in his n· shall the Gentiles trust. "
18: 5 one such little child in my n· "
20 are gathered together in my n·, "
21: 9 that cometh in the n· of the Lord; "
23:39 that cometh in the n· of the Lord. "
24: 5 many shall come in my n·, saying, "
27:32 a man of Cyrene, Simon by n·: him "
28:19 them in the n· of the Father, and of "
M'r 5: 9 What is thy n·? And he answered, "
9 My n· is Legion: for we are many. "
22 of the synagogue, Jairus by n·; "

M'r 6:14 (for his n· was spread abroad:) and 3686
9:37 one of such children in my n·, "
38 saw one casting out devils in thy n·, "
39 which shall do a miracle in my n·, "
41 a cup of water to drink in my n·, * "
11: 9 that cometh in the n· of the Lord: "
10 that cometh in the n· of the Lord:* "
13: 6 many shall come in my n·, saying, "
16:17 In my n· shall they cast out devils; "
Lu 1: 5 of Aaron, and her n· was Elisabeth. "
13 son, and thou shalt call his n· John. "
27 to a man whose n· was Joseph, of "
27 David; and the virgin's n· was Mary. "
31 a son, and shalt call his n· Jesus. "
49 me great things; and holy is his n·. "
59 Zacharias, after the n· of his father. "
61 thy kindred that is called by this n·. "
63 and wrote, saying, His n· is John. "
2:21 the child, his n· was called Jesus, "
25 Jerusalem, whose n· was Simeon; "
6:22 and cast out your n· as evil, for the "
8:30 asked him, saying, What is thy n·? "
9:48 receive this child in my n· receiveth "
49 saw one casting out devils in thy n·; "
10:17 are subject unto us through thy n·. "
11: 2 art in heaven, Hallowed be thy n·. "
13:35 that cometh in the n· of the Lord. "
19:38 that cometh in the n· of the Lord: "
21: 8 many shall come in my n·, saying, "
24:18 one of them, whose n· was Cleopas,* "
47 be preached in his n· among all "
Joh 1: 6 sent from God, whose n· was John. "
12 even to them that believe on his n·: "
2:23 feast day, many believed in his n·, "
3:18 not believed in the n· of the only "
5:43 I am come in my Father's n·, and "
43 if another shall come in his own n·, "
10: 3 he calleth his own sheep by n·, and "
25 works that I do in my Father's n·, "
12:13 that cometh in the n· of the Lord. "
28 Father, glorify thy n·. Then came "
14:13 whatsoever ye shall ask in my n·, "
14 If ye shall ask any thing in my n·, "
26 whom the Father will send in my n·, "
15:16 ye shall ask of the Father in my n·, "
16:23 ye shall ask the Father in my n·, he "
24 have ye asked nothing in my n·: "
26 At that day ye shall ask in my n·: "
17: 6 manifested thy n· unto the men "
11 keep through thine own n· those "
12 in the world, I kept them in thy n·: "
26 I have declared unto them thy n·, "
18:10 ear. The servant's n· was Malchus. "
20:31 ye might have life through his n·. "
Ac 2:21 shall call on the n· of the Lord shall "
38 one of you in the n· of Jesus Christ "
3: 6 the n· of Jesus Christ of Nazareth "
16 his n· through faith in his n· hath "
4: 7 or by what n·, have ye done this? "
10 the n· of Jesus Christ of Nazareth, "
12 there is none other n· under heaven "
17 henceforth to no man in this n·. "
18 at all nor teach in the n· of Jesus. "
30 by the n· of thy holy child Jesus. "
5:28 that ye should not teach in this n·? "
40 should not speak in the n· of Jesus, "
41 worthy to suffer shame for his n·. "
7:58 man's feet, whose n· was Saul. *2564
8:12 of God, and the n· of Jesus Christ, 3686
16 baptized in the n· of the Lord Jesus.) "
9:14 to bind all that call on thy n·. "
15 to bear my n· before the Gentiles, "
21 called on this n· in Jerusalem, "
27 at Damascus in the n· of Jesus. "
29 boldly in the n· of the Lord Jesus, "
10:43 that through his n· whosoever "
48 to be baptized in the n· of the Lord. "
13: 6 a Jew, whose n· was Bar-jesus: "
8 (for so is his n· by interpretation) "
15:14 take out of them a people for his n·. "
17 upon whom my n· is called, saith "
26 lives for the n· of our Lord Jesus "
16:18 in the n· of Jesus Christ to come out "
19: 5 baptized in the n· of the Lord Jesus. "
13 spirits the n· of the Lord Jesus, "
17 n· of the Lord Jesus was magnified. "
21:13 Jerusalem for the n· of the Lord "
22:16 sins, calling on the n· of the Lord. "
26: 9 things contrary to the n· of Jesus of "
28: 7 the island, whose n· was Publius; * "
Ro 1: 5 faith among all nations, for his n·:* "
2:24 the n· of God is blasphemed among "
9:17 and that my n· might be declared "
10:13 shall call upon the n· of the Lord "
15: 9 the Gentiles, and sing unto thy n·. "
1Co 1: 2 call upon the n· of Jesus Christ "
10 by the n· of our Lord Jesus Christ, "
13 were ye baptized in the n· of Paul? "
15 that I had baptized in mine own n·. "
5: 4 In the n· of our Lord Jesus Christ, "
6:11 in the n· of the Lord Jesus, and by "
Eph 1:21 and every n· that is named, not "
5:20 in the n· of our Lord Jesus Christ; "
Ph'p 2: 9 him a n· which is above every n·: "
10 That at the n· of Jesus every knee "
Col 3:17 do all in the n· of the Lord Jesus, "
2Th 1:12 That the n· of our Lord Jesus "
3: 6 in the n· of our Lord Jesus Christ, "
1Ti 6: 1 that the n· of God and his doctrine "
2Ti 2:19 one that nameth the n· of Christ "
Heb 1: 4 a more excellent n· than they. "
2:12 declare thy n· unto my brethren, "
6:10 which ye have shewed toward his n·, "
13:15 of our lips giving thanks to his n·. "
Jas 2: 7 n· by the which ye are called? "
5:10 have spoken in the n· of the Lord,

Jas 5:14 him with oil in the *n'* of the Lord: 3686
1Pe 4:14 be reproached for the *n'* of Christ, "
1Jo 3:23 believe on the *n'* of his Son Jesus "
5:13 believe on the *n'* of the Son of God;* "
13 believe on the *n'* of the Son of God. "
3Jo 14 thee. Greet the friends by *n'*. "
Rev 2:13 thou holdest fast my *n'*, and hast "
17 and in the stone a new *n'* written, "
3: 1 that thou hast a *n'* that thou livest, "
5 not blot out his *n'* out of the book "
5 will confess his *n'* before my Father, "
8 word, and hast not denied my *n'*. "
12 *n'* of my God, and the *n'* of the city "
12 I will write upon him my new *n'*. "
6: 8 his *n'* that sat on him was Death, "
8:11 *n'* of the star is called Wormwood: "
9:11 whose *n'* in the Hebrew tongue is "
11 Greek tongue hath his *n'* Apollyon. "
11:18 and them that fear thy *n'*, small and "
13: 1 upon his heads the *n'* of blasphemy.* "
6 against God, to blaspheme his *n'*, "
17 had the mark, or the *n'* of the beast, "
17 the beast, or the number of his *n'*. "
14: 1 having his Father's *n'* written in "
11 receiveth the mark of his *n'*. "
15: 2 and over the number of his *n'*, "
4 O Lord, and glorify thy *n'*? for thou "
16: 9 and blasphemed the *n'* of God, "
17: 5 upon her forehead was a *n'* written, "
19:12 and he had a *n'* written, that no "
13 his *n'* is called The Word of God. "
16 and on his thigh a *n'* written, King "
22: 4 his *n'* shall be in their foreheads. "

named See also SURNAMED.
Ge 23:16 which he had *n'* in the audience 1696
27:36 Is not he rightly *n'* Jacob? 7121,8034
48:16 and let my name be *n'* on them, 7121
Jos 2: 1 into an harlot's house, *n'* Rahab, *8034
1Sa 4:21 And she *n'* the child I-chabod, 7121
17: 4 *n'* Goliath, of Gath, whose height 8034
22:20 the son of Ahitub, *n'* Abiathar, "
2Ki 17:34 of Jacob, whom he *n'* Israel; "
1Ch 23:14 sons were *n'* of the tribe of Levi. 7121
Ec 6:10 which hath been is *n'* already, *8034,
Isa 61: 6 shall be *n'* the Priests of the Lord: "
Jer 44:26 my name shall no more be *n'* in the "
Da 5:12 whom the king *n'* Belteshazzar: 8036
Am 6: 1 which are *n'* chief of the nations, *5344
Mic 2: 7 thou that art *n'* the house of Jacob,*559
M't 9: 9 a man, *n'* Matthew, sitting at the 3004
27:57 a rich man of Arimathæa, *n'* Joseph,3686
M'r 14:32 a place which was *n'* Gethsemane: "
15: 7 there was one *n'* Barabbas, which *3004
Lu 1: 5 a certain priest *n'* Zacharias, of 3686
26 unto a city of Galilee, *n'* Nazareth, "
2:21 which was so *n'* of the angel *2564
5:27 forth, and saw a publican, *n'* Levi, 3686
6:13 twelve, whom also he *n'* apostles; 3687
14 Simon, (whom he also *n'* Peter,) "
8:41 there came a man *n'* Jairus, and he 3686
10:38 woman *n'* Martha received him into "
16:20 was a certain beggar *n'* Lazarus, "
19: 2 there was a man *n'* Zacchæus, *2564
23:50 behold, there was a man *n'* Joseph,3686
Joh 3: 1 of the Pharisees, *n'* Nicodemus, "
11: 1 a certain man was sick, *n'* Lazarus, *
49 And one of them, *n'* Caiaphas, being *
Ac 5: 1 But a certain man *n'* Ananias, 3686
34 a Pharisee, *n'* Gamaliel, a doctor "
9:10 disciple at Damascus, *n'* Ananias; "
12 vision a man *n'* Ananias coming in, "
33 he found a certain man *n'* Æneas, "
36 Joppa a certain disciple *n'* Tabitha, "
11:28 stood up one of them *n'* Agabus, "
12:13 damsel came to hearken, *n'* Rhoda. "
16: 1 disciple was there, *n'* Timotheus, "
14 woman *n'* Lydia, a seller of purple, "
17:34 a woman *n'* Damaris, and others "
18: 2 Jew *n'* Aquila, born in Pontus, "
7 a certain man's house, *n'* Justus, "
24 And a certain Jew *n'* Apollos, born "
19:24 man *n'* Demetrius, a silversmith, "
20: 9 a certain young man *n'* Eutychus, "
21:10 Judæa a certain prophet, *n'* Agabus. "
24: 1 with a certain orator *n'* Tertullus,* "
27: 1 other prisoners unto one *n'* Julius,3686
Ro 15:20 gospel, not where Christ was *n'*, 3687
1Co 5: 1 so much as *n'* among the Gentiles,* "
Eph 1:21 and every name that is *n'*, not only "
3:15 family in heaven and earth is *n'*, "
5: 3 let it not be once *n'* among you, "

namely
Le 1:10 be of the flocks, *n'*, of the sheep, *
Nu 1:32 Of the children of Joseph, *n'*, of the
9:15 *n'*, the tent of the testimony: *
31: 8 that were slain; *n'*, Evi, and Rekem,*
De 4:43 *N'*, Bezer in the wilderness, in the
13: 7 *N'*, of the gods of the people which*
20:17 *n'*, the Hittites, and the Amorites, the*
J'g 3: 3 *N'*, five lords of the Philistines, and
8:35 to the house of Jerubbaal, *n'*, Gideon,*
1Ch 6:57 they gave the cities of Judah, *n'*, *
61 tribe, *n'*, out of the half tribe of *
9:23 *n'*, the house of the tabernacle, by*
23: 6 the sons of Levi, *n'*, Gershon, Kohath,*
Ezr 10:18 *n'*, of the sons of Jeshua the son of
Ne 12:35 *n'*, Zechariah the son of Jonathan, the*
Es 8:12 *n'*, upon the thirteenth day of the
Ec 5:13 *n'*, riches kept for the owners thereof
Isa 7:20 *n'*, by them beyond the river, by *
Jer 26:22 *n'*, Elnathan the son of Achbor, and
M'r 12:31 And the second is like, *n'* this, Thou*
Ac 15:22 *n'*, Judas surnamed Barsabas, and
Ro 13: 9 *n'*, Thou shalt love thy neighbour 1722

name's
1Sa 12:22 his people for his great *n'* sake: 8034
1Ki 8:41 out of a far country for thy *n'* sake; "
2Ch 6:32 a far country for thy great *n'* sake, "
Ps 23: 3 of righteousness for his *n'* sake. "
25:11 For thy *n'* sake, O Lord, pardon "
31: 3 therefore for thy *n'* sake lead me, "
79: 9 away our sins, for thy *n'* sake. "
106: 8 he saved them for his *n'* sake, that "
109:21 O God the Lord, for thy *n'* sake: "
143:11 Quicken me, O Lord, for thy *n'* sake: "
Isa 48: 9 For my *n'* sake will I defer mine "
66: 5 cast you out for my *n'* sake, said, "
Jer 14: 7 us, do thou it for thy *n'* sake: "
21 Do not abhor us, for thy *n'* sake, "
Eze 20: 9, 14 But I wrought for my *n'* sake, "
22 and wrought for my *n'* sake, that it "
44 wrought with you for my *n'* sake, "
36:22 but for mine holy *n'* sake, which ye * "
M't 10:22 hated of all men for my *n'* sake: 3686
19:29 children, or lands, for my *n'* sake, "
24: 9 hated of all nations for my *n'* sake. "
M'k 13:13 be hated of all men for my *n'* sake: "
Lu 21:12 kings and rulers for my *n'* sake. "
17 be hated of all men for my *n'* sake. "
Joh 15:21 they do unto you for my *n'* sake, "
Ac 9:16 he must suffer for my *n'* sake. "
1Jo 2:12 are forgiven you for his *n'* sake. "
3Jo 7 that for his *n'* sake they went forth,* "
Re 2: 3 and for my *n'* sake hast laboured, "

names
Ge 2:20 Adam gave *n'* to all cattle, and to 8034
25:13 are the *n'* of the sons of Ishmael, "
13 by their *n'*, according to their "
16 of Ishmael, and these are their *n'*, "
26:18 called their *n'* after the *n'* by which "
36:10 are the *n'* of Esau's sons; Eliphaz "
40 the *n'* of the dukes that came of "
40 after their places, by their *n'*; Duke "
46: 8 are the *n'* of the children of Israel, "
Ex 1: 1 are the *n'* of the children of Israel, "
6:16 these are the *n'* of the sons of Levi "
28: 9 them the *n'* of the children of Israel: "
10 Six of their *n'* on one stone, and the "
10 six *n'* of the rest on the other stone, "
11 with the *n'* of the children of Israel: "
12 shall bear their *n'* before the Lord "
21 with the *n'* of the children of Israel, "
21 twelve, according to their *n'*, like "
29 bear the *n'* of the children of Israel "
39: 6 with the *n'* of the children of Israel. "
14 to the *n'* of the children of Israel, "
14 twelve, according to their *n'*, like "
Nu 1: 2 with the number of their *n'*, every "
5 *n'* of the men that shall stand with "
17 which are expressed by their *n'*: * "
18, 20, 22, 24, 26, 28, 30, 32, 34, 36, 38, 40, "
42 according to the number of the *n'*, "
3: 2 are the *n'* of the sons of Aaron; "
3 are the *n'* of the sons of Aaron, the "
17 were the sons of Levi by their *n'*; "
18 are the *n'* of the sons of Gershon "
40 and take the number of their *n'*. "
43 firstborn males by the number of *n'*, "
13: 4 these were their *n'*: of the tribe "
16 *n'* of the men which Moses sent "
26:33 and the *n'* of the daughters of "
53 according to the number of *n'*. "
55 the *n'* of the tribes of their fathers "
27: 1 these are the *n'* of his daughters; "
32:38 (their *n'* being changed,) and "
38 gave other *n'* unto the cities which "
34:17 These are the *n'* of the men which "
19 the *n'* of the men are these: of the "
De 12: 3 the *n'* of them out of that place, * "
Jos 17: 3 these are the *n'* of his daughters, "
1Sa 14:49 the *n'* of his two daughters were "
17:13 the *n'* of his three sons that went "
2Sa 5:14 *n'* of those that were born unto him "
23: 8 These be the *n'* of the mighty men "
1Ki 4: 8 And these are their *n'*: The son of "
1Ch 4:38 mentioned by their *n'* were princes "
6:17 be the *n'* of the sons of Gershom; "
65 cities, which are called by their *n'*.* "
8:38 had six sons, whose *n'* are these, "
9:44 had six sons, whose *n'* are these, "
14: 4 are the *n'* of his children which he "
23:24 by number of *n'* by their polls, that "
Ezr 5: 4 What are the *n'* of the men that 8036
10 We asked their *n'* also, to certify "
10 we might write the *n'* of the men "
8:13 whose *n'* are these, Eliphelet, 8034
10:16 and all of them by their *n'*, were "
Ps 16: 4 nor take up their *n'* into my lips. "
49:11 call their lands after their own *n'*. "
147: 4 he calleth them all by their *n'*. "
Isa 40:26 he calleth them all by *n'* by the* "
Eze 23: 4 the *n'* of them were Aholah the "
4 were their *n'*; Samaria is Aholah, "
48: 1 Now these are the *n'* of the tribes. "
31 after the *n'* of the tribes of Israel: "
Da 1: 7 the prince of the eunuchs gave *n'*: "
Ho 2:17 I will take away the *n'* of Baalim "
Zec 13: 2 will cut off the *n'* of the idols out of "
M't 10: 2 the *n'* of the twelve apostles are 3686
Lu 10:20 your *n'* are written in heaven. "
Ac 1:15 (the number of the *n'* together were* "
18:15 if it be a question of words and *n'*, "
Ph'p 4: 3 whose *n'* are in the book of life. "
Re 3: 4 hast a few *n'* even in Sardis which "
13: 8 whose *n'* are not written in the * "
17: 3 full of *n'* of blasphemy, having "
8 whose *n'* were not written in the * "
21:12 angels, and *n'* written thereon, "
12 are the *n'* of the twelve tribes of the "
14 them the *n'* of the twelve apostles 3686

nameth
2Ti 2:19 one that *n'* the name of Christ 3687

Nangæ See NAGGE.

Naomi (*na'-o-mee*) See also NAOMI'S.
Ru 1: 2 and the name of his wife *N'*, and 5281
8 *N'* said unto her two daughters in "
11 *N'* said, Turn again, my daughters: "
19 them, and they said, Is this *N'*? "
20 them, Call me not *N'*, call me Mara: "
21 why then call ye me *N'*, seeing the "
22 So *N'* returned, and Ruth the "
2: 1 *N'* had a kinsman of her husband's, "
2 Ruth the Moabitess said unto *N'*, "
6 damsel that came back with *N'* "
20 *N'* said unto her daughter in law, "
20 *N'* said unto her, The man is near "
22 *N'* said unto Ruth her daughter in "
3: 1 *N'* her mother in law said unto her, "
4: 3 he said unto the kinsman, *N'*, that "
5 buyest the field of the hand of *N'*, "
9 and Mahlon's, of the hand of *N'*. "
14 women said unto *N'*, Blessed be "
16 *N'* took the child, and laid it in her "
17 saying, There is a son born to *N'*; "

Naomi's (*na'-o-meze*)
Ru 1: 3 And Elimelech *N'* husband died; 5281

Naphish (*na'-fish*) See also NEPHISH.
Ge 25:15 Tema, Jetur, *N'*, and Kedemah: 5305
1Ch 1:31 Jetur, *N'*, and Kedemah. These "

Naphtali (*naf'-ta-li*) See also NEPHTHALIM.
Ge 30: 8 and she called his name *N'*. 5321
35:25 Rachel's handmaid; Dan, and *N'*: "
46:24 And the sons of *N'*; Jahzeel, and "
49:21 *N'* is a hind let loose: he giveth "
Ex 1: 4 Dan, and *N'*, Gad, and Asher. "
Nu 1:15 Of *N'*; Ahira the son of Enan. "
42 Of the children of *N'*, throughout "
43 of them, even of the tribe of *N'*, "
2:29 Then the tribe of *N'*: and the "
29 captain of the children of *N'* shall "
7:78 Ahira...prince of the children of *N'*, "
10:27 of the children of *N'* was Ahira "
13:14 Of the tribe of *N'*, Nahbi the son of "
26:48 the sons of *N'* after their families: "
50 These are the families of *N'* "
34:28 of the tribe of the children of *N'*, "
De 27:13 Asher, and Zebulun, Dan, and *N'*. "
33:23 of *N'* he said, O *N'*, satisfied with "
34: 2 all *N'*, and the land of Ephraim, "
Jos 19:32 lot came out to the children of *N'*, "
32 for the children of *N'* according to "
39 children of *N'* according to their "
20: 7 Kedesh in Galilee in mount *N'*, "
21: 6 and out of the tribe of *N'*, and out "
32 out of the tribe of *N'*, Kedesh in "
J'g 1:33 did *N'* drive out the inhabitants "
4: 6 thousand men of the children of *N'* "
10 called Zebulun and *N'* to Kedesh; "
5:18 Zebulun and *N'* were a people that "
6:35 and unto Zebulun, and unto *N'*; "
7:23 themselves together out of *N'*, and "
1Ki 4:15 Ahimaaz was in *N'*; he also took "
7:14 a widow's son of the tribe of *N'*, "
15:20 Cinneroth, with all the land of *N'*. "
2Ki 15:29 all the land of *N'*, and carried them "
1Ch 2: 2 Joseph, and Benjamin, *N'*, Gad, "
6:62 and out of the tribe of *N'*, and out "
76 And out of the tribe of *N'*; Kedesh "
7:13 The sons of *N'*; Jahziel, and Guni, "
12:34 And of *N'* a thousand captains, and "
40 unto Issachar and Zebulun and *N'*, "
27:19 of *N'*, Jerimoth the son of Azriel: "
2Ch 16: 4 and all the store cities of *N'*. "
34: 6 and Simeon, even unto *N'*, with "
Ps 68:27 of Zebulun, and the princes of *N'*. "
Isa 9: 1 land of Zebulun and the land of *N'*, "
Eze 48: 3 unto the west side, a portion for *N'*. "
4 And by the border of *N'*, from the "
34 one gate of Asher, one gate of *N'*. "

Naphtuhim (*naf'-too-him*)
Ge 10:13 Anamim, and Lehabim, and *N'*, 5320
1Ch 1:11 Anamim, and Lehabim, and *N'*, "

napkin
Lu 19:20 which I have kept laid up in a *n'*: 4676
Joh 11:44 face was bound about with a *n'*. "
20: 7 And the *n'*, that was about his head, "

Narcissus (*nar-sis'-sus*)
Ro 16:11 that be of the household of *N'*, 3488

nard See SPIKENARD.

narrow See also NARROWED; NARROWER.
Nu 22:26 further, and stood in a *n'* place, 6862
Jos 17:15 mount Ephraim be too *n'* for thee. 213
1Ki 6: 4 he made windows of *n'* lights. * 331
Pr 23:27 and a strange woman is a *n'* pit. 6862
Isa 49:19 even now be too *n'* by reason of *3334
Eze 40:16 *n'* windows to the little chambers,* 331
41:16 posts, and the *n'* windows, and the* "
26 were *n'* windows and palm trees * "
M't 7:14 is the gate, and *n'* is the way, *2346

narrowed
1Ki 6: 6 he made *n'* rests round about, †‡4052

narrower
Isa 28:20 covering *n'* than that he can wrap 6887

narrowly
Job 13:27 and lookest *n'* unto all my paths; *8104
Isa 14:16 that see thee shall *n'* look upon thee,

Nathan (*na'-than*) See also NATHAN-MELECH.
2Sa 5:14 Shammuah, and Shobab, and *N'*, 5416
7: 2 the king said unto *N'* the prophet, "
3 And *N'* said unto the king, Go, do "

2Sa 7: 4 the word of the Lord came unto N·, 5416
17 vision, so did N· speak unto David."
12: 1 And the Lord sent N· unto David. "
5 he said to N·, As the Lord liveth, "
7 And N· said to David, Thou art the"
13 David said unto N·, I have sinned "
13 N· said unto David, The Lord also "
15 And N· departed unto his house. "
25 sent by the hand of N· the prophet;"
23: 36 Igal the son of N· of Zobah, Bani "
1Ki 1: 8 N· the prophet, and Shimei, and "
10 N· the prophet, and Benaiah, and "
11 N· spake unto Bath-sheba the "
22 king, N· the prophet also came in. "
23 saying, Behold N· the prophet. "
24 And N· said, My lord, O king, hast "
32 the priest, and N· the prophet, and"
34 priest and N· the prophet anoint "
38, 44 the priest, and N· the prophet, "
45 N· the prophet have anointed him "
4: 5 the son of N· was over the officers: "
5 Zabud the son of N· was principal "
1Ch 2: 36 Attai begat N·, and N· begat "
3: 5 Shimea, and Shobab, and N·, and "
11: 38 Joel the brother of N·, Mibhar the "
14: 4 and Shobab, N·, and Solomon. "
17: 1 that David said to N· the prophet, "
2 N· said unto David, Do all that is "
3 word of God came to N·, saying, "
15 vision, so did N· speak unto David."
29: 29 and in the book of N· the prophet, "
2Ch 9: 29 in the book of N· the prophet, and "
29: 25 king's seer, and N· the prophet: "
Ezr 8: 16 for N·, and for Zechariah, and for "
10: 39 Shelemiah, and N·, and Adaiah, "
Ps 51: title N· the prophet came unto him, "
Zec 12: 12 the family of the house of N· a part,"
Lu 3: 31 which was the son of N·, which 3481

Nathanael (*na-than'-a-el*) See also BARTHOLOMEW.
Joh 1: 45 Philip findeth N·, and saith unto 3482
46 N· said unto him, Can there any "
47 Jesus saw N· coming to him, and "
48 N· saith unto him, Whence knowest"
49 N· answered and saith unto him, "
21: 2 Didymus, and N· of Cana in Galilee,"

Nathan-melech (*na"-than-me'-lek*)
2Ki 23: 11 chamber of N· the chamberlain, 5419

nation See also NATIONS.
Ge 12: 2 I will make of thee a great n·, and 1471
15: 14 also that n·, whom they shall serve, "
17: 20 and I will make him a great n·. "
18: 18 become a great and mighty n·, and "
20: 4 wilt thou slay also a righteous n·? "
21: 13 of the bondwoman will I make a n·, "
18 for I will make him a great n·. "
35: 11 a n· and a company of nations shall "
46: 3 I will there make of thee a great n·:"
Ex 9: 24 land of Egypt since it became a n·. "
19: 6 kingdom of priests, and an holy n·. "
21: 8 to sell her unto a strange n· he *5971
32: 10 and I will make of thee a great n·. 1471
33: 13 consider that this n· is thy people. "
34: 10 done in all the earth, nor in any n·: "
Le 18: 26 neither any of your own n·, nor any*249
20: 23 not walk in the manners of the n·, 1471
Nu 14: 12 and will make of thee a greater n· "
De 4: 6 Surely this great n· is a wise and "
7 what n· is there so great, who hath "
8 what n· is there so great, that hath "
34 a n· from the midst of another n·, "
9: 14 I will make of thee a n· mightier "
26: 5 with a few, and became there a n·, "
28: 33 shall a n· which thou knowest not 5971
36 unto a n· which neither thou nor 1471
49 Lord shall bring a n· against thee "
49 a n· whose tongue thou shalt not "
50 A n· of fierce countenance, which "
32: 21 them to anger with a foolish n·. "
28 For they are a n· void of counsel, "
2Sa 7: 23 what one n· in the earth is like thy "
1Ki 18: 10 there is no n· or kingdom, whither "
10 took an oath of the kingdom and n·,"
2Ki 17: 29 every n· made gods of their own, "
29 every n· in their cities wherein they"
1Ch 16: 20 And when they went from n· to n·, "
17: 21 what one n· in the earth is like thy "
2Ch 15: 6 n· was destroyed of n·, and city of "
32: 15 for no god of any n· or kingdom was"
Job 34: 29 done against a n·, or against a man"
Ps 33: 12 Blessed is the n· whose God is the "
43: 1 my cause against an ungodly n·: "
83: 4 let us cut them off from being a n·; "
105: 13 they went from one n· to another, "
106: 5 rejoice in the gladness of thy n·, "
147: 20 He hath not dealt so with any n·: "
Pr 14: 34 Righteousness exalteth a n·: but "
Isa 1: 4 Ah sinful n·, a people laden with "
2: 4 n· shall not lift up sword against n·,"
9: 3 Thou hast multiplied the n·, and "
10: 6 send him against an hypocritical n·,"
14: 32 answer the messengers of the n·? "
18: 2 to a n· scattered and peeled, to a "
2 a n· meted out and trodden down, "
7 a n· meted out and trodden under "
26: 2 that the righteous n· which keepeth"
15 Thou hast increased the n·, O Lord,"
15 O Lord, thou hast increased the n·:"
49: 7 to him whom the n· abhorreth, to "
51: 4 and give ear unto me, O my n·: 3816
55: 5 shalt call a n· that thou knowest 1471
58: 2 as a n· that did righteousness, and "
60: 12 n· and kingdom that will not serve "
22 and a small one a strong n·: I the "
65: 1 n· that was not called by my name. "
Isa 66: 8 or shall a n· be born at once? for as 1471
Jer 2: 11 Hath a n· changed their gods, which"
5: 9 my soul be avenged on such a n· as "
15 I will bring a n· upon you from far, "
15 it is a mighty n·, it is an ancient n·, "
15 a n· whose language thou knowest "
29 my soul be avenged on such a n· as "
6: 22 a great n· shall be raised from the "
7: 28 is a n· that obeyeth not the voice of "
9: 9 my soul be avenged on such a n· as "
12: 17 pluck up and destroy that n·, saith "
18: 7 I shall speak concerning a n·, and "
8 If that n·, against whom I have "
9 I shall speak concerning a n·, and "
25: 12 the king of Babylon, and that n·, "
32 evil shall go forth from n· to n·, and "
27: 8 the n· and kingdom which will not "
8 that n· will I punish, saith the Lord,"
13 against the n· that will not serve "
31: 36 shall cease from being a n· before "
33: 24 that they should be no more a n· "
48: 2 and let us cut it off from being a n·. "
49: 31 get you up unto the wealthy n·, "
36 shall be no n· whither the outcasts "
50: 3 there cometh up a n· against her, "
41 a great n·, and many kings shall be "
La 4: 17 watched for a n· that could not save "
Eze 2: 3 a rebellious n· that hath rebelled * "
37: 22 I will make them one n· in the land "
Da 3: 29 every people, n·, and language, 524
8: 22 shall stand up out of the n·, 1471
12: 1 as never was since there was a n· "
Joe 1: 6 For a n· is come up upon my land, "
Am 6: 14 I will raise up against you a n·, O "
Mic 4: 3 n· shall not lift...sword against n·, "
7 that was cast far off a strong n·: "
Hab 1: 6 Chaldeans, that bitter and hasty n·,"
Zep 2: 1 gather together, O n· not desired; "
5 sea coast, the n· of the Cherethites!"
Hag 2: 14 So is this people, and so is this n· "
Mal 3: 9 have robbed me, even this whole n·."
M't 21: 43 to a n· bringing forth the fruits 1484
24: 7 For n· shall rise against n·, and "
M'r 7: 26 a Greek, a Syrophenician by n·; *1085
13: 8 For n· shall rise against n·, and 1484
Lu 7: 5 he loveth our n·, and he hath built "
21: 10 unto them, N· shall rise against n·, "
23: 2 found this fellow perverting the n·, "
Joh 11: 48 take away both our place and n·. "
50 and that the whole n· perish not. "
51 that Jesus should die for that n·; "
52 And not for that n· only, but that "
18: 35 Thine own n· and the chief priests "
Ac 2: 5 men, out of every n· under heaven. "
7: 7 n· to whom they shall be in bondage"
10: 22 report among all the n· of the Jews,"
28 or come unto one of another n·; 246
35 in every n· he that feareth him, 1484
24: 2 worthy deeds are done unto this n· "
10 of many years a judge unto this n·, "
17 I came to bring alms to my n·, and "
26: 4 among mine own n· at Jerusalem, "
28: 19 that I had ought to accuse my n· of."
Ro 10: 19 and by a foolish n· I will anger you."
Ga 1: 14 many my equals in mine own n·, *1085
Ph'p 2: 15 of a crooked and perverse n·, *1074
1Pe 2: 9 an holy n·, a peculiar people; 1484
Re 5: 9 and tongue, and people, and n·; "
14: 6 every n·, and kindred, and tongue, "

nations
Ge 10: 5 after their families, in their n·. 1471
20 in their countries, and in their n·. "
31 in their lands, after their n·. "
32 after their generations, in their n·: "
32 were the n· divided in the earth "
14: 1 king of Elam, and Tidal king of n·;*"
9 Elam, and with Tidal king of n·, * "
17: 4 thou shalt be a father of many n·. "
5 father of many n· have I made thee."
6 I will make n· of thee, and kings "
16 and she shall be a mother of n·; "
18: 18 the n· of the earth shall be blessed "
22: 18 all the n· of the earth be blessed; "
25: 16 twelve princes according to their n·. 523
23 Two n· are in thy womb, and two 1471
26: 4 all the n· of the earth be blessed; "
27: 29 thee, and n· bow down to thee: 3816
35: 11 a company of n· shall be of thee, 1471
48: 19 seed shall become a multitude of n·."
Ex 34: 24 I will cast out the n· before thee, "
Le 18: 24 for in all these the n· are defiled "
28 spued out the n· that were before* "
Nu 14: 15 the n· which have heard the fame "
23: 9 shall not be reckoned among the n·."
24: 8 he shall eat up the n· his enemies, "
20 Amalek was the first of the n·; "
De 2: 25 the n· that are under the whole *5971
4: 6 understanding...the sight of the n·,* "
19 unto all n· under the whole heaven."
27 shall scatter you among the n·, "
38 To drive out n· from before thee 1471
7: 1 hath cast out many n· before thee, "
1 seven n· greater and mightier than "
17 These n· are more than I; how can "
22 God will put out those n· before thee"
8: 20 As the n· which the Lord destroyeth"
9: 1 possess n· greater and mightier than"
4, 5 but for the wickedness of these n· "
11: 23 will the Lord drive out all these n· "
23 possess greater n· and mightier than"
12: 2 the n· which ye shall possess served"
29 God shall cut off the n· from before "
30 How did these n· serve their gods? "
14: 2 all the n· that are upon the earth.*5971
15: 6 and thou shalt lend unto many n·, 1471
6 and thou shalt reign over many n·, "
De 17: 14 like as all the n· that are about me; 1471
18: 9 after the abominations of those n·. "
14 these n·, which thou shalt possess, "
19: 1 Lord thy God hath cut off the n·, "
20: 15 are not of the cities of these n·. "
26: 19 And to make thee high above all n· "
28: 1 on high above all n· of the earth: "
12 and thou shalt lend unto many n·, "
37 all n· whither the Lord shall lead *5971
65 among these n· shalt thou find no 1471
29: 16 and how we came through the n· "
18 to go and serve the gods of these n·;"
24 Even all n· shall say, Wherefore "
30: 1 call them to mind among all the n·, "
3 and gather thee from all the n·, *5971
31: 3 destroy these n· from before thee, 1471
32: 8 the Most High divided to the n· their"
43 Rejoice, O ye n·, with his people: "
Jos 12: 23 one; the king of the n· of Gilgal, "
23: 3 God hath done unto all these n· "
4 divided unto you by lot these n· that"
4 with all the n· that I have cut off, "
7 That ye come not among these n·, "
9 from before you great n· and strong:"
12 cleave unto the remnant of these n·,"
13 no more drive out any of these n· "
J'g 2: 21 n· which Joshua left when he died: "
23 Therefore the Lord left those n·, "
3: 1 these are the n· which the Lord left,"
1Sa 8: 5 a king to judge us like all the n·. "
20 That we also may be like all the n·;"
27: 8 those n· were of old the inhabitants
2Sa 7: 23 Egypt, from the n· and their gods? 1471
8: 11 dedicated of all n· which he subdued;"
1Ki 4: 31 his fame was in all n· round about. "
11: 2 n· concerning which the Lord said "
14: 24 to all the abominations of the n· "
2Ki 17: 26 The n· which thou hast removed, "
33 manner of the n· whom they carried"
41 So these n· feared the Lord, and "
18: 33 of the gods of the n· delivered at all"
19: 12 Have the gods of the n· delivered "
17 destroyed the n· and their lands, "
21: 9 to do more evil than did the n· "
1Ch 14: 17 brought the fear of him upon all n·."
16: 24 marvellous works among all n·. *5971
31 and let men say among the n·, The 1471
17: 21 by driving out n· from before thy "
18: 11 that he brought from all these n·; "
2Ch 7: 20 and a byword among all n·. *5971
13: 9 manner of the n· of other lands? * "
32: 13 the gods of the n· of those lands 1471
14 there among all the gods of those n·"
17 the gods of the n· of other lands "
23 was magnified in the sight of all n· "
Ezr 4: 10 the rest of the n· whom the great 524
Ne 1: 8 scatter you abroad among the n·:*5971
9: 22 gavest them kingdoms and n·, * "
13: 26 among many n· was there no king 1471
Job 12: 23 He increaseth the n·, and destroyeth"
23 he enlargeth the n·, and straiteneth"
Ps 9: 17 hell, and all the n· that forget God. "
20 n· may know themselves to be but "
22: 27 the kindreds of the n· shall worship"
28 he is the governor among the n·. "
47: 3 us, and the n· under our feet. 3816
57: 9 I will sing unto thee among the n·. "
66: 7 for ever; his eyes behold the n·: 1471
67: 2 thy saving health among all n·. "
4 let the n· be glad and sing for joy: 3816
4 and govern the n· upon earth. "
72: 11 before him: all n· shall serve him. 1471
17 in him: all n· shall call him blessed."
82: 8 earth: for thou shalt inherit all n·. "
86: 9 All n·...thou hast made shall come "
96: 5 all the gods of the n· are idols: *5971
106: 27 their seed also among the n·, and 1471
34 They did not destroy the n·, *5971
108: 3 praises unto thee among the n·. 3816
113: 4 The Lord is high above all n·, and 1471
117: 1 O praise the Lord, all ye n·: praise "
118: 10 All n· compassed me about: but in "
135: 10 smote great n·, and slew mighty "
Pr 24: 24 people curse, n· shall abhor him: 3816
Isa 2: 2 hills; and all n· shall flow unto it. 1471
4 And he shall judge among the n·, "
5: 26 lift up an ensign to the n· from far, "
9: 1 beyond Jordan, in Galilee of the n·. "
10: 7 to destroy and cut off n· not a few. "
11: 12 he shall set up an ensign for the n·, "
13: 4 kingdoms of n· gathered together: "
14: 6 he that ruled the n· in anger, is "
9 their thrones all the kings of the n·."
12 ground, which didst weaken the n·! "
18 the kings of the n·, even all of them,"
26 is stretched out upon all the n·. "
17: 12 and to the rushing of n·, that make 3816
13 The n· shall rush like the rushing of "
23: 3 revenue; and she is a mart of n·. 1471
25: 3 city of the terrible n· shall fear thee."
7 the vail that is spread over all n·. "
29: 7 the multitude of all the n· that fight"
8 shall the multitude of all the n· be, "
30: 28 sift the n· with the sieve of vanity: "
33: 3 up of thyself the n· were scattered. "
34: 1 Come near, ye n·, to hear; and "
2 of the Lord is upon all n·, and his "
36: 18 any of the gods of the n· delivered "
37: 12 Have the gods of the n· delivered "
18 Assyria have laid waste all the n·,* 776
40: 15 the n· are as a drop of a bucket, 1471
17 All n· before him are as nothing; "
41: 2 to his foot, gave the n· before him, "
43: 9 Let all the n· be gathered together, "
45: 1 holden, to subdue n· before him; "
20 ye that are escaped of the n·; they "

Isa 52:10 holy arm in the eyes of all the n'; 1471
15 So shall he sprinkle many n'; the "
55: 5 n' that knew not thee shall run * "
60:12 those n' shall be utterly wasted. "
61:11 to spring forth before all the n'. "
64: 2 the n' may tremble at thy presence!"
66:18 I will gather all n' and tongues; "
19 that escape of them unto the n', "
20 the Lord out of all n' upon horses, "
Jer 1: 5 ordained thee a prophet unto the n'."
10 have this day set thee over the n' "
3:17 all the n' shall be gathered unto it, "
19 goodly heritage of the hosts of n'? "
4: 2 and the n' shall bless themselves in"
16 Make ye mention to the n'; behold, "
6:18 Therefore hear, ye n', and know, "
9:26 for all these n' are uncircumcised, "
10: 7 would not fear thee, O King of n'? "
7 among all the wise men of the n', "
10 and the n' shall not be able to abide"
22: 8 And many n' shall pass by this city "
25: 9 against all these n' round about, "
11 and these n' shall serve the king "
13 hath prophesied against all the n'. "
14 many n' and great kings shall serve"
15 and cause all the n', to whom I send"
17 and made all the n' to drink, unto "
31 Lord hath a controversy with the n',"
26: 6 a curse to all the n' of the earth. "
27: 7 all n' shall serve him, and his son, "
7 many n' and great kings shall serve"
11 the n' that bring their neck under* "
28:11 of Babylon from the neck of all n' "
14 iron upon the neck of all these n', "
29:14 I will gather you from all the n', "
18 among all the n' whither I have "
30:11 I make a full end of all n' whither I "
31: 7 shout among the chief of the n': "
10 Hear the word of the Lord, O ye n', "
33: 9 honour before all the n' of the earth."
36: 2 Judah, and against all the n', from "
43: 5 that were returned from all n', "
44: 8 among all the n' of the earth? "
46:12 The n' have heard of thy shame, "
28 I will make a full end of all the n' "
50: 2 Declare ye among the n',...publish, "
9 an assembly of great n' from the "
12 the hindermost of the n' shall be a "
23 become a desolation among the n'! "
46 and the cry is heard among the n'. "
51: 7 the n' have drunken of her wine; "
7 her wine; therefore the n' are mad."
20 thee will I break in pieces the n', "
27 blow the trumpet among the n', "
27 prepare the n' against her, call "
28 Prepare against her the n' with the "
41 an astonishment among the n'! "
44 the n' shall not flow together any "
La 1: 1 that she was great among the n', "
Eze 5: 5 I have set it in the midst of the n' "
6 into wickedness more than the n', "
7 multiplied more than the n' that "
7 according to the judgments of the n'"
8 midst of thee in the sight of the n'. "
14 a reproach among the n' that are "
15 unto the n' that are round about "
6: 8 escape the sword among the n', "
9 shall remember me among the n' "
12:15 I shall scatter them among the n', "
19: 4 The n' also heard of him; he was "
8 the n' set against him on every "
25:10 not be remembered among the n'. "
26: 3 and will cause many n' to come up "
5 and it shall become a spoil to the n'."
28: 7 upon thee, the terrible of the n': "
29:12 scatter the Egyptians among the n',"
15 exalt itself any more above the n': "
15 they shall no more rule over the n'. "
30:11 the terrible of the n', shall be "
23, 26 scatter...Egyptians among...n', "
31: 6 under his shadow dwelt all great n'. "
12 And strangers, the terrible of the n',"
16 I made the n' to shake at the sound"
32: 2 Thou art like a young lion of the n',"
9 bring thy destruction among the n',"
12 the terrible of the n', all of them: "
16 the daughters of the n' shall lament"
18 and the daughters of the famous n',"
35:10 said, These two n' and these two "
36:13 up men, and hast bereaved thy n';* "
14 neither bereave thy n' any more, * "
15 thou cause thy n' to fall any more,* "
37:22 and they shall be no more two n', "
38: 8 but it is brought forth out of the n',*"
12 that are gathered out of the n', "
23 be known in the eyes of many n', "
39:27 in them in the sight of many n'; "
Da 3: 4 O people, n', and languages, 524
7 the people, the n',...the languages, "
4: 1 unto all people, n', and languages, "
5:19 him, all people, n', and languages, "
6:25 Darius wrote unto all people, n', "
7:14 that all people, n', and languages, "
Ho 8:10 they have hired among the n', 1471
9:17 shall be wanderers among the n'. "
Joe 3: 2 I will also gather all n', and will "
2 they have scattered among the n', "
Am 6: 1 which are named chief of the n', to "
9: 9 the house of Israel among all n', "
Mic 4: 2 many n' shall come, and say, Come, "
3 people,...rebuke strong n' afar off; "
11 many n' are gathered against thee, "
7:16 n' shall see and be confounded at "
Na 3: 4 selleth n' through her whoredoms, "
5 I will shew the n' thy nakedness, "
Hab 1:17 not spare continually to slay the n'?"
Hab 2: 5 but gathereth unto him all n', and 1471
8 thou hast spoiled many n', all the "
3: 6 beheld, and drove asunder the n'; "
Zep 2:14 midst of her, all the beasts of the n':"
3: 6 I have cut off the n': their towers "
8 determination is to gather the n', "
Hag 2: 7 And I will shake all n', and the "
7 and the desire of all n' shall come: "
Zec 2: 8 me unto the n' which spoiled you: "
11 many n' shall be joined to the Lord "
7:14 all the n' whom they knew not. "
8:22 n' shall come to seek the Lord of "
23 hold out of all languages of the n', "
12: 9 n' that come against Jerusalem. "
14: 2 gather all n' against Jerusalem to "
3 go forth, and fight against those n', "
16 n' which came against Jerusalem "
19 punishment of all n' that come not "
Mal 3:12 all n' shall call you blessed: for ye "
M't 24: 9 ye shall be hated of all n' for my 1484
14 the world for a witness unto all n'; "
25:32 before him shall be gathered all n': "
28:19 Go ye therefore, and teach all n', "
M'r 11:17 called of all n' the house of prayer! "
13:10 first be published among all n'. "
Lu 12:30 do the n' of the world seek after: "
21:24 shall be led away captive into all n': "
25 and upon the earth distress of n', "
24:47 preached in his name among all n', "
Ac 13:19 when he had destroyed seven n' in "
14:16 all n' to walk in their own ways. "
17:26 made of one blood all n' of men * "
Ro 1: 5 obedience to the faith among all n', "
4:17 made thee a father of many n',) "
18 become the father of many n', "
16:26 known to all n' for the obedience "
Ga 3: 8 In thee shall all n' be blessed. "
Re 2:26 him will I give power over the n': "
7: 9 no man could number, of all n', * "
10:11 many peoples, and n', and tongues, "
11: 9 people...kindreds...tongues and n' "
18 the n' were angry, and thy wrath "
12: 5 was to rule all n' with a rod of iron:"
13: 7 all kindreds, and tongues, and n'.* "
14: 8 she made all n' drink of the wine "
15: 4 for all n' shall come and worship "
16:19 parts, and the cities of the n' fell: "
17:15 peoples, and multitudes, and n', "
18: 3 For all n' have drunk of the wine "
23 thy sorceries were all n' deceived. "
19:15 that with it he should smite the n': "
20: 3 he should deceive the n' no more, "
8 and shall go out to deceive the n' "
21:24 And the n' of them which are saved "
26 glory and honour of the n' into it. "
22: 2 tree were for the healing of the n'. "

native
Jer 22:10 no more, nor see his n' country. 4138

nativity
Ge 11:28 father Terah in the land of his n', 4138
Ru 2:11 thy mother, and the land of thy n', "
Jer 46:16 people and to the land of our n', "
Eze 16: 3 and thy n' is of the land of Canaan;"
4 as for thy n', in the day thou wast "
21:30 wast created, in the land of thy n'.*4351
23:15 of Chaldea, the land of their n': 4138

natural
De 34: 7 not dim, nor his n' force abated. 3893
Ro 1:26 women did change the n' use into 5446
27 leaving the n' use of the woman, "
31 without n' affection, implacable,
11:21 spared not the n' branches, 2596,5449
24 these, which be the n' branches," "
1Co 2:14 But the n' man receiveth not the 5591
15:44 It is sown a n' body; it is raised a "
44 There is a n' body, and there is a "
46 is spiritual, but that which is n'; "
2Ti 3: 3 Without n' affection, trucebreakers,
Jas 1:23 beholding his n' face in a glass: 1083
2Pe 2:12 But these, as n' brute beasts, made*5446

naturally
Ph'p 2:20 who will n' care for your state. *1108
Jude 10 what they know n', as brute beasts,5447

nature
Ro 1:26 use into that which is against n': 5449
2:14 do by n' the things contained in the "
27 not uncircumcision which is by n', "
11:24 of the olive tree which is wild by n', "
24 and wert graffed contrary to n' into "
1Co 11:14 Doth not even n' itself teach you, "
Ga 2:15 We who are Jews by n', and not "
4: 8 unto them which by n' are no gods. "
Eph 2: 3 were by n' the children of wrath, "
Heb 2:16 he took not on him the n' of angels;*
Jas 3: 6 and setteth on fire the course of n';1078
2Pe 1: 4 be partakers of the divine n', 5449

naught See also NOUGHT.
2Ki 2:19 water is n', and the ground barren.7451
Pr 20:14 It is n', it is n', saith the buyer: "

naughtiness
1Sa 17:28 pride, and the n' of thine heart; 7455
Pr 11: 6 shall be taken in their own n'. *1942
Jas 1:21 all filthiness and superfluity of n',*2549

naughty
Pr 6:12 A n' person, a wicked man, *1100
17: 4 a liar giveth ear to a n' tongue. *1942
Jer 24: 2 the other basket had very n' figs, *7451

Naum (*na'-um*) See also NAHUM.
Lu 3:25 of Amos, which was the son of N',*3486

navel
Job 40:16 his force is in the n' of his belly. *8306
Pr 3: 8 It shall be health to thy n', and 8270
Ca 7: 2 Thy n' is like a round goblet, ‡8326
Eze 16: 4 thou wast born thy n' was not cut,8270

naves
1Ki 7:33 axletrees, and their n', and their *1354

navy
1Ki 9:26 King Solomon made a n' of ships 590
27 Hiram sent in the n' his servants, "
10:11 the n' also of Hiram, that brought "
22 a n' of Tharshish with the n' of "
22 once in three years came the n' of "

nay See also NO.
Ge 18:15 he said, N'; but thou didst laugh.3808
23:11 N', my lord, hear me: the field give"
33:10 Jacob said, N', I pray thee, if now 408
42:10 N', my lord, but to buy food are 3808
12 N', but to see the nakedness of "
Nu 22:30 do so unto thee? And he said, N'. "
Jos 5:14 said, N'; but as captain of the host"
24:21 said unto Joshua, N'; but we will "
J'g 12: 5 thou an Ephraimite? If he said, N';"
19:23 N', my brethren,...I pray you, do 408
23 n', I pray you, do not so wickedly;*
Ru 1:13 n', my daughters; for it grieveth me 408
1Sa 2:16 N'; but thou shalt give it me now:
24 N', my sons; for it is no good 408
8:19 N'; but we will have a king over 3808
10:19 unto him, N', but set a king over "
12:12 N'; but a king shall reign over us: 3808
2Sa 13:12 N', my brother, do not force me; 408
25 N', my son, let us not all now go, "
16:18 Hushai said unto Absalom, N'; 3808
24:24 the king said unto Araunah, N'; "
1Ki 2:17 (for he will not say thee n',) that he give
20 I pray thee, say me not n'. And *6440
20 my mother: for I will not say thee n'.*
2:30 he said, N'; but I will die here. 3808
3:22 And the other woman said, N'; but"
23 saith, N'; but thy son is the dead, "
2Ki 3:13 king of Israel said unto him, N': 408
4:16 said, N', my lord, thou man of God, "
20:10 n', but let the shadow return 3808
1Ch 21:24 And king David said to Ornan, N': "
Jer 6:15 n', they were not at all ashamed, 1571
8:12 n', they were not at all ashamed, "
M't 5:37 communication be, Yea, yea; N', n': 3756
13:29 he said, N'; lest while ye gather "
Lu 12:51 I tell you, N'; but rather division: 3780
13: 3, 5 tell you, N': but, except ye repent,"
16:30 And he said, N', father Abraham: "
Joh 7:12 N'; but he deceiveth the people. *3756
Ac 16:37 n' verily; but let them come "
Ro 3:27 works? N'; but by the law of faith.3780
7: 7 N', I had not known sin, but by the*235
8:37 N', in all these things we are more "
9:20 N' but, O man, who art thou that 3304
1Co 6: 8 N', ye do wrong, and defraud, and 235
12:22 N', much more those members of the"
2Co 1:17 there should be yea yea, and n' n'? 3756
18 word toward you was not yea and n'."
19 was not yea and n', but in him was "
Jas 5:12 your yea be yea; and your n', n'; "

Nazarene (*naz-a-reen'*) See also NAZARENES.
M't 2:23 prophets, He shall be called a N'. 3480

Nazarenes (*naz-a-reens'*)
Ac 24: 5 a ringleader of the sect of the N': 3480

Nazareth (*naz'-a-reth*) See also NAZARENE.
M't 2:23 came and dwelt in a city called N':3478
4:13 And leaving N', he came and dwelt "
21:11 Jesus the prophet of N' of Galilee. "
26:71 fellow was also with Jesus of N'. * "
M'r 1: 9 that Jesus came from N' of Galilee,"
24 to do with thee, thou Jesus of N'? "
10:47 he heard that it was Jesus of N', "
14:67 thou also wast with Jesus of N'. * "
16: 6 Ye seek Jesus of N', which was * "
Lu 1:26 unto a city of Galilee, named N', "
2: 4 from Galilee, out of the city of N', "
39 into Galilee, to their own city N'. "
51 down with them, and came to N', "
4:16 he came to N', where he had been "
34 to do with thee, thou Jesus of N'? "
18:37 told him, that Jesus of N' passeth by."
24:19 Concerning Jesus of N', which was "
Joh 1:45 Jesus of N', the son of Joseph. "
46 any good thing come out of N'? "
18: 5 They answered him, Jesus of N'. "
7 seek ye? And they said, Jesus of N'."
19:19 Jesus Of N' The King Of The Jews. "
Ac 2:22 Jesus of N', a man approved of God"
3: 6 In the name of Jesus Christ of N' "
4:10 by the name of Jesus Christ of N', "
6:14 this Jesus of N' shall destroy this "
10:38 How God anointed Jesus of N' with"
22: 8 me, I am Jesus of N', whom thou "
26: 9 contrary to the name of Jesus of N'."

Nazarite (*naz'-a-rite*) See also NAZARITES.
Nu 6: 2 themselves to vow a vow of a N', *5139
13 And this is the law of the N', when* "
18 the N' shall shave the head of his* "
19 put them upon the hands of the N',*"
20 after that the N' may drink wine.* "
21 the law of the N' who hath vowed,*"
J'g 13: 5 the child shall be a N' unto God * "
7 for the child shall be a N' to God * "
16:17 I have been a N' unto God from my*"

Nazarites (*naz'-a-rites*)
La 4: 7 Her N' were purer than snow, *5139
Am 2:11 and of your young men for N'. * "
12 But ye gave the N' wine to drink;* "

Neah (*ne'-ah*)
Jos 19:13 out to Remmon-methoar to N': 5269

Neapolis (*ne-ap'-o-lis*)
Ac 16:11 and the next day to *N*'; 3496
near See also NEARER; NEXT; NIGH.
Ge 12:11 was come *n*' to enter into Egypt, 7126
18:23 Abraham drew *n*', and said, Wilt 5066
19: 9 Lot, and came *n*' to break the door. "
20 this city is *n*' to flee unto, and it is 7138
20: 4 Abimelech had not come *n*' her: 7126
27:21 unto Jacob, Come *n*', I pray thee, 5066
22 Jacob went *n*' unto Isaac his father; "
25 Bring it *n*' to me, and I will eat of "
25 he brought it *n*' to him, and he did "
26 Come *n*' now, and kiss me, my son. "
27 he came *n*', and kissed him: and he "
29:10 Jacob went *n*', and rolled the stone "
33: 3 until he came *n*' to his brother. "
6 Then the handmaidens came *n*', "
7 Leah also with her children came *n*', "
7 after came Joseph *n*' and Rachel, "
37:18 even before he came *n*' unto them, 7126
43:19 came *n*' to the steward of Joseph's 5066
44:18 Then Judah came *n*' unto him, and "
45: 4 brethren, Come *n*' to me, I pray you. "
4 they came *n*'. And he said, I am "
10 and thou shalt be *n*' unto me, thou, 7138
48:10 And he brought them *n*' unto him; 5066
13 and brought them *n*' unto him. "
Ex 12:48 then let him come *n*' and keep it; 7126
13:17 Philistines, although that was *n*'; 7138
14:20 the one came not *n*' the other all 7126
16: 9 of Israel, Come *n*' before the Lord: "
19:22 also, which come *n*' to the Lord, 5066
20:21 drew *n*' unto the thick darkness "
24: 2 Moses alone shall come *n*' the Lord: "
28:43 come *n*' unto the altar to minister "
30:20 come *n*' to the altar to minister, "
40:32 when they came *n*' unto the altar, 7126
Le 9: 5 all the congregation drew *n*' and "
10: 4 Come *n*', carry your brethren from "
5 So they went *n*', and carried them "
18: 6 to any that is *n*' of kin to him, to 7607
12 she is thy father's *n*' kinswoman. "
13 she is thy mother's *n*' kinswoman. "
17 for they are her *n*' kinswomen: 7608
20:19 he uncovereth his *n*' kin: they 7607
21: 2 for his kin, that is *n*' unto him, 7138
Nu 3: 6 Bring the tribe of Levi *n*', and "
5:16 the priest shall bring her *n*', and "
16: 5 cause him to come *n*' unto him: 7126
5 will he cause to come *n*' unto him. "
9 to bring you *n*' to himself to do 7138
10 he hath brought thee *n*' to him, "
40 come *n*' to offer incense before 7126
17:13 cometh any thing *n*' unto the 7138
26: 3 of Moab by Jordan *n*' Jericho, saying,*
63 plains of Moab by Jordan *n*' Jericho.*
31:12 Moab, which are by Jordan *n*' Jericho.*
48 of hundreds, came *n*' unto Moses; 5066
32:16 they came *n*' unto him, and said, "
33:50 plains of Moab by Jordan *n*' Jericho,*
34:15 this side Jordan *n*' Jericho eastward,*
36: 1 came *n*', and spake before Moses, 5066
13 plains of Moab by Jordan *n*' Jericho.*
De 1:22 ye came *n*' unto me every one of 7126
4:11 ye came *n*' and stood under the "
5:23 that ye came *n*' unto me, even all "
27 Go thou *n*', and hear all that the "
16:21 any trees *n*' unto the altar of the * 681
21: 5 the sons of Levi shall come *n*'; 5066
25:11 the wife of the one draweth *n*' for 7126
Jos 3: 4 come not *n*' unto it, that ye may "
10:24 Come *n*', put your feet upon the "
24 they came *n*', and put their feet "
15:46 all that lay *n*' Ashdod, with their *3027
17: 4 they came *n*' before Eleazar the 7126
18:13 *n*' the hill that lieth on the south *5921
21: 1 Then came *n*' the heads of the 5066
J'g 18:22 were in the houses *n*' to Micah's 5973
19:13 and let us draw *n*' to one of these 7126
20:24 And the children of Israel came *n*' "
34 knew not that evil was *n*' them. *5060
Ru 2:20 The man is *n*' of kin unto us, one *7138
3: 9 handmaid; for thou art a *n*' kinsman. "
12 it is true that I am thy *n*' kinsman: "
1Sa 4:19 was with child, *n*' to be delivered: "
7:10 the Philistines drew *n*' to battle 5066
9:18 then Saul drew *n*' to Samuel in the "
10:20 all the tribes of Israel to come *n*', 7126
21 the tribe of Benjamin to come *n*' by "
14:36 Let us draw *n*' hither unto God. "
38 Draw ye *n*' hither, all the chief of *5066
17:16 the Philistine drew *n*' morning and "
40 and he drew *n*' to the Philistine. "
41 Philistine came on and drew *n*' 7126
30:21 when David came *n*' to the people, 5066
2Sa 1:15 and said, Go *n*', and fall upon him. "
14:30 See Joab's field is *n*' mine, and he 413
18:25 And he came apace, and drew *n*'. 7126
19:42 the king is *n*' of kin to us: 7138
20:16 Come *n*' hither, that I may speak 7126
17 And when he was come *n*' unto her, "
1Ki 8:46 the land of the enemy, far or *n*'; 7138
18:30 all the people, Come *n*' unto me. 5066
30 all the people came *n*' unto him. "
36 Elijah the prophet came *n*', and "
21: 2 because it is *n*' unto my house: 7138
22:24 the son of Chenaanah went *n*', and 5066
2Ki 4:27 Gehazi came *n*' to thrust her away. "
5:13 And his servants came *n*', and "
2Ch 6:36 captives unto a land far off or *n*'; 7138
18:23 the son of Chenaanah came *n*', 5066
21:16 that were *n*' the Ethiopians: *3027
29:31 come *n*' and bring sacrifices and 5066
Es 5: 2 So Esther drew *n*', and touched 7126
9: 1 drew *n*' to be put in execution, 5060
Job 31:37 a prince would I go *n*' unto him. 7126
Job 33:22 his soul draweth *n*' unto the grave, 7126
41:16 One is so *n*' to another, that no air 5066
Ps 22:11 not far from me; for trouble is *n*'; 7138
32: 9 bridle, lest they come *n*' unto thee. 7126
73:28 is good for me to draw *n*' to God: 7132
75: 1 name is *n*' thy wondrous works 7138
107:18 draw *n*' unto the gates of death. 5060
119:151 Thou art *n*', O Lord; and all thy *7138
169 Let my cry come *n*' before thee, 7126
148:14 of Israel, a people *n*' unto him. 7138
Pr 7: 8 through the street *n*' her corner; 681
10:14 of the foolish is *n*' destruction. *7138
27:10 for better is a neighbour that is *n*' "
Isa 13:22 and her time is *n*' to come, and her "
26:17 *n*' the time of her delivery, is in 7126
29:13 draw *n*' me with their mouth, and *5066
33:13 ye that are *n*', acknowledge my 7138
34: 1 Come *n*', ye nations, to hear; and 7126
41: 1 let them come *n*'; then let them 5066
1 let us come *n*' together to 7126
5 of the earth were afraid, drew *n*', "
45:20 draw *n*' together, ye that are 5066
21 Tell ye, and bring them *n*'; yea, let *"
46:13 I bring *n*' thy righteousness; it 7126
48:16 Come ye *n*' unto me, hear ye this; "
50: 8 He is *n*' that justifieth me; who 7138
8 adversary? let him come *n*' to me. 5066
51: 5 My righteousness is *n*'; my 7138
54:14 for it shall not come *n*' thee. 7126
55: 6 call ye upon him while he is *n*': 7138
56: 1 for my salvation is *n*' to come, and "
57: 3 But draw *n*' hither, ye sons of the 7126
19 is far off, and to him that is *n*', 7138
65: 5 come not *n*' to me; for I am holier 5066
Jer 12: 2 thou art *n*' in their mouth, and 7138
25:26 the kings of the north, far and *n*', "
30:21 will cause him to draw *n*', and he 7126
42: 1 even unto the greatest, came *n*', 5066
46: 3 and shield, and draw *n*' to battle. "
48:16 calamity of Moab is *n*' to come, 7138
24 cities of the land of Moab, far or *n*'. "
52:25 that were *n*' the king's person, *7200
La 3:57 Thou drewest *n*' in the day that I 7126
4:18 our end is *n*', our days are fulfilled; "
Eze 6:12 that is *n*' shall fall by the sword; 7138
7: 7 is come, the day of trouble is *n*', "
12 time is come, the day draweth *n*': 5060
9: 1 charge over the city to draw *n*', 7126
6 come not *n*' any man upon whom 5066
11: 3 Which say, It is not *n*'; let us 7138
18: 6 come *n*' to a menstruous woman, 7126
22: 4 hast caused thy days to draw *n*', "
5 Those that be *n*', and those that 7138
30: 3 For the day is *n*', even the day of "
3 the day of the Lord is *n*', a cloudy "
40:46 *n*' to the Lord to minister unto 7131
44:13 they shall not come *n*' unto me, 5066
13 come *n*' to any of my holy things, "
15 *n*' to me to minister unto me, 7126
16 and they shall come *n*' to my table, "
45: 4 come *n*' to minister unto the Lord: 7131
Da 3: 8 time certain Chaldeans came *n*', 7127
26 *n*' to the mouth of the burning "
6:12 came *n*', and spake before the king "
7:13 they brought him *n*' before him. "
16 I came *n*' unto one of them that "
8:17 So he came *n*' where I stood: and 681
9: 7 and unto all Israel, that are *n*', 7138
Joe 3: 9 let all the men of war draw *n*'; 5066
14 the day of the Lord is *n*' in the 7138
Am 6: 3 the seat of violence to come *n*'; 5066
Ob 15 day of the Lord is *n*' upon all the 7138
Zep 1:14 great day of the Lord is *n*', it is *n*', "
3: 2 Lord; she drew not *n*' to her God. 7126
Mal 3: 5 I will come *n*' to you to judgment; "
M't 21:34 when the time of the fruit drew *n*', *1448*
24:33 these things, know that it is *n*', **1451*
M'r 13:28 leaves, ye know that summer is *n*': *"
Lu 15: 1 Then drew *n*' unto him all the *1448*
18:40 when he was come *n*', he asked him, "
19:41 when he was come *n*', he beheld * "
21: 8 the time draweth *n*': go ye not * "
22:47 drew *n*' unto Jesus to kiss him. "
24:15 Jesus himself drew *n*', and went "
Joh 3:23 baptizing in Ænon *n*' to Salim, *1451*
4: 5 *n*' to the parcel of ground that *4139*
11:54 a country *n*' to the wilderness, *1451*
Ac 7:31 and as he drew *n*' to behold it, the *4334*
8:29 Philip, Go *n*', and join thyself to this "
9: 3 journeyed, he came *n*' Damascus: **1448*
10:24 together his kinsmen and *n*' friends. *316*
21:33 chief captain came *n*', and took him, *1448*
23:15 ever he come *n*', are ready to kill him. "
27:27 that they drew *n*' to some country; *4317*
Heb 10:22 Let us draw *n*' with a true heart *4334*
nearer
Ru 3:12 there is a kinsman *n*' than I. 7138
Ro 13:11 is our salvation *n*' than when we *1452*
Neariah (*ne-a-ri'-ah*) See also NAGGE.
1Ch 3:22 and Bariah, and *N*', and Shaphat, 5294
23 And the sons of *N*'; Elioenai, and "
4:42 and *N*', and Rephaiah, and Uzziel, "
neath See BENEATH; UNDERNEATH.
Nebai (*ne'-bahee*)
Ne 10:19 Hariph, Anathoth, *N*', *5109
Nebaioth (*ne-bah'-yoth*) See also NEBAJOTH.
1Ch 1:29 The firstborn of Ishmael, *N*'; 5032
Isa 60: 7 the rams of *N*' shall minister unto "
Nebajoth (*ne-ba'-joth*) See also NEBAIOTH.
Ge 25:13 the firstborn of Ishmael, *N*'; and *5032
28: 9 son, the sister of *N*', to be his wife. * "
36: 3 Ishmael's daughter, sister of *N*'. * "
Neballat (*ne-bal'-lat*)
Ne 11:34 Hadid, Zeboim, *N*', 5041
Nebat (*ne'-bat*)
1Ki 11:26 And Jeroboam the son of *N*', an 5028
12: 2 when Jeroboam the son of *N*', who "
15 unto Jeroboam the son of *N*'. "
15: 1 of king Jeroboam the son of *N*' "
16: 3 house of Jeroboam the son of *N*'. "
26 the way of Jeroboam the son of *N*'. "
31 the sins of Jeroboam the son of *N*', "
21:22 house of Jeroboam the son of *N*', "
22:52 the way of Jeroboam the son of *N*', "
2Ki 3: 3 the sins of Jeroboam the son of *N*', "
9: 9 house of Jeroboam the son of *N*', "
10:29 the sins of Jeroboam the son of *N*', "
13: 2, 11 sins of Jeroboam the son of *N*', "
14:24 the sins of Jeroboam the son of *N*'. "
15: 9, 18, 24, 28 of Jeroboam the son of *N*', "
17:21 made Jeroboam the son of *N*' king: "
23:15 which Jeroboam the son of *N*', who "
2Ch 9:29 against Jeroboam the son of *N*'? "
10: 2 when Jeroboam the son of *N*', who "
15 spake...to Jeroboam the son of *N*'. "
13: 6 Yet Jeroboam the son of *N*', the "
Nebo (*ne'-bo*) See also PISGAH; SAMGAR-NEBO.
Nu 32: 3 and Shebam, and *N*', and Beon, 5015
38 *N*', and Baal-meon, (their names "
33:47 mountains of Abarim, before *N*'. "
De 32:49 mount *N*', which is in the land of "
34: 1 of Moab unto the mountain of *N*', "
1Ch 5: 8 dwelt in Aroer, even unto *N*' and "
Ezr 2:29 The children of *N*', fifty and two. "
10:43 the sons of *N*'; Jeiel, Mattithiah, "
Ne 7:33 men of the other *N*', fifty and two. "
Isa 15: 2 Moab shall howl over *N*', and over "
46: 1 Bel boweth down, *N*' stoopeth, "
Jer 48: 1 Woe unto *N*'! for it is spoiled: "
22 upon *N*', and upon Beth-diblathaim, "
Nebuchadnezzar (*neb-u-kad-nez'-zar*) See also NEBUCHADREZZAR.
2Ki 24: 1 *N*' king of Babylon came up, and 5019
10 servants of *N*' king of Babylon "
11 *N*' king of Babylon came against "
25: 1 that *N*' king of Babylon came, he, "
8 is the nineteenth year of king *N*' "
22 whom *N*' king of Babylon had left, "
1Ch 6:15 and Jerusalem by the hand of *N*'. "
2Ch 36: 6 Against him came up *N*' king of "
7 *N*' also carried of the vessels of the "
10 king *N*' sent, and brought him to "
13 he also rebelled against king *N*', "
Ezr 1: 7 which *N*' had brought forth out of "
2: 1 whom *N*' the king of Babylon had "
5:12 he gave them into the hand of *N*' 5020
14 which *N*' took out of the temple "
6: 5 *N*' took forth out of the temple "
Ne 7: 6 *N*' the king of Babylon had carried 5019
Es 2: 6 *N*' the king of Babylon had carried "
Jer 27: 6 all these lands into the hand of *N*'. "
8 which will not serve the same *N*' "
20 Which *N*' king of Babylon took not, "
28: 3 that *N*' king of Babylon took away "
11 Even so will I break the yoke of *N*' "
14 they may serve *N*' king of Babylon; "
29: 1 whom *N*' had carried away captive "
3 of Judah sent unto Babylon to *N*' "
34: 1 when *N*' king of Babylon, and all "
39: 5 up to *N*' king of Babylon to Riblah "
Da 1: 1 came *N*' king of Babylon unto "
18 eunuchs brought them in before *N*'. "
2: 1 the second year of the reign of *N*', "
1 *N*' dreamed dreams, wherewith "
28 maketh known to the king *N*' 5020
46 the king *N*' fell upon his face, and "
3: 1 *N*' the king made an image of gold, "
2 *N*' the king sent to gather together "
2 the image which *N*' the king had "
3 image that *N*' the king had set up; "
3 the image that *N*' had set up. "
5 image that *N*' the king hath set up: "
7 image that *N*' the king had set up. "
9 They spake and said to the king *N*', "
13 *N*' in his rage and fury commanded "
14 *N*' spake and said unto them, Is it "
16 O *N*', we are not careful to answer "
19 Then was *N*' full of fury, and the "
24 Then *N*' the king was astonied, "
26 *N*' came near to the mouth of the "
28 *N*' spake, and said, Blessed be the "
4: 1 *N*' the king, unto all people, "
4 I *N*' was at rest in mine house, and "
18 This dream I king *N*' have seen. "
28 All this came upon the king *N*'. "
31 O king *N*', to thee it is spoken; The "
33 was the thing fulfilled upon *N*': "
34 days I *N*' lifted up mine eyes unto "
37 I *N*' praise and extol and honour "
5: 2 which his father *N*' had taken out "
11 whom the king *N*' thy father, the "
18 God gave *N*' thy father a kingdom, "
Nebuchadrezzar (*neb-u-kad-rez'-zar*) See also NEBUCHADNEZZAR.
Jer 21: 2 *N*' king of Babylon maketh war 5019
7 the hand of *N*' king of Babylon, "
22:25 the hand of *N*' king of Babylon, "
24: 1 that *N*' king of Babylon had carried "
25: 1 the first year of *N*' king of Babylon; "
9 *N*' the king of Babylon, my servant, "
29:21 deliver them into the hand of *N*' "
32: 1 which was the eighteenth year of *N*'. "
28 Chaldeans, and into the hand of *N*' "
35:11 when *N*' king of Babylon came up "
37: 1 whom *N*' king of Babylon made "
39: 1 came *N*' king of Babylon and all "
11 *N*' king of Babylon gave charge "
43:10 I will send and take *N*' the king of "

Jer 44:30 king of Judah into the hand of N. 5019
46: 2 N. king of Babylon smote in the "
13 N. king of Babylon should come "
26 into the hand of N. king of Babylon, "
49:28 N. king of Babylon shall smite, "
30 for N. king of Babylon hath taken "
50:17 N. king of Babylon hath broken "
51:34 N. the king of Babylon hath "
52: 4 N. king of Babylon came, he and "
12 the nineteenth year of N. king of "
28 the people whom N. carried away "
29 In the eighteenth year of N. he "
30 the three and twentieth year of N. "
Eze 26: 7 I will bring upon Tyrus N. king of "
29:18 N. king of Babylon caused his army "
19 will give the land of Egypt unto N. "
30:10 to cease by the hand of N. king of "

Nebushasban (*neb-u-shas'-ban*)
Jer 39:13 captain of the guard sent, and N.,*5021

Nebuzar-adan (*neb-u-zar'-a-dan*)
2Ki 25: 8 came N., captain of the guard, a 5018
11 did N. the captain of the guard "
20 N. captain of the guard took these, "
Jer 39: 9 Then N. the captain of the guard "
10 N. the captain of the guard left of "
11 to N. the captain of the guard, "
13 So N. the captain of the guard sent, "
40: 1 that N. the captain of the guard "
41:10 whom N. the captain of the guard "
43: 6 that N. the captain of the guard "
52:12 came N., captain of the guard, "
15 N. the captain of the guard carried "
16 But N. the captain of the guard left "
26 N. the captain of the guard took "
30 N. the captain of the guard carried "

necessary
Job 23:12 his mouth more than my n. food. 2706
Ac 13:46 It was n. that the word of God *316*
15:28 burden than these n. things; *1876*
28:10 such things as were n. *4314,3588,5532*
1Co 12:22 seem to be more feeble, are n.: *316*
2Co 9: 5 Therefore I thought it n. to exhort "
Ph'p 2:25 Yet I supposed it n. to send to you "
Tit 3:14 maintain good works for n. uses, "
Heb 9:23 was therefore n. that the patterns *318*

necessities
Ac 20:34 hands have ministered unto my n.,*5532*
2Co 6: 4 much patience, in affliction, in n., *318*
12:10 reproaches, in n., in persecutions, "

necessity See also NECESSITIES.
Lu 23:17 (For of n. he must release one *2192,318*
Ro 12:13 Distributing to the n. of saints; *5532*
1Co 7:37 stedfast in his heart, having no n., *318*
9:16 for n. is laid upon me; yea, woe is "
2Co 9: 7 not grudgingly, or of n.: for God "
Ph'p 4:16 sent once and again unto my n. *5532*
Ph'm 14 not be as it were of n., but willingly.*318*
Heb 7:12 there is made of n. a change also "
8: 3 wherefore it is of n. that this man* *316*
9:16 there must also of n. be the death *318*

Necho (*ne'-ko*) See also PHARAOH-NECHOH.
2Ch 35:20 N. king of Egypt came up to fight*5224
22 the words of N. from the mouth of* "
36: 4 N. took Jehoahaz his brother, and* "

Nechoh See NECHO.

neck See also NECKS; STIFFNECKED.
Ge 27:16 and upon the smooth of his n.: 6677
40 shalt break his yoke from off thy n. "
33: 4 and fell on his n., and kissed him: "
41:42 and put a gold chain about his n.; "
45:14 fell upon his brother Benjamin's n., "
14 and Benjamin wept upon his n. "
46:29 fell on his n., and he wept on his n. "
49: 8 shall be in the n. of thine enemies;6203
Ex 13:13 it, then shalt thou break his n. "
34:20 not, then shalt thou break his n. "
Le 5: 8 and wring off his head from his n., "
De 21: 4 shall strike off the heifer's n. there "
28:48 put a yoke of iron upon thy n. 6677
31:27 thy rebellion, and thy stiff n.: 6203
1Sa 4:18 and his n. brake, and he died: for 4665
2Ki 17:14 like to the n. of their fathers, that 6203
2Ch 36:13 he stiffened his n., and hardened "
Ne 9:29 hardened their n., and would not "
Job 15:26 runneth upon him, even on his n., 6677
16:12 he hath also taken me by my n., 6203
39:19 thou clothed his n. with thunder? 6677
41:22 In his n. remaineth strength, and "
Ps 75: 5 on high: speak not with a stiff n. "
Pr 1: 9 thy head, and chains about thy n. 1621
3: 3 bind them about thy n.; write "
22 unto thy soul, and grace to thy n. "
6:21 heart, and tie them about thy n. "
29: 1 often reproved hardeneth his n., 6203
Ca 1:10 jewels, thy n. with chains of gold. 6677
4: 4 Thy n. is like the tower of David "
9 eyes, with one chain of thy n. "
7: 4 Thy n. is as a tower of ivory; "
Isa 8: 8 over, he shall reach even to the n.; "
10:27 and his yoke from off thy n., and "
30:28 shall reach to the midst of the n., "
48: 4 and thy n. is an iron sinew, and 6203
52: 2 thyself from the bands of thy n., 6677
66: 3 a lamb, as if he cut off a dog's n.; 6202
Jer 7:26 their ear, but hardened their n.: "
17:23 their ear, but made their n. stiff, "
27: 2 yokes, and put them upon thy n., 6677
8 will not put their n. under the yoke "
11 that bring their n. under the yoke "
28:10 from off the prophet Jeremiah's n., "
11 n. of all nations within the space "
12 off the n. of the prophet Jeremiah, "
Jer 28:14 a yoke of iron upon the n. of all 6677
30: 8 will break his yoke from off thy n., "
La 1:14 wreathed, and come up upon my n.: "
Eze 16:11 thy hands, and a chain on thy n. 1627
Da 5: 7, 16, 29 chain of gold about his n., 6676
Hos 10:11 but I passed over upon her fair n.: "
Hab 3:13 the foundation unto the n. Selah. "
M't 18: 6 were hanged about his n., and that *5137*
M'r 9:42 were hanged about his n., and he "
Lu 15:20 and fell on his n., and kissed him. "
17: 2 were hanged about his n., and he "
Ac 15:10 a yoke upon the n. of the disciples, "
20:37 and fell on Paul's n., and kissed him, "

necks
Jos 10:24 feet upon the n. of these kings. 6677
24 put their feet upon the n. of them. "
J'g 5:30 the n. of them that take the spoil? "
8:21 that were on their camels' n. "
26 that were about their camels' n. "
2Sa 22:41 given me the n. of mine enemies,*6203
2Ki 17:14 not hear, but hardened their n., * "
Ne 3: 5 put not their n. to the work of 6677
9:16 proudly, and hardened their n., *6203
17 but hardened their n., and in their* "
Ps 18:40 given me the n. of mine enemies;* "
Isa 3:16 walk with stretched forth n. and 1627
Jer 19:15 they have hardened their n., that*6203
27:12 Bring your n. under the yoke of 6677
La 5: 5 Our n. are under persecution: we "
Eze 21:29 upon the n. of them that are slain, "
Mic 2: 3 which ye shall not remove your n.; "
Ro 16: 4 for my life laid down their own n.: *5137*

necromancer
De 18:11 spirits, or a wizard, or a n. 1875,4191

Nedabiah (*ned-a-bi'-ah*)
1Ch 3:18 Jecaniah, Hoshama, and N. 5072

need See also NEEDED; NEEDEST; NEEDETH; NEEDFUL; NEEDS.
De 15: 8 lend him sufficient for his n., in 4270
1Sa 21:15 Have I n. of mad men, that ye *2638
2Ch 2:16 Lebanon, as much as thou shalt n.:*6878
20:17 Ye shall not n. to fight in this battle:
Ezr 6: 9 that which they have n. of, both 2818
Pr 31:11 that he shall have no n. of spoil. *2637
M't 3:14 I have n. to be baptized of thee, *5532*
6: 8 knoweth what things ye have n. of, "
32 that ye have n. of all these things. *5535*
9:12 be whole n. not a physician, *2192,5532*
14:16 They n. not depart; give ye them" "
21: 3 shall say The Lord hath n. of them; "
26:65 further n. have we of witnesses? "
M'r 2:17 whole have no n. of the physician, "
25 what David did, when he had n., "
11: 3 ye that the Lord hath n. of him; "
14:63 n. we any further witnesses? *2192,* "
Lu 5:31 that are whole n. not a physician; "
9:11 healed them that had n. of healing. "
12:30 that ye have n. of these things. *5535*
15: 7 which n. no repentance. *2192,5532*
19:31 Because the Lord hath n. of him. "
34 they said, The Lord hath n. of him. "
22:71 What n. we any further witness?*2192,* "
Joh 13:29 that we have n. of against the feast; "
Ac 2:45 to all men, as every man had n. "
4:35 every man according as he had n. "
Ro 16: 2 business she hath n. of you: for *5535*
1Co 7:36 and n. so require, let him do what *3784*
12:21 the hand, I have no n. of thee: *5532*
21 to the feet, I have no n. of you. "
24 For our comely parts have no n.: "
2Co 3: 1 or n. we, as some others, epistles *5535*
Ph'p 4:12 both to abound and to suffer n. *
19 my God shall supply all your n. *5532*
1Th 1: 8 we n. not to speak any thing. *2192,* "
4: 9 love ye n. not that I write unto you: "
5: 1 ye have no n. that I write unto you. "
Heb 4:16 and find grace to help in time of n.*2121*
5:12 ye have n. that one teach you *5532*
12 are become such as have n. of milk, "
7:11 further n. was there that another "
10:36 For ye have n. of patience, that, "
1Pe 1: 6 though now for a season, if n. be, *1163*
1Jo 2:27 n. not that any man teach you:*2192,5532*
3:17 and seeth his brother have n., and "
Re 3:17 with goods, and have n. of nothing; "
21:23 And the city had no n. of the sun, "
22: 5 they n. no candle, neither light*2192,* "

needed
Joh 2:25 n. not that any should testify *2192,5532*
Ac 17:25 hands, as though he n. any thing, *4326*

neededst
Joh 16:30 n. not that any man should ask*2192,5532*

needeth
Ge 33:15 And he said, What n. it? let me find
Lu 11: 8 and give him as many as he n. *5535*
Joh 13:10 n. not save to wash his feet, *2192,5532*
Eph 4:28 he may have to give to him that n.* "
2Ti 2:15 workman that n. not to be ashamed,*422*
Heb 7:27 Who n. not daily, as those high*2192,318*

needful
Ezr 7:20 be n. for the house of thy God, 2819
Lu 10:42 But one thing is n.: and Mary hath*5532*
Ac 15: 5 That it was n. to circumcise them, *1163*
Ph'p 1:24 abide in the flesh is more n. for you.*316*
Jas 2:16 things which are n. to the body; *2006*
Jude 3 it was n. for me to write unto you,* *318*

needle See also NEEDLE'S; NEEDLEWORK.
M't 19:24 camel to go through the eye of a n.,*4476*
M'r 10:25 camel to go through the eye of a n.,* "

needle's
Lu 18:25 for a camel to go through a n. eye,*4476*

needlework
Ex 26:36 linen, wrought with n. *4639,7551
27:16 fine twined linen, wrought with n.:* "
28:39 thou shalt make the girdle of n. * "
36:37 scarlet and fine twined linen, of n.:* "
38:18 for the gate of the court was n., * "
39:29 blue, and purple, and scarlet, of n.;* "
J'g 5:30 a prey of divers colours of n., *7553
30 divers colours of n. on both sides,* "
Ps 45:14 unto the king in raiment of n.: * "

needs
Ge 31:30 though thou wouldest n. be gone,
2Sa 14:14 For we must n. die, and are as waters
Jer 10: 5 they must n. be borne, because they
M't 18: 7 for it must n. be that offences *318*
M'r 13: 7 for such things must n. be; but the
Lu 14:18 and I must n. go and see it: *318*
Joh 4: 4 he must n. go through Samaria.
Ac 1:16 this scripture must n. have been *
17: 3 that Christ must n. have suffered,*
21:22 the multitude must n. come *3843*
Ro 13: 5 ye must n. be subject, not only *318*
1Co 5:10 then must ye n. go out of the world.
2Co 11:30 If I must n. glory, I will glory of

needy
De 15:11 to thy poor, and to thy n., in thy land.34
24:14 an hired servant that is poor and n., "
Job 24: 4 They turn the n. out of the way: "
14 with the light killeth the poor and n., "
Ps 9:18 the n. shall not alway be forgotten: "
12: 5 of the poor, for the sighing of the n., "
35:10 the n. from him that spoileth him? "
37:14 to cast down the poor and n., and to "
40:17 But I am poor and n.; yet the Lord "
70: 5 I am poor and n.: make haste unto "
72: 4 he shall save the children of the n., "
12 shall deliver the n. when he crieth; "
13 He shall spare the poor and n., and "
13 and shall save the souls of the n. "
74:21 let the poor and n. praise thy name. "
82: 3 do justice to the afflicted and n. *7326
4 Deliver the poor and n.: rid them 34
86: 1 Lord, hear me: for I am poor and n. "
109:16 but persecuted the poor and n. man, "
22 For I am poor and n., and my heart "
113: 7 and lifteth the n. out of the dunghill; "
Pr 30:14 earth, and the n. from among men. "
31: 9 plead the cause of the poor and n. "
20 forth her hands to the n. "
Isa 10: 2 turn aside the n. from judgment, 1800
14:30 and the n. shall lie down in safety: 34
25: 4 a strength to the n. in his distress, "
26: 6 the poor, and the steps of the n. 1800
32: 7 even when the n. speaketh right. 34
41:17 When the poor and n. seek water, "
Jer 5:28 the right of the n. do they not judge. "
22:16 judged the cause of the poor and n.; "
Eze 16:49 the hand of the poor and n. "
18:12 Hath oppressed the poor and n., "
22:29 and have vexed the poor and n.: "
Am 4: 1 oppress the poor, which crush the n., "
8: 4 this, O ye that swallow up the n., "
6 and the n. for a pair of shoes; "

neesings
Job 41:18 By his n. a light doth shine, and ‡5846

Neginah (*neg'-i-nah*) See also NEGINOTH.
Ps 61: *title* To the chief Musician upon N. *5058

Neginoth (*neg'-i-noth*) See also NEGINAH.
Ps 4: *title* To the chief Musician on N. *5058
6: *title* To the chief Musician on N. * "
54: *title* To the chief Musician on N., * "
55: *title* To the chief Musician on N., * "
67: *title* To the chief Musician on N., * "
76: *title* To the chief Musician on N., * "

neglect See also NEGLECTED; NEGLECTING.
M't 18:17 And if he shall n. to hear them, *3878*
17 but if he n. to hear the church, let* "
1Ti 4:14 N. not the gift that is in thee, *272*
Heb 2: 3 escape, if we n. so great salvation; "

neglected
Ac 6: 1 were n. in the daily ministration. *3865*

neglecting
Col 2:23 and humility, and n. of the body; * *857*

negligent
2Ch 29:11 My sons, be not now n.: for the 7952
2Pe 1:12 I will not be n. to put you always * *272*

Nego See ABED-NEGO.

Nehelamite (*ne-hel'-am-ite*)
Jer 29:24 also speak to Shemaiah the N., 5161
31 Lord concerning Shemaiah the N.; "
32 I will punish Shemaiah the N., "

Nehemiah (*ne-he-mi'-ah*)
Ezr 2: 2 with Zerubbabel: Jeshua, N., 5166
Ne 1: 1 words of N. the son of Hachaliah. "
3:16 him repaired N. the son of Azbuk, "
7: 7 came with Zerubbabel, Jeshua, N., "
8: 9 N., which is the Tirshatha, and "
10: 1 that sealed were, N., the Tirshatha, "
12:26 and in the days of N. the governor, "
47 in the days of N., gave the portions "

Nehiloth (*ne'-hi-loth*)
Ps 5: *title* To the chief Musician upon N. 5155

Nehum (*ne'-hum*) See also REHUM.
Ne 7: 7 Bilshan, Mispereth, Bigvai, N. 5149

Nehushta (*ne-hush'-tah*)
2Ki 24: 8 And his mother's name was N., 5179

Nehushtan (*ne-hush'-tan*)
2Ki 18: 4 incense to it: and he called it N. 5180

Neiel (ne-i'-el)
Jos 19:27 and N', and goeth out to Cabul 5272

neighbour See also NEIGHBOUR'S; NEIGHBOURS.
Ex 3:22 woman shall borrow of her n', 7934
11: 2 let every man borrow of his n', 7453
2 and every woman of her n', jewels 7468
12: 4 him and his n' next unto his house 7934
20:16 bear false witness against thy n'. 7453
21:14 come presumptuously upon his n', "
22: 7 man shall deliver unto his n' money "
9 he shall pay double unto his n'. "
10 If a man deliver unto his n' an ass, "
14 if a man borrow ought of his n', "
32:27 companion, and every man his n'. 7138
Le 6: 2 and lie unto his n' in that which 5997
2 violence, or hath deceived his n'; "
19:13 Thou shalt not defraud thy n', 7453
15 shalt thou judge thy n'. 5997
16 stand against the blood of thy n': 7453
17 shalt in any wise rebuke thy n', 5997
18 thou shalt love thy n' as thyself: 7453
24:19 a man cause a blemish in his n'; 5997
25:14 And if thou sell ought unto thy n', "
15 the jubile thou shalt buy of thy n', "
De 4:42 which should kill his n' unawares, 7453
5:20 bear false witness against thy n'. "
15: 2 that lendeth ought unto his n' shall "
2 he shall not exact it of his n', or of "
19: 4 Whoso killeth his n' ignorantly, "
5 man goeth into the wood with his n' "
5 lighteth upon his n', that he die; "
11 But if any man hate his n', and lie "
22:26 when a man riseth against his n', "
23:25 into the standing corn of thy n', * "
27:24 be he that smiteth his n' secretly. "
Jos 20: 5 because he smote his n' unwittingly, "
Ru 4: 7 off his shoe, and gave it to his n': "
1Sa 15:28 and hath given it to a n' of thine, "
28:17 given it to thy n', even to David: "
2Sa 12:11 and give them unto thy n', and he "
1Ki 8:31 If any man trespass against his n', "
20:35 said unto his n' in the word of the* "
2Ch 6:22 If a man sin against his n', and an "
Job 12: 4 I am as one mocked of his n', who "
16:21 God, as a man pleadeth for his n'! "
Ps 12: 2 speak vanity every one with his n': "
15: 3 his tongue, nor doeth evil to his n',* "
3 up a reproach against his n'. 7138
101: 5 Whoso privily slandereth his n', 7453
Pr 3:28 Say not unto thy n', Go, and come "
29 Devise not evil against thy n', "
11: 9 with his mouth destroyeth his n': "
12 is void of wisdom despiseth his n': "
12:26 is more excellent than his n': "
14:20 poor is hated even of his own n': "
21 He that despiseth his n' sinneth: "
16:29 A violent man enticeth his n', and "
18:17 his n' cometh and searcheth him. "
19: 4 the poor is separated from his n'. * "
21:10 his n' findeth no favour in his eyes.* "
24:28 Be not a witness against thy n' "
25: 8 when thy n' hath put thee to shame. "
9 Debate thy cause with thy n' "
18 beareth false witness against his n' "
26:19 So is the man that deceiveth his n', "
27:10 better is a n' that is near than a 7934
29: 5 that flattereth his n' spreadeth a 7453
Ec 4: 4 for this a man is envied of his n'. "
Isa 3: 5 by another, and every one by his n': "
19: 2 and every one against his n'; "
41: 6 They helped every one his n'; and "
Jer 6:21 the n' and his friend shall perish. 7934
7: 5 between a man and his n'; 7453
9: 4 Take ye heed every one of his n', "
4 every n' will walk with slanders. "
5 they will deceive every one his n', "
8 speaketh peaceably to his n' with "
20 and every one her n' lamentation. 7468
22: 8 they shall say every man to his n', 7453
23:27 which they tell every man to his n', "
30 my words every one from his n'. "
35 shall ye say every one to his n', and "
31:34 teach no more every man his n', "
34:15 liberty every man to his n'; and ye "
17 brother, and every man to his n': "
49:18 Gomorrah and the n' cities thereof, 7934
50:40 Gomorrah and the n' cities thereof, "
Hab 2:15 unto him that giveth his n' drink, 7453
Zec 3:10 ye call every man his n' under the "
8:10 all men every one against his n'. "
16 ye every man the truth to his n'; "
17 evil in your hearts against his n'; "
14:13 every one on the hand of his n', and "
13 rise up against the hand of his n'. "
M't 5:43 been said, Thou shalt love thy n', 4139
19:19 Thou shalt love thy n' as thyself. "
22:39 Thou shalt love thy n' as thyself. "
M'r 12:31 Thou shalt love thy n' as thyself. "
33 and to love his n' as himself, is "
Lu 10:27 all thy mind; and thy n' as thyself. "
29 said unto Jesus, And who is my n'? "
36 was n' unto him that fell among "
Ac 7:27 he that did his n' wrong thrust him "
Ro 13: 9 Thou shalt love thy n' as thyself. "
10 Love worketh no ill to his n': "
15: 2 Let every one of us please his n' "
Gal 5:14 Thou shalt love thy n' as thyself. "
Eph 4:25 speak every man truth with his n': "
Heb 8:11 shall not teach every man his n', * "
Jas 2: 8 Thou shalt love thy n' as thyself, "

neighbour's
Ex 20:17 Thou shalt not covet thy n' house, 7453
17 thou shalt not covet thy n' wife, "
17 his ass, nor any thing that is thy n'. "
22: 8 have put his hand unto his n' goods. "
22:11 not put his hand unto his n' goods; 7453
26 If thou at all take thy n' raiment "
Le 18:20 not lie carnally with thy n' wife, to 5997
20:10 adultery with his n' wife, 7453
25:14 or buyest ought of thy n' hand, ye 5997
De 5:21 shalt thou desire thy n' wife, 7453
21 shalt thou covet thy n' house, his "
21 his ass, or any thing that is thy n'. "
19:14 shalt not remove thy n' landmark, "
22:24 he hath humbled his n' wife: "
23:24 thou comest into thy n' vineyard, "
25 a sickle unto thy n' standing corn. "
27:17 he that removeth his n' landmark. "
Job 31: 9 or if I have laid wait at my n' door; "
Pr 6:29 So he that goeth in to his n' wife; "
25:17 thy foot from thy n' house; lest he "
Jer 5: 8 every one neighed after his n' wife. "
22:13 useth his n' service without wages, "
Eze 18: 6 neither hath defiled his n' wife, "
11 mountains, and defiled his n' wife, "
15 Israel, hath not defiled his n' wife, "
22:11 abomination with his n' wife; and "
33:26 and ye defile every one his n' wife: "
Zec 11: 6 the men every one into his n' hand, "

neighbours See also NEIGHBOURS'.
Jos 9:16 they heard that they were their n', 7138
Ru 4:17 the women her n' gave it a name, 7934
2Ki 4: 3 vessels abroad of all thy n', even "
Ps 28: 3 which speak peace to their n', but 7453
31:11 but especially among my n', and 7934
44:13 makest us a reproach to our n', a "
79: 4 We are become a reproach to our n', "
12 And render unto our n' sevenfold "
80: 6 Thou makest us a strife unto our n': "
89:41 him: he is a reproach to his n'. "
Jer 12:14 against all mine evil n', that touch "
49:10 his brethren, and his n', and he is "
Eze 16:26 the Egyptians thy n', great of flesh; "
22:12 thou hast greedily gained of thy n' 7453
23: 5 her lovers, on the Assyrians her n', 7138
12 doted upon the Assyrians her n', "
Lu 1:58 And her n' and her cousins heard 4040
14:12 thy kinsmen, nor thy rich n'; lest 1069
15: 6 calleth together his friends and n', "
9 she calleth her friends and her n' "
Joh 9: 8 The n' therefore, and they which "

neighbours'
Jer 29:23 adultery with their n' wives, and 7453

neighed
Jer 5: 8 every one n' after his neighbour's 6670

neighing See also NEIGHINGS.
Jer 8:16 sound of the n' of his strong ones; 4684

neighings
Jer 13:27 seen thine adulteries, and thy n', 4684

neither
Ge 9:11 n' shall all flesh be cut off any more 3808
11 n' shall there any more be a flood "
17: 5 N' shall thy name any more be "
19:17 thee, n' stay thou in all the plain; 408
21:26 this thing: n' didst thou tell me, 3808
26 me, n' yet heard I of it, but to day. "
22:12 n' do thou any thing unto him: 408
24:16 n' had any man known her: and 3808
29: 7 n' is it time that the cattle should "
39: 9 n' hath he kept back any thing from "
45: 6 there shall n' be earing nor harvest. 369
Ex 4: 8 n' hearken to the voice of the first 3808
9 signs, n' hearken unto thy voice, "
10 n' heretofore, nor since thou hast 1571
5: 2 Lord, n' will I let Israel go. *1571,3808
23 n' hast thou delivered thy people "
7:22 n' did he hearken unto them; as * "
23 n' did he set his heart to this also. "
8:32 also, n' would he let the people go.* "
9:29 n' shall there be any more hail; "
35 n' would he let the children of * "
10: 6 n' thy fathers, nor thy fathers' "
14 as they, n' after them shall be such. "
23 n' rose any from his place for three "
12:39 n' had...prepared...victual. 1571, "
46 n' shall ye break a bone thereof. "
13: 7 n' shall there be leaven seen with "
16:24 n' was there any worm therein. "
20:23 n' shall ye make unto you gods of* "
26 N' shalt thou go up by steps unto "
22:21 n' vex a stranger, nor oppress him:* "
25 n' shalt thou lay upon him usury. "
31 n' shall ye eat any flesh that is torn* "
23: 2 n' shalt thou speak in a cause to "
2 N' shalt thou countenance a poor "
13 n' let it be heard out of thy mouth. "
18 n' shall the fat of my sacrifice "
24: 2 n' shall the people go up with him. "
30: 9 n' shall ye pour drink offering * "
32 n' shall ye make any other like it, "
32:18 n' is it the voice of them that cry for 369
34: 3 n' let any man be seen throughout 408
3 n' let the flocks nor herds feed "
24 n' shall any man desire thy land, 3808
28 he did n' eat bread, nor drink water. "
36: 6 Let n' man nor woman make any 408
Le 2:13 n' shalt thou suffer the salt of the 3808
3:17 that ye eat n' fat nor blood. "
5:11 n' shall he put any frankincense "
7:18 n' shall it be imputed unto him that "
10: 6 n' rend your clothes; lest ye die, and "
11:43 n' shall ye make yourselves unclean "
44 n' shall ye defile yourselves with "
17:12 n' shall any stranger...eat blood. "
18: 3 n' shall ye walk in their ordinances. "
17 n' shalt thou take her son's * "
18 N' shalt thou take a wife to her * "
21 n' shalt thou profane the name of "
23 N' shalt thou lie with any beast to* "
Le 18:23 n' shall any woman stand before a 3808
26 n' any of your own nation, nor any "
19: 9 n' shalt thou gather the gleanings of "
10 n' shalt thou gather every grape of 3808
11 Ye shall not steal, n' deal falsely, "
11 deal falsely, n' lie one to another. * "
12 n' shalt thou profane the name of thy* "
13 not defraud thy neighbour, n' rob* 3808
16 n' shalt thou stand against the "
19 n' shall a garment mingled of linen "
26 n' shall ye use enchantment, nor "
27 n' shalt thou mar the corners of thy "
31 n' seek after wizards, to be defiled* 408
21: 5 n' shall they shave off the corner 3808
7 n' shall they take a woman put away "
11 N' shall he go in to any dead body, "
12 N' shall he go out of the sanctuary, "
15 N' shall he profane his seed among* "
22:24 n' shall ye make any offering "
25 N' from a stranger's hand shall ye "
32 N' shall ye profane my holy name;* "
23:14 ye shall eat n' bread, nor parched "
22 n' shalt thou gather any gleaning "
25: 4 thou shalt n' sow thy field, nor "
5 n' gather the grapes of thy vine * "
11 n' reap that which groweth of itself "
26: 1 n' rear you up a standing image, "
1 n' shall ye set up any image of "
6 n' shall the sword go through your "
20 n' shall the trees of the land yield "
44 them away, n' will I abhor them, "
27:33 good or bad, n' shall he change it: "
Nu 1:49 n' take the sum of them among the "
5:13 n' she be taken with the manner; "
11:19 days, n' ten days, nor twenty days; "
14: 9 n' fear ye the people of the land; 408
23 n' shall any of them that provoked 3808
16:15 them, n' have I hurt one of them. "
18: 3 that n' they, nor ye also, die. 3808,1571
20 n' shalt thou have any part among 3808
22 N' must the children of Israel * "
32 n' shall ye pollute the holy things* "
20: 5 n' is there any water to drink. 369
17 n' will we drink of the water of thy 3808
21: 5 is no bread, n' is there any water;* 369
23:19 n' the son of man, that he should
21 n' hath he seen perverseness in 3808
23 n' is there any divination against "
25 N' curse them at all, nor bless 1571, "
35:23 not his enemy, n' sought his harm: "
36: 9 N' shall the inheritance remove * "
De 1:21 thee; fear not, n' be discouraged. 408
29 Dread not, n' be afraid of them. 3808
42 unto them, Go not up, n' fight; "
2: 9 n' contend with them in battle: 408
27 I will n' turn unto the right hand 3808
4: 2 n' shall ye diminish ought from it, "
28 n' see, nor hear, nor eat, nor smell. "
31 not forsake thee, n' destroy thee, "
5:18 N' shalt thou commit adultery. "
19 N' shalt thou steal. "
20 N' shalt thou bear false witness "
21 N' shalt thou desire thy neighbour's "
21 n' shalt thou covet thy neighbour's "
7: 3 N' shalt thou make marriages with "
16 them: n' shalt thou serve their gods; "
26 N' shalt thou bring an abomination* "
8: 3 not, n' did thy fathers know; "
4 old upon thee, n' did thy foot swell, "
9: 9 I n' did eat bread nor drink water: "
18 I did n' eat bread, nor drink water, "
13: 8 n' shall thine eye pity him, "
8 eye pity him, n' shalt thou spare, "
8 spare, n' shalt thou conceal him: "
16: 4 n' shall there any thing of the flesh, "
19 not respect persons, n' take a gift: "
22 N' shalt thou set thee up any image; "
17:17 N' shall he multiply wives to "
17 n' shall he greatly multiply...silver "
18:16 n' let me see this great fire any more, "
20: 3 n' be ye terrified because of them; 408
21: 4 valley, which is n' eared nor sown, 3808
7 this blood, n' have our eyes seen it. "
22: 5 n' shall a man put on a woman's "
24: 5 n' shall he be charged with any "
15 n' shall the sun go down upon it; "
16 n' shall the children be put to death "
26:13 commandments, n' have I forgotten "
14 n' have I taken away ought thereof "
28:36 n' thou nor thy fathers have known;* "
39 n' drink of the wine, nor gather the "
64 n' thou nor thy fathers have known,* "
65 n' shall...sole of thy foot have rest:* "
29: 6 n' have ye drunk wine or strong "
14 N' with you only do I make this "
30:11 not hidden from thee, n' is it far off. "
13 N' is it beyond the sea, that thou "
31: 8 he will not fail thee, n' forsake thee: "
8 thee: fear not, n' be dismayed. "
32:28 n' is there any understanding in * 369
39 n' is there any that can deliver out of* "
33: 9 n' did...acknowledge his brethren, 3808
Jos 1: 9 be not afraid, n' be thou dismayed: 408
2:11 n' did...remain any more courage 3808
5: 1 n' was there spirit in them any more, "
12 n' had the children of Israel manna "
6:10 n' shall any word proceed out of your "
7:12 n' will I be with you any more, * "
8: 1 Fear not, n' be thou dismayed: 408
11:14 them, n' left they any to breathe. 3808
23: 7 n' make mention of the name of "
7 n' serve them, nor bow yourselves "
J'g 1:27 N' did Manasseh drive out the * "
29 N' did Ephraim drive out the * "
30 N' did Zebulun drive out the * "
31 N' did Asher drive out the * "

J'g 1:33 N· did Naphtali drive out the *3808
2:23 n· delivered he them into the hand "
6: 4 for Israel, n· sheep, nor ox, nor ass.
8:23 you, n· shall my son rule over you:3808
35 N· shewed they kindness to the "
11:34 her he had n· son nor daughter. 369
13: 6 he was, n· told he me his name: 3808
7 drink, n· eat any unclean thing: * 408
14 n· let her drink wine or strong drink,"
23 n· would he have shewed us all 3808
20: 8 n· will we any of us turn into his "
Ru 2: 8 n· go from hence, but abide 1571, "
1Sa 1:15 I have drunk n· wine nor strong "
2: 2 n· is there any rock like our God. 369
3: 7 n· was the word of the Lord yet
4:20 answered not, n· did she regard it.3808
5: 5 n· the priests of Dagon, nor any "
12: 4 n· hast thou taken ought of any "
13:22 was n· sword nor spear found in the"
16: 8, 9 N· hath the Lord chosen 1571, "
20:27 to meat, n· yesterday, nor to-day? 1571
21: 8 n· brought my sword nor my 1571,3808
24:11 is n· evil nor transgression in mine 369
25: 7 n· was there ought missing unto 3808
15 not hurt, n· missed we any thing, "
26:12 man saw it, nor knew it, n· awaked:369
27: 9 and left n· man nor woman alive, 3808
11 saved n· man nor woman alive, "
28: 6 n· by dreams, nor by Urim, nor by 1571
15 n· by prophets, nor by dreams: "
30:15 that thou wilt n· kill me, nor deliver518
19 n· small nor great, n· sons nor 4480
19 n· spoil, nor anything that they had "
2Sa 1:21 dew, n· let there be rain, upon you,*408
2:28 no more, n· fought they any more.3808
7:10 n· shall the children of wickedness "
22 n· is there any God beside thee, 369
12:17 not, n· did he eat bread with them.3808
13:22 his brother Amnon n· good nor bad:"
14: 7 n· name nor remainder upon the 1115
14 n· doth God respect any person: 3808
18: 3 n· if half of us died, will they care 518
19: 6 regardest n· princes nor servants:* 369
19 n· do thou remember that which thy408
24 n· dressed his feet, nor trimmed 3808
20: 1 n· have we inheritance in the son of"
21: 4 n· for us shalt thou kill any man in 369
10 n· the birds of the air to rest on 3808
24:24 n· will I offer burnt offerings unto "
1Ki 3:11 n· hast asked riches for thyself, "
26 Let it be n· mine nor thine, 1571, "
5: 4 that there is n· adversary nor evil 369
6: 7 there was n· hammer nor axe nor 3808
7:47 n· was the weight of the brass found*"
11: 2 n· shall they come in unto you: "
12:16 n· have we inheritance in the son of"
13: 8, 16 n· will I eat bread nor drink water"
16:11 n· of his kinsfolks, nor of his friends.
17:14 waste, n· shall the cruse of oil fail,3808
16 not, n· did the cruse of oil fail, "
18:29 was n· voice, nor any to answer, 369
22:31 Fight n· with small nor great, save3808
2Ki 3:17 not see wind, n· shall ye see rain; "
4:23 it is n· new moon, nor sabbath. "
31 but there was n· voice, nor hearing.369
5:17 offer n· burnt offering nor sacrifice3808
6:19 is not the way, n· is this the city: "
7:10 was no man there, n· voice of man, 369
10:14 forty men; n· left he any of them. 3808
12: 8 n· to repair the breaches of the 1115
13: 7 N· did he leave of the people to *3808
23 n· cast he them from his presence "
17:34 n· do they after their statutes, or 369
38 forget; n· shall ye fear other gods.3808
18:30 N· let Hezekiah make you trust in 408
21: 8 N· will I make the feet of Israel 3808
23:25 n· after him arose there any like "
1Ch 4:27 n· did all their family multiply, like"
17: 9 n· shall the children of wickedness "
20 n· is there any God beside thee, 369
19:19 n· would the Syrians help the 3808
27:24 n· was the number put in the "
2Ch 1:11 enemies, n· yet hast asked long life;"
12 n· shall there any after thee have "
6: 5 n· chose I any man to be a ruler "
9: 9 n· was there any such spice as the "
13:20 N· did Jeroboam recover strength "
20:12 n· know we what to do: but our "
25: 4 n· shall the children die for the "
26:18 n· shall it be for thine honour from "
30: 3 n· had the people gathered "
32:15 on this manner, n· yet believe him: 408
33: 8 N· will I any more remove the foot3808
34: 2 declined n· to the right hand, nor * "
28 n· shall thine eyes see all the evil "
35:18 n· did all the kings of Israel keep "
Ezr 9:12 n· take their daughters unto your 408
10:13 n· is this a work of one day or two:3808
Ne 2:12 n· told I any man what my God had"
12 n· was there any beast with me, 369
16 n· had I as yet told it to the Jews, 3808
4:11 They shall not know, n· see, till we "
23 So n· I, nor my brethren, nor my 369
5: 5 n· is it in our power to redeem them;"
16 this wall, n· bought we any land: 3808
8:10 n· be ye sorry; for the joy of the 408
11 for the day is holy; n· be ye grieved. "
9:17 n· were mindful of thy wonders 3808
19 n· the pillar of fire by night, to shew
34 N· have our kings, our princes, 3808
35 n· turned they from their wicked "
Es 2: 7 for she had n· father nor mother, 369
3: 8 people; n· keep they the king's laws:"
4:16 n· eat nor drink three days, night 408
Job 3: 4 n· let the light shine upon it. "
9 n· let it see the dawning of the day: "
Job 3:26 I was not in safety, n· had I rest, 3808
26 n· was I quiet; yet trouble came. "
5: 4 n· is there any to deliver them. 369
6 n· doth trouble spring out of the 3808
21 n· shalt...be afraid of destruction "
22 n· shalt thou be afraid of the beasts408
7:10 n· shall his place know him any 3808
8:20 man, n· will he help the evil doers: "
9:33 N· is there any daysman betwixt* "
15:29 n· shall his substance continue, "
29 n· shall he prolong the perfection "
18:19 He shall n· have son nor nephew "
20: 9 n· shall his place any more behold "
21: 9 n· is the rod of God upon them. "
23:12 N· have I gone back from the * "
17 n· hath he covered the darkness from
28:13 n· is it found in the land of the 3808
15 n· shall silver be weighed for the "
19 n· shall it be valued with pure gold."
31:30 N· have I suffered my mouth to sin*"
32: 9 n· do the aged understand judgment.*
14 n·...answer him with...speeches. 3808
21 n· let me give flattering titles unto "
33: 7 n· shall my hand be heavy upon "
9 innocent; n· is there iniquity in me."
34:12 n·...the Almighty pervert judgment."
35:13 n· will the Almighty regard it. "
36:26 n· can the number of his years be* "
39: 7 n· regardeth he the crying of the "
17 n·...imparted to her understanding."
22 n· turneth he back from the sword."
24 n· believeth he that it is the sound "
Ps 5: 4 n· shall evil dwell with thee. * "
16:10 n· wilt thou suffer thine Holy One "
18:37 n· did I turn again till they were "
22:24 n· hath he hid his face from him; "
26: 4 n· will I go in with dissemblers. "
27: 9 leave me not, n· forsake me, O God 408
33:17 n·...deliver any by...great strength.3808
35:19 n· let them wink with the eye that hate
37: 1 n· be thou envious against the 408
38: 1 n· chasten me in thy hot displeasure. "
3 n· is there any rest in my bones 369
44: 3 n· did their own arm save them: 3808
6 my bow, n· shall my sword save me."
17 n· have we dealt falsely in thy "
18 n· have our steps declined from thy "
55:12 n· was it he that hated me that 3808
69:15 n· let the deep swallow me up, and 408
73: 5 n· are they plagued like other men.3808
74: 9 n· is there among us any that "
75: 6 promotion cometh n· from the east,"
78:37 n· were...steadfast in his covenant. "
81: 9 n· shalt thou worship any strange "
82: 5 know not, n· will they understand; "
86: 8 n· are there any works like unto 369
91:10 n· shall any plague come nigh thy3808
92: 6 not; n· doth a fool understand this."
94: 7 n· shall the God of Jacob regard it. "
14 n· will he forsake his inheritance. "
103: 9 n· will he keep his anger for ever. "
109:12 n· let there be any to favour his 408
115: 7 n· speak they through their throat.3808
17 n· any that go down into silence. "
121: 4 Israel shall n· slumber nor sleep. 3804
129: 8 N· do they which go by say, The 3808
131: 1 n· do I exercise myself in great "
135:17 n· is there any breath in their 369
Pr 2:19 n· take they hold of the paths of life.
3:11 n· be weary of his correction: 408
25 n· of the desolation of the wicked,
4: 5 n· decline from the words of my 408
6:25 n· let her take thee with her eyelids."
35 n· will he rest content, though 3808
15:12 him: n· will he go unto the wise. * "
22:22 n· oppress the afflicted in the gate: "
23: 6 n· desire thou his dainty meats: 408
24: 1 evil men, n· desire to be with them: "
19 n· be thou envious at the wicked; "
27:10 n· go into thy brother's house in the*"
30: 3 I n· learned wisdom, nor have the 3808
8 give me n· poverty nor riches; feed 408
Ec 1:11 n· shall there be any remembrance3808
4: 8 he hath n· child nor brother: 1571,369
8 n· is his eye satisfied with riches; 3808
8 n· saith he, For whom do I labour,*
5: 6 n· say thou before the angel, that 408
6:10 n· may he contend with him that 3808
7:16 much; n· make thyself over wise: 408
17 much wicked, n· be thou foolish: "
8: 8 n· hath...power in the day of death:369
8 n· shall wickedness deliver those 3808
13 n· shall he prolong his days, which "
16 there is that n· day nor night 1571,369
9: 5 n· have they any more a reward; for "
6 n· have they any more a portion for "
11 n· yet bread to the wise, nor yet 3808
Ca 8: 7 love, n· can the floods drown it: "
Isa 1: 6 n· bound up, n· mollified with "
23 n· doth the cause of the widow "
2: 4 n· shall they learn war any more. "
7 n· is there...end of their treasures; "
7 n· is there any end of their chariots:"
3: 7 my house is n· bread nor clothing: 369
5:12 n· consider the operation of his 3808
27 n· shall the girdle of their loins be "
7: 4 n· be fainthearted for the two tails 408
7 stand, n· shall it come to pass. 3808
12 not ask, n· will I tempt the Lord. "
8:12 n· fear ye their fear, nor be afraid. "
9:13 n· do they seek the Lord of hosts. "
17 n·...have mercy on their fatherless "
10: 7 not so, n· doth his heart think so; "
11: 3 n· reprove after the hearing of his "
13:20 n· shall it be dwelt in from "
20 n· shall the Arabian pitch tent "
Isa 13:20 n· shall the shepherds make their 3808
16:10 singing, n· shall there be shouting; "
17: 8 n· shall respect that which his "
19:15 N· shall there be any work for "
22:11 n· had respect unto him that "
23: 4 n· do I nourish up young men, nor "
26:18 n· have the inhabitants of the 1077
28:27 n· is a cart wheel turned about upon"
29:22 n· shall his face now wax pale. 3808
31: 1 One of Israel, n· seek the Lord! "
33:20 n· shall any of the cords thereof 1077
21 n· shall gallant ship pass thereby. 3808
36:15 N· let Hezekiah make you trust in 408
40:28 earth, fainteth not, n· is weary? 3808
42: 8 n· my praise to graven images. "
24 n· were they obedient unto his law.3808
43: 2 n· shall the flame kindle upon thee. "
10 formed, n· shall there be after me. "
18 things, n· consider the things of old.408
23 n· hast thou honoured me with 3808
24 n· hast thou filled me with the fat "
44: 8 Fear ye not, n· be afraid: have not 408
19 heart, n· is there knowledge nor 3808
47: 7 n· didst remember the latter end "
8 n· shall I know the loss of children:"
49:10 n· shall the heat nor sun smite "
50: 5 not rebellious, n· turned away back."
51: 7 n· be ye afraid of their revilings. 408
18 n· is there any that taketh her by 369
53: 9 n· was any deceit in his mouth. 3808
54: 4 n· be thou confounded; for thou 408
10 n· shall the covenant of my peace 3808
55: 8 n· are your ways my ways, saith "
56: 3 N· let the son of the strangers, 408
3 n· let the eunuch say, Behold, I am "
57:16 n· will I be always wroth: for the 3808
59: 1 n· his ear heavy, that it cannot hear."
6 n· shall they cover themselves with "
9 from us, n· doth justice overtake us:"
60:19 n· for brightness shall the moon "
20 n· shall thy moon withdraw itself: "
62: 4 n·...thy land any more be termed "
64: 4 n· hath the eye seen, O God, besides"
9 n· remember iniquity for ever: 408
66:19 my fame, n· have seen my glory; 3808
24 die, n· shall their fire be quenched; "
Jer 2: 6 N· said they, Where is the Lord "
3:16 the Lord: n· shall it come to mind: "
16 n· shall they remember it; "
16 n· shall they visit it; "
16 n· shall that be done any more. "
17 n· shall they walk any more after "
4:28 repent, n· will I turn back from it. "
5:12 not he; n· shall evil come upon us; "
12 n· shall we see sword nor famine: "
15 n· understandest what they say. "
24 N· say they in their heart, Let us "
6:15 ashamed, n· could they blush:1571, "
7: 6 n· walk after other gods to your "
16 n· lift up cry nor prayer for them, 408
16 them, n· make intercession to me: "
31 them not, n· came it into my heart.3808
8:12 all ashamed, n· could they blush: "
9:10 n· can men hear the voice of the "
13 obeyed my voice, n· walked therein;"
16 n· they nor their fathers have "
23 n· let the mighty man glory in his 408
10: 5 n· also is it in them to do good. 1571,369
11:14 n· lift up a cry or prayer for them: 408
14:13 sword, n· shall ye have famine; 3808
14 not, n· have I commanded them, "
14 them, n· spake unto them: "
15:10 I have n· lent on usury, nor men * "
16: 2 a wife, n· shalt thou have sons or "
4 lamented; n· shall they be buried; "
5 n· go to lament nor bemoan them: "
6 n· shall men lament for them, nor "
7 N· shall men tear themselves for "
7 n· shall men give them the cup of "
13 know not, n· ye nor your fathers; "
17 n· is their iniquity hid from mine 3808
17: 8 n· shall cease from yielding fruit. "
16 n· have I desired the woeful day; "
22 N· carry forth a burden out of your"
22 the sabbath day, n· do ye any work,"
23 obeyed not, n· inclined their ear, "
18:23 n· blot out their sin from thy sight,408
19: 4 n· they nor their fathers have *3808
5 spake it, n· came it into my mind: "
21: 7 them, n· have pity, nor have mercy. "
22: 3 n· shed innocent blood in this place.408
10 ye not for the dead, n· bemoan him; "
23: 4 n· shall they be lacking, saith the 3808
25:33 lamented, n· gathered, nor buried; "
29: 8 n· hearken to your dreams which 408
32 n· shall he behold the good that I 3808
30:10 n· be dismayed, O Israel: for, lo, I 408
32:23 thy voice, n· walked in thy law; 3808
35 them not, n· came it into my mind, "
33:18 N· shall the priests the Levites "
22 n· the sand of the sea measured: "
34:14 not unto me, n· inclined their ear. "
35: 6 drink no wine, n· ye nor your sons "
7 N· shall ye build house, nor sow 3808
9 n· have we vineyard, nor field, nor "
36:24 n· the king, nor any of his servants "
37: 2 n· he, nor his servants, nor the 3808
38:16 n· will I give thee into the hand of 518
42:13 n· obey the voice of the Lord your*1115
44: 3 knew not, n· they, ye, nor your fathers.
10 n· have they feared, nor walked in 3808
48:11 n· hath he gone into captivity: "
49:18 n· shall a son of man dwell in it. "
31 which have n· gates nor bars "
50:39 n· shall it be dwelt in from "
40 n· shall any son of man dwell "

Jer 51:43 *n'* doth any son of man pass 3808
62 remain in it, *n'* man nor beast, 1115
Eze 2: 6 them, *n'* be afraid of their words, 408
3: 9 not, *n'* be dismayed at their looks, 3808
4:14 *n'* came there abominable flesh into "
5: 7 *n'* have kept my judgments, "
7 *n'* have done according to the "
11 thee; *n'* shall mine eye spare, 1571
11 eye spare, *n'* will I have any pity. *3808
7: 4 not spare thee, *n'* will I have pity: "
9 shall not spare, *n'* will I have pity: "
11 *n'* shall there be wailing for them. "
13 *n'* shall any strengthen himself in "
19 their souls, *n'* fill their bowels: "
8:18 shall not spare, *n'* will I have pity: "
9: 5 not your eye spare, *n'* have ye pity: 408
10 shall not spare, *n'* will I have pity, 3808
11:11 *n'* shall ye be the flesh in the midst
12 *n'* executed my judgments, but 3808
13: 5 *n'* made up the hedge for the house of
9 *n'* shall they be written in the 3808
9 *n'* shall they enter into the land of "
15 is no more, *n'* they that daubed it; 369
14:11 *n'* be polluted any more with all 3808
16 shall deliver *n'* sons nor daughters; 518
18 shall deliver *n'* sons nor daughters, 3808
20 shall deliver *n'* son nor daughter; 518
16: 4 *n'* wast thou washed in water to 3808
16 shall not come, *n'* shall it be so. "
49 *n'* did she strengthen the hand of "
51 *N'* hath Samaria committed half of "
17:17 *N'* shall Pharaoh with his mighty "
18: 6 *n'* hath lifted up his eyes to the "
6 *n'* hath defiled his neighbour's "
6 *n'* hath come near to a menstruous "
8 usury, *n'* hath taken any increase, "
15 *n'* hath lifted up his eyes to the "
16 *N'* hath oppressed any, hath not "
16 pledge, *n'* hath spoiled by violence, "
20 *n'* shall the father bear the iniquity "
20: 8 *n'* did they forsake the idols of "
17 *n'* did I make an end of them in the "
18 *n'* observe their judgments, nor 408
21 *n'* kept my judgments to do them, 3808
22:26 *n'* have they shewed difference "
23: 8 *N'* left she her whoredoms brought "
24:14 *n'* will I spare, *n'* will I repent; "
16 yet *n'* shalt thou mourn nor weep, "
16 weep, *n'* shall thy tears run down. "
29:11 *n'* shall it be inhabited forty years. "
15 *n'* shall it exalt itself any more "
31:14 *n'* shoot up their top among the "
14 *n'* their trees stand up in their * "
32:13 *n'* shall the foot of man trouble "
33:12 *n'* shall the righteous be able to live "
34: 4 *n'* have ye healed that which was "
4 *n'* have ye bound up that which was "
4 *n'* have ye brought again that which "
4 *n'* have ye sought that which was "
8 *n'* did my shepherds search for my "
10 flock; *n'* shall the shepherds feed "
28 *n'* shall the beast of the land devour "
29 *n'* bear the shame of the heathen "
36:14 *n'* bereave thy nations any more, "
15 *N'* will I cause men to hear in thee "
15 *n'* shalt thou bear the reproach of "
15 *n'* shalt thou cause thy nations to "
37:22 *n'* shall they be divided into two "
23 *N'* shall they defile themselves any "
38:11 walls, and having *n'* bars nor gates, 369
39:10 *n'* cut down any out of the forests; 3808
29 *N'* will I hide my face any more "
43: 7 more defile, *n'* they, nor their kings, "
44:20 *N'* shall they shave their heads, 3808
21 *N'* shall any priest drink wine, "
22 *N'* shall they take for their wives a "
47:12 fade, *n'* shall the fruit thereof be "
48:14 they shall not sell of it, *n'* exchange, "
Da 3:27 *n'* were their coats changed, nor 3809
6: 4 *n'* was there any error or fault found "
18 *n'* were instruments of musick "
8: 4 *n'* was there any that could deliver 369
9: 6 *N'* have we hearkened unto thy 3808
10 *N'* have we obeyed the voice of the "
10: 3 *n'* came flesh nor wine in my mouth, "
3 *n'* did I anoint myself at all, till "
17 in me, *n'* is there breath left in me. "
11: 6 *n'* shall he stand, nor his arm: but "
15 withstand, *n'* his chosen people, 369
15 *n'* shall there be any strength to "
17 not stand on his side, *n'* be for him. 3808
20 destroyed, *n'* in anger, nor in battle. "
37 *N'* shall he regard the God of his "
Ho 2: 2 not my wife, *n'* am I her husband: "
4:15 Gilgal, *n'* go ye up to Beth-aven, 408
9: 4 *n'* shall they be pleasing unto him: 3808
14: 3 *n'* will we say any more to the work "
Joe 2: 2 like, *n'* shall be any more after it, "
8 *N'* shall one thrust another; they "
Am 2:14 *n'* shall the mighty deliver himself: "
15 *N'* shall he stand that handleth the "
15 *n'* shall he that rideth the horse "
5:22 *n'* will I regard the peace offerings "
7:14 prophet, *n'* was I a prophet's son; "
Ob 12 *n'* shouldest thou have rejoiced * 408
12 *n'* shouldest thou have spoken "
14 *N'* shouldest thou have stood in the* "
14 *n'* shouldest thou have delivered up* "
Jon 3: 7 Let *n'* man nor beast, herd nor 369
4:10 not laboured, *n'* madest it grow; 3808
Mic 2: 3 your necks; *n'* shall ye go haughtily: "
4: 3 *n'* shall they learn war any more. "
12 *n'* understand they his counsel: "
Hab 2: 5 a proud man, *n'* keepeth at home,* "
3:17 *n'* shall fruit be in the vines; 369
Zep 1:12 will not do good, *n'* will he do evil. 3808
Zep 1:18 *N'* their silver nor their gold shall 3808
3:13 *n'* shall a deceitful tongue be found "
Zec 8:10 *n'* was there any peace to him that 369
11:16 *n'* shall seek the young one, nor 3808
13: 4 *n'* shall they wear a rough garment "
Mal 1:10 *n'* do ye kindle fire on mine altar * "
10 *n'* will I accept an offering at your "
3:11 *n'* shall your vine cast her fruit "
4: 1 shall leave them *n'* root nor branch.
M't 5:15 *N'* do men light a candle, and put 3761
34 *n'* by heaven; for it is God's throne: 3383
35 *n'* by Jerusalem; for it is the city * "
36 *N'* shalt thou swear by thy head, "
6:15 *n'* will your Father forgive your 3761
20 *n'* moth nor rust doth corrupt, and 3777
26 *n'* do they reap, nor gather into 3761
28 grow; they toil not, *n'* do they spin: "
7: 6 *n'* cast ye your pearls before swine, 3366
18 *n'* can a corrupt tree bring forth 3761
9:17 *N'* do men put new wine into old "
10: 9 Provide *n'* gold, nor silver, nor *3361
10 your journey, *n'* two coats, *n'* shoes, 3366
11:18 John came *n'* eating nor drinking, 3383
27 *n'* knoweth any man the Father, 3761
12: 4 *n'* for them which were with him, "
19 *n'* shall any man hear his voice in "
32 be forgiven him, *n'* in this world, 3777
32 world, *n'* in the world to come. * "
13:13 hear not, *n'* do they understand. 3761
16: 9 *n'* remember the five loaves of the "
10 *N'* the seven loaves of the four "
21:27 *N'* tell I you by what authority I do "
22:16 *n'* carest thou for any man: *2532,3756
30 *n'* marry, nor...given in marriage, 3777
46 *n'* durst any man from that day 3761
23:10 *N'* be ye called masters: for one 3366
13 men: for ye *n'* go in yourselves, *3761
13 *n'* suffer ye them that are entering 3756
24:18 *N'* let him which is in the field *3361
20 the winter, *n'* on the sabbath day: 3366
25:13 ye know *n'* the day nor the hour *3383
M'r 4:22 *n'* was any thing kept secret, but 3761
5: 4 *n'* could any man tame him. *2532,3762
8:14 *n'* had they in the ship with * "
17 perceive ye not yet, *n'* understand? 3761
26 *N'* go into the town, nor tell it to *3366
11:26 *n'* will your Father which is in *3761
33 *N'* do I tell you by what authority * "
12:21 her, and died, *n'* left he any seed: * "
24 scriptures, *n'* the power of God? *3366
25 *n'* marry, nor...given in marriage; 3777
13:11 shall speak, *n'* do ye premeditate: *3366
15 *n'* enter therein, to take any thing* "
19 unto this time, *n'* shall be. *3756,3361
32 heaven, *n'* the Son, but the Father. 3761
14:40 *n'* wist they what to answer *2532,3756
59 But *n'* so did their witness agree *3761
68 *n'* understand I what thou sayest.* "
16: 8 *n'* said they any thing to any *2532,3762
13 residue: *n'* believed they them. 3761
Lu 1:15 *n'* wine nor strong drink; *3756,3361
3:14 to no man, *n'* accuse any falsely; 3366
6:43 *n'* doth a corrupt tree bring forth *3761
7: 7 *n'* thought I myself worthy to come "
33 came *n'* eating bread nor drinking* 3383
8:17 *n'* any thing hid, that shall not be* 3761
27 *n'* abode in any house, but in* 2532,3756
43 *n'* could be healed of any, * "
9: 3 journey, *n'* staves, nor scrip, *n'* 3383
3 *n'* scrip, *n'* bread, *n'* money; "
3 money; *n'* have two coats apiece. "
10: 4 Carry *n'* purse, nor scrip, nor *3361
11:33 secret place, *n'* under a bushel, 3761
12: 2 *n'* hid, that shall not be known. "
22 *n'* for the body, what ye shall put *3366
24 ravens: for they *n'* sow nor reap; *3756
24 which *n'* have storehouse nor barn;* "
29 drink, *n'* be ye of doubtful mind. 3361
33 approacheth, *n'* moth corrupteth. 3761
47 *n'* did according to his will, shall *3366
14:12 thy brethren, *n'* thy kinsmen, nor* "
35 It is *n'* fit for the land, nor yet for 3777
15:29 *n'* transgressed I at any time thy *3763
16:26 *n'* can they pass to us, that would *3366
31 *n'* will they be persuaded, though 3761
17:21 *N'* shall they say, Lo here! or, lo "
18: 2 feared not God, *n'* regarded man: *3366
34 *n'* knew they the things which* 2532,3756
20: 8 *N'* tell I you by what authority I 3761
21 *n'* acceptest thou the person *2532,3756
35 *n'* marry, nor...given in marriage: 3777
36 *N'* can they die any more: for "
Joh 1:25 Christ, nor Elias, *n'* that prophet?
3:20 light, *n'* cometh to the light, *2532,3756
4:15 thirst not, *n'* come hither to draw. 3366
21 shall *n'* in this mountain, nor yet 3777
5:37 *n'* heard his voice at any time, nor "
6:24 was not there, *n'* his disciples, 3761
7: 5 *n'* did his brethren believe in him.* "
8:11 *N'* do I condemn thee: go, and sin "
19 Ye *n'* know me, nor my Father: if 3777
42 *n'* came I of myself, but he sent 3761
9: 3 *N'* hath this man sinned, nor his 3777
10:28 *n'* shall any man pluck them *2532,3756
13:16 *n'* he that is sent greater than he 3761
14:17 it seeth him not, *n'* knoweth him:
27 be troubled, *n'* let it be afraid. 3366
17:20 *N'* pray I for these alone, but for
Ac 2:27 *n'* wilt thou suffer thine Holy One 3761
31 *n'* his flesh did see corruption.
4:12 *N'* is there salvation in any *2532,3756
32 *n'* said any of them that ought of *3761
34 *N'* was there any among them "
8:21 Thou hast *n'* part nor lot in this 3756
9: 9 sight, and *n'* did eat nor drink. 3761
15:10 *n'* our fathers nor we were able to 3777
Ac 16:21 us to receive, *n'* to observe, being *3761
17:25 *N'* is worshipped with men's "
19:37 which are *n'* robbers of churches, 3777
20:24 *n'* count I my life dear unto *3761
21:21 *n'* to walk after the customs. 3366
23: 8 resurrection, *n'* angel, nor spirit: "
12 they would *n'* eat nor drink till 3385
21 they will *n'* eat nor drink till they "
24:12 they *n'* found me in the temple 3777
12 any man, *n'* raising up the people,* 2228
12 *n'* in the synagogue, nor in the * "
13 *N'* can they prove the things "
18 in the temple, *n'* with multitude, *3756
25: 8 *N'* against the law of the Jews, 3777
8 *n'* against the temple, nor yet * "
27:20 when *n'* sun nor stars in many 3383
28:21 We *n'* received letters out of Judæa 3777
21 *n'* any of the brethren that came * "
Ro 1:21 him not as God, *n'* were thankful; 2228
2:28 *n'* is that circumcision, which is 3761
4:19 *n'* yet the deadness of Sarah's womb: *
6:13 *N'* yield ye your members as 3366
8: 7 to the law of God, *n'* indeed can be. 3761
38 *n'* death, nor life, nor angels, nor 3777
9: 7 *N'*, because they are the seed of 3761
11 *n'* having done any good or evil, 3366
14:21 It is good *n'* to eat flesh, nor to *3361
1Co 2: 9 *n'* have entered into the heart *2532,3756
14 *n'* can he know them, because* "
3: 2 bear it, *n'* yet now are ye able. *235,3777
7 *n'* is he that planteth any thing, "
7 *n'* he that watereth; but God that "
5: 8 *n'* with the leaven of malice and 3366
6: 9 *n'* fornicators, nor idolaters, nor 3777
8: 8 for *n'*, if we eat, are we the better;* "
8 *n'*, if we eat not, are we the worse. "
9:15 *n'* have I written these things, that it *
10: 7 *N'* be ye idolaters, as were some 3366
8 *N'* let us commit fornication, as "
9 *N'* let us tempt Christ, as some of "
10 *N'* murmur ye, as some of them "
32 *n'* to the Jews, nor to the Gentiles,*
11: 9 *N'* was the man created for 2532,3756
11 *n'* is the man without the woman,* 3777
11 *n'* the woman without the man, "
16 custom, *n'* the churches of God. 3761
15:50 of God; *n'* doth corruption inherit "
Ga 1: 1 *n'* by man, but by Jesus Christ, and "
12 For I *n'* received it of man, "
12 *n'* was I taught it, but by the Lord* 3777
17 *N'* went I up to Jerusalem to them 3761
2: 3 *N'* Titus, who was with me, being a* "
3:28 There is *n'* Jew nor Greek, there 3756
28 there is *n'* bond nor free, there is "
28 there is *n'* male nor female: for ye* "
5: 6 *n'* circumcision availeth any thing, 3777
6:13 For *n'* they themselves who are *3761
15 *n'* circumcision availeth any thing, 3777
Eph 4:27 *N'* give place to the devil. 3383
5: 4 *N'* filthiness, nor foolish *2532,3756
6: 9 *n'* is there respect of persons* " "
Ph'p 2:16 run in vain, *n'* laboured in vain. 3761
Col 3:11 Where there is *n'* Greek nor Jew, *3756
1Th 2: 5 *n'* at any time used we flattering 3777
6 glory, *n'* of you, nor yet of others, "
2Th 2: 2 *n'* by spirit, nor by word, nor by *3383
3: 8 *N'* did we eat any man's bread for 3761
10 would not work, *n'* should he eat. 3366
1Ti 1: 4 *N'* give heed to fables and endless "
7 understanding *n'* what they say, 3383
5:22 *n'* be partaker of other men's sins: 3366
Heb 4:13 *N'* is there any creature that* 2532,3756
7: 3 *n'* beginning of days, nor end of 3383
9:12 *N'* by the blood of goats and *3761
18 *n'* the first testament was dedicated* "
10: 8 not, *n'* hadst pleasure therein;
Jas 1:13 evil, *n'* tempteth he any man: *2532,3762
17 variableness, *n'* shadow of turning. 2228
5:12 brethren, swear not, *n'* by heaven, 3383
12 *n'* by earth, *n'* by any other oath: * "
1Pe 2:22 *n'* was guile found in his mouth: 3761
3:14 of their terror, *n'* be troubled; 3366
5: 3 *N'* as being lords over God's "
2Pe 1: 8 shall *n'* be barren nor unfruitful *3756
1Jo 2:15 *n'* the things that are in the world. 3366
3: 6 hath not seen him, *n'* known him. 3761
10 God, *n'* he that loveth not his brother.
18 us not love in word, *n'* in tongue; 3366
2Jo 10 your house, *n'* bid him God speed:* "
3Jo 10 *n'* doth he himself receive the 3777
Re 3:15 works, that thou art *n'* cold nor hot: "
16 art lukewarm, and *n'* cold nor hot, "
5: 3 nor in earth, *n'* under the earth, *3761
3 to open the book, *n'* to look thereon.* "
4 read the book, *n'* to look thereon. *3777
7: 3 Hurt not the earth, *n'* the sea, nor 3383
16 no more, *n'* thirst any more; 3761
16 *n'* shall the sun light on them, nor "
9: 4 *n'* any green thing, *n'* any tree; but
20 which *n'* can see, nor hear, nor 3777
21 *N'* repented they of their *2532,3756
12: 8 *n'* was there place found any more 3777
20: 4 worshipped the beast, *n'* his image,
4 *n'*...received his mark upon *2532,3756
21: 4 more death, *n'* sorrow, nor crying, 3777
4 *n'* shall there be any more pain: for*
23 sun, *n'* of the moon, to shine in it: 3761
27 *n'* whatsoever worketh abomination,*
22: 5 need no candle, *n'* light of the sun;

Nekeb (*ne'-keb*)
Jos 19:33 *N'*, and Jabneel, unto Lakum; *5346

Nekoda (*ne-ko'-dah*)
Ezr 2:48 of Rezin, the children of *N'*, 5353
60 children of *N'*, six hundred fifty "

Ne 7:50 of Rezin, the children of N', 5353
62 children of N', six hundred forty "
Nemuel (*ne-mu'-el*) See also JEMUEL; NEMUELITES.
Nu 26: 9 sons of Eliab; N', and Dathan, 5241
12 of N', the family of the Nemuelites: "
1Ch 4:24 sons of Simeon were, N' and Jamin, "
Nemuelites (*ne-mu'-el-ites*)
Nu 26:12 of Nemuel, the family of the N': 5242
Nepheg (*ne'-feg*)
Ex 6:21 sons of Izhar; Korah, and N', and 5298
2Sa 5:15 Ibhar also, and Elishua, and N', "
1Ch 3: 7 And Nogah, and N', and Japhia, "
14: 6 And Nogah, and N', and Japhia, "
nephew See also NEPHEWS.
Job 18:19 neither have son nor n' among *5220
Isa 14:22 and son, and n', saith the Lord. * "
nephews
J'g 12:14 he had forty sons and thirty n', *1121
1Ti 5: 4 if any widow have children or n', *1549
Nephish (*ne'-fish*) See also NAPHISH.
1Ch 5:19 Hagarites, with Jetur, and N', *5305
Nephishesim (*ne-fish'-e-sim*) See also NEPHUSIM.
Ne 7:52 of Meunim, the children of N', *5300
Nephthalim (*nef'-tha-lim*) See also NAPHTALI.
M't 4:13 in the borders of Zabulon and N': *3508
15 and the land of N', by the way of * "
Re 7: 6 N' were sealed twelve thousand. * "
Nephtoah (*nef-to'-ah*)
Jos 15: 9 the fountain of the water of N', 5318
18:15 went out to the well of waters of N': "
Nephusim (*ne-fu'-sim*) See also NEPHISHESIM.
Ezr 2:50 of Mehunim, the children of N', *5304
Ner (*nur*)
1Sa 14:50 Abner, the son of N', Saul's uncle.5369
51 N' the father of Abner was the son "
26: 5 Abner the son N', the captain of "
14 and to Abner the son of N', saying, "
2Sa 2: 8 Abner the son of N', captain of "
12 And Abner the son of N', and the "
3:23 son of N' came to the king, and he "
25 Thou knowest Abner the son of N', "
28 the blood of Abner the son of N': "
37 king to slay Abner the son of N'. "
1Ki 2: 5 unto Abner the son of N', and unto "
32 Abner the son of N', captain of the "
1Ch 8:33 N' begat Kish, and Kish begat Saul, "
9:36 Kish, and Baal, and N', and Nadab, "
39 N' begat Kish; and Kish begat "
26:28 and Abner the son of N', and Joab "
Nereus (*ne'-re-us*)
Ro 16:15 Salute Philologus, and Julia, N', 3517
Nergal (*nur'-gal*) See also NERGAL-SHAREZER.
2Ki 17:30 and the men of Cuth made N', and 5370
Nergal-sharezer (*nur''-gal-sha-re'-zur*)
Jer 39: 3 sat in the middle gate, even N', 5371
3 N', Rab-mag, with all the residue "
13 N', Rab-mag, and all the king of "
Neri (*ne'-ri*)
Lu 3:27 Salathiel, which was the son of N',3518
Neriah (*ne-ri'-ah*)
Jer 32:12, 16 unto Baruch the son of N', 5374
36: 4 called Baruch the son of N': and "
8 Baruch the son of N' did according "
14 the son of N' took the roll in his "
32 to Baruch the scribe, the son of N'; "
43: 3 son of N' setteth thee on against us, "
6 prophet, and Baruch the son of N'. "
45: 1 spake unto Baruch the son of N', "
51:59 commanded Seraiah the son of N', "
Nero (*ne'-ro*)
2Ti *subscr.* when Paul was brought before N'3505
nest See also NESTS.
Nu 24:21 and thou puttest thy n' in a rock. 7064
De 22: 6 If a bird's n' chance to be before "
32:11 As an eagle stirreth up her n', "
Job 29:18 Then I said, I shall die in my n', "
39:27 command, and make her n' on high? "
Ps 84: 3 the swallow a n' for herself, where "
Pr 27: 8 a bird that wandereth from her n', "
Isa 10:14 as a n' the riches of the people: "
16: 2 a wandering bird cast out of the n', "
34:15 shall the great owl make her n', 7077
Jer 22:23 that makest thy n' in the cedars, "
48:28 like the dove that maketh her n' in "
49:16 make thy n' as high as the eagle, 7064
Ob 4 thou set thy n' among the stars, "
Hab 2: 9 that he may set his n' on high, that "
nests
Ps 104:17 Where the birds make their n': as 7077
Eze 31: 6 heaven made their n' in his boughs, "
M't 8:20 and the birds of the air have n'; 2682
Lu 9:58 holes, and birds of the air have n'; "
net See also NETS; NETWORK.
Ex 27: 4 upon the n' shalt thou make four 7568
5 the n' may be even to the midst of "
Job 18: 8 he is cast into a n' by his own feet, "
19: 6 hath compassed me with his n'. 4685
Ps 9:15 in the n' which they hid is their 7568
10: 9 when he draweth him into his n'. "
25:15 he shall pluck my feet out of the n'. "
31: 4 me out of the n' that they have laid "
35: 7 they hid for me their n' in a pit, "
8 n' that he hath hid catch himself: "
57: 6 have prepared a n' for my steps; "
66:11 Thou broughtest us into the n'; 4685
140: 5 have spread a n' by the wayside; 7568
Pr 1:17 n' is spread in the sight of any bird.7568
12:12 wicked desireth the n' of evil men:4686
29: 5 spreadeth a n' for his feet. 7568
Ec 9:12 fishes that are taken in an evil n', 4686
Isa 51:20 the streets, as a wild bull in a n': 4364
La 1:13 he hath spread a n' for my feet, he7568
Eze 12:13 My n' also will I spread upon him, "
17:20 And I will spread my n' upon him, "
19: 8 and spread their n' over him: he "
32: 3 I will therefore spread out my n' "
3 they shall bring thee up in my n'. 2764
Ho 5: 1 and a n' spread upon Tabor. 7568
7:12 go, I will spread my n' upon them; "
Mic 7: 2 every man his brother with a n'. 2764
Hab 1:15 they catch them in their n', and "
16 they sacrifice unto their n', and "
17 Shall they therefore empty their n', "
M't 4:18 brother, casting a n' into the sea: 293
13:47 the kingdom of heaven is like a n',4522
M'r 1:16 brother, casting a n' into the sea: 293
Lu 5: 5 at thy word I will let down the n'. *1350
6 of fishes: and their n' break. * "
Joh 21: 6 Cast the n' on the right side of the "
8 cubits,) dragging the n' with fishes. "
11 drew the n' to the land full of fishes, "
11 many, yet was not the n' broken. "
Nethaneel (*ne-than'-e-el*)
Nu 1: 8 of Issachar; N' the son of Zuar. *5417
2: 5 N' the son of Zuar shall be captain* "
7:18 the second day N' the son of Zuar, * "
23 the offering of N' the son of Zuar.* "
10:15 Issachar was N' the son of Zuar. * "
1Ch 2:14 N' the fourth, Raddai the fifth, * "
15:24 N', and Amasai, and Zechariah, * "
24: 6 Shemaiah the son of N' the scribe,* "
26: 4 Sacar the fourth, and N' the fifth,* "
2Ch 17: 7 to N', and to Michaiah, to teach in* "
35: 9 and Shemaiah and N', his brethren,* "
Ezr 10:22 Ishmael, N', Jozabad, and Elasah.* "
Ne 12:21 Hashabiah; of Jedaiah, N'. * "
36 N', and Judah, Hanani, with the * "
Nethaniah (*neth-a-ni'-ah*)
2Ki 25:23 even Ishmael the son of N', and 5418
25 month, that Ishmael the son of N', "
1Ch 25: 2 and N', and Asarelah, the sons of "
12 The fifth to N', he, his sons, and "
2Ch 17: 8 Levites, even Shemaiah, and N', "
Jer 36:14 princes sent Jehudi the son of N', "
40: 8 Mizpah, even Ishmael the son of N', "
14 Ishmael the son of N' to slay thee? "
15 I will slay Ishmael the son of N', "
41: 1 Ishmael the son of N' the son of "
2 arose Ishmael the son N', and the "
6 Ishmael the son of N' went forth "
7 Ishmael the son of N' slew them, "
9 Ishmael the son of N' filled it with "
10 Ishmael the son of N' carried them "
11 Ishmael the son of N' had done, "
12 to fight with Ishmael the son of N', "
15 But Ishmael the son of N' escaped "
16 from Ishmael the son of N', from "
18 the son of N' had slain Gedaliah "
nether See also NETHERMOST.
Ex 19:17 stood at the n' part of the mount. 8482
De 24: 6 take the n' or the upper millstone*7347
Jos 15:19 upper springs, and the n' springs. 8482
16: 3 the coast of Beth-horon the n', 8481
18:13 the south side of the n' Beth-horon. "
J'g 1:15 upper springs and the n' springs. 8482
1Ki 9:17 Gezer, and Beth-horon the n', 8481
1Ch 7:24 who built Beth-horon the n', and "
2Ch 8: 5 the upper, and Beth-horon the n', "
Job 41:24 hard as a piece of the n' millstone.8482
Eze 31:14 death, to the n' parts of the earth, "
16 in the n' parts of the earth. "
18 Eden unto the n' parts of the earth: "
32:18 unto the n' parts of the earth, with "
24 into the n' parts of the earth, which "
nethermost
1Ki 6: 6 n' chamber was five cubits broad, 8481
Nethinims (*neth'-in-ims*)
1Ch 9: 2 the priests, Levites, and the N'. *5411
Ezr 2:43 The N': the children of Ziha, the* "
58 All the N', and the children of * "
70 and the N', dwelt in their cities, * "
7: 7 and the N', unto Jerusalem, in the* "
24 N', or ministers of this house of *5412
8:17 his brethren the N', at the place *5411
20 Also of the N', whom David and * "
20 two hundred and twenty N': all * "
Ne 3:26 Moreover the N' dwelt in Ophel, * "
31 Malchiah...unto the place of the N'.* "
7:46 The N': the children of Ziha, the* "
60 All the N', and the children of * "
73 people, and the N', and all Israel,* "
10:28 the porters, the singers, the N', * "
11: 3 and the N', and the children of * "
21 But the N' dwelt in Ophel: and * "
21 Ziha and Gispa were over the N'. * "
Netophah (*ne-to'-fah*) See also NETOPHATHITE.
Ezr 2:22 The men of N', fifty and six. 5199
Ne 7:26 The men of Beth-lehem and N', "
Netophathi (*ne-to'-fa-thi*) See also NETOPHATHITE.
Ne 12:28 and from the village of N'; *5200
Netophathite (*ne-to'-fa-thite*) See also NETOPHATHI; NETOPHATHITES.
2Sa 23:28 the Ahohite, Maharai the N', 5200
29 Heleb the son of Baanah, a N', "
2Ki 25:23 the son of Tanhumeth the N', "
1Ch 11:30 Maharai the N', Heled the son "
30 Heled the son of Baanah the N', "
1Ch 27:13 tenth month was Maharai the N', 5200
15 twelfth month was Heldai the N', "
Jer 40: 8 sons of Ephai the N', and Jezaniah "
Netophathites (*ne-to'-fa-thites*)
1Ch 2:54 of Salma; Beth-lehem, and the N',5200
9:16 dwelt in the villages of the N'. "
nets
1Ki 7:17 n' of checker work, and wreaths 7638
Ps 141:10 the wicked fall into their own n', 4365
Ec 7:26 whose heart is snares and n', and 2764
Isa 19: 8 that spread n' upon the waters 4364
Eze 26: 5 be a place for the spreading of n' 2764
14 shalt be a place to spread n' upon; "
47:10 shall be a place to spread forth n'; "
M't 4:20 they straightway left their n', and 1350
21 their father, mending their n'; and "
M'r 1:18 straightway they forsook their n', "
19 were in the ship mending their n'. "
Lu 5: 2 them, and were washing their n'. "
4 and let down your n' for a draught. "
nettles
Job 30: 7 under the n' they were gathered 2738
Pr 24:31 n' had covered the face thereof, "
Isa 34:13 n' and brambles in the fortresses 7057
Ho 9: 6 their silver, n' shall possess them: "
Zep 2: 9 the breeding of n', and saltpits, 2738
network See also NETWORKS.
Ex 27: 4 for it a grate of n' of brass; 4639,7568
38: 4 for the altar a brasen grate of n', "
1Ki 7:18 rows round about upon the one n',7639
20 the belly which was by the n': and "
42 rows of pomegranates for one n', "
Jer 52:22 n' and pomegranates upon the "
23 all the pomegranates upon the n' "
networks
1Ki 7:41 the two n', to cover the two bowls 7639
42 pomegranates for the two n', even "
Isa 19: 9 and they that weave n', shall be *2355
never See also NEVERTHELESS.
Ge 34:12 Ask me n' so much dowry and gift,
41:19 such as I n' saw in all the land of 3808
Le 6:13 upon the altar; it shall n' go out. * "
Nu 19: 2 and upon which n' came yoke: "
De 15:11 poor shall n' cease out of the land: "
J'g 2: 1 n' break my covenant with 3808,5769
14: 3 n' a woman among the daughters 369
16: 7 green withs that were n' dried, 3808
11 new ropes that were n' occupied, * "
2Sa 12:10 sword shall n' depart 3808,5704,5769
2Ch 18: 7 he n' prophesied good unto me, 369
Job 3:16 as infants which n' saw light. 3808
9:30 and make my hands n' so clean; 1253
21:25 soul, and n' eateth with pleasure. 3808
Ps 10: 6 for I shall n' be in adversity. *1755
11 his face; he will n' see it. 1074,5331
15: 5 these things shall n' be moved.3808,5769
30: 6 I said, I shall n' be moved. "
31: 1 let me n' be ashamed: 408,3808
49:19 they shall n' see light. 5704,5331,
55:22 n' suffer the righteous to be 3808,5769
58: 5 of charmers, charming n' so wisely.
71: 1 trust: let me n' be put to 408,5769
119:93 I will n' forget thy precepts: 5769,3808
Pr 10:30 righteous shall n' be removed: " 1077
27:20 Hell and destruction are n' full; 3808
20 the eyes of man are n' satisfied. "
30:15 three things that are n' satisfied, "
Isa 13:20 It shall n' be inhabited, 3808,5331
14:20 seed of evildoers shall n' be * " 5769
25: 2 be no city; it shall n' be built.5769,3808
56:11 dogs which can n' have enough, "
62: 6 shall n' hold their peace day nor "
63:19 thou n' barest rule over them;5769
Jer 33:17 shall n' want a man to sit upon "
Eze 16:63 and n' open thy mouth any more "
26:21 shalt thou n' be found again, 3808,5769
27:36 and n' shalt be any more. 5704, "
28:19 and n' shalt thou be any "
Da 2:44 which shall n' be destroyed: 5957,3809
12: 1 such as n' was since there was a 3808
Joe 2:26, 27 and my people shall n' be 3808,5769
Am 8: 7 n' forget any of their works. 518,5331
14 shall fall, and n' rise up again. 3808
Hab 1: 4 judgment doth n' go forth: 3808,5331
M't 7:23 I n' knew you: depart from me, 3763
9:33 saying, It was n' so seen in Israel. "
21:16 have ye n' read, Out of the mouth "
42 Did ye n' read in the scriptures, "
26:33 of thee, yet I will n' be offended. "
27:14 answered him to n' a word; *3761,1520
M'r 2:12 We n' saw it on this fashion. 3763
25 Have ye n' read what David did, "
3:29 hath n' forgiveness, 3756,1519,3588,165
9:43, 45 fire that n' shall be quenched: 3756
11: 2 colt tied, whereon n' man sat;*3762,4455
14:21 that man if he had n' been born. *3756
Lu 15:29 and yet thou n' gavest me a kid, 3763
19:30 tied, whereon yet n' man sat: *3762
23:29 and the wombs that n' bare, 3756
29 and the paps which n' gave suck. "
53 wherein n' man before was laid. 3764
Joh 4:14 give...shall n' thirst; 3364,1519,3588,165
6:35 that cometh to me shall n' hunger;* "
35 believeth on me shall n' thirst.3364,4455
7:15 man letters, having n' learned? 3361
46 N' man spake like this man. 3763
8:33 n' in bondage to any man: 3762,4455
51 saying,...shall n' see 3364,1519,3588,165
52 shall n' taste of death. " " " "
10:28 shall n' perish, neither " " " "
11:26 believeth in me shall n' " " " "
13: 8 Thou shalt n' wash my " " " "
19:41 wherein was n' man yet laid. 3764
Ac 10:14 n' eaten any thing that is common3763

Ac 14: 8 mother's womb, who *n'* had walked: *3763*
1Co 13: 8 Charity *n'* faileth: but whether "
2Ti 3: 7 *n'* able to come to the knowledge *3368*
Heb 10: 1 can *n'* with those sacrifices which *3763*
11 which can *n'* take away sins: "
13: 5 I will *n'* leave thee, nor forsake *3364*
2Pe 1:10 these things, ye shall *n'* fall: *3364,4219*

nevertheless
Ex 32:34 *n'* in the day when I visit I will
Le 11: 4 *N'* these shall ye not eat of them 389
36 *N'* a fountain or pit, wherein there "
Nu 13:28 *N'* the people be strong that dwell *657
14:44 *n'* the ark of the covenant of the
18:15 *n'* the firstborn of man shalt thou 389
24:22 *N'* the Kenite shall be wasted, 3588, 518
31:23 *n'* it shall be purified with the 389
De 14: 7 *N'* these ye shall not eat of them "
23: 5 *N'* the Lord thy God would not
Jos 13:13 *N'* the children of Israel expelled not
14: 8 *N'* my brethren that went up with
J'g 1:33 *n'* the inhabitants of Beth-shemesh
2:16 *N'* the Lord raised up judges, which *
1Sa 8:19 *N'* the people refused to obey the *
15:35 *n'* Samuel mourned for Saul: and *3588
20:26 *N'* Saul spake not any thing that
29: 6 day: *n'* the lords favour thee not.
2Sa 5: 7 *N'* David took the strong hold of
17:18 *N'* a lad saw them, and told Absalom: *
23:16 *n'* he would not drink thereof. *
1Ki 8:19 *N'* thou shalt not build the house; 7535
15: 4 *N'* for David's sake did the Lord 3588
14 *n'* Asa's heart was perfect with 7535
23 *N'* in the time of his old age he * "
22:43 *n'* the high places were not taken * 389
2Ki 2:10 *n'*, if thou see me when I am taken
3: 3 *N'* he cleaved unto the sins of 7535
13: 6 *N'* they departed not from the sins 389
23: 9 *N'* the priests of the high places
1Ch 11: 5 *N'* David took the castle of Zion,
21: 4 *N'* the king's word prevailed against
2Ch 12: 8 *N'* they shall be his servants; 3588
15:17 *n'* the heart of Asa was perfect all 7535
19: 3 *N'* there are good things found in 61
30:11 *N'* divers of Asher and Manasseh 389
33:17 *N'* the people did sacrifice still in 61
35:22 *N'* Josiah would not turn his face
Ne 4: 9 *N'* we made our prayer unto our God, *
9:26 *N'* they were disobedient, and
31 *N'* for thy great mercies' sake thou
13:26 *n'* even him did outlandish women 1571
Es 5:10 *N'* Haman refrained himself: and
Ps 31:22 *n'* thou heardest the voice of my 403
49:12 *N'* man being in honour abideth *
73:23 *N'* I am continually with thee:
78:36 *N'* they did flatter him with their *
89:33 *N'* my lovingkindness will I not *
106: 8 *N'* he saved them for his name's
44 *N'* he regarded their affliction, when
Pr 19:21 *n'* the counsel of the Lord, that *
Ec 9:16 *n'* the poor man's wisdom is despised,
Isa 9: 1 *N'* the dimness shall not be such *3588
Jer 5:18 *N'* in those days, saith the Lord, *1571
26:24 *N'* the hand of Ahikam the son of * 389
28: 7 *N'* hear thou now this word that I "
36:25 *N'* Elnathan and Delaiah and *1571
Eze 16:60 *N'* I will remember my covenant
20:17 *N'* mine eye spared them from
22 *N'* I withdrew mine hand, and
33: 9 *N'*, if thou warn the wicked of his
Da 4:15 *N'* leave the stump of his roots in 1297
Jon 1:13 *N'* the men rowed hard to bring it to
M't 14: 9 *n'* for the oath's sake, and them *
26:39 *n'* not as I will, but as thou wilt. *4133*
64 *n'* I say unto you, Hereafter shall "
M'r 14:36 *n'* not what I will, but what thou * *235*
Lu 5: 5 *n'* at thy word I will let down the **1161*
13:33 *N'* I must walk to day, and **4133*
18: 8 *N'* when the Son of man cometh, * "
22:42 *n'* not my will, but thine, be done. "
Joh 11:15 may believe; *n'* let us go unto him. *235*
12:42 *N'* among the chief rulers *3676,3305*
16: 7 *N'* I tell you the truth; It is *235*
Ac 14:17 *N'* he left not himself without **2544*
27:11 *N'* the centurion believed the **1161*
Ro 5:14 *N'* death reigned from Adam to *235*
15:15 *N'*, brethren, I have written the **1161*
1Co 7: 2 *N'*, to avoid fornication, let every * "
28 *N'* such shall have trouble in the * "
37 *N'* he that standeth stedfast in his * "
9:12 *N'* we have not used this power; *235*
11:11 *N'* neither is the man without the **4133*
2Co 3:16 *N'*, when it shall turn to the Lord, **1161*
7: 6 *N'* God, that comforteth those that *235*
12:16 *n'*, being crafty, I caught you with * "
Ga 2:20 *n'* I live; yet not I, but Christ †‡*1161*
4:30 *N'* what saith the scripture? Cast * *235*
Eph 5:33 *N'*, let every one of you...so love *4133*
Ph'p 1:24 *N'* to abide in the flesh is more **1161*
3:16 *N'*, whereto we have already **4133*
2Ti 1:12 *n'* I am not ashamed: for I know * *235*
2:19 *N'* the foundation of God standeth **3305*
Heb 12:11 *n'* afterward it yieldeth the **1161*
2Pe 3:13 *N'* we, according to his promise, * "
Re 2: 4 *N'* I have somewhat against thee, * *235*

new See also NEWBORN; NEWS; RENEW.
Ex 1: 8 arose up a *n'* king over Egypt, 2319
Le 23:16 a *n'* meat offering unto the Lord. "
26:10 forth the old because of the *n'*. "
Nu 16:30 But if the Lord make a *n'* thing, 1278
28:26 a *n'* meat offering unto the Lord, 2319
De 20: 5 is there that hath built a *n'* house, "
22: 8 When thou buildest a *n'* house, "
24: 5 When a man hath taken a *n'* wife, "
32:17 not, to *n'* gods that came newly up, "
Jos 9:13 of wine, which we filled, were *n'*; "
J'g 5: 8 They chose *n'* gods; then was war 2319
15:13 they bound him with two *n'* cords, "
15 he found a *n'* jawbone of an ass, ‡2961
16:11 If they bind me fast with *n'* ropes 2319
12 Delilah therefore took *n'* ropes, "
1Sa 6: 7 Now therefore make a *n'* cart, and "
20: 5 Behold, to morrow is the *n'* moon, 2320
18 To morrow is the *n'* moon: and "
24 and when the *n'* moon was come, "
2Sa 6: 3 set the ark of God upon a *n'* cart, 2319
3 sons of Abinadab, drave the *n'* cart." "
21:16 he being girded with a *n'* sword, "
1Ki 11:29 had clad himself with a *n'* garment; "
30 Ahijah caught the *n'* garment that "
2Ki 2:20 Bring me a *n'* cruse, and put salt "
4:23 it is neither *n'* moon, nor sabbath. 2320
1Ch 13: 7 carried the ark of God in a *n'* cart 2319
23:31 in the *n'* moons, and on the set 2320
2Ch 2: 4 on the *n'* moons, and on the solemn "
8:13 on the *n'* moons, and on the solemn "
20: 5 of the Lord, before the *n'* court, 2319
31: 3 and for the *n'* moons, and for the 2320
Ezr 3: 5 offering, both of the *n'* moons, and "
6: 4 stones, and a row of *n'* timber: 2323
Ne 10:33 of the sabbaths, of the *n'* moons, 2320
39 offering of the corn, of the *n'* wine, 8492
13: 5 the tithes of the corn, the *n'* wine, ‡ "
12 tithe of the corn and the *n'* wine ‡ "
Job 32:19 it is ready to burst like *n'* bottles. 2319
Ps 33: 3 Sing unto him a *n'* song; play "
40: 3 hath put a *n'* song in my mouth, "
81: 3 up the trumpet in the *n'* moon, 2320
96: 1 O sing unto the Lord a *n'* song: 2319
98: 1 O sing unto the Lord a *n'* song; for "
144: 9 I will sing a *n'* song unto thee, O "
149: 1 Sing unto the Lord a *n'* song, and "
Pr 3:10 presses...burst out with *n'* wine. 8492
Ec 1: 9 there is no *n'* thing under the sun. 2319
10 it may be said, See, this is *n'*? it "
Ca 7:13 of pleasant fruits, *n'* and old, which "
Isa 1:13 the *n'* moons and sabbaths, the 2320
14 Your *n'* moons and your appointed "
24: 7 The *n'* wine mourneth, the vine 8492
41:15 a *n'* sharp threshing instrument 2319
42: 9 to pass, and *n'* things do I declare: "
10 Sing unto the Lord a *n'* song, and "
43:19 Behold, I will do a *n'* thing; now it "
48: 6 shewed thee *n'* things from this "
62: 2 thou shalt be called by a *n'* name, "
65: 8 the *n'* wine is found in the cluster, 8492
17 create *n'* heavens and a *n'* earth: 2319
66:22 as the *n'* heavens and the *n'* earth, "
23 that from one *n'* moon to another, 2320
Jer 26:10 down in the entry of the *n'* gate 2319
31:22 hath created a *n'* thing in the earth, "
31 I will make a *n'* covenant with the "
36:10 at the entry of the *n'* gate of the "
La 3:23 They are *n'* every morning: great "
Eze 11:19 I will put a *n'* spirit within you; "
18:31 make you a *n'* heart and a *n'* spirit: "
36:26 A *n'* heart also will I give you, and "
26 a *n'* spirit will I put within you: "
45:17 in the feasts, and in the *n'* moons, 2320
46: 1 day of the *n'* moon it shall be opened. "
3 the sabbaths and in the *n'* moons. "
6 in the day of the *n'* moon it shall be "
47:12 shall bring forth *n'* fruit according 1069
Ho 2:11 her feast days, her *n'* moons, and 2320
4:11 and *n'* wine take away the heart. 8492
9: 2 and the *n'* wine shall fail in her. "
Joe 1: 5 because of the *n'* wine; for it is cut *
10 the *n'* wine is dried up, the oil 8492
3:18 mountains shall drop down *n'* wine, *
Am 8: 5 When will the *n'* moon be gone, 2320
Hag 1:11 upon the *n'* wine,...upon the oil. ‡8492
Zec 9:17 cheerful, and *n'* wine the maids. "
M't 9:16 of *n'* cloth unto an old garment, for **46*
17 men put *n'* wine into old bottles: *3501*
17 they put *n'* wine into...bottles, "
17 they put...wine into *n'* bottles, **2537*
13:52 of his treasure things *n'* and old. "
26:28 this is my blood of the *n'* testament, * "
29 that day when I drink it *n'* with you " "
27:60 And laid it in his own *n'* tomb, which " "
M'r 1:27 is this? What *n'* doctrine is this? "
2:21 piece of *n'* cloth on an old garment: **46*
21 else the *n'* piece that filled it up **2537*
22 putteth *n'* wine into old bottles: *3501*
22 else the *n'* wine doth burst...bottles, * "
22 *n'* wine must be put into...bottles. *3501*
22 wine must be put into *n'* bottles. **2537*
14:24 is my blood of the *n'* testament, * "
25 I drink it *n'* in the kingdom of God. "
16:17 they shall speak with *n'* tongues; "
Lu 5:36 piece of a *n'* garment upon an old; "
36 then both the *n'* maketh a rent, and "
36 of the *n'* agreeth not with the old. "
37 putteth *n'* wine into old bottles; *3501*
37 else the *n'* wine will burst...bottles, "
38 *n'* wine must be put into...bottles; "
38 wine must be put into *n'* bottles; **2537*
39 old wine straightway desireth *n'*: "
22:20 This cup is the *n'* testament in my "
Joh 13:34 A *n'* commandment I give unto you, "
19:41 and in the garden a *n'* sepulchre, "
Ac 2:13 These men are full of *n'* wine. *1098*
17:19 we know what this *n'* doctrine, *2537*
21 to tell, or to hear some *n'* thing.) "
1Co 5: 7 that ye may be a *n'* lump, as ye *3501*
11:25 This cup is the *n'* testament in my *2537*
2Co 3: 6 able ministers of the *n'* testament; "
5:17 be in Christ, he is a *n'* creature: "
17 behold, all things are become *n'*. "
Ga 6:15 uncircumcision, but a *n'* creature. "
Eph 2:15 in himself of twain one *n'* man, "
4:24 that ye put on the *n'* man, which "
Col 2:16 or of the *n'* moon, or of the sabbath *3561*
3:10 have put on the *n'* man, which is *3501*
Heb 8: 8 I will make a *n'* covenant with the *2537*
13 A *n'* covenant, he hath made the "
9:15 the mediator of the *n'* testament, "
10:20 By a *n'* and living way, which he *4372*
12:24 the mediator of the *n'* covenant, *3501*
2Pe 3:13 look for *n'* heavens and a *n'* earth, *2537*
1Jo 2: 7 I write no *n'* commandment unto "
8 *n'* commandment I write unto you, "
2Jo 5 I wrote a *n'* commandment unto "
Re 2:17 and in the stone a *n'* name written, "
3:12 city of my God,...is *n'* Jerusalem, "
12 I will write upon him my *n'* name. "
5: 9 they sung a *n'* song, saying, Thou "
14: 3 And they sung as it were a *n'* song "
21: 1 I saw a *n'* heaven and a *n'* earth: "
2 I...saw the holy city, *n'* Jerusalem, "
5 said, Behold, I make all things *n'*. "

newborn
1Pe 2: 2 As *n'* babes, desire the sincere *738*

newly
De 32:17 new gods that came *n'* up, whom *7138
J'g 7:19 they had but *n'* set the watch: 6965

new-moon See NEW and MOON.

newness
Ro 6: 4 we also should walk in *n'* of life. *2538*
7: 6 that we should serve in *n'* of spirit, "

news
Pr 25:25 so is good *n'* from a far country. 8052

next
Ge 17:21 thee at this set time in the *n'* year. 312
Ex 12: 4 his neighbour *n'* unto his house 7138
Nu 2: 5 those that do pitch *n'* unto him shall
11:32 all that night, and all the *n'* day, 4283
27:11 his kinsman that is *n'* to him of 7138
De 21: 3 city which is *n'* unto the slain man, * "
6 city, that are *n'* unto the slain man, * "
Ru 2:20 of kin unto us, one of our *n'* kinsmen. *
1Sa 17:13 *n'* unto him Abinadab, and the 4932
23:17 Israel, I shall be *n'* unto thee;
30:17 unto the evening of the *n'* day. 4283
2Ki 6:29 I said unto her on the *n'* day, Give 312
1Ch 5:12 Joel the chief,...Shapham the *n'*, *4932
16: 5 the chief, and *n'* to him Zechariah, * "
2Ch 17:15 And *n'* to him was Jehohanan 5921, 3027
16 *n'* him was Amasiah the son of " "
18 And *n'* him was Jehozabad, and " "
28: 7 Elkanah that was *n'* to the king. 4932
31:12 and Shimei his brother was the *n'*. * "
15 and *n'* him were Eden, and 5921, 3027
Ne 3: 2 *n'* unto him builded the men of " "
2 *n'* to them builded Zaccur the " "
4 *n'*...them repaired Meremoth " "
4 *n'*...them repaired Meshullam " "
4 *n'* unto them repaired Zadok " "
5 *n'* unto them the Tekoites " "
7 *n'* unto them repaired Melatiah " "
8 *N'* unto him repaired Uzziel the " "
8 *N'*...also repaired Hananiah " "
9 *n'*...them repaired Rephaiah " "
10 *n'* unto them repaired Jedaiah " "
10 *n'* unto him repaired Hattush " "
12 *n'* unto him repaired Shallum " "
17 *N'*...him repaired Hashabiah, " "
19 And *n'* to him repaired Ezer the " "
13:13 *n'* to them was Hanan...son of " "
Es 1:14 the *n'* unto him was Carshena, 7138
10: 3 Jew was *n'* unto king Ahasuerus, 4932
Jon 4: 7 when the morning rose the *n'* day, 4283
M't 27:62 Now the *n'* day, that followed the **1887*
M'r 1:38 Let us go into the *n'* towns, that I *2192*
Lu 9:37 that on the *n'* day, when they were *1836*
Joh 1:29 *n'* day John seeth Jesus coming **1887*
35 the *n'* day after John stood, and * "
12:12 On the *n'* day much people that * "
Ac 4: 3 put them in hold unto the *n'* day: * *839*
7:26 the *n'* day he shewed himself unto **1966*
13:42 preached to them the *n'* sabbath. *3342*
44 the *n'* sabbath day came almost *2064*
14:20 *n'* day he departed with Barnabas **1887*
16:11 Samothracia,...*n'* day to Neapolis; **1966*
20:15 came the *n'* day over against Chios; * "
15 the *n'* day we arrived at Samos, *2087*
15 and the *n'* day we came to Miletus. **2192*
21: 8 the *n'* day we that were of Paul's **1887*
26 the *n'* day purifying himself with *2192*
25: 6 the *n'* day sitting on the judgment **1887*
27: 3 the *n'* day we touched at Sidon. *2087*
18 the *n'* day they lightened the ship; *1836*
28:13 we came the *n'* day to Puteoli: **1206*

Neziah (*ne-zi'-ah*)
Ezr 2:54 children of *N'*, the children of 5335
Ne 7:56 children of *N'*, the children of "

Nezib (*ne'-zib*)
Jos 15:43 Jiphtah, and Ashnah, and *N'*, 5334

Nibhaz (*nib'-haz*)
2Ki 17:31 the Avites made *N'* and Tartak, 5026

Nibshan (*nib'-shan*)
Jos 15:62 And *N'*, and the city of Salt, and 5044

Nicanor (*ni-ca'-nor*)
Ac 6: 5 Prochorus, and *N'*, and Timon, *3527*

Nicodemus (*nic-o-de'-mus*)
Joh 3: 1 a man of the Pharisees, named *N'*, *3530*
4 *N'* saith unto him, How can a man "
9 *N'* answered and said unto him, "
7:50 *N'* saith unto them, (he that came "
19:39 And there came also *N'*, which at "

Nicolaitanes (*nic-o-la'-i-tans*)
Re 2: 6 thou hatest the deeds of the *N'*, **3531*
15 that hold the doctrine of the *N'*. * "

Nicolas (*nic'-o-las*)
Ac 6: 5 and *N*· a proselyte of Antioch: *3532*
Nicopolis (*ni-cop'-o-lis*)
Tit 3:12 diligent to come unto me to *N*·: *3533*
subscr. Cretians, from *N*· of Macedonia.*"

Niger (*ni'-jur*) See also SIMEON.
Ac 13: 1 and Simeon that was called *N*·. *3526*
nigh See also NEAR.
Ge 47:29 time drew *n*· that Israel must die:*7126
Ex 3: 5 Draw not *n*· hither: put off thy "
14:10 when Pharaoh drew *n*·, the children "
24: 2 Lord: but they shall not come *n*·;* 5066
32:19 soon as he came *n*· unto the camp, 7126
34:30 they were afraid to come *n*· him. 5066
32 all the children of Israel came *n*·: "
Le 10: 3 be sanctified in them that come *n*· 7138
21: 3 sister a virgin, that is *n*· unto him, *"
21 shall come *n*· to offer the offerings 5066
21 not come *n*· to offer the bread of "
23 nor come *n*· unto the altar, because "
25:49 any that is *n*· of kin unto him of 7607
Nu 1:51 stranger that cometh *n*· shall be 7126
3:10, 38 stranger that cometh *n*· shall be "
8:19 children of Israel come *n*· unto 5066
18: 3 they shall not come *n*· the vessels 7126
4 a stranger shall not come *n*· unto "
7 stranger that cometh *n*· shall be "
22 come *n*· the tabernacle of the "
24:17 I shall behold him, but not *n*·: there "
De 1: 7 unto all the places *n*· thereunto, 7934
2:19 when thou comest *n*· over against 7126
4: 7 who hath God so *n*· unto them, as "
13: 7 *n*· unto thee, or far off from thee, "
20: 2 when ye are come *n*· unto the battle, "
10 thou comest *n*· unto a city to fight "
22: 2 if thy brother be not *n*· unto thee, "
30:14 But the word is very *n*· unto thee, "
Jos 8:11 went up, and drew *n*·, and came 5066
1Sa 17:48 came and drew *n*· to meet David, 7126
2Sa 10:13 Joab drew *n*·, and the people that 5066
11:20 approached ye so *n*· unto the city "
21 why went ye *n*· the wall? then say 5066
15: 5 any man came *n*· to him to do him 7126
1Ki 2: 1 the days of David drew *n*· that he "
8:59 be *n*· unto the Lord our God day and "
1Ch 12:40 Moreover they that were *n*· them, "
19:14 drew *n*· before the Syrians unto 5066
Es 9:20 king Ahasuerus, both *n*· and far, 7126
Ps 32: 6 they shall not come *n*· unto him. * 5060
34:18 *n*· unto them that are of a broken 7126
69:18 Draw *n*· unto my soul, and "
73: 2 gone; my steps had well *n*· slipped. 4952
85: 9 his salvation is *n*· them that fear 7138
88: 3 my life draweth *n*· unto the grave. 5060
91: 7 but it shall not come *n*· thee. 5066
10 any plague come *n*· thy dwelling. 7126
119:150 draw *n*· that follow after mischief "
145:18 *n*· unto all them that call upon him, 7138
Pr 5: 8 come not *n*· the door of her house: 7126
Ec 12: 1 nor the years draw *n*·, when thou 5060
Isa 5:19 of the Holy One of Israel draw *n*· 7126
Joe 2: 1 Lord cometh, for it is *n*· at hand; "
M't 15: 8 draweth *n*· unto me with their *1448
29 came *n*· unto the sea of Galilee; *3844*
21: 1 when they drew *n*· unto Jerusalem, *1448*
24:32 ye know that summer is *n*·: *1451*
M'r 2: 4 not come *n*· unto him for the press, "
5:11 there was *n*· unto the mountains *4314
21 him: and he was *n*· unto the sea. *3844
11: 1 And when they came *n*· to Jerusalem, "
13:29 come to pass, know that it is *n*·, *1451*
Lu 7:12 when he came *n*· to the gate of *1448
10: 9, 11 kingdom of God is come *n*· unto "
15:25 as he came and drew *n*· to the house, "
18:35 as he was come *n*· unto Jericho, "
19:11 because he was *n*· to Jerusalem, *1451*
29 when he was come *n*· to Bethphage *1448*
37 when he was come *n*·, even now at "
21:20 that the desolation thereof is *n*·. * "
28 for your redemption draweth *n*·. "
30 that summer is now *n*· at hand. *1451*
31 the kingdom of God is *n*· at hand. "
22: 1 feast of unleavened bread drew *n*·, *1448*
24:28 And they drew *n*· unto the village, "
Joh 6: 4 a feast of the Jews, was *n*·. *1451
19 sea, and drawing *n*· unto the ship: "
23 *n*· unto the place where they did "
11:18 Bethany was *n*· unto Jerusalem, "
55 the Jews' passover was *n*· at hand:*"
19:20 Jesus was crucified...*n*· to the city: "
42 for the sepulchre was *n*· at hand. "
Ac 7:17 the time of the promise drew *n*·, *1448*
9:38 as Lydda was *n*· to Joppa, and the *1451*
10: 9 drew *n*· unto the city, Peter went *1448*
22: 6 was come *n*· unto Damascus about "
27: 8 *n*· whereunto was the city of Lasea. *1451*
Ro 10: 8 The word is *n*· thee, even in thy "
Eph 2:13 are made *n*· by the blood of Christ. "
17 afar off, and to them that were *n*·. "
Ph'p 2:27 indeed he was sick *n*· unto death: *3897*
30 work of Christ he was *n*· unto death, *1448*
Heb 6: 8 rejected, and is *n*· unto cursing; *1451*
7:19 by the which we draw *n*· unto God. *1448*
Jas 4: 8 Draw *n*· to God, and he will draw *n*·"
5: 8 the coming of the Lord draweth *n*·.*"

night See also MIDNIGHT; NIGHTS; YESTERNIGHT.
Ge 1: 5 and the darkness he called *N*·. 3915
14 to divide the day from the *n*·; and "
16 the lesser light to rule the *n*·: he "
18 to rule over the day and over the *n*·, "
8:22 and day and *n*· shall not cease. "
14:15 he and his servants, by *n*·, and smote "
19: 2 tarry all *n*·, and wash your feet, and ye "
2 but we will abide in the street all *n*·. "
Ge 19: 5 men which came in to thee this *n*·? 3915
33 made their father drink wine that *n*·: "
34 make him drink wine this *n*· also; "
35 made their father drink wine that *n*· "
20: 3 came to Abimelech in a dream by *n*·, "
24:54 that were with him, and tarried all *n*·; "
26:24 appeared unto him the same *n*·, 3915
28:11 tarried there all *n*·, because the sun "
30:15 Therefore he shall lie with thee to *n*· 3915
16 And he lay with her that *n*·. "
31:24 Laban the Syrian in a dream by *n*·, "
39 stolen by day, or stolen by *n*·. "
40 consumed me, and the frost by *n*·; "
54 bread, and tarried all *n*· in the mount. "
32:13 And he lodged there that same *n*·; 3915
21 lodged that *n*· in the company. "
22 he rose up that *n*·, and took his two "
40: 5 each man his dream in one *n*·, each "
41:11 And we dreamed a dream in one *n*·, "
46: 2 God spake...in the visions of the *n*·, "
49:27 and at *n*· he shall divide the spoil.*6153
Ex 10:13 land all that day, and all that *n*·; 3915
12: 8 they shall eat the flesh in that *n*·, "
12 through the land of Egypt this *n*·, "
30 And Pharaoh rose up in the *n*·, he, "
31 called for Moses and Aaron by *n*·, "
42 It is a *n*· to be much observed unto "
42 that *n*· of the Lord to be observed "
13:21 by *n*· in a pillar of fire, to give "
21 them light; to go by day and *n*·; "
22 by day, nor the pillar of fire by *n*·, "
14:20 it gave light by *n*· to these: so that "
20 came not near the other all the *n*·. "
21 by a strong east wind all that *n*·, "
40:38 and fire was on it by *n*·, in the sight "
Le 6: 9 the burning upon the altar all *n*· "
20 morning, and half thereof at *n*·. 6153
8:35 day and *n*· seven days, and keep 3915
11:16 And the owl, and the *n*· hawk, and 8464
19:13 abide with thee all *n*· until...morning. 3915
Nu 9:16 and the appearance of fire by *n*·. 3915
21 whether it was by day or by *n*· that "
11: 9 dew fell upon the camp in the *n*·, "
32 up all that day, and all that *n*·, and "
14: 1 cried; and the people wept that *n*·. "
14 cloud, and in a pillar of fire by *n*·. "
22: 8 said unto them, Lodge here this *n*·, "
19 tarry ye also here this *n*·, that I "
20 And God came unto Balaam at *n*·, "
De 1:33 in fire by *n*·, to shew you by what "
14:15 the owl, and the *n*· hawk, and the 8464
16: 1 thee forth out of Egypt by *n*·. 3915
4 even, remain all *n*· until the morning. "
21:23 shall not remain all *n*· upon the tree, "
23:10 that chanceth him by *n*·, then 3915
28:66 and thou shalt fear day and *n*·, and "
Jos 1: 8 shalt meditate therein day and *n*·, "
2: 2 there came men in hither to *n*· of "
4: 3 place, where ye shall lodge this *n*·. "
8: 3 valour, and sent them away by *n*·. "
9 Joshua lodged that *n*· among the "
13 Joshua went that *n*· into the midst "
10: 9 and went up from Gilgal all *n*·. "
J'g 6:25 And it came to pass the same *n*·, "
27 do it by day, that he did it by *n*·. "
40 And God did so that *n*·: for it was "
7: 9 And it came to pass the same *n*·, "
9:32 Now therefore up by *n*·, thou and "
34 people that were with him, by *n*·, "
16: 2 laid wait for him all *n*· in the gate "
2 and were quiet all the *n*·, saying, "
19: 6 content, I pray thee, and tarry all *n*·, "
9 evening, I pray you tarry all *n*·: "
10 But the man would not tarry that *n*·, "
13 to one of these places to lodge all *n*·, "
25 and abused her all the *n*· until 3915
20: 5 house round about upon me by *n*·, "
Ru 1:12 I should have an husband also to *n*·, "
3: 2 he winnoweth barley to *n*· in the "
13 Tarry this *n*·, and it shall be in "
1Sa 14:34 every man his ox with him that *n*·, "
36 go down after the Philistines by *n*·, "
15:11 and he cried unto the Lord all *n*·. "
16 the Lord hath said to me this *n*·. "
19:10 and David fled, and escaped that *n*·. "
11 If thou save not thy life to *n*·, to "
24 naked all that day and all that *n*·. "
25:16 a wall unto us both by *n*· and day, "
26: 7 Abishai came to the people by *n*·: "
28: 8 and they came to the woman by *n*·: "
20 no bread all the day, nor all the *n*·. "
25 rose up, and went away that *n*·. "
31:12 valiant men arose, and went all *n*·, "
2Sa 2:29 and his men walked all that *n*· "
32 And Joab and his men went all *n*·, "
4: 7 them away through the plain all *n*·. "
7: 4 And it came to pass that *n*·, that "
12:16 went in, and lay all *n*· upon the earth. "
17: 1 and pursue after David this *n*·: 3915
16 Lodge not this *n*· in the plains of "
19: 7 not tarry one with thee this *n*·: "
21:10 day, nor the beasts of the field by *n*·. "
1Ki 3: 5 to Solomon in a dream by *n*·: and "
19 this woman's child died in the *n*·; "
8:29 open toward this house *n*· and day, "
59 unto the Lord our God day and *n*·, "
2Ki 6:14 they came by *n*·, and compassed "
7:12 the king arose in the *n*·, and said "
8:21 and he arose by *n*·, and smote the "
19:35 it came to pass that *n*·, that the "
25: 4 all the men of war fled by *n*· by the "
1Ch 9:33 employed in that work day and *n*·. "
17: 3 it came to pass the same *n*·, that "
2Ch 1: 7 In that *n*· did God appear unto "
6:20 open upon this house day and *n*·, "
7:12 Lord appeared to Solomon by *n*·. "
2Ch 21: 9 he rose up by *n*·, and smote the 3915
35:14 burnt offerings and the fat until *n*·; "
Ne 1: 6 I pray before thee now, day and *n*·, "
2:12 I arose in the *n*·, I and some few "
13 I went out by *n*· by the gate of the "
15 went I up in the *n*· by the brook, "
4: 9 a watch against them day and *n*·, "
22 in the *n*· they may be a guard to us, "
6:10 in the *n*· will they come to slay "
9:12 in the *n*· by a pillar of fire, to give "
19 neither the pillar of fire by *n*·, to "
Es 4:16 eat nor drink three days, *n*· or day: "
6: 1 On that *n*· could not the king sleep, "
Job 3: 3 the *n*· in which it was said, There "
6 As for that *n*·, let darkness seize "
7 let that *n*· be solitary, let no joyful "
4:13 thoughts from the visions of the *n*·, "
5:14 grope in the noonday as in the *n*·. "
7: 4 shall I arise, and the *n*· be gone? 6153
17:12 They change the *n*· into day: the 3915
20: 8 chased away as a vision of the *n*·. "
24:14 needy, and in the *n*· is as a thief. "
26:10 the day and *n*· come to an end. *2822
27:20 stealeth him away in the *n*·. 3915
29:19 the dew lay all *n*· upon my branch. "
30:17 bones are pierced in me in the *n*· 3915
33:15 In a dream, in a vision of the *n*·, "
34:25 and he overturneth them in the *n*·, "
35:10 maker, who giveth songs in the *n*·; "
36:20 Desire not the *n*·, when people are "
Ps 1: 2 law doth he meditate day and *n*·. "
6: 6 all the *n*· make I my bed to swim; "
16: 7 also instruct me in the *n*· seasons. "
17: 3 thou hast visited me in the *n*·; thou "
19: 2 and *n*· unto *n*· sheweth knowledge. "
22: 2 and in the *n*· season, and am not "
30: 5 weeping may endure for a *n*·, but 6153
32: 4 day and *n*· thy hand was heavy 3915
42: 3 have been my meat day and *n*·, "
8 in the *n*· his song shall be with "
55:10 Day and *n*· they go about it upon "
74:16 day is thine, the *n*· also is thine: "
77: 2 my sore ran in the *n*·, and ceased "
6 to remembrance my song in the *n*·: "
78:14 and all the *n*· with a light of fire. "
88: 1 I have cried day and *n*· before thee: "
90: 4 is past, and as a watch in the *n*·. "
91: 5 not be afraid for the terror by *n*·; "
92: 2 and thy faithfulness every *n*·, "
104:20 Thou makest darkness, and it is *n*·: "
105:39 and fire to give light in the *n*·. "
119:55 O Lord, in the *n*·, and have kept "
148 Mine eyes prevent the *n*· watches, "
121: 6 thee by day, nor the moon by *n*·. 3915
134: 1 which by *n*· stand in the house of "
136: 9 The moon and stars to rule by *n*·: "
139:11 even the *n*· shall be light about me. "
12 thee; but the *n*· shineth as the day: "
Pr 7: 9 evening, in the black and dark *n*·: "
31:15 She riseth also while it is yet *n*·, "
18 her candle goeth not out by *n*·. "
Ec 2:23 his heart taketh not rest in the *n*·. "
8:16 neither day nor *n*· seeth sleep with "
Ca 1:13 he shall lie all *n*· betwixt my breasts.* "
3: 1 By *n*· on my bed I sought him 3915
8 his thigh because of fear in the *n*·. "
5: 2 my locks with the drops of the *n*·. "
Isa 4: 5 the shining of a flaming fire by *n*·: "
5:11 that continue until *n*·, till wine 5399
15: 1 in the *n*· Ar of Moab is laid waste, 3915
1 in the *n*· Kir of Moab is laid waste, "
16: 3 make thy shadow as the *n*· in the "
21: 4 the *n*· of my pleasure hath he *5399
11, 11 Watchman, what of the *n*·? 3915
12 morning cometh, and also the *n*·: "
26: 9 soul have I desired thee in the *n*·; "
27: 3 hurt it, I will keep it *n*· and day. "
28:19 it pass over, by day and by *n*·: "
29: 7 shall be as a dream of a *n*· vision. "
30:29 Ye shall have a song, as in the *n*· "
34:10 shall not be quenched *n*· nor day; "
38:12, 13 from day even to *n*· wilt thou "
59:10 stumble at noon day as in the *n*·; *5399
60:11 they shall not be shut day nor *n*·; 3915
62: 6 never hold their peace day nor *n*·: "
Jer 6: 5 Arise, and let us go by *n*·, and let "
9: 1 that I might weep day and *n*· for "
14: 8 that turneth aside to tarry for a *n*·? "
17 run down with tears *n*· and day, 3915
16:13 shall ye serve other gods day and *n*·; "
31:35 and of the stars for a light by *n*·, "
33:20 and my covenant of the *n*·, and that "
20 not be day and *n*· in their seasons; "
25 my covenant be not with day and *n*·, "
36:30 the heat, and in the *n*· to the frost. "
39: 4 and went forth out of the city by *n*·, "
49: 9 if thieves by *n*·, they will destroy "
52: 7 went forth out of the city by *n*· by "
La 1: 2 She weepeth sore in the *n*·, and her "
2:18 run down like a river day and *n*·: "
19 Arise, cry out in the *n*·: in the "
Da 2:19 revealed unto Daniel in a *n*· vision. 3916
5:30 In that *n*· was Belshazzar the king "
6:18 palace, and passed the *n*· fasting: 956
7: 2 I was in my vision by *n*·, and, 3916
7 After this I saw in the *n*· visions, "
13 I saw in the *n*· visions, and, behold, "
Ho 4: 5 also shall fall with thee in the *n*·, 3915
7: 6 their baker sleepeth all the *n*·; in "
Joe 1:13 lie all *n*· in sackcloth, ye ministers of "
Am 5: 8 and maketh the day dark with *n*·: 3915
Ob 5 thieves came to thee, if robbers by *n*·, "
Jon 4:10 up in a *n*·, and perished in a *n*·: "
Mic 3: 6 Therefore *n*· shall be unto you, "
Zec 1: 8 I saw by *n*·, and behold a man "
14: 7 not day, nor *n*·: but it shall come "

M't 2:14 young child and his mother by n'. 3571
14:25 in the fourth watch of the n' Jesus "
26:31 be offended because of me this n': "
34 That this n', before the cock crow, "
27:64 his disciples come by n', and steal* "
28:13 Say ye, His disciples came by n', "
M'r 4:27 should sleep, and rise n' and day, "
5: 5 always, n' and day, he was in the "
6:48 about the fourth watch of the n' he "
14:27 be offended because of me this n':* "
30 thee, That this day, even in this n', "
Lu 2: 8 keeping watch over their flock by n'. "
37 fastings and prayers n' and day. "
5: 5 we have toiled all the n', and have "
6:12 continued all n' in prayer to God. 1273
12:20 this n' thy soul shall be required 3571
17:34 in that n' there shall be two men "
18: 7 which cry day and n' unto him, "
21:37 at n' he went out, and abode in the "
Joh 3: 2 same came to Jesus by n', and said "
7:50 (he that came to Jesus by n', being* "
9: 4 the n' cometh, when no man can "
11:10 But if a man walk in the n', he "
13:30 immediately out: and it was n'. "
19:39 at the first came to Jesus by n', and "
21: 3 and that n' they caught nothing. "
Ac 5:19 angel...by n' opened the prison "
9:24 watched the gates day and n' to "
25 Then the disciples took him by n', "
12: 6 the same n' Peter was sleeping "
16: 9 vision appeared to Paul in the n'; "
33 took them the same hour of the n', "
17:10 sent away Paul and Silas by n' unto "
18: 9 spake the Lord to Paul in the n' by "
20:31 not to warn every one n' and day "
23:11 the n' following the Lord stood by "
23 hundred, at the third hour of the n'; "
31 brought him by n' to Antipatris. "
26: 7 serving God day and n', hope to "
27:23 there stood by me this n' the angel "
27 when the fourteenth n' was come, "
Ro 13:12 The n' is far spent, the day is at "
1Co 11:23 same n' in which he was betrayed "
2Co 11:25 a n' and a day I have been in the 3574
1Th 2: 9 labouring n' and day, because we 3571
3:10 N' and day praying exceedingly "
5: 2 Lord so cometh as a thief in the n'. "
5 we are not of the n', nor of darkness. "
7 For they that sleep sleep in the n'; "
7 be drunken are drunken in the n'. "
2Th 3: 8 with labour and travail n' and day, "
1Ti 5: 5 supplications and prayers n' and "
2Ti 1: 3 of thee in my prayers n' and day; "
2Pe 3:10 Lord will come as a thief in the n';* "
Re 4: 8 they rest not day and n', saying, "
7:15 serve him day and n' in his temple: "
8:12 third part of it, and the n' likewise. "
12:10 them before our God day and n'. "
14:11 they have no rest day nor n', who "
20:10 be tormented day and n' for ever "
21:25 day: for there shall be no n' there. "
22: 5 And there shall be no n' there; and "

night-hawk See NIGHT and HAWK.

nights
Ge 7: 4 the earth forty days and forty n'; 3915
12 the earth forty days and forty n'. "
Ex 24:18 the mount forty days and forty n'. "
34:28 the Lord forty days and forty n'; "
De 9: 9 the mount forty days and forty n', "
11 the end of forty days and forty n', "
18 at the first, forty days and forty n': "
25 the Lord forty days and forty n', "
10:10 first time, forty days and forty n'; "
1Sa 30:12 any water, three days and three n'. "
1Ki 19: 8 of that meat forty days and forty n' "
Job 2:13 ground seven days and seven n', "
7: 3 wearisome n' are appointed to me. "
Isa 21: 8 and I am set in my ward whole n': "
Jon 1:17 of the fish three days and three n'. "
M't 4: 2 had fasted forty days and forty n', 3571
12:40 and three n' in the whale's belly; "
40 three n' in the heart of the earth. "

night-vision See NIGHT and VISION.

night-watches See NIGHT and WATCHES.

Nimrah (nim'-rah) See also BETH-NIMRAH.
Nu 32: 3 N', and Heshbon, and Elealeh, 5247

Nimrim (nim'-rim)
Isa 15: 6 the waters of N' shall be desolate: 5249
Jer 48:34 waters also of N' shall be desolate. "

Nimrod (nim'-rod)
Ge 10: 8 Cush begat N': he began to be a 5248
9 N' the mighty hunter before the "
1Ch 1:10 Cush begat N': he began to be "
Mic 5: 6 land of N' in the entrances thereof: "

Nimshi (nim'-shi)
1Ki 19:16 the son of N' shalt thou anoint 5250
2Ki 9: 2 son of Jehoshaphat the son of N', "
14 son of Jehoshaphat the son of N' "
20 the driving of Jehu the son of N'; "
2Ch 22: 7 against Jehu the son of N', whom "

nine See also NINETEEN.
Ge 5: 5 that Adam lived were n' hundred 8672
8 of Seth were n' hundred and twelve "
11 of Enos were n' hundred and five "
14 of Cainan were n' hundred and ten "
20 of Jared were n' hundred sixty and "
27 were n' hundred sixty and n' years: "
9:29 of Noah were n' hundred and fifty "
11:19 Reu two hundred and n' years, and "
24 Nahor lived n' and twenty years, "
17: 1 Abram was ninety years old and n', "
24 Abraham was ninety years...and n', "
Ex 38:24 offering, was twenty and n' talents, 8672
Le 25: 8 be unto thee forty and n' years. "
Nu 1:23 Simeon, were fifty and n' thousand "
2:13 fifty and n' thousand and three "
29:26 And on the fifth day n' bullocks, "
34:13 to give unto the n' tribes, and to "
De 3:11 n' cubits was the length thereof, "
Jos 13: 7 an inheritance unto the n' tribes, "
14: 2 for the n' tribes, and for the half "
15:32 the cities are twenty and n', with "
44 n' cities with their villages. "
54 Zior; n' cities with their villages. "
21:16 n' cities out of those two tribes. "
J'g 4: 3 he had n' hundred chariots of iron; "
13 even n' hundred chariots of iron, "
2Sa 24: 8 Jerusalem at the end of n' months "
2Ki 14: 2 and reigned twenty and n' years in "
15:13 the n' and thirtieth year of Uzziah "
17 n' and thirtieth year of Azariah "
17: 1 in Samaria over Israel n' years. "
18: 2 he reigned twenty and n' years in "
1Ch 3: 8 and Eliada, and Eliphelet, n'. "
9: 9 n' hundred and fifty and six. "
2Ch 25: 1 he reigned twenty and n' years in "
29: 1 he reigned n' and twenty years in "
Ezr 1: 9 of silver, n' and twenty knives, "
2: 8 of Zattu, n' hundred forty and five. "
36 n' hundred seventy and three. "
42 in all an hundred thirty and n'. "
Ne 7:38 thousand n' hundred and thirty. "
39 n' hundred seventy and three. "
11: 1 and n' parts to dwell in other cities. "
8 Sallai, n' hundred twenty and eight. "
M't 18:12 he not leave the ninety and n', and 1768
13 and n' which went not astray. "
Lu 15: 4 ninety and n' in the wilderness, "
7 over ninety and n' just persons, "
17:17 ten cleansed? but where are the n'? 1767

nine hundred See NINE and HUNDRED.

nineteen
Ge 11:25 an hundred and n' years, 8672,6240
Jos 19:38 n' cities with their villages. " "
2Sa 2:30 of David's servants n' men and " "

nineteenth
2Ki 25: 8 which is the n' year of king 8672,6240
1Ch 24:16 The n' to Pethahiah, the " "
25:26 The n' to Mallothi, he, his sons, " "
Jer 52:12 the n' year of Nebuchadrezzar " "

ninety
Gen 5: 9 Enos lived n' years, and begat 8673
17 eight hundred n' and five years: "
30 Noah five hundred n' and five years, "
17: 1 when Abram was n' years old and "
17 Sarah, that is n' years old, bear? "
24 Abraham was n' years old and nine, "
1Sa 4:15 Now Eli was n' and eight years old; "
1Ch 9: 6 their brethren, six hundred and n'. "
Ezr 2:16 of Ater of Hezekiah, n' and eight. "
20 The children of Gibbar, n' and five. "
58 were three hundred n' and two. "
8:35 for all Israel, n' and six rams, "
Ne 7:21 of Ater of Hezekiah, n' and eight. "
25 The children of Gibeon, n' and five. "
60 were three hundred n' and two. "
Jer 52:23 there were n' and six pomegranates "
Eze 4: 5 days, three hundred and n' days: "
9 hundred and n' days shalt thou eat "
41:12 and the length thereof n' cubits. "
Da 12:11 thousand two hundred and n' days. "
M't 18:12 doth he not leave the n' and nine, 1768
13 n' and nine which went not astray. "
Lu 15: 4 doth not leave the n' and nine in "
7 than over n' and nine just persons, "

Nineve (nin'-e-ve) See also NINEVEH; NINEVITES.
Lu 11:32 The men of N' shall rise up in *3535

Nineveh (nin'-e-veh) See also NINEVE.
Ge 10:11 forth Asshur, and builded N', and 5210
12 And Resen between N' and Calah: "
2Ki 19:36 and returned, and dwelt at N'. "
Isa 37:37 and returned, and dwelt at N'. "
Jon 1: 2 go to N', that great city, and cry "
3: 2 Arise, go unto N', that great city, "
3 So Jonah arose, and went unto N', "
3 N' was an exceeding great city of "
4 days, and N' shall be overthrown. "
5 So the people of N' believed God, "
6 word came unto the king of N', and "
7 published through N' by the decree "
4:11 should not I spare N', that great "
Na 1: 1 The burden of N'. The book of the "
2: 8 N' is of old like a pool of water: "
3: 7 thee, and say, N' is laid waste: "
Zep 2:13 will make N' a desolation, and dry "
M't 12:41 men of N' shall rise in judgment 3536

Ninevites (nin'-e-vites)
Lu 11:30 as Jonas was a sign unto the N', 3536

ninth
Le 23:32 in the n' day of the month at even, 8672
25:22 yet of old fruit until the n' year; 8671
Nu 7:60 On the n' day Abidan the son of "
2Ki 17: 6 In the n' year of Hoshea the king "
18:10 is the n' year of Hoshea king of 8672
25: 1 to pass in the n' year of his reign, 8671
3 on the n' day of the fourth month 8672
1Ch 12:12 the eighth, Elzabad the n', 8671
24:11 The n' to Jeshuah, the tenth to "
25:16 The n' to Mattaniah, he, his sons, "
27:12 The n' captain for the n' month was "
2Ch 16:12 Asa in the thirty and n' year of 8672
Ezr 10: 9 It was the n' month, on the 8671
Jer 36: 9 king of Judah, in the n' month "
Jer 36:22 in the winterhouse in the n' month: 8671
39: 1 In the n' year of Zedekiah king of "
2 the n' day of the month, the city 8672
52: 4 to pass in the n' year of his reign, 8671
6 in the n' day of the month, the 8672
Eze 24: 1 Again in the n' year, in the tenth 8671
Hag 2:10, 18 twentieth day of the n' month, "
Zec 7: 1 in the fourth day of the n' month, "
M't 20: 5 out about the sixth and n' hour, 1766
27:45 over all the land unto the n' hour. "
46 the n' hour Jesus cried with a loud "
M'r 15:33 the whole land until the n' hour. "
34 the n' hour Jesus cried with a loud "
Lu 23:44 over all the earth until the n' hour. "
Ac 3: 1 hour of prayer, being the n' hour. "
10: 3 vision evidently about the n' hour "
30 and at the n' hour I prayed in my "
Re 21:20 the eighth, beryl; the n', a topaz; "

Nisan (ni'-san) See also ABIB.
Ne 2: 1 it came to pass in the month N', 5212
Es 3: 7 first month, that is, the month N', "

Nisroch (nis'-rok)
2Ki 19:37 worshipping in the house of N' 5268
Isa 37:38 worshipping in the house of N' "

Nissi See JEHOVAH-NISSI.

nitre
Pr 25:20 as vinegar upon n', so is he that 5427
Jer 2:22 though thou wash thee with n', * "

no See also NAY; NONE; NOTHING.
Ge 8: 9 dove found n' rest for the sole of 3808
9:15 waters shall n' more become a flood "
11:30 Sarai was barren; she had n' child. 369
13: 8 unto Lot, Let there be n' strife, 408
15: 3 to me thou hast given n' seed: and, 3808
16: 1 Abram's wife bare him n' children: "
26:29 That thou wilt do us n' hurt, as we "
30: 1 that she bare Jacob n' children, 369
31:50 my daughters, n' man is with us; 3808
32:28 name shall be called n' more Jacob, "
37:22 said unto them, Shed n' blood, but "
22 and lay n' hand upon him; that he "
24 was empty, there was n' water in it. "
32 whether it be thy son's coat or n'. * "
38:21 There was n' harlot in this place. "
22 there was n' harlot in this place. "
26 And he knew her again n' more. "
40: 8 and there is n' interpreter of it. * 369
41:44 thee shall n' man lift up his hand 3808
42:11 true men, thy servants are n' spies. "
31 We are true men; we are n' spies: "
34 shall I know that ye are n' spies, "
44:23 you, ye shall see my face n' more. "
45: 1 there stood n' man with him, while "
47: 4 have n' pasture for their flocks; 369
13 there was n' bread in all the land; "
Ex 2:12 when he saw that there was n' man, "
3:19 you go, n', not by a mighty hand. 3808
5: 7 n' more give the people straw to "
16 is n' straw given unto thy servants, 369
18 there shall n' straw be given you, 3808
8:22 that n' swarms of flies shall be 1115
9:26 of Israel were, was there n' hail. 3808
28 be n' more mighty thunderings and* "
28 you go, and ye shall stay n' longer. "
10:14 there were n' such locusts as they, "
28 heed to thyself, see my face n' more; "
29 I will see thy face again n' more. "
12:16 n' manner of work shall be done in "
19 be n' leaven found in your houses: "
43 there shall n' stranger eat thereof: "
48 n' uncircumcised person shall eat "
13: 3 shall n' leavened bread be eaten. "
7 n' leavened bread be seen with thee, "
14:11 there were n' graves in Egypt, hast 369
13 see them again n' more for ever. 3808
15:22 wilderness, and found n' water. "
16: 4 they will walk in my law, or n'. "
18 he that gathered little had n' lack; "
19 n' man leave of it till the morning. 408
29 n' man go out of his place on the "
17: 1 n' water for the people to drink. 369
20: 3 have n' other gods before me. *3808
21: 8 strange nation...shall have n' power, "
22 her, and yet n' mischief follow: "
22: 2 there shall n' blood be shed for him. 369
10 or driven away, n' man seeing it: "
23: 8 And thou shalt take n' gift: for 3808
13 make n' mention of the name of "
32 shalt make n' covenant with them, "
30: 9 offer n' strange incense thereon, "
12 there be n' plague among them, "
33: 4 and n' man did put on him his "
20 for there shall n' man see me, and* "
34: 3 n' man shall come up with thee, "
7 will by n' means clear the guilty; "
14 thou shalt worship n' other god: "
17 shalt make thee n' molten gods. "
35: 3 shall kindle n' fire throughout your "
Le 2:11 N' meat offering, which ye shall "
11 for ye shall burn n' leaven, nor any "
5:11 he shall put n' oil upon it, neither "
6:30 And n' sin offering, whereof any of "
7:23 ye shall eat n' manner of fat, of ox, "
24 use: but ye shall in n' wise eat of it. "
26 ye shall eat n' manner of blood, "
11:12 Whatsoever hath n' fins or scales 369
12: 4 she shall touch n' hallowed thing, 3808
13:21 there be n' white hairs therein, and 369
26 be n' white hair in the bright spot, "
26 it be n' lower than the other skin, "
31 and that there is n' black hair in it; "
32 and there be in it n' yellow hair, 3808
16:17 shall be n' man in the tabernacle "
29 do n' work at all, whether it be one "

Le 17: 7 shall *n'* more offer their sacrifices 3808
12 *N'* soul of you shall eat blood, "
14 eat the blood of *n'* manner of flesh: "
19: 15, 35 Ye shall do *n'* unrighteousness "
20: 14 there be *n'* wickedness among you. "
21: 3 him, which hath had *n'* husband: "
22: 10 *n'* stranger eat of the holy thing: "
13 or divorced, and have *n'* child, and 369
13 there shall *n'* stranger eat thereof. 3808
21 there shall be *n'* blemish therein. "
23: 3 ye shall do *n'* work therein: it is the "
7, 8, 21 ye shall do *n'* servile work 3605, "
25 Ye shall do *n'* servile work "
28 shall do *n'* work in that same day: "
31 Ye shall do *n'* manner of work: it "
35, 36 ye shall do *n'* servile work 3605, "
25: 31 which have *n'* wall round about 369
36 Take thou *n'* usury of him, or 408
26: 1 you *n'* idols nor graven image, 3808
37 have *n'* power to stand before your "
27: 26 firstling, *n'* man shall sanctify it; "
28 *n'* devoted thing...shall be sold 3605, "
Nu 1: 53 be *n'* wrath upon the congregation "
3: 4 of Sinai, and they had *n'* children: "
5: 8 have *n'* kinsmen to recompense the 369
13 and there be *n'* witness against her. "
15 he shall pour *n'* oil upon it, nor 3808
19 If *n'* man have lain with thee, and "
6: 3 shall drink *n'* vinegar of wine, or "
5 shall *n'* rasor come upon his head: "
6 Lord...shall come at *n'* dead body.* "
8: 19 be *n'* plague among the children of "
25 thereof, and shall serve *n'* more: "
26 the charge, and shall do *n'* service. "
14: 18 by *n'* means clearing the guilty. "
16: 40 that *n'* stranger, which is not of the "
18: 5 be *n'* wrath any more upon the "
20 have *n'* inheritance in their land, "
23 of Israel they have *n'* inheritance. "
24 they shall have *n'* inheritance. "
32 ye shall bear *n'* sin by reason of it, "
19: 2 without spot, wherein is *n'* blemish, 369
15 hath *n'* covering bound upon it, is "
20: 5 it is *n'* place of seed, or of figs, or 3808
21: 5 there is *n'* bread, neither is there 369
22: 26 where was *n'* way to turn either to "
23: 23 there is *n'* enchantment against 3808
26: 33 the son of Hepher had *n'* sons, but "
62 was *n'* inheritance given them "
27: 3 in his own sin, and had *n'* sons. "
4 family, because he hath *n'* son? 369
8 If a man die, and have *n'* son, then "
9 And if he have *n'* daughter, then ye "
10 And if he have *n'* brethren, then ye "
11 And if his father have *n'* brethren, "
17 as sheep which have *n'* shepherd. "
28: 18 shall do *n'* manner of servile work 3808
25 ye shall do *n'* servile work. 3605, "
26 ye shall do *n'* servile work: "
29: 1 ye shall do *n'* servile work: it is "
12 ye shall do *n'* servile work, and "
35 ye shall do *n'* servile work "
33: 14 was *n'* water for the people to drink. "
35: 31 shall take *n'* satisfaction for the life "
32 ye shall take *n'* satisfaction for him "
De 1: 39 *n'* knowledge between good and evil, "
2: 5 *n'*, not so much as a foot breadth; "
3: 26 speak *n'* more unto me of this 408
4: 12 the words, but saw *n'* similitude; 369
15 ye saw *n'* manner of similitude on 3808
5: 22 great voice: and he added *n'* more. "
7: 2 shalt make *n'* covenant with them, "
16 eye shall have *n'* pity upon them:* "
24 there shall *n'* man be able to stand "
8: 2 keep his commandments, or *n'*. "
15 drought, where there was *n'* water; 369
10: 9 Levi hath *n'* part nor inheritance 3808
16 heart, and be *n'* more stiffnecked. "
11: 17 that there be *n'* rain, and that the "
25 *n'* man shall be able to stand before "
12: 12 as he hath *n'* part nor inheritance 369
13: 11 do *n'* more any such wickedness 3808
14: 27, 29 he hath *n'* part nor inheritance 369
15: 4 there shall be *n'* poor among you; 3808
19 do *n'* work with the firstling of thy "
16: 3 Thou shalt eat *n'* leavened bread "
4 shall be *n'* leavened bread seen "
8 God: thou shalt do *n'* work therein. "
17: 13 and do *n'* more presumptuously. "
16 henceforth return *n'* more that way. "
18: 1 the tribe of Levi, shall have *n'* part "
2 they have *n'* inheritance among "
19: 20 commit *n'* more any such evil "
20: 12 if it will make *n'* peace with thee, "
21: 14 be, if thou have *n'* delight in her, "
22: 26 the damsel *n'* sin worthy of death: 369
23: 14 he see *n'* unclean thing in thee, 3808
17 be *n'* whore of the daughters of "
22 to vow, it shall be *n'* sin in thee. "
24: 1 that she find *n'* favour in his eyes, "
6 *N'* man shall take the nether or the "
25: 5 one of them die, and have *n'* child, 369
28: 26 and *n'* man shall fray them away.* "
29 and *n'* man shall save thee. * "
32 shall be *n'* might in thine hand. * "
65 nations shalt thou find *n'* ease, 3808
68 Thou shalt see it *n'* more again: "
68 and *n'* man shall buy you. 369
31: 2 I can *n'* more go out and come in: 3808
32: 12 there was *n'* strange god with him. 369
20 children in whom is *n'* faith. 3808
39 am he, and there is *n'* god with me: 369
34: 6 *n'* man knoweth of his sepulchre 3808
Jos 8: 20 they had *n'* power to flee this way "
31 which *n'* man hath lift up any iron: "
10: 14 there was *n'* day like that before it "

Jos 11: 20 that they might have *n'* favour, 1115
14: 4 they gave *n'* part unto the Levites 3808
17: 3 the son of Manasseh, had *n'* sons, "
18: 7 Levites have *n'* part among you; "
22: 25 Gad; ye have *n'* part in the Lord: 369
27 come, Ye have *n'* part in the Lord. "
23: 9 *n'* man hath been able to stand 3808
13 God will *n'* more drive out any of "
J'g 2: 2 *n'* league with the inhabitants of "
4: 20 man here? that thou shalt say, *N'*. 369
5: 19 they took *n'* gain of money. 3808
6: 4 and left *n'* sustenance for Israel, "
8: 28 they lifted up their heads *n'* more. "
10: 13 I will deliver you *n'* more. "
11: 39 had vowed; and she knew *n'* man.‡ "
13: 5 *n'* rasor shall come on his head: "
7 now drink *n'* wine nor strong drink, 408
21 of the Lord did *n'* more appear 3808
15: 13 they spake unto him, saying, *N'*; "
17: 6 days there was *n'* king in Israel, 369
18: 1 there was *n'* king in Israel: and in "
7 was *n'* magistrate in the land, that "
7 and had *n'* business with any man. "
10 where there is *n'* want of any thing "
28 And there was *n'* deliverer, because "
28 had *n'* business with any man; and "
19: 1 when there was *n'* king in Israel, "
15 was *n'* man that took them into his "
18 *n'* man that receiveth me to house. "
19 there is *n'* want of any thing. "
30 *n'* such deed done nor seen from 3808
21: 12 virgins, that had known *n'* man by "
25 days there was *n'* king in Israel; 369
1Sa 1: 2 but Hannah had *n'* children. "
11 shall *n'* rasor come upon his head. 3808
15 answered and said, *N'*, my lord, "
18 her countenance was *n'* more sad. "
2: 3 Talk *n'* more so exceeding proudly; 408
9 by strength shall *n'* man prevail. 3808
24 for it is *n'* good report that I hear: "
3: 1 days; there was *n'* open vision. 369
6: 7 on which there hath come *n'* yoke, 3808
7: 13 *n'* more into the coast of Israel: "
10: 14 we saw that they were *n'* where, * 369
27 him, and brought him *n'* presents. 3808
11: 3 then, if there be *n'* man to save us, *369
13: 19 Now there was *n'* smith found 3808
14: 6 is *n'* restraint to the Lord to save 369
26 *n'* man put his hand to his mouth: "
15: 35 Samuel came *n'* more to see Saul 3808
17: 32 Let *n'* man's heart fail because of 408
50 was *n'* sword in the hand of David. 369
18: 2 would let him go *n'* more home to 3808
20: 15 *n'*, not when the Lord hath cut off "
21 there is peace to thee, and *n'* hurt; 369
34 eat *n'* meat the second day of the 3808
21: 1 thou alone, and *n'* man with thee? 369
2 Let *n'* man know any thing of the 408
4 *n'* common bread under mine hand, 369
6 *n'* bread there but the shewbread, 3808
9 for there is *n'* other save that here. 369
25: 31 this shall be *n'* grief unto thee, 3808
26: 12 gat them away, and *n'* man saw it, 369
21 for I will *n'* more do thee harm. 3808
27: 4 he sought *n'* more again for him. "
28: 10 there shall *n'* punishment happen 518
15 me, and answereth me *n'* more, 3808
20 and there was *n'* strength in him; "
20 he had eaten *n'* bread all the day, "
29: 3 found *n'* fault in him since he fell "
30: 4 they had *n'* more power to weep. 369
12 he had eaten *n'* bread, nor drunk 3808
2Sa 1: 21 let there be *n'* dew, neither let 408
2: 28 and pursued after Israel *n'* more, 3808
6: 23 the daughter of Saul had *n'* child "
7: 10 of their own, and move *n'* more; "
12: 6 thing, and because he had *n'* pity. "
13: 12 *n'* such thing ought to be done in "
16 said unto him, There is *n'* cause: * 408
14: 25 head there was *n'* blemish in him. 3808
15: 3 there is *n'* man deputed of the king 369
26 I have *n'* delight in thee; behold, 3808
18: 13 there is *n'* matter hid from the king, "
18 I have *n'* son to keep my name in 369
20 day thou shalt bear *n'* tidings, 3808
22 that thou hast *n'* tidings ready? 369
20: 1 We have *n'* part in David, neither "
10 Amasa took *n'* heed to the sword 3808
21: 4 will have *n'* silver nor gold of Saul, 369
17 go *n'* more out with us to battle, 3808
1Ki 1: 1 with clothes, but he gat *n'* heat. "
3: 2 was *n'* house built unto the name "
18 *n'* stranger with us in the house, 369
22 said, *N'*; but the dead is thy son, 3808
26 living child, and in *n'* wise slay it. 408
27 living child, and in *n'* wise slay it: 3808
6: 18 was cedar; there was *n'* stone seen. 369
8: 16 I chose *n'* city out of all the tribes 3808
23 Israel, there is *n'* God like thee, 369
35 is shut up, and there is *n'* rain, 3808
46 there is *n'* man that sinneth not,) 369
9: 22 did Solomon make *n'* bondmen: 3808
10: 5 there was *n'* more spirit in her. "
10 there came *n'* more such abundance "
12 there came *n'* such almug trees, nor "
13: 9 Eat *n'* bread, nor drink water, nor "
17 shalt eat *n'* bread nor drink water "
22 Eat *n'* bread, and drink *n'* water; 408
17: 7 there had been *n'* rain in the land. 3808
17 that there was *n'* breath left in him. "
18: 10 there is *n'* nation or kingdom, 518
23, 23 on wood, and put *n'* fire under: 3808
25 your gods, but put *n'* fire under. "
26 there was *n'* voice, nor any that 369
21: 4 his face, and would eat *n'* bread. 3808
5 so sad, that thou eatest *n'* bread? 369

1Ki 22: 17 These have *n'* master: let them 3808
18 prophesy *n'* good concerning me, "
47 There was then *n'* king in Edom: 369
2Ki 1: 16 is *n'* God in Israel to inquire of his "
17 of Judah; because he had *n'* son. 3808
2: 12 And he saw him *n'* more: and he "
3: 9 there was *n'* water for the host, and "
4: 14 she hath *n'* child, and her husband 369
41 And there was *n'* harm in the pot. 3808
5: 15 that there is *n'* God in all the earth, 369
25 Thy servant went *n'* whither. 3808
6: 23 came *n'* more into the land of Israel. "
7: 5 behold, there was *n'* man there. 369
10 there was *n'* man there, neither "
9: 35 *n'* more of her than the skull, and 3808
10: 31 Jehu took *n'* heed to walk in the law "
12: 7 receive *n'* more money of your 408
8 to receive *n'* more money of the 1115
17: 4 *n'* present to the king of Assyria, 3808
19: 18 were *n'* gods, but the work of men's "
22: 7 was *n'* reckoning made with them "
23: 10 that *n'* man might make his son or 1115
18 alone; let *n'* man move his bones. 408
25 him was there *n'* king before him, 3808
25: 3 *n'* bread for the people of the land. "
1Ch 2: 34 Now Sheshan had *n'* sons, but "
12: 17 there is *n'* wrong in mine hands, "
16: 21 suffered *n'* man to do them wrong: "
22 and do my prophets *n'* harm. 408
17: 9 place, and shall be moved *n'* more; 3808
22: 16 and the iron, there is *n'* number. 369
23: 22 Eleazar died, and had *n'* sons, but 3808
26 shall *n'* more carry the tabernacle, 369
24: 2 their father, and had *n'* children: 3808
28 came Eleazar, who had *n'* sons. "
2Ch 6: 5 I chose *n'* city among all the tribes "
14 is *n'* God like thee in the heaven, 369
26 is shut up, and there is *n'* rain, 3808
36 there is *n'* man which sinneth not,) 369
7: 13 up heaven that there be *n'* rain, 3808
8: 9 Solomon make *n'* servants for his "
9: 4 there was *n'* more spirit in her. "
13: 9 a priest of them that are *n'* gods. "
14: 6 and he had *n'* war in those years; 369
11 or with them that have *n'* power: "
15: 5 was *n'* peace to him that went out, "
19 was *n'* more war unto the five and 3808
17: 10 made *n'* war against Jehoshaphat. "
18: 16 sheep that have *n'* shepherd: and 369
16 These have *n'* master; let them 3808
19: 7 *n'* iniquity with the Lord our God, 369
20: 12 *n'* might against this great company "
21: 19 people made *n'* burning for him, 3808
22: 9 *n'* power to keep still the kingdom. 369
32: 15 *n'* god of any nation or kingdom 3808
35: 18 was *n'* passover like to that kept "
36: 16 people, till there was *n'* remedy. 369
17 *n'* compassion upon young man or 3808
Ezr 4: 16 *n'* portion on this side of the river. 3809
9: 14 should be *n'* remnant nor escaping? 369
10: 6 he did eat *n'* bread, nor drink 3808
Ne 2: 14 there was *n'* place for the beast 369
17 that we be *n'* more a reproach. 3808
20 ye have *n'* portion, nor right, nor 369
6: 1 there was *n'* breach left therein; 3808
8 *n'* such things done as thou sayest, "
13: 19 there should *n'* burden be brought "
21 came they *n'* more on the Sabbath. "
26 was there *n'* king like him, who was "
Es 1: 19 Vashti come *n'* more before king "
2: 14 came in unto the king *n'* more, "
5: 12 let *n'* man come in with the king "
8: 8 king's ring, may *n'* man reverse. 369
9: 2 and *n'* man could withstand them; 3808
Job 3: 7 let *n'* joyful voice come therein. 408
4: 18 he put *n'* trust in his servants; 3808
5: 19 seven there shall *n'* evil touch thee. "
7: 7 mine eye shall *n'* more see good. "
8 hath seen me shall see me *n'* more. "
9 the grave shall come up *n'* more. "
10 shall return *n'* more to his house, "
9: 25 they flee away, they see *n'* good. "
10: 18 the ghost, and *n'* eye had seen me! "
11: 3 shall *n'* man make thee ashamed? 369
12: 2 *N'* doubt but ye are the people, 551
14 man, and there can be *n'* opening. 3808
24 a wilderness where there is *n'* way. "
13: 4 ye are all physicians of *n'* value. 457
14: 12 till the heavens be *n'* more, they 1115
15: 3 wherewith he can do *n'* good? 3808
15 he putteth *n'* trust in his saints; "
19 *n'* stranger passed among them. "
28 in houses which *n'* man inhabiteth, "
16: 18 blood, and let my cry have *n'* place. 408
18: 17 shall have *n'* name in the street. 3808
19: 7 aloud, but there is *n'* judgment. "
16 servant, and he gave me *n'* answer; "
20: 9 saw him shall see him *n'* more; "
21 shall *n'* man look for his goods. "
23: 6 *N'*; but he would put strength in * "
24: 7 they have *n'* covering in the cold. 369
15 saying, *N'* eye shall see me: and 3808
20 he shall be *n'* more remembered; "
22 riseth up, and *n'* man is sure of life. "
26: 2 thou the arm that hath *n'* strength? "
3 counselled him that hath *n'* wisdom? "
6 and destruction hath *n'* covering. 369
28: 18 *N'* mention shall be made of coral, 3808
30: 13 my calamity, they have *n'* helper. "
17 season: and my sinews take *n'* rest. "
32: 3 because they had found *n'* answer, "
5 there was *n'* answer in the mouth 369
15 amazed, they answered *n'* more: 3808
16 stood still, and answered *n'* more;) "
19 belly is as wine which hath *n'* vent; "
34: 22 is *n'* darkness, nor shadow of death, 369

Job 34:32 done iniquity, I will do *n'* more. 3808
36:16 place, where there is *n'* straitness; "
19 *n'* not gold, nor all the forces of * "
38:11 shalt thou come, but *n'* further: "
26 on the earth, where *n'* man is; on "
26 wilderness, wherein there is *n'* man;"
40: 5 twice; but I will proceed *n'* further."
41: 8 remember the battle, do *n'* more. 408
16 that *n'* air can come between them.3808
42: 2 that *n'* thought can be withholden "
15 all the land were *n'* women found "
Ps 3: 2 There is *n'* help for him in God. 369
5: 9 is *n'* faithfulness in their mouth; "
6: 5 in death there is *n'* remembrance of "
10:18 man of...earth may *n'* more oppress.1077
14: 1 said in his heart, There is *n'* God. 369
3 is none that doeth good, *n'*, not one.
4 workers of iniquity *n'* knowledge?3808
19: 3 There is *n'* speech nor language, 369
22: 6 But I am a worm, and *n'* man; a 3808
23: 4 I will fear *n'* evil: for thou art with "
32: 2 and in whose spirit there is *n'* guile.369
9 mule, which have *n'* understanding:"
33:16 is *n'* king saved by the multitude of "
34: 9 is *n'* want to them that fear him. "
36: 1 is *n'* fear of God before his eyes. "
38: 3 There is *n'* soundness in my flesh "
7 there is *n'* soundness in my flesh. "
14 and in whose mouth are *n'* reproofs. "
39:13 before I go hence, and be *n'* more. "
40:17 make *n'* tarrying, O my God. 408
41: 8 he lieth he shall rise up *n'* more. 3808
50: 9 will take *n'* bullock out of thy house."
53: 1 said in his heart, There is *n'* God. 369
3 is none that doeth good, *n'*, not one.
4 workers of iniquity *n'* knowledge?3808
5 in great fear, where *n'* fear was: "
55:19 Because they have *n'* changes, 369
63: 1 thirsty land, where *n'* water is; 1097
69: 2 mire, where there is *n'* standing: 369
70: 5 O Lord, make *n'* tarrying. 408
72:12 also, and him that hath *n'* helper. 369
73: 4 there are *n'* bands in their death: "
74: 9 signs: there is *n'* more any prophet:"
77: 7 and will he be favourable *n'* more?3808
78:64 their widows made *n'* lamentation. "
81: 9 shall *n'* strange god be in thee; "
83: 4 may be *n'* more in remembrance. "
84:11 *n'* good thing will he withhold from "
88: 4 am as a man that hath *n'* strength:369
5 whom thou rememberest *n'* more:3808
91:10 There shall *n'* evil befall thee, "
92:15 there is *n'* unrighteousness in him. "
101: 3 *n'* wicked thing before mine eyes: "
102:27 and thy years shall have *n'* end. "
103:16 thereof shall know it *n'* more. "
104:35 and let the wicked be *n'* more. 369
105:14 suffered *n'* man to do them wrong:3808
15 and do my prophets *n'* harm. 408
107: 4 way; they found *n'* city to dwell in.3808
40 wilderness, where there is *n'* way. "
119: 3 They also do *n'* iniquity: they walk "
142: 4 was *n'* man that would know me: 369
4 failed me; *n'* man cared for my soul."
143: 2 shall *n'* man living be justified. 3808
144:14 that there be *n'* breaking in, nor 369
14 be *n'* complaining in our streets. "
146: 3 son of man, in whom there is *n'* help."
Pr 1:24 out my hand, and *n'* man regarded; "
3:30 if he have done thee *n'* harm. 3808
6: 7 Which having *n'* guide, overseer, 369
8:24 When there were *n'* depths, I was "
24 *n'* fountains abounding with water. "
10:22 and he addeth *n'* sorrow with it. 3808
25 passeth, so is the wicked *n'* more: 369
11:14 Where *n'* counsel is, the people fall: "
12:21 shall *n'* evil happen to the just: 3808
28 pathway thereof there is *n'* death. 408
14: 4 Where *n'* oxen are, the crib is 369
17:16 seeing he hath *n'* heart to it? "
20 a froward heart findeth *n'* good: 3808
21 and the father of a fool hath *n'* joy. "
18: 2 hath *n'* delight in understanding, "
21:10 findeth *n'* favour in his eyes. "
30 is *n'* wisdom nor understanding nor369
22:24 Make *n'* friendship with an angry 408
24:20 be *n'* reward to the evil man; the 3808
25:28 hath *n'* rule over his own spirit is* 369
26:20 Where *n'* wood is, there the fire * 657
20 so where there is *n'* talebearer, the 369
28: 1 wicked flee when *n'* man pursueth: "
3 sweeping rain which leaveth *n'* food."
17 flee to the pit; let *n'* man stay him. 408
24 and saith, It is *n'* transgression; 369
29: 9 he rage or laugh, there is *n'* rest. "
18 Where there is *n'* vision, the people "
30:20 saith, I have done *n'* wickedness. 3808
27 The locusts have *n'* king, yet go 369
31 against whom there is *n'* rising up. 510
31: 7 and remember his misery *n'* more.3808
11 that he shall have *n'* need of spoil. "
Ec 1: 9 there is *n'* new thing under the sun.369
11 is *n'* remembrance of former things;"
2:11 there was *n'* profit under the sun. "
16 there is *n'* remembrance of the wise "
3:11 *n'* man can find out the work that*1097
12 know that there is *n'* good in them,*369
19 a man hath *n'* preeminence above a "
4: 1 and they had *n'* comforter; and on "
1 power; but they had *n'* comforter. "
8 yet is there *n'* end of all his labour; "
13 who will *n'* more be admonished. *3808
16 There is *n'* end of all the people, 369
5: 4 for he hath *n'* pleasure in fools: "
6: 3 and also that he have *n'* burial; 3808
6 told, yet he hath seen *n'* good: "

Ec 7:21 Also take *n'* heed unto all words *3808
8: 5 commandment shall feel *n'* evil 3808
8 There is *n'* man that hath power 369
8 there is *n'* discharge in that war; "
15 hath *n'* better thing under the sun, "
9: 1 *n'* man knoweth either love or * "
8 and let thy head lack *n'* ointment. *408
10 for there is *n'* work, nor device, nor369
15 yet *n'* man remembered that same3808
10:11 and a babbler is *n'* better. 369
20 not the king, *n'* not in thy thought;408
12: 1 say, I have *n'* pleasure in them; 369
12 making many books there is *n'* end; "
Ca 4: 7 my love; there is *n'* spot in thee. "
5: 6 him, but he gave me *n'* answer. 3808
8: 8 sister, and she hath *n'* breasts: 369
Isa 1: 6 head there is *n'* soundness in it; "
13 Bring *n'* more vain oblations; 3808
30 and as a garden that hath *n'* water.369
5: 6 clouds that they rain *n'* rain upon it.
8 field to field, till there be *n'* place, 675
13 because they have *n'* knowledge:*1097
8:20 because there is *n'* light in them. 369
9: 7 and peace there shall be *n'* end, "
17 have *n'* joy in their young men, *3808
19 fire: *n'* man shall spare his brother."
10:15 lift up itself, as if it were *n'* wood.* "
20 shall *n'* more again stay upon him "
13:14 as a sheep that *n'* man taketh up: 369
18 shall have *n'* pity on the fruit of 3808
14: 8 *n'* feller is come up against us. "
15: 6 faileth, there is *n'* green thing. "
16:10 vineyards there shall be *n'* singing, "
10 tread out *n'* wine in their presses; "
19: 7 be driven away, and be *n'* more. 369
23: 1 that there is *n'* house, *n'* entering in:
10 Tarshish: there is *n'* more strength.369
12 Thou shalt *n'* more rejoice, O thou3808
12 there also shalt thou have *n'* rest. "
24:10 is shut up, that *n'* man may come in.
25: 2 a palace of strangers to be *n'* city;
26:21 and shall *n'* more cover her slain. 3808
27:11 it is a people of *n'* understanding: "
11 them will shew them *n'* favour. "
28: 8 so that there is *n'* place clean. 1097
29:16 it, He had *n'* understanding? 3808
30: 7 help in vain, and to *n'* purpose: 7385
16 ye said, *N'*; for we will flee upon 3808
19 thou shalt weep *n'* more: he will "
32: 5 shall be *n'* more called liberal, nor "
33: 8 the cities, he regardeth *n'* man. * "
21 shall go *n'* galley with oars, 1077
34:16 *n'* one of these shall fail, none 3808
35: 9 *N'* lion shall be there, nor any "
37:19 they were *n'* gods, but the work of "
38:11 I shall behold man *n'* more with the"
40:20 impoverished that he hath *n'* "
28 *n'* searching of his understanding. 369
29 *n'* might he increaseth strength. "
41:28 I beheld, and there was *n'* man; "
28 and there was *n'* counsellor, that, "
43:10 me there was *n'* God formed, 3808
11 and beside me there is *n'* saviour. 369
12 was *n'* strange god among you: "
24 me *n'* sweet cane with money, 3808
44: 6 last; and beside me there is *n'* God.369
8 yea, there is *n'* God; I know not any."
12 he drinketh *n'* water, and is faint. 3808
45: 5 else, there is *n'* God besides me: 369
9 or thy work, He hath *n'* hands? "
14 there is none else, there is *n'* God. 657
20 have *n'* knowledge that set up the 3808
21 and there is *n'* God else beside me;369
47: 1 there is *n'* throne, O daughter of the* "
1 thou shalt *n'* more be called tender3808
5 thou shalt *n'* more be called, The "
6 thou didst shew them *n'* mercy; "
48:22 There is *n'* peace, saith the Lord, 369
50: 2 when I came, was there *n'* man? "
2 or have I *n'* power to deliver? behold,"
2 stinketh, because there is *n'* water, "
10 in darkness, and hath *n'* light? let "
51:22 thou shalt *n'* more drink it again: 3808
52: 1 there shall *n'* more come unto thee "
11 thence, touch *n'* unclean thing; 408
53: 2 he hath *n'* form nor comeliness; 3808
2 *n'* beauty that we should desire him."
9 because he had done *n'* violence, "
54: 9 waters of Noah should *n'* more go over
17 *N'* weapon that is formed against 3808
55: 1 and he that hath *n'* money; come 369
57: 1 and *n'* man layeth it to heart: and "
10 saidst thou not, There is *n'* hope:
21 There is *n'* peace, saith my God, to 369
58: 3 and thou takest *n'* knowledge? 3808
59: 8 is *n'* judgment in their goings: 369
10 and we grope as if we had *n'* eyes: "
15 him that there was *n'* judgment. "
16 And he saw that there was *n'* man, "
16 that there was *n'* intercessor: "
60:15 so that *n'* man went through thee, "
18 Violence shall *n'* more be heard in3808
19 The sun shall be *n'* more thy light "
20 Thy sun shall *n'* more go down; "
62: 4 shalt *n'* more be termed Forsaken; "
7 give him *n'* rest, till he establish, 408
8 *n'* more give thy corn to be meat 518
65:19 of weeping shall be *n'* more heard 3808
20 shall be *n'* more thence an infant "
Jer 2: 6 a land that *n'* man passed through,*"
6 and where *n'* man dwelt? "
11 their gods, which are yet *n'* gods? "
13 cisterns, that can hold *n'* water. "
25 but thou saidst, There is *n'* hope:*
25 *n'*; for I have loved strangers, and 3808
30 they received *n'* correction: your "

Jer 2:31 we will come *n'* more unto thee? 3808
3: 3 and there hath been *n'* latter rain; "
16 the Lord, they shall say *n'* more, "
4:22 to do good they have *n'* knowledge. "
23 the heavens, and they had *n'* light. 369
25 and, lo, there was *n'* man, and all "
5: 7 sworn by them that are *n'* gods: 3808
6:10 reproach; they have *n'* delight in it."
14 peace; when there is *n'* peace. 369
23 they are cruel, and have *n'* mercy;3808
7:32 it shall *n'* more be called Tophet, "
32 in Tophet, till there be *n'* place. 369
8: 6 *n'* man repented...of his wickedness,"
11 Peace, peace; when there is *n'* peace."
13 there shall be *n'* grapes on the vine, "
15 looked for peace, but *n'* good came; "
22 Is there *n'* balm in Gilead? is there "
22 is there *n'* physician there? why "
10:14 and there is *n'* breath in them. 3808
11:19 name may be *n'* more remembered:"
23 there shall be *n'* remnant of them: "
12:11 because *n'* man layeth it to heart. 369
12 the land: *n'* flesh shall have peace. "
14: 3 to the pits, and found *n'* water; 3808
4 for there was *n'* rain in the earth, "
5 it, because there was *n'* grass. "
6 did fail, because there was *n'* grass.369
19 us, and there is *n'* healing for us? "
19 for peace, and there is *n'* good; and "
16:14 that it shall *n'* more be said, The 3808
19 things, wherein there is *n'* profit. 369
20 himself, and they are *n'* gods? 3808
17:21 bear *n'* burden on the sabbath day, 408
24 in *n'* burden through the gates of 1115
24 sabbath day, to do *n'* work therein;"
18:12 There is *n'* hope: but we will walk "
19: 6 shall *n'* more be called Tophet, 3808
11 till there be *n'* place to bury. "
22: 3 do *n'* wrong, do *n'* violence to the 408
10 for he shall return *n'* more, nor 3808
12 and shall see this land *n'* more. "
28 he a vessel wherein is *n'* pleasure? 363
30 *n'* man of his seed shall prosper, 3808
23: 4 and they shall fear *n'* more, nor be "
7 shall *n'* more say, The Lord liveth, "
17 heart, *N'* evil shall come upon you."
36 the Lord shall ye mention *n'* more; "
25: 6 hands; and I will do you *n'* hurt. "
27 and spue, and fall, and rise *n'* more,"
35 shepherds shall have *n'* way to flee,4480
30: 8 and strangers shall *n'* more serve 3808
13 up: thou hast *n'* healing medicines.369
17 Zion, whom *n'* man seeketh after. "
31:29 those days they shall say *n'* more, 3808
34 shall teach *n'* more every man his "
34 I will remember their sin *n'* more. "
33:24 be *n'* more a nation before them. "
35: 6 they said, We will drink *n'* wine: 3808
6 Ye shall drink *n'* wine, neither ye, "
8 us, to drink *n'* wine all our days, 1115
36:19 and let *n'* man know where ye be. 408
38: 6 the dungeon there was *n'* water, 369
9 there is *n'* more bread in the city. "
24 Let *n'* man know of these words, 408
39:12 well to him, and do him *n'* harm; "
40:15 and *n'* man shall know it: 3808
41: 4 Gedaliah, and *n'* man knew it, "
42:14 Saying, *N'*; but we will go into the "
14 where we shall see *n'* war, nor hear"
18 and ye shall see this place *n'* more. "
44: 2 and *n'* man dwelleth therein, 369
5 burn *n'* incense unto other gods. 1115
17 and were well, and saw *n'* evil. 3808
22 that the Lord could *n'* longer bear. "
26 my name shall *n'* more be named 518
45: 3 in my sighing, and I find *n'* rest. 3808
48: 2 shall be *n'* more praise of Moab: 369
8 city, and *n'* city shall escape: 3808
33 their shouting shall be *n'* shouting. "
38 like a vessel wherein is *n'* pleasure.369
49: 1 Hath Israel *n'* sons? hath he *n'* heir?"
7 Is wisdom *n'* more in Teman? is "
18 *n'* man shall abide there, neither 3808
33 there shall *n'* man abide there, nor "
36 there shall be *n'* nation whither the "
50:14 shoot at her, spare *n'* arrows: for 408
39 be *n'* more inhabited for ever; 3808
40 so shall *n'* man abide there, neither"
51:17 and there is *n'* breath in them. "
43 a land wherein *n'* man dwelleth, "
52: 6 there was *n'* bread for the people "
La 1: 3 the heathen, she findeth *n'* rest: "
6 like harts that find *n'* pasture, and "
9 wonderfully: she had *n'* comforter.369
2: 9 the Gentiles: the law is *n'* more; * "
9 also find *n'* vision from the Lord, 3808
18 give thyself *n'* rest; let not the 408
4: 4 and *n'* man breaketh it unto them. 369
6 and *n'* hands stayed on her. 3808
15 They shall *n'* more sojourn there. "
16 he will *n'* more regard them: they "
22 will *n'* more carry thee away into "
5: 5 we labour, and have *n'* rest. "
Eze 12:23 shall *n'* more use it as a proverb in "
24 shall be *n'* more any vain vision "
25 it shall be *n'* more prolonged: for "
13:10 and there was *n'* peace; and one 369
15 The wall is *n'* more, neither they "
16 and there is *n'* peace, saith the Lord "
21 shall be *n'* more in your hand to 3808
23 ye shall see *n'* more vanity, nor "
14:11 of Israel may go *n'* more astray "
15 *n'* man may pass through because1097
15: 5 whole, it was meet for *n'* work: 3808
16:34 and *n'* reward is given unto thee: "
41 also shalt give *n'* hire any more. "

Eze 16: 42 quiet, and will be *n·* more angry. 3808
18: 32 I have *n·* pleasure in the death of "
19: 9 voice should *n·* more be heard upon "
14 hath *n·* strong rod to be a sceptre "
20: 39 pollute ye my holy name *n·* more "
21: 13 it shall be *n·* more, saith the Lord "
27 it shall be *n·* more, until he come "
32 thou shalt be *n·* more remembered: "
22: 26 put *n·* difference between the holy "
24: 6 by piece; let *n·* lot fall upon it. "
17 make *n·* mourning for the dead, "
27 speak, and shall be *n·* more dumb: "
26: 13 thy harps shall be *n·* more heard. "
14 thou shalt be built *n·* more: for I "
21 terror, and thou shalt be *n·* more: 369
28: 3 there is *n·* secret...they can hide 3808
9 thou shalt be a man, and *n·* God, * "
24 shall be *n·* more a pricking brier "
29: 11 *N·* foot of man shall pass through "
15 shall *n·* more rule over the nations. "
16 shall be *n·* more the confidence of "
18 yet had he *n·* wages, nor his army, "
30: 13 there shall be *n·* more a prince of "
33: 11 I have *n·* pleasure in the death of 518
22 opened, and I was *n·* more dumb. 3808
34: 5 because there is *n·* shepherd: and 1097
8 because there was *n·* shepherd, 369
22 they shall *n·* more be a prey; and 3808
28 they shall *n·* more be a prey to the "
29 shall be *n·* more consumed with "
36: 12 shalt *n·* more henceforth bereave "
14 thou shalt devour men *n·* more, "
29 it, and lay *n·* famine upon you. "
30 receive *n·* more reproach of famine "
37: 8 but there was *n·* breath in them. 369
22 they shall be *n·* more two nations, 3808
39: 10 shall take *n·* wood out of the field, "
43: 7 the house of Israel *n·* more defile, "
44: 2 *n·* man shall enter in by it; because* "
9 *N·* stranger, uncircumcised in "
17 and *n·* wool shall come upon them, "
25 come at *n·* dead person to defile "
25 sister that hath had *n·* husband, "
28 give them *n·* possession in Israel: "
45: 8 shall *n·* more oppress my people. "
Da 1: 4 Children in whom was *n·* blemish, 369
2: 10 therefore there is *n·* king, 3606,3809
35 *n·* place was found for them: "
3: 25 of the fire, and they have *n·* hurt; "
27 whose bodies the fire had *n·* power, "
29 is *n·* other God that can deliver "
4: 9 and *n·* secret troubleth thee, 3606 "
6: 2 the king should have *n·* damage. "
15 is, That *n·* decree nor statute 3606 "
22 O king, have I done *n·* hurt. "
23 *n·* manner of hurt was found 3606 "
8: 4 *n·* beasts might stand before him, 3808
7 was *n·* power in the ram to stand "
10: 3 I ate *n·* pleasant bread, neither "
8 there remained *n·* strength in me: "
8 corruption,...I retained *n·* strength. "
16 and I have retained *n·* strength. "
17 there remained *n·* strength in me, "
Ho 1: 6 I will *n·* more have mercy upon the "
2: 16 and shalt call me *n·* more Baali. "
17 shall *n·* more be remembered by "
4: 1 there is *n·* truth, nor mercy, nor 369
4 Yet let *n·* man strive, nor reprove 408
6 that thou shalt be *n·* priest to me: "
8: 7 the whirlwind: it hath *n·* stalk: 369
7 the bud shall yield *n·* meal: if so be "
8 as a vessel wherein is *n·* pleasure. "
9: 15 I will love them *n·* more; all their 3808
16 dried up, they shall bear *n·* fruit: 1077
10: 3 We have *n·* king, because we feared 369
13: 4 thou shalt know *n·* god but me: 3808
4 for there is *n·* saviour beside me. 369
Joe 1: 18 because they have *n·* pasture; yea, "
2: 19 will *n·* more make you a reproach 3808
3: 17 shall *n·* strangers pass through her "
Am 3: 4 in the forest, when he hath *n·* prey? 369
5 the earth, where *n·* gin is for him: "
5: 2 is fallen; she shall *n·* more rise: 3808
20 very dark, and *n·* brightness in it? "
6: 10 and he shall say, *N·*. Then shall 657
7: 14 I was *n·* prophet, neither was I a 3808
9: 15 they shall *n·* more be pulled up out "
Mic 3: 7 lips; for there is *n·* answer of God. 369
4: 9 is there *n·* king in thee? is thy "
5: 12 shalt have *n·* more soothsayers: 3808
13 shalt *n·* more worship the work of "
7: 1 there is *n·* cluster to eat: my soul 369
Na 1: 12 thee, I will afflict thee *n·* more. 3808
14 that *n·* more of thy name be sown: "
15 wicked shall *n·* more pass through "
2: 13 messengers shall *n·* more be heard. "
3: 18 and *n·* man gathereth them. * 369
19 There is *n·* healing of thy bruise; "
Hab 1: 14 that have *n·* ruler over them? 3808
2: 19 is *n·* breath at all in the midst of it. 369
3: 17 fields shall yield *n·* meat; and the 3808
17 there shall be *n·* herd in the stalls: "
Zep 2: 5 that there shall be *n·* inhabitant. 369
3: 5 but the unjust knoweth *n·* shame. 3808
6 so that there is *n·* man, that there 1097
11 thou shalt *n·* more be haughty 3808
Hag 2: 12 the priests answered and said, *N·*. "
Zec 1: 21 so that *n·* man did lift up his head: "
4: 5, 13 these be? And I said, *N·*, my lord. "
7: 14 that *n·* man passed through nor "
8: 10 there was *n·* hire for man, nor any 3808
17 neighbour; and love *n·* false oath: "
9: 8 *n·* oppressor shall pass through "
11 out of the pit wherein is *n·* water. "
10: 2 because there was *n·* shepherd. 639
11: 6 I will *n·* more pity the inhabitants 3808

Zec 13: 2 they shall *n·* more be remembered: 3808
5 he shall say, I am *n·* prophet, I am "
14: 11 shall be *n·* more utter destruction; "
17 even upon them shall be *n·* rain. "
18 and come not, that have *n·* rain; * "
21 shall be *n·* more the Canaanite in "
Mal 1: 10 I have *n·* pleasure in you, saith 639
M't 5: 18 shall in *n·* wise pass from the law, 3364
20 in *n·* case enter into the kingdom "
26 shalt by *n·* means come out thence, "
6: 1 otherwise ye have *n·* reward of 3756
24 *N·* man can serve two masters: 3762
25 Take *n·* thought for your life, *3361
31 Therefore take *n·* thought, saying, * "
34 Take...*n·* thought for the morrow: "
8: 4 unto him, See thou tell *n·* man; 3367
10 so great faith, *n·*, not in Israel. 3761
28 *n·* man might pass by that way. 3361
9: 16 *N·* man putteth a piece of new 3762
30 saying, See that *n·* man know it. "
36 as sheep having *n·* shepherd. *3361
10: 19 *n·* thought how or what ye shall * "
42 shall in *n·* wise lose his reward. 3364
11: 27 *n·* man knoweth the Son, but the 3762
12: 39 there shall *n·* sign be given to it, 3756
13: 5 they had *n·* deepness of earth: 3361
6 they had *n·* root, they withered "
16: 4 there shall *n·* sign be given unto it, 3756
7 is because we have taken *n·* bread. "
8 because ye have brought *n·* bread? "
20 tell *n·* man that he was Jesus the 3762
17: 8 they saw *n·* man, save Jesus only. "
9 Tell the vision to *n·* man, until the "
19: 6 are *n·* more twain, but one flesh. 3765
18 Thou shalt do *n·* murder, Thou *3756
20: 7 Because *n·* man hath hired us. 3762
13 said, Friend, I do thee *n·* wrong: 3756
21: 19 unto it, Let *n·* fruit grow on thee 3370
22: 23 say that there is *n·* resurrection, 3361
24 If a man die, having *n·* children, "
25 having *n·* issue, left his wife unto "
46 *n·* man was able to answer him a 3762
23: 9 And call *n·* man your father upon 3361
24: 4 Take heed that *n·* man deceive you. "
21 to this time, *n·*, nor ever shall be. "
22 there should *n·* flesh be saved: 3756,3956
36 that day and hour knoweth *n·* man, 3762
36 *n·*, not the angels of heaven, but *3761
25: 3 lamps, and took *n·* oil with them: 3756
42 an hungred, and ye gave me *n·* meat: "
42 thirsty, and ye gave me *n·* drink: "
26: 55 temple, and ye laid *n·* hold on me.* "
M'r 1: 45 could *n·* more openly enter into 3370
2: 2 was *n·* room to receive them, "
2 *n·*, not so much as about the door: "
17 have *n·* need of the physician, but 3756
21 *N·* man also seweth a piece of 3762
22 *n·* man putteth new wine into old "
3: 27 *N·* man can enter into a strong "
4: 5 because it had *n·* depth of earth: 3361
6 because it had *n·* root, it withered "
7 choked it, and it yielded *n·* fruit. 3756
17 have *n·* root in themselves, and so "
40 how is it that ye have *n·* faith? * "
5: 3 and *n·* man could bind him, 3762
3 bind him, *n·*, not with chains, 3777
37 he suffered *n·* man to follow him, 3762
43 that *n·* man should know it; and 3367
6: 5 he could there do *n·* mighty work, 3762
8 *n·* scrip, *n·* bread, *n·* money in 3361
31 had *n·* leisure so much as to eat. 3761
7: 12 suffer him *n·* more to do ought for 3765
24 and would have *n·* man know it: 3762
36 them that they should tell *n·* man: 3367
8: 12 shall *n·* sign be given unto this 1487
16 It is because we have *n·* bread. 3756
17 ye, because ye have *n·* bread? "
30 they should tell *n·* man of him. 3367
9: 3 *n·* fuller on earth can white them. 3756
8 saw *n·* man any more, save Jesus 3762
9 tell *n·* man what things they had 3367
25 him, and enter *n·* more into him. 3370
39 *n·* man which shall do a miracle 3762
10: 8 are *n·* more twain, but one flesh. 3765
29 is *n·* man that hath left house, or 3762
11: 14 *N·* man eat fruit of thee hereafter 3367
12: 14 art true, and carest for *n·* man: *3762
18 which say there is *n·* resurrection 3361
19 behind him, and leave *n·* children, "
20 took a wife, and dying left *n·* seed. 3756
22 the seven had her, and left *n·* seed: "
34 *n·* man after that durst ask him 3762
13: 11 take *n·* thought beforehand what *3361
20 days, *n·* flesh should be saved: 3756,3956
32 and that hour knoweth *n·* man, 3762
32 *n·*, not the angels which are in heaven, *
14: 25 I will drink *n·* more of the fruit of 3765
Lu 1: 7 they had *n·* child, because that 3756
33 his kingdom there shall be *n·* end. "
2: 7 was *n·* room for them in the inn. "
3: 13 Exact *n·* more than that which is 3367
14 Do violence to *n·* man, neither "
4: 24 *N·* prophet is accepted in his own 3762
5: 14 he charged him to tell *n·* man: but 3367
36 *N·* man putteth a piece of a new 3762
37 *n·* man putteth new wine into old "
39 *N·* man also having drunk old wine "
7: 9 so great faith, *n·*, not in Israel. 3761
44 gavest me *n·* water for my feet: 3756
45 Thou gavest me *n·* kiss: but this "
8: 13 and these have *n·* root, which for a "
14 and bring *n·* fruit to perfection. "
16 *N·* man, when he hath lighted a 3762
27 and ware *n·* clothes, neither abode 3756
51 he suffered *n·* man to go in, save *3762
56 should tell *n·* man what was done. 3367

Lu 9: 13 We have *n·* more but five loaves 3756
21 them to tell *n·* man that thing; 3367
36 and told *n·* man in those days any 3762
62 *N·* man, having put his hand to the "
10: 4 and salute *n·* man by the way. 3367
22 *n·* man knoweth who the Son is, 3762
11: 20 *n·* doubt the kingdom of God is * 686
29 and there shall *n·* sign be given it. 3756
33 *N·* man, when he hath lighted a 3762
36 of light, having *n·* part dark, 3365,5100
12: 4 have *n·* more that they can do. 3756
11 ye *n·* thought how or what thing *3361
17 I have *n·* room where to bestow *3756
22 Take *n·* thought for your life, *3361
33 not, where *n·* thief approacheth, 3756
13: 11 and could in *n·* wise lift up herself. 3361
15: 7 persons, which need *n·* repentance. 3756
16 eat: and *n·* man gave unto him. 3762
19, 21 am *n·* more worthy to be called 3765
16: 2 thou mayest be *n·* longer steward. 3756
13 *N·* servant can serve two masters: 3762
18: 17 child shall in *n·* wise enter therein. 3364
29 is *n·* man that hath left house, or 3762
20: 22 to give tribute unto Cæsar, or *n·*? *3756
31 and they left *n·* children, and died. "
22: 36 and he that hath *n·* sword, let him *3361
53 forth *n·* hands against me: *3756
23: 4 people, I find *n·* fault in this man. 3762
14 have found *n·* fault in this man "
15 *N·*, nor yet Herod: for I sent 235
22 found *n·* cause of death in him: 3762
Joh 1: 18 *N·* man hath seen God at any time; "
21 prophet? And he answered, *N·*. 3756
47 Israelite...in whom is *n·* guile! "
2: 3 saith unto him, They have *n·* wine. "
3: 2 for *n·* man can do these miracles 3762
13 *n·* man hath ascended up to heaven, "
32 *n·* man receiveth his testimony. "
4: 9 *n·* dealings with the Samaritans. 3756
17 and said, I have *n·* husband. "
17 hast well said, I have *n·* husband: "
27 *n·* man said, What seekest thou? 3762
38 whereon ye bestowed *n·* labour: *3756
44 hath *n·* honour in his own country. "
5: 7 I have *n·* man, when the water is "
14 sin *n·* more, lest a worse thing 3370
22 For the Father judgeth *n·* man, *3762
6: 37 to me I will in *n·* wise cast out. 3364
44 *N·* man can come to me, except 3762
53 his blood, ye have *n·* life in you. *3756
65 that *n·* man can come unto me, 3762
66 and walked *n·* more with him. 3765
7: 4 *n·* man...doeth any thing in secret, 3762
13 *n·* man spake openly of him for fear "
18 and *n·* unrighteousness is in him. 3756
27 *n·* man knoweth whence he is. 3762
30 but *n·* man laid hands on him, "
44 but *n·* man laid hands on him. "
52 out of Galilee ariseth *n·* prophet. 3756
8: 10 hath *n·* man condemned thee? 3762
11 She said, *N·* man, Lord. And "
11 condemn thee: go, and sin *n·* more. 3370
15 after the flesh; I judge *n·* man. 3762
20 and *n·* man laid hands on him; for "
37 my word hath *n·* place in you. *3756
44 because there is *n·* truth in him. "
9: 4 cometh, when *n·* man can work. 3762
25 Whether he be a sinner or *n·*, I know *
41 were blind, ye should have *n·* sin: 3756
10: 18 *N·* man taketh it from me, but I 3762
29 *n·* man is able to pluck them out "
41 and said, John did *n·* miracle: "
11: 10 because there is *n·* light in him. *3756
54 walked *n·* more openly among 3765
13: 8 not, thou hast *n·* part with me. 3756
28 *n·* man at the table knew for what 3762
14: 6 *n·* man cometh unto the Father, "
19 and the world seeth me *n·* more; 3765
15: 4 *n·* more can ye, except ye abide *3761
13 Greater love hath *n·* man than 3762
22 they have *n·* cloke for their sin. 3756
16: 10 Father, and ye see me *n·* more; 3765
21 remembereth *n·* more the anguish, "
22 your joy *n·* man taketh from you. 3762
25 shall *n·* more speak...in proverbs, 3765
29 plainly, and speakest *n·* proverb. 3762
17: 11 now I am *n·* more in the world, 3765
18: 38 them, I find in him *n·* fault at all. 3762
19: 4 know that I find *n·* fault in him. "
6 him: for I find *n·* fault in him. 3756
9 But Jesus gave him *n·* answer. "
11 have *n·* power at all against me, "
15 We have *n·* king but Cæsar. "
21: 5 any meat? They answered him, *N·*. "
Ac 1: 20 and let *n·* man dwell therein: 3361
4: 17 spread *n·* further among the people, "
17 henceforth to *n·* man in this name. 3367
5: 13 durst *n·* man join himself to them: 3762
23 opened, we found *n·* man within. "
7: 5 *n·*, not so much as to set his foot on: "
5 him, when as yet he had *n·* child. 3756
11 and our fathers found *n·* sustenance. "
8: 39 that the eunuch saw him *n·* more: 3765
9: 7 hearing a voice, but seeing *n·* man. 3367
8 eyes were opened, he saw *n·* man: *3762
10: 34 God is *n·* respecter of persons: 3756
12: 18 *n·* small stir among the soldiers, "
13: 28 found *n·* cause of death in him, 3367
34 *n·* more to return to corruption, 3370
37 raised again, saw *n·* corruption. 3756
41 which ye shall in *n·* wise believe, 3364
15: 2 Barnabas had *n·* small dissension 3756
9 *n·* difference between us and them, 3762
24 we gave *n·* such commandment: 3756
28 you *n·* greater burden than these 3367
16: 28 Do thyself *n·* harm: for we are all "

Ac 18:10 n' man shall set on thee to hurt 3762
15 I will be n' judge of such matters.*3756
19:23 arose n' small stir about that way. "
24 n' small gain unto the craftsmen; "
26 saying that they be n' gods, which "
40 n' cause whereby we may give *3367
20:25 ye all,...shall see my face n' more. 3765
33 I have coveted n' man's silver, or 3762
38 they should see his face n' more. 3765
21:25 that they observe n' such thing, *3367
39 Cilicia, a citizen of n' mean city: 3756
23: 8 say that there is n' resurrection, 3361
9 We find n' evil in this man: but if 3762
22 See thou tell n' man that thou hast3367
25:10 to the Jews have I done n' wrong, 3762
11 n' man may deliver me unto them. "
26 I have n' certain thing to write 3756
27:20 and n' small tempest lay on us, "
22 shall be n' loss of any man's life 3762
28: 2 people shewed us n' little kindness:3756
4 N' doubt this man is a murderer, "
5 into the fire, and felt n' harm. 3762
6 and saw n' harm come to him, *3367
18 there was n' cause of death in me. "
31 confidence, n' man forbidding him. 209
Ro 2:11 is n' respect of person with God. 3756
3: 9 are we better than they? N', "
9 we better than they?...in n' wise: 3843
10 There is none righteous, n', not one: "
12 is none that doeth good, n', not one. "
18 There is n' fear of God before 3756
20 n' flesh be justified in his 3756,3956
22 believe: for there is n' difference: 3756
4:15 wrath: for where n' law is, there "
15 law is, there is n' transgression. *3761
5:13 not imputed when there is n' law. 3361
6: 9 from the dead dieth n' more; 3765
9 hath n' more dominion over him. "
7: 3 so that she is n' adulteress, though3361
17 Now then it is n' more I that do it, 3765
18 my flesh) dwelleth n' good thing: 3756
20 it is n' more I that do it, but sin 3765
8: 1 therefore now n' condemnation 3762
10:12 is n' difference between the Jew 3756
19 jealousy by them that are n' people, "
11: 6 grace, then is it n' more of works: 3765
6 otherwise grace is n' more grace. "
6 of works, then is it n' more grace:* "
6 otherwise work is n' more work. * "
12:17 Recompense to n' man evil for evil. 3367
13: 1 For there is n' power but of God: 3756
8 Owe n' man any thing, but to love 3367
10 worketh n' ill to his neighbour: 3756
14: 7 and n' man dieth to himself. *3762
13 that n' man put a stumblingblock 3361
15:23 now having n' more place in these 3370
1Co 1: 7 So that ye come behind in n' gift; 3367
10 there be n' divisions among you; 3361
29 n' flesh...glory in his presence. 3361,3956
2:11 things of God knoweth n' man, *3762
15 yet he himself is judged of n' man. "
3:11 other foundation can n' man lay "
18 Let n' man deceive himself. If 3367
21 Therefore let n' man glory in men. "
4: 6 that n' one of you be puffed up for 3361
11 and have n' certain dwellingplace; 790
5:11 with such an one n' not to eat.
6: 5 n', not one that shall be able to *
7:25 virgins I have n' commandment 3756
37 in his heart, having n' necessity, 3361
8:13 I will eat n' flesh while the world 3364
9:10 For our sakes, n' doubt, this is *1063
10:13 hath n' temptation taken you but 3756
24 Let n' man seek his own, but 3367
25, 27 asking n' question for conscience"
11:16 we have n' such custom, neither 3756
12: 3 that n' man speaking by the Spirit3762
3 that n' man can say that Jesus is "
21 to the hand, I have n' need of thee:3756
21 to the feet, I have n' need of you. "
24 For our comely parts have n' need: "
25 should be n' schism in the body; 3361
13: 5 easily provoked, thinketh n' evil; 3756
14: 2 for n' man understandeth him; 3762
28 But if there be n' interpreter, let 3361
15:12 there is n' resurrection of the dead?3756
13 there be n' resurrection of the dead, "
16: 2 there be n' gatherings when I come. 3361
11 Let n' man therefore despise him: "
2Co 2:13 I had n' rest in my spirit, because 3756
3:10 had n' glory in this respect, by *3761
5:16 know we n' man after the flesh: 3762
16 henceforth know we him n' more. 3765
21 to be sin for us, who knew n' sin; 3361
6: 3 Giving n' offence in any thing, 3367
7: 2 us; we have wronged n' man, 3762
2 we have corrupted n' man; we have"
2 man, we have defrauded n' man. "
5 our flesh had n' rest, but we were "
8:15 had gathered little had n' lack. 3756
20 that n' man should blame us in 3361
11: 9 I was chargeable to n' man: *3762
10 n' man shall stop me of this 3756,
14 And n' marvel; for Satan himself "
15 it is n' great thing if his ministers "
16 again, Let n' man think me a fool; 3367
13: 7 pray to God that ye do n' evil; 3361,
Ga 2: 5 by subjection, n', not for an hour;*
6 were, it maketh n' matter to me: 3762
6 God accepteth n' man's person:) *3756
16 law shall n' flesh be justified. 3756,3956
3:11 that n' man is justified by the law 3762
15 n' man disannulleth, or addeth "
18 the law, it is n' more of promise: 3765
25 are n' longer under a schoolmaster."
4: 7 art n' more a servant, but a son; "

Ga 4: 8 them which by nature are n' gods. 3361
5: 4 Christ is become of n' effect unto *2673
23 against such there is n' law. 3756
6:17 henceforth let n' man trouble me: 3367
Eph 2:12 having n' hope, and without God 3361
19 therefore ye are n' more strangers3765
4:14 we henceforth be n' more children, 3370
28 Let him that stole steal n' more: "
29 Let n' corrupt communication3956,3361
5: 5 ye know, that n' whoremonger," 3756
6 Let n' man deceive you with vain 3367
11 n' fellowship with the unfruitful 3361
29 For n' man ever yet hated his own 3762
Ph'p 2: 7 But made himself of n' reputation,*5013
20 For I have n' man likeminded, 3762
3: 3 have n' confidence in the flesh. 3756
4:15 n' church communicated with me 3762
Col 2:16 Let n' man therefore judge you in 3361
18 n' man beguile you of your reward3367
3:25 and there is n' respect of persons. 3756
1Th 3: 1 when we could n' longer forbear, 3370
3 n' man should be moved by these 3367
5 when I could n' longer forbear, 3370
4: 6 n' man go beyond and defraud his 3361
13 even as others which have n' hope. "
5: 1 have n' need that I write unto you. 3756
2Th 2: 3 Let n' man deceive you by any 3361
3:14 have n' company with him, that "
1Ti 1: 3 that they teach n' other doctrine, * "
3: 3 Not given to wine, n' striker, not * "
4:12 Let n' man despise thy youth; but 3367
5:22 Lay hands suddenly on n' man, "
23 Drink n' longer water, but use a 3370
6:16 which n' man can approach unto;*3762
16 whom n' man hath seen, nor can see: "
2Ti 2: 4 N' man that warreth entangleth "
14 strive not about words to n' profit, "
3: 9 they shall proceed n' further: for 3756
4:16 answer n' man stood with me, 3762
Tit 1: 7 not given to wine, n' striker, not 3361
2: 8 having n' evil thing to say of you. 3367
15 authority. Let n' man despise thee."
3: 2 To speak evil of n' man, to be "
2 man, to be n' brawlers, but gentle,* 269
Heb 5: 4 n' man taketh this honour unto 3756
6:13 he could sware by n' greater, he *3762
7:13 of which n' man gave attendance "
8: 7 should n' place have been sought 3756
12 will I remember n' more. 3364
9:17 otherwise it is of n' strength at all*3361
22 shedding of blood is n' remission. 3756
10: 2 had n' more conscience of sins. 3367
6 for sin thou hast had n' pleasure. 3756
17 iniquities will I remember n' more. 3361
18 there is n' more offering for sin. 3765
26 remaineth n' more sacrifice for sins,"
38 soul shall have n' pleasure in him. 3756
12:11 Now n' chastening for the *3956
14 without which n' man shall see the3762
17 for he found n' place of repentance, 3756
13:10 whereof they have n' right to eat "
14 here we have n' continuing city, * "
Jas 1:11 the sun is n' sooner risen with a *
13 Let n' man say when he is tempted, 3367
17 with whom is n' variableness, 3756
2:11 Now if thou commit n' adultery, * "
13 mercy, that hath shewed n' mercy; 3361
3: 8 the tongue can n' man tame; it is 3762
12 so can n' fountain both yield salt * "
1Pe 2:22 Who did n' sin, neither was guile 3756
3:10 his lips that they speak n' guile: 3361
4: 2 That he n' longer should live the 3370
2Pe 1:20 n' prophecy of the scripture 3956,3756
1Jo 1: 5 and in him is n' darkness at all. "
8 If we say that we have n' sin, we "
2: 7 I write n' new commandment unto "
19 n' doubt have continued with us:*
21 and that n' lie is of the truth. 3956,3756
27 and his truth, and is n' lie, and "
3: 5 our sins; and in him is n' sin. "
7 children, let n' man deceive you: *3367
15 n' murderer hath eternal life 3956,3756
4:12 N' man hath seen God at any 3762
18 There is n' fear in love; but 3756
3Jo 4 n' greater joy than to hear that my* "
Re 2:17 which n' man knoweth saving he 3762
3: 7 openeth, and n' man shutteth, * "
7 and shutteth, and n' man openeth;*"
8 open door, and n' man can shut it:*"
11 hast, that n' man take thy crown. 3367
12 and he shall go n' more out: and I 3364
5: 3 n' man in heaven, nor in earth, 3762
4 because n' man was found worthy "
7: 9 which n' man could number, of all "
16 They shall hunger n' more, 3756
10: 6 that there should be time n' longer:"
13:17 And that n' man might buy or sell, 3361
14: 3 and n' man could learn that song 3762
5 in their mouth was found n' guile: 3756
11 they have n' rest day nor night, "
15: 8 and n' man was able to enter into *3762
17:12 have received n' kingdom as yet; 3768
18: 7 I sit a queen, and am n' widow, 3756
7 widow, and shall see n' sorrow. 3364
11 n' man buyeth their merchandise 3762
14 thou shalt find them n' more at all. 3364
21 and shall be found n' more at all. "
22 shall be heard n' more at all in thee;"
22 n' craftsman, of whatsoever 3956,
22 shall be heard n' more at all in thee:"
23 shall shine n' more at all in thee; "
23 bride shall be heard n' more at all "
19:12 name written, that n' man knew, 3762
20: 3 should deceive the nations n' more, 3361
6 the second death hath n' power, 3756
11 there was found n' place for them. "

Re 21: 1 away; and there was n' more sea. 3756
4 and there shall be n' more death, "
22 And I saw n' temple therein: for "
23 And the city had n' need of the sun,"
25 for there shall be n' night there. "
27 there shall in n' wise enter into it 3364
22: 3 And there shall be n' more curse: 3756
5 And there shall be n' night there; "

No (*no*) See also POPULOUS.
Jer 46:25 will punish the multitude of N', 4996
Eze 30:14 and will execute judgments in N'. "
15 I will cut off the multitude of N'. "
16 pain, and N' shall be rent asunder, "
Na 3: 8 Art thou better than populous N',* "

Noadiah (*no-a-di'-ah*)
Ezr 8:33 Jeshua, and N' the son of Binnui,*5129
Ne 6:14 and on the prophetess N', and the "

Noah (*no'-ah*) See also NOAH'S; NOE.
Ge 5:29 he called his name N', saying, 5146
30 after he begat N' five hundred "
32 And N' was five hundred years old:"
32 N' begat Shem, Ham, and Japheth."
6: 8 N' found grace in the eyes of the "
9 These are the generations of N': "
9 N' was a just man and perfect in "
9 and N' walked with God. "
10 N' begat three sons, Shem, Ham, "
13 And God said unto N', The end of "
22 Thus did N'; according to all that "
7: 1 the Lord said unto N', Come thou "
5 N' did according unto all that the "
6 N' was six hundred years old when"
7 N' went in, and his sons, and his "
9 two and two unto N' into the ark, "
9 female, as God had commanded N'. "
13 In the selfsame day entered N', "
13 Ham, and Japheth, the sons of N', "
15 they went in unto N' into the ark, "
23 N' only remained alive, and they "
8: 1 God remembered N', and every "
6 N' opened the window of the ark "
11 so N' knew that the waters were "
13 N' removed the covering of the ark,"
15 And God spake unto N', saying, "
18 N' went forth, and his sons, and "
20 N' builded an altar unto the Lord; "
9: 1 God blessed N' and his sons, and "
8 God spake unto N', and to his sons"
17 God said unto N', This is the token"
18 the sons of N', that went forth of "
19 These are the three sons of N': and"
20 N' began to be an husbandman, "
24 N' awoke from his wine, and knew "
28 And N' lived after the flood three "
29 the days of N' were nine hundred "
10: 1 the generations of the sons of N', "
32 are the families of the sons of N', "
Nu 26:33 Zelophehad were Mahlah, and N', 5270
27: 1 of his daughters; Mahlah, N', "
36:11 N', the daughters of Zelophehad, "
Jos 17: 3 of his daughters, Mahlah, and N', "
1Ch 1: 4 N', Shem, Ham, and Japheth. 5146
Isa 54: 9 is as the waters of N' unto me: "
9 waters of N' should no more go "
Eze 14:14 three men, N', Daniel, and Job, "
20 Though N', Daniel, and Job, were "
Heb11: 7 By faith N', being warned of God 3575
1Pe 3:20 of God waited in the days of N', "
2Pe 2: 5 but saved N' the eighth person, a "

Noah's (*no'-ahz*)
Ge 7:11 the six hundredth year of N' life, 5146
13 and N' wife, and three wives of his "

Nob (*nob*)
1Sa 21: 1 came David to N' to Abimelech 5011
22: 9 I saw the son of Jesse coming to N', "
11 house, the priests that were in N': "
19 And N', the city of the priests, smote"
Ne 11:32 And at Anathoth, N', Ananiah, "
Isa 10:32 yet shall he remain at N' that day: "

Nobah (*no'-bah*) See also KENAH; NOPHAH.
Nu 32:42 And N' went and took Kenath, 5025
42 called it N', after his own name. "
J'g 8:11 dwelt in tents on the east of N' "

noble See also NOBLEMAN; NOBLES.
Ezr 4:10 whom the great and n' Asnapper 3358
Es 6: 9 one of the king's most n' princes, 6579
Jer 2:21 Yet I had planted thee a n' vine, wholly
Ac 17:11 These were more n' than those in 2104
24: 3 and in all places, most n' Felix, *2903
26:25 said, I am not mad, most n' Festus;*"
1Co 1:26 mighty, not many n', are called; 2104

nobleman
Lu 19:12 A certain n' went into a far 2104,444
Joh 4:46 there was a certain n', whose son 937
49 The n' saith unto him, Sir, come "

nobles
Ex 24:11 the n' of the children of Israel 678
Nu 21:18 the n' of the people digged it, by 5081
J'g 5:13 have dominion over the n' among 117
1Ki 21: 8 to the n' that were in his city, 2715
11 the elders and the n' who were the "
2Ch 23:20 captains of hundreds, and the n', 117
Ne 2:16 nor to the priests, nor to the n', 2715
3: 5 but their n' put not their necks to 117
4:14 rose up, and said unto the n', and 2715
19 And I said unto the n', and to the "
5: 7 I rebuked the n', and the rulers, and"
6:17 the n' of Judah sent many letters "
7: 5 heart to gather together the n', "
10:29 clave to their brethren, their n', 117
13:17 I contended with the n' of Judah, 2715
Es 1: 3 n' and princes of the provinces, 6579
Job 29:10 The n' held their peace, and their 5057

Ps 83:11 Make their *n'* like Oreb, and like 5081
149: 8 and their *n'* with fetters of iron; 3513
Pr 8:16 By me princes rule, and *n'*, even 5081
Ec 10:17 when thy king is the son of *n'*, and2715
Isa 13: 2 may go into the gates of the *n'*. 5081
34:12 call the *n'* thereof to the kingdom, 2715
43:14 have brought down all their *n'*, *1281
Jer 14: 3 their *n'* have sent their little ones to117
27:20 the *n'* of Judah and Jerusalem; 2715
30:21 their *n'* shall be of themselves, * 117
39: 6 Babylon slew all the *n'* of Judah. 2715
Jon 3: 7 the decree of the king and his *n'*, 1419
Na 3:18 thy *n'* shall dwell in the dust: thy* 117

Nod (*nod*)
Ge 4:16 dwelt in the land of *N'*, on the 5113

Nodab (*no'-dab*)
1Ch 5:19 with Jetur, and Nephish, and *N'*. 5114

Noe (*no'-e*) See also NOAH.
M't 24:37 as the days of *N'* were, so shall *3575
38 day that *N'* entered into the ark, * "
Lu 3:36 which was the son of *N'*, which * "
17:26 as it was in the days of *N'*, so shall*"
27 day that *N'* entered into the ark, * "

Nogah (*no'-gah*)
1Ch 3: 7 And *N'*, and Nepheg, and Japhia, 5052
14: 6 And *N'*, and Nepheg, and Japhia,

Nohah (*no'-hah*)
1Ch 8: 2 *N'* the fourth, and Rapha the fifth.5119

noise See also NOISED.
Ex 20:18 and the *n'* of the trumpet, and the*6963
32:17 Joshua heard the *n'* of the people "
17 There is a *n'* of war in the camp. "
18 the *n'* of them that sing do I hear. "
Jos 6:10 nor make any *n'* with your voice,*8085
J'g 5:11 delivered from the *n'* of archers 6963
1Sa 4: 6 heard the *n'* of the shout, they "
6 meaneth the *n'* of this great shout "
14 when Eli heard the *n'* of the crying,"
14 What meaneth the *n'* of this tumult?"
14:19 the *n'* that was in the host of the *1995
1Ki 1:41 *n'* of the city being in an uproar? 6963
45 This is the *n'* that ye have heard. "
2Ki 7: 6 the Syrians to hear a *n'* of chariots,"
6 *n'* of horses, even the *n'* of a great "
11:13 Athaliah heard the *n'* of the guard "
1Ch 15:28 making a *n'* with psalteries and *8085
2Ch 23:12 when Athaliah heard the *n'* of the 6963
Ezr 3:13 discern the *n'* of the shout of joy "
13 the *n'* of the weeping of the people:"
13 shout, and the *n'* was heard afar off."
Job 36:29 or the *n'* of his tabernacle? *8663
33 *n'* thereof sheweth concerning it, 7452
37: 2 Hear attentively the *n'* of his voice,7267
Ps 33: 3 song; play skilfully with a loud *n'*.8643
42: 7 deep at the *n'* of thy waterspouts: 6963
55: 2 in my complaint, and make a *n'*; *1949
59: 6 they make a *n'* like a dog, and go 1993
14 let them make a *n'* like a dog, "
65: 7 Which stilleth the *n'* of the seas, *7588
7 *n'* of their waves, and the tumult of*"
66: 1 Make a joyful *n'* unto God, all ye
81: 1 make a joyful *n'* unto the God of
93: 4 than the *n'* of many waters, yea, *6963
95: 1 let us make a joyful *n'* to the rock of
2 a joyful *n'* unto him with psalms.
98: 4 Make a joyful *n'* unto the Lord, all
4 make a loud *n'*, and rejoice, and *6476
6 make a joyful *n'* before the Lord, the
100: 1 Make a joyful *n'* unto the Lord, all ye
Isa 9: 5 of the warrior is with confused *n'*,*
13: 4 *n'* of a multitude in the mountains,6963
4 tumultuous *n'* of the kingdoms of "
14:11 the grave, and the *n'* of thy viols: 1998
17:12 make a *n'* like the *n'* of the seas; *1993
24: 8 the *n'* of them that rejoice endeth,7588
18 who fleeth from the *n'* of the fear 6963
25: 5 bring down the *n'* of strangers, as 7588
29: 6 and with earthquake, and great *n'*,6963
31: 4 abase himself for the *n'* of them: 1995
33: 3 At the *n'* of the tumult the people 6963
66: 6 A voice of *n'* from the city, a voice*7588
Jer 4:19 my heart maketh a *n'* in me; I *1993
29 flee for the *n'* of the horsemen 6963
10:22 Behold, the *n'* of the bruit is come,*"
11:16 with the *n'* of a great tumult he "
25:31 A *n'* shall come even to the ends of7588
46:17 Pharaoh king of Egypt is but a *n'*; "
47: 3 the *n'* of the stamping of the hoofs6963
49:21 is moved at the *n'* of their fall; "
21 at the cry the *n'* thereof was heard "
50:46 At the *n'* of the taking of Babylon "
51:55 a *n'* of their voice is uttered: 7588
La 2: 7 a *n'* in the house of the Lord, 6963
Eze 1:24 went, I heard the *n'* of their wings, "
24 like the *n'* of great waters, as the "
24 of speech, as the *n'* of an host: "
3:13 I heard also the *n'* of the wings of "
13 the *n'* of the wheels over against "
13 them, and a *n'* of a great rushing. "
19: 7 thereof, by the *n'* of his roaring. "
26:10 shake at the *n'* of the horsemen, "
13 cause the *n'* of thy songs to cease;1995
37: 7 as I prophesied, there was a *n'*, 6963
43: 2 voice was like a *n'* of many waters:*"
Joe 2: 5 Like the *n'* of chariots on the tops of"
5 like the *n'* of a flame of fire that "
Am 5:23 away from me the *n'* of thy songs;1995
Mic 2:12 make a great *n'* by reason of the 1949
Na 3: 2 The *n'* of a whip, and the *n'* of the 6963
Zep 1:10 the *n'* of a cry from the fish gate, "
Zec 9:15 and make a *n'* as through wine; "
M't 9:23 minstrels and...people make a *n'*, *2350
2Pe 3:10 shall pass away with a great *n'*, 4500
Re 6: 1 heard, as it were the *n'* of thunder,*5456

noised
Jos 6:27 his fame was *n'* throughout all the*
M'r 2: 1 it was *n'* that he was in the house. 191
Lu 1:65 all these sayings were *n'* abroad 1255
Ac 2: 6 when this was *n'* abroad, the*1096,5408

noisome
Ps 91: 3 fowler, and from the *n'* pestilence.1942
Eze 14:15 I cause *n'* beasts to pass through 7451
21 the *n'* beast, and the pestilence,
Re 16: 2 fell a *n'* and grievous sore upon the2556

Non (*non*) See also NUN.
1Ch 7:27 *N'* his son, Jehoshuah his son. *5126

none See also NO and ONE.
Ge 23: 6 *n'* of us shall withhold from 376,3808
28:17 is *n'* other but the house of God, 369
39: 9 is *n'* greater in this house than I; "
11 there was *n'* of the men of the house"
41: 8 there was *n'* that could interpret "
15 and there is *n'* that can interpret it: "
24 was *n'* that could declare it to me. "
39 there is *n'* so discreet and wise as "
Ex 8:10 is *n'* like unto the Lord our God. "
9:14 there is *n'* like me in all the earth. "
24 *n'* like it in all the land of Egypt *3808
11: 6 such as there was *n'* like it, nor "
12:22 *n'* of you shall go out at the door of "
15:26 put *n'* of these diseases upon thee, "
16:26 the sabbath, in it there shall be *n'*. "
27 for to gather, and they found *n'*. "
23:15 *n'* shall appear before me empty:) "
34:20 *n'* shall appear before me empty. "
Le 18: 6 *N'* of you shall approach to any376,"
21: 1 shall *n'* be defiled for the dead "
22:30 leave *n'* of it until the morrow: "
25:26 if the man have *n'* to redeem it, and"
26: 6 down, and *n'* shall make you afraid:369
17 ye shall flee when *n'* pursueth you. "
36 they shall fall when *n'* pursueth. "
37 before a sword, when *n'* pursueth: "
27:29 *N'* devoted, which shall be 3606,3808
Nu 7: 9 the sons of Kohath he gave *n'*: "
9:12 leave *n'* of it unto the morning, nor "
21:35 until there was *n'* left him alive: 1115
30: 8 she bound her soul, of *n'* effect: *6565
32:11 Surely *n'* of the men that came up "
De 2:34 of every city, we left *n'* to remain: 3808
3: 3 smote him until *n'* was left to him 1115
4:35 God; there is *n'* else beside him. 369
39 the earth beneath: there is *n'* else. "
5: 7 shalt have *n'* other gods before me. "
7:15 *n'* of the evil diseases of Egypt, 3808
22:27 cried, and there was *n'* to save her. 369
28:31 thou shalt have *n'* to rescue them. "
66 have *n'* assurance of thy life: 3808
32:36 and there is *n'* shut up, or left. 657
33:26 is *n'* like unto the God of Jeshurun,369
Jos 6: 1 Israel: *n'* went out, and *n'* came in. "
8:22 let *n'* of them remain or escape. 1115
9:23 *n'* of you be freed from being *3808
10:21 *n'* moved his tongue against any "
28 were therein; he let *n'* remain: "
30 therein; he let *n'* remain in it; "
33 he had left him *n'* remaining. 1115
37 he left *n'* remaining, according "
39 therein; he left *n'* remaining: as "
40 he left *n'* remaining, but utterly "
11: 8 they left them *n'* remaining, 1115
13 Israel burned *n'* of them, save 3808
22 *n'* of the Anakims left in the land "
13:14 of Levi he gave *n'* inheritance; "
14: 3 gave *n'* inheritance among them. "
J'g 19:28 let us be going. But *n'* answered. 369
21: 8 came *n'* to the camp from 3808,376
9 were *n'* of the inhabitants of 369, "
Ru 4: 4 is *n'* to redeem it beside thee: and 369
1Sa 2: 2 There is *n'* holy as the Lord: for "
2 for there is *n'* besides thee: neither "
3:19 *n'* of his words fall to the ground. 3808
10:24 *n'* like him among all the people? 369
14:24 *n'* of the people tasted any food. 3808
21: 9 David said, There is *n'* like that; 369
22: 8 is *n'* that sheweth me that my son "
8 is *n'* of you that is sorry for me, or 369
2Sa 7:22 for there is *n'* like thee, neither is "
14: 6 and there was *n'* to part them, but "
19 *n'* can turn to the right hand or to 376
25 was *n'* to be so much praised 3808, "
18:12 Beware that *n'* touch the young man
22:42 looked, but there was *n'* to save; 369
1Ki 3:12 there was *n'* like thee before thee,3808
8:60 is God, and that there is *n'* else. 369
10:21 were of pure gold; *n'* were of silver:"
12:20 was *n'* that followed the house of 3808
15:22 all Judah; *n'* was exempted: 369
21:25 But there was *n'* like unto Ahab, 3808
2Ki 5:16 I will receive *n'*. And he urged him
6:12 his servants said, *N'*, my lord, O 3808
9:10 and there shall be *n'* to bury her. 369
15 let *n'* go forth nor escape out of the408
10:11 until he left him *n'* remaining. 1115
19 his priests; let *n'* be wanting: 376,408
23 be here with you *n'* of the servants
25 and slay them; let *n'* come forth. 408
17:18 was *n'* left but the tribe of Judah 3808
18: 5 after him was *n'* like him among "
24:14 *n'* remained, save the poorest sort "
1Ch 15: 2 *N'* ought to carry the ark of God "
17:20 O Lord, there is *n'* like thee, 369
23:17 Eliezer had *n'* other sons; but 3808
29:15 a shadow, and there is *n'* abiding.* 369
2Ch 1:12 such as *n'* of the kings have had 3808
9:11 *n'* such seen before in the land of "
20 were of pure gold: *n'* were of silver;*369
10:16 we have *n'* inheritance in the son *369
16: 1 let *n'* go out or come in to Asa *1115

2Ch 20: 6 that *n'* is able to withstand thee? 369
24 fallen to the earth, and *n'* escaped. "
23: 6 let *n'* come into the house of the 408
19 that *n'* which was unclean in any 3808
Ezr 8:15 found there *n'* of the sons of Levi. "
Ne 4:23 *n'* of us put off our clothes, saving 369
Es 1: 8 *n'* did compel: for so the king had "
4: 2 *n'* might enter into the king's gate "
Job 1: 8 there is *n'* like him in the earth, "
2: 3 there is *n'* like him in the earth, "
13 and *n'* spake a word unto him: for "
3: 9 dark; let it look for light but have *n'*,"
10: 7 there is *n'* that can deliver out of "
11:19 down, and *n'* shall make thee afraid;"
18:15 tabernacle, because it is *n'* of his: 1097
20:21 There shall *n'* of his meat be left;* 369
29:12 and him that had *n'* to help him. 3808
32:12 was *n'* of you that convinced Job, 369
35:10 *n'* saith, Where is God my maker, 3808
12 they cry, but *n'* giveth answer, "
41:10 *N'* is so fierce that dare stir him up:"
Ps 7: 2 pieces, while there is *n'* to deliver. 369
10:15 his wickedness till thou find *n'*. 1077
14: 1 works, there is *n'* that doeth good. 369
3 is *n'* that doeth good, no, not one. "
18:41 cried, but there was *n'* to save them:"
22:11 is near; for there is *n'* to help. "
29 and *n'* can keep alive his own soul.3808
25: 3 *n'* that wait on thee be ashamed: "
33:10 devices of the people of *n'* effect. 5106
34:22 *n'* of them that trust in him shall 3808
37:31 heart; *n'* of his steps shall slide. "
49: 7 *N'* of them can by any means 376, "
50:22 pieces, and there be *n'* to deliver. 369
53: 1 iniquity: there is *n'* that doeth good."
3 there is *n'* that doeth good, no, not "
69:20 some to take pity, but there was *n'*; "
20 and for comforters, but I found *n'*.3808
25 and let *n'* dwell in their tents. 408
71:11 him; for there is *n'* to deliver him. 369
73:25 is *n'* upon earth that I desire 3808
76: 5 *n'* of the men of might have found "
79: 3 and there was *n'* to bury them. 369
81:11 voice; and Israel would *n'* of me. 3808
86: 8 the gods there is *n'* like unto thee, 369
107:12 fell down, and there was *n'* to help. "
109:12 be *n'* to extend mercy unto him: 408
Pr 1:25 and would *n'* of my reproof: 3808
30 They would *n'* of my counsel: they "
2:19 *N'* that go unto her return again, "
3:31 and choose *n'* of his ways. 408
Ca 4: 2 twins, and *n'* is barren among them.369
Isa 1:31 together, and *n'* shall quench them. "
5:27 *N'* shall be weary nor stumble
27 them; *n'* shall slumber nor sleep; 3808
29 away safe, and *n'* shall deliver it. 369
10:14 there was *n'* that moved the wing, 3808
14: 6 is persecuted, and *n'* hindereth. 1097
31 *n'* shall be alone in his appointed 369
17: 2 down, and *n'* shall make them afraid."
22:22 so he shall open, and *n'* shall shut; "
22 and he shall shut, and *n'* shall open. "
34:10 *n'* shall pass through it for ever and "
12 the kingdom, but *n'* shall be there, "
16 fail, *n'* shall want her mate: 802,3808
41:17 needy seek water, and there is *n'*, 369
26 yea, there is *n'* that sheweth, "
26 yea, there is *n'* that declareth, "
26 there is *n'* that heareth your words. "
42:22 are for a prey, and *n'* delivereth; "
22 for a spoil, and *n'* saith, Restore. "
43:13 is *n'* that can deliver out of my hand:"
44:19 And *n'* considereth in his heart, 3808
45: 5 I am the Lord, and there is *n'* else, 369
6 west, that there is *n'* beside me. 657
6 I am the Lord, and there is *n'* else. 369
14 and there is *n'* else, there is no God. "
18 I am the Lord; and there is *n'* else. "
21 a Saviour; there is *n'* beside me. "
22 for I am God, and there is *n'* else. "
46: 9 for I am God, and there is *n'* else; "
9 I am God, and there is *n'* like me, 657
47: 8 heart, I am, and *n'* else besides me; "
10 thou hast said, *n'* seeth me. Thy 369
10 heart, I am, and *n'* else besides me.657
15 to his quarter; *n'* shall save thee. 369
50: 2 I called, was there *n'* to answer? "
51:18 is *n'* to guide her among all the sons"
57: 1 *n'* considering that the righteous is "
59: 4 *n'* calleth for justice, nor any "
11 look for judgment, but there is *n'*; "
63: 3 people there was *n'* with me; *369,376
5 looked, and there was *n'* to help; 369
5 that there was *n'* to uphold: "
64: 7 is *n'* that calleth upon thy name, "
66: 4 when I called, *n'* did answer; "
Jer 4: 4 fire, and burn that *n'* can quench it, "
22 and they have *n'* understanding: 3808
7:33 and *n'* shall fray them away. 369
9:10 *n'* can pass through them; 1097,376
12 that *n'* passeth through? 1997
22 and *n'* shall gather them. 369
10: 6 as there is *n'* like unto thee, O Lord "
7 kingdoms, there is *n'* like unto thee."
20 there is *n'* to stretch forth my tent "
13:19 be shut up, and *n'* shall open them: "
14:16 they shall have *n'* to bury them, "
21:12 and burn that *n'* can quench it, "
23:14 *n'* doth return from...wickedness: 1115
30: 7 day is great, so that *n'* is like it: 369
10 quiet, and *n'* shall make him afraid. "
13 There is *n'* to plead thy cause, that "
34: 9 *n'* should serve himself of them, 1115
10 *n'* should serve themselves of them "
35:14 for unto this day they drink *n'*, 3808
36:30 shall have *n'* to sit upon the throne "

Jer 42:17 n· of them shall remain or escape 3808
44: 7 Judah, to leave you n· to remain; 1115
14 that n· of the remnant of Judah, 3808
14 n· shall return but such as shall "
46:27 ease, and n· shall make him afraid. 369
48:33 n· shall tread with shouting; 3808
49: 5 and n· shall gather up him that 369
50: 3 and n· shall dwell therein; they 3808
9 man; n· shall return in vain. "
20 sought for, and there shall be n·; 369
29 round about; let n· thereof escape:408
32 and fall, and n· shall raise him up: 369
51:62 that n· shall remain in it, neither 1115
La 1: 2 lovers she hath n· to comfort her: 369
4 n· come to the solemn feasts: all 1997
7 of the enemy, and n· did help her: 369
17 and there is n· to comfort her: the "
21 I sigh: there is n· to comfort me: "
2:22 of the Lord's anger n· escaped 3808
5: 8 is n· that doth deliver us out of 369
Eze 7:11 n· of them shall remain, nor of 3808
14 ready; but n· goeth to the battle: 369
25 seek peace, and there shall be n·. "
12:28 n· of my words be prolonged any 3808
16: 5 N· eye pitied thee, to do any of "
34 n· followeth thee to commit "
18: 7 pledge, hath spoiled n· by violence, "
22:30 not destroy it: but I found n·. "
31:14 end that n· of all the trees by the "
33:16 N· of his sins...he hath committed "
28 that n· shall pass through. 369
34: 6 n· did search or seek after them. "
28 and n· shall make them afraid. "
39:26 land, and n· made them afraid. "
28 left n· of them any more there. 3808
Da 1:19 them all was found n· like Daniel, "
2:11 n· other that can shew it before 3809
4:35 n· can stay his hand, or say unto "
6: 4 could find n· occasion nor fault; "
8: 7 n· that could deliver the ram out 3808
27 at the vision, but n· understood it. 369
10:21 is n· that holdeth with me in these "
11:16 and n· shall stand before him: and "
45 to his end, and n· shall help him. "
12:10 n· of the wicked shall understand;3808
Ho 2:10 and n· shall deliver her out of mine "
5:14 take away and n· shall rescue him. 369
7: 7 n· among them that calleth unto "
11: 7 High, n· at all would exalt him. 3808
12: 8 n· iniquity in me that were sin. "
Joe 2:27 the Lord your God, and n· else: 369
Am 5: 2 land; there is n· to raise her up. "
6 there be n· to quench it in Beth-el. "
Ob 7 there is n· understanding in him. "
Mic 2: 5 n· that shall cast a cord by lot in 3808
3:11 us? n· evil can come upon us. * "
4: 4 n· shall make them afraid: for the 369
5: 8 in pieces, and n· can deliver. "
7: 2 and there is n· upright among men: "
Na 2: 8 they cry; but n· shall look back. "
9 for there is n· end of the store and "
11 whelp, and n· make them afraid? "
3: 3 and there is n· end of their corpses; "
Zep 2:15 I am, and there is n· beside me: 657
3: 6 streets waste, that n· passeth by: 1097
6 man, that there is n· inhabitant. 369
13 and n· shall make them afraid. "
Hag 1: 6 ye clothe you, but there is n· warm; "
Zec 7:10 let n· of you imagine evil against 408
8:17 let n· of you imagine evil in your "
Mal 2:15 let n· deal treacherously against "
M't 12:43 places, seeking rest, and findeth n·.3756
15: 6 commandment of God of n· effect * 208
19:17 there is n· good but one, that is, *3762
26:60 But found n·: yea, though many *3756
60 witnesses came, yet found they n·.* "
M'r 7:13 Making...word of God of n· effect * 208
10:18 is n· good but one, that is, God. 3762
12:31 is n· other commandment greater 3756
32 God; and there is n· other but he: "
14:55 to put him to death; and found n·.* "
Lu 1:61 is n· of thy kindred that is called 3762
3:11 him impart to him that hath n·; 3361
4:26 unto n· of them was Elias sent, 3762
27 n· of them was cleansed, saving "
11:24 seeking rest; and finding n·, he 3361
13: 6 sought fruit thereon, and found n·,3756
7 fruit on this fig tree, and find n·: "
14:24 n· of those men which were bidden3762
18:19 n· is good, save one, that is, God. "
34 they understood n· of these things: "
Joh 6:22 that there was n· other boat there,3756
7:19 n· of you keepeth the law? Why go3762
8:10 saw n· but the woman, he said 3367
15:24 the works which n· other man did, 3762
16: 5 n· of you asketh me, Whither goest "
17:12 and n· of them is lost, but the son* "
18: 9 thou gavest me have I lost n·. * "
21:12 n· of the disciples durst ask him, "
Ac 3: 6 said, Silver and gold have I n·; 3756
4:12 is n· other name under heaven 3777
7: 5 he gave him n· inheritance in it, 3756
8:16 yet he was fallen upon n· of them: 3762
24 n· of these things which ye have 3367
11:19 word to n· but unto the Jews only. "
18:17 Gallio cared for n· of these things. 3762
20:24 But n· of these things move * "
24:23 forbid n· of his acquaintance to *3367
25:11 but if there be n· of these things 3762
18 they brought n· accusation of such*"
26:22 saying n· other things than those* "
26 persuaded that n· of these5100,3756, "
Ro 3:10 there is n· righteous, no, not one: 3756
11 There is n· that understandeth, "
11 there is n· that seeketh after God. "
12 there is n· that doeth good, no, not "

Ro 4:14 and the promise made of n· effect:2673
8: 9 the Spirit of Christ, he is n· of his. 3756
9: 6 word of God hath taken n· effect. *1601
14: 7 For n· of us liveth to himself, and 3762
1Co 1:14 thank God that I baptized n· of you,"
17 cross...should be made of n· effect.*2758
2: 8 n· of the princes of this world 3762
7:29 wives be as though they had n·; 3361
8: 4 there is n· other God but one. *3762
9:15 But I have used n· of these things: "
10:32 Give n· offence, neither to...Jews, * 677
14:10 n· of them is without signification.*3762
2Co 1:13 we write n· other things unto you, 3756
Ga 1:19 But other of the apostles saw I n·, "
3:17 make the promise of n· effect. 208
5:10 ye will be n· otherwise minded: 3762
1Th 5:15 n· render evil for evil unto any3361,5100
1Ti 5:14 give n· occasion to the adversary 3361
1Pe 4:15 let n· of you suffer as a murderer, 3387
1Jo 2:10 is n· occasion of stumbling in him.3756
Re 2:10 Fear n· of those things which thou*3367
24 put upon you n· other burden. "

noon See also AFTERNOON; NOONDAY; NOONTIDE.
Ge 43:16 men shall dine with me at n·. 6672
25 present against Joseph came at n·: "
2Sa 4: 5 Ish-bosheth, who lay on a bed at n·."
1Ki 18:26 Baal from morning even until n·, "
27 it came to pass at n·, that Elijah "
20:16 And they went out at n·. But "
2Ki 4:20 he sat on her knees till n·, and then"
Ps 55:17 Evening, and morning, and at n·,* "
Ca 1: 7 thou makest thy flock to rest at n·: "
Isa 58:10 and thy darkness be as the n· day: "
59:10 we stumble at n· day as in the "
Jer 6: 4 her; arise, and let us go up at n·. "
Am 8: 9 will cause the sun to go down at n·, "
Zep 2: 4 shall drive out Ashdod at the n· day,"
Ac 22: 6 nigh unto Damascus about n·, 3314

noonday See also NOON and DAY.
De 28:29 And thou shalt grope at n·, as the 6672
Job 5:14 and grope in the n· as in the night. "
11:17 age shall be clearer than the n·; "
Ps 37: 6 light, and thy judgment as the n·. "
91: 6 the destruction that wasteth at n·. "
Isa 16: 3 as the night in the midst of the n·; "
Jer 15: 8 of the young men a spoiler at n·: "

noontide
Jer 20:16 and the shouting at n·; 6256,6672

Noph (*nof*) See also MEMPHIS.
Isa 19:13 the princes of N· are deceived; 5297
Jer 2:16 the children of N· and Tahapanes "
44: 1 and at Tahpanhes, and at N·, and "
46:14 publish in N· and in Tahpanhes: "
19 for N· shall be waste and desolate "
Eze 30:13 their images to cease out of N·; "
16 and N· shall have distresses daily. "

Nophah (*no'-fah*) See also NOBAH.
Nu 21:30 them waste even unto N·, which 5302

nor
Ge 21:23 me, n· with my son, n· with my son's
45: 5 grieved, n· angry with yourselves, 408
6 shall neither be earing n· harvests.
49:10 Judah, n· a lawgiver from between
Ex 4: 1 me, n· hearken unto my voice: 3808
10 n· since thou hast spoken unto thy1571
10: 6 thy fathers, n· thy father's fathers 3808
11: 6 none like it, n· be like it any more. "
12: 9 of it raw, n· sodden at all with water, "
13:22 by day, n· the pillar of fire by night,*
20: 5 thyself to them, n· serve them: 3808
10 thou, n· thy son, n· thy daughter,
10 thy manservant, n· thy maidservant,
10 n· thy cattle, n· thy stranger that is
17 n· his manservant, n· his maidservant,
17 n· his ox, n· his ass, n· any thing that is
22:21 vex a stranger, n· oppress him: *3808
28 n· curse the ruler of thy people. "
23:24 gods, n· serve them, n· do after their"
26 nothing cast their young, n· be barren,
32 covenant with them, n· with their gods.
30: 9 n· burnt sacrifice, n· meat offering;
34: 3 n· herds feed before that mount. 408
10 in all the earth, n· in any nation;
28 neither eat bread, n· drink water. 3808
36: 6 n· woman make any more work 408
Le 2:11 shall burn no leaven, n· any honey,
3:17 that ye eat neither fat n· blood.
10: 9 Do not drink wine n· strong drink,
9 n· thy sons with thee, when ye go
11:12 hath no fins n· scales in the waters,
26 clovenfooted, n· cheweth the cud. 369
12: 4 thing, n· come into the sanctuary, 3808
13:34 n· be in sight deeper than the skin;*
17:16 wash them not, n· bathe his flesh; 3808
18:26 your own nation, n· any stranger that
19: 4 n· make to yourselves molten 3808
14 n· put a stumblingblock before the "
15 n· honour the person of the mighty: "
18 n· bear any grudge against the "
20 redeemed, n· freedom given her; "
26 use enchantment, n· observe times. "
28 dead, n· print any marks upon you: "
20:19 sister, n· of thy father's sister;
21: 5 n· make...cuttings in their flesh. 3808
10 his head, n· rend his clothes; "
11 n· defile himself for his father, or "
12 n· profane the sanctuary of his God; "
23 vail, n· come nigh unto the altar, "
22:22 n· make an offering by fire of them "
23:14 n· parched corn, n· green ears, until
25: 4 thy field, n· prune thy vineyard. 3808
11 n· gather the grapes in it of thy vine"
20 not sow, n· gather in our increase. "
37 n· lend him thy victuals for increase."

Le 26: 1 shall make no idols n· graven image,*
27:10 shall not alter it, n· change it, a 3808
Nu 5:15 it, n· put frankincense thereon; "
6: 3 n· eat moist grapes, or dried. "
9:12 morning, n· break any bone of it: "
11:19 one day, n· two days, n· five days, "
19 neither ten days, n· twenty days; "
18: 3 that neither they, n· ye also, die. "
20:17 turn to the right hand, n· to the left, "
23:25 them at all, n· bless them at all. 3808
De 1:45 your voice, n· give ear unto you. "
2:19 them not, n· meddle with them: 408
27 turn unto the right hand n· to the left.
37 n· unto any place of the river Jabbok,*
37 n· unto the cities in the mountains,*
37 n· unto whatsoever the Lord our God*
4:28 see, n· hear, n· eat, n· smell. 3808
31 thee, n· forget the covenant of thy "
5: 9 thyself unto them, n· serve them: "
14 work, thou, n· thy son, n· thy daughter,
14 n· thy manservant, n· thy maidservant,
14 n· thine ox, n· thine ass, n· any of thy
14 n· thy servant that is within thy gates;
7: 2 them, n· shew mercy unto them: 3808
3 n· his daughter shalt thou take "
7 his love upon you, n· choose you, "
25 n· take it unto thee, lest thou be "
9: 9 did eat bread n· drink water: 3808
18 neither eat bread, n· drink water, "
23 him not, n· hearkened to his voice. "
27 n· to their wickedness, n· to their sin:
10:17 not persons, n· taketh reward: 3808
12:12 hath no part n· inheritance with you.
17 n· any of thy vows which thou vowest,
17 n· thy freewill offerings, or heave
32 add thereto, n· diminish from it. 3808
13: 6 hast not known, thou, n· thy fathers;
8 unto him, n· hearken unto him; 3808
14: 1 n· make any baldness between your"
8 flesh, n· touch their dead carcase.* "
27 hath no part n· inheritance with thee.
29 hath no part n· inheritance with thee,)
15: 7 n· shut thine hand from thy poor 3808
19 n· shear the firstling of thy sheep. "
17:11 thee, to the right hand, n· to the left.
16 n· cause the people to return to 3808
18: 1 no part n· inheritance with Israel:
22 thing follow not, n· come to pass, 3808
21: 4 which is neither eared n· sown, and "
22:30 wife, n· discover his father's skirt.* "
23: 6 seek their peace n· their prosperity
17 n· a sodomite of the sons of Israel.*3808
24:17 the stranger, n· of the fatherless:
17 n· take a widow's raiment to 3808
26:14 n· given ought thereof for the dead:"
28:36 neither thou n· thy father have known;
39 of the wine, n· gather the grapes; 3808
50 old, n· shew favour to the young: "
64 neither thou n· thy fathers have known,
29:23 n· beareth, n· any grass groweth 3808
31: 6 fear not, n· be afraid of them: for 408
6 will not fail thee, n· forsake thee. 3808
33: 9 brethren, n· knew his own children:"
34: 7 dim, n· his natural force abated. "
Jos 1: 5 I will not fail thee, n· forsake thee. "
6:10 shall not shout, n· make any noise "
10:25 Fear not, n· be dismayed, be strong408
13:13 Geshurites, n· the Maachathites: "
22:19 the Lord, n· rebel against us, in "
26 for burnt offering, n· for sacrifice: 3808
28 for burnt offerings, n· for sacrifices;"
23: 7 gods, n· cause to swear by them, "
7 them, n· bow yourselves unto them:"
24:12 with thy sword, n· with thy bow.
19 your transgressions n· your sins.
J'g 1:27 her towns, n· Taanach and her towns,
27 n· the inhabitants of Dor and her
27 n· the inhabitants of Ibleam and her
27 n· the inhabitants of Megiddo and her
30 n· the inhabitants of Nahalol; but the
31 n· the inhabitants of Zidon, n· of Ahlab,
31 n· of Achzib, n· of Helbah,
31 n· of Aphik, n· of Rehob:
33 n· the inhabitants of Beth-anath;
2:10 not the Lord, n· yet the works 1571
19 doings, n· from their stubborn way.
6: 4 Israel, neither sheep, n· ox, n· ass.
11:15 n· the land of the children of Ammon:
34 he had neither son n· daughter. 176
13: 4 and drink not wine n· strong drink,
7 now drink no wine n· strong drink,
14 drink, n· eat any unclean thing: 408
23 n· would as at this time have told 3908
14:16 not told it my father n· my mother, "
19:30 was no such deed done n· seen from"
1Sa 1:15 drunk neither wine n· strong drink,
3:14 with sacrifice n· offering for ever.
5: 5 n· any that come into Dagon's house,
12: 4 not defrauded us, n· oppressed us,3808
21 which cannot profit n· deliver; for "
13:22 n· spear found in the hand of any of
15:29 of Israel will not lie n· repent: 3808
20:27 meat, neither yesterday, n· to day?1571
31 not be established, n· thy kingdom.
21: 8 my sword n· my weapons with me,1571
22:15 n· to all the house of my father:
24:11 there is neither evil n· transgression
25:31 thee, n· offence of heart unto my lord,
26:12 no man saw it, n· knew it, neither 369
27: 9 and left neither man n· woman alive,
11 saved neither man n· woman alive,
28: 6 dreams, n· by Urim, n· by prophets.1571
15 neither by prophets, n· by dreams: "
18 n· executedst his fierce wrath *3808
20 no bread all the day, n· all the night.
30:12 no bread, n· drunk any water, 3808

1Sa 30:15 n· deliver me into the hands of my 518
19 small n· great, neither sons n· 5703
19 n· any thing that they had taken "
2Sa 1:21 rain, upon you, n· fields of offerings:*
2:19 not to the right hand n· to the left
3:34 bound, n· thy feet put into fetters:3808
13:22 brother Amnon neither good n· bad:
14: 7 name n· remainder upon the earth.
19: 6 regardest neither princes n· servants:*
24 n· trimmed his beard, n· washed 3808
21: 4 n· gold of Saul, n· of his house; *
10 n· the beasts of the field by night.
1Ki 3: 8 numbered n· counted for multitude.
11 n· hast asked the life of thine 3808
26 Let it be neither mine n· thine, but
5: 4 neither adversary n· evil occurrent.369
6: 7 that there was neither hammer n· axe
7 n· any tool of iron heard in the house,
8: 5 told n· numbered for multitude. 3808
57 let him not leave us, n· forsake us: 408
10:12 trees, n· were seen unto this day. 3808
12:24 up, n· fight against your brethren "
13: 8 will I eat bread n· drink water in "
9 Eat no bread, n· drink water, "
9 n· turn again by the same way * "
16 return with thee, n· go in with thee:
16 bread n· drink water with thee in 3808
17 eat no bread n· drink water there, "
17 n· turn again to go by the way that "
28 eaten the carcase, n· torn the ass. "
16:11 of his kinsfolks, n· of his friends.
17: 1 shall not be dew n· rain these years,
18:26 was no voice, n· any that answered.369
29 n· any to answer, n· any that
20: 8 Hearken not unto him, n· consent.*3808
22:31 Fight neither with small n· great,
2Ki 3:14 not look toward thee, n· see thee. 518
4:23 is neither new moon, n· Sabbath. 3808
31 there was neither voice, n· hearing.369
5:17 offering n· sacrifice unto other gods,
6:10 himself there, not once n· twice. 3808
9:15 go forth n· escape out of the city *
14: 6 n· the children be put to death for3808
26 n· any left, n· any helper for Israel.*369
17:35 gods, n· bow yourselves to them, 3808
35 n· serve them, n· sacrifice to them: "
18: 5 Judah, n· any that were before him.
12 would not hear them, n· do them. 3808
19:32 this city, n· shoot an arrow there, "
32 n· come before it with shield, * "
32 with shield, n· cast a bank against it.
20:13 in his house, n· in all his dominion,
23:22 Israel, n· in all the days of the kings
22 of Israel, n· of the kings of Judah;
1Ch 21:24 n· offer burnt offerings without cost.
22:13 courage; dread not, n· be dismayed.*408
23:26 n· any vessels of it for the service *
28:20 fear not, n· be dismayed: for the 408
20 will not fail thee, n· forsake thee. 3808
2Ch 1:11 or honour, n· the life of thine enemies,
5: 6 told n· numbered for multitude. 3808
6:14 thee in the heaven, n· in the earth;*
11: 4 up, n· fight against your brethren:3808
15: 5 that went out, n· to him that came in,
19: 7 n· respect of persons, n· taking of gifts.
20:15 afraid n· dismayed by reason of * 408
17 fear not, n· be dismayed; to morrow "
21:12 n· in the ways of Asa king of Judah,
29: 7 incense n· offered burnt offerings 3808
32: 7 n· dismayed for the king of Assyria,408
7 n· for all the multitude that is with
15 n· persuade you on this manner, 408
34: 2 to the right hand, n· to the left. *
Ezr 9:12 n· seek their peace or their wealth3808
14 should be no remnant n· escaping?
10: 6 did eat no bread, n· drink water: 3808
Ne 1: 7 n· the statutes, n· the judgments,
2:16 Jews, n· to the priests, n· to the nobles,
16 n· to the rulers, n· to the rest that did
20 no portion, n· right, n· memorial, in
4:23 I, n· my brethren, n· my servants,
23 n· the men of the guard which
7:61 their father's house, n· their seed,
8: 9 your God; mourn not, n· weep. 408
9:31 consume them, n· forsake them; 3808
34 priests, n· our fathers, kept thy law,"
34 thy law, n· hearkened unto thy "
10:30 n· take their daughters for our "
13:25 n· take their daughters unto your 518
Es 2: 7 for she had neither father n· mother,
10 not shewed her people n· her kindred:
20 yet shewed her kindred n· her people;
3: 2 bowed not, n· did him reverence. 3808
5 bowed not, n· did him reverence,
4:16 neither eat n· drink three days, 408
5: 9 stood not up, n· moved for him, 3808
9:28 n· the memorial of them perish "
Job 1:22 not, n· charged God foolishly. "
3:10 womb, n· hid sorrow from mine eyes.
7:19 n· let me alone till I swallow 3808
14:12 n· be raised out of their sleep. "
18:19 son n· nephew among his people, "
19 n· any remaining in his dwellings. "
24:13 n· abide in the paths thereof. "
27: 4 n· my tongue utter deceit. * 518
28: 8 it, n· the fierce lion passed by it. 3808
34:19 n· regardeth the rich more than "
22 no darkness, n· shadow of death, 369
36:19 gold, n· all the forces of strength.*3808
41:12 n· his power, n· his comely proportion.
26 spear, the dart, n· the habergeon.
Ps 1: 1 n· standeth in the way of sinners, 3808
1 n· sitteth in the seat of the scornful."
5 n· sinners in the congregation of the
15: 3 n· doeth evil to his neighbour, 3808
3 n· taketh up a reproach against his "

Ps 15: 5 n· taketh reward against the 3808
16: 4 n· take up their names into my 1077
19: 3 There is no speech n· language, 369
22:24 despised n· abhorred the affliction 3808
24: 4 unto vanity, n· sworn deceitfully.* "
25: 7 of my youth, n· my transgression:
26: 9 sinners, n· my life with bloody men:
28: 5 Lord, n· the operation of his hands,
37:25 forsaken, n· his seed begging bread.
33 n· condemn him when he is 3808
40: 4 proud, n· such as turn aside to lies."
49: 7 n· give to God a ransom for him: "
50: 9 thy house, n· he goats out of thy folds.
59: 3 my transgression, n· for my sin, 3808
66:20 my prayer, n· his mercy from me.
75: 6 n· from the west, n· from the south,
78:42 n· the day when he delivered them
89:22 n· the son of wickedness afflict him.3808
33 n· suffer my faithfulness to fail. "
34 n· alter the thing that is gone out of"
91: 5 n· for the arrow that flieth by day;
6 N· for the pestilence that walketh *
6 n· for the destruction that wasteth at
103:10 n· rewarded us according to our 3808
121: 4 Israel shall neither slumber n· sleep."
6 thee by day, n· the moon by night.
129: 7 n· he that bindeth sheaves his bosom.
131: 1 not haughty, n· mine eyes lofty: 3808
132: 3 of my house, n· go up into my bed;
144:14 be no breaking in, n· going out; * 369
146: 3 trust in princes, n· in the son of man,
Pr 4:27 not to the right hand n· to the left:
5:13 n· inclined mine ear to them that 3808
6: 4 thine eyes, n· slumber to thine eyelids.
8:26 had not made the earth, n· the fields,
26 n· the highest part of the dust of the
17:26 good, n· to strike princes for equity.
21:30 no...n· understanding n· counsel 369
30: 3 n· have the knowledge of the holy.*
8 give me neither poverty n· riches;
31: 3 n· thy ways to that which destroyeth
4 wine; n· for princes strong drink: 408
Ec 1: 8 n· the ear filled with hearing. 3808
3:14 to it, n· any thing taken from it: 369
4: 8 yea, he hath neither child n· brother:
5:10 n· he that loveth abundance with
6: 5 seen the sun, n· known any thing:3808
8:16 neither day n· night seeth sleep
9:10 n· device, n· knowledge, n· wisdom,
11 swift, n· the battle to the strong, 3808
11 n·...riches to men of understanding,"
11 n· yet favour to men of skill; "
11: 5 n· how the bones do grow in the womb
12: 1 n· the years draw nigh, when thou†
2 n· the clouds return after the rain:*
Ca 2: 7 n· awake my love, till he please. 518
3: 5 n· awake my love, till he please. "
8: 4 n· awake my love, until he please.
Isa 3: 7 house is neither bread n· clothing: 369
5: 6 it shall not be pruned, n· digged; 3808
27 be weary n· stumble among them; "
27 none shall slumber n· sleep; "
27 n· the latchet of their shoes be "
8:12 fear ye their fear, n· be afraid. "
11: 9 not hurt n· destroy in all my holy "
14:21 they do not rise, n· possess the land,*
21 n· fill the face of the world with cities.*
22: 2 with the sword, n· dead in battle. *3808
23: 4 travail not, n· bring forth children, "
4 up young men, n· bring up virgins.
18 shall not be treasured n· laid up; 3808
28:28 n· break it with the wheel of his cart,*
28 n· bruise it with his horsemen. *3808
30: 5 not profit them, n· be an help "
5 be an help n· profit, but a shame, "
31: 4 n· abase himself for the noise of "
32: 5 n· the churl said to be bountiful. "
34:10 It shall not be quenched night n· day;
35: 9 n· any ravenous beast shall go up 1077
37:33 this city, n· shoot an arrow there, 3808
33 n· come before it with shields, * "
33 n· cast a bank against it. "
39: 2 in his house, n· in all his dominion,
40:16 n· the beasts thereof sufficient for 369
42: 2 He shall not cry, n· lift up, 3808
2 n· cause his voice to be heard in the"
4 He shall not fail n· be discouraged,"
43:23 n· wearied thee with incense. "
44: 9 witnesses; they see not, n· know; 1077
19 knowledge n· understanding to 3808
20 n· say, Is there not a lie in my right"
45:13 captives, not for price n· reward, "
17 shall not be ashamed n· confounded"
46: 7 n· save him out of his trouble. "
47:14 coal to warm at, n· fire to sit before it.
48: 1 not in truth, n· in righteousness. 3808
19 cut off n· destroyed from before me."
49:10 They shall not hunger n· thirst; "
10 shall the heat n· sun smite them: "
51:14 pit, n· that his bread should fail. * "
52:12 go out with haste, n· go by flight: * "
53: 2 he hath no form n· comeliness; and"
54: 9 not be wroth with thee, n· rebuke thee.
57:11 me, n· laid it to thy heart? 3808
58:13 ways, n· finding thine own pleasure,
13 n· speaking thine own words:
59: 4 justice, n· any pleadeth for truth:* 369
21 mouth, n· out of the mouth of thy seed,
21 n· out of the mouth of thy seed's seed,
60:11 they shall not be shut day n· night;
18 wasting n· destruction within thy
62: 6 never hold their peace day n· night:
64: 4 not heard, n· perceived by the ear,3808
65:17 be remembered, n· come into mind. "
19 heard in her, n· the voice of crying.
20 n· an old man that hath not filled his

Isa 65:23 in vain, n· bring forth for trouble;3808
25 not hurt n· destroy in all my holy "
Jer 4:11 my people, not to fan, n· to cleanse,"
5: 4 Lord, n· the judgment of their God.
12 neither shall we see sword n· famine:
6:19 my words, n· to my law, but rejected it.*
20 n· your sacrifices sweet unto me. 3808
25 into the field, n· walk by the way; 408
7:16 lift up cry n· prayer for them, "
22 n· commanded them in the day 3808
24 hearkened not, n· inclined their ear, "
26 not unto me, n· inclined their ear, "
28 their God, n· receiveth correction: "
32 n· the valley of the son of Hinnom,
8: 2 not be gathered, n· be buried; 3808
13 on the vine, n· figs on the fig tree, 369
9:16 they n· their fathers have known:
11: 8 obeyed not, n· inclined their ear, 3808
13:14 not pity, n· spare, n· have mercy,
14:16 wives, n· their sons, n· their daughters:
15:10 n· men have lent to me on usury,;*3808
17 assembly of the mockers, n· rejoiced;
16: 2 shalt thou have sons n· daughters*
5 go to lament n· bemoan them: for*3808
6 lament for them, n· cut themselves,"
6 n· make themselves bald for them: "
13 know not, neither ye n· your fathers;
17:21 n· bring it in by the gates of
23 not hear, n· receive instruction. *1115
18:18 the priest, n· counsel from the wise,
18 the wise, n· the word from the prophet.
19: 4 they n· their fathers have known,*
4 have known, n· the kings of Judah,*
5 I commanded not, n· spake it, 3808
6 n· The valley of the son of Hinnom,
20: 9 n· speak any more in his name. 3808
21: 7 neither have pity, n· have mercy.
22: 3 stranger, the fatherless, n· the widow,
10 no more, n· see his native country.
23: 4 shall fear no more, n· be dismayed,3808
32 sent them not, n· commanded them:"
25: 4 n· inclined your ear to hear. "
33 neither gathered, n· buried; "
35 n· the principal of the flock to escape.
27: 9 n· to your diviners, n· to...dreamers,
9 n· to...enchanters, n· to...sorcerers,
31:40 n· thrown down any more for ever.3808
35: 6 wine, neither ye, n· your sons for ever:
7 shall ye build house, n· sow seed, 3808
7 n· plant vineyard, n· have any:
8 our wives, our sons, n· our daughters;
9 N· to build houses for us to dwell 1115
9 have we vineyard, n· field, n· seed:
15 your ear, n· hearkened unto me. 3808
36:24 not afraid, n· rent their garments, "
24 the king, n· any of his servants that
37: 2 he, n· his servants, n· the people of the
19 come against you, n· against this land?
42:14 n· hear the sound of the trumpet, 3808
14 trumpet, n· have hunger of bread; "
21 n· any thing for the which he hath*
44: 3 not, neither they, ye, n· your fathers.
5 n· inclined their ear to turn from 3808
10 have they feared, n· walked in my "
10 in my law, n· in my statutes,
23 voice of the Lord, n· walked in...law,3808
23 n· in his statutes, n· in his testimonies;
46: 6 away, n· the mighty man escape; 408
49:31 which have neither gates n· bars 3808
33 n· any son of man dwell in it. * "
51: 5 been forsaken, n· Judah of his God,
26 a corner, n· a stone for foundations;
62 remain in it, neither man n· beast,
La 2:22 anger none escaped n· remained:*
3:33 n· grieve the children of men.
Eze 2: 6 n· be dismayed at their looks, 408
3:18 n· speakest to warn the wicked 3808
19 wickedness, n· from his wicked way,
7:11 n· of their multitude, n· of any of 3808
12 buyer rejoice, n· the seller mourn: 408
12:24 any vain vision n· flattering divination
13:23 more vanity, n· divine divinations:3808
14:16 deliver neither sons n· daughters; 508
18 shall deliver neither sons n· daughters,
20 deliver neither son n· daughter; 518
16: 4 not salted at all, n· swaddled at all.3808
47 n· done after their abominations:
48 hath not done, she n· her daughters,
18:17 hath not received usury n· increase,
20:18 n· defile yourselves with their idols:408
44 n· according to your corrupt doings,
22:24 cleansed, n· rained upon in the day3808
23:27 n· remember Egypt any more. "
24:16 neither shalt thou mourn n· weep, "
22 your lips, n· eat the bread of men. "
23 ye shall not mourn n· weep; but ye"
28:24 n· any grieving thorn of all that are
29: 5 be brought together, n· gathered: 3808
11 n· foot of beast shall pass through "
18 yet had he no wages, n· his army,
32:13 n· the hoofs of beasts trouble them.3808
37:23 idols, n· with their detestable things,
23 n· with any of their transgressions:
38:11 walls, and having neither bars n· gates,
43: 7 defile, neither they, n· their kings,
7 n· by the carcases of their kings in*
44: 9 in heart, n· uncircumcised in flesh,*
13 n· to come near to any of my holy
20 n· suffer their locks to grow long; 3808
22 a widow, n· her that is put away:
48:14 n· alienate the firstfruits of the 3808
Da 1: 8 n· with the wine which he drank:
2:10 there is no king, lord, n· ruler,
3:12, 14, 18, n· worship the golden image3809
27 n· was an hair of their head singed,"
27 n· the smell of fire had passed on

Da 3:28 n· worship any god, except their 3809
5: 8 n· make known to the king the
10 n· let thy countenance be changed:408
23 which see not, n· hear, n· know; 3809
6: 4 could find none occasion n· fault; "
13 n· the decree that thou hast signed,
15 n· statute which the king establisheth
10: 3 came flesh n· wine in any mouth, 3808
11: 4 n· according to his dominion which"
6 neither shall he stand, n· his arm:
20 neither in anger, n· in battle. 3808
24 have not done, n· his fathers' fathers;
37 of his fathers, n· the desire of women,
37 n· regard any god: for he shall 3808
Hos 1: 7 by bow, n· by sword, n· by battle,
7 battle, by horses, n· by horsemen.
10 cannot be measured n· numbered;3808
4: 1 because there is no truth, n· mercy,369
1 n· knowledge of God in the land.
4 no man strive, n· reprove another:*408
14 n· your spouses when they commit
15 n· swear, The Lord liveth. 408
5: 13 you, n· cure you of your wound. *3808
7: 10 their God, n· seek him for all this. "
Am 5: 5 not Beth-el, n· enter into Gilgal, "
8: 11 of bread, n· a thirst for water, but "
9: 10 evil shall not overtake n· prevent us.
Ob 13 n·...laid hands on their substance 408
Jon 3: 7 man n· beast, herd n· flock, taste any
7 let them not feed, n· drink water: 408
Mic 5: 7 n· waiteth for the sons of men. 3808
Zep 1: 6 the Lord, n· enquired for him. "
18 silver n· their gold shall be able to1571
3: 13 not do iniquity, n· speak lies; 3808
Zec 1: 4 did not hear, n· hearken unto me, "
4: 6 Not by might, n· by power, but by "
7: 10 not the widow, n· the fatherless, the
10 the stranger, n· the poor; and let
10 no man passed through n· returned:
8: 10 hire for man, n· any hire for beast; 369
11: 16 one, n· heal that that is broken, 3808
16 n· feed that that standeth still: but*"
14: 6 the light shall not be clear, n· dark:*
7 to the Lord, not day, n· night: *3808
Mal 4: 1 leave them neither root n· branch.
M't 5: 35 N· by the earth; for it is his 3383
6: 20 neither moth n· rust doth corrupt,3777
20 do not break through n· steal: 3761
25 n· yet for your body, what ye shall 3366
26 do they reap, n· gather into barns;3761
10: 9 neither gold, n· silver, n· brass in 3366
10 N· scrip for your journey, neither*3361
10 coats, neither shoes, n· yet staves: 3366
14 receive you, n· hear your words, "
24 n· the servant above his lord. 3761
11: 18 came neither eating n· drinking, 3383
12: 19 He shall not strive, n· cry; neither3761
22: 29 scriptures, n· the power of God. 3366
30 marry, n· are given in marriage, 3777
24: 21 this time, no, n· ever shall be. 3364,3761
25: 13 day n· the hour wherein the Son of "
M'r 6: 11 shall not receive you, n· hear you,*3366
8: 26 town, n· tell it to any in the town.* "
12: 25 marry, n· are given in marriage; 3777
Lu 1: 15 drink neither wine n· strong drink;2532
6: 44 n· of a bramble bush gather they 3761
7: 33 eating bread n· drinking wine; 3383
9: 3 staves, n· scrip, neither bread, "
10: 4 neither purse, n· scrip, n· shoes: *3361
12: 24 for they neither sow n· reap; *3761
24 neither have storehouse n· barn; "
14: 12 not thy friends, n· thy brethren, 3364
12 kinsmen, n· thy rich neighbours; "
35 for the land, n· yet for the dunghill;3777
17: 23 go not after them, n· follow them. 3364
18: 4 I fear not God, n· regard man; 3756
20: 35 marry, n· are given in marriage: 3777
21: 15 not be able to gainsay n· resist. *3761
22: 68 will not answer me, n· let me go. *2228
23: 15 No, n· yet Herod: for I sent you to 3761
Joh 1: 13 of blood, n· of the will of the flesh, "
13 n· of the will of man, but of God. "
25 thou be not that Christ, n· Elias, *3777
4: 21 this mountain, n· yet at Jerusalem, "
5: 37 at any time, n· seen his shape. "
8: 19 neither know me, n· my Father: "
9: 3 this man sinned, n· his parents: "
11: 50 N· consider that it is expedient 3761
12: 40 n· understand with their hearts, *2532
16: 3 have not known the Father, n· me.3761
Ac 4: 18 all n· teach in the name of Jesus. 3366
8: 21 neither part n· lot in this matter: 3761
9: 9 sight, and neither did eat n· drink. "
13: 27 n· yet the voices of the prophets 2532
15: 10 fathers n· we were able to bear? 3777
19: 37 n· yet blasphemers of your goddess."
23: 8 neither angel, n· spirit: but the 3383
12, 21 neither eat n· drink till they had
24: 12 in the synagogues, n· in the city: 3777
18 with multitude, n· with tumult. 3761
25: 8 the temple, n· yet against Cæsar, 3777
27: 20 neither sun n· stars in many days 3383
Ro 8: 38 neither death, n· life, n· angels, 3777
38 n· principalities, n· powers, "
38 n· things present, n· things to come,"
39 N· height, n· depth, n· any other "
9: 16 willeth, n· of him that runneth, 3761
14: 21 to eat flesh, n· to drink wine, 3366
21 n· any thing whereby thy brother "
1Co 2: 6 n· of the princes of this world, that3761
9 hath not seen, n· ear heard, *2532, 3756
6: 9 n· idolaters, n· adulterers, 3777
9 n· effeminate, n· abusers of "
10 N· thieves, n· covetous, "
10 n· drunkards, n· revilers, 3756
10 n· extortioners, shall inherit the

1Co 10: 32 n· to the Gentiles, n· to the church*2532
12: 21 n· again the head to the feet, I *2228
2Co 4: 2 n· handling the word of God 3366
7: 12 n· for his cause...suffered wrong, 3761
Ga 3: 28 There is neither Jew n· Greek, "
28 there is neither bond n· free, "
28 there is neither male n· female: "
4: 14 flesh ye despised not, n· rejected; "
5: 6 any thing, n· uncircumcision; 3777
6: 15 any thing, n· uncircumcision, but "
Eph 5: 4 Neither filthiness,n· foolish talking,2532
4 n· jesting, which are not *2228
5 n· unclean person, n· covetous man,"
Col 3: 11 there is neither Greek n· Jew, 2532
11 circumcision n· uncircumcision, "
11 Barbarian, Scythian, bond n· free:*
1Th 2: 3 not of deceit, n· of uncleanness, 3761
3 of uncleanness, n· of guile, 3777
5 know, n· a cloke of covetousness; "
6 N· of men sought we glory, neither "
6 n· yet of others, when we might have"
5: 5 not of the night, n· of darkness. 3761
2Th 2: 2 n· by word, n· by letter as from us,*3383
1Ti 1: 7 they say, n· whereof they affirm. "
2: 12 n· to usurp authority over the 3761
6: 16 no man hath seen, n· can see: to "
17 n· trust in uncertain riches, but *3366
2Ti 1: 8 of our Lord, n· of me his prisoner: "
Heb 7: 3 beginning of days, n· end of life; 3383
9: 25 N· yet that he should offer himself3761
12: 5 n· faint when thou art rebuked of 3366
18 n· unto blackness, and darkness, *2532
13: 5 never leave thee, n· forsake *3761, 3364
2Pe 1: 8 neither be barren n· unfruitful in 3761
Re 3: 15 that thou art neither cold n· hot: 3777
16 lukewarm, and neither cold n· hot, "
5: 3 no man in heaven, n· in earth, *3761
7: 1 n· on the sea, n· on any tree. *3383
3 neither the sea, n· the trees, till "
16 the sun light on them, n· any heat.3761
9: 20 neither can see, n· hear, n· walk: 3777
21 their murders, n· of their sorceries,"
21 sorceries, n· of their fornication, "
21 their fornication, n· of their thefts. "
14: 11 and they have no rest day n· night,*2532
21: 4 death, neither sorrow, n· crying, 3777

north See also NORTHERN; NORTHWARD.
Ge 28: 14 and to the n·, and to the south: 6828
Ex 26: 20 n· side there shall be twenty boards:"
35 shalt put the table on the n· side. "
27: 11 for the n· side in length there shall "
36: 25 which is toward the n· corner, "
38: 11 for the n· side the hangings were an"
Nu 2: 25 camp of Dan shall be on the n· side "
34: 7 And this shall be your n· border: "
9 this shall be your n· border: "
35: 5 on the n· side two thousand cubits; "
Jos 8: 11 and pitched on the n· side of Ai: "
13 host that was on the n· of the city, "
11: 2 were on the n· of the mountains, "
15: 5 their border in the n· quarter was "
6 along by the n· of Beth-arabah; "
10 which is Chesalon, on the n· side, "
16: 6 sea to Michmethah on the n· side; "
17: 9 also was on the n· side of the river, "
10 met together in Asher on the n·, "
18: 5 shall abide in their coasts on the n·."
12 their border on the n· side was from"
12 to the side of Jericho on the n· side,"
16 in the valley of the giants on the n·,*"
17 And was drawn from the n·, and "
19 were at the n· bay of the salt sea "
19: 14 compasseth it on the n· side to "
27 toward the n· side of Beth-emek, * "
24: 30 on the n· side of the hill of Gaash. "
J'g 2: 9 on the n· side of the hill Gaash. "
7: 1 Midianites were on the n· side "
21: 19 which is on the n· side of Beth-el, "
1Ki 7: 25 oxen, three looking toward the n·, "
2Ki 16: 14 put it on the n· side of the altar. "
1Ch 9: 24 toward the east, west, n·, and south."
2Ch 4: 4 oxen, three looking toward the n·, "
Job 26: 7 He stretcheth out the n· over the "
37: 9 whirlwind: and cold out of the n·. 4215
22 Fair weather cometh out of the n·:6828
Ps 48: 2 mount Zion, on the sides of the n·, "
89: 12 n· and the south thou hast created "
107: 3 from the n·, and from the south. "
Pr 25: 23 The n· wind driveth away rain: "
Ec 1: 6 and turneth about unto the n·; "
11: 3 toward the south, or toward the n·, "
Ca 4: 16 Awake, O n· wind; and come, thou "
Isa 14: 13 congregation, in the sides of the n·:"
31 shall come from the n· a smoke, "
41: 25 I have raised up one from the n·, "
43: 6 I will say to the n·, Give up; and to "
49: 12 these from the n· and from the west;"
Jer 1: 13 the face thereof is toward the n·. "
14 Out of the n· an evil shall break "
15 families of the kingdoms of the n·, "
3: 12 proclaim these words toward the n·,"
18 out of the land of the n· to the land "
4: 6 for I will bring evil from the n·, and"
6: 1 for evil appeareth out of the n·, and"
22 people cometh from the n· country, "
10: 22 commotion out of the n· country, "
13: 20 behold them that come from the n·:"
16: 15 of Israel from the land of the n·, "
23: 8 of Israel out of the n· country, "
25: 9 and take all the families of the n·, "
26 all the kings of the n·, far and near, "
31: 8 will bring them from the n· country,"
46: 6 stumble, and fall toward the n· by "
10 hath a sacrifice in the n· country "
20 cometh; it cometh out of the n·. "
24 into the hand of the people of the n·."

Jer 47: 2 Behold, waters rise up out of the n·,6828
50: 3 out of the n·....cometh up a nation "
9 great nations from the n· country: "
41 a people shall come from the n·, "
51: 48 shall come unto her from the n·, "
Eze 1: 4 a whirlwind came out of the n·, "
8: 3 gate that looketh toward the n·; "
5 eyes now the way toward the n·. "
5 mine eyes the way toward the n·, "
14 house which was toward the n·; "
9: 2 gate, which lieth toward the n·, "
20: 47 all faces from the south to the n· "
21: 4 all flesh from the south to the n·: "
26: 7 a king of kings, from the n·, with "
32: 30 There be the princes of the n·, all "
38: 6 of Togarmah of the n· quarters, "
15 from thy place out of the n· parts, "
39: 2 cause thee to come up from the n· parts,"
40: 20 court that looked toward the n·, "
23 over against the gate toward the n·,"
35 And he brought me to the n· gate, "
40 goeth up to the entry of the n· gate,"
44 which was at the side of the n· gate;"
44 having the prospect toward the n·. "
46 whose prospect is toward the n· "
41: 11 one door toward the n·, and another"
42: 1 utter court, the way toward the n·: "
1 before the building toward the n·. "
2 an hundred cubits was the n· door, "
4 cubit; and their doors toward the n·."
11 chambers which were toward the n·,"
13 The n· chambers and the south "
17 measured the n· side, five hundred "
44: 4 brought...me the way of the n· gate "
46: 9 entering in by the way of the n· gate "
9 go forth by the way of the n· gate: "
19 priests, which looked toward the n·:"
47: 15 of the land toward the n· side, from"
17 Damascus, and the n· northward, "
17 of Hamath. And this is the n· side. "
48: 1 From the n· end to the coast of the "
10 toward the n· five and twenty "
16 the n· side four thousand and five "
17 toward the n· two hundred and "
30 goings out of the city on the n· side,"
Da 11: 6 shall come to the king of the n· to "
7 the fortress of the king of the n·, "
8 more years than the king of the n·. "
11 him, even with the king of the n·: "
13 For the king of the n· shall return, "
15 So the king of the n· shall come, "
40 and the king of the n· shall come "
44 tidings...out of the n· shall trouble "
Am 8: 12 and from the n· even to the east, "
Zep 2: 13 stretch out his hand against the n·, "
Zec 2: 6 and flee from the land of the n·, "
6: 6 therein go forth into the n· country;"
8 these that go toward the n· country"
8 quieted my spirit in the n· country."
14: 4 half...shall remove toward the n·, "
Lu 13: 29 from the n·, and from the south, 1005
Ac 27: 12 toward the south west and n· west. 5566
Re 21: 13 on the n· three gates; on the south1005

northern
Jer 15: 12 Shall iron break the n· iron and *6828
Joe 2: 20 far off from you the n· army, 6830

northward See also NORTH and TOWARD.
Ge 13: 14 from the place where thou art n·, 6828
Ex 40: 22 upon the side of the tabernacle n·. "
Le 1: 11 shall kill it on the side of the altar n·"
Nu 3: 35 pitch on the side of the tabernacle n·."
De 2: 3 mountain long enough: turn you n·."
3: 27 lift up thine eyes westward, and n·,"
Jos 13: 3 even unto the borders of Ekron n·, "
15: 7 and so n·, looking toward Gilgal, "
8 end of the valley of the giants n·: "
11 went out unto the side of Ekron n·:"
17: 10 n· it was Manasseh's, and the sea "
18: 18 the side over against Arabah n·, "
19 along to the side of Beth-hoglah n·:"
J'g 12: 1 themselves together, and went n·, "
1Sa 14: 5 situate n· over against Michmash,*"
1Ch 26: 14 cast lots; and his lot came out n·. "
17 n· four a day, southward four a day,"
Eze 8: 5 behold n· at the gate of the altar "
40: 19 an hundred cubits eastward and n·.*"
47: 2 he me out of the way of the gate n·, "
17 of Damascus, and the north n·. "
48: 1 the border of Damascus n·, to the "
31 three gates n·; one gate of Reuben,"
Da 8: 4 the ram pushing westward, and n·, "

north-west See NORTH and WEST.

nose See also NOSES.
Le 21: 18 or a lame, or he that hath a flat n·, 2763
2Ki 19: 28 I will put my hook in thy n·, and 639
Job 40: 24 eyes: his n· pierceth through snares."
41: 2 Canst thou put an hook into his n·? "
Pr 30: 33 the wringing of the n· bringeth forth"
Ca 7: 4 thy n· is as the tower of Lebanon "
8 and the smell of thy n· like apples;*"
Isa 3: 21 The rings, and n· jewels, "
37: 29 therefore will I put my hook in thy n·,"
65: 5 These are a smoke in my n·, a fire "
Eze 8: 17 lo, they put the branch to their n·. "
23: 25 they shall take away thy n· and thine"

nose-jewels See NOSE and JEWELS.

noses
Ps 115: 6 n· have they, but they smell not: 639
Eze 39: 11 it shall stop the n· of the passengers:*

nostrils
Ge 2: 7 into his n· the breath of life; and 639
7: 22 in whose n· was the breath of life, "
Ex 15: 8 with the blast of thy n· the waters "
Nu 11: 20 month, until it come out at your n·, "

2Sa 22: 9 There went up a smoke out of his n', 639
16 at the blast of the breath of his n'. "
Job 4: 9 by the breath of his n' are they * "
27: 3 and the spirit of God is in my n'; "
39: 20 the glory of his n' is terrible. *5170
41: 20 Out of his n' goeth smoke, as out 5156
Ps 18: 8 went up a smoke out of his n', 639
15 at the blast of the breath of thy n'. "
Isa 2: 22 from man, whose breath is in his n': "
La 4: 20 The breath of our n', the anointed "
Am 4: 10 your camps to come up unto your n': "

not See in the APPENDIX; also CANNOT; NOTWITHSTANDING.

notable
Da 8: 5 goat had a n' horn between his 2380
8 and for it came up four n' ones "
M't 27: 16 a n' prisoner, called Barabbas. 1978
Ac 2: 20 great and n' day of the Lord come: 2016
4: 16 indeed a n' miracle hath been done 1110

note See also NOTABLE; NOTED.
Isa 30: 8 in a table, and n' it in a book, *2710
Ro 16: 7 who are of n' among the apostles, 1978
2Th 3: 14 n' that man, and have no company 4593

noted
Da 10: 21 is n' in the scripture of truth: *7559

nothing See also NAUGHT.
Ge 11: 6 n' will be restrained from 3808,3605
19: 8 only unto these men do n'; for " 1697
29 have done unto thee n' but good, 7535
40: 15 and here also have I done n' 3808,3972
Ex 9: 4 n' die of all that is the children's 3808
12: 10 ye shall let n' of it remain until "
20 Ye shall eat n' leavened; in all your "
16: 18 that gathered much had n' over, "
21: 2 seventh he shall go out free for n'. 2600
22: 3 if he have n', then he shall be sold 369
23: 26 There shall n' cast their young, *3808
Nu 6: 4 eat n' that is made of the vine tree, "
11: 6 is n' at all, beside this manna, *369,3605
16: 26 and touch n' of theirs, lest ye 408, "
22: 16 Let n', I pray thee, hinder thee 408
De 2: 7 with thee; thou hast lacked n'. 3808
20: 16 save alive n' that breatheth: 3808,3605
22: 26 the damsel thou shalt do n'; " 1697
28: 55 he hath n' left him in the siege 3605
Jos 11: 15 left n' undone of all that the 3808,1697
J'g 3: 2 such as before knew n' thereof; 3808
7: 14 is n' else save the sword of Gideon 369
14: 6 and he had n' in his hand: 3972, "
1Sa 3: 18 every whit, and hid n' from him. 3808
20: 2 father will do n' either great 3808,1697
22: 15 thy servant knew n' of all this, " "
25: 21 so that n' was missed of all that " 3972
36 she told him n', less or more, " 1697
27: 1 there is n' better for me than that 369
30: 19 And there was n' lacking to them, 3808
2Sa 12: 3 But the poor man had n', save 369,3605
24: 24 offer...that which doth cost me n'. 2600
1Ki 4: 27 in his month: they lacked n'. 3808,1697
8: 9 There was n' in the ark save the 369
10: 21 n' accounted of in the days of 3808,3972
11: 22 country? And he answered, N'. 3808
18: 43 looked, and said, There is n'. 3808,3972
22: 16 tell me n' but that which is true 3808
2Ki 10: 10 fall unto the earth n' of the word of "
20: 13 there was n' in his house, nor 3808,1697
15 there is n' among my treasures "
17 n' shall be left, saith the Lord. 3808, "
2Ch 5: 10 There was n' in the ark save the 369
9: 2 n' hid from Solomon which *3808,1697
18: 15 thou say n' but the truth to me 3808
Ne 2: 2 this is n' else but sorrow of heart. 369
5: 8 peace, and found n' to answer. *3808
12 them, and will require n' of them; "
8: 10 unto them for whom n' is prepared: "
9: 21 wilderness, so that they lacked n'; "
Es 2: 15 required n' but what Hegai 3808,1697
5: 13 Yet all this availeth me n', so long 369
6: 3 There is n' done for him. 3808,1697
10 n' fail of all that thou hast spoken. "
Job 6: 18 aside; they go to n', and perish. *8414
21 now ye are n'; ye see my casting 3808
8: 9 are but of yesterday, and know n', "
24: 25 liar, and make my speech n' worth? 408
26: 7 and hangeth the earth upon n'. 1099
34: 9 It profiteth a man n' that he 3808
Ps 19: 6 is n' hid from the heat thereof. 369
39: 5 and mine age is as n' before thee: "
49: 17 dieth he shall carry n' away: 3808,3605
119: 165 law: and n' shall offend them. * 369
Pr 8: 8 is n' froward or perverse in them. "
9: 13 is simple, and knoweth n'. 1077,4100
10: 2 Treasures of wickedness profit n': 3808
13: 4 the sluggard desireth, and hath n': 369
7 himself rich, yet hath n': 3808,3605
20: 4 shall he beg in harvest and have n'. 369
22: 27 If thou hast n' to pay, why should * "
Ec 2: 24 There is n' better for a man, than "
3: 14 n' can be put to it, nor any thing "
22 is n' better, than that a man should "
5: 14 and there is n' in his hand. 3808,3972
15 and shall take n' of his labour, " "
6: 2 so that he wanteth n' for his soul 369
7: 14 man should find n' after him. *3808,3972
Isa 34: 12 and all her princes shall be n'. 657
39: 2 there was n' in his house, nor 3808,1697
4 is n' among my treasures that " "
6 n' shall be left, saith the Lord. " "
40: 17 All nations before him are as n'; 369
17 counted to him less than n', 657,8414
41: 11 confounded: they shall be as n'; 369
12 that war against thee shall be as n', "
24 Behold, ye are of n', and your work "
29 are all vanity; their works are n':* 657
44: 10 image that is profitable for n'? 1115
Jer 10: 24 anger, lest thou bring me to n'. 4591
13: 7 it was profitable for n'. 3808,3605
10 girdle, which is good for n'. " "
32: 17 there is n' too hard for thee: 1697
23 n' of all that thou commandedst 3808
38: 14 thee a thing; hide n' from me. 408,1697
39: 10 of the people, which had n', 3808,3972
42: 4 I will keep n' back from you. " 1697
50: 26 her utterly: let n' of her be left. 408
La 1: 12 Is it n' to you, all ye that pass by? 3808
Eze 13: 3 their own spirit, and have seen n'! 1115
Da 4: 35 of the earth are reputed as n': 3809
Joe 2: 3 yea, and n' shall escape them. *3808
Am 3: 4 out of his den, if he have taken n'? 1115
5 earth, and have taken n' at all? 3808
7 the Lord God will do n', but 3808,1697
Hag 2: 3 your eyes in comparison of it as n'? 369
M't 5: 13 it is thenceforth good for n', but to 3762
10: 26 there is n' covered, that shall not "
15: 32 three days, and have n' to eat: 3756,5100
17: 20 n' shall be impossible unto you. 3762
21: 19 found n' thereon, but leaves only, "
23: 16 shall swear by the temple, it is n'; "
18 shall swear by the altar, it is n'; "
26: 62 said unto him, Answerest thou n'? "
27: 12 priests and elders, he answered n'. "
19 thou n' to do with that just man: 3367
24 Pilate saw that he could prevail n', 3762
M'r 1: 44 See thou say n' to any man: but 3367
4: 22 there is n' hid, which shall not 3756,5100
5: 26 was n' bettered, but rather grew 3367
6: 8 should take n' for their journey, "
36 for they have n' to eat. *3756,5100
7: 15 There is n' from without a man, 3762
8: 1 and having n' to eat, Jesus called 3385
2 three days, and have n' to eat: 3756,5100
9: 29 This kind can come forth by n', 3762
11: 13 came to it, he found n' but leaves; "
14: 60 Jesus, saying, Answerest thou n'? "
61 he held his peace, and answered n'. "
15: 3 things: but he answered n'. *3756, "
4 again, saying, Answerest thou n'? "
5 But Jesus yet answered n'; so that* "
Lu 1: 37 n' shall be impossible. *3756,3956,4487
4: 2 And in those days he did eat n': 3762
5: 5 all the night, and have taken n': "
6: 35 and lend, hoping for n' again; *3367
7: 42 And when they had n' to pay, he *3361
8: 17 n' is secret, that shall not be made 3756
9: 3 Take n' for your journey, neither 3367
10: 19 n' shall by any means hurt you. 3762
11: 6 I have n' to set before him? 3756,3739
12: 2 there is n' covered, that shall not 3762
22: 35 ye any thing? And they said, N'. "
23: 9 words; but he answered him n'. "
15 n' worthy of death is done unto him. "
41 but this man hath done n' amiss. "
Joh 3: 27 A man can receive n', except it be "
4: 11 Sir, thou hast n' to draw with, 3777
5: 19 The Son can do n' of himself, but 3762
30 I can of mine own self do n': 3756, "
6: 12 that remain, that n' be lost. 3361,5100
39 hath given me I should lose n', 3361,848
63 quickeneth; the flesh profiteth n': 3762
7: 26 boldly, and they say n' unto him. "
8: 28 I am he, and that I do n' of myself; "
54 I honour myself, my honour is n': "
9: 33 man were not of God, he could do n'. "
11: 49 unto them, Ye know n' at all, 3756
12: 19 Perceive ye how ye prevail n'? 3762
14: 30 world cometh, and hath n' in me. "
15: 5 fruit: for without me ye can do n'. "
16: 23 And in that day ye shall ask me n'. "
24 have ye asked n' in my name: "
18: 20 resort; and in secret have I said n'. "
21: 3 and that night they caught n'. "
Ac 4: 14 them, they could say n' against it. "
21 finding n' how they might punish 3367
10: 20 and go with them, doubting n': "
11: 8 n' common or unclean hath 3956,3763
12 me go with them, n' doubting. *3367
17: 21 spent their time in n' else, but 3762
19: 36 to be quiet, and to do n' rashly. 3367
20: 20 kept back n' that was profitable *3762
21: 24 informed concerning thee, are n'; * "
23: 14 will eat n' until we have slain Paul. 3367
29 to have n' laid to his charge worthy "
25: 25 had committed n' worthy of death, "
26: 31 This man doeth n' worthy of death 3762
27: 33 continued fasting, having taken n'. 3367
28: 17 committed n' against the people, 3762
Ro 14: 14 that there is n' unclean of itself: "
1Co 1: 19 will bring to n' the understanding* 114
4: 4 For I know n' by myself; yet am I 3762
5 Therefore judge n' before the time. 3385
7: 19 Circumcision is n', and 3762
19 and uncircumcision is n', but the "
8: 2 he knoweth n' yet as he ought to * "
4 that an idol is n' in the world, * "
9: 16 the gospel, I have n' to glory of: 3756
13: 2 and have not charity, I am n'. 3762
3 not charity, it profiteth me n'. "
2Co 6: 10 as having n', and yet possessing 3367
7: 9 might receive damage by us in n'. "
8: 15 had gathered much had n' over; 3756
12: 11 for in n' am I behind the very 3762
11 chiefest apostles, though I be n'. "
13: 8 we can do n' against the truth, 3756,5100
Ga 2: 6 in conference added n' to me: 3762
4: 1 a child, differeth n' from a servant, "
5: 2 Christ shall profit you n'. "
6: 3 to be something, when he is n', 3367
Ph'p 1: 20 that in n' I shall be ashamed, 3762
28 in n' terrified by your adversaries: 3367
2: 3 Let n' be done through strife or "
4: 6 Be careful for n'; but in every thing 3367
1Th 4: 12 and that ye may have lack of n'. "
1Ti 4: 4 God is good, and n' to be refused, 3762
5: 21 another, doing n' by partiality. 3367
6: 4 He is proud, knowing n', but doting "
7 For we brought n' into this world, 3762
7 certain we can carry n' out. *3761,5100
Tit 1: 15 defiled and unbelieving is n' pure; 3762
3: 13 that n' be wanting unto them. 3367
Ph'm 14 without thy mind would I do n'; 3762
Heb 2: 8 he left n' that is not put under him. "
7: 14 of which tribe Moses spake n' "
19 For the law made n' perfect, but the "
Jas 1: 4 be perfect and entire, wanting n'. 3367
6 let him ask in faith, n' wavering: "
3Jo 7 forth, taking n' of the Gentiles. "
Re 3: 17 with goods, and have need of n'; 3762

notice
2Sa 3: 36 all the people took n' of it, and it 5234
2Co 9: 5 bounty, whereof ye had n' before, *4293

notwithstanding
Ex 16: 20 N' they hearkened not unto Moses;
21: 21 N', if he continue a day or two, he 389
Le 25: 32 N' the cities of the Levites, and *
27: 28 N' no devoted thing, that a man * 389
Nu 26: 11 N' the children of Korah died not.
55 N' the land shall be divided by lot:
De 1: 26 N' ye would not go up, but rebelled*
12: 15 N' thou mayest kill and eat flesh 7535
Jos 22: 19 N', if the land of your possession* 389
J'g 4: 9 n' the journey that thou takest shall 657
9: 5 n' yet Jotham the youngest son
1Sa 2: 25 N' they hearkened not unto the
20: 8 n', if there be in me iniquity, slay*
29: 9 n' the princes of the Philistines 389
2Sa 24: 4 N' the king's word prevailed against
1Ki 11: 12 N' in thy days I will not do it for 389
2Ki 17: 14 N' they would not hear, but
23: 26 N' the Lord turned not from the 389
2Ch 6: 9 N' thou shalt not build the house; *7535
32: 26 N' Hezekiah humbled himself for
Jer 35: 14 n' I have spoken unto you, rising*
Eze 20: 21 N' the children rebelled against me:*
Mic 7: 13 N' the land shall be desolate *
M't 2: 22 n', being warned of God in a dream,*
11: 11 n' he that is least in the kingdom *
17: 27 N', lest we should offend them, *
Lu 10: 11 n' be ye sure of this, that the *4133
20 N' in this rejoice not, that the * "
Ac 15: 34 N' it pleased Silas to abide there *
24: 4 N', that I be not further tedious *
Ph'p 1: 18 n', every way, whether in *4133
4: 14 N' ye have well done, that ye did * "
1Ti 2: 15 N' she shall be saved in childbearing,*
2Ti 4: 17 N' the Lord stood with me, and *
Jas 2: 16 n' ye give them not those things *
Rev 2: 20 N' I have a few things against thee,*235

nought See also NAUGHT; NOTHING.
Ge 29: 15 thou therefore serve me for n'? 2600
De 13: 17 cleave n' of the cursed thing 408,3972
15: 9 brother, and thou givest him n'; 3808
28: 63 destroy you, and to bring you to n'; *8045
Ne 4: 15 had brought their counsel to n'. 6565
Job 1: 9 said, Doth Job fear God for n'? 2600
8: 22 place of the wicked shall come to n'. *369
14: 18 the mountain falling cometh to n', 5034
22: 6 a pledge from thy brother for n', 2600
Ps 33: 10 the counsel of the heathen to n': 6331
44: 12 Thou sellest thy people for n', 3808,1952
Pr 1: 25 ye have set at n' all my counsel, 6544
Isa 8: 10 together, and it shall come to n'; 6565
29: 20 the terrible one is brought to n', 656
21 turn aside the just for a thing of n'. 8414
41: 12 be as nothing, and as a thing of n'. 657
24 of nothing, and your work of n': 659
49: 4 I have spent my strength for n', 8414
52: 3 Ye have sold yourselves for n'; 2600
5 my people is taken away for n'? "
Jer 14: 14 and a thing of n', and the deceit of 434
Am 5: 5 and Beth-el shall come to n'. 205
6: 13 which rejoice in a thing of n', 3808,1697
Mal 1: 10 you that would shut the doors for n'? "
10 ye kindle fire on mine altar for n'. 2600
M'r 9: 12 many things, and be set at n'. 1847
Lu 23: 11 with his men of war set him at n', 1848
Ac 4: 11 is the stone which was set at n' of "
5: 36 were scattered, and brought to n'. 3762
38 work be of men, it will come to n': *2647
19: 27 craft is in danger to be set at n'; * 557
Ro 14: 10 why dost thou set at n' thy brother? 1848
1Co 1: 28 not, to bring to n' things that are: 2673
2: 6 of this world, that come to n': "
2Th 3: 8 did we eat any man's bread for n'; 1432
Re 18: 17 hour so great riches is come to n'. *2049

nourish See also NOURISHED; NOURISHETH; NOURISHING.
Ge 45: 11 And there will I n' thee; for yet 3557
50: 21 I will n' you, and your little ones. "
Isa 7: 21 a man shall n' a young cow, and 2421
23: 4 neither do I n' up young men, nor *1431
44: 14 an ash, and the rain doth n' it. "

nourished
Ge 47: 12 And Joseph n' his father, and his 3557
2Sa 12: 3 which he had bought and n' up: 2421
Isa 1: 2 I have n' and brought up children. 1431
Eze 19: 2 n' her whelps among young lions. 7235
Ac 7: 20 n' up in his father's house three 397
21 him up, and n' him for her own son. "
12: 20 their country was n' by the king's *5142
1Ti 4: 6 n' up in the words of faith and of 1789
Jas 5: 5 ye have n' your hearts, as in a day 5142
Re 12: 14 her place, where she is n' for a time, "

nourisher
Ru 4: 15 thy life, and a n' of thine old age: 3557

nourisheth
Eph 5:29 n' and cherisheth it, even as the 1625
nourishing
Da 1: 5 so n' them three years, that at the*1431
nourishment
Col 2:19 having n' ministered, and knit *2023
novice
1Ti 3: 6 Not a n', lest being lifted up with 3504
now
Ge 2:23 This is n' bone of my bones, and 6471
3: 1 N' the serpent was more subtil than
22 and n', lest he put forth his hand, 6258
4:11 n' art thou cursed from the earth, "
10: 1 N' these are the generations of the
11: 6 n' nothing will be restrained from 6258
27 N' these are the generations of
12: 1 N' the Lord had said unto Abram, Get
11 Behold n', I know...thou art a fair 4994
19 n' therefore behold thy wife, take 6258
13:14 Lift up n' thine eyes, and look from
15: 5 Look n' toward heaven, and tell 4994
16: 1 N' Sarai, Abram's wife, bare him no
2 n', the Lord hath restrained me 4994
18: 3 if n' I have found favour in thy "
11 N' Abraham and Sarah were old and
21 I will go down n', and see whether4994
27, 31 Behold n', I have taken upon me"
19: 2 Behold n', my lords, turn in, I pray "
8 Behold n', I have two daughters "
9 n' will we deal worse with thee, 6288
19 Behold n', thy servant hath found 4994
20 Behold n', this city is near to flee "
20: 7 N'...restore the man his wife; 6258
21:23 N' therefore swear unto me here "
22:12 for n' I know that thou fearest God,"
24:49 n' if ye will deal kindly and truly "
25:12 N' these are the generations of
26:22 n' the Lord hath made room for us,6258
28 Let there be n' an oath betwixt us,4994
29 thou art n' the blessed of the Lord.6258
27:26 Come near n', and kiss me, my son.4994
36 n' he hath taken...my blessing. 6258
37 shall I do n' unto thee, my son? * 645
43 N' therefore, my son, obey my 6258
29:32 n' therefore my husband will love "
34 N' this time will my husband 6471, "
35 said, N' will I praise the Lord:*"
30:20 n' will my husband dwell with me,6471
30 it is n' increased unto a multitude;*
30 n' when shall I provide for mine 6258
31:12 Lift up n' thine eyes, and see, all 4994
13 n' arise, get thee out from this 6258
16 n' then, whatsoever God hath said "
25 N' Jacob had pitched his tent in the
28 hast n' done foolishly in so doing. 6258
30 n', though thou wouldest needs be "
34 N' Rachel had taken the images, and
42 hadst sent me away n' empty. *6258
44 N' therefore come thou, let us "
32: 4 Laban, and stayed there until n': "
10 and n' I am become two bands. "
33:10 n' I have found grace in thy sight, 4994
15 Let me n' leave with thee some of "
34: 5 n' his sons were with his cattle in the*
35:22 N' the sons of Jacob were twelve:
36: 1 N' these are the generations of Esau,
37: 3 N' Israel loved Joseph more than all
20 Come n' therefore, and let us slay 6258
32 know n' whether it be thy son's 4994
42: 1 N' when Jacob saw that there was
43:10 surely n' we had returned this 6258
11 If it must be so n', do this; take of 645
44:10 N' also let it be according unto 6258
30 N' therefore when I come to thy "
33 N' therefore, I pray thee, let thy "
45: 5 N' therefore be not grieved, nor "
8 So n' it was not you that sent me "
19 N' thou art commanded, this do ye;
46:30 N' let me die, since I have seen 6471
34 from our youth even until n', both 6258
47: 4 n' therefore, we pray thee, let thy "
48: 5 And n' thy two sons, Ephraim and "
10 N' the eyes of Israel were dim for age,
50: 4 n' I have found grace in your eyes,4994
5 N' therefore let me go up, I pray 6258
17 Forgive, I pray...n', the trespass 4994
17 n', we pray...forgive the trespass "
21 N' therefore fear ye not: I will 6258
Ex 1: 1 N' these are the names of the children
8 N' there arose up a new king over
2:15 N' when Pharaoh heard this thing,
16 N' the priest of Midian had seven
3: 1 N' Moses kept the flock of Jethro
3 I will n' turn aside, and see this 4994
9 N' therefore, behold, the cry of 6258
10 Come n' therefore, and I will send "
18 n' let us go, we beseech thee, three "
4: 6 Put n' thine hand into thy bosom. 4994
12 N' therefore go, and I will be with6258
5: 5 the people of the land n' are many, "
18 Go therefore n', and work; for "
6: 1 N' shalt thou see what I will do to "
9:15 For n' I will stretch out my hand, "
18 foundation thereof even until n'. "
19 Send therefore n', and gather thy "
10:17 N' therefore forgive, I pray thee, "
11: 2 Speak n' in the ears of the people, 4994
12:40 N' the sojourning of the children of
16:36 N' an omer is the tenth part of an
18:11 N' I know that the Lord is greater6258
19 Hearken n' unto my voice, I will "
19: 5 N' therefore, if ye will obey my "
21: 1 N' these are the judgments which
29:38 N' this is that which thou shalt offer

Ex 32:10 N' therefore let me alone, that my 6258
30 and n' I will go up unto the Lord; "
32 n', if thou wilt forgive their sin—; "
34 Therefore n' go, lead the people "
33: 5 n' put off thy ornaments from thee, "
13 N' therefore, I pray thee, if I have "
13 shew me n' thy way, that I may 4994
34: 9 n' I have found grace in thy sight, "
Nu 11: 6 But n' our soul is dried away: 6258
23 shalt see n' whether my word shall "
12: 3 (N' the man Moses was very meek,
6 Hear n' my words: If there be a 4994
13 Heal her n', O God, I beseech thee.*"
13:20 N' the time was the time of the
22 (N' Hebron was built seven years
14:15 N' if thou shalt kill all this people as
17 n', I beseech thee, let the power of6258
19 people, from Egypt even until n'. 2008
22 tempted me n' these ten times, *2088
25 (N' the Amalekites and the Canaanites
41 Wherefore n' do ye transgress the 2088
16: 1 N' Korah, the son of Izhar, the son of
49 N' they that died in the plague were
20:10 Hear n', ye rebels; must we fetch 4994
22: 4 N' shall this company lick up all 6258
6 Come n' therefore, I pray thee, "
11 the earth: come n', curse me them;"
19 N' therefore, I pray you, tarry ye "
22 N' he was riding upon his ass, and his
29 hand, for n' would I kill thee. 6258
33 surely n' also I had slain thee, and "
34 n' therefore, if it displease thee, I "
38 have I n' any power at all to say "
24:11 Therefore n' flee thou to thy place: "
14 n', behold, I go unto my people: "
17 I shall see him, but not n': I shall "
25:14 N' the name of the Israelite that was
31:17 N' therefore kill every male 6258
43 (N' the half that pertained unto the
32: 1 N' the children of Reuben and the
De 2:13 N' rise up, said I, and get you 6258
4: 1 N' therefore hearken, O Israel, "
32 ask n' of the days that are past, 4994
5:25 N' therefore why should we die? 6258
6: 1 N' these are the commandments, the
10:12 n', Israel, what doth the Lord thy 6258
22 n' the Lord thy God hath made thee"
26:10 And n', behold, I have brought the "
31:19 N' therefore write ye this song for "
21 even n', before I have brought ‡3117
32:39 See n' that I, even I, am he, and 6258
Jos 1: 1 N' after the death of Moses the
2 n' therefore arise, go over this 6258
2:12 N' therefore, I pray you, swear "
3:12 N' therefore take you twelve men "
5: 5 N' all the people that came out *3588
14 the host of the Lord am I n' come. 6258
6: 1 N' Jericho was straitly shut up
7:19 tell me n' what thou hast done; 4994
8:11 n' there was a valley between them
9: 6 n' therefore make ye a league 6258
11 n' make ye a league with us. "
12 but n', behold, it is dry, and it is "
17 N' their cities were Gibeon, and
19 n' therefore we may not touch 6258
23 N' therefore ye are cursed, and "
25 n', behold, we are in thine hand; "
10: 1 N' it came to pass, when Adoni-zedec
12: 1 N' these are the kings of the land,
13: 1 N' Joshua was old and stricken in
7 N' therefore divide this land for 6258
14:10 n', behold, the Lord hath kept me "
10 n', lo, I am this day fourscore and "
11 even so is my strength n', for war, "
12 N' therefore give me this mountain,"
17: 8 N' Manasseh had the land of *
18:21 N' the cities of the tribe of the children
22: 4 n' the Lord your God hath given 6258
4 n' return ye, and get you unto your "
7 N' to the one half of the tribe of
26 Let us n' prepare to build us an 4994
31 n' ye have delivered the children of 227
24:14 N' therefore fear the Lord, and 6258
23 N' therefore put away, said he, the "
J'g 1: 1 N' after the death of Joshua it came*
8 N' the children of Judah had fought*
10 (n' the name of Hebron before was
23 (N' the name of the city before was
3: 1 N' these are the nations which the
4:11 N' Heber the Kenite, which was of
6:13 n' the Lord hath forsaken us, and 6258
17 If n' I have found grace in thy 4994
39 it n' be dry only upon the fleece; "
7: 3 N' therefore go to, proclaim in 6288
8: 2 I done n' in comparison of you? "
6 and Zalmunna n' in thine hand, 6258
10 N' Zebah and Zalmunna were in
15 and Zalmunna n' in thine hand, 6258
9:16 N' therefore, if ye have done truly "
32 N' therefore up by night, thou and "
38 Where is n' thy mouth, wherewith 645
38 go out, I pray n', and fight with 6258
11: 1 N' Jephthah the Gileadite was a
7 and why are ye come unto me n' 6258
8 Therefore we turn again to thee n', "
13 n' therefore restore those lands "
23 So n' the Lord God of Israel hath "
25 n' art thou anything better than "
12: 6 they unto him, Say n' Shibboleth: 4994
13: 3 Behold n', thou art barren, and "
4 N' therefore beware, I pray thee,6258
7 n' drink no wine nor strong drink, "
12 said, N' let thy words come to pass. "
14: 2 n' therefore get her for me to wife. "
12 I will n' put forth a riddle unto 4994
15: 3 N' shall I be more blameless than*6471

J'g 15:18 n' shall I die for thirst, and fall 6258
16: 9 N' there were men lying in wait,
10 n' tell me, I pray thee, wherewith 6258
27 N' the house was full of men and
17: 3 n' therefore I will restore it unto 6258
13 N' know I that the Lord will do me"
18:14 n' therefore consider what ye have "
19: 9 n' the day draweth toward evening,4994
18 am n' going to the house of the Lord;
22 N' as they were making their hearts*
24 them I will bring out n', and 4994
20: 3 (N' the children of Benjamin heard
9 n' this shall be the thing which 6258
13 N' therefore deliver us the men, "
38 N' there was an appointed sign
21: 1 N' the men of Israel had sworn in
Ru 1: 1 N' it came to pass in the days when*
2: 2 Let me n' go to the field, and 4994
7 even from the morning until n', 6258
3: 2 and n' is not Boaz of our kindred, "
11 n', my daughter, fear not; I will do"
12 n' it is true...I am thy near kinsman:"
4: 7 N' this was the manner in former time
18 n' these are the generations of Pharez:
1Sa 1: 1 N' there was a certain man of
9 N' Eli the priest sat upon a seat by a
13 N' Hannah, she spake in her heart;
2:12 N' the sons of Eli were the sons of
16 but thou shalt give it me n': 3588,6258
22 N' Eli was very old, and heard all that
30 n' the Lord saith, Be it far from 6258
3: 7 N' Samuel did not yet know the Lord,
4: 1 n' Israel went out against the
15 N' Eli was ninety and eight years old;
6: 7 N' therefore make a new cart, and6258
8: 2 N' the name of his firstborn was Joel;
5 n' make us a king to judge us like6258
9 N' therefore hearken unto their "
9: 1 N' there was a man of Benjamin,
3 Take n' one of the servants with 4994
6 Behold n', there is in this city a "
9 he that is n' called a prophet was 3117
12 make haste n', for he came to day 6258
13 N' therefore get you up; for about "
15 N' the Lord had told Samuel in his
10:19 N' therefore present yourselves 6258
12: 2 n', behold, the king walketh before "
7 N' therefore stand still, that I may "
10 n' deliver us out of the hand of our "
13 N' therefore behold the king whom"
16 N'...stand and see this great thing,"
13:12 come down n' upon me to Gilgal, "
13 n' would the Lord have established"
14 n' thy kingdom shall not continue: "
19 N' there was no smith found
14: 1 N' it came to pass upon a day, that
17 Number n', and see who is gone 4994
30 there not been n' a much greater 6258
49 N' the sons of Saul were Jonathan,
15: 1 n' therefore hearken thou unto 6258
3 N' go and smite Amalek, and "
25 N' therefore, I pray thee, pardon "
30 yet honour me n', I pray thee, "
16:12 N' he was ruddy, and withal of a
15 Behold n', an evil spirit from God 4994
16 our Lord n' command thy servants,"
17 Provide me n' a man that can play "
17: 1 N' the Philistines gathered together
12 N' David was the son of that
17 Take n' for thy brethren an ephah 4994
19 N' Saul, and they, and all the men of
29 David said, What have I n' done? 6258
18:22 n' therefore be the king's son in "
19: 2 n' therefore, I pray thee, take heed "
20:29 and n', if I have found favour in "
31 n' send and fetch him unto me, "
36 Run, find out n' the arrows which4994
21: 3 N'...what is under thine hand?
7 N' a certain man of the servants of
22: 6 (n' Saul abode in Gibeah under a tree
7 Hear n', ye Benjamites; will the 4994
12 said, Hear n', thou son of Ahitub.
23:20 N' therefore, O king, come down 6258
24:20 And n', behold, I know well that "
21 Swear n' therefore unto me by the "
25: 3 N' the name of the man was Nabal;
7 n' I have heard that thou hast 6258
7 n' thy shepherds which were with us,
10 be many servants n' a days that break
17 N' therefore know and consider 6258
21 N' David had said, Surely in vain have
26 N' therefore, my lord, as the Lord6258
26 n' let thine enemies, and they that "
27 And n' this blessing which thine "
26: 8 n' therefore let me smite him, I "
11 take thou n' the spear that is at his "
16 n' see where the king's spear is, "
19 N' therefore, I pray thee, let my "
20 N' therefore, let not my blood fall "
27: 1 I shall n' perish one day by the "
5 have n' found grace in thine eyes, 4994
28: 3 N' Samuel was dead, and all Israel
22 N' therefore, I pray thee, hearken6258
29: 1 N' the Philistines gathered together
7 Wherefore n' return, and go in 6258
10 n' rise up early in the morning "
31: 1 N' the Philistines fought against
2Sa 1: 1 N' it came to pass after the death of
2: 6 n' the Lord shew kindness and 6258
7 n' let your hands be strengthened, "
14 Let the young men n' arise, and *4994
3: 1 N' there was long war between the
18 N' then do it: for the Lord hath 6258
4:11 not therefore n' require his blood "
7: 2 See n', I dwell in an house of 4994
8 N' therefore so shalt thou say 6258

2Sa 7:25 *n*·, O Lord God, the word that thou 6258
28 *n*·, O Lord God, thou art that God, "
9: 6 *N*· when Mephibosheth, the son of*
10 *N*· Ziba had fifteen sons and twenty
12:10 *N*· therefore the sword shall 6258
23 *n*· he is dead, wherefore should "
28 *N*· therefore gather the rest of the "
13: 7 Go *n*· to thy brother Amnon's 4994
13 *N*· therefore, I pray thee, speak 6258
17 Put *n*· this woman out from me, 4994
20 but hold *n*· thy peace, my sister: 6258
24 said, Behold *n*·, thy servant hath 4994
25 Nay, my son, let us not all *n*· go, * "
28 *N*· Absalom had commanded his
28 *n*· when Amnon's heart is merry 4994
33 *N*· therefore let not my lord the 6258
14: 1 *N*· Joab the son of Zeruiah perceived
2 and put on *n*· mourning apparel, *4994
15 *N*· therefore that I am come to 6258
15 I will *n*· speak unto the king; it 4994
17 the king shall *n*· be comfortable: "
18 said, Let my lord the king *n*· speak. "
21 Behold *n*·, I have done this thing: "
32 *n*·...let me see the king's face; 6258
15:34 so will I *n*· also be thy servant: "
16:11 more *n*· may this Benjamite do it? "
17: 1 Let me *n*· choose out twelve 4994
5 Call *n*· Hushai the Archite also, "
9 he is hid *n*· in some pit, or in some6258
16 *N*· therefore send quickly, and tell "
17 *N*· Jonathan and Ahimaaz stayed by
18: 3 *n*· thou art worth ten thousand of 6258
3 therefore *n*· it is better that than "
18 *N*· Absalom in his lifetime had taken
19 Let me *n*· run, and fear the king 4994
19: 7 *N*· therefore arise, go forth, and 6258
7 befell thee from thy youth until *n*·. "
9 and *n*· he is fled out of the land for "
10 *N*· therefore why speak ye not a "
32 *N*· Barzillai was a very aged man,
20: 6 *N*· shall Sheba the son of Bichri 6258
23 *N*· Joab was over all the host of
21: 2 (*N*· the Gibeonites were not of the
23: 1 *N*· these be the last words of David.
24: 2 go *n*· through all the tribes of 4994
3 *N*· the Lord thy God add unto the
10 and *n*·, I beseech thee, O Lord, 6258
13 *n*· advise, and see what answer I "
14 fall *n*· into the hand of the Lord; 4994
16 is enough: stay *n*· thine hand. 6258
1Ki 1: 1 *N*· king David was old and stricken
12 *N*· therefore come, let me, I pray 6258
18 And *n*·, behold, Adonijah reigneth; "
18 *n*·, my lord the king, thou knowest*
2: 1 *N*· the days of David drew nigh that
9 *N*·...hold him not guiltless: for 6258
16 *n*· I ask one petition of thee, deny "
24 *N*· therefore, as the Lord liveth, "
3: 7 And *n*·, O Lord my God, thou hast "
5: 4 *n*· the Lord my God hath given me "
6 *N*· therefore command thou that "
8:25 Therefore *n*·, Lord God of Israel, "
9:11 (*N*· Hiram the king of Tyre had
10:14 *N*· the weight of gold that came to
12: 4 *n*· therefore make thou the 6258
11 *n*· whereas my father did lade you "
16 *n*· see to thine own house, David. "
26 *N*· shall the kingdom return to the "
13: 6 Intreat *n*· the face of the Lord 4994
11 *N*· there dwelt an old prophet in
14:14 that day: but what? even *n*·. 6258
29 *N*· the rest of the acts of Rehoboam,
15: 1 *N*· in the eighteenth year of king
7 *N*· the rest of the acts of Abijam, and*
31 *N*· the rest of the acts of Nadab, and
16: 5 *N*· the rest of the acts of Baasha,
14 *N*· the rest of the acts of Elah, and
20 *N*· the rest of the acts of Zimri, and
27 *N*· the rest of the acts of Omri which
17:24 *N*· by this I know that thou art a 6258
18: 3 (*N*· Obadiah feared the Lord greatly:
11, 14 *n*· thou sayest, Go, tell thy 6258
19 *N*· therefore send, and gather to "
43 And said to his servant, Go up *n*·, 4994
19: 4 *n*·, O Lord, take away my life; 6258
20:31 Behold *n*·, we have heard that the 4994
33 *N*· the men did diligently observe
21: 7 Dost thou *n*· govern the kingdom 6258
22:13 Behold *n*·, the words of the 4994
23 *N*· therefore, behold, the Lord 6258
39 *N*· the rest of the acts of Ahab, and
45 *N*· the rest of the acts of Jehoshaphat,
2Ki 1: 4 *N*· therefore thus saith the Lord,
5 Why are ye *n*· turned back? *2088
14 my life *n*· be precious in thy sight. 6258
18 *N*· the rest of the acts of Ahaziah
2:16 *n*·, there be with thy servants 4994
3: 1 *N*· Jehoram the son of Ahab began to
15 But *n*· bring me a minstrel. And 6258
23 *n*· therefore, Moab, to the spoil. "
4: 1 *N*· there cried a certain woman of
9 Behold *n*·, I perceive that this is 4994
13 Say *n*· unto her, Behold, thou hast "
26 Run *n*·, I pray thee, to meet her, 6258
5: 1 *N*· Naaman, captain of the host of
6 *N*· when this letter is come unto 6258
8 let him come *n*· to me, and he 4994
15 *n*· I know that there is no god in
15 *n*· therefore, I pray thee, take a 6258
22 even *n*· there be come to me from "
6: 1 Behold *n*·, the place where we 4994
7: 4 *N*· therefore come, and let us fall 6258
9 *n*· therefore come, that we may go "
12 will *n*· shew you what the Syrians 4994
19 *N*·, behold, if the Lord should make
8: 6 she left the land, even until *n*·. 6258

2Ki 9:12 they said, It is false; tell us *n*·. 4994
14 (*N*· Joram had kept Ramoth-gilead,
26 *N*· therefore take and cast him 6258
34 Go, see *n*· this cursed woman, and 4994
10: 2 *N*· as soon as this letter cometh 6258
6 *N*· the king's sons, being seventy
10 Know *n*· that there shall fall unto 645
19 *N*· therefore call unto me all the 6258
34 *N*· the rest of the acts of Jehu, and all
12: 7 *n*· therefore receive no more 6258
13:14 *N*· Elisha was fallen sick of his
19 *n*· thou shalt smite Syria...thrice. 6258
14:15 *N*· the rest of the acts of Jehoash
19 *N*· they made a conspiracy against*
28 *N*· the rest of the acts of Jeroboam,
15:36 *N*· the rest of the acts of Jotham,
16:19 *N*· the rest of the acts of Ahaz which
18: 1 *N*· it came to pass in the third year
13 *N*· in the fourteenth year of king
19 them, Speak ye *n*· to Hezekiah, 4994
20 *N*· on whom dost thou trust, that 6258
21 *N*·, behold, thou trustest upon the "
23 *N*· therefore, I pray thee, give "
25 Am I *n*· come up without the Lord "
19:19 *N*· therefore, O Lord our God, I "
25 *n*· have I brought it to pass, that "
20: 3 remember *n*· how I have walked 4994
21:17 *N*· the rest of the acts of Manasseh,
25 *N*· the rest of the acts of Amon which
22:14 (*n*· she dwelt in Jerusalem in the
23:28 *N*· the rest of the acts of Josiah, and
24: 5 *N*· the rest of the acts of Jehoiakim,
25: 4 (*n*· the Chaldees were against the
11 *N*· the rest of the people that were*
1Ch 1:32 *N*· the sons of Keturah, Abraham's*
43 *N*· these are the kings that reigned
2:34 *N*· Sheshan had no sons, but
42 *N*· the sons of Caleb the brother of*
3: 1 *N*· these were the sons of David,
5: 1 *N*· the sons of Reuben the firstborn*
6:54 *N*· these are their dwelling places
7: 1 *N*· the sons of Issachar were, Tola,*
8: 1 *N*· Benjamin begat Bela his firstborn,*
9: 2 *N*· the first inhabitants that dwelt in
10: 1 *N*· the Philistines fought against
11:15 *N*· three of the thirty captains went*
12: 1 *N*· these are they that came to David
14: 1 *N*· Hiram king of Tyre sent *
4 *N*· these are the names of his *
17: 1 *N*· it came to pass, as David sat in*
7 *N*· therefore thus shalt thou say 6258
23 Therefore *n*·, Lord, let the thing "
26 And *n*·, Lord, thou art God, and "
27 *N*· therefore let it please thee to "
18: 1 *N*· after this it came to pass, that*
9 *N*· when Tou king of Hamath heard*
19: 1 *N*· it came to pass after this, that*
10 *N*· when Joab saw that the battle
21: 8 but *n*·, I beseech thee, do away 6258
12 *N*· therefore advise thyself what "
13 let me fall *n*· into the hand of the ‡4994
15 is enough, stay *n*· thine hand. 6258
20 *N*· Ornan was threshing wheat.
22: 5 *n*· make preparations for it. So *4994
11 *N*·, my son, the Lord be with 6258
14 *N*·, behold, in my trouble I have
19 *N*· set your heart and your soul 6258
23: 3 *N*· the Levites were numbered from*
14 *N*· concerning Moses the man of God,*
24: 1 *N*· these are the divisions of the sons*
7 *N*· the first lot came forth to
25: 9 *N*· the first lot came forth for Asaph
27: 1 *N*· the children of Israel after their
28: 8 *N*· therefore in the sight of all 6258
10 Take heed *n*·; for the Lord hath "
29: 2 *N*· I have prepared with all my might
13 *N*· therefore, our God, we thank 6258
17 *n*· have I seen with joy thy people, "
20 *N*· bless the Lord your God. And 4994
29 *N*· the acts of David the king, first
2Ch 1: 9 *N*·, O Lord God, let thy promise 6258
10 me *n*· wisdom and knowledge, "
2: 7 Send me *n*· therefore a man cunning "
13 And *n*· I have sent a cunning man, "
15 *N*· therefore the wheat, and the
3: 3 *N*· these are the things wherein
6: 7 *N*· it was in the heart of David my
16 *N*· therefore, O Lord God of Israel, 6258
17 *N*· then, O Lord God of Israel, let "
40 *N*·, my God, let, I beseech thee, "
41 *N*· therefore arise, O Lord God, "
7: 1 *N*· when Solomon had made an end
15 *N*· mine eyes shall be open, and 6258
16 For *n*· have I chosen and sanctified "
8:16 *N*· all the work of Solomon was
9:13 *N*· the weight of gold that came to
29 *N*· the rest of the acts of Solomon,
10: 4 *n*· therefore ease thou somewhat 6258
16 *n*·, David, see to thine own house. "
12:15 *N*· the acts of Rehoboam, first and
13: 1 *N*· in the eighteenth year of king*
8 And *n*· ye think to withstand the 6258
15: 3 *N*· for a long season Israel hath been
18: 1 *N*· Jehoshaphat had riches and
22 *N*· therefore, behold, the Lord 6258
30 *N*· the king of Syria had commanded
19: 7 *n*· let the fear of the Lord be 6258
20:10 *n*·, behold, the children of Ammon "
34 *N*· the rest of the acts of Jehoshaphat,
21: 1 *N*· Jehoshaphat slept with his fathers,*
4 *N*· when Jehoram was risen up to
23:12 *N*· when Athaliah heard the noise of*
24:11 *N*· it came to pass, that at what time*
17 *N*· after the death of Jehoiada came
27 *N*· concerning his sons, and the
25: 3 *N*· it came to pass, when the

2Ch 25:14 *N*· it came to pass, after that
19 abide *n*· at home; why shouldest 6258
26 *N*· the rest of the acts of Amaziah,
27 *N*· after the time that Amaziah did
26:22 *N*· the rest of the acts of Uzziah, first
27: 7 *N*· the rest of the acts of Jotham, and
28:10 And *n*· ye purpose to keep under 6258
11 *N*· hear me therefore, and deliver "
26 *N*· the rest of his acts and of all his
29: 5 Levites, sanctify *n*· yourselves, 6258
10 *N*· it is in mine heart to make a "
11 My sons, be not *n*· negligent: for "
17 *N*· they began on the first day of the
31 *N*·...have consecrated yourselves 6258
30: 8 *N*· be ye not stiffnecked, as your "
31: 1 *N*· when all this was finished, all
32:15 *N*· therefore let not Hezekiah 6258
32 *N*· the rest of the acts of Hezekiah,
33:14 *N*· after this he built a wall without
18 *N*· the rest of the acts of Manasseh,
34: 8 *N*· in the eighteenth year of his reign,
22 (*n*· she dwelt in Jerusalem in the
35: 3 serve *n*· the Lord your God, and 6258
26 *N*· the rest of the acts of Josiah, and
36: 8 *N*· the rest of the acts of Jehoiakim,
22 *N*· in the first year of Cyrus king of
Ezr 1: 1 *N*· in the first year of Cyrus king of
2: 1 *N*· these are the children of the
3: 8 *N*· in the second year of their coming
4: 1 *N*· when the adversaries of Judah and
13 Be it known *n*· unto the king, that, 3705
14 *N*· because we have maintenance "
21 Give ye *n*· commandment to cause "
22 Take heed *n*· that ye fail not to do*
23 *N*· when the copy of king * 116
5:16 until *n*· hath it been in building, 3705
17 *N*· therefore, if it seem good to the "
6: 6 *N*· therefore, Tatnai, governor "
7: 1 *N*· after these things, in the reign of
11 *N*· this is the copy of the letter that
8: 1 These are *n*· the chief of their fathers,
33 *N*· on the fourth day was the silver*
9: 1 *N*· when these things were done, the
8 And *n*· for a little space grace hath 6258
10 *n*·, O our God, what shall we say "
12 *N*·...give not your daughters unto "
10: 1 *N*· when Ezra had prayed, and when
2 land: yet *n*· there is hope in Israel 6258
3 *N*·...let us make a covenant with "
11 *N*· therefore make confession unto "
14 Let *n*· our rulers of all the 4994
Ne 1: 6 Let thine ear *n*· be attentive, and "
6 which I pray before thee *n*·, day *3117
10 *N*· these are thy servants and thy
11 let *n*· thine ear be attentive to the 4994
2: 1 *N*· I had not been beforetime sad in
9 *N*· the king had sent captains of the
4: 3 *N*· Tobiah the Ammonite was by him,
5: 5 *n*· our flesh is as the flesh of our 6258
18 *N*· that which was prepared for me
6: 1 *N*· it came to pass, when Sanballat,
7 *n*· shall it be reported to the king 6258
6 Come *n*· therefore, and let us take "
9 *N*· therefore, O God, strengthen my "
7: 1 *N*· it came to pass, when the wall was
4 *N*· the city was large and great: but
9: 1 *N*· in the twenty and fourth day of
32 *N*· therefore, our God, the great, 6258
10: 1 *N*· those that sealed were, Nehemiah,
11: 3 *N*· these are the chief of the province
12: 1 *N*· these are the priests and the
13: 3 *N*· it came to pass, when they had*
Es 1: 1 *N*· it came to pass in the days of
2: 5 *N*· in Shushan the palace there was a*
12 *N*· when every maid's turn was come
15 *N*· when the turn of Esther, the
3: 4 *N*· it came to pass, when they spake
5: 1 *N*· it came to pass on the third day,
6: 4 *N*· Haman was come into the outward
6 *N*· Haman thought in his heart, To
9: 1 *N*· in the twelfth month, that is, the
12 *n*· what is thy petition? and it shall
Job 1: 6 *N*· there was a day when the sons of
11 But put forth thine hand *n*·, and 4994
2: 5 But put forth thine hand *n*·, and "
11 *N*· when Job's three friends heard of
3:13 For *n*· should I have lain still and 6258
4: 5 But *n*· it is come upon thee, and "
12 *N*· a thing was secretly brought to me,
5: 1 Call *n*·, if there be any that will 4994
6: 3 For *n*· it would be heavier than the 6258
21 For *n*· ye are nothing; ye see my "
28 *N*· therefore be content, look upon "
7:21 for *n*· shall I sleep in the dust; and "
8: 6 surely *n*· he would awake for thee, "
9:25 *N*· my days are swifter than a post:
12: 7 But ask *n*· the beasts, and they 4994
13: 6 Hear *n*· my reasoning, and hearken "
18 Behold *n*·, I have ordered my cause; "
19 for *n*·, if I hold my tongue, I shall 6258
14:16 For *n*· thou numberest my steps: "
16: 7 But *n*· he hath made me weary: "
19 Also *n*·, behold, my witness is in "
17: 3 Lay down *n*·, put me in a surety 4994
10 you all, do ye return, and come *n*·: "
15 And where is *n*· my hope? as for * 645
19: 6 Know *n*· that God hath overthrown "
23 Oh that my words were *n*· written! "
22:21 Acquaint *n*· thyself with him, and 4994
24:25 if it be not so *n*·, who will make 645
30: 1 *n*· they that are younger than I 6258
9 And *n*· am I their song, yea, I am "
16 *n*· my soul is poured out upon me; "
32:14 *N*· he hath not directed his words *
33: 2 *n*· I have opened my mouth, my 4994
34:16 If *n*· thou hast understanding, hear

Job 35:15 But *n'*, because it is not so, he hath 6258
37:21 And *n'* men see not the bright light "
38: 3 Gird up *n'* thy loins like a man; 4994
40: 7 Gird up thy loins *n'* like a man: I "
10 Deck thyself *n'* with majesty and "
15 Behold *n'* behemoth, which I made "
16 Lo *n'*, his strength is in his loins, "
42: 5 ear: but *n'* mine eye seeth thee. 6258
8 take unto you *n'* seven bullocks "
Ps 2:10 Be wise *n'* therefore, O ye kings: be"
12: 5 sighing of the needy, *n'* will I arise,"
17:11 have *n'* compassed us in our steps: "
20: 6 *N'* know I that the Lord saveth his"
27: 6 And *n'* shall mine head be lifted up "
37:25 I have been young, and *n'* am old; yet
39: 7 And *n'*, Lord, what wait I for? my 6258
41: 8 and *n'* that he lieth he shall rise up no
50:22 *N'* consider this, ye that forget 4994
71:18 *N'* also when I am old and *
74: 6 *n'* they break down the carved 6258
115: 2 say, Where is *n'* their God? 4994
116:14, 18 pay my vows unto the Lord *n'** "
118: 2 Let Israel *n'* say, that his mercy "
3 Let the house of Aaron *n'* say, that "
4 Let them *n'* that fear the Lord say, "
25 Save *n'*, I beseech thee, O Lord: O "
25 I beseech thee, send *n'* prosperity. "
119:67 astray: but *n'* have I kept thy word.6258
122: 8 I will *n'* say, Peace be within thee.4994
124: 1 was on our side, *n'* may Israel say; "
129: 1 from my youth, may Israel *n'* say: "
Pr 5: 7 Hear me *n'* therefore, O ye 6258
6: 3 Do this *n'*, my son, and deliver 645
7:12 *N'* is she without, *n'* in the streets,6471
24 Hearken unto me *n'* therefore, O 6258
8:32 *N'* therefore hearken unto me, O "
Ec 2: 1 Go to *n'*, I will prove thee with 4994
16 which *n'* is in the days to come *3528
3:15 That which hath been is *n'*; and * "
9: 6 and their envy, is *n'* perished; "
7 for God *n'* accepteth thy works. * "
15 *N'* there was found in it a poor wise
12: 1 Remember *n'* thy Creator in the days*
Ca 3: 2 I will rise *n'*, and go about the 4994
7: 8 *N'* also thy breasts shall be as * "
Isa 1:18 Come *n'*, and let us reason "
21 lodged in it; but *n'* murderers. 6258
5: 1 *N'* will I sing to my wellbeloved *4994
3 *n'*, O inhabitants of Jerusalem, 6258
5 *n'* go to; I will tell you what I will "
7: 3 Go forth *n'* to meet Ahaz, thou, 4994
8: 7 *N'* therefore, behold, the Lord "
16:14 *n'* the Lord hath spoken, saying, 6258
19:12 men? and let them tell thee *n'*, 4994
22: 1 What aileth thee *n'*, that thou art 645
28:22 *N'* therefore be ye not mockers. 6258
29:22 Jacob shall not *n'* be ashamed, "
30: 8 *N'* go, write it before them in a "
31: 3 *N'* the Egyptians are men, and not
33:10 *N'* will I rise, saith the Lord; 6258
10 the Lord; *n'* will I be exalted; "
10 be exalted; *n'* will I lift up myself. "
36: 1 *N'* it came to pass in the fourteenth
4 Say ye *n'* to Hezekiah, Thus saith 4994
5 *n'* on whom dost thou trust, that 6258
8 *N'* therefore give pledges, I pray "
10 And am I *n'* come up without the "
37:20 *N'* therefore, O Lord our God, save"
38: 3 Remember *n'*, O Lord, I beseech 4994
42:14 *n'* will I cry like a travailing woman; "
43: 1 *n'* thus saith the Lord that created6258
19 *n'* it shall spring forth; shall ye not"
44: 1 Yet *n'* hear, O Jacob my servant; "
47: 8 hear *n'* this, thou that art given to "
12 Stand *n'* with thine enchantments,4994
13 Let *n'* the astrologers, the "
48: 7 They are created *n'*, and not from 6258
16 and *n'* the Lord God, and his Spirit,"
49: 5 *n'*, saith the Lord that formed me "
19 even *n'* be too narrow by reason "
51:21 hear *n'* this, thou afflicted, and 4994
52: 5 *N'* therefore, what have I here, 6258
64: 8 *n'*, O Lord, thou art our father; we "
Jer 2:18 *n'* what hast thou to do in the way "
4:12 *n'* also will I give sentence against "
31 Woe is me *n'*! for my soul is 4994
5: 1 and see *n'*, and know, and seek in "
21 Hear *n'* this, O foolish people, and "
24 Let us *n'* fear the Lord our God, "
7:12 But go ye *n'* unto my place which "
13 *n'*, because ye have done all these "
14:10 he will *n'* remember their iniquity, "
17:15 the word of the Lord? let it come *n'*."
18:11 *N'* therefore go to, speak to the 6258
11 return...*n'* every one from his evil 4994
13 Ask ye *n'* among the heathen, who "
20: 1 *N'* Pashur the son of Immer the
25: 5 Turn ye again *n'* every one from 4994
26: 8 *N'* it came to pass, when Jeremiah*
13 Therefore *n'* amend your ways 6258
27: 6 And *n'* have I given all these lands "
16 shall *n'* shortly be brought again "
18 *n'* make intercession to the Lord 4994
28: 7 hear thou *n'* this word that I speak "
15 Hear *n'*, Hananiah; The Lord hath"
29: 1 *N'* these are the words of the letter
30: 6 Ask ye *n'*, and see whether a man 4994
32:16 *N'* when I had delivered the evidence
36 *n'* therefore thus saith the Lord, 6258
34:10 *N'* when all the princes, and all the*
15 ye were *n'* turned, and had done 3117
35:15 Return ye *n'* every man from his 4994
36:15 Sit down *n'*, and read it in our ears."
16 *N'* it came to pass, when they had
17 Tell us *n'*, How didst thou write 4994
22 *N'* the king sat in the winterhouse in

Jer 37: 3 Pray *n'* unto the Lord our God for 4994
4 *N'* Jeremiah came in and went out
19 Where are *n'* your prophets which
20 hear *n'*, I pray thee, O my lord the6254
38: 7 *N'* when Ebed-melech the Ethiopian,
12 Put *n'* these old cast clouts and 4994
25 Declare unto us *n'* what thou hast "
39:11 *N'* Nebuchadrezzar king of Babylon
15 *N'* the word of the Lord came unto
40: 3 *N'* the Lord hath brought it, and*
4 *n'*, behold, I loose thee this day 6258
5 *N'* while he was not yet gone back, he
7 *N'* when all the captains of the forces
41: 1 *N'* it came to pass in the seventh
9 *N'* the pit wherein Ishmael had cast
13 *N'* it came to pass, that when all the
42:15 *n'* therefore hear the word of the 6258
21 *n'* I have this day declared it to you;*
22 *N'* therefore know certainly that 6258
44: 7 Therefore *n'* thus saith the Lord,
45: 3 Woe is me *n'*! for the Lord hath 4994
52: 7 (*n'* the Chaldeans were by the city
12 *N'* in the fifth month, in the tenth day
Eze 1: 1 *N'* it came to pass in the thirtieth
15 *N'* as I beheld the living creatures,
7: 3 *N'* is the end come upon thee, 6258
8 *N'* will I shortly pour out my fury "
8: 5 Son of man, lift up thine eyes *n'* 4994
8 me, Son of man, dig *n'* in the wall: "
10: 3 *N'* the cherubims stood on the right
16: 8 *N'* when I passed by thee, and looked
17:12 Say *n'* to the rebellious house, 4994
18:14 *N'*, lo, if he beget a son, that seeth all
25 Hear *n'*, O house of Israel; Is not 4994
19: 5 *N'* when she saw that she had waited,
13 *n'* she is planted in the wilderness,6258
22: 2 *N'*, thou son of man, wilt thou judge,*
23:43 Will they *n'* commit whoredoms 6258
26: 2 be replenished, *n'* she is laid waste:
18 *N'* shall the isles tremble in the 6258
27: 2 *N'*, thou son of man, take up a *
33:22 *N'* the hand of the Lord was upon me
38:12 desolate places that are *n'* inhabited,
39:25 *N'* will I bring again the captivity6258
41:12 *N'* the building that was before the*
42: 5 *N'* the upper chambers were shorter:
15 *N'* when he had made an end of
43: 9 *N'* let them put away their 6258
46:12 *N'* when the prince shall prepare*3588
47: 7 *N'* when I had returned, behold, at
48: 1 *N'* these are the names of the tribes.
Da 1: 6 *N'* among these were of the children
9 *N'* God had brought Daniel into favour
18 *N'* at the end of the days that the king*
2:23 made known unto me *n'* what we 3705
23 *n'* made known unto us the king's* "
3:15 *N'* if ye be ready that at what time "
4:18 *N'* thou, O Belteshazzar, declare*
37 *N'* I Nebuchadnezzar praise and 3705
5:10 *N'* the queen by reason of the words
12 *n'* let Daniel be called, and he will 3705
15 *n'* the wise men, the astrologers, "
16 *n'* if thou canst read the writing, "
6: 8 *N'*, O king, establish the decree, "
10 *N'* when Daniel knew that the *1768
16 *N'* the king spake and said unto 116
8:18 *N'* as he was speaking with me, I was
22 *N'* that being broken, whereas four*
9:15 And *n'*, O Lord our God, that hast 6258
17 *N'* therefore, O our God, hear the "
22 I am *n'* come forth to give thee skill"
10:11 for unto thee am I *n'* sent: "
14 *N'* I am come to make thee
20 *n'* will I return to fight with the 6258
11: 2 And *n'* will I shew thee the truth.
34 *N'* when they shall fall, they shall be
Ho 1: 8 *N'* when she had weaned Lo-ruhamah,
2: 7 then was it better with me than *n'*.6258
10 *n'* will I discover her lewdness in "
4:16 *n'* the Lord will feed them as a lamb"
5: 3 for *n'*, O Ephraim, thou committest
7 *n'* shall a month devour them 6258
7: 2 *n'* their own doings have beset them
8: 8 *n'* shall they be among the Gentiles as
10 *n'* will I gather them, and they 6258
13 *n'* will he remember their iniquity, "
10: 2 *n'* shall they be found faulty: he "
3 *n'* they shall say, We have no king, "
13: 2 And *n'* they sin more and more, and"
Am 6: 7 Therefore *n'* shall they go captive "
7:16 *N'* therefore hear thou the word "
Jon 1: 1 *N'* the word of the Lord came unto
17 *N'* the Lord...prepared a great fish*
3: 3 *N'* Nineveh was an exceeding great
4: 3 *n'*, O Lord, take, I beseech thee, 6258
Mic 4: 9 *N'* why dost thou cry out aloud? is "
10 *n'* shalt thou go...out of the city, "
11 *N'* also many nations are gathered "
5: 1 *N'* gather thyself in troops, O "
4 *n'* shall he be great unto the ends "
6: 1 Hear ye *n'* what the Lord saith; 4994
5 remember *n'* what Balak king of "
7: 4 *n'* shall be their perplexity. 6258
10 *n'* shall she be trodden down as the"
Na 1:13 *n'* will I break his yoke from off "
Hag 1: 5 *N'* therefore thus saith the Lord of "
2: 2 Speak *n'* to Zerubbabel the son of 4994
3 and how do ye see it *n'*? is it not 6258
4 Yet *n'* be strong, O Zerubbabel, "
11 Ask *n'* the priests concerning the 4994
15 *n'*, I pray...consider from this day "
18 Consider *n'* from this day and * "
Zec 1: 4 Turn ye *n'* from your evil ways, "
3: 3 *N'* Joshua was clothed with filthy
8 Hear *n'*, O Joshua the high priest,4994
5: 5 Lift up *n'* thine eyes, and see what "

Zec 8:11 *n'* I will not be unto the residue 6258
9: 8 for *n'* have I seen with mine eyes. "
Mal 1: 8 offer it *n'* unto thy governor; will 4994
9 *n'*, I pray you, beseech God that 6258
2: 1 *n'*, O ye priests, this commandment"
3:10 and prove me *n'* herewith, saith 4994
15 And *n'* we call the proud happy; 6258
M't 1:18 *N'* the birth of Jesus Christ was on*1161*
22 *N'* all this was done, that it might "
2: 1 *N'* when Jesus was born in "
3:10 *n'* also the ax is laid unto the root *2236*
15 Suffer it to be so *n'*: for thus it *737*
4:12 *N'* when Jesus had heard that *1161*
8:18 *N'* when Jesus saw great "
9:18 saying, My daughter is even *n'* dead:*737*
10: 2 *N'* the names of the twelve *1161*
11: 2 *N'* when John had heard in the "
12 until *n'* the kingdom of heaven *737*
14:15 place, and the time is *n'* past; **2236*
24 But the ship was *n'* in the midst of "
15:32 continue with me *n'* three days, "
21:18 *N'* in the morning as he returned *1161*
22:25 *N'* there were with us seven "
24:32 *N'* learn a parable of the fig tree; "
26: 6 *N'* when Jesus was in Bethany, in "
17 *N'* the first day of the feast of "
20 *N'* when the even was come, he sat"
45 Sleep on *n'*, and take your rest: *3063*
48 *N'* he that betrayed him gave *1161*
53 that I cannot *n'* pray to my Father,**737*
65 *n'* ye have heard his blasphemy. *3568*
69 *N'* Peter sat without in the palace:*1161*
27:15 *N'* at that feast the governor was "
42 him *n'* come down from the cross, *3568*
43 let him deliver him *n'*, if he will "
45 *N'* from the sixth hour there was *1161*
54 *N'* when the centurion, and they "
62 *N'* the next day, that followed the "
28:11 *N'* when they were going, behold, "
M'r 1:14 *N'* after that John was put in "
16 *N'* as he walked by the sea of Galilee,*
4:37 into the ship, so that it was *n'* full. *2235*
5:11 *N'* there was there nigh unto the *1161*
6:35 when the day was *n'* far spent, *2236*
35 place, and *n'* the time is far passed:"
8: 2 have *n'* been with me three days, "
14 *N'* the disciples had forgotten to **2532*
10:30 an hundredfold *n'* in this time, *3568*
11:11 *n'* the eventide was come, he went *2236*
12:20 *N'* there were seven brethren: and**3767*
13:12 *N'* the brother shall betray the **1161*
28 *N'* learn a parable of the fig tree: "
14:41 Sleep on *n'*, and take your rest: it *3063*
15: 6 *N'* at that feast he released unto *1161*
32 Christ...descend *n'* from the cross, *3568*
42 And *n'* when the even was come, *2236*
16: 9 *N'* when Jesus was risen early the *1161*
Lu 1: 7 both were *n'* well stricken in years.
57 *N'* Elisabeth's full time came that *1161*
2:15 Let us *n'* go even unto Bethlehem, *1211*
29 *n'* lettest thou thy servant depart *3568*
41 *N'* his parents went to Jerusalem**2532*
3: 1 *N'* in the fifteenth year of the reign*1161*
9 *n'* also the axe is laid unto the root *2236*
21 *N'* when all the people were *1161*
4:40 *N'* when the sun was setting, all * "
5: 4 *N'* when he had left speaking, he * "
6:21 Blessed are ye that hunger *n'*: for *3568*
21 Blessed are ye that weep *n'*: for ye "
25 Woe unto you that laugh *n'*! for ye"
7: 1 *N'* when he had ended all his **1161*
6 he was *n'* not far from the house, *2236*
12 *N'* when he came nigh to the gate *1161*
39 *N'* when the Pharisee which had "
8:11 *N'* the parable is this: The seed is "
22 *N'* it came to pass on a certain day,*2532*
38 *N'* the man out of whom the devils**1161*
9: 7 *N'* Herod the tetrarch heard of all "
10:36 which *n'* of these three, thinkest **3767*
38 *N'* it came to pass, as they went, *1161*
11: 7 the door is *n'* shut, and my *2236*
39 *N'* do ye Pharisees make clean the*3568*
14:17 Come; for all things are *n'* ready. *2236*
15:25 *N'* his elder son was in the field: *1161*
16:25 *n'* he is comforted, and thou art *3568*
18:22 *N'* when Jesus heard these things,**1161*
19:37 even *n'* at the descent of the mount*2236*
42 *n'* they are hid from thine eyes. *3568*
20:37 *N'* that the dead are raised, even **1161*
21:30 when they *n'* shoot forth, ye see *2236*
30 that summer is *n'* nigh at hand. "
22: 1 *N'* the feast of unleavened bread *1161*
36 But *n'*, he that hath a purse, let *3568*
23:47 *N'* when the centurion saw what**1161*
24: 1 *N'* upon the first day of the week,**2532*
Joh 1:44 *N'* Philip was of Bethsaida, the *1161*
2: 8 Draw out *n'*, and bear unto the *3568*
10 hast kept the good wine until *n'*. *737*
23 *N'* when he was in Jerusalem at *1161*
4: 6 *N'* Jacob's well was there. Jesus* "
18 he whom thou *n'* hast is not thy *3568*
23 the hour cometh, and *n'* is, when "
42 *N'* we believe, not because of thy *3765*
43 *N'* after two days he departed **1161*
51 And as he was *n'* going down, his *2236*
5: 2 *N'* there is at Jerusalem by the *1161*
6 been *n'* a long time in that case, *2236*
25 The hour is coming, and *n'* is, *3568*
6:10 *N'* there was much grass in the *1160*
16 And when even was *n'* come, his *
17 it was *n'* dark, and Jesus was not *2236*
7: 2 *N'* the Jews' feast of tabernacles *1161*
14 *N'* about the midst of the feast **2236*
8: 5 *N'* Moses in the law commanded *1161*
40 But *n'* ye seek to kill me, a man *3568*
52 *N'* we know that thou hast a devil."

Joh 9:19 blind? how then doth he n' see? 737
21 by what means he n' seeth, we 3568
25 that, whereas I was blind, n' I see. 737
31 N' we know that God heareth not*1161
41 n' ye say, We see; therefore your 3568
11: 1 N' a certain man was sick, named 1161
5 N' Jesus loved Martha, and her "
18 N' Bethany was nigh...Jerusalem, "
22 that even n', whatsoever thou wilt 3568
30 N' Jesus was not yet come into the1161
57 N' both the chief priests and the "
12:27 N' is my soul troubled; and what 3568
31 N' is the judgment of this world: "
31 n' shall the prince of this world be "
13: 1 N' before the feast of the passover,1161
2 devil having n' put into the heart *2236
7 What I do thou knowest not n'; 737
19 N' I tell you before it come, that,* "
23 N' there was leaning on Jesus' *1161
28 N' no man at the table knew for "
31 N' is the Son of man glorified, 3568
33 ye cannot come; so n' I say to you. 737
36 go, thou canst not follow me n'; 3568
37 Lord, why cannot I follow thee n'? 737
14:29 n' I have told you before it come 3568
15: 3 N' ye are clean through the word*2236
22 n' they have no cloke for their sin. 3568
24 n' have they both seen and hated "
16: 5 n' I go my way to him that sent me; "
12 you, but ye cannot bear them n'. 737
19 N' Jesus knew that they were *3767
22 ye n' therefore have sorrow: but I 3568
29 Lo, n' speakest thou plainly, and "
30 N' are we sure that thou knowest "
31 answered them, Do ye n' believe? 737
32 the hour cometh, yea, is n' come, 3568
17: 5 n', O Father, glorify thou me with "
7 N' they have known that all things "
11 And n' I am no more in the world,*3765
13 And n' come I to thee; and these 3568
18:14 N' Caiaphas was he, which gave 1161
24 N' Annas had sent him bound *3767
36 n' is my kingdom not from hence. 3568
40 N' Barabbas was a robber. 1161
19:23 n' the coat was without seam, woven "
25 N' there stood by the cross of Jesus* "
28 all things were n' accomplished, 2236
29 N' there was set a vessel full of *3767
41 N' in the place where he was 1161
21: 4 when the morning was n' come, 2236
6 n' they were not able to draw it 3765
7 N' when Simon Peter heard *3767
10 the fish which ye have n' caught. 3568
14 This is n' the third time that Jesus2236
Ac 1:18 N' this man purchased a field 3767
2: 6 N' when this was noised abroad, 1161
33 this, which ye n' see and hear. *3568
37 N' when they heard this they were1161
3: 1 N' Peter and John went up together "
17 n', brethren, I wot that through 3568
4: 3 next day: for it was n' eventide. 2236
13 N', when they saw the boldness of1161
29 n', Lord, behold their threatenings:3568
5:24 N' when the high priest and the 1161
38 n' I say unto you, Refrain from 3568
7: 4 into this land, wherein ye n' dwell. "
11 N' there came a dearth all over 1161
34 n' come, I will send thee into 3568
52 whom ye have been n' the betrayers "
8:14 N' when the apostles which were 1161
9:36 N' there was at Joppa a certain "
10: 5 n' send men to Joppa, and call for 3568
17 N' while Peter doubted in himself 1161
33 N' therefore are we all here 3568
11:19 N' they which were scattered *3767
12: 1 N' about that time Herod the king1161
11 N' I know of a surety, that the 3568
18 N' as soon as it was day, there 1161
13: 1 N' there were in the church that "
11 n', behold, the hand of the Lord is 3568
13 N' when Paul and his company 1161
34 n' no more to return to corruption, he
43 N' when the congregation was 1161
15:10 N' therefore why tempt ye God, to3568
16:36 n' therefore depart, and go in peace. "
37 n' do they thrust us out privily? "
17: 1 N' when they had passed through 1161
16 N' while Paul waited for them at "
30 n' commandeth all men everywhere3568
18:14 was n' about to open his mouth, *1161
20:22 n', behold, I go bound in the spirit3568
25 And n', behold, I know that ye all, "
32 n', brethren, I commend you to God, "
21: 3 N' when we had discovered *1161
22: 1 ye my defence which I make n' 3568
16 n' why tarriest thou? arise, and "
23:15 N' therefore ye with the counsel "
21 and n' are they ready, looking for a "
24:13 things whereof they n' accuse me. "
17 N' after many years I came to 1161
25: 1 N' when Festus was come into *3767
26: 6 n' I stand and am judged for the 3568
17 Gentiles, unto whom n' I send thee,* "
27: 9 N' when much time was spent, and*1161
9 when sailing was n' dangerous, 2235
9 the fast was n' already past, "
22 And n' I exhort you to be of good 3568
Ro 1:10 if by any means n' at length I 2236
13 N' I would not have you ignorant,*1161
3:19 N' we know that what things soever "
21 But n' the righteousness of God 3568
4: 4 N' to him that worketh is the 1161
19 not his own body n' dead, when 2236
23 N' it was not written for his sake 1161
5: 9 being n' justified by his blood, 3568
11 we have n' received the atonement. "

Ro 6:19 even so n' yield your members 3568
21 things whereof ye are n' ashamed? "
22 But n' being made free from sin, 3570
7: 6 n' we are delivered from the law, "
17 N' then it is no more I that do it, "
20 N' if I do that I would not, it is no*1161
8: 1 therefore n' no condemnation to 3568
9 N' if any man have not the Spirit*1161
22 in pain together until n'. 3568
11:12 N' if the fall of them be the riches 1161
30 God, yet have n' obtained mercy 3568
31 so have these also n' not believed, "
13:11 n' it is high time to awake out of 2236
11 for n' is our salvation nearer than 3568
14:15 n' walkest thou not charitably. *3765
15: 5 N' the God of patience and 1161
8 N' I say that Jesus Christ was a *1160
13 N' the God of hope fill you with all1161
23 n' having no more place in these 3570
25 n' I go unto Jerusalem to minister "
30 N' I beseech you, brethren, for the1161
33 N' the God of peace be with you all. "
16:17 N' I beseech you, brethren, mark "
25 N' to him that is of power to stablish "
26 But n' is made manifest, and by 3568
1Co 1:10 N' I beseech you, brethren, by the1161
12 N' this I say, that every one of you "
2:12 N' we have received, not the spirit* "
3: 2 bear it, neither yet n' are ye able. 3568
8 N' he that planteth and he that 1161
12 N' if any man build upon this * "
4: 7 n' if thou didst receive it, why *2532
8 N' ye are full, n' ye are rich, ye *2236
18 N' some are puffed up, as though I1161
5:11 n' I have written unto you not to 3570
6: 7 N' therefore there is utterly a *2236
13 N' the body is not for fornication,*1161
7: 1 N' concerning the things whereof ye "
14 unclean; but n' are they holy. 3568
8: 1 N' as touching things offered unto1161
9:25 N' they do it to obtain a...crown; 3767
10: 6 N' these things were our examples,1161
11 N' all these things happened unto "
11: 2 N' I praise you, brethren, that ye "
17 N' in this that I declare unto you I* "
12: 1 N' concerning spiritual gifts, "
4 N' there are diversities of gifts, but "
18 n' hath God set the members every3570
20 But n' are they many members, 3568
27 N' ye are the body of Christ, and 1161
13:12 n' we see through a glass, darkly; 737
12 N' I know in part; but then shall I "
13 And n' abideth faith, hope, charity,3570
14: 6 N', brethren, if I come unto you "
15:12 N' if Christ be preached that he 1161
20 n' is Christ risen from the dead, 3570
50 N' this I say, brethren, that flesh 1161
16: 1 N' concerning the collection for the "
5 N' I will come unto you, when I * "
7 I will not see you n' by the way; 737
10 N' if Timotheus come, see that he 1161
2Co 1:21 N' he which stablisheth us with you "
2:14 N' thanks be unto God, which * "
3:17 N' the Lord is that Spirit: and "
5: 5 N' he that hath wrought us for the "
16 yet n' henceforth know we him no 3568
20 N' then we are ambassadors for *3767
6: 2 behold, n' is the accepted time; 3568
2 behold, n' is the day of salvation.) "
13 N' for a recompence in the same, 1161
7: 9 N' I rejoice, not that ye were made3568
8:11 N' therefore perform the doing of*3570
14 n' at this time your abundance *3568
22 but n' much more diligent, upon 3570
9:10 N' he that ministereth seed to *1161
10: 1 N' I Paul myself beseech you by the "
12: 6 but n' I forbear, lest any man should*
13: 2 being absent n' I write to them 3568
7 N' I pray to God that ye do no evil;1161
Ga 1: 9 As we said before, so say I n' again,737
10 For do I n' persuade men, or God? "
20 N' the things which I write unto 2236
23 n' preacheth the faith which once 3568
2:20 the life which I n' live in the flesh "
3: 3 are ye n' made perfect by the flesh? "
16 N' to Abraham and his seed were 1161
20 N' a mediator is not a mediator of "
4: 1 N' I say, That the heir, as long as*2236
9 But n', after that ye have known 3568
20 I desire to be present with you n', 737
25 to Jerusalem which n' is, and is 3568
28 N' we, brethren, as Isaac was, are1161
29 after the Spirit, even so it is n'. 3568
5:19 N' the works of the flesh are 1161
Eph 2: 2 the spirit that n' worketh in the 3568
13 But n' in Christ Jesus ye who 3570
19 N'...ye are no more strangers *3767
3: 5 n' revealed unto his holy apostles 3568
10 n' unto the principalities and "
20 N' unto him that is able to do 1161
4: 9 (N' that he ascended, what is it but "
5: 8 but n' are ye light in the Lord: 3568
Ph'p 1: 5 gospel from the first day until n'; "
20 so n' also Christ shall be magnified "
30 saw in me, and n' hear to be in me. "
2:12 but n' much more in my absence, "
3:18 n' tell you even weeping, that they "
4:10 n' at the last your care of me hath 2236
15 N' ye Philippians know also, that *1161
20 N' unto God and our Father be glory "
Col 1:21 works, yet n' hath he reconciled 3570
24 n' rejoice in my sufferings for you,3568
26 n' is made manifest to his saints: 3570
3: 8 n' ye also put off all these; anger, "
1Th 3: 6 n' when Timotheus came from you 737
8 For n' we live, if ye stand fast in 3568

1Th 3:11 N' God himself and our Father, and1161
5:14 N' we exhort you, brethren, warn* "
2Th 2: 1 N' we beseech you, brethren, by the "
6 And n' ye know what withholdeth 3568
7 only he who n' letteth will let, 737
16 N' our Lord Jesus Christ himself, 1161
3: 6 N' we command you, brethren, in "
12 N' them that are such we command "
16 N' the Lord of peace himself give "
1Ti 1: 5 N' the end of the commandment is* "
17 N' unto the King eternal, immortal,* "
4: 1 N' the Spirit speaketh expressly, * "
8 promise of the life that n' is, and 3568
5: 5 N' she that is a widow indeed, and1161
2Ti 1:10 But is n' made manifest by the 3568
3: 8 N' as Jannes and Jambres *1161
4: 6 For I am n' ready to be offered, *2236
Ph'm 9 n' also a prisoner of Jesus Christ. 3570
11 but n' profitable to thee and to me: "
16 Not n' as a servant, but above a *3765
Heb 2: 8 n' we see not yet all things put 3568
7: 4 N' consider how great this man 1161
8: 1 N' of the things which we have "
6 But n' hath he obtained a more 3570
13 N' that which decayeth and *1161
9: 5 we cannot n' speak particularly. 3568
6 N' when these things were thus 1161
24 n' to appear in the presence of 3568
26 n' once in the end of the world hath "
10:18 N' where remission of these is, 1161
38 N' the just shall live by faith: but* "
11: 1 N' faith is the substance of things "
16 n' they desire a better country, 3570
12:11 N' no chastening for the present *1161
26 n' he hath promised, saying, Yet 3568
13:20 N' the God of peace, that brought 1161
Jas 4:13 Go to n', ye that say, To day or 3568
16 n' ye rejoice in your boastings: all "
5: 1 Go to n', ye rich men, weep and "
1Pe 1: 6 though n' for a season, if need be, 737
8 in whom, though n' ye see him not, "
12 which are n' reported unto you by 3568
2:10 people, but are n' the people of God: "
10 mercy, but n' have obtained mercy. "
25 are n' returned unto the Shepherd "
3:21 even baptism doth also n' save us "
2Pe 2: 3 n' of a long time lingereth not,
3: 1 beloved, I n' write unto you; in 2236
7 and the earth, which are n', 3568
18 him be glory both n' and for ever. "
1Jo 2: 8 past, and the true light n' shineth.*2235
9 brother, is in darkness even until n'.737
18 even n' are there many antichrists;3568
28 n', little children, abide in him; "
3: 2 Beloved, n' are we the sons of God, "
4: 3 even n' already is it in the world. "
2Jo 5 And n' I beseech thee, lady, not as "
Jude 24 N' unto him that is able to keep 1161
25 and power, both n' and ever. 3568
Re 12:10 N' is come salvation, and strength,737

now-a-days See NOW and DAYS.

no-wise See NO and WISE.

number See also NUMBERED; NUMBERETH; NUMBERING; NUMBERS.

Ge 13:16 man can n' the dust of the earth, 4487
15: 5 stars, if thou be able to n' them: †5608
34:30 being few in n', they shall gather 4557
41:49 numbering; for it was without n'. "
Ex 12: 4 it according to the n' of the souls; 4373
16:16 according to the n' of your persons;4557
23:26 land: the n' of thy days I will fulfil. "
30:12 children of Israel after their n', *6485
Le 15:13 he shall n' to himself seven days 5608
28 she shall n' to herself seven days, "
23:16 seventh sabbath shall ye n' fifty "
25: 8 thou shalt n' seven sabbaths of "
15 to the n' of years after the jubile 4557
15 unto the n' of years of the fruits "
16 to the n' of the years of the fruits "
50 be according unto the n' of years, "
26:22 your cattle, and make you few in n'; "
Nu 1: 2 fathers, with the n' of their names,4557
3 shall n' them by their armies. 6485
18, 20, 22, 24, 26, 28, 30, 32, 34, 36, 38, 40,
42 according to the n' of the names,4557
49 thou shalt not n' the tribe of Levi, 6485
3:15 N' the children of Levi after the "
15 old and upward shalt thou n' them. "
22 according to the n' of all the males,4557
28 In the n' of all the males, from a "
34 according to the n' of all the males, "
40 N' all the firstborn of the males of6485
40 and take the n' of their names. 4557
43 firstborn males by the n' of names, "
48 odd n' of them is to be redeemed. 5736
4:23 fifty years old shalt thou n' them; 6485
29 shalt n' them after their families, "
30 fifty years old shalt thou n' them, "
37 which Moses and Aaron did n' * "
41 whom Moses and Aaron did n' * "
14:29 of you, according to your whole n',4557
34 n' of the days in which ye searched "
15:12 According to the n'...ye...prepare, "
12 do to every one according to their n'. "
23:10 the n' of the fourth part of Israel? "
26:53 according to the n' of names. "
29:18, 21, 24, 27, 30, 33, 37 shall be according to their n', after the "
31:36 was in n' three hundred thousand "
De 4:27 be left few in n' among the heathen, "
7: 7 ye were more in n' than any people; "
16: 9 Seven weeks shalt thou n' unto 5608
9 begin to n' the seven weeks from "
25: 2 to his fault, by a certain n'. 4557
28:62 And ye shall be left few in n', whereas

De 32: 8 the *n*' of the children of Israel. 4557
Jos 4: 5, 8 *n*' of the tribes of the children of "
J'g 6: 5 and their camels were without *n*': "
7: 6 the *n*' of them that lapped, putting "
12 and their camels were without *n*', "
21: 23 them wives, according to their *n*', "
1Sa 6: 4 *n*' of the lords of the Philistines: "
18 *n*' of all the cities of the Philistines "
14: 17 *N*' now, and see who is gone from 6485
2Sa 2: 15 over by *n*' twelve of Benjamin, 4557
21: 20 foot six toes, four and twenty in *n*'; "
24: 1 to say, Go, *n*' Israel and Judah. 4487
2 Beer-sheba, and *n*' ye the people, 6485
2 I may know the *n*' of the people. *4557
4 the king, to *n*' the people of Israel. 6485
9 the sum of the *n*' of the people *4662
1Ki 18: 31 to the *n*' of the tribes of the sons of 4557
20: 25 And *n*' thee an army, like the army 4487
1Ch 7: 2 whose *n*' was in the days of David 4557
9 And the *n*' of them, after their 3187
40 *n*' throughout the genealogy 4557, "
11: 11 *n*' of the mighty men whom David 4557
21: 1 and provoked David to *n*' Israel. 4487
2 Go, *n*' Israel from Beer-sheba even 5608
2 and bring the *n*' of them to me, *4557
5 the sum of the *n*' of the people *4662
22: 16 brass, and the iron, there is no *n*'. 4557
23: 3 their *n*' by their polls, man by man, "
24 counted by *n*' of names by their "
31 feasts, by *n*', according to the order "
25: 1 the *n*' of the workmen according to "
7 the *n*' of them, with their brethren "
27: 1 the children of Israel after their *n*', "
23 But David took not the *n*' of them "
24 the son of Zeruiah began to *n*', 4487
24 was the *n*' put in the account of 4557
2Ch 12: 3 people were without *n*' that came "
26: 11 according to the *n*' of their account "
12 whole *n*' of the chief of the fathers "
29: 32 And the *n*' of the burnt offerings, "
30: 24 *n*' of priests sanctified themselves. "
35: 7 to the *n*' of thirty thousand, and 4557
Ezr 1: 9 And this is the *n*' of them: thirty "
2: 2 the *n*' of the men of the people of "
3: 4 the daily burnt offerings by *n*', "
6: 17 to the *n*' of the tribes of Israel. 4510
8: 34 By *n*' and by weight of every one: 4557
Ne 7: 7 *n*', I say, of the men of the people "
Es 9: 11 day the *n*' of those that were slain "
Job 1: 5 according to the *n*' of them all. "
3: 6 not come into the *n*' of the months. "
5: 9 marvellous things without *n*': "
9: 10 out; yea, and wonders without *n*'. "
14: 5 the *n*' of his months are with thee, "
15: 20 and the *n*' of years is hidden to the "
21: 21 the *n*' of his months is cut off in the "
25: 3 Is there any *n*' of his armies? and "
31: 37 unto him the *n*' of my steps; as a "
34: 24 in pieces mighty men without *n*', *2714
36: 26 can the *n*' of his years be searched 4557
38: 21 because the *n*' of thy days is great? "
37 Who can *n*' the clouds in wisdom? 5608
39: 2 Canst thou *n*' the months that they "
Ps 90: 12 So teach us to *n*' our days, that 4487
105: 12 they were but a few men in *n*'; 4557
34 caterpillars, and that without *n*', "
139: 18 they are more in *n*' than the sand: "
147: 4 He telleth the *n*' of the stars; he 4557
Ca 6: 8 concubines, and virgins without *n*'. "
Isa 21: 17 the residue of the *n*' of archers, "
40: 26 that bringeth out their host by *n*': "
65: 11 the drink offering unto that *n*'. *4507
12 will I *n*' you to the sword, and ye *4487
Jer 2: 28 according to the *n*' of thy cities 4557
32 have forgotten me days without *n*'. "
11: 13 For according to the *n*' of thy cities "
13 according to the *n*' of the streets "
44: 28 a small *n*' that escape the sword * "
Eze 4: 4 according to the *n*' of the days that "
5 according to the *n*' of the days, "
9 according to the *n*' of the days that "
5: 3 shalt also take thereof a few in *n*', "
Da 9: 2 by books the *n*' of the years, "
Ho 1: 10 the *n*' of the children of Israel shall "
Joe 1: 6 my land, strong, and without *n*', "
Na 3: 3 of slain, and a great *n*' of carcases;* "
M'r 10: 46 disciples and a great *n*' of people, *3793
Lu 22: 3 being of the *n*' of the twelve. 706
Joh 6: 10 sat down, in *n*' about five thousand. "
Ac 1: 15 (the *n*' of names together were *3793
4: 4 the *n*' of the men was about five 706
5: 36 to whom a *n*' of men, about four "
6: 1 the *n*' of the disciples was multiplied, "
7 the *n*' of the disciples multiplied in 706
11: 21 and a great *n*' believed, and turned "
16: 5 the faith, and increased in *n*' daily. "
Ro 9: 27 the *n*' of the children of Israel be 706
2Co 10: 12 dare not make ourselves of the *n*', 1469
1Ti 5: 9 not a widow be taken into the *n*' *2639
Re 5: 11 the *n*' of them was ten thousand 706
7: 4 I heard the *n*' of them which were "
9 multitude, which no man could *n*', 705
9: 16 the *n*' of the army of the horsemen 706
16 and I heard the *n*' of them. "
13: 17 of the beast, or the *n*' of his name. "
18 count the *n*' of the beast: for it is "
18 the beast: for it is the *n*' of a man; "
18 his *n*' is Six hundred threescore "
15: 2 mark, and over the *n*' of his name, "
20: 8 *n*' of whom is as the sand of the sea. "

numbered
Ge 13: 16 then shall thy seed also be *n*'. 4487
16: 10 it shall not be *n*' for multitude. 5608
32: 12 which cannot be *n*' for multitude. "
Ex 30: 13, 14 among them that are *n*', 6485
38: 25 And the silver of them that were *n*' "
26 for every one that went to be *n*', "
Nu 1: 19 so he *n*' them in the wilderness of "
21 Those that were *n*' of them, even "
22 fathers, those that were *n*' of them, "
23, 25, 27, 29, 31, 33, 35, 37, 39, 41, 43
Those that were *n*' of them, "
44 These are those that were *n*', "
44 which Moses and Aaron *n*', and the "
45 So were all those that were *n*' of "
46 they that were *n*' were six hundred "
47 fathers were not *n*' among them. "
2: 4 and those that were *n*' of them, "
6, 8 and those that were *n*' thereof, "
9 that were *n*' in the camp of Judah "
11 and those that were *n*' thereof, "
13, 15 and those that were *n*' of them, "
16 that were *n*' in the camp of Reuben "
19, 21, 23 those that were *n*' of them, "
24 All that were *n*' of the camp of "
26, 28, 30 those that were *n*' of them, "
31 that were *n*' in the camp of Dan "
32 were *n*' of the children of Israel by "
32 all those that were *n*' of the camps "
33 the Levites were not *n*' among the "
3: 16 And Moses *n*' them according to the "
22 that were *n*' of them, according to "
22 that were *n*' of them were seven "
34 And those that were *n*' of them, "
39 that were *n*' of the Levites, which "
39 Levites, which Moses and Aaron *n*' "
42 Moses *n*', as the Lord commanded "
43 of those that were *n*' of them, were "
4: 34 *n*' the sons of the Kohathites after "
36 those that were *n*' of them by their "
37 they that were *n*' of the families "
38 And those that were *n*' of the sons "
40 Even those that were *n*' of them, "
41 they that were *n*' of the families of "
42 those that were *n*' of the families of "
44 Even those that were *n*' of them "
45 those that were *n*' of the families "
45 Moses and Aaron *n*' according to "
46 those that were *n*' of the Levites, "
46 Aaron and the chief of Israel *n*', "
48 Even those that were *n*' of them, "
49 they were *n*' by the hand of Moses, "
49 thus were they *n*' of him, as the "
7: 2 and were over them that were *n*', "
14: 29 all that were *n*' of you, according "
26: 7 that were *n*' of them were forty and "
18, 22, 25, 27, 34 that were *n*' of them, "
37 according to those that were *n*' of "
41 that were *n*' of them were forty "
43 to those that were *n*' of them, "
47 to those that were *n*' of them; "
50 and they that were *n*' of them were "
51 the *n*' of the children of Israel, six "
54 to those that were *n*' of him. "
57 are they that were *n*' of the Levites "
62 that were *n*' of them were twenty "
62 were not *n*' among the children of "
63 are they that were *n*' by Moses and "
63 who *n*' the children of Israel in the "
64 Moses and Aaron the priest *n*', "
64 when they *n*' the children of Israel "
Jos 8: 10 and *n*' the people, and went up, he "
J'g 20: 15 the children of Benjamin were *n*' "
15 were *n*' seven hundred chosen men. "
17 were *n*' four hundred thousand "
21: 9 For the people were *n*', and, behold, "
1Sa 11: 8 And when he *n*' them in Bezek, the "
13: 15 Saul *n*' the people that were present "
14: 17 when they had *n*', behold, Jonathan "
15: 4 together, and *n*' them in Telaim, "
2Sa 18: 1 David *n*' the people that were with "
24: 10 after that he had *n*' the people. 5608
1Ki 3: 8 be *n*' nor counted for multitude. 4487
8: 5 not be told nor *n*' for multitude. "
20: 15 he *n*' the young men of the princes *6485
15 after them he *n*' all the people, * "
26 year, that Ben-hadad *n*' the Syrians, * "
27 children of Israel were *n*', and were * "
2Ki 3: 6 the same time, and *n*' all Israel. * "
1Ch 21: 17 commanded the people to be *n*'? 4487
23: 3 the Levites were *n*' from the age 5608
27 the Levites were *n*' from twenty 4557
2Ch 2: 17 Solomon *n*' all the strangers that 5608
17 David his father had *n*' them; and "
5: 6 not be told nor *n*' for multitude. 4487
25: 5 he *n*' them from twenty years old 6485
Ezr 1: 8 and *n*' them unto Sheshbazzar, the 5608
Ps 40: 5 them, they are more than can be *n*'. "
Ec 1: 15 which is wanting cannot be *n*'. 4487
Isa 22: 10 have *n*' the houses of Jerusalem, 5608
53: 12 he was *n*' with the transgressors; 4487
Jer 33: 22 the host of heaven cannot be *n*', 5608
Da 5: 26 God hath *n*' thy kingdom, and 4483
Ho 1: 10 which cannot be measured nor *n*'; 5608
M't 10: 30 very hairs of your head are all *n*'. 705
M'r 15: 28 he was *n*' with the transgressors. *3049
Lu 12: 7 very hairs of your head are all *n*'. 705
Ac 1: 17 For he was *n*' with us, and had 2674
26 he was *n*' with the eleven apostles. 4785

numberest
Ex 30: 12 the Lord, when thou *n*' them; 6485
12 among them, when thou *n*' them. "
Job 14: 16 For now thou *n*' my steps: dost 5608

numbering
Ge 41: 49 sea, very much, until he left *n*'; 5608
2Ch 2: 17 after the *n*' wherewith David his 5610

numbers
1Ch 12: 23 the *n*' of the bands that were 4557
2Ch 17: 14 the *n*' of them according to the *6486
Ps 71: 15 for I know not the *n*' thereof. 5615

Nun (*nun*) See also NON.
Ex 33: 11 his servant Joshua, the son of *N*'. 5126
Nu 11: 28 Joshua the son of *N*', the servant "
13: 8 of Ephraim, Oshea the son of *N*'. "
16 Moses called Oshea the son of *N*' "
14: 6 Joshua the son of *N*', and Caleb "
30 Jephunneh,...Joshua the son of *N*'. "
38 Joshua the son of *N*', and Caleb "
26: 65 Jephunneh,...Joshua the son of *N*'. "
27: 18 Take thee Joshua the son of *N*', a "
32: 12 Kenezite, and Joshua the son of *N*': "
28 Joshua the son of *N*', and the chief "
34: 17 priest, and Joshua the son of *N*'. "
De 1: 38 But Joshua the son of *N*', which "
31: 23 gave Joshua the son of *N*' a charge, "
32: 44 he, and Hoshea the son of *N*'. "
34: 9 the son of *N*' was full of the spirit "
Jos 1: 1 spake unto Joshua the son of *N*', "
2: 1 Joshua the son of *N*' sent out of "
23 and came to Joshua the son of *N*', "
6: 6 the son of *N*' called the priests, "
14: 1 priest, and Joshua the son of *N*', "
17: 4 before Joshua the son of *N*', and "
19: 49 inheritance to Joshua the son of *N*' "
51 priest, and Joshua the son of *N*', "
21: 1 and unto Joshua the son of *N*', "
24: 29 Joshua the son of *N*', the servant "
J'g 2: 8 Joshua the son of *N*', the servant of "
1Ki 16: 34 he spake by Joshua the son of *N*'. "
Ne 8: 17 the days of Jeshua the son of *N*' "

nurse See also NURSED; NURSING.
Ge 24: 59 Rebekah their sister, and her *n*', 3243
35: 8 But Deborah Rebekah's *n*' died, and "
Ex 2: 7 to thee a *n*' of the Hebrew women, "
7 that she may *n*' the child for thee? "
9 this child away, and *n*' it for me, "
Ru 4: 16 her bosom, and became *n*' unto it. 539
2Sa 4: 4 and his *n*' took him up, and fled: "
2Ki 11: 2 they hid him, even him and his *n*', 3243
2Ch 22: 11 him and his *n*' in a bedchamber. "
1Th 2: 7 as a *n*' cherisheth her children; 5162

nursed
Ex 2: 9 woman took the child, and *n*' it. 5134
Isa 60: 4 daughters shall be *n*' at thy side. * 539

nursing
Nu 11: 12 as a *n*' father beareth the sucking 539
Isa 49: 23 And kings shall be thy *n*' fathers, "
23 and their queens thy *n*' mothers: 3243

nurture
Eph 6: 4 *n*' and admonition of the Lord. *3809

nuts
Ge 43: 11 spices, and myrrh, *n*', and almonds: 992
Ca 6: 11 went down into the garden of *n*' to 93

Nymphas (*nim'-fas*)
Col 4: 15 which are in Laodicea, and *N*', 3564

O.

O See in the APPENDIX; also OH.

oak See also OAKS.
Ge 35: 4 Jacob hid them under the *o*' which 424
8 buried beneath Beth-el under an *o*': 437
Jos 24: 26 set it up there under an *o*', that was 427
J'g 6: 11 under an *o*' which was in Ophrah, 424
19 brought it out unto him under the *o*', "
2Sa 18: 9 under the thick boughs of a great *o*', "
9 and his head caught hold of the *o*', "
10 I saw Absalom hanged in an *o*'. "
14 was yet alive in the midst of the *o*'. "
1Ki 13: 14 and found him sitting under an *o*': "
1Ch 10: 12 buried their bones under the *o*' in "
Isa 1: 30 shall be as an *o*' whose leaf fadeth, 424
6: 13 and as an *o*', whose substance is in 437
44: 14 taketh the cypress and the *o*', which "
Eze 6: 13 and under every thick *o*', the place 424

oaks
Isa 1: 29 be ashamed of the *o*' which ye have 352
2: 13 up, and upon all the *o*' of Bashan, 437
Eze 27: 6 Of the *o*' of Bashan have they made "
Ho 4: 13 hills, under *o*' and poplars and elms, "
Am 2: 9 and he was strong as the *o*'; yet I "
Zec 11: 2 howl, O ye *o*' of Bashan; for the "

oar See also OARS.
Eze 27: 29 And all that handle the *o*', the 4880

oars
Isa 33: 21 wherein shall go no galley with *o*', 7885
Eze 27: 6 Bashan have they made thine *o*'; 4880

oath See also OATH'S; OATHS.
Ge 24: 8 shalt be clear from this my *o*': 7621
41 shalt thou be clear from this my *o*', 423
41 one, thou shalt be clear from my *o*'. "
26: 3 I will perform the *o*' which I 7621
28 Let there be now an *o*' betwixt us, 423
50: 25 Joseph took an *o*' of the children 7650
Ex 22: 11 an *o*' of the Lord be between them 7621
Le 5: 4 a man shall pronounce with an *o*', "
Nu 5: 19 priest shall charge her by an *o*', *7650

Nu 5:21 the woman with an o· of cursing, 7621
21 Lord make thee a curse and an o· "
30: 2 swear an o· to bind his soul with a "
10 her soul by a bond with an o·; "
13 every binding o· to afflict the soul, "
De 7: 8 he would keep the o· which he had "
29:12 into his o·, which the Lord thy God 423
14 do I make this covenant and this o·; "
Jos 2:17 will be blameless of this thine o· 7621
20 then we will be quit of thine o· "
9:20 because of the o· which we sware "
J'g 21: 5 had made a great o· concerning him "
1Sa 14:26 mouth: for the people feared the o·. "
27 charged the people with the o·: 7650
28 straitly charged...people with an o·. "
2Sa 21: 7 Lord's o· that was between them, 7621
1Ki 2:43 thou not kept the o· of the Lord, "
8:31 an o· be laid upon him to cause him 423
31 o· come before thine altar in this * "
18:10 he took an o· of the kingdom and 7650
2Ki 11: 4 took an o· of them in the house of "
1Ch 16:16 Abraham, and of his o· unto Isaac; 7621
2Ch 6:22 an o· be laid upon him to make him 423
22 the o· come before the altar in this* "
15:15 And all Judah rejoiced at the o·: 7621
Ne 5:12 priests, and took an o· of them, 7650
10:29 entered into a curse, and into an o·, 7621
Ps 105: 9 Abraham, and his o· unto Isaac; "
Ec 8: 2 and that in regard of the o· of God. "
9: 2 sweareth, as he that feareth an o·. "
Jer 11: 5 That I may perform the o· which I "
Eze 16:59 despised the o· in breaking the 423
17:13 him, and hath taken an o· of him: "
16 whose o· he despised, and whose "
18 he despised the o· by breaking the "
19 surely mine o· that he hath despised, "
Da 9:11 the o· that is written in the law of 7621
Zec 8:17 his neighbour; and love no false o·: "
M't 14: 7 he promised with an o· to give her 3727
26:72 he denied with an o·, I do not know "
Lu 1:73 o· which he sware to our father "
Ac 2:30 God had sworn with an o· to him, "
23:21 have bound themselves with an o·,* 332
Heb 6:16 an o· for confirmation is to them 3727
17 his counsel, confirmed it by an o·: "
7:20 without an o· he was made priest: 3728
21 priests were made without an o·; "
21 but this with an o· by him that said "
28 the word of the o·, which was since "
Jas 5:12 the earth, neither by any other o·: 3727

oath's
M't 14: 9 nevertheless for the o· sake, and *3727
M'r 6:26 yet for his o· sake, and for their * "

oaths
Eze 21:23 sight, to them that have sworn o·: 7621
Hab 3: 9 according to the o· of the tribes, "
M't 5:33 perform unto the Lord thine o·: 3727

Obadiah (*o-ba-di'-ah*)
1Ki 18: 3 And Ahab called O·, which was the 5662
3 (Now O· feared the Lord greatly: "
4 O· took an hundred prophets, and "
5 And Ahab said unto O·, Go into the "
6 O· went another way by himself. "
7 And as O· was in the way, behold, "
16 So O· went to meet Ahab, and told "
1Ch 3:21 the sons of Arnan, the sons of O·, "
7: 3 Michael, and O·, and Joel, Ishiah, "
8:38 and Sheariah, and O·, and Hanan. "
9:16 O· the son of Shemaiah, the son of "
44 and Sheariah, and O·, and Hanan: "
12: 9 Ezer the first, O· the second, Eliab "
27:19 Of Zebulun, Ishmaiah the son of O·: "
2Ch 17: 7 and to O·, and to Zechariah, and to "
34:12 overseers...were Jahath and O·, "
Ezr 8: 9 O· the son of Jehiel, and with him "
Ne 10: 5 Harim, Meremoth, O·, "
12:25 O·, Meshullam, Talmon, Akkub, "
Ob 1 The vision of O·. Thus saith the "

Obal (*o'-bal*)
Ge 10:28 And O·, and Abimael, and Sheba, 5745

Obed (*o'-bed*) See also OBED-EDOM.
Ru 4:17 and they called his name O·: he 5744
21 begat Boaz, and Boaz begat O·, "
22 O· begat Jesse, and Jesse begat "
1Ch 2:12 Boaz begat O·, and O· begat Jesse, "
37 begat Ephlal, and Ephlal begat O·, "
38 And O· begat Jehu, and Jehu begat "
11:47 and O·, and Jasiel the Mesobaite. "
26: 7 and O·, Elzabad, whose brethren "
2Ch 23: 1 and Azariah the son of O·, and "
M't 1: 5 begat O· of Ruth; and O· begat 5601
Lu 3:32 of Jesse, which was the son of O·, "

Obed-edom (*o''-bed-e'-dom*)
2Sa 6:10 into the house of O· the Gittite. 5654
11 continued in the house of O· the "
11 the Lord blessed O·, and all his "
12 Lord hath blessed the house of O·, "
12 from the house of O· into the city of "
1Ch 13:13 carried it aside into the house of O· "
14 God remained with the family of O· "
14 the Lord blessed the house of O·. "
15:18 and O·, and Jeiel, the porters. "
21 and O·, and Jeiel, and Azaziah, with "
24 O· and Jehiah were doorkeepers "
25 Lord out of the house of O· with joy. "
16: 5 and Eliab, and Benaiah, and O·: "
38 O· with their brethren, threescore "
38 O· also the son of Jeduthun and "
26: 4 Moreover the sons of O· were, "
8 All these of the sons of O·: they and "
8 were threescore and two of O·. "
15 To O· southward; and to his sons "
2Ch 25:24 found in the house of God with O·, "

obedience See also DISOBEDIENCE.
Ro 1: 5 o· to the faith among all nations, 5218
5:19 so by the o· of one shall many be "
6:16 death, or of o· unto righteousness? "
16:19 For your o· is come abroad unto all "
26 to all nations for the o· of faith: "
1Co 14:34 are commanded to be under o·, *5293
2Co 7:15 he remembereth the o· of you all, 5218
10: 5 every thought to the o· of Christ; "
6 when your o· is fulfilled. "
Ph'm 21 Having confidence in thy o· I wrote "
Heb 5: 8 yet learned he o· by the things "
1Pe 1: 2 unto o· and sprinkling of the blood "

obedient See also DISOBEDIENT.
Ex 24: 7 Lord...said will we do, and be o·. 8085
Nu 27:20 the children of Israel may be o·. * "
De 4:30 and shalt be o· unto his voice; * "
8:20 ye would not be o· unto the voice * "
2Sa 22:45 they hear, they shall be o· unto me.* "
Pr 25:12 so is a wise reprover upon an o· ear. "
Isa 1:19 If ye be willing and o·, ye shall eat "
42:24 neither were they o· unto his law. "
Ac 6: 7 of the priests were o· to the faith. 5219
Ro 15:18 to make the Gentiles o·, by word *5218
2Co 2: 9 whether ye be o· in all things. 5255
Eph 6: 5 o· to them that are your masters 5219
Ph'p 2: 8 and became o· unto death, even 5255
Tit 2: 5 good, o· to their own husbands, *5293
9 to be o· unto their own masters, * "
1Pe 1:14 As o· children, not fashioning *5218

obeisance
Ge 37: 7 about, and made o· to my sheaf. 7812
9 moon and the eleven stars made o· "
43:28 down their heads, and made o·. "
Ex 18: 7 meet his father in law, and did o·, "
2Sa 1: 2 that he fell to the earth, and did o·. "
14: 4 her face to the ground, and did o·, "
15: 5 man came nigh to him to do him o·, "
1Ki 1:16 Bath-sheba bowed, and did o· unto "
2Ch 24:17 of Judah, and made o· to the king. "

obey See also DISOBEYED; OBEYED; OBEYETH; OBEYING.
Ge 27: 8 my son, o· my voice according to 8085
13 only o· my voice, and go fetch me "
43 my son, o· my voice; and arise, flee "
Ex 5: 2 should o· his voice to let Israel go?* "
19: 5 if ye will o· my voice indeed, and "
23:21 Beware of him, and o· his voice, * "
22 if thou shalt indeed o· his voice, * "
De 11:27 if ye o· the commandments of the* "
28 if ye will not o· the commandments* "
13: 4 commandments, and o· his voice, "
21:18 will not o· the voice of his father, "
20 rebellious, he will not o· our voice; "
27:10 o· the voice of the Lord thy God, "
28:62 wouldest not o· the voice of the * "
30: 2 shalt o· his voice according to all "
8 return and o· the voice of the Lord, "
20 and that thou mayest o· his voice, "
Jos 24:24 we serve, and his voice will we o·. "
1Sa 8:19 refused to o· the voice of Samuel;* "
12:14 serve him, and o· his voice, and not* "
15 ye will not o· the voice of the Lord,* "
15:19 didst thou not o· the voice of the "
22 to o· is better than sacrifice, and to "
Ne 9:17 refused to o·, neither were mindful "
Job 36:11 If they o· and serve him, they shall* "
12 But if they o· not, they shall perish* "
Ps 18:44 they hear of me, they shall o· me: "
Pr 30:17 and despiseth to o· his mother, 3349
Isa 11:14 children of Ammon shall o· them. 4928
Jer 7:23 O· my voice, and I will be your *8085
11: 4 O· my voice, and do them, according "
7 and protesting, saying, O· my voice. "
12:17 if they will not o·, I will utterly * "
18:10 in my sight, that it o· not my voice, "
26:13 o· the voice of the Lord your God; "
35:14 but o· their father's commandment: "
38:20 O·, I beseech thee, the voice of the "
42: 6 we will o· the voice of the Lord our "
6 when we o· the voice of the Lord "
13 neither o· the voice of the Lord your "
Da 7:27 dominions shall serve and o· him. 8086
9:11 that they might not o· thy voice; 8085
Zec 6:15 diligently o· the voice of the Lord "
M't 8:27 even the winds and the sea o· him! 5219
M'r 1:27 unclean spirits, and they do o· him. "
4:41 even the wind and the sea o· him? "
Lu 8:25 winds and water, and they o· him. "
17: 6 in the sea; and it should o· you. † "
Ac 5:29 ought to o· God rather than men. 3980
32 God hath given to them that o· him. "
7:39 our fathers would not o·, *5255,1036
Ro 2: 8 and do not o· the truth, but 544
8 the truth, but o· unrighteousness, 3982
6:12 ye should o· it in the lusts thereof. 5219
16 yield yourselves servants to o·, *5218
16 his servants ye are to whom ye o·; 5219
Ga 3: 1 that ye should not o· the truth, *3982
5: 7 that ye should not o· the truth? "
Eph 6: 1 Children, o· your parents in the 5219
Col 3:20 Children, o· your parents in all "
22 o· in all things your masters "
2Th 1: 8 that o· not the gospel of our Lord "
3:14 if any man o· not our word by this* "
Tit 3: 1 to o· magistrates, to be ready to *3980
Heb 5: 9 salvation unto all them that o· 5219
13:17 O· them that have the rule over 3982
Jas 3: 3 horses' mouths, that they may o· "
1Pe 3: 1 if any o· not the word, they also 544
4:17 them that o· not the gospel of God? "

obeyed See also DISOBEYED; OBEYEDST.
Ge 22:18 because thou hast o· my voice. 8085
26: 5 Because that Abraham o· my voice, "
28: 7 Jacob o· his father and his mother, 8085
Jos 5: 6 they o· not the voice of the Lord: * "
22: 2 o· my voice in all that I commanded* "
J'g 2: 2 but ye have not o· my voice: why * "
6:10 dwell: but ye have not o· my voice.* "
1Sa 15:20 Yea, I have o· the voice of the Lord, "
24 the people, and o· their voice. "
28:21 thine handmaid hath o· thy voice,* "
1Ki 20:36 hast not o· the voice of the Lord, "
2Ki 18:12 they o· not the voice of the Lord "
1Ch 29:23 prospered; and all Israel o· him. "
2Ch 11: 4 they o· the words of the Lord, and* "
Pr 5:13 have not o· the voice of my teachers, "
Jer 3:13 ye have not o· my voice, saith the "
25 have not o· the voice of the Lord our "
9:13 and have not o· my voice, neither "
11: 8 Yet they o· not, nor inclined their "
17:23 they o· not, neither inclined their * "
32:23 but they o· not thy voice, neither "
34:10 more, then they o·, and let them go. "
35: 8 we o· the voice of Jonadab the son "
10 we have dwelt in tents, and have o·, "
18 o· the commandment of Jonadab "
40: 3 the Lord, and have not o· his voice, "
42:21 not o· the voice of the Lord your "
43: 4 o· not the voice of the Lord, to dwell "
7 they o· not the voice of the Lord: "
44:23 have not o· the voice of the Lord, "
Da 9:10 Neither have we o· the voice of the "
14 he doeth: for we o· not his voice. "
Zep 3: 2 She o· not the voice; she received "
Hag 1:12 o· the voice of the Lord their God, "
Ac 5:36 as many as o· him, were scattered, 3982
37 as many as o· him, were dispersed. "
Ro 6:17 have o· from the heart that form *5219
10:16 they have not all o· the gospel. * "
Ph'p 2:12 my beloved, as ye have always o·, "
Heb 11: 8 By faith Abraham,...o·; "
1Pe 3: 6 Even as Sara o· Abraham, calling "

obeyedst
1Sa 28:18 thou o· not the voice of the Lord, 8085
Jer 22:21 youth, that thou o· not my voice. "

obeyeth
Isa 50:10 that o· the voice of his servant, 8085
Jer 7:28 a nation that o· not the voice of the* "
11: 3 Cursed be the man that o· not the * "

obeying
J'g 2:17 o· the commandments of the Lord; 8085
1Sa 15:22 as in o· the voice of the Lord? "
1Pe 1:22 purified your souls in o· the truth *5218

Obil (*o'-bil*)
1Ch 27:30 Over the camels also was O· the 179

object
Ac 24:19 o·, if they had ought against me. *2723

oblation See also OBLATIONS.
Le 2: 4 thou bring an o· of a meat offering 7133
5, 7 if thy o· be a meat offering baken "
12 for the o· of the firstfruits, ye shall "
13 every o· of thy meat offering shalt "
3: 1 And if his o· be a sacrifice of peace "
7:14 one out of the whole o· for an heave "
29 shall bring his o· unto the Lord of "
22:18 that will offer his o· for all his vows, "
Nu 18: 9 every o· of theirs, every meat "
31:50 We have therefore brought an o· "
Isa 19:21 and shall do sacrifice and o·; yea, 4503
40:20 so impoverished that he hath no o· 8641
66: 3 he that offereth an o·, as if he 4503
Jer 14:12 they offer burnt offering and an o·,‡ "
Eze 44:30 every o· of all, of every sort of 8641
45: 1 ye shall offer an o· unto the Lord, "
6 against the o· of the holy portion: "
7 side of the o· of the holy portion, "
7 before the o· of the holy portion, "
13 This is the o· that ye shall offer; "
16 give this o· for the prince in Israel. "
48: 9 The o· that ye shall offer unto the "
10 for the priests, shall be this holy o·; "
12 this o· of the land that is offered 8642
18 against the o· of the holy portion 8641
20 All the o· shall be five and twenty "
20 shall offer the holy o· foursquare, "
21 and on the other of the holy o·, "
21 five and twenty thousand of the o· "
21 and it shall be the holy o·; and the "
Da 2:46 should offer an o· and sweet odours 4541
9:21 about the time of the evening o·. 4503
27 the sacrifice and the o· to cease, "

oblations
Le 7:38 children of Israel to offer their o· 7133
2Ch 31:14 to distribute the o· of the Lord, 8641
Isa 1:13 Bring no more vain o·; incense is 4503
Eze 20:40 and the firstfruits of your o·, 4864
44:30 of every sort of your o·, shall be 8641

Oboth (*o'-both*)
Nu 21:10 set forward, and pitched in O·. 88
11 they journeyed from O·, and pitched "
33:43 from Punon, and pitched in O·. "
44 they departed from O·, and pitched "

obscure
Pr 20:20 shall be put out in o· darkness. * 380

obscurity
Isa 29:18 eyes of the blind shall see out of o·, 652
58:10 then shall thy light rise in o·, and *2822
59: 9 we wait for light, but behold o·; * "

observation
Lu 17:20 of God cometh not with o·: 3907

observe See also OBSERVED; OBSERVEST; OBSERVETH.
Ex 12:17 o· the feast of unleavened bread; 8104
17 ye o· this day in your generations "
24 shall o· this thing for an ordinance "

Ex 31:16 o· the sabbath throughout their 6213
34:11 O· thou that which I command 8104
22 thou shalt o· the feast of weeks, 6213
Le 19:26 ye use enchantment, nor o· times.*6049
37 shall ye o· all my statutes, and 8104
Nu 28: 2 shall ye o· to offer unto me in their "
De 5:32 shall o· to do therefore as the Lord "
6: 3 O Israel, and o· to do it; that it "
25 o· to do all these commandments "
8: 1 commandments...shall ye o· to do, "
11:32 ye shall o· to do all the statutes "
12: 1 which ye shall o· to do in the land, "
28 O· and hear all these words which "
32 soever I command you, o· to do it: "
15: 5 to o· to do all these commandments"
16: 1 O· the mouth of Abib, and keep the "
12 thou shalt o· and do these statutes. "
13 shalt o· the feast of tabernacles 6213
17:10 thou shalt o· to do according to all8104
24: 8 of leprosy, that thou o· diligently, "
8 them, so ye shall o· to do. "
28: 1 to o· and to do...his commandments"
13 thee this day, to o· and to do them: "
15 to o· to do all his commandments "
58 wilt not o· to do all the words of "
31:12 o· to do all the words of this law: "
32:46 command your children to o· to do, "
Jos 1: 7, 8 thou mayest o· to do according to"
J'g 13:14 all that I commanded her let her o·."
1Ki 20:33 Now the men did diligently o· *5172
2Ki 17:37 ye shall o· to do for evermore; 8104
21: 8 only if they will o· to do according "
2Ch 7:17 and shalt o· my statutes and my "
Ne 1: 5 him and o· his commandments: * "
10:29 to o· and do all the commandments* "
Ps 105:45 That they might o· his statutes, * "
107:43 is wise, and will o· these things, * "
119:34 I shall o· it with my whole heart. "
Pr 23:26 and let thine eyes o· my ways. *5341
Jer 8: 7 the swallow o· the time of their 8104
Eze 20:18 neither o· their judgments, nor "
37:24 and o· my statutes, and do them. "
Ho 13: 7 as a leopard by the way will I o· *7789
Jon 2: 8 They that o· lying vanities forsake*8104
M't 23: 3 whatsoever they bid you o·, that *5083
3 that o· and do; but do not ye "
28:20 Teaching them to o· all things "
Ac 16:21 to receive, neither to o·, being 4160
21:25 that they o· no such thing, save *5083
Ga 4:10 Ye o· days, and months, and 3906
1Ti 5:21 that thou o· these things without 5442

observed
Ge 37:11 him; but his father o· the saying.*8104
Ex 12:42 is a night to be much o· unto the 8107
42 is that night of the Lord to be o· of "
Nu 15:22 not o· all these commandments, 6213
De 33: 9 they have o· thy word, and kept 8104
2Sa 11:16 to pass, when Joab o· the city, * "
2Ki 21: 6 through the fire, and o· times, *6049
2Ch 33: 6 also he o· times, and used "
Ho 14: 8 I have heard him, and o· him: I *7789
M'r 6:20 just man and a holy, and o· him; *4933
10:20 all these have I o· from my youth. 5442

observer See also OBSERVERS.
De 18:10 an o· of times, or an enchanter, *6049

observers
De 18:14 hearkened unto o· of times, and *6049

observest
Isa 42:20 many things, but thou o· not; 8104

observeth
Ec 11: 4 He that o· the wind shall not sow; 8104

obstinate
De 2:30 his spirit, and made his heart o·, 553
Isa 48: 4 Because I knew that thou art o·, 7186

obtain See also OBTAINED; OBTAINETH; OBTAINING.
Ge 16: 2 be that I may o· children by her. 1129
Pr 8:35 and shall o· favour of the Lord. 6329
Isa 35:10 they shall o· joy and gladness, and5381
51:11 they shall o· gladness and joy; and "
Da 11:21 and o· the kingdom by flatteries. 2388
M't 5: 7 merciful: for they shall o· mercy. 1653
Lu 20:35 accounted worthy to o· that world,*5177
Ro 11:31 mercy they also may o· mercy. 1653
1Co 9:24 the prize? So run, that ye may o·. 2638
25 do it to o· a corruptible crown; 2983
1Th 5: 9 to o· salvation by our Lord Jesus *4047
2Ti 2:10 that they may also o· the salvation5177
Heb 4:16 that we may o· mercy, and find *2983
11:35 might o· a better resurrection: 5177
Jas 4: 2 and desire to have, and cannot o·: 2013

obtained
Ne 13: 6 certain days o· I leave of the king:*7592
Es 2: 9 him, and she o· kindness of him; 5375
15 Esther o· favour in the sight of all "
17 she o· grace and favour in his "
5: 2 that she o· favour in his sight: "
Ho 2:23 upon her that had not o· mercy; "
Ac 1:17 and had o· part of this ministry. *2975
22:28 With a great sum o· I this freedom.2932
26:22 Having therefore o· help of God, I 5177
27:13 that they had o· their purpose, 2902
Ro 11: 7 Israel hath not o· that which he 2013
7 but the election hath o· it, and the "
30 o· mercy through their unbelief: 1653
1Co 7:25 one that hath o· mercy of the Lord "
Eph 1:11 also we have o· an inheritance, *2820
1Ti 1:13 but I o· mercy, because I did it 1653
16 Howbeit for this cause I o· mercy, "
Heb 1: 4 by inheritance o· a more excellent*2816
6:15 endured, he o· the promise. 2013
8: 6 he o· a more excellent ministry, 5177
Heb 9:12 o· eternal redemption for us. 2147
11: 2 by it the elders o· a good report. *3140
4 o· witness that he was righteous, * "
33 o· promises, stopped the mouths of2013
39 o· a good report through faith, *3140
1Pe 2:10 of God: which had not o· mercy, 1653
10 but now have o· mercy. "
2Pe 1: 1 that have o· like precious faith 2975

obtaineth
Pr 12: 2 A good man o· favour of the Lord:*6329
18:22 thing, and o· favour of the Lord. "

obtaining
2Th 2:14 to the o· of the glory of our Lord 4047

occasion See also OCCASIONED; OCCASIONS.
Ge 43:18 that he may seek o· against us, and 1556
J'g 9:33 do to them as thou shalt find o·. 4672
14: 4 sought an o· against...Philistines: 8385
1Sa 10: 7 thee, that thou do as o· serve thee;4672
2Sa 12:14 given great o· to the enemies of the
Ezr 7:20 which thou shalt have o· to bestow,5308
Jer 2:24 in her o· who can turn her away? 8385
Eze 18: 3 have o· any more to use this proverb
Da 6: 4 sought to find o· against Daniel 5931
4 they could find none o· nor fault; "
5 not find any o· against this Daniel, "
Ro 7: 8, 11 taking o· by the commandment, 874
14:13 or an o· to fall in his brother's way.4625
2Co 5:12 give you o· to glory on our behalf, 874
8: 8 by o· of the forwardness of others,*1223
11:12 cut off o· from them which desire o·;874
Ga 5:13 use not liberty for an o· to the flesh, "
1Ti 5:14 give none o· to the adversary to "
1Jo 2:10 is none o· of stumbling in him. 4625

occasioned
1Sa 22:22 o· the death of all the persons 5437

occasions
De 22:14 And give o· of speech against her,*5949
17 hath given o· of speech against her,*"
Job 33:10 Behold, he findeth o· against me, 8569

occupation
Ge 46:33 and shall say, What is your o·? 4639
47: 3 unto his brethren, What is your o·? "
Jon 1: 8 What is thine o·? and whence 4399
Ac 18: 3 by their o· they were tentmakers.*5078
19:25 together with the workmen of like o·,

occupied
Ex 38:24 the gold that was o· for the work *6213
J'g 16:11 new ropes that never were o·,6213,4399
Eze 27:16 they o· in thy fairs with emeralds,*5414
19 going to and fro o· in thy fairs: * "
21 they o· with thee in lambs, and *5503
22 they o· in thy fairs with chief of *5414
Heb 13: 9 them that have been o· therein. 4043

occupiers
Eze 27:27 and the o· of thy merchandise, ‡6148

occupieth
1Co 14:16 that o· the room of unlearned * 378

occupy See also OCCUPIED; OCCUPIETH.
Eze 27: 9 in thee to o· thy merchandise. ‡6148
Lu 19:13 and said unto them, O· till I come.*4231

occurrent
1Ki 5: 4 is neither adversary nor evil o·. ‡6294

Ocran (*o'-cran*)
Nu 1:13 Of Asher; Pagiel the son of O·. *5918
2:27 Asher shall be Pagiel the son of O·.*"
7:72 Pagiel the son of O·, prince of the* "
77 the offering of Pagiel the son of O·.*"
10:26 of Asher was Pagiel the son of O·.* "

odd
Nu 3:48 the o· number...is to be redeemed,5736

Oded (*o'-ded*)
2Ch 15: 1 came upon Azariah the son of O·: 5752
8 and the prophecy of O· the prophet, "
28: 9 Lord was there, whose name was O·:"

odious
1Ch 19: 6 had made themselves o· to David, 887
Pr 30:23 o· woman when she is married; 8130

odour See also ODOURS.
Joh 12: 3 filled with the o· of the ointment. 3744
Ph'p 4:18 an o· of a sweet smell, a sacrifice "

odours
Le 26:31 smell the savour of your sweet o·. 5207
2Ch 16:14 bed which was filled with sweet o·1314
Es 2:12 and six months with sweet o·, and "
Jer 34: 5 thee, so shall they burn o· for thee;*
Da 2:46 an oblation and sweet o· unto him.5208
Re 5: 8 golden vials full of o·, which are *2368
18:13 cinnamon, and o·, and ointments,* "

of See in the APPENDIX; also HEREOF; OFF; THEREOF; WHEREOF.

off See also OFFSCOURING; OFFSPRING.
Ge 7: 4 from o· the face of the earth. 5921
8: 3 waters returned from o· the earth "
7 were dried up from o· the earth. "
8 from o· the face of the ground; "
11 mouth was an olive leaf pluckt o·:
11 were abated from o· the earth. 5921
13 were dried up from o· the earth: "
9:11 shall all flesh be cut o· any more by
11: 8 and they left o· to build the city.
17:14 soul shall be cut o· from his people;
22 he left o· talking with him, and God
21:16 down over against him a good way o·,
22: 4 up his eyes, and saw the place afar o·.
24:64 saw Isaac, she lighted o· the camel.5921
27:40 break his yoke from o· thy neck. "
37:18 And when they saw him afar o·, even
Ge 38:14 her widow's garments o· from her. 5921
40:19 lift up thy head from o· thee, "
19 shall eat thy flesh from o· thee. "
41:42 took o· his ring from his hand,
44: 4 out of the city, and not yet far o·,
Ex 2: 4 his sister stood afar o·, to wit what
3: 5 put o· thy shoes from o· thy feet; for
4:25 and cut o· the foreskin of her son,
9:15 thou shalt be cut o· from the earth.
12:15 that soul shall be cut o· from Israel.
19 shall be cut o· from the congregation
14:25 And took o· their chariot wheels, that
20:18 saw it, they removed, and stood afar o·
21 the people stood afar o·, and Moses
23:23 the Jebusites; and I will cut them o·.
24: 1 of Israel; and worship ye afar o·.
30:33, 38 shall even be cut o· from his people.
31:14 shall be cut o· from among his people.
32: 2 Break o· the golden earrings, which are
3 people brake o· the golden earrings
24 hath any gold, let them break it o·.
33: 5 now put o· thy ornaments from thee,
7 the camp, afar o· from the camp,
34:34 he took the vail o·, until he came out.
Le 1:15 and wring o· his head, and burn it on
3: 9 he take o· hard by the backbone; *
4: 8 take o· from it...the fat of the bullock
10 As it was taken o· from the bullock
31 fat is taken away from o· the sacrifice
5: 8 and wring o· his head from his neck,
6:11 And he shall put o· his garments, and
7:20, 21 soul shall be cut o· from his people.
25 it shall be cut o· from his people.
27 soul shall be cut o· from his people.
34 from o· the sacrifices of their peace*
8:28 took them from o· their hands, 5921
13:40 man whose hair is fallen o· his head,
41 hair fallen o· from the part of his head
14: 8 shave o· all his hair, and wash himself
9 he shall shave all his hair o· his head
9 even all his hair he shall shave o·:
41 that they scrape o· without the city
16:12 coals of fire from o· the altar 5921
23 shall put o· the linen garments, which
17: 4 shall be cut o· from among his people:
9 shall be cut o· from among his people.
10 will cut him o· from among his people.
14 whosoever eateth it shall be cut o·.
18:29 be cut o· from among their people.
19: 8 shall be cut o· from among his people.
20: 3 will cut him o· from among his people;
5 against his family, and will cut him o·,
6 will cut him o· from among his people.
17 be cut o· in the sight of their people:
18 be cut o· from among their people.
21: 5 they shave o· the corner of their beard,
22: 3 shall be cut o· from my presence:
23:29 shall be cut o· from among his people.
Nu 2: 2 far o· about the tabernacle of the*
4:18 Cut ye not o· the tribe of the families
7:89 unto him from o· the mercy seat *5921
9:10 or be in a journey afar o·, yet he shall
13 shall be cut o· from among his people:
10:11 taken up from o· the tabernacle *5921
12:10 departed from o· the tabernacle; * "
15:30 shall be cut o· from among his people.
31 that soul shall utterly be cut o·;
16:46 put fire therein from o· the altar. 5921
19:13 that soul shall be cut o· from Israel:
20 cut o· from among the congregation.
De 4:26 utterly perish from o· the land 5921
6:15 thee from o· the face of the earth. "
12:29 shall cut o· the nations from before
13: 7 nigh unto thee, or far o· from thee,
19: 1 Lord thy God hath cut o· the nations,
20:15 cities which are very far o· from thee,
21: 4 strike o· the heifer's neck there in the*
13 of her captivity from o· her, 5921
23: 1 or hath his privy member cut o·,
25: 9 loose his shoe from o· his foot, 5921
12 Then thou shalt cut o· her hand, thine
28:21 consumed thee from o· the land, 5921
63 shall be plucked from o· the land "
30:11 hidden from thee, neither is it far o·.
Jos 3:13 the waters of Jordan shall be cut o·
16 the salt sea, failed, and were cut o·:
4: 7 the waters of Jordan were cut o·
7 the waters of Jordan were cut o·
5: 9 the reproach of Egypt from o· you.5921
15 loose thy shoe from o· thy foot; for "
7: 9 and cut o· our name from the earth:
10:27 they took them down o· the trees, 5921
11:21 and cut o· the Anakims from the
15:18 and she lighted o· her ass; and 5921
23: 4 with all the nations that I have cut o·,
13 ye perish from o· this good land 5921
15 you from o· this good land which "
16 quickly from o· the good land "
J'g 1: 6 caught him, and cut o· his thumbs
7 thumbs and their great toes cut o·,
14 and she lighted from o· her ass; 5921
4:15 lighted down from o· his chariot, * "
5:26 smote Sisera, she smote o· his head,*
13:20 toward heaven from o· the altar, 5921
15:14 his bands loosed from o· his hands. "
16:12 from o· his arms like a thread.
19 caused him to shave o· the seven locks
21: 6 is one tribe cut o· from Israel this day.
Ru 2:20 Lord, who hath not left o· his kindness
4: 7 a man plucked o· his shoe, and gave it
8 it for thee. So he drew o· his shoe.
10 that the name of the dead be not cut o·
1Sa 2:31 come, that I will cut o· thine arm,
33 I shall not cut o· from mine altar,
4:18 fell from o· the seat backward by 5921
5: 4 hands were cut o· upon the threshold;

1Sa 6: 5 will lighten his hand from o' you, 5921
5 and from o' your gods, "
5 and from o' your land. "
17:39 them. And David put them o' him."
51 him, and cut o' his head therewith.
19:24 And he stripped o' his clothes also,
20:15 cut o' thy kindness from my house
15 when the Lord hath cut o' the enemies
24: 4 and cut o' the skirt of Saul's robe
5 because he had cut o' Saul's skirt.
11 for in that I cut o' the skirt of thy robe,
21 thou wilt not cut o' my seed after me,
25:23 lighted o' the ass, and fell before 5921
26:13 and stood on the top of an hill afar o';
28: 9 hath cut o' those that have familiar
31: 9 And they cut o' his head, and
9 and stripped o' his armour, and
2Sa 4:12 and cut o' their hands and their feet,
7: 9 have cut o' all thine enemies out of
10: 4 shaved o' the one half of their beards,
4 cut o' their garments in the middle,
11: 2 that David arose from o' his bed, 5921
24 shooters shot from o' the wall upon "
12:30 their king's crown from o' his head, "
15:17 and tarried in a place that was far o'.*
16: 9 over, I pray thee, and take o' his head.
20:22 cut o' the head of Sheba the son of
1Ki 9: 7 will I cut o' Israel out of the land
11:16 he had cut o' every male in Edom:)
13:34 house of Jeroboam, even to cut it o'
34 it from o' the face of the earth.
14:10 will cut o' from Jeroboam him that*
14 cut o' the house of Jeroboam that day:
15:21 that he left o' building of Ramah, and
18: 4 Jezebel cut o' the prophets of the Lord,
20:11 boast himself as he that putteth it o'.
21:21 and will cut o' from Ahab him that
2Ki 1:16 shalt not come down o' that bed on*
2: 7 went, and stood to view afar o':
4:25 man of God saw her afar o', that he
9: 8 and I will cut o' from Ahab him that
16:17 Ahaz cut o' the borders of the bases,
17 removed the laver from o' them; 5921
17 the sea from o' the brasen oxen "
18:16 cut o' the gold from the doors of the
23:27 and will cast o' this city Jerusalem
1Ch 17: 8 have cut o' all thine enemies from
19: 4 and cut o' their garments in the midst
20: 2 of their king from o' his head, 5921
28: 9 forsake him, he will cast thee o' for ever.
2Ch 6:36 captives unto a land far o' or near;
11:14 cast them o' from executing the
16: 5 he left o' building of Ramah, and let
20:25 which they stripped o' for themselves,
22: 7 anointed to cut o' the house of Ahab.
26:21 was cut o' from the house of the Lord:
32:21 angel, which cut o' all the mighty men
Ezr 3:13 and the noise was heard afar o'.
9: 3 plucked o' the hair of my head and of
Ne 4:23 none of us put o' our clothes, saving
23 every one put them o' for washing.*
5:10 I pray you, let us leave o' this usury.
12:43 joy of Jerusalem was heard...afar o'.
13:25 and plucked o' their hair, and made
Es 8: 2 And the king took o' his ring, which
Job 2:12 lifted up their eyes afar o', and knew
4: 7 or where were the righteous cut o'?
6: 9 let loose his hand, and cut me o'!
8:14 Whose hope shall be cut o', and whose*
9:27 I will leave o' my heaviness, and
11:10 If he cut o', and shut up, or gather*
15: 4 Yea, thou castest o' fear, and *
33 shake o' his unripe grape as the vine,
33 shall cast o' his flower as the olive.
17:11 my purposes are broken o', even the
18:16 and above shall his branch be cut o'.
21:21 of his months is cut o' in the midst?
23:17 I was not cut o' before the darkness,
24:24 cut o' as the tops of the ears of corn.
32:15 no more: they left o' speaking. *
36:20 when people are cut o' in their place.
25 may see it; man may behold it afar o'.
39:25 and he smelleth the battle afar o',
29 the prey, and her eyes behold afar o'.
Ps 10: 1 Why standest thou afar o', O Lord?
12: 3 Lord shall cut o' all flattering lips,
30:11 thou hast put o' my sackcloth, and
31:22 I am cut o' from before thine eyes:
34:16 cut o' the remembrance of them from
36: 3 he hath left o' to be wise, and to do
37: 9 For evildoers shall be cut o': but
22 that be cursed of him shall be cut o'.
28 the seed of the wicked shall be cut o'.
34 when the wicked are cut o', thou shalt
38 the end of the wicked shall be cut o'.
38:11 sore; and my kinsman stand afar o'.
43: 2 why dost thou cast me o'? why go I
44: 9 But thou hast cast o', and put us to
23 O Lord? arise, cast us not o' for ever.
54: 5 enemies: cut them o' in thy truth.*
55: 7 Lo, then would I wander far o', and
60: 1 O God, thou hast cast us o', thou hast
10 thou, O God, which hadst cast us o'?
65: 5 of them that are afar o' upon the sea:
71: 9 Cast me not o' in the time of old age;
74: 1 why hast thou cast us o' for ever?
75:10 horns of the wicked also will I cut o';
76:12 He shall cut o' the spirit of princes:
77: 7 Will the Lord cast o' for ever? and will
83: 4 let us cut them o' from being a nation;
88: 5 and they are cut o' from thy hand.
14 why castest thou o' my soul? why
16 over me; thy terrors have cut me o'.
89:38 But thou hast cast o' and abhorred,
90:10 for it is soon cut o', and we fly away.*
94:14 the Lord will not cast o' his people.
Ps 94:23 cut them o' in their...wickedness;
23 the Lord our God shall cut them o'.
101: 5 his neighbour, him will I cut o':
8 I may cut o' all the wicked doers from
108:11 not thou, O God, who hast cast us o'?
109:13 Let his posterity be cut o'; and in the
15 he may cut o' the memory of them
138: 6 but the proud he knoweth afar o'.*
139: 2 understandest my thought afar o'.
143:12 of thy mercy cut o' mine enemies,
Pr 2:22 wicked shall be cut o' from the earth,
17:14 leave o' contention, before it be
23:18 thine expectation shall not be cut o'.
24:14 and thy expectation shall not be cut o'.
26: 6 the hand of a fool cutteth o' the feet,
27:10 that is near than a brother far o'.
30:14 to devour the poor from o' the earth,
Ec 7:24 That which is far o', and exceeding
Ca 5: 3 I have put o' my coat; how shall I put
Isa 6: 6 with the tongs from o' the altar: 5921
9:14 will cut o' from Israel head and tail,
10: 7 heart to destroy and cut o' nations
27 taken away from o' thy shoulder, 5921
27 and his yoke from o' thy neck, "
11:13 adversaries of Judah shall be cut o':
14:22 cut o' from Babylon the name, and
25 shall his yoke depart from o' them,5921
25 depart from o' their shoulders. "
15: 2 be baldness, and every beard cut o'.
17:13 rebuke them, and they shall flee far o',
18: 5 cut o' the sprigs with pruning hooks,
20: 2 the sackcloth from o' thy loins, 5921
2 and put o' thy shoe from thy foot.
22:25 that was upon it shall be cut o':
23: 7 feet shall carry her afar o' to sojourn.
25: 8 wipe away tears from o' all faces; 5921
8 he take away from o' all the earth: "
27:11 withered, they shall be broken o':
12 beat o' from the channel of the river
29:20 all that watch for iniquity are cut o':
33: 9 and Carmel shake o' their fruits.
13 Hear, ye that are far o', what I have
17 behold the land that is very far o'.*
34: 4 as the leaf falleth o' from the vine, and
38:10 I said in the cutting o' of my days,*
12 cut o' like a weaver my life: he will*
12 he will cut me o' with pining sickness:
46:13 it shall not be far o', and my salvation
47:11 thou shalt not be able to put it o':*
48: 9 refrain for thee, that I cut thee not o'.
19 his name should not have been cut o'
50: 6 to them that plucked o' the hair:
53: 8 for he was cut o' out of the land of the
55:13 everlasting sign...shall not be cut o'.
56: 5 everlasting name,...shall not be cut o'.
57: 9 and didst send thy messengers far o',
19 Peace, peace to him that is far o', and
59:11 for salvation, but it is far o' from us.
14 backward, and justice standeth afar o':
66: 3 a lamb, as if he cut o' a dog's neck;*
19 to the isles afar o', that have not heard
Jer 7:28 perished,...is cut o' from their mouth.
29 Cut o' thine hair, O Jerusalem,...cast
9:21 to cut o' the children from without,
11:19 cut him o' from the land of the living,
23:23 saith the Lord, and not a God afar o'?
24:10 they be consumed from o' the land5921
28:10 o' the prophet Jeremiah's neck, "
12 o' the neck of the prophet Jeremiah,"
16 thee from o' the face of the earth; "
30: 8 break his yoke from o' thy neck, "
31:10 and declare it in the isles afar o', and
37 I will also cast o' all the seed of Israel
33:24 he hath even cast them o'? thus they
38:27 So they left o' speaking with him; for
44: 7 to cut o' from you man and woman,
8 that ye might cut yourselves o', and
11 you for evil, and to cut o' all Judah.
18 since we left o' to burn incense to the
46:27 behold, I will save thee from afar o',*
47: 4 And to cut o' from Tyrus and Zidon
5 Askelon is cut o' with the remnant of*
48: 2 let us cut it o' from being a nation.
25 The horn of Moab is cut o', and his
49:26 men of war shall be cut o' in that day,*
30 Flee, get you far o', dwell deep, O ye
50:16 Cut o' the sower from Babylon, and
30 men of war shall be cut o' in that day,*
51: 6 be not cut o' in her iniquity; for this is
50 remember the Lord afar o', and let *
62 to cut it o', that none shall remain in
La 2: 3 He hath cut o' in his fierce anger all
7 The Lord hath cast o' his altar, he
3:17 removed my soul far o' from peace:
31 For the Lord will not cast o' for ever:
53 have cut o' my life in the dungeon,
54 mine head; then I said, I am cut o'.
Eze 6:12 that is far o' shall die of the pestilence;
8: 6 I should go far o' from my sanctuary?
10:18 departed from o' the threshold of *5921
11:16 cast them far o' among the heathens,
12:27 of the times that are afar o'.
14: 8 will cut him o' from the midst of my
13 and will cut o' man and beast from it:
17 so that I cut o' man and beast from it:
19 blood, to cut o' from it man and beast:
21 to cut o' from it man and beast?
17: 4 cropped o' the top of his young twigs,
9 and cut o' the fruit thereof, that it
17 building forts, to cut o' many persons:
22 I will crop o' from the top of his young
18:17 hath taken o' his hand from the poor,*
21: 3 will cut o' from thee the righteous and
4 I will cut o' from thee the righteous
26 the diadem, and take o' the crown:
23:34 thereof,...pluck o' thine own breasts:*
Eze 25: 7 and I will cut thee o' from the people,
13 and will cut o' man and beast from it;
16 and I will cut o' the Cherethims, and
26:16 and put o' their broidered garments:
29: 8 and cut o' man and beast out of thee.
30:15 and I will cut o' the multitude of No.
31:12 terrible of the nations, have cut him o',
35: 7 will cut o' from him that passeth out
37:11 is lost: we are cut o' for our parts.
44:19 shall put o' their garments wherein
Da 4:14 down the tree, and cut o' his branches,
27 and break o' thy sins by righteousness,
9: 7 that are near, and that are far o',
26 two weeks shall Messiah be cut o',
Ho 4:10 have left o' to take heed to the Lord.
8: 3 hath cast o' the thing that is good:
4 them idols, that they may be cut o'.
5 Thy calf, O Samaria, hath cast thee o';
10: 7 Samaria, her king is cut o' as the foam
15 the king of Israel utterly be cut o'.
11: 4 take o' the yoke on their jaws, 5921
Joe 1: 5 wine; for it is cut o' from your mouth.
9 is cut o' from the house of the Lord;
16 Is not the meat cut o' before our eyes,
2:20 far o' from you the northern army,
3: 8 to the Sabeans, to a people far o':
Am 1: 5 cut o' the inhabitant from the plain of
8 cut o' the inhabitant from Ashdod,
11 and did cast o' all pity, and his anger
2: 3 I will cut o' the judge from the midst
3:14 the horns of the altar shall be cut o',
5: 7 leave o' righteousness in the earth,*
9: 8 it from o' the face of the earth; 5921
Ob 5 (how art thou cut o'!) would they not
9 of Esau may be cut o' by slaughter.
10 and thou shalt be cut o' for ever.
14 to cut o' those of his that did escape;
Mic 2: 8 ye pull o' the robe with the garment
3: 2 who pluck o' the skin from o' them,
2 their flesh from o' their bones; 5921
3 and flay their skin from o' them; "
4: 3 rebuke strong nations afar o'; and
7 that was cast far o' a strong nation:
5: 9 and all thine enemies shall be cut o'.
10 cut o' thy horses out of the midst of
11 And I will cut o' the cities of thy land,
12 cut o' witchcrafts out of thine hand;
13 Thy graven images also will I cut o',
Na 1:13 will I break his yoke from o' thee, 5921
14 thy gods will I cut o' the graven image
15 through thee; he is utterly cut o'.
2:13 I will cut o' thy prey from the earth,
3:15 the sword shall cut thee o', it shall eat
Hab 2:10 thy house by cutting o' many people,
3:17 the flock shall be cut o' from the fold,
Zep 1: 2 all things from o' the land, 5921,6440
3 cut o' [] man from o' the land, "
4 I will cut o' the remnant of Baal from
11 all they that bear silver are cut o'.
3: 6 I have cut o' the nations: their towers
7 their dwelling should not be cut o',
Zec 5: 3 every one that stealeth shall be cut o'†
3 every one that sweareth shall be cut o'†
6:15 that are far o' shall come and build
9: 6 will cut o' the pride of the Philistines.
10 I will cut o' the chariot from Ephraim,
10 and the battle bow shall be cut o';
10: 6 be as though I had not cast them o':
11: 8 Three shepherds also I cut o' in one
9 that is to be cut o', let it be cut o';
16 shall not visit those that be cut o',
13: 2 cut o' the names of the idols out of the
8 parts therein shall be cut o' and die;
14: 2 shall not be cut o' from the city.
Mal 2:12 will cut o' the man that doeth this,
M't 5:30 thy right hand offend thee, cut it o',1581
8:30 a good way o' from them a herd 575
10:14 city, shake o' the dust of your feet.1621
18: 8 or thy foot offend thee, cut them o',1581
26:51 high priest's, and smote o' his ear. 851
58 Peter followed him afar o' unto the 575
27:31 they took the robe o' from him, 1562
55 women were...beholding afar o', * 575
M'r 5: 6 when he saw Jesus afar o', he ran* "
6:11 shake o' the dust under your feet 1621
9:43 And if thy hand offend thee, cut it o':609
45 And if thy foot offend thee, cut it o' "
11: 8 cut down branches o' the trees *1537
13 seeing a fig tree afar o' having leaves,
14:47 of the high priest, and cut o' his ear, 609
54 Peter followed him afar o', even 575
15:20 they took o' the purple from him, 609
40 were also women looking on afar o':*575
Lu 10:11 on us, do we wipe o' against you: 631
14:32 while the other is yet a great way o',
15:20 But when he was yet a great way o',568
16:23 and seeth Abraham afar o', and 575
17:12 that were lepers, which stood afar o':
18:13 publican, standing afar o', would not
22:50 high priest, and cut o' his right ear.851
54 house. And Peter followed afar o'.
23:49 him from Galilee, stood afar o',
Joh 11:18 Jerusalem, about fifteen furlongs o'.575
18:10 servant, and cut o' his right ear. 609
26 his kinsman whose ear Peter cut o', "
Ac 2:39 to all that are afar o', even as many
7:33 Put o' thy shoes from thy feet: for 3089
12: 7 his chains fell o' from his hands. 1601
13:51 shook o' the dust of their feet 1621
16:22 the magistrates rent o' their clothes,4048
22:23 cried out, and cast o' their clothes,4496
27:32 soldiers cut o' the ropes of the boat,*609
32 ropes of the boat, and let her fall o'.1601
28: 5 he shook o' the beast into the fire, 660
Ro 11:17 if some of the branches be broken o' 1575
19 The branches were broken o', that I "

Ro 11:20 of unbelief they were broken o', 1575
22 otherwise thou also shalt be cut o'.1581
13:12 let us...cast o' the works of darkness,659
2Ch 11:12 I may cut o' occasion from them 1581
Ga 5:12 ye were even cut o' which trouble you.*609
Eph 2:13 were far o' are made nigh by the 3112
17 peace to you which were afar o', and "
4:22 ye put o' concerning the former 659
Col 2:11 putting o' the body of the sins of the554
3: 8 But now ye also put o' all these; * 659
9 put o' the old man with his deeds; 554
1Ti 5:12 they have cast o' their first faith. * 114
Heb 11:13 but having seen them afar o', and were
2Pe 1: 9 things is blind, and cannot see afar o',*
14 I must put o' this my tabernacle, 595
Re 18:10 Standing afar o' for the fear of her 575
15 shall stand afar o' for the fear of "
17 many as trade by sea, stood afar o', "

offence See also OFFENCES.
1Sa 25:31 thee, nor o' of heart unto my lord,4383
Isa 8:14 a rock of o' to both the houses of "
Ho 5:15 till they acknowledge their o', and 816
M't 16:23 Satan: thou art an o' unto me: *4625
18: 7 that man by whom the o' cometh!* "
Ac 24:16 conscience void of o' toward God, 677
Ro 5:15 not as the o', so also is the free *3900
15 through...o' of one many be dead,* "
17 if by one man's o' death reigned* "
18 as by the o' of one judgment came* "
20 entered, that the o' might abound.* "
9:33 a stumblingstone and rock of o': 4625
14:20 for that man who eateth with o'. 4348
1Co 10:32 Give none o', neither to the Jews,* 677
2Co 6: 3 Giving no o' in any thing, that the*4349
11: 7 committed an o' in abasing myself*266
Ga 5:11 then is the o' of the cross ceased. *4625
Ph'p 1:10 and without o' till the day of Christ;677
1Pe 2: 8 of stumbling, and a rock of o', 4625

offences
Ec 10: 4 for yielding pacifieth great o'. 2399
M't 18: 7 Woe unto the world because of o'!*4625
7 for it must needs be that o' come* "
Lu 17: 1 impossible but that o' will come: * "
Ro 4:25 Who was delivered for our o', and*3900
5:16 the free gift is of many o' unto * "
16:17 them which cause divisions and o'*4625

offend See also OFFENDED.
Job 34:31 I will not o' any more: 2254
Ps 73:15 I should o' against the generation*898
119:165 law: and nothing shall o' them. *4383
Jer 2: 3 all that devour him shall o'; evil * 816
50: 7 We o' not, because they have sinned‡"
Ho 4:15 play the harlot, yet let not Judah o';"
Hab 1:11 he shall pass over, and o', imputing*"
M't 5:29 if thy right eye o' thee, pluck it *4624
30 if thy right hand o' thee, cut it off,* "
13:41 of his kingdom all things that o', *4625
17:27 lest we should o' them, go thou to*4624
18: 6 shall o' one of these little ones * "
8 if thy hand or thy foot o' thee, cut* "
9 And if thine eye o' thee, pluck it * "
M'r 9:42 shall o' one of these little ones * "
43 And if thy hand o' thee, cut it off:* "
45 And if thy foot o' thee, cut it off: * "
47 And if thine eye o' thee, pluck it * "
Lu 17: 2 should o' one of these little ones.* "
Joh 6:61 said unto them, Doth this o' you?* "
1Co 8:13 if meat make my brother to o', * "
13 lest I make my brother to o'. * "
Jas 2:10 the whole law, yet o' in one point,*4417
3: 2 For in many things we o' all. * "
2 If any man o' not in word, the * "

offended
Ge 20: 9 what have I o' thee, that thou *2398
40: 1 baker had o' their lord the king of "
2Ki 18:14 saying, I have o'; return from me: "
2Ch 28:13 have o' against the Lord already,* 819
Pr 18:19 A brother o' is harder to be won 6586
Jer 37:18 What have I o' against thee, or *2398
Eze 25:12 and hath greatly o', and revenged 816
Ho 13: 1 but when he o' in Baal, he died. "
M't 11: 6 whosoever shall not be o' in me. *4624
13:21 of the word, by and by he is o'. * "
57 And they were o' in him. But Jesus* "
15:12 thou that the Pharisees were o', * "
24:10 And then shall many be o', and * "
26:31 All ye shall be o' because of me * "
33 Though all men shall be o' because* "
33 of thee, yet will I never be o'. * "
M'r 4:17 sake, immediately they are o'. * "
6: 3 with us? And they were o' at him. * "
14:27 All ye shall be o' because of me * "
29 Although all shall be o', yet will not‡"
Lu 7:23 whosoever shall not be o' in me. * "
Joh 16: 1 unto you, that ye should not be o'.* "
Ac 25: 8 Cæsar, have I o' any thing at all. * 264
Ro 14:21 brother stumbleth, or is o', or *4624
2Co 11:29 weak? who is o', and I burn not? * "

offender See also OFFENDERS.
Isa 29:21 That make a man an o' for a word,2398
Ac 25:11 if I be an o', or have committed * 91

offenders
1Ki 1:21 son Solomon shall be counted o'. 2400

offer See also OFFERED; OFFERETH; OFFERING.
Ge 22: 2 o' him there for a burnt offering 5927
Ex 22:29 not delay to o' the first of thy ripe
23:18 not o' the blood of my sacrifice 2076
29:36 thou shalt o' every day a bullock 6213
38 which thou shalt o' upon the altar;"
39 lamb thou shalt o' in the morning; "
39 other lamb thou shalt o' at even: "
41 other lamb thou shalt o' at even, "
30: 9 o' no strange incense thereon, 5927
34:25 not o' the blood of my sacrifice 7819
Ex 35:24 that did o' an offering of silver 7311
Le 1: 3 him o' a male without blemish: 7126
3 shall o' it of his own voluntary will "
2: 1 when any will o' a meat offering * "
12 ye shall o' them unto the Lord: "
13 thine offerings thou shalt o' salt. "
14 o' a meat offering of thy firstfruits "
14 thou shalt o' for the meat offering "
3: 1 offering, if he o' it of the herd; "
1 he shall o' it without blemish before"
3 shall o' of the sacrifice of the peace"
6 he shall o' it without blemish. "
7 If he o' a lamb for his offering, then"
7 then shall he o' it before the Lord. "
9 o' of the sacrifice of the peace "
12 then he shall o' it before the Lord. "
14 he shall o' thereof his offering, "
4:14 shall o' a young bullock for the sin."
5: 8 who shall o' that which is for the sin"
10 o' the second for a burnt offering, 6213
6:14 Aaron shall o' it before the Lord, 7126
20 which they shall o' unto the Lord in"
21 shalt thou o' for a sweet savour "
22 is anointed in his stead shall o' it: 6213
7: 3 he shall o' of it all the fat thereof; 7126
11 which he shall o' unto the Lord. "
12 If he o' it for a thanksgiving, then "
12 o' with the sacrifice of thanksgiving"
13 o' for his offering leavened bread "
14 o' one out of the whole oblation "
25 men o' an offering made by fire unto"
38 to o' their oblations unto the Lord, "
9: 2 and o' them before the Lord. "
7 o' thy sin offering, and thy burnt 6213
7 o' the offering of the people, and "
12: 7 Who shall o' it before the Lord, 7126
14:12 o' him for a trespass offering, and "
19 the priest shall o' the sin offering, 6213
20 priest shall o' the burnt offering 5927
30 shall o' the one of the turtledoves,6213
15:15 And the priest shall o' them, the "
30 shall o' the one for a sin offering, "
16: 6 o' his bullock of the sin offering, *7126
9 fell, and o' him for a sin offering. 6213
24 forth, and o' his burnt offering, "
17: 4 to o' an offering unto the Lord 7126
5 which they o' in the open field, *2076
5 o' them for peace offerings unto * "
7 o' their sacrifices unto devils, * "
9 to o' it unto the Lord; even that 6213
19: 5 ye o' a sacrifice of peace offerings 2076
5 Lord, ye shall o' it at your own will."
6 be eaten the same day ye o' it, 2077
21: 6 bread of their God, they do o': 7126
17 approach to o' the bread of his God."
21 nigh to o' the offerings of the Lord "
21 nigh to o' the bread of his God. "
22:15 Israel, which they o' unto the Lord;7311
18 that will o' his oblation for all his*7126
18 will o' unto the Lord for a burnt "
19 Ye shall o' at your own will a male
20 a blemish, that shall ye not o': 7126
22 ye shall not o' these unto the Lord, "
23 thou o' for a freewill offering; 6213
24 not o' unto the Lord that which 7126
25 shall ye o' the bread of your God "
29 when ye will o' a sacrifice of *2076
29 the Lord, o' it at your own will. * "
23: 8 shall o' an offering made by fire 7126
12 ye shall o' that day when ye wave 6213
16 shall o' a new meat offering unto 7126
18 shall o' with the bread seven lambs* "
25, 27, 36, 36, 37 o' an offering...by fire "
27:11 do not o' a sacrifice unto the Lord,* "
Nu 5:25 the Lord, and o' it upon the altar:* "
6:11 shall o' the one for a sin offering, 6213
14 shall o' his offering unto the Lord, 7126
16 shall o' his sin offering, and his 6213
17 shall o' the ram for a sacrifice of "
17 shall o' also his meat offering, and "
7:11 They shall o' their offering, each 7126
18 of Zuar, prince of Issachar, did o': "
24 of the children of Zebulun, did o':* "
30 of the children of Reuben, did o':* "
36 of the children of Simeon, did o': *
8:11 Aaron shall o' the Levites before 5130
12 shalt o' the one for a sin offering, 6213
13 o' them for an offering unto the 5130
15 them, and o' them for an offering. "
9: 7 not o' an offering of the Lord in 7126
15: 7 o' the third part of an hin of wine, "
14 will o' an offering made by fire, 6213
19 ye shall o' up an heave offering 7311
20 o' up a cake of the first of your "
24 shall o' one young bullock for a 6213
16:40 come near to o' incense before *
18:12 which they shall o' unto the Lord,*5414
19 children of Israel o' unto the Lord,7311
24 they o' as an heave offering unto "
26 shall o' up an heave offering of it "
28 ye also shall o' an heave offering "
29 ye shall o' every heave offering of "
28: 2 o' unto me in their due season. 7126
3 which ye shall o' unto the Lord; "
4 lamb shalt thou o' in the morning,6213
4 other lamb shalt thou o' at even; "
8 other lamb shalt thou o' at even: "
8 thou shalt o' it, a sacrifice made by "
11 ye shall o' a burnt offering unto 7126
19 ye shall o' a sacrifice made by fire "
20 tenth deals shall ye o' for a bullock,6213
21 A several tenth deal shalt thou o' for"
23 o' these beside the burnt offering "
24 this manner ye shall o' daily, "
27 ye shall o' the burnt offering for 7126
31 shall o' them beside the continual 6213
Nu 29: 2 shall o' a burnt offering for a sweet6213
8 shall o' a burnt offering unto the 7126
13 And ye shall o' a burnt offering, a "
17 shall o' twelve young bullocks, two
36 But ye shall o' a burnt offering, 7126
De 12:13 thou o' not thy burnt offerings in 5927
14 thou shalt o' thy burnt offerings, "
27 thou shalt o' thy burnt offerings, 6213
18: 3 from them that o' a sacrifice, 2076
27: 6 o' burnt offerings thereon unto 5927
7 thou shalt o' peace offerings, and*2076
33:19 shall o' sacrifices of righteousness: "
Jos 22:23 o' thereon burnt offering or meat 5927
23 if to o' peace offerings thereon, let 6213
J'g 3:18 made an end to o' the present, *7126
6:26 o' a burnt sacrifice with the wood 5927
11:31 I will o' it up for a burnt offering. "
13:16 if thou wilt o' a burnt offering, 6213
16 thou must o' it unto the Lord. 5927
16:23 o' a great sacrifice unto Dagon 2076
1Sa 1:21 went up to o' unto the Lord the "
2:19 husband to o' the yearly sacrifice. "
28 to o' upon mine altar, to burn *5927
10: 8 unto thee, to o' burnt offerings, "
2Sa 24:12 the Lord, I o' thee three things; 5190
22 take and o' up what seemeth good 5927
24 will I o' burnt offerings unto the "
1Ki 3: 4 did Solomon o' upon that altar. "
9:25 did Solomon o' burnt offerings "
13: 2 upon thee shall he o' the priests *2076
2Ki 5:17 o' neither burnt offering nor 6213
10:24 to o' sacrifices and burnt offerings, "
1Ch 16:40 o' burnt offerings unto the Lord 5927
21:10 the Lord, I o' thee three things: 5186
24 nor o' burnt offerings without 5927
23:31 o' all burnt sacrifices unto the "
29:14 should be able to o' so willingly
17 here, to o' willingly unto thee.
2Ch 23:18 o' the burnt offerings of the Lord, 5927
24:14 to minister, and to o' withal, and "
29:21 to o' them on the altar of the Lord. "
27 to o' the burnt offering upon the "
35:12 o' unto the Lord, as it is written 7126
16 o' burnt offerings upon the altar 5927
Ezr 3: 2 to o' burnt offerings thereon, as it "
6 o' burnt offerings unto the Lord. "
6:10 may o' sacrifices of sweet savours 7127
7:17 and o' them upon the altar of the "
Job 42: 8 and o' up for yourselves a burnt 5927
Ps 4: 5 O' the sacrifices of righteousness, 2076
16: 4 offerings of blood will I not o', 5258
27: 6 o' in his tabernacle sacrifices of 2076
50:14 O' unto God thanksgiving; and "
51:19 they o' bullocks upon thine altar. 5927
66:15 will o' unto thee burnt sacrifices of "
15 I will o' bullocks with goats. 6213
72:10 Sheba and Seba shall o' gifts. 7126
116:17 I will o' to thee the sacrifice of 2076
Isa 57: 7 wentest thou up to o' sacrifice. "
Jer 11:12 gods unto whom they o' incense:
14:12 o' burnt offering and an oblation, 5927
33:18 before me to o' burnt offerings, "
Eze 6:13 where they did o' sweet savour 5414
20:31 For when ye o' your gifts, when 5375
43:18 o' burnt offerings thereon, and to 5927
22 second day thou shalt o' a kid 7126
23 thou shalt o' a young bullock "
24 thou shalt o' them before the Lord,*"
24 o' them up for a burnt offering 5927
44: 7 o' my bread, the fat and the blood,7126
15 o' unto me the fat and the blood, "
27 he shall o' his sin offering, saith "
45: 1 shall o' an oblation unto the Lord.7311
13 is the oblation that ye shall o'; "
14 ye shall o' the tenth part of a bath*
46: 4 offering that the prince shall o' 7126
48: 8 be the offering which ye shall o' 7311
9 oblation that ye shall o' unto the "
20 o' the holy oblation foursquare, "
Da 2:46 o' an oblation and sweet odours 5260
Ho 9: 4 not o' wine offerings to the Lord, 5258
Am 4: 5 And o' a sacrifice of thanksgiving 6999
5:22 Though ye o' me burnt offerings 5927
Hag 2:14 which they o' there is unclean. 7126
Mal 1: 7 Ye o' polluted bread upon mine 5066
8 if ye o' the blind for sacrifice, is it "
8 if ye o' the lame and sick, is it not "
8 o' it now unto thy governor; will *7126
3: 3 may o' unto the Lord an offering 5066
M't 5:24 and then come and o' thy gift. 4374
8: 4 o' the gift that Moses commanded, "
M'r 1:44 o' for thy cleansing those things "
Lu 2:24 to o' a sacrifice according to that 1325
5:14 o' for thy cleansing, according as 4374
6:29 on the one cheek o' also the other;3930
11:12 an egg, will he o' him a scorpion? 1929
Heb 5: 1 o' both gifts and sacrifices 4374
3 so also for himself, to o' for sins. "
7:27 to o' up sacrifice, first for his own 399
8: 3 ordained to o' gifts and sacrifices:4374
3 man have somewhat also to o'. "
4 that o' gifts according to the law: "
9:25 that he should o' himself often, "
13:15 let us o' the sacrifice of praise to 399
1Pe 2: 5 to o' up spiritual sacrifices, "
Re 8: 3 o' it with the prayers of all saints 1325

offered
Ge 8:20 o' burnt offerings on the altar. 5927
22:13 and o' him up for a burnt offering "
31:54 o' sacrifice upon the mount, and 2076
46: 1 and o' sacrifices unto the God of his"
Ex 24: 5 of Israel, which o' burnt offerings,5927
32: 6 o' burnt offerings, and brought "
35:22 man that o'...an offering of gold 5130
22 every man...o' an offering of gold*
40:29 o' upon it the burnt offering and 5927

Le 7: 8 burnt offering which he hath o'. 7126
15 eaten the same day that it is o'; *7133
9: 15 slew it, and o' it for sin, as the 2398
16 and o' it according to the manner. 6213
10: 1 o' strange fire before the Lord, 7126
19 day have they o' their sin offering "
16: 1 when they o' before the Lord, and* "
Nu 3: 4 they o' strange fire before the Lord," "
7: 2 over them that were numbered, o': "
10 o' for dedicating of the altar in "
10 o' their offering before the altar. "
12 he that o' his offering the first day "
19 He o' for his offering one silver "
42 prince of the children of Gad, o': *
48 prince of the children of Ephraim, o':*
54 On the eighth day o' Gamaliel the*
60 prince of the children of Benjamin, o':*
66 prince of the children of Dan, o': *
72 prince of the children of Asher, o':*
78 prince of the children of Naphtali, o':*
8: 21 and Aaron o' them as an offering 5130
16: 35 and fifty men that o' incense. 7126
38 for they o' them before the Lord, "
39 they that were burnt had o'; and "
22: 40 And Balak o' oxen and sheep, *2076
23: 2 and Balaam o' on every altar a 5927
4 o' upon every altar a bullock and "
14, 30 o' a bullock and a ram on every "
26: 61 o' strange fire before the Lord. 7126
28: 15 offering unto the Lord shall be o', 6213
24 o' beside the continual burnt "
31: 52 gold of the offering that they o' 7311
Jos 8: 31 they o' thereon burnt offerings 5927
J'g 5: 2 the people willingly o' themselves.
9 o' themselves willingly among the
6: 28 bullock was o' upon the altar 5927
13: 19 o' it upon a rock unto the Lord: "
20: 26 and o' burnt offerings and peace "
21: 4 and o' burnt offerings and peace "
1Sa 1: 4 the time was that Elkanah o', *2076
2: 13 that, when any man o' sacrifice,
6: 14 o' the kine a burnt offering unto 5927
15 of Beth-shemesh o' burnt offerings "
7: 9 lamb, and o' it for a burnt offering "
13: 9 And he o' the burnt offering. "
12 therefore, and o' a burnt offering. "
2Sa 6: 17 David o' burnt offerings and peace "
15: 12 from Giloh, while he o' sacrifices. 2076
24: 25 and o' burnt offerings and peace 5927
1Ki 3: 15 Lord, and o' up burnt offerings,
15 o' peace offerings, and made a 6213
8: 62 him, o' sacrifice before the Lord. 2076
63 And Solomon o' a sacrifice of peace "
63 he o' unto the Lord, two and twenty"
64 there he o' burnt offerings, and 6213
12: 32 in Judah, and he o' upon the altar.*5927
33 So he o' upon the altar which he* "
33 he o' upon the altar, and burnt * "
22: 43 the people o' and burnt incense *2076
2Ki 3: 20 when the meat offering was o', *5927
27 o' him for a burnt offering upon "
16: 12 to the altar, and o' thereon. "
1Ch 6: 49 his sons o' upon the altar of the 6999
15: 26 they o' seven bullocks and seven *2076
16: 1 they o' burnt sacrifices and peace 7126
21: 26 and o' burnt offerings and peace 5927
29: 6 of the king's work, o' willingly,
9 rejoiced, for that they o' willingly,
9 with perfect heart they o' willingly
17 have willingly o' all these things:
21 o' burnt offerings unto the Lord, 5927
2Ch 1: 6 o' a thousand burnt offerings upon "
4: 6 such things as they o' for the *4639
7: 4 o' sacrifices before the Lord. 2076
5 And king Solomon o' a sacrifice of "
7 there he o' burnt offerings, and the6213
8: 12 Solomon o' burnt offerings unto 5927
15: 11 o' unto the Lord the same time, *2076
17: 16 willingly o' himself unto the Lord;
24: 14 And they o' burnt offerings in the 5927
29: 7 incense nor o' burnt offerings "
Ezr 1: 6 beside all that was willingly o'.
2: 68 o' freely for the house of God to
3: 3 they o' burnt offerings thereon 5927
4 o' the daily burnt offerings by number,
5 o' the continual burnt offering, *
5 willingly o' a freewill offering 5068
6: 3 the place where they o' sacrifices,*1684
17 o' at the dedication of this house 7127
7: 15 freely o' unto the God of Israel, 5069
8: 25 all Israel there present, had o': 7311
35 o' burnt offerings unto the God of 7126
10: 19 they o' a ram of the flock for their
Ne 11: 2 willingly o' themselves to dwell at
12: 43 that day they o' great sacrifices, 2076
Job 1: 5 o' burnt offerings according to 5927
Isa 57: 6 thou hast o' a meat offering. "
66: 3 oblation, as if he o' swine's blood;* "
Jer 32: 29 they have o' incense unto Baal, 6999
Eze 20: 28 and they o' there their sacrifices, 2076
48: 12 this oblation of the land that is o'*8641
Da 11: 18 the reproach o' by him to cease;
Am 5: 25 Have ye o' unto me sacrifices and*5066
Jon 1: 16 o' a sacrifice unto the Lord, and 2076
Mal 1: 11 in every place incense shall be o' 5066
Ac 7: 41 and o' sacrifice unto the idol, and* *321*
42 have ye o' to me slain beasts and **4374*
8: 18 was given, he o' them money,
15: 29 ye abstain from meats o' to idols,**1494*
21: 25 themselves from things o' to idols,*"
26 until that an offering should be o' *4374*
1Co 8: 1 as touching things o' unto idols, **1494*
4 are o' in sacrifice unto idols, "
7 eat it as a thing o' unto an idol; * "
10 those things which are o' to idols;* "
10: 19 o' in sacrifice to idols is any thing?*"

1Co 10: 28 This is o' in sacrifice unto idols, *1494*
Ph'p 2: 17 and if I be o' upon the sacrifice *4689*
2Ti 4: 6 For I am now ready to be o', and "
Heb 5: 7 when he had o' up prayers and *4374*
7: 27 he did once, when he o' up himself.
9: 7 which he o' for himself, and for **4374*
9 were o' both gifts and sacrifices,
14 o' himself without spot to God, *4374*
28 once o' to bear the sins of many; "
10: 1 they o' year by year continually * "
2 they not have ceased to be o'? "
8 therein; which are o' by the law; "
12 he had o' one sacrifice for sins "
11: 4 By faith Abel o' unto God a more "
17 when he was tried, o' up Isaac: "
17 o' up his only begotten son, * "
Jas 2: 21 when he had o' Isaac his son upon *399*

offereth
Le 6: 26 The priest that o' it for sin shall 2398
7: 8 that o' any man's burnt offering 7126
9 shall be the priest's that o' it. "
16 same day that he o' his sacrifice: "
18 it be imputed unto him that o' it: "
29 He that o' the sacrifice of his peace "
33 o' the blood of the peace offerings, "
17: 8 that o' a burnt offering or sacrifice,5926
21: 8 for he o' the bread of thy God: he 7126
22: 21 o' a sacrifice of peace offerings unto"
Nu 15: 4 that o' his offering unto the Lord "
Ps 50: 23 Whoso o' praise glorifieth me: 2076
Isa 66: 3 he that o' an oblation, as if he 5927
Jer 48: 35 him that o' in the high places, and "
Mal 2: 12 that o' an offering unto the Lord 5066

offering See also OFFERINGS.
Ge 4: 3 the ground an o' unto the Lord. 4503
4 respect unto Abel and to his o': "
5 and to his o' he had not respect. "
22: 2 and offer him there for a burnt o'
3 and clave the wood for the burnt o',
6 took the wood of the burnt o', and
7 where is the lamb for a burnt o'?
8 himself a lamb for a burnt o': so
13 a burnt o' in the stead of his son.
35: 14 and he poured a drink o' thereon,
Ex 18: 12 took a burnt o' and sacrifices for
25: 2 Israel, that they bring me an o': 8641
2 with his heart ye shall take my o'. "
3 the o' which ye shall take of them; "
29: 14 without the camp: it is a sin o'.
18 it is a burnt o' unto the Lord: it is
18 an o' made by fire unto the Lord.
24 for a wave o' before the Lord.
25 them upon the altar for a burnt o',
25 an o' made by fire unto the Lord.
26 wave it for a wave o' before the Lord:
27 sanctify the breast of the wave o',
27 shoulder of the heave o', which is 8641
28 of Israel; for it is an heave o': "
28 be an heave o' from the children "
28 even their heave o' unto the Lord. "
36 every day a bullock for a sin o'
40 of an hin of wine for a drink o'.
41 to the meat o' of the morning, 4503
41 according to the drink o' thereof,
41 an o' made by fire unto the Lord.
42 This shall be a continual burnt o'
30: 9 nor burnt sacrifice, nor meat o'; 4503
9 neither shall ye pour drink o'
10 year with the blood of the sin o'
13 shekel shall be the o' of the Lord. 8641
14 shall give an o' unto the Lord. "
15 when they give an o' unto the Lord,"
20 minister, to burn o' made by fire
28 altar of burnt o' with all his vessels,
31: 9 the altar of burnt o' with all his
35: 5 among you an o' unto the Lord: 8641
5 let him bring it, an o' of the Lord; "
16 The altar of burnt o', with his
21 they brought the Lord's o' to the 8641
22 that offered offered an o' of gold
24 did offer an o' of silver and brass 8641
24 and brass brought the Lord's o': "
29 of Israel brought a willing o' unto
36: 3 they received of Moses all the o', 8641
6 work for the o' of the sanctuary. "
38: 1 altar of burnt o' of shittim wood:
24 holy place, even the gold of the o', 8573
29 the brass of the o' was seventy "
40: 6 set the altar of the burnt o' before
10 anoint the altar of the burnt o',
29 the altar of burnt o' by the door
29 offered upon it the burnt o' and the
29 and offered upon it...the meat o'; 4503
Le 1: 2 of you bring an o' unto the Lord, *7133
2 ye shall bring your o' of the cattle,*"
3 If his o' be a burnt sacrifice of the* "
4 upon the head of the burnt o';
6 he shall flay the burnt o', and cut
9 an o' made by fire, of a sweet
10 if his o' be of the flocks, namely, *7133
13 an o' made by fire, of a sweet
14 for his o' to the Lord be of fowls, *7133
14 he shall bring his o' of turtledoves,*"
17 an o' made by fire, of a sweet
2: 1 will offer a meat o' unto the Lord, 7133
1 Lord, his o' shall be of fine flour;* "
2 to be an o' made by fire, of a sweet
3 of the meat o' shall be Aaron's 4503
4 of a meat o' baken in the oven, "
5 be a meat o' baken in a pan, it "
6 pour oil thereon: it is a meat o'. "
7 be a meat o' baken in a fryingpan, "
8 thou shalt bring the meat o' that is "
9 priest shall take from the meat o' "
9 it is an o' made by fire, of a sweet

Le 2: 10 is left of the meat o' shall be 4503
11 No meat o', which ye shall bring "
11 in any o' of the Lord made by fire.
13 thy meat o' shalt thou season 4503
13 to be lacking from thy meat o': "
14, 14 offer a meat o' of thy firstfruits "
15 thereon: it is a meat o'. "
16 is an o' made by fire unto the Lord.
3: 1 oblation be a sacrifice of peace o',*
2 his hand upon the head of his o',*7133
3 offer of the sacrifice of the peace o',*
3 an o' made by fire unto the Lord;
5 it is an o' made by fire, of a sweet
6 if his o' for a sacrifice of peace *7133
6 sacrifice of peace o' unto the Lord*
7 If he offer a lamb for his o', then *7133
8 his hand upon the head of his o',* "
9 offer of the sacrifice of the peace o'*
9 an o' made by fire unto the Lord;
11 it is the food of the o' made by fire
12 if his o' be a goat, then he shall *7133
14 And he shall offer thereof his o', * "
14 an o' made by fire unto the Lord;
16 it is the food of the o' made by fire
4: 3 blemish unto the Lord for a sin o'.
7 bottom of the altar of the burnt o',
8 fat of the bullock for the sin o';
10 upon the altar of the burnt o'.
18 bottom of the altar of the burnt o',
20 did with the bullock for a sin o',
21 it is a sin o' for the congregation.
23 he shall bring his o', a kid of the *7133
24 where they kill the burnt o' before
24 before the Lord: it is a sin o'.
25 take of the blood of the sin o' with
25 the horns of the altar of burnt o',
25 bottom of the altar of burnt o'.
28 he shall bring his o', a kid of the *7133
29 hand upon the head of the sin o',
29 and slay the sin o' in the place of
29 in the place of the burnt o'.
30 the horns of the altar of burnt o',
32 And if he bring a lamb for a sin o',7133
33 hand upon the head of the sin o',
33 and slay it for a sin o', in the
33 place where they kill the burnt o'.
34 blood of the sin o' with his finger,
34 the horns of the altar of burnt o',
5: 6 bring his trespass o' unto the Lord 817
6 or a kid of the goats, for a sin o';
7 one for a sin o', and the other
7 and the other for a burnt o'.
8 that which is for the sin o' first,
9 sprinkle of the blood of the sin o'
9 bottom of the altar: it is a sin o'.
10 offer the second for a burnt o',
11 that sinned shall bring for his o' 7133
11 an ephah of fine flour for a sin o';
11 thereon: for it is a sin o'.
12 fire unto the Lord: it is a sin o'.
13 shall be the priest's, as a meat o', 4503
15 of the sanctuary, for a trespass o':
16 him with the ram of the trespass o',
18 thy estimation, for a trespass o', unto
19 It is a trespass o': he hath certainly
6: 5 in the day of his trespass o'. *
6 bring his trespass o' unto the Lord,
6 with thy estimation, of a trespass o',
9 This is the law of the burnt o':
9 It is the burnt o', because of the
10 with the burnt o' on the altar, and
12 lay the burnt o' in order upon it;
14 And this is the law of the meat o': 4503
15 the flour of the meat o', and of the "
15 which is upon the meat o', and "
17 it is most holy, as is the sin o',
17 most holy, as is...the trespass o'.
20 is the o' of Aaron and of his sons,*7133
20 fine flour for a meat o' perpetual, 4503
21 and the baken pieces of the meat o' "
23 every meat o' for the priest shall be"
25 saying, This is the law of the sin o':
25 place where the burnt o' is killed
25 the sin o' be killed before the Lord:
30 no sin o', whereof any of the blood
7: 1 this is the law of the trespass o':
2 place where they kill the burnt o'
2 shall they kill the trespass o': and
5 upon the altar for an o' made by fire
5 fire unto the Lord: it is a trespass o'.
7 As the sin o' is, so is the trespass
7 so is the trespass o': there is one
8 that offereth any man's burnt o',
8 the burnt o' which he hath offered.
9 meat o' that is baken in the oven, 4503
10 every meat o', mingled with oil, "
13 offer for his o' leavened bread *7133
14 for an heave o' unto the Lord, and8641
16 if the sacrifice of his o' be a vow, *7133
16 or a voluntary o', it shall be eaten the
25 offer an o' made by fire unto the Lord,
30 waved for a wave o' before the Lord.
32 for an heave o' of the sacrifices of 8641
37 This is the law of the burnt o',
37 This is the law of...the meat o', 4503
37 This is the law of...the sin o',
37 This is the law of...the trespass o',
8: 2 and a bullock for the sin o', and
14 brought the bullock for the sin o':
14 head of the bullock for the sin o'.
18 brought the ram for the burnt o': 5930
21 an o' made by fire unto the Lord;
27 them for a wave o' before the Lord.
28 on the altar upon the burnt o':
28 an o' made by fire unto the Lord.
29 waved it for a wave o' before the Lord:

Le 9: 2 Take thee a young calf for a sin o',
2 and a ram for a burnt o', without
3 ye a kid of the goats for a sin o';
3 without blemish, for a burnt o';
4 and a meat o' mingled with oil: 4503
7 unto the altar, and offer thy sin o',
7 and thy burnt o', and make an
7 and offer the o' of the people, and*7133
8 slew the calf of the sin o', which
10 caul above the liver of the sin o',
12 he slew the burnt o'; and Aaron's
13 presented the burnt o' unto him,
14 them upon the burnt o' on the altar.
15 And he brought the people's o', *7133
15 took the goat, which was the sin o'
16 he brought the burnt o', and offered it
17 he brought the meat o', and took 4503
21 waved for a wave o' before the Lord;
22 and came down from o' of the sin 6213
22 of the sin o', and the burnt
22 and the burnt o', and peace offerings.
24 upon the altar the burnt o' and
10: 12 Take the meat o' that remaineth 4503
15 wave it for a wave o' before the Lord;
16 sought the goat of the sin o', and,
17 have ye not eaten the sin o' in the
19 day have they offered their sin o'
19 and their burnt o' before the Lord;
19 if I had eaten the sin o' to day,
12: 6 of the first year for a burnt o',
6 or a turtledove, for a sin o', unto
8 pigeons; the one for the burnt o',
8 and the other for a sin o': and
14: 10 deals of fine flour for a meat o',
12 lamb, and offer him for a trespass o',
12 them for a wave o' before the Lord:
13 place where he shall kill the sin o'
13 and the burnt o', in the holy place:
13 for as the sin o' is the priest's,
13 so is the trespass o': it is most holy:
14 some of the blood of the trespass o',
17 upon the blood of the trespass o':
19 the priest shall offer the sin o',
19 he shall kill the burnt o':
20 the priest shall offer the burnt o'
20 and the meat o' upon the altar: 4503
21 lamb for a trespass o' to be waved,
21 mingled with oil for a meat o', 4503
22 and the one shall be a sin o',
22 and the other a burnt o'.
24 take the lamb of the trespass o',
24 them for a wave o' before the Lord:
25 shall kill the lamb of the trespass o',
25 some of the blood of the trespass o',
28 place of the blood of the trespass o':
31 is able to get, the one for a sin o',
31 and the other for a burnt o', with
31 with the meat o': and the priest 4503
15: 15 offer them, the one for a sin o',
15 and the other for a burnt o'; and
30 shall offer the one for a sin o',
30 and the other for a burnt o'; and
16: 3 with a young bullock for a sin o',
3 and a ram for a burnt o'.
5 two kids of the goats for a sin o',
5 and one ram for a burnt o'.
6 shall offer his bullock of the sin o',
9 lot fell, and offer him for a sin o'.
11 bring the bullock of the sin o',
11 kill the bullock of the sin o' which
15 shall he kill the goat of the sin o',
24 come forth, and offer his burnt o',
24 and the burnt o' of the people, and
25 fat of the sin o' shall he burn upon
27 And the bullock for the sin o', and
27 and the goat for the sin o', whose
17: 4 to offer an o' unto the Lord before*7133
8 offereth a burnt o' or sacrifice,
19: 21 bring his trespass o' unto the Lord,
21 even a ram for a trespass o'.
22 with the ram of the trespass o' before
22: 12 not eat of an o' of the holy things. 8641
18 offer unto the Lord for a burnt o';
21 or a freewill o' in beeves or sheep,
22 nor make an o' by fire of them
23 mayest thou offer for a freewill o';
24 neither shall ye make any o' thereof*
27 an o' made by fire unto the Lord.
23: 8 an o' made by fire unto the Lord
12 year for a burnt o' unto the Lord.
13 meat o' thereof shall be two tenth 4503
13 an o' made by fire unto the Lord for a
13 drink o' thereof shall be of wine,
14 have brought an o' unto your God:*7133
15 ye brought the sheaf of the wave o';
16 offer a new meat o' unto the Lord. 4503
18 be for a burnt o' unto the Lord,
18 with their meat o', and their 4503
18 even an o' made by fire, of sweet
19 one kid of the goats for a sin o',
20 for a wave o' before the Lord,
25, 27 an o' made by fire unto the Lord.
36, 36 an o' made by fire unto the Lord:
37 an o' made by fire unto the Lord,
37 unto the Lord, a burnt o',
37 and a meat o', a sacrifice, 4503
24: 7 even an o' made by fire unto the Lord.
27: 9 men bring an o' unto the Lord, *7133
Nu 4: 16 incense, and the daily meat o', 4503
5: 9 every o' of all the holy things of 8641
15 and he shall bring her o' for her, 7133
15 thereon; for it is an o' of jealousy, 4503
15 o' of memorial, bringing iniquity "
18 the o' of memorial in her hands, "
18 which is the jealousy o': and the "
25 jealousy o' out of a woman's hand, "

Nu 5: 25 shall wave the o' before the Lord, 4503
26 shall take an handful of the o', "
6: 11 shall offer the one for a sin o',
11 and the other for a burnt o', and
12 of the first year for a trespass o':
14 shall offer his o' unto the Lord, *7133
14 without blemish for a burnt o', and
14 year without blemish for a sin o',
15 and their meat o', and their drink 4503
16 Lord, and shall offer his sin o',
16 offer his sin...and his burnt o':
17 priest shall offer also his meat o', 4503
17 also his meat...and his drink o'.
20 them for a wave o' before the Lord:
21 o' unto the Lord for...separation, *7133
7: 3 brought their o' before the Lord, * "
10 offered their o' before the altar. * "
11 They shall offer their o', each * "
12 he that offered his o' the first day* "
13 his o' was one silver charger, the * "
13 mingled with oil for a meat o': 4503
15 of the first year, for a burnt o':
16 One kid of the goats for a sin o':
17 this was the o' of Nahshon the *7133
19 for his o' one silver charger, the * "
19 mingled with oil for a meat o': 4503
21 of the first year, for a burnt o':
22 One kid of the goats for a sin o':
23 was the o' of Nethaneel the son *7133
25 His o' was one silver charger, the* "
25 mingled with oil for a meat o': 4503
27 of the first year, for a burnt o':
28 One kid of the goats for a sin o':
29 the o' of Eliab the son of Helon. *7133
31 His o' was one silver charger of * "
31 mingled with oil for a meat o': 4503
33 of the first year, for a burnt o':
34 One kid of the goats for a sin o':
35 this was the o' of Elizur the son of 7133
37 His o' was one silver charger, * "
37 mingled with oil for a meat o': 4503
39 of the first year, for a burnt o':
40 One kid of the goats for a sin o':
41 this was the o' of Shelumiel the *7133
43 His o' was one silver charger of the* "
43 mingled with oil for a meat o': 4503
45 of the first year, for a burnt o':
46 One kid of the goats for a sin o':
47 this was the o' of Eliasaph the *7133
49 His o' was one silver charger, the* "
49 mingled with oil for a meat o': 4503
51 of the first year, for a burnt o':
52 One kid of the goats for a sin o':
53 this was the o' of Elishama the *7133
55 His o' was one silver charger of * "
55 mingled with oil for a meat o': 4503
57 of the first year, for a burnt o':
58 One kid of the goats for a sin o':
59 this was the o' of Gamaliel the *7133
61 His o' was one silver charger, the* "
61 mingled with oil for a meat o': 4503
63 of the first year, for a burnt o':
64 One kid of the goats for a sin o':
65 this was the o' of Abidan the son *7133
67 His o' was one silver charger, the* "
67 mingled with oil for a meat o': 4503
69 of the first year, for a burnt o':
70 One kid of the goats for a sin o':
71 this was the o' of Ahiezer the son*7133
73 His o' was one silver charger, the* "
73 mingled with oil for a meat o': 4503
75 of the first year, for a burnt o':
76 One kid of the goats for a sin o':
77 this was the o' of Pagiel the son *7133
79 His o' was one silver charger, the* "
79 mingled with oil for a meat o': 4503
81 of the first year, for a burnt o':
82 One kid of the goats for a sin o':
83 this was the o' of Ahira the son of*7133
87 the burnt o' were twelve bullocks,
87 year twelve, with their meat o': 4503
87 kids of the goats for sin o' twelve.
8: 8 a young bullock with his meat o', 4503
8 bullock shalt thou take for a sin o'.
11 for an o' of the children of Israel, 8573
12 shalt offer the one for a sin o',
12 other for a burnt o', unto the Lord,
13 offer them for an o' unto the Lord. 8573
15 them, and offer them for an o'. "
21 them as an o' before the Lord; and "
9: 7 we may not offer an o' of the Lord*7133
13 he brought not the o' of the Lord * "
15: 3 will make an o' by fire unto the Lord
3 Lord, a burnt o', or a sacrifice in
3 or in a freewill o', or in your
4 that offereth his o' unto the Lord*7133
4 bring a meat o' of a tenth deal of 4503
5 of an hin of wine for a drink o' shalt
5 with the burnt o' or sacrifice, for one
6 prepare for a meat o' two tenth 4503
7 for a drink o' thou shalt offer the
8 preparest a bullock for a burnt o',
9 a meat o' of three tenth deals of 4503
10 for a drink o' half an hin of wine,
10 o' made by fire, of a sweet savour
13 after this manner, in o'...by fire, 7126
13, 14 an o' made by fire, of a sweet
19 offer up an heave o' unto the Lord. 8641
20 first of your dough for an heave o': "
20 the heave o' of the threshingfloor, "
21 an heave o' in your generations. "
24 one young bullock for a burnt o',
24 unto the Lord, with his meat o', 4503
24 and his drink o', according to the
24 One kid of the goats for a sin o'.
25 and they shall bring their o', a *7133

Nu 15: 25 and their sin o' before the Lord,
27 goat of the first year for a sin o'.
16: 15 Respect not thou their o': I have 4503
18: 9 of theirs, every meat o' of theirs, "
9 and every sin o' of theirs, and
9 every trespass o' of theirs, which they
11 the heave o' of their gift, with all 8641
17 their fat for an o' made by fire,
24 they offer as an heave o' unto the 8641
26 ye shall offer up an heave o' of it "
27 your heave o' shall be reckoned "
28 offer an heave o' unto the Lord "
28 Lord's heave o' to Aaron the priest. "
29 offer every heave o' of the Lord, "
23: 3 unto Balak, Stand by thy burnt o',
15 Balak, Stand here by thy burnt o',
17 he stood by his burnt o', and the
28: 2 My o', and my bread for my *7133
3 This is the o' made by fire which ye
3 by day, for a continual burnt o'.
5 of an ephah of flour for a meat o', 4503
6 a continual burnt o', which was
7 the drink o' thereof shall be the
7 unto the Lord for a drink o'.
8 as the meat o' of the morning, 4503
8 and as the drink o' thereof, thou
9 tenth deals of flour for a meat o', 4503
9 with oil, and the drink o' thereof:
10 is the burnt o' of every sabbath,
10 beside the continual burnt o',
10 and his drink o'.
11 offer a burnt o' unto the Lord;
12, 12 tenth deals of flour...a meat o', 4503
13 oil for a meat o' unto one lamb; "
13 for a burnt o' of a sweet savour, a
14 is the burnt o' of every month
15 one kid of the goats for a sin o'
15 beside the continual burnt o',
15 and his drink o'.
19 made by fire for a burnt o' unto
20 meat o' shall be of flour mingled 4503
22 one goat for a sin o', to make an
23 the burnt o' in the morning,
23 which is for a continual burnt o'.
24 beside the continual burnt o',
24 and his drink o'.
26 when ye bring a new meat o' unto 4503
27 the burnt o' for a sweet savour
28 meat o' of flour mingled with oil, 4503
31 beside the continual burnt o',
31 and his meat o', (they shall be 4503
29: 2 offer a burnt o' for a sweet savour
3 meat o' shall be of flour mingled
5 one kid of the goats for a sin o',
6 Beside the burnt o' of the month,
6 and his meat o', 4503
6 and the daily burnt o',
6 and his meat o', 4503
8 offer a burnt o' unto the Lord for a
9 meat o' shall be of flour mingled 4503
11 One kid of the goats for a sin o';
11 beside the sin o' of atonement,
11 and the continual burnt o',
11 and the meat o' of it, and their 4503
13 offer a burnt o', a sacrifice made
14 meat o' shall be of flour mingled 4503
16 And one kid of the goats for a sin o';
16 beside the continual burnt o',
16 his meat o', 4503
16 and his drink o'.
18 And their meat o' and their drink 4503
19 one kid of the goats for a sin o';
19 beside the continual burnt o', and
19 and the meat o' thereof, and their 4503
21 And their meat o' and their drink "
22 And one goat for a sin o'; beside
22 beside the continual burnt o',
22 and his meat o', 4503
22 and his drink o'.
24 Their meat o' and their drink 4503
25 And one kid of the goats for a sin o';
25 beside the continual burnt o',
25 his meat o', 4503
25 and his drink o'.
27 And their meat o' and their drink 4503
28 And one goat for a sin o'; beside
28 beside the continual burnt o',
28 and his meat o', 4503
28 and his drink o'.
30 And their meat o' and their drink 4503
31 And one goat for a sin o'; beside
31 beside the continual burnt o',
31 his meat o', 4503
31 and his drink o'.
33 And their meat o' and their drink 4503
34 And one goat for a sin o'; beside
34 beside the continual burnt o',
34 his meat o', 4503
34 and his drink o'.
36 ye shall offer a burnt o', a sacrifice
37 Their meat o' and their drink 4503
38 And one goat for a sin o'; beside
38 beside the continual burnt o',
38 and his meat o', 4503
38 and his drink o'.
31: 29 for an heave o' of the Lord. 8641
41 which was the Lord's heave o', "
52 the gold of the o' that they offered "
De 12: 11 and the heave o' of your hand, and "
17 offerings, or heave o' of thine hand: "
16: 10 with a tribute of a freewill o'
23: 23 a freewill o', according as thou hast
Jos 22: 23 to offer thereon burnt o' or meat
23 offer thereon burnt...or meat o', 4503
26 an altar, not for burnt o', nor for
J'g 11: 31 and I will offer it up for a burnt o'.

J'g 13:16 and if thou wilt offer a burnt o·, *
19 Manoah took a kid with a meat o·,4503
23 would not have received a burnt o·
23 and a meat o· at our hands, 4503
1Sa 2:17 for men abhorred the o· of the Lord."
29 ye at my sacrifice and at mine o·, "
3:14 purged with sacrifice nor o· for ever."
6: 3 in any wise return him a trespass o·:
4 What shall be the trespass o· which
8 which ye return him for a trespass o·,
14 offered the kine a burnt o· unto
17 returned for a trespass o· unto the
7: 9 lamb, and offered it for a burnt o·
10 as Samuel was o· up the burnt 5927
10 the burnt o·, the Philistines drew
13: 9 said, Bring hither a burnt o· to me,
9 And he offered the burnt o·.
10 soon as he had made an end of o· 5927
10 the burnt o·, behold, Samuel
12 therefore, and offered a burnt o·.
26:19 against me, let him accept an o·: 4503
2Sa 6:18 as David had made an end of o· 5927
1Ki 18:29, 36 the o· of the evening sacrifice, "
2Ki 3:20 when the meat o· was offered, 4503
27 offered him for a burnt o· upon
5:17 offer neither burnt o· nor sacrifice
10:25 soon as he had made an end of o· 6213
25 the burnt o·, that Jehu said to the
16:13 And he burnt his burnt o·, and his
13 and his meat o·, and poured his 4503
13 and poured his drink o·, and
15 altar burn the morning burnt o·,
15 and the evening meat o·, and the 4503
15 burnt sacrifice, and his meat o·,
15 with the burnt o· of all the people
15 meat o·, and their drink offerings;4503
15 it all the blood of the burnt o·,
1Ch 6:49 upon the altar of the burnt o·,
16: 2 when David had made an end of o·5927
29 bring an o·, and come before him:4503
40 upon the altar of the burnt o·
21:23 and the wheat for the meat o·; 4503
26 by fire upon the altar of burnt o·.
29 and the altar of the burnt o·, were at
22: 1 this is the altar of the burnt o· for
23:29 and for the fine flour for meat o·, 4503
2Ch 4: 6 as they offered for the burnt o·
7: 1 and consumed the burnt o· and the
8:13 o· according to the commandment5927
29:18 and the altar of burnt o·, with all the
21 goats, for a sin o· for the kingdom,
23 goats for the sin o· before the king
24 king commanded that the burnt o·
24 and the sin o· should be made for
27 offer the burnt o· upon the altar.
27 And when the burnt o· began, the
28 until the burnt o· was finished.
29 when they had made an end of o·, 5927
32 all these were for a burnt o· to the
35 drink offerings for every burnt o·.
30:22 o· peace offerings, and making 2076
35:14 Aaron were busied in o· of burnt 5927
Ezr 1: 4 freewill o· for the house of God
3: 5 offered the continual burnt o·,
5 that willingly offered a freewill o·
6:17 for a sin o· for all Israel, twelve
7:16 with the freewill o· of the people,
16 o· willingly for the house of their God
8:25 even the o· of the house of our God,8641
28 silver and the gold are a freewill o·
35 twelve he goats for a sin o·:
35 this was a burnt o· unto the Lord.
Ne 10:33 and for the continual meat o·, 4503
33 and for the continual burnt o· of the
34 for the wood o·, to bring it into 7133
39 shall bring the o· of the corn, 8641
13: 9 the meat o· and the frankincense.*4503
31 And for the wood o·, at times 7133
Job 42: 8 offer up for yourselves a burnt o·;
Ps 40: 6 and o· thou didst not desire; 4503
6 burnt o·...hast thou not required.
6 and sin o· hast thou not required.
51:16 thou delightest not in burnt o·.
19 with burnt o· and whole burnt o·:
96: 8 bring an o·, and come into his 4503
Isa 40:16 beasts sufficient for a burnt o·.
43:23 caused thee to serve with an o·, *4503
53:10 shalt make his soul an o· for sin,
57: 6 them hast thou poured a drink o·,
6 thou hast offered a meat o·. *4503
61: 8 I hate robbery for burnt o·; *
65:11 furnish the drink o· unto that number.
66:20 brethren for an o· unto the Lord 4503
20 bring an o· in a clean vessel into ‡ "
Jer 11:17 me to anger in o· incense unto Baal.
14:12 when they offer burnt o· and an
Eze 20:28 the provocation of their o·: 7133
40:38 where they washed the burnt o·.
39 side, to slay thereon the burnt o· and
39 to slay thereon...the sin o· and
39 to slay thereon...the trespass o·.
42 of hewn stone for the burnt o·,
42 slew the burnt o· and the sacrifice.
43 the tables was the flesh of the o·. *7133
42:13 most holy things, and the meat o·,4503
13 and the sin o·, and the
13 and the trespass o·; for the place
43:19 a young bullock for a sin o·.
21 take the bullock also of the sin o·,
22 goats without blemish for a sin o·;
24 shall offer them up for a burnt o·
25 every day a goat for a sin o·:
44:11 they shall slay the burnt o· and
27 he shall offer his sin o·, saith the
29 They shall eat the meat o·, and 4503
29 They shall eat...the sin o·, and

Eze 44:29 They shall eat...the trespass o·;
45:15 pastures of Israel; for a meat o·, 4503
15 and for a burnt o·, and for peace
17 he shall prepare the sin o·,
17 he shall prepare...the meat o·, 4503
17 he shall prepare...the burnt o·,
19 shall take of the blood of the sin o·,
22 of the land a bullock for a sin o·.
23 prepare a burnt o· to the Lord,
23 kid of the goats daily for a sin o·.
24 he shall prepare a meat o· of an 4503
25 seven days, according to the sin o·,
25 and according to the burnt o·, and
25 and according to the meat o·, and 4503
46: 2 priests shall prepare his burnt o·
4 the burnt o· that the prince shall offer
5 the meat o· shall be an ephah for 4503
5 and the meat o· for the lambs as he "
7 And he shall prepare a meat o·, an "
11 the meat o· shall be an ephah to a "
12 shall prepare a voluntary burnt o·
12 he shall prepare his burnt o· and
13 Thou shalt daily prepare a burnt o·
14 And thou shalt prepare a meat o· 4503
14 a meat o· continually by a perpetual"
15 prepare the lamb, and the meat o·, "
15 morning for a continual burnt o·.
20 priests shall boil the trespass o·
20 priests shall boil...the sin o·,
20 where they shall bake the meat o·;4503
48: 8 be the o· which ye shall offer of *8641
Joe 1: 9 The meat o· and the 4503
9 drink o· is cut off from the house
13 my God: for the meat o· and the 4503
13 drink o· is withholden from the
2:14 behind him; even a meat o· and a 4503
14 drink o· unto the Lord your God.
Zep 3:10 my dispersed, shall bring mine o·.4503
Mal 1:10 neither will I accept an o· at your "
11 unto my name, and a pure o·: "
13 thus ye brought an o·: should I "
2:12 and him that offereth an o· unto the"
13 he regardeth not the o· any more, "
3: 3 the Lord an o· in righteousness. * "
4 the o· of Judah and Jerusalem be "
Lu 23:36 coming to him, and o· him vinegar,4374
Ac 21:26 until that an o· should be offered 4376
Ro 15:16 the o· up of the Gentiles might be "
Eph 5: 2 hath given himself for us an o· and "
Heb10: 5 Sacrifice and o· thou wouldest not, "
8 Sacrifice and o· and burnt offerings*"
8 and o· for sin thou wouldest not, *
10 through the o· of the body of Jesus4376
11 o· oftentimes the same sacrifices, 4374
14 by one o· he hath perfected for ever4376
18 these is, there is no more o· for sin."

offerings
Ge 8:20 and offered burnt o· on the altar.
Ex 10:25 give us also sacrifices and burnt o·,
20:24 shalt sacrifice thereon thy burnt o·,
24 thy peace o·, thy sheep, and thine
24: 5 Israel, which offered burnt o·, and
5 sacrificed peace o· of oxen unto 2077
29:28 of the sacrifice of their peace o·,
32: 6 the morrow, and offered burnt o·,
6 and brought peace o·; and the people
36: 3 brought yet unto him free o· every
Le 2: 3, 10 the o· of the Lord made by fire.
13 with all thine o·...shalt offer salt. 7133
4:10 bullock of the sacrifice of peace o·:
26 the fat of the sacrifice of peace o·:
31 from off the sacrifice of peace o·;
35 from the sacrifice of the peace o·;
35 the o· made by fire unto the Lord:
5:12 the o· made by fire unto the Lord:
6:12 thereon the fat of the peace o·.
17 their portion of my o· made by fire;
18 the o· of the Lord made by fire:
7:11 the law of the sacrifice of peace o·,
13 of thanksgiving of his peace o·.
14 sprinkleth the blood of the peace o·.
15, 18 of the sacrifice of his peace o·
20, 21 flesh of the sacrifice of peace o·,
29 offereth the sacrifice of his peace o·
29 of the sacrifice of his peace o·.
30 the o· of the Lord made by fire,
32 of the sacrifices of your peace o·.
33 offereth the blood of the peace o·,
34 off the sacrifices of their peace o·,
35 out of the o· of the Lord made by fire,
37 of the sacrifice of the peace o·;
9: 4 a bullock and a ram for peace o·,
18 the ram for a sacrifice of peace o·,
22 the burnt offering, and peace o·.
10:12 the o· of the Lord made by fire,
14 out of the sacrifices of peace o· of the
15 with the o· made by fire of the fat,
17: 5 offer them for peace o· unto the 2077
19: 5 offer a sacrifice of peace o· unto
21: 6 for the o· of the Lord made by fire,
21 the o· of the Lord made by fire:
22:18 vows, and for all his freewill o·, which
21 offereth a sacrifice of peace o· unto
23:18 and their drink o·, even an
19 year for a sacrifice of peace o·.
37 offering, a sacrifice, and drink o·,
38 and beside all your freewill o·,
24: 9 of the o· of the Lord made by fire
Nu 6:14 ram without blemish for peace o·,
15 meat offering, and their drink o·.
17 the ram for a sacrifice of peace o·
18 under the sacrifice of the peace o·.
7:17, 23, 29, 35, 41, 47, 53, 59, 65, 71, 77,
83 And for a sacrifice of peace o·,
88 oxen for the sacrifice of the peace o·
10:10 the trumpets over your burnt o·,

Nu 10:10 over the sacrifices of your peace o·;
15: 8 a vow, or peace o· unto the Lord:
18: 8 mine heave o· of all the hallowed 8641
11 the wave o· of the children of Israel:
19 All the heave o· of the holy things,8641
28:14 their drink o· shall be half an hin
31 without blemish) and their drink o·.
29: 6 meat offering, and their drink o·,
11 offering of it, and their drink o·.
18 and their drink o· for the bullocks, for
19 offering thereof, and their drink o·.
21, 24, 27, 30, 33 and their drink o· for
the bullocks,
37 and their drink o· for the bullock,
39 your vows, and your freewill o·,
39 for your burnt o·, and for your
39 for your meat o·, and for your 4503
39 and for your drink o·, and for your
39 and for your peace o·.
De 12: 6 ye shall bring your burnt o·, and
6 tithes, and heave o· of your hand,*
6 your vows, and your freewill o·,
11 your burnt o·, and your sacrifices,
13 offer not thy burnt o· in every place
14 there thou shalt offer thy burnt o·,
17 thou vowest, freewill o·, or heave
27 And thou shalt offer thy burnt o·,
18: 1 eat the o· of the Lord made by fire,
27: 6 shalt not offer burnt o· thereon
7 thou shalt offer peace o·, and shalt
32:38 drank the wine of their drink o·? *
Jos 8:31 they offered thereon burnt o· unto
31 unto the Lord, and sacrificed peace o·.
22:23 or if to offer peace o· thereon, let 2077
27 Lord before him with our burnt o·,
27 sacrifices, and with our peace o·;
28 not for burnt o·, nor for sacrifices;*
29 to build an altar for burnt o·, for *
29 for meat o·, or for sacrifices, *4503
J'g 20:26 until even, and offered burnt o·
26 and peace o· before the Lord.
21: 4 an altar, and offered burnt o· and
4 an altar, and offered...peace o·.
1Sa 2:28 thy father all the o· made by fire of
29 chiefest of all the o· of Israel my 4503
6:15 of Beth-shemesh offered burnt o·
10: 8 down unto thee, to offer burnt o·,
8 to sacrifice sacrifices of peace o·:
11:15 sacrificed sacrifices of peace o·
13: 9 burnt offering to me, and peace o·.
15:22 Lord as great delight in burnt o·
2Sa 1:21 be rain, upon you, nor fields of o·: 8641
6:17 for it: and David offered burnt o·
17 and peace o· before the Lord.
18 made an end of offering burnt o· *
18 and peace o·, he blessed the people
24:24 neither will I offer burnt o· unto
25 unto the Lord, and offered burnt o·
25 and peace o·. So the Lord was
1Ki 3: 4 a thousand burnt o· did Solomon
15 the Lord, and offered up burnt o·,
15 and offered peace o·, and made a
8:63 offered a sacrifice of peace o·,
64 for there he offered burnt o·, *
64 for there he offered...and meat o·,*4503
64 and the fat of the peace o·:
64 too little to receive the burnt o·, *
64 too little to receive the...meat o·, *4503
64 and the fat of the peace o·.
9:25 year did Solomon offer burnt o·
25 and peace o· upon the altar which he
2Ki 10:24 in to offer sacrifices and burnt o·,
16:13 sprinkled the blood of his peace o·
15 meat offering, and their drink o·;
1Ch 16: 1 sacrifices and peace o· before God.
2 an end of offering the burnt o· and*
2 and the peace o·, he blessed the people
40 To offer burnt o· unto the Lord
21:23 give thee the oxen also for burnt o·,
24 nor offer burnt o· without cost. *
26 unto the Lord, and offered burnt o·
26 and peace o·, and called upon the
29:21 and offered burnt o· unto the Lord,
21 with their drink o·, and sacrifices
2Ch 1: 6 a thousand burnt o· upon it.
2: 4 the burnt o· morning and evening,
7: 7 Lord: for there he offered burnt o·,
7 and the fat of the peace o·, because
7 was not able to receive the burnt o·,*
7 and the meat o·, and the fat. *4503
8:12 Then Solomon offered burnt o·
23:18 to offer the burnt o· of the Lord
24:14 And they offered burnt o· in the house
29: 7 nor offered burnt o· in the holy place
31 bring sacrifices and thank o· into the
31 brought in sacrifices and thank o·;
31 as were of a free heart burnt o·.
32 And the number of the burnt o·,
34 they could not flay all the burnt o·:
35 the burnt o· were in abundance,
35 with the fat of the peace o·, and
35 drink o· for every burnt offering.
30:15 and brought in the burnt o· into the
22 feast seven days, offering peace o·,2077
31: 2 the priests and Levites for burnt o·
2 and for peace o·, to minister, and
3 of his substance for the burnt o·,
3 the morning and evening burnt o·,
3 and the burnt o· for the sabbaths,
10 the people began to bring the o· *8641
12 brought in the o· and the tithes * "
14 was over the freewill o· of God,
33:16 and sacrificed thereon peace o· 2077
16 and thank o·, and commanded *
35: 7 and kids, all for the passover o·,
8 unto the priests for the passover o·

2Ch 35: 9 gave unto the Levites for passover o'
12 they removed the burnt o', that they
13 but the other holy o' sod they in pots,
14 were busied in offering of burnt o'
16 to offer burnt o' upon the altar of
Ezr 3: 2 to offer burnt o' thereon, as it is
3 they offered burnt o' thereon unto
3 even burnt o' morning and evening.
4 and offered the daily burnt o' by
6 they to offer burnt o' unto the Lord.
6: 9 for the burnt o' of the God of heaven,
7:17 rams, lambs, with their meat o' 4503
17 and their drink o', and offer them
8:35 offered burnt o' unto the God of Israel,
Ne 10:33 for the sin o' to make an atonement
37 firstfruits of our dough, and our o',8641
12:44 for the treasures, for the o', for "
13: 5 aforetime they laid the meat o', 4503
5 porters; and the o' of the priests. "
Job 1: 5 offered burnt o' according to the
Ps 16: 4 their drink o' of blood will I not offer,
20: 3 Remember all thy o', and accept 4503
50: 8 for thy sacrifices or thy burnt o',
66:13 go into thy house with burnt o':
119:108 thee, the freewill o' of my mouth,
Pro 7:14 I have peace o' with me; this day
Isa 1:11 I am full of the burnt o' of rams,
43:23 me the small cattle of thy burnt o';
56: 7 their burnt o' and their sacrifices
Jer 6:20 your burnt o' are not acceptable,
7:18 pour out drink o' unto other gods,5262
21 Put your burnt o' unto your
22 concerning burnt o' or sacrifices:
17:26 from the south, bringing burnt o',
26 and sacrifices, and meat o', and 4503
19: 5 sons with fire for burnt o' unto
13 out drink o' unto other gods.
32:29 out drink o' unto other gods,
33:18 a man before me to offer burnt o',
18 and to kindle meat o', and to do †4503
41: 5 with o' and incense in their hand,† "
44:17, 18 to pour out drink o' unto her,
19 and poured out drink o' unto her,
19 and pour out drink o' unto her,
25 and to pour out drink o' unto her:
Eze 20:28 poured out there their drink o'.
40 and there will I require your o', 8641
43:18 make it, to offer burnt o' thereon,
27 the priests shall make your burnt o'
27 upon the altar, and your peace o';
45:15 burnt offering, and for peace o', to
17 the prince's part to give burnt o',
17 and meat o', 4503
17 and drink o', in the feasts, and in
17 the peace o', to make reconciliation
46: 2 burnt offering and his peace o', and
12 or peace o' voluntarily unto the
12 burnt offering and his peace o', as he
Hos 6: 6 of God more than burnt o'.
8:13 flesh for the sacrifices of mine o', 1890
9: 4 shall not offer wine o' to the Lord,
Am 4: 5 proclaim and publish the free o':
5:22 Though ye offer me burnt o' and
22 meat o', I will not accept them: 4503
22 the peace o' of your fat beasts.
25 o' in the wilderness forty years, 4503
Mic 6: 6 I come before him with burnt o',
Mal 3: 8 we robbed thee? In tithes and o'. 8641
M'r 12:33 all whole burnt o' and sacrifices. 3646
Lu 21: 4 cast in unto the o' of God: *1435
Ac 24:17 bring alms to my nation, and o'. 4376
Heb10: 6 In burnt o' and sacrifices for sin 3646
8 and burnt o' and offering for sin "

office See also OFFICES.
Ge 41:13 me he restored unto mine o', and 3653
Ex 1:16 the o' of a midwife to the Hebrew
28: 1 minister unto me in the priest's o',
3, 4, 41 unto me in the priest's o'.
29: 1 minister unto me in the priest's o':
9 and the priest's o' shall be theirs for
44 minister to me in the priest's o'.
30:30 minister unto me in the priest's o'.
31:10 sons, to minister in the priest's o',
35:19 sons, to minister in the priest's o'.
39:41 to minister in the priest's o'.
40:13 minister unto me in the priest's o'.
15 minister unto me in the priest's o':
Le 7:35 unto the Lord in the priest's o';
16:32 in the priest's o' in his father's *
Nu 3: 3 to minister in the priest's o'.
4 ministered in the priest's o' in the
10 they shall wait on their priest's o': *
4:16 And to the o' of Eleazar the son of*6486
18: 7 keep your priest's o' for every thing*
7 I have given your priest's o' unto you*
De 10: 6 in the priest's o' in his stead.
1Ch 6:10 priest's o' in the temple that
32 waited on their o' according to 5656
9:22 the seer did ordain in their set o'.
26 were in their set o', and were over
31 had the set o' over the things that
23:28 their o' was to wait on the sons of 4612
24: 2 Ithamar executed the priest's o'.
2Ch 11:14 from executing the priest's o' unto
24:11 was brought unto the king's o' by 6486
31:15 the cities of the priests, in their set o',
18 for in their set o' they sanctified
Ne 13:13 and their o' was to distribute unto *
Ps 109: 8 few; and let another take his o'. 6486
Eze 44:13 to do the o' of a priest unto me,
Lu 1: 8 while he executed the priest's o' 2407
9 to the custom of the priest's o', 2405
Ro 11:13 of the Gentiles, I magnify mine o':1248
12: 4 all members have not the same o':4234
1Ti 3: 1 If a man desire the o' of a bishop, 1984
10 let them use the o' of a deacon, *1247
13 that have used the o' of a deacon *1247
Heb 7: 5 receive the o' of the priesthood, 2405

officer See also OFFICERS.
Ge 37:36 unto Potiphar, an o' of Pharaoh's, 5631
39: 1 and Potiphar, an o' of Pharaoh,
J'g 9:28 of Jerubbaal? and Zebul his o'? 6496
1Ki 4: 5 the son of Nathan was principal o',*5324
19 the only o' which was in the land. 5333
22: 9 the king of Israel called an o', and 5631
2Ki 8: 6 appointed unto her a certain o', "
25:19 he took an o' that was set over the "
2Ch 24:11 priest's o' came and emptied the 6496
M't 5:25 the judge deliver thee to the o', 5257
Lu 12:58 the judge deliver thee to the o', 4233
58 and the o' cast thee into prison. "

officers
Ge 40: 2 was wroth against two of his o', 5631
7 asked Pharaoh's o' that were with "
41:34 let him appoint o' over the land, *6496
Ex 5: 6 of the people, and their o', saying,7860
10 of the people went out, and their o', "
14 And the o' of the children of Israel, "
15 the o' of the children of Israel came "
19 the o' of the children of Israel did "
Nu 11:16 of the people, and o' over them; "
31:14 was wroth with the o' of the host, 6485
48 o' which were over thousands of "
De 1:15 tens, and o' among your tribes. 7860
16:18 Judges and o' shalt thou make thee "
20: 5 the o' shall speak unto the people, "
8 the o' shall speak further unto the "
9 when the o' have made an end of "
29:10 your o', with all the men of Israel, "
31:28 elders of your tribes, and your o', "
Jos 1:10 Joshua commanded the o' of the "
3: 2 that the o' went through the host; "
8:33 all Israel, and their elders, and o', "
23: 2 for their judges, and for their o', "
24: 1 for their judges, and for their o'; "
1Sa 8:15 give to his o', and to his servants. 5631
1Ki 4: 5 the son of Nathan was over the o':5324
7 had twelve o' over all Israel, which "
27 those o' provided victual for king "
28 they unto the place where the o' were, "
5:16 the chief of Solomon's o' which 5324
9:23 o' that were over Solomon's work, "
2Ki 11:15 the hundreds, the o' of the host, *6485
18 priest appointed o' over the house 6486
24:12 and his princes, and his o': and 5631
15 king's wives, and his o', and the "
1Ch 23: 4 six thousand were o' and judges: 7860
26:29 over Israel, for o' and judges. "
30 o' among them of Israel on this *6486
27: 1 their o' that served the king in 7860
28: 1 with the o', and with the mighty 5631
2Ch 8:10 the chief of king Solomon's o', 5324
18: 8 of Israel called for one of his o', *5631
19:11 the Levites shall be o' before you. 7860
34:13 there were scribes, and o', and "
Es 1: 8 to all the o' of his house, that 7227
2: 3 king appoint o' in all the provinces6496
9: 3 o' of the king, helped the Jews; *6213
Isa 60:17 I will also make thy o' peace, and 6486
Jer 29:26 be o' in the house of the Lord, 6496
Joh 7:32 chief priests sent o' to take him. 5257
45 came the o' of the chief priests and "
46 The o' answered, Never man spake "
18: 3 received a band of men and o' from "
12 and o' of the Jews took Jesus, and "
18 the servants and o' stood there, "
22 one of the o' which stood by struck "
19: 6 priests therefore and o' saw him, "
Ac 5:22 But when the o' came, and found "
26 Then went the captain with the o', "

offices
1Sa 2:36 pray thee, into one of the priest's o',
1Ch 24: 3 according to their o' in their *6486
2Ch 7: 6 And the priests waited on their o':4931
23:18 the o' of the house of the Lord 6486
Ne 13:14 of my God, and for the o' thereof.*4929

offscouring
La 3:45 made us as the o' and refuse in 5501
1Co 4:13 the o' of all things unto this day. 4067

offspring
Job 5:25 thine o' as the grass of the earth. 6631
21: 8 and their o' before their eyes. "
27:14 o' shall not be satisfied with bread. "
31: 8 eat; yea, let my o' be rooted out. * "
Isa 22:24 o' and the issue, all vessels of small "
44: 3 and my blessing upon thine o': "
48:19 the o' of thy bowels like the gravel "
61: 9 and their o' among the people: "
65:23 the Lord, and their o' with them. "
Ac 17:28 have said, For we are also his o'. 1085
29 then as we are the o' of God, we "
Re 22:16 I am the root and the o' of David, "

oft See also OFTEN; OFTTIMES.
2Ki 4: 8 as o' as he passed by, he turned 1767
Job 21:17 How o' is the candle of...wicked put out!
17 how o' cometh their destruction upon*
Ps 78:40 How o' did they provoke him in
M't 9:14 do we and the Pharisees fast o', 4183
17:15 into the fire, and o' into the water.*4178
18:21 how o' shall my brother sin against4212
M'r 7: 3 they wash their hands o', eat not, *4435
Ac 26:11 And I punished them o' in every *4178
1Co 11:25 this do ye, as o' as ye drink it, in 3740
2Co 11:23 more frequent, in deaths o'. 4178
2Ti 1:16 he o' refreshed me, and was not "
Heb 6: 7 in the rain that cometh o' upon it, "

often See also OFTENER; OFTENTIMES.
Pr 29: 1 He, that being o' reproved hardeneth
Mal 3:16 they that feared the Lord spake o' one*
M't 23:37 how o' would I have gathered thy 4212
M'r 5: 4 been o' bound with fetters and 4178
Lu 5:33 the disciples of John fast o', and 4437
13:34 how o' would I have gathered thy 4212
1Co 11:26 For as o' as ye eat this bread, and 3740
2Co 11:26 In journeyings o', in perils of "
27 watchings o', in hunger and thirst, "
27 fastings o', in cold and nakedness. "
Ph'p 3:18 walk, of whom I have told you o', "
1Ti 5:23 sake and thine o' infirmities. 4437
Heb 9:25 that he should offer himself o', as 4178
26 For then must he o' have suffered "
Re 11: 6 with all plagues, as o' as they will.3740

oftener
Ac 24:26 wherefore he sent for him the o', 4437

oftentimes See also OFTTIMES.
Job 33:29 these things worketh God o' *6471,7969
Ec 7:22 For o' also thine own heart 7227
Lu 8:29 o' it had caught him: and he 4183,5550
Ro 1:13 o' I purposed to come unto you, 4178
2Co 8:22 o' proved diligent in many things,* "
Heb10:11 and offering o' the same sacrifices, "

ofttimes
M't 17:15 for o' he falleth into the fire, and 4178
M'r 9:22 o' it hath cast him into the fire, "
Joh 18: 2 Jesus o' resorted thither with his "

Og (*og*)
Nu 21:33 O' the king of Bashan went out 5747
32:33 the kingdom of O' king of Bashan, "
De 1: 4 and O' the king of Bashan, which "
3: 1 O' the king of Bashan came out "
3 God delivered into our hands O' "
4 the kingdom of O' in Bashan. "
10 of the kingdom of O' in Bashan. "
11 only O' king of Bashan remained "
13 Bashan, being the kingdom of O', "
4:47 and the land of O' king of Bashan, "
29: 7 and O' the king of Bashan, came "
31: 4 as he did to Sihon and to O', kings "
Jos 2:10 Sihon and O', whom ye utterly "
9:10 and to O' king of Bashan, which "
12: 4 the coast of O' king of Bashan, "
13:12 All the kingdom of O' in Bashan, "
30 the kingdom of O' king of Bashan, "
31 of the kingdom of O' in Bashan, "
1Ki 4:19 and of O' king of Bashan; and he "
Ne 9:22 and the land of O' king of Bashan. "
Ps 135:11 and O' king of Bashan, and all the "
136:20 And O' the king of Bashan: for his "

oh
Ge 18:30, 32 O' let not the Lord be angry, 4994
19:18 unto them, O', not so, my Lord: "
20 O', let me escape thither, (is it not "
44:18 O' my lord, let thy servant, I pray 994
Ex 32:31 O', this people have sinned a great 577
J'g 6:13 O' my Lord, if the Lord be with us, 994
15 O' my Lord, wherewith shall I save "
1Sa 1:26 O' my lord, as thy soul liveth, my "
2Sa 15: 4 O' that I were made judge in the land,
23:15 O' that one would give me drink of the
1Ch 4:10 O' that thou wouldest bless me 518
11:17 O' that one would give me drink of the
Job 6: 2 O' that my grief were thoroughly 3863
8 O' that I might have my request; and
10:18 O' that I had given up the ghost, and *
11: 5 O' that God would speak, and open his
19:23 O' that my words were now written!
23 o' that they were printed in a book!
23: 3 O' that I knew where I might find him!
29: 2 O' that I were as in months past, as in
31:31 O' that we had of his flesh! we cannot*
35 O' that one would hear me! behold,
Ps 6: 4 o' save me for thy mercies' sake. *
7: 9 O' let the wickedness of the 4994
14: 7 O' that the salvation of Israel were
31:19 O' how great is thy goodness, which
53: 6 O' that the salvation of Israel were
55: 6 O' that I had wings like a dove! for
81:13 O' that my people had hearkened 3863
107: 8, 15, 21, 31 O' that men would praise
Isa 64: 1 O' that thou wouldest rend the 3863
Jer 9: 1 O' that my head were waters, and
2 O' that I had in the wilderness a
44: 4 O', do not this abominable thing 4994

Ohad (*o'-had*)
Ge 46:10 Jemuel, and Jamin, and O', and 161
Ex 6:15 Jemuel, and Jamin, and O', and "

Ohel (*o'-hel*)
1Ch 3:20 And Hashubah, and O', and 169

oil See also OILED.
Ge 28:18 and poured o' upon the top of it. 8081
35:14 thereon, and he poured o' thereon. "
Ex 25: 6 O' for the light, spices for "
6 spices for anointing o', and for "
27:20 pure o' olive beaten for the light, "
29: 2 cakes unleavened tempered with o', "
2 wafers unleavened anointed with o': "
7 shalt thou take the anointing o', "
21 the altar, and of the anointing o', "
40 fourth part of an hin of beaten o'; "
30:24 sanctuary, and of o' olive an hin: "
25 make it an o' of holy ointment, an "
25 it shall be an holy anointing o', "
31 be an holy anointing o' unto me "
31:11 the anointing o', and sweet incense "
35: 8 And o' for the light, and spices for "
8 and spices for anointing o', and for "
14 his lamps, with the o' for the light, "
15 and the anointing o', and the sweet "
28 And spice, and o' for the light, "
28 and for the anointing o', and for "
37:29 And he made the holy anointing o', "

Ex 39: 37 vessels thereof, and the o' for light, 8081
38 and the anointing o', and the sweet "
40: 9 thou shalt take the anointing o', "
Le 2: 1 he shall pour o' upon it, and put "
2 and of the o' thereof, with all the "
4 cakes of fine flour mingled with o', "
4 unleavened wafers anointed with o'. "
5 flour unleavened, mingled with o'. "
6 it in pieces, and pour o' thereon: "
7 shall be made of fine flour with o'. "
15 And thou shalt put o' upon it, and "
16 thereof, and part of the o' thereof, "
5: 11 he shall put no o' upon it, neither "
6: 15 meat offering, and of the o' thereof, "
21 In a pan it shall be made with o'; "
7: 10 meat offering, mingled with o', "
12 unleavened cakes mingled with o', "
12 unleavened wafers anointed with o', "
12 and cakes mingled with o', of fine "
8: 2 the garments, and the anointing o', "
10 Moses took the anointing o', and "
12 he poured of the anointing o' upon "
30 Moses took of the anointing o', and "
9: 4 meat offering mingled with o': for "
10: 7 anointing o' of the Lord is upon you. "
14: 10 mingled with o', and one log of o'. "
12 trespass offering, and the log of o', "
15 shall take some of the log of o', and "
16 shall dip his right finger in the o' "
16 sprinkle of the o' with his finger "
17 the rest of the o' that is in his hand "
18 the remnant of the o' that is in the "
21 deal of fine flour mingled with o' "
21 for a meat offering, and a log of o'; "
24 trespass offering, and the log of o', "
26 priest shall pour of the o' into the "
27 some of the o' that is in his left "
28 priest shall put of the o' that is in "
29 rest of the o' that is in the priest's "
21: 10 head the anointing o' was poured, "
12 the crown of the anointing o' of his "
23: 13 deals of fine flour mingled with o', "
24: 2 pure o' olive beaten for the light, "
Nu 4: 9 snuffdishes, and all the o' vessels "
16 pertaineth the o' for the light, "
16 meat offering, and the anointing o' "
5: 15 he shall pour no o' upon it, nor put "
6: 15 cakes of fine flour mingled with o', "
15 unleavened bread anointed with o', "
7: 13, 19, 25, 31, 37, 43, 49, 55, 61, 67, 73, 79
mingled with o' for a meat offering: "
8: 8 even fine flour mingled with o', and "
11: 8 of it was as the taste of fresh o'. "
15: 4 with the fourth part of an hin of o'. "
6 with the third part of an hin of o'. "
9 flour mingled with half an hin of o'. "
18: 12 the best of the o', and all the best of "
28: 5 fourth part of an hin of beaten o'. "
9, 12, 12 meat offering, mingled with o', "
13 tenth deal of flour mingled with o' "
20 shall be of flour mingled with o': "
28 offering of flour mingled with o', "
29: 3, 9, 14 be of flour mingled with o', "
35: 25 was anointed with the holy o'. "
De 7: 13 corn, and thy wine, and thine o', 3323
8: 8 a land of o' olive, and honey; 8081
11: 14 corn, and thy wine, and thine o'. 3323
12: 17 thy corn, or of thy wine, or of thy o', "
14: 23 corn, of thy wine, and of thine o', "
18: 4 corn, of thy wine, and of thine o', "
28: 40 not anoint thyself with the o'; 8081
51 leave thee either corn, wine, or o', 3323
32: 13 rock, and o' out of the flinty rock; 8081
33: 24 and let him dip his foot in o'. "
1Sa 10: 1 Samuel took a vial of o', and poured "
16: 1 fill thine horn with o', and go, I will "
13 Then Samuel took the horn of o', "
2Sa 1: 21 he had not been anointed with o'. "
14: 2 anoint not thyself with o', but be as "
1Ki 1: 39 the priest took an horn of o' out of "
5: 11 and twenty measures of pure o': "
17: 12 in a barrel, and a little o' in a cruse: "
14 neither shall the cruse of o' fail, "
16 not, neither did the cruse of o' fail, "
2Ki 4: 2 thing in the house, save a pot of o'. "
6 a vessel more. And the o' stayed. "
7 Go, sell the o', and pay thy debt, "
9: 1 take this box of o' in thine hand, "
3 Then take the box of o', and pour it "
6 and he poured the o' on his head, "
18: 32 a land of o' olive and of honey, 3323
1Ch 9: 29 flour, and the wine, and the o', 8081
12: 40 bunches of raisins, and wine, and o', "
27: 28 over the cellars of o' was Joash: "
2Ch 2: 10 and twenty thousand baths of o'. "
15 the barley, the o', and the wine, "
11: 11 store of victual, and of o' and wine. "
31: 5 of corn, wine, and o', and honey, 3323
32: 28 increase of corn, and wine, and o'; "
Ezr 3: 7 meat, and drink, and o', unto them 8081
6: 9 salt, wine, and o', according to 4887
7: 22 to an hundred baths of o', and salt "
Neh 5: 11 the corn, the wine, and the o', that 3323
10: 37 of wine and of o', unto the priests, "
39 the new wine, and the o', unto the "
13: 5 new wine, and the o', which was "
12 wine and the o' unto the treasuries, "
Es 2: 12 wit, six months with o' of myrrh, 8081
Job 24: 11 Which make o' within their walls, 6671
29: 6 rock poured me out rivers of o'; 8081
Ps 23: 5 thou anointest my head with o'; "
45: 7 anointed thee with...o' of gladness "
55: 21 his words were softer than o', yet "
89: 20 with my holy o' have I anointed him: "
92: 10 I shall be anointed with fresh o'. "
104: 15 o' to make his face to shine, and "
Ps 109: 18 water, and like o' into his bones. 8081
141: 5 it shall be an excellent o', which "
Pr 5: 3 and her mouth is smoother than o': "
21: 17 he that loveth wine and o' shall not "
20 and o' in the dwelling of the wise; "
Isa 41: 19 and the myrtle, and the o' tree; "
61: 3 ashes, the o' of joy for mourning, "
Jer 31: 12 for wine, and for o', and for the 3323
40: 10 wine, and summer fruits, and o', 8081
41: 8 of barley, and of o', and of honey. "
Eze 16: 9 thee, and I anointed thee with o'. "
13 eat fine flour, and honey, and o': "
18 hast set mine o' and mine incense "
19 thee, fine flour, and o', and honey, "
23: 41 hast set mine incense and mine o'. "
27: 17 and honey, and o', and balm. "
32: 14 and cause their rivers to run like o', "
45: 14 the ordinance of o', the bath of o', "
24 ram, and an hin of o' for an ephah. "
25 offering, and according to the o'. "
46: 5, 7, 11 and an hin of o' to an ephah. "
14 and the third part of an hin of o', to "
15 and the meat offering, and the o', "
Ho 2: 5 and my flax, mine o' and my drink. "
8 I gave her corn, and wine, and o', 3323
22 the corn, and the wine, and the o'; "
12: 1 and o' is carried into Egypt. 8081
Joe 1: 10 is dried up, the o' languisheth. 3323
2: 19 send you corn, and wine, and o', "
24 shall overflow with wine and o'. "
Mic 6: 7 with ten thousands of rivers of o'? 8081
15 thou shalt not anoint thee with o'; "
Hag 1: 11 the new wine and upon the o', 3323
2: 12 bread or pottage, or wine, or o', or 8081
Zec 4: 12 empty the golden o' out of themselves? "
M't 25: 3 lamps, and took no o' with them: *1637*
4 wise took o' in their vessels with "
8 Give us of your o'; for our lamps "
M'r 6: 13 anointed with o' many that were "
Lu 7: 46 My head with o' thou didst not "
10: 34 his wounds, pouring in o' and wine, "
16: 6 he said, An hundred measures of o'. "
Heb 1: 9 anointed thee with...o' of gladness "
Jas 5: 14 anointing him with o' in the name "
Re 6: 6 thou hurt not the o' and the wine. "
18: 13 and wine, and o', and fine flour, and "

oiled
Ex 29: 23 bread, and one cake of o' bread, 8081
Le 8: 26 a cake of o' bread, and one wafer, "

oil-olive See OIL and OLIVE.

oil-tree See OIL and TREE.

ointment See also OINTMENTS.
Ex 30: 25 shalt make it an oil of holy o', an o' 4888
25 an o' compound after the art *7545
2Ki 20: 13 the spices, and the precious o', *8081
1Ch 9: 30 sons of the priests made the o' of *4842
Job 41: 31 he maketh the sea like a pot of o'. ‡4841
Ps 133: 2 like the precious o' upon the head, *8081
Pr 27: 9 O' and perfume rejoice the heart: ‡ "
16 and the o' of his right hand, which* "
Ec 7: 1 name is better than precious o'; "
9: 8 white; and let thy head lack no o'. ‡ "
10: 1 flies cause the o' of the apothecary ‡ "
Ca 1: 3 thy name is as o' poured forth, ‡ "
Isa 1: 6 bound up, neither mollified with o'. * "
39: 2 and the spices, and the precious o', * "
57: 9 thou wentest to the king with o', ‡ "
M't 26: 7 alabaster box of very precious o', *3464*
9 For this o' might have been sold for "
12 she hath poured this o' on my body, "
M'r 14: 3 alabaster box of o' of spikenard "
4 Why was this waste of the o' made? "
Lu 7: 37 brought an alabaster box of o', "
38 feet, and anointed them with the o'. "
46 hath anointed my feet with o'. "
Joh 11: 2 which anointed the Lord with o', "
12: 3 Mary a pound of o' of spikenard, "
3 was filled with the odour of the o'. "
5 Why was not this o' sold for three "

ointments
Ca 1: 3 of the savour of thy good o' thy ‡8081
4: 10 the smell of thine o' than all spices! ‡ "
Am 6: 6 anoint themselves with the chief o': "
Lu 23: 56 and prepared spices and o'; and *3464*
Re 18: 13 cinnamon, and odours, and o', and "

old See also ELDER; ELDEST.
Ge 5: 32 Noah was five hundred years o': 1121
6: 4 mighty men which were of o', 5769
7: 6 Noah was six hundred years o' 1121
11: 10 Shem was an hundred years o', "
12: 4 Abram was seventy and five years o' "
15: 9 Take...an heifer of three years o', 8027
9 and a she goat of three years o', "
9 and a ram of three years o', and a "
15 shalt be buried in a good o' age. 7872
16: 16 was fourscore and six years o', 1121
17: 1 when Abram was ninety years o' "
12 he that is eight days o' shall be "
17 him that is an hundred years o'? "
17 Sarah, that is ninety years o', bear? 1323
24 Abraham was ninety years o' and 1121
25 Ishmael...was thirteen years o', "
18: 11 Now Abraham and Sarah were o' 2205
12 After I am waxed o' shall I have 1086
12 pleasure, my lord being o' also? 2204
13 a surety bear a child, which am o'? "
19: 4 house round, both o' and young, 2205
31 unto the younger, Our father is o', 2204
21: 2 bare Abraham a son in his o' age, 2208
4 his son Isaac being eight days o', 1121
5 Abraham was an hundred years o', "
7 have born him a son in his o' age. 2208
23: 1 and seven and twenty years o': *2416
24: 1 Abraham was o', and well stricken 2204
Ge 24: 36 son to my master when she was o': 2209
25: 8 ghost, and died in a good o' age, 7872
8 an o' man, and full of years; and 2205
20 Isaac was forty years o' when he 1121
26 Isaac was threescore years o' when "
26: 34 Esau was forty years o' when he "
27: 1 when Isaac was o', and his eyes 2204
2 I am o', I know not the day of my "
35: 29 people, being o' and full of days: 2205
37: 2 Joseph, being seventeen years o', 1121
3 he was the son of his o' age: 2208
41: 46 Joseph was thirty years o' when 1121
43: 27 well, the o' man of whom ye spake? 2205
44: 20 We have a father, an o' man, and "
20 a child of his o' age, a little one; 2208
47: 8 Jacob, How o' art thou? *3117, 8140, 3117
49: 9 as a lion, and as an o' lion; *3833
50: 26 being an hundred and ten years o': 1121
Ex 7: 7 Moses was fourscore years o', and "
7 Aaron fourscore and three years o', "
10: 9 go with our young and with our o', 2205
30: 14 from twenty years o' and above, 1121
38: 26 from twenty years o' and upward, "
Le 13: 11 It is an o' leprosy in the skin of 3462
19: 32 and honour the face of the o' man, 2205
25: 22 eat yet of o' fruit until the ninth 3465
22 come in ye shall eat of the o' store. "
26: 10 And ye shall eat o' store, and bring 3462
10 forth the o' because of the new. 3465
27: 3 years o' even unto sixty years o', 1121
5 years o' even unto twenty years o', "
6 a month o' even unto five years o', "
7 it be from sixty years o' and above; "
Nu 1: 3 From twenty years o' and upward, "
18, 20, 22, 24, 26, 28, 30, 32, 34, 36, 38, 40,
42, 45 from twenty years o' and "
3: 15 male from a month o' and upward "
22, 28, 34, 39, 40, 43 from a month o'
and upward, "
4: 3 From thirty years o' and upward "
3 even unto fifty years o', all that "
23 From thirty years o' and upward "
23 until fifty years o' shalt thou "
30 From thirty years o' and upward "
30 even unto fifty years o' shalt thou "
35 From thirty years o' and upward "
35 even unto fifty years o', every one "
39 From thirty years o' and upward "
39 even unto fifty years o', every one "
43 From thirty years o' and upward "
43 even unto fifty years o', every one "
47 From thirty years o' and upward "
47 even unto fifty years o', every one "
8: 24 from twenty and five years o' and "
14: 29 from twenty years o' and upward, "
18: 16 from a month o' shalt thou redeem, "
26: 2 from twenty years o' and upward, "
4 from twenty years o' and upward; "
62 males from a month o' and upward: "
32: 11 from twenty years o' and upward, "
33: 39 and twenty and three years o' "
De 2: 20 giants dwelt therein in o' time; *6440
8: 4 raiment waxed not o' upon thee, 1086
19: 14 they of o' time have set in thine 7223
28: 50 not regard the person of the o', 2205
29: 5 clothes are not waxen o' upon you, 1086
5 shoe is not waxen o' upon thy foot. "
31: 2 an hundred and twenty years o'; 1121
32: 7 Remember the days of o', consider 5769
34: 7 an hundred and twenty years o' 1121
Jos 5: 11 did eat of the o' corn of the land ‡5669
12 after they had eaten of the o' corn ‡ "
6: 21 man and woman, young and o', 5288
9: 4 and took o' sacks upon their asses, 1087
4 and wine bottles, o', and rent, and "
5 And o' shoes and clouted upon their "
5 feet, and o' garments upon them; "
13 shoes are become o' by reason of 1086
13: 1 Now Joshua was o' and stricken in 2204
1 Thou art o' and stricken in years, "
14: 7 Forty years o' was I when Moses 1121
10 this day fourscore and five years o'. "
23: 1 that Joshua waxed o' and stricken 2204
2 them, I am o' and stricken in age: "
24: 2 the other side of the flood in o' time, 5769
29 being an hundred and ten years o'. 1121
J'g 2: 8 being an hundred and ten years o'. "
6: 25 the second bullock of seven years o', "
8: 32 Gideon...died in a good o' age, 7872
19: 16 came an o' man from his work 2205
17 and the o' man said, Whither goest "
20 And the o' man said, Peace be with "
22 the master of the house, the o' man, "
Ru 1: 12 I am too o' to have an husband. 2204
4: 15 and a nourisher of thine o' age: 7872
1Sa 2: 22 Now Eli was very o', and heard 2204
31 not be an o' man in thine house. 2205
32 not be an o' man in thine house for "
4: 15 Eli was ninety and eight years o'; 1121
18 for he was an o' man, and heavy. 2204
8: 1 came to pass, when Samuel was o', "
5 Behold, thou art o', and thy sons "
12: 2 and I am o' and grayheaded; and, "
17: 12 man went among men for an o' man "
27: 8 nations were of o' inhabitants 5769
28: 14 she said, An o' man cometh up; 2205
2Sa 2: 10 Saul's son was forty years o' when 1121
4: 4 was five years o' when the tidings "
5: 4 David was thirty years o' when he "
19: 32 aged man, even fourscore years o': "
35 I am this day fourscore years o': "
20: 18 They were wont to speak in o' time, 7223
1Ki 1: 1 king David was o' and stricken in 2204
15 chamber: and the king was very o'; "
11: 4 to pass, when Solomon was o', 2209
12: 6 consulted with the o' men, that 2205

1Ki 12: 8 forsook the counsel of the o' men 2205
13 forsook the o' men's counsel that "
13:11 dwelt an o' prophet in Beth-el; "
25 the city where the o' prophet dwelt."
29 and the o' prophet came to the city, "
14:21 was forty and one years o' when 1121
15:23 time of his o' age he was diseased 2209
22:42 was thirty and five years o' when 1121
2Ki 4:14 no child, and her husband is o'. 2204
8:17 Thirty and two years o' was he 1121
26 and twenty years o' was Ahaziah "
11:21 Seven years o' was Jehoash when "
14: 2 He was twenty and five years o' "
21 Azariah, which was sixteen years o'."
15: 2 Sixteen years o' was he when he "
33 Five and twenty years o' was he "
16: 2 Twenty years o' was Ahaz when he "
18: 2 Twenty and five years o' was he "
21: 1 Manasseh was twelve years o' when"
19 Amon was twenty and two years o' "
22: 1 Josiah was eight years o' when he "
23:31 was twenty and three years o' when"
36 was twenty and five years o' when "
24: 8 Jehoiachin was eighteen years o' "
18 was twenty and one years o' when "
1Ch 2:21 when he was threescore years o'; "
4:40 they of Ham had dwelt there of o'.*6440
23: 1 So when David was o' and full of 2204
27 from twenty years o' and above: 1121
27:23 from twenty years o' and under: "
29:28 And he died in a good o' age, full 7872
2Ch 10: 6 took counsel with the o' men that 2205
8 the counsel which the o' men gave "
13 forsook the counsel of the o' men, "
12:13 was one and forty years o' when 1121
20:31 was thirty and five years o' when "
21: 5 was thirty and two years o' when "
20 Thirty and two years o' was he "
22: 2 Forty and two years o' was Ahaziah"
24: 1 Joash was seven years o' when he "
15 But Jehoiada waxed o', and was 2204
15 an hundred and thirty years o' 1121
25: 1 was twenty and five years o' when "
5 from twenty years o' and above, "
26: 1 Uzziah, who was sixteen years o', "
3 Sixteen years o' was Uzziah when "
27: 1 was twenty and five years o' when "
8 was five and twenty years o' when "
28: 1 was twenty years o' when he began "
29: 1 he was five and twenty years o', "
31:16 from three years o' and upward, "
17 from twenty years o' and upward, "
33: 1 Manasseh was twelve years o' "
21 Amon was two and twenty years o' "
34: 1 Josiah was eight years o' when he "
36: 2 was twenty and three years o' when"
5 was twenty and five years o' when "
9 Jehoiachin was eight years o' when"
11 was one and twenty years o' when "
17 o' man, or him that stooped for 2205
Ezr 3: 8 from twenty years o' and upward, 1121
4:15 within the same of o' time: 5957
19 this city of o' time hath made "
Ne 3: 6 o' gate repaired Jehoiada the son 3465
9:21 their clothes waxed not o', and 1086
12:39 Ephraim, and above the o' gate, 3465
46 the days of David and Asaph of o' 6924
Es 3:13 all Jews, both young and o', little 2205
Job 4:11 o' lion perisheth for lack of prey, "
14: 8 root thereof wax o' in the earth, 2204
20: 4 Knowest thou not this of o', since 5703
21: 7 do the wicked live, become o', yea,6275
22:15 the o' way which wicked men have5769
30: 2 me, in whom o' age was perished?*
32: 6 I am young, and ye are very o'; 3453
42:17 died, being o' and full of days. 2205
Ps 6: 7 it waxeth o' because of all mine 6275
25: 6 for they have been ever of o'. 5769
32: 3 my bones waxed o' through my 1086
37:25 have been young, and now am o'; 2204
44: 1 in their days, in the times of o'. 6924
55:19 them, even he that abideth of o'. "
68:33 of heavens, which were of o'; "
71: 9 me not off in the time of o' age; 2209
18 when I am o' and grayheaded, O "
74: 2 which thou hast purchased of o'; 6924
12 For God is my King of o', working "
77: 5 I have considered the days of o', "
11 will remember thy wonders of o'. "
78: 2 I will utter dark sayings of o': "
92:14 still bring forth fruit in o' age; 7872
93: 2 Thy throne is established of o': 227
102:25 Of o' hast thou laid the foundation6440
26 them shall wax o' like a garment;1086
119:52 remembered thy judgments of o', 5769
152 have known of o' that thou hast 6924
143: 5 I remember the days of o'; I "
148:12 maidens; o' men, and children: 2205
Pro 8:22 of his way, before his works of o'. 227
17: 6 children are the crown of o' men; 2205
20:29 beauty of o' men is the gray head. "
22: 6 when he is o', he will not depart 2204
23:10 Remove not the o' landmark; and*5769
22 not thy mother when she is o'. 2204
Ec 1:10 it hath been already of o' time, 5769
4:13 child than an o' and foolish king, 2205
Ca 7:13 of pleasant fruits, new and o', 3465
Isa 15: 5 Zoar, an heifer of three years o': *7992
20: 4 Ethiopians captives, young and o',2205
22:11 walls for the water of the o' pool: 3465
25: 1 thy counsels of o' are faithfulness 7350
30: 6 whence come...young and o' lion, *3918
33 For Tophet is ordained of o'; yea, 865
43:18 neither consider the things of o'. 6931
46: 4 And even to your o' age I am he; 2209
9 Remember the former things of o':5769
Isa 50: 9 all shall wax o' as a garment; 1086
51: 6 earth shall wax o' like a garment, "
9 days, in the generations of o'. *5769
57:11 not I held my peace even of o', and* "
58:12 shall build the o' waste places: "
61: 4 they shall build the o' wastes, "
63: 9 and carried them all the days of o'. "
11 Then he remembered the days of o'. "
65:20 an o' man that hath not filled his 2205
20 shall die an hundred years o'; 1121
20 sinner being an hundred years o' "
Jer 2:20 of o' time I have broken thy yoke, 5769
6:16 and see, and ask for the o' paths, "
28: 8 been before me and before thee of o' "
31: 3 The Lord hath appeared of o' unto7350
13 both young men and o' together: 2205
38:11 o' cast clouts and o' rotten rags, 1094
12 Put now these o' cast clouts and "
46:26 be inhabited, as in the days of o', 6924
48:34 as an heifer of three years o': *7992
51:22 I break in pieces o' and young; 2205
52: 1 was one and twenty years o' when 1121
La 1: 7 that she had in the days of o', 6924
2:17 had commanded in the days of o': "
21 The young and the o' lie on the 2205
3: 4 and my skin hath he made o'; 1086
6 places, as they that be dead of o'.*5769
5:21 turned; renew our days as of o'. 6924
Eze 9: 6 Slay utterly o' and young, both 2205
23:43 her that was o' in adulteries, 1087
25:15 to destroy it for the o' hatred; *5769
26:20 the pit, with the people of o' time, "
20 the earth, in places desolate of o', "
36:11 settle you after your o' estates, *6927
38:17 of whom I have spoken in o' time 6931
Da 5:31 about threescore and two years o'.1247
Joe 1: 2 Hear this, ye o' men, and give ear,2205
2:28 your o' men shall dream dreams, "
Am 9:11 I will build it as in the days of o': 5769
Mic 5: 2 goings forth have been from of o', 6924
6: 6 offerings, with calves of a year o'? 1121
7:14 and Gilead, as in the days of o'. 5769
20 our fathers from the days of o'. 6924
Na 2: 8 But Nineveh is of o' like a pool of 3117
11 the lion, even the o' lion, walked, *
Zec 8: 4 yet o' men and o' women dwell in 2205
Mal 3: 4 as in the days of o', and as in 5769
M't 2:16 from two years o' and under, 1332
5:21 that it was said by them of o' time, 744
27 that it was said by them of o' time,* "
33 hath been said by them of o' time, "
9:16 of new cloth unto an o' garment, 3820
17 men put new wine into o' bottles: "
13:52 of his treasure things new and o'. "
M'r 2:21 of new cloth on an o' garment: "
21 filled it up taketh away from the o'."
22 putteth new wine into o' bottles: "
Lu 1:18 for I am an o' man, and my wife 4246
36 also conceived a son in her o' age: 1094
2:42 And when he was twelve years o', "
5:36 of a new garment upon an o'; 3820
36 the new agreeth not with the o'. "
37 putteth new wine into o' bottles; "
39 No man also having drunk o' wine "
39 new: for he saith, The o' is better. "
9: 8 one of the o' prophets was risen 744
19 one of the o' prophets is risen again."
12:33 yourselves bags which wax not o',3822
Joh 3: 4 can a man be born when he is o'? 1088
8:57 Thou art not yet fifty years o', and "
21:18 when thou shalt be o', thou shalt 1095
Ac 2:17 your o' men shall dream dreams: 4245
4:22 For the man was above forty years o', "
7:23 when he was full forty years o', it 5550
15:21 Moses of o' time hath in every city 744
21:16 Mnason of Cyprus, an o' disciple, * "
Ro 4:19 he was about an hundred years o',1541
6: 6 our o' man is crucified with him, 3820
1Co 5: 7 Purge out therefore the o' leaven, "
8 not with o' leaven, neither with the "
2Co 3:14 in the reading of the o' testament; "
5:17 creature: o' things are past away; 744
Eph 4:22 That ye put off...the o' man, which3820
Col 3: 9 that ye have put off the o' man "
1Ti 4: 7 refuse profane and o' wives' fables,1126
5: 9 number under threescore years o', "
Heb 1:11 shall wax o' as doth a garment; 3822
8:13 covenant, he hath made the first o'. "
13 that which decayeth and waxeth o'*1095
1Pe 3: 5 in the o' time the holy women also,4218
2Pe 1: 9 he was purged from his o' sins. 3819
21 came not in o' time by the will of*4218
2: 5 spared not the o' world, but saved* 744
3: 5 word of God the heavens were of o',1597
1Jo 2: 7 an o' commandment which ye had 3820
7 The o' commandment is the word "
Jude 4 who were before of o' ordained to 3819
Re 12: 9 that o' serpent, called the Devil, 744
20: 2 that o' serpent, which is the Devil, "

old age See OLD and AGE.

oldness
Ro 7: 6 and not in the o' of the letter. 3821

olive See also OLIVES; OLIVEYARDS.
Ge 8:11 in her mouth was an o' leaf pluckt2132
Ex 27:20 that they bring thee pure oil o' "
30:24 the sanctuary, and of oil o' an hin: "
Le 24: 2 they bring unto thee pure oil o' "
De 6:11 o' trees, which thou plantedst not; "
8: 8 a land of oil o', and honey; "
24:20 When thou beatest thine o' tree, "
28:40 Thou shalt have o' trees throughout"
40 for thine o' shall cast his fruit. "
J'g 9: 8 they said unto the o' tree, Reign "
9 But the o' tree said unto them, "
1Ki 6:23 he made two cherubims of o' tree,8081
1Ki 6:31 the oracle he made doors of o' tree:8081
32 The two doors also were of o' tree; "
33 door of the temple posts of o' tree, "
2Ki 18:32 a land of oil o' and of honey, 2132
1Ch 27:28 over the o' trees and the sycomore "
Ne 8:15 and fetch o' branches, and pine "
Job 15:33 shall cast off his flower as the o'. "
Ps 52: 8 am like a green o' tree in the house "
128: 3 thy children like o' plants round "
Isa 17: 6 in it, as the shaking of an o' tree, "
24:13 shall be as the shaking of an o' tree, "
Jer 11:16 called thy name, A green o' tree, "
Hos 14: 6 his beauty shall be as the o' tree, "
Am 4: 9 trees and your o' trees increased, "
Hab 3:17 the labour of the o' shall fail, and "
Hag 2:19 the pomegranate, and the o' tree, "
Zec 4: 3 two o' trees by it, one upon the right"
11 What are these two o' trees upon "
12 What be these two o' branches "
Ro 11:17 and thou, being a wild o' tree, wert 65
17 the root and fatness of the o' tree;1636
24 if thou wert cut out of the o' tree 65
24 to nature into a good o' tree: 2565
24 be graffed into their own o' tree? 1636
Jas 3:12 tree, my brethren, bear o' berries? "
Re 11: 4 These are the two o' trees, and the "

olive-berries See OLIVE and BERRIES.

olive-branches See OLIVE and BRANCHES.

oliv -leaf See OLIVE and LEAF.

olives
J'g 15: 5 corn, with the vineyards and o'. *2132
Mic 6:15 thou shalt tread the o', but thou "
Zec 14: 4 in that day upon the mount of O', "
4 the mount of O' shall cleave in the "
M't 21: 1 Bethphage, unto the mount of O', 1636
24: 3 And as he sat upon the mount of O'. "
26:30 they went out into the mount of O'. "
M'r 11: 1 and Bethany, at the mount of O', "
13: 3 And as he sat upon the mount of O' "
14:26 they went out into the mount of O'. "
Lu 19:29 the mount called the mount of O',‡ "
37 at the descent of the mount of O', "
21:37 that is called the mount of O'. ‡ "
22:39 as he was wont, to the mount of O'; "
Joh 8: 1 Jesus went unto the mount of O'. "

Olivet See also MOUNT and OLIVES.
2Sa 15:30 up by the ascent of mount O', *2132
Ac 1:12 from the mount called O', which 1638

olive-tree See OLIVE and TREE.

oliveyard See also OLIVEYARDS.
Ex 23:11 with thy vineyard and with thy o'.2132

oliveyards
Jos 24:13 vineyard and o' which ye planted 2132
1Sa 8:14 and your o', even the best of them, "
2Ki 5:26 and to receive garments, and o', "
Ne 5:11 vineyards, their o', and their houses, "
9:25 o', and fruit trees in abundance: "

Olympas (*o-lim'-pas*)
Ro 16:15 and O', and all the saints which 3632

Omar (*o'-mar*)
Ge 36:11 sons of Eliphaz were Teman, O', 201
15 duke Teman, duke O', duke Zepho, "
1Ch 1:36 The sons of Eliphaz; Teman, and O'. "

Omega (*o'-me-gah*)
Re 1: 8 I am Alpha and O', the beginning 5598
11 I am Alpha and O', the first and * "
21: 6 I am Alpha and O', the beginning "
22:13 I am Alpha and O', the beginning "

omer See also OMERS.
Ex 16:16 an o' for every man, according to 6016
18 when they did mete it with an o', "
32 Fill an o' of it to be kept for your * "
33 a pot, and put an o' full of manna* "
36 an o' is the tenth part of an ephah. "

omers
Ex 16:22 much bread, two o' for one man: 6016

omitted
M't 23:23 o'...weightier matters of the law, * 863

omnipotent
Re 19: 6 for the Lord God o' reigneth. *3841

Omri (*om'-ri*)
1Ki 16:16 made O',...captain of the host, king6018
17 O' went up from Gibbethon, and all "
21 him king; and half followed O'. "
22 people that followed O' prevailed "
22 so Tibni died, and O' reigned. "
23 began O' to reign over Israel, twelve"
25 O' wrought evil in the eyes of the "
27 rest of the acts of O' which he did "
28 O' slept with his fathers, and was "
29 began Ahab the son of O' to reign "
29 Ahab the son of O' reigned over "
30 Ahab the son of O' did evil in the "
2Ki 8:26 Athaliah, the daughter of O' king "
1Ch 7: 8 and O', and Jerimoth, and Abiah, "
9: 4 the son of Ammihud, the son of O', "
27:18 of Issachar, O' the son of Michael: "
2Ch 22: 2 was Athaliah the daughter of O'. "
Mic 6:16 the statutes of O' are kept, and all "

on See also ANON; ONWARD; THEREON; UPON; WHEREON.
Ge 2: 2 o' the seventh day God ended his work
2 he rested o' the seventh day from all
4:15 Cain, vengeance shall be taken o' him
16 in the land of Nod, o' the east of Eden.
6: 1 multiply o' the face of the earth, 5921
6 that he had made man o' the earth,
8: 4 o' the seventeenth day of the month,
5 month, o' the first day of the month.

Ge 8: 9 o' the face of the whole earth: 5921
14 o' the seven and twentieth day of the
20 offered burnt offerings o' the altar.
12: 8 unto a mountain o' the east of Beth-el,
8 Beth-el o' the west, and Hai o' the east:
9 going o' still toward the south.
13: 3 he went o' his journeys from the south
4 Abram called o' the name of the Lord.
14: 15 which is o' the left hand of Damascus.
17: 3 Abram fell o' his face: and God 5921
18: 5 your hearts; after that ye shall pass o':
16 with them to bring them o' the way.
19: 2 rise up early, and go o' your ways.
34 And it came to pass o' the morrow,
20: 9 brought o' me and o' my kingdom5921
21: 14 Hagar, putting it o' her shoulder, "
33 called there o' the name of the Lord,
22: 4 Then o' the third day Abraham lifted
9 him o' the altar upon the wood. 5921
24: 33 mine errand. And he said, Speak o'.
45 with her pitcher o' her shoulder; 5921
25: 26 and his hand took hold o' Esau's heel;
28: 12 behold a ladder set up o' the earth,
12 of God ascending and descending o' it.
20 bread to eat, and raiment to put o',
29: 1 Then Jacob went o' his journey, and
31: 22 it was told Laban o' the third day that
32: 1 Jacob went o' his way, and the angels
19 O' this manner shall ye speak unto
33: 4 fell o' his neck, and kissed him: 5921
14 and I will lead o' softly, according as
16 Esau returned that day o' his way
34: 25 And it came to pass o' the third day,
37: 23 of many colours that was o' him; 5921
38: 9 wife, that he spilled it o' the ground,
19 put o' the garments of her widowhood.
40: 14 think o' me when it shall be well with*
16 three white baskets o' my head: 5921
19 thee, and shall hang thee o' a tree; "
43: 31 himself, and said, Set o' bread.
32 And they set o' for him by himself,
44: 14 they fell before him o' the ground.
34 evil that shall come o' my father.
46: 29 fell o' his neck, and wept o' his neck5921
48: 16 and let my name be named o' them,
49: 26 they shall be o' the head of Joseph,
26 and o' the crown of the head of him
Ex 1: 10 Come o', let us deal wisely with them;*
2: 6 And she had compassion o' him, 5921
11 brethren, and looked o' their burdens:
4: 3 And he said, Cast it o' the ground.
3 he cast it o' the ground, and it became
6: 28 came to pass o' the day when the Lord
8: 4 the frogs shall come up both o' thee,*
12: 7 and strike it o' the two side posts 5921
7 o' the upper door post of the houses,"
11 your shoes o' your feet, and your staff
18 o' the fourteenth day of the month at
23 lintel, and o' the two side posts, 5921
29 of Pharaoh that sat o' his throne "
37 six hundred thousand o' foot that
14: 16 Israel shall go o' dry ground through
22, 29 o' their right hand, and o' their
15: 14 hold o' the inhabitants of Palestina.
19 children of Israel went o' dry land in
16: 1 o' the fifteenth day of the second
5 o' the sixth day they shall prepare
14 as the hoar frost o' the ground. 5921
22 o' the sixth day they gathered twice
26 but o' the seventh day, which is the
27 some of the people o' the seventh day
29 he giveth you o' the sixth day the
29 go out of his place o' the seventh day.
17: 5 Moses, Go o' before the people,
9 I will stand o' the top of the hill 5921
12 up his hands, the one o' the one side,
12 and the other o' the other side; and
18: 13 it came to pass o' the morrow, that
19: 4 how I bare you o' eagles' wings, 5921
16 to pass o' the third day in the morning,
18 mount Sinai was altogether o' a smoke,
20 Sinai, o' the top of the mount: * 413
21: 30 be laid o' him a sum of money, 5921
22: 30 o' the eighth day thou shalt give it me.
23: 12 o' the seventh day thou shalt rest:
24: 6 the blood he sprinkled o' the altar.5921
8 and sprinkled it o' the people, and "
17 devouring fire o' the top of the mount
25: 19 And make one cherub o' the one end, *
19 and the other cherub o' the other end:*
19 the cherubims o' the two ends thereof.
20 stretch forth their wings o' high,
26 that are o' the four feet thereof. 5921
26: 10 loops o' the edge of the one curtain "
13 And a cubit o' the one side,
13 and a cubit o' the other side of that
13 o' this side and o' that side, to cover
18 boards o' the south side southward.*
20 o' the north side there shall be
35 table o' the side of the tabernacle 5921
35 put the table o' the north side. "
27: 12 breadth of the court o' the west side
13 o' the east side eastward shall be fifty
15 o' the other side shall be hangings*
28: 9 grave o' them the names of the 5921
10 Six of their names o' one stone, "
10 names of the rest o' the other stone,"
23 put the two rings o' the two ends "
24 two rings which are o' the ends of 413
25 put them o' the shoulderpieces of 5921
27 them o' the two sides of the ephod "
37 thou shalt put it o' a blue lace, that"
29: 9 sons, and put the bonnets o' them:
30 shall put them o' seven days,
31: 17 and o' the seventh day he rested, and
32: 6 And they rose up early o' the morrow,

Ex 32: 15 tables were written o' both their sides;
15 o' the one side and o' the other were
22 people, that they are set o' mischief.
26 Who is o' the Lord's side? let him
30 And it came to pass o' the morrow,
33: 4 man did put o' him his ornaments.
19 will shew mercy o' whom I will shew
34: 21 but o' the seventh day thou shalt rest:
33 them, he put a vail o' his face. 5921
35: 2 o' the seventh day there shall be to
36: 11 he made loops of blue o' the edge*5921
37: 7 o' the two ends of the mercy seat; *
8 One cherub o' the end o' this side, and*
8 cherub o' the other end o' that side:*
8 the cherubims o' the two ends thereof.*
9 spread out their wings o' high,
38: 2 horns thereof o' the four corners *5921
7 the rings o' the sides of the altar, "
9 o' the south side southward the *
15 o' this hand and that hand, were
39: 7 o' the shoulders of the ephod, 5921
17 o' the ends of the breastplate. * "
18 put them o' the shoulderpieces of "
19 o' the two ends of the breastplate,* "
19 o' the side of the ephod inward. * 413
20 them o' the two sides of the ephod 5921
31 fasten it o' high upon the mitre; *
40: 2 O' the first day of the first month
17 o' the first day of the month, that the
20 set the staves o' the ark, and put 5921
24 o' the side of the tabernacle "
38 by day, and fire was o' it by night,*
Le 1: 8 o' the fire which is upon the altar:5921
9 the priest shall burn all o' the altar,
11 shall kill it o' the side of the altar 5921
12 order o' the wood that is o' the fire "
15 off his head, and burn it o' the altar;
16 it beside the altar o' the east part,
2: 12 not be burnt o' the altar for a sweet413
3: 4 kidneys, and the fat that is o' them,5921
5 Aaron's sons shall burn it o' the altar
5 upon the wood that is o' the fire: 5921
4: 12 burn him o' the wood with fire: "
5: 12 thereof, and burn it o' the altar,
6: 10 shall put o' his linen garment,
10 the burnt offering o' the altar, 5921
11 and put o' other garments, and
12 priest shall burn wood o' it every
7: 4 and the fat that is o' them, which 5921
16 o' the morrow also the remainder of it
17 sacrifice o' the third day shall be burnt
18 be eaten at all o' the third day,
8: 26 wafer, and put them o' the fat, 5921
28 o' the altar upon the burnt offering:
9: 1 came to pass o' the eighth day, that
14 upon the burnt offering o' the altar.
24 shouted, and fell o' their faces. 5921
11: 2 all the beasts that are o' the earth. "
27 manner of beasts that go o' all four,"
34 o' which such water cometh shall "
13: 3 priest shall look o' the plague in
3 the priest shall look o' him, and
5 shall look o' him the seventh day:
6 look o' him again the seventh day:
21, 26 But if the priest look o' it, and,
31 look o' the plague of the scall, and,
32 the priest shall look o' the plague:
34 the priest shall look o' the scall:
36 Then the priest shall look o' him:
51 look o' the plague o' the seventh
55 the priest shall look o' the plague,*
14: 9 it shall be o' the seventh day, that
10 o' the eighth day he shall take two
37 he shall look o' the plague, and,
15: 6 And he that sitteth o' any thing 5921
14 o' the eighth day he shall take to him
23 if it be o' her bed, or o' any thing 5921
29 o' the eighth day she shall take unto
16: 4 He shall put o' the holy linen coat,
4 flesh in water, and so put them o'.
10 goat, o' which the lot fell to be 5921
23 put o' when he went into the holy
24 and put o' his garments, and come
29 o' the tenth day of the month, ye shall
30 o' that day shall the priest make an
32 shall put o' the linen clothes, even
19: 6 day ye offer it, and o' the morrow:
7 if it be eaten at all o' the third day,
20: 25 thing that creepeth o' the ground,
21: 10 consecrated to put o' the garments,
22: 30 O' the same day it shall be eaten up;
23: 6 o' the fifteenth day of the same
11 o' the morrow after the sabbath the
21 shall proclaim o' the selfsame day,
27 o' the tenth day of this seventh month
35 O' the first day shall be an holy
36 o' the eighth day shall be an holy
39 o' the first day shall be a sabbath,
39 o' the eighth day shall be a sabbath.
40 take you o' the first day the boughs
24: 6 set them in two rows, six o' a row,
7 it may be o' the bread for a memorial,*
25: 9 of the jubile to sound o' the tenth
Nu 1: 1 o' the first day of the second month, in
18 congregation together o' the first day
2: 3 o' the east side toward the rising of
10 O' the south side shall be the
18 O' the west side shall be the standard
3: 10 shall wait o' their priest's office: *
13 o' the day that I smote all the firstborn
29, 35 pitch o' the side of the tabernacle5921
4: 12 skins, and shalt put them o' a bar: "
6: 9 o' the seventh day shall he shave it.
10 o' the eighth day he shall bring two
23 O' this wise ye shall bless the
7: 1 it came to pass o' the day that Moses

Nu 7: 11 their offering, each prince o' his day,
18 O' the second day Nathaneel the son
24 O' the third day Eliab the son of
30 O' the fourth day Elizur the son of
36 O' the fifth day Shelumiel the son of
42 O' the sixth day Eliasaph the son of
48 O' the seventh day Elishama the son
54 O' the eighth day offered Gamaliel the
60 O' the ninth day Abidan the son of
66 O' the tenth day Ahiezer the son of
72 O' the eleventh day Pagiel the son of
78 O' the twelfth day Ahira the son of
8: 17 o' the day that I smote every firstborn
9: 5 kept the passover o' the fourteenth
6 not keep the passover o' that day:
6 Moses and before Aaron o' that day:
15 o' the day that the tabernacle was
10: 5 the camps that lie o' the east parts
6 the camps that lie o' the south side
11 it came to pass o' the twentieth day
11: 31 it were a day's journey o' this side,
31 were a day's journey o' the other side,
14: 5 Moses and Aaron fell o' their faces5921
16: 27 Dathan, and Abiram, o' every side:
41 o' the morrow all the congregation
46 off the altar, and put o' incense, *
47 he put o' incense, and made an
17: 8 o' the morrow Moses went into the
19: 12 o' the seventh day he shall be clean:
12 purify himself with it o' the third day,
19 o' the third day, and o' the seventh
19 o' the seventh day he shall purify
20: 19 any thing else, go through o' my feet.
21: 13 and pitched o' the other side of Arnon,
22: 1 Moab o' this side Jordan by Jericho.*
24 vineyards, a wall being o' this side,
24 this side, and a wall o' that side.
31 down his head, and fell flat o' his face.
41 it came to pass o' the morrow, that*
23: 2 o' every altar a bullock and a ram.
14, 30 a bullock and a ram o' every altar.
24: 20 And when he looked o' Amalek,
21 he looked o' the Kenites, and took
28: 9 o' the sabbath day two lambs of the
25 o' the seventh day ye shall have an holy
29: 1 o' the first day of the month, ye shall
7 shall have o' the tenth day of this
12 o' the fifteenth day of the seventh
17 o' the second day ye shall offer twelve
20 And o' the third day eleven bullocks,
23 And o' the fourth day ten bullocks, two
26 And o' the fifth day nine bullocks, two
29 And o' the sixth day eight bullocks,
32 o' the seventh day seven bullocks, two
35 O' the eighth day ye shall have a
30: 12 them void o' the day he heard them;*
31: 19 and your captives o' the third day,
19 third day, and o' the seventh day.
24 wash your clothes o' the seventh day,
32: 19 with them o' yonder side Jordan,
19 to us o' this side Jordan eastward.
32 of our inheritance o' this side Jordan*
33: 3 o' the fifteenth day of the first month;
3 o' the morrow after the passover the
34: 4 of Akrabbim, and pass o' to Zin: *
4 and shall go o' to Hazar-addar, *
4 and pass o' to Azmon: *
9 And the border shall go o' to Ziphron,*
11 to Riblah, o' the east side of Ain;
15 their inheritance o' this side Jordan*
35: 5 city o' the east side two thousand *
5 and o' the south side two thousand*
5 and o' the west side two thousand*
5 and o' the north side two thousand*
14 give three cities o' this side Jordan,*
De 1: 1 unto all Israel o' this side Jordan*
3 month, o' the first day of the month,
5 O' this side Jordan, in the land of*
41 o' every man his weapons of war,
2: 28 only I will pass through o' my feet;
3: 8 the land that was o' this side Jordan,*
4: 15 o' the day that the Lord spake unto
17 of any beast that is o' the earth,
18 any thing that creepeth o' the ground,
41 severed three cities o' this side Jordan*
46 O' this side Jordan, in the valley over*
47 were o' this side Jordan toward the*
49 the plain o' this side Jordan eastward,*
6: 9 posts of thy house, and o' thy gates.*
7: 25 the silver or gold that is o' them, 5921
9: 10 o' them was written according to "
10: 2 I will write o' the tables the words "
4 he wrote o' the tables, according to "
11: 30 they not o' the other side Jordan, by*
16: 8 o' the seventh day shall be a solemn
21: 19 father and his mother lay hold o' him,
22 and thou hang him o' a tree: 5921
22: 5 man put o' a woman's garment:
6 way in any tree, or o' the ground, 5921
28 and lay hold o' her, and lie with her,
23: 11 shall be, when evening cometh o',
26: 7 voice, and looked o' our affliction, *
27: 2 o' the day when ye shall pass over
28: 1 set thee o' high above all nations 5921
2 these blessings shall come o' thee,*"
30: 7 and o' them that hate thee, which "
32: 11 them, beareth them o' her wings: "
13 ride o' the high places of the earth,"
22 set o' fire the foundations of the
41 mine hand take hold o' judgment;
33: 26 help, and in his excellency o' the sky.
Jos 1: 14 Moses gave you o' this side Jordan;*
15 servant gave you o' this side Jordan*
2: 10 that were o' the other side Jordan,*
19 his blood shall be o' our head, if any
3: 17 of the Lord stood firm o' dry ground

Jos 3:17 Israelites passed over o' dry ground,
4:14 O' that day the Lord magnified
19 up out of Jordan o' the tenth day
22 came over this Jordan o' dry land.
5: 1 were o' the side of Jordan westward,*
10 kept the passover o' the fourteenth
11 the old corn of the land o' the morrow
12 And the manna ceased o' the morrow
14 Joshua fell o' his face to the earth, 413
6: 7 Pass o', and compass the city, and
7 armed pass o' before the ark of the "
8 horns passed o' before the Lord, "
9 the priests going o', and blowing *
13 before the ark of the Lord went o' "
13 priests going o', and blowing with* "
15 And it came to pass o' the seventh day,
15 o' that day they compassed the city
7: 2 Beth-aven, o' the east side of Beth-el,
7 and dwelt o' the other side Jordan! *
8: 8 city, that ye shall set the city o' fire:
9 Beth-el and Ai, o' the west side of Ai:
11 and pitched o' the north side of Ai:
12 and Ai, o' the west side of the city.
13 host that was o' the north of the city,
13 liers in wait o' the west of the city,
19 and hasted and set the city o' fire.
22 some o' this side, and some o' that
24 all fallen o' the edge of the sword,*
29 he hanged o' a tree until eventide:5921
33 stood o' this side the ark and o' that
9: 1 kings which were o' this side Jordan,*
12 of our houses o' the day we came forth
17 came unto their cities o' the third day.
10:26 and hanged them o' five trees: 5921
32 Israel, which took it o' the second day,
35 they took it o' that day, and smote
11: 2 were o' the north of the mountains,
2 and in the borders of Dor o' the west,
3 Canaanite o' the east and o' the west,
12: 1 their land o' the other side Jordan*
1 Hermon, and all the plain o' the east:*
3 to the sea of Chinneroth o' the east,*
3 the plain, even the salt sea o' the east,*
7 smote o' this side Jordan o' the west,*
13:16 is o' the bank of the river Arnon, *5921
27 sea of Chinnereth o' the other side*
32 of Moab, o' the other side Jordan,*
14: 3 an half tribe o' the other side Jordan:*
9 And Moses sware o' that day, saying,
15: 3 and ascended up o' the south side
7 which is o' the south side of the river:
10 which is Chesalon, o' the north side,*
10 and passed o' to Timnah: *
16: 1 unto the water of Jericho o' the east,
5 inheritance o' the east side was *
6 the sea to Michmethah o' the north
6 passed by it o' the east to Janohah;
17: 5 which were o' the other side Jordan;*
7 went along o' the right hand unto* 413
8 Tappuah o' the border of Manasseh "
9 also was o' the north side of the river,
10 met together in Asher o' the north,
10 and in Issachar o' the east.
18: 5 shall abide in their coast o' the south,
5 shall abide in their coasts o' the north.
7 inheritance beyond Jordan o' the east,*
12 border o' the north side was from
12 to the side of Jericho o' the north side,
13 lieth o' the south side of the nether
15 and the border went out o' the west,*
16 in the valley of the giants o' the north,*
16 to the side of Jebusi o' the south, *
20 was the border of it o' the east side.
19:13 passeth o' along o' the east to *
14 it o' the north side to Hannathon:
27 goeth out to Cabul o' the left hand,
34 reacheth to Zebulun o' the south side,
34 reacheth to Asher o' the west side,
20: 8 o' the other side Jordan by Jericho*
22: 4 gave you o' the other side Jordan.*
7 brethren o' this side Jordan westward.*
20 o' all the congregation of Israel? *5921
24: 2 dwelt o' the other side of the flood*
8 which dwelt o' the other side Jordan;*
14 served o' the other side of the flood,*
15 were o' the other side of the flood,*
30 o' the north side of the hill of Gaash.
J'g 1: 8 of the sword, and set the city o' fire.
2: 9 o' the north side of the hill Gaash.
3:25 lord was fallen down dead o' the earth.
4:15 his chariot, and fled away o' his feet.
17 fled away o' his feet to the tent of
23 God subdued o' that day Jabin the
5: 1 Barak the son of Abinoam o' that day,
10 Speak, ye that ride o' white asses, ye
15 he was sent o' foot into the valley.*
17 Asher continued o' the sea shore, and*
30 colours of needlework o' both sides,
6:32 o' that day he called him Jerubbaal,
37 if the dew be o' the fleece only, 5921
38 for he rose up early o' the morrow,
40 there was dew o' all the ground. 5921
7: 1 were o' the north side of them, by
17 them, Look o' me, and do likewise:
18 also o' every side of all the camp,
25 to Gideon o' the other side Jordan.*
8:11 dwelt in tents o' the east of Nobah
21 that were o' their camels' necks.
26 that was o' the kings of Midian, 5921
34 of all their enemies o' every side:
9: 8 went forth o' a time to anoint a king
42 And it came to pass o' the morrow,
48 took it, and laid it o' his shoulder, 5921
49 and set the hold o' fire upon them;
10: 4 sons that rode o' thirty ass colts, 5921
8 that were o' the other side Jordan*

J'g 11:18 pitched o' the other side of Arnon,
12:14 o' threescore and ten ass colts: 5921
13: 5 no rasor shall come o' his head: * "
19 and Manoah and his wife looked o'.
20 And Manoah and his wife looked o' it,
20 and fell o' their faces to the 5921
14: 9 in his hands, and went o' eating,
15, 17 came to pass o' the seventh day,
18 of the city said unto him o' the seventh
15: 5 when he had set the brands o' fire,
18 and called o' the Lord, and said, 413
16:29 and o' which it was borne up, *5921
19: 1 o' the side of mount Ephraim,
5 o' the fourth day, when they arose
8 early in the morning o' the fifth day
9 to morrow get you early o' your way,
14 they passed o' and went their way;
29 a knife, and laid hold o' his concubine,
20:30 the children of Benjamin o' the third
48 also they set o' fire all the cities that
21: 4 And it came to pass o' the morrow,
19 which is o' the north side of Beth-el,
19 o' the east side of the highway that
19 Shechem, and o' the south of Lebonah.
Ru 1: 7 went o' the way to return unto the
2: 3 hap was to light o' a part of the field
9 Let thine eyes be o' the field that they
10 she fell o' her face, and bowed 5921
3:15 of barley, and laid it o' her: "
1Sa 1:11 look o' the affliction of thine handmaid,
2:26 And the child Samuel grew o', and
34 two sons, o' Hophni and Phinehas; 413
5: 3 of Ashdod arose early o' the morrow,
4 arose early o' the morrow morning,
5 tread o' the threshold of Dagon 5921
6: 4 plague was o' you all, and o' your lords.
7 o' which there hath come no yoke,5921
15 and put them o' the great stone: 413
7: 6 before the Lord, and fasted o' that day,
10 with a great thunder o' that day
9:20 days ago, set not thy mind o' them;
20 o' whom is all the desire of Israel?*
20 Is it not o' thee, and o' all thy father's*
27 o' before us, (and he passed o',)
10: 3 thou go o' forward from thence,
11: 2 O' this condition will I make a
7 fear of the Lord fell o' the people, 5921
11 And it was so o' the morrow, that Saul
12:11 hand of your enemies o' every side,
13: 5 sand which is o' the sea shore in 5921
14: 1 garrison, that is o' the other side.
4 there was a sharp rock o' the one side,
4 and a sharp rock o' the other side:
16 they went o' beating down one *
19 Philistines went o' and increased:
24 I may be avenged o' mine enemies.
32 calves, and slew them o' the ground:
40 he unto all Israel, Be ye o' one side,
40 my son will be o' the other side.
47 against all his enemies o' every side,
15:12 is gone about, and passed o', and
16 And he said unto him, Say o'.
18 the Lord sent thee o' a journey, and
16: 6 were come, that he looked o' Eliab,
7 Look not o' his countenance, or 413
7 or o' the height of his stature;
7 looketh o' the outward appearance,
7 but the Lord looketh o' the heart.
16 who is a cunning player o' an harp:
17: 3 stood o' a mountain o' the one side,413
3 stood o' a mountain o' the other "
41 Philistine came o' and drew near
18:10 And it came to pass o' the morrow,
24 saying, O' this manner spake David.
19:23 and he went o', and prophesied,
20:20 shoot three arrows o' the side thereof,
21 the arrows are o' this side of thee,
27 And it came to pass o' the morrow,
41 fell o' his face to the ground, and
21:13 scrabbled o' the doors of the gate, 5921
22:18 and slew o' that day fourscore and five
23:19 which is o' the south of Jeshimon?
21 Lord; for ye have compassion o' me.
24 the plain o' the south of Jeshimon. 413
26 Saul went o' this side of the mountain,
26 his men o' that side of the mountain:
24: 7 out of the cave, and went o' his way.
25:13 men, Gird ye o' every man his sword.
13 they girded o' every man his sword;
13 and David also girded o' his sword:
14 our master; and he railed o' them.*
18 of figs, and laid them o' asses. 5921
19 Go o' before me; behold, I come
20 it was so, as she rode o' the ass, 5921
23 and fell before David o' her face, "
41 bowed herself o' her face to the earth,*
26:13 and stood o' the top of an hill afar 5921
25 So David went o' his way, and Saul*
27:11 Lest they should tell o' us, saying,5921
28: 8 himself, and put o' other raiment,
20 fell straightway all along o' the earth,*
22 strength; when thou goest o' thy way.
29: 2 Philistines passed o' by hundreds,
2 his men passed o' in the rereward
30: 1 were come to Ziklag o' the third day,
2 them away, and went o' their way.*
31: 7 were o' the other side of the valley,
7 that were o' the other side Jordan,*
8 And it came to pass o' the morrow,
2Sa 1: 2 It came even to pass o' the third day,
10 the bracelet that was o' his arm, 5921
11 Then David took hold o' his clothes,
24 who put o' ornaments of gold upon
2:13 the one o' the one side of the pool.5921
13 other o' the other side of the pool. "
21 lay thee hold o' one of the young men,

2Sa 2:25 and stood o' the top of an hill. 5921
3:12 sent messengers to David o' his behalf,
29 Let it rest o' the head of Joab, *5921
29 Joab, and o' all his father's house:*413
29 is a leper, or that leaneth o' a staff,
29 or that falleth o' the sword, or that*
4: 5 who lay o' a bed at noon. *
7 lay o' his bed in his bedchamber, *5921
5: 8 David said o' that day, Whosoever
10 And David went o', and grew great,*
6: 5 o' all manner of instruments made of*
5 even o' harps, and o' psalteries, and*
5 o' timbrels,...o' cornets,...o' cymbals.*
8: 7 were o' the servants of Hadadezer, 413
9: 3 yet a son, which is lame o' his feet.
6 come unto David, he fell o' his face,5921
13 table; and was lame o' both his feet.
11:13 at even he went out to lie o' his bed
12:18 And it came to pass o' the seventh day,
30 and it was set o' David's head. 5921
13: 5 Lay thee down o' thy bed, and make"
19 Tamar put ashes o' her head, and "
19 of divers colours that was o' her, "
19 and laid her hand o' her head, "
19 her head, and went o' crying. *
31 his garments, and lay o' the earth;
14: 2 and put o' now mourning apparel,
3 and speak o' this manner unto him.
4 she fell o' her face to the ground, 5921
9 be o' me, and o' my father's house: "
12 lord the king. And he said, Say o'.
14 and are as water spilt o' the ground,
22 Joab fell to the ground o' his face, 413
26 because the hair was heavy o' him,5921
30 hath barley there; go and set it o' fire.
30 Absalom's servants set the field o' fire.
31 have thy servants set my field o' fire?
33 bowed himself o' his face to the 5921
15: 6 And o' this manner did Absalom to all
18 his servants passed o' beside him;
18 Gath, passed o' before the king.
33 If thou passest o' with me, then
16: 2 be for the king's household to ride o';
6 were o' his right hand and o' his left.
12 the Lord will look o' mine affliction,
13 Shimei went along o' the hill's side
17:12 as the dew falleth o' the ground: 5921
19:40 Then the king went o' to Gilgal,
40 and Chimham went o' with him: *
20: 8 Joab's garment that he had put o' was
13 all the people went o' after Joab,
21:10 birds of the air to rest o' them 5921
20 that had o' every hand six fingers,
20 and o' every foot six toes, four and
22: 4 I will call o' the Lord, who is worthy*
49 also hast lifted me up o' high *
23: 1 man who was raised up o' high,
24: 5 in Aroer, o' the right side of the city
20 servants coming o' toward him:
20 the king o' his face upon the ground.*
1Ki 1:20 shall sit o' the throne of my lord 5921
27 who should sit o' the throne of my lord
46 Solomon sitteth o' the throne of 5921
48 hath given one to sit o' my throne "
50 caught hold o' the horns of the altar.
51 caught hold o' the horns of the altar,
2: 4 a man o' the throne of Israel. 5921
5 and in his shoes that were o' his feet.
14 unto thee. And she said, Say o'.
15 that all Israel set their faces o' me,5921
16 And she said unto him, Say o'.
19 her, and sat down o' his throne, 5921
19 and she sat o' his right hand.
20 said unto her, Ask o', my mother:
24 o' the throne of David my father, 5921
28 caught hold o' the horns of the altar.
37 be, that o' the day thou goest out,
42 certain, o' the day thou goest out,
3: 6 him a son to sit o' his throne, as 5921
4:24 all the region o' this side the river,
24 all the kings o' this side the river:
24 peace o' all sides round about him.
29 the sand that is o' the sea shore. 5921
5: 3 which were about him o' every side,
4 God hath given me rest o' every side,
6:10 o' the house with timber of cedar,
15 covered them o' the inside with wood,
16 twenty cubits o' the sides of the house,
7: 3 beams, that lay o' forty five pillars,*
9 so o' the outside toward the great 5704
28 work of the bases was o' this manner:
29 o' the borders that were between 5921
35 o' the top of the base the ledges "
36 o' the plates of the ledges thereof, "
36 o' the borders thereof, he graved "
39 bases o' the right side of the house, "
39 five o' the left side of the house: "
39 he set the sea o' the right side of the
41 were o' the top of the two pillars; 5921
43 bases, and ten lavers o' the bases; "
49 of pure gold, five o' the right side,
49 and five o' the left, before the oracle,
8:20 and sit o' the throne of Israel, 5921
23 heaven above, or o' earth beneath, "
25 sight to sit o' the throne of Israel; "
27 will God indeed dwell o' the earth? "
50 they may have compassion o' them:
54 arose...from kneeling o' his knees 5921
66 O' the eighth day he sent the people
9:26 o' the shore of the Red sea, in the 5921
10: 9 to set thee o' the throne of Israel: "
19 and there were stays o' either side
19 o' the place of the seat, and two *413
20 twelve lions stood there o' the one side
20 and o' the other upon the six steps:
11:30 the new garment that was o' him, 5921

1Ki 12:32 o' the fifteenth day of the month, like
13: 4 from the altar, saying, Lay hold o' him.
14:23 o' every high hill, and under 5921
16:11 soon as he sat o' his throne, that he "
24 and built o' the hill, and called the 853
18: 7 he knew him, and fell o' his face, 5921
23, 23 and lay it o' wood, and put no fire "
24 And call ye o' the name of your gods,
24 and I will call o' the name of the Lord:
25 and call o' the name of your gods, but
26 and called o' the name of Baal from
33 pieces, and laid him o' the wood, 5921
33 pour it o' the burnt sacrifice and on "
39 people saw it, they fell o' their faces: "
46 the hand of the Lord was o' Elijah; 413
19: 6 there was a cake baken o' the coals,
15 Go, return o' thy way to the wilderness
20:11 Let not him that girdeth o' his harness
20 king of Syria escaped o' an horse 5921
31 put sackcloth o' our loins, and rope
32 So they girded sackcloth o' their loins,
32 and put ropes o' their heads, and
21: 9, 12 set Naboth o' high among the
22:10 of Judah sat each o' his throne, 5921
10 having put o' their robes, *
19 I saw the Lord sitting o' his throne, 5921
19 standing by him o' his right hand and
19 his right hand and o' his left.
20 And one said o' this manner,
20 and another said o' that manner.
24 and smote Micaiah o' the cheek, 5921
30 battle; but put thou o' thy robes.
2Ki 1: 4, 6 that bed o' which thou art gone up,*
9 behold, he sat o' the top of an hill. 5921
13 and fell o' his knees before Elijah, "
16 that bed o' which thou art gone up,*
2: 6 leave thee. And they two went o'.
8 they two went over o' dry ground.
11 as they still went o', and talked,
15 spirit of Elijah doth rest o' Elisha. 5921
24 he turned back, and looked o' them,*
3:11 water o' the hands of Elijah. 5921
21 that were able to put o' armour,
22 water o' the other side as red as
25 o' every good piece of land cast every
4: 8 And it fell o' a day, that Elisha passed
10 little chamber, I pray thee, o' the wall;
11 it fell o' a day, that he came thither
18 it fell o' a day, that he went out to his
20 he sat o' her knees till noon, and 5921
21 him o' the bed of the man of God,
31 Gehazi passed o' before them, and
38 Set o' the great pot, and seethe
5: 2 and she waited o' Naaman's wife.
11 and call o' the name of the Lord his
18 and he leaneth o' my hand, and I 5921
6:29 I said unto her o' the next day, Give
31 head of Elisha...shall stand o' him 5921
7: 2 lord o' whose hand the king leaned "
17 the lord o' whose hand he leaned to "
8:12 their strong holds wilt thou set o' fire,
15 And it came to pass o' the morrow,
15 in water, and spread it o' his face, 5921
9: 3 box of oil, and pour it o' his head, "
6 and he poured the oil o' his head, 413
13 it under him o' the top of the stairs, "
17 watchman o' the tower in Jezreel, 5921
18 went one o' horseback to meet him,
19 sent out a second o' horseback, which
32 and said, Who is o' my side? who? 854
33 o' the wall, and o' the horses. 413
10: 3 and set him o' his father's throne, 5921
15 he lighted o' Jehonadab the son of 854
30 shall sit o' the throne of Israel. 5921
11: 5 of you that enter in o' the sabbath shall
7 of all you that go forth o' the sabbath,
9 that were to come in o' the sabbath,
9 that should go out o' the sabbath,
16 they laid hands o' her; and she went
19 he sat o' the throne of the kings. 5921
12: 9 o' the right side as one cometh into
15 money to be bestowed o' workmen:*
13:21 revived, and stood up o' his feet. 5921
23 had compassion o' them, and had
14: 4 and burnt incense o' the high places.*
20 And they brought him o' horses: *5921
15: 4 burnt incense still o' the high places.*
12 shall sit o' the throne of Israel *5921
16: 4 o' the hills, and under every green "
14 put it o' the north side of the altar. "
18:14 which thou puttest o' me will I bear. "
20 o' whom dost thou trust, that thou "
21 o' which if a man lean, it will go into*"
21 of Egypt unto all that trust o' him. "
23 be able o' thy part to set riders upon
24 put thy trust o' Egypt for chariots 5921
26 of the people that are o' the wall. "
27 me to the men which sit o' the wall, "
19:22 and lifted up thine eyes o' high?
26 as the grass o' the house tops, and as
20: 5 o' the third day thou shalt go up unto
7 laid it o' the boil, and he recovered. 5921
23: 8 which were o' a man's left hand at "
12 were o' the top of the upper chamber "
13 were o' the right hand of the mount
25: 3 o' the ninth day of the fourth month
8 o' the seventh day of the month,
27 o' the seven and twentieth day of the
1Ch 4:10 And Jabez called o' the God of Israel,
6:32 then they waited o' their office
39 Asaph, who stood o' his right hand, 5921
44 of Merari stood o' the left hand: "
49 offering, and o' the altar of incense,*"
78 o' the other side Jordan by Jericho,*"
78 o' the east of Jordan, were given them
10: 5 fell likewise o' the sword, and died. 5921

1Ch 10: 8 And it came to pass o' the morrow,
12:18 Thine are we, David, and o' thy side,
37 And o' the other side of Jordan, of the
40 brought bread o' asses, and o' camels,
40 and o' mules, and o' oxen, and meat,
13: 6 Lord,...whose name is called o' it.*
14: 2 his kingdom was lifted up o' high,
15:20 with psalteries o' Alamoth; *5921
21 harps o' the Sheminith to excel. * "
16: 7 o' that day David delivered first this
18: 7 were o' the servants of Hadarezer, 5921
20: 6 six o' each hand, and six o' each foot:
21:17 be o' me and o' my father's house:*
17 not o' thy people, that they should be
22:18 he not given you rest o' every side?
23:28 was to wait o' the sons of Aaron
31 the new moons, and o' the set feasts,
26:30 them of Israel o' this side Jordan *
29:15 our days o' the earth are as a 5921
21 the Lord, o' the morrow after that day,
22 and drink before the Lord o' that day
23 Solomon sat o' the throne of the 5921
25 o' any king before him in Israel. "
2Ch 2: 4 o' the sabbaths, and o' the new moons,
4 and o' the solemn feasts of the Lord
3: 7 and graved cherubims o' the walls. 5921
13 they stood o' their feet, and their "
15 chapiter that was o' the top of each "
16 put them o' the heads of the pillars; "
16 and put them o' the chains.
17 the pillars...one o' the right hand,
17 and the other o' the left; and called
17 name of that o' the right hand Jachin,
17 and the name of that o' the left Boaz.
4: 6 lavers, and put five o' the right hand,
6 and five o' the left, to wash in them:
7 candlesticks...five o' the right hand,
7 and five o' the left.
8 ten tables,...five o' the right side,
8 and five o' the left.
10 he set the sea o' the right side of the
12 were o' the top of the two pillars, 5921
12 which were o' the top of the pillars; "
13 pomegranates o' the two wreaths;*
13 rows of pomegranates o' each wreath,*
6:10 and am set o' the throne of Israel, 5921
18 deed dwell with men o' the earth? "
7: 6 the priests waited o' their offices:*
10 o' the three and twentieth day of the
22 of Egypt, and laid hold o' other gods,
8:12 offerings unto the Lord o' the altar 5921
13 o' the sabbaths, and o' the new moons,
13 and o' the solemn feasts, three times
9: 8 in thee to set thee o' his throne, 5921
18 stays o' each side of the sitting place,
19 twelve lions stood there o' the one side
19 and o' the other upon the six steps.
10:12 came to Rehoboam o' the third day,*
12 Come again to me o' the third day. *
11:12 strong, having Judah...o' his side.*
14: 7 he hath given us rest o' every side.
11 for we rest o' thee, and in thy 5921
16: 7 thou hast relied o' the king of Syria, "
7 and not relied o' the Lord thy God, "
8 because thou didst rely o' the Lord, "
17:19 These waited o' the king, beside
18: 9 sat either of them o' his throne, 5921
18 o' [5921] his right hand and o' his left.
24 Behold, thou shalt see o' that day
29 battle; but put thou o' thy robes.
20: 2 from beyond the sea o' this side Syria;*
19 of Israel with a loud voice o' high.*
26 And o' the fourth day they assembled
29 of God was o' all the kingdoms 5921
23: 4 part of you entering o' the sabbath,
8 that were to come in o' the sabbath,
8 that were to go out o' the sabbath:
15 So they laid hands o' her; and when*
24:25 slew him o' his bed, and he died: 5921
26:15 o' the towers and upon the bulwarks, "
27: 3 o' the wall of Ophel he built much.
28: 4 o' the hills, and under every green 5921
29:17 began o' the first day of the first month
17 o' the eighth day of the month came
21 offer them o' the altar of the Lord. 5921
22 the blood, and sprinkled it o' the altar:
30:15 o' the fourteenth day of the second
32:15 nor persuade you o' this manner,
17 to rail o' the Lord God of Israel,
18 of Jerusalem that were o' the wall, 5921
22 other, and guided them o' every side.
33:14 o' the west side of Gihon, in the valley,
34: 4 that were o' high above them,
35: 1 o' the fourteenth day of the first
36:15 o' his people, and o' his dwelling 5921
Ezr 4:10 the rest that are o' this side the river,*
11 the men o' this side the river, and*
16 have no portion o' this side the river.*
5: 3, 6 governor o' this side the river, and*
6 which were o' this side the river, sent*
8 the walls, and this work goeth fast o',
6:13 Tatnai, governor o' this side the river,*
15 o' the third day of the month Adar, 5705
7: 9 and o' the first day of the fifth month
8:31 o' the twelfth day of the first month,
33 Now o' the fourth day was the silver
36 the governors o' this side the river:*
10: 9 o' the twentieth day of the month;
Ne 2:14 went o' to the gate of the fountain, 413
3: 7 of the governor o' this side the river,*
13 cubits o' the wall unto the dung gate.*
4:13 the wall, and o' the higher places,*
17 They which builded o' the wall, and*
22 a guard to us, and labour o' the day,*
6:14 and o' the prophetess Noadiah, and*
8: 4 and Maaseiah, o' his right hand; 5921

Ne 8: 4 and o' his left hand, Pedaiah, and
13 And o' the second day were gathered
18 and o' the eighth day was a solemn
9:10 Pharaoh, and o' all his servants,
10 and o' all the people of his land:
11 the midst of the sea o' the dry land;
32 that hath come upon us, o' our kings,
32 o' our princes, and o' our priests, and
32 o' our prophets, and o' our fathers,
32 and o' all thy people, since the time
10:31 victuals o' the sabbath day to sell,
31 o' the sabbath, or o' the holy day:
12:31 went o' the right hand upon the wall
13: 1 O' that day they read in the book of
15 treading wine presses o' the sabbath,
15 into Jerusalem o' the sabbath day;
16 sold o' the sabbath unto the children
19 be brought in o' the sabbath day.
21 ye do so again, I will lay hands o' you.
21 came they no more o' the sabbath.
Es 1: 2 Ahasuerus sat o' the throne of his 5921
10 O' the seventh day, when the heart of
11 beauty: for she was fair to look o'.
2:14 o' the morrow she returned into the
21 to lay hand o' the king Ahasuerus.
23 they were both hanged o' a tree: 5921
3: 6 scorn to lay hands o' Mordecai alone;
12 o' the thirteenth day of the first
4: 1 and put o' sackcloth with ashes,
5: 1 Now it came to pass o' the third day,
1 Esther put o' her royal apparel,
6: 1 O' that night could not the king sleep,
2 to lay hand o' the king Ahasuerus.
4 to hang Mordecai o' the gallows 5921
9 bring him o' horseback through
11 brought him o' horseback through*
7: 2 said unto Esther o' the second day
10 hanged Haman o' the gallows 5921
8: 1 O' that day did the king Ahasuerus
9 Sivan, o' the three and twentieth day
10 sent letters by posts o' horseback,
10 riders o' mules, camels, and young
13 avenge themselves o' their enemies.
14 hastened and pressed o' by the king's
9: 1 o' the thirteenth day of the same,
2 to lay hand o' such as sought their
10 o' the spoil laid they not their hand.
11 O' that day the number of those that
15 o' the fourteenth day also of the
15 o' the prey they laid not their hand.
16 they laid not their hands o' the prey.
17 O' the thirteenth day of the month
17 o' the fourteenth day of the same
18 together o' the thirteenth day thereof,
18 and o' the fourteenth day thereof;
18 and o' the fifteenth day of the same
25 should be hanged o' the gallows. 5921
Job 1:10 about all that he hath o' every side?
4:13 when deep sleep falleth o' men, 5921
5:11 set up o' high those that be low;
9:11 he passeth o' also, but I perceive
13:13 and let come o' me what will.
15:26 runneth upon him, even o' his neck,*
27 maketh collops of fat o' his flanks.‡
16:16 and o' my eyelids is the shadow of 5921
19 heaven, and my record is o' high.
17: 9 righteous also shall hold o' his way,
18:11 shall make him afraid o' every side,
19:10 He hath destroyed me o' every side,
21: 3 and after that I have spoken, mock o'.
6 trembling taketh hold o' my flesh.
23: 9 O' the left hand, where he doth work,
9 he hideth himself o' the right hand,
24:20 the worm shall feed sweetly o' him;
27:17 but the just shall put it o', and the
20 Terrors take hold o' him as waters,*
29: 9 and laid their hand o' their mouth.
14 I put o' righteousness, and it
24 If I laughed o' them, they believed 413
31: 2 of the Almighty from o' high?
36: 2 I have yet to speak o' God's behalf.
7 with kings are they o' the throne;*
16 which should be set o' thy table
17 judgment and justice take hold o' thee.
37: 6 to the snow, Be thou o' the earth;
39:18 time she lifteth up herself o' high,
21 goeth o' to meet the armed men. *
27 command, and make her nest o' high?
28 She dwelleth and abideth o' the rock,
40:12 Look o' every one that is proud, and
Ps 4: *title* To the chief Musician o' Neginoth,
6: *title* To the chief Musician o' Neginoth
7: 7 therefore return thou o' high.
12: 8 The wicked walk o' every side, when
21: 3 a crown of pure gold o' his head.
22: 8 He trusted o' the Lord that he * 413
25: 3 that wait o' thee be ashamed: *
5 o' thee do I wait all the day. *
21 preserve me; for I wait o' thee. *
27:14 Wait o' the Lord: be of good *
14 heart: wait, I say, o' the Lord. *
31:13 fear was o' every side: while they took
35:17 Lord, how long wilt thou look o'?
37:34 Wait o' the Lord, and keep his *
48: 2 mount Zion, o' the sides of the north,
49:14 the grave; death shall feed o' them;*
52: 9 and I will wait o' thy name; for *
54: *title* To the chief Musician o' Neginoth,
55: *title* To the chief Musician o' Neginoth,
57: 4 even among them that are set o' fire,
63: 6 meditate o' thee in the night watches.
65:12 the little hills rejoice o' every side.*
66: 6 went through the flood o' foot:
67: *title* To the chief Musician o' Neginoth,
68:18 Thou hast ascended o' high, thou
21 one as goeth o' still in his trespasses,

Ps 68:25 the players o' instruments followed*
69: 6 Let not them that wait o' thee, O *
29 salvation, O God, set me up o' high.
71:21 and comfort me o' every side. *
75: 5 Lift not up your horn o' high:
76: *title* To the chief Musician o' Neginoth,
78:53 And he led them o' safely so that *
79: 1 they have laid Jerusalem o' heaps.
81: 3 appointed, o' our solemn feast day.
82: 5 they walk o' in darkness: all the *
83:14 the flame setteth the mountains o' fire;
87: 7 players o' instruments shall be there:*
91:14 I will set him o' high, because he hath
92:11 shall see my desire o' mine enemies,
93: 4 The Lord o' high is mightier than
104:32 He looketh o' the earth, and it
107:41 Yet setteth he the poor o' high from
113: 5 Lord our God, who dwelleth o' high,
118: 6 The Lord is o' my side; I will not fear:
119:59 I thought o' my ways, and turned my
84 thou execute judgment o' them that
143 and anguish have taken hold o' me:
124: 1, 2 been the Lord who was o' our side,
142: 4 I looked o' my right hand, and beheld,
143: 5 I meditate o' all thy works;
5 I muse o' the work of thy hands.
Pr 4:25 Let thine eyes look right o', and let
5: 5 to death; her steps take hold o' hell.
9:14 o' a seat in the high places of the 5921
15 who go right o' their ways:
14:21 he that hath mercy o' the poor, happy
31 honoureth him hath mercy o' the poor.
15:14 mouth of fools feedeth o' foolishness.
20:22 but wait o' the Lord, and he shall‡
22: 3 simple pass o', and are punished.
27:12 simple pass o', and are punished.
18 he that waiteth o' his master
Ec 2: 3 and to lay hold o' folly, till I might see
11 I looked o' all the works that my hands
11 o' the labour that I had laboured to do:
4: 1 o' the side of their oppressors there
Ca 2:12 The flowers appear o' the earth; the
3: 1 By night o' my bed I sought him 5921
5: 3 off my coat; how shall I put it o'?
Isa 7:25 o' all hills that shall be digged with*
9:17 have mercy o' their fatherless and
20 he shall snatch o' the right hand, 5921
20 and he shall eat o' the left hand, "
10:12 upon mount Zion and o' Jerusalem,
11: 8 shall play o' the hole of the asp, 5921
8 put his hand o' the cockatrice' den. "
13:18 have no pity o' the fruit of the womb;
14: 1 the Lord will have mercy o' Jacob,
15: 2 o' all their heads shall be baldness,
3 o' the tops of their houses, and in 5921
16:12 Moab is weary o' the high place, "
18: 3 the world, and dwellers o' the earth,
3 lifteth up an ensign o' the mountains;
22:16 him out a sepulchre o' high,
24:18 the windows from o' high are open,
21 of the high ones that are o' high,
25: 6 fat things, a feast of wine o' the lees,
6 of wines o' the lees well refined.
26: 3 peace, whose mind is stayed o' thee:
5 down them that dwell o' high; 4791
27:11 the women come, and set them o' fire;
11 them will not have mercy o' them,*
28: 1 are o' the head of the fat valleys of
4 is o' the head of the fat valley, 5921
20 that a man can stretch himself o' it:
30:17 and as an ensign o' an hill. 5921
31: 1 and stay o' horses, and trust in "
4 the young lion roaring o' his prey, "
32:15 be poured upon us from o' high,
19 shall hail, coming down o' the forest;*
33: 5 exalted; for he dwelleth o' high:
16 He shall dwell o' high: his place of
36: 5 now o' whom dost thou trust, that5921
6 of this broken reed, o' Egypt; * "
8 be able o' thy part to set riders upon
9 put thy trust o' Egypt for chariots5921
11 of the people that are o' the wall. "
37:23 and lifted up thine eyes o' high? the
27 as the grass o' the housetops, and as
40:26 Lift up your eyes o' high, and
42:25 it hath set him o' fire round about,
44:20 He feedeth o' ashes: a deceived heart
47: 1 of Babylon, sit o' the ground: 5921
48:14 he will do his pleasure o' Babylon, and
14 and his arm shall be o' the Chaldeans.
49:10 hath mercy o' them shall lead them,
15 compassion o' the son of her womb?
18 bind them o' thee, as a bride doeth.*
51: 5 and o' mine arm shall they trust. 413
9 put o' strength, O arm of the Lord;
52: 1 awake; put o' thy strength, O Zion;
1 put o' thy beautiful garments, O
53: 6 hath laid o' him the iniquity of us all.
54: 3 forth o' the right hand and o' the left;
8 kindness will I have mercy o' thee,
10 the Lord that hath mercy o' thee.
56: 2 the son of man that layeth hold o' it;*
57:17 he went o' frowardly in the way
58: 4 your voice to be heard o' high.
13 doing thy pleasure o' my holy day;
59:17 For he put o' righteousness as a
17 put o' the garments of vengeance
60: 7 up with acceptance o' mine altar, 5921
10 in my favour have I had mercy o' thee.
63: 7 all that the Lord hath bestowed o' us,
7 which he hath bestowed o' them
Jer 4: 7 destroyer of the Gentiles is o' his way;
5: 9, 29 soul be avenged o' such a nation
6:23 They shall lay hold o' bow and spear;
25 of the enemy and fear is o' every side.
7:29 up a lamentation o' high places; 5921
Jer 8:13 there shall be no grapes o' the vine,
13 nor figs o' the fig tree, and the leaf
21 astonishment hath taken hold o' me.
9: 9 my soul be avenged o' such a nation
10:25 the families that call not o' thy name:
11:20 let me see thy vengeance o' them: for
12:15 and have compassion o' them, and will
13: 2 girdle...and put it o' my loins. *5921
27 thine abominations o' the hills in "
15:10 I have neither lent o' usury, nor men
10 nor men have lent to me o' usury; yet
17:11 As the partridge sitteth o' eggs, and*
21 bear no burden o' the sabbath day,
22 out of your houses o' the sabbath day,
24 gates of this city o' the sabbath day,
25 riding in chariots and o' horses, they,
27 gates of Jerusalem o' the sabbath day;
18: 3 he wrought a work o' the wheels. 5921
20: 3 And it came to pass o' the morrow,
10 defaming of many, fear o' every side.
10 and we shall take our revenge o' him.
12 let me see thy vengeance o' them:
22: 4 riding in chariots and o' horses, he,
23:12 they shall be driven o', and fall
25:29 to bring evil o' the city which is called*
30 The Lord shall roar from o' high,
30: 6 man with his hands o' his loins, 5921
18 and have mercy o' his dwellingplaces;
31:29 children's teeth are set o' edge.
30 grape, his teeth shall be set o' edge.
32:29 shall come and set fire o' this city,*
33:26 to return, and have mercy o' them.
36:22 there was a fire o' the hearth burning*
23 into the fire that was o' the hearth,*413
23 in the fire that was o' the hearth.*5921
38:22 Thy friends have set thee o', and
43: 3 of Neriah setteth thee o' against us,
12 as a shepherd putteth o' his garment;
46: 4 spears, and put o' the brigandines.
48:11 and he hath settled o' his lees, and 413
49:23 there is sorrow o' the sea; it cannot be
24 flee, and fear hath seized o' her:
29 cry unto them, Fear is o' every side.
50: 6 turned them away o' the mountains:
19 he shall feed o' Carmel and Bashan,
52:23 and six pomegranates o' a side;
La 1: 2 and her tears are o' her cheeks: 5921
2:21 young and the old lie o' the ground in
4: 6 moment, and no hands stayed o' her.*
Eze 1: 8 their wings o' their four sides; 5921
10 the face of a lion, o' the right side: 413
10 had the face of an ox o' the left side;
23 two, which covered o' this side,
23 two, which covered o' that side,
3:23 of Chebar: and I fell o' my face. 5921
4: 6 lie again o' thy right side, and thou "
7:16 and shall be o' the mountains like 413
11:23 which is o' the east side of the city.
16:11 thy hands, and a chain o' thy neck.5921
12 I put a jewel o' thy forehead, and* "
15 fornications o' every one that passed
33 they may come unto thee o' every side
18: 2 children's teeth are set o' edge?
19: 8 nations set against him o' every side
21:16 o' the right hand, or o' the left, *
23: 5 doted o' her lovers, o' the Assyrians413
7 and with all o' whom she doted:
22 bring them against thee o' every side;
24: 3 Set o' a pot, set it o', and also pour
10 Heap o' wood, kindle the fire, consume
17 put o' thy shoes upon thy feet, and*
25: 9 his cities which are o' his frontiers,
26:17 their terror to be o' all that haunt it!
28:23 by the sword upon her o' every side;
31: 4 the deep set him o' high with her rivers*
33:32 and can play well o' an instrument:
36: 3 and swallowed you up o' every side,
37:21 and will gather them o' every side,
39: 6 I will send a fire o' Magog, and among
9 shall set o' fire and burn the weapons,*
11 the passengers o' the east of the sea:
17 gather yourselves o' every side to my
40: 2 was as the frame of a city o' the south.
5 a wall o' the outside of the house
10 three o' this side, and three o' that
10 measure o' this side and o' that side.
12 was one cubit o' this side, and the
12 space was one cubit o' that side:
12 chambers were six cubits o' this side,
12 and six cubits o' that side.
21 three o' this side and three o' that side;
26 it had palm trees, one o' this side,
26 and another o' that side, upon the
34, 37 o' this side, and o' that side:
39 the gate were two tables o' this side,
39 and two tables o' that side, to slay
40 o' the other side, which was at the 413
41 Four tables were o' this side, and four
41 tables o' that side, by the side of the
48 of the porch, five cubits o' this side,
48 and five cubits o' that side:
48 the gate was three cubits o' this side,
48 and three cubits o' that side.
49 pillars by the posts, one o' this side,
49 and another o' that side.
41: 1 posts, six cubits broad o' the one side,
1 and six cubits broad o' the other side,
2 door were five cubits o' the one side,
2 and five cubits o' the other side: and
5, 10 round about the house o' every side.
15 o' the one side and o' the other side,
16 round about o' their three stories,
19 toward the palm tree o' the one side,
19 toward the palm tree o' the other side:
20 made, and o' the wall of the temple.*
25 o' them, o' the doors of the temple, 413
Eze 41:26 o' the one side and o' the other side,
26 o' the sides of the porch, and upon 413
42: 7 court o' the forepart of the chambers,*
9 was the entry o' the east side, as one
14 and shall put o' other garments,
43:20 and put it o' the four horns of it, 5921
20 and o' the four corners of the settle,413
22 o' the second day thou shalt offer a kid
44:19 they shall put o' other garments;
45: 7 o' the one side and o' the other side of
46: 1 but o' the sabbath it shall be opened,
12 offerings, as he did o' the sabbath day:
19 was a place o' the two sides westward.
47: 2 there ran out waters o' the right side.
2 trees o' the one side and o' the other.
12 o' this side and o' that side, shall
48:16 o' the east side four thousand and
30 goings out of the city o' the north side,
Da 3:27 the smell of fire had passed o' them.
6:14 set his heart o' Daniel to deliver 5922
7: 5 it raised up itself o' one side, and it
8: 5 west o' the face of the whole earth,*
18 I was in a deep sleep o' my face *5921
10: 9 was I in a deep sleep o' my face, and"
11:17 she shall not stand o' his side, neither*
31 And arms shall stand o' his part, and
12: 5 one o' this side of the bank of the
5 o' that side of the bank of the river.
Ho 4: 8 set their heart o' their iniquity. 413
5: 1 ye have been a snare o' Mizpah, and*
6: 3 if we follow o' to know the Lord:
10: 5 priests thereof that rejoiced o' it, *5921
8 thistle shall come up o' their altars;"
8 Cover us; and to the hills, Fall o' us."
11: 4 that take off the yoke o' their jaws, "
6 the sword shall abide o' his cities,*
12: 1 Ephraim feedeth o' wind, and
6 and wait o' thy God continually. ‡
Joe 2: 5 chariots o' the tops of mountains 5921
7 shall march every one o' his ways,
32 shall call o' the name of the Lord
Am 1: 7 I will send a fire o' the wall of Gaza,
10 I will send a fire o' the wall of Tyrus,
2: 7 of the earth o' the head of the poor,
5:19 leaned his hand o' the wall, and a 5921
Ob 11 that thou stoodest o' the other side,
12 have looked o' the day of thy brother
13 not have looked o' their affliction
13 have laid hands o' their substance
21 saviours shall come up o' mount Zion
Jon 3: 5 put o' sackcloth, from the greatest
4: 5 and sat o' the east side of the city, and
10 Thou hast had pity o' the gourd, 5921
Mic 2:13 and the Lord o' the head of them.*
Na 1: 2 will take vengeance o' his adversaries,
Hab 1:13 evil, and canst not look o' iniquity: 413
2: 9 that he may set his nest o' high,
15 mayest look o' their nakedness! 5921
16 spewing shall be o' thy glory. * "
3:10 and lifted up his hands o' high.
19 singer o' my stringed instruments.
Zep 1: 9 those that leap o' the threshold, *5921
12 men that are settled o' their lees: "
Zec 1:12 thou not have mercy o' Jerusalem
12 and o' the cities of Judah,
5: 3 cut off as o' this side according to it;
3 cut off as o' that side according to it.
10: 5 riders o' horses shall be confounded.
12: 6 o' the right hand and o' the left: 5921
13: 9 they shall call o' my name, and I will
14: 4 which is before Jerusalem o' the east,
13 every one o' the hand of his neighbour,
Mal 1:10 kindle fire o' mine altar for nought.
M't 1:18 of Jesus Christ was o' this wise: *3779*
20 while he thought o' these things, *1760*
4: 5 him o' a pinnacle of the temple, *1909*
21 And going o' from thence, he saw
5:14 A city that is set o' an hill cannot *1883*
15 a bushel, but o' a candlestick; *1909*
28 whosoever looketh o' a woman to
39 shall smite thee o' thy right cheek,*1909*
45 to rise o' the evil and...the good, "
45 the evil and o' the good, and sendeth*
45 rain o' the just and...the unjust. *1909*
45 the just and o' the unjust. *
6:25 your body, what ye shall put o'. *1746*
9: 2 sick of the palsy, lying o' a bed: *1909*
6 hath power o' earth to forgive sins, "
27 Thou son of David, have mercy o' us.
36 moved with compassion o' them, **4012*
10:29 them shall not fall o' the ground *1909*
34 I am come to send peace o' earth: "
12: 1 that time Jesus went o' the sabbath
5 that o' the sabbath days the priests
10 it lawful to heal o' the sabbath days?
11 if it fall into a pit o' the sabbath day,
11 will he not lay hold o' it, and lift it out?
12 lawful to do well o' the sabbath days.
13: 2 whole multitude stood o' the shore.*1909*
14: 3 For Herod had laid hold o' John,
13 followed him o' foot out of...cities. *3979*
19 multitude to sit down o' the grass,*1909*
25 went unto them, walking o' the sea.*"
26 disciples saw him walking o' the sea,"
28 bid me come unto thee o' the water.*"
29 walked o' the water, to go to Jesus.*"
15:22 Have mercy o' me, O Lord, thou son
32 have compassion o' the multitude,*1909*
35 multitude to sit down o' the ground. "
16:19 whatsoever thou shalt bind o' earth"
19 whatsoever thou shalt loose o' earth"
17: 6 they fell o' their face, and were sore"
15 Lord, have mercy o' my son: for he is
18:18 Whatsoever ye shall bind o' earth, *1909*
18 whatsoever ye shall loose o' earth, "
19 if two of you shall agree o' earth as"

M't 18:28 and he laid hands o' him, and took
33 had compassion o' thy fellow servant,
33 even as I had pity o' thee?
19:13 he should put his hands o' them, 2007
15 And he laid his hands o' them, and "
20:21 sit, the one o' thy right hand, 1537
21 and the other o' the left, in thy
23 sit o' my right hand, and o' my left, "
30, 31 Have mercy o' us, O Lord, thou
34 So Jesus had compassion o' them, and*
21: 7 and put o' them their clothes, and 1883
19 fruit grow o' thee henceforward *1537
38 and let us seize o' his inheritance.*
44 whosoever shall fall o' this stone 1909
44 o' whomsoever it shall fall, it will "
46 when they sought to lay hands o' him,
22:11 had not o' a wedding garment: 1746
40 O' these two commandments hang 1722
44 Sit thou o' my right hand, till I 1537
23: 4 and lay them o' men's shoulders; 1909
24:17 is o' the housetop not come down "
20 winter, neither o' the sabbath day: 1722
25:33 set the sheep o' his right hand, 1537
33 right hand, but the goats o' the left."
34 say unto them o' his right hand, "
41 say also unto them o' the left hand, "
26: 5 Not o' the feast day, lest there be *1722
7 poured it o' his head, as he sat at *1909
12 poured this ointment o' my body,* "
39 and fell o' his face, and prayed, "
45 Sleep o' now, and take your rest:
50 they, and laid hands o' Jesus, 1909
55 the temple, and ye laid no hold o' me.*
57 they that had laid hold o' Jesus led*
64 sitting o' the right hand of power,*1537
27:19 was set down o' the judgment seat, 1909
25 blood be o' us, and o' our children. "
28 him, and put o' him a scarlet robe. 4060
30 reed, and smote him o' the head. 1519
31 and put his own raiment o' him, 1746
38 with him, one o' the right hand, 1537
38 right hand, and another o' the left. "
48 vinegar, and put it o' a reed, and 4060
M'r 1:21 o' the sabbath day he entered into
2:10 hath power o' earth to forgive sins, 1909
12 We never saw it o' this fashion.
21 of new cloth o' an old garment: 1909
23 the corn fields o' the sabbath day; 1722
24 why do they o' the sabbath day that"
3: 2 would heal him o' the sabbath day;
4 lawful to do good o' the sabbath days,
5 had looked round about o' them with
9 that a small ship should wait o' him 4342
21 of it, they went out to lay hold o' him:
34 looked round about o' them which sat
4: 1 was by the sea o' the land. 1909
5 And some fell o' stony ground, "
8 And other fell o' good ground, *1519
16 which are sown o' stony ground; *1909
20 which are sown o' good ground; * "
21 and not to be set o' a candlestick? "
38 part of the ship, asleep o' a pillow: "
5:19 and hath had compassion o' thee.
23 thee, come and lay thy hands o' her, 2007
6: 9 sandals; and not put o' two coats. 1746
21 Herod o' his birthday made a supper
47 the sea, and he alone o' the land. 1909
8: 2 I have compassion o' the multitude, "
6 people to sit down o' the ground: "
23 when he had spit o' his eyes, and 1519
33 about and looked o' his disciples,*
9: 3 no fuller o' earth can white them. 1909
20 he fell o' the ground, and wallowed "
22 have compassion o' us, and help us."
40 is not against us is o' our part. 5228
10:37 we may sit, one o' thy right hand, 1537
37 other o' thy left hand, in thy glory. "
40 But to sit o' my right hand and "
40 o' my left hand is not mine to give; "
47 thou son of David, have mercy o' me.
48 Thou son of David, have mercy o' me.
11: 7 and cast their garments o' him; 1911
12 o' the morrow, when they were come
12:12 And they sought to lay hold o' him,
36 Sit thou o' my right hand, till I 1537
13:15 that is o' the housetop not go down 1909
14: 2 Not o' the feast day, lest there be *1722
3 box, and poured it o' his head. *2596
6 hath wrought a good work o' me. 1722
35 and fell o' the ground, and prayed 1909
41 Sleep o' now, and take your rest:
46 they laid their hands o' him, and 1909
51 and the young men laid hold o' him:
62 sitting o' the right hand of power,*1537
65 And some began to spit o' him, and 1716
15:19 they smote him o' the head with a reed,
20 and put his own clothes o' him, and 1746
27 thieves; the one o' his right hand, 1537
27 hand, and the other o' his left.
29 that passed by railed o' him, wagging
36 of vinegar, and put it o' a reed, and 4060
40 were also women looking o' afar off:*
16: 5 young man sitting o' the right side, 1722
18 they shall lay hands o' the sick, 1909
19 and sat o' the right hand of God. *1537
Lu 1:11 standing o' the right side of the altar"
25 the days wherein he looked o' me, 1896
50 his mercy is o' them that fear him
59 o' the eighth day they came to 1722
65 fear came o' all that dwelt round 1909
78 the dayspring from o' high hath visited
2:14 o' earth peace, good will toward 1909
4: 9 set him o' a pinnacle of the temple, "
16 the synagogue o' the sabbath day, 1722
20 the synagogue were fastened o' him.
31 taught them o' the sabbath days. 1722

Lu 5:12 who seeing Jesus fell o' his face, 1909
17 it came to pass o' a certain day, 1722
6: 1 came to pass o' the second sabbath "
2 lawful to do o' the sabbath days? "
6 to pass also o' another sabbath, "
7 he would heal o' the sabbath day; "
9 lawful o' the sabbath days to do good,
20 lifted up his eyes o' his disciples, 1519
29 him smiteth thee o' the one cheek 1909
48 and laid the foundation o' a rock:* "
7:13 saw her, he had compassion o' her, "
16 And there came a fear o' all: and they
40 thee. And he saith, Master, say o'.
8: 8 And other fell o' good ground, and*1519
13 They o' the rock are they, which, 1909
15 that o' the good ground are they, *1722
16 but setteth it o' a candlestick, 1909
22 it came to pass o' a certain day, 1722
23 down a storm of wind o' the lake; 1519
32 swine feeding o' the mountain: 1722
9:37 came to pass, that o' the next day, "
10:11 which cleaveth o' us, we do wipe off*
19 tread o' serpents and scorpions, *1883
31 him, he passed by o' the other side.
32 at the place, came and looked o' him,*
32 and passed by o' the other side.
33 saw him, he had compassion o' him,*
34 and set him o' his own beast, and 1909
35 o' the morrow when he departed, "
37 He that shewed mercy o' him. 3326
11:33 a bushel, but o' a candlestick, 1909
12:22 for the body, what ye shall put o'. 1746
49 am come to send fire o' the earth:*1519
51 I am come to give peace o' earth?*1722
13: 7 come seeking fruit o' this fig tree, "
10 of the synagogues o' the sabbath. "
13 And he laid his hands o' her: and *2007
14 that Jesus had healed o' the sabbath
15 be healed, and not o' the sabbath day.
15 o' the sabbath loose his ox or his ass
16 from this bond o' the sabbath day?
14: 1 Pharisees to eat bread o' the sabbath
3 Is it lawful to heal o' the sabbath day?
5 pull him out o' the sabbath day? 1722
15: 5 he layeth it o' his shoulders, 1909
20 and fell o' his neck, and kissed him."
22 the best robe, and put it o' him; 1746
22 o' his hand, and shoes o' his feet: 1519
16:24 Father Abraham, have mercy o' me,
17:13 said, Jesus, Master, have mercy o' us.
16 fell down o' his face at his feet, *1909
18: 8 shall he find faith o' the earth? "
32 spitefully entreated,...spitted o': *1716
38 thou son of David, have mercy o' me.
39 Thou Son of David, have mercy o' me.
19:43 and keep thee in o' every side, 3840
20: 1 to pass, that o' one of those days, 1722
18 o' whomsoever it shall fall, it will 1909
19 hour sought to lay hands o' him; "
42 my Lord, Sit thou o' my right hand, 1537
21:12 they shall lay their hands o' you, 1909
35 dwell o' the face of the whole earth. 1909
22:21 betrayeth me is with me o' the table."
30 o' thrones judging the twelve tribes"
64 they struck him o' the face, and *
69 sit o' the right hand of the power*1537
23:26 and o' him they laid the cross, that 2007
30 say to the mountains, Fall o' us; 1909
33 malefactors, one o' the right hand, 1537
33 right hand, and the other o' the left."
39 which were hanged railed o' him,
54 preparation,...the sabbath drew o'. 2020
24:49 be endued with power from o' high.
Joh 1:12 to them that believe o' his name: 1519
33 descending, and remaining o' him, *1909
2:11 and his disciples believed o' him. 1519
3:18 believeth o' him is not condemned: "
36 believeth o' the Son hath everlasting"
36 the wrath of God abideth o' him. 1909
4: 6 his journey, sat thus o' the well: "
35 up your eyes, and look o' the fields;
39 the Samaritans...believed o' him 1519
5: 9 o' the same day was the sabbath. 1722
16 these things o' the sabbath day.
24 and believeth o' him that sent me,*
6: 2 he did o' them that were diseased. 1909
19 they see Jesus walking o' the sea,* "
22 which stood o' the other side of the sea
25 found him o' the other side of the sea,
29 believe o' him whom he hath sent. 1519
35 believeth o' me shall never thirst. "
40 seeth the Son, and believeth o' him, "
47 believeth o' me hath everlasting * "
7:22 ye o' the sabbath day circumcise 1722
23 a man o' the sabbath day receive "
23 whit whole o' the sabbath day? "
30 but no man laid hands o' him, 1909
31 of the people believed on him, 1519
38 He that believeth o' me, as the "
39 that believe o' him should receive: "
44 but no man laid hands o' him. 1909
48 of the Pharisees believed o' him? 1519
8: 6 with his finger wrote o' the ground, "
8 down, and wrote o' the ground.
20 and no man laid hands o' him; for his*
30 these words, many believed o' him. 1519
31 to those Jews which believed o' him,*
9: 6 spat o' the ground, and made clay 5476
35 thou believe o' the Son of God? 1519
36 Lord, that I might believe o' him? "
10:42 And many believed o' him there. "
11:45 which Jesus did, believed o' him. "
48 alone, all men will believe o' him: "
12:11 went away, and believed o' Jesus. "
12 O' the next day much people that

Joh 12:15 cometh, sitting o' an ass's colt. 1909
37 them, yet they believed not o' him: 1519
42 rulers also many believed o' him; "
44 and said, He that believeth o' me, "
44 believeth not o' me, but o' him that "
46 believeth o' me should not abide in "
13:22 the disciples looked one o' another,"
23 leaning o' Jesus' bosom one of his*1722
25 He then lying o' Jesus' breast 1909
14:12 He that believeth o' me, the works 1519
16: 9 sin, because they believe not o' me; "
17: 4 I have glorified thee o' the earth: 1909
20 believe o' me through their word; 1519
19: 2 of thorns, and put it o' his head, 2007
2 and they put o' him a purple robe,*4016
18 other with him, o' either side one, 1782
19 a title, and put it o' the cross. 1909
31 upon the cross o' the sabbath day,*1722
37 look o' him whom they pierced. 1519
20:22 had said this, he breathed o' them, 1720
21: 1 and o' this wise shewed he himself.
4 come, Jesus stood o' the shore: 1519
6 net o' the right side of the ship, "
20 also leaned o' his breast at supper, 1909
Ac 2:18 And o' my servants and "
18 o' my handmaidens I will pour "
21 shall call o' the name of the Lord 1941
25 for he is o' my right hand, that I 1537
30 up Christ to sit o' his throne; *1909
34 Lord, Sit thou o' my right hand, 1537
3: 4 him with John, said, Look o' us. 1519
12 or why look ye so earnestly o' us, 1909
4: 3 they laid hands o' them, and put
5 And it came to pass o' the morrow, 1909
22 o' whom this miracle of healing
5: 5 great fear came o' all them that * "
15 and laid them o' beds and couches, "
18 laid their hands o' the apostles, "
30 whom ye slew and hanged o' a tree."
6: 6 prayed, they laid...hands o' them. 2007
15 council, looking stedfastly o' him, 1519
7: 5 no, not so much as to set his foot o':
6 And God spake o' this wise, That his
54 gnashed o' him with their teeth. 1909
55 standing o' the right hand of God, 1537
56 standing o' the right hand of God. "
8:17 laid they their hands o' them, 1909
18 laying o' of the apostles' hands 1936
19 o' whomsoever I lay hands, he may 2007
36 And as they went o' their way, 2596
39 and he went o' his way rejoicing.
9:12 putting his hand o' him, that he 2007
14 to bind all that call o' thy name. *
17 and putting his hands o' him said, 1909
21 called o' this name in Jerusalem, 1941
10: 4 And when he looked o' him, he was*
7 soldier of them that waited o' him 4342
9 O' the morrow, as they went o' their
19 While Peter thought o' the vision, 4012
23 o' the morrow Peter went away with
39 they slew and hanged o' a tree: 1909
44 Holy Ghost fell o' all them which "
45 o' the Gentiles also was poured out "
11:15 Holy Ghost fell o' them, as o' us at "
17 us, who believed o' the Lord Jesus "
12: 7 he smote Peter o' the side, and raised
8 thyself, and bind o' thy sandals. 5265
10 out, and passed o' through one street;
13: 3 and laid their hands o' them, 2007
9 Holy Ghost, set his eyes o' him, 1519
11 fell o' him a mist and a darkness; 1909
14 into the synagogue o' the sabbath day,
15 exhortation for the people, say o'.
34 he said o' this wise, I will give you
36 fell o' sleep, and was laid unto his
14:10 voice, Stand upright o' thy feet. 1909
23 the Lord, o' whom they believed. 1519
15: 3 being brought o' their way by the
16:13 o' the sabbath we went out of the city
31 Believe o' the Lord Jesus Christ, 1909
17: 5 and set all the city o' an uproar,
26 to dwell o' all the face of the earth, 1909
18: 8 believed o' the Lord with all his *
10 man shall set o' thee to hurt thee: 2007
19: 4 believe o' him which should come 1519
4 after him, that is, o' Christ Jesus. "
6 the Holy Ghost came o' them; and 1909
16 the evil spirit was leaped o' them, "
17 fear fell o' them all, and the name* "
20: 7 them, ready to depart o' the morrow;
10 Paul went down, and fell o' him, 1968
37 wept sore, and fell o' Paul's neck, 1909
21: 3 Cyprus, we left it o' the left hand,
5 brought us o' our way, with wives 1909
5 we kneeled down o' the shore, and "
23 men which have a vow o' them; "
27 the people, and laid hands o' him, "
40 licence Paul stood o' the stairs, "
22:16 calling o' the name of the Lord. 1941
19 them that believed o' thee: 1909
30 O' the morrow, because he would
23: 2 by him to smite him o' the mouth.
24 beasts, that they may set Paul o', 1913
32 O' the morrow they left the horsemen
25: 6 day sitting o' the judgment seat 1909
17 any delay o' the morrow I sat "
17 I sat o' the judgment seat, "
23 o' the morrow, when Agrippa was
27:20 and no small tempest lay o' us, 1945
33 while the day was coming o', Paul
44 And the rest, some o' boards, 1909
44 some o' broken pieces of the ship. "
28: 3 of sticks, and laid them o' the fire, "
3 the heat, and fastened o' his hand. 2510
4 venomous beast hang o' his hand,*1537
8 laid his hands o' him, and healed 2007

Ro 4: 5 believeth o' him that justifieth the 1909
24 if we believe o' him that raised up "
9: 15 I will have mercy o' whom I will
15 will have compassion o' whom I will
18 hath he mercy o' whom he will have
23 his glory o' the vessels of mercy, *1909
33 whosoever believeth o' him shall "
10: 6 is of faith speaketh o' this wise, Say*
11 Whosoever believeth o' him shall 1909
14 they call o' him in whom they have 1941
11: 22 God: o' them which fell, severity;*1909
12: 7 let us wait o' our ministering: *1722
7 or he that teacheth, o' teaching; * "
8 he that exhorteth, o' exhortation:* "
20 shalt heap coals of fire o' his head.*1909
13: 12 let us put o' the armour of light. 1746
14 put ye o' the Lord Jesus Christ, "
15: 3 that reproached thee fell o' me. *1909
24 be brought o' my way thitherward
16: 6 who bestowed much labour o' us. 1519
19 am glad therefore o' your behalf: *1909
1Co 1: 4 my God always o' your behalf, for *4012
11: 10 woman to have power o' her head 1909
14: 25 so falling down o' his face he will "
15: 53 must put o' incorruption, 1746
53 this mortal must put o' immortality."
54 shall have put o' incorruption, "
54 mortal shall have put o' immortality,"
16: 6 bring me o' my journey whithersoever
17 that which was lacking o' your part
2Co 1: 11 be given by many o' our behalf. 5228
16 be brought o' my way toward Judæa.
4: 8 We are troubled o' every side, yet 1722
5: 12 occasion to glory o' our behalf, 5228
6: 7 o' the right hand and o' the left,
7: 5 but we were troubled o' every side;1722
8: 1 o' the churches of Macedonia; * "
24 and of our boasting o' your behalf.5228
10: 7 ye look o' things after the outward*991
11: 20 if a man smite you o' the face. 1519
Ga 3: 13 is every one that hangeth o' a tree:1909
14 might come o' the Gentiles *1519
27 into Christ have put o' Christ. 1746
6: 16 peace be o' them, and mercy, and*1909
Eph 1: 10 in heaven, and which are o' earth; "
4: 8 When he ascended up o' high, he 5311
24 And that ye put o' the new man, 1746
6: 3 thou mayest live long o' the earth.1909
11 Put o' the whole armour of God, 1746
14 o' the breastplate of righteousness;"
Ph'p 1: 29 not only to believe o' him, but also1519
2: 4 not every man o' his own things, but*
4 every man also o' the things of others.*
27 mercy o' him; and not o' him only,
27 o' me also, lest I should have sorrow
4: 8 be any praise, think o' these things.
Col 3: 1 sitteth o' the right hand of God. 1722
2 affection o' things above, not o' things
2 things above, not...o' the earth. *1909
6 o' the children of disobedience: * "
10 And have put o' the new man, which1746
12 Put o' therefore, as the elect of God,"
14 above all these things put o' charity,
1Th 5: 8 putting o' the breastplate of faith 1746
2Th 1: 8 vengeance o' them that know not God,*
1Ti 1: 16 believe o' him to life everlasting. 1909
18 prophecies...went before o' thee, * "
3: 16 believed o' in the world, received up
5: 22 Lay hands suddenly o' no man, 2007
6: 12 lay hold o' eternal life, whereunto 1949
19 they may lay hold o' eternal life. "
2Ti 1: 6 thee by the putting o' of my hands.1936
2: 22 call o' the Lord out of a pure heart.1941
Tit 3: 6 Which he shed o' us abundantly 1909
13 lawyer and Apollos o' their journey
Ph'm 18 ought, put that o' mine account; 1677
Heb 1: 3 sat down o' the right hand of the 1722
3 right hand of the Majesty o' high; "
13 Sit o' my right hand, until I make 1537
2: 16 not o' him the nature of angels; †‡1949
16 took o' him the seed of Abraham.†‡"
4: 4 place of the seventh day o' this wise,
5: 2 can have compassion o' the ignorant,*
2 and o' them that are out of the way;*
6: 1 let us go o' unto perfection; not
2 baptisms, and of laying o' of hands,1936
8: 1 o' the right hand of the throne of 1722
4 if he were o' the earth, he should 1909
9: 10 carnal ordinances, imposed o' them* "
10: 12 sat down o' the right hand of God; 1722
11: 13 strangers and pilgrims o'...earth. 1909
12: 25 refused him that spoke o' earth, "
Jas 3: 6 and setteth o' fire the cause of nature;
6 of nature; and it is set o' fire of hell.
4: 14 know not what shall be o' the morrow.
5: 5 have lived in pleasure o' the earth,1909
17 and it rained not o' the earth by the"
1Pe 1: 17 And if ye call o' the Father, who 1941
2: 6 that believeth o' him shall not be 1909
24 our sins in his own body o' the tree,*"
3: 3 of gold, or of putting o' of apparel;1745
22 and is o' the right hand of God; 1722
4: 14 o' their part he is evil spoken of, *2596
14 but o' your part he is glorified. * "
16 let him glorify God o' this behalf. *1722
2Pe 3: 12 being o' fire shall be dissolved,
1Jo 3: 23 should believe o' the name of his Son*
5: 10 He that believeth o' the Son of God1519
13, 13 believe o' the name of the Son "
3Jo 6 if thou bring forward o' their journey
Jude 20 up yourselves o' your most holy faith,
Re 1: 10 was in the Spirit o' the Lord's day, 1722
3: 3 I will come o' thee as a thief, and *1909
4: 2 heaven, and one sat o' the throne. "
4 had o' their heads crowns of gold. "
9 thanks to him that sat o' the throne,"

Re 4: 10 before him that sat o' the throne, 1909
5: 1 hand of him that sat o' the throne "
1 written within and o' the backside, "
10 and we shall reign o' the earth. * "
13 is in heaven, and o' the earth, and 1722
6: 2 and he that sat o' him had a bow;*1909
5 he that sat o' him had a pair of "
8 name that sat o' him was Death, *1883
10 o' [575] them that dwell o'...earth? 1909
16 the mountains and rocks, Fall o' us,"
16 of him that sitteth o' the throne, "
7: 1 angels standing o' the four corners*"
1 wind should not blow o' the earth, "
1 the earth, nor o' the sea, nor "
1 the sea, nor o' any tree. * "
11 before the throne o' their faces, "
15 he that sitteth o' the throne shall "
16 neither shall the sun light o' them,*"
9: 7 and o' their heads were as it were "
17 and them that sat o' them, having "
10: 2 sea, and his left foot o' the earth, * "
11: 10 them that dwelt o' the earth. "
16 which sat before God o' their seats, "
13: 13 down from heaven o' the earth in* 1519
14 them that dwell o' the earth by 1909
14 to them that dwell o' the earth, "
14: 1 a Lamb stood o' the mount Sion, "
6 unto them that dwell o' the earth, "
14 having o' his head a golden crown, "
15 voice to him that sat o' the cloud, "
16 And he that sat o' the cloud thrust "
16 thrust in his sickle o' the earth; * "
15: 2 stand o' the sea of glass, having * "
17: 8 dwell o' the earth shall wonder, "
9 o' which the woman sitteth. "
18: 19 they cast dust o' their heads, and "
20 for God hath avenged you o' her. 1537
19: 4 God that sat o' the throne, saying, 1909
12 and o' his head were many crowns;*"
16 hath o' his vesture and o' his thigh "
18 and of them that sit o' them, and * "
19 against him that sat o' the horse, * "
20: 2 he laid hold o' the dragon, that old
6 o' such the second death hath no *1909
9 up o' the breadth of the earth, * "
11 white throne, and him that sat o' it,*"
21: 13 O' the east three gates; 575
13 O' the north three gates; "
13 o' the south three gates; "
13 and o' the west three gates. "
22: 2 and o' either side of the river, was 1909

On (*on*)
Ge 41: 45 daughter of Poti-pherah priest of O'.204
50 daughter of Poti-pherah priest of O' "
46: 20 daughter of Poti-pherah priest of O' "
Nu 16: 1 and O', the son of Peleth, sons of 203

Onam (*o'-nam*)
Ge 36: 23 and Ebal, Shepho, and O'. 208
1Ch 1: 40 and Ebal, Shephi, and O'. "
2: 26 Atarah; she was the mother of O'. "
28 the sons of O' were, Shammai, and "

Onan (*o'-nan*)
Ge 38: 4 a son; and she called his name O'. 209
8 Judah said unto O', Go in unto thy "
9 O' knew that the seed should not be "
46: 12 the sons of Judah; Er, and O', and "
12 and O' died in the land of Canaan. "
Nu 26: 19 The sons of Judah were Er and O': "
19 and O' died in the land of Canaan. "
1Ch 2: 3 The sons of Judah; Er, and O', and "

once
Ge 18: 32 and I will speak yet but this o': 6471
Ex 10: 17 I pray thee, my sin only this o', "
30: 10 upon the horns of it o' in a year 259
10 o' in the year shall he make "
Le 16: 34 of Israel for all their sins o' a year. "
Nu 13: 30 Let us go up at o', and possess it;
De 7: 22 mayest not consume them at o', 4118
Jos 6: 3 and go round about the city o'. 259
11 compassed the city, going about it o': "
14 day they compassed the city o', "
J'g 6: 39 me, and I will speak but this o': 6471
39 prove,...but this o' with the fleece; "
16: 18 Come up this o', for he hath shewed"
28 me, I pray thee, only this o', O God,"
28 be at o' avenged of the Philistines
1Sa 26: 8 spear even to the earth at o', *6471,259
1Ki 10: 22 o' in three years came the navy of "
2Ki 6: 10 saved himself there, not o' nor twice."
2Ch 9: 21 every three years o' came the ships "
Ne 5: 18 and o' in ten days store of all sorts 996
13: 20 lodged without Jerusalem o' or 6471
Job 33: 14 For God speaketh o', yea twice, yet 259
40: 5 O' have I spoken; but I will not "
Ps 62: 11 God hath spoken o'; twice have I "
74: 6 carved work thereof at o' with axes*
76: 7 in thy sight when o' thou art angry?227
89: 35 O' have I sworn by my holiness that259
Pr 28: 18 perverse in his ways shall fall at o'. "
Isa 42: 14 I will destroy and devour at o'. *3162
66: 8 or shall a nation be born at o'? 6471
Jer 10: 18 inhabitants of the land at this o',* "
13: 27 made clean? when shall it o' be? *5750
16: 21 I will this o' cause them to know, 6471
Hag 2: 6 Yet o', it is a little while, and I will 259
Lu 13: 25 When o' the master of the house is risen
23: 18 they cried out all at o', saying, *3826
Ro 6: 10 that he died, he died unto sin o': 2178
7: 9 I was alive without the law o': but4218
1Co 15: 6 above five hundred brethren at o';2178
2Co 11: 25 I beaten with rods, o' was I stoned, 530
Ga 1: 23 the faith which o' he destroyed. 4218
Eph 5: 3 let it not be o' named among you,*3366
Ph'p 4: 16 o' and again unto my necessity. 530
1Th 2: 18 unto you, even I Paul, o' and again; "

Heb 6: 4 for those who were o' enlightened, 530
7: 27 for this he did o', when he offered 2178
9: 7 the high priest alone o' every year, 530
12 he entered in o' into the holy place,2178
26 o' in the end of the world hath he 530
27 it is appointed unto men o' to die, "
28 So Christ was o' offered to bear the "
10: 2 worshippers o' purged should have "
10 the body of Jesus Christ o' for all. 2178
12: 26 o' more I shake not the earth only, 530
27 this word, Yet o' more, signifieth the"
1Pe 3: 18 Christ also hath o' suffered for sins, "
20 when o' the longsuffering of God * "
Jude 3 faith which was o' delivered unto the"
5 though ye o' knew this, how that the"

one See also NONE; ONE'S; ONES.
Ge 1: 9 be gathered together unto o' place, 259
2: 21 he took o' of his ribs, and closed up "
24 his wife: and they shall be o' flesh. "
3: 6 a tree to be desired to make o' wise,
22 the man is become as o' of us, to 259
4: 14 every o' that findeth me shall slay*
19 the name of the o' was Adah, and 259
10: 5 every o' after his tongue, after their376
8 began to be a mighty o' in the earth.
25 sons: the name of o' was Peleg; 259
11: 1 was of o' language, and of o' speech."
3 they said o' to another, Go to, let us376
6 Lord said, Behold, the people is o', 259
6 and they have all o' language; and "
7 not understand o' another's speech.376
13: 11 themselves the o' from the other.
14: 13 And there came o' that had escaped,
15: 3 lo, o' born in my house is mine heir.
10 laid each piece o' against another: *
19: 9 This o' fellow came in to sojourn, 259
14 But he seemed as o' that mocked
20 to flee unto, and it is a little o':
20 escape thither, (is it not a little o'?)
21: 15 cast the child under o' of the shrubs.259
22: 2 upon o' of the mountains which I "
25: 23 the o' people shall be stronger than
26: 10 o' of the people might lightly have 259
26 and Ahuzzath o' of his friends, and*
31 morning, and sware o' to another: 376
27: 29 cursed be every o' that curseth thee,
38 Hast thou but o' blessing, my 259
45 deprived also of you both in o' day? "
30: 33 every o' that is not speckled and 3605
35 and every o' that had some white in it,
31: 49 when we are absent o' from another.376
32: 8 If Esau come to the o' company, 259
33: 13 if men should overdrive them o' day,"
34: 14 sister to o' that is uncircumcised; 376
16 you, and we will become o' people. 259
22 dwell with us, to be o' people, "
37: 19 they said o' to another, Behold, this376
38: 28 that the o' put out his hand: and
40: 5 each man his dream in o' night, 259
41: 5 ears of corn came up upon o' stalk, "
11 And we dreamed a dream in o' night,"
22 seven ears came up in o' stalk, full "
25 The dream of Pharaoh is o': God "
26 are seven years: the dream is o'. "
38 Can we find such a o' as this is, a man
42: 1 sons, Why do ye look o' upon another?
11 We are all o' man's sons; we are 259
13 the sons of o' man in the land of "
13 day with our father, and o' is not. "
16 Send o' of you, and let him fetch "
19 let o' of your brethren be bound in "
21 And they said o' to another, We are376
27 And as o' of them opened his sack 259
28 saying o' to another, What is this 376
32 o' is not, and the youngest is this 259
33 leave o' of your brethren here with "
43: 33 the men marvelled o' at another. 376
44: 20 and a child of his old age, a little o';
28 And the o' went out from me, and 259
47: 21 to cities from o' end of the borders
48: 1 o' told Joseph, Behold, thy father is
2 o' told Jacob, and said, Behold, thy son
22 given to thee o' portion above thy 259
49: 16 people, as o' of the tribes of Israel. "
28 every o' according to his blessing 376
Ex 1: 15 the name of the o' was Shiphrah, 259
2: 6 This is o' of the Hebrews' children.
11 smiting an Hebrew, o' of his brethren.
6: 25 o' of the daughters of Putiel to wife;
8: 31 his people; there remained not o'. 259
9: 6 of the children of Israel died not o'. "
7 not o' of the cattle of the Israelites "
10: 5 o' cannot be able to see the earth:
19 remained not o' locust in all the 259
23 They saw not o' another, neither 376
11: 1 o' plague more upon Pharaoh, 259
12: 18 until the o' and twentieth day of the"
30 house where there was not o' dead.
46 In o' house shall it be eaten; thou 259
48 shall be as o' that is born in the land:
49 O' law shall be to him that is 259
14: 7 and captains over every o' of them.*
20 o' came not near the other all the 2088
28 remained not so much as o' of them.259
16: 15 they said o' to another, It is manna:376
22 much bread, two omers for o' man:259
17: 12 o' [259] on the o' side, and the other2088
18: 3 the name of the o' was Gershom; 259
16 I judge between o' and another, * 376
21: 18 and o' smite another with a stone, or
35 And if o' man's ox hurt another's,
23: 29 out from before thee in o' year; 259
24: 3 the people answered with o' voice, "
25: 12 two rings shall be in the o' side of it,"
19 make o' [259] cherub on the o' end,2088
20 their faces shall look o' to another:

Ex 25:32 of the candlestick out of the o' side,259
33 a knop and a flower in o' branch; "
36 shall be o' beaten work of pure gold."
26: 2 length of o' curtain shall be eight * "
2 breadth of o' curtain four cubits: * "
2 every o' of the curtains shall have * "
2 the curtains shall have o' measure.259
3 be coupled together o' to another; 802
3 shall be coupled o' to another. "
4 blue upon the edge of the o' curtain259
5 shalt thou make in the o' curtain, "
5 loops may take hold o' of another. 802
6 taches: and it shall be o' tabernacle.259
8 length of o' curtain shall be thirty* "
8 breadth of o' curtain four cubits: * "
8 curtains shall be all of o' measure. 259
10 loops on the edge of the o' curtain "
11 the tent together, that it may be o'. "
13 And a cubit on the o' side, and a cubit
16 shall be the breadth of o' board. * 259
17 tenons shall there be in o' board, * "
17 set in order o' against another: 802
19 two sockets under o' board for his 259
21 two sockets under o' board, and two "
24 above the head of it unto o' ring: "
25 two sockets under o' board, and two "
26 of the o' side of the tabernacle, "
27: 9 an hundred cubits long for o' side: "
14 The hangings of o' side of the gate
28:10 Six of their names on o' stone, and 259
21 every o' with his name shall they be376
29: 1 Take o' young bullock, and two 259
3 thou shalt put them into o' basket, "
15 Thou shalt also take o' ram; and "
23 o' loaf of bread, and o' cake of oiled "
23 and o' wafer out of the basket of the "
39 The o' lamb thou shalt offer in the "
40 And with the o' lamb a tenth deal of "
30:13 every o' that passeth among them that
14 Every o' that passeth among them
31:14 every o' that defileth it shall surely be
32:15 on the o' side and on the other were
33: 7 that every o' which sought the Lord
34:15 and o' call thee, and thou eat of his
35:21 every o' whose heart stirred him up,
21 and every o' whom his spirit made
24 Every o' that did offer an offering of
36: 2 even every o' whose heart stirred him
9 length of o' curtain was twenty and*259
9 breadth of o' curtain four cubits: * "
9 the curtains were all of o' size. 259
10 the five curtains o' unto another: "
10 curtains he coupled o' unto another."
11 loops of blue on the edge of o' curtain"
12 Fifty loops made he in o' curtain, "
12 the loops held o' curtain to another. "
13 coupled the curtains o' unto another"
13 taches: so it became o' tabernacle. "
15 of o' curtain was thirty cubits, * "
15 cubits was the breadth of o' curtain:*"
15 the eleven curtains were of o' size. "
18 the tent together, that it might be o'."
21 breadth of a board o' cubit and a half.*
22 O' board had two tenons, equally * 259
22 equally distant o' from another: "
24 under o' board for his two tenons, "
26 silver; two sockets under o' board, "
29 at the head thereof, to o' ring: "
31 of the o' side of the tabernacle, "
33 boards from the o' end to the other.
37: 3 even two rings upon the o' side of it,259
6 o' cubit and half the breadth thereof.*
7 beaten out of o' piece made he them,*
8 O' cherub on the end on this side, 259
9 seat, with their faces o' to another;376
18 candlestick out of the o' side thereof,
19 fashion of almonds in o' branch, 259
22 it was o' beaten work of pure gold.
38:14 The hangings of the o' side of the gate
26 every o' that went to be numbered,
39:14 of a signet, every o' with his name, 376
Le 4:27 if any o' of the common people sin 5315
5: 4 then he shall be guilty in o' of these.259
5 shall be guilty in o' of these things, "
7 o' for a sin offering, and the other "
13 sin that he hath sinned in o' of these,*"
6:18 every o' that toucheth them shall be*
7: 7 there is o' law for them: the priest 259
10 Aaron have, o' as much as another.376
14 offer o' out of the whole oblation 259
8:26 he took o' unleavened cake, and a "
26 a cake of oiled bread, and o' wafer, "
12: 8 the o' for the burnt offering, and the "
13: 2 or unto o' of his sons the priests: "
14: 5 that o' of the birds be killed "
10 and o' ewe lamb of the first year "
10 mingled with oil, and o' log of oil. "
12 And the priest shall take o' he lamb,"
21 take o' lamb for a trespass offering "
21 o' tenth deal of fine flour mingled "
22 the o' shall be a sin offering, and the"
30 shall offer the o' of the turtledoves, "
31 the o' for a sin offering, and the "
50 And he shall kill the o' of the birds "
15:15 the o' for a sin offering, and the "
30 shall offer the o' for a sin offering, "
16: 5 and o' ram for a burnt offering. "
8 o' lot for the Lord, and the other lot "
27 o' carry forth without the camp; *
29 whether it be o' of your own country,*
17:15 whether it be o' of your own country,*
18:30 any o' of these abominable customs,*
19: 8 every o' that eateth it shall bear his
11 falsely, neither lie o' to another. 376
34 be unto you as o' born among you,*
20: 9 every o' that curseth his father or 376

Le 22:28 kill it and her young both in o' day.259
23:18 and o' young bullock, and two rams:"
19 ye shall sacrifice o' kid of the goats "
24: 5 two tenth deals shall be in o' cake. "
22 Ye shall have o' manner of law, as "
22 stranger, as for o' of your own country:*
25:14 ye shall not oppress o' another: 376
17 not therefore oppress o' another; "
46 shall not rule o' over another with "
48 o' of his brethren may redeem him:259
26:26 shall bake your bread in o' oven, "
37 And they shall fall o' upon another,376
Nu 1: 4 every o' head of the house of his "
41 were forty and o' thousand and 259
44 each o' was for the house of his "
2:16 fifty and o' thousand and four "
28 forty and o' thousand and five "
34 every o' after their families, 376
4:19 appoint them every o' to his service "
30, 35, 39, 43 every o' that entereth into
47 every o' that came to do the service
49 every o' according to his service, 376
5: 2 and every o' that hath an issue, and
6:11 shall offer the o' for a sin offering, 259
14 o' he lamb of the first year without "
14 o' ewe lamb of the first year without "
14 o' ram without blemish for peace "
19 and o' unleavened cake out of the "
19 and o' unleavened wafer, and shall "
7: 3 of the princes, and for each o' an ox:
13 his offering was o' silver charger, 259
13 o' silver bowl of seventy shekels, "
14 O' spoon of ten shekels of gold, full "
15 O' young bullock, o' ram, o' lamb "
16 O' kid of the goats for a sin offering:"
19 for his offering o' silver charger, "
19 o' silver bowl of seventy shekels, "
20 O' spoon of gold of ten shekels, full "
21 O' young bullock, o' ram, o' lamb "
22 O' kid of the goats for a sin offering:"
25 His offering was o' silver charger, "
25 o' silver bowl of seventy shekels, "
26 O' golden spoon of ten shekels, full "
27 O' young bullock, o' ram, o' lamb "
28 O' kid of the goats for a sin offering:"
31 His offering was o' silver charger of "
31 o' silver bowl of seventy shekels, "
33 O' golden spoon of ten shekels, full "
33 O' young bullock, o' ram, o' lamb "
34 O' kid of the goats for a sin offering:"
37 His offering was o' silver charger, "
37 o' silver bowl of seventy shekels, "
38 O' golden spoon of ten shekels, full "
39 O' young bullock, o' ram, o' lamb "
40 O' kid of the goats for a sin offering:"
43 His offering was o' silver charger "
44 O' golden spoon of ten shekels, full "
45 O' young bullock, o' ram, o' lamb "
46 O' kid of the goats for a sin offering:"
49 His offering was o' silver charger "
49 o' silver bowl of seventy shekels, "
50 O' golden spoon of ten shekels, full "
51 O' young bullock, o' ram, o' lamb "
52 O' kid of the goats for a sin offering:"
55 His offering was o' silver charger of "
55 o' silver bowl of seventy shekels, "
56 O' golden spoon of ten shekels, full "
57 O' young bullock, o' ram, o' lamb "
58 O' kid of the goats for a sin offering:"
61 His offering was o' silver charger, "
61 o' silver bowl of seventy shekels, "
62 O' golden spoon of ten shekels, full "
63 O' young bullock, o' ram, o' lamb "
64 O' kid of the goats for a sin offering:"
67 His offering was o' silver charger, "
67 o' silver bowl of seventy shekels, "
68 O' golden spoon of ten shekels, full "
69 O' young bullock, o' ram, o' lamb "
70 O' kid of the goats for a sin offering:"
73 His offering was o' silver charger, "
73 o' silver bowl of seventy shekels, "
74 O' golden spoon of ten shekels, full "
75 O' young bullock, o' ram, o' lamb "
76 O' kid of the goats for a sin offering:"
79 His offering was o' silver charger, "
79 o' silver bowl of seventy shekels, "
80 O' golden spoon of ten shekels, full "
81 O' young bullock, o' ram, o' lamb "
82 O' kid of the goats for a sin offering:"
89 the voice of o' speaking unto him *
8:12 shalt offer the o' for a sin offering, 259
9:14 ye shall have o' ordinance, both for "
10: 4 if they blow but with o' trumpet, "
11:19 Ye shall not eat o' day, nor two days,"
26 the name of the o' was Eldad, and "
28 o' of his young men, answered and "
12:12 Let her not be as o' dead, of whom "
13: 2 man, every o' a ruler among them. "
23 a branch with o' cluster of grapes, 259
14: 4 And they said o' to another, Let us 376
15 shalt kill all this people as o' man, 259
15: 5 offering or sacrifice, for o' lamb. * "
11 be done for o' bullock, or for o' ram,*"
12 ye do to every o' according to their "
15 O' ordinance shall be both for you "
16 O' law and o' manner shall be for "
24 o' young bullock for a burnt offering,"
24 o' kid of the goats for a sin offering. "
29 o' law for him that sinneth through "
16: 3 the congregation are holy, every o'
15 I have not taken o' ass from them, 259
15 neither have I hurt o' of them. "
22 shall o' man sin, and wilt thou be "
17: 3 o' rod shall be for the head of the "
6 every o' of their princes gave him a
6 a rod apiece, for each prince o', 259

Nu 18:11 every o' that is clean in thy house
13 every o' that is clean in thine house
19: 3 and o' shall slay her before his face:
5 o' shall burn the heifer in his sight;
16 whosoever toucheth o' that is slain
18 bone, or o' slain, or o' dead, or a grave:*
21: 8 that every o' that is bitten, when he
25: 5 Slay ye every o' his men that were 376
6 o' of the children of Israel came and "
26:54 to every o' shall his inheritance be "
28: 4 The o' lamb shalt thou offer in the 259
7 fourth part of an hin for the o' lamb:"
11 and o' ram, seven lambs of the first "
12 mingled with oil, for o' bullock; * "
12 mingled with oil, for o' ram; "
13 for a meat offering unto o' lamb; * "
15 o' kid of the goats for a sin offering "
19 o' ram, and seven lambs of the first "
22 o' goat for a sin offering, to make "
27 o' ram, seven lambs of the first year;"
28 three tenth deals unto o' bullock, * "
28 two tenth deals unto o' ram, * "
29 A several tenth deal unto o' lamb,* "
30 And o' kid of the goats, to make an "
29: 2 o' young bullock, o' ram, and seven "
4 And o' tenth deal for "
4 tenth deal for o' lamb, throughout* "
5 o' kid of the goats for a sin offering,"
8 o' young bullock, o' ram, and seven "
9 and two tenth deals to o' ram, "
10 A several tenth deal for o' lamb, * "
11 O' kid of the goats for a sin offering;"
16, 19 And o' kid of the goats for a sin "
22 o' goat for a sin offering; beside the "
25 o' kid of the goats for a sin offering;"
28, 31, 34 And o' goat for a sin offering;"
36 o' bullock, o' ram, seven lambs of "
38 o' goat for a sin offering; beside the"
31:28 o' soul of five hundred, both of the "
30 thou shalt take o' portion of fifty, of "
34 threescore and o' thousand asses, "
39 Lord's tribute was threescore and o' "
47 Moses took o' portion of fifty, both "
49 and there lacketh not o' man of us, "
34:18 shall take o' prince of every tribe, 259
35: 8 every o' shall give of his cities unto 376
15 o' that killeth any person unawares "
30 o' witness shall not testify against 259
36: 7 for every o' of the children of Israel376
8 be wife unto o' of the family of the 259
9 remove from o' tribe to another tribe; "
9 every o' of the tribes of the children 376
De 1:22 ye came near unto me every o' of you,
23 twelve men of you, o' of a tribe: 259
35 there shall not o' of these men of 376
2:36 there was not o' city too strong for us:*
4: 4 are alive every o' of you this day.
32 from the o' side of heaven unto the
42 that fleeing unto o' of these cities he259
6: 4 Israel: The Lord our God is o' Lord: "
12:14 Lord shall choose in o' of thy tribes, "
13: 7 from the o' end of the earth even unto
12 shalt hear say in o' of thy cities, 259
15: 7 a poor man of o' of thy brethren "
17: 6 at the mouth of o' witness he shall "
15 o' from among thy brethren shalt thou
18:10 any o' that maketh his son or his
19: 5 he shall flee unto o' of those cities,259
11 die, and fleeth into o' of these cities: "
15 O' witness shall not rise up against "
21:15 two wives, o' beloved, and another "
23:16 he shall choose in o' of thy gates, "
24: 5 but he shall be free at home o' year,"
25: 5 dwell together, and o' of them die, "
11 men strive together o' with another,"
11 and the wife of the o' draweth near "
28: 7 shall come out against thee o' way, "
25 shalt go out o' way against them, "
57 And toward her young o' that cometh
32:30 How should o' chase a thousand, 259
33: 3 every o' shall receive of thy words.
8 and thy Urim be with thy holy o',
Jos. 9: 2 and with Israel, with o' accord. 259
10: 2 a great city, as o' of the royal cities,"
42 land did Joshua take at o' time, "
12: 9 The king of Jericho, o'; "
9 of Ai, which is beside Beth-el, o'; "
10 The king of Jerusalem, o'; "
10 the king of Hebron, o'; "
11 The king of Jarmuth, o'; "
11 the king of Lachish, o'; "
12 The king of Eglon, o'; "
12 the king of Gezer, o'; "
13 The king of Debir, o'; "
13 the king of Geder, o'; "
14 The king of Hormah, o'; "
14 the king of Arad, o'; "
15 The king of Libnah, o'; "
15 The king of Adullam, o'; "
16 The king of Makkedah, o'; "
16 the king of Beth-el, o'; "
17 The king of Tappuah, o'; "
17 the king of Hepher, o'; "
18 The king of Aphek, o'; "
18 the king of Lasharon, o'; "
19 The king of Madon, o'; "
19 the king of Hazor, o'; "
20 The king of Shimron-meron, o'; "
20 the king of Achshaph, o'; "
21 The king of Taanach, o'; "
21 the king of Megiddo, o'; "
22 The king of Kedesh, o'; "
22 the king of Jokneam of Carmel, o'; "
23 king of Dor in the coast of Dor, o'; "
23 the king of the nations of Gilgal, o';"
24 The king of Tirzah, o'; "

Jos 12:24 all the kings thirty and o'. 259
13:31 to the o' half of the children of Machir*
17:14 Why hast thou given me but o' lot 259
14 and o' portion to inherit, seeing I "
17 thou shalt not have o' lot only: "
20: 4 that doth flee unto o' of those cities "
21:42 cities were every o' with their suburbs
22: 7 the o' half of the tribe of Manasseh
14 each o' was an head of the house of376
23:10 O' man of you shall chase a 259
14 not o' thing hath failed of all the "
14 and not o' thing hath failed thereof. "
J'g 6:16 smite the Midianites as o' man. 259
29 they said o' to another, Who hath 376
31 because o' hath cast down his altar.
7: 5 Every o' that lappeth of the water
5 every o' that boweth down upon his
8:18 each o' resembled the children of a 259
9: 2 over you, or that o' reign over you? "
5 and ten persons, upon o' stone: "
18 and ten persons, upon o' stone, "
10:18 princes of Gilead said o' to another,376
11:35 thou art o' of them that trouble me: "
12: 7 was buried in o' of the cities of Gilead. "
16: 5 will give thee every o' of us eleven 376
29 of the o' with his right hand, and of259
17: 5 and consecrated o' of his sons, who "
11 man was unto him as o' of his sons. "
18:19 be a priest unto the house of o' man,"
19:13 let us draw near to o' of these places"
20: 1 was gathered together as o' man, "
8 And all the people arose as o' man, "
11 the city, knit together as o' man. "
16 every o' could sling stones at an hair
31 o' goeth up to the house of God, 259
21: 3 be to day o' tribe lacking in Israel? "
6 o' tribe cut off from Israel this day. "
8 What o' is there of the tribes of "
Ru 1: 4 the name of the o' was Orpah, and "
2:13 like unto o' of thine handmaidens. "
20 kin unto us, o' of our next kinsmen.
3:14 rose up before o' could know another.
4: 1 Ho, such a o'! turn aside, sit down 492
1Sa 1: 2 the name of the o' was Hannah, 259
24 and o' ephah of flour, and a bottle of"
2:25 If o' man sin against another, the
34 in o' day they shall die both of them.259
36 every o' that is left in thine house
36 thee, into o' of the priests' offices, 259
3:11 every o' that heareth it shall tingle.
6: 4 for o' plague was on you all, and on259
17 the Lord; for Ashdod o', for Gaza o';"
17 Askelon o', for Gath o', for Ekron o';"
9: 3 now o' of the servants with thee, "
10: 3 o' carrying three kids, and another "
11 people said o' to another, What is 376
12 o' of the same place answered and "
11: 7 and they came out with o' consent. 259
13: 1 Saul reigned o' year; and when he had*
17 o' company turned unto the way 259
14: 4 was a sharp rock on the o' side, 2088
4 the name of the o' was Bozez, and 259
5 The forefront of the o' was situate "
16 they went on beating down o' another.*
28 Then answered o' of the people, and
40 Be ye on o' side, and I and Jonathan259
45 there shall not o' hair of his head fall
16:18 Then answered o' of the servants, 259
17: 3 stood on a mountain on the o' side,2088
7 o' bearing a shield went before him.*
36 Philistine shall be as o' of them, 259
18: 7 women answered o' another as they
21 my son in law in the o' of the twain.*
19:22 And o' said, Behold, they be at Naioth
20:15 every o' from the face of the earth. 376
41 times: and they kissed o' another,
41 wept o' with another, until David
21:11 did they not sing o' to another of him
22: 2 And every o' that was in distress, 376
2 and every o' that was in debt, and "
2 and every o' that was discontented, "
7 son of Jesse give every o' of you fields
20 o' of the sons of Ahimelech the son 259
25:14 o' of the young men told Abigail, "
26:15 came o' of the people in to destroy "
22 let o' of the young men come over "
27: 1 perish o' day by the hand of Saul: "
29: 5 they sang o' to another in dances,
2Sa 1:15 David called o' of the young men, 259
2:13 the o' [428] on the o' side of the pool,2088
16 And they caught every o' his fellow376
21 thee hold on o' of the young men, 259
25 and became o' troop, and stood on "
27 every o' from following his brother.376
3:13 o' thing I require of thee, that is, 259
29 house of Joab o' that hath an issue,
4: 2 the name of the o' was Baanah, 259
10 When o' told me, saying, Behold, Saul
6:19 as men, to every o' a cake of bread,376
19 departed every o' to his house. "
20 o' of the vain fellows shamelessly 259
7:23 what o' nation in the earth is like "
8: 2 and with o' full line to keep alive.
9:11 at my table, as o' of the king's sons.259
10: 4 and shaved off o' half of their beards,
11: 3 o' said, Is not this Bath-sheba, the
25 the sword devoureth o' as well as 2088
12: 1 There were two men in o' city; the 259
1 city; the o' rich, and the other poor."
3 had nothing, save o' little ewe lamb,"
13:13 shalt be as o' of the fools in Israel. "
30 sons, and there is not o' of them left."
14: 6 but the o' smote the other, and slew "
11 not o' hair of thy son fall to the earth.
12 speak o' word unto my lord the king.*
13 speak this thing as o' which is faulty,
2Sa 14:27 and o' daughter, whose name was 259
15: 2 Thy servant is o' of the tribes of "
31 And o' told David, saying, Ahithophel
17:12 there shall not be left so much as o'.259
13 be not o' small stone found there. 1571
22 lacked not o' of them that was not 259
18:17 all Israel fled every o' to his tent. 376
19: 7 not tarry o' with thee this night: * "
14 Judah, even as the heart of o' man;259
20:11 And o' of Joab's men stood by him, 376
12 every o' that came by him stood still.
19 I am o' of them that are peaceable and*
23: 8 hundred, whom he slew at o' time. 259
9 o' of the three mighty men with David,
15 Oh that o' would give me drink of the
24 brother of Joab was o' of the thirty;
24:12 choose thee o' of them, that I may 259
1Ki 1:48 hath given o' to sit on my throne this
2:16 I ask o' petition of thee, deny me 259
20 I desire o' small petition of thee; "
3:17 And the o' woman said, O my lord, "
17 I and this woman dwell in o' house; "
23 The o' saith, This is my son that 2063
25 half to the o', and half to the other.259
4:22 Solomon's provision for o' day was "
6:24 five cubits was the o' wing of the "
24 from the uttermost part of the o' wing
25 were of o' measure and o' size. 259
26 of the o' cherub was ten cubits, and "
27 so that the wing of the o' touched "
27 touched the o' wall, and the wing
27 touched o' another in the midst of 3671
34 leaves of the o' door were folding, 259
7: 7 from o' side of the floor to the other.*
16 of the o' chapiter was five cubits, 259
17 seven for the o' chapiter, and seven "
18 round about upon the o' network, "
23 cubits from the o' brim to the other:*
27 cubits was the length of o' base, 259
34 to the four corners of o' base: and* "
36 to the proportion of every o', * 376
37 o' casting, o' measure, and o' size. 259
38 o' laver contained forty baths: and "
38 upon every o' of the ten bases o' laver."
42 of pomegranates for o' network, * "
44 o' sea, and twelve oxen under the "
8:56 o' word of all his good promise, "
9: 8 every o' that passeth by it shall be
10:14 that came to Solomon in o' year 259
16 shekels of gold went to o' target. "
17 pound of gold went to o' shield: "
20 twelve lions stood...on the o' side 2088
11:13 give o' tribe to thy son for David my259
32 have o' tribe for my servant David's "
36 And unto his son will I give o' tribe, "
12:29 And he set the o' in Beth-el, and the "
30 went to worship before the o', even "
13:33 and he became o' of the priests of the*
14:21 was forty and o' years old when he 259
15:10 And forty and o' years reigned he in"
16:11 left him not o' that pisseth against a*
18: 6 Ahab went o' way by himself, and 259
23 choose o' bullock for themselves, "
25 you o' bullock for yourselves, and "
40 of Baal; let not o' of them escape. 376
19: 2 not thy life as the life of o' of them 259
20:20 And they slew every o' his man: 376
29 thousand footmen in o' day. 259
22: 8 There is yet o' man, Micaiah the "
13 good unto the king with o' mouth: "
13 thee, be like the word of o' of them, "
20 And o' said on this manner, and
28 Hearken, O people, every o' of you.*
38 o' washed the chariot in the pool of*
2Ki 3:11 o' of the king of Israel's servants 259
23 and they have smitten o' another:* 376
4:22 o' of the young men, and o' of the 259
39 o' went out into the field to gather "
5: 4 o' went in, and told his lord, saying,
6: 3 o' said, Be content, I pray thee, and259
5 as o' was felling a beam, the axe "
12 o' of his servants said, None, my "
7: 3 they said o' to another, Why sit we 376
6 and they said o' to another, Lo, the "
8 they went into o' tent, and did eat 259
9 they said o' to another, We do not 376
13 o' of his servants answered and 259
8:26 he reigned o' year in Jerusalem. "
9: 1 prophet called o' of the children of "
11 and o' said unto him, Is all well?
18 went o' on horseback to meet him,
10:21 was full from o' end to another.
12: 4 of every o' that passeth the account,*
9 side as o' cometh into the house of 376
14: 8 let us look o' another in the face.
11 looked o' another in the face at
23 and reigned forty and o' years. 259
17:27 Carry thither o' of the priests whom "
28 Then o' of the priests whom they "
18:24 turn away the face of o' captain of "
31 vine, and every o' of his fig tree, 376
31 drink ye every o' the waters of his "
21:16 Jerusalem from o' end to another;
22: 1 thirty and o' years in Jerusalem. 259
23:35 every o' according to his taxation, 376
24:18 was twenty and o' years old when he259
25:16 two pillars, o' sea, and the bases "
17 height of the o' pillar was eighteen "
1Ch 1:19 sons: the name of the o' Peleg; "
9:31 Mattithiah, o' of the Levites,
10:13 of o' that had a familiar spirit,
11:11 hundred slain by him at o' time. 259
12 who was o' of the three mighties.
17 o' would give me drink of the water
12:14 o' of the least was over an hundred,*259
25 war, seven thousand and o' hundred.
1Ch 12:38 of o' heart to make David king. 259
16: 3 And he dealt to every o' of Israel, 376
3 to every o' a loaf of bread, and a
20 from o' kingdom to another people;
17: 5 and from o' tabernacle to another.
21 what o' nation in the earth is like 259
21:10 things: choose thee o' of them, that "
23:11 therefore they were in o' reckoning, "
24: 5 divided by lot, o' sort with another; 428
6 o' of the Levites, wrote them before*
6 o' principal household being taken 259
6 Eleazar, and o' taken for Ithamar.
17 The o' and twentieth to Jachin, the 259
25:28 The o' and twentieth to Hothir, he, "
26:12 having wards o' against another,*
27:18 Elihu, o' of the brethren of David:
29: 7 o' hundred thousand talents of iron.*
2Ch 3:11 o' wing of the...cherub was five * 259
11 wing of the o' cherub was five cubits,
12 o' wing of the other cherub was five*
17 o' on the right hand, and the other 259
4:15 O' sea, and twelve oxen under it. "
5:13 trumpeters and singers were as o', "
13 o' sound to be heard in praising and "
6:29 every o' shall know his own sore * "
7:21 to every o' that passeth by it; so
9: 6 o' half of the greatness of thy wisdom*
13 that came to Solomon in o' year 259
15 of beaten gold went to o' target. "
16 shekels of gold went to o' shield. "
19 twelve lions stood there on the o' side
12:13 was o' and forty years old when he 259
16:13 died in the o' and fortieth year of "
18: 7 There is yet o' man, by whom we "
8 Israel called for o' of his officers,* "
12 good to the king with o' assent; "
12 be like o' of theirs, and speak thou "
19 o' spake saying after this manner, and
20:23 every o' helped to destroy another.
22: 2 he reigned o' year in Jerusalem. 259
25:17 Come, let us see o' another in the face.
21 and they saw o' another in the face,
26:11 Hananiah, o' of the king's captains.
28: 6 and twenty thousand in o' day, 259
30:12 was to give them o' heart to do the "
17 for every o' that was not clean,
18 saying, The good Lord pardon every o'
31:16 every o' that entereth into the house
32:12 Ye shall worship before o' altar, 259
34: 1 in Jerusalem o' and thirty years. "
35:24 in o' of the sepulchres of his fathers.*
36:11 Zedekiah was o' and twenty years 259
Ezr 2: 1 and Judah, every o' unto his city; 376
26 Gaba, six hundred twenty and o'. 259
69 and o' thousand drams of gold,
69 and o' hundred priests' garments.
3: 1 together as o' man to Jerusalem. 259
5 every o' that willingly offered a
5:14 and they were delivered unto o',
6: 5 every o' to his place, and place them
8:34 By number and by weight of every o':*
9: 4 every o' that trembled at the words of
11 filled it from o' end to another with
10: 2 o' of the sons of Elam, answered and
13 is this a work of o' day or two: for 259
Ne 1: 2 Hanani, o' of my brethren, came, he "
3: 8 the son of o' of the apothecaries,
28 every o' over against his house. 376
4:15 to the wall, every o' unto his work. "
17 every o' with...hands wrought in
17 with o' of his hands wrought in the 259
18 every o' had his sword girded by 376
19 upon the wall, o' far from another.
22 Let every o' with his servant lodge 376
23 every o' put them off for washing. "
5: 7 exact usury, every o' of his brother. "
18 prepared for me daily was o' ox and259
6: 2 together in some o' of the villages
7: 3 every o' in his watch, and every o' 376
6 and to Judah, every o' unto his city;"
30 Gaba, six hundred twenty and o'. 259
37 Ono, seven hundred twenty and o'. "
63 took o' of the daughters of Barzillai*
8: 1 themselves together as o' man 259
16 every o' upon the roof of his house,376
9: 3 their God o' fourth part of the day;*
10:28 every o' having knowledge, and having
11: 1 cast lots, to bring o' of ten to dwell 259
3 dwelt every o' in his possession in 376
14 Zabdiel, the son of o' of the great men.*
20 Judah, every o' in his inheritance. 376
12:31 o' went on the right hand upon the
13:10 work, were fled every o' to his field.376
30 Levites, every o' in his business; "
Es 1: 7 being diverse o' from another,) 3627
3:13 children and women, in o' day, even259
4: 5 Hatach, o' of the king's chamberlains,
11 is o' law of his to put him to death,259
6: 9 to the hand of o' of the king's most376
7: 9 o' of the chamberlains, said before 259
8:12 o' day in all the provinces of king "
9:19 of sending portions o' to another. 376
22 of sending portions o' to another, "
Job 1: 1 o' that feared God, and eschewed evil.
4 in their houses, every o' his day; 376
8 o' that feareth God, and escheweth
2: 3 o' that feareth God, and escheweth
10 Thou speakest as o' of the foolish 259
11 came every o' from his own place; 376
12 they rent every o' his mantle, and "
5: 2 man, and envy slayeth the silly o'.
6:10 concealed the words of the Holy O'.
26 and the speeches of o' that is desperate,
9: 3 cannot answer him o' of a thousand.259
22 This is o' thing, therefore I said it. "
12: 4 I am as o' mocked of his neighbour,

Job 13: 9 as o· mocketh another, do ye so mock
14: 3 open thine eyes upon such an o·,
4 thing out of an unclean? not o·. 259
16: 21 o· might plead for a man with God,*
17: 10 I cannot find o· wise man among you.*
19: 11 me unto him as o· of his enemies.
21: 23 O· dieth in his full strength, being
23: 13 he is in o· mind, and who can turn 259
24: 6 They reap every o· his corn in the*
17 if o· know them, they are in the terrors*
29: 25 as o· that comforteth the mourners.
31: 15 did not o· fashion us in the womb? 259
35 Oh that o· would hear me! behold,
33: 23 interpreter, o· among a thousand, 259
40: 11 and behold every o· that is proud, and
12 Look on every o· that is proud,
41: 9 shall not o· be cast down even at the
16 O· is so near to another, that no air 259
17 They are joined o· to another, they 376
32 o· would think the deep to be hoary.
42: 11 and every o· an earring of gold. 376
Ps 12: 2 They speak vanity every o· with his "
14: 3 is none that doeth good, no, not o·. 259
16: 10 thine Holy O· to see corruption.
27: 4 O· thing have I desired of the Lord,259
29: 9 doth every o· speak of his glory.
32: 6 For this shall every o· that is godly
34: 20 bones: not o· of them is broken. 259
35: 14 as o· that mourneth for his mother.
49: 16 thou afraid when o· is made rich, 376
50: 21 I was altogether such an o· as thyself:
53: 3 Every o· of them is gone back: they
3 is none that doeth good, no, not o·. 259
58: 8 let every o· of them pass away: *
63: 11 every o· that sweareth by him shall
64: 6 inward thought of every o· of them,376
68: 21 hairy scalp of such an o· as goeth on
30 every o· submit himself with pieces of
71: 18 thy power to every o· that is to come.
22 the harp, O thou Holy O· of Israel.
73: 20 As a dream when o· awaketh; so,
75: 7 he putteth down o· and setteth up
78: 41 and limited the Holy O· of Israel.
65 the Lord awaked as o· out of sleep,
82: 7 men, and fall like o· of the princes. 259
83: 5 consulted together with o· consent:
84: 7 every o· of them in Zion appeareth
89: 10 Rahab in pieces, as o· that is slain;
18 the Holy O· of Israel is our king.
19 spakest in vision to thy holy o·, *
19 laid help upon o· that is mighty;
19 exalted o· chosen out of the people.
105: 13 they went from o· nation to another,*
13 from o· kingdom to another people;
37 not o· feeble person among their
106: 11 there was not o· of them left. 259
115: 8 so is every o· that trusteth in them.
119: 160 every o· of thy righteous judgments
162 thy word, as o· that findeth great spoil.
128: 1 Blessed is every o· that feareth the
135: 18 so is every o· that trusteth in them.
137: 3 saying, Sing us o· the songs of Zion.
141: 7 as when o· cutteth and cleaveth wood
145: 4 O· generation shall praise thy works
Pr 1: 14 among us; let us all have o· purse: 259
19 the ways of every o· that is greedy of
3: 18 happy is every o· that retaineth her.
6: 11 thy poverty come as o· that travelleth,*
28 Can o· go upon hot coals, and his 376
8: 30 by him, as o· brought up with him:
15: 12 scorner loveth not o· that reproveth*
16: 5 Every o· that is proud in heart is an
17: 14 strife is as when o· letteth out water:
19: 25 reprove o· that hath understanding,
20: 6 proclaim every o· his own goodness:376
21: 5 every o· that is hasty only to want.
22: 26 Be not thou o· of them that strike
24: 34 poverty come as o· that travelleth;*
26: 17 like o· that taketh a dog by the ears.
Ec 1: 4 O· generation passeth away, and
2: 14 o· event happeneth to them all. 259
3: 19 even o· thing befalleth them: as 2088
19 as the o· dieth, so dieth the other;
19 they have all o· breath; so that a 259
20 All go unto o· place; all are of the "
4: 8 There is o· alone, and there is not a "
9 Two are better than o·; because "
10 they fall, the o· will lift up his fellow:"
11 heat: but how can o· be warm alone?"
12 if o· prevail against him, two shall * "
5: 18 and comely for o· to eat and to drink,
6: 6 no good: do not all go to o· place? 259
7: 14 set the o· over against the other, 2088
27 counting o· by o·, to find out the 259
28 o· man among a thousand have I "
8: 9 a time wherein o· man ruleth over
9: 2 there is o· event to the righteous, 259
3 that there is o· event unto all: yea, "
18 but o· sinner destroyeth much good."
10: 3 he saith to every o· that he is a fool.
15 labour of the foolish wearieth every o·
12: 11 which are given from o· shepherd. 259
Ca 1: 7 as o· that turneth aside by the flocks
2: 10 Rise up, my love, my fair o·, and come
13 Arise, my love, my fair o·, and come
4: 2 whereof every o· bear twins, and none
9 my heart with o· of thine eyes, 259
9 thine eyes, with o· chain of thy neck."
6: 6 whereof every o· beareth twins, "
6 there is not o· barren among them.* "
9 My dove, my undefiled is but o·; "
9 she is the only o· of her mother, "
9 choice o· of her that bare her. "
8: 10 in his eyes as o· that found favour.
11 every o· for the fruit thereof was to376
Isa 1: 4 provoked the Holy O· of Israel

Isa 1: 23 every o· loveth gifts, and followeth
24 Lord of hosts, the mighty O· of Israel,
2: 12 shall be upon every o· that is proud*
12 and upon every o· that is lifted up;*
20 made each o· for himself to worship,*
3: 5 be oppressed, every o· by another, 376
5 and every o· by his neighbour: the "
4: 1 women shall take hold of o· man, 259
3 even every o· that is written among
5: 10 acres of vineyard shall yield o· bath,259
19 counsel of the Holy O· of Israel
24 the word of the Holy O· of Israel.
30 and if o· look unto the land, behold
6: 2 seraphims: each o· had six wings; 259
3 o· cried unto another, and said, Holy,
6 Then flew o· of the seraphims unto259
7: 22 every o· eat that is left in the land.
9: 14 and tail, branch and rush, in o· day.259
17 every o· is an hypocrite and an evildoer,
10: 17 fire, and his Holy O· for a flame:
17 his thorns and his briers in o· day; 259
20 Lord, the Holy O· of Israel, in truth.
34 and Lebanon shall fall by a mighty o·.
12: 6 for great is the Holy O· of Israel
13: 8 they shall be amazed o· at another;376
14 and flee every o· into his own land.*
15 Every o· that is found shall be thrust
15 every o· that is joined unto them
14: 18 in glory, every o· in his own house. 376
32 shall o· then answer the messengers
15: 3 and in their streets, every o· shall howl,
16: 7 howl for Moab, every o· shall howl: for
17: 7 respect to the Holy O· of Israel.
19: 2 fight every o· against his brother, 376
2 and every o· against his neighbour; "
17 every o· that maketh mention thereof
18 o· shall be called, The city of 259
20 send them a saviour, and a great o·,*
23: 15 according to the days of o· king: 259
27: 12 ye shall be gathered o· by o·, O ye "
28: 2 the Lord hath a mighty and strong o·,
29: 4 be, as of o· that hath a familiar spirit,
11 men deliver to o· that is learned,
19 rejoice in the Holy O· of Israel.
20 terrible o· is brought to nought,
23 and sanctify the Holy O· of Jacob,
30: 11 cause the Holy O· of Israel to cease
12 thus saith the Holy O· of Israel,
15 Lord God, the Holy O· of Israel;
17 O· thousand shall flee at the rebuke259
17 shall flee at the rebuke of o·; at the "
29 when o· goeth with a pipe to come
29 to the mighty O· of Israel. *
31: 1 not unto the Holy O· of Israel,
33: 20 not o· of the stakes thereof shall ever*
34: 15 be gathered, every o· with her mate.
16 no o· of these shall fail, none shall 259
36: 9 turn away the face of o· captain of "
16 and eat ye every o· of his vine, 376
16 and every o· of his fig tree, and "
16 drink ye every o· the waters of his "
37: 23 even against the Holy O· of Israel.
40: 25 shall I be equal? saith the Holy O·.
26 is strong in power; not o· faileth. 376
41: 6 They helped every o· his neighbour;"
6 every o· said to his brother, Be of "
14 redeemer, the Holy O· of Israel.
16 shalt glory in the Holy O· of Israel.
20 the Holy O· of Israel hath created it.
25 I have raised up o· from the north,
43: 3 the Holy O· of Israel, thy Saviour:
7 every o· that is called by my name:
14 redeemer, the Holy O· of Israel;
15 I am the Lord, your Holy O·, the
44: 5 O· shall say, I am the Lord's; and
45: 11 the Lord, the Holy O· of Israel,
24 Surely, shall o· say, in the Lord have
46: 7 o· shall cry unto him, yet can he not
47: 4 is his name, the Holy O· of Israel.
9 come to thee in a moment in o· day,259
15 wander every o· to his quarter; 376
48: 17 Redeemer, the Holy O· of Israel;
49: 7 Redeemer of Israel, and his Holy O·,
7 the Holy O· of Israel, and he shall
26 thy Redeemer, the Mighty O· of Jacob.
53: 6 turned every o· to his own way; 376
54: 5 Redeemer the Holy O· of Israel;
55: 1 Ho, every o· that thirsteth, come ye
5 and for the Holy O· of Israel; for
56: 6 every o· that keepeth the sabbath
11 their own way, every o· for his gain,376
57: 2 each o· walking in his uprightness.
15 lofty O· that inhabiteth eternity,
60: 9 God, and to the Holy O· of Israel,
14 The Zion of the Holy O· of Israel.
16 thy Redeemer, the mighty O· of Jacob.
22 A little o· shall become a thousand,
22 and a small o· a strong nation:
65: 8 and o· saith, Destroy it not; for a
66: 8 be made to bring forth in o· day? 259
13 As o· whom his mother comforteth,376
17 in the gardens, behind o· tree in the259
23 that from o· new moon to another,
23 and from o· sabbath to another,
Jer 1: 15 shall set every o· his throne at the 376
3: 14 I will take you o· of a city, and two 259
5: 6 every o· that goeth out thence shall be
8 morning: every o· neighed after his376
6: 3 they shall feed every o· in his place. "
13 them every o· is given to covetousness;
13 the priest every o· dealeth falsely.
8: 6 every o· turned to his course, as the
10 for every o· from the least even unto
10 the priest every o· dealeth falsely.
9: 4 ye heed every o· of his neighbour, 376
5 will deceive every o· his neighbour, "

Jer 9: 8 o· speaketh peaceably to his
20 every o· her neighbour lamentation.
10: 3 for o· cutteth a tree out of the forest,
11: 8 walked every o· in the imagination 376
12: 12 devour from the o· end of the land
13: 14 will dash them o· against another. 376
15: 10 yet every o· of them doth curse me.
16: 12 walk every o· after the imagination376
18: 11 return ye now every o· from his evil "
12 we will every o· do the imagination "
16 every o· that passeth thereby shall be
19: 8 every o· that passeth thereby shall be
9 eat every o· the flesh of his friend 376
11 as o· breaketh a potter's vessel, that
20: 7 in derision daily, every o· mocketh me.
11 is with me as a mighty terrible o·:
22: 7 thee, every o· with his weapons: 376
23: 17 they say unto every o· that walketh
30 steal my words every o· from his 376
35 ye say every o· to his neighbour, "
35 and every o· to his brother, What "
24: 2 O· basket had very good figs, even 259
25: 5 now every o· from his evil way, 376
26 north, far and near, o· with another, "
33 at that day from o· end of the earth
30: 14 with the chastisement of a cruel o·, for
31: 30 But every o· shall die for his own 376
32: 19 give every o· according to his ways, "
39 will give them o· heart, and o· way,259
34: 10 every o· should let his manservant,376
10 every o· his maidservant, go free, "
17 liberty, every o· to his brother, and "
35: 2 into o· of the chambers, and give 259
36: 7 will return every o· from his evil way:
16 they were afraid both o· and other, 376
38: 7 o· of the eunuchs which was in the* "
46: 16 to fall, yea, o· fell upon another: "
49: 17 every o· that goeth by it shall be
50: 13 every o· that goeth by Babylon shall
16 shall turn every o· to his people, 376
16 shall flee every o· to his own land.
29 Lord, against the Holy O· of Israel.
42 every o· put in array, like a man to the
51: 5 sin against the Holy O· of Israel.
9 go every o· into his own country: 376
31 O· post shall run to meet another, and
31 and o· messenger to meet another, to
31 that his city is taken at o· end, *
46 a rumour shall both come o· year, and
56 every o· of their bows is broken: for*
52: 1 Zedekiah was o· and twenty years 259
20 o· sea, and twelve brasen bulls that "
21 of o· pillar was eighteen cubits; "
22 height of o· chapiter was five cubits, "
Eze 1: 6 And every o· had four faces, and "
6 faces, and every o· had four wings. "
9 wings were joined o· to another; 802
9 they went every o· straight forward.376
11 wings of every o· were joined o· to "
12 they went every o· straight forward:"
15 behold o· wheel upon the earth by 259
16 and they four had o· likeness: and "
23 straight, the o· toward the other: 802
23, 23 every o· had two, which covered376
28 and I heard a voice of o· that spake.
3: 13 creatures that touched o· another, 802
4: 8 turn thee from o· side to another,
9 fitches, and put them in o· vessel, 259
17 and be astonied o· with another, 376
7: 16 mourning, every o· for his iniquity. "
9: 2 o· man among them was clothed 259
10: 7 o· cherub stretched forth his hand
9 o· wheel by...cherub, and another 259
10 wheel by o· cherub, and another
10 they four had o· likeness, as if a 259
14 every o· had four faces: the first face*
19 every o· stood at the door of the east*
21 Every o· had four faces apiece, and259
21 faces apiece, and every o· four wings;"
22 they went every o· straight forward.376
11: 5 into your mind, every o· of them. *
19 And I will give them o· heart, and 259
13: 10 and o· built up a wall, and, lo, others
14: 7 For every o· of the house of Israel, 376
15: 7 they shall go out from o· fire, and *
16: 15 on every o· that passed by; his it was.
25 thy feet to every o· that passed by,
44 Behold, every o· that useth proverbs
17: 22 top of his young twigs a tender o·,
18: 10 the like to any o· of these things, 259
30 every o· according to his ways, 376
19: 3 she brought up o· of her whelps: 259
20: 39 Go ye, serve ye every o· his idols, 376
21: 16 Go thee o· way or other, either on the*
19 shall come forth out of o· land: 259
22: 6 every o· were in thee to their power376
11 And o· hath committed abomination
23: 2 women, the daughters of o· mother:259
13 defiled, that they took both o· way, "
24: 23 and mourn o· toward another. 376
31: 11 hand of the mighty o· of the heathen;
33: 20 judge...every o· after his own ways. 376
21 o· that had escaped out of Jerusalem
24 Abraham was o·, and he inherited 259
26 ye defile every o· his neighbour's 376
30 houses, and speak o· to another, 2297
30 every o· to his brother, saying, 376
32 song of o· that hath a pleasant voice,
34: 23 will set up o· shepherd over them, 259
37: 16 son of man, take thee o· stick, and
17 join them o· to another into o· stick;"
17 they shall become o· in thine hand. "
19 of Judah, and make them o· stick, "
19 and they shall be o· in mine hand. "
22 make them o· nation in the land "
22 o· king shall be king to them all: "

Eze 37: 24 and they all shall have o· shepherd:259
39: 7 am the Lord, the Holy O· in Israel.
40: 5 the breadth of the building, o· reed;259
5 and the height, o· reed. "
6 the gate, which was o· reed broad; "
6 the gate, which was o· reed broad. "
7 little chamber was o· reed long, "
7 and o· reed broad; and between the "
7 of the gate within was o· reed. "
8 porch of the gate within, o· reed. "
10 they three were of o· measure: and "
10 posts had o· measure on this side "
12 the little chamber was o· cubit on "
12 and the space was o· cubit on that side; "
13 from the roof of o· little chamber to "
26 it had palm trees, o· on this side, 259
42 an half broad, and o· cubit high: "
44 o· at the side of the east gate having "
49 o· on this side, and another on that "
41: 1 six cubits broad on the o· side,
2 were five cubits on the o· side, and
6 o· over another, and thirty in order;
11 was left, o· door toward the north, 259
15 the galleries thereof on the o· side
19 toward the palm tree on the o· side,
21 the appearance of the o· as the *
24 two leaves for the o· door, and two 259
26 and palm trees on the o· side and on
42: 4 breadth inward, a way of o· cubit; 259
9 as o· goeth into them from the utter
12 the east, as o· entereth into them.
43: 14 two cubits, and the breadth o· cubit.*259
14 four cubits, and the breadth o· cubit;
45: 7 be for the prince on the o· side and
7 be over against o· of the portions, 259
11 and the bath shall be of o· measure, "
15 o· lamb out of the flock, out of two "
20 the month for every o· that erreth, 376
46: 12 o· shall then open him the gate that
12 his going forth o· shall shut the gate.
17 his inheritance to o· of his servants,259
22 four corners were of o· measure. "
47: 7 many trees on the o· side and on the
14 inherit it, o· as well as another: 376
48: 1 of Hethlon, as o· goeth to Hamath,*
8 in length as o· of the other parts, 259
21 on the o· side and on the other of the
31 gates northward; o· gate of Reuben,259
31 o· gate of Judah, o· gate of Levi. "
32 three gates; and o· gate of Joseph, "
32 o· gate of Benjamin, o· gate of Dan. "
33 and three gates; o· gate of Simeon, "
33 o· gate of Issachar, o· gate of Zebulun."
34 their three gates; o· gate of Gad, "
34 o· gate of Asher, o· gate of Naphtali."
Da 2: 9 there is but o· decree for you: 2298
43 they shall not cleave o· to another,1836
3: 19 heat the furnace o· seven times 2298
4: 13 and an holy o· came down from
19 was astonied for o· hour, and his *2298
23 and an holy o· coming down from
5: 6 knees smote o· against another. 1668
7: 3 the sea, diverse o· from another.
5 and it raised up itself on o· side, 2298
13 o· like the Son of man came with the
16 near unto o· of them that stood 2298
8: 3 but o· was higher than the other. 259
9 out of o· of them came forth a little "
13 Then I heard o· saint speaking, and "
9: 27 the covenant with many for o· week:"
10: 13 withstood me o· and twenty days: "
13 lo, Michael, o· of the chief princes, "
16 o· like the similitude of the sons of
18 touched me o· like the appearance
11: 5 shall be strong, and o· of his princes;
7 roots shall o· stand up in his estate,
10 and o· shall certainly come, and
27 they shall speak lies at o· table; 259
12: 1 every o· that shall be found written in
5 the o· on this side of the bank of 259
6 o· said to the man clothed in linen,
Ho 1: 11 and appoint themselves o· head, 259
4: 3 every o· that dwelleth therein shall
11: 9 and Holy O· in the midst of thee:
Joe 2: 7 shall march every o· on his ways, 376
8 Neither shall o· thrust another;
8 shall walk every o· in his path: 1397
Am 3: 5 o· take up a snare from the earth,*
4: 7 I caused it to rain upon o· city, and259
7 o· piece was rained upon, and the "
8 three cities wandered unto o· city, "
6: 9 if there remain ten men in o· house, "
12 rock? will o· plow there with oxen?
8: 8 every o· mourn that dwelleth therein?
Ob 9 every o· of the mount of Esau may 376
11 even thou wast as o· of them. 259
Jon 1: 7 And they said every o· to his fellow,376
3: 8 turn every o· from his evil way, and "
Mic 2: 4 shall o· take up a parable against you,*
4: 5 every o· in the name of his god, 376
Na 1: 11 There is o· come out of thee, that
2: 4 shall justle o· against another in the‡
Hab 1: 12 O Lord my God, mine Holy O·? 6918
3: 3 and the Holy O· from mount Paran."
Zep 2: 11 every o· from his place, even all 376
15 every o· that passeth by her shall hiss,
3: 9 Lord, to serve him with o· consent. 259
Hag 2: 1 o· and twentieth day of the month, "
12 If o· bear holy flesh in the skirt of
13 If o· that is unclean by a dead body
16 o· came to an heap of twenty measures,
16 o· came to the pressfat for to draw
22 every o· by the sword of his brother.376
Zec 3: 9 upon o· stone shall be seven eyes: 259
9 the iniquity of that land in o· day. "
4: 3 o· upon the right side of the bowl, "

Zec 5: 3 every o· that stealeth shall be cut off
3 every o· that sweareth shall be cut off
8: 10 men every o· against his neighbour.376
21 the inhabitants of o· city shall go to259
10: 1 rain, to every o· grass in the field. 376
11: 6 every o· into his neighbour's hand, "
7 two staves; the o· I called Beauty, 259
8 shepherds...I cut off in o· month; "
9 rest eat every o· the flesh of another.802
16 neither shall seek the young o·, nor*
12: 10 as o· mourneth for his only son, and
10 as o· that is in bitterness for his
13: 4 be ashamed every o· of his vision, 376
6 And o· shall say unto him, What are
14: 7 But it shall be o· day which shall be 259
9 there be o· Lord, and his name o·. "
13 lay hold every o· on the hand of his 376
16 that every o· that is left of all the
Mal 2: 3 and o· shall take you away with it.*
10 Have we not all o· father? hath 259
10 hath not o· God created us? why do "
15 And did not he make o·? Yet had he "
15 And wherefore o·? That he might "
16 for o· covereth violence with his *
17 Every o· that doeth evil is good in the
3: 16 the Lord spake often o· to another:376
M't 3: 3 voice of o· crying in the wilderness,
5: 18 heaven and earth pass, o· jot or 1520
18 o· tittle shall in no wise pass 3391
19 shall break o· of these least
29, 30 should o· of thy members perish,1520
36 not make o· hair white or black. 3391
6: 24 for either he will hate the o·, and 1520
24 or else he will hold to the o·, and "
27 can add o· cubit unto his stature? "
29 was not arrayed like o· of these. "
7: 8 every o· that asketh receiveth; and
21 Not every o· that saith unto me,
26 every o· that heareth these sayings
29 he taught them as o· having authority,
10: 29 and o· of them shall not fall on the 1520
42 o· of these little ones a cup of cold "
12: 6 place is o· greater than the temple.
11 that shall have o· sheep, and if it 1520
22 unto him o· possessed with a devil,
29 can o· enter into a strong man's 5100
47 Then o· said unto him, Behold, thy "
13: 19 When any o· heareth the word of
19 then cometh the wicked o·, and
38 are the children of the wicked o·;
46 had found o· pearl of great price, 1520
16: 14 Jeremias, or o· of the prophets. "
17: 4 here three tabernacles, o· for thee, 3391
4 and o· for Moses, and o· for Elias. "
18: 5 shall receive o· such little child in 1520
6 shall offend o· of these little ones "
9 for thee to enter into life with o· eye,3442
10 despise not o· of these little ones; 1520
12 o· of them be gone astray, doth he "
14 o· of these little ones should perish."
16 then take with thee o· or two more, "
24 o· was brought unto him, which "
28 and found o· of his fellowservants, "
35 forgive not every o· his brother
19: 5 and they twain shall be o· flesh? 3391
6 they are no more twain, but o· flesh."
16 o· came and said unto him, Good 1520
17 is none good but o·, that is, God: "
29 And every o· that hath forsaken
20: 12 last have wrought but o· hour, and3391
13 he answered o· of them, and said, 1520
21 may sit, the o· on thy right hand, "
21: 24 I also will ask you o· thing, which if"
35 took his servants, and beat o·, and 3739
22: 5 went their ways, o· to his farm,3588,3303
35 o· of them, which was a lawyer, 1520
23: 4 not move them with o· of their fingers.*
8 for o· is your Master, even Christ; 1520
9 for o· is your Father, which is in "
10 for o· is your Master, even Christ. "
15 sea and land to make o· proselyte, "
24: 2 not be left here o· stone upon another,
10 and shall betray o· another, 240
10 another, and shall hate o· another. "
31 from o· end of heaven to the other.
40, 41 o· shall be taken, and the other1520
25: 15 unto o· he gave five talents, 3739,3303
15 to another two, and to another o·; 1520
18 he that had received o· went and "
24 he which had received the o· talent "
29 every o· that hath shall be given,
32 separate them o· from another, as 240
40 it unto o· of the least of these my 1520
45 did it not to o· of the least of these. "
26: 14 Then o· of the twelve, called Judas "
21 you, that o· of you shall betray me. "
22 every o· of them to say unto him,
40 ye not watch with me o· hour? 3391
47 lo, Judas, o· of the twelve, came, 1520
51 o· of them which were with Jesus "
73 Peter, Surely thou also art o· of them;
27: 38 o· on the right hand, and another 1520
48 And straightway o· of them ran, "
M'r 1: 3 voice of o· crying in the wilderness,
7 cometh o· mightier than I after me,*
22 taught them as o· that had authority,*
24 who thou art, the Holy O· of God.
2: 3 bringing o· sick of the palsy, which*
4: 41 said o· to another, What manner 240
5: 22 o· of the rulers of the synagogue, 1520
6: 15 prophet, or as o· of the prophets. "
7: 14 Hearken unto me every o· of you,*
32 bring unto him o· that was deaf,
8: 14 ship with them more than o· loaf. 1520
28 and others, O· of the prophets. "
9: 5 three tabernacles; o· for thee, 3391

M'r 9: 5 and o· for Moses, and o· for Elias.
10 questioning o· with another what*
17 o· of the multitude answered and 1520
26 and he was as o· dead; insomuch
37 receive o· of such children in my 1520
38 o· casting out devils in thy name, 5100
42 shall offend o· of these little ones 1520
47 into the kingdom of God with o· 3442
49 every o· shall be salted with fire,
50 and have peace o· with another. 240
10: 8 And they twain shall be o· flesh: 3391
8 are no more twain, but o· flesh.
17 came o· running, and kneeled to 1520
18 is none good but o·, that is, God. "
21 O· thing thou lackest: go thy way, "
37 we may sit, o· on thy right hand, "
11: 29 I will also ask of you o· question, "
12: 6 Having yet therefore o· son, his "
28 o· of the scribes came, and having "
29 The Lord our God is o· Lord: "
32 there is o· God; and there is none "
13: 1 o· of his disciples saith unto him, "
2 not be left o· stone upon another,
14: 10 Judas Iscariot, o· of the twelve, 1520
18 O· of you which eateth with me "
19 to say unto him o· by o·, Is it I? "
20 It is o· of the twelve, that dippeth "
37 couldest thou not watch o· hour? 3391
43 cometh Judas, o· of the twelve, 1520
47 o· of them that stood by drew a "
66 o· of the maids of the high priest: 3391
69 that stood by, This is o· of them.
70 to Peter, Surely thou art o· of them:
15: 6 he released unto them o· prisoner, 1520
7 And there was o· named Barabbas,
21 they compel o· Simon a Cyrenian, 5100
27 the o· on his right hand, and the 1520
36 o· ran and filled a sponge full of "
Lu 2: 3 taxed, every o· into his own city.
15 the shepherds said o· to another, 240
36 there was o· Anna, a prophetess,
3: 4 voice of o· crying in the wilderness,
16 but o· mightier than I cometh, the*
4: 34 who thou art; the Holy O· of God.
40 laid his hands on every o· of them,1520
5: 3 And he entered into o· of the ships, "
6: 9 unto them, I will ask you o· thing;5100
11 communed o· with another what 240
29 on the o· cheek offer also the other;
40 every o· that is perfect shall be as
7: 8 I say unto o·, Go, and he goeth; 5129
32 calling o· to another, and saying, 240
36 o· of the Pharisees desired him 5100
41 the o· owed five hundred pence, 1520
8: 25 wondered, saying o· to another, 240
42 For he had o· only daughter, about*
49 cometh o· from the ruler of the 5100
9: 8 o· of the old prophets was risen 1520
19 that o· of the old prophets is risen 5100
33 three tabernacles; o· for thee, 3391
33 and o· for Moses, and o· for Elias: "
43 wondered every o· at all things *3956
49 o· casting out devils in thy name; 5100
10: 42 But o· thing is needful: and Mary 1520
11: 1 o· of his disciples said unto him, 5100
4 forgive every o· that is indebted
10 every o· that asketh receiveth; and
45 Then answered o· of the lawyers, 5100
46 burdens with o· of your fingers. 1520
12: 1 that they trode o· upon another, he 240
6 not o· of them is forgotten before 1520
13 o· of the company said unto him, 5100
25 can add to his stature o· cubit? *1520
27 was not arrayed like o· of these. "
52 shall be five in o· house divided, "
13: 10 teaching in o· of the synagogues 3391
15 not each o· of you on the sabbath
23 Then said o· unto him, Lord, are 5100
14: 1 house of o· of the chief Pharisees "
15 o· of them that sat at meat with "
18 o· consent began to make excuse. 3391
15: 4 he lose o· of them, doth not leave 1520
7 over o· sinner that repenteth, more "
8 if she lose o· piece, doth not light 3391
10 God over o· sinner that repenteth. 1520
19 make me as o· of thy hired servants."
26 he called o· of the servants, and "
16: 5 called every o· of his lord's debtors "
13 either he will hate the o·, and love "
13 or else he will hold to the o·, and "
17 than o· tittle of the law to fail. 3391
30 if o· went unto them from the dead,5100
31 though o· rose from the dead.
17: 2 should offend o· of these little ones.1520
15 And o· of them, when he saw that "
22 shall desire to see o· of the days of3391
24 out of the o· part under heaven,
34 there shall be two men in o· bed; 3391
34 the o· shall be taken, and the 1520
35 the o· shall be taken, and the 3391
36 the o· shall be taken, and the 1520
18: 10 the o· a Pharisee, and the other a "
14 for every o· that exalteth himself
19 none is good, save o·, that is, God. 1520
22 Yet lackest thou o· thing: sell all "
19: 26 unto every o· which hath shall be
44 leave in thee o· stone upon another;
20: 1 on o· of those days, as he taught 3391
3 I will also ask you o· thing; and *1520
21: 6 shall not be left o· stone upon another,
22: 36 him sell his garment, and buy o·. *
47 was called Judas, o· of the twelve, 1520
50 o· of them smote the servant of the "
59 about the space of o· hour after 3391
23: 14 as o· that perverteth the people: and
17 release o· unto them at the feast.)*1520

Lu 23:26 away, they laid hold upon o· Simon, 5100
33 o· on the right hand, and the 3739,3303
39 o· of the malefactors which were 1520
24:17 these that ye have o· to another, 240
18 the o· of them, whose name was 1520
32 they said o· to another, Did not our 240
Joh 1:23 voice of o· crying in the wilderness,
26 there standeth o· among you, whom
40 O· of the two which heard John 1520
3: 8 so is every o· that is born of the
20 every o· that doeth evil hateth the
4:33 said the disciples o· to another, 240
37 O· soweth, and another reapeth. 243
5:44 which receive honour o· of another, 240
45 there is o· that accuseth you, even
6: 7 every o· of them may take a little.
8 O· of his disciples, Andrew, Simon 1520
22 save that o· whereinto his disciples "
40 every o· which seeth the Son, and
70 you twelve, and o· of you is a devil? 1520
71 betray him, being o· of the twelve. "
7:21 unto them, I have done o· work, "
50 Jesus by night, being o· of them,) "
8: 9 went out o· by o·, beginning at the "
18 am o· that bear witness of myself,*
41 we have o· Father, even God. 1520
50 there is o· that seeketh and judgeth.
9:25 o· thing I know, that, whereas I 1520
32 the eyes of o· that was born blind.*
10:16 there shall be o· fold, and 3391
16 there shall be...o· shepherd. 1520
30 I and my Father are o·. "
11:49 o· of them, named Caiaphas, being "
50 o· man should die for the people, "
52 together in o· the children of God "
12: 2 Lazarus was o· of them that sat at "
4 o· of his disciples, Judas Iscariot, "
48 my words, hath o· that judgeth him:
13:14 also ought to wash o· another's feet. 240
21 you, that o· of you shall betray me. 1520
22 the disciples looked o· on another, 240
23 on Jesus' bosom o· of his disciples, 1520
34 unto you, That ye love o· another; 240
34 you, that ye also love o· another. "
35 if ye have love o· to another. "
15:12 That ye love o· another, as I have "
17 you, that ye love o· another. "
17:11 me, that they may be o·, as we are. 1520
21 That they all may be o·; as thou, "
21 thee, that they also may be o· in us:*"
22 they may be o·, even as we are o·: "
23 they may be made perfect in o·; "
18:14 o· man should die for the people. "
17 thou also o· of this man's disciples?
22 o· of the officers which stood by 1520
25 Art not thou also o· of his disciples?
26 O· of the servants of the high 1520
37 Every o· that is of the truth
39 release unto you o· at the passover: 1520
19:18 on either side o·, and Jesus in the
34 But o· of the soldiers with a spear 1520
20:12 the o· at the head, and the other at "
24 Thomas, o· of the twelve, called
21:25 if they should be written every o·, "
Ac 1:14 continued with o· accord in prayer 3661
22 must o· be ordained to be a witness 1520
2: 1 they were all with o· accord in *3661
1 all with...accord in o· place. 3858,848
7 marvelled, saying o· to another, 240
12 in doubt, saying o· to another, 243
27 thine Holy O· to see corruption.
38 and be baptized every o· of you in
46 daily with o· accord in the temple, 3661
3:14 ye denied the Holy O· and the Just,
26 turning away every o· of you from
4:24 their voice to God with o· accord, 3661
32 were of o· heart and of...soul:
32 were of...heart and of o· soul: *3391
5:12 with o· accord in Solomon's porch. 3661
16 and they were healed every o·.
25 came o· and told them, saying, 5100
34 stood there up o· in the council, a "
7:24 seeing o· of them suffer wrong, he "
26 would have set them at o· again, 1515
26 why do ye wrong o· to another? 240
52 before of the coming of the Just O·; of
57 and ran upon him with o· accord, 3661
8: 6 the people with o· accord gave heed"
9 that himself was some great o·:
9:11 the house of Judas for o· called Saul,
43 in Joppa with o· Simon a tanner. 5100
10: 2 o· that feared God with all his house,
5 men to Joppa, and call for o· Simon,
6 lodgeth with o· Simon a tanner, 5100
22 a just man, and o· that feareth God,
28 or come unto o· of another nation;
32 the house of o· Simon a tanner by the*
11:28 stood up o· of them named Agabus, 1520
12:10 and passed on through o· street; 3391
20 they came with o· accord to him, 3661
13:25 there cometh o· after me, whose
35 thine Holy O· to see corruption.
15:25 being assembled with o· accord, 3661
39 departed asunder o· from the other: 240
17: 7 that there is another king, o· Jesus.
26 hath made of o· blood all nations 1520
27 he be not far from every o· of us: "
18: 7 o· that worshipped God, whose house
12 made insurrection with o· accord 3661
19: 9 daily in the school of o· Tyrannus.* 5100
14 there were seven sons of o· Sceva, a
29 with o· accord into the theatre. 3661
32 cried o· thing, and some another: 3303
34 all with o· voice about the space of 3391
38 let them implead o· another. 240
20:31 ceased not to warn every o· night 1520

Ac 21: 6 had taken our leave o· of another, *240
7 and abode with them o· day. 3391
8 evangelist, which was o· of the seven;
16 with them o· Mnason of Cyprus, 5100
26 be offered for every o· of them. 1520
34 some cried o· thing, and some another,
22:12 And o· Ananias, a devout man 5100
14 know his will, and see that Just O·,
23: 6 that the o· part were Sadducees, 1520
17 Paul called o· of the centurions "
24:21 Except it be for this o· voice, that 3391
25:19 and of o· Jesus, which was dead, 5100
27: 1 other prisoners unto o· named Julius,*
2 o· Aristarchus, a Macedonian of *
28: 2 a fire, and received us every o·, *
13 after o· day the south wind blew, 3391
25 that Paul had spoken o· word, 1520
Ro 1:16 salvation to every o· that believeth;
27 in their lust o· toward another; 240
2:15 accusing or...excusing o· another;) "
28 is not a Jew, which is o· outwardly;
29 But he is a Jew, which is o· inwardly;
3:10 There is none righteous, no, not o·: 1520
12 is none that doeth good, no, not o·. "
30 Seeing it is o· God, which shall "
5: 7 for a righteous man will o· die: 5100
12 as by o· man sin entered into the 1520
15 the offence of o· many be dead, "
15 which is by o· man, Jesus Christ, "
16 not as it was by o· that sinned, so "
16 was by o· to condemnation, but the "
17 by o· man's offence death reigned "
17 man's offence death reigned by o·; "
17 reign in life by o·, Jesus Christ.) "
18 by the offence of o· judgment came "
18 the righteousness of o· the free gift "
19 as by o· man's disobedience many "
19 by the obedience of o· shall many be "
9:10 Rebecca also had conceived by o·, "
21 lump to make o· vessel unto honour,
10: 4 law for righteousness to every o· 3956
12: 4 have many members in o· body, 1520
5 being many, are o· body in Christ, "
5 every o· members...of another. * "
5 members o· of another. 240
10 kindly affectioned o· to another "
10 in honour preferring o· another; "
16 of the same mind o· toward another."
13: 8 any thing, but to love o· another: "
14: 5 O· man esteemeth...day above 3739,3303
5 man esteemeth o· day above another:
12 every o· of us shall give account of
13 not...judge o· another any more: 240
19 wherewith o· may edify another. "
15: 2 every o· of us please his neighbour
5 be likeminded o· toward another 240
6 That ye may with o· mind...mouth 3661
6 with...mind and o· mouth glorify 1520
7 Wherefore receive ye o· another, 240
14 able also to admonish o· another. "
16:16 Salute o· another with an holy kiss. "
1Co 1:12 that every o· of you saith, I am of
3: 4 For while o· saith, I am of Paul; 5100
8 and he that watereth are o·: 1520
4: 6 no o· of you be puffed up for o· "
5: 1 o· should have his father's wife. 5100
5 To deliver such an o· unto Satan
11 with such an o· no not to eat.
6: 5 not o· that shall be able to judge
7 ye go to law with o· another. 1438
16 is joined to an harlot is o· body? 1520
16 two, saith he, shall be o· flesh. 3391
17 is joined unto the Lord is o· spirit. 1520
7: 5 Defraud ye not o· the other, except 240
7 o· after this manner, and 3739,3303
17 as the Lord hath called every o·, so*
25 as o· that hath obtained mercy of the
8: 4 there is none other God but o·. 1520
6 But to us there is but o· God, the "
6 o· Lord Jesus Christ, by whom are "
9:24 run all, but o· receiveth the prize? "
26 fight I, not as o· that beateth the air:*
10: 8 and fell in o· day three and twenty 3391
17 many are o· bread, and o· body: 1520
17 are all partakers of that o· bread. "
11: 5 is even all o· as if she were shaven. "
20 come together...into o· place, *3588,846
21 eating every o· taketh before other
21 o· is hungry, and another is 3739,3303
33 together to eat, tarry o· for another. 240
12: 8 For to o· is given by the Spirit 3739,3303
11 that o· and the selfsame Spirit, 1520
12 as the body is o·, and hath many "
12 the members of that o· body, being "
12 many, are o· body: so also is Christ. "
13 For by o· Spirit are we all baptized "
13 into o· body, whether we be Jews or"
13 been all made to drink o· Spirit. "
14 For the body is not o· member, but "
18 every o· of them in the body, as it "
19 if they were all o· member, where "
20 many members, yet but o· body. "
25 have the same care o· for another. 240
26 whether o· member suffer, all the 1520
26 or o· member be honoured, all the "
14:23 be come together into o· place,*3588,846
24 come in o· that believeth not, or 5100
24 or o· unlearned, he is convinced of*
26 every o· of you hath a psalm, hath
27 by course; and let o· interpret. 1520
31 For ye may all prophesy o· by 2596, "
31 ye may all prophesy...by o·, "
15: 8 of me also, as of o· born out of due time.
39 there is o· kind of flesh of men, 243
40 the glory of the celestial is o·, and 2087
41 There is o· glory of the sun, and 243

1Co 15:41 o· star differeth from another star in
16: 2 every o· of you lay by him in store,
16 to every o· that helpeth with us,
20 ye o· another with an holy kiss. 240
2Co 2: 7 such a o· should be swallowed up
5:10 every o· may receive the things done
14 that if o· died for all, then were all 1520
10:11 Let such an o· think this, that,
11: 2 have espoused you to o· husband, 1520
24 received I forty stripes save o·. 3391
12: 2 o· caught up to the third heaven.
5 Of such an o· will I glory: yet of
13:11 be of o· mind, live in peace; and 3588,846
12 Greet o· another with an holy kiss. 240
Ga 3:10 Cursed is every o· that continueth
13 Cursed is every o· that hangeth on
16 as of o·, And to thy seed, which is 1520
20 not a mediator of o·, but God is o·. "
28 for ye are all o· in Christ Jesus. "
4:22 o· by a bondmaid, the other by a "
24 the o· from the mount Sinai, which 3391
5:13 flesh, but by love serve o· another. 240
14 all the law is fulfilled in o· word, 1520
15 if ye bite and devour o· another, 240
15 ye be not consumed o· of another. "
17 are contrary the o· to the other: so "
26 o· another, envying o· another. "
6: 1 restore such an o· in the spirit of
2 Bear ye o· another's burdens, and 240
Eph 1:10 gather together in o· all things *
2:14 who hath made both o·, and hath 1520
15 in himself of twain o· new man, so "
16 both unto God in o· body by the "
18 access by o· Spirit unto the Father. "
4: 2 forbearing o· another in love; 240
4 There is o· body, and o· Spirit, even 1520
4 called in o· hope of your calling; 3391
5 O· Lord,...faith, o· baptism, 1520
5 Lord, o· faith,...baptism, 3391
6 O· God and Father of all, who is 1520
7 unto every o· of us is given grace
25 for we are members o· of another. 240
32 And be ye kind o· to another, "
32 forgiving o· another, even as God 1438
5:21 Submitting yourselves o· to another 240
31 wife, and they two shall be o· flesh. 3391
33 let every o· of you in particular
Ph'p 1:16 The o· preach Christ of contention, 3303
27 that ye stand fast in o· spirit, with 1520
27 with o· mind striving together 3391
2: 2 the same love, being of o· accord, 4861
2 love, being...of o· mind. 3888,1520
3:13 this o· thing I do, forgetting those "
Col 3: 9 Lie not o· to another, seeing that 240
13 Forbearing o· another, and "
13 forgiving o· another, if any man *1438
15 also ye are called in o· body; and 1520
16 and admonishing o· another in 1438
4: 9 and beloved brother, who is o· of you.
12 Epaphras, who is o· of you, a servant
1Th 2:11 and charged every o· of you, as a 1520
3:12 abound in love o· toward another, 240
4: 4 every o· of you should know how
9 taught of God to love o· another. 240
18 comfort o· another with these words."
5:11 edify o· another, even as also ye 1520
2Th 1: 3 charity of every o· of you all toward"
1Ti 2: 5 there is o· God, and o· mediator "
3: 2 husband of o· wife, vigilant, sober, 3391
12 deacons be the husbands of o· wife, "
5: 9 having been the wife of o· man, 1520
21 without preferring o· before another,*
2Ti 2:19 every o· that nameth the name of
Tit 1: 6 blameless, the husband of o· wife, 3391
12 O· of themselves, even a prophet 5100
3: 3 envy, hateful, and hating o· another. 240
Ph'm 9 being such an o· as Paul the aged,
Heb 2: 6 But o· in a certain place testified, 5100
11 who are sanctified are all of o·: 1520
3:13 exhort o· another daily, while it 1438
5:12 ye have need that o· teach you again
13 For every o· that useth milk is
6:11 every o· of you do shew the same
10:12 he had offered o· sacrifice for sins 3391
14 by o· offering he hath perfected for "
24 us consider o· another to provoke 240
25 but exhorting o· another: and so much
11:12 Therefore sprang there even of o·, 1520
12:16 who for o· morsel of meat sold his 3391
13:14 continuing city,...we seek o· to come.*
Jas 2:10 yet offend in o· point, he is guilty 1520
16 o· of you say unto them, Depart in 5100
19 believest that there is o· God; thou 1520
4:11 Speak not evil o· of another, 240
12 There is o· lawgiver, who is able to 1520
5: 9 Grudge not o· against another, 240
16 Confess your faults o· to another, "
16 pray o· for another, that ye may be "
19 the truth, and o· convert him; 5100
1Pe 1:22 love o· another with a pure heart 240
3: 8 Finally, be ye all of o· mind, having*3675
8 having compassion o· for another,*
4: 9 hospitality o· to another without 240
10 minister the same o· to another, *1438
5: 5 all of you be subject o· to another, 240
14 Greet ye o· another with a kiss of "
2Pe 3: 8 be not ignorant of this o· thing, 1520
8 that o· day is with the Lord as a 3391
8 and a thousand years as o· day. "
1Jo 1: 7 have fellowship o· with another, "
2:13 ye have overcome the wicked o·.
14 and ye have overcome the wicked o·.
20 ye have an unction from the Holy O·,
29 every o· that doeth righteousness
3:11 that we should love o· another. 240
12 Not as Cain, who was of that wicked o·,

1Jo 3:23 and love o' another, as he gave us 240
4: 7 Beloved, let us love o' another: for "
7 every o' that loveth is born of God,
11 ye ought also to love o' another. 240
12 If we love o' another, God dwelleth "
5: 1 every o' that loveth him that begat*
7 Ghost: and these three are o'. *1520
8 blood: and these three agree in o'. "
18 and that wicked o' toucheth him not.
2Jo 5 beginning, that we love o' another. 240
Re 1:13 midst...o' like unto the Son of man,
2:23 I will give unto every o' of you
4: 2 in heaven, and o' sat on the throne.
5: 5 And o' of the elders saith unto me, 1520
8 having every o' of them harps, and
6: 1 the Lamb opened o' of the seals, 3391
1 o' of the four beasts saying, Come 1520
4 that they should kill o' another: 240
11 robes were given unto every o' of
7:13 o' of the elders answered, saying 1520
9:12 O' woe is past; and, behold, there*3391
11:10 and shall send gifts o' to another; 240
13: 3 I saw o' of his heads as it were 3391
14:14 cloud o' sat like unto the Son of man,
15: 7 o' of the four beasts gave unto the 1520
17: 1 there came o' of the seven angels "
10 five are fallen, and o' is, and the "
12 as kings o' hour with the beast. 3391
13 These have o' mind, and shall give "
18: 8 shall her plagues come in o' day, "
10 in o' hour is thy judgment come. "
17 in o' hour so great riches is come "
19 for in o' hour is she made desolate. "
21: 9 unto me o' of the seven angels 1520
21 every several gate was of o' pearl: "

one's
Ac 16:26 and every o' bands were loosed.

ones
Ge 34:29 all their little o', and their wives took
43: 8 we, and thou, and also our little o'.
45:19 the land of Egypt for your little o',
46: 5 their little o', and their wives, in the
47:24 and for food for your little o'.
50: 8 only their little o', and their flocks,
21 I will nourish you, and your little o'.
Ex 10:10 as I will let you go, and your little o':
24 let your little o' also go with you.
Nu 14:31 But your little o', which ye said should
31: 9 of Midian captives, and their little o',
17 kill every male among the little o',
32:16 our cattle, and cities for our little o':
17 little o' shall dwell in the fenced cities
24 Build your cities for your little o', and
26 Our little o', our wives, our flocks, and
De 1:39 your little o', which ye said should be a
2:34 women, and the little o', of every city,
3:19 But your wives, and your little o', and
20:14 But the women, and the little o', and
22: 6 whether they be young o', or eggs, and
29:11 Your little o', your wives, and thy
Jos 1:14 Your wives, your little o', and your
8:35 with the women, and the little o', and
J'g 5:22 the pransings of their mighty o'.
18:21 and put the little o' and the cattle
2Sa 15:22 and all the little o' that were with him.
1Ch 16:13 ye children of Jacob, his chosen o'.
Ezr 8:21 and for our little o', and for all our
Es 8:11 assault them, both little o' and women,
Job 21:11 send forth their little o' like a flock,
38:41 when his young o' cry unto God, they
39: 3 bring forth their young o', they cast*
4 Their young o' are in good liking, they
16 She is hardened against her young o',
30 Her young o' also suck up blood: and
Ps 10:10 that the poor may fall by his strong o'.
137: 9 dasheth thy little o' against the stones.
Pr 1:22 How long, ye simple o', will ye love
7: 7 among the simple o', I discerned
Isa 5:17 the waste places of the fat o' shall
10:16 hosts, send among his fat o' leanness;
33 high o' of stature shall be hewn down;*
11: 7 their young o' shall lie down together:
13: 3 I have commanded my sanctified o', I
3 called my mighty o' for mine anger.*
14: 9 thee, even all the chief o' of the earth;
24:21 shall punish the host of the high o'
25: 4 the blast of the terrible o' is as a storm
5 of the terrible o' shall be brought low.
29: 5 of the terrible o' shall be as chaff that
32:11 be troubled, ye careless o': strip you,
33: 7 valiant o' shall cry without: their
57:15 to revive the heart of the contrite o'.
Jer 2:33 also taught the wicked o' thy ways.*
8:16 sound of the neighing of his strong o';
14: 3 have sent their little o' to the waters:
48: 4 her little o' have caused a cry to be
45 of the head of the tumultuous o'. 1121
La 4: 3 they give suck to their young o':
Da 4:17 the demand by the word of the holy o':
8: 8 for it came up four notable o' *
11:17 and upright o' with him; thus shall he
Joe 3:11 cause thy mighty o' to come down,
Zec 4:14 These are the two anointed o', that†
13: 7 will turn mine hand upon the little o'.
M't 10:42 of these little o' a cup of cold water
18: 6 shall offend one of these little o' which
10 ye despise not one of these little o';
14 one of these little o' should perish.
M'r 9:42 shall offend one of these little o' that
10:42 their great o' exercise authority upon

Onesimus (*o-nes'-i-mus*)
Col 4: 9 O', a faithful and beloved brother, 3682
subscr. Colossians by Tychicus and O'.* "
Ph'm 10 I beseech thee for my son O', * "
subscr. to Philemon, by O' a servant.* "

Onesiphorus (*o-ne-sif'-o-rus*)
2Ti 1:16 give mercy unto the house of O'; 3683
4:19 Aquila, and the household of O'. "

Oni See BEN-ONI.

onions
Nu 11: 5 leeks, and the o', and the garlick: 1211

only
Ge 6: 5 his heart was o' evil continually. 7535
7:23 Noah o' remained alive, and they 389
22: 2 now thy son, thine o' son Isaac, 3173
12 thy son, thine o' son from me 3162
16 withheld thy son, thine o' son: 3173
34:22 O' herein will the men consent 389
23 o' let us consent unto them, and "
41:40 o' in the throne will I be greater 7535
47:22 O' the land of the priests bought "
26 except the land of the priests o', 905
50: 8 o' their little ones, and their 7535
Ex 8:11 they shall remain in the river o'. "
9:26 O' in the land of Goshen, where "
21:19 o' he shall pay for the loss of his "
22:20 unto any god, save unto the Lord o',905
27 For that is his covering o', it is his "
Le 21:23 O' he shall not go in unto the vail, 389
27:26 O' the firstling of the beasts, which "
Nu 1:49 O' thou shalt not number the tribe "
12: 2 indeed spoken o' by Moses? 7535
14: 9 O' rebel not ye against the Lord, 389
18: 3 o' they shall not come nigh the
20:19 I will o', without doing any thing 7535
22:35 o' the word that I shall speak unto
31:22 O' the gold, and the silver, the * 389
36: 6 o' to the family of the tribe of their
De 2:28 o' I will pass through on my feet; 7535
35 O' the cattle we took for a prey "
37 O' unto the land of the children of "
3:11 o' Og king of Bashan remained of "
4: 9 O' take heed to thyself, and keep "
12 similitude; o' ye heard a voice. 2108
8: 3 that man doth not live by bread o', 905
10:15 O' the Lord had a delight in thy 7535
12:16 O' ye shall not eat the blood; ye "
23 O' be sure that thou eat not the "
26 O' thy holy things which thou hast, "
15: 5 O' if thou carefully hearken unto "
23 O' thou shalt not eat the blood "
20:20 O' the trees which thou knowest "
22:25 man o' that lay with her shall die: 905
28:13 and thou shalt be above o', and 7535
29, 33 thou shalt be o' oppressed and 389
29:14 with you o' do I make this covenant905
Jos 1: 7 O' be thou strong and very 7535
17 o' the Lord thy God be with thee, "
18 o' be strong and of a good courage. "
6:15 o' on that day they compassed the "
17 o' Rahab the harlot shall live, she "
24 o' the silver, and the gold, and the "
8: 2 o' the spoil thereof, and the cattle "
27 O' the cattle and the spoil of that "
11:13 none of them, save Hazor o'; 905
22 o' in Gaza, in Gath, and in Ashdod,7535
13: 6 o' divide thou it by lot unto the "
14 O' unto the tribe of Levi he gave "
17:17 thou shalt not have one lot o':
J'g 3: 2 O' that the generations of the 7535
6:37 and if the dew be on the fleece o', 905
39 it now be dry o' upon the fleece,
40 for it was dry upon the fleece o',
10:15 deliver us o', we pray thee, this 389
11:34 she was his o' child; beside her 3173
16:28 and strengthen me,...o' this once, 389
19:20 me; o' lodge not in the street. 7535
1Sa 1:13 o' her lips moved, but her voice
23 o' the Lord establish his word. 389
5: 4 o' the stump of Dagon was left to 7535
7: 3 unto the Lord, and serve him o': 905
4 Ashtaroth, and served the Lord o'. "
12:24 O' fear the Lord, and serve him in 389
18:17 o' be thou valiant for me, and fight "
20:14 shalt not o' while yet I live shew me
39 o' Jonathan and David knew the 389
2Sa 13:32 king's sons; for Ammon o' is dead:905
33 are dead: for Ammon o' is dead. "
17: 2 flee; and I will smite the king o':
23:10 returned after him o' to spoil. 389
1Ki 3: 2 O' the people sacrificed in high 7535
3 o' he sacrificed and burnt incense "
4:19 o' officer which was in the land. 259
8:39 (for thou, even thou o', knowest 905
12:20 David, but the tribe of Judah o'. "
14: 8 to do that o' which was right in 7535
13 he o' of Jeroboam shall come to 905
15: 5 save o' in the matter of Uriah the 7535
18:22 even I o', remain a prophet of the 905
19:10, 14 and I, even I o', am left; and "
22:31 save o' with the king of Israel. "
2Ki 3:25 o' in Kir-haraseth left they the stones
10:23 but the worshippers of Baal o'. 905
17:18 none left but the tribe of Judah o'. "
19:19 thou art the Lord God, even thou o'. "
21: 8 o' if they will observe to do 7535
1Ch 22:12 O' the Lord give thee wisdom and
2Ch 2: 6 save o' to burn sacrifice before him?
18:30 save o' with the king of Israel. 905
33:17 yet unto the Lord their God o'. 7535
Ezr 10:15 O' Jonathan the son of Asahel and 389
Es 1:16 not done wrong to the king o' 905
Job 1:12 o' upon himself put not forth 7535
15, 16, 17, 19 I o' am escaped alone 7535
13:20 O' do not two things unto me: 389
34:29 a nation, or against a man o': *3162
Ps 4: 8 Lord, o' makest me dwell in safety.*910
51: 4 Against thee, thee o', have I sinned,905
62: 2 He o' is my rock and my salvation; 389
4 They o' consult to cast him down
Ps 62: 5 My soul, wait thou o' upon God; 389
6 He o' is my rock and my salvation: "
71:16 thy righteousness, even of thine o'.905
72:18 who o' doeth wondrous things. "
91: 8 O' with thine eyes shalt thou 7535
Pr 4: 3 tender and o' beloved in the sight 3173
11:23 desire of the righteous is o' good: 389
13:10 O' by pride cometh contention: 7535
14:23 of the lips tendeth o' to penury. 389
17:11 An evil man seeketh o' rebellion: "
21: 5 diligent tend o' to plenteousness; "
5 every one that is hasty o' to want. "
Ec 7:29 this o' have I found, that God hath 905
Ca 6: 9 she is the o' one of her mother, she
Isa 4: 1 o' let us be called by thy name, to 7535
26:13 by thee o' will we make mention 905
28:19 o' to understand the report. *7535
37:20 thou art the Lord, even thou o'. 905
Jer 3:13 O' acknowledge thine iniquity, 389
6:26 thee mourning, as for an o' son, 3173
32:30 children of Judah have o' done evil 389
30 have o' provoked me to anger with "
Eze 7: 5 God; An evil, an o' evil, behold, is 259
14:16 they o' shall be delivered, but the 905
18 o' shall be delivered themselves.
44:20 they shall o' poll their heads. 3697
Am 3: 2 You o' have I known of all the 7535
8:10 it as the mourning of an o' son, 3173
Zec 12:10 one mourneth for his o' son, and
M't 4:10 God, and him o' shalt thou serve. 3441
5:47 And if ye salute your brethren o', 3440
8: 8 speak the word o', and my servant "
10:42 a cup of cold water o' in the name "
12: 4 with him, but o' for the priests? 3441
14:36 o' touch the hem of his garment: 3440
17: 8 they saw no man, save Jesus o'. 3441
21:19 nothing thereon, but leaves o', 3440
21 not o' do this which is done to the "
24:36 of heaven, but my Father o'. 3441
M'r 2: 7 who can forgive sins but God o'? *1520
5:36 Be not afraid, o' believe, 3440
6: 8 for their journey, save a staff o'; "
9: 8 save Jesus o' with themselves. 3441
Lu 4: 8 God, and him o' shalt thou serve. "
7:12 the o' son of his mother, and she 3439
8:42 For he had one o' daughter, about "
50 Fear not: believe o', and she shall 3440
9:38 my son: for he is mine o' child. 3439
24:18 thou o' a stranger in Jerusalem, *3441
Joh 1:14 as of the o' begotten of the Father,)3439
18 the o' begotten Son, which is in the "
3:16 he gave his o' begotten Son, that "
18 name of the o' begotten Son of God. "
5:18 he not o' had broken the sabbath, 3440
44 honour that cometh from God o'? 3441
11:52 And not for that nation o', but 3440
12: 9 they came not for Jesus' sake o', "
13: 9 Lord, not my feet o', but also my "
17: 3 might know thee the o' true God, 3441
Ac 8:16 o' they were baptized in the name 3440
11:19 word to none but unto the Jews o'. "
18:25 knowing o' the baptism of John. "
19:27 not o' this our craft is in danger to "
21:13 I am ready not to be bound o', but "
25 save o' that they keep themselves from*
26:29 not o' thou, but also all that hear 3440
27:10 not o' of the lading and ship, but "
Ro 1:32 not o' do the same, but have "
3:29 Is he the God of the Jews o'? is he "
4: 9 then upon the circumcision o', or "
12 who are not of the circumcision o',3440
16 not to that o' which is of the law, "
5: 3 And not o' so, but we glory in "
11 not o' so, but we also joy in God "
8:23 And not o' they, but ourselves also, "
9:10 And not o' this; but when Rebecca "
24 not of the Jews o', but also of the "
13: 5 needs be subject, not o' for wrath, "
16: 4 unto whom not o' I give thanks, 3441
27 To God o' wise, be glory through
1Co 7:39 to whom she will; o' in the Lord. 3440
9: 6 Or I o' and Barnabas, have not we 3441
14:36 from you? or came it unto you o'?* "
15:19 If in this life o' we have hope in 3440
2Co 7: 7 And not by his coming o', but by "
8:10 not o' to do, but also to be forward "
19 And not that o', but who was also "
21 not o' in the sight of the Lord, but "
9:12 not o' supplieth the want of the "
Ga 1:23 they had heard o', That he which "
2:10 O' they would that we should "
3: 2 This o' would I learn of you, "
4:18 not o' when I am present with you. "
5:13 o' use not liberty for an occasion to "
6:12 o' lest they...suffer persecution "
Eph 1:21 not o' in this world, but also in that "
Phil 1:27 O' let your conversation be as it "
29 not o' to believe on him, but also to "
2:12 obeyed, not as in my presence o', "
27 and not on him o', but on me also, "
4:15 giving and receiving, but ye o'. 3441
Col 4:11 These o' are my fellowworkers "
1Th 1: 5 came not unto you in word o', but 3440
8 not o' in Macedonia and Achaia, "
2: 8 not the gospel of God o', but also "
2Th 2: 7 o' he who now letteth will let, until "
1Ti 1:17 the o' wise God, be honour and 3441
5:13 not o' idle, but tattlers also and 3440
6:15 is the blessed and o' Potentate, 3441
16 Who o' hath immortality, dwelling "
2Ti 2:20 there are not o' vessels of gold and3440
4: 8 and not to me o', but unto all them "
11 O' Luke is with me. Take Mark. 3441
Heb 9:10 stood o' in meats and drinks, and 3440
11:17 offered up his o' begotten son, 3439
12:26 once more I shake not the earth o',3440

Jas 1:22 of the word, and not hearers o·, 3440
2:24 man is justified, and not by faith o·. "
1Pe 2:18 not o· to the good and gentle, but "
1Jo 2: 2 and not fo: ours o·, but also for "
4: 9 God sent his o· begotten Son into 3439
5: 6 not by water o·, but by water and 3440
2Jo 1: 1 and not I o·, but also all they that 3441
Jude 4 denying the o· Lord God, and our "
25 To the o· wise God our Saviour, be "
Re 9: 4 o· those men which have not the "
15: 4 for thou o· art holy: for all nations "

only-begotten See ONLY and BEGOTTEN.

Ono (o'-no)
1Ch 8:12 who built O·, and Lod, with the 207
Ezr 2:33 The children of Lod, Hadid, and O·. "
Ne 6: 2 one of the villages in the plain of O·. "
7:37 The children of Lod, Hadid, and O·. "
11:35 Lod, and O·, the valley of craftsmen."

onward
Ex 40:36 of Israel went o· in all their journeys:

onycha (on'-e-kah)
Ex 30:34 stacte, and o·, and galbanum; 7827

onyx (o'-nix)
Ge 2:12 there is bdellium and the o· stone.7718
Ex 25: 7 O· stones, and stones to be set in "
28: 9 And thou shalt take two o· stones, "
20 the fourth row a beryl, and an o·, "
35: 9 o· stones, and stones to be set for "
27 And the rulers brought o· stones, "
39: 6 they wrought o· stones inclosed in "
13 row, a beryl, an o·, and a jasper: "
1Ch 29: 2 o· stones, and stones to be set, "
Job 28:16 gold of Ophir, with the precious o·, "
Eze 28:13 the beryl, the o·, and the jasper, "

open See also OPENED; OPENEST; OPENETH; OPENING.
Ge 1:20 in the o· firmament of heaven. 6440
38:14 sat in an o· place, which is by the 5869
Ex 21:33 if a man shall o· a pit, or if a man 6605
Le 14: 7 living bird loose into the o· field. 6440
53 bird out of the city into the o· fields,"
17: 5 which they offer in the o· field, even"
Nu 8:16 instead of such as o· every womb,*6363
16:30 and the earth o· her mouth, and 6475
19:15 And every o· vessel, which hath no6605
16 slain with a sword in the o· fields, 6440
24: 3 man whose eyes are o· hath said: 8365
4 a trance, but having his eyes o·: 1540
15 man whose eyes are o· hath said: 8365
16 a trance, but having his eyes o·: 1540
De 15: 8 shalt o· thine hand wide unto him,6605
11 shalt o· thine hand wide unto thy "
20:11 answer of peace, and o· unto thee, "
28:12 shall o· unto thee his good treasure,"
Jos 8:17 they left the city o·, and pursued "
10:22 O· the mouth of the cave, and bring"
1Sa 3: 1 those days; there was no o· vision.‡6555
2Sa 11:11 lord, are encamped in the o· fields;6440
1Ki 6:18 carved with knops and o· flowers: 6358
29 palm trees and o· flowers, within "
32 and palm trees and o· flowers, and "
35 and palm trees and o· flowers: "
8:29 thine eyes may be o· toward this 6605
52 That thine eyes may be o· unto the "
2Ki 6:17 Lord, I pray thee, o· his eyes, that 6491
20 Lord, o· the eyes of these men, "
9: 3 Then o· the door, and flee, and 6605
13:17 he said, O· the window eastward. "
19:16 o·, Lord, thine eyes, and see: and 6491
2Ch 6:20 That thine eyes may be o· upon 6605
40 let, I beseech thee, thine eyes be o·,"
7:15 Now mine eyes shall be o·, and "
Ne 1: 6 and thine eyes o·, that thou mayest "
6: 5 time with an o· letter in his hand; "
Job 11: 5 speak, and o· his lips against thee; "
14: 3 dost thou o· thine eyes upon such 6491
32:20 I will o· my lips and answer. 6605
34:26 men in the o· sight of others; 4725
35:16 doth Job o· his mouth in vain; 6475
41:14 Who can o· the doors of his face? 6605
Ps 5: 9 their throat is an o· sepulchre; they"
34:15 and his ears are o· unto their cry.
49: 4 I will o· my dark saying upon the 6605
51:15 O Lord, o· thou my lips; and my "
78: 2 I will o· my mouth in a parable: "
81:10 o· thy mouth wide, and I will fill it.
118:19 O·...the gates of righteousness: 6605
119:18 O· thou mine eyes, that I may 1540
Pr 13:16 but a fool layeth o· his folly. *6566
20:13 o· thine eyes, and thou shalt be 6491
27: 5 O· rebuke is better than secret 1540
31: 8 O· thy mouth for the dumb in the 6605
9 O· thy mouth, judge righteously, "
Ca 5: 2 O· to me, my sister, my love, my "
5 I rose up to o· to my beloved; and "
Isa 9:12 shall devour Israel with o· mouth. 3605
22:22 so he shall o·, and none shall shut;6605
22 and he shall shut, and none shall o·."
24:18 the windows from on high are o·, * "
26: 2 O· ye the gates, that the righteous "
28:24 doth he o· and break the clods of "
37:17 o· thine eyes, O Lord, and see: and6491
41:18 I will o· rivers in high places, and 6605
42: 7 To o· the blind eyes, to bring out 6491
45: 1 to o· before him the two leaved 6605
8 let the earth o·, and let them bring "
60:11 thy gates shall be o· continually; "
Jer 5:16 Their quiver is as an o· sepulchre, "
9:22 fall as dung upon the o· field, and 6440
13:19 shut up, and none shall o· them: 6605
32:11 custom, and that which was o·: 1540
14 and this evidence which is o·; and "
19 thine eyes are o· upon all the ways6491
50:26 utmost border, o· her storehouses:6605

Eze 2: 8 o· thy mouth, and eat that I give 6475
3:27 I will o· thy mouth, and thou shalt6605
16: 5 thou wast cast out in the o· field, 6440
63 and never o· thy mouth any more 6610
21:22 to o· the mouth in the slaughter, 6605
25: 9 I will o· the side of Moab from the "
29: 5 thou shalt fall upon the o· fields; 6440
32: 4 cast thee forth upon the o· field, "
33:27 him that is in the o· field will I give"
37: 2 were very many in the o· valley; "
12 I will o· your graves, and cause 6605
39: 5 Thou shalt fall upon the o· field: 6440
46:12 one shall then o· him the gate that6605
Da 6:10 and his windows being o· in his 6606
9:18 o· thine eyes, and behold our 6491
Na 3:13 set wide o· unto thine enemies: 6605
Zec 11: 1 O· thy doors, O Lebanon, that the "
12: 4 I will o· mine eyes upon the house6491
Mal 3:10 I will not o· you the windows of 6605
M't 13:35 I will o· my mouth in parables; I 455
25:11 virgins, saying, Lord, Lord, o· to us."
Lu 12:36 they may o· unto him immediately. "
13:25 door, saying, Lord, Lord, o· unto us;"
Joh 1:51 Hereafter ye shall see heaven o·, * "
10:21 Can a devil o· the eyes of the blind? "
Ac 16:27 sleep, and seeing the prison doors o·,"
18:14 Paul was now about to o· his mouth,"
19:38 the law is o·, and there are deputies:71
26:18 To o· their eyes, and to turn them 455
Ro 3:13 Their throat is an o· sepulchre; "
2Co 3:18 with o· face beholding as in a glass*343
6:11 our mouth is o· unto you, our heart 455
Eph 6:19 that I may o· my mouth boldly,1722,457
Col 4: 3 that God would o· unto us a door of455
1Ti 5:24 men's sins are o· beforehand, *4271
Heb 6: 6 afresh, and put him to an o· shame.3856
1Pe 3:12 and his ears are o· unto their prayers:*
Re 3: 8 I have set before thee an o· door, *455
20 man hear my voice, and o· the door,"
5: 2 Who is worthy to o· the book, and to"
3 no man...was able to o· the book, "
4 worthy to o· and to read the book, "
5 hath prevailed to o· the book, and "
9 the book, and to o· the seals thereof:"
10: 2 he had in his hand a little book o·: "
8 and take the little book which is o· "

opened
Ge 3: 5 thereof, then your eyes shall be o·,6491
7 And the eyes of them both were o·, "
4:11 which hath o· her mouth to receive6475
7:11 the windows of heaven were o·. 6605
8: 6 that Noah o· the window of the ark "
21:19 God o· her eyes, and she saw a 6491
29:31 Leah was hated, he o· her womb: 6605
30:22 hearkened to her, and o· her womb."
41:56 Joseph o· all the storehouses, and "
42:27 as one of them o· his sack to give "
43:21 we o· our sacks, and, behold, every "
44:11 ground, and o· every man his sack."
Ex 2: 6 she had o· it, she saw the child: "
Nu 16:32 earth o· her mouth, and swallowed "
22:28 the Lord o· the mouth of the ass, "
31 the Lord o· the eyes of Balaam, 1540
26:10 earth o· her mouth, and swallowed6605
De 11: 6 earth o· her mouth, and swallowed6475
J'g 3:25 he o· not the doors of the parlour;6605
25 they took a key, and o· them: "
4:19 she o· a bottle of milk, and gave "
11:35 I have o· my mouth unto the Lord,6475
36 hast o· thy mouth unto the Lord, "
19:27 o· the doors of the house, and went6605
1Sa 3:15 o· the doors of the house of the Lord."
2Ki 4:35 times, and the child o· his eyes. 6491
6:17 Lord o· the eyes of the young man; "
20 Lord o· their eyes, and they saw; "
9:10 And he o· the door and fled. 6605
13:17 window eastward. And he o· it. "
15:16 because they o· not to him, "
2Ch 29: 3 o· the doors of the house of the Lord."
Ne 7: 3 Let not the gates of Jerusalem be o·"
8: 5 Ezra o· the book in the sight of all "
5 when he o· it, all the people stood "
13:19 that they should not be o· till after "
Job 3: 1 After this o· Job his mouth, and "
29:23 they o· their mouth wide as for the6473
31:32 but I o· my doors to the traveller. 6605
33: 2 Behold, now I have o· my mouth, "
38:17 Have the gates of death been o· *1540
Ps 35:21 they o· their mouth wide against
39: 9 I was dumb, I o· not my mouth; 6605
40: 6 mine ears hast thou o·: burnt 3738
78:23 above, and o· the doors of heaven,6605
105:41 He o· the rock, and the waters "
106:17 earth o· and swallowed up Dathan, "
109: 2 the mouth of the deceitful are o· "
119:131 I o· my mouth, and panted: 6473
Ca 5: 6 I o· to my beloved; but my beloved6605
Isa 5:14 o· her mouth without measure: 6473
10:14 moved the wing, or o· the mouth, 6475
14:17 o· not the house of his prisoners?*6605
35: 5 the eyes of the blind shall be o·, 6491
48: 8 time that thine ear was not o·: 6605
50: 5 The Lord God hath o· mine ear, "
53: 7 afflicted, yet he o· not his mouth: "
Jer 20:12 for unto thee have I o· my cause.*1540
50:25 The Lord hath o· his armoury, 6605
La 2:16 enemies have o· their mouths 6475
3:46 our enemies have o· their mouths "
Eze 1: 1 the heavens were o·, and I saw 6605
3: 2 I o· my mouth, and he caused me to"
16:25 and hast o· thy feet to every one 6589
24:27 In that day shall thy mouth be o· 6605
33:22 had o· my mouth, until he came to "
22 and my mouth was o·, and I was no"
37:13 when I have o· your graves, O my "
44: 2 gate shall be shut, it shall not be o·,"

Eze 46: 1 on the sabbath it shall be o·, and in6605
1 day of the new moon it shall be o·. "
Da 7:10 was set, and the books were o·. 6606
10:16 then I o· my mouth, and spake, 6605
Na 2: 6 The gates of the rivers shall be o·, "
Zec 13: 1 shall be a fountain o· to the house "
M't 2:11 when they had o· their treasures, *455
3:16 the heavens were o· unto him, and "
5: 2 he o· his mouth, and taught them, "
7: 7 knock, and it shall be o· unto you: "
8 to him that knocketh it shall be o·. "
9:30 their eyes were o·; and Jesus straitly"
17:27 and when thou hast o· his mouth, "
20:33 him, Lord, that our eyes may be o·. "
27:52 graves were o·; and many bodies "
M'r 1:10 he saw the heavens o·, and the *4977
7:34 him, Ephphatha, that is, Be o·. 1272
35 straightway his ears were o·, and "
Lu 1:64 his mouth was o· immediately, 455
3:21 and praying, the heaven was o·, "
4:17 And when he had o· the book, he 380
11: 9 knock, and it shall be o· unto you. 455
10 to him that knocketh it shall be o·. "
24:31 their eyes were o·, and they knew 1272
32 while he o· to us the scriptures? "
45 Then o· he their understanding, "
Joh 9:10 unto him, How were thine eyes o·? 455
14 Jesus made the clay, and o· his eyes."
17 of him, that he hath o· thine eyes? "
21 who hath o· his eyes, we know not: "
26 did he to thee? how o· he thine eyes?"
30 he is, and yet he hath o· mine eyes. "
32 that any man o· the eyes of one that "
11:37 man, which o· the eyes of the blind, "
Ac 5:19 Lord by night o· the prison doors, "
23 when we had o·, we found no man "
7:56 Behold, I see the heavens o·, and "
8:32 his shearer, so o· he not his mouth:*"
35 Then Philip o· his mouth, and began"
9: 8 when his eyes were o·, he saw no "
40 she o· her eyes: and when she saw "
10:11 saw heaven o·, and a certain vessel "
34 Then Peter o· his mouth, and said, "
12:10 which o· to them of his own accord: "
14 she o· not the gate for gladness, but "
16 and when they had o· the door, and "
14:27 o· the door of faith unto the Gentiles."
16:14 whose heart the Lord o·, that she 1272
26 immediately all the doors were o·, 455
1Co 16: 9 door and effectual is o· unto me, "
2Co 2:12 a door was o· unto me of the Lord, "
Heb 4:13 all things are naked and o· unto 5136
Re 4: 1 behold, a door was o· in heaven: 455
6: 1 when the Lamb o· one of the seals, "
3 And when he had o· the second seal,"
5 And when he had o· the third seal, "
7 And when he had o· the fourth seal, "
9 And when he had o· the fifth seal, "
12 when he had o· the sixth seal, "
8: 1 And when he had o· the seventh seal,"
9: 2 And he o· the bottomless pit; and "
11:19 the temple of God was o· in heaven, "
12:16 earth o· her mouth, and swallowed "
13: 6 o· his mouth in blasphemy against "
15: 5 of the testimony in heaven was o·: "
19:11 And I saw heaven o·, and behold a "
20:12 before God; and the books were o·: "
12 another book was o·, which is the "

openest
Ps 104:28 thou o· thine hand, they are filled 6605
145:16 Thou o· thine hand, and satisfiest "

openeth
Ex 13: 2 whatsoever o· the womb among 6363
12 unto the Lord all that o· the matrix,"
15 to the Lord all that o· the matrix, "
34:19 All that o· the matrix is mine; and "
Nu 3:12 all the firstborn that o· the matrix "
18:15 thing that o· the matrix in all flesh, "
Job 27:19 he o· his eyes, and he is not. 6491
33:16 he o· the ears of men, and sealeth 1540
36:10 He o· also their ear to discipline, "
15 and o· their ears in oppression. "
Ps 38:13 dumb man that o· not his mouth. 6605
146: 8 The Lord o· the eyes of the blind: 6491
Pr 13: 3 he that o· wide his lips shall have 6589
24: 7 he o· not his mouth in the gate. 6605
31:26 She o· her mouth with wisdom; "
Isa 53: 7 is dumb, so he o· not his mouth. * "
Eze 20:26 the fire all that o· the womb, 6363
Lu 2:23 Every male that o· the womb shall1272
Joh 10: 3 To him the porter o·; and the sheep455
Re 3: 7 he that o·, and no man shutteth; "
7 and shutteth, and no man o·; "

opening See also OPENINGS.
1Ch 9:27 and the o· thereof every morning 4668
Job 12:14 up a man, and there can be no o·. 6605
Pr 8: 6 o· of my lips shall be right things. 4669
Isa 42:20 o· the ears, but he heareth not. *6491
61: 1 o· of the prison to them that are 6495
Eze 29:21 will give thee the o· of the mouth 6610
Ac 17: 3 O· and alleging, that Christ must 1272

openings
Pr 1:21 concourse, in the o· of the gates: *6607

openly
Ge 38:21 that was o· by the way side? *5879
Ps 98: 2 righteousness hath he o· shewed in
M't 6: 4 shall reward thee o·. *1722,5318
6 secret shall reward thee o·.* " "
18 secret, shall reward thee o·.* " "
M'r 1:45 no more o· enter into the city, 5320
8:32 And he spake that saying o·. 3954
Joh 7: 4 himself seeketh to be known o·.1722,"
10 not o·, but as it were in secret. *5320

Joh 7:13 no man spake o· of him for fear of 3954
11:54 walked no more o· among the Jews;"
18:20 I spake o· to the world; I ever "
Ac 10:40 the third day, and shewed him o·;*1717
16:37 have beaten us o· uncondemned, *1219
Col 2:15 he made a shew of them o·, 1722,3954

operation See also OPERATIONS.
Ps 28: 5 the Lord, nor the o· of his hands, 4639
Isa 5:12 neither consider the o· of his hands."
Col 2:12 through the faith of the o· of God,*1753

operations
1Co 12: 6 there are diversities of o·, but it is*1755

Ophel (o'-fel)
2Ch 27: 3 on the wall of O· he built much. 6077
33:14 and compassed about O·, and raised"
Ne 3:26 the Nethinims dwelt in O·, unto "
27 lieth out, even unto the wall of O·. "
11:21 But the Nethinims dwelt in O·: "

Ophir (o'-fur)
Ge 10:29 And O·, and Havilah, and Jobab: 211
1Ki 9:28 they came to O·, and fetched from "
10:11 Hiram, that brought gold from O·, "
11 brought in from O· great plenty of "
22:48 ships of Tharshish to go to O· for "
1Ch 1:23 And O·, and Havilah, and Jobab. "
29: 4 talents of gold, of the gold of O·, "
2Ch 8:18 with the servants of Solomon to O·, "
9:10 which brought gold from O·, brought"
Job 22:24 the gold of O· as the stones of the "
28:16 cannot be valued with the gold of O·,"
Ps 45: 9 did stand the queen in gold of O·. "
Isa 13:12 man than the golden wedge of O·. "

Ophni (of'-ni)
Jos 18:24 Chephar-haammonai, and O·, and 6078

Ophrah (of'-rah) See also APHRAH.
Jos 18:23 And Avim, and Parah, and O·, 6084
J'g 6:11 sat under an oak which was in O·, "
24 it is yet in O· of the Abi-ezrites. "
8:27 and put it in his city, even in O·: "
32 sepulchre of Joash his father, in O· "
9: 5 went unto his father's house at O·, "
1Sa 13:17 unto the way that leadeth to O·, "
1Ch 4:14 And Meonothai begat O·: and "

opinion See also OPINIONS.
Job 32: 6 and durst not shew you mine o·. 1843
10 to me; I also will shew mine o·. "
17 my part, I also will shew mine o·. "

opinions
1Ki 18:21 How long halt ye between two o·? 5587

opportunity
M't 26:16 time he sought o· to betray him. 2120
Lu 22: 6 sought o· to betray him unto them "
Ga 6:10 As we have therefore o·, let us do 2540
Ph'p 4:10 were also careful, but ye lacked o·. 170
Heb11:15 have had o· to have returned. 2540

oppose See also OPPOSED; OPPOSEST; OPPOSETH.
2Ti 2:25 instructing those that o· themselves;475

opposed
Ac 18: 6 And when they o· themselves, and 498

opposest
Job 30:21 hand thou o· thyself against me. *7852

opposeth
2Th 2: 4 Who o· and exalteth himself above 480

oppositions
1Ti 6:20 and o· of science falsely so called: 477

oppress See also OPPRESSED; OPPRESSETH; OPPRESSING.
Ex 3: 9 wherewith the Egyptians o· them. 3905
22:21 neither vex a stranger, nor o· him: "
23: 9 Also thou shalt not o· a stranger: "
Le 25:14 hand, ye shall not o· one another:*3238
17 shall not therefore o· one another;*"
De 23:16 him best: thou shalt not o· him. "
24:14 Thou shalt not o· an hired servant6231
J'g 10:12 and the Maonites, did o· you; 3905
Job 10: 3 unto thee that thou shouldest o·, 6231
Ps 10:18 man of the earth may no more o·.*6206
17: 9 From the wicked that o· me, from†7703
119:122 for good: let not the proud o· me.6231
Pr 22:22 neither o· the afflicted in the gate:1792
Isa 49:26 I will feed them that o· thee with 3238
Jer 7: 6 If ye o· not the stranger, the 6231
30:20 and I will punish all that o· them. 3905
Eze 45: 8 shall no more o· my people; and 3238
Ho 12: 7 are in his hand: he loveth to o·. 6231
Am 4: 1 which o· the poor, which crush the "
Mic 2: 2 so they o· a man and his house, "
Zec 7:10 o· not the widow, nor the fatherless,"
Mal 3: 5 that o· the hireling in his wages, "
Jas 2: 6 Do not rich men o· you, and draw 2616

oppressed
De 28:29 thou shalt be only o· and spoiled 6231
33 thou shalt be only o· and crushed "
J'g 2:18 by reason of them that o· them 3905
4: 3 mightily o· the children of Israel. "
6: 9 out of the hand of all that o· you, "
10: 8 and o· the children of Israel: 7533
1Sa 10:18 kingdoms, and of them that o· you:3905
12: 3 whom have I o·? or of whose hand7533
4 hast not defrauded us, nor o· us, "
2Ki 13: 4 because the king of Syria o· them.3905
22 But Hazael king of Syria o· Israel "
2Ch 16:10 And Asa o· some of the people 7533
Job 20:19 o· and hath forsaken the poor; "
35: 9 they make the o· to cry: they cry out
Ps 9: 9 also will be a refuge for the o·, 1790
10:18 To judge the fatherless and the o·, "
74:21 O let not the o· return ashamed: "

Ps 103: 6 and judgment for all that are o·. 6231
106:42 Their enemies also o· them, and 3905
146: 7 executeth judgment for the o·: 6231
Ec 4: 1 the tears of such as were o·, "
Isa 1:17 seek judgment, relieve the o·, 2541
3: 5 And the people shall be o·, every 5065
23:12 no more rejoice, O thou o· virgin, 6231
38:14 O Lord, I am o·; undertake for me.6234
52: 4 Assyrian o· them without cause. 6231
53: 7 He was o·, and he was afflicted, 5065
58: 6 to let the o· go free, and that ye 7533
Jer 50:33 and the children of Judah were o· 6231
Eze 18: 7 hath not o· any, but hath restored*3238
12 Hath o· the poor and needy, hath* "
16 Neither hath o· any, hath not * "
18 because he cruelly o·, spoiled his 6231
22:29 have o· the stranger wrongfully. "
Ho 5:11 Ephraim is o· and broken in "
Am 3: 9 and the o· in the midst thereof. *6217
Ac 7:24 and avenged him that was o·, and 2669
10:38 all that were o· of the devil; 2616

oppresseth
Nu 10: 9 against the enemy that o· you, 6887
Ps 56: 1 me up; he fighting daily o· me. 3905
Pr 14:31 He that o· the poor reproacheth 6231
22:16 He that o· the poor to increase his "
28: 3 A poor man that o· the poor is like "

oppressing
Jer 46:16 our nativity, from the o· sword. 3238
50:16 for fear of the o· sword they shall "
Zep 3: 1 filthy and polluted, to the o· city! "

oppression See also OPPRESSIONS.
Ex 3: 9 the o· wherewith the Egyptians 3906
De 26: 7 and our labour, and our o·: "
2Ki 13: 4 he saw the o· of Israel, because the "
Job 36:15 and openeth their ears in o·. "
Ps 12: 5 For the o· of the poor, for the *7701
42: 9 because of the o· of the enemy? 3906
43: 2 because of the o· of the enemy? "
44:24 forgettest our affliction and our o·? "
55: 3 because of the o· of the wicked: 6125
62:10 Trust not in o·, and become not 6233
73: 8 and speak wickedly concerning o·: "
107:39 brought low through o·, affliction, 6115
119:134 Deliver me from the o· of man: 6233
Ec 5: 8 If thou seest the o· of the poor, "
7: 7 Surely o· maketh a wise man mad;*"
Isa 5: 7 for judgment, but behold o·; 4939
30:12 despise this word, and trust in o· 6233
54:14 thou shalt be far from o·; for thou "
59:13 speaking o· and revolt, concerning "
Jer 6: 6 she is wholly o· in the midst of her. "
22:17 and for o·, and for violence, to do it."
Eze 22: 7 they dealt by o· with the stranger: "
29 people of the land have used o·, "
46:18 of the people's inheritance by o·, *3238

oppressions
Job 35: 9 By reason of the multitude of o· 6217
Ec 4: 1 the o· that are done under the sun: "
Isa 33:15 he that despiseth the gain of o·, 4642

oppressor See also OPPRESSORS.
Job 3:18 they hear not the voice of the o·. *5065
15:20 number of years is hidden to the o·.6184
Ps 72: 4 and shall break in pieces the o·. 6231
Pr 3:31 Envy thou not the o·, and * 376,2555
28:16 understanding is also a great o·: 4642
Isa 9: 4 of his shoulder, the rod of his o·, 5065
14: 4 and say, How hath the o· ceased! "
51:13 day because of the fury of the o·, 6693
13 and where is the fury of the o·? "
Jer 21:12 spoiled out of the hand of the o·, 6231
22: 3 spoiled out of the hand of the o·: 6216
25:38 because of the fierceness of the o·,*3238
Zec 9: 8 no o· shall pass through them 5065
10: 4 bow, out of him every o· together.* "

oppressors
Job 27:13 and the heritage of o·, which they 6184
Ps 54: 3 and o· seek after my soul: they * "
119:121 justice: leave me not to mine o·. 6231
Ec 4: 1 side of their o· there was power; "
Isa 3:12 children are their o·, and women 5065
14: 2 and they shall rule over their o·. "
16: 4 o· are consumed out of the land. 7429
19:20 unto the Lord because of the o·, 3905

or See also NOR.
Ge 13: 9 o· if thou depart to the right hand,
17:12 o· bought with money of any stranger,
24:21 his journey prosperous o· not.
49 to the right hand, o· to the left. 176
50 cannot speak unto thee bad o· good. "
26:11 that toucheth this man o· his wife
27:21 thou be my very son Esau o· not.
30: 1 Give me children, o· else I die.
31:14 yet any portion o· inheritance for us
24, 29 to Jacob either good o· bad. 5704
39 stolen by day, o· stolen by night.
43 daughters, o· unto their children 176
50 o· if thou shalt take other wives *
37: 8 o· shalt thou indeed have dominion
32 whether it be thy son's coat o· no.
39:10 her, to lie by her, o· to be with her.
41:44 no man lift up his hand o· foot in
42:16 o· else by the life of Pharaoh
44: 8 of thy lord's house silver o· gold? 176
16 speak? o· how shall we clear ourselves?
19 Have ye a father, o· a brother? 176
Ex 4:11 mouth? o· who maketh the dumb, "
11 o· deaf, o· the seeing, o· the blind? "
5: 3 with pestilence, o· with the sword. "
10:15 the trees, o· in the herbs of the field,
11: 7 his tongue, against man o· beast: 5704
12: 5 out from the sheep, o· from the goats:

Ex 12:19 he be a stranger, o· born in the land.
16: 4 they will walk in my law, o· no.
17: 7 Is the Lord among us, o· not?
19:12 the mount, o· touch the border of it:
13 whether it be beast o· man, it shall
13 surely be stoned, o· shot through; 176
20: 4 o· any likeness of any thing that is*
4 o· that is in the earth beneath, o· that
21: 4 have born him sons o· daughters; 176
6 to the door, o· unto the door post; "
15 that smiteth his father, o· his mother,
16 him, o· if he be found in his hand,
17 that curseth his father, o· his mother,
18 with a stone, o· with his fist, and 176
20 man smite his servant, o· his maid, "
21 if he continue a day o· two, he "
26 his servant, o· the eye of his maid, "
27 tooth, o· his maidservant's tooth; "
28 If an ox gore a man o· a woman, "
29 he hath killed a man o· woman; "
31 a son, o· have gored a daughter, "
32 a manservant o· a maidservant; "
33 o· if a man shall dig a pit, and not "
33 it, and an ox o· an ass fall therein; "
36 O· if it be known that the ox hath "
22: 1 ox, o· a sheep, and kill it, o· sell it; "
4 whether it be ox, o· ass, o· sheep; 5704
5 a field o· vineyard to be eaten, and 176
6 o· the standing corn, o· the field, be "
7 neighbour money o· stuff to keep, "
9 o· for any manner of lost thing,
10 o· an ox, o· a sheep, o· any beast, to176
10 o· be hurt, o· driven away, no man "
14 it be hurt, o· die, the owner thereof "
22 afflict any widow, o· fatherless child.
23: 4 enemy's ox o· his ass going astray, 176
28:43 o· when they come near unto the "
29:34 the consecrations, o· of the bread, "
30:20 o· when they come near to the altar176
33 o· whosoever putteth any of it upon a
34:19 whether ox o· sheep, that is male.*
Le 1:10 o· of the goats, for a burnt sacrifice;176
14 of turtledoves, o· of young pigeons. "
2: 4 o· unleavened wafers anointed with
3: 1 whether it be a male o· female, he
6 male o· female, he shall offer it 176
4:23 O· if his sin, wherein he hath * "
28 O· if his sin, which he hath sinned,* "
5: 1 whether he hath seen o· known of it;"
2 O· if a soul touch any unclean thing,"
2 o· a carcase of unclean cattle, "
2 o· the carcase of unclean creeping "
3 O· if he touch the uncleanness of "
4 O· if a soul swear, pronouncing with"
4 his lips to do evil, o· to do good, "
6 lamb o· a kid of the goats, for a sin "
7,11 turtledoves, o· two young pigeons,"
6: 2 him to keep, o· in fellowship, "
2 o· in a thing taken away by violence,"
2 o· hath deceived his neighbour; "
3 O· have found that which was lost, "
4 away, o· the thing which he hath "
4 o· that which was delivered him to "
4 o· the lost thing which he found, "
5 O· all that about which he hath "
7:16 be a vow, o· a voluntary offering, it "
21 man, o· any unclean beast, o· any "
23 of fat, of ox, o· of sheep, o· of goat.
26 whether it be of fowl o· of beast, in
11: 4 cud, o· of them that divide the hoof:
32 wood, o· raiment, o· skin, o· sack, 176
35 it be oven, o· ranges for pots, they
36 fountain o· pit, wherein there is plenty
42 o· whatsoever hath more feet 5704
12: 6 fulfilled, for a son, o· for a daughter,
6 young pigeon, o· a turtledove, for a176
7 that hath born a male o· a female. "
8 two turtles, o· two young pigeons; "
13: 2 a rising, a scab, o· bright spot, and "
2 o· unto one of his sons the priests: "
16 O· if the raw flesh turn again, and "
19 white rising, o· a bright spot, white,"
24 O· if there be any flesh, in the skin "
24 spot, somewhat reddish, o· white; "
29 If a man o· woman have a plague "
29 plague upon the head o· the beard; "
30 a leprosy upon the head o· beard. "
38 o· also a woman have in the skin of "
42 in the bald head, o· bald forehead, "
42 his bald head, o· his bald forehead. "
43 bald head, o· in his bald forehead, "
47 garment, o· a linen garment; "
48 warp, o· woof; of linen, o· of woollen;"
48 skin, o· in any thing made of skin; "
49 o· reddish in the garment, o·...skin, "
49 o· in the woof, o· in any thing of skin;"
51 warp, o· in the woof, o· in a skin, "
51 o· in any work that is made of *
52 o· woof, in woollen o· in linen, o· any176
53 o· in the woof, o· in any thing of skin;"
56 of the garment, o· out of the skin, "
56 o· out of the warp, o· out of the woof:"
57 o· in the woof, o· in any thing of "
58 o· woof, o· whatsoever thing of skin "
59 o· linen, either in the warp, o· woof, "
59 o· any thing of skins, to pronounce "
59 clean, o· to pronounce it unclean. "
14:22 turtledoves, o· two young pigeons, "
30 o· of the young pigeons, such as he "
37 hollow strakes, greenish o· reddish, "
15: 3 o· his flesh be stopped from his "
14 turtledoves, o· two young pigeons, "
23 o· on any thing whereon she sitteth, "
25 o· if it run beyond the time of her "
29 two turtles, o· two young pigeons, "
16:29 o· a stranger that sojourneth among

Le 17: 3 an ox, o' lamb, o' goat, in the camp,176
3 o' that killeth it out of the camp,
8 o' of the strangers which sojourn
8 a burnt offering o' sacrifice, 176
10, 13 o' of the strangers that sojourn
13 catcheth any beast o' fowl that may176
15 o' that which was torn with beasts,
15 of your own country, o' a stranger,
18: 7 father, o' the nakedness of thy mother,*
9 father, o' daughter of thy mother, 176
9 be born at home, o' born abroad, "
10 o' of thy daughter's daughter, even "
17 o' her daughter's daughter, to
19: 35 in meteyard, in weight, o' in measure.
20: 2 o' of the strangers that sojourn in
9 curseth his father o' his mother shall
9 cursed his father o' his mother;
17 o' his mother's daughter, and see 176
25 o' by fowl, o' by any manner of living
27 A man also o' woman that hath a 176
27 o' that is a wizard, shall surely be put
21: 7 a wife that is a whore, o' profane;
11 for his father, o' for his mother;
14 o' a divorced woman, o' profane,
14 o' an harlot, these shall he not take:*
18 blind man, o' a lame, o' he that 176
18 flat nose, o' any thing superfluous, "
19 O' a man that is brokenfooted, "
19 is brokenfooted, o' brokenhanded, "
20 O' crookbackt, o' a dwarf, "
20 o' that hath a blemish in his eye, "
20 a blemish in his eye, o' be scurvy,
20 o' scabbed, o' hath his stones 176
22: 4 is a leper, o' hath a running issue; "
4 o' a man whose seed goeth from him;"
5 O' whosoever toucheth any creeping"
5 o' a man of whom he may take "
8 dieth of itself, o' is torn with beasts,
10 of the priest, o' an hired servant,
13 daughter be a widow, o' divorced,
16 O' suffer them to bear the iniquity of*
18 Israel, o' of the strangers in Israel,
19 beeves, of the sheep, o' of the goats.
21 o' a freewill offering in beeves 176
21 a freewill offering in beeves o' sheep,
22 o' broken, o' maimed, o' having a 176
22 o' scurvy, o' scabbed, ye shall not "
23 bullock o' a lamb that hath any thing
23 superfluous o' lacking in his parts,
24 is bruised, o' crushed, o' broken, o' cut;
27 a bullock, o' a sheep, o' a goat, is 176
28 whether it be cow o' ewe, ye shall "
25: 14 o' buyest ought of thy neighbour's "
35 he be a stranger, o' a sojourner; that*
36 thou no usury of him, o' increase: but
47 sojourner o' stranger wax rich by thee,
47 the stranger o' sojourner by thee,
49 o' his uncle's son, may redeem him,176
49 o' any that is nigh of kin unto him
49 o' if he be able, he may redeem 176
26: 15 o' if your soul abhor my judgments,*
27: 10 good for a bad, o' a bad for a good: 176
12 value it, whether it be good o' bad:
14 estimate it, whether it be good o' bad:
20 o' if he have sold the field to
26 whether it be ox o' sheep: it is the 176
27 o' if it be not redeemed, then it
28 possession, shall be sold o' redeemed:
30 o' of the fruit of the tree, is the Lord's:
32 the tithe of the herd, o' of the flock,
33 not search whether it be good o' bad,
Nu 5: 6 a man o' woman shall commit any 176
14 o' if the spirit of jealousy come upon"
30 O' when the spirit of jealousy "
6: 2 either man o' woman shall separate "
3 of wine, o' vinegar of strong drink,
3 grapes, nor eat moist grapes, o' dried.
7 for his father, o' for his mother,
7 for his brother, o' for his sister, when
10 two turtles, o' two young pigeons, 176
9: 10 o' of your posterity shall be unclean
10 o' be in a journey afar off, yet he 176
21 o' by night that the cloud was taken*
22 O' whether it were two days, *
22 o' a month, o' a year, that the cloud176
11: 8 it in mills, o' beat it in a mortar, "
22 o' shall all the fish of the sea be
23 shall come to pass unto thee o' not.
13: 18 be strong o' weak, few o' many;
19 dwell in, whether it be good o' bad;
19 whether in tents, o' in strong holds;
20 whether it be fat o' lean, whether
20 there be wood therein o' not.
14: 2 o' would God we had died in this
15: 3 o' a sacrifice in performing a vow, 176
3 a vow, o' in a freewill offering,
3 o' in your solemn feasts, to make a "
3 the Lord, of the herd, o' of the flock:"
5 with the burnt offering o' sacrifice, "
6 O' for a ram, thou shalt prepare for"
8 o' for a sacrifice in performing a vow,"
8 o' peace offering unto the Lord: "
11 for one bullock, o' for one ram,
11 o' for a lamb, o' a kid. 176
14 o' whosoever be among you in your "
30 he be born in the land, o' a stranger,
16: 14 o' given us inheritance of fields and*
29 o' if they be visited after the 176
18: 15 whether it be of men o' beasts, shall*"
17 of a cow, o' the firstling of a sheep,
17 o' the firstling of a goat, thou shalt176
19: 16 the open fields, o' a dead body,
16 o' a bone of a man,
16 o' a grave, shall be unclean seven
18 that touched a bone, o' one slain,
18 o' one dead, o' a grave: 176

Nu 20: 5 it is no place of seed, o' of figs,
5 o' of vines, o' of pomegranates;
17 the fields, o' through the vineyards,
21: 22 into the fields, o' into the vineyards;
22: 18 Lord my God, to do less o' more. 176
26 either to the right hand o' to the left.
23: 8 o' how shall I defy, whom the Lord*
19 o' hath he spoken, and shall he not
24: 13 good o' bad of mine own mind; 176
30: 2 o' swear an oath to bind his soul "
5 o' of her bonds wherewith she hath
6 o' uttered ought out of her lips, 176
10 o' bound her soul by a bond with an"
13 it, o' her husband may make it void,
14 o' all her bonds, which are upon "
32: 19 on yonder side Jordan, o' forward;*
35: 18 O' if he smite him with an hand 176
20 o' hurl at him by laying of wait, "
21 O' in enmity smite him with his "
22 o' have cast upon him any thing "
23 O' with any stone, wherewith a "
De 3: 24 God is there in heaven o' in earth,
4: 16 the likeness of male o' female, 176
23, 25 image, o' the likeness of any thing,*
32 is, o' hath been heard like it? 176
34 O' hath God assayed to go and take"
5: 8 image, o' any likeness of any thing*
8 above, o' that is in the earth beneath,
8 o' that is in the waters beneath the
21 o' his manservant, o' his maidservant,
21 ox, o' his ass, o' any thing that is thy
32 aside to the right hand o' to the left.
7: 14 be male o' female barren among you,
14 among you, o' among your cattle.
25 the silver o' gold that is on them,
8: 2 keep his commandments, o' no.
9: 5 o' for the uprightness of thine heart,
12: 17 thy corn, o' of thy wine, o' of thy oil,
17 o' the firstlings of thy herds,
17 o' of thy flock, nor any of thy vows
17 o' heave offering of thine hand: *
13: 1 prophet, o' a dreamer of dreams, 176
1 and giveth thee a sign o' a wonder, "
2 the sign o' the wonder come to pass,
3 prophet, o' that dreamer of dreams:176
5 prophet, o' that dreamer of dreams,"
6 mother, o' thy son, o' thy daughter,
6 daughter, o' the wife of thy bosom,176
6 o' thy friend, which is as thine own "
7 nigh unto thee, o' far off from thee, "
14: 21 o' thou mayest sell it unto an alien: "
24 o' if the place be too far from thee,*
26 for oxen, o' for sheep, o' for wine,
26 o' for strong drink,
26 o' for whatsoever thy soul desireth:
15: 2 it of his neighbour, o' of his brother;*
12 man, o' an Hebrew woman, be sold 176
21 therein, as if it be lame, o' blind,
21 o' have any ill blemish, thou shalt*
17: 1 bullock, o' sheep, wherein is blemish,
1 o' any evilfavouredness: for that
2 man o' woman, that hath wrought
3 sun, o' moon, o' any of the host of 176
5 bring forth that man o' that woman,"
5 gates, even that man o' that woman,"
6 two witnesses, o' three witnesses, "
12 the Lord thy God, o' unto the judge,"
20 to the right hand, o' to the left:
18: 3 sacrifice, whether it be ox o' sheep;
10 son o' his daughter to pass through
10 o'...useth divinations, o' an observer*
10 of times, o' an enchanter, o' a witch,
11 O' a charmer, o' a consulter with
11 spirits, o' a wizard, o' a necromancer.
20 o' that shall speak in the name of
19: 15 man for any iniquity, o' for any sin,
15 o' at the mouth of three witnesses,
21: 18 his father, o' the voice of his mother,
22: 1 brother's ox o' his sheep go astray, 176
2 o' if thou know him not, then thou
4 ass o' his ox fall down by the way, 176
6 way in any tree, o' on the ground, "
6 whether they be young ones, o' eggs,"
6 upon the young, o' upon the eggs, "
23: 1 o' hath his privy member cut off,
3 An Ammonite o' Moabite shall not
18 o' the price of a dog, into the house of
24: 3 o' if the latter husband die, which 176
6 o' the upper millstone to pledge:
7 merchandise of him, o' selleth him;
14 o' of thy strangers that are in thy
27: 15 maketh any graven o' molten image,
16 light by his father o' his mother.
22 o' the daughter of his mother. 176
28: 14 day, to the right hand, o' to the left,
51 leave thee either corn, wine, o' oil,
51 o' the increase of thy kine, *
51 o' flocks of thy sheep, until he have
29: 6 have ye drunk wine o' strong drink:
18 man, o' woman, o' family, o' tribe,176
32: 36 and there is none shut up, o' left.
Jos 1: 7 it to the right hand o' to the left,
5: 13 thou for us, o' for our adversaries?
7: 3 two o' three thousand men go up 176
8: 17 was not a man left in Ai o' Beth-el,
20 power to flee this way o' that way:
22 let none of them remain o' escape.
10: 14 no day like that before it o' after it,
22: 22 in rebellion, o' if in transgression
23 o' if to offer thereon burnt offering
23 burnt offering o' meat offering,
23 o' if to offer peace offerings thereon,
28 so say to us o' to our generations in
29 for meat offerings, o' for sacrifices,
23: 6 to the right hand o' to the left;
24: 15 flood, o' the gods of the Amorites,

J'g 2: 22 as their fathers did keep it, o' not.
5: 8 a shield o' spear seen among forty
30 prey; to every man a damsel o' two;*
9: 2 you, o' that one reign over you?
11: 25 o' did he ever fight against them,
13: 14 let her drink wine o' strong drink,
14: 3 brethren, o' among all my people,
6 he told not his father o' his mother
18: 19 o' that thou be a priest unto a 176
19: 13 all night, in Gibeah, o' in Ramah. "
20: 28 my brother, o' shall I cease?
21: 22 fathers o' their brethren come 176
Ru 1: 16 o' to return from following after thee:*
3: 10 young men, whether poor o' rich.
1Sa 2: 14 pan, o' kettle, o' caldron, o' pot; 176
6: 12 aside to the right hand o' to the left;
12: 3 I taken? o' whose ass have I taken?
3 I taken? o' whom have I defrauded?
3 o' of whose hand have I received any
13: 19 make them swords o' spears: 176
14: 6 Lord to save by many o' by few. "
52 any strong man, o' any valiant man,
16: 7 o' on the height of his stature;
18: 18 life, o' my father's family in Israel,
20: 2 do nothing either great o' small, 176
10 o' what if thy father answer thee* "
12 to-morrow any time, o' the third day,
21: 3 mine hand, o' what there is present.176
8 under thine hand spear o' sword? "
22: 8 o' sheweth unto me that my son hath
15 nothing of all this, less o' more. 176
25: 31 o' that my lord hath avenged himself:
36 she told him nothing, less o' more,
26: 10 him; o' his day shall come to die; 176
10 o' he shall descend into battle, and
18 I done? o' what evil is in mine hand?
29: 3 with me these days, o' these years,176
30: 2 slew not any, either great o' small,*
2Sa 2: 21 to thy right hand o' to thy left, 176
3: 29 that hath an issue, o' that is a leper,
29 is a leper, o' that leaneth on a staff,
29 staff, o' that falleth on the sword,
23 on the sword, o' that lacketh bread.
35 if I taste bread, o' aught else, till 176
14: 19 turn to the right hand o' to the left
15: 4 man which hath any suit o' cause
21 whether in death o' life, even there
17: 9 in some pit, o' in some other place: 176
19: 35 taste what I eat o' what I drink? 854
42 cost? o' hath he given us any gift?
20: 20 that I should swallow up o' destroy.
24: 13 o' wilt thou flee three months before
13 o' that there be three days' pestilence
1Ki 3: 7 I know not how to go out o' come in.
8: 23 in heaven above, o' on earth beneath,
37 locust, o' if there be caterpiller;
38 any man, o' by all thy people Israel,
46 the land of the enemy, far o' near; 176
9: 6 from following me, ye o' your children,
15: 17 suffer any to go out o' come in to Asa
18: 10 there is no nation o' kingdom, whither
27 o' he is pursuing, o' he is on a journey,
27 a journey, o' peradventure he sleepeth,
20: 18 o' whether they be come out for war,
39 o' else thou shalt pay a talent of 176
21: 2 o', if it seem good to thee, I will give"
6 o' else, if it please thee, I will give
22: 6 to battle, o' shall I forbear?
15 to battle, o' shall we forbear?
2Ki 2: 16 some mountain, o' into some valley.176
21 thence any more death o' barren land.
4: 13 king, o' to the captain of the host? 176
6: 27 barnfloor, o' out of the winepress? "
9: 32 to him out two o' three eunuchs.
12: 13 any vessels of gold, o' vessels of silver,
13: 19 have smitten five o' six times; 176
17: 34 statutes, o' after their ordinances,
34 o' after the law and commandment
20: 9 degrees, o' go back ten degrees?
22: 2 to the right hand o' to the left.
23: 10 son o' his daughter to pass through
1Ch 21: 12 o' three months to be destroyed
12 o' else three days the sword of the
2Ch 1: 11 not asked riches, wealth, o' honour,
6: 28 o' mildew, locust o' caterpillers;
28 sore o' whatsoever sickness there be;
29 what prayer o' what supplication *
29 of any man, o' of all thy people Israel,
36 captives unto a land far off o' near;176
7: 13 o' if I command the locusts to
13 o' if I send pestilence among my
8: 15 matter, o' concerning the treasures.
14: 11 o' with them that have no power:*
15: 13 to death, whether small o' great, 5704
13 great, whether man o' woman. "
16: 1 let none go out o' come in to Asa king
18: 5, 14 to battle, o' shall I forbear?
30 Fight ye not with small o' great, * 854
20: 9 judgment, o' pestilence, o' famine,
32: 15 for no god of any nation o' kingdom
36: 17 upon young man o' maiden,
17 old man, o' him that stooped for age:
Ezr 7: 24 o' ministers of this house of God,
24 to impose toll, tribute, o' custom,
26 be unto death, o' to banishment, 2006
26 o' to confiscation of goods, "
26 of goods, o' imprisonment.
9: 12 nor seek their peace o' their wealth
10: 13 is this a work of one day o' two:
Ne 2: 16 not whether I went, o' what I did;
5: 8 brethren? o' shall they be sold unto us?*
10: 31 bring ware o' any victuals on the
31 on the sabbath, o' on the holy day:
13: 20 without Jerusalem once o' twice.
25 unto your sons, o' for yourselves.
Es 4: 11 whosoever, whether man o' woman,

Es 4:16 eat nor drink three days, night o· day:
8: 6 o· how can I endure to see the
9:12 o· what is thy request further? and it
Job 3:12 o· why the breasts that I should suck?
15 O· with princes that had gold, who 176
16 O· as an hidden untimely birth I had"
4: 7 o· where were the righteous cut off?
6: 5 o· loweth the ox over his fodder?
6 o· is there any taste in the white of
12 of stones? o· is my flesh of brass?
22 o·, Give a reward for me of your
23 O·, Deliver me from the enemy's
23 o·, Redeem me from the hand of the
7:12 Am I a sea, o· a whale, that thou
8: 3 o· doth the Almighty pervert justice?
10: 4 flesh? o· seest thou as man seeth?
11:10 off, and shut up, o· gather together,*
12: 8 O· speak to the earth, and it shall 176
13: 9 o· as one man mocketh another, do
22 o· let me speak, and answer thou 176
15: 3 o· with speeches wherewith he can do
7 o· wast thou made before the hills?
16: 3 o· what emboldeneth thee that thou176
22: 3 o· is it gain to him, that thou
11 O· darkness, that thou canst not 176
25: 4 o· how can he be clean that is born of
28:16 the precious onyx, o· the sapphire.
18 shall be made of coral, o· of pearls:
31: 5 o· if my foot hath hasted to deceit;
9 o· if I have laid wait at my neighbour's*
13 my manservant o· of my maidservant,
16 o· have caused the eyes of the widow
17 O· have eaten my morsel myself
19 clothing, o· any poor without covering;
24 o· have said to the fine gold, Thou art*
26 o· the moon walking in brightness;
27 o· my mouth hath kissed my hand:*
29 o· lifted up myself when evil found
34 o· did the contempt of families terrify*
38 o· that the furrows likewise thereof*
39 o· have caused the owners thereof to
32:12 Job, o· that answered his words:
34:13 o· who hath disposed the whole world?
29 a nation, o· against a man only:
33 thou refuse, o· whether thou choose;*
35: 6 o· if thy transgressions be multiplied,*
7 o· what receiveth he of thine hand? 176
36:23 o· who can say, Thou hast wrought
29 clouds, o· the noise of his tabernacle?*
37:13 correction, o· for his land, o· for mercy.
38: 5 o· who hath stretched the line upon176
6 o· who laid the corner stone thereof;"
8 O· who shut up the sea with doors,
16 o· hast thou walked in the search of
17 o· hast thou seen the doors of the
21 o· because the number of thy days is*
22 o· hast thou seen the treasures of the
25 o· the way for the lightning of thunder;
28 o· who hath begotten the drops of 176
31 o· loose the bands of Orion? "
32 o· canst thou guide Arcturus with his
36 o· who hath given understanding 176
37 o· who can stay the bottles of heaven,
39 o· fill the appetite of the young lions,
39: 1 o· canst thou mark when the hinds do
2 o· knowest thou the time when they
5 o· who hath loosed the bands of the
9 to serve thee, o· abide by thy crib?
10 o· will he harrow the valleys after
11 o· wilt thou leave thy labour to him?
13 o· wings and feathers unto the *
15 o· that the wild beast may break them.
40: 9 o· canst thou thunder with a voice like*
41: 1 o· his tongue with a cord which thou
2 o· bore his jaw through with a thorn?
5 o· wilt thou bind him for thy maidens?
7 irons? o· his head with fish spears?
13 o· who can come to him with his *
20 as out of a seething pot o· caldron.*
Ps 24: 3 o· who shall stand in his holy place?*
32: 9 Be ye not as the horse, o· as the mule,
35:14 he had been my friend o· brother:
44:20 o· stretched out our hands to a strange
50: 8 thy sacrifices o· thy burnt offerings,*
13 of bulls, o· drink the blood of goats?
16 o· that thou shouldest take my *
66: *title* the chief Musician, A Song o· Psalm.*
67: *title* on Neginoth, A Psalm o· Song.
68: *title* Musician, A Psalm o· Song of David.*
69:31 than an ox o· bullock that hath horns*
75: *title* A Psalm o· Song of Asaph. *
76: *title* A Psalm o· Song of Asaph. *
87: *title* A Psalm o· Song for the sons of *
88: *title* A Song o· Psalm for the sons of *
11 o· thy faithfulness in destruction?*
89: 8 o· to thy faithfulness round about*
90: 2 o· ever thou hadst formed the earth
92: *title* A Psalm o· Song for the sabbath day.*
94:16 o· who will stand up for me against*
108: *title* A Song o· Psalm of David. *
120: 3 o· what shall be done unto thee, thou*
131: 1 matters, o· in things too high for me.
132: 4 mine eyes, o· slumber to mine eyelids,
139: 7 o· whither shall I flee from thy
144: 3 o· the son of man, that thou makest
Pr 6: 7 having no guide, overseer, o· ruler,
7:22 o· as a fool to the correction of the
8: 8 nothing froward o· perverse in them.
23 the beginning, o· ever the earth was.
20:20 curseth his father o· his mother,
22:26 o· of them that are sureties for debts.
23:34 o· as he that lieth upon the top of a
28:24 robbeth his father o· his mother, and
29: 9 whether he rage o· laugh, there is no
30: 4 up into heaven, o· descended? *
9 o· lest I be poor and steal, and take

Pr 30:32 o· if thou hast thought evil, lay
Ec 2:19 he shall be a wise man o· a fool? 176
25 o· who else can hasten here unto, more
5:12 whether he eat little o· much: but
9: 1 no man knoweth either love o· hatred
11: 3 o· toward the north, in the place
6 shall prosper, either this o· that, 176
6 o· whether they both shall be alike
12: 2 sun, o· the light, o· the moon, o· the‡
6 O· ever the silver cord be loosed, ‡5704
6 o· the golden bowl be broken, ‡
6 o· the pitcher be broken at the ‡
6 o· the wheel broken at the cistern.‡
14 it be good, o· whether it be evil.
Ca 2: 9 is like a roe o· a young hart: 176
17 be thou like a roe o· a young hart
6:12 O· ever I was aware, my soul made me‡
8:14 thou like to a roe o· to a young hart176
Isa 1:11 bullocks, o· of lambs, o· of he goats.
7:11 the depth, o· in the height above. 176
10:14 wing, o· opened the mouth, o· peeped.
15 o· shall the saw magnify itself *
15 o· as if the staff should lift up itself,
17: 6 two o· three berries in the top of the
6 four o· five in the outmost fruitful
8 made, either the groves, o· the images.
19:15 head o· tail, branch o· rush, may do.
27: 5 O· let him take hold of my strength,176
7 o· is he slain according to the
29: 8 o· as when a thirsty man dreameth,
16 o· shall the thing framed say of him
30:14 o· to take water withal out of the pit.
38:14 Like a crane o· a swallow, so did I
40:13 o· being his counseller hath taught
18 o· what likeness will ye compare unto
25 ye liken me, o· shall I be equal? *
41:22 them; o· declare us things for to come.
23 do good, o· do evil, that we may be
42:19 o· deaf, as my messenger that I sent?
43: 9 o· let them hear, and say, It is truth.
44:10 a god, o· molten a graven image
45: 9 thou? o· thy work, He hath no hands?
10 o· to the woman, What hast thou
49:24 o· the lawful captive delivered?
50: 1 o· which of my creditors is it to 176
2 o· have I no power to deliver?
57:11 hast thou been afraid o· feared, *
66: 8 o· shall a nation be born at once? *
Jer 2:18 o· what hast thou to do in the way of
32 her ornaments, o· a bride her attire?
7:22 burnt offerings o· sacrifices:
11:14 neither lift up a cry o· prayer for them:*
19 like a lamb o· an ox that is brought*
13:23 his skin, o· the leopard his spots?
14:22 o· can the heavens give showers?
15: 5 o· who shall bemoan thee?
5 o· who shall go aside to ask how thou
16: 7 for their father o· for their mother.
10 against us? o· what is our iniquity?
10 o· what is our sin that we have
18:14 o· shall the cold flowing waters that
20:17 o· that my mother might have been*
21:13 us? o· who shall enter into our
22:18 saying, Ah my brother! o·, Ah sister!
18 him, saying, Ah lord! o·, Ah his glory!
23:33 people, o· the prophet, o· a priest, 176
32:43 It is desolate without man o· beast;
34: 9 being an Hebrew o· an Hebrewess,
36:23 Jehudi had read three o· four leaves,
37:18 against thee, o· against thy servants,
18 thy servants, o· against this people,
40: 5 o· go wheresoever it seemeth 176
42: 6 it be good, o· whether it be evil, we
17 none of them shall remain o· escape
44:14 sojourn there, shall escape o· remain,
28 words shall stand, mine, o· theirs.
48:24 cities of the land of Moab, far o· near.
Eze 2: 5 hear, o· whether they will forbear,
7 hear, o· whether they will forbear:
3:11 hear o· whether they will forbear.
4:14 dieth of itself, o· is torn in pieces;
14: 7 o· of the stranger that sojourneth in
17 O· if I bring a sword upon that 176
19 O· if I send a pestilence into that "
15: 2 o· than a branch which is among *
3 o· will men take a pin of it to hang
17: 9 without great power o· many people
15 o· shall he break the covenant, and be*
21:16 Go thee one way o· other, either on the*
16 either on the right hand, o· on the left,*
22:14 o· can thine hands be strong, in the
34: 6 and none did search o· seek after them.
44:22 o· a widow that had a priest before.
25 but for father, o· for mother,
25 o· for son, o· for daughter, for brother,
25 o· for sister that hath had no husband,
31 o· torn, whether it be fowl o· beast.
46:12 burnt offering o· peace offerings
Da 2:10 magician, o· astrologer, o· Chaldean.
4:19 dream, o· the interpretation thereof,
35 o· say unto him, What doest thou?
6: 4 there any error o· fault found in him.
7, 12 ask a petition of any God o· man
24 o· ever they came at the bottom of‡
11:29 not be as the former, o· as the latter.*
Joe 1: 2 o· even in the days of your fathers?
Am 3:12 lion two legs, o· a piece of an ear; 176
4: 8 two o· three cities wandered unto one
5:19 o· went into the house, and leaned his
6: 2 o· their border greater than your
Mic 6: 7 o· with ten thousands of rivers of oil?
Hag 2:12 his skirt do touch bread, o· pottage,
12 o· wine, o· oil, o· any meat, shall it be
Zec 8:10 to him that went out o· came in
Mal 1: 8 with thee, o· accept thy person? 176
2:13 o· receiveth it with good will at your *

Mal 2:17 o·, Where is the God of judgment? 2228
M't 5:17 destroy the law, o· the prophets: 2228
18 one jot o· one tittle shall in no wise "
36 not make one hair white o· black. "
6:24 o· else he will hold to the one, and "
25 ye shall eat, o· what ye shall drink; "
31 we eat? o·, What shall we drink? 2228
31 o·, Wherewithal shall we be clothed?"
7: 4 O· how wilt thou say to thy brother,"
9 O· what man is there of you, whom "
10 O· if he ask a fish, will he give him2532
16 of thorns, o· figs of thistles? 2228
9: 5 thee; o· to say, Arise, and walk? "
10:11 And into whatsoever city o· town ye"
14 ye depart out of that house o· city, "
19 thought how o· what ye shall speak:"
37 He that loveth father o· mother "
37 he that loveth son o· daughter more"
11: 3 come, o· do we look for another? "
12: 5 O· have ye not read in the law, how"
25 every city o· house divided against "
29 O· else how can one enter into a "
33 o· else make the tree corrupt, and "
13:21 tribulation o· persecution ariseth "
15: 4 He that curseth father o· mother, "
5 say to his father o· his mother, It "
6 honour not his father o· his mother,*"
16:14 Jeremias, o· one of the prophets. "
26 soul? o· what shall a man give in "
17:25 the earth take custom o· tribute? "
25 their own children, o· of strangers?"
18: 8 if thy hand o· thy foot offend thee, "
8 to enter into life halt o· maimed, "
8 than having two hands o· two feet "
16 take with thee one o· two more, "
16 the mouth of two o· three witnesses"
20 For where two o· three are gathered"
19:29 houses, o· brethren, o· sisters, "
29 o· father, o· mother, "
29 father,...mother, o· wife, * "
29 o· children, o· lands, for my name's "
21:25 was it from heaven, o· of men? "
22:17 to give tribute unto Cæsar, o· not? "
23:17 o· the temple that sanctifieth the "
19 o· the altar that sanctifieth the "
24:23 you, Lo, here is Christ, o· there; "
25:37 o· thirsty, and gave thee drink? "
38 thee in? o· naked, and clothed thee?"
39 O· when saw we thee sick, * "
39 o· in prison, and came unto thee? "
44 hungred, o· athirst, o· a stranger, "
44 o· naked, o· sick, o· in prison, and "
27:17 o· Jesus which is called Christ? "
M'r 2: 9 o· to say, Arise, and take up thy "
3: 4 on the sabbath days, o· to do evil? "
4 to save life, o· to kill? But they "
33 Who is my mother, o· my brethren?*"
4:17 affliction o· persecution ariseth "
21 under a bushel, o· under a bed? "
30 o· with what comparison shall we "
6:15 a prophet, o· as one of the prophets.*"
56 into villages, o· cities, o· country, "
7:10 Whoso curseth father o· mother, let"
11 shall say to his father o· mother, It "
12 ought for his father o· his mother; "
8:37 O· what shall a man give in * "
10:29 that hath left house, o· brethren, "
29 o· sisters, o· father, o· mother, "
29 father,...mother, o· wife, * "
29 o· children, o· lands, for my sake, "
11:30 was it from heaven, o· of men? "
12:14 to give tribute to Cæsar, o· not? "
15 Shall we give, o· shall we not give? "
13:21 Lo, here is Christ; o·, lo, he is there;"
35 cometh, at even, o· at midnight, "
35 at midnight, o· at the cockcrowing,"
35 the cockcrowing, o· in the morning:"
Lu 2:24 turtledoves, o· two young pigeons. "
3:15 whether he were the Christ, o· not;*
5:23 o· to say, Rise up and walk? 2228
6: 9 days to do good, o· to do evil? "
9 evil? to save life, o· to destroy it? "
7:19, 20 come? o· look we for another? "
8:16 vessel, o· putteth it under a bed; "
9:25 and lose himself, o· be cast away? "
11:11 o· if ye ask a fish, will he for a fish "
12 O· if he shall ask an egg, will 2228,2532
12:11 how o· what thing ye shall answer,2228
11 shall answer, o· what ye shall say: "
14 me a judge o· a divider over you? "
29 shall eat, o· what ye shall drink, * "
38 watch, o· come in the third watch,2532
41 this parable unto us, o· even to all?2228
13: 4 O· those eighteen, upon whom the "
15 loose his ox o· his ass from the stall,"
14: 5 have an ass o· an ox fallen into a pit,"
12 thou makest a dinner o· a supper, "
31 O· what king, going to make war "
32 O· else, while the other is yet a 1161
16:13 o· else he will hold to the one, and 2228
17: 7 servant plowing o· feeding cattle, "
21 shall they say, Lo here! o·, lo there!"
23 say to you, See here; o·, see there:*"
18:11 o· even as this publican. "
29 o· parents, o· brethren, o· wife, "
29 o· children, for the kingdom of God's"
20: 2 o· who is he that gave thee this "
4 was it from heaven, o· of men? "
22 to give tribute unto Cæsar, o· no? "
22:27 sitteth at meat, o· he that serveth? "
Joh 2: 6 two o· three firkins apiece. "
4:27 o·, Why talkest thou with her? "
6:19 five and twenty o· thirty furlongs, "
7:17 God, o· whether I speak of myself. "
48 of the rulers o· of the Pharisees "
9: 2 did sin, this man, o· his parents, "

Joh 9:21 o' who hath opened his eyes, we 2228
25 Whether he be a sinner o' no, I know*
13:29 o', that he should give something 2228
14:11 o' else believe me for the very 1161
18:34 o' did others tell it thee of me? 2228
Ac 1: 7 to know the times o' the seasons, "
3:12 o' why look ye so earnestly on us, "
12 by our own power o' holiness we "
4: 7 By what power, o' by what name, "
34 were possessors of lands o' houses "
5:38 this counsel o' this work be of men, "
7:49 o' what is the place of my rest? "
8:34 of himself, o' of some other man? "
9: 2 whether they were men o' women, 2532
10:14 thing that is common o' unclean. *2228
28 o' come unto one of another nation; "
28 call any man common o' unclean. "
11: 8 for nothing common o' unclean hath "
17:21 to tell, o' to hear some new thing.) 2532
29 like unto gold, o' silver, o' stone, 2228
18:14 of wrong o' wicked lewdness, "
19:12 the sick handkerchiefs o' aprons, "
20:33 no man's silver, o' gold, o' apparel. "
23: 9 a spirit o' an angel hath spoken to "
15 o' ever he come near, are ready to 4253
29 worthy of death o' of bonds. 2228
24:20 O' else let these same here say, if "
23 to minister o' come unto him. * "
25:11 o' have committed any thing *2532
26:31 worthy of death o' of bonds. 2228
28: 6 o' fallen down dead suddenly: "
17 people, o' customs of our fathers, "
21 shewed o' spake any harm of thee. "
Ro 2: 4 O' despisest thou the riches of his "
15 accusing o' else excusing one "
3: 1 o' what profit is there of "
4: 9 o' upon the uncircumcision also? "
10 circumcision, o' in uncircumcision? "
13 was not to Abraham, o' to his seed, "
6:16 o' of obedience unto righteousness? "
8:35 o' distress, o' persecution, o' famine, "
35 o' nakedness, o' peril, o' sword? "
9:11 having done any good o' evil, that "
10: 7 O', Who shall descend into the deep? "
11:34 o' who hath been his counsellor? "
35 O' who hath first given to him, and "
12: 7 O' ministry, let us wait on our 1535
7 o' he that teacheth, on teaching; "
8 O' he that exhorteth, on "
14: 4 own master he standeth o' falleth. 2228
8 whether we live therefore, o' die, 5037
10 o' why dost thou set at nought 2228
13 a stumblingblock o' an occasion "
21 brother stumbleth, o' is offended,* "
21 is offended, o' is made weak. * "
1Co 1:13 o' were ye baptized in the name of "
2: 1 excellency of speech o' of wisdom, "
3:22 Paul, o' Apollos, o' Cephas, 1535
22 o' the world, o' life, o' death, "
22 o' things present, o' things to come; "
4: 3 of you, o' of man's judgment: 2228
21 come unto you with a rod, o' in love, "
5:10 this world, o' with the covetous, * "
10 the covetous, o' extortioners, "
10 the covetous, o' with idolaters; "
11 be a fornicator, o' covetous, "
11 o' an idolater, o' a railer, "
11 o' a drunkard, o' an extortioner; "
7:11 o' be reconciled to her husband: "
15 A brother o' a sister is not under "
16 o' how knowest thou, O man, "
8: 5 whether in heaven o' in earth, 1535
9: 6 O' I only and Barnabas, have not 2228
7 o' who feedeth a flock, and eateth "
8 o' saith not the law the same also? "
10 O' saith he it altogether for our "
10:19 o' that which is offered in sacrifice* "
31 eat, o' drink, o' whatsoever ye do, 1535
11: 4 Every man praying o' prophesying, 2228
5 woman that prayeth o' prophesieth "
6 for a woman to be shorn o' shaven, "
22 o' despise ye the church of God, "
12:13 whether we be Jews o' Gentiles, 1535
13 whether we be bond or free; "
26 o' one member be honoured, all "
13: 1 brass, o' a tinkling cymbal. 2228
14: 6 by revelation, o' by knowledge, "
6 o' by prophesying, o' by doctrine? "
7 giving sound, whether pipe o' harp, 1535
7 be known what is piped o' harped? 2228
23 that are unlearned, o' unbelievers, "
24 believeth not, o' one unlearned, "
27 be by two, o' at the most by three, "
29 the prophets speak two o' three, "
36 from you, o' came it unto you only? "
37 himself to be a prophet, o' spiritual, "
15:11 whether it were I o' they, so we 1535
37 of wheat, o' of some other grain: 2228
2Co 1: 6 o' whether we be comforted, it is 1535
13 than what ye read o' acknowledge; 2228
17 o' the things that I purpose, do I "
3: 1 o' need we, as some others, 2228,3361
1 o' letters of commendation from 2228
5: 9 that, whether present o' absent, 1535
10 done, whether it be good o' bad. "
13 o' whether we be sober, it is for your "
6:15 o' what part hath he that believeth 2228
8:23 o' our brethren be enquired of, 1535
9: 7 not grudgingly, o' of necessity: 2228
10:12 o' compare ourselves with some "
11: 4 o' if ye receive another spirit, which "
4 o' another gospel, which ye have "
12: 2 o' whether out of the body I cannot 1535
3 in the body, o' out of the body, "
6 me to be, o' that he heareth of me. 2228
13: 1 the mouth of two o' three witnesses 2532

Ga 1: 8 o' an angel from heaven, preach 2228
10 do I now persuade men, o' God? "
10 o' do I seek to please men? for if I "
2: 2 I should run, o' had run, in vain. "
3: 2, 5 the law, o' by the hearing of faith? "
15 disannulleth, o' addeth thereto. "
4: 9 God, o' rather are known of God, 1161
Eph 3:20 above all that we ask o' think, 2228
5: 3 all uncleanness, o' covetousness, "
27 spot, o' wrinkle, o' any such thing; "
6: 8 Lord, whether he be bond o' free. 1535
Ph'p 1:18 whether in pretence, o' in truth, "
20 whether it be by life, o' by death. "
27 come and see you, o' else be absent, "
2: 3 done through strife o' vainglory; 2228
Col 1:16 they be thrones, o' dominions, 1535
16 o' principalities, o' powers: "
20 things in earth, o' things in heaven. "
2:16 judge you in meat, o' in drink, 2228
16 o' in respect of a holyday, "
16 o' of the new moon, o'...the sabbath "
3:17 ye do in word o' in deed, do all in "
1Th 2:19 hope, o' joy, o' crown of rejoicing? "
5:10 that, whether we wake o' sleep, 1535
2Th 2: 2 shaken in mind, o' be troubled, *3383
4 called God, o' that is worshipped; 2228
15 whether by word, o' our epistle. 1535
1Ti 2: 9 o' gold, o' pearls, o' costly array; 2228
5: 4 widow have children o' nephews, "
16 any man o' woman that believeth* "
19 but before two o' three witnesses. "
Tit 1: 6 not accused of riot o' unruly. "
3:12 Artemas unto thee, o' Tychicus, "
Ph'm 18 wronged thee, o' oweth thee ought, "
Heb 2: 6 o' the son of man, that thou visitest "
10:28 under two o' three witnesses: "
12:16 any fornicator, o' profane person, "
20 o' thrust through with a dart: * "
Jas 2: 3 o' sit here under my footstool: "
15 If a brother o' sister be naked, and "
4:13 To day o' to morrow we will go into "
15 we shall live, and do this, o' that. "
1Pe 1:11 what, o' what manner of time the "
2:14 O' unto governors, as unto them 1535
3: 3 of gold, o' of putting on of apparel; 2228
9 evil for evil, o' railing for railing: "
4:15 o' as a thief, o' as an evildoer, "
15 o' as a busybody in other men's "
Re 2: 5, 16 o' else I will come unto thee 1161
3:15 I would thou wert cold o' hot:) 2228
13:16 right hand, o' in their foreheads: "
17 that no man might buy o' sell, save "
17 the mark, o' the name of the beast,* "
17 beast, o' the number of his name. "
14: 9 mark in his forehead, o' in his hand, "
20: 4 their foreheads, o' in their hands; *2532
21:27 abomination, o' maketh a lie: * "

oracle See also ORACLES.
2Sa 16:23 had enquired at the o' of God: 1697
1Ki 6: 5 both of the temple and of the o': 1687
16 them for it within, even for the o', "
19 And the o' he prepared in the house "
20 the o' in the forepart was twenty "
21 by the chains of gold before the o'; "
22 altar that was by the o' he overlaid "
23 the o' he made two cherubims of "
31 entering of the o' he made doors "
7:49 and five on the left, before the o', "
8: 6 his place, into the o' of the house, "
8 out in the holy place before the o', "
2Ch 3:16 he made chains, as in the o', and "
4:20 after the manner before the o', of "
5: 7 his place, to the o' of the house, "
9 seen from the ark before the o'; "
Ps 28: 2 up my hands toward thy holy o'. "

oracles
Ac 7:38 the lively o' to give unto us: 3051
Ro 3: 2 were committed the o' of God. "
Heb 5:12 the first principles of the o' of God; "
1Pe 4:11 let him speak as the o' of God; "

oration
Ac 12:21 throne, and made an o' unto them. 1215

orator
Isa 3: 3 artificer, and the eloquent o'. 3908
Ac 24: 1 with a certain o' named Tertullus, 4489

orchard See also ORCHARDS.
Ca 4:13 plants are an o' of pomegranates, 6508

orchards
Ec 2: 5 I made me gardens and o', and I *6508

ordain See ORDAINED; ORDAINETH.
1Ch 9:22 the seer did o' in their set office. 3245
17: 9 Also I will o' a place for my people *7760
Isa 26:12 Lord, thou wilt o' peace for us: 8239
1Co 7:17 walk. And so o' I in all churches. 1299
Ti 1: 5 and o' elders in every city, as I *2525

ordained
Nu 28: 6 was o' in mount Sinai for a sweet 6213
1Ki 12:32 And Jeroboam o' a feast in the eighth "
33 o' a feast unto the children of Israel: "
2Ki 23: 5 had o' to burn incense in the 5414
2Ch 11:15 And he o' him priests for the high *5975
23:18 with singing, as it was o' by David.* "
29:27 the instruments o' by David king of* "
Es 9:27 The Jews o', and took upon them, 6965
Ps 8: 2 thou o' strength because of thine *3245
3 and the stars, which thou hast o'; 3559
81: 5 This he o' in Joseph for a *7760
132:17 have o' a lamp for mine anointed. 6186
Isa 30:33 Tophet is o' of old; yea, for the * "
Jer 1: 5 and I o' thee a prophet unto the 5414
Da 2:24 Arioch, whom the king had o' *4483
Hab 1:12 thou hast o' them for judgment; 7760
M'r 3:14 o' twelve, that they should be with *4160

Joh 15:16 I have chosen you, and o' you, *5087
Ac 1:22 must one be o' to be a witness *1096
10:42 was o' of God to be the Judge of 3724
13:48 as were o' to eternal life believed. 5021
14:23 when they had o' them elders in *5500
16: 4 were o' of the apostles and elders 2919
17:31 by that man whom he hath o'; 3724
Ro 7:10 which was o' to life, I found to be *
13: 1 the powers that be are o' of God. 5021
1Co 2: 7 God o' before the world unto our *4304
9:14 Lord o' that they which preach *1299
Ga 3:19 was o' by angels in the hand of a "
Eph 2:10 o' that we should walk in them. *4282
1Ti 2: 7 Whereunto I am o' a preacher, *5087
2Ti *subscr.* o' the first bishop of the church *5500
Tit *subscr.* o' the first bishop of the church* "
Heb 5: 1 o' for men in things pertaining to *2525
8: 3 every high priest is o' to offer gifts* "
9: 6 when these things were thus o', *2680
Jude 4 who were before of old o' to this †‡4270

ordaineth
Ps 7:13 he o' his arrows against the *6466

order See also ORDERED; ORDERETH; ORDERINGS.
Ex 26:17 set in o' one against another: *7947
27:21 Aaron and his sons shall o' it from 6186
39:37 even with the lamps to be set in o', 4634
40: 4 the table, and set in o' the things 6186
4 that are to be set in o' upon it; *6187
23 And he set the bread in o' upon it 6186
Le 1: 7 lay the wood in o' upon the fire: "
8 and the fat, in o' upon the wood "
12 and the priest shall lay them in o' "
6:12 lay the burnt offering in o' upon it; "
24: 3 shall Aaron o' it from the evening "
4 shall o' the lamps upon the pure "
8 every sabbath he shall set it in o' "
Jos 2: 6 she had laid in o' upon the roof. "
J'g 13:12 How shall we o' the child, and †‡4941
2Sa 17:23 city, and put his household in o', 6680
1Ki 18:33 And he put the wood in o', and cut 6186
14 he said, Who shall o' the battle? * 631
2Ki 20: 1 the Lord, Set thine house in o'; 6680
23: 4 and the priests of the second o', "
1Ch 6:32 their office according to their o'. 4941
15:13 we sought him not after the due o'.* "
23:31 according to the o' commanded * "
25: 2 according to the o' of the king. 3027
6 according to the king's o' to Asaph, "
2Ch 8:14 according to the o' of David his *4941
13:11 shewbread also set they in o' upon
29:35 house of the Lord was set in o'. 3559
Job 10:22 shadow of death, without any o', 5468
23: 4 I would o' my cause before him, 6186
33: 5 set thy words in o' before me, "
37:19 o' our speech by reason of darkness. "
Ps 40: 5 be reckoned up in o' unto thee: "
50:21 and set them in o' before thine eyes. "
110: 4 ever after the o' of Melchizedek. 1700
119:133 O' my steps in thy word: and let 3559
Ec 12: 9 out, and set in o' many proverbs. 8626
Isa 9: 7 kingdom, to o' it, and to establish *3559
38: 1 the Lord, Set thine house in o': 6680
44: 7 declare it, and set it in o' for me, 6186
Jer 46: 3 O' ye the buckler and shield, and ‡ "
Eze 41: 6 over another, and thirty in o'; 6471
Lu 1: 1 in o' a declaration of those things *1299
3 to write unto thee in o', most 2517
8 before God in the o' of his course, 5010
Ac 11: 4 and expounded it by o' unto them, 2517
18:23 of Galatia and Phrygia in o', "
1Co 11:34 rest will I set in o' when I come. 1299
14:40 things be done decently and in o'. 5010
15:23 every man in his own o': Christ 5001
16: 1 as I have given o' to the churches 1299
Col 2: 5 joying and beholding your o', and 5010
Tit 1: 5 set in o' the things that are wanting, 1930
Heb 5: 6 ever after the o' of Melchisedec. 5010
10 priest after the o' of Melchisedec. "
6:20 ever after the o' of Melchisedec. "
7:11 rise after the o' of Melchisedec, "
11 not be called after the o' of Aaron? "
17 ever after the o' of Melchisedec. "
21 ever after the o' of Melchisedec:) * "

ordered
J'g 6:26 top of this rock, in the o' place, *4634
2Sa 23: 5 covenant, o' in all things, and 6186
Job 13:18 I have o' my cause; I know that I* "
Ps 37:23 of a good man are o' by the Lord: *3559

ordereth
Ps 50:23 to him that o' his conversation 7760

orderings
1Ch 24:19 the o' of them in their service to *6486

orderly See also DISORDERLY.
Ac 21:24 that thou thyself also walkest o', 4748

ordinance See also ORDINANCES.
Ex 12:14 keep it a feast by an o' for ever. 2708
17 your generations by an o' for ever. "
24 observe this thing for an o' to thee 2706
43 This is the o' of the passover: 2708
13:10 therefore keep this o' in his season "
15:25 for them a statute and an o', and 4941
Le 18:30 Therefore shall ye keep mine o', *4931
22: 9 They shall therefore keep mine o',* "
Nu 9:14 according to the o' of the passover,* 2708
14 ye shall have one o', both for the * "
10: 8 shall be to you for an o' for ever "
15:15 One o' shall be both for you of the* "
15 an o' for ever in your generations:* "
18: 8 and to thy sons, by an o' for ever. *2706
19: 2 This is the o' of the law which the *2708
31:21 This is the o' of the law which the* "
Jos 24:25 a statute and an o' in Shechem. 4941
1Sa 30:25 it a statute and an o' for Israel "
2Ch 2: 4 This is an o' for ever to Israel.

2Ch 35:13 with fire according to the o': but 4941
25 and made them an o' in Israel: 2706
Ezr 3:10 after the o' of David king of Israel.*3027
Ps 99: 7 and the o' that he gave them. *2706
Isa 24: 5 the laws, changed the o', broken "
58: 2 forsook not the o' of their God: 4941
Eze 45:14 Concerning the o' of oil, the bath *2706
46:14 by a perpetual o' unto the Lord. 2708
Mal 3:14 is it that we have kept his o', 4931
Ro 13: 2 the power, resisteth the o' of God: *1296*
1Pe 2:13 Submit...to every o' of man for *2937*
ordinances
Ex 18:20 thou shalt teach them o' and laws,*2706
Le 18: 3 neither shall ye walk in their o'. *2708
4 and keep mine o', to walk therein:*"
Nu 9:12 all the o' of the passover they shall*"
2Ki 17:34 or after their o', or after the law 4941
37 And the statutes, and the o', and "
2Ch 33: 8 and the o' by the hand of Moses. "
Ne 10:32 Also we made o' for us, to charge 4687
Job 38:33 Knowest thou the o' of heaven? 2708
Ps 119:91 this day according to thine o': 4941
Isa 58: 2 they ask of me the o' of justice; "
Jer 31:35 the o' of the moon and of the stars 2708
36 If those o' depart from before me, 2706
33:25 not appointed the o' of heaven and2708
Eze 11:20 and keep mine o', and do them: 4941
43:11 all the o' thereof, and all the forms2708
11 and all the o' thereof, and do them. "
18 These are the o' of the altar in the "
44: 5 concerning all the o' of the house "
Mal 3: 7 ye are gone away from mine o', 2706
Lu 1: 6 and o' of the Lord blameless. *1345*
1Co 11: 2 keep the o', as I delivered them to**3862*
Eph 2:15 commandments contained in o'; *1378*
Col 2:14 Blotting out the handwriting of o' "
20 in the world, are ye subject to o', *1379*
Heb 9: 1 had also o' of divine service, and *1345*
10 divers washings, and carnal o', "
ordinary
Eze 16:27 and have diminished thine o' food,2706
Oreb (*o'-reb*)
J'g 7:25 of the Midianites, *O'* and Zeeb; 6157
25 and they slew *O'* upon the rock *O'*, "
25 brought the heads of *O'* and Zeeb to"
8: 3 the princes of Midian, *O'* and Zeeb:"
Ps 83:11 Make their nobles like *O'*, and like "
Isa 10:26 slaughter of Midian at the rock of *O'*:"
Oregim See JAARE-OREGIM.
Oren (*o'-ren*)
1Ch 2:25 and Bunah, and *O'*, and Ozem, and 767
organ See also ORGANS.
Ge 4:21 such as handle the harp and o'. *5748
Job 21:12 and rejoice at the sound of the o'.* "
30:31 and my o' into the voice of them * "
organs
Ps 150: 4 with stringed instruments and o'.*5748
Orion (*o-ri'-on*)
Job 9: 9 Arcturus, *O'*, and Pleiades, and 3685
38:31 Pleiades, or loose the bands of *O'*? "
Am 5: 8 that maketh the seven stars and *O'*,"
ornament See also ORNAMENTS.
Pr 1: 9 be an o' of grace unto thy head, *3880
4: 9 give to thine head an o' of grace: * "
25:12 of gold, and an o' of fine gold, 2481
Isa 30:22 the o' of thy molten images of gold:*642
49:18 thee with them all, as with an o', 5716
Eze 7:20 As for the beauty of his o', he set "
1Pe 3: 4 the o' of a meek and quiet spirit, *
ornaments
Ex 33: 4 and no man did put on him his o'. 5716
5 now put off thy o' from thee, that "
6 stripped themselves of their o' by "
J'g 8:21 and took away the o' that were on*7720
26 beside o', and collars, and purple* "
2Sa 1:24 put on o' of gold upon your apparel.5716
Isa 3:18 their tinkling o' about their feet, *5914
20 bonnets, and the o' of the legs, *6807
61:10 decketh himself with o', *6287
Jer 2:32 Can a maid forget her o', or a 5716
4:30 thou deckest thee with o' of gold, "
Eze 16: 7 and thou art come to excellent o':* "
11 I decked thee also with o', and I "
23:40 eyes, and deckedst thyself with o', "
Ornan (*or'-nan*) See also ARAUNAH.
1Ch 21:15, 18 threshingfloor of *O'* the Jebusite.771
20 *O'* turned back, and saw the angel; "
20 Now *O'* was threshing wheat. "
21 as David came to *O'*, *O'* looked and "
22 Then David said to *O'*, Grant me the"
23 *O'* said unto David, Take it to thee, "
24 So David said to *O'*, Nay; but I will "
25 So David gave to *O'* for the place six"
28 threshingfloor of *O'* the Jebusite, "
2Ch 3: 1 threshingfloor of *O'* the Jebusite. "
Orpah (*or'-pah*)
Ru 1: 4 the name of the one was *O'*, and 6204
14 and *O'* kissed her mother in law; "
orphans
La 5: 3 We are o' and fatherless, our 3490
Osee (*o'-see*) See also HOSEA; JOSHUA; OSHEA.
Ro 9:25 As he saith also in *O'*, I will call **5617*
Oshea (*o-she'-ah*) See also HOSHEA; OSEE.
Nu 13: 8 of Ephraim, *O'* the son of Nun. *1954
16 called *O'* the son of Nun Jehoshua.*"
ospray
Le 11:13 and the ossifrage, and the o', 5822
De 14:12 and the ossifrage, and the o', "
ossifrage
Le 11:13 eagle, and the o', and the ospray, 6538
De 14:12 eagle, and the o', and the ospray. "

ostrich See also OSTRICHES.
Job 39:13 wings and feathers unto the o'? †‡5133
ostriches
La 4: 3 cruel, like the o' in the wilderness.3283
other See also ANOTHER; OTHERS; OTHERWISE.
Ge 4:19 and the name of the o' Zillah. 8145
8:10, 12 And he stayed yet o' seven days;312
13:11 themselves the one from the o'. 251
28:17 is none o' but the house of God,
29:27 serve with me yet seven o' years. 312
30 served with him yet seven o' years. "
31:50 if thou shalt take o' wives beside *
32: 8 then the o' company which is left*
41: 3 seven o' kine came up after them 312
3 stood by the o' kine upon the brink
19 seven o' kine came up after them, 312
43:14 he may send away your o' brother, "
22 o' money have we brought down in "
47:21 of Egypt even to the o' end thereof.
Ex 1:15 and the name of the o' Puah: 8145
4: 7 it was turned again as his o' flesh.
14:20 one came not near the o' all the 2088
17:12 one side, and the o' on the...side; 259
12 one side, and the...on the o' side; 2088
18: 4 And the name of the o' was Eliezer;259
7 asked each o' of their welfare; 7453
20: 3 shalt have no o' gods before me. 312
23:13 no mention of the name of o' gods, "
25:12 and two rings in the o' side of it. 8145
19 one end, and the o' cherub on the* 259
19 and the...cherub on the o' end: 2088
32 the candlestick out of the o' side: 8145
33 made like almonds in the o' branch,259
26: 3 o' five curtains shall be coupled one to
13 and a cubit on the o' side of that 2088
27 of the o' side of the tabernacle, 8145
27:15 on the o' side shall be hangings "
28:10 the o' six names of the rest on the*
10 names of the rest on the o' stone,
25 the o' two ends of the two wreathen
27 two o' rings of gold thou shalt make,*
27 against the o' coupling thereof, *
29:19 And thou shalt take the o' ram; 8145
39 the o' lamb thou shalt offer at even:"
41 the o' lamb thou shalt offer at even,"
30:32 neither shall ye make any o' like it,*
32:15 and on the o' were they written. 2088
34:14 For thou shalt worship no o' god: 312
36:10 and the o' five curtains he coupled
25 for the o' side of the tabernacle, *8145
32 of the o' side of the tabernacle, "
33 boards from the one end to the o'. "
37: 3 and two rings upon the o' side of it. "
8 cherub on the o' end of that side:
18 out of the o' side thereof: 8145
38:15 for the o' side of the court gate, "
39:20 And they made two o' golden rings,*
20 over against the o' coupling thereof,*
Le 5: 7 and the o' for a burnt offering. 259
6:11 put on o' garments, and carry forth312
7:24 beasts, may be used in any o' use:
8:22 And he brought the o' ram, the 8145
11:23 But all o' flying creeping things, which*
12: 8 and the o' for a sin offering: 259
13:26 and it be no lower than the o' skin, but*
14:22 offering, and the o' a burnt offering.259
31 and the o' for a burnt offering, "
42 they shall take o' stones, and put 312
42 and he shall take o' morter, and "
15:15, 30 and the o' for a burnt offering; 259
16: 8 and the o' lot for the scapegoat. "
18:18 beside the o' in her life time.
20:24 have separated you from o' people.*
26 and have severed you from o' people,*
25:53 the o' shall not rule with rigour over*
Nu 6:11 and the o' for a burnt offering, 259
8:12 and the o' for a burnt offering, "
10:21 and the o' did set up the tabernacle
11:26 and the name of the o' Medad: 8145
31 were a day's journey on the o' side,3541
21:13 and pitched on the o' side of Arnon,5676
28: 4, 8 o' lamb shalt thou offer at even;8145
36: 3 to any of the sons of the o' tribes 259
De 4:32 the one side of heaven unto the o',
5: 7 shalt have none o' gods before me. 312
6:14 Ye shall not go after o' gods, of the "
7: 4 me, that they may serve o' gods: "
8:19 walk after o' gods, and serve them, "
11:16 and ye turn aside, and serve o' gods,"
28 to go after o' gods, which ye have not"
30 Are they not on the o' side Jordan,*5676
13: 2 Let us go after o' gods, which thou 312
6 Let us go and serve o' gods, which "
7 even unto the o' end of the earth;
13 Let us go and serve o' gods, which 312
17: 3 And hath gone and served o' gods, "
18:20 shall speak in the name of o' gods, "
28:14 to go after o' gods to serve them. "
36 and there shalt thou serve o' gods, "
64 one end of the earth even unto the o';
64 and there thou shalt serve o' gods, 312
29:26 For they went and served o' gods, "
30:17 and worship o' gods, and serve them;"
31:18 in that they are turned unto o' gods."
20 then will they turn unto o' gods, "
Jos 2:10 Amorites,...on the o' side Jordan,*5676
7: 7 and dwelt on the o' side Jordan! * "
8:22 the o' issued out of the city against428
11:19 of Gibeon: all o' they took in battle.*
12: 1 their land on the o' side Jordan *5676
13:27 on the o' side Jordan eastward. * "
32 of Moab, on the o' side Jordan, * "
14: 3 an half tribe on the o' side Jordan:* "
17: 5 which were on the o' side Jordan;* "
20: 8 And on the o' side Jordan by Jericho*"

Jos 21:27 out of the o' half tribe of Manasseh*
22: 4 Lord gave you on...o' side Jordan.*5676
7 unto the o' half thereof gave Joshua
23:16 have gone and served o' gods, and 312
24: 2 dwelt on the o' side of the flood in*5676
2 of Nachor: and they served o' gods.312
3 from the o' side of the flood, *5676
8 which dwelt on the o' side Jordan;*"
14 served on the o' side of the flood, * "
15 that were on the o' side of the flood,* "
16 forsake the Lord, to serve o' gods;*312
J'g 2:12 followed o' gods, of the gods of the "
17 they went a whoring after o' gods, "
19 in following o' gods to serve them, "
7: 7 and let all the o' people go every man*
25 to Gideon on the o' side Jordan. *5676
9:44 and the two o' companies ran upon all*
10: 8 that were on the o' side Jordan in*5676
13 forsaken me, and served o' gods: 312
11:18 and pitched on the o' side of Arnon,5676
13:10 unto me, that came unto me the o' day.
16:17 become weak, and be like any o' man.
20 I will go out as at o' times before,
29 hand, and of the o' with his left. 259
20:30 array against Gibeah, as at o' times.
31 kill, as at o' times, in the highways,
31 and the o' to Gibeah in the field, 259
Ru 1: 4 and the name of the o' Ruth: 8145
2:22 they meet thee not in any o' field. 312
1Sa 1: 2 and the name of the o' Peninnah: 8145
3:10 and called as at o' times, Samuel,
8: 8 forsaken me, and served o' gods, 312
14: 1 garrison, that is on the o' side. *5676
4 and a sharp rock on the o' side: 2088
4 and the name of the o' Seneh. 259
5 o' southward over against Gibeah. "
40 my son will be on the o' side.
17: 3 stood on a mountain on the o' side:2088
18:10 played with his hand, as at o' times:*
19:21 he sent o' messengers, and they 312
20:25 king sat upon his seat, as at o' times,
21: 9 for there is no o' save that here. 312
26:13 Then David went over to the o' side,5676
19 the Lord, saying, Go, serve o' gods.312
28: 8 himself, and put on o' raiment,
30:20 which they drave before those o' cattle,
31: 7 were on the o' side of the valley, 5676
7 they that were on the o' side Jordan,*"
2Sa 1:24 clothed you in scarlet, with o' delights,*
2:13 the o' on the...side of the pool. 428
13 the...on the o' side of the pool. 2088
4: 2 and the name of the o' Rechab, 8145
12: 1 city; the one rich, and the o' poor. 259
13:16 this evil is...greater than the o' 312
14: 6 but the one smote the o', and slew 259
17: 9 now in some pit, or in some o' place:
24:22 and o' instruments of the oxen for*
1Ki 3:22 the o' woman said, Nay; but the 312
23 the o' saith, Nay; but thy son is 2063
25 half to the one, and half to the o'. 259
26 But the o' said, Let it be neither 2063
6:24 cubits the o' wing of the cherub: 8145
24 unto the uttermost part of the o' 3671
25 And the o' cherub was ten cubits: 8145
26 and so was it of the o' cherub. "
27 of the o' cherub touched the o' wall;"
34 the two leaves of the o' door were "
7: 6 the o' pillars and the thick beam were*
7 from one side of the floor to the o'.*
16 height of the o' chapiter was five 8145
17 and seven for the o' chapiter. "
18 and so did he for the o' chapiter. "
20 round about upon the o' chapiter. "
23 cubits from the one brim to the o':*
9: 6 but go and serve o' gods, and 312
9 and have taken hold upon o' gods, "
10:20 one side and on the o' upon the six2088
11: 4 turned away his heart after o' gods:312
10 that he should not go after o' gods: "
12:29 Beth-el, and the o' put he in Dan. 259
14: 9 hast gone and made thee o' gods, 312
18:23 I will dress the o' bullock, and lay 259
20:29 pitched one over against the o' 428
2Ki 3:22 saw the water on the o' side as red*5048
5:17 offering nor sacrifice unto o' gods, 312
12: 7 Jehoiada the priest, and the o' priests,
17: 7 of Egypt, and had feared o' gods, 312
35 Ye shall not fear o' gods, nor bow "
37 and ye shall not fear o' gods. "
38 forget; neither shall ye fear o' gods. "
22:17 have burned incense unto o' gods, "
1Ch 6:78 on the o' side Jordan by Jericho, *5676
9:32 And o' of their brethren, of the *
12:37 And on the o' side of Jordan, of the 5676
23:17 Eliezer had none o' sons; but the 312
2Ch 3:11 o' wing was likewise five cubits,
11 reaching to the wing of the o' cherub."
12 one wing of the o' cherub was five 259
12 the o' wing was five cubits also, 312
12 joining to the wing of the o' cherub."
17 right hand, and the o' on the left; 259
7:19 you, and shall go and serve o' gods,312
22 laid hold on o' gods, and worshipped"
9:19 and on the o' upon the six steps. 2088
13: 9 the manner of the nations of o' lands?
20: 1 with them o' beside the Ammonites,*
25:12 And o' ten thousand left alive did the
28:25 places to burn incense unto o' gods,312
29:34 and until the o' priests had sanctified*
30:23 took counsel to keep o' seven days: 312
23 they kept o' seven days with gladness.
32:13 done unto all the people of o' lands?*
17 gods of the nations of o' lands have*
22 from the hand of all o', and guided
34:12 and o' of the Levites, all that could
25 have burned incense unto o' gods, 312

2Ch 35: 13 the o· holy offerings sod they in pots.*
Ezr 1: 10 and ten, and o· vessels a thousand. 312
2: 31 The children of the o· Elam, a "
Ne 3: 11 repaired the o· piece, and...tower *8145
20 earnestly repaired the o· piece, * "
4: 16 o· half of them held both the spears,*
17 with the o· hand held a weapon. 259
5: 5 o· men have our lands...vineyards. 312
7: 33 The men of the o· Nebo, fifty and "
34 children of the o· Elam, a thousand "
12: 38 the o· company of them that gave 8145
Es 9: 16 the o· Jews that were in the king's7605
Job 8: 12 down, it withereth before any o· herb.
24: 24 they are taken out of the way as all o·.
Ps 73: 5 They are not in trouble as o· men;
5 neither are they plagued like o· men.
85: 10 and peace have kissed each o·.
Ec 3: 19 as the one dieth, so dieth the o·; 2088
6: 5 this hath more rest than the o·. "
7: 14 set the one over against the o·. "
Isa 26: 13 o· lords beside thee have had dominion
49: 20 shalt have, after thou hast lost the o·,*
Jer 1: 16 have burned incense unto o· gods, 312
7: 6 walk after o· gods to your hurt: "
9 after o· gods whom ye know not; "
18 out drink offerings unto o· gods. "
11: 10 went after o· gods to serve them: "
13: 10 walk after o· gods, to serve them, "
16: 11 have walked after o· gods, and have "
13 shall ye serve o· gods day and night;"
19: 4 burned incense in it unto o· gods, "
13 out drink offerings unto o· gods. "
22: 9 and worshipped o· gods, and served "
24: 2 o· basket had very naughty figs, 259
25: 6 go not after o· gods to serve them, 312
33 even unto the o· end of the earth: "
32: 20 and in Israel, and among o· men; and
29 out drink offerings unto o· gods, 312
35: 15 go not after o· gods to serve them, "
36: 16 they were afraid both one and o·, *7453
44: 3 burn incense, and to serve o· gods, 312
5 to burn no incense unto o· gods. "
8 burning incense unto o· gods in the"
15 had burned incense unto o· gods, "
Eze 1: 23 straight, the one toward the o·: 269
16: 34 from o· women in thy whoredoms,
21: 16 Go thee one way or o·, either on the*
40: 6 the o· threshold of the gate, which 259
40 on the o· side, which was at the 312
41: 1 and six cubits on the o· side, which6311
2 side, and five cubits on the o· side: "
15 on the o· side, an hundred cubits, "
19 toward the palm tree on the o· side:"
21 the one as the appearance of the o·.*
24 door, and two leaves for the o· door.312
26 on the one side and on the o· side, 6311
42: 14 shall put on o· garments, and shall 312
44: 19 and they shall put on o· garments; "
45: 7 and on the o· side of the oblation 2088
47: 7 trees on the one side and on the o·. "
48: 8 in length as one of the o· parts, from *
21 and on the o· of the holy oblation, 2088
Da 2: 11 there is none o· that can shew it 321
44 shall not be left to o· people, but * "
3: 21 and their hats, and their o· garments,*
29 is no o· God that can deliver after 321
7: 20 and of the o· which came up, and 317
8: 3 but one was higher than the o·, 8145
12: 5 behold, there stood o· two, the one 312
5 the o· on that side of the bank of 259
Ho 3: 1 who look to o· gods, and love 312
9: 1 not, O Israel, for joy, as o· people:*
13: 10 where is any o· that may save thee in*
Ob 11 day...thou stoodest on the o· side, 5048
Zec 4: 3 the o· upon the left side thereof. 259
11: 7 Beauty, and the o· I called Bands; "
14 Then I cut asunder mine o· staff, 8145
M't 4: 21 he saw o· two brethren, James the 243
5: 39 right cheek, turn to him the o· also. "
6: 24 will hate the one, and love the o·; 2087
24 hold to the one, and despise the o·. "
8: 18 to depart unto the o· side. 4008
28 when he was come to the o· side "
12: 13 it was restored whole, like as the o·.243
45 with himself seven o· spirits 2087
13: 8 But o· fell into good ground, and * 243
14: 22 to go before him unto the o· side, 4008
16: 5 disciples were come to the o· side, "
20: 21 the o· on the left, in thy kingdom.*1520
21: 36 he sent o· servants more than the 243
41 his vineyard unto o· husbandmen, "
22: 4 Again, he sent forth o· servants, "
23: 23 and not to leave the o· undone. 2548
24: 31 from one end of heaven to the o·. 1565
40, 41 shall be taken, and the o· left. 1520
25: 11 Afterward came also the o· virgins,3062
16 and made them o· five talents. 243
17 received two, he also gained o· two. "
20 came and brought o· five talents, "
22 gained two o· talents beside them. "
27: 61 Mary Magdalene, and the o· Mary, "
28: 1 Mary Magdalene and the o· Mary to "
M'r 3: 5 hand was restored whole as the o·.* "
4: 8 o· fell on good ground, and did yield*"
19 the lusts of o· things entering in, 3062
35 Let us pass over unto the o· side. 4008
36 were also with him o· little ships. 243
5: 1 over unto the o· side of the sea, 4008
21 again by ship unto the o· side, "
6: 45 to the o· side before unto Bethsaida,"
7: 4 And many o· things there be, which243
8 and many o· such like things ye do.*"
8: 13 ship again departed to the o· side. 4008
10: 37 hand, and the o· on thy left hand, 1520
12: 31 is none o· commandment greater 243
32 God; and there is none o· but he: "

M'r 15: 27 right hand, and the o· on his left. *1520
41 and many o· women which came up243
Lu 3: 18 many o· things in his exhortation 2087
4: 43 kingdom of God to o· cities also: "
5: 7 partners, which were in the o· ship, "
6: 10 hand was restored whole as the o·.*243
29 on the one cheek offer also the o·; "
7: 41 hundred pence, and the o· fifty. 2087
8: 8 And o· fell on good ground, and "
22 over unto the o· side of the lake. 4008
10: 1 Lord appointed o· seventy also, 2087
31 saw him, he passed by on the o· side.492
32 on him, and passed by on the o· side."
11: 26 seven o· spirits more wicked than 2087
42 and not to leave the o· undone. 2548
14: 32 while the o· is yet a great way off, 846
16: 13 will hate the one, and love the o·; 2087
13 hold to the one, and despise the o·. "
17: 24 unto the o· part under heaven; so
34 be taken, and the o· shall be left. 2087
35 one shall be taken, and the o· left. "
36 one shall be taken, and the o· left.* "
18: 10 a Pharisee, and the o· a publican. "
11 thee, that I am not as o· men are, *3062
14 house justified rather than the o·: 1565
22: 65 many o· things blasphemously 2087
23: 32 And there were also two o·, * "
33 right hand, and the o· on the left. 3739
40 But the o· answering rebuked him,2087
24: 10 o· women that were with them, 3062
Joh 4: 38 o· men laboured, and ye are entered*243
6: 22 stood on the o· side of the sea 4008
22 that there was none o· boat there, 243
23 came o· boats from Tiberias nigh* "
25 him on the o· side of the sea, 4008
10: 1 but climbeth up some o· way, the 237
16 o· sheep I have, which are not of 243
15: 24 the works which none o· man did, "
18: 16 Then went out that o· disciple, "
19: 18 crucified him, and two o· with him.* "
32 the o· which was crucified with him. "
20: 2 to the o· disciple, whom Jesus loved, "
3 went forth, and that o· disciple, and "
4 and the o· disciple did outrun Peter,"
8 Then went in also that o· disciple, "
12 at the head, and the o· at the feet,*1520
25 o· disciples therefore said unto him,243
30 And many o· signs truly did Jesus "
21: 2 Zebedee, and two o· of his disciples. "
8 the o· disciples came in a little ship;"
25 also many o· things which Jesus did,"
Ac 2: 4 began to speak with o· tongues, 2087
40 with many o· words did he testify "
4: 12 Neither is there salvation in any o·:243
12 none o· name under heaven given 2087
5: 29 Peter and the o· apostles answered*
8: 34 of himself, or of some o· man? 2087
15: 2 Barnabas, and certain o· of them, 243
39 departed asunder one from the o·: 240
17: 9 security of Jason, and of the o·, *3062
18 o· some, He seemeth to be a setter
19: 39 any thing concerning o· matters, 2087
23: 6 Sadducees, and the o· Pharisees, "
26: 22 saying none o· things than those *1622
27: 1 Paul and certain o· prisoners unto2087
Ro 1: 13 also, even as among o· Gentiles. *3062
8: 39 nor any o· creature, shall be able 2087
13: 9 if there be any o· commandment, "
1Co 1: 16 know not whether I baptized any o·.243
3: 11 o· foundation can no man lay than "
7: 5 Defraud ye not one the o·, except it240
8: 4 that there is none o· God but one.*2087
9: 5 as well as o· apostles, and as the *3062
10: 29 I say, not thine own, but of the o·:*2087
11: 21 one taketh before o· his own supper:
14: 17 well, but the o· is not edified. 2087
21 With men of o· tongues and...lips *2084
21 With men of...tongues and o· lips 2087
29 two or three, and let the o· judge. * 243
15: 37 of wheat, or of some o· grain: 3062
2Co 1: 13 we write none o· things unto you, 243
2: 16 and to the o· the savour of life unto 3739
8: 13 I mean not that o· men be eased, * 243
10: 15 that is, of o· men's labours; but 245
11: 8 I robbed o· churches, taking wages 243
12: 13 ye were inferior to o· churches, *3062
13: 2 and to all o·, that, if I come again,* "
Ga 1: 8 any o· gospel unto you than that...we
9 any o· gospel unto you than that ye
19 But o· of the apostles saw I none, 2087
2: 13 the o· Jews dissembled likewise *3062
4: 22 bondmaid, the o· by a freewoman.*1520
5: 17 these are contrary the one to the o·:240
Eph 3: 5 in o· ages was not made known 2087
4: 17 henceforth walk not as o· Gentiles*3062
Ph'p 1: 13 all the palace, and in all o· places;* "
17 But the o· of love, knowing that I am
2: 3 esteem o· better than themselves. 240
4 any o· man thinketh that he hath 243
4: 3 and with o· my fellowlabourers, *3062
2Th 1: 3 you all toward each o· aboundeth;*240
1Ti 1: 3 that they teach no o· doctrine, *2085
10 be any o· thing that is contrary to 2087
5: 22 be partakers of o· men's sins: 245
Jas 5: 12 the earth, neither by any o· oath: 243
1Pe 4: 15 as a busybody in o· men's matters. 244
2Pe 3: 16 as they do also the o· scriptures, 3062
Re 2: 24 will put upon you none o· burden. 243
8: 13 by reason of the o· voices of the 3062
17: 10 one is, and the o· is not yet come; 243

others
Job 8: 19 and out of the earth shall o· grow. 312
31: 10 and let o· bow down upon her. "
34: 24 number, and set o· in their stead. "
26 as wicked men in the open sight of o·;
Ps 49: 10 perish, and leave their wealth to o·.312

Pr 5: 9 Lest thou give thine honour unto o·,312
Ec 7: 22 thou thyself likewise hast cursed o·. "
Isa 56: 8 Yet will I gather o· to him, beside
Jer 6: 12 houses shall be turned unto o·, with312
8: 10 will I give their wives unto o·, and "
Eze 9: 5 to the o· he said in mine hearing, 428
13: 6 and they have made o· to hope that*
10 o· daubed it with untempered morter:*
Da 7: 19 which was diverse from all the o·,*
11: 4 plucked up, even for o· beside those.312
M't 5: 47 only, what do ye more than o·?
15: 30 dumb, maimed, and many o·, and 2087
16: 14 and o·, Jeremias, or one of the "
20: 3 o· standing idle in the marketplace,243
6 went out, and found o· standing idle,"
21: 8 o· cut down branches from the trees,"
26: 67 o· smote him with the palms of *3588
27: 42 He saved o·; himself he cannot 243
M'r 6: 15 O· said, That it is Elias. "
15 And o· said, That it is a prophet, or "
8: 28 Elias; and o·, One of the prophets. "
11: 8 o· cut down branches off the trees, "
12: 5 and him they killed, and many o·; "
9 and will give the vineyard unto o·. "
15: 31 He saved o·; himself he cannot save."
Lu 5: 29 of publicans and of o· that sat down "
8: 3 and many o·, which ministered 2087
10 but to o· in parables; that seeing *3062
9: 8 of o·, that one of the old prophets 243
19 o· say, that one of the old prophets "
11: 16 And o·, tempting him, sought of 2087
18: 9 were righteous, and despised o·: 3062
20: 16 and shall give the vineyard to o·. 243
23: 35 He saved o·; let him save himself, "
24: 1 prepared, and certain o· with them.*
Joh 7: 12 He is a good man: o· said, Nay; 243
41 O· said, This is the Christ. But "
9: 9 This is he: o· said, He is like him: "
16 O· said, How can a man that is a "
10: 21 O· said, These are not the words of "
12: 29 o· said, An angel spake to him. "
18: 34 thyself, or did o· tell it thee of me? "
Ac 2: 13 O· mocking said, These men are 2087
15: 35 word of the Lord, with many o· also."
17: 32 and o· said, We will hear thee again3588
34 named Damaris, and o· with them.2087
28: 9 o· also, which had diseases in the*3062
1Co 9: 2 If I be not an apostle unto o·, yet 243
12 If o· be partakers of this power over"
27 means, when I have preached to o·, "
14: 19 by my voice I might teach o· also, "
2Co 3: 1 or need we, as some o·, epistles of *
8: 8 occasion of the forwardness of o·, 2087
Eph 2: 3 the children of wrath, even as o·. *3062
Ph'p 2: 4 man also on the things of o·. 2087
1Th 2: 6 glory, neither of you, nor yet of o·, 243
4: 13 even as o· which have no hope. *3062
5: 6 let us not sleep, as do o·; but let * "
1Ti 5: 20 before all, that o· also may fear. "
2Ti 2: 2 who shall be able to teach o· also. 2087
Heb 9: 25 place every year with blood of o·:* 245
11: 35 and o· were tortured, not accepting243
36 o· had trial of cruel mockings and 2087
Jude 23 And o· save with fear, pulling *3739

otherwise
2Sa 18: 13 O· I should have wrought 176
1Ki 1: 21 O· it shall come to pass, when my
2Ch 30: 18 passover o· than it was written. 3808
Ps 38: 16 lest o· they should rejoice over me:*
M't 6: 1 o· ye have no reward of your *1490
Lu 5: 36 if o·, then both the new maketh a* "
Ro 11: 6 works: o· grace is no more grace. 1893
6 grace: o· work is no more work. * "
22 o· thou also shalt be cut off.
2Co 11: 16 if o·, yet as a fool receive me, that*1490
Ga 5: 10 that ye will be none o· minded: 243
Ph'p 3: 15 if in any thing ye be o· minded, 2088
1Ti 5: 25 and they that are o· cannot be hid. 247
6: 3 If any man teach o·, and consent 2085
Heb 9: 17 o· it is of no strength at all while *1893

Othni (*oth'-ni*)
1Ch 26: 7 The sons of Shemaiah; O·, and 6273

Othniel (*oth'-ne-el*)
Jos 15: 17 O· the son of Kenaz, the brother 6274
J'g 1: 13 And O· the son of Kenaz, Caleb's "
3: 9 even O· the son of Kenaz, Caleb's "
11 and O· the son of Kenaz died. "
1Ch 4: 13 And the sons of Kenaz; O·, and "
13 and the sons of O·; Hathath. "
27: 15 Heldai the Netophathite, of O·: "

ouches
Ex 28: 11 make them to be set in o· of gold.‡4865
13 And thou shalt make o· of gold; ‡ "
14 fasten...wreathen chains to the o·.‡ "
25 thou shalt fasten in the two o·, and‡"
39: 6 onyx stones inclosed in o· of gold,‡ "
13 they were inclosed in o· of gold in‡ "
16 they made two o· of gold, and two‡ "
18 chains they fastened in the two o·,‡ "

ought See also AUGHT; NOUGHT; OUGHTEST.
Ge 34: 7 which thing o· not to be done.
39: 6 he knew not o· he had, save *3972
47: 18 there is not o· left in the sight of my*
Ex 5: 8 ye shall not diminish o· thereof: *
11 yet not o· of your work shall be *1697
19 shall not minish o· from your bricks*
12: 46 shalt not carry forth o· of the flesh*
22: 14 if a man borrow o· of his neighbour,*
29: 34 o· of the flesh of the consecrations,*
Le 4: 2, 27 things which o· not to be done,*
11: 25 whosoever beareth o· of the carcase*
19: 6 and if o· remain until the third day,*
25: 14 if thou sell o· unto thy neighbour,*4465
14 or buyest o· of thy neighbour's hand.*

Le 27:31 man will at all redeem o' of his tithes,*
Nu 15:24 if o' be committed by ignorance
30 the soul that doeth o' presumptuously,*
30: 6 vowed, or uttered o' out of her lips,*
De 4: 2 neither shall ye diminish o' from it, *
15: 2 that lendeth o' unto his neighbour*
26:14 neither have I taken away o' thereof*
14 nor given o' thereof for the dead:*
Jos 21:45 failed not o' of any good thing *1697
Ru 1:17 if o' but death part thee and me. *
1Sa 12: 4 taken o' of any man's hand. *3972
5 have not found o' in my hand. * "
25: 7 there o' missing unto them, * "
30:22 we will not give them o' of the spoil*
2Sa 3:35 if I taste bread, or o' else, *3972
13:12 no such thing o' to be done in Israel:*
14:10 said, Whosoever saith o' unto thee,*
19 o' that my lord the king hath spoken:*
1Ch 12:32 times, to know what Israel o' to do;
15: 2 None o' to carry the ark of God but
2Ch 13: 5 O' ye not to know that the Lord God
Ne 5: 9 o' ye not to walk in the fear of God
Ps 76:11 presents unto him that o' to be feared.
M't 5:23 thy brother hath o' against thee; *5100
21: 3 And if any man say o' unto you, * "
23:23 these o' ye to have done, and not *1163
M'r 7:12 do o' for his father or his mother;*3762
8:23 him, he asked him if he saw o'. *5100
11:25 forgive, if ye have o' against any:* "
13:14 prophet, standing where it o' not, 1163
Lu 11:42 these o' ye to have done, and not to"
12:12 in the same hour what we o' to say."
13:14 six days in which men o' to work: "
16 o' not this woman, being a daughter"
18: 1 that men o' always to pray, and not"
24:26 O' not Christ to have suffered * "
Joh 4:20 the place where men o' to worship. "
33 any man brought him o' to eat? *
13:14 also o' to wash one another's feet. 3784
19: 7 a law, and by our law he o' to die, "
Ac 4:32 o' of the things which he possessed*5100
5:29 o' to obey God rather than men. *1163
17:29 o' not to think that the Godhead *3784
19:36 ye o' to be quiet, and to do nothing1163
20:35 labouring ye o' to support the weak, "
21:21 o' not to circumcise their children,*
24:19 Who o' to have been here before 1163
19 object, if they had o' against me. *5100
25:10 seat, where I o' to be judged: 1163
24 that he o' not to live any longer. "
26: 9 I o' to do many things contrary to "
28:19 I had o' to accuse my nation of. *5100
Ro 8:26 what we should pray for as we o': 1163
12: 3 more highly than he o' to think; "
15: 1 strong o' to bear the infirmities of 3784
1Co 8: 2 nothing yet as he o' to know. 1163
11: 7 indeed o' not to cover his head, 3784
10 cause o' the woman to have power "
2Co 2: 3 from them of whom I o' to rejoice;1163
7 ye o' rather to forgive him, and *
12:11 for I o' to have been commended 3784
14 o' not to lay up for the parents, "
Eph 5:28 So o' men to love their wives as "
6:20 may speak boldly, as I o' to speak. 1163
Col 4: 4 make it manifest, as I o' to speak. "
6 how ye o' to answer every man. "
1Th 4: 1 how ye o' to walk and to please God,"
2Th 3: 7 know how ye o' to follow us: "
1Ti 5:13 speaking things which they o' not. "
Tit 1:11 teaching things which they o' not, "
Ph'm 18 wronged thee, or oweth thee o', *5100
Heb 2: 1 o' to give the more earnest heed 1163
5: 3 by reason hereof he o', as for the *3784
12 for the time ye o' to be teachers, "
Jas 3:10 these things o' not so to be. 5534
4:15 For that ye o' to say, If the Lord will
2Pe 3:11 what manner of persons o' ye to be1163
1Jo 2: 6 o' himself also so to walk, even as 3784
3:16 we o' to lay down our lives for the "
4:11 us, we o' also to love one another. "
3Jo 8 We therefore o' to receive such, that"

oughtest
1Ki 2: 9 knowest what thou o' to do unto him;
M't 25:27 o' therefore to have put my money1163
Ac 10: 6 shall tell thee what thou o' to do. "
1Ti 3:15 know how thou o' to behave thyself "

our See in the APPENDIX; also OURS; OURSELVES.

ours See also OURSELVES.
Ge 26:20 herdmen, saying, The water is o':
31:16 hath taken from our father, that is o',
34:23 and every beast of theirs be o'?
Nu 32:32 on this side Jordan may be o'. *
1Ki 22: 3 Know ye that Ramoth in Gilead is o',
Eze 36: 2 even the ancient high places are o' in
M'r 12: 7 and the inheritance shall be o'. 2257
Lu 20:14 that the inheritance may be o'. "
1Co 1: 2 Christ our Lord, both theirs and o':"
2Co 1:14 as ye also are o' in the day of the "
Tit 3:14 let o' also learn to maintain good *2251
1Jo 2: 2 and not for o' only, but also for "

ourselves
Ge 37:10 to bow down o' to thee to the earth?
44:16 we speak? or how shall we clear o'?
Nu 32:17 we o' will go ready armed before 587
De 2:35 we took cattle for a prey unto o',
3: 7 of the cities, we took for a prey to o'.
1Sa 14: 8 and we will discover o' unto them.
1Ch 19:13 and let us behave o' valiantly for our*
Ezr 4: 3 but we o' together will build unto 587
8:21 we might afflict o' before our God,
Ne 10:32 to charge o' yearly with the third
Job 34: 4 let us know among o' what is good.
Ps 83:12 Let us take to o' the houses of God
Ps 100: 3 that hath made us, and not we o';* 587
Pr 7:18 morning: let us solace o' with loves.
Isa 28:15 and under falsehood have we hid o':
56:12 and we will fill o' with strong drink;
Jer 50: 5 Come, and let us join o' to the Lord*
Lu 22:71 we o' have heard of his own mouth.
Joh 4:42 for we have heard him o', and know
Ac 6: 4 will give o' continually to prayer, *
23:14 have bound o' under a great curse,1438
Ro 8:23 but o' also, which have the first fruits
23 of the Spirit, even we o' groan
23 groan within o', waiting for the 1438
15: 1 of the weak, and not to please o'. "
1Co 11:31 For if we would judge o', we should"
2Co 1: 4 we o' are comforted of God.
9 we had the sentence of death in o',1438
9 that we should not trust in o', but "
3: 1 Do we begin again to commend o'? "
5 that we are sufficient of o' to think "
5 to think any thing as of o'; but our "
4: 2 commending o' to every man's "
5 For we preach not o', but Christ "
5 o' your servants for Jesus' sake. "
5:12 we commend not o' again unto you,"
13 whether we be beside o', it is to God:
6: 4 approving o' as the ministers of 1438
7: 1 let us cleanse o' from all filthiness "
10:12 we dare not make o' of the number,*"
12 or compare o' with some that "
14 stretch not o' beyond our measure. "
12:19 think ye that we excuse o' unto you?
Ga 2:17 if...we o' also are found sinners, is
1Th 2:10 we behaved o' among you that believe:
2Th 1: 4 we o' glory in you in the churches 846
3: 7 behaved not o' disorderly among you;
9 to make o' an ensample unto you 1438
Tit 3: 3 we o' also were sometimes foolish,*2249
Heb10:25 the assembling of o' together, ‡1438
1Jo 1: 8 we deceive o', and the truth is not "

out See in the APPENDIX; also OUTCAST; OUTER; OUTGOINGS; OUTLANDISH; OUTLIVED; OUTMOST; OUTRAGEOUS; OUTRUN; OUTSIDE; OUTSTRETCHED; OUTWARD; OUTWENT; THEREOUT; THROUGHOUT; UTMOST; UTTER; WITHOUT.

outcast See also OUTCASTS.
Jer 30:17 they called thee an O', saying, 5080

outcasts
Ps 147: 2 gathereth together the o' of Israel.1760
Isa 11:12 and shall assemble the o' of Israel, "
16: 3 hide the o'; bewray not him that 5080
4 Let mine o' dwell with thee, Moab; "
27:13 and the o' in the land of Egypt, "
56: 8 which gathereth the o' of Israel 1760
Jer 49:36 the o' of Elam shall not come. 5080

outer See also UTTER.
Eze 10: 5 was heard even to the o' court, 2435
M't 8:12 shall be cast out into o' darkness: 1857
22:13 and cast him into o' darkness; "
25:30 servant into o' darkness: there "

outgoings
Jos 17: 9 and the o' of it were at the sea: *8444
18 and the o' of it shall be thine: * "
18:19 o' of the border were at the north* "
19:14 the o' thereof are in the valley of * "
22 o' of their border were at Jordan:* "
29 the o' thereof are at the sea from * "
33 and the o' thereof were at Jordan:* "
Ps 65: 8 the o' of the morning and evening4161

outlandish
Ne 13:26 him did o' women cause to sin. *5237

outlived
J'g 2: 7 the elders that o' Joshua, 748,3117,310

outmost See also UTMOST.
Ex 26:10 curtain that is o' in the coupling, 7020
Nu 34: 3 o' coast of the salt sea eastward: *7097
De 30: 4 out unto the o' parts of heaven, * "
Isa 17: 6 in the o' fruitful branches thereof,

outrageous
Pr 27: 4 Wrath is cruel, and anger is o'; ‡7858

outrun
Joh 20: 4 the other disciple did o' Peter,*4370,5032

outside
J'g 7:11 unto the o' of the armed men *7097
17 when I come to the o' of the camp,* "
19 came unto the o' of the camp in the*"
1Ki 7: 9 on the o' toward the great court. 2351
Eze 40: 5 behold a wall on the o' of the house"
M't 23:25 ye make clean the o' of the cup 1855
26 the o' of them may be clean also. 1623
Lu 11:39 make clean the o' of the cup and 1855

outstretched
De 26: 8 a mighty hand, and with an o' arm, 5186
Jer 21: 5 fight against you with an o' hand "
27: 5 by my great power by my o' arm, "

outward
Nu 35: 4 from the wall of the city and o' 2435
1Sa 16: 7 man looketh on the o' appearance,5869
1Ch 26:29 for the o' business over Israel, 2435
Ne 11:16 had the oversight of the o' business"
Es 6: 4 Haman was come into the o' court "
Eze 40:17 brought he me into the o' court, "
20 the gate of the o' court that looked*"
34 arches...were toward the o' court;* "
44: 1 way of the gate of the o' sanctuary* "
M't 23:27 which indeed appear beautiful o',*1855
Ro 2:28 which is o' in the flesh: 1722,3588,5318
2Co 4:16 though our o' man perish, yet the 1854
10: 7 on things after the o' appearance?*4383
1Pe 3: 3 o' adorning of plaiting the hair, 1855

outwardly
M't 23:28 so ye also o' appear righteous 1855
Ro 2:28 is not a Jew, which is one o'; 1722,5318

outwent
M'k 6:33 out of all cities, and o' them, and 4281

oven See also OVENS.
Le 2: 4 of a meat offering baken in the o', 8574
7: 9 offering that is baken in the o', "
11:35 whether it be o', or ranges for pots, "
26:26 shall bake your bread in one o', "
Ps 21: 9 Thou shalt make them as a fiery o'* "
La 5:10 skin was black like an o' because "
Ho 7: 4 as an o' heated by the baker, who "
6 made ready their heart like an o', "
7 They are all hot as an o', and have "
Mal 4: 1 cometh, that shall burn as an o'; * "
M't 6:30 and to morrow is cast into the o', 2823
Lu 12:28 and to morrow is cast into the o'; "

ovens
Ex 8: 3 and into thine o', and into thy 8574

over See also MOREOVER; OVERCHARGE; OVERCOME; OVERDRIVE; OVERFLOW; OVERLAY; OVERLIVED; OVERMUCH; OVERPASS; OVERPLUS; OVERRAN; OVERSEE; OVERSHADOW; OVERSIGHT; OVERSPREAD; OVERTAKE; OVERTHROW; OVERTURN; OVERWHELM; PASSOVER.
Ge 1:18 to rule o' the day and o' the night,
26 have dominion o' the fish of the sea,
26 o' the fowl of the air, and o' the cattle,
26 o' all the earth, and o' every creeping
28 o' the fish of the sea, and o' the fowl
28 and o' every living thing that moveth
3:16 thy husband, and he shall rule o' thee.
4: 7 his desire, and thou shalt rule o' him.
8: 1 made a wind to pass o' the earth, 5921
9:14 when I bring a cloud o' the earth, "
21:16 and sat her down o' against him 5048
16 she sat o' against him, and lift up "
24: 2 house, that ruled o' all that he had,
25:25 out red, all o' like an hairy garment;
27:29 be lord o' thy brethren, and let thy
31:21 he rose up, and passed o' the river,5674
52 I will not pass o' this heap to thee, "
52 thou shalt not pass o' this heap and"
32:10 my staff I passed o' this Jordan; "
16 Pass o' before me, and put a space "
21 So went the present o' before him: "
22 and passed o' the ford Jabbok. "
23 them o' the brook, and sent o' that "
31 as he passed o' Penuel the sun rose "
33: 3 And he passed o' before them, and "
14 thee, pass o' before his servant: "
36:31 any king o' the children of Israel.
37: 8 Shalt thou indeed reign o' us? 5921
8 thou indeed have dominion o' us? "
39: 4 made him overseer o' his house, 5921
5 his house, and o' all that he had, "
41:33 and set him o' the land of Egypt. "
34 let him appoint officers o' the land, "
40 Thou shalt be o' my house, and "
41 set thee o' all the land of Egypt. "
43 him ruler o' all the land of Egypt. "
45 went out o' all the land of Egypt. "
56 was o' all the face of the earth: "
42: 6 Joseph was...governor o' the land, "
47: 6 then make them rulers o' my cattle. "
20 the famine prevailed o' them: * "
26 made it a law o' the land of Egypt* "
49:22 whose branches run o' the wall: "
Ex 1: 8 there arose up a new king o' Egypt,"
11 they did set o' them taskmasters "
2:14 thee a prince and a judge o' us? "
5:14 taskmasters had set o' them, "
8: 5 hand with thy rod o' the streams, "
5 o' the rivers, and o' the ponds, and "
6 his hand o' the waters of Egypt; "
9 said unto Pharaoh, Glory o' me: "
10:12 out thine hand o' the land of Egypt "
13 forth his rod o' the land of Egypt, "
14 went up o' all the land of Egypt, "
21 be darkness o' the land of Egypt, "
12:13 I see the blood, I will pass o' you, "
23 the Lord will pass o' the door, and "
27 passed o' the houses of the children"
14: 2 the sea, o' against Baal-zephon: *6440
7 and captains o' every one of them.5921
16 stretch out thine hand o' the sea, "
21 stretched out his hand o' the sea; "
26 Stretch out thine hand o' the sea, "
27 stretched forth his hand o' the sea, "
15:16 till thy people pass o', O Lord, 5674
16 till the people pass o', which thou "
16:18 gathered much had nothing o', 5736
23 that which remaineth o' lay up for "
18:21 and place such o' them, to be 5921
25 and made them heads o' the people,"
25:27 O' against the border shall the *5980
37 may give light o' against it. 5921,5676
26:12 o' the backside of the tabernacle. 5921
13 hang o' the sides of the tabernacle "
35 candlestick o' against the table on5227
28:27 o' against the other coupling 5980
36:14 hair for the tent o' the tabernacle:5921
37: 9 with their wings o' the mercy seat,5980
14 O' against the border were the rings,"
39:20 o' against the other coupling "
40:19 abroad the tent o' the tabernacle, 5921
24 congregation, o' against the table,5227
36 taken up from o' the tabernacle, 5921
Le 14: 5 an earthen vessel o' running water:"
6 was killed o' the running water: "
50 an earthen vessel o' running water:"
16:21 confess o' him all the iniquities of "
25:43 shalt not rule o' him with rigour:

Le 25:46 but o' your brethren the children of
46 not rule one o' another with rigour.
53 shall not rule with rigour o' him
26:16 I will even appoint o' you terror,
17 they that hate you shall reign o' you;
Nu 1:50 the Levites o' the tabernacle of 5921
50 and o' all the vessels thereof, and "
50 and o' all things that belong to it: "
3:32 be chief o' the chief of the Levites,*
49 of them that were o' and above 5736
4: 6 shall spread o' it a cloth wholly of 4605
5:30 him, and he be jealous o' his wife,
7: 2 were o' them that were numbered,5975
8: 2 o' against the candlestick. *5922,6440
3 o' against the candlestick, * "
10:10 trumpets o' your burnt offerings, 5921
10 o' the sacrifices of your peace offerings;
14 o' his host was Nahshon the son of5921
15, 16 o' the host of the tribe of the "
18 o' his host was Elizur the son of "
19, 20 o' the host of the tribe of the "
22 o' his host was Elishama the son of "
23, 24 o' the host of the tribe of the "
25 o' his host was Ahiezer the son of "
26, 27 o' the host of the tribe of the "
11:16 of the people, and officers o' them;
14:14 that thy cloud standeth o' them, 5921
16:13 thyself altogether a prince o' us? "
22: 5 earth, and they abide o' against me:
25:15 he was head o' a people, and of a *
27:16 set a man o' the congregation, 5921
31:14 with the captains o' thousands, and*
14 and captains o' hundreds which came*
48 which were o' thousands of the host,
32: 5 and bring us not o' Jordan. 5674
7 from going o' into the land which "
21 will go all of you armed o' Jordan "
27 But thy servants will pass o', every "
29 will pass with you o' Jordan, every "
30 will not pass o' with you armed, "
32 will pass o' armed before the Lord "
33:51 When ye are passed o' Jordan into "
35:10 ye be come o' Jordan into the land "
De 1: 1 the plain o' against the Red sea, 4136
13 and I will make them rulers o' you.
15 and made them heads o' you, 5921
15 o' thousands,...captains o' hundreds,*
15 captains o' fifties, and captains o' tens,*
2:13 and get you o' the brook Zered. 5674
13 And we went o' the brook Zered. "
14 we were come o' the brook Zered, "
18 Thou art to pass o' through Ar, the "
19 o' against the children of Ammon,4136
24 and pass o' the river Arnon: 5674
29 until I shall pass o' Jordan into the"
3:18 pass o' armed before your brethren"
25 let me go o', and see the good land "
27 for thou shalt not go o' this Jordan."
28 he shall go o' before this people, "
29 in the valley o' against Beth-peor. 4136
4:14 land whither ye go o' to possess it.5674
21 that I should not go o' Jordan, and "
22 this land, I must not go o' Jordan: "
22 but ye shall go o', and possess that "
26 ye go o' Jordan to possess it; ye "
46 in the valley o' against Beth-peor, 4136
9: 1 to pass o' Jordan this day, to go 5674
3 God is he that goeth o' before thee;"
11:30 the champaign o' against Gilgal, 4136
31 ye shall pass o' Jordan to go in to 5674
12:10 when ye go o' Jordan, and dwell "
15: 6 and thou shalt reign o' many nations,
6 but they shall not reign o' thee.
17:14 I will set a king o' me, like as all 5921
15 in any wise set him king o' thee, "
15 shalt thou set king o' thee: thou "
15 mayest not set a stranger o' thee, "
21: 6 shall wash their hands o' the heifer"
24:20 thou shalt not go o' the boughs again:
27: 2 day when ye shall pass o' Jordan 5674
3 this law, when thou art passed o', "
4 shall be when ye be gone o' Jordan,"
12 when ye are come o' Jordan; "
28:23 And thy heaven that is o' thy head5921
36 king which thou shalt set o' thee. "
63 Lord rejoiced o' you to do you good,"
63 will rejoice o' you to destroy you, "
30: 9 the Lord will again rejoice o' thee "
9 good, as he rejoiced o' thy fathers: "
13 Who shall go o' the sea for us, and5674
18 passest o' Jordan...to possess it. "
31: 2 Thou shalt not go o' this Jordan. "
3 he will go o' before thee, and he "
3 Joshua, he shall go o' before thee, "
13 ye go o' Jordan to possess it. "
15 stood o' the door of the tabernacle.5921
32:11 her nest, fluttereth o' her young, "
47 ye go o' Jordan to possess it. 5674
49 that is o' against Jericho; 5921,6440
34: 1 that is o' against Jericho. "
4 but thou shalt not go o' thither. 5674
6 of Moab, o' against Beth-peor: 4136
Jos 1: 2 arise, go o' this Jordan, thou, 5674
11 days ye shall pass o' this Jordan "
2:23 passed o', and came to Joshua the "
3: 1 lodged there before they passed o'. "
6 and pass o' before the people. And "
11 all the earth passeth o' before you "
14 from their tents, to pass o' Jordan, "
16 passed o' right against Jericho. "
17 Israelites passed o' on dry ground, "
17 people were passed clean o' Jordan."
4: 1 people were clean passed o' Jordan,"
3 ye shall carry them o' with you, "
5 Pass o' before the ark of the Lord "
7 when it passed o' Jordan, the "

Jos 4: 8 and carried them o' with them unto5674
10 the people hasted and passed o'. "
11 all the people were clean passed o', "
11 that the ark of the Lord passed o', "
12 tribe of Manasseh, passed o' armed "
13 prepared for war passed o' before "
18 flowed o' all his banks, as they did5921
22 came o' this Jordan on dry land. 5674
23 before you, until ye were passed o', "
23 before us, until we were gone o': "
5: 1 of Israel, until we were passed o'. "
13 there stood a man o' against him 5048
7: 7 all brought this people o' Jordan, 5674
26 o' him a great heap of stones unto5921
8:31 o' which no man hath lift up any * "
33 of them o' against mount Gerizim,*413
33 them o' against mount Ebal; *413,4136
9: 1 great sea o' against Lebanon.* " "
18:13 went o' from thence toward Luz, *5674
17 which is o' against the going up 5227
18 toward the side o' against Arabah 4136
22:11 o' against the land of Canaan,*413,
19 pass ye o' unto the land of the 5674
24:11 ye went o' Jordan, and came unto "
J'g 3:28 and suffered not a man to pass o'. "
5:13 dominion o' the nobles among
13 made me have dominion o' the mighty.*
6:33 gathered together, and went o', 5674
8: 4 came to Jordan, and passed o', "
22 Rule thou o' us, both thou, and thy
23 said unto them, I will not rule o' you,
23 neither shall my son rule o' you:
23 the Lord shall rule o' you.
9: 2 and ten persons, reign o' you, or that
2 or that one reign o' you? remember
8 a time to anoint a king o' them; 5921
8 the olive tree, Reign thou o' us. "
9 and go to be promoted o' the trees? "
10 fig tree, Come thou, and reign o' us."
11 and go to be promoted o' the trees? "
12 vine, Come thou, and reign o' us. "
13 and go to be promoted o' the trees? "
14 Come thou, and reign o' us. "
15 in truth ye anoint me king o' you, "
18 king o' the men of Shechem: "
22 had reigned three years o' Israel, "
26 brethren, and went o' to Shechem:5674
10: 9 of Ammon passed o' Jordan to "
18 head o' all the inhabitants of Gilead.
11: 8 head o' all the inhabitants of Gilead.
11 him head and captain o' them: 5921
29 and he passed o' Gilead, and 5674
29 and passed o' Mizpeh of Gilead, "
29 o' unto the children of Ammon: "
32 So Jephthah passed o' unto the "
12: 1 passedst thou o' to fight against "
3 passed o' against the children of "
5 were escaped said, Let me go o'; "
14: 4 the Philistines had dominion o' Israel.
15:11 that the Philistines are rulers o' us?
19:10 and came o' against Jebus, which 5227
12 Israel; we will pass o' to Gibeah. 5674
20:43 down with ease o' against Gibeah 5227
Ru 2: 5 servant that was set o' the reapers,5921
6 servant that was set o' the reapers "
3: 9 thy skirt o' thine handmaid; for "
1Sa 2: 1 mouth is enlarged o' mine enemies;"
8: 1 that he made his sons judges o' Israel.
7 that I should not reign o' them. 5921
9 the king that shall reign o' them.
11 of the king that shall reign o' you:
12 o' thousands, and captains o' fifties;*
19 but we will have a king o' us; 5921
9:16 to be captain o' my people Israel, "
17 of this same shall reign o' my people.
10: 1 to be captain o' his inheritance? 5921
19 unto him, Nay, but set a king o' us. "
11:12 he that said, Shall Saul reign o' us? "
12: 1 me, and have made a king o' you. "
12 Nay; but a king shall reign o' us: "
13 the Lord hath set a king o' you. "
14 also the king that reigneth o' you "
13: 1 he had reigned two years o' Israel, "
7 of the Hebrews went o' Jordan to 5674
14 him to be captain o' his people, 5921
14: 1, 4 go o' to the Philistines' garrison,5674
5 northward o' against Michmash, *4136
5 other southward o' against Gibeah.*"
6 and let us go o' unto the garrison 5674
8 we will pass o' unto these men, and"
23 battle passed o' unto Beth-aven. "
47 Saul took the kingdom o' Israel, 5921
15: 1 anoint thee to be king o' his people, "
1 to anoint thee to be king...o' Israel; "
7 that is o' against Egypt. *5921,6440
17 Lord anointed thee king o' Israel?5921
26 thee from being king o' Israel. "
35 he had made Saul king o' Israel. "
16: 1 him from reigning o' Israel? fill "
17:50 David prevailed o' the Philistine 4480
18: 5 Saul set him o' the men of war, 5921
13 made him his captain o' a thousand;
19:20 standing as appointed o' them, 5921
22: 2 he became a captain o' them: and "
9 was set o' the servants of Saul, * "
23:17 and thou shalt be king o' Israel, "
25:30 have appointed thee ruler o' Israel; "
26:13 David went o' to the other side, 5674
22 let one of the young men come o' "
27: 2 passed o' with the six hundred men"
30:10 could not go o' the brook Besor. "
2Sa 1:17 lamentation o' Saul,...o' Jonathan 5921
24 daughters of Israel, weep o' Saul, 413
2: 4 David king o' the house of Judah. 5921
7 have anointed me king o' them. "
8 and brought him o' to Mahanaim;5674

2Sa 2: 9 king o' Gilead, and o' the Ashurites,413
9 and o' Jezreel, and o' Ephraim, 1591
9 and o' Benjamin, and o' all Israel.5921
10 when he began to reign o' Israel, "
11 in Hebron o' the house of Judah "
15 arose and went o' by number 5674
29 the plain, and passed o' Jordan, "
3:10 of David o' Israel and o' Judah, 5921
17 in times past to be king o' you: "
21 reign o' all that thine heart desireth.
33 And the king lamented o' Abner, 413
34 all the people wept again o' him. 5921
4:12 them up o' the pool in Hebron. * "
5: 2 when Saul was king o' us, thou "
2 thou shalt be a captain o' Israel. "
3 they anointed David king o' Israel."
5 he reigned o' Judah seven years "
5 thirty and three years o' all Israel "
12 had established him king o' Israel, "
17 had anointed David king o' Israel, "
23 o' against the mulberry trees. 4136
6:21 me ruler o' the people of the Lord,5921
21 the people of the Lord, o' Israel: "
7: 8 to be ruler o' my people, o' Israel: "
11 judges to be o' my people Israel, "
26 Lord of hosts is the God o' Israel: "
8:15 And David reigned o' all Israel; "
16 the son of Zeruiah was o' the host; "
18 Benaiah...was o' both the Cherethites
10:17 together, and passed o' Jordan, 5674
12: 7 I anointed thee king o' Israel, 5921
15:22 David said to Ittai, Go and pass o'.5674
22 Ittai the Gittite passed o', and all "
23 voice, and all the people passed o': "
23 himself passed o' the brook Kidron,"
23 all the people passed o', toward the "
16: 9 let me go o', I pray thee, and take "
13 on the hill's side o' against him, 5980
17:16 wilderness, but speedily pass o'; 5674
19 a covering o' the well's mouth, 5921
20 be gone o' the brook of water. 5674
21 and pass quickly o' the water: "
22 him, and they passed o' Jordan: "
22 them that was not gone o' Jordan. "
24 And Absalom passed o' Jordan, "
18: 1 and captains of hundreds o' them. 5921
8 o' the face of all the country: "
24 went up to the roof o' the gate * 413
33 up to the chamber o' the gate, 5921
19:10 Absalom, whom we anointed o' us, "
15 to conduct the king o' Jordan. 5674
17 went o' Jordan before the king. *6743
18 there went o' a ferry boat to carry5674
18 to carry o' the king's household, "
18 the king, as he was come o' Jordan;"
22 that I am this day king o' Israel? 5921
31 and went o' Jordan with the king, 5674
31 the king, to conduct him o' Jordan. "
33 Come thou o' with me, and I will "
36 will go a little way o' Jordan with "
37 let him go o' with my lord the king;"
38 Chimham shall go o' with me, and "
39 And all the people went o' Jordan. "
39 And when the king was come o', the"
41 David's men with him, o' Jordan? "
20:21 shall be thrown to thee o' the wall.1157
23 Joab was o' all the host of Israel: 413
23 Benaiah...was o' the Cherethites 5921
23 Cherethites and o' the Pelethites: "
24 And Adoram was o' the tribute: "
22:30 by my God have I leaped o' a wall. "
23: 3 He that ruleth o' men must be just, "
23 And David set him o' his guard. 413
24: 5 And they passed o' Jordan, and 5674
1Ki 1:34 anoint him there king o' Israel: 5921
35 to be ruler o' Israel and o' Judah. "
2:11 days that David reigned o' Israel "
35 of Jehoiada in his room o' the host:"
37 and passest o' the brook Kidron, 5674
4: 1 Solomon was king o' all Israel. 5921
4 the son of Jehoiada was o' the host:"
5 son of Nathan was o' the officers: "
6 And Ahishar was o' the household: "
6 the son of Abda was o' the tribute. "
7 had twelve officers o' all Israel, "
21 And Solomon reigned o' all kingdoms
24 o' all the region on this side the river,
24 o' all the kings on this side the river:
5: 7 a wise son o' this great people. 5921
14 and Adoniram was o' the levy. "
16 officers which were o' the work, "
16 which ruled o' the people that wrought
6: 1 year of Solomon's reign o' Israel, 5921
7:20 o' against the belly which was by*5980
39 eastward o' against the south. *4136
8: 7 two wings o' the place of the ark, 413
16 David to be o' my people Israel. 5921
9:23 officers that were o' Solomon's work,"
23 bear rule o' the people that wrought
11:24 and became captain o' a band, when
25 Israel, and reigned o' Syria. 5921
28 o' all the charge of the house of Joseph.
37 and shalt be king o' Israel. 5921
42 reigned in Jerusalem o' all Israel "
12:17 Judah, Rehoboam reigned o' them. "
18 Adoram, who was o' the tribute; "
20 and made him king o' all Israel: "
13:30 mourned o' him, saying, Alas, my "
14: 2 that I should be king o' this people."
7 thee prince o' my people Israel, "
14 shall raise him up a king o' Israel, "
15: 1 of Nebat reigned Abijam o' Judah."
9 king of Israel reigned Asa o' Judah."
25 Nadab...began to reign o' Israel "
25 and reigned o' Israel two years. "
33 to reign o' all Israel in Tirzah,

1Ki 16: 2 thee prince o' my people Israel; 5921
8 Elah...to reign o' Israel in Tirzah, "
16 king o' Israel that day in the camp. "
18 and burnt the king's house o' him "
23 Judah began Omri to reign o' Israel, "
29 began Ahab...to reign o' Israel: "
29 Ahab...reigned o' Israel in Samaria "
19: 15 anoint Hazael to be king o' Syria: "
16 thou anoint to be king o' Israel: "
20: 29 pitched one o' against the other 5227
22: 31 captains that had rule o' his chariots,*
41 of Asa began to reign o' Judah 5921
51 began to reign o' Israel in Samaria "
51 and reigned two years o' Israel. "
2Ki 2: 8 they two went o' on dry ground. 5674
9 to pass, when they were gone o', "
14 and thither: and Elisha went o'. "
3: 1 began to reign o' Israel in Samaria5921
5: 11 and strike his hand o' the place, 413
8: 13 that thou shalt be king o' Syria. 5921
20 and made a king o' themselves. "
21 So Joram went o' to Zair, and all 5674
9: 3 have anointed thee king o' Israel. 5921
6 anointed thee king o' the people 413
6 people of the Lord, even o' Israel. "
12 I have anointed thee king o' Israel. "
29 began Ahaziah to reign o' Judah. 5921
10: 5 And he that was o' the house, and "
5 he that was o' the city, the elders "
22 unto him that was o' the vestry, "
36 Jehu reigned o' Israel in Samaria "
11: 3 And Athaliah did reign o' the land. "
4 and fetched the rulers o' hundreds,
9 And the captains o' the hundreds did
10 to the captains o' hundreds did the
18 officers o' the house of the Lord. 5921
19 And he took the rulers o' hundreds,
13: 1, 10 to reign o' Israel in Samaria ,5921
14 and wept o' his face, and said, O my"
15: 5 the king's son was o' the house, "
8 reign o' Israel in Samaria six "
17 the son of Gadi to reign o' Israel, "
23, 27 to reign o' Israel in Samaria, "
17: 1 of Elah to reign in Samaria o' Israel"
18: 18, 37 which was o' the household, "
19: 2 which was o' the household, "
21: 13 will stretch o' Jerusalem the line of"
25: 19 that was set o' the men of war, "
22 o' them he made Gedaliah...ruler. "
1Ch 1: 43 king reigned o' the children of Israel;
5: 11 of Gad dwelt o' against them. 5048
6: 31 David set o' the service of song 5921
8: 32 in Jerusalem, o' against them. 5048
9: 19 were o' the work of the service, 5921
19 being o' the host of the Lord, "
20 was the ruler o' them in time past, "
26 o' the chambers and treasuries "
31 o' the things that were made in the "
32 were o' the shewbread, to prepare "
38 o' against their brethren. 5048
11: 2 shalt be ruler o' my people Israel. 5921
3 they anointed David king o' Israel, "
25 and David set him o' his guard. "
12: 4 among the thirty, and o' the thirty; "
14 one of the least was o' an hundred,*
14 and the greatest o' a thousand. *
15 are they that went o' Jordan in 5674
38 to make David king o' all Israel: 5921
14: 2 had confirmed him king o' Israel, "
8 was anointed king o' all Israel, "
14 o' against the mulberry trees. 4136
15: 25 and the captains o' thousands, went to
17: 7 be ruler o' my people Israel: 5921
10 judges to be o' my people Israel. "
18: 14 So David reigned o' all Israel, and "
15 the son of Zeruiah was o' the host; "
17 was o' the Cherethites and the "
19: 17 all Israel, and passed o' Jordan, 5674
21: 16 hand stretched out o' Jerusalem. 5921
22: 10 of his kingdom o' Israel for ever. "
23: 1 Solomon his son king o' Israel. "
24: 31 cast lots o' against their brethren*5980
31 o' against their younger brethren.* "
26: 20 Ahijah was o' the treasures of the 5921
20 o' the treasures of the dedicated
22 which were o' the treasures of the5921
26 brethren were o' all the treasures "
26 captains o' thousands and hundreds,
29 for the outward business o' Israel,5921
32 made rulers o' the Reubenites, the "
27: 2 O' the first course for the first "
4 o' the course of the second month "
16 Furthermore o' the tribes of Israel:"
25 And o' the king's treasures was "
25 and o' the storehouses in the fields,"
26 o' them that did the work of the "
27 And o' the vineyards was Shimei "
27 o' the increase of the vineyards for "
28 o' the olive trees and the sycomore "
28 and o' the cellars of oil was Joash: "
29 o' the herds that fed in Sharon was "
29 o' the herds that were in the valleys"
30 O' the camels also was Obil the "
30 and o' the asses was Jehdeiah the "
31 And o' the flocks was Jaziz the "
28: 1 and the captains o' the thousands,*
1 and captains o' the hundreds, and*
1 the stewards o' all the substance and
4 to be king o' Israel for ever: 5921
4 me to make me king o' all Israel: "
5 the kingdom of the Lord o' Israel. "
29: 3 o' and above all that I have prepared"
12 of thee, and thou reignest o' all: 4605
26 son of Jesse reigned o' all Israel. 5921
27 time that he reigned o' Israel was "
30 and the times that went o' him, 5674

1Ch 29: 30 o' Israel, and o' all the kingdoms of5921
2Ch 1: 9 thou hast made me king o' a people"
11 o' whom I have made thee king: "
13 congregation, and reigned o' Israel."
2: 11 he hath made thee king o' them. "
4: 10 the east end, o' against the south.*4136
5: 8 their wings o' the place of the ark,5921
6: 5 to be a ruler o' my people Israel: "
6 David to be o' my people Israel. "
36 them o' before their enemies, *6440
8: 10 and fifty, that bare rule o' the people.
9: 8 made he thee king o' them, to do 5921
26 And he reigned o' all the kings from
30 Jerusalem o' all Israel forty years.5921
10: 17 Judah, Rehoboam reigned o' them. "
18 Hadoram that was o' the tribute; "
13: 1 began Abijah to reign o' Judah. "
5 gave the kingdom o' Israel to David"
19: 11 chief priest is o' you in all matters "
20: 6 rulest not thou o' all the kingdoms of
27 made them to rejoice o' their enemies.
31 Jehoshaphat reigned o' Judah: he5921
22: 12 and Athaliah reigned o' the land. "
23: 14 of hundreds that were set o' the host,
25: 5 and made them captains o' thousands,*
5 and captains o' hundreds, according*
26: 21 his son was o' the king's house, 5921
31: 12 o' which Cononiah the Levite was "
14 was o' the freewill offerings of God, "
32: 6 he set captains of war o' the people,"
11 to give o' yourselves to die by famine
34: 13 were o' the bearers of burdens, 5921
36: 4 Eliakim his brother king o' Judah "
10 his brother king o' Judah and "
Ezr 4: 10 and noble Asnapper brought o', 1541
20 mighty kings also o' Jerusalem, 5922
20 ruled o' all countries beyond the
9: 6 are increased o' our head, and 4605
Ne 2: 7 convey me o' till I come...Judah; *5674
3: 10 even o' against the house. And 5048
16 o' against the sepulchres of David, "
19 piece o' against the going up to the "
23 and Hashub o' against their house. "
25 o' against the turning of the wall, "
26 the place o' against the water gate "
27 o' against the great tower that "
28 every one o' against his house. "
29 son of Immer o' against his house. "
30 of Berechiah o' against his chamber."
31 o' against the gate of Miphkad, and"
5: 15 servants bare rule o' the people: 5921
7: 2 of the palace, charge o' Jerusalem: "
3 one to be o' against his house. 5048
9: 28 so that they had the dominion o' them:
37 the kings whom thou hast set o' us5921
37 they have dominion o' our bodies, "
37 and o' our cattle, at their pleasure, "
11: 9 of Senuah was second o' the city. "
21 and Gispa were o' the Nethinims. "
22 the singers were o' the business of5048
12: 8 which was o' the thanksgiving, he 5921
9 o' against them in the watches. 5048
24 their brethren o' against them, 5980
24 man of God, ward o' against ward.*"
37 gate, which was o' against them, 5048
38 gave thanks went o' against them,*4136
44 o' the chambers for the treasures,5921
13: 13 I made treasurers o' the treasuries, "
26 God made him king o' all Israel: "
Es 1: 1 o' an hundred and seven and twenty
3: 12 that were o' every province, and 5921
5: 1 house, o' against the king's house:5227
1 o' against the gate of the house. "
8: 2 Mordecai o' the house of Haman. 5921
9: 1 Jews hoped to have power o' them, "
1 had rule o' them that hated them;)
Job 6: 5 or loweth the ox o' his fodder? 5921
7: 12 that thou settest a watch o' me? "
14: 16 dost thou not watch o' my sin? "
16: 11 me o' into the hands of the wicked.*"
26: 7 out the north o' the empty place, "
34: 13 hath given him a charge o' the earth?
41: 34 king o' all the children of pride. 5921
42: 11 comforted him o' all the evil that * "
Ps 8: 6 dominion o' the works of thy hands;
12: 4 lips are our own: who is lord o' us?
13: 2 mine enemy be exalted o' me? 5921
18: 29 and by my God have I leaped o' a wall.
19: 13 let them not have dominion o' me:
23: 5 my head with oil; my cup runneth o'.
25: 2 let not mine enemies triumph o' me.
27: 12 not o' unto the will of mine enemies:
30: 1 hast not made my foes to rejoice o' me.
35: 19 enemies wrongfully rejoice o' me:
24 and let them not rejoice o' me.
38: 4 iniquities are gone o' mine head: 5674
16 otherwise they should rejoice o' me:
41: 11 enemy doth not triumph o' me. 5921
42: 7 and thy billows are gone o' me. "
47: 2 he is a great King o' all the earth. "
8 God reigneth o' the heathen: God "
49: 14 upright shall have dominion o' them
60: 8 o' Edom will I cast out my shoe: *5921
65: 13 valleys...are covered o' with corn; 5848
66: 12 hast caused men to ride o' our heads;
68: 34 his excellency is o' Israel, and his 5921
78: 50 gave their life o' to the pestilence;5462
62 his people o' also unto the sword; "
83: 18 art the most high o' all the earth. 5921
88: 16 Thy fierce wrath goeth o' me; thy 5674
91: 11 shall give his angels charge o' thee, "
103: 16 For the wind passeth o' it, and it 5674
19 heavens; and his kingdom ruleth o' all.
104: 9 bound that they may not pass o'; 5674
106: 41 they that hated them ruled o' them.
108: 9 o' Edom will I cast out my shoe; *5921

Ps 108: 9 o' Philistia will I triumph.
109: 6 Set thou a wicked man o' him: and5921
110: 6 wound the heads o' many countries.*"
118: 18 hath not given me o' unto death. 5414
119: 133 any iniquity have dominion o' me.
124: 4 the stream had gone o' our soul: 5674
5 proud waters had gone o' our soul. "
145: 9 tender mercies are o' all his works.5921
Pr 17: 2 A wise servant shall have rule o' a son
19: 10 for a servant to have rule o' princes.
11 glory to pass o' a transgression. 5921
20: 26 and bringeth the wheel o' them. "
22: 7 The rich ruleth o' the poor, and the
24: 31 lo, it was all grown o' with thorns, 5927
25: 28 that hath no rule o' his own spirit is*
28: 15 a wicked ruler o' the poor people. 5921
Ec 1: 12 I the Preacher was king o' Israel "
2: 19 yet shall he have rule o' all my labour
7: 14 hath set...one o' against the other, 5980
16 Be not righteous o' much; neither7235
16 neither make thyself o' wise: why3148
17 Be not o' much wicked, neither be 7235
8: 8 power o' the spirit to retain the spirit;
9 one man ruleth o' another to his own
Ca 2: 4 and his banner o' me was love. 5921
11 is past, the rain is o' and gone; 2498
Isa 3: 4 princes, and babes shall rule o' them.
12 oppressors, and women rule o' them.
8: 7 shall come up o' all his channels, 5921
7 channels, and go o' all his banks: "
8 he shall overflow and go o', he *5674
10: 29 They are gone o' the passage: they "
11: 15 he shake his hand o' the river, 5921
15 and make men go o' dryshod. 1869
14: 2 and they shall rule o' their oppressors.
15: 2 shall howl o' Nebo, and o' Medeba: 5921
16: 8 out, they are gone o' the sea. 5674
19: 4 Egyptians will I give o' into the 5534
4 and a fierce king shall rule o' them,
16 of hosts, which he shaketh o' it. 5921
22: 15 Shebna, which is o' the house, and "
23: 2 of Zidon, that pass o' the sea, 5674
6 Pass ye o' to Tarshish; howl, ye "
11 stretched out his hand o' the sea, 5921
12 of Zidon: arise, pass o' to Chittim ;5674
25: 7 of the covering cast o' all people, 5921
7 vail that is spread o' all nations. "
26: 13 beside thee have had dominion o' us:
28: 19 by morning shall it pass o', *5674
31: 5 it; and passing o' he will preserve it.
9 he shall pass o' to his strong hold*5674
35: 8 the unclean shall not pass o' it; "
36: 3 son, which was o' the house, 5921
22 Hilkiah, that was o' the household, "
37: 2 Eliakim, who was o' the household,"
40: 19 goldsmith spreadeth it o' with gold,
27 is passed o' from my God? *5674
41: 2 him, and made him rule o' kings?
45: 14 stature, shall come o' unto thee, 5674
14 in chains they shall come o', and "
47: 2 the thigh, pass o' the rivers. * "
51: 10 a way for the ransomed to pass o'? "
23 Bow down, that we may go o': "
23 as the street, to them that went o'. "
52: 5 that rule o' them make them to howl,
54: 9 should no more go o' the earth; 5674
62: 5 bridegroom rejoiceth o' the bride, 5921
5 so shall thy God rejoice o' thee. "
63: 19 thou never barest rule o' them; they
Jer 1: 10 this day set thee o' the nations 5921
10 and o' the kingdoms, to root out, "
2: 10 pass o' the isles f Chittim, and 5674
5: 6 leopard shall watch o' their cities:†5921
22 roar, yet can they not pass o' it? 5674
6: 17 Also I set watchmen o' you, 5921
13: 21 to be captains, and as chief o' thee: "
15: 3 I will appoint o' them four kinds, "
23: 4 And I will set up shepherds o' them"
31: 28 that like as I have watched o' them,"
28 so will I watch o' them, to build, "
39 shall yet go forth o' against it *5048
32: 41 rejoice o' them to do them good, 5921
33: 26 to be rulers o' the seed of Abraham,413
40: 5 made governor o' the cities of Judah,
11 that he had set o' them Gedaliah 5921
41: 2 Babylon had made governor o' the land.
10 to go o' to the Ammonites. 5674
43: 10 spread his royal pavilion o' them. 5921
44: 27 I will watch o' them for evil, "
48: 32 thy plants are gone o' the sea, 5674
40 shall spread his wings o' Moab. * 413
49: 19 man, that I may appoint o' her? "
22 and spread his wings o' Bozrah: *5921
50: 44 man, that I may appoint o' her? 413
La 2: 17 thine enemy to rejoice o' thee, 5921
3: 54 Waters flowed o' mine head; then I "
5: 8 Servants have ruled o' us: there is
Eze 1: 20, 21 were lifted up o' against them:*5980
22 stretched forth o' their heads 5921
25 firmament that was o' their heads, "
26 firmament that was o' their heads "
3: 13 of the wheels o' against them, *5980
9: 1 them that have charge o' the city to
10: 1 o' them as it were a sapphire *5921
2 and scatter them o' the city. "
4 stood o' the threshold of the house;"
18 house, and stood o' the cherubims. "
19 God of Israel was o' them above. "
11: 22 God of Israel was o' them above. "
16: 8 and I spread my skirt o' thee, and "
27 have stretched out my hand o' thee,"
19: 8 and spread their net o' him: he
20: 33 fury poured out, will I rule o' you:
27: 32 for thee, and lament o' thee, 5921
29: 15 shall no more rule o' the nations. "
32: 3 therefore spread out my net o' thee"

Eze 32: 8 of heaven will I make dark o· thee.5921
31 be comforted o· all his multitude, "
34: 23 I will set up one shepherd o· them, "
37: 24 my servant shall be king o· them; "
40: 18 o· against the length of the gates *5980
23 was o· against the gate toward the5048
41: 6 one o· another, and thirty in order;413
15 o· against the separate place *413,6440
16 three stories, o· against the door, 5048
42: 1 was o· against the separate place, "
3 O· against the twenty cubits which "
3 o· against the pavement which was"
7 without o· against the chambers, 5980
10 o· against the separate place,*413,6440
10 and o· against the building. *
45: 6 o· against the oblation of the holy*5980
7 be o· against one of the portions, * "
46: 9 but shall go forth o· against it. *5226
47: 5 a river that I could not pass o·: *5674
5 a river that could not be passed o·.*"
20 a man come o· against Hamath. 5227
48: 13 o· against the border of the *5980
15 o· against the five and twenty*5922,6440
18, 18 o· against the oblation of the *5980
21, 21 o· against the five and *5922,6440
21 o· against the portions for the *5980
Da 1: 11 had set o· Daniel, Hananiah, 5921
2: 38 and hath made thee ruler o· them all.
39 which shall bear rule o· all the earth.
48 o· the whole province of Babylon, 5922
48 o· all the wise men of Babylon. "
49 o· the affairs of the province of "
3: 12 o· the affairs of the province of 5921
4: 16 and let seven times pass o· him. 5922
17 setteth up o· it the basest of men. "
23 field, till seven times pass o· him; "
25, 32 seven times shall pass o· thee, "
5: 5 wrote o· against the candlestick 6903
21 appointeth o· it whomsoever he 5922
6: 1 to set o· the kingdom an hundred "
1 should be o· the whole kingdom;*
2 And o· these three presidents; 5924
3 to set him o· the whole realm. 5922
9: 1 o· the realm of the Chaldeans; 5921
11: 39 he shall cause them to rule o· many,
40 and shall overflow and pass o·. *5674
43 o· the treasures of gold and of silver,
43 o· all the precious things of Egypt:
Ho 10: 5 people thereof shall mourn o· it, 5921
11 I passed o· upon her fair neck: 5674
12: 4 he had power o· the angel, and 413
Joe 2: 17 that the heathen should rule o· them:
Ob 12 rejoiced o· the children of Judah
Jon 2: 3 and thy waves passed o· me. 5674
4: 6 and made it to come up o· Jonah, 5921
6 it might be a shadow o· his head, "
Mic 3: 6 sun shall go down o· the prophets,*"
6 and the day shall be dark o· them. "
4: 7 Lord shall reign o· them in mount "
Na 3: 19 thee shall clap their hands o· thee: "
Hab 1: 11 and he shall pass o·, and offend, 5674
14 things, that have no ruler o· them?
2: 19 it is laid o· with gold and silver,
Zep 3: 17 he will rejoice o· thee with joy; 5921
17 he will joy o· thee with singing. "
Hag 1: 10 heaven o· you is stayed from dew,* "
Zec 1: 21 up their horn o· the land of Judah* 413
5: 3 o· the face of the whole earth: 5921
9: 14 And the Lord shall be seen o· them,"
14: 9 Lord shall be king o· all the earth: "
M't 2: 9 o· where the young child was. 1883
9: 1 passed o·, and came into his own 1276
10: 23 have gone o· the cities of Israel, *5055
14: 34 And when they were gone o·, they 1276
20: 25 Gentiles exercise dominion o· them,
21: 2 Go into the village o· against you, 561
24: 45 hath made ruler o· his household, 1909
47 make him ruler o· all his goods. "
25: 21 hast been faithful o· a few things, "
21 make thee ruler o· many things: "
23 hast been faithful o· a few things, "
23 make thee ruler o· many things: "
27: 37 set up o· his head his accusation 1883
45 there was darkness o· all the land 1909
61 sitting o· against the sepulchre. 561
M'r 4: 35 Let us pass o· unto the other side. 1330
5: 1 o· unto the other side of the sea, *
21 Jesus was passed o· again by ship 1276
6: 7 gave them power o· unclean spirits;
53 And when they had passed o·, they 1276
10: 42 are accounted to rule o· the Gentiles
42 Gentiles exercise lordship o· them;
11: 2 into the village o· against you: 2713
12: 41 Jesus sat o· against the treasury, "
13: 3 of Olives o· against the temple, "
15: 26 of his accusation was written o·, 1924
33 was darkness o· the whole land 1909
39 which stood o· against him, 1537,1727
Lu 1: 33 o· the house of Jacob for ever; 1909
2: 8 watch o· their flock by night. "
4: 10 give his angels charge o· thee, *4012
39 he stood o· her, and rebuked the 1883
6: 38 shaken together, and running o·, 5240
8: 22 o· unto the other side of the lake. 1330
26 which is o· against Galilee. 495
9: 1 power and authority o· all devils, 1909
10: 19 and o· all the power of the enemy: "
11: 42 pass o· judgment and...love of God:3928
44 that walk o· them are not aware 1883
12: 14 me a judge or a divider o· you? 1909
42 shall make ruler o· his household, "
44 make him ruler o· all that he hath. "
15: 7 o· one sinner that repenteth, "
7 more than o· ninety and nine just "
10 God o· one sinner that repenteth. "
19: 14 not have this man to reign o· us. "
Lu 19: 17 have thou authority o· ten cities. 1883
19 to him, Be thou also o· five cities. "
27 not that I should reign o· them, 1909
30 ye into the village o· against you; 2713
41 he beheld the city, and wept o· it, 1909
22: 25 Gentiles exercise lordship o· them;
23: 38 written o· him in letters of Greek, 1909
44 was a darkness o· all the earth "
Joh 6: 1 Jesus went o· the sea of Galilee, *4008
13 remained o· and above unto them 4052
17 o· the sea toward Capernaum. 4008
17: 2 thou hast given him power o· all flesh,
18: 1 his disciples o· the brook Cedron, 4008
Ac 6: 3 we may appoint o· this business. 1909
7: 10 made him governor o· Egypt and "
11 there came a dearth o· all the land "
16 were carried o· into Sychem, and 3346
27 thee a ruler and a judge o· us? 1909
8: 2 made great lamentation o· him. "
16: 9 Come o· into Macedonia, and help 1224
18: 23 went o· all the country of Galatia *1330
19: 13 call o· them which had evil spirits 1909
20: 2 when he had gone o· those parts, *1330
15 the next day o· against Chios; and 481
28 o· the which the Holy Ghost hath *1722
21: 2 a ship sailing o· unto Phenicia, 1276
27: 5 we had sailed o· the sea of Cilicia *1277
7 were come o· against Cnidus, the 2596
7 under Crete, o· against Salmone;
Ro 1: 28 gave them o· to a reprobate mind,*3860
5: 14 even o· them that had not sinned 1909
6: 9 death hath no more dominion o· him.
14 sin shall not have dominion o· you:
7: 1 hath dominion o· a man as long as he
9: 5 who is o· all, God blessed for ever. 1909
21 Hath not the potter power o· the clay,
10: 12 the same Lord o· all is rich unto all*
15: 12 shall rise to reign o· the Gentiles;
1Co 7: 37 but hath power o· his own will, *4012
9: 12 be partakers of this power o· you,
2Co 1: 24 that we have dominion o· your faith,
3: 13 Moses, which put a vail o· his face,*1909
8: 15 had gathered much had nothing o·;4121
11: 2 am jealous o· you with godly jealousy:
Eph 1: 22 him to be the head o· all things to 5228
4: 19 themselves o· unto lasciviousness,*3860
Col 2: 15 them openly, triumphing o· them in it.
1Th 3: 7 were comforted o· you in all our 1909
5: 12 you, and are o· you in the Lord, 4291
1Ti 2: 12 nor to usurp authority o· the man, but
Heb 2: 7 set him o· the works of thy hands: 1909
3: 6 Christ as a son o· his own house; "
9: 5 And o· it the cherubims of glory *5231
10: 21 an high priest o· the house of God;1909
13: 7 them which have the rule o· you,
17 Obey them that have the rule o· you,
24 all them that have the rule o· you,
Jas 5: 14 let them pray o· him, anointing 1909
1Pe 3: 12 of the Lord are o· the righteous, * "
5: 3 as being lords o· God's heritage, 2634
Jude 7 giving themselves o· to fornication,1608
Re 2: 26 will I give power o· the nations: 1909
6: 8 o· the fourth part of the earth, "
9: 11 they had a king o· them, which is "
11: 6 o· waters to turn them to blood, "
10 the earth shall rejoice o· them, "
13: 7 was given him o· all kindreds, and "
14: 18 the altar, which had power o· fire; "
15: 2 had gotten the victory o· the beast, *1537
2 and o· his image, and o· his mark,* "
2 and o· the number of his name, * "
16: 9 which hath power o· these plagues:1909
17: 18 reigneth o· the kings of the earth. "
18: 11 earth shall weep and mourn o· her; "
20 Rejoice o· her, thou heaven, and ye "

overcame
Ac 19: 16 o· them, and prevailed against *2634
Re 3: 21 even as I also o·, and am set down 3528
12: 11 o· him by the blood of the Lamb, "

overcharge See also OVERCHARGED.
2Co 2: 5 in part: that I may not o· you all. *1912

overcharged
Lu 21: 34 your hearts be o· with surfeiting, 925

overcome See also OVERCAME; OVERCOMETH.
Ge 49: 19 Gad, a troop shall o· him: *1464
19 but he shall o· at the last. * "
Ex 32: 18 of them that cry for being o·: but 2476
Nu 13: 30 it; for we are well able to o· it. 3201
22: 11 I shall be able to o· them, and *3898
2Ki 16: 5 Ahaz, but could not o· him.
Ca 6: 5 from me, for they have o· me: 7292
Isa 28: 1 of them that are o· with wine! 1986
Jer 23: 9 like a man whom wine hath o·, 5674
Lu 11: 22 shall come upon him, and o· him, 3528
Joh 16: 33 of good cheer; I have o· the world. "
Ro 3: 4 mightest o· when thou art judged.* "
12: 21 Be not o· of evil, "
21 but o· evil with good. "
2Pe 2: 19 for of whom a man is o·, of the 2274
20 again entangled therein, and o·, "
1Jo 2: 13 because ye have o· the wicked one.3528
14 and ye have o· the wicked one. "
4: 4 little children, and have o· them: "
Re 11: 7 and shall o· them, and kill them. "
13: 7 with the saints, and to o· them: "
17: 14 Lamb, and the Lamb shall o· them:"

overcometh
1Jo 5: 4 is born of God o· the world: and 3528
4 is the victory that o· the world, * "
5 Who is he that o· the world, but "
Re 2: 7 To him that o· will I give to eat of "
11 He that o· shall not be hurt of the "
17 To him that o· will I give to eat of "
Re 2: 26 he that o·, and keepeth my works 3528
3: 5 He that o·, the same shall be "
12 Him that o· will I make a pillar in "
21 To him that o· will I grant to sit "
21: 7 He that o· shall inherit all things; "

overdrive
Ge 33: 13 if men should o· them one day, 1849

overflow See also OVERFLOWED; OVERFLOWETH; OVERFLOWING; OVERFLOWN.
De 11: 4 water of the Red sea to o· them 6687
Ps 69: 2 waters, where the floods o· me. 7857
15 Let not the waterflood o· me, * "
Isa 8: 8 he shall o· and go over, he shall "
10: 22 decreed shall o· with righteousness.*"
28: 17 waters shall o· the hiding place. "
43: 2 the rivers, they shall not o· thee: "
Jer 47: 2 shall o· the land, and all that is * "
Da 11: 10 one shall certainly come, and o·, "
26 destroy him, and his army shall o·: "
40 and shall o· and pass over. "
Joe 2: 24 the fats shall o· with wine and oil. 7783
3: 13 for the press is full, the fats o·; "

overflowed
Ps 78: 20 gushed out, and the streams o·; 7857
2Pe 3: 6 was, being o· with water, perished:2626

overfloweth
Jos 3: 15 Jordan o· all his banks all the 4390

overflowing
Job 28: 11 He bindeth the floods from o·; *1065
38: 25 watercourse for the o· of waters, *7858
Isa 28: 2 a flood of mighty waters o·, shall 7857
15, 18 when the o· scourge shall pass "
30: 28 And his breath, as an o· stream, "
Jer 47: 2 and shall be an o· flood, and shall "
Eze 13: 11 there shall be an o· shower; and "
13 be an o· shower in mine anger, "
38: 22 an o· rain, and great hailstones, "
Hab 3: 10 the o· of the water passed by: the*2230

overflown
1Ch 12: 15 when it had o· all his banks; and ‡4390
Job 22: 16 foundation was o· with a flood: *3332
Da 11: 22 shall they be o· from before him, *7857

overlaid
Ex 26: 32 of shittim wood o· with gold: 6823
36: 34 he o· the boards with gold, and "
34 the bars, and o· the bars with gold. "
36 wood, and o· them with gold: "
38 and he o· their chapiters and their "
37: 2 And he o· it with pure gold within "
4 wood, and o· them with gold. "
11 he o· it with pure gold, and made "
15 o· them with gold, to bear the table."
26 And he o· it with pure gold, both "
28 wood, and o· them with gold. "
38: 2 the same: and he o· it with brass. "
6 wood, and o· them with brass. "
28 o· their chapiters, and filleted them."
1Ki 3: 19 in the night; because she o· it. 7901
6: 20 and he o· it with pure gold; and 6823
21 Solomon o· the house within with "
21 the oracle; and he o· it with gold. "
22 the whole house he o· with gold, "
22 altar...by the oracle he o· with gold."
28 And he o· the cherubims with gold. "
30 floor of the house he o· with gold, "
32 flowers, and o· them with gold, "
10: 18 ivory, and o· it with the best gold. "
2Ki 18: 16 Hezekiah king of Judah had o·, "
2Ch 3: 4 and he o· it within with pure gold. "
5 which he o· with fine gold, and set 2645
7 He o· also the house, the beams, "
8 cubits: and he o· it with fine gold, "
9 o· the upper chambers with gold. "
10 work, and o· them with gold. 6823
4: 9 and o· the doors of them with brass. "
9: 17 of ivory, and o· it with pure gold. "
Ca 5: 14 as bright ivory o· with sapphires. 5968
Heb 9: 4 covenant o· round about with gold,4028

overlay See also OVERLAID.
Ex 25: 11 thou shalt o· it with pure gold, 6823
11 within and without shalt thou o· it, "
13 wood, and o· them with gold. "
24 thou shalt o· it with pure gold, and "
28 wood, and o· them with gold. "
26: 29 thou shalt o· the boards with gold, "
29 thou shalt o· the bars with gold. "
37 o· them with gold, and their hooks "
27: 2 and thou shalt o· it with brass. "
6 wood, and o· them with brass. "
30: 3 shalt o· it with pure gold, the top "
5 wood, and o· them with gold. "
1Ch 29: 4 to o· the walls of the houses 2902

overlaying
Ex 38: 17 the o· of their chapiters of silver; 6826
19 the o· of their chapiters and their "

overlived
Jos 24: 31 the elders that o· Joshua, *748,3117,310

overmuch
2Co 2: 7 be swallowed up with o· sorrow. 4055

overpass See also OVERPAST.
Jer 5: 28 they o· the deeds of the wicked: 5674

overpast
Ps 57: 1 until these calamities be o·. 5674
Isa 26: 20 until the indignation be o·. "

overplus
Le 25: 27 and restore the o· unto the man to5736

overran
2Sa 18: 23 way of the plain, and o· Cushi. 5674

overrunning
Na 1: 8 But with an o' flood he will make 5674
oversee
1Ch 9:29 also were appointed to o' the vessels,*
2Ch 2: 2 and six hundred to o' them. 5329
overseer See also OVERSEERS.
Ge 39: 4 he made him o' over his house, 6485
5 he had made him o' in his house, "
Ne 11: 9 the son of Zichri was their o': 6496
14 their o' was Zabdiel, the son of one "
22 o' also of the Levites at Jerusalem "
12:42 sang loud, with Jezrahiah their o'. "
Pr 6: 7 having no guide, o', or ruler, 7860
overseers
2Ch 2:18 o' to set the people a work. 5329
31:13 o' under the hand of Cononiah 6496
34:12 the o' of them were Jahath and 6485
13 o' of all that wrought the work in*5329
17 it into the hand of the o', and to 6485
Ac 20:28 the Holy Ghost hath made you o',*1985
overshadow See also OVERSHADOWED.
Lu 1:35 power of the Highest shall o' thee:1982
Ac 5:15 Peter passing by might o' some "
overshadowed
M't 17: 5 behold, a bright cloud o' them: 1982
M'r 9: 7 there was a cloud that o' them: * "
Lu 9:34 there came a cloud, and o' them: "
oversight
Ge 43:12 hand; peradventure it was an o': 4870
Nu 3:32 o' of them that keep the charge of 6486
4:16 the o' of all the tabernacle, and of* "
2Ki 12:11 the o' of the house of the Lord: 6485
22: 5 the o' of the house of the Lord: "
9 the o' of the house of the Lord. "
1Ch 9:23 had the o' of the gates of the house6485
2Ch 34:10 the o' of the house of the Lord, 6485
Ne 11:16 had the o' of the outward business5921
13: 4 having the o' of the chamber of *5414
1Pe 5: 2 among you, taking the o' thereof, 1983
overspread See also OVERSPREADING.
Ge 9:19 of them was the whole earth o'. 5310
overspreading
Da 9:27 and for the o' of abominations he *3671
overtake See also OVERTAKE; OVERTAKETH.
Ge 44: 4 when thou dost o' them, say unto 5381
Ex 15: 9 enemy said, I will pursue, I will o', "
De 19: 6 while his heart is hot, and o' him, "
28: 2 shall come on thee, and o' thee, "
15 shall come upon thee, and o' thee: "
45 and shall pursue thee, and o' thee, "
Jos 2: 5 them quickly; for ye shall o' them. "
1Sa 30: 8 after this troop? shall I o' them? "
8 for thou shalt surely o' them, and "
2Sa 15:14 lest he o' us suddenly, and bring "
Isa 59: 9 from us, neither doth justice o' us: "
Jer 42:16 sword, which ye feared, shall o' you"
Ho 2: 7 lovers, but she shall not o' them; "
10: 9 children of iniquity did not o' them." "
Am 9:10 evil shall not o' nor prevent us. 5066
13 the plowman shall o' the reaper, "
1Th 5: 4 that day should o' you as a thief. 2638
overtaken
Ps 18:37 mine enemies, and o' them: *5381
Ga 6: 1 Brethren, if a man be o' in a fault, 4301
overtaketh
1Ch 21:12 sword of thine enemies o' thee; 5381
overthrew
Ge 19:25 And he o' those cities, and all the 2015
29 he o' the cities in which Lot dwelt. "
Ex 14:27 and the Lord o' the Egyptians in 5287
De 29:23 which the Lord o' in his anger, 2015
Ps 136:15 But o' Pharaoh and his host in the5286
Isa 13:19 God o' Sodom and Gomorrah, 4114
Jer 20:16 be as the cities which the Lord o', 2015
50:40 As God o' Sodom and Gomorrah 4114
Am 4:11 as God o' Sodom and Gomorrah. 4114
M't 21:12 o' the tables of...moneychangers, 2690
M'r 11:15 o' the tables of the moneychangers, "
Joh 2:15 changers' money, and o' the tables;390
overthrow See also OVERTHREW; OVERTHROWETH; OVERTHROWN.
Ge 19:21 also, that I will not o' this city, 2015
29 sent Lot out of the midst of the o',2018
Ex 23:24 but thou shalt utterly o' them, 2040
De 12: 3 ye shall o' their altars, and break*5422
29:23 therein, like the o' of Sodom, and 4114
2Sa 10: 3 and to spy it out, and to o' it? 2015
11:25 strong against the city, and o' it: 2040
1Ch 19: 3 and to o', and to spy out the land? 2015
Ps 106:26 to o' them in the wilderness: 5307
27 To o' their seed also among the "
140: 4 have purposed to o' my goings. *1760
11 hunt the violent man to o' him. 4073
Pr 18: 5 to o' the righteous in judgment. *5186
Jer 49:18 in the o' of Sodom and Gomorrah 4114
Hag 2:22 I will o' the throne of kingdoms, 2015
22 I will o' the chariots, and those "
Ac 5:39 if it be of God, ye cannot o' it; 2647
2Ti 2:18 already; and o' the faith of some. 396
2Pe 2: 6 condemned them with an o', 2692
overthroweth
Job 12:19 away spoiled, and o' the mighty. 5557
Pr 13: 6 but wickedness o' the sinner. "
21:12 but God o' the wicked for their * "
22:12 o' the words of the transgressor. "
29: 4 but he that receiveth gifts o' it. 2040
overthrown
Ex 15: 7 hast o' them that rose up against*2040
J'g 9:40 and many were o' and wounded, *5307
2Sa 17: 9 some of them be o' at the first. * "
2Ch 14:13 and the Ethiopians were o', that *5307
Job 19: 6 Know now that God hath o' me, *5791
Ps 141: 6 judges are o' in stony places, *8058
Pr 11:11 it is o' by the mouth of the wicked.2040
12: 7 The wicked are o', and are not: 2015
14:11 house of the wicked shall be o': 8045
Isa 1: 7 it is desolate, as o' by strangers. 4114
Jer 18:23 but let them be o' before thee; 3782
La 4: 6 that was o' as in a moment, and 2015
Da 11:41 and many countries shall be o': 3782
Am 4:11 I have o' some of you, as God 2015
Jon 3: 4 days, and Nineveh shall be o'. "
1Co 10: 5 for they were o' in the wilderness. 2693
overtook
Ge 31:23 they o' him in the mount Gilead. 1692
25 Then Laban o' Jacob. Now *5381
44: 6 And he o' them, and he spake unto "
Ex 14: 9 and o' them encamping by the sea, "
J'g 18:22 and o' the children of Dan. 1692
20:42 but the battle o' them; and them * "
2Ki 25: 5 and o' him in the plains of Jericho:5381
Jer 39: 5 o' Zedekiah in the plains of Jericho:"
52: 8 o' Zedekiah in the plains of Jericho;"
La 1: 3 o' her between the straits. "
overturn See also OVERTURNED; OVERTURNETH.
Job 12:15 them out, and they o' the earth. 2015
Eze 21:27 I will o', o', o', it: and it shall be 5754
overturned
J'g 7:13 and o' it, that the tent lay along. *2015
overturneth
Job 9: 5 not: which o' them in his anger; 2015
28: 9 he o' the mountains by the roots. "
34:25 and he o' them in the night, so "
overwhelm See also OVERWHELMED.
Job 6:27 Yea, ye o' the fatherless, and ye *5307
overwhelmed
Ps 55: 5 upon me, and horror hath o' me. 3680
61: 2 unto thee, when my heart is o': 5848
77: 3 and my spirit was o'. Selah. "
78:53 not: but the sea o' their enemies. 3680
102: *title* of the afflicted, when he is o', 5848
124: 4 Then the waters had o' us, the 7857
142: 3 When my spirit was o' within me, 5848
143: 4 is my spirit o' within me; my "
owe See also OWED; OWEST; OWETH.
Ro 13: 8 O' no man any thing, but to love 3784
owed
M't 18:24 o' him ten thousand talents. 3781
28 which o' him an hundred pence: 3784
Lu 7:41 the one o' five hundred pence, and "
owest
M't 18:28 saying, Pay me that thou o'. 3784
Lu 16: 5 How much o' thou unto my lord? "
7 another, And how much o' thou? "
Ph'm 19 o' unto me even thine own self 4359
oweth
Ph'm 18 wronged thee, or o' thee ought, 3784
owl See also OWLS.
Le 11:16 the o', and the night hawk, *1323,3284
17 the little o', and the cormorant, 3563
17 the cormorant, and the great o', 3244
De 14:15 the o', and the night hawk, *1323,3284
16 the little o', and the...swan, 3563
16 and the great o', and the swan, 3244
Ps 102: 6 I am like an o' of the desert. 3563
Isa 34:11 the o' also and the raven shall 3244
14 screech o' also shall rest there, *3917
15 shall the great o' make her nest, *7091
owls
Job 30:29 and a companion to o'. *1323,3284
Isa 13:21 and o' shall dwell there, and* " "
34:13 dragons, and a court for o'. * " "
43:20 me, the dragons and the o': * " "
Jer 50:39 and the o' shall dwell therein:* " "
Mic 1: 8 and mourning as the o'. * " "
own See also OWNETH.
Ge 1:27 So God created man in his o' image,
30:25 that I may go unto mine o' place, and
30 shall I provide for mine o' house also?
40 and he put his o' flocks by themselves,
47:24 four parts shall be your o', for seed
Ex 5:16 but the fault is in thine o' people.
18:27 and he went his way into his o' land.
21:36 for ox; and the dead shall be his o'.
22: 5 man's field; of the best of his o' field,
5 and of the best of his o' vineyard,
32:13 to whom thou swarest by thine o' self,
Le 1: 3 shall offer it of his o' voluntary will *
7:30 His o' hands...bring the offerings
14:15 into the palm of his o' left hand: 3548
26 into the palm of his o' left hand: "
16:29 it be one of your o' country, or a * 249
17:15 whether it be one of your o' country,*"
18:10 for theirs is thine o' nakedness.
26 neither any of your o' nation, nor* 249
19: 5 Lord, ye shall offer it at your o' will.*
21:14 take a virgin of his o' people to wife.
22:19 offer at your o' will a male without*
29 unto the Lord, offer it at your o' will. *
24:22 as for one of your o' country: for I*249
25: 5 which groweth of its o' accord of thy*
41 and shall return unto his o' family,
Nu 1:52 their tents, every man by his o' camp,
52 and every man by his o' standard,
2: 2 shall pitch by his o' standard, with
10:30 but I will depart to mine o' land, and
13:33 were in our o' sight as grasshoppers,
15:39 that ye seek not after your o' heart
39 and your o' eyes, after which ye use to
16:28 have not done them of mine o' mind.
38 of these sinners against their o' souls,
24:13 do either good or bad of mine o' mind:
Nu 27: 3 but died in his o' sin, and had no sons.
32:42 and called it Nobah, after his o' name.
36: 9 shall keep himself to his o' inheritance.
De 3:14 and called them after his o' name,
12: 8 man whatsoever is right in his o' eyes.
13: 6 or thy friend, which is as thine o' soul,
22: 2 shalt bring it unto thine o' house, *
23:24 eat grapes thy fill at thine o' pleasure;
24:13 sleep in his o' raiment, and bless thee:*
16 shall be put to death for his o' sin.
28:53 shalt eat the fruit of thine o' body,
33: 9 brethren, nor knew his o' children:
Jos 7:11 have put it even among their o' stuff.
20: 6 come unto his o' city, and unto his
6 and unto his o' house, unto the city
J'g 2:19 they ceased not from their o' doings,*
7: 2 saying, Mine o' hand hath saved me.
8:29 Joash went and dwelt in his o' house.
17: 6 that which was right in his o' eyes.
21:25 that which was right in his o' eyes.
Ru 4: 6 lest I mar mine o' inheritance:
1Sa 2:20 And they went unto their o' home.
5:11 and let it go again to his o' place,
6: 9 way of his o' coast to Beth-shemesh,
13:14 sought him a man after his o' heart,
14:46 the Philistines went to their o' place.
15:17 thou wast little in thine o' sight,
18: 1 Jonathan loved him as his o' soul.
3 because he loved him as his o' soul.
20:17 for he loved him as he loved his o' soul.
30 the son of Jesse to thine o' confusion,
25:26 avenging thyself with thine o' hand,
33 avenging myself with mine o' hand.
39 wickedness of Nabal upon his o' head.
28: 3 buried him in Ramah,...in his o' city.
2Sa 4:11 a righteous person in his o' house
6:22 and will be base in mine o' sight:
7:10 they may dwell in a place of their o',
21 sake, and according to thine o' heart,
12: 3 it did eat of his o' meat, and drank of
3 drank of his o' cup, and lay in his
4 take of his o' flock and of his o' herd,
11 against thee out of thine o' house,
20 then he came to his o' house; and
14:24 said, Let him turn to his o' house,
24 So Absalom returned to his o' house,
18:13 wrought falsehood against mine o' life:*
18 he called the pillar after his o' name:
19:28 them that did eat at thine o' table.
30 come again in peace unto his o' house.
37 that I may die in mine o' city, and be
39 him; and he returned unto his o' place.
23:21 hand, and slew him with his o' spear.
1Ki 1:12 that thou mayest save thine o' life, and
33 my son to ride upon mine o' mule,
2:23 spoken this word against his o' life.
26 thee to Anathoth, unto thine o' fields;
32 return his blood upon his o' head,
34 buried in his o' house in the wilderness.
37 thy blood shall be upon thine o' head.
44 thy wickedness upon thine o' head;
3: 1 made an end of building his o' house,
7: 1 Solomon was building his o' house
8:38 every man the plague of his o' heart,
9:15 house of the Lord, and his o' house,
10: 6 I heard in mine o' land of thy acts
11:19 him to wife the sister of his o' wife,
21 that I may go to mine o' country.
22 thou seekest to go to thine o' country?
12:16 now see to thine o' house, David.
33 which he had devised of his o' heart;
13:30 And he laid his carcase in his o' grave;
14:12 therefore, get thee to thine o' house:*
17:19 abode, and laid him upon his o' bed.
22:36 city, and every man to his o' country.*
2Ki 3:27 him, and returned to their o' land.
4:13 I dwell among mine o' people.
12:18 and his o' hallowed things, and all the
14: 6 man shall be put to death for his o' sin.
17:23 away out of their o' land to Assyria
29 every nation made gods of their o',
33 the Lord, and served their o' gods,
18:27 they may eat their o' dung, and drink
27 and drink their o' piss with you?
31 then eat ye every man of his o' vine,*
32 you away to a land like your o' land,
19: 7 and shall return to his o' land; and
7 him to fall by the sword in his o' land.
34 this city, to save it, for mine o' sake,
20: 6 I will defend this city for mine o' sake,
21:18 buried in the garden of his o' house,
23 him, and slew the king in his o' house.
23:30 and buried him in his o' sepulchre.
1Ch 11:23 hand, and slew him with his o' spear.
17:19 according to thine o' heart, hast thou
21 went to redeem to be his o' people,*
22 thou make thine o' people for ever;
29: 3 I have of mine o' proper good, of gold
14 and of thine o' have we given thee.
16 of thine hand, and is all thine o'.
2Ch 6:23 his way upon his o' head;
29 know his o' sore and his o' grief,
7:11 in his o' house, he prosperously
8: 1 house of the Lord, and his o' house,
9: 5 I heard in mine o' land of thine acts,
12 and went away to her o' land, she
10:16 and now, David, see to thine o' house.
16:14 they buried him in his o' sepulchres,
25: 4 but every man shall die for his o' sin.
15 their o' people out of thine hand?
31: 1 to his possession, into their o' cities.
32:21 with shame of face to his o' land.
21 they that came forth of his o' bowels
33:20 and they buried him in his o' house:
24 him, and slew him in his o' house.
Ezr 7:13 are minded of their o' freewill to

Ne 4: 4 their reproach upon their o' head.
6: 8 feignest them out of thine o' heart.
16 were much cast down in their o' eyes:
Es 1:22 man should bear rule in his o' house,
2: 7 were dead, took for his o' daughter.
9:25 Jews, should return upon his o' head,
Job 2:11 they came every one from his o' place;
5:13 taketh the wise in their o' craftiness:
9:20 mine o' mouth shall condemn me:
31 and mine o' clothes shall abhor me.
13:15 maintain mine o' ways before him.*
15: 6 Thine o' mouth condemneth thee, and
6 yea, thine o' lips testify against thee.
18: 7 his o' counsel shall cast him down.
8 For he is cast into a net by his o' feet,
19:17 the children's sake of mine o' body.*
20: 7 shall perish for ever like his o' dung:
32: 1 he was righteous in his o' eyes.
40:14 that thine o' right hand can save thee.
Ps 4: 4 commune with your o' heart upon
5:10 let them fall by their o' counsels;
7:16 mischief shall return upon his o' head,
16 shall come down upon his o' pate.
9:15 which they hid is their o' foot taken.
16 is snared in the work of his o' hands.
12: 4 our lips are our o': who is lord over
15: 4 He that sweareth to his o' hurt, and
20: 4 Grant thee according to thine o' heart,*
21:13 exalted, Lord, in thine o' strength:*
22:29 and none can keep alive his o' soul.*
33:12 he hath chosen for his o' inheritance.
35:13 prayer returned into mine o' bosom.
36: 2 he flattereth himself in his o' eyes,
37:15 sword shall enter into their o' heart,
41: 9 mine o' familiar friend, in whom I
44: 3 land in possession by their o' sword,
3 neither did their o' arm save them:
45:10 forget also thine o' people, and thy
49:11 call their lands after their o' names.
50:20 thou slanderest thine o' mother's son.
64: 8 their o' tongue to fall upon themselves:
67: 6 God, even our o' God, shall bless us.
74:22 Arise, O God, plead thine o' cause:
77: 6 I commune with mine o' heart: and
78:29 for he gave them their o' desire; *
52 his o' people to go forth like sheep,
81:12 gave them up unto their o' hearts' lust:
12 and they walked in their o' counsels.
94:23 bring upon them their o' iniquity,
23 cut them off in their o' wickedness;
106:39 were they defiled with their o' works,*
39 a whoring with their o' inventions.*
40 that he abhorred his o' inheritance.*
109:29 their o' confusion as with a mantle.
138: 8 forsake not the works of thine o' hands.
140: 9 mischief of their o' lips cover them.
Pr 1:18 And they lay wait for their o' blood;
18 they lurk privily for their o' lives.
31 they eat of the fruit of their o' way,
31 and be filled with their o' devices.
3: 5 lean not unto thine o' understanding.
7 Be not wise in thine o' eyes: fear the
5:15 Drink waters out of thine o' cistern,
15 running waters out of thine o' well.
6:32 that doeth it destroyeth his o' soul.
8:36 that sinneth...wrongeth his o' soul:
11: 5 wicked shall fall by his o' wickedness.
6 shall be taken in their o' naughtiness.
17 merciful man doeth good to his o' soul:
19 evil pursueth it to his o' death.
29 He that troubleth his o' house shall
12:15 way of a fool is right in his o' eyes:
14:10 heart knoweth his o' bitterness; 5315
14 in heart shall be filled with his o' ways:
20 poor is hated even of his o' neighbour:
15:27 greedy of gain troubleth his o' house;
32 instruction despiseth his o' soul:
16: 2 ways of a man are clean in his o' eyes;
18:11 as an high wall in his o' conceit.
17 is first in his o' cause seemeth just;*
19: 8 that getteth wisdom loveth his o' soul:
16 commandment keepeth his o' soul;*
20: 2 to anger sinneth against his o' soul.
6 proclaim every one his o' goodness:
24 a man then understand his o' way?*
21: 2 way of a man is right in his o' eyes:
23: 4 be rich: cease from thine o' wisdom.
25:27 to search their o' glory is not glory.
28 he that hath no rule over his o' spirit*
26: 5 lest he be wise in his o' conceit.
12 thou a man wise in his o' conceit?
16 sluggard is wiser in his o' conceit
27: 2 praise thee, and not thine o' mouth;
2 a stranger, and not thine o' lips.
28:10 he shall fall himself into his o' pit:
11 rich man is wise in his o' conceit;
26 that trusteth in his o' heart is a fool:
29:24 partner with a thief hateth his o' soul:
30:12 that are pure in their o' eyes, and yet
31:31 let her o' works praise her in the gates.*
Ec 1:16 I communed with mine o' heart,
3:22 a man should rejoice in his o' works;*
4: 5 hands together, and eateth his o' flesh.
7:22 thine o' heart knoweth that thou thyself
8: 9 ruleth over another to his o' hurt.*
Ca 1: 6 but mine o' vineyard have I not kept.
Isa 2: 8 worship the work of their o' hands,
8 that which their o' fingers have made:
4: 1 saying, We will eat our o' bread,
1 and wear our o' apparel: only let us
5:21 them that are wise in their o' eyes,
21 eyes, and prudent in their o' sight!
9:20 eat every man the flesh of his o' arm:
13:14 shall every man turn to his o' people,
14 and flee every one into his o' land.
14: 1 Israel, and set them in their o' land:

Isa 23: 7 her o' feet shall carry her afar off to*
31: 7 which your o' hands have made unto
36:12 they may eat their o' dung, and drink
12 dung, and drink their o' piss with you?
16 every one the waters of his o' cistern;
17 you away to a land like your o' land,
37: 7 a rumour, and return to his o' land;
7 to fall by the sword in his o' land.
35 this city to save it for mine o' sake,
43:25 thy transgressions for mine o' sake,
44: 9 they are their o' witnesses; they see
48:11 mine o' sake, even for mine o' sake,
49:26 that oppress thee with their o' flesh;
26 shall be drunken with their o' blood,
56:11 they all look to their o' way, every one
58: 7 hide not thyself from thine o' flesh?
13 honour him, not doing thine o' ways,
13 nor finding thine o' pleasure,
13 nor speaking thine o' words:
63: 5 mine o' arm brought salvation unto
65: 2 was not good; after their o' thoughts;
66: 3 Yea, they have chosen their o' ways,
Jer 2:19 Thine o' wickedness shall correct
30 o' sword hath devoured your prophets,
7:19 to the confusion of their o' faces?
9:14 after the imagination of their o' heart,
18:12 but we will walk after our o' devices,
23: 8 and they shall dwell in their o' land.
16 they speak a vision of their o' heart,
17 after the imagination of their o' heart,
26 prophets of the deceit of their o' heart;
25: 7 works of your hands to your o' hurt.
14 to the works of their o' hands. *
27:11 will I let remain still in their o' land,
30:18 shall be builded upon her o' heap,
31:17 shall come again to their o' border.
30 every one shall die for his o' iniquity:
37: 7 return to Egypt into their o' land.
42:12 cause you to return to your o' land.
44: 9 their wives, and your o' wickedness,
17 thing goeth forth out of our o' mouth,*
46:16 and let us go again to our o' people,
50:16 they shall flee every one to his o' land.
51: 9 let us go every one into his o' country:
52:27 away captive out of his o' land. *
La 4:10 women have sodden their o' children:
Eze 11:21 their way upon their o' heads,
13: 2 that prophesy out of their o' hearts,
3 prophets, that follow their o' spirit,
17 which prophesy out of their o' heart;
14: 5 the house of Israel in their o' heart,
14 should deliver but their o' souls
20 shall but deliver their o' souls
16: 6 saw thee polluted in thine o' blood,*
15 thou didst trust in thine o' beauty,*
52 bear thine o' shame for thy sins that
54 thou mayest bear thine o' shame,
17:19 will I recompense upon his o' head.
20:26 And I polluted them in their o' gifts,
43 shall lothe yourselves in your o' sight
22:31 their o' way have I recompensed upon
23:34 thereof, and pluck off thine o' breasts:*
29: 3 My river is mine o', and I have made
33:10 every man for his o' life, in the day
33: 4 his blood shall be upon his o' head.
13 if he trust to his o' righteousness,*
34:13 and will bring them to their o' land,
36:17 house of Israel dwelt in their o' land,
17 they defiled it by their o' way and by*
24 and will bring you into your o' land.
31 shall ye remember your o' evil ways,*
31 shall lothe yourselves in your o' sight
32 and confounded for your o' ways,*
37:14 and I shall place you in your o' land:
21 and bring them into their o' land:
39:28 have gathered them unto their o' land,
46:18 inheritance out of his o' possession:
Da 3:28 worship any god, except their o' God.
6:17 the king sealed it with his o' signet,
8:24 be mighty, but not by his o' power:
9:19 defer not, for thine o' sake, O my God:
11: 9 and shall return into his o' land.
16 shall do according to his o' will, 7522
18 a prince for his o' behalf shall cause
18 without his o' reproach he shall cause
19 face toward the fort of his o' land:
28 do exploits, and return to his o' land.
Ho 7: 2 now their o' doings have beset them
10: 6 shall be ashamed of his o' counsel.
11: 6 them, because of their o' counsels.
13: 2 according to their o' understanding,
Joe 3: 4 your recompence upon your o' head;
7 your recompence upon your o' head:
Am 6:13 taken to us horns by our o' strength?
7:11 led away captive out of their o' land.*
Ob 15 shall return upon thine o' head.
Jon 2: 8 lying vanities forsake their o' mercy.
Mic 7: 6 enemies are the men of his o' house.
Hag 1: 9 ye run every man unto his o' house.
Zec 5:11 and set there upon her o' base.
11: 5 and their o' shepherds pity them not.
12: 6 be inhabited again in her o' place,
Mal 3:17 a man spareth his o' son that serveth
M't 2:12 departed into their o' country another
7: 3 not the beam that is in thine o' eye?
4 and, behold, a beam is in thine o' eye?
5 cast out the beam out of thine o' eye;
9: 1 over, and came into his o' city. 2398
10:36 foes shall be they of his o' household.
13:54 he was come into his o' country,
57 in his o' country, and in his o' house.
16:26 whole world, and lose his o' soul?*
17:25 of their o' children, or of strangers?*
20:15 to do what I will with mine o'?
25:14 who called his o' servants, and 2398
27 have received mine o' with usury.

M't 27:31 and put his o' raiment on him, and*
60 And laid it in his o' new tomb, which
M'k 6: 1 and came into his o' country;
4 but in his o' country and among
4 among his o' kin, and in his o' house.
7: 9 that ye may keep your o' tradition.*
8: 3 away fasting to their o' houses, *
36 whole world, and lose his o' soul?*
15:20 and put his o' clothes on him, *2398
Lu 1:23 he departed to his o' house. *
56 and returned to her o' house. *
2: 3 be taxed, every one into his o' city,2398
35 sword pierce through thy o' soul also
39 into Galilee, to their o' city Nazareth.
4:24 is accepted in his o' country.
5:25 lay, and departed to his o' house,*
29 him a great feast in his o' house:*
6:41 the beam that is in thine o' eye? 2398
42 not the beam that is in thine o' eye?
42 out first the beam out of thine o' eye,
44 every tree is known by his o' fruit.2398
8:39 Return to thine o' house, and shew*
9:26 when he shall come in his o' glory,
10:34 and set him on his o' beast, and 2398
14:26 and his o' life also, he cannot be my1438
16:12 shall give you that which is your o'?
18: 7 shall not God avenge his o' elect, *
19:22 Out of thine o' mouth will I judge thee,
23 have required mine o' with usury?*
21:30 know of your o' selves that summer
22:71 ourselves have heard of his o' 1438
Joh 1:11 He came unto his o', and his
11 and his o' received him not.
41 first findeth his o' brother Simon,
4:41 more believed because of his o' word;*
44 hath no honour in his o' country. 2398
5:30 I can of mine o' self do nothing: *
30 I seek not mine o' will, but the
43 another shall come in his o' name,2398
6:38 not to do mine o' will, but the will
7:18 of himself seeketh his o' glory: 2398
53 every man went unto his o' house.
8: 9 being convicted by their o' conscience,*
44 a lie, he speaketh of his o': 2398
50 I seek not mine o' glory: there is
10: 3 he calleth his o' sheep by name, 2398
4 when he putteth forth his o' sheep, "
12 whose o' the sheep are not, "
13: 1 loved his o' which were in the world, "
15:19 world, the world would love his o': "
16:32 be scattered, every man to his o', "
17: 5 glorify thou me with thine o' self 4572
11 keep through thine o' name those*
18:35 Thine o' nation and the chief priests
19:27 disciple took her unto his o' home.2398
20:10 away again unto their o' home. 1438
Ac 1: 7 Father hath put in his o' power. 2398
25 that he might go to his o' place. "
2: 6 them speak in his o' language. "
8 we every man in our o' tongue, "
3:12 by our o' power or holiness we had "
4:23 they went to their o' company, "
32 which he possessed was his o'; "
5: 4 it remained, was it not thine o'?
4 sold, was it not in thine o' power?*
7:21 and nourished him for her o' son. 1438
41 In the works of their o' hands. *
12:10 opened to them of his o' accord: 848
13:22 a man after mine o' heart, which *
36 he had served his o' generation by2398
14:16 all nations to walk in their o' ways. 848
15:22 send chosen men of their o' company*
17:28 also of your o' poets have said, 2596
18: 6 Your blood be upon your o' heads;
20:28 hath purchased with his o' blood. 2398
30 Also of your o' selves shall men arise,
21:11 and bound his o' hands and feet, 848
25:19 against him of their o' superstition,2398
26: 4 mine o' nation at Jerusalem,
27:19 day we cast out with our o' hands 849
28:30 years in his o' hired house, and 2398
Ro 1:24 through the lusts of their o' hearts,*
24 to dishonour their o' bodies between
4:19 he considered not his o' body now 1438
8: 3 God sending his o' Son in the
32 that spared not his o' Son, but 2398
10: 3 to establish their o' righteousness, "
11:24 be graffed into their o' olive tree? "
25 should be wise in your o' conceits;1438
12:16 Be not wise in your o' conceits.
14: 4 to his o' master he standeth or 2398
5 be fully persuaded in his o' mind. "
16: 4 my life laid down their o' necks: 1438
18 our Jesus Christ, but their o' belly: "
1Co 1:15 I had baptized in mine o' name. *
3: 8 man shall receive his o' reward 2398
8 reward according to his o' labour.
19 taketh the wise in their o' craftiness.*
4: 3 yea, I judge not mine o' self. 1683
12 labour, working with our o' hands:2398
6:14 also raise up us by his o' power. * 848
18 sinneth against his o' body. 2398
19 of God, and ye are not your o'? 1438
7: 2 let every man have his o' wife, and *
2 every woman have her o' husband.2398
4 wife hath not power of her o' body, "
4 hath not power of his o' body, but "
35 And this I speak for your o' profit; 846
37 but hath power over his o' will, 2398
9: 7 warfare any time at his o' charges? "
10:24 Let no man seek his o', but every 1438
29 Conscience, I say, not thine o', but of"
33 not seeking mine o' profit, but the 1683
11:21 taketh before other his o' supper: 2398
13: 5 seeketh not her o', is not easily 1438
15:23 But every man in his o' order: 2398

1Co 11:38 him, and to every seed his *o'* body.*2398*
16:21 of me Paul with mine *o'* hand. *1699*
2Co 6:12 ye are straitened in your *o'* bowels.
8:5 gave their *o'* selves to the Lord,
17 of his *o'* accord he went unto you. *830*
11:26 in perils by mine *o'* countrymen, in*
13:5 be in the faith, prove your *o'* selves.
5 Know ye not your *o'* selves, how that
Ga 1:14 many my equals in mine *o'* nation,
4:15 would have plucked out your *o'* eyes,*
6:4 let every man prove his *o'* work, *1438*
5 man shall bear his *o'* burden. *2398*
11 unto you with mine *o'* hand.
Eph 1:11 after the counsel of his *o'* will: * *848*
20 set him at his *o'* right hand in the* "
5:22 yourselves unto your *o'* husbands,*2398*
24 the wives be to their *o'* husbands * "
28 love their wives as their *o'* bodies. *1438*
29 no man ever yet hated his *o'* flesh; "
Ph'p 2:4 not every man on his *o'* things,
12 work out your *o'* salvation with fear "
21 For all seek their *o'*, not the
3:9 having mine *o'* righteousness, *1699*
Col 3:18 yourselves unto your *o'* husbands,*2398*
1Th 2:8 of God only, but also our *o'* souls, *1438*
14 like things of your *o'* countrymen, *2398*
15 Lord Jesus, and their *o'* prophets,* "
4:11 be quiet, and to do your *o'* business," "
11 and to work with your *o'* hands, * "
2Th 3:12 they work, and eat their *o'* bread. *1438*
17 of Paul with mine *o'* hand, which
1Ti 1:2 Timothy, my *o'* son in the faith: **1103*
3:4 One that ruleth well his *o'* house, *2398*
5 know not how to rule his *o'* house, "
12 children and their *o'* houses well. "
5:8 if any provide not for his *o'*, and "
8 specially for those of his *o'* house, "
6:1 count their *o'* masters worthy of "
2Ti 1:9 according to his *o'* purpose and "
3:2 men shall be lovers of their *o'* selves,*
4:3 after their *o'* lusts shall they heap *2398*
Tit 1:4 *o'* son after the common faith: **1103*
12 even a prophet of their *o'*, said, *2398*
2:5 good, obedient to their *o'* husbands," "
9 be obedient unto their *o'* masters, "
Ph'm 12 him, that is, mine *o'* bowels: *
19 have written it with mine *o'* hand,
19 unto me even thine *o'* self besides. *4572*
Heb 2:4 Holy Ghost, according to his *o'* will? "
3:6 Christ as a son over his *o'* house; *848*
4:10 also hath ceased from his *o'* works,* "
7:27 up sacrifice, first for his *o'* sins, *2398*
9:12 but by his *o'* blood he entered in "
12:10 chastened...after their *o'* pleasure;**848*
13:12 the people with his *o'* blood, *2398*
Jas 1:14 he is drawn away of his *o'* lust, and "
18 Of his *o'* will begat he us with the
22 hearers only, deceiving your *o'* selves.
26 tongue, but deceiveth his *o'* heart,* *848*
1Pe 2:24 Who his *o'* self bare our sins in his "
24 our sins in his *o'* body on the tree,*
3:1 in subjection to your *o'* husbands; *2398*
5 subjection unto their *o'* husbands: "
2Pe 2:12 perish in their *o'* corruption; * *848*
13 themselves with their *o'* deceivings* "
22 dog is turned to his *o'* vomit again;*2398*
3:3 scoffers, walking after their *o'* lusts," "
16 scriptures, unto their *o'* destruction." "
17 fall from your *o'* stedfastness.
1Jo 3:12 Because his *o'* works were evil, and*
Jude 6 but left their *o'* habitation, he **2398*
13 sea, foaming out their *o'* shame; *1438*
16 walking after their *o'* lusts; and * *848*
18 walk after their *o'* ungodly lusts. *1438*
Re 1:5 us from our sins in his *o'* blood, * *848*

owner See also OWNERS.
Ex 21:28 but the *o'* of the ox shall be quit. 1167
29 and it hath been testified to his *o'*, "
29 and his *o'* also shall be put to death." "
34 The *o'* of the pit shall make it good," "
34 give money unto the *o'* of them; "
36 and his *o'* hath not kept him in; he "
22:11 and the *o'* of it shall accept thereof, "
12 shall make restitution unto the *o'* "
14 the *o'* thereof being not with it, he "
15 the *o'* thereof be with it, he shall not" "
1Ki 16:24 the name of Shemer, *o'* of the hill, 113
Isa 1:3 The ox knoweth his *o'*, and the 7069
Ac 27:11 the master and the *o'* of the ship, *3490*

owners
Job 31:39 the *o'* thereof to lose their life: 1167
Pr 1:19 taketh away the life of the *o'* "
Ec 5:11 good is there to the *o'* thereof, * "
13 riches kept for the *o'* thereof to * "
Lu 19:33 the *o'* thereof said unto them, *2962*

owneth
Le 14:35 And he that *o'* the house shall come
Ac 21:11 bind the man that *o'* this girdle, *2076*

ox See also OXEN.
Ex 20:17 nor his *o'*, nor his ass, nor any 7794
21:28 If an *o'* gore a man or a woman, "
28 then the *o'* shall be surely stoned, "
28 the owner of the *o'* shall be quit. "
29 *o'* were wont to push with his horn "
29 the *o'* shall be stoned, and his "
32 If the *o'* shall push a manservant "
32 silver, and the *o'* shall be stoned. "
33 and an *o'* or an ass fall therein; "
35 And if one man's *o'* hurt another's, "
35 then they shall sell the live *o'*, and "
35 the dead *o'* also they shall divide.* "
36 the *o'* hath used to push in time 7794
36 in; he shall surely pay *o'* for *o'*; "
22:1 If a man shall steal an *o'*, or a "
1 he shall restore five oxen for an *o'*, "
4 whether it be *o'*, or ass, or sheep; "
9 whether it be for *o'*, for ass, for "
10 his neighbour an ass, or an *o'*, or "
23:4 meet thine enemy's *o'* or his ass "
12 that thine *o'* and thine ass may "
34:19 thy cattle, whether *o'* or sheep, "
Le 7:23 shall eat no manner of fat, of *o'*, "
17:3 that killeth an *o'*, or lamb, or goat, "
27:26 whether it be *o'*, or sheep: it is the "
Nu 7:3 princes, and for each one an *o'*: "
22:4 as the *o'* licketh up the grass of the "
De 5:14 thine *o'*, nor thine ass, nor any of "
21 his *o'*, or his ass, or any thing that "
14:4 ye shall eat: the *o'*, the sheep, and "
5 and the wild *o'*, and the chamois.*8377
18:3 sacrifice, whether it be *o'* or sheep;7794
22:1 brother's *o'* or his sheep go astray, "
4 thy brother's ass or his *o'* fall down "
10 not plow with an *o'* and an ass "
25:4 shalt not muzzle the *o'* when he "
28:31 Thine *o'* shall be slain before thine "
Jos 6:21 and *o'*, and sheep, and ass, with the "
J'g 3:31 hundred men with an *o'* goad: 1241
6:4 for Israel, neither sheep, nor *o'*, 7794
1Sa 12:3 whose *o'* have I taken? or whose ass "
14:34 Bring me hither every man his *o'*, "
34 brought every man his *o'* with him "
15:3 infant and suckling, *o'* and sheep, "
Ne 5:18 was one *o'* and six choice sheep; "
Job 6:5 or loweth the *o'* over his fodder? "
24:3 take the widow's *o'* for a pledge. "
40:15 thee; he eateth grass as an *o'*. 1241
Ps 69:31 please the Lord better than an *o'* 7794
106:20 similitude of an *o'* that eateth grass." "
Pr 7:22 as an *o'* goeth to the slaughter, or "
14:4 increase is by the strength of the *o'*." "
15:17 a stalled *o'* and hatred therewith. "
Isa 1:3 The *o'* knoweth his owner, and the "
11:7 the lion shall eat straw like the *o'*. 1241
32:20 the feet of the *o'* and the ass. 7794
66:3 He that killeth an *o'* is as if he slew "
Jer 11:19 I was like a lamb or an *o'* that is * 441
Eze 1:10 they four had the face of an *o'* on 7794
Lu 13:15 the sabbath loose his *o'* or his ass *1016*
14:5 an ass or an *o'* fallen into a pit, "
1Co 9:9 not muzzle the mouth of the *o'* that" "
1Ti 5:18 not muzzle the *o'* that treadeth out "

oxen
Ge 12:16 and he had sheep, and *o'*, and he 1241
20:14 Abimelech took sheep, and *o'*, and "
21:27 And Abraham took sheep and *o'*, "
32:5 And I have *o'*, and asses, flocks, 7794
34:28 took their sheep, and their *o'*, and*1241
Ex 9:3 upon the *o'*, and upon the sheep: "
20:24 offerings, thy sheep, and thine *o'*: "
22:1 he shall restore five *o'* for an ox, "
30 shalt thou do with thine *o'*, and 7794
24:5 peace offerings of *o'* unto the Lord.6499
Nu 7:3 six covered wagons, and twelve *o'*;1241
6 Moses took the wagons and the *o'*, "
7 Two wagons and four *o'* he gave "
8 four wagons and eight *o'* he gave "
7:17, 23, 29, 35, 41, 47, 53, 59, 65, 71, 77,
83 two *o'*, five rams, five he goats, 1241
87 All the *o'* for the burnt offering "
88 all the *o'* for the sacrifice of the "
22:40 Balak offered *o'* and sheep, and sent" "
23:1 and prepare me here seven *o'* and*6499
De 14:26 for *o'*, or for sheep, or for wine, or 1241
Jos 7:24 and his *o'*, and his asses, and his 7794
1Sa 11:7 he took a yoke of *o'*, and hewed 1241
7 so shall it be done unto his *o'*. "
14:14 land, which a yoke of *o'* might plow.*
32 took sheep, and *o'*, and calves, and1241
15:9 the best of the sheep, and of the *o'*, "
14 the lowing of the *o'* which I hear? "
15 the best of the sheep and of the *o'*, "
21 took of the spoil, sheep and *o'*, the "
22:19 *o'*, and asses, and sheep, with the 7794
27:9 took away the sheep, and the *o'*, 1241
2Sa 6:6 took hold of it; for the *o'* shook it. "
13 paces, he sacrificed *o'* and fatlings.*7794
24:22 here be *o'* for burnt sacrifice, and 1241
22 instruments of the *o'* for wood. "
24 and the *o'* for fifty shekels of silver. "
1Ki 1:9 Adonijah slew sheep and *o'* and fat "
19 And he hath slain *o'* and fat cattle7794
25 hath slain *o'* and fat cattle and sheep" "
4:23 Ten fat *o'*, and twenty *o'* out of the1241
7:25 It stood upon twelve *o'*, three "
29 were lions, *o'*, and cherubims: "
29 and beneath the lions and *o'* were "
44 sea, and twelve *o'* under the sea; "
8:5 sacrificing sheep and *o'*, that could "
63 two and twenty thousand *o'*, and an" "
19:19 was plowing with twelve yoke of *o'* "
20 And he left the *o'*, and ran after 1241
21 took a yoke of *o'*, and slew them, "
21 flesh with the instruments of the *o'*," "
2Ki 5:26 vineyards, and sheep, and *o'*, and "
16:17 the brasen *o'* that were under it, "
1Ch 12:40 and on mules, and on *o'*, and meat, "
40 and wine, and oil, and *o'*, and sheep" "
13:9 hold the ark; for the *o'* stumbled. "
21:23 thee the *o'* also for burnt offerings, "
2Ch 4:3 under it was the similitude of *o'*, "
3 Two rows of *o'* were cast, when it "
4 It stood upon twelve *o'*, three "
15 One sea, and twelve *o'* under it. "
5:6 sacrificed sheep and *o'*, which could" "
7:5 of twenty and two thousand *o'*, "
15:11 had brought, seven hundred *o'* and "
18:2 Ahab killed sheep and *o'* for him in "
29:33 six hundred *o'* and three thousand "
31:6 brought in the tithe of *o'* and sheep, "
35:8 small cattle, and three hundred *o'*. "
9 small cattle, and five hundred *o'*. "
12 Moses. And so did they with the *o'*. "
Job 1:3 camels, and five hundred yoke of *o'*," "
14 The *o'* were plowing, and the asses" "
42:12 camels, and a thousand yoke of *o'*, "
Ps 8:7 All sheep and *o'*, yea, and the beasts504
144:14 our *o'* may be strong to labour; 441
Pr 14:4 Where no *o'* are, the crib is clean: 5091
Isa 7:25 shall be for the sending forth of *o'*,7794
22:13 joy and gladness, slaying *o'*, and 1241
30:24 The *o'* likewise and the young asses504
Jer 51:23 the husbandman and his yoke of *o'*;
Da 4:25, 32 make thee to eat grass as *o'*, 8450
33 and did eat grass as *o'*, and his "
5:21 they fed him with grass like *o'*, and "
Am 6:12 rock? will one plow there with *o'*? 1241
M't 22:4 my *o'* and my fatlings are killed, *5022*
Lu 14:19 I have bought five yoke of *o'*, and *1016*
Joh 2:14 that sold *o'* and sheep and doves, "
15 temple, and the sheep, and the *o'*; "
Ac 14:13 *o'* and garlands unto the gates, *5022*
1Co 9:9 corn. Doth God take care for *o'*? *1016*

ox-goad See OX and GOAD.

Ozem (*o'-zem*)
1Ch 2:15 *O'* the sixth, David the seventh: 684
25 and Oren, and *O'*, and Ahijah.

Ozias (*o-zi'-as*) See also UZZIAH.
M't 1:8 begat Joram, and Joram begat *O'*;**3604*
9 And *O'* begat Joatham; and * "

Ozni (*oz'-ni*) See also OZNITES.
Nu 26:16 Of *O'*, the family of the Oznites: 244

Oznites (*oz'-nites*)
Nu 26:16 Of Ozni, the family of the *O'*: of 244

P.

Paaneah See ZAPH-NATH-PAANEAH.

Paarai (*pa'-ar-ahee*) See also NOARAI.
2Sa 23:35 the Carmelite, *P'* the Arbite, 6474

Pacatiana (*pa-ca-she-a'-nah*)
1Ti *subscr.* is the chiefest city of Phrygia *P'*. *3818*

paces See also APACE.
2Sa 6:13 ark of the Lord had gone six *p'*, 6806

pacified
Es 7:10 Then was the king's wrath *p'*. 7918
Eze 16:63 when I am *p'* toward thee for all *3722

pacifieth
Pr 21:14 A gift in secret *p'* anger: and a 3711
Ec 10:4 for yielding *p'* great offences. *3240

pacify See also PACIFIED; PACIFIETH.
Pr 16:14 death: but a wise man will *p'* it. 3722

Padan (*pa'-dan*) See also PADAN-ARAM.
Ge 48:7 as for me, when I came from *P'*, *6307

Padan-aram (*pa''-dan-a'-ram*)
Ge 25:20 of Bethuel the Syrian of *P'*, *6307
28:2 go to *P'*, to the house of Bethuel * "
5 he went to *P'* unto Laban, son of * "
6 Jacob, and sent him away to *P'*; * "
7 his mother, and was gone to *P'*; * "
31:18 which he had gotten in *P'*, for to go* "
33:18 of Canaan, when he came from *P'*;* "
35:9 again when he came out of *P'*, and* "
26 which were born to him in *P'*. * "
46:15 which she bare unto Jacob in *P'*, * "

paddle
De 23:13 shalt have a *p'* upon thy weapon; 3489

Padon (*pa'-don*)
Ezr 2:44 of Siaha, the children of *P'*, 6303
Ne 7:47 children of Sia, the children of *P'*. "

Pagiel (*pa'-ghe-el*)
Nu 1:13 Of Asher; *P'* the son of Ocran. 6295
2:27 Asher shall be *P'* the son of Ocran." "
Nu 7:72 eleventh day *P'* the son of Ocran, 6295
77 the offering of *P'* the son of Ocran." "
10:26 of Asher was *P'* the son of Ocran. "

Pahath-moab (*pa''-hath-mo'-ab*)
Ezr 2:6 children of *P'*, of the children 6355
8:4 Of the sons of *P'*; Elihoenai the "
10:30 And of the sons of *P'*; Adna, and "
Ne 3:11 and Hashub the son of *P'*, repaired" "
7:11 The children of *P'*, of the children "
10:14 The chief of the people; Parosh, *P'*," "

Pai (*pa'-i*) See also PAU.
1Ch 1:50 and the name of his city was *P'*; 6464

paid See also PAYED.
Ezr 4:20 and custom, was *p'* unto them. 3052
Jon 1:3 so he *p'* the fare thereof, and went 5414
M't 5:26 thou hast *p'* the uttermost farthing.*591*
Lu 12:59 till thou hast *p'* the very last mite.

pain See also PAINED; PAINFUL; PAINS.
Job 14:22 his flesh upon him shall have *p'*, 3510

Job 15: 20 wicked man travaileth with p· all his
33: 19 He is chastened also with p· upon 4341
19 multitude of his bones with strong p·:*
Ps 25: 18 upon mine affliction and my p·; *5999
48: 6 and p·, as of a woman in travail. 2427
Isa 13: 8 in p· as a woman that travaileth: 2342
21: 3 are my loins filled with p·: pangs *2479
26: 17 the time of her delivery, is in p·, 2342
18 been with child, we have been in p·, "
66: 7 before her p· came, she was 2256
Jer 6: 24 and p·, as of a woman in travail. *2427
12: 13 they have put themselves to p·, 2470
15: 18 Why is my p· perpetual, and my 3511
22: 23 the p· as of a woman in travail! 2427
30: 23 fall with p· upon the head of the *2342
51: 8 take balm for her p·, if so be she 4341
Eze 30: 4 and great p· shall be in Ethiopia, *2479
9 great p· shall come upon them, * "
16 Sin shall have great p·, and No *2342
Mic 4: 10 Be in p·, and labour to bring forth, "
Na 2: 10 and much p· is in all loins, and the *2479
Ro 8: 22 and travaileth in p· together until now.
Re 16: 10 they gnawed their tongues for p·, 4192
21: 4 neither shall there be any more p·:*"

pained
Ps 55: 4 My heart is sore p· within me: and2342
Isa 23: 5 be sorely p· at the report of Tyre. "
Jer 4: 19 bowels! I am p· at my very heart; 3176
Joe 2: 6 face the people shall be much p·: *2342
Re 12: 2 in birth, and p· to be delivered. * 928

painful
Ps 73: 16 to know this, it was too p· for me; 5999

painfulness
2Co 11: 27 In weariness and p·, in watchings*3449

pains
1Sa 4: 19 travailed; for her p· came upon her. 6735
Ps 116: 3 the p· of hell gat hold upon me: 4712
Ac 2: 24 up, having loosed the p· of death:*5604
Re 16: 11 because of their p· and their sores, 4192

painted See also PAINTEDST.
2Ki 9: 30 she p· her face, and tired her 7760, 6320
Jer 22: 14 with cedar, and p· with vermilion. 4886

paintedst
Eze 23: 40 p· thy eyes, and deckedst thyself 3583

painting
Jer 4: 30 thou rentest thy face with p·, in *6320

pair See also REPAIR.
Am 2: 6 silver, and the poor for a p· of shoes;
8: 6 and the needy for a p· of shoes;
Lu 2: 24 A p· of turtledoves, or two young 2201
Re 6: 5 had a p· of balances in his hand. *2218

palace See also PALACES.
1Ki 16: 18 into the p· of the king's house, * 759
21: 1 hard by the p· of Ahab king of 1964
2Ki 15: 25 in the p· of the king's house, with* 759
20: 18 in the p· of the king of Babylon. 1964
1Ch 29: 1 p· is not for man, but for the Lord 1002
19 these things, and to build the p·, "
2Ch 9: 11 of the Lord, and to the king's p·, *1004
Ezr 4: 14 maintenance from the king's p·, 1964
6: 2 p· that is in the province of the 1002
Ne 1: 1 year, as I was in Shushan the p·, "
2: 8 make beams for the gates of the p·*"
7: 2 and Hananiah the ruler of the p·,* "
Es 1: 2 which was in Shushan the p·, "
5 were present in Shushan the p·, "
5 of the garden of the king's p·; 1055
2: 3 young virgins unto Shushan the p·, 1002
5 Now in Shushan the p· there was a "
8 together unto Shushan the p·, to "
3: 15 decree was given in Shushan the p·. "
7: 7 his wrath went into the p· garden: 1055
8 king returned out of the p· garden "
8: 14 was given at Shushan the p·. 1002
9: 6 in Shushan the p· the Jews slew "
11 that were slain in Shushan the p· "
12 hundred men in Shushan the p·, "
Ps 45: 15 they shall enter into the king's p·. 1964
144: 12 after the similitude of a p·: "
Ca 8: 9 will build upon her a p· of silver: *2918
Isa 25: 2 a p· of strangers to be no city; it 759
39: 7 in the p· of the king of Babylon. 1964
Jer 30: 18 p· shall remain after the manner 759
Da 1: 4 in them to stand in the king's p·, 1964
4: 4 house, and flourishing in my p·: 1965
29 he walked in the p· of the kingdom "
5: 5 of the wall of the king's p·: and "
6: 18 Then the king went to his p·, and "
8: 2 that I was at Shushan in the p·, 1002
11: 45 shall plant the tabernacles of the p· 643
Am 4: 3 and ye shall cast them into the p·, *2038
Na 2: 6 and the p· shall be dissolved. 1964
M't 26: 3 unto the p· of the high priest, who*833
58 afar off unto the high priest's p·, * "
69 Now Peter sat without in the p·: * "
M'r 14: 54 even into the p· of the high priest: * "
66 And as Peter was beneath in the p·,* "
Lu 11: 21 strong man armed keepeth his p·,* "
Joh 18: 15 Jesus into the p· of the high priest.* "
Ph'p 1: 13 in Christ are manifest in all the p·, *4232

palaces
2Ch 36: 19 burnt all the p· thereof with fire, 759
Ps 45: 8 and cassia, out of the ivory p·, 1964
48: 3 is known in her p· for a refuge. 759
13 well her bulwarks, consider her p·; "
78: 69 he built his sanctuary like high p·,* "
122: 7 walls, and prosperity within thy p·. 759
Pr 30: 28 with her hands, and is in kings' p·. 1964
Isa 13: 22 and dragons in their pleasant p·: "
23: 13 they raised up the p· thereof; and 759
32: 14 Because the p· shall be forsaken; 759
34: 13 And thorns shall come up in her p·, "
Jer 6: 5 by night, and let us destroy her p·. "
9: 21 and is entered into our p·, to cut off "
17: 27 it shall devour the p· of Jerusalem, "
49: 27 shall consume the p· of Ben-hadad. "
La 2: 5 he hath swallowed up all her p·: "
7 of the enemy the walls of her p·; "
Eze 19: 7 he knew their desolate p·, and he laid
25: 4 and they shall set their p· in thee, *2918
Ho 8: 14 and it shall devour the p· thereof.* 759
Am 1: 4 shall devour the p· of Ben-hadad. "
7 which shall devour the p· thereof: "
10 which shall devour the p· thereof. "
12 which shall devour the p· of Bozrah. "
14 it shall devour the p· thereof, with "
2: 2 and it shall devour the p· of Kirioth: "
5 it shall devour the p· of Jerusalem. "
3: 9 Publish in the p· at Ashdod, and "
9 and in the p· in the land of Egypt, "
10 up violence and robbery in their p·. "
11 thee, and thy p· shall be spoiled. "
6: 8 I abhor...Jacob, and hate his p·: "
Mic 5: 5 and when he shall tread in our p·, "

Palal (*pa'-lal*)
Ne 3: 25 P· the son of Uzai, over against 6420

pale
Isa 29: 22 neither shall his face now wax p·. 2357
Re 6: 8 I looked, and behold a p· horse: 5515

paleness
Jer 30: 6 and all faces are turned into p·? 3420

Palestina (*pal-es-ti'-nah*) See also PALESTINE; PHILISTIA.
Ex 15: 14 hold on the inhabitants of P·. *6429
Isa 14: 29 Rejoice not thou, whole P·, because*"
31 city; thou, whole P·, art dissolved:*"

Palestine (*pal'-es-tine*) See also PALESTINA.
Joe 3: 4 Zidon, and all the coasts of P·? *6429

Palet See BETH-PALET.

Pallu (*pal'-lu*) See also PALLUITES; PHALLU.
Ex 6: 14 Hanoch, and P·, Hezron, and 6396
Nu 26: 5 of P·, the family of the Palluites: "
8 And the sons of P·; Eliab. "
1Ch 5: 3 Hanoch, and P·, Hezron, and "

Palluites (*pal'-lu-ites*)
Nu 26: 5 of Pallu, the family of the P·: 6384

palm See also PALMS.
Ex 15: 27 and threescore and ten p· trees: 8558
Le 14: 15, 26 into the p· of his own left hand: 3709
23: 40 branches of p· trees, goodly trees, 8558
Nu 33: 9 and threescore and ten p· trees; "
De 34: 3 Jericho, the city of p· trees, unto "
J'g 1: 16 went up out of the city of p· trees "
3: 13 and possessed the city of p· trees. "
4: 5 under the p· tree of Deborah 8560
1Ki 6: 29, 32 cherubims and p· trees and open 8561
32 cherubims, and upon the p· trees. "
35 cherubims and p· trees and open "
7: 36 cherubims, lions, and p· trees, "
2Ch 3: 5 and set thereon p· trees and chains. "
28: 15 to Jericho, the city of p· trees, 8558
Ne 8: 15 myrtle branches, and p· branches, "
Ps 92: 12 shall flourish like the p· tree: "
Ca 7: 7 This thy stature is like to a p· tree, "
8 I said, I will go up to the p· tree, "
Jer 10: 5 They are upright as the p· tree, 8560
Eze 40: 16 and upon each post were p· trees. 8561
22 and their arches, and their p· trees, "
26 and it had p· trees, one on this side, "
31, 34, 37 p· trees were upon the posts "
41: 18 made with cherubims and p· trees, "
18 that a p· tree was between a cherub "
19 toward the p· tree on the one side, "
19 toward the p· tree on the other side: "
20 were cherubims and p· trees made, "
25 cherubims and p· trees, like as were "
26 were narrow windows and p· trees "
Joe 1: 12 the p· tree also, and the apple tree, 8558
Joh 12: 13 Took branches of p· trees, and 5404
18: 22 struck Jesus with the p· of his *4475

palm-branches See PALM and BRANCHES.

palmerworm
Joe 1: 4 That which the p· hath left hath 1501
2: 25 and the caterpiller, and the p·, "
Am 4: 9 increased, the p· devoured them: "

palms
1Sa 5: 4 both the p· of his hands were cut 3709
2Ki 9: 35 the feet, and the p· of her hands. "
Isa 49: 16 graven...upon the p· of my hands; "
Da 10: 10 knees and upon the p· of my hands. "
M't 26: 67 smote him with...p· of their hands, 4474
M'r 14: 65 smote him with...p· of their hands.*4475
Re 7: 9 robes, and p· in their hands; 5404

palm-tree See PALM and TREE.

palsies
Ac 8: 7 and many taken with p·, and that*3886

palsy See also PALSIES.
M't 4: 24 lunatick, and those that had...p·; *3885
8: 6 servant lieth at home sick of the p·, "
9: 2 brought to him a man sick of the p·, "
2 faith said unto the sick of the p·; "
6 (then saith he to the sick of the p·,) "
M'r 2: 3 him, bringing one sick of the p·, "
4 bed wherein the sick of the p· lay. "
5 he said unto the sick of the p·, Son, "
9 easier to say to the sick of the p·, "
10 sins, (he saith to the sick of the p·,) "
Lu 5: 18 a man which was taken with a p·: *3886
5: 24 (he said unto the sick of the p·,) I *3886
Ac 9: 33 eight years, and was sick of the p·. *"

Palti (*pal'-ti*)
Nu 13: 9 of Benjamin, P· the son of Raphu. 6406

Paltiel (*pal'-te-el*) See also PHALTIEL.
Nu 34: 26 of Issachar, P· the son of Azzan. 6409

Paltite (*pal'-tite*) See also PELONITE.
2Sa 23: 26 Helez the P·, Ira the son of 6407

Pamphylia (*pam-fil'-e-ah*)
Ac 2: 10 Phrygia, and P·, in Egypt, and 3828
13: 13 Paphos, they came to Perga in P·: "
14: 24 Pisidia, they came to P·. "
15: 38 who departed from them from P·, "
27: 5 sailed over the sea of Cilicia and P·, "

pan See also PANS; FRYINGPANS.
Le 2: 5 be a meat offering baken in a p·. 4227
6: 21 In a p· it shall be made with oil; "
7: 9 and in the p·, shall be the priest's "
1Sa 2: 14 he struck it into the p·, or kettle, 3595
2Sa 13: 9 she took a p·, and poured them 4958
1Ch 23: 29 for that which is baked in the p·, 4227
Eze 4: 3 take thou unto thee an iron p·, "

pangs
Isa 13: 8 p· and sorrows shall take hold of 6735
21: 3 p· have taken hold upon me, as "
3 the p· of a woman that travaileth: "
26: 17 in pain, and crieth out in her p·; 2256
Jer 22: 23 thou be when p· come upon thee, "
48: 41 as the heart of a woman in her p·. 6887
49: 22 as the heart of a woman in her p·. "
50: 43 and p· as of a woman in travail. 2427
Mic 4: 9 p· have taken thee as a woman in "

Pannag (*pan'-nag*)
Eze 27: 17 market wheat of Minnith, and P·, 6436

pans See also FRYINGPANS.
Ex 27: 3 make his p· to receive his ashes, *5518
Nu 11: 8 baked it in p·, and made cakes of *6517
1Ch 9: 31 things that were made in the p·. 2281
2Ch 35: 13 in caldrons, and in p·, and divided 6745

pant See also PANTED; PANTETH.
Am 2: 7 That p· after the dust of the earth 7602

panted
Ps 119: 131 I opened my mouth, and p·: for I 7602
Isa 21: 4 My heart p·, fearfulness †8582

panteth
Ps 38: 10 My heart p·, my strength faileth *5503
42: 1 the hart p· after the water brooks, 6165
1 so p· my soul after thee, O God. "

paper
Isa 19: 7 The p· reeds by the brooks, by the*6169
2Jo 12 would not write with p· and ink: 5489

paper-reeds See PAPER and REEDS.

Paphos (*pa'-fos*)
Ac 13: 6 had gone through the isle unto P·, 3974
13 and his company loosed from P·, "

paps
Eze 23: 21 Egyptians for the p· of thy youth. *7699
Lu 11: 27 the p· which thou hast sucked *3149
23: 29 and the p· which never gave suck.* "
Re 1: 13 about the p· with a golden girdle.* "

parable See also PARABLES.
Nu 23: 7 And he took up his p·, and said, 4912
18 he took up his p·, and said, Rise up, "
24: 3, 15 And he took up his p·, and said, "
20 he took up his p·, and said, Amalek "
21 took up his p·, and said, Strong is "
23 he took up his p·, and said, Alas, "
Job 27: 1 Moreover Job continued his p·, "
29: 1 Moreover Job continued his p·, "
Ps 49: 4 I will incline mine ear to a p·: I will "
78: 2 I will open my mouth in a p·: I will "
Pr 26: 7, 9 so is a p· in the mouth of fools. "
Eze 17: 2 speak a p· unto the house of Israel; "
24: 3 utter a p· unto the rebellious house, "
Mic 2: 4 shall one take up a p· against you, "
Hab 2: 6 all these take up a p· against him, "
M't 13: 18 ye therefore the p· of the sower. 3850
24, 31 Another p· put he forth unto "
33 Another p· spake he unto them; "
34 without a p· spake he not unto them; "
36 Declare unto us the p· of the tares "
15: 15 unto him, Declare unto us this p·. "
21: 33 Hear another p·: There was a "
24: 32 Now learn a p· of the fig tree; When "
M'r 4: 10 with the twelve asked of him the p·.* "
13 unto them, Know ye not this p·? "
34 without a p· spake he not unto them: "
7: 17 asked him concerning the p·. "
12: 12 he had spoken the p· against them: "
13: 28 Now learn a p· of the fig tree; When "
Lu 5: 36 And he spake also a p· unto them; "
6: 39 And he spake a p· unto them, Can "
8: 4 out of every city, he spake by a p·: "
9 him, saying, What might this p· be? "
11 Now the p· is this: The seed is the "
12: 16 he spake a p· unto them, saying, "
41 Lord, speakest thou this p· unto us, "
13: 6 He spake also this p·; A certain "
14: 7 he put forth a p· to those which "
15: 3 he spake this p· unto them, saying, "
18: 1 he spake a p· unto them to this end, "
9 And he spake this p· unto certain "
19: 11 he added and spake a p·, because "
20: 9 he to speak to the people this p·; "
19 had spoken this p· against them. "
21: 29 And he spake to them a p·; Behold "
Joh 10: 6 This p· spake Jesus unto them 3942

parables
Eze 20:49 say of me, Doth he not speak p'? 4912
M't 13: 3 many things unto them in p', 3850
10 Why speakest thou unto them in p'?"
13 Therefore speak I to them in p': "
34 Jesus unto the multitude in p'; "
35 saying, I will open my mouth in p'; "
53 when Jesus had finished these p', "
21:45 and Pharisees had heard his p', "
22: 1 and spake unto them again by p', "
M'r 3:23 and said unto them in p', How can "
4: 2 he taught them many things by p', "
11 all these things are done in p': "
13 and how then will ye know all p'? "
33 many such p' spake he the word "
12: 1 he began to speak unto them by p'. "
Lu 8:10 but to others in p'; that seeing they"

paradise
Lu 23:43 To day shalt thou be with me in p'. 3857
2Co 12: 4 How that he was caught up into p', "
Re 2: 7 is in the midst of the p' of God. "

Parah (pa'-rah)
Jos 18:23 And Avim, and P', and Ophrah, 6511

paramours
Eze 23:20 she doted upon their p', whose 6370

Paran (pa'-ran) See also EL-PARAN.
Ge 21:21 he dwelt in the wilderness of P': 6290
Nu 10:12 cloud rested in the wilderness of P'."
12:16 and pitched in the wilderness of P'."
13: 3 them from the wilderness of P': "
26 unto the wilderness of P', to "
De 1: 1 Red sea, between P', and Tophel, "
33: 2 he shined forth from mount P', and"
1Sa 25: 1 went down to the wilderness of P'. "
1Ki 11:18 arose out of Midian, and came to P':"
18 they took men with them out of P':"
Hab 3: 3 and the Holy One from mount P'. "

Parbar (par'-bar)
1Ch 26:18 At P' westward, four at the 6503
18 at the causeway, and two at P'. "

parcel
Ge 33:19 he bought a p' of a field, where he 2513
Jos 24:32 in a p' of ground which Jacob bought"
Ru 4: 3 selleth a p' of land, which was our "
1Ch 11:13 was a p' of ground full of barley; * "
14 themselves in the midst of that p',* "
Joh 4: 5 the p' of ground that Jacob gave 5564

parched
Le 23:14 eat neither bread, nor p' corn, nor 7039
Jos 5:11 and p' corn in the selfsame day. "
Ru 2:14 he reached her p' corn, and she 7039
1Sa 17:17 brethren an ephah of this p' corn, "
25:18 and five measures of p' corn, and an"
2Sa 17:28 and barley, and flour, and p' corn, "
28 beans, and lentiles, and p' pulse, "
Isa 35: 7 p' ground shall become a pool, *8273
Jer 17: 6 shall inhabit the p' places in the 2788

parchments
2Ti 4:13 the books, but especially the p'. 3200

pardon See also PARDONED; PARDONETH.
Ex 23:21 will not p' your transgressions: 5375
34: 9 and p' our iniquity and our sin, 5545
Nu 14:19 P', I beseech thee, the iniquity of "
1Sa 15:25 I pray thee, p' my sin, and turn 5375
2Ki 5:18 this thing the Lord p' thy servant, 5545
18 Lord p' thy servant in this thing. "
24: 4 blood; which the Lord would not p'."
2Ch 30:18 The good Lord p' every one 3722
Ne 9:17 but thou art a God ready to p', 5547
Job 7:21 dost thou not p' my transgression, 5375
Ps 25:11 O Lord, p' mine iniquity; for it is 5545
Isa 55: 7 our God, for he will abundantly p'. "
Jer 5: 1 seeketh the truth; and I will p' it. "
7 How shall I p' thee for this? thy "
33: 8 and I will p' all their iniquities, "
50:20 for I will p' them whom I reserve. "

pardoned
Nu 14:20 I have p' according to thy word: 5545
Isa 40: 2 that her iniquity is p': for she 7521
La 3:42 have rebelled: thou hast not p'. 5545

pardoneth
Mic 7:18 like unto thee, that p' iniquity, 5375

pare
De 21:12 shave her head, and p' her nails; 6213

parents
M't 10:21 shall rise up against their p', and 1118
M'r 13:12 shall rise up against their p', and "
Lu 2:27 the p' brought in the child Jesus, "
41 his p' went to Jerusalem every year"
8:56 And her p' were astonished: but he"
18:29 hath left house, or p', or brethren, "
21:16 ye shall be betrayed both by p', "
Joh 9: 2 who did sin, this man, or his p', "
3 hath this man sinned, nor his p': "
18 until they called the p' of him that "
20 His p' answered them and said, We "
22 These words spake his p', because "
23 Therefore said his p', He is of age; "
Ro 1:30 of evil things, disobedient to p', "
2Co 12:14 ought not to lay up for the p', but "
14 but the p' for the children. "
Eph 6: 1 Children, obey your p' in the Lord: "
Col 3:20 obey your p' in all things: for "
1Ti 5: 4 at home, and to requite their p': 4269
2Ti 3: 2 disobedient to p', unthankful, 1118
Heb 11:23 was hid three months of his p', 3962

Parez See RIMMON-PAREZ.

parlour See also PARLOURS.
J'g 3:20 and he was sitting in a summer p',‡5944
23 shut the doors of the p' upon him,‡ "
24 the doors of the p' were locked, ‡ "
25 he opened not the doors of the p';‡ "
1Sa 9:22 and brought them into the p', and*3957

parlours
1Ch 28:11 and of the inner p' thereof, and of*2315

Parmashta (par-mash'-tah)
Es 9: 9 And P', and Arisai, and Aridai, 6534

Parmenas (par'-me-nas)
Ac 6: 5 and Timon, and P', and Nicolas a 3937

Parnach (par'-nak)
Nu 34:25 Zebulun, Elizaphan the son of P'. 6535

Parosh (pa'-rosh) See also PHAROSH.
Ezr 2: 3 The children of P', two thousand 6551
10:25 of the sons of P'; Ramiah, and "
Ne 3:25 After him Pedaiah the son of P'. "
7: 8 The children of P', two thousand "
10:14 The chief of the people; P', "

Parshandatha (par-shan'-da-thah)
Es 9: 7 P', and Dalphon, and Aspatha, 6577

part See also APART; DEPART; FOREPART; IMPART; PARTAKEST; PARTED; PARTETH; PARTING; PARTS.
Ge 41:34 up the fifth p' of the land of Egypt
47:24 shall give the fifth p' unto Pharaoh,*
26 that Pharaoh should have the fifth p';*
Ex 16:36 an omer is the tenth p' of an ephah.
19:17 stood at the nether p' of the mount.
29:26 the Lord: and it shall be thy p'. *4490
40 the fourth p' of an hin of beaten oil;
40 and the fourth p' of an hin of wine for
Le 1:16 cast it beside the altar on the east p',
2: 6 Thou shalt p' it in pieces, and pour 6626
16 of it, p' of the beaten corn thereof, and
16 and p' of the oil thereof, with all the
5:11 his offering the tenth p' of an ephah
16 and shall add the fifth p' thereto, and
6: 5 shall add the fifth p' more thereto,
20 the tenth p' of an ephah of fine flour
7:33 have the right shoulder for his p'. 4940
8:29 of consecration it was Moses' p'; * "
11:35 whereupon any p' of their carcase
37 And if any p' of their carcase fall upon*
38 any p' of their carcase fall thereon,*
13:41 from the p' of his head toward his face,
22:14 he shall put the fifth p' thereof unto it,
23:13 be of wine, the fourth p' of an hin.
27:13 fifth p' thereof unto thy estimation.
15 he shall add the fifth p' of the money
16 unto the Lord some p' of a field of
19 he shall add the fifth p' of the money
27 and shall add a fifth p' of it thereto:
31 shall add thereto the fifth p' thereof.
Nu 5: 7 and add unto it the fifth p' thereof,
15 tenth p' of an ephah of barley meal;
15: 4 with the fourth p' of an hin of oil.
5 the fourth p' of an hin of wine for
6 with the third p' of an hin of oil.
7 offer the third p' of an hin of wine,
18:20 thou have any p' among them: *2506
20 I am thy p' and thine inheritance* "
26 the Lord, even a tenth p' of the tithe.*
29 even the hallowed p' thereof out of it.
22:41 might see the utmost p' of the people.
23:10 the number of the fourth p' of Israel?
13 shalt see but the utmost p' of them,
28: 5 And a tenth p' of an ephah of flour
5 the fourth p' of an hin of beaten oil.
7 fourth p' of an hin for the one lamb:
14 and the third p' of an hin unto a ram,
14 the fourth p' of an hin unto a lamb:
De 10: 9 Levi hath no p' nor inheritance *2506
12:12 no p' nor inheritance with you. * "
14:27 no p' nor inheritance with thee. * "
29 no p' nor inheritance with thee,) * "
18: 1 no p' nor inheritance with Israel:* "
33:21 he provided the first p' for himself,
Jos 14: 4 they gave no p' unto the Levites *2506
15: 1 the uttermost p' of the south coast.
5 the sea at the uttermost p' of Jordan:*
13 a p' among the children of Judah,*2506
18: 7 the Levites have no p' among you;* "
19: 9 for the p' of the children of Judah* "
22:25 ye have no p' in the Lord: so shall* "
27 to come, Ye have no p' in the Lord. "
Ru 1:17 if ought but death p' thee and me. 6504
2: 3 hap was to light on a p' of the field*2513
3:13 perform unto thee the p' of a kinsman,
13 well; let him do the kinsman's p':
13 will not do the p' of a kinsman to thee,
13 will I do the p' of a kinsman to thee,
1Sa 9: 8 the fourth p' of a shekel of silver:
14: 2 tarried in the uttermost p' of Gibeah
23:20 and our p' shall be to deliver him into
30:24 as his p' is that goeth down to the*2506
24 his p' be that tarrieth by the stuff:* "
24 by the stuff: they shall p' alike. *2505
2Sa 14: 6 there was none to p' them, but 5337
18: 2 sent forth a third p' of the people
2 and a third p' under the hand of Ittai
20: 1 We have no p' in David, neither *2506
1Ki 6:24 the uttermost p' of the one wing unto
24 the uttermost p' of the other were ten
31 side posts were a fifth p' of the wall.
33 of olive tree, a fourth p' of the wall.
2Ki 6:25 the fourth p' of a cab of dove's dung
7: 5 come to the uttermost p' of the camp
8 came to the uttermost p' of the camp,
11: 5 A third p' of you that enter in on the
6 a third p' shall be at the gate of Sur:
2Ki 11: 6 and a third p' at the gate behind the
18:23 be able on thy p' to set riders upon
1Ch 12:29 the greatest p' of them had kept the
2Ch 23: 4 A third p'...entering on the sabbath,
5 And a third p' shall be at the king's
5 and a third p' at the gate of the
29:16 went into the inner p' of the house
Ne 1: 9 unto the uttermost p' of the heaven,
3: 9 ruler of the half p' of Jerusalem. *6418
12 ruler of the half p' of Jerusalem, * "
14 the ruler of p' of Beth-haccerem;* "
15 the ruler of p' of Mizpah; he * "
16 the ruler of the half p' of Beth-zur,* "
17 of the half p' of Keilah, in his p'. * "
18 the ruler of the half p' of Keilah. * "
5:11 also the hundredth p' of the money,
9: 3 Lord their God one fourth p' of the day;
3 and another fourth p' they confessed,
10:32 yearly with the third p' of a shekel
Job 32:17 I said, I will answer also my p', 2506
41: 6 p' him among the merchants? 2673
Ps 5: 9 their inward p' is very wickedness;
22:18 p' my garments among them, 2505
51: 6 hidden p' thou shalt make me to know
118: 7 The Lord taketh my p' with them*
Pr 8:26 highest p' of the dust of the world.*
31 in the habitable p' of his earth; *
17: 2 shall have p' of the inheritance 2505
Isa 7:18 uttermost p' of the rivers of Egypt,
24:16 From the uttermost p' of the earth
36: 8 able on thy p' to set riders upon them.
44:16 He burneth p' thereof in the fire; 2677
16 with p' thereof he eateth flesh; "
19 I have burned p' of it in the fire; "
Eze 4:11 by measure, the sixth p' of an hin:
5: 2 Thou shalt burn with fire a third p'
2 and thou shalt take a third p', and
2 a third p' thou shalt scatter in the
12 A third p' of thee shall die with the
12 third p' shall fall by the sword round
12 scatter a third p' into all the winds,
39: 2 and leave but the sixth p' of thee,*
45:11 may contain the tenth p' of an homer,
11 the ephah the tenth p' of an homer:
13, 13 sixth p' of an ephah of an homer
14 offer the tenth p' of a bath out of the
17 prince's p' to give burnt offerings,
46:14 morning, the sixth p' of an ephah,
14 and the third p' of an hin of oil, to
Da 1: 2 with p' of the vessels of the house 7117
2:33 his feet p' of iron and p' of clay. 4481
41 p' of potters' clay, and p' of iron, "
42 the toes of the feet were p' of iron, "
42 p' of clay, so the kingdom shall be "
5: 5 the king saw the p' of the hand 6447
24 the p' of the hand sent from him; "
Joe 2:20 his hinder p' toward the utmost sea,
Am 7: 4 great deep, and did eat up a p'. *2506
Zec 13: 9 bring the third p' through the fire,
M'r 4:38 he was in the hinder p' of the ship,*
9:40 he that is not against us is on our p'.*
13:27 from the uttermost p' of the earth
27 to the uttermost p' of heaven.
Lu 10:42 Mary hath chosen that good p', 3310
11:36 be full of light, having no p' dark, 3313
39 but your inward p' is full of ravening
17:24 out of the one p' under heaven,
24 unto the other p' under heaven;
Joh 13: 8 thee not, thou hast no p' with me. 3313
19:23 four parts, to every soldier a p'; "
Ac 1: 8 unto the uttermost p' of the earth.
17 had obtained p' of this ministry. *2819
25 he may take p' of this ministry * "
5: 2 And kept back p' of the price, his wife
2 brought a certain p', and laid it at 3313
3 keep back p' of the price of the land?
8:21 neither p' nor lot in this matter: 3310
14: 4 and p' held with the Jews,
4 and p' with the apostles.
16:12 chief city of that p' of Macedonia,*3310
19:32 more p' knew not wherefore they were
23: 6 that the one p' were Sadducees, 3313
9 were of the Pharisees' p' arose, "
27:12 the more p' advised to depart thence
41 hinder p' was broken with the *4403
Ro 11:25 in p' is happened to Israel, until 3313
1Co 12:24 honour to that p' which lacked:
13: 9 know in p', and we prophesy in p'. 3313
10 which is in p' shall be done away. "
12 now I know in p'; but then shall I "
15: 6 the greater p' remain unto this 4119
16:17 lacking on your p' they have supplied.
2Co 1:14 ye have acknowledged us in p', 3313
2: 5 he hath not grieved me, but in p': "
6:15 or what p' hath he that believeth 3310
Eph 4:16 in the measure of every p', 3313
Tit 2: 8 is of the contrary p' may be ashamed,
Heb 2:14 likewise took p' of the same; *3348
7: 2 Abraham gave a tenth p' of all; 3307
1Pe 4:14 on their p' he is evil spoken of, but on*
14 of, but on your p' he is glorified. *
Re 6: 8 them over the fourth p' of the earth,
8: 8 the third p' of the sea became blood;
9 And the third p' of the creatures
9 and the third p' of the ships were
10 fell upon the third p' of the rivers,
11 the third p' of the waters became
12 the third p' of the sun was smitten,
12 smitten, and the third p' of the moon,
12 moon, and the third p' of the stars;
12 as the third p' of them was darkened,
12 the day shone not for a third p' of it,
9:15 year, for to slay the third p' of men.
18 three was the third p' of men killed,
11:13 and the tenth p' of the city fell, and in
12: 4 the third p' of the stars of heaven,

Re 20: 6 hath p· in the first resurrection: 3313
21: 8 liars, shall have their p· in the lake "
22: 19 away his p· out of the book of life, "

partaker See also PARTAKERS.
Ps 50: 18 and hast been p· with adulterers. 2506
1Co 9: 10 in hope should be p· of his hope. *3348
23 I might be p· thereof with you. 4791
10: 30 if I by grace be a p·, why am I evil*3348
1Ti 5: 22 neither be p· of other men's sins: 2841
2Ti 1: 8 be thou p· of the afflictions of the *4777
2: 6 must be first p· of the fruits. *3335
1Pe 5: 1 a p· of the glory that shall be 2844
2Jo 11 God speed is p· of his evil deeds. *2841

partakers
M't 23: 30 we would not have been p· with 2844
Ro 15: 27 made p· of their spiritual things, 2841
1Co 9: 12 be p· of this power over you, are *3348
13 at the altar are p· with the altar? *4829
10: 17 for we are all p· of that one bread.*3348
18 eat of the sacrifices p· of the altar?*2844
21 ye cannot be p· of the Lord's table,*3348
2Co 1: 7 that as ye are p· of the sufferings, 2844
Eph 3: 6 p· of his promise in Christ by the 4830
5: 7 Be not ye therefore p· with them. "
Ph'p 1: 7 gospel, ye are all p· of my grace. 4791
Col 1: 12 us meet to be p· of the inheritance 3310
1Ti 6: 2 and beloved, p· of the benefit. * 482
Heb 2: 14 as the children are p· of flesh and *2841
3: 1 p· of the heavenly calling, consider3353
14 For we are made p· of Christ, if we "
6: 4 were made p· of the Holy Ghost, "
12: 8 whereof all are p·, then are ye "
10 we might be p· of his holiness. 3335
1Pe 4: 13 ye are p· of Christ's sufferings; 2841
2Pe 1: 4 might be p· of the divine nature, 2844
Re 18: 4 that ye be not p· of her sins, and *4790

partakest
Ro 11: 17 them p· of the root and fatness*1096,4791

parted See also DEPARTED; IMPARTED.
Ge 2: 10 and from thence it was p·, and 6504
2Ki 2: 11 of fire, and p· them both asunder; "
14 waters, they p· hither and thither:*2673
Job 38: 24 By what way is the light p·, which 2505
Joe 3: 2 among the nations, and p· my land. "
M't 27: 35 and p· his garments, casting lots:*1266
35 They p· my garments among them, "
M'r 15: 24 they p· his garments, casting lots * "
Lu 23: 34 they p· his raiment, and cast lots. "
24: 51 he was p· from them, and carried 1339
Joh 19: 24 They p· my raiment among them, 1266
Ac 2: 45 p· them to all men, as every man "

parteth
Le 11: 3 Whatsoever p· the hoof, and is 6536
De 14: 6 And every beast that p· the hoof, "
Pr 18: 18 cease, and p· between the mighty. 6504

Parthians (*par-the'-uns*)
Ac 2: 9 P·, and Medes, and Elamites, and 3934

partial
Mal 2: 9 but have been p· in the law, *5375,6440
Jas 2: 4 Are ye not then p· in yourselves, *1252

partiality
1Ti 5: 21 another, doing nothing by p·. 4346
Jas 3: 17 of mercy and good fruits, without p·,*87

particular
1Co 12: 27 of Christ, and members in p·. *3313
Eph 5: 33 every one of you in p· so love *3588,1520

particularly
Ac 21: 19 he declared p· what *1520,1538,2596
Heb 9: 5 we cannot now speak p·. *2596,3313

parties
Ex 22: 9 cause of both p· shall come before the

parting See also DEPARTING.
Eze 21: 21 Babylon stood at the p· of the way, 517

partition
1Ki 6: 21 made a p· by the chains of gold. *5674
Eph 2: 14 broken down the middle wall of p· 5418

partly
Da 2: 42 shall be p· strong, and p· broken. 7118
1Co 11: 18 you; and I p· believe it. 3313,5100
Heb 10: 33 P·, whilst ye were made a 5124,3303
33 p·, whilst ye became companions" 1161

partner See also PARTNERS.
Pr 29: 24 Whoso is p· with a thief hateth his2505
2Co 8: 23 he is my p· and fellowhelper 2844
Ph'm 17 If thou count me therefore a p·, "

partners
Lu 5: 7 And they beckoned unto their p·, 3353
10 Zebedee, which were p· with Simon.2844

partridge
1Sa 26: 20 as when one doth hunt a p· in the 7124
Jer 17: 11 the p· sitteth on eggs, and hatcheth "

parts
Ge 47: 24 four p· shall be your own, for seed 3027
Ex 33: 23 hand, and thou shalt see my back p·:*
Le 1: 8 Aaron's sons, shall lay the p·, the *5409
22: 23 thing superfluous or lacking in his p·,
Nu 10: 5 lie on the east p· shall go forward.*
11: 1 were in the uttermost p· of the camp.*
31: 27 divide the prey into two p·; between
De 19: 3 giveth thee to inherit, into three p·,
30: 4 out unto the outmost p· of heaven,
Jos 18: 5 they shall divide it into seven p·: *2506
6 describe the land into seven p·, * "
9 it by cities into seven p· in a book,* "
1Sa 5: 9 they had emerods in their secret p·.*
2Sa 19: 43 and said, We have ten p· in the king,
1Ki 6: 38 throughout all the p· thereof, and 1697
7: 25 and all their hinder p· were inward.
16: 21 of Israel divided into two p·: 2677
2Ki 11: 7 two p· of all you that go forth on *3027
2Ch 4: 4 and all their hinder p· were inward.
Ne 11: 1 nine p· to dwell in other cities. 3027
Job 26: 14 these are p· of his ways: but how*7098
38: 36 hath put wisdom in the inward p·?
41: 12 I will not conceal his p·, nor his * 905
Ps 2: 8 uttermost p· of the earth for thy
51: 6 thou desirest truth in the inward p·:
63: 9 shall go into the lower p· of the earth.
65: 8 dwell in the uttermost p· are afraid
78: 66 he smote his enemies in the hinder p·:*
136: 13 which divided the Red sea into p·:*1506
139: 9 dwell in the uttermost p· of the sea;
15 wrought in the lowest p· of the earth.
Pr 18: 8 into the innermost p· of the belly.
20: 27 searching all the inward p· of the belly.
30 so do stripes the inward p· of the belly.
26: 22 into the innermost p· of the belly.
Isa 3: 17 the Lord will discover their secret p·.
16: 11 and mine inward p· for Kir-haresh.
44: 23 shout, ye lower p· of the earth:
Jer 31: 33 I will put my law in their inward p·,
34: 18 and passed between the p· thereof,1335
19 passed between the p· of the calf; "
Eze 26: 20 set thee in the low p· of the earth,
31: 14 death, to the nether p· of the earth,
16 comforted in the nether p· of the earth.
18 Eden unto the nether p· of the earth:
32: 18 unto the nether p· of the earth, with
24 into the nether p· of the earth, which
38: 15 from thy place out of the north p·, 3411
39: 2 thee to come up from the north p·, "
48: 8 in length as one of the other p·, *2506
Zec 13: 8 two p· therein shall be cut off and 6310
M't 2: 22 he turned aside into the p· of Galilee:
12: 42 from the uttermost p· of the earth to*
M'r 8: 10 came into the p· of Dalmanutha. 3313
Lu 11: 31 came from the utmost p· of the earth*
Joh 19: 23 his garments, and made four p·, 3313
Ac 2: 10 and in the p· of Libya about Cyrene," "
20: 2 when he had gone over those p·, "
Ro 15: 23 having no more place in these p·, *2825
1Co 12: 23 our uncomely p· have more abundant
24 For our comely p· have no need: but
Eph 4: 9 first into the lower p· of the earth? 3313
Re 16: 19 great city was divided into three p·, "

Paruah (*par'-u-ah*)
1Ki 4: 17 Jehoshaphat the son of P·, in 6515

Parvaim (*par-va'-im*)
2Ch 3: 6 and the gold was gold of P·. 6516

Pas See PAS-DAMMIM.

Pasach (*pa'-sak*)
1Ch 7: 33 sons of Japhlet; P·, and Bimhal, 6457

Pas-dammim (*pas-dam'-mim*)
1Ch 11: 13 He was with David at P·, and 6450

Paseah (*pa-se'-ah*) See also PHASEAH.
1Ch 4: 12 Eshton begat Beth-rapha, and P·, 6454
Ezr 2: 49 children of Uzza, the children of P·, "
Ne 3: 6 repaired Jehoiada the son of P·, "

Pashur (*pash'-ur*)
1Ch 9: 12 the son of Jeroham, the son of P·,*6583
Ezr 2: 38 The children of P·, a thousand two* "
10: 22 And of the sons of P·; Elioenai, * "
Ne 7: 41 The children of P·, a thousand two* "
10: 3 P·, Amariah, Malchijah, * "
11: 12 the son of P·, the son of Malchiah,* "
Jer 20: 1 P· the son of Immer the priest, * "
2 P· smote Jeremiah the prophet, * "
3 P· brought forth Jeremiah out of* "
3 Lord hath not called thy name P·,* "
6 P·,...all that dwell in thine house* "
21: 1 king Zedekiah sent unto him P· * "
38: 1 and Gedaliah the son of P·, and * "
1 and P· the son of Malchiah, * "

pass See also COMPASS; OVERPASS; PASSED; PASSEST; PASSETH; PASSING; PASSOVER; PAST; TRESPASS.
Ge 4: 14 it shall come to p·, that every one
6: 1 it came to p·, when men began to
7: 10 it came to p· after seven days, that
8: 1 made a wind to p· over the earth, 5674
6 came to p· at the end of forty days,
13 it came to p· in the six hundredth
18: 3 p· not away, I pray thee, from thy 5674
5 hearts; after that ye shall p· on: "
24: 52 And it came to p·, that, when
25: 11 to p· after the death of Abraham,
26: 8 came to p·, when he had been there
27: 1 And it came to p·, that when Isaac
30 it came to p·, as soon as Isaac had
40 it shall come to p· when thou shalt
29: 10 came to p·, when Jacob saw Rachel
13 it came to p·, when Laban heard
23 it came to p· in the evening, that
25 it came to p· that in the morning,
30: 25 And it came to p·, when Rachel had
32 will p· through all thy flock to day,5674
41 And it came to p·, whensoever the
31: 10 it came to p· at the time that the
52 I will not p· over this heap to thee,5674
52 thou shalt not p· over this heap "
32: 16 P· over before me, and put a space "
33: 14 thee, p· over before his servant: "
34: 25 And it came to p· on the third day,
35: 18 And it came to p·, as her soul was
22 it came to p·, when Israel dwelt in
37: 23 And it came to p·, when Joseph was
38: 1 And it came to p· at that time, that
Ge 38: 9 and it came to p·, when he went in
24 And it came to p· about three months
27 And it came to p· in the time of her
28 And it came to p·, when she travailed,
29 it came to p·, as he drew back his
39: 5 And it came to p· from the time that he
7 And it came to p· after these things,
10 And it came to p·, as she spake to
11 And it came to p· about this time,
13 And it came to p·, when she saw that
15 And it came to p·, when he heard that
18 And it came to p·, as I lifted up my
19 And it came to p·, when his master
40: 1 And it came to p· after these things,
20 And it came to p· the third day, which
41: 1 And it came to p· at the end of two
8 And it came to p· in the morning
13 And it came to p·, as he interpreted
32 and God will shortly bring it to p·.6213
42: 35 And it came to p· as they emptied
43: 2 it came to p·, when they had eaten
21 it came to p·, when we came to the
44: 24 And it came to p· when we came up
31 It shall come to p·, when he seeth
46: 33 it shall come to p·, when Pharaoh shall
47: 24 And it shall come to p· in the increase,
48: 1 And it came to p· after these things,
50: 20 to bring to p·, as it is this day, 6213
Ex 1: 10 and it come to p·, that, when there
21 it came to p·, because the midwives
2: 11 it came to p· in those days, when
23 And it came to p· in process of time,
3: 21 it shall come to p·, that, when ye go,
4: 8, 9 come to p·, if they will not believe
24 it came to p· by the way in the inn,
6: 28 it came to p· on the day when the
12: 12 For I will p· through the land of *5674
13 I see the blood, I will p· over you, 6452
23 the Lord will p· through to smite 5674
23 the Lord will p· over the door, and 6452
25 And it shall come to p·, when ye be
26 And it shall come to p·, when your
29 it came to p·, that at midnight the
41 it came to p· at the end of the four
41 even the selfsame day it came to p·,
51 And it came to p· the selfsame day,
13: 15 came to p·, when Pharaoh would
17 it came to p·, when Pharaoh had
14: 24 it came to p·, that in the morning
15: 16 till thy people p· over, O Lord, 5674
16 till the people p· over, which thou "
16: 5 come to p·, that on the sixth day
10 And it came to p·, as Aaron spake
13 came to p·, that at even the quails
22 it came to p·, that on the sixth day
27 it came to p·, that there went out
17: 11 And it came to p· when Moses held up
18: 13 And it came to p· on the morrow,
19: 16 it came to p· on the third day in the
22: 27 it shall come to p·, when he crieth
32: 19 it came to p·, as soon as he came
30 it came to p· on the morrow, that
33: 7 it came to p·, that every one which
8 it came to p·, when Moses went out
9 And it came to p·, as Moses entered
19 make all my goodness p· before 5674
22 come to p·, while my glory passeth
22 thee with my hand while I p· by: *5674
34: 29 it came to p·, when Moses came
40: 17 it came to p· in the first month in
Le 9: 1 came to p· on the eighth day, that
18: 21 seed p· through the fire to Molech,5674
Nu 5: 27 come to p·, that, if she be defiled,
7: 1 came to p· on the day that Moses
10: 35 And it came to p·, when the ark set
11: 23 shall come to p· unto thee or not.
25 it came to p·, that, when the spirit
16: 31 came to p·, as he had made an end
42 came to p·, when the congregation
17: 5 it shall come to p·, that the man's rod,
8 it came to p·, that on the morrow
20: 17 Let us p·, I pray thee, through thy 5674
17 we will not p· through the fields, or "
18 Thou shalt not p· by me, lest I "
21: 8 come to p·, that every one that is
9 came to p·, that if a serpent had
22 Let me p· through thy land: we 5674
23 Israel to p· through his border: "
22: 41 it came to p· on the morrow, that
26: 1 it came to p· after the plague, that
27: 7 of their father to p· unto them. 5674
8 his inheritance to p· unto his "
32: 27 But thy servants will p· over, every "
29 will p· with you over Jordan, every "
30 will not p· over with you armed, "
32 We will p· over armed before the "
33: 55 then it shall come to p·, that those
56 come to p·, that I shall do unto you,
34: 4 of Akrabbim, and p· on to Zin: 5674
4 Hazar-addar, and p· on to Azmon: "
De 1: 3 it came to p· in the fortieth year,
2: 4 Ye are to p· through the coast of 5674
16 it came to p·, when all the men of
18 Thou art to p· over through Ar, 5674
24 and p· over the river Arnon: "
27 Let me p· through thy land: I will "
28 only I will p· through on my feet; "
29 shall p· over Jordan into the land "
30 Sihon...would not let us p· by him: "
3: 18 ye shall p· over armed before your "
5: 23 it came to p·, when ye heard the
7: 12 it shall come to p·, if ye hearken to
9: 1 Thou art to p· over Jordan this 5674
11 it came to p· at the end of forty days
11: 13 And it shall come to p·, if ye shall
29 it shall come to p·, when the Lord

De 11:31 ye shall p' over Jordan to go in to 5674
13: 2 the sign or the wonder come to p',
18:10 daughter to p' through the fire, 5674
19 shall come to p', that whosoever
22 thing follow not, nor come to p',
24: 1 it come to p' that she find no favour
27: 2 day when ye shall p' over Jordan 5674
28: 1 it shall come to p', if thou shalt
15 it shall come to p', if thou wilt not
63 it shall come to p', that as the Lord
29:19 it come to p', when he heareth the
30: 1 it shall come to p', when all these
31:21 shall come to p', when many evils
24 it came to p', when Moses made an
Jos 1: 1 it came to p', that the Lord spake
11 P' through the host, and command5674
11 ye shall p' over this Jordan, to go
14 but ye shall p' before your brethren"
2: 5 it came to p' about the time of
3: 2 it came to p' after three days, that
6 and p' over before the people. 5674
13 come to p', as soon as the soles of
14 it came to p', when the people 5674
14 from their tents, to p' over Jordan, "
4: 1 it came to p', when all the people
5 P' over before the ark of the 5674
11 it came to p', when all the people
18 And it came to p', when the priests
5: 1 it came to p', when all the kings of
8 And it came to p', when they had
13 it came to p', when Joshua was by
6: 5 come to p', that when they make a*
7 P' on, and compass the city, and 5674
7 let him that is armed p' on before "
8 it came to p', when Joshua had
15 And it came to p' on the seventh day,
16 And it came to p' at the seventh time,
20 came to p', when the people heard
8: 5 come to p', when they come out
14 it came to p', when the king of Ai
24 came to p', when Israel had made
9: 1 it came to p', when all the kings
16 came to p' at the end of three days
10: 1 it came to p', when Adoni-zedec
11 came to p', as they fled from before
20 And it came to p', when Joshua and
24 And it came to p', when they brought
27 And it came to p' at the time of the
11: 1 And it came to p', when Jabin king
15:18 it came to p', as she came unto him,
17:13 it came to p', when the children of
21:45 the house of Israel; all came to p'. 935
22:19 then p' ye over unto the land of 5674
23: 1 it came to p' a long time after that
14 all are come to p' unto you, and
15 come to p', that as all good things
24:29 And it came to p' after these things,
J'g 1: 1 the death of Joshua it came to p',
14 And it came to p', when she came
28 And it came to p', when Israel was
2: 4 it came to p', when the angel of the
19 it came to p', when the judge was
3:27 And it came to p', when he was come,
28 and suffered not a man to p' over. 5674
6: 7 it came to p', when the children of
25 And it came to p' the same night,
7: 9 And it came to p' the same night,
8:33 it came to p', as soon as Gideon was
9:42 it came to p' on the morrow, that
11: 4 And it came to p' in process of time,
17 Let me, I pray thee, p' through thy5674
19 Let us p', we pray thee, through "
20 But Sihon trusted not Israel to p' "
35 And it came to p', when he saw her,
39 it came to p' at the end of two months,
13:12 said, Now let thy words come to p'. 935
17 when thy sayings come to p' we may"
20 it came to p', when the flame went
14:11 And it came to p', when they saw him,
15 And it came to p' on the seventh day,
15: 1 But it came to p' in a while after,
17 it came to p', when he had made an
16: 4 it came to p' afterward, that he loved
16 it came to p', when she pressed him
25 it came to p', when their hearts were
19: 1 And it came to p' in those days, when
5 And it came to p' on the fourth day,
12 Israel; we will p' over to Gibeah. 5674
21: 3 why is this come to p' in Israel,
4 And it came to p' on the morrow, that
Ru 1: 1 Now it came to p' in the days when
19 it came to p', when they were come
3: 8 And it came to p' at midnight, that
1Sa 1:12 And it came to p', as she continued
20 it came to p', when the time was
2:36 it shall come to p', that every one
3: 2 it came to p' at that time, when Eli
4:18 And it came to p', when he made
5:10 And it came to p', as the ark of God
7: 2 And it came to p', while the ark abode
8: 1 it came to p', when Samuel was old,
9: 6 that he saith cometh surely to p':
26 it came to p' about the spring of
27 Bid the servant p' on before us, 5674
10: 5 it shall come to p', when thou art
11 it came to p', when all that knew him
11:11 and it came to p', that they which
13:10 it came to p', that as soon as he had
22 So it came to p' in the day of battle,
14: 1 Now it came to p' upon a day, that*
8 we will p' over unto these men, 5674
19 And it came to p', while Saul talked
16: 6 And it came to p', when they were
8 and made him p' before Samuel. 5674
9 Then Jesse made Shammah to p' by."
10 made seven of his sons to p' before "

1Sa 16:16 shall come to p', when the evil spirit
23 it came to p', when the evil spirit
17:48 it came to p', when the Philistine
18: 1 it came to p', when he had made an
6 it came to p' as they came, when
10 And it came to p' on the morrow, that
19 came to p' at the time when Merab
30 it came to p', after they went forth,
20:27 And it came to p' on the morrow,
35 it came to p' in the morning, that
23: 6 And it came to p', when Abiathar
23 it shall come to p', if he be in the land,
24: 1 And it came to p', when Saul was
5 it came to p' afterward, that David's
16 And it came to p', when David had
25:30 it shall come to p', when the Lord
37 it came to p' in the morning, when
38 it came to p' about ten days after,
28: 1 And it came to p' in those days, that
30: 1 And it came to p', when David and his
31: 8 it came to p' on the morrow, when
2Sa 1: 1 it came to p' after the death of Saul,
2 It came even to p' on the third day,
2: 1 it came to p' after this, that David
23 it came to p', that as many as came
3: 6 And it came to p', while there was
4: 4 it came to p', as she made haste to
7: 1 it came to p', when the king sat in
4 And it came to p' that night, that
8: 1 it came to p', that David smote the
10: 1 came to p' after this, that the king
11: 1 And it came to p', after the year
2 came to p' in an eveningtide, that
14 it came to p' in the morning, that
16 it came to p', when Joab observed
12:18 it came to p' on the seventh day,
31 them p' through the brickkiln: 5674
13: 1 And it came to p' after this, that
23 came to p' after two full years, that
30 came to p', while they were in the
36 came to p', as soon as he had made
15: 1 And it came to p' after this, that
22 David said to Ittai, Go and p' over.5674
32 came to p', that when David was
16:16 it came to p', when Hushai the
17: 9 will come to p', when some of them
16 speedily p' over; lest the king be 5674
21 it came to p', after they were
21 and p' quickly over the water: for5674
27 came to p', when David was come
19:25 it came to p', when he was come
21:18 it came to p' after this, that there
1Ki 1:21 come to p', when my lord the king
2:39 came to p' at the end of three years,
3:18 came to p' the third day after that
5: 7 it came to p', when Hiram heard
6: 1 it came to p' in the four hundred
8:10 And it came to p', when the priests
9: 1 it came to p', when Solomon had
10 it came to p' at the end of twenty
11: 4 came to p', when Solomon was old,
15 it came to p', when David was in
29 it came to p' at that time when
12: 2 came to p', when Jeroboam the son
20 it came to p', when all Israel heard
13: 4 it came to p', when king Jeroboam
20 it came to p', as they sat at the table,
23 it came to p', after he had eaten
31 came to p', after he had buried him,
32 of Samaria, shall surely come to p'.
14:25 came to p' in the fifth year of king
15:21 it came to p', when Baasha heard
29 came to p', when he reigned, that
16:11 came to p', when he began to reign,
18 it came to p', when Zimri saw that
31 it came to p', as if it had been a
17: 7 it came to p' after a while, that the
17 came to p' after these things, that
18: 1 it came to p' after many days, that
6 between them to p' throughout it:5674
12 come to p', as soon as I am gone
17 came to p', when Ahab saw Elijah,
27 it came to p' at noon, that Elijah
29 came to p', when midday was past,
36 And it came to p' at the time of the
44 came to p' at the seventh time, that
45 came to p' in the mean while, that
19:17 come to p', that him that escapeth
20:12 came to p', when Benhadad heard
26 came to p' at the return of the year,
21: 1 it came to p' after these things,
15 it came to p', when Jezebel heard
16 came to p', when Ahab heard that
27 came to p', when Ahab heard those
22: 2 it came to p' in the third year, that
32, 33 came to p', when the captains of
2Ki 2: 1 And it came to p', when the Lord
9 it came to p', when they were gone
11 it came to p', as they still went on,
3: 5 came to p', when Ahab was dead,
15 it came to p', when the minstrel
20 it came to p' in the morning, when
4: 6 it came to p', when the vessels were
25 it came to p', when the man of God
40 came to p', as they were eating of
5: 7 came to p', when the king of Israel
6: 9 that thou p' not such a place; for 5674
20 came to p', when they were come
24 And it came to p' after this, that
30 it came to p', when the king heard
7:18 came to p' as the man of God had
8: 3 came to p' at the seven years' end,
5 it came to p', as he was telling the
15 came to p' on the morrow, that he
9:22 came to p', when Joram saw Jehu,
10: 7 it came to p', when the letter came

2Ki 10: 9 it came to p' in the morning, that
25 came to p', as soon as he had made
13:21 came to p', as they were burying a
14: 5 came to p', as soon as the kingdom
15:12 generation. And so it came to p'.
16: 3 made his son to p' through...fire, 5674
17:17 their daughters to p' through...fire, "
18: 1 it came to p' in the third year of
9 it came to p' in the fourth year of
19: 1 it came to p', when king Hezekiah
25 now have I brought it to p', that
35 it came to p', that night, that the
37 came to p', as he was worshipping
20: 4 it came to p', afore Isaiah was gone
21: 6 made his son p' through the fire. 5674
22: 3 came to p' in the eighteenth year
11 it came to p', when the king had
23:10 daughter to p' through the fire to 5674
24:20 it came to p' in Jerusalem and
25: 1 it came to p' in the ninth year of
25 it came to p' in the seventh month,
27 it came to p' in the seventh and
1Ch 10: 8 it came to p' on the morrow, when
15:26 it came to p', when God helped the
29 And it came to p', as the ark of the
17: 1 it came to p', as David sat in his
3 it came to p' the same night, that
11 it shall come to p', when thy days
18: 1 after this it came to p', that David
19: 1 Now it came to p' after this, that
20: 1 it came to p', that after the year
4 it came to p' after this, that there
2Ch 5:11 And it came to p', when the priests
13 came even to p', as the trumpeters
8: 1 it came to p' at the end of twenty
10: 2 it came to p', when Jeroboam the
12: 1 it came to p', when Rehoboam had
2 it came to p', that in the fifth year
13:15 it came to p', that God smote
16: 5 came to p', when Baasha heard it,
18:31 it came to p', when the captains of
32 came to p', that, when the captains
20: 1 came to p' after this also, that the
21:19 came to p', that in process of time,
22: 8 came to p', that, when Jehu was
24: 4 it came to p' after this, that Joash
11 came to p', that at what time the *
23 came to p' at the end of the year,
25: 3 came to p', when the kingdom was
14 came to p', after that Amaziah was
16 came to p', as he talked with him,
33: 6 his children to p' through the fire 5674
34:19 it came to p', when the king had
Ne 1: 1 it came to p' in the month Chisleu,
4 it came to p', when I heard these
2: 1 it came to p' in the month Nisan,
14 beast that was under me to p'. 5674
4: 1 came to p', that when Sanballat
7 it came to p', that when Sanballat,
12 it came to p', that when the Jews
15 it came to p', when our enemies
16 it came to p' from that time forth,
6: 1 Now it came to p', when Sanballat,
16 it came to p', that when all our
7: 1 it came to p', when the wall was
13: 3 it came to p', when they had heard
19 came to p', that when the gates of
Es 1: 1 came to p' in the days of Ahasuerus,
2: 8 came to p', when the king's...decree
3: 4 came to p', when they spake daily
5: 1 it came to p' on the third day, that
Job 6:15 the stream of brooks they p' away;5674
11:16 remember it as waters that p' away:*"
14: 5 his bounds that he cannot p'; "
19: 8 fenced up my way that I cannot p', "
34:20 troubled at midnight, and p' away: "
Ps 37: 5 him; and he shall bring it to p'. 6213
7 who bringeth wicked devices to p'. "
58: 8 let every one of them p' away: *1980
78:13 and caused them to p' through; 5674
80:12 which p' by the way do pluck her? "
89:41 All that p' by the way spoil him: he "
104: 9 a bound that they may not p' over: "
136:14 made Israel to p through the midst"
148: 6 made a decree which shall not p'. "
Pr 4:15 Avoid it, p' not by it, turn from it, "
15 turn from it, and p' away. "
8:29 should not p' his commandment: * "
16:30 his lips he bringeth evil to p'. 3615
19:11 glory to p' over a transgression. 5674
22: 3 but the simple p' on,...are punished."
27:12 but the simple p' on,...are punished."
Isa 2: 2 it shall come to p' in the last days,
3:24 come to p', that instead of sweet
4: 3 shall come to p', that he that is left
7: 1 it came to p' in the days of Ahaz the
7 stand, neither shall it come to p'.
18, 21 it shall come to p' in that day,
22 shall come to p', for the abundance
23 And it shall come to p' in that day,
8: 8 And he shall p' through Judah; *2498
21 they shall p' through it, hardly 5674
21 come to p', that when they shall
10:12 shall come to p', that when the Lord
20, 27 it shall come to p' in that day,
11:11 And it shall come to p' in that day,
14: 3 And it shall come to p' in the day
24 have thought, so shall it come to p';
16:12 it shall come to p', when it is seen
17: 4 And in that day it shall come to p',
21: 1 whirlwinds in...south p' through; *2498
22: 7 shall come to p', that thy choicest
20 And it shall come to p' in that day,
23: 2 of Zidon, that p' over the sea, 5674
6 P' ye over to Tarshish; howl, ye "
10 P' through thy land as a river, O "

Isa 23:12 arise, p· over to Chittim; there also5674
15 come to p· in that day, that Tyre
17 come to p· after the end of seventy
24:18 And it shall come to p· that he who
21 And it shall come to p· in that day,
27:12, 13 it shall come to p· in that day,
28:15, 18 the overflowing scourge shall p·5674
19 morning by morning shall it p· over, "
21 bring to p· his act, his strange act. "
30:32 where the grounded staff shall p·*4569
31: 9 he shall p· over to his strong hold 5674
33:21 neither...gallant ship p· thereby. "
34:10 none shall p· through it for ever "
35: 8 the unclean shall not p· over it; "
36: 1 came to p· in the fourteenth year
37: 1 it came to p·, when king Hezekiah
26 now have I brought it to p·, that
38 came to p·, as he was worshipping
42: 9 the former things are come to p·,
46:11 spoken it, I will also bring it to p·;
47: 2 the thigh, p· over the rivers. 5674
48: 3 suddenly, and they came to p·.
5 it came to p· I shewed it thee: lest
51:10 a way for the ransomed to p· over?5674
65:24 come to p·, that before they call,
66:23 it shall come to p·, that from one
Jer 2:10 For p· over the isles of Chittim, 5674
3: 9 it came to p· through the lightness
16 come to p·, when ye be multiplied
4: 9 it shall come to p· at that day, saith
5:19 shall come to p·, when ye shall say,
22 perpetual decree,...it cannot p· it: 5674
22 they roar, yet can they not p· over it?"
8:13 them shall p· away from them. "
9:10 so that none can p· through them:* "
13: 6 it came to p· after many days, that
15: 2 it shall come to p·, if they say unto
14 thee to p· with thine enemies into 5674
16:10 shall come to p·, when thou shalt
17:24 come to p·, if ye diligently hearken
20: 3 it came to p· on the morrow, that
22: 8 many nations shall p· by this city, 5674
25:12 come to p·, when seventy years
26: 8 it came to p·, when Jeremiah had
27: 8 it shall come to p·, that the nation
28: 1 it came to p· the same year, in the
9 of the prophet shall come to p·,
30: 8 shall come to p· in that day, saith
31:28 shall come to p·, that like as I have
32:24 thou hast spoken is come to p·;
35 daughters to p· through the fire 5674
33:13 flocks p· again under the hands of "
35:11 came to p·, when Nebuchadrezzar
36: 1 it came to p· in the fourth year of
9 And it came to p· in the fifth year of
16 it came to p·, when they had heard
23 it came to p·, that when Jehudi had
37:11 came to p·, that when the army of
39: 4 came to p·, that when Zedekiah the
41: 1 it came to p· in the seventh month,
4 came to p· the second day after he
6 and it came to p·, as he met them,
13 came to p·, that when all the people
42: 4 come to p· that whatsoever thing
7 And it came to p· after ten days,
16 it shall come to p·, that the sword,
43: 1 it came to p·, that when Jeremiah
49:39 shall come to p· in the latter days,
51:43 neither doth any son of man p· 5674
52: 3 came to p· in Jerusalem and Judah,
4 came to p· in the ninth year of his
31 came to p· in the seven and thirtieth
La 1:12 it nothing to you, all ye that p· by?5674
2:15 that p· by clap their hands at thee; "
3:37 and it cometh to p·, when the Lord
44 our prayer should not p· through. 5674
4:21 cup also shall p· through unto thee: "
Eze 1: 1 it came to p· in the thirtieth year,
3:16 came to p· at the end of seven days,
5: 1 and cause it to p· upon thine head 5674
14 thee, in the sight of all that p· by. "
17 and blood shall p· through thee; "
8: 1 And it came to p· in the sixth year,
9: 8 came to p·, while they were slaying
10: 6 And it came to p· that when he had
11:13 it came to p·, when I prophesied,
12:25 I shall speak shall come to p·; *6213
14:15 noisome beasts to p· through the 5674
15 no man may p· through because "
16:21 to cause them to p· through the fire"
23 And it came to p· after all thy
20:26 caused to p· through the fire all 5674
31 your sons to p· through the fire, "
37 will cause you to p· under the rod, "
21: 7 cometh, and shall be brought to p·,*
23:37 to p· for them through the fire, to 5674
24:14 it shall come to p·, and I will do it;
26: 1 it came to p· in the eleventh year,
29:11 No foot of man shall p· through it,5964
11 nor foot of beast shall p· through it,"
17 And it came to p· in the seven and
30:20 it came to p· in the eleventh year,
31: 1 it came to p· in the eleventh year,
32: 1 it came to p· in the twelfth year, in
17 came to p· also in the twelfth year,
19 Whom dost thou p· in beauty? go
33:21 it came to p· in the twelfth year of
28 desolate,...none shall p· through. 5674
33 And when this cometh to p·, (lo, it
37: 2 me to p· by them round about: 5674
38:10 come to p·, that at the same time
18 it shall come to p· at the same time
39:11 shall come to p· in that day, that
15 the passengers that p· through the5674
44:17 And it shall come to p·, that when*
46:21 and caused me to p· by the four 5674
Eze 47: 5 was a river that I could not p· over:*5674
9 it shall come to p·, that every thing
10 it shall come to p·, that the fishers
22 come to p·, that ye shall divide it by
23 shall come to p·, that in what tribe
Da 2:29 what should come to p· hereafter:
29 to thee what shall come to p·.
45 what shall come to p· hereafter:
4:16 and let seven times p· over him. 2499
23 field, till seven times p· over him; "
25, 32 and seven times shall p· over thee,"
7:14 dominion, which shall not p· away,5709
8: 2 came to p·, when I saw, that I was
15 came to p·, when I, even I Daniel,
11:10 and overflow, and p· through: 5674
40 and shall overflow and p· over. "
Ho 1: 5 shall come to p· at that day, that
10 shall come to p·, that in the place
2:21 come to p· in that day, I will hear,
Joe 2:28 it shall come to p· afterward, that
32 it shall come to p·, that whosoever
3:17 shall no strangers p· through her 5674
18 it shall come to p· in that day, that
Am 5: 5 Gilgal, and p· not to Beer-sheba: 5674
17 for I will p· through thee, saith the "
6: 2 P· ye unto Calneh, and see; and "
9 come to p·, if there remain ten
7: 2 it came to p·, that when they had
8 not again p· by them any more: 5674
8: 2 not again p· by them any more. "
9 And it shall come to p· in that day,
Jon 4: 8 came to p·, when the sun did arise,
Mic 1:11 P· ye away, thou inhabitant of 5674
2: 8 the garment from them that p· by "
13 and their king shall p· before them,*"
4: 1 in the last days it shall come to p·,
5:10 And it shall come to p· in that day,
Nah 1:12 down, when he shall p· through. 5674
15 wicked shall no more p· through "
3: 7 come to p·, that all they that look
Hab 1:11 mind change, and he shall p· over,5674
Zep 1: 8 shall come to p· in the day of the
10 And it shall come to p· in that day,*
12 And it shall come to p· at that time,
2: 2 before the day p· as the chaff, 5674
Zec 3: 4 caused thine iniquity to p· from "
6:15 And this shall come to p·, if ye will
7: 1 it came to p· in the fourth year of
13 it is come to p·, that as he cried,
8:13 it shall come to p·, that as ye were
20 yet come to p·, that there shall come
23 shall come to p·, that ten men shall
9: 8 and no oppressor shall p· through5674
10:11 p· through the sea with affliction, "
12: 9 it shall come to p· in that day, that
13: 2 And it shall come to p· in that day,
2 the unclean spirit to p· out of the 5674
3 it shall come to p·, that when any
4 it shall come to p· in that day, that
8 it shall come to p·, that in all the land,
14: 6, 13 it shall come to p· in that day, that
16 it shall come to p·, that every one that
M't 5:18 Till heaven and earth p·, one jot 3928
18 one tittle shall in no wise p· from "
7:28 came to p·, when Jesus had ended
8:28 that no man might p· by that way. 3928
9:10 came to p·, as Jesus sat at meat in
11: 1 came to p·, when Jesus had made
13:53 it came to p·, that when Jesus had
19: 1 it came to p·, that when Jesus had
24: 6 all these things must come to p·,
34 This generation shall not p·, till all3928
35 Heaven and earth shall p· away, "
35 but my words shall not p· away. "
26: 1 And it came to p·, when Jesus had
39 possible, let this cup p· from me: 3928
42 Father, if this cup may not p· away "
M'r 1: 9 it came to p· in those days, that
2:15 it came to p·, that, as Jesus sat at
23 it came to p·, that he went through
4: 4 came to p·, as he sowed, some fell
35 Let us p· over unto the other side.*1330
11:23 which he saith shall come to p·;
13:29 shall see these things come to p·,
30 this generation shall not p·, till all 3928
31 Heaven and earth shall p· away: "
31 but my words shall not p· away. "
14:35 the hour might p· from him. "
Lu 1: 8 came to p·, that while he executed
23 came to p·, that, as soon as the days
41 it came to p·, that, when Elisabeth
59 came to p·, that on the eighth day
2: 1 And it came to p· in those days, that
15 came to p·, as the angels were gone
15 see this thing which is come to p·,
46 it came to p·, that after three days
3:21 it came to p·, that Jesus also being
5: 1 it came to p·, that, as the people
12 came to p·, when he was in a certain
17 it came to p· on a certain day, as he
6: 1 it came to p· on the second sabbath
6 came to p· also on another sabbath,
12 it came to p· in those days, that he
7:11 it came to p· the day after, that he
8: 1 And it came to p· afterward, that
22 it came to p· on a certain day, that
40 it came to p·, that, when Jesus was*
9:18 came to p·, as he was alone praying,
28 it came to p· about an eight days
33 came to p·, as they departed from
37 it came to p·, that on the next day,
51 came to p·, when the time was come
57 came to p·, that, as they went in the*
10:38 it came to p·, as they went, that he*
11: 1 came to p·, that, as he was praying
14 came to p·, when the devil was gone
Lu 11:27 came to p·, as he spake these things,
42 p· over judgment and the love of 3928
12:55 will be heat; and it cometh to p·.
14: 1 it came to p·, as he went into the
16:17 easier for heaven and earth to p·, 3928
22 it came to p·, that the beggar died,
26 which would p· from hence to you 1224
26 neither can they p· to us, that *1276
17:11 And it came to p·, as he went to
14 it came to p·, that, as they went,
18:35 it came to p·, that as he was come
36 And hearing the multitude p· by, *1279
19: 4 see him: for he was to p· that way.1330
15 it came to p·, that when he was
29 it came to p·, when he was come
20: 1 it came to p·, that on one of those
21: 7 when these things shall come to p·?
9 these things must first come to p·;
28 these things begin to come to p·,
31 when ye see these things come to p·,
32 This generation shall not p· away, 3928
33 Heaven and earth shall p· away: "
33 but my words shall not p· away. "
36 these things that shall come to p·,
24: 4 it came to p·, as they were much
12 himself at that which was come to p·.
15 And it came to p·, that, while they
18 are come to p· there in these days?
30 it came to p·, as he sat at meat with
51 it came to p·, while he blessed them,
Joh 13:19 when it is come to p·, ye may believe
14:29 I have told you before it come to p·,
29 that, when it is come to p·, ye might
15:25 But this cometh to p·, that the word
Ac 2:17 it shall come to p· in the last days,*
21 it shall come to p·, that whosoever*
3:23 it shall come to p·, that every soul,*
4: 5 it came to p· on the morrow, that
9:32 And it came to p·, as Peter passed 1330
37 it came to p· in those days, that
43 it came to p·, that he tarried many
11:26 And it came to p·, that a whole year
28 came to p· in the days of Claudius
14: 1 it came to p· in Iconium, that they
16:16 it came to p·, as we went to prayer,
18:27 he was disposed to p· into Achaia, 1330
19: 1 came to p·, that, while Apollos was
21: 1 it came to p·, that after we were
22: 6 it came to p·, that, as I made my
17 it came to p·, that, when I was come
27:44 so it came to p·, that they escaped
28: 8 came to p·, that the father of Publius*
17 it came to p·, that after three days
Ro 9:26 it shall come to p·, that in the place*
1Co 7:36 if she p· the flower of her age, *5230
15:54 shall be brought to p· the saying
16: 5 I shall p· through Macedonia: 1330
5 for I do p· through Macedonia. "
2Co 1:16 And to p· by you into Macedonia, "
1Th 3: 4 even as it came to p·, and ye know.
Jas 1:10 of the grass he shall p· away. 3928
1Pe 1:17 p· the time of your sojourning here 390
2Pe 3:10 the heavens shall p· away with a 3928
Re 1: 1 which must shortly come to p·;

passage See also PASSAGES.
Nu 20:21 Edom refused to give Israel p· 5674
Jos 22:11 at the p· of the children of Israel. *1552
1Sa 13:23 went out to the p· of Michmash. *4569
Isa 10:29 They are gone over the p·: they * "

passages
J'g 12: 5 Gileadites took the p· of Jordan *4569
6 and slew him at the p· of Jordan: * "
1Sa 14: 4 between the p·, by which Jonathan*"
Jer 22:20 cry from the p·: for all thy lovers*5676
51:32 And that the p· are stopped, and 4569

passed See also COMPASSED; PASSEDST; PAST; TRESPASSED.
Ge 12: 6 And Abram p· through the land 5674
15:17 a burning lamp that p· between "
31:21 he rose up, and p· over the river, "
32:10 with my staff I p· over this Jordan; "
22 sons, and p· over the ford Jabbok. "
31 as he p· over Penuel the sun rose "
33: 3 he p· over before them, and bowed "
37:28 p· by Midianites merchantmen; "
Ex 12:27 p· over the houses of the children 6452
34: 6 And the Lord p· by before him, 5674
Nu 14: 7 which we p· through to search it "
20:17 left, until we have p· thy borders. "
33: 8 and p· through the midst of the sea "
51 are p· over Jordan into the land of* "
De 2: 8 when we p· by from our brethren "
8 and p· by the way of the wilderness"
27: 3 of this law, when thou art p· over, "
29:16 the nations through which ye p· by; "
Jos 2:23 p· over, and came to Joshua the "
3: 1 lodged there before they p· over. "
4 ye have not p· this way heretofore. "
16 people p· over...against Jericho. "
17 the Israelites p· over on dry ground,"
17 people were p· clean over Jordan. "
4: 1 people were clean p· over Jordan, "
7 when it p· over Jordan, the waters "
10 and the people hasted and p· over. "
11 all the people were clean p· over, "
11 the ark of the Lord p· over, and the "
12 tribe of Manasseh, p· over armed "
13 thousand prepared for war p· over "
23 until ye were p· over, as the Lord "
5: 1 until we were p· over, that their "
6: 8 priests...p· on before the Lord, "
10:29 Then Joshua p· from Makkedah, "
31 And Joshua p· from Libnah, and "
34 Lachish Joshua p· unto Eglon, "

Jos 15: 3 and p' along to Zin, and ascended 5674
3 and p' along to Hezron, and went "
4 From thence it p' toward Azmon, "
6 p'...by the north of Beth-arabah; "
7 the border p' toward the waters of "
10 and p' along unto the side of mount"
10 and p' on to Timnah: "
11 p' along to mount Baalah, and went"
16: 6 and p' by it on the east to Janohah;"
18: 9 men went and p' through the land, "
18 And p' along toward the side over "
19 And the border p' along to the side "
24:17 all the people through whom we p':"
J'g 3:26 and p' beyond the quarries, and "
8: 4 Gideon came to Jordan, and p' over,"
10: 9 children of Ammon p' over Jordan "
11:29 he p' over Gilead, and Manasseh, "
29 and p' over Mizpeh of Gilead, and "
29 p' over unto the children of Ammon."
32 Jephthah p' over unto the children "
12: 3 and p' over against the children of "
18:13 p' thence unto mount Ephraim, "
19:14 And they p' on and went their way;"
1Sa 9: 4 And he p' through mount Ephraim, "
4 and p' through the land of Shalisha,"
4 they p' through the land of Shalim, "
4 p' through the land of...Benjamites,"
27 pass on before us, (and he p' on,) "
14:23 the battle p' over unto Beth-aven. "
15:12 and p' on, and gone down to Gilgal."
27: 2 p' over with the six hundred men "
29: 2 the Philistines p' on by hundreds, "
2 and his men p' on in the rereward "
2Sa 2:29 the plain, and p' over Jordan, and "
10:17 Israel together, and p' over Jordan."
15:18 all his servants p' on beside him; "
18 from Gath, p' on before the king. "
22 And Ittai the Gittite p' over, and all"
23 voice, and all the people p' over: "
23 himself p' over the brook Kidron, "
23 Kidron, and all the people p' over, "
17:22 with him, and they p' over Jordan: "
24 And Absalom p' over Jordan, he "
24: 5 they p' over Jordan, and pitched "
1Ki 13:25 And, behold, men p' by, and saw the"
19:11 And, behold, the Lord p' by, and a "
19 and Elijah p' by him, and cast his "
20:39 as the king p' by, he cried unto the "
2Ki 4: 8 on a day, that Elisha p' to Shunem, "
8 that as oft as he p' by, he turned "
31 Gehazi p' on before them, and laid "
6:30 and he p' by upon the wall, and the*"
14: 9 there p' by a wild beast that was "
1Ch 19:17 all Israel, and p' over Jordan, and "
2Ch 9:22 king Solomon p' all the kings of *1431
25:18 and there p' by a wild beast that 5674
30:10 So the posts p' from city to city "
Job 4:15 Then a spirit p' before my face; 2498
9:26 are p' away as the swift ships: "
15:19 and no stranger p' among them. 5674
28: 8 it, nor the fierce lion p' by it. 5710
Ps 18:12 was before him his thick clouds p',5674
37:36 Yet he p' away, and, lo, he was "
48: 4 assembled, they p' by together. "
90: 9 all our days are p' away in thy 6437
Ca 3: 4 but a little that I p' from them, 5674
Isa 10:28 come to Aiath, he is p' to Migron; "
40:27 judgment is p' over from my God? "
41: 3 He pursued them, and p' safely; * "
Jer 2: 6 a land that no man p' through, and "
11:15 and the holy flesh is p' from thee? "
34:18 and p' between the parts thereof, "
19 p' between the parts of the calf; "
46:17 he hath p' the time appointed. * "
Eze 16: 6 when I p' by thee, and saw thee "
8 Now when I p' by thee, and looked "
15 on every one that p' by; his it "
25 thy feet to every one that p' by, "
36:34 in the sight of all that p' by. "
47: 5 a river that could not be p' over. "
Da 3:27 the smell of fire had p' on them. 5709
6:18 to his palace, and p' the night fasting:
Hos 10:11 but I p' over upon her fair neck: I 5674
Jon 2: 3 billows and thy waves p' over me. "
Mic 2:13 up, and have p' through the gate, "
Na 3:19 not thy wickedness p' continually? "
Hab 3:10 the overflowing of the water p' by: "
Zec 7:14 no man p' through nor returned: "
M't 9: 1 entered into a ship, and p' over, *1276
9 And as Jesus p' forth from thence,3855
30 when they heard that Jesus p' by,* "
27:39 And they that p' by reviled him, 3899
M'r 2:14 as he p' by, he saw Levi the son 3855
5:21 Jesus was p' over again by ship *1276
6:35 place, and now the time is far p': * "
48 sea, and would have p' by them. 3928
53 And when they had p' over, they *1276
9:30 thence, and p' through Galilee; 3899
11:20 as they p' by, they saw the fig tree "
15:21 one Simon a Cyrenian, who p' by,*3855
29 And they that p' by railed on him, 3899
Lu 10:31 saw him, he p' by on the other side.492
32 him, and p' by on the other side. "
17:11 p' through the midst of Samaria *1330
19: 1 entered and p' through Jericho. * "
Joh 5:24 but is p' from death unto life. 3327
8:59 the midst of them, and so p' by. *3855
9: 1 and as Jesus p' by, he saw a man "
Ac 9:32 Peter p' throughout all quarters. *1330
12:10 out, and p' on through one street; 4281
14:24 they had p' throughout Pisidia, 1330
15: 3 p' through Phenice and Samaria, "
17: 1 they had p' through Amphipolis 1353
23 For as I p' by, and beheld your 1330
19: 1 Paul having p' through the upper "
21 when he had p' through Macedonia "
Ro 5:12 so death p' upon all men, for that 1330
1Co 10: 1 cloud, and all p' through the sea; "
2Co 5:17 old things are p' away; behold, all3928
Heb 4:14 priest, that is p' into the heavens, 1330
11:29 faith they p' through the Red sea 1224
1Jo 3:14 we have p' from death unto life. 3327
Re 21: 1 and the first earth were p' away; 3928
4 for the former things are p' away. 565

passedst
J'g 12: 1 p' thou over to fight against the 5674

passengers
Pr 9:15 p' who go right on their ways:*5674,1870
Eze 39:11 the valley of the p' on the east of *5674
11 and it shall stop the noses of the p':* "
14 land to bury with the p' those that* "
15 the p' that pass through the land,* "

passest See also COMPASSEST.
De 3:21 all the kingdoms whither thou p',*5674
30:18 p' over Jordan to go to possess it. "
2Sa 15:33 If thou p' on with me, then thou "
1Ki 2:37 out, and p' over the brook Kidron, "
Isa 43: 2 When thou p' through the waters, "

passeth See also COMPASSETH.
Ex 30:13 them, every one that p' among 5674
14 Every one that p' among them that "
33:22 while my glory p' by, that I will put"
Le 27:32 whatsoever p' under the rod, the "
Jos 3:11 p' over before you into Jordan. "
16: 2 p' along unto the borders of Archi* "
19:13 from thence p' on along on the east*"
1Ki 9: 8 one that p' by it shall be astonished,"
2Ki 4: 9 of God, which p' by us continually. "
12: 4 of every one that p' the account, * "
2Ch 7:21 to every one that p' by it; so that "
Job 9:11 he p' on also, but I perceive him 2498
14:20 for ever against him, and he p': 1980
30:15 my welfare p' away as a cloud. *5674
37:21 the wind p', and cleanseth them. "
Ps 8: 8 p' through the paths of the seas. "
78:39 a wind that p' away, and cometh 1980
103:16 For the wind p' over it, and it is 5674
144: 4 days are as a shadow that p' away. "
Pr 10:25 As the whirlwind p', so is the "
26:17 He that p' by, and meddleth with "
Ec 1: 4 One generation p' away, and *1980
Isa 29: 5 shall be as chaff that p' away: 5674
Jer 9:12 wilderness, that none p' through? "
13:24 scatter them as the stubble that p' "
18:16 that p' thereby shall be astonished, "
19: 8 that p' thereby shall be astonished "
Eze 35: 7 and cut off from it him that p' out "
Ho 13: 3 and as the early dew that p' away,1980
Mic 7:18 and p' by the transgression of the 5674
Zep 2:15 every one that p' by her shall hiss, "
3: 6 their streets waste, that none p' by:"
Zec 9: 8 army, because of him that p' by, * "
Lu 18:37 that Jesus of Nazareth p' by. 3928
1Co 7:31 the fashion of this world p' away. 3855
Eph 3:19 love of Christ, which p' knowledge,5235
Ph'p 4: 7 God, which p' all understanding, 5242
1Jo 2:17 the world p' away, and the lust 3855

passing See also COMPASSING; TRESPASSING.
J'g 19:18 We are p' from Beth-lehem-judah 5674
2Sa 1:26 was wonderful, p' the love of women.
15:24 people had done p' out of the city. 5674
2Ki 6:26 king of Israel was p' by upon the "
Ps 84: 6 Who p' through the valley of Baca "
Pr 7: 8 P' through the street near her "
Isa 31: 5 and p' over he will preserve it. * "
Eze 39:14 p' through the land to bury with * "
Lu 4:30 he p' through the midst of them 1330
Ac 5:15 the shadow of Peter p' by might *2064
8:40 p' through he preached in all the 1330
16: 8 p' by Mysia came down to Troas. 3928
27: 8 hardly p' it, came unto a place *3881

passion See also PASSIONS; COMPASSION.
Ac 1: 3 shewed himself alive after his p' 3958

passions See also COMPASSIONS.
Ac 14:15 We also are men of like p' with you,3663
Jas 5:17 a man subject to like p' as we are, "

passover See also PASSOVERS.
Ex 12:11 eat it in haste: it is the Lord's p'. 6453
21 to your families, and kill the p'. "
27 It is the sacrifice of the Lord's p', "
43 This is the ordinance of the p': "
48 and will keep the p' to the Lord, "
34:25 of the p' be left unto the morning. "
Le 23: 5 first month at even is the Lord's p'. "
Nu 9: 2 keep the p' at his appointed season."
4 Israel, that they should keep the p'. "
5 kept the p' on the fourteenth day "
6 could not keep the p' on that day: "
10 he shall keep the p' unto the Lord. "
12 ordinances of the p' they shall keep"
13 and forbeareth to keep the p', "
14 and will keep the p' unto the Lord; "
14 according to the ordinance of the p', "
28:16 first month is the p' of the Lord. "
33: 3 morrow after the p' the children "
De 16: 1 keep the p' unto the Lord thy God: "
2 shalt therefore sacrifice the p' "
5 Thou mayest not sacrifice the p' "
6 thou shalt sacrifice the p' at even, "
Jos 5:10 kept the p' on the fourteenth day "
11 land on the morrow after the p', "
2Ki 23:21 Keep the p' unto the Lord your God,"
22 there was not holden such a p' from"
23 this p' was holden to the Lord in "
2Ch 30: 1 to keep the p' unto the Lord God "
2 to keep the p' in the second month. "
2Ch 30: 5 to keep the p' unto the Lord God 6453
15 killed the p' on the fourteenth day "
18 yet did they eat the p' otherwise "
35: 1 Josiah kept a p' unto the Lord in "
1 killed the p' on the fourteenth day "
6 kill the p', and sanctify yourselves, "
7 and kids, all for the p' offerings, "
8 unto the priests for the p' offerings "
9 unto the Levites for p' offerings "
11 they killed the p', and the priests "
13 And they roasted the p' with fire "
16 to keep the p', and to offer burnt "
17 that were present kept the p' at that"
18 was no p' like to that kept in Israel "
18 keep such a p' as Josiah kept, "
19 the reign of Josiah was this p' kept."
Ezr 6:19 children of the captivity kept the p' "
20 killed the p' for all the children of "
Eze 45:21 of the month, ye shall have the p', "
M't 26: 2 after two days is the feast of the p',3957
17 we prepare for thee to eat the p'? "
18 I will keep the p' at thy house with "
19 them; and they made ready the p'. "
M'r 14: 1 two days was the feast of the p', "
12 when they killed the p', his disciples"
12 prepare that thou mayest eat the p'?"
14 I shall eat the p' with my disciples? "
16 them: and they made ready the p'. "
Lu 2:41 every year at the feast of the p'. "
22: 1 drew nigh, which is called the P'. "
7 bread, when the p' must be killed. "
8 Go and prepare us the p', that we "
11 I shall eat the p' with my disciples? "
13 them: and they made ready the p'. "
15 I have desired to eat this p' with you"
Joh 2:13 And the Jews' p' was at hand, and "
23 when he was in Jerusalem at the p', "
6: 4 the p', a feast of the Jews, was nigh."
11:55 And the Jews' p' was nigh at hand: "
55 went...up to Jerusalem before the p'."
12: 1 Jesus six days before the p' came to"
13: 1 Now before the feast of the p', when"
18:28 but that they might eat the p'. "
39 release unto you one at the p': "
19:14 And it was the preparation of the p'."
1Co 5: 7 Christ our p' is sacrificed for us: "
Heb 11:28 Through faith he kept the p', and "

passovers
2Ch 30:17 the charge of the killing of the p' 6453

past See also OVERPASSED; PASSED.
Ge 50: 4 the days of his mourning were p', 5674
Ex 21:29 to push with his horn in time p', 8032
36 the ox hath used to push in time p'," "
Nu 21:22 way, until we be p' thy borders. *5674
De 2:10 Emims dwelt therein in times p', *
4:32 ask now of the days that are p', 7223
42 and hated him not in times p'; and8032
19: 4 whom he hated not in time p'; "
6 as he hated him not in time p'. "
1Sa 15:32 Surely the bitterness of death is p'.5493
19: 7 was in his presence, as in times p'.*8032
2Sa 3:17 for David in times p' to be king "
5: 2 in time p', when Saul was king over"
11:27 And when the mourning was p', 5493
16: 1 when David was a little p' the top 5674
1Ki 18:29 came to pass when midday was p', "
1Ch 9:20 was the ruler over them in time p', "
11: 2 time p', even when Saul was king, 8032
Job 9:10 doeth great things p' finding out; 369
14:13 me secret, until thy wrath be p', 7725
17:11 My days are p', my purposes are 5674
29: 2 Oh that I were as in months p', *6924
Ps 90: 4 are but as yesterday when it is p', 5674
Ec 3:15 God requireth that which is p'. *7291
Ca 2:11 the winter is p', the rain is over 5674
Jer 8:20 harvest is p', the summer is ended, "
M't 14:15 place, and the time is now p'; 3928
M'r 16: 1 when the sabbath was p', Mary 1230
Lu 9:36 the voice was p', Jesus was found *1096
Ac 12:10 p' the first and the second ward, 1330
14:16 in times p' suffered all nations *3944
27: 9 because the fast was...already p', 3928
Ro 3:25 the remission of sins that are p', *4266
11:30 in times p' have not believed God,
33 and his ways p' finding out! 421
Ga 1:13 heard of my conversation in time p'
23 he which persecuted us in times p'*
5:21 as I have also told you in time p',*4302
Eph 2: 2 Wherein in time p' ye walked
3 all had our conversation in times p'*
11 that ye, being in time p' Gentiles *
4:19 Who being p' feeling have given 524
2Ti 2:18 that the resurrection is p' already;1096
Ph'm 11 in time p' was to thee unprofitable,*
Heb 1: 1 spake in time p' unto the fathers *3819
11:11 of a child when she was p' age, 3844
1Pe 2:10 Which in time p' were not a people,
4: 3 the time p' of our life may suffice 3928
1Jo 2: 8 because the darkness is p', and *3855
Re 9:12 One woe is p'; and, behold, there 565
11:14 The second woe is p'; and, behold, "

pastor See also PASTORS.
Jer 17:16 have not hastened from being a p'*7462

pastors
Jer 2: 8 p' also transgressed against me, *7462
3:15 will give you p' according to mine* "
10:21 p' are become brutish, and have * "
12:10 Many p'...destroyed my vineyard, * "
22:22 The wind shall eat up all thy p', * "
23: 1 Woe be unto the p' that destroy * "
2 against the p' that feed my people;*"
Eph 4:11 and some, p' and teachers; 4166

pasture See also PASTURES.
Ge 47: 4 servants have no p' for their flocks ;4829
1Ch 4:39 valley, to seek p' for their flocks. "
40 And they found fat p' and good, and "
41 there was p' there for their flocks. "
Job 39: 8 range of the mountains is his p'. "
Ps 74: 1 smoke against the sheep of thy p'?4830
79:13 we, thy people and sheep of thy p' "
95: 7 the people of his p', and the sheep "
100: 3 his people, and the sheep of his p'. "
Isa 32:14 a joy of wild asses, a p' of flocks; 4829
Jer 23: 1 and scatter the sheep of my p'! 4830
25:36 for the Lord hath spoiled their p'. "
La 1: 6 become like harts that find no p', 4829
Eze 34:14 I will feed them in a good p', and "
14 and in a fat p' shall they feed upon "
18 you to have eaten up the good p', "
31 ye my flock, the flock of my p', 4830
Ho 13: 6 According to their p', so were they "
Joe 1:18 perplexed, because they have no p';4829
Joh 10: 9 shall go in and out, and find p'. 3542

pastures
1Ki 4:23 and twenty oxen out of the p', 7471
Ps 23: 2 maketh me to lie down in green p':4999
65:12 drop upon the p' of the wilderness: "
13 The p' are clothed with flocks; 3733
Isa 30:23 day shall thy cattle feed in large p'. "
49: 9 their p' shall be in all high places.*4830
Eze 34:18 your feet the residue of your p'? *4829
45:15 hundred, out of the fat p' of Israel;4945
Joe 1:19 devoured the p' of the wilderness, 4999
20 devoured the p' of the wilderness. "
2:22 the p' of the wilderness do spring, "

Patara (*pat'-a-rah*)
Ac 21: 1 Rhodes, and from thence unto P': 3959

pate
Ps 7:16 shall come down upon his own p'. 6936

path See also PATHS; PATHWAY.
Ge 49:17 an adder in the p', that biteth the 734
Nu 22:24 angel of the Lord stood in a p' of *4934
Job 28: 7 is a p' which no fowl knoweth, and5410
30:13 They mar my p', they set forward "
41:32 He maketh a p' to shine after him; "
Ps 16:11 Thou wilt shew me the p' of life: 734
27:11 O Lord, and lead me in a plain p', "
77:19 sea, and thy p' in the great waters,*7635
119:35 Make me to go in the p' of thy 5410
105 my feet, and a light unto my p'. "
139: 3 Thou compassest my p' and my 734
142: 3 me, then thou knewest my p'. 5410
Pr 1:15 them; refrain thy foot from their p': "
2: 9 and equity; yea, every good p'. 4570
4:14 Enter not into the p' of the wicked,734
18 the p' of the just is as the shining "
26 Ponder the p' of thy feet, and let 4570
5: 6 shouldest ponder the p' of life, 734
Isa 26: 7 dost weigh the p' of the just. 4570
30:11 of the way, turn aside out of the p',734
40:14 taught him in the p' of judgment, "
43:16 and a p' in the mighty waters; 5410
Joe 2: 8 shall walk every one in his p': 4546

Pathros (*path'-ros*) See also PATHRUSIM.
Isa 11:11 and from Egypt, and from P', and6624
Jer 44: 1 at Noph, and in the country of P'. "
15 dwelt in the land of Egypt, in P', "
Eze 29:14 them to return into the land of P', "
30:14 And I will make P' desolate, and "

Pathrusim (*path-ru'-sim*)
Ge 10:14 And P', and Casluhim, (out of 6625
1Ch 1:12 And P', and Casluhim, (of whom "

paths
Job 6:18 p' of their way are turned aside; * 734
8:13 So are the p' of all that forget God; "
13:27 lookest narrowly unto all my p'; "
19: 8 and he hath set darkness in my p'.5410
24:13 thereof, nor abide in the p' thereof. "
33:11 the stocks, he marketh all my p'. 734
38:20 know the p' to the house thereof? 5410
Ps 8: 8 passeth through the p' of the seas. 734
17: 4 me from the p' of the destroyer. * "
5 Hold up my goings in thy p', that 4570
23: 3 me in the p' of righteousness for "
25: 4 thy ways, O Lord; teach me thy p'. 734
10 All the p' of the Lord are mercy "
65:11 goodness; and thy p' drop fatness.4570
Pr 2: 8 He keepeth the p' of judgment, and734
13 leave the p' of uprightness, to walk "
15 and they froward in their p': 4570
18 death, and her p' unto the dead. "
19 take they hold of the p' of life. 734
20 and keep the p' of the righteous. "
3: 6 him, and he shall direct thy p'. "
17 and all her p' are peace. 5410
4:11 wisdom; I have led thee in right p'.4570
7:25 her ways, go not astray in her p'. 5410
8: 2 by the way in the places of the p'. "
20 in the midst of the p' of judgment: "
Isa 2: 3 his ways, and we will walk in his p':734
3:12 err, and destroy the way of thy p'. "
42:16 in p' that they have not known: 5410
58:12 The restorer of p' to dwell in. "
59: 7 and destruction are in their p'. 4546
8 they have made them crooked p': 5410
Jer 6:16 and ask for the old p', where is the "
18:15 in their ways from the ancient p', 7635
15 walk in p', in a way not cast up; *5410
La 3: 9 stone, he hath made my p' crooked. "
Ho 2: 6 wall, that she shall not find her p'. "
Mic 4: 2 ways, and we will walk in his p': 734
M't 3: 3 of the Lord, make his p' straight. 5147
M'r 1: 3 of the Lord, make his p' straight. "
Lu 3: 4 of the Lord, make his p' straight. "
Heb 12:13 made straight p' for your feet, lest5163

pathway
Pr 12:28 in the p' thereof...is no death.1870,5410

patience
M't 18:26 Lord, have p' with me, and I will 3114
29 Have p' with me, and I will pay "
Lu 8:15 it, and bring forth fruit with p'. 5281
21:19 In your p' possess ye your souls. "
Ro 5: 3 that tribulation worketh p'; "
4 And p', experience; and experience, "
8:25 not, then do we with p' wait for it. "
15: 4 p' and comfort of the scriptures "
5 Now the God of p' and consolation "
2Co 6: 4 the ministers of God, in much p', in "
12:12 were wrought among you in all p', "
Col 1:11 unto all p' and longsuffering with "
1Th 1: 3 and p' of hope in our Lord Jesus "
2Th 1: 4 for your p' and faith in all your "
1Ti 6:11 godliness, faith, love, p', meekness. "
2Ti 3:10 faith, longsuffering, charity, p', "
Tit 2: 2 sound in faith, in charity, in p'. "
Heb 6:12 faith and p' inherit the promises. 3115
10:36 For ye have need of p', that, after 5281
12: 1 let us run with p' the race that is "
Jas 1: 3 the trying of your faith worketh p'. "
4 But let p' have her perfect work, "
5: 7 and hath long p' for it, until he *3114
10 of suffering affliction, and of p'. 3115
11 Ye have heard of the p' of Job, 5281
2Pe 1: 6 temperance p'; and to p' godliness; "
Re 1: 9 the kingdom and p' of Jesus Christ, "
2: 2 works, and thy labour, and thy p', "
3 hast p', and for my name's sake "
19 faith, and thy p', and thy works; "
3:10 thou hast kept the word of my p', "
13:10 it the p' and the faith of the saints. "
14:12 Here is the p' of the saints: here "

patient
Ec 7: 8 p' in spirit is better than the proud 750
Ro 2: 7 by p' continuance in well doing *5281
12:12 in hope; p' in tribulation; 5278
1Th 5:14 the weak, be p' toward all men. *3114
2Th 3: 5 and into the p' waiting for Christ.*5281
1Ti 3: 3 p', not a brawler, not covetous; *1933
2Ti 2:24 gentle unto all men, apt to teach, p',*420
Jas 5: 7 Be p' therefore, brethren, unto the3114
8 Be ye also p'; stablish your hearts: "

patiently
Ps 37: 7 in the Lord, and wait p' for him: 2342
40: 1 I waited p' for the Lord; and he 6960
Ac 26: 3 I beseech thee to hear me p'. 3116
Heb 6:15 And so, after he had p' endured, 3114
1Pe 2:20 for your faults, ye shall take it p'? 5278
20 ye take it p', this is acceptable with "

Patmos (*pat'-mos*)
Re 1: 9 was in the isle that is called P', 3963

patriarch See also PATRIARCHS.
Ac 2:29 speak unto you of the p' David, 3966
Heb 7: 4 the p' Abraham gave the tenth of "

patriarchs
Ac 7: 8 and Jacob begat the twelve p'. 3966
9 And the p', moved with envy, sold "

patrimony
De 18: 8 which cometh of the sale of his p'.5921,1

Patrobas (*pat'-ro-bas*)
Ro 16:14 P', Hermes, and the brethren 3969

pattern See also PATTERNS.
Ex 25: 9 after the p' of the tabernacle, and 8403
9 the p' of all the instruments thereof, "
40 p',...shewed thee in the mount. "
Nu 8: 4 the p' which the Lord had shewed 4758
Jos 22:28 the p' of the altar of the Lord, 8403
2Ki 16:10 fashion of the altar, and the p' of it, "
1Ch 28:11 p' of the porch, and of the houses "
12 the p' of all that he had by the spirit, "
18 and gold for the p' of the chariot of "
19 me, even all the works of this p'. "
Eze 43:10 and let them measure the p'. 8508
1Ti 1:16 p' to them which should hereafter*5296
Tit 2: 7 showing thyself a p' of good works:*5179
Heb 8: 5 the p' shewed to thee in the mount. "

patterns
Heb 9:23 p' of things in the heavens should*5262

Pau (*pa'-u*) See also PAI.
Ge 36:39 and the name of his city was P'; 6464

Paul (*pawl*) See also PAUL'S; PAULUS; SAUL.
Ac 13: 9 Saul, (who also is called P',) filled 3972
13 when P' and his company loosed "
16 Then P' stood up, and beckoning "
43 followed P' and Barnabas: who, "
45 things which were spoken by P', "
46 Then P' and Barnabas waxed bold, "
50 raised persecution against P' and "
14: 9 The same heard P' speak: who "
11 the people saw what P' had done, "
12 and P', Mercurius, because he was "
14 when the apostles, Barnabas and P', "
19 having stoned P', drew him out of "
15: 2 P' and Barnabas had no small "
2 determined that P' and Barnabas, "
12 gave audience to Barnabas and P', "
22 to Antioch with P' and Barnabas; "
25 with our beloved Barnabas and P', "
35 P' also and Barnabas continued in "
36 P' said unto Barnabas, Let us go "
38 P' thought not good to take him "
40 And P' chose Silas, and departed, "
16: 3 would P' have to go forth with him; "
9 vision appeared to P' in the night; "
14 the things which were spoken of P'. "
17 The same followed P' and us, and "
Ac 16:18 But P', being grieved, turned and 3972
19 they caught P' and Silas, and drew "
25 at midnight P' and Silas prayed, "
28 P' cried with a loud voice, saying, "
29 and fell down before P' and Silas, "
36 this saying to P', The magistrates "
37 But P' said unto them, They have "
17: 2 And P', as his manner was, went in "
4 and consorted with P' and Silas; "
10 sent away P' and Silas by night "
13 God was preached of P' at Berea, "
14 sent away P' to go as it were to the "
15 they that conducted P' brought him "
16 while P' waited for them at Athens, "
22 P' stood in the midst of Mars' hill, "
33 So P' departed from among them. "
18: 1 After these things P' departed from* "
5 P' was pressed in the spirit, and "
9 spake the Lord to P' in the night by "
12 with one accord against P', and "
14 when P' was now about to open his "
18 And P' after this tarried there yet a "
19: 1 P' having passed through the upper "
4 Then said P', John verily baptized "
6 when P' had laid his hands upon "
11 miracles by the hands of P': "
13 you by Jesus whom P' preacheth. "
15 Jesus I know, and P' I know; but "
21 P' purposed in the spirit, when he "
26 this P' hath persuaded and turned "
30 And when P' would have entered in "
20: 1 P' called unto him the disciples, "
7 P' preached unto them, ready to "
9 as P' was long preaching, he sunk "
10 And P' went down, and fell on him, "
13 there intending to take in P': for "
16 P'...determined to sail by Ephesus, "
21: 4 who said to P' through the Spirit, "
13 Then P' answered, What mean ye "
18 P' went in with us unto James; "
26 P' took the men, and the next day "
29 P' had brought into the temple.) "
30 they took P', and drew him out of "
32 the soldiers, they left beating of P'. "
37 as P' was to be led into the castle, "
39 But P' said, I am a man which am "
40 P' stood on the stairs, and beckoned "
22:25 P' said unto the centurion that "
28 And P' said, But I was free born. "
30 and brought P' down, and set him "
23: 1 P', earnestly beholding the council, "
3 Then said P' unto him, God shall "
5 Then said P', I wist not, brethren, "
6 P' perceived that the one part were "
10 lest P' should have been pulled in "
11 Be of good cheer, P': and said, * "
12 eat nor drink till they had killed P'. "
14 eat nothing until we have slain P'. "
16 entered into the castle, and told P'. "
17 P' called one of the centurions unto "
18 P' the prisoner called me unto him, "
20 wouldest bring down P' to morrow "
24 that they may set P' on, and bring "
31 took P', and brought him by night "
33 presented P' also before him. "
24: 1 informed the governor against P'. "
10 Then P', after that the governor "
23 commanded a centurion to keep P',* "
24 he sent for P', and heard him "
26 should have been given him of P', "
27 the Jews a pleasure, left P' bound. "
25: 2 the Jews informed him against P', "
4 P' should be kept at Cæsarea, and "
6 seat commanded P' to be brought. "
7 grievous complaints against P', * "
9 answered P', and said, Wilt thou go "
10 Then said P', I stand at Cæsar's "
19 dead, whom P' affirmed to be alive. "
21 P' had appealed to be reserved "
23 morrow...P' was brought forth. "
26: 1 Then Agrippa said unto P', Thou "
1 P' stretched forth the hand, and "
24 P', thou art beside thyself; much "
28 Agrippa said unto P', Almost thou "
29 P' said, I would to God, that not "
27: 1 they delivered P' and certain other "
3 Julius courteously entreated P', "
9 already past, P' admonished them, "
11 things which were spoken by P'. "
21 P' stood forth in the midst of them, "
24 Fear not, P'; thou must be brought "
31 P' said to the centurion and to the "
33 P' besought them all to take meat, "
43 the centurion, willing to save P', "
28: 3 P' had gathered a bundle of sticks, "
8 to whom P' entered in, and prayed, "
15 whom when P' saw, he thanked "
16 P' was suffered to dwell by himself "
17 days P' called the chief of the Jews* "
25 after that P' had spoken one word, "
30 P' dwelt two whole years in his * "
Ro 1: 1 P', a servant of Jesus Christ, called "
1Co 1: 1 P', called to be an apostle of Jesus "
12 every one of you saith, I am of P'; "
13 was P' crucified for you? or were "
13 were ye baptized in the name of P'? "
3: 4 For while one saith, I am of P'; "
5 Who then is P', and who is Apollos, "
22 Whether P', or Apollos, or Cephas, "
16:21 of me P' with mine own hand. "
2Co 1: 1 P', an apostle of Jesus Christ by the "
10: 1 Now I P' myself beseech you by "
Ga 1: 1 P', an apostle, (not of men, neither "
5: 2 Behold, I P' say unto you, that if "
Eph 1: 1 P', an apostle of Jesus Christ by "
3: 1 For this cause I P', the prisoner of "

Ph'p 1: 1 P· and Timotheus, the servants of 3972
Col 1: 1 P·, an apostle of Jesus Christ by "
23 whereof I P· am made a minister: "
4:18 salutation by the hand of me P·. "
1Th 1: 1 P·, and Silvanus, and Timotheus, "
2:18 you, even I P·, once and again; "
2Th 1: 1 P·, and Silvanus, and Timotheus, "
3:17 The salutation of P· with mine own "
1Ti 1: 1 P·, an apostle of Jesus Christ by "
2Ti 1: 1 P·, an apostle of Jesus Christ by "
subscr. P· was brought before Nero "
Tit 1: 1 P·, a servant of God, and an "
Ph'm 1 P·, a prisoner of Jesus Christ, and "
9 being such an one as P· the aged, "
19 I P· have written it with mine own "
2Pe 3:15 even as our beloved brother P· "

Paul's (*pawls*)
Ac 19:29 P· companions in travel, they 3972
20:37 fell on P· neck, and kissed him, "
21: 8 that were of P· company departed,* "
11 took P· girdle, and bound his own "
23:16 And when P· sister's son heard of "
25:14 declared P· cause unto the king, "

Paulus See also PAUL.
Ac 13: 7 deputy of the country, Sergius P·, 3972

paved
Ex 24:10 were a p· work of a sapphire stone, 3840
Ca 3:10 midst thereof being p· with love, 7528

pavement
2Ki 16:17 it, and put it upon a p· of stones. 4837
2Ch 7: 3 faces to the ground upon the p·, 7531
Es 1: 6 a p· of red, and blue, and white, "
Eze 40:17 p· made for the court round about: "
17 thirty chambers were upon the p·. "
18 And the p· by the side of the gates "
18 of the gates was the lower p·. "
42: 3 p· which was for the utter court, "
Joh 19:13 in a place that is called the P·, 3038

pavilion See also PAVILIONS.
Ps 18:11 his p· round about him were dark 5521
27: 5 he shall hide me in his p·: in the 5520
31:20 shalt keep them secretly in a p· 5521
Jer 43:10 shall spread his royal p· over them. 8237

pavilions
2Sa 22:12 he made darkness p· round about 5521
1Ki 20:12 drinking, he and the kings in the p·, "
16 drinking himself drunk in the p·, "

paw See also PAWETH; PAWS.
1Sa 17:37 delivered me out of...p· of the lion, 3027
37 and out of the p· of the bear, he will "

paweth
Job 39:21 He p· in the valley, and rejoiceth 2658

paws
Le 11:27 And whatsoever goeth upon his p·, 3709

pay See also PAID; PAYED; PAYETH; REPAY.
Ex 21:19 he shall p· for the loss of his time, 5414
22 he shall p· as the judges determine. "
36 he shall surely p· ox for ox; and 7999
22: 7 thief be found, let him p· double. "
9 p· double unto his neighbour. "
17 p· money according to the dowry 8254
Nu 20:19 thy water, then I will p· for it: 5414, 4377
De 23:21 thou shalt not slack to p· it: for 7999
2Sa 15: 7 let me go and p· my vow, which I "
1Ki 20:39 else thou shalt p· a talent of silver. 8254
2Ki 4: 7 Go, sell the oil, and p· thy debt, 7999
2Ch 8: 8 make to p· tribute until this day. *5927
27: 5 children of Ammon p· unto him, *7725
Ezr 4:13 will they not p· toll, tribute, and 5415
Es 3: 9 will p· ten thousand talents of silver 8254
4: 7 that Haman had promised to p· to "
Job 22:27 thee, and thou shalt p· thy vows. 7999
Ps 22:25 p· my vows before them that fear "
50:14 and p· thy vows unto the most High: "
66:13 offerings: I will p· thee my vows, "
76:11 Vow, and p· unto the Lord your God: "
116:14, 18, p· my vows unto the Lord now "
Pr 19:17 he hath given will he p· him again. "
22:27 If thou hast nothing to p·, why "
Ec 5: 4 a vow unto God, defer not to p· it; "
4 p· that which thou hast vowed. "
5 thou shouldest vow and not p·. "
Jon 2: 9 I will p· that that I have vowed. "
M't 17:24 Doth not your master p· tribute? 5055
18:25 forasmuch as he had not to p·, his 591
26 with me, and I will p· thee all. "
28 saying, P· me that thou owest. "
29 with me, and I will p· thee all. "
30 prison, till he should p· the debt. "
34 should p· all that was due unto him. "
23:23 for ye p· tithe of mint and anise and *586
Lu 7:42 when they had nothing to p·, he 591
Ro 13: 6 For this cause p· ye tribute also: 5055

payed See also PAID; REPAYED.
Pr 7:14 me; this day have I p· my vows. *7999
Heb 7: 9 tithes, p· tithes in Abraham. *1183

payeth See also REPAYETH.
Ps 37:21 borroweth, and p· not again: 7999

payment
M't 18:25 that he had, and p· to be made. 591

Pazzez See BETH-PAZZEZ.

peace See also PEACEABLE; PEACEMAKERS.
Ge 15:15 thou shalt go to thy fathers in p·; 7965
24:21 man wondering at her held his p·, 2790
26:29 and have sent thee away in p·: 7965
31 and they departed from him in p·. "
28:21 again to my father's house in p·; "
34: 5 Jacob held his p· until they were 2790
41:16 give Pharaoh an answer of p·. 7965
43:23 And he said, P· be to you, fear not: "
44:17 get you up in p· unto your father. "
Ex 4:18 And Jethro said to Moses, Go in p·. "
14:14 you, and ye shall hold your p·. 2790
18:23 shall also go to their place in p·. 7965
20:24 offerings, and thy p· offerings, 8002
24: 5 sacrificed p· offerings of oxen unto "
29:28 of the sacrifice of their p· offerings, "
32: 6 offerings, and brought p· offerings; "
Le 3: 1 be a sacrifice of p· offering, if he "
3 of the sacrifice of the p· offering "
6 a sacrifice of p· offering unto the "
9 of the sacrifice of the p· offering "
4:10 of the sacrifice of p· offerings: and "
26 fat of the sacrifice of p· offerings: "
31 off the sacrifice of p· offerings: and "
35 the sacrifice of the p· offerings; "
6:12 thereon the fat of the p· offerings. "
7:11 law of the sacrifice of p· offerings, "
13 of thanksgiving of his p· offerings. "
14 the blood of the p· offerings. "
15, 18 of the sacrifice of his p· offerings "
20, 21 of the sacrifice of p· offerings, "
29 the sacrifice of his p· offerings unto "
29 of the sacrifice of his p· offerings. "
32 the sacrifices of your p· offerings. "
33 the blood of the p· offerings, and "
34 the sacrifices of their p· offerings, "
37 of the sacrifice of the p· offerings; "
9: 4 bullock and a ram for p· offerings, "
18 ram for a sacrifice of p· offerings, "
22 the burnt offering, and p· offerings. "
10: 3 glorified. And Aaron held his p·. 1826
14 out of the sacrifices of p· offerings 8002
17: 5 them for p· offerings unto the Lord. "
19: 5 ye offer a sacrifice of p· offerings "
22:21 offereth a sacrifice of p· offerings "
23:19 year for a sacrifice of p· offerings. "
26: 6 I will give p· in the land, and ye 7965
Nu 6:14 without blemish for p· offerings, 8002
17 ram for a sacrifice of p· offerings "
18 the sacrifice of the p· offerings. "
26 upon thee, and give thee p·. 7965
7:17, 23, 29, 35, 41, 47, 53, 59, 65, 71, 77, 83
sacrifice of p· offerings, two oxen, 8002
88 for the sacrifice of the p· offerings "
10:10 the sacrifices of your p· offerings; "
15: 8 vow, or p· offerings unto the Lord: "
25:12 give unto him my covenant of p·: 7965
29:39 offerings, and for your p· offerings. 8002
30: 4 her father shall hold his p· at her; 2790
7 held his p· at her in the day that "
11 held his p· at her, and disallowed her "
14 hold his p· at her from day to day; "
14 he held his p· at her in the day "
De 2:26 king of Heshbon with words of p·, 7965
20:10 against it, then proclaim p· unto it. "
11 if it make thee answer of p·, and "
12 if it will make no p· with thee, but 7999
23: 6 Thou shalt not seek their p· nor 7965
27: 7 And thou shalt offer p· offerings, 8002
29:19 I shall have p·, though I walk in 7965
Jos 8:31 Lord, and sacrificed p· offerings. 8002
9:15 Joshua made p· with them, and 7965
10: 1 Gibeon had made p· with Israel, 7999
4 for it hath made p· with Joshua "
21 to Joshua at Makkedah in p·: 7965
11:19 There was not a city that made p· 7999
22:23 or if to offer p· offerings thereon, 8002
27 sacrifices, and with our p· offerings; "
J'g 4:17 was p· between Jabin the king of 7965
6:23 him, P· be unto thee; fear not: "
8: 9 When I come again in p·, I will "
11:31 I return in p· from the children of "
18: 6 the priest said unto them, Go in p·: "
19 they said unto him, Hold thy p·, 2790
19:20 the old man said, P· be with thee; 7965
20:26 and p· offerings before the Lord. 8002
21: 4 burnt offerings and p· offerings. "
1Sa 1:17 Eli answered and said, Go in p·: 7965
7:14 p· between Israel and the Amorites. "
10: 8 sacrifice sacrifices of p· offerings: 8002
27 no presents. But he held his p·. 2790
11:15 sacrificed sacrifices of p· offerings 8002
13: 9 offering to me, and p· offerings. "
20: 7 is well; thy servant shall have p·: 7965
13 away, that thou mayest go in p·: "
21 for there is p· to thee, and no hurt; "
42 Jonathan said to David, Go in p·, "
25: 6 in prosperity, P· be both to thee, "
6 and p· be to thine house, "
6 and p· be unto all that thou hast. "
35 Go up in p· to thine house; see, I "
29: 7 now return, and go in p·, that thou "
2Sa 3:21 Abner away; and he went in p·. "
22 him away, and he was gone in p·. "
23 him away, and he is gone in p·. "
6:17 and p· offerings before the Lord. 8002
18 burnt offerings and p· offerings, "
10:19 made p· with Israel, and served 7999
13:20 but hold now thy p·, my sister: he 2790
15: 9 the king said unto him, Go in p·. 7965
27 return into the city in p·, and your "
17: 3 so all the people shall be in p·. "
19:24 until the day he came again in p·. "
30 again in p· unto his own house. "
24:25 burnt offerings and p· offerings. 8002
1Ki 2: 5 shed the blood of war in p·, and 7965
6 head go down to the grave in p·. "
33 there be p· for ever from the Lord. "
3:15 offered p· offerings, and made a 8002
4:24 and he had p· on all sides round 7965
5:12 p· between Hiram and Solomon; "
8:63 offered a sacrifice of p· offerings, 8002
64 and the fat of the p· offerings: "
1Ki 8:64 and the fat of the p· offerings. 8002
9:25 p· offerings upon the altar which "
20:18 Whether they be come out for p·, 7965
22:17 every man to his house in p·. "
27 of affliction, until I come in p·. "
28 If thou return at all in p·, the Lord "
44 Jehoshaphat made p· with the 7999
2Ki 2: 3, 5 Yea, I know it; hold ye your p·. 2814
5:19 And he said unto him, Go in p·. 7965
7: 9 good tidings, and we hold our p·: 2814
9:17 them, and let him say, Is it p·? 7965
18 said, Thus saith the king, Is it p·? "
18 What hast thou to do with p·? "
19 said, Thus saith the king, Is it p·? "
19 What hast thou to do with p·? "
22 Jehu, that he said, Is it p·, Jehu? "
22 And he answered, What p·, so long "
31 Had Zimri p·, who slew his master? "
16:13 the blood of his p· offerings, 8002
18:36 But the people held their p·, and 2790
20:19 good, if p· and truth be in my days? 7965
22:20 be gathered into thy grave in p·; "
1Ch 12:18 son of Jesse: p·, p· be unto thee, "
18 thee, and p· be to thine helpers; "
16: 1 offered...p· offerings before God. 8002
2 burnt offerings and the p· offerings, "
19:19 made p· with David, and became 7999
21:26 burnt offerings and p· offerings, 8002
22: 9 give p· and quietness unto Israel 7965
2Ch 7: 7 and the fat of p· offerings, 8002
15: 5 was no p· to him that went out, 7965
18:16 return...every man to his house in p·. "
26 of affliction, until I return in p·. "
27 If thou certainly return in p·, then "
19: 1 of Judah returned to his house in p· "
29:35 with the fat of the p· offerings, 8002
30:22 seven days, offering p· offerings, "
31: 2 burnt offerings and for p· offerings, "
33:16 p· offerings and thank offerings, "
34:28 be gathered to thy grave in p·, 7965
Ezr 4:17 unto the rest beyond the river, P·, 8001
5: 7 thus; Unto Darius the king, all p·. "
7:12 unto Ezra the priest,...perfect p·, "
9:12 nor seek their p· or their wealth 7965
Ne 5: 8 Then held they their p·, and found 2790
8:11 Hold your p·, for the day is holy; 2013
Es 4:14 if thou altogether holdest thy p· 2790
9:30 with words of p· and truth, 7965
10: 3 and speaking p· to all his seed. "
Job 5:23 of the field shall be at p· with thee 7999
24 that thy tabernacle shall be in p·; 7965
11: 3 thy lies make men hold their p·? 2790
13: 5 ye would altogether hold your p·! "
13 Hold your p·, let me alone, that I "
22:21 now thyself with him, and be at p·: 7999
25: 2 he maketh p· in his high places. 7965
29:10 The nobles held their p·, and their *6963
33:31 me: hold thy p·, and I will speak. 2790
33 hold thy p·, and I shall teach thee "
Ps 4: 8 both lay me down in p·, and sleep: 7965
7: 4 unto him that was at p· with me; 7999
28: 3 which speak p· to their neighbours, 7965
29:11 Lord will bless his people with p·. "
34:14 and do good; seek p·, and pursue it. "
35:20 For they speak not p·: but they "
37:11 themselves in the abundance of p·. "
37 for the end of that man is p·. "
39: 2 dumb with silence, I held my p·, 2814
12 hold not thy p· at my tears: for I 2790
55:18 He that delivered my soul in p· 7965
20 against such as be at p· with him: "
72: 3 mountains...bring p· to the people, "
7 abundance of p· so long as the moon "
83: 1 hold not thy p·, and be not still, 2790
85: 8 he will speak p· unto his people, 7965
10 righteousness and p· have kissed "
109: 1 Hold not thy p·, O God of my 2790
119:165 Great p· have they which love 7965
120: 6 long dwelt with him that hateth p·. "
7 I am for p·: but when I speak, they "
122: 6 Pray for the p· of Jerusalem: they "
7 P· be within thy walls, and "
8 I will now say, P· be within thee. "
125: 5 iniquity: but p· shall be upon Israel. "
128: 6 children, and p· upon Israel. "
147:14 He maketh p· in thy borders, and "
Pr 3: 2 long life, and p·, shall they add to "
17 and all her paths are p·. "
7:14 I have p· offerings with me; this 8002
11:12 of understanding holdeth his p·. 2790
12:20 but to the counsellers of p· is joy. 7965
16: 7 his enemies to be at p· with him. 7999
17:28 Even a fool, when he holdeth his p·, 2790
Ec 3: 8 a time of war, and a time of p·. 7965
Isa 9: 6 Father, The Prince of P·. "
7 increase of his government and p· "
26: 3 wilt keep him in perfect p·, whose "
12 Lord, thou wilt ordain p· for us: "
27: 5 that he may make p· with me; "
5 me; and he shall make p· with me. "
32:17 work of righteousness shall be p·; "
33: 7 the ambassadors of p· shall weep "
36:21 they held their p·, and answered 2790
38:17 for p· I had great bitterness: but 7965
39: 8 shall be p· and truth in my days. "
42:14 I have long time holden my p·; 2814
45: 7 I make p·, and create evil: I the 7965
48:18 then had thy p· been as a river, and "
22 There is no p·, saith the Lord, unto "
52: 7 good tidings, that publisheth p·; "
53: 5 chastisement of our p· was upon "
54:10 the covenant of my p· be removed, "
13 great shall be the p· of thy children. "
55:12 with joy, and be led forth with p·: "
57: 2 He shall enter into p·: they shall "
11 have not I held my p· even of old, 2814

Isa 57:19 *P*, *p* to him that is far off, and to 7965
21 There is no *p*, saith my God, to the "
59: 8 The way of *p* they know not; and "
8 goeth therein shall not know *p*. "
60:17 I will also make thy officers *p*, and "
62: 1 Zion's sake will I not hold my *p*, 2814
6 never hold their *p* day nor night: "
64:12 wilt thou hold thy *p*, and afflict us "
66:12 I will extend *p* to her like a river, 7965
Jer 4:10 Ye shall have *p*; whereas the sword "
19 I cannot hold my *p*, because thou 2790
6:14 saying, *P*, *p*; when there is no *p*. 7965
8:11 saying, *P*, *p*; when there is no *p*. "
15 We looked for *p*, but no good came; "
12: 5 if in the land of *p*, wherein thou "
12 of the land: no flesh shall have *p*. "
14:13 will give you assured *p* in this place. "
19 looked for *p*, and there is no good; "
16: 5 taken away my *p* from this people, "
23:17 Lord hath said, Ye shall have *p*; "
28: 9 prophet which prophesieth of *p*, "
29: 7 seek the *p* of the city whither I have "
7 in the *p* thereof shall ye have *p*. "
11 thoughts of *p*, and not of evil, to "
30: 5 of trembling, of fear, and not of *p*. "
33: 6 the abundance of *p* and truth. "
34: 5 But thou shalt die in *p*: and with "
43:12 he shall go forth from thence in *p*. "
La 3:17 removed my soul far off from *p*: "
Eze 7:25 they shall seek *p*, and there shall "
13:10 saying, *P*; and there was no *p*; "
16 which see visions of *p* for her, and "
16 there is no *p*, saith the Lord God. "
34:25 make with them a covenant of *p*, "
37:26 make a covenant of *p* with them; "
43:27 the altar, and your *p* offerings; 8002
45:15 burnt offering, and for *p* offerings, "
17 burnt offering, and the *p* offerings, "
46: 2 burnt offering and his *p* offerings, "
12 burnt offering or *p* offerings "
12 burnt offering and his *p* offerings, "
Da 4: 1 earth: *P* be multiplied unto you. 8001
6:25 earth: *P* be multiplied unto you. "
8:25 and by *p* shall destroy many: *7962
10:19 *p* be unto thee, be strong, yea, be 7965
Am 5:22 the *p* offerings of your fat beasts. 8002
Ob 7 men that were at *p* with thee have 7965
Mic 3: 5 bite with their teeth, and cry, *P*; "
5: 5 this man shall be the *p*, when the "
Na 1:15 good tidings, that publisheth *p*! "
Zep 1: 7 Hold thy *p* at the presence of the 2013
Hag 2: 9 in this place will I give *p*, saith 7965
Zec 6:13 the counsel of *p* shall be between "
8:10 was there any *p* to him that went "
16 execute...judgment of truth and *p* "
19 therefore love the truth and *p*. "
9:10 he shall speak *p* unto the heathen: "
Mal 2: 5 covenant...with him of life and *p*; "
6 he walked with me in *p* and equity, "
M't 10:13 worthy, let your *p* come upon it: *1515*
13 worthy, let your *p* return to you. "
34 that I am come to send *p* on earth: "
34 I came not to send *p*, but a sword. "
20:31 because they should hold their *p*: *4623*
26:63 But Jesus held his *p*. And the high "
M'r 1:25 Hold thy *p*, and come out of him. *5392*
3: 4 or to kill? But they held their *p*. *4623*
4:39 and said unto the sea, *P*, be still. "
5:34 go in *p*, and be whole of thy plague. *1515*
9:34 But they held their *p*: for by the *4623*
50 and have *p* one with another. *1518*
10:48 him that he should hold his *p*: *4623*
14:61 held his *p*, and answered nothing. "
Lu 1:79 to guide our feet into the way of *p*. *1515*
2:14 on earth *p*, good will toward men. "
29 lettest thou thy servant depart in *p*, "
4:35 Hold thy *p*, and come out of him. *5392*
7:50 faith hath saved thee; go in *p*. *1515*
8:48 hath made thee whole; go in *p*. "
10: 5 enter, first say, *P* be to this house. "
6 And if the son of *p* be there, your "
6 your *p* shall rest upon it: if not, it "
11:21 his palace, his goods are in *p*: "
12:51 that I am come to give *p* on earth? "
14: 4 And they held their *p*. And he *2270*
32 and desireth conditions of *p*. *1515*
18:39 him, that he should hold his *p*: *4623*
19:38 *p* in heaven,...glory in the highest. *1515*
40 if these should hold their *p*, the *4623*
42 things which belong unto thy *p*! *1515*
20:26 at his answer, and held their *p*. *4601*
24:36 saith unto them, *P* be unto you. *1515*
Joh 14:27 *P* I leave with you, my *p* I give "
16:33 you, that in me ye might have *p*. "
20:19 saith unto them, *P* be unto you. "
21 Jesus to them again, *P* be unto you: "
26 the midst, and said, *P* be unto you. "
Ac 10:36 preaching *p* by Jesus Christ: "
11:18 held their *p*, and glorified God, *2270*
12:17 with the hand to hold their *p*, *4601*
20 desired *p*; because their country *1515*
15:13 after they had held their *p*, James *4601*
33 were let go in *p* from the brethren *1515*
16:36 now therefore depart, and go in *p*. "
18: 9 but speak, and hold not thy *p*: *4623*
Ro 1: 7 Grace to you and *p* from God our *1515*
2:10 But glory, honour, and *p*, to every "
3:17 the way of *p* have they not known: "
5: 1 we have *p* with God through our "
8: 6 be spiritually minded is life and *p*. "
10:15 that preach the gospel of *p*, and * "
14:17 but righteousness, and *p*, and joy "
19 after the things which make for *p*, "
15:13 you with all joy and *p* in believing, "
33 Now the God of *p* be with you all. "
16:20 God of *p* shall bruise Satan under "
1Co 1: 3 Grace be unto you, and *p*, from God *1515*
7:15 cases: but God hath called us to *p*. "
14:30 sitteth by, let the first hold his *p*. **4601*
33 the author of confusion, but of *p*, *1515*
16:11 but conduct him forth in *p*, that he "
2Co 1: 2 to you and *p* from God our Father, "
13:11 comfort, be of one mind, live in *p*; *1518*
11 of love and *p* shall be with you. *1515*
Ga 1: 3 Grace be to you and *p* from God "
5:22 the fruit of the Spirit is love, joy, *p*, "
6:16 *p* be on them, and mercy, and upon "
Eph 1: 2 Grace be to you, and *p*, from God "
2:14 For he is our *p*, who hath made "
15 twain one new man, so making *p*; "
17 preached *p* to you which were afar "
4: 3 unity of the Spirit in the bond of *p*. "
6:15 the preparation of the gospel of *p*; "
23 *P* be to the brethren, and love "
Ph'p 1: 2 Grace be unto you, and *p*, from God "
4: 7 the *p* of God, which passeth all "
9 and the God of *p* shall be with you. "
Col 1: 2 Grace be unto you, and *p*, from God "
20 made *p* through the blood of his *1517*
3:15 the *p* of God rule in your hearts, *1515*
1Th 1: 1 Grace be unto you, and *p*, from God "
5: 3 when they shall say, *P* and safety; "
13 And be at *p* among yourselves. *1518*
23 And the very God of *p* sanctify you *1515*
2Th 1: 2 Grace unto you, and *p*, from God "
3:16 the Lord of *p* himself give you *p* "
1Ti 1: 2 mercy, and *p*, from God our Father "
2Ti 1: 2 mercy, and *p*, from God the Father "
2:22 righteousness, faith, charity, *p*, "
Tit 1: 4 mercy, and *p*, from God the Father "
Ph'm 3 Grace to you, and *p*, from God our "
Heb 7: 2 King of Salem, which is, King of *p*; "
11:31 she had received the spies with *p*. "
12:14 Follow *p* with all men, and "
13:20 the God of *p*, that brought again "
Jas 2:16 Depart in *p*, be ye warmed and "
3:18 is sown in *p* of them that make *p*. "
1Pe 1: 2 Christ: Grace unto you, and *p*, be "
3:11 good; let him seek *p*, and ensue it. "
5:14 *P* be with you all that are in Christ "
2Pe 1: 2 Grace and *p* be multiplied unto "
3:14 that ye may be found of him in *p*, "
2Jo 3 Grace be with you, mercy, and *p*, "
3Jo 14 *P* be to thee. Our friends salute "
Jude 2 you, and *p*, and love, be multiplied. "
Re 1: 4 Grace be unto you, and *p*, from him "
6: 4 thereon to take *p* from the earth, "

peaceable
Ge 34:21 These men are *p* with us; 8003
2Sa 20:19 that are *p* and faithful in Israel: 7999
1Ch 4:40 land was wide, and quiet, and *p*; 7961
Isa 32:18 shall dwell in a *p* habitation, and 7965
Jer 25:37 the *p* habitations are cut down "
1Ti 2: 2 we may lead a quiet and *p* life in **2272*
Heb 12:11 the *p* fruit of righteousness unto *1516*
Jas 3:17 first pure, then *p*, gentle, and easy "

peaceably
Ge 37: 4 and could not speak *p* unto him. 7965
J'g 11:13 now...restore those lands again *p*. "
21:13 Rimmon, and to call *p* unto them. * "
1Sa 16: 4 coming, and said, Comest thou *p*? "
5 And he said, *P*: I am come to "
1Ki 2:13 And she said, Comest thou *p*? "
13 And he said, *P*. "
1Ch 12:17 If ye be come *p* unto me to help me, "
Jer 9: 8 one speaketh *p* to his neighbour "
Da 11:21 he shall come in *p*, and obtain *7962
24 He shall enter *p* even upon the "
Ro 12:18 lieth in you, live *p* with all men. **1518*

peacemakers
M't 5: 9 Blessed are the *p*: for they shall *1518*

peace-offering See PEACE and OFFERING.

peacocks
1Ki 10:22 and silver, ivory, and apes, and *p*. 8500
2Ch 9:21 and silver, ivory, and apes, and *p*. "
Job 39:13 thou the goodly wings unto the *p*? *7443

pearl See also PEARLS.
M't 13:46 he had found one *p* of great price, *3135*
Re 21:21 every several gate was of one *p*: "

pearls
Job 28:18 shall be made of coral, or of *p*: *1378
M't 7: 6 cast ye your *p* before swine, *3135*
13:45 a merchant man, seeking goodly *p*: "
1Ti 2: 9 hair, or gold, or *p*, or costly array; "
Re 17: 4 gold and precious stones and *p*, "
18:12 and precious stones, and of *p*, and "
16 gold, and precious stones, and *p*! * "
21:21 the twelve gates were twelve *p*; "

peculiar
Ex 19: 5 ye shall be a *p* treasure unto me ‡5459
De 14: 2 thee to be a *p* people unto himself, ‡ "
26:18 thee this day to be his *p* people, ‡ "
Ps 135: 4 and Israel for his *p* treasure. ‡ "
Ec 2: 8 and the *p* treasure of kings and of "
Tit 2:14 a *p* people, zealous of good works. **4041*
1Pe 2: 9 an holy nation, a *p* people; **1519,4047*

Pedahel (*ped'-a-hel*)
Nu 34:28 Naphtali, *P* the son of Ammihud. 6300

Pedahzur (*pe-dah'-zur*)
Nu 1:10 Manasseh; Gamaliel the son of *P*. 6301
2:20 shall be Gamaliel the son of *P*. "
7:54 day offered Gamaliel the son of *P*. "
59 offering of Gamaliel the son of *P*. "
10:23 was Gamaliel the son of *P*. "

Pedaiah (*pe-dah'-yah*)
2Ki 23:36 the daughter of *P* of Rumah. 6305
1Ch 3:18 Malchiram also, and *P*, and 6305
19 the sons of *P* were, Zerubbabel, "
27:20 of Manasseh, Joel the son of *P*: "
Ne 3:25 After him *P* the son of Parosh. "
8: 4 on his left hand, *P*, and Mishael, "
11: 7 the son of Joed, the son of *P*, the "
13:13 the scribe, and of the Levites, *P*: "

pedigrees
Nu 1:18 they declared their *p* after their 3205

peeled See also PILLED.
Isa 18: 2 to a nation scattered and *p*, to a *4178
7 of a people scattered and *p*, and * "
Eze 29:18 bald, and every shoulder was *p*: ‡4803

peep See also PEEPED.
Isa 8:19 and unto wizards that *p*, and that *6850

peeped
Isa 10:14 wing, or opened the mouth, or *p*. *6850

Pekah (*pe'-kah*)
2Ki 15:25 But *P* the son of Remaliah, a 6492
27 *P* the son of Remaliah began to "
29 In the days of *P* king of Israel "
30 made a conspiracy against *P* the "
31 And the rest of the acts of *P*, and "
32 In the second year of *P* the son of "
37 Syria, and *P* the son of Remaliah. "
16: 1 In the seventeenth year of *P* the "
5 *P* son of Remaliah king of Israel "
2Ch 28: 6 For *P* the son of Remaliah slew in "
Isa 7: 1 *P* the son of Remaliah, king of "

Pekahiah (*pe-ka-hi'-ah*)
2Ki 15:22 *P* his son reigned in his stead. 6494
23 *P* the son of Menahem began to "
26 And the rest of the acts of *P*, and "

Pekod (*pe'-kod*)
Jer 50:21 and against the inhabitants of *P*: 6489
Eze 23:23 all the Chaldeans, *P*, and Shoa, "

Pelaiah (*pel-a-i'-ah*)
1Ch 3:24 and Eliashib, and *P*, and Akkub, 6411
Ne 8: 7 *P*, and the Levites, caused the "
10:10 Shebaniah, Hodijah, Kelita, *P*, "

Pelaliah (*pel-a-li'-ah*)
Ne 11:12 the son of Jeroham, the son of *P*, 6421

Pelatiah (*pel-a-ti'-ah*)
1Ch 3:21 the sons of Hananiah; *P*, and 6410
4:42 having for their captains *P*, and "
Ne 10:22 *P*, Hanan, Anaiah, "
Eze 11: 1 and *P* the son of Benaiah, princes "
13 that *P* the son of Benaiah died. "

Peleg (*pe'-leg*) See also PHALEG.
Ge 10:25 two sons; the name of one was *P*; 6389
11:16 four and thirty years, and begat *P*: "
17 And Eber lived after he begat *P* "
18 *P* lived thirty years, and begat "
19 *P* lived after he begat Reu two "
1Ch 1:19 sons: the name of the one was *P*; "
25 Eber, *P*, Reu, "

Pelet (*pe'-let*) See also BETH-PALET.
1Ch 2:47 Gesham, and *P*, and Ephah, and 6404
12: 3 and *P*, the sons of Azmaveth; "

Peleth (*pe'-leth*)
Nu 16: 1 and On, the son of *P*, sons of 6431
1Ch 2:33 the sons of Jonathan; *P*, and "

Pelethites (*pel'-e-thites*)
2Sa 8:18 both the Cherethites and the *P*; 6432
15:18 and all the *P*, and all the Gittites, "
20: 7 the *P*, and all the mighty men: "
23 the Cherethites and over the *P*: "
1Ki 1:38 and the *P*, went down, and caused "
44 the Cherethites, and the *P*, and "
1Ch 18:17 over the Cherethites and the *P*; "

pelican
Le 11:18 and the *p*, and the gier eagle, 6893
De 14:17 And the *p*, and the gier eagle, and "
Ps 102: 6 I am like a *p* of the wilderness: "

Pelonite (*pel'-o-nite*) See also PALTITE
1Ch 11:27 the Harorite, Helez the *P*, 6397
36 the Mecherathite, Ahijah the *P*, "
27:10 seventh month was Helez the *P*. "

pen See also PENKNIFE.
J'g 5:14 they that handle the *p* of the *7626
Job 19:24 they were graven with an iron *p* 5842
Ps 45: 1 tongue is the *p* of a ready writer. "
Isa 8: 1 roll, and write in it with a man's *p* 2747
Jer 8: 8 it; the *p* of the scribes is in vain. 5842
17: 1 Judah is written with a *p* of iron, "
3Jo 13 with ink and *p* write unto thee: *2563*

pence
M't 18:28 which owed him an hundred *p*: ‡*1220*
M'r 14: 5 for more than three hundred *p*, ‡ "
Lu 7:41 the one owed five hundred *p*, and ‡ "
10:35 he took out two *p*, and gave them ‡ "
Joh 12: 5 ointment sold for three hundred *p*, ‡ "

Peniel (*pe-ni'-el*) See also PENUEL.
Ge 32:30 called the name of the place *P*: 6439

Peninnah (*pe-nin'-nah*)
1Sa 1: 2 and the name of the other *P*: 6444
2 and *P* had children, but Hannah "
4 offered, he gave to *P* his wife, "

penknife
Jer 36:23 leaves, he cut it with the *p*, and 8593

penny See also PENNYWORTH; PENCE.
M't 20: 2 with the labourers for a *p* a day, ‡*1220*
9 hour, they received every man a *p*. ‡ "
10 likewise received every man a *p*. ‡ "
13 not thou agree with me for a *p*? ‡ "

M't 22:19 And they brought unto him a p'. ‡1220
M'r 12:15 bring me a p', that I may see it. ‡ "
Lu 20:24 Shew me a p'. Whose image and‡ "
Re 6: 6 A measure of wheat for a p', and ‡ "
6 three measures of barley for a p'; ‡ "

pennyworth
M'r 6:37 and buy two hundred p' of bread, ‡1220
Joh 6: 7 Two hundred p' of bread is not ‡ "

Pentecost (*pen'-te-cost*)
Ac 2: 1 the day of P' was fully come, 4005
20:16 to be at Jerusalem the day of P'. "
1Co 16: 8 I will tarry at Ephesus until P'. "

Penuel (*pe-nu'-el*) See also PENIEL.
Ge 32:31 as he passed over P' the sun rose 6439
J'g 8: 8 he went up thence to P', and spake "
8 and the men of P' answered him "
9 he spake also unto the men of P', "
17 And he beat down the tower of P', "
1Ki 12:25 went out from thence, and built P'. "
1Ch 4: 4 and P' the father of Gedor, and "
8:25 and P', the sons of Shashak; "

penury
Pr 14:23 talk of the lips tendeth only to p'. 4270
Lu 21: 4 but she of her p' hath cast in all *5303

people See also PEOPLE'S; PEOPLES.
Ge 11: 6 Lord said, Behold, the p' is one, 5971
14:16 and the women also, and the p'. "
17:14 soul shall be cut off from his p'; "
16 nations; kings of p' shall be of her. "
19: 4 all the p' from every quarter: "
23: 7 bowed himself to the p' of the land, "
11 in the presence of the sons of my p' "
12 bowed down himself before the p' "
13 the audience of the p' of the land, "
25: 8 years; and was gathered to his p'. "
17 died; and was gathered unto his p'. "
23 and two manner of p' shall be *3816
23 the one p' shall be stronger than "
23 be stronger than the other p'; and "
26:10 one of the p' might lightly have 5971
11 And Abimelech charged all his p', "
27:29 Let p' serve thee, and nations bow "
28: 3 thou mayest be a multitude of p';* "
29: 1 into the land of the p' of the east. *1121
32: 7 divided the p' that was with him, 5971
34:16 you, and we will become one p'. "
22 for to dwell with us, to be one p', "
35: 6 and all the p' that were with him. "
29 was gathered unto his p', being "
41:40 thy word shall all my p' be ruled: "
55 the p' cried to Pharaoh for bread: "
42: 6 and he it was that sold to all the p' "
47:21 as for the p', he removed them to "
23 Then Joseph said unto the p', "
48: 4 will make of thee a multitude of p';* "
19 know it: he also shall become a p', "
49:10 shall the gathering of the p' be. * "
16 Dan shall judge his p', as one of "
29 I am to be gathered unto my p': "
33 and was gathered unto his p'. "
50:20 is this day, to save much p' alive. "
Ex 1: 9 And he said unto his p', Behold, "
9 the p' of the children of Israel are "
20 the p' multiplied, and waxed very "
22 And Pharaoh charged all his p', "
3: 7 surely seen the affliction of my p' "
10 bring forth my p' the children of * "
12 thou hast brought forth the p' out "
21 will give this p' favour in the sight "
4:16 be thy spokesman unto the p': "
21 that he shall not let the p' go. "
30 did the signs in the sight of the p'. "
31 And the p' believed: and when they "
5: 1 Let my p' go, that they may hold a "
4 Aaron, let the p' from their works? "
5 the p' of the land now are many, "
6 same day the taskmasters of the p', "
7 Ye shall no more give the p' straw "
10 the taskmasters of the p' went out, "
10 officers, and they spake to the p', "
12 So the p' were scattered abroad "
16 but the fault is in thine own p'. "
22 hast thou so evil entreated this p'? "
23 name, he hath done evil to this p'; "
23 hast thou delivered thy p' at all. "
6: 7 I will take you to me for a p', and I "
7: 4 and my p' the children of Israel, "
14 he refuseth to let the p' go. "
16 Let my p' go, that they may serve "
8: 1 Let my p' go, that they may serve "
3 of thy servants, and upon thy p', "
4 up both on thee, and upon thy p', "
8 the frogs from me, and from my p'; "
8 and I will let the p' go, that they "
9 and for thy servants, and for thy p', "
11 from thy servants, and from thy p'; "
20 Let my p' go, that they may serve "
21 Else, if thou wilt not let my p' go, "
21 upon thy servants, and upon thy p', "
22 of Goshen, in which my p' dwell, "
23 division between my p' and thy p': "
29 from his servants, and from his p' "
29 the p' go to sacrifice to the Lord. "
31 from his servants, and from his p'; "
32 also, neither would he let the p' go. "
9: 1 Let my p' go, that they may serve "
7 and he did not let the p' go. "
13 Let my p' go, that they may serve "
14 upon thy servants, and upon thy p'; "
15 I may smite thee and thy p' with "
17 exaltest thou thyself against my p', "
27 and I and my p' are wicked. "

Ex 10: 3 let my p' go, that they may serve 5971
4 Else, if thou refuse to let my p' go, "
11: 2 Speak now in the ears of the p', and "
3 the Lord gave the p' favour in the "
3 servants, and in the sight of the p'. "
8 out, and all the p' that follow thee: "
12:27 p' bowed the head and worshipped. "
31 get you forth from among my p', "
33 Egyptians were urgent upon the p', "
34 p' took their dough before it was "
36 the Lord gave the p' favour in the "
13: 3 Moses said unto the p', Remember "
17 when Pharaoh had let the p' go, "
17 Lest peradventure the p' repent "
18 God led the p' about, through the "
22 of fire by night, from before the p'. "
14: 5 the king of Egypt that the p' fled: "
5 servants was turned against the p', "
6 chariot, and took his p' with him: "
13 Moses said unto the p', Fear ye "
31 the p' feared the Lord, and believed "
15:13 in thy mercy hast led forth the p' "
14 p' shall hear, and be afraid: sorrow* "
16 still as a stone; till thy p' pass over, "
16 O Lord, till the p' pass over, which "
24 the p' murmured against Moses, "
16: 4 and the p' shall go out and gather "
27 there went out some of the p' on "
30 So the p' rested on the seventh day. "
17: 1 was no water for the p' to drink. "
2 the p' did chide with Moses, and "
3 the p' thirsted there for water; and "
3 the p' murmured against Moses, "
4 What shall I do unto this p'? they "
5 Go on before the p', and take with "
6 out of it, that the p' may drink. "
13 discomfited Amalek and his p' with "
18: 1 for Moses, and for Israel his p', "
10 hath delivered the p' from under "
13 that Moses sat to judge the p': and "
13 and the p' stood by Moses from the "
14 in law saw all that he did to the p', "
14 thing that thou doest to the p'? "
14 and all the p' stand by thee from "
15 the p' come unto me to enquire of "
18 thou, and this p' that is with thee: "
19 Be thou for the p' to God-ward, "
21 provide out of all the p' able men, "
22 let them judge the p' at all seasons: "
23 this p' shall also go to their place "
25 and made them heads over the p', "
26 they judged the p' at all seasons: "
19: 5 treasure unto me above all p': for* "
7 and called for the elders of the p', "
8 all the p' answered together, and "
8 Moses returned the words of the p' "
9 that the p' may hear when I speak "
9 Moses told the words of the p' unto "
10 Go unto the p', and sanctify them "
11 come down in the sight of all the p' "
12 set bounds unto the p' round about, "
14 down from the mount unto the p', "
14 sanctified the p'; and they washed "
15 said unto the p', Be ready against "
16 that all the p' that was in the camp "
17 Moses brought forth the p' out of "
21 Go down, charge the p', lest they "
23 The p' cannot come up to mount "
24 let not the priests and the p' break "
25 Moses went down unto the p', and "
20:18 all the p' saw the thunderings, and "
18 when the p' saw it, they removed, "
20 Moses said unto the p', Fear not: "
21 the p' stood afar off, and Moses "
22:25 If thou lend money to any of my p' "
28 gods, nor curse the ruler of thy p'. "
23:11 that the poor of thy p' may eat: and "
27 will destroy all the p' to whom thou "
24: 2 neither shall the p' go up with him. "
3 Moses came and told the p' all the "
3 and all the p' answered with one "
7 and read in the audience of the p': "
8 blood, and sprinkled it on the p', "
30:33 shall even be cut off from his p'. "
38 shall even be cut off from his p'. "
31:14 shall be cut off from among his p'. "
32: 1 when the p' saw that Moses delayed "
1 p' gathered themselves together "
3 the p' brake off the golden earrings "
6 the p' sat down to eat and to drink, "
7 for thy p', which thou broughtest "
9 unto Moses, I have seen this p', "
9 and, behold, it is a stiffnecked p': "
11 thy wrath wax hot against thy p', "
12 repent of this evil against thy p'. "
14 which he thought to do unto his p'. "
17 Joshua heard the noise of the p' as "
21 Aaron, What did this p' unto thee, "
22 thou knowest the p', that they are "
25 Moses saw that the p' were naked; "
28 there fell of the p' that day about "
30 Moses said unto the p', Ye have "
31 Oh, this p' have sinned a great sin, "
34 lead the p' unto the place of which "
35 the Lord plagued the p', because "
33: 1 the p' which thou hast brought up "
3 for thou art a stiffnecked p': lest I "
4 when the p' heard these evil tidings, "
5 of Israel, Ye are a stiffnecked p': "
8 all the p' rose up, and stood every "
10 And all the p' saw the cloudy pillar "
10 all the p' rose up and worshipped, "
12 sayest unto me, Bring up this p': "
13 consider that this nation is thy p'. "
16 that I and thy p' have found grace "
16 shall we be separated, I and thy p', "

Ex 33:16 from all the p' that are upon the 5971
34: 9 among us; for it is a stiffnecked p'; "
10 before all thy p' I will do marvels, "
10 all the p' among which thou art "
36: 5 p' bring much more than enough "
6 p' were restrained from bringing. "
Le 4: 3 sin according to the sin of the p'; "
27 if any one of the common p' sin "
7:20, 21 soul shall be cut off from his p'. "
25 eateth it shall be cut off from his p'. "
27 that soul shall be cut off from his p'. "
9: 7 for thyself, and for the p': and "
7 and offer the offering of the p', and "
15 which was the sin offering for the p', "
18 offerings, which was for the p': and "
22 lifted up his hand toward the p', "
23 and came out, and blessed the p': "
23 of the Lord appeared unto all the p'. "
24 when all the p' saw, they shouted, "
10: 3 before all the p' I will be glorified. "
6 lest wrath come upon all the p': *5712
16:15 the sin offering, that is for the p', 5971
24 and the burnt offering of the p', "
24 atonement for himself, and...the p'. "
33 for all the p' of the congregation. "
17: 4 shall be cut off from among his p': "
9 shall be cut off from among his p'. "
10 will cut him off from among his p'. "
18:29 shall be cut off from among their p'. "
19: 8 shall be cut off from among his p'. "
16 down as a talebearer among thy p': "
18 against the children of thy p', but "
20: 2 the p' of the land shall stone him "
3 will cut him off from among his p'; "
4 the p' of the land do any ways hide "
5 with Molech, from among their p'. "
6 will cut him off from among his p'. "
17 cut off in the sight of their p':1121, "
18 shall be cut off from among their p'. "
24 have separated you from other p'.* "
26 severed you from other p', that ye* "
21: 1 defiled for the dead among his p': "
4 being a chief man among his p', to "
14 take a virgin of his own p' to wife. "
15 he profane his seed among his p': "
23:29 shall be cut off from among his p'. "
30 will I destroy from among his p'. "
26:12 be your God, and ye shall be my p'. "
Nu 5:21 a curse and an oath among thy p', "
27 shall be a curse among her p'. "
9:13 shall be cut off from among his p': "
11: 1 And when the p' complained, it "
2 the p' cried unto Moses; and when "
8 the p' went about, and gathered it, "
10 Then Moses heard the p' weep "
11 the burden of all this p' upon me? "
12 Have I conceived all this p'? have I "
13 I have flesh to give unto all this p'? "
14 am not able to bear all this p' alone, "
16 knowest to be the elders of the p', "
17 bear the burden of the p' with thee, "
18 And say thou unto the p', Sanctify "
21 The p', among whom I am, are six "
24 told the p' the words of the Lord, "
24 seventy men of the elders of the p', "
29 that all the Lord's p' were prophets, "
32 the p' stood up all that day, and all "
33 the Lord was kindled against the p', "
33 Lord smote the p' with a very great "
34 there they buried the p' that lusted. "
35 the p' journeyed...unto Hazeroth; "
12:15 p' journeyed not till Miriam was "
16 the p' removed from Hazeroth, and "
13:18 p' that dwelleth therein, whether "
28 p' be strong that dwell in the land, "
30 Caleb stilled the p' before Moses, "
31 be not able to go up against the p'; "
32 the p' that we saw in it are men of a "
14: 1 cried; and the p' wept that night. "
9 neither fear ye the p' of the land; "
11 How long will this p' provoke me? "
13 broughtest up this p' in thy might "
14 that thou Lord art among this p', "
15 shalt kill all this p' as one man, "
16 Lord was not able to bring this p' "
19 the iniquity of this p' according "
19 and as thou hast forgiven this p', "
39 Israel: and the p' mourned greatly. "
15:26 seeing all the p' were in ignorance. "
30 shall be cut off from among his p'. "
16:41 Ye have killed the p' of the Lord. "
47 plague was begun among the p': "
47 and made an atonement for the p'. "
20: 1 and the p' abode in Kadesh; and "
3 And the p' chode with Moses, and "
20 came out against him with much p', "
24 Aaron shall be gathered unto his p': "
26 Aaron shall be gathered unto his p', "
21: 2 If thou wilt indeed deliver this p' 5971
4 of the p' was much discouraged "
5 And the p' spake against God, and "
6 sent fiery serpents among the p', "
6 and they bit the p'; and much "
6 and much p' of Israel died. "
7 Therefore the p' came to Moses, "
7 us. And Moses prayed for the p'. "
16 Gather the p' together, and I will "
18 the nobles of the p' digged it, by the "
23 Sihon gathered all his p' together, "
29 thou art undone, O p' of Chemosh: "
33 out against them, he, and all his p', "
34 him into thy hand, and all his p', "
35 him, and his sons, and all his p', "
22: 3 And Moab was sore afraid of the p', "
5 of the land of the children of his p', "
5 there is a p' come out from Egypt; "

Nu 22: 6 I pray thee, curse me this p'; for 5971
11 there is a p' come out of Egypt, "
12 them; thou shalt not curse the p': "
17 I pray thee, curse me this p'. "
41 might see the utmost part of the p'. "
23: 9 the p' shall dwell alone, and shall "
24 the p' shall rise up as a great lion, "
24: 14 And now, behold, I go unto my p': "
14 I will advertise thee what this p' "
14 shall do to thy p' in the latter days. "
25: 1 p' began to commit whoredom with "
2 called the p' unto the sacrifices of "
2 p' did eat, and bowed down to their "
4 Take all the heads of the p', and "
15 he was head over a p', and of a 523
26: 4 Take the sum of the p', from twenty
27: 13 also shalt be gathered unto thy p', 5971
31: 2 shalt thou be gathered unto thy p'. "
3 Moses spake unto the p', saying, "
32: 15 and ye shall destroy all this p'. "
33: 14 was no water for the p' to drink. "
De 1: 28 The p' is greater and taller than we; "
2: 4 And command thou the p', saying, "
10 a p' great, and many, and tall, as "
16 and dead from among the p', "
21 A p' great, and many, and tall, as "
32 out against us, he and all his p', "
33 him, and his sons, and all his p'. "
3: 1 out against us, he and all his p', "
2 I will deliver him, and all his p', "
3 the king of Bashan, and all his p': "
28 for he shall go over before this p', "
4: 6 is a wise and understanding p'. "
10 Gather me the p' together, and I "
20 to be unto him a p' of inheritance, "
33 Did ever p' hear the voice of God "
5: 28 the voice of the words of this p', "
6: 14 the gods of the p' which are round* "
7: 6 thou art an holy p' unto the Lord "
6 to be a special p' unto himself, "
6 above all p' that are upon the face* "
7 were more in number than any p'; "
7 for ye were the fewest of all p': * "
14 Thou shalt be blessed above all p': * "
16 thou shalt consume all the p' which* "
19 all the p' of whom thou art afraid.* "
9: 2 A p' great and tall, the children of "
6 for thou art a stiffnecked p'. "
12 for thy p' which thou hast brought "
13 I have seen this p', and, behold, it "
13 and, behold, it is a stiffnecked p': "
26 not thy p' and thine inheritance, "
27 unto the stubbornness of this p', "
29 are thy p' and thine inheritance, "
10: 11 take thy journey before the p', that "
15 even you above all p', as it is this * "
13: 7 of the gods of the p' which are * "
9 afterwards the hand of all the p'. "
14: 2 thou art an holy p' unto the Lord "
2 hath chosen thee to be a peculiar p' "
21 thou art an holy p' unto the Lord "
16: 18 judge the p' with just judgment. "
17: 7 afterward the hands of all the p'. "
13 And all the p' shall hear, and fear, "
16 cause the p' to return to Egypt, "
18: 3 be the priest's due from the p', "
20: 1 a p' more than thou, be not afraid "
2 approach and speak unto the p', "
5 the officers shall speak unto the p', "
8 shall speak further unto the p', and "
9 an end of speaking unto the p', "
9 captains of the armies to lead the p'. "
11 that all the p' that is found therein "
16 of the cities of these p', which the* "
21: 8 merciful, O Lord, unto thy p' Israel, "
8 lay not innocent blood unto thy p' of "
26: 15 from heaven, and bless thy p' Israel, "
18 thee this day to be his peculiar p', "
19 mayest be an holy p' unto the Lord "
27: 1 elders of Israel commanded the p', "
9 thou art become the p' of the Lord "
11 Moses charged the p' the same day, "
12 upon mount Gerizim to bless the p', "
15 the p' shall answer and say, Amen. "
16, 17, 18, 19, 20, 21, 22, 23, 24, 25, 26
And all the p' shall say, Amen. "
28: 9 thee an holy p' unto himself, as he "
10 all p' of the earth shall see that * "
32 shall be given unto another p', and "
64 shall scatter thee among all p', * "
29: 13 thee to day for a p' unto himself, "
31: 7 must go with this p' unto the land "
12 Gather the p' together, men, and "
16 and this p' will rise up, and go a "
32: 6 the Lord, O foolish p' and unwise? "
8 set the bounds of the p' according "
9 For the Lord's portion is his p'; "
21 with those which are not a p'; "
36 Lord shall judge his p', and repent "
43 Rejoice, O ye nations, with his p': "
43 unto his land, and to his p'. "
44 of this song in the ears of the p', "
50 up, and be gathered unto thy p'; as "
50 Hor, and was gathered unto his p': "
33: 3 Yea, he loved the p'; all his saints† "
5 the heads of the p' and the tribes of "
7 Judah, and bring him unto his p': "
17 he shall push the p' together to the "
19 shall call the p' unto the mountain:* "
21 he came with the heads of the p', "
29 O p' saved by the Lord, the shield "
Jos 1: 2 thou, and all this p', unto the land "
6 unto this p' shalt thou divide for an "
10 commanded the officers of the p', "
11 the host, and commanded the p', "
3: 3 they commanded the p', saying, "

Jos 3: 5 Joshua said unto the p', Sanctify 5971
6 and pass over before the p'. And "
6 covenant, and went before the p'. "
14 the p' removed from their tents, to "
14 ark of the covenant before the p'; "
16 and the p' passed over right against "
17 p' were passed clean over Jordan. *1471
4: 1 p' were clean passed over Jordan,* "
2 Take you twelve men out of the p', 5971
10 Joshua to speak unto the p', "
10 and the p' hasted and passed over. "
11 all the p' were clean passed over, "
11 priests, in the presence of the p'. "
19 And the p' came up out of Jordan "
24 all the p' of the earth might know* "
5: 4 All the p' that came out of Egypt, "
5 p' that came out were circumcised: "
5 p' that were born in the wilderness "
6 all the p' that were men of war, *1471
8 had done circumcising all the p', * "
6: 5 p' shall shout with a great shout; 5971
5 the p' shall ascend up every man "
7 And he said unto the p', Pass on, "
8 Joshua had spoken unto the p', "
10 And Joshua had commanded the p', "
16 Joshua said unto the p', Shout; for "
20 p' shouted when the priests blew "
20 p' heard the sound of the trumpet, "
20 the p' shouted with a great shout, "
20 so that the p' went up into the city, "
7: 3 unto him, Let not all the p' go up; "
3 not all the p' to labour thither; "
4 went up thither of the p' about "
5 the hearts of the p' melted, and "
7 at all brought this p' over Jordan, "
13 sanctify the p', and say, Sanctify "
8: 1 take all the p' of war with thee, "
1 the king of Ai, and his p', and his "
3 Joshua arose, and all the p' of war, "
5 p' that are with me, will approach "
9 lodged that night among the p'. "
10 and numbered the p', and went up, "
10 elders of Israel, before the p' to Ai. "
11 And all the p',...went up, and drew "
11 even the p' of war that were with * "
13 when they had set the p', even all 5971
14 to battle, he and all his p', at a "
16 the p' that were in Ai were called "
20 the p' that fled to the wilderness "
33 they should bless the p' of Israel. "
10: 7 he, and all the p' of war with him, "
13 stayed, until the p' had avenged *1471
21 p' returned to the camp to Joshua 5971
33 and Joshua smote him and his p', "
11: 4 all their hosts with them, much p' "
7 came, and all the p' of war with him, "
14: 8 made the heart of the p' melt: but "
17: 14 I am a great p', forasmuch as the "
15 If thou be a great p', then get thee "
17 Thou art a great p', and hast great "
24: 2 Joshua said unto all the p', Thus "
16 p' answered and said, God forbid "
17 the p' through whom we passed: * "
18 drave out from before us all the p', * "
19 Joshua said unto the p', Ye cannot "
21 p' said unto Joshua, Nay; but we "
22 And Joshua said unto the p', Ye are "
24 p' said unto Joshua, The Lord our "
25 made a covenant with the p' that "
27 Joshua said unto all the p', Behold, "
28 Joshua let the p' depart, every man "
J'g 1: 16 they went and dwelt among the p'. "
2: 4 p' lifted up their voice, and wept. "
6 when Joshua had let the p' go, the "
7 the p' served the Lord all the days "
12 the gods of the p' that were round* "
20 p' hath transgressed my covenant*1471
3: 18 away the p' that bare the present. 5971
4: 13 and all the p' that were with him, "
5: 2 the p' willingly offered themselves. "
9 themselves willingly among the p'. "
11 the p' of the Lord go down to the "
13 over the nobles among the p': the "
14 thee, Benjamin, among thy p'; * "
18 were a p' that jeoparded their lives "
7: 1 the p' that were with him, rose up "
2 The p' that are with thee are too "
3 go to, proclaim in the ears of the p', "
3 of the p' twenty and two thousand; "
4 Gideon, The p' are yet too many; "
5 down the p' unto the water: and "
6 the rest of the p' bowed down upon "
7 the other p' go every man unto his "
8 the p' took victuals in their hand, "
8: 5 of bread unto the p' that follow me; "
9: 29 to God this p' were under my hand! "
32 thou and the p' that is with thee, "
33 when he and the p' that is with him "
34 the p' that were with him, by night, "
35 up, and the p' that were with him, "
36 And when Gaal saw the p', he said "
36 there come p' down from the top of "
37 come p' down by the middle of the "
38 this the p' that thou hast despised? "
42 that the p' went out into the field; "
43 took the p', and divided them into "
43 p' were come forth out of the city; "
44 ran upon all the p'...in the fields, * "
45 he took the city, and slew the p' 5971
48 and all the p' that were with him; "
48 said unto the p' that were with him, "
49 all the p' likewise cut down every "
10: 18 the p' and princes of Gilead said "
11: 11 the p' made him head and captain "
20 Sihon gathered all his p' together, "
21 and all his p' into the hand of Israel, "

J'g 11: 23 Amorites from before his p' Israel, 5971
12: 2 I and my p' were at great strife with "
14: 3 never a woman...among all my p', "
16 a riddle unto the children of my p', "
17 the riddle to the children of her p'. "
16: 24 when the p' saw him, they praised "
30 upon the lords, and upon all the p' "
18: 7 came to Laish, and saw the p' "
10 ye shall come unto a p' secure, and "
20 and went in the midst of the p'. "
27 Laish, unto a p' that were at quiet "
20: 2 the chief of all the p', even all the "
2 in the assembly of the p' of God, "
8 all the p' arose as one man, saying, "
10 to fetch victual for the p', that they "
16 Among all this p' there were seven "
22 the p' the men of Israel encouraged "
26 all the p', went up, and came unto "
31 Benjamin went out against the p', "
31 they began to smite of the p', and "
21: 2 the p' came to the house of God, and "
4 the morrow, that the p' rose early, "
9 the p' were numbered, and, behold, "
15 the p' repented them for Benjamin, "
Ru 1: 6 the Lord had visited his p' in giving "
10 we will return with thee unto thy p'. "
15 sister in law is gone...unto her p', "
16 thy p' shall be my p', and thy God "
2: 11 unto a p' which thou knewest not "
3: 11 all the city of my p' doth know that "
4: 4 and before the elders of my p'. If "
9 unto the elders, and unto all the p', "
11 all the p' that were in the gate, and "
1Sa 2: 13 the priest's custom with the p' was, "
23 of your evil dealings by all this p'. "
24 ye make the Lord's p' to transgress. "
29 of all the offerings of Israel my p'? "
4: 3 the p' were come into the camp, "
4 So the p' sent to Shiloh, that they "
17 also a great slaughter among the p', "
5: 10 of Israel to us, to slay us and our p'. "
11 that it slay us not, and our p': for "
6: 6 did they not let the p' go, and they "
19 he smote of the p' fifty thousand 5971
19 the p' lamented, because the Lord "
19 Lord had smitten many of the p' "
8: 7 Hearken unto the voice of the p' "
10 the words of the Lord unto the p' "
19 the p' refused to obey the voice of "
21 Samuel heard all the words of the p', "
9: 2 he was higher than any of the p'. "
12 there is a sacrifice of the p' to day "
13 for the p' will not eat until he come, "
16 him to be captain over my p' Israel, "
16 save my p' out of the hand of the "
16 I have looked upon my p', because "
17 this same shall reign over my p'. "
24 since I said, I have invited the p'. "
10: 11 the p' said one to another, What is "
17 And Samuel called the p' together "
23 when he stood among the p', he was "
23 higher than any of the p' from his "
24 Samuel said to all the p', See ye him "
24 is none like him among all the p'? "
24 the p' shouted, and said, God save "
25 Samuel told the p' the manner of the "
25 Samuel sent all the p' away, every "
11: 4 the tidings in the ears of the p': "
4 all the p' lifted up their voices, and "
5 What aileth the p' that they weep? "
7 the fear of the Lord fell on the p', "
11 put the p' in three companies; and "
12 the p' said unto Samuel, Who is he "
14 said Samuel to the p', Come, and let "
15 all the p' went to Gilgal; and there "
12: 6 Samuel said unto the p', It is the "
18 all the p' greatly feared the Lord "
19 all the p' said unto Samuel, Pray "
20 Samuel said unto the p', Fear not: "
22 the Lord will not forsake his p' for "
22 pleased the Lord to make you his p'. "
13: 2 the rest of the p' he sent every man "
4 p' were called together after Saul "
5 p' as the sand which is on the sea "
6 a strait, (for the p' were distressed,) "
6 the p' did hide themselves in caves, "
7 all the p' followed him trembling. "
8 and the p' were scattered from him. "
11 that the p' were scattered from me, "
14 him to be captain over his p', "
15 numbered the p' that were present "
16 the p' that were present with them, "
22 found in the hand of any of the p' "
14: 2 the p' that were with him were "
3 the p' knew not that Jonathan was "
15 in the field, and among all the p': "
17 said Saul unto the p' that were with "
20 Saul and all the p' that were with "
24 for Saul had adjured the p', saying, "
24 so none of the p' tasted any food. "
26 the p' were come into the wood, "
26 mouth: for the p' feared the oath. "
27 father charged the p' with the oath: "
28 Then answered one of the p', and "
28 straitly charged the p' with an oath, "
28 this day. And the p' were faint. "
30 haply the p' had eaten freely to day "
31 Aijalon: and the p' were very faint. "
32 the p' flew upon the spoil, and took "
32 the p' did eat them with the blood. "
33 Behold, the p' sin against the Lord, "
34 Disperse yourselves among the p', "
34 all the p' brought every man his ox "
38 near hither, all the chief of the p': "
39 was not a man among all the p' that "
40 p' said unto Saul, Do what seemeth "

1Sa 14:41 were taken: but the p' escaped. 5971
45 p' said unto Saul, Shall Jonathan "
45 p' rescued Jonathan, that he died "
15: 1 anoint thee to be king over his p'. "
4 Saul gathered the p' together, and "
8 utterly destroyed all the p' with "
9 Saul and the p' spared Agag, and "
15 the p' spared the best of the sheep "
21 the p' took of the spoil, sheep and "
24 because I feared the p', and obeyed "
30 thee, before the elders of my p', "
17:27 p' answered him after this manner, "
30 the p' answered him again after the "
18: 5 accepted in the sight of all the p', "
13 went out and came in before the p'. "
23: 8 Saul called all the p' together to "
26: 5 the p' pitched round about him. "
7 Abishai came to the p' by night: "
7 Abner and the p' lay...about him. "
14 David cried to the p', and to Abner "
15 came one of the p' in to destroy the "
27:12 his p' Israel utterly to abhor him; "
30: 4 David...the p' that were with him "
6 for the p' spake of stoning him, "
6 soul of all the p' was grieved, every "
21 to meet the p' that were with him: "
21 when David came near to the p', he "
31: 9 of their idols, and among the p'. "
2Sa 1: 4 that the p' are fled from the battle, "
4 many of the p' also are fallen and "
12 his son, and for the p' of the Lord, "
2:26 bid the p' return from following "
27 in the morning the p' had gone up, "
28 a trumpet, and all the p' stood still, "
30 he had gathered all the p' together, "
3:18 I will save my p' Israel out of the "
31 David said to Joab, and to all the p' "
32 grave of Abner; and all the p' wept. "
34 And all the p' wept again over him. "
35 the p' came to cause David to eat "
36 all the p' took notice of it, and it "
36 the king did pleased all the p'. "
37 all the p' and all Israel understood "
5: 2 Thou shalt feed my p' Israel, and "
12 kingdom for his p' Israel's sake. "
6: 2 David arose,...went with all the p' "
18 he blessed the p' in the name of the "
19 And he dealt among all the p', even "
19 p' departed every one to his house. "
21 me ruler over the p' of the Lord, "
7: 7 I commanded to feed my p' Israel, "
8 to be ruler over my p', over Israel: "
10 appoint a place for my p' Israel, "
11 judges to be over my p' Israel, and "
23 nation in the earth is like thy p', "
23 whom God went to redeem for a p' "
23 for thy land, before thy p', which "
24 confirmed to thyself thy p' Israel "
24 Israel to be a p' unto thee for ever: "
8:15 judgment and justice unto all his p'. "
10:10 the rest of the p' he delivered into "
12 and let us play the men for our p', "
13 and the p' that were with him, "
11: 7 how Joab did, and how the p' did, "
17 and there fell some of the p' of the "
12:28 gather the rest of the p' together, "
29 David gathered all the p' together, "
31 he brought forth the p' that were "
31 David and all the p' returned unto "
13:34 there came much p' by the way of "
14:13 such a thing against the p' of God? "
15 because the p' have made me afraid: "
15:12 for the p' increased continually "
17 went forth, and all the p' after him, "
23 and all the p' passed over: the king "
23 all the p' passed over, toward the "
24 until all the p' had done passing "
30 all the p' that was with him covered "
16: 6 all the p' and all the mighty men "
14 and all the p' that were with him, "
15 Absalom, and all the p' the men of "
18 this p', and all the men of Israel, "
17: 2 the p' that are with him shall flee; "
3 will bring back all the p' unto thee: "
3 so all the p' shall be in peace. "
8 war, and will not lodge with the p'. "
9 There is a slaughter among the p' "
16 and all the p' that are with him. "
22 and all the p' that were with him, "
29 and for the p' that were with him, "
29 The p' is hungry, and weary, and "
18: 1 David numbered the p' that were "
2 sent forth a third part of the p' "
2 And the king said unto the p', I will "
3 the p' answered, Thou shalt not go "
4 all the p' came out by hundreds "
5 all the p' heard when the king gave "
6 p' went out into the field against "
7 Where the p' of Israel were slain "
8 wood devoured more p' that day "
16 and the p' returned from pursuing "
16 Israel: for Joab held back the p'. "
19: 2 into mourning unto all the p': "
2 p' heard say that day how the king "
3 the p' gat them by stealth that day "
3 p' being ashamed steal away when "
8 they told unto all the p', saying, "
8 And all the p' came before the king: "
9 all the p' were at strife throughout "
39 And all the p' went over Jordan. "
40 the p' of Judah conducted the king, "
40 king, and also half the p' of Israel. "
20:12 man saw that all the p' stood still, "
13 the p' went on after Joab, to pursue 376
15 p' that were with Joab battered 5971
22 the woman went unto all the p' in "

2Sa 22:28 And the afflicted p' thou wilt save: 5971
44 from the strivings of my p', thou "
44 p' which I knew not shall serve me. "
48 bringeth down the p' under me, * "
23:10 p' returned after him only to spoil. "
11 and the p' fled from the Philistines. "
24: 2 Beer-sheba, and number ye the p', "
2 I may know the number of the p'. "
3 the Lord thy God add unto the p', "
4 king, to number the p' of Israel. "
9 up the sum of the number of the p' "
10 after that he had numbered the p'. "
15 there died of the p' from Dan even "
16 to the angel that destroyed the p', "
17 he saw the angel that smote the p', "
21 plague may be stayed from the p'. "
1Ki 1:39 the p' said, God save king Solomon. "
40 And all the p' came up after him, "
40 the p' piped with pipes, and rejoiced "
3: 2 the p' sacrificed in high places, "
8 thy servant is in the midst of thy p' "
8 which thou hast chosen, a great p', "
9 understanding heart to judge thy p', "
9 able to judge this thy so great a p'? "
4:34 And there came of all p' to hear the* "
5: 7 David a wise son over this great p'. "
16 ruled over the p' that wrought in "
6:13 and will not forsake my p' Israel. "
8:16 that I brought forth my p' Israel "
16 chose David to be over my p' Israel. "
30 thy servant, and of thy p' Israel, "
33 When thy p' Israel be smitten down "
34 and forgive the sin of thy p' Israel, "
36 of thy servants, and of thy p' Israel, "
36 land, which thou hast given to thy p' "
38 by any man, or by all thy p' Israel, "
41 stranger, that is not of thy p' Israel, "
43 p' of the earth may know thy name,* "
43 to fear thee, as do thy p' Israel; "
44 If thy p' go out to battle against "
50 And forgive thy p' that have sinned "
51 be thy p', and thine inheritance, "
52 the supplication of thy p' Israel, "
53 from among all the p' of the earth,* "
56 hath given rest unto his p' Israel, "
59 cause of his p' Israel at all times, "
60 all the p' of the earth may know, * "
66 the eighth day he sent the p' away: "
66 his servant, and for Israel his p'. "
9: 7 proverb and a byword among all p':* "
20 p' that were left of the Amorites, "
23 bare rule over the p' that wrought "
12: 5 again to me. And the p' departed. "
6 advise that I may answer this p'? "
7 thou wilt be a servant unto this p' "
9 give ye that we may answer this p', "
10 Thus shalt thou speak unto this p' "
12 and all the p' came to Rehoboam "
13 the king answered the p' roughly, "
15 the king hearkened not unto the p'; "
16 the p' answered the king, saying, "
23 to the remnant of the p', saying, "
27 If this p' go up to do sacrifice in "
27 then shall the heart of this p' turn "
30 the p' went to worship before the "
31 made priests of the lowest of the p', "
13:33 made again of the lowest of the p' "
14: 2 that I should be king over this p'. "
7 I exalted thee from among the p', "
7 made thee prince over my p' Israel, "
16: 2 made thee prince over my p' Israel; "
2 and hast made my p' Israel to sin, "
15 And the p' were encamped against "
16 p' that were encamped heard say, "
21 p' of Israel divided into two parts: "
21 half of the p' followed Tibni the son "
22 the p' that followed Omri prevailed "
22 against the p' that followed Tibni "
18:21 Elijah came unto all the p', and "
21 the p' answered him not a word. "
22 Then said Elijah unto the p', I, "
24 the p' answered and said, It is well "
30 Elijah said unto all the p', Come "
30 And all the p' came near unto him. "
37 that this p' may know that thou art "
39 when all the p' saw it, they fell on "
19:21 gave unto the p', and they did eat. "
20: 8 all the p' said unto him, Hearken "
10 for all the p' that follow me. "
15 after them he numbered all the p', "
42 go for his life, and thy p' for his p'. "
21: 9 set Naboth on high among the p': "
12 set Naboth on high among the p'. "
13 Naboth, in the presence of the p', "
22: 4 I am as thou art, my p' as thy p', "
28 Hearken, O p', every one of you. * "
43 for the p' offered and burnt incense "
2Ki 3: 7 I am as thou art, my p' as thy p', "
4:13 I dwell among mine own p'. "
41 Pour out for the p', that they may "
42 Give unto the p', that they may eat. "
43 Give the p', that they may eat: for "
6:18 Smite this p', I pray thee, with 1471
30 the p' looked, and, behold, he had 5971
7:16 the p' went out, and spoiled the "
17, 20 p' trode upon him in the gate. "
8:21 and the p' fled into their tents. "
9: 6 have anointed thee king over the p' "
10: 9 said to all the p', Ye be righteous: "
18 Jehu gathered all the p' together, "
11:13 the noise of the guard and of the p', "
13 came to the p' into the temple of "
14 and all the p' of the land rejoiced, "
17 Lord and the king and the p', that "
17 that they should be the Lord's p'; "
17 between the king also and the p'. "

2Ki 11:18 all the p' of the land went into the 5971
19 guard, and all the p' of the land; "
20 And all the p' of the land rejoiced. "
12: 3 p' still sacrificed and burnt incense "
8 to receive no more money of the p', "
13: 7 did he leave of the p' to Jehoahaz "
14: 4 p' did sacrifice and burnt incense "
21 all the p' of Judah took Azariah, "
15: 4 the p' sacrificed and burnt incense "
5 house, judging the p' of the land. "
10 smote him before the p', and slew "
35 p' sacrificed and burned incense "
16: 9 and carried the p' of it captive to Kir,
15 offering of all the p' of the land, 5971
18:26 ears of the p' that are on the wall. "
36 But the p' held their peace, and "
20: 5 tell Hezekiah the captain of my p', "
21:24 the p' of the land slew all them that "
24 p' of the land made Josiah his son "
22: 4 keepers...have gathered of the p': "
13 and for the p', and for all Judah, "
23: 2 and all the p', both small and great: "
3 And all the p' stood to the covenant. "
6 the graves of the children of the p'. "
21 And the king commanded all the p', "
30 the p' of the land took Jehoahaz "
35 and the gold of the p' of the land, "
24:14 the poorest sort of the p' of the land. "
25: 3 was no bread for the p' of the land. "
11 Now the rest of the p' that were left "
19 which mustered the p' of the land, "
19 threescore men of the p' of the land "
22 for the p' that remained in the land "
26 And all the p', both small and great, "
1Ch 5:25 after the gods of the p' of the land,* "
10: 9 unto their idols, and to the p'. "
11: 2 Thou shalt feed my p' Israel, and "
2 shalt be ruler over my p' Israel. "
13 p' fled from before the Philistines. "
13: 4 was right in the eyes of all the p'. "
14: 2 up on high, because of his p' Israel. "
16: 2 blessed the p' in the name of the "
8 known his deeds among the p'. * "
20 from one kingdom to another p'; "
26 For all the gods of the p' are idols:* "
28 ye kindreds of the p', give unto the* "
36 p' said, Amen, and praised the Lord. "
43 p' departed every man to his house: "
17: 6 whom I commanded to feed my p', "
7 shouldest be ruler over my p' Israel: "
9 will ordain a place for my p' Israel, "
10 commanded judges to be over my p' "
21 in the earth is like thy p' Israel, "
21 went to redeem to be his own p', "
21 driving out nations...before thy p', "
22 thy p' Israel didst thou make thine "
22 thou make thine own p' for ever; "
18:14 judgment and justice among...his p'. "
19: 7 the king of Maachah and his p'; "
11 the rest of the p' he delivered unto "
13 let us behave...valiantly for our p', "
14 Joab and the p' that were with him "
20: 3 brought out the p' that were in it, "
3 all the p' returned to Jerusalem. "
21: 2 to Joab and to the rulers of the p', "
3 Lord make his p' an hundred times "
5 gave the sum of the number of the p' "
17 commanded the p' to be numbered? "
17 but not on thy p', that they should "
22 plague may be stayed from the p'. "
22:18 before the Lord, and before his p'. "
23:25 of Israel hath given rest unto his p', "
28: 2 Hear me, my brethren, and my p': "
21 princes and all the p' will be wholly "
29: 9 Then the p' rejoiced, for that they "
14 But who am I, and what is my p', "
17 and now have I seen with joy thy p', "
18 the thoughts of the heart of thy p', "
2Ch 1: 9 king over a p' like the dust of the "
10 go out and come in before this p': "
10 who can judge this thy p', that is so "
11 that thou mayest judge my p', over "
2:11 Because the Lord hath loved his p', "
18 overseers to set the p' a work. "
6: 5 forth my p' out of the land of Egypt "
5 man to be a ruler over my p' Israel: "
6 have chosen David to be over my p' "
21 of thy servant, and of thy p' Israel, "
24 if thy p' Israel be put to the worse "
25 and forgive the sin of thy p' Israel, "
27 the sin of thy servants, and of thy p' "
27 given unto thy p' for an inheritance. "
29 of any man, or of all thy p' Israel, "
32 which is not of thy p' Israel, but is "
33 that all p' of the earth may know * "
33 and fear thee, as doth thy p' Israel, "
34 If thy p' go out to war against their "
39 forgive thy p' which have sinned "
7: 4 Then the king and all the p' offered "
5 the king and all the p' dedicated "
10 he sent the p' away unto their tents, "
10 and to Solomon, and to Israel his p'. "
13 if I send pestilence among my p'; "
14 If my p', which are called by my "
8: 7 the p' that were left of the Hittites, "
10 and fifty, that bare rule over the p'. "
10: 5 three days. And the p' departed. "
6 ye me to return answer to this p'? "
7 If thou be kind to this p', and please "
9 we may return answer to this p', "
10 Thus shalt thou answer the p' that "
12 So Jeroboam and all the p' came to "
15 the king hearkened not unto the p': "
16 the p' answered the king, saying, "
12: 3 p' were without number that came "
13:17 And Abijah and his p' slew them "

2Ch 14: 13 Asa and the p' that were with him 5971
16: 10 And Asa oppressed some of the p' "
17: 9 cities of Judah, and taught the p'. "
18: 2 and for the p' that he had with him, "
3 am as thou art, and my p' as thy p'; "
27 And he said, Hearken, all ye p'. * "
19: 4 he went out again through the p' "
20: 7 of this land before thy p' Israel, "
21 when he had consulted with the p', "
25 Jehoshaphat and his p' came to take "
33 the p' had not prepared their hearts "
21: 14 plague will the Lord smite thy p', "
19 And his p' made no burning for him, "
23: 5 all the p' shall be in the courts of "
6 the p' shall keep the watch of the "
10 he set all the p', every man having "
12 Athaliah heard the noise of the p' "
12 she came to the p' into the house "
13 and all the p' of the land rejoiced, "
16 between him, and between all the p', "
16 that they should be the Lord's p'. "
17 all the p' went to the house of Baal, "
20 nobles, and the governors of the p', "
20 and all the p' of the land, and "
21 And all the p' of the land rejoiced: "
24: 10 the princes and all the p' rejoiced, "
20 priest, which stood above the p', "
23 destroyed all the princes of the p' "
23 the princes...from among the p', "
25: 11 And Amaziah...led forth his p', and "
15 thou sought after the gods of the p', "
15 which could not deliver their own p' "
26: 1 all the p' of Judah took Uzziah, "
21 house, judging the p' of the land. "
27: 2 And the p' did yet corruptly. "
29: 36 Hezekiah rejoiced, and all the p', "
36 that God had prepared the p': for "
30: 3 neither had the p' gathered "
13 assembled at Jerusalem much p' "
18 a multitude of the p', even many of "
20 to Hezekiah, and healed the p'. "
27 Levites arose and blessed the p': "
31: 4 he commanded the p' that dwelt in "
8 blessed the Lord, and his p' Israel. "
10 the p' began to bring the offerings "
10 for the Lord hath blessed his p'; 5971
32: 4 was gathered much p' together "
6 he set captains of war over the p', "
8 And the p' rested themselves upon "
13 done unto all the p' of other lands?* "
14 that could deliver his p' out of mine "
15 able to deliver his p' out of mine "
17 not delivered their p' out of mine "
17 the God of Hezekiah deliver his p' "
18 unto the p' of Jerusalem that were "
19 the gods of the p' of the earth, * "
33: 10 spake to Manasseh, and to his p': "
17 the p' did sacrifice still in the high "
25 the p' of the land slew all them that "
25 p' of the land made Josiah his son "
34: 30 and all the p', great and small: "
35: 3 Lord your God, and his p' Israel, "
5 families of your brethren the p', 1121, "
7 And Josiah gave to the p', of " "
8 princes gave willingly unto the p', "
12 of the families of the p', to 1121, "
13 them speedily among all the p'. " "
36: 1 the p' of the land took Jehoahaz the "
14 priests, and the p', transgressed "
15 because he had compassion on his p', "
16 of the Lord arose against his p', "
23 is there among you of all his p'? "
Ezr 1: 3 is there among you of all his p'? "
2: 2 of the men of the p' of Israel: "
70 and the Levites, and some of the p', "
3: 1 p' gathered themselves together "
3 because of the p' of those countries: "
11 the p' shouted with a great shout, "
13 the p' could not discern the noise "
13 the noise of the weeping of the p': "
13 for the p' shouted with a loud shout, "
4: 4 p' of the land weakened the hands "
4 the hands of the p' of Judah, and "
5: 12 carried the p' away into Babylon. 5972
6: 12 dwell there destroy all kings and p',* "
7: 13 that all they of the p' of Israel, and "
16 with the freewill offering of the p', "
25 may judge all the p' that are beyond "
8: 15 I viewed the p', and the priests, 5971
36 they furthered the p', and the house "
9: 1 The p' of Israel, and the priests, "
1 separated...from...p' of the lands, * "
2 mingled with...p' of those lands: * "
11 the filthiness of the p' of the lands,* "
14 with the p' of these abominations?* "
10: 1 children: for the p' wept very sore. "
2 strange wives of the p' of the land:* "
9 p' sat in the street of the house of "
11 separate...from the p' of the land, * "
13 But the p' are many, and it is a time "
Ne 1: 10 these are thy servants and thy p', "
4: 6 for the p' had a mind to work. "
13 I even set the p' after their families "
14, 19 rulers, and to the rest of the p', "
22 at the same time said I unto the p', "
5: 1 And there was a great cry of the p' "
13 the p' did according to this promise. "
15 me were chargeable unto the p', "
15 their servants bare rule over the p': "
18 the bondage was heavy upon this p'. "
19 to all that I have done for this p'. "
7: 4 but the p' were few therein, and the "
5 nobles, and the rulers, and the p', "
7 number,...of...men of the p' of Israel "
72 that which the rest of the p' gave "
73 and the singers, and some of the p', "

Ne 8: 1 p' gathered themselves together 5971
3 ears of all the p' were attentive "
5 the book in the sight of all the p'; "
5 (for he was above all the p';) when "
5 he opened it, all the p' stood up: "
6 And all the p' answered, Amen, "
7 caused the p' to understand the law: "
7 law: and the p' stood in their place. "
9 and the Levites that taught the p', "
9 said unto all the p', This day is holy "
9 For all the p' wept, when they heard "
11 So the Levites stilled all the p', "
12 all the p' went their way to eat, and "
13 the chief of the fathers of all the p', "
16 So the p' went forth, and brought "
9: 10 and on all the p' of his land: "
24 their kings, and the p' of the land,* "
30 into the hand of the p' of the lands.* "
32 on our fathers, and on all thy p', "
10: 14 The chief of the p'; Parosh, "
28 And the rest of the p', the priests, "
28 separated...from the p' of the lands* "
30 daughters unto the p' of the land,* "
31 And if the p' of the land bring ware* "
34 the priests, the Levites, and the p', "
11: 1 rulers of the p' dwelt at Jerusalem: "
1 the rest of the p' also cast lots, to "
2 And the p' blessed all the men, that "
24 in all matters concerning the p'. "
12: 30 purified themselves, and...the p', "
38 and the half of the p' upon the wall, "
13: 1 of Moses in the audience of the p'; "
24 according to the language of each p'. "
Es 1: 5 the king made a feast unto all the p' "
11 shew...p' and...princes her beauty:* "
16 the p' that are in all the provinces* "
22 and to every p' after their language, "
22 to the language of every p'. "
2: 10 Esther had not shewed her p' nor "
20 yet shewed her kindred nor her p'; "
3: 6 had shewed him the p' of Mordecai: "
6 Ahasuerus, even the p' of Mordecai. "
8 is a certain p' scattered abroad and "
8 among the p' in all the provinces * "
8 their laws are diverse from all p'; "
11 silver is given to thee, the p' also, "
12 to the rulers of every p' of every "
12 to every p' after their language; "
14 province was published unto all p',* "
4: 8 make request before him for her p'. "
11 p' of the king's provinces, do know, "
7: 3 petition, and my p' at my request: "
4 For we are sold, I and my p', to be "
8: 6 the evil that shall come unto my p'? "
9 unto every p' after their language, "
11 all the power of the p' and province "
13 province was published unto all p',* "
17 of the p' of the land became Jews;* "
9: 2 for the fear of them fell upon all p'.* "
10: 3 seeking the wealth of his p', and "
Job 12: 2 No doubt but ye are the p', and "
24 of the chief of the p' of the earth, "
17: 6 made me also a byword of the p'; "
18: 19 have son nor nephew among his p', "
34: 20 the p' shall be troubled at midnight, "
30 reign not, lest the p' be ensnared. "
36: 20 when p' are cut off in their place. * "
31 For by them judgeth he the p'; he* "
Ps 2: 1 and the p' imagine a vain thing? *3816
3: 6 be afraid of ten thousands of p', 5971
8 Lord: thy blessing is upon thy p'. "
7: 7 congregation of the p' compass *3816
8 The Lord shall judge the p': *5971
9: 8 shall minister judgment to the p' *3816
11 declare among the p' his doings. 5971
14: 4 who eat up my p' as they eat bread, "
7 back the captivity of his p', Jacob "
18: 27 For thou wilt save the afflicted p'; "
43 me from the strivings of the p'; "
43 a p' whom I have not known shall "
47 me, and subdueth the p' under me.* "
22: 6 of men, and despised of the p'. "
31 righteousness unto a p' that shall "
28: 9 Save thy p', and bless thine "
29: 11 Lord will give strength unto his p'; "
11 Lord will bless his p' with peace. "
33: 10 the devices of the p' of none effect.* "
12 p' whom he hath chosen for his own "
35: 18 I will praise thee among much p'. "
44: 2 thou didst afflict the p', and cast *3816
12 Thou sellest thy p' for nought, and 5971
14 shaking of the head among the p'. *3816
45: 5 whereby the p' fall under thee. *5971
10 forget also thine own p', and thy "
12 the rich among the p' shall intreat "
17 shall the p' praise thee for ever and* "
47: 1 O clap your hands, all ye p'; shout;* "
3 He shall subdue the p' under us, * "
9 The princes of the p' are gathered* "
9 even the p' of the God of Abraham: "
49: 1 Hear this, all ye p'; give ear, all * "
50: 4 the earth, that he may judge his p'. "
7 Hear, O my p', and I will speak; "
53: 4 who eat up my p' as they eat bread: "
6 back the captivity of his p', Jacob "
56: 7 in thine anger cast down the p', * "
57: 9 praise thee, O Lord, among the p':* "
59: 11 Slay them not, lest my p' forget: "
60: 3 hast shewed thy p' hard things: "
62: 8 ye p', pour out your heart before "
65: 7 waves, and the tumult of the p'. *3816
66: 8 O bless our God, ye p', and make *5971
67: 3 Let the p' praise thee, O God; let* "
3 O God; let all the p' praise thee. * "
4 thou shalt judge the p' righteously,* "
5 Let the p' praise thee, O God; let* "

Ps 67: 5 O God; let all the p' praise thee. *5971
68: 7 thou wentest forth before thy p', "
22 bring my p' again from the depths of* "
30 the bulls, with the calves of the p',* 5971
30 thou the p' that delight in war. * "
35 strength and power unto his p'. "
72: 2 judge thy p' with righteousness, "
3 shall bring peace to the p', and the "
4 He shall judge the poor of the p', "
73: 10 Therefore his p' return hither: and "
74: 14 and gavest him to be meat to the p' "
18 the foolish p' have blasphemed thy "
77: 14 declared thy strength among the p'.* "
15 with thine arm redeemed thy p', "
20 Thou leddest thy p' like a flock by "
78: 1 Give ear, O my p', to my law: "
20 also? can he provide flesh for his p'? "
52 his own p' to go forth like sheep, "
62 gave his p' over also unto the sword; "
71 brought him to feed Jacob his p', "
79: 13 we thy p' and sheep of thy pasture "
80: 4 angry against the prayer of thy p'? "
81: 8 O my p', and I will testify unto thee: "
11 p' would not hearken to my voice; "
13 Oh that my p' had hearkened unto "
83: 3 taken crafty counsel against thy p', "
85: 2 hast forgiven the iniquity of thy p', "
6 that thy p' may rejoice in thee? "
8 for he will speak peace unto his p', "
87: 6 count when he writeth up the p', * "
89: 15 the p' that know the joyful sound: "
19 exalted one chosen out of the p'. "
50 the reproach of all the mighty p';* "
94: 5 They break in pieces thy p', O "
8 ye brutish among the p': and ye "
14 For the Lord will not cast off his p', "
95: 7 we are the p' of his pasture, and "
10 It is a p' that do err in their heart, "
96: 3 heathen, his wonders among all p'.* "
7 O ye kindreds of the p', give unto* "
10 he shall judge the p' righteously. * "
13 and the p' with his truth. * "
97: 6 and all the p' see his glory. * "
98: 9 the world, and the p' with equity.* "
99: 1 Lord reigneth; let the p' tremble:* "
2 and he is high above all the p'. * "
100: 3 we are his p', and the sheep of his "
102: 18 the p' which shall be created shall "
22 When the p' are gathered together,* "
105: 1 known his deeds among the p'. * "
13 from one kingdom to another p'; * "
20 even the ruler of the p', and let * "
24 he increased his p' greatly; and "
25 He turned their heart to hate his p',* "
40 The p' asked, and he brought quails,* "
43 he brought forth his p' with joy, 5971
44 they inherited the labour of the p';* 3816
106: 4 that thou bearest unto thy p': *5971
40 of the Lord kindled against his p', "
48 let all the p' say, Amen. Praise ye "
107: 32 also in the congregation of the p', "
108: 3 praise thee, O Lord, among the p':* "
110: 3 Thy p' shall be willing in the day "
111: 6 He hath shewed his p' the power of "
9 He sent redemption unto his p': he "
113: 8 even with the princes of his p'. "
114: 1 from a p' of strange language; "
116: 14 now in the presence of all his p'. "
18 now in the presence of all his p', "
117: 1 ye nations: praise him, all ye p'. * 523
125: 2 so the Lord is round about his p' 5971
135: 12 an heritage unto Israel his p'. "
14 the Lord will judge his p', and he "
136: 16 led his p' through the wilderness: "
144: 2 who subdueth my p' under me. "
15 Happy is that p', that is in such a "
15 happy is that p', whose God is the "
148: 11 Kings of the earth, and all p'; *3816
14 also exalteth the horn of his p', 5971
14 of Israel, a p' near unto him. "
149: 4 the Lord taketh pleasure in his p': "
7 and punishments upon the p'; *3816
Pr 11: 14 Where no counsel is, the p' fall: 5971
14: 26 corn, the p' shall curse him: but 3816
28 of p' is the king's honour: but in 5971
28 the want of p' is the destruction 3816
34 but sin is a reproach to any p'. "
24: 24 him shall the p' curse, nations *5971
28: 15 is a wicked ruler over the poor p'. "
29: 2 are in authority, the p' rejoice: but "
2 wicked beareth rule, the p' mourn. "
18 there is no vision, the p' perish: "
30: 25 The ants are a p' not strong, yet "
Ec 4: 16 There is no end of all the p', even "
12: 9 he still taught the p' knowledge; "
Isa 1: 3 not know, my p' doth not consider. "
4 nation, a p' laden with iniquity, "
10 law of our God, ye p' of Gomorrah. "
2: 3 many p' shall go and say, Come * "
4 nations, and shall rebuke many p':* "
6 Therefore thou hast forsaken thy p' "
3: 5 And the p' shall be oppressed, every "
7 make me not a ruler of the p'. "
12 As for my p', children are their "
12 O my p', they which lead thee cause "
13 plead, and standeth to judge the p'.* "
14 judgment with the ancients of his p', "
15 What mean ye that ye beat my p' "
5: 13 my p' are gone into captivity, "
25 of the Lord kindled against his p', "
6: 5 the midst of a p' of unclean lips: "
9 Go, and tell this p', Hear ye indeed, "
10 Make the heart of this p' fat, and "
7: 2 heart of his p', as the trees of the "
8 be broken, that it be not a p'. "
17 bring upon thee, and upon thy p', "

Isa 8: 6 p' refuseth the waters of Shiloah 5971
9 Associate yourselves, O ye p', and* "
11 should not walk in the way of this p'. "
12 all them to whom this p' shall say, "
19 should not a p' seek unto their God? "
9: 2 The p' that walked in darkness have "
9 the p' shall know, even Ephraim "
13 the p' turneth not unto him that "
16 the leaders of this p' cause them to "
19 p' shall be as the fuel of the fire: "
10: 2 the right from the poor of my p', "
6 against the p' of my wrath will I "
13 have removed the bounds of the p',* "
14 as a nest the riches of the p': * "
22 though thy p' Israel be as the sand "
24 O my p' that dwellest in Zion, be "
11: 10 shall stand for an ensign of the p';* "
11 to recover the remnant of his p', "
16 highway for the remnant of his p', "
12: 4 declare his doings among the p', * "
13: 4 The noise...like as of a great p'; "
14 shall every man turn to his own p', "
14: 2 the p' shall take them, and bring * "
6 He who smote the p' in wrath with* "
20 destroyed thy land, and slain thy p': "
32 the poor of his p' shall trust in it. "
17: 12 Woe to the multitude of many p', * "
18: 2 to a p' terrible from their beginning "
7 hosts of a p' scattered and peeled, "
7 a p' terrible from their beginning "
19: 25 saying, Blessed be Egypt my p', "
22: 4 spoiling of the daughter of my p'. "
23: 13 this p' was not, till the Assyrian "
24: 2 as with the p', so with the priest; "
4 haughty p' of the earth do languish. "
13 the midst of the land among the p',* "
25: 3 shall the strong p' glorify thee, the "
6 make unto...p' a feast of fat things,* "
7 of the covering cast over all p', * "
8 rebuke of his p' shall he take away "
26: 11 be ashamed for their envy at the p';* "
20 p', enter thou into thy chambers, "
27: 11 for it is a p' of no understanding: "
28: 5 beauty, unto the residue of his p', "
11 tongue will he speak to this p'. "
14 rule this p' which is in Jerusalem. "
29: 13 p' draw near me with their mouth, "
14 a marvellous work among this p', "
30: 5 all ashamed of a p' that could not "
6 to a p' that shall not profit them. "
9 That this is a rebellious p', lying "
19 For the p' shall dwell in Zion at "
26 bindeth up the breach of his p', and "
28 bridle in the jaws of the p', causing* "
32: 13 Upon the land of my p' shall come "
18 my p' shall dwell in a peaceable "
33: 3 the noise of the tumult the p' fled;* "
12 p' shall be as the burnings of lime:* "
19 Thou shalt not see a fierce p', "
19 a p' of a deeper speech than thou "
24 the p' that dwell therein shall be "
34: 1 hearken, ye p': let the earth hear,*3816
5 and upon the p' of my curse, to 5971
36: 11 ears of the p' that are on the wall. "
40: 1 comfort ye my p', saith your God. "
7 upon it: surely the p' is grass. "
41: 1 let the p' renew their strength: *3816
42: 5 he that giveth breath unto the p' 5971
6 give thee for a covenant of the p', "
22 But this is a p' robbed and spoiled; "
43: 4 men for thee, and p' for thy life. *3816
8 Bring...the blind p' that have eyes,5971
9 and let the p' be assembled: who*3816
20 the desert, to give drink to my p', 5971
21 This p' have I formed for myself; "
44: 7 since I appointed the ancient p'? "
47: 6 I was wroth with my p', I have "
49: 1 hearken, ye p', from far; The Lord*3816
8 give thee for a covenant of the p', 5971
13 for the Lord hath comforted his p', "
22 and set up my standard to the p':* "
51: 4 Hearken unto me, my p'; and give "
4 to rest for a light of the p'. * "
5 and mine arms shall judge the p';* "
7 the p' in whose heart is my law; "
16 and say unto Zion, Thou art my p'. "
22 that pleadeth the cause of his p', "
52: 4 My p' went down aforetime into "
5 my p' is taken away for nought? "
6 my p' shall know my name: "
9 for the Lord hath comforted his p', "
53: 8 for the transgression of my p' was "
55: 4 given him for a witness to the p', *3816
4 leader and commander to the p'. * "
56: 3 utterly separated me from his p': 5971
7 called an house of prayer for all p'.* "
57: 14 block out of the way of my p'. "
58: 1 shew my p' their transgression, "
60: 2 earth, and gross darkness the p': 3816
21 Thy p' also shall be all righteous: 5971
61: 9 and their offspring among the p':* "
62: 10 gates; prepare ye the way of the p'; "
10 stones; lift up a standard for the p'.* "
12 they shall call them, The holy p', "
63: 3 of the p' there was none with me:* "
6 tread down the p' in mine anger, * "
8 they are my p', children that will "
11 the days of old, Moses, and his p', "
14 so didst thou lead thy p', to make "
18 p' of thy holiness have possessed "
64: 9 we beseech thee, we are all thy p'. "
65: 2 all the day unto a rebellious p', "
3 A p' that provoketh me to anger "
10 in, for my p' that have sought me. "
18 a rejoicing, and her p' a joy. "
19 in Jerusalem, and joy in my p': "

Isa 65: 22 days of a tree are the days of my p',5971
Jer 1: 18 and against the p' of the land. "
2: 11 my p' have changed their glory for "
13 my p' have committed two evils; "
31 wherefore say my p', We are lords; "
32 yet my p' have forgotten me days "
4: 10 thou hast greatly deceived this p' "
11 it be said to this p' and to Jerusalem, "
11 toward the daughter of my p', not "
22 For my p' is foolish, they have not "
5: 14 this p' wood, and it shall devour "
21 Hear now this, O foolish p', and "
23 But this p' hath a revolting and a "
26 among my p' are found wicked men: "
31 and my p' love to have it so: and "
6: 14 of the daughter of my p' slightly, "
19 I will bring evil upon this p', even "
21 lay stumblingblocks before this p', "
22 a p' cometh from the north country, "
26 O daughter of my p', gird thee with "
27 tower and a fortress among my p', "
7: 12 for the wickedness of my p' Israel. "
16 Therefore pray not thou for this p', "
23 be your God, and ye shall be my p': "
33 carcases of this p' shall be meat for "
8: 5 is this p' of Jerusalem slidden back "
7 but my p' know not the judgment of "
11 of the daughter of my p' slightly, "
19 of the cry of the daughter of my p' "
21 the daughter of my p' am I hurt; "
22 of the daughter of my p' recovered? "
9: 1 the slain of the daughter of my p'! "
2 I might leave my p', and go from "
7 I do for the daughter of my p'? "
15 I will feed them, even this p', with "
10: 3 For the customs of the p' are vain:* "
11: 4 so shall ye be my p', and I will be "
14 pray not thou for this p', neither "
12: 14 have caused my p' Israel to inherit; "
16 diligently learn the ways of my p', "
16 they taught my p' to swear by Baal; "
16 they be built in the midst of my p'. "
13: 10 This evil p', which refuse to hear "
11 they might be unto me for a p', and "
14: 10 Thus saith the Lord unto his p', "
11 Pray not for this p' for their good. "
16 the p' to whom they prophesy shall "
17 virgin daughter of my p' is broken "
15: 1 mind could not be toward this p': "
7 I will destroy my p', since they "
20 unto this p' a fenced brazen wall. "
16: 5 taken away my peace from this p', "
10 shalt shew these p' all these words, "
17: 19 in the gate of the children of the p', "
18: 15 Because my p' hath forgotten me, "
19: 1 and take of the ancients of the p', "
11 so will I break this p' and this city, "
14 Lord's house; and said to all the p', "
21: 7 the p', and such as are left in this "
8 unto this p' thou shalt say, Thus "
22: 2 thy p' that enter in by these gates: "
4 he, and his servants, and his p'. "
23: 2 against the pastors that feed my p'; "
13 and caused my p' Israel to err. "
22 had caused my p' to hear my words, "
27 to cause my p' to forget my name "
32 and cause my p' to err by their lies, "
32 they shall not profit this p' at all, "
33 when this p', or the prophet, or a "
34 prophet, and the priest, and the p', "
24: 7 they shall be my p', and I will be "
25: 1 concerning all the p' of Judah in "
2 spake unto all the p' of Judah, and "
19 and his princes, and all his p'; "
20 And all the mingled p', and all the "
24 mingled p' that dwell in the desert, "
26: 7 the p' heard Jeremiah speaking 5971
8 end of speaking...unto all the p', "
8 prophets and all the p' took him, "
9 p' were gathered against Jeremiah "
11 unto the princes and to all the p', "
12 unto all the princes and to all the p', "
16 said the princes and all the p' unto "
17 spake to all the assembly of the p', "
18 and spake to all the p' of Judah, "
23 into the graves of the common p'. "
24 hand of the p' to put him to death. "
27: 12 and serve him and his p', and live. "
13 Why will ye die, thou and thy p', by "
16 to the priests and to all this p', "
28: 1 of the priests and of all the p', "
5 and in the presence of all the p' that "
7 ears, and in the ears of all the p'; "
11 spake in the presence of all the p', "
15 thou makest this p' to trust in a lie. "
29: 1 to all the p' whom Nebuchadnezzar "
16 all the p' that dwelleth in this city, "
25 all the p' that are at Jerusalem, "
32 have a man to dwell among this p'; "
32 the good that I will do for my p', "
30: 3 again the capitivity of my p' Israel "
22 ye shall be my p', and I will be your "
31: 1 of Israel, and they shall be my p'. "
2 The p' which were left of the sword "
7 Lord, save thy p', the remnant of "
14 my p' shall be satisfied with my "
33 their God, and they shall be my p'. "
32: 21 brought forth thy p' Israel out of "
38 And they shall be my p', and I will "
42 all this great evil upon this p', so "
33: 24 thou not what this p' have spoken, "
24 they have despised my p', that they "
34: 1 all the p', fought against Jerusalem,* "
8 had made a covenant with all the p' "
10 when all the princes, and all the p', "
19 priests, and all the p' of the land, "

Jer 35: 16 this p' hath not hearkened unto me:5971
36: 6 words of the Lord in...ears of the p' "
7 hath pronounced against this p'. "
9 the Lord to all the p' in Jerusalem, "
9 the p' that came from the cities of "
10 house, in the ears of all the p'. "
13 read the book in the ears of the p'. "
14 thou hast read in the ears of the p', "
37: 2 nor the p' of the land, did hearken "
4 in and went out among the p': "
12 thence in the midst of the p'. "
18 thy servants, or against this p', "
38: 1 had spoken unto all the p', saying, "
4 the hands of all the p', in speaking "
4 seeketh not the welfare of this p', "
39: 8 and the houses of the p', with fire, "
9 the remnant of the p' that remained "
9 the rest of the p' that remained. "
10 the guard left of the poor of the p', "
14 home: so he dwelt among the p'. "
40: 5 and dwell with him among the p': "
6 among the p' that were left in the "
41: 10 the residue of the p' that were in "
10 all the p' that remained in Mizpah, "
13 all the p' which were with Ishmael "
14 p' that Ishmael had carried away "
16 the remnant of the p' whom he had "
42: 1 the p' from the least even unto the "
8 all the p' from the least even to the "
43: 1 end of speaking unto all the p' all "
4 p', obeyed not the voice of the Lord, "
44: 15 p' that dwelt in the land of Egypt, "
20 Then Jeremiah said unto all the p', "
20 all the p' which had given him that "
21 princes, and the p' of the land, did "
24 Jeremiah said unto all the p', and "
46: 16 let us go again to our own p', and to "
24 into the hand of the p' of the north. "
48: 42 shall be destroyed from being a p', "
46 the p' of Chemosh perisheth: for "
49: 1 Gad, and his p' dwell in his cities? "
50: 6 My p' hath been lost sheep: their "
16 they shall turn every one to his p', "
37 mingled p' that are in the midst of "
41 a p' shall come from the north, and5971
51: 45 My p', go ye out of the midst of her, "
58 the p' shall labour in vain, and the* "
52: 6 was no bread for the p' of the land. "
15 captive certain of the poor of the p', "
15 residue of the p' that remained in "
25 who mustered the p' of the land; "
25 men of the p' of the land, that were "
28 p' whom Nebuchadrezzar carried "
La 1: 1 city sit solitary, that was full of p'! "
7 p' fell into the hand of the enemy, "
11 All her p' sigh, they seek bread; "
18 hear, I pray you, all p', and behold* "
2: 11 of the daughter of my p'; "
3: 14 I was a derision to all my p'; and "
45 and refuse in the midst of the p'. * "
48 of the daughter of my p'. "
4: 3 the daughter of my p' is become "
6 daughter of my p' is greater than "
10 of the daughter of my p'. "
Eze 3: 5 not sent to a p' of a strange speech "
6 to many p' of a strange speech and* "
11 unto the children of thy p', and "
7: 27 the p' of the land shall be troubled: "
11: 1 the son of Benaiah, princes of the p'. "
17 will even gather you from the p', and* "
20 they shall be my p', and I will be "
12: 19 say unto the p' of the land, Thus "
13: 9 not be in the assembly of my p', "
10 because they have seduced my p', "
17 against the daughters of thy p', "
18 Will ye hunt the souls of my p', and* "
19 will ye pollute me among my p' for "
19 lying to my p' that hear your lies? "
21 and deliver my p' out of your hand, "
23 deliver my p' out of your hand: "
14: 8 him off from the midst of my p'; "
9 him from the midst of my p' Israel. "
11 they may be my p', and I may be "
17: 9 many p' to pluck it up by the roots "
15 might give him horses and much p'. "
18: 18 which is not good among his p', lo, "
20: 34 I will bring you out from the p', * "
35 you into the wilderness of the p', * "
41 when I bring you out from the p',* "
21: 12 for it shall be upon my p', it shall "
12 of the sword shall be upon my p': "
22: 29 p' of the land have used oppression, "
23: 24 and with an assembly of p', which* "
24: 18 spake unto the p' in the morning: "
19 the p' said unto me, Wilt thou not "
25: 7 I will cut thee off from the p', and* "
14 Edom by the hand of my p' Israel: "
26: 2 broken that was the gates of the p';* "
7 and companies, and much p'. "
11 he shall slay thy p' by the sword, "
20 into the pit, with the p' of old time, "
27: 3 merchant of the p' for many isles,* "
33 of the seas, thou filledst many p';* "
36 merchants among the p' shall hiss* "
28: 19 that know thee among the p' shall* "
25 p' among whom they are scattered,* "
29: 13 gather the Egyptians from the p' * "
30: 5 all the mingled p', and Chub, and
11 He and his p' with him, the 5971
31: 12 the p' of the earth are gone down* "
32: 3 thee with a company of many p'; * "
9 will also vex the hearts of many p',* "
10 will make many p' amazed at thee,* "
33: 2 speak to the children of thy p', and "
2 p' of the land take a man of their "
3 blow the trumpet, and warn the p'; "

Eze 33: 6 trumpet, and the p' be not warned; 5971
12 say unto the children of thy p', The "
17 Yet the children of thy p' say, The "
30 children of thy p' still are talking "
31 come unto thee as the p' cometh, "
31 they sit before thee as my p', and "
34: 13 I will bring them out from the p', "
30 even the house of Israel, are my p', "
36: 3 talkers, and are an infamy of the p': "
8 yield your fruit to my p' of Israel; "
12 walk upon you, even my p' Israel; "
15 the reproach of the p' any more, * "
20 These are the p' of the Lord, and "
28 ye shall be my p', and I will be your "
37: 12 O my p', I will open your graves, "
13 have opened your graves, O my p', "
18 children of thy p' shall speak unto "
23 so shall they be my p', and I will "
27 their God, and they shall be my p'. "
38: 6 his bands: and many p' with thee.* "
8 gathered out of many p', against * "
9 thy bands, and many p' with thee. "
12 the p' that are gathered out of the "
14 my p' of Israel dwelleth safely, "
15 and many p' with thee, all of them* "
16 come up against my p' of Israel, "
22 the many p' that are with him, an* "
39: 4 bands, and the p' that is with thee:* "
7 known in the midst of my p' Israel; "
13 all the p' of the land shall bury "
27 brought them again from the p', * "
42: 14 those things which are for the p'. "
44: 11 sacrifice for the p', and they shall "
19 even into the utter court to the p', "
19 shall not sanctify the p' with their "
23 shall teach my p' the difference "
45: 8 shall no more oppress my p'; and "
9 away your exactions from my p', "
16 the p' of the land shall give this "
22 prepare for himself and all the p' "
46: 3 the p' of the land shall worship at "
9 when the p' of the land shall come "
18 my p' be not scattered every man "
20 the utter court, to sanctify the p'. "
24 shall boil the sacrifice of the p'. "
Da 2: 44 kingdom...not be left to other p'. 5972
3: 4 O p', nations, and languages, "
7 all the p' heard the sound of the * "
7 all the p', the nations, and the * "
29 That every p', nation,...language, "
4: 1 the king, unto all p', nations, and* "
5: 19 him, all p', nations, and languages,* "
6: 25 Darius wrote unto all p', nations, * "
7: 14 that all p', nations, and languages, "
27 be given to the p' of the saints of "
8: 24 destroy the mighty and the holy p'. 5971
9: 6 fathers, and to all the p' of the land. "
15 that hast brought thy p' forth out "
16 Jerusalem and thy p' are become "
19 and thy p' are called by thy name. "
20 my sin and the sin of my p' Israel, "
24 upon thy p' and upon thy holy "
26 the p' of the prince that shall come "
10: 14 what shall befall thy p' in the "
11: 14 the robbers of thy p' shall exalt "
15 neither his chosen p', neither shall "
23 become strong with a small p'. 1471
32 but the p' that do know their God 5971
33 among the p' shall instruct many: "
12: 1 standeth for the children of thy p': "
1 that time thy p' shall be delivered, "
7 to scatter the power of the holy p', "
Ho 1: 9 for ye are not my p', and I will not "
10 Ye are not my p', there it shall be "
2: 23 say to them which were not my p', "
23 Thou art my p'; and they shall say, "
4: 4 for thy p' are as they that strive "
6 My p' are destroyed for lack of "
8 They eat up the sin of my p', and "
9 there shall be, like p', like priest: "
12 My p' ask counsel at their stocks, "
14 p' that doth not understand shall "
6: 11 I returned the captivity of my p'. "
7: 8 hath mixed himself among the p';* "
9: 1 not, O Israel, for joy, as other p':* "
10: 5 the p' thereof shall mourn over it, "
10 p' shall be gathered against them,* "
14 shall a tumult arise among thy p', "
11: 7 my p' are bent to backsliding from "
Joe 2: 2 a great p' and a strong; there hath "
5 as a strong p' set in battle array. "
6 face the p' shall be much pained: * "
16 Gather the p', sanctify the "
17 Spare thy p', O Lord, and give not "
17 should they say among the p', * "
18 jealous for his land, and pity his p'. "
19 will answer and say unto his p', "
26, 27 my p' shall never be ashamed. "
3: 2 there for my p' and for my heritage "
3 And they have cast lots for my p'; "
8 to the Sabeans, to a p' far off: *1471
16 the Lord will be the hope of his p', 5971
Am 1: 5 p' of Syria shall go into captivity "
3: 6 the city, and the p' not be afraid? "
7: 8 in the midst of my p' Israel: "
15 Go, prophesy unto my p' Israel. "
8: 2 end is come upon my p' of Israel; "
9: 10 All the sinners of my p' shall die "
14 bring again the captivity of my p' "
Ob 13 have entered into the gate of my p' "
Jon 1: 8 country? and of what p' art thou? "
3: 5 So the p' of Nineveh believed God, 582
Mic 1: 2 Hear, all ye p'; hearken, O earth,*5971
9 he is come unto the gate of my p', "
2: 4 hath changed the portion of my p': "
8 Even of late my p' is risen up as an "

Mic 2: 9 women of my p' have ye cast out 5971
11 shall even be the prophet of this p'. "
3: 3 Who also eat the flesh of my p', and "
5 the prophets that make my p' err, "
4: 1 the hills; and p' shall flow unto it.* "
3 he shall judge among many p', * "
5 p' will walk every one in the name* "
13 thou shalt beat in pieces many p':* "
5: 7 of many p' as a dew from the Lord,* "
8 in the midst of many p' as a lion * "
6: 2 hath a controversy with his p', and "
3 O my p', what have I done unto "
5 O my p', remember now what "
16 shall bear the reproach of my p'. "
7: 14 Feed thy p' with thy rod, the flock "
Na 3: 13 p' in the midst of thee are women: "
18 p' is scattered upon the mountains, "
Hab 2: 5 and heapeth unto him all p': * "
8 remnant of the p' shall spoil thee;* "
10 thy house by cutting off many p', * "
13 the p' shall labour in the very fire,* "
13 and the p' shall weary themselves*3816
3: 13 forth for the salvation of thy p', 5971
16 when he cometh up unto the p', he "
Zep 1: 11 all the merchant p' are cut down; "
2: 8 they have reproached my p', and "
9 residue of my p' shall spoil them, "
9 remnant of my p' shall possess *1471
10 magnified themselves against...p' 5971
3: 9 I turn to the p' a pure language, * "
12 of thee an afflicted and poor p', "
20 a praise among all p' of the earth,* "
Hag 1: 2 This p' say, The time is not come, "
12 with the remnant of the p', obeyed "
12 and the p' did fear before the Lord. "
13 in the Lord's message unto the p', "
14 spirit of all the remnant of the p'; "
2: 2 priest, and to the residue of the p', "
4 and be strong, all ye p' of the land, "
14 So is this p', and so is this nation "
Zec 2: 11 in that day, and shall be my p': "
7: 5 Speak unto all the p' of the land, "
8: 6 the remnant of this p' in these days, "
7 I will save my p' from the east "
8 shall be my p', and I will be their "
11 not be unto the residue of this p' as "
12 remnant of this p' to possess all "
20 that there shall come p', and the * "
22 many p' and strong nations shall * "
9: 16 in that day as the flock of his p': "
10: 9 And I will sow them among the p':* "
11: 10 which I had made with all the p'. * "
12: 2 unto all the p' round about, when* "
3 a burdensome stone for all p': all* "
3 though all the p' of the earth be *1471
4 smite every horse of the p' with *5971
6 shall devour all the p' round about,* "
13: 9 hear them: I will say, It is my p': "
14: 2 residue of the p' shall not be cut off "
12 Lord will smite all the p' that have* "
Mal 1: 4 The p' against whom the Lord hath "
2: 9 base before all the p', according "
M't 1: 21 shall save his p' from their sins. 2992
2: 4 and scribes of the p' together, he "
6 Governor,...shall rule my p' Israel. "
4: 16 The p' which sat in darkness saw "
23 all manner of disease among the p'. "
24 they brought unto him all sick p' * "
25 great multitudes of p' from Galilee, * "
7: 28 p' were astonished at his doctrine:*3793
9: 23 and the p' making a noise, "
25 when the p' were put forth, he went* "
35 and every disease among the p'. *2992
12: 23 all the p' were amazed, and said, *3793
46 While he yet talked to the p', "
14: 13 and when the p' had heard thereof,* "
15: 8 p' draweth nigh unto me with their 2992
21: 23 the elders of the p' came unto him "
26 shall say, Of men; we fear the p';*3793
26: 3 scribes, and the elders of the p', 2992
5 there be an uproar among the p'. "
47 chief priests and elders of the p'. "
27: 1 and elders of the p' took counsel "
15 to release unto the p' a prisoner, *3793
25 Then answered all the p', and said, 2992
64 him away, and say unto the p', "
M'r 5: 21 side, much p' gathered unto him:*3793
24 and much p' followed him, and * "
6: 33 And the p' saw them departing, and "
34 saw much p', and was moved with* "
45 while he sent away the p'. "
7: 6 p' honoureth me with their lips, 2992
14 he had called all the p' unto him, *3793
17 entered into the house from the p',* "
8: 6 commanded the p' to sit down on* "
6 and they did set them before the p'.* "
34 he had called the p' unto him with* "
9: 15 And straightway all the p', when * "
25 Jesus saw that the p' came running* "
10: 1 and the p' resort unto him again;* "
46 disciples and a great number of p',* "
11: 18 p' was astonished at his doctrine * "
32 say, Of men; they feared the p': 2992
12: 12 lay hold on him, but feared the p';*3793
37 the common p' heard him gladly. "
41 beheld how the p' cast money into* "
14: 2 lest there be an uproar of the p'. 2992
15: 11 But the chief priests moved the p',*3793
15 so Pilate, willing to content the p',* "
Lu 1: 10 multitude of the p' were praying 2992
17 ready a p' prepared for the Lord. "
21 And the p' waited for Zacharias, "
68 hath visited and redeemed his p', "
77 knowledge of salvation unto his p' "
2: 10 great joy, which shall be to all p'. "
31 prepared before the face of all p';* "

Lu 2: 32 and the glory of thy p' Israel. 2992
3: 10 And the p' asked him, saying, *3793
15 And as the p' were in expectation, 2992
18 preached he unto the p'. "
21 Now when all the p' were baptized, "
4: 42 the p' sought him, and came unto*3793
5: 1 p' pressed upon him to hear the * "
3 and taught the p' out of the ship, * "
6: 17 multitude of p' out of all Judæa 2992
7: 1 sayings in the audience of the p', "
9 said unto the p' that followed *3793
11 went with him, and much p'. * "
12 much p' of the city was with her. "
16 and, That God hath visited his p'. 2992
24 speak unto the p' concerning *3793
29 And all the p' that heard him, and 2992
8: 4 And when much p' were gathered*3793
40 the p' gladly received him: for * "
42 as he went the p' thronged him. * "
47 declared unto him before all the p'*2992
9: 11 And the p', when they knew it, *3793
13 go and buy meat for all this p'. 2992
18 saying, Whom say the p' that I *3793
37 from the hill, much p' met him. * "
11: 14 dumb spake; and the p' wondered.* "
29 when the p' were gathered thick * "
12: 1 an innumerable multitude of p', * "
54 he said also to the p', When ye see* "
13: 14 said unto the p', There are six days* "
17 p' rejoiced for all the glorious * "
18: 43 all the p', when they saw it, gave 2992
19: 47 chief of the p' sought to destroy "
48 the p' were very attentive to hear "
20: 1 as he taught the p' in the temple, "
6 say, Of men; all the p' will stone us: "
9 he to speak to the p' this parable; "
19 and they feared the p': for they "
26 take hold of his words before the p': "
45 in the audience of all the p' he said "
21: 23 in the land, and wrath upon this p'. "
38 all the p' came early in the morning "
22: 2 kill him; for they feared the p'. "
66 the elders of the p' and the chief "
23: 4 to the chief priests and to the p', *3793
5 He stirreth up the p', teaching 2992
13 priests and the rulers and the p', "
14 me, as one that perverteth the p': "
27 followed him a great company of p', "
35 And the p' stood beholding. And "
48 And all the p' that came together *3793
24: 19 and word before God and all the p': 2992
Joh 6: 22 p' which stood on the other side *3793
24 p' therefore saw that Jesus was * "
7: 12 much murmuring among the p' * "
12 said, Nay; but he deceiveth the p':* "
20 p' answered and said, Thou hast a* "
31 many of the p' believed on him, * "
32 heard that the p' murmured such * "
40 Many of the p', therefore, when * "
43 was a division among the p' * "
49 this p' who knoweth not the law are* "
8: 2 all the p' came unto him; and he sat 2992
11: 42 because of the p' which stand by I*3793
50 that one man should die for the p', 2992
12: 9 Much p' of the Jews therefore knew 3793
12 next day much p' that were come to* "
17 The p' therefore that was with him* "
18 For this cause the p' also met him,* "
29 The p' therefore, that stood by, and* "
34 p' answered him, We have heard * "
18: 14 that one man should die for the p'. 2992
Ac 2: 47 and having favour with all the p'. "
3: 9 the p' saw him walking and praising "
11 all the p' ran together unto them in "
12 he answered unto the p', Ye men of "
23 be destroyed from among the p'. "
4: 1 And as they spake unto the p', the "
2 grieved that they taught the p', and "
8 Ye rulers of the p', and elders of "
10 you all, and to all the p' of Israel, "
17 it spread no further among the p', "
21 punish them, because of the p': for "
25 and the p' imagine vain things? * "
27 p' of Israel, were gathered together,* "
5: 12 and wonders wrought among the p'; "
13 them: but the p' magnified them. "
20 and speak in the temple to the p' "
25 in the temple, and teaching the p'. "
26 they feared the p', lest they should "
34 had in reputation among all the p', "
37 and drew away much p' after him: "
6: 8 wonders and miracles among the p'. "
12 stirred up the p', and the elders, "
7: 17 the p' grew and multiplied in Egypt, "
34 seen the affliction of my p' "
8: 6 the p' with one accord gave heed *3793
9 and bewitched the p' of Samaria, 1484
10: 2 which gave much alms to the p', 2992
41 Not to all the p', but unto witnesses "
42 commanded us to preach unto the p', "
11: 24 much p' was added unto the Lord. 3793
26 with the church, and taught much p'. "
12: 4 Easter to bring him forth to the p'. 2992
11 expectation of the p' of the Jews. "
22 the p' gave a shout, saying, It is 1218
13: 15 any word of exhortation for the p', 2992
17 God of this p' of Israel chose our "
17 exalted the p' when they dwelt as "
24 of repentance to all the p' of Israel. "
31 who are his witnesses unto the p'. "
14: 11 the p' saw what Paul had done, *3793
13 have done sacrifice with the p'. "
14 and ran in among the p', crying out,* "
18 scarce restrained they the p', that,* "
19 who persuaded the p', and, having* "
15: 14 take out of them a p' for his name. 2992

Ac 17: 5 sought to bring them out to the p'. 1218
8 And they troubled the p' and the *3793
13 thither also, and stirred up the p'.* "
18: 10 thee: for I have much p' in this city. 2992
19: 4 saying unto the p', that they should "
26 and turned away much p', saying 3793
30 would have entered in unto the p', 1218
33 have made his defence unto the p'. "
35 the townclerk had appeased the p',*3793
21: 27 stirred up all the p', and laid hands*"
28 against the p', and the law, and 2992
30 was moved, and the p' ran together: "
35 soldiers for the violence of the p'. *3793
36 For the multitude of the p' followed 2992
39 thee, suffer me to speak unto the p'. "
40 beckoned with the hand unto the p'. "
23: 5 not speak evil of the ruler of thy p'. "
24: 12 neither raising up the p', neither in*3793
26: 17 Delivering thee from the p', and 2992
23 should shew light unto the p', and "
28: 2 barbarous p' shewed us no little *
17 committed nothing against the p', 2992
26 Go unto this p', and say, Hearing ye "
27 the heart of this p' is waxed gross,* "
Ro 9: 25 also in Osee, I will call them my p', "
25 which were not my p'; and her "
26 said unto them, Ye are not my p'; "
10: 19 to jealousy by them that are no p',*1484
21 a disobedient and gainsaying p'. 2992
11: 1 then, Hath God cast away his p'? "
2 God hath not cast away his p' which "
15: 10 Rejoice, ye Gentiles, with his p'. "
11 Gentiles; and laud him, all ye p'. * "
1Co 10: 7 The p' sat down to eat and drink, "
14: 21 other lips will I speak unto this p'; "
2Co 6: 16 their God, and they shall be my p'. "
Tit 2: 14 a peculiar p', zealous of good works. "
Heb 2: 17 reconciliation for the sins of the p'. "
4: 9 therefore a rest to the p' of God. "
5: 3 as for the p', so also for himself, to "
7: 5 to take tithes of the p' according "
11 (for under it the p' received the law,) "
8: 10 God, and they shall be to me a p': "
9: 7 himself, and for the errors of the p': "
19 spoken every precept to all the p' "
19 sprinkled...the book, and all the p'. "
10: 30 again, The Lord shall judge his p'. "
11: 25 suffer affliction with the p' of God, "
13: 12 sanctify the p' with his own blood, "
1Pe 2: 9 an holy nation, a peculiar p'; that "
10 Which in time past were not a p', "
10 but are now the p' of God: which "
2Pe 2: 1 false prophets also among the p', "
Jude 5 having saved the p' out of...Egypt, "
Re 5: 9 and tongue, and p', and nation; "
7: 9 and kindreds, and p', and tongues,* "
11: 9 And they of the p' and kindreds and* "
14: 6 and kindred, and tongue, and p', "
18: 4 Come out of her, my p', that ye be "
19: 1 a great voice of much p' in heaven,*3793
21: 3 with them, and they shall be his p',*2992

people's
Le 9: 15 And he brought the p' offering, 5971
Eze 46: 18 shall not take of the p' inheritance "
M't 13: 15 For this p' heart is waxed gross, 2992
Heb 7: 27 his own sins, and then for the p': * "

peoples
Re 10: 11 prophesy again before many p', 2992
17: 15 where the whore sitteth, are p', and "

Peor (*pe'-or*) See also BAAL-PEOR; BETH-PEOR; PEOR'S.
Nu 23: 28 Balaam unto the top of P', 6465
25: 18 beguiled you in the matter of P', "
31: 16 against the Lord in the matter of P'. "
Jos 22: 17 Is the iniquity of P' too little for us, "

Peor's
Nu 25: 18 the day of the plague for P' sake.*6465

peradventure
Ge 18: 24 P' there be fifty righteous within 194
28 P' there shall lack five of the fifty "
29 P' there shall be forty found there. "
30 P' there shall thirty be found there. "
31 P' there shall be twenty found there. "
32 P' ten shall be found there. And "
31: 31 P' thou wouldest take by force *6435
32: 20 his face; p' he will accept of me. 194
38: 11 Lest p' he die also, as his brethren*
42: 4 said, Lest p' mischief befall him.
43: 12 your hand; p' it was an oversight: 194
44: 34 lest p' I see the evil that shall come*
50: 15 Joseph will p' hate us, and will *3863
Ex 13: 17 God said, Lest p' the people repent
32: 30 p' I shall make an atonement for 194
Nu 22: 6 p' I shall prevail, that we may smite "
11 p' I shall be able to overcome them, "
23: 3 p' the Lord will come to meet me: "
27 p' it will please God that thou mayest "
Jos 9: 7 P' ye dwell among us; and how "
1Sa 6: 5 p' he will lighten his hand from off "
9: 6 p' he can shew us our way that we "
1Ki 18: 5 p' we may find grass to save the "
27 p' he sleepeth, and must be awaked. "
20: 31 of Israel: p' he will save thy life. "
2Ki 2: 16 lest p' the Spirit of the Lord hath "
Jer 20: 10 P' he will be enticed, and we shall 194
Ro 5: 7 yet p' for a good man some would 5029
2Ti 2: 25 if God p' will give them repentance 3379

Perazim (*per'-a-zim*) See also BAAL-PERAZIM.
Isa 28: 21 Lord shall rise up as in mount P'.

perceive See also PERCEIVED; PERCEIVEST; PERCEIVETH; PERCEIVING.
De 29: 4 hath not given you an heart to p'.*3045
Jos 22: 31 day we p' that the Lord is among us,*3045
1Sa 12: 17 p' and see that your wickedness is* "
2Sa 19: 6 for this day I p', that if Absalom "
2Ki 4: 9 I p' that this is an holy man of God. "
Job 9: 11 he passeth on also, but I p' him not. 995
23: 8 and backward, but I cannot p' him:* "
Pr 1: 2 to p' the words of understanding;*
Ec 3: 22 I p' that there is nothing better, *7200
Isa 6: 9 not; and see ye indeed, but p' not. 3045
33: 19 deeper speech than thou canst p';‡8085
M't 13: 14 seeing ye shall see, and shall not p': 1492
M'r 4: 12 seeing they may see, and not p'; "
7: 18 Do ye not p', that whatsoever thing 3539
8: 17 p' ye not yet, neither understand? "
Lu 8: 46 I p' that virtue is gone out of me. *1097
Joh 4: 19 Sir, I p' that thou art a prophet. 2334
12: 19 P' ye how ye prevail nothing? * "
Ac 8: 23 For I p' that thou art in the gall of*3708
10: 34 I p' that God is no respecter of 2638
17: 22 I p' that in all things ye are too 2334
27: 10 I p'...this voyage will be with hurt "
28: 26 and seeing ye shall see, and not p': 1492
2Co 7: 8 p' that the same epistle hath made*991
1Jo 3: 16 Hereby p' we the love of God, *1097

perceived
Ge 19: 33, 35 he p' not when she lay down, *3045
J'g 6: 22 Gideon p' that he was an angel *7200
1Sa 3: 8 And Eli p' that the Lord had called 995
28: 14 And Saul p' that it was Samuel, 3045
2Sa 5: 12 David p'...the Lord had established "
12: 19 David p' that the child was dead: 995
14: 1 p' that the king's heart was toward 3045
1Ki 22: 33 p' that it was not the king of Israel*7200
1Ch 14: 2 David p'...the Lord had confirmed*3045
2Ch 18: 32 p'...it was not the king of Israel, *7200
Ne 6: 12 I p' that God had not sent him; *5234
16 p' that this work was wrought of 3045
13: 10 p' that the portions of the Levites "
Es 4: 1 Mordecai p' all that was done, * "
Job 38: 18 thou p' the breadth of the earth? * 995
Ec 1: 17 I p' that this also is vexation of 3045
2: 14 and I myself p' also that one event "
Isa 64: 4 have not heard, nor p' by the ear, 238
Jer 23: 18 and hath p' and heard his word ? *7200
38: 27 him; for the matter was not p'. 8085
M't 16: 8 Which when Jesus p', he said unto*1097
21: 45 they p' that he spake of them. "
22: 18 Jesus p' their wickedness, and said "
M'r 2: 8 when Jesus p' in his spirit that *1921
Lu 1: 22 they p' that he had seen a vision "
5: 22 when Jesus p' their thoughts, he * "
9: 45 hid from them, that they p' it not:* 143
20: 19 p' that he had spoken this parable 1097
23 But he p' their craftiness, and said 2657
Joh 6: 15 p'...they would come and take him*1097
Ac 4: 13 p' that they were unlearned and 2638
23: 6 p'...the one part were Sadducees, 1097
29 I p' to be accused of questions of *2147
Ga 2: 9 p' the grace that was given unto 1097

perceivest
Pr 14: 7 p' not in him the lips of knowledge*3045
Lu 6: 41 p' not the beam that is in thine *2657

perceiveth
Job 14: 21 low, but he p' it not of them. 995
33: 14 once, yea twice, yet man p' it not.*7789
Pr 31: 18 p' that her merchandise is good: 2938

perceiving
M'r 12: 28 p' that he had answered them well,*1492
Lu 9: 47 Jesus, p' the thought of their heart,* "
Ac 14: 9 p' that he had faith to be healed, * "

perdition
Joh 17: 12 of them is lost, but the son of p'; 684
Ph'p 1: 28 is to them an evident token of p', "
2Th 2: 3 of sin be revealed, the son of p'; "
1Ti 6: 9 drown men in destruction and p'. "
Heb 10: 39 not of them who draw back unto p'; "
2Pe 3: 7 of judgment and p' of ungodly men. "
Re 17: 8 of the bottomless pit, and go into p': "
11 is of the seven, and goeth into p'. "

Peres (*pe'-res*) See also UPHARSIN.
Da 5: 28 P'; Thy kingdom is divided, and 6537

Peresh (*pe'-resh*)
1Ch 7: 16 a son, and she called his name P'; 6570

Perez (*pe'-rez*) See also PEREZ-UZZAH; PHARES.
1Ch 27: 3 Of the children of P' was the chief 6557
Ne 11: 4 of Mahalaleel, of the children of P'; "
6 sons of P' that dwelt at Jerusalem "

Perez-uzza (*pe''-rez-uz'-zah*) See also PEREZ-UZZAH.
1Ch 13: 11 that place is called P' to this day. 6560

Perez-uzzah (*pe''-rez-uz'-zah*) See also PEREZ-UZZA.
2Sa 6: 8 name of the place P' to this day. 6560

perfect See also PERFECTED; PERFECTING; UNPERFECT.
Ge 6: 9 Noah was a just man and p' in his 8549
17: 1 walk before me, and be thou p'. "
Le 22: 21 sheep, it shall be p' to be accepted; "
De 18: 13 shalt be p' with the Lord thy God. "
25: 15 shalt have a p' and just weight, 8003
15 a p' and just measure shalt thou "
32: 4 He is the Rock, his work is p': 8549
1Sa 14: 41 Lord God of Israel, Give a p' lot. * "
2Sa 22: 31 As for God, his way is p'; the word "
33 power: and he maketh my way p'. "
1Ki 8: 61 Let your heart therefore be p' 8003
11: 4 his heart was not p' with the Lord "
15: 3 his heart was not p' with the Lord "
14 nevertheless Asa's heart was p' "
2Ki 20: 3 thee in truth and with a p' heart, "
1Ch 12: 38 came with a p' heart to Hebron, 8003
28: 9 serve him with a p' heart and with "
29: 9 with p' heart they offered willingly "
19 unto Solomon my son a p' heart, "
2Ch 4: 21 made he of gold, and that p' gold; 4357
15: 17 heart of Asa was p' all his days. 8003
16: 9 them whose heart is p' toward him. "
19: 9 faithfully, and with a p' heart. "
25: 2 of the Lord, but not with a p' heart. "
Ezr 7: 12 unto Ezra the priest,...p' peace, 1585
Job 1: 1 and that man was p' and upright, 8535
8 a p' and an upright man, one that "
2: 3 a p' and an upright man, one that "
8: 20 God will not cast away a p' man, "
9: 20 if I say, I am p', it shall also prove "
21 Though I were p', yet would I not "
22 destroyeth the p' and the wicked "
22: 3 that thou makest thy ways p'? 8552
36: 4 he that is p' in knowledge is with 8549
37: 16 of him which is p' in knowledge? "
Ps 18: 30 As for God, his way is p': the "
32 strength, and maketh my way p'. "
19: 7 law of the Lord is p', converting "
37: 37 Mark the p' man, and behold the 8535
64: 4 they may shoot in secret at the p': "
101: 2 behave myself wisely in a p' way. 8549
2 within my house with a p' heart. 8537
6 he that walketh in a p' way, he 8549
138: 8 will p' that which concerneth me: 1584
139: 22 I hate them with p' hatred: I 8503
Pr 2: 21 land, and the p' shall remain in it. 8549
4: 18 more and more unto the p' day. 3559
11: 5 righteousness of the p' shall direct 8549
Isa 18: 5 when the bud is p', and the sour *8552
26: 3 Thou wilt keep him in p' peace, whose
38: 3 thee in truth and with a p' heart, 8003
42: 19 who is blind as he that is p', and *7999
Eze 16: 14 it was p' through my comeliness, 3632
27: 3 thou hast said, I am of p' beauty, "
11 they have made thy beauty p'. *3634
28: 12 full of wisdom, and p' in beauty. 3632
15 Thou wast p' in thy ways from the 8549
M't 5: 48 Be ye therefore p', even as your 5046
48 your Father which is in heaven is p'. "
19: 21 If thou wilt be p', go and sell that "
Lu 1: 3 having had p' understanding of all*199
6: 40 that is p' shall be as his master. *2675
Joh 17: 23 that they may be made p' in one; *5048
Ac 3: 16 hath given him this p' soundness 3647
22: 3 p' manner of the law of the fathers,*195
24: 22 more p' knowledge of that way, * 197
Ro 12: 2 and acceptable, and p', will of God. 5046
1Co 2: 6 wisdom among them that are p': ‡ "
13: 10 But when that which is p' is come, "
2Co 12: 9 strength is made p' in weakness. 5048
13: 11 Be p', be of good comfort, be of *2675
Ga 3: 3 are ye now made p' by the flesh? *2005
Eph 4: 13 unto a p' man, unto the measure *5046
Ph'p 3: 12 attained, either were already p': 5048
15 Let us therefore, as many as be p', 5046
Col 1: 28 every man p' in Christ Jesus: "
4: 12 that ye may stand p' and complete "
1Th 3: 10 might p' that which is lacking 2675
2Ti 3: 17 That the man of God may be p', * 739
Heb 2: 10 the captain of their salvation p' 5048
5: 9 And being made p', he became the "
7: 19 For the law made nothing p', but "
9: 9 make him that did the service p', "
11 a greater and more p' tabernacle, 5046
10: 1 make the comers thereunto p'. 5048
11: 40 without us should not be made p'. "
12: 23 to the spirits of just men made p'. "
13: 21 Make you p' in every good work 2675
Jas 1: 4 But let patience have her p' work, 5046
4 be p' and entire, wanting nothing. "
17 and every p' gift is from above, "
25 looketh into the p' law of liberty, "
2: 22 and by works was faith made p'? 5048
3: 2 not in word, the same is a p' man, 5046
1Pe 5: 10 suffered a while, make you p', 2675
1Jo 4: 17 Herein is our love made p', that 5048
18 but p' love casteth out fear: 5046
18 that feareth is not made p' in love. 5048
Re 3: 2 have not found thy works p' †‡4137

perfected
2Ch 8: 16 So the house of the Lord was p'. 8003
24: 13 and the work was p' by them, 5927, 724
Eze 27: 4 thy builders have p' thy beauty. 3634
M't 21: 16 and sucklings thou hast p' praise? 2675
Lu 13: 32 and the third day I shall be p'. 5048
Heb 10: 14 by one offering he hath p' for ever "
1Jo 2: 5 in him verily is the love of God p': "
4: 12 in us, and his love is p' in us. "

perfecting
2Co 7: 1 p' holiness in the fear of God. 2005
Eph 4: 12 For the p' of the saints, for the 2677

perfection See also PERFECTNESS.
Job 11: 7 find out the Almighty unto p'? 8503
15: 29 shall he prolong the p' thereof †‡4512
28: 3 darkness, and searcheth out all p':*8503
Ps 50: 2 Out of Zion, the p' of beauty, 4359
119: 96 I have seen an end of all p': 8502
Isa 47: 9 shall come upon thee in their p' *8537
La 2: 15 The p' of beauty, The joy of the 3632
Lu 8: 14 this life, and bring no fruit to p'. 5052
2Co 13: 9 this also we wish, even your p'. *2676
Heb 6: 1 of Christ, let us go on unto p'; 5051
7: 11 p' were by the Levitical priesthood, 5050

perfectly
Jer 23: 20 latter days ye shall consider it p'. 998
M't 14: 36 as touched were made p' whole. *1295
Ac 18: 26 unto him the way of God more p'.* 197
23: 15 would enquire something more p'* "

Ac 23:20 enquire somewhat of him more p'.* 197
1Co 1:10 but that ye be p' joined together *2675
1Th 5: 2 know p' that the day of the Lord 199

perfectness See also PERFECTION.
Col 3:14 on charity, which is the bond of p'.5047

perform See also PERFORMED; PERFORMETH; PERFORMING.
Ge 26: 3 I will p' the oath which I sware *6965
Ex 18:18 art not able to p' it thyself alone. 6213
Nu 4:23 all that enter in to p' the service, *6633
De 4:13 which he commanded you to p', 6213
9: 5 may p' the word which the Lord *6965
23:23 of thy lips thou shalt keep and p';*6213
25: 5 p' the duty of an husband's brother
7 p' the duty of my husband's brother.
Ru 3:13 p' unto thee the part of a kinsman,
1Sa 3:12 day I will p' against Eli all things 6965
2Sa 14:15 p' the request of his handmaid. 6213
1Ki 6:12 then will I p' my word with thee, *6965
12:15 Lord, that he might p' his saying,* "
2Ki 23: 3 to p' the words of this covenant "
24 he might p' the words of the law,* "
2Ch 10:15 that the Lord might p' his word, * "
34:31 to p' the words of the covenant 6213
Es 5: 8 my petition, and to p' my request, "
Job 5:12 their hands cannot p' their enterprise.
Ps 21:11 device, which they are not able to p'.
61: 8 ever, that I may daily p' my vows. 7999
119:106 I have sworn, and I will p' it, *6965
112 heart to p' thy statutes alway, 6213
Isa 9: 7 zeal of the Lord of hosts will p' this."
19:21 vow a vow unto the Lord, and p' it.7999
44:28 and shall p' all my pleasure: "
Jer 1:12 for I will hasten my word to p' it. 6213
11: 5 p' the oath which I have sworn *6965
28: 6 Lord p' thy words which thou hast "
29:10 and p' my good word toward you, "
33:14 will p' that good thing which I have"
44:25 We will surely p' our vows that 6213
25 your vows, and surely p' your vows."
Eze 12:25 will I say the word, and will p' it, "
Mic 7:20 Thou wilt p' the truth to Jacob, 5414
Na 1:15 thy solemn feasts, p' thy vows: 7999
M't 5:33 shalt p' unto the Lord thine oaths: 591
Lu 1:72 p' the mercy promised to our *4160
Ro 4:21 promised, he was able also to p'. "
7:18 how to p' that which is good I find*2716
2Co 8:11 Now therefore p' the doing of it; *2005
Ph'p 1: 6 will p' it until the day of Jesus * "

performance
Lu 1:45 there shall be a p' of those things *5050
2Co 8:11 so there may be a p' also out of *2005

performed
1Sa 15:11 hath not p' my commandments. 6965
13 p' the commandment of the Lord. "
2Sa 21:14 p' all that the king commanded. 6213
1Ki 8:20 And the Lord hath p' his word *6965
2Ch 6:10 The Lord therefore hath p' his word"
Ne 9: 8 and hast p' thy words; for thou art "
Es 1:15 she hath not p' the commandment*6213
5: 6 half of the kingdom it shall be p'. "
7: 2 and it shall be p', even to the half "
Ps 65: 1 and unto thee shall the vow be p'. 7999
Isa 10:12 the Lord hath p' his whole work 1214
Jer 23:20 have p' the thoughts of his heart: 6965
30:24 he have p' the intents of his heart: "
34:18 not p' the words of the covenant "
35:14 The words of Jonadab...are p'; "
16 p' the commandment of their father."
51:29 purpose of the Lord shall be p' * "
Eze 37:14 the Lord have spoken it, and p' it, 6213
Lu 1:20 day that these things shall be p', *1096
2:39 p' all things according to the law *5055
Ro 15:28 When therefore I have p' this, *2005

performeth
Ne 5:13 that p' not this promise, even thus6965
Job 23:14 p' the thing that is appointed for 7999
Ps 57: 2 unto God that p' all things for me.1584
Isa 44:26 p' the counsel of his messengers; 7999

performing
Nu 15: 3 offering, or a sacrifice in p' a vow,*6381
8 or for a sacrifice in p' a vow, * "

perfume See also PERFUMED; PERFUMES.
Ex 30:35 And thou shalt make it a p', a *7004
37 for the p' which thou shalt make,* "
Pr 27: 9 Ointment and p' rejoice the heart: "

perfumed
Pr 7:17 have p' my bed with myrrh, aloes, 5130
Ca 3: 6 p' with myrrh and frankincense, 6999

perfumes
Isa 57: 9 and didst increase thy p', and 7547

Perga (pur'-gah)
Ac 13:13 they came to P' in Pamphylia: 4011
14 when they departed from P', they "
14:25 they had preached the word in P'. "

Pergamos (pur'-ga-mos)
Re 1:11 and unto P', and unto Thyatira, *4010
2:12 angel of the church in P' write; * "

perhaps
Ac 8:22 if p' the thought of thine heart may 686
2Co 2: 7 lest p' such...should be swallowed*3381
Ph'm 15 For p' he...departed for a season, 5029

Perida (per-i'-dah) See also PERUDA.
Ne 7:57 of Sophereth, the children of P'. 6514

peril See also PERILS.
La 5: 9 gat our bread with the p' of our lives,
Ro 8:35 or nakedness, or p', or sword? 2794

perilous
2Ti 3: 1 the last days p' times shall come. *5467

perils
2Co 11:26 in p' of waters, in p' of robbers, 2794
26 in p' by mine own countrymen, "
26 p' by the heathen, in p' in the city, "
26 in the city, in p' in the wilderness, "
26 in the wilderness, in p' in the sea, "
26 the sea, in p' among false brethren;"

perish See also PERISHED; PERISHETH; PERISHING.
Ge 41:36 land p' not through the famine. 3772
Ex 19:21 Lord to gaze, and many of them p'.5307
21:26 or the eye of his maid, that it p'; *7843
Le 26:38 And ye shall p' among the heathen, 6
Nu 17:12 Behold, we die, we p', we all p'. * "
24:20 latter end shall be that he p' for ever.*8
24 Eber, and he also shall p' for ever.* "
De 4:26 shall soon utterly p' from off the land6
8:19 you this day that ye shall surely p'. "
20 so shall ye p'; because ye would not "
11:17 ye p' quickly from off the good land "
26: 5 A Syrian ready to p' was my father, "
28:20 destroyed, and until thou p' quickly; "
22 they shall pursue thee until thou p'. "
30:18 you this day, that ye shall surely p', "
Jos 23:13 until ye p' from off this good land "
16 shall p' quickly from off the good "
J'g 5:31 So let all thine enemies p', O Lord: "
1Sa 26:10 shall descend into battle, and p'. 5595
27: 1 p' one day by the hand of Saul: "
2Ki 9: 8 For the whole house of Ahab shall p':6
Es 3:13 to kill, and to cause to p', all Jews, "
4:16 according to the law: and if I p', I p'. "
7: 4 to be destroyed, to be slain, and to p'. "
8:11 to destroy, to slay, and to cause to p', "
9:28 nor the memorial of them p' from 5486
Job 3: 3 Let the day p' wherein I was born, 6
4: 9 By the blast of God they p', and by "
20 p' for ever without any regarding it. "
6:18 aside; they go to nothing, and p'. "
8:13 and the hypocrite's hope shall p': "
18:17 His remembrance shall p' from the "
20: 7 he shall p' for ever like his own dung "
29:13 blessing of him that was ready to p' "
31:19 have seen any p' for want of clothing "
34:15 All flesh shall p' together, and man1478
36:12 they shall p' by the sword, and 5674
Ps 1: 6 but the way of the ungodly shall p'. 6
2:12 lest he be angry, and ye p' from the "
9: 3 they shall fall and p' at thy presence."
18 expectation of the poor shall not p' "
37:20 the wicked shall p', and the enemies "
41: 5 When shall he die, and his name p'? "
49:10 the fool and the brutish person p', "
12 not: he is like the beasts that p'. 1820
20 not, is like the beasts that p'. "
68: 2 let the wicked p' at...presence of God.6
73:27 they that are far from thee shall p': "
80:16 p' at the rebuke of thy countenance. "
83:17 let them be put to shame and p': "
92: 9 Lord, for, lo, thine enemies shall p'; "
102:26 They shall p', but thou shalt endure: "
112:10 the desire of the wicked shall p'. "
146: 4 in that very day his thoughts p'. "
Pr 10:28 expectation of the wicked shall p'. "
11: 7 man dieth, his expectation shall p': "
10 the wicked p', there is shouting. "
19: 9 and he that speaketh lies shall p'. "
21:28 A false witness shall p': but the man "
28:28 when they p', the righteous increase. "
29:18 there is no vision, the people p': *6544
31: 6 drink unto him that is ready to p', 6
Ec 5:14 But those riches p' by evil travail: "
Isa 26:14 and made all their memory to p'. "
27:13 ready to p' in the land of Assyria, "
29:14 wisdom of their wise men shall p', "
41:11 they that strive with thee shall p'. "
60:12 that will not serve thee shall p'; "
Jer 4: 9 that the heart of the king shall p', "
6:21 neighbour and his friend shall p'. "
10:11 they shall p' from the earth, and 7
15 time of their visitation they shall p'. 6
18:18 the law shall not p' from the priest, "
27:10 drive you out, and ye should p'. "
15 drive you out, and that ye might p', "
40:15 and the remnant in Judah p'? "
48: 8 the valley also shall p', and the plain "
51:18 time of their visitation they shall p'. "
Eze 7:26 but the law shall p' from the priest, "
25: 7 cause thee to p' out of the countries: "
Da 2:18 Daniel and his fellows should not p' 7
Am 1: 8 the remnant of the Philistines shall p'.6
2:14 the flight shall p' from the swift, "
3:15 the houses of ivory shall p', and the "
Jon 1: 6 will think upon us, that we p' not. "
14 let us not p' for this man's life, and "
3: 9 from his fierce anger, that we p' not? "
Zec 9: 5 and the king shall p' from Gaza, "
M't 5:29, 30 one of thy members should p', 622
8:25 him, saying, Lord, save us: we p'. "
9:17 wine runneth out, and the bottles p': "
18:14 one of these little ones should p'. "
26:52 the sword shall p' with the sword. "
M'r 4:38 Master, carest thou not that we p'? "
Lu 5:37 be spilled, and the bottles shall p'. "
8:24 saying, Master, master, we p'. "
13: 3, 5 repent, ye shall all likewise p'. "
33 that a prophet p' out of Jerusalem. "
15:17 and to spare, and I p' with hunger! "
21:18 shall not an hair of your head p'. "
Joh 3:15 believeth in him should not p', * "
16 believeth in him should not p', "
10:28 and they shall never p', neither "
11:50 and that the whole nation p' not. "
Ac 8:20 Thy money p' with thee, 1510,1519,684
13:41 ye despisers, and wonder, and p': 853
Ro 2:12 law shall also p' without law: 622
1Co 1:18 cross is to them that p' foolishness;†"
8:11 shall the weak brother p', for whom*"
2Co 2:15 that are saved, and in them that p':†"
4:16 but though our outward man p', *1311
Col 2:22 Which all are to p' with the using;5356
2Th 2:10 unrighteousness in them that p'; † 622
Heb 1:11 They shall p'; but thou remainest; "
2Pe 2:12 utterly p' in their own corruption;*2704
3: 9 not willing that any should p', but 622

perished
Nu 16:33 p' from among the congregation. 6
21:30 Heshbon is p' even unto Dibon, "
Jos 22:20 man p' not alone in his iniquity. 1478
2Sa 1:27 fallen, and the weapons of war p'! 6
Job 4: 7 thee, who ever p', being innocent? "
30: 2 profit me, in whom old age was p'? "
Ps 9: 6 their memorial is p' with them. "
10:16 the heathen are p' out of his land. "
83:10 Which p' at En-dor: they became 8045
119:92 should then have p' in mine affliction.6
Ec 9: 6 hatred, and their envy, is now p'; "
Jer 7:28 truth is p', and is cut off from their "
48:36 riches that he hath gotten are p'. "
49: 7 is counsel p' from the prudent? "
La 3:18 and my hope is p' from the Lord: "
Joe 1:11 because the harvest of the field is p'. "
Jon 4:10 up in a night, and p' in a night: "
Mic 4: 9 no king in thee? is thy counsellor p'? "
7: 2 The good man is p' out of the earth: "
M't 8:32 into the sea, and p' in the waters. 599
Lu 11:51 p' between the altar and the temple:622
Ac 5:37 he also p'; and all, even as many "
1Co 15:18 are fallen asleep in Christ are p'. "
Heb 11:31 By faith the harlot Rahab p' not 4881
2Pe 3: 6 being overflowed with water, p': 622
Jude 11 and p' in the gainsaying of Core. "

perisheth
Job 4:11 The old lion p' for lack of prey, and 6
Pr 11: 7 and the hope of unjust men p'. "
Ec 7:15 just man that p' in his righteousness."
Isa 57: 1 righteous p', and no man layeth "
Jer 9:12 for what the land p' and is burned up*"
48:46 the people of Chemosh p': for thy * "
Joh 6:27 Labour not for the meat which p', 622
Jas 1:11 and the grace of the fashion of it p': "
1Pe 1: 7 more precious than of gold that p', "

perishing
Job 33:18 and his life from p' by the sword. 5674

Perizzite (per'-iz-zite) See also PERIZZITES.
Ge 13: 7 the P' dwelled then in the land, 6522
Ex 33: 2 and the Hittite, and the P', "
34:11 and the Hittite, and the P'. "
Jos 9: 1 Amorite, the Canaanite, the P', "
11: 3 P', and...Jebusite in the mountains,"

Perizzites (per'-iz-zites)
Ge 15:20 Hittites, and the P', and the *6522
34:30 among the Canaanites and the P': "
Ex 3: 8 the P', and the Hivites, and the * "
17 the P', and the Hivites, and the * "
23:23 and the Hittites, and the P', and* "
De 7: 1 the P', and the Hivites, and the * "
20:17 and the P', the Hivites, and the * "
Jos 3:10 and the P', and the Girgashites, * "
12: 8 the P', the Hivites, and the * "
17:15 in the land of the P' and of the "
24:11 the Amorites, and the P', and the* "
J'g 1: 4 Canaanites and the P' into their "
5 slew the Canaanites and the P'. "
3: 5 Hittites, and Amorites, and P', * "
1Ki 9:20 P', Hivites, and Jebusites, which "
2Ch 8: 7 the P', and the Hivites, and the "
Ezr 9: 1 the Canaanites, the Hittites, the P',"
Ne 9: 8 Hittites, the Amorites, and the P',*"

perjured
1Ti 1:10 for liars, for p' persons, and if *1965

permission
1Co 7: 6 But I speak this by p', and not of ‡4774

permit See also PERMITTED.
1Co 16: 7 a while with you, if the Lord p'. 2010
Heb 6: 3 And this will we do, if God p'. "

permitted
Ac 26: 1 Thou art p' to speak for thyself. 2010
1Co 14:34 it is not p' unto them to speak; "

pernicious
2Pe 2: 2 many shall follow their p' ways; *684

perpetual
Ge 9:12 is with you, for p' generations: 5769
Ex 29: 9 shall be theirs for a p' statute: "
30: 8 a p' incense before the Lord 8548
31:16 generations, for a p' covenant. 5769
Le 3:17 a p' statute for your generations "
6:20 fine flour for a meat offering p'. *8548
24: 9 Lord made by fire by a p' statute. 5769
25:34 sold; for it is their p' possession. "
Nu 19:21 it shall be a p' statute unto them, "
Ps 9: 6 destructions are come to a p' end:*5331
74: 3 thy feet unto the p' desolations; "
78:66 he put them to a p' reproach. 5769
Jer 5:22 bound of the sea by a p' decree, "
8: 5 slidden back by a p' backsliding? 5331
15:18 Why is my pain p', and my wound "
18:16 land desolate, and a p' hissing; 5769
23:40 and a p' shame, which shall not "
25: 9 and an hissing, and p' desolations. "
12 and will make it p' desolations. "
49:13 the cities thereof shall be p' wastes. * "
50: 5 to the Lord in a p' covenant that * "

Jer 51: 39 and sleep a *p'* sleep, and not wake, 5769
57 shall sleep a *p'* sleep, and not wake, "
Eze 35: 5 Because thou hast had a *p'* hatred, "
9 will make thee *p'* desolations, and "
46: 14 by a *p'* ordinance unto the Lord. "
Hab 3: 6 scattered, the *p'* hills did bow: * "
Zep 2: 9 and saltpits, and a *p'* desolation: "

perpetually
1Ki 9: 3 mine heart shall be there *p'*. 3605, 3117
2Ch 7: 16 mine heart shall be there *p'*. "
Am 1: 11 all pity, and his anger did tear *p'*, 5703

perplexed
Es 3: 15 drink; but the city Shushan was *p'*. 943
Joe 1: 18 the herds of cattle are *p'*, because "
Lu 9: 7 And he was *p'*, because that it was 1280
24: 4 as they were much *p'* thereabout, "
2Co 4: 8 we are *p'*, but not in despair; 639

perplexity
Isa 22: 5 and of *p'* by the Lord God of hosts 3998
Mic 7: 4 cometh; now shall be their *p'*. "
Lu 21: 25 earth distress of nations, with *p'*; 640

persecute See also PERSECUTED; PERSECUTEST; PERSECUTING.
Job 19: 22 Why do ye *p'* me as God, and are 7291
28 Why *p'* we him, seeing the root of "
Ps 7: 1 save me from all them that *p'* me,* "
5 Let the enemy *p'* my soul, and * "
10: 2 in his pride doth *p'* the poor: *1814
31: 15 enemies,...from them that *p'* me. 7291
35: 3 the way against them that *p'* me: * "
6 let the angel of the Lord *p'* them.* "
69: 26 they *p'* him who thou hast smitten; "
71: 11 forsaken him; *p'* and take him; "
83: 15 So *p'* them with thy tempest, and* "
119: 84 judgment on them that *p'* me? "
86 they *p'* me wrongfully; help thou "
Jer 17: 18 them be confounded that *p'* me, "
29: 18 I will *p'* them with the sword, *7291, 310
La 3: 66 *P'* and destroy them in anger *7291
M't 5: 11 men shall revile you, and *p'* you, 1377
44 despitefully use you, and *p'* you; "
10: 23 when they *p'* you in this city, flee "
23: 34 and *p'* them from city to city: "
Lu 11: 49 of them they shall slay and *p'*: 1559
21: 12 their hands on you, and *p'* you, 1377
Joh 5: 16 therefore did the Jews *p'* Jesus, "
15: 20 me, they will also *p'* you; "
Ro 12: 14 Bless them which *p'* you: bless, and "

persecuted
De 30: 7 that hate thee, which *p'* thee. 7291
Ps 109: 16 but *p'* the poor and needy man, "
119: 161 have *p'* me without a cause: but "
143: 3 For the enemy hath *p'* my soul; he "
Isa 14: 6 ruled the nations in anger, is *p'*, *4783
La 3: 43 covered with anger, and *p'* us: *7291
M't 5: 10 are *p'* for righteousness' sake: 1377
12 so *p'* they the prophets which were "
Joh 15: 20 If they have *p'* me, they will also "
Ac 7: 52 prophets have not your fathers *p'*?* "
22: 4 And I *p'* this way unto the death, "
26: 11 I *p'* them even unto strange cities. "
1Co 4: 12 we bless; being *p'*, we suffer it: "
15: 9 because I *p'* the church of God. "
2Co 4: 9 *P'*, but not forsaken; cast down, * "
Ga 1: 13 measure I *p'* the church of God, "
23 he which *p'* us in times past now "
4: 29 *p'* him that was born after the "
1Th 2: 15 own prophets, and have *p'* us; *1559
Re 12: 13 *p'* the woman which brought forth 1377

persecutest
Ac 9: 4 him, Saul, Saul, why *p'* thou me? 1377
5 said, I am Jesus whom thou *p'*: "
22: 7 me, Saul, Saul, why *p'* thou me? "
8 Jesus of Nazareth, whom thou *p'*. "
26: 14 Saul, Saul, why *p'* thou me? it is "
15 he said, I am Jesus whom thou *p'*. "

persecuting
Ph'p 3: 6 Concerning zeal, *p'* the church; 1377

persecution See also PERSECUTIONS.
La 5: 5 Our necks are under *p'*: we *7291
M't 13: 21 or *p'* ariseth because of the word, 1375
M'r 4: 17 or *p'* ariseth for the word's sake, "
Ac 8: 1 was a great *p'* against the church "
11: 19 the *p'* that arose about Stephen *2347
13: 50 and raised *p'* against Paul and 1375
Ro 8: 35 shall tribulation, or distress, or *p'*, "
Ga 5: 11 circumcision, why do I...suffer *p'*?*1377
6: 12 suffer *p'* for the cross of Christ. * "
2Ti 3: 12 godly in Christ Jesus shall suffer *p'*." "

persecutions
M'r 10: 30 and children, and lands, with *p'*; 1375
2Co 12: 10 *p'*, in distresses for Christ's sake: "
2Th 1: 4 faith in all your *p'* and tribulations "
2Ti 3: 11 *P'*, afflictions, which came unto me "
11 at Lystra; what *p'* I endured: "

persecutor See also PERSECUTORS.
1Ti 1: 13 before a blasphemer, and a *p'*, 1376

persecutors
Ne 9: 11 *p'* thou threwest into the deeps, *7291
Ps 7: 13 his arrows against the *p'*. *1814
119: 157 are my *p'* and mine enemies; 7291
142: 6 very low: deliver me from my *p'*; "
Jer 15: 15 me, and revenge me of my *p'*; "
20: 11 therefore my *p'* shall stumble, and "
La 1: 3 all her *p'* overtook her between "
4: 19 Our *p'* are swifter than the eagles* "

perseverance
Eph 6: 18 with all *p'* and supplication for 4343

Persia (*per'-she-ah*) See also ELAM; PERSIAN.
2Ch 36: 20 the reign of the kingdom of *P'*: 6539
22 the first year of Cyrus king of *P'*, "
22 up the spirit of Cyrus king of *P'*, "
23 Thus saith Cyrus king of *P'*, All the "
Ezr 1: 1 the first year of Cyrus king of *P'*, "
1 up the spirit of Cyrus king of *P'*, "
2 saith Cyrus king of *P'*, The Lord "
8 did Cyrus king of *P'* bring forth "
3: 7 that they had of Cyrus king of *P'*. "
4: 3 the king of *P'* hath commanded us. "
5 all the days of Cyrus king of *P'*, "
5 the reign of Darius king of *P'*. "
7 wrote...unto Artaxerxes king of *P'*; "
24 of the reign of Darius king of *P'*. 6540
6: 14 Darius, and Artaxerxes king of *P'*. "
7: 1 the reign of Artaxerxes king of *P'*, 6539
9: 9 us in the sight of the kings of *P'*, "
Es 1: 3 the power of *P'* and Media, the "
14 the seven princes of *P'* and Media, "
18 shall the ladies of *P'* and Media say "
10: 2 of the kings of Media and *P'*? "
Eze 27: 10 They of *P'* and of Lud and of Phut "
38: 5 *P'*, Ethiopia, and Libya with them; "
Da 8: 20 are the kings of Media and *P'*. "
10: 1 the third year of Cyrus king of *P'* "
13 But the prince of the kingdom of *P'* "
13 remained...with the kings of *P'*. "
20 to fight with the prince of *P'*: "
11: 2 stand up yet three kings in *P'*; "

Persian (*per'-she-un*) See also PERSIANS.
Ne 12: 22 to the reign of Darius the *P'*. 6542
Da 6: 28 and in the reign of Cyrus the *P'*. 6523

Persians (*pur'-she-uns*) See also ELAMITES.
Es 1: 19 the laws of the *P'* and the Medes, 6539
Da 5: 28 and given to the Medes and *P'*. 6540
6: 8, 12 to the law of the Medes and *P'*, "
15 that the law of the Medes and *P'* is, "

Persis (*pur'-sis*)
Ro 16: 12 Salute the beloved *P'*, which 4069

person See also PERSONS.
Ge 39: 6 Joseph was a goodly *p'*, and well *
Ex 12: 48 no uncircumcised *p'* shall eat thereof.
Le 19: 15 not respect the *p'* of the poor, 6440
15 nor honour the *p'* of the mighty: "
Nu 5: 6 the Lord, and that *p'* be guilty; *5315
19: 17 for an unclean *p'* they shall take of*
18 And a clean *p'* shall take hyssop, 376, 120
22 whatsoever the unclean *p'* toucheth
31: 19 whosoever hath killed any *p'*, and 5315
35: 11 which killeth any *p'* at unawares. "
15 one that killeth any *p'* unawares "
30 Whoso killeth any *p'*, the murderer "
30 shall not testify against any *p'* to "
De 15: 22 and the clean *p'* shall eat it alike,*
27: 25 reward to slay an innocent *p'*. 5315
28: 50 shall not regard the *p'* of the old, 6440
Jos 20: 3 that killeth any *p'* unawares and 5315
9 that whosoever killeth any *p'* at "
1Sa 9: 2 of Israel a goodlier *p'* than he: 376
16: 18 prudent in matters, and a comely *p'*, "
25: 35 voice, and have accepted thy *p'*. 6440
2Sa 4: 11 men have slain a righteous *p'* in 376
14: 14 neither doth God respect any *p'*: *5315
17: 11 thou go to battle in thine own *p'*. 6440
Job 13: 8 Will ye accept his *p'*? will ye ‡ "
22: 29 up; and he shall save the humble *p'*.
32: 21 I pray you, accept any man's *p'*, 6440
Ps 15: 4 In whose eyes a vile *p'* is contemned;*
49: 10 the fool and the brutish *p'* perish, *
101: 4 from me: I will not know a wicked *p'*.*
105: 37 not one feeble *p'* among their tribes.
Pr 6: 12 A naughty *p'*, a wicked man, 120
18: 5 to accept the *p'* of the wicked, 6440
24: 8 shall be called a mischievous *p'*. 1167
28: 17 violence to the blood of any *p'* 5315
Isa 32: 5 The vile *p'* shall be no more called‡
6 the vile *p'* will speak villany, and his‡
Jer 43: 6 every *p'* that Nebuzar-adan the 5315
52: 25 them that were near the king's *p'*, *6440
Eze 16: 5 to the lothing of thy *p'*, in the day 5315
33: 6 and take any *p'* from among them, "
44: 25 shall come at no dead *p'* to defile 120
Da 11: 21 in his estate shall stand up a vile *p'*,
Mal 1: 8 or accept thy *p'*? saith the Lord 6440
M't 22: 16 thou regardest not the *p'* of men. 4383
27: 24 innocent of the blood of this just *p'*: * "
M'r 12: 14 thou regardest not the *p'* of men, 4383
Lu 20: 21 neither acceptest thou the *p'* of any, "
1Co 5: 13 from among yourselves that wicked *p'*.*
2Co 2: 10 forgave I it in the *p'* of Christ; 4383
Ga 2: 6 to me: God accepteth no man's *p'*:) "
Heb 1: 3 and the express image of his *p'*, *5287
12: 16 any fornicator, or profane *p'*, as Esau,
2Pe 2: 5 but saved Noah the eighth *p'*, a *

persons
Ge 14: 21 said unto Abram, Give me the *p'*, 5315
36: 6 and all the *p'* of his house, and his* "
Ex 16: 16 according to the number of your *p'*; "
Le 27: 2 the *p'* shall be for the Lord by thy "
Nu 19: 18 and upon the *p'* that were there, "
31: 28 soul of five hundred, both of the *p'*, 120
30 take one portion of fifty, of the *p'*, of "
35 and two thousand *p'* in all, 5315
40 the *p'* were sixteen thousand; "
40 tribute was thirty and two *p'*. "
46 And sixteen thousand *p'*;) "
De 1: 17 shall not respect *p'* in judgment; 6440
10: 17 which regardeth not *p'*, nor taketh "
22 Egypt with threescore and ten *p'*; 5315
16: 19 thou shalt not respect *p'*, neither 6440
J'g 9: 2 which are threescore and ten *p'*, 376
4 Abimelech hired vain and light *p'*, *582

J'g 9: 5 being threescore and ten *p'*, upon 376
18 threescore and ten *p'*, upon one "
20: 39 of the men of Israel about thirty *p'*: "
1Sa 9: 22 bidden, which were about thirty *p'*. "
22: 18 five *p'* that did wear a linen ephod. "
22 of all the *p'* of thy father's house. 5315
2Ki 10: 6 the king's sons, being seventy *p'*, 376
7 slew seventy *p'*, and put their heads "
2Ch 19: 7 nor respect of *p'*, nor taking of 6440
Job 13: 10 you, if ye do secretly accept *p'*. "
34: 19 that accepteth not the *p'* of princes, "
Ps 26: 4 I have not sat with vain *p'*, neither ‡4962
82: 2 and accept the *p'* of the wicked? 6440
Pr 12: 11 he that followeth vain *p'* is void of
24: 23 not good to have respect of *p'* in 6440
28: 19 after vain *p'* shall have poverty
21 To have respect of *p'* is not good: 6440
Jer 52: 29 eight hundred thirty and two *p'*: 5315
30 seven hundred forty and five *p'*: "
30 the *p'* were four thousand and six "
La 4: 16 respected not the *p'* of the priests, 6440
Eze 17: 17 building forts, to cut off many *p'*: 5315
27: 13 traded the *p'* of men and vessels "
Jon 4: 11 are more than sixscore thousand *p'* 120
Zep 3: 4 are light and treacherous *p'*: 582
Mal 1: 9 means: will he regard your *p'*? 6440
Lu 15: 7 than over ninety and nine just *p'*,
Ac 10: 34 that God is no respecter of *p'*: 4381
17: 17 with the Jews, and with the devout *p'*,
Ro 2: 11 there is no respect of *p'* with God. 4382
2Co 1: 11 upon us by the means of many *p'* *4383
Eph 6: 9 is there respect of *p'* with him. 4382
Col 3: 25 done: and there is no respect of *p'*. "
1Ti 1: 10 for liars, for perjured *p'*, and if *678
Jas 2: 1 Lord of glory, with respect of *p'*. 4382
9 if ye have respect to *p'*, ye commit 4380
1Pe 1: 17 who without respect of *p'* judgeth 678
2Pe 3: 11 what manner of *p'* ought ye to be in
Jude 16 having men's *p'* in admiration 4383

persuade See also PERSUADED; PERSUADEST; PERSUADETH; PERSUADING.
1Ki 22: 20 Who shall *p'* Ahab, that he may *6601
21 the Lord, and said, I will *p'* him. * "
22 Thou shalt *p'* him, and prevail * "
2Ch 32: 11 Doth not Hezekiah *p'* you to give 5496
15 you, nor *p'* you on this manner, "
Isa 36: 18 Beware lest Hezekiah *p'* you, "
M't 28: 14 we will *p'* him, and secure you. 3982
2Co 5: 11 the terror of the Lord, we *p'* men; "
Ga 1: 10 For do I now *p'* men, or God? or †‡ "

persuaded
2Ch 18: 2 and *p'* him to go up with him to *5496
Pr 25: 15 By long forbearing is a prince *p'*, 6601
M't 27: 20 and elders *p'* the multitude that 3982
Lu 16: 31 neither will they be *p'*, though one "
20: 6 they be *p'* that John was a prophet. "
Ac 13: 43 *p'* them to continue in the grace of* "
14: 19 who *p'* the people, and, having "
18: 4 and *p'* the Jews and the Greeks. "
19: 26 *p'* and turned away much people, "
21: 14 And when he would not be *p'*, we "
26: 26 I am *p'* that none of these things "
Ro 4: 21 And being fully *p'* that, what he *4135
8: 38 For I am *p'*, that neither death, 3982
14: 5 man be fully *p'* in his own mind. *4135
14 and am *p'* by the Lord Jesus, that 3982
15: 14 also am *p'* of you, my brethren, "
2Ti 1: 5 and I am *p'* that in thee also. "
12 and am *p'* that he is able to keep "
Heb 6: 9 we are *p'* better things of you, and "
11: 13 were *p'* of them, and embraced * "

persuadest
Ac 26: 28 thou *p'* me to be a Christian. *3982

persuadeth
2Ki 18: 32 unto Hezekiah, when he *p'* you, 5496
Ac 18: 13 This fellow *p'* men to worship God 374

persuading
Ac 19: 8 and *p'* the things concerning the 3982
28: 23 *p'* them concerning Jesus, both out "

persuasion
Ga 5: 8 *p'* cometh not of him that calleth 3988

pertain See also APPERTAIN; PERTAINED; PERTAINETH; PERTAINING; PURTENANCE.
Le 7: 20 peace offerings, that *p'* unto the Lord,
21 offerings, which *p'* unto the Lord,
1Sa 25: 22 if I leave of all that *p'* to him by the
Ro 15: 17 in those things which *p'* to God. *
1Co 6: 3 much more things that *p'* to this life?
2Pe 1: 3 unto us all things that *p'* unto life

pertained
Nu 31: 43 half that *p'* unto the congregation*
Jos 24: 33 in a hill that *p'* to Phinehas his son,*
J'g 6: 11 that *p'* unto Joash the Abi-ezrite:
1Sa 25: 21 was missed of all that *p'* unto him:
2Sa 2: 15 which *p'* to Ish-bosheth the son of*
9: 9 *p'* to Saul and to all his house. 1961
16: 4 are all that *p'* unto Mephibosheth.*
1Ki 4: 10 to him *p'* Sochoh, and all the land of
12 to him *p'* Taanach and Megiddo, and*
13 to him *p'* the towns of Jair the son of
13 to him also *p'* the region of Argob,
7: 48 all the vessels that *p'* unto the house*
2Ki 24: 7 all that *p'* to the king of Egypt.
1Ch 9: 27 thereof every morning *p'* to them.
11: 31 that *p'* to the children of Benjamin,*
2Ch 12: 4 the fenced cities which *p'* to Judah,
34: 33 that *p'* to the children of Israel,

pertaineth
Le 14: 32 get that which *p'* to his cleansing.
Nu 4: 16 the priest *p'* the oil for the light, *
De 22: 5 wear that which *p'* unto a man. 3627

1Sa 27: 6 Ziklag p' unto the kings of Judah 1961
2Sa 6:12 Obed-edom, and all that p' unto him, "
Ro 9: 4 to whom p' the adoption, and the*
Heb 7:13 are spoken p' to another tribe, *3348

pertaining
Jos 13:31 were p' unto the children of Machir*
1Ch 26:32 every matter p' to God, and affairs
Ac 1: 3 things p' to the kingdom of God: *4012
Ro 4: 1 as p' to the flesh, hath found? *
1Co 6: 4 judgments of things p' to this life,
Heb 2:17 high priest in things p' to God,
5: 1 ordained for men in things p' to God,
9: 9 perfect, as p' to the conscience; *

Peruda (*per'-u-dah*) See also PERIDA.
Ezr 2:55 of Sophereth, the children of P', 6514

perverse
Nu 22:32 because thy way is p' before me: 3399
De 32: 5 are a p' and crooked generation. 6141
1Sa 20:30 son of the p' rebellious woman, 5753
Job 6:30 my taste discern p' things? *1942
9:20 perfect, it shall also prove me p'. 6140
Pr 4:24 and p' lips put far from thee. 3891
8: 8 is nothing froward or p' in them. 6141
12: 8 is of a p' heart shall be despised. 5753
14: 2 is p' in his ways despiseth him. 3868
17:20 a p' tongue falleth into mischief. 2015
19: 1 he that is p' in his lips, and...a fool 6141
23:33 thine heart shall utter p' things. *8419
28: 6 he that is p' in his ways, though 6141
18 p' in his ways shall fall at once. 6140
Isa 19:14 The Lord hath mingled a p' spirit *5773
M't 17:17 said, O faithless and p' generation, 1294
Lu 9:41 said, O faithless and p' generation, "
Ac 20:30 men arise, speaking p' things, to "
Ph'p 2:15 midst of a crooked and p' nation, "
1Ti 6: 5 P' disputings of men of corrupt *3859

perversely
2Sa 19:19 that which thy servant did p' the 5753
1Ki 8:47 We have sinned, and have done p', "
Ps 119:78 for they dealt p' with me without *5791

perverseness
Nu 23:21 neither hath he seen p' in Israel: 5999
Pr 11: 3 p' of transgressors shall destroy 5558
15: 4 p' therein is a breach in the spirit. "
Isa 30:12 trust in oppression and p', and 3868
59: 3 your tongue hath muttered p'. *5766
Eze 9: 9 of blood, and the city full of p': *4297

pervert See also PERVERTED; PERVERTETH; PERVERTING.
De 16:19 and p' the words of the righteous. 5557
24:17 p' the judgment of the stranger, *5186
Job 8: 3 Doth God p' judgment? 5791
3 or doth the Almighty p' justice? "
34:12 will the Almighty p' judgment. "
Pr 17:23 bosom to p' the ways of judgment. 5186
31: 5 forget...law, and p' the judgment 8138
Mic 3: 9 abhor judgment, and p' all equity. 6140
Ac 13:10 to p' the right ways of the Lord? 1294
Ga 1: 7 and would p' the gospel of Christ 3344

perverted
1Sa 8: 3 and took bribes, and p' judgment. 5186
Job 33:27 sinned, and p'...which was right, 5753
Isa 47:10 thy knowledge, it hath p' thee; 7725
Jer 3:21 they have p' their way, and they 5753
23:36 p' the words of the living God, 2015

perverteth
Ex 23: 8 and p' the words of the righteous. 5557
De 27:19 cursed be he that p' the judgment *5186
Pr 10: 9 that p' his ways shall be known. 6140
19: 3 foolishness of man p' his way: *5557
Lu 23:14 unto me, as one that p' the people; 654

perverting
Ec 5: 8 violent p' of judgment and justice*
Lu 23: 2 We found this fellow p' the nation, 1294

pestilence See also PESTILENCES.
Ex 5: 3 he fall upon us with p', or with the 1698
9:15 smite thee and thy people with p'; "
Le 26:25 I will send the p' among you; and "
Nu 14:12 I will smite them with the p', and "
De 28:21 shall make the p' cleave unto thee, "
2Sa 24:13 there be three days' p' in thy land? "
15 So the Lord sent a p' upon Israel "
1Ki 8:37 be in the land famine, if there be p', "
1Ch 21:12 even the p', in the land, and the "
14 So the Lord sent p' upon Israel: "
2Ch 6:28 if there be p', if there be blasting, "
7:13 or if I send p' among my people; "
20: 9 sword, judgment, or p', or famine, "
Ps 78:50 but gave their life over to the p'; "
91: 3 fowler, and from the noisome p'. "
6 for the p' that walketh in darkness; "
Jer 14:12 and by the famine, and by the p'. "
21: 6 they shall die of a great p'. "
7 as are left in this city from the p', "
9 and by the famine, and by the p', "
24:10 famine, and the p', among them, "
27: 8 with the famine, and with the p', "
13 sword, by the famine, and by the p', "
28: 8 of war, and of evil, and of p'. "
29:17 the sword, the famine, and the p', "
18 the famine, and with the p', and "
32:24 famine, and of the p': and what "
36 and by the famine, and by the p'; "
34:17 sword, to the p', and to the famine; "
38: 2 sword, by the famine, and by the p': "
42:17 sword, by the famine, and by the p': "
22 sword, by the famine, and by the p', "
44:13 sword, by the famine, and by the p': "
Eze 5:12 A third part...shall die with the p', "
17 p' and blood shall pass through "
6:11 sword, by the famine, and by the p'. 1698
12 He that is far off shall die of the p'; "
7:15 and the p' and the famine within: "
15 famine and p' shall devour him. "
12:16 from the famine, and from the p'; "
14:19 Or if I send a p' into that land, and "
21 the noisome beast, and the p', to "
28:23 I will send into her p', and blood "
33:27 and in the caves shall die of the p'. "
38:22 against him with p' and with blood; "
Am 4:10 I have sent among you the p' after "
Hab 3: 5 Before him went the p', and "

pestilences
M't 24: 7 p', and earthquakes, in divers *3061
Lu 21:11 divers places, and famines, and p'; "

pestilent
Ac 24: 5 have found this man a p' fellow, 3061

pestle
Pr 27:22 a mortar among wheat with a p', 5940

Peter (*pe'-tur*) See also CEPHAS; PETER'S; SIMON.
M't 4:18 And Simon called P', and Andrew 4074
10: 2 The first, Simon, who is called P', "
14:28 P' answered him and said, Lord, "
29 when P' was come down out of the "
15:15 Then answered P' and said unto "
16:16 And Simon P' answered and said, "
18 That thou art P', and upon this "
22 P' took him, and began to rebuke "
23 said unto P', Get thee behind me, "
17: 1 Jesus taketh P', James, and John "
4 Then answered P', and said unto "
24 received tribute money came to P', "
26 P' saith unto him, Of strangers. * "
18:21 Then came P' to him, and said, "
19:27 answered P' and said unto him, "
26:33 P' answered and said unto him, "
35 P' said unto him, Though I should "
37 P' and the two sons of Zebedee, "
40 saith unto P', What, could ye not "
58 P' followed him afar off unto the "
69 Now P' sat without in the palace: "
73 said to P', Surely thou also art one "
75 P' remembered the word of Jesus, "
M'r 3:16 And Simon he surnamed P'; "
5:37 to follow him, save P', and James, "
8:29 P' answereth and saith unto him, "
32 P' took him, and began to rebuke "
33 he rebuked P', saying, Get thee "
9: 2 Jesus taketh with him P', and "
5 P' answered and said to Jesus, "
10:28 P' began to say unto him, Lo, we "
11:21 P' calling to remembrance saith "
13: 3 P' and James and John...Andrew "
14:29 P' said unto him, Although all "
33 he taketh with him P' and James "
37 saith unto P', Simon, sleepest thou? "
54 P' followed him afar off, even into "
66 P' was beneath in the palace, there "
67 when she saw P' warming himself, "
70 said again to P', Surely thou art "
72 P' called to mind the word that "
16: 7 tell his disciples and P' that he "
Lu 5: 8 When Simon P' saw it, he fell down "
6:14 Simon, (whom he also named P',) "
8:45 P' and they that were with him "
51 suffered no man to go in, save P', "
9:20 P' answering said, The Christ of "
28 he took P' and John and James, "
32 But P' and they that were with him "
33 P' said unto Jesus, Master, it is "
12:41 P' said unto him, Lord, speakest "
18:28 Then P' said, Lo, we have left all, "
22: 8 And he sent P' and John, saying, "
34 I tell thee, P', the cock shall not "
54 house. And P' followed afar off. "
55 together, P' sat down among them. "
58 them. And P' said, Man, I am not. "
60 P' said, Man, I know not what thou "
61 Lord turned, and looked upon P'. "
61 P' remembered the word of the "
62 And P' went out, and wept bitterly.* "
24:12 Then arose P', and ran unto the "
Joh 1:44 Bethsaida,...city of Andrew and P'. "
6:68 Simon P' answered him, Lord, to "
13: 6 Then cometh he to Simon P': and "
6 P' saith unto him, Lord, dost thou* "
8 P' saith unto him, Thou shalt 4074
9 Simon P' saith unto him, Lord, not "
24 Simon P' therefore beckoned to "
36 Simon P' said unto him, Lord, "
37 P' said unto him, Lord, why cannot "
18:10 Simon P' having a sword drew it, "
11 said Jesus unto P', Put up thy "
15 And Simon P' followed Jesus, and "
16 P' stood at the door without. Then "
16 kept the door, and brought in P'. "
17 damsel that kept the door unto P', "
18 P' stood with them, and warmed "
25 And Simon P' stood and warmed "
26 his kinsman whose ear P' cut off, "
27 P' then denied again: and "
20: 2 runneth, and cometh to Simon P', "
3 P' therefore went forth, and that "
4 the other disciple did outrun P', "
6 cometh Simon P' following him, "
21: 2 together Simon P', and Thomas "
3 Simon P' saith unto them, I go a "
7 loved saith unto P', It is the Lord. "
7 P' heard that it was the Lord, "
11 Simon P' went up, and drew the "
15 Jesus saith to Simon P', Simon, "
17 P' was grieved because he said "
20 P', turning about, seeth the "
Joh 21:21 P' seeing him saith to Jesus, Lord, 4074
Ac 1:13 where abode both P', and James, "
15 P' stood up in the midst of the "
2:14 P', standing up with the eleven, "
37 unto P' and to the rest of the "
38 Then P' said unto them, Repent, "
3: 1 P' and John went up together into "
3 seeing P' and John about to go "
4 P', fastening his eyes upon him "
6 P' said, Silver and gold have I "
11 which was healed held P' and John, "
12 when P' saw it he answered unto "
4: 8 P', filled with the Holy Ghost, said "
13 saw the boldness of P' and John, "
19 P' and John answered and said "
5: 3 P' said, Ananias, why hath Satan "
8 P' answered unto her, Tell me "
9 P' said unto her, How is it that "
15 the shadow of P' passing by might "
29 P' and the other apostles answered "
8:14 they sent unto them P' and John: "
20 But P' said unto him, Thy money "
9:32 P' passed throughout all quarters, "
34 P' said unto him, Æneas, Jesus "
38 disciples had heard that P' was "
39 Then P' arose and went with them. "
40 P' put them all forth, and kneeled "
40 and when she saw P', she sat up. "
10: 5 one Simon, whose surname is P': "
9 P' went up upon the housetop to "
13 voice to him, Rise, P'; kill and eat. "
14 P' said, Not so, Lord; for I have "
17 P' doubted in himself what this "
18 which was surnamed P', were "
19 While P' thought on the vision, the "
21 P' went down to the men which "
23 morrow P' went away with them,* "
25 as P' was coming in, Cornelius met "
26 P' took him up, saying, Stand up; "
32 Simon, whose surname is P'; "
34 P' opened his mouth, and said, Of "
44 P' yet spake these words, the Holy "
45 as many as came with P', "
46 magnify God. Then answered P', "
11: 2 P' was come up to Jerusalem, "
4 P' rehearsed the matter from the "
7 unto me, Arise, P'; slay and eat. "
13 for Simon, whose surname is P'; "
12: 3 proceeded further to take P' also. "
5 P' therefore was kept in prison: "
6 P'...sleeping between two soldiers, "
7 he smote P' on the side, and raised "
11 when P' was come to himself, he "
13 as P' knocked at the door of the * "
14 told how P' stood before the gate. "
16 But P' continued knocking: and "
18 soldiers, what was become of P'. "
Ga 1:18 I went up to Jerusalem to see P', * "
2: 7 of the circumcision was unto P'; "
8 he that wrought effectually in P' "
11 But when P' was come to Antioch,* "
14 I said unto P' before them all, * "
1Pe 1: 1 P', an apostle of Jesus Christ, "
2Pe 1: 1 Simon P', a servant and an apostle "

Peter's (*pe'-turz*)
M't 8:14 Jesus was come into P' house, 4074
Joh 1:40 him, was Andrew, Simon P' brother. "
6: 8 Andrew, Simon P' brother, saith "
Ac 12:14 And when she knew P' voice, she "

Pethahiah (*peth-a-hi'-ah*)
1Ch 24:16 nineteenth to P', the twentieth 6611
Ezr 10:23 Kelaiah, (the same is Kelita,) P', "
Ne 9: 5 Hodijah, Shebaniah, and P', said, "
11:24 And P' the son of Meshezabeel, of "

Pethor (*pe'-thor*)
Nu 22: 5 unto Balaam the son of Beor to P', 6604
De 23: 4 Balaam the son of Beor of P' of "

Pethuel (*pe-thu'-el*)
Joe 1: 1 that came to Joel the son of P'. 6602

petition See also PETITIONS.
1Sa 1:17 God of Israel grant thee thy p' 7596
27 Lord hath given me my p' which I "
1Ki 2:16 I ask one p' of thee, deny me not. "
20 said, I desire one small p' of thee; "
Es 5: 6 What is thy p'? and it shall be "
7 and said, My p' and my request is; "
8 if it please the king to grant my p', "
7: 2 What is thy p', queen Esther? and "
3 let my life be given me at my p', "
9:12 now what is thy p'? and it shall be "
Da 6: 7 shall ask a p' of any God or man 1159
12 that shall ask a p' of any God or man
13 maketh his p' three times a day. 1159

petitions
Ps 20: 5 banners: the Lord fulfil all thy p'. 4862
1Jo 5:15 have the p' that we desired of him. 155

Peulthai (*pe-ul'-thahee*)
1Ch 26: 5 the seventh, P' the eighth: *6469

Phalec (*fa'-lek*) See also PELEG.
Lu 3:35 which was the son of P', which *5317

Phallu (*fal'-lu*) See also PALLU.
Ge 46: 9 sons of Reuben; Hanoch, and P', *6396

Phalti (*fal'-ti*) See also PHALTIEL.
1Sa 25:44 his daughter, David's wife, to P' *6406

Phaltiel (*fal'-te-el*) See also PHALTI.
2Sa 3:15 even from P' the son of Laish. *6409

Phanuel (*fan-u'-el*)
Lu 2:36 a prophetess, the daughter of P'. 5323

Pharaoh (*fa'-ra-o*) See also PHARAOH'S; PHARAOH-HOPHRA; PHARAOH-NECHO.
Ge 12:15 The princes also of P· saw her, 6547
15 and commended her before P·:
17 the Lord plagued P· and his house "
18 P· called Abram, and said, What is "
20 P· commanded his men concerning "
39: 1 Potiphar, an officer of P·, captain* "
40: 2 P· was wroth against two of his "
13 days shall P· lift up thine head, "
14 and make mention of me unto P·, "
17 of all manner of bakemeats for P·; "
19 three days shall P· lift up thy head "
41: 1 of full two years, that P· dreamed: "
4 favoured and fat kine. So P· awoke. "
7 and P· awoke, and, behold, it was a "
8 and P· told them his dream; but "
8 that could interpret them unto P·. "
9 Then spake the chief butler unto P·, "
10 P· was wroth with his servants, "
14 Then P· sent and called Joseph, "
14 his raiment, and came in unto P·. "
15 And P· said unto Joseph, I have "
16 Joseph answered P·, saying, It is "
16 shall give P· an answer of peace. "
17 P· said unto Joseph, In my dream, "
25 And Joseph said unto P·, "
25 The dream of P· is one: God hath "
25 shewed P· what he is about to do. "
28 thing which I have spoken unto P·: "
28 is about to do he sheweth unto P·. "
32 dream was doubled unto P· twice; "
33 let P· look out a man discreet and "
34 Let P· do this, and let him appoint "
35 lay up corn under the hand of P·, "
37 the thing was good in the eyes of P·, "
38 P· said unto his servants, Can we "
39 P· said unto Joseph, Forasmuch as "
41 P· said unto Joseph, See, I have set "
42 P· took off his ring from his hand, "
44 And P· said unto Joseph, I am P·, "
45 And P· called Joseph's name "
46 years old when he stood before P· "
46 went out from the presence of P·, "
55 the people cried to P· for bread: "
55 P· said unto all the Egyptians, Go "
42:15 By the life of P· ye shall not go forth "
16 by the life of P· surely ye are spies. "
44:18 servant: for thou art even as P·. "
45: 2 and the house of P· heard. "
8 he hath made me a father to P·, "
16 pleased P· well, and his servants. "
17 P· said unto Joseph, Say unto thy "
21 to the commandment of P·, "
46: 5 which P· had sent to carry him. "
31 I will go up, and shew P·, and say "
33 to pass, when P· shall call you, "
47: 1 Joseph came and told P·, and said, "
2 men, and presented them unto P·. "
3 P· said unto his brethren, What is "
3 they said unto P·, Thy servants "
4 They said moreover to P·, For to "
5 P· spake unto Joseph, saying, Thy "
7 before P·: and Jacob blessed P·. "
8 P· said unto Jacob, How old art "
9 Jacob said unto P·, The days of the "
10 And Jacob blessed P·, and went "
10 and went out from before P·. "
11 of Rameses, as P· had commanded. "
19 our land will be servants unto P·: "
20 bought all the land of Egypt for P·; "
22 had a portion assigned them of P·, "
22 did eat their portion which P· gave "
23 have bought you this day...for P·: "
24 ye shall give the fifth part unto P·, "
26 that P· should have the fifth part; "
50: 4 Joseph spake unto the house of P·, "
4 speak, I pray you, in the ears of P·, "
6 P· said, Go up, and bury thy father, "
7 him went up all the servants of P·, "
Ex 1:11 they built for P· treasure cities, "
19 the midwives said unto P·, Because "
22 P· charged all his people, saying, "
2: 5 daughter of P· came down to wash "
15 Now when P· heard this thing, he "
15 Moses fled from the face of P·, and "
3:10 I will send thee unto P·, that thou "
11 Who am I, that I should go unto P·, "
4:21 thou do all those wonders before P·, "
22 thou shalt say unto P·, Thus saith "
5: 1 and Aaron went in, and told P·, "
2 P· said, Who is the Lord, that I "
5 P· said, Behold, the people of the "
6 And P· commanded the same day "
10 Thus saith P·, I will not give you "
15 of Israel came and cried unto P·, "
20 way, as they came forth from P·: "
21 to be abhorred in the eyes of P·, "
23 I came to P· to speak in thy name, "
6: 1 shalt thou see what I will do to P·: "
11 Go in, speak unto P· king of Egypt, "
12 how then shall P· hear me, who am "
13 Israel, and unto P· king of Egypt, "
27 which spake to P· king of Egypt, "
29 speak thou unto P· king of Egypt "
30 and how shall P· hearken unto me? "
7: 1 See, I have made thee a god to P·: "
2 thy brother shall speak unto P·, "
4 But P· shall not hearken unto you, "
7 old, when they spake unto P·. "
9 When P· shall speak unto you, "
9 Take thy rod, and cast it before P·, "
10 Moses and Aaron went in unto P·, "
10 Aaron cast down his rod before P·, "
11 Then P· also called the wise men "
15 Get thee unto P· in the morning; "
Ex 7:20 were in the river, in the sight of P·, 6547
23 P· turned and went into his house, "
8: 1 Go unto P·, and say unto him, Thus "
8 P· called for Moses and Aaron, "
9 Moses said unto P·, Glory over me: "
12 and Aaron went out from P·: "
12 which he had brought against P·. "
15 when P· saw that there was respite, "
19 Then the magicians said unto P·, "
20 the morning, and stand before P·; "
24 swarm of flies into the house of P·, "
25 P· called for Moses and for Aaron, "
28 P· said, I will let you go, that ye "
29 swarms of flies may depart from P·, "
29 let not P· deal deceitfully any more "
30 And Moses went out from P·, and "
31 the swarms of flies from P·, "
32 P· hardened his heart at this time "
9: 1 Go in unto P·, and tell him, Thus "
7 P· sent, and, behold, there was not "
7 And the heart of P· was hardened, "
8 toward...heaven in the sight of P·. "
10 of the furnace, and stood before P·; "
12 the Lord hardened the heart of P·, "
13 stand before P·, and say unto him, "
20 the Lord among the servants of P· "
27 P· sent, and called for Moses and "
33 Moses went out of the city from P·, "
34 when P· saw that the rain and the "
35 heart of P· was hardened, neither "
10: 1 said unto Moses, Go in unto P·: "
3 Moses and Aaron came in unto P·, "
6 himself, and went out from P·. "
8 Aaron were brought again unto P·: "
16 P· called for Moses and Aaron in "
18 he went out from P·, and intreated "
24 P· called unto Moses, and said, Go "
28 P· said unto him, Get thee from "
11: 1 I bring one plague more upon P·, "
5 firstborn of P· that sitteth upon his "
8 went out from P· in a great anger. "
9 P· shall not hearken unto you; "
10 did all these wonders before P·: "
12:29 the firstborn of P· that sat on his "
30 P· rose up in the night, he, and all "
13:15 P· would hardly let us go, that the "
17 when P· had let the people go, that "
14: 3 P· will say of the children of Israel, "
4 I will be honoured upon P·, and "
5 heart of P· and of his servants was "
8 The Lord hardened the heart of P· "
9 all the horses and chariots of P·, "
10 when P· drew nigh, the children of "
17 and I will get me honour upon P·, "
18 I have gotten me honour upon P·, "
28 all the host of P· that came into the "
15:19 the horse of P· went in with his "
18: 4 delivered me from the sword of P·: "
8 all that the Lord had done unto P· "
10 and out of the hand of P·, who hath "
De 6:22 and sore, upon Egypt, upon P·, and "
7: 8 from the hand of P· king of Egypt. "
18 what the Lord thy God did unto P·, "
11: 3 did in the midst of Egypt unto P· "
29: 2 eyes in the land of Egypt unto P·, "
34:11 to do in the land of Egypt to P·, and "
1Sa 6: 6 and P· hardened their hearts? "
1Ki 3: 1 made affinity with P· king of Egypt, "
9:16 P· king of Egypt had gone up, and "
11: 1 together with the daughter of P·, "
18 to Egypt, unto P· king of Egypt; "
19 great favour in the sight of P·, so "
20 household among the sons of P·. "
21 Hadad said to P·, Let me depart, "
22 Then P· said unto him, But what "
2Ki 17: 7 under the hand of P· king of Egypt, "
18:21 so is P· king of Egypt unto all that "
23:35 gave the silver and the gold to P·; "
35 to the commandment of P·: "
1Ch 4:18 sons of Bithiah the daughter of P·, "
2Ch 8:11 the daughter of P· out of the city of "
Ne 9:10 signs and wonders upon P·, and "
Ps 135: 9 the midst of thee, O Egypt, upon P·, "
136:15 P· and his host in the Red sea: "
Isa 19:11 wise counsellers of P· is become "
11 how say ye unto P·, I am the son of "
30: 2 themselves in the strength of P·, "
3 the strength of P· be your shame, "
36: 6 so is P· king of Egypt to all that "
Jer 25:19 P· king of Egypt, and his servants, "
46:17 P· king of Egypt is but a noise; "
25 punish the multitude of No, and P·, "
25 even P·, and all them that trust in "
47: 1 before that P· smote Gaza. "
Eze 17:17 shall P· with his mighty army and "
29: 2 thy face against P· king of Egypt; "
3 I am against thee, P· king of Egypt, "
30:21 have broken the arm of P· king of "
22 I am against P· king of Egypt, "
25 and the arms of P· shall fall down; "
31: 2 speak unto P· king of Egypt, and "
18 This is P· and all his multitude, "
32: 2 lamentation for P· king of Egypt, "
31 P· shall see them, and shall be "
31 even P· and all his army slain by the "
32 even P· and all his multitude, "
Ac 7:10 in the sight of P· king of Egypt; 5328
13 kindred was made known unto P·. "
Ro 9:17 For the scripture saith unto P·, "

Pharaoh-hophra (*fa''-ra-o-hof'-rah*)
Jer 44:30 I will give P· king of Egypt into 6548

Pharaoh-necho (*fa''-ra-o-ne'-ko*) See also PHARAOH-NECHOH.
Jer 46: 2 against the army of P· king of *6549

Pharaoh-nechoh (*fa''-ra-o-ne'-ko*) See also PHARAOH-NECHO.
2Ki 23:29 P· king of Egypt went up against *6549
33 P· put him in bands at Riblah in * "
34 P· made Eliakim the son of Josiah* "
35 to his taxation, to give it unto P·. * "

Pharaoh's (*fa'-ra-oze*)
Ge 12:15 woman was taken into P· house. 6547
37:36 unto Potiphar, an officer of P·, and "
40: 7 he asked P· officers that were with "
11 P· cup was in my hand: and I took "
11 and pressed them into P· cup, "
11 and I gave the cup into P· hand. "
13 shalt deliver P· cup into his hand, "
20 third day, which was P· birthday, "
21 and he gave the cup into P· hand: "
45:16 fame thereof was heard in P· house, "
47:14 brought the money into P· house. "
20 over them: so the land became P·. "
25 my lord, and we will be P· servants. "
26 priests only, which became not P·. "
Ex 2: 7 Then said his sister to P· daughter, "
8 And P· daughter said unto her, Go. "
9 P· daughter said unto her, Take "
10 she brought him unto P· daughter, "
5:14 P· taskmasters had set over them, "
7: 3 And I will harden P· heart, and "
13 And he hardened P· heart, that he "
14 P· heart was hardened, he refuseth "
22 P· heart was hardened, neither "
8:19 and P· heart was hardened, and he "
10: 7 P· servants said...How long "
11 were driven out from P· presence. "
20, 27 the Lord hardened P· heart, "
11: 3 Egypt, in the sight of P· servants, "
10 the Lord hardened P· heart, so that "
14: 4 I will harden P· heart, that he shall "
23 sea, even all P· horses, his chariots, "
15: 4 P· chariots and...hosts hath he cast "
De 6:21 We were P· bondmen in Egypt; "
1Sa 2:27 they were in Egypt in P· house? "
1Ki 3: 1 and took P· daughter, and brought "
7: 8 made also an house for P· daughter, "
9:24 P· daughter came up out of the city "
11:20 Tahpenes weaned in P· house: "
20 and Genubath was in P· household "
Ca 1: 9 company of horses in P· chariots. "
Jer 37: 5 P· army was come...out of Egypt: "
7 P· army, which has come forth to "
11 Jerusalem for fear of P· army, from "
43: 9 which is at the entry of P· house "
Eze 30:24 but I will break P· arms, and he * "
Ac 7:21 P· daughter took him up, and 5328
Heb 11:24 be called the son of P· daughter; "

Phares (*fa'-rez*) See also PHAREZ.
M't 1: 3 And Judas begat P· and Zara of *5329
3 P· begat Esrom; and Esrom begat* "
Lu 3:33 Esrom, which was the son of P·, * "

Pharez (*fa'-rez*) See also PEREZ; PHARES; PHARZITES.
Ge 38:29 therefore his name was called P·.*6557
46:12 and Shelah, and P·, and Zarah: * "
12 sons of P· were Hezron and Hamul.* "
Nu 26:20 of P·, the family of the Pharzites:* "
21 sons of P· were; of Hezron, the * "
Ru 4:12 thy house be like the house of P·,* "
18 the generations of P·: P· begat * "
1Ch 2: 4 his daughter in law bare him P· * "
5 sons of P·; Hezron, and Hamul. * "
4: 1 P·, Hezron, and Carmi, and Hur, * "
9: 4 children of P· the son of Judah. * "

Pharisee (*far'-i-see*) See also PHARISEE'S; PHARISEES.
M't 23:26 Thou blind P·, cleanse first that 5330
Lu 7:39 the P· which had bidden him saw it, "
11:37 P· besought him to dine with him: "
38 when the P· saw it, he marveled "
18:10 one a P·, and the other a publican. "
11 The P· stood and prayed thus with "
Ac 5:34 a P·, named Gamaliel, a doctor of "
23: 6 Men and brethren, I am a P·, "
6 the son of a P·: of the hope and * "
26: 5 sect of our religion I lived a P·. "
Ph'p 3: 5 as touching the law, a P·; "

Pharisee's (*far'-i-seze*)
Lu 7:36 he went into the P· house, and sat 5330
37 Jesus sat at meat in the P· house, "

Pharisees (*far'-i-seze*) See also PHARISEES'.
M't 3: 7 saw many of the P· and Sadducees 5330
5:20 righteousness of the scribes and P·, "
9:11 when the P· saw it, they said unto* "
14 Why do we and the P· fast oft, but "
34 the P· said, He casteth out devils "
12: 2 But when the P· saw it, they said, "
14 the P· went out, and held a council "
24 when the P· heard it, they said, "
38 certain of the scribes and of the P· "
15: 1 Then came to Jesus scribes and P·, "
12 thou that the P· were offended, "
16: 1 P· also with the Sadducees came, "
6, 11 beware of the leaven of the P· "
12 but of the doctrine of the P· and of "
19: 3 P· also came unto him, tempting "
21:45 and P· had heard his parables, "
22:15 Then went the P·, and took counsel "
34 the P· had heard that he had put "
41 the P· were gathered together, "
23: 2 scribes and the P· sit in Moses' "
13, 14, 15, 23, 25, 27, 29 P·, hypocrites! "
27:62 chief priests and P· came together "
M'r 2:16 the scribes and P· saw him eat with "
18 of John and of the P· used to fast: "
18 disciples of John and of the P· fast, "
24 P· said unto him, Behold, why do "

M'r 3: 6 the P· went forth, and straightway 5330
7: 1 came together unto him the P·, "
3 For the P·, and all the Jews, except "
5 Then the P· and scribes asked him, "
8: 11 P· came...and began to question "
15 beware of the leaven of the P·, "
10: 2 the P· came to him, and asked him, "
12: 13 send unto him certain of the P· "
Lu 5: 17 were P· and doctors of the law "
21 scribes and the P· began to reason, "
30 their scribes and P· murmured "
33 likewise the disciples of the P·; "
6: 2 certain of the P· said unto them, "
7 the scribes and P· watched him, "
7: 30 P· and lawyers rejected the counsel "
36 one of the P· desired him that he "
11: 39 do ye P· make clean the outside of "
42 woe unto you, P·! for ye tithe mint "
43 Woe unto you, P·! for ye love the "
44 Woe unto you, scribes and P·, "
53 P· began to urge him vehemently, "
12: 1 Beware ye of the leaven of the P·, "
13: 31 day there came certain of the P·, "
14: 1 house of one of the chief P· to eat "
3 spake unto the lawyers and P·, "
15: 2 And the P· and scribes murmured, "
16: 14 P· also, who were covetous, heard "
17: 20 when he was demanded of the P·, "
19: 39 the P· from among the multitude "
Joh 1: 24 which were sent were of the P·. "
3: 1 man of the P·, named Nicodemus, "
4: 1 Lord knew how the P· had heard "
7: 32 P· heard that the people murmured "
32 P· and...chief priests sent officers "
45 officers to the chief priests and P·; "
47 answered them the P·, Are ye also "
48 rulers or of the P· believed on him? "
8: 3 and P· brought unto him a woman "
13 The P· therefore said unto him, "
9: 13 They brought to the P· him that "
15 the P· also asked him how he had "
16 said some of the P·, This man is not "
40 some of the P· which were with him "
11: 46 went their ways to the P·, and told "
47 gathered the chief priests and...P· "
57 the P· had given a commandment, "
12: 19 The P· therefore said among "
42 of the P· they did not confess him, "
18: 3 officers from the...priests and P·, "
Ac 15: 5 of the sect of the P· which believed, "
23: 6 were Sadducees, and the other P·, "
7 a dissension between the P· and "
8 nor spirit: but the P· confess both. "

Pharisees' (*far'-i-seez*)
Ac 23: 9 scribes that were of the P· part 5330

Pharosh (*fa'-rosh*)
Ezr 8: 3 of Shechaniah, of the sons of P·; *6551

Pharpar (*far'-par*)
2Ki 5: 12 and P·, rivers of Damascus, 6554

Pharzites (*far'-zites*)
Nu 26: 20 of Pharez, the family of the P·: of *6558

Phaseah (*fa-se'-ah*) See also PASEAH.
Ne 7: 51 of Uzza, the children of P·, *6454

Phebe (*fe'-be*)
Ro 16: 1 I commend unto you P· our sister, *5402
subscr. sent by P· servant of the church at* "

Phelet See BETH-PHELET.

Phenice (*fe-ni'-se*) See also PHENICIA.
Ac 11: 19 Stephen travelled as far as P·, *5403
15: 3 passed through P· and Samaria, * "
27: 12 means they might attain to P·, *5405

Phenicia (*fe-nish'-e-ah*) See also PHENICE.
Ac 21: 2 finding a ship sailing...unto P·, *5403

phial See VIAL.

Phichol (*fi'-kol*)
Ge 21: 22 P· the chief captain of his host *6369
32 P· the chief captain of his host, * "
26: 26 P· the chief captain of his army. * "

Philadelphia (*fil-a-del'-fe-ah*)
Re 1: 11 and unto Sardis, and unto P·, and 5359
3: 7 angel of the church in P· write; "

Philemon (*fi-le'-mon*)
Ph'm 1 unto P· our dearly beloved, and 5371
subscr. Written from Rome to P·, by * "

Philetus (*fi-le'-tus*)
2Ti 2: 17 of whom is Hymenæus and P·; 5372

Philip (*fil'-ip*) See also PHILIP'S.
M't 10: 3 P·, and Bartholomew; Thomas, 5376
M'k 3: 18 Andrew, and P·, and Bartholomew, "
Lu 3: 1 his brother P· tetrarch of Ituræa "
6: 14 and John, P· and Bartholomew, "
Joh 1: 43 findeth P·, and saith unto him, "
44 Now P· was of Bethsaida, the city "
45 P· findeth Nathanael, and saith "
46 P· saith unto him, Come and see. "
48 Before that P· called thee, when "
6: 5 he saith unto P·, Whence shall we "
7 P· answered him, Two hundred "
12: 21 same came therefore to P·, which "
22 P· cometh and telleth Andrew: and "
22 and again Andrew and P· tell Jesus. "
14: 8 P· saith unto him, Lord, shew us "
9 yet hast thou not known me, P·? "
Ac 1: 13 P·, and Thomas, Bartholomew, "
6: 5 P·, and Prochorus, and Nicanor, "
8: 5 P· went down to...city of Samaria, "
6 unto those things which P· spake, "
12 when they believed P· preaching "
13 baptized, he continued with P·, "
Ac 8: 26 angel of the Lord spake unto P·, 5376
29 Then the Spirit said unto P·, Go "
30 P· ran thither to him, and heard "
31 he desired P· that he would come "
34 And the eunuch answered P·, and "
35 P· opened his mouth, and began "
37 P· said, If thou believest with all * "
38 the water, both P· and the eunuch; "
39 Spirit of the Lord caught away P·, "
40 But P· was found at Azotus: and "
21: 8 into the house of P· the evangelist, "

Philippi (*fil-ip'-pi*) See also PHILIPPIANS.
M't 16: 13 into the coasts of Cæsarea P·, 5375
M'r 8: 27 into the towns of Cæsarea P·: "
Ac 16: 12 And from thence to P·, which is 5375
20: 6 And we sailed away from P· after "
1Co *subscr.* Corinthians was written from P·* "
2Co *subscr.* Corinthians was written from P·,* "
Ph'p 1: 1 in Christ Jesus which are at P·, "
1Th 2: 2 as ye know, at P·, we were bold in "

Philippians (*fil-ip'-pe-uns*)
Ph'p 4: 15 Now ye P· know also, that in the 5374
subscr. It was written to the P· from Rome*

Philip's (*fil'-ips*)
M't 14: 3 Herodias' sake, his brother P· wife. 5376
M'r 6: 17 Herodias' sake, his brother P· wife: "
Lu 3: 19 for Herodias his brother P· wife, * "

Philistia (*fil-is'-te-ah*) See also PALESTINE; PHILISTINE.
Ps 60: 8 P·, triumph thou because of me. 6429
87: 4 behold P·, and Tyre, with Ethiopia; "
108: 9 my shoe; over P· will I triumph. "

Philistim (*fil-is'-tim*) See also PHILISTINES.
Ge 10: 14 Casluhim, (out of whom came P·,)*6430

Philistine (*fil-is'-tin*) See also PHILISTINES.
1Sa 17: 8 am not I a P·, and ye servants to 6430
10 P· said, I defy the armies of Israel "
11 Israel heard those words of the P·, "
16 P· drew near morning and evening, "
23 up the champion, the P· of Gath, "
26 done to the man that killeth this P·, "
26 for who is this uncircumcised P·, "
32 will go and fight with this P·. "
33 art not able to go against this P· "
36 uncircumcised P· shall be as one "
37 me out of the hand of this P·. "
40 hand: and he drew near to the P·. "
41 P· came on and drew near unto "
42 P· looked about, and saw David, "
43 the P· said unto David, Am I a dog, "
43 the P· cursed David by his gods. "
44 the P· said to David, Come to me, "
45 said David to the P·, Thou comest "
48 the P· arose, and came and drew "
48 toward the army to meet the P·. "
49 and smote the P· in his forehead, "
50 prevailed over the P· with a sling, "
50 and smote the P·, and slew him; "
51 David ran, and stood upon the P·, "
54 And David took the head of the P·, "
55 saw David go forth against the P·, "
57 from the slaughter of the P·, "
57 before Saul with the head of the P· "
18: 6 from the slaughter of the P·, "
19: 5 life in his hand, and slew the P·, "
21: 9 The sword of Goliath the P·, whom "
22: 10 him the sword of Goliath the P·. "
2Sa 21: 17 and smote the P·, and killed him. "

Philistines (*fil-is'-tinz*) See also PHILISTIM; PHILISTINES'.
Ge 21: 32 returned into the land of the P·. 6430
26: 1 unto Abimelech king of the P· "
8 Abimelech king of the P· looked "
14 servants: and the P· envied him. "
15 P· had stopped them, and filled "
18 the P· had stopped them after the "
Ex 13: 17 the way of the land of the P·, "
23: 31 sea even unto the sea of the P·, "
Jos 13: 2 all the borders of the P·, and all "
3 five lords of the P·; the "
J'g 3: 3 Namely, five lords of the P·, and "
31 slew of the P· six hundred men "
10: 6 the gods of the P·, and forsook the "
7 sold them into the hands of the P·, "
11 of Ammon, and from the P·? "
13: 1 into the hand of the P· forty years. "
5 Israel out of the hand of the P·. "
14: 1 Timnath of the daughters of the P·. "
2 Timnath of the daughters of the P·: "
3 a wife of the uncircumcised P·? "
4 sought an occasion against the P·: "
4 the P· had dominion over Israel. "
15: 3 I be more blameless than the P·, "
5 go into the standing corn of the P·, "
6 the P· said, Who hath done this? "
6 the P· came up, and burnt her and "
9 P· went up, and pitched in Judah, "
11 not that the P· are rulers over us? "
12 deliver thee into the hand of the P·. "
14 Lehi, the P· shouted against him: "
20 judged Israel in the days of the P· "
16: 5 lords of the P· came up unto her, "
8 lords of the P· brought up to her "
9, 12, 14 The P· be upon thee, Samson. "
18 and called for the lords of the P·, "
18 lords of the P· came up unto her, "
20 The P· be upon thee, Samson. "
21 P· took him, and put out his eyes, "
23 the lords of the P· gathered them "
27 all the lords of the P· were there; "
28 may be at once avenged of the P· "
30 Samson said, Let me die with the P·. "
1Sa 4: 1 went out against the P· to battle, 6430
1 and the P· pitched in Aphek. "
2 P· put themselves in array against "
2 Israel was smitten before the P·: "
3 smitten us to day before the P·? "
6 when the P· heard the noise of the "
7 the P· were afraid, for they said, "
9 quit yourselves like men, O ye P·, "
10 P· fought, and Israel was smitten, "
17 and said, Israel is fled before the P·, "
5: 1 And the P· took the ark of God, and "
2 When the P· took the ark of God, "
8 and gathered all the lords of the P· "
11 together all the lords of the P·, and "
6: 1 the country of the P· seven months. "
2 the P· called for the priests and "
4 the number of the lords of the P·: "
12 the lords of the P· went after them "
16 the five lords of the P· had seen it, "
17 emerods which the P· returned for "
18 the number of all the cities of the P· "
21 P· have brought again the ark of "
7: 3 deliver you out of the hand of the P·. "
7 P· heard that the children of Israel "
7 the lords of the P· went up against "
7 heard it, they were afraid of the P·. "
8 save us out of the hand of the P·. "
10 the P· drew near to battle against "
10 thunder on that day upon the P·, "
11 pursued the P·, and smote them, "
13 So the P· were subdued, and they "
13 hand of the Lord was against the P· "
14 which the P· had taken from Israel "
14 deliver out of the hand of the P·. "
9: 16 my people out of the hand of the P·: "
10: 5 where is the garrison of the P·: "
12: 9 Hazor, and into the hand of the P·, "
13: 3 smote the garrison of the P· that "
3 was in Geba, and the P· heard of it. "
4 had smitten a garrison of the P·, "
4 had in abomination with the P·. "
5, 11 the P· gathered themselves "
12 P· will come down now upon me to "
16 but the P· encamped in Michmash. "
17 camp of the P· in three companies: "
19 for the P· said, Lest the Hebrews "
20 the Israelites went down to the P·, "
23 the garrison of the P· went out to "
14: 11 unto the garrison of the P·: and "
11 the P· said, Behold, the Hebrews "
19 of the P· went on and increased: "
21 Hebrews that were with the P· "
22 when they heard that the P· fled, "
30 greater slaughter among the P·? "
31 they smote the P· that day from "
36 us go down after the P· by night, "
37 God, Shall I go down after the P·? "
46 went up from following the P·: "
46 and the P· went to their own place. "
47 kings of Zobah, and against the P·: "
52 war against the P· all the days of "
17: 1 P· gathered together their armies "
2 the battle in array against the P·. "
3 P· stood on a mountain on the one "
4 champion out of the camp of the P·, "
19 valley of Elah, fighting with the P·. "
21 the P· had put the battle in array, "
23 name, out of the armies of the P·, "
46 carcases of the hosts of the P· this "
51 P· saw their champion was dead, "
52 and shouted, and pursued the P·, "
52 the wounded of the P· fell down by "
53 returned from chasing after the P·, "
18: 17 let the hand of the P· be upon him. "
21 hand of the P· may be against him. "
25 but an hundred foreskins of the P·, "
25 David fall by the hand of the P·. "
27 slew of the P· two hundred men; "
30 the princes of the P· went forth: "
19: 8 fought with the P·, and slew them "
23: 1 Behold, the P· fight against Keilah, "
2 Shall I go and smite these P·? "
2 Go, and smite the P·, and save "
3 against the armies of the P·? "
4 will deliver the P· into thine hand. "
5 to Keilah, and fought with the P·, "
27 for the P· have invaded the land. "
28 David, and went against the P·: "
24: 1 was returned from following the P·, "
27: 1 escape into the land of the P·; and "
7 David dwelt in the country of the P· "
11 dwelleth in the country of the P·. "
28: 1 P· gathered their armies together "
4 P· gathered themselves together, "
5 when Saul saw the host of the P·, "
15 for the P· make war against me, "
19 with thee into the hand of the P·: "
19 of Israel into the hand of the P·. "
29: 1 the P· gathered together all their "
2 the lords of the P· passed on by "
3 Then said the princes of the P·, "
3 said unto the princes of the P·, Is "
4 of the P· were wroth with him; "
4 the princes of the P· said unto him, "
7 displease not the lords of the P·. "
9 the princes of the P· have said, He "
11 to return into the land of the P·. "
11 And the P· went up to Jezreel. "
30: 16 had taken out of the land of the P·, "
31: 1 Now the P· fought against Israel: "
1 of Israel fled from before the P·, "
2 the P· followed hard upon Saul and "
2 P· slew Jonathan, and Abinadab, "
7 and the P· came and dwelt in them. "
8 when the P· came to strip the slain, "
9 into the land of the P· round about, "

1Sa 31:11 that which the P· had done to Saul: 6430
2Sa 1:20 lest the daughters of the P· rejoice, "
3:14 for an hundred foreskins of the P·. "
18 Israel out of the hand of the P·, and "
5:17 P· heard that they had anointed "
17 all the P· came up to seek David; "
18 The P· also came and spread "
19 saying, Shall I go up to the P·? "
19 deliver the P· into thine hand. "
22 And the P· came up yet again, and "
24 thee, to smite the host of the P·. "
25 smote the P· from Geba until thou "
8: 1 smote the P·, and subdued them: "
1 out of the hand of the P·. "
12 children of Ammon, and of the P·, "
19: 9 us out of the hand of the P·; "
21:12 where the P· had hanged them, "
12 the P· had slain Saul in Gilboa: "
15 P· had yet war again with Israel; "
15 him, and fought against the P·: "
18 again a battle with the P· at Gob: "
19 again a battle in Gob with the P·, "
23: 9 with David, when they defied the P· "
10 smote the P· until his hand was "
11 P·...gathered together into a troop, "
11 and the people fled from the P·. "
12 and defended it, and slew the P·: "
13 of the P· pitched in the valley "
14 of the P· was then in Beth-lehem. "
16 brake through the host of the P·, "
1Ki 4:21 the river unto the land of the P·, "
15:27 which belonged to the P·; "
16:15 which belonged to the P·. "
2Ki 8: 2 sojourned in the land of the P· "
3 returned out of the land of the P·: "
18: 8 He smote the P·, even unto Gaza, "
1Ch 1:12 Casluhim, (of whom came the P·,) "
10: 1 Now the P· fought against Israel; "
1 of Israel fled from before the P·, "
2 the P· followed hard after Saul, "
2 P· slew Jonathan, and Abinadab, "
7 and the P· came and dwelt in them. "
8 the P· came to strip the slain, "
9 and sent into the land of the P. "
11 all that the P· had done to Saul, "
11:13 the P· were gathered together "
13 the people fled from before the P·. "
14 and delivered it, and slew the P·; "
15 host of the P· encamped in the "
18 brake through the host of the P·, "
12:19 with the P· against Saul to battle: "
19 lords of the P· upon advisement "
14: 8 P· heard that David was anointed "
8 all the P· went up to seek David. "
9 the P· came and spread themselves "
10 Shall I go up against the P·? "
13 the P· yet again spread themselves "
15 thee to smite the host of the P·. "
16 smote the host of the P· from "
18: 1 David smote the P·, and subdued "
1 towns out of the hand of the P·. "
11 Ammon, and from the P·, and from "
20: 4 arose war at Gezer with the P·; "
5 there was war again with the P·; "
2Ch 9:26 river even unto the land of the P·, "
17:11 P· brought Jehoshaphat presents, "
21:16 Jehoram the spirit of the P·, "
26: 6 warred against the P·, and brake "
6 about Ashdod, and among the P·. "
7 God helped him against the P·, "
28:18 The P· also had invaded the cities "
Ps 56: title when the P· took him in Gath. "
83: 7 P· with the inhabitants of Tyre; * "
Isa 2: 6 and are soothsayers like the P·, "
9:12 Syrians before, and the P· behind; "
11:14 shoulders of the P· toward the west; "
Jer 25:20 all the kings of the land of the P·, "
47: 1 the prophet against the P·, "
4 day that cometh to spoil all the P·, "
4 the Lord will spoil the P·, the "
Eze 16:27 the daughters of the P·, which are "
57 the daughters of the P·, which "
25:15 the P· have dealt by revenge, "
16 stretch out mine hand upon the P·, "
Am 1: 8 remnant of the P· shall perish, "
6: 2 then go down to Gath of the P·: "
9: 7 P· from Caphtor, and the Syrians "
Ob 19 and they of the plain the P·: and "
Zep 2: 5 O Canaan, the land of the P·, I will "
Zec 9: 6 I will cut off the pride of the P·. "

Philistines' (*fil-is'-tinz*)
Ge 21:34 Abraham sojourned in the P· land 6430
1Sa 14: 1 let us go over to the P· garrison, "
4 to go over unto the P· garrison, "
1Ch 11:16 P· garrison was then at Beth-lehem. "

Philologus (*fil-ol'-o-gus*)
Ro 16:15 Salute P·, and Julia, Nereus, and 5378

philosophers
Ac 17:18 Then certain p· of the Epicureans, 5386

philosophy
Col 2: 8 spoil you through p· and...deceit 5385

Phinehas (*fin'-e-has*) See also PHINEHAS'.
Ex 6:25 she bare him P·: these are the 6372
Nu 25: 7 And when P·, the son of Eleazar, "
11 P·, the son of Eleazar, the son of "
31: 6 P· the son of Eleazar the priest, "
Jos 22:13 P· the son of Eleazar the priest, "
30 when P· the priest, and the princes "
31 P· the son of Eleazar the priest "
32 P· the son of Eleazar the priest, "
24:33 a hill that pertained to P· his son, "
J'g 20:28 P·, the son of Eleazar, the son of "
1Sa 1: 3 the two sons of Eli, Hophni and P·, "
2:34 thy two sons, on Hophni and P·; 6372
4: 4 the two sons of Eli, Hophni and P·, "
11 of Eli, Hophni and P·, were slain. "
17 sons also, Hophni and P·, are dead, "
14: 3 Ichabod's brother, the son of P·, "
1Ch 6: 4 Eleazar begat P·, P· begat Abishua, "
50 Aaron; Eleazar his son, P· his son, "
9:20 P· the son of Eleazar was the ruler "
Ezr 7: 5 The son of Abishua, the son of P·, "
8: 2 Of the sons of P·; Gershom: of the "
33 with him was Eleazar the son of P·; "
Ps 106:30 stood up P·,...executed judgment: "

Phinehas' (*fin'-e-has*)
1Sa 4:19 And his daughter in law, P· wife, 6372

Phlegon (*fle'-gon*)
Ro 16:14 Salute Asyncritus, P·, Hermas, 5393

Phœbe See PHEBE.

Phœnice See PHENICE.

Phœnicia See PHENICIA.

Phœnician See PHENICIAN.

Phrygia (*frij'-e-ah*)
Ac 2:10 P·, and Pamphylia, in Egypt, and 5435
16: 6 when they had gone throughout P· "
18:23 all the country of Galatia and P· "
1Ti *subscr.* chiefest city of P· Pacatiana. "

Phurah (*fu'-rah*)
J'g 7:10 go thou with P· thy servant down *6513
11 went he down with P· his servant* "

Phut (*fut*) See also PUT.
Ge 10: 6 and Mizraim, and P·, and Canaan. *6316
Eze 27:10 of Persia and of Lud and of P· * "

Phuvah (*fu'-vah*) See also PUAH.
Ge 46:13 sons of Issachar; Tola, and P·, *6312

Phygellus (*fi-jel'-lus*)
2Ti 1:15 of whom are P· and Hermogenes. *5436

phylacteries
M't 23: 5 they make broad their p·, and 5440

physician See also PHYSICIANS.
Jer 8:22 in Gilead; is there no p· there? 7495
M't 9:12 They that be whole need not a p·, 2395
M'r 2:17 are whole have no need of the p·, "
Lu 4:23 me this proverb, P·, heal thyself: "
5:31 They that are whole need not a p·; "
Col 4:14 Luke, the beloved p·, and Demas, "

physicians
Ge 50: 2 commanded his servants the p· 7495
2 and the p· embalmed Israel. "
2Ch 16:12 sought not to the Lord, but to the p·. "
Job 13: 4 of lies, ye are all p· of no value. "
M'r 5:26 suffered many things of many p·, 2395
Lu 8:43 had spent all her living upon p·, "

Pi See PI-BESETH; PI-HAHIROTH.

Pi-beseth (*pi-be'-zeth*)
Eze 30:17 The young men of Aven and of P· 6364

pick
Pr 30:17 ravens of the valley shall p· it out, 5365

pictures
Nu 33:52 destroy all their p·, and destroy *4906
Pr 25:11 is like apples of gold in p· of silver. ‡* "
Isa 2:16 Tarshish,...upon all pleasant p·. *7914

piece See also APIECE; PIECES.
Ge 15:10 laid each p· one against another: *1335
Ex 37: 7 of gold, beaten out of one p· made *4749
Nu 10: 2 of a whole p· shalt thou make them: * "
J'g 9:53 woman cast a p· of a millstone *6400
1Sa 2:36 crouch to him for a p· of silver and 95
36 that I may eat a p· of bread. *6595
30:12 gave him a p· of a cake of figs, 6400
2Sa 6:19 of bread, and a good p· of flesh, * 829
11:21 a woman cast a p· of a millstone *6400
23:11 a p· of ground full of lentiles: *2513
2Ki 3:19 and mar every good p· of land with "
25 on every good p· of land cast every "
1Ch 16: 3 of bread, and a good p· of flesh, * 829
Ne 3:11 repaired the other p·, and the *4060
19 another p· over against the going * "
20 earnestly repaired the other p·, * "
21 Urijah the son of Koz another p·, * "
24 the son of Henadad another p·, * "
27 the Tekoites repaired another p·, * "
30 the sixth son of Zalaph, another p·. * "
Job 41:24 as a p· of the nether millstone. *6400
42:11 man also gave him a p· of money, "
Pr 6:26 a man is brought to a p· of bread: 3603
28:21 for a p· of bread that man will 6595
Ca 4: 3 are like a p· of a pomegranate 6400
6: 7 As a p· of a pomegranate are thy "
Jer 37:21 give him daily a p· of bread out *3603
Eze 24: 4 thereof into it, even every good p·, 5409
6 bring it out p· by p·; let no lot fall "
Am 3:12 the lion two legs, or a p· of an ear; 915
4: 7 one p· was rained upon, and the
7 p· whereupon it rained not withered.
M't 9:16 putteth a p· of new cloth unto an 1915
17:27 mouth, thou shalt find a p· of money: *
M'r 2:21 seweth a p· of new cloth on an old 1915
21 the new p· that filled it up taketh *4138
Lu 5:36 putteth a p· of a new garment upon 1915
36 the p· that was taken out of the "
14:18 I have bought a p· of ground, and *
15: 8 if she lose one p·, doth not light a 1406
9 have found the p· which I had lost. "
24:42 gave him a p· of a broiled fish, 3313

pieces See also SHOULDERPIECES.
Ge 15:17 that passed between those p·, 1506
20:16 thy brother a thousand p· of silver:
33:19 father, for an hundred p· of money.
37:28 Ishmeelites for twenty p· of silver:
33 Joseph is without doubt rent in p·.
44:28 and I said, Surely he is torn in p·;
45:22 he gave three hundred p· of silver,
Ex 15: 6 Lord, hath dashed in p· the enemy.
22:13 If it be torn in p·, then let him bring
29:17 And thou shalt cut the ram in p·, 5409
17 put them unto his p·, and unto his "
Le 1: 6 burnt offering, and cut it into his p·. "
12 he shall cut it into his p·, with his "
2: 6 Thou shalt part it in p·, and pour 6595
6:21 the baken p· of the meat offering
8:20 he cut the ram into p·; and Moses 5409
20 the head, and the p·, and the fat. "
9:13 with the p· thereof, and the head: * "
Jos 24:32 Shechem for an hundred p· of silver:
J'g 9: 4 him threescore and ten p· of silver
16: 5 of us eleven hundred p· of silver.
19:29 with her bones, into twelve p·, 5409
20: 6 my concubine, and cut her in p·,
1Sa 2:10 of the Lord shall be broken to p·;
11: 7 yoke of oxen, and hewed them in p·,
15:33 Samuel hewed Agag in p· before the
1Ki 11:30 on him, and rent it in twelve p·: 7168
31 to Jeroboam, Take thee ten p·: "
18:23 and cut it in p·, and lay it on wood,
33 and cut the bullock in p·, and laid
19:11 brake in p· the rocks before the Lord;
2Ki 2:12 clothes, and rent them in two p·. 7168
5: 5 silver, and six thousand p· of gold,
6:25 was sold for fourscore p· of silver,
25 of dove's dung for five p· of silver.
11:18 and his images brake they in p·
18: 4 brake in p· the brasen serpent that
23:14 he brake in p· the images, and cut
24:13 cut in p· all the vessels of gold which
25:13 did the Chaldees break in p·, and
2Ch 23:17 brake his altars and his images in p·,
25:12 that they all were broken in p·.
28:24 cut in p· the vessels of the house of*
31: 1 brake the images in p·, and cut
34: 4 the molten images, he brake in p·,
Job 16:12 me by my neck, and shaken me to p·,
19: 2 soul, and brake me in p· with words?
34:24 brake in p· mighty men without
40:18 His bones are as strong p· of brass;*
Ps 2: 9 dash them in p· like a potter's vessel.
7: 2 my soul like a lion, rending it in p·,
50:22 that forget God, lest I tear you in p·,
58: 7 his arrows, let them be as cut in p·.*
68:30 submit himself with p· of silver: 7518
72: 4 and shall break in p· the oppressor.
74:14 breakest the heads of leviathan in p·,
89:10 Thou hast broken Rahab in p·, as one
94: 5 They break in p· thy people, O Lord,
Ca 8:11 was to bring a thousand p· of silver.
Isa 3:15 mean ye that ye beat my people to p·,*
8: 9 ye shall be broken in p·; and give ear,
9 and ye shall be broken in p·; gird
9 yourselves,...ye shall be broken in p·.
13:16 children also shall be dashed to p·
18 also shall dash the young men to p·;
30:14 potter's vessel that is broken in p·;
45: 2 I will break in p· the gates of brass,
Jer 5: 6 goeth out thence shall be torn in p·:
23:29 hammer that breaketh the rock in p·?
50: 2 Merodach is broken in p·; her idols*
2 her images are broken in p·. *
51:20 thee will I break in p· the nations,
21 break in p· the horse and his rider;
21 break in p· the chariot and his rider;
22 will I break in p· man and woman;
22 will I break in p· old and young;
22 break in p· the young man and the
23 break in p· with thee the shepherd and
23 will I break in p· the husbandman
23 I break in p· captains and rulers.
La 3:11 aside my ways, and pulled me in p·:
Eze 4:14 that dieth of itself, or is torn in p·;*
13:19 of barley and for p· of bread, 6595
24: 4 Gather the p· thereof into it, even 5409
Da 2: 5 ye shall be cut in p·, and your 1917
34 of iron and clay, and brake them to p·.
35 and the gold, broken to p· together,
40 forasmuch as iron breaketh in p· and
40 these, shall it break in p· and bruise.
44 it shall break in p· and consume all
45 and that it break in p· the iron, the
3:29 and Abed-nego, shall be cut in p·, 1917
6:24 and brake all their bones in p· or
7: 7 it devoured and brake in p·, and
19 which devoured, brake in p·, and
23 shall tread it down, and break it in p·.
Ho 3: 2 her to me for fifteen p· of silver,
8: 6 of Samaria shall be broken in p·.
10:14 mother was dashed in p· upon her
13:16 their infants shall be dashed in p·,
Mic 1: 7 images thereof shall be beaten to p·,
3: 3 their bones, and chop them in p·,
4:13 thou shalt beat in p· many people:
5: 8 treadeth down, and teareth in p·,
Na 2: 1 He that dasheth in p· is come up
12 The lion did tear in p· enough for his
3:10 young children also were dashed in p·
Zec 11:12 for my price thirty p· of silver.
13 And I took the thirty p· of silver, and
16 the fat, and tear their claws in p·.
12: 3 themselves with it shall be cut in p·,*
M't 26:15 with him for thirty p· of silver.
27: 3 brought again the thirty p· of silver
5 cast down the p· of silver in the
6 the chief priests took the silver p·,
9 And they took the thirty p· of silver
M'r 5: 4 by him, and the fetters broken in p·,

Lu 15: 8 what woman having ten p' of silver, 1406
Ac 19: 19 found it fifty thousand p' of silver.
23: 10 should have been pulled in p' of 1288
27: 44 and some on broken p' of the ship.*

pierce See also PIERCED; PIERCETH; PIERCING.
Nu 24: 8 p' them through with his arrows.*4272
2Ki 18: 21 it will go into his hand, and p' it: 5344
Isa 36: 6 it will go into his hand, and p' it: "
Lu 2: 35 shall p' through thy own soul also,) 1330

pierced
J'g 5: 26 had p' and stricken through his 4272
Job 30: 17 My bones are p' in me in the night 5365
Ps 22: 16 me: they p' my hands and my feet. 738
Zec 12: 10 look upon me whom they have p'. 1856
Joh 19: 34 soldiers with a spear p' his side, 3572
37 shall look on him whom they p'. 1574
1Ti 6: 10 p' themselves through with many 4044
Re 1: 7 him, and they also which p' him: 1574

pierceth
Job 40: 24 eyes: his nose p' through snares.*5344

piercing See also PIERCINGS.
Isa 27: 1 punish leviathan the p' serpent, *1281
Heb 4: 12 p' even to the dividing asunder of 1338

piercings
Pr 12: 18 speaketh like the p' of a sword: 4094

piety
1Ti 5: 4 them learn first to show p' at 2151

pigeon See also PIGEONS.
Ge 15: 9 and a turtledove, and a young p'. 1469
Le 12: 6 and a young p', or a turtledove, 3123

pigeons
Le 1: 14 of turtledoves, or of young p'. 3123
5: 7, 11 two turtledoves, or two young p', "
12: 8 bring two turtles, or two young p'; "
14: 22 two turtledoves, or two young p', "
30 the turtledoves, or of the young p', "
15: 14 two turtledoves, or two young p', "
29 her two turtles, or two young p', "
Nu 6: 10 bring two turtles, or two young p', "
Lu 2: 24 of turtledoves, or two young p'. 4058

Pi-hahiroth (pi-ha-hi'-roth)
Ex 14: 2 they turn and encamp before P', 6367
9 sea, beside P', before Baal-zephon."
Nu 33: 7 Etham, and turned again unto P', "
8 And they departed from before P',*"

Pilate (pi'-lut)
M't 27: 2 him to Pontius P' the governor. 4091
13 said P' unto him, Hearest thou not "
17 P' said unto them, Whom will ye "
22 P' saith unto them, What shall I do"
24 When P' saw that he could prevail "
58 went to P', and begged the body of "
58 Then P' commanded the body to be"
62 Pharisees came together unto P', "
65 P' said unto them, Ye have a "
M'r 15: 1 him away, and delivered him to P'. "
2 P' asked him, Art thou the King of"
4 And P' asked him again, saying, "
5 nothing; so that P' marvelled. "
9 P' answered them, saying, Will ye "
12 P' answered and said again unto "
14 P' said unto them, Why, what evil "
15 And so P', willing to content the "
43 went in boldly unto P', and craved "
44 P' marvelled if he were already "
Lu 3: 1 Pontius P' being governor of "
13: 1 blood P' had mingled with their "
23: 1 of them arose, and led him unto P'. "
3 And P' asked him, saying, Art thou"
4 said P' to the chief priests and to "
6 When P' heard of Galilee, he asked"
11 robe, and sent him again to P'. "
12 P' and Herod were made friends "
13 P', when he had called together "
20 P' therefore, willing to release "
24 P' gave sentence that it should be "
52 This man went unto P', and begged"
Joh 18: 29 P' then went out unto them, and "
31 Then said P' unto them, Take ye "
33 P' entered into the judgment hall "
35 P' answered, Am I a Jew? Thine "
37 P' therefore said unto him, Art thou"
38 P' saith unto him, What is truth? "
19: 1 Then P' therefore took Jesus, and "
4 P' therefore went forth again, and "
5 P' saith unto them, Behold the man! "
6 P' saith unto them, Take ye him, 4091
8 P' therefore heard that saying, "
10 Then saith P' unto him, Speakest "
12 thenceforth P' sought to release "
13 P' therefore heard that saying, "
15 P' saith unto them, Shall I crucify "
19 P' wrote a title, and put it on the "
21 the chief priests of the Jews to P', "
22 P' answered, What I have written "
31 besought P' that their legs might "
38 besought P' that he might take "
38 of Jesus: and P' gave him leave. "
Ac 3: 13 denied him in the presence of P', "
4: 27 both Herod, and Pontius P', with "
13: 28 they P' that he should be slain. "
1Ti 6: 13 before Pontius P' witnessed a good"

Pildash (pil'-dash)
Ge 22: 22 and Hazo, and P', and Jidlaph, 6394

pile
Isa 30: 33 p' thereof is fire and much wood; 4071
Eze 24: 9 will even make the p' for fire great."

Pileha (pil'-e-hah)
Ne 10: 24 Hallohesh, P', Shobek, *6401

Pileser See TIGLATH-PILESER.

pilgrim See PILGRIMS.

pilgrimage
Ge 47: 9 The days of the years of my p' are 4033
9 my fathers in the days of their p'. "
Ex 6: 4 land of Canaan, the land of their p',*"
Ps 119: 54 my songs in the house of my p'. "

pilgrims
Heb 11: 13 strangers and p' on the earth. 3927
1Pe 2: 11 I beseech you as strangers and p', "

pillar See also PILLARS.
Ge 19: 26 him, and she became a p' of salt. 5333
28: 18 his pillows, and set it up for a p', 4676
22 this stone, which I have set for a p',"
31: 13 where thou anointedst the p', and "
45 took a stone, and set it up for a p'. "
51 this heap, and behold this p', which"
52 this p' be witness, that I will not "
52 not pass over this heap and this p' "
35: 14 And Jacob set up a p' in the place "
14 talked with him, even a p' of 4678
20 And Jacob set a p' upon her grave: 4676
20 that is the p' of Rachel's grave 4678
Ex 13: 21 them by day in a p' of a cloud, to 5982
21 by night in a p' of fire, to give them "
22 took not away the p' of the cloud "
22 by day, nor the p' of fire by night, "
14: 19 the p' of the cloud went from before "
24 through the p' of fire and of the "
33: 9 the cloudy p' descended, and stood "
10 the people saw the cloudy p' stand "
Nu 12: 5 Lord came down in the p' of the "
14: 14 them, by day time in a p' of a cloud, "
14 and in a p' of fire by night. "
De 31: 15 the tabernacle in a p' of a cloud: "
15 p' of the cloud stood over the door "
J'g 9: 6 of the p' that was in Shechem. 5324
20: 40 out of the city with a p' of smoke, 5982
2Sa 18: 18 and reared up for himself a p', 4678
18 he called the p' after his own name:"
1Ki 7: 21 set up the right p', and called the 5982
21 he set up the left p', and called "
2Ki 11: 14 the king stood by a p', as the "
23: 3 the king stood by a p', and made a "
25: 17 the one p' was eighteen cubits, "
17 the second p' with wreathen work. "
2Ch 23: 13 the king stood at his p' at the "
Ne 9: 12 them in the day by a cloudy p'; "
12 and in the night by a p' of fire, "
19 p' of the cloud departed not from "
19 neither the p' of fire by night, to "
Ps 99: 7 spake unto them in the cloudy p': "
Isa 19: 19 a p' at the border thereof to the 4676
Jer 1: 18 defenced city, and an iron p', and 5982
52: 21 of one p' was eighteen cubits; "
22 The second p' also and the "
1Ti 3: 15 the p' and ground of the truth. 4769
Re 3: 12 a p' in the temple of my God, "

pillars
Ex 24: 4 p', according to the twelve tribes 4676
26: 32 it upon four p' of shittim wood 5982
37 hanging five p' of shittim wood, "
27: 10 twenty p' thereof and their twenty "
10 the hooks of the p', and their fillets "
11 twenty p' and their twenty sockets "
11 hooks of the p' and their fillets of "
12 their p' ten, and their sockets ten. "
14, 15 their p' three, and their sockets "
16 p' shall be four, and their sockets "
17 All the p' round about the court "
35: 11 his bars, his p', and his sockets, "
17 his p', and their sockets, and the "
36: 36 thereunto four p' of shittim wood, "
38 the five p' of it with their hooks: "
38: 10 Their p' were twenty, and their "
10 the hooks of the p' and their fillets "
11 their p' were twenty, and their "
11 hooks of the p' and their fillets of "
12 their p' ten, and their sockets ten; "
12 hooks of the p' and their fillets of "
14, 15 their p' three, and their sockets "
17 the sockets for the p' were of brass; "
17 hooks of the p' and their fillets of "
17 all the p' of the court were filleted "
19 their p' were four, and their sockets"
28 shekels he made hooks for the p', "
39: 33 bars, and his p', and his sockets; "
40 his p', and his sockets, and the "
40: 18 bars thereof, and reared up his p'. "
Nu 3: 36 and the p' thereof, and the sockets "
37 the p' of the court round about, "
4: 31 bars thereof, and the p' thereof, "
32 the p' of the court round about, "
De 12: 3 break their p', burn their groves 4676
J'g 16: 25 and they set him between the p'. 5982
26 Suffer me that I may feel the p' "
29 took hold of the two middle p' "
1Sa 2: 8 the p' of the earth are the Lord's, 4690
1Ki 7: 2 upon four rows of cedar p', 5982
2 with cedar beams upon the p'. "
3 lay on forty five p', fifteen in a row. "
6 And he made a porch of p'; the "
6 the other p' and the thick beam "
15 he cast two p' of brass, of eighteen "
16 to set upon the tops of the p': "
17 which were upon the top of the p'; "
18 And he made the p', and two rows "
19 the top of the p' were of lily work "
20 And the chapiters upon the two p' "
21 the p' in the porch of the temple: "
22 the top of the p' was lily work: "
22 so was the work of the p' finished. "
41 The two p', and the two bowls of "

1Ki 7: 41 that were on the top of the two p'; 5982
41 which were upon the top of the p'; "
42 the chapiters that were upon the p'; "
10: 12 king made of the almug trees p' 4552
2Ki 18: 16 p' which Hezekiah king of Judah 547
25: 13 p' of brass that were in the house 5982
16 The two p', one sea, and the bases "
1Ch 18: 8 made the brasen sea, and the p', "
2Ch 3: 15 he made before the house two p' "
16 put them on the heads of the p'; "
17 reared up the p' before the temple, "
4: 12 the two p', and the pommels, and "
12 were on the top of the two p', "
12 which were on the top of the p'; "
13 chapiters which were upon the p'. "
Es 1: 6 to silver rings and p' of marble: "
Job 9: 6 place, and the p' thereof tremble. "
26: 11 The p' of heaven tremble and are "
Ps 75: 3 are dissolved: I bear up the p' of it."
Pr 9: 1 she hath hewn out her seven p': "
Ca 3: 6 of the wilderness like p' of smoke, 8490
10 He made the p' thereof of silver, 5982
5: 15 His legs are as p' of marble, set "
Jer 27: 19 concerning the p', and concerning "
52: 17 p' of brass that were in the house "
20 The two p', one sea, and twelve "
21 concerning the p', the height of "
Eze 40: 49 and there were p' by the posts, one "
42: 6 had not p' as the p' of the courts: "
Joe 2: 30 blood, and fire, and p' of smoke. 8490
Ga 2: 9 and John, who seemed to be p', 4769
Re 10: 1 the sun, and his feet as p' of fire: "

pilled See also PEELED.
Ge 30: 37 and p' white strakes in them, and*6478
38 rods which he had p' before the * "

pillow See also PILLOWS.
1Sa 19: 13 a p' of goats' hair for his bolster, 3523
16 a p' of goats' hair for his bolster. "
M'r 4: 38 part of the ship, asleep on a p': 4344

pillows
Ge 28: 11 that place, and put them for his p',*4763
18 the stone that he had put for his p',*"
Eze 13: 18 women that sew p' in all armholes, 3704
20 I am against your p', wherewith ye "

Pilneser See TILGATH-PILNESER.

pilots
Eze 27: 8 that were in thee, were thy p'. 2259
27 thy mariners, and thy p', thy "
28 at the sound of the cry of thy p'. "
29 all the p' of the sea, shall come "

Piltai (pil'-tahee)
Ne 12: 17 of Miniamin, of Moadiah, P'; 6408

pin See also PINS.
J'g 16: 14 she fastened it with the p', and 3489
14 went away with the p' of the beam, "
Eze 15: 3 take a p' of it to hang any vessel "

pine See also PINETH; PINING.
Le 26: 39 that are left of you shall p' away 4743
39 shall they p' away with them. "
Ne 8: 15 fetch olive branches, and p' *6086, 8081
Isa 41: 19 the desert the fir tree, and the p', 8410
60: 13 unto thee, the fir tree, the p' tree, "
La 4: 9 these p' away, stricken through 2100
Eze 24: 23 shall p' away for your iniquities, 4743
33: 10 upon us, and we p' away in them, "

pineth
M'r 9: 18 with his teeth, and p' away; 3583

pining
Isa 38: 12 he will cut me off with p' sickness:*1803

pinnacle
M't 4: 5 setteth him on a p' of the temple, 4419
Lu 4: 9 and set him on a p' of the temple, "

Pinon (pi'-non)
Ge 36: 41 Aholibamah, duke Elah, duke P', 6373
1Ch 1: 52 Aholibamah, duke Elah, duke P', "

pins
Ex 27: 19 thereof, and all the p' thereof, and 3489
19 the p' of the court shall be of brass."
35: 18 The p' of the tabernacle, and the "
18 the p' of the court, and their cords, "
38: 20 all the p' of the tabernacle, and of "
31 and all the p' of the tabernacle, "
31 all the p' of the court round about. "
39: 40 his cords, and his p', and all the "
Nu 3: 37 and their p', and their cords. "
4: 32 and their p', and their cords, "
Isa 3: 22 the wimples, and the crisping p', *

pipe See also PIPED; PIPES.
1Sa 10: 5 with a tabret, and a p', and a harp, 2485
Isa 5: 12 viol, the tabret, and p', and wine, "
30: 29 one goeth with a p' to come into the"
1Co 14: 7 giving sound, whether p' or harp, 836

piped
1Ki 1: 40 and the people p' with pipes, and 2490
M't 11: 17 We have p' unto you, and ye have 832
Lu 7: 32 We have p' unto you, and ye have "
1Co 14: 7 it be known what is p' or harped? "

pipers
Re 18: 22 harpers, and musicians, and of p',* 834

pipes
1Ki 1: 40 and the people piped with p', and 2485
Jer 48: 36 heart shall sound for Moab like p', "
36 mine heart shall sound like p' for "
Eze 28: 13 of thy tabrets and of thy p' was 5345
Zec 4: 2 seven p' to the seven lamps, which 4166
12 two golden p' empty the golden *6804

Piram (*pi'-ram*)
Jos 10: 3 and unto P' king of Jarmuth, and 6502

Pirathon (*pir'-a-thon*) See also PIRATHONITE.
J'g 12:15 was buried in P' in the land of 6552

Pirathonite (*pir'-a-thon-ite*)
J'g 12:13 son of Hillel, a P', judged Israel. 6553
15 Abdon the son of Hillel the P' died, "
2Sa 23:30 Benaiah the P', Hiddai of the "
1Ch 11:31 of Benjamin, Benaiah the P', "
27:14 month was Benaiah the P', of the "

Pisgah (*piz'-gah*) See also ASHDOTH-PISGAH; NEBO.
Nu 21:20 top of P', which looketh toward 6449
23:14 field of Zophim, to the top of P', "
De 3:27 Get thee up into the top of P', and "
4:49 the plain, under the springs of P'. "
34: 1 the top of P', that is over against "

Pisidia (*pi-sid'-e-ah*)
Ac 13:14 they came to Antioch in P', and *4099*
14:24 they had passed throughout P', "

Pison (*pi'-son*)
Ge 2:11 The name of the first is P': that *6376

Pispah (*piz'-pah*)
1Ch 7:38 Jephunneh, and P', and Ara. *6462

piss See also PISSETH.
2Ki 18:27 and drink their own p' with you? *7890
Isa 36:12 and drink their own p' with you? * "

pisseth
1Sa 25:22, 34 any that p' against the wall. *8366
1Ki 14:10 him that p' against the wall, and * "
16:11 him not one that p' against a wall,* "
21:21 Ahab him that p' against the wall,* "
2Ki 9: 8 Ahab him that p' against the wall,* "

pit See also PITS.
Ge 37:20 him, and cast him into some p', * 953
22 but cast him into this p' that is in "
24 took him, and cast him into a p': "
24 p' was empty, there was no water "
28 and lifted up Joseph out of the p', "
29 And Reuben returned unto the p'; "
29 behold, Joseph was not in the p'; "
Ex 21:33 And if a man shall open a p', or "
33 if a man shall dig a p', and not cover "
34 owner of the p' shall make it good, "
Le 11:36 Nevertheless a fountain or p', "
Nu 16:30 they go down quick into the p'; ‡7585
33 went down alive into the p', and ‡ "
2Sa 17: 9 he is hid now in some p', or in 6354
18:17 cast him into a great p' in the wood, "
23:20 and slew a lion in the midst of a p' 953
2Ki 10:14 slew them at the p' of the shearing "
1Ch 11:22 slew a lion in a p' in a snowy day. "
Job 17:16 go down to the bars of the p', ‡7585
33:18 keepeth back his soul from the p', 7845
24 him from going down to the p': "
28 his soul from going into the p', "
30 To bring back his soul from the p', "
Ps 7:15 He made a p', and digged it, and 953
9:15 heathen are sunk down in the p' 7845
28: 1 like them that go down into the p'. 953
30: 3 that I should not go down to the p'. "
9 blood, when I go down to the p'? 7845
35: 7 they hid for me their net in a p', "
40: 2 me up also out of an horrible p', 953
55:23 down into the p' of destruction: 875
57: 6 they have digged a p' before me, 7882
69:15 let not the p' shut her mouth upon 875
88: 4 with them that go down into the p':953
6 Thou hast laid me in the lowest p', "
94:13 the p' be digged for the wicked. 7845
143: 7 unto them that go down into the p'.953
Pr 1:12 as those that go down into the p': "
22:14 of strange women is a deep p': 7745
23:27 a strange woman is a narrow p'. 875
26:27 Whoso diggeth a p' shall fall 7845
28:10 shall fall himself into his own p': 7816
17 doeth violence...shall flee to the p'; 953
Ec 10: 8 He that diggeth a p' shall fall into 1475
Isa 14:15 down to hell, to the sides of the p'. 953
19 that go down to the stones of the p'; "
24:17 Fear, and the p', and the snare, 6354
18 noise of...fear shall fall into the p'; "
18 cometh up out of the midst of the p'"
22 as prisoners are gathered in the p', 953
30:14 to take water withal out of the p'.*1360
38:17 it from the p' of corruption: 7845
18 that go down into the p' cannot hope953
51: 1 hole of the p' whence ye are digged. "
14 that he should not die in the p', 7845
Jer 18:20 they have digged a p' for my soul. 7745
22 have digged a p' to take me, 7743,7882
41: 7 cast them into the midst of the p', 953
9 the p' wherein Ishmael had cast all "
48:43 Fear, and the p', and the snare, 6354
44 from the fear shall fall into the p'; "
44 and he that getteth up out of the p' "
Eze 19: 4 he was taken in their p', and 7845
8 over him: he was taken in their p'. "
26:20 with them that descend into the p', 953
20 with them that go down to the p', "
28: 8 shall bring thee down to the p', 7845
31:14 with them that go down to the p'. 953
16 with them that descend into the p': "
32:18 with them that go down into the p'; "
23 graves are set in the sides of the p', "
24 with them that go down to the p'. "
25 with them that go down to the p': "
29, 30 with them that go down to the p'. "
Zec 9:11 out of the p' wherein is no water. "
M't 12:11 it fall into a p' on the sabbath day, *999*
Lu 14: 5 an ass or an ox fallen into a p', **5421*

Re 9: 1 given the key of the bottomless p'. *5421*
2 And he opened the bottomless p'; "
2 there arose a smoke out of the p', "
2 by reason of the smoke of the p'. "
11 is the angel of the bottomless p', *
11: 7 ascendeth out of the bottomless p'*
17: 8 ascend out of the bottomless p', and*
20: 1 having the key of the bottomless p'*
3 And cast him into the bottomless p',*

pitch See also PITCHED.
Ge 6:14 shalt p' it within and without 3722
14 it within and without with p'. 3724
Ex 2: 3 daubed it with slime and with p', 2203
Nu 1:52 of Israel shall p' their tents, 2583
53 the Levites shall p' round about ‡ "
2: 2 shall p' by his own standard, ‡ "
2 of the congregation shall they p'. ‡ "
3 Judah p' throughout their armies:*"
5 And those that do p' next unto him‡"
12 And those which p' by him shall be‡"
3:23 shall p' behind the tabernacle ‡ "
29, 35 p' on the side of the tabernacle‡ "
De 1:33 you out a place to p' your tents in, "
Jos 4:20 of Jordan, did Joshua p' in Gilgal.*6965
Isa 13:20 neither shall the Arabian p' tent 167
34: 9 thereof shall be turned into p', 2203
9 thereof shall become burning p'. "
Jer 6: 3 shall p' their tents against her 8628

pitched
Ge 12: 8 east of Beth-el, and p' his tent, 5186
13:12 and p' his tent toward Sodom. * 167
26:17 p' his tent in the valley of Gerar, *2583
25 an altar...and p' his tent there: 5186
31:25 Jacob had p' his tent in the mount:8628
25 Laban...p' in the mount of Gilead.‡ "
33:18 and p' his tent before the city. *2583
Ex 17: 1 p' in Rephidim: and there was no‡ "
19: 2 and had p' in the wilderness; and‡ "
33: 7 and p' it without the camp, *5186
Nu 1:51 when the tabernacle is to be p', 2583
2:34 so they p' by their standards, and‡ "
9:17 children of Israel p' their tents. * "
18 commandment of the Lord they p':*"
12:16 and p' in the wilderness of Paran.‡ "
21:10 Israel set forward, and p' in Oboth.‡"
11 p' at Ije-abarim, in the wilderness‡ "
12 and p' in the valley of Zared. ‡ "
13 and p' on the other side of Arnon,‡ "
22: 1 and p' in the plains of Moab on this‡"
33: 5 from Rameses, and p' in Succoth. ‡ "
6 from Succoth, and p' in Etham, ‡ "
7 and they p' before Migdol. ‡ "
8 of Etham, and p' in Marah. ‡ "
9 ten palm trees; and they p' there.‡ "
15 and p' in the wilderness of Sinai. ‡ "
16 Sinai, and p' in Kibroth-hattaavah.‡"
18 from Hazeroth, and p' in Rithmah.‡"
19 Rithmah, and p' in Rimmon-parez.‡"
20 Rimmon-parez, and p' in Libnah.‡ "
21 from Libnah, and p' at Rissah. ‡ "
22 from Rissah, and p' in Kehelathah.‡"
23 and p' in mount Shapher. ‡ "
25 Haradah, and p' in Makheloth. ‡ "
27 from Tahath, and p' at Tarah. ‡ "
28 from Tarah, and p' in Mithcah. ‡ "
29 from Mithcah,...p' in Hashmonah.‡ "
31 Moseroth, and p' in Bene-jaakan. ‡ "
33 Hor-hagidgad, and p' in Jotbathah.‡"
36 and p' in the wilderness of Zin, ‡ "
37 Kadesh, and p' in mount Hor; ‡ "
41 mount Hor, and p' in Zalmonah. ‡ "
42 from Zalmonah, and p' in Punon. ‡ "
43 from Punon, and p' in Oboth. ‡ "
44 from Oboth, and p' in Ije-abarim,‡ "
45 from Iim, and p' in Dibon-gad. ‡ "
47 and p' in the mountains of Abarim,‡"
48 p' in the plains of Moab by Jordan‡ "
49 p' by Jordan, from Beth-jesimoth ‡ "
Jos 8:11 and p' on the north side of Ai: ‡ "
11: 5 p' together at the waters of Merom,‡"
J'g 4:11 and p' his tent unto the plain of 5186
6:33 and p' in the valley of Jezreel. ‡2583
7: 1 and p' beside the well of Harod: ‡ "
11:18 and p' on the other side of Arnon,‡ "
20 and p' in Jahaz, and fought against‡ "
15: 9 the Philistines...p' in Judah, ‡ "
18:12 and p' in Kirjath-jearim, in Judah:*"
1Sa 4: 1 battle, and p' beside Eben-ezer; ‡ "
1 and the Philistines p' in Aphek. ‡ "
13: 5 they came up, and p' in Michmash,‡"
17: 1 p' between Shochoh and Azekah ‡ "
2 p' by the valley of Elah, and set the‡"
26: 3 And Saul p' in the hill of Hachilah,‡"
5 to the place where Saul had p': ‡ "
5 and the people p' round about him.‡"
28: 4 and came and p' in Shunem: and‡ "
4 together, and they p' in Gilboa. ‡ "
29: 1 p' by a fountain which is in Jezreel.‡ "
2Sa 6:17 tabernacle that David had p' for it:5186
17:26 Absalom p' in the land of Gilead. ‡2583
23:13 p' in the valley of Rephaim. * "
24: 5 passed over Jordan, and p' in Aroer,‡"
1Ki 20:27 children of Israel p' before them * "
29 they p' one over against the other,* "
2Ki 25: 1 Jerusalem, and p' against it; * "
1Ch 15: 1 the ark of God, and p' it for a tent. 5186
16: 1 of the tent that David had p' for it: "
19: 7 who came and p' before Medeba. ‡2583
2Ch 1: 4 had p' a tent for it at Jerusalem. 5186
Jer 52: 4 Jerusalem, and p' against it, *2583
Heb 8: 2 which the Lord p', and not man. *4078*

pitcher See also PITCHERS.
Ge 24:14 Let down thy p', I pray thee, that 3537
15 with her p' upon her shoulder. "

Ge 24:16 well, and filled her p', and came up. 3537
17 thee, drink a little water of thy p'. "
18 and let down her p' upon her hand, "
20 and emptied her p' into the trough, "
43 a little water of thy p' to drink; "
45 forth with her p' on her shoulder; "
46 let down her p' from her shoulder, "
Ec 12: 6 or the p' be broken at the fountain, "
M'r 14:13 you a man bearing a p' of water: *2765*
Lu 22:10 meet you, bearing a p' of water; "

pitchers
J'g 7:16 every man's hand, with empty p', 3537
16 and lamps within the p'. "
19 and brake the p' that were in their "
20 brake the p', and held the lamps "
La 4: 2 are they esteemed as earthen p', 5035

Pithom (*pi'-thom*)
Ex 1:11 treasure cities, P' and Raamses. 6619

Pithon (*pi'-thon*)
1Ch 8:35 the sons of Micah were, P', and 6377
9:41 the sons of Micah were, P', and "

pitied
Ps 106:46 He made them also to be p' of all 7356
La 2: 2 of Jacob, and hath not p': 2550
17 hath thrown down, and hath not p':"
21 anger; thou hast killed, and not p'. "
3:43 thou hast slain, thou hast not p'. "
Eze 16: 5 None eye p' thee, to do any of 2347

pitieth
Ps 103:13 Like as a father p' his children, 7355
13 so the Lord p' them that fear him. "
Eze 24:21 eyes, and that which your soul p'; 4263

pitiful
La 4:10 The hands of the p' women have 7362
Jas 5:11 the Lord is very p', and of tender **4184*
1Pe 3: 8 love as brethren, be p', be **2155*

pits See also SALTPITS; SLIMEPITS.
1Sa 13: 6 rocks, and in high places, and in p'.953
Ps 119:85 The proud have digged p' for me, 7882
140:10 be cast into the fire; into deep p', "
Jer 2: 6 through a land of deserts and...p', 7745
14: 3 they came to the p', and found no ‡1356
La 4:20 the Lord, was taken in their p', 7825

pity See also PITIED; PITIETH; PITIFUL.
De 7:16 eye shall have no p' upon them: 2347
13: 8 neither shall thine eye p' him, "
19:13 Thine eye shall not p' him, but thou"
21 thine eye shall not p'; but life shall"
25:12 her hand, thine eye shall not p' her. "
2Sa 12: 6 thing, and because he had no p'. 2550
Job 6:14 is afflicted p' should be shewed *2617
19:21 Have p' upon me, have p' upon me,2603
Ps 69:20 I looked for some to take p', but 5110
Pr 19:17 He that hath p' upon the poor 2603
28: 8 it for him that will p' the poor. "
Isa 13:18 no p' on the fruit of the womb; 7355
63: 9 and in his p' he redeemed them; 2551
Jer 13:14 I will not p', nor spare, nor have 2550
15: 5 For who shall have p' upon thee, O "
21: 7 neither have p', nor have mercy. "
Eze 5:11 spare, neither will I have any p'. "
7: 4 spare thee, neither will I have p': "
9 not spare, neither will I have p': "
8:18 not spare, neither will I have p': "
9: 5 your eye spare, neither have ye p': "
10 not spare, neither will I have p', "
36:21 But I had p' for mine holy name, "
Joe 2:18 for his land, and p' his people. "
Am 1:11 the sword, and did cast off all p', 7356
Jon 4:10 Thou hast had p' on the gourd, 2347
Zec 11: 5 their own shepherds p' them not. 2550
6 no more p' the inhabitants of the "
M't 18:33 fellowservant,...I had p' on thee? **1653*

place See also BURYINGPLACE; COUCHINGPLACE; DWELLINGPLACE; FEEDINGPLACE; MARKETPLACE; PLACED; PLACES; THRESHINGPLACE.
Ge 1: 9 be gathered together unto one p', 4725
12: 6 the land unto the p' of Sichem, "
13: 3 unto the p' where his tent had been "
4 Unto the p' of the altar, which he "
14 look from the p' where thou art "
18:24 spare the p' for the fifty righteous "
26 will spare all the p' for their sakes. "
33 and Abraham returned unto his p'. "
19:12 the city, bring them out of this p': "
13 we will destroy this p', because the "
14 and said, Up, get you out of this p'; "
27 p' where he stood before the Lord: "
20:11 the fear of God is not in this p'; "
13 at every p' whither we shall come, "
21:31 he called that p' Beer-sheba; "
22: 3 the p' of which God had told him. "
4 up his eyes, and saw the p' afar off. "
9 the p' which God had told him of; "
14 the name of that p' Jehovah-jireh: "
26: 7 men of the p' asked him of his wife;"
7 men of the p' should kill me for "
28:11 he lighted upon a certain p', and "
11 he took of the stones of that p', and "
11 and lay down in that p' to sleep. "
16 Surely the Lord is in this p'; and I "
17 and said, How dreadful is this p'! "
19 called the name of that p' Beth-el: "
29: 3 upon the well's mouth in his p'. "
22 together all the men of the p', and "
30:25 that I may go unto mine own p', "
31:55 departed, and returned unto his p'. "
32: 2 the name of that p' Mahanaim. "
30 called the name of the p' Peniel: "
33:17 the name of the p' is called Succoth. "
35: 7 altar, and called the p' El-beth-el: "

Ge 35:13 in the p' where he talked with him.4725
14 in the p' where he talked with him, "
15 the p' where God spake with him, "
38:14 herself, and sat in an open p', *6607
21 Then he asked the men of that p', 4725
21 said, There was no harlot in this p'.*
22 also the men of the p' said, that 4725
22 that there was no harlot in this p'.*
39:20 p' where the king's prisoners were4725
40: 3 the p' where Joseph was bound. "
13 head, and restore thee unto thy p':*3653
48: 9 whom God hath given me in this p'.*
50:19 Fear not: for am I in the p' of God?
Ex 3: 5 p' whereon thou standest is holy 4725
8 unto the p' of the Canaanites, and "
10:23 rose any from his p' for three days: 8478
13: 3 the Lord brought you out from this p':
15:17 the p', O Lord, which thou hast 4349
16:29 abide ye every man in his p', let no 8478
29 let no man go out of his p' on the 4725
17: 7 called the name of the p' Massah, "
18:21 p' such over them, to be rulers of 7760
23 shall also go to their p' in peace. 4725
21:13 thee a p' whither he shall flee. "
23:20 into the p' which I have prepared. "
26:33 between the holy p' and the most holy.
34 of the testimony in the most holy p'.
28:35 he goeth in unto the holy p' before the
43 the altar to minister in the holy p';
29:30 congregation to minister in the holy p'.
31 and seethe his flesh in the holy p'.4725
31:11 oil, and sweet incense for the holy p':
32:34 lead the people unto the p' of which
33:21 there is a p' by me, and thou shalt4725
35:19 to do service in the holy p', the holy
38:24 work in all the work of the holy p',*
39: 1 to do service in the holy p', and made
41 to do service in the holy p', and the
Le 1:16 east part, by the p' of the ashes, 4725
4:12 without the camp unto a clean p', "
24 kill it in the p' where they kill the "
29 in the p' of the burnt offering. "
33 sin offering in the p' where they kill "
6:11 without the camp unto a clean p'. "
16 shall it be eaten in the holy p'; "
25 the p' where the burnt offering is "
26 in the holy p' shall it be eaten, in "
27 it was sprinkled in the holy p'. "
30 to reconcile withal in the holy p', "
7: 2 In the p' where they kill the burnt4725
6 it shall be eaten in the holy p': it "
10:13 shall eat it in the holy p', because "
14 shoulder shall ye eat in a clean p'; "
17 eaten the sin offering in the holy p', "
18 not brought in within the holy p':*
18 indeed have eaten it in the holy p',*
13:19 p' of the boil...be a white rising, 4725
28 And if the bright spot stay in his p',8478
14:13 the p' where he shall kill the sin 4725
13 the burnt offering, in the holy p': "
28 the p' of the blood of the trespass "
40 shall cast them into an unclean p' "
41 without the city into an unclean p':"
42 put them in the p' of those stones:8478
45 out of the city into an unclean p'. 4725
16: 2 times into the holy p' within the vail
3 shall Aaron come into the holy p':
16 make an atonement for the holy p',
17 make an atonement in the holy p',
20 an end of reconciling the holy p',
23 put on when he went into the holy p',
24 his flesh with water in the holy p',4725
27 make atonement in the holy p',
24: 9 they shall eat in the holy p': 4725
Nu 2:17 man in his p' by their standards. 3027
9:17 p' where the cloud abode, there 4725
10:14 In the first p' went the standard of
29 journeying unto the p' of which 4725
33 to search out a resting p' for them.
11: 3 the name of the p' Taberah: 4725
34 of that p' Kibroth-hattaavah: "
13:24 p' was called the brook Eschol, "
14:40 p' which the Lord hath promised: "
18:10 In the most holy p' shalt thou eat it:*
31 ye shall eat it in every p', ye and 4725
19: 9 without the camp in a clean p', "
20: 5 to bring us in unto this evil p'? "
5 it is no p' of seed, or of figs, or of "
21: 3 called the name of the p' Hormah. "
22:26 and stood in a narrow p', where "
23: 3 thee. And he went to an high p'.*
13 thee, with me unto another p', 4725
27 I will bring thee unto another p'; "
24:11 Therefore now flee thou to thy p': "
25 and went and returned to his p': "
28: 7 holy p' shalt thou cause the strong
32: 1 behold, the p' was a p' for cattle; 4725
17 have brought them unto their p': "
33:54 be in the p' where his lot falleth; *
De 1:31 went, until ye come into this p'. 4725
33 you out a p' to pitch your tents "
2:37 unto any p' of the river Jabbok, *3027
9: 7 until ye came into this p', ye 4725
11: 5 until ye came into this p'; "
24 Every p' whereon the soles of your "
12: 3 the names of them out of that p'. "
5 p' which the Lord your God shall "
11 a p' which the Lord your God shall "
13 thy burnt offerings in every p' that "
14 the p' which the Lord shall choose "
18 p' which the Lord thy God shall "
21 the p' which the Lord thy God hath "
26 the p' which the Lord shall choose:"
14:23 before the Lord thy God, in the p' "
23 choose to p' his name there, *7931
24 or if the p' be too far from thee, 4725

De 14:25 unto the p' which the Lord thy God4725
15:20 by year in the p' which the Lord "
16: 2 the p' which the Lord shall choose "
2 shall choose to p' his name there.*7931
6 at the p' which the Lord thy God 4724
6 shall choose to p' his name in, *7931
7 shalt roast and eat it in the p' 4725
11 in the p' which the Lord thy God "
11 hath chosen to p' his name there.*7931
15 p' which the Lord shall choose: 4725
16 in the p' which he shall choose; "
17: 8 arise, and get thee up into the p' "
10 they of that p' which the Lord "
18: 6 the p' which the Lord shall choose;"
21:19 city, and unto the gate of his p'; "
23:12 have a p' also without the camp, "
16 p' which he shall choose in one of "
26: 2 go unto the p' which the Lord "
2 shall choose to p' his name there.*7931
9 hath brought us into this p', and 4725
27:15 and putteth it in a secret p'. *
29: 7 And when ye came unto this p', 4725
31:11 in the p' which he shall choose, "
Jos 1: 3 Every p' that the sole of your foot "
3: 3 then ye shall remove from your p', "
4: 3 of the p' where the priests' feet stood
3 leave them in the lodging p', where ye
8 unto the p' where they lodged, and
9 p' where the feet of the priests which
18 of Jordan returned unto their p', 4725
5: 9 the name of the p' is called Gilgal "
15 p' whereon thou standest is holy. "
7:26 p' was called, The valley of Achor, "
8:19 arose quickly out of their p', and "
9:27 in the p' which he should choose. "
20: 4 give him a p', that he may dwell "
J'g 2: 5 called the name of that p' Bochim: "
6:26 top of this rock, in the ordered p',*4634
7: 7 people go every man unto his p'. 4725
21 stood every man in his p' round 8478
9:55 departed every man unto his p'. 4725
11:19 thee through thy land into my p'. "
15:17 and called that p' Ramath-lehi. "
19 an hollow p' that was in the jaw,
17: 8 to sojourn where he could find a p':
9 I go to sojourn where I may find a p'.
18: 3 and what makest thou in this p'?
10 p' where there is no want of any 4725
12 called that p' Mahaneh-dan unto "
19:16 men of the p' were Benjamites. "
28 rose up, and gat him unto his p'. "
20:22 p' where they put themselves in "
33 of Israel rose up out of their p', "
36 Israel gave p' to the Benjamites,
21:19 in a p' which is on the north side of*
Ru 1: 7 forth out of the p' where she was, 4725
3: 4 mark the p' where he shall lie, "
4:10 and from the gate of his p': ye are "
1Sa 3: 2 Eli was laid down in his p', and his "
9 Samuel went and lay down in his p'."
5: 3 Dagon, and set him in his p' again. "
11 let it go again to his own p', that it "
6: 2 wherewith we shall send it to his p'. "
9:12 of the people to day in the high p':
13 before he go up to the high p' to eat:
14 them, for to go up to the high p'.
19 go up before me unto the high p';
22 sit in the chiefest p' among them 4725
25 down from the high p' into the city,
10: 5 coming down from the high p' with a
12 And one of the same p' answered and
13 prophesying, he came to the high p'.
12: 8 and made them dwell in this p'. 4725
14: 9 we will stand still in our p', and 8478
46 Philistines went to their own p'. 4725
15:12 behold, he set him up a p', and is *3027
19: 2 and abide in a secret p', and hide
20:19 p' where thou didst hide thyself 4725
25 side, and David's p' was empty. "
27 month, that David's p' was empty: "
37 lad was come to the p' of the arrow "
41 arose out of a p' toward the south,
21: 2 my servants to such and such a p'.4725
23:22 and see his p' where his haunt is, "
28 called that p' Sela-hammahlekoth. "
26: 5 to the p' where Saul had pitched: "
5 David beheld the p' where Saul lay,"
25 way, and Saul returned to his p'. "
27: 5 them give me a p' in some town "
29: 4 he may go again to his p' which "
2Sa 2:16 p' was called Helkath-hazzurim, "
23 there, and died in the same p': 8478
23 came to the p' where Asahel fell 4725
5:20 name of that p' Baal-perazim. "
6: 8 the name of the p' Perez-uzzah "
17 ark of the Lord, and set it in his p', "
7:10 I will appoint a p' for my people "
10 they may dwell in a p' of their own,8478
11:16 assigned Uriah unto a p' where 4725
15:17 tarried in a p' that was far off. *1004
19 return to thy p', and abide with *4725
21 what p' my lord the king shall be, "
17: 9 in some pit, or in some other p': "
12 come upon him in some p' where he"
18:18 called unto this day, Absalom's p'.*3027
19:39 and he returned unto his own p'. 4725
22:20 brought me forth also into a large p':
23: 7 burned with fire in the same p'. 7675
1Ki 3: 4 for that was the great high p': a
4:12 unto the p' that is beyond Jokneam:
28 brought they unto the p' where 4725
5: 9 the p' that thou shalt appoint me, "
6:16 the oracle, even for the most holy p'.
7:50 of the inner house, the most holy p',
8: 6 covenant of the Lord unto his p', 4725
6 to the most holy p', even under the

1Ki 8: 7 two wings over the p' of the ark, 4725
8 out in the holy p' before the oracle,
10 priests were come out of the holy p',
13 a settled p' for thee to abide in for
21 I have set there a p' for the ark, 4725
29 the p' of which thou hast said, My "
29 servant shall make toward this p'. "
30 when they shall pray toward this p':"
30 hear thou in heaven thy dwelling p':"
35 if they pray toward this p', and "
39 thou in heaven thy dwelling p', 4349
43 Hear thou in heaven thy dwelling p',"
49 prayer...in heaven thy dwelling p', "
10:19 on either side on the p' of the seat,4725
11: 7 build an high p' for Chemosh, the
13: 8 bread nor drink water in this p': 4725
16 drink water with thee in this p': "
22 bread and drunk water in the p', "
20:24 kings away, every man out of his p',"
21:19 p' where dogs licked the blood of "
22:10 in a void p' in the entrance of the "
2Ki 5:11 and strike his hand over the p', and"
6: 1 p' where we dwell with thee is too "
2 let us make us a p' there, where we "
6 fell it? And he shewed him the p'. "
8 and such a p' shall be my camp. "
9 Beware that thou pass not such a p';"
10 king of Israel sent to the p' which "
18:25 Lord against this p' to destroy it? "
22:16 Behold, I will bring evil upon this p',"
17 shall be kindled against this p', and"
19 what I spake against this p', and "
20 evil which I will bring upon this p'. "
23:15 the high p' which Jeroboam the son of
15 altar and the high p' he brake down,
15 burned the high p', and stamped it
1Ch 6:32 the dwelling p' of the tabernacle of*
49 for all the work of the p' most holy,
13:11 p' is called Perez-uzza to this day. 4725
14:11 the name of that p' Baal-perazim. "
15: 1 and prepared a p' for the ark of God,"
3 up the ark of the Lord unto his p', "
12 unto the p' that I have prepared for it.
16:27 and gladness are in his p'. 4725
39 Lord in the high p' that was at Gibeon,
17: 9 ordain a p' for my people Israel, 4725
9 and they shall dwell in their p', and8478
21:22 me the p' of this threshingfloor, 4725
25 to Ornan for the p' six hundred "
29 that season in the high p' at Gibeon.
23:32 and the charge of the holy p', and the
28:11 and of the p' of the mercy seat, 1004
2Ch 1: 3 to the high p' that was at Gibeon;
4 p' which David had prepared for it:
13 to the high p' that was at Gibeon
3: 1 p' that David had prepared in the 4725
4:22 doors thereof for the most holy p',
5: 7 covenant of the Lord unto his p', 4725
7 into the most holy p', even under the
8 their wings over the p' of the ark, 4725
11 priests were come out of the holy p':
6: 2 and a p' for thy dwelling for ever. 4349
20 the p' whereof thou hast said that 4725
20 thy servant prayeth toward this p'. "
21 they shall make toward this p': "
21 hear thou from thy dwelling p', even"
26 yet if they pray toward this p', and "
30 thou from heaven thy dwelling p', 4349
33, 39 even from thy dwelling p', and "
40 the prayer that is made in this p'. 4725
41 arise, O Lord God, into thy resting p',
7:12 have chosen this p' to myself for 4725
15 the prayer that is made in this p'. "
9:18 stays on each side of the sitting p', "
18: 9 they sat in a void p' at the entering in
20:26 name of the same p' was called, 4725
24:11 it, and carried it to his p' again. "
29: 5 forth the filthiness out of the holy p'.
7 in the holy p' unto the God of Israel.
30:16 they stood in their p' after their 5977
27 came up to his holy dwelling p', *
34:24 I will bring evil upon this p', and 4725
25 shall be poured out upon this p', "
27 heardest his words against this p', "
28 evil that I will bring upon this p', "
31 the king stood in his p', and made 5977
35: 5 stand in the holy p' according to the
10 the priests stood in their p', and 5977
15 the sons of Asaph were in their p',4612
36:15 on his people, and on his dwelling p':
Ezr 1: 4 whosoever remaineth in any p' 4725
4 men of his p' help him with silver, "
2:68 house of God to set it up in his p': 4349
5:15 house of God be builded in his p'. 870
6: 3 the p' where they offered sacrifices, "
5 at Jerusalem, every one to his p', "
5 and p' them in the house of God' *5182
7 build this house of God in his p'. 870
8:17 Iddo the chief at the p' Casiphia, 4725
17 the Nethinims, at the p' Casiphia, "
9: 8 and to give us a nail in his holy p', "
Ne 1: 9 unto the p' that I have chosen to "
2: 3 the p' of my fathers' sepulchres, 1004
14 there was no p' for the beast that 4725
3:16 p' over against the sepulchres of David,
26 p' over against the water gate toward
31 son unto the p' of the Nethinims, *1004
4:20 In what p'...ye hear the sound of 4725
8: 7 and the people stood in their p'. 5977
9: 3 they stood up in their p', and read "
13:11 together, and set them in their p'. "
Es 2: 9 best p' of the house of the women.
4:14 arise to the Jews from another p';4725
7: 8 into the p' of the banquet of wine;1004
Job 2:11 came every one from his own p'; 4725
6:17 they are consumed out of their p'. "

Job 7:10 shall his p' know him any more. 4725
8:17 heap, and seeth the p' of stones. 1004
18 If he destroy him from his p', then4725
22 the dwelling p' of the wicked shall*
9: 6 shaketh the earth out of her p', 4725
14:18 and the rock is removed out of his p'. "
16:18 blood, and let my cry have no p'. "
18: 4 the rock be removed out of his p'? "
21 the p' of him that knoweth not God. "
20: 9 shall his p' any more behold him. "
26: 7 out the north over the empty p', *8414
27:21 a storm hurleth him out of his p'. 4725
23 and shall hiss him out of his p'. "
28: 1 and a p' for gold where they fine it. "
6 stones of it are the p' of sapphires: "
12, 20 is the p' of understanding? "
23 and he knoweth the p' thereof. "
36:16 thee out of the strait into a broad p',
20 when people are cut off in their p'.8478
37: 1 my heart...is moved out of his p'. 4725
38:10 And brake up for it my decreed p',*
12 the dayspring to know his p'; 4725
19 darkness, where is the p' thereof, "
39:28 the crag of the rock, and the strong p'.*
40:12 tread down the wicked in their p'.*8478
Ps 18:11 He made darkness his secret p'; his
19 me forth also into a large p'; 4800
24: 3 or who shall stand in his holy p'? 4725
26: 8 p' where thine honour dwelleth. "
12 My foot standeth in an even p'; in
32: 7 Thou art my hiding p'; thou shalt
33:14 the p' of his habitation he looketh 4349
37:10 shalt diligently consider his p', 4725
44:19 broken us in the p' of dragons, "
46: 4 holy p' of the tabernacles of the most
52: 5 pluck thee out of thy dwelling p', *
66:12 broughtest us out into a wealthy p'.
68:17 them, as in Sinai, in the holy p'. *
74: 7 the dwelling p' of thy name to the
76: 2 and his dwelling p' in Zion.
79: 7 and laid waste his dwelling p'. *
81: 7 thee in the secret p' of thunder:
90: 1 Lord, thou hast been our dwelling p'
91: 1 He that dwelleth in the secret p' of
103:16 p' thereof shall know it no more. 4725
104: 8 the p' which thou hast founded for "
118: 5 me, and set me in a large p'.
119:114 Thou art my hiding p' and my
132: 5 until I find out a p' for the Lord, 4725
Pr 1:21 She crieth in the chief p' of concourse,
14:26 his children shall have a p' of refuge.
15: 3 eyes of the Lord are in every p', 4725
24:15 righteous; spoil not his resting p':
25: 6 stand not in the p' of great men: 4725
27: 8 man that wandereth from his p'. "
Ec 1: 5 hasteth to his p' where he arose.
7 p' from whence the rivers come,
3:16 under the sun the p' of judgment,
16 p' of righteousness, that iniquity
20 All go unto one p'; all are of the
6: 6 no good: do not all go to one p'?
8:10 and gone from the p' of the holy,
10: 4 up against thee, leave not thy p';
6 dignity, and the rich sit in low p'.
11: 3 in the p' where the tree falleth, 4725
Isa 4: 5 every dwelling p' of mount Zion, *
6 and for a p' of refuge, and for a *
5: 8 field to field, till there be no p', *4725
7:23 that every p' shall be, where there "
13:13 earth shall remove out of her p', "
14: 2 them, and bring them to their p': "
16:12 that Moab is weary on the high p',
18: 4 I will consider in my dwelling p'
7 the p' of the name of the Lord of 4725
22:23 fasten him as a nail in a sure p'; "
25 nail that is fastened in the sure p' "
25: 5 strangers, as the heat in a dry p';
26:21 cometh out of his p' to punish the 4725
28: 8 so that there is no p' clean.
17 waters shall overflow the hiding p'.
25 barley and the rie in their p'? 1367
30:32 p' where the grounded staff shall *
32: 2 a man shall be as an hiding p' from
2 as rivers of water in a dry p', as the
19 and the city shall be low in a low p'.*
33:16 his p' of defence shall be the
21 will be unto us a p' of broad rivers4725
34:14 there, and find for herself a p' of rest.
35: 1 solitary p' shall be glad for them;
45:19 secret, in a dark p' of the earth: 4725
46: 7 carry him, and set him in his p', 8478
7 from his p' shall he not remove: 4725
13 and I will p' salvation in Zion for 5414
49:20 ears, The p' is too straight for me:4725
20 give p' to me that I may dwell. "
54: 2 Enlarge the p' of thy tent, and let "
56: 5 p' and a name better than of sons*3027
57:15 I dwell in the high and holy p', with
60:13 beautify the p' of my sanctuary; 4725
13 make the p' of my feet glorious. "
65:10 valley of Achor a p' for the herds to
66: 1 and where is the p' of my rest? 4725
Jer 4: 7 he is gone forth from his p' to "
26 lo, the fruitful p' was a wilderness,*
6: 3 they shall feed every one in his p'. 3027
7: 3 will cause you to dwell in this p'. 4725
6 shed not innocent blood in this p', "
7 will I cause you to dwell in this p', "
12 unto my p' which was in Shiloh, "
14 unto the p' which I gave to you "
20 shall be poured out upon this p', "
32 bury in Tophet, till there be no p'. "
9: 2 lodging p' of wayfaring men; that I
13: 7 took the girdle from the p' where 4725
14:13 give you assured peace in this p'. "
16: 2 have sons or daughters in this p'. "

Jer 16: 3 daughters that are born in this p', 4725
9 will cause to cease out of this p' "
17:12 is the p' of our sanctuary. "
18:14 waters that come from another p' be*
19: 3 I will bring evil upon this p', the 4725
4 me, and have estranged this p', "
4 this p' with the blood of innocents; "
6 p' shall no more be called Tophet, "
7 of Judah and Jerusalem in this p'; "
11 Tophet, till there be no p' to bury. "
12 Thus will I do unto this p', saith "
13 shall be defiled as the p' of Tophet, "
22: 3 shed innocent blood in this p'. "
11 which went forth out of this p'; "
12 he shall die in the p' whither they "
24: 5 whom I have sent out of this p' into "
27:22 up, and restore them to this p'. "
28: 3 will I bring again into this p' all "
3 of Babylon took away from this p', "
4 will bring again to this p' Jeconiah "
6 captive, from Babylon into this p'. "
29:10 in causing you to return to this p'. "
14 bring you again into the p' whence "
32:37 will bring them again unto this p', "
33:10 there shall be heard in this p', "
12 Again in this p', which is desolate "
38: 9 like to die for hunger in the p' 8478
40: 2 pronounced this evil upon this p'. 4725
42:18 and ye shall see this p' no more. "
22 in the p' whither ye desire to go "
44:29 I will punish you in this p', that ye "
51:62 thou hast spoken against this p', "
Eze 3:12 the glory of the Lord from his p'. "
6:13 the p' where they did offer sweet "
7:22 they shall pollute my secret p':
10:11 p' whither the head looked they 4725
12: 3 from thy p' to another p' in their "
16:24 also built unto thee an eminent p',
24 made thee an high p' in every street.
25 thy high p' at every head of the way,
31 eminent p' in the head of every way,
31 makest thine high p' in every street;
39 shall throw down thine eminent p',
17:16 the p' where the king dwelleth 4725
20:29 is the high p' whereunto ye go?
21:19 choose thou a p', choose it at the 3027
30 I will judge thee in the p' where 4725
26: 5 shall be a p' for the spreading of nets
14 shalt be a p' to spread nets upon;
37:14 I shall p' you in your own land: 3241
26 I will p' them, and multiply them, 5414
38:15 come from thy p' out of the north 4725
39:11 give unto Gog a p' there of graves "
41: 4 unto me, This is the most holy p'.
9 was the p' of the side chambers 1004
11 were toward the p' that was left,
11 the breadth of the p' that was left 4725
12 the separate p' at the end toward the
13 and the separate p', and the building,
14 and of the separate p' toward the east,
15 the separate p' which was behind it,
42: 1 that was over against the separate p',
10 over against the separate p', and over
13 which are before the separate p', they
13 trespass offering; for the p' is holy.4725
14 shall they not go out of the holy p'
20 the sanctuary and the profane p'.*
43: 7 Son of man, the p' of my throne, 4725
7 the p' of the soles of my feet, where "
13 this shall be the higher p' of the altar.*
21 he shall burn it in the appointed p' of
44:13 my holy things, in the most holy p':*
45: 3 the sanctuary and the most holy p'.*
4 it shall be a p' for their houses, 4725
4 and an holy p' for the sanctuary.
46:19 there was a p' on the two sides 4725
20 the p' where the priests shall boil "
47:10 they shall be a p' to spread forth nets;
48:15 shall be a profane p' for the city, for*
Da 2:35 no p' was found for them: and the 870
8:11 p' of his sanctuary was cast down.4349
11:31 they shall p' the abomination that*5414
Ho 1:10 p' where it was said unto them, 4725
4:16 will feed them as a lamb in a large p'.
5:15 I will go and return to my p', till 4725
9:13 Tyrus, is planted in a pleasant p':
11:11 and I will p' them in their houses,*3427
13:13 p' of the breaking forth of children.
Joe 3: 7 I will raise them out of the p' 4725
Am 8: 3 be many dead bodies in every p'; "
Mic 1: 3 the Lord cometh forth out of his p'. "
4 that are poured down a steep p'.
Na 1: 8 an utter end of the p' thereof, 4725
3:17 p' is not known where they are. "
Zep 1: 4 the remnant of Baal from this p', "
2:11 worship him every one from his p', "
15 a p' for beasts to lie down in! every
Hag 2: 9 and in this p' will I give peace, 4725
Zec 6:12 and he shall grow up out of his p', 8478
10: 6 I will bring them again to p' them;*3427
10 and p' shall not be found for them.
12: 6 be inhabited again in her own p', 8478
14:10 be lifted up, and inhabited in her p',
10 gate unto the p' of the first gate, 4725
Mal 1:11 in every p' incense shall be offered "
M't 8:32 violently down a steep p' into the sea,*
9:24 He said unto them, Give p': for the 402
12: 6 in this p' is one...than the temple. *5602
14:13 by ship into a desert p' apart: 5117
15 This is a desert p', and the time is "
35 the men of that p' had knowledge "
17:20 Remove hence to yonder p'; and it
24:15 the prophet, stand in the holy p', 5117
26:36 them unto a p' called Gethsemane,5564
52 Put up again thy sword into his p':5117
27:33 come unto a p' called Golgotha, "

M't 27:33 that is to say, a p' of a skull, 5117
28: 6 Come see the p' where the Lord lay. "
M'r 1:35 departed into a solitary p', and "
5:13 violently down a steep p' into the sea,*
6:10 p' soever ye enter into an house, *3699
10 abide till ye depart from that p'. *1564
31 yourselves apart into a desert p', 5117
32 they departed into a desert p' by "
35 This is a desert p', and now the "
11: 4 without in a p' where two ways met;*
12: 1 and digged a p' for the winefat, and*
14:32 to a p' which...named Gethsemane:5564
15:22 bring him unto the p' Golgotha, 5117
22 being interpreted, The p' of a skull. "
16: 6 behold the p' where they laid him. "
Lu 4:17 found the p' where it was written, "
37 went out into every p' of the country "
42 departed and went into a desert p': "
8:33 violently down a steep p' into the *
9:10 aside privately into a desert p' *5117
12 for we are here in a desert p'. "
10: 1 his face into every city and p', "
32 a Levite, when he was at the p', "
11: 1 as he was praying in a certain p', "
33 a candle, putteth it in a secret p', *
14: 9 and say to thee, Give this man p'; 5117
16:28 also come into this p' of torment. "
19: 5 And when Jesus came to the p', he "
22:40 when he was at the p', he said unto "
23: 5 beginning from Galilee to this p' 5602
33 And when they were come to the p',5117
Joh 4:20 in Jerusalem is the p' where men "
5:13 away, a multitude being in that p'. "
6:10 there was much grass in the p'. "
23 unto the p' where they did eat "
8:37 my word hath no p' in you. *5562
10:40 p' where John at first baptized; 5117
11: 6 still in the same p' where he was. "
30 in that p' where Martha met him. "
41 from the p' where the dead was laid.*
48 take away both our p' and nation. 5117
14: 2 you. I go to prepare a p' for you. "
3 if I go and prepare a p' for you, "
18: 2 which betrayed him, knew the p': "
19:13 in a p' that is called the Pavement, "
17 his cross went forth into a p' "
17 called the p' of a skull, which is 5117
20 the p' where Jesus was crucified "
41 the p' where he was crucified there "
20: 7 wrapped together in a p' by itself. "
Ac 1:25 fell, that he might go to his own p'. "
2: 1 were all with one accord in one p'. "
4:31 the p' was shaken where they 5117
6:13 words against this holy p', and the "
14 of Nazareth shall destroy this p', "
7: 7 come forth, and serve me in this p'. "
33 the p' where thou standest is holy "
49 Lord: or what is the p' of my rest? "
8:32 p' of the scripture which he read 4042
12:17 departed, and went into another p'.5117
21:12 and they of that p', besought him 1786
28 people, and the law, and this p': 5117
28 and hath polluted this holy p'. "
25:23 was entered into the p' of hearing, 201
27: 8 a p' which is called The fair havens;5117
41 into a p' where two seas met, "
Ro 9:26 p' where it was said unto them, "
12:19 but rather give p' unto wrath: "
15:23 having no more p' in these parts, "
1Co 1: 2 that in every p' call upon the name "
11:20 come together therefore into one p',*
14:23 church be come together into one p',*
2Co 2:14 his knowledge by us in every p'. 5117
Ga 2: 5 whom we gave p' by subjection, 1502
Eph 4:27 Neither give p' to the devil. 5117
1Th 1: 8 in every p' your faith to God-ward "
Heb 2: 6 But one in a certain p' testified, *
4: 4 spake in a certain p' of the seventh*
5 And in this p' again, If they shall
5: 6 As he saith also in another p', Thou
8: 7 no p' have been sought for the 5117
9:12 he entered in once into the holy p',
25 high priest entereth into the holy p'
11: 8 he was called to go out into a p' 5117
12:17 for he found no p' of repentance, "
Jas 2: 3 Sit thou here in a good p'; and
3:11 at the same p' sweet water and *3692
2Pe 1:19 a light that shineth in a dark p', 5117
Re 2: 5 thy candlestick out of this p', "
12: 6 she hath a p' prepared of God, "
8 was their p' found any more "
14 into her p', where she is nourished "
16:16 a p' called in the Hebrew tongue "
20:11 and there was found no p' for them. "

placed
Ge 3:24 he p' at the east of the garden of 7931
47:11 And Joseph p' his father and his 3427
1Ki 12:32 and he p' in Beth-el the priests of 5975
2Ki 17: 6 p' them in Halah and in Habor by 3427
24 p' them in the cities of Samaria "
26 p' in the cities of Samaria, know "
2Ch 1:14 which he p' in the chariot cities, 3240
4: 8 p' them in the temple, five on the "
17: 2 he p' forces in all the fenced cities 5414
Job 20: 4 old, since man was p' upon earth, 7760
Ps 78:60 the tent which he p' among men; 7931
Isa 5: 8 they may be p' alone in the midst *3427
Jer 5:22 have p' the sand for the bound of 776
Eze 17: 5 he p' it by great waters, and set 3947

places See also MARKETPLACES.
Ge 28:15 keep thee in all p' whither thou goest,*
36:40 to their families after their p', 4725
Ex 20:24 p' where I record my name I will * "
25:27 be for p' of the staves to bear the 1004
26:29 rings of gold for p' for the bars: "

Ex 30: 4 they shall be for p' for the staves 1004
36: 34 rings of gold to be p' for the bars, "
37: 14 p' for the staves to bear the table. "
27 p' for the staves to bear it withal. "
38: 5 of brass, to be p' for the staves. "
Le 26: 30 I will destroy your high p', and cut
Nu 21: 28 the lords of the high p' of Arnon.
22: 41 him up into the high p' of Baal,
33: 52 and quite pluck down all their high p':
De 1: 7 and unto all the p' nigh thereunto,
12: 2 Ye shall utterly destroy all the p', 4725
32: 13 ride on the high p' of the earth,
33: 29 thou shalt tread upon their high p'.
Jos 5: 8 they abode in their p' in the camps*8478
J'g 5: 11 of archers in the p' of drawing water,
18 the death in the high p' of the field
19: 13 one of these p' to lodge all night, 4725
20: 33 Israel came forth out of their p', * "
1Sa 7: 16 and judged Israel in all those p'. "
13: 6 in rocks, and in high p', and in pits.*
23: 23 of all the lurking p' where he hideth
30: 31 to all the p' where David himself 4725
2Sa 1: 19 of Israel is slain upon thy high p':
25 thou wast slain in thine high p'.
7: 7 In all the p' wherein I have walked
22: 34 feet: and setteth me upon my high p'.
46 shall be afraid out of their close p'.
1Ki 3: 2 Only the people sacrificed in high p',
3 only he...burnt incense in high p'.
12: 31 And he made an house of high p', and
32 priests of the high p' which he...made.
13: 2 he offer the priests of the high p'
32 against all the houses of the high p'
33 lowest...people, priests of the high p':
33 one of the priests of the high p'.
14: 23 For they also built them high p', and
15: 14 But the high p' were not removed:
22: 43 the high p' were not taken away;
43 and burnt incense yet in the high p'.
2Ki 12: 3 But the high p' were not taken away:
3 and burnt incense in the high p'.
14: 4 the high p' were not taken away:
4 and burnt incense on the high p'.
15: 4 that the high p' were not removed:
4 and burnt incense still on the high p'.
35 the high p' were not removed:
35 burned incense still in the high p'.
16: 4 burnt incense in the high p', and on
17: 9 built them high p' in all their cities,
11 they burnt incense in all the high p',
29 put them in the houses of the high p'
32 lowest of them priests of the high p'
32 for them in the houses of the high p'.
18: 4 He removed the high p', and brake the
22 whose high p' and...altars Hezekiah
19: 24 I dried up all the rivers of besieged p'.*
21: 3 For he built up again the high p'
23: 5 in the high p' in the cities of Judah,
5 and in the p' round about Jerusalem;
8 defiled the high p' where the priests
8 brake down the high p' of the gates
9 the priests of the high p' came not up
13 high p' that were before Jerusalem,
14 filled their p' with...bones of men. 4725
19 all the houses of the high p' that were
20 he slew all the priests of the high p'
1Ch 6: 54 dwelling p' throughout their castles
2Ch 8: 11 the p' are holy, whereunto the ark of
11: 15 ordained him priests for the high p',
14: 3 of the strange gods, and the high p',
5 away...the high p' and the images:
15: 17 But the high p' were not taken away
17: 6 he took away the high p' and groves
20: 33 the high p' were not taken away:
21: 11 he made high p' in the mountains
28: 4 burnt incense in the high p', and on
25 he made high p' to burn incense
31: 1 threw down the high p' and the altars
32: 12 taken away his high p' and his altars,
33: 3 For he built again the high p' which
17 people did sacrifice still in the high p',
19 and the p' wherein he built high 4725
19 wherein he built high p', and set up
34: 3 purge...Jerusalem from the high p',
Ne 4: 12 From all p' whence ye shall return4725
13 set I in the lower p' behind the wall,*"
13 and on the higher p', I even set
12: 27 sought the Levites out of all...p', 4725
Job 3: 14 built desolate p' for themselves; 2723
20: 26 darkness shall be hid in his secret p':*
21: 28 are the dwelling p' of the wicked ?* 168
25: 2 him, he maketh peace in his high p'.
37: 8 into dens, and remain in their p'. *4585
Ps 10: 8 in the lurking p' of the villages:
8 in the secret p' doth he murder the
16: 6 lines are fallen unto me in pleasant p';
17: 12 were a young lion lurking in secret p'.
18: 33 feet, and setteth me upon my high p'.
45 and be afraid out of their close p'.
49: 11 their dwelling p' to all generations;
68: 35 thou art terrible out of thy holy p':
73: 18 thou didst set them in slippery p':
74: 20 the dark p' of the earth are full of the
78: 58 provoked him...with their high p',
95: 4 his hand are the deep p' of the earth:
103: 22 works in all p' of his dominion: 4725
105: 41 they ran in the dry p' like a river.
109: 10 bread also out of their desolate p'.
110: 6 shall fill the p' with the dead bodies;
135: 6 in earth, in the seas, and all deep p'.*
141: 6 judges are overthrown in stony p'.*3027
Pr 8: 2 She standeth in the top of high p',
2 by the way in the p' of the paths. *1004
9: 3 crieth upon the highest p' of the city,
14 on a seat in the high p' of the city,
Ca 2: 14 the rock, in the secret p' of the stairs,*

Isa 5: 17 and the waste p' of the fat ones shall
15: 2 to Bajith, and to Dibon, the high p',
32: 18 sure dwellings, and in quiet resting p';
36: 7 whose high p' and...altars Hezekiah
37: 25 up all the rivers of the besieged p'.*
40: 4 made straight, and the rough p' plain:
41: 18 I will open rivers in high p', and *
44: 26 I will raise up the decayed p' thereof:
45: 2 and make the crooked p' straight:
3 and hidden riches of secret p',
49: 9 their pastures shall be in all high p'.*
19 For thy waste and thy desolate p',
51: 3 he will comfort all her waste p'; and
52: 9 together, ye waste p' of Jerusalem:
58: 12 be of thee shall build the old waste p':
14 to ride upon the high p' of the earth,
59: 10 we are in desolate p' as dead men.*
Jer 3: 2 Lift up thine eyes unto the high p',*
21 A voice was heard upon the high p',*
4: 11 wind of the high p' in the wilderness*
12 a full wind from those p' shall come*
5: 1 and seek in the broad p' thereof, if
7: 29 and take up a lamentation on high p';*
31 they have built the high p' of Tophet,
8: 3 in all the p' whither I have driven 4725
12: 12 The spoilers are come upon all high p'*
13: 17 my soul shall weep in secret p' for*
14: 6 wild asses did stand in the high p',*
17: 3 to the spoil, and thy high p' for sin,
6 but shall inhabit the parched p' in the
26 and from the p' about Jerusalem, 5439
19: 5 have built also the high p' of Baal,
23: 10 the pleasant p' of the wilderness are*
24 Can any hide himself in secret p' that
24: 9 all p' whither I shall drive them. 4725
26: 18 of the house as the high p' of a forest.
29: 14 all the p' whither I have driven 4725
32: 35 And they built the high p' of Baal,
44 and in the p' about Jerusalem, and in
33: 13 and in the p' about Jerusalem, and in
40: 12 all p' whither they were driven, 4725
45: 5 for a prey in all p' whither thou "
48: 35 him that offereth in the high p', and*
49: 10 bare, I have uncovered his secret p',
La 2: 6 hath destroyed his p' of the assembly:*
3: 6 He hath set me in dark p', as they that
10 in wait, and as a lion in secret p'.
Eze 6: 3 you, and I will destroy your high p'.
6 and the high p' shall be desolate;
7: 24 and their holy p' shall be defiled.
16: 16 and deckedst thy high p' with divers
39 and shall break down thy high p':
21: 2 and drop thy word toward the holy p',*
26: 20 parts of the earth, in p' desolate of old,
34: 12 deliver them out of all p' where 4725
13 in all the inhabited p' of the country.
26 the p' round about my hill a blessing;
36: 2 even the ancient high p' are ours in
36 that I the Lord build the ruined p',
38: 12 desolate p' that are now inhabited,
20 and the steep p' shall fall, and every
43: 7 of their kings in their high p'.
46: 23 was made with boiling p' under the
24 These are the p' of them that boil,*1004
47: 11 But the miry p' thereof and the
Da 11: 24 upon the fattest p' of the province;
Ho 9: 6 the pleasant p' for their silver, nettles*
10: 8 The high p' also of Aven, the sin of
Am 4: 6 and want of bread in all your p': 4725
13 upon the high p' of the earth,
7: 9 the high p' of Isaac shall be desolate,
Mic 1: 3 tread upon the high p' of the earth.
5 and what are the high p' of Judah?
3: 12 the house as the high p' of the forest.
Hab 3: 19 make me to walk upon mine high p'.
Zec 3: 7 I will give thee p' to walk among *
Mal 1: 4 will return and build the desolate p';
M't 12: 43 he walketh through dry p', seeking5117
13: 5 Some fell upon stony p', where they
20 that received the seed into stony p',
24: 7 and earthquakes, in divers p'. 5117
M'r 1: 45 city, but was without in desert p': "
13: 8 shall be earthquakes in divers p', "
Lu 11: 24 he walketh through dry p', seeking "
21: 11 earthquakes shall be in divers p', "
Ac 24: 3 We accept it always, and in all p', 3837
Eph 1: 3 blessings in heavenly p' in Christ:
20 his own right hand in the heavenly p',
2: 6 in heavenly p' in Christ Jesus:
3: 10 in heavenly p' might be known by
6: 12 spiritual wickedness in high p'.
Ph'p 1: 13 all the palace, and in all other p';*
Heb 9: 24 into the holy p' made with hands,*
Re 6: 14 island were moved out of their p'. 5117

plague See also PLAGUED; PLAGUES.
Ex 11: 1 bring one p' more upon Pharaoh, 5061
12: 13 p' shall not be upon you to destroy5063
30: 12 that there be no p' among them,
Le 13: 2 of his flesh like the p' of leprosy; 5061
3 shall look on the p' in the skin of
3 the hair in the p' is turned white, "
3 p' in sight be deeper than the skin "
3 skin of his flesh, it is a p' of leprosy:"
4 up him that hath the p' seven days:"
5 if the p' in his sight be at a stay, "
5 and the p' spread not in the skin; "
6 behold, if the p' be somewhat dark, "
6 p' spread not in the skin, the priest "
9 When the p' of leprosy is in a man, "
12 hath the p' from his head even to "
13 pronounce him clean that hath...p': "
17 if the p' be turned into white; then "
17 pronounce him clean that hath...p':"
20 p' of leprosy broken out of the boil."
22 pronounce him unclean: it is a p'. "

Le 13: 25, 27 unclean: it is the p' of leprosy. 5061
29 or woman have a p' upon the head "
30 Then the priest shall see the p': and, "
31 the priest look on the p' of the scall,"
31 up him that hath the p' of the scall "
32 day the priest shall look on the p': "
44 unclean; his p' is in his head. "
45 And the leper in whom the p' is, his "
46 days wherein the p' shall be in him "
47 garment...that the p' of leprosy is in,"
49 if the p' be greenish or reddish in "
49 it is a p' of leprosy, and shall be "
50 the priest shall look upon the p', "
50 up it that hath the p' seven days: "
51 look on the p' on the seventh day: "
51 if the p' be spread in the garment, "
51 the p' is a fretting leprosy; it is "
52 thing of skin, wherein the p' is: "
53 the p' be not spread in the garment,"
54 wash the thing wherein the p' is, "
55 the priest shall look on the p', after "
55 the p' have not changed his colour, "
55 colour, and the p' be not spread; "
56 the p' be somewhat dark after the "
57 it is a spreading p': thou shalt burn*
57 shalt burn that wherein the p' is 5061
58 if the p' be departed from them, "
59 This is the law of the p' of leprosy "
14: 3 if the p' of leprosy be healed in the "
32 him in whom is the p' of leprosy, "
34 I put the p' of leprosy in a house of "
35 there is as it were a p' in the house:"
36 the priest go into it to see the p', "
37 he shall look on the p', and, behold, "
37 if the p' be in the walls of the house"
39 p' be spread in the walls of the "
40 away the stones in which the p' is, "
43 if the p' come again, and break out "
44 if the p' be spread in the house, it "
48 the p' hath not spread in the house,"
48 clean, because the p' is healed. "
54 law for all manner of p' of leprosy. "
Nu 8: 19 there be no p' among the children 5063
11: 33 the people with a very great p'. 4347
14: 37 died by the p' before the Lord. 4046
16: 46 from the Lord; the p' is begun. 5063
47 the p' was begun among the people: "
48 the living; and the p' was stayed. 4046
49 Now they that died in the p' were "
50 congregation: and the p' was stayed."
25: 8 p' was stayed from the children of "
9 and those that died in the p' were "
18 slain in the day of the p' for Peor's "
26: 1 it came to pass after the p', that the"
31: 16 was a p' among the congregation "
De 24: 8 Take heed in the p' of leprosy, that5061
28: 61 Also every sickness, and every p', 4347
Jos 22: 17 was a p' in the congregation of the5063
1Sa 6: 4 for one p' was on you all, and on 4046
2Sa 24: 21 p' may be stayed from the people. "
25 and the p' was stayed from Israel. "
1Ki 8: 37 of their cities; whatsoever p', 5061
38 every man the p' of his own heart, "
1Ch 21: 22 p' may be stayed from the people. 4046
2Ch 21: 14 p' will the Lord smite thy people, "
Ps 89: 23 face, and p' them that hate him. *5063
91: 10 neither shall any p' come nigh thy 5061
106: 29 and the p' brake in upon them. 4046
30 judgment: and so the p' was stayed."
Zec 14: 12 this shall be the p' wherewith the "
15 be the p' of the horse, of the mule, "
15 shall be in these tents, as this p'. "
18 there shall be the p', wherewith the "
M'r 5: 29 that she was healed of that p'. 3148
34 go in peace, and be whole of thy p'. "
Re 16: 21 God because of the p' of the hail; 4127
21 the p' thereof was exceeding great. "

plagued
Ge 12: 17 Lord p' Pharaoh and his house 5060
Ex 32: 35 the Lord p' the people, because *5062
Jos 24: 5 I p' Egypt, according to that which "
1Ch 21: 17 thy people, that they should be p'.4046
Ps 73: 5 neither are they p' like other men.5060
14 all the day long have I been p', "

plagues
Ge 12: 17 plagued Pharaoh...with great p' 5061
Ex 9: 14 at this time send all my p' upon 4046
Le 26: 21 seven times more p' upon you 4347
De 28: 59 Lord will make thy p' wonderful, "
59 and the p' of thy seed, even great p',"
29: 22 when they see the p' of that land, "
1Sa 4: 8 smote the Egyptians with all the p' "
Jer 19: 8 hiss because of all the p' thereof. "
49: 17 and shall hiss at all the p' thereof. "
50: 13 be astonished, and hiss at all her p'."
Ho 13: 14 O death, I will be thy p'; O grave, 1698
M'r 3: 10 to touch him, as many as had p'. 3148
Lu 7: 21 many of their infirmities and p', "
Re 9: 20 which were not killed by these p' 4127
11: 6 and to smite the earth with all p'.* "
15: 1 angels having the seven last p'; "
6 of the temple, having the seven p', "
8 seven p' of the seven angels were "
16: 9 which hath power over these p': "
18: 4 and that ye receive not of her p'. "
8 shall her p' come in one day, death,"
21: 9 seven vials full of the seven last p', "
22: 18 God shall add unto him the p' that "

plain See also PLAINS.
Ge 11: 2 found a p' in the land of Shinar; 1237
12: 6 of Sichem, unto the p' of Moreh. * 436
13: 10 and beheld all the p' of Jordan, 3603
11 Lot chose him all the p' of Jordan; "
12 Lot dwelled in the cities of the p', "

Ge 13:18 came and dwelt in the p' of Mamre,*436
14:13 for he dwelt in the p' of Mamre the* "
19:17 neither stay thou in all the p'; 3603
25 those cities, and all the p', and all "
28 and toward all the land of the p', "
29 God destroyed the cities of the p', "
25:27 Jacob was a p' man, dwelling in 8535
De 1: 1 in the p' over against the Red sea,*6160
7 places nigh thereunto, in the p', * "
2: 8 the way of the p' from Elath, and* "
3:10 the cities of the p', and all Gilead, 4334
17 p' also, and Jordan, and the coast*6160
17 even unto the sea of the p', even the*"
4:43 the wilderness, in the p' country, 4334
49 p' on this side Jordan eastward, *6160
49 even unto the sea of the p', under* "
34: 3 p' of the valley of Jericho, the city 3603
Jos 3:16 down toward the sea of the p', *6160
8:14 at a time appointed, before the p';* "
11:16 Goshen, and the valley, and the p',* "
12: 1 Hermon, and all the p' on the east:* "
3 the p' to the sea of Chinneroth on* "
3 and unto the sea of the p', even the*"
13: 9 all the p' of Medeba unto Dibon; 4334
16 the river, and all the p' by Medeba; "
17 and all her cities that are in the p'; "
21 all the cities of the p', and all the "
20: 8 Bezer in the wilderness upon the p' "
J'g 4:11 his tent unto the p' of Zaanaim, * 436
9: 6 by the p' of the pillar that was in * "
37 come along by the p' of Meonenim.* "
11:33 and unto the p' of the vineyards, * 58
1Sa 10: 3 thou shalt come to the p' of Tabor,*436
23:24 the p' on the south of Jeshimon. *6160
2Sa 2:29 all that night through the p', * "
4: 7 them away through the p' all night.*"
15:28 tarry in the p' of the wilderness, * "
18:23 Ahimaaz ran by the way of the p', 3603
1Ki 7:46 In the p' of Jordan did the king "
20:23 let us fight against them in the p', 4334
25 we will fight against them in the p'."
2Ki 14:25 of Hamath unto the sea of the p', *6160
25: 4 king went the way toward the p'. * "
2Ch 4:17 In the p' of Jordan did the king 3603
Ne 3:22 the priests, the men of the p'. "
6: 2 one of the villages in the p' of Ono.1237
12:28 p' country round about Jerusalem,3603
Ps 27:11 lead me in a p' path, because of 4334
Pr 8: 9 all p' to him that understandeth, 5228
15:19 way of the righteous is made p'. *5549
Isa 28:25 he hath made p' the face thereof, ‡7737
40: 4 straight, and the rough places p': 1237
Jer 17:26 of Benjamin, and from the p', *8219
21:13 of the valley, and rock of the p', 4334
39: 4 and he went out the way of the p'.*6160
48: 8 and the p' shall be destroyed, as 4334
21 is come upon the p' country; "
52: 7 they went by the way of the p'. *6160
Eze 3:22 Arise, go forth into the p', and I 1237
23 arose, and went forth into the p': "
8: 4 to the vision that I saw in the p'. "
Da 3: 1 he set it up in the p' of Dura, in the1236
Am 1: 5 the inhabitant from the p' of Aven,*1237
Ob 19 and they of the p' the Philistines:*8219
Hab 2: 2 vision, and make it p' upon tables, 874
Zec 4: 7 thou shalt become a p': and he 4334
7: 7 inhabited the south and the p'? *8219
14:10 All the land shall be turned as a p'*6160
M'r 7:35 tongue was loosed, and he spake p'.*3723
Lu 6:17 and stood in the p', and the *5117,3977

plainly
Ex 21: 5 if the servant shall p' say, I love 559
De 27: 8 all the words of this law very p'. 874
1Sa 2:27 p' appear unto the house of thy *1540
10:16 He told us p' that the asses were 5046
Ezr 4:18 sent unto us hath been p' read 6568
Isa 32: 4 shall be ready to speak p'. 6703
Joh 10:24 If thou be the Christ, tell us p'. 3954
11:14 Then said Jesus unto them p', "
16:25 I shall shew you p' of the Father. "
29 him, Lo, now speakest thou p', "
Heb 11:14 declare p' that they seek a country.*1718

plainness
2Cor 3:12 hope, we use great p' of speech: *3954

plains
Ge 18: 1 unto him in the p' of Mamre: * 436
Nu 22: 1 and pitched in the p' of Moab on 6160
26: 3 spake with them in the p' of Moab "
63 children of Israel in the p' of Moab by"
31:12 unto the camp at the p' of Moab, "
33:48 and pitched in the p' of Moab by "
49 unto Abel-shittim in the p' of Moab."
50 spake unto Moses in the p' of Moab "
35: 1 spake unto Moses in the p' of Moab "
36:13 children of Israel in the p' of Moab "
De 11:30 Gilgal, beside the p' of Moreh? * 436
34: 1 Moses went up from the p' of Moab6160
8 wept for Moses in the p' of Moab "
Jos 4:13 unto battle, to the p' of Jericho. "
5:10 month at even in the p' of Jericho. "
11: 2 and of the p' south of Chinneroth,* "
12: 8 and in the p', and in the springs, * "
13:32 for inheritance in the p' of Moab, "
2Sa 17:16 night in the p' of the wilderness, * "
2Ki 25: 5 overtook him in the p' of Jericho: "
1Ch 27:28 trees that were in the low p' was *8219
2Ch 9:27 trees that are in the low p' in * "
26:10 in the low country, and in the p': *4334
Jer 39: 5 Zedekiah in the p' of Jericho: 6160
52: 8 Zedekiah in the p' of Jericho; "

plaister See also PLAISTERED.
Le 14:42 morter, and shall p' the house. 2902
De 27: 2 great stones, and p' them with 7874
De 27: 2 great stones, and...them with p': 7875
4 Ebal, and thou shalt p' them with 7874
4 Ebal, and thou shalt...them with p'.7875
Isa 38:21 and lay it for a p' upon the boil, 4799
Da 5: 5 p' of the wall of the king's palace: 1528

plaistered
Le 14:43 the house, and after it is p'; 2902
48 the house, after the house was p': "

plaiting See also PLATTED.
1Pe 3: 3 outward adorning of p' the hair, 1708

planes
Isa 44:13 he fitteth it with p', and he 4741

planets
2Ki 23: 5 and to the p', and to all the hosts 4208

planks
1Ki 6:15 floor of the house with p' of fir. *6763
Eze 41:25 thick p' upon the face of...porch *6086
26 of the house, and thick p'. *5646

plant See also PLANTED; PLANTETH; PLANTING; PLANTS; SUPPLANT.
Ge 2: 5 every p' of the field before it was 7880
Ex 15:17 shalt bring them in, and p' them 5193
De 16:21 shalt not p' thee a grove of any "
28:30 thou shalt p' a vineyard, and shalt "
39 Thou shalt p' vineyards, and dress "
2Sa 7:10 my people Israel, and will p' them, "
2Ki 19:29 sow ye, and reap, and p' vineyards, "
1Ch 17: 9 my people Israel, and will p' them, "
Job 14: 9 and bring forth boughs like a p'. 5194
Ps 107:37 sow the fields, and p' vineyards, 5193
Ec 3: 2 a time to p', and a time to pluck up "
Isa 5: 7 the men of Judah his pleasant p': 5194
17:10 shalt thou p' pleasant plants, and 5193
11 shalt thou make thy p' to grow, *5194
37:30 ye, and reap, and p' vineyards, 5193
41:19 will p' in the wilderness the cedar,5414
51:16 that I may p' the heavens, and lay5193
53: 2 grow up before him as a tender p', "
65:21 they shall p' vineyards, and eat 5193
22 they shall not p', and another eat: "
Jer 1:10 to throw down, to build, and to p'. "
2:21 art turned into the degenerate p' of "
18: 9 a kingdom, to build and to p' it; 5193
24: 6 and I will p' them, and not pluck "
29: 5 p' gardens, and eat the fruit of them;"
28 p' gardens, and eat the fruit of them."
31: 5 yet p' vines upon the mountains "
5 the planters shall p', and shall eat "
28 over them, to build, and to p', saith "
32:41 I will p' them in this land assuredly"
35: 7 nor sow seed, nor p' vineyard, nor "
42:10 I will p' you, and not pluck you up: "
Eze 17:22 p' it upon an high mountain and 8362
23 of the height of Israel will I p' it: "
28:26 build houses, and p' vineyards; 5193
34:29 raise up for them a p' of renown, *4302
36:36 and p' that that was desolate: 5193
Da 11:45 p' the tabernacles of his palace "
Am 9:14 and they shall p' vineyards, and "
15 and I will p' them upon their land, "
Zep 1:13 and they shall p' vineyards, but not"
M't 15:13 p', which my heavenly Father 5451

plantation
Eze 17: 7 water it by the furrows of her p'. 4302

planted See also PLANTEDST; SUPPLANTED.
Ge 2: 8 Lord God p' a garden eastward 5193
9:20 husbandman, and he p' a vineyard: "
21:33 Abraham p' a grove in Beer-sheba, "
Le 19:23 shall have p' all manner of trees "
Nu 24: 6 lign aloes which the Lord hath p', "
De 20: 6 man is he that hath p' a vineyard, "
Jos 24:13 oliveyards which ye p' not do ye eat."
Ps 1: 3 shall be like a tree p' by the rivers8362
80: 8 cast out the heathen, and p' it. *5193
15 which thy right hand hath p', and "
92:13 that be p' in the house of the 8362
94: 9 He that p' the ear, shall he not 5193
104:16 of Lebanon, which he hath p'; "
Ec 2: 4 me houses; I p' me vineyards: "
5 and I p' trees in them of all kinds of"
3: 2 a time to pluck up that which is p'; "
Isa 5: 2 p' it with the choicest vine, and "
40:24 they shall not be p'; yea, they shall "
Jer 2:21 I had p' thee a noble vine, wholly "
11:17 the Lord of hosts, that p' thee, hath"
12: 2 Thou hast p' them, yea, they have "
17: 8 shall be as a tree p' by the waters,8362
45: 4 which I have p' I will pluck up, 5193
Eze 17: 5 of the land, and p' it in a fruitful field; "
8 It was p' in a good soil by great 8362
10 behold, being p', shall it prosper? "
19:10 in thy blood, p' by the waters: "
13 And now she is p' in the wilderness,"
Ho 9:13 Tyrus, is p' in a pleasant place: "
Am 5:11 ye have p' pleasant vineyards, but 5193
M't 15:13 my heavenly Father hath not p', 5452
21:33 which p' a vineyard, and hedged it "
M'r 12: 1 A certain man p' a vineyard, and "
Lu 13: 6 had a fig tree p' in his vineyard; "
17: 6 the root, and be thou p' in the sea; "
28 they sold, they p', they builded; "
20: 9 A certain man p' a vineyard, and "
Ro 6: 5 p' together in the likeness of his *4854
1Co 3: 6 I have p', Apollos watered; but 5452

plantedst
De 6:11 and olive trees, which thou p' not;5193
Ps 44: 2 with thy hand, and p' them; how * "

planters
Jer 31: 5 the p' shall plant, and shall eat 5193

planteth
Pr 31:16 of her hands she p' a vineyard. 5193
Isa 44:14 he p' an ash, and the rain doth "
1Co 3: 7 neither is he that p' any thing, 5452
8 Now he that p' and he that watereth"
9: 7 who p' a vineyard, and eateth not "

planting See also PLANTINGS.
Isa 60:21 the branch of my p', the work of 4302
61: 3 the p' of the Lord, that he might "

plantings
Mic 1: 6 the field, and as p' of a vineyard: 4302

plants
1Ch 4:23 that dwelt among p' and hedges: *5194
Ps 128: 3 children like olive p' round about 8363
144:12 our sons may be as p' grown up 5195
Ca 4:13 p' are...orchard of pomegranates,*7973
Isa 16: 8 broken down the principal p' 8291
17:10 shalt thou plant pleasant p', and 5194
Jer 48:32 thy p' are gone over the sea, they *5189
Eze 31: 4 rivers running round about...p', *4302

plaster See PLAISTER.

plat See also PLAITING; PLATTED.
2Ki 9:26 I will requit thee in this p', saith 2513
26 cast him into the p' of ground, "

plate See also PLATES.
Ex 28:36 thou shalt make a p' of pure gold, 6731
39:30 they made the p' of the holy crown "
Le 8: 9 forefront, did he put the golden p', "

plates
Ex 39: 3 they did beat the gold into thin p', 6341
Nu 16:38 let them make them broad p' for "
39 were made broad p' for a covering* "
1Ki 7:30 brasen wheels, and p' of brass: *5633
36 For on the p' of the ledges thereof,3871
Jer 10: 9 Silver spread into p' is brought from

platted See also PLAITING.
M't 27:29 they had p' a crown of thorns, *4120
M'r 15:17 p' a crown of thorns, and put it * "
Joh 19: 2 the soldiers p' a crown of thorns, * "

platter
M't 23:25 outside of the cup and of the p', 3953
26 that which is within the cup and p'."
Lu 11:39 the outside of the cup and the p'; 4094

play See also PLAYED; PLAYETH; PLAYING.
Ex 32: 6 and to drink, and rose up to p'. 6711
De 22:21 to p' the whore in her father's house:
1Sa 16:16 he shall p' with his hand, and 5059
17 me now a man that can p' well, "
21:15 to p' the mad man in my presence?
2Sa 2:14 men now arise, and p' before us. 7832
6:21 therefore will I p' before the Lord. "
10:12 and let us p' the men for our people,
Job 40:20 where all the beasts of the field p'.7832
41: 5 thou p' with him as with a bird? "
Ps 33: 3 p' skilfully with a loud noise. 5059
104:26 thou hast made to p' therein. *7832
Isa 11: 8 shall p' on the hole of the asp, 8173
Eze 33:32 and can p' well on an instrument: 5059
Ho 3: 3 thou shalt not p' the harlot, and thou
4:15 p' the harlot, yet let not Judah offend;
1Co 10: 7 eat and drink, and rose up to p'. 3815

played See also DISPLAYED; PLAYEDST.
Ge 38:24 daughter in law hath p' the harlot;
J'g 19: 2 concubine p' the whore against him,
1Sa 16:23 an harp, and p' with his hand: 5059
18: 7 answered one another as they p', *7832
10 David p' with his hand, as at other5059
19: 9 and David p' with his hand. "
26:21 I have p' the fool, and have erred
2Sa 6: 5 house of Israel p' before the Lord 7832
2Ki 3:15 came to pass, when the minstrel p',5059
1Ch 13: 8 David and all Israel p' before God 7832
Jer 3: 1 thou hast p' the harlot with many
6 tree, and there hath p' the harlot.
8 not, but went and p' the harlot also.
Eze 16:28 Thou hast p' the whore also with the
28 yea, thou hast p' the harlot with them,
23: 5 Aholah p' the harlot when she was
19 had p' the harlot in the land of Egypt.
Ho 2: 5 For their mother hath p' the harlot:

playedst
Eze 16:15 p' the harlot because of thy renown,
16 p' the harlot thereupon: the like

player See also PLAYERS.
1Sa 16:16 who is a cunning p' on a harp: 5059

players
Ps 68:25 p' on instruments followed after; *5059
87: 7 p' on instruments shall be there: *2490

playeth
Eze 23:44 go in unto a woman that p' the harlot:*

playing
Le 21: 9 she profane herself by p' the whore,
1Sa 16:18 Beth-lehemite that is cunning in p',5059
1Ch 15:29 saw king David dancing and p': 7832
Ps 68:25 were the damsels p' with timbrels.
Jer 2:20 tree thou wanderest, p' the harlot.
Eze 16:41 cause thee to cease from p' the harlot,
Zec 8: 5 boys and girls p' in the streets 7832

plea
De 17: 8 between p' and p', and between 1779

plead See also IMPLEAD; PLEADED; PLEADETH; PLEADINGS.
J'g 6:31 Will ye p' for Baal? will ye save *7378
31 he that will p' for him, let him be * "
31 let him p' for himself, because one* "

J'g 6:32 Let Baal p' against him, because *7378
1Sa 24:15 and p' my cause, and deliver me * "
Job 9:19 who shall set me a time to p'? *
13:19 Who is he that will p' with me? *7378
16:21 one might p' for a man with God, *3198
19: 5 and p' against me my reproach: * "
23: 6 Will he p' against me with his *7378
Ps 35: 1 P' my cause, O Lord, with them * "
Pr 43: 1 Judge me, O God, and p' my cause "
74:22 Arise, O God, p' thine own cause: "
119:154 P' my cause, and deliver me: "
22:23 the Lord will p' their cause, and "
23:11 he shall p' their cause with thee. "
31: 9 p' the cause of the poor and needy.*1777
Isa 1:17 the fatherless, p' for the widow. 7378
3:13 The Lord standeth up to p', and ‡ "
43:26 remembrance: let us p' together: 8199
66:16 will the Lord p' with all flesh: ‡ "
Jer 2: 9 I will yet p' with you, saith the ‡7378
9 your children's children will I p'. ‡ "
29 Wherefore will ye p' with me? ye ‡ "
35 I will p' with thee, because thou *8199
12: 1 thou, O Lord, when I p' with thee:‡7378
25:31 he will p' with all flesh; he will 8199
30:13 There none to p' thy cause, that 1777
50:34 he shall thoroughly p' their cause, 7378
51:36 Behold, I will p' thy cause, and take"
Eze 17:20 and will p' with him there for his 8199
20:35 will I p' with you face to face. "
36 so will I p' with you, saith the Lord "
38:22 will p' against him with pestilence‡ "
Ho 2: 2 P' with your mother, p': for she is‡7378
Joel 3: 2 p' with them there for my people *8199
Mic 6: 2 people, and he will p' with Israel. 3198
7: 9 until he p' my cause, and execute 7378

pleaded
1Sa 25:39 the Lord that hath p' the cause 7378
La 3:58 thou hast p' the causes of my soul; "
Eze 20:36 Like as I p' with your fathers in 8199

pleadeth
Job 16:21 as a man p' for his neighbour! *
Isa 51:22 that p' the cause of his people, 7378
59: 4 for justice, nor any p' for truth: 8199

pleadings
Job 13: 6 and hearken to the p' of my lips. 7379

pleasant
Ge 2: 9 every tree that is p' to the sight, 2530
3: 6 it was p' to the eyes, and a tree *8378
49:15 good, and the land that it was p'; 5276
2Sa 1:23 and Jonathan were lovely and p' 5273
26 very p' hast thou been unto me: 5276
1Ki 20: 6 whatsoever is p' in thine eyes, 4261
2Ki 2:19 situation of this city is p', as my 2896
2Ch 32:27 and for all manner of p' jewels; *2532
Ps 16: 6 are fallen unto me in p' places; 5273
81: 2 the p' harp with the psaltery. "
106:24 they despised the p' land, they 2532
133: 1 how p' it is for brethren to dwell 5273
135: 3 praises unto his name; for it is p'. "
147: 1 praises unto our God; for it is p': "
Pr 2:10 and knowledge is p' to thy soul; 5276
5:19 be as the loving hind and p' roe; 2580
9:17 and bread eaten in secret is p'. 5276
15:26 the words of the pure are p' words.5278
16:24 P' words are as an honeycomb, "
22:18 p' thing if thou keep them within 5273
24: 4 with all precious and p' riches. "
Ec 11: 7 a p' thing it is for the eyes to 2896
Ca 1:16 thou art fair, my beloved, yea, p': 5273
4:13 of pomegranates, with p' fruits; *4022
16 his garden, and eat his p' fruits. * "
7: 6 How fair and how p' art thou, O 5276
13 gates are all manner of p' fruits, *4022
Isa 2:16 Tarshish, and upon all p' pictures.2532
5: 7 the men of Judah his p' plant: 8191
13:22 and dragons in their p' palaces: 6027
17:10 shalt thou plant p' plants, and 2532
32:12 for the teats, for the p' fields, 2531
54:12 and all thy borders of p' stones. ‡2656
64:11 all our p' things are laid waste. 4261
Jer 3:19 and give thee a p' land, a goodly 2532
12:10 p' portion a desolate wilderness. "
23:10 p' places of the wilderness are *4999
25:34 and ye shall fall like a p' vessel. 2532
31:20 my dear son? is he a p' child? ‡8191
La 1: 7 all her p' things that she had in 4262
10 his hand upon all her p' things: 4621
11 have given their p' things for meat4622
2: 4 slew all that were p' to the eye "
Eze 26:12 walls, and destroy thy p' houses: 2532
33:32 song of one that hath a p' voice, 3303
Da 8: 9 the east, and toward the p' land. 6643
10: 3 I ate no p' bread, neither came 2530
11:38 precious stones, and p' things. "
Ho 9: 6 p' places for their silver, nettles 4261
13 Tyrus, is planted in a p' place: 5116
13:15 the treasure of all p' vessels. 2532
Joe 3: 5 temples my goodly p' things: ‡4261
Am 5:11 ye have planted p' vineyards, but 2531
Mic 2: 9 ye cast out from their p' houses; 8588
Na 2: 9 glory out of all the p' furniture. ‡2532
Zec 7:14 for they laid the p' land desolate. "
Mal 3: 4 of Judah and Jerusalem be p' 6148

pleasantness
Pr 3:17 Her ways are ways of p', and all 5278

please See also DISPLEASE; PLEASED; PLEASETH; PLEASING.
Ex 21: 8 If she p' not her master, who 7451,5869
Nu 23:27 peradventure it will p' God 3477, "
1Sa 20:13 if it p' my father to do thee evil, 3190
2Sa 7:29 p' thee to bless the house of thy 2974
1Ki 21: 6 else, if it p' thee, I will give thee 2655
1Ch 17:27 p' thee to bless the house of thy *2974
2Ch 10: 7 kind to this people, and p' them, 7521
Ne 2: 5 If it p' the king, and if thy servant2895
7 If it p' the king, let letters be "
Es 1:19 it p' the king, let there go a royal "
3: 9 If it p' the king, let it be written "
5: 8 it p' the king to grant my petition, "
7: 3 if it p' the king, let my life be given "
8: 5 it p' the king, and if I have found 2896
9:13 If it p' the king, let it be granted "
Job 6: 9 it would p' God to destroy me; 2974
20:10 children shall seek to p' the poor,*7521
Ps 69:31 shall p' the Lord better than an ox3190
Pr 16: 7 When a man's ways p' the Lord, 7521
Ca 2: 7 up, nor awake my love, till he p'. 2654
3: 5 up, nor awake my love, till he p'. "
8: 4 up, nor awake my love, until he p'. "
Isa 2: 6 p' themselves in the children of *5606
55:11 shall accomplish that which I p', 2654
56: 4 and choose the things that p' me, "
Joh 8:29 do always those things that p' him.*701
Ro 8: 8 that are in the flesh cannot p' God. 700
15: 1 the weak, and not to p' ourselves. "
2 Let every one of us p' his neighbour"
1Co 7:32 the Lord, how he may p' the Lord: "
33 the world, how he may p' his wife. "
34 world, how she may p' her husband. "
10:33 Even as I p' all men in all things, "
Ga 1:10 men, or God? or do I seek to p' men?"
1Th 2:15 they p' not God, and are contrary "
4: 1 how ye ought to walk and to p' God, "
2Ti 2: 4 he may p' him who hath chosen him "
Tit 2: 9 to p' them well in all things; *2001,1511*
Heb11: 6 faith it is impossible to p' him: *2100

pleased See also DISPLEASED.
Ge 28: 8 daughters of Canaan p' not 7451,5869
33:10 of God, and thou wast p' with me. 7521
34:18 And their words p' Hamor, 3190,5869
45:16 and it p' Pharaoh well, and his "
Nu 24: 1 Balaam saw that it p' the Lord 2895
De 1:23 And the saying p' me well: 3190,5869
Jos 22:30 of Manasseh spake, it p' them. " "
33 thing p' the children of Israel; " "
J'g 13:23 If the Lord was p' to kill us, he 2654
14: 7 and she p' Samson well. 3477,5869
1Sa 12:22 hath p' the Lord to make you his 2974
18:20 Saul, and the thing p' him. 3477,5869
26 it p' David well to be the king's " "
2Sa 3:36 notice of it, and it p' them: 3190, "
36 whatsoever the king did p' all2896, "
17: 4 the saying p' Absalom well. 3477, "
19: 6 day, then it had p' thee well. " "
1Ki 3:10 the speech p' the Lord, that 3190, "
9: 1 desire which he was p' to do, 2654
12 him; and they p' him not. 3477,5869
2Ch 30: 4 the thing p' the king and all * "
Ne 2: 6 So it p' the king to send me; and I3190
Es 1:21 p' the king and the princes; 3190,5869
2: 4 And the thing p' the king; " "
9 And the maiden p' him, and " "
5:14 And the thing p' Haman; and he 3190
Ps 40:13 Be p', O Lord, to deliver me: O 7521
51:19 shalt thou be p' with the sacrifices*2654
115: 3 hath done whatsoever he hath p'. "
135: 6 Whatsoever the Lord p', that did "
Isa 42:21 Lord is well p' for his righteousness'"
53:10 Yet it p' the Lord to bruise him; "
Da 6: 1 It p' Darius to set over the 8232
Jon 1:14 O Lord, hast done as it p' thee. 2654
Mic 6: 7 Lord be p' with thousands of rams,7521
Mal 1: 8 will he be p' with thee, or accept "
M't 3:17 beloved Son, in whom I am well p'.*2106*
12:18 beloved, in whom my soul is well p': *700*
14: 6 danced before them, and p' Herod. *700*
17: 5 beloved Son, in whom I am well p';*2106*
M'r 1:11 beloved Son, in whom I am well p'. "
6:22 came in, and danced, and p' Herod *700*
Lu 3:22 beloved Son; in thee I am well p'. *2106*
Ac 6: 5 the saying p' the whole multitude: *700*
12: 3 And because he saw it p' the Jews, *701*
15:22 Then p' it the apostles and elders,*1380
34 it p' Silas to abide there still. * "
Ro 15: 3 For even Christ p' not himself; *700*
26 For it hath p' them of Macedonia *2106
27 It hath p' them verily; and their * "
1Co 1:21 it p' God by the foolishness of "
7:12 and she be p' to dwell with him, *4909
13 if he be p' to dwell with her, let * "
10: 5 many of them God was not well p':*2106*
12:18 in the body, as it hath p' him. *2309*
15:38 giveth it a body as it hath p' him, "
Gal 1:10 for if I yet p' men, I should not be* *700*
15 But when it p' God, who separated*2106
Col 1:19 it p' the Father that in him should* "
Heb11: 5 had this testimony, that he p' God.*2100
13:16 with such sacrifices God is well p'. "
2Pe 1:17 beloved son, in whom I am well p'.*2106*

pleasers See MENPLEASERS.

pleaseth
Ge 16: 6 hand; do to her as it p' thee.*2896,5869
20:15 thee: dwell where it p' thee. "
J'g 14: 3 for me; for she p' me well. 3477, "
Es 2: 4 the maiden which p' the king 3190, "
Ec 7:26 whoso p' God shall escape 2896,6440
8: 3 for he doeth whatsoever p' him. 2654

pleasing See also WELLPLEASING.
Es 8: 5 the king, and I be p' in his eyes, 2896
Ho 9: 4 neither shall they be p' unto him: 6148
Col 1:10 walk worthy of the Lord unto all p',*699*
1Th 2: 4 not as p' men, but God, which trieth*700*
1Jo 3:22 those things that are p' in his sight.*701*

pleasure See also DISPLEASURE; PLEASURES.
Ge 18:12 I am waxed old shall I have p', 5730
De 23:24 eat grapes thy fill at thine own p';5315
1Ch 29:17 heart, and hast p' in uprightness. 7521
Ezr 5:17 and let the king send his p' to us 7470
10:11 God of your fathers, and do his p':7522
Ne 9:37 and over our cattle, at their p'. "
Es 1: 8 do according to every man's p'. "
Job 21:21 For what p' hath he in his house 2656
25 soul, and never eateth with p'. *2896
22: 3 Is it any p' to the Almighty, that 2656
Ps 5: 4 God that hath p' in wickedness: 2655
35:27 p' in the prosperity of his servant. "
51:18 Do good in thy good p' unto Zion: 7522
102:14 thy servants take p' in her stones, 7521
103:21 ye ministers of his, that do his p'. 7522
105:22 To bind his princes at his p'; and 5315
111: 2 of all them that have p' therein. 2656
147:10 taketh not p' in the legs of a man. 7521
11 Lord taketh p' in them that fear "
149: 4 the Lord taketh p' in his people: "
Pr 21:17 that loveth p' shall be a poor man;8057
Ec 2: 1 therefore enjoy p': and, behold, 2896
5: 4 pay it; for he hath no p' in fools: 2656
12: 1 thou shalt say, I have no p' in them;"
Isa 21: 4 the night of my p' hath he turned*2837
44:28 and shall perform all my p': 2656
46:10 shall stand, and I will do all my p': "
48:14 he will do his p' on Babylon, and "
53:10 p' of the Lord shall prosper in his "
58: 3 in the day of your fast ye find p', "
13 from doing thy p' on my holy day; "
13 own ways, nor finding thine own p'. "
Jer 2:24 snuffeth up the wind at her p';*185,5315
22:28 is he a vessel wherein is no p'? 2656
34:16 he had set at liberty at their p'. 5315
48:38 like a vessel wherein is no p'. 2656
Eze 16:37 with whom thou hast taken p', 6148
18:23 Have I any p' at all that the wicked2654
32 no p' in the death of him that dieth,"
33:11 no p' in the death of the wicked; "
Ho 8: 8 as a vessel wherein is no p'. 2656
Hag 1: 8 I will take p' in it, and I will be 7521
Mal 1:10 I have no p' in you, saith the Lord 2656
Lu 12:32 your Father's good p' to give you *2106*
Ac 24:27 willing to shew the Jews a p', *5485
25: 9 Festus, willing to do the Jews a p',* "
Ro 1:32 but have p' in them that do them.*4909
2Co 12:10 Therefore I take p' in infirmities, *2106*
Eph 1: 5 according to the good p' of his will,*2107*
9 according to his good p' which he "
Ph'p 2:13 both to will and to do of his good p'."
2Th 1:11 all the good p' of his goodness, * "
2:12 but had p' in unrighteousness. *2106*
1Ti 5: 6 But she that liveth in p' is dead *4684*
Heb10: 6 sacrifices...thou hast had no p'. *2106*
8 not, neither hadst p' therein; "
38 my soul shall have no p' in him. "
12:10 chastened...after their own p';*3588,1380
Jas 5: 5 Ye have lived in p' on the earth, *5171
2Pe 2:13 count it p' to riot in the day time. *2237*
Re 4:11 and for thy p' they are and were *2307

pleasures
Job 36:11 in prosperity, and their years in p'.5273
Ps 16:11 hand there are p' for evermore. "
36: 8 them drink of the river of thy p'. 5730
Isa 47: 8 thou that art given to p', that 5719
Lu 8:14 cares and riches and p' of this life, *2237*
2Ti 3: 4 lovers of p' more than lovers of *5569
Tit 3: 3 serving divers lusts and p', living *2237*
Heb11:25 to enjoy the p' of sin for a season; "

pledge See also PLEDGES.
Ge 38:17 Wilt thou give me a p', till thou 6162
18 he said, What p' shall I give thee? "
20 his p' from the woman's hand: "
Ex 22:26 thy neighbour's raiment to p', 2254
De 24: 6 nether or the upper millstone to p': "
6 for he taketh a man's life to p'. "
10 go into his house to fetch his p'. 5667
11 bring out the p' abroad unto thee. "
12 thou shalt not sleep with his p': "
13 shalt deliver him the p' again when"
17 take the widow's raiment to p': 2254
1Sa 17:18 brethren fare, and take their p'. 6161
Job 22: 6 taken a p' from thy brother for *2254
24: 3 they take the widow's ox for a p'. "
9 breast, and take a p' of the poor. "
Pr 20:16 a p' of him for a strange woman. "
27:13 a p' of him for a strange woman. "
Eze 18: 7 hath restored to the debtor his p', 2258
12 hath not restored the p', and hath "
16 hath not withholden the p', neither "
33:15 If the wicked restore the p', give "
Am 2: 8 clothes laid to p' by every altar, 2254

pledges
2Ki 18:23 give p' to my lord...king of Assyria,6148
Isa 36: 8 give p', I pray thee, to my master "

Pleiades (*ple'-ya-dez*)
Job 9: 9 maketh Arcturus, Orion, and P', 3598
38:31 bind the sweet influences of P'. "

plenish See REPLENISH.

plenteous
Ge 41:34 of Egypt in the seven p' years. 7647
47 And in the seven p' years the earth "
De 28:11 Lord shall make thee p' in goods, 3498
30: 9 make thee p' in every work of thine"
2Ch 1:15 gold at Jerusalem as p' as stones,*
Ps 86: 5 p' in mercy unto all them that call‡7227
15 and p' in mercy and truth. ‡ "
103: 8 slow to anger, and p' in mercy. ‡ "
130: 7 and with him is p' redemption. 7235
Isa 30:23 earth, and it shall be fat and p': 8082
Hab 1:16 portion is fat, and their meat p': 1277
M't 9:37 The harvest truly is p', but the *4183*

plenteousness
Ge 41: 53 the seven years of *p'*, that was in *7647
Pr 21: 5 of the diligent tend only to *p'*; 4195

plentiful
Ps 68: 9 Thou, O God, didst send a *p'* rain, 5071
Isa 16: 10 away, and joy out of the *p'* field; 3759
Jer 2: 7 I brought you into a *p'* country, "
48: 33 gladness is taken from the *p'* field,* "

plentifully
Job 26: 3 hast thou *p'* declared the thing 7230
Ps 31: 23 and *p'* rewardeth the proud doer. 3499
Lu 12: 16 certain rich man brought forth *p'*: *2164*

plenty See also PLENTIFUL.
Ge 27: 28 the earth, and *p'* of corn and wine: 7230
41: 29 come seven years of great *p'* 7647
30 the *p'* shall be forgotten in the land "
31 *p'* shall not be known in the land "
Le 11: 36 pit, wherein there is *p'* of water, *4723
1Ki 10: 11 Ophir great *p'* of almug trees, 7235
2Ch 31: 10 enough to eat, and have left *p'*: 7230
Job 22: 25 and thou shalt have *p'* of silver. *8443
37: 23 in judgment, and in *p'* of justice: *7230
Pr 3: 10 So shall thy barns be filled with *p'*, 7647
28: 19 his land shall have *p'* of bread: 7646
Jer 44: 17 for then had we *p'* of victuals, and "
Joe 2: 26 And ye shall eat in *p'*, and be 398

plot See PLAT

plotteth
Ps 37: 12 The wicked *p'* against the just, 2161

plough See also PLOW.
Lu 9: 62 man, having put his hand to the *p'*, *723*

plow See also EAR; PLOUGH; PLOWED; PLOWETH; PLOWING; PLOWMAN; PLOWSHARES.
De 22: 10 Thou shalt not *p'* with an ox and 2790
1Sa 14: 14 land, which a yoke of oxen might *p'*.*
Job 4: 8 I have seen, they that *p'* iniquity, 2790
Pr 20: 4 sluggard will not *p'* by reason of "
Isa 28: 24 the plowman *p'* all day to sow? "
Ho 10: 11 Judah shall *p'*, and Jacob shall "
Am 6: 12 rock? will one *p'* there with oxen? "
1Co 9: 10 he that ploweth should *p'* in hope; *722*

plowed
J'g 14: 18 If ye had not *p'* with my heifer, 2790
Ps 129: 3 The plowers *p'* upon my back: "
Jer 26: 18 Zion shall be *p'* like a field, and "
Ho 10: 13 Ye have *p'* wickedness, ye have "
Mic 3: 12 Zion for your sake be *p'* as a field, "

plowers
Ps 129: 3 The *p'* plowed upon my back: they 2790

ploweth
1Co 9: 10 he that *p'* should plow in hope; *722*

plowing
1Ki 19: 19 was *p'* with twelve yoke of oxen 2790
Job 1: 14 The oxen were *p'*, and the asses "
Pr 21: 4 and the *p'* of the wicked, is sin. *5215
Lu 17: 7 having a servant *p'* or feeding *722*

plowman See also PLOWMEN.
Isa 28: 24 Doth the *p'* plow all day to sow? ‡2790
Am 9: 13 the *p'* shall overtake the reaper, "

plowmen
Isa 61: 5 sons of the alien shall be your *p'* 406
Jer 14: 4 *p'* were ashamed, they covered their "

plowshares
Isa 2: 4 shall beat their swords into *p'*, and 855
Joe 3: 10 Beat your *p'* into swords, and your "
Mic 4: 3 shall beat their swords into *p'*, and "

pluck See also PLUCKED; PLUCKETH; PLUCKT.
Le 1: 16 *p'* away his crop with his feathers, *5493
Nu 33: 52 *p'* down all their high places: *8045
De 23: 25 thou mayest *p'* the ears with thine 6998
2Ch 7: 20 will I *p'* them up by the roots out 5428
Job 24: 9 *p'* the fatherless from the breast, 1497
Ps 25: 15 he shall *p'* my feet out of the net. 3318
52: 5 *p'* thee out of thy dwelling place, 5255
74: 11 right hand? *p'* it out of thy bosom. 3615
80: 12 which pass by the way do *p'* her? 717
Ec 3: 2 time to *p'* up that which is planted; 6131
Jer 12: 14 I will *p'* them out of their land, 5428
14 and *p'* out the house of Judah from "
17 *p'* up and destroy that nation, * "
18: 7 to *p'* up, and to pull down, and to "
22: 24 hand, yet would I *p'* thee thence; 5423
24: 6 plant them, and not *p'* them up. 5428
31: 28 to *p'* up, and to break down, and to "
42: 10 will plant you, and not *p'* you up: "
45: 4 which I have planted I will *p'* up, "
Eze 17: 9 to *p'* it up by the roots thereof. ‡5375
23: 34 *p'* off thine own breasts: and *5423
Mic 3: 2 *p'* off their skin from off them, 1497
5: 14 And I will *p'* up thy groves out of 5428
M't 5: 29 right eye offend thee, *p'* it out, *1808*
12: 1 and began to *p'* the ears of corn, *5089*
18: 9 thine eye offend thee, *p'* it out, *1807*
M'r 2: 23 they went, to *p'* the ears of corn. *5089*
9: 47 if thine eye offend thee, *p'* it out: *1544*
Joh 10: 28 any man *p'* them out of my hand. * *726*
29 to *p'* them out of my Father's hand.* "

plucked See also PLUCKT.
Ex 4: 7 *p'* it out of his bosom, and, behold, *3318
De 28: 63 ye shall be *p'* from off the land 5255
Ru 4: 7 a man *p'* off his shoe, and gave it *8025
2Sa 23: 21 *p'* the spear out of the Egyptian's 1497
1Ch 11: 23 *p'* the spear out of the Egyptian's "
Ezr 9: 3 *p'* off the hair of my head and of 4803
Ne 13: 25 *p'* off their hair, and made them "
Job 29: 17 and *p'* the spoil out of his teeth. 7993

Isa 50: 6 cheeks to them that *p'* off the hair: 4803
Jer 6: 29 for the wicked are not *p'* away. 5423
12: 15 I have *p'* them out I will return, 5428
31: 40 it shall not be *p'* up, nor thrown "
Eze 19: 12 she was *p'* up in fury, she was cast "
Da 7: 4 till the wings thereof were *p'*, 4804
8 the first horns *p'* up by the roots: 6132
11: 4 for his kingdom shall be *p'* up, 5428
Am 4: 11 a firebrand *p'* out of the burning: 5337
Zec 3: 2 not this a brand *p'* out of the fire? "
M'r 5: 4 had been *p'* asunder by him, and *1288*
Lu 6: 1 his disciples *p'* the ears of corn, *5089*
17: 6 Be thou *p'* up by the root, and be *1610*
Ga 4: 15 would have *p'* out your own eyes, *1846*
Jude 12 twice dead, *p'* up by the roots; *1610*

plucketh
Pr 14: 1 foolish *p'* it down with her hands. 2040

pluckt See also PLUCKED.
Ge 8: 11 her mouth was an olive leaf *p'* off: 2965

plumbline
Am 7: 7 made by a *p'*, with a *p'* in his hand. 594
8 what seest thou? And I said, A *p'*. "
8 I will set a *p'* in the midst of my "

plummet
2Ki 21: 13 and the *p'* of the house of Ahab: 4949
Isa 28: 17 line, and righteousness to the *p'*: "
Zec 4: 10 shall see the *p'* in the hand of 68,913

plunge
Job 9: 31 Yet shalt thou *p'* me in the ditch, 2881

plus See OVERPLUS.

ply See REPLY; SUPPLY.

Pochereth (*po-ke'-reth*)
Ezr 2: 57 the children of *P'* of Zebaim, *6380
Ne 7: 59 the children of *P'* of Zebaim, * "

poets
Ac 17: 28 also of your own *p'* have said, *4163*

point See also APPOINT; POINTED; POINTS.
Ge 25: 32 said, Behold, I am at the *p'* to die: 1980
Nu 34: 7 ye shall *p'* out for you mount Hor: *8376
8 mount Hor ye shall *p'* out your * "
10 ye shall *p'* out your east border * 184
Jer 17: 1 and with the *p'* of a diamond: 6856
Eze 21: 15 have set the *p'* of the sword against 19
M'r 5: 23 daughter lieth at the *p'* of death: *2079*
Joh 4: 47 son: for he was at the *p'* of death. *3195*
Jas 2: 10 yet offend in one *p'*, he is guilty of all.

pointed See also APPOINTED.
Job 41: 30 sharp *p'* things upon the mire. *2742

points
Ec 5: 16 in all *p'* as he came, so shall he 5980
Heb 4: 15 was in all *p'* tempted like as we are,

poison
De 32: 24 with the *p'* of serpents of the dust. 2534
33 Their wine is the *p'* of dragons, and "
Job 6: 4 *p'* whereof drinketh up my spirit: "
20: 16 He shall suck the *p'* of asps: the 7219
Ps 58: 4 Their *p'* is like the *p'* of a serpent: 2534
140: 3 adders' *p'* is under their lips. "
Ro 3: 13 the *p'* of asps is under their lips: *2447*
Jas 3: 8 an unruly evil, full of deadly *p'*. "

pole
Nu 21: 8 fiery serpent, and set it upon a *p'*: *5251
9 of brass, and put it upon a *p'*, * "

policy
Da 8: 25 through his *p'*...shall cause craft 7922

polished
Ps 144: 12 *p'* after the similitude of a palace: *2404
Isa 49: 2 hid me, and made me a *p'* shaft; 1305
Da 10: 6 his feet like in colour to *p'* brass, *7044

polishing
La 4: 7 rubies, their *p'* was of sapphire: 1508

poll See also POLLED; POLLS.
Nu 3: 47 take five shekels apiece by the *p'*, 1538
Eze 44: 20 they shall only *p'* their heads. ‡3697
Mic 1: 16 *p'* thee for thy delicate children; ‡1494

polled
2Sa 14: 26 And when he *p'* his head, (for it ‡1548
26 at every year's end that he *p'* it; ‡ "
26 heavy on him, therefore he *p'* it:) ‡ "

polls
Nu 1: 2 names, every male by their *p'*; 1538
18 years old and upward, by their *p'*. "
20, 22 number of the names, by their *p'*, "
1Ch 23: 3 their number by their *p'*, man by "
24 by number of names by their *p'*, "

pollute See also POLLUTED; POLLUTING.
Nu 18: 32 neither shall ye *p'* the holy things *2490
35: 33 So ye shall not *p'* the land wherein 2610
Jer 7: 30 is called by my name, to *p'* it. *2930
Eze 7: 21 for a spoil; and they shall *p'* it. *2490
22 and they shall *p'* my secret place: * "
13: 19 And will ye *p'* me among my people * "
20: 31 ye *p'* yourselves with all your idols, 2930
39 *p'* ye my holy name no more with *2490
39: 7 I will not let them *p'* my holy name * "
44: 7 to *p'* it, even my house, when ye "
Da 11: 31 shall *p'* the sanctuary of strength, * "

polluted
Ex 20: 25 thy tool upon it, thou hast *p'* it. 2490
2Ki 23: 16 burned...upon the altar, and *p'* it, *2930
2Ch 36: 14 *p'* the house of the Lord, which he "
Ezr 2: 62 as *p'*, put from the priesthood. 1351
Ne 7: 64 as *p'*, put from the priesthood. "

Ps 106: 38 and the land was *p'* with blood. 2610
Isa 47: 6 I have *p'* mine inheritance, and *2490
48: 11 how should my name be *p'*? and I * "
Jer 2: 23 How canst thou say, I am not *p'*, I *2930
3: 1 shall not that land be greatly *p'*? 2610
2 and thou hast *p'* the land with thy "
34: 16 But ye turned and *p'* my name, *2490
La 2: 2 he hath *p'* the kingdom and the "
4: 14 have *p'* themselves with blood, so 1351
Eze 4: 14 soul hath not been *p'*; for, from 2930
14: 11 neither be *p'* any more with all * "
16: 6 saw thee *p'* in thine own blood, * 947
22 naked and bare,...*p'* in thy blood. * "
20: 9 should not be *p'* before...heathen, *2490
13 and my sabbaths they greatly *p'*: * "
14 should not be *p'* before...heathen, * "
16 my statutes, but *p'* my sabbaths: * "
21 they *p'* my sabbaths: then I said, * "
22 be *p'* in the sight of the heathen, * "
24 had *p'* my sabbaths, and their eyes * "
26 I *p'* them in their own gifts, in 2930
30 Are ye *p'* after the manner of your * "
23: 17 she was *p'* with them, and her mind "
30 because thou art *p'* with their idols. "
36: 18 idols wherewith they had *p'* it: "
Ho 6: 8 iniquity, and is *p'* with blood. *6121
9: 4 all that eat thereof shall be *p'*: 2930
Am 7: 17 and thou shalt die in a *p'* land: *2931
Mic 2: 10 because it is *p'*, it shall destroy *2930
Zep 3: 1 Woe to her that is filthy and *p'*, to 1351
4 her priests have *p'* the sanctuary, *2490
Mal 1: 7 Ye offer *p'* bread upon mine altar; 1351
7 ye say, Wherein have we *p'* thee? "
12 The table of the Lord is *p'*; and the "
Ac 21: 28 temple,...hath *p'* this holy place. *2840*

polluting
Isa 56: 2, 6 keepeth the sabbath from *p'* it, *2490

pollution See POLLUTIONS.
Eze 22: 10 her that was set apart for *p'*. †‡2931

pollutions
Ac 15: 20 that they abstain from *p'* of idols, *234*
2Pe 2: 20 have escaped the *p'* of the world *3393*

Pollux (*pol'-lux*)
Ac 28: 11 whose sign was Castor and *P'*. *1359*

pomegranate See POMEGRANATES.
Ex 28: 34 bell and a *p'*, a golden bell and a *p'*, 7416
39: 26 A bell and a *p'*, a bell and a *p'*, "
1Sa 14: 2 under a *p'* tree which is in Migron: "
Ca 4: 3 thy temples are like a piece of a *p'* "
6: 7 As a piece of a *p'* are thy temples "
8: 2 spiced wine of the juice of my *p'*. "
Joe 1: 12 the *p'* tree, the palm tree also, and "
Hag 2: 19 the *p'*, and the olive tree, hath not "

pomegranate-tree See POMEGRANATE and TREE.

pomegranates
Ex 28: 33 thou shalt make *p'* of blue, and of 7416
39: 24 upon the hems of the robe *p'* of blue, "
25 and put the bells between the *p'* "
25 robe, round about between the *p'*; "
Nu 13: 23 they brought of the *p'*, and of the "
20: 5 or of figs, or of vines, or of *p'*; "
De 8: 8 and vines, and fig trees, and *p'*; "
1Ki 7: 18 that were upon the top, with *p'*: * "
20 upon the two pillars had *p'* also above, *
20 and the *p'* were two hundred in 7416
42 And four hundred *p'* for the two "
42 two rows of *p'* for one network, "
2Ki 25: 17 *p'* upon the chapiter round about, "
2Ch 3: 16 and made an hundred *p'*, and put "
4: 13 hundred *p'* on the two wreaths; "
13 two rows of *p'* on each wreath, "
Ca 4: 13 Thy plants are an orchard of *p'*, "
6: 11 vine flourished, and the *p'* budded. "
7: 12 grape appear, and the *p'* bud forth: "
Jer 52: 22 *p'* upon the chapiters round about, "
22 and the *p'* were like unto these. "
23 were ninety and six *p'* on a side; "
23 and all the *p'* upon the network "

pommels
2Ch 4: 12 and the *p'*, and the chapiters *1543
12, 13 cover the two *p'* of the chapiters * "

pomp
Isa 5: 14 and their multitude, and their *p'*, 7588
14: 11 Thy *p'* is brought down to the 1347
Eze 7: 24 make the *p'* of the strong to cease; * "
30: 18 the *p'* of her strength shall cease * "
32: 12 they shall spoil the *p'* of Egypt, "
33: 28 the *p'* of her strength shall cease; * "
Ac 25: 23 come, and Bernice, with great *p'*, *5325*

ponder See PONDERED; PONDERETH.
Pr 4: 26 *P'* the path of thy feet, and let all *6424
5: 6 thou shouldest *p'* the path of life, * "

pondered
Lu 2: 19 things, and *p'* them in her heart. *4820*

pondereth
Pr 5: 21 the Lord, and he *p'* all his goings. *6424
21: 2 eyes: but the Lord *p'* the hearts. *8505
24: 12 not he that *p'* the heart consider it? * "

ponds
Ex 7: 19 upon their rivers, and upon their *p'*, *98
8: 5 over the rivers, and over the *p'*, * "
Isa 19: 10 all that make sluices and *p'* for fish. *99

Pontius (*pon'-she-us*)
M't 27: 2 him to *P'* Pilate the governor. *4194*
Lu 3: 1 *P'* Pilate being governor of Judæa, "
Ac 4: 27 both Herod, and *P'* Pilate, with the "
1Ti 6: 13 before *P'* Pilate witnessed a good "

Pontus (*pon'-tus*)
Ac 2: 9 and Cappadocia, in *P'*, and Asia, *4195*
18: 2 Jew named Aquila, born in *P'*, "
1Pe 1: 1 strangers scattered throughout *P'*,"

pool See also POOLS.
2Sa 2:13 met together by the *p'* of Gibeon: 1295
13 the one on the one side of the *p'*, "
13 other on the other side of the *p'*. "
4:12 them up over the *p'* in Hebron. "
1Ki 22:38 the chariot in the *p'* of Samaria; "
2Ki 18:17 by the conduit of the upper *p'*, "
20:20 how he made a *p'*, and a conduit, "
Ne 2:14 the fountain, and to the king's *p'*: "
3:15 *p'* of Siloah by the king's garden, "
16 and to the *p'* that was made, and "
Isa 7: 3 end of the conduit of the upper *p'* "
22: 9 together the waters of the lower *p'*. "
11 two walls for the water of the old *p'*: "
35: 7 parched ground shall become a *p'*, 98
36: 2 by the conduit of the upper *p'* 1295
41:18 make the wilderness a *p'* of water, 98
Na 2: 8 Nineveh is...like a *p'* of water: 1295
Joh 5: 2 there is...by the sheep market a *p'*, *2861*
4 down at a certain season into the *p'*, "
7 is troubled, to put me into the *p'*: "
9: 7 him, Go, wash in the *p'* of Siloam, "
11 Go to the *p'* of Siloam, and wash:* "

pools
Ex 7:19 and upon all their *p'* of water, *4723
Ps 84: 6 a well; the rain also filleth the *p'*.*1293
Ec 2: 6 I made me *p'* of water, to water 1295
Isa 14:23 for the bittern, and *p'* of water: 98
42:15 islands, and I will dry up the *p'*. "

poor See also POORER; POOREST.
Ge 41:19 kine...*p'* and very ill favoured and 1800
Ex 22:25 lend...to any of my people that is *p'* 6041
23: 3 shalt thou countenance a *p'* man 1800
6 not wrest the judgment of thy *p'* 34
11 that the *p'* of thy people may eat: "
30:15 more, and the *p'* shall not give less 1800
Le 14:21 if he be *p'*, and cannot get so much;"
19:10 leave them for the *p'* and stranger: 6041
15 not respect the person of the *p'*, 1800
23:22 thou shalt leave them unto the *p'*, 6041
25:25 If thy brother be waxen *p'*, and 4134
35 And if thy brother be waxen *p'*, and"
39 that dwelleth by thee be waxen *p'*, "
47 brother that dwelleth by him wax *p'*, "
De 15: 4 there shall be no *p'* among you; 34
7 If there be among you a *p'* man "
7 shut thine hand from thy *p'* brother:"
9 eye be evil against thy *p'* brother, "
11 *p'* shall never cease out of the land: "
11 to thy *p'*, and to thy needy, in thy*6041
24:12 And if the man be *p'*, thou shalt not"
14 oppress an hired servant that is *p'* "
15 he is *p'*, and setteth his heart upon "
J'g 6:15 my family is *p'* in Manasseh, and *1800
Ru 3:10 not young men, whether *p'* or rich. "
1Sa 2: 7 The Lord maketh *p'*, and maketh 3423
8 raiseth up the *p'* out of the dust, 1800
18:23 seeing that I am a *p'* man, and 7326
2Sa 12: 1 city; the one rich, and the other *p'*. "
3 But the *p'* man had nothing, save "
4 took the *p'* man's lamb, and dressed"
2Ki 25:12 *p'* of the land to be vinedressers *1803
Es 9:22 one to another, and gifts to the *p'*. 34
Job 5:15 he saveth the *p'* from the sword, * "
16 So the *p'* hath hope, and iniquity 1800
20:10 children shall seek to please the *p'*,*"
19 oppressed and hath forsaken the *p'*; "
24: 4 *p'* of the earth hide themselves 6035
9 breast, and take a pledge of the *p'*. 6041
14 rising with the light killeth the *p'* "
29:12 I delivered the *p'* that cried, and "
16 I was a father to the *p'*: and the * 34
30:25 was not my soul grieved for the *p'*?* "
31:16 withheld the *p'* from their desire, 1800
19 clothing, or any *p'* without covering;*34
34:19 the rich more than the *p'*? 1800
28 the cry of the *p'* to come unto him, "
36: 6 wicked: but giveth right to the *p'*.*6041
15 delivereth the *p'* in his affliction, * "
Ps 9:18 expectation of the *p'* shall not 6035,
10: 2 in his pride doth persecute the *p'*: "
8 eyes are privily set against the *p'*.*2489
9 he lieth in wait to catch the *p'*: 6041
9 doth catch the *p'* when he draweth "
10 the *p'* may fall by his strong ones.*2489
14 *p'* committeth himself unto thee; * "
12: 5 For the oppression of the *p'*, 6041
14: 6 have shamed the counsel of the *p'*, "
34: 6 This *p'* man cried, and the Lord "
35:10 deliverest the *p'* from him that is too"
10 the *p'* and the needy from him that "
37:14 bow, to cast down the *p'* and needy,"
40:17 I am *p'* and needy; yet the Lord "
41: 1 is he that considereth the *p'*: 1800
49: 2 low and high, rich and *p'*, together. 34
68:10 prepared of thy goodness for the *p'*. 6041
69:29 But I am *p'* and sorrowful: let thy "
33 For the Lord heareth the *p'*, and * 34
70: 5 I am *p'* and needy: make haste 6041
72: 2 and thy *p'* with judgment. "
4 He shall judge the *p'* of the people, "
12 *p'* also, and him that had no helper."
13 He shall spare the *p'* and needy, 1800
74:19 forget not...congregation of thy *p'* 6041
21 the *p'* and needy praise thy name. "
82: 3 Defend the *p'* and fatherless: do 1800
4 Deliver the *p'* and needy: rid them "
86: 1 hear me: for I am *p'* and needy. 6041
107:41 Yet setteth he the *p'* on high from* 34
109:16 persecuted the *p'* and needy man, 6041
Ps 109:22 For I am *p'* and needy, and my 6041
31 stand at the right hand of the *p'*, * 34
112: 9 dispersed, he hath given to the *p'*;* "
113: 7 raiseth up the *p'* out of the dust, 1800
132:15 I will satisfy her *p'* with bread. 34
140:12 the afflicted, and the right of the *p'*.* "
Pr 10: 4 He becometh *p'* that dealeth with 7326
15 the destruction of the *p'* is their 1800
13: 7 there is that maketh himself *p'*, 7326
8 but the *p'* heareth not rebuke. "
23 Much food is in the tillage of the *p'*:"
14:20 The *p'* is hated even of his own "
21 he that hath mercy on the *p'*, 6035,6041
31 that oppresseth the *p'* reproacheth 1800
31 him hath mercy on the *p'*. * 34
17: 5 Whoso mocketh the *p'* reproacheth 7326
18:23 The *p'* useth intreaties; but the "
19: 1 Better is the *p'* that walketh in his "
4 *p'* is separated from his neighbour. 1800
7 brethren of the *p'* do hate him: 7326
17 that hath pity upon the *p'* lendeth 1800
22 and a *p'* man is better than a liar. 7326
21:13 stoppeth his ears at...cry of the *p'*, 1800
17 loveth pleasure shall be a *p'* man: 4270
22: 2 The rich and *p'* meet together: 7326
7 The rich ruleth over the *p'*, and the"
9 he giveth of his bread to the *p'*. 1800
16 that oppresseth the *p'* to increase "
22 Rob not the *p'*, because he is *p'*: "
28: 3 A *p'* man that oppresseth the *7326
3 A...man that oppresseth the *p'* 1800
6 Better is the *p'* that walketh in his "
8 it for him that will pity the *p'*. "
11 but the *p'* that hath understanding "
15 a wicked ruler over the *p'* people. "
27 that giveth unto the *p'* shall not 7326
29: 7 considereth the cause of the *p'*: 1800
13 The *p'* and the deceitful man meet 7326
14 king that faithfully judgeth the *p'*, 1800
30: 9 or lest I be *p'*, and steal, and take 3423
14 devour the *p'* from off the earth, 6041
31: 9 plead the cause of the *p'* and needy."
20 She stretched out her hand to the *p'*;"
Ec 4:13 Better is a *p'* and a wise child 4542
14 born in his kingdom becometh *p'*. 7326
5: 8 thou seest the oppression of the *p'*, "
6: 8 what hath the *p'*, that knoweth to 6041
9:15 was found in it a *p'* wise man, 4542
15 remembered that same *p'* man. "
16 the *p'* man's wisdom is despised, "
Isa 3:14 spoil of the *p'* is in your houses. 6041
15 pieces, and grind the faces of the *p'*?"
10: 2 the right from the *p'* of my people, "
30 be heard unto Laish, O *p'* Anathoth."
11: 4 righteousness shall he judge the *p'*, 1800
14:30 the firstborn of the *p'* shall feed, "
32 *p'* of his people shall trust in it. *6041
25: 4 thou hast been a strength to the *p'*, 1800
26: 6 it down, even the feet of the *p'*, 6041
29:19 the *p'* among men shall rejoice in 34
32: 7 to destroy the *p'* with lying *6035,6041
41:17 When the *p'* and needy seek water, "
58: 7 *p'* that are cast out to thy house? "
66: 2 that is *p'* and of a contrite spirit, "
Jer 2:34 of the souls of the *p'* innocents: 34
5: 4 said, Surely these are *p'*; they are 1800
20:13 delivered the soul of the *p'* from the*34
22:16 He judged the cause of the *p'* and 6041
39:10 guard left of the *p'* of the people, 1800
40: 7 and of the *p'* of the land, of them *1803
52:15 certain of the *p'* of the people, and* "
16 the *p'* of the land for vinedressers* "
Eze 16:49 the hand of the *p'* and needy. 6041
18:12 Hath oppressed the *p'* and needy, "
17 hath taken off his hand from the *p'*,"
22:29 and have vexed the *p'* and needy: "
Da 4:27 by shewing mercy to the *p'*; if it 6033
Am 2: 6 silver, and the *p'* for a pair of shoes;*34
7 of the earth on the head of the *p'*, 1800
4: 1 which oppress the *p'*, which crush "
5:11 as your treading is upon the *p'*, and"
12 turn aside the *p'* in the gate from * 34
8: 4 the *p'* of the land to fail, 6035,6041
6 That we may buy the *p'* for silver, 1800
Hab 3:14 was as to devour the *p'* secretly. 6041
Zep 3:12 of thee an afflicted and *p'* people, 1800
Zec 7:10 widow,...the stranger, nor the *p'*; 6041
11: 7 even you, O *p'* of the flock. "
11 *p'* of the flock that waited upon me "
M't 5: 3 Blessed are the *p'* in spirit: for *4434*
11: 5 the *p'* have the gospel preached to "
19:21 that thou hast, and give to the *p'*, "
26: 9 sold for much, and given to the *p'*. "
11 For ye have the *p'* always with you;"
M'r 10:21 thou hast, and give to the *p'*, and "
12:42 there came a certain *p'* widow, and "
43 this *p'* widow hath cast more in, "
14: 5 and have been given to the *p'*. "
7 ye have the *p'* with you always, and"
Lu 4:18 me to preach the gospel to the *p'*; "
6:20 Blessed be ye *p'*: for yours is the "
7:22 to the *p'* the gospel is preached. "
14:13 thou makest a feast, call the *p'*, the"
21 and bring in hither the *p'*, and the "
18:22 hast, and distribute unto the *p'*, "
19: 8 half of my goods I give to the *p'*; "
21: 2 *p'* widow casting in thither two *3998*
3 *p'* widow hath cast in more than *4434*
Joh 12: 5 hundred pence, and given to the *p'*? "
6 he said, not that he cared for the *p'*;"
8 the *p'* always ye have with you; but"
13:29 he should give something to the *p'*. "
Ro 15:26 *p'* saints which are at Jerusalem. "
1Co 13: 3 I bestow all my goods to feed the *p'*, "
2Co 6:10 as *p'*, yet making many rich; as *4434*
8: 9 yet for your sakes he became *p'*, *4433*
2Co 9: 9 abroad; he hath given to the *p'*: *3993*
Ga 2:10 that we should remember the *p'*; *4434*
Jas 2: 2 in also a *p'* man in vile raiment; "
3 say to the *p'*, Stand thou there, or "
5 not God chosen the *p'* of this world "
6 But ye have despised the *p'*. Do "
Re 3:17 miserable, and *p'*, and blind, and "
13:16 great, rich and *p'*, free and bond, "

poorer
Le 27: 8 if he be *p'* than thy estimation, 4134

poorest
2Ki 24:14 *p'* sort of the people of the land. 1803

poplar See also POPLARS.
Ge 30:37 Jacob took him rods of green *p'*, 3839

poplars
Ho 4:13 hills, under oaks and *p'* and elms, 3839

populous
De 26: 5 a nation, great, mighty, and *p'*: 7227
Na 3: 8 Art thou better than *p'* No, that * 527

Poratha (*por'-a-thah*)
Es 9: 8 And *P'*, and Adalia, and Aridatha, 6334

porch See also PORCHES.
J'g 3:23 Ehud went forth through the *p'*, 4528
1Ki 6: 3 *p'* before the temple of the house, 197
7: 6 he made a *p'* of pillars; the length "
6 and the *p'* was before them: and the"
7 Then he made a *p'* for the throne "
7 judge, even the *p'* of judgment: "
8 had another court within the *p'*, "
8 had taken to wife, like unto this *p'*. "
12 Lord, and for the *p'* of the house. "
19 pillars were of lily work in the *p'*, "
21 the pillars in the *p'* of the temple: "
1Ch 28:11 to Solomon...the pattern of the *p'*, "
2Ch 3: 4 *p'* that was in the front of the house,"
8:12 which he had built before the *p'*, "
15: 8 that was before the *p'* of the Lord. "
29: 7 have shut up the doors of the *p'*, and"
17 came they to the *p'* of the Lord: "
Eze 8:16 between the *p'* and the altar, were "
40: 7 *p'* of the gate within was one reed. "
8 He measured also the *p'* of the gate "
9 Then measured he the *p'* of the gate,"
9 and the *p'* of the gate was inward. "
15 the face of the *p'* of the inner gate "
39 in the *p'* of the gate were two tables,"
40 which was at the *p'* of the gate, "
48 brought me to the *p'* of the house, "
48 measured each post of the *p'*, five "
49 length of the *p'* was twenty cubits, "
41:25 thick planks upon the face of the *p'* "
26 the other side, on the sides of the *p'*,"
44: 3 he shall enter by the way of the *p'* "
46: 2 shall enter by the way of the *p'* of "
8 he shall go in by the way of the *p'* "
Joe 2:17 weep between the *p'* and the altar, "
M't 26:71 when he was gone out into the *p'*, *4440*
M'r 14:68 And he went out into the *p'*; and *4259*
Joh 10:23 in the temple in Solomon's *p'*. *4745*
Ac 3:11 in the *p'* that is called Solomon's, "
5:12 all with one accord in Solomon's *p'*."

porches
Eze 41:15 temple, and the *p'* of the court; 197
Joh 5: 2 tongue Bethesda, having five *p'*. *4745*

Porcius (*por'-she-us*)
Ac 24:27 after two years *P'* Festus came *4201*

port See also REPORT; SUPPORT.
Ne 2:13 dragon well, and to the dung *p'*, 8179

porter See also PORTERS.
2Sa 18:26 the watchman called unto the *p'*, 7778
2Ki 7:10 and called unto the *p'* of the city: "
1Ch 9:21 was *p'* of the door of the tabernacle "
2Ch 31:14 the *p'* toward the east, was over the"
M'r 13:34 and commanded the *p'* to watch. *2377*
Joh 10: 3 To him the *p'* openeth; and the "

porters
2Ki 7:11 he called the *p'*; and they told it 7778
1Ch 9:17 the *p'* were, Shallum, and Akkub, "
18 *p'* in the companies of the children "
22 were chosen to be *p'* in the gates "
24 In four quarters were the *p'*, "
26 these Levites, the four chief *p'*, "
15:18 and Obed-edom, and Jeiel, the *p'*.* "
16:38 of Jeduthun and Hosah to be *p'*: * "
42 And the sons of Jeduthun were *p'*.*8179
23: 5 Moreover four thousand were *p'*;*7778
26: 1 Concerning the divisions of the *p'*:*"
12 these were the divisions of the *p'*,* "
19 These are the divisions of the *p'* * "
2Ch 8:14 *p'* also by their courses at every * "
23: 4 the Levites, shall be *p'* of the doors;"
19 set the *p'* at the gates of the house "
34:13 were scribes, and officers, and *p'*. "
35:15 and the *p'* waited at every gate; they"
Ezr 2:42 children of the *p'*: the children of "
70 people, and the singers, and the *p'*, "
7: 7 Levites, and the singers, and the *p'*,"
24 priests and Levites, singers, *p'*, 8652
10:24 and of the *p'*; Shallum, and 7778
Ne 7: 1 *p'* and the singers and the Levites "
45 The *p'*: the children of Shallum, "
73 priests, and the Levites, and the *p'*, "
10:28 the priests, the Levites, the *p'*, the "
39 the priests that minister, and the *p'*,"
11:19 Moreover the *p'*, Akkub, Talmon, "
12:25 were *p'* keeping the ward at the "
45 the *p'* kept the ward of their God, "
47 portions of the singers and the *p'*, "
13: 5 Levites, and the singers, and the *p'*;"

portion See also PORTIONS.
Ge 14: 24 the p' of the men which went with 2506
24 and Mamre; let them take their p'. "
31: 14 yet any p' or inheritance for us in "
47: 22 the priests had a p' assigned them 2706
22 did eat their p' which Pharaoh gave "
48: 22 to thee one p' above thy brethren, 7926
Le 6: 17 given it unto them for their p' of 2506
7: 35 This is the p' of the anointing of Aaron, "
Nu 31: 30 thou shalt take one p' of fifty, of the *270
36 p' of them that went out to war, 2506
47 Moses took one p' of fifty, both of * 270
De 21: 17 a double p' of all that he hath: 6310
32: 9 For the Lord's p' is his people; 2506
33: 21 in a p' of the lawgiver, was he 2513
Jos 17: 14 but one lot and one p' to inherit, *2256
19: 9 of the p' of the children of Judah * "
1Sa 1: 5 unto Hannah he gave a worthy p'; 4490
9: 23 Bring the p' which I gave thee, of "
1Ki 12: 16 What p' have we in David? neither 2506
2Ki 2: 9 double p' of thy spirit be upon me. 6310
9: 10 eat Jezebel in the p' of Jezreel, 2506
21 met him in the p' of Naboth the 2513
25 him in the p' of the field of Naboth "
36 In the p' of Jezreel shall dogs eat 2506
37 face of the field in the p' of Jezreel; "
2Ch 10: 16 saying, What p' have we in David? "
28: 21 For Ahaz took away a p' out of the 2505
31: 3 also the king's p' of his substance 4521
4 p' of the priests and the Levites, "
16 his daily p' for their service in *1697
Ezr 4: 16 have no p' on this side the river. 2508
Ne 2: 20 but ye have no p', nor right, nor 2506
11: 23 a certain p' should be for the singers,*
12: 47 and the porters, every day his p': *1697
Job 20: 29 the p' of a wicked man from God, 2506
24: 18 their p' is cursed in the earth: he 2513
26: 14 but how little a p' is heard of him? *1697
27: 13 the p' of a wicked man with God, 2506
31: 2 what p' of God is there from above? "
Ps 11: 6 this shall be the p' of their cup. 4521
16: 5 Lord is the p' of mine inheritance 4490
17: 14 which have their p' in this life, 2506
63: 10 sword: they shall be a p' for foxes. 4521
73: 26 of my heart, and my p' for ever. 2506
119: 57 Thou art my p', O Lord: I have "
142: 5 and my p' in the land of the living. "
Pr 31: 15 and a p' to her maidens. *2706
Ec 2: 10 this was my p' of all my labour. 2506
21 therein shall he leave it for his p'. "
3: 22 in his own works; for that is his p': "
5: 18 God giveth him: for it is his p'. "
19 to eat thereof, and to take his p', "
9: 6 neither have they any more a p' "
9 for that is thy p' in this life, and in "
11: 2 Give a p' to seven, and also to eight; "
Isa 17: 14 This is the p' of them that spoil us, "
53: 12 I divide him a p' with the great, "
57: 6 stones of the stream is thy p'; 2506
61: 7 they shall rejoice in their p': "
Jer 10: 16 p' of Jacob is not like them: for he "
12: 10 have trodden my p' under foot, 2513
10 pleasant p' a desolate wilderness. "
13: 25 the p' of thy measures from me, 4490
51: 19 The p' of Jacob is not like them; 2506
52: 34 day a p' until the day of his death, 1697
La 3: 24 The Lord is my p', saith my soul; 2506
Eze 45: 1 unto the Lord, an holy p' of the land: "
4 The holy p' of the land shall be for "
6 against the oblation of the holy p': "
7 And a p' shall be for the prince on the* "
7 other side of the oblation of the holy p',* "
7 before the oblation of the holy p', and* "
48: 1 are his sides east and west, a p' for Dan: "
2 side unto the west side, a p' for Asher. "
3 unto the west side, a p' for Naphtali. "
4 unto the west side, a p' for Manasseh. "
5 unto the west side, a p' for Ephraim. "
6 unto the west side, a p' for Reuben. "
7 unto the west side, a p' for Judah. "
18 against the oblation of the holy p'* "
18 against the oblation of the holy p';* "
23 west side, Benjamin shall have a p'. "
24 the west side, Simeon shall have a p'. "
25 side unto the west side, Issachar a p'. "
26 side unto the west side, Zebulun a p'. "
27 east side unto the west side, Gad a p'. "
Da 1: 8 with the p' of the king's meat, nor *6598
13 eat of the p' of the king's meat: * "
15 did eat the p' of the king's meat. * "
16 took away the p' of their meat, and* "
4: 15 let his p' be with the beasts in the 2508
23 let his p' be with the beasts of the "
11: 26 they that feed of the p' of his meat *6598
Mic 2: 4 hath changed the p' of my people: 2506
Hab 1: 16 by them their p' is fat, and their "
Zec 2: 12 Lord shall inherit Judah his p' in "
M't 24: 51 him his p' with the hypocrites: *3313*
Lu 12: 42 their p' of meat in due season? *4620*
46 him his p' with the unbelievers. *3313*
15: 12 give me the p' of goods that falleth "

portions
De 18: 8 shall have like p' to eat, besides 2506
Jos 17: 5 fell ten p' to Manasseh, besides *2256
1Sa 1: 4 her sons and her daughters, p': 4490
2Ch 31: 19 give p' to all the males among the "
Ne 8: 10 and send p' unto them for whom "
12 and to send p', and to make great "
12: 44 p' of the law for the priests and 4521
47 gave the p' of the singers and the "
13: 10 the p' of the Levites had not been "
Es 9: 19 and of sending p' one to another. 4490
22 and of sending p' one to another, "
Eze 45: 7 shall be over against one of the p', 2506
47: 13 Israel: Joseph shall have two p'. 2256

Eze 48: 21 over against the p' for the prince: 2506
29 these are their p', saith the Lord 4256
Ho 5: 7 month devour them with their p'. *2506

portray See POURTRAY.

possess See also DISPOSSESS; POSSESSED; POSSESSEST; POSSESSETH; POSSESSING.
Ge 22: 17 shall p' the gate of his enemies; 3423
24: 60 let thy seed p' the gate of those "
Le 20: 24 give it unto you to p' it, a land that "
Nu 13: 30 Let us go up at once, and p' it; "
14: 24 he went; and his seed shall p' it. "
27: 11 of his family, and he shall p' it: "
33: 53 I have given you the land to p' it. "
De 1: 8 p' the land which the Lord sware "
21 go up and p' it, as the Lord God of* "
39 will I give it, and they shall p' it. "
2: 24 begin to p' it, and contend with "
31 begin to p', that thou mayest "
3: 18 hath given you this land to p' it: "
20 until they also p' the land which "
4: 1 go in and p' the land which the "
5 in the land whither ye go to p' it. "
14 the land whither ye go over to p' it. "
22 shall go over, and p' that good land. "
26 ye go over Jordan to p' it; ye shall "
5: 31 the land which I give them to p' it. "
33 days in the land which ye shall p'. "
6: 1 in the land whither ye go to p' it: "
18 mayest go in and p' the good land "
7: 1 the land whither thou goest to p' it, "
8: 1 and go in and p' the land which the "
9: 1 p' nations greater and mightier ‡ "
4 hath brought me in to p' this land: "
5 heart, dost thou go to p' their land: "
6 land to p' it for thy righteousness; "
23 and p' the land which I have given "
10: 11 they may go in and p' the land, "
11: 8 be strong, and go in and p' the land, "
8 the land, whither ye go to p' it; "
10 whither thou goest in to p' it, is "
11 the land, whither ye go to p' it, is a "
23 p' greater nations and mightier "
29 the land whither thou goest to p' it, "
31 over Jordan to go in to p' the land "
31 you, and ye shall p' it, and dwell "
12: 1 of thy fathers giveth thee to p' it, "
2 nations which ye shall p' served * "
29 whither thou goest to p' them, and* "
15: 4 thee for an inheritance to p' it: "
17: 14 shalt p' it, and shalt dwell therein, "
18: 14 these nations, which thou shalt p',* "
19: 2, 14 Lord thy God giveth thee to p' it. "
21: 1 Lord thy God giveth thee to p' it, "
23: 20 land whither thou goest to p' it. "
25: 19 giveth thee an inheritance to p' it, "
28: 21 land, whither thou goest to p' it. "
63 land whither thou goest to p' it. "
30: 5 possessed, and thou shalt p' it; "
16 land whither thou goest to p' it. "
18 passest over Jordan to go to p' it. "
31: 3 before thee, and thou shalt p' them:* "
13 whither ye go over Jordan to p' it. "
32: 47 whither ye go over Jordan to p' it. "
33: 23 p' thou the west and the south. "
Jos 1: 11 this Jordan, to go in to p' the land, "
11 Lord your God giveth you to p' it. "
18: 3 long are ye slack to go to p' the land, "
23: 5 ye shall p' their land, as the Lord "
24: 4 gave unto Esau mount Seir, to p' it; "
8 hand, that ye might p' their land; * "
J'g 2: 6 unto his inheritance to p' the land. "
11: 23 Israel, and shouldest thou p' it? "
24 Wilt not thou p' that which "
24 Chemosh thy god giveth thee to p'? "
24 out from before us, them will we p'. "
18: 9 to go, and to enter to p' the land. "
1Ki 21: 18 whither he is gone down to p' it. * "
1Ch 28: 8 that ye may p' this good land, and "
Ezr 9: 11 The land, unto which ye go to p' it, "
Neh 9: 15 they should go in to p' the land "
23 that they should go in to p' it. "
Job 7: 3 I made to p' months of vanity, 5157
13: 26 to p' the iniquities of my youth. *3423
Isa 14: 2 house of Israel shall p' them in 5157
21 do not rise, nor p' the land, nor 3423
34: 11 and the bittern shall p' it; the owl "
17 they shall p' it forever, from "
57: 13 his trust in me shall p' the land, 5157
61: 7 their land they shall p'...double: 3423
Jer 30: 3 their fathers, and they shall p' it. "
Eze 7: 24 and they shall p' their houses; "
33: 25 blood: and shall ye p' the land? "
26 wife: and shall ye p' the land? "
35: 10 shall be mine, and we will p' it; "
36: 12 and they shall p' thee, and thou "
Da 7: 18 p' the kingdom for ever, even for 2631
Ho 9: 6 their silver, nettles shall p' them: 3423
Am 2: 10 to p' the land of the Amorite. "
9: 12 they may p' the remnant of Edom, "
Ob 17 of Jacob shall p' their possessions. "
19 south shall p' the mount of Esau; "
19 they shall p' the fields of Ephraim, "
19 and Benjamin shall p' Gilead. "
20 shall p' that of the Canaanites, "
20 shall p' the cities of the south. 423
Hab 1: 6 p' the dwellingplaces that are not "
Zep 2: 9 remnant of my people shall p' *5157
Zec 8: 12 this people to p' all these things. * "
Lu 18: 12 I give tithes of all that I p'. *2932*
21: 19 In your patience p' ye your souls.* "
1Th 4: 4 p' his vessel in sanctification and "

possessed See also DISPOSSESSED.
Nu 21: 24 and p' his land from Arnon unto 3423
35 them alive: and they p' his land. "

De 3: 12 this land which we p' at that time, *3423
4: 47 they p' his land, and the land of Og* "
30: 5 the land which thy fathers p', "
Jos 1: 15 they also have p' the land which "
12: 1 p' their land on the other side "
13: 1 yet very much land to be p'. "
19: 47 the edge of the sword, and p' it, "
21: 43 and they p' it, and dwelt therein. "
22: 9 possession, whereof they were p', 270
J'g 3: 13 and p' the city of palm trees. 3423
11: 21 p' all the land of the Amorites, "
22 p' all the coasts of the Amorites, "
2Ki 17: 24 p' Samaria, and dwelt in the cities "
Neh 9: 22 so they p' the land of Sihon, and "
24 children went in and p' the land, "
25 p' houses full of all goods, wells "
Ps 139: 13 For thou hast p' my reins: thou ‡7069
Pr 8: 22 Lord p' me in the beginning of "
Isa 63: 18 people of thy holiness have p' it 3423
Jer 32: 15 shall be p' again in this land. *7069
23 And they came in, and p' it; but 3423
Da 7: 22 that the saints p' the kingdom. 2631
M't 4: 24 those which were p' with devils, *1139*
8: 16 many that were p' with devils: "
28 there met him two p' with devils, "
33 befallen to the p' of the devils. "
9: 32 him a dumb man p' with a devil. "
12: 22 one p' with a devil, blind, and "
M'r 1: 32 and them that were p' with devils. "
5: 15 see him that was p' with the devil, "
16 to him that was p' with the devil, "
18 had been p' with the devil prayed "
Lu 8: 36 was p' of the devils was healed. "
Ac 4: 32 aught of the things which he p' *5224*
8: 7 of many that were p' with them: *2192*
16: 16 damsel p' with a spirit of divination* "
1Co 7: 30 that buy, as though they p' not; *2722*

possessest
De 26: 1 and p' it, and dwellest therein; 3423

possesseth
Nu 36: 8 daughter, that p' an inheritance 3423
Lu 12: 15 abundance of...things which he p'. *5224*

possessing
2Co 6: 10 nothing, and yet p' all things. *2722*

possession See also POSSESSIONS.
Ge 17: 8 Canaan, for an everlasting p'; 272
23: 4 me a p' of a buryingplace with you, "
9 p' of a buryingplace amongst you. "
18 Unto Abraham for a p' in the 4736
20 Abraham for a p' of a buryingplace 272
26: 14 had p' of flocks, and p' of herds, *4735
36: 43 habitations in the land of their p': 272
47: 11 them a p' in the land of Egypt, "
48: 4 seed after thee for an everlasting p'. "
49: 30 Hittite for a p' of a buryingplace. "
50: 13 the field for a p' of a buryingplace "
Le 14: 34 Canaan, which I give to you for a p', "
34 in a house of the land of your p'; "
25: 10 shall return every man unto his p', "
13 shall return every man unto his p'. "
24 all the land of your p' ye shall grant "
25 and hath sold away some of his p', "
27 it; that he may return unto his p'. "
28 and he shall return unto his p'. "
32 the houses of the cities of their p', "
33 the city of his p', shall go out in the "
33 p' among the children of Israel. "
34 be sold; for it is their perpetual p'. "
41 unto the p' of his fathers shall he "
45 your land: and they shall be your p'. "
46 after you, to inherit them for a p'; "
27: 16 some part of a field of his p', then "
21 the p' thereof shall be the priest's. "
22 which is not of the fields of his p'; "
24 whom the p' of the land did belong. "
28 his p' shall be sold or redeemed: "
Nu 24: 18 And Edom shall be a p', Seir also 3424
18 Seir also shall be a p' for his "
26: 56 According to the lot shall the p' *5159
27: 4 Give unto us therefore a p' among 272
7 shalt surely give them a p' of an "
32: 5 be given unto thy servants for a p', "
22 shall be your p' before the Lord. "
29 them the land of Gilead for a p': "
32 p' of our inheritance on this side "
35: 2 the inheritance of their p' cities to * "
8 of the p' of the children of Israel: "
28 shall return into the land of his p'. "
De 2: 5 mount Seir unto Esau for a p'. 3425
9 not give thee of their land for a p'; "
9 unto the children of Lot for a p'. "
12 land of his p', which the Lord gave "
19 of the children of Ammon any p'; "
19 it unto the children of Lot for a p'. "
3: 20 ye return every man unto his p', "
11: 6 the substance that was in their p', *7272
32: 49 unto the children of Israel for a p': 272
Jos 1: 15 return unto the land of your p', 3425
12: 6 gave it for a p' unto the Reubenites, "
7 for a p' according to their divisions; "
13: 29 this was the p' of the half tribe of * "
21: 12 the son of Jephunneh for his p'. 272
41 the p' of the children of Israel were "
22: 4 unto the land of your p', which "
7 Moses had given p' in Bashan: "
9 to the land of their p', whereof they 272
19 if the land of your p' be unclean, "
19 unto the land of the p' of the Lord, "
19 dwelleth, and take p' among us: 270
1Ki 21: 15 p' of the vineyard of Naboth the 3423
16 the Jezreelite, to take p' of it. "
19 Hast thou killed, and also taken p'? "
1Ch 28: 1 p' of the king, and of his sons, *4735

2Ch 11:14 left their suburbs and their p', 272
20:11 to come to cast us out of thy p', 3425
31: 1 every man to his p', into their 272
Ne 11: 3 every one in his p' in their cities, "
Ps 2: 8 parts of the earth for thy p'. "
44: 3 got not the land in p' by their own3423
69:35 may dwell there, and have it in p'. "
83:12 ourselves the houses of God in p'. "
Pr 28:10 shall have good things in p'. *5157
Isa 14:23 also make it a p' for the bittern, 4180
Eze 11:15 unto us is this land given in p'. 4181
25: 4 to the men of the east for a p', "
10 and will give them in p', that the "
36: 2 ancient high places are ours in p': "
3 might be a p' unto the residue of "
5 appointed my land into their p' "
44:28 them no p' in Israel: I am their p'. 272
45: 5 for a p' for twenty chambers. "
6 ye shall appoint the p' of the city "
7 and of the p' of the city, before the "
7 before the p' of the city, from the "
8 In the land shall be his p' in Israel: "
46:16 it shall be their p' by inheritance. "
18 to thrust them out of their p'; but "
18 sons inheritance out of his own p': "
18 not scattered every man from his p'. "
48:20 foursquare, with the p' of the city. "
21 and of the p' of the city, over "
22 Moreover, from the p' of the Levites, "
22 Levites, and from the p' of the city, "
Ac 5: 1 with Sapphira his wife, sold a p', 2933
7: 5 he would give it to him for a p', 2697
45 Jesus into the p' of the Gentiles, "
Eph 1:14 redemption of the purchased p', 4047

possessions
Ge 34:10 therein, and get you p' therein. 270
47:27 and they had p' therein, and grew, "
Nu 32:30 have p' among you in the land "
1Sa 25: 2 Maon, whose p' were in Carmel; 4639
1Ch 7:28 And their p' and habitations were, 272
9: 2 that dwelt in their p' in their cities "
2Ch 32:29 cities, and p' of flocks and herds in4735
Ec 2: 7 great p' of great and small cattle "
Ob 17 of Jacob shall possess their p'. 4180
M't 19:22 sorrowful: for he had great p'. 2933
M'r 10:22 grieved: for he had great p'. "
Ac 2:45 And sold their p' and goods, and "
28: 7 quarters were p' of the chief man *5564

possessor See also POSSESSORS.
Ge 14:19 high God, p' of heaven and earth: 7069
22 God, the p' of heaven and earth, "

possessors
Zec 11: 5 Whose p' slay them, and hold 7069
Ac 4:34 p' of lands or houses sold them, 2935

possible See also IMPOSSIBLE.
M't 19:26 but with God all things are p'. 1415
24:24 if it were p', they shall deceive "
26:39 if it be p', let this cup pass from me: "
M'r 9:23 things are p' to him that believeth. "
10:27 God: for with God all things are p'. "
13:22 seduce, if it were p', even the elect. "
14:35 if it were p', the hour might pass "
36 Father, all things are p' unto thee; "
Lu 18:27 impossible with men are p' with God. "
Ac 2:24 not p' that he should be holden of it. "
20:16 it were p' for him, to be at Jerusalem "
27:39 if it were p', to thrust in the ship. *1410
Ro 12:18 If it be p', as much as lieth in you, 1415
Ga 4:15 if it had been p', ye would have "
Heb 10: 4 it is not p' that the blood of bulls * 102

post See also POSTS.
Ex 12: 7 on the upper door p' of the houses,*4947
21: 6 to the door, or unto the door p'; 4201
1Sa 1: 9 upon a seat by a p' of the temple "
Job 9:25 Now my days are swifter than a p':7323
Jer 51:31 One p' shall run to meet another, "
Eze 40:14 the p' of the court round about the 352
16 and upon each p' were palm trees. "
48 and measured each p' of the porch, "
41: 3 and measured the p' of the door, two "
43: 8 their p' by my posts, and the wall 4201
46: 2 and shall stand by the p' of the gate, "

posterity
Ge 45: 7 to preserve you a p' in the earth, *7611
Nu 9:10 you or of your p' shall be unclean*1755
1Ki 16: 3 I will take away the p' of Baasha,* 310
3 and the p' of his house; and will * "
21:21 will take away thy p', and will cut* "
Ps 49:13 yet their p' approve their sayings.* "
109:13 Let his p' be cut off; and in the 319
Da 11: 4 and not to his p', nor according to "
Am 4: 2 hooks, and your p' with fishhooks.* "

posts
Ex 12: 7 and strike it on the two side p' 4201
22 and the two side p' with the blood "
23 the lintel, and on the two side p', "
De 6: 9 write them upon the p' of thy house, "
11:20 write them upon the door p' of "
J'g 16: 3 gate of the city, and the two p', "
1Ki 6:31 lintel and side p' were a fifth part "
33 for the door of the temple p' of olive "
7: 5 all the doors and p' were square, "
2Ch 3: 7 beams, the p', and...walls thereof, *5592
30: 6 p' went with the letters from the 7323
10 the p' passed from city to city "
Es 3:13 the letters were sent by p' into all "
15 The p' went out, being hastened by "
8:10 and sent letters by p' on horseback, "
14 So the p' that rode upon mules and "
Pr 8:34 waiting at the p' of my doors. 4201
Isa 6: 4 the p' of the door moved at the * 520
57: 8 Behind the doors also and the p' 4201

Eze 40: 9 and the p' thereof, two cubits; and 352
10 p' had one measure on this side and "
14 made also p' of threescore cubits, "
16 p' within the gate round about, "
21 the p' thereof and the arches thereof "
24 he measured the p' thereof and the "
26 on that side, upon the p' thereof. "
29 chambers thereof, and the p' thereof, "
31 palm trees were upon the p' thereof: "
33 chambers thereof, and the p' thereof, "
34 palm trees were upon the p' thereof, "
36 chambers thereof, the p' thereof, "
37 p' thereof were toward the utter "
37 palm trees were upon the p' thereof, "
38 thereof were by the p' of the gates, "
49 there were pillars by the p', one on "
41: 1 measured the p', six cubits broad on "
16 door p', and the narrow windows,*5592
21 The p' of the temple were squared,4201
43: 8 their post by my p', and the wall* "
45:19 and put it upon the p' of the house, "
19 upon the p' of the gate of the inner "
Am 9: 1 the door, that the p' may shake: *5592

pot See also POTS; POTSHERD; WASHPOT; WATERPOT.
Ex 16:33 Take a p', and put an omer full of6803
Le 6:28 if it be sodden in a brasen p', it *3627
J'g 6:19 and he put the broth in a p', and 6517
1Sa 2:14 pan, or kettle, or caldron, or p'; "
2Ki 4: 2 thing in the house, save a p' of oil. 610
38 his servant, Set on the great p', 5518
39 shred them into the p' of pottage: "
40 man of God, there is death in the p'. "
41 meal. And he cast it into the p'; "
41 And there was no harm in the p'. "
Job 41:20 as out of a seething p' or caldron. 1731
31 maketh the deep to boil like a p': 5518
31 the sea like a p' of ointment. *
Pr 17: 3 The fining p' is for silver, and the 4715
27:21 As the fining p' for silver, and the "
Ec 7: 6 the crackling of thorns under a p', 5518
Jer 1:13 I said, I see a seething p'; and the* "
Eze 24: 3 Set on a p', set it on, and also * "
6 to the p' whose scum is therein, "
Mic 3: 3 chop them in pieces, as for the p', "
Zec 14:21 every p' in Jerusalem and in Judah "
Heb 9: 4 was the golden p' that had manna,4713

potent See IMPOTENT.

potentate
1Ti 6:15 who is the blessed and only P', the1413

Poti See POTI-PHERAH.

Potiphar (*pot'i-far*)
Ge 37:36 sold him into Egypt unto P', an 6318
39: 1 P', an officer of Pharaoh, captain "

Poti-pherah (*po-tif'e-rah*)
Ge 41:45 the daughter of P' priest of On. *6319
50 the daughter of P' priest of On bare*"
46:20 the daughter of P' priest of On bare*"

pots See also WATERPOTS.
Ex 16: 3 when we sat by the flesh p', and 5518
38: 3 p', and the shovels, and the basons, "
Le 11:35 whether it be oven, or ranges for p', "
1Ki 7:45 the p', and the shovels, and the 5518
2Ki 25:14 the p', and the shovels, and the "
2Ch 4:11 And Huram made the p', and the "
16 The p' also, and the shovels, and the "
35:13 other holy offerings sod they in p', "
Ps 58: 9 Before your p' can feel the thorns, "
68:13 Though ye have lien among the p',*8240
81: 6 hands were delivered from the p'.*1731
Jer 35: 5 of the Rechabites p' full of wine, *1375
Zec 14:20 p' in the Lord's house shall be like5518
M'r 7: 4 p', brasen vessels, and of tables. 3582
8 men, as the washing of p' and cups:*"

potsherd See also POTSHERDS.
Job 2: 8 he took him a p' to scrape himself 2789
Ps 22:15 My strength is dried up like a p'; "
Pr 26:23 and a wicked heart are like a p' * "
Isa 45: 9 Let the p' strive with the potsherds "

potsherds
Isa 45: 9 Let the potsherd strive with the p' 2789

pottage
Ge 25:29 And Jacob sod p': and Esau came 5138
25:30 I pray thee, with that same red p'; "
34 gave Esau bread and p' of lentiles;5138
2Ki 4:38 and seethe p' for the sons of the "
39 and shred them into the pot of p': "
40 pass, as they were eating of the p', "
Hag 2:12 with his skirt do touch bread, or p'," "

potter See also POTTER'S; POTTERS.
Isa 41:25 morter, and as the p' treadeth clay.3335
64: 8 we are the clay, and thou our p'; "
Jer 18: 4 was marred in the hand of the p': "
4 as seemed good to the p' to make it. "
6 cannot I do with you as this p'? "
La 4: 2 the work of the hands of the p'! "
Zec 11:13 said unto me, Cast it unto the p': "
13 cast them to the p' in the house of "
Ro 9:21 not the p' power over the clay, 2763
Re 2:27 as the vessels of a p' shall they be 2764

potter's
Ps 2: 9 them in pieces like a p' vessel. 3335
Isa 29:16 shall be esteemed as the p' clay: * "
Jer 18: 2 Arise, and go down to the p' house, "
3 I went down to the p' house, and, "
6 Behold, as the clay is in the p' hand, "
19: 1 Go and get a p' earthen bottle, and "
11 city, as one breaketh a p' vessel, "

Da 2:41 part of p' clay, and part of iron, 3353
M't 27: 7 bought with them the p' field, to 2763
10 And gave them for the p' field, as "

potters See also POTTERS'.
1Ch 4:23 These were the p', and those that 3335

potters'
Isa 30:14 p' vessel that is broken in pieces;*3335

pound See also POUNDS.
1Ki 10:17 three p' of gold went to one shield:‡4488
Ezr 2:69 five thousand p' of silver, and one "
Ne 7:71 and two hundred p' of silver. "
72 gold, and two thousand p' of silver, "
Lu 19:16 thy p' hath gained ten pounds. 3414
18 thy p' hath gained five pounds. "
20 here is thy p', which I have kept "
24 Take from him the p', and give it to "
Joh 12: 3 a p' of ointment of spikenard, 3046
19:39 aloes, about a hundred p' weight. "

pounds
Lu 19:13 servants, and delivered them ten p',3414
16 Lord, thy pound hath gained ten p'. "
18 Lord, thy pound hath gained five p'. "
24 and give it to him that hath ten p'. "
25 said unto him, Lord, he hath ten p'. "

pour See also POURED; POURETH; POURING.
Ex 4: 9 river, and p' it upon the dry land: 8210
29: 7 and p' it upon his head, and anoint3332
12 p' all the blood beside the bottom 8210
30: 9 shall ye p' drink offering thereon. 5258
Le 2: 1 and he shall p' oil upon it, and put3332
6 part it in pieces, and p' oil thereon: "
4: 7 shall p' all the blood of the bullock8210
18 p' out all the blood at the bottom "
25 shall p' out his blood at the bottom "
30 p' out all the blood thereof at the "
34 shall p' out all the blood thereof at "
14:15 p' it into the palm of his own left 3332
18 he shall p' upon the head of him *5414
26 priest shall p' of the oil into the 3332
41 they shall p' out the dust that they8210
17:13 shall even p' out the blood thereof, "
Nu 5:15 he shall p' no oil upon it, nor put 3332
24: 7 p' the water out of his buckets, *5140
De 12:16 shall p' it upon the earth as water.8210
24 shalt p' it upon the earth as water. "
15:23 shalt p' it upon the ground as water. "
J'g 6:20 this rock, and p' out the broth. "
1Ki 18:33 and p' it on the burnt sacrifice, 3332
2Ki 4: 4 p' out into all those vessels, and "
41 P' out for the people, that they may "
9: 3 the box of oil, and p' it on his head, "
Job 36:27 they p' down rain according to the*2212
Ps 42: 4 things, I p' out my soul in me: 8210
62: 8 p' out your heart before him: God "
69:24 P' out thine indignation upon them, "
79: 6 P' out thy wrath upon the heathen "
Pr 1:23 I will p' out my spirit unto you, I 5042
Isa 44: 3 p' water upon him that is thirsty, 3332
3 I will p' my spirit upon thy seed, "
45: 8 the skies p' down righteousness: 5140
Jer 6:11 p' it out upon the children abroad,8210
7:18 to p' out drink offerings unto other5258
10:25 P' out thy fury upon the heathen 8210
14:16 will p' their wickedness upon them. "
18:21 p' out their blood by the force of *5064
44:17,18,19,25 p' out drink offerings unto5258
La 2:19 p' out thine heart like water 8210
Eze 7: 8 I shortly p' out my fury upon thee, "
14:19 and p' out my fury upon it in blood, "
20: 8 I will p' out my fury upon them, "
13 p' out my fury upon them in the "
21 I would p' out my fury upon them, "
21:31 p' out mine indignation upon thee, "
24: 3 set it on, and also p' water into it: 3332
30:15 And I will p' my fury upon Sin, the8210
Ho 5:10 p' out my wrath upon them like "
Joe 2:28 will p' out my spirit upon all flesh; "
29 those days will I p' out my spirit. "
Mic 1: 6 I will p' down the stones thereof 5064
Zep 3: 8 to p' upon them mine indignation,8210
Zec 12:10 I will p' upon the house of David, "
Mal 3:10 heaven, and p' you out a blessing, 7324
Ac 2:17 p' out of my Spirit upon all flesh: 1632
18 p' out in those days of my Spirit; "
Re 16: 1 p' out the vials of the wrath of God "

poured See also POUREDST.
Ge 28:18 pillar, and p' oil upon the top of it.3332
35:14 and he p' a drink offering thereon,5258
14 and he p' oil thereon. 3332
Ex 9:33 the rain was not p' upon the earth.5413
30:32 Upon man's flesh shall it not be p',3251
Le 4:12 place, where the ashes are p' out, 8211
12 where the ashes are p' out shall he "
8:12 And he p' of the anointing oil upon3332
15 p' the blood at the bottom of the "
9: 9 p' out the blood at the bottom of "
21:10 whose head the anointing oil was p'," "
Nu 28: 7 cause the strong wine to be p' *5258
De 12:27 p' out upon the altar of the Lord 8210
1Sa 1:15 p' out my soul before the Lord. "
7: 6 water, and p' it out before the Lord, "
10: 1 vial of oil, and p' it upon his head,3332
2Sa 13: 9 a pan, and p' them out before him; "
23:16 thereof, but p' it out unto the Lord.5258
1Ki 13: 3 that are upon it shall be p' out. 8210
5 and the ashes p' out from the altar, "
2Ki 3:11 p' water on the hands of Elijah. 3332
4: 5 the vessels to her; and she p' out. "
40 So they p' out for the men to eat. "
9: 6 he p' the oil on his head, and said "
16:13 p' his drink offering, and sprinkled5258
1Ch 11:18 drink of it, but p' it out to the Lord. "

2Ch 12: 7 my wrath shall not be p' out upon 5413
34:21 wrath of the Lord that is p' out upon "
25 my wrath shall be p' out upon this "
Job 3:24 roarings are p' out like the waters. "
10:10 Hast thou not p' me out as milk, "
29: 6 the rock p' me out rivers of oil; 6694
30:16 now my soul is p' out upon me; 8210
Ps 22:14 I am p' out like water, and all my "
45: 2 grace is p' into thy lips: therefore 3332
77:17 The clouds p' out water: the skies 2229
142: 2 p' out my complaint before him; *8210
Ca 1: 3 thy name is as ointment p' forth, 7324
Isa 26:16 they p' out a prayer when thy 6694
29:10 hath p' out upon you the spirit 5258
32:15 spirit be p' upon us from on high, 6168
42:25 p' upon him the fury of his anger, 8210
53:12 hath p' out his soul unto death: 6168
57: 6 hast thou p' a drink offering, thou 8210
Jer 7:20 my fury shall be p' out upon this 5413
19:13 p' out drink offerings unto other 5258
32:29 p' out drink offerings unto other "
42:18 and my fury hath been p' forth 5413
18 so shall my fury be p' forth upon "
44: 6 fury and mine anger was p' forth, "
19 p' out drink offerings unto her, 5258
La 2: 4 Zion: he p' out his fury like fire. 8210
11 my liver is p' upon the earth, for "
12 p' out into their mothers' bosom. "
4: 1 p' out in the top of every street. "
11 he hath p' out his fierce anger, and "
Eze 16:36 Because thy filthiness was p' out, "
20:28 p' out there their drink offerings. 5258
33 with fury p' out, will I rule over 8210
34 out arm, and with fury p' out. "
22:22 Lord have p' out my fury upon you. "
31 I p' out mine indignation upon "
23: 8 and p' their whoredom upon her. "
24: 7 she p' it not upon the ground, to "
36:18 Wherefore I p' my fury upon them "
39:29 p' out my spirit upon the house "
Da 9:11 therefore the curse is p' upon us, 5413
27 shall be p' upon the desolate. "
Mic 1: 4 waters that are p' down a steep 5064
Na 1: 6 his fury is p' out like fire, and the 5413
Zep 1:17 blood shall be p' out as dust, and 8210
M't 26: 7 ointment, and p' it on his head, 2708
12 hath p' this ointment on my body, 906
M'r 14: 3 the box, and p' it on his head. 2708
Joh 2:15 and p' out the changers' money, 1632
Ac 10:45 p' out the gift of the Holy Ghost. 1632
Re 14:10 p' out without mixture into the *2767
16: 2 p' out his vial upon the earth; 1632
3 angel p' out his vial upon the sea; "
4 p' out his vial upon the rivers and "
8 angel p' out his vial upon the sun; "
10 angel p' out his vial upon the seat "
12 p' out his vial upon the great river "
17 angel p' out his vial into the air; "

pouredst
Eze 16:15 p' out thy fornications on every 8210

poureth
Job 12:21 He p' contempt upon princes, and 8210
16:13 p' out my gall upon the ground. "
20 mine eye p' out tears unto God. 1811
Ps 75: 8 p' out of the same: but the dregs 5064
102: title p' out his complaint before the 8210
107:40 He p' contempt upon princes, and "
Pr 15: 2 mouth of fools p' out foolishness. 5042
28 of the wicked p' out evil things. "
Am 5: 8 p' them out upon the face of the 8210
9: 6 p' them out upon the face of the "
Joh 13: 5 After that he p' water into a bason, 906

pouring
Eze 9: 8 p' out of thy fury upon Jerusalem? 8210
Lu 10:34 p' in oil and wine, and set him on his

pourtray See also POURTRAYED.
Eze 4: 1 and p' it upon the city, even 2710

pourtrayed
Eze 8:10 p' upon the wall round about. 2707
23:14 she saw men p' upon the wall, "
14 the Chaldeans p' with vermilion, 2710

poverty
Ge 45:11 and all that thou hast, come to p'. 3423
Pr 6:11 thy p' come as one that travelleth, 7389
10:15 destruction of the poor is their p'. "
11:24 than is meet, but it tendeth to p'. *4270
13:18 P' and shame shall be to him that 7389
20:13 not sleep, lest thou come to p'; 3423
23:21 and the glutton shall come to p': "
24:34 thy p' come as one that travelleth; 7389
28:19 vain persons shall have p' enough. "
22 not that p' shall come upon him. *2639
30: 8 give me neither p' nor riches; 7389
31: 7 Let him drink, and forget his p', "
2Co 8: 2 deep p' abounded unto the riches 4432
9 ye through his p' might be rich. "
Re 2: 9 thy works, and tribulation, and p', "

powder See also POWDERS.
Ex 32:20 it in the fire, and ground it to p', 1854
De 28:24 the rain of thy land p' and dust: 80
2Ki 23: 6 and stamped it small to p', and 6083
6 the p' thereof upon the graves of "
15 stamped it small to p', and burned 1854
2Ch 34: 7 beaten the graven images into p', 1854
M't 21:44 shall fall, it will grind him to p'. *3039
Lu 20:18 shall fall, it will grind him to p'. * "

powders
Ca 3: 6 with all p' of the merchant? 81

power See also POWERFUL; POWERS.
Ge 31: 6 with all my p' I have served your 3581
29 the p' of my hand to do you hurt: 410
32:28 prince hast p' with God and with *8280
49: 3 dignity, and the excellency of p': 5794
Ex 9:16 up, for to shew in thee my p'; 3581
15: 6 O Lord, is become glorious in p': "
21: 8 strange nation he shall have no p', 4910
32:11 the land of Egypt with great p', 3581
Le 26:19 will break the pride of your p'; 5797
37 p' to stand before your enemies. 8617
Nu 14:17 let the p' of my lord be great, 3581
22:38 now any p' at all to say any thing? 3201
De 4:37 with his mighty p' out of Egypt; 3581
8:17 My p' and the might of mine hand "
18 that giveth thee p' to get wealth, "
9:29 broughtest out by thy mighty p' "
32:36 he seeth that their p' is gone, and 3027
Jos 8:20 p' to flee this way or that way: "
17:17 a great people, and hast great p': 3581
1Sa 9: 1 a Benjamite, a mighty man of p'. *2428
30: 4 until they had no more p' to weep. 3581
2Sa 22:33 God is my strength and p': and *2428
2Ki 17:36 the land of Egypt with great p' 3581
19:26 their inhabitants were of small p', 3027
1Ch 20: 1 Joab led forth the p' of the army, 2428
29:11 and the p', and the glory, and the 1369
12 in thine hand is p' and might; 3581
2Ch 14:11 or with them that have no p': * "
20: 6 in thine hand is there not p' and "
22: 9 no p' to keep still the kingdom. "
25: 8 God hath p' to help, and to cast "
26:13 that made war with mighty p', to "
32: 9 Lachish, and all his p' with him,) 4475
Ezr 4:23 them to cease by force and p'. 2429
8:22 his p' and his wrath is against all 5797
Ne 1:10 hast redeemed by thy great p', 3581
5: 5 is it in our p' to redeem them; 3027
Es 1: 3 p' of Persia and Media, the nobles 2428
8:11 p' of the people and province that "
9: 1 Jews hoped to have p' over them, *7980
10: 2 the acts of his p' and of his might, 8633
Job 1:12 all that he hath is in thy p'; only 3027
5:20 in war from the p' of the sword. "
21: 7 old, yea, are mighty in p'? 2428
23: 6 against me with his great p'? 3581
24:22 draweth also the mighty with his p': "
26: 2 thou helped him that is without p'? "
12 He divideth the sea with his p', "
14 but the thunder of his p' who can 1369
36:22 Behold, God exalteth by his p': 3581
37:23 he is excellent in p', and in "
41:12 not conceal his parts, nor his p', *1369
Ps 21:13 so will we sing and praise thy p'. "
22:20 my darling from the p' of the dog. 3027
37:35 I have seen the wicked in great p', 6184
49:15 my soul from the p' of the grave: 3027
59:11 scatter them by thy p'; and bring 2428
16 But I will sing of thy p'; yea, I *5797
62:11 this; that p' belongeth unto God. "
63: 2 To see thy p' and thy glory, so as I "
65: 6 mountains; being girded with p': *1369
66: 3 through the greatness of thy p' 5797
7 He ruleth by his p' for ever; his 1369
68:35 giveth strength and p' unto his 8592
71:18 thy p' to every one that is to come. *1369
78:26 by his p' he brought in the south 5797
79:11 according to the greatness of thy p' 2220
90:11 knoweth the p' of thine anger? 5797
106: 8 make his mighty p' to be known. 1369
110: 3 shall be willing in the day of thy p', 2428
111: 6 his people the p' of his works, 3581
145:11 thy kingdom, and talk of thy p'; 1369
147: 5 Great is our Lord, and of great p': 3581
150: 1 him in the firmament of his p'. 5797
Pr 3:27 it is in the p' of thine hand to do it. 410
18:21 and life are in the p' of the tongue: 3027
Ec 4: 1 of their oppressors there was p'; 3581
5:19 hath given him p' to eat thereof, 7980
6: 2 God giveth him not p' to eat thereof, "
8: 4 the word of a king is, there is p': 7983
8 no man that hath p' over the spirit 7989
8 hath he p' in the day of death: 7983
Isa 37:27 their inhabitants were of small p', 3027
40:26 might, for that he is strong in p'; 3581
29 He giveth p' to the faint; and to "
43:17 and horse, the army and the p'; 5808
47:14 deliver...from the p' of the flame: 3027
50: 2 redeem? or have I no p' to deliver? 3581
Jer 10:12 He hath made the earth by his p', "
27: 5 my great p' and by my outstretched "
32:17 by thy great p' and stretched out "
51:15 He hath made the earth by his p', "
Eze 17: 9 without great p' or many people ‡2220
22: 6 in thee to their p' to shed blood. * "
30: 6 pride of her p' shall come down: 5797
Da 2:37 given thee a kingdom, p', and 2632
3:27 whose bodies the fire had no p', 7981
4:30 kingdom by the might of my p', 2632
6:27 Daniel from the p' of the lions. 3028
8: 6 ran unto him in the fury of his p'. 3581
7 there was no p' in the ram to stand "
22 out of the nation, but not in his p'. "
24 And his p' shall be mighty, but not "
24 be mighty, but not by his own p': "
11: 6 shall not retain the p' of the arm;* "
25 shall stir up his p' and his courage "
43 have p' over the treasures of gold 4910
12: 7 to scatter the p' of the holy people, 3027
Ho 12: 3 his strength he had p' with God: 8280
4 Yea, he had p' over the angel, and 7786
13:14 ransom...from the p' of the grave; 3027
Mic 2: 1 because it is in the p' of their hand. 410
3: 8 I am full of p' by the spirit of the 3581
Na 1: 3 is slow to anger, and great in p', "
2: 1 loins, strong, fortify thy p' mightily. "
Hab 1:11 imputing this his p' unto his god. * "
2: 9 be delivered from the p' of evil! *3709
3: 4 and there was the hiding of his p'. 5797
Zec 4: 6 Not by might, nor by p', but by my 3581
9: 4 he will smite her p' in the sea; 2428
M't 6:13 kingdom, and the p', and the glory, *1411
9: 6 Son of man hath p' on earth to ‡1849
8 which had given such p' unto men. ‡ "
10: 1 he gave them p' against unclean * "
22:29 the scriptures, nor the p' of God. 1411
24:30 of heaven with p' and great glory. "
26:64 man sitting on the right hand of p', "
28:18 All p' is given unto me in heaven *1849
M'r 2:10 Son of man hath p' on earth to ‡ "
3:15 And to have p' to heal sicknesses,* "
6: 7 gave them p' over unclean spirits;* "
9: 1 the kingdom of God come with p'. 1411
12:24 scriptures, neither the p' of God? "
13:26 the clouds with great p' and glory. "
14:62 man sitting on the right hand of p', "
Lu 1:17 him in the spirit and p' of Elias, to "
35 p' of the Highest shall overshadow "
4: 6 All this p' will I give thee, and the *1849
14 returned in the p' of the Spirit into 1411
32 doctrine: for his word was with p'. *1849
36 authority and p' he commandeth 1411
5:17 p' of the Lord was present to heal "
24 Son of man hath p' upon earth to ‡1849
9: 1 p' and authority over all devils, 1411
43 amazed at the mighty p' of God. *3168
10:19 unto you p' to tread on serpents *1849
19 and over all the p' of the enemy: 1411
12: 5 hath killed hath p' to cast into hell; 1849
20:20 p' and authority of the governor. * 746
21:27 of man coming in a cloud with p' 1411
22:53 your hour, and the p' of darkness. 1849
69 on the right hand of the p' of God. 1411
24:49 be endued with p' from on high. "
Joh 1:12 he p' to become the sons of God, *1849
10:18 I have p' to lay it down, and I "
18 and I have p' to take it again. "
17: 2 hast given him p' over all flesh, * "
19:10 not that I have p' to crucify thee, "
10 thee, and have p' to release thee? "
11 have no p' at all against me, "
Ac 1: 7 the Father hath put in his own p'.* "
8 But ye shall receive p', after that 1411
3:12 by our own p' or holiness we had "
4: 7 By what p', or by what name, have "
33 great p' gave the apostles witness "
5: 4 sold, was it not in thine own p'? 1849
6: 8 Stephen, full of faith and p', did 1411
8:10 This man is the great p' of God. "
19 Saying, Give me also this p', that 1849
10:38 with the Holy Ghost and with p': 1411
26:18 and from the p' of Satan unto God, 1849
Ro 1: 4 to be the Son of God with p', 1411
16 it is the p' of God unto salvation "
20 even his eternal p' and Godhead; "
9:17 that I might shew my p' in thee, "
21 not the potter p' over the clay, *1849
22 wrath, and to make his p' known, 1415
13: 1 For there is no p' but of God: the 1849
2 therefore resisteth the p', "
3 thou then not be afraid of the p'? "
15:13 through the p' of the Holy Ghost. 1411
19 by the p' of the Spirit of God; so "
16:25 to him that is of p' to stablish you *1410
1Co 1:18 which are saved it is the p' of God. 1411
24 Christ the p' of God, and the "
2: 4 demonstration of...Spirit and of p': "
5 of men, but in the p' of God. "
4:19 which are puffed up, but the p'. "
20 of God is not in word, but in p'. "
5: 4 with the p' of our Lord Jesus Christ, "
6:12 not be brought under the p' of any. 1850
14 will also raise up us by his own p'. 1411
7: 4 wife hath not p' of her own body, 1850
4 hath not p' of his own body, but "
37 but hath p' over his own will, and 1849
9: 4 Have we not p' to eat and to drink? "
5 Have we not p' to lead...a sister, * "
6 have not we p' to forbear working?* "
12 be partakers of this p' over you, * "
12 we have not used this p'; but * "
18 I abuse not my p' in the gospel. * "
11:10 the woman to have p' on her head* "
15:24 all rule and all authority and p'. 1411
43 in weakness; it is raised in p': "
2Co 4: 7 excellency of the p' may be of God, "
6: 7 the word of truth, by the p' of God, "
8: 3 For to their p', I bear record, yea, "
3 beyond their p' they were willing "
12: 9 the p' of Christ may rest upon me.* "
13: 4 yet he liveth by the p' of God. "
4 him by the p' of God toward you. "
10 according to the p' which the Lord *1849
Eph 1:19 the exceeding greatness of his p' 1411
19 to the working of his mighty p', *2904
21 all principality, and p', and might, *1849
2: 2 to the prince of the p' of the air, ‡ "
3: 7 by the effectual working of his p'. 1411
20 to the p' that worketh in us, "
6:10 Lord, and in the p' of his might. *2904
Ph'p 3:10 him, and the p' of his resurrection, 1411
Col 1:11 according to his glorious p', unto 2904
13 us from the p' of darkness, and 1849
2:10 the head of all principality and p': "
1Th 1: 5 but also in p', and in the Holy 1411
2Th 1: 9 Lord, and from the glory of his p'; *2479
11 and the work of faith with p': 1411
2: 9 all p' and signs and lying wonders, "
3: 9 Not because we have not p', but to *1849
1Ti 6:16 be honour and p' everlasting. 2904
2Ti 1: 7 of p', and of love, and of a sound 1411
8 gospel according to the p' of God; "
3: 5 but denying the p' thereof: from "
Heb 1: 3 all things by the word of his p', "
2:14 him that had the p' of death, that 2904

Heb 7:16 but after the p' of an endless life. 1411
1Pe 1: 5 kept by the p' of God through faith "
2Pe 1: 3 as his divine p' hath given unto us "
16 you the p' and coming of our Lord "
2:11 are greater in p' and might, bring 2479
Jude 25 and majesty, dominion and p', 1849
Re 2:26 will I give p' over the nations: * "
4:11 to receive glory and honour and p':1411
5:12 Lamb that was slain to receive p', "
13 and honour, and glory, and p', be *2904
6: 4 p' was given to him that sat thereon*
8 p' was given unto them over the *1849
7:12 p', and might, be unto our God 1411
9: 3 and unto them was given p', as 1849
3 the scorpions of the earth have p'. "
10 p' was to hurt men five months. "
19 their p' is in their mouth, and in "
11: 3 I will give p' unto my two witnesses,*
6 have p' to shut heaven, that it 1849
6 have p' over waters to turn them to"
17 hast taken to thee thy great p', 1411
12:10 our God, and the p' of his Christ: *1849
13: 2 the dragon gave him his p', and 1411
4 which gave p' unto the beast: and*1849
5 p' was given unto him to continue* "
7 and p' was given him over all * "
12 he exerciseth all the p' of the first* "
14 miracles which he had p' to do in *1325
15 And he had p' to give life unto the* "
14:18 the altar, which had p' over fire; 1849
15: 8 the glory of God, and from his p'; 1411
16: 8 p' was given unto him to scorch men*
9 which hath p' over these plagues: 1849
17:12 receive p' as kings one hour with * "
13 p' and strength unto the beast. 1411
18: 1 from heaven, having great p'; *1849
19: 1 honour, and p', unto the Lord our 1411
20: 6 such the second death hath no p', 1849

powerful

Ps 29: 4 The voice of the Lord is p'; the 3581
2Co 10:10 his letters,...are weighty and p'; *2478
Heb 4:12 the word of God is quick, and p', *1756

powers

M't 24:29 p' of the heavens shall be shaken:1411
M'r 13:25 the p' that are in heaven shall be "
Lu 12:11 unto magistrates, and p', take ye *1849
21:26 the p' of heaven shall be shaken. 1411
Ro 8:38 angels, nor principalities, nor p', "
13: 1 soul be subject unto the higher p'. 1849
1 the p' that be are ordained of God. "
Eph 3:10 and p' in heavenly places might be "
6:12 against principalities, against p', "
Col 1:16 dominions, or principalities, or p': "
2:15 having spoiled principalities and p'," "
Ti 3: 1 be subject to principalities and p',* "
Heb 6: 5 and the p' of the world to come, 1411
1Pe 3:22 p' being made subject unto him. "

practices

2Pe 2:14 they have exercised with covetous p';*

practise See also PRACTICES; PRACTISED.

Ps 141: 4 to p' wicked works with men that *5953
Isa 32: 6 to p' hypocrisy, and to utter error 6213
Da 8:24 and shall prosper, and p', and shall*"
Mic 2: 1 when the morning is light, they p' it."

practised

1Sa 23: 9 Saul secretly p' mischief against *2790
Da 8:12 ground; and it p', and prospered.*6213

Prætorium (*pre-to'-re-um*)

M'r 15:16 him away into the hall, called P'; 4232

praise See also PRAISED; PRAISES; PRAISETH; PRAISING.

Ge 29:35 she said, Now will I p' the Lord: 3034
49: 8 art he whom thy brethren shall p': "
Le 19:24 shall be holy to p' the Lord withal.1974
De 10:21 He is thy p', and he is thy God, 8416
26:19 in p', and in name, and in honour; "
J'g 5: 2 P' ye the Lord for the avenging *1288
3 will sing p' to the Lord God of Israel.
1Ch 16: 4 and p' the Lord God of Israel: 1984
35 thy holy name, and glory in thy p'.8416
23: 5 made, said David, to p' therewith. 1984
30 morning to thank and p' the Lord, "
25: 3 to give thanks and to p' the Lord.* "
29:13 thee, and p' thy glorious name. "
2Ch 7: 6 the king had made to p' the Lord,*3034
8:14 p' and minister before the priests,1984
20:19 stood up to p' the Lord God of "
21 should p' the beauty of holiness, "
21 the army, and to say, P' the Lord;*3034
22 when they began to sing and to p',8416
23:13 and such as taught to sing p'. 1984
29:30 Levites to sing p' unto the Lord "
31: 2 to p' in the gates of the tents of the "
Ezr 3:10 p' the Lord, after the ordinance of "
Ne 9: 5 exalted above all blessing and p'. 8416
12:24 to p' and to give thanks, according1984
46 songs of p' and thanksgiving unto8416
Ps 7:17 I will p' the Lord according to his*3034
17 sing p' to the name of the Lord
9: 1 I will p' thee, O Lord, with my *3034
2 I will sing p' to thy name, O thou
14 I may shew forth all thy p' in the 8416
21:13 so will we sing and p' thy power. 2167
22:22 of the congregation will I p' thee. 1984
23 Ye that fear the Lord, p' him; all "
25 My p' shall be of thee in the great 8416
26 shall p' the Lord that seek him: 1984
28: 7 and with my song will I p' him. 3034
30: 9 Shall the dust p' thee? shall it "
12 that my glory may sing p' to thee,
33: 1 for p' is comely for the upright. 8416
2 P' the Lord with harp: sing unto*3034
34: 1 his p' shall continually be in my 8416
Ps 35:18 I will p' thee among much people.1984
28 and of thy p' all the day long. 8416
40: 3 my mouth, even p' unto our God: "
42: 4 with the voice of joy and p', with 8426
5 shall yet p' him for the help of 3034
11 for I shall yet p' him, who is the "
43: 4 upon the harp will I p' thee, O God "
5 for I shall yet p' him, who is the "
44: 8 day long, and p' thy name for ever.*"
45:17 shall the people p' thee for ever * "
48:10 thy p' unto the ends of the earth: 8416
49:18 and men will p' thee, when thou 3034
50:23 Whoso offereth p' glorifieth me: *8426
51:15 my mouth shall shew forth thy p'.8416
52: 9 I will p' thee for ever, because *3034
54: 6 I will p' thy name, O Lord; for it is*"
56: 4 In God I will p' his word, in God I 1984
10 In God will I p' his word: in the "
10 in the Lord will I p' his word. "
57: 7 is fixed: I will sing and give p'. *2167
9 I will p' thee, O Lord, among the *3034
61: 8 I sing p' unto thy name for ever,
63: 3 than life, my lips shall p' thee. 7623
5 shall p' thee with joyful lips: 1984
65: 1 P' waiteth for thee, O God, in 8416
66: 2 of his name: make his p' glorious. "
8 make the voice of his p' to be heard:"
67: 3 Let the people p' thee, O God; let 3034
3 O God; let all the people p' thee. "
5 Let the people p' thee, O God; let "
5 O God; let all the people p' thee. "
69:30 p' the name of God with a song, 1984
34 Let the heaven and earth p' him, "
71: 6 my p' shall be continually of thee. 8416
8 Let my mouth be filled with thy p' "
14 will yet p' thee more and more. "
22 will also p' thee with the psaltery, 3034
74:21 the poor and needy p' thy name. 1984
76:10 the wrath of man shall p' thee: 3034
79:13 forth thy p' to all generations. 8416
86:12 I will p' thee, O Lord my God, with3034
88:10 shall the dead arise and p' thee? "
89: 5 the heavens shall p' thy wonders, "
98: 4 noise, and rejoice, and sing p'. *
99: 3 p' thy great and terrible name; 3034
100: *title* A Psalm of p'. *8426
4 and into his courts with p': 8416
102:18 shall be created shall p' the Lord. 1984
21 in Zion, and his p' in Jerusalem; 8416
104:33 I will sing p' to my God while I
35 Lord, O my soul. P' ye the Lord.1984
105:45 and keep his laws. P' ye the Lord. "
106: 1 P' ye the Lord. O give thanks "
2 who can shew forth all his p'? 8416
12 they his words; they sang his p'. "
47 holy name, and to triumph in thy p'."
48 people say, Amen. P' ye the Lord.1984
107: 8, 15, 21, 31 Oh that men would p' 3034
32 and p' him in the assembly of the 1984
108: 1 I will sing and give p', even with *2167
3 I will p' thee, O Lord, among the *3034
109: 1 not thy peace, O God of thy p'; 8416
30 p' the Lord with my mouth; *3034
30 will p' him among the multitude. 1984
111: 1 P' ye the Lord. I will "
1 p' the Lord with my whole heart, *3034
10 his p' endureth for ever. 8416
112: 1 P' ye the Lord. Blessed is the 1984
113: 1 P' ye the Lord. P', O ye servants "
1 the Lord, p' the name of the Lord. "
9 mother of children. P' ye the Lord."
115:17 The dead p' not the Lord, neither "
18 forth...for evermore. P' the Lord. "
116:19 thee, O Jerusalem. P' ye the Lord."
117: 1 O p' the Lord, all ye nations: "
1 ye nations: p' him, all ye people. *7623
2 endureth for ever. P' ye the Lord.1984
118:19 into them, and I will p' the Lord: *3034
21 I will p' thee: for thou hast heard* "
28 Thou art my God, and I will p' thee:*"
119: 7 p' thee with uprightness of heart, * "
164 Seven times a day do I p' thee 1984
171 My lips shall utter p', when thou 8416
175 my soul live, and it shall p' thee; 1984
135: 1 P' ye the Lord. P' ye the name "
1 p' him, O ye servants of the Lord. "
3 P' the Lord; for the Lord is good: "
21 at Jerusalem. P' ye the Lord. "
138: 1 will p' thee with my whole heart: *3034
1 the gods will I sing p' unto thee. *2167
2 p' thy name for...lovingkindness *3034
4 the kings of the earth shall p' thee,*"
139:14 I will p' thee; for I am fearfully * "
142: 7 of prison, that I may p' thy name:* "
145: *title* David's Psalm of p'. 8416
2 I will p' thy name for ever and 1984
4 generation shall p' thy works to *7623
10 All thy works shall p' thee, O *3034
21 shall speak the p' of the Lord: 8416
146: 1 P' ye the Lord. P' the Lord, O 1984
2 While I live I will p' the Lord: I will"
10 all generations. P' ye the Lord. "
147: 1 P' ye the Lord: for it is good to "
1 it is pleasant; and p' is comely. 8416
7 sing p' upon the harp unto our "
12 P' the Lord, O Jerusalem; 7623
12 Jerusalem; p' thy God, O Zion. 1984
20 not known them. P' ye the Lord. "
148: 1 P' ye the Lord. P' ye the Lord. "
1 the heavens: p' him in the heights."
2 P' ye him, all his angels: "
2 his angels: p' ye him, all his hosts. "
3 P' ye him, sun and moon: "
3 moon: p' him, all ye stars of light: "
4 P' him, ye heavens of heavens, and"
5 Let them p' the name of the Lord: "
Ps 148: 7 P' the Lord from the earth, ye 1984
13 Let them p' the name of the Lord: "
14 people, the p' of all his saints; 8416
14 near unto him. P' ye the Lord. 1984
149: 1 P' ye the Lord. Sing unto the Lord"
1 and his p' in the congregation of 8416
3 Let them p' his name in the 1984
9 have all his saints. P' ye the Lord."
150: 1 P' ye the Lord. "
1 P' God in his sanctuary: "
1 p' him in the firmament of his "
2 P' him for his mighty acts; "
2 p' him according to his excellent "
3 P' him with the sound of the "
3 p' him with the psaltery and harp. "
4 P' him with the timbrel and dance:"
4 p' him with stringed instruments "
5 P' him upon the loud cymbals: "
5 p' him upon the high sounding "
6 that hath breath p' the Lord. "
6 the Lord. P' ye the Lord. "
Pr 27: 2 Let another man p' thee, and not "
21 for gold; so is a man to his p'. 4110
28: 4 that forsake the law p' the wicked:1984
31:31 her own works p' her in the gates. "
Isa 12: 1 O Lord, I will p' thee: though *3034
4 P' the Lord, call upon his name, * "
25: 1 I will p' thy name; for thou hast "
38:18 For the grave cannot p' thee, death "
19 living, the living, he shall p' thee, "
42: 8 neither my p' to graven images. 8416
10 his p' from the end of the earth, "
12 and declare his p' in the islands. "
43:21 myself; they shall shew forth my p'."
48: 9 and for my p' will I refrain for thee,"
60:18 walls Salvation, and thy gates P'. "
61: 3 garment of p' for the spirit of "
11 p' to spring forth before all the "
62: 7 make Jerusalem a p' in the earth. "
9 it shall eat it, and p' the Lord; 1984
Jer 13:11 and for a p', and for a glory: 8416
17:14 I shall be saved: for thou art my p'."
26 sacrifices of p' unto the house of *8426
20:13 p' ye the Lord: for he hath 1984
31: 7 p' ye, and say, O Lord, save thy "
33: 9 a p' and an honour before all the 8416
11 P' the Lord of hosts: for the Lord*3034
11 shall bring the sacrifice of p' into *8426
48: 2 shall be no more p' of Moab: 8416
49:25 is the city of p' not left, the city of "
51:41 how is the p' of the whole earth "
Da 2:23 I thank thee, and p' thee, O thou 7624
4:37 Now I Nebuchadnezzar p' and extol"
Joe 2:26 p' the name of the Lord your God,1984
Hab 3: 3 and the earth was full of his p'. 8416
Zep 3:19 get them p' and fame in every land "
20 and a p' among all people of the "
M't 21:16 sucklings thou hast perfected p'? 136
Lu 18:43 when they saw it, gave p' unto God. "
19:37 rejoice and p' God with a loud voice134
Joh 9:24 said unto him, Give God the p': we*1391
12:43 For they loved the p' of men more* "
43 of men more than the p' of God. * "
Ro 2:29 whose p' is not of men, but of God.1868
13: 3 and thou shalt have p' of the same: "
15:11 again, P' the Lord, all ye Gentiles; 134
1Co 4: 5 shall every man have p' of God. 1868
11: 2 Now I p' you, brethren, that ye 1867
17 I p' you not, that ye come together "
22 shall I p' you in this? I p' you not. "
2Co 8:18 brother, whose p' is in the gospel 1868
Eph 1: 6 To the p' of the glory of his grace, "
12 to the p' of his glory, who first "
14 possession, unto the p' of his glory. "
Ph'p 1:11 Christ, unto the glory and p' of God."
4: 8 if there be any p', think on these "
Heb 2:12 the church will I sing p' unto thee.5214
13:15 let us offer the sacrifice of p' to God133
1Pe 1: 7 be found unto p' and honour and 1868
2:14 and for the p' of them that do well. "
4:11 whom be p' and dominion for ever1391
Re 19: 5 P' our God, all ye his servants, 134

praised

J'g 16:24 people saw him, they p' their god:1984
2Sa 14:25 none to be so much p' as Absalom "
22: 4 on the Lord, who is worthy to be p':"
1Ch 16:25 is the Lord, and greatly to be p': "
36 people said, Amen, and p' the Lord."
23: 5 four thousand p' the Lord with the "
2Ch 5:13 p' the Lord, saying, For he is good: "
7: 3 and worshipped, and p' the Lord,*3034
6 when David p' by their ministry; 1984
30:21 Levites and the priests p' the Lord "
Ezr 3:11 great shout, when they p' the Lord,"
Ne 5:13 said, Amen, and p' the Lord. "
Ps 18: 3 the Lord, who is worthy to be p': "
48: 1 greatly to be p' in the city of our "
72:15 continually;...daily shall he be p'.*1288
96: 4 Lord is great, and greatly to be p':1984
113: 3 same the Lord's name is to be p'. "
145: 3 is the Lord, and greatly to be p'; "
Pr 31:30 feareth the Lord, she shall be p'. "
Ec 4: 2 I p' the dead which are already 7623
Ca 6: 9 the concubines, and they p' her. 1984
Isa 64:11 house, where our fathers p' thee, is "
Da 4:34 I p' and honoured him that liveth 7624
5: 4 drank wine, and p' the gods of gold,"
23 thou hast p' the gods of silver, and "
Lu 1:64 loosed, and he spake, and p' God. *2127

praiseth

Pr 31:28 her husband also, and he p' her. 1984

praising

2Ch 5:13 heard in p' and thanking the Lord;1984
23:12 the people running and p' the king."

Ezr 3:11 p' and giving thanks unto the Lord;1984
Ps 84: 4 thy house: they will be still p' thee."
Lu 2:13 heavenly host, p' God, and saying, 134
20 glorifying and p' God for all the "
24:53 in the temple, p' and blessing God.* "
Ac 2:47 P' God, and having favour with all "
3: 8 walking, and leaping, and p' God. "
9 people saw him walking and p' God:"

praises
Ex 15:11 fearful in p', doing wonders? 8416
2Sa 22:50 and I will sing p' unto thy name. "
2Ch 29:30 And they sang p' with gladness, 1984
Ps 9:11 Sing p' to the Lord, which "
18:49 heathen,...sing p' unto thy name. "
22: 3 that inhabitest the p' of Israel. 8416
27: 6 yea, I will sing p' unto the Lord. "
47: 6 Sing p' to God, sing p': "
6 sing p' unto our King, sing p'. "
7 sing ye p' with understanding. "
56:12 O God: I will render p' unto thee.*8426
68: 4 unto God, sing p' to his name: "
32 the earth; O sing p' unto the Lord; "
75: 9 I will sing p' to the God of Jacob. "
78: 4 p' of the Lord, and his strength, 8416
92: 1 to sing p' unto thy name, O most "
108: 3 I will sing p' unto thee among the* "
135: 3 Lord is good: sing p' unto his name; "
144: 9 ten strings will I sing p' unto thee. "
146: 2 I will sing p' unto my God while I "
147: 1 it is good to sing p' unto our God; "
149: 3 sing p' unto him with the timbrel "
6 the high p' of God be in their mouth. "
Isa 60: 6 shew forth the p' of the Lord. 8416
63: 7 and the p' of the Lord, according "
Ac 16:25 prayed, and sang p' unto God: *
1Pe 2: 9 shew forth the p' of him who hath* 703

pransing See also PRANSINGS.
Na 3: 2 the p' horses, and of the jumping 1725

pransings
J'g 5:22 broken by the means of the p'. 1726
22 the p' of their mighty ones. "

prating
Pr 10: 8 but a p' fool shall fall. 8193
10 sorrow: but a p' fool shall fall. "
3Jo 10 p' against us with malicious 5396

pray See also PRAYED; PRAYETH; PRAYING.
Ge 12:13 Say, I p' thee, thou art my sister: 4994
13: 8 Let there be no strife, I p' thee, "
9 separate thyself, I p' thee, from me:"
16: 2 I p' thee, go in unto my maid; it "
18: 3 pass not away, I p' thee, from thy "
4 a little water, I p' you, be fetched.* "
19: 2 now, my lords, turn in, I p' you, "
7 said, I p' you, brethren, do not so "
8 let me, I p' you, bring them out "
20: 7 he shall p' for thee, and thou shalt6419
23:13 if thou wilt give it, I p' thee, hear 3863
25:30 said to Jacob, Feed me, I p' thee, 4994
27:19 I p' thee, sit and eat of my venison,"
21 Come near, I p' thee, that I may "
30:14 Give me, I p' thee, of thy son's "
27 I p' thee, if I have found favour in* "
32:11 Deliver me, I p' thee, from the hand"
29 said, Tell me, I p' thee, thy name. "
33:10 Jacob said, Nay, I p' thee, if now I "
11 Take, I p' thee, my blessing that is "
14 Let my lord, I p' thee, pass over "
34: 8 I p' you give her him to wife. "
37: 6 Hear, I p' you, this dream which I "
14 Go, I p' thee, see whether it be well*"
16 tell me, I p' thee, where they feed "
38:16 Go to, I p' thee, let me come in unto"
40: 8 to God? tell me them, I p' you. "
14 shew kindness, I p' thee, unto me, "
44:33 I p' thee, let thy servant abide "
45: 4 brethren, Come near to me, I p' you."
47: 4 we p' thee, let thy servants dwell in "
29 put, I p' thee, thy hand under my "
29 bury me not, I p' thee, in Egypt: "
50: 4 speak, I p' you, in the ears of "
5 let me go up, I p' thee, and bury my"
17 Forgive, I p' thee now, the trespass577
17 we p' thee, forgive the trespass of 4994
Ex 4:13 O my Lord, send, I p' thee, by "
18 Let me go, I p' thee, and return "
5: 3 let us go, we p' thee, three days' "
10:17 forgive, I p' thee, my sin only this "
32:32 blot me, I p' thee, out of thy book "
33:13 therefore, I p' thee, if I have found "
34: 9 let my Lord, I p' thee, go among us;"
Nu 10:31 he said, Leave us not, I p' thee; "
11:15 kill me, I p' thee, out of hand, if I "
16: 8 Hear, I p' you, ye sons of Levi: * "
26 Depart, I p' you, from the tents of "
20:17 Let us pass, I p' thee, through thy "
21: 7 p' unto the Lord, that he take 6419
22: 6 therefore, I p' thee, curse me this 4994
16 Let nothing, I p' thee, hinder thee "
17 therefore, I p' thee, curse me this "
19 I p' you, tarry ye also here this "
23:13 him, Come, I p' thee, with me unto "
27 Come, I p' thee, I will bring thee "
De 3:25 I p' thee, let me go over, and see the"
Jos 2:12 I p' you, swear unto me by the Lord,"
7:19 give, I p' thee, glory to the Lord "
J'g 1:24 Shew us, we p' thee, the entrance "
4:19 Give me, I p' thee, a little water to "
6:18 Depart not hence, I p' thee, until I "
39 let me prove, I p' thee, but this "
8: 5 Give, I p' you, loaves of bread unto "
9: 2 Speak, I p' you, in the ears of all the"
38 go out, I p' now, and fight with "
10:15 deliver us only, we p' thee, this day."
11:17 Let me, I p' thee, pass through thy "
J'g 11:19 Let us pass, we p' thee, through thy4994
13: 4 beware, I p' thee, and drink not wine"
15 I p' thee, let us detain thee, until "
15: 2 take her, I p' thee, instead of her. "
16: 6 Tell me, I p' thee, wherein thy great"
10 now tell me, I p' thee, wherewith "
28 Lord God, remember me, I p' thee, "
28 strengthen me, I p' thee, only this "
18: 5 Ask counsel, we p' thee, of God, "
19: 6 Be content, I p' thee, and tarry all "
8 said, Comfort thine heart, I p' thee."
9 evening, I p' you tarry all night: "
11 Come, I p' thee, and let us turn in "
23 nay, I p' you, do not so wickedly; "
Ru 2: 7 I p' you, let me glean and gather "
1Sa 2:36 Put me, I p' thee, into one of the "
3:17 I p' thee hide it not from me: God "
7: 5 I will p' for you unto the Lord. 6419
9:18 Tell me, I p' thee, where the seer's4994
10:15 Tell me, I p' thee, what Samuel "
12:19 P' for thy servants unto the Lord 6419
23 the Lord in ceasing to p' for you: "
14:29 see, I p' you, how mine eyes have 4994
15:25 I p' thee, pardon my sin, and turn "
30 honour me now, I p' thee, before "
16:22 Let David, I p' thee, stand before "
19: 2 now therefore, I p' thee, take heed "
20:29 Let me go, I p' thee; for our family "
29 let me get away, I p' thee, and see "
22: 3 my mother, I p' thee, come forth, "
23:22 Go, I p' you, prepare yet, and know "
25: 8 give, I p' thee, whatsoever cometh "
24 let thine handmaid, I p' thee, speak"
25 Let not my lord, I p' thee, regard "
26: 8 let me smite him, I p' thee, with the"
11 I p' thee, take thou now the spear "
19 I p' thee, let my lord the king hear "
28: 8 said, I p' thee, divine unto me by the"
22 I p' thee, hearken thou also unto "
30: 7 I p' thee, bring me hither the ephod."
2Sa 1: 4 went the matter? I p' thee, tell me. "
9 Stand, I p' thee, upon me, and slay "
7:27 in his heart to p' this prayer unto 6419
13: 5 him, I p' thee, let my sister Tamar4994
6 I p' thee, let Tamar my sister come, "
13 I p' thee, speak unto the king; for "
26 I p' thee, let my brother Amnon go "
14: 2 I p' thee, feign thyself to be a "
11 I p' thee, let the king remember the"
12 Let thine handmaid, I p' thee, "
18 Hide not from me, I p' thee, the "
15: 7 I p' thee, let me go and pay my vow,"
16: 9 go over, I p' thee, and take off his "
18:22 let me, I p' thee, also run after "
19:37 Let thy servant, I p' thee, turn back"
20:16 say, I p' you, unto Joab, Come near "
24:17 let thine hand, I p' thee, be against "
1Ki 1:12 let me, I p' thee, give thee counsel, "
2:17 I p' thee, unto Solomon the king, "
20 of thee; I p' thee, say me not nay.*
8:26 let thy word, I p' thee, be verified, 4994
30 they shall p' toward this place: 6419
33 confess thy name, and p', and make"
35 if they p' toward this place, and "
42 when he shall come and p' toward "
44 and shall p' unto the Lord toward "
48 p' unto thee toward their land, which"
13: 6 p' for me, that my hand may be "
14: 2 wife, Arise, I p' thee, and disguise 4994
17:10 Fetch me, I p' thee, a little water in"
11 Bring me, I p' thee, a morsel of "
21 I p' thee, let this child's soul come "
19:20 Let me, I p' thee, kiss my father "
20: 7 I p' you, and see how this man "
31 let us, I p' thee, put sackcloth on "
32 Ben-hadad saith, I p' thee, let me "
37 Smite me, I p' thee. And the man "
22: 5 Enquire, I p' thee, at the word of "
13 let thy word, I p' thee, be like the "
2Ki 1:13 O man of God, I p' thee, let my life, "
2: 2 unto Elisha, Tarry here, I p' thee; "
4 him, Elisha, tarry here, I p' thee; "
6 said unto him, Tarry, I p' thee, "
9 And Elisha said, I p' thee, let a "
19 said unto Elisha, Behold, I p' thee, "
4:10 chamber, I p' thee, on the wall; "
22 Send me, I p' thee, one of the young"
26 Run now, I p' thee, to meet her, and"
5: 7 wherefore consider, I p' you, and "
15 I p' thee, take a blessing of thy "
17 I p' thee, be given to thy servant "
22 them, I p' thee, a talent of silver, "
6: 2 Let us go, we p' thee, unto Jordan, "
17 said, Lord, I p' thee, open his eyes, "
18 Smite this people, I p' thee, with "
7:13 Let some take, I p' thee, five of the "
8: 4 Tell me, I p' thee, all the great "
18:23 therefore, I p' thee, give pledges "
1Ch 17:25 hath found in his heart to p' 6419
21:17 let thine hand, I p' thee, O Lord 4994
2Ch 6:24 p' and make supplication before 6419
26 p' toward this place, and confess "
32 if they come and p' in this house; "
34 they p' unto thee toward this city "
37 turn and p' unto thee in the land *2603
38 p' toward their land, which thou 6419
7:14 humble themselves, and p', and seek"
18: 4 Enquire, I p' thee, at the word of 4994
12 let thy word therefore, I p' thee, be "
Ezr 6:10 p' for the life of the king, and of 6739
Ne 1: 6 I p' before thee now, day and 6419
11 prosper, I p' thee, thy servant this 4994
5:10 I p' you, let us leave off this usury. "
11 Restore, I p' you, to them, even this"
Job 6:29 Return, I p' you, let it not be "
8: 8 enquire, I p' thee, of the former age."
Job 21:15 should we have, if we p' unto him?6293
22:22 Receive, I p' thee, the law from his4994
32:21 Let me not, I p' you, accept any "
33: 1 Job, I p' thee, hear my speeches, and "
26 He shall p' unto God, and he will *6279
42: 8 my servant Job shall p' for you: 6419
Ps 5: 2 and my God: for unto thee will I p'."
32: 6 this shall every one that is godly p' "
55:17 and morning, and at noon will I p'*7878
122: 6 P' for the peace of Jerusalem: they7592
Isa 5: 3 of Judah, judge, I p' you, betwixt 4994
16:12 shall come to his sanctuary to p'; 6419
29:11 Read this, I p' thee: and he saith, 4994
36: 8 give pledges, I p' thee, to my master"
11 Speak, I p' thee, unto thy servants "
45:20 and p' unto a god that cannot save.6419
Jer 7:16 p' not thou for this people, neither "
11:14 p' not thou for this people, neither "
14:11 P' not for this people for their good."
21: 2 Enquire, I p' thee, of the Lord for 4994
29: 7 and p' unto the Lord for it: for in 6419
12 ye shall go and p' unto me, and I "
32: 8 Buy my field, I p' thee, that is in 4994
37: 3 P' now unto the Lord our God for 6419
20 hear now, I p' thee, O my lord the 4994
20 let my supplication, I p' thee, be "
40:15 Let me go, I p' thee, and I will slay "
42: 2 p' for us unto the Lord thy God, 6419
4 I will p' unto the Lord your God "
20 P' for us unto the Lord our God; "
La 1:18 hear, I p' you, all people, and 4994
Eze 33:30 Come, I p' you, and hear what is the"
Jon 1: 8 Tell us, we p' thee, for whose cause "
4: 2 said, I p' thee, O Lord, was not this577
Mic 3: 1 Hear, I p' you, O heads of Jacob, 4994
9 Hear this, I p' you, ye heads of the "
Hag 2:15 now, I p' you, consider from this "
Zec 7: 2 their men, to p' before the Lord, *2470
8:21 us go speedily to p' before the Lord,*"
22 Jerusalem, and...p' before the Lord.*"
Mal 1: 9 now, I p' you, beseech God that 4994
M't 5:44 p' for them which despitefully use 4336
6: 5 to p' standing in the synagogues "
6 p' to thy Father which is in secret; "
7 when ye p', use not vain repetitions,*"
9 After this manner therefore p' ye: "
9:38 P' ye therefore the Lord of the 1189
14:23 up into a mountain apart to p': 4336
19:13 put his hands on them and p': "
24:20 p' ye that your flight be not in the "
26:36 ye here, while I go and p' yonder. "
41 Watch and p', that ye enter not into"
53 that I cannot now p' to my Father,*3870
M'r 5:17 they began to p' him to depart out* "
23 I p' thee, come and lay thy hands on
6:46 he departed into a mountain to p'. 4336
11:24 things ye desire, when ye p', believe"
13:18 p' ye that your flight be not in the "
33 watch and p': for ye know not "
14:32 disciples, Sit ye here, while I shall p'."
38 Watch ye and p', lest ye enter into "
Lu 6:12 he went out into a mountain to p', "
28 p' for them which despitefully use "
9:28 and went up into a mountain to p'. "
10: 2 p' ye therefore the Lord of the 1189
11: 1 unto him, Lord, teach us to p', 4336
2 When ye p', say, Our Father which "
14:18 see it: I p' thee have me excused. 2065
19 them: I p' thee have me excused. "
16:27 I p' thee therefore, father, that thou"
18: 1 men ought always to p', and not 4336
10 went up into the temple to p'; "
21:36 ye therefore, and p' always, that *1189
22:40 P' that ye enter not into 4336
46 and p', lest ye enter into temptation."
Joh 14:16 I will p' the Father, and he shall 2065
16:26 that I will p' the Father for you: "
17: 9 I p' for them: I p' not for the "
15 I p' not that thou shouldest take "
20 Neither p' I for these alone, but "
Ac 8:22 this thy wickedness, and p' God, 1189
24 P' ye to the Lord for me, that "
34 I p' thee, of whom speaketh the "
10: 9 went up upon the housetop to p' 4336
24: 4 I p' thee that thou wouldest hear *3870
27:34 I p' you to take some meat: for * "
Ro 8:26 we should p' for as we ought: 4336
1Co 11:13 comely that a woman p' unto God "
14:13 tongue p' that he may interpret. "
14 if I p' in an unknown tongue, my "
15 it then? I will p' with the spirit, "
15 will p' with the understanding also:"
2Co 5:20 we p' you in Christ's stead, be ye *1189
13: 7 Now p' to God that ye do no evil; 2172
Ph'p 1: 9 And this I p', that your love may 4336
Col 1: 9 do not cease to p' for you, and to "
1Th 5:17 P' without ceasing. "
23 I p' God your whole spirit and soul*
25 Brethren, p' for us. 4336
2Th 1:11 we p' always for you, that our God "
3: 1 brethren, p' for us, that the word "
1Ti 2: 8 therefore that men p' every where, "
2Ti 4:16 I p' God that it may not be laid to*
Heb 13:18 P' for us: for we trust we have 4336
Jas 5:13 among you afflicted? let him p'. "
14 let them p' over him, anointing "
16 p' one for another, that ye may 2172
1Jo 5:16 I do not say that he shall p' for it.*2065

prayed
Ge 20:17 So Abraham p' unto God: and 6419
Nu 11: 2 when Moses p' unto the Lord, "
21: 7 us. And Moses p' for the people. "
De 9:20 I p' for Aaron also the same time. "
26 I p' therefore unto the Lord, and "
1Sa 1:10 p' unto the Lord, and wept sore. "

1Sa 1:27 For this child I p'; and the Lord 6419
2: 1 Hannah p', and said, My heart "
8: 6 us. And Samuel p' unto the Lord. "
2Ki 4:33 them twain, and p' unto the Lord. "
6:17 Elisha p', and said, Lord, I pray "
18 Elisha p' unto the Lord, and said, "
19:15 Hezekiah p' before the Lord, and "
20 That which thou hast p' to me "
20: 2 to the wall, and p' unto the Lord, "
2Ch 30:18 But Hezekiah p' for them, saying, "
32:20 of Amoz, p' and cried to heaven. "
24 the death, and p' unto the Lord: "
33:13 p' unto him: and he was intreated "
Ezr 10: 1 Now when Ezra had p', and when "
Ne 1: 4 and p' before the God of heaven. "
2: 4 So I p' to the God of heaven. "
Job 42:10 Job, when he p' for his friends: "
Isa 37:15 Hezekiah p' unto the Lord, saying, "
21 Whereas thou hast p' to me "
38: 2 the wall, and p' unto the Lord, "
Jer 32:16 Neriah, I p' unto the Lord, saying, "
Da 6:10 p', and gave thanks before his 6739
9: 4 And I p' unto the Lord my God, 6419
Jon 2: 1 Jonah p' unto the Lord his God "
4: 2 And he p' unto the Lord, and said, "
M't 26:39 fell on his face, and p', saying, O *4336*
42 away the second time, and p', "
44 p' the third time, saying the same "
M'r 1:35 a solitary place, and there p'. "
5:18 p' him that he might be with him.**3870*
14:35 and p' that, if it were possible, *4336*
39 went away, and p', and spake the "
Lu 5: 3 p' him that he would thrust out a **2065*
16 himself into the wilderness, and p'.*4336*
9:29 And as he p', the fashion of his * "
18:11 stood and p' thus with himself, "
22:32 p' for thee, that thy faith fail not:**1189*
41 cast, and kneeled down and p', *4336*
44 in an agony he p' more earnestly: "
Joh 4:31 his disciples p' him, saying, *2065*
Ac 1:24 And they p', and said, Thou, Lord,*4336*
4:31 And when they had p', the place *1189*
6: 6 when they had p', they laid their *4336*
8:15 p' for them, that they might receive"
9:40 forth, and kneeled down, and p'; "
10: 2 to the people, and p' to God alway.*1189*
30 the ninth hour I p' in my house, **4336*
48 p' they him to tarry certain days. *2065*
13: 3 when they had fasted and p', and *4336*
14:23 p' with fasting, they commended "
16: 9 man of Macedonia, and p' him, **3870*
25 Paul and Silas p', and sang **4336*
20:36 kneeled down, and p' with them all. "
21: 5 kneeled down on the shore, and p'. "
22:17 while I p' in the temple, I was in a "
23:18 p' me to bring this young man **2065*
28: 8 Paul entered in, and p', and laid *4336*
Jas 5:17 he p' earnestly that it might not "
18 he p' again, and the heaven gave "

prayer See also PRAYERS.
2Sa 7:27 heart to pray this p' unto thee. 8605
1Ki 8:28 thou respect unto the p' of thy "
28 hearken unto the cry and to the p', "
29 p' which thy servant shall make "
38 p' and supplication soever be made"
45 hear thou in heaven their p' and "
49 Then hear thou their p' and their "
54 made an end of praying all this p' "
9: 3 him, I have heard thy p' and thy "
2Ki 19: 4 lift up thy p' for the remnant that "
20: 5 I have heard thy p', I have seen "
2Ch 6:19 Have respect therefore to the p' "
19 to the p' which thy servant prayeth "
20 to hearken unto the p' which thy "
29 p' or what supplication soever "
35 hear thou from the heavens their p' "
39 their p' and their supplications, "
40 attent unto the p' that is made in "
7:12 I have heard thy p', and have "
15 unto the p' that is made in this "
30:27 and their p' came up to his holy "
33:18 Manasseh, and his p' unto his God, "
19 His p' also, and how God was "
Ne 1: 6 hear the p' of thy servant, which "
11 attentive to the p' of thy servant, "
11 and to the p' of thy servants, who "
4: 9 Nevertheless we made our p' unto 6419
11:17 begin the thanksgiving in p': and 8605
Job 15: 4 and restrainest p' before God. *7878
16:17 mine hands: also my p' is pure. 8605
22:27 Thou shalt make thy p' unto him, 6279
Ps 4: 1 mercy upon me, and hear my p'. 8605
5: 3 will I direct my p' unto thee, and
6: 9 the Lord will receive my p'. 8605
17: *title* A p' of David. "
1 give ear unto my p', that goeth "
35:13 p' returned into mine own bosom. "
39:12 Hear my p', O Lord, and give ear "
42: 8 p' unto the God of my life. "
54: 2 Hear my p', O God; give ear to the "
55: 1 Give ear to my p', O God; and hide "
61: 1 my cry, O God; attend unto my p'. "
64: 1 Hear my voice, O God, in my p': *7879
65: 2 O thou that hearest p', unto thee 8605
66:19 attended to the voice of my p'. "
20 which hath not turned away my p', "
69:13 for me, my p' is unto thee, O Lord, "
72:15 p' also shall be made for him *6419
80: 4 against the p' of thy people? 8605
84: 8 O Lord God of hosts, hear my p': "
86: *title* A p' of David. "
6 Give ear, O Lord, unto my p'; "
88: 2 Let my p' come before thee: incline"
13 morning shall my p' prevent thee. "
90: *title* A p' of Moses the man of God. "

Ps 102: *title* A p' of the afflicted, when he is 8605
1 Hear my p', O Lord, and let my "
17 will regard the p' of the destitute, "
17 and not despise their p'. "
109: 4 but I give myself unto p'. "
7 and let his p' become sin. "
141: 2 Let my p' be set forth before thee "
5 yet my p' also shall be in their "
142: *title* David; A P' when he was in "
143: 1 Hear my p', O Lord, give ear to my "
Pr 15: 8 the p' of the upright is his delight. "
29 he heareth the p' of the righteous. "
28: 9 his p' shall be an abomination. "
Isa 26:16 poured out a p' when...chastening 3908
37: 4 thy p' for the remnant that is left. 8605
38: 5 I have heard thy p', I have seen "
56: 7 them joyful in my house of p': "
7 house shall be called an house of p' "
Jer 7:16 neither lift up cry nor p' for them, "
11:14 neither lift up a cry or p' for them: "
La 3: 8 and shout, he shutteth out my p'. "
44 that our p' should not pass through."
Da 9: 3 seek by p' and supplications, with "
13 we not our p' before the Lord our*2470
17 God, hear the p' of thy servant, 8605
21 whiles I was speaking in p', even "
Jon 2: 7 my p' came in unto thee, into thine"
Hab 3: 1 A p' of Habakkuk the prophet "
M't 17:21 not out but by p' and fasting. **4335*
21:13 shall be called the house of p'; but "
22 whatsoever ye shall ask in p', "
23:14 and for a pretence make long p': **4336*
M'r 9:29 by nothing, but by p' and fasting. *4335*
11:17 called of all nations the house of p'?"
Lu 1:13 not, Zacharias: for thy p' is heard;**1162*
6:12 continued all night in p' to God. *4335*
19:46 My house is the house of p': but ye "
22:45 when he rose up from p', and was "
Ac 1:14 one accord in p' and supplication, "
3: 1 the hour of p', being the ninth hour."
6: 4 will give ourselves continually to p', "
10:31 And said, Cornelius, thy p' is heard, "
12: 5 but p' was made without ceasing of"
16:13 where p' was wont to be made; "
16 as we went to p', a certain damsel "
Ro 10: 1 desire and p' to God for Israel is, **1162*
12:12 continuing instant in p'; *4335*
1Co 7: 5 give yourselves to fasting and p'; "
2Co 1:11 also helping together by p' for us,**1162*
9:14 by their p' for you, which long after*"
Eph 6:18 Praying always with all p' and *4335*
Ph'p 1: 4 Always in every p' of mine for you**1162*
19 to my salvation through your p', * "
4: 6 every thing by p' and supplication *4335*
Col 4: 2 Continue in p', and watch in the "
1Ti 4: 5 sanctified by...word of God and p'. *1783*
Jas 5:15 the p' of faith shall save the sick, *2171*
16 fervent p' of a righteous man **1162*
1Pe 4: 7 therefore sober, and watch unto p'.*4335*

prayers
Ps 72:20 p' of David the son of Jesse are 8605
Isa 1:15 when ye make many p', I will not "
M'r 12:40 and for a pretence make long p': *4336*
Lu 2:37 with fastings and p' night and day.**1162*
5:33 of John fast often, and make p', * "
20:47 and for a shew make long p': *4336*
Ac 2:42 and in breaking of bread, and in p'.*4335*
10: 4 Thy p' and thine alms are come up "
Ro 1: 9 mention of you always in my p'; "
15:30 with me in your p' to God for me; "
Eph 1:16 making mention of you in my p'; "
Col 4:12 labouring fervently for you in p', "
1Th 1: 2 making mention of you in our p'; "
1Ti 2: 1 supplications, p', intercessions, and "
5: 5 continueth in supplications and p' "
2Ti 1: 3 have remembrance of thee in my p'**1162*
Ph'm 4 mention of thee always in my p', *4335*
22 through your p' I shall be given "
Heb 5: 7 he had offered up p'...supplications*1162*
1Pe 3: 7 life; that your p' be not hindered. *4335*
12 and his ears are open unto their p':**1162*
Re 5: 8 odours, which are the p' of saints. *4335*
8: 3 offer it with the p' of all saints upon"
4 came with the p' of the saints, "

prayest
M't 6: 5 when thou p', thou shalt not be as**4336*
6 when thou p', enter into thy closet, "

prayeth
1Ki 8:28 thy servant p' before thee to day: 6419
2Ch 6:19 which thy servant p' before thee: "
20 thy servant p' toward this place. * "
Isa 44:17 and worshippeth it, and p' unto it, "
Ac 9:11 Saul, of Tarsus: for, behold, he p', *4336*
1Co 11: 5 every woman that p' or prophesieth*"
14:14 my spirit p', but my understanding "

praying
1Sa 1:12 she continued p' before the Lord, 6419
26 stood by thee here, p' unto the Lord."
1Ki 8:54 Solomon had made an end of p' all "
2Ch 7: 1 Solomon had made an end of p', "
Da 6:11 and found Daniel p' and making *1156
9:20 And whiles I was speaking, and p',6419
M'r 11:25 And when ye stand p', forgive, if ye*4336*
Lu 1:10 people were p' without at the time "
3:21 Jesus also being baptized, and p', "
9:18 it came to pass, as he was alone p', "
11: 1 as he was p' in a certain place, "
Ac 11: 5 I was in the city of Joppa p': and in"
12:12 many were gathered together p'. "
1Co 11: 4 Every man p' or prophesying, "
2Co 8: 4 P' us with much intreaty that we **1189*
Eph 6:18 P' always with all prayer and *4336*
Col 1: 3 Lord Jesus Christ, p' always for you,"

Col 4: 3 p' also for us, that God would open*4336*
1Th 3:10 Night and day p' exceedingly that *1189*
Jude 20 holy faith, p' in the Holy Ghost, *4336*

preach See also PREACHED; PREACHEST; PREACHETH; PREACHING.
Ne 6: 7 prophets to p' of thee at Jerusalem,7121
Isa 61: 1 anointed me to p' good tidings 1319
Jon 3: 2 p' unto it the preaching that I bid 7121
M't 4:17 From that time Jesus began to p', *2784*
10: 7 as ye go, p', saying, The kingdom of"
27 ear, that p' ye upon the housetops.*"
11: 1 to teach and to p' in their cities. "
M'r 1: 4 p' the baptism of repentance for the*"
38 next towns, that I may p' there also:"
3:14 that he might send them forth to p',"
16:15 and p' the gospel to every creature. "
Lu 4:18 me to p' the gospel to the poor; *2097*
18 to p' deliverance to the captives, **2784*
19 p' the acceptable year of the Lord.* "
43 I must p' the kingdom of God to *2097*
9: 2 he sent them to p' the kingdom of *2784*
60 thou and p' the kingdom of God. **1229*
Ac 5:42 not to teach and p' Jesus Christ. *2097*
10:42 he commanded us to p' unto the *2784*
14:15 and p' unto you that ye should turn**2097*
15:21 hath in every city them that p' him,*2784*
16: 6 Holy Ghost to p' the word in Asia,**2980*
10 us for to p' the gospel unto them. *2097*
17: 3 this Jesus, whom I p' unto you, is**2605*
Ro 1:15 I am ready to p' the gospel to you *2097*
10: 8 is, the word of faith, which we p'; *2784*
15 shall they p', except they be sent? "
15 of them that p' the gospel of peace,**2097*
15:20 so have I strived to p' the gospel, "
1Co 1:17 not to baptize, but to p' the gospel: "
23 But we p' Christ crucified, unto the*2784*
9:14 they which p' the gospel should **2605*
16 For though I p' the gospel, I have *2097*
16 woe is unto me, if I p' not the gospel!"
18 when I p' the gospel, I may make "
15:11 they, so we p', and so ye believed. *2784*
2Co 2:12 I came to Troas to p' Christ's gospel,*
4: 5 For we p' not ourselves, but Christ*2784*
10:16 p' the gospel in the regions beyond*2097*
Ga 1: 8 p' any other gospel unto you than "
9 man p' any other gospel unto you * "
16 I might p' him among the heathen; "
2: 2 which I p' among the Gentiles, *2784*
5:11 if I yet p' circumcision, why do I "
Eph 3: 8 I should p' among the Gentiles the*2097*
Ph'p 1:15 Some indeed p' Christ even of envy*2784*
16 The one p' Christ of contention, **2605*
Col 1:28 we p', warning every man, Whom * "
2Ti 4: 2 P' the word; be instant in season,*2784*
Re 14: 6 to p' unto them that dwell on the **2097*

preached
Ps 40: 9 have p' righteousness in the great*1319
M't 11: 5 the poor have the gospel p' to them.*2097*
24:14 be p' in all the world for a witness *2784*
26:13 this gospel shall be p' in the whole "
M'r 1: 7 And p', saying, There cometh one "
39 And he p' in their synagogues * "
2: 2 and he p' the word unto them. **2980*
6:12 and p' that men should repent. *2784*
14: 9 this gospel shall be p' throughout "
16:20 they went forth, and p' every where, "
Lu 3:18 exhortation p' he unto the people. *2097*
4:44 And he p' in the synagogues of **2784*
7:22 raised, to the poor the gospel is p'.*2097*
16:16 that time the kingdom of God is p', "
20: 1 in the temple, and p' the gospel, "
24:47 should be p' in his name among all*2784*
Ac 3:20 which before was p' unto you: **4296*
4: 2 p' through Jesus the resurrection**2605*
8: 5 Samaria, and p' Christ unto them.**2784*
25 testified and p' the word of the **2980*
25 p' the gospel in many villages of *2097*
35 scripture, and p' unto him Jesus. "
40 he p' in all the cities, till he came "
9:20 he p' Christ in the synagogues, **2784*
27 how he had p' boldly at Damascus*3954*
10:37 after the baptism which John p'; *2784*
13: 5 they p' the word of God in the **2605*
24 John had first p' before his coming*4296*
38 p' unto you the forgiveness of sins:**2605*
42 be p' to them the next sabbath. **2980*
14: 7 And there they p' the gospel. *2097*
21 they had p' the gospel to that city, "
25 they had p' the word in Perga, **2980*
15:36 where we have p' the word of the **2605*
17:13 that the word of God was p' of Paul*"
18 because he p' unto them Jesus. *2097*
20: 7 Paul p' unto them, ready to depart*1256*
Ro 15:19 have fully p' the gospel of Christ. *4137*
1Co 9:27 when I have p' to others, I myself *2784*
15: 1 you the gospel which I p' unto you,*2097*
2 keep in memory what I p' unto you,"
12 if Christ be p' that he rose from the*2784*
2Co 1:19 who was p' among you by us, even "
11: 4 Jesus, whom we have not p', * "
7 I have p' to you the gospel of God *2097*
Ga 1: 8 that which we have p' unto you, "
11 the gospel which was p' of me is not"
3: 8 p' before the gospel unto Abraham,*4283*
4:13 I p' the gospel unto you at the *2097*
Eph 2:17 came and p' peace to you which "
Ph'p 1:18 pretence, or in truth, Christ is p';**2605*
Col 1:23 which was p' to every creature *2784*
1Th 2: 9 we p' unto you the gospel of God. "
1Ti 3:16 p' unto the Gentiles, believed on in "
Heb 4: 2 For unto us was the gospel p', as *2097*
2 but the word p' did not profit them,**189*
6 and they to whom it was first p'. *2097*
1Pe 1:12 them that have p' the gospel unto "
25 which by the gospel is p' unto you. "

1Pe 3:19 and p' unto the spirits in prison; *2784*
4: 6 for this cause was the gospel p' *2097*

preacher
Ec 1: 1 words of the P', the son of David, 6953
2 Vanity of vanities, saith the P', "
12 I the P' was king over Israel in "
7:27 this have I found, saith the p', "
12: 8 Vanity of vanities, saith the p'; all "
9 because the p' was wise, he still "
10 p' sought to find out acceptable "
Ro 10:14 how shall they hear without a p'? *2784*
1Ti 2: 7 I am ordained a p', and an apostle, *2783*
2Ti 1:11 I am appointed a p', and an apostle, "
2Pe 2: 5 eighth person, a p' of righteousness, "

preachest
Ro 2:21 that p' a man should not steal, *2784*

preacheth
Ac 19:13 you by Jesus whom Paul p'. *2784*
2Co 11: 4 if he that cometh p' another Jesus, "
Ga 1:23 now p' the faith which once he *2097*

preaching
Jon 3: 2 unto it the p' that I bid thee. 7150
M't 3: 1 p' in the wilderness of Judæa, *2784*
4:23 and p' the gospel of the kingdom, "
9:35 and p' the gospel of the kingdom, "
12:41 they repented at the p' of Jonas; *2782*
M'r 1:14 p' the gospel of the kingdom of *2784*
Lu 3: 3 p' the baptism of repentance for "
8: 1 p' and shewing the glad tidings of "
9: 6 p' the gospel, and healing every *2097*
11:32 they repented at the p' of Jonas; *2782*
Ac 8: 4 went every where p' the word. *2097*
12 believed Philip p' the things "
10:36 Israel, p' peace by Jesus Christ: "
11:19 p' the word to none but unto the *2980
20 the Grecians, p' the Lord Jesus. *2097*
15:35 and p' the word of the Lord, with "
20: 9 as Paul was long p', he sunk down *1256*
25 have gone p' the kingdom of God, *2784*
28:31 P' the kingdom of God, and "
Ro 16:25 gospel, and the p' of Jesus Christ, *2782*
1Co 1:18 For the p' of the cross is to them *3056
21 by the foolishness of p' to save *2782*
2: 4 my p' was not with enticing words "
15:14 be not risen, then is our p' vain, "
2Co 10:14 to you also in p' the gospel of Christ:*
2Ti 4:17 me the p' might be fully known, *2782
Tit 1: 3 manifested his word through p', * "

precept See also PRECEPTS.
Isa 28:10 p' must be upon p', p' upon p'; 6673
13 unto them p' upon p', p' upon p'; "
29:13 me is taught by the p' of men: *4687
M'r 10: 5 your heart he wrote you this p'. *1785
Heb 9:19 Moses had spoken every p' to all * "

precepts
Ne 9:14 and commandedst them p', *4687
Ps 119: 4 commanded us to keep thy p' 6490
15 I will meditate in thy p', and have "
27 to understand the way of thy p': "
40 I have longed after thy p': quicken "
45 walk at liberty: for I seek thy p'. "
56 This I had, because I kept thy p'. "
63 thee, and of them that keep thy p'. "
69 keep thy p' with my whole heart. "
78 cause: but I will meditate in thy p'. "
87 earth; but I forsook not thy p'. "
93 I will never forget thy p': for with "
94 save me; for I have sought thy p'. "
100 the ancients, because I keep thy p'. "
104 thy p' I get understanding: "
110 for me: yet I erred not from thy p'. "
128 I esteem all thy p' concerning all "
134 of man: so will I keep thy p'. "
141 despised: yet do not I forget thy p'. "
159 Consider how I love thy p': "
168 kept thy p' and thy testimonies: "
173 help me; for I have chosen thy p'. "
Jer 35:18 and kept all his p', and done 4687
Da 9: 5 even by departing from thy p' and "

precious
Ge 24:53 and to her mother p' things. 4030
De 33:13 for the p' things of heaven, for 4022
14 p' fruits brought forth by the sun, "
14 p' things put forth by the moon, "
15 for the p' things of the lasting hills, "
16 for the p' things of the earth and "
1Sa 3: 1 of the Lord was p' in those days; 3368
26:21 my soul was p' in thine eyes this 3365
2Sa 12:30 a talent of gold with the p' stones:3368
1Ki 10: 2 and very much gold, and p' stones: "
10 very great store, and p' stones: "
11 plenty of almug trees, and p' stones. "
2Ki 1:13 thy servants, be p' in thy sight. 3365
14 let my life now be p' in thy sight. "
20:13 all the house of his p' things, 5238
13 the spices, and the p' ointment, 2896
1Ch 20: 2 and there were p' stones in it; 3368
29: 2 all manner of p' stones, and marble "
8 they with whom p' stones were found "
2Ch 3: 6 garnished the house with p' stones 3368
9: 1 gold in abundance, and p' stones: "
9 great abundance, and p' stones: "
10 brought algum trees and p' stones. "
20:25 the dead bodies, and p' jewels, 2530
21: 3 and of gold, and of p' things, with 4030
32:27 and for gold, and for p' stones, 3368
Ezr 1: 6 with beasts, and with p' things, 4030
8:27 vessels of fine copper, p' as gold. 2530
Job 28:10 and his eyes seeth every p' thing. 3366
16 gold of Ophir, with the p' onyx, 3368
Ps 49: 8 the redemption of their soul is p',*3365
72:14 and p' shall their blood be in his "

Ps 116:15 P' in the sight of the Lord is the 3368
126: 6 and weepeth, bearing p' seed, *4901
133: 2 It is like the p' ointment upon the 2896
139:17 How p' also are thy thoughts 3365
Pr 1:13 We shall find all p' substance, we 3368
3:15 She is more p' than rubies: and all "
6:26 adulteress will hunt for the p' life. "
12:27 substance of a diligent man is p'. "
17: 8 A gift is as a p' stone in the eyes 2580
20:15 lips of knowledge are a p' jewel. 3366
24: 4 with all p' and pleasant riches. 3368
Ec 7: 1 name is better than p' ointment; 2896
Isa 13:12 a man more p' than fine gold; *3365
28:16 a tried stone, a p' corner stone, 3368
39: 2 them the house of his p' things, 5238
2 the spices, and the p' ointment, 2896
43: 4 Since thou wast p' in my sight, 3365
Jer 15:19 take forth the p' from the vile, 3368
20: 5 and all the p' things thereof, and 3366
La 4: 2 The p' sons of Zion, comparable to 3368
Eze 22:25 taken the treasure and p' things; 3366
27:20 Dedan...thy merchant in p' clothes 2667
22 and with all p' stones, and gold. 3368
28:13 every p' stone was thy covering, "
Da 11: 8 p' vessels of silver and of gold; 2532
38 and silver, and with p' stones, 3368
43 over all the p' things of Egypt: 2530
M't 26: 7 alabaster box of very p' ointment, *927*
M'r 14: 3 of ointment of spikenard very p'; *4185
1Co 3:12 silver, p' stones, wood, hay, *5093
Jas 5: 7 waiteth for the p' fruit of the earth, "
1Pe 1: 7 more p' than of gold that perisheth, "
19 But with the p' blood of Christ, as "
2: 4 of men, but chosen of God, and p', *1784*
6 Sion a chief corner stone, elect, p': "
7 therefore which believe he is p': *5092
2Pe 1: 1 that have obtained like p' faith *2472*
4 exceeding great and p' promises *5093*
Re 17: 4 decked with gold and p' stones and "
18:12 silver, and p' stones, and of pearls, "
12 all manner vessels of most p' wood, "
16 decked with gold, and p' stones, and "
21:11 light was like unto a stone most p' "
19 with all manner of p' stones. "

predestinate See also PREDESTINATED.
Ro 8:29 also did p' to be conformed to the *4309
30 whom he did p', them he also * "

predestinated
Eph 1: 5 Having p' us unto the adoption *4309
11 being p' according to the purpose * "

preeminence
Ec 3:19 a man hath no p' above a beast: 4195
Col 1:18 all things he might have the p'. *4409*
3Jo 9 loveth to have the p' among them, *5383*

prefer See also PREFERRED; PREFERRING.
Ps 137: 6 If I p' not Jerusalem above my 5927

preferred
Es 2: 9 he p' her and her maids unto the 8138
Da 6: 3 this Daniel was p' above the 5330
Joh 1:15 cometh after me is p' before me: *1096*
27 coming after me is p' before me, * "
30 a man which is p' before me: * "

preferring
Ro 12:10 love; in honour p' one another; *4285*
1Ti 5:21 without p' one before another, *4299

premeditate
M'r 13:11 ye shall speak, neither do ye p': *3191

preparation See also PREPARATIONS.
1Ch 22: 5 will therefore now make p' for it. 3559
Na 2: 3 flaming torches in the day of his p', "
M't 27:62 that followed the day of the p', *3904*
M'r 15:42 was come, because it was the p', "
Lu 23:54 And that day was the p', and the "
Joh 19:14 And it was the p' of the passover, "
31 because it was the p', that the "
42 because of the Jews' p' day; "
Eph 6:15 with the p' of the gospel of peace; *2091*

preparations
Pr 16: 1 The p' of the heart in man, and 4633

prepare See also PREPARED; PREPAREST; PREPARETH; PREPARING.
Ex 15: 2 God, and I will p' him an habitation;*
16: 5 they shall p' that which they bring 3559
Nu 15: 5 a drink offering shalt thou p' with 6213
6 thou shalt p' for a meat offering "
12 to the number that ye shall p', so "
23: 1 p' me here seven oxen and seven 3559
29 and p' me here seven bullocks and "
De 19: 3 Thou shalt p' thee a way, and "
Jos 1:11 people, saying, P' you victuals; "
22:26 Let us now p' to build us an altar, 6213
1Sa 7: 3 p' your hearts unto the Lord, and 3559
23:22 I pray you, p' ye, and know and * "
1Ki 18:44 Ahab, P' thy chariot, and get thee *631
1Ch 9:32 shewbread, to p' it every sabbath. 3559
29:18 and p' their heart unto thee: and "
2Ch 2: 9 to p' me timber in abundance: "
31:11 to p' chambers in the house of the "
35: 4 p' yourselves by the houses of your "
6 yourselves, and p' your brethren, "
Es 5: 8 banquet that I shall p' for them, 6213
Job 8: 8 p' thyself to the search of their *3559
11:13 If thou p' thine heart, and stretch* "
27:16 dust, and p' raiment as the clay; "
17 He may p' it, but the just shall put "
Ps 10:17 thou wilt p' their heart, thou wilt "
59: 4 p' themselves without my fault: "
61: 7 O p' mercy and truth, which may 4487
107:36 they may p' a city for habitation; 3559
Pr 24:27 P' thy work without, and make it "

Pr 30:25 they p' their meat in the summer;*3559
Isa 14:21 P' slaughter for his children for "
21: 5 P' the table, watch in the 6186
40: 3 P' ye the way of the Lord, make 6437
20 to p' a graven image, that shall *3559
57:14 ye up, p' the way, take up the 6437
62:10 p' ye the way of the people; cast "
65:11 that p' a table for that troop, and 6186
Jer 6: 4 P' ye war against her; arise, and 6942
12: 3 p' them for the day of slaughter. "
22: 7 I will p' destroyers against thee, "
46:14 Stand fast, and p' thee; for the 3559
51:12 the watchmen, p' the ambushes: "
27 p' the nations against her, call 6942
28 P' against her the nations with the "
Eze 4:15 thou shalt p' thy bread therewith. 6213
12: 3 man, p' thee stuff for removing, "
35: 6 I will p' thee unto blood, and blood "
38: 7 and p' for thyself, thou, and all thy 3559
43:25 thou p' every day a goat for a sin 6213
25 they shall also p' a young bullock, 3559
45:17 he shall p' the sin offering, and the "
22 day shall the prince p' for himself "
23 p' a burnt offering to the Lord, "
24 shall p' a meat offering of an ephah "
46: 2 priests shall p' his burnt offering "
7 And he shall p' a meat offering, an "
12 shall p' a voluntary burnt offering "
12 he shall p' his burnt offering and "
13 Thou shalt daily p' a burnt offering "
13 thou shalt p' it every morning. "
14 thou shalt p' a meat offering for it "
15 Thus shall they p' the lamb, and "
Joe 3: 9 P' war, wake up the mighty men, 6942
Am 4:12 thee, p' to meet thy God, O Israel. 3559
Mic 3: 5 they even p' war against him. 6942
Mal 3: 1 and he shall p' the way before me:6437
M't 3: 3 P' ye the way of the Lord, make *2090
11:10 which shall p' thy way before thee. *2680*
26:17 p' for thee to eat the passover? *2090
M'r 1: 2 which shall p' thy way before thee. *2680*
3 P' ye the way of the Lord, make *2090
14:12 Where wilt thou that we go and p'* "
Lu 1:76 face of the Lord to p' his ways; * "
3: 4 P' ye the way of the Lord, make * "
7:27 which shall p' thy way before thee. *2680*
22: 8 Go and p' us the passover, that we *2090
9 him, Where wilt thou that we p'? * "
Joh 14: 2 told you. I go to p' a place for you. "
3 And if I go and p' a place for you, "
1Co 14: 8 who shall p' himself to the battle? *3903*
Ph'm 22 p' me also a lodging: for I trust *2090*

prepared See also PREPAREDST; UNPREPARED.
Ge 24:31 I have p' the house, and room for 6437
27:17 and the bread, which she had p', 6213
Ex 12:39 neither had they p' for themselves "
23:20 into the place which I have p'. 3559
Nu 21:27 the city of Sihon be built and p': "
23: 4 unto him, I have p' seven altars, 6186
Jos 4: 4 he had p' of the children of Israel, 3559
13 forty thousand p' for war passed *2502
2Sa 15: 1 Absalom p' him chariots and 6213
1Ki 1: 5 he p' him chariots and horsemen, "
5:18 so they p' timber and stones to 3559
6:19 the oracle he p' in the house within, "
2Ki 6:23 he p' great provision for them: 3739
1Ch 12:39 for their brethren had p' for them.*3559
15: 1 and p' a place for the ark of God, "
3 his place, which he had p' for it. "
12 unto the place that I have p' for it. "
22: 3 And David p' iron in abundance for "
5 So David p' abundantly before his "
14 I have p' for the house of the Lord "
14 timber also and stone have I p'; "
29: 2 Now I have p' with all my might for "
3 all that I have p' for the holy house, "
16 we have p' to build thee an house "
2Ch 1: 4 the place which David had p' for it: "
3: 1 in the place that David had p' in * "
8:16 Now all the work of Solomon was p' "
12:14 he p' not his heart to seek the Lord.* "
16:14 spices p' by the apothecaries' art: 7543
17:18 thousand ready p' for the war. 2502
19: 3 hast p' thine heart to seek God. *3559
20:33 people had not p' their hearts unto* "
26:14 Uzziah p' for them throughout all "
27: 6 p' his ways before the Lord his God.* "
29:19 his transgression, have we p' and "
36 people, that God had p' the people: "
31:11 of the Lord; and they p' them, "
35:10 the service was p', and the priests "
14 the Levites p' for themselves, "
15 brethren the Levites p' for them. "
16 So all the service of the Lord was p' "
20 this when Josiah had p' the temple, "
Ezr 7:10 Ezra had p' his heart to seek the law "
Ne 5:18 was p' for me daily was one ox 6213
18 also the fowls were p' for me, and "
8:10 unto them for whom nothing is p': 3559
13: 5 had p' for him a great chamber, 6213
Es 5: 4 the banquet that I have p' for him. "
5 to the banquet that Esther had p'. "
12 banquet that she had p' but myself; "
6: 4 the gallows that he had p' for him. 3559
14 the banquet that Esther had p'. 6213
7:10 the gallows that he had p' for 3559
Job 28:27 it; he p' it, yea, and searched it out.* "
29: 7 city, when I p' my seat in the street! "
Ps 7:13 also p' for him the instruments "
9: 7 he hath p' his throne for judgment. "
57: 6 They have p' a net for my steps; * "
68:10 God, hast p' of thy goodness for * "
74:16 thou hast p' the light and the sun. "
103:19 hath p' his throne in the heavens; * "
Pr 8:27 When he p' the heavens, I was "

Pr 19:29 Judgments are p· for scorners, and3559
21:31 The horse is p· against the day of "
Isa 30:33 of old; yea, for the king it is p·; * "
64: 4 p· for him that waiteth for him. *6213
Eze 23:41 bed, and a table p· before it, 6186
28:13 thy pipes was p· in thee in the day3559
38: 7 Be thou p·, and prepare for thyself, "
Da 2: 9 have p· lying and corrupt words 2164
Ho 2: 8 and gold, which they p· for Baal. *6213
6: 3 going forth is p· as the morning; *3559
Jon 1:17 p· a great fish to swallow up 4487
4: 6 And the Lord God p· a gourd, and "
7 God p· a worm when the morning "
8 that God p· a vehement east wind; "
Na 2: 5 and the defence shall be p·. 3559
Zep 1: 7 the Lord hath p· a sacrifice, he hath"
M't 20:23 for whom it is p· of my Father. 2090
22: 4 Behold, I have p· my dinner: my * "
25:34 inherit the kingdom p· for you from"
41 fire, p· for the devil and his angels: "
M'r 10:40 be given to them for whom it is p·. "
14:15 upper room furnished and p·: *2092
Lu 1:17 ready a people p· for the Lord. 2680
2:31 p· before the face of all people; 2090
12:47 his lord's will, and p· not himself,* "
23:56 and p· spices and ointments; "
24: 1 the spices which they had p·, and "
Ro 9:23 which he had afore p· unto glory, 4282
1Co 2: 9 hath p· for them that love him. 2090
2Ti 2:21 use, and p· unto every good work. "
Heb10: 5 not, but a body hast thou p· me: *2675
11: 7 p· an ark to the saving of his house;2680
16 God: for he hath p· for them a city.2090
Re 8: 6 trumpets p· themselves to sound. "
9: 7 like unto horses p· unto battle; "
15 which were p· for an hour, and a "
12: 6 where she hath a place p· of God, "
16:12 the kings of the east might be p·. * "
21: 2 p· as a bride adorned for her * "

preparedst
Ps 80: 9 Thou p· room before it, and didst 6437

preparest
Nu 15: 8 thou p· a bullock for a burnt 6213
Ps 23: 5 Thou p· a table before me in the 6186
65: 9 thou p· them corn, when thou *3559

prepareth
2Ch 30:19 That p· his heart to seek God, the*3559
Job 15:35 vanity, and their belly p· deceit. "
Ps 147: 8 who p· rain for the earth, who "

preparing
Ne 13: 7 in p· him a chamber in the courts 6213
1Pe 3:20 while the ark was a p·, wherein 2680

presbytery
1Ti 4:14 laying on of the hands of the p·. 4244

prescribed
Isa 10: 1 grievousness which they have p·;*3789

prescribing
Ezr 7:22 and salt without p· how much. 3792

presence
Ge 3: 8 from the p· of the Lord God 6440
4:16 Cain went out from the p· of the "
16:12 dwell in the p· of all his brethren. "
23:11 in the p· of the sons of my people 5869
18 in the p· of the children of Heth, "
25:18 died in the p· of all his brethren. *6440
27:30 out from the p· of Isaac his father, "
41:46 went out from the p· of Pharaoh, "
45: 3 for they were troubled at his p·. "
47:15 for why should we die in thy p·? 5048
Ex 10:11 driven out from Pharaoh's p·. 5869
33:14 My p· shall go with thee, and I 6440
15 If thy p· go not with me, carry us "
35:20 departed from the p· of Moses. "
Le 22: 3 soul shall be cut off from my p·: * "
Nu 20: 6 Moses and Aaron went from the p· "
De 25: 9 unto him in the p· of the elders, 5869
Jos 4:11 the priests, in the p· of the people. 6440
8:32 in the p· of the children of Israel. "
1Sa 18:11 David avoided out of his p· twice. "
19: 7 he was in his p·, as in times past. "
10 he slipped away out of Saul's p·, "
21:15 to play the mad man in my p·? 5921
2Sa 16:19 I not serve in the p· of his son? 6440
19 as I have served in thy father's p·, "
19 so will I be in thy p·. "
24: 4 went out from the p· of the king, to "
1Ki 1:28 And she came into the king's p·, "
8:22 in the p· of all the congregation 5048
12: 2 fled from the p· of king Solomon, 6440
21:13 against Naboth in the p· of the 5048
2Ki 3:14 that I regard the p· of Jehoshaphat6440
5:27 his p· a leper as white as snow. "
13:23 cast he them from his p· as yet. "
24:20 he had cast them out from his p·, "
25:19 of them that were in the king's p·,* "
1Ch 16:27 Glory and honour are in his p·; * "
33 wood sing out at the p· of the Lord,*"
24:31 Aaron in the p· of David the king, "
2Ch 6:12 the p· of all the congregation of 5048
9:23 earth sought the p· of Solomon, 6440
10: 2 from the p· of Solomon the king, "
20: 9 and in thy p·, (for thy name is in "
34: 4 down the altars of Baalim in his p·;"
Ne 2: 1 not been beforetime sad in his p·. "
Es 1:10 in the p· of Ahasuerus the king. "
8:15 went out from the p· of the king "
Job 1:12 went forth from the p· of the Lord. "
2: 7 Satan forth from the p· of the Lord."
23:15 Therefore am I troubled at his p·: "
Ps 9: 3 they shall fall and perish at thy p·. "
Ps 16:11 of life: in thy p· is fulness of joy; 6440
17: 2 sentence come forth from thy p·; "
23: 5 me in the p· of mine enemies: 5048
31:20 hide them in the secret of thy p· 6440
51:11 Cast me not away from thy p·; and "
68: 2 the wicked perish at the p· of God. "
8 also dropped at the p· of God: "
8 itself was moved at the p· of God, "
95: 2 before his p· with thanksgiving, "
97: 5 like wax at the p· of the Lord, "
5 p· of the Lord of the whole earth. "
100: 2 come before his p· with singing. "
114: 7 thou earth, at the p· of the Lord, "
7 at the p· of the God of Jacob; "
116:14 Lord now in the p· of all his people.5048
139: 7 whither shall I flee from thy p·? 6440
140:13 the upright shall dwell in thy p·. "
Pr 14: 7 Go from the p· of a foolish man, 5048
17:18 surety in the p· of his friend. 6440
25: 6 forth thyself in the p· of the king, "
7 be put lower in the p· of the prince "
Isa 1: 7 strangers devour it in your p·, and5048
19: 1 of Egypt shall be moved at his p·, 6440
63: 9 and the angel of his p· saved them: "
64: 1 mountains might flow...at thy p·, "
2 the nations may tremble at thy p·! "
3 mountains flowed down at thy p·. "
Jer 4:26 broken down at the p· of the Lord, "
5:22 will ye not tremble at my p·, which "
23:39 fathers, and cast you out of my p·: "
28: 1 the p· of the priests and of all the 5869
5 Hananiah in the p· of the priests, "
5 and in the p· of all the people that "
11 spake in the p· of all the people, "
32:12 and in the p· of the witnesses that "
52: 3 he had cast them out from his p·, 6440
Eze 38:20 of the earth, shall shake at my p·, "
Da 2:27 answered in the p· of the king, 6925
Jon 1: 3 Tarshish from the p· of the Lord, 6440
3 Tarshish from the p· of the Lord. "
10 he fled from the p· of the Lord, "
Na 1: 5 and the earth is burned at his p·, "
Zep 1: 7 thy peace at the p· of the Lord God:"
Lu 1:19 that stand in the p· of God; 1799
13:26 We have eaten and drunk in thy p·, "
14:10 in the p· of them that sit at meat "
15:10 there is joy in the p· of the angels "
Joh 20:30 did Jesus in the p· of his disciples, "
Ac 3:13 and denied him in the p· of Pilate,*4383
16 soundness in the p· of you all. 561
19 come from the p· of the Lord; 4383
5:41 departed from the p· of the council, "
27:35 thanks to God in the p· of them 1799
1Co 1:29 That no flesh should glory in his p·.*"
2Co 10: 1 who in p· am base among you, 4383
10 but his bodily p· is weak, and his 3952
Ph'p 2:12 always obeyed, not as in my p· only,"
1Th 2:17 from you for a short time in p·, 4383
19 in the p· of our Lord Jesus Christ*1715
2Th 1: 9 from the p· of the Lord, and from *4383
Heb 9:24 to appear in the p· of God for us: * "
Jude 24 faultless before the p· of his glory 2714
Re 14:10 in the p· of the holy angels, and in 1799
10 angels, and in the p· of the Lamb: "

present See also PRESENTED; PRESENTING; PRESENTS.
Ge 32:13 came to his hand a p· for Esau 4503
18 it is a p· sent unto my lord Esau: "
20 I will appease him with the p· that "
21 So went the p· over before him: and"
33:10 then receive my p· at my hand: for "
43:11 carry down the man a p·, a little "
15 the men took that p·, and they took "
25 made ready the p· against Joseph "
26 brought him the p· which was in "
Ex 34: 2 Sinai, and p· thyself there to me 5324
Lev 14:11 p· the man that is to be made *5975
16: 7 goats, and p· them before the Lord*"
27: 8 shall p· himself before the priest,* "
11 shall p· the beast before the priest:*"
Nu 3: 6 p· them before Aaron the priest, * "
De 31:14 p· yourselves in the tabernacle of 3320
J'g 3:15 sent a p· unto Eglon the king of 4503
17 he brought the p· unto Eglon king "
18 he had made an end to offer the p·, "
18 away the people that bare the p·. "
6:18 bring forth my p·, and set it before "
1Sa 9: 7 is not a p· to bring to the man of 8670
10:19 p· yourselves before the Lord by 3320
13:15 the people that were p· with him, 4672
16 the people that were p· with them, "
21: 3 in mine hand, or what there is p·. "
30:26 a p· for you of the spoil of the 1293
2Sa 20: 4 three days, and be thou here p·. 5975
1Ki 9:16 a p· unto his daughter, Solomon's*7964
10:25 they brought every man his p·, 4503
15:19 unto thee a p· of silver and gold; 7810
20:27 were numbered, and were all p·, *3557
2Ki 8: 8 Take a p· in thine hand, and go, 4503
9 took a p· with him, even of every "
16: 8 it for a p· to the king of Assyria. 7810
17: 4 no p· to the king of Assyria, as he 4503
18:31 an agreement with me by a p·, *1293
20:12 letters and a p· unto Hezekiah: 4503
1Ch 29:17 joy thy people, which are p· here, 4672
2Ch 5:11 all the priests...p· were sanctified, "
9:24 they brought every man his p·, 4503
29:29 all that were p· with him bowed 4672
30:21 that were p· at Jerusalem kept the "
31: 1 all Israel that were p· went out to "
34:32 all that were p· in Jerusalem and * "
33 all that were p· in Israel to serve, * "
35: 7 for all that were p·, to the number "
17 that were p· kept the passover at "
18 all Judah and Israel that were p·, "
Ezr 8:25 all Israel there p·, had offered: "
Es 1: 5 the people that were p· in Shushan4672
4:16 all the Jews that are p· in Shushan, "
Job 1: 6 to p· themselves before the Lord, 3320
2: 1 to p· themselves before the Lord, "
1 them to p· himself before the Lord. "
Ps 46: 1 strength, a very p· help in trouble.4672
Isa 18: 7 the p· be brought unto the Lord of7862
36:16 an agreement with me by a p·, *1293
39: 1 sent letters and a p· to Hezekiah: 4503
Jer 36: 7 p· their supplication before the 5307
42: 9 ye sent me to p· your supplication "
Eze 27:15 for a p· horns of ivory and ebony.* 814
Da 9:18 p· our supplications before thee 5307
Ho 10: 6 Assyria for a p· to king Jareb: 4503
Lu 2:22 Jerusalem, to p· him to the Lord; 3936
5:17 of the Lord was p· to heal them. *
13: 1 There were p· at that season some 3918
Joh 14:25 unto you, being yet p· with you. *3306
Ac 10:33 are we all here p· before God, to 3918
21:18 James; and all the elders were p·.3854
25:24 all men which are here p· with us, 4840
28: 2 because of the p· rain, and because2186
Ro 7:18 for to will is p· with me; but how 3873
21 would do good, evil is p· with me. "
8:18 sufferings of this p· time are not 3568
38 nor things p·, nor things to come, 1764
11: 5 then at this p· time also there is a 3568
12: 1 ye p· your bodies a living sacrifice,3936
1Co 3:22 or things p·, or things to come; 1764
4:11 unto this p· hour we both hunger, 737
5: 3 as absent in body, but p· in spirit, 3918
3 have judged...as though I were p·, "
7:26 that this is good for the p· distress,‡1764
15: 6 greater part remain unto this p·, * 737
2Co 4:14 by Jesus, and shall p· us with you. 3936
5: 8 body, and to be p· with the Lord. *1736
9 that, whether p· or absent, we may*"
10: 2 when I am p· with that confidence,3918
11 we be also in deed when we are p·. "
11: 2 I may p· you as a chaste virgin to 3936
9 And when I was p· with you, and 3918
13: 2 as if I were p·, the second time; "
10 being p· I should use sharpness, "
Ga 1: 4 deliver us from this p· evil world, 1764
4:18 not only when I am p· with you. 3918
20 I desire to be p· with you now, and "
Eph 5:27 p· it to himself a glorious church, 3936
Col 1:22 p· you holy and unblameable and "
28 may p· every man perfect in Christ "
2Ti 4:10 me, having loved this p· world, 3568
Tit 2:12 and godly, in this p· world; "
Heb 9: 9 was a figure for the time then p·, 1764
12:11 no chastening for the p· seemeth 3918
2Pe 1:12 and be established in the p· truth.* "
Jude 24 and to p· you faultless before the *2476

presented
Ge 46:29 Goshen, and p· himself unto him; 7200
47: 2 men, and p· them unto Pharaoh. 3322
Le 2: 8 when it is p· unto the priest, he 7126
7:35 p· them to minister unto the Lord "
9:12 sons p· unto him the blood, *4672
13 they p· the burnt offering unto him,*"
18 sons p· unto him the blood, * "
16:10 be the scapegoat, shall be p· alive *5975
De 31:14 p· themselves in the tabernacle of 3320
Jos 24: 1 and they p· themselves before God. "
J'g 6:19 unto him under the oak, and p· it. 5066
20: 2 p· themselves in the assembly of 3320
1Sa 17:16 evening, and p· himself forty days. "
Jer 38:26 I p· my supplication before the 5307
Eze 20:28 they p· the provocation of their 5414
M't 2:11 treasures, they p· unto him gifts; *4374
Ac 9:41 saints and widows, p· her alive. 3936
23:33 governor, p· Paul also before him. "

presenting
Da 9:20 p· my supplication before the Lord5307

presently
1Sa 2:16 Let them not fail to burn the fat p·,3117
Pr 12:16 A fool's wrath is p· known: but a "
M't 21:19 And p· the fig tree withered away.*3916
26:53 shall p· give me more than twelve*3936
Ph'p 2:23 Him therefore I hope to send p·, *1824

presents
1Sa 10:27 him, and brought him no p·. *4503
1Ki 4:21 brought p·, and served Solomon "
2Ki 17: 3 his servant, and gave him p·. "
2Ch 17: 5 Judah brought to Jehoshaphat p·; "
11 brought Jehoshaphat p·, and "
32:23 and p· to Hezekiah king of Judah:*4030
Ps 68:29 shall kings bring p· unto thee. 7862
72:10 and of the isles shall bring p·: 4503
76:11 bring p· unto him that ought to be7862
Mic 1:14 thou give p· to Moresheth-gath: *7964

preserve See also PRESERVED; PRESERVEST; PRESERVETH.
Ge 19:32, 34 we may p· seed of our father. 2421
45: 5 did send me before you to p· life. 4241
7 to p· you a posterity in the earth, 7760
De 6:24 that he might p· us alive, as it is 2421
Ps 12: 7 p· them from this generation for 5341
16: 1 P· me, O God: for in thee do I put 8104
25:21 integrity and uprightness p· me; 5341
32: 7 thou shalt p· me from trouble; "
40:11 and thy truth continually p· me. "
41: 2 The Lord will p· him, and keep 8104
61: 7 and truth, which may p· him. 5341
64: 1 p· my life from fear of the enemy. "
79:11 p· thou those that are appointed to3498
86: 2 P· my soul; for I am holy: O thou 8104
121: 7 The Lord shall p· thee from all evil:*"
7 he shall p· thy soul. * "
8 Lord shall p· thy going out and thy*"
140: 1 man: p· me from the violent man; 5341

Ps 140: 4 wicked; p' me from the violent man;5341
Pr 2:11 Discretion shall p' thee, *8104
4: 6 her not, and she shall p' thee: "
14: 3 the lips of the wise shall p' them. "
20:28 Mercy and truth p' the king: and 5341
22:12 The eyes of the Lord p' knowledge, "
Isa 31: 5 it; and passing over he will p' it. 4422
49: 8 and I will p' thee, and give thee 5341
Jer 49:11 children, I will p' them alive; 2421
Lu 17:33 shall lose his life shall p' it. *2225*
2Ti 4:18 p' me unto his heavenly kingdom: *4982*

preserved

Ge 32:30 God face to face, and my life is p'. 5337
Jos 24:17 p' us in all the way wherein we 8104
1Sa 30:23 who hath p' us, and delivered the "
2Sa 8: 6, 14 p' David whithersoever he *3467
1Ch 18: 6, 13 p' David whithersoever he went.*"
Job 10:12 thy visitation hath p' my spirit. 8104
29: 2 as in the days when God p' me; * "
Ps 37:28 they are p' for ever: but the seed "
Isa 49: 6 and to restore the p' of Israel: 5336
Ho 12:13 Egypt, and by a prophet was he p'.8104
M't 9:17 into new bottles, and both are p'. *4933*
Lu 5:38 into new bottles; and both are p'. * "
1Th 5:23 be p' blameless unto the coming *5083*
Jude 1 and p' in Jesus Christ, and called:* "

preserver

Job 7:20 I do unto thee, O thou p' of men? *5341

preservest

Ne 9: 6 is therein, and thou p' them all; 2421
Ps 36: 6 O Lord, thou p' man and beast. 3467

preserveth

Job 36: 6 He p' not the life of the wicked: 2421
Ps 31:23 for the Lord p' the faithful, and 5341
97:10 he p' the souls of his saints; he 8104
116: 6 The Lord p' the simple: I was "
145:20 The Lord p' all them that love him:"
146: 9 The Lord p' the strangers; he "
Pr 2: 8 and p' the way of his saints. * "
16:17 he that keepeth his way p' his soul."

presidents

Da 6: 2 And over these three p'; of whom 5632
3 preferred above the p' and princes, "
4 the p' and princes sought to find "
6 these p' and princes assembled "
7 All the p' of the kingdom, the "

press See also PRESSED; PRESSES; PRESSETH; PRESSFAT; OPPRESS; WINEPRESS.

Joe 3:13 for the p' is full, the fats overflow;*1660
Hag 2:16 draw out fifty vessels out of the p',*6333
M'r 2: 4 not come nigh unto him for the p',*3793*
5:27 came in the p' behind, and touched*"
30 him, turned him about in the p', * "
Lu 8:19 could not come at him for the p'. * "
45 multitude throng thee and p' thee,**598*
19: 3 could not for the p', because he *3793*
Ph'p 3:14 I p' toward the mark for the prize *1377*

pressed See also OPPRESSED.

Ge 19: 3 And he p' upon them greatly; and*6484
9 they p' sore upon the man, even "
40:11 and p' them into Pharaoh's cup, 7818
J'g 16:16 she p' him daily with her words, 6693
2Sa 13:25 he p' him: howbeit he would not 6555
27 But Absalom p' him, that he let "
Es 8:14 p' on by the king's commandment.1765
Eze 23: 3 there were their breasts p', and 4600
Am 2:13 Behold, I am p' under you, as a *5781
13 as a cart is p' that is full of sheaves.*"
M'r 3:10 they p' upon him for to touch him,*1968*
Lu 5: 1 people p' upon him to hear the *1945*
6:38 good measure, p' down, and shaken*4085*
Ac 18: 5 Paul was p' in the spirit, and **4912*
2Co 1: 8 that we were p' out of measure, * *916*

presses See also WINEPRESSES.

Ne 13:15 treading wine p' on the sabbath, *1660
Pr 3:10 p' shall burst out with new wine. *3342
Isa 16:10 shall tread out no wine in their p'; "

presseth See also OPPRESSETH.

Ps 38: 2 in me, and thy hand p' me sore. 5181
Lu 16:16 preached, and every man p' into it.**971*

pressfat

Hag 2:16 one came to the p' for to draw *3342

presume See also PRESUMED.

De 18:20 shall p' to speak a word in my *2102
Es 7: 5 that durst p' in his heart to do so? 4390

presumed

Nu 14:44 they p' to go up unto the hill top: 6075

presumptuous

Ps 19:13 thy servant also from p' sins; 2086
2Pe 2:10 P' are they, selfwilled, they are **5113*

presumptuously

Ex 21:14 man come p' upon his neighbour, 2102
Nu 15:30 But the soul that doeth ought p', *3027
De 1:43 and went p' up into the hill, *2102
17:12 And the man that will do p', and 2087
13 and fear, and do no more p'. 2102
18:22 the prophet hath spoken it p': 2087

pretence

M't 23:14 and for a p' make long prayer: **4392*
M'r 12:40 for a p' make long prayers: these "
Ph'p 1:18 whether in p', or in truth, Christ is "

Pretorium See PRÆTORIUM.

prevail See also PREVAILED; PREVAILEST; PREVAILETH.

Ge 7:20 cubits upward did the waters p'; 1396
Nu 22: 6 peradventure I shall p', that we 3201
J'g 16: 5 what means we may p' against him, "
1Sa 2: 9 for by strength shall no man p'. 1396
1Sa 17: 9 but if I p' against him, and kill him,3201
26:25 great things, and also shalt still p'. "
1Ki 22:22 shalt persuade him, and p' also: "
2Ch 14:11 God; let not man p' against thee. 6113
18:21 entice him, and thou shalt also p':3201
Es 6:13 thou shalt not p' against him, but "
Job 15:24 they shall p' against him, as a king8630
18: 9 the robber shall p' against him. *2388
Ps 9:19 Arise, O Lord; let not man p': let 5810
12: 4 With our tongue will we p'; our 1396
65: 3 Iniquities p' against me: as for our "
Ec 4:12 if one p' against him, two shall 8630
Isa 7: 1 it, but could not p' against it. 3898
16:12 to pray; but he shall not p'. 3201
42:13 he shall p' against his enemies. *1396
47:12 to profit, if so be thou mayest p'. 6206
Jer 1:19 but they shall not p' against thee;3201
5:22 themselves, yet can they not p'; "
15:20 they shall not p' against thee: for I "
20:10 enticed, and we shall p' against him,"
11 stumble, and they shall not p': "
Da 11: 7 deal against them, and shall p': 2388
M't 16:18 gates of hell shall not p' against it.*2729*
27:24 Pilate saw...he could p' nothing, **5623*
Joh 12:19 Perceive ye how ye p' nothing? "

prevailed

Ge 7:18 the waters p', and were increased 1396
19 the waters p' exceedingly upon the "
24 And the waters p' upon the earth "
30: 8 with my sister, and I have p': 3201
32:25 he saw that he p' not against him, "
28 with God and with men, and has p'."
47:20 because the famine p' over them:*2388
49:26 blessings of thy father have p' 1396
Ex 17:11 held up his hand, that Israel p': "
11 he let down his hand, Amalek p'. "
J'g 1:35 the hand of the house of Joseph p',3513
3:10 p' against Chushan-rishathaim. 5810
4:24 and p' against Jabin the king of 7186
6: 2 hand of Midian p' against Israel: 5810
1Sa 17:50 So David p' over the Philistine 2388
2Sa 11:23 Surely the men p' against us, 1396
24: 4 the king's word p' against Joab, 2388
1Ki 16:22 the people that followed Omri p' "
2Ki 25: 3 the famine p' in the city, and there*"
1Ch 5: 2 For Judah p' above his brethren, 1396
21: 4 the king's word p' against Joab. 2388
2Ch 8: 3 to Hamath-zobah, and p' against it."
13:18 children of Judah p', because they 553
27: 5 Ammonites, and p' against them. 2388
Ps 13: 4 enemy say, I have p' against him; 3201
129: 2 yet they have not p' against me. "
Jer 20: 7 art stronger than I, and hast p': "
38:22 thee on, and have p' against thee: "
La 1:16 desolate, because the enemy p'. 1396
Da 7:21 the saints, and p' against them; 3202
Ho 12: 4 had power over the angel, and p': 3201
Ob 7 deceived thee, and p' against thee; "
Lu 23:23 them and of the chief priests p'. *2729*
Ac 19:16 p' against them, so that they fled *2480*
20 grew the word of God, and p'. "
Re 5: 5 David hath p' to open the book, **3528*
12: 8 p' not; neither was their place *2480*

prevailest

Job 14:20 Thou p' for ever against him, 8630

prevaileth

La 1:13 my bones, and it p' against them: 7287

prevent See also PREVENTED; PREVENTEST.

Job 3:12 Why did the knees p' me? or why*6923
Ps 59:10 The God of my mercy shall p' me:‡ "
79: 8 thy tender mercies speedily p' us;‡ "
88:13 morning shall my prayer p' thee. * "
119:148 Mine eyes p' the night watches,†‡ "
Am 9:10 evil shall not overtake nor p' us. "
1Th 4:15 shall not p' them which are asleep.**5348*

prevented

2Sa 22: 6 about; the snares of death p' me;*6923
19 p' me in the day of my calamity: * "
Job 30:27 not: the days of affliction p' me. * "
41:11 Who hath p' me, that I should * "
Ps 18: 5 about: the snares of death p' me.* "
18 They p' me in the day of my * "
119:147 I p' the dawning of the morning,‡ "
Isa 21:14 p' with their bread him that fled. * "
M't 17:25 come into the house, Jesus p' him,**4399*

preventest

Ps 21: 3 thou p' him with the blessings ‡6923

prey

Ge 49: 9 from the p', my son, thou art gone2964
27 morning he shall devour the p', 5706
Nu 14: 3 and our children should be a p'? 957
31 ones, which ye said should be a p', "
23:24 not lie down until he eat of the p', 2964
31:11 took all the spoil, and all the p', 4455
12 brought the captives, and the p', "
26 Take the sum of the p' that was "
27 And divide the p' into two parts; "
32 the p' which the men of war had 957
De 1:39 ones, which ye said should be a p', "
2:35 we took for a p' unto ourselves, 962
3: 7 cities, we took for a p' to ourselves, "
Jos 8: 2 ye take for a p' unto yourselves: "
27 Israel took for a p' unto themselves, "
11:14 Israel took for a p' unto themselves;"
J'g 5:30 have they not divided the p'; to *7998
30 to Sisera a p' of divers colours, * "
30 p' of divers colours of needlework, "
8:24, 25 every man the earrings of his p'.*"
2Ki 21:14 they shall become a p' and a spoil 957
Ne 4: 4 for a p' in the land of captivity: †‡ 961
Es 3:13 to take the spoil of them for a p'. 962
8:11 to take the spoil of them for a p', "
Es 9:15 on the p' they laid not their hand.* 961
16 they laid not their hands on the p'.*"
Job 4:11 old lion perisheth for lack of p', 2964
9:26 as the eagle that hasteth to the p'. 400
24: 5 work; rising betimes for a p': *2964
38:39 Wilt thou hunt the p' for the lion? "
39:29 thence she seeketh the p', and her 400
Ps 17:12 as a lion that is greedy of his p', 2963
76: 4 excellent than the mountains of p'.2964
104:21 The young lions roar after their p', "
124: 6 not given us as a p' to their teeth. "
Pr 23:28 She also lieth in wait as for a p', *2863
Isa 5:29 lay hold of the p', and shall carry 2964
10: 2 that widows may be their p', and *7998
6 to take the p', and to tread them 957
31: 4 the young lion roaring on his p', 2964
33:23 is the p' of a great spoil divided; 5706
23 spoil divided; the lame take the p'.957
42:22 they are for a p', and none "
49:24 the p' be taken from the mighty, 4455
25 p' of the terrible shall be delivered: "
59:15 from evil maketh himself a p': 7997
Jer 21: 9 his life shall be unto him for a p'. 7998
30:16 p' upon thee will I give for a p'. 962
38: 2 he shall have his life for a p', and 7998
39:18 thy life shall be for a p' unto thee: "
45: 5 life will I give unto thee for a p' in "
Eze 7:21 the hands of the strangers for a p',957
19: 3 and it learned to catch the p'; 2964
6 lion, and learned to catch the p', "
22:25 like a roaring lion ravening the p'; "
27 like wolves ravening the p', to shed"
26:12 and make a p' of thy merchandise: 962
29:19 and take her spoil, and take her p';957
34: 8 because my flock became a p', and "
22 and they shall no more be a p'; "
28 shall no more be a p' to the heathen,"
36: 4 became a p' and derision to the "
5 minds, to cast it out for a p'. "
38:12 To take a spoil, and to take a p'; "
13 gathered thy company to take a p'? "
Da 11:24 he shall scatter among them the p',961
Am 3: 4 in the forest, when he hath no p'? 2964
Na 2:12 filled his holes with p', and his dens"
13 I will cut off thy p' from the earth, "
3: 1 robbery; the p' departeth not; "
Zep 3: 8 the day that I rise up to the p': 5706

price See also PRICES; PRISED.

Le 25:16 thou shalt increase the p' thereof, 4736
16 thou shalt diminish the p' of it: "
50 p' of his sale shall be according 3701
51 give again the p' of his redemption "
52 him again the p' of his redemption. "
De 23:18 the p' of a dog, into the house of *4242
2Sa 24:24 I will surely buy it of thee at a p': "
1Ki 10:28 received the linen yarn at a p'. "
1Ch 21:22 shalt grant it me for the full p': 3701
24 I will verily buy it for the full p': "
2Ch 1:16 received the linen yarn at a p'. 4242
Job 28:13 Man knoweth not the p' thereof; 6187
15 be weighed for the p' thereof. 4242
18 the p' of wisdom is above rubies. 4901
Ps 44:12 increase thy wealth by their p'. 4242
Pr 17:16 a p' in the hand of a fool to get "
27:26 the goats are the p' of the field. "
31:10 for her p' is far above rubies. 4377
Isa 45:13 my captives, not for p' nor reward,4242
55: 1 without money and without p'. "
Jer 15:13 will I give to the spoil without p', "
Zec 11:12 If you think good, give me my p';*7939
12 for my p' thirty pieces of silver. "
13 a goodly p' that I was prised at of 3365
M't 13:46 had found one pearl of great p', *4186*
27: 6 because it is the p' of blood. *5092*
9 the p' of him that was valued, "
Ac 5: 2 kept back part of the p', his wife "
3 keep back part of the p' of the land?"
19:19 and they counted the p' of them, "
1Co 6:20 For ye are bought with a p': "
7:23 Ye are bought with a p'; be not ye "
1Pe 3: 4 is in the sight of God of great p'. *4185*

priced See PRISED.

prices

Ac 4:34 p' of the things that were sold, *5092*

pricked

Ps 73:21 grieved, and I was p' in my reins. 8150
Ac 2:37 they were p' in their heart, and *2669*

pricking

Eze 28:24 shall be no more a p' brier unto 3992

pricks

Nu 33:55 be p' in your eyes, and thorns 7899
Ac 9: 5 for thee to kick against the p'. *2759*
26:14 for thee to kick against the p'. * "

pride

Le 26:19 I will break the p' of your power; 1347
1Sa 17:28 I know thy p', and the 2087
2Ch 32:26 humbled himself for the p' of his 1363
Job 33:17 purpose, and hide p' from man. 1466
35:12 because of the p' of evil men. 1347
41:15 His scales are his p', shut up 1346
34 a king over all the children of p'. 7830
Ps 10: 2 wicked in his p' doth persecute 1346
4 through the p' of his countenance,1363
31:20 thy presence from the p' of man: *7407
36:11 the foot of p' come against me, 1346
59:12 them even be taken in their p': 1347
73: 6 p' compasseth them about as a 1346
Pr 8:13 p', and arrogancy, and the evil 1344
11: 2 p' cometh, then cometh shame: 2087
13:10 Only by p' cometh contention: but "
14: 3 mouth of the foolish is a rod of p': 1346
16:18 P' goeth before destruction, and 1347

Pr 29:23 man's p' shall bring him low: but 1346
Isa 9: 9 in the p' and stoutness of heart,
16: 6 We have heard of the p' of Moab; 1347
6 even of his haughtiness, and his p', "
23: 9 it, to stain the p' of all glory, "
25:11 he shall bring down their p' 1346
28: 1 Woe to the crown of p', to the 1348
3 The crown of p', the drunkards of "
Jer 13: 9 will I mar the p' of Judah, 1347
9 and the great p' of Jerusalem. "
17 weep in secret places for your p'; 1466
48:29 We have heard the p' of Moab, (he 1347
29 and his arrogancy, and his p', "
49:16 thee, and the p' of thine heart, 2087
Eze 7:10 hath blossomed, p' hath budded. "
16:49 Sodom, p', fulness of bread, and 1347
56 thy mouth in the day of thy p', "
30: 6 and the p' of her power shall come "
Da 4:37 those that walk in p' he is able 1466
5:20 his mind hardened in p', he was *2103
Ho 5: 5 the p' of Israel doth testify to his 1347
7:10 the p' of Israel testifieth to his "
Ob 3 p' of thine heart hath deceived 2087
Zep 2:10 This shall they have for their p', 1347
3:11 them that rejoice in thy p', and *1346
Zec 9: 6 cut off the p' of the Philistines. 1347
10:11 the p' of Assyria shall be brought "
11: 3 for the p' of Jordan is spoiled. "
M'r 7:22 eye, blasphemy, p', foolishness: 5243
1Ti 3: 6 being lifted up with p' he fall into*5187
1Jo 2:16 lust of the eyes, and the p' of life,* 212

priest See also PRIESTHOOD; PRIEST'S; PRIESTS.
Ge 14:18 was the p' of the most high God. 3548
41:45 daughter of Poti-pherah p' of On. "
50 of Poti-pherah p' of On bare unto "
46:20 of Poti-pherah p' of On bare unto "
Ex 2:16 p' of Midian had seven daughters: "
3: 1 father in law, the p' of Midian: "
18: 1 Jethro, the p' of Midian, Moses' "
29:30 that son that is p' in his stead "
31:10 holy garments for Aaron the p', "
35:19 holy garments for Aaron the p', "
38:21 Ithamar, son to Aaron the p'. "
39:41 holy garments for Aaron the p', "
Le 1: 7 Aaron the p' shall put fire upon the "
9 the p' shall burn all on the altar, "
12 p' shall lay them in order on the "
13 p' shall bring it all, and burn it "
15 the p' shall bring it unto the altar, "
17 the p' shall burn it upon the altar, "
2: 2 p' shall burn the memorial of it "
8 when it is presented unto the p', "
9 p' shall take from the meat offering "
16 the p' shall burn the memorial of it, "
3:11 the p' shall burn it upon the altar: "
16 p' shall burn them upon the altar: "
4: 3 p' that is anointed do sin according "
5 p' that is anointed shall take of the "
6 p' shall dip his finger in the blood, "
7 p' shall put some of the blood upon "
10 p' shall burn them upon the altar "
16 p' that is anointed shall bring of "
17 p' shall dip his finger in some of "
20 the p' shall make an atonement for "
25 the p' shall take of the blood of the "
26 p' shall make an atonement for him "
30 p' shall take of the blood thereof "
31 p' shall make an atonement for him, "
34 p' shall take of the blood of the sin "
35 p' shall burn them upon the altar, "
35 p' shall make an atonement for his "
5: 6 p' shall make an atonement for him "
8 shall bring them unto the p', who "
10 p' shall make an atonement for him "
12 Then shall he bring it to the p', and "
12 the p' shall take his handful of it, "
13 p' shall make an atonement for him "
16 thereto, and give it unto the p': "
16 p' shall make an atonement for him "
18 for a trespass offering, unto the p': "
18 p' shall make an atonement for him "
6: 6 for a trespass offering, unto the p': "
7 p' shall make an atonement for him "
10 p' shall put on his linen garment, "
12 the p' shall burn wood on it every "
22 the p' of his sons that is anointed "
23 offering for the p' shall be wholly "
26 The p' that offereth it for sin shall "
7: 5 p' shall burn them upon the altar "
7 the p' that maketh atonement "
8 p' that offereth any man's burnt "
8 p' shall have to himself the skin "
31 p' shall burn the fat upon the altar: "
32 ye give unto the p' for an heave "
34 unto Aaron the p' and unto his sons "
12: 6 of the congregation, unto the p': "
8 p' shall make an atonement for her, "
13: 2 shall be brought unto Aaron the p', "
3 p' shall look on the plague in the "
3 p' shall look on him, and pronounce "
4 p' shall shut up him that hath the "
5 p' shall look on him the seventh "
5 p' shall shut him up seven days "
6 the p' shall look on him again the "
6 the p' shall pronounce him clean: "
7 that he hath been seen of the p' for "
7 he shall be seen of the p' again: "
8 if the p' see that, behold, the scab "
8 p' shall pronounce him unclean: "
9 he shall be brought unto the p'; "
10 And the p' shall see him: and, "
11 p' shall pronounce him unclean, "
12 foot wheresoever the p' looketh; "
13 Then the p' shall consider: and "
15 the p' shall see the raw flesh, and "
Le 13:16 white, he shall come unto the p'; 3548
17 And the p' shall see him: and, "
17 the p' shall pronounce him clean "
19 reddish, and it be shewed to the p'; "
20 when the p' seeth it, behold, it be "
20 p' shall pronounce him unclean: "
21 if the p' look on it, and, behold, "
21 p' shall shut him up seven days: "
22 the p' shall pronounce him unclean: "
23 the p' shall pronounce him clean. "
25 the p' shall look upon it: and, "
25 p' shall pronounce him unclean: "
26 if the p' look on it, and, behold, "
26 p' shall shut him up seven days: "
27 p' shall look upon him the seventh "
27 p' shall pronounce him unclean: "
28 the p' shall pronounce him clean: "
30 the p' shall see the plague: and, "
30 p' shall pronounce him unclean: "
31 p' look upon the plague of the scall, "
31 p' shall shut up him that hath the "
32 the p' shall look on the plague: "
33 p' shall shut up him that hath the "
34 day the p' shall look on the scall: "
34 the p' shall pronounce him clean: "
36 p' shall look on him: and, behold, "
36 p' shall not seek for yellow hair; "
37 the p' shall pronounce him clean. "
39 Then the p' shall look: and, behold, "
43 p' shall look upon it: and, behold, "
44 the p' shall pronounce him utterly "
49 and shall be shewed unto the p': "
50 the p' shall look upon the plague, "
53 if the p' shall look, and, behold, the "
54 p' shall command that they wash "
55 And the p' shall look on the plague, "
56 And if the p' look, and, behold, the "
14: 2 He shall be brought unto the p': "
3 p' shall go forth out of the camp; "
3 p' shall look, and, behold, if the "
4 the p' command to take for him "
5 p' shall command that one of the "
11 the p' that maketh him clean shall "
12 the p' shall take one he lamb, and "
14 the p' shall take some of the blood "
14 p' shall put it upon the tip of the "
15 p' shall take some of the log of oil, "
16 the p' shall dip his right finger in "
17 the p' put upon the tip of the right "
18 the p' shall make an atonement for "
19 p' shall offer the sin offering, and "
20 the p' shall offer the burnt offering "
20 p' shall make an atonement for him, "
23 day for his cleansing unto the p', "
24 the p' shall take the lamb of the "
24 the p' shall wave them for a wave "
25 the p' shall take some of the blood "
26 p' shall pour of the oil into the palm "
27 the p' shall sprinkle with his right "
28 the p' shall put of the oil that is in "
31 p' shall make an atonement for him "
35 shall come and tell the p', saying, "
36 the p' shall command that they "
36 before the p' go into it to see the "
36 the p' shall go in to see the house: "
38 the p' shall go out of the house to "
39 the p' shall come again the seventh "
40 the p' shall command that they "
44 the p' shall come and look, and, "
48 if the p' shall come in, and look "
48 p' shall pronounce the house clean, "
15:14 and give them unto the p': "
15 the p' shall offer them, the one for "
15 p' shall make an atonement for him "
29 pigeons, and bring them unto the p', "
30 the p' shall offer the one for a sin "
30 the p' shall make an atonement "
16:30 shall the p' make an atonement for*
32 the p', whom he shall anoint, and 3548
17: 5 unto the p', and offer them for "
6 And the p' shall sprinkle the blood "
19:22 p' shall make an atonement for him "
21: 9 daughter of any p', if she profane "
10 the high p' among his brethren, "
21 blemish of the seed of Aaron the p' "
22:10 a sojourner of the p', or an hired * "
11 if the p' buy any soul with his "
14 it unto the p' with the holy thing. "
23:10 first fruits of...harvest unto the p': "
11 the sabbath the p' shall wave it. "
20 the p' shall wave them with the "
20 shall be holy to the Lord for the p'. "
27: 8 shall present himself before the p', "
8 the p' shall value him; according "
8 that vowed shall the p' value him. "
11 present the beast before the p': "
12 the p' shall value it, whether it be "
12 who art the p', so shall it be. "
14 the p' shall estimate it, whether it "
14 the p' shall estimate it, so shall it "
18, 23 the p' shall reckon unto him the "
Nu 3: 6 present them before Aaron the p', "
32 Eleazar the son of Aaron the p' "
4:16 of Eleazar the son of Aaron the p' "
28, 33 Ithamar the son of Aaron the p'. "
5: 8 even to the p'; beside the ram of * "
9 which they bring unto the p', shall "
10 whatsoever any man giveth the p', "
15 the man bring his wife unto the p', "
16 the p' shall bring her near, and set "
17 the p' shall take holy water in an "
17 and of the dust...the p' shall take, "
18 the p' shall set the woman before "
18 p' shall have in his hand the bitter "
19 the p' shall charge her by an oath, 3548
21 p' shall charge the woman with an "
Nu 5:21 the p' shall say unto the woman, 3548
23 the p' shall write these curses in a "
25 p' shall take the jealousy offering "
26 the p' shall take an handful of the "
30 p' shall execute upon her all this "
6:10 or two young pigeons, to the p', to "
11 the p' shall offer the one for a sin "
16 p' shall bring them before the Lord, "
17 p' shall offer also his meat offering, "
19 p' shall take the sodden shoulder "
20 the p' shall wave them for a wave "
20 this is holy for the p', with the wave "
7: 8 of Ithamar the son of Aaron the p'. "
15:25 p' shall make an atonement for all "
28 p' shall make an atonement for the "
16:37 Eleazar the son of Aaron the p', "
39 Eleazar the p' took the brasen "
18:28 heave offering to Aaron the p'. "
19: 3 shall give her unto Eleazar the p', "
4 And Eleazar the p' shall take of her "
6 the p' shall take cedar wood, and "
7 Then the p' shall wash his clothes, "
7 p' shall be unclean until the even. "
25: 7 the son of Aaron the p', saw it, he "
11 son of Aaron the p', hath turned "
26: 1 Eleazar the son of Aaron the p', "
3 and Eleazar the p' spake with them "
63 by Moses and Eleazar the p', who "
64 Moses and Aaron the p' numbered, "
27: 2 Moses, and before Eleazar the p', "
19 And set him before Eleazar the p', "
21 he shall stand before Eleazar the p', "
22 and set him before Eleazar the p', "
31: 6 Phinehas the son of Eleazar the p', "
12 unto Moses, and Eleazar the p', and "
13 Moses, and Eleazar the p', and all "
21 Eleazar the p' said unto the men of "
26 and Eleazar the p', and the chief "
29 give it unto Eleazar the p', for an "
31 and Eleazar the p' did as the Lord "
41 unto Eleazar the p', as the Lord "
51, 54 and Eleazar the p' took the gold "
32: 2 unto Moses, and to Eleazar the p', "
28 Moses commanded Eleazar the p', "
33:38 the p' went up into mount Hor at "
34:17 Eleazar the p', and Joshua the son "
35:25 in it unto the death of the high p', "
28 until the death of the high p': "
28 after the death of the high p' the "
32 the land, until the death of the p'. "
De 17:12 will not hearken unto the p' that "
18: 3 shall give unto the p' the shoulder, "
20: 2 p' shall approach and speak unto "
26: 3 thou shalt go unto the p' that shall "
4 p' shall take the basket out of thine "
Jos 14: 1 which Eleazar the p', and Joshua "
17: 4 came near before Eleazar the p', "
19:51 which Eleazar the p', and Joshua "
20: 6 until the death of the high p' that "
21: 1 the Levites unto Eleazar the p', "
4 the children of Aaron the p', which "
13 gave to the children of Aaron the p' "
22:13 Phinehas the son of Eleazar the p', "
30 And when Phinehas the p', and the "
31 the son of Eleazar the p' said unto "
32 Phinehas the son of Eleazar the p', "
J'g 17: 5 one of his sons, who became his p'. "
10 and be unto me a father and a p', "
12 the young man became his p', and "
13 seeing I have a Levite to my p'. "
18: 4 and hath hired me, and I am his p'. "
6 p' said unto them, Go in peace: "
17 p' stood in the entering of the gate "
18 said the p' unto them, What do ye? "
19 us, and be to us a father and a p': "
19 for thee to be a p' unto the house of "
19 be a p' unto a tribe and a family in "
24 my gods which I made, and the p', "
27 had made, and the p' which he had, "
1Sa 1: 9 Now Eli the p' sat upon a seat by a "
2:11 unto the Lord before Eli the p'. "
14 the fleshhook brought up the p' took "
15 Give flesh to roast for the p'; for "
28 all the tribes of Israel to be my p', "
35 And I will raise me up a faithful p', "
14: 3 son of Eli, the Lord's p' in Shiloh, "
19 while Saul talked unto the p', that "
19 Saul said unto the p', Withdraw "
36 Then said the p', Let us draw near "
21: 1 David to Nob to Ahimelech the p': "
2 David said unto Ahimelech the p', "
4 the p' answered David, and said, "
5 David answered the p', and said "
6 So the p' gave him hallowed bread: "
9 the p' said, The sword of Goliath "
22:11 king sent to call Ahimelech the p', "
23: 9 he said to Abiathar the p', Bring "
30: 7 And David said to Abiathar the p', "
2Sa 15:27 king said also unto Zadok the p', "
1Ki 1: 7 and with Abiathar the p': and "
8 But Zadok the p', and Benaiah the "
19 of the king, and Abiathar the p', "
25 of the host, and Abiathar the p'; "
26 me thy servant, and Zadok the p', "
32 David said, Call me Zadok the p', "
34 let Zadok the p' and Nathan the "
38 So Zadok the p', and Nathan the "
39 Zadok the p' took an horn of oil out "
42 the son of Abiathar the p' came: "
44 with him Zadok the p', and Nathan "
45 And Zadok the p' and Nathan the "
2:22 for him, and for Abiathar the p', "
26 unto Abiathar the p' said the king, "
27 thrust out Abiathar from being p' "
35 Zadok the p' did the king put in the "
4: 2 Azariah the son of Zadok the p'. "

2Ki 11: 9 that Jehoiada the p' commanded: 3548
9 and came to Jehoiada the p'. "
10 did the p' give king David's spears "
15 Jehoiada the p' commanded the "
15 p' had said, Let her not be slain in "
18 slew Mattan the p' of Baal before "
18 p' appointed officers over the house "
12: 2 Jehoiada the p' instructed him. "
7 Jehoash called for Jehoiada the p', "
9 Jehoiada the p' took a chest, and "
10 scribe and the high p' came up, "
16: 10 the p' the fashion of the altar, "
11 And Urijah the p' built an altar "
11 Urijah the p' made it against king "
15 Ahaz commanded Urijah the p', "
16 Thus did Urijah the p', according "
22: 4 Go up to Hilkiah the high p', that "
8 And Hilkiah the high p' said unto "
10 the p' hath delivered me a book. "
12 king commanded Hilkiah the p', "
14 So Hilkiah the p', and Ahikam, and "
23: 4 commanded Hilkiah the high p', "
24 the book that Hilkiah the p' found "
25: 18 the guard took Seraiah the chief p', "
18 Zephaniah the second p', and the "
1Ch 16: 39 Zadok the p', and his brethren the "
24: 6 the princes, and Zadok the p', and "
27: 5 the son of Jehoiada, a chief p': "
29: 22 chief governor, and Zadok to be p'. "
2Ch 13: 9 be a p' of them that are no gods. "
15: 3 without a teaching p', and without "
19: 11 Amariah the chief p' is over you in "
22: 11 the wife of Jehoiada the p', (for she "
23: 8 Jehoiada the p' had commanded, "
8 Jehoiada the p' dismissed not the "
9 Jehoiada the p' delivered to the "
14 Jehoiada the p' brought out the "
14 For the p' said, Slay her not in the "
17 slew Mattan the p' of Baal before "
24: 2 all the days of Jehoiada the p'. "
20 the son of Jehoiada the p', which "
25 of the sons of Jehoiada the p', "
26: 17 Azariah the p' went in after him, "
20 And Azariah the chief p', and all "
31: 10 Azariah the chief p' of the house of "
34: 9 they came to Hilkiah the high p', "
14 Hilkiah the p' found a book of the "
18 the p' hath given me a book. "
Ezr 2: 63 till there stood up a p' with Urim "
7: 5 the son of Aaron the chief p': "
11 Artaxerxes gave unto Ezra the p', "
12 unto Ezra the p', a scribe of the 3549
21 whatsoever Ezra the p', the scribe 3548
8: 33 Meremoth the son of Uriah the p'; "
10: 10 Ezra the p' stood up, and said unto "
16 Ezra the p', with certain chief of "
Ne 3: 1 high p' rose up with his brethren "
20 the house of Eliashib the high p'. "
7: 65 till there stood up a p' with Urim "
8: 2 Ezra the p' brought the law before "
9 and Ezra the p' the scribe, and the "
10: 38 p' the son of Aaron shall be with "
12: 26 and of Ezra the p', the scribe. "
13: 4 before this, Eliashib the p', having "
13 the treasuries, Shelemiah the p', "
28 the son of Eliashib the high p', was "
Ps 110: 4 art a p' for ever after the order of "
Isa 8: 2 witnesses to record, Uriah the p', "
24: 2 as with the people, so with the p'; "
28: 7 the p' and the prophet have erred "
Jer 6: 13 from the prophet even unto the p' "
8: 10 from the prophet even unto the p' "
14: 18 and the p' go about into a land "
18: 18 the law shall not perish from the p', "
20: 1 Pashur the son of Immer the p', "
21: 1 the son of Maaseiah the p', saying, "
23: 11 both prophet and p' are profane; "
33 the prophet, or a p', shall ask thee, "
34 the p', and the people, that shall "
29: 25 son of Maaseiah the p', and to all "
26 The Lord hath made thee p' in the "
26 in the stead of Jehoiada the p', "
29 Zephaniah the p' read this letter in "
37: 3 the son of Maaseiah the p' to the "
52: 24 the guard took Seraiah the chief p', "
24 and Zephaniah the second p', and "
La 2: 6 of his anger the king and the p'. "
20 the p' and the prophet be slain in "
Eze 1: 3 came expressly unto Ezekiel the p', "
7: 26 the law shall perish from the p', "
44: 13 to do the office of a p' unto me, 3547
21 Neither shall any p' drink wine, 3548
22 or a widow that had a p' before. "
30 unto the p' the first of your dough, "
45: 19 p' shall take of the blood of the sin "
Hos 4: 4 are as they that strive with the p'. "
6 that thou shalt be no p' to me: 3547
9 there shall be, like people, like p': 3548
Am 7: 10 the p' of Beth-el sent to Jeroboam "
Hag 1: 1, 12, 14 son of Josedech, the high p', "
2: 2 the son of Josedech, the high p', "
4 son of Josedech, the high p'; "
Zec 3: 1 he shewed me Joshua the high p' "
8 Hear now, O Joshua the high p', "
6: 11 the son of Josedech, the high p'; "
13 he shall be a p' upon his throne: "
M't 8: 4 shew thyself to the p', and offer 2409
26: 3 unto the palace of the high p', who 749
57 him away to Caiaphas the high p', "
62 And the high p' arose, and said unto "
63 the high p' answered and said unto "
65 Then the high p' rent his clothes, "
M'r 1: 44 shew thyself to the p', and offer for 2409
2: 26 in the days of Abiathar the high p', 749
14: 47 smote a servant of the high p', and "
53 they led Jesus away to the high p': "

M'r 14: 54 even into the palace of the high p': 749
60 the high p' stood up in the midst, "
61 Again the high p' asked him, and "
63 Then the high p' rent his clothes, "
66 one of the maids of the high p': "
Lu 1: 5 a certain p' named Zacharias, of 2409
5: 14 and shew thyself to the p', and offer "
10: 31 there came down a certain p' that "
22: 50 smote the servant of the high p', 749
Joh 11: 49 being the high p' that same year, "
51 but being high p' that year, he "
18: 13 was the high p' that same year. "
15 disciple was known unto the high p', "
15 Jesus into the palace of the high p'. "
16 which was known unto the high p', "
19 The high p' then asked Jesus of his "
22 Answerest thou the high p' so? "
24 him bound unto Caiaphas the high p'. "
26 One of the servants of the high p', "
Ac 4: 6 Annas the high p', and Caiaphas, "
6 were of the kindred of the high p', 748
5: 17 Then the high p' rose up, and all 749
21 But the high p' came, and they that "
24 the high p' and the captain of the* "
27 council: and the high p' asked them, "
7: 1 Then said the high p', Are these "
9: 1 of the Lord, went unto the high p', "
14: 13 Then the p' of Jupiter, Which was 2409
22: 5 the high p' doth bear me witness, 749
23: 2 the high p' Ananias commanded "
4 said, Revilest thou God's high p'? "
5 brethren, that he was the high p': "
24: 1 Ananias the high p' descended with "
25: 2 high p' and the chief of the Jews * "
Heb 2: 17 a merciful and faithful high p' in "
3: 1 and High P' of our profession, "
4: 14 then that we have a great high p', "
15 For we have not an high p' which "
5: 1 every high p' taken from among "
5 not himself to be made an high p'; "
6 Thou art a p' forever after the 2409
10 of God an high p' after the order of 749
6: 20 made an high p' for ever after the "
7: 1 p' of the most high God, who met 2409
3 of God; abideth a p' continually. "
11 p' should rise after the order of "
15 of Melchisedec...ariseth another p', "
17 Thou art a p' for ever after the "
20 not without an oath he was made p':* "
21 Thou art a p' for ever after the 2409
26 such an high p' became us, who is 749
8: 1 We have such an high p', who is set "
3 For every high p' is ordained to "
4 on earth, he should not be a p', 2409
9: 7 went the high p' alone once every 749
11 But Christ being come an high p' of "
25 high p' entereth into the holy place "
10: 11 p' standeth daily ministering and 2409
21 an high p' over the house of God; "
13: 11 sanctuary by the high p' for sin, 749

priesthood

Ex 40: 15 shall surely be an everlasting p' 3550
Nu 16: 10 with thee: and seek ye the p' also? "
18: 1 shall bear the iniquity of your p'. "
25: 13 the covenant of an everlasting p'; "
Jos 18: 7 p' of the Lord is their inheritance: "
Ezr 2: 62 they, as polluted, put from the p'. "
Ne 7: 64 they, as polluted, put from the p'. "
13: 29 because they have defiled the p', "
29 and the covenant of the p', and of "
Heb 7: 5 who receive the office of the p', *2405
11 perfection were by the Levitical p', 2420
12 For the p' being changed, there is "
14 Moses spake nothing concerning p'.*"
24 ever, hath an unchangeable p'. "
1Pe 2: 5 up a spiritual house, an holy p', 2406
9 a chosen generation, a royal p', "

priest's

Ex 28: 1 minister unto me in the p' office, 3547
3, 4 minister unto me in the p' office. "
41 minister unto me in the p' office. "
29: 1 minister unto me in the p' office: "
9 the p' office shall be theirs for a *3550
44 to minister to me in the p' office. 3547
30: 30 minister unto me in the p' office. "
31: 10 sons, to minister in the p' office, "
35: 19 sons, to minister in the p' office. "
39: 41 garments, to minister in the p' office. "
40: 13 minister unto me in the p' office. "
15 minister unto me in the p' office: "
Le 5: 13 the remnant shall be the p', as a 3548
7: 9 pan, shall be the p' that offereth it. "
14 shall be the p' that sprinkleth the "
35 unto the Lord in the p' office; 3547
14: 13 for as the sin offering is the p', so 3548
18, 29 oil that is in the p' hand he shall "
16: 32 to minister in the p' office in his *3547
22: 12 the p' daughter also be married 3548
13 if the p' daughter be a widow, or "
27: 21 possession thereof shall be the p'. "
Nu 3: 3 to minister in the p' office. 3547
4 Ithamar ministered in the p' office "
10 they shall wait on their p' office: *3550
18: 7 with thee shall keep your p' office* "
7 I have given your p' office unto you* "
De 10: 6 his son ministered in the p' office 3547
18: 3 be the p' due from the people, 3548
J'g 18: 20 And the p' heart was glad, and he "
1Sa 2: 13 the p' custom with the people was* "
13 the p' servant came, while the flesh "
15 p' servant came, and said to the "
36 into one of the p' offices, that I 3550
1Ch 6: 10 that executed the p' office in the 3547
24: 2 and Ithamar executed the p' office. "
2Ch 11: 14 from executing the p' office unto "

2Ch 24: 11 and the high p' officer came and 3548
Eze 44: 30 of your oblations, shall be the p':* "
Mal 2: 7 the p' lips should keep knowledge, "
M't 26: 51 struck a servant of the high p', * 749
58 him afar off unto the high p' palace.*"
Lu 1: 8 executed the p' office before God 2407
9 to the custom of the p' office, 2405
22: 54 brought him into the high p' house. 749
Joh 18: 10 it, and smote the high p' servant, "

priests See also PRIESTS'.

Ge 47: 22 the land of the p' bought he not; 3548
22 the p' had a portion assigned them "
26 except the land of the p' only, "
Ex 19: 6 shall be unto me a kingdom of p', "
22 let the p' also, which come near "
24 the p' and the people break through "
Le 1: 5 the p', Aaron's sons, shall bring "
8 And the p', Aaron's sons, shall lay "
11 the p', Aaron's sons, shall sprinkle "
2: 2 bring it to Aaron's sons the p': "
3: 2 Aaron's sons the p' shall sprinkle "
6: 29 the males among the p' shall eat "
7: 6 Every male among the p' shall eat "
13: 2 or unto one of his sons the p': "
16: 33 shall make an atonement for the p', "
21: 1 Speak unto the p' the sons of Aaron, "
Nu 3: 3 Aaron, the p' which were anointed, "
10: 8 sons of Aaron, the p', shall blow "
De 17: 9 shalt come unto the p' the Levites, "
18 which is before the p' the Levites: "
18: 1 The p' the Levites, and all the "
19: 17 before the p' and the judges, which "
21: 5 p' the sons of Levi shall come near; "
24: 8 the p' the Levites shall teach you: "
27: 9 Moses and the p' the Levites spake "
31: 9 it unto the p' the sons of Levi, "
Jos 3: 3 and the p' the Levites bearing it, "
6 Joshua spake unto the p', saying, "
8 command the p' that bear the ark "
13 feet of the p' that bear the ark of "
14 p' bearing the ark of the covenant "
15 feet of the p' that bare the ark were "
17 p' that bare the ark of the covenant "
4: 9 the feet of the p' which bare the ark "
10 For the p' which bare the ark stood "
11 of the Lord passed over, and the p', "
16 Command the p' that bear the ark "
17 Joshua therefore commanded the p', "
18 p' that bare the ark of the covenant "
6: 4 p' shall bear before the ark seven "
4 the p' shall blow with the trumpets. "
6 Joshua the son of Nun called the p', "
6 let seven p' bear seven trumpets of "
8 seven p' bearing the seven trumpets "
9 the p' that blew with the trumpets, "
9 p' going on, and blowing with the "
12 the p' took up the ark of the Lord. "
13 seven p' bearing seven trumpets "
13 p' going on, and blowing with the 3548
16 the p' blew with the trumpets, "
20 shouted when the p' blew with the "
8: 33 that side before the p' the Levites, "
21: 19 of the children of Aaron, the p', "
J'g 18: 30 his sons were p' to the tribe of Dan "
1Sa 1: 3 the p' of the Lord, were there. "
5: 5 neither the p' of Dagon, nor any "
6: 2 Philistines called for the p' and the "
22: 11 house, the p' that were in Nob: "
17 Turn, and slay the p' of the Lord; "
17 hand to fall upon the p' of the Lord. "
18 Turn thou, and fall upon the p'. "
18 turned, and he fell upon the p', "
19 Nob, the city of the p', smote he "
21 that Saul had slain the Lord's p'. "
2Sa 8: 17 the son of Abiathar, were the p'; "
15: 35 thee Zadok and Abiathar the p'? "
35 it to Zadok and Abiathar the p'. "
17: 15 unto Zadok and to Abiathar the p', "
19: 11 to Zadok and to Abiathar the p', "
20: 25 and Zadok and Abiathar were the p': "
1Ki 4: 4 and Zadok and Abiathar were the p': "
8: 3 came, and the p' took up the ark. "
4 did the p' and the Levites bring up. "
6 the p' brought in the ark of the "
10 p' were come out of the holy place, "
11 the p' could not stand to minister "
12: 31 made p' of the lowest of the people, "
32 in Beth-el the p' of the high places "
13: 2 he offer the p' of the high places "
33 lowest of the people p' of the high "
33 one of the p' of the high places. "
2Ki 10: 11 men, and his kinfolks, and his p', "
19 Baal, all his servants, and all his p': "
12: 4 And Jehoash said to the p', All the "
5 Let the p' take it to them, every "
6 p' had not repaired the breaches of "
7 the priest, and the other p', and "
8 p' consented to receive no more "
9 p' that kept the door put therein "
17: 27 Carry thither one of the p' whom "
28 Then one of the p' whom they had "
32 of them p' of the high places, "
19: 2 the elders of the p', covered with "
23: 2 the p', and the prophets, and all "
4 p' of the second order, and the "
5 put down the idolatrous p', whom "
8 the p' out of the cities of Judah, 3548
8 where the p' had burned incense, "
9 p' of the high places came not up "
20 And he slew all the p' of the high "
1Ch 9: 2 p', Levites, and the Nethinims. "
10 And of the p'; Jedaiah, and "
30 sons of the p' made the ointment "
13: 2 p' and Levites which are in their "
15: 11 for Zadok and Abiathar the p', "

1Ch 15: 14 the p' and the Levites sanctified 3548
24 the p', did blow with the trumpets "
16: 6 and Jahaziel the p' with trumpets "
39 the priest, and his brethren the p', "
18: 16 the son of Abiathar, were the p'; "
23: 2 Israel, with the p' and the Levites. "
24: 6, 31 the chief of the fathers of the p' "
28: 13, 21 courses of the p' and the Levites, "
2Ch 4: 6 the sea was for the p' to wash in. "
9 he made the court of the p', and "
5: 5 the p' and the Levites bring up. "
7 the p' brought in the ark of the "
11 p' were come out of the holy place: "
11 p' that were present were sanctified, "
12 them an hundred and twenty p' "
14 p' could not stand to minister by "
6: 41 thy p', O Lord God, be clothed with "
7: 2 p' could not enter into the house "
6 the p' waited on their offices: the "
6 p' sounded trumpets before them, "
8: 14 courses of the p' to their service, "
14 and minister before the p', as "
15 of the king unto the p' and Levites "
11: 13 the p' and the Levites that were "
15 he ordained him p' for the high "
13: 9 ye not cast out the p' of the Lord, "
9 made you p' after the manner of "
10 the p', which minister unto the "
12 his p' with sounding trumpets to "
14 and the p' sounded with the "
17: 8 them Elishama and Jehoram, p'. "
19: 8 set of the Levites, and of the p', "
23: 4 of the p' and of the Levites, shall "
6 save the p', and they that minister "
18 by the hand of the p' the Levites, "
24: 5 together the p' and the Levites, "
26: 17 fourscore p' of the Lord, that "
18 to the p' the sons of Aaron, that "
19 while he was wroth with the p', "
19 before the p' in the house of the "
20 all the p', looked upon him, and, "
29: 4 brought in the p' and the Levites, "
16 p' went into the inner part of the "
21 the p' the sons of Aaron to offer "
22 the p' received the blood, and "
24 the p' killed them, and they made "
26 and the p' with the trumpets. "
34 the p' were too few, so that they "
34 other p' had sanctified themselves: "
34 to sanctify themselves than the p'. "
30: 3 because the p' had not sanctified "
15 p' and the Levites were ashamed, "
16 the p' sprinkled the blood, which "
21 the p' praised the Lord day by day, "
24 a great number of p' sanctified "
25 with the p' and the Levites, and all "
27 p' the Levites arose and blessed "
31: 2 appointed the courses of the p' "
2 p' and Levites for burnt offerings "
4 to give the portion of the p' and "
9 Hezekiah questioned with the p' "
15 in the cities of the p', in their set "
17 the genealogy of the p' by the "
19 the sons of Aaron the p', which "
19 to all the males among the p', and to "
34: 5 burnt the bones of the p' upon "
30 the p', and the Levites, and all the "
35: 2 he set the p' in their charges, and "
8 willingly unto the people, to the p', "
8 gave unto the p' for the passover "
10 and the p' stood in their place, "
11 p' sprinkled the blood from their "
14 for themselves, and for the p': "
14 the p' the sons of Aaron were "
14 and for the p' the sons of Aaron. "
18 the p', and the Levites, and all "
36: 14 the chief of the p', and the people, "
Ezr 1: 5 and the p', and the Levites, with "
2: 36 The p': the children of Jedaiah, "
61 And of the children of the p': the "
70 So the p', and the Levites, and "
3: 2 his brethren the p', and Zerubbabel "
8 remnant of their brethren the p' "
10 set the p' in their apparel with "
12 many of the p' and Levites and "
6: 9 to the appointment of the p' which 3549
16 of Israel, the p', and the Levites, "
18 they set the p' in their divisions, "
20 p' and the Levites were purified 3548
20 for their brethren the p', and for "
7: 7 children of Israel, and of the p', "
13 of his p' and Levites, in my realm, 3549
16 of the p', offering willingly for the "
24 touching any of the p' and Levites, "
8: 15 I viewed the people, and the p', 3548
24 twelve of the chief of the p', "
29 them before the chief of the p' and "
30 So took the p' and the Levites the "
9: 1 The people of Israel, and the p', "
7 have we, our kings, and our p', "
10: 5 arose Ezra, and made the chief p', "
18 among the sons of the p' there were "
Ne 2: 16 told it to the Jews, nor to the p', "
3: 1 rose up with his brethren the p', "
22 after him repaired the p', the men "
28 above the horse gate repaired the p', "
5: 12 Then I called the p', and took an "
7: 39 The p': the children of Jedaiah, of "
63 And of the p': the children of "
73 So the p', and the Levites, and the "
8: 13 the p', and the Levites, unto Ezra "
9: 32 on our princes, and on our p', and "
34 our p', nor our fathers, kept thy "
38 Levites, and p', seal unto it. "
10: 8 Shemaiah: these were the p'. "
28 the p', the Levites, the porters, the "
Ne 10: 34 we cast the lots among the p', the 3548
36 p' that minister in the house of "
37 unto the p', to the chambers of the "
39 and the p' that minister, and the "
11: 3 Israel, the p', and the Levites, and "
10 Of the p': Jedaiah the son of "
20 p', and the Levites, were in all the "
12: 1 these are the p', and the Levites "
7 These were the chief of the p' and "
12 the days of Joiakim were p', the "
22 also the p', to the reign of Darius "
30 And the p' and the Levites purified "
41 And the p'; Eliakim, Maaseiah, "
44 of the law for the p' and Levites: "
44 for Judah rejoiced for the p' and "
13: 5 porters; and the offerings of the p'. "
30 appointed the wards of the p' and "
Ps 78: 64 Their p' fell by the sword; and "
99: 6 Moses and Aaron among his p', and "
132: 9 p' be clothed with righteousness; "
16 also clothe her p' with salvation: "
Isa 37: 2 elders of the p' covered with "
61: 6 shall be named the P' of the Lord: "
66: 21 take of them for p' and for Levites, "
Jer 1: 1 of the p' that were in Anathoth in "
18 against the p' thereof, and against "
2: 8 The p' said not, Where is the Lord? "
26 and their p', and their prophets, "
4: 9 the p' shall be astonished, and the "
5: 31 the p' bear rule by their means; "
8: 1 the bones of the p', and the bones "
13: 13 and the p', and the prophets, and "
19: 1 and of the ancients of the p'; "
26: 7, 8 the p' and the prophets and all "
11 Then spake the p' and the prophets "
16 unto the p' and to the prophets; "
27: 16 I spake to the p' and to all this "
28: 1 in the presence of the p' and of all "
5 Hananiah in the presence of the p', "
29: 1 to the p', and to the prophets, and "
25 the priest, and to all the p', saying, "
31: 14 the soul of the p' with fatness, "
32: 32 their p', and their prophets, and "
33: 18 Neither shall the p' the Levites "
21 and with the Levites the p', my "
34: 19 the eunuchs, and the p', and all "
48: 7 forth into captivity with his p' and "
49: 3 his p' and his princes together. "
La 1: 4 p' sigh, her virgins are afflicted, "
19 my p' and mine elders gave up the "
4: 13 the iniquities of her p', that have "
16 respected not the persons of the p', "
Eze 22: 26 Her p' have violated my law, and "
40: 45 is for the p', the keepers of the "
46 is toward the north is for the p', "
42: 13 the p' that approach unto the Lord "
14 When the p' enter therein, then "
43: 19 shalt give to the p' the Levites "
24 the p' shall cast salt upon them, "
27 p' shall make your burnt offerings "
44: 15 But the p' the Levites, the sons of "
31 p' shall not eat of any thing that is "
45: 4 of the land shall be for the p' the "
46: 2 p' shall prepare his burnt offering "
19 into the holy chambers of the p', "
20 p' shall boil the trespass offering "
48: 10 even for the p', shall be this holy "
11 be for the p' that are sanctified of "
13 over against the border of the p' "
Ho 5: 1 Hear ye this, O p'; and hearken, ye "
6: 9 so the company of p' murder in the "
10: 5 the p' thereof that rejoiced on it, 3649
Joe 1: 9 the p', the Lord's ministers, mourn. 3548
13 yourselves, and lament, ye p': "
2: 17 Let the p', the ministers of the "
Mic 3: 11 p' thereof teach for hire, and the "
Zep 1: 4 of the Chemarims with the p'; "
3: 4 her p' have polluted the sanctuary, "
Hag 2: 11 Ask now the p' concerning the law, "
12 And the p' answered and said, No. "
13 p' answered and said, It shall be "
Zec 7: 3 unto the p' which were in the house "
5 to the p', saying, When ye fasted "
Mal 1: 6 you, O p', that despise my name. "
2: 1 O ye p', this commandment is for "
M't 2: 4 gathered all the chief p' and scribes 749
12: 4 were with him, but only for the p'? 2409
5 the p' in the temple profane the "
16: 21 the elders and chief p' and scribes, 749
20: 18 shall be betrayed unto the chief p' "
21: 15 when the chief p' and scribes saw "
23 chief p' and the elders of the people "
45 chief p' and Pharisees had heard "
26: 3 assembled together the chief p', "
14 Iscariot, went unto the chief p', "
47 the chief p' and elders of the people. "
59 Now the chief p', and elders, and "
27: 1 the chief p' and elders of the people "
3 of silver to the chief p' and elders, "
6 the chief p' took the silver pieces, "
12 accused of the chief p' and elders, "
20 chief p' and elders persuaded the "
41 also the chief p' mocking him, with "
62 the chief p' and Pharisees came "
28: 11 and shewed unto the chief p' all the "
M'r 2: 26 is not lawful to eat but for the p', 2409
8: 31 of the chief p', and scribes, and be 749
10: 33 shall be delivered unto the chief p', "
11: 18 the scribes and chief p' heard it, "
27 there come to him the chief p', and "
14: 1 the chief p' and the scribes sought "
10 went unto the chief p' to betray "
43 from the chief p' and the scribes "
53 him were assembled all the chief p' "
55 And the chief p' and all the council "
15: 1 the chief p' held a consultation with "
M'r 15: 3 the chief p' accused him of many 749
10 the chief p' had delivered him for "
11 But the chief p' moved the people, "
31 also the chief p' mocking said "
Lu 3: 2 and Caiaphas being the high p', the* "
6: 4 lawful to eat but for the p' alone? 2409
9: 22 rejected of the elders and chief p' 749
17: 14 Go shew yourselves unto the p'. 2409
19: 47 But the chief p' and the scribes 749
20: 1 the chief p' and the scribes came "
19 the chief p' and the scribes the same "
22: 2 the chief p' and scribes sought how "
4 with the chief p' and captains, how "
52 Then Jesus said unto the chief p', "
66 the chief p' and the scribes came "
23: 4 Then said Pilate to the chief p' and "
10 the chief p' and scribes stood and "
13 together the chief p' and the rulers "
23 voices...of the chief p' prevailed. * "
24: 20 chief p' and our rulers delivered "
Joh 1: 19 the Jews sent p' and Levites from 2409
7: 32 the Pharisees and the chief p' sent 749
45 came the officers to the chief p' and "
11: 47 Then gathered the chief p' and the "
57 both the chief p' and the Pharisees "
12: 10 But the chief p' consulted that they "
18: 3 from the chief p' and Pharisees, "
35 Thine own nation and the chief p' "
19: 6 the chief p' therefore and officers "
15 The chief p' answered, We have no "
21 The chief p' of the Jews to Pilate, "
Ac 4: 1 spake unto the people, the p', and 2409
23 the chief p' and elders had said 749
5: 24 and the chief p' heard these things, "
6: 7 the p' were obedient to the faith. 2409
9: 14 authority from the chief p' to bind 749
21 bring them bound unto the chief p'? "
19: 14 a Jew, and chief of the p', which did* "
22: 30 and commanded the chief p' and all "
23: 14 they came to the chief p' and elders, "
25: 15 chief p' and the elders of the Jews "
26: 10 received authority from the chief p'; "
12 and commission from the chief p', "
Heb 7: 21 p' were made without an oath: 2409
23 they truly were many p', because "
27 needeth not daily, as those high p', 749
28 men high p' which have infirmity; "
8: 4 that there are p' that offer gifts *2409
9: 6 the p' went always into the first "
Re 1: 6 made us kings and p' unto God "
5: 10 us unto our God kings and p': and "
20: 6 they shall be p' of God and of "

priests'
Jos 4: 3 place where the p' feet stood firm, 3548
18 the soles of the p' feet were lifted "
2Ki 12: 16 house of the Lord: it was the p'. "
Ezr 2: 69 and one hundred p' garments. "
Ne 7: 70 hundred and thirty p' garments. "
72 threescore and seven p' garments. "
12: 35 of the p' sons with trumpets; "

prince See also PRINCE'S; PRINCES; PRINCESS.
Ge 23: 6 thou art a mighty p' among us: 5387
32: 28 as a p' hast thou power with God and *
34: 2 p' of the country, saw her, he 5387
Ex 2: 14 thee a p' and a judge over us? 8269
Nu 7: 11 their offering, each p' on his day, 5387
18 the son of Zuar, p' of Issachar, "
24 p' of the children of Zebulun, did "
30 p' of the children of Reuben, did "
36 p' of the children of Simeon, did "
42 p' of the children of Gad, offered: "
48 p' of the children of Ephraim, "
54 p' of the children of Manasseh: "
60 p' of the children of Benjamin, "
66 p' of the children of Dan, offered: "
72 p' of the children of Asher, offered: "
78 p' of the children of Naphtali, "
16: 13 thou make thyself altogether a p' 8328
17: 6 him a rod apiece, for each p' one, 5387
25: 14 a p' of a chief house among the "
18 the daughter of a p' of Midian, "
34: 18 ye shall take one p' of every tribe, "
22 the p' of the tribe of the children of "
23 the p' of the children of Joseph, for "
24, 25, 26, 27, 28 the p' of the tribe of "
Jos 22: 14 of each chief house a p' throughout "
2Sa 3: 38 p' and a great man fallen this day 8269
1Ki 11: 34 make him p' all the days of his 5387
14: 7 and made thee p' over my people 5057
16: 2 and made thee p' over my people "
1Ch 2: 10 p' of the children of Judah; 5387
5: 6 he was p' of the Reubenites. "
Ezr 1: 8 unto Sheshbazzar, the p' of Judah. "
Job 21: 28 say, Where is the house of the p'? 5081
31: 37 as a p' would I go near unto him. 5057
Pr 14: 28 people is the destruction of the p'. 7333
17: 7 fool: much less do lying lips a p'. 5081
19: 6 will intreat the favour of the p': * "
25: 7 put lower in the presence of the p' "
15 forbearing is a p' persuaded, *7101
28: 16 p' that wanteth understanding 5057
Isa 9: 6 everlasting Father,...P' of Peace. 8269
Jer 51: 59 And this Seraiah was a quiet p'. * "
Eze 7: 27 the p' shall be clothed with 5387
12: 10 This burden concerneth the p' in "
12 p' that is among them shall bear "
21: 25 profane wicked p' of Israel, whose "
28: 2 of man, say unto the p' of Tyrus, 5057
30: 13 no more a p' in the land of Egypt: 5387
34: 24 servant David a p' among them; "
37: 25 my servant David shall be their p'. "
38: 2 the chief p' of Meshech and Tubal, "
3 the chief p' of Meshech and Tubal: "
39: 1 chief p' of Meshech and Tubal: "
44: 3 It is for the p'; the p', he shall sit "

Eze 45: 7 a portion shall be for the p· on the 5387
16 this oblation for the p· in Israel. "
22 shall the p· prepare for himself and "
46: 2 the p· shall enter by the way of the "
4 offering that the p· shall offer unto "
8 when the p· shall enter, he shall go "
10 p· in the midst of them, when they "
12 the p· shall prepare a voluntary "
16 p· give a gift unto any of his sons, "
17 after it shall return to the p·: but "
18 the p· shalt not take of the people's "
48: 21 And the residue shall be for the p·, "
21 over against the portions for the p·: "
22 of Benjamin, shall be for the p·. "
Da 1: 7 the p· of the eunuchs gave names: 8269
8 requested of the p· of the eunuchs "
9 love with the p· of the eunuchs. "
10 p· of the eunuchs said unto Daniel, "
11 whom the p· of the eunuchs had set "
18 p· of the eunuchs brought them in "
8: 11 himself even to the p· of the host, "
25 stand up against the P· of princes; "
9: 25 unto the Messiah the P· shall be 5057
26 people of the p· that shall come "
10: 13 the p· of the kingdom of Persia 8269
20 return to fight with the p· of Persia: "
20 lo, the p· of Grecia shall come. "
21 these things, but Michael your p·. "
11: 18 a p· for his own behalf shall cause 7101
22 yea, also the p· of the covenant. 5057
12: 1 p· which standeth for the children 8269
Ho 3: 4 without a king, and without a p·, "
Mic 7: 3 p· asketh, and the judge asketh for "
M't 9: 34 devils through the p· of the devils. 758
12: 24 by Beelzebub the p· of the devils. "
M'r 3: 22 by the p· of the devils casteth he out "
Joh 12: 31 shall the p· of this world be cast out. "
14: 30 the p· of this world cometh, and hath "
16: 11 the p· of this world is judged. "
Ac 3: 15 killed the P· of life, whom God hath 747
5: 31 right hand to be a P· and a Saviour, "
Eph 2: 2 to the p· of the power of the air, 758
Re 1: 5 and the p· of the kings of the earth.* "

prince's
Ca 7: 1 thy feet with shoes, O p· daughter! 5081
Eze 45: 17 the p· part to give burnt offerings, 5387
48: 22 in the midst of that which is the p·, "

princes
Ge 12: 15 The p· also of Pharaoh saw her, 8269
17: 20 twelve p· shall he beget, and I will 5387
25: 16 twelve p· according to their nations. "
Nu 1: 16 p· of the tribes of their fathers, "
44 the p· of Israel, being twelve men: "
7: 2 the p· of Israel, heads of the house "
2 who were the p· of the tribes, and "
3 a wagon for two of the p·, and for "
10 the p· offered for dedicating of the "
10 the p· offered their offering before "
84 it was anointed, by the p· of Israel: "
10: 4 then the p·, which are heads of the "
16: 2 and fifty p· of the assembly, famous "
17: 2 of all their p· according to the house "
6 of their p· gave him a rod apiece, "
21: 18 The p· digged the well, the nobles 8269
22: 8 the p· of Moab abode with Balaam. "
13 said unto the p· of Balak, Get you "
14 p· of Moab rose up, and they went "
15 Balak sent yet again p·, more, and "
21 ass, and went with the p· of Moab. "
35 Balaam went with the p· of Balak. "
40 and to the p· that were with him. "
23: 6 sacrifice, he, and all the p· of Moab. "
17 and the p· of Moab with him. "
27: 2 the p· and all the congregation, 5387
31: 13 all the p· of the congregation, went "
32: 2 unto the p· of the congregation, "
36: 1 before Moses, and before the p·, "
Jos 9: 15 p· of the congregation sware unto "
18 p· of the congregation had sworn "
18 murmured against their p·. "
19 p· said unto all the congregation, "
21 p· said unto them, Let them live; "
21 as the p· had promised them. "
13: 21 Moses smote with the p· of Midian,* "
17: 4 the son of Nun, and before the p·, "
22: 14 And with him ten p·, of each chief "
30 p· of the congregation and heads of "
32 the p·, returned from the children "
J'g 5: 3 O ye kings; give ear, O ye p·; I, 7336
15 p· of Issachar were with Deborah; 8269
7: 25 two p· of the Midianites, Oreb and "
8: 3 into your hands the p· of Midian, "
6 And the p· of Succoth said, Are the "
14 unto him the p· of Succoth, and "
10: 18 p· of Gilead said one to another, "
1Sa 2: 8 to set them among p·, and to make 5081
18: 30 Then the p· of the Philistines went 8269
29: 3 Then said the p· of the Philistines, "
3 said unto the p· of the Philistines, "
4 the p· of the Philistines were wroth "
4 p· of the Philistines said unto him, "
9 the p· of the Philistines have said, "
2Sa 10: 3 p· of the children of Ammon said "
19: 6 regardest neither p· nor servants: "
1Ki 4: 2 these were the p· which he had; "
9: 22 his p·, and his captains, and rulers "
20: 14 men of the p· of the provinces. "
15 numbered the young men of the p· "
17 p· of the provinces went out first; "
19 p· of the provinces came out of the "
2Ki 11: 14 p· and the trumpeters by the king,* "
24: 12 and his p·, and his officers: and the "
14 all the p·, and all the mighty men "
1Ch 4: 38 mentioned by their names were p· 5387
7: 40 men of valour, chief of the p·. "
19: 3 p· of the children of Ammon said 8269
22: 17 also commanded all the p· of Israel "
23: 2 together all the p· of Israel, with "
24: 6 them before the king, and the p·, "
27: 22 were the p· of the tribes of Israel.* "
28: 1 David assembled all the p· of Israel, "
1 p· of the tribes, and the captains of "
21 also the p· and all the people will be* "
29: 6 p· of the tribes of Israel, and the "
24 And all the p·, and the mighty men, "
2Ch 12: 5 Rehoboam, and to the p· of Judah, "
6 p· of Israel and the king humbled "
17: 7 he sent to his p·, even to Ben-hail, "
21: 4 and divers also of the p· of Israel. "
9 Jehoram went forth with his p·, * "
22: 8 and found the p· of Judah, and the "
23: 13 p· and the trumpets by the king: * "
24: 10 the p· and all the people rejoiced, "
17 came the p· of Judah, and made "
23 destroyed all the p· of the people "
28: 14 and the spoil before the p· and all "
21 the house of the king, and of the p·, "
29: 30 p· commanded the Levites to sing "
30: 2 king had taken counsel, and his p·, "
6 and his p· throughout all Israel and "
12 of the king and of the p·, by the "
24 the p· gave to the congregation a "
31: 8 when Hezekiah and the p· came and "
32: 3 He took counsel with his p· and his "
31 ambassadors of the p· of Babylon, "
35: 8 p· gave willingly unto the people, "
36: 18 treasures of the king, and of his p·; "
Ezr 7: 28 and before all the king's mighty p·. "
8: 20 David and the p· had appointed for "
9: 1 things were done, the p· came to me, "
2 the hand of the p· and rulers hath "
10: 8 according to the counsel of the p· "
Ne 9: 32 on our kings, on our p·, and on our "
34 Neither have our kings, our p·, our "
38 our p·, Levites, and priests, seal "
12: 31 Then I brought up the p· of Judah "
32 and half of the p· of Judah, "
Es 1: 3 made a feast unto all his p· and his "
3 the nobles and p· of the provinces, "
11 the people and the p· her beauty: "
14 the seven p· of Persia and Media, "
16 before the king and the p·, Vashti "
16 king only, but also to all the p·, "
18 say this day unto all the king's p·, "
21 saying pleased the king and the p·; "
2: 18 made a great feast unto all his p· "
3: 1 set his seat above all the p· that "
5: 11 advanced him above the p· and "
6: 9 of one of the king's most noble p·, "
Job 3: 15 Or with p· that had gold, who filled "
12: 19 He leadeth p· away spoiled, and *3548
21 poureth contempt upon p·, and 5081
29: 9 The p· refrained talking, and laid 8269
34: 18 wicked? and to p·, Ye are ungodly? *5081
19 accepteth not the persons of p·, 8269
Ps 45: 16 mayest make p· in all the earth. "
47: 9 The p· of the people are gathered 5081
68: 27 the p· of Judah and their council, 8269
27 the p· of Zebulun, and the p· of "
31 P· shall come out of Egypt; 2831
76: 12 He shall cut off the spirit of p·: 5057
82: 7 men, and fall like one of the p·. 8269
83: 11 yea, all their p· as Zebah, and as 5257
105: 22 To bind his p· at his pleasure; 8269
107: 40 He poureth contempt upon p·, 5081
113: 8 That he may set him with p·, "
8 even with the p· of his people. "
118: 9 than to put confidence in p·. "
119: 23 P· also did sit and speak against 8269
161 P· have persecuted me without a "
146: 3 Put not your trust in p·, nor in the 5081
148: 11 p·, and all judges of the earth: 8269
Pr 8: 15 kings reign, and p· decree justice. 7336
16 By me p· rule, and nobles, even 8269
17: 26 good, nor to strike p· for equity. *5081
19: 10 for a servant to have rule over p·. 8269
28: 2 of a land many are the p· thereof: "
31: 4 wine; nor for p· strong drink: 7336
Ec 10: 7 p· walking as servants upon the 8269
16 and thy p· eat in the morning! "
17 and thy p· eat in due season, for "
Isa 1: 23 Thy p· are rebellious, and "
3: 4 I will give children to be their p·, "
14 of his people, and the p· thereof: "
10: 8 Are not my p· altogether kings? "
19: 11 p· of Zoan are fools, the counsel "
13 The p· of Zoan are become fools, "
13 p· of Noph are deceived; they have "
21: 5 arise, ye p·, and anoint the shield. "
23: 8 whose merchants are p·, whose "
30: 4 For his p· were at Zoan, and his "
31: 9 his p· shall be afraid of the ensign, "
32: 1 and p· shall rule in judgment. "
34: 12 and all her p· shall be nothing. "
40: 23 bringeth the p· to nothing; he 7336
41: 25 come upon p· as upon morter, *5461
43: 28 profaned the p· of the sanctuary, 8269
49: 7 p· also shall worship, because of "
Jer 1: 18 against the p· thereof, against the "
2: 26 they, their kings, their p·, and their "
4: 9 perish, and the heart of the p·; "
8: 1 the bones of his p·, and the bones "
17: 25 p· sitting upon the throne of David, "
25 and their p·, the men of Judah, "
24: 1 the p· of Judah, with the carpenters "
8 the king of Judah, and his p·, "
25: 18 kings thereof, and the p· thereof, "
19 and his servants, and his p·, and all "
26: 10 the p· of Judah heard these things, "
11 and the prophets unto the p· and to "
12 spake Jeremiah unto all the p· and "
16 Then said the p· and all the people 8269
21 men, and all the p·, heard his words, "
29: 2 p· of Judah and Jerusalem, and the "
32: 32 their kings, their p·, their priests, "
34: 10 Now when all the p· and all the "
19 The p· of Judah, and the p· of "
21 king of Judah and his p· will I give "
35: 4 was by the chamber of the p·, which "
36: 12 all the p· sat there, even Elishama "
12 son of Hananiah, and all the p·. "
14 all the p· sent Jehudi the son of "
19 Then said the p· unto Baruch, Go, "
21 p· which stood beside the king. "
37: 14 and brought him to the p·. "
15 the p· were wroth with Jeremiah, "
38: 4 the p· said unto the king, We "
17 unto the king of Babylon's p·, "
18, 22 forth to the king of Babylon's p·, "
22 forth to the king of Babylon's p·, "
25 if the p· hear that I have talked "
27 came all the p· unto Jeremiah, and "
39: 3 p· of the king of Babylon came in, "
3 residue of the p· of the king of "
13 and all the king of Babylon's p·; *7227
41: 1 the p· of the king, even ten men * "
44: 17 our fathers, our kings, and our p·, 8269
21 fathers, your kings, and your p·, "
48: 7 captivity with his priests and his p· "
49: 3 and his priests and his p· together. "
38 from thence the king and the p·, "
50: 35 of Babylon, and upon her p·, and "
51: 57 And I will make drunk her p·, and "
52: 10 also all the p· of Judah in Riblah. "
La 1: 6 her p· are become like harts that "
2: 2 the kingdom and the p· thereof. "
9 her p· are among the Gentiles: the "
5: 12 P· are hanged up by their hand: "
Eze 11: 1 son of Benaiah, p· of the people. "
17: 12 the king thereof, and the p· thereof, "
19: 1 a lamentation for the p· of Israel, 5387
21: 12 shall be upon all the p· of Israel: "
22: 6 Behold, the p· of Israel, every one "
27 Her p· in the midst thereof are like 8269
23: 15 heads, all of them p· to look to, 7991
26: 16 all the p· of the sea shall come 5387
27: 21 all the p· of Kedar, they occupied "
32: 29 is Edom, her kings, and all her p·, "
30 There be the p· of the north, all of 5257
39: 18 the blood of the p· of the earth, 5387
45: 8 my p· shall no more oppress my "
9 Let it suffice you, O p· of Israel: "
Da 1: 3 of the king's seed, and of the p·; *6579
3: 2 king sent to gather together the p·, *324
3 Then the p·, the governors, and * "
27 the p·, governors, and captains, * "
5: 2 that the king, and his p·, his wives, *7261
3 and the king, and his p·, his wives, * "
6: 1 an hundred and twenty p·, which * 324
2 p· might give accounts unto them, * "
3 above the presidents and p·, * "
4 the presidents and p· sought to find * "
6 these presidents and p· assembled * "
7 the governors, and the p·, the * "
8: 25 stand up against the Prince of p·; 8269
9: 6 our kings, our p·, and our fathers, "
8 to our kings, to our p·, and to our "
10: 13 Michael, one of the chief p·, came "
11: 5 shall be strong, and one of his p·; "
8 their p·, and with their precious *5257
Ho 5: 10 p· of Judah were like them that 8269
7: 3 and the p· with their lies. "
5 the p· have made him sick with "
16 their p· shall fall by the sword for "
8: 4 have made p·, and I knew it not: "
10 for the burden of the king of p·. "
9: 15 no more: all their p· are revolters. "
13: 10 thou saidst, Give me a king and p·? "
Am 1: 15 captivity, he and his p· together, "
2: 3 slay all the p· thereof with him, "
Mic 3: 1 and ye p· of the house of Israel; *7101
9 p· of the house...Israel, that abhor* "
Hab 1: 10 the p· shall be a scorn unto them: 7336
Zep 1: 8 will punish the p·, and the king's 8269
3: 3 p· within her are roaring lions; "
M't 2: 6 not the least among the p· of Juda: 2232
20: 25 that the p· of the Gentiles exercise* 758
1Co 2: 6 nor of the p· of this world, that * "
8 none of the p· of this world knew: * "

princess See also PRINCESSES.
La 1: 1 and p· among the provinces, how 8282

princesses
1Ki 11: 3 he had seven hundred wives, p·, 8282

principal
Ex 30: 23 thou also unto thee p· spices, *7218
Le 6: 5 restore it in the p·, and shall add * "
Nu 5: 7 his trespass with the p· thereof, * "
1Ki 4: 5 the son of Nathan was p· officer, *3548
2Ki 25: 19 the p· scribe of the host, which *8269
1Ch 24: 6 one p· household being taken for * 1
31 the p· fathers over against their *7218
Ne 11: 17 p· to begin the thanksgiving in * "
Pr 4: 7 Wisdom is the p· thing; therefore 7225
Isa 16: 8 have broken down the p· plants *8291
28: 25 and cast in the p· wheat and the *7795
Jer 25: 34 in the ashes, ye p· of the flock: 117
35 nor the p· of the flock to escape. "
36 an howling of the p· of the flock, "
52: 25 and the p· scribe of the host who *8269
Mic 5: 5 shepherds, and eight p· men. 5257
Ac 25: 23 and p· men of the city, 3588,2596,1851,5607

principalities
Jer 13: 18 your p· shall come down, even *4761
Ro 8: 38 nor p·, nor powers, nor things 746
Eph 3: 10 now unto the p· and powers in "

Eph 6:12 but against *p'*, against powers, 746
Col 1:16 or dominions, or *p'*, or powers: "
2:15 And having spoiled *p'* and powers, "
Tit 3: 1 mind to be subject to *p'* and powers,*"

principality See also PRINCIPALITIES.
Eph 1:21 Far above all *p'*, and power, and * 746
Col 2:10 is the head of all *p'* and power: "

principles
Heb 5:12 the first *p'* of the oracles of God; 4747
6: 1 leaving the *p'* of the doctrine of 746

print See also PRINTED.
Le 19:28 dead, nor *p'* any marks upon you: 5414
Job 13:27 a *p'* upon the heels of my feet. †‡2707
Joh 20:25 in his hands the *p'* of the nails, 5179
25 my finger into the *p'* of the nails, "

printed
Job 19:23 oh that they were *p'* in a book! *2710

Prisca (*pris'-cah*) See also PRISCILLA.
2Ti 4:19 Salute *P'* and Aquila, and the 4251

Priscilla (*pris-sil'-lah*) See also PRISCA.
Ac 18: 2 come from Italy, with his wife *P'*; 4252
18 and with him *P'* and Aquila; "
26 when Aquila and *P'* had heard, "
Ro 16: 3 Greet *P'* and Aquila my helpers * "
1Co 16:19 Aquila and *P'* salute you much * "

prised
Zec 11:13 price that I was *p'* at of them. 3365

prison See also IMPRISONED; PRISONS.
Ge 39:20 and put him into the *p'*, a 1004,5470
20 and he was there in the *p'*. " "
21 sight of the keeper of the *p'*. " "
22 the keeper of the *p'* committed " "
22 prisoners that were in the *p'*; " "
23 keeper of the *p'* looked not to " "
40: 3 into the *p'*, the place where " "
5 which were bound in the *p'*. " "
42:16 ye shall be kept in *p'*, that your *
19 be bound in the house of your *p'*: 4929
J'g 16:21 and he did grind in the *p'* house. 631
25 for Samson out of the *p'* house: "
1Ki 22:27 Put this fellow in the *p'*, and 1004,3608
2Ki 17: 4 him up, and bound him in *p'*. " "
25:27 king of Judah out of *p'*; " "
29 And changed his *p'* garments: " "
2Ch 16:10 seer, and put him in a *p'* house; 4115
18:26 Put this fellow in the *p'*, and 1004,3608
Ne 3:25 that was by the court of the *p'* *4307
12:39 and they stood still in the *p'* gate.* "
Ps 142: 7 Bring my soul out of *p'*, that I 4525
Ec 4:14 out of *p'* he cometh to reign, 1004,612
Isa 24:22 and shall be shut up in the *p'*, 4525
42: 7 bring out the prisoners from the *p'*,*"
7 in darkness out of the *p'* house. 3608
22 and they are hid in *p'* houses: "
53: 8 He was taken from *p'* and from *6115
61: 1 opening of the *p'* to them that are 6495
Jer 29:26 thou shouldest put him in *p'* and *4115
32: 2 was shut up in the court of the *p'*,*4307
8 came to me in the court of the *p'* * "
12 Jews that sat in the court of the *p'*.*"
33: 1 yet shut up in the court of the *p'*,* "
37: 4 they had not put him into *p'*. 1004,3608
15 in *p'* in the house of Jonathan " 612
15 for they had made that the *p'*. " 3608
18 that ye have put me in *p'*? "
21 Jeremiah into the court of the *p'*,*4307
21 remained in the court of the *p'*. * "
38: 6 that was in the court of the *p'*: and*"
13 remained in the court of the *p'*. * "
28 abode in the court of the *p'* until * "
39:14 Jeremiah out of the court of the *p'*,*"
15 was shut up in the court of the *p'*,* "
52:11 in *p'* till the day of his death. 1004,6486
31 brought him forth out of *p'*, 3608
33 And changed his *p'* garments: "
M't 4:12 heard that John was cast into *p'*, *3860
5:25 officer, and thou be cast into *p'*. 5438
11: 2 John had heard in the *p'* the works 1201
14: 3 put him in *p'* for Herodias' sake, 5438
10 sent, and beheaded John in the *p'*. "
18:30 went and cast him into *p'*, till he "
25:36 I was in *p'*, and ye came unto me. "
39 when saw we thee sick, or in *p'*, "
43 sick, and in *p'*, and ye visited me "
44 or sick, or in *p'*, and did not "
M'r 1:14 after that John was put in *p'*, *3860
6:17 bound him in *p'* for Herodias' sake, 5438
27 went and beheaded him in the *p'*, "
Lu 3:20 all, that he shut up John in *p'*. "
12:58 and the officer cast thee into *p'*. "
22:33 ready to go with thee, both into *p'*, "
23:19 and for murder, was cast into *p'*.) "
25 and murder was cast into *p'*, "
Joh 3:24 For John was not yet cast into *p'*. "
Ac 5:18 and put them in the common *p'*. *5084
19 Lord by night opened the *p'* doors, 5438
21 to the *p'* to have them brought. *1201
22 and found them not in the *p'*, 5438
23 The *p'* truly found we shut with *1201
25 the men whom ye put in *p'* are 5438
8: 3 women committed them to *p'*. "
12: 4 he put him in *p'*, and delivered "
5 Peter therefore was kept in *p'*: "
6 keepers before the door kept the *p'*,"
7 and a light shined in the *p'*: and he 3612
17 had brought him out of the *p'*. 5438
16:23 they cast them into *p'*, charging "
24 thrust them into the inner *p'*, and "
26 foundations...the *p'* were shaken: *1201
27 keeper of the *p'* awaking out of *1200
27 and seeing the *p'* doors open, he 5438
36 keeper of the *p'* told this saying to *1200
Ac 16:37 Romans, and have cast us into *p'*; 5438
40 And they went out of the *p'*, and "
26:10 of the saints did I shut up in *p'*, * "
1Pe 3:19 preached unto the spirits in *p'*; "
Re 2:10 devil shall cast some of you into *p'*, "
20: 7 Satan shall be loosed out of his *p'*, "

prisoner See also FELLOWPRISONER; PRISONERS.
Ps 79:11 the sighing of the *p'* come before 616
102:20 To hear the groaning of the *p'*; 615
M't 27:15 to release unto the people a *p'*, 1198
16 they had then a notable *p'*, called "
M'r 15: 6 he released unto them one *p'*, "
Ac 23:18 Paul the *p'* called me unto him, and "
25:27 to me unreasonable to send a *p'*, "
28:17 was I delivered *p'* from Jerusalem "
Eph 3: 1 Paul, the *p'* of Jesus Christ for you "
4: 1 I therefore, the *p'* of the Lord, "
2Ti 1: 8 of our Lord, nor of me his *p'*: "
Ph'm 1 Paul, a *p'* of Jesus Christ, and "
9 and now also a *p'* of Jesus Christ. "

prisoners See also FELLOWPRISONERS.
Ge 39:20 where the king's *p'* were bound: 615
22 all the *p'* that were in the prison; "
Nu 21: 1 Israel, and took some of them *p'*. *7628
Job 3:18 There the *p'* rest together; they 615
Ps 69:33 the poor, and despiseth not his *p'*. "
146: 7 hungry. The Lord looseth the *p'*: 631
Isa 10: 4 they shall bow down under the *p'*, 616
14:17 that opened not the house of his *p'*?615
20: 4 Assyria lead away...Egyptians *p'*, *7628
24:22 as *p'* are gathered in the pit, and 616
42: 7 to bring out the *p'* from the prison, "
49: 9 That thou mayest say to the *p'*, Go*631
La 3:34 his feet all the *p'* of the earth, 615
Zec 9:11 have sent forth thy *p'* out of the pit "
12 to the strong hold, ye *p'* of hope: "
Ac 16:25 unto God: and the *p'* heard them. 1198
27 supposing that the *p'* had been fled. "
27: 1 delivered Paul and certain other *p'* 1202
42 soldiers' counsel was to kill the *p'*, "
28:16 delivered the *p'* to the captain of *1198

prison-house See PRISON and HOUSE.

prisons
Lu 21:12 up to the synagogues, and into *p'*, 5438
Ac 22: 4 delivering into *p'* both men and "
2Co 11:23 in *p'* more frequent, in deaths oft. "

private See also PRIVY.
2Pe 1:20 is of any *p'* interpretation. 2398

privately See also PRIVILY.
M't 24: 3 disciples came unto him *p'*, 2596,2398
M'r 6:32 into a desert place by ship *p'*. * " "
9:28 his disciples asked him *p'*, Why " "
13: 3 John and Andrew asked him *p'*, " "
Lu 9:10 aside *p'* into a desert place * " "
10:23 and said *p'*, Blessed are the eyes" "
Ac 23:19 and went with him aside *p'*, and" "
Gal 2: 2 but *p'* to them which were of " "

privily See also PRIVATELY.
J'g 9:31 messengers unto Abimelech *p'*, *8649
1Sa 24: 4 cut off the skirt of Saul's robe *p'*. 3909
Ps 10: 8 his eyes are *p'* set against the poor. 6845
11: 2 *p'* shoot at the upright in heart. * 652
31: 4 net that they have laid *p'* for me: 2934
64: 5 they commune of laying snares *p'*; "
101: 5 Whoso *p'* slandereth his neighbour, 5643
142: 3 have they *p'* laid a snare for me. *2934
Pr 1:11 let us lurk *p'* for the innocent without
18 blood; they lurk *p'* for their own lives.
M't 1:19 was minded to put her away *p'*. 2977
2: 7 when he had *p'* called the wise men, "
Ac 16:37 and now do they thrust us out *p'*? "
Gal 2: 4 came in *p'* to spy out our liberty 3922
2Pe 2: 1 who *p'* shall bring in damnable 3918

privy See also PRIVATE.
De 23: 1 or hath his *p'* member cut off, 8212
1Ki 2:44 which thine heart is *p'* to, that 3045
Eze 21:14 entereth into their *p'* chambers. *2314
Ac 5: 2 price, his wife also being *p'* to it, 4894

prize See also PRISED.
1Co 9:24 run all, but one receiveth the *p'*? 1017
Ph'p 3:14 mark for the *p'* of the high calling "

probate See REPROBATE.

proceed See also PROCEEDED; PROCEEDETH; PROCEEDING.
Ex 25:35 that *p'* out of the candlestick. *3318
Jos 6:10 any word *p'* out of your mouth, "
2Sa 7:12 which shall *p'* out of thy bowels, "
Job 40: 5 yea, twice; but I will *p'* no further. 3254
Isa 29:14 I will *p'* to do a marvellous work "
51: 4 for a law shall *p'* from me, and I *3318
Jer 9: 3 for they *p'* from evil to evil, and "
30:19 out of them shall *p'* thanksgiving "
21 shall *p'* from the midst of them; "
Hab 1: 7 their dignity shall *p'* of themselves." "
M't 15:18 things which *p'* out of the mouth 1607
19 out of the heart *p'* evil thoughts, *1831
M'r 7:21 the heart of men, *p'* evil thoughts, 1607
Eph 4:29 communication *p'* out...your mouth, "
2Ti 3: 9 they shall *p'* no further: for their 4298

proceeded
Nu 30:12 then whatsoever *p'* out of her lips 4161
32:24 which hath *p'* out of your mouth. 3318
J'g 11:36 which hath *p'* out of thy mouth; "
Job 36: 1 Elihu also *p'*, and said, 3254
Lu 4:22 words which *p'* out of his mouth. 1607
Joh 8:42 for I *p'* forth and came from God; *1831
Ac 12: 3 he *p'* further to take Peter also. 4369
Re 4: 5 out of the throne *p'* lightnings *1607
19:21 which sword *p'* out of his mouth: * "

proceedeth
Ge 24:50 The thing *p'* from the Lord: we 3318
Nu 30: 2 to all that *p'* out of his mouth. "
De 8: 3 word that *p'* out of the mouth of 4161
1Sa 24:13 Wickedness *p'* from the wicked: *3318
Ec 10: 5 as an error which *p'* from the ruler: "
La 3:38 most High *p'* not evil and good? * "
Hab 1: 4 therefore wrong judgment *p'*. * "
M't 4: 4 word that *p'* out of the mouth of 1607
Joh 15:26 truth, which *p'* from the Father, "
Jas 3:10 mouth *p'* blessing and cursing. *1831
Re 11: 5 fire *p'* out of their mouth, and 1607

proceeding
Re 22: 1 crystal, *p'* out of the throne of God 1607

process
Ge 4: 3 And in *p'* of time it came to pass, 7093
38:12 *p'* of time the daughter of Shuah 7235
Ex 2:23 it came to pass in *p'* of time, that *7227
J'g 11: 4 it came to pass in *p'* of time, that *
2Ch 21:19 it came to pass, that in *p'* of time,

Prochorus (*prok'-o-rus*)
Ac 6: 5 Philip, and *P'*, and Nicanor, and 4402

proclaim See also PROCLAIMED; PROCLAIMETH; PROCLAIMING.
Ex 33:19 and I will *p'* the name of the Lord 7121
Le 23: 2 ye shall *p'* to be holy convocations, "
4 which ye shall *p'* in their seasons. "
21 And ye shall *p'* on the selfsame day,*"
37 ye shall *p'* to be holy convocations, "
25:10 *p'* liberty throughout all the land "
De 20:10 against it, then *p'* peace unto it. "
J'g 7: 3 *p'* in the ears of the people, saying, "
1Ki 21: 9 *P'* a fast, and set Naboth on high "
2Ki 10:20 *P'* a solemn assembly for Baal. *6942
Ne 8:15 publish and *p'* in all their cities, 5674
Es 6: 9 of the city, and *p'* before him, 7121
Pr 20: 6 will *p'* every one his own goodness: "
Isa 61: 1 to *p'* liberty to the captives, and "
2 *p'* the acceptable year of the Lord, "
Jer 3:12 Go and *p'* these words toward the "
7: 2 *p'* there this word, and say, Hear "
11: 6 *P'* all these words in the cities of "
19: 2 *p'* there the words that I shall tell "
34: 8 Jerusalem, to *p'* liberty unto them; "
17 I *p'* a liberty for you, saith the Lord, "
Joe 3: 9 *P'* ye this among the Gentiles; "
Am 4: 5 *p'* and publish the free offerings: "

proclaimed
Ex 34: 5 there, and *p'* the name of the Lord. 7121
6 Lord passed by before him, and *p'*, "
36: 6 it to be *p'* throughout the camp, 5674
1Ki 21:12 They *p'* a fast, and set Naboth on 7121
2Ki 10:20 assembly for Baal. And they *p'* it. "
23:16 man of God *p'*, who *p'* these words. "
17 *p'* these things that thou hast done "
2Ch 20: 3 and *p'* a fast throughout all Judah. "
Ezr 8:21 Then I *p'* a fast there, at the river "
Es 6:11 *p'* before him, Thus shall it be done "
Isa 62:11 the Lord hath *p'* unto the end of 8085
Jer 36: 9 that they *p'* a fast before the Lord 7121
Jon 3: 5 and *p'* a fast, and put on sackcloth, "
7 he caused it to be *p'* and published *2199
Lu 12: 3 shall be *p'* upon the housetops. 2784

proclaimeth
Pr 12:23 the heart of fools *p'* foolishness. 7121

proclaiming
Jer 34:15 in *p'* liberty every man to his 7121
17 *p'* liberty, every one to his brother,*"
Re 5: 2 strong angel *p'* with a loud voice, 2784

proclamation
Ex 32: 5 and Aaron made *p'*, and said, To 7121
1Ki 15:22 king Asa made a *p'* throughout 8085
22:36 went a *p'* throughout the host *7440
2Ch 24: 9 they made a *p'* through Judah 6963
30: 5 make *p'* throughout all 5674,6963
36:22 he made a *p'* throughout all " "
Ezr 1: 1 he made a *p'* throughout all his " "
10: 7 they made *p'* throughout " "
Da 5:29 and made a *p'* concerning him, 3745

procure See also PROCURED; PROCURETH.
Jer 26:19 we *p'* great evil against our souls. *6213
33: 9 all the prosperity that I *p'* unto it. "

procured
Jer 2:17 Hast thou not *p'* this unto thyself, 6213
4:18 way and thy doings have *p'* these "

procureth
Pr 11:27 diligently seeketh good *p'* favour: *1245

produce
Isa 41:21 *P'* your cause, saith the Lord; 7126

profane See also PROFANED; PROFANETH; PROFANING.
Le 18:21 shalt thou *p'* the name of thy God: 2490
19:12 shalt thou *p'* the name of thy God: "
20: 3 sanctuary, and to *p'* my holy name. "
21: 4 among his people, to *p'* himself. "
6 and not *p'* the name of their God: "
7 take a wife that is a whore, or *p'*; 2491
9 *p'* herself by playing the whore, 2490
12 nor *p'* the sanctuary of his God; "
14 widow, or a divorced woman, or *p'*, 2491
15 he *p'* his seed among his people: 2490
23 that he *p'* not my sanctuaries: for "
22: 2 that they *p'* not my holy name in "
9 it, and die therefore, if they *p'* it: "
15 they shall not *p'* the holy things of "
32 Neither shall ye *p'* my holy name; "
Ne 13:17 that ye do, and *p'* the sabbath day? "
Jer 23:11 both prophet and priest are *p'*; 2610
Eze 21:25 thou, *p'* wicked prince of Israel, *2491

Eze 22:26 between the holy and p', neither *2455
23:39 day into my sanctuary to p' it; 2490
24:21 Behold, I will p' my sanctuary, "
28:16 cast thee as p' out of the mountain "
42:20 the sanctuary and the p' place. *2455
44:23 difference between the holy and p'.* "
48:15 shall be a p' place for the city, for* "
Am 2: 7 same maid, to p' my holy name: 2490
M't 12: 5 priests in the temple p' the sabbath,953
Ac 24: 6 hath gone about to p' the temple: "
1Ti 1: 9 and for sinners, for unholy and p', 952
4: 7 But refuse p' and old wives' fables, "
6:20 avoiding p' and vain babblings, and "
2Ti 2:16 But shun p' and vain babblings: "
Heb12:16 be any fornicator, or p' person, "

profaned
Le 19: 8 hath p' the hallowed thing of the 2490
Ps 89:39 thou hast p' his crown by casting "
Isa 43:28 I have p' the princes of the * "
Eze 22: 8 things, and hast p' my sabbaths. "
26 law, and have p' mine holy things: "
26 sabbaths, and I am p' among them. "
23:38 day, and have p' my sabbaths. "
25: 3 my sanctuary, when it was p'; "
36:20 they went, they p' my holy name, "
21 Israel had p' among the heathen, "
22 ye have p' among the heathen, "
23 which was p' among the heathen, "
23 ye have p' in the midst of them; "
Mal 1:12 But ye have p' it, in that ye say, * "
2:11 hath p' the holiness of the Lord "

profaneness
Jer 23:15 the prophets of Jerusalem is p' ‡2613

profaneth
Le 21: 9 the whore, she p' her father: she 2490

profaning
Ne 13:18 upon Israel by p' the sabbath. 2490
Mal 2:10 by p' the covenant of our fathers? "

profess See also PROFESSED; PROFESSING.
De 26: 3 him, I p' this day unto the Lord 5046
M't 7:23 then will I p' unto them, I never 3670
Tit 1:16 They p' that they know God; but "

professed
2Co 9:13 for your p' subjection unto the *3671
1Ti 6:12 hast p' a good profession before *3670

professing
Ro 1:22 P' themselves to be wise, they 5335
1Ti 2:10 becometh women p' godliness) 1861
6:21 some p' have erred concerning the "

profession
1Ti 6:12 good p' before many witnesses. *3671
Heb 3: 1 Apostle and High Priest of our p',* "
4:14 Son of God, let us hold fast our p'.* "
10:23 Let us hold fast the p' of our faith* "

profit See also PROFITABLE; PROFITED; PROFITETH; PROFITING.
Ge 25:32 what p' shall this birthright do to me?
37:26 What p' is it if we slay our brother,1215
1Sa 12:21 which cannot p' nor deliver; for 3276
Es 3: 8 for the king's p' to suffer them. 7737
Job 21:15 what p' should we have, if we 3276
30: 2 the strength of their hands p' me, "
35: 3 and, What p' shall I have, if I be 3276
8 righteousness may p' the son of man. "
Ps 30: 9 What p' is there in my blood, when1215
Pr 10: 2 of wickedness p' nothing: but 3276
11: 4 Riches p' not in the day of wrath: "
14:23 In all labour there is p': but the 4195
Ec 1: 3 What p' hath a man of all his 3504
2:11 and there was no p' under the sun. "
3: 9 What p' hath he that worketh in "
5: 9 the p' of the earth is for all: the "
16 and what p' hath he that hath "
7:11 is p' to them that see the sun. 3148
Isa 30: 5 a people that could not p' them. 3276
5 nor be an help nor p', but a shame, "
6 to a people that shall not p' them. "
44: 9 their delectable things shall not p';* "
47:12 if so be thou shalt be able to p', if "
48:17 thy God which teacheth thee to p'. "
57:12 works; for they shall not p' thee. "
Jer 2: 8 walked after things that do not p'. "
11 glory for that which doth not p'. "
7: 8 trust in lying words, that cannot p'. "
12:13 themselves to pain, but shall not p': "
16:19 and things wherein there is no p'. "
23: : they shall not p' this people at all, "
Mal 3:14 what p' is it that we have kept his 1215
M'r 8:36 For what shall it p' a man, if he 5623
Ro 3: 1 what p' is there of circumcision? 5622
1Co 7:35 And this I speak for your own p'; 4851
10:33 things, not seeking mine own p', "
33 p' of many, that they may be saved. "
12: 7 is given to every man to p' withal. "
14: 6 what shall I p' you, except I shall 5623
Ga 5: 2 Christ shall p' you nothing. "
2Ti 2:14 strive not about words to no p', 5539
Heb 4: 2 word preached did not p' them, 5623
12:10 he for our p', that we might be 4851
Jas 2:14 What doth it p', my brethren, 3786
16 to the body; what doth it p'? "

profitable See also UNPROFITABLE.
Job 22: 2 Can a man be p' unto God, as he 5532
2 is wise may be p' unto himself? "
Ec 10:10 but wisdom is p' to direct. 3504
Isa 44:10 image that is p' for nothing? 3276
Jer 13: 7 was marred, it was p' for nothing. 6743
M't 5:29, 30 it is p' for thee that one of thy 4851
Ac 20:20 back nothing that was p' unto you, "
1Ti 4: 8 godliness is p' unto all things, 5624
2Ti 3:16 and is p' for doctrine, for reproof, "
2Ti 4:11 for he is p' to me for the ministry.*2173
Tit 3: 8 things are good and p' unto men. 5624
Ph'm 11 but now p' to thee and to me: 2173

profited
Job 33:27 which was right, and it p' me not;7737
M't 15: 5 thou mightest be p' by me; 5623
16:26 For what is a man p', if he shall "
M'r 7:11 thou mightest be p' by me; he "
Ga 1:14 And p' in the Jews' religion above*4298
Heb13: 9 p' them that have been occupied 5623

profiteth
Job 34: 9 It p' a man nothing that he 5532
Hab 2:18 What p' the graven image that the3276
Joh 6:63 the flesh p' nothing: the words 5623
Ro 2:25 circumcision verily p', if thou keep "
1Co 13: 3 have not charity, it p' me nothing. "
1Ti 4: 8 For bodily exercise p' little: *5624,2076

profiting
1Ti 4:15 that thy p' may appear to all. *4297

profound
Ho 5: 2 revolters are p' to make slaughter,*6009

progenitors
Ge 49:26 blessings of my p' unto the utmost 2029

prognosticators
Isa 47:13 stargazers, the monthly p', stand 3045

prolong See also PROLONGED; PROLONGETH.
De 4:26 shall not p' your days upon it, but 748
40 mayest p' thy days upon the earth, "
5:33 ye may p' your days in the land "
11: 9 ye may p' your days in the land, "
17:20 he may p' his days in his kingdom, "
22: 7 and that thou mayest p' thy days. "
30:18 shall not p' your days upon the land," "
32:47 ye shall p' your days in the land, "
Job 6:11 mine end, that I should p' my life?* "
15:29 neither shall he p' the perfection†‡5186
Ps 61: 6 Thou wilt p' the king's life: and 3254
Pr 28:16 covetousness shall p' his days. 748
Ec 8:13 neither shall he p' his days, which "
Isa 53:10 seed, he shall p' his days, and the "

prolonged
De 5:16 that thy days may be p', and that* 748
6: 2 life; and that thy days may be p'. "
Pr 28: 2 the state thereof shall be p'. "
Ec 8:12 his days be p', yet surely I know * "
Isa 13:22 come, and her days shall not be p'.4900
Eze 12:22 The days are p', and every vision 748
25 it shall be no more p': for in your*4900
28 shall none of my words be p' any * "
Da 7:12 lives were p' for a season and 754,3052

prolongeth
Pr 10:27 The fear of the Lord p' days: but 3254
Ec 7:15 a wicked man that p' his life in 748

promise See also PROMISED; PROMISES; PROMISING.
Nu 14:34 and ye shall know my breach of p'.*
1Ki 8:56 failed one word of all his good p', 1697
2Ch 1: 9 let thy p' unto David my father be "
Ne 5:12 should do according to this p'. "
13 performeth not this p', even thus "
13 the people did according to this p'. "
Ps 77: 8 doth his p' fail for evermore? 562
105:42 he remembered his holy p', and 1697
Lu 24:49 the p' of my Father upon you: 1860
Ac 1: 4 but wait for the p' of the Father, "
2:33 Father, the p' of the Holy Ghost, "
39 For the p' is unto you, and to your "
7:17 when the time of the p' drew nigh, "
13:23 according to his p', raised unto "
32 p' which was made unto the fathers, "
23:21 ready, looking for a p' from thee. "
26: 6 for the hope of the p' made of God "
7 Unto which p' our twelve tribes, "
Ro 4:13 For the p', that he should be the 1860
14 and the p' made of none effect: "
16 the end the p' might be sure to all "
20 He staggered not at the p' of God "
9: 8 children of the p' are counted for "
9 this is the word of p', At this time "
Ga 3:14 the p' of the Spirit through faith. "
17 should make the p' of none effect. "
18 be of the law, it is no more of p': "
18 but God gave it to Abraham by p'. "
19 come to whom the p' was made; 1861
22 that the p' by faith of Jesus Christ1860
29 and heirs according to the p'. "
4:23 he of the freewoman was by p'. "
28 as Isaac was, are the children of p'. "
Eph 1:13 sealed with that holy Spirit of p', "
2:12 from the covenants of p', having "
3: 6 partakers of his p' in Christ by the "
6: 2 is the first commandment with p'; "
1Ti 4: 8 having p' of the life that now is, "
2Ti 1: 1 the p' of life which is in Christ "
Heb 4: 1 a p' being left us of entering into "
6:13 when God made p' to Abraham, 1861
15 endured, he obtained the p'. 1860
17 to shew unto the heirs of p' the "
9:15 the p' of eternal inheritance. "
10:36 of God, ye might receive the p'. "
11: 9 faith he sojourned in the land of p', "
9 the heirs with him of the same p': "
39 through faith, received not the p': "
2Pe 2:19 While they p' them liberty, they *1861
3: 4 Where is the p' of his coming? 1860
9 is not slack concerning his p', "
13 according to his p', look for new 1862
1Jo 2:25 the p' that he hath promised us, 1860

promised See also PROMISEDST.
Ex 12:25 according as he hath p', that ye 1696
Nu 14:40 place which the Lord hath p': 559
De 1:11 and bless you, as he hath p' you!) 1696
6: 3 Lord God of thy fathers hath p' "
9:28 into the land which he p' them, "
10: 9 as the Lord thy God p' him. * "
12:20 thy border, as he hath p' thee, and "
15: 6 God blesseth thee, as he p' thee: "
19: 8 land which he p' to give unto thy "
23:23 thou hast p' with thy mouth. "
26:18 peculiar people, as he hath p' thee, "
27: 3 God of thy fathers hath p' thee. "
Jos 9:21 as the princes had p' them. * "
22: 4 unto your brethren, as he p' them:* "
23: 5 Lord your God hath p' unto you. "
10 fighteth for you, as he hath p' you.* "
15 the Lord your God p' you; which * "
2Sa 7:28 p' this goodness unto thy servant: "
1Ki 2:24 hath made me an house, as he p', "
5:12 Solomon wisdom, as he p' him: "
8:20 throne of Israel, as the Lord p', "
56 Israel, according to all that he p': "
56 which he p' by the hand of Moses "
9: 5 as I p' to David thy father, saying, "
2Ki 8:19 as he p' him to give him alway a 559
1Ch 17:26 p' this goodness unto thy servant: 1696
2Ch 6:10 throne of Israel, as the Lord p', "
15 that which thou hast p' him; and * "
16 which thou hast p' him, saying, "
21: 7 as he p' to give a light to him and 559
Ne 9:23 which thou hadst p' to their fathers,* "
Es 4: 7 money that Haman had p' to pay "
Jer 32:42 all the good that I have p' them. 1696
33:14 that good thing which I have p' * "
M't 14: 7 he p' with an oath to give her 3670
M'r 14:11 glad, and p' to give him money. 1861
Lu 1:72 perform the mercy p' to our fathers,*
22: 6 he p', and sought opportunity to *1843
Ac 7: 5 yet he p' that he would give it... him1861
Ro 1: 2 he had p' afore by his prophets 4279
4:21 what he had p', he was able also 1861
Tit 1: 2 God, that cannot lie, p' before the "
Heb10:23 wavering; (...he is faithful that p';) "
11:11 judged him faithful who had p'. "
12:26 now he hath p', saying, Yet once "
Jas 1:12 Lord hath p' to them that love him. "
2: 5 kingdom which he hath p' to them "
1Jo 2:25 promise that he hath p' us, even "

promisedst
1Ki 8:24 David my father that thou p' him:*1696
25 David my father that thou p' him,* "
Ne 9:15 p' them that they should go in to * 559

promises
Ro 9: 4 and the service of God, and the p'; 1860
15: 8 the p' made unto the fathers: "
2Co 1:20 For all the p' of God in him are yea, "
7: 1 Having therefore these p', dearly "
Gal 3:16 and his seed were the p' made. "
21 the law then against the p' of God? "
Heb 6:12 faith and patience inherit the p'. "
7: 6 and blessed him that had the p'. "
8: 6 was established upon better p'. "
11:13 faith, not having received the p', "
17 he that had received the p' offered "
33 obtained p', stopped the mouths of "
2Pe 1: 4 exceeding great and precious p': 1862

promising
Eze 13:22 his wicked way, by p' him life: *2421

promote See also PROMOTED.
Nu 22:17 I will p' thee unto very great 3513
37 able indeed to p' thee to honour? "
24:11 to p' thee unto great honour; but "
Es 3: 1 did king Ahasuerus p' Haman 1431
Pr 4: 8 Exalt her, and she shall p' thee: 7311

promoted
J'g 9: 9, 11, 13 go to be p' over the trees? *5128
Es 5:11 wherein the king had p' him, 1431
Da 3:30 Then the king p' Shadrach, 6744

promotion
Ps 75: 6 p' cometh neither from the east, *7311
Pr 3:35 but shame shall be the p' of fools. "

pronounce See also PRONOUNCED; PRONOUNCING.
Le 5: 4 that a man shall p' with an oath, * 981
13: 3 look on him, and p' him unclean.
6 the skin, the priest shall p' him clean:
8 then the priest shall p' him unclean:
11 and the priest shall p' him unclean,
13 he shall p' him clean that hath the
15 raw flesh, and p' him to be unclean:
17 then the priest shall p' him clean
20 the priest shall p' unclean: it is a
22 then the priest shall p' him unclean:
23 and the priest shall p' him clean.
25 the priest shall p' him unclean:
27 then the priest shall p' him unclean:
28 and the priest shall p' him clean; for
30 then the priest shall p' him unclean:
34 then the priest shall p' him clean:
37 and the priest shall p' him clean.
44 priest shall p' him utterly unclean;
59 to p' it clean, or to p' it unclean.
14: 7 and shall p' him clean, and shall let
48 the priest shall p' the house clean,
J'g 12: 6 he could not frame to p' it right. 1696

pronounced
Ne 6:12 he p' this prophecy against me: 1696
Jer 11:17 hath p' evil against thee, for the "
16:10 p' all this great evil against us? "
18: 8 nation, against whom I have p', * "
19:15 the evil that I have p' against it, "
25:13 words which I have p' against it, "
26:13 evil that he hath p' against you. "
19 evil which he had p' against them? "
34: 5 for I have p' the word, saith the * "

Jer 35:17 evil that I have p' against them: 1696
36: 7 Lord hath p' against this people. "
18 He p' all these words unto me 7126
31 evil that I have p' against them; 1691
40: 2 hath p' this evil upon this place. "

pronouncing
Le 5: 4 swear, p' with his lips to do evil, * 981

proof See also PROOFS; REPROOF.
2Co 2: 9 that I might know the p' of you, 1382
8:24 p' of your love, and of our boasting 1732
13: 3 a p' of Christ speaking in me, 1382
Ph'p 2:22 But ye know the p' of him, that, "
2Ti 4: 5 make full p' of thy ministry. *4135

proofs See also REPROOFS.
Ac 1: 3 his passion by many infallible p', 5039

proper
1Ch 29: 3 I have of mine own p' good, of *5459
Ac 1:19 field is called in their p' tongue, *2398
1Co 7: 7 every man hath his p' gift of God,* "
Heb11:23 they saw he was a p' child; * 791

prophecies
1Co 13: 8 whether there be p', they shall 4394
1Ti 1:18 the p' which went before on thee, "

prophecy See also PROPHECIES.
2Ch 9:29 in the p' of Ahijah the Shilonite, 5016
15: 8 and the p' of Oded the prophet, "
Ne 6:12 he pronounced this p' against me: "
Pr 30: 1 the son of Jakeh, even the p': *4853
31: 1 the p' that his mother taught him.* "
Da 9:24 to seal up the vision and p', and 5030
M't 13:14 them is fulfilled the p' of Esaias, 4394
Ro 12: 6 that is given to us, whether p', "
1Co 12:10 working of miracles; to another p'; "
13: 2 though I have the gift of p', and "
1Ti 4:14 in thee, which was given thee by p', "
2Pe 1:19 have also a more sure word of p'; 4397
20 that no p' of the scripture is of any 4394
21 For the p' came not in old time by "
Re 1: 3 they that hear the words of this p', "
11: 6 it rain not in the days of their p': "
19:10 testimony of Jesus is the spirit of p'. "
22: 7 the sayings of the p' of this book. "
10 the sayings of the p' of this book: "
18 the words of the p' of this book, "
19 the words of the book of this p', "

prophesied
Nu 11:25 spirit rested upon them, they p', 5012
26 tabernacle: and they p' in the camp. "
1Sa 10:10 upon him, and he p' among them. "
11 he p' among the prophets, that the "
18:10 and he p' in the midst of the house: "
19:20 of Saul, and they also p'. "
21 messengers, and they p' likewise. "
21 the third time, and they p' also. "
23 he went on, and p', until he came "
24 p' before Samuel in like manner, "
1Ki 18:29 and they p' until the time of the "
22:10 all the prophets p' before them. "
12 all the prophets p' so, saying, Go "
1Ch 25: 2 p' according to the order of the "
3 also p' with a harp, to give thanks "
2Ch 18: 7 for he never p' good unto me, but "
9 all the prophets p' before them. "
11 And all the prophets p' so, saying, "
20:37 p' Eliezer...against Jehoshaphat, "
Ezr 5: 1 p' unto the Jews that were in 5013
Jer 2: 8 and the prophets p' by Baal, and 5012
20: 1 that Jeremiah p' these things. * "
6 friends, to whom thou hast p' lies. "
23:13 they p' in Baal, and caused my "
21 not spoken to them, yet they p'. "
25:13 hath p' against all the nations. "
26: 9 thou p' in the name of the Lord, "
11 for he hath p' against this city, as "
18 Micah the Morasthite p' in the days "
20 man that p' in the name of the Lord, "
20 who p' against this city and against "
28: 6 thy words which thou hast p', "
8 old p' both against many countries, "
29:31 that Shemaiah hath p' unto you, "
37:19 your prophets which p' unto you, "
Eze 11:13 to pass, when I p', that Pelatiah "
37: 7 So I p' as I was commanded: "
7 and as I p', there was a noise, and "
10 So I p' as he commanded me, and "
38:17 which p' in those days many years "
Zec 13: 4 one of his vision, when he hath p';* "
M't 7:22 Lord, have we not p' in thy name?* 4395
11:13 prophets and the law p' until John. "
M'r 7: 6 Well hath Esaias p' of you * "
Lu 1:67 the Holy Ghost, and p', saying, "
Joh 11:51 he p' that Jesus should die for that "
Ac 19: 6 and they spake with tongues, and p'. "
1Co 14: 5 with tongues, but rather that ye p':* "
1Pe 1:10 who p' of the grace that should "
Jude 14 Adam, p' of these, saying, Behold, "

prophesieth
Jer 28: 9 The prophet which p' of peace, 5012
Eze 12:27 he p' of the times that are far off. "
Zec 13: 3 thrust him through when he p'. "
1Co 11: 5 or p' with her head uncovered *4395
14: 3 But he that p' speaketh unto men "
4 but he that p' edifieth the church. "
5 greater is he that p' than he that "

prophesy See also PROPHESIED; PROPHESIETH; PROPHESYING.
Nu 11:27 and Medad do p' in the camp. 5012
1Sa 10: 5 before them; and they shall p': * "
6 thou shalt p' with them, and shalt "
1Ki 22: 8 he doth not p' good concerning me, "
18 would p' no good concerning me, "
1Ch 25: 1 who should p' with harps, with 5012
2Ch 18:17 he would not p' good unto me, but "
Isa 30:10 P' not unto us right things, speak 2372
10 unto us smooth things, p' deceits: "
Jer 5:31 The prophets p' falsely, and the 5012
11:21 P' not in the name of the Lord, "
14:14 The prophets p' lies in my name: "
14 they p' unto you a false vision and "
15 the prophets that p' in my name, "
16 the people to whom they p' shall be "
19:14 whither the Lord had sent him to p'; "
23:16 words of the prophets that p' unto "
25 said, that p' lies in my name, "
26 heart of the prophets that p' lies? "
32 against them that p' false dreams, "
25:30 p' thou against them all these "
26:12 sent me to p' against this house "
27:10 For they p' a lie unto you, to remove "
14 Babylon: for they p' a lie unto you. "
15 Lord, yet they p' a lie in my name; "
15 and the prophets that p' unto you. "
16 of your prophets that p' unto you, "
16 Babylon: for they p' a lie unto you. "
29: 9 p' falsely unto you in my name: "
21 p' a lie unto you in my name; "
32: 3 Wherefore dost thou p', and say, "
Eze 4: 7 and thou shalt p' against it. "
6: 2 of Israel, and p' against them, "
11: 4 p' against them, p', O son of man. "
13: 2 p' against the prophets of Israel "
2 the prophets of Israel that p', "
2 unto them that p' out of their own "
16 the prophets of Israel which p' "
17 daughters of thy people, which p' "
17 heart; and p' thou against them, "
20:46 p' against the forest of the south "
21: 2 and p' against the land of Israel, * "
9 Son of man, p', and say, Thus saith "
14 son of man, p', and smite thine "
28 son of man, p' and say, Thus saith "
25: 2 Ammonites, and p' against them; "
28:21 against Zidon, and p' against it, "
29: 2 king of Egypt, and p' against him, "
30: 2 Son of man, p' and say, Thus saith "
34: 2 p' against the shepherds of Israel, "
2 p', and say unto them, Thus saith "
35: 2 mount Seir, and p' against it, "
36: 1 p' unto the mountains of Israel, "
3 Therefore p' and say, Thus saith "
6 P' therefore concerning the land of "
37: 4 P' upon these bones, and say unto "
9 P' unto the wind, p', son of man, "
12 Therefore p' and say unto them, "
38: 2 and Tubal, and p' against him, "
14 son of man, p' and say unto Gog, "
39: 1 thou son of man, p' against Gog, "
Joe 2:28 sons and your daughters shall p', "
Am 2:12 the prophets, saying, P' not. "
3: 8 God hath spoken, who can but p'? "
7:12 and there eat bread, and p' there: "
13 p' not again any more at Beth-el: "
15 me, Go, p' unto my people Israel. "
16 Thou sayest, P' not against Israel, "
Mic 2: 6 P' ye not, say they to them that 5197
6 say they to them that p': they shall "
6 they shall not p' to them, that they "
11 I will p' unto thee of wine and of "
Zec 13: 3 that when any shall yet p', then "
M't 15: 7 well did Esaias p' of you, saying, 4395
26:68 P' unto us, thou Christ, Who is he "
M'r 14:65 him, and to say unto him, P': "
Lu 22:64 P', who is it that smote thee? "
Ac 2:17 sons and your daughters shall p', "
18 of my Spirit; and they shall p': "
21: 9 daughters, virgins, which did p'. "
Ro 12: 6 let us p' according to the proportion "
1Co 13: 9 we know in part, and we p' in part. 4395
14: 1 gifts, but rather that ye may p'. "
24 if all p', and there come in one that "
31 For ye may all p' one by one, that "
39 covet to p', and forbid not to speak "
Re 10:11 Thou must p' again before many "
11: 3 shall p' a thousand two hundred "

prophesying See also PROPHESYINGS.
1Sa 10:13 when he had made an end of p', 5012
19:20 the company of the prophets p', "
Ezr 6:14 prospered through the p' of Haggai 5017
1Co 11: 4 Every man praying or p', having 4395
14: 6 or by knowledge, or by p', or by 4394
22 but p' serveth not for them that "

prophesyings
1Th 5:20 Despise not p'. 4394

prophet See also PROPHETESS; PROPHET'S; PROPHETS.
Ge 20: 7 for he is a p', and he shall pray for 5030
Ex 7: 1 Aaron thy brother shall be thy p'. "
Nu 12: 6 If there be a p' among you, I the "
De 13: 1 If there arise among you a p', or a "
3 hearken unto the words of that p', "
5 that p', or that dreamer of dreams, "
18:15 thy God will raise up unto thee a P' "
18 I will raise them up a P' from "
20 But the p', which shall presume to "
20 of other gods, even that p' shall die. "
22 When a p' speaketh in the name of "
22 p' hath spoken it presumptuously: "
34:10 arose not a p' since in Israel like "
J'g 6: 8 Lord sent a p' unto the children of "
1Sa 3:20 established to be a p' of the Lord. "
9: 9 a P' was before time called a Seer.) "
22: 5 p' Gad said unto David, Abide not "
2Sa 7: 2 the king said unto Nathan the p', "
12:25 sent by the hand of Nathan the p': "
24:11 of the Lord came unto the p' Gad, "
1Ki 1: 8 Nathan the p', and Shimei, and Rei, "
1Ki 1:10 Nathan the p', and Benaiah, and 5030
22 the king, Nathan the p' also came "
23 king, saying, Behold Nathan the p'. "
32 the priest, and Nathan the p', and "
34 Nathan the p' anoint him there "
38, 44 and Nathan the p', and Benaiah "
45 Nathan the p' have anointed him "
11:29 p' Ahijah the Shilonite found him "
13:11 there dwelt an old p' in Beth-el; "
18 him, I am a p' also as thou art; "
20 unto the p' that brought him back: "
23 the p' whom he had brought back. "
25 in the city where the old p' dwelt. "
26 when the p' that brought him back "
29 the p' took up the carcase of the "
29 and the old p' came to the city, to "
14: 2 there is Ahijah the p', which told "
18 hand of his servant Ahijah the p'. "
16: 7 by the hand of the p' Jehu the son "
12 against Baasha by Jehu the p', "
18:22 I only, remain a p' of the Lord; "
36 Elijah the p' came near, and said, "
19:16 thou anoint to be p' in thy room. "
20:13 there came a p' unto Ahab king of "
22 the p' came to the king of Israel, "
38 So the p' departed, and waited for "
22: 7 Is there not here a p' of the Lord "
2Ki 3:11 Is there not here a p' of the Lord, "
5: 3 were with the p' that is in Samaria! "
8 know that there is a p' in Israel. "
13 if the p' had bid thee do some great "
6:12 but Elisha, the p' that is in Israel, "
9: 1 the p' called one of the children of "
4 even the young man the p', went to "
14:25 Jonah the son of Amittai, the p', "
19: 2 to Isaiah the p' the son of Amoz. "
20: 1 the p' Isaiah the son of Amoz came "
11 Isaiah the p' cried unto the Lord: "
14 Then came Isaiah the p' unto king "
23:18 of the p' that came out of Samaria. "
1Ch 17: 1 David said to Nathan the p', Lo, I "
29:29 and in the book of Nathan the p', "
2Ch 9:29 in the book of Nathan the p', and "
12: 5 came Shemaiah the p' to Rehoboam, "
15 in the book of Shemaiah the p', and "
13:22 written in the story of the p' Iddo. "
15: 8 and the prophecy of Oded the p', "
18: 6 Is there not here a p' of the Lord "
21:12 a writing to him from Elijah the p', "
25:15 he sent unto him a p', which said "
16 Then the p' forbare, and said, I "
26:22 did Isaiah the p', the son of Amoz, "
28: 9 a p' of the Lord was there, whose "
29:25 the king's seer, and Nathan the p': "
32:20 p' Isaiah the son of Amoz, prayed "
32 written in the vision of Isaiah the p', "
35:18 from the days of Samuel the p'; "
36:12 Jeremiah the p' speaking from the "
Ezr 5: 1 Haggai the p', and Zechariah the 5029
6:14 the prophesying of Haggai the p' "
Ps 51: *title* Nathan the p' came unto him, 5030
74: 9 there is no more any p': neither is "
Isa 3: 2 man of war, the judge, and the p', "
9:15 the p' that teacheth lies, he is the "
28: 7 the priest and the p' have erred "
37: 2 unto Isaiah the p' the son of Amoz. "
38: 1 Isaiah the p' the son of Amoz came "
39: 3 Isaiah the p' unto king Hezekiah, "
Jer 1: 5 ordained thee a p' unto the nations. "
6:13 from the p' even unto the priest "
8:10 from the p' even unto the priest "
14:18 both the p' and the priest go about "
18:18 the wise, nor the word from the p'. "
20: 2 Pashur smote Jeremiah the p', and "
23:11 both p' and priest are profane; yea, "
28 The p' that hath a dream, let him "
33 or the p', or a priest shall ask thee, "
34 And as for the p', and the priest, "
37 Thus shalt thou say to the p', What "
25: 2 Jeremiah the p' spake unto all the "
28: 1 Hananiah the son of Azar the p', "
5 p' Jeremiah said unto...p' Hananiah "
6 Even the p' Jeremiah said, Amen: "
9 The p' which prophesieth of peace, "
9 the word of the p' shall come to "
9 then shall the p' be known, that "
10 Hananiah the p' took the yoke "
10 from off the p' Jeremiah's neck, "
11 And the p' Jeremiah went his way. "
12 Lord came unto Jeremiah the p', * "
12 the p' had broken the yoke 5030
12 off the neck of the p' Jeremiah, "
15 p' Jeremiah unto Hananiah the p', "
17 So Hananiah the p' died the same "
29: 1 that Jeremiah the p' sent from "
26 is mad, and maketh himself a p', 5012
27 which maketh himself a p' to you? "
29 in the ears of Jeremiah the p'. 5030
32: 2 Jeremiah the p' was shut up in the "
34: 6 Jeremiah the p' spake all these "
36: 8 Jeremiah the p' commanded him, "
26 the scribe and Jeremiah the p': "
37: 2 which he spake by the p' Jeremiah. "
3 the priest to the p' Jeremiah, "
6 of the Lord unto the p' Jeremiah, "
13 he took Jeremiah the p', saying, "
38: 9 they have done to Jeremiah the p', "
10 take up Jeremiah the p' out of the "
14 took Jeremiah the p' unto him into "
42: 2 And said unto Jeremiah the p', Let, "
4 Jeremiah the p' said unto them, I "
43: 6 and Jeremiah the p', and Baruch "
45: 1 that Jeremiah the p' spake unto "
46: 1 Lord which came to Jeremiah the p' "
13 the Lord spake to Jeremiah the p', "
47: 1 Lord that came to Jeremiah the p' "

Jer 49:34 came to Jeremiah the p' against 5030
50: 1 the Chaldeans by Jeremiah the p'. "
51:59 which Jeremiah the p' commanded "
La 2:20 the priest and the p' be slain in the "
Eze 2: 5 there hath been a p' among them. "
7:26 shall they seek a vision of the p'; "
14: 4 his face, and cometh to the p'; "
7 cometh to a p' to enquire of him "
9 And if the p' be deceived when he "
9 I the Lord have deceived that p', "
10 the punishment of the p' shall be "
33:33 that a p' hath been among them. "
Da 9: 2 the Lord came to Jeremiah the p', "
Ho 4: 5 p' also shall fall with thee in the "
9: 7 the p' is a fool, the spiritual man "
8 the p' is a snare of a fowler in all "
12:13 by a p' the Lord brought Israel out "
13 and by a p' was he preserved. "
Am 7:14 I was no p', neither was I a "
Mic 2:11 shall even be the p' of this people. 5197
Hab 1: 1 which Habakkuk the p' did see. 5030
3: 1 A prayer of Habakkuk the p' upon "
Hag 1: 1 word of the Lord by Haggai the p' "
3 word of the Lord by Haggai the p', "
12 and the words of Haggai the p', "
2: 1 word of the Lord by the p' Haggai, "
10 word of the Lord by Haggai the p', "
Zec 1: 1, 7 Berechiah, the son of Iddo the p'," "
13: 5 shall say, I am no p', I am an "
Mal 4: 5 Behold, I will send you Elijah the p' "
M't 1:22 was spoken of the Lord by the p', 4396
2: 5 for thus it is written by the p', "
15 was spoken of the Lord by the p', "
17 which was spoken by Jeremy the p'," "
3: 3 that was spoken of by the p' Esaias," "
4:14 spoken by Esaias the p', saying, "
8:17 which was spoken by Esaias the p', "
10:41 a p' in the name of a p' shall receive "
11: 9 what went ye out for to see? A p'? "
9 I say unto you, and more than a p'. "
12:17 which was spoken by Esaias the p', "
39 to it, but the sign of the p' Jonas: "
13:35 which was spoken by the p', "
57 A p' is not without honour, save in "
14: 5 because they counted him as a p'. "
16: 4 unto it, but the sign of the p' Jonas.* "
21: 4 which was spoken by the p', "
11 This is Jesus the p' of Nazareth of "
26 people; for all hold John as a p'. "
46 because they took him for a p'. "
24:15 spoken of by Daniel the p', stand in "
27: 9 which was spoken by Jeremy the p'," "
35 which was spoken by the p', They* "
M'r 6: 4 A p' is not without honour, but in "
15 others said, That it is a p', or as one "
11:32 John, that he was a p' indeed. "
13:14 spoken of by Daniel the p', * "
Lu 1:76 be called the p' of the Highest: "
3: 4 book of the words of Esaias the p', "
4:17 unto him the book of the p' Esaias. "
24 No p' is accepted in his own "
27 Israel in the time of Eliseus the p'; "
7:16 a great p' is risen up among us; "
26 what went ye out for to see? A p'? "
26 unto you, and much more than a p'. "
28 a greater p' than John the Baptist:* "
39 This man, if he were a p', would "
11:29 it, but the sign of Jonas the p'. * "
13:33 that a p' perish out of Jerusalem. "
20: 6 be persuaded that John was a p'. "
24:19 which was a p' mighty in deed and "
Joh 1:21 Art thou that p'? And he answered, "
23 of the Lord, as said the p' Esaias. "
25 Christ, nor Elias, neither that p'? "
4:19 Sir, I perceive that thou art a p'. "
44 that a p' hath no honour in his own "
6:14 p' that should come into the world. "
7:40 said, Of a truth this is the P'. "
52 look: for out of Galilee ariseth no p'. "
9:17 thine eyes? He said, He is a p'. "
12:38 of Esaias the p' might be fulfilled, "
Ac 2:16 which was spoken by the p' Joel; "
30 being a p', and knowing that God "
3:22 A p' shall the Lord your God raise "
23 soul, which will not hear that p', "
7:37 A p' shall the Lord your God raise "
48 made with hands; as saith the p', "
8:28 in his chariot read Esaias the p'. "
30 and heard him read the p' Esaias, "
34 of whom speaketh the p' this? of "
13: 6 sorcerer, a false p', a Jew, whose 5578
20 fifty years, until Samuel the p'. 4396
21:10 Judæa a certain p', named Agabus. "
28:25 the Holy Ghost by Esaias the p' "
1Co 14:37 If any man think himself to be a p'," "
Tit 1:12 even a p' of their own, said, The "
2Pe 2:16 voice forbad the madness of the p'. "
Re 16:13 out of the mouth of the false p'. 5578
19:20 the false p' that wrought miracles "
20:10 where the beast and the false p' are, "

prophetess

Ex 15:20 Miriam the p', the sister of Aaron, 5031
J'g 4: 4 Deborah, a p', the wife of Lapidoth," "
2Ki 22:14 went unto Huldah the p', the wife "
2Ch 34:22 appointed, went to Huldah the p', "
Ne 6:14 and on the p' Noadiah, and the rest "
Isa 8: 3 And I went unto the p'; and she "
Lu 2:36 was one Anna, a p', the daughter 4398
Re 2:20 Jezebel, which calleth herself a p', "

prophet's

Am 7:14 neither was I a p' son; but I was a 5030
M't 10:41 prophet shall receive a p' reward; 4396

prophets

Nu 11:29 that all the Lord's people were p', 5030
1Sa 10: 5 meet a company of p' coming down 5030
10 behold, a company of p' met him; "
11 he prophesied among the p', then "
11 Kish? Is Saul also among the p'? "
12 proverb, Is Saul also among the p'? "
19:20 they saw the company of the p' "
24 they say, Is Saul also among the p'? "
28: 6 by dreams, nor by Urim, nor by p'. "
15 more, neither by p', nor by dreams: "
1Ki 18: 4 Jezebel cut off the p' of the Lord, "
4 Obadiah took an hundred p', and "
13 Jezebel slew the p' of the Lord, "
13 an hundred men of the Lord's p' "
19 p' of Baal four hundred and fifty, "
19 the p' of the groves four hundred, "
20 gathered the p' together unto "
22 Baal's p' are four hundred and fifty "
25 said unto the p' of Baal, Choose "
40 unto them, Take the p' of Baal; let "
19: 1 how he had slain all the p' with the "
10, 14 and slain thy p' with the sword; "
20:35 man of the sons of the p' said unto "
41 discerned him that he was of the p'. "
22: 6 of Israel gathered the p' together, "
10 all the p' prophesied before them. "
12 all the p' prophesied so, saying, Go "
13 the p' declare good unto the king "
22 lying spirit in...mouth of all his p'. "
23 in the mouth of all these thy p', "
2Ki 2: 3 sons of the p' that were at Beth-el "
5 sons of the p' that were at Jericho "
7 fifty men of the sons of the p' went, "
15 And when the sons of the p' which "
3:13 get thee to the p' of thy father, "
13 to the p' of thy mother. And the "
4: 1 of the wives of the sons of the p' "
38 sons of the p' were sitting before "
38 seethe pottage for the sons of the p'. "
5:22 young men of the sons of the p': "
6: 1 the sons of the p' said unto Elisha, "
9: 1 called one of the children of the p', "
7 the blood of my servants the p', "
10:19 call unto me all the p' of Baal, all "
17:13 against Judah, by all the p', and * "
13 I sent to you by my servants the p'. "
23 had said by all his servants the p'. "
21:10 Lord spake by his servants the p', "
23: 2 the priests, and the p', and all the "
24: 2 he spake by his servants the p'. "
1Ch 16:22 anointed, and do my p' no harm. "
2Ch 18: 5 together of p' four hundred men, "
9 all the p' prophesied before them. "
11 all the p' prophesied so, saying, Go "
12 the p' declare good to the king "
21 lying spirit in...mouth of all his p'. "
22 spirit in the mouth of these thy p', "
20:20 believe his p', so shall ye prosper. "
24:19 Yet he sent p' to them, to bring "
29:25 commandment of the Lord by...p'. "
36:16 his words, and misused his p', "
Ezr 5: 1 Then the p', Haggai the prophet, 5029
2 were the p' of God helping them. "
9:11 commanded by thy servants the p', 5030
Ne 6: 7 hast also appointed p' to preach "
14 the rest of the p', that would have "
9:26 slew thy p' which testified against "
30 against them by thy spirit in thy p': "
32 and on our priests, and on our p', "
Ps 105:15 anointed, and do my p' no harm. "
Isa 29:10 the p' and your rulers, the seers "
30:10 to the p', Prophesy not unto us 2374
Jer 2: 8 the p' prophesied by Baal, and 5030
26 and their priests, and their p', "
30 own sword hath devoured your p', "
4: 9 astonished, and the p' shall wonder. "
5:13 And the p' shall become wind, and "
31 The p' prophesy falsely, and the "
7:25 unto you all my servants the p', "
8: 1 the bones of the p', and the bones "
13:13 the priests, and the p', and all the "
14:13 the p' say unto them, Ye shall not "
14 The p' prophesy lies in my name: "
15 p' that prophesy in my name, and "
15 famine shall those p' be consumed. "
23: 9 me is broken because of the p'; "
13 seen folly in the p' of Samaria; "
14 seen also in the p' of Jerusalem "
15 Lord of hosts concerning the p'; "
15 the p' of Jerusalem is profaneness "
16 not unto the words of the p' that "
21 I have not sent these p', yet they "
25 I have heard what the p' said, that "
26 this be in the heart of the p' that "
26 p' of the deceit of their own heart; "
30, 31 I am against the p', saith the "
25: 4 unto you all his servants the p', "
26: 5 the words of my servants the p', "
7, 8 So the priests and the p' and all "
11 Then spake the priests and the p' "
16 people unto the priests and to the p'; "
27: 9 hearken not ye to your p', nor to "
14 not unto the words of the p' that "
15 and the p' that prophesy unto you. "
16 of your p' that prophesy unto you, "
18 But if they be p', and if the word "
28: 8 The p' that have been before me "
29: 1 and to the priests, and to the p', and "
8 Let not your p' and your diviners, "
15 hath raised us up p' in Babylon; "
19 unto them by my servants the p', "
32:32 and their p', and the men of Judah, "
35:15 unto you all my servants the p', "
37:19 Where are now your p' which "
44: 4 unto you all my servants the p', "
La 2: 9 her p' also find no vision from the "
14 Thy p' have seen vain and foolish "
La 4:13 For the sins of her p', and the 5030
Eze 13: 2 prophesy against the p' of Israel "
3 Woe unto the foolish p', that follow "
4 p' are like the foxes in the deserts. "
9 be upon the p' that see vanity, "
16 the p' of Israel which prophesy "
22:25 conspiracy of her p' in the midst "
28 her p' have daubed them with "
38:17 time by my servants the p' of Israel, "
Da 9: 6 hearkened unto thy servants the p', "
10 set before us by his servants the p'. "
Ho 6: 5 have I hewed them by the p'; "
12:10 I have also spoken by the p', and I "
10 by the ministry of the p'. "
Am 2:11 And I raised up of your sons for p'," "
12 and commanded the p', saying, "
3: 7 his secret unto his servants the p'. "
Mic 3: 5 the p' that make my people err, "
6 the sun shall go down over the p', "
11 the p' thereof divine for money: "
Zep 3: 4 Her p' are light and treacherous "
Zec 1: 4 whom the former p' have cried, "
5 and the p', do they live for ever? "
6 I commanded my servants the p', "
7: 3 and to the p', saying, Should I weep "
7 Lord hath cried by the former p', "
12 sent in his spirit by the former p': "
8: 9 these words by the mouth of the p'," "
13: 2 cause the p' and the unclean spirit "
4 the p' shall be ashamed every one "
M't 2:23 which was spoken by the p', 4396
5:12 so persecuted they the p' which "
17 come to destroy the law, or the p': "
7:12 them: for this is the law and the p'. "
15 Beware of false p', which come to 5578
11:13 For all the p' and the law 4396
13:17 that many p' and righteous men "
16:14 others, Jeremias, or one of the p'. "
22:40 hang all the law and the p'. "
23:29 ye build the tombs of the p', and "
30 with them in the blood of the p'. "
31 children of them which killed the p'. "
34 behold, I send unto you p', and "
37 thou that killest the p', and stonest "
24:11 And many false p' shall rise, and 5578
24 and false p', and shall shew great "
26:56 of the p' might be fulfilled. 4396
M'r 1: 2 As it is written in the p', Behold, * "
6:15 it is a prophet, or as one of the p'. "
8:28 Elias; and others, One of the p'. "
13:22 false Christs and false p' shall rise, 5578
Lu 1:70 spake by the mouth of his holy p', 4396
6:23 did their fathers unto the p'. "
26 so did their fathers to the false p'. 5578
9: 8 one of the old p' was risen again. 4396
19 one of the old p' is risen again. "
10:24 many p' and kings have desired "
11:47 ye build the sepulchres of the p', "
49 I will send them p' and apostles, "
50 That the blood of all the p', which "
13:28 all the p', in the kingdom of God, "
34 Jerusalem, which killeth the p', "
16:16 The law and the p' were until John: "
29 him, They have Moses and the p'; "
31 If they hear not Moses and the p', "
18:31 all things that are written by the p' "
24:25 believe all that the p' have spoken: "
27 beginning at Moses and all the p', "
44 in the law of Moses, and in the p', "
Joh 1:45 law, and the p', did write, Jesus of "
6:45 It is written in the p', And they "
8:52 Abraham is dead, and the p'; and "
53 and the p' are dead: whom makest "
Ac 3:18 shewed by the mouth of all his p', "
21 by the mouth of all his holy p' "
24 and all the p' from Samuel and "
25 Ye are the children of the p', and of "
7:42 it is written in the book of the p', "
52 Which of the p' have not your "
10:43 To him give all the p' witness, that "
11:27 days came p' from Jerusalem unto "
13: 1 Antioch certain p' and teachers; "
15 the reading of the law and the p' "
27 nor yet the voices of the p' which "
40 you, which is spoken of in the p'; "
15:15 to this agree the words of the p'; "
32 being p' also themselves, exhorted "
24:14 written in the law and in the p': "
26:22 which the p' and Moses did say "
27 Agrippa, believest thou the p'? "
28:23 and out of the p', from morning till "
Ro 1: 2 by his p' in the holy scriptures,) "
3:21 witnessed by the law and the p'; "
11: 3 Lord, they have killed thy p', and "
16:26 the scriptures of the p', according 4397
1Co 12:28 apostles, secondarily p', thirdly 4396
29 are all p'? are all teachers? are all "
14:29 Let the p' speak two or three, and "
32 spirits of the p' are subject to the p'. "
Eph 2:20 foundation of the apostles and p', "
3: 5 holy apostles and p' by the Spirit; "
4:11 gave some, apostles; and some, p'; "
1Th 2:15 the Lord Jesus, and their own p', "
Heb 1: 1 past unto the fathers by the p', "
11:32 also, and Samuel, and of the p': "
Jas 5:10 the p', who have spoken in the "
1Pe 1:10 salvation the p' have enquired "
2Pe 2: 1 there were false p' also among 5578
3: 2 were spoken before by the holy p', 4396
1Jo 4: 1 many false p' are gone out into 5578
Re 10: 7 declared to his servants the p'. 4396
11:10 these two p' tormented them that "
18 reward unto thy servants the p', "
16: 6 shed the blood of saints and p', and "
18:20 heaven, and ye holy apostles and p'; "
24 was found the blood of p', and of "

Re 22: 6 Lord God of the holy p', sent his 4396
9 and of thy brethren the p', and "

propitiation
Ro 3:25 a p' through faith in his blood, 2435
1Jo 2: 2 he is the p' for our sins: and not 2434
4:10 his Son to be the p' for our sins. "

proportion
1Ki 7:36 according to the p' of every one, *4626
Job 41:12 nor his power, nor his comely p'. ‡6187
Ro 12: 6 according to the p' of faith; 356

proselyte See also PROSELYTES.
M't 23:15 sea and land to make one p', and 4339
Ac 6: 5 and Nicolas a p' of Antioch: "

proselytes
Ac 2:10 strangers of Rome, Jews and p', 4339
13:43 and religious p' followed Paul and "

prospect
Eze 40:44 and their p' was toward the south:6440
44 having the p' toward the north. "
45 whose p' is toward the south, "
46 whose p' is toward the north "
42:15 gate whose p' is toward the east, "
43: 4 gate whose p' is toward the east. "

prosper See also PROSPERED; PROSPERETH.
Ge 24:40 angel with thee, and p' thy way; 6743
42 if now thou do p' my way which I "
39: 3 made all that he did to p' in his "
23 he did, the Lord made it to p'. "
Nu 14:41 of the Lord? but it shall not p'. "
De 28:29 and thou shalt not p' in thy ways: "
29: 9 that ye may p' in all that ye do. 7919
Jos 1: 7 p' whithersoever thou goest. * "
1Ki 2: 3 mayest p' in all that thou doest, "
22:12 Go up to Ramoth-gilead, and p': 6743
15 Go, and p', for the Lord shall "
1Ch 22:11 p' thou, and build the house of the "
13 Then shalt thou p', if thou takest "
2Ch 13:12 of your fathers; for ye shall not p'. "
18:11 Go up to Ramoth-gilead, and p': "
14 Go ye up, and p', and they shall be "
20:20 believe his prophets, so shall ye p'. "
24:20 that ye cannot p'? because ye have "
26: 5 the Lord, God made him to p'. "
Ne 1: 11 and p', I pray thee, thy servant this"
2:20 The God of heaven, he will p' us; "
Job 12: 6 The tabernacles of robbers p', and7951
Ps 1: 3 and whatsoever he doeth shall p'. 6743
73:12 the ungodly, who p' in the world;*7951
122: 6 they shall p' that love thee. "
Pr 28:13 covereth his sins shall not p.: 6743
Ec 11: 6 knowest not whether shall p', 3787
Isa 53:10 of the Lord shall p' in his hand. 6743
54:17 that is formed against thee shall p';"
55:11 p' in the thing whereto I sent it. "
Jer 2:37 and thou shalt not p' in them. "
5:28 cause of the fatherless, yet they p'; "
10:21 therefore they shall not p', and all*7919
12: 1 doth the way of the wicked p'? 6743
20:11 for they shall not p': their *7919
22:30 man that shall not p' in his days: 6743
30 for no man of his seed shall p', "
23: 5 a King shall reign and p', and *7919
32: 5 the Chaldeans, ye shall not p'. 6743
La 1: 5 are the chief, her enemies p'; 7951
Eze 16:13 and thou didst p' into a kingdom. 6743
17: 9 Shall it p'? shall he not pull up "
10 being planted, shall it p'? shall it "
15 Shall he p'? shall he escape that "
Da 8:24 shall p', and practise, and shall "
25 shall cause craft to p' in his hand; "
11:27 it shall not p': for yet the end shall "
36 shall p' till the indignation be "
3Jo 2 thou mayest p' and be in health, 2137

prospered
Ge 24:56 seeing the Lord hath p' my way; 6743
J'g 4:24 hand of the children of Israel p', *1980
2Sa 11: 7 people did, and how the war p'. 7965
2Ki 18: 7 and he p' whithersoever he went 7919
1Ch 29:23 of David his father, and p'; 6743
2Ch 14: 7 every side. So they built and p'. "
31:21 he did it with all his heart, and p'. "
32:30 And Hezekiah p' in all his works. "
Ezr 6:14 they p' through the prophesying 6744
Job 9: 4 himself against him, and hath p'? 7999
Da 6:28 Daniel p' in the reign of Darius, 6744
8:12 ground; and it practised, and p'. 6743
1Co 16: 2 him in store, as God hath p' him, *2137

prospereth
Ezr 5: 8 fast on, and p' in their hands. 6744
Ps 37: 7 because of him who p' in his way, 6743
Pr 17: 8 whithersoever it turneth, it p'. 7919
3Jo 2 be in health, even as thy soul p'. 2137

prosperity
De 23: 6 not seek their peace nor their p' 2896
1Sa 25: 6 shall ye say to him that liveth in p',
1Ki 10: 7 and p' exceedeth the fame which 2896
Job 15:21 in p' the destroyer shall come 7965
36:11 they shall spend their days in p', 2896
Ps 30: 6 in my p' I said, I shall never be 7961
35:27 pleasure in the p' of his servant. 7965
73: 3 when I saw the p' of the wicked. "
118:25 Lord, I beseech thee, send now p'. 6743
122: 7 walls, and p' within thy palaces. 7962
Pr 1:32 the p' of fools shall destroy them. "
Ec 7:14 In the day of p' be joyful, but in 2896
Jer 22:21 I spake unto thee in thy p'; but 7962
33: 9 all the p' that I procure unto it. *7965
La 3:17 far off from peace: I forgat p'. 2896
Zec 1:17 My cities through p' shall yet be "
7: 7 was inhabited and in p', and 7961

prosperous
Ge 24:21 had made his journey p' or not. 6743
39: 2 Joseph, and he was a p' man; "
Jos 1: 8 then thou shalt make thy way p', "
J'g 18: 5 our way which we go shall be p'. "
Job 8: 6 habitation of thy righteousness p'.7999
Isa 48:15 him, and he shall make his way p'.6743
Zec 8:12 For the seed shall be p'; the vine *7965
Ro 1:10 I might have a p' journey by the 2137

prosperously
2Ch 7:11 in his own house, he p' effected. 6743
Ps 45: 4 majesty ride p' because of truth "

prostitute
Le 19:29 Do not p' thy daughter, to cause *2490

protection
De 32:38 up and help you, and be your p'. 5643

protest See also PROTESTED; PROTESTING.
Ge 43: 3 The man did solemnly p' unto us, 5749
1Sa 8: 9 howbeit yet p' solemnly unto them, "
1Co 15:31 I p' by your rejoicing which I have3513

protested
1Ki 2:42 by the Lord, and p' unto thee, 5749
Jer 11: 7 I earnestly p' unto your fathers in "
Zec 3: 6 angel of the Lord p' unto Joshua, "

protesting
Jer 11: 7 rising early and p', saying, Obey 5749

proud
Job 9:13 the p' helpers do stoop under him.*7293
26:12 he smiteth through the p'. * "
38:11 here shall thy p' waves be stayed? 1347
40:11 and behold every one that is p', 1343
12 Look on every one that is p', and "
Ps 12: 3 tongue that speaketh p' things: *1419
31:23 plentifully rewarded the p' doer. 1346
40: 4 respecteth not the p', nor such as 7295
86:14 the p' are risen against me, and 2086
94: 2 earth: render a reward to the p'. 1343
101: 5 look and a p' heart will not I suffer.7342
119:21 rebuked the p' that are cursed. 2086
51 p' have had me greatly in derision:"
69 p' have forged a lie against me: but"
78 Let the p' be ashamed; for they "
85 The p' have digged pits for me, "
122 good: let not the p' oppress me. "
123: 4 and with the contempt of the p'. 1349
124: 5 p' waters had gone over our soul. 2121
138: 6 but the p' he knoweth afar off. *1364
140: 5 p' have hid a snare for me, and 1343
Pr 6:17 A p' look, a lying tongue, and *7311
15:25 will destroy the house of the p': 1343
16: 5 Every one that is p' in heart is an 1362
19 to divide the spoil with the p'. 1343
21: 4 high look, and a p' heart, and the 7342
24 P' and haughty scorner is his 2086
24 name, who dealeth in p' wrath. *2087
28:25 He that is of a p' heart stirreth up*7342
Ec 7: 8 is better than the p' in spirit. 1362
Isa 2:12 upon every one that is p' and lofty,1343
13:11 the arrogancy of the p' to cease, 2086
16: 6 the pride of Moab; he is very p': 1341
Jer 13:15 hear me, and give ear; be not p': "
43: 2 and all the p' men, saying unto 2086
48:29 of Moab, (he is exceeding p') 1343
50:29 hath been p' against the Lord, 2102
31 am against thee, O thou most p', 2087
32 the most p' shall stumble and fall, "
Hab 2: 5 he is a p' man, neither keepeth *3093
Mal 3:15 now we call the p' happy; yea, 2086
4: 1 all the p', yea, and all that do "
Lu 1:51 the p' in the imagination of their 5244
Ro 1:30 of God, despiteful, p', boasters, * "
1Ti 6: 4 He is p', knowing nothing, but *5187
2Ti 3: 2 p', blasphemers, disobedient to *5244
Jas 4: 6 God resisteth the p', but giveth "
1Pe 5: 5 God resisteth the p', and giveth "

proudly
Ex 18:11 the thing wherein they dealt p' 2102
1Sa 2: 3 Talk no more so exceeding p'; let 1364
Ne 9:10 that they dealt p' against them. 2102
16 But they and our fathers dealt p', "
29 yet they dealt p', and hearkened "
Ps 17:10 with their mouth they speak p'. 1348
31:18 which speak grievous things p' *1346
Isa 3: 5 the child shall behave himself p' 7292
Ob 12 spoken p' in the day of distress. 1431

prove See also PROVED; PROVETH; PROVING; APPROVE; REPROVE.
Ex 16: 4 that I may p' them, whether they 5254
20:20 Fear not: for God is come to p' you,"
De 8: 2 to humble thee, and to p' thee, to "
16 thee, and that he might p' thee, "
33: 8 whom thou didst p' at Massah, "
J'g 2:22 through them I may p' Israel, "
3: 1 to p' Israel by them, even as many "
4 they were to p' Israel by them, to "
6:39 let me p', I pray thee, but this once "
1Ki 10: 1 came to p' him with hard questions."
2Ch 9: 1 to p' Solomon with hard questions "
Job 9:20 perfect, it shall also p' me perverse.
Ps 26: 2 Examine me, O Lord, and p' me; 5254
Ec 2: 1 Go to now, I will p' thee with mirth,"
Da 1:12 P' thy servants, I beseech thee, ten"
Mal 3:10 p' me now herewith, saith the Lord974
Lu 14:19 yoke of oxen, and I go to p' them: 1381
Joh 6: 6 And this he said to p' him: for he 3985
Ac 24:13 Neither can they p' the things 3936
25: 7 Paul, which they could not p'. 584
Ro 12: 2 that ye may p' what is that good, 1381
2Co 8: 8 and to p' the sincerity of your love.*"
13: 5 be in the faith; p' your own selves. "

Ga 6: 4 But let every man p' his own work,1381
1Th 5:21 P' all things; hold fast that which "

proved See also APPROVED; REPROVED.
Ge 42:15 Hereby ye shall be p': By the life 974
16 prison, that your words may be p', "
Ex 15:25 ordinance, and there he p' them, 5254
1Sa 17:39 assayed to go; for he had not p' it. "
39 with these; for I have not p' them. "
Ps 17: 3 Thou hast p' mine heart; thou hast974
66:10 thou, O God, hast p' us: thou hast "
81: 7 I p' thee at the waters of Meribah. "
95: 9 me, p' me, and saw my work. "
Ec 7:23 All this have I p' by wisdom: I 5254
Da 1:14 this matter, and p' them ten days. "
Ro 3: 9 we have before p' both Jews and *4256
2Co 8:22 p' diligent in many things, but 1381
1Ti 3:10 let these also first be p'; then let "
Heb 3: 9 your fathers tempted me, p' me, "

provender
Ge 24:25 have both straw and p' enough, 4554
32 gave straw and p' for the camels, "
42:27 opened his sack to give his ass p' in "
43:24 feet; and he gave their asses p'. "
J'g 19:19 is both straw and p' for our asses; "
21 house, and gave p' unto the asses:*1101
Isa 30:24 ear the ground shall eat clean p', 1098

proverb See also PROVERBS.
De 28:37 become an astonishment, a p', 4912
1Sa 10:12 Therefore it became a p', Is Saul "
24:13 As saith the p' of the ancients, "
1Ki 9: 7 Israel shall be a p' and a byword "
2Ch 7:20 to be a p' and a byword among all "
Ps 69:11 and I became a p' to them. "
Pr 1: 6 To understand a p', and the "
Isa 14: 4 take up this p' against the king of* "
Jer 24: 9 to be a reproach and a p', a taunt "
Eze 12:22 that p' that ye have in the land of "
23 I will make this p' to cease, and they"
23 no more use it as a p' in Israel; 4911
14: 8 and will make him a sign and a p'.4912
16:44 shall use this p' against thee, 4911
18: 2 ye use this p' concerning the land "
3 any more to use this p' in Israel. "
Hab 2: 6 and a taunting p' against him, 2420
Lu 4:23 Ye will surely say unto me this p',*3850
Joh 16:29 thou plainly, and speakest no p'. ‡3942
2Pe 2:22 unto them according to the true p', "

proverbs
Nu 21:27 Wherefore they that speak in p' 4911
1Ki 4:32 And he spake three thousand p': 4912
Pr 1: 1 The p' of Solomon the son of David,"
10: 1 The p' of Solomon. A wise son "
25: 1 These are also p' of Solomon, which"
Ec 12: 9 out, and set in order many p'. "
Eze 16:44 every one that useth p' shall use 4911
Joh 16:25 have I spoken unto you in p': 3942
25 shall no more speak unto you in p',‡"

proveth See also APPROVETH; REPROVETH.
De 13: 3 for the Lord your God p' you, to 5254

provide See also PROVIDED; PROVIDETH; PROVIDING.
Ge 22: 8 God will p' himself a lamb for a 7200
30:30 shall I p' for mine own house also?6213
Ex 18:21 p' out of all the people able men, 2372
1Sa 16:17 P' me now a man that can play 7200
2Ch 2: 7 whom David my father did p'. 3559
Ps 78:20 can he p' flesh for his people? "
M't 10: 9 P' neither gold, nor silver, nor *2932
Lu 12:33 p' yourselves bags which wax not*4160
Ac 23:24 And p' them beasts, that they may 3936
Ro 12:17 P' things honest in the sight of *4306
1Ti 5: 8 But if any p' not for his own, and * "

provided
De 33:21 And he p' the first part for himself,7200
1Sa 16: 1 I have p' me a king among his sons. "
2Sa 19:32 he had p' the king of sustenance
1Ki 4: 7 which p' victuals for the king and his
27 p' victual for king Solomon, and
2Ch 32:29 he p' him cities, and possessions 6213
Ps 65: 9 corn, when thou hast so p' for it. *3559
Lu 12:20 things be, which thou hast p'? *2090
Heb 11:40 God having p' some better thing 4265

providence
Ac 24: 2 done unto this nation by thy p', 4307

provideth
Job 38:41 Who p' for the raven his food? 3559
Pr 6: 8 P' her meat in the summer, and "

providing
2Co 8:21 P' for honest things, not only in *4306

province See also PROVINCES.
Ezr 2: 1 the children of the p' that went up4082
5: 8 that we went into the p' of Judea, 4083
6: 2 that is in the p' of the Medes, 4082
7:16 canst find in all the p' of Babylon, "
Ne 1: 3 The remnant that are left...in the p'"
7: 6 These are the children of the p', "
11: 3 are the chief of the p' that dwelt in "
Es 1:22 into every p' according to the "
3:12 governors that were over every p', "
12 rulers of every people of every p' "
14 commandment...given in every p' "
4: 3 And in every p', whithersoever the "
8: 9 unto every p' according to the "
11 the power of the people and p' that "
13 commandment...given in every p' "
17 And in every p', and in every city, "
9:28 family, every p', and every city; "
Ec 5: 8 of judgment and justice in a p', "
Da 2:48 ruler over the whole p' of Babylon,4083
49 over the affairs of the p' of Babylon:"

Da 3: 1 plain of Dura, in the p' of Babylon. 4083
12 over the affairs of the p' of Babylon, "
30 Abed-nego, in the p' of Babylon. 4082
8: 2 the palace, which is the p' of Elam; "
11: 24 upon the fattest places of the p'; "
Ac 23: 34 letter, he asked of what p' he was. *1885*
25: 1 when Festus was come into the p', "

provinces
1Ki 20: 14 young men of the princes of the p'. 4082
15 young men of the princes of the p', "
17 princes of the p' went out first; "
19 of the princes of the p' came out "
Ezr 4: 15 and hurtful unto kings and p', 4083
Es 1: 1 hundred and seven and twenty p':) 4082
3 the nobles and princes of the p', "
16 in all the p' of the king Ahasuerus. "
22 he sent letters into all the king's p', "
2: 3 in all the p' of his kingdom, that "
18 and he made a release to the p', and "
3: 8 people in all the p' of thy kingdom; "
13 sent by posts into all the king's p', "
4: 11 the people of the king's p', do know, "
8: 5 Jews which are in all the king's p': "
9 and rulers of the p' which are from "
9 hundred twenty and seven p', unto "
12 day in all the p' of king Ahasuerus, "
9: 2 all the p' of the king Ahasuerus, "
3 And all the rulers of the p', and the "
4 went out throughout all the p': "
12 done in the rest of the king's p'? "
16 Jews that were in the king's p' "
20 in all the p' of the king Ahasuerus, "
30 and seven p' of the kingdom of "
Ec 2: 8 treasure of kings and of the p': "
La 1: 1 nations, and princess among the p', "
Eze 19: 8 him on every side from the p', "
Da 3: 2 the rulers of the p', to come to the "
3 and all the rulers of the p', were "

proving See also APPROVING.
Ac 9: 22 p' that this is very Christ. *4822*
Eph 5: 10 P' what is acceptable unto...Lord. *1381*

provision
Ge 42: 25 and to give them p' for the way: 6720
45: 21 and gave them p' for the way. "
Jos 9: 5 of their p' was dry and mouldy. 6718
12 our bread we took hot for our p' 6679
1Ki 4: 7 man his month in a year made p'. 3557
22 Solomon's p' for one day was 3899
2Ki 6: 23 he prepared great p' for them: 3740
1Ch 29: 19 for the which I have made p'. 3559
Ps 132: 15 I will abundantly bless her p': 6718
Da 1: 5 them a daily p' of the king's meat,*1697
Ro 13: 14 and make not p' for the flesh, to *4307*

provocation See also PROVOCATIONS.
1Ki 15: 30 Israel sin, by his p' wherewith he 3708
21: 22 for the p' wherewith thou hast "
Job 17: 2 not mine eye continue in their p'? 4784
Ps 95: 8 not your heart, as in the p', and *4808
Eze 20: 28 presented the p' of their offering: 3708
Heb 3: 8 not your hearts, as in the p', in *3894*
15 harden not your hearts, as in the p'. "

provocations
2Ki 23: 26 of all the p' that Manasseh had 3708
Ne 9: 18 Egypt, and had wrought great p'; 5007
26 to thee, and they wrought great p'. "

provoke See also PROVOKED; PROVOKETH; PROVOKING.
Ex 23: 21 and obey his voice, p' him not; 4843
Nu 14: 11 How long will this people p' me? *5006
De 4: 25 Lord thy God, to p' him to anger: "
9: 18 of the Lord, to p' him to anger. "
31: 20 gods, and serve them, and p' me, *5006
29 to p' him to anger through the "
32: 21 I will p' them to anger with a "
1Ki 14: 9 molten images, to p' me to anger, "
16: 2 to p' me to anger with their sins; "
26 sin, to p' the Lord God of Israel to anger "
33 to p' the Lord God of Israel to anger "
2Ki 17: 11 things to p' the Lord to anger: "
17 of the Lord, to p' him to anger. "
21: 6 of the Lord, to p' him to anger. "
22: 17 they might p' me to anger with all "
23: 19 had made to p' the Lord to anger, "
2Ch 33: 6 of the Lord, to p' him to anger. "
34: 25 that they might p' me to anger "
Job 12: 6 and they that p' God are secure; 7264
Ps 78: 40 did they p' him in the wilderness,*4784
Isa 3: 8 Lord, to p' the eyes of his glory. "
Jer 7: 18 that they may p' me to anger. "
19 Do they p' me to anger? saith the "
19 not p' themselves to the confusion of "
11: 17 p' me to anger in offering incense* "
25: 6 p' me not to anger with the works "
7 ye might p' me to anger with the "
32: 29 unto other gods, to p' me to anger. "
32 they have done to p' me to anger. "
44: 3 have committed to p' me to anger, "
8 p' me unto wrath with the works "
Eze 8: 17 have returned to p' me to anger: "
16: 26 thy whoredoms, to p' me to anger. "
Lu 11: 53 to p' him to speak of many things: *653*
Ro 10: 19 saith, I will p' you to jealousy by *3863*
11: 11 Gentiles, for to p' them to jealousy. "
14 any means I may p' to emulation "
1Co 10: 22 Do we p' the Lord to jealousy? are "
Eph 6: 4 p' not your children to wrath: *3949*
Col 3: 21 p' not your children to anger, *2042*
Heb 3: 16 when they had heard, did p': *3893*
10: 24 to p' unto love and to good works: *3948*

provoked See also PROVOKEDST.
Nu 14: 23 any of them that p' me see it: *5006
16: 30 that these men have p' the Lord. * "

De 9: 8 in Horeb ye p' the Lord to wrath,
22 ye p' the Lord to wrath.
32: 16 p' him to jealousy with strange *3707
16 abominations p' they him to anger.
21 p' me to anger with their vanities:
J'g 2: 12 them, and p' the Lord to anger.
1Sa 1: 6 And her adversary also p' her sore, 3707
7 so she p' her; therefore she wept; "
1Ki 14: 22 they p' him to jealousy with their sins
15: 30 p' the Lord God of Israel to anger.
21: 22 thou hast p' me to anger,
22: 53 p' to anger the Lord God of Israel,
2Ki 21: 15 have p' me to anger, since the day
23: 26 that Manasseh had p' him withal. 3707
1Ch 21: 1 and p' David to number Israel. *5496
2Ch 28: 25 and p' to anger the Lord God of his
Ezr 5: 12 p' the God of heaven unto wrath, 7265
Ne 4: 5 have p' thee to anger before the
Ps 78: 56 tempted and p' the most high *4784
58 p' him to anger with their high
106: 7 but p' him at the sea, even at the *4784
29 they p' him to anger with their
33 Because they p' his spirit, so that *4784
43 but they p' him with their counsel.*"
Isa 1: 4 have p' the Holy One of Israel *5006
Jer 8: 19 p' me to anger with their graven
32: 30 Israel have only p' me to anger
Ho 12: 14 Ephraim p' him to anger most
Zec 8: 14 when your fathers p' me to wrath,
1Co 13: 5 is not easily p', thinketh no evil; *3947*
2Co 9: 2 and your zeal hath p' very many. **2042*

provokedst
De 9: 7 thou p' the Lord thy God to wrath

provoketh
Pr 20: 2 whoso p' him to anger sinneth 5674
Isa 65: 3 A people that p' me to anger
Eze 8: 3 of jealousy, which p' to jealousy.

provoking
De 32: 19 because of the p' of his sons, and *3707
1Ki 14: 15 their groves, p' the Lord to anger.
16: 7 in p' him to anger with the work of*
13 p' the Lord God of Israel to anger*
Ps 78: 17 by p' the most High in the *4784
Ga 5: 26 p' one another, envying one *4292*

prudence
2Ch 2: 12 a wise son, endued with p' and *7922
Pr 8: 12 I wisdom dwell with p', and find *6195
Eph 1: 8 toward us in all wisdom and p'; *5428*

prudent
1Sa 16: 18 a man of war, and p' in matters, 995
Pr 12: 16 but a p' man covereth shame. 6175
23 A p' man concealeth knowledge: "
13: 16 p' man dealeth with knowledge: "
14: 8 wisdom of the p' is to understand "
15 but the p' man looketh well to his "
18 the p' are crowned with knowledge. "
15: 5 he that regardeth reproof is p'. *6191
16: 21 wise in heart shall be called p': 995
18: 15 heart of the p' getteth knowledge; "
19: 14 and a p' wife is from the Lord. 7919
22: 3 A p' man foreseeth the evil, and 6175
27: 12 A p' man foreseeth the evil, and * "
Isa 3: 2 and the p', and the ancient, *7080
5: 21 eyes, and p' in their own sight! 995
10: 13 for I am p': and I have removed ‡ "
29: 14 the understanding of their p' men "
Jer 49: 7 is counsel perished from the p'? is "
Ho 14: 9 p', and he shall know them? for the "
Am 5: 13 p' shall keep silence in that time; 7919
M't 11: 25 these things from the wise and p',*4908
Lu 10: 21 these things from the wise and p',* "
Ac 13: 7 country, Sergius Paulus, a p' man;*"
1Co 1: 19 the understanding of the p'. ‡ "

prudently
Isa 52: 13 my servant shall deal p', he shall *7919

prune See also PRUNED; PRUNING.
Le 25: 3 years thou shalt p' thy vineyard, 2168
4 sow thy field, nor p' thy vineyard. "

pruned
Isa 5: 6 it shall not be p', nor digged; 2167

pruning See also PRUNINGHOOKS.
Isa 18: 5 cut off the sprigs with p' hooks, 4211

pruninghooks See also PRUNING and HOOKS.
Isa 2: 4 and their spears into p': 4211
Joe 3: 10 swords, and your p' into spears: "
Mic 4: 3 and their spears into p': "

psalm See also PSALMS.
1Ch 16: 7 David delivered first this p' to thank*
Ps 3: *title* A P' of David, when he fled from 4210
4: *title* on Neginoth, A P' of David. "
5: *title* upon Nehiloth, A P' of David. "
6: *title* upon Sheminith, A P' of David. "
8: *title* upon Gittith, A P' of David. "
9: *title* upon Muth-labben, A P' of David. "
11: *title* chief Musician, A P' of David. "
12: *title* upon Sheminith, A P' of David. 4210
13: *title* chief Musician, A P' of David. "
14: *title* chief Musician, A P' of David. "
15: *title* A P' of David. 4210
18: *title* A P' of David, the servant of the "
19: *title* chief Musician, A P' of David. "
20: *title* chief Musician, A P' of David. "
21: *title* chief Musician, A P' of David. "
22: *title* Aijeleth Shahar, A P' of David. "
23: *title* A P' of David. "
24: *title* A P' of David. "
25: *title* A P' of David. "
26: *title* A P' of David. "
27: *title* A P' of David. "
28: *title* A P' of David. "

Ps 29: *title* A P' of David. 4210
30: *title* A P' and Song at the dedication "
31: *title* the chief Musician, A P' of David. "
32: *title* A P' of David, Maschil. "
34: *title* A P' of David, when he changed "
35: *title* A P' of David. "
36: *title* A P' of David the servant of the "
37: *title* A P' of David. "
38: *title* A P' of David, to bring to 4210
39: *title* even to Jeduthun, A P' of David. "
40: *title* chief Musician, A P' of David. "
41: *title* chief Musician, A P' of David. "
47: *title* A P' for the sons of Korah. "
48: *title* and P' for the sons of Korah. "
49: *title* A P' for the sons of Korah. "
50: *title* A P' of Asaph. "
51: *title* A P' of David, when Nathan the "
52: *title* A P' of David, when Doeg the *
53: *title* Mahalath, Maschil, A P' of David.*
54: *title* A P' of David, when the Ziphims*
55: *title* Maschil, A P' of David. *
61: *title* upon Neginah, A P' of David.
62: *title* to Jeduthun, A P' of David. 4210
63: *title* A P' of David, when he was in "
64: *title* chief Musician, A P' of David. "
65: *title* A P' and Song of David. "
66: *title* the chief Musician, A Song or P'. "
67: *title* on Neginoth, A P' or Song. "
68: *title* Musician, A P' or Song of David. "
69: *title* Shoshannim, A P' of David. "
70: *title* A P' of David, to bring to "
72: *title* A P' for Solomon. 4210
73: *title* A P' of Asaph. "
75: *title* A P' or Song of Asaph. "
76: *title* Neginoth, A P' or Song of Asaph. "
77: *title* to Jeduthun, A P' of Asaph. "
79: *title* A P' of Asaph. "
80: *title* A P' of Asaph. "
81: *title* upon Gittith, A P' of Asaph. "
2 Take a P', and bring hither the 2172
82: *title* A P' of Asaph. 4210
83: *title* A Song or P' of Asaph. "
84: *title* A P' for the sons of Korah. "
85: *title* A P' for the sons of Korah. "
87: *title* A P' or Song for the sons of "
88: *title* A Song or P' for the sons of "
92: *title* A P' or Song for the sabbath day. "
98: *title* A P'. "
5 the harp, and the voice of a p'. *2172
100: *title* A P' of praise. 4210
101: *title* A P' of David. "
103: *title* A P' of David. "
108: *title* A Song or P' of David. 4210
109: *title* chief Musician, A P' of David. "
110: *title* A P' of David. "
138: *title* A P' of David. "
139: *title* chief Musician, A P' of David. 4210
140: *title* chief Musician, A P' of David. "
141: *title* A P' of David. "
143: *title* A P' of David. "
144: *title* A P' of David. "
145: *title* David's P' of praise. "
Ac 13: 33 it is also written in the second p', *5568*
35 Wherefore he saith also in another p', "
1Co 14: 26 every one of you hath a p', hath a *5568*

psalmist
2Sa 23: 1 Jacob, and the sweet p' of Israel, 2158

psalms
1Ch 16: 9 Sing unto him, sing p' unto him, *2167
Ps 95: 2 a joyful noise unto him with p'. 2158
105: 2 Sing unto him, sing p' unto him: *2167
Lu 20: 42 himself saith in the book of P', *5568*
24: 44 and in the p', concerning me. "
Ac 1: 20 it is written in the book of P', Let "
Eph 5: 19 Speaking to yourselves in p' and "
Col 3: 16 admonishing one another in p' and "
Jas 5: 13 Is any merry? let him sing p'. *5567*

psalteries
2Sa 6: 5 even on harps, and on p', and on 5035
1Ki 10: 12 harps also and p' for singers: there "
1Ch 13: 8 and with harps, and with p', and "
15: 16 musick, p' and harp and cymbals, "
20 and Benaiah, with p' on Alamoth; "
28 making a noise with p' and harps. "
16: 5 and Jeiel with p' and with harps; 3627
25: 1 prophesy with harps, with p', 5035
6 with cymbals, p', and harps, for "
2Ch 5: 12 having cymbals and p' and harps, "
9: 11 and harps and p' for singers: and "
20: 28 they came to Jerusalem with p' and "
29: 25 with p', and with harps, according "
Ne 12: 27 with cymbals, p', and with harps. "

psaltery See also PSALTERIES.
1Sa 10: 5 from the high place with a p', 5035
Ps 33: 2 sing unto him with the p' and an "
57: 8 awake, p' and harp: I myself will "
71: 22 also praise thee with the p', even 3627
81: 2 the pleasant harp with the p'. 5035
92: 3 of ten strings, and upon the p'; "
108: 2 Awake, p' and harp: I myself will "
144: 9 upon a p' and an instrument of ten "
150: 3 praise him with the p' and harp. "
Da 3: 5 p', dulcimer, and all kinds of 6460
7 p', and all kinds of musick, "
10, 15 p', and dulcimer, and all kinds "

Ptolemais (*tol-e-ma'-is*) See also ACCHO.
Ac 21: 7 from Tyre, we came to P', and *4424*

Pua (*pu'-ah*) See also PUAH.
Nu 26: 23 of P', the family of the Punites: *6312

Puah (*pu'-ah*) See also PHUVAH; PUA; PUNITES.
Ex 1: 15 and the name of the other P': 6326
J'g 10: 1 Tola the son of P', the son of 6312
1Ch 7: 1 sons of Issachar were, Tola, and P'. "

public See PUBLICK.
publican See also PUBLICANS.
M't 10: 3 Thomas, and Matthew the p'; 5057
18:17 thee as an heathen man and a p'. "
Lu 5:27 and saw a p', named Levi, sitting "
18:10 one a Pharisee, and the other a p'. "
11 adulterers, or even as this p'. "
13 And the p', standing afar off, would "
publicans
M't 5:46 ye? do not even the p' the same? 5057
47 others? do not even the p' so? * "
9:10 many p' and sinners came and sat "
11 Why eateth your Master with p' and "
11:19 a friend of p' and sinners. "
21:31 That the p' and the harlots go into "
32 the p' and the harlots believed him: "
M'r 2:15 house, many p' and sinners sat also "
16 saw him eat with p' and sinners, "
16 and drinketh with p' and sinners? "
Lu 3:12 Then came also p' to be baptized, "
5:29 there was a great company of p' "
30 eat and drink with p' and sinners? "
7:29 the p', justified God, being baptized "
34 a friend of p' and sinners! "
15: 1 Then drew near unto him all the p' "
19: 2 which was the chief among the p'.* 754
publick
M't 1:19 willing to make her a p' example. *3856
publickly
Ac 18:28 convinced the Jews, and that p', *1219
20:20 shewed you, and have taught you p',* "
publish See also PUBLISHED; PUBLISHETH.
De 32: 3 I will p' the name of the Lord: *7121
1Sa 31: 9 to p' it in the house of their idols,*1319
2Sa 1:20 p' it not in the streets of Askelon; "
Ne 8:15 p' and proclaim in all their cities, 8085
Ps 26: 7 That I may p' with the voice of * "
Jer 4: 5 and p' in Jerusalem; and say, Blow "
16 behold, p' against Jerusalem, that "
5:20 house of Jacob, and p' it in Judah, "
31: 7 p' ye, praise ye, and say, O Lord, "
46:14 Declare ye in Egypt,...p' in Migdol, "
14 and p' in Noph and in Tahpanhes: "
50: 2 ye among the nations, and p', "
2 up a standard; p', and conceal not: "
Am 3: 9 P' in the palaces at Ashdod, and in "
4: 5 proclaim and p' the free offerings: "
M'r 1:45 went out, and began to p' it much, 2784
5:20 began to p' in Decapolis how great "
published
Es 1:20 be p' throughout all his empire, 8085
22 that it should be p' according to *1696
3:14 province was p' unto all people, 1540
8:13 province was p' unto all people, "
Ps 68:11 the company of those that p' it. *1319
Jon 3: 7 p' through Nineveh by the decree 559
M'r 7:36 the more a great deal they p' it; 2784
13:10 must first be p' among all nations.* "
Lu 8:39 and p' throughout the whole city "
Ac 10:37 which was p' throughout all Judæa, 1096
13:49 And the word of the Lord was p' *1308
publisheth
Isa 52: 7 good tidings, that p' peace; 8085
7 tidings of good, that p' salvation; "
Jer 4:15 p' affliction from mount Ephraim. "
Na 1:15 good tidings, that p' peace! "
Publius (*pub'-le-us*)
Ac 28: 7 of the island, whose name was P'; 4196
8 the father of P' lay sick of a fever "
Pudens (*pu'-denz*)
2Ti 4:21 Eubulus greeteth thee, and P'. 4227
puffed
1Co 4: 6 that no one of you be p' up for one 5448
18 Now some are p' up, as though I "
19 the speech of them which are p' up, "
5: 2 ye are p' up, and have not rather "
13: 4 vaunteth not itself, is not p' up, "
Col 2:18 vainly p' up by his fleshly mind, "
puffeth
Ps 10: 5 for all his enemies, he p' at them. 6315
12: 5 in safety from him that p' at him.* "
1Co 8: 1 Knowledge p' up, but charity 5448
Puhites (*pu'-hites*)
1Ch 2:53 the Ithrites, and the P', and the *6336
Pul (*pul*)
2Ki 15:19 And P' the king of Assyria came 6322
19 gave P' a thousand talents of "
1Ch 5:26 stirred up the spirit of P' king of "
Isa 66:19 nations, to Tarshish, P', and Lud, "
pull See also PULLED; PULLING.
1Ki 13: 4 he could not p' it in again to him.*7725
Ps 31: 4 P' me out of the net that they *3318
Isa 22:19 thy state shall he p' thee down. 2040
Jer 1:10 to root out, and to p' down, and to*5422
12: 3 p' them out like sheep for the 5423
18: 7 and to p' down, and to destroy it;*5422
24: 6 them, and not p' them down; 2040
42:10 build you, and not p' you down, "
Eze 17: 9 shall he not p' up the roots 5423
Mic 2: 8 p' off the robe with the garment *6584
M't 7: 4 p' out the mote out of thine eye; *1544
Lu 6:42 p' out the mote that is in thine eye,* "
42 to p' out the mote that is in thy "
12:18 I will p' down my barns, and build 2507
14: 5 p' him out on the sabbath day? * 385
pulled
Ge 8: 9 p' her in unto him into the ark. *4026
19:10 and p' Lot into the house to them,* 935
Ezr 6:11 timber be p' down from his house, 5256
La 3:11 my ways, and p' me in pieces: 6582
Am 9:15 no more be p' up out of their land*5428
Zec 7:11 and p' away the shoulder, and 5414
Ac 23:10 Paul should have been p' in pieces*1288
pulling
2Co 10: 4 to the p' down of strong holds;) *2506
Jude 23 with fear, p' them out of the fire; * 726
pulpit
Ne 8: 4 the scribe stood upon a p' of wood, 4026
pulse
2Sa 17:28 beans, and lentiles, and parched p',
Da 1:12 and let them give us p' to eat, and 2235
16 should drink; and gave them p'. "
punish See also PUNISHED.
Le 26:18 I will p' you seven times more for*3256
24 p' you yet seven times for your *5221
Pr 17:26 Also to p' the just is not good, nor 6064
Isa 10:12 will p' the fruit of the stout heart 6485
13:11 I will p' the world for their evil, and "
24:21 shall p' the host of the high ones "
26:21 to p' the inhabitants of the earth "
27: 1 p' leviathan the piercing serpent, "
Jer 9:25 that I will p' all them which are "
11:22 of hosts, Behold, I will p' them: "
13:21 thou say when he shall p' thee? * "
21:14 I will p' you according to the fruit "
23:34 I will even p' that man and his "
25:12 that I will p' the king of Babylon, "
27: 8 that nation will I p', saith the Lord, "
29:32 I will p' Shemaiah the Nehelamite, "
30:20 and I will p' all that oppress them. "
36:31 I will p' him and his seed and his "
44:13 I will p' them that dwell in the land "
29 I will p' you in this place, that ye "
46:25 I will p' the multitude of No, and "
50:18 I will p' the king of Babylon and "
51:44 And I will p' Bel in Babylon, and * "
Ho 4: 9 I will p' them for their ways, and "
14 I will not p' your daughters when "
12: 2 will p' Jacob according to his ways; "
Am 3: 2 I will p' you for all your iniquities.* "
Zep 1: 8 I will p' the princes, and the king's "
9 day also will I p' all those that leap "
12 p' the men that are settled on their "
Zec 8:14 As I thought to p' you, when your*7489
Ac 4:21 how they might p' them, because 2849
punished See also UNPUNISHED.
Ex 21:20 his hand; he shall be surely p'. 5358
21 a day or two, he shall not be p': "
22 he shall be surely p', according as*6064
Ezr 9:13 hast p' us less than our iniquities 2820
Job 31:11 it is an iniquity to be p' by the judges.
28 were an iniquity to be p' by the judge:
Pr 21:11 When the scorner is p', the simple 6064
22: 3 but the simple pass on, and are p'.* "
27:12 but the simple pass on, and are p'.* "
Jer 44:13 as I have p' Jerusalem, by the 6485
50:18 as I have p' the king of Assyria. "
Zep 3: 7 not be cut off, howsoever I p' them:* "
Zec 10: 3 the shepherds, and I p' the goats:* "
Ac 22: 5 unto Jerusalem, for to be p'. 5097
26:11 I p' them oft in every synagogue, * "
2Th 1: 9 p'...everlasting destruction *1349,5099
2Pe 2: 9 unto the day of judgment to be p':*2849
punishment See also PUNISHMENTS.
Ge 4:13 My p' is greater than I can bear. 5771
Le 26:41, 43 accept of the p' of their iniquity: "
1Sa 28:10 there shall no p' happen to thee for "
Job 31: 3 strange p' to the workers of iniquity?*
Pr 19:19 man of great wrath shall suffer p':*6066
La 3:39 a man for the p' of his sins? 2399
4: 6 p' of the iniquity of the daughter *5771
6 than the p' of the sin of Sodom, *2403
22 p' of thine iniquity...accomplished, 5771
Eze 14:10 shall bear the p' of their iniquity:* "
10 the p' of the prophet shall be even* "
10 as the p' of him that seeketh unto* "
Am 1: 3, 6, 9, 11, 13 I will not turn away the p'
2: 1, 4, 6 will not turn away the p' thereof;
Zec 14:19 This shall be the p' of Egypt, and 2403
19 the p' of all nations that come not "
M't 25:46 shall go away into everlasting p': 2851
2Co 2: 6 Sufficient to such a man is this p', 2009
Heb 10:29 Of how much sorer p', suppose ye, 5098
1Pe 2:14 sent by him for the p' of evildoers,*1557
punishments
Job 19:29 bringeth the p' of the sword, 5771
Ps 149: 7 upon the heathen, and p' upon the "
Punites (*pu'-nites*)
Nu 26:23 of Pua, the family of the P': 6324
Punon (*pu'-non*)
Nu 33:42 Zalmonah, and pitched in P'. 6325
43 they departed from P', and pitched "
Pur (*pur*) See also PURIM.
Es 3: 7 they cast P', that is, the lot, 6332
9:24 and had cast P', that is, the lot, to "
26 days Purim after the name of P'. "
purchase See also PURCHASED.
Ge 49:32 The p' of the field and of the cave*4735
Le 25:33 if a man p' of the Levites, then the*1350
Jer 32:11 So I took the evidence of the p', 4736
12 I gave the evidence of the p' unto "
12 that subscribed the book of the p', "
14 evidences, this evidence of the p', "
16 the evidence of the p' unto Baruch "
1Ti 3:13 p' to themselves a good degree, *4046
purchased
Ge 25:10 Abraham p' of the sons of Heth: 7069
Ex 15:16 pass over, which thou hast p'. "
Ru 4:10 of Mahlon, have I p' to be my wife, "
Ps 74: 2 which thou hast p' of old; the rod of 7069
78:54 which his right hand had p'. "
Ac 1:18 man p' a field with the reward of *2932
8:20 gift of God may be p' with money.* "
20:28 he hath p' with his own blood. 4046
Eph 1:14 redemption of the p' possession. *4047
pure See also PURER.
Ex 25:11 thou shalt overlay it with p' gold, 2889
17 shalt make a mercy seat of p' gold: "
24 thou shalt overlay it with p' gold, "
29 of p' gold shalt thou make them. "
31 shalt make a candlestick of p' gold: "
36 shall be one beaten work of p' gold. "
38 thereof, shall be of p' gold. "
39 a talent of p' gold shall he make it, "
27:20 p' oil olive beaten for the light, 2134
28:14 two chains of p' gold at the ends; 2889
22 ends of wreathen work of p' gold. "
36 thou shalt make a plate of p' gold, "
30: 3 shalt overlay it with p' gold, the top "
23 of p' myrrh five hundred shekels, *1865
34 sweet spices with p' frankincense: 2134
35 tempered together, p' and holy: 2889
31: 8 and the p' candlestick with all his "
37: 2 he overlaid it with p' gold within "
6 he made the mercy seat of p' gold: "
11 And he overlaid it with p' gold, and "
16 covers to cover withal, of p' gold. "
17 made the candlestick of p' gold: of "
22 it was one beaten work of p' gold. "
23 and his snuffdishes, of p' gold. "
24 Of a talent of p' gold made he it, "
26 he overlaid it with p' gold, both the "
29 and the p' incense of sweet spices, "
39:15 ends, of wreathen work of p' gold. "
25 they made bells of p' gold, and put "
30 plate of the holy crown of p' gold, "
37 The p' candlestick, with the lamps "
Le 24: 2 bring unto thee p' oil olive beaten 2134
4 the lamps upon the p' candlestick 2889
6 upon the p' table before the Lord. "
7 p' frankincense upon each row, 2134
De 32:14 drink the p' blood of the grape. *2561
2Sa 22:27 the p' thou wilt shew thyself p'; 1305
1Ki 5:11 and twenty measures of p' oil: 3795
6:20 he overlaid it with p' gold; and so 5462
21 the house within with p' gold; "
7:49 candlesticks of p' gold, five on the "
50 spoons, and the censers of p' gold; "
10:21 forest of Lebanon were of p' gold; "
1Ch 28:17 Also p' gold for the fleshhooks, 2889
2Ch 3: 4 he overlaid it within with p' gold. "
4:20 before the oracle, of p' gold; 5462
22 spoons, and the censers, of p' gold: "
9:17 ivory, and overlaid it with p' gold. 2889
20 forest of Lebanon were of p' gold: 5462
13:11 they in order upon the p' table; 2889
Ezr 6:20 all of them were p', and killed the "
Job 4:17 a man be more p' than his Maker? 2891
8: 6 If thou wert p' and upright; surely 2134
11: 4 thou hast said, My doctrine is p', "
16:17 in mine hands: also my prayer is p'. "
25: 5 the stars are not p' in his sight. 2141
28:19 shall it be valued with p' gold. 2889
Ps 12: 6 words of the Lord are p' words: "
18:26 the p' thou wilt shew thyself p'; 1305
19: 8 commandment of the Lord is p', 1249
21: 3 settest a crown of p' gold on his *6337
24: 4 hath clean hands, and a p' heart; 1249
119:140 Thy word is very p': therefore 6884
Pr 15:26 the words of the p' are pleasant 2889
20: 9 heart clean, I am p' from my sin? 2891
11 whether his work be p', and 2134
21: 8 but as for the p', his work is right. "
30: 5 Every word of God is p': he is a *6884
12 a generation that are p' in their 2889
Da 7: 9 hair of his head like the p' wool: 5343
Mic 6:11 Shall I count them p' with the 2135
Zep 3: 9 turn to the people a p' language, 1305
Mal 1:11 unto my name, and a p' offering: 2889
M't 5: 8 Blessed are the p' in heart: for 2513
Ac 20:26 I am p' from the blood of all men. "
Ro 14:20 All things indeed are p'; but it is * "
Ph'p 4: 8 are just, whatsoever things are p', 53
1Ti 1: 5 is charity out of a p' heart, and of 2513
3: 9 of the faith in a p' conscience. "
5:22 of other men's sins: keep thyself p'. 53
2Ti 1: 3 my forefathers with p' conscience, 2513
2:22 call on the Lord out of a p' heart. "
Tit 1:15 Unto the p' all things are p': but "
15 and unbelieving is nothing p'; "
Heb 10:22 our bodies washed with p' water. "
Jas 1:27 P' religion and undefiled before "
3:17 wisdom that is from above is first p', 53
1Pe 1:22 love one another with a p' heart *2513
2Pe 3: 1 I stir up your p' minds by way *1506
1Jo 3: 3 purifieth himself, even as he is p'. 53
Re 15: 6 clothed in p' and white linen, and 2513
21:18 and the city was p' gold, like unto "
21 street of the city was p' gold, as it "
22: 1 he shewed me a p' river of water * "
purely
Isa 1:25 and p' purge away the dross, and*1252
pureness
Job 22:30 delivered by the p' of thine hands.*1252
Pr 22:11 He that loveth p' of heart, for the 2890
2Co 6: 6 By p', by knowledge, by 54
purer
La 4: 7 Her Nazarites were p' than snow, 2141
Hab 1:13 art of p' eyes than to behold evil, 2889
purge See also PURGED; PURGETH; PURGING; PURIFY.
2Ch 34: 3 year he began to p' Judah and 2891
Ps 51: 7 P' me with hyssop, and I shall be 2398

Ps 65: 3 thou shalt *p'* them away. ‡3722
79: 9 deliver us, and *p'* away our sins. ‡ "
Isa 1: 25 and purely *p'* away thy dross, and 6884
Eze 20: 38 *p'* out from among you the rebels, 1305
43: 20 thus shalt thou cleanse and *p'* it. *3722
26 Seven days shall they *p'* the altar* "
Da 11: 35 to *p'*, and to make them white, *1305
Mal 3: 3 and *p'* them as gold and silver, ‡2212
M't 3: 12 he will thoroughly *p'* his floor, *1245
Lu 3: 17 he will thoroughly *p'* his floor, * "
1Co 5: 7 *P'* out therefore the old leaven, 1571
2Ti 2: 21 If a man therefore *p'* himself from "
Heb 9: 14 *p'* your conscience from dead *2511

purged
1Sa 3: 14 shall not be *p'* with sacrifice nor 3722
2Ch 34: 8 when he had *p'* the land, and the 2891
Pr 16: 6 mercy and truth iniquity is *p'*: 3722
Isa 4: 4 have *p'* the blood of Jerusalem 1740
6: 7 is taken away, and thy sin *p'*. ‡3722
22: 14 iniquity shall not be *p'* from you ‡ "
27: 9 shall the iniquity of Jacob be *p'*; ‡ "
Eze 24: 13 lewdness: because I have *p'* thee, ‡2891
13 not *p'*, thou shalt not be *p'* from ‡ "
Heb 1: 3 had by himself *p'* our sins, *4160,2512
9: 22 are by the law *p'* with blood; *2511
10: 2 worshippers once *p'* should have *2508
2Pe 1: 9 that he was *p'* from his old sins. *2512

purgeth
Joh 15: 2 he *p'* it, that it may bring forth *2508

purging
M'r 7: 19 into the draught, *p'* all meats? *2511

purification See also PURIFICATIONS.
Nu 19: 9 of separation: it is a *p'* for sin. *2403
17 of the burnt heifer of *p'* for sin. * "
2Ch 30: 19 to the *p'* of the sanctuary. 2893
Ne 12: 45 their God, and the ward of the *p'*, "
Es 2: 3 their things for *p'* be given them: 8562
9 speedily gave her her things for *p'*, "
Lu 2: 22 And when the days of her *p'* 2512
Ac 21: 26 accomplishment of the days of *p'*, 49

purifications
Es 2: 12 days of their *p'* accomplished, 4795

purified
Le 8: 15 with his finger, and *p'* the altar, 2398
Nu 8: 21 And the Levites were *p'*, and they "
31: 23 nevertheless it shall be *p'* with the "
2Sa 11: 4 she was *p'* from her uncleanness: 6942
Ezr 6: 20 priests and the Levites were *p'* 2891
Ne 12: 30 and the Levites *p'* themselves, "
30 *p'* the people, and the gates, and "
Ps 12: 6 furnace of earth, *p'* seven times. 2212
Da 12: 10 Many shall be *p'*, and made *1305
Ac 24: 18 Asia found me *p'* in the temple, 48
Heb 9: 23 heavens should be *p'* with these; *2511
1Pe 1: 22 ye have *p'* your souls in obeying 48

purifier
Mal 3: 3 sit as a refiner and *p'* of silver: 2891

purifieth
Nu 19: 13 and *p'* not himself, defileth the 2398
1Jo 3: 3 hath this hope in him *p'* himself, 48

purify See also PURGE; PURIFIED; PURIFIETH; PURIFYING.
Nu 19: 12 *p'* himself with it on the third day, 2398
12 if he *p'* not himself the third day, "
19 the seventh day he shall *p'* himself, "
20 unclean, and shall not *p'* himself, "
31: 19 *p'* both yourselves and your "
20 *p'* all your raiment, and all that is "
Job 41: 25 of breakings they *p'* themselves. * "
Isa 66: 17 and *p'* themselves in the gardens 2891
Eze 43: 26 shall they purge the altar and *p'* it; "
Mal 3: 3 and he shall *p'* the sons of Levi, "
Joh 11: 55 the passover, to *p'* themselves. 48
Ac 21: 24 take, and *p'* thyself with them, "
Tit 2: 14 *p'* unto himself a peculiar people, 2511
Jas 4: 8 *p'* your hearts, ye double minded. 48

purifying
Le 12: 4 blood of her *p'* three and thirty 2893
4 the days of her *p'* be fulfilled. 2892
5 blood of her *p'* three score and 2893
6 the days of her *p'* are fulfilled, 2892
Nu 8: 7 Sprinkle water of *p'* upon them, *2403
1Ch 23: 28 and in the *p'* of all holy things, 2893
Es 2: 12 things for the *p'* of the women;) 8562
Joh 2: 6 manner of the *p'* of the Jews, 2512
3: 25 disciples and the Jews about *p'*. "
Ac 15: 9 them, *p'* their hearts by faith. *2511
21: 26 the next day *p'* himself with them 48
Heb 9: 13 sanctifieth to the *p'* of the flesh: *2514

Purim (*pu'-rim*) See also PUR.
Es 9: 26 called these days *P'* after the 6332
28 these days of *P'* should not fail "
29 confirm this second letter of *P'*. "
31 To confirm these days of *P'* in "
32 confirmed these matters of *P'*; "

purity
1Ti 4: 12 charity, in spirit, in faith, in *p'*. 47
5: 2 the younger as sisters, with all *p'*. "

purloining
Tit 2: 10 Not *p'*, but shewing all good 3557

purple
Ex 25: 4 And blue, and *p'*, and scarlet, and 713
26: 1 and blue, and *p'*, and scarlet: "
31 shalt make a vail of blue, and *p'*, "
36 door of the tent, of blue, and *p'*, "
27: 16 of twenty cubits, of blue, and *p'*, "
28: 5 gold, and blue, and *p'*, and scarlet, "
6 ephod of gold, of blue, and of *p'*, "
Ex 28: 8 even of gold, of blue, and *p'*, and 713
15 make it; of gold, of blue, and of *p'*, "
33 pomegranates of blue, and of *p'*, "
35: 6 And blue, and *p'*, and scarlet, and "
23 with whom was found blue, and *p'*, "
25 had spun, both of blue, and of *p'*, "
35 in blue, and in *p'*, in scarlet, and "
36: 8 twined linen, and blue, and *p'*, and "
35 he made a vail of blue, and *p'*, and "
37 tabernacle door of blue, and *p'*, and "
38: 18 was needlework, of blue, and *p'*, "
23 an embroiderer in blue, and in *p'*, "
39: 1 of the blue, and *p'*, and scarlet, and "
2 and *p'*, and scarlet, and fine twined "
3 work it in the blue, and in the *p'*, "
5 of gold, blue, and *p'*, and scarlet, "
8 and *p'*, and scarlet, and fine twined "
24 robe pomegranates of blue, and *p'*, "
29 fine twined linen, and blue, and *p'*, "
Nu 4: 13 and spread a *p'* cloth thereon: "
J'g 8: 26 *p'* raiment that was on the kings of "
2Ch 2: 7 and in iron, and in *p'*, and crimson, 710
14 in *p'*, in blue, and in fine linen, 713
3: 14 vail of blue, and *p'*, and crimson, "
Es 1: 6 with cords of fine linen and *p'* to "
8: 15 a garment of fine linen and *p'*: "
Pr 31: 22 tapestry; her clothing is silk and *p'*. "
Ca 3: 10 the covering of it of *p'*, the midst "
7: 5 and the hair of thine head like *p'*; "
Jer 10: 9 blue and *p'* is their clothing: they "
Eze 27: 7 blue and *p'* from the isles of Elishah "
16 emeralds, *p'*, and broidered work, "
M'r 15: 17 they clothed him with *p'*, and 4209
20 they took off the *p'* from him, and "
Lu 16: 19 was clothed in *p'* and fine linen, "
Joh 19: 2 and they put on him a *p'* robe, 4210
5 crown of thorns, and the *p'* robe. "
Ac 16: 14 Lydia, a seller of *p'*, of the city of 4211
Re 17: 4 arrayed in *p'* and scarlet colour, 4209
18: 12 and fine linen, and *p'*, and silk, "
16 was clothed in fine linen, and *p'*, 4210

purpose See also PURPOSED; PURPOSES; PURPOSETH; PURPOSING.
Ru 2: 16 of the handfuls of *p'* for her, and *7997
1Ki 5: 5 I *p'* to build an house unto the 559
2Ch 28: 10 ye *p'* to keep under the children "
Ezr 4: 5 against them, to frustrate their *p'*, 6098
Ne 8: 4 which they had made for the *p'*; 1697
Job 33: 17 may withdraw man from his *p'*, 4639
Pr 20: 18 *p'* is established by counsel: and 4284
Ec 3: 1 to every *p'* under the heaven: 2656
17 a time there for every *p'* and for "
8: 6 Because to every *p'* there is time "
Isa 1: 11 To what *p'* is the multitude of your
14: 26 is the *p'* that is purposed upon 6098
30: 7 shall help in vain, and to no *p'*: 7385
Jer 6: 20 To what *p'* cometh there to me incense
26: 3 which I *p'* to do unto them because 2803
36: 3 evil which I *p'* to do unto them; "
49: 30 hath conceived a *p'* against you. 4284
51: 29 *p'* of the Lord shall be performed * "
Da 6: 17 that the *p'* might not be changed *6640
M't 26: 8 saying, To what *p'* is this waste?
Ac 11: 23 with *p'* of heart they would cleave 4286
26: 16 I have appeared unto thee for this *p'*,*
27: 13 that they had obtained their *p'*, 4286
43 Paul, kept them from their *p'*; 1013
Ro 8: 28 are the called according to his *p'*. 4286
9: 11 the *p'* of God according to election "
17 Even for this same *p'* have I raised
2Co 1: 17 lightness? or the things that I *p'*, 1011
17 do I *p'* according to the flesh, that "
Eph 1: 11 *p'* of him who worketh all things 4286
3: 11 the eternal *p'* which he purposed "
6: 22 I have sent unto you for the same *p'*,
Col 4: 8 I have sent unto you for the same *p'*,
2Ti 1: 9 but according to his own *p'* and 4286
3: 10 doctrine, manner of life, *p'*, faith, "
1Jo 3: 8 For this *p'* the Son...was manifested,*

purposed
2Ch 32: 2 that he was *p'* to fight against 6440
Ps 17: 3 I am *p'* that my mouth shall not 2161
140: 4 have *p'* to overthrow my goings. 2803
Isa 14: 24 as I have *p'*, so shall it stand: 3289
26 that is *p'* upon the whole earth: "
27 For the Lord of hosts hath *p'*, and "
19: 12 Lord of hosts hath *p'* upon Egypt. "
23: 9 The Lord of hosts hath *p'* it, to "
46: 11 pass; I have *p'* it, I will also do it. 3335
Jer 4: 28 I have *p'* it, and will not repent, 2161
49: 20 hath *p'* against the inhabitants 2803
50: 45 that he hath *p'* against the land of "
La 2: 8 The Lord hath *p'* to destroy the "
Da 1: 8 Daniel *p'* in his heart that he 7760
Ac 19: 21 Paul *p'* in the spirit, when he had 5087
20: 3 he *p'* to return through *1096,1106
Ro 1: 13 oftentimes I *p'* to come unto you, 4388
Eph 1: 9 which he hath *p'* in himself:
3: 11 which he *p'* in Christ Jesus our 4160

purposes
Job 17: 11 my *p'* are broken off, even the 2154
Pr 15: 22 Without counsel *p'* are 4284
Isa 19: 10 shall be broken in the *p'* thereof, *8356
Jer 49: 20 and his *p'*, that he hath purposed 4284
50: 45 and his *p'*, that he hath purposed "

purposeth
2Co 9: 7 according as he *p'* in his heart, *4255

purposing
Ge 27: 42 doth comfort himself, *p'* to kill thee.

purse See also PURSES.
Pr 1: 14 among us; let us all have one *p'*: 3599
M'r 6: 8 no bread, no money in their *p'*: 2223
Lu 10: 4 Carry neither *p'*, nor scrip, nor 905
Lu 22: 35 I sent you without *p'*, and scrip, 905
36 he that hath a *p'*, let him take it, "

purses
M't 10: 9 nor silver, nor brass in your *p'*. 2223

pursue See also ENSUE; PURSUED; PURSUETH; PURSUING.
Ge 35: 5 did not *p'* after the sons of Jacob. 7291
Ex 15: 9 The enemy said, I will *p'*, I will "
De 19: 6 avenger of the blood *p'* the slayer, "
28: 22 they shall *p'* thee until thou perish. "
45 shall *p'* thee, and overtake thee, "
Jos 2: 5 *p'* after them quickly; for ye shall "
8: 16 called together to *p'* after them: "
10: 19 *p'* after your enemies, and smite "
20: 5 the avenger of blood *p'* after him, "
1Sa 24: 14 after whom dost thou *p'*? after a "
25: 29 Yet a man is risen to *p'* thee, and "
26: 18 my lord thus *p'* after his servant? "
30: 8 Shall I *p'* after this troop? shall I "
8 *P'*: for thou shalt surely overtake "
2Sa 17: 1 I will arise and *p'* after David this "
20: 6 lord's servants, and *p'* after him, "
7, 13 *p'* after Sheba the son of Bichri. "
24: 13 thine enemies, while they *p'* thee? "
Job 13: 25 and wilt thou *p'* the dry stubble? "
30: 15 they *p'* my soul as the wind: and * "
Ps 34: 14 and do good; seek peace, and *p'* it. "
Isa 30: 16 shall they that *p'* you be swift. "
Jer 48: 2 Madmen; the sword shall *p'* thee. 3212
Eze 35: 6 blood, and blood shall *p'* thee: 7291
6 blood, even blood shall *p'* thee: "
Ho 8: 3 is good: the enemy shall *p'* him. "
Am 1: 11 did *p'* his brother with the sword, "
Na 1: 8 and darkness shall *p'* his enemies. "

pursued
Ge 14: 14 eighteen, and *p'* them unto Dan. 7291
15 and *p'* them unto Hobah, which "
31: 23 *p'* after him seven days' journey; "
36 thou hast so hotly *p'* after me? 1814
Ex 14: 8 he *p'* after the children of Israel: 7291
9 But the Egyptians *p'* after them, "
23 And the Egyptians *p'*, and went in "
De 11: 4 overflow them as they *p'* after you, "
Jos 2: 7 the men *p'* after them the way to "
7 they which *p'* after them were gone "
8: 16 and they *p'* after Joshua, and were "
17 the city open, and *p'* after Israel. "
24: 6 the Egyptians *p'* after your fathers "
J'g 1: 6 they *p'* after him, and caught him, "
4: 16 Barak *p'* after the chariots, and "
22 as Barak *p'* Sisera, Jael came out "
7: 23 and *p'* after the Midianites. "
25 and *p'* Midian, and brought the "
8: 12 he *p'* after them, and took the two "
20: 45 *p'* hard after them unto Gidom, *1692
1Sa 7: 11 and *p'* the Philistines, and smote 7291
17: 52 shouted, and *p'* the Philistines, "
23: 25 he *p'* after David in the wilderness "
30: 10 David *p'*, he and four hundred "
2Sa 2: 19 And Asahel *p'* after Abner; and in "
24 also and Abishai *p'* after Abner: "
28 and *p'* after Israel no more, neither "
20: 10 Abishai his brother *p'* after Sheba "
22: 38 I have *p'* mine enemies, and "
1Ki 20: 20 Syrians fled; and Israel *p'* them: "
2Ki 25: 5 of the Chaldees *p'* after the king, "
2Ch 13: 19 Abijah *p'* after Jeroboam, and took "
14: 13 were with him *p'* them unto Gerar: "
Ps 18: 37 I have *p'* mine enemies, and * "
Isa 41: 3 He *p'* them, and passed safely; * "
Jer 39: 5 the Chaldeans' army *p'* after them, "
52: 8 the Chaldeans *p'* after the king, "
La 4: 19 they *p'* us upon the mountains, *1814

pursuer See also PURSUERS.
La 1: 6 without strength before the *p'*. 7291

pursuers
Jos 2: 16 mountain, lest the *p'* meet you; 7291
16 days, until the *p'* be returned: "
22 days, until the *p'* were returned: "
22 *p'* sought them throughout all the "
8: 20 turned back upon the *p'*. "

pursueth
Le 26: 17 ye shall flee when none *p'* you. 7291
36 and they shall fall when none *p'*. "
37 were before a sword, when none *p'*: "
Pr 11: 19 tendeth to life: so he that *p'* evil
19 *p'* it to his own death. *
13: 21 Evil *p'* sinners: but to the 7291
19: 7 he *p'* them with words, yet they "
28: 1 The wicked flee when no man *p'*: "

pursuing
J'g 8: 4 were with him, faint, yet *p'* them. 7291
5 I am *p'* after Zebah and Zalmunna, "
1Sa 23: 28 Saul returned from *p'* after David, "
2Sa 3: 22 David and Joab came from *p'* a troop,*
18: 16 returned from *p'* after Israel: 7291
1Ki 18: 27 he is talking, or he is *p'*, or he is *7873
22: 33 that they turned back from *p'* him. 310
2Ch 18: 32 turned back again from *p'* him. "

purtenance See also PERTAIN.
Ex 12: 9 his legs, and with the *p'* thereof. *7130

push See PUSHED; PUSHING.
Ex 21: 29 ox were wont to *p'* with his horn *5056
32 ox shall *p'* a manservant or a *5055
36 ox hath used to *p'* in time past, *5056
De 33: 17 *p'* the people together to the ends 5055
1Ki 22: 11 these shalt thou *p'* the Syrians, "
2Ch 18: 10 *p'* Syria until they be consumed. "
Job 30: 12 they *p'* away my feet, and they *7971
Ps 44: 5 thee will we *p'* down our enemies: 5055
Da 11: 40 the king of the south *p'* at him: * "

pushed
Eze 34: 21 p' all the diseased with your *5055
pushing
Da 8: 4 I saw the ram p' westward, and 5055
put See also PUTTEST; PUTTETH; PUTTING.
Ge 2: 8 there he p' the man whom he had 7760
15 p' him into the garden of Eden to 3240
3: 15 I will p' enmity between thee and 7896
22 lest he p' forth his hand, and take 7971
8: 9 he p' forth his hand, and took her, "
19: 10 But the men p' forth their hand, "
24: 2 P', I pray thee, thy hand under 7760
9 the servant p' his hand under the "
47 I p' the earring upon her face, and "
26: 11 his wife shall surely be p' to death.
27: 15 p' them upon Jacob her younger 3847
16 she p' the skins of the kids of the "
28: 11 and p' them for his pillows, and 7760
18 stone that he had p' for his pillows,"
20 bread to eat, and raiment to p' on,3847
29: 3 p' the stone again upon the well's 7725
30: 40 he p' his own flocks by themselves,7896
40 p' them not unto Laban's cattle. "
42 were feeble, he p' them not in: 7760
31: 34 p' them in the camel's furniture, "
32: 16 p' a space betwixt drove and drove."
33: 2 And he p' the handmaids and their "
35: 2 P' away the strange gods that are5493
37: 34 p' sackcloth upon his loins, and 7760
38: 14 she p' her widow's garments off 5493
19 and p' on the garments of her 3847
28 that the one p' out his hand: and 5414
39: 4 all that he had he p' into his hand. "
20 him, and p' him into the prison, "
40: 3 he p' them in ward in the house of "
15 should p' me into the dungeon. 7760
41: 10 p' me in ward in the captain of the5414
42 and p' it upon Joseph's hand, and "
42 and p' a gold chain about his neck;7760
42: 17 he p' them altogether into ward 622
43: 22 who p' our money in our sacks. 7760
44: 1 p' every man's money in his sack's "
2 p' my cup, the silver cup, in the "
46: 4 shall p' his hand upon thine eyes. 7896
47: 29 p', I pray thee, thy hand under my7760
48: 18 p' thy right hand upon his head. "
50: 26 and he was p' in a coffin in Egypt. 3455
Ex 2: 3 pitch, and p' the child therein; 7760
3: 5 p' off thy shoes from off thy feet, 5394
22 ye shall p' them upon your sons, 7760
4: 4 P' forth thine hand, and take it by7971
4 he p' forth his hand, and caught it, "
6 P' now thine hand into thy bosom. 935
6 he p' his hand into his bosom: and "
7 P' thine hand into thy bosom 7725
7 p' his hand into his bosom again; "
15 him, and p' words in his mouth: 7760
21 which I have p' in thine hand: "
5: 21 to p' a sword in their hand to slay 5414
8: 23 p' a division between my people 7760
11: 7 doth p' a difference between the
12: 15 shall p' away leaven out of your 7673
15: 26 I will p' none of these diseases 7760
16: 33 and p' an omer full of manna 5414
17: 12 took a stone, and p' it under him, 7760
14 utterly p' out the remembrance 4229
19: 12 the mount shall be surely p' to death:
21: 12 that he die, shall be surely p' to death.
15 his mother, shall be surely p' to death.
16 hand, he shall surely be p' to death.
17 his mother, shall surely be p' to death.
29 and his owner also shall be p' to death.
22: 5 and shall p' in his beast, and shall*7971
8 whether he have p' his hand unto "
11 not p' his hand unto his neighbour's"
19 a beast shall surely be p' to death.
23: 1 p' not thine hand with the wicked 7896
24: 6 of the blood, and p' it in basons; 7760
25: 12 and p' them in the four corners 5414
14 shalt p' the staves into the rings 935
16 shalt p' into the ark the testimony5414
21 p' the mercy seat above upon the "
21 the ark thou shalt p' the testimony "
26 p' the rings in the four corners that"
26: 11 and p' the taches into the loops, 935
34 p' the mercy seat upon the ark of 5414
35 p' the table on the north side. "
27: 5 p' it under the compass of the altar "
7 the staves shall be p' into the rings,935
28: 12 shalt p' the two stones upon the 7760
23 p' the two rings on the two ends 5414
24 shalt p' the two wreathen chains "
25 p' them on the shoulderpieces of the"
26 shalt p' them upon the two ends 7760
27 p' them on the two sides of the 5414
30 p' in the breastplate of judgment "
37 thou shalt p' it on a blue lace, that7760
41 p' them upon Aaron thy brother, 3847
29: 3 shalt p' them into one basket, 5414
5 p' upon Aaron the coat, and the 3847
6 shalt p' the mitre upon his head,*7760
6 p' the holy crown upon the mitre.5414
8 his sons, and p' coats upon them. 3847
9 sons, and p' the bonnets on them:*2280
10 p' their hands upon the head of 5564
12 p' it upon the horns of the altar 5414
15 p' their hands upon the head of *5564
17 p' them unto his pieces, and unto 5414
19 p' their hands upon the head of *5564
20 p' it upon the tip of the right ear 5414
24 shalt p' all in the hands of Aaron, 7760
30 stead shall p' them on seven days,3847
30: 6 p' it before the vail that is by the 5414
18 p' it between the tabernacle of the "
18 and thou shalt p' water therein. "
Ex 30: 36 p' of it before the testimony in the5414
31: 6 are wise hearted I have p' wisdom, "
14 defileth it shall surely be p' to death:
15 day, he shall surely be p' to death.
32: 27 P' every man his sword by his 7760
33: 4 man did p' on him his ornaments. 7896
5 now p' off thy ornaments from 3381
22 I will p' thee in a clift of the rock, 7760
34: 33 with them, he p' a vail on his face.5414
35 and Moses p' the vail upon his face7725
35: 2 work therein shall be p' to death.
34 hath p' in his heart that he may 5414
36: 1 in whom the Lord p' wisdom and "
2 heart the Lord had p' wisdom, "
37: 5 he p' the staves into the rings by 935
13 p' the rings upon the four corners "
38: 7 he p' the staves into the rings on 935
39: 7 he p' them on the shoulders of the7760
16 p' the two rings in the two ends of5414
17 they p' the two wreathen chains of "
18 p' them on the shoulderpieces of "
19 p' them on the two ends of the 7760
20 and p' them on the two sides of the5414
25 gold, and p' the bells between the "
40: 3 p' therein the ark of the testimony,7760
5 p' the hanging of the door to the "
7 altar, and shalt p' water therein. 5414
13 p' upon Aaron the holy garments, 3847
18 p' in the bars thereof, and reared 5414
19 p' the covering of the tent above 7760
20 and p' the testimony into the ark, 5114
20 and p' the mercy seat above upon "
22 he p' the table in the tent of the "
24 he p' the candlestick in the tent of7760
26 p' the golden altar in the tent of the"
29 he p' the altar of burnt offering by* "
30 p' water there, to wash withal. 5414
Le 1: 4 he shall p' his hand upon the head*5564
7 priest shall p' fire upon the altar, 5414
2: 1 it, and p' frankincense thereon: "
15 thou shalt p' oil upon it, and lay "
4: 7, 18 p' some of the blood upon the "
25, 30, 34 p' it upon the horns of the "
5: 11 offering; he shall p' no oil upon it,7760
11 he p' any frankincense thereon: 5414
6: 10 shall p' on his linen garment, 3847
10 breeches shall he p' upon his "
10 he shall p' them beside the altar. 7760
11 And he shall p' off his garments, 6584
11 and p' on other garments, and 3847
12 in it; it shall not be p' out: and *3518
8: 7 And he p' upon him the coat, and 5414
7 and p' the ephod upon him, and he "
8 he p' the breastplate upon him: *7760
8 p' in the breastplate the Urim and5414
9 he p' the mitre upon his head; *7760
9 forefront, did he p' the golden * "
13 sons, and p' coats upon them, and*3847
13 girdles,...p' bonnets upon them; *2280
15 p' it upon the horns of the altar 5414
23 p' it upon the tip of Aaron's right "
24 p' of the blood upon the tip of "
26 one wafer, and p' them on the fat,*7760
27 And he p' all upon Aaron's hands, 5414
9: 9 p' it upon the horns of the altar, "
20 p' the fat upon the beasts, and he 7760
10: 1 his censer, and p' fire therein, 5414
1 and p' incense thereon, and *7760
10 p' difference between holy and
11: 32 it must be p' into water, and it 935
38 if any water be p' upon the seed, 5414
13: 45 p' a covering upon his upper lip, *
14: 14 p' it upon the tip of the right ear 5414
17 p' upon the tip of the right ear "
25 p' it upon the tip of the right ear "
28 shall p' of the oil that is in his "
29 shall p' upon the head of him that "
34 p' the plague of leprosy in a house "
42 p' them in the place of those stones;935
15: 19 she shall be p' apart seven days: *5079
16: 4 He shall p' on the holy linen coat, 3847
4 flesh in water, and so p' them on. "
13 shall p' the incense upon the fire 5414
18 p' it upon the horns of the altar "
23 shall p' off the linen garments, 6584
23 which he p' on when he went into 3847
24 and p' on his garments, and come "
32 and shall p' on the linen clothes, "
18: 19 is p' apart for her uncleanness. *5079
19: 14 p' a stumblingblock before the 5414
20 they shall not be p' to death,
20: 2 he shall surely be p' to death: the
9 shall be surely p' to death: he hath
10 adulteress shall surely be p' to death.
11 of them shall surely be p' to death;
12 of them shall surely be p' to death:
13 they shall surely be p' to death;
15 beast, he shall surely be p' to death:
16 they shall surely be p' to death; their
25 p' difference between clean beasts*
27 is a wizard, shall surely be p' to death:
21: 7 woman p' away from her husband:1644
10 consecrated to p' on the garments,3847
22: 14 p' the fifth part thereof unto it, 3254
24: 7 p' pure frankincense upon each 5414
12 And they p' him in ward, that the 3240
16 he shall surely be p' to death, and all
16 name of the Lord, shall be p' to death.
17 any man shall surely be p' to death.
21 killeth a man, he shall be p' to death.
26: 8 of you shall p' ten thousand to flight:*
27: 29 redeemed; but shall surely be p' to
Nu 1: 51 that cometh nigh shall be p' to death.
3: 10, 38 cometh nigh shall be p' to death.
4: 6 shall p' thereon the covering of 5414
6 and shall p' in the staves thereof. 7760
Nu 4: 7 p' thereon the dishes, and the 5414
8 and shall p' in the staves thereof. 7760
10 they shall p' it, and all the vessels5414
10 skins, and shall p' it upon a bar. "
11 and shall p' to the staves thereof: 7725
12 p' them in a cloth of blue, and 5414
12 skins, and shall p' them on a bar: "
14 they shall p' upon it all the vessels "
14 skins, and p' to the staves of it. 7760
5: 2 p' out of the camp every leper, 7971
3 male and female shall ye p' out, "
3 without the camp shall ye p' them; "
4 and p' them out without the camp: "
15 it, nor p' frankincense thereon; 5414
17 take, and p' it into the water: "
18 p' the offering of memorial in her "
6: 18 p' it in the fire which is under the "
19 p' them upon the hands of the "
27 they shall p' my name upon the 7760
8: 10 p' their hands upon the Levites: *5564
11: 17 thee, and will p' it upon them; 7760
29 the Lord would p' his spirit upon 5414
15: 34 they p' him in ward, because it 3240
35 The man shall be surely p' to death:
38 p' upon the fringe of the borders 5414
16: 7 And p' fire therein,
7 p' incense in them before the 7760
14 thou p' out the eyes of these men? 5365
17 his censer, and p' incense in them,5414
18 his censer, and p' fire in them, "
46 Take a censer, and p' fire therein "
46 off the altar, and p' on incense, *7760
47 and he p' on incense, and made an5414
18: 7 that cometh nigh shall be p' to death.
19: 17 running water shall be p' thereto 5414
20: 26, 28 and p' them upon Eleazar his 3847
21: 9 of brass, and p' it upon a pole, and*7760
23: 5 Lord p' a word in Balaam's mouth, "
12 the Lord hath p' in my mouth? * "
16 and p' a word in his mouth, and "
27: 20 shalt p' some of thine honour upon5414
35: 16, 17, 18 shall surely be p' to death.
21 smote him shall surely be p' to death;
30 shall be p' to death by the mouth of*
31 but he shall be surely p' to death.
36: 3 shall be p' to the inheritance of *3254
4 their inheritance be p' unto the * "
De 2: 25 I begin to p' the dread of thee 5414
7: 15 will p' none of the evil diseases of 7760
22 thy God will p' out those nations *5394
10: 2 and thou shalt p' them in the ark. 7760
5 p' the tables in the ark which I had "
11: 29 shalt p' the blessing upon mount *5414
12: 5 your tribes to p' his name there, 7760
7 in all that ye p' your hand unto, 4916
21 hath chosen to p' his name there 7760
13: 5 of dreams shall be p' to death;
5 p' the evil away from the midst of 1197
9 be first upon him to p' him to death,
16: 9 beginnest to p' the sickle to the corn.
17: 6 that is worthy of death be p' to death;
6 witness he shall not be p' to death,
7 be first upon him to p' him to death,
7 p' the evil away from among you. 1197
12 shalt p' away the evil from Israel. "
18: 18 will p' my words in his mouth; 5414
19: 13 p' away the guilt of innocent 1197
19 p' the evil away from among you. "
21: 9 p' away the guilt of innocent blood "
13 p' the raiment of her captivity 5493
21 p' evil away from among you; 1197
22 he be to be p' to death, and thou hang
22: 5 a man p' on a woman's garment: 3847
19 may not p' her away all his days. 7971
21 p' evil away from among you. 1197
22 thou p' away evil from Israel. "
24 shalt p' away evil from among you."
29 may not p' her away all his days. 7971
23: 24 thou shalt not p' any in thy vessel.5414
24: 7 p' evil away from among you. 1197
16 fathers shall not be p' to death for the
16 children be p' to death for the fathers:
16 shall be p' to death for his own sin.
25: 6 his name be not p' out of Israel. *4229
26: 2 shalt p' it in a basket, and shalt 7760
28: 14 p' a yoke of iron upon the neck 5414
30: 7 thy God will p' all these curses "
31: 19 p' it in their mouths, that this 7760
26 law, and p' it in the side of the ark "
32: 30 two p' ten thousand to flight, except
33: 10 they shall p' incense before thee, 7760
14 precious things p' forth by the *1645
Jos 1: 18 him, he shall be p' to death:
6: 24 they p' into the treasury of the 5414
7: 6 and p' dust upon their heads. 5927
11 p' it even among their own stuff. 7760
10: 24 p' your feet upon the necks of "
24 p' their feet upon the necks of "
17: 13 they p' the Canaanites to tribute; 5414
24: 7 he p' darkness between you and 7760
14 and p' away the gods which your 5493
23 p' away, said he, the strange gods "
J'g 1: 28 they p' the Canaanites to tribute, 7760
3: 21 And Ehud p' forth his left hand, 7971
5: 26 She p' her hand to the nail, and her"
6: 19 flour: the flesh he p' in a basket, 7760
19 he p' the broth in a pot, and
21 angel of the Lord p' forth the end 7971
31 be p' to death whilst it is yet morning:
37 p' a fleece of wool in the floor; and3322
7: 16 p' a trumpet in every man's hand,5414
8: 27 p' it in his city, even in Ophrah: 3322
9: 15 and p' your trust in my shadow; ‡
26 of Shechem p' their confidence in him.
49 and p' them to the hold, and set 7760
10: 16 p' away the strange gods from 5493

J'g 12: 3 I p' my life in my hands, and 7760
14: 12 I will now p' forth a riddle unto 2330
13 P' forth thy riddle, that we may "
16 p' forth a riddle unto the children "
15: 4 and p' a firebrand in the midst 7760
15 and p' forth his hand, and took it, 7971
16: 3 p' them upon his shoulders, and 7760
21 took him, and p' out his eyes, and 5365
18: 7 p' them to shame in any thing; 3637
21 p' the little ones and the cattle 7760
20: 13 Gibeah, that we may p' them to death, 13 and p' away evil from Israel. 1197
20 Israel p' themselves in array to fight*
22 p' themselves in array the first day.*
30 p' themselves in array against Gibeah,*
33 p' themselves in array at Baal-tamar:*
21: 5 saying, He shall surely be p' to death.
Ru 3: 3 and p' thy raiment upon thee, 7760
1Sa 1: 14 p' away thy wine from thee. 5493
2: 36 P' me, I pray thee, into one of the 5596
4: 2 Philistines p' themselves in array,
6: 8 p' the jewels of gold, which ye 7760
15 and p' them on the great stone: "
7: 3 then p' away the strange gods and 5493
4 did p' away Baalim and Ashtaroth, "
8: 16 asses, and p' them to his work. 6213
11: 11 p' the people in three companies; 7760
12 men, that we may p' them to death.
13 not a man be p' to death this day:
14: 26 no man p' his hand to his mouth: 5381
27 he p' forth the end of the rod that 7971
27 and p' his hand to his mouth; and 7725
17: 21 Philistines had p' the battle in array,
38 p' an helmet of brass upon his 5414
39 them. And David p' them off him. 5493
40 p' them in a shepherd's bag which 7760
49 And David p' his hand in his bag, 7971
54 but he p' his armour in his tent. 7760
19: 5 For he did p' his life in his hand, "
13 p' a pillow of goat's hair for his "
21: 6 to p' hot bread in the day when it "
22: 17 king would not p' forth their hand 7971
24: 10 will not p' forth mine hand against "
28: 3 p' away those that had familiar 5493
8 himself, and p' on other raiment, 3847
21 I have p' my life in my hand, and 7760
31: 10 they p' his armour in the house of "
2Sa 1: 24 who p' on ornaments of gold upon 5927
3: 34 bound, nor thy feet p' into fetters, 5056
6: 6 Uzzah p' forth his hand to the ark 7971
7: 15 Saul, whom I p' away before thee. 5493
8: 2 two lines measured he to p' to death,
6 David p' garrisons in Syria of 7760
14 And he p' garrisons in Edom; "
14 all Edom p' he garrisons, and all "
10: 8 p' the battle in array at the entering
9 p' them in array against the Syrians:
10 that he might p' them in array
12: 13 Lord also hath p' away thy sin; 5674
31 therein, and p' them under saws, 7760
13: 17 P' now this woman out from me, 7971
19 Tamar p' ashes on her head, and 3947
14: 2 and p' on now mourning apparel, 3847
3 Joab p' the words in her mouth. 7760
19 he p' all these words in the mouth "
15: 5 he p' forth his hand, and took him, 7971
17: 23 p' his household in order, and hanged*
18: 12 would I not p' forth mine hand 7971
19: 21 not Shimei be p' to death for this,
22 there any man be p' to death this day
20: 3 p' them in ward, and fed them, 5414
21: 9 were p' to death in the days of harvest,
1Ki 2: 5 p' the blood of war upon his girdle 5414
8 not p' thee to death with the sword.
24 Adonijah shall be p' to death this day.
26 will not at this time p' thee to death,
35 the king p' Benaiah the son of 5414
35 priest did the king p' in the room of "
5: 3 p' them under the soles of his feet. "
7: 39 he p' five bases on the right side * "
51 p' among the treasures of the house "
8: 9 which Moses p' there at Horeb, 3240
9: 3 built, to p' my name there for ever; 7760
10: 17 p' them in the house of the forest 5414
24 which God had p' in his heart. "
11: 36 chosen me to p' my name there. 7760
12: 4 heavy yoke which he p' upon us, 5414
9 thy father did p' upon us lighter? "
29 Beth-el, and the other p' he in Dan. "
13: 4 p' forth his hand from the altar, 7971
4 hand, which he p' forth against "
14: 21 of Israel, to p' his name there. 7760
18: 23, 23 on wood, and p' no fire under: "
25 of your gods, but p' no fire under. "
33 And he p' the wood in order, and 6186
42 and p' his face between his knees, 7760
20: 6 they shall p' it in their hand, and "
24 and p' captains in their rooms: "
31 pray thee, p' sackcloth on our loins, "
32 loins, and p' ropes on their heads,
21: 27 and p' sackcloth upon his flesh, 7760
22: 10 throne, having p' on their robes, *3847
23 hath p' a lying spirit in the mouth 5414
27 P' this fellow in the prison, and 7760
30 battle; but p' thou on thy robes. 3847
2Ki 2: 20 a new cruse, and p' salt therein. 7760
3: 2 he p' away the image of Baal that 5493
21 all that were able to p' on armour, 2296
4: 34 and p' his mouth upon his mouth, 7760
6: 7 he p' out his hand, and took it. 7971
9: 13 and p' it under him on the top of 7760
10: 7 and p' their heads in baskets, and "
11: 12 king's son, and p' the crown upon 5414
12: 9 p' therein all the money that was "
10 p' up in bags, and told the money 6695
13: 16 P' thine hand upon the bow. 7392
2Ki 13: 16 And he p' his hand upon it: and 7760
16 Elisha p' his hands upon the king's*"
14: 6 not be p' to death for the children, 4191
6 be p' to death for the fathers; "
6 shall be p' to death for his own sin:*"
12 was p' to the worse before Israel;
16: 14 p' it on the north side of the altar. 5414
17 p' it upon a pavement of stones. "
17: 29 p' them in the houses of the high 3240
18: 11 p' them in Halah and in Habor 5148
24 p' thy trust on Egypt for chariots and
19: 28 I will p' my hook in thy nose, and 7760
21: 4 In Jerusalem will I p' my name. "
7 Israel, will I p' my name for ever: "
23: 5 he p' down the idolatrous priests, 7673
24 did Josiah p' away, that he might 1197
33 p' him in bands at Riblah in the
33 p' the land to a tribute of an hundred
25: 7 p' out the eyes of Zedekiah, and 5786
1Ch 5: 20 because they p' their trust in him.
10: 10 p' his armour in the house of their 7760
12: 15 and they p' to flight all them of the "
13: 9 Uzza p' forth his hand to hold the 7971
10 because he p' his hand to the ark: "
18: 6 p' garrisons in Syria-damascus; 7760
13 And he p' garrisons in Edom; and "
19: 9 and p' the battle in array before the
10 p' them in array against the Syrians.
16 they were p' to the worse before Israel,
17 when David had p' the battle in array
19 saw that they were p' to the worse
21: 27 and he p' up his sword again into 7725
27: 24 was the number p' in the account 5927
2Ch 1: 5 he p' before the tabernacle of the *7760
2: 14 device which shall be p' to him, 5414
3: 16 p' them on the heads of the pillars; "
16 and p' them on the chains. "
4: 6 and p' five on the right hand, and "
5: 1 p' he among the treasures of the "
10 two tables which Moses p' therein "
6: 11 in it have I p' the ark, wherein is *7760
20 thou wouldest p' thy name there; "
24 thy people Israel be p' to the worse*
9: 16 And the king p' them in the house 5414
23 wisdom,...God had p' in his heart. "
10: 4 his heavy yoke that he p' upon us, "
9 yoke that thy father did p' upon us? "
11 father p' a heavy yoke upon you, *6006
11 you, I will p' more to your yoke: *3254
11: 11 holds, and p' captains in them, 5414
12 several city he p' shields and spears,
12: 13 of Israel, to p' his name there. 7760
15: 8 p' away the abominable idols out 5674
13 God of Israel should be p' to death,
16: 10 and p' him in a prison house; for 5414
17: 19 whom the king p' in the fenced "
18: 22 hath p' a lying spirit in the mouth "
26 P' this fellow in the prison, and 7760
29 battle; but p' thou on thy robes. 3847
22: 11 and p' him and his nurse in a 5414
23: 7 the house, he shall be p' to death:*
11 son, and p' upon him the crown, 5414
25: 22 was p' to the worse before Israel,
29: 7 and p' out the lamps, and have not 3518
33: 7 Israel, will I p' my name for ever: 7760
14 p' captains of war in all the fenced "
34: 10 p' it in the hand of the workmen *5414
35: 3 P' the holy ark in the house which "
24 p' him in the second chariot that 7392
36: 3 Egypt p' him down at Jerusalem, *5493
7 p' them in his temple at Babylon. 5414
22 his kingdom, and p' it also in writing,
Ezr 1: 1 his kingdom, and p' it also in writing,
7 p' them in the house of his gods; 5414
2: 62 as polluted, p' from the priesthood.
6: 12 shall p' to their hand to alter and 7972
7: 27 p' such a thing as this in the king's 5414
10: 3 our God to p' away all the wives, 3318
19 they would p' away their wives;
Ne 2: 12 p' in my heart to do at Jerusalem: 5414
3: 5 p' not their necks to the work of 935
4: 23 me, none of us p' off our clothes, 6584
23 every one p' them off for washing. *7973
6: 14 that would have p' me in fear.
19 Tobiah sent letters to p' me in fear.
7: 5 And my God p' into mine heart to 5414
64 as polluted, p' from the priesthood.
Es 4: 1 and p' on sackcloth with ashes, 3847
11 is one law of his to p' him to death,
5: 1 Esther p' on her royal apparel, 3847
8: 3 to p' away the mischief of Haman 5674
9: 1 decree drew near to be p' in execution,
Job 1: 11 But p' forth thine hand now, and 7971
12 himself p' not forth thine hand. "
2: 5 But p' forth thine hand now, and "
4: 18 Behold, he p' no trust in his servants;*
11: 14 be in thine hand, p' it far away,
13: 14 and p' my life in mine hand? 7760
17: 3 now, p' me in a surety with thee;*
18: 5 light of the wicked shall be p' out, 1846
6 his candle shall be p' out with him. "
19: 13 hath p' my brethren far from me,
21: 17 is the candle of the wicked p' out! 1846
22: 23 p' away iniquity far from thy
23: 6 but he would p' strength in me. *7760
27: 17 but the just shall p' it on, and the 3847
29: 14 I p' on righteousness, and it
38: 36 p' wisdom in the inward parts? 7896
41: 2 thou p' an hook into his nose? 7760
Ps 2: 12 are all they that p' their trust in him.‡
4: 5 and p' your trust in the Lord.
7 Thou hast p' gladness in my heart, 5414
5: 11 that p' their trust in thee rejoice:‡
7: 1 Lord my God, in thee do I p' my trust:‡
8: 6 hast p' all things under his feet: 7896
9: 5 thou hast p' out their name for *4229
Ps 9: 10 thy name will p' their trust in thee:
20 P' them in fear, O Lord: that the 7896
11: 1 In the Lord p' I my trust: how say ye‡
16: 1 O God: for in thee do I p' my trust.‡
17: 7 them which p' their trust in thee from‡
18: 22 not p' away his statutes from me. 5493
25: 20 be ashamed; for I p' my trust in thee.‡
27: 9 p' not thy servant away in anger: 5186
30: 11 thou hast p' off my sackcloth, and*6605
31: 1 In thee, O Lord, do I p' my trust; let
18 Let the lying lips be p' to silence; *
35: 4 and p' to shame that seek after my†
36: 7 p' their trust under the shadow of thy*
40: 3 hath p' a new song in my mouth, 5414
14 and p' to shame that wish me evil.*
44: 7 hast p' them to shame that hated us.
9 thou hast cast off, and p' us to shame;
53: 5 thou hast p' them to shame, because
55: 20 He hath p' forth his hands against 7971
56: 4 his word, in God I have p' my trust;
8 p' thou my tears into thy bottle: 5414
11 In God have I p' my trust: I will not
70: 2 backward, and p' to confusion, *
71: 1 In thee, O Lord, do I p' my trust: ‡
1 trust: let me never be p' to confusion.†
73: 28 I have p' my trust in the Lord God, *7896
78: 66 p' them to a perpetual reproach. 5414
83: 17 yea, let them be p' to shame, and*
88: 8 hast p' away mine acquaintance 7368
18 and friend hast thou p' far from me, "
118: 8 the Lord than to p' confidence in man.
9 Lord than to p' confidence in princes.
119: 31 O Lord, p' me not to shame.
125: 3 the righteous p' forth their hands 7971
146: 3 P' not your trust in princes, nor in
Pr 4: 24 P' away from thee a froward 5493
24 and perverse lips p' far from thee. 7368
8: 1 understanding p' forth her voice? 5414
13: 9 lamp of the wicked shall be p' out. 1846
20: 20 shall be p' out in obscure darkness. "
23: 2 And p' a knife to thy throat, if thou 7760
24: 20 of the wicked shall be p' out. 1846
25: 6 P' not forth thyself in the 1921
7 shouldest be p' lower in the presence
8 thy neighbour hath p' thee to shame.
10 he that heareth it p' thee to shame,*
30: 5 unto them that p' their trust in him.†‡
Ec 3: 14 nothing can be p' to it, nor any 3254
10: 10 then must he p' to more strength: 1396
11: 10 and p' away evil from thy flesh: 5674
Ca 5: 3 I have p' off my coat; how shall I 6584
3 my coat; how shall I p' it on? 3847
4 beloved p' in his hand by the hole 7971
Isa 1: 16 p' away the evil of your doings 5493
5: 20 p' darkness for light, and light for 7760
20 that p' bitter for sweet, and sweet "
10: 13 p' down the inhabitants like a *3381
11: 8 p' his hand on the cockatrice' den. 1911
20: 2 and p' off thy shoe from thy foot. 2502
36: 9 p' thy trust on Egypt for chariots and
37: 29 will I p' my hook in thy nose, and 7760
42: 1 I have p' my spirit upon him: he 5414
43: 26 P' me in remembrance: let us plead
47: 11 thou shalt not be able to p' it off: 3722
50: 1 divorcement, whom I have p' away? 7971
1 transgressions is your mother p' "
51: 9 p' on strength, O arm of the Lord; 3847
16 I have p' my words in thy mouth, 7760
23 p' it into the hand of them that
52: 1 awake; p' on thy strength, O Zion; 3847
1 p' on thy beautiful garments, O "
53: 10 he hath p' him to grief: when thou
54: 4 for thou shalt not be p' to shame:
59: 17 For he p' on righteousness as a 3847
17 he p' on the garments of vengeance "
21 which I have p' in thy mouth, 7760
63: 11 that p' his holy Spirit within him? "
Jer 1: 9 Then the Lord p' forth his hand, 7971
9 I have p' my words in thy mouth. 5414
3: 1 If a man p' away his wife, and she 7971
8 I had p' her away, and given her "
19 How shall I p' thee among the 7896
4: 1 p' away thine abominations out of 5493
7: 21 P' your burnt offerings unto your*5595
8: 14 the Lord our God hath p' us to silence,
12: 13 they have p' themselves to pain, but
13: 1 girdle, and p' it upon thy loins, 7760
1 thy loins, and p' it not in water. "
2 of the Lord, and p' it on my loins. "
18: 21 and let their men be p' to death; *2026
20: 2 and p' him in the stocks that were 5414
26: 15 that if ye p' me to death, ye shall
19 and all Judah p' him at all to death?
21 the king sought to p' him to death:
24 hand of the people to p' him to death.
27: 2 yokes, and p' them upon thy neck, 5414
8 not p' their neck under the yoke of "
28: 14 p' a yoke of iron upon the neck of "
29: 26 thou shouldest p' him in prison, "
31: 33 will p' my law in their inward parts, "
32: 14 p' them in an earthen vessel, that "
40 I will p' my fear in their hearts, "
37: 4 for they had not p' him into prison. "
15 p' him in prison in the house of "
18 that ye have p' me in prison? "
38: 4 thee, let this man be p' to death:
7 had p' Jeremiah in the dungeon; 5414
12 P' now these old cast clouts and 7760
15 wilt thou not surely p' me to death?
16 I will not p' thee to death, neither will
25 us, and we will not p' thee to death;
39: 7 Moreover he p' out Zedekiah's 5786
18 because thou hast p' thy trust in me.
40: 10 and p' them in your vessels, and 7760
43: 3 that they might p' us to death, and
46: 4 spears, and p' on the brigandines. 3847

Jer 47: 6 p' up thyself into thy scabbard, 622
50:14 P' yourselves in array against *
42 every one p' in array, like a man to
52:11 he p' out the eyes of Zedekiah; 5786
11 p' him in prison till the day of his 5411
27 p' them to death in Riblah in the land
Eze 3:25 they shall p' bands upon thee, *5414
4: 9 and p' them in one vessel, and "
8: 3 p' forth the form of an hand, and 7971
17 they p' the branch to their nose. "
10: 7 p' it into the hands of him that 5414
11:19 I will p' a new spirit within you; "
14: 3 and p' the stumblingblock of their "
16:11 I p' bracelets upon thy hands, and "
12 I p' a jewel on thy forehead, and "
14 which I had p' upon thee, 7760
17: 2 Son of man, p' forth a riddle, and 2330
19: 9 they p' him in ward in chains, and 5414
22:26 p' no difference between the holy and
23:42 p' bracelets upon their hands, and 5414
24:17 p' on thy shoes upon thy feet, and 7760
26:16 p' off their broidered garments: 6584
29: 4 I will p' hooks in thy jaws, and I 5414
30:13 will p' a fear in the land of Egypt. "
21 to p' a roller to bind it, to make it 7760
24 and p' my sword in his hand: but 5414
25 p' my sword into the hand of the "
32: 7 when I shall p' thee out, I will *3518
25 p' in the midst of them that be 5414
36:26 a new spirit will I p' within you: "
27 I will p' my spirit within you, and "
37: 6 p' breath in you, and ye shall live; "
14 shall p' my spirit in you, and ye "
19 and will p' them with him, even "
38: 4 back, and p' hooks into thy jaws, "
42:14 and shall p' on other garments, 3847
43: 9 let them p' away their whoredom, 7368
20 and p' it on the four horns of it, 5414
44:19 they shall p' off their garments 6584
19 they shall p' on other garments; 3847
22 a widow, nor her that is p' away: 1644
45:19 p' it upon the posts of the house, 5414
Da 5:19 and whom he would he p' down. 8214
29 and p' a chain of gold about his neck,
Ho 2: 2 therefore p' away her whoredoms 5493
Joe 3:13 P' ye in the sickle, for the harvest 7971
Am 6: 3 Ye that p' far away the evil day, and
Jon 3: 5 a fast, and p' on sackcloth, from 3847
Mic 2:12 will p' them together as the sheep 7760
7: 5 p' ye not confidence in a guide:
Zep 3:19 where they have been p' to shame.*
Hag 1: 6 wages to p' it into a bag with holes.
M't 1:19 was minded to p' her away privily. 630
5:15 candle, and p' it under a bushel, 5087
31 Whosoever shall p' away his wife, 630
32 whosoever shall p' away his wife, * "
6:25 for your body, what ye shall p' on. 1749
8: 3 And Jesus p' forth his hand, and *1614
9:16 that which is p' in to fill it up taketh*
17 do men p' new wine into old bottles: 906
17 they p' new wine into new bottles, "
25 when the people were p' forth, he 1544
10:21 and cause them to be p' to death. 2289
12:18 I will p' my spirit upon him, and 5087
13:24, 31 parable p' he forth unto them, *3908
14: 3 p' him in prison for Herodias' sake, 5087
5 he would have p' him to death, 615
19: 3 for a man to p' away his wife for 630
6 together, let not man p' asunder. 5562
7 divorcement, and to p' her away? 630
8 suffered you to p' away your wives: "
9 Whosoever shall p' away his wife, "
9 marrieth her which is p' away doth "
13 he should p' his hands on them, *2007
21: 7 and p' on them their clothes, and "
22:34 had p' the Sadducees to silence,
25:27 p' my money to the exchangers, 906
26:52 P' up again thy sword into his 654
59 against Jesus, to p' him to death; 2289
27: 1 against Jesus, to p' him to death: "
6 for to p' them into the treasury, 906
28 him, and p' on him a scarlet robe. 4060
29 thorns, they p' it upon his head, 2007
31 and p' his own raiment on him, 1746
48 p' it on a reed, and gave him to 4060
M'r 1:14 after that John was p' in prison, *3860
41 compassion, p' forth his hand, *1614
2:22 wine must be p' into new bottles. 906
4:21 brought to be p' under a bushel, 5087
5:40 But when he had p' them all out, 1544
6: 9 sandals; and not p' on two coats. 1746
7:32 beseech him to p' his hand upon *2007
33 p' his fingers into his ears, and he 906
M'r 8:23 p' his hands upon him, he asked *2007
25 p' his hands again upon his eyes, * "
10: 2 for a man to p' away his wife? 630
4 divorcement, and to p' her away. "
9 together, let not man p' asunder. 5562
11 shall p' away his wife, and marry 630
12 woman shall p' away her husband, "
16 p' his hands upon them, and *5087
13:12 shall cause them to be p' to death. 2289
14: 1 him by craft, and p' him to death.* 615
55 against Jesus to p' him to death; 2289
15:17 thorns, and p' it about his head, 4060
20 p' his own clothes on him, and led 1746
36 full of vinegar, and p' it on a reed, 4060
Lu 1:52 He hath p' down the mighty from 2507
5:13 he p' forth his hand, and touched *1614
38 new wine must be p' into new 906
8:54 p' them all out, and took her by *1544
9:62 having p' his hand to the plough, 1911
12:22 for the body, what ye shall p' on. 1746
14: 7 And he p' forth a parable to those *3004
15:22 the best robe, and p' it on him; 1746
22 p' a ring on his hand, and shoes on 1325
16: 4 I am p' out of the stewardship, 3179
18 that is p' away from her husband 630
18:33 scourge him, and p' him to death:* 615
21:16 shall they cause to be p' to death. 2289
23:32 led with him to be p' to death. 337
Joh 5: 7 troubled, to p' me into the pool: 906
9:15 He p' clay upon mine eyes, and I 2007
22 he should be p' out of the synagogue.
11:53 together for to p' him to death. 615
12: 6 bag, and bare what was p' therein. 906
10 might p' Lazarus also to death; 615
42 should be p' out of the synagogue: 1096
13: 2 now p' into the heart of Judas 906
16: 2 shall p' you out of the synagogues: 4160
18:11 P' up thy sword into the sheath: 906
31 for us to p' any man to death: 615
19: 2 of thorns, and p' it on his head, 2007
2 and they p' on him a purple robe, *4016
19 a title, and p' it on the cross. 5087
29 vinegar, and p' it upon hyssop, 4060
29 and p' it to his mouth. *4374
20:25 p' my finger into the print of the 906
Ac 1: 7 Father hath p' in his own power. *5087
4: 3 p' them in hold unto the next day: "
5:18 and p' them in the common prison. "
25 the men whom ye p' in prison are "
34 p' the apostles forth a little space; 4160
7:33 P' off thy shoes from thy feet: *3089
9:40 But Peter p' them all forth, and 1544
12: 4 him, he p' him in prison, 5087
19 that they should be p' to death. 520
13:46 seeing ye p' it from you, and judge *683
15: 9 p' no difference between us and *1252
10 to p' a yoke upon the neck of the 2007
26:10 when they were p' to death, I gave 337
27: 6 into Italy; and he p' us therein. 1688
Ro 13:12 let us p' on the armour of light. 1746
14 But p' ye on the Lord Jesus Christ, "
14:13 that no man p' a stumblingblock 5087
1Co 5:13 p' away from among yourselves 1808
7:11 not the husband p' away his wife.* 863
12 with him, let him not p' her away.* "
13:11 a man, I p' away childish things. 2673
15:24 he shall have p' down all rule and* "
25 hath p' all enemies under his feet. 5087
27 hath p' all things under his feet. 5293
27 saith all things are p' under him, "
27 which did p' all things under him.* "
28 subject unto him that p' all things* "
53 corruptible must p'...incorruption, 1746
53 this mortal must p' on immortality. "
54 shall have p' on incorruption, and "
54 mortal shall have p' on immortality. "
2Co 3:13 which p' a vail over his face, that 5087
8:16 which p' the same earnest care *1325
Ga 3:27 into Christ have p' on Christ. 1746
Eph 1:22 hath p' all things under his feet, 5293
4:22 That ye p' off concerning the former 659
24 that ye p' on the new man, which 1746
31 evil speaking, be p' away from you, 142
6:11 P' on the whole armour of God, 1746
Col 3: 8 also p' off all these; anger, wrath, 659
9 p' off the old man with his deeds; 554
10 have p' on the new man, which is 1746
12 P' on therefore, as the elect of God, "
14 above all these things p' on charity,
1Th 2: 4 to be p' in trust with the gospel, *4160
1Ti 1:19 having p' away concerning faith * 683
4: 6 p' the brethren in remembrance 5294
2Ti 1: 6 I p' thee in remembrance that 363
2Ti 2:14 things p' them in remembrance, 5279
Tit 3: 1 P' them in mind to be subject to "
Ph'm 18 ought, p' that on mine account; 1677
Heb 2: 5 p' in subjection the world to come, *5293
8 p' all things in subjection under his "
8 he p' all in subjection under him, * "
8 nothing that is not p' under him. * 506
8 not yet all things p' under him. *5293
13 again, I will p' my trust in him. 3982
6: 6 and p' him to an open shame. 3856
8:10 I will p' my laws into their mind, 1325
9:26 to p' away sin by the sacrifice of 115
10:16 I will p' my laws into their hearts, 1325
Jas 3: 3 we p' bits in the horses' mouths, 906
1Pe 2:15 may p' to silence the ignorance of 5392
3:18 being p' to death in the flesh, but 2289
2Pe 1:12 to p' you always in remembrance 5279
14 I must p' off this my tabernacle, * 595
Jude 5 therefore p' you in remembrance, 5279
Re 2:24 p' upon you none other burden: * 906
11: 9 dead bodies to be p' in graves. *5087
17:17 p' in their hearts to fulfil his will, 1325

Put (*put*) See also PHUT.
1Ch 1: 8 sons of Ham; Cush,...Mizraim, P', 6316
Na 3: 9 P' and Lubim were thy helpers. "

Puteoli (*pu-te'-o-li*)
Ac 28:13 and we came the next day to P': 4223

Putiel (*pu'-te-el*)
Ex 6:25 one of the daughters of P' to wife; 6317

putrifying
Isa 1: 6 wounds, and bruises, and p' sores: *2961

puttest
Nu 24:21 and thou p' thy nest in a rock. *7760
De 12:18 all that thou p' thine hands unto. 4916
15:10 in all that thou p' thine hands unto. "
2Ki 18:14 which thou p' on me will I bear. 5414
Job 13:27 Thou p' my feet also in the stocks, 7760
Ps 119:119 Thou p' away all the wicked of 7673
Hab 2:15 that p' thy bottle to him, and *5596

putteth
Ex 30:33 p' any of it upon a stranger, shall 5414
Nu 22:38 word that God p' in my mouth, 7760
De 25:11 and p' forth her hand, and taketh 7971
27:15 and p' it in a secret place. *7760
1Ki 20:11 boast himself as he that p' it off. 6605
Job 15:15 Behold, he p' no trust in his saints;
28: 9 p' forth his hand upon the rock; 7971
33:11 He p' my feet in the stocks, he 7760
Ps 15: 5 He that p' not out his money to 5414
75: 7 he p' down one, and setteth up 8213
Pr 28:25 he that p' his trust in the Lord shall be
29:25 whoso p' his trust in the Lord shall be
Ca 2:13 fig tree p' forth her green figs, *2590
Isa 57:13 he that p' his trust in me shall ‡
Jer 43:12 as a shepherd p' on his garment; 5844
La 3:29 He p' his mouth in the dust; if so *5414
Eze 14: 4, 7 p' the stumblingblock of his 7760
Mic 3: 5 he that p' not into their mouths, 5414
M't 9:16 p' a piece of new cloth unto an old 1911
24:32 is yet tender, and p' forth leaves, 1631
M'r 2:22 no man p' new wine into old bottles: 906
4:29 immediately he p' in the sickle, 649
13:28 is yet tender, and p' forth leaves, 1631
Lu 5:36 p' a piece of a new garment upon 1911
37 man p' new wine into old bottles; 906
8:16 with a vessel, or p' it under a bed; 5087
11:33 a candle, p' it in a secret place, "
16:18 Whosoever p' away his wife, and 630
Joh 10: 4 when he p' forth his own sheep, *1544

putting
Ge 21:14 p' it on her shoulder, and the 7760
Le 16:21 p' them...the head of the goat, *5414
J'g 7: 6 lapped, p' their hand to their mouth,
Isa 58: 9 p' forth of the finger, and speaking 7971
Mal 2:16 Israel, saith that he hateth p' away: "
Ac 9:12 coming in,...p' his hand on him, *2007
17 p' his hands on him said, Brother * "
19:33 the Jews p' him forward. And 4261
Ro 15:15 as p' you in mind, because of the 1878
Eph 4:25 Wherefore p' away lying, speak 659
Col 2:11 p' off the body of the sins of the 555
1Th 5: 8 p' on the breastplate of faith and 1746
1Ti 1:12 faithful, p' me into the ministry; *5087
2Ti 1: 6 in thee by the p' on of my hands. *1936
1Pe 3: 3 of gold, or of p' on of apparel; 1745
21 the p' away of the filth of the flesh, 595
2Pe 1:13 you up by p' you in remembrance; 5279

pygarg
De 14: 5 the wild goat, and the p', and the 1787

Q.

quails
Ex 16:13 pass, that at even the q' came up, 7958
Nu 11:31 brought q' from the sea, and let
32 next day, and they gathered the q': "
Ps 105:40 people asked, and he brought q', "

quake See also EARTHQUAKE; QUAKED; QUAKING.
Joe 2:10 The earth shall q' before them; *7264
Na 1: 5 The mountains q' at him, and the 7493
M't 27:51 and the earth did q', and the rocks 4579
Heb 12:21 said, I exceedingly fear and q':) 1790

quaked
Ex 19:18 and the whole mount q' greatly. 2729
1Sa 14:15 also trembled, and the earth q': 7264

quaking
Eze 12:18 Son of man, eat thy bread with q', 7494
Da 10: 7 but a great q' fell upon them, so 2731

quantity
Isa 22:24 and the issue, all vessels of small q'.*

quarrel
Le 26:25 avenge the q' of my covenant: *5359
2Ki 5: 7 see how he seeketh a q' against me. 579
M'r 6:19 Herodias had a q' against him, *1758
Col 3:13 if any man have a q' against any: *3437

quarries
J'g 3:19 from the q' that were by Gilgal, 6456
26 and passed beyond the q', and "

quarter See also QUARTERS.
Ge 19: 4 all the people from every q': 7098
Nu 34: 3 q' shall be from the wilderness 6285
Jos 15: 5 north q' was from the bay of the sea "
18:14 of Judah: this was the west q'. "
15 the south q' was from the end of "
Isa 47:15 shall wander every one to his q'; 5676
56:11 every one for his gain, from his q'. 7098
M'r 1:45 they came to him from every q'. 3836

quarters
Ex 13: 7 leaven seen with thee in all thy q'. *1366
De 22:12 upon the four q' of thy vesture, *3671
1Ch 9:24 In four q' were the porters, *7307
Jer 49:36 winds from the four q' of heaven, 7098
Eze 38: 6 of Togarmah of the north q', *3411
Ac 9:32 as Peter passed throughout all q',*
16: 3 the Jews which were in those q': *5117
28: 7 In the same q' were possessions * "
Re 20: 8 are in the four q' of the earth, *1137

Quartus (*quar'-tus*)
Ro 16:23 saluteth you, and Q' a brother. 2890

quaterniens
Ac 12: 4 delivered him to four q' of soldiers 5069

queen See also QUEENS.
1Ki 10: 1 the q' of Sheba heard of the fame 4436
4 when the q' of Sheba had seen all "
10 which the q' of Sheba gave to king "
13 unto the q' of Sheba all her desire, "
11: 19 wife, the sister of Tahpenes the q'. 1377
15: 13 even her he removed from being q', "
2Ki 10: 13 the king and the children of the q'. "
2Ch 9: 1 q' of Sheba heard of the fame of 4436
3 q' of Sheba had seen the wisdom of "
9 the q' of Sheba gave king Solomon. "
12 Solomon gave to the q' of Sheba all "
15: 16 he removed her from being q', 1377
Ne 2: 6 me, (the q' also sitting by him,) 7694
Es 1: 9 Vashti the q' made a feast for the 4436
11 bring Vashti the q' before the king "
12 the q' Vashti refused to come at the "
15 do unto the q' Vashti according to "
16 Vashti the q' hath not done wrong "
17 deed of the q' shall come abroad "
17 Vashti the q' to be brought in "
18 have heard of the deed of the q'. "
2: 4 which pleaseth the king be q' 4427
17 and made her q' instead of Vashti. "
22 who told it unto Esther the q'; 4436
4: 4 was the q' exceedingly grieved; "
5: 2 Esther the q' standing in the court, "
3 her, What wilt thou, q' Esther? "
12 the q' did let no man come in with "
7: 1 came to banquet with Esther the q'. "
2 What is thy petition, q' Esther? "
3 Esther the q' answered and said, "
5 said unto Esther the q', Who is he, "
6 afraid before the king and the q'. "
7 request for his life to Esther the q'; "
8 Will he force the q' also before me "
8: 1 Jews' enemy unto Esther the q'. "
7 Ahasuerus said unto Esther the q', "
9: 12 the king said unto Esther the q', "
29 Then Esther the q', the daughter of "
31 Esther the q' had enjoined them, "
Ps 45: 9 right hand did stand the q' in gold 7694
Jer 7: 18 to make cakes to the q' of heaven, 4446
13: 18 Say unto the king and to the q', *1377
29: 2 king, and the q', and the eunuchs,* "
44: 17 incense unto the q' of heaven, 4446
18 to burn incense to the q' of heaven, "
19 burned incense to the q' of heaven, "
25 to burn incense to the q' of heaven, "
Da 5: 10 the q' by reason of the words of 4433
10 the q' spake and said, O king, live "
M't 12: 42 The q' of the south shall rise up in 938
Lu 11: 31 The q' of the south shall rise up in "
Ac 8: 27 under Candace q' of the Ethiopians, "
Re 18: 7 for she saith in her heart, I sit a q', "

queens
Ca 6: 8 are threescore q', and fourscore 4436
9 yea, the q' and the concubines, and "
Isa 49: 23 and their q' thy nursing mothers: 8282

quench See also QUENCHED; UNQUENCHABLE.
2Sa 14: 7 they shall q' my coal which is left, 3518
21: 17 that thou q' not the light of Israel. "
Ps 104: 11 the wild asses q' their thirst. 7665
Ca 8: 7 Many waters cannot q' love, 3518
Isa 1: 31 together, and none shall q' them. "
42: 3 the smoking flax shall he not q': "
Jer 4: 4 fire, and burn that none can q' it, "
21: 12 fire, and burn that none can q' it, "
Am 5: 6 there be none to q' it in Beth-el. "
M't 12: 20 and smoking flax shall he not q', 4570
Eph 6: 16 q' all the fiery darts of the wicked. "
1Th 5: 19 Q' not the Spirit. "

quenched
Nu 11: 2 unto the Lord, the fire was q'. *8257
2Ki 22: 17 this place, and shall not be q'. 3518
2Ch 34: 25 this place, and shall not be q'. "
Ps 118: 12 they are q' as the fire of thorns: 1846
Isa 34: 10 It shall not be q' night nor day; 3518
43: 17 they are extinct, they are q' as tow. "
66: 24 die, neither shall their fire be q'; "
Jer 7: 20 it shall burn, and shall not be q'. "
17: 27 of Jerusalem, and it shall not be q'. "
Eze 20: 47 the flaming flame shall not be q', "
48 have kindled it: it shall not be q'. "
M'r 9: 43 into the fire that never shall be q':* 762
44 dieth not, and the fire is not q'. *4570
45 into the fire that never shall be q':* 762
46 dieth not, and the fire is not q'. *4570
48 dieth not, and the fire is not q'. "
Heb 11: 34 Q' the violence of fire, escaped the "

question See also QUESTIONED; QUESTIONING; QUESTIONS.
M't 22: 35 which was a lawyer, asked him a q', "
M'r 8: 11 began to q' with him, seeking of 4802
9: 16 the scribes, What q' ye with them? "
11: 29 I will also ask of you one q', and 3056
12: 34 man after that durst ask him any q': "
Lu 20: 40 they durst not ask him any q' at all. "
Joh 3: 25 there arose a q' between some of *2214
Ac 15: 2 apostles and elders about this q'. 2213
18: 15 if it be a q' of words and names, * "
19: 40 we are in danger to be called in q'*1458
23: 6 of the dead I am called in q'. 2919
24: 21 I am called in q' by you this day. "
1Co 10: 25 asking no q' for conscience sake: "
27 asking no q' for conscience sake. "

questioned
2Ch 31: 9 Hezekiah q' with the priests and 1875
M'r 1: 27 that they q' among themselves, 4802
Lu 23: 9 he q' with him in many words; 1905

questioning
M'r 9: 10 q' one with another what the 4802
14 them, and the scribes q' with them. "

questions
1Ki 10: 1 came to prove him with hard q'. 2420
3 And Solomon told her all her q': 1697
2Ch 9: 1 to prove Solomon with hard q' at 2420
2 And Solomon told her all her q': 1697
M't 22: 46 that day forth ask him any more q'. "
Lu 2: 46 hearing them, and asking them q'. 1905
Ac 23: 29 to be accused of q' of their law, 2213
25: 19 But had certain q' against him of "
20 I doubted of such manner of q', *2214
26: 3 to be expert in all customs and q' 2213
1Ti 1: 4 genealogies, which minister q', *2214
6: 4 about q' and strifes of words, * "
2Ti 2: 23 But foolish and unlearned q' avoid,* "
Tit 3: 9 avoid foolish q', and genealogies, * "

quick See also ALIVE; LIVING; QUICKSANDS.
Le 13: 10 there be q' raw flesh in the rising; 4241
24 q' flesh that burneth have a white "
Nu 16: 30 and they go down q' into the pit; *2416
Ps 55: 15 and let them go down q' into hell:* "
124: 3 they had swallowed us up q', when* "
Isa 11: 3 shall make him of q' understanding
Ac 10: 42 to be the Judge of q' and dead. 2198
2Ti 4: 1 shall judge the q' and the dead at "
Heb 4: 12 the word of God is q', and powerful,* "
1Pe 4: 5 ready to judge the q' and the dead. "

quicken See also QUICKENED; QUICKENETH; QUICKENING.
Ps 71: 20 sore troubles, shalt q' me again, 2421
80: 18 q' us, and we will call upon thy "
119: 25 q' thou me according to thy word. "
37 vanity; and q' thou me in thy way. "
40 q' me in thy righteousness. "
88 Q' me after thy lovingkindness; so "
107 q' me, O Lord, according unto thy "
149 q' me according to thy judgment. "
154 me: q' me according to thy word. "
156 q' me according to thy judgments. "
159 q' me, O Lord, according to thy "
143: 11 Q' me, O Lord, for thy name's sake; "
Ro 8: 11 also q' your mortal bodies by his 2227

quickened
Ps 119: 50 affliction: for thy word hath q' me. 2421
93 for with them thou hast q' me. "
1Co 15: 36 that which thou sowest is not q', 2227
Eph 2: 1 you hath he q', who were dead *
5 hath q' us together with Christ, 4806
Col 2: 13 flesh, hath he q' together with him,* "
1Pe 3: 18 in the flesh, but q' by the Spirit: 2227

quickeneth
Joh 5: 21 raiseth up the dead, and q' them; 2227
21 even so the Son q' whom he will. "
6: 63 It is the spirit that q'; the flesh "
Ro 4: 17 even God, who q' the dead, and "
1Ti 6: 13 the sight of God, who q' all things, "

quickening
1Co 15: 45 last Adam was made a q' spirit. *2227

quickly
Ge 18: 6 Make ready q' three measures of 4116
27: 20 is it that thou hast found it so q', "
Ex 32: 8 turned aside q' out of the way 4118
Nu 16: 46 go q' unto the congregation, and 4120
De 9: 3 them out, and destroy them q', 4118
12 get thee down q' from hence; "
12 they are q' turned aside out of the "
16 had turned aside q' out of the way "
11: 17 lest ye perish q' from off the good 4120
28: 20 and until thou perish q'; because 4118
Jos 2: 5 pursue after them q'; for ye shall "
8: 19 the ambush arose q' out of their 4120
10: 6 come up to us q', and save us, and "
23: 16 ye shall perish q' from off the good "
J'g 2: 17 they turned q' out of the way 4118
1Sa 20: 19 then thou shalt go down q', and 3966
2Sa 17: 16 Now therefore send q', and tell 4120
18 they went both of them away q', "
21 Arise, and pass q' over the water: "
2Ki 1: 11 hath the king said, Come down q'. "
2Ch 18: 8 Fetch q' Micaiah the son of Imla. 4116
Ec 4: 12 a threefold cord is not q' broken. 4120
M't 5: 25 Agree with thine adversary q', 5035
28: 7 And go q', and tell his disciples "
8 departed q' from the sepulchre "
M'r 16: 8 they went out q', and fled from the* "
Lu 14: 21 Go out q' into the streets and 5030
16: 6 and sit down q', and write fifty. "
Joh 11: 29 she arose q', and came unto him. 5035
13: 27 unto him, That thou doest, do q'. 5032
Ac 12: 7 him up, saying, Arise up q'. 1722,5034
22: 18 get thee q' out of Jerusalem: " "
Re 2: 5 or else I will come unto thee q', *5035
16 or else I will come unto thee q', "
3: 11 Behold, I come q': hold that fast "
11: 14 behold, the third woe cometh q'. "
22: 7 Behold, I come q': blessed is he "
12 I come q'; and my reward is with "
20 saith, Surely I come q'. Amen. "

quicksands
Ac 27: 17 lest they should fall into the q', *4950

quiet See also DISQUIET; QUIETED; QUIETETH.
J'g 16: 2 were q' all the night, saying, In 2790
18: 7 of the Zidonians, q' and secure; 8252
27 a people that were at q' and secure: "
2Ki 11: 20 rejoiced, and the city was in q': "
1Ch 4: 40 the land was wide, and q', and "
2Ch 14: 1 his days the land was q' ten years. "
5 the kingdom was q' before him. "
20: 30 the realm of Jehoshaphat was q': "
23: 21 the city was q', after that they had "
Job 3: 13 should I have lain still and been q', "
26 had I rest, neither was I q'; 5117
21: 23 being wholly at ease and q'. 7961
Ps 35: 20 them that are q' in the land. 7282
107: 30 are they glad because they be q'; 8367
Pr 1: 33 and shall be q' from fear of evil. 7599
Ec 9: 17 of wise men are heard in q' more 5183
Isa 7: 4 Take heed, and be q'; fear not, 8252
14: 7 whole earth is at rest, and is q': "
32: 18 dwellings, and in q' resting places; 7600
33: 20 shall see Jerusalem a q' habitation," "
Jer 30: 10 shall be in rest, and be q', and 7599
47: 6 how long will it be ere thou be q'? 8252
7 How can it be q', seeing the Lord "
49: 23 sorrow on the sea; it cannot be q'. "
51: 59 And this Seraiah was a q' prince. *4496
Eze 16: 42 be q', and will be no more angry. 8252
Na 1: 12 Though they be q', and likewise *8003
Ac 19: 36 ye ought to be q', and to do 2687
1Th 4: 11 that ye study to be q', and to do 2270
1Ti 2: 2 may lead a q' and peaceable life 2263
1Pe 3: 4 ornament of a meek and q' spirit, 2272

quieted
Ps 131: 2 I have behaved and q' myself, 1826
Zec 6: 8 have q' my spirit in the north 5117

quieteth
Job 37: 17 he q' the earth by the south wind? *8252

quietly
2Sa 3: 27 in the gate to speak with him q', 7987
La 3: 26 q' wait for the salvation of the Lord.

quietness
J'g 8: 28 the country was in q' forty years *8252
1Ch 22: 9 will give peace and q' unto Israel 8253
Job 20: 20 he shall not feel q' in his belly, 7961
34: 29 When he giveth q', who then can 8252
Pr 17: 1 is a dry morsel, and q' therewith, 7962
Ec 4: 6 Better is an handful with q', than 5183
Isa 30: 15 in q' and in confidence shall be 8252
32: 17 q' and assurance for ever. "
Ac 24: 2 that by thee we enjoy great q', *1515
2Th 3: 12 that with q' they work, and eat 2271

quit See also ACQUIT.
Ex 21: 19 shall he that smote him be q': 5352
28 the owner of the ox shall be q'. 5355
Jos 2: 20 then we will be q' of thine oath * "
1Sa 4: 9 and q' yourselves like men, 1961
9 q' yourselves like men, and fight.
1Co 16: 13 faith, q' you like men, be strong. 407

quite
Ge 31: 15 and hath q' devoured also our money.
Ex 23: 24 and q' break down their images. *
Nu 17: 10 q' take away their murmurings *3615
33: 52 q' plucked down all their high places:*
2Sa 3: 24 hast sent him away, and he is q' gone?
Job 6: 13 and is wisdom driven q' from me? 5080
Hab 3: 9 Thy bow was made q' naked, 6181

quiver See also QUIVERED.
Ge 27: 3 thy weapons, thy q' and thy bow, 8522
Job 39: 23 The q' rattleth against him, the 827
Ps 127: 5 Happy is the man that hath his q' "
Isa 22: 6 Elam bare the q' with chariots of "
49: 2 shaft; in his q' hath he hid me; "
Jer 5: 16 Their q' is as an open sepulchre, "
La 3: 13 of his q' to enter into my reins. "

quivered
Hab 3: 16 trembled; my lips q' at the voice: 6750

R.

Raamah (*ra'-a-mah*)
Ge 10: 7 and Havilah, and Sabtah, and R', 7484
7 the sons of R'; Sheba, and Dedan. "
1Ch 1: 9 and Havilah, and Sabta, and R', * "
9 the sons of R'; Sheba, and Dedan. "
Eze 27: 22 The merchants of Sheba and R', "

Raamiah (*ra-a-mi'-ah*)
Ne 7: 7 Azariah, R', Nahamani, Mordecai, 7485

Raamses (*ra-am'-seze*) See also RAMESES.
Ex 1: 11 treasure cities, Pithom, and R'. 7486

Rab See RAB-MAG; RAB-SARIS; RAB-SHAKEH.

Rabbah (*rab'-bah*) See also RABBATH.
Jos 13: 25 unto Aroer that is before R'; 7237
15: 60 which is Kirjath-jearim, and R'; "
2Sa 11: 1 children of Ammon,...besieged R'. "
12: 26 And Joab fought against R' of the "
27 I have fought against R', and have "
29 went to R', and fought against it, "
17: 27 that Shobi the son of Nahash of R' "
1Ch 20: 1 Ammon, and came and besieged R'. "
1 Joab smote R', and destroyed it. "
Jer 49: 2 an alarm of war to be heard in R' "
3 cry, ye daughters of R', gird you "
Eze 25: 5 I will make R' a stable for camels, 7237
Am 1: 14 will kindle a fire in the wall of R', "

Rabbath (*rab'-bath*) See also RABBAH.
De 3: 11 in R' of the children of Ammon? *7237
Eze 21: 20 that the sword may come to R' * "

Rabbi (*rab'-bi*) See also RABBONI.
M't 23: 7 and to be called of men, R', R'. 4461
8 But be not ye called R': for one is "
Joh 1: 38 They said unto him, R', (which is "
49 him, R', thou art the Son of God; "
3: 2 R', we know...thou art a teacher "

Joh 3:26 *R'*, he that was with thee beyond *4461*
6:25 *R'*, when camest thou hither? "
Rabbim See Bath-rabbim.
Rabbith (*rab'-bith*)
Jos 19:20 And *R'*, and Kishion, and Abez, 7245
Rabboni (*rab-bo'-ni*) See also Rabbi.
Joh 20:16 herself, and saith unto him, *R'*; *4462*
Rab-mag (*rab'-mag*)
Jer 39: 3 Rab-saris, Nergal-sharezer, *R'*, 7248
13 *R'*, and all the king of Babylon's "
Rab-saris (*rab'-sa-ris*)
2Ki 18:17 of Assyria sent Tartan and *R'* 7249
Jer 39: 3 *R'*, Nergal-sharezer, Rab-mag, "
13 *R'*, and Nergal-sharezer, Rab-mag, "
Rab-shakeh (*rab'-sha-keh*) See also Rabshakeh.
2Ki 18:17 and *R'* from Lachish to king *7262
19 *R'* said unto them, Speak ye now * "
26 unto *R'*, Speak, I pray thee, to thy* "
27 *R'* said unto them, Hath my master* "
28 Then *R'* stood and cried with a loud* "
37 and told him the words of *R'*. * "
19: 4 God will hear all the words of *R'*,* "
8 So *R'* returned, and found the king* "
Rabshakeh (*rab'-sha-keh*) See also Rab-shakeh.
Isa 36: 2 *R'* from Lachish to Jerusalem 7262
4 *R'* said unto them, Say ye now to "
11 *R'*, Speak, I pray thee, unto thy "
12 *R'* said, Hath my master sent me "
13 *R'* stood, and cried with a loud "
22 rent, and told him the words of *R'*. "
37: 4 thy God will hear the words of *R'*, "
8 So *R'* returned, and found the king "
Raca (*ra'-cah*)
M't 5:22 shall say to his brother, *R'*, shall *4469*
race
Ps 19: 5 as a strong man to run a *r'*. * 734
Ec 9:11 the *r'* is not to the swift, nor the 4793
1Co 9:24 they which run in a *r'* run all, but *4712*
Heb12: 1 patience the *r'* that is set before us, *73*
Rachab (*ra'-kab*) See also Rahab.
M't 1: 5 Salmon begat Booz of *R'*; and *4477
Rachal (*ra'-kal*)
1Sa 30:29 And to them which were in *R'*, 7403
Rachel (*ra'-chel*) See also Rachel's; Rahel.
Ge 29: 6 *R'* his daughter cometh with the 7354
9 *R'* came with her father's sheep: "
10 Jacob saw *R'* the daughter of Laban "
11 Jacob kissed *R'*, and lifted up his "
12 And Jacob told *R'* that he was her "
16 the name of the younger was *R'*. "
17 *R'* was beautiful and well favoured. "
18 And Jacob loved *R'*; and said, I "
18 will serve thee seven years for *R'* "
20 Jacob served seven years for *R'*; "
25 did I not serve with thee for *R'*? "
28 gave him *R'* his daughter to wife "
29 And Laban gave to *R'* his daughter "
30 he went in also unto *R'*, and he "
30 he loved also *R'* more than Leah, "
31 her womb: but *R'* was barren. "
30: 1 when *R'* saw that she bare Jacob "
1 *R'* envied her sister; and said unto "
2 Jacob's anger...kindled against *R'*: "
6 *R'* said, God hath judged me, and "
8 And *R'* said, With great wrestlings "
14 *R'* said to Leah, Give me, I pray "
15 And *R'* said, Therefore he shall lie "
22 And God remembered *R'*, and God "
25 pass, when *R'* had borne Joseph, "
31: 4 Jacob sent and called *R'* and Leah "
14 *R'* and Leah answered and said "
19 and *R'* had stolen the images that "
32 knew not that *R'* had stolen them. "
34 Now *R'* had taken the images, and "
33: 1 children unto Leah, and unto *R'*, "
2 and *R'* and Joseph hindermost. "
7 after came Joseph near and *R'*, "
35:16 and *R'* travailed, and she had hard "
19 *R'* died, and was buried in the way "
24 sons of *R'*; Joseph, and Benjamin: "
46:19 The sons of *R'*, Jacob's wife; "
22 These are the sons of *R'*, which "
25 Laban gave unto *R'* his daughter, "
48: 7 *R'* died by me in the land of Canaan "
Ru 4:11 thine house like *R'* and like Leah, "
M't 2:18 *R'* weeping for her children, and *4478*
Rachel's (*ra'-chelz*)
Ge 30: 7 Bilhah *R'* maid conceived again, 7354
31:33 tent, and entered into *R'* tent. "
35:20 that is the pillar of *R'* grave unto "
25 the sons of Bilhah, *R'* handmaid; "
1Sa 10: 2 shalt find two men by *R'* sepulchre "
Raddai (*rad'-dahee*)
1Ch 2:14 Nethaneel the fourth, *R'* the fifth, 7288
rafters
Ca 1:17 house are cedar, and our *r'* of fir. 7351
rag See ragged; rags.
Ragau (*ra'-gaw*) See also Reu.
Lu 3:35 Saruch, which was the son of *R'*, *4466
rage See also outrageous; raged; rageth; raging.
2Ki 5:12 he turned and went away in a *r'*. 2534
19:27 coming in, and thy *r'* against me.*7264
28 Because thy *r'* against me and thy* "
2Ch 16:10 for he was in a *r'* with him because 2197
28: 9 slain them in a *r'* that reacheth "
Job 39:24 the ground with fierceness and *r'*: 7267
40:11 Cast abroad the *r'* of thy wrath: *5678
Ps 2: 1 Why do the heathen *r'*, and the 7283
Ps 7: 6 because of the *r'* of mine enemies: 5678
Pr 6:34 For jealousy is the *r'* of a man: 2534
29: 9 whether he *r'* or laugh, there is *7264
Isa 37:28 coming in, and thy *r'* against me.* "
29 Because thy *r'* against me, and thy* "
Jer 46: 9 ye horses; and *r'*, ye chariots; 1984
Da 3:13 Nebuchadnezzar in his *r'* and 7266
Ho 7:16 sword for the *r'* of their tongue: 2195
Na 2: 4 The chariots shall *r'* in the streets, 1984
Ac 4:25 Why did the heathen *r'*, and the *5433*
raged
Ps 46: 6 The heathen *r'*, the kingdoms 1993
rageth
Pr 14:16 but the fool *r'*, and is confident. *5674
ragged
Isa 2:21 into the tops of the *r'* rocks, for fear
raging
Ps 89: 9 Thou rulest the *r'* of the sea: *1348
Pr 20: 1 is a mocker, strong drink is *r'*: *1993
Jon 1:15 and the sea ceased from her *r'*. 2197
Lu 8:24 the wind and the *r'* of the water: *2830*
Jude 13 *R'* waves of the sea, foaming out * *66*
rags
Pr 23:21 shall clothe a man with *r'*. 7168
Isa 64: 6 righteousnesses are as filthy *r'*; * 899
Jer 38:11 old cast clouts and old rotten *r'*, 4418
12 and rotten *r'* under thine armholes "
Raguel (*ra-gu'-el*)
Nu 10:29 unto Hobab, the son of *R'* the *7467
Rahab (*ra'-hab*) See also Rachab.
Jos 2: 1 into an harlot's house, named *R'*, 7343
3 the king of Jericho sent unto *R'*, "
6:17 only *R'* the harlot shall live, she "
23 spies went in, and brought out *R'*, "
25 Joshua saved *R'* the harlot alive, "
Ps 87: 4 make mention of *R'* and Babylon 7294
89:10 Thou hast broken *R'* in pieces, as "
Isa 51: 9 Art thou not it that hath cut *R'*, "
Heb11:31 By faith the harlot *R'* perished *4460*
Jas 2:25 was not *R'* the harlot justified by "
Raham (*ra'-ham*)
1Ch 2:44 And Shema begat *R'*, the father of 7357
Rahel (*ra'-hel*) See Rachel.
Jer 31:15 *R'* weeping for her children *7354
rail See also railed; railing.
2Ch 32:17 also letters to *r'* on the Lord God 2778
railed
1Sa 25:14 our master; and he *r'* on them. *5860
M'r 15:29 And they that passed by *r'* on him, *987*
Lu 23:39 which were hanged *r'* on him, "
railer
1Co 5:11 idolater, or a *r'*, or a drunkard, *3060*
railing See also railings.
1Pe 3: 9 rendering evil for evil, or *r'* for *r'*: *3059*
2Pe 2:11 bring not *r'* accusation against *989*
Jude 9 bring against him a *r'* accusation, *988*
railings
1Ti 6: 4 whereof cometh envy, strife, *r'*, evil *988*
raiment
Ge 24:53 of gold, and *r'*, and gave them to 899
27:15 goodly *r'* of her eldest son Esau, ‡ "
27 and he smelled the smell of his *r'*, "
28:20 me bread to eat, and *r'* to put on, "
41:14 changed his *r'*, and came in unto 8071
45:22 he gave each man changes of *r'*; "
22 of silver, and five changes of *r'*. "
Ex 3:22 of silver, and jewels of gold, and *r'*: "
12:35 of silver, and jewels of gold, and *r'*: "
21:10 her food, her *r'*, and her duty of 3682
22: 9 for ass, for sheep, for *r'*, or for any 8008
26 take thy neighbour's *r'* to pledge,* "
27 only, it is his *r'* for his skin: *8071
Le 11:32 it be any vessel of wood, or *r'*, or 899
Nu 31:20 purify all your *r'*, and all that is * "
De 8: 4 Thy *r'* waxed not old upon thee, 8071
10:18 stranger, in giving him food and *r'*. "
21:13 the *r'* of her captivity from off her, "
22: 3 and so shalt thou do with his *r'*; * "
24:13 that he may sleep in his own *r'*, *8008
17 nor take a widow's *r'* to pledge: 899
Jos 22: 8 with iron, and with very much *r'*: 8008
J'g 3:16 under his *r'* upon his right thigh. 4055
8:26 purple *r'* that was on the kings of 899
Ru 3: 3 thee, and put thy *r'* upon thee, 8071
1Sa 28: 8 and put on other *r'*, and he went, 899
2Ki 5: 5 pieces of gold, and ten changes of *r'*. "
7: 8 gold, and *r'*, and went and hid it; "
2Ch 9:24 vessels of gold, and *r'*, harness, 8008
Es 4: 4 and she sent *r'* to clothe Mordecai, 899
Job 27:16 dust, and prepare *r'* as the clay; 4403
Ps 45:14 unto the king in *r'* of needlework: *7553
Isa 14:19 as the *r'* of those that are slain, *3830
63: 3 and I will stain all my *r'*. 4403
Eze 16:13 thy *r'* was of fine linen, and silk, "
Zec 3: 4 will clothe thee with change of *r'*.*4254
M't 3: 4 John had his *r'* of camel's hair, *1742*
6:25 than meat, and the body than *r'*? "
28 And why take ye thought for *r'*? "
11: 8 for to see? A man clothed in soft *r'*? *2440*
17: 2 and his *r'* was white as the light. * "
27:31 put his own *r'* on him, and led him* "
28: 3 and his *r'* white as snow: *1742*
M'r 9: 3 his *r'* became shining, exceeding *2440*
Lu 7:25 to see? A man clothed in soft *r'*? "
9:29 his *r'* was white and glistering. *2441*
10:30 thieves, which stripped him of his *r'*,* "
12:23 meat, and the body is more than *r'*. *1742*
23:34 they parted his *r'*, and cast lots. *2440*
Joh 19:24 They parted my *r'* among them, * "
Ac 18: 6 he shook his *r'*, and said unto them, *2440*
22:20 kept the *r'* of them that slew him.* "
1Ti 6: 8 And having food and *r'* let us be *4629*
Jas 2: 2 come in also a poor man in vile *r'*; *2066*
Re 3: 5 same shall be clothed in white *r'*; *2440*
18 and white *r'*, that thou mayest be* "
4: 4 elders sitting, clothed in white *r'*;* "
rain See also rainbow; rained.
Ge 2: 5 not caused it to *r'* upon the earth, 4305
7: 4 I will cause it to *r'* upon the earth "
12 the *r'* was upon the earth forty 1653
8: 2 the *r'* from heaven was restrained; "
Ex 9:18 cause it to *r'* a very grievous hail, 4305
33 *r'* was not poured upon the earth. 4306
34 when Pharaoh saw that the *r'* and "
16: 4 will *r'* bread from heaven for you; 4305
Le 26: 4 I will give you *r'* in due season, *1653
De 11:11 drinketh water of the *r'* of heaven: 4306
14 I will give you the *r'* of your land "
14 in his due season, the first *r'* and 4456
14 and the latter *r'*, that thou mayest 3138
17 up the heaven, that there be no *r'*, 4306
28:12 the *r'* unto thy land in his season, "
24 make the *r'* of thy land powder and "
32: 2 My doctrine shall drop as the *r'*, my "
2 the small *r'* upon the tender herb, 8164
1Sa 12:17 and he shall send thunder and *r'*; 4306
18 the Lord sent thunder and *r'* that "
2Sa 1:21 neither let there be *r'*, upon you, "
23: 4 the earth by clear shining after *r'*. "
1Ki 8:35 is shut up, and there is no *r'*, "
36 and give *r'* upon thy land, which "
17: 1 shall not be dew nor *r'* these years, "
7 there had been no *r'* in the land. 1653
14 the Lord sendeth *r'* upon the earth. "
18: 1 and I will send *r'* upon the earth. 4306
41 is a sound of abundance of *r'*. 1653
44 thee down, that the *r'* stop thee not. "
45 and wind, and there was a great *r'*. "
2Ki 3:17 see wind, neither shall ye see *r'*; "
2Ch 6:26 is shut up, and there is no *r'*, 4306
27 send *r'* upon thy land, which thou "
7:13 shut up heaven, that there be no *r'*, "
Ezr 10: 9 of this matter, and for the great *r'*. 1653
13 it is a time of much *r'*, and we are "
Job 5:10 Who giveth *r'* upon the earth, and 4306
20:23 *r'* it upon him while he is eating. 4305
28:26 When he made a decree for the *r'*, 4306
29:23 they waited for me as for the *r'*; "
23 mouth wide as for the latter *r'*. 4456
36:27 they pour down *r'* according to the 4306
37: 6 to the small *r'*, and to the great *r'* 1653
38:26 To cause it to *r'* on the earth, 4305
28 Hath the *r'* a father? or who hath 4306
Ps 11: 6 Upon the wicked he shall *r'* snares, 4305
68: 9 didst send a plentiful *r'*, whereby 1653
72: 6 come down like *r'* upon the mown 4306
84: 6 a well; the *r'* also filleth the pools. 4175
105:32 He gave them hail for *r'*, and 1653
135: 7 he maketh lightnings for the *r'*; 4306
147: 8 who prepareth *r'* for the earth, "
Pr 16:15 favour is as a cloud of the latter *r'*. 4456
25:14 is like clouds and wind without *r'*. 1653
23 The north wind driveth away *r'*: so "
26: 1 and as *r'* in harvest, so honour is 4306
28: 3 sweeping *r'* which leaveth no food. "
Ec 11: 3 If the clouds be full of *r'*, they 1653
12: 2 nor the clouds return after the *r'*: "
Ca 2:11 is past, the *r'* is over and gone; "
Isa 4: 6 a covert from storm and from *r'*. 4306
5: 6 the clouds that they *r'* no 4305
6 clouds that they...no *r'* upon it. 4306
30:23 shall he give the *r'* of thy seed, "
44:14 an ash, and the *r'* doth nourish it. 1653
55:10 For as the *r'* cometh down, and the "
Jer 3: 3 and there hath been no latter *r'*; 4456
5:24 the Lord our God, that giveth *r'*, 1653
10:13 he maketh lightnings with *r'*, and 4306
14: 4 for there was no *r'* in the earth, 1653
22 of the Gentiles that can cause *r'*? "
51:16 he maketh lightnings with *r'*, and 4306
Eze 1:28 is in the cloud in the day of *r'*, 1653
38:22 I will *r'* upon him, and upon his 4305
22 an overflowing *r'*, and great *1653
Ho 6: 3 and he shall come unto us as the *r'*, "
3 as the latter and former *r'* unto the 3384
10:12 and *r'* righteousness upon you. "
Joe 2:23 you the former *r'* moderately, 4175
23 cause to come down for you the *r'*, 1653
23 down for you...the former *r'*, 4175
23 the latter *r'* in the first month. 4456
Am 4: 7 have withholden the *r'* from you, 1653
7 I caused it to *r'* upon one city, 4305
7 it not to *r'* upon another city: "
Zec 10: 1 Ask ye of the Lord *r'* in the time of 4306
1 of the latter *r'*; so the Lord shall 4456
1 and give them showers of *r'*, to 4306
14:17 even upon them shall be no *r'*. "
18 not up, and come not, that have no *r'*;* "
M't 5:45 sendeth *r'* on the just and on the *1026*
7:25, 27 And the *r'* descended, and the *1028*
Ac 14:17 and gave us *r'* from heaven, and *5205*
28: 2 because of the present *r'*, and "
Heb 6: 7 the earth which drinketh in the *r'* "
Jas 5: 7 he receive the early and latter *r'*. "
17 earnestly that it might not *r'*: *1026*
18 again, and the heaven gave *r'*, *5205*
Re 11: 6 it *r'* not in the days of their *1026, 5205*
rainbow
Re 4: 3 was a *r'* round about the throne, *2463*
10: 1 a *r'* was upon his head, and his "
rained
Ge 19:24 *r'* upon Sodom and Gomorrah 4305
Ex 9:23 *r'* hail upon the land of Egypt. "
Ps 78:24 *r'* down manna upon them to eat, "

Ps 78:27 He r' flesh also upon them as dust,4305
Eze 22:24 r' upon in the day of indignation.1656
Am 4: 7 one piece was r' upon, and the 4305
7 whereupon it r' not withered. "
Lu 17:29 r' fire and brimstone from heaven,*1026*
Jas 5:17 r' not on the earth for the space of "

rainy
Pr 27:15 r' day and contentious woman are5464

raise See also RAISED; RAISETH; RAISING.
Ge 38: 8 her, and r' up seed to thy brother. 6965
Ex 23: 1 Thou shalt not r' a false report: *5375
De 18:15 God will r' up unto thee a Prophet6965
18 I will r' them up a Prophet from "
25: 7 to r' up unto his brother a name "
Jos 8:29 r' thereon a great heap of stones,* "
Ru 4: 5, 10 r' up the name of the dead upon "
1Sa 2:35 will r' me up a faithful priest, that "
2Sa 12:11 I will r' up evil against thee out of "
17 him, to r' him up from the earth: "
1Ki 14:14 Lord shall r' him up a king over "
1Ch 17:11 that I will r' up thy seed after thee,*"
Job 3: 8 ready to r' up their mourning. *5782
19:12 and r' up their way against me. *5549
30:12 they r' up against me the ways of* "
Ps 41:10 merciful unto me, and r' me up, 6965
Isa 15: 5 shall r' up a cry of destruction. 5782
29: 3 and I will r' forts against thee. 6965
44:26 and I will r' up the decayed places "
49: 6 servant to r' up the tribes of Jacob, "
58:12 thou shalt r' up the foundation "
61: 4 shall r' up the former desolations, "
Jer 23: 5 r' unto David a righteous Branch, "
30: 9 king, whom I will r' up unto them. "
50: 9 I will r' and cause to come up *5782
32 fall, and none shall r' him up: 6965
51: 1 I will r' up against Babylon, and 5782
Eze 23:22 will r' up thy lovers against thee, "
34:29 I will r' up for them a plant of 6965
Ho 6: 2 in the third day he will r' us up, and"
Joe 3: 7 I will r' them out of the place *5782
Am 5: 2 land; there is none to r' her up. 6965
6:14 I will r' up against you a nation, "
9:11 day will I r' up the tabernacle of "
11 I will r' up his ruins, and I will "
Mic 5: 5 we r' against him seven shepherds, "
Hab 1: 3 that r' up strife and contention. *5375
6 lo, I r' up the Chaldeans, that 6965
Zec 11:16 will r' up a shepherd in the land, "
M't 3: 9 to r' up children unto Abraham. *1453*
10: 8 sick, cleanse the lepers, r' the dead, "
22:24 and r' up seed unto his brother. *450*
M'r 12:19 and r' up seed unto his brother. *1817*
Lu 3: 8 to r' up children unto Abraham. *1453*
20:28 and r' up seed unto his brother. *1817*
Joh 2:19 and in three days I will r' it up. *1453*
6:39 r' it up again at the last day. *450*
40, 44, 54 will r' him up at the last day. "
Ac 2:30 r' up Christ to sit on his throne; * "
3:22 shall the Lord your God r' up unto "
7:37 shall the Lord your God r' up unto "
26: 8 you, that God should r' the dead? *1453*
1Co 6:14 will also r' up us by his own power.*1825*
2Co 4:14 Jesus shall r' up us also by Jesus, *1453*
Heb 11:19 that God was able to r' him up, "
Jas 5:15 sick, and the Lord shall r' him up; "

raised
Ex 9:16 for this cause have I r' thee up, *5975
Jos 5: 7 whom he r' up in their stead, 6965
7:26 r' over him a great heap of stones "
J'g 2:16 Nevertheless the Lord r' up judges, "
18 when the Lord r' them up judges, "
3: 9 r' up a deliverer to the children of "
15 the Lord r' them up a deliverer, "
2Sa 23: 1 the man who was r' up on high, "
1Ki 5:13 Solomon r' a levy out of all Israel;5927
9:15 the levy which king Solomon r'; "
2Ch 32: 5 and r' it up to the towers, and "
33:14 and r' it up a very great height, 1361
Ezr 1: 5 all them whose spirit God had r',*5782
Job 14:12 awake, nor be r' out of their sleep.* "
Ca 8: 5 I r' thee up under the apple tree:* "
Isa 14: 9 r' up from their thrones all the 6965
23:13 they r' up the palaces thereof; *6209
41: 2 Who r' up the righteous man from5782
25 have r' up one from the north, and "
45:13 I have r' him up in righteousness, "
Jer 6:22 a great nation shall be r' from the "
25:32 a great whirlwind shall be r' from "
29:15 The Lord hath r' us up prophets 6965
50:41 many kings shall be r' up from *5782
51:11 the Lord hath r' up the spirit of * "
Da 7: 5 and it r' up itself on one side, 6966
Am 2:11 I r' up of your sons for prophets, 6965
Zec 2:13 is r' up out of his holy habitation.*5782
9:13 and r' up thy sons, O Zion, against* "
M't 1:24 Joseph being r' from sleep did as *1326*
11: 5 the deaf hear, the dead are r' up, *1453*
16:21 and be r' again the third day. "
17:23 the third day he shall be r' again. "
Lu 1:69 r' up an horn of salvation for us "
7:22 the deaf hear, the dead are r', to "
9:22 be slain, and be r' the third day. "
20:37 Now that the dead are r', even "
Joh 12: 1 dead, whom he r' from the dead. "
9 whom he had r' from the dead. "
17 r' him from the dead, bare record. "
Ac 2:24 Whom God hath r' up, having *450*
32 This Jesus hath God r' up, whereof* "
3:15 whom God hath r' from the dead; *1453*
26 God, having r' up his Son Jesus, *450*
4:10 whom God r' from the dead, even *1453*
5:30 God of our fathers r' up Jesus, "
10:40 Him God r' up the third day, and "
12: 7 r' him up, saying, Arise up quickly.* "
13:22 he r' up unto them David to be "
23 r' unto Israel a Saviour, Jesus: *1453*
30 But God r' him from the dead: "
33 in that he hath r' up Jesus again; *450*
34 that he r' him up from the dead, "
37 he, whom God r' again, saw no *1453*
50 r' persecution against Paul and *1892*
17:31 that he hath r' him from the dead. *450*
Ro 4:24 believe on him that r' up Jesus *1453*
25 was r' again for our justification. "
6: 4 as Christ was r' up from the dead "
9 Christ being r' from the dead dieth "
7: 4 to him who is r' from the dead, "
8:11 him that r' up Jesus from the dead"
11 he that r' up Christ from the dead "
9:17 same purpose have I r' thee up, *1825*
10: 9 God hath r' him from the dead, *1453*
1Co 6:14 God hath both r' up the Lord, and "
15:15 of God that he r' up Christ: "
15 whom he r' not up, if so be that the"
16 dead rise not, then is not Christ r': "
17 Christ be not r', your faith is vain; "
35 will say, How are the dead r' up? "
42 corruption, it is r' in incorruption: "
43 sown in dishonour, it is r' in glory: "
43 sown in weakness; it is r' in power: "
44 body; it is r' a spiritual body. "
52 dead shall be r' incorruptible, and "
2Co 4:14 that he which r' up the Lord "
Ga 1: 1 Father, who r' him from the dead;) "
Eph 1:20 when he r' him from the dead, and "
2: 6 hath r' us up together, and made *4891*
Col 2:12 who hath r' him from the dead. *1453*
1Th 1:10 whom he r' from the dead, even "
2Ti 2: 8 seed of David was r' from the dead* "
Heb 11:35 received their dead r' to life again:*386*
1Pe 1:21 God, that r' him up from the dead,*1453*

raiser
Da 11:20 up in his estate a r' of taxes *5674

raiseth
1Sa 2: 8 He r' up the poor out of the dust, 6965
Job 41:25 When he r' up himself, the 7613
Ps 107:25 and r' the stormy wind, which 5975
113: 7 r' up the poor out of the dust, 6965
145:14 r' up all those that be bowed down.2210
146: 8 r' them that are bowed down: "
Joh 5:21 For as the Father r' up the dead, *1453*
2Co 1: 9 but in God which r' the dead: "

raising
Ho 7: 4 from r' after he hath kneaded *5872
Ac 24:12 neither r' up the people, *4160,1999*

raisins
1Sa 25:18 an hundred clusters of r', and two6778
30:12 cake of figs, and two clusters of r': "
2Sa 16: 1 an hundred bunches of r', and an "
1Ch 12:40 cakes of figs, and bunches of r', and"

Rakem (*ra'-kem*)
1Ch 7:16 and his sons were Ulam and R'. 7552

Rakkath (*rak'-kath*)
Jos 19:35 Hammath, R', and Chinnereth, 7557

Rakkon (*rak'-kon*)
Jos 19:46 And Me-jarkon, and R', with the 7542

ram See also RAM; RAM'S; RAMS.
Ge 15: 9 and a r' of three years old, and a 352
22:13 r' caught in a thicket by his horns: "
13 Abraham went and took the r', and "
Ex 29:15 Thou shalt also take one r'; and "
15 their hands upon the head of the r'. "
16 And thou shalt slay the r', and thou "
17 thou shalt cut the r' in pieces, and "
18 burn the whole r' upon the altar: "
19 And thou shalt take the other r'; "
19 their hands upon the head of the r'. "
20 Then shalt thou kill the r', and take "
22 thou shalt take of the r' the fat and "
22 for it is a r' of consecration: "
26 of the r' of Aaron's consecration, "
27 of the r' of the consecration, even of "
31 shalt take the r' of the consecration, "
32 his sons shall eat the flesh of the r', "
Le 5:15 unto the Lord a r' without blemish "
16 with the r' of the trespass offering, "
18 he shall bring a r' without blemish "
6: 6 r' without blemish out of the flock, "
8:18 the r' for the burnt offering: "
18 their hands upon the head of the r'. "
20 And he cut the r' into pieces; and "
21 burnt the whole r' upon the altar: "
22 the other r', the r' of consecration: "
22 their hands upon the head of the r'. "
29 the r' of consecration it was Moses' "
9: 2 a r' for a burnt offering, without "
4 bullock and a r' for peace offerings, "
18 bullock and the r' for a sacrifice of "
19 the fat of the bullock and of the r', "
16: 3 and a r' for a burnt offering. "
5 and one r' for a burnt offering. "
19:21 even a r' for a trespass offering. "
22 with the r' of the trespass offering "
Nu 5: 8 the r' of the atonement, whereby an "
6:14 one r' without blemish for peace "
17 he shall offer the r' for a sacrifice of "
19 take the sodden shoulder of the r', "
7:15, 21, 27, 33, 39, 45, 51, 57, 63, 69, 75, 81
One young bullock, one r', one "
15: 6 Or for a r', thou shalt prepare for a "
11 or for one r', or for a lamb, or a kid. "
23: 2 on every altar a bullock and a r'. "
4 upon every altar a bullock and a r'. "
14, 30 a bullock and a r' on every altar. "
28:11 two young bullocks, and one r', "
12 mingled with oil, for one r'; "
14 the third part of an hin unto a r', "
Nu 28:19 two young bullocks, and one r', and352
20 bullock, and two tenth deals for a r'; "
27 two young bullocks, one r', seven "
28 bullock, two tenth deals unto one r', "
29: 2 one young bullock, one r', and seven "
3 bullock, and two tenth deals for a r', "
8 one young bullock, one r', and seven "
9 and two tenth deals to one r', "
14 two tenth deals to each r' of the two "
36 one bullock, one r', seven lambs of "
37 offerings for the bullock, for the r', "
Ezr 10:19 a r' of the flock for their trespass. "
Eze 43:23 a r' out of the flock without blemish. "
25 and a r' out of the flock, without "
45:24 and an ephah for a r', and an hin of "
46: 4 blemish, and a r' without blemish. "
5 offering shall be an ephah for a r', "
6 blemish, and six lambs, and a r': "
7 an ephah for a r', and for the lambs "
11 an ephah to a r', and to the lambs "
Da 8: 3 the river a r' which had two horns: "
4 I saw the r' pushing westward, and "
6 came to the r' that had two horns, "
7 I saw him come close unto the r', "
7 and smote the r', and brake his two "
7 and there was no power in the r' to "
7 could deliver the r' out of his hand. "
20 The r' which thou sawest having "

Ram (*ram*)
Ru 4:19 Hezron begat R', and R' begat 7410
1Ch 2: 9 Jerahmeel, and R', and Chelubai. "
10 And R' begat Amminadab; and "
25 of Hezron were, R' the firstborn, "
27 And the sons of R' the firstborn "
Job 32: 2 the Buzite, of the kindred of R': "

Rama (*ra'-mah*) See also RAMAH.
M't 2:18 In R' was there a voice heard, *4471*

Ramah (*ra'-mah*) See also RAMA; RAMATH.
Jos 18:25 Gibeon, and R', and Beeroth, 7414
19:29 And then the coast turneth to R', "
36 And Adamah, and R', and Hazor, "
J'g 4: 5 between R' and Beth-el in mount "
19:13 lodge all night, in Gibeah, or in R'. "
1Sa 1:19 and came to their house to R': and "
2:11 Elkanah went to R' to his house. "
7:17 And his return was to R'; for there "
8: 4 and came to Samuel unto R', "
15:34 Then Samuel went to R'; and Saul "
16:13 So Samuel rose up, and went to R'. "
19:18 came to Samuel to R', and told him "
19 Behold, David is at Naioth in R'. "
22 Then went he also to R', and came "
22 Behold, they be at Naioth in R'. "
23 he went thither to Naioth in R': and "
23 until he came to Naioth in R'. "
20: 1 David fled from Naioth in R', and "
22: 6 abode in Gibeah under a tree in R', "
25: 1 and buried him in his house at R'. "
28: 3 buried him in R', even in his own "
1Ki 15:17 up against Judah, and built R', "
21 that he left off building of R', and "
22 and they took away the stones of R', "
2Ki 8:29 the Syrians had given him at R', "
2Ch 16: 1 up against Judah, and built R', to "
5 he left off building of R', and let his "
6 they carried away the stones of R', "
22: 6 wounds which were given him at R', "
Ezr 2:26 The children of R' and Gaba, six "
Ne 7:30 men of R' and Gaba, six hundred "
11:33 Hazor, R', Gittaim, "
Isa 10:29 R' is afraid; Gibeah of Saul is fled. "
Jer 31:15 the Lord; A voice was heard in R', "
40: 1 the guard had let him go from R', "
Ho 5: 8 in Gibeah, and the trumpet in R': "

Ramath (*ra'-math*) See also RAMAH; RAMATHAIM-ZOPHIM; RAMATHITE; RAMATH-LEHI; RAMATH-MIZPEH; RAMOTH-GILEAD.
Jos 19: 8 to Baalath-beer, R' of the south. *7418

Ramathaim-zophim (*ram-a-tha''-im-zo'-fim*)
1Sa 1: 1 there was a certain man of R', of 7436

Ramathite (*ra'-math-ite*)
1Ch 27:27 the vineyards was Shimei the R': 7435

Ramath-lehi (*ra''-math-le'-hi*)
J'g 15:17 his hand, and called that place R'.7437

Ramath-mizpeh (*ra''-math-miz'-peh*)
Jos 13:26 And from Heshbon unto R', and 7434

Rameses (*ram'-e-seze*) See also RAAMSES.
Ge 47:11 best of the land, in the land of R', 7486
Ex 12:37 journeyed from R' to Succoth, "
Nu 33: 3 And they departed from R' in the "
5 children of Israel removed from R', "

Ramiah (*ra-mi'-ah*)
Ezr 10:25 sons of Parosh; R', and Jeziah, 7422

Ramoth (*ra'-moth*) See also JARMUTH; RAMAH; RAMOTH-GILEAD; REMETH.
De 4:43 and R' in Gilead, of the Gadites; 7216
Jos 20: 8 R' in Gilead out of the tribe of Gad, "
21:38 R' in Gilead with her suburbs, to be "
1Sa 30:27 to them which were in south R', 7418
1Ki 22: 3 Know ye that R' in Gilead is ours,*7216
1Ch 6:73 And R' with her suburbs, and Anem "
80 R' in Gilead with her suburbs, and "
Ezr 10:29 Adaiah, Jashub, and Sheal, and R'.*3406

Ramoth-gilead (*ra''-moth-ghil'-e-ad*)
1Ki 4:13 The son of Geber, in R'; to him 7433
22: 4 thou go with me to battle to R'? "
6 Shall I go against R' to battle, or "
12 saying, Go up to R', and prosper: "
15 shall we go against R' to battle, or "
20 that he may go up and fall at R'? "
29 the king of Judah went up to R'. "

2Ki 8:28 against Hazael king of Syria in R': 7433
9: 1 of oil in thine hand, and go to R': "
4 young man the prophet, went to R'. "
14 (Now Joram had kept R', he and all "
2Ch 18: 2 him to go up with him to R'. "
3 Judah, Wilt thou go with me to R'? "
5 Shall we go to R' to battle, or shall "
11 saying, Go up to R', and prosper: "
14 shall we go to R' to battle, or shall "
19 that he may go up and fall at R'? "
28 the king of Judah went up to R'. "
22: 5 against Hazael king of Syria at R': "

rampart
La 2: 8 the r' and the wall to lament; 2426
Na 3: 8 whose r' was the sea, and her wall "

ram's
Jos 6: 5 make a long blast with the r' horn, 3104

rams See also RAMS'.
Ge 31:10 r' which leaped upon the cattle *6260
12 r' which leap upon the cattle * "
38 and the r' of the flock have I not 352
32:14 two hundred ewes, and twenty r', "
Ex 29: 1 and two r' without blemish, "
3 with the bullock, and the two r'. "
35:23 red skins of r', and badgers' skins,* "
Le 8: 2 for the sin offering, and two r', "
23:18 and one young bullock, and two r': "
Nu 7:17, 23, 29, 35, 41, 47, 53, 59, 65, 71, 77,
83 five r', five he goats, five lambs of "
87 were twelve bullocks, the r' twelve, "
88 and four bullocks, the r' sixty, "
23: 1 me here seven oxen and seven r'. "
29 here seven bullocks and seven r'. "
29:13 thirteen young bullocks, two r', and "
14 deals to each ram of the two r', "
17 offer twelve young bullocks, two r', "
18 offerings for the bullocks, for the r', "
20 third day eleven bullocks, two r', "
21 offerings for the bullocks, for the r', "
23 the fourth day ten bullocks, two r', "
24 offerings for the bullocks, for the r', "
26 the fifth day nine bullocks, two r', "
27 offerings for the bullocks, for the r', "
29 eight bullocks, two r', and fourteen "
30 offerings for the bullocks, for the r', "
32 seven bullocks, two r', and fourteen "
33 offerings for the bullocks, for the r', "
De 32:14 and r' of the breed of Bashan, and "
1Sa 15:22 and to hearken than the fat of r'. "
2Ki 3: 4 an hundred thousand r', with the "
1Ch 15:26 offered seven bullocks and seven r'. "
29:21 a thousand bullocks, a thousand r', "
2Ch 13: 9 with a young bullock and seven r' "
17:11 thousand and seven hundred r', "
29:21 brought seven bullocks, and seven r', "
22 when they had killed the r', they "
32 an hundred r', and two hundred "
Ezr 6: 9 of, both young bullocks, and r', 1798
17 two hundred r', four hundred "
7:17 with this money bullocks, r', "
8:35 ninety and six r', seventy and 352
Job 42: 8 now seven bullocks and seven r', "
Ps 66:15 of fatlings, with the incense of r'; "
114: 4 The mountains skipped like r', and "
6 mountains, that ye skipped like r'; "
Isa 1:11 am full of the burnt offerings of r', "
34: 6 with the fat of the kidneys of r': "
60: 7 the r' of Nebaioth shall minister "
Jer 51:40 slaughter, like r' with he goats. "
Eze 4: 2 set battering r' against it round 3733
21:22 battering r' against the gates, "
27:21 occupied with thee in lambs, and r', 352
34:17 between the r' and the he goats. "
39:18 of r', of lambs, and of goats, of "
45:23 and seven r' without blemish daily "
Mic 6: 7 be pleased with thousands of r', "

rams'
Ex 25: 5 And r' skins dyed red, and badgers' 352
26:14 for the tent of r' skins dyed red, "
35: 7 And r' skins dyed red, and badgers' "
36:19 for the tent of r' skins dyed red, "
39:34 the covering of r' skins dyed red, "
Jos 6: 4 ark seven trumpets of r' horns: 3104
6 bear seven trumpets of r' horns "
8 the seven trumpets of r' horns "
13 bearing seven trumpets of r' horns "

ran See also OVERRAN.
Ge 18: 2 he r' to meet them from the tent 7323
7 Abraham r' unto the herd, and "
24:17 And the servants r' to meet her, "
20 and r' again unto the well to draw "
28 the damsel r', and told them of her "
29 Laban r' out unto the man, unto "
29:12 son: and she r' and told her father. "
13 son, that he r' to meet him, and "
33: 4 Esau r' to meet him, and embraced "
Ex 9:23 the fire r' along upon the ground; 1980
Nu 11:27 there r' a young man, and told 7323
16:47 and r' into the midst of the "
Jos 7:22 and they r' unto the tent; and, "
8:19 they r' as soon as he had stretched "
J'g 7:21 and all the host r', and cried, and "
9:44 other companies r' upon all the *6584
13:10 the woman made haste, and r', 7323
1Sa 3: 5 And he r' unto Eli, and said, Here "
4:12 And there r' a man of Benjamin "
10:23 they r' and fetched him thence: and "
17:22 and r' into the army, and came and "
48 and r' toward the army to meet the "
51 Therefore David r', and stood upon "
20:36 And as the lad r', he shot an arrow "
2Sa 18:21 bowed himself unto Joab, and r'. "
23 Ahimaaz r' by the way of the plain, "
1Ki 2:39 of the servants of Shimei r' away 1272
1Ki 18:35 the water r' round about the altar; 7323
46 r' before Ahab to the entrance of "
19:20 left the oxen, and r' after Elijah, "
22:35 the blood r' out of the wound into 3332
2Ch 32: 4 the brook that r' through the *7857
Ps 77: 2 my sore r' in the night, and *5064
105:41 r' in the dry places like a river. 1980
133: 2 that r' down upon the beard, even 3331
Jer 23:21 sent these prophets, yet they r': 7323
Eze 1:14 living creatures r' and returned 7519
47: 2 r' out waters on the right side. 6379
Da 8: 6 r' unto him in the fury of his 7323
M't 8:32 swine r' violently down a steep *3729
27:48 straightway one of them r', and 5143
M'r 5: 6 afar off, he r' and worshipped him, "
13 r' violently down a steep place *3729
6:33 r' afoot thither out of all cities, 4936
55 And r' through that whole region 4063
15:36 one r' and filled a spunge full of 5143
Lu 8:33 herd r' violently down a steep *3729
15:20 r', and fell on his neck, and kissed 5143
19: 4 he r' before, and climbed up into 4390
24:12 Peter, and r' unto the sepulchre; 5143
Joh 20: 4 So they r' both together: and the "
Ac 3:11 people r' together unto them in 4936
7:57 and r' upon him with one accord,*3729
8:30 And Philip r' thither to him, and 4370
12:14 the gate for gladness, but r' in, 1532
14:14 r' in among the people, crying out,*1530
21:30 and the people r' together: and 4890
32 centurions, and r' down unto them: 2701
27:41 they r' the ship aground; and the 2027
Jude 11 and r' greedily after the error of 1632

rang
1Sa 4: 5 shout, so that the earth r' again. 1949
1Ki 1:45 rejoicing, so that the city r' again. "

range See also RANGING; RANGES.
Job 39: 8 The r' of the mountains is his 3491

ranges
Le 11:35 whether it be oven, or r' for pots, *3600
2Ki 11: 8 he that cometh within the r', let *7713
15 Have her forth without the r': and* "
2Ch 23:14 Have her forth of the r': and * "

ranging
Pr 28:15 As a roaring lion, and a r' bear; 8264

rank See also RANKS.
Ge 41: 5 up upon one stalk, r' and good. 1277
7 devoured the seven r' and full ears. "
Nu 2:16 they shall set forth in the second r'.* "
24 they shall go forward in the third r'.* "
1Ch 12:33 thousand, which could keep r': *5737
38 men of war, that could keep r', *4634

ranks
1Ki 7: 4, 5 was against light in three r'. 6471
Joe 2: 7 and they shall not break their r': 734
M'r 6:40 And they sat down in r', by 4237

ransom See also RANSOMED.
Ex 21:30 the r' of his life whatsoever is *6306
30:12 give every man a r' for his soul 3724
Job 33:24 down to the pit: I have found a r'. "
36:18 then a great r' cannot deliver thee. "
Ps 49: 7 nor give to God a r' for him: "
Pr 6:35 He will not regard any r'; neither "
13: 8 The r' of a man's life are his riches: "
21:18 The wicked shall be a r' for the "
Isa 43: 3 I gave Egypt for thy r', Ethiopia "
Ho 13:14 I will r' them from the power of 6299
M't 20:28 and to give his life a r' for many. 3083
M'r 10:45 and to give his life a r' for many. "
1Ti 2: 6 Who gave himself a r' for all, to be 487

ransomed
Isa 35:10 the r' of the Lord shall return, 6299
51:10 sea a way for the r' to pass over? *1350
Jer 31:11 r' him from the hand of him that * "

Rapha (ra'-fah) See also BETH-RAPHA; REPHAIAH.
1Ch 8: 2 Nohah the fourth, and R' the fifth. 7498
37 R' was his son, Eleasah his son, * "

Raphu (ra'-fu)
Nu 13: 9 of Benjamin, Palti the son of R'. 7505

rare
Da 2:11 a r' thing that the king requireth, 3358

rase
Ps 137: 7 R' it, r' it, even to the foundation 6168

rash
Ec 5: 2 Be not r' with thy mouth, and let 926
Isa 32: 4 r' shall understand knowledge, 4116

rashly
Ac 19:36 to be quiet, and to do nothing r'. *4312

rasor
Nu 6: 5 shall no r' come upon his head: 8593
J'g 13: 5 and no r' shall come on his head: 4177
16:17 hath not come a r' upon mine head; "
1Sa 1:11 shall no r' come upon his head. "
Ps 52: 2 like a sharp r', working deceitfully. 8593
Isa 7:20 Lord shave with a r' that is hired, "
Eze 5: 1 take thee a barber's r', and cause it "

rate
Ex 16: 4 and gather a certain r' every day, *1697
1Ki 10:25 horses, and mules, a r' year by year. "
2Ki 25:30 of the king, a daily r' for every day, * "
2Ch 8:13 Even after a certain r' every day, * "
9:24 horses, and mules, a r' year by year. "

rather
Jos 22:24 have not r' done it for fear of this
2Sa 10: 3 hath not David r' sent his servants*
2Ki 5:13 how much r' then, when he saith to
Job 7:15 strangling, and death r' than my life,
32: 2 he justified himself r' than God.
Job 36:21 hast thou chosen r' than affliction.
Ps 52: 3 lying r' than to speak righteousness.
84:10 I had r' be a doorkeeper in the 977
Pr 8:10 and knowledge r' than choice gold. 408
16:16 understanding r' to be chosen than
17:12 a man, r' than a fool in his folly. 408
22: 1 A good name is r' to be chosen than
1 loving favour r' than silver and gold.
M't 10: 6 But go r' to the lost sheep of the 3123
28 r' fear him which is able to destroy "
18: 8 r' than having two hands or two 2228
9 r' than having two eyes to be cast "
25: 9 go ye r' to them that sell, and buy 3123
27:24 but that r' a tumult was made, he "
M'r 5:26 nothing bettered, but r' grew worse, "
15:11 should r' release Barabbas unto "
Lu 10:20 but r' rejoice, because your names "
11:28 Yea r', blessed are they that hear 3304
41 r' give alms of such things as ye *4133
12:31 But r' seek ye the kingdom of God;* "
51 I tell you, Nay; but r' division: 2228
17: 8 And will not r' say unto him, Make
18:14 to his house justified r' than the other:
Joh 3:19 men loved darkness r' than light, 3123
Ac 5:29 We ought to obey God r' than men. "
Ro 3: 8 And not r', (as we be slanderously*
8:34 died, yea r', that is risen again, 3123
11:11 r' through their fall salvation is come*
12:19 but r' give place unto wrath: for *
14:13 but judge this r', that no man put 3123
1Co 5: 2 puffed up, and have not r' mourned, "
6: 7 Why do ye not r' take wrong? why "
7 r' suffer yourselves to be defrauded? "
7:21 thou mayest be made free, use it r'. "
9:12 this power over you, are not we r'? "
14: 1 gifts, but r' that ye may prophesy. "
5 tongues, but r' that ye prophesied: "
19 I had r' speak five words with my 2309
2Co 2: 7 ye ought r' to forgive him, and 3123
3: 8 of the spirit be r' glorious? "
5: 8 r' to be absent from the body, and "
12: 9 will I r' glory in my infirmities, "
Ga 4: 9 known God, or r' are known of God, "
Eph 4:28 but r' let him labour, working with "
5: 4 convenient: but r' giving of thanks. "
11 of darkness, but r' reprove them. "
Ph'p 1:12 fallen out r' unto the furtherance of "
1Ti 1: 4 r' than godly edifying which is in "
4: 7 exercise thyself r' unto godliness.*
6: 2 but r' do them service, because 3123
Ph'm 9 Yet for love's sake I r' beseech thee, "
Heb 11:25 Choosing r' to suffer affliction with "
12: 9 r' be in subjection unto the Father "
13 of the way; but let it r' be healed. "
13:19 But I beseech you the r' to do this,*4056
2Pe 1:10 Wherefore the r', brethren, give *3123

rattleth
Job 39:23 The quiver r' against him, the 7439

rattling
Na 3: 2 the noise of the r' of the wheels, 7494

raven See also RAVENING; RAVENS; RAVIN.
Ge 8: 7 And he sent forth a r', which went *6158
Le 11:15 Every r' after his kind; "
De 14:14 And every r' after his kind, "
Job 38:41 Who provideth for the r' his food? "
Ca 5:11 locks are bushy, and black as a r'. "
Isa 34:11 owl also and the r' shall dwell in it: "

ravens
1Ki 17: 4 the r' to feed thee there. 6158
6 the r' brought him bread and flesh "
Ps 147: 9 food, and to the young r' which cry. "
Pr 30:17 the r' of the valley shall pick it out, "
Lu 12:24 Consider the r': for they neither 2876

ravening
Ps 22:13 mouths, as a r' and a roaring lion. 2963
Eze 22:25 like a roaring lion r' the prey; they "
27 are like wolves r' the prey, to shed "
M't 7:15 but inwardly they are r' wolves. 727
Lu 11:39 part is full of r' and wickedness. * 724

ravenous
Isa 35: 9 there, nor any r' beast shall go up 6530
46:11 Calling a r' bird from the east, the 5861
Eze 39: 4 give thee unto the r' birds of every "

ravin See also RAVENING.
Ge 49:27 Benjamin shall r' as a wolf: in the *2963
Na 2:12 with prey, and his dens with r'. 2966

ravished
Pr 5:19 be thou r' always with her love. 7686
20 son, be r' with a strange woman, "
Ca 4: 9 Thou hast r' my heart, my sister, 3823
9 thou hast r' my heart with one of "
Isa 13:16 shall be spoiled, and their wives r'. 7693
La 5:11 They r' the women in Zion, and 6031
Zec 14: 2 houses rifled, and the women r'; 7693

raw
Ex 12: 9 Eat not of it r', nor sodden at all 4995
Le 13:10 be quick r' flesh in the rising; 2416
14 But when r' flesh appeareth in him, "
15 the priest shall see the r' flesh, and "
15 for the r' flesh is unclean: it is a "
16 Or if the r' flesh turn again, and be "
1Sa 2:15 have sodden flesh of thee, but r'. "

raze See RASE.

razor See RASOR.

reach See also REACHED; REACHETH; REACHING.
Ge 11: 4 tower, whose top may r' unto heaven; "
Ex 26:28 boards shall r' from end to end. *1272
28:42 even unto the thighs shall they r': 1961
Le 26: 5 threshing shall r' unto the vintage, 5381
5 vintage shall r' unto...sowing time: "
Nu 34:11 shall r' unto the side of the sea of 4229
35: 4 shall r' from the wall of the city and*

Job 20: 6 and his head r· unto the clouds; 5060
Isa 8: 8 over, he shall r· even to the neck; "
Jer 48:32 they r· even to the sea of Jazer: the*"
Zec 14: 5 the mountains shall r· unto Azal: "
Joh 20:27 R· hither thy finger, and behold 5342
27 r· hither thy hand, and thrust it "
2Co 10:13 us, a measure to r· even unto you. 2185

reached
Ge 28:12 and the top of it r· to heaven: and 5060
Jos 19:11 Maralah, and r· to Dabbasheth, 6293
11 r· to the river...before Jokneam; "
Ru 2:14 and he r· her parched corn, and 6642
Da 4:11 the height thereof r· unto heaven, 4291
20 whose height r· unto the heaven, "
2Co 10:14 as though we r· not unto you: for 2185
Re 18: 5 For her sins have r· unto heaven, 190

reacheth
Nu 21:30 unto Nophah, which r· unto Medeba.
Jos 19:22 And the coast r· to Tabor, and *6293
26 and r· to Carmel westward, and to* "
27 and r· to Zebulun, and to the valley*"
34 and r· to Zebulun on the south side,*"
34 and r· to Asher on the west side, * "
2Ch 28: 9 in a rage that r· up unto heaven. *5060
Ps 36: 5 thy faithfulness r· unto the clouds.
108: 4 and thy truth r· unto the clouds.
Pr 31:20 r· forth her hands to the needy. 7971
Jer 4:10 the sword r· unto the soul. 5060
18 because it r· unto thine heart. "
51: 9 for her judgment r· unto heaven, "
Da 4:22 is grown, and r· unto heaven, 4291

reaching
2Ch 3:11 cubits, r· to the wall of the house: 5060
11 r· to the wing of the other cherub. "
12 cubits, r· to the wall of the house: "
Ph'p 3:13 r· forth unto those things which *1901

read See READEST; READETH; READING.
Ex 24: 7 r· in the audience of the people: 7121
De 17:19 r· therein all the days of his life: "
31:11 shalt r· this law before all Israel "
Jos 8:34 he r· all the words of the law, "
35 which Joshua r· not before all the "
2Ki 5: 7 the king of Israel had r· the letter, "
19:14 hand of the messengers, and r· it: "
22: 8 the book to Shaphan, and he r· it. "
10 And Shaphan r· it before the king. "
16 which the king of Judah hath r·: "
23: 2 he r· in their ears all the words of "
2Ch 34:18 And Shaphan r· it before the king. "
24 have r· before the king of Judah: "
30 he r· in their ears all the words of "
Ezr 4:18 hath been plainly r· before me. 7123
23 Artaxerxes' letter was r· before "
Ne 8: 3 And he r· therein before the street 7121
8 they r· in the book in the law of God "
18 he r· in the book of the law of God. "
9: 3 r· in the book of the law of the Lord "
13: 1 day they r· in the book of Moses "
Es 6: 1 and they were r· before the king. "
Isa 29:11, 12 R· this, I pray thee: and he saith, "
34:16 out of the book of the Lord, and r·: "
37:14 hand of the messengers, and r· it: "
Jer 29:29 Zephaniah the priest r· this letter "
36: 6 Therefore go thou, and r· in the roll, "
6 shalt r· them in the ears of all Judah "
10 r· Baruch in the book the words of "
13 when Baruch r· the book in the ears "
14 roll wherein thou hast r· in the ears "
15 Sit down now, and r· it in our ears. "
15 ears. So Baruch r· it in our ears. "
21 Jehudi r· it in the ears of the king, "
23 Jehudi had r· three or four leaves, "
51:61 see, and shalt r· all these words; "
Da 5: 7 Whosoever shall r· this writing, 7123
8 but they could not r· the writing, "
15 that they should r· this writing, "
16 now if thou canst r· the writing, and "
17 I will r· the writing unto the king, "
M't 12: 3 Have ye not r· what David did, 314
5 Or have ye not r· in the law, how "
19: 4 Have ye not r·, that he which made "
21:16 have ye never r·, Out of the mouth "
42 Did ye never r· in the scriptures, "
22:31 have ye not r· that which was spoken "
M'r 2:25 Have ye never r· what David did, "
12:10 And have ye not r· this scripture; "
26 have ye not r· in the book of Moses, "
Lu 4:16 sabbath day, and stood up for to r·. "
6: 3 Have ye not r· so much as this, what "
Joh 19:20 This title then r· many of the Jews: "
Ac 8:28 in his chariot r· Esaias the prophet.* "
30 heard him r· the prophet Esaias, * "
32 the scripture which he r· was this,* "
13:27 prophets which are r· every sabbath "
15:21 being r· in the synagogues every "
31 when they had r·, they rejoiced "
23:34 when the governor had r· the letter, "
2Co 1:13 than what ye r· or acknowledge; "
3: 2 our hearts, known and r· of all men: "
15 even unto this day, when Moses is r·, "
Eph 3: 4 when ye r·, ye may understand my "
Col 4:16 when this epistle is r· among you, "
16 that it be r· also in the church of the "
16 r· the epistle from Laodicea. "
1Th 5:27 be r· unto all the holy brethren. "
Re 5: 4 worthy to open and to r· the book,* "

readest
Lu 10:26 is written in the law? how r· thou? 314
Ac 8:30 Understandest thou what thou r·? "

readeth
Hab 2: 2 tables, that he may run that r· it. 7121
M't 24:15 (whoso r·, let him understand:) 314
M'r 13:14 (let him that r· understand,) then "
Re 1: 3 Blessed is he that r·, and they that "

readiness
Ac 17:11 received the word with all r· of 4288
2Co 8:11 that as there was a r· to will, so "
10: 6 a r· to revenge all disobedience, 2092

reading
Ne 8: 8 caused them to understand the r·. 4744
Jer 36: 8 r· in the book...words of the Lord 7121
51:63 hast made an end of r· this book, "
Ac 13:15 the r· of the law and the prophets 320
2Co 3:14 away in the r· of the old testament; "
1Ti 4:13 Till I come, give attendance to r·, "

ready See also ALREADY.
Ge 18: 6 Make r· quickly three measures 4116
43:16 men home, and slay, and make r·; 3559
25 made r· the present against Joseph "
46:29 And Joseph made r· his chariot, 631
Ex 14: 6 he made r· his chariot, and took "
17: 4 they be almost r· to stone me. 5750
19:11 And be r· against the third day: 3559
15 people, Be r· against the third day: "
34: 2 And be r· in the morning, and come "
Nu 32:17 But we ourselves will go r· armed 2363
De 1:41 ye were r· to go up into the hill. *1951
26: 5 Syrian r· to perish was my father,
Jos 8: 4 far from the city, but be ye all r·: 3559
J'g 6:19 Gideon went in, and made r· a kid,
13:15 we shall have made r· a kid for thee.
1Sa 25:18 and five sheep r· dressed, and five
2Sa 15:15 thy servants are r· to do whatsoever
18:22 that thou hast no tidings r·? *4672
1Ki 6: 7 was built of stone made r· before 8003
2Ki 9:21 And Joram said, Make r·. 631
21 And his chariot was made r·.
1Ch 12:23 bands that were r· armed to the war,*
24 eight hundred, r· armed to the war.*
28: 2 and had made r· for the building: 3559
2Ch 17:18 thousand r· prepared for the war.
35:14 they made r· for themselves, *3559
Ezr 7: 6 a r· scribe in the law of Moses, 4106
Ne 9:17 but thou art a God r· to pardon,
Es 3:14 they should be r· against that day. 6264
8:13 Jews should be r· against that day "
Job 3: 8 are r· to raise up their mourning. "
12: 5 He that is r· to slip with his feet 3559
15:23 day of darkness is r· at his hand. "
24 him, as a king r· to the battle. 6264
28 which are r· to become heaps. 6257
17: 1 are extinct, the graves are r· for me.
18:12 destruction shall be r· at his side. 3559
29:13 blessing of him that was r· to perish
32:19 it is r· to burst like new bottles.
Ps 7:12 hath bent his bow, and made it r·. 3559
11: 2 make r· their arrow upon the string, "
21:12 thou shalt make r· thine arrows "
38:17 I am r· to halt, and my sorrow is "
45: 1 tongue is the pen of a r· writer. 4106
86: 5 Lord, art good, and r· to forgive;
88:15 and r· to die from my youth up:
Pr 24:11 and those that are r· to be slain; 4131
31: 6 drink unto him that is r· to perish,
Ec 5: 1 be more r· to hear, than to give *7138
Isa 27:13 r· to perish in the land of Assyria,
30:13 shall be to you as a breach r· to fall,
32: 4 shall be r· to speak plainly. 4116
38:20 The Lord was r· to save me: therefore
41: 7 saying, It is r· for the sodering: 2896
51:13 as if he were r· to destroy? and 3559
Eze 7:14 the trumpet, even to make all r·; "
Da 3:15 if ye be r· that at what time ye 6263
Ho 7: 6 made r· their heart like an oven, 7126
M't 22: 4 are killed, and all things are r·: 2092
8 The wedding is r·, but they which "
24:44 Therefore be ye also r·: for in such "
25:10 they that were r· went in with him "
26:19 and they made r· the passover. 2090
M'r 14:15 prepared: there make r· for us. "
16 and they made r· the passover. "
38 The spirit truly is r·, but the flesh*4289
Lu 1:17 r· a people prepared for the Lord. 2090
7: 2 unto him, was sick, and r· to die. *3195
9:52 Samaritans, to make r· for him. 2090
12:40 Be ye therefore r· also: for the 2092
14:17 Come; for all things are now r·. "
17: 8 Make r· wherewith I may sup, 2090
22:12 room furnished: there make r·. "
13 and they made r· the passover. "
33 Lord, I am r· to go with thee, both*2092
Joh 7: 6 come: but your time is alway r·. "
Ac 10:10 they made r·, he fell into a trance. 3903
20: 7 r· to depart on the morrow; and 3195
21:13 I am r· not to be bound only, but 2093
23:15 he come near, are r· to kill him. 2092
21 now are they r·, looking for a "
23 Make r· two hundred soldiers to 2090
Ro 1:15 am r· to preach the gospel to you 4289
2Co 8:19 and declaration of your r· mind: *4288
9: 2 Achaia was r· a year ago; and *3903
3 that, as I said, ye may be r·: * "
5 that the same might be r·, as a 2092
10:16 line of things made r· to our hand. "
12:14 third time I am r· to come to you; 2093
1Ti 6:18 in good works, r· to distribute, 2130
2Ti 4: 6 For I am now r· to be offered, and*4689
Tit 3: 1 to be r· to every good work, 2092
Heb 8:13 waxeth old is r· to vanish away. 1451
1Pe 1: 5 r· to be revealed in the last time. 2092
3:15 and be r· always to give an answer "
4: 5 r· to judge the quick and the dead. 2093
5: 2 for filthy lucre, but of a r· mind; 4289
Re 3: 2 which remain, that are r· to die: 3195
12: 4 the woman...r· to be delivered, * "
19: 7 and his wife hath made herself r·. 2090

Reaia (re-ah'-yah) See also HAROEH; REAIAH.
1Ch 5: 5 Micah his son, R· his son, Baal his*7211

Reaiah (re-ah'-yah) See also REAIA.
1Ch 4: 2 And R· the son of Shobal begat 7211
Ezr 2:47 of Gahar, the children of R·, "
Ne 7:50 The children of R·, the children of "

realm
2Ch 20:30 the r· of Jehoshaphat was quiet: 4438
Ezr 7:13 his priests and Levites, in my r·, 4437
23 wrath against the r· of the king "
Da 1:20 astrologers that were in all his r·. 4438
6: 3 to set him over the whole r·. 4437
9: 1 king over the r· of the Chaldeans; 4438
11: 2 stir up all against the r· of Grecia. "

reap See also REAPED; REAPEST; REAPETH; REAPING.
Le 19: 9 ye r· the harvest of your land, 7114
9 shalt not wholly r· the corners of
23:10 and shall r· the harvest thereof, 7114
22 ye r· the harvest of your land, "
25: 5 of thy harvest thou shalt not r·, "
11 neither r· that which groweth of "
Ru 2: 9 eyes be on the field that they do r·, "
1Sa 8:12 his ground, and to r· his harvest, "
2Ki 19:29 in the third year sow ye, and r·, "
Job 4: 8 and sow wickedness, r· the same. "
24: 6 r· every one his corn in the field: "
Ps 126: 5 that sow in tears shall r· in joy. "
Pr 22: 8 soweth iniquity shall r· vanity: "
Ec 11: 4 regardeth the clouds shall not r·. "
Isa 37:30 in the third year sow ye, and r·, "
Jer 12:13 sown wheat, but shall r· thorns: * "
Ho 8: 7 and they shall r· the whirlwind: "
10:12 in righteousness, r· in mercy; "
Mic 6:15 shalt sow, but thou shalt not r·; "
M't 6:26 neither do they r·, nor gather 2325
25:26 I r· where I sowed not, and gather "
Lu 12:24 ravens: for they neither sow nor r·; "
Joh 4:38 to r· that whereon ye bestowed no "
1Co 9:11 if we shall r· your carnal things? "
2Co 9: 6 sparingly shall r· also sparingly; "
6 bountifully shall r·...bountifully. "
Ga 6: 7 man soweth, that shall he also r·. "
8 shall of the flesh r· corruption; "
8 of the Spirit r· life everlasting. "
9 for in due season we shall r·, if we "
Re 14:15 Thrust in thy sickle, and r·: for "
15 for the time is come for thee to r·; "

reaped
Ho 10:13 wickedness, ye have r· iniquity; 7114
Jas 5: 4 who have r· down your fields, * 270
4 the cries of them which have r· 2325
Re 14:16 the earth; and the earth was r·. "

reaper See also REAPERS.
Am 9:13 the plowman shall overtake the r·, 7114

reapers
Ru 2: 3 gleaned in the field after the r·: 7114
4 said unto the r·, The Lord be with "
5 his servant that was set over the r·, "
6 the servant that was set over the r·, "
7 after the r· among the sheaves: "
14 And she sat beside the r·: and he "
2Ki 4:18 he went out to his father to the r·. "
M't 13:30 I will say to the r·, Gather ye 2327
39 world; and the r· are the angels. "

reapest
Le 23:22 corners of thy field when thou r·, *7114
Lu 19:21 and r· that thou didst not sow. 2325

reapeth
Isa 17: 5 and r· the ears with his arm; 7114
Joh 4:36 he that r· receiveth wages, and 2325
36 he that r· may rejoice together. "
37 true, One soweth, and another r·. "

reaping
1Sa 6:13 were r· their wheat harvest in the 7114
M't 25:24 r· where thou hast not sown, and 2325
Lu 19:22 down, and r· that I did not sow: "

rear See also REARED; REREWARD.
Ex 26:30 thou shalt r· up the tabernacle 6965
Le 26: 1 neither r· you up a standing image, "
2Sa 24:18 Go up, r· an altar unto the Lord in "
Joh 2:20 wilt thou r· it up in three days? *1453

reared
Ex 40:17 that the tabernacle was r· up. 6965
18 Moses r· up the tabernacle, and "
18 bars thereof, and r· up his pillars. "
33 And he r· up the court round about "
Nu 9:15 day that the tabernacle was r· up "
2Sa 18:18 and r· up for himself a pillar, 5324
1Ki 16:32 And he r· up an altar for Baal in 6965
2Ki 21: 3 and he r· up altars for Baal, and "
2Ch 3:17 And he r· up the pillars before the "
33: 3 and he r· up altars for Baalim, and "

reason See also REASONABLE; REASONED; REASONING; REASONS.
Ge 41:31 in the land by r· of that famine 6440
47:13 Canaan fainted by r· of the famine. 4480
Ex 2:23 Israel sighed by r· of the bondage, "
23 up unto God by r· of the bondage, "
3: 7 cry by r· of their taskmasters; 6440
8:24 corrupted by r· of the swarm of flies. "
Nu 9:10 shall be unclean by r· of a dead body, "
18: 8 I given them by r· of the anointing, "
32 And ye shall bear no sin by r· of 5921
De 5: 5 for ye were afraid by r· of the fire, *6440
23:10 that is not clean by r· of uncleanness
Jos 9:13 old by r· of the very long journey.
J'g 2:18 by r· of them that oppressed them
1Sa 12: 7 may r· with you before the Lord *8199
1Ki 9:15 this is the r· of the levy which 1697
2Ch 5:14 stand to minister by r· of the 6440
20:15 by r· of this great multitude; "
21:15 fall out by r· of the sickness day 4480
19 fell out by r· of his sickness: 5973

Job 6:16 which are blackish by r· of the ice,4480
9:14 choose out my words to r· with him?
13: 3 and I desire to r· with God. 3198
15: 3 Should he r· with unprofitable talk?"
17: 7 Mine eye also is dim by r· of sorrow,
31:23 and by r· of his highness I could not
35: 9 By r· of the multitude of oppressions
9 cry out by r· of the arm of the mighty.
37:19 our speech by r· of darkness. 6440
Ps 38: 8 have roared by r· of the disquietness
44:16 by r· of the enemy and avenger. 6440
78:65 man that shouteth by r· of wine.
88: 9 eye mourneth by r· of affliction: 4480
90:10 if by r· of strength they be fourscore
102: 5 By r· of the voice of my groaning my
Pr 20: 4 will not plow by r· of the cold;
26:16 seven men that can render a r·. 2940
Ec 7:25 out wisdom, and the r· of things, 2808
Isa 1:18 Come now, and let us r· together, 3198
49:19 too narrow by r· of the inhabitants,*
Eze 19:10 full of branches by r· of many waters.
21:12 terrors by r· of the sword shall be* 413
26:10 By r· of the abundance of his horses
27:12, 16 thy merchant by r· of the multitude
28:17 wisdom by r· of thy brightness: 5921
Da 4:36 time my r· returned unto me; *4486
5:10 by r· of the words of the king and 6903
8:12 daily sacrifice by r· of transgression,*
Jon 2: 2 I cried by r· of mine affliction unto the
Mic 2:12 noise by r· of the multitude of men.
M't 16: 8 why r· ye among yourselves, 1260
M'r 2: 8 Why r· ye these things in your "
8:17 Why r· ye, because ye have no "
Lu 5:21 and the Pharisees began to r·, "
22 them, What r· ye in your hearts? "
Joh 6:18 sea arose by r· of a great wind that
12:11 by r· of him many of the Jews 1223
Ac 6: 2 It is not r· that we should leave the*701
18:14 r· would that I should bear with 3056
Ro 8:20 by r· of him who hath subjected 1223
2Co 3:10 by r· of the glory that excelleth. 1752
Heb 5: 3 by r· hereof he ought, as for the 1223
14 who by r· of use have their senses "
7:23 suffered to continue by r· of death:*
1Pe 3:15 a r· of the hope that is in you with3056
2Pe 2: 2 by r· of whom the way of truth 1223
Re 8:13 earth by r· of the other voices of 1537
9: 2 by r· of the smoke of the pit. "
18:19 in the sea by r· of her costliness! "

reasonable See also UNREASONABLE.
Ro 12: 1 unto God, which is your r· service.‡3050

reasoned
M't 16: 7 they r· among themselves, saying,1260
21:25 they r· among themselves, saying, "
M'r 2: 8 that they so r· among themselves, "
8:16 they r· among themselves, saying, "
11:31 they r· with themselves, saying, If 3049
Lu 20: 5 they r· with themselves, saying, If 4817
14 they r· among themselves, saying,1260
24:15 they communed together and r·, *4802
Ac 17: 2 r· with them out of the scriptures, 1256
18: 4 r· in the synagogue every sabbath, "
19 synagogue, and r· with the Jews. "
24:25 And as he r· of righteousness, "

reasoning
Job 13: 6 Hear now my r·, and hearken to 8433
M'r 2: 6 sitting there, and r· in their hearts,1260
12:28 having heard them r· together, *4802
Lu 9:46 Then there arose a r· among them,1261
Ac 28:29 had great r· among themselves. *4803

reasons
Job 32:11 I gave ear to your r·, whilst ye 8394
Isa 41:21 bring forth your strong r·, saith the

Reba (*Re'-bah*)
Nu 31: 8 Hur, and R·, five kings of Midian: 7254
Jos 13:21 and R·, which were dukes of Sihon, "

Rebecca (*re-bek'-kah*) See also REBEKAH.
Ro 9:10 R· also had conceived by one, even4479

Rebekah (*re-bek'-kah*) See also REBECCA; REBEKAH'S.
Ge 22:23 Bethuel begat R·: these eight 7259
24:15 R· came out, who was born to "
29 R· had a brother, and his name was"
30 he heard the words of R· his sister,"
45 R· came forth with her pitcher on "
51 R· is before thee, take her, and go, "
53 and raiment, and gave them to R·: "
58 they called R·, and said unto her, "
59 they sent away R· their sister, and "
60 they blessed R·, and said unto her, "
61 R· arose, and her damsels, and they"
61 servant took R·, and went his way. "
64 R· lifted up her eyes, and when she "
67 took R·, and she became his wife; "
25:20 years old when he took R· to wife, "
21 of him, and R· his wife conceived. "
28 of his venison: but R· loved Jacob. "
26: 7 of the place should kill me for R·; "
8 was sporting with R· his wife. "
35 grief of mind unto Isaac and to R·. "
27: 5 R· heard when Isaac spake to Esau "
6 And R· spake unto Jacob her son, "
11 Jacob said to R· his mother, Behold, "
15 And R· took goodly raiment of her "
42 Esau her elder son were told to R·: "
46 R· said to Isaac, I am weary of my "
28: 5 the Syrian, the brother of R·, "
49:31 they buried Isaac and R· his wife; "

Rebekah's (*re-bek'-kahz*)
Ge 29:12 brother, and that he was R· son: 7259
35: 8 But Deborah R· nurse died, and "

rebel See also REBELLED; REBELLEST; REBELS.
Nu 14: 9 Only r· not ye against the Lord. 4775
Jos 1:18 doth r· against thy commandment,4784
22:16 r· this day against the Lord? 4775
18 seeing ye r· to day against the Lord,"
19 but r· not against the Lord, nor "
19 against the Lord, nor r· against us,"
29 God forbid that we should r· against"
1Sa 12:14 not r· against the commandment 4784
15 but r· against the commandment "
Ne 2:19 ye do? will ye r· against the king? 4775
6: 6 that thou and the Jews think to r·: "
Job 24:13 of those that r· against the light; "
Isa 1:20 But if ye refuse and r·, ye shall be 4784
Ho 7:14 and wine, and they r· against me. 5493

rebelled
Ge 14: 4 and in the thirteenth year they r·. 4775
Nu 20:24 because ye r· against my word at 4784
27:14 ye r· against my commandment in "
De 1:26, 43 but r· against the commandment"
9:23 ye r· against the commandment of4784
1Ki 12:19 So Israel r· against the house of 6586
2Ki 1: 1 Then Moab r· against Israel after "
3: 5 Moab r· against the king of Israel. "
7 king of Moab hath r· against me: "
18: 7 he r· against the king of Assyria, 4775
24: 1 then he turned and r· against him. "
20 Zedekiah r· against the king of "
2Ch 10:19 And Israel r· against the house of 6856
13: 6 up, and hath r· against his lord. 4775
36:13 r· against king Nebuchadnezzar, "
Ne 9:26 disobedient, and r· against thee, "
Ps 5:10 for they have r· against thee. 4784
105:28 and they r· not against his word. "
107:11 they r· against the words of God, "
Isa 1: 2 and they have r· against me. 6586
63:10 they r·, and vexed his holy Spirit: 4784
Jer 52: 3 Zedekiah r· against the king of 4775
La 1:18 r· against his commandment: 4784
20 for I have grievously r·: abroad "
3:42 We have transgressed and have r·: "
Eze 2: 3 nation that hath r· against me: 4775
17:15 he r· against him in sending his "
20: 8 they r· against me, and would not 4784
13 r· against me in the wilderness: "
21 the children r· against me: they "
Da 9: 5 have r·, even by departing from 4775
9 though we have r· against him; "
Ho 13:16 for she hath r· against her God: 4784

rebellest
2Ki 18:20 trust, that thou r· against me? *4775
Isa 36: 5 trust, that thou r· against me? * "

rebellion
De 31:27 I know thy r·, and thy stiff neck: 4805
Jos 22:22 if it be in r·, or if in transgression 4777
1Sa 15:23 For r· is as the sin of witchcraft, 4805
Ezr 4:19 r· and sedition have been made 4776
Ne 9:17 in their r· appointed a captain to 4805
Job 34:37 For he addeth r· unto his sin, he 6588
Pr 17:11 An evil man seeketh only r·: 4805
Jer 28:16 hast taught r· against the Lord. 5627
29:32 he hath taught r· against the Lord. "

rebellious
De 9: 7 ye have been r· against the Lord. 4784
24 Ye have been r· against the Lord "
21:18 a man have a stubborn and r· son, "
20 This our son is stubborn and r·, he "
31:27 ye have been r· against the Lord; "
1Sa 20:30 son of the perverse r· woman, do 4780
Ezr 4:12 building the r· and the bad city, 4779
15 and know that this city is a r· city, "
Ps 66: 7 let not the r· exalt themselves. 5637
68: 6 but the r· dwell in a dry land. "
18 yea, for the r· also, that the Lord "
78: 8 a stubborn and r· generation; a 4784
Isa 1:23 princes are r·, and companions of 5637
30: 1 Woe to the r· children, saith the "
9 this is a r· people, lying children, 4805
50: 5 I was not r·, neither turned away 4784
65: 2 hands all the day unto a r· people, 5637
Jer 4:17 she hath been r· against me, saith 4784
5:23 hath a revolting and a r· heart; "
Eze 2: 3 to a r· nation that hath rebelled 4775
5 (for they are a r· house,) yet shall 4805
6 looks, though they be a r· house. "
7 will forbear: for they are most r·. "
8 Be not thou r· like that r· house; "
3: 9 looks, though they be a r· house. "
26 a reprover: for they are a r· house. "
27 forbear: for they are a r· house. "
12: 2 dwellest in the midst of a r· house, "
2 hear not: for they are a r· house. "
3 consider, though they be a r· house."
9 the house of Israel, the r· house, "
25 O r· house, will I say the word, and "
17:12 Say now to the r· house, Know ye "
24: 3 utter a parable unto the r· house, "
44: 6 thou shalt say to the r·, even to the "

rebels
Nu 17:10 kept for a token against the r·; *4805
20:10 Hear now, ye r·; must we fetch 4784
Eze 20:38 purge out from among you the r·, 4775

rebuke See also REBUKED; REBUKES; REBUKETH; REBUKING; UNREBUKABLE.
Le 19:17 in any wise r· thy neighbour, and 3198
De 28:20 upon thee cursing, vexation and r·,4045
Ru 2:16 may glean them, and r· her not. 1605
2Ki 19: 3 day is a day of trouble, and of r·, 8433
1Ch 12:17 our fathers look thereon, and r· it.3198
Ps 6: 1 O Lord, r· me not in thine anger, "
18:15 were discovered at thy r·, O Lord, 1606
38: 1 O Lord, r· me not in thy wrath: 3198
68:30 R· the company of spearmen, the 1605
76: 6 At thy r·, O God of Jacob, both the1606
80:16 perish at the r· of thy countenance. "
104: 7 At thy r· they fled; at the voice of "
Pr 9: 8 r· a wise man, and he will love *3198
13: 1 but a scorner heareth not r·. 1606
8 riches: but the poor heareth not r·.*"
24:25 them that r· him shall be delight, 3198
27: 5 Open r· is better than secret love. 8433
Ec 7: 5 is better to hear the r· of the wise, 1606
Isa 2: 4 and shall r· many people: †‡3198
17:13 God shall r· them, and they shall 1605
25: 8 r· of his people shall he take away*2781
30:17 shall flee at the r· of one; at the 1606
17 at the r· of five shall ye flee: till ye "
37: 3 day is a day of trouble, and of r·, 8433
50: 2 behold, at my r· I dry up the sea, I 1606
51:20 fury of the Lord, the r· of thy God. "
54: 9 be wroth with thee, nor r· thee. 1605
66:15 fury, and his r· with flames of fire. 1606
Jer 15:15 for thy sake I have suffered r·. *2781
Ho 5: 9 shall be desolate in the day of r·: 8433
Mic 4: 3 and r· strong nations afar off; †‡3198
Zec 3: 2 The Lord r· thee, O Satan; even 1605
2 hath chosen Jerusalem r· thee: "
Mal 3:11 r· the devourer for your sakes, and "
M't 16:22 took him, and began to r· him, 2008
M'r 8:32 took him, and began to r· him. "
Lu 17: 3 trespass against thee, r· him; and "
19:39 unto him, Master, r· thy disciples. "
Ph'p 2:15 the sons of God, without r·, in the* 298
1Ti 5: 1 R· not an elder, but intreat him as 1969
20 Them that sin r· before all, that *1651
2Ti 4: 2 r·, exhort with all longsuffering 2008
Tit 1:13 Wherefore r· them sharply, that *1651
2:15 exhort, and r· with all authority. * "
Jude 9 but said, The Lord r· thee. 2008
Re 3:19 many as I love, I r· and chasten: *1651

rebuked
Ge 31:42 my hands, and r· thee yesternight.3198
37:10 and his father r· him, and said 1605
Ne 5: 7 and I r· the nobles, and the rulers,*7378
Ps 9: 5 Thou hast r· the heathen, thou 1605
106: 9 He r· the Red sea also, and it was "
119:21 hast r· the proud that are cursed, "
M't 8:26 and r· the winds and the sea; and 2008
17:18 And Jesus r· the devil; and he "
19:13 pray: and the disciples r· them. "
20:31 the multitude r· them, because they"
M'r 1:25 And Jesus r· him, saying, Hold thy "
4:39 he arose, and r· the wind, and said "
8:33 he r· Peter, saying, Get thee behind"
9:25 he r· the foul spirit, saying unto "
10:13 his disciples r· those that brought "
Lu 4:35 And Jesus r· him, saying, Hold thy "
39 and r· the fever; and it left her: "
8:24 he arose, and r· the wind and the "
9:42 Jesus r· the unclean spirit, and "
55 he turned, and r· them, and said, "
18:15 his disciples saw it, they r· them. "
39 they which went before r· him, "
23:40 But the other answering r· him, * "
Heb 12: 5 nor faint when thou art r· of him:*1651
2Pe 2:16 But was r· for his iniquity: the 2192,1649

rebuker
Ho 5: 2 I have been a r· of them all. 4148

rebukes
Ps 39:11 When thou with r· dost correct 8433
Eze 5:15 and in fury and in furious r·. "
25:17 upon them with furious r·; and "

rebuketh
Pr 9: 7 he that r· a wicked man getteth *3198
28:23 He that r· a man afterwards shall "
Am 5:10 They hate him that r· in the gate,* "
Na 1: 4 He r· the sea, and maketh it dry, 1605

rebuking
2Sa 22:16 discovered, at the r· of the Lord, *1606
Lu 4:41 he r· them suffered them not to 2008

Recah (*re'-kah*)
1Ch 4:12 These are the men of R·. 7397

recall
La 3:21 This I r· to my mind, therefore 7725

receipt
M't 9: 9 Matthew, sitting at...r· of custom:*5058
M'r 2:14 Alphæus sitting at the r· of custom,* "
Lu 5:27 Levi, sitting at the r· of custom: * "

receive See also RECEIVED; RECEIVETH; RECEIVING.
Ge 4:11 mouth to r· thy brother's blood 3947
33:10 then r· my present at my hand: "
38:20 to r· his pledge from the woman's "
Ex 27: 3 make his pans to r· his ashes, *1878
29:25 thou shalt r· them of their hands, 3947
Nu 18:28 ye r· of the children of Israel; "
De 9: 9 the mount to r· the tables of stone, "
33: 3 every one shall r· of thy words. 5375
1Sa 10: 4 which thou shalt r· of their hands.3947
2Sa 18:12 r· a thousand shekels of silver in 8254
1Ki 5: 9 there, and thou shalt r· them: 5375
8:64 too little to r· the burnt offerings, 3557
2Ki 5:16 whom I stand, I will r· none. 3947
26 to r· money, and to r· garments, "
12: 7 r· no more money of your * "
8 to r· no more money of the people,* "
2Ch 7: 7 not able to r· the burnt offerings, 3557
Job 2:10 we r· good at the hand of God, 6901
10 of God, and shall we not r· evil? "
22:22 R·, I pray thee, the law from his 3947
27:13 they shall r· of the Almighty. "
Ps 6: 9 the Lord will r· my prayer. "
24: 5 r· the blessing from the Lord, 5375
49:15 of the grave: for he shall r· me. 3947
73:24 and afterward r· me to glory. "
75: 2 When I shall r· the congregation I* "
Pr 1: 3 To r· the instruction of wisdom, "
2: 1 My son, if thou wilt r· my words, "

Pr 4:10 Hear, O my son, and r' my sayings;3947
8:10 R' my instruction, and not silver; "
10: 8 The wise...will r' commandments: "
19:20 Hear counsel, and r' instruction. 6901
Isa 57: 6 Should I r' comfort in these? *5162
Jer 5: 3 they have refused to r' correction:3947
9:20 your ear r' the word of his mouth, "
17:23 might not hear, nor r' instruction. "
32:33 have not hearkened to r' instruction." "
35:13 Will ye not r' instruction to hearken"
Eze 3:10 speak unto thee r' in thine heart, "
16:61 when thou shalt r' thy sisters, thine"
36:30 shall r' no more reproach of famine"
Da 2: 6 ye shall r' of me gifts and rewards6902
Ho 10: 6 Ephraim shall r' shame, and 3947
14: 2 all iniquity, and r' us graciously: * "
Mic 1:11 he shall r' of you his standing. * "
Zep 3: 7 fear me, thou wilt r' instruction; "
Mal 3:10 shall not be room enough to r' it.
M't 10:14 whosoever shall not r' you, nor 1209
41 shall r' a prophet's reward; and 2983
41 shall r' a righteous man's reward. "
11: 5 blind r' their sight, and the lame 308
14 if ye will r' it, this is Elias, which 1209
18: 5 whoso shall r' one such little child "
19:11 All men cannot r' this saying, save5562
12 that is able to r' it, let him r' it. "
29 shall r' an hundredfold, and shall 2983
20: 7 is right, that shall ye r'. * "
21:22 ask in prayer, believing, ye shall r'. "
34 that they might r' the fruits of it. "
23:14 ye shall r' the greater damnation.* "
M'r 2: 2 there was no room to r' them, *5562
4:16 immediately r' it with gladness; 2983
20 such as hear the word, and r' it, *3858
6:11 whosoever shall not r' you, nor 1209
9:37 shall r' one of such children in "
37 whosoever shall r' me, receiveth not*"
10:15 shall not r' the kingdom of God as "
30 he shall r' an hundredfold now in 2983
51 Lord, that I might r' my sight. 308
11:24 ye pray, believe that ye r' them, †2983
12: 2 he might r' from the husbandmen "
40 these shall r' greater damnation. "
Lu 6:34 to them of whom ye hope to r', 618
34 lend to sinners, to r' as much again. "
8:13 they hear, r' the word with joy; 1209
9: 5 whosoever will not r' you, when ye "
48 shall r' this child in my name "
48 whosoever shall r' me receiveth "
53 they did not r' him, because his "
10: 8 city ye enter, and they r' you, eat "
10 they r' you not, go your ways out "
16: 4 they may r' me into their houses. "
9 they may r' you into everlasting "
18:17 shall not r' the kingdom of God as "
30 not r' manifold more in this present618
41 said, Lord, that I may r' my sight. 308
42 Jesus said unto him, R' thy sight: "
19:12 to r' for himself a kingdom, and 2983
20:47 same shall r' greater damnation. "
23:41 for we r' the due reward of our 618
Joh 3:11 seen; and ye r' not our witness. 2983
27 A man can r' nothing, except it be "
5:34 But I r' not testimony from man: "
41 I r' not honour from men. "
43 Father's name, and ye r' me not: "
43 in his own name, him ye will r'. "
44 which r' honour one of another, "
7:23 the sabbath day r' circumcision, * "
39 they that believe on him should r': "
14: 3 again, and r' you unto myself; 3880
17 whom the world cannot r', because2983
16:14 for he shall r' of mine, and shall "
24 ask, and ye shall r', that your joy "
20:22 unto them, R' ye the Holy Ghost: "
Ac 1: 8 But ye shall r' power, after that the"
2:38 shall r' the gift of the Holy Ghost. "
3: 5 expecting to r' something of them. "
21 Whom the heaven must r' until 1209
7:59 and saying, Lord Jesus, r' my spirit. "
8:15 that they might r' the Holy Ghost:2983
19 hands, he may r' the Holy Ghost. "
9:12 on him, that he might r' his sight. 308
17 that thou mightest r' thy sight, and "
10:43 in him shall r' remission of sins. 2983
16:21 which are not lawful for us to r', 3858
18:27 exhorting the disciples to r' him: 588
20:35 is more blessed to give than to r'. 2983
22:13 unto me, Brother Saul, r' thy sight.308
18 r' thy testimony concerning me. 3858
26:18 they may r' forgiveness of sins, 2983
Ro 5:17 they which r' abundance of grace "
13: 2 shall r' to themselves damnation. "
14: 1 that is weak in the faith r' ye, 4355
15: 7 r' ye one another, as Christ also "
16: 2 That ye r' her in the Lord, as 4327
1Co 3: 8 man shall r' his own reward 2983
14 thereupon, he shall r' a reward. "
4: 7 hast thou that thou didst not r'? "
7 thou didst r' it, why dost thou glory, "
14: 5 that the church may r' edifying. "
2Co 5:10 r' the things done in his body, 2865
6: 1 ye r' not the grace of God in vain. 1209
17 unclean thing; and I will r' you, 1523
7: 2 R' us; we have wronged no man, *5562
9 might r' damage by us in nothing.*2210
8: 4 intreaty that we would r' the gift,*1209
11: 4 or if ye r' another spirit, which ye 2983
16 as a fool r' me, that I may boast 1209
Ga 3:14 might r' the promise of the Spirit 2983
4: 5 we might r' the adoption of sons. 618
Eph 6: 8 the same shall he r' of the Lord, 2865
Ph'p 2:29 R' him therefore in the Lord with 4327
Col 3:24 r' the reward of the inheritance: 618
25 r' for the wrong which he hath 2865

Col 4:10 if he come unto you, r' him;) 1209
1Ti 5:19 an elder r' not an accusation, but 3858
Ph'm 12 thou therefore r' him, that is, *4355
15 that thou shouldest r' him for ever:*568
17 a partner, r' him as myself. 4355
Heb 7: 5 who r' the office of the priesthood,2983
8 And here men that die r' tithes; "
9:15 might r' the promise of eternal "
10:36 of God, ye might r' the promise. 2865
11: 8 should after r' for an inheritance, 2983
Jas 1: 7 he shall r' any thing of the Lord. "
12 is tried, he shall r' the crown of life, "
21 r' with meekness the engrafted 1209
3: 1 shall r' the greater condemnation. 2983
4: 3 Ye ask, and r' not, because ye ask "
5: 7 until he r' the early and latter rain. "
1Pe 5: 4 r' a crown of glory that fadeth not 2865
2Pe 2:13 r' the reward of unrighteousness.* "
1Jo 3:22 whatsoever we ask, we r' of him, 2983
5: 9 If we r' the witness of men, the "
2Jo 8 but that we r' a full reward. 618
10 r' him not into your house, neither2983
3Jo 8 We therefore ought to r' such, that*618
10 doth he himself r' the brethren, 1926
Re 4:11 to r' glory and honour and power:2983
5:12 Lamb that was slain to r' power, "
13:16 to r' a mark in their right hand, 1325
14: 9 r' his mark in his forehead, or in *2983
17:12 but r' power as kings one hour with "
18: 4 and that ye r' not of her plagues. "

received See also RECEIVEDST.
Ge 26:12 land, and r' in the same year an *4672
Ex 32: 4 And he r' them at their hand, and 3947
36: 3 they r' of Moses all the offering, "
Nu 12:14 after that let her be r' in again. 622
23:20 I have r' commandment to bless: 3947
34:14 fathers, have r' their inheritance; "
14 have r' their inheritance: "
15 half tribe have r' their inheritance "
36: 3, 4 the tribe whereunto they are r':*1961
Jos 13: 8 Gadites have r' their inheritance, 3947
18: 2 had not yet r' their inheritance. *2505
7 have r' their inheritance beyond 3947
J'g 13:23 would not have r' a burnt offering "
1Sa 12: 3 of whose hand have I r' any bribe "
25:35 So David r' of her hand that which "
1Ki 10:28 merchants r' the linen yarn at a "
2Ki 19:14 Hezekiah r' the letter of the hand "
1Ch 12:18 David r' them, and made them 6901
2Ch 1:16 merchants r' the linen yarn at a 3947
4: 5 r' and held three thousand baths. 2388
29:22 and the priests r' the blood, and 6901
30:16 they r' at the hand of the Levites. "
Es 4: 4 from him: but he r' it not. 6901
Job 4:12 and mine ear r' a little thereof. 3947
Ps 68:18 thou hast r' gifts for men; yea, for "
Pr 24:32 looked upon it, and r' instruction. "
Isa 37:14 And Hezekiah r' the letter from the "
40: 2 for she hath r' of the Lord's hand "
Jer 2:30 children; they r' no correction: "
Eze 18:17 hath not r' usury nor increase, "
Zep 3: 2 she r' not correction; she trusted "
M't 10: 8 freely ye have r', freely give. 2983
13:19 he which r' seed by the way side. *4687
20 that r' the seed into stony places, * "
22 also that r' seed among the thorns*"
23 that r' seed into the good ground * "
17:24 they that r' tribute money came to2983
20: 9 hour, they r' every man a penny. "
10 that they should have r' more; * "
10 they likewise r' every man a penny. "
11 And when they had r' it, they "
34 and immediately their eyes r' sight.308
25:16 he that had r' the five talents went2983
17 And likewise he that had r' two, "
18 But he that had r' one went and 2983
20 so he that had r' five talents came "
22 also that had r' two talents came "
24 which had r' the one talent came "
27 have r' mine own with usury. 2865
M'r 7: 4 which they have r' to hold, as the 3880
10:52 And immediately he r' his sight, 308
15:23 with myrrh: but he r' it not. 2983
16:19 he was r' up into heaven, and sat on353
Lu 6:24 for ye have r' your consolation. 568
8:40 returned, the people gladly r' him:*588
9:11 he r' them, and spake unto them *1209
51 was come that he should be r' up, 354
10:38 Martha r' him into her house. 5264
15:27 he hath r' him safe and sound. 618
18:43 And immediately he r' his sight, 308
19: 6 came down, and r' him joyfully. 5264
15 returned, having r' the kingdom, 2983
Joh 1:11 his own, and his own r' him not. 3880
12 as many as r' him, to them gave 2983
16 And of his fulness have all we r', "
3:33 He that hath r' his testimony hath "
4:45 the Galilæans r' him, having seen 1209
6:21 they willingly r' him into the ship:*2983
9:11 I went and washed, and I r' sight. 308
15 asked him how he had r' his sight. "
18 he had been blind, and r' his sight, "
18 parents of him that had r' his sight. "
10:18 This commandment have I r' of 2983
13:30 He then having r' the sop went "
17: 8 they have r' them, and have known "
18: 3 then, having r' a band of men and "
19:30 Jesus therefore had r' the vinegar, "
Ac 1: 9 a cloud r' him out of their sight. 5274
2:33 and having r' of the Father the 2983
41 gladly r' his word were baptized: 588
3: 7 feet and ancle bones r' strength. 4732
7:38 r' the lively oracles to give unto us:1209
53 r' the law by the disposition of 2983
8:14 Samaria had r' the word of God, 1209
17 them, and they r' the Holy Ghost. 2983

Ac 9:18 he r' sight forthwith, and arose, 308
19 And when he had r' meat, he was*2983
10:16 vessel was r' up again into heaven.353
47 r' the Holy Ghost as well as we? 2983
11: 1 Gentiles had also r' the word of 1209
15: 4 they were r' of the church, and of 588
16:24 Who, having r' such a charge, 2983
17: 7 Whom Jason hath r': and these 5264
11 they r' the word with all readiness1209
19: 2 Have ye r' the Holy Ghost since ye*2983
20:24 which I have r' of the Lord Jesus, "
21:17 the brethren r' us gladly. 1209
22: 5 from whom also I r' letters unto "
26:10 r' authority from the chief priests;2983
28: 2 fire, and r' us every one, because 4355
7 who r' us, and lodged us three days324
21 We neither r' letters out of Judæa 1209
30 and r' all that came in unto him, 588
Ro 1: 5 we have r' grace and apostleship, 2983
4:11 And he r' the sign of circumcision, "
5:11 we have now r' the atonement. "
8:15 ye have not r' the spirit of bondage "
15 ye have r' the Spirit of adoption, "
14: 3 that eateth: for God hath r' him. 4355
15: 7 as Christ also r' us to the glory of "
1Co 2:12 Now we have r', not the spirit of 2983
4: 7 glory, as if thou hadst not r' it? "
11:23 I have r' of the Lord that which 3880
15: 1 which also ye have r', and wherein "
3 you first of all that which I also r', "
2Co 4: 1 as we have r' mercy, we faint not;*1653
7:15 with fear and trembling ye r' him. 1209
11: 4 which ye have not r', or another *2983
24 times r' I forty stripes save one. "
Ga 1: 9 unto you than that ye have r', 3880
12 For I neither r' it of man, neither* "
3: 2 R' ye the Spirit by the works of 2983
4:14 but r' me as an angel of God, even1209
Ph'p 4: 9 ye have both learned, and r', and 3880
18 having r' of Epaphroditus the 1209
Col 2: 6 ye have therefore r' Christ Jesus 3880
4:10 whom ye r' commandments: if 2983
17 which thou hast r' in the Lord, 3880
1Th 1: 6 r' the word in much affliction, 1209
2:13 when ye r' the word of God which 3880
13 ye r' it not as the word of men, *1209
4: 1 as ye have r' of us how ye ought 3880
2Th 2:10 they r' not the love of the truth, 1209
3: 6 the tradition which he r' of us. 3880
1Ti 3:16 on in the world, r' up into glory. 353
4: 3 which God hath created to be r' 3336
4 if it be r' with thanksgiving: 2983
Heb 2: 2 r' a just recompense of reward; "
7: 6 from them r' tithes of Abraham, 1183
11 (for under it the people r' the law,)3549
10:26 r' the knowledge of the truth, 2983
11:11 Sara herself r' strength to conceive"
13 not having r' the promises, but "
17 he that had r' the promises offered 324
19 whence also he r' him in a figure.*2865
31 she had r' the spies with peace. 1209
35 Women r' their dead raised to life 2983
39 through faith, r' not the promise: 2865
Jas 2:25 when she had r' the messengers, 5264
1Pe 1:18 vain conversation r' by tradition *
4:10 As every man hath r' the gift, even2983
2Pe 1:17 he r' from God the Father honour "
1Jo 2:27 anointing which ye have r' of him "
2Jo 4 we have r' a commandment from "
Re 2:27 shivers: even as I r' of my Father. "
3: 3 how thou hast r' and heard, and "
17:12 which have r' no kingdom as yet; "
19:20 that had r' the mark of the beast, "
20: 4 r' his mark upon their foreheads, "

receivedst
Lu 16:25 in thy lifetime r' thy good things, 618

receiver
Isa 33:18 is the scribe? where is the r'? *8254

receiveth
J'g 19:18 is no man that r' me to house. * 622
Job 35: 7 him? or what r' he of thine hand? 3947
Pr 21:11 wise is instructed, he r' knowledge."
29: 4 but he that r' gifts overthroweth it.*
Jer 7:28 Lord their God, nor r' correction:*3947
Mal 2:13 or r' it with good will at your hand. "
M't 7: 8 For every one that asketh r'; and 2983
10:40 He that r' you r' me, and he 1209
40 that r' me r' him that sent me. "
41 He that r' a prophet in the name 2983
41 he that r' a righteous man in the "
13:20 the word, and anon with joy r' it; "
18: 5 such little child in my name r' me. 1209
M'r 9:37 little children in my name, r' me: "
37 shall receive me, r' not me, but "
Lu 9:48 receive this child in my name r' me: "
48 receive me r' him that sent me: "
11:10 every one that asketh r'; and he 2983
15: 2 This man r' sinners, and eateth 4327
Joh 3:32 and no man r' his testimony. 2983
4:36 And he that reapeth r' wages, and "
12:48 and r' not my words, hath one that "
13:20 that r' whomsoever I send r' me; "
20 he that r' me r' him that sent me. "
1Co 2:14 the natural man r' not the things 1209
9:24 race run all, but one r' the prize? 2983
Heb 6: 7 it is dressed, r' blessing from God:3335
7: 8 but there he r' them, of whom it is* "
9 Levi also, who r' tithes, payed 2983
12: 6 scourgeth every son whom he r'. 3858
3Jo 9 among them, r' us not. 1926
Re 2:17 man knoweth saving he that r' it. 2983
14:11 whosoever r' the mark of his name."

receiving
2Ki 5:20 not r' at his hands that which he 3947

Ac 17:15 r· a commandment unto Silas and 2983
Ro 1:27 r· in themselves that recompence 618
11:15 what shall the r· of them be, but 4356
Ph'p 4:15 me as concerning giving and r·, 3028
Heb12:28 Wherefore we r· a kingdom which 3880
1Pe 1: 9 R· the end of your faith, even the 2865

Rechab (*re'-kab*) See also RECHABITES.
2Sa 4: 2 and the name of the other R·, 7394
5 sons of Rimmon...R· and Baanah, "
6 R· and Baanah his brother escaped. "
9 R· and Baanah his brother, the "
2Ki 10:15 the son of R· coming to meet him: "
23 went, and Jehonadab the son of R·, "
1Ch 2:55 the father of the house of R·. "
Ne 3:14 repaired Malchiah the son of R·, "
Jer 35: 6 of R· our father commanded us, "
8 the voice of Jonadab the son of R· "
14 words of Jonadab the son of R·, "
16 the son of R· have performed the "
19 the son of R· shall not want a man "

Rechabites (*rek'-ab-ites*)
Jer 35: 2 Go unto the house of the R·, and 7397
3 and the whole house of the R·; "
5 house of the R· pots full of wine, "
18 said unto the house of the R·, "

Rechokim See JONATH-ELEM-RECHOKIM.

reckon See also RECKONED; RECKONETH; RECKONING.
Le 25:50 he shall r· with him that bought 2803
27:18 priest shall r· unto him the money "
23 priest shall r· unto him the worth "
Nu 4:32 name ye shall r· the instruments *6485
Eze 44:26 they shall r· unto him seven days. 5608
M't 18:24 And when he had begun to r·, one 4868
Ro 6:11 r· ye also yourselves to be dead 3049
8:18 For I r· that the sufferings of this "

reckoned
Nu 18:27 offering shall be r· unto you, 2803
23: 9 shall not be r· among the nations. "
2Sa 4: 2 Beeroth also was r· to Benjamin: "
2Ki 12:15 they r· not with the men, into "
1Ch 5: 1 and the genealogy is not to be r· 3187
7 of their generations was r·, were "
17 All these were r· by genealogies in "
7: 5 r· in all by their genealogies "
7 and were r· by their genealogies "
9: 1 all Israel were r· by genealogies; "
22 These were r· by their genealogy in "
2Ch 31:19 to all that were r· by genealogies "
Ezr 2:62 those that were r· by genealogy, "
8: 3 and with him were r· by genealogy "
Ne 7: 5 that they might be r· by genealogy. "
64 those that were r· by genealogy, "
Ps 40: 5 cannot be r· up in order unto thee: *
Isa 38:13 I r· till morning, that, as a lion, *7737
Lu 22:37 was r· among the transgressors: 3049
Ro 4: 4 is the reward not r· of grace, but "
9 say that faith was r· to Abraham "
10 How was it then r·? when he was "

reckoneth
M't 25:19 cometh, and r· with them. *4868,3056

reckoning
2Ki 22: 7 there was no r· made with them 2803
1Ch 23:11 they were in one r·, according to 6486

recommended
Ac 14:26 had been r· to the grace of God *3860
15:40 being r· by the brethren unto the * "

recompence See also RECOMPENCES; RECOMPENSE.
De 32:35 me belongeth vengeance, and r·; 8005
Job 15:31 vanity: for vanity shall be his r·. 8545
Pr 12:14 the r· of a man's hands shall be *1576
Isa 35: 4 vengeance, even God with a r·; he "
59:18 his adversaries, r· to his enemies; "
18 to the islands he will repay r·. "
66: 6 that rendereth r· to his enemies. "
Jer 51: 6 he will render unto her a r·. "
La 3:64 Render unto them a r·, O Lord, "
Hos 9: 7 the days of r· are come; Israel 7966
Joe 3: 4 will ye render me a r·? and if ye 1576
4 return your r· upon your own head; "
Lu 14:12 thee again, and a r· be made thee.* 468
Ro 1:27 r· of their error which was meet. * 489
11: 9 stumblingblock...a r· unto them: * 468
2Co 6:13 Now for a r· in the same, (I speak * 489
Heb 2: 2 received a just r· of reward; *3405
10:35 which hath great r· of reward. * "
11:26 respect unto the r· of the reward. * "

recompences
Isa 34: 8 year of r· for the controversy of *7966
Jer 51:56 for the Lord God of r· shall surely 1578

recompense See also RECOMPENCE; RECOMPENSED; RECOMPENSEST; RECOMPENSING.
Nu 5: 7 he shall r· his trespass with the *7725
8 if the man have no kinsman to r· * "
Ru 2:12 The Lord r· thy work, and a full 7999
2Sa 19:36 king r· it me with such a reward? 1580
Job 34:33 he will r· it, whether thou refuse,*7999
Pr 20:22 Say not thou, I will r· evil; but "
Isa 65: 6 but will r·, even r· into their bosom, "
Jer 16:18 And first I will r· their iniquity "
25:14 r· them according to their deeds, "
50:29 r· her according to her work; "
Eze 7: 3 and will r· upon thee all thine *5414
4 I will r· thy ways upon thee, and * "
8 and will r· thee for all thine * "
9 I will r· thee according to thy ways* "
9:10 will r· their way upon their head.* "
11:21 r· their way upon their own heads,* "
16:43 will r· thy way upon thine head,* "
17:19 even it will I r· upon his own head.* "
23:49 they shall r· your lewdness upon "

Ho 12: 2 to his doings will he r· him. 7725
Joe 3: 4 if ye r· me, swiftly and speedily 1580
Lu 14:14 they cannot r· thee: for thou shalt 467
Ro 12:17 R· to no man evil for evil. Provide*591
2Th 1: 6 with God to r· tribulation to them 467
Heb10:30 unto me, I will r·, saith the Lord. "

recompensed
Nu 5: 8 the trespass be r· unto the Lord, 7725
2Sa 22:21 of my hands hath he r· me. "
25 Lord hath r· me according to my "
Ps 18:20 of my hands hath he r· me. "
24 the Lord r· me according to my "
Pr 11:31 righteous shall be r· in the earth: 7999
Jer 18:20 Shall evil be r· for good? for they "
Eze 22:31 way have I r· upon their heads, *5414
Lu 14:14 thou shalt be r· at the resurrection 467
Ro 11:35 and it shall be r· unto him again? "

recompensest
Jer 32:18 and r· the iniquity of the fathers 7999

recompensing
2Ch 6:23 by r· his way upon his own head;*5414

reconcile See also RECONCILED; RECONCILING.
Le 6:30 to r· withal in the holy place, *3722
1Sa 29: 4 he r· himself unto his master? 7521
Eze 45:20 simple: so shall ye r· the house. *3722
Eph 2:16 r· both unto God in one body by the 604
Col 1:20 him to r· all things unto himself; "

reconciled
M't 5:24 first be r· to thy brother, and then 1259
Ro 5:10 r· to God by the death of his Son, 2644
10 much more, being r·, we shall be "
1Co 7:11 unmarried, or be r· to her husband: "
2Co 5:18 of God, who hath r· us to himself by "
20 in Christ's stead, be ye r· to God. "
Col 1:21 wicked works, yet now hath he r· 604

reconciliation
Le 8:15 sanctified it, to make r· upon it. *3722
2Ch 29:24 made r· with their blood upon the 2398
Eze 45:15 offerings, to make r· for them, *3722
17 to make r· for the house of Israel.* "
Da 9:24 and to make r· for iniquity, and to "
2Co 5:18 hath given to us the ministry of r·; 2643
19 committed unto us the word of r·. "
Heb 2:17 make r· for the sins of the people.*2433

reconciling
Le 16:20 made an end of r· the holy place, *3722
Ro 11:15 of them be the r· of the world, 2643
2Co 5:19 Christ, r· the world unto himself, 2644

record See also RECORDED; RECORDS.
Ex 20:24 where I r· my name I will come 2142
De 30:19 heaven and earth to r· this day *5749
31:28 heaven and earth to r· against "
1Ch 16: 4 and to r·, and to thank and praise*2142
Ezr 6: 2 and therein was a r· thus written: 1799
Job 16:19 in heaven, and my r· is on high. *7717
Isa 8: 2 unto me faithful witnesses to r·, 5749
Joh 1:19 And this is the r· of John, when *3141
32 John bare r·, saying, I saw the *3140
34 bare r· that this is the Son of God.* "
8:13 him, Thou bearest r· of thyself; * "
13 of thyself; thy r· is not true. *3141
14 Though I bear r· of myself, yet *3140
14 of myself, yet my r· is true: for *3141
12:17 raised him from the dead, bare r·.*3140
19:35 And he that saw it bare r·, and * "
35 his r· is true: and he knoweth * 3141
Ac 20:26 I take you to r· this day, that I am*3143
Ro 10: 2 bear them r· that they have a zeal*3140
2Co 1:23 I call God for a r· upon my soul, *3144
8: 3 I bear r·, yea, and beyond their *3140
Ga 4:15 For I bear you r·, that, if it had * "
Ph'p 1: 8 For God is my r·, how greatly I *3144
Col 4:13 For I bear him r·, that he hath a *3140
1Jo 5: 7 are three that bear r· in heaven, * "
10 the r· that God gave of his Son. *3141
11 this is the r·, that God hath given * "
3Jo 12 itself: yea, and we also bear r·; *3140
12 and ye know that our r· is true. *3141
Re 1: 2 Who bare r· of the word of God, *3140

recorded
Ne 12:22 were r· chief of the fathers: also 3789

recorder
2Sa 8:16 the son of Ahilud was r·; 2142
20:24 the son of Ahilud was r·: "
1Ki 4: 3 the son of Ahilud, the r·. "
2Ki 18:18 and Joah the son of Asaph the r·. "
37 and Joah the son of Asaph the r·, "
1Ch 18:15 Jehoshaphat the son of Ahilud, r·. "
2Ch 34: 8 and Joah the son of Joahaz the r·, "
Isa 36: 3 and Joah, Asaph's son, the r·. "
22 and Joah, the son of Asaph, the r·, "

records
Ezr 4:15 may be made in the book of the r· 1799
15 thou find in the book of the r·, "
Es 6: 1 the book of r· of the chronicles; 2146

recount
Na 2: 5 He shall r· his worthies: they *2142

recover See also RECOVERED; RECOVERING.
J'g 11:26 did ye not r· them within that 5337
1Sa 30: 8 them, and without fail r· all. "
2Sa 8: 3 went to r· his border at the river 7725
2Ki 1: 2 whether I shall r· of this disease. 2421
5: 3 for he would r· him of his leprosy. 622
6 thou mayest r· him of his leprosy. "
7 unto me to r· a man of his leprosy? "
11 hand over the place, and r· the leper. "
8: 8, 9 saying, Shall I r· of this disease? 2421
10 him, Thou mayest certainly r·: "
14 me that thou shouldest surely r·. "
2Ch 13:20 Neither did Jeroboam r· strength 6113
14:13 that they could not r· themselves; 4241

Ps 39:13 spare me, that I may r· strength, 1082
Isa 11:11 to r· the remnant of his people, 7069
38:16 so wilt thou r· me, and make me to 2492
21 upon the boil, and he shall r·. 2421
Ho 2: 9 will r· my wool and my flax given*5337
M'r 16:18 on the sick, and they shall r·. 2192,2573
2Ti 2:26 may r· themselves out of the snare 366

recovered
1Sa 30:18 r· all that the Amalekites had 5337
19 had taken to them: David r· all. *7725
22 ought of the spoil that we have r·, 5337
2Ki 13:25 him, and r· the cities of Israel. 7725
14:28 how he r· Damascus, and Hamath, "
16: 6 time Rezin king of Syria r· Elath "
20: 7 and laid it on the boil, and he r·. 2421
Isa 38: 9 sick, and was r· of his sickness: "
39: 1 that he had been sick, and was r·. 2388
Jer 8:22 of the daughter of my people r·? 5927
41:16 whom he had r· from Ishmael the 7725

recovering
Lu 4:18 r· of sight to the blind, to set at 309

red See also RED; REDDISH.
Ge 25:25 And the first came out r·, all over 132
30 thee, with that same r· pottage; 122
49:12 His eyes shall be r· with wine, and 2447
Ex 25: 5 rams' skins dyed r·, and badgers' 119
26:14 for the tent of rams' skins dyed r·, "
35: 7 rams' skins dyed r·, and badgers' "
23 r· skins of rams, and badgers' skins, "
36:19 for the tent of rams' skins dyed r·, "
39:34 the covering of rams' skins dyed r·, "
Nu 19: 2 bring thee a r· heifer without spot, 122
2Ki 3:22 on the other side as r· as blood: "
Es 1: 6 upon a pavement of r·, and blue, 923
Ps 75: 8 there is a cup, and the wine is r·; *2560
Pr 23:31 thou upon the wine when it is r·, 119
Isa 1:18 though they be r· like crimson, "
27: 2 unto her, A vineyard of r· wine. *2561
63: 2 art thou r· in thine apparel, and 122
Na 2: 3 of his mighty men is made r·, 119
Zec 1: 8 behold a man riding upon a r· horse, 122
8 behind him were there r· horses, "
6: 2 In the first chariot were r· horses; "
M't 16: 2 be fair weather: for the sky is r·. 4449
3 to day: for the sky is r· and lowring. "
Re 6: 4 out another horse that was r·: 4450
12: 3 behold a great r· dragon, having "

Red See also RED.
Ex 10:19 and cast them into the R· sea; 5488
13:18 way the wilderness of the R· sea: "
15: 4 also are drowned in the R· sea. "
22 brought Israel from the R· sea, "
23:31 will set thy bounds from the R· sea "
Nu 14:25 wilderness by the way of the R· sea. "
21: 4 mount Hor by the way of the R· sea, "
14 What he did in the R· sea, and 5492
33:10 Elim, and encamped by the R· sea. 5488
11 And they removed from the R· sea, "
De 1: 1 the plain over against the R· sea, *5489
40 wilderness by...way of the R· sea. 5488
2: 1 wilderness by the way of the R· sea, "
11: 4 the water of the R· sea to overflow "
Jos 2:10 dried up the water of the R· sea "
4:23 Lord your God did to the R· sea, "
24: 6 and horsemen unto the R· sea. "
J'g 11:16 the wilderness unto the R· sea, "
1Ki 9:26 on the shore of the R· sea, in the "
Ne 9: 9 heardest their cry by the R· sea; "
Ps 106: 7 him at the sea, even at the R· sea. "
9 He rebuked the R· sea also, and it "
22 and terrible things by the R· sea. "
136:13 which divided the R· sea into parts: "
15 Pharaoh and his host in the R· sea: "
Jer 49:21 noise...was heard in the R· sea. "
Ac 7:36 land of Egypt, and in the R· sea, 2281
Heb11:29 passed through the R· sea as by dry "

reddish See also RED.
Le 13:19 spot, white, and somewhat r·, 125
24 bright spot, somewhat r·, or white; "
42 a white r· sore; it is a leprosy "
43 if the rising of the sore be white r· "
49 be greenish or r· in the garment, "
14:37 with hollow strakes, greenish or r·, "

redeem See also REDEEMED; REDEEMETH; REDEEMING.
Ex 6: 6 r· you with a stretched out arm, 1350
13:13 firstling of an ass thou shalt r· 6299
13 if thou wilt not r· it, then thou shalt "
13 firstborn of man...shalt thou r·. "
15 all the firstborn of my children I r·. "
34:20 firstling of an ass thou shalt r· "
20 if thou r· him not, then shalt thou "
20 firstborn of thy sons thou shalt r·. "
Le 25:25 and if any of his kin come to r· it, 1350
25 he r· that which his brother sold. "
26 And if the man have none to r· it, "
26 and himself be able to r· it; 1353
29 he may r· it within a whole year "
29 within a full year may he r· it. * "
32 may the Levites r· at any time. "
48 one of his brethren may r· him: 1350
49 or his uncle's son, may r· him, "
49 unto him of his family may r· him; "
49 or if he be able, he may r· himself. 1353
27:13 But if he will at all r· it, then he 1350
15 that sanctified it will r· his house, "
19 that sanctified the field will...r· it, "
20 And if he will not r· the field, or if "
27 he shall r· it according to thine *6299
31 will at all r· ought of his tithes, 1350
Nu 18:15 firstborn of man shalt thou...r·, 6299
15 of unclean beasts shalt thou r·. "
16 from a month old shalt thou r·, "
17 firstling of a goat, thou shalt not r·; "

Ru 4: 4 If thou wilt *r·* it, *r·* it: but 1350
4 if thou wilt not *r·* it, then tell me, "
4 there is none to *r·* it beside thee; "
4 after thee. And he said, I will *r·* it. "
6 I cannot *r·* it for myself, lest I mar "
6 *r·* thou my right to thyself; * "
6 for I cannot *r·* it. "
2Sa 7:23 whom God went to *r·* for a people 6299
1Ch 17:21 God went to *r·* to be his own people, "
Ne 5: 5 neither is it in our power to *r·* them; * "
Job 5:20 famine he shall *r·* thee from death: 6299
6:23 *R·* me from the hand of the mighty? "
Ps 25:22 *R·* Israel, O God, out of all his "
26:11 *r·* me, and be merciful unto me. "
44:26 and *r·* us for thy mercies' sake. "
49: 7 can by any means *r·* his brother, "
15 God will *r·* my soul from the power "
69:18 Draw nigh unto my soul, and *r·* it: 1350
72:14 He shall *r·* their soul from deceit "
130: 8 *r·* Israel from all his iniquities. 6299
Isa 50: 2 shortened at all, that it cannot *r·*? 6304
Jer 15:21 I will *r·* thee out of the hand of 6299
Ho 13:14 grave; I will *r·* them from death: 1350
Mic 4:10 shall *r·* thee from the hand of thine "
Ga 4: 5 To *r·* them that were under the *1805*
Tit 2:14 he might *r·* us from all iniquity *3084*

redeemed See also REDEEMEDST.
Ge 48:16 Angel which *r·* me from all evil, 1350
Ex 15:13 led forth the people...thou hast *r·*: "
21: 8 then shall he let her be *r·*: 6299
Le 19:20 not at all *r·*, nor freedom given her; "
25:30 *r·* within the space of a full year, 1350
31 they may be *r·*, and they shall go 1353
48 After that he is sold he may be *r·* "
54 And if he be not *r·* in these years, 1350
27:20 man, it shall not be *r·* any more. "
27 if it be not *r·*, then it shall be sold "
28 devoted thing,...shall be sold or *r·*: "
29 None devoted,...shall be *r·*; 6299
33 shall be holy; it shall not be *r·*. 1350
Nu 3:46 And for those that are to be *r·* of *6302
48 the odd number of them is to be *r·*, "
49 them that were *r·* by the Levites: 6306
51 the money of them that were *r·* "
18:16 that are to be *r·* from a month old 6299
De 7: 8 *r·* you out of the house of bondmen, "
9:26 thou hast *r·* through thy greatness, "
13: 5 *r·* you out of the house of bondage, "
15:15 and the Lord thy God *r·* thee: "
21: 8 people Israel, whom thou hast *r·*, "
24:18 the Lord thy God *r·* thee thence: "
2Sa 4: 9 hath *r·* my soul out of all adversity, "
1Ki 1:29 hath *r·* my soul out of all distress, "
1Ch 17:21 whom thou hast *r·* out of Egypt? * "
Ne 1:10 thou hast *r·* by thy great power, "
5: 8 have *r·* our brethren the Jews, 7069
Ps 31: 5 hast *r·* me, O Lord God of truth. 6299
71:23 and my soul, which thou hast *r·*. "
74: 2 inheritance, which thou hast *r·*; 1350
77:15 hast with thine arm *r·* thy people, "
106:10 *r·* them from the hand of the enemy. "
107: 2 Let the *r·* of the Lord say so, whom "
2 hath *r·* from the hand of the enemy; "
136:24 And hath *r·* us from our enemies: *6561
Isa 1:27 Zion shall be *r·* with judgment, 6299
29:22 saith the Lord, who *r·* Abraham, "
35: 9 there; but the *r·* shall walk there: 1350
43: 1 Fear not: for I have *r·* thee, I have "
44:22 return unto me; for I have *r·* thee. "
23 for the Lord hath *r·* Jacob, and "
48:20 The Lord hath *r·* his servant Jacob. "
51:11 the *r·* of the Lord shall return, *6299
52: 3 and ye shall be *r·* without money. 1350
9 his people, he hath *r·* Jerusalem. "
62:12 The holy people, The *r·* of the Lord: "
63: 4 and the year of my *r·* is come. "
9 his love and in his pity he *r·* them; "
Jer 31:11 For the Lord hath *r·* Jacob, and *6299
La 3:58 of my soul; thou hast *r·* my life. 1350
Ho 7:13 though I have *r·* them, yet they *6299
Mic 6: 4 *r·* thee out of the house of servants; "
Zec 10: 8 for I have *r·* them: and they shall "
Lu 1:68 hath visited and *r·* his people, **4160,3085*
24:21 he which should have *r·* Israel: **3084*
Ga 3:13 Christ hath *r·* us from the curse *1805*
1Pe 1:18 not *r·* with corruptible things, *3084*
Re 5: 9 and hast *r·* us to God by thy blood* *59*
14: 3 which were *r·* from the earth. * "
4 These were *r·* from among men, * "

redeemedst
2Sa 7:23 which thou *r·* to thee from Egypt, 6299

redeemer
Job 19:25 I know that my *r·* liveth, and that 1350
Ps 19:14 O Lord, my strength, and my *r·*. "
78:35 rock, and the high God their *r·*. "
Pr 23:11 For their *r·* is mighty; he shall "
Isa 41:14 saith the Lord, and thy *r·*, the Holy "
43:14 Thus saith the Lord, your *r·*, the "
44: 6 Israel, and his *r·* the Lord of hosts; "
24 Thus saith the Lord, thy *r·*, and he "
47: 4 As for our *r·*, the Lord of hosts is his "
48:17 Thus saith the Lord, thy *R·*, the "
49: 7 the *R·* of Israel, and his Holy One, "
26 Lord am thy Saviour and thy *R·*, "
54: 5 and thy *R·* the Holy One of Israel; "
8 on thee, saith the Lord thy *R·*. "
59:20 And the *R·* shall come to Zion, and "
60:16 Lord am thy Saviour and thy *R·*, "
63:16 thou, O Lord, art our father, our *r·*; "
Jer 50:34 Their *R·* is strong; The Lord of "

redeemeth
Ps 34:22 Lord *r·* the soul of his servants: 6299
103: 4 Who *r·* thy life from destruction; 1350

redeeming
Ru 4: 7 concerning *r·* and concerning 1353
Eph 5:16 *R·* the time, because the days are *1805*
Col 4: 5 them that are without, *r·* the time. "

redemption
Le 25:24 ye shall grant a *r·* for the land. 1353
51 shall give again the price of his *r·* "
52 give him again the price of his *r·*. "
Nu 3:49 Moses took the *r·* money of them 6306
Ps 49: 8 (For the *r·* of their soul is precious, "
111: 9 He sent *r·* unto his people: he 6304
130: 7 mercy, and with him is plenteous *r·*. "
Jer 32: 7 the right of *r·* is thine to buy it. 1353
8 the *r·* is thine; buy it for thyself. "
Lu 2:38 that looked for *r·* in Jerusalem. *3085*
21:28 heads; for your *r·* draweth nigh. *629*
Ro 3:24 through the *r·* that is in Christ Jesus: "
8:23 adoption, to wit, the *r·* of our body. "
1Co 1:30 and sanctification, and *r·*: "
Eph 1: 7 whom we have *r·* through his blood, "
14 the *r·* of the purchased possession, "
4:30 ye are sealed unto the day of *r·*. "
Col 1:14 whom we have *r·* through his blood, "
Heb 9:12 having obtained eternal *r·* for us. *3085*
15 for the *r·* of the transgressions that *629*

redness
Pr 23:29 cause? who hath *r·* of eyes? 2498

redound
2Co 4:15 of many *r·* to the glory of God. **4052*

Red-sea See RED and SEA.

reed See also REEDS.
1Ki 14:15 as a *r·* is shaken in the water, 7070
2Ki 18:21 upon the staff of this bruised *r·*, "
Job 40:21 shady trees, in the covert of the *r·*, "
Isa 36: 6 in the staff of this broken *r·*, on "
42: 3 A bruised *r·* shall he not break, and "
Eze 29: 6 a staff of *r·* to the house of Israel. "
40: 3 in his hand, and a measuring *r·*; "
5 a measuring *r·* of six cubits long "
5 the breadth of the building, one *r·*; "
5 and the height, one *r·*. "
6 of the gate, which was one *r·* broad; "
6 the gate, which was one *r·* broad. "
7 was one *r·* long, and one *r·* broad; "
7 porch of the gate within was one *r·*. "
8 the porch of the gate within, one *r·*. "
41: 8 were a full *r·* of six great cubits. "
42:16 east side with the measuring *r·*, "
16, 17 the measuring *r·* round about, "
18 reeds, with the measuring *r·*. "
19 reeds with the measuring *r·*. "
M't 11: 7 to see? A *r·* shaken with the wind? *2563*
12:20 A bruised *r·* shall he not break, and "
27:29 head, and a *r·* in his right hand: "
30 took the *r·*, and smote him on the "
48 it with vinegar, and put it on a *r·*, "
M'r 15:19 smote him on the head with a *r·*, "
36 full of vinegar, and put it on a *r·*, "
Lu 7:24 to see? A *r·* shaken with the wind? "
Re 11: 1 was given me a *r·* like unto a rod: "
21:15 talked with me had a golden *r·* to "
16 he measured the city with the *r·*, "

reeds
Isa 19: 6 up: the *r·* and flags shall wither. 7070
7 The paper *r·* by the brooks, by the*
35: 7 shall be grass with *r·* and rushes. 7070
Jer 51:32 the *r·* they have burned with fire, 98
Eze 42:16 measuring reed, five hundred *r·*, 7070
17 the north side, five hundred *r·*, "
18 the south side, five hundred *r·*, "
19 side, and measured five hundred *r·* "
20 round about, five hundred *r·* long,* "
45: 1 length of five and twenty thousand *r·*, "
48: 8 five and twenty thousand *r·* in breadth, "

reel
Ps 107:27 They *r·* to and fro, and stagger 2287
Isa 24:20 earth shall *r·* to and fro like a *5128

Reelaiah (*re-el-ah'-yah*)
Ezr 2: 2 Seraiah, *R·*, Mordecai, Bilshan, 7480

refine See also REFINED.
Zec 13: 9 will *r·* them as silver is refined, 6884

refined
1Ch 28:18 for the altar of incense *r·* gold 2212
29: 4 seven thousand talents of *r·* silver, "
Isa 25: 6 of wines on the lees well *r·*. "
48:10 I have *r·* thee, but not with silver; 6884
Zec 13: 9 and will refine them as silver is *r·*, "

refiner See also REFINER'S.
Mal 3: 3 he shall sit as a *r·* and purifier of 6884

refiner's
Mal 3: 2 for he is like a *r·* fire, and like 6884

reformation
Heb 9:10 on them until the time of *r·*. *1357*

reformed
Le 26:23 if ye will ot be *r·* by me by these 3256

refrain See also REFRAINED; REFRAINETH.
Ge 45: 1 Joseph could not *r·* himself before 662
Job 7:11 I will not *r·* my mouth; I will 2820
Pr 1:15 them; *r·* thy foot from their path: 4513
Ec 3: 5 and a time to *r·* from embracing; 7368
Isa 48: 9 for my praise will I *r·* for thee, 2413
64:12 Wilt thou *r·* thyself for these things, 662
Jer 31:16 *R·* thy voice from weeping, and 4513
Ac 5:38 *R·* from these men, and let them *868*
1Pe 3:10 let him *r·* his tongue from evil, *3973*

refrained
Ge 43:31 *r·* himself, and said, Set on bread. 662
Es 5:10 Nevertheless Haman *r·* himself: "
Job 29: 9 The princes *r·* talking, and laid 6113
Ps 40: 9 I have not *r·* my lips, O Lord, thou 3607
119:101 *r·* my feet from every evil way, 3601
Isa 42:14 I have been still, and *r·* myself: 662
Jer 14:10 they have not *r·* their feet, 2820

refraineth
Pr 10:19 sin: but he that *r·* his lips is wise. 2820

refresh See also REFRESHED; REFRESHETH; REFRESHING.
1Ki 13: 7 home with me, and *r·* thyself, 5582
Ac 27: 3 unto his friends to *r·* himself. *1958,5177*
Ph'm 20 the Lord: *r·* my bowels in the Lord. *373*

refreshed
Ex 23:12 and the stranger, may be *r·*. 5314
31:17 seventh day he rested, and was *r·*. "
1Sa 16:23 so Saul was *r·*, and was well, and 7304
2Sa 16:14 weary, and *r·* themselves there. 5314
Job 32:20 I will speak, that I may be *r·*: 7304
Ro 15:32 of God, and may with you be *r·*. *4875*
1Co 16:18 they have *r·* my spirit and yours: *373*
2Co 7:13 because his spirit was *r·* by you all. "
2Ti 1:16 he oft *r·* me, and was not ashamed *404*
Ph'm 7 bowels of the saints are *r·* by thee, *373*

refresheth
Pr 25:13 for he *r·* the soul of his masters. 7725

refreshing
Isa 28:12 weary to rest; and this is the *r·*: 4774
Ac 3:19 the times of *r·* shall come from *403*

refuge
Nu 35: 6 there shall be six cities for *r·*, 4733
11 you cities to be cities of *r·* for you; "
12 shall be unto you cities for *r·* from "
13 give six cities shall ye have for *r·*. "
14 Canaan, which shall be cities of *r·*. "
15 These six cities shall be a *r·*, both "
25 shall restore him to the city of his *r·*, "
26 out the border of the city of his *r·*, "
27 the borders of the city of his *r·*, "
28 remained in the city of his *r·* until "
32 him that is fled to the city of his *r·*, "
De 33:27 The eternal God is thy *r·*, and *4585
Jos 20: 2 Appoint out for you cities of *r·*, 4733
3 your *r·* from the avenger of blood. "
21:13, 21, 27, 32, 38 city of *r·* for the slayer; "
2Sa 22: 3 my high tower, and my *r·*, my 4498
1Ch 6:57 Hebron, the city of *r·*, and Libnah 4733
67 gave unto them, of the cities of *r·*, "
Ps 9: 9 also will be a *r·* for the oppressed, *4869
9 oppressed, a *r·* in times of trouble.* "
14: 6 poor, because the Lord is his *r·*. 4268
46: 1 God is our *r·* and strength, a very "
7, 11 us; the God of Jacob is our *r·*. 4869
48: 3 is known in her palaces for a *r·*. "
57: 1 of thy wings will I make my *r·*, 2620
59:16 and *r·* in the day of my trouble. 4498
62: 7 my strength, and my *r·*, is in God. 4268
8 before him: God is a *r·* for us. "
71: 7 many; but thou art my strong *r·*. "
91: 2 Lord, He is my *r·* and my fortress: "
9 hast made the Lord, which is my *r·*, "
94:22 and my God is the rock of my *r·*. "
104:18 high hills are a *r·* for the wild goats; "
142: 4 *r·* failed me; no man cared for 4498
5 Thou art my *r·* and my portion in 4268
Pr 14:26 his children shall have a place of *r·*. "
Isa 4: 6 for a place of *r·*, and for a covert "
25: 4 a *r·* from the storm, a shadow from "
28:15 for we have made lies our *r·*, and "
17 hail shall sweep away the *r·* of lies, "
Jer 16:19 and my *r·* in the day of affliction, 4498
Heb 6:18 have fled for *r·* to lay hold upon the *2703*

refuse See also REFUSED; REFUSETH.
Ex 4:23 if thou *r·* to let him go, behold, I *3985
8: 2 if thou *r·* to let them go, behold, I 3986
9: 2 if thou *r·* to let them go, and wilt "
10: 3 long wilt thou *r·* to humble thyself 3985
4 if thou *r·* to let my people go, 3986
16:28 *r·* ye to keep my commandments 3985
22:17 utterly *r·* to give her unto him, "
1Sa 15: 9 every thing that was vile and *r·*, 4549
Job 34:33 whether thou *r·*, or whether thou *3988
Pr 8:33 and be wise, and *r·* it not. 6544
21: 7 because they *r·* to do judgment. 3985
25 him; for his hands *r·* to labour. "
Isa 1:20 But if ye *r·* and rebel, ye shall be "
7:15 that he may know to *r·* the evil, 3988
16 the child shall know to *r·* the evil, "
Jer 8: 5 hold fast deceit, they *r·* to return. 3985
9: 6 through deceit they *r·* to know me, "
13:10 people, which *r·* to hear my words, 3987
25:28 *r·* to take the cup at thine hand to 3985
38:21 But if thou *r·* to go forth, this is 3986
La 3:45 and *r·* in the midst of the people. 3973
Am 8: 6 yea, and sell the *r·* of the wheat? 4651
Ac 25:11 worthy of death, I *r·* not to die: *3868*
1Ti 4: 7 *r·* profane and old wives' fables, "
5:11 But the younger widows *r·*: for "
Heb 12:25 that ye *r·* not him that speaketh. "

refused See also REFUSEDST.
Ge 37:35 but he *r·* to be comforted; and he 3985
39: 8 he *r·*, and said unto his master's "
48:19 his father *r·*, and said, I know it, "
Nu 20:21 Edom *r·* to give Israel passage "
1Sa 8:19 the people *r·* to obey the voice of "
16: 7 stature; because I have *r·* him: *3988
28:23 But he *r·*, and said, I will not eat. 3985
2Sa 2:23 Howbeit he *r·* to turn aside: "
13: 9 out before him; but he *r·* to eat. "
1Ki 20:35 thee. And the man *r·* to smite him. "
21:15 which he *r·* to give thee for money: "
2Ki 5:16 he urged him to take it; but he *r·*. "
Ne 9:17 *r·* to obey, neither were mindful of "
Es 1:12 Vashti *r·* to come at the king's "
Job 6: 7 things that my soul *r·* to touch are* "

Ps 77: 2 not: my soul *r'* to be comforted. 3985
78:10 of God, and *r'* to walk in his law: "
67 he *r'* the tabernacle of Joseph, 3988
118:22 The stone which the builders *r'* is* "
Pr 1:24 Because I have called, and ye *r'*; 3985
Isa 54: 6 wife of youth, when thou wast *r'*,*3988
Jer 5: 3 they have *r'* to receive correction:3985
3 a rock; they have *r'* to return. "
11:10 which *r'* to hear my words; and "
31:15 *r'* to be comforted for her children,*"
50:33 them fast; they *r'* to let them go.* "
Eze 5: 6 they have *r'* my judgments and *3988
Ho 11: 5 king, because they *r'* to return. 3985
Zec 7:11 But they *r'* to hearken, and pulled "
Ac 7:35 Moses whom they *r'*, saying, Who *720*
1Ti 4: 4 God is good, and nothing to be *r'*,* *579*
Heb11:24 *r'* to be called the son of Pharaoh's*720*
12:25 escaped not who *r'* him that spake*3868*

refusedst
Jer 3: 3 forehead, thou *r'* to be ashamed. 3985

refuseth
Ex 7:14 hardened, he *r'* to let the people go.3985
Nu 22:13 the Lord *r'* to give me leave to go "
14 said, Balaam *r'* to come with us. "
De 25: 7 My husband's brother *r'* to raise up"
Pr 10:17 but he that *r'* reproof erreth. *5800
13:18 shall be to him that *r'* instruction:6544
15:32 He that *r'* instruction despiseth "
Isa 8: 6 people *r'* the waters of Shiloah 3988
Jer 15:18 incurable, which *r'* to be healed? 3985

regard See also REGARDED; REGARDEST; REGARDETH; REGARDING.
Ge 45:20 Also *r'* not your stuff; 5869,2347,5921
Ex 5: 9 and let them not *r'* vain words. 8159
Le 19:31 *R'* not them that have familiar *6437
De 28:50 shall not *r'* the person of the old, 5375
1Sa 4:20 answered not, neither did she *r'* it.3820
25:25 I pray thee, *r'* this man of Belial, * "
2Sa 13:20 is thy brother; *r'* not this thing. "
2Ki 3:14 I *r'* the presence of Jehoshaphat 5375
Job 3: 4 let not God *r'* it from above, ‡1875
35:13 neither will the Almighty *r'* it. 7789
36:21 Take heed, *r'* not iniquity: for 6437
Ps 28: 5 they *r'* not the works of the Lord, 995
31: 6 hated them that *r'* lying vanities: 8104
66:18 If I *r'* iniquity in my heart, the 7200
94: 7 neither shall the God of Jacob *r'* it.*995
102:17 will *r'* the prayer of the destitute,*6437
Pr 5: 2 That thou mayest *r'* discretion, *8104
6:35 He will not *r'* any ransom; 5375,6440
Ec 8: 2 that in *r'* of the oath of God. 5921,1700
Isa 5:12 they *r'* not the work of the Lord, 5027
13:17 which shall not *r'* silver; and as 2803
La 4:16 he will no more *r'* them: they 5027
Da 11:37 shall he *r'* the God of his fathers, 995
37 desire of women, nor *r'* any god: "
Am 5:22 will I *r'* the peace offerings of 5027
Hab 1: 5 and *r'*, and wonder marvellously: "
Mal 1: 9 means: will he *r'* your persons? *5375
Lu 18: 4 I fear not God, nor *r'* man; *1788*
Ac 8:11 to him they had *r'*, because that **4337*
Ro 14: 6 day, to the Lord he doth not *r'* it.**5426*

regarded
Ex 9:21 that *r'* not the word of the Lord 3820
1Ki 18:29 nor any to answer, nor any that *r'*.7182
1Ch 17:17 *r'* me according to the estate of a 7200
Ps 106:44 Nevertheless he *r'* their affliction, "
Pr 1:24 out my hand, and no man *r'*; 7181
Da 3:12 men, O king, have not *r'* thee:7761,2942
Lu 1:48 he hath *r'* the low estate of his **1914*
18: 2 feared not God, neither *r'* man: *1788*
Heb 8: 9 and I *r'* them not, saith the Lord. *272*

regardest
2Sa 19: 6 thou *r'* neither princes nor servants:*
Job 30:20 I stand up, and thou *r'* me not. * 995
M't 22:16 for thou *r'* not the person of men. *991*
M'r 12:14 for thou *r'* not the person of men,

regardeth
De 10:17 *r'* not persons, nor taketh reward:5375
Job 34:19 nor *r'* the rich more than the poor?5234
39: 7 *r'* he the crying of the driver. *8085
Pr 12:10 man *r'* the life of his beast: 3045
13:18 that *r'* reproof shall be honoured. 8104
15: 5 but he that *r'* reproof is prudent. "
29: 7 but the wicked *r'* not to know it. * 995
Ec 5: 8 that is higher than the highest *r'*;8104
11: 4 that *r'* the clouds shall not reap. 7200
Isa 33: 8 despised the cities, he *r'* no man. 2803
Da 6:13 of Judah, *r'* not thee, O king, 7761,2942
Mal 2:13 he *r'* not the offering any more, 6437
Ro 14: 6 *r'* the day, *r'* it unto the Lord; *5426*
6 he that *r'* not the day, to the Lord* "

regarding
Job 4:20 perish for ever without any *r'* it. 7760
Ph'p 2:30 nigh unto death, not *r'* his life, **3851*

Regem (*re'-ghem*) See also REGEM-MELECH.
1Ch 2:47 sons of Jahdai; *R'*, and Jotham, 7276

Regem-melech (*re''-ghem-me'-lek*)
Zec 7: 2 Sherezer and *R'*, and their men, 7278

regeneration
M't 19:28 the *r'* when the Son of man shall *3824*
Tit 3: 5 he saved us, by the washing of *r'*, "

region See also REGIONS.
De 3: 4 all the *r'* of Argob, the kingdom of2256
13 the *r'* of Argob, with all Bashan, "
1Ki 4:11 of Abinadab, in all the *r'* of Dor; *5299
13 *r'* of Argob, which is in Bashan, 2256
24 over all the *r'* on this side the river,
M't 3: 5 and all the *r'* round about Jordan,*4066*
4:16 sat in the *r'* and shadow of death *5561*
M'r 1:28 all the *r'* round about Galilee. *4066*
6:55 through that whole *r'* round about," "
Lu 3: 1 and of the *r'* of Trachonitis, and *5561*
4:14 through all the *r'* round about. *4066*
7:17 throughout all the *r'* round about. "
Ac 13:49 published throughout all the *r'*. *5561*
14: 6 unto the *r'* that lieth round about: *4066*
16: 6 Phrygia and the *r'* of Galatia, and *5561*

regions
Ac 8: 1 throughout the *r'* of Judæa and *5561*
2Co 10:16 preach the gospel in the *r'* beyond* "
11:10 this boasting in the *r'* of Achaia. *2825*
Ga 1:21 I came into the *r'* of Syria and "

register
Ezr 2:62 sought their *r'* among those that 3791
Ne 7: 5 I found a *r'* of the genealogy of *5612
64 sought their *r'* among those that 3791

Rehabiah (*re-hab-i'-ah*)
1Ch 23:17 sons of Eliezer were, *R'* the chief. 7345
17 but the sons of *R'* were very many. "
24:21 Concerning *R'*: of the sons of *R'*, "
26:25 *R'* his son, and Jeshaiah his son, "

rehearse See also REHEARSED.
Ex 17:14 and *r'* it in the ears of Joshua: 7760
J'g 5:11 shall they *r'* the righteous acts of 8567

rehearsed
1Sa 8:21 he *r'* them in the ears of the Lord.1696
17:31 spake, they *r'* them before Saul: 5046
Ac 11: 4 But Peter *r'* the matter from the * *756*
14:27 they *r'* all that God had done with *312*

Rehob (*re'-hob*) See also BETH-REHOB.
Nu 13:21 from the wilderness of Zin unto *R'*,7340
Jos 19:28 Hebron, and *R'*, and Hammon, and "
30 Ummah also, and Aphek, and *R'*: "
21:31 suburbs, and *R'* with her suburbs; "
J'g 1:31 of Helbah, nor of Aphik, nor of *R'*: "
2Sa 8: 3 also Hadadezer, the son of *R'*, king "
12 spoil of Hadadezer, the son of *R'*, "
10: 8 Syrians of Zobah, and of *R'*, and "
1Ch 6:75 suburbs, and *R'* with her suburbs: "
Ne 10:11 Micha, *R'*, Hashabiah, "

Rehoboam (*re-ho-bo'-am*) See also ROBOAM.
1Ki 11:43 *R'* his son reigned in his stead. 7346
12: 1 *R'* went to Shechem: for all Israel "
3 of Israel came, and spake unto *R'*, "
6 king *R'* consulted with the old men, "
12 the people came to *R'* the third day, "
17 of Judah, *R'* reigned over them. "
18 king *R'* sent Adoram, who was over "
18 king *R'* made speed to get him up "
21 when *R'* was come to Jerusalem, "
21 to bring the kingdom again to *R'* "
23 Speak unto *R'*, the son of Solomon, "
27 lord, even unto *R'* king of Judah, "
27 and go again to *R'* king of Judah. "
14:21 *R'* the son of Solomon reigned in "
21 *R'* was forty and one years old when "
25 to pass in the fifth year of king *R'*, "
27 king *R'* made in their stead brasen "
29 Now the rest of the acts of *R'*, and "
30 was war between *R'* and Jeroboam "
31 And *R'* slept with his fathers, and "
15: 6 was war between *R'* and Jeroboam "
1Ch 3:10 Solomon's son was *R'*, Abia his son, "
2Ch 9:31 and *R'* his son reigned in his stead. "
10: 1 And *R'* went to Shechem: for to "
3 all Israel came and spake to *R'*, "
6 *R'* took counsel with the old men "
12 and all the people came to *R'* on "
13 *R'* forsook the counsel of the old "
17 of Judah, *R'* reigned over them. "
18 *R'* sent Hadoram that was over the "
18 *R'* made speed to get him up to his "
11: 1 when *R'* was come to Jerusalem, "
1 bring the kingdom again to *R'*. "
3 Speak unto *R'* the son of Solomon, "
5 *R'* dwelt in Jerusalem, and built "
17 made *R'* the son of Solomon strong, "
18 *R'* took him Mahalath the daughter "
21 *R'* loved Maachah the daughter of "
22 *R'* made Abijah the son of Maachah "
12: 1 *R'* had established the kingdom, "
2 that in the fifth year of king *R'* "
5 came Shemaiah the prophet to *R'*, "
10 king *R'* made shields of brass, and "
13 So king *R'* strengthened himself in "
13 for *R'* was one and forty years old "
15 Now the acts of *R'*, first and last, "
15 wars between *R'* and Jeroboam "
16 *R'* slept with his fathers, and was "
13: 7 strengthened themselves against *R'* "
7 *R'* was young and tenderhearted, "

Rehoboth (*re'-ho-both*)
Ge 10:11 Nineveh, and the city *R'*, and *7344
26:22 and he called the name of it *R'*; "
36:37 Saul of *R'* by the river reigned in "
1Ch 1:48 Shaul of *R'* by the river reigned in "

Rehum (*re'-hum*) See also NEHUM.
Ezr 2: 2 Mizpar, Bigvai, *R'*, Baanah. 7348
4: 8 *R'* the chancellor and Shimshai "
9 Then wrote *R'* the chancellor, and "
17 an answer unto *R'* the chancellor, "
23 letter was read before *R'*, and "
Ne 3:17 the Levites, *R'* the son of Bani. "
10:25 *R'*, Hashabnah, Maaseiah, "
12: 3 Shechaniah, *R'*, Meremoth, "

Rei (*re'-i*)
1Ki 1: 8 the prophet, and Shimei, and *R'*. 7472

reign See also REIGNED; REIGNEST; REIGNETH; REIGNING.
Ge 37: 8 him, Shalt thou indeed *r'* over us? 4427
Ex 15:18 The Lord shall *r'* for ever and ever.4427
Le 26:17 that hate you shall *r'* over you; *7287
De 15: 6 thou shalt *r'* over many nations, *4910
6 but they shall not *r'* over thee. * "
J'g 9: 2 threescore and ten persons, *r'* over*"
2 you, or that one *r'* over you? "
8 the olive tree, *R'* thou over us. 4427
10 fig tree, Come thou, and *r'* over us. "
12 the vine, Come thou, and *r'* over us. "
14 bramble, Come thou, and *r'* over us. "
1Sa 8: 7 me, that I should not *r'* over them.*"
9 of the king that shall *r'* over them. "
11 of the king that shall *r'* over you: "
9:17 this same shall *r'* over my people.*6113
11:12 that said, Shall Saul *r'* over us? 4427
12:12 Nay; but a king shall *r'* over us: "
2Sa 2:10 forty years old when he began to *r'* "
3:21 *r'* over all that thine heart desireth. "
5: 4 thirty years old when he began to *r'*, "
1Ki 1:11 not heard that Adonijah...doth *r'*, "
13 Solomon thy son shall *r'* after me, "
13 throne? why then doth Adonijah *r'*? "
17 Solomon thy son shall *r'* after me, "
24 Adonijah shall *r'* after me, and he "
30 Solomon thy son shall *r'* after me, "
2:15 their faces on me, that I should *r'*: "
6: 1 year of Solomon's *r'* over Israel, "
11:37 *r'* according to all that thy soul "
14:21 one years old when he began to *r'*, "
15:25 And Nadab...began to *r'* over Israel "
33 began Baasha...to *r'* over all Israel "
16: 8 began Elah...to *r'* over Israel in "
11 came to pass, when he began to *r'*, "
15 did Zimri *r'* seven days in Tirzah. "
23 began Omri to *r'* over Israel, twelve "
29 began Ahab...to *r'* over Israel: "
22:41 Jehoshaphat...to *r'* over Judah "
42 five years old when he began to *r'*; "
51 Ahaziah...began to *r'* over Israel "
2Ki 3: 1 Jehoram...began to *r'* over Israel "
8:16 Jehoram the son...began to *r'*. "
17 old was he when he began to *r'*; "
25 did Ahaziah...begin to *r'*. "
26 was Ahaziah when he began to *r'*; "
9:29 began Ahaziah to *r'* over Judah. "
11: 3 And Athaliah did *r'* over the land.* "
21 was Jehoash when he began to *r'*. "
12: 1 year of Jehu Jehoash began to *r'*; "
13: 1 son of Jehu began to *r'* over Israel "
10 began Jehoash...to *r'* over Israel in "
14: 2 five years old when he began to *r'*, "
23 Jeroboam...began to *r'* in Samaria, "
15: 1 son of Amaziah king of Judah to *r'*. "
2 old was he when he began to *r'*, "
8 did Zachariah...*r'* over Israel in "
13 Shallum...son of Jabesh began to *r'* "
17 the son of Gadi to *r'* over Israel, "
23 Pekahiah...began to *r'* over Israel "
27 Pekah...began to *r'* over Israel "
32 son of Uzziah king of Judah to *r'*. "
33 old was he when he began to *r'*, "
16: 1 Ahaz...son of Jotham...began to *r'*. "
2 old was Ahaz when he began to *r'*, "
17: 1 began Hoshea...to *r'* in Samaria "
18: 1 that Hezekiah...began to *r'*. "
2 old was he when he began to *r'*, "
21: 1 twelve years old...he began to *r'*, "
19 two years old when he began to *r'*, "
22: 1 eight years old when he began to *r'*, "
23:31 years old when he began to *r'*; "
33 that he might not *r'* in Jerusalem; "
36 five years old when he began to *r'*; "
24: 8 years old when he began to *r'*, "
12 him in the eighth year of his *r'*. "
18 one years old when he began to *r'*, "
25: 1 to pass in the ninth year of his *r'*, "
27 in the year that he began to *r'* did "
1Ch 4:31 their cities unto the *r'* of David. "
26:31 the fortieth year of the *r'* of David 4438
29:30 With all his *r'* and his might, and "
2Ch 1: 8 hast made me to *r'* in his stead. *4427
3: 2 month, in the fourth year of his *r'*.4438
12:13 years old when he began to *r'*, 4427
13: 1 began Abijah to *r'* over Judah. "
15:10 the fifteenth year of the *r'* of Asa. 4438
19 and thirtieth year of the *r'* of Asa. "
16: 1 and thirtieth year of the *r'* of Asa "
12 the thirty and ninth year of his *r'* "
13 the one and fortieth year of his *r'*.4427
17: 7 third year of his *r'* he sent to his "
20:31 five years old when he began to *r'*, "
21: 5 two years old when he began to *r'*, "
20 old was he when he began to *r'*, "
22: 2 was Ahaziah when he began to *r'*, "
23: 3 Behold, the king's son shall *r'*, as "
24: 1 seven years old when he began to *r'*. "
25: 1 five years old when he began to *r'*, "
26: 3 was Uzziah when he began to *r'*, "
27: 1 five years old when he began to *r'*, "
8 years old when he began to *r'*, "
28: 1 years old when he began to *r'*, "
29: 1 Hezekiah began to *r'* when he was "
3 He in the first year of his *r'*, in the "
19 king Ahaz in his *r'* did cast away 4438
33: 1 years old when he began to *r'*, 4427
21 years old when he began to *r'*, "
34: 1 eight years old when he began to *r'*, "
3 in the eighth year of his *r'*, while "
8 the eighteenth year of his *r'*, when "
35:19 eighteenth year of the *r'* of Josiah 4438
36: 2 years old when he began to *r'*, 4427
5 five years old when he began to *r'*, "
9 eight years old when he began to *r'*, "
11 years old when he began to *r'*, "
20 the *r'* of the kingdom of Persia: "
Ezr 4: 5 the *r'* of Darius king of Persia, 4438

Ezr 4: 6 And in the r· of Ahasuerus, in the 4438
6 in the beginning of his r·, wrote "
24 the second year of the r· of Darius 4437
6:15 in the sixth year of the r· of Darius "
7: 1 in the r· of Artaxerxes king of 4438
8: 1 in the r· of Artaxerxes the king. "
Ne 12:22 to the r· of Darius the Persian. "
Es 1: 3 In the third year of his r·, he made 4427
2:16 in the seventh year of his r·. 4438
Job 34:30 That the hypocrite r· not, lest the 4427
Ps 146:10 The Lord shall r· for ever, even thy "
Pr 8:15 By me kings r·, and princes decree "
Ec 4:14 For out of prison he cometh to r·;* "
Isa 24:23 the Lord of hosts shall r· in mount "
32: 1 a king shall r· in righteousness, "
Jer 1: 2 in the thirteenth year of his r·. "
22:15 Shalt thou r·, because thou closest "
23: 5 and a King shall r· and prosper, "
26: 1 beginning of the r· of Jehoiakim 4468
27: 1 beginning of the r· of Jehoiakim 4467
28: 1 the beginning of the r· of Zedekiah "
33:21 have a son to r· upon his throne; 4427
49:34 the r· of Zedekiah king of Judah, 4438
51:59 in the fourth year of his r·. 4427
52: 1 years old when he began to r·, "
4 to pass in the ninth year of his r·, "
31 in the first year of his r· lifted up 4438
Da 1: 1 third year of the r· of Jehoiakim "
2: 1 year of the r· of Nebuchadnezzar "
6:28 this Daniel prospered in the r· of 4437
28 and in the r· of Cyrus the Persian. "
8: 1 year of the r· of king Belshazzar 4438
9: 2 In the first year of his r· I Daniel 4427
Mic 4: 7 shall r· over them in mount Zion "
M't 2:22 that Archelaus did r· in Judæa in* 936
Lu 1:33 r· over the house of Jacob for ever; "
3: 1 year of the r· of Tiberius Cæsar, 2231
19:14 not have this man to r· over us. 936
27 would not that I should r· over them, "
Ro 5:17 shall r· in life by one, Jesus Christ.) "
21 grace r· through righteousness unto "
6:12 Let not sin...r· in your mortal body, "
15:12 shall rise to r· over the Gentiles; * 757
1Co 4: 8 us: and I would to God ye did r·, 936
8 that we also might r· with you. 4821
15:25 For he must r·, till he hath put all 936
2Ti 2:12 suffer, we shall also r· with him: 4821
Re 5:10 and we shall r· on the earth. 936
11:15 and he shall r· for ever and ever. "
20: 6 shall r· with him a thousand years. "
22: 5 and they shall r· for ever and ever. "

reigned
Ge 36:31 kings that r· in the land of Edom, 4427
31 before there r· any king over the "
32 Bela the son of Beor r· in Edom: "
33 and Jobab...r· in his stead. "
34 and Husham...r· in his stead. "
35 and Hadad...r· in his stead: "
36 Samlah of Masrekah r· in his stead. "
37 died, and Saul... r· in his stead. "
38 the son of Achbor r· in his stead. "
39 died, and Hadar r· in his stead: "
Jos 12: 5 And r· in mount Hermon, and in *4910
13:10 Amorites, which r· in Heshbon, 4427
12 which r· in Ashtaroth and in Edrei, "
21 the Amorites, which r· in Heshbon, "
J'g 4: 2 king of Canaan, that r· in Hazor; "
9:22 Abimelech had r· three years over*7786
1Sa 13: 1 Saul r· one year; and when he had*4427
1 he had r· two years over Israel, "
2Sa 2:10 reign over Israel, and r· two years. "
5: 4 to reign, and he r· forty years. "
5 he r· over Judah seven years and "
5 he r· thirty and three years over "
8:15 And David r· over all Israel; and "
10: 1 and Hanun his son r· in his stead. "
16: 8 Saul, in whose stead thou hast r·; "
1Ki 2:11 that David r· over Israel were forty "
11 seven years r· he in Hebron, and "
11 and three years r· he in Jerusalem. "
4:21 And Solomon r· over all kingdoms*4910
11:24 dwelt therein, and r· in Damascus. 4427
25 abhorred Israel, and r· over Syria. "
42 Solomon r· in Jerusalem over all "
43 Rehoboam his son r· in his stead. "
12:17 of Judah, Rehoboam r· over them. "
14:19 how he warred, and how he r·, "
20 the days which Jeroboam r· were "
20 and Nadab his son r· in his stead. "
21 And Rehoboam...r· in Judah. "
21 he r· seventeen years in Jerusalem, "
31 And Abijam his son r· in his stead. "
15: 1 son of Nebat r· Abijam over Judah.* "
2 Three years r· he in Jerusalem. "
8 and Asa his son r· in his stead. "
9 king of Israel r· Asa over Judah. "
10 and one years r· he in Jerusalem. "
24 Jehoshaphat his son r· in his stead. "
25 Judah, and r· over Israel two years. "
28 slay him, and r· in his stead. "
29 it came to pass, when he r·, that he* "
16: 6 and Elah his son r· in his stead. "
10 king of Judah, and r· in his stead. "
22 so Tibni died, and Omri r·. "
23 years: six years r· he in Tirzah. "
28 and Ahab his son r· in his stead. "
29 Ahab the son of Omri r· over Israel "
22:40 Ahaziah his son r· in his stead. "
42 and he r· twenty and five years in "
50 Jehoram his son r· in his stead. "
51 Judah, and r· two years over Israel. "
2Ki 1:17 And Jehoram r· in his stead in the "
3: 1 king of Judah, and r· twelve years. "
27 that should have r· in his stead. "
8:15 he died: and Hazael r· in his stead. "
2Ki 8:17 and he r· eight years in Jerusalem. 4427
24 and Ahaziah his son r· in his stead. "
26 and he r· one year in Jerusalem. "
10:35 Jehoahaz his son r· in his stead. 4427
36 the time that Jehu r· over Israel "
12: 1 and forty years r· he in Jerusalem. "
21 Amaziah his son r· in his stead. "
13: 1 in Samaria, and r· seventeen years. "
9 and Joash his son r· in his stead. 4427
10 in Samaria, and r· sixteen years. "
24 Ben-hadad his son r· in his stead. 4427
14: 1 r· Amaziah the son of Joash king* "
2 and r· twenty and nine years in "
16 Jeroboam his son r· in his stead. "
23 Samaria, and r· forty and one years. "
29 Zachariah his son r· in his stead. 4427
15: 2 and he r· two and fifty years in "
7 and Jotham his son r· in his stead. "
10 and slew him, and r· in his stead. "
13 and he r· a full month in Samaria. "
14 and slew him, and r· in his stead. "
17 Israel, and r· ten years in Samaria. "
22 Pekahiah his son r· in his stead. 4427
23 Israel in Samaria, and r· two years. "
25 he killed him, and r· in his room. 4427
27 in Samaria, and r· twenty years. "
30 and slew him, and r· in his stead. 4427
33 he r· sixteen years in Jerusalem. "
38 and Ahaz his son r· in his stead. "
16: 2 and r· sixteen years in Jerusalem, "
20 Hezekiah his son r· in his stead. "
18: 2 and he r· twenty and nine years in "
19:37 Esarhaddon his son r· in his stead. "
20:21 Manasseh his son r· in his stead. "
21: 1 r· fifty and five years in Jerusalem. "
18 and Amon his son r· in his stead. "
19 and he r· two years in Jerusalem. "
26 and Josiah his son r· in his stead. "
22: 1 and he r· thirty and one years in "
23:31 he r· three months in Jerusalem. "
36 he r· eleven years in Jerusalem. "
24: 6 Jehoiachin his son r· in his stead. "
8 he r· in Jerusalem three months. "
18 he r· eleven years in Jerusalem. "
1Ch 1:43 kings that r· in the land of Edom "
43 before any king r· over the children "
44 Jobab the son...r· in his stead. "
45 Husham...r· in his stead. "
46 Hadad the son...r· in his stead. "
47 Samlah of Masrekah r· in his stead. "
48 Shaul of Rehoboth...r· in his stead. "
49 the son of Achbor r· in his stead. "
50 was dead, Hadad r· in his stead: "
3: 4 he r· seven years and six months: "
4 he r· thirty and three years. "
18:14 So David r· over all Israel, and "
19: 1 died, and his son r· in his stead. "
29:26 David the son...r· over all Israel. "
27 he r· over Israel was forty years; "
27 seven years r· he in Hebron, and "
27 and three years r· he in Jerusalem. "
28 and Solomon his son r· in his stead. "
2Ch 1:13 congregation, and r· over Israel. "
9:26 And he r· over all the kings from *4910
30 Solomon r· in Jerusalem over all 4427
31 Rehoboam his son r· in his stead. "
10:17 of Judah, Rehoboam r· over them. "
12:13 himself in Jerusalem, and r·: for "
13 he r· seventeen years in Jerusalem. "
16 and Abijah his son r· in his stead. "
13: 2 He r· three years in Jerusalem. "
14: 1 and Asa his son r· in his stead. "
17: 1 Jehoshaphat his son r· in his stead. "
20:31 And Jehoshaphat r· over Judah: he "
31 he r· twenty and five years in "
21: 1 Jehoram his son r· in his stead. "
5 and he r· eight years in Jerusalem. "
20 and he r· in Jerusalem eight years. "
22: 1 son of Jehoram king of Judah r·. "
2 and he r· one year in Jerusalem. "
12 and Athaliah r· over the land. "
24: 1 and he r· forty years in Jerusalem. "
27 Amaziah his son r· in his stead. "
25: 1 and he r· twenty and nine years in "
26: 3 r· fifty and two years in Jerusalem. "
23 and Jotham his son r· in his stead. "
27: 1 he r· sixteen years in Jerusalem. "
8 and r· sixteen years in Jerusalem. "
9 and Ahaz his son r· in his stead. "
28: 1 he r· sixteen years in Jerusalem: "
27 Hezekiah his son r· in his stead. "
29: 1 and he r· nine and twenty years in "
32:33 Manassah his son r· in his stead. "
33: 1 and he r· fifty and five years in "
20 and Amon his son r· in his stead. "
21 and r· two years in Jerusalem. "
34: 1 he r· in Jerusalem one and thirty "
36: 2 he r· three months in Jerusalem. "
5 he r· eleven years in Jerusalem: "
8 Jehoiachin his son r· in his stead. "
9 he r· three months and ten days in "
11 and r· eleven years in Jerusalem. "
Es 1: 1 (this is Ahasuerus which r·, from "
Isa 37:38 Esar-haddon his son r· in his stead. "
Jer 22:11 r· instead of Josiah his father, "
37: 1 Zedekiah...r· instead of Coniah "
52: 1 he r· eleven years in Jerusalem. "
Ro 5:14 death r· from Adam to Moses, even 936
17 one man's offence death r· by one; "
21 as sin hath r· unto death, even so "
1Co 4: 8 ye have r· as kings without us: ‡ "
Re 11:17 thee thy great power, and hast r·. * "
20: 4 and r· with Christ a thousand years. "

reignest
1Ch 29:12 come of thee, and thou r· over all;*4910

reigneth
1Sa 12:14 and also the king that r· over you 4427
2Sa 15:10 shall say, Absalom r· in Hebron. * "
1Ki 1:18 now, behold, Adonijah r·; and now. "
1Ch 16:31 among the nations, The Lord r·. "
Ps 47: 8 God r· over the heathen: God "
93: 1 The Lord r·, he is clothed with "
96:10 the heathen that the Lord r·: "
97: 1 The Lord r·; let the earth rejoice; "
99: 1 The Lord r·; let the people "
Pr 30:22 For a servant when he r·; and a * "
Isa 52: 7 that saith unto Zion, Thy God r·! "
Re 17:18 which r· over the kings of the 2192,932
19: 6 for the Lord God omnipotent r·. 936

reigning
1Sa 16: 1 rejected him from r· over Israel?*4427

reins
Job 16:13 he cleaveth my r· asunder, and 3629
19:27 my r· be consumed within me. "
Ps 7: 9 God trieth the hearts and r·. "
16: 7 my r· also instruct me in the night "
26: 2 prove me; try my r· and my heart. "
73:21 grieved, and I was pricked in my r·. "
139:13 For thou hast possessed my r·: "
Pr 23:16 my r· shall rejoice, when thy lips "
Isa 11: 5 faithfulness the girdle of his r·. 2504
Jer 11:20 that triest the r· and the heart, 3629
12: 2 their mouth, and far from their r·. "
17:10 Lord search the heart, I try the r·, "
20:12 and seest the r· and the heart, let "
La 3:13 of his quiver to enter into my r·. "
Re 2:23 which searcheth the r· and hearts: 3510

reject See also REJECTED; REJECTETH.
Ho 4: 6 I will also r· thee, and thou shalt 3988
M'r 6:26 sat with him, he would not r· her. 114
7: 9 well ye r· the commandment of God, "
Tit 3:10 first and second admonition r·; *3868

rejected
1Sa 8: 7 they have not r· thee, but they 3988
7 they have r· me, that I should not "
10:19 And ye have this day r· your God, "
15:23 thou hast r· the word of the Lord, "
23 hath also r· thee from being king. "
26 thou hast r· the word of the Lord, "
26 Lord hath r· thee from being king "
16: 1 r· him from reigning over Israel? "
2Ki 17:15 And they r· his statutes, and his "
20 the Lord r· all the seed of Israel, "
Isa 53: 3 He is despised and r· of men; a 2310
Jer 2:37 the Lord hath r· thy confidences, 3988
6:19 my words, nor to my law, but r· it. "
30 because the Lord hath r· them. "
7:29 the Lord hath r· and forsaken the "
8: 9 they have r· the word of the Lord; "
14:19 Hast thou utterly r· Judah? hath "
La 5:22 thou hast utterly r· us; thou art "
Ho 4: 6 because thou hast r· knowledge, I "
M't 21:42 The stone which the builders r·, 593
M'r 8:31 and be r· of the elders, and of the "
12:10 The stone which the builders r· is "
Lu 7:30 and lawyers r· the counsel of God 114
9:22 be r· of the elders and chief priests 593
17:25 things, and be r· of this generation. "
20:17 The stone which the builders r·, "
Ga 4:14 in my flesh ye despised not, nor r·; 1609
Heb 6: 8 beareth thorns and briers is r·, 96
12:17 inherited the blessing, he was r·: 593

rejecteth
Joh 12:48 He that r· me, and receiveth not 114

rejoice See also REJOICED; REJOICEST; REJOICETH; REJOICING.
Le 23:40 shall r· before the Lord your God 8055
De 12: 7 shall r· in all that ye put your hand "
12 shall r· before the Lord your God, "
18 shalt r· before the Lord your God "
14:26 and thou shalt r·, thou, and thine "
16:11 shalt r· before the Lord thy God, "
14 thou shalt r· in thy feast, thou, and "
15 therefore thou shalt surely r·. * "
26:11 thou shalt r· in every good thing 8056
27: 7 and r· before the Lord thy God. 8055
28:63 Lord will r· over you to destroy 7797
30: 9 will again r· over thee for good, "
32:43 R, O ye nations, with his people: 7442
33:18 R, Zebulun, in thy going out; 8055
J'g 9:19 this day, then r· ye in Abimelech, "
19 and let him also r· in you: "
16:23 unto Dagon their god, and to r·: 8057
1Sa 2: 1 because I r· in thy salvation. 8055
19: 5 thou sawest it, and didst r·: "
2Sa 1:20 the daughters of the Philistines r·, "
1Ch 16:10 heart of them r· that seek the Lord. "
31 be glad, and let the earth r·: 1523
32 let the fields r·, and all that is *5970
2Ch 6:41 and let thy saints r· in goodness. 8055
20:27 made them to r· over their enemies. "
Ne 12:43 had made them r· with great joy: "
Job 3:22 Which r· exceedingly, and are glad, "
20:18 be, and he shall not r· therein. 5965
21:12 and r· at the sound of the organ. 8055
Ps 2:11 with fear, and r· with trembling. 1523
5:11 that put their trust in thee r·: 8055
9: 2 I will be glad and r· in thee: I will*5970
14 of Zion: I will r· in thy salvation. 1523
13: 4 trouble me r· when I am moved. "
5 my heart shall r· in thy salvation. "
14: 7 Jacob shall r·, and Israel shall be "
20: 5 We will r· in thy salvation, and in*7442
21: 1 salvation how greatly shall he r·! 1523
30: 1 not made my foes to r· over me. 8055
31: 7 I will be glad and r· in thy mercy: "
32:11 Be glad in the Lord, and r·, ye 1524

Ps 33: 1 R' in the Lord, O ye righteous: 7442
21 For our heart shall r' in him, 8055
35: 9 Lord: it shall r' in his salvation. 7797
19 enemies wrongfully r' over me: 8055
24 and let them not r' over me. "
26 together that r' at mine hurt: "
38:16 otherwise they should r' over me: 8056
40:16 Let all those that seek thee r' 7797
48:11 Let mount Zion r', let the 8055
51: 8 bones...thou hast broken may r'. 1523
53: 6 Jacob shall r', and Israel shall be "
58:10 righteous shall r' when he seeth 8055
60: 6 I will r', I will divide Shechem, *5937
63: 7 the shadow of thy wings will I r'. 7442
11 But the king shall r' in God; 8055
65: 8 outgoings of the morning...to r'. 7442
12 the little hills r' on every side. *1524
66: 6 on foot: there did we r' in him. 8055
68: 3 be glad; let them r' before God: *5970
3 yea, let them exceedingly r'. 7797
4 name Jah, and r' before him. *5937
70: 4 Let all those that seek thee r' and 7797
71:23 My lips shall greatly r' when I sing7442
85: 6 that thy people may r' in thee? 8055
86: 4 R' the soul of thy servant: for unto "
89:12 and Hermon shall r' in thy name. 7442
16 thy name shall they r' all the day: 1523
42 hast made all his enemies to r'. 8055
90:14 we may r' and be glad all our days.7442
96:11 Let the heavens r', and let the *8056
12 shall all the trees of the wood r' *7442
97: 1 Lord reigneth; let the earth r'; 1523
12 R' in the Lord, ye righteous; and*8055
98: 4 make a loud noise, and r', and *7442
104:31 the Lord shall r' in his works. 8055
105: 3 heart of them r' that seek the Lord."
106: 5 may r' in the gladness of thy nation."
107:42 The righteous shall see it, and r':* "
108: 7 I will r', I will divide Shechem, *5937
109:28 ashamed; but let thy servant r'. 8055
118:24 made; we will r' and be glad in it.1523
119:162 I r' at thy word, as one that 7797
149: 2 Israel r' in him that made him: 8055
Pr 2:14 Who r' to do evil, and delight 8056
5:18 and r' with the wife of thy youth. 8055
23:15 wise, my heart shall r', even mine.* "
16 Yea, my reins shall r', when thy 5937
24 father of the righteous shall...r': 1523
25 and she that bare thee shall r'. "
24:17 R' not when thine enemy falleth, 8055
27: 9 Ointment and perfume r' the heart:"
28:12 When righteous men do r', there *5970
29: 2 are in authority, the people r': 8055
6 but the righteous doth sing and r'. "
31:25 and she shall r' in time to come. *7832
Ec 3:12 but for a man to r', and to do good8055
22 a man should r' in his own works; "
4:16 that come after shall not r' in him. "
5:19 his portion, and to r' in his labour; "
11: 8 live many years, and r' in them all; "
9 R', O young man, in thy youth; "
Ca 1: 4 we will be glad and r' in thee, we "
Isa 8: 6 r' in Rezin and Remaliah's son; 4885
9: 3 men r' when they divide the spoil. 1523
13: 3 even them that r' in my highness.*5947
14: 8 Yea, the fir trees r' at thee, and 8055
29 R' not thou, whole Palestina, "
23:12 Thou shalt no more r', O thou 5937
24: 8 the noise of them that r' endeth, 5947
25: 9 will be glad and r' in his salvation.8055
29:19 poor among men shall r' in the 1523
35: 1 and the desert shall r', and blossom"
2 and r' even with joy and singing: "
41:16 thou shalt r' in the Lord, and shalt "
61: 7 they shall r' in their portion: 7442
10 I will greatly r' in the Lord, my 7797
62: 5 bride, so shall thy God r' over thee."
65:13 my servants shall r', but ye shall 8055
18 But be ye glad and r' for ever in 1523
19 And I will r' in Jerusalem, and joy "
66:10 R' ye with Jerusalem, and be glad8055
10 r' for joy with her, all ye that 7797
14 your heart shall r', and your bones "
Jer 31:13 shall the virgin r' in the dance, 8057
13 make them r' from their sorrow. "
32:41 I will r' over them to do them good,7797
51:39 them drunken, that they may r', 5937
La 2:17 caused thine enemy to r' over thee,8055
4:21 R' and be glad, O daughter of 7797
Eze 7:12 let not the buyer r', nor the seller 8055
35:15 As thou didst r' at the inheritance8057
Ho 9: 1 R' not, O Israel, for joy, as other 8055
Joe 2:21 Fear not, O land; be glad and r': "
23 Zion, and r' in the Lord your God: "
Am 6:13 Ye which r' in a thing of nought, "
Mic 7: 8 R' not against me, O mine enemy:8056
Hab 1:15 therefore they r' and are glad. *8055
3:18 Yet I will r' in the Lord, I will joy 5937
Zep 3:11 of them that r' in thy pride, *5947
14 be glad and r' with all the heart, O5937
17 save, he will r' over thee with joy;7797
Zec 2:10 Sing and r', O daughter of Zion: 8055
4:10 for they shall r', and shall see the "
9: 9 R' greatly, O daughter of Zion; 1523
10: 7 heart shall r' as through wine: 8055
7 their heart shall r' in the Lord. *1523
M't 5:12 R', and be exceeding glad: for 5463
Lu 1:14 and many shall r' at his birth. "
6:23 R' ye in that day, and leap for joy: "
10:20 Notwithstanding in this r' not, "
20 but rather r', because your names "
15: 6 R' with me; for I have found my 4796
9 R' with me; for I have found the "
19:37 began to r' and praise God with a 5463
Joh 4:36 and he that reapeth may r' together."
5:35 willing for a season to r' in his light.21
Joh 14:28 If ye loved me, ye would r', *5463
16:20 and lament, but the world shall r': "
22 you again, and your heart shall r', "
Ac 2:26 Therefore did my heart r', and *2165
Ro 5: 2 and r' in hope of the glory of God. 2744
12:15 R' with them that do r', and weep 5463
15:10 R', ye Gentiles, with his people. 2165
1Co 7:30 and they that r', as though they 5463
12:26 all the members r' with it. 4796
2Co 2: 3 from them of whom I ought to r'; 5463
7: 9 I r', not that ye were made sorry, "
16 I r' therefore that I have confidence"
Ga 4:27 R', thou barren that bearest not; 2165
Ph'p 1:18 I therein do r', yea, and will r'. 5463
2:16 that I may r' in the day of Christ, *2745
17 faith, I joy, and r' with you all. 4796
18 cause also do ye joy, and r' with me."
28 when ye see him again, ye may r', 5463
3: 1 Finally, my brethren, r' in the Lord."
3 the spirit, and r' in Christ Jesus, *2744
4: 4 R' in the Lord alway: 5463
4 and again I say, R'. "
Col 1:24 Who now r' in my sufferings for "
1Th 5:16 R' evermore. "
Jas 1: 9 Let the brother of low degree r' *2744
4:16 But now ye r' in your boastings: * "
1Pe 1: 6 Wherein ye greatly r', though now 21
8 ye r' with joy unspeakable and full "
4:13 r', inasmuch as ye are partakers 5463
Re 11:10 upon the earth shall r' over them, "
12:12 r', ye heavens, and ye that dwell 2165
18:20 R' over her, thou heaven, and ye "
19: 7 Let us be glad and r', and give * 21

rejoiced
Ex 18: 9 And Jethro r' for all the goodness 2302
De 28:63 Lord r' over you to do you good, 7797
30: 9 for good, as he r' over thy fathers: "
J'g 19: 3 saw him, he r' to meet him. 8055
1Sa 6:13 and saw the ark, and r' to see it. "
11:15 and all the men of Israel r' greatly. "
1Ki 1:40 with pipes, and r' with great joy, 8056
5: 7 words of Solomon,...he r' greatly 8055
2Ki 11:14 and all the people of the land r', 8056
20 And all the people of the land r', 8055
1Ch 29: 9 the people r', for that they offered "
9 David...also r' with great joy. "
2Ch 15:15 And all Judah r' at the oath: for "
23:13 and all the people of the land r', 8056
21 And all the people of the land r': 8055
24:10 the princes and all the people r' "
29:36 And Hezekiah r', and all the people,"
30:25 Israel, and that dwelt in Judah, r'. "
Ne 12:43 offered great sacrifices, and r': "
43 the wives also and the children r': "
44 for Judah r' for the priests and 8057
Es 8:15 city of Shushan r' and was glad. *6670
Job 31:25 I r' because my wealth was great,8055
29 If I r' at the destruction of him "
Ps 35:15 But in mine adversity they r', and "
97: 8 and the daughters of Judah r' 1523
119:14 r' in the way of thy testimonies, 7797
Ec 2:10 for my heart r' in all my labour: 8055
Jer 15:17 assembly of the mockers, nor r'; 5937
50:11 Because ye were glad,because ye r'.*"
Eze 25: 6 r' in heart with all thy despite 8055
Ho 10: 5 the priests thereof that r' on it, 1523
Ob 12 thou have r' over the children of *8055
M't 2:10 they r' with exceeding great joy. 5463
Lu 1:47 my spirit hath r' in God my Saviour.21
58 upon her; and they r' with her. 4796
10:21 In that hour Jesus r' in spirit, 21
13:17 people r' for all the glorious things5463
Joh 8:56 father Abraham r' to see my day: 21
Ac 7:41 r' in the works of their own hands.2165
15:31 read, they r' for the consolation. 5463
16:34 he set meat before them, and r', 21
1Co 7:30 that rejoice, as though they r' not;5463
2Co 7: 7 toward me; so that I r' the more. "
Ph'p 4:10 But I r' in the Lord greatly, that * "
2Jo 4 I r' greatly that I found of thy "
3Jo 3 For I r' greatly, when the brethren "

rejoicest
Jer 11:15 when thou doest evil, then thou r'.5937

rejoiceth
1Sa 2: 1 and said, My heart r' in the Lord,*5970
Job 39:21 the valley, and r' in his strength: 7797
Ps 16: 9 my heart is glad, and my glory r': 1523
19: 5 r' as a strong man to run a race. 7797
28: 7 therefore my heart greatly r'; 5937
Pr 11:10 with the righteous, the city r': 5970
13: 9 The light of the righteous r': but 8055
15:30 The light of the eyes r' the heart: "
29: 3 Whoso loveth wisdom r' his father: "
Isa 5:14 he that r', shall descend into it. 5938
62: 5 the bridegroom r' over the bride, 4885
64: 5 meetest him that r' and worketh 7797
Eze 35:14 When the whole earth r', I will 8055
M't 18:13 he r' more of that sheep, than of 5463
Joh 3:29 r'...because of the bridegroom's "
1Co 13: 6 R' not in iniquity,
6 but r' in the truth; 4796
Jas 2:13 and mercy r' against judgment. *2620

rejoicing
1Ki 1:45 they are come up from thence r', 8056
2Ch 23:18 with r' and with singing, as it was8057
Job 8:21 laughing, and thy lips with r'. *8643
Ps 19: 8 of the Lord are right, r' the heart: 8055
45:15 and r' shall they be brought: 1524
107:22 and declare his works with r'. *7440
118:15 The voice of r' and salvation is in "
119:111 for they are the r' of my heart. 8342
126: 6 doubtless come again with r', *7440
Pr 8:30 his delight, r' always before him; 7832
Pr 8:31 R' in the habitable part of his 7832
Isa 65:18 I create Jerusalem a r', and her 1525
Jer 15:16 me the joy and r' of mine heart: 8057
Hab 3:14 their r' was as to devour the poor 5951
Zep 2:15 is the r' city that dwelt carelessly,*5947
Lu 15: 5 he layeth it on his shoulders, r'. 5463
Ac 5:41 r' that they were counted worthy to"
8:39 more: and he went on his way r'. "
Ro 12:12 R' in hope; patient in tribulation; "
1Co 15:31 by your r' which I have in Christ *2746
2Co 1:12 For our r' is this, the testimony of* "
14 that we are your r', even as ye also*2745
6:10 As sorrowful, yet always r'; as 5463
Ga 6: 4 shall he have r' in himself alone, *2745
Ph'p 1:26 your r' may be more abundant in * "
1Th 2:19 is our hope, or joy, or crown of r'?*2746
Heb 3: 6 r' of the hope firm unto the end. *2745
Jas 4:16 your boastings: all such r' is evil.*2746

Rekem (re'-kem)
Nu 31: 8 were slain; namely, Evi, and R', 7552
Jos 13:21 the princes of Midian, Evi, and R', "
18:27 And R', and Irpeel, and Taralah, "
1Ch 2:43 and Tappuah, and R', and Shema. "
44 Jorkoam: and R' begat Shemmai. "

release See also RELEASED.
De 15: 1 seven years thou shalt make a r'. 8059
2 And this is the manner of the r': "
2 unto his neighbour shall r' it; 8058
2 because it is called the Lord's r'. 8059
3 thy brother thine hand shall r'; 8058
9 year, the year of r', is at hand; 8059
31:10 in the solemnity of the year of r', "
Es 2:18 and he made a r' to the provinces, 2010
M't 27:15 to r' unto the people a prisoner, 630
17 will ye that I r' unto you? Barabbas,"
21 the twain will ye that I r' unto you?"
M'r 15: 9 I r' unto you the King of the Jews? "
11 rather r' Barabbas unto them. "
Lu 23:16 therefore chastise him, and r' him. "
17 must r' one unto them at the feast.)*"
18 this man, and r' unto us Barabbas: "
20 Pilate therefore, willing to r' Jesus, "
Joh 18:39 r' unto you one at the passover: "
39 I r' unto you the King of the Jews? "
19:10 thee, and have power to r' thee? "
12 thenceforth Pilate sought to r' him: "

released
M't 27:26 Then r' he Barabbas unto them: 630
M'r 15: 6 feast he r' unto them one prisoner,* "
15 the people, r' Barabbas unto them, "
Lu 23:25 And he r' unto them him that for "

relied
2Ch 13:18 they r' upon the Lord God of their8172
16: 7 thou hast r' on the king of Syria, "
7 and not r' on the Lord thy God, "

relief
Ac 11:29 to send r' unto the brethren 1248

relieve See also RELIEVED; RELIEVETH.
Le 25:35 then thou shalt r' him: yea, *2388
Isa 1:17 seek judgment, r' the oppressed, 833
La 1:11 things for meat to r' the soul: *7725
16 comforter that should r' my soul is*"
19 sought their meat to r' their souls.*"
1Ti 5:16 let them r' them, and let not the 1884
16 that it may r' them that are widows"

relieved
1Ti 5:10 feet, if she have r' the afflicted, 1884

relieveth
Ps 146: 9 he r' the fatherless and widow: 5749

religion
Ac 26: 5 sect of our r' I lived a Pharisee. 2356
Ga 1:13 in time past in the Jews' r', how 2454
14 profited in the Jews' r' above many2454
Jas 1:26 own heart, this man's r' is vain. 2356
27 Pure r' and undefiled before God "

religious
Ac 13:43 many of the Jews and r' proselytes*4576
Jas 1:26 any man among you seem to be r',2357

rely See also RELIED.
2Ch 16: 8 because thou didst r' on the Lord,8172

remain See also REMAINED; REMAINEST; REMAINETH; REMAINING.
Ge 38:11 R' a widow at thy father's house, 3427
Ex 8: 9 that they may r' in the river only? 7604
11 they shall r' in the river only. "
12:10 nothing of it r' until the morning: 3498
23:18 shall the fat of my sacrifice r' 3885
29:34 of the bread, r' unto the morning, 3498
Le 19: 6 ought r' until the third day, it shall"
25:28 r' in the hand of him that...bought1961
52 r' but few years unto the year of 7604
27:18 according to the years that r', 3498
Nu 33:55 those which ye let r' of them shall "
De 2:34 of every city, we left none to r': *8300
16: 4 r' all night until the morning. 3885
19:20 which r' shall hear, and fear, and 7604
21:13 and shall r' in thine house, and 3427
23 His body shall not r' all night 3885
Jos 1:14 shall r' in the land which Moses *3427
2:11 r' any more courage in any man, 6965
8:22 they let none of them r' or escape.8300
10:27 mouth, which r' until this very day.*
28 that were therein; he let none r' *8300
30 were therein; he let none r' in it; "
23: 4 you by lot these nations that r', 7604
7 nations, these that r' among you; "
12 even these that r' among you, and "
J'g 5:17 and why did Dan r' in ships? 1481
21: 7, 16 do for wives for them that r', 3498
1Sa 20:19 hand, and shalt r' by the stone Ezel.3427
1Ki 11:16 (For six months did Joab r' there* "
18:22 I only, r' a prophet of the Lord; *3498

2Ki 7:13 thee, five of the horses that r', 7604
Ezr 9:15 for we r' yet escaped, as it is this * "
Job 21:32 grave, and shall r' in the tomb. *8245
27:15 that r' of him shall be buried in 8300
37: 8 go into dens, and r' in their places.7931
Ps 55: 7 far off, and r' in the wilderness. *3885
Pr 2:21 land, and the perfect shall r' in it. 3498
21:16 r' in the congregation of the dead.*5117
Isa 10:32 yet shall he r' at Nob that day: he*5975
32:16 righteousness r' in the fruitful *3427
44:13 man; that it may r' in the house. * "
65: 4 Which r' among the graves, and * "
66:22 I will make, shall r' before me, 5975
22 shall your seed and your name r'. "
Jer 8: 3 residue...that r' of this evil family,7604
3 r' in all the places whither I have "
17:25 and this city shall r' for ever. 3427
24: 8 of Jerusalem, that r' in this land, 7604
27:11 will I let r' still in their own land, 3241
19 of the vessels that r' in this city, *3498
21 the vessels that r' in the house of * "
30:18 palace shall r' after the manner 3427
38: 4 the men of war that r' in this city, 7604
42:17 none of them shall r' or escape 8300
44: 7 Judah, to leave you none to r'; *7611
14 shall escape or r', that they should8300
51:62 that none shall r' in it, neither *3427
Eze 7:11 none of them shall r', nor of their
17:21 and they that r' shall be scattered 7604
31:13 all the fowls of the heaven r', *7931
32: 4 all the fowls of the heaven to r' * "
39:14 that r' upon the face of the earth, 3498
Am 6: 9 if there r' ten men in one house, "
Ob 14 that did r' in the day of distress. 8300
Zec 5: 4 shall r' in the midst of his house, *3885
12:14 All the families that r', every 7604
Lu 10: 7 And in the same house r', eating 3306
Joh 6:12 Gather up the fragments that r', 4052
15:11 that my joy might r' in you, and *3306
16 fruit, and that your fruit should r':*"
19:31 bodies should not r' upon the cross"
1Co 7:11 if she depart, let her r' unmarried, "
15: 6 the greater part r' unto this present,"
1Th 4:15 and r' unto the coming of the Lord*4035
17 are alive and r' shall be caught up*"
Heb12:27 which cannot be shaken may r'. 3306
1Jo 2:24 from the beginning shall r' in you,*"
Re 3: 2 strengthen the things which r', 3062

remainder
Ex 29:34 thou shalt burn the r' with fire: 3498
Le 6:16 the r' thereof shall Aaron and his* "
7:16 also the r' of it shall be eaten: * "
17 the r' of the flesh of the sacrifice * "
2Sa 14: 7 name nor r' upon the earth. 7611
Ps 76:10 the r' of wrath shalt thou restrain.*"

remained
Ge 7:23 Noah only r' alive, and they that *7604
14:10 they that r' fled to the mountain. "
Ex 8:31 from his people; there r' not one. "
10:15 there r' not any green thing in 3498
19 r' not one locust in all the coasts 7604
14:28 there r' not so much as one of them."
Nu 11:26 r' two of the men in the camp, "
35:28 have r' in the city of his refuge 3427
36:12 their inheritance r' in the tribe 1961
De 3:11 only Og king of Bashan r' of the 7604
4:25 ye shall have r' long in the land, *3462
Jos 10:20 the rest which r' of them entered 8277
11:22 in Gath, and in Ashdod, there r'. *7604
13:12 who r' of the remnant of the giants:*"
18: 2 r' among the children of Israel 3498
21:20 which r' of the children of Kohath,*"
26 of the children of Kohath that r'. * "
J'g 7: 3 and there r' ten thousand. 7604
1Sa 11:11 they which r' were scattered, so that"
23:14 r' in a mountain in the wilderness3427
24: 3 his men r' in the sides of the cave.*"
2Sa 13:20 Tamar r' desolate in her brother "
1Ki 22:46 which r' in the days of his father 7604
2Ki 10:11 Jehu slew all that r' of the house of"
17 he slew all that r' unto Ahab in "
13: 6 there r' the grove also in Samaria.)5975
24:14 none r', save the poorest sort of 7604
25:22 as for the people that r' in the land*"
1Ch 13:14 ark of God r' with the family of 3427
Ec 2: 9 also my wisdom r' with me. 5975
Jer 34: 7 cities r' of the cities of Judah. 7604
37:10 there r' but wounded men among "
16 Jeremiah had r' there many days;3427
21 Thus Jeremiah r' in the court of the"
38:13 and Jeremiah r' in the court of the "
39: 9 of the people that r' in the city, 7604
9 with the rest of the people that r'. "
41:10 all the people that r' in Mizpah, * "
48:11 therefore his taste r' in him, and *5975
51:30 fight, they have r' in their holds: *3427
52:15 of the people that r' in the city, *7604
La 2:22 Lord's anger none escaped nor r': 8300
Eze 3:15 r' there astonished among them *3427
Da 10: 8 and there r' no strength in me: 7604
13 I r' there with the kings of Persia. 3498
17 there r' no strength in me, 5975
M't 11:23 it would have r' until this day. 3306
14:20 fragments that r' twelve baskets 4052
Lu 1:22 unto them, and r' speechless. 1265
9:17 that r' to them twelve baskets. 4052
Joh 6:13 which r' over and above unto them "
Ac 5: 4 Whiles it r', was it not thine own? 3306
27:41 stuck fast, and r' unmovable, but "

remainest
La 5:19 Thou, O Lord, r' for ever; thy *3427
Heb 1:11 They shall perish; but thou r'; *1265

remaineth
Ge 8:22 While the earth r', seedtime and 3117
Ex 10: 5 which r' unto you from the hail, 7604
Ex 12:10 which r' of it until the morning 3498
16:23 that which r' over lay up for you 5736
26:12 the remnant that r' of the curtains "
12 the half curtain that r', shall hang "
13 r' in the length of the curtains of "
Le 8:32 And that which r' of the flesh and 3498
10:12 Take the meat offering that r' of "
16:16 that r' among them in the midst *7931
Nu 24:19 shall destroy him that r' of...city. *8300
Jos 8:29 heap of stones, that r' unto this day.*
13: 1 there r' yet very much land to be 7604
2 This is the land that yet r': all the "
J'g 5:13 made him that r' have dominion *8300
1Sa 6:18 which stone r' unto this day in the
16:11 There r' yet the youngest, and, 7604
1Ch 17: 1 the covenant of the Lord r' under*
Ezr 1: 4 whosoever r' in any place where *7604
Job 19: 4 erred, mine error r' with myself. 3885
21:34 your answers there r' falsehood? 7604
41:22 In his neck r' strength, and *3885
Isa 4: 3 he that r' in Jerusalem, shall be 3498
Jer 38: 2 He that r' in this city shall die by 3427
47: 4 and Zidon every helper that r': 8300
Eze 6:12 he that r' and is besieged shall die7604
Hag 2: 5 so my spirit r' among you: fear ye*5975
Zec 9: 7 he that r', even he, shall be for *7604
Joh 9:41 say, We see; therefore your sin r'.3306
1Co 7:29 it r', that both they that have 3588,3063
2Co 3:11 more that which r' is glorious. 3306
14 for until this day r' the same vail "
9: 9 poor: his righteousness r' for ever.*"
Heb 4: 6 it r' that some must enter therein, 620
9 r' therefore a rest to the people of "
10:26 there r' no more sacrifice for sins, "
1Jo 3: 9 his seed r' in him: and he cannot*3306

remaining
Nu 9:22 upon the tabernacle, r' thereon, *7931
De 3: 3 him until none was left to him r'. 8300
Jos 10:33 until he had left him none r'. "
37 he left none r', according to all that"
39 he left none r': as he had done to "
40 left none r', but utterly destroyed "
11: 8 them, until they left them none r'. "
21:40 r' of the families of the Levites, *3498
2Sa 21: 5 r' in any of the coasts of Israel, 3320
2Ki 10:11 priests, until he left him none r'. 8300
1Ch 9:33 who r' in the chambers were free:*
Job 18:19 people, nor any r' in his dwellings.8300
Ob 18 not be any r' of the house of Esau; "
Joh 1:33 Spirit descending, and r' on him, *3306

Remaliah (*rem-a-li'-ah*) See also REMALIAH'S.
2Ki 15:25 Pekah the son of *R'*, a captain of 7425
27 Pekah the son of *R'* began to reign"
30 against Pekah the son of *R'*, and "
32 Pekah the son of *R'* king of Israel "
37 of Syria, and Pekah the son of *R'*. "
16: 1 year of Pekah the son of *R'*, "
5 and Pekah son of *R'* king of Israel "
2Ch 28: 6 Pekah the son of *R'* slew in Judah "
Isa 7: 1 Pekah the son of *R'*, king of Israel, "
4 with Syria, and of the son of *R'*. "
5 Syria, Ephraim, and the son of *R'*, "

Remaliah's (*rem-a-li'-ahs*)
Isa 7: 9 and the head of Samaria is *R'* son.7425
8: 6 and rejoice in Rezin and *R'* son; "

remedy
2Ch 36:16 his people, till there was no r'. 4832
Pr 6:15 shall he be broken without r'. "
29: 1 be destroyed, and that without r'. "

remember See also REMEMBERED; REMEMBEREST; REMEMBERETH; REMEMBERING.
Ge 9:15 And I will r' my covenant, which 2142
16 I may r' the everlasting covenant "
40:23 did not the chief butler r' Joseph, "
41: 9 saying, I do r' my faults this day: "
Ex 13: 3 *R'* this day, in which ye came out "
20: 8 *R'* the sabbath day, to keep it holy. "
32:13 *R'* Abraham, Isaac, and Israel, thy "
Le 26:42 will I r' my covenant with Jacob, "
42 covenant with Abraham will I r'; "
42 and I will r' the land. "
45 will for their sakes r' the covenant "
Nu 11: 5 We r' the fish, which we did eat in "
15:39 and r' all the commandments of the"
40 That ye may r', and do all my "
De 5:15 And r' that thou wast a servant in "
7:18 but shalt well r' what the Lord thy "
8: 2 And thou shalt r' all the way which"
18 thou shalt r' the Lord thy God: for "
9: 7 *R'*, and forget not, how thou "
27 *R'* thy servants, Abraham, Isaac, "
15:15 shalt r' that thou wast a bondman "
16: 3 thou mayest r' the day when thou "
12 shalt r' that thou wast a bondman "
24: 9 *R'* what the Lord thy God did unto "
18, 22 shalt r'...thou wast a bondman "
25:17 *R'* what Amalek did unto thee by "
32: 7 *R'* the days of old, consider the "
Jos 1:13 *R'* the word which Moses the "
J'g 9: 2 r' also that I am your bone and "
16:28 r' me, I pray thee, and strengthen "
1Sa 1:11 and r' me, and not forget thine "
15: 2 I r' that which Amalek did to *6485
25:31 my lord, then r' thine handmaid. 2142
2Sa 14:11 let the king r' the Lord thy God, "
19:19 neither do thou r' that which thy "
2Ki 9:25 r' how that, when I and thou rode "
20: 3 r' now how I have walked before "
1Ch 16:12 *R'* his marvellous works that he "
2Ch 6:42 r' the mercies of David thy servant."
Ne 1: 8 *R'*, I beseech thee, the word that "
4:14 r' the Lord, which is great and "
13:14 *R'* me, O my God, concerning this, "
Ne 13:22 *R'* me, O my God, concerning this 2142
29 *R'* them, O my God, because they "
31 *R'* me, O my God, for good. "
Job 4: 7 *R'*, I pray thee, who ever perished, "
7: 7 O r' that my life is wind: mine eye "
10: 9 *R'*, I beseech thee, that thou hast "
11:16 and r' it as waters that pass away: "
14:13 appoint me a set time, and r' me! "
21: 6 Even when I r' I am afraid, and "
36:24 *R'* that thou magnify his work, "
41: 8 upon him, r' the battle, do no more."
Ps 20: 3 *R'* all thy offerings, and accept thy "
7 r' the name of the Lord our God. * "
22:27 All the ends of the world shall r' "
25: 6 *R'*, O Lord, thy tender mercies and "
7 *R'* not the sins of my youth, nor "
7 r' thou me for thy goodness' sake, "
42: 4 When I r' these things, I pour out "
6 I r' thee from the land of Jordan, "
63: 6 When I r' thee upon my bed, and "
74: 2 *R'* thy congregation, which thou "
18 *R'* this, that the enemy hath "
22 r' how the foolish man reproacheth"
77:10 I will r' the years of the right hand "
11 I will r' the works of the Lord: * "
11 surely I will r' thy wonders of old. "
79: 8 r' not against us former iniquities: "
89:47 *R'* how short my time is: wherefore"
50 *R'*, Lord, the reproach of thy "
103:18 to those that r' his commandments "
105: 5 *R'* his marvellous works that he "
106: 4 *R'* me, O Lord, with the favour that "
119:49 *R'* the word unto thy servant, upon "
132: 1 r' David, and all his afflictions: "
137: 6 If I do not r' thee, let my tongue "
7 *R'*, O Lord, the children of Edom "
143: 5 I r' the days of old; I meditate on "
Pr 31: 7 poverty, and r' his misery no more. "
Ec 5:20 not much r' the days of his life; "
11: 8 yet let him r' the days of darkness; "
12: 1 *R'* now thy Creator in the days of "
Ca 1: 4 we will r' thy love more than wine:*"
Isa 38: 3 *R'* now, O Lord, I beseech thee, "
43:18 *R'* ye not the former things, neither"
25 own sake, and will not r' thy sins. "
44:21 *R'* these, O Jacob and Israel; for "
46: 8 *R'* this, and shew yourselves men: "
9 *R'* the former things of old: for I "
47: 7 neither didst r' the latter end of it. "
54: 4 and shalt not r' the reproach of thy "
64: 5 those that r' thee in thy ways: "
9 O Lord, neither r' iniquity for ever:"
Jer 2: 2 I r' thee, the kindness of thy "
3:16 to mind: neither shall they r' it; "
14:10 he will now r' their iniquity, and "
21 r', break not thy covenant with us. "
15:15 r' me, and visit me, and revenge "
17: 2 Whilst their children r' their altars"
18:20 *R'* that I stood before thee to speak"
31:20 him, I do earnestly r' him still: "
34 and I will r' their sin no more. "
44:21 did not the Lord r' them, and came"
51:50 r' the Lord afar off, and let "
La 5: 1 *R'*, O Lord, what is come upon us: "
Eze 6: 9 you shall r' me among the nations "
16:60 Nevertheless I will r' my covenant "
61 shalt r' thy ways, and be ashamed, "
63 thou mayest r', and be confounded,"
20:43 And there shall ye r' your ways, "
23:27 unto them, nor r' Egypt any more. "
36:31 Then shall ye r' your own evil ways,"
Ho 7: 2 that I r' all their wickedness: "
8:13 now will he r' their iniquity, and "
9: 9 therefore he will r' their iniquity, "
Mic 6: 5 r' now what Balak king of Moab "
Hab 3: 2 make known; in wrath r' mercy. "
Zec 10: 9 they shall r' me in far countries; "
Mal 4: 4 *R'* ye the law of Moses my servant, "
M't 16: 9 neither r' the five loaves of the 3421
27:63 Sir, we r' that that deceiver said, 3415
M'r 8:18 hear ye not? and do ye not r'? 3421
Lu 1:72 and to r' his holy covenant; 3415
16:25 Son, r' that thou in thy lifetime "
17:32 *R'* Lot's wife. 3421
23:42 r' me when thou comest into thy 3415
24: 6 r' how he spake unto you when he "
Joh 15:20 *R'* the word that I said unto you, 3421
16: 4 ye may r' that I told you of them. "
Ac 20:31 r', that by the space of three years "
35 to r' the words of the Lord Jesus, "
1Co 11: 2 that ye r' me in all things, and 3415
Ga 2:10 would that we should r' the poor; 3421
Eph 2:11 Wherefore r', that ye being in time "
Col 4:18 *R'* my bonds. Grace be with you. "
1Th 2: 9 For ye r', brethren, our labour and "
2Th 2: 5 *R'* ye not, that, when I was yet with"
2Ti 2: 8 *R'* that Jesus Christ of the seed of "
Heb 8:12 their iniquities will I r' no more. 3415
10:17 sins and iniquities will I r' no more."
13: 3 *R'* them that are in bonds, as 3403
7 *R'* them which have the rule over 3421
3Jo 10 will r' his deeds which he doeth, *5279
Jude 17 r' ye the words which were spoken3415
Re 2: 5 *R'* therefore from whence thou art3421
3: 3 *R'* therefore how thou hast received"

remembered
Ge 8: 1 And God r' Noah, and every living2142
19:29 that God r' Abraham, and sent Lot "
30:22 And God r' Rachel, and God "
42: 9 And Joseph r' the dreams which he"
Ex 2:24 God r' his covenant with Abraham, "
6: 5 and I have r' my covenant. "
Nu 10: 9 shall be r' before the Lord your God, "
J'g 8:34 children of Israel r' not the Lord "
1Sa 1:19 Hannah his wife; and the Lord r' "
2Ch 24:22 Joash the king r' not the kindness "

Es 2: 1 r· Vashti, and what she had done, 2142
9:28 these days should be r· and kept "
Job 24:20 he shall be no more r·; and "
Ps 45:17 name to be r· in all generations: "
77: 3 I r· God, and was troubled: I * "
78:35 they r· that God was their rock, "
39 For he r· that they were but flesh; "
42 They r· not his hand, nor the day "
98: 3 He hath r· his mercy and his truth "
105: 8 He hath r· his covenant for ever, "
42 For he r· his holy promise, and "
106: 7 r· not the multitude of thy mercies; "
45 And he r· for them his covenant, "
109:14 Let the iniquity of his fathers be r· "
16 that he r· not to shew mercy, but "
111: 4 made his wonderful works to be r·:2143
119:52 I r· thy judgments of old, O Lord; 2142
55 I have r· thy name, O Lord, in the "
136:23 Who r· us in our low estate: for his "
137: 1 yea, we wept, when we r· Zion. "
Ec 9:15 yet no man r· that same poor man. "
Isa 23:16 many songs, that thou mayest be r·. "
57:11 thou hast lied, and hast not r· me, "
63:11 Then he r· the days of old, Moses, "
65:17 and the former shall not be r·, nor "
Jer 11:19 that his name may be no more r·. "
La 1: 7 Jerusalem r· in the days of her * "
2: 1 r· not his footstool in the day of his "
Eze 3:20 which he hath done shall not be r·; "
16:22, 43 hast not r· the days of thy youth, "
21:24 ye have made your iniquity to be r·, "
32 thou shalt be no more r·: for I the "
25:10 that the Ammonites may not be r· "
33:13 his righteousnesses shall not be r·; "
Ho 2:17 shall no more be r· by their name.* "
Am 1: 9 and r· not the brotherly covenant: "
Jon 2: 7 soul fainted within me I r· the Lord: "
Zec 13: 2 land, and they shall no more be r·: "
M't 26:75 And Peter r· the word of Jesus, 3415
Lu 22:61 And Peter r· the word of the Lord, 5279
24: 8 And they r· his words, 3415
Joh 2:17 his disciples r· that it was written, "
22 his disciples r· that he had said this "
12:16 then r· they that these things were "
Ac 11:16 Then r· I the word of the Lord, how "
Re 18: 5 and God hath r· her iniquities. 3421

rememberest
Ps 88: 5 the grave, whom thou r· no more: 2142
M't 5:23 and there r· that thy brother hath 3415

remembereth
Ps 9:12 inquisition for blood, he r· them: 2142
103:14 our frame; he r· that we are dust. "
La 1: 9 she r· not her last end; therefore* "
Joh 16:21 child, she r· no more the anguish, 3421
2Co 7:15 he r· the obedience of you all, how 363

remembering
La 3:19 R· mine affliction and my misery,*2142
1Th 1: 3 R· without ceasing your work of 3421

remembrance See also REMEMBRANCES.
Ex 17:14 utterly put out the r· of Amalek 2143
Nu 5:15 memorial, bringing iniquity to r·.2142
De 25:19 shalt blot out the r· of Amalek 2143
32:26 I would make the r· of them to cease "
2Sa 18:18 have no son to keep my name in r·:2142
1Ki 17:18 come unto me to call my sin to r·, "
Job 18:17 His r· shall perish from the earth, 2143
Ps 6: 5 For in death there is no r· of thee: "
30: 4 thanks at the r· of his holiness. * "
34:16 to cut off the r· of them from the "
38: *title* A Psalm of David, to bring to r·. 2142
70: *title* A Psalm of David, to bring to r·. "
77: 6 I call to r· my song in the night: "
83: 4 name of Israel may be no more in r·. "
97:12 thanks at the r· of his holiness. *2143
102:12 and thy r· unto all generations. †‡ "
112: 6 righteous shall be in everlasting r·. "
Ec 1:11 There is no r· of former things; 2146
11 any r· of things that are to come "
2:16 there is no r· of the wise more than "
Isa 26: 8 thy name, and to the r· of thee. ††2143
43:26 Put me in r·: let us plead together:2142
57: 8 the posts hast thou set up thy r·:*2146
La 3:20 My soul hath them still in r·, 2142
Eze 21:23 but he will call to r· the iniquity, "
24 because,...that ye are come to r·, "
23:19 calling to r· the days of her youth,* "
21 thou calledst to r· the lewdness of 6485
29:16 which bringeth their iniquity to r·,2142
Mal 3:16 a book of r· was written before 2146
M'r 11:21 Peter calling to r· saith unto him, 363
Lu 1:54 servant Israel, in r· of his mercy;*3415
22:19 given for you: this do in r· of me. 364
Joh 14:26 and bring all things to your r·, 5279
Ac 10:31 and thine alms are had in r· in the 3415
1Co 4:17 shall bring you into r· of my ways 363
11:24 broken for you: this do in r· of me. 364
25 do ye, as oft as ye drink it, in r· of me. "
Ph'p 1: 3 thank...God upon every r· of you, 3417
1Th 3: 6 that ye have good r· of us always, "
1Ti 4: 6 the brethren in r· of these things,*5294
2Ti 1: 3 I have r· of thee in my prayers 3417
5 I call to r· the unfeigned faith *5280
6 I put thee in r· that thou stir up 363
2:14 Of these things put them in r·, 5279
Heb 10: 3 there is a r· again made of sins 364
32 But call to r· the former days, in 363
2Pe 1:12 you always in r· of these things, 5179
13 stir you up by putting you in r·; 5280
15 to have these things always in r·. 3418
3: 1 up your pure minds by way of r·: 5280
Jude 5 I will therefore put you in r·, 5179
Re 16:19 Babylon came in r· before God, *3415

remembrances
Job 13:12 Your r· are like unto ashes, your *2146

Remeth (*re'-meth*) See also RAMOTH; JARMUTH.
Jos 19:21 And R·, and En-gannim, and 7432

remission
M't 26:28 is shed for many for the r· of sins. 859
M'r 1: 4 of repentance for the r· of sins. "
Lu 1:77 his people by the r· of their sins, "
3: 3 of repentance for the r· of sins; "
24:47 and r· of sins should be preached "
Ac 2:38 of Jesus Christ for the r· of sins, "
10:43 in him shall receive r· of sins. "
Ro 3:25 for the r· of sins that are past, *3929
Heb 9:22 without shedding of blood is no r·. 859
10:18 Now where r· of these is, there is no "

remit See also REMITTED.
Joh 20:23 Whose soever sins ye r·, they are * 863

remitted
Joh 20:23 ye remit, they are r· unto them; * 863

Remmon (*rem'-mon*) See also REMMON-METHOAR; RIMMON.
Jos 19: 7 R·, and Ether, and Ashan; four *7417

Remmon-methoar (*rem''-mon-meth'-o-ar*)
Jos 19:13 and goeth out to R· to Neah; *7417

remnant
Ex 26:12 r· that remaineth of the curtains *5629
Le 2: 3 r· of the meat offering shall be *3498
5:13 the r· shall be the priest's, as a meat "
14:18 r· of the oil that is in the priest's *3498
De 3:11 remained of the r· of giants; 3499
28:54 r· of his children which he shall "
Jos 12: 4 which was of the r· of the giants, "
13:12 remained of the r· of the giants: "
23:12 cleave unto the r· of these nations, "
2Sa 21: 2 but of the r· of the Amorites; and "
1Ki 12:23 to the r· of the people, saying, * "
14:10 the r· of the house of Jeroboam, * 310
22:46 the r· of the sodomites, which 3499
2Ki 19: 4 lift up thy prayer for the r· that 7611
30 r· that is escaped of the house of 7604
31 of Jerusalem shall go forth a r·, 7611
21:14 forsake the r· of mine inheritance, "
25:11 with the r· of the multitude, did *3499
1Ch 6:70 of the r· of the sons of Kohath. *3498
2Ch 30: 6 and he will return to the r· of you, 7604
34: 9 and of all the r· of Israel, and of 7611
Ezr 3: 8 r· of their brethren the priests *7605
9: 8 our God, to leave us a r· to escape, 7611
14 should be no r· nor escaping? "
Ne 1: 3 r· that are left of the captivity 7604
Job 22:20 the r· of them the fire consumeth. 3499
Isa 1: 9 had left unto us a very small r·, 8300
10:20 in that day, that the r· of Israel, 7605
21 The r· shall return, even the r· of "
22 sea, yet a r· of them shall return: "
11:11 time to recover the r· of his people, "
16 an highway for the r· of his people, "
14:22 the name, and r·, and son, and "
30 famine, and he shall slay thy r·. 7611
15: 9 Moab, and upon the r· of the land. "
16:14 r· shall be very small and feeble. 7605
17: 3 from Damascus, and the r· of Syria: "
37: 4 lift up thy prayer for the r· that is 7611
31 r· that is escaped of the house of 7604
32 of Jerusalem shall go forth a r·, 7611
46: 3 and all the r· of the house of Israel, "
Jer 6: 9 glean the r· of Israel as a vine: "
11:23 there shall be no r· of them: for "
15:11 Verily it shall be well with thy r·;*8293
23: 3 will gather the r· of my flock out 7611
25:20 and Ekron, and the r· of Ashdod, "
31: 7 save thy people, the r· of Israel. "
39: 9 captive...the r· of the people that *3499
40:11 of Babylon had left a r· of Judah, 7611
15 and the r· in Judah perish? "
41:16 the r· of the people whom he had "
42: 2 Lord thy God, even for all this r·; "
15 word of the Lord, ye r· of Judah; "
19 concerning you, O ye r· of Judah; "
43: 5 took all the r· of Judah, that were "
44:12 I will take the r· of Judah, that "
14 none of the r· of Judah, which are "
28 all the r· of Judah, that are gone "
47: 4 the r· of the country of Caphtor. "
5 cut off with the r· of their valley: "
Eze 5:10 whole r· of thee will I scatter into "
6: 8 Yet will I leave a r·, that ye may 3498
11:13 make a full end of the r· of Israel?7611
14:22 therein shall be left a r· that shall 6413
23:25 thy r· shall fall by the sword: they*319
25:16 and destroy the r· of the sea coast. 7611
Joe 2:32 in the r· whom the Lord shall call. 8300
Am 1: 8 r· of the Philistines shall perish, 7611
5:15 be gracious unto the r· of Joseph. "
9:12 they may possess the r· of Edom, "
Mic 2:12 will surely gather the r· of Israel; "
4: 7 I will make her that halted a r·, "
5: 3 r· of his brethren shall return *3499
7 r· of Jacob shall be in the midst 7611
8 the r· of Jacob shall be among the "
7:18 of the r· of his heritage? "
Hab 2: 8 all the r· of the people shall spoil 3499
Zep 1: 4 I will cut off the r· of Baal from 7605
2: 7 for the r· of the house of Judah; 7611
9 r· of my people shall possess 3499
3:13 r· of Israel shall not do iniquity, 7611
Hag 1:12 with all the r· of the people, obeyed "
14 spirit of all the r· of the people; "
Zec 8: 6 in the eyes of the r· of this people "
12 the r· of this people to possess all "
M't 22: 6 And the r· took his servants, and *3062
Ro 9:27 of the sea, a r· shall be saved: 2640
11: 5 is a r· according to the election of 3005
Re 11:13 the r· were affrighted, and gave *3062
12:17 make war with the r· of her seed, * "
19:21 the r· were slain with the sword of* "

remove See also REMOVED; REMOVETH; REMOVING.
Ge 48:17 to r· it from Ephraim's head unto 5493
Nu 36: 7 of Israel r· from tribe to tribe: 5437
9 the inheritance r· from one tribe "
De 19:14 not r· thy neighbour's landmark, 5253
Jos 3: 3 then ye shall r· from your place, 5265
J'g 9:29 hand! then would I r· Abimelech. 5493
2Sa 6:10 So David would not r· the ark of "
2Ki 23:27 will r· Judah also out of my sight, "
24: 3 to r· them out of his sight, for the "
2Ch 33: 8 will I any more r· the foot of Israel "
Job 24: 2 Some r· the landmarks; they 5472
27: 5 not r· mine integrity from me. *5493
Ps 36:11 not the hand of the wicked r· me.*5110
39:10 R· thy stroke away from me: I 5493
119:22 R· from me reproach...contempt; *1556
29 R· from me the way of lying: and 5493
Pr 4:27 nor to the left: r· thy foot from evil. "
5: 8 R· thy way far from her, and come 7368
22:28 R· not the ancient landmark, 5253
23:10 R· not the old landmark; and "
30: 8 R· far from me vanity and lies: 7368
Ec 11:10 r· sorrow from thy heart, and put 5493
Isa 13:13 the earth shall r· out of her place,*7493
46: 7 from his place shall he not r·: 4185
Jer 4: 1 my sight, then shalt thou not r·. *5110
27:10 you, to r· you far from your land; 7368
32:31 should r· it from before my face 5493
50: 3 they shall r·, they shall depart, *5110
8 R· out of the midst of Babylon, and* "
Eze 12: 3 r· by day in their sight; and thou 1540
3 r· from thy place to another place "
21:26 R· the diadem, and take off the 5493
45: 9 r· violence and spoil, and execute "
Ho 5:10 were like them that r· the bound: 5253
Joe 2:20 r· far off from you the northern 7368
3: 6 r· them far from their border. "
Mic 2: 3 which ye shall not r· your necks; 4185
Zec 3: 9 I will r· the iniquity of that land in "
14: 4 mountain shall r· toward the north, "
M't 17:20 R· hence to yonder place; and it 3327
20 to yonder place; and it shall r·; "
Lu 22:42 be willing, r· this cup from me: 3911
1Co 13: 2 faith, so that I could r· mountains,3179
Re 2: 5 r· thy candlestick out of his place,*2795

removed
Ge 8:13 Noah r· the covering of the ark, 5493
12: 8 he r· from thence unto a mountain 6275
13:18 Then Abram r· his tent, and came* 167
26:22 he r· from thence, and digged 6275
30:35 he r· that day the he goats that 5493
47:21 he r· them to cities from one end 5674
Ex 8:31 and he r· the swarms of flies from 5493
14:19 angel r·...and went behind them; 5265
20:18 when the people saw it, they r·, *5128
Nu 12:16 the people r· from Hazeroth, and *5265
21:12, 13 From thence they r·, and pitched* "
33: 5 children of Israel r· from Rameses,* "
7 they r· from Etham, and turned * "
9 they r· from Marah, and came unto* "
10 they r· from Elim, and encamped* "
11 And they r· from the Red sea, and* "
14 they r· from Alush, and encamped* "
16 they r· from the desert of Sinai, * "
21 they r· from Libnah, and pitched * "
24 they r· from mount Shapher, and * "
25 they r· from Haradah, and pitched* "
26 And they r· from Makheloth, and * "
28 they r· from Tarah, and pitched in* "
32 And they r· from Bene-jaakan, and* "
34 And they r· from Jotbathah, and * "
36 And they r· from Ezion-gaber, and* "
37 they r· from Kadesh, and pitched * "
46 And they r· from Dibon-gad, and * "
47 they r· from Almon-diblathaim, * "
De 28:25 be r· into all the kingdoms of the *2189
Jos 3: 1 they r· from Shittim, and came to 5265
14 when the people r· from their tents, "
1Sa 6: 3 why his hand is not r· from you. 5493
18:13 Saul r· him from him, and made "
2Sa 20:12 he r· Amasa out of the highway *5437
13 he was r· out of the highway, 3014
1Ki 15:12 r· all the idols that his fathers 5493
13 even her he r· from being queen, "
14 But the high places were not r·: "
2Ki 15: 4 Save that...high places were not r·:* "
35 Howbeit...high places were not r·:* "
16:17 and r· the laver from off them; "
17:18 and r· them out of his sight: there "
23 the Lord r· Israel out of his sight, "
26 The nations which thou hast r·, *1540
18: 4 He r· the high places, and brake 5493
23:27 as I have r· Israel, and will cast off "
1Ch 8: 6 and they r· them to Manahath: *1540
7 and Ahiah, and Gera, he r· them, * "
2Ch 15:16 king, he r· her from being queen, 5493
35:12 And they r· the burnt offerings, "
Job 14:18 and the rock is r· out of his place. 6275
18: 4 shall the rock be r· out of his place? "
19:10 mine hope hath he r· like a tree. *5265
36:16 would he have r· thee out of the *5496
Ps 46: 2 we fear, though the earth be r·, *4171
81: 6 I r· his shoulder from the burden:5493
103:12 far hath he r· our transgressions 7368
104: 5 that it should not be r· for ever. *4131
125: 1 as mount Zion, which cannot be r·,* "
Pr 10:30 The righteous shall never be r·: "
Isa 6:12 the Lord have r· men far away, 7368
10:13 I have r· the bounds of the people,5493
31 Madmenah is r·; the inhabitants *5074
22:25 fastened in the sure place be r·, *4185
24:20 and shall be r· like a cottage; and*5110
26:15 r· it far unto all the ends of the *7368
29:13 but have r· their heart far from me, "
30:20 yet shall not thy teachers be r· *3670

Isa 33:20 the stakes thereof shall ever be r'.*5265
38:12 r' from me as a shepherd's tent: *1556
54:10 shall depart, and the hills be r'; 4131
10 the covenant of my peace be r', "
Jer 15: 4 them to be r' into all kingdoms of*2189
24: 9 them to be r' into all the kingdoms*"
29:18 them to be r' to all the kingdoms * "
34:17 you to be r' into all the kingdoms* "
La 1: 8 sinned; therefore she is r': *5206
3:17 hast r' my soul far off from peace:2186
Eze 7:19 streets, and their gold shall be r':*5079
23:46 give them to be r' and spoiled. *2189
36:17 the uncleanness of a r' woman. †‡5079
Am 6: 7 stretched themselves shall be r'. *5493
Mic 2: 4 how hath he r' it from me! *4185
7:11 in that day shall the decree be far r'. "
M't 21:21 Be thou r', and be thou cast into * 142
M'r 11:23 Be thou r', and be thou cast into * "
Ac 7: 4 was dead, he r' him into this land, 3351
13:22 when he had r' him, he raised up 3179
Ga 1: 6 I marvel that ye are so soon r' *3346

removeth
De 27:17 that r' his neighbour's landmark. 5253
Job 9: 5 r' the mountains, and they know 6275
12:20 r' away the speech of the trusty, 5493
Ec 10: 9 Whoso r' stones shall be hurt *5265
Da 2:21 he r' kings, and setteth up kings: 5709

removing
Ge 30:32 r' from thence all the speckled 5493
Isa 49:21 a captive, and r' to and fro? and * "
Eze 12: 3 of man, prepare thee stuff for r', 1473
4 day in their sight, as stuff for r': "
Heb 12:27 r' of those things that are shaken, 3331

Remphan (*rem'-fan*)
Ac 7:43 the star of your god R', figures *4481

rend See also RENDING; RENT.
Ex 39:23 about the hole, that it should not r'.*
Le 10: 6 neither r' your clothes; lest ye 6533
13:56 he shall r' it out of the garment, 7167
21:10 his head, nor r' his clothes; 6533
2Sa 3:31 R' your clothes, and gird you with 7167
1Ki 11:11 surely r' the kingdom from thee, "
12 will r' it out of the hand of thy son. "
13 I will not r' away all the kingdom; "
31 r' the kingdom out of the hand of "
2Ch 34:27 and didst r' thy clothes, and weep* "
Ec 3: 7 A time to r', and a time to sew; a "
Isa 64: 1 that thou wouldest r' the heavens, "
Eze 13:11 fall; and a stormy wind shall r' it.1234
13 r' it with a stormy wind in my fury;"
29: 7 break, and r' all their shoulder: "
Ho 13: 8 and will r' the caul of their heart, 7167
Joe 2:13 And r' your heart, and not your "
M't 7: 6 feet, and turn again and r' you. 4486
Joh 19:24 Let us not r' it, but cast lots for it,4977

render See also RENDERED; RENDEREST; RENDERETH; RENDERING.
Nu 18: 9 which they shall r' unto me, shall 7725
De 32:41 will r' vengeance to mine enemies, "
43 r' vengeance to his adversaries, "
J'g 9:57 did God r' upon their heads: and* "
1Sa 26:23 r' to every man his righteousness "
2Ch 6:30 r' unto every man according unto 5415
Job 33:26 r' unto man his righteousness. *7725
34:11 work of a man shall he r' unto him,7999
Ps 28: 4 hands; r' to them their desert. 7725
38:20 They also that r' evil for good are 7999
56:12 God: I will r' praises unto thee. "
79:12 r' unto our neighbours sevenfold 7725
94: 2 earth: r' a reward to the proud. "
116:12 What shall I r' unto the Lord for "
Pr 24:12 not he r' to every man according to "
29 r' to the man according to his work."
26:16 seven men that can r' a reason. "
Isa 66:15 to r' his anger with fury, and his "
Jer 51: 6 he will r' unto her a recompence. 7999
24 I will r' unto Babylon and to all "
La 3:64 R' unto them a recompence, O 7725
Ho 14: 2 so will we r' the calves of our lips. 7999
Joe 3: 4 will ye r' me a recompence? and if "
Zec 9:12 that I will r' double unto thee; 7725
M't 21:41 r' him the fruits in their seasons. 591
22:21 R' therefore unto Cæsar the things "
M'r 12:17 R' to Cæsar the things that are "
Lu 20:25 R' therefore unto Cæsar the things "
Ro 2: 6 will r' to every man according to his "
13: 7 R' therefore to all their dues: "
1Co 7: 3 Let the husband r' unto the wife due"
1Th 3: 9 what thanks can we r' to God again467
5:15 that none r' evil for evil unto any 591

rendered
J'g 9:56 r' the wickedness of Abimelech, *7725
2Ki 3: 4 and r' unto the king of Israel an "
2Ch 32:25 Hezekiah r' not again according to "
Pr 12:14 man's hands shall be r' unto him. "

renderest
Ps 62:12 r' to every man according to his 7999

rendereth
Isa 66: 6 that r' recompence to his enemies.7999

rendering
1Pe 3: 9 Not r' evil for evil, or railing for 591

rending
Ps 7: 2 my soul like a lion, r' it in pieces, 6561

renew See also RENEWED; RENEWEST; RENEWING.
1Sa 11:14 Gilgal, and r' the kingdom there. 2318
Ps 51:10 and r' a right spirit within me. "
Isa 40:31 the Lord shall r' their strength; 2498
41: 1 and let the people r' their strength:"
La 5:21 be turned; r' our days as of old. 2318
Heb 6: 6 to r' them again unto repentance: 340

renewed
2Ch 15: 8 and r' the altar of the Lord, that 2318
Job 29:20 and my bow was r' in my hand. 2498
Ps 103: 5 thy youth is r' like the eagle's. 2318
2Co 4:16 the inward man is r' day by day. 341
Eph 4:23 be r' in the spirit of your mind; 365
Col 3:10 which is r' in knowledge after the 341

renewest
Job 10:17 Thou r' thy witnesses against me, 2318
Ps 104:30 and thou r' the face of the earth. "

renewing
Ro 12: 2 transformed by the r' of your mind,342
Tit 3: 5 regeneration,...r' of the Holy Ghost; "

renounced
2Co 4: 2 But have r' the hidden things of 550

renown See also RENOWNED.
Ge 6: 4 men which were of old, men of r'. 8034
Nu 16: 2 in the congregation, men of r': "
Eze 16:14 thy r' went forth among...heathen "
15 the harlot because of thy r', and "
34:29 I will raise up for them a plant of r',"
39:13 it shall be to them a r' the day that "
Da 9:15 hast gotten thee r', as at this day; "

renowned
Nu 1:16 were the r' of the congregation, *7121
Isa 14:20 seed of evildoers shall never be r'.* "
Eze 23:23 and rulers great lords and r', all * "
26:17 the r' city, which wast strong in 1984

rent See also RENTEST.
Ge 37:29 in the pit; and he r' his clothes. 7167
33 is without doubt r' in pieces. 2963
34 And Jacob r' his clothes, and put 7167
44:13 they r' their clothes, and laded "
Ex 28:32 of an habergeon, that it be not r'. "
Le 13:45 his clothes shall be r', and his 6533
Nu 14: 6 searched the land, r' their clothes:7167
Jos 7: 6 Joshua r' his clothes, and fell to the"
9: 4 and wine bottles, old, and r', and 1234
13 were new; and behold, they be r': "
J'g 11:35 he saw her, that he r' his clothes, 7167
14: 6 him, and he r' him as he would 8156
6 as he would have r' a kid, and he "
1Sa 4:12 the same day with his clothes r', 7167
15:27 the skirt of his mantle, and it r'. "
28 The Lord hath r' the kingdom of "
28:17 Lord hath r' the kingdom out of "
2Sa 1: 2 camp from Saul with his clothes r', "
11 hold on his clothes, and r' them; "
13:19 r' her garment of divers colours "
31 stood by with their clothes r'. "
15:32 came to meet him with his coat r', "
1Ki 1:40 earth r' with the sound of them. 1234
11:30 on him, and r' it in twelve pieces: 7167
13: 3 the altar shall be r', and the ashes "
5 the altar also was r', and the ashes "
14: 8 And r' the kingdom away from the "
19:11 and strong wind r' the mountains,6561
21:27 those words, that he r' his clothes,7167
2Ki 2:12 clothes, and r' them in two pieces. "
5: 7 the letter, that he r' his clothes, "
8 the king of Israel had r' his clothes, "
8 Wherefore hast thou r' thy clothes? "
6:30 the woman, that he r' his clothes; "
11:14 Athaliah r' her clothes, and cried, "
17:21 r' Israel from the house of David; "
18:37 to Hezekiah with their clothes r', "
19: 1 heard it, that he r' his clothes, "
22:11 of the law, that he r' his clothes. "
19 hast r' thy clothes, and wept before"
2Ch 23:13 Then Athaliah r' her clothes, and "
34:19 of the law, that he r' his clothes. "
Ezr 9: 3 I r' my garment and my mantle, "
5 and having r' my garment and my "
Es 4: 1 Mordecai r' his clothes, and put on "
Job 1:20 Then Job arose, and r' his mantle, "
2:12 they r' every one his mantle, and "
26: 8 the cloud is not r' under them. 1234
Isa 3:24 and instead of a girdle a r'; and *5364
36:22 to Hezekiah with their clothes r'. 7167
37: 1 heard it, that he r' his clothes, "
Jer 36:24 not afraid, nor r' their garments, "
41: 5 beards shaven, and their clothes r', "
Eze 30:16 and No shall be r' asunder, and *1234
M't 9:16 garment, and the r' is made worse.4978
26:65 Then the high priest r' his clothes,1284
27:51 veil of the temple was r' in twain 4977
51 earth did quake, and the rocks r'; "
M'r 2:21 the old, and the r' is made worse. 4978
9:26 the spirit cried, and r' him sore, *4682
14:63 Then the high priest r' his clothes,1284
15:38 veil of the temple was r' in twain 4977
Lu 5:36 then both the new maketh a r', and* "
23:45 the veil of the temple was r' in the "
Ac 14:14 they r' their clothes, and ran in 1284
16:22 the magistrates r' off their clothes,4048

rentest
Jer 4:30 thou r' thy face with painting. *7167

repair See also REPAIRED; REPAIRING.
2Ki 12: 5 them r' the breaches of the house,2388
7 Why r' ye not the breaches of the "
8 to r' the breaches of the house. "
12 hewed stone to r' the breaches of "
12 was laid out for the house to r' it. 2393
22: 5 to r' the breaches of the house. 2388
6 and hewn stone to r' the house. "
2Ch 24: 4 Joash was minded to r' the house 2318
5 money to r' the house of your God2388
12 and carpenters to r' the house of *2318
34: 8 to r' the house of the Lord his 2388
10 Lord, to r' and amend the house: 918
Ezr 9: 9 and to r' the desolations thereof, 5975
Isa 61: 4 and they shall r' the waste cities, 2318

repaired
J'g 21:23 r' the cities, and dwelt in them. *1129
1Ki 11:27 and r' the breaches of the city of *5462
18:30 r' the altar of the Lord that was 7495
2Ki 12: 6 not r' the breaches of the house. 2388
14 r' therewith the house of the Lord. "
1Ch 11: 8 and Joab r' the rest of the city. 2421
2Ch 29: 3 house of the Lord, and r' them. 2388
32: 5 r' Millo in the city of David, and * "
33:16 he r' the altar of the Lord, and *1129
Ne 3: 4 next unto them r' Meremoth the 2388
4 next unto them r' Meshullam the "
4 next unto them r' Zadok the son of "
5 next unto them the Tekoites r'; "
6 the old gate r' Jehoida the son of "
7 them r' Melatiah the Gibeonite, "
8 next unto him r' Uzziel the son of "
8 Next unto him also r' Hananiah the"
9 next unto them r' Rephaiah the son"
10 next unto them r' Jedaiah the son "
10 next unto him r' Hattush the son of"
11 r' the other piece, and the tower of "
12 next unto him r' Shallum the son "
13 The valley gate r' Hanun, and the "
14 the dung gate r' Malchiah the son "
15 gate of the fountain r' Shallun the "
16 After him r' Nehemiah the son of "
17 after him r' the Levites, Rehum the"
17 Next unto him r' Hashabiah, the "
18 After him r' their brethren, Bavai "
19 And next to him r' Ezer the son of "
20 Zabbai earnestly r' the other piece, "
21 After him r' Meremoth the son of "
22 after him r' the priests, the men of "
23 After him r' Benjamin and Hashub "
23 After him r' Azariah the son of "
24 After him r' Binnui the son of "
27 them the Tekoites r' another piece, "
28 above the horse gate r' the priests, "
29 After them r' Zadok the son of "
29 After him r' also Shemaiah the son "
30 After him r' Hananiah the son of "
30 After him r' Meshullam the son of "
31 After him r' Malchiah the "
32 the sheep gate r' the goldsmiths "

repairer
Isa 58:12 The r' of the breach, The restorer 1443

repairing
2Ch 24:27 and the r' of the house of God. *3247

repay See also REPAYED; REPAYETH.
De 7:10 him, he will r' him to his face. 7999
Job 21:31 shall r' him what he hath done? "
41:11 prevented me, that I should r' him?"
Isa 59:18 accordingly he will r', fury to his "
18 the islands he will r' recompence. "
Lu 10:35 when I come again, I will r' thee. 591
Ro 12:19 is mine; I will r', saith the Lord. * 467
Ph'm 19 with mine own hand, I will r' it: 661

repayed
Pr 13:21 to the righteous good shall be r'. *7999

repayeth
De 7:10 r' them that hate him to their 7999

repeateth
Pr 17: 9 he that r' a matter separateth *8138

repent See also REPENTED; REPENTEST; REPENTETH; REPENTING.
Ex 13:17 the people r' when they see war, 5162
32:12 r' of this evil against thy people. "
Nu 23:19 the son of man, that he should r': "
De 32:36 and r' himself for his servants, "
1Sa 15:29 Strength of Israel will not lie nor r':"
29 he is not a man, that he should r'. "
1Ki 8:47 and r', and make supplication *7725
Job 42: 6 myself, and r' in dust and ashes. 5162
Ps 90:13 it r' thee concerning thy servants. "
110: 4 Lord hath sworn, and will not r', "
135:14 r' himself concerning his servants. "
Jer 4:28 I have purposed it, and will not r',* "
18: 8 r' of the evil that I thought to do "
10 my voice, then I will r' of the good, "
26: 3 that I may r' me of the evil, which "
13 and the Lord will r' him of the evil "
42:10 I r' me of the evil that I have done "
Eze 14: 6 R', and turn...from your idols; *7725
18:30 R', and turn yourselves from all * "
24:14 will I spare, neither will I r'; 5162
Joe 2:14 knoweth if he will return and r', "
Jon 3: 9 Who can tell if God will turn and r'," "
M't 3: 2 R' ye: for the kingdom of heaven 3340
4:17 R': for the kingdom of heaven is at "
M'r 1:15 hand: r' ye, and believe the gospel. "
6:12 and preached that men should r'. "
Lu 13: 3, 5 except ye r', ye shall all likewise "
16:30 them from the dead, they will r'. "
17: 3 him; and if he r', forgive him. "
4 saying, I r'; thou shalt forgive him."
Ac 2:38 R', and be baptized every one of you"
3:19 R' ye therefore, and be converted, "
8:22 R' therefore of this thy wickedness,"
17:30 all men every where to r': "
26:20 that they should r' and turn to God,"
2Co 7: 8 I do not r', though I did r': for I *3338
Heb 7:21 The Lord sware and will not r', "
Re 2: 5 whence thou art fallen, and r', and3340
5 out of his place, except thou r'. "
16 R'; or else I will come unto thee "
21 her space to r' of her fornication; "
22 except they r' of their deeds. "
3: 3 and heard, and hold fast, and r'. "
19 be zealous therefore, and r'. "

repentance
Ho 13:14 r' shall be hid from mine eyes. 5164
M't 3: 8 Bring forth...fruits meet for r': 3341

M't 3:11 baptize you with water unto r·: 3341
9:13 the righteous, but sinners to r·. * "
M'r 1: 4 and preach the baptism of r· for the "
2:17 the righteous, but sinners to r·. * "
Lu 3: 3 preaching the baptism of r· for the "
8 Bring forth...fruits worthy of r·, "
5:32 call the righteous, but sinners to r·. "
15: 7 nine just persons, which need no r·. "
24:47 And that r· and remission of sins "
Ac 5:31 to give r· to Israel, and forgiveness "
11:18 to the Gentiles granted r· unto life. "
13:24 the baptism of r· to all the people "
19: 4 baptized with the baptism of r·, "
20:21 r· toward God, and faith toward "
26:20 to God, and do works meet for r·. "
Ro 2: 4 goodness of God leadeth thee to r·? "
11:29 and calling of God are without r·. 278
2Co 7: 9 sorry, but that ye sorrowed to r·: 3341
10 For godly sorrow worketh r· to "
2Ti 2:25 God peradventure will give them r· "
Heb 6: 1 laying again the foundation of r· "
6 to renew them again unto r·; "
12:17 for he found no place of r·, though‡ "
2Pe 3: 9 but that all should come to r·. "

repented
Ge 6: 6 r· the Lord that he had made man 5162
Ex 32:14 Lord r· of the evil which he thought "
J'g 2:18 for it r· the Lord because of their "
21: 6 children of Israel r·...for Benjamin "
15 the people r· them for Benjamin, "
1Sa 15:35 Lord r· that he had made Saul king "
2Sa 24:16 the Lord r· him of the evil, and said "
1Ch 21:15 beheld, and he r· him of the evil, "
Ps 106:45 r· according to the multitude of his "
Jer 8: 6 no man r· him of his wickedness,* "
20:16 the Lord overthrew, and r· not: "
26:19 the Lord r· him of the evil which "
31:19 Surely after that I was turned, I r·; "
Am 7: 3 Lord r· for this: It shall not be, "
6 Lord r· for this: This also shall not "
Jon 3:10 God r· of the evil, that he had said "
Zec 8:14 saith the Lord of hosts, and I r· not: "
M't 11:20 were done, because they r· not: 3340
21 would have r· long ago in sackcloth "
12:41 they r· at the preaching of Jonas; "
21:29 not: but afterward he r·, and went. 3338
32 ye had seen it, r· not afterward, * "
27: 3 that he was condemned, r· himself, "
Lu 10:13 they had a great while ago r·, 3340
11:32 they r· at the preaching of Jonas; "
2Co 7:10 worketh repentance...not to be r· of: *278
12:21 and have not r· of the uncleanness 3340
Re 2:21 of her fornication; and she r· not.* "
9:20 r· not of the works of their hands, "
21 Neither r· they of their murders "
16: 9 and they r· not to give him glory. "
11 sores, and r· not of their deeds. "

repentest
Jon 4: 2 kindness, and r· thee of the evil. 5162

repenteth
Ge 6: 7 it r· me that I have made them. 5162
1Sa 15:11 It r· me that I have set up Saul to "
Joe 2:13 kindness, and r· him of the evil. "
Lu 15: 7 in heaven over one sinner that r·. 3340
10 angels...over one sinner that r·. "

repenting See also REPENTINGS.
Jer 15: 6 destroy thee; I am weary with r·. 5162

repentings
Ho 11: 8 me, my r· are kindled together. *5150

repetitions
M't 6: 7 But when ye pray, use not vain r·. 945

Rephael (*re'-fa-el*)
1Ch 26: 7 sons of Shemaiah; Othni, and R·, 7501

Rephah (*re'-fah*)
1Ch 7:25 And R· was his son, also Resheph, 7506

Rephaiah (*ref-a-i'-ah*) See also RAPHA; RHESA.
1Ch 3:21 the sons of R·, the sons of Arnan, 7509
4:42 and Neariah, and R·, and Uzziel, "
7: 2 sons of Tola; Uzzi, and R·, and "
9:43 Moza begat Binea; and R· his son, "
Ne 3: 9 them repaired R· the son of Hur, "

Rephaim (*re-fa'-im*) See also REPHAIMS.
2Sa 5:18, 22 themselves in the valley of R·. 7497
23:13 pitched in the valley of R·. "
1Ch 11:15 encamped in the valley of R·. "
14: 9 themselves in the valley of R·. "
Isa 17: 5 gathereth ears in the valley of R·. "

Rephaims (*re-fa'-ims*) See also REPHAIM.
Ge 14: 5 and smote the R· in Ashteroth *7497
15:20 and the Perizzites, and the R·, * "

Rephidim (*ref'-i-dim*)
Ex 17: 1 of the Lord, and pitched in R·: 7508
8 and fought with Israel in R·. "
19: 2 For they were departed from R·, "
Nu 33:14 and encamped at R·, where was no "
15 And they departed from R·, and "

replenish See also REPLENISHED.
Ge 1:28 and multiply, and r· the earth, and 4390
9: 1 and multiply, and r· the earth. "

replenished
Isa 2: 6 because they be r· from the east, *4390
23: 2 that pass over the sea, have r·. "
Jer 31:25 and I have r· every sorrowful soul. "
Eze 26: 2 I shall be r·, now she is laid waste: "
27:25 wast r·, and made very glorious "

repliest
Ro 9:20 who art thou that r· against God? 470

report See also REPORTED.
Ge 37: 2 brought unto his father their evil r·. 1681
Ex 23: 1 Thou shalt not raise a false r·: 8088
Nu 13:32 brought up an evil r· of the land 1681
14:37 bring up the evil r· upon the land, "
De 2:25 who shall hear r· of thee, and shall 8088
1Sa 2:24 for it is no good r· that I hear: 8052
1Ki 10: 6 was a true r· that I heard in mine 1697
2Ch 9: 5 was a true r· which I heard in mine "
Ne 6:13 might have matter for an evil r·, 8034
Pr 15:30 a good r· maketh the bones fat. *8052
Isa 23: 5 As at the r· concerning Egypt, 8088
5 be sorely pained at the r· of Tyre. "
28:19 a vexation...to understand the r·. *8052
53: 1 Who hath believed our r·? and to ‡ "
Jer 20:10 R·, say they, and we will r· it. All *5046
50:43 king of Babylon hath heard the r· *8088
Joh 12:38 Lord, who hath believed our r·? 189
Ac 6: 3 among you seven men of honest r·, 3140
10:22 and of good r· among all the nation* "
22:12 having a good r· of all the Jews * "
Ro 10:16 Lord, who hath believed our r·? 189
1Co 14:25 and r· that God is in you of a truth. *518
2Co 6: 8 By honour and dishonour, by evil r· 1426
8 and good r·: as deceivers, and yet 2162
Ph'p 4: 8 whatsoever things are of good r·; 2163
1Ti 3: 7 he must have a good r· of them *3141
Heb 11: 2 it the elders obtained a good r·. *3140
39 obtained a good r· through faith, * "
3Jo 12 Demetrius hath good r· of all men,* "

reported
Ne 6: 6 It is r· among the heathen, and 8085
7 and now shall it be r· to the king "
19 they r· his good deeds before me,* 559
Es 1:17 in their eyes, when it shall be r·, "
Eze 9:11 inkhorn by his side, r· the matter, 7725
M't 28:15 commonly r· among the Jews is *1310
Ac 4:23 and r· all that the chief priests and 518
16: 2 was well r· of by the brethren 3140
Ro 3: 8 (as we be slanderously r·, and as 987
1Co 5: 1 It is r· commonly that there is 191
1Ti 5:10 Well r· of for good works; if she 3140
1Pe 1:12 which are now r· unto you by them *312

reproach See also REPROACHED; REPROACHES; REPROACHEST; REPROACHETH; REPROACHFULLY.
Ge 30:23 said, God hath taken away my r·: 2781
34:14 for that were a r· unto us: "
Jos 5: 9 have I rolled away the r· of Egypt "
Ru 2:15 among the sheaves, and r· her not: 3637
1Sa 11: 2 and lay it for a r· upon all Israel. 2781
17:26 and taketh away the r· from Israel? "
25:39 hath pleaded the cause of my r· "
2Ki 19: 4 hath sent to r· the living God; ‡2778
16 hath sent him to r· the living God. "
Ne 1: 3 are in great affliction and r·: 2781
2:17 Jerusalem, that we be no more a r·. "
4: 4 turn their r· upon their own head, "
5: 9 the r· of the heathen our enemies? "
6:13 evil report, that they might r· me. 2778
Job 19: 5 me, and plead against me my r·: 2781
20: 3 I have heard the check of my r·, *3639
27: 6 my heart shall not r· me so long 2778
Ps 15: 3 up a r· against his neighbour. 2781
22: 6 a r· of men, and despised of the "
31:11 I was a r· among all mine enemies, "
39: 8 make me not the r· of the foolish. "
42:10 in my bones, mine enemies r· me; 2778
44:13 makest us a r· to our neighbours, 2781
57: 3 and save me from the r· of him *2778
69: 7 for thy sake I have borne r·; 2781
10 soul with fasting, that was to my r·. "
19 Thou hast known my r·, and my "
20 R· hath broken my heart; and I "
71:13 be covered with r· and dishonour "
74:10 how long shall the adversary r·? 2778
78:66 he put them to a perpetual r·. 2781
79: 4 are become a r· to our neighbours, "
12 sevenfold into their bosom their r·, "
89:41 him: he is a r· to his neighbours. "
50 Remember,...the r· of thy servants; "
50 bosom the r· of all the mighty people; "
102: 8 Mine enemies r· me all the day; 2778
109:25 I became also a r· unto them: 2781
119:22 Remove from me r· and contempt; "
39 Turn away my r· which I fear: for "
Pr 6:33 his r· shall not be wiped away. "
14:34 but sin is a r· to any people. 2617
18: 3 contempt, and with ignominy r·. 2781
19:26 causeth shame, and bringeth r·. 2659
22:10 yea, strife and r· shall cease. *7036
Isa 4: 1 by thy name, to take away our r·. 2781
30: 5 profit, but a shame, and also a r·. "
37: 4 hath sent to r· the living God, and ‡2778
17 hath sent to r· the living God. ‡ "
51: 7 fear ye not the r· of men, neither 2781
54: 4 remember the r· of thy widowhood "
Jer 6:10 word of the Lord is unto them a r·; "
20: 8 the word of the Lord was made a r·, "
23:40 bring an everlasting r· upon you, "
24: 9 be a r· and a proverb, a taunt and "
29:18 an hissing, and a r·, among all the "
31:19 I did bear the r· of my youth. "
42:18 astonishment, and a curse, and a r·; "
44: 8 a r· among all the nations of the "
12 astonishment, and a curse, and a r·. "
49:13 shall become a desolation, a r·, a "
51:51 because we have heard r·: shame "
La 3:30 smiteth him: he is filled full with r·. "
61 Thou hast heard their r·, O Lord, "
5: 1 us: consider, and behold our r·. "
Eze 5:14 a r· among the nations that are "
15 So it shall be a r· and a taunt, an "
16:57 of thy r· of the daughters of Syria, "
21:28 Ammonites, and concerning their r·; "
22: 4 I made thee a r· unto the heathen, "
36:15 bear the r· of the people any more, "
30 shall receive no more r· of famine "
Da 9:16 become a r· to all that are about us. "
11:18 cause the r· offered by him to cease; 2781
18 without his own r· he shall cause it "
Ho 12:14 his r· shall his Lord return unto "
Joe 2:17 give not thine heritage to r·, that "
19 make you a r· among the heathen: "
Mic 6:16 ye shall bear the r· of my people. "
Zep 2: 8 I have heard the r· of Moab, and "
3:18 to whom the r· of it was a burden. "
Lu 1:25 to take away my r· among men. 3681
6:22 and shall r· you, and cast out your 3679
2Co 11:21 I speak as concerning r·, as though *819
1Ti 3: 7 fall into r· and...snare of the devil. 3680
4:10 we both labour and suffer r·, *3679
Heb 11:26 Esteeming the r· of Christ greater 3680
13:13 without the camp, bearing his r·. "

reproached
2Ki 19:22 hast thou r· and blasphemed? ‡2778
23 messengers thou hast r· the Lord,‡ "
Job 19: 3 These ten times have ye r· me: ye 3637
Ps 55:12 it was not an enemy that r· me; 2778
69: 9 reproaches of them that r· thee are* "
74:18 this, that the enemy hath r·, O Lord, "
79:12 wherewith they have r· thee, O Lord. "
89:51 Wherewith thine enemies have r·, "
51 they have r· the footsteps of thine "
Isa 37:23 hast thou r· and blasphemed? ‡ "
24 thy servants hast thou r· the Lord,‡ "
Zep 2: 8 whereby they have r· my people, "
10 have r· and magnified themselves "
Ro 15: 3 reproaches of them that r· thee 3679
1Pe 4:14 If ye be r· for the name of Christ, "

reproaches
Ps 69: 9 the r· of them that reproached thee 2781
Isa 43:28 Jacob to the curse, and Israel to r·. *1421
Ro 15: 3 The r· of them that reproached thee 3679
2Co 12:10 take pleasure in infirmities, in r·, *5196
Heb 10:33 both by r· and afflictions; and 3680

reproachest
Lu 11:45 Master, thus saying thou r· us also. 5195

reproacheth
Nu 15:30 a stranger, the same r· the Lord; *1442
Ps 44:16 For the voice of him that r· and 2778
74:22 how the foolish man r· thee daily. 2781
119:42 to answer him that r· me: for 2778
Pr 14:31 oppresseth the poor r· his Maker: "
17: 5 mocketh the poor r· his Maker: "
27:11 that I may answer him that r· me. "

reproachfully
Job 16:10 smitten me upon the cheek r·; 2781
1Ti 5:14 to the adversary to speak r·. *5484, 3059

reprobate See also REPROBATES.
Jer 6:30 R· silver shall men call them, *3988
Ro 1:28 God gave them over to a r· mind, 96
2Ti 3: 8 minds, r· concerning the faith. "
Tit 1:16 and unto every good work r·. "

reprobates
2Co 13: 5 Christ is in you, except ye be r·? * 96
6 ye shall know that we are not r·. * "
7 which is honest, though we be as r·.* "

reproof See also REPROOFS.
Job 26:11 and are astonished at his r·. *1606
Pr 1:23 Turn you at my r·: behold, I will 8433
25 counsel, and would none of my r·: "
30 my counsel: they despised all my r·. "
5:12 and my heart despised r·; "
10:17 but he that refuseth r· erreth. "
12: 1 but he that hateth r· is brutish. "
13:18 that regardeth r· shall be honoured. "
15: 5 but he that regardeth r· is prudent. "
10 way: and he that hateth r· shall die. "
31 The ear that heareth the r· of life "
32 heareth r· getteth understanding. "
17:10 A r· entereth more into a wise *1606
29:15 The rod and r· give wisdom: but 8433
2Ti 3:16 for doctrine, for r·, for correction, 1650

reproofs
Ps 38:14 and in whose mouth are no r·. 8433
Pr 6:23 r· of instruction are the way of life: "

reprove See also REPROVED; REPROVETH; UNREPROVABLE.
2Ki 19: 4 will r· the words which the Lord *3198
Job 6:25 but what doth your arguing r·? "
26 Do ye imagine to r· words, and the "
13:10 He will surely r· you, if ye do "
22: 4 Will he r· thee for fear of thee? will* "
Ps 50: 8 I will not r· thee for thy sacrifices "
21 I will r· thee, and set them in order "
141: 5 and let him r· me; it shall be an "
Pr 9: 8 R· not a scorner, lest he hate thee: "
19:25 and r· one that hath understanding, "
30: 6 lest he r· thee, and thou be found a ‡
Isa 11: 3 r· after the hearing of his ears: ‡
4 r· with equity for the meek of the ‡
37: 4 will r· the words which the Lord ‡
Jer 2:19 and thy backslidings shall r· thee: "
Ho 4: 4 let no man strive, nor r· another: "
Joh 16: 8 is come, he will r· the world of sin, *1651
Eph 5:11 of darkness, but rather r· them. "
2Ti 4: 2 r·, rebuke, exhort with all "

reproved
Ge 20:16 with all other: thus she was r·. *3198
21:25 Abraham r· Abimelech because "
1Ch 16:21 yea, he r· kings for their sakes, "
Ps 105:14 yea, he r· kings for their sakes; "
Pr 29: 1 being often r· hardeneth his neck, 8433
Jer 29:27 why hast thou not r· Jeremiah 1605
Hab 2: 1 what I shall answer when I am r·. *8433
Lu 3:19 being r· by him for Herodias his 1651
Joh 3:20 light, lest his deeds should be r·. "
Eph 5:13 that are r· are made manifest by "

reprover
Pr 25:12 is a wise r' upon an obedient ear. 3198
Eze 3:26 dumb, and shalt not be to them a r': "
reproveth
Job 40: 2 he that r' God, let him answer it. *3198
Pr 9: 7 He that r' a scorner getteth to 3256
15:12 scorner loveth not one that r' him: *3198
Isa 29:21 a snare for him that r' in the gate, "
reputation
Ec 10: 1 is in r' for wisdom and honour. *3368
Ac 5:34 had in r' among all the people, *5093
Ga 2: 2 privately to them which were of r',*1380
Ph'p 2: 7 But made himself of no r', and *2758
29 gladness; and hold such in r': *1784
reputed
Job 18: 3 as beasts, and r' vile in your sight?*
Da 4:35 of the earth are r' as nothing: 2804
request See also REQUESTED; REQUESTS.
J'g 8:24 them, I would desire a r' of you, 7596
2Sa 14:15 perform the r' of his handmaid. 1697
22 hath fulfilled the r' of his servant. "
Ezr 7: 6 the king granted him all his r', 1246
Ne 2: 4 me, For what dost thou make r'? 1245
Es 4: 8 make r' before him for her people. "
5: 3 queen Esther? and what is thy r'? 1246
6 and what is thy r'? even to the half "
7 and said, My petition and my r' is; "
8 my petition, and to perform my r', "
7: 2 and what is thy r'? and it shall be "
3 petition, and my people at my r': "
7 Haman stood up to make r' for his 1245
9:12 what is thy r' further? and it shall 1246
Job 6: 8 Oh that I might have my r'; and 7596
Ps 21: 2 not withholden the r' of his lips. 782
106:15 he gave them their r'; but sent 7596
Ro 1:10 Making r', if by any means now at 1189
Ph'p 1: 4 for you all making r' with joy, *1162
requested
J'g 8:26 of the golden earrings that he r' 7592
1Ki 19: 4 he r' for himself that he might die; "
1Ch 4:10 God granted him that which he r'. "
Da 1: 8 he r' the prince of the eunuchs 1245
2:49 Then Daniel r' of the king, and he 1156
requests
Ph'p 4: 6 let your r' be made known unto God. 155
require See also REQUIRED; REQUIREST; REQUIRETH; REQUIRING.
Ge 9: 5 your blood of your lives will I r'; 1875
5 the hand of every beast will I r' it, "
5 brother will I r' the life of man. "
31:39 of it; of my hand didst thou r' it. 1245
43: 9 of my hand shalt thou r' him: if I "
De 10:12 doth the Lord thy God r' of thee, 7592
18:19 in my name, I will r' it of him. 1875
23:21 thy God will surely r' it of thee; "
Jos 22:23 thereon, let the Lord himself r' it; 1245
1Sa 20:16 the Lord even r' it at the hand of "
2Sa 3:13 but one thing I r' of thee, that is, 7592
4:11 now r' his blood of your hand, and 1245
19:38 whatsoever thou shalt r' of me, 977
1Ki 8:59 at all times, as the matter shall r': 3117
1Ch 21: 3 then doth my lord r' this thing? 1245
2Ch 24:22 The Lord look upon it, and r' it. 1875
Ezr 7:21 the God of heaven, shall r' of you, 7592
8:22 ashamed to r' of the king a band *7592
Ne 5:12 them, and will r' nothing of them; 1245
Ps 10:13 in his heart, Thou wilt not r' it. 1875
Eze 3:18, 20 blood will I r' at thine hand. 1245
20:40 there will I r' your offerings, and 1875
33: 6 blood will I r' at the watchman's "
8 his blood will I r' at thine hand. 1245
34:10 I will r' my flock at their hand, 1875
Mic 6: 8 and what doth the Lord r' of thee, "
1Co 1:22 the Jews r' a sign, and the Greeks* 154
7:36 and need so r', let him do what he 1096
required
Ge 42:22 behold, also his blood is r'. 1875
Ex 12:36 lent unto them such things as they r'.*
1Sa 21: 8 the king's business r' haste. 1961
2Sa 12:20 when he r', they set bread before 7592
1Ch 16:37 continually, as every day's work r': 3117
2Ch 8:14 priests, as the duty of every day r': "
24: 6 hast thou not r' of the Levites to 1875
Ezr 3: 4 as the duty of every day r'; 3117
Ne 5:18 r' not I the bread of the governor,*1245
Es 2:15 she r' nothing but what Hegai the "
Ps 40: 6 and sin offering hast thou not r'. 7592
137: 3 us away captive r' of us a song; "
3 they that wasted us r' of us mirth, "
Pr 30: 7 Two things have I r' of thee; deny*7592
Isa 1:12 who hath r' this at your hand, to 1245
Lu 11:50 world, may be r' of this generation; 1567
51 It shall be r' of this generation. "
12:20 night thy soul shall be r' of thee: 523
48 is given, of him shall be much r': 2212
19:23 have r' mine own with usury? 4238
23:24 that it should be as they r'. * 155
1Co 4: 2 Moreover it is r' in stewards, that 2212
requirest
Ru 3:11 I will do to thee all that thou r': * 559
requireth
Ec 3:15 and God r' that which is past. *1245
Da 2:11 it is a rare thing that the king r', 7593
requiring
Lu 23:23 voice, r' that he might be crucified.*154
requite See also REQUITED; REQUITING.
Ge 50:15 and will certainly r' us all the evil 7725
De 32: 6 Do ye thus r' the Lord, O foolish 1580
2Sa 2: 6 and I will also r' you this kindness, 6213
16:12 the Lord will r' me good for his 7725
2Ki 9:26 I will r' thee in this plat, saith the 7999
Ps 10:14 and spite, to r' it with thy hand: †5414
41:10 raise me up, that I may r' them. 7999
Jer 51:56 God of recompences shall surely r'. "
1Ti 5: 4 at home, and to r' their parents: 287,591
requited
J'g 1: 7 as I have done, so God hath r' me. 7999
1Sa 25:21 and he hath r' me evil for good. *7725
requiting
2Ch 6:23 by r' the wicked, by recompensing 7725
rereward
Nu 10:25 which was the r' of all the camps* 622
Jos 6: 9 and the r' came after the ark, the* "
13 but the r' came after the ark of the* "
1Sa 29: 2 passed on in the r' with Achish. * 314
Isa 52:12 the God of Israel will be your r'. * 622
58: 8 the glory of the Lord shall be thy r'.* "
rescue See also RESCUED; RESCUETH.
De 28:31 thou shalt have none to r' them. *3467
Ps 35:17 look on? r' my soul from their 7725
Ho 5:14 take away, and none shall r' him.*5337
rescued
1Sa 14:45 So the people r' Jonathan, that he 6299
30:18 away: and David r' his two wives. 5337
Ac 23:27 came I with an army, and r' him, 1807
rescueth
Da 6:27 He delivereth and r', and he 5338
resemblance
Zec 5: 6 is their r' through all the earth. 5869
resemble See also RESEMBLED.
Lu 13:18 like? and whereunto shall I r' it? *3666
resembled
J'g 8:18 each one r' the children of a king. 8389
Resen (*re'-zen*)
Ge 10:12 R' between Nineveh and Calah: 7449
reserve See also RESERVED; RESERVETH.
Jer 3: 5 Will he r' his anger for ever? will*5201
50:20 for I will pardon them whom I r'.*7604
2Pe 2: 9 to r' the unjust unto the day of *5083
reserved
Ge 27:36 thou not r' a blessing for me? 680
Nu 18: 9 most holy things, r' from the fire:
J'g 21:22 we r' not to each man his wife 3947
Ru 2:18 gave to her that she had r' after *3498
2Sa 8: 4 r' of them for an hundred chariots. "
1Ch 18: 4 but r' of them an hundred chariots. "
Job 21:30 is r' to the day of destruction? 2820
38:23 Which I have r' against the time of "
Ac 25:21 be r' unto the hearing of Augustus,*5083
Ro 11: 4 I have r' to myself seven thousand*2641
1Pe 1: 4 not away, r' in heaven for you, 5083
2Pe 2: 4 darkness, to be r' unto judgment; "
17 the mist of darkness is r' for ever. "
3: 7 r' unto fire against the day of "
Jude 6 hath r' in everlasting chains under* "
13 to whom is r' the blackness of "
reserveth
Jer 5:24 r' unto us the appointed weeks of 8104
Na 1: 2 and he r' wrath for his enemies. 5201
Resheph (*re'-shef*)
1Ch 7:25 Rephah was his son, also R', and 7566
residue
Ex 10: 5 eat the r' of that which is escaped, 3499
1Ch 6:66 And the r' of the families of the sons*
Ne 11:20 the r' of Israel, of the priests, and 7605
Isa 21:17 the r' of the number of archers, the "
28: 5 of beauty, unto the r' of his people, "
38:10 am deprived of the r' of my years. 3499
44:17 the r' thereof he maketh a god, 7611
19 the r' thereof an abomination? 3499
Jer 8: 3 r' of them that remain of this evil 7611
15: 9 the r' of them will I deliver to the "
24: 8 the r' of Jerusalem, that remain in "
27:19 the r' of the vessels that remain in 3499
29: 1 Jerusalem unto the r' of the elders "
39: 3 the r' of the princes of the king of*7611
41:10 all the r' of the people that were "
52:15 r' of the people that remained in 3499
Eze 9: 8 wilt thou destroy all the r' of Israel 7611
23:25 thy r' shall be devoured by the fire. 319
34:18 your feet the r' of your pastures? 3499
18 ye must foul the r' with your feet? 3498
36: 3 unto the r' of the heathen, 7611
4 derision to the r' of the heathen "
5 against the r' of the heathen, and "
48:18 And the r' in length over against 3498
21 And the r' shall be for the prince, "
Da 7: 7 stamped the r' with the feet of it: 7606
19 and stamped the r' with his feet; "
Zep 2: 9 r' of my people shall spoil them, 7611
Hag 2: 2 and to the r' of the people, saying,* "
Zec 8:11 be unto the r' of this people as in * "
14: 2 r' of the people shall not be cut off 3499
Mal 2:15 Yet had he the r' of the spirit. 7605
M'r 16:13 they went and told it unto the r': *3062
Ac 15:17 r' of the men might seek after the 2645
resist See also RESISTED; RESISTETH.
Zec 3: 1 at his right hand to r' him. *7853
M't 5:39 I say unto you, That ye r' not evil: 436
Lu 21:15 shall not be able to gainsay nor r'.* "
Ac 6:10 were not able to r' the wisdom and* "
7:51 ears, ye do always r' the Holy Ghost: 496
Ro 13: 2 and they that r' shall receive to * 436
2Ti 3: 8 Moses, so do these also r' the truth:* "
Jas 4: 7 R' the devil, and he will flee from "
5: 6 the just; and he doth not r' you. 498
1Pe 5: 9 Whom r' stedfast in the faith, * 436
resisted
Ro 9:19 find fault? For who hath r' his will?*436
Heb 12: 4 Ye have not yet r' unto blood, 478
resisteth
Ro 13: 2 Whosoever therefore r' the power, 498
2 r' the ordinance of God: and they* 436
Jas 4: 6 God r' the proud, but giveth grace 498
1Pe 5: 5 God r' the proud, and giveth grace "
resolved
Lu 16: 4 I am r' what to do, that, when I 1097
resort See also RESORTED.
Ne 4:20 trumpet, r' ye thither unto us: 6908
Ps 71: 3 whereunto I may continually r': 935
M'r 10: 1 and the people r' unto him again;*4848
Joh 18:20 whither the Jews always r'; *4905
resorted
2Ch 11:13 r' to him out of all their coasts. 3320
M'r 2:13 and all the multitude r' unto him, 2064
Joh 10:41 many r' unto him, and said, John* "
18: 2 Jesus ofttimes r' thither with his 4863
Ac 16:13 unto the women which r' thither.*4905
respect See also RESPECTED; RESPECTETH.
Ge 4: 4 And the Lord had r' unto Abel 8159
5 and to his offering he had not r'. "
Ex 2:25 Israel, and God had r' unto them.*3045
Le 19:15 not r' the person of the poor, 5375
26: 9 For I will have r' unto you, and 6437
Nu 16:15 Lord, R' not thou their offering: "
De 1:17 shall not r' persons in judgment; 5234
16:19 thou shalt not r' persons, neither "
2Sa 14:14 neither doth God r' any person: *5375
1Ki 8:28 have thou r' unto the prayer of 6437
2Ki 13:23 had r' unto them, because of his "
2Ch 6:19 Have r' therefore to the prayer of "
19: 7 Lord our God, nor r' of persons, 4856
Ps 74:20 Have r' unto the covenant: for 5027
119: 6 have r' unto all thy commandments. "
15 precepts, and have r' unto thy ways. "
117 r' unto thy statutes continually. 8159
138: 6 yet hath he r' unto the lowly: 7200
Pr 24:23 have r' of persons in judgment. 5234
28:21 To have r' of persons is not good: "
Isa 17: 7 have r' to the Holy One of Israel. 7200
17: 8 r' that which his fingers have made. "
22:11 r' unto him that fashioned it long "
Ro 2:11 there is no r' of persons with God. 4382
2Co 3:10 glorious had no glory in this r', 3313
Eph 6: 9 is there r' of persons with him. 4382
Ph'p 4:11 Not that I speak in r' of want: for 2596
Col 2:16 or in r' of an holyday, or of the 3313
3:25 and there is no r' of persons. 4382
Heb 11:26 had r' unto the recompence of the* 578
Jas 2: 1 Lord of glory, with r' of persons. 4382
3 r' to him that weareth the gay *1914
9 But if ye have r' to persons, ye 4380
1Pe 1:17 who without r' of persons judgeth 678
respected
La 4:16 r' not the persons of the priests, 5375
respecter
Ac 10:34 that God is no r' of persons: 4381
respecteth
Job 37:24 r' not any that are wise of heart. *7200
Ps 40: 4 and r' not the proud, nor such as 6437
respite
Ex 8:15 Pharaoh saw that there was r', 7309
1Sa 11: 3 Give us seven days' r', that we 7503
rest See also RESTED; RESTETH; RESTING; RESTS.
Ge 8: 9 dove found no r' for the sole of her 4494
18: 4 and r' yourselves under the tree. 8172
30:36 Jacob fed the r' of Laban's flocks. 3498
49:15 he saw that r' was good, and the *4496
Ex 5: 5 make them r' from their burdens. 7673
16:23 is the r' of the holy sabbath unto 7677
23:11 thou shalt let it r' and lie still; 8058
12 on the seventh day thou shalt r': 7673
12 thine ox and thine ass may r', and 5117
28:10 names of the r' on the other stone,*3498
31:15 the seventh is the sabbath of r', 7677
33:14 with thee, and I will give thee r'. 5117
34:21 on the seventh day thou shalt r': 7673
21 time and in harvest thou shalt r'. "
35: 2 day, a sabbath of r' to the Lord: 7677
Le 5: 9 r' of the blood shall be wrung out 7604
14:17 r' of the oil that is in his hand 3499
29 r' of the oil that is in the priest's 3498
16:31 shall be a sabbath of r' unto you, 7677
23: 3 seventh day is the sabbath of r', "
32 shall be unto you a sabbath of r', "
25: 4 be a sabbath of r' unto the land, "
5 for it is a year of r' unto the land. "
26:34 then shall the land r', and enjoy 7673
35 long as it lieth desolate it shall r'; "
35 it did not r' in your sabbaths, when "
Nu 31: 8 beside the r' of them that were slain;
32 r' of the prey which the men of *3499
De 3:13 the r' of Gilead, and all Bashan, "
20 have given r' unto your brethren, 5117
5:14 maidservant may r' as well as thou. "
12: 9 ye are not as yet come to the r' 4496
10 he giveth you r' from all your 5117
25:19 God hath given thee r' from all "
28:65 shall the sole of thy foot have r': 4494
Jos 1:13 Lord your God hath given you r', 5117
15 Lord have given your brethren r', "
3:13 shall r' in the waters of Jordan, "
10:20 the r' which remained of them *8300
13:27 the r' of the kingdom of Sihon 3499
14:15 And the land had r' from war. 8252
17: 2 the r' of the children of Manasseh 3498
6 the r' of Manasseh's sons had the "
21: 5 the r' of the children of Kohath "
34 the r' of the Levites, out of the "
44 Lord gave them r' round about, 5117
22: 4 hath given r' unto your brethren, "
23: 1 the Lord had given r' unto Israel "

J'g 3:11 And the land had r· forty years. 8252
30 the land had r· fourscore years. "
5:31 And the land had r· forty years. "
7: 6 the r· of the people bowed down 3499
8 he sent all the r· of Israel every man*
Ru 1: 9 grant you that ye may find r·, 4496
3: 1 shall I not seek r· for thee, that 4494
18 the man will not be in r·, until he 8252
1Sa 13: 2 the r· of the people he sent every 3499
15:15 the r· we have utterly destroyed. 3498
2Sa 3:29 Let it r· on the head of Joab, and *2342
7: 1 the Lord had given him r· round 5117
11 thee to r· from all thine enemies. "
10:10 the r· of the people he delivered 3499
12:28 gather the r· of the people together, "
21:10 the birds of the air to r· on them 5117
1Ki 5: 4 the Lord my God hath given me r· "
8:56 that hath given r· unto his people 4496
11:41 the r· of the acts of Solomon, and 3499
14:19 the r· of the acts of Jeroboam, how "
29 the r· of the acts of Rehoboam, and "
15: 7 Now the r· of the acts of Abijam, "
23 The r· of all the acts of Asa, and "
31 Now the r· of the acts of Nadab, "
16: 5 Now the r· of the acts of Baasha, "
14 Now the r· of the acts of Elah, and "
20 Now the r· of the acts of Zimri, "
27 Now the r· of the acts of Omri "
20:30 But the r· fled to Aphek, into the 3498
22:39 Now the r· of the acts of Ahab, 3499
45 the r· of the acts of Jehoshaphat, "
2Ki 1:18 Now the r· of the acts of Ahaziah "
2:15 spirit of Elijah doth r· on Elisha. 5117
4: 7 thou and thy children of the r·. 3498
8:23 And the r· of the acts of Joram, 3499
10:34 Now the r· of the acts of Jehu, and "
12:19 And the r· of the acts of Joash, and "
13: 8 Now the r· of the acts of Jehoahaz, "
12 And the r· of the acts of Joash, and "
14:15 the r· of the acts of Jehoash which "
18 the r· of the acts of Amaziah, are "
28 the r· of the acts of Jeroboam, and "
15: 6 And the r· of the acts of Azariah, "
11 And the r· of the acts of Zachariah, "
15 the r· of the acts of Shallum, and "
21 And the r· of the acts of Menahem, "
26 And the r· of the acts of Pekahiah, "
31 the r· of the acts of Pekah, and all "
36 Now the r· of the acts of Jotham, "
16:19 the r· of the acts of Ahaz which he "
20:20 And the r· of the acts of Hezekiah, "
21:17 the r· of the acts of Manasseh, and "
25 the r· of the acts of Amon which he "
23:28 the r· of the acts of Josiah, and all "
24: 5 the r· of the acts of Jehoiakim, and "
25:11 r· of the people that were left in "
1Ch 4:43 smote the r· of the Amalekites *7611
6:31 Lord, after that the ark had r·. 4494
77 r· of the children of Merari were 3498
11: 8 Joab repaired the r· of the city. 7605
12:38 r· also of Israel were of one heart 7611
16:41 and the r· that were chosen, who 7605
19:11 r· of the people he delivered unto 3499
22: 9 to thee, who shall be a man of r·; 4496
9 give him r· from all his enemies, 5117
18 he not given you r· on every side? "
23:25 hath given r· unto his people, that "
24:20 r· of the sons of Levi were these: 3498
28: 2 build an house of r· for the ark of 4496
2Ch 9:29 Now the r· of the acts of Solomon, 7605
13:22 And the r· of the acts of Abijah, 3499
14: 6 for the land had r·, and he had no 8252
6 because the Lord had given him r·.5117
7 he hath given us r· on every side. "
11 for we r· on thee, and in thy *8172
15:15 Lord gave them r· round about. 5117
20:30 his God gave him r· round about. "
34 the r· of the acts of Jehoshaphat, 3499
24:14 they brought the r· of the money 7605
25:26 Now the r· of the acts of Amaziah,3499
26:22 the r· of the acts of Uzziah, first "
27: 7 the r· of the acts of Jotham, and "
28:26 r· of his acts and of all his ways, "
32:32 the r· of the acts of Hezekiah, "
33:18 the r· of the acts of Manasseh, and "
35:26 the r· of the acts of Josiah, and "
36: 8 the r· of the acts of Jehoiakim, "
Ezr 4: 3 the r· of the chief of the fathers 7605
7 and the r· of their companions, "
9 and the r· of their companions; 7606
10 r· of the nations whom the great "
10 r· that are on this side the river, "
17 r· of their companions that dwell "
17 and unto the r· beyond the river, "
6:16 r· of the children of the captivity, "
7:18 the r· of the silver and the gold, "
Ne 2:16 nor to the r· that did the work. 3499
4:14, 19 to the r· of the people, "
6: 1 and the r· of our enemies, heard "
14 and the r· of the prophets, that "
7:72 which the r· of the people gave 7611
9:28 But after they had r·, they did evil5117
10:28 the r· of the people, the priests, 7605
11: 1 the r· of the people also cast lots, to"
Es 9:12 in the r· of the king's provinces? "
16 and had r· from their enemies, 5118
Job 3:13 have slept: then had I been at r·, 5117
17 and there the weary be at r·. "
18 There the prisoners r· together; *7599
26 was not in safety, neither had I r·,*8252
11:18 thou shalt take thy r· in safety. 7901
14: 6 Turn from him, that he may r·, 2308
17:16 when our r· together is in the dust.5183
30:17 season: and my sinews take no r·.7901
Ps 16: 9 my flesh also shall r· in hope. *7931
17:14 leave the r· of their substance to 3499
37: 7 R· in the Lord, and wait patiently 1826
38: 3 neither is there any r· in my bones*7965
55: 6 then would I fly away, and be at r·.7931
94:13 r· from the days of adversity, 8252
95:11 they should not enter into my r·. 4496
116: 7 Return unto thy r·, O my soul; for "
125: 3 the rod of the wicked shall not 5117
132: 8 Arise, O Lord, into thy r·; thou, *4496
14 This is my r· for ever: here will I* "
Pr 6:35 neither will he r· content, though thou
29: 9 he rage or laugh, there is no r·. 5183
17 thy son, and he shall give thee r·:5117
Ec 2:23 his heart taketh not r· in the night.
6: 5 this hath more r· than the other. 5183
Ca 1: 7 makest thy flock to r· at noon: 7257
Isa 7:19 shall r· all of them in the desolate 5117
10:19 the r· of the trees of his forest *7605
11: 2 spirit of the Lord shall r· upon 5117
10 seek: and his r· shall be glorious.*4496
14: 3 shall give thee r· from thy sorrow,5117
7 whole earth is at r·, and is quiet: "
18: 4 I will take my r·, and I will *8252
23:12 there also shalt thou have no r·. 5117
25:10 shall the hand of the Lord r·, "
28:12 said, This is the r· wherewith 4496
12 ye may cause the weary to r·; 5117
30:15 returning and r· shall ye be saved;5183
34:14 screech owl also shall r· there, *7280
14 and find for herself a place of r·. 4494
51: 4 my judgment to r· for a light of *7280
57: 2 they shall r· in their beds, each 5117
20 troubled sea, when it cannot r·, 8252
62: 1 for Jerusalem's sake I will not r·, "
7 give him no r·, till he establish, 1824
63:14 Spirit of the Lord caused him to r·:5117
66: 1 and where is the place of my r·? 4496
Jer 6:16 and ye shall find r· for your souls.4771
30:10 shall return, and shall be in r·, *8252
31: 2 when I went to cause him to r·. 7280
39: 9 the r· of the people that remained.*3499
45: 3 in my sighing, and I find no r·. 4496
46:27 return, and be in r· and at ease, *8252
47: 6 into thy scabbard, r·, and be still. 7280
50:34 that he may give r· to the land, "
52:15 and the r· of the multitude. *3499
La 1: 3 the heathen, she findeth no r·: 4494
2:18 day and night: give thyself no r·;*6314
5: 5 we labour, and have no r·. 5117
Eze 5:13 cause my fury to r· upon them, † "
16:42 make my fury toward thee to r·, † "
21:17 and I will cause my fury to r·: † "
24:13 caused my fury to r· upon thee. † "
38:11 I will go to them that are at r·, *8252
44:30 the blessing to r· in thine house. 5117
45: 8 r· of the land shall they give to the*
48:23 As for the r· of the tribes, from the3499
Da 2:18 the r· of the wise men of Babylon. 7606
4: 4 Nebuchadnezzar was at r· in mine7954
7:12 As concerning the r· of the beasts,7606
12:13 thou shalt r·, and stand in thy lot 5117
Mic 2:10 depart; for this is not your r·: 4496
Hab 3:16 I might r· in the day of trouble: 5117
Zep 3:17 he will r· in his love, he will joy 2790
Zec 1:11 the earth sitteth still, and is at r·. 8252
9: 1 Damascus shall be the r· thereof:*4496
11: 9 let the r· eat every one the flesh *7604
M't 11:28 heavy laden, and I will give you r·. 373
29 and ye shall find r· unto your souls.372
12:43 places, seeking r·, and finding none. "
26:45 Sleep on now, and take your r·: 373
27:49 The r· said, Let be, let us see 3062
M'r 6:31 into a desert place, and r· a while: 373
14:41 Sleep on now, and take your r·: "
Lu 10: 6 there, your peace shall r· upon it: 1879
11:24 through dry places, seeking r·; 372
12:26 why take ye thought for the r·? 3062
24: 9 unto the eleven, and to all the r·. "
Joh 11:13 had spoken of taking of r· in sleep.2838
Ac 2:26 also my flesh shall r· in hope: *2681
37 Peter and to the r· of the apostles, 3062
5:13 of the r· durst no man join himself "
7:49 or what is the place of my r·? 2663
9:31 had the churches r· throughout *1515
27:44 And the r·, some on boards, and 3062
Ro 11: 7 obtained it, and the r· were blinded "
1Co 7:12 But to the r· speak I, not the Lord: "
11:34 r· will I set in order when I come. "
2Co 2:13 I had no r· in my spirit, because I* 425
7: 5 Macedonia, our flesh had no r·, * "
12: 9 power of Christ may r· upon me. 1981
2Th 1: 7 to you who are troubled r· with us, 425
Heb 3:11 They shall not enter into my r·.) 2663
18 they should not enter into his r·, "
4: 1 being left us of entering into his r·,"
3 which have believed do enter into r·,"
3 if they shall enter into my r·: "
4 God did r· the seventh day from *2664
5 If they shall enter into my r·. 2663
8 For if Jesus had given them r·, 2664
9 therefore a r· to the people of God.4520
10 For he that is entered into his r·, 2663
11 labour therefore to enter into that r·,"
1Pe 4: 2 live the r· of his time in the flesh 1954
Re 2:24 I say, and unto the r· in Thyatira, 3062
4: 8 and they r· not day and night, 2192,372
6:11 should r· yet for a little season, 373
9:20 r· of the men which were not killed3062
14:11 and they have no r· day nor night, 372
13 that they may r· from their labours;373
20: 5 the r· of the dead lived not again 3062

rested

Ge 2: 2 he r· on the seventh day from all 7673
3 that in it he had r· from all his work"
8: 4 the ark r· in the seventh month, 5117
Ex 10:14 and r· in all the coasts of Egypt: "
16:30 the people r· on the seventh day. 7673
20:11 in them is, and r· the seventh day:5117
31:17 and on the seventh day he r·, and 7673
Nu 9:18 tabernacle they r· in their tents. *2583
23 of the Lord they r· in the tents, * "
10:12 the cloud r· in the wilderness of *7931
36 when it r·, he said, Return, O Lord,5117
11:25 when the spirit r· upon them, they "
26 Medad: and the spirit r· upon them; "
Jos 11:23 tribes. And the land r· from war.*8252
1Ki 6:10 they r· on the house with timber of270
2Ch 32: 8 r· themselves upon the words of 5564
Es 9:17 fourteenth day of the same r· they,5118
18 fifteenth day of the same they r·, "
22 the Jews r· from their enemies, "
Job 30:27 My bowels boiled, and r· not: the*1826
Lu 23:56 and r· the sabbath day according 2270

restest

Ro 2:17 art called a Jew, and r· in the law,1879

resteth

Job 24:23 him to be in safety, whereon he r·;*8172
Pr 14:33 Wisdom r· in the heart of him that5117
Ec 7: 9 for anger r· in the bosom of fools. "
1Pe 4:14 spirit of glory and of God r· upon 373

resting See also RESTINGPLACE.

Nu 10:33 to search out a r· place for them. 4496
2Ch 6:41 O Lord God, into thy r· place, thou,5118
Pr 24:15 righteous; spoil not his r· place: 7258
Isa 32:18 dwellings, and in quiet r· places; 4496

restingplace See also RESTING and PLACE.

Jer 50: 6 hill, they have forgotten their r·. 7258

restitution

Ex 22: 3 he should make full r·; if he have 7999
5 his own vineyard, shall he make r·. "
6 kindled...fire shall surely make r·. "
12 he shall make r· unto the owner "
Job 20:18 to his substance shall the r· be, *8545
Ac 3:21 until the times of r· of all things, * 605

restore See also RESTORED; RESTORETH.

Ge 20: 7 r· the man his wife; for he is a 7725
7 if thou r· her not, know thou that "
40:13 head, and r· thee unto thy place: "
42:25 r· every man's money into his sack, "
Ex 22: 1 he shall r· five oxen for an ox, and *7999
4 ass, or sheep; he shall r· double. * "
Le 6: 4 r· that which he took violently 7725
5 he shall even r· it in the principal,7999
24:21 that killeth a beast, he shall r· it:* "
25:27 r· the overplus unto the man to 7725
28 But if he be not able to r· it to him,*"
Nu 35:25 r· him to the city of his refuge, "
De 22: 2 and thou shalt r· it to him again. "
J'g 11:13 r· those lands again peaceably. "
17: 3 now therefore I will r· it unto thee. "
1Sa 12: 3 eyes therewith? and I will r· it you. "
2Sa 9: 7 will r· thee all the land of Saul thy "
12: 6 And he shall r· the lamb fourfold, 7999
16: 3 r· me the kingdom of my father. 7725
1Ki 20:34 took from thy father, I will r·; "
2Ki 8: 6 R· all that was hers, and all the "
Ne 5:11 R·, I pray you, to them, even this "
12 Then said they, We will r· them, "
Job 20:10 and his hands shall r· their goods.* "
18 which he laboured for shall he r·, "
Ps 51:12 R· unto me the joy of thy "
Pr 6:31 he be found, he shall r· sevenfold; 7999
Isa 1:26 I will r· thy judges as at the first, 7725
42:22 for a spoil, and none saith, R·. "
49: 6 and to r· the preserved of Israel: "
57:18 r· comforts unto him and to his 7999
Jer 27:22 them up, and r· them to this place.7725
30:17 For I will r· health unto thee, and 5927
Eze 33:15 If the wicked r· the pledge, give 7725
Da 9:25 to r· and to build Jerusalem unto "
Joe 2:25 I will r· to you the years that the 7999
M't 17:11 shall first come, and r· all things. 600
Lu 19: 8 false accusation, I r· him fourfold. 591
Ac 1: 6 r· again the kingdom to Israel? 600
Ga 6: 1 r· such an one in the spirit of 2675

restored

Ge 20:14 and r· him Sarah his wife. 7725
40:21 And he r· the chief butler unto his "
41:13 me he r· unto mine office, and him "
42:28 My money is r·; and, lo, it is even "
De 28:31 and shall not be r· to thee: thy "
J'g 17: 3 had r· the eleven hundred shekels "
4 he r· the money unto his mother; "
1Sa 7:14 taken from Israel were r· to Israel, "
1Ki 13: 6 that my hand may be r· me again. "
6 the king's hand was r· him again, "
2Ki 8: 1 whose son he had r· to life, 2421
5 how he had r· a dead body to life, "
5 woman, whose son he had r· to life, "
5 is her son, whom Elisha r· to life. "
14:22 He built Elath, and r· it to Judah, 7725
25 He r· the coast of Israel from the "
2Ch 8: 2 which Huram had r· to Solomon,*5414
26: 2 He built Eloth, and r· it to Judah,7725
Ezr 6: 5 be r·, and brought again unto the 8421
Ps 69: 4 I r· that which I took not away. 7725
Eze 18: 7 but hath r· to the debtor his pledge, "
12 hath not r· the pledge, and hath "
M't 12:13 it was r· whole, like as the other. 600
M'r 3: 5 his hand was r· whole as the other. "
8:25 and he was r·, and saw every man "
Lu 6:10 his hand was r· whole as the other. "
Heb 13:19 that I may be r· to you the sooner. "

restorer

Ru 4:15 shall be unto thee a r· of thy life, 7725
Isa 58:12 breach, The r· of paths to dwell in. "

restoreth

Ps 23: 3 He r· my soul: he leadeth me in 7725
M'r 9:12 cometh first, and r· all things; 600

restrain See also RESTRAINED; RESTRAINEST.
Job 15: 8 dost thou r· wisdom to thyself? ‡1639
Ps 76:10 remainder of wrath shalt thou r·.*2296
restrained
Ge 8: 2 and the rain from heaven was r·; 3607
11: 6 now nothing will be r· from them.*1219
16: 2 the Lord hath r· me from bearing:6113
Ex 36: 6 the people were r· from bringing. 3607
1Sa 3:13 vile, and he r· them not. 3543
Isa 63:15 mercies toward me? are they r·? 662
Eze 31:15 and I r· the floods thereof, and 4513
Ac 14:18 sayings scarce r· they the people. 2664
restrainest
Job 15: 4 off fear, and r· prayer before God. 1639
restraint
1Sa 14: 6 there is no r· to the Lord to save 4622
rests
1Ki 6: 6 he made narrowed r· round about,†‡
resurrection
M't 22:23 which say that there is no r·, and 386
28 in the r· whose wife shall she be of "
30 For in the r· they neither marry, "
31 But as touching the r· of the dead, "
27:53 came out the graves after his r·, 1454
M'r 12:18 Sadducees, which say there is no r·;386
23 In the r· therefore, when they shall "
Lu 14:14 be recompensed at the r· of the just."
20:27 which deny that there is any r·; "
33 in the r· whose wife of them is she? "
35 that world, and the r· from the dead,"
36 of God, being the children of the r·. "
Joh 5:29 have done good, unto the r· of life; "
29 done evil, unto the r· of damnation. "
11:24 rise again in the r· at the last day. "
25 unto her, I am the r·, and the life: "
Ac 1:22 to be a witness with us of his r·. "
2:31 this before spake of the r· of Christ, "
4: 2 through Jesus the r· from the dead. "
33 witness of the r· of the Lord Jesus: "
17:18 preached unto them Jesus, and...r·. "
32 when they heard of the r· of the dead,"
23: 6 of the hope and r· of the dead I am "
8 Sadducees say that there is no r·, "
24:15 that there shall be a r· of the dead, "
21 Touching the r· of the dead I am "
Ro 1: 4 of holiness, by the r· from the dead:"
6: 5 be also in the likeness of his r·: "
1Co 15:12 you that there is no r· of the dead? "
13 But if there be no r· of the dead, then"
21 by man came also the r· of the dead."
42 So also is the r· of the dead. It is "
Ph'p 3:10 know him, and the power of his r·, "
11 attain unto the r· of the dead. 1815
2Ti 2:18 saying that the r· is past already; 386
Heb 6: 2 of r· of the dead, and of eternal "
11:35 that they might obtain a better r·: "
1Pe 1: 3 lively hope by the r· of Jesus Christ "
3:21 God,) by the r· of Jesus Christ: "
Re 20: 5 were finished. This is the first r·. "
6 is he that hath part in the first r·: "
retain See also RETAINED; RETAINETH.
Job 2: 9 Dost thou still r· thine integrity? *2388
Pr 4: 4 Let thine heart r· my words: keep 8551
11:16 honour: and strong men r· riches,‡"
Ec 8: 8 over the spirit to r· the spirit; 3607
Da 11: 6 shall not r· the power of the arm; 6113
Joh 20:23 whose soever sins ye r·, they are 2902
Ro 1:28 like to r· God in their knowledge,*2192
retained
J'g 7: 8 and r· those three hundred men: 2388
19: 4 the damsel's father, r· him; and "
Da 10: 8 corruption, and I r· no strength. 6113
16 upon me, and I have r· no strength.*"
Joh 20:23 soever sins ye retain, they are r·. 2902
Ph'm 13 Whom I would have r· with me, *2722
retaineth
Pr 3:18 and happy is every one that r· her.8551
11:16 A gracious woman r· honour: and‡ "
Mic 7:18 he r· not his anger for ever, 2388
retire See also RETIRED.
2Sa 11:15 and r· ye from him, that he may be7725
Jer 4: 6 r·, stay not: for I will bring 5756
retired
J'g 20:39 the men of Israel r· in the battle, *2015
2Sa 20:22 they r· from the city, every man *6327
return See also RETURNED; RETURNETH; RETURNING.
Ge 3:19 bread, till thou r· unto the ground;7725
19 art, and unto dust shalt thou r·. "
14:17 after his r· from the slaughter of "
16: 9 R· to thy mistress, and submit "
18:10 said, I will certainly r· unto thee "
14 time appointed I will r· unto thee, "
31: 3 R· unto the land of thy fathers, and"
13 r· unto the land of thy kindred. "
32: 9 R· unto thy country, and to thy "
Ex 4:18 r· unto my brethren which are in "
19 in Midian, Go, r· into Egypt: "
21 When thou goest to r· into Egypt, "
13:17 they see war, and they r· to Egypt: "
Le 25:10 r· every man unto his possession, "
10 shall r· every man unto his family. "
13 r· every man unto his possession. "
27 that he may r· unto his possession. "
28 he shall r· unto his possession. "
41 and shall r· unto his own family, "
41 of his fathers shall he r·. "
27:24 the field shall r· unto him of whom "
Nu 10:36 said, R·, O Lord, unto the many "
14: 3 not better for us to r· into Egypt? "
4 captain, and let us r· into Egypt. "
23: 5 R· unto Balak, and thus thou shalt "
32:18 We will not r· unto our houses, "
Nu 32:22 then afterward ye shall r·, and be 7725
35:28 slayer shall r· into the land of his "
De 3:20 r· every man unto his possession, "
17:16 nor cause the people to r· to Egypt,"
16 henceforth r· no more that way. "
20: 5 let him go and r· to his house, "
6 let him also go and r· unto his "
7, 8 him go and r· unto his house, "
30: 2 shalt r· unto the Lord thy God, and "
3 will r· and gather thee from all the "
8 thou shalt r· and obey the voice of "
Jos 1:15 r· unto the land of your possession,"
20: 6 then shall the slayer r·, and come "
22: 4 therefore now r· ye, and get you *6437
8 R· with much riches unto your 7725
J'g 7: 3 let him r· and depart early from "
11:31 I r· in peace from the children "
Ru 1: 6 might r· from the country of Moab:"
7 way to r· unto the land of Judah. "
8 Go, r· each to her mother's house: "
10 will r· with thee unto thy people. "
15 gods: r· thou after thy sister in law."
16 or to r· from following after thee: "
1Sa 6: 3 any wise r· him a trespass offering:"
4 offering which we shall r· to him? "
8 ye r· him for a trespass offering. "
7: 3 If ye do r· unto the Lord with all "
17 And his r· was to Ramah; for 8666
9: 5 with him, Come, and let us r·; 7725
15:26 unto Saul, I will not r· with thee: "
26:21 r·, my son David: for I will no "
29: 4 Make this fellow r·, that he may "
7 Wherefore now r·, and go in peace,"
11 to r· into the land of the Philistines."
2Sa 2:26 r· from following their brethren? "
3:16 Then said Abner unto him, Go, r·. "
10: 5 your beards be grown, and then r·. "
12:23 him, but he shall not r· to me. "
15:19 r· to thy place, and abide with the "
20 r· thou, and take back thy brethren:"
27 r· into the city in peace, and your "
34 if thou r· to the city, and say unto "
19:14 R· thou, and all thy servants. "
24:13 I shall r· to him that sent me. "
1Ki 2:32 r· his blood upon his own head, "
33 blood...r· upon the head of Joab, "
44 r· thy wickedness upon thine own "
8:48 r· unto thee with all their heart, "
12:24 r· every man to his house; for this "
26 kingdom r· to the house of David: "
13:16 I may not r· with thee, nor go in "
19:15 r· on thy way to the wilderness of "
20:22 r· of the year the king of Syria 8666
26 came to pass at the r· of the year, "
22:17 r· every man to his house in peace.7725
28 If thou r· at all in peace, the Lord "
2Ki 18:14 I have offended; r· from me: that "
19: 7 and shall r· to his own land; and I "
33 he came, by the same shall he r·, "
20:10 shadow r· backward ten degrees. "
1Ch 19: 5 your beards be grown, and then r·. "
2Ch 6:24 shall r· and confess thy name, and* "
38 they r· to thee with all their heart "
10: 6 give ye me to r· answer to this "
9 we may r· answer to this people, "
11: 4 r· every man to his house: for this "
18:16 let them r·...every man to his house"
26 of affliction, until I r· in peace. "
27 If thou certainly r· in peace, then "
30: 6 he will r· to the remnant of you, "
9 face from you, if ye r· unto him. "
Ne 2: 6 be? and when wilt thou r·? "
4:12 From all places whence ye shall r· "
9:17 a captain to r· to their bondage: "
Es 4:15 Esther bade them r· Mordecai this "
9:25 Jews, should r· upon his own head, "
Job 1:21 and naked shall I r· thither: the "
6:29 R·, I pray you, let it not be iniquity;"
29 yea, r· again, my righteousness is "
7:10 He shall r· no more to his house, "
10:21 Before I go whence I shall not r·, "
15:22 believeth not that he shall r· out of "
16:22 go the way whence I shall not r·. "
17:10 for you all, do ye r·, and come now: "
22:23 If thou r· to the Almighty, thou "
33:25 shall r· to the days of his youth: * "
36:10 that they r· from iniquity. "
39: 4 go forth, and r· not unto them. "
Ps 6: 4 R·, O Lord, deliver my soul: oh "
10 them r· and be ashamed suddenly.*"
7: 7 sakes therefore r· thou on high. "
16 His mischief shall r· upon his own "
59: 6 They r· at evening: they make a "
14 And at evening let them r·; and "
73:10 Therefore his people r· hither: "
74:21 let not the oppressed r· ashamed: "
80:14 R·, we beseech thee, O God of * "
90: 3 and sayest, R·, ye children of men. "
13 R·, O Lord, how long? and let it "
94:15 shall r· unto righteousness: and "
104:29 they die, and r· to their dust. "
116: 7 R· unto thy rest, O my soul; for "
Pr 2:19 None that go unto her r· again, "
26:27 rolleth a stone, it will r· upon him. "
Ec 1: 7 rivers come, thither they r· again.* "
5:15 shall he r· to go as he came, and * "
12: 2 nor the clouds r· after the rain: "
7 the dust r· to the earth as it was: "
7 shall r· unto God who gave it. "
Ca 6:13 R·, r·, O Shulamite; "
13 r·, r·, that we may look upon thee. "
Isa 6:13 it shall be a tenth, and it shall r·, * "
10:21 The remnant shall r·, even the "
22 yet a remnant of them shall r·: "
19:22 and they shall r· even to the Lord, "
21:12 will enquire, enquire ye: r·, come.* "
Isa 35:10 the ransomed of the Lord shall r·,7725
37: 7 a rumour, and r· to his own land; "
34 he came, by the same shall he r·, "
44:22 r· unto me; for I have redeemed "
45:23 in righteousness, and shall not r·, "
51:11 the redeemed of the Lord shall r·, "
55: 7 and let him r· unto the Lord, and "
11 it shall not r· unto me void, but it "
63:17 R· for thy servants' sake, the tribes"
Jer 3: 1 man's, shall he r· unto her again? "
1 r· again unto me, saith the Lord. "
12 R·, thou backsliding Israel, saith "
22 R·, ye backsliding children, and I "
4: 1 If thou wilt r·, O Israel, saith the "
1 Lord, r· unto me: and if thou wilt "
5: 3 than a rock; they have refused to r·."
8: 4 shall he turn away, and not r·? "
5 hold fast deceit, they refuse to r·. "
12:15 I have plucked them out I will r·, "
15: 7 since they r· not from their ways.* "
19 If thou r·, then will I bring thee "
19 my mouth: let them r· unto thee; "
19 but r· not thou unto them. "
18:11 r· ye now every one from his evil "
22:10 for he shall r· no more, nor see his "
11 He shall not r· thither any more: "
27 land whereunto they desire to r·, "
27 thither shall they not r·. "
23:14 none doth r· from his wickedness: "
20 The anger of the Lord shall not r·, "
24: 7 r· unto me with their whole heart. "
29:10 in causing you to r· to this place. "
30: 3 I will cause them to r· to the land "
10 Jacob shall r·, and shall be in rest, "
24 fierce anger of the Lord shall not r·, "
31: 8 a great company shall r· thither. "
32:44 for I will cause their captivity to r·."
33: 7 and the captivity of Israel to r·, "
11 cause to r· the captivity of the land,"
26 for I will cause their captivity to r·."
34:11 whom they had let go free, to r·, "
16 set at liberty at their pleasure, to r·,"
22 and cause them to r· to this city; "
35:15 R· ye now every man from his evil "
36: 3 may r· every man from his evil way;"
7 will r· every one from his evil way, "
37: 7 shall r· to Egypt into their own land."
20 not to r· to the house of Jonathan "
38:26 cause me to r· to Jonathan's house, "
42:12 cause you to r· to your own land. "
44:14 should r· into the land of Judah, "
14 have a desire to r· to dwell there: "
14 shall r· but such as shall escape. "
28 shall r· out of the land of Egypt "
46:27 and Jacob shall r·, and be in rest "
50: 9 expert man; none shall r· in vain. "
Eze 7:13 the seller shall not r· to that which "
13 multitude...which shall not r·; "
13:22 should not r· from his wicked way, "
16:55, 55 shall r· to their former estate, "
55 shall r· to your former estate. "
18:23 not that he should r· from his ways, "
21: 5 sheath: it shall not r· any more. "
30 Shall I cause it to r· into his sheath?"
29:14 to r· into the land of Pathros, "
35: 9 and thy cities shall not r·: *3427
46: 9 shall not r· by the way of the gate 7725
17 after it shall r· to the prince: but "
47: 6 me to r· to the brink of the river. "
Da 10:20 now will I r· to fight with the "
11: 9 and shall r· into his own land. "
10 then shall he r·, and be stirred up, "
13 For the king of the north shall r·, "
28 r· into his land with great riches; "
28 do exploits, and r· to his own land. "
29 At the time appointed he shall r·, "
30 he shall be grieved, and r·, and "
30 shall even r·, and have intelligence "
Ho 2: 7 I will go and r· to my first husband;"
9 Therefore will I r·, and take away* "
3: 5 shall the children of Israel r·, and "
5:15 I will go and r· to my place, till they"
6: 1 Come, and let us r· unto the Lord: "
7:10 do not r· to the Lord their God, * "
16 They r·, but not to the most High: "
8:13 their sins: they shall r· to Egypt. "
9: 3 but Ephraim shall r· to Egypt, and "
11: 5 shall not r· into the land of Egypt, "
5 his king, because they refused to r·."
9 I will not r· to destroy Ephraim: "
12:14 reproach shall his Lord r· unto him."
14: 1 O Israel, r· unto the Lord thy God; "
7 dwell under his shadow shall r·; "
Joe 2:14 knoweth if he will r· and repent, * "
3: 4 speedily will I r· your recompence "
7 and will r· your recompence upon "
Ob 15 thy reward shall r· upon thine own "
Mic 1: 7 they shall r· to the hire of an harlot."
5: 3 the remnant of his brethren shall r·"
Mal 1: 4 r· and build the desolate places; "
3: 7 R· unto me, and I will r· unto you, "
7 But ye said, Wherein shall we r·? "
18 Then shall ye r·, and discern "
M't 2:12 that they should not r· to Herod, 344
10:13 not worthy, let your peace r· to you.1994
12:44 will r· into my house from whence "
24:18 let him which is in the field r· back "
Lu 8:39 R· to thine own house, and shew 5290
11:24 r· unto my house whence I came * "
12:36 when he will r· from the wedding; 360
17:31 field, let him likewise not r· back. 1994
19:12 to receive...a kingdom, and to r·. 5290
Ac 13:34 now no more to r· to corruption, "
15:16 After this I will r·, and will build 390
18:21 but I will r· again unto you, if God 344
20: 3 purposed to r· through Macedonia. 5290

returned
Ge 8: 3 the waters r' from off the earth 7725
9 and she r' unto him into the ark, "
12 dove; which r' not again unto him "
14: 7 they r', and came to En-mishpat, "
18: 33 and Abraham r' unto his place. "
21: 32 r' into the land of the Philistines. "
22: 19 So Abraham r' unto his young men. "
31: 55 departed, and r' unto his place. "
32: 6 the messengers r' to Jacob, saying, "
33: 16 So Esau r' that day on his way unto "
37: 29 And Reuben r' unto the pit; and, "
30 he r' unto his brethren, and said, "
38: 22 he r' to Judah, and said, I cannot "
42: 24 r' to them again, and communed "
43: 10 now we had r' this second time. "
18 the money that was r' in our sacks "
44: 13 every man his ass, and r' to the city. "
50: 14 And Joseph r' into Egypt, he, and "
Ex 4: 18 And Moses went and r' to Jethro his "
20 ass, and he r' to the land of Egypt: "
5: 22 And Moses r' unto the Lord, and "
14: 27 and the sea r' to his strength when "
28 And the waters r', and covered the "
19: 8 Moses r' the words of the people * "
32: 31 And Moses r' unto the Lord, and "
34: 31 all the rulers of the congregation r' "
Le 22: 13 and is r' unto her father's house, as "
Nu 13: 25 they r' from searching of the land "
14: 36 sent to search the land, who r', "
16: 50 Aaron r' unto Moses unto the door "
23: 6 he r' unto him, and, lo, he stood "
24: 25 up, and went and r' to his place: "
De 1: 45 And ye r' and wept before the Lord: "
Jos 2: 16 three days, until the pursuers be r': "
22 days, until the pursuers were r': "
23 So the two men r', and descended "
4: 18 waters of Jordan r' unto their place "
6: 14 the city once, and r' into the camp: "
7: 3 And they r' to Joshua, and said "
8: 24 that all the Israelites r' unto Ai, "
10: 15 And Joshua r', and all Israel with "
21 And all the people r' to the camp "
38, 43 Joshua r', and all Israel with "
22: 9 and the half tribe of Manasseh r', "
32 r' from the children of Reuben, and "
J'g 2: 19 they r', and corrupted themselves* "
5: 29 her, yea, she r' answer to herself, "
7: 3 r' of the people twenty and two "
15 r' into the host of Israel, and said, "
8: 13 the son of Joash r' from battle "
11: 39 that she r' unto her father, who did "
14: 8 And after a time he r' to take her, "
21: 23 went and r' unto their inheritance. "
Ru 1: 22 So Naomi r',...Ruth the Moabitess, "
22 r' out of the country of Moab: "
1Sa 1: 19 worshipped before the Lord, and r', "
6: 16 it, they r' to Ekron the same day. "
17 Philistines r' for a trespass offering "
17: 15 David went and r' from Saul to feed* "
53 r' from chasing after...Philistines, "
57 r' from the slaughter of...Philistine, "
18: 6 r' from the slaughter of...Philistine, "
23: 28 Saul r' from pursuing after David, "
24: 1 r' from following the Philistines, "
25: 39 hath r' the wickedness of Nabal "
26: 25 on his way, and Saul r' to his place. "
27: 9 apparel, and r', and came to Achish. "
2Sa 1: 1 David was r' from the slaughter of "
22 and the sword of Saul r' not empty. "
2: 30 And Joab r' from following Abner: "
3: 16 unto him, Go, return. And he r'. "
27 when Abner was r' to Hebron, Joab "
6: 20 David r' to bless his household. "
8: 13 he r' from smiting of the Syrians "
10: 14 So Joab r' from the children of "
11: 4 and she r' unto her house. "
12: 31 all the people r' unto Jerusalem. "
14: 24 So Absalom r' to his own house, *5437
16: 8 hath r' upon thee all the blood of 7725
17: 3 whom thou seekest is as if all r': "
20 not find them, they r' to Jerusalem. "
18: 16 the people r' from pursuing after "
19: 15 So the king r', and came to Jordan. "
39 him; and he r' unto his own place. "
20: 22 Joab r' to Jerusalem unto the king. "
23: 10 people r' after him only to spoil. "
1Ki 12: 24 r' to depart, according to the word "
13: 10 r' not by the way that he came to "
33 Jeroboam r' not from his evil way, "
19: 21 And he r' back from him, and took "
2Ki 2: 25 and from thence he r' to Samaria. "
3: 27 from him, and r' to their own land. "
4: 35 he r', and walked in the house "
5: 15 And he r' to the man of God, he and "
7: 15 And the messengers r', and told the "
8: 3 that the woman r' out of the land "
9: 15 king Joram was r' to be healed in "
14: 14 and hostages, and r' to Samaria. "
19: 8 Rab-shakeh r', and found the king "
36 and went and r', and dwelt at "
23: 20 upon them, and r' to Jerusalem. "
1Ch 16: 43 and David r' to bless his house. 5437
20: 3 and all the people r' to Jerusalem. 7725
2Ch 10: 2 it, that Jeroboam r' out of Egypt. "
11: 4 r' from going against Jeroboam. "
14: 15 in abundance, and r' to Jerusalem. "
19: 1 Jehoshaphat the king of Judah r' "
8 when they r' to Jerusalem. "
20: 27 Then they r', every man of Judah "
22: 6 And he r' to be healed in Jezreel "
25: 10 and they r' home in great anger. "
24 hostages also, and r' to Samaria. "
28: 15 brethren: then they r' to Samaria. "
31: 1 Then all the children of Israel r', "
32: 21 he r' with shame of face to his own "
2Ch 34: 7 land of Israel, he r' to Jerusalem. 7725
9 Benjamin;...they r' to Jerusalem.* "
Ezr 5: 5 and then they r' answer by letter 8421
11 thus they r' us answer, saying, We "
Ne 2: 15 the gate of the valley, and so r'. 7725
4: 15 we r' all of us to the wall, every one "
9: 28 yet when they r', and cried unto "
Es 2: 14 the morrow she r' into the second "
7: 8 the king r' out of the palace garden "
Ps 35: 13 my prayer r' into mine own bosom. "
60: *title* when Joab r', and smote of Edom "
78: 34 r' and enquired early after God. "
Ec 4: 1 So I r', and considered all the "
7 Then I r', and I saw vanity under "
9: 11 I r', and saw under the sun, that "
Isa 37: 8 So Rabshakeh r', and found the "
37 went and r', and dwelt at Nineveh. "
38: 8 So the sun r' ten degrees, by which "
Jer 3: 7 Turn thou unto me. But she r' not. "
14: 3 they r' with their vessels empty; * "
40: 12 Even all the Jews r' out of all places "
41: 14 from Mizpah cast about and r', ‡ "
43: 5 that were r' from all nations, "
Eze 1: 14 And the living creatures ran and r' "
8: 17 have r' to provoke me to anger: * "
47: 7 Now when I had r', behold, at the "
Da 4: 34 mine understanding r' unto me, "
36 same time my reason r' unto me; "
36 honour and brightness r' unto me; "
Ho 6: 11 I r' the captivity of my people. * "
Am 4: 6, 8, 9, 10, 11 have ye not r' unto me, "
Zec 1: 6 and they r' and said, Like as the * "
16 I am r' to Jerusalem with mercies: "
7: 14 that no man passed through nor r': "
8: 3 I am r' unto Zion, and will dwell in "
M't 21: 18 as he r' into the city, he hungered. 1877
M'r 14: 40 when he r', he found them asleep *5290
Lu 1: 56 months, and r' to her own house. "
2: 20 the shepherds r', glorifying and 1994
39 they r' into Galilee, to their own 5290
43 as they r', the child Jesus tarried * "
4: 1 of the Holy Ghost r' from Jordan, "
14 Jesus r' in the power of the Spirit "
8: 37 up into the ship, and r' back again. "
40 to pass, that, when Jesus was r', "
9: 10 the apostles, when they were r', "
10: 17 And the seventy r' again with joy, "
17: 18 found that r' to give glory to God, "
19: 15 came to pass, that when he was r', *1880
23: 48 done, smote their breasts, and r'. 5290
56 And they r', and prepared spices "
24: 9 r' from the sepulchre, and told all "
33 the same hour, and r' to Jerusalem, "
52 and r' to Jerusalem with great joy: "
Ac 1: 12 Then r' they unto Jerusalem from "
5: 22 not in the prison, they r', and told, 390
8: 25 r' to Jerusalem, and preached the 5290
12: 25 and Saul r' from Jerusalem, when "
13: 13 John departing from them r' to "
14: 21 they r' again to Lystra, and to "
21: 6 took ship; and they r' home again. "
23: 32 to go with him, and r' to the castle: "
Ga 1: 17 and r' again unto Damascus. "
Heb 11: 15 have had opportunity to have r'. * 344
1Pe 2: 25 but are now r' unto the Shepherd 1994

returneth
Ps 146: 4 goeth forth, he r' to his earth; 7725
Pr 26: 11 As a dog r' to his vomit, "
11 so a fool r' to his folly. *8138
Ec 1: 6 the wind r' again according to his 7725
Isa 55: 10 from heaven, and r' not thither, "
Eze 35: 7 that passeth out and him that r'. "
Zec 9: 8 by, and because of him that r': * "

returning
Isa 30: 15 In r' and rest shall ye be saved; 7729
Lu 7: 10 r' to the house, found the servant 5290
Ac 8: 28 Was r', and sitting in his chariot "
Heb 7: 1 r' from the slaughter of the kings, "

Reu (*re'-u*) See also RAGAU.
Ge 11: 18 lived thirty years, and begat R': 7466
19 Peleg lived after he begat R' two "
20 And R' lived two and thirty years, "
21 R' lived after he begat Serug two "
1Ch 1: 25 Eber, Peleg, R',

Reuben (*ru'-ben*) See also REUBENITE.
Ge 29: 32 a son, and she called his name R': 7205
30: 14 And R' went in the days of wheat "
35: 22 that R' went and lay with Bilhah "
23 sons of Leah; R', Jacob's firstborn, "
37: 21 R' heard it, and he delivered him "
22 R' said unto them, Shed no blood, "
29 And R' returned unto the pit; and, "
42: 22 R' answered them, saying, Spake I "
37 R' spake unto his father, saying, "
46: 8 Jacob and his sons: R', Jacob's "
9 the sons of R'; Hanoch, and Phallu, "
48: 5 as R' and Simeon, they shall be "
49: 3 R', thou art my firstborn, my "
Ex 1: 2 R', Simeon, Levi, and Judah, "
6: 14 sons of R' the firstborn of Israel: "
14 Carmi: these be the families of R'. "
Nu 1: 5 the tribe of R'; Elizur the son of "
20 the children of R', Israel's eldest "
21 tribe of R', were forty and six "
2: 10 be the standard of the camp of R' "
10 captain of the children of R' shall "
16 were numbered in the camp of R' "
7: 30 prince of the children of R', did "
10: 18 the standard of the camp of R' set "
13: 4 tribe of R', Shammua the son of "
16: 1 son of Peleth, sons of R', took men: "
26: 5 R', the eldest son of Israel: "
5 children of R'; Hanoch, of whom "
32: 1 Now the children of R' and the "
Nu 32: 2 the children of R' came and spake 7205
6 to the children of R', Shall your "
25 children of R' spake unto Moses, "
29 children of R' will pass with your "
31 the children of R' answered, saying, "
33 of Gad and to the children of R', "
37 the children of R' built Heshbon, "
34: 14 For the tribe of the children of R' 7206
De 11: 6 the sons of Eliab, the son of R': 7205
27: 13 R', Gad, and Asher, and Zebulun, "
33: 6 Let R' live, and not die; and let not "
Jos 4: 12 And the children of R', and the "
13: 15 unto the tribe of the children of R' "
23 border of the children of R' was "
23 the inheritance of the children of R' "
15: 6 to the stone of Bohan the son of R': "
18: 7 and Gad, and R', and half the tribe "
17 to the stone of Bohan the son of R', "
20: 8 upon the plain out of the tribe of R', "
21: 7 families had out of the tribe of R', "
36 out of the tribe of R', Bezer with "
22: 9 children of R' and the children "
10, 11 children of R' and the children "
13 Israel sent unto the children of R', "
15 they came unto the children of R', "
21 Then the children of R' and the "
25 ye children of R' and children of "
30 the words that the children of R' "
31 priest said unto the children of R', "
32 returned from the children of R', "
33 the children of R' and Gad dwelt. "
34 the children of R' and the children "
J'g 5: 15, 16 divisions of R' there were great "
1Ch 2: 1 are the sons of Israel; R', Simeon, "
5: 1 the sons of R' the firstborn of Israel, "
3 I say, of R' the firstborn of Israel "
18 The sons of R', and the Gadites, "
6: 63 their families, out of the tribe of R', "
78 given them out of the tribe of R', "
Eze 48: 6 unto the west side, a portion for R'. "
7 And by the border of R', from the "
31 one gate of R', one gate of Judah, "
Re 7: 5 of R' were sealed twelve thousand. 4502

Reubenite (*ru'-ben-ite*) See also REUBENITES.
1Ch 11: 42 Adina the son of Shiza the R', a 7206

Reubenites (*ru'-ben-ites*)
Nu 26: 7 These are the families of the R': 7206
De 3: 12 cities thereof, gave I unto the R' "
16 unto the R' and unto the Gadites "
4: 43 in the plain country, of the R'; and "
29: 8 it for an inheritance unto the R', "
Jos 1: 12 And to the R', and to the Gadites, "
12: 6 it for a possession unto the R', and "
13: 8 With whom the R' and the Gadites "
22: 1 Then Joshua called the R', and the "
2Ki 10: 33 the Gadites, and the R', and the "
1Ch 5: 6 captive: he was prince of the R'. "
26 he carried them away, even the R', "
11: 42 a captain of the R', and thirty with "
12: 37 the other side of Jordan, of the R', "
26: 32 king David made rulers over the R', "
27: 16 the ruler of the R' was Eliezer the "

Reuel (*re-u'-el*) See also DEUEL; JETHRO; RAGUEL.
Ge 36: 4 Eliphaz; and Bashemath bare R'; 7467
10 R' the son of Bashemath the wife of "
13 these are the sons of R'; Nahath, "
17 these are the sons of R' Esau's son; "
17 these are the dukes that came of R' "
Ex 2: 18 when they came to R' their father, "
Nu 2: 14 shall be Eliasaph the son of R'. "
1Ch 1: 35 The sons of Esau; Eliphaz, R', and "
37 The sons of R'; Nahath, Zerah, "
9: 8 the son of R', the son of Ibnijah:

Reumah (*re-u'-mah*)
Ge 22: 24 his concubine, whose name was R', 7208

reveal See also REVEALED; REVEALETH.
Job 20: 27 The heaven shall r' his iniquity; 1540
Jer 33: 6 will r' unto them the abundance of "
Da 2: 47 seeing thou couldest r' this secret. 1541
M't 11: 27 to whomsoever the Son will r' him. 601
Lu 10: 22 and he to whom the Son will r' him. "
Ga 1: 16 To r' his Son in me, that I might "
Ph'p 3: 15 God shall r' even this unto you. "

revealed
De 29: 29 those things which are r' belong 1540
1Sa 3: 7 word of the Lord yet r' unto him. "
21 for the Lord r' himself to Samuel "
2Sa 7: 27 hast r' to thy servant, saying, I will "
Isa 22: 14 it was r' in mine ears by the Lord "
23: 1 the land of Chittim it is r' to them. "
40: 5 the glory of the Lord shall be r', "
53: 1 to whom is the arm of the Lord r'? "
56: 1 and my righteousness to be r'. "
Jer 11: 20 for unto thee have I r' my cause. "
Da 2: 19 was the secret r' unto Daniel in a 1541
30 is not r' to me for any wisdom "
10: 1 Persia a thing was r' unto Daniel, 1540
M't 10: 26 covered, that shall not be r'; and * 601
11: 25 and hast r' them unto babes. "
16: 17 and blood hath not r' it unto thee, "
Lu 2: 26 r' unto him by the Holy Ghost, 5537
35 thoughts of many hearts may be r'. 601
10: 21 and hast r' them unto babes: * "
12: 2 nothing covered, that shall not be r'; "
17: 30 the day when the Son of man is r'. "
Joh 12: 38 hath the arm of the Lord been r'? "
Ro 1: 17 righteousness of God r' from faith "
18 the wrath of God is r' from heaven "
8: 18 the glory which shall be r' in us. "
1Co 2: 10 hath r' them unto us by his Spirit: "
3: 13 it, because it shall be r' by fire; "
14: 30 If any thing be r' to another that * "
Ga 3: 23 faith which should afterwards be r'. "

Eph 3: 5 as it is now r· unto his holy apostles601
2Th 1: 7 when the Lord Jesus shall be r· from602
2: 3 and that man of sin be r·, the son 601
6 that he might be r· in his time. "
8 then shall that Wicked be r·, whom "
1Pe 1: 5 ready to be r· in the last time. "
12 Unto whom it was r·, that not unto "
4: 13 when his glory shall be r·, ye may* 602
5: 1 of the glory that shall be r·: 601

revealer
Da 2: 47 and a r· of secrets, seeing thou 1541

revealeth
Pr 11: 13 A talebearer r· secrets: but he 1540
20: 19 about as a talebearer r· secrets: "
Da 2: 22 He r· the deep and secret things: 1541
28 is a God in heaven that r· secrets, "
29 he that r· secrets maketh known to "
Am 3: 7 he r· his secret unto his servants 1540

revelation See also REVELATIONS.
Ro 2: 5 and r· of the righteous judgment of 602
16: 25 according to the r· of the mystery, "
1Co 14: 6 I shall speak to you either by r·, or "
26 doctrine, hath a tongue, hath a r·, "
Ga 1: 12 it, but by the r· of Jesus Christ. "
2: 2 And I went up by r·, and "
Eph 1: 17 unto you the spirit of wisdom and r· "
3: 3 How that by r· he made known unto "
1Pe 1: 13 unto you at the r· of Jesus Christ; "
Re 1: 1 The R· of Jesus Christ, which God "

revelations
2Co 12: 1 come to visions and r· of the Lord. 602
7 through the abundance of the r·, "

revellings
Ga 5: 21 drunkenness, r·, and such like: 2970
1Pe 4: 3 r·, banquetings, and abominable "

revenge See also REVENGED; REVENGES; REVENGETH; REVENGING.
Jer 15: 15 me, and r· me of my persecutors;*5358
20: 10 and we shall take our r· on him. 5360
Eze 25: 15 the Philistines hath dealt by r·, "
2Co 7: 11 desire, yea, what zeal, yea, what r· !*1557
10: 6 readiness to r· all disobedience, *1556

revenged
Eze 25: 12 and r· himself upon them; 5358

revenger See also REVENGERS.
Nu 35: 19 The r· of blood himself shall slay *1350
21 r· of blood shall slay the murderer.*"
24 between the slayer and...r· of blood*"
25 out of the hand of the r· of blood, * "
27 the r· of blood find him without * "
27 and the r· of blood kill the slayer;* "
Ro 13: 4 a r· to execute wrath upon him *1558

revengers
2Sa 14: 11 suffer the r· of blood to destroy *1350

revenges
De 32: 42 beginning of r· upon the enemy. *6546

revengeth
Na 1: 2 God is jealous, and the Lord r·; *5358
2 the Lord r·, and is furious; the * "

revenging
Ps 79: 10 r· of the blood of thy servants *5360

revenue See also REVENUES.
Ezr 4: 13 shalt endamage the r· of the kings.*674
Pr 8: 19 gold; and my r· than choice silver.8393
Isa 23: 3 the harvest of the river is her r·; "

revenues
Pr 15: 6 in the r· of the wicked is trouble. 8393
16: 8 than great r· without right. "
Jer 12: 13 shall be ashamed of your r· because*"

reverence See also REVERENCED.
Le 19: 30 sabbaths, and r· my sanctuary: 3372
26: 2 my sabbaths, and r· my sanctuary: "
2Sa 9: 6 he fell on his face, and did r·. *7812
1Ki 1: 31 and did r· to the king, and said, "
Es 3: 2 Mordecai bowed not, nor did him r·."
5 Mordecai bowed not, nor did him r·,"
Ps 89: 7 to be had in r· of all them that *3372
M't 21: 37 son, saying, They will r· my son. 1788
M'r 12: 6 them, saying, They will r· my son. "
Lu 20: 13 they will r· him when they see him."
Eph 5: 33 wife see that she r· her husband. *5399
Heb 12: 9 us, and we gave them r·: 1788
28 acceptably with r· and godly fear: 127

reverenced
Es 3: 2 king's gate, bowed, and r· Haman:*7812

reverend
Ps 111: 9 ever: holy and r· is his name. 3372

reverse
Nu 23: 20 hath blessed; and I cannot r· it. 7725
Es 8: 5 to r· the letters devised by Haman "
8 the king's ring, may no man r·. "

revile See also REVILED; REVILEST; REVILINGS.
Ex 22: 28 Thou shalt not r· the gods, nor 7043
M't 5: 11 are ye, when men shall r· you, *3679

reviled
M't 27: 39 And they that passed by r· him, * 987
M'r 15: 32 were crucified with him r· him. *3679
Joh 9: 28 Then they r· him, and said, Thou 3058
1Co 4: 12 being r·, we bless; being "
1Pe 2: 23 Who, when he was r·,...not again; "
23 Who when he was...,r· not again; 486

revilers
1Co 6: 10 nor r·, nor extortioners, shall 3060

revilest
Ac 23: 4 said, R· thou God's high priest? 3058

revilings
Isa 51: 7 neither be ye afraid of their r·. 1421
Zep 2: 8 the r· of the children of Ammon, "

revive See also REVIVED; REVIVING.
Ne 4: 2 r· the stones out of the heaps of 2421
Ps 85: 6 Wilt thou not r· us again: that thy*"
138: 7 midst of trouble, thou wilt r· me: "
Isa 57: 15 to r· the spirit of the humble, and "
15 r· the heart of the contrite ones. "
Ho 6: 2 after two days will he r· us: in the "
14: 7 They shall r· as the corn, and grow "
Hab 3: 2 r· thy work in the midst of the "

revived
Ge 45: 27 the spirit of Jacob their father r·: 2421
J'g 15: 19 his spirit came again, and he r·. "
1Ki 17: 22 came into him again, and he r·. "
2Ki 13: 21 touched the bones of Elisha, he r·. "
Ro 7: 9 the commandment came, sin r·, 326
14: 9 Christ both died, and rose, and r·, * "

reviving
Ezr 9: 8 give us a little r· in our bondage. 4241
9 to give us a r·, to set up the house "

revolt See also REVOLTED; REVOLTING.
2Ch 21: 10 did Libnah r· from under his hand;6586
Isa 1: 5 more? ye will r· more and more: 5627
59: 13 God, speaking oppression and r·, "

revolted
2Ki 8: 20 Edom r· from under the hand of 6586
22 Yet Edom r· from under the hand "
22 Then Libnah r· at the same time.* "
2Ch 21: 8 In his days the Edomites r· from "
10 So the Edomites r· from under the "
Isa 31: 6 children of Israel have deeply r·. 5627
Jer 5: 23 heart; they are r· and gone. 5493

revolters
Jer 6: 28 They are all grievous r·, walking 5637
Ho 5: 2 the r· are profound to make a 7846
9: 15 no more: all their princes are r·. 5637

revolting
Jer 5: 23 hath a r· and a rebellious heart: 5637

reward See also REWARDED; REWARDETH; REWARDS.
Ge 15: 1 shield, and thy exceeding great r·.7939
Nu 18: 31 r· for your service in the tabernacle"
De 10: 17 not persons, nor taketh r·: 7810
27: 25 r· to slay an innocent person: "
32: 41 and will r· them that hate me. *7999
Ru 2: 12 a full r· be given thee of the Lord 4909
1Sa 24: 19 Lord r· thee good for that thou 7999
2Sa 3: 39 the Lord shall r· the doer of evil "
4: 10 have given him a r· for his tidings:1309
19: 36 recompense it me with such a r·? 1578
1Ki 13: 7 thyself, and I will give thee a r·. 4991
2Ch 20: 11 Behold, I say, how they r· us, to 1580
Job 6: 22 a r· for me of your substance? *7809
7: 2 hireling looketh for the r· of his work:*
Ps 15: 5 taketh r· against the innocent. 7810
19: 11 keeping of them there is great r·. 6118
40: 15 them be desolate for a r· of their * "
54: 5 shall r· evil unto mine enemies: *7725
58: 11 there is a r· for the righteous: 6529
70: 3 for a r· of their shame that say, *6118
91: 8 and see the r· of the wicked. 8011
94: 2 earth: render a r· to the proud. *1576
109: 20 this be the r· of mine adversaries 6468
127: 3 the fruit of the womb is his r·. 7939
Pr 11: 18 righteousness shall be a sure r·. 7938
21: 14 a r· in the bosom strong wrath. *7810
24: 14 then there shall be a r·, and thy 319
20 shall be no r· to the evil man; "
25: 22 head, and the Lord shall r· thee. 7999
Ec 4: 9 have a good r· for their labour. 7939
9: 5 neither have they any more a r·; "
Isa 3: 11 r· of his hands shall be given him.1576
5: 23 Which justify the wicked for r·, 7810
40: 10 behold, his r· is with him, and his 7939
45: 13 not for price nor r·, saith the Lord7810
62: 11 his r· is with him, and his work 7939
Jer 40: 5 guard gave him victuals and a r·,*4864
Eze 16: 34 and in that thou givest a r·, * 868
34 and no r· is given unto thee, * "
Ho 4: 9 ways, and r· them their doings. 7725
9: 1 loved a r· upon every cornfloor. * 868
Ob 15 thy r· shall return upon thine own*1576
Mic 3: 11 heads thereof judge for r·, and 7810
7: 3 and the judge asketh for a r·; 7966
M't 5: 12 for great is your r· in heaven: for 3408
46 which love you, what r· have ye? "
6: 1 ye have no r· of your Father which "
2 I say unto you, They have their r·. "
4 secret himself shall r· thee openly.*591
5 say unto you, They have their r·. 3408
6 seeth in secret shall r· thee openly.* 591
16 I say unto you, They have their r·.3408
18 seeth in secret, shall r· thee openly.*591
10: 41 shall receive a prophet's r·; and 3408
41 shall receive a righteous man's r·. "
42 you, he shall in no wise lose his r·. "
16: 27 he shall r· every man according * 591
M'r 9: 41 unto you, he shall not lose his r·. 3408
Lu 6: 23 behold, your r· is great in heaven: "
35 your r· shall be great, and ye shall "
23: 41 we receive the due r· of our deeds: 514
Ac 1: 18 a field with the r· of iniquity; 3408
Ro 4: 4 worketh is the r· not reckoned of "
1Co 3: 8 every man shall receive his own r· "
14 thereupon, he shall receive a r·. "
9: 17 do this thing willingly, I have a r·: "
18 What is my r· then? Verily that, "
Col 2: 18 Let no man beguile you of your r·*2603
3: 24 receive the r· of the inheritance: * 469
1Ti 5: 18 The labourer is worthy of his r·. *3408
2Ti 4: 14 the Lord r· him according to his * 591
Heb 2: 2 received a just recompence of r·; 3405
10: 35 hath a great recompence of r·. "
11: 26 unto the recompence of the r·. "
2Pe 2: 13 receive the r· of unrighteousness,*3408
2Jo 8 but that we receive a full r·. "
Jude 11 after the error of Balaam for r·, * "
Re 11: 18 shouldest give r· unto thy servants "
18: 6 R· her even as she rewarded you,* 591
22: 12 my r· is with me, to give every 3408

rewarded
Ge 44: 4 Wherefore have ye r· evil for good?7999
1Sa 24: 17 thou hast r· me good, whereas *1580
17 whereas I have r· thee evil. * "
2Sa 22: 21 The Lord r· me according to my "
2Ch 15: 7 weak: for your work shall be r·. 7939
Ps 7: 4 I have r· evil unto him that was 1580
18: 20 The Lord r· me according to my "
35: 12 They r· me evil for good to the *7999
103: 10 r· us according to our iniquities. 1580
109: 5 And they have r· me evil for good,7760
Pr 13: 13 the commandment shall be r·. 7999
Isa 3: 9 they have r· evil unto themselves. 1580
Jer 31: 16 for thy work shall be r·, saith the 7939
Re 18: 6 Reward her even as she r· you, * 591

rewarder
Heb 11: 6 a r· of them that diligently seek 3406

rewardeth
Job 21: 19 he r· him, and he shall know it. *7999
Ps 31: 23 and plentifully r· the proud doer. "
137: 8 r· thee as thou hast served us. "
Pr 17: 13 Whoso r· evil for good, evil shall 7725
26: 10 formed all things both r· the fool,*7936
10 the fool, and r· transgressors. * "

rewards
Nu 22: 7 the r· of divination in their hand;
Isa 1: 23 gifts, and followeth after r·: 8021
Da 2: 6 ye shall receive of me gifts and r· 5023
5: 17 thyself, and give thy r· to another; "
Ho 2: 12 These are my r· that my lovers * 866

Rezeph *(re'-zef)*
2Ki 19: 12 as Gozan, and Haran, and R·, and7530
Isa 37: 12 as Gozan, and Haran, and R·, and "

Rezia *(re-zi'-ah)*
1Ch 7: 39 Ulla; Arah, and Haniel, and R·. *7525

Rezin *(re'-zin)*
2Ki 15: 37 against Judah, R·...king of Syria, 7526
16: 5 Then R· king of Syria and Pekah "
6 At that time R· king of Syria "
9 people...captive to Kir, and slew R·. "
Ezr 2: 48 The children of R·, the children of "
Ne 7: 50 of Reaiah, the children of R·, the "
Isa 7: 1 that R· the king of Syria and Pekah "
4 the fierce anger of R· with Syria, "
8 and the head of Damascus is R·; "
8: 6 rejoice in R· and Remaliah's son; "
9: 11 shall set up the adversaries of R· "

Rezon *(re'-zon)*
1Ki 11: 23 adversary, R· the son of Eliadah, 7331

Rhegium *(re'-je-um)*
Ac 28: 13 fetched a compass, and came to R·:4484

Rhesa *(re'-sah)* See also REPHAIAH.
Lu 3: 27 which was the son of R·, which 4488

Rhoda *(ro'-dah)*
Ac 12: 13 damsel came to hearken, named R·4498

Rhodes *(rodes)*
Ac 21: 1 and the day following unto R·, 4499

rib See also RIBBAND; RIBS.
Ge 2: 22 And the r·,...made he a woman, 6763
2Sa 2: 23 spear smote him under the fifth r·,*
3: 27 smote him there under the fifth r·,*
4: 6 they smote him under the fifth r·:*
20: 10 smote him therewith in the fifth r·,*

Ribai *(rib'-ahee)*
2Sa 23: 29 Ittai the son of R· out of Gibeah 7380
1Ch 11: 31 Ithai the son of R· of Gibeah, that "

ribband
Nu 15: 38 fringe of the borders a r· of blue: *6616

ribbon See RIBBAND.

Riblah *(rib'-lah)*
Nu 34: 11 go down from Shepham to R·, 7247
2Ki 23: 33 put him in bands at R· in the land "
25: 6 up to the king of Babylon to R·; "
20 them to the king of Babylon to R·: "
21 and slew them at R· in the land of "
Jer 39: 5 to R· in the land of Hamath, where "
6 slew the sons of Zedekiah in R· "
52: 9 to R· in the land of Hamath; "
10 slew...the princes of Judah in R·. "
26 them to the king of Babylon to R·. "
27 and put them to death in R· in the "

ribs
Ge 2: 21 took one of his r·, and closed up 6763
Da 7: 5 it had three r· in the mouth of it 5967

rich See also ENRICH; RICHER; RICHES.
Ge 13: 2 And Abram was very r· in cattle, 3513
14: 23 shouldest say, I...made Abram r·: 6238
Ex 30: 15 The r· shall not give more, and 6223
Le 25: 47 a sojourner or stranger wax r· 5381
Ru 3: 10 young men, whether poor or r·. 6223
1Sa 2: 7 Lord maketh poor, and maketh r·:6238
2Sa 12: 1 the one r·, and the other poor. 6223
2 r· man had exceeding many flocks "
4 came a traveller unto the r· man, "
Job 15: 29 He shall not be r·, neither shall 6238
27: 19 The r· man shall lie down, but he 6223
34: 19 nor regardeth the r· more than 7771
Ps 45: 12 r· among the people shall intreat 6223
49: 2 low and high, r· and poor, together."
16 thou afraid when one is made r·, 6238
Pr 10: 4 the hand of the diligent maketh r·, "
15 r· man's wealth is his strong city: 6223

Pr 10:22 blessing of the Lord, it maketh r', 6238
13: 7 There is that maketh himself r', "
14:20 but the r' hath many friends. 6223
18:11 r' man's wealth is his strong city, "
23 but the r' answereth roughly. "
21:17 loveth wine and oil shall not be r'. 6238
22: 2 The r' and poor meet together: 6223
7 The r' ruleth over the poor, and "
16 he that giveth to the r', shall surely "
23: 4 Labour not to be r': cease from 6238
28: 6 is perverse...though he be r'. 6223
11 r' man is wise in his own conceit; "
20 he that maketh haste to be r' shall 6238
22 hasteth to be r' hath an evil eye, *1952
Ec 5:12 abundance of the r' will not suffer 6223
10: 6 dignity, and the r' sit in low place. "
20 curse not the r' in thy bedchamber: "
Isa 53: 9 wicked, and with the r' in his death; "
Jer 5:27 are become great, and waxen r'. 6238
9:23 not the r' man glory in his riches: 6223
Eze 27:24 in chests of r' apparel, bound with
Ho 12: 8 Ephraim said, Yet I am become r', 6238
Mic 6:12 the r' men...are full of violence, 6223
Zec 11: 5 Blessed be the Lord; for I am r': 6238
M't 19:23 a r' man shall hardly enter into 4145
24 than for a r' man to enter into the "
27:57 there came a r' man of Arimathæa, "
M'r 10:25 than for a r' man to enter into the "
12:41 many that were r' cast in much. "
Lu 1:53 the r' he hath sent empty away. 4147
6:24 But woe unto you that are r'! 4145
12:16 The ground of a certain r' man "
21 himself, and is not r' toward God. 4147
14:12 kinsmen, nor thy r' neighbours; 4145
16: 1, 19 There was a certain r' man, "
21 which fell from the r' man's table: "
22 r' man also died, and was buried; "
18:23 very sorrowful: for he was very r'. "
25 than for a r' man to enter into the "
19: 2 among the publicans, and he was r'. "
21: 1 saw the r' men casting their gifts "
Ro 10:12 is r' unto all that call upon him. 4147
1Co 4: 8 Now ye are full, now ye are r', ye "
2Co 6:10 as poor, yet making many r'; 4148
8: 9 though he was r', yet for your 4145
9 through his poverty might be r'. 4147
Eph 2: 4 God, who is r' in mercy, for his 4145
1Ti 6: 9 that will be r' fall into temptation 4147
17 Charge them that are r' in this 4145
18 that they be r' in good works, 4147
Jas 1:10 But the r', in that he is made low: 4145
11 So also shall the r' man fade away "
2: 5 the poor of this world r' in faith, "
6 Do not r' men oppress you, and "
5: 1 Go to now, ye r' men, weep and "
Re 2: 9 and poverty, (but thou art r') "
3:17 Because thou sayest, I am r', and "
18 in the fire, that thou mayest be r'; 4147
6:15 the r' men, and the chief captains, 4145
13:16 great, r' and poor, free and bond, "
18: 3 merchants of the earth...waxed r' 4147
15 things, which were made r' by her, "
19 were made r' all that had ships "

richer
Da 11: 2 fourth shall be far r' than they all: 6238

riches
Ge 31:16 the r' which God hath taken from 6239
36: 7 their r' were more than that they *7399
Jos 22: 8 Return with much r' unto your *5233
1Sa 17:25 king will enrich him with great r', 6239
1Ki 3:11 neither hast asked r' for thyself, "
13 hast not asked, both r', and honour: "
10:23 exceeded...kings of the earth for r' "
1Ch 29:12 Both r' and honour come of thee, "
28 old age, full of days, r', and honour: "
2Ch 1:11 not asked r', wealth, or honour, "
12 I will give thee r', and wealth, and "
9:22 passed...the kings of the earth in r' "
17: 5 he had r' and honour in abundance. "
18: 1 Jehoshaphat had r' and honour in "
20:25 both r' with the dead bodies, and 7399
32:27 Hezekiah had exceeding much r' 6239
Es 1: 4 the r' of his glorious kingdom and "
5:11 told them of the glory of his r', and "
Job 20:15 He hath swallowed down r', and 2428
36:19 Will he esteem thy r'? no, not gold, 7769
Ps 37:16 better than the r' of many wicked. *1995
39: 6 he heapeth up r', and knoweth not who
49: 6 boast...in the multitude of their r'; 6239
52: 7 trusted in the abundance of his r', "
62:10 if r' increase, set not your heart 2428
73:12 in the world; they increase in r'. "
104:24 them all: the earth is full of thy r'. 7075
112: 3 and r' shall be in his house: 6239
119:14 testimonies, as much as in all r'. 1952
Pr 3:16 in her left hand r' and honour. 6239
8:18 R' and honour are with me; yea, "
18 yea, durable r' and righteousness. 1952
11: 4 R' profit not in the day of wrath: "
16 honour: and strong men retain r'. 6239
28 He that trusteth in his r' shall fall: "
13: 7 himself poor, yet hath great r'. *1952
8 ransom of a man's life are his r': 6239
14:24 The crown of the wise is their r'; "
19:14 House and r' are the inheritance 1952
22: 1 rather to be chosen than great r', 6239
4 and the fear of the Lord are r', and "
16 oppresseth the poor to increase his r', *
23: 5 r' certainly make themselves wings: "
24: 4 with all precious and pleasant r'. 1952
27:24 For r' are not for ever: and doth 2633
30: 8 give me neither poverty nor r'; 6239
Ec 4: 8 neither is his eye satisfied with r': "
5:13 r' kept for the owners thereof to "
14 But those r' perish by evil travail: "
Ec 5:19 whom God hath given r' and wealth, 6239
6: 2 A man to whom God hath given r', "
9:11 nor yet r' to men of understanding, "
Isa 8: 4 r' of Damascus and the spoil of 2428
10:14 found as a nest the r' of the people: "
30: 6 carry their r' upon the shoulders of "
45: 3 and hidden r' of secret places, 4301
61: 6 ye shall eat the r' of the Gentiles, *2428
Jer 9:23 not the rich man glory in his r': 6239
17:11 he that getteth r', and not by right, "
48:36 r'...he hath gotten are perished. *3502
Eze 26:12 they shall make a spoil of thy r', 2428
27:12 of the multitude of all kind of r'; 1952
18 making, for the multitude of all r'; "
27 r', and thy fairs, thy merchandise, "
33 earth with the multitude of thy r' "
28: 4 thou hast gotten thee r', and hast 2428
5 traffick hast thou increased thy r', "
5 heart is lifted up because of thy r': "
Da 11: 2 through his r' he shall stir up all 6239
13 a great army and with much r'. *7399
24 them the prey, and spoil, and r': * "
28 return into his land with great r'; * "
M't 13:22 world, and the deceitfulness of r', 4149
M'r 4:19 world, and the deceitfulness of r', "
10:23 they that have r' enter into the 5536
24 that trust in r' to enter into the "
Lu 8:14 are choked with cares and r' and 4149
16:11 will commit to your trust the true r'? "
18:24 they that have r' enter into the 5536
Ro 2: 4 Or despisest thou the r' of his 4149
9:23 make known the r' of his glory on "
11:12 fall of them be the r' of the world, "
12 diminishing of them the r' of the "
33 depth of the r' both of the wisdom "
2Co 8: 2 unto the r' of their liberality. "
Eph 1: 7 according to the r' of his grace; "
18 r' of the glory of his inheritance in "
2: 7 shew the exceeding r' of his grace "
3: 8 the unsearchable r' of Christ; "
16 according to the r' of his glory, to "
Ph'p 4:19 to his r' in glory by Christ Jesus. "
Col 1:27 the r' of the glory of this mystery "
2: 2 unto all r' of the full assurance of "
1Ti 6:17 nor trust in uncertain r', but in the "
Heb 11:26 reproach of Christ greater r' "
Jas 5: 2 Your r' are corrupted, and your "
Re 5:12 was slain to receive power, and r', "
18:17 hour so great r' is come to nought. "

richly
Col 3:16 the word of Christ dwell in you r' 4146
1Ti 6:17 who giveth us r' all things to enjoy; "

rid
Ge 37:22 he might r' him out of their hands, *5337
Ex 6: 6 I will r' you out of their bondage, "
Le 26: 6 will r' evil beasts out of the land, *7673
Ps 82: 4 needy: r' them out of the hand of *5337
144: 7 r' me, and deliver me out of great *6475
11 R' me, and deliver me from the * "

riddance
Le 23:22 not make clean r' of the corners *3615
Zep 1:18 for he shall make even a speedy r' *3617

ridden
Nu 22:30 ass, upon which thou hast r' ever 7392

riddle
J'g 14:12 I will now put forth a r' unto you: 2420
13 Put forth thy r', that we may hear "
14 not in three days expound the r'. "
15 that he may declare unto us the r', "
16 thou hast put forth a r' unto the "
17 she told the r' to the children of her "
18 heifer, ye had not found out my r'. "
19 unto them which expounded the r'. "
Eze 17: 2 Son of man, put forth a r', and "

ride See also RIDDEN; RIDETH; RIDING; RODE.
Ge 41:43 he made him to r' in the second 7392
De 32:13 He made him r' on the high places "
J'g 5:10 Speak, ye that r' on white asses, ye "
2Sa 16: 2 be for the king's household to r' on; "
19:26 me an ass, that I may r' thereon, "
1Ki 1:33 cause Solomon my son to r' upon "
38 Solomon to r' upon king David's "
44 caused him to r' upon the king's "
2Ki 10:16 So they made him r' in his chariot. "
Job 30:22 thou causest me to r' upon it, and "
Ps 45: 4 And in thy majesty r' prosperously "
66:12 caused men to r' over our heads; "
Isa 30:16 We will r' upon the swift; therefore "
58:14 and I will cause thee to r' upon the "
Jer 6:23 they r' upon horses, set in array "
50:42 they shall r' upon horses, every one "
Ho 10:11 I will make Ephraim to r'; Judah* "
14: 3 save us; we will not r' upon horses: "
Hab 3: 8 thou didst r' upon thine horses and "
Hag 2:22 chariots, and those that r' in them; "

rider See also RIDERS.
Ge 49:17 so that his r' shall fall backward. 7392
Ex 15: 1, 21 horse and his r' hath he thrown "
Job 39:18 she scorneth the horse and his r'. "
Jer 51:21 break in pieces the horse and his r'; "
21 in pieces the chariot and his r'; "
Zec 12: 4 and his r' with madness: and I "

riders
2Ki 18:23 on thy part to set r' upon them. 7392
Es 8:10 r' on mules, camels, and young * "
Isa 36: 8 on thy part to set r' upon them. "
Hag 2:22 and their r' shall come down, "
Zec 10: 5 r' on horses shall be confounded. "

rideth
Le 15: 9 what saddle soever he r' upon that 7392
De 33:26 who r' upon the heaven in thy help, "
Es 6: 8 and the horse that the king r' upon, "
Ps 68: 4 r' upon the heavens by his name "
Ps 68:33 r' upon the heavens of heavens, 7392
Isa 19: 1 the Lord r' upon a swift cloud, and "
Am 2:15 he that r' the horse deliver himself. "

ridges
Ps 65:10 Thou waterest the r' thereof *8525

riding
Nu 22:22 Now he was r' upon his ass, and 7392
2Ki 4:24 slack not thy r' for me, except I bid "
Jer 17:25 r' in chariots and on horses, they, "
22: 4 r' in chariots and on horses, he, and "
Eze 23: 6 men, horsemen r' upon horses. "
12 horsemen r' upon horses, all of them "
23 all of them r' upon horses. "
38:15 all of them r' upon horses, a great "
Zec 1: 8 behold a man r' upon a red horse, "
9: 9 lowly, and r' upon an ass, and "

rie
Ex 9:32 wheat and the r' were not smitten: *3698
Isa 28:25 barley and the r' in their place? * "

rifled
Zec 14: 2 shall be taken, and the houses r', 8155

right See also ARIGHT; UPRIGHT.
Ge 13: 9 left hand, then I will go to the r'; 3231
9 if thou depart to the r' hand, then 3225
18:25 the Judge of all the earth do r'? 4941
24:48 which had led me in the r' way to 571
49 that I may turn to the r' hand, or 3225
48:13 Ephraim in his r' hand toward "
13 left hand toward Israel's r' hand, "
14 Israel stretched out his r' hand, "
17 r' hand upon the head of Ephraim, "
18 put thy r' hand upon his head. "
Ex 14:22, 29 wall unto them on their r' hand, "
15: 6 Thy r' hand, O Lord, is become "
6 thy r' hand, O Lord, hath dashed "
12 Thou stretchedst out thy r' hand, "
26 do that which is r' in his sight, 3477
29:20 upon the tip of the r' ear of Aaron, "
20 the tip of the r' ear of his sons, 3233
20 upon the thumb of their r' hand, "
20 upon the great toe of their r' foot, "
22 is upon them, and the r' shoulder; "
Le 7:32 r' shoulder shall ye give unto the 3225
33 have the r' shoulder for his part. "
8:23 it upon the tip of Aaron's r' ear, 3233
23 upon the thumb of his r' hand, "
23 upon the great toe of his r' foot. "
24 blood upon the tip of their r' ear, "
24 upon the thumbs of their r' hands, "
24 upon the great toes of their r' feet: "
25 and their fat, and the r' shoulder: 3225
26 the fat, and upon the r' shoulder: "
9:21 the r' shoulder Aaron waved for "
14:14 put it upon the tip of the r' ear 3233
14 and upon the thumb of his r' hand, "
14 and upon the great toe of his r' foot: "
16 dip his r' finger in the oil that is in "
17 priest put upon the tip of the r' ear "
17 and upon the thumb of his r' hand, "
17 and upon the great toe of his r' foot, "
25 it upon the tip of the r' ear of him "
25 and upon the thumb of the r' hand, "
25 and upon the great toe of his r' foot: "
27 shall sprinkle with his r' finger "
28 upon the tip of the r' ear of him "
28 and upon the thumb of his r' hand, "
28 and upon the great toe of his r' foot, "
Nu 18:18 and as the r' shoulder are thine. 3225
20:17 will not turn to the r' hand nor to "
22:26 either to the r' hand or to the left. "
27: 7 daughters of Zelophehad speak r': 3651
De 2:27 neither turn unto the r' hand nor 3225
5:32 aside to the r' hand or to the left. "
6:18 do that which is r' and good in the 3477
12: 8 whatsoever is r' in his own eyes. "
25 do that which is r' in the sight of "
28 that which is good and r' in the "
13:18 to do that which is r' in the eyes of "
17:11 thee, to the r' hand, nor to the left. 3225
20 to the r' hand, or to the left: "
21: 9 which is r' in the sight of the Lord. 3477
17 the r' of the firstborn is his. 4941
28:14 day, to the r' hand, or to the left, 3225
32: 4 without iniquity, just and r' is he. 3477
33: 2 from his r' hand went a fiery law 3225
Jos 1: 7 turn not from it to the r' hand or to "
3:16 people passed over r' against Jericho.
9:25 seemeth good and r' unto thee to 3477
17: 7 border went along on the r' hand 3225
23: 6 not aside therefrom to the r' hand "
J'g 3:16 under his raiment upon his r' thigh. "
21 took the dagger from his r' thigh, "
5:26 r' hand to the workmen's hammer: "
7:20 trumpets in their r' hands to blow "
12: 6 could not frame to pronounce it r'. 3651
16:29 one with his r' hand, and of the 3225
17: 6 every man did that which was r' 3477
21:25 every man did that which was r' in "
Ru 4: 6 redeem thou my r' to thyself; for I 1353
1Sa 6:12 turned not aside to the r' hand or 3225
11: 2 I may thrust out all your r' eyes, "
12:23 teach you the good and the r' way: 3477
2Sa 2:19 he turned not to the r' hand nor 3225
21 Turn thee aside to thy r' hand or to "
14:19 none can turn to the r' hand or to 3231
15: 3 See, thy matters are good and r'; 5228
16: 6 mighty men were on his r' hand 3225
19:28 What r' therefore have I yet to cry 6666
43 we have also more r' in David than ye:
20: 9 beard with the r' hand to kiss him. 3225
24: 5 r' side of the city that lieth in the "
1Ki 2:19 mother; and she sat on his r' hand. "
6: 8 was in the r' side of the house: 3233
7:21 he set up the r' pillar, and called "

1Ki 7:39 bases on the r' side of the house, 3225
39 the sea on the r' side of the house 3233
49 five on the r' side, and five on the 3225
11:33 do that which is r' in mine eyes, 3477
38 and do that is r' in my sight, to "
14: 8 to do that only which is r' in mine "
15: 5 David did that which was r' in the "
11 Asa did that which was r' in the "
22:19 standing by him on his r' hand and 3225
43 that which was r' in the eyes of 3477
2Ki 10:15 Is thine heart r', as my heart is "
30 executing that which is r' in mine "
11:11 from the r' corner of the temple to 3233
12: 2 Jehoash did that which was r' in 3477
9 it beside the altar, on the r' side 3225
14: 3 did that which was r' in the sight 3477
15: 3, 34 that which was r' in the sight "
16: 2 did not that which was r' in the "
17: 9 things that were not r' against the 3651
18: 3 did that which was r' in the sight 3477
22: 2 And that which was r' in the sight "
2 turned not aside to the r' hand or 3225
23:13 were on the r' hand of the mount "
1Ch 6:39 Asaph, who stood on his r' hand, "
12: 2 could use both the r' hand and 3231
13: 4 the thing was r' in the eyes of all 3477
2Ch 3:17 one on the r' hand, and the other 3225
17 of that on the r' hand Jachin, 3227
4: 6 lavers, and put five on the r' hand, 3225
7 five on the r' hand, and five on the "
8 five on the r' side, and five on the "
10 set the sea on the r' side of the 3233
14: 2 did that which was good and r' in 3477
18:18 of heaven standing on his r' hand 3225
20:32 that which was r' in the sight of 3477
23:10 from the r' side of the temple to 3233
24: 2 Joash did that which was r' in the 3477
25: 2 did that which was r' in the sight of "
26: 4 did that which was r' in the sight of "
27: 2 did that which was r' in the sight of "
28: 1 he did not that which was r' in the "
29: 2 did that which was r' in the sight of "
31:20 that which was good and r' and "
34: 2 did that which was r' in the sight of "
2 declined neither to the r' hand, 3225
Ezr 8:21 God, to seek of him a r' way for us, *3477
Ne 2:20 but ye have no portion, nor r', nor 6666
8: 4 and Maaseiah, on his r' hand; 3225
9:13 and gavest them r' judgments, 3477
33 for thou hast done r', but we have* 571
12:31 one went on the r' hand upon the 3225
Es 8: 5 the thing seem r' before the king, 3787
Job 6:25 How forcible are r' words! but *3476
23: 9 he hideth himself on the r' hand, 3225
30:12 Upon my r' hand rise the youth; "
33:27 and perverted that which was r', 3477
34: 6 Should I lie against my r'? my 4941
17 Shall even he that hateth r' govern? "
23 will not lay upon man more than r'; *
35: 2 Thinkest thou this to be r', that 4941
36: 6 wicked: but giveth r' to the poor. "
40:14 thine own r' hand can save thee. 3225
42: 7 spoken of me the thing that is r', 3559
8 spoken of me the thing which is r', "
Ps 9: 4 maintained my r' and my cause; 4941
4 satest in the throne judging r'. *6664
16: 8 he is at my r' hand, I shall not 3225
11 at thy r' hand there are pleasures "
17: 1 Hear the r', O Lord, attend unto 6664
7 O thou that savest by thy r' hand 3225
18:35 and thy r' hand hath holden me up, "
19: 8 The statutes of the Lord are r', 3477
20: 6 the saving strength of his r' hand. 3225
21: 8 thy r' hand shall find out those that "
26:10 and their r' hand is full of bribes. "
33: 4 For the word of the Lord is r'; and 3477
44: 3 but thy r' hand, and thine arm, 3225
45: 4 thy r' hand shall teach thee terrible "
6 of thy kingdom is a r' sceptre. *4334
9 thy r' hand did stand the queen 3225
46: 5 shall help her, and that r' early. 6437
48:10 r' hand is full of righteousness. 3225
51:10 and renew a r' spirit within me. 3559
60: 5 save with thy r' hand, and hear 3225
63: 8 thee: thy r' hand upholdeth me. "
73:23 thou hast holden me by my r' hand. "
74:11 thou thy hand, even thy r' hand? "
77:10 of the r' hand of the most High. "
78:37 their heart was not r' with him, 3559
54 which his r' hand had purchased. 3225
80:15 which thy r' hand hath planted, "
17 be upon the man of thy r' hand, "
89:13 thy hand, and high is thy r' hand. "
25 sea, and his r' hand in the rivers. "
42 up the r' hand of his adversaries; "
91: 7 and ten thousand at thy r' hand; "
98: 1 his r' hand, and his holy arm, hath "
107: 7 he led them forth by the r' way, *3477
108: 6 save with thy r' hand, and answer 3225
109: 6 and let Satan stand at his r' hand. "
31 stand at the r' hand of the poor, "
110: 1 Sit thou at my r' hand, until I make "
5 The Lord at thy r' hand shall strike "
118:15 r' hand of the Lord doeth valiantly. "
16 The r' hand of the Lord is exalted: "
16 r' hand of the Lord doeth valiantly. "
119:75 Lord, that thy judgments are r', *6664
128 esteem all thy precepts...to be r'; 3474
121: 5 Lord is thy shade upon thy r' hand. 3225
137: 5 let my r' hand forget her cunning. "
138: 7 and thy r' hand shall save me. "
139:10 and thy r' hand shall hold me. "
140:12 the afflicted, and the r' of the poor. 4941
142: 4 I looked on my r' hand, and beheld, 3225
144: 8, 11 r' hand is a r' hand of falsehood. "
Pr 3:16 Length of days is in her r' hand; "
Pr 4:11 I have led thee in r' paths. *3476
25 Let thine eyes look r' on, and let 5227
27 Turn not to the r' hand nor to the 3225
8: 6 opening of my lips...be r' things. 4339
9 r' to them that find knowledge. 3477
9:15 passengers...go r' on their ways: 3474
12: 5 thoughts of the righteous are r': *4941
15 way of a fool is r' in his own eyes: 3477
14:12 There is a way which seemeth r' "
16: 8 than great revenues without r'. *4941
13 they love him that speaketh r'. 3477
25 There is a way that seemeth r' "
20:11 work be pure, and whether it be r'. "
21: 2 Every way of a man is r' in his own "
8 but as for the pure, his work is r'. "
23:16 when thy lips speak r' things. 4339
24:26 his lips that giveth a r' answer. 5228
27:16 and the ointment of his r' hand, 3225
Ec 4: 4 all travail, and every r' work, *3788
10: 2 wise man's heart is at his r' hand; 3225
Ca 2: 6 and his r' hand doth embrace me. "
8: 3 and his r' hand should embrace me. "
Isa 9:20 And he shall snatch on the r' hand, "
10: 2 to take away the r' from the poor 4941
30:10 Prophesy not unto us r' things, 5229
21 when ye turn to the r' hand, and 541
32: 7 even when the needy speaketh r'. 4941
41:10 the r' hand of my righteousness. 3225
13 Lord thy God will hold thy r' hand, "
44:20 Is there not a lie in my r' hand? "
45: 1 Cyrus, whose r' hand I have holden, "
19 I declare things that are r'. 4339
48:13 r' hand...spanned the heavens: 3225
54: 3 shalt break forth on the r' hand "
62: 8 Lord hath sworn by his r' hand, "
63:12 led them by the r' hand of Moses "
Jer 2:21 thee a noble vine, wholly a r' seed: 571
5:28 r' of the needy do they not judge. 4941
17:11 he that getteth riches, and not by r', "
16 which came out of my lips was r' *5227
22:24 were the signet upon my r' hand, 3225
23:10 is evil, and their force is not r'. "
32: 7 r' of redemption is thine to buy it. 4941
8 for the r' of inheritance is thine, "
34:15 and had done r' in my sight, in 3477
49: 5 be driven out every man r' forth; 6440
La 2: 3 he hath drawn back his r' hand 3225
4 with his r' hand as an adversary, "
3:35 To turn aside the r' of a man 4941
Eze 1:10 the face of a lion, on the r' side: 3225
4: 6 them, lie again on thy r' side, 3227
10: 3 the cherubims stood on the r' side 3225
16:46 sister, that dwelleth at thy r' hand, "
18: 5 and do that which is lawful and r', 6666
19 done that which is lawful and r', "
21 and do that which is lawful and r', "
27 doeth that which is lawful and r', "
21:16 way or other, either on the r' hand, 3231
22 At his r' hand was the divination 3225
27 until he come whose r' it is; 4941
33:14 and do that which is lawful and r'; 6666
16 done that which is lawful and r'; "
19 and do that which is lawful and r', "
39: 3 arrows to fall out of thy r' hand. 3225
47: 1 from the r' side of the house, 3233
2 there ran out waters on the r' side. "
Da 12: 7 held up his r' hand and his left 3225
Ho 14: 9 for the ways of the Lord are r', 3477
Am 3:10 they know not to do r', saith the 5229
5:12 the poor in the gate from their r'. "
Jon 4:11 discern between their r' hand and 3225
Hab 2:16 cup of the Lord's r' hand shall be "
Zec 3: 1 and Satan standing at his r' hand "
4: 3 one upon the r' side of the bowl, "
11 upon the r' side of the candlestick "
11:17 upon his arm and upon his r' eye: "
17 his r' eye shall be utterly darkened. "
12: 6 on the r' hand and on the left: "
Mal 3: 5 turn aside the stranger from his r', "
M't 5:29 if thy r' eye offend thee, pluck it 1188
30 if thy r' hand offend thee, cut it off, "
39 shall smite thee on thy r' cheek, "
6: 3 hand know what thy r' hand doeth. "
20: 4 whatsoever is r' I will give you. 1342
7 and whatsoever is r', that shall ye* "
21 may sit, the one on thy r' hand, 1188
23 but to sit on my r' hand, and on my "
22:44 Sit thou on my r' hand, till I make "
25:33 shall set the sheep on his r' hand, "
34 King say unto them on his r' hand, "
26:64 man sitting on the r' hand of power, "
27:29 his head, and a reed in his r' hand: "
38 one on the r' hand, and another on "
M'r 5:15 and clothed, and in his r' mind: 4993
10:37 we may sit, one on thy r' hand, 1188
40 But to sit on my r' hand and on my "
12:36 Sit thou on my r' hand, till I make "
14:62 man sitting on the r' hand of power, "
15:27 one on his r' hand, and the other "
16: 5 a young man sitting on the r' side, "
19 and sat on the r' hand of God. "
Lu 1:11 standing on the r' side of the altar "
6: 6 a man whose r' hand was withered. "
8:35 Jesus, clothed, and in his r' mind: 4993
10:28 unto him, Thou hast answered r': 3723
12:57 yourselves judge ye not what is r'? 1342
20:42 my Lord, Sit thou on my r' hand, 1188
22:50 high priest, and cut off his r' ear. "
69 on the r' hand of the power of God. "
23:33 one on the r' hand, and the other "
Joh 18:10 servant, and cut off his r' ear. "
21: 6 the net on the r' side of the ship, "
Ac 2:25 my face, for he is on my r' hand, "
33 being by the r' hand of God exalted, "
34 my Lord, Sit thou on my r' hand, "
3: 7 And he took him by the r' hand, "
Ac 4:19 Whether it be r' in the sight of 1342
5:31 hath God exalted with his r' hand 1188
7:55 standing on the r' hand of God, "
56 standing on the r' hand of God. "
8:21 thy heart is not r' in the sight of 2117
13:10 to pervert the r' ways of the Lord? "
Ro 8:34 who is even at the r' hand of God, 1188
2Co 6: 7 righteousness on the r' hand and on "
Ga 2: 9 gave...the r' hands of fellowship; "
Eph 1:20 and set him at his own r' hand in "
6: 1 parents in the Lord: for this is r'. 1342
Col 3: 1 sitteth on the r' hand of God. 1188
Heb 1: 3 the r' hand of the Majesty on high; "
13 he at any time, Sit on my r' hand, "
8: 1 is set on the r' hand of the throne of "
10:12 sat down on the r' hand of God; "
12: 2 at the r' hand of the throne of God. "
13:10 whereof they have no r' to eat 1849
1Pe 3:22 and is on the r' hand of God; 1188
2Pe 2:15 Which have forsaken the r' way, 2117
Re 1:16 he had in his r' hand seven stars: 1188
17 And he laid his r' hand upon me, "
20 which thou sawest in my r' hand, "
2: 1 the seven stars in his r' hand, "
5: 1 I saw in the r' hand of him that sat "
7 took the book out of the r' hand of "
10: 2 and he set his r' foot upon the sea, "
13:16 to receive a mark in their r' hand, "
22:14 they may have r' to the tree of life, 1849

righteous See also UNRIGHTEOUS.
Ge 7: 1 thee have I seen r' before me in 6662
18:23 Wilt thou also destroy the r' with "
24 Peradventure there be fifty r' "
24 place for the fifty r' that are therein? "
25 to slay the r' with the wicked: and "
25 that the r' should be as the wicked, "
26 If I find in Sodom fifty r' within the "
28 there shall lack five of the fifty r': "
20: 4 Lord, wilt thou slay also a r' nation? "
38:26 She hath been more r' than I; 6663
Ex 9:27 Lord is r', and I and my people 6662
23: 7 the innocent and r' slay thou not: "
8 and perverteth the words of the r'. "
Nu 23:10 Let me die the death of the r', and 3477
De 4: 8 judgments so r' as all this law, 6662
16:19 wise, and pervert the words of the r'. "
25: 1 then they shall justify the r', and "
J'g 5:11 rehearse the r' acts of the Lord, 6666
11 the r' acts toward the inhabitants "
1Sa 12: 7 all the r' acts of the Lord, which he "
24:17 to David, Thou art more r' than I: 6662
2Sa 4:11 wicked men have slain a r' person "
1Ki 2:32 who fell upon two men more r' and "
8:32 and justifying the r', to give him "
2Ki 10: 9 and said to all the people, Ye be r': "
2Ch 6:23 and by justifying the r', by giving "
12: 6 and they said, The Lord is r'. "
Ezr 9:15 O Lord God of Israel, thou art r': "
Ne 9: 8 performed thy words; for thou art r': "
Job 4: 7 or where were the r' cut off? * "
9:15 though I were r', yet would I not 6663
10:15 if I be r', yet will I not lift up my "
15:14 of a woman, that he should be r'? "
17: 9 The r' also shall hold on his way, 6662
22: 3 to the Almighty, that thou art r'? 6663
19 The r' see it, and are glad: and 6662
23: 7 the r' might dispute with him; *3477
32: 1 because he was r' in his own eyes. 6662
34: 5 For Job hath said, I am r': and 6663
35: 7 If thou be r', what givest thou him? "
36: 7 withdraweth not...eyes from the r': 6662
40: 8 me, that thou mayest be r'? *6663
Ps 1: 5 in the congregation of the r'. 6662
6 the Lord knoweth the way of the r': "
5:12 For thou, Lord, wilt bless the r'; "
7: 9 for the r' God trieth the hearts and "
11 God judgeth the r', and God is "
11: 3 be destroyed, what can the r' do? "
5 The Lord trieth the r': but the "
7 the r' Lord loveth righteousness; "
14: 5 God is in the generation of the r'. "
19: 9 Lord are true and r' altogether. 6663
31:18 and contemptuously against the r'. 6662
32:11 glad in the Lord, and rejoice, ye r': "
33: 1 Rejoice in the Lord, O ye r': for "
34:15 eyes of the Lord are upon the r', "
17 The r' cry, and the Lord heareth, "
19 Many are the afflictions of the r': 6662
21 that hate the r' shall be desolate. "
35:27 be glad, that favour my r' cause: 6664
37:16 little that a r' man hath is better 6662
17 but the Lord upholdeth the r'. "
21 the r' sheweth mercy, and giveth. "
25 yet have I not seen the r' forsaken, "
29 The r' shall inherit the land, and "
30 mouth of the r' speaketh wisdom, "
32 The wicked watcheth the r', and "
39 But the salvation of the r' is of the "
52: 6 The r' also shall see, and fear, and "
55:22 never suffer the r' to be moved. "
58:10 The r' shall rejoice when he seeth "
11 Verily there is a reward for the r': "
64:10 The r' shall be glad in the Lord, "
68: 3 let the r' be glad; let them rejoice "
69:28 and not be written with the r'. "
72: 7 In his days shall the r' flourish; "
75:10 horns of the r' shall be exalted. "
92:12 The r' shall flourish like the palm "
94:21 together against the soul of the r', "
97:11 Light is sown for the r', and "
12 Rejoice in the Lord, ye r'; and give "
107:42 The r' shall see it, and rejoice: *3477
112: 4 and full of compassion, and r'. 6662
6 the r' shall be in everlasting "
116: 5 Gracious is the Lord, and r'; yea, "
118:15 is in the tabernacles of the r': "

Ps 118: 20 Lord, into which the r· shall enter. 6662
119: 7 have learned thy r· judgments. 6664
62 thee because of thy r· judgments. "
106 that I will keep thy r· judgments. "
137 R· art thou, O Lord, and upright 6662
138 that thou hast commanded are r· *6664
160 thy r· judgments endureth for ever. "
164 thee because of thy r· judgments. "
125: 3 not rest upon the lot of the r·; 6662
3 lest the r· put forth their hands "
129: 4 Lord is r·: he hath cut asunder "
140: 13 r· shall give thanks unto thy name: "
141: 5 Let the r· smite me; it shall be a "
142: 7 the r· shall compass me about; for "
145: 17 The Lord is r· in all his ways, and "
146: 8 bowed down: the Lord loveth the r·: "
Pr 2: 7 layeth up sound wisdom for the r·: *3477
20 men, and keep the paths of the r·. 6662
3: 32 Lord: but his secret is with the r·. *3477
10: 3 suffer the soul of the r· to famish: 6662
11 mouth of a r· man is a well of life: "
16 labour of the r· tendeth to life: "
21 The lips of the r· feed many: but "
24 the desire of the r· shall be granted. "
25 the r· is an everlasting foundation. "
28 hope of the r· shall be gladness: "
30 The r· shall never be removed: but "
32 The lips of the r· know what is "
11: 8 The r· is delivered out of trouble, "
10 When it goeth well with the r·, the "
21 seed of the r· shall be delivered. "
23 The desire of the r· is only good: "
28 the r· shall flourish as a branch. "
30 The fruit of the r· is a tree of life; "
31 the r· shall be recompensed in the "
12: 3 root of the r· shall not be moved. "
5 The thoughts of the r· are right: "
7 but the house of the r· shall stand. "
10 A r· man regardeth the life of his "
12 but the root of the r· yieldeth fruit. "
26 The r· is more excellent than his "
13: 5 A r· man hateth lying: but a "
9 The light of the r· rejoiceth: but "
21 but to the r· good shall be repayed. "
25 The r· eateth to the satisfying of "
14: 9 but among the r· there is favour. *3477
19 the wicked at the gates of the r·. 6662
32 but the r· hath hope in his death. "
15: 6 house of the r· is much treasure: "
19 the way of the r· is made plain. *3477
28 heart of the r· studieth to answer: 6662
29 but he heareth the prayer of the r· "
16: 13 R· lips are the delight of kings; 6664
18: 5 to overthrow the r· in judgment. 6662
10 the r· runneth into it, and is safe. "
21: 12 The r· man wisely considereth the "
18 wicked shall be a ransom for the r·. "
26 but the r· giveth and spareth not. "
23: 24 The father of the r· shall greatly "
24: 15 man, against the dwelling of the r·; "
24 saith unto the wicked, Thou art r·; "
25: 26 A r· man falling down before the "
28: 1 but the r· are bold as a lion. "
10 Whoso causeth the r· to go astray *3477
12 When r· men do rejoice, there is 6662
28 when they perish, the r· increase. "
29: 2 When the r· are in authority, the "
6 but the r· doth sing and rejoice. "
7 r· considereth the cause of the poor: "
16 but the r· shall see their fall. "
Ec 3: 17 God shall judge the r· and the "
7: 16 Be not r· over much; neither make "
8: 14 according to the work of the r·: "
9: 1 that the r·, and the wise, and their "
2 there is one event to the r·, and to "
Isa 3: 10 Say ye to the r·, that it shall be well "
5: 23 away the righteousness of the r· "
24: 16 we heard songs, even glory to the r·. "
26: 2 r· nation which keepeth the truth "
41: 2 Who raised up the r· man from the 6664
26 that we may say, He is r·? yea, 6662
53: 11 shall my r· servant justify many; "
57: 1 r· perisheth, and no man layeth "
1 the r· is taken away from the evil "
60: 21 Thy people also shall be all r·: they "
Jer 12: 1 R· art thou, O Lord, when I plead "
20: 12 O Lord of hosts, that triest the r·, "
23: 5 will raise unto David a r· Branch, "
La 1: 18 Lord is r·; for I have rebelled "
Eze 3: 20 When a r· man doth turn from his "
21 if thou warn the r· man, that the "
21 that the r· sin not, and he doth not "
13: 22 have made the heart of the r· sad, "
16: 52 they are more r· than thou: yea, 6663
18: 20 the righteousness of the r· shall be 6662
24 when the r· turneth away from his "
26 When a r· man turneth away from "
21: 3 off from thee the r· and the wicked. "
4 off from thee the r· and the wicked, "
23: 45 the r· men, they shall judge them "
33: 12 righteousness of the r· shall not "
12 neither shall the r· be able to live "
13 When I shall say to the r·, that he "
18 r· turneth from his righteousness, "
Da 9: 14 Lord our God is r· in all his works "
Am 2: 6 because they sold the r· for silver, "
Hab 1: 4 wicked doth compass about the r·; "
13 the man that is more r· than he? "
Mal 3: 18 between the r· and the wicked, "
M't 9: 13 for I am not come to call the r·, but 1342
10: 41 a r· man in the name of a r· man "
41 shall receive a r· man's reward. "
13: 17 r· men have desired to see those "
43 shall the r· shine forth as the sun "
23: 28 also outwardly appear r· unto men. "
29 and garnish the sepulchres of the r·. "
M't 23: 35 all the r· blood shed upon the earth, 1342
35 blood of r· Abel unto the blood of "
25: 37 Then shall the r· answer him, "
46 but the r· into life eternal. "
M'r 2: 17 I came not to call the r·, but sinners "
Lu 1: 6 And they were both r· before God, "
5: 32 I came not to call the r·, but sinners "
18: 9 in themselves that they were r·, "
23: 47 saying, Certainly this was a r· man. "
Joh 7: 24 appearance, but judge r· judgment. "
17: 25 O r· Father, the world hath not "
Ro 2: 5 and revelation of the r· judgment of 1341
3: 10 There is none r·, no, not one: 1342
5: 7 scarcely for a r· man will one die: "
19 of one shall many be made r·. "
2Th 1: 5 token of the r· judgment of God, "
6 Seeing it is a r· thing with God to "
1Ti 1: 9 the law is not made for a r· man, "
2Ti 4: 8 which the Lord, the r· judge, shall "
Heb 11: 4 he obtained witness that he was r·, "
Jas 5: 16 prayer of a r· man availeth much. "
1Pe 3: 12 the eyes of the Lord are over the r·, "
4: 18 if the r· scarcely be saved, where "
2Pe 2: 8 that r· man dwelleth among them, "
8 vexed his r· soul from day to day "
1Jo 2: 1 the Father, Jesus Christ the r·: "
29 If ye know that he is r·, ye know "
3: 7 righteousness is r·, even as he is r·. "
12 were evil, and his brother's r·. "
Re 16: 5 Thou art r·, O Lord, which art, and "
7 true and r· are thy judgments. "
19: 2 For true and r· are his judgments: "
22: 11 be filthy still: and he that is r·, "
11 let him be r· still: and he that is *1344

righteously See also UNRIGHTEOUSLY.
De 1: 16 judge r· between every man and 6664
Ps 67: 4 for thou shalt judge the people r·. *4334
96: 10 he shall judge the people r·. *4339
Pr 31: 9 Open thy mouth, judge r·, and 6664
Isa 33: 15 He that walketh r·, and speaketh 6666
Jer 11: 20 O Lord of hosts, that judgest r·, 6664
Tit 2: 12 we should live soberly, r·, and 1346
1Pe 2: 23 himself to him that judgeth r·: "

righteousness See also RIGHTEOUSNESS'; RIGHTEOUSNESSES; UNRIGHTEOUSNESS.
Ge 15: 6 and he counted it to him for r·. 6666
30: 33 shall my r· answer for me in time "
Le 19: 15 but in r· shalt thou judge thy 6664
De 6: 25 it shall be our r·, if we observe 6666
9: 4 For my r· the Lord hath brought "
5 Not for thy r·, or for the "
6 good land to possess it for thy r·; "
24: 13 it shall be r· unto thee before the "
33: 19 they shall offer sacrifices of r·: 6664
1Sa 26: 23 Lord render to every man his r· 6666
2Sa 22: 21 rewarded me according to my r·: "
25 recompensed me according to my r·; "
1Ki 3: 6 before thee in truth, and in r·, and "
8: 32 to give him according to his r·. "
2Ch 6: 23 by giving him according to his r·. "
Job 6: 29 yea, return again, my r· is in it. *6664
8: 6 the habitation of thy r· prosperous. "
27: 6 My r· I hold fast, and will not let it 6666
29: 14 I put on r·, and it clothed me: my 6664
33: 26 for he will render unto man his r·. 6666
35: 2 saidst, My r· is more than God's? 6664
8 thy r· may profit the son of man. 6666
36: 3 and will ascribe r· to my Maker. 6664
Ps 4: 1 me when I call, O God of my r·: "
5 Offer the sacrifices of r·, and put "
5: 8 Lead me, O Lord, in thy r· because 6666
7: 8 me, O Lord, according to my r·, 6664
17 praise the Lord according to his r·: "
9: 8 And he shall judge the world in r·, "
11: 7 For the righteous Lord loveth r·; 6666
15: 2 walketh uprightly, and worketh r·, 6664
17: 15 for me, I will behold thy face in r·: "
18: 20 rewarded me according to my r·: "
24 recompensed me according to my r·, "
22: 31 shall declare his r· unto a people 6666
23: 3 he leadeth me in the paths of r· 6664
24: 5 r· from the God of his salvation. 6666
31: 1 be ashamed: deliver me in thy r·. "
33: 5 He loveth r· and judgment: the "
35: 24 my God, according to thy r·; 6664
28 my tongue shall speak of thy r· "
36: 6 Thy r· is like the great mountains; 6666
10 and thy r· to the upright in heart. "
37: 6 bring forth thy r· as the light, 6664
40: 9 I have preached r· in the great "
10 not hid thy r· within my heart; 6666
45: 4 of truth and meekness and r·; 6664
7 lovest r·, and hatest wickedness: "
48: 10 earth: thy right hand is full of r·. "
50: 6 the heavens shall declare his r·: "
51: 14 tongue shall sing aloud of thy r·. 6666
19 pleased with the sacrifices of r·, 6664
52: 3 and lying rather than to speak r·. "
58: 1 Do ye...speak r·, O congregation? "
65: 5 things in r· wilt thou answer us, "
69: 27 and let them not come into thy r·. 6666
71: 2 Deliver me in thy r·, and cause me "
15 My mouth shall shew forth thy r· "
16 I will make mention of thy r·, even "
19 Thy r· also, O God, is very high, "
24 My tongue also shall talk of thy r· "
72: 1 and thy r· unto the king's son. "
2 He shall judge thy people with r·, 6664
3 people, and the little hills, by r·. 6666
85: 10 r· and peace have kissed each 6664
11 r· shall look down from heaven. "
13 R· shall go before him; and shall "
88: 12 thy r· in the land of forgetfulness? 6666
89: 16 and in thy r· shall they be exalted. "
Ps 94: 15 But judgment shall return unto r·: 6664
96: 13 he shall judge the world with r·, "
97: 2 r· and judgment are the habitation "
6 The heavens declare his r·, and "
98: 2 his r· hath he openly shewed in 6666
9 with r· shall he judge the world, 6664
99: 4 thou executest judgment and r· in 6666
103: 6 Lord executeth r· and judgment * "
17 and his r· unto children's children; "
106: 3 and he that doeth r· at all times. "
31 counted unto him for r· unto all "
111: 3 and his r· endureth for ever. "
112: 3 house: and his r· endureth for ever. "
9 the poor; his r· endureth for ever; "
118: 19 Open to me the gates of r·: but 6664
119: 40 precepts: quicken me in thy r·. 6666
123 and for the word of thy r·. *6664
142 Thy r· is an everlasting 6666
142 is an everlasting r·, and thy law 6664
144 r· of my testimonies is everlasting: * "
172 for all thy commandments are r·. "
132: 9 let thy priests be clothed with r·; "
143: 1 answer me, and in thy r·. 6666
145: 7 goodness, and shall sing of thy r·. "
Pr 2: 9 Then shalt thou understand r·, 6664
8: 8 the words of my mouth are in r·; "
18 me; yea, durable riches and r·. 6666
20 I lead in the way of r·, in the "
10: 2 but r· delivereth from death. "
11: 4 but r· delivereth from death. "
5 r· of the perfect shall direct his "
6 r· of the upright shall deliver them: "
18 to him that soweth r· shall be a "
19 As r· tendeth to life: so he that "
12: 17 speaketh truth sheweth forth r·: 6664
28 In the way of r· is life; and in the 6666
13: 6 R· keepeth him that is upright in "
14: 34 R· exalteth a nation: but sin is a "
15: 9 loveth him that followeth after r·. "
16: 8 Better is a little with r· than great "
12 for the throne is established by r·. "
31 if it be found in the way of r·. "
21: 21 that followeth after r· and mercy "
21 mercy findeth life, r·, and honour. "
25: 5 throne shall be established in r·. 6664
Ec 3: 16 the place of r·, that iniquity was "
7: 15 just man that perisheth in his r·, "
Isa 1: 21 r· lodged in it; but now murderers. "
26 The city of r·, the faithful city. "
27 judgment,...her converts with r·. 6666
5: 7 oppression; for r·, but behold a cry. "
16 is holy shall be sanctified in r·. "
23 take away the r· of the righteous "
10: 22 decreed shall overflow with r·. "
11: 4 with r· shall he judge the poor, 6664
5 r· shall be the girdle of his loins, "
16: 5 seeking judgment, and hasting r·. "
26: 9 inhabitants of the world...learn r·. "
10 wicked, yet will he not learn r·: "
28: 17 to the line, and r· to the plummet: 6666
32: 1 Behold, a king shall reign in r·, 6664
16 and r· remain in the fruitful field. 6666
17 And the work of r· shall be peace; "
17 and the effect of r· quietness and "
33: 5 filled Zion with judgment and r·. "
41: 10 thee with the right hand of my r·. 6664
42: 6 I the Lord have called thee in r·, "
45: 8 and let the skies pour down r·: "
8 and let r· spring up together; 6666
13 I have raised him up in r·, and I 6664
19 I the Lord speak r·, I declare "
23 word...gone out of my mouth in r·, 6666
24 in the Lord have I r· and strength: "
46: 12 stoutheated, that are far from r·: "
13 I bring near my r·; it shall not be "
48: 1 Israel, but not in truth, nor in r·. "
18 and thy r· as the waves of the sea: "
51: 1 ye that follow after r·, ye that 6664
5 My r· is near; my salvation is "
6 and my r· shall not be abolished. 6666
7 Hearken unto me, ye that know r·, 6664
8 but my r· shall be for ever, and 6666
54: 14 In r· shalt thou be established: "
17 their r· is of me, saith the Lord. "
56: 1 to come, and my r· to be revealed. "
57: 12 I will declare thy r·, and thy works; "
58: 2 my ways, as a nation that did r·, "
8 and thy r· shall go before thee; 6664
59: 16 him; and his r·, it sustained him. 6666
17 For he put on r· as a breastplate, "
60: 17 officers peace, and thine exactors r·. "
61: 3 they might be called trees of r·, 6664
10 covered me with the robe of r·, 6666
11 so the Lord God will cause r· and "
62: 1 r· thereof go forth as brightness, 6664
2 And the Gentiles shall see thy r·, "
63: 1 I that speak in r·, mighty to save. 6666
64: 5 him that rejoiceth and worketh r·, 6664
Jer 4: 2 in truth, in judgment, and in r·; 6666
9: 24 lovingkindness, judgment, and r·, "
22: 3 Execute ye judgment and r·, and "
23: 6 he shall be called, The Lord Our R·. 6664
33: 15 Branch of r· to grow up unto David; 6666
15 execute judgment and r· in the "
16 shall be called, The Lord our r·. 6664
51: 10 Lord hath brought forth our r·: 6666
Eze 3: 20 man doth turn from his r·, and "
20 his r· which he hath done shall *6666
14: 14 but their own souls by their r·, "
20 deliver their own souls by their r·. "
18: 20 the r· of the righteous shall be upon "
22 in his r·...he hath done he shall live. "
24 righteous turneth away from his r·, "
24 All his r· that he hath done shall * "
26 righteous man turneth...from his r·, "
33: 12 r· of the righteous shall not deliver "

Eze 33: 12 righteous be able to live for his r' in
13 if he trust to his own r', and 6666
18 the righteous turneth from his r', "
Da 4: 27 and break off thy sins by r', and 6665
9: 7 O Lord, r' belongeth unto thee, 6666
16 O Lord, according to all thy r', I "
24 to bring in everlasting r', and to 6664
12: 3 that turn many to r' as the stars 6663
Ho 2: 19 I will betroth thee unto me in r', 6664
10: 12 Sow to yourselves in r', reap in 6666
12 till he come and reign r' upon you.6664
Am 5: 7 and leave off r' in the earth, 6666
24 waters, and r' as a mighty stream. "
6: 12 and the fruit of r' into hemlock: "
Mic 6: 5 ye may know the r' of the Lord. * "
7: 9 the light, and I shall behold his r'. "
Zep 2: 3 seek r', seek meekness: it may be6664
Zec 8: 8 be their God, in truth and in r'. 6666
Mal 3: 3 offer unto the Lord an offering in r'."
4: 2 Sun of r' arise with healing in his "
M't 3: 15 thus it becometh us to fulfil all r'. *1343*
5: 6 which do hunger and thirst after r': "
20 I say unto you, That except your r'"
20 shall exceed the r' of the scribes "
6: 33 the kingdom of God, and his r'; "
21: 32 John came unto you in the way of r', "
Lu 1: 75 In holiness and r' before him, all "
Joh 16: 8 reprove the world of sin, and of r', "
10 Of r', because I go to my Father, "
Ac 10: 35 he feareth him, and worketh r', is "
13: 10 of the devil, thou enemy of all r', "
17: 31 which he will judge the world in r' "
24: 25 as he reasoned of r', temperance, "
Ro 1: 17 therein is the r' of God revealed "
2: 26 keep the r' of the law, shall not **1345*
3: 5 commend the r' of God, what shall*1343*
21 But now r' of God without the law "
22 Even the r' of God which is by faith"
25 to declare his r' for the remission "
26 To declare, I say, at this time his r':"
4: 3 and it was counted unto him for r'. "
5 ungodly, his faith is counted for r'. "
6 man, unto whom God imputeth r' "
9 was reckoned to Abraham for r'. "
11 a seal of the r' of the faith which "
11 that r' might be imputed unto them"
13 the law, but through the r' of faith. "
22 it was imputed to him for r'. "
5: 17 receive abundance...of the gift of r' "
18 by the r' of one the free gift came *1345*
21 so might grace reign through r' *1343*
6: 13 as instruments of r' unto God. "
16 unto death, or of obedience unto r'?"
18 sin, ye became the servants of r'. "
19 yield your members servants to r' "
20 servants of sin, ye were free from r'."
8: 4 the r' of the law might be fulfilled**1345*
10 but the Spirit is life because of r'. *1343*
9: 28 the work, and cut it short in r': * "
30 followed not after r',...attained to r',"
30 even the r' which is of faith. "
31 which followed after the law of r', "
31 hath not attained to the law of r'.* "
10: 3 For they being ignorant of God's r', "
3 going about to establish their own r',"
3 not submitted...unto the r' of God. "
4 Christ is the end of the law for r' "
5 describeth the r' which is of the law,"
6 But the r' which is of faith speaketh"
10 the heart man believeth unto r'; "
14: 17 r', and peace, and joy in the Holy "
1Co 1: 30 is made unto us wisdom, and r', "
15: 34 Awake to r', and sin not; for ††*1346*
2Co 3: 9 ministration of r' exceed in glory. *1343*
5: 21 might be made the r' of God in him."
6: 7 the armour of r' on the right hand "
14 for what fellowship hath r' with "
9: 9 the poor: his r' remaineth for ever. "
10 and increase the fruits of your r';) "
11: 15 transformed as the ministers of r'; "
Ga 2: 21 if r' come by the law, then Christ "
3: 6 and it was accounted to him for r'. "
21 r' should have been by the law. "
5: 5 wait for the hope of r' by faith. "
Eph 4: 24 is created in r' and true holiness. "
5: 9 is in all goodness and r' and truth;)"
6: 14 and having on the breastplate of r'; "
Ph'p 1: 11 Being filled with the fruits of r', "
3: 6 touching the r' which is in the law, "
9 not having mine own r', which is of"
9 the r' which is of God by faith: "
1Ti 6: 11 and follow after r', godliness, faith,"
2Ti 2: 22 but follow r', faith, charity, peace, "
3: 16 for correction, for instruction in r':"
4: 8 there is laid up for me a crown of r',"
Tit 3: 5 Not by works of r' which we have "
Heb 1: 8 a sceptre of r' is the sceptre of thy**2118*
9 hast loved r', and hated iniquity; *1343*
5: 13 milk is unskilful in the word of r': "
7: 2 being by interpretation King of r', "
11: 7 heir of the r' which is by faith. "
33 wrought r', obtained promises, "
12: 11 it yieldeth the peaceable fruit of r' "
Jas 1: 20 of man worketh not the r' of God. "
2: 23 and it was imputed unto him for r': "
3: 18 And the fruit of r' is sown in peace "
1Pe 2: 24 dead to sins, should live unto r': "
2Pe 1: 1 the r' of God and our Saviour Jesus"
2: 5 the eighth person, a preacher of r', "
21 not to have known the way of r', "
3: 13 a new earth, wherein dwelleth r'. "
1Jo 2: 29 every one that doeth r' is born of "
3: 7 he that doeth r' is righteous, even "
10 whosoever doeth not r' is not of God,"
Re 19: 8 for the fine linen is the r' of saints.**1345*
11 in r' he doth judge and make war. *1343*

righteousness'
Ps 143: 11 for thy r' sake bring my soul out *6666
Isa 42: 21 is well pleased for his r' sake; 6664
M't 5: 10 which are persecuted for r' sake: *1343*
1Pe 3: 14 But and if ye suffer for r' sake, "

righteousnesses
Isa 64: 6 and all our r' are as filthy rags; 6666
Eze 33: 13 all his r' shall not be remembered ;*"
Da 9: 18 supplications before thee for our r', "

rightly See also UPRIGHTLY.
Ge 27: 36 he said, Is not he r' named Jacob?3588
Lu 7: 43 said unto him, Thou hast r' judged*3723*
20: 21 that thou sayest and teachest r', "
2Ti 2: 15 ashamed, r' dividing the word of truth.*

rigour
Ex 1: 13 children of Israel to serve with r':6531
14 they made them serve, was with r'."
Le 25: 43 Thou shalt not rule over him with r';"
46 not rule one over another with r'. "
53 other shall not rule with r' over him"

Rimmon (*rim'-mon*) See also EN-RIMMON; GATH-RIMMON; RIMMON-PAREZ.
Jos 15: 32 and Shilhim, and Ain, and R': 7417
J'g 20: 45 the wilderness unto the rock of R': "
47 to the wilderness unto the rock R', "
47 abode in the rock R' four months. "
21: 13 Benjamin that were in the rock R', "
2Sa 4: 2 the sons of R' a Beerothite, of the "
5, 9 the sons of R' the Beerothite, "
2Ki 5: 18 master goeth into the house of R' "
18 I bow myself in the house of R': "
18 bow down myself in the house of R', "
1Ch 4: 32 villages were, Etam, and Ain, R', "
6: 77 R' with her suburbs, Tabor with * "
Zec 14: 10 Geba to R' south of Jerusalem: "

Rimmon-parez (*rim"-mon-pa'-rez*)
Nu 33: 19 from Rithmah, and pitched at R'.*7428
20 And they departed from R', and "

ring See also EARRING; RANG; RINGLEADER; RINGS; RINGSTRAKED.
Ge 41: 42 Pharaoh took off his r' from his 2885
Ex 26: 24 above the head of it unto one r': "
36: 29 at the head thereof, to one r': "
Es 3: 10 the king took his r' from his hand, "
12 and sealed with the king's r'. "
8: 2 And the king took off his r', which "
8 name, and seal it with the king's r':"
8 name, and sealed with the king's r',"
10 and sealed it with the king's r', and"
Lu 15: 22 put a r' on his hand, and shoes on *1146*
Jas 2: 2 assembly a man with a gold r', *5554*

ringleader
Ac 24: 5 a r' of the sect of the Nazarenes: 4414

rings See also EARRINGS.
Ex 25: 12 shalt cast four r' of gold for it, 2885
12 two r' shall be in the one side of it, "
12 and two r' in the other side of it. "
14 thou shalt put the staves into the r' "
15 staves shall be in the r' of the ark: "
26 shalt make for it four r' of gold, "
26 and put the r' in the four corners "
27 against the border shall the r' be "
26: 29 make their r' of gold for places for "
27: 4 four brasen r' in the four corners "
7 the staves shall be put into the r', "
28: 23 upon the breastplate two r' of gold,"
23 shalt put the two r' on the two ends"
24 wreathen chains of gold in the two r'"
26 And thou shalt make two r' of gold,"
27 two other r' of gold thou shalt make,"
28 shall bind the breastplate by the r' "
28 unto the r' of the ephod with a lace "
30: 4 two golden r' shalt thou make to it "
35: 22 bracelets, and earrings, and r', and "
36: 34 made their r' of gold to be places "
37: 3 And he cast for it four r' of gold, to "
3 even two r' upon the one side of it, "
3 and two r' upon the other side of it."
5 he put the staves into the r' by the "
13 And he cast for it four r' of gold, "
13 put the r' upon the four corners "
14 Over against the border were the r',"
27 he made two r' of gold for it under "
38: 5 he cast four r' for the four ends of "
7 he put the staves into the r' on the "
39: 16 two ouches of gold, and two gold r'; "
16 and put the two r' in the two ends of"
17 wreathen chains of gold in the two r'"
19 they made two r' of gold, and put "
20 And they made two other golden r', "
21 did bind the breastplate by his r' "
21 unto the r' of the ephod with a lace"
Nu 31: 50 chains, and bracelets, r', earrings, "
Es 1: 6 to silver r' and pillars of marble: 1550
Ca 5: 14 His hands are as gold r' set with "
Isa 3: 21 The r', and nose jewels, 2885
Eze 1: 18 As for their r', they were so high ‡1354
18 and their r' were full of eyes round‡"

ringstraked
Ge 30: 35 he goats that were r' and spotted, 6124
39 brought forth cattle r', speckled, "
40 the faces of the flocks toward the r',"
31: 8 said thus, The r' shall be thy hire; "
8 then bare all the cattle r'. "
10 leaped upon the cattle were r', "
12 which leap upon the cattle are r', "

Rinnah (*rin'-nah*)
1Ch 4: 20 of Shimon were, Amnon, and R'. 7441

rinsed
Le 6: 28 be both scoured, and r' in water. 7857
15: 11 and hath not r' his hands in water, "
12 vessel of wood shall be r' in water. "

riot See also RIOTING.
Tit 1: 6 faithful children not accused of r' *810*
1Pe 4: 4 with them to the same excess of r', "
2Pe 2: 13 count it pleasure to r' in the day **5172*

rioting
Ro 13: 13 not in r' and drunkenness, not in **2970*

riotous
Pr 23: 20 among r' eaters of flesh: *2151
28: 7 is a companion of r' men shameth* "
Lu 15: 13 wasted his substance with r' living.*811*

rip See also RIPPED.
2Ki 8: 12 and r' up their women with child. 1234

ripe See also FIRSTRIPE; UNRIPE.
Ge 40: 10 clusters...brought forth r' grapes: 1310
Ex 22: 29 delay to offer the first of thy r' fruits.*
Jer 24: 2 figs, even like the figs that are first r':
Joe 3: 13 in the sickle, for the harvest is r': 1310
Re 14: 15 for the harvest of the earth is r'. †*3583*
18 earth; for her grapes are fully r'. *187*

ripening
Isa 18: 5 the sour grape is r' in the flower, 1580

Riphath (*ri'-fath*)
Ge 10: 3 sons of Gomer; Ashkenaz, and R',7384
1Ch 1: 6 sons of Gomer; Ashchenaz, and R',*"

ripped
2Ki 15: 16 the women...with child he r' up. 1234
Ho 13: 16 women with child shall be r' up. "
Am 1: 13 have r' up the women with child of "

rise See also ARISE; RISEN; RISEST; RISETH; RISING; ROSE.
Ge 19: 2 and ye shall r' up early, and go on7925
31: 35 that I cannot r' up before thee; 6965
Ex 8: 20 R' up early in the morning, and 7925
9: 13 R' up early in the morning, and "
12: 31 R' up, and get you forth from 6965
21: 19 If he r' again, and walk abroad "
Le 19: 32 shalt r' up before the hoary head, "
Nu 10: 35 R' up, Lord, and let thine enemies "
22: 20 call thee, r' up, and go with them; "
23: 18 R' up, Balak, and hear; hearken "
24 people shall r' up as a great lion, "
24: 17 a Sceptre shall r' out of Israel, and "
De 2: 13 Now r' up, said I, and get you over "
24 R' ye up, take your journey, and "
19: 11 wait for him, and r' up against him, "
15 One witness shall not r' up against "
16 false witness r' up against any man"
28: 7 thine enemies that r' up against "
29: 22 your children that shall r' up after "
31: 16 and this people will r' up, and go a "
32: 38 let them r' up and help you, and be "
33: 11 loins of them that r' against him, "
11 hate him, that they r' not again. "
Jos 8: 7 ye shall r' up from the ambush, and"
18: 4 they shall r', and go through the * "
J'g 8: 21 said, R' thou, and fall upon us: "
9: 33 r' early, and set upon the city: 7925
20: 38 make a great flame with smoke r' 5927
1Sa 22: 13 he should r' against me, to lie in 6965
24: 7 suffered them not to r' against Saul."
29: 10 r' up early in the morning with thy7925
2Sa 12: 21 dead, thou didst r' and eat bread. 6965
18: 32 that r' against thee to do thee hurt. "
2Ki 16: 7 of Israel, which r' up against me. "
Ne 2: 18 they said, Let us r' up and build. "
Job 20: 27 the earth shall r' up against him. "
30: 12 Upon my right hand r' the youth; "
Ps 3: 1 many are they that r' up against me."
17: 7 from those that r' up against them."
18: 38 them that they were not able to r': "
48 above those that r' up against me: "
27: 3 though war should r' against me, "
35: 11 False witnesses did r' up; they laid"
36: 12 down, and shall not be able to r'. "
41: 8 that he lieth he shall r' up no more."
44: 5 them under that r' up against us. "
59: 1 from them that r' up against me. "
74: 23 tumult of those that r' up against "
92: 11 of the wicked that r' up against me."
94: 16 r' up for me against the evildoers? "
119: 62 At midnight I will r' to give thanks "
127: 2 It is vain for you to r' up early, to "
139: 21 not I grieved with those that r' up 8618
140: 10 pits, that they r' not up again. 6965
Pr 24: 22 their calamity shall r' suddenly; "
28: 12 but when the wicked r', a man is "
28 When the wicked r', men hide "
Ec 10: 4 spirit of the ruler r' up against 5927
12: 4 shall r' up at the voice of the bird,6965
Ca 2: 10 R' up, my love, my fair one, and "
3: 2 I will r' now, and go about the city "
Isa 5: 11 Woe unto them that r' up early in 7925
14: 21 that they do not r', nor possess the6965
22 I will r' up against them, saith the "
24: 20 and it shall fall, and not r' again. "
26: 14 they are deceased, they shall not r':"
28: 21 the Lord shall r' up as in mount "
32: 9 R' up, ye women that are at ease; "
33: 10 Now will I r', saith the Lord; now* "
43: 17 lie down together, they shall not r':"
54: 17 tongue that shall r' against thee in "
58: 10 then shall thy light r' in obscurity,2224
Jer 25: 27 and spue, and fall, and r' no more,6965
37: 10 they r' up every man in his tent, "
47: 2 waters r' up out of the north, and 5927
49: 14 against her, and r' up to the battle.6965
51: 1 of them that r' up against me, * "
64 shall not r' from the evil that I will "
La 1: 14 from whom I am not able to r' up.* "
Da 7: 24 another shall r' after them; and *6966
Am 5: 2 is fallen; she shall no more r': she6965
7: 9 r' against the house of Jeroboam "

Am 8: 8 and it shall r· up wholly as a flood; 5927
14 shall fall, and never r· up again. 6965
9: 5 it shall r· up wholly like a flood; 5927
Ob 1 let us r· up against her in battle. 6965
Na 1: 9 affliction shall not r· up the second "
Hab 2: 7 Shall they not r· up suddenly that "
Zep 3: 8 the day that I r· up to the prey: for "
Zec 14: 13 shall r· up against the hand of his 5927
M't 5: 45 he maketh his sun to r· on the evil 393
10: 21 and the children shall r· up against 1881
12: 41 men of Nineveh shall r· in judgment *450
42 south shall r· up in the judgment 1453
20: 19 and the third day he shall r· again. *450
24: 7 For nation shall r· against nation, 1453
11 And many false prophets shall r·, * "
26: 46 R·, let us be going: behold, he is at* "
27: 63 After three days I will r· again. "
M'r 3: 26 And if Satan r· up against himself, *450
4: 27 should sleep, and r· night and day, 1453
8: 31 and after three days r· again. 450
9: 31 be killed, he shall r· the third day. "
10: 34 and the third day he shall r· again. "
49 Be of good comfort, r·; he calleth 1453
12: 23 when they shall r·, whose wife * 450
25 when they shall r· from the dead, "
26 as touching the dead, that they r·: *1453
13: 8 For nation shall r· against nation, "
12 shall r· up against their parents, 1881
22 Christs and false prophets shall r·, *1453
14: 42 R· up, let us go; lo, he that * "
Lu 5: 23 thee; or to say, R· up and walk? * "
6: 8 R· up, and stand forth in the midst. "
11: 7 in bed; I cannot r· and give thee. 450
8 Though he will not r· and give 1453
8 he will r· and give him as many as *450
31 queen of the south shall r· up in 1453
32 Nineve shall r· up in the judgment *450
12: 54 ye see a cloud r· out of the west, * 393
18: 33 and the third day he shall r· again. 450
21: 10 Nation shall r· against nation, 1453
22: 46 r· and pray, lest ye enter into 450
24: 7 crucified, and the third day r· again. "
46 to r· from the dead the third day: "
Joh 5: 8 unto him, R·, take up thy bed, and *1453
11: 23 her, Thy brother shall r· again. 450
24 I know that he shall r· again in the "
20: 9 he must r· again from the dead. "
Ac 3: 6 name of Jesus...of Nazareth r· up *1453
10: 13 to him, R·, Peter; kill, and eat. 450
26: 16 r·, and stand upon thy feet: for I * "
23 first that should r· from the dead. * 386
Ro 15: 12 shall r· to reign over the Gentiles; * 450
1Co 15: 15 up, if so be that the dead r· not. *1453
16 if the dead r· not,...is not Christ * "
29 the dead, if the dead r· not at all? * "
32 advantageth it me, if the dead r· * "
1Th 4: 16 the dead in Christ shall r· first: 450
Heb 7: 11 that another priest should r· after * "
Re 11: 1 R·, and measure the temple of 1453
13: 1 saw a beast r· up out of the sea, * 305

risen See also ARISEN.
Ge 19: 23 The sun was r· upon the earth 3318
Ex 22: 3 If the sun be r· upon him, there 2224
Nu 32: 14 ye are r· up in your fathers' stead, 6965
J'g 9: 18 ye are r· up against my father's "
Ru 2: 15 when she was r· up to glean, Boaz "
1Sa 25: 29 Yet a man is r· to pursue thee, and "
2Sa 14: 7 the whole family is r· against thine "
1Ki 8: 20 I am r· up in the room of David my "
2Ki 6: 15 the servant...of God was r· early, "
2Ch 6: 10 am r· up in the room of David my "
13: 6 Solomon the son of David, is r· up, * "
21: 4 Jehoram was r· up to the kingdom "
Ps 20: 8 but we are r·, and stand upright. "
27: 12 witnesses are r· up against me, "
54: 3 strangers are r· up against me, "
86: 14 the proud are r· against me, and "
Isa 60: 1 glory of the Lord is r· upon thee. 2224
Eze 7: 11 Violence is r· up into a rod of 6965
47: 5 for the waters were r·, waters to 1342
Mic 2: 8 my people is r· up as an enemy: 6965
M't 11: 11 hath not r· a greater than John 1453
14: 2 Baptist; he is r· from the dead; "
17: 9 the Son of man be r· again from 450
26: 32 But after I am r· again, I will go *1453
27: 64 the people, He is r· from the dead: "
28: 6 He is not here: for he is r·, as he "
7 his disciples that he is r· from the "
M'r 6: 14 John the Baptist was r· from the "
16 beheaded: he is r· from the dead. "
9: 9 Son of man were r· from the dead. 450
14: 28 after that I am r·, I will go before *1453
16: 6 he is r·; he is not here: behold the "
9 Jesus was r· early the first day of 450
14 had seen him after he was r·. 1453
Lu 7: 16 a great prophet is r· up among us; * "
9: 7 that John was r· from the dead; "
8 of the old prophets was r· again. 450
19 one of the old prophets is r· again. "
13: 25 the master of the house is r· up, 1453
24: 6 He is not here, but is r·: remember "
34 The Lord is r· indeed, and hath "
Joh 2: 22 therefore he was r· from the dead, * "
21: 14 after that he was r· from the dead. "
Ac 17: 3 suffered,...r· again from the dead; * 450
Ro 8: 34 died, yea rather, that is r· again, *1453
1Co 15: 13 of the dead, then is Christ not r·: * "
14 And if Christ be not r·, then is our* "
20 But now is Christ r· from the dead, * "
Col 2: 12 r· with him through the faith of *4891
3: 1 If ye then be r· with Christ, seek * "
Jas 1: 11 sun is...r· with a burning heat, * 393

risest
De 6: 7 liest down, and when thou r· up. 6965
11: 19 liest down, and when thou r· up. "

riseth See also ARISETH.
De 22: 26 a man r· against his neighbour, 6965
Jos 6: 26 r· up and buildeth this city Jericho: "
2Sa 23: 4 when the sun r·, even a morning 2224
Job 9: 7 commandeth the sun, and it r· not; "
14: 12 So man lieth down, and r· not: 6965
24: 22 he r· up, and no man is sure of life. "
27: 7 he that r· up against me as the "
31: 14 then shall I do when God r· up? "
Pr 24: 16 falleth seven times, and r· up again: "
31: 15 She r· also while it is yet night, and "
Isa 47: 11 shalt not know from whence it r·: *7837
Jer 46: 8 Egypt r· up like a flood, and his 5927
Mic 7: 6 daughter r· up against her mother, 6965
Joh 13: 4 He r· from supper, and laid aside 1453

rising See also ARISING; SUNRISING; UPRISING.
Le 13: 2 have in the skin of his flesh a r·, 7613
10 if the r· be white in the skin, and "
10 there be quick raw flesh in the r·; "
19 place of the boil there be a white r·, "
28 it is a r· of the burning, and the "
43 the r· of the sore be white reddish "
14: 56 for a r·, and for a scab, and for a "
Nu 2: 3 east side toward the r· of the sun *4217
Jos 12: 1 Jordan toward the r· of the sun, * "
2Ch 36: 15 r· up betimes, and sending; 7925
Ne 4: 21 spears from the r· of the morning 5927
Job 16: 8 my leanness r· up in me beareth *6965
24: 5 their work; r· betimes for a prey: *7836
14 murderer r· with the light killeth *6965
Ps 50: 1 the earth from the r· of the sun 4217
113: 3 From the r· of the sun unto the "
Pr 27: 14 r· early in the morning, it shall be 7925
30: 31 against whom there is no r· up. 510
Isa 41: 25 from the r· of the sun shall he call 4217
45: 6 may know from the r· of the sun, "
59: 19 and his glory from the r· of the sun. "
60: 3 kings to the brightness of thy r·. 2225
Jer 7: 13 r· up early and speaking, but ye 7925
25 r· up early and sending them: "
11: 7 r· early and protesting, saying, "
25: 3 unto you, r· early and speaking; "
4 the prophets, r· early and sending "
26: 5 both r· up early, and sending them, "
29: 19 r· up early and sending them; "
32: 33 r· up early and teaching them, yet "
35: 14 unto you, r· early and speaking; "
15 r· up early and sending them, "
44: 4 the prophets, r· early and sending "
La 3: 63 sitting down, and their r· up; 7012
Mal 1: 11 from the r· of the sun even unto 4217
M'r 1: 35 r· up a great while before day, he * 450
9: 10 the r· from the dead should mean. 305
16: 2 the sepulchre at the r· of the sun. * 393
Lu 2: 34 and r· again of many in Israel; 386

Rissah (*ris'-sah*)
Nu 33: 21 from Libnah, and pitched at R·. 7446
22 And they journeyed from R·, and "

rites
Nu 9: 3 according to all the r· of it, and *2708

Rithmah (*rith'-mah*)
Nu 33: 18 Hazeroth, and pitched in R·. 7575
19 And they departed from R·, and "

river See also RIVER'S; RIVERS.
Ge 2: 10 a r· went out of Eden to water the 5104
13 the name of the second r· is Gihon: "
14 name of the third r· is Hiddekel: "
14 And the fourth r· is Euphrates. "
15: 18 I given this land, the r· of Egypt "
18 unto the great r·, the r· Euphrates: "
31: 21 he rose up, and passed over the r·, "
36: 37 Saul of Rehoboth by the r· reigned "
41: 1 and, behold, he stood by the r·. 2975
2 came up out of the r· seven...kine "
3 came up after them out of the r·, "
3 other kine upon the brink of the r·. "
17 I stood upon the bank of the r·: "
18 came up out of the r· seven kine, "
Ex 1: 22 Every son...ye shall cast into the r·, "
2: 5 came down to wash herself at the r·; "
4: 9 shalt take of the water of the r·, "
9 water...thou takest out of the r· "
7: 17 upon the waters which are in the r·, "
18 the fish that is in the r· shall die, "
18 and the r· shall stink; and the "
18 lothe to drink of the water of the r·. "
20 smote the waters that were in the r·, "
20 all the waters that were in the r·, "
21 And the fish that was in the r· died; "
21 and the r· stank, and the Egyptians "
21 could not drink...the water of the r·; "
24 digged round about the r· for water "
24 could not drink...the water of the r·. "
25 that the Lord had smitten the r·. "
8: 3 And the r· shall bring forth frogs "
9 they may remain in the r· only? "
11 they shall remain in the r· only. "
17: 5 rod, wherewith thou smotest the r·, "
23: 31 and from the desert unto the r·: 5104
Nu 22: 5 by the r· of the land of the children "
34: 5 from Azmon unto the r· of Egypt, *5158
De 1: 7 unto the great r·, the r· Euphrates. 5104
2: 24 and pass over the r· Arnon: *5158
36 is by the brink of the r· of Arnon, * "
36 and from the city that is by the r·, * "
37 nor unto any place of the r· Jabbok, "
3: 8 from the r· of Arnon unto mount * "
12 Aroer, which is by the r· Arnon, * "
16 from Gilead even unto the r· Arnon* "
16 the border even unto the r· Jabbok, "
4: 48 is by the bank of the r· Arnon, * "
11: 24 from the r·, the r· Euphrates, even 5104
Jos 1: 4 unto the great r·, the r· Euphrates, "
12: 1 from the r· Arnon unto mount *5158

Jos 12: 2 is upon the bank of the r· Arnon, *5158
2 and from the middle of the r·, and* "
2 even unto the r· Jabbok, which is "
13: 9 is upon the bank of the r· Arnon, * "
9 city that is in the midst of the r·, * "
16 that is on the bank of the r· Arnon, * "
16 city that is in the midst of the r·, * "
15: 4 and went out unto the r· of Egypt: * "
7 which is on the south side of the r·: "
47 the r· of Egypt, and the great sea, * "
16: 8 westward unto the r· Kanah; * "
17: 9 the r· Kanah, southward of the r·: * "
9 was on the north side of the r·, "
19: 11 to the r· that is before Jokneam; * "
J'g 4: 7 will draw...to the r· Kishon Sisera, "
13 Harosheth...unto the r· of Kishon. "
5: 21 The r· of Kishon swept them away, "
21 that ancient r·, the r· Kishon. "
2Sa 8: 3 his border at the r· Euphrates. 5104
10: 16 Syrians that were beyond the r·: "
17: 13 city, and...will draw it into the r·, 5158
24: 5 lieth in the midst of the r· of Gad, * "
1Ki 4: 21 from the r· unto the land of the 5104
24 all the region on this side the r·, "
24 over all the kings on this side the r·: "
8: 65 of Hamath unto the r· of Egypt, *5158
14: 15 shall scatter them beyond the r·, 5104
2Ki 10: 33 Aroer, which is by the r· Arnon, *5158
17: 6 and in Habor by the r· of Gozan, 5104
18: 11 and in Habor by the r· of Gozan, "
23: 29 king of Assyria to the r· Euphrates: "
24: 7 had taken from the r· of Egypt *5158
7 unto the r· Euphrates all that "
1Ch 1: 48 Shaul of Rehoboth by the r· 5104
5: 9 wilderness from the r· Euphrates: "
26 and Hara, and to the r· Gozan, "
18: 3 his dominion by the r· Euphrates. "
19: 16 Syrians that were beyond the r·: "
2Ch 7: 8 of Hamath unto the r· of Egypt. *5158
9: 26 from the r· even unto the land of 5104
Ezr 4: 10 rest that are on this side the r·, 5103
11 servants the men on this side the r·, "
16 have no portion on this side the r·. "
17 and unto the rest beyond the r·, "
20 over all countries beyond the r·; "
5: 3, 6 governor on this side the r·, "
6 Apharsachites,...on this side the r·, "
6: 6 Tatnai, governor beyond the r·, "
6 Apharsachites,...beyond the r·, "
8 even of the tribute beyond the r·, "
13 Tatnai, governor on this side the r·, "
7: 21 treasurers which are beyond the r·, "
25 the people that are beyond the r·, "
8: 15 to the r· that runneth to Ahava; 5104
21 a fast there, at the r· of Ahava, "
31 we departed from the r· of Ahava "
36 to the governors on this side the r·: "
Ne 2: 7, 9 to the governors beyond the r·, "
3: 7 of the governor on this side the r·. "
Job 40: 23 drinketh up a r·, and hasteth not: "
Ps 36: 8 drink of the r· of thy pleasures. 5158
46: 4 There is a r·, the streams whereof 5104
65: 9 enrichest it with the r· of God, 6388
72: 8 and from the r· unto the ends of 5104
80: 11 sea, and her branches unto the r·. "
105: 41 they ran in the dry places like a r·. "
Isa 7: 20 namely, by them beyond the r·, "
8: 7 up upon them the waters of the r·, "
11: 15 shall he shake his hand over the r·, "
19: 5 the r· shall be wasted and dried up. "
23: 3 seed of Sihor, the harvest of the r·, *2975
10 Pass through thy land as a r·, O * "
27: 12 channel of the r· unto the stream 5104
48: 18 then had thy peace been as a r·, "
66: 12 I will extend peace to her like a r·, "
Jer 2: 18 to drink the waters of the r·? "
17: 8 spreadeth out her roots by the r·, 3105
46: 2 which was by the r· Euphrates in 5104
6 the north by the r· Euphrates. "
10 north country by the r· Euphrates. "
La 2: 18 let tears run down like a r· day 5158
Eze 1: 1 the captives by the r· of Chebar, 5104
3 of the Chaldeans by the r· Chebar; "
3: 15 that dwelt by the r· of Chebar, and "
23 which I saw by the r· of Chebar: "
10: 15 that I saw by the r· of Chebar. "
20 God of Israel by the r· of Chebar; "
22 faces...I saw by the r· of Chebar, "
29: 3 My r· is mine own, and I have 2975
9 The r· is mine, and I have made it. "
43: 3 vision...I saw by the r· Chebar; 5104
47: 5 was a r· that I could not pass over: 5158
5 a r· that could not be passed over. "
6 me to return to the brink of the r·. "
7 bank of the r· were very many trees "
9 shall live whither the r· cometh. "
12 by the r· upon the bank thereof, on "
19 in Kadesh, the r· to the great sea.* "
48: 28 and to the r· toward the great sea.* "
Da 8: 2 vision, and I was by the r· of Ulai. 180
3 there stood before the r· a ram "
6 I had seen standing before the r·, "
10: 4 as I was by the side of the great r·, 5104
12: 5 on this side of the bank of the r·, 2975
5 on that side of the bank of the r·. "
6, 7 was upon the waters of the r·, "
Am 6: 14 unto the r· of the wilderness. *5158
Mic 7: 12 from the fortress even to the r·, 5104
Zec 9: 10 from the r· even to the ends of the "
10: 11 all the deeps of the r· shall dry up: *2975
M'r 1: 5 baptized of him in the r· of Jordan. 4215
Ac 16: 13 we went out of the city by a r· side, "
Re 9: 14 bound in the great r· Euphrates. "
16: 12 vial upon the great r· Euphrates; "
22: 1 shewed me a pure r· of water of life, "
2 of it, and on either side of the r·, "

river's
Ex 2: 3 laid it in the flags by the r' brink. 2975
5 maidens walked...by the r' side; * "
7:15 thou shalt stand by the r' brink "
Nu 24: 6 forth, as gardens by the r' side, *5104

rivers
Ex 7:19 upon their streams, upon their r',*2975
8: 5 over the r', and over the ponds, * "
Le 11: 9 waters, in the seas, and in the r', 5158
10 scales in the seas, and in the r', "
De 10: 7 to Jotbath, a land of r' of waters. * "
2Ki 5:12 and Pharpar, r' of Damascus, 5104
19:24 up all the r' of besieged places. 2975
Job 20:17 He shall not see the r', the floods, 6390
28:10 cutteth out r' among the rocks; *2975
29: 6 the rock poured me out r' of oil; ‡6388
Ps 1: 3 a tree planted by the r' of water, * 5104
74:15 flood: thou driedst up mighty r'. 5104
78:16 caused waters to run down like r'. "
44 had turned their r' into blood; 2975
89:25 sea, and his right hand in the r'. 5104
107:33 He turneth r' into a wilderness, "
119:136 R' of waters run down mine ‡6388
137: 1 By the r' of Babylon, there we sat 5104
Pr 5:16 and r' of waters in the streets. ‡6388
21: 1 hand of the Lord, as the r' of water:* "
Ec 1: 7 All the r' run into the sea; yet the 5158
7 the place from whence the r' come, "
Ca 5:12 eyes of doves by the r' of waters, * 650
Isa 7:18 uttermost part of the r' of Egypt, 2975
18: 1 which is beyond the r' of Ethiopia:5104
2 whose land the r' have spoiled! "
7 whose land the r' have spoiled, to "
19: 6 And they shall turn the r' far away;"
30:25 r' and streams of waters in the ‡6388
32: 2 as rivers of water in a dry place, ‡ "
33:21 a place of broad r' and streams; 5103
37:25 all the r' of the besieged places. 2975
41:18 I will open r' in high places, and 5103
42:15 and I will make the r' islands, and "
43: 2 and through the r', they shall not "
19 the wilderness, and r' in the desert."
20 the wilderness, and r' in the desert."
44:27 Be dry, and I will dry up thy r': "
47: 2 uncover the thigh, pass over the r'."
50: 2 the sea, I make the r' a wilderness:"
Jer 31: 9 them to walk by the r' of waters 5158
46: 7 whose waters are moved as the r'?5104
8 his waters are moved like the r'; "
La 3:48 runneth down with r' of water ‡6388
Eze 6: 3 hills, to the r', and to the valleys;* 650
29: 3 that lieth in the midst of his r', 2975
4 will cause the fish of thy r' to stick "
4 thee up out of the midst of thy r', "
4 and all the fish of thy r' shall stick "
5 thee and all the fish of thy r': "
10 am against thee, and against thy r',"
30:12 And I will make the r' dry, and sell"
31: 4 r' running round about his plants, 5104
4 little r' unto all the trees. *8585
12 are broken by all the r' of the land;*650
32: 2 and thou camest forth with thy r',5104
2 with thy feet, and fouledst their r'. "
6 and the r' shall be full of thee. * 650
14 and cause their r' to run like oil, 5104
34:13 the mountains of Israel by the r',* 650
35: 8 and in all thy r', shall they fall that*"
36: 4, 6 hills, to the r', and to the valleys,*"
47: 9 whithersoever the r' shall come, 5158
Joe 1:20 for the r' of waters are dried up, * 650
3:18 r' of Judah shall flow with waters,* "
Mic 6: 7 or with ten thousands of r' of oil? 5158
Na 1: 4 it dry, and drieth up all the r': 5104
2: 6 The gates of the r' shall be opened, "
3: 8 No, that was situate among the r', 2975
Hab 3: 8 the Lord displeased against the r'?5104
8 was thine anger against the r'? was"
9 Thou didst cleave the earth with r'."
Zep 3:10 From beyond the r' of Ethiopia my "
Joh 7:38 belly shall flow r' of living water. 4215
Re 8:10 it fell upon the third part of the r', "
16: 4 poured out his vial upon the r' and "

Rizpah (riz'-pah)
2Sa 3: 7 a concubine, whose name was R', 7532
21: 8 the king took the two sons of R' "
10 And R' the daughter of Aiah took "
11 told David what R'...had done. "

road
1Sa 27:10 Whither have ye made a r' to day?*6584

roar See also ROARED; ROARETH; ROARING; UPROAR.
1Ch 16:32 Let the sea r', and the fulness 7481
Ps 46: 3 waters thereof r' and be troubled, 1993
74: 4 Thine enemies r' in the midst of *7580
96:11 let the sea r', and the fulness 7481
98: 7 Let the sea r', and the fulness "
104:21 The young lions r' after their prey,7580
Isa 5:29 lion, they shall r' like young lions: "
29 yea, they shall r', and lay hold of 5098
30 that day they shall r' against them "
42:13 a man of war: he shall cry, yea, r';*6873
59:11 We r' all like bears, and mourn 1993
Jer 5:22 though they r', yet can they not "
25:30 The Lord shall r' from on high, 7580
30 mightily r' upon his habitation; "
31:35 the sea when the waves thereof r';1993
50:42 their voice shall r' like the sea, and*"
51:38 They shall r' together like lions: 7580
55 her waves do r' like great waters, 1993
Ho 11:10 the Lord: he shall r' like a lion: 7580
10 when he shall r', then the children "
Joe 3:16 The Lord also shall r' out of Zion, "
Am 1: 2 he said, The Lord will r' from Zion,"
3: 4 Will a lion r' in the forest, when he "

roared
J'g 14: 5 a young lion r' against him. 7580
Ps 38: 8 r' by reason of the disquietness of‡ "
Isa 51:15 divided the sea, whose waves r': *1993
Jer 2:15 The young lions r' upon him, and 7580
Am 3: 8 The lion hath r', who will not fear? "

roareth
Job 37: 4 After it a voice r': he thundereth 7580
Jer 6:23 mercy; their voice r' like the sea; 1993
Re 10: 3 a loud voice, as when a lion r': 3455

roaring See also ROARINGS.
Job 4:10 The r' of the lion, and the voice of7581
Ps 22: 1 me, and from the words of my r'? ‡ "
13 as a ravening and a r' lion. 7580
32: 3 my bones waxed old through my r'‡7581
Pr 19:12 king's wrath is as the r' of a lion; 5099
20: 2 fear of a king is as the r' of a lion: "
28:15 As a r' lion, and a ranging bear; 5098
Isa 5:29 Their r' shall be like a lion, they 7581
30 shall roar...like the r' of the sea: 5100
31: 4 and the young lion r' on his prey,*1897
Eze 19: 7 thereof, by the noise of his r'. 7581
22:25 like a r' lion ravening the prey; 7580
Zep 3: 3 princes within her are r' lions; "
Zec 11: 3 a voice of the r' of young lions; 7581
Lu 21:25 the sea and the waves r'; 2278
1Pe 5: 8 devil, as a r' lion, walketh about, 5612

roarings
Job 3:24 r' are poured out like the waters. ‡7581

roast See also ROASTED; ROASTETH.
Ex 12: 8 the flesh in that night, r' with fire,6748
9 at all with water, but r' with fire; "
De 16: 7 And thou shalt r' and eat it in the 1310
1Sa 2:15 Give flesh to r' for the priest; for 6740
Isa 44:16 He roasteth r', and is satisfied: 6748

roasted
2Ch 35:13 And they r' the passover with fire 1310
Isa 44:19 I have r' flesh, and eaten it: and 6740
Jer 29:22 whom the king of Babylon r' in the7033

roasteth
Pr 12:27 slothful man r' not that which he 2760
Isa 44:16 he r' roast, and is satisfied: yea, 6740

rob See also ROBBED; ROBBETH.
Le 19:13 thy neighbour, neither r' him: 1497
26:22 which shall r' you of your children,7921
1Sa 23: 1 and they r' the threshingfloors. 8154
Pr 22:22 R' not the poor, because he is 1497
Isa 10: 2 that they may r' the fatherless! 962
17:14 us, and the lot of them that r' us. "
Eze 39:10 and r' those that robbed them, saith "
Mal 3: 8 Will a man r' God? Yet ye have 6906

robbed
J'g 9:25 they r' all that came along that 1497
2Sa 17: 8 as a bear r' of her whelps in the 7909
Ps 119:61 bands of the wicked have r' me: *5749
Pr 17:12 Let a bear r' of her whelps meet a 7909
Isa 10:13 and have r' their treasures, and I 8154
42:22 But this is a people r' and spoiled; 962
Jer 50:37 her treasures; and they shall be r'. "
Eze 33:15 pledge, give again that he had r', 1500
39:10 rob those that r' them, saith the 962
Mal 3: 8 man rob God? Yet ye have r' me. *6906
8 ye say, Wherein have we r' thee? "
9 for ye have r' me, even this whole* "
2Co 11: 8 I r' other churches, taking wages 4813

robber See also ROBBERS.
Job 5: 5 r' swalloweth up their substance. *6782
18: 9 the r' shall prevail against him. * "
Eze 18:10 If he beget a son that is a r', a 6530
Joh 10: 1 way, the same is a thief and a r'. 3027
18:40 Barabbas. Now Barabbas was a r'. "

robbers
Job 12: 6 The tabernacles of r' prosper, and 7703
Isa 42:24 for a spoil, and Israel to the r'? 962
Jer 7:11 become a den of r' in your eyes? 6530
Eze 7:22 for the r' shall enter into it, and * "
Da 11:14 the r' of thy people shall exalt * "
Ho 6: 9 And as troops of r' wait for a man, "
7: 1 and the troop of r' spoileth without. "
Ob 5 thieves came to thee, if r' by night,7703
Joh 10: 8 came before me are thieves and r':3027
Ac 19:37 which are neither r' of churches, 2417
2Co 11:26 in perils of waters, in perils of r', 3027

robbery
Ps 62:10 and become not vain in r': if 1498
Pr 21: 7 The r' of the wicked shall destroy*7701
Isa 61: 8 I hate r' for burnt offering; and 1498
Eze 22:29 used oppression, and exercised r', "
Am 3:10 violence and r' in their palaces. 7701
Na 3: 1 city! it is all full of lies and r'; the*6563
Ph'p 2: 6 it not r' to be equal with God: †‡ 725

robbeth
Pr 28:24 Whoso r' his father or his mother,1497

robe See also ROBES; WARDROBE.
Ex 28: 4 and a r', and a broidered coat, 4598
31 make the r' of the ephod all of blue."
34 upon the hem of the r' round about."
29: 5 the coat, and the r' of the ephod, "
39:22 the r' of the ephod of woven work, "
23 was an hole in the midst of the r', "
24 they made upon the hems of the r' "
25 upon the hem of the r', round "
26 round about the hem of the r' to "
Le 8: 7 clothed him with the r', and put "
1Sa 18: 4 Jonathan stripped himself of the r' "
24: 4 cut off the skirt of Saul's r' privily. "
11 see the skirt of thy r' in my hand: "
11 in that I cut off the skirt of thy r', "
1Ch 15:27 David was clothed with a r' of fine "
Job 29:14 my judgment was as a r' and a "
Isa 22:21 And I will clothe him with thy r'. 3801
61:10 me with the r' of righteousness, 4598
Jon 3: 6 and he laid his r' from him, and 155
Mic 2: 8 ye pull off the r' with the garment 145
M't 27:28 him, and put on him a scarlet r'. 5511
31 they took the r' off from him, and "
Lu 15:22 Bring forth the best r', and put it 4749
23:11 and arrayed him in a gorgeous r',*2066
Joh 19: 2 and they put on him a purple r', *2440
5 crown of thorns, and the purple r'.*"

robes
2Sa 13:18 for with such r' were the king's 4598
1Ki 22:10 his throne, having put on their r', 899
30 the battle; but put thou on thy r'. "
2Ch 18: 9 on his throne, clothed in their r', "
29 the battle; but put thou on thy r'. "
Eze 26:16 thrones, and lay away their r', 4598
Lu 20:46 which desire to walk in long r', 4749
Re 6:11 white r' were given unto every one*"
7: 9 clothed with white r', and palms in "
13 these which are arrayed in white r'?"
14 have washed their r', and made "

Roboam (ro-bo'-am) See also REHOBOAM.
M't 1: 7 Solomon begat R'; and R' begat *4497

rock See also ROCKS.
Ex 17: 6 thee there upon the r' in Horeb; 6697
6 and thou shalt smite the r', and "
33:21 me, and thou shalt stand upon a r':"
22 I will put thee in a clift of a r', and "
Nu 20: 8 ye unto the r' before their eyes: 5553
8 forth to them water out of the r': "
10 congregation together before the r',"
10 we fetch you water out of this r'? "
11 with his rod he smote the r' twice: "
24:21 and thou puttest thy nest in a r'. "
De 8:15 forth water out of the r' of flint; 6697
32: 4 He is the R', his work is perfect: "
13 him to suck honey out of the r', 5553
13 and oil out of the flinty r'; 6697
15 esteemed the R' of his salvation. "
18 Of the R' that begat thee thou art "
30 except their R' had sold them, and "
31 For their r' is not as our R', even "
37 gods, their r' in whom they trusted,"
J'g 1:36 from the r', and upward. 5553
6:20 cakes, and lay them upon this r', "
21 there rose up fire out of the r', 6697
26 thy God upon the top of this r', *4581
7:25 they slew Oreb upon the r' Oreb, 6697
13:19 offered it upon a r' unto the Lord: "
15: 8 dwelt in the top of the r' Etam. 5553
11 went to the top of the r' Etam, "
13 and brought him up from the r'. "
20:45 wilderness unto the r' of Rimmon: "
47 wilderness unto the r' Rimmon, "
47 and abode in the r' Rimmon four "
21:13 that were in the r' Rimmon, and "
1Sa 2: 2 is there any r' like our God. 6697
14: 4 was a sharp r' on the one side, *5553
4 and a sharp r' on the other side: * "
23:25 wherefore he came down into a r', "
2Sa 21:10 and spread it for her upon the r', 6697
22: 2 said, The Lord is my r', and my 5553
3 The God of my r'; in him will I 6697
32 and who is a r', save our God? "
47 Lord liveth; and blessed be my r'; "
47 the God of the r' of my salvation. "
23: 3 said, the R' of Israel spake to me, "
1Ch 11:15 went down to the r' to David, into "
2Ch 25:12 them unto the top of the r', and 5553
12 them down from the top of the r', "
Ne 9:15 them out of the r' for their thirst, "
Job 14:18 the r' is removed out of his place. 6697
18: 4 the r' be removed out of his place? "
19:24 iron pen and lead in the r' for ever!"
24: 8 embrace the r' for want of a shelter."
28: 9 putteth forth his hand upon the r';2496
29: 6 the r' poured me out rivers of oil; 6697
39: 1 wild goats of the r' bring forth? 5553
28 dwelleth and abideth on the r', ‡ "
28 upon the crag of the r', and the ‡ "
Ps 18: 2 The Lord is my r', and my fortress, "
31 Lord? or who is a r' save our God?6697
46 Lord liveth; and blessed be my r'; "
27: 5 me; he shall set me up upon a r'. "
28: 1 Unto thee will I cry, O Lord my r'; "
31: 2 be thou my strong r', for an house "
3 thou art my r' and my fortress; 5553
40: 2 clay, and set my feet upon a r', "
42: 9 I will say unto God my r', Why hast"
61: 2 lead me to the r' that is higher 6697
62: 2 He only is my r' and my salvation: "
6 He only is my r' and my salvation: "
7 the r' of my strength, and my "
71: 3 thou art my r' and my fortress. 5553
78:16 brought streams also out of the r', "
20 he smote the r', that the waters 6697
35 remembered that God was their r', "
81:16 with honey out of the r' should I "
89:26 God, and the r' of my salvation. "
92:15 he is my r', and there is no "
94:22 And my God is the r' of my refuge. "
95: 1 noise to the r' of our salvation. "
105:41 He opened the r', and the waters "
114: 8 turned the r' into a standing water, "
Pr 30:19 the way of a serpent upon a r'; "
Ca 2:14 that are in the clefts of the r', in 5553
Isa 2:10 Enter into the r', and hide thee 6697
8:14 stumbling and for a r' of offence "
10:26 slaughter of Midian at...r' of Oreb: "
17:10 mindful of the r' of thy strength, "
22:16 an habitation for himself in a r'? 5553
32: 2 shadow of a great r' in a weary land."
42:11 let the inhabitants of the r' sing, * "
48:21 the waters to flow out of the r' for 6697

Isa 48:21 he clave the r' also, and the waters 6697
51: 1 unto the r' whence ye are hewn, "
Jer 5: 3 made their faces harder than a r'; 5553
13: 4 and hide it there in a hole of the r'. "
18:14 snow...from the r' of the field? 6697
21:13 of the valley, and r' of the plain, "
23:29 hammer that breaketh the r' in 5553
48:28 the cities, and dwell in the r', and "
49:16 that dwellest in the clefts of the r'. "
Eze 24: 7 her; she set it upon the top of a r'; "
8 set her blood upon the top of a r', "
26: 4 and make her like the top of a r'. "
14 will make thee like the top of a r': "
Am 6:12 Shall horses run upon the r'? will "
Ob 3 that dwellest in the clefts of the r', "
M't 7:24 which built his house upon a r': 4073
25 not: for it was founded upon a r'. "
16:18 upon this r' I will build my church; "
27:60 which he had hewn out in the r': "
M'r 15:46 sepulchre...was hewn out of a r', "
Lu 6:48 and laid the foundation on a r': "
48 it: for it was founded upon a r'. * "
8: 6 And some fell upon a r'; and as "
13 They on the r' are they, which, "
Ro 9:33 a stumblingstone and r' of offence: "
1Co 10: 4 they drank of that spiritual R' that "
4 them: and that R' was Christ. "
1Pe 2: 8 a r' of offence, even to them which "

rocks
Nu 23: 9 from the top of the r' I see him, 6697
1Sa 13: 6 caves, and in thickets, and in r', 5553
24: 2 men upon the r' of the wild goats. 6697
1Ki 19:11 brake in pieces the r' before the 5553
Job 28:10 cutteth out rivers among the r'; 6697
30: 6 caves of the earth, and in the r'. 3710
Ps 78:15 He clave the r' in the wilderness, 6697
104:18 goats; and the r' for the conies. 5553
Pr 30:26 make they their houses in the r': "
Isa 2:19 shall go into the holes of the r', 6697
21 To go into the clefts of the r', and "
21 and into the tops of the ragged r', 5553
7:19 valleys, and in the holes of the r', "
33:16 shall be the munitions of r': "
57: 5 valleys under the clifts of the r'? "
Jer 4:29 and climb up upon the r': every 3710
16:16 hill, and out of the holes of the r'. 5553
51:25 and roll thee down from the r', "
Na 1: 6 the r' are thrown down by him. 6697
M't 27:51 earth did quake, and the r' rent; 4073
Ac 27:29 we should have fallen upon r', *5138, 5117
Re 6:15 and in the r' of the mountains; 4073
16 And said to the mountains and r', "

rod See also RODS.
Ex 4: 2 in thine hand? And he said, A r'. 4294
4 it, and it became a r' in his hand: "
17 shalt take this r' in thine hand, "
20 and Moses took the r' of God in his "
7: 9 Take thy r', and cast it before "
10 and Aaron cast down his r' before "
12 they cast down every man his r', "
12 Aaron's r' swallowed up their rods. "
15 r' which was turned to a serpent "
17 smite with the r'...in mine hand "
19 Say unto Aaron, Take thy r', and "
20 he lifted up the r', and smote the "
8: 5 Stretch forth thine hand with thy r' "
16 Stretch out thy r', and smite the "
17 stretched out his hand with his r', "
9:23 stretched...his r' toward heaven: "
10:13 stretched forth his r' over the land "
14:16 but lift thou up thy r', and stretch "
17: 5 and thy r', wherewith thou smotest "
9 with the r' of God in mine hand. "
21:20 his servant, or his maid, with a r', 7626
Le 27:32 of whatsoever passeth under the r', "
Nu 17: 2 and take of every one of them a r' *4294
2 thou every man's name upon his r'. "
3 Aaron's name upon the r' of Levi: "
3 for one r' shall be for the head of "
5 the man's r', whom I shall choose, "
6 their princes gave him a r' apiece,* "
6 r' of Aaron was among their rods. "
8 r' of Aaron for the house of Levi "
9 looked, and took every man his r'. "
10 Bring Aaron's r' again before the "
20: 8 Take the r', and gather thou the "
9 Moses took the r' from before the "
11 with his r' he smote the rock twice: "
1Sa 14:27 end of the r' that was in his hand, "
43 end of the r' that was in mine hand, "
2Sa 7:14 chasten him with the r' of man, 7626
Job 9:34 Let him take his r' away from me, "
21: 9 neither is the r' of God upon them. "
Ps 2: 9 shalt break them with a r' of iron; "
23: 4 r' and thy staff they comfort me. "
74: 2 the r' of thine inheritance, which* "
89:32 their transgression with the r', "
110: 2 the r' of thy strength out of Zion: 4294
125: 3 the r' of the wicked shall not rest *7626
Pr 10:13 a r' is for the back of him that is "
13:24 that spareth his r' hateth his son: "
14: 3 mouth of...foolish is a r' of pride: 2415
22: 8 and the r' of his anger shall fail. 7626
15 r' of correction shall drive it far "
23:13 for if thou beatest him with the r', "
14 Thou shalt beat him with the r', "
26: 3 the ass, and a r' for the fool's back. "
29:15 The r' and reproof give wisdom: "
Isa 9: 4 shoulder, the r' of his oppressor, "
10: 5 the r' of mine anger, and the staff "
15 r' should shake itself against them "
24 he shall smite thee with a r', and "
26 and as his r' was upon the sea, so 4294
11: 1 forth a r' out of the stem of Jesse, 2415
4 smite the earth with the r' of his 7626

Isa 14:29 r' of him that smote thee is broken: 7626
28:27 a staff, and the cummin with a r'. "
30:31 beaten down, which smote with a r'. "
Jer 1:11 I said, I see a r' of an almond tree. 4731
10:16 Israel is the r' of his inheritance: *7626
48:17 staff broken, and the beautiful r'! 4731
51:19 Israel is the r' of his inheritance: *7626
La 3: 1 seen affliction by the r' of his wrath. "
Eze 7:10 the r' hath blossomed, pride hath 4294
11 is risen up into a r' of wickedness: "
19:14 is gone out of a r' of her branches,* "
14 hath no strong r' to be a sceptre "
20:37 cause you to pass under the r', 7626
21:10 it contemneth the r' of my son, as "
13 if the sword contemn even the r'? "
Mic 5: 1 smite the judge of Israel with a r' "
6: 9 hear ye the r', and who hath 4294
7:14 Feed thy people with thy r', the 7626
1Co 4:21 shall I come unto you with a r', or 4464
Heb 9: 4 Aaron's r' that budded, and the "
Re 2:27 shall rule them with a r' of iron; "
11: 1 was given me a reed like unto a r': "
12: 5 to rule all nations with a r' of iron: "
19:15 he shall rule them with a r' of iron: "

Rodanim See DODANIM.

rode
Ge 24:61 and they r' upon the camels, and 7392
J'g 10: 4 had thirty sons that r' on thirty ass "
12:14 that r' on threescore and ten ass "
1Sa 25:20 And it was so, as she r' on the ass, "
42 and arose, and r' upon an ass, "
30:17 young men, which r' upon camels, "
2Sa 18: 9 Absalom r' upon a mule, and the "
22:11 he r' upon a cherub, and did fly: "
1Ki 13:13 him the ass: and he r' thereon, "
18:45 And Ahab r', and went to Jezreel. "
2Ki 9:16 So Jehu r' in a chariot, and went to "
25 I and thou r' together after Ahab "
Ne 2:12 me, save the beast that I r' upon. "
Es 8:14 the posts that r' upon mules and "
Ps 18:10 he r' upon a cherub, and did fly: "

rods
Ge 30:37 Jacob took him r' of green poplar, 4731
37 white appear which was in the r'. "
38 he set the r' which he had pilled "
39 the flocks conceived before the r', "
41 Jacob laid the r' before the eyes of "
41 they might conceive among the r'. "
Ex 7:12 Aaron's rod swallowed up their r'. 4294
Nu 17: 2 house of their fathers, twelve r': "
6 fathers' houses, even twelve r': "
6 rod of Aaron was among their r'. "
7 laid up the r' before the Lord in "
9 Moses brought out all the r' from "
Eze 19:11 strong r' for the sceptres of them "
12 her strong r' were broken and "
2Co 11:25 Thrice was I beaten with r', once 4463

roe See also ROEBUCK; ROES.
2Sa 2:18 was as light of foot as a wild r'. 6643
Pr 5:19 the loving hind and pleasant r'; *3280
6: 5 Deliver thyself as a r' from the 6643
Ca 2: 9 beloved is like a r' or a young hart "
17 be thou like a r' or a young hart "
8:14 thou like to a r' or to a young hart "
Isa 13:14 And it shall be as the chased r', "

roebuck See also ROEBUCKS.
De 12:15 as of the r', and as of the hart. *6643
22 as the r' and the hart is eaten, so* "
14: 5 The hart, and the r', and the "
15:22 it alike, as the r', and as the hart.* "

roebucks
1Ki 4:23 harts, and r', and fallowdeer, *6643

roes
1Ch 12: 8 were as swift as the r' upon the 6643
Ca 2: 7 by the r', and by the hinds of the "
3: 5 by the r', and by the hinds of the "
4: 5 like two young r' that are twins, *6646
7: 3 like two young r' that are twins. * "

Rogel See EN-ROGEL.

Rogelim (*ro'-ghel-im*)
2Sa 17:27 and Barzillai the Gileadite of R', 7274
19:31 the Gileadite came down from R', "

Rohgah (*ro'-gah*)
1Ch 7:34 the sons of Shamer; Ahi, and R', 7303

Roi See LAHAI-ROI.

roll See also ROLLED; ROLLETH; ROLLING; ROLLS.
Ge 29: 8 and till they r' the stone from the 1556
Jos 10:18 R' great stones upon the mouth of "
1Sa 14:33 r' a great stone unto me this day. "
Ezr 6: 2 in the province of the Medes, a r', 4040
Isa 8: 1 Take thee a great r', and write in *1549
Jer 36: 2 Take thee a r' of a book, and write 4039
4 unto him, upon a r' of a book, "
6 and read in the r', which thou hast "
14 Take in thine hand the r' wherein "
14 Baruch...took the r' in his hand, "
20 they laid up the r' in the chamber "
21 king sent Jehudi to fetch the r': "
23 until all the r' was consumed in "
25 king that he would not burn the r': "
27 that the king had burned the r', "
28 Take thee again another r', and "
28 words that were in the first r', "
29 Thou hast burned this r', saying, "
32 Then took Jeremiah another r', "
51:25 and r' thee down from the rocks, 1556
Eze 2: 9 and, lo, a r' of a book was therein; 4040
3: 1 eat this r', and go speak unto the "
2 and he caused me to eat that r'. "
3 fill thy bowels with this r' that I "

Mic 1:10 of Aphrah r' thyself in the dust. *6428
Zec 5: 1 and looked, and behold a flying r'. 4040
2 I see a flying r'; the length thereof "
M'r 16: 3 Who shall r' us away the stone 617

rolled
Ge 29: 3 they r' the stone from the well's 1556
10 r' the stone from the well's mouth, "
Jos 5: 9 I r' away the reproach of Egypt "
Job 30:14 they r' themselves upon me. * "
Isa 9: 5 noise, and garments r' in blood; "
34: 4 the heavens shall be r' together as "
M't 27:60 and he r' a great stone to the door 4351
28: 2 came and r' back the stone from 617
M'r 15:46 and r' a stone unto the door of the 4351
16: 4 saw that the stone was r' away: 617
Lu 24: 2 stone r' away from the sepulchre. "
Re 6:14 as a scroll when it is r' together; 1507

roller
Eze 30:21 to put a r' to bind it, to make it 2848

rolleth
Pr 26:27 he that r' a stone, it will return 1556

rolling
Isa 17:13 a r' thing before the whirlwind. *1534

rolls
Ezr 6: 1 was made in the house of the r', 5609

Romamti-ezer (*romam''-ti-e'-zur*)
1Ch 25: 4 Giddalti, and R', Joshbekashah, 7320
31 The four and twentieth to R', he, "

Roman (*ro'-mun*) See also ROMANS.
Ac 22:25 you to scourge a man that is a R', 4514
26 thou doest: for this man is a R'. "
27 Tell me, art thou a R'? He said, "
29 after he knew that he was a R', and "
23:27 having understood that he was a R'. "

Romans (*ro'-muns*)
Joh 11:48 R' shall come and take away both 4514
Ac 16:21 neither to observe, being R'. "
37 us openly uncondemned, being R', "
38 when they heard that they were R'. "
25:16 not the manner of the R' to deliver "
28:17 Jerusalem into the hands of the R'. "
Ro *subscr.* Written to the R' from * "

Rome (*rome*) See also ROMAN.
Ac 2:10 and strangers of R', Jews and 4516
18: 2 all Jews to depart from R':) and "
19:21 have been there, I must also see R'. "
23:11 must thou bear witness also at R'. "
28:14 days: and so we went toward R'. "
16 And when we came to R', the "
Ro 1: 7 To all that be in R', beloved of God, "
15 gospel to you that are at R' also. "
Ga *subscr.* the Galatians written from R'. * "
Eph *subscr.* from R' unto the Ephesians * "
Ph'p *subscr.* to the Philippians from R' by * "
Col *subscr.* Written from R' to the * "
2Ti 1:17 when he was in R', he sought me "
subscr. was written from R', when * "
Ph'm *subscr.* Written from R' to Philemon,* "

roof See also ROOFS.
Ge 19: 8 they under the shadow of my r'. 6982
De 22: 8 shalt make a battlement for thy r', 1406
Jos 2: 6 them up to the r' of the house, and "
6 she had laid in order upon the r'. "
8 she came up unto them upon the r'; "
J'g 16:27 upon the r' about three thousand "
2Sa 11: 2 upon the r' of the king's house: "
2 and from the r' he saw a woman "
18:24 the watchman went up to the r' "
Ne 8:16 every one upon the r' of his house, "
Job 29:10 cleaved to the r' of their mouth. 2441
Ps 137: 6 cleave to the r' of my mouth; if I "
Ca 7: 9 r' of thy mouth like the best wine* "
La 4: 4 cleaveth to the r' of his mouth for "
Eze 3:26 cleave to the r' of thy mouth, "
40:13 r' of one little chamber to the r' of 1406
M't 8: 8 thou shouldest come under my r': 4721
M'r 2: 4 uncovered the r' where he was: "
Lu 7: 6 thou shouldest enter under my r': "

roofs
Jer 19:13 upon whose r' they have burned 1406
32:29 upon whose r' they have offered "

room See also ROOMS.
Ge 24:23 is there r' in thy father's house 4725
25 straw...enough, and r' to lodge in. "
31 the house, and r' for the camels. "
26:22 now the Lord hath made r' for us, 7337
2Sa 19:13 me continually in the r' of Joab. 8478
1Ki 2:35 of Jehoiada in his r' over the host: "
35 the king put in the r' of Abiathar. "
5: 1 him king in the r' of his father: "
5 I will set upon thy throne in thy r', "
8:20 I am risen up in the r' of David my "
2Ki 15:25 he killed him, and reigned in his r'.* "
23:34 king in the r' of Josiah his father, "
2Ch 26: 1 king in the r' of his father Amaziah. "
Ps 31: 8 thou hast set my feet in a large r'. 4800
80: 9 Thou preparedst r' before it, and "
Pr 18:16 A man's gift maketh r' for him, 7337
Mal 3:10 shall not be r' enough to receive it. "
M't 2:22 Judæa in the r' of his father Herod, 473
M'r 2: 2 there was no r' to receive them, 5562
14:15 shew you a large upper r' furnished 508
Lu 2: 7 there was no r' for them in the 5117
12:17 have no r' where to bestow my fruits?* "
14: 8 sit not down in the highest r'; lest 4411
9 with shame to take the lowest r'. *5117
10 go sit down in the lowest r'; that * "
22 commanded, and yet there is r'. "
22:12 shew you a large upper r' furnished: "
Ac 1:13 in, they went up into an upper r', *5253
24:27 Porcius Festus came into Felix' r': *1240
1Co 14:16 occupieth the r' of the unlearned *5117

rooms
Ge 6:14 r· shalt thou make in the ark, and 7064
1Ki 20:24 place, and put captains in their r·:*8478
1Ch 4:41 unto this day, and dwelt in their r·:*"
M't 23: 6 love the uppermost r· at feasts, *4411
M'r 12:39 and the uppermost r· at feasts: * "
Lu 14: 7 how they chose out the chief r·; * "
20:46 synagogues,...the chief r· at feasts;*"

root See also ROOTED; ROOTS.
De 29:18 among you a r· that beareth gall 8328
J'g 5:14 there a r· of them against Amalek; "
1Ki 14:15 r· up Israel out of this good land, 5428
2Ki 19:30 of Judah shall yet again take r· 8328
Job 5: 3 I have seen the foolish taking r·: 8327
14: 8 the r· thereof wax old in the earth,8328
19:28 the r· of the matter is found in me? "
29:19 r· was spread out by the waters, "
31:12 and would r· out all mine increase.8327
Ps 52: 5 and r· thee out of the land of the "
80: 9 didst cause it to take deep r·, and it"
Pr 12: 3 r· of the righteous shall not be 8328
12 r· of the righteous yieldeth fruit. "
Isa 5:24 so their r· shall be as rottenness, "
11:10 that day there shall be a r· of Jesse, "
14:29 out of the serpent's r· shall come "
30 I will kill thy r· with famine, and he"
27: 6 that come of Jacob to take r·: 8327
37:31 house of Judah shall again take r·8328
40:24 their stock shall not take r· in the 8327
53: 2 and as a r· out of a dry ground: 8328
Jer 1:10 to r· out, and to pull down, and to*5428
12: 2 yea, they have taken r·: they grow,8327
Eze 31: 7 for his r· was by great waters. 8328
Ho 9:16 their r· is dried up, they shall bear "
Mal 4: 1 leave them neither r· nor branch. "
M't 3:10 ax is laid unto the r· of the trees: 4491
13: 6 and because they had no r·, they "
21 Yet hath he not r· in himself, but "
29 ye r· up also the wheat with them. 1610
M'r 4: 6 because it had no r·, it withered 4491
17 And have no r· in themselves, and "
Lu 3: 9 axe is laid unto the r· of the trees: "
8:13 these have no r·, which for a while "
17: 6 Be thou plucked up by the r·, and *1610
Ro 11:16 and if the r· be holy, so are the 4491
17 of the r· and fatness of the olive "
18 bearest not the r·, but the r· thee. "
15:12 There shall be a r· of Jesse, and he "
1Ti 6:10 love of money is the r· of all evil: "
Heb12:15 lest any r· of bitterness springing "
Re 5: 5 the tribe of Juda, the R· of David, "
22:16 the r· and the offspring of David, "

rooted
De 29:28 the Lord r· them out of their land 5428
Job 18:14 His confidence shall be r· out of his5423
31: 8 eat; yea, let my offspring be r· out.8327
Pr 2:22 transgressors shall be r· out of it. 5255
Zep 2: 4 day, and Ekron shall be r· up. 6131
M't 15:13 hath not planted, shall be r· up. 1610
Eph 3:17 ye, being r· and grounded in love, 4492
Col 2: 7 R· and built up in him, and "

roots
2Ch 7:20 will I pluck them up by the r· out 5428
Job 8:17 His r· are wrapped about the heap,8328
18:16 His r· shall be dried up beneath, "
28: 9 overturneth the mountains by the r·. "
30: 4 and juniper r· for their meat. "
Isa 11: 1 a Branch shall grow out of his r·: "
Jer 17: 8 spreadeth out her r· by the river, "
Eze 17: 6 and the r· thereof were under him: "
7 vine did bend her r· toward him, "
9 shall he not pull up the r· thereof, "
9 to pluck it up by the r· thereof. "
Da 4:15 the stump of his r· in the earth, 8330
23 leave the stump of the r· thereof in "
26 to leave the stump of the tree r·; "
7: 8 first horns plucked up by the r·: 6132
11: 7 out of a branch of her r· shall one 8328
Ho 14: 5 and cast forth his r· as Lebanon. "
Am 2: 9 from above, and his r· from beneath."
M'r 11:20 the fig tree dried up from the r·. 4491
Jude 12 twice dead, plucked up by the r·; 1610

rope See also ROPES.
Isa 5:18 and sin as it were with a cart r·: 5688

ropes
J'g 16:11 If they bind me fast with new r· 5688
12 Delilah therefore took new r·, and "
2Sa 17:13 shall all Israel bring r· to that city,2256
1Ki 20:31 on our loins, and r· upon our heads."
32 loins, and put r· on their heads, "
Ac 27:32 soldiers cut off the r· of the boat, 4979

rose See also AROSE.
Ge 4: 8 r· up against Abel his brother, 6965
18:16 And the men r· up from thence, "
19: 1 Lot seeing them r· up to meet them;"
20: 8 Abimelech r· early in the morning,7925
21:14 Abraham r· up early in the morning, "
32 then Abimelech r· up, and Phichol6965
22: 3 And Abraham r· up early in the 7925
3 and r· up, and went unto the place6965
19 they r· up and went together to "
24:54 and they r· up in the morning, and "
25:34 drink, and r· up, and went his way: "
26:31 they r· up betimes in the morning,7925
28:18 Jacob r· up early in the morning, "
31:17 Then Jacob r· up, and set his sons6965
21 he r· up, and passed over the river, "
55 early in the morning Laban r· up, 7925
32:22 he r· up that night, and took his 6965
31 over Penuel the sun r· upon him, 2224
37:35 daughters r· up to comfort him; 6965
43:15 and r· up, and went down to Egypt, "
46: 5 And Jacob r· up from Beer-sheba: "
Ex 10:23 neither r· any from his place for 6965
12:30 And Pharaoh r· up in the night, he, "
15: 7 hast overthrown them that r· up * "
24: 4 and r· up early in the morning, 7925
13 And Moses r· up, and his minister 6965
32: 6 And they r· up early on the morrow,7925
6 eat and to drink, and r· up to play.6965
33: 8 that all the people r· up, and stood "
10 the people r· up and worshipped, "
34: 4 Moses r· up early in the morning, 7925
Nu 14:40 And they r· up early in the morning, "
16: 2 And they r· up before Moses, with6965
25 Moses r· up and went unto Dathan "
22:13 And Balaam r· up in the morning, "
14 And the princes of Moab r· up, and "
21 And Balaam r· up in the morning, "
24:25 And Balaam r· up, and went and "
25: 7 r· up from among the congregation."
De 33: 2 and r· up from Seir unto them; 2224
Jos 3: 1 Joshua r· early in the morning; 7925
16 the waters...r· up upon an heap 6965
6:12 Joshua r· early in the morning, 7925
15 they r· early about the dawning of "
7:16 Joshua r· up early in the morning, "
8:10 Joshua r· up early in the morning, "
14 that they hasted and r· up early, "
J'g 6:21 and there r· up fire out of the rock,*5927
38 for he r· up early on the morrow, 7925
7: 1 Gideon,...r· up early, and pitched "
9:34 And Abimelech r· up, and all the 6965
35 and Abimelech r· up, and the people"
43 he r· up against them, and smote "
19: 5 morning, that he r· up to depart: "
7, 9 when the man r· up to depart, "
10 but he r· up and departed, and came"
27 And her lord r· up in the morning, "
28 the man r· up, and gat him unto his"
20: 5 the men of Gibeah r· against me, "
19 the children of Israel r· up in the "
33 men of Israel r· up out of their place,"
21: 4 the people r· early, and built there 7925
Ru 3:14 she r· up before one could know 6965
1Sa 1: 9 Hannah r· up after they had eaten "
19 they r· up in the morning early, 7925
15:12 when Samuel r· early to meet Saul "
16:13 Samuel r· up, and went to Ramah.6965
17:20 David r· up early in the morning, 7925
24: 7 But Saul r· up out of the cave, and6965
28:25 Then they r· up, and went away "
29:11 So David...r· up early to depart 7925
2Sa 15: 2 And Absalom r· up early, and stood"
18:31 of all them that r· up against thee.6965
22:40 them that r· up...hast thou subdued"
49 above them that r· up against me:*"
1Ki 1:49 and r· up, and went every man his "
2:19 And the king r· up to meet her, and"
3:21 I r· in the morning to give my child"
21:16 r· up to go down to the vineyard "
2Ki 3:22 they r· up early in the morning, 7925
24 r· up and smote the Moabites, so 6965
7: 5 And they r· up in the twilight, to "
8:21 r· by night, and smote the Edomites"
2Ch 20:20 And they r· early in the morning, 7925
21: 9 r· up...and smote the Edomites 6965
26:19 leprosy even r· up in his forehead*2224
28:15 men...expressed by name r· up, 6965
29:20 Then Hezekiah the king r· early, *7925
Ezr 1: 5 Then r· up the chief of the fathers 6965
5: 2 Then r· up Zerubbabel the son of "
10: 6 Ezra r· up from before the house "
Ne 3: 1 Then Eliashib the high priest r· up "
4:14 And I looked, and r· up, and said "
Job 1: 5 and r· up early in the morning, 7925
Ps 18:39 subdued under me those that r· up6965
124: 2 our side, when men r· up against us:"
Ca 2: 1 I am the r· of Sharon, and the lily 2261
5: 5 I r· up to open to my beloved; 6965
Isa 35: 1 rejoice, and blossom as the r·. 2261
Jer 26:17 Then r· up certain of the elders 6965
La 3:62 lips of those that r· up against me, "
Da 3:24 was astonied, and r· up in haste, "
8:27 I r· up, and did the king's business;"
Jon 1: 3 Jonah r· up to flee unto Tarshish "
4: 7 when the morning r· the next day,5927
Zep 3: 7 they r· early, and corrupted all 7925
M'r 10:50 garment, r·, and came to Jesus. * 450
Lu 4:29 r· up, and thrust him out of the city, "
5:25 immediately he r· up before them, "
28 he left all, r· up, and followed him. "
16:31 though one r· from the dead. * "
22:45 And when he r· up from prayer, and "
24:33 And they r· up the same hour, and "
Joh 11:31 that she r· up hastily and went out, "
Ac 5:17 Then the high priest r· up, and all "
36 For before these days r· up Theudas,"
37 After this man r· up Judas of "
10:41 with him after he r· from the dead. "
14:20 him, he r· up, and came into the city:"
15: 5 r· up certain of the sect of the 1817
7 Peter r· up, and said unto them, 450
16:22 r· up together against them: and 4911
26:30 the king r· up, and the governor, 450
Ro 14: 9 this end Christ both died, and r·, * "
1Co 10: 7 to eat and drink, and r· up to play. "
15: 4 and that he r· again the third day*1453
12 preached that he r· from the dead,* "
2Co 5:15 which died for them, and r· again. "
1Th 4:14 that Jesus died and r· again, even 450
Re 19: 3 her smoke r· up for ever and ever.* 305

Rosh (*rosh*)
Ge 46:21 and R·, Muppim, and Huppim, 7220

rot See also ROTTEN.
Nu 5:21 doth make thy thigh to r·, and thy *5307
22 belly to swell, and thy thigh to r·:* "
27 shall swell, and her thigh shall r·:* "
Pr 10: 7 the name of the wicked shall r·. 7537
Isa 40:20 chooseth a tree that will not r·; he "

rotten
Job 13:28 he, as a r· thing, consumeth, as a 7538
41:27 iron as straw,...brass as r· wood. 7539
Jer 38:11 old cast clouts and old r· rags, 4418
12 old cast clouts and r· rags under "
Joe 1:17 The seed is r· under their clods, *5685

rottenness
Pr 12: 4 ashamed is as r· in his bones. 7538
14:30 flesh: but envy the r· of the bones. "
Isa 5:24 so their root shall be as r·, and 4716
Ho 5:12 and to the house of Judah as r·. 7538
Hab 3:16 r· entered into my bones, and I "

rough
De 21: 4 down the heifer unto a r· valley, * 386
Isa 27: 8 he stayeth his r· wind in the day 7186
40: 4 straight, and the r· places plain: 7406
Jer 51:27 to come up as the r· caterpillers. 5569
Da 8:21 the r· goat is the king of Grecia: 8163
Zec 13: 4 wear a r· garment to deceive: *8181
Lu 3: 5 the r· ways shall be made smooth;5138

roughly
Ge 42: 7 them, and spake r· unto them; 7186
30 spake r· to us, and took us for spies"
1Sa 20:10 what if thy father answer thee r·? "
1Ki 12:13 the king answered the people r·, "
2Ch 10:13 And the king answered them r·; "
Pr 18:23 but the rich answereth r·. 5794

round
Ge 19: 4 compassed the house r·, both old 5921
23:17 that were in all the borders r· 5439
35: 5 the cities that were r· about them, "
37: 7 your sheaves stood r· about, and 5437
41:48 which was r· about every city, 5439
Ex 7:24 Egyptians digged r· about the river"
16:13 the dew lay r· about the host. "
14 there lay a small r· thing, as 2636
19:12 bounds unto the people r· about, 5439
25:11 upon it a crown of gold r· about. "
24 thereto a crown of gold r· about. "
25 border of an hand breadth r· about,"
25 crown to the border thereof r· "
27:17 All the pillars r· about the court "
28:32 woven work r· about the hole of it, "
33 scarlet, r· about the hem thereof; "
33 of gold between them r· about: "
34 upon the hem of the robe r· about. "
29:16 sprinkle it r· about upon the altar. "
20 the blood upon the altar r· about. "
30: 3 the sides thereof r· about, and the "
3 unto it a crown of gold r· about. "
37: 2 made a crown of gold to it r· about."
11 thereunto a crown of gold r· about. "
12 border of an handbreadth r· about;"
12 for the border thereof r· about. "
26 the sides thereof r· about, and the "
26 unto it a crown of gold r· about. "
38:16 the hangings of the court r· about "
20 and of the court r· about, were of "
31 the sockets of the court r· about, "
31 all the pins of the court r· about. "
39:23 with a band r· about the hole, that "
25 of the robe, r· about between the "
26 r· about the hem of the robe to "
40: 8 thou shalt set up the court r· about,"
33 the court r· about the tabernacle "
Le 1: 5 and sprinkle the blood r· about "
11 shall sprinkle his blood r· about "
3: 2 the blood upon the altar r· about. "
8 the blood thereof r· about upon the"
13 the blood thereof upon the altar r· "
7: 2 he sprinkle r· about upon the altar. "
8:15 upon the horns of the altar r· about"
19, 24 the blood upon the altar r· about."
9:12 sprinkled r· about upon the altar. "
18 sprinkled upon the altar r· about. "
14:41 house to be scraped within r· about."
16:18 upon the horns of the altar r· about."
19:27 not r· the corners of your heads, 5362
25:31 which have no wall r· about them 5439
44 the heathen that are r· about you; "
Nu 1:50 encamp r· about the tabernacle. "
53 the Levites shall pitch r· about the "
3:26 and by the altar r· about, and the "
37 the pillars of the court r· about, "
4:26 which is...by the altar r· about, "
32 the pillars of the court r· about, "
11:24 set them r· about the tabernacle. "
31 the other side, r· about the camp, "
32 for themselves r· about the camp. "
16:34 all Israel that were r· about them "
22: 4 lick up all that are r· about us, as "
32:33 the cities of the country r· about. "
34:12 with the coasts thereof r· about. "
35: 2 suburbs for the cities r· about "
4 a thousand cubits r· about. "
De 6:14 the people which are r· about you; "
12:10 from all your enemies r· about, "
13: 7 the people which are r· about you, "
21: 2 which are r· about him that is slain:"
25:19 from all thine enemies r· about, "
Jos 6: 3 war, and go r· about the city once.*5362
7: 9 and shall environ us r·, and cut 5921
15:12 of the children of Judah r· about 5439
18:20 by the coasts thereof r· about, "
19: 8 the villages...r· about these cities "
21:11 with the suburbs thereof r· about it."
42 with their suburbs r· about them: "
44 the Lord gave them rest r· about, "
23: 1 from all their enemies r· about, "
J'g 2:12 the people that were r· about them,"
14 the hands of their enemies r· about,"
7:21 man in his place r· about the camp:"

J'g 19:22 of Belial, beset the house r· about, 5437
20: 5 beset the house r· about upon me "
29 set liers in wait r· about Gibeah. 5439
43 inclosed the Benjamites r· about, 3803
1Sa 14:21 camp from the country r· about, 5439
23:26 compassed David and his men r· about
26: 5 the people pitched r· about him. 5439
7 and the people lay r· about him. "
31: 9 the land of the Philistines r· about, "
2Sa 5: 9 And David built r· about from Millo "
7: 1 rest r· about from all his enemies; "
22:12 darkness pavilions r· about him, "
1Ki 3: 1 and the wall of Jerusalem r· about. "
4:24 had peace on all sides r· about him. "
31 fame was in all nations r· about. "
6: 5 house he built chambers r· about, "
5 the walls of the house r· about, "
5 and he made chambers r· about: "
6 he made narrowed rests r· about, "
29 walls of the house r· about with 4524
7:12 the great court r· about was with 5439
18 and two rows r· about upon the one "
20 hundred in rows r· about upon the "
23 it was r· all about, and his 5696
23 thirty cubits did compass it r· 5439
24 under the brim of it r· about there "
24 cubit, compassing the sea r· about: "
31 the mouth thereof was r· after the 5696
31 their borders, foursquare, not r·. "
35 a r· compass of half a cubit high: "
36 every one, and additions r· about. 5439
10:19 top of the throne was r· behind: 5696
18:35 the water ran r· about the altar; 5439
2Ki 6:17 and chariots of fire r· about Elisha. "
11: 8 ye shall compass the king r· about, "
11 in his hand, r· about the king, "
17:15 heathen that were r· about them, "
23: 5 in the places r· about Jerusalem; 4524
25: 1 they built forts against it r· about. 5439
4 were against the city r· about:) and "
10 the walls of Jerusalem r· about. "
17 upon the chapiter r· about, all of "
1Ch 4:33 their villages that were r· about "
6:55 and the suburbs thereof r· about it. "
9:27 lodged r· about the house of God, "
10: 9 the land of the Philistines r· about, "
11: 8 the city r· about, even from Millo "
22: 9 rest from all his enemies r· about: "
28:12 of all the chambers r· about, of the "
2Ch 4: 2 from brim to brim, r· in compass, 5696
2 of thirty cubits did compass it r· 5439
3 which did compass it r· about: ten "
3 cubit, compassing the sea r· about. "
14:14 smote all the cities r· about Gerar; "
15:15 the Lord gave them rest r· about. "
17:10 lands that were r· about Judah, "
20:30 for his God gave him rest r· about. "
23: 7 shall compass the king r· about, "
10 the temple, by the king r· about. "
34: 6 with their mattocks r· about. "
Ne 12:28 plain country r· about Jerusalem, "
29 them villages r· about Jerusalem. "
Job 10: 8 fashioned me together r· about; "
16:13 His archers compass me r· about, 5437
19:12 encamp r· about my tabernacle. 5439
22:10 snares are r· about thee, and "
37:12 turned r· about by his counsels: 4524
41:14 his teeth are terrible r· about. 5439
Ps 3: 6 themselves against me r· about. "
18:11 his pavilion r· about him were "
22:12 bulls of Bashan have beset me r·. 3803
27: 6 above mine enemies r· about me: 5439
34: 7 encampeth r· about them that fear "
44:13 to them that are r· about us. "
48:12 about Zion, and go r· about her: 5362
50: 3 be very tempestuous r· about him. 5439
59: 6, 14 dog, and go r· about the city. 5437
76:11 be r· about him bring presents 5439
78:28 camp, r· about their habitations. "
79: 3 like water r· about Jerusalem; "
4 to them that are r· about us. "
88:17 r· about me daily like water; 5437
89: 8 to thy faithfulness r· about thee? 5439
97: 2 and darkness are r· about him: "
3 burneth up his enemies r· about. "
125: 2 mountains are r· about Jerusalem, "
2 so the Lord is r· about his people "
128: 3 like olive plants r· about thy table. "
Ca 7: 2 navel is like a r· goblet, which 5469
Isa 3:18 and their r· tires like the moon, *7720
15: 8 gone r· about the borders of Moab; 5362
29: 3 I will camp against thee r· about, 1754
42:25 it hath set him on fire r· about, 5439
49:18 Lift up thine eyes r· about, and "
60: 4 Lift up thine eyes r· about, and see: "
Jer 1:15 against all the walls thereof r· about, "
4:17 are they against her r· about; "
6: 3 their tents against her r· about; "
12: 9 the birds r· about are against her; "
21:14 shall devour all things r· about it. "
25: 9 against all these nations r· about, "
46: 5 for fear was r· about, saith the *
14 sword shall devour r· about thee. "
50:14 in array against Babylon r· about: "
15 Shout against her r· about: she "
29 the bow, camp against it r· about; "
32 it shall devour all r· about him. "
51: 2 they shall be against her r· about. "
52: 4 and built forts against it r· about. "
7 Chaldeans were by the city r· about:) "
14 all the walls of Jerusalem r· about. "
22 upon the chapiters r· about, all "
23 network were an hundred r· about. "
La 1:17 adversaries should be r· about him: "
2: 3 fire, which devoureth r· about. "
22 a solemn day my terrors r· about,* "

Eze 1:18 full of eyes r· about them four. 5439
27 the appearance of fire r· about "
27 and it had brightness r· about. "
28 of the brightness r· about. "
4: 2 battering rams against it r· about. "
5: 5 and countries that are r· about her. "
6 the countries that are r· about her: "
7 the nations that are r· about you, "
7 the nations that are r· about you; "
12 fall by the sword r· about thee; "
14, 15 nations that are r· about thee, "
6: 5 your bones r· about your altars. "
13 their idols r· about their altars, "
8:10 pourtrayed upon the wall r· about. "
10:12 wheels, were full of eyes r· about, "
11:12 the heathen that are r· about you. "
16:37 gather them r· about against thee,* "
57 Syria, and all that are r· about her, "
57 which despise thee r· about. "
23:24 and shield and helmet r· about: "
27:11 army were upon thy walls r· about, "
11 shields upon thy walls r· about; "
28:24 thorn of all that are r· about them, "
26 that despise them r· about them; "
31: 4 rivers running r· about his plants, "
32:23 her company is r· about her grave: "
24 her multitude r· about her grave, "
25, 26 her graves are r· about him: "
34:26 and the places r· about my hill a "
36: 4 the residue...that are r· about; "
36 the heathen that are left r· about "
37: 2 me to pass by them r· about: and, "
40: 5 the outside of the house r· about, "
14 post of the court r· about the gate. "
16 posts within the gate r· about, "
16 windows were r· about inward: "
17 pavement...for the court r· about: "
25 and in the arches thereof r· about, "
29 and in the arches thereof r· about: "
30 the arches r· about were five and "
33 and in the arches thereof r· about: "
36 and the windows to it r· about: "
43 an hand broad, fastened r· about: "
41: 5 r· about the house on every side. "
6 for the side chambers r· about, "
7 still upward r· about the house: "
8 the height of the house r· about: "
10 twenty cubits r· about the house "
11 was left was five cubits r· about. "
12 was five cubits thick r· about, and "
16 galleries r· about on their three "
16 door, cieled with wood r· about, "
17 by all the wall r· about within and "
19 through all the house r· about. "
42:15 the east, and measured it r· about. "
16, 17 the measuring reed r· about. "
20 it had a wall r· about, five hundred "
43:12 the whole limit thereof r· about "
13 by the edge thereof r· about shall "
20 and upon the border r· about: "
45: 1 in all the borders thereof r· about. "
2 in breadth, square r· about; and "
2 and fifty cubits r· about for the "
46:23 a row of building r· about in them, "
23 r· about them four, and it was "
23 places under the rows r· about. "
48:35 It was r· about eighteen thousand "
Joe 3:11 gather yourselves together r· about: "
12 to judge all the heathen r· about. "
Am 3:11 shall be even r· about the land; "
Jon 2: 5 the depth closed me r· about, the 5437
Na 3: 8 that had the waters r· about it, 5439
Zec 2: 5 be unto her a wall of fire r· about, "
7: 7 and the cities thereof r· about her, "
12: 2 unto all the people r· about, when "
6 shall devour all the people r· about, "
14:14 wealth of all the heathen r· about "
M't 3: 5 all the region r· about Jordan, 4066
14:35 out into all that country r· about, "
21:33 vineyard, and hedged it r· about, *
M'r 1:28 all the region r· about Galilee. 4066
3: 5 had looked r· about on them with 4017
34 he looked r· about on them which 2943
5:32 he looked r· about to see her that 4017
6: 6 And he went r· about the villages, 2943
36 may go into the country r· about, "
55 that whole region r· about, and 4066
9: 8 when they had looked r· about, 4017
10:23 Jesus looked r· about, and saith "
11:11 looked r· about upon all things, "
Lu 1:65 on all that dwelt r· about them: 4039
2: 9 glory of the Lord shone r· about 4034
4:14 through all the region r· about. 4066
37 every place of the country r· about. "
6:10 looking r· about upon them all, he "
7:17 throughout all the region r· about. 4066
8:37 country of the Gadarenes r· about "
9:12 the towns and country r· about, 2943
19:43 compass thee r·, and keep thee in 4033
Joh 10:24 Then came the Jews r· about him, 2944
Ac 5:16 the cities r· about unto Jerusalem, 4038
9: 3 there shined r· about him a light 4015
14: 6 the region that lieth r· about: 4066
20 the disciples stood r· about him, 2944
22: 6 heaven a great light r· about me. 4015
25: 7 from Jerusalem stood r· about, 4026
26:13 of the sun, shining r· about me 4034
Ro 15:19 and r· about unto Illyricum, I 2943
Heb 9: 4 overlaid r· about with gold, 3840
Re 4: 3 was a rainbow r· about the throne, 2943
4 r· about the throne were four and "
6 and r· about the throne, were four "
5:11 many angels r· about the throne "
7:11 angels stood r· about the throne, "

rouse
Ge 49: 9 an old lion; who shall r· him up? 6965

rovers
1Ch 12:21 David against the band of the r·:

row See also ROWED; ROWING; ROWS.
Ex 28:17 the first r· shall be a sardius, a 2905
17 carbuncle: this shall be the first r·. "
18 the second r· shall be an emerald, a "
19 the third r· a ligure, an agate, and "
20 the fourth r· a beryl, and an onyx, "
39:10 the first r· was a sardius, a topaz, "
10 a carbuncle: this was the first r·. "
11 second r·, an emerald, a sapphire, "
12 the third r·, a ligure, an agate, and "
13 the fourth r·, a beryl, an onyx, and "
Le 24: 6 set them in two rows, six on a r·, 4635
7 put pure frankincense upon each r·. "
1Ki 6:36 stone, and a r· of cedar beams. *2905
7: 3 on forty five pillars, fifteen in a r·. "
12 stones, and a r· of cedar beams, "
Ezr 6: 4 stones, and a r· of good timber: *5073
Eze 46:23 there was a r· of building round 2905

rowed
Jon 1:13 men r· hard to bring it to the land; 2864
Joh 6:19 they had r· about five and twenty 1643

rowers
Eze 27:26 Thy r· have brought thee into 7751

rowing
M'r 6:48 And he saw them toiling in r·; for 1643

rows
Ex 28:17 of stones, even four r· of stones: 2905
39:10 And they set in it four r· of stones: "
Le 24: 6 And thou shalt set them in two r·, 4634
1Ki 6:36 court with three r· of hewed stone, *2905
7: 2 upon four r· of cedar pillars, with "
4 And there were windows in three r·, "
12 was with three r· of hewed stones, "
18 two r· round about upon the one "
20 were two hundred in r· round about "
24 the knops were cast in two r·, when "
42 r· of pomegranates for one network, "
2Ch 4: 3 Two r· of oxen were cast, when it "
13 r· of pomegranates on each wreath, "
Ezr 6: 4 With three r· of great stones, and *5073
Ca 1:10 are comely with r· of jewels, *8447
Eze 46:23 with boiling places under the r· 2918

royal
Ge 49:20 fat, and he shall yield r· dainties. 4428
Jos 10: 2 great city, as one of the r· cities, 4467
1Sa 27: 5 thy servant dwell in the r· city with "
2Sa 12:26 of Ammon, and took the r· city. 4410
1Ki 10:13 Solomon gave her of his r· bounty. 4428
2Ki 11: 1 arose and destroyed all the seed r·. 4467
25:25 the son of Elishama, the seed r·, 4410
1Ch 29:25 such r· majesty as had not been 4438
2Ch 22:10 the seed r· of the house of Judah. 4467
Es 1: 7 r· wine in abundance, according 4438
9 feast for the women in the r· house "
11 before the king with the crown r·, "
19 go a r· commandment from him, "
19 king give her r· estate unto another "
2:16 king Ahasuerus into his house r· "
17 he set the r· crown upon her head, "
5: 1 Esther put on her r· apparel, and "
1 upon his r· throne in the r· house, "
6: 8 Let the r· apparel be brought "
8 crown r· which is set upon his head: "
8:15 in r· apparel of blue and white, "
Isa 62: 3 r· diadem in the hand of thy God. 4410
Jer 41: 1 the son of Elishama, of the seed r·, "
43:10 spread his r· pavilion over them. 8237
Da 6: 7 together to establish a r· statute, 4430
Ac 12:21 Herod, arrayed in r· apparel, sat 937
Jas 2: 8 If ye fulfill the r· law according to "
1Pe 2: 9 a r· priesthood, an holy nation, a 934

rubbing
Lu 6: 1 did eat, r· them in their hands. 5597

rubbish
Ne 4: 2 heaps of the r· which are burned? 6083
10 is decayed, and there is much r·; "

rubies
Job 28:18 the price of wisdom is above r·. 6443
Pr 3:15 She is more precious than r·: and "
8:11 For wisdom is better than r·; and "
20:15 There is gold, and a multitude of r·: "
31:10 woman? for her price is far above r·. "
La 4: 7 were more ruddy in body than r·, "

rudder
Ac 27:40 the sea, and loosed the r· bands, *4079

ruddy
1Sa 16:12 Now he was r·, and withal of a 132
17:42 for he was but a youth, and r·, and "
Ca 5:10 My beloved is white and r·, the 122
La 4: 7 were more r· in body than rubies, 119

rude
2Co 11: 6 But though I be r· in speech, yet 2399

rudiments
Col 2: 8 after the r· of the world, and not 4747
20 be dead...from the r· of the world, "

rue
Lu 11:42 for ye tithe the mint and r· and all 4076

Rufus (*ru'-fus*)
M'r 15:21 the father of Alexander and R·, 4504
Ro 16:13 Salute R· chosen in the Lord, and "

Ruhamah (*ru-ha'-mah*) See also LO-RUHAMAH.
Ho 2: 1 Ammi; and to your sisters, R·. 7355

ruin See also RUINED; RUINS.
Ps 89:40 hast brought his strong holds to r·. 4288
Pr 24:22 who knoweth the r· of them both? *6365
26:28 and a flattering mouth worketh r·. 4072
Isa 3: 6 and let this r· be under thy hand: 4384

Isa 23:13 thereof; and he brought it to r'. 4654
25: 2 city an heap; of a defenced city a r': "
Eze 18:30 so iniquity shall not be your r'. 4383
27:27 midst of the seas in...day of thy r'.4658
31:13 Upon his r' shall all the fowls of the "
Lu 6:49 and the r' of that house was great.4485

ruined
Isa 3: 8 For Jerusalem is r', and Judah is 3782
Eze 36:35 and r' cities are become fenced, 2040
36 that I the Lord build the r' places, "

ruinous
2Ki 19:25 waste fenced cities into r' heaps. 5327
Isa 17: 1 a city, and it shall be a r' heap. 4654
37:26 waste defenced cities into r' heaps.5327

ruins
Eze 21:15 faint, and their r' be multiplied: *4383
Am 9:11 and I will raise up his r', and I will2034
Ac 15:16 I will build again the r' thereof, 2679

rule See also RULED; RULEST; RULETH; RULING; UNRULY.
Ge 1:16 the greater light to r' the day, 4475
16 and the lesser light to r' the night: "
18 to r' over the day and over the 4910
3:16 husband, and he shall r' over thee. "
4: 7 desire, and thou shalt r' over him. "
Le 25:43 shalt not r' over him with rigour; 7287
46 r' one over another with rigour; "
53 shall not r' with rigour over him in"
J'g 8:22 R' thou over us, both thou, and 4910
23 unto them, I will not r' over you, "
23 neither shall my son r' over you: "
23 you: the Lord shall r' over you. "
1Ki 9:23 which bare r' over the people that7287
22:31 captains that had r' over his chariots,*
2Ch 8:10 fifty, that bare r' over the people. 7287
Ne 5:15 servants bare r' over the people: 7980
Es 1:22 should bare r' in his own house, 8323
9: 1 Jews had r' over them that hated 7980
Ps 110: 2 r' thou in the midst of thine 7287
136: 8 The sun to r' by day: for his 4475
9 The moon and stars to r' by night: "
Pr 8:16 By me princes r', and nobles, 8323
12:24 hand of the diligent shall bare r':4910
17: 2 servant shall have r' over a son that"
19:10 a servant to have r' over princes. "
25:28 hath no r' over his own spirit is *4623
29: 2 but when the wicked beareth r', 4910
Ec 2:19 he have r' over all my labour 7980
Isa 3: 4 and babes shall r' over them. 4910
12 oppressors,...women r' over them. "
14: 2 they shall r' over their oppressors.7287
19: 4 a fierce king shall r' over them, 4910
28:14 r' this people which is in Jerusalem."
32: 1 and princes shall r' in judgment. 8323
40:10 and his arm shall r' for him: 4910
41: 2 him, and made him r' over kings?7287
52: 5 r' over them make them to howl, 4910
63:19 thou never barest r' over them; "
Jer 5:31 priests bare r' by their means; 7287
Eze 19:11 the sceptres of them that bare r', 4910
14 no strong rod to be a sceptre to r'. "
20:33 poured out, will I r' over you: *4427
29:15 shall no more r' over the nations. 7287
Da 2:39 shall bare r' over all the earth. 7981
4:26 known that the heavens do r'. 7990
11: 3 that shall r' with great dominion, 4910
39 shall cause them to r' over many, "
Joe 2:17 the heathen should r' over them: "
Zec 6:13 shall sit and r' upon his throne; "
M't 2: 6 that shall r' my people Israel. *4165
M'r 10:42 accounted to r' over the Gentiles 757
1Co 15:24 he shall have put down all r' and 746
2Co 10:13 the r' which God hath distributed*2583
15 you according to our r' abundantly,*"
Ga 6:16 many as walk according to this r', "
Ph'p 3:16 let us walk by the same r', let us "
Col 3:15 the peace of God r' in your hearts,1018
1Ti 3: 5 know not how to r' his own house,4291
5:17 the elders that r' well be counted "
Heb 13: 7 them which have the r' over you, 2233
17 Obey them that have...r' over you, "
24 Salute all...that have...r' over you, "
Re 2:27 shall r' them with a rod of iron; 4165
12: 5 r' all nations with a rod of iron: "
19:15 he shall r' them with a rod of iron: "

ruled
Ge 24: 2 house, that r' over all that he had,4910
41:40 word shall all my people be r': 5401
Jos 12: 2 and r' from Aroer, which is upon 4910
Ru 1: 1 in the days when the judges r', *8199
1Ki 5:16 which r' over the people that *7287
1Ch 26: 6 that r' throughout the house of 4474
Ezr 4:20 which have r' over all countries 7990
Ps 106:41 that hated them r' over them. 4910
Isa 14: 6 he that r' the nations in anger, is 7287
La 5: 8 Servants have r' over us: there is*4910
Eze 34: 4 and with cruelty have ye r' them. 7287
Da 5:21 God r' in the kingdom of men, *7990
11: 4 to his dominion which he r': 4910

ruler See also RULER'S; RULERS.
Ge 41:43 he made him r' over all the land of *
43:16 he said to the r' of his house, *834,5921
45: 8 a r' throughout all the land of 4910
Ex 22:28 nor curse the r' of thy people. 5387
Le 4:22 When a r' hath sinned, and done "
Nu 13: 2 a man, every one a r' among them.*"
J'g 9:30 Zebul the r' of the city heard the 8269
1Sa 25:30 appointed thee r' over Israel; *5057
2Sa 6:21 me r' over the people of the Lord,* "
7: 8 the sheep, to be r' over my people,*"
20:26 Jairite was a chief r' about David.*
1Ki 1:35 appointed him to be r' over Israel*5057
11:28 made him r' over all the charge *6485
2Ki 25:22 them he made Gedaliah...r', * "
1Ch 5: 2 and of him came the chief r'; but*5057
9:11 the r' of the house of God; "
20 Phinehas...was the r' over them in "
11: 2 shalt be r' over my people Israel. * "
17: 7 be r' over my people Israel: * "
26:24 Shebuel...was r' of the treasures. "
27: 4 his course was Mikloth also the r': "
16 r' of the Reubenites was Eliezer the"
28: 4 he hath chosen Judah to be the r';*"
2Ch 6: 5 to be a r' over my people Israel: * "
7:18 fail thee a man to be r' in Israel. 4910
11:22 to be r' among his brethren: for 5057
19:11 the r' of the house of Judah, for "
26:11 the scribe and Maaseiah the r', *7860
31:12 which Cononiah the Levite was r',5057
13 Azariah the r' of the house of God. "
Ne 3: 9 r' of the half part of Jerusalem. 8269
12 r' of the half part of Jerusalem, he "
14 the r' of part of Beth-haccerem; "
15 Col-hozeh, the r' of part of Mizpah;"
16 the r' of the half part of Beth-zur, "
17 the r' of the half part of Keilah. "
18 the r' of the half part of Keilah. "
19 son of Jeshua, the r' of Mizpah, "
7: 2 and Hananiah the r' of the palace, "
11:11 was the r' of the house of God. 5057
Ps 68:27 is little Benjamin with their r', 7287
105:20 the r' of the people, and let him 4910
21 house, and r' of all his substance: "
Pr 6: 7 having no guide, overseer, or r', "
23: 1 When thou sittest to eat with a r', "
28:15 is a wicked r' over the poor people."
29:12 If a r' hearken to lies, all his "
Ec 10: 4 the spirit of the r' rise up against "
5 which proceedeth from the r': 7989
Isa 3: 6 be thou our r', and let this ruin 7101
7 make me not a r' of the people. "
16: 1 Send ye the lamb to the r' of the 4910
Jer 51:46 violence in the land, r' against r'. "
Da 2:10 there is no king, lord, nor r', that 7990
38 hath made thee r' over them all. *7981
48 him r' over the whole province of* "
5: 7, 16 be the third r' in the kingdom. "
29 be the third r' in the kingdom. 7990
Mic 5: 2 unto me that is to be r' in Israel; 4910
Hab 1:14 things, that have no r' over them? "
M't 9:18 came a certain r', and worshipped 758
24:45 hath made r' over his household, *2525
47 make him r' over all his goods. * "
25:21, 23 make thee r' over many things:*"
M'r 5:35 from the r' of the synagogue's 752
36 saith unto the r' of the synagogue, "
38 house of the r' of the synagogue, "
Lu 8:41 and he was a r' of the synagogue: 758
49 the r' of the synagogue's house, 752
12:42 shall make r' over his household,*2525
44 make him r' over all that he hath.* "
13:14 the r' of the synagogue answered 752
18:18 And a certain r' asked him, saying,758
Joh 2: 9 When the r' of the feast had tasted755
3: 1 named Nicodemus, a r' of the Jews:758
Ac 7:27 made thee a r' and a judge over us? "
35 Who made thee a r' and a judge? "
35 God send to be a r' and a deliverer "
18: 8, 17 the chief r' of the synagogue, 752
23: 5 speak evil of the r' of thy people. 758

ruler's
Pr 29:26 Many seek the r' favour; but every4910
M't 9:23 when Jesus came into the r' house, 758

rulers
Ge 47: 6 then make them r' over my cattle. 8269
Ex 16:22 the r' of the congregation came 5387
18:21 r' of thousands, and r' of hundreds,8269
21 r' of fifties, and r' of tens: "
25 r' of thousands, r' of hundreds, "
25 r' of fifties, and r' of tens. "
34:31 the r' of the congregation returned5387
35:27 And the r' brought onyx stones, "
De 1:13 and I will make them r' over you.*7218
J'g 15:11 that the Philistines are r' over us? 4910
2Sa 8:18 and David's sons were chief r'. *
2Ki 10: 1 to Samaria, unto the r' of Jezreel, 8269
11: 4 and fetched the r' over hundreds,* "
19 And he took the r' over hundreds,* "
1Ch 21: 2 to Joab and to the r' of the people,* "
26:32 David made r' over...Reubenites, *6485
27:31 these were the r' of the substance 8269
29: 6 with the r' of the king's work, "
2Ch 29:20 and gathered the r' of the city, and*"
35: 8 Jethiel, r' of the house of God, 5057
Ezr 9: 2 r' hath been chief in this trespass.5461
10:14 r' of all the congregation stand, *8269
Ne 2:16 the r' knew not whither I went, 5461
16 nor to the nobles, nor to the r', nor "
4:14 said unto the nobles, and to the r', "
16 the r' were behind all the house of8269
19 unto the nobles, and to the r', and5461
5: 7 I rebuked the nobles, and the r', "
17 hundred and fifty of the Jews and r', "
7: 5 together the nobles, and the r', and"
11: 1 And the r' of the people dwelt *8269
12:40 I, and the half of the r' with me: 5461
13:11 Then contended I with the r', and "
Es 3:12 to the r' of every people of every 8269
8: 9 deputies and r' of the provinces * "
9: 3 And all the r' of the provinces, and*"
Ps 2: 2 and the r' take counsel together, 7336
Isa 1:10 word of the Lord, ye r' of Sodom; 7101
14: 5 wicked, and the sceptre of the r'. 4910
22: 3 All thy r' are fled together, they 7101
29:10 prophets and your r', the seers *7218
49: 7 abhorreth, to a servant of r', 4910
Jer 33:26 to be r' over the seed of Abraham, "
51:23 I break in pieces captains and r'. *5461
28 all the r' thereof, and all the land* "
57 and her r', and her mighty men: *5461
Eze 23: 6 clothed with blue, captains and r'. "
12 and r' clothed most gorgeously, "
23 captains and r', great lords and "
Da 3: 2 and all the r' of the provinces, to 7984
3 and all the r' of the provinces, were"
Ho 4:18 her r' with shame do love, Give ye.4043
M'r 5:22 one of the r' of the synagogue, 752
13: 9 before r' and kings for my sake, *2232
Lu 21:12 kings and r' for my name's sake. * "
23:13 priests and the r' and the people, 758
35 the r' also with them derided him, "
24:20 chief priests and our r' delivered "
Joh 7:26 Do the r' know indeed that this is "
48 of the r' or of the Pharisees believed"
12:42 among the chief r'...many believed "
Ac 3:17 ye did it, as did also your r'. "
4: 5 their r', and elders, and scribes, "
8 Ye r' of the people, and elders of "
26 and the r' were gathered together "
13:15 the r' of the synagogue sent unto 752
27 dwell at Jerusalem, and their r', 758
14: 5 also of the Jews with their r', to use "
16:19 into the marketplace unto the r', "
17: 6 brethren unto the r' of the city, 4173
8 the people and the r' of the city, "
Ro 13: 3 r' are not a terror to good works, 758
Eph 6:12 against the r' of the darkness of 2888

rulest
2Ch 20: 6 r' not thou over all the kingdoms*4910
Ps 89: 9 Thou r' the raging of the sea: when"

ruleth
2Sa 23: 3 He that r' over men must be just, 4910
Ps 59:13 let them know that God r' in Jacob "
66: 7 He r' by his power for ever; his "
103:19 and his kingdom r' over all. "
Pr 16:32 he that r' his spirit than he that "
22: 7 The rich r' over the poor, and the "
Ec 8: 9 wherein one man r' over another*7980
9:17 the cry of him that r' among fools.4910
Da 4:17, 25, 32 that the most High r' in the7980
Ho 11:12 but Judah yet r' with God, and is 7300
Ro 12: 8 he that r', with diligence; he that 4291
1Ti 3: 4 One that r' well his own house, "

ruling
2Sa 23: 3 must be just, r' in the fear of God.*4910
Jer 22:30 David, and r' any more in Judah. "
1Ti 3:12 r' their children and their own 4291

Rumah (*ru'-mah*) See also ARUMAH.
2Ki 23:36 the daughter of Pedaiah of R'. 7316

rumbling
Jer 47: 3 at the r' of his wheels, the fathers 1995

rumour See also RUMOURS.
2Ki 19: 7 and he shall hear a r', and shall ‡8052
Isa 37: 7 he shall hear a r', and return to ‡ "
Jer 49:14 I have heard a r' from the Lord, ‡ "
51:46 fear for the r' that shall be heard ‡ "
46 a r' shall both come one year, and‡ "
46 in another year shall come a r', and‡"
Eze 7:26 mischief, and r' shall be upon r'; "
Ob 1 We have heard a r' from the Lord,* "
Lu 7:17 And this r' of him went forth *3056

rumours
M't 24: 6 shall hear of wars and r' of wars: 189
M'r 13: 7 shall hear of wars and r' of wars, "

rump
Ex 29:22 take of the ram the fat and the r',* 451
Le 3: 9 the fat thereof, and the whole r', it* "
7: 3 the r', and the fat that covereth the*"
8:25 And he took the fat, and the r', and*"
9:19 the bullock and of the ram, the r', * "

run See also RAN; RUNNEST; RUNNETH; RUNNING; OUTRUN.
Ge 49:22 whose branches r' over the wall: 6805
Le 15: 3 whether his flesh r' with his issue,7325
25 or if it r' beyond the time of her *2100
J'g 18:25 lest angry fellows r' upon thee, *6293
1Sa 8:11 some shall r' before his chariots. 7323
17:17 and r' to the camp to thy brethren;*"
20: 6 that he might r' to Beth-lehem his "
36 R', find out now the arrows which "
2Sa 15: 1 and fifty men to r' before him. "
18:19 Let me now r', and bear the king "
22 me, I pray thee, also r' after Cushi. "
22 Wherefore wilt thou r', my son, "
23 But howsoever, said he, let me r'. "
23 And he said unto him, R'. Then "
22:30 by thee I have r' through a troop: "
1Ki 1: 5 and fifty men to r' before him. "
2Ki 4:22 that I may r' to the man of God, "
26 R' now, I pray thee, to meet her, "
5:20 r' after him, and take somewhat "
2Ch 16: 9 the eyes of the Lord r' to and fro 7751
Ps 18:29 by thee I have r' through a troop; 7323
19: 5 rejoiceth as a strong man to r' a "
58: 7 as waters which r' continually: *1980
59: 4 They r' and prepare themselves 7323
78:16 waters to r' down like rivers. 3381
104:10 valleys, which r' among the hills. 1980
119:32 r' the way of thy commandments, 7323
136 of waters r' down mine eyes, 3381
Pr 1:16 For their feet r' to evil, and make 7323
Ec 1: 7 All the rivers r' into the sea; yet 1980
Ca 1: 4 Draw me, we will r' after thee: 7323
Isa 33: 4 of locusts shall he r' upon them. *8264
40:31 they shall r', and not be weary; 7323
55: 5 that knew not thee shall r' unto thee"
59: 7 Their feet r' to evil, and they make "
Jer 5: 1 R'...to and fro through the streets 7751
9:18 our eyes may r' down with tears, 3381
12: 5 If thou hast r' with the footmen, 7323
13:17 weep sore, and r' down with tears,3381

Jer 14:17 Let mine eyes r· down with tears 3381
49: 3 and r· to and fro by the hedges; 7751
19 I will suddenly make him r· away 7323
50:44 I will make them suddenly r· away "
51:31 One post shall r· to meet another, "
La 2:18 let tears r· down like a river day 3381
Eze 24:16 neither shall thy tears r· down. 935
32:14 and cause their rivers to r· like oil, 3212
Da 12: 4 many shall r· to and fro, and 7751
Joe 2: 4 and as horsemen, so shall they r·. 7323
7 They shall r· like mighty men; they" "
9 They shall r· to and fro in the city;*8264
9 they shall r· upon the wall, they 7323
Am 5:24 let judgment r· down as waters, *1556
6:12 Shall horses r· upon the rock? 7323
8:12 shall r· to and fro to seek the word 7751
Na 2: 4 they shall r· like the lightnings. 7323
Hab 2: 2 that he may r· that readeth it. "
Hag 1: 9 ye r· every man unto his own house. "
Zec 2: 4 R·, speak to this young man, saying, "
4:10 r· to and fro through the whole 7751
M't 28: 8 did r· to bring his disciples word. *5143
1Co 9:24 that they which r· in a race r· all, "
24 prize? So r·, that ye may obtain. "
26 therefore so r·, not as uncertainly; "
Ga 2: 2 means I should r·, or had r·, in vain. "
5: 7 Ye did r· well; who did hinder you* "
Ph'p 2:16 that I have not r· in vain, neither "
Heb 12: 1 let us r· with patience the race that "
1Pe 4: 4 strange that ye r· not with them to 4936

runner See FORERUNNER.

runnest
Pr 4:12 and when thou r·, thou shalt not 7323

runneth
Ezr 8:15 to the river that r· to Ahava; 935
Job 15:26 He r· upon him, even on his neck, 7323
16:14 breach, he r· upon me like a giant. "
Ps 23: 5 my head with oil; my cup r· over. 7310
147:15 earth: his word r· very swiftly. 7323
Pr 18:10 the righteous r· into it, and is safe. 7323
La 1:16 eye, mine eye r· down with water, 3381
3:48 Mine eye r· down with rivers of "
M't 9:17 bottles break, and the wine r· out,*1632
Joh 20: 2 Then she r·, and cometh to Simon 5143
Ro 9:16 him that willeth, nor of him that r·, "

running See also OVERRUNNING.
Le 14: 5 in an earthen vessel over r· water: 2416
6 that was killed over the r· water: "
50 in an earthen vessel over r· water: "
51 the slain bird, and in the r· water, "
52 of the bird, and with the r· water, "
15: 2 hath a r· issue out of his flesh, *2100
13 and bathe his flesh in r· water, and 2416
22: 4 is a leper, or hath a r· issue; *2100
Nu 19:17 r· water shall be put thereto in a 2416
2Sa 18:24 looked, and behold a man r· alone. 7323
26 the watchman saw another man r·: "
26 said, Behold another man r· alone. "
27 the r· of the foremost is like 4794
27 the r· of Ahimaaz the son of Zadok. "
2Ki 5:21 Naaman saw him r· after him, he 7323
2Ch 23:12 noise of the people r· and praising "
Pr 5:15 r· waters out of thine own well. 5140
6:18 feet that be swift in r· to mischief, 7323
Isa 33: 4 as the r· to and fro of locusts shall*4944
Eze 31: 4 rivers r· round about his plants, *1980
M'r 9:15 amazed, and r· to him saluted him. 4370
25 that the people came r· together, 1998
10:17 there came one r·, and kneeled to*4370
Lu 6:38 and shaken together, and r· over, 5240
Ac 27:16 And r· under a certain island 5295
Re 9: 9 of many horses r· to battle. *5143

rush See also BULRUSH; RUSHED; RUSHES; RUSHETH; RUSHING.
Job 8:11 Can the r· grow up without mire? 1573
Isa 9:14 Israel head and tail, branch and r·, 100
17:13 nations shall r· like the rushing of 7582
19:15 head or tail, branch or r·, may do. 100

rushed
J'g 9:44 Abimelech...r· forward, and stood 6584
20:37 in wait hasted, and r· upon Gibeah; "
Ac 19:29 they r· with one accord into the 3729

rushes See also BULRUSHES.
Isa 35: 7 shall be grass with reeds and r·. 1573

rusheth
Jer 8: 6 as the horse r· into the battle. 7857

rushing
Isa 17:12 and to the r· of nations, that make 7588
12 of nations, that make a r· like the*7582
12 like the r· of mighty waters! 7588
13 rush like the r· of many waters: "
Jer 47: 3 at the r· of his chariots, and at the 7494
Eze 3:12 behind me a voice of a great r·, "
13 them, and a noise of a great r·. "
Ac 2: 2 from heaven as of a r· mighty wind, 5342

rust
M't 6:19 where moth and r· doth corrupt, 1035
20 neither moth nor r· doth corrupt, "
Jas 5: 3 the r· of them shall be a witness 2447

Ruth (rooth)
Ru 1: 4 and the name of the other R·: 7327
14 in law; but R· clave unto her. "
16 R· said, Intreat me not to leave "
22 returned, and R· the Moabitess, "
2: 2 R· the Moabitess said unto Naomi, "
8 Then said Boaz unto R·, Hearest "
21 R· the Moabitess said, He said unto "
22 Naomi said unto R· her daughter "
3: 9 answered, I am R· thine handmaid: "
4: 5 must buy it also of R· the Moabitess, "
10 R· the Moabitess,...wife of Mahlon, "
13 Boaz took R·, and she was his wife: "
M't 1: 5 and Booz begat Obed of R·; and 4503

rye See RIE.

S.

sabachthani (sa-bak'-tha-ni)
M't 27:46 loud voice, saying, Eli, Eli, lama s·? 4518
M'r 15:34 voice, saying, Eloi, Eloi, lama s·? "

Sabaoth (sab'-a-oth)
Ro 9:29 Except the Lord of S· had left us a 4519
Jas 5: 4 into the ears of the Lord of s·. "

Sabas See BARSABAS.

sabbath See also SABBATHS.
Ex 16:23 rest of the holy s· unto the Lord: 7676
25 for to day is a s· unto the Lord: "
26 on the seventh day, which is the s·, "
29 that the Lord hath given you the s·, "
20: 8 Remember the s· day, to keep it holy. "
10 seventh day is the s· of the Lord thy "
11 the Lord blessed the s· day, and "
31:14 Ye shall keep the s· therefore; for it "
15 but in the seventh is the s· of rest, "
15 whosoever doeth any work in the s· "
16 shall keep the s·, to observe the s· "
35: 2 an holy day, a s· of rest to the Lord: "
3 kindle no fire...upon the s· day. "
Le 16:31 It shall be a s· of rest unto you, and "
23: 3 but the seventh day is the s· of rest, "
3 s· of the Lord in all your dwellings. "
11 morrow after the s· the priest shall "
15 you from the morrow after the s·, "
16 unto the morrow after the seventh s· "
24 shall ye have a s·, a memorial of *7677
32 It shall be unto you a s· of rest, 7676
32 unto even, shall ye celebrate your s·. "
39 on the first day shall be a s·, and *7677
39 on the eighth day shall be a s·. * "
24: 8 Every s· he shall set it in order 7676
25: 2 then shall the land keep a s· unto "
4 shall be a s· of rest unto the land, "
4 a s· for the Lord: thou shalt neither "
6 s· of the land shall be meat for you; "
Nu 15:32 gathered sticks upon the s· day. "
28: 9 And on the s· day two lambs of the "
10 is the burnt offering of every s·, "
De 5:12 Keep the s· day to sanctify it, as the "
14 seventh day is the s· of the Lord "
15 commanded thee to keep the s· day. "
2Ki 4:23 it is neither new moon, nor s·. "
11: 5 part of you that enter in on the s· "
7 of all you that go forth on the s·, "
9 men that were to come in on the s·, "
9 them that should go out on the s·, "
16:18 covert for the s· that they had built "
1Ch 9:32 shewbread, to prepare it every s·. "
2Ch 23: 4 third part of you entering on the s·, "
8 men that were to come in on the s·, "
8 them that were to go out on the s·: "
36:21 as she lay desolate she kept s·, 7673
Ne 9:14 And madest known...thy holy s·, 7676
10:31 ware or any victuals on the s· day "
31 would not buy it of them on the s·, "
13:15 treading wine presses on the s·, "
15 brought into Jerusalem on the s· "
16 sold on the s· unto the children of "
17 that ye do, and profane the s· day? "
18 more wrath...by profaning the s·. "
19 began to be dark before the s·, "
19 not be opened till after the s·: "
19 burden be brought in on the s· day. "
21 forth came they no more on the s·. "
22 keep the gates, to sanctify the s· day. "
Ps 92: title A Psalm or Song for the s· day. "
Isa 56: 2, 6 keepeth the s· from polluting it. "
Isa 58:13 thou turn away thy foot from the s·, 7676
13 and call the s· a delight, the holy of "
66:23 another, and from one s· to another, "
Jer 17:21 and bear no burden on the s· day, "
22 burden out of your houses on the s· "
22 hallow...the s· day, as I commanded "
24 the gates of this city on the s· day, "
24 but hallow the s· day, to do no work "
27 hearken unto me to hallow the s· "
27 gates of Jerusalem on the s· day; "
Eze 46: 1 but on the s· it shall be opened, and "
4 shall offer unto the Lord in the s· "
12 offerings, as he did on the s· day: "
Am 8: 5 and the s·, that we may set forth "
M't 12: 1 Jesus went on the s· day through 4521
2 is not lawful to do upon the s· day: "
5 how that on the s· days the priests "
5 in the temple profane the s·, and are "
8 of man is Lord even of the s· day. "
10 Is it lawful to heal on the s· days? "
11 and if it fall into a pit on the s· day, "
12 is lawful to do well on the s· days. "
24:20 in the winter, neither on the s· day: "
28: 1 In the end of the s·, as it began to "
M'r 1:21 s· day he entered...the synagogue, "
2:23 through the corn fields on the s· "
24 on the s·...that which is not lawful? "
27 The s· was made for man, and not "
27 for man, and not man for the s·: "
28 Son of man is Lord also of the s·. "
3: 2 he would heal him on the s· day; "
4 it lawful to do good on the s· days, "
6: 2 And when the s· day was come, "
15:42 that is, the day before the s·, 4315
16: 1 And when the s· was past, Mary 4521
Lu 4:16 into the synagogue on the s· day, "
31 and taught them on the s· days. "
6: 1 pass on the second s· after the first, "
2 is not lawful to do on the s· days? "
5 Son of man is Lord also of the s·. "
6 it came to pass also on another s·, "
7 whether he would heal on the s· "
9 lawful on the s· days to do good, or "
13:10 in one of the synagogues on the s·. "
14 that Jesus had healed on the s· day, "
14 and be healed, and not on the s· day. "
15 one of you on the s· loose his ox or "
16 loosed from this bond on the s· day? "
14: 1 Pharisees to eat bread on the s· day, "
3 Is it lawful to heal on the s· day? "
5 straightway pull him out on the s· "
23:54 the preparation, and the s· drew on. "
56 and rested the s· day according to "
Joh 5: 9 and on the same day was the s·. "
10 It is the s· day: it is not lawful for "
16 had done these things on the s· day. "
18 he not only had broken the s·, but "
7:22 ye on the s· day circumcise a man. "
23 on the s· day receive circumcision, "
23 man every whit whole on the s· day? "
9:14 s· day when Jesus made the clay, "
16 because he keepeth not the s· day. "
19:31 remain upon the cross on the s· day, "
31 (for that s· day was an high day,) "
Ac 1:12 from Jerusalem a s· day's journey. "
13:14 into the synagogue on the s· day, "
27 prophets which are read every s· "
42 be preached to them the next s·. "
44 next s· day came almost the whole "
15:21 read in the synagogues every s· day. "
Ac 16:13 on the s· we went out of the city by 4521
17: 2 three s· days reasoned with them "
18: 4 reasoned in the synagogue every s·, "
Col 2:16 of the new moon, or of the s· days: "

sabbath-day See SABBATH and DAY.

sabbaths
Ex 31:13 Verily my s· ye shall keep: for it 7676
Le 19: 3 and his father, and keep my s·: "
30 Ye shall keep my s·, and reverence "
23:15 offering; seven s· shall be complete: "
38 Beside the s· of the Lord, and beside "
25: 8 thou shalt number seven s· of years "
8 the space of the seven s· of years "
26: 2 Ye shall keep my s·, and reverence "
34 Then shall the land enjoy her s·, "
34 shall the land rest, and enjoy her s·. "
35 because it did not rest in your s·, "
43 left of them, and shall enjoy her s·, "
1Ch 23:31 sacrifices unto the Lord in the s·, "
2Ch 2: 4 on the s·, and on the new moons, "
8:13 on the s·, and on the new moons, "
31: 3 and the burnt offerings for the s·, "
36:21 until the land had enjoyed her s·: "
Ne 10:33 of the s·, of the new moons, for the "
Isa 1:13 the new moons and s·, the calling* "
56: 4 unto the eunuchs that keep my s·, "
La 1: 7 saw her, and did mock at her s·. *4868
2: 6 feasts and s· to be forgotten in *7676
Eze 20:12 Moreover also I gave them my s·, "
13 and my s· they greatly polluted: "
16 in my statutes, but polluted my s·: "
20 And hallow my s·; and they shall be "
21 they polluted my s·: then I said, "
24 statutes, and had polluted my s·, "
22: 8 things, and hast profaned my s·. "
26 and have hid their eyes from my s·, "
23:38 same day, and have profaned my s·. "
44:24 and they shall hallow my s·. "
45:17 and in the new moons, and in the s·, "
46: 3 in the s· and in the new moons. "
Ho 2:11 her new moons, and her s·, and all "

Sabeans (sab-e'-uns)
Job 1:15 And the S· fell upon them, and 7614
Isa 45:14 and of the S·, men of stature, 5436
Eze 23:42 brought S· from the wilderness, *5433
Joe 3: 8 and they shall sell them to the S·,*7615

Sabta (sab'-tah) See also SABTAH.
1Ch 1: 9 Seba, and Havilah, and S·, and 5454

Sabtah (sab'-tah) See also SABTA.
Ge 10: 7 Seba, and Havilah, and S·, and 5454

Sabtecha (sab'-te-kah) See also SABTECHAH.
1Ch 1: 9 Sabta, and Raamah, and S·. *5455

Sabtechah (sab'-te-kah) See also SABTECHA.
Ge 10: 7 Sabtah, and Raamah, and S·: *5455

Sacar (sa'-kar) See also SHARAR.
1Ch 11:35 Ahiam the son of S· the Hararite, 7940
26: 4 Joah the third, and S· the fourth, "

sack See also SACKBUT; SACKCLOTH; SACK'S; SACKS.
Ge 42:25 every man's money into his s·, 8242
27 as one of them opened his s· to give "
28 restored; and, lo, it is even in my s·: 572
35 bundle of money was in his s·: 8242
43:21 money was in the mouth of his s·, 572
44:11 down every man his s· to the ground, "
11 and opened every man his s·. "

Ge 44:12 the cup was found in Benjamin's s'.572
Le 11:32 of wood, or raiment, or skin, or s',8242

sackbut
Da 3: 5, 7, 10, 15 of the cornet, flute, harp, s',5443

sackcloth See also SACKCLOTHES.
Ge 37:34 clothes, put s' upon his loins, and 8242
2Sa 3:31 your clothes, and gird you with s', "
21:10 Rizpah the daughter of Aiah took s', "
1Ki 20:31 us, I pray thee, put s' on our loins, "
32 So they girded s' on their loins, "
21:27 clothes, and put s' upon his flesh, "
27 and fasted, and lay in s', and went "
2Ki 6:30 he had s' within upon his flesh. "
19: 1 clothes, and covered himself with s'," "
2 elders of the priests, covered with s'," "
1Ch 21:16 of Israel, who were clothed in s', "
Es 4: 1 clothes, and put on s' with ashes, "
2 into the king's gate clothed with s'. "
3 and many lay in s' and ashes. "
4 and to take away his s' from him: "
Job 16:15 I have sewed s' upon my skin, and "
Ps 30:11 thou hast put off my s', and girded "
35:13 they were sick, my clothing was s': "
69:11 I made s' also my garment; and I "
Isa 3:24 of a stomacher a girding of s'; "
15: 3 they shall gird themselves with s': "
20: 2 and loose the s' from off thy loins, "
22:12 to baldness, and to girding with s': "
32:11 you bare, and gird s' upon your loins. "
37: 1 and covered himself with s', and 8242
2 elders of the priests covered with s'," "
50: 3 and I make s' their covering. "
58: 5 to spread s' and ashes under him? "
Jer 4: 8 gird you with s', lament and howl: "
6:26 gird thee with s', and wallow thyself "
48:37 be cuttings, and upon the loins s'. "
49: 3 of Rabbah, gird you with s'; lament, "
La 2:10 they have girded themselves with s': "
Eze 7:18 shall also gird themselves with s', "
27:31 bald for thee, and gird them with s'," "
Da 9: 3 with fasting, and s', and ashes: "
Joe 1: 8 Lament like a virgin girded with s' "
13 come, lie all night in s', ye ministers "
Am 8:10 and I will bring up s' upon all loins, "
Jon 3: 5 proclaimed a fast, and put on s', "
6 and covered him with s', and sat in "
8 man and beast be covered with s', "
M't 11:21 repented long ago in s' and ashes. 4526
Lu 10:13 repented, sitting in s' and ashes. "
Re 6:12 the sun became black as s' of hair, "
11: 3 and threescore days, clothed in s'. "

sackclothes
Ne 9: 1 with fasting, and with s', and *8242

sack's
Ge 42:27 for, behold, it was in his s' mouth.*572
44: 1 every man's money in his s' mouth. "
2 cup, in the s' mouth of the youngest," "

sacks See also SACKS'.
Ge 42:25 Joseph commanded to fill their s'*3672
35 to pass as they emptied their s', 8242
43:12 the money...in the mouth of your s',572
18 money that was returned in our s' "
21 that we opened our s', and, behold, "
22 tell who put our money in our s'. "
23 hath given you treasure in your s': "
44: 1 saying, Fill the men's s' with food, "
Jos 9: 4 and took old s' upon their asses, 8242

sacks'
Ge 44: 8 which we found in our s' mouths, 572

sacrifice See also SACRIFICED; SACRIFICES; SACRIFICETH; SACRIFICING.
Ge 31:54 Jacob offered s' upon the mount, 2077
Ex 3:18 we may s' to the Lord our God. 2076
5: 3 and s' unto the Lord our God; lest "
8 Let us go and s' to our God. "
17 Let us go and do s' to the Lord. "
8: 8 go, they may do s' unto the Lord. "
25 Go ye, s' to your God in the land. "
26 we shall s' the abomination of the "
26 shall we s' the abomination of the "
27 and s' to the Lord our God, as he "
28 ye may s' to the Lord your God in "
29 the people go to s' to the Lord. "
10:25 we may s' unto the Lord our God. 2077
12:27 It is the s' of the Lord's passover, "
13:15 I s' to the Lord all that openeth 2076
20:24 s' thereon thy burnt offerings, "
23:18 not offer the blood of my s' with 2077
18 shall the fat of my s' remain until 2282
29:28 of the s' of their peace offerings, *2077
30: 9 incense thereon, nor burnt s', nor* "
34:15 and do s' unto their gods, and 2076
15 call thee, and thou eat of his s'; 2077
25 the blood of my s' with leaven; "
25 the s' of the feast of the passover be "
Le 1: 3 offering be a burnt s', of the herd,*
9 to be a burnt s', an offering made*
10 or of the goats, for a burnt s'; he*
13 it is a burnt s', an offering made *
14 if the burnt s' for his offering to *
17 it is a burnt s', an offering made by*
3: 1 oblation be a s' of peace offering, 2077
3 offer of the s' of the peace offering "
5 it on the altar upon the burnt s', *
6 offering for a s' of peace offering 2077
9 offer of the s' of the peace offering "
4:10 bullock of the s' of peace offerings: "
26 the fat of the s' of peace offerings: "
31 from off the s' of peace offerings; "
35 from the s' of the peace offerings; "
7:11 law of the s' of peace offerings, "
12 offer with the s' of thanksgiving "
13 bread with the s' of thanksgiving "

Le 7:15 the flesh of the s' of his peace 2077
16 if the s' of his offering be a vow, "
16 same day that he offereth his s': "
17 the remainder of the flesh of the s' "
18 flesh of the s' of his peace offerings "
20, 21 flesh of the s' of peace offerings, "
29 offereth the s' of his peace offerings "
29 of the s' of his peace offerings. "
37 of the s' of the peace offerings; "
8:21 a burnt s' for a sweet savour, *
9: 4 offerings, to s' before the Lord; 2076
17 beside the burnt s' of the morning.*
18 the ram for a s' of peace offerings,2077
17: 8 offereth a burnt offering or s', "
19: 5 if ye offer a s' of peace offerings "
22:21 offereth a s' of peace offerings unto "
29 ye will offer a s' of thanksgiving "
23:19 ye shall s' one kid of the goats* 6213
19 year for a s' of peace offerings. 2077
37 a meat offering, a s', and drink "
27:11 they do not offer a s' unto the Lord,*7133
Nu 6:17 the ram for a s' of peace offerings*2077
18 it in the fire which is under the s' "
7:17, 23, 29, 35, 41, 47, 53, 59, 65, 71, 77,
83 for a s' of peace offerings, two "
88 all the oxen for the s' of the peace "
15: 3 or a s' in performing a vow, or in "
5 with the burnt offering or s', for "
8 or for a s' in performing a vow, or "
25 s' made by fire unto the Lord, and* "
23: 6 he stood by his burnt s', he, and *
28: 6 a s' made by fire unto the Lord. *
8 thou shalt offer it, a s' made by fire,*
13 a s' made by fire unto the Lord. *
19 ye shall offer a s' made by fire for a*
24 the meat of the s' made by fire, of*
29: 6 a s' made by fire unto the Lord. *
13, 36 a s' made by fire, of a sweet *
De 15:21 shalt not s' it unto the Lord thy 2076
16: 2 shalt therefore s' the passover "
5 Thou mayest not s' the passover "
6 thou shalt s' the passover at even, "
17: 1 shalt not s' unto the Lord thy God "
18: 3 people, from them that offer a s', 2077
33:10 whole burnt s' upon thine altar. *
Jos 22:26 not for burnt offering, nor for s': 2077
J'g 6:26 offer a burnt s' with the wood of *
16:23 a great s' unto Dagon their god, 2077
1Sa 1: 3 to s' unto the Lord of hosts in 2076
21 offer unto the Lord the yearly s', 2077
2:13 that, when any man offered s', the "
19 her husband to offer the yearly s'. "
29 Wherefore kick ye at my s' and at "
3:14 shall not be purged with s' nor "
9:12 s' of the people to day in the high "
13 come, because he doth bless the s'; "
10: 8 to s' sacrifices of peace offerings: 2076
15:15 oxen, to s' unto the Lord thy God; "
21 s' unto the Lord thy God in Gilgal. "
22 to obey is better than s', and to 2077
16: 2 say, I am come to s' to the Lord. 2076
3 call Jesse to the s', and I will 2077
5 I am come to s' unto the Lord: 2076
5 and come with me to the s'. 2077
5 sons, and called them to the s'. "
20: 6 there is a yearly s' there for all the "
29 our family hath a s' in the city; "
2Sa 24:22 here be oxen for burnt s', and *
1Ki 3: 4 king went to Gibeon to s' there; 2076
8:62 him, offered s' before the Lord. 2077
63 And Solomon offered a s' of peace "
12:27 this people go up to do s' in the "
18:29 the offering of the evening s', *4503
33 and pour it on the burnt s', and *
36 of the offering of the evening s', *4503
38 fell, and consumed the burnt s', *
2Ki 5:17 neither burnt offering nor s' unto*2077
10:19 I have a great s' to do to Baal; "
14: 4 as yet the people did s' and burnt*2076
16:15 offering, and the king's burnt s', *
15 and all the blood of the s': *2077
17:35 nor serve them, nor s' to them: 2076
36 worship, and to him shall ye do s'. "
2Ch 2: 6 save only to burn s' before him? *
7: 5 And king Solomon offered a s' of 2077
12 place to myself for an house of s'. "
11:16 to s' unto the Lord God of their 2076
28:23 will I s' to them, that they may "
33:17 people did s'...in the high places, "
Ezr 4: 2 we do s' unto him since the days of "
9: 4 I sat astonied until...evening s'. *4503
5 at the evening s' I arose up from * "
Ne 4: 2 will they s'? will they make an 2076
Ps 20: 3 offerings, and accept thy burnt s'; "
40: 6 S' and offering thou didst not 2077
50: 5 made a covenant with me by s'. "
51:16 For thou desirest not s'; else "
54: 6 I will freely s' unto thee: I will 2076
107:22 And let them s' the sacrifices of "
116:17 offer to thee...s' of thanksgiving, 2077
118:27 bind the s' with cords, even unto 2282
141: 2 up of my hands as the evening s'. 4503
Pr 15: 8 s' of the wicked is an abomination 2077
21: 3 acceptable to the Lord than s'. "
27 s' of the wicked is abomination: "
Ec 5: 1 hear, than to give the s' of fools: "
Isa 19:21 day, and shall do s' and oblation; "
34: 6 the Lord hath a s' in Bozrah, and "
57: 7 thither wentest thou up to offer s'. "
Jer 33:11 that shall bring the s' of praise *
18 offerings, and to do s' continually.2077
46:10 the Lord God of hosts hath a s' in "
Eze 39:17 yourselves on every side to my s' "
17 that I do s' for you, even a great 2076
17 s' upon the mountains of Israel, 2077
19 s' which I have sacrificed for you. 2076

Eze 40:42 slew the burnt offering and the s'. 2077
44:11 offering and the s' for the people, "
46:24 house shall boil the s' of the people." "
Da 8:11 by him the daily s' was taken away,*
12 daily s' by reason of transgression,*
13 the vision concerning the daily s',*
9:27 s' and the oblation to cease, 2077
11:31 and shall take away the daily s', *
12:11 the daily s' shall be taken away, *
Ho 3: 4 and without a s', and without an 2077
4:13 s' upon the tops of the mountains,2076
14 whores, and they s' with harlots: "
6: 6 For I desired mercy, and not s'; 2077
8:13 They s' flesh for the sacrifices of 2076
12:11 vanity: they s' bullocks in Gilgal; "
13: 2 the men that s' kiss the calves. "
Am 4: 5 a s' of thanksgiving with leaven, "
Jon 1:16 and offered a s' unto the Lord, 2077
2: 9 will s' unto thee with the voice of 2076
Hab 1:16 Therefore they s' unto their net, * "
Zep 1: 7 for the Lord hath prepared a s', 2077
8 pass in the day of the Lord's s', "
Zec 14:21 they that s' shall come and take 2076
Mal 1: 8 And if ye offer the blind for s', is it "
M't 9:13 I will have mercy, and not s': for 2378
12: 7 I will have mercy, and not s', ye "
M'r 9:49 every s' shall be salted with salt. * "
Lu 2:24 And to offer a s' according to that "
Ac 7:41 and offered s' unto the idol, and "
14:13 and would have done s' with the 2380
18 they had not done s' unto them. "
Ro 12: 1 ye present your bodies a living s', 2378
1Co 8: 4 that are offered in s' unto idols, 1494
10:19 is offered in s' to idols is any thing?* "
20 the things which the Gentiles s', 2380
20 they s' to devils, and not to God: "
28 This is offered in s' unto idols, eat 1494
Eph 5: 2 for us an offering and a s' to God 2378
Ph'p 2:17 the s' and service of your faith, "
4:18 s' acceptable, wellpleasing to God. "
Heb 7:27 to offer up s', first for his own sins,* "
9:26 to put away sin by the s' of himself. "
10: 5 S' and offering thou wouldest not, "
8 S' and offering and burnt offerings "
12 after he had offered one s' for sins "
26 remaineth no more s' for sins, "
11: 4 God a more excellent s' than Cain, "
13:15 let us offer the s' of praise to God "

sacrificed See also SACRIFICEDST.
Ex 24: 5 s' peace offerings of oxen unto the 2076
32: 8 it, and have s' thereunto, and said, "
De 32:17 They s' unto devils, not to God; to "
Jos 8:31 the Lord, and s' peace offerings. "
J'g 2: 5 and they s' there unto the Lord. "
1Sa 2:15 said to the man that s', Give flesh "
6:15 s' sacrifices the same day unto the "
11:15 and there they s' sacrifices of peace "
2Sa 6:13 six paces, he s' oxen and fatlings. "
1Ki 3: 2 Only the people s' in high places, "
3 only he s' and burnt incense in high "
11: 8 incense and s' unto their gods. "
2Ki 12: 3 the people still s' and burnt incense "
15: 4 the people s' and burnt incense still "
35 the people s' and burned incense "
16: 4 he s' and burnt incense in the high "
17:32 which s' for them in the houses of 6213
1Ch 21:28 the Jebusite, then he s' there. 2076
29:21 they s' sacrifices unto the Lord, and "
2Ch 5: 6 s' sheep and oxen, which could not* "
28: 4 He s' also and burnt incense in the "
23 he s' unto the gods of Damascus, "
33:16 and s' thereon peace offerings and* "
22 Amon s' unto all the carved images "
34: 4 graves of them that...s' unto them. "
Ps 106:37 s' their sons and their daughters "
38 they s' unto the idols of Canaan: "
Eze 16:20 thou s' unto them to be devoured. "
39:19 sacrifice which I have s' for you. "
Ho 11: 2 they s' unto Baalim, and burned "
1Co 5: 7 Christ our passover is s' for us: 2380
Re 2:14 to eat things s' unto idols, and to 1494
20 and to eat things s' unto idols. "

sacrificedst
De 16: 4 which thou s' the first day at even,*2076

sacrifices
Ge 46: 1 and offered s' unto the God of his 2077
Ex 10:25 give us also s' and burnt offerings, "
18:12 a burnt offering and s' for God: "
Le 7:32 of the s' of your peace offerings. "
34 off the s' of their peace offerings, "
10:13 of the s' of the Lord made by fire: *
14 out of the s' of peace offerings of 2077
17: 5 children of Israel may bring their s'," "
7 no more offer their s' unto devils, "
Nu 10:10 over the s' of your peace offerings; "
25: 2 the people unto the s' of their gods: "
28: 2 my bread for my s' made by fire, *
De 12: 6 and your s', and your tithes, and 2077
11 your burnt offerings, and your s', "
27 the blood of thy s' shall be poured "
32:38 Which did eat the fat of their s', and "
33:19 they shall offer s' of righteousness: "
Jos 13:14 s' of the Lord...of Israel made by fire*
22:27 with our s', and with our peace 2077
28 not for burnt offerings, nor for s';* "
29 for meat offerings, or for s', beside* "
1Sa 6:15 sacrificed s' the same day unto the "
10: 8 to sacrifice s' of peace offerings: "
11:15 they sacrificed s' of peace offerings "
15:22 delight in burnt offerings and s', as "
2Sa 15:12 even from Giloh, while he offered s'." "
2Ki 10:24 they went in to offer s' and burnt "
1Ch 16: 1 they offered burnt s' and peace "
23:31 to offer all burnt s' unto the Lord *
29:21 they sacrificed s' unto the Lord, 2077

1Ch 29:21 and s' in abundance for all Israel:2077
2Ch 7: 1 the burnt offerings and the s'; and "
4 people offered s' before the Lord.* "
13:11 every evening burnt s' and sweet "
29:31 bring s' and thank offerings into 2077
31 the congregation brought in s' and "
Ezr 6: 3 the place where they offered s', 1685
10 they may offer s' of sweet savours
Ne 12:43 that day they offered great s', 2077
Ps 4: 5 Offer the s' of righteousness, and "
27: 6 I offer in his tabernacle s' of joy; "
50: 8 I will not reprove thee for thy s' or "
51:17 The s' of God are a broken spirit: "
19 with the s' of righteousness, with "
66:15 unto thee burnt s' of fatlings, with*
106:28 and ate the s' of the dead. 2077
107:22 sacrifice the s' of thanksgiving, and"
Pr 17: 1 than an house full of s' with strife.* "
Isa 1:11 the multitude of your s' unto me? "
29: 1 ye year to year; let them kill s'. *2282
43:23 hast thou honoured me with thy s'.2077
24 thou filled me with the fat of thy s': "
56: 7 s' shall be accepted upon mine "
Jer 6:20 nor your s' sweet unto me. "
7:21 your burnt offerings unto your s'. "
22 concerning burnt offerings or s': "
17:26 bringing burnt offerings, and s', and"
26 incense, and bringing s' of praise, "
Eze 20:28 and they offered there their s', 2077
40:41 tables, whereupon they slew their s'. "
Ho 4:19 be ashamed because of their s'. 2077
8:13 flesh for the s' of mine offerings, "
9: 4 their s' shall be unto them as the "
Am 4: 4 and bring your s' every morning, "
5:25 ye offered unto me s' and offerings "
M'r 12:33 all whole burnt offerings and s'. 2378
Lu 13: 1 Pilate had mingled with their s'. "
Ac 7:42 offered to me slain beasts and s' "
1Co 10:18 which eat of the s' partakers of the "
Heb 5: 1 may offer both gifts and s' for sins: "
8: 3 is ordained to offer gifts and s': "
9: 9 were offered both gifts and s', that "
23 with better s' than these. "
10: 1 can never with those s' which they "
3 in those s' there is a remembrance "
6 In burnt offerings and s' for sin thou "
11 offering oftentimes the same s', 2378
13:16 with such s' God is well pleased. "
1Pe 2: 5 to offer up spiritual s', acceptable "

sacrificeth
Ex 22:20 He that s' unto any god, save unto2076
Ec 9: 2 him that s', and to him that s' not: "
Isa 65: 3 s' in gardens, and burneth incense* "
66: 3 he that s' a lamb, as if he cut off a "
Mal 1:14 s' unto the Lord a corrupt thing: "

sacrificing
1Ki 8: 5 s' sheep and oxen, that could not 2076
12:32 s' unto the calves that he had made:"

sacrilege
Ro 2:22 idols, dost thou commit s'? *2416

sad
Ge 40: 6 them, and, behold, they were s'. 2196
1Sa 1:18 and her countenance was no more s'.
1Ki 21: 5 Why is thy spirit so s', that thou 5620
Ne 2: 1 been beforetime s' in his presence.7451
2 Why is thy countenance s', seeing "
3 should not my countenance be s', 7489
Eze 13:22 made the heart of the righteous s'*3512
22 whom I have made s'; and 3510
M't 6:16 hypocrites, of a s' countenance: 4659
M'r 10:22 he was s' at that saying, and went*4768
Lu 24:17 to another, as ye walk, and are s'? 4659

saddle See also SADDLED.
Le 15: 9 what s' soever he rideth upon that4817
2Sa 19:26 I will s' me an ass, that I may ride2280
1Ki 13:13 said unto his sons, S' me the ass. "
27 to his sons, saying, S' me the ass. "

saddled
Ge 22: 3 in the morning, and s' his ass, 2280
Nu 22:21 in the morning, and s' his ass, "
J'g 19:10 there were with him two asses s', "
2Sa 16: 1 met him, with a couple of asses s', "
17:23 he s' his ass, and arose, and gat him"
1Ki 2:40 And Shimei arose, and s' his ass, "
13:13 So they s' him the ass: and he rode"
23 that he s' for him the ass, to wit, "
27 Saddle me the ass. And they s' him."
2Ki 4:24 Then she s' an ass, and said to her "

Sadducees (*sad'-du-sees*)
M't 3: 7 saw many of the Pharisees and S' 4523
16: 1 Pharisees also with the S' came, "
6 leaven of the Pharisees and...S'. "
11 leaven of the Pharisees and...S'? "
12 doctrine of the Pharisees and...S'. "
22:23 The same day came to him the S', "
34 that he had put the S' to silence, "
M'r 12:18 Then come unto him the S', which "
Lu 20:27 Then came to him certain of the S', "
Ac 4: 1 captain of the temple, and the S', "
5:17 (which is the sect of the S',) and "
23: 6 perceived that the one part were S', "
7 between the Pharisees and the S': "
8 S' say that there is no resurrection, "

sadly
Ge 40: 7 Wherefore look ye so s' to day? 7451

sadness
Ec 7: 3 by the s' of the countenance the 7455

Sadoc (*sa'-dok*)
M't 1:14 begat S'; and S' begat Achim; 4524

safe See also SAFEGUARD.
1Sa 12:11 on every side, and ye dwelled s'. * 983
2Sa 18:29, 32 Is the young man Absalom s'?*7965
Job 21: 9 Their houses are s' from fear, 7965
Ps 119:117 Hold...me up, and I shall be s': 3467
Pr 18:10 runneth into it, and is safe. 7682
29:25 his trust in the Lord shall be s'. "
Isa 5:29 prey, and shall carry it away s', 6403
Eze 34:27 and they shall be s' in their land, * 983
Lu 15:27 he hath received him s' and sound.5198
Ac 23:24 and bring him s' unto Felix the 1295
27:44 pass, that they escaped all s' to land."
Ph'p 3: 1 is not grievous, but for you it is s'. 809

safeguard
1Sa 22:23 but with me thou shalt be in s'. 4931

safely
Le 26: 5 the full, and dwell in your land s'. 983
1Ki 4:25 And Judah and Israel dwelt s', every"
Ps 78:53 he led them on s' so that they feared "
Pr 1:33 hearkeneth unto me shall dwell s'.* "
3:23 Then shalt thou walk in thy way s'.*"
31:11 of her husband doth s' trust in her.*
Isa 41: 3 He pursued them, and passed s'; 7965
Jer 23: 6 be saved, and Israel shall dwell s': 983
32:37 and I will cause them to dwell s': "
33:16 saved, and Jerusalem shall dwell s':"
Eze 28:26 And they shall dwell s' therein, and*"
34:25 they shall dwell s' in the wilderness,*"
28 they shall dwell s', and none shall * "
38: 8 and they shall dwell s' all of them.* "
11 them that are at rest, that dwell s',* "
14 my people of Israel dwelleth s', * "
39:26 when they dwelt s' in their land, * "
Ho 2:18 and will make them to lie down s'. "
Zec 14:11 but Jerusalem shall be s' inhabited. "
M'r 14:44 take him, and lead him away s': 806
Ac 16:23 charging the jailor to keep them s': "

safety
Le 25:18 and ye shall dwell in the land in s'. 983
19 eat your fill, and dwell therein in s'. "
De 12:10 round about, so that ye dwell in s'; "
33:12 beloved of the Lord shall dwell in s' "
28 Israel then shall dwell in s' alone: "
Job 3:26 I was not in s', neither had I rest,*7951
5: 4 His children are far from s', and 3468
11 which mourn may be exalted to s'. "
11:18 and thou shalt take thy rest in s'. 983
24:23 Though it be given him to be in s',* "
Ps 4: 8 Lord, only makest me dwell in s'. "
12: 5 set him in s' from him that puffeth3468
33:17 An horse is a vain thing for s': 8668
Pr 11:14 multitude of counsellers there is s'."
21:31 day of battle: but s' is of the Lord.*"
24: 6 multitude of counsellers there is s'. "
Isa 14:30 and the needy shall lie down in s': 983
Ac 5:23 prison...found we shut with all s'. 803
1Th 5: 3 when they shall say, Peace and s'; "

saffron
Ca 4:14 Spikenard and s'; calamus and 3750

said See also SAIDST.
Ge 1: 3 And God s', Let there be light: and559
6 God s', Let there be a firmament in "
9 God s', Let the waters under the "
11 God s', Let the earth bring forth "
14 God s', Let there be lights in the "
20 God s', Let the waters bring forth "
24 God s', Let the earth bring forth "
26 And God s', Let us make man in our"
28 God s' unto them, Be fruitful, and "
29 God s', Behold, I have given you "
2:18 God s', It is not good that the man "
23 Adam s', This is now bone of my "
3: 1 And he s' unto the woman, Yea, "
1 hath God s', Ye shall not eat of every "
2 And the woman s' unto the serpent, "
3 God hath s', Ye shall not eat of it, "
4 And the serpent s' unto the woman, "
9 and s' unto him, Where art thou? "
10 And he s', I heard thy voice in the "
11 And he s', Who told thee that thou "
12 And the man s', The woman whom "
13 the Lord God s' unto the woman, "
13 the woman s', The serpent beguiled "
14 the Lord God s' unto the serpent, "
16 Unto the woman he s', I will greatly"
17 And unto Adam he s', Because thou "
22 the Lord God s', Behold, the man "
4: 1 and s', I have gotten a man from the"
6 And the Lord s' unto Cain, Why art "
9 And the Lord s' unto Cain, Where is"
9 thy brother? And he s', I know not:"
10 And he s', What hast thou done? "
13 Cain s'...My punishment is greater "
15 And the Lord s' unto him, Therefore"
23 And Lamech s' unto his wives, Adah"
25 For God, s' she, hath appointed me "
6: 3 And the Lord s', My spirit shall not559
7 And the Lord s', I will destroy man "
13 And God s' unto Noah, The end of all"
7: 1 the Lord s' unto Noah, Come thou "
8:21 Lord s' in his heart, I will not again "
9: 1 and s' unto them, Be fruitful, and "
12 And God s', This is the token of the "
17 God s' unto Noah, This is the token "
25 he s', Cursed be Canaan; a servant "
26 he s', Blessed be the...God of Shem, "
10: 9 it is s', Even as Nimrod the mighty "
11: 3 they s' one to another, Go to, let us "
4 they s', Go to, let us build us a city. "
6 Lord s', Behold, the people is one, "
12: 1 Lord had s' unto Abram, Get thee "
7 and s', Unto thy seed will I give this"
11 that he s' unto Sarai his wife, Behold"
18 Pharaoh called Abram, and s', What"
13: 8 Abram s' unto Lot, Let there be no "
14 Lord s' unto Abram, after that Lot "
Ge 14:19 and s', Blessed be Abram of the 559
21 the king of Sodom s' unto Abram, "
22 And Abram s' to the king of Sodom, "
15: 2 Abram s', Lord God, What wilt thou"
3 Abram s', Behold, to me thou hast "
5 and s', Look now toward heaven, and"
5 he s' unto him, So shall thy seed be. "
7 he s' unto him, I am the Lord that "
8 he s', Lord God, Whereby shall I "
9 he s' unto him, Take me an heifer "
13 he s' unto Abram, Know of a surety "
16: 2 Sarai s' unto Abram, Behold now, "
5 Sarai s' unto Abram, My wrong be "
6 Abram s' unto Sarai, Behold, thy "
8 he s', Hagar, Sarai's maid, whence "
8 And she s', I flee from the face of my"
9, 10, 11 angel of the Lord s' unto her, "
13 for she s', Have I also here looked "
17: 1 s' unto him, I am the Almighty God;"
9 God s' unto Abraham, Thou shalt "
15 God s' unto Abraham, As for Sarai "
17 laughed, and s' in his heart, Shall a "
18 And Abraham s' unto God, O that "
19 And God s', Sarah thy wife shall bear"
23 day, as God had s' unto him. 1696
18: 3 And s', My Lord, if now I have found559
5 And they s', So do, as thou hast s'.1696
6 into the tent unto Sarah, and s', 559
9 they s' unto him, Where is Sarah "
9 And he s', Behold, in the tent. "
10 And he s', I will certainly return "
13 And the Lord s' unto Abraham, "
15 he s', Nay; but thou didst laugh. "
17 And the Lord s', Shall I hide from "
20 And the Lord s', Because the cry of "
23 Abraham drew near, and s', Wilt "
26 the Lord s', If I find in Sodom fifty "
27 Abraham answered and s', Behold "
28 And he s', If I find there forty and "
29 and s', Peradventure there shall be "
29 And he s', I will not do it for forty's "
30 he s' unto him, Oh let not the Lord "
30 And he s', I will not do it, if I find "
31 And he s', Behold now, I have taken"
31 And he s', I wi l not destroy it for "
32 he s', Oh let not the Lord be angry, "
32 And he s', I will not destroy it for "
19: 2 he s', Behold now, my lords, turn in, "
2 they s', Nay; but we will abide in "
5 called unto Lot, and s' unto him, "
7 And s', I pray you, brethren, do not "
9 s', Stand back. And they s' again, "
12 And the men s' unto Lot, Hast thou "
14 and s', Up, get you out of this place;"
17 he s', Escape for thy life; look not "
18 And Lot s' unto them, Oh, not so, "
21 And he s' unto him, See, I have "
31, 34 the firstborn s' unto the younger,"
20: 2 Abraham s' of Sarah his wife, She is"
3 a dream by night, and s' to him, "
4 and he s', Lord, wilt thou slay also a"
5 S' he not unto me, She is my sister?"
5 even she herself s', He is my brother:"
6 God s' unto him in a dream, Yea, "
9 s' unto him, What hast thou done "
10 Abimelech s' unto Abraham, What "
11 And Abraham s', Because I thought, "
13 I s' unto her, This is thy kindness "
15 Abimelech s', Behold, my land is "
16 And unto Sarah he s', Behold, I have"
21: 1 the Lord visited Sarah as he had s', "
6 And Sarah s', God hath made me to "
7 she s', [559] Who would have s' unto4448
10 Wherefore she s' unto Abraham, 559
12 God s' unto Abraham, Let it not be "
12 in all that Sarah hath s' unto thee,* "
16 for she s', Let me not see the death "
17 and s' unto her, What aileth thee, "
24 And Abraham s', I will swear. "
26 Abimelech s', I wot not who hath "
29 Abimelech s' unto Abraham, What "
30 he s', For these seven ewe lambs "
22: 1 tempt Abraham, and s' unto him, "
1 and he s', Behold, here I am. "
2 he s', Take now thy son, thine only "
7 unto Abraham his father, and s', My"
7 and he s', Here am I, my son. "
7 he s', Behold the fire and the wood: "
8 And Abraham s', My son, God will "
11 s', Abraham,...and he s', Here am I. "
12 he s', Lay not thine hand upon the "
14 as it is s' to this day, In the mount "
16 And s', By myself have I sworn, "
24: 2 Abraham s' unto his eldest servant "
5 servant s' unto him, Peradventure "
6 Abraham s' unto him, Beware thou "
12 And he s', O Lord God of my master "
17 the servant ran to meet her, and s', "
18 And she s', Drink, my lord: and she"
19 she s', I will draw water for thy "
23 And s', Whose daughter art thou? "
24 she s' unto him, I am the daughter "
25 She s' moreover unto him, We have "
27 he s', Blessed be the Lord God of "
31 he s', Come in, thou blessed of the "
33 he s', I will not eat, until I have told"
33 mine errand, And he s', Speak on. "
34 And he s', I am Abraham's servant. "
39 I s' unto my master, Peradventure "
40 And he s' unto me, The Lord, before"
42 and s', O Lord God of my master "
45 and I s' unto her, Let me drink, I "
46 and s', Drink, and I will give thy "
47 and s', Whose daughter art thou? "
47 she s', The daughter of Bethuel, "
50 Laban and Bethuel answered and s',"

Ge 24:54 and he s', Send me away unto my 559
55 her brother and her mother s', Let "
56 he s' unto them, Hinder me not, "
57 And they s', We will call the damsel, "
58 s' unto her, Wilt thou go with this "
58 And she s', I will go. "
60 blessed Rebekah, and s' unto her, "
65 she had s' unto the servant, What "
65 the servant had s', It is my master: "
25:22 she s', If it be so, why am I thus? "
23 the Lord s' unto her, Two nations "
30 Esau s' to Jacob, Feed me, I pray "
31 And Jacob s', Sell me this day thy "
32 Esau s', Behold, I am at the point "
33 And Jacob s', Swear to me this day; "
26: 2 Lord appeared unto him, and s', Go, "
7 he s', She is my sister: for he feared "
7 s' he, the men of the place should "
9 And Abimelech called Isaac, and s', "
9 And Isaac s' unto him, Because I s', "
10 And Abimelech s', What is this thou "
16 Abimelech s' unto Isaac, Go from "
22 he s', For now the Lord hath made "
24 and s', I am the God of Abraham "
27 And Isaac s' unto them, Wherefore "
28 And they s', We saw certainly that "
28 and we s', Let there be now an oath "
32 s' unto him, We have found water. "
27: 1 eldest son, and s' unto him, My son: "
1 he s' unto him, Behold, here am I "
2 he s', Behold now, I am old, I know "
11 And Jacob s' to Rebekah his mother, "
13 his mother s' unto him, Upon me be "
18 unto his father, and s', My father: "
18 and he s', Here am I; who art thou, "
19 And Jacob s' unto his father, I am "
20 And Isaac s' unto his son, How is it "
20 And he s', Because the Lord thy God "
21 And Isaac s' unto Jacob, Come near, "
22 s', The voice is Jacob's voice, but "
24 he s', Art thou my very son Esau? "
24 my very son Esau? And he s', I am. "
25 he s', Bring it near to me, and I will "
26 his father Isaac s' unto him, Come "
27 s', See, the smell of my son is as the "
31 and s' unto his father, Let my father "
32 Isaac his father s' unto him, Who "
32 he s', I am thy son, thy firstborn "
33 trembled very exceedingly, and s', "
34 s' unto his father, Bless me, even "
35 And he s', Thy brother came with "
36 And he s', Is not he rightly named "
36 And he s', Hast thou not reserved a "
37 Isaac answered and s' unto Esau, "
38 Esau s' unto his father, Hast thou "
39 Isaac his father answered and s' "
41 Esau s' in his heart, The days of "
42 and s' unto him, Behold, thy brother "
46 Rebekah s' to Isaac, I am weary of "
28: 1 s' unto him, Thou shalt not take a "
13 s', I am the Lord God of Abraham "
16 and he s', Surely the Lord is in this "
17 and s', How dreadful is this place! "
29: 4 Jacob s' unto them, My brethren, "
4 And they s', Of Haran are we. "
5 he s' unto them, Know ye Laban the "
5 And they s', We know him. "
6 And he s' unto them, Is he well? "
6 And they s', He is well: and, behold, "
7 he s', Lo, it is yet high day, neither "
8 And they s', We cannot, until all the "
14 Laban s' to him, Surely thou art my "
15 Laban s' unto Jacob, Because thou "
18 and s', I will serve thee seven years "
19 Laban s', It is better that I give her "
21 Jacob s' unto Laban, Give me my "
25 he s' to Laban, What is this thou "
26 Laban s', It must not be so done in "
32 she s', Surely the Lord hath looked "
33 and s', Because the Lord hath heard "
34 s', Now this time will my husband "
35 she s', Now will I praise the Lord: "
30: 1 s' unto Jacob, Give me children, or "
2 and he s', Am I in God's stead, who "
3 she s', Behold my maid Bilhah, go "
6 Rachel s', God hath judged me, and "
8 Rachel s', With great wrestlings "
11 Leah s', A troop cometh: and she "
13 And Leah s', Happy am I, for the "
14 Rachel s' to Leah, Give me, I pray "
15 she s' unto her, Is it a small matter "
15 And Rachel s', Therefore he shall lie "
16 and s', Thou must come in unto me; "
18 And Leah s', God hath given me my "
20 Leah s', God hath endued me with a "
23 and s', God hath taken away my "
24 and s', The Lord shall add to me "
25 that Jacob s' unto Laban, Send me "
27 And Laban s' unto him, I pray thee, "
28 And he s', Appoint me thy wages, "
29 he s' unto him, Thou knowest how I "
31 And he s', What shall I give thee? "
31 Jacob s', Thou shalt not give me "
34 Laban s', Behold, I would it might "
31: 3 the Lord s' unto Jacob, Return unto "
5 s' unto them, I see your father's "
8 If he s' thus, The speckled shall be "
8 if he s' thus, The ringstraked shall "
11 saying, Jacob: And I s', Here am I. "
12 And he s', Lift up now thine eyes, "
14 s' unto him, Is there yet any portion "
16 whatsoever God hath s' unto thee, "
24 s' unto him, Take heed that thou "
26 Laban s' to Jacob, What hast thou "
31 Jacob answered and s' to Laban, "
31 for I s', Peradventure thou wouldest "

Ge 31:35 And she s' to her father, Let it not 559
36 and Jacob answered and s' to Laban, "
43 Laban answered and s' unto Jacob, "
46 Jacob s' unto his brethren, Gather "
48 And Laban s', This heap is a witness "
49 he s', The Lord watch between me "
51 Laban s' to Jacob, Behold this heap, "
32: 2 Jacob saw them, he s', This is God's "
8 s', If Esau come to the one company, "
9 And Jacob s', O God of my father "
16 s' unto his servants, Pass over "
20 he s', I will appease him with the "
26 And he s', Let me go, for the day "
26 he s', I will not let thee go, except "
27 he s' unto him, What is thy name? "
27 is thy name? And he s', Jacob. "
28 he s', Thy name shall be called no "
29 s', Tell me, I pray thee, thy name. "
29 he s', Wherefore is it that thou dost "
33: 5 and s', Who are those with thee? "
5 he s', The children which God hath "
8 he s', What meanest thou by all this "
8 he s', These are to find grace in the "
9 Esau s', I have enough, my brother; "
10 And Jacob s', Nay, I pray thee, if now "
12 And he s', Let us take our journey, "
13 And he s' unto him, My lord knoweth "
15 Esau s', Let me now leave with thee "
15 And he s', What needeth it? let me "
34:11 Shechem s' unto her father and unto "
13 s', because he had defiled Dinah *1696
14 And they s' unto them, We cannot 559
30 And Jacob s' to Simeon and Levi, "
31 And they s', Should he deal with our "
35: 1 And God s' unto Jacob, Arise, go up "
2 Then Jacob s' unto his household, "
10 God s' unto him, Thy name is Jacob: "
11 And God s' unto him, I am God "
17 the midwife s' unto her, Fear not; "
37: 6 And he s' unto them, Hear, I pray "
8 his brethren s' to him, Shalt thou "
9 s', Behold, I have dreamed a dream "
10 his father rebuked him, and s' "
13 And Israel s' unto Joseph, Do not "
13 them. And he s' to him, Here am I. "
14 And he s' to him, Go, I pray thee, "
16 he s', I seek my brethren: tell me, I "
17 And the man s', They are departed "
19 And they s' one to another, Behold, "
21 hands; and s', Let us not kill him. "
22 And Reuben s' unto them, Shed no "
26 Judah s' unto his brethren, What "
30 brethren, and s', The child is not; "
32 father; and s', This have we found: "
33 And he knew it, and s', It is my son's "
35 and he s', For I will go down into the "
38: 8 And Judah s' unto Onan, Go in unto "
11 s' Judah to Tamar his daughter in "
11 for he s', Lest peradventure he die "
16 s', Go to, I pray thee, let me come in "
16 And she s', What wilt thou give me, "
17 he s', I will send thee a kid from the "
17 she s', Wilt thou give me a pledge, "
18 he s', What pledge shall I give thee? "
18 And she s', Thy signet, and thy "
21 And they s', There was no harlot "
22 to Judah, and s', I cannot find her; "
22 men of the place s', that there was "
23 Judah s', Let her take it to her, lest "
24 And Judah s', Bring her forth, and "
25 she s', Discern, I pray thee, whose "
26 Judah acknowledged them, and s', "
29 and she s', How hast thou broken "
39: 7 Joseph; and she s', Lie with me. "
8 refused, and s' unto his master's wife, "
40: 8 they s' unto him, We have dreamed "
8 And Joseph s' unto them, Do not "
9 and s' to him, In my dream, behold, "
12 And Joseph s' unto him, This is the "
16 he s' unto Joseph, I also was in my "
18 Joseph answered and s', This is the "
41:15 And Pharaoh s' unto Joseph, I have "
17 Pharaoh s' unto Joseph, In my *1696
25 Joseph s' unto Pharaoh, The dream 559
38 Pharaoh s' unto his servants, Can we "
39 Pharaoh s' unto Joseph, Forasmuch "
41 Pharaoh s' unto Joseph, See, I have "
44 And Pharaoh s' unto Joseph, I am "
51 God, s' he, hath made me forget all "
54 come, according as Joseph had s': 559
55 Pharaoh s' unto all the Egyptians, "
42: 1 Jacob s' unto his sons, Why do ye "
2 And he s', Behold, I have heard that "
4 for he s', Lest peradventure mischief "
7 he s' unto them, Whence come ye? "
7 they s', From the land of Canaan to "
9 s' unto them, Ye are spies; to see "
10 they s' unto him, Nay, my lord, but "
12 he s' unto them, Nay, but to see the "
13 And they s', Thy servants are twelve "
14 Joseph s' unto them, That is it that "
18 Joseph s' unto them the third day, "
21 they s' one to another, We are verily, "
28 he s' unto his brethren, My money is "
31 we s' unto him, We are true men; "
33 s' unto us, Hereby shall I know that "
36 Jacob their father s' unto them, Me "
38 he s', My son shall not go down with "
43: 2 father s' unto them, Go again, buy "
5 man s' unto us, Ye shall not see my "
6 Israel s', Wherefore dealt ye so ill "
7 they s', The man asked us straitly of "
8 And Judah s' unto Israel his father, "
11 father Israel s' unto them, If it must "
16 he s' to the ruler of his house, Bring "
18 they s', Because of the money that "

Ge 43:20 And s', O sir, we came indeed down 559
23 And he s', Peace be to you, fear not: "
27 welfare, and s', Is your father well, "
29 and s', Is this your younger brother, "
29 he s', God be gracious unto thee, my "
31 and refrained himself, and s', Set on "
44: 4 far off, Joseph s' unto his steward, "
7 they s' unto him, Wherefore saith "
10 he s', Now also let it be according "
15 Joseph s' unto them, What deed is "
16 Judah s', What shall we say unto my "
17 he s', God forbid that I should do so: "
18 and s', Oh my lord, let thy servant, "
20 And we s' unto my lord, We have a "
22 we s' unto my lord, The lad cannot "
25 our father s', Go again, and buy us a "
26 And we s', We cannot go down: if "
27 my father s' unto us, Ye know that "
28 and I s', Surely he is torn in pieces; "
45: 3 Joseph s' unto his brethren, I am "
4 Joseph s' unto his brethren, Come "
4 And he s', I am Joseph your brother, "
17 Pharaoh s' unto Joseph, Say unto "
24 he s' unto them, See that ye fall not "
27 words of Joseph, which he had s'. 1697
28 Israel s', It is enough; Joseph my 559
46: 2 s', Jacob, Jacob. And he s', Here am "
3 And he s', I am God, the God of thy "
30 Israel s' unto Joseph, Now let me "
31 And Joseph s' unto his brethren, and "
47: 1 and s', My father and my brethren, "
3 Pharaoh s' unto his brethren, What "
3 s' unto Pharaoh, Thy servants are "
4 They s' moreover unto Pharaoh, For "
8 Pharaoh s' unto Jacob, How old art "
9 Jacob s' unto Pharaoh, The days of "
15 unto Joseph, and s', Give us bread: "
16 Joseph s', Give your cattle; and I "
18 s' unto him, We will not hide it "
23 Joseph s' unto the people, Behold, "
25 they s', Thou hast saved our lives: "
29 and s' unto him, If now I have found "
30 in their buryingplace. And he s', "
30 I will do as thou hast s'. 1697
31 And he s', Swear unto me. And he 559
48: 2 one told Jacob, and s', Behold, thy "
3 And Jacob s' unto Joseph, God "
4 s' unto me, Behold, I will make thee "
8 Joseph's sons, and s', Who are these? "
9 Joseph s' unto his father, They are "
9 he s', Bring them, I pray thee, unto "
11 And Israel s' unto Joseph, I had not "
15 blessed Joseph, and s', God, before "
18 Joseph s' unto his father, Not so, my "
19 his father refused, and s', I know it, "
21 Israel s' unto Joseph, Behold, I die: "
49: 1 s', Gather yourselves together, that "
29 he charged them, and s' unto them, "
50: 6 And Pharaoh s', Go up, and bury thy "
11 s', This is a grievous mourning "
15 they s', Joseph will peradventure "
18 they s', Behold, we be thy servants. "
19 And Joseph s' unto them, Fear not: "
24 Joseph s' unto his brethren, I die: "
Ex 1: 9 he s' unto his people, Behold, the "
16 And he s', When ye do the office of "
18 and s' unto them, Why have ye done "
19 midwives s' unto Pharaoh, Because "
2: 6 and s', This is one of the Hebrews' "
7 s' his sister to Pharaoh's daughter, "
8 Pharaoh's daughter s' to her, Go. "
9 And Pharaoh's daughter s' unto her, "
10 she s', Because I drew him out of the "
13 and he s' to him that did the wrong, "
14 he s', Who made thee a prince and "
14 Moses feared, and s', Surely this "
18 he s', How is it that ye are come so "
19 they s', An Egyptian delivered us "
20 he s' unto his daughters, And where "
22 he s', I have been a stranger in a "
3: 3 And Moses s', I will now turn aside, "
4 and s', Moses, Moses. And he s', "
5 And he s', Draw not nigh hither: "
6 he s', I am the God of thy father, "
7 And the Lord s', I have surely seen "
11 And Moses s' unto God, Who am I, "
12 And he s', Certainly I will be with "
13 And Moses s' unto God, Behold, "
14 And God s' unto Moses, I Am That I "
14 and he s', Thus shalt thou say unto "
15 God s' moreover unto Moses, Thus "
17 And I have s', I will bring you up "
4: 1 Moses answered and s', But, behold, "
2 the Lord s' unto him, What is that "
2 in thine hand? And he s', A rod. "
3 And he s', Cast it on the ground. "
4 Lord s' unto Moses, Put forth thine "
6 Lord s' furthermore unto him, Put "
7 he s', Put thine hand into thy bosom "
10 Moses s' unto the Lord, O my Lord, "
11 Lord s' unto him, Who hath made "
13 And he s', O my Lord, send, I pray "
14 and he s', Is not Aaron the Levite "
18 and s' unto him, Let me go, I pray "
18 And Jethro s' to Moses, Go in peace. "
19 Lord s' unto Moses in Midian, Go, "
21 Lord s' unto Moses, When thou goest "
25 and s', Surely a bloody husband art "
26 she s', A bloody husband thou art, "
27 And the Lord s' to Aaron, Go into the "
5: 2 And Pharaoh s', Who is the Lord, "
3 And they s', The God of the Hebrews "
4 And the king of Egypt s' unto them, "
5 And Pharaoh s', Behold, the people "
17 But he s', Ye are idle, ye are idle: "
19 after it was s', Ye shall not minish "

Ex 5:21 they s' unto them, The Lord look 559
22 returned unto the Lord, and s', Lord, "
6: 1 Lord s' unto Moses, Now shalt thou "
2 and s' unto him, I am the Lord: "
26 to whom the Lord s', Bring out the "
30 Moses s' before the Lord, Behold, I "
7: 1 Lord s' unto Moses, See, I have made "
13 not unto them; as the Lord had s'.*1696
14 the Lord s' unto Moses, Pharaoh's 559
22 not unto them; as the Lord had s'.*1696
8: 8 and s', Intreat the Lord, that he 559
9 Moses s' unto Pharaoh, Glory over "
10 And he s', To morrow. "
10 he s', Be it according to thy word: "
15 not unto them; as the Lord had s'.*1696
16 the Lord s' unto Moses, Say unto 559
19 the magicians s' unto Pharaoh, 1696
19 not unto them, as the Lord had s'.* "
20 the Lord s' unto Moses, Rise up 559
25 and s', Go ye, sacrifice to your God "
26 And Moses s', It is not meet so to do; "
28 And Pharaoh s', I will let you go, "
29 And Moses s', Behold, I go out from "
9: 1 the Lord s' unto Moses, Go in unto "
8 Lord s' unto Moses and unto Aaron, "
13 And the Lord s' unto Moses, Rise up "
22 the Lord s' unto Moses, Stretch out "
27 and said unto them, I have sinned "
29 And Moses s' unto him, As soon as I "
10: 1 the Lord s' unto Moses, Go in unto "
3 and s' unto him, Thus saith the Lord "
7 And Pharaoh's servants s' unto him, "
8 he s' unto them, Go, serve the Lord "
9 Moses s', We will go with our young "
10 he s' unto them, Let the Lord be so "
12 the Lord s' unto Moses, Stretch out "
16 and he s', I have sinned against the "
21 the Lord s' unto Moses, Stretch out "
24 and s', Go ye, serve the Lord; "
25 Moses s', Thou must give us also "
28 Pharaoh s' unto him, Get thee from "
29 Moses s', Thou hast spoken well, "
11: 1 Lord s' unto Moses, Yet will I bring "
4 And Moses s', Thus saith the Lord, "
9 Lord s' unto Moses, Pharaoh shall "
12:21 and s' unto them, Draw out and take "
31 and s', Rise up, and get you forth "
31 go, serve the Lord, as ye have s'. 1696
32 flocks and your herds, as ye have s'," "
33 for they s', We be all dead men. 559
43 the Lord s' unto Moses and Aaron, "
13: 3 Moses s' unto the people, Remember "
17 for God s', Lest peradventure the "
14: 5 And they s', Why have we done this, "
11 they s' unto Moses, Because there "
13 And Moses s' unto the people, Fear "
15 the Lord s' unto Moses, Wherefore "
25 so that the Egyptians s', Let us flee "
26 the Lord s' unto Moses, Stretch out "
15: 9 The enemy s', I will pursue, I will "
26 And s', If thou will diligently hearken "
16: 3 the children of Israel s' unto them, "
4 Then s' the Lord unto Moses, Behold, "
6 And Moses and Aaron s' unto all the "
8 And Moses s', This shall be, when "
15 they s' one to another, It is manna: "
15 And Moses s' unto them, This is the "
19 And Moses s', Let no man leave of it "
23 he s' unto them, This is that which "
23 the Lord hath s', To morrow is the 1696
25 And Moses s', Eat that to day; for 559
28 the Lord s' unto Moses, How long "
32 Moses s', This is the thing which "
33 Moses s' unto Aaron, Take a pot, "
17: 2 and s', Give us water that we may "
2 And Moses s' unto them, Why chide "
3 murmured against Moses, and s', "
5 the Lord s' unto Moses, Go on before "
9 Moses s' unto Joshua, Choose us "
10 Joshua did as Moses had s' to him, "
14 Lord s' unto Moses, Write this for a "
16 he s', Because the Lord hath sworn "
18: 3 for he s', I have been an alien in a "
4 God of my father, s' he, was mine help, "
6 s' unto Moses, I thy father in law 559
10 And Jethro s', Blessed be the Lord, "
14 he s', What is this thing that thou "
15 And Moses s' unto his father in law, "
17 And Moses' father in law s' unto him, "
24 in law, and did all that he had s'. "
19: 8 people answered together, and s', All "
9 the Lord s' unto Moses, Lo, I come "
10 the Lord s' unto Moses, Go unto the "
15 And he s' unto the people, Be ready "
21 the Lord s' unto Moses, Go down, "
23 Moses s' unto the Lord, The people "
24 the Lord s' unto him, Away, get thee "
20:19 And they s' unto Moses, Speak thou "
20 Moses s' unto the people, Fear not: "
22 Lord s' unto Moses, Thus thou shalt "
23:13 in all things that I have s' unto you "
24: 1 he s' unto Moses, Come up unto the "
3 answered with one voice, and s', All "
3 which the Lord hath s' will we do.*1696
7 the people: and they s', All that the 559
7 that the Lord hath s' will we do, *1696
8 and s', Behold the blood of the 559
12 Lord s' unto Moses, Come up to me "
14 he s' unto the elders, Tarry ye here "
30:34 Lord s' unto Moses, Take unto thee "
32: 1 and s' unto him, Up, make us gods, "
2 And Aaron s' unto them, Break off "
4 they s', These be thy gods, O Israel, "
5 Aaron made proclamation, and s', "
7 Lord s' unto Moses, Go, get thee 1696
8 and s', These be thy gods, O Israel, 559

Ex 32: 9 the Lord s' unto Moses, I have seen 559
11 and s', Lord, why doth thy wrath "
17 he s' unto Moses, There is a noise of "
18 And he s', It is not the voice of them "
21 And Moses s' unto Aaron, What did "
22 And Aaron s', Let not the anger of "
23 For they s' unto me, Make us gods, "
24 I s' unto them, Whosoever hath any "
26 and s', Who is on the Lord's side? "
27 he s' unto them, Thus saith the Lord "
29 Moses had s', Consecrate yourselves "
30 Moses s' unto the people, Ye have "
31 and s', Oh, this people have sinned "
33 the Lord s' unto Moses, Whosoever "
33: 1 the Lord s' unto Moses, Depart, *1696
5 Lord had s' unto Moses, Say unto 559
12 Moses s' unto the Lord, See, thou "
12 thou hast s', I know thee by name, "
14 And he s', My presence shall go with "
15 And he s' unto him, If thy presence "
17 Lord s' unto Moses, I will do this "
18 he s', I beseech thee, shew me thy "
19 he s', I will make all my goodness "
20 he s', Thou canst not see my face: "
21 the Lord s', Behold, there is a place "
34: 1 Lord s' unto Moses, Hew thee two "
9 And he s', If now I have found grace "
10 he s', Behold, I make a covenant: "
27 Lord s' unto Moses, Write thou these "
35: 1 s' unto them, These are the words "
30 Moses s' unto the children of Israel, "
Le 8: 5 Moses s' unto the congregation, "
31 Moses s' unto Aaron, and to his sons, "
9: 2 he s' unto Aaron, Take thee a young "
6 And Moses s', This is the thing "
7 And Moses s' unto Aaron, Go unto "
10: 3 Then Moses s' unto Aaron, This is it "
4 and s' unto them, Come near, carry "
5 out of the camp; as Moses had s'. 1696
6 And Moses s' unto Aaron, and unto 559
19 Aaron s' unto Moses, Behold, this*1696
16: 2 Lord s' unto Moses, Speak unto 559
17:12 I s' unto the children of Israel, No "
14 I s' unto the children of Israel, Ye "
20:24 I have s' unto you, Ye shall inherit "
21: 1 Lord s' unto Moses, Speak unto the "
Nu 3:40 Lord s' unto Moses, Number all the "
7:11 the Lord s' unto Moses, They shall "
9: 7 men s' unto him, We are defiled by "
8 Moses s' unto them, Stand still, and "
10:29 Moses s' unto Hobab, the son of "
29 unto the place of which the Lord s', "
30 he s' unto him, I will not go; but I "
31 he s', Leave us not, I pray thee; "
35 Moses s', Rise up, Lord, and let "
36 when it rested, he s', Return, O Lord, "
11: 4 and s', Who shall give us flesh to "
11 Moses s' unto the Lord, Wherefore "
16 Lord s' unto Moses, Gather unto me "
21 Moses s', The people, among whom "
21 thou hast s', I will give them flesh, "
23 Lord s' unto Moses, Is the Lord's "
27 s', Eldad and Medad do prophesy "
28 and s', My lord Moses, forbid them. "
29 Moses s' unto him, Enviest thou for "
12: 2 And they s', Hath the Lord indeed "
6 he s', Hear now my words: If there "
11 Aaron s' unto Moses, Alas, my lord, "
14 Lord s' unto Moses, If her father "
13:17 s' unto them, Get you up this way "
27 s', We came unto the land whither "
30 s', Let us go up at once, and possess "
31 men that went up with him s', We be "
14: 2 whole congregation s' unto them, "
4 they s' one to another, Let us make "
11 Lord s' unto Moses, How long will "
13 Moses s' unto the Lord, Then the "
20 Lord s', I have pardoned according "
31 ones, which ye s' should be a prey, "
35 I the Lord have s', I will surely do*1696
41 Moses s', Wherefore now do ye 559
15:35 Lord s' unto Moses, The man shall "
16: 3 and against Aaron, and s' unto them, "
8 Moses s' unto Korah, Hear, I pray "
12 which s', We will not come up: "
15 s' unto the Lord, Respect not thou "
16 Moses s' unto Korah, Be thou and "
22 fell upon their faces, and s', O God, "
28 Moses s', Hereby ye shall know that "
34 for they s', Lest the earth swallow "
40 as the Lord s' to him by the hand*1696
46 And Moses s' unto Aaron, Take a 559
17:10 Lord s' unto Moses, Bring Aaron's "
18: 1 Lord s' unto Aaron, Thou and thy "
24 I have s' unto them, Among the "
20:10 s' unto them, Hear now, ye rebels; "
18 Edom s' unto him, Thou shalt not "
19 children of Israel s' unto him, We "
20 he s', Thou shalt not go through. "
21: 2 vowed a vow unto the Lord, and s', "
7 people came to Moses, and s', We "
8 Lord s' unto Moses, Make thee a "
14 it is s' in the book of the wars of "
34 Lord s' unto Moses, Fear him not: "
22: 4 Moab s' unto the elders of Midian, "
8 he s' unto them, Lodge here this "
9 And God came unto Balaam, and s', "
10 Balaam s' unto God, Balak the son "
12 God s' unto Balaam, Thou shalt not "
13 s' unto the princes of Balak, Get "
14 went unto Balak, and s', Balaam "
16 they came to Balaam, and s' to him, "
18 answered and s' unto the servants "
20 Balaam at night, and s' unto him, "
28 she s' unto Balaam, What have I "
29 Balaam s' unto the ass, Because "

Nu 22:30 the ass s' unto Balaam, Am not I 559
30 do so unto thee? And he s', Nay. "
32 the angel of the Lord s' unto him, "
34 Balaam s' unto the angel of the "
35 angel of the Lord s' unto Balaam, "
37 Balak s' unto Balaam, Did I not "
38 And Balaam s' unto Balak, Lo, I am "
23: 1 Balaam s' unto Balak, Build me "
3 Balaam s' unto Balak, Stand by thy "
4 and he s' unto him, I have prepared "
5 s', Return unto Balak, and thus "
7 And he took up his parable, and s', "
11 Balak s' unto Balaam, What hast "
12 And he answered and s', Must I not "
13 Balak s' unto him, Come, I pray "
15 he s' unto Balak, Stand here by my "
16 s', Go again unto Balak, and say "
17 Balak s' unto him, What hath the "
18 and s', Rise up, Balak, and hear; "
19 hath he s', and shall he not do it? "
23 it shall be s' of Jacob and of Israel, "
25 Balak s' unto Balaam, Neither curse "
26 Balaam answered and s' unto Balak, "
27 Balak s' unto Balaam, Come, I pray "
29 Balaam s' unto Balak, Build me "
30 Balak did as Balaam had s', and "
24: 3 And he took up his parable and s', "
3 Balaam the son of Beor hath s', *5002
3 man whose eyes are open hath s':* "
4 He hath s', which heard the words* "
10 Balak s' unto Balaam, I called thee 559
12 Balaam s' unto Balak, Spake I not "
15 he took up his parable, and s', "
15 Balaam the son of Beor hath s', *5002
15 man whose eyes are open hath s':* "
16 hath s', which heard the words of* "
20 and s', Amalek was the first of the 559
21 s', Strong is the dwellingplace, and "
23 s', Alas, Who shall live when God "
25: 4 And the Lord s' unto Moses, Take "
5 Moses s' unto the judges of Israel, "
26:65 For the Lord had s' of them, They "
27:12 Lord s' unto Moses, Get thee up "
18 the Lord s' unto Moses, Take thee "
31:15 Moses s' unto them, Have ye saved "
21 the priest s' unto the men of war "
49 they s' unto Moses, Thy servants "
32: 5 s' they, if we have found grace in "
6 Moses s' unto the children of Gad "
16 s', We will build sheepfolds here "
20 Moses s' unto them, If ye will do "
29 Moses s' unto them, If the children "
31 Lord hath s' unto thy servants, so 1696
36: 2 they s', The Lord commanded my 559
5 the sons of Joseph hath s' well. *1696
De 1:14 ye answered me, and s', The thing 559
20 I s' unto you, Ye are come unto the "
21 of thy fathers hath s' unto thee; *1696
22 and s', We will send men before us, 559
25 s', It is a good land which the Lord "
27 s', Because the Lord hated us, he "
29 I s' unto you, Dread not, neither "
39 ones, which ye s' should be a prey, "
41 s' unto me, We have sinned against "
42 Lord s' unto me, Say unto them, Go "
2: 9 Lord s' unto me, Distress not the "
13 rise up, s' I, and get you over the "
31 Lord s' unto me, Behold, I have 559
3: 2 Lord s' unto me, Fear him not: for "
26 Lord s' unto me, Let it suffice thee; "
4:10 when the Lord s' unto me, Gather "
5: 1 s' unto them, Hear, O Israel, the "
24 And ye s', Behold, the Lord our God "
28 Lord s' unto me, I have heard the "
28 have well s' all that they have spoken. "
9: 3 as the Lord hath s' unto thee. *1696
12 Lord s' unto me, Arise, get thee 559
25 Lord had s' he would destroy you. "
26 and s', O Lord God, destroy not thy "
10: 1 s' unto me, Hew the two tables of "
11 Lord s' unto me, Arise, take thy "
11:25 tread upon, as he hath s' unto you.*1696
17:16 as the Lord hath s' unto you, Ye 559
18: 2 as he hath s' unto them. *1696
17 Lord s' unto me, They have well 559
29: 2 s' unto them, Ye have seen all that "
13 as he hath s' unto thee, and as he*1696
31: 2 he s' unto them, I am an hundred 559
2 also the Lord hath s' unto me, "
3 before thee, as the Lord hath s'. *1696
7 s' unto him in the sight of all Israel,559
14, 16 the Lord s' unto Moses, Behold, "
23 the son of Nun a charge, and s', Be "
32:20 he s', I will hide my face from them, "
26 I s', I would scatter them into "
46 he s' unto them, Set your hearts "
33: 2 he s', The Lord came from Sinai, "
7 s', Hear, Lord, the voice of Judah, "
8 And of Levi he s', Let thy Thummim "
9 Who s' unto his father and to his "
12 of Benjamin he s', The beloved of "
13 of Joseph he s', Blessed of the Lord "
18 of Zebulun he s', Rejoice, Zebulun, "
20 And of Gad he s', Blessed be he that "
22 of Dan he s', Dan is a lion's whelp: "
23 And of Naphtali he s', O Naphtali, "
24 of Asher he s', Let Asher be blessed "
34: 4 Lord s' unto him, This is the land "
Jos 1: 3 unto you, as I s' unto Moses. *1696
2: 4 s' thus, There came men unto me, 559
9 she s' unto the men, I know that "
16 she s' unto them, Get you to the "
17 And the men s' unto her, We will be "
21 she s', According unto your words, "
24 they s' unto Joshua, Truly the Lord "
3: 5 Joshua s' unto the people, Sanctify "

Jos 3: 7 Lord s' unto Joshua, This day will 559
9 Joshua s' unto the children of Israel, "
10 Joshua s', Hereby ye shall know "
4: 5 Joshua s' unto them, Pass over "
5: 2 that time the Lord s' unto Joshua, "
9 Lord s' unto Joshua, This day have "
13 s' unto him, Art thou for us, or for "
14 he s', Nay; but as captain of the "
14 did worship, and s' unto him, what "
15 captain of the Lord's host s' unto "
6: 2 Lord s' unto Joshua, See, I have "
6 called the priests, and s' unto them, "
7 he s' unto the people, Pass on, and "
16 Joshua s' unto the people, Shout; "
22 Joshua had s' unto the two men "
7: 3 returned to Joshua, and s' unto him, "
7 And Joshua s', Alas, O Lord God, "
10 Lord s' unto Joshua, Get thee up; "
19 Joshua s' unto Achan, My son, give, "
20 s', Indeed I have sinned against "
25 Joshua s', Why hast thou troubled "
8: 1 the Lord s' unto Joshua, Fear not, "
18 Lord s' unto Joshua, Stretch out "
9: 6 And s' unto him, and to the men of "
7 men of Israel s' unto the Hivites, "
8 s' unto Joshua, We are thy servants. "
8 Joshua s' unto them, Who art ye? "
9 they s' unto him, From a very far "
19 princes s' unto all the congregation, "
21 the princes s' unto them, Let them "
24 And they answered Joshua, and s', "
10: 8 Lord s' unto Joshua, Fear them not: "
12 s' in the sight of Israel, Sun, stand "
18 Joshua s', Roll great stones upon "
22 s' Joshua, Open the mouth of the "
24 s' unto the captains of the men of "
25 Joshua s' unto them, Fear not, nor "
11: 6 Lord s' unto Joshua, Be not afraid "
23 to all that the Lord s' unto Moses; *1696
13: 1 the Lord s' unto him, Thou art old 559
14, 33 inheritance, as he s' unto them. 1696
14: 6 Caleb...the Kenezite s' unto him, 559
6 thing that the Lord s' unto Moses *1696
10 as he s', these forty and five years, * "
12 to drive them out, as the Lord s'. * "
15: 16 s', He that smiteth Kirjath-sepher, 559
18 Caleb s' unto her, What wouldest "
17: 16 children of Joseph s', The hill is not "
18: 3 Joshua s' unto the children of Israel, "
22: 2 s' unto them, Ye have kept all that "
21 s' unto the heads of the thousands *1696
26 we s', Let us now prepare to build 559
28 s' we, that it shall be, when they "
31 the priest s' unto the children of "
23: 2 s' unto them, I am old and stricken "
24: 2 Joshua s' unto all the people, Thus "
16 people answered and s', God forbid "
19 And Joshua s' unto the people, Ye "
21 people s' unto Joshua, Nay; but we "
22 Joshua s' unto the people, Ye are "
22 And they s', We are witnesses. "
23 put away, s' he, the strange gods "
24 people s' unto Joshua, the Lord 559
27 And Joshua s' unto all the people, "
J'g 1: 2 And the Lord s', Judah shall go up: "
3 Judah s' unto Simeon his brother, "
7 Adoni-bezek s', Threescore and ten "
12 And Caleb s', He that smiteth "
14 Caleb s' unto her, What wilt thou? "
15 she s' unto him, Give me a blessing: "
20 Hebron unto Caleb, as Moses s': *1696
24 they s' unto him, Shew us, we pray 559
2: 1 s', I made you to go up out of Egypt, "
1 I s', I will never break my covenant "
3 Wherefore I also s', I will not drive "
15 them for evil, as the Lord had s', *1696
20 and he s', Because that this people 559
3: 19 s', I have a secret errand unto thee, "
19 thee, O king: who s', Keep silence. "
20 and Ehud s', I have a message from "
24 they s', Surely he covereth his feet "
28 he s' unto them, Follow after me: "
4: 6 s' unto him, Hath not the Lord God "
8 Barak s' unto her, If thou wilt go "
9 she s', I will surely go with thee: "
14 Deborah s' unto Barak, Up; for this "
18 s' unto him, Turn in, my lord, turn "
19 he s' unto her, Give me, I pray thee, "
20 he s' unto her, Stand in the door of "
22 s' unto him, Come, and I will shew "
5: 23 ye Meroz, s' the angel of the Lord, "
6: 8 which s' unto them, Thus saith the "
10 I s' unto you, I am the Lord your "
12 s' unto him, The Lord is with thee, "
13 Gideon s' unto him, Oh my Lord, if "
14 s', Go in this thy might, and thou "
15 And he s' unto him, Oh my Lord, "
16 the Lord s' unto him, Surely I will "
17 he s' unto him, If now I have found "
18 he s', I will tarry until thou come "
20 the angel of God s' unto him, Take "
22 Gideon s', Alas, O Lord God! for "
23 the Lord s' unto him, Peace be unto "
25 that the Lord s' unto him, Take thy "
27 did as the Lord had s' unto him: *1696
29 they s' one to another, Who hath 559
29 they s', Gideon the son of Joash "
30 the men of the city s' unto Joash, "
31 Joash s' unto all that stood against "
36 Gideon s' unto God, If thou wilt "
36 by mine hand, as thou hast s', *1696
37 by mine hand, as thou hast s'. * "
39 Gideon s' unto God, Let not thine 559
7: 2, 4 Lord s' unto Gideon, The people "
5 the Lord s' unto Gideon, Every one "
7 the Lord s' unto Gideon, By the "

J'g 7: 9 that the Lord s' unto him, Arise, 559
13 s', Behold, I dreamed a dream, and, "
14 his fellow answered and s', This is "
15 the host of Israel, and s', Arise; "
17 he s' unto them, Look on me, and "
8: 1 the men of Ephraim s' unto him, "
2 he s' unto them, What have I done "
3 toward him, when he had s' that. 1696
5 he s' unto the men of Succoth, 559
6 princes of Succoth s', Are the hands "
7 Gideon s', Therefore when the Lord "
15 s', Behold Zebah and Zalmunna, "
18 s' he unto Zebah and Zalmunna, "
19 he s', They were my brethren, even "
20 he s' unto Jether his firstborn, Up, "
21 Zebah and Zalmunna s', Rise thou, "
22 the men of Israel s' unto Gideon, "
23 Gideon s' unto them, I will not rule "
24 Gideon s' unto them, I would desire "
9: 3 Abimelech; for they s', He is our "
7 s' unto them, Hearken unto me, ye "
8 s' unto the olive tree, Reign thou "
9 olive tree s' unto them, Should I "
10 trees s' to the fig tree, Come thou, "
11 the fig tree s' unto them, Should I "
12 s' the trees unto the vine, Come "
13 vine s' unto them, Should I leave "
14 s' all the trees unto the bramble, "
15 And the bramble s' unto the trees, "
28 Gaal the son of Ebed s', Who is "
29 s' to Abimelech, Increase the army, "
36 he s' to Zebul, Behold, there come "
36 Zebul s' unto him, Thou seest the "
37 Gaal spake again and s', See there "
38 s' Zebul unto him, Where is now "
48 s' unto the people that were with "
54 s' unto him, Draw thy sword, and "
10: 11 Lord s' unto the children of Israel, "
15 children of Israel s' unto the Lord, "
18 princes of Gilead s' one to another, "
11: 2 s' unto him, Thou shalt not inherit "
6 they s' unto Jephthah, Come, and be "
7 And Jephthah s' unto the elders of "
8 elders of Gilead s' unto Jephthah, "
9 And Jephthah s' unto the elders of "
10 elders of Gilead s' unto Jephthah, "
15 s' unto him, Thus saith Jephthah, "
19 Israel s' unto him, Let us pass, we "
30 and s', If thou shalt without fail "
35 clothes, and s', Alas, my daughter! "
36 she s' unto him, My father, if thou "
37 And she s' unto her father, Let this "
38 And he s', Go. And he sent her away "
12: 1 and s' unto Jephthah, Wherefore "
2 Jephthah s' unto them, I and my "
4 because they s', Ye Gileadites are "
5 Ephraimites which were escaped s', "
5 men of Gilead s' unto him, Art thou "
5 thou an Ephraimite? If he s', Nay; "
6 Then s' they unto him, Say now "
6 he s' Sibboleth: for he could not "
13: 3 s' unto her, Behold now, thou art "
7 he s' unto me, Behold, thou shalt "
8 s', O my Lord, let the man of God "
10 s' unto him, Behold, the man hath "
11 s' unto him, Art thou the man that "
11 unto the woman, And he s', I am. "
12 Manoah s', Now let thy words come "
13 angel of the Lord s' unto Manoah, "
13 I s' unto the woman let her beware. "
15 Manoah s' unto the angel of the "
16 angel of the Lord s' unto Manoah, "
17 Manoah s' unto the angel of the "
18 the angel of the Lord s' unto him, "
22 Manoah s' unto his wife, We shall "
23 his wife s' unto him, If the Lord "
14: 2 and s', I have seen a woman in "
3 father and his mother s' unto him, "
3 Samson s' unto his father, Get her "
12 Samson s' unto them, I will now "
13 s' unto him, Put forth thy riddle, "
14 he s' unto them, Out of the eater "
15 s' unto Samson's wife, Entice thy "
16 and s', Thou dost but hate me, and "
16 And he s' unto her, Behold, I have "
18 the men of the city s' unto him on "
18 s' unto them, If ye had not plowed "
15: 1 he s', I will go in to my wife into the "
2 And her father s', I verily thought "
3 Samson s' concerning them, Now "
6 the Philistines s', Who hath done "
7 Samson s' unto them, Though ye "
10 the men of Judah s', Why are ye "
11 and s' to Samson, Knowest thou not "
11 he s' unto them, As they did unto "
12 they s' unto him, We are come down "
12 Samson s' unto them, Swear unto "
16 Samson s', With the jawbone of an "
18 called on the Lord, and s', Thou hast "
16: 5 and s' unto her, Entice him, and see "
6 And Delilah s' to Samson, Tell me, I "
7 Samson s' unto her, If they bind "
9 she s' unto him, The Philistines be "
10 Delilah s' unto Samson, Behold, "
11 he s' unto her, If they bind me fast "
12 and s' unto him, The Philistines be "
13 Delilah s' unto Samson, Hitherto "
13 And he s' unto her, If thou weavest "
14 s' unto him, The Philistines be upon "
15 she s' unto him, How canst thou "
17 her all his heart, and s' unto her, "
20 she s', The Philistines be upon thee, "
20 awoke out of his sleep, and s', I will "
23, 24 they s', Our god hath delivered "
25 that they s', Call for Samson, that he "
26 Samson s' unto the lad that held "

J'g 16: 28 and s', O Lord God, remember me, 559
30 And Samson s', Let me die with the "
17: 2 he s' unto his mother, The eleven "
2 his mother s', Blessed be thou of "
3 his mother s', I had wholly "
9 Micah s' unto him, Whence comest "
9 he s' unto him, I am a Levite of "
10 Micah s' unto him, Dwell with me, "
13 Then s' Micah, Now know I that the "
18: 2 s' unto them, Go, search the land: "
3 and s' unto him, Who brought thee "
4 he s' unto them, Thus and thus "
5 they s' unto him, Ask counsel, we "
6 priest s' unto them, Go in peace: "
8 brethren s' unto them, What say "
9 they s', Arise, that we may go up "
14 s' unto their brethren, Do ye know "
18 s' the priest unto them, What do "
19 they s' unto him, Hold thy peace, "
23 and s' unto Micah, What aileth thee, "
24 he s', Ye have taken away my gods "
25 children of Dan s' unto him, Let "
19: 5 damsel's father s' said unto his son "
6 the damsel's father had s' unto the "
8 damsel's father s', Comfort thine "
9 the damsel's father, s' unto him, "
11 servant s' unto his master, Come, I "
12 his master s' unto him, We will not "
13 he s' unto his servant, Come, and let "
17 the old man s', Whither goest thou? "
18 And he s' unto him, We are passing "
20 the old man s', Peace be with thee; "
23 and s' unto them, Nay, my brethren, "
28 he s' unto her, Up, and let us be "
30 s', There was no such deed done "
20: 3 Then s' the children of Israel, Tell "
4 slain, answered and s', I came into "
18 and s', Which of us shall go up first "
18 the Lord s', Judah shall go up first. "
23 And the Lord s', Go up against him. "
28 Lord s', Go up; for to morrow I will "
32 of Benjamin s', They are smitten "
32 children of Israel s', Let us flee, and "
39 s', Surely they are smitten down "
21: 3 s', O Lord God of Israel, why is this "
5 children of Israel s', Who is there "
6 s', There is one tribe cut off from "
8 And they s', What one is there of the "
16 the elders of the congregation s', "
17 s', There must be an inheritance "
19 they s', Behold, there is a feast of "
Ru 1: 8 Naomi s' unto her two daughters "
10 s' unto her, Surely we will return "
11 And Naomi s', Turn again, my "
15 she s', Behold, thy sister in law is "
16 Ruth s', Intreat me not to leave "
19 them, and they s', Is this Naomi? "
20 And she s' unto them, Call me not "
2: 2 Ruth the Moabitess s' unto Naomi, "
2 she s' unto her, Go, my daughter. "
4 s' unto the reapers, The Lord be "
5 Then s' Boaz unto his servant that "
6 over the reapers answered and s', "
7 she s', I pray you, let me glean and "
8 s' Boaz unto Ruth, Hearest thou "
10 and s' unto him, Why have I found "
11 Boaz answered and s' unto her, It "
13 she s', Let me find favour in thy "
14 Boaz s' unto her, At mealtime come "
19 And her mother in law s' unto her, "
19 s', The man's name with whom I "
20 Naomi s' unto her daughter in law, "
20 And Naomi s' unto her, The man is "
21 Ruth...s', He s' unto me also, "
22 Naomi s' unto Ruth her daughter "
3: 1 Then Naomi her mother in law s' "
5 she s' unto her, All that thou sayest "
9 And he s', Who art thou? And she "
10 he s', Blessed be thou of the Lord, "
14 he s', Let it not be known that a "
15 he s', Bring the vail that thou hast "
16 she s', Who art thou, my daughter? "
17 she s', These six measure of barley "
17 he s' to me, Go not empty unto thy "
18 s' she, Sit still, my daughter, until "
4: 1 unto whom he s', Ho, such a one! "
2 the city, and s', Sit ye down here. "
3 he s' unto the kinsman, Naomi, that "
4 thee. And he s', I will redeem it. "
5 Then s' Boaz, What day thou buyest "
6 kinsman s', I cannot redeem it for "
8 the kinsman s' unto Boaz, Buy it "
9 Boaz s' unto the elders, and unto all "
11 and the elders, s', We are witnesses. "
14 woman s' unto Naomi, Blessed be "
1Sa 1: 8 s' Elkanah her husband to her, "
11 she vowed a vow, and s', O Lord of "
14 Eli s' unto her, How long wilt thou "
15 Hannah answered and s', No, my "
17 Eli answered and s', Go in peace: "
18 And she s', Let thine handmaid find "
22 she s' unto her husband, I will not "
23 Elkanah her husband s' unto her, "
26 And she s', Oh my lord, as thy soul "
2: 1 Hannah prayed, and s', My heart "
15 s' to the man that sacrificed, Give "
16 if any man s' unto him, Let them "
20 s', The Lord give thee seed of this "
23 he s' unto them, Why do ye such "
27 of God unto Eli, and s' unto him, "
30 I s' indeed that thy house, and the "
3: 5 he ran unto Eli, and s', Here am I; "
5 he s', I called not; lie down again. "
6, 8 went to Eli, and s', Here am I; "
9 Therefore Eli s' unto Samuel, Go, "
11 the Lord s' to Samuel, Behold, I "

1Sa 3:16 called Samuel, and s', Samuel, my 559
17 he s', What is the thing that the "
17 that the Lord hath s' unto thee? *1696
17 all the things that he s' unto thee.* "
18 And he s', It is the Lord: let him 559
4: 3 the elders of Israel s', Wherefore "
6 they s', What meaneth the noise of "
7 they s', God is come into the camp. "
7 And they s', Woe unto us! for there "
14 he s', What meaneth the noise of "
16 the man s' unto Eli, I am he that "
16 he s', What is there done, my son? "
17 the messenger answered and s', "
20 that stood by her s' unto her, 1696
22 she s', The glory is departed from 559
5: 7 they s', The ark of the God of Israel "
8 and s', What shall we do with the "
11 s', Send away the ark of the God of "
6: 3 they s', If ye send away the ark of "
4 s' they, What shall be the trespass "
20 the men of Beth-shemesh s', Who is "
7: 5 And Samuel s', Gather all Israel to "
6 and s' there, We have sinned against "
8 the children of Israel s' to Samuel, "
8: 5 s' unto him, Behold, thou art old, "
6 they s', Give us a king to judge us. "
7 Lord s' unto Samuel, Hearken unto "
11 he s', This will be the manner of the "
19 they s', Nay; but we will have a king "
22 the Lord s' to Samuel, Hearken unto "
22 Samuel s' unto the men of Israel, Go "
9: 3 Kish s' to Saul his son, Take now "
5 s' to his servant that was with him, "
6 s' unto him, Behold now, there is in "
7 s' Saul to his servant, But, behold, "
8 servant answered Saul again, and s'. "
10 s' [559] Saul to his servant, Well s'; 1697
11 and s' unto them, Is the seer here? 559
12 they answered them, and s', He is; "
17 Lord s' unto him, Behold the man 6030
18 s', Tell me, I pray thee, where the 559
19 Samuel answered Saul, and s', I am "
21 and s', Am not I a Benjamite, of the "
23 Samuel s' unto the cook, Bring the "
23 of which I s' unto thee, Set it by thee. "
24 Samuel s', Behold that which is left! "
24 hath it been kept for thee since I s', "
27 Samuel s' to Saul, Bid the servant "
10: 1 and s', Is it not because the Lord "
11 then the people s' one to another, "
12 and s', But who is their father? "
14 Saul's uncle s' unto him and to his "
14 And he s', To seek the asses: and "
15 And Saul's uncle s', Tell me, I pray "
15 pray thee, what Samuel s' unto you. "
16 Saul s' unto his uncle, He told us "
18 s' unto the children of Israel, Thus "
19 ye have s' unto him, Nay, but set a "
24 Samuel s' to all the people, See ye "
24 shouted, and s', God save the king. "
27 children of Belial s', How shall this "
11: 1 the men of Jabesh s' unto Nahash, "
3 elders of Jabesh s' unto him, Give "
5 and Saul s', What aileth the people "
9 s' unto the messengers that came, "
10 the men of Jabesh s', To morrow we "
12 And the people s' unto Samuel, Who "
12 Who is he that s', Shall Saul reign "
13 And Saul s', There shall not a man "
14 s' Samuel to the people, Come, and "
12: 1 Samuel s' unto all Israel, Behold, I "
1 your voice in all that ye s' unto me, "
4 they s', Thou hast not defrauded "
5 And he s' unto them, The Lord is "
6 Samuel s' unto the people, It is the "
10 the Lord, and s', We have sinned, "
12 ye s' unto me, Nay; but a king shall "
19 all the people s' unto Samuel, Pray "
20 Samuel s' unto the people, Fear not: "
13: 9 And Saul s', Bring hither a burnt "
11 Samuel s', What hast thou done? "
11 And Saul s', Because I saw that the "
12 Therefore s' I, The Philistines will "
13 Samuel s' to Saul, Thou hast done "
19 Philistines s', Lest the Hebrews "
14: 1 son of Saul s' unto the young man "
6 And Jonathan s' to the young man "
7 And his armourbearer s' unto him, "
8 Then s' Jonathan, Behold, we will "
11 Philistines s', Behold, the Hebrews "
12 and s', Come up to us, and we will "
12 Jonathan s' unto his armourbearer, "
17 Then s' Saul unto the people that "
18 Saul s' unto Ahiah, Bring hither the "
19 Saul s' unto the priest, Withdraw "
28 answered one of the people, and s', "
29 Then s' Jonathan, My father hath "
33 he s', Ye have transgressed: roll "
34 Saul s', Disperse yourselves among "
36 Saul s', Let us go down after the "
36 they s', Do whatsoever seemeth good "
36 Then s' the priest, Let us draw near "
38 And Saul s', Draw ye near hither, "
40 Then s' he unto all Israel, Be ye on "
40 the people s' unto Saul, Do what "
41 Therefore Saul s' unto the Lord God "
42 And Saul s', Cast lots between me "
43 Then Saul s' to Jonathan, Tell me "
43 and s', I did but taste a little honey "
45 And the people s' unto Saul, Shall "
15: 1 Samuel also s' unto Saul, The Lord "
6 And Saul s' unto the Kenites, Go, "
13 Saul s' unto him, Blessed be thou of "
14 Samuel s', What meaneth then this "
15 Saul s', They have brought them "
16 Then Samuel s' unto Saul, Stay, and "

1Sa 15:16 the Lord hath s' to me this night. 1696
16 And he s' unto him, Say on. 559
17 Samuel s', When thou wast little in "
18 Lord sent thee on a journey, and s', "
20 Saul s' unto Samuel, Yea, I have "
22 Samuel s', Hath the Lord as great "
24 Saul s' unto Samuel, I have sinned: "
26 And Samuel s' unto Saul, I will not "
28 And Samuel s' unto him, The Lord "
30 he s', I have sinned: yet honour "
32 Then s' Samuel, Bring ye hither to "
32 And Agag s', Surely the bitterness of "
33 Samuel s', As thy sword hath made "
16: 1 And the Lord s' unto Samuel, How "
2 Samuel s', How can I go? if Saul "
2 And the Lord s', Take an heifer with "
4 and s', Comest thou peaceably? "
5 And he s', Peaceably: I am come to "
6 and s', Surely the Lord's anointed is "
7 But the Lord s' unto Samuel, Look "
8, 9 s', Neither hath the Lord chosen "
10 And Samuel s' unto Jesse, The Lord "
11 Samuel s' unto Jesse, Are here all "
11 And he s', There remaineth yet the "
11 And Samuel s' unto Jesse, Send and "
12 And the Lord s', Arise, anoint him: "
15 And Saul's servants s' unto him, "
17 Saul s' unto his servants, Provide "
18 and s', Behold, I have seen a son of "
19 s', Send me David thy son, which is "
17: 8 and s' unto them, Why are ye come "
10 the Philistine s', I defy the armies "
17 Jesse s' unto David his son, Take "
25 the men of Israel s', Have ye seen "
28 and he s', Why camest thou down "
29 David s', What have I now done? "
32 And David s' to Saul, Let no man's "
33 Saul s' to David, Thou art not able "
34 David s' unto Saul, Thy servant kept "
37 David s' moreover, The Lord that "
37 And Saul s' unto David, Go, and the "
39 David s' unto Saul, I cannot go with "
43 the Philistine s' unto David, Am I a "
44 Philistine s' to David, Come to me, "
45 Then s' David to the Philistine, "
55 he s' unto Abner, the captain of the "
55 And Abner s', As thy soul liveth, O "
56 the king s', Enquire thou whose "
58 Saul s' to him, Whose son art thou, "
18: 7 s', Saul hath slain his thousands, "
8 and he s', They have ascribed unto "
11 for he s', I will smite David even to "
17 Saul s' to David, Behold my elder "
17 Saul s', Let not mine hand be upon "
18 And David s' unto Saul, Who am I? "
21 Saul s', I will give him her, that she "
21 Saul s' to David, Thou shalt this day "
23 David s', Seemeth it to you a light "
25 Saul s', Thus shall ye say to David, "
19: 4 and s' unto him, Let not the king sin "
14 to take David, she s', He is sick. "
17 And Saul s' unto Michal, Why hast "
17 answered Saul, He s' unto me, Let "
22 s', Where are Samuel and David? "
22 one s', Behold, they be at Naioth in "
20: 1 and s' before Jonathan, What have I "
2 And he s' unto him, God forbid; "
3 David sware moreover, and s', Thy "
4 s' Jonathan unto David, Whatsoever "
5 s' unto Jonathan, Behold, to morrow "
9 Jonathan s', Far be it from thee: for "
10 s' David to Jonathan, Who shall tell "
11 Jonathan s' unto David, Come, and "
12 Jonathan s' unto David, O Lord God "
18 Jonathan s' to David, To morrow is "
27 and Saul s' unto Jonathan his son, "
29 And he s', Let me go, I pray thee; "
30 and he s' unto him, Thou son of the "
32 Saul his father, and s' unto him, "
36 he s' unto his lad, Run, find out now "
37 Jonathan cried after the lad, and s', "
40 s' unto him, Go, carry them to the "
42 Jonathan s' to David, Go in peace, "
21: 1 and s' unto him, Why art thou alone, "
2 David s' unto Ahimelech the priest, "
2 hath s' unto me, Let no man know "
4 the priest answered David, and s', "
5 David answered the priest, and s', "
8 And David s' unto Ahimelech, And is "
9 the priest s', The sword of Goliath "
9 David s', There is none like that; "
11 the servants of Achish s' unto him, "
14 Then s' Achish unto his servants, "
22: 3 he s' unto the king of Moab, Let my "
5 And the prophet Gad s' unto David, "
7 Then Saul s' unto his servants that "
9 s', I saw the son of Jesse coming to "
12 And Saul s', Hear now, thou son of "
13 And Saul s' unto him, Why have ye "
14 answered the king, and s', And who "
16 the king s', Thou shalt surely die, "
17 king s' unto the footmen that stood "
18 the king s' to Doeg, Turn thou, and "
22 David s' unto Abiathar, I knew it "
23: 2 Lord s' unto David, Go, and smite "
3 David's men s' unto him, Behold, we "
4 Lord answered him and s', Arise, go "
7 And Saul s', God hath delivered him "
9 he s' to Abiathar the priest, Bring "
10 s' David, O Lord God of Israel, thy "
11 And the Lord s', He will come down. "
12 s' David, Will the men of Keilah "
12 Lord s', They will deliver thee up. "
17 And he s' unto him, Fear not: for "
21 Saul s', Blessed be ye of the Lord; "
24: 4 And the men of David s' unto him, "

1Sa 24: 4 day of which the Lord s' unto thee; 559
6 And he s' unto his men, The Lord "
9 And David s' to Saul, Wherefore "
10 I s', I will not put forth mine hand "
16 Saul s', Is this thy voice, my son "
17 And he s' to David, Thou art more "
25: 5 and David s' unto the young men, "
10 and s', Who is David? and who is the "
13 David s' unto his men, Gird ye on "
19 And she s' unto her servants, Go on "
21 Now David had s', Surely in vain "
24 fell at his feet, and s', Upon me, my "
32 And David s' to Abigail, Blessed be "
35 s' unto her, Go up in peace to thine "
39 he s', Blessed be the Lord, that hath "
41 on her face to the earth, and s', "
26: 6 answered David and s' to Ahimelech "
6 Abishai s', I will go down with thee. "
8 Then s' Abishai to David, God hath "
9 And David s' to Abishai, Destroy "
10 David s' furthermore, As the Lord "
14 Then Abner answered and s', Who "
15 And David s' to Abner, Art not thou "
17 s', Is this thy voice, my son David? "
17 David s', It is my voice, my lord, O "
18 he s', Wherefore doth my lord thus "
21 Then s' Saul, I have sinned: return, "
22 David answered and s', Behold the "
25 Saul s' to David, Blessed be thou, "
27: 1 And David s' in his heart, I shall "
5 David s' unto Achish, If I have now "
10 Achish s', Whither have ye made a "
10 And David s', Against the south of "
28: 1 And Achish s' unto David, Know thou "
2 And David s' to Achish, Surely thou "
2 And Achish s' to David, Therefore "
7 Then s' Saul unto his servants, Seek "
7 And his servants s' to him, Behold, "
8 he s', I pray thee, divine unto me "
9 And the woman s' unto him, Behold, "
11 s' the woman, Whom shall I bring "
11 And he s', Bring me up Samuel. "
13 the king s' unto her, Be not afraid: "
13 the woman s' unto Saul, I saw gods "
14 he s' unto her, What form is he of? "
14 And she s', an old man cometh up; "
15 And Samuel s' to Saul, Why hast "
16 Then s' Samuel, Wherefore then "
21 s' unto him, Behold, thine handmaid "
23 he refused, and s', I will not eat. "
29: 3 s' the princes of the Philistines, "
3 s' unto the princes of the Philistines, "
4 princes of the Philistines s' unto "
6 Achish called David, and s' unto "
8 And David s' unto Achish, But what "
9 Achish answered and s' to David, I "
9 the princes of the Philistines have s', "
30: 7 And David s' to Abiathar the priest, "
13 And David s' unto him, To whom "
13 he s', I am a young man of Egypt, "
15 David s' to him, Canst thou bring "
15 he s', Swear unto me by God, that "
20 cattle, and s', This is David's spoil. "
22 s', Because they went not with us, "
23 Then s' David, Ye shall not do so, "
31: 4 Then s' Saul unto his armourbearer, "
2Sa 1: 3 And David s' unto him, From whence "
3 he s' unto him, Out of the camp of "
4 David s' unto him, How went the "
5 David s' unto the young man that "
6 And the young man that told him s', "
8 And he s' unto me, Who art thou? "
9 He s' unto me again, Stand, I pray "
13 David s' unto the young man that "
14 David s' unto him, How wast thou "
15 and s', Go near, and fall upon him. "
16 And David s' unto him, thy blood "
2: 1 And the Lord s' unto him, Go up. "
1 David s', Whither shall I go up? "
1 And he s', Unto Hebron. "
5 and said unto them, Blessed be ye "
14 And Abner s' to Joab, Let the young "
14 us. And Joab s', Let them arise. "
20 him, and s', Art thou Asahel? "
21 Abner s' to him, Turn thee aside "
22 And Abner s' again to Asahel, Turn "
26 s', Shall the sword devour for ever? "
27 And Joab s', As God liveth, unless "
3: 7 And Ish-bosheth s' to Abner, "
8 and s', Am I a dog's head, which "
13 he s', Well; I will make a league "
16 Then s' Abner unto him, Go, return. "
21 Abner s' unto David, I will arise "
24 Joab came to the king, and s', "
28 he s', I and my kingdom are "
31 And David s' to Joab, and to all the "
33 and s', Died Abner as a fool dieth? "
38 And the king s' unto his servants, "
4: 8 s' to the king, Behold the head of "
9 and s' unto them, As the Lord liveth, "
5: 2 and the Lord s' to thee, Thou shalt "
8 David s' on that day, Whosoever "
8 Wherefore they s', The blind and "
19 And the Lord s' unto David, Go up: "
20 and David smote them there, and s', "
23 Lord, he s', Thou shalt not go up; "
6: 9 s', How shall the ark of the Lord "
20 and s', How glorious was the king "
21 David s' unto Michal, It was before "
7: 2 king s' unto Nathan the prophet, "
3 Nathan s' to the king, Go, do all "
18 and he s', Who am I, O Lord God? "
25 it for ever, and do as thou hast s'. *169
9: 1 David s', Is there...any that is left 55
2 the king s' unto him, Art thou Ziba? "
2 And he s', Thy servant is he.

2Sa 9: 3 king s', Is there not yet any of the 559
3 And Ziba s' unto the king, Jonathan "
4 the king s' unto him, Where is he? "
4 Ziba s' unto the king, Behold, he is "
6 David s', Mephibosheth. And he "
7 And David s' unto him, Fear not: "
8 himself, and s', What is thy servant, "
9 s' unto him, I have given unto thy "
11 s' Ziba unto the king, According to "
11 Mephibosheth, s' the king, he shall "
10: 2 s' David, I will shew kindness unto 559
3 s' unto Hanun their lord, Thinkest "
5 the king s', Tarry at Jericho until "
11 he s', If the Syrians be too strong for "
11: 3 And one s', Is not this Bath-sheba, "
5 told David, and s', I am with child. "
8 David s' to Uriah, Go down to thy "
10 David s' unto Uriah, Camest thou "
11 Uriah s' unto David, the ark, and "
12 David s' to Uriah, Tarry here to-day "
23 messenger s' unto David, Surely the "
25 Then David s' unto the messenger, "
12: 1 s' unto him, There were two men in "
5 he s' to Nathan, As the Lord liveth, "
7 Nathan s' to David, Thou art the "
13 David s' unto Nathan, I have sinned "
13 And Nathan s' unto David, The Lord "
18 they s', Behold, while the child was "
19 David s' unto his servants, Is the "
19 child dead? And they s', He is dead. "
21 Then s' his servants unto him, What "
22 he s', While the child was yet alive, "
22 for I s', Who can tell whether God "
27 s', I have fought against Rabbah, "
13: 4 he s' unto him, Why art thou, being "
4 Amnon s' unto him, I love Tamar, "
5 Jonadab s' unto him, Lay thee down "
6 Amnon s' unto the king, I pray thee, "
9 Amnon s', Have out all men from me. "
10 Amnon s' unto Tamar, Bring the "
11 s' unto her, Come lie with me, my "
15 Amnon s' unto her, Arise, be gone. "
16 she s' unto him, There is no cause: "
17 s', Put now this woman out from me, "
20 Absalom her brother s' unto her, "
24 and s', Behold now, thy servant hath "
25 king s' to Absalom, Nay, my son, "
26 Then s' Absalom, If not, I pray thee, "
26 the king s' unto him, Why should he "
32 s', Let not my lord suppose that they "
35 Jonadab s' unto the king, Behold, "
35 come: as thy servant s', so it is. 1697
14: 2 s' unto her, I pray thee, feign thyself 559
4 did obeisance, and s', Help, O king. "
5 king s' unto her, What aileth thee? "
7 they s', Deliver him that smote his "
8 the king s' unto the woman, Go to "
9 woman of Tekoah s' unto the king, "
10 the king s', Whosoever saith ought "
11 Then s' she, I pray thee, let the "
11 he s', As the Lord liveth, there shall "
12 the woman s', Let thine handmaid, I "
12 my lord the king. And he s', Say on. "
13 the woman s', Wherefore then hast "
15 thy handmaid s', I will now speak "
17 thine handmaid s', The word of my "
18 the king answered and s' unto the "
18 the woman s', Let my lord the king "
19 the king s', Is not the hand of Joab "
19 the woman answered and s', As thy "
21 the king s' unto Joab, Behold now, "
22 and Joab s', To day thy servant "
24 the king s', Let him turn to his own "
30 he s' unto his servants, See, Joab's "
31 s' unto him, Wherefore have thy "
15: 2 him, and s', Of what city art thou? "
2 And he s', Thy servant is of one of "
3 And Absalom s' unto him, See, thy "
4 Absalom s' moreover, Oh that I were "
7 Absalom s' unto the king, I pray "
9 the king s' unto him, Go in peace. "
14 And David s' unto all his servants "
15 the king's servants s' unto the king, "
19 Then s' the king to Ittai the Gittite, "
21 And Ittai answered the king, and s', "
22 David s' to Ittai, Go and pass over. "
25 king s' unto Zadok, Carry back the "
27 king s' also unto Zadok the priest, "
31 David s', O Lord, I pray thee, turn "
33 Unto whom David s', If thou passest "
16: 2 the king s' unto Ziba, What meanest "
2 Ziba s', The asses be for the king's "
3 king s', And where is thy master's "
3 Ziba s' unto the king, Behold, he "
8 for he s', To day shall the house of "
4 s' the king to Ziba, Behold, thine are "
4 And Ziba s', I humbly beseech thee "
7 And thus s' Shimei when he cursed, "
9 Then s' Abishai the son of Zeruiah "
10 king s', What have I to do with you, "
10 Lord hath s' unto him, Curse David. "
11 David s' to Abishai, and to all his "
16 Hushai s' unto Absalom, God save "
17 And Absalom s' to Hushai, Is this thy "
18 Hushai s' unto Absalom, Nay; but "
20 Then s' Absalom to Ahithophel, Give "
21 Ahithophel s' unto Absalom, Go in "
17: 1 Ahithophel s' unto Absalom, Let me "
5 Then s' Absalom, Call now Hushai "
7 And Hushai s' unto Absalom, The "
8 s' Hushai, Thou knowest thy father "
14 Absalom and all the men of Israel s', "
15 s' Hushai unto Zadok and...Abiathar "
20 they s', Where is Ahimaaz and "
20 woman s' unto them, They be gone "
21 and s' unto David, Arise, and pass "

2Sa 17: 29 for they s', The people is hungry, 559
18: 2 king s' unto the people, I will surely "
4 king s' unto them, What seemeth "
10 and s',...I saw Absalom hanged in "
11 And Joab s' unto the man that told "
12 And the man s' unto Joab, Though I "
14 Then s' Joab, I may not tarry thus "
18 for he s', I have no son to keep my "
19 Then s' Ahimaaz the son of Zadok, "
20 And Joab s' unto him, Thou shalt not "
21 s' Joab to Cushi, Go tell the king "
22 Then s' Ahimaaz the son of Zadok yet "
22 Joab s', Wherefore wilt thou run, "
23 But howsoever, s' he, let me run. "
23 And he s' unto him, Run. Then 559
25 the king s', If he be alone, there is "
26 and s', Behold another man running "
26 the king s', He also bringeth tidings. "
27 And the watchman s', Me thinketh "
27 the king s', He is a good man, and "
28 and s' unto the king, All is well. "
28 and s', Blessed be the Lord thy God, "
29 king s', Is the young man Absalom "
30 And the king s' unto him, Turn aside, "
31 Cushi s', Tidings, my lord the king: "
32 king s' unto Cushi, Is the young man "
33 went, thus he s', O my son Absalom, "
19: 5 to the king, and s', Thou hast shamed "
19 And s' unto the king, Let not my lord "
21 the son of Zeruiah answered and s', "
22 David s', What have I to do with you, "
23 Therefore the king s' unto Shimei, "
25 king s' unto him, Wherefore wentest "
26 for thy servant s', I will saddle me "
29 the king s' unto him, Why speakest "
29 I have s', Thou and Ziba divide the* "
30 And Mephibosheth s' unto the king, "
33 And the king s' unto Barzillai, Come "
34 Barzillai s' unto the king, How long "
41 and s' unto the king, Why have our "
43 and s', We have ten parts in the king, "
20: 1 and s', We have no part in David, "
4 s' the king to Amasa, Assemble me "
6 David s' to Abishai, Now shall Sheba "
9 Joab s' to Amasa, Art thou in health, "
11 and s', He that favoureth Joab, and "
17 her, the woman s', Art thou Joab? "
17 she s' unto him, Hear the words of "
20 And Joab answered and s', Far be it, "
21 woman s' unto Joab, Behold his head "
21: 2 the Gibeonites, and s' unto them; "
3 David s' unto the Gibeonites, What "
4 Gibeonites s' unto him, We will have "
4 he s', What ye shall say, that will I "
6 And the king s', I will give them. "
22: 2 And he s', The Lord is my rock, and "
23: 1 David the son of Jesse s', and the* 5002
1 and the sweet psalmist of Israel, s',* "
3 The God of Israel s', the Rock of 559
15 David longed, and s', Oh that one "
17 And he s', Be it far from me, O Lord, "
24: 2 For the king s' to Joab the captain of "
3 Joab s' unto the king, Now the Lord "
10 David s' unto the Lord, I have sinned "
13 and s' unto him, Shall seven years of "
14 David s' unto Gad, I am in a great "
16 and s' to the angel that destroyed "
17 and s', Lo, I have sinned, and I have "
18 and s' unto him, Go up, rear an altar "
21 Araunah s', Wherefore is my lord "
21 David s', To buy the threshingfloor "
22 Araunah s' unto David, Let my lord "
23 Araunah s' unto the king, The Lord "
24 And the king s' unto Araunah, Nay; "
1Ki 1: 2 Wherefore his servants s' unto him, "
16 the king s', What wouldest thou? "
17 And she s' unto him, My lord, thou "
24 And Nathan s', My lord, O king, hast "
24 hast thou s', Adonijah shall reign "
28 king David answered and s', Call me "
29 the king sware, and s', As the Lord "
31 and s', Let my lord king David live "
32 king David s', Call me Zadok the "
33 king also s' unto them, Take with "
36 answered the king, and s', Amen: "
39 people s', God save king Solomon. "
41 he s', Wherefore is this noise of the "
42 Adonijah s' unto him, Come in; for "
43 Jonathan...s' to Adonijah, Verily our "
48 thus s' the king, Blessed be the Lord "
52 Solomon s', If he will shew himself a "
53 and Solomon s' unto him, Go to thine "
2: 4 there shall not fail thee (s' he) a man "
13 and she s', Comest thou peaceably? "
13 And he s', Peaceably. "
14 He s' moreover, I have somewhat to "
14 say unto thee. And she s', Say on. "
15 he s', Thou knowest...the kingdom "
16 not. And she s' unto him, Say on. "
17 And he s', Speak, I pray thee, unto "
18 Bath-sheba s', Well; I will speak for "
20 she s', I desire one small petition "
20 king s' unto her, Ask on, my mother: "
21 she s', Let Abishag the Shunammite "
22 answered and s' unto his mother, "
26 unto Abiathar the priest s' the king, "
30 and s' unto him, Thus saith the king, "
30 And he s', Nay; but I will die here. "
30 Thus s' Joab,...thus he answered 1696
31 And the king s' unto him, 559
31 Do as he hath s', and fall upon him, 1696
36 and s' unto him, Build thee an 559
38 Shimei s' unto the king, The saying "
38 as my lord the king hath s', so will 1696
42 and s' unto him, Did I not make thee 559
44 The king s' moreover to Shimei, "

1Ki 3: 5 God s', Ask what I shall give thee. 559
6 Solomon s', Thou hast shewed unto "
11 God s' unto him, Because thou hast "
17 one woman s', O my lord, I and this "
22 other woman s', Nay; but the living "
22 this s', No; but the dead is thy son. "
23 Then s' the king, The one saith, "
24 And the king s', Bring me a sword. "
25 the king s', Divide the living child "
26 and she s', O my lord, give her the "
26 But the other s', Let it be neither "
27 king answered and s', Give her the "
5: 7 and s', Blessed be the Lord this day, "
8: 12 Lord s' that he would dwell in the "
15 he s', Blessed be the Lord God of "
18 the Lord s' unto David my father, "
23 he s', Lord God of Israel, there is no "
29 place of which thou hast s', My name "
9: 3 the Lord s' unto him, I have heard "
13 he s', What cities are these which "
10: 6 And she s' to the king, It was a true "
11: 2 Lord s' unto the children of Israel, "
11 Wherefore the Lord s' unto Solomon, "
21 Hadad s' to Pharaoh, Let me "
22 Pharaoh s' unto him, But what hast "
31 he s' to Jeroboam, Take thee ten "
12: 5 And he s' unto them, Depart yet for "
6 and s', How do ye advise that I may "
9 And he s' unto them, What counsel "
26 And Jeroboam s' in his heart, Now "
28 And s' unto them, It is too much for "
13: 2 and s', O altar, altar, thus saith the "
6 and s' unto the man of God, Intreat "
7 the king s' unto the man of God, 1696
8 the man of God s' unto the king, If 559
12 their father s' unto them, What 1696
13 And he s' unto his sons, Saddle me 559
14 he s' unto him, Art thou the man of "
14 camest from Judah? And he s', I am. "
15 Then he s' unto him, Come home "
16 he s', I may not return with thee, "
17 For it was s' to me by the word of 1697
18 He s' unto him, I am a prophet also 559
26 he s', It is the man of God, who was "
14: 2 And Jeroboam s' to his wife, Arise, "
5 the Lord s' unto Ahijah, Behold, the "
6 that he s', Come in, thou wife of "
17: 1 s' unto Ahab, As the Lord God of "
10 and s', Fetch me, I pray thee, a little "
11 s', Bring me, I pray thee, a morsel of "
12 she s', As the Lord thy God liveth, "
13 And Elijah s' unto her, Fear not; go "
13 go and do as thou hast s': but make "
18 And she s' unto Elijah, What have I "
19 And he s' unto her, Give me thy son. "
20 And he cried unto the Lord, and s', "
21 s', O Lord my God, I pray thee, let "
23 and Elijah s', See, thy son liveth. "
24 the woman s' to Elijah, Now by this "
18: 5 And Ahab s' unto Obadiah, Go into "
7 and s', Art thou that my lord Elijah? "
9 And he s', What have I sinned, that "
10 and when they s', He is not there; he "
15 And Elijah s', As the Lord of hosts "
17 Ahab s' unto him, Art thou he that "
21 s', How long halt ye between two "
22 Then s' Elijah unto the people, I, "
24 all the people answered and s', It is "
25 Elijah s' unto the prophets of Baal, "
27 Elijah mocked them, and s', Cry "
30 Elijah s' unto all the people, Come "
33 and s', Fill four barrels with water, "
34 And he s', Do it the second time. "
34 And he s', Do it the third time. And "
36 and s', Lord God of Abraham, Isaac, "
39 they s', The Lord, he is the God; the "
40 And Elijah s' unto them, Take the "
41 Elijah s' unto Ahab, Get thee up, eat "
43 s' to his servant, Go up now, look "
43 and looked, and s', There is nothing. "
43 And he s', Go again seven times. "
44 he s', Behold, there ariseth a little "
44 And he s', Go up, say unto Ahab, "
19: 4 s', It is enough; now, O Lord, take "
5 him, and s' unto him, Arise and eat. "
7 touched him, and s', Arise and eat; "
9 and he s' unto him, What doest thou "
10 he s', I have been very jealous for "
11 And he s', Go forth, and stand upon "
13 and s', What doest thou here, Elijah? "
14 he s', I have been very jealous for "
15 Lord s' unto him, Go, return on thy "
20 ran after Elijah, and s', Let me, I "
20 And he s' unto him, Go back again: "
20: 2 s' unto him, Thus saith Ben-hadad, "
4 of Israel answered and s', My lord, "
5 and s', Thus speaketh Ben-hadad, "
7 s', Mark, I pray you, and see how "
8 all the people s' unto him, Hearken "
9 Wherefore he s' unto the messengers "
10 and s', The gods do so unto me, and "
11 of Israel answered and s', Tell him, "
12 that he s' unto his servants, Set "
14 And Ahab s', By whom? And he s', "
14 he s', Who shall order the battle? "
18 he s', Whether they be come out for "
22 s' unto him, Go, strengthen thyself, "
23 servants of the king of Syria s' unto "
28 unto the king of Israel, and s', Thus "
28 Syrians have s', The Lord is God of 559
31 servants s' unto him, Behold now, "
32 s', Thy servant Ben-hadad saith, "
32 And he s', Is he yet alive? he is my "
33 and they s', Thy brother Ben-hadad. "
33 Then he s', Go ye, bring him. Then "
34 Ben-hadad s' unto him, The cities, "

1Ki 20:34 Then s' Ahab, I will send thee away
35 the sons of the prophets s' unto his 559
36 s' he unto him, Because thou hast "
37 man, and s', Smite me, I pray thee. "
39 he s', Thy servant went out into the "
39 me, and s', Keep this man: if by any "
40 king of Israel s' unto him, So shall "
42 he s' unto him, Thus saith the Lord, "
21: 3 Naboth s' to Ahab, The Lord forbid "
4 for he had s', I will not give thee the "
5 s' unto him, Why is thy spirit so 1696
6 he s' unto her, Because I spake "
6 s' unto him, Give me thy vineyard 559
7 Jezebel his wife s' unto him, Dost "
15 that Jezebel s' to Ahab, Arise, take "
20 Ahab s' to Elijah, Hast thou found "
22: 3 king of Israel s' unto his servants, "
4 he s' unto Jehoshaphat, Wilt thou go "
4 Jehoshaphat s' to the king of Israel, "
5 And Jehoshaphat s' unto the king of "
6 and s' unto them, Shall I go against "
6 they s', Go up; for the Lord shall "
7 Jehoshaphat s', Is there not here a "
8 king of Israel s' unto Jehoshaphat, "
8 Jehoshaphat s', Let not the king say "
9 and s', Hasten hither Micaiah the "
11 and he s', Thus saith the Lord, With "
14 And Micaiah s', As the Lord liveth, "
15 And the king s' unto him, Micaiah, "
16 king s' unto him, How many times "
17 And he s', I saw all Israel scattered "
17 the Lord s', These have no master: "
18 king of Israel s' unto Jehoshaphat, "
19 he s', Hear thou therefore the word "
20 Lord s', Who shall persuade Ahab, "
20 one s' on this manner, and another "
20 and another s' on that manner. "
21 Lord, and s', I will persuade him. "
22 the Lord s' unto him, Wherewith? "
22 And he s', I will go forth, and I will "
22 And he s', Thou shalt persuade him, "
24 and s', Which way went the Spirit of "
25 And Micaiah s', Behold, thou shalt "
26 the king of Israel s', Take Micaiah, "
28 And Micaiah s', If thou return at all "
28 he s', Hearken, O people, every one "
30 king of Israel s' unto Jehoshaphat, "
32 that they s', Surely it is the king of "
34 he s' unto the driver of his chariot, "
49 Then s' Ahaziah the son of Ahab "
2Ki 1: 2 and s' unto them, Go, enquire of "
3 the angel of the Lord s' to Elijah 1696
5 he s' unto them, Why are ye now 559
6 And they s' unto him, There came a "
6 and s' unto us, Go, turn again unto "
7 he s' unto them, What manner of 1696
8 And he s', It is Elijah the Tishbite. 559
9 God, the king hath s', Come down. 1696
10 And Elijah answered and s' to the "
11 And he answered and s' unto him, "
11 thus hath the king s', Come down 559
12 Elijah answered and s' unto them, 1696
13 besought him, and s' unto him, O "
15 the angel of the Lord s' unto Elijah, "
16 And he s' unto him, Thus saith the "
2: 2 Elijah s' unto Elisha, Tarry here, I 559
2 And Elisha s' unto him, As the Lord "
3 and s' unto him, Knowest thou that "
3 he s', Yea, I know it; hold ye your "
4 Elijah s' unto him, Elisha, tarry "
4 And he s', As the Lord liveth, and as "
5 and s' unto him, Knowest thou that "
6 And Elijah s' unto him, Tarry, I pray "
6 he s', As the Lord liveth, and as thy "
9 that Elijah s' unto Elisha, Ask what "
9 Elisha s', I pray thee, let a double "
10 And he s', Thou hast asked a hard "
14 smote the waters, and s', Where is "
15 they s', The spirit of Elijah doth rest "
16 And they s' unto him, Behold now, "
16 valley. And he s', Ye shall not send. "
17 till he was ashamed, he s', Send. "
18 he s' unto them, Did I not say unto "
19 the men of the city s' unto Elisha, "
20 And he s', Bring me a new cruse, "
21 and s', Thus saith the Lord, I have "
23 s' unto him, Go up, thou bald head; "
3: 7 And he s', I will go up: I am as thou "
8 he s', Which way shall we go up? "
10 the king of Israel s', Alas! that the "
11 Jehoshaphat s', Is there not here a "
11 and s', Here is Elisha the son of "
12 And Jehoshaphat s', The word of the "
13 Elisha s' unto the king of Israel, "
13 the king of Israel s' unto him, Nay: "
14 And Elisha s', As the Lord of hosts "
16 he s', Thus saith the Lord, Make "
23 And they s', This is blood: the kings "
4: 2 Elisha s' unto her, What shall I do "
2 she s', Thine handmaid hath not "
3 Then he s', Go, borrow thee vessels "
6 she s' unto her son, Bring me yet a "
6 he s' unto her, There is not a vessel "
7 And he s', Go, sell the oil, and pay "
9 she s' unto her husband, Behold "
12 And he s' to Gehazi his servant, Call "
13 he s' unto him, Say now unto her, "
14 he s', What then is to be done for "
15 he s', Call her. And when he had "
16 he s', About this season, according "
16 she s', Nay, my lord, thou man of "
17 season that Elisha had s' unto her, 1696
19 he s' unto his father, My head, my 559
19 And he s' to a lad, Carry him to his "
22 s', Send me, I pray thee, one of the "
23 he s', Wherefore wilt thou go to him "

2Ki 4:23 And she s', It shall be well. 559
24 and s' to her servant, Drive, and go "
25 he s' to Gehazi his servant, Behold, "
27 the man of God s', Let her alone; "
28 she s', Did I desire a son of my lord? "
29 he s' to Gehazi, Gird up thy loins, "
30 mother of the child s', As the Lord "
36 Gehazi, and s', Call this Shunammite. "
36 unto him, he s', Take up thy son. "
38 he s' unto his servant, Set on the "
40 and s', O thou man of God, there is "
41 But he s', Then bring meal. And he "
41 he s', Pour out for the people, that "
42 he s', Give unto the people, that they "
43 his servitor s', What, should I set "
43 He s' again, Give the people, that "
5: 3 she s' unto her mistress, Would God "
4 thus s' the maid that is of the land 1696
5 king of Syria s', Go to, go, and I 559
7 s', Am I God, to kill and to make "
11 away, and s', Behold, I thought, "
13 s', My father, if the prophet had bid "
15 and he s', Behold, now I know that "
16 But he s', As the Lord liveth, before "
17 Naaman s', Shall there not then, I "
19 And he s' unto him, Go in peace. "
20 servant of Elisha, the man of God, s', "
21 to meet him, and s', Is all well? "
22 And he s', All is well. My master "
23 Naaman s', Be content, take two "
25 Elisha s' unto him, Whence comest "
25 he s', Thy servant went no whither. "
26 he s' unto him, Went not mine heart "
6: 1 sons of the prophets s' unto Elisha, "
3 And one s', Be content, I pray thee, "
5 he cried, and s', Alas, master! for it "
6 the man of God s', Where fell it? "
7 Therefore s' he, Take it up to thee, "
11 s' unto them, Will ye not shew me "
12 one of his servants s', None, my lord, "
13 he s', Go and spy where he is, that "
15 his servant s' unto him, Alas, my "
17 Elisha prayed, and s', Lord, I pray "
18 s', Smite this people, I pray thee, "
19 Elisha s' unto them, This is not the "
20 that Elisha s', Lord, open the eyes "
21 the king of Israel s' unto Elisha, "
27 he s', If the Lord do not help thee, "
28 king s' unto her, What aileth thee? "
28 This woman s' unto me, Give thy "
29 I s' unto her on the next day, Give "
31 Then he s', God do so and more also "
32 he s' to the elders, See ye how this "
33 he s', Behold, this evil is of the Lord; "
7: 1 Then Elisha s', Hear ye the word of "
2 answered the man of God, and s', "
2 he s', Behold, thou shalt see it with "
3 they s' one to another, Why sit we "
6 they s' one to another, Lo, the king "
9 Then they s' one to another, We do "
12 s' unto his servants, I will now shew "
13 one of his servants answered and s', "
17 he died, as the man of God had s', 1696
19 answered the man of God, and s', 559
19 he s', Behold, thou shalt see it with "
8: 5 Gehazi s', My lord, O king, this is "
8 And the king s' unto Hazael, Take a "
9 s', Thy son Ben-hadad king of Syria "
10 And Elisha s' unto him, Go, say unto "
12 Hazael s', Why weepeth my lord? "
13 Hazael s', But what, is thy servant "
14 who s' to him, What s' Elisha to "
9: 1 and s' unto him, Gird up thy loins, "
5 he s', I have an errand to thee, "
5 And Jehu s', Unto which of all us? "
5 And he s', To thee, O captain. "
6 s' unto him, Thus saith the Lord "
11 and one s' unto him, Is all well? "
11 he s' unto them, Ye know the man, "
12 And they s', It is false; tell us now. "
12 he s', Thus and thus spake he to me, "
15 Jehu s', If it be your minds, then let "
17 as he came, and s', I see a company. "
17 And Joram s', Take an horseman, "
18 s', Thus saith the king, Is it peace? "
18 Jehu s', What hast thou to do with "
19 s', Thus saith the king, Is it peace? "
21 Joram s', Make ready. And his "
22 Jehu, that he s', Is it peace, Jehu? "
23 s' to Ahaziah, There is treachery, O "
25 s' Jehu to Bidkar his captain, Take "
27 s', Smite him also in the chariot. "
31 she s', Had Zimri peace, who slew "
32 window, and s', Who is on my side? "
33 he s', Throw her down. So they "
34 s', Go, see now this cursed woman, "
36 he s', This is the word of the Lord, "
10: 4 and s', Behold, two kings stood not "
8 he s', Lay ye them in two heaps at "
9 s' to all the people, Ye be righteous: "
13 king of Judah, and s', Who are ye? "
14 he s', Take them alive. And they "
15 s' to him, Is thine heart right, as "
16 he s', Come with me, and see my "
18 s' unto them, Ahab served Baal a "
20 Jehu s', Proclaim a solemn assembly "
22 s' unto him that was over the vestry, "
23 s' unto the worshippers of Baal, "
24 s', If any of the men whom I have "
25 that Jehu s' to the guard and to the "
30 Lord s' unto Jehu, Because thou "
11:12 hands, and s', God save the king. "
15 s' unto them, Have her forth without "
15 priest had s', Let her not be slain "
12: 4 Jehoash s' to the priests, All the "
7 s' unto them, Why repair ye not the "

2Ki 13:14 and s', O my father, my father! the 559
15 Elisha s' unto him, Take bow and "
16 he s' to the king of Israel, Put thine "
17 he s', Open the window eastward. "
17 opened it. Then Elisha s', Shoot. "
17 And he s', The arrow of the Lord's "
18 he s', Take the arrows. And he took "
18 he s' unto the king of Israel, Smite "
19 and s', Thou shouldest have smitten "
14:27 s' not that he would blot out the 1696
17:12 the Lord had s' unto them, Ye shall 559
23 s'...all his servants the prophets. *1696
18:19 Rab-shakeh s' unto them, Speak 559
22 hath s' to Judah and Jerusalem, Ye "
25 The Lord s' to me, Go up against "
26 Then s' Eliakim the son of Hilkiah, "
27 Rab-shakeh s' unto them, Hath my "
19: 3 And they s' unto him, Thus saith "
6 And Isaiah s' unto them, Thus shall "
15 and s', O Lord God of Israel, which "
23 and hast s', With the multitude of "
20: 1 s' unto him, Thus saith the Lord, "
7 And Isaiah s', Take a lump of figs. "
8 Hezekiah s' unto Isaiah, What shall "
9 Isaiah s', This sign shalt thou have "
14 s' unto him, What s' these men? "
14 Hezekiah s', They are come from a "
15 he s', What have they seen in thine "
16 Isaiah s' unto Hezekiah, Hear the "
19 Then s' Hezekiah unto Isaiah, Good "
19 And he s', Is it not good, if peace "
21: 4 of which the Lord s', In Jerusalem "
7 of which the Lord s' to David, and "
22: 8 the high priest s' unto Shaphan the "
9 s', Thy servants have gathered the "
15 And she s' unto them, Thus saith "
23:17 he s', What title is that that I see? "
18 he s', Let him alone; let no man "
27 the Lord s', I will remove Judah "
27 which, I s', My name shall be there. "
24:13 of the Lord, as the Lord had s'. 1696
25:24 s' unto them, Fear not to be the 559
1Ch 10: 4 Then s' Saul to his armourbearer, "
11: 2 the Lord thy God s' unto thee, Thou "
5 inhabitants of Jebus s' to David, "
6 David s', Whosoever smiteth the "
17 David longed, and s', Oh that one "
19 s', My God forbid it me, that I should "
12:17 answered and s' unto them, If ye be "
18 and he s', Thine are we, David, and on
13: 2 David s' unto all the congregation 559
4 congregation s' that they would do "
14:10 the Lord s' unto him, Go up; for I "
11 Then David s', God hath broken in "
14 God s' unto him, Go not up after "
15: 2 Then David s', None ought to carry "
12 s' unto them, Ye are the chief of the "
16:36 all the people s', Amen, and praised "
17: 1 that David s' to Nathan the prophet, "
2 Then Nathan s' unto David, Do all "
16 David...s', Who am I, O Lord God, "
23 for ever, and do as thou hast s'. *1696
19: 2 David s', I will shew kindness unto 559
3 the children of Ammon s' to Hanun, "
5 the king s', Tarry at Jericho until "
12 he s', If the Syrians be too strong "
21: 2 David s' to Joab and to the rulers "
8 David s' unto God, I have sinned "
11 Gad came to David, and s' unto him, "
13 David s' unto Gad, I am in a great "
15 s' to the angel that destroyed, It is "
17 David s' unto God, Is it not I that "
22 David s' to Ornan, Grant me the "
22 Ornan s' unto David, Take it to thee, "
24 And king David s' to Ornan, Nay; "
22: 1 David s', This is the house of the "
5 David s', Solomon my son is young "
7 David s' to Solomon, My son, as for "
11 thy God, as he hath s' of thee. *1696
23: 5 instruments which I made, s' David, "
25 David s', The Lord God of Israel 559
27:23 Lord had s' he would increase Israel "
28: 2 and s', Hear me, my brethren, and "
3 God s' unto me, Thou shalt not build "
6 he s' unto me, Solomon thy son, he "
19 All this, s' David, the Lord made me "
20 David s' to Solomon...Be strong 559
29: 1 David...s' unto all the congregation, "
10 David s', Blessed be thou, Lord God "
20 And David s' to all the congregation, "
2Ch 1: 7 and s' unto him, Ask what I shall "
8 Solomon s' unto God, Thou hast "
11 God s' to Solomon, Because this was "
2:12 Huram s' moreover, Blessed be the "
6: 1 Then s' Solomon, The Lord hath * "
1 Lord hath s' that he would dwell "
4 he s', Blessed be the Lord God of "
8 But the Lord s' to David my father, "
14 And s', O Lord God of Israel, there "
20 hast s'...thou wouldest put thy name "
7:12 and s' unto him, I have heard thy "
8:11 for he s', My wife shall not dwell in "
9: 5 And she s' to the king, It was a true "
10: 5 he s' unto them, Come again unto "
9 he s' unto them, What advice give "
12: 5 and s' unto them, Thus saith the "
6 and they s', The Lord is righteous. "
13: 4 and s', Hear me, thou Jeroboam, and "
14: 7 he s' unto Judah, Let us build these "
11 and s', Lord, it is nothing with thee "
15: 2 and s' unto him, Hear ye me, Asa, "
16: 7 s' unto him, Because thou hast "
18: 3 And Ahab...s' unto Jehoshaphat "
4 And Jehoshaphat s' unto the king of "
5 and s' unto them, Shall we go to "
5 they s', Go up; for God will deliver "

2Ch 18: 6 Jehoshaphat s', Is there not here a 559
7 king of Israel s' unto Jehoshaphat, "
7 Jehoshaphat s', Let not the king say "
8 and s', Fetch quickly Micaiah the "
10 and s', Thus saith the Lord, With "
13 Micaiah s', As the Lord liveth, even "
14 king s' unto him, Micaiah, shall we "
14 And he s', Go ye up, and prosper, "
15 king s' unto him, How many times "
16 he s', I did see all Israel scattered "
16 the Lord s', These have no master; "
17 the king of Israel s' to Jehoshaphat, "
18 Again he s', Therefore hear the word "
19 the Lord s', Who shall entice Ahab "
20 the Lord, and s', I will entice him. "
20 the Lord s' unto him, Wherewith? "
21 he s', I will go out, and be a lying "
21 the Lord s', Thou shalt entice him, "
23 and s', Which way went the Spirit "
24 Micaiah s', Behold, thou shalt see "
25 king of Israel s', Take ye Micaiah, "
27 Micaiah s', If thou certainly return "
27 And he s', Hearken, all ye people. "
29 king of Israel s' unto Jehoshaphat, "
31 that they s', It is the king of Israel. "
33 therefore he s' to his chariot man, "
19: 2 s' to king Jehoshaphat, Shouldest "
6 And s' to the judges, Take heed what "
20: 6 And s', O Lord God of our fathers, "
15 he s', Hearken ye, all Judah, and ye "
20 Jehoshaphat stood and s', Hear me, "
22: 9 s' they, he is the son of Jehoshaphat, "
23: 3 he s' unto them, Behold, the king's "
3 Lord hath s' of the sons of David.*1696
11 him, and s', God save the king. 559
13 Athaliah rent her clothes, and s', "
14 and s' unto them, Have her forth of "
14 priest s', Slay her not in the house "
24: 5 and s' to them, Go out unto the cities "
6 and s' unto him, Why hast thou not "
20 and s' unto them, Thus saith God, "
22 died, he s', The Lord look upon it, "
25: 9 Amaziah s' to the man of God, But "
15 a prophet, which s' unto him, Why "
16 the king s' unto him, Art thou made "
16 the prophet forbare, and s', I know "
26: 18 and s' unto him, It appertaineth not "
23 for they s', He is a leper: and "
28: 9 and s' unto them, Behold, because "
13 And s' unto them, Ye shall not bring "
23 he s', Because the gods of the kings "
29: 5 s' unto them, Hear me, ye Levites, "
18 and s', We have cleansed all the "
31 Hezekiah answered and s', Now ye "
33: 4 Lord had s', In Jerusalem shall my "
7 God had s' to David and to Solomon "
34: 15 Hilkiah answered and s' to Shaphan "
35: 3 And s' unto the Levites that taught "
23 the king s' to his servants, Have me "
Ezr 2: 63 Tirshatha s' unto them, that they "
4: 2 and s' unto them, Let us build with "
3 s' unto them, Ye have nothing to do "
5: 3 and s' thus unto them, Who hath 560
4 s' we unto them after this manner,* "
9 s' unto them thus, Who commanded "
15 And s' unto him, Take these vessels, "
8: 28 I s' unto them, Ye are holy unto 559
9: 6 And s', O my God, I am ashamed "
10: 2 answered and s' unto Ezra, We have "
10 s' unto them, Ye have transgressed "
12 the congregation answered and s' "
12 As thou hast s', so must we do. 1697
Ne 1: 3 they s' unto me, The remnant that 559
5 And s', I beseech thee, O Lord God "
2: 2 the king s' unto me, Why is thy "
3 s' unto the king, Let the king live "
4 king s' unto me, For what dost thou "
5 I s' unto the king, If it please the "
6 the king s' unto me, (the queen also "
7 I s' unto the king, If it please the "
17 s' I unto them, Ye see the distress "
18 they s', Let us rise up and build. "
19 s', What is this thing that ye do? "
20 s' unto them, The God of heaven, "
4: 2 and s', What do these feeble Jews? "
3 he s', Even that which they build, "
10 And Judah s', The strength of the "
11 adversaries s', They shall not know, "
12 they s' unto us ten times, From all "
14, 19 s' unto the nobles, and to...rulers, "
22 the same time s' I unto the people, "
5: 2 For there were that s', We, our sons, "
3 were that s', We have mortgaged "
4 were also that s', We have borrowed "
7 and s' unto them, Ye exact usury, "
8 I s' unto them, We after our ability "
9 Also I s', It is not good that ye do: "
12 Then s' they, We will restore them, "
13 I shook my lap, and s', So God shake "
13 And all the congregation s', Amen, "
6: 10 he s', Let us meet together in the "
11 I s', Should such a man as I flee? "
7: 3 I s' unto them, Let not the gates of "
65 And the Tirshatha s' unto them, "
8: 9 s' unto all the people, This day is "
10 he s' unto them, Go your way, eat "
9: 5 s', Stand up and bless the Lord your "
18 and s', This is thy God that brought "
13: 11 and s', Why is the house of God "
17 and s' unto them, What evil thing is "
21 and s' unto them, Why lodge ye "
Es 1: 13 Then the king s' to the wise men, "
2: 2 Then s' the king's servants that "
3: 3 s' unto Mordecai, Why transgressest "
8 Haman s' unto king Ahasuerus, "
11 king s' unto Haman, The silver is "

Es 5: 3 s' the king unto her, What wilt thou, 559
5 king s', Cause Haman to make haste, "
5 that he may do as Esther hath s'. 1697
6 king s' unto Esther at the banquet 559
7 answered Esther, and s', My petition "
8 do to morrow as the king hath s'. 1697
12 Haman s' moreover, Yea, Esther 559
14 s' Zeresh his wife and all his friends "
6: 3 king s', What honour and dignity "
3 s' the king's servants that ministered "
4 And the king s', Who is in the court? "
5 king's servants s' unto him, Behold, "
5 And the king s', Let him come in. "
6 king s' unto him, What shall be done "
10 the king s' to Haman, Make haste, "
10 as thou hast s', and do even so to 1696
13 s' his wise men and Zeresh his wife 559
7: 2 And the king s' again unto Esther "
3 Esther the queen answered and s', "
5 king Ahasuerus answered and s' "
6 And Esther s', The adversary and "
8 s' the king, Will he force the queen "
9 chamberlains, s' before the king, * "
9 the king s', Hang him thereon. "
8: 5 And s', If it please the king, and if "
7 king Ahasuerus s' unto Esther the "
9: 12 the king s' unto Esther the queen, "
13 Then s' Esther, If it please the king, "
Job 1: 5 Job s', It may be that my sons have "
7 Lord s' unto Satan, Whence comest "
7 Satan answered the Lord, and s', "
8 the Lord s' unto Satan, Hast thou "
9 s', Doth Job fear God for nought? "
12 the Lord s' unto Satan, Behold, all "
14 and s', The oxen were plowing, and "
16 and s', The fire of God is fallen from "
17 s', The Chaldeans made out three "
18 and s', Thy sons and thy daughters "
21 s', Naked came I out of my mother's "
2: 2 Lord s' unto Satan, From whence "
2 Satan answered the Lord, and s', "
3 the Lord s' unto Satan, Hast thou "
4 the Lord, and s', Skin for skin, yea, "
6 And the Lord s' unto Satan, Behold, "
9 s' his wife unto him, Dost thou still "
10 But he s' unto her, Thou speakest "
3: 2 And Job spake, and s', "
3 the night in which it was s', There "
4: 1 the Temanite answered and s', "
6: 1 But Job answered and s', "
8: 1 answered Bildad the Shuhite, and s', "
9: 1 Then Job answered and s', "
22 This is one thing, therefore I s' it,* "
11: 1 Zophar the Naamathite, and s', "
4 thou hast s', My doctrine is pure, * "
12: 1 And Job answered and s', "
15: 1 Eliphaz the Temanite, and s', "
16: 1 Then Job answered and s', "
17: 14 I have s' to corruption, Thou art 7121
18: 1 answered Bildad...Shuhite, and s', 559
19: 1 Then Job answered and s', "
20: 1 Zophar the Naamathite, and s', "
21: 1 But Job answered and s', "
22: 1 the Temanite answered and s', "
17 Which s' unto God, Depart from us: "
23: 1 Then Job answered and s', "
25: 1 answered Bildad the Shuhite, and s', "
26: 1 But Job answered and s', "
27: 1 Job continued his parable, and s', "
28: 28 unto man he s', Behold, the fear of "
29: 1 Job continued his parable, and s', "
18 Then I s', I shall die in my nest, and "
31: 24 or have s' to the fine gold, Thou art "
31 If the men of my tabernacle s' not, "
32: 6 the Buzite answered and s', I am "
7 I s', Days should speak, and "
10 I s', Hearken to me; I also will shew "
17 I s', I will answer also my part, I * "
34: 1 Furthermore Elihu answered and s', 559
5 For Job hath s', I am righteous: and "
9 For he hath s', It profiteth a man "
31 Surely it is meet to be s' unto God, "
35: 1 Elihu spake moreover, and s', "
36: 1 Elihu also proceeded, and s', "
38: 1 Job out of the whirlwind, and s', "
11 s', Hitherto shalt thou come, but no "
40: 1 the Lord answered Job, and s', "
3 Then Job answered the Lord, and s', "
6 Job out of the whirlwind, and s', "
42: 1 Then Job answered the Lord, and s', "
7 Lord s' to Eliphaz the Temanite, "
Ps 2: 7 Lord hath s' unto me, Thou art my "
10: 6 s' in his heart, I shall not be moved: "
11 s' in his heart, God hath forgotten:* "
13 hath s' in his heart, Thou wilt not* "
12: 4 s', With our tongue will we prevail; "
14: 1 The fool hath s' in his heart, There "
16: 2 s' unto the Lord, Thou art my Lord: "
18: *title* from the hand of Saul: And he s', "
27: 8 heart s' unto thee, Thy face, Lord, "
30: 6 I s', I shall never be moved. "
31: 14 O Lord: I s', Thou art my God. "
22 I s' in my haste, I am cut off from "
32: 5 I s', I will confess my transgressions "
35: 21 s', Aha, aha, our eye hath seen it. "
38: 16 I s', Hear me, lest otherwise they "
39: 1 I s', I will take heed to my ways, "
40: 7 Then s' I, Lo, I come: in the volume "
41: 4 I s', Lord, be merciful unto me: heal "
52: *title* s' unto him, David is come to the "
53: 1 The fool hath s' in his heart, There "
54: *title* and s' to Saul, Doth not David hide "
55: 6 And I s', Oh that I had wings like a "
68: 22 The Lord s', I will bring again from "
74: 8 s' in their hearts, Let us destroy "
75: 4 I s' unto the fools, Deal not "

Ps 77: 10 And I s', This is my infirmity: but I 559
78: 19 they s', Can God furnish a table in "
82: 6 I have s', Ye are gods; and all of "
83: 4 They have s', Come, and let us cut "
12 Who s', Let us take to ourselves the "
87: 5 of Zion it shall be s', This and that "
89: 2 I have s', Mercy shall be built up for "
94: 18 When I s', My foot slippeth; thy "
95: 10 s', It is a people that do err in their "
102: 24 I s', O my God, take me not away in "
106: 23 he s' that he would destroy them, "
110: 1 Lord s' unto my Lord, Sit thou at 5002
116: 11 I s' in my haste, All men are liars. 559
119: 57 I have s' that I would keep thy "
122: 1 I was glad when they s' unto me, "
126: 2 then s' they among the heathen, The "
137: 7 who s', Rase it, rase it, even to the "
140: 6 I s' unto the Lord, Thou art my God: "
142: 5 I s', Thou art my refuge and my "
Pr 4: 4 taught me also, and s' unto me, "
7: 13 with an impudent face s' unto him, "
25: 7 better it is that it be s' unto thee, "
Ec 1: 10 any thing whereof it may be s', "
2: 1 I s' in mine heart, Go to now, I will "
2 I s' of laughter, It is mad: and of "
15 s' I in my heart, As it happeneth "
15 I s' in my heart, that this also is 1696
3: 17 I s' in mine heart, God shall judge 559
18 I s' in mine heart concerning the "
7: 23 I s', I will be wise; but it was far "
8: 14 I s' that this also is vanity. "
9: 16 Then s' I, Wisdom is better than "
Ca 2: 10 My beloved spake, and s' unto me, "
3: 3 to whom I s', Saw ye him whom my "
7: 8 I s', I will go up to the palm tree, I 559
Isa 5: 9 In mine ears s' the Lord of hosts, Of a*
6: 3 s', Holy, holy, holy, is the Lord of 559
5 s' I, Woe is me! for I am undone; "
7 s', Lo, this hath touched thy lips; "
8 Then s' I, Here am I; send me. "
9 And he s', Go, and tell this people, "
11 Then s' I, Lord, how long? And he "
7: 3 s' the Lord unto Isaiah, Go forth now "
12 But Ahaz s', I will not ask, neither "
13 And he s', Hear ye now, O house of "
8: 1 Moreover the Lord s' unto me, Take "
3 s' the Lord to me, Call his name "
14: 13 thou hast s' in thine heart, I will * "
18: 4 For so the Lord s' unto me, I will "
20: 3 And the Lord s', Like as my servant "
21: 6 For thus hath the Lord s' unto me, "
9 And he answered and s', Babylon is "
12 watchman s', The morning cometh, "
16 For thus hath the Lord s' unto me, "
22: 4 s' I, Look away from me; I will weep "
23: 12 he s', Thou shalt no more rejoice, O "
24: 16 But I s', My leanness, my leanness, "
25: 9 it shall be s' in that day, Lo, this "
28: 12 To whom he s', This is the rest "
15 Because ye have s', We have made "
29: 13 Wherefore the Lord s', Forasmuch "
30: 16 But ye s', No; for we will flee upon "
32: 5 nor the churl s' to be bountiful. "
36: 4 Rabshakeh s' unto them, Say ye now "
7 and s' to Judah and to Jerusalem, "
10 the Lord s' unto me, Go up against "
11 Then s' Eliakim and Shebna and "
12 But Rabshakeh s', Hath my master "
13 s', Hear ye the words of the great "
37: 3 And they s' unto him, Thus saith "
6 Isaiah s' unto them, Thus shall ye "
24 and hast s', By the multitude of my "
38: 1 s' unto him, Thus saith the Lord, "
3 and s', Remember now, O Lord, I "
10 I s' in the cutting off of my days, I "
11 I s', I shall not see the Lord, even "
21 Isaiah had s', Let them take a lump "
22 Hezekiah also had s', What is the "
39: 3 s' unto him, What s' these men? "
3 Hezekiah s', They had come from a "
4 Then s' he, What have they seen in "
5 Then s' Isaiah to Hezekiah, Hear "
8 Then s' Hezekiah to Isaiah, Good is "
8 He s' moreover, For there shall be "
40: 6 The voice s', Cry. And he s', What "
41: 6 every one s' to his brother, Be of "
9 s' unto thee, Thou art my servant; "
45: 19 I s' not unto the seed of Jacob, Seek "
47: 10 thou hast s', None seeth me. Thy "
10 thou hast s' in thine heart, I am, "
49: 3 s' unto me, Thou art my servant, O "
4 Then I s', I have laboured in vain, I "
6 he s', It is a light thing that thou * "
14 But Zion s', The Lord hath forsaken "
51: 23 which have s' to my soul, Bow down, "
63: 8 he s', Surely they are my people, "
65: 1 I s', Behold me, behold me, unto a "
66: 5 sake, s', Let the Lord be glorified: "
Jer 1: 6 Then s' I, Ah, Lord God! behold, I "
7 the Lord s' unto me, Say not, I am "
9 the Lord s' unto me, Behold, I have "
11 I s', I see a rod of an almond tree. "
12 s' the Lord unto me, Thou hast well "
13 I s', I see a seething pot; and the "
14 Then the Lord s' to me, Out of the "
2: 6 Neither s' they, Where is the Lord "
8 priests s' not, Where is the Lord? "
3: 6 Lord s' also unto me in the days of "
7 I s' after she had done all these "
11 Lord s' unto me, The backsliding "
19 But I s', How shall I put thee among "
19 I s', Thou shalt call me, My father; "
4: 10 Then s' I, Ah, Lord God! surely "
11 time shall it be s' to this people "
27 Lord s', The whole land shall be * "
5: 4 Therefore I s', Surely these are "

Jer 5:12 belied the Lord, and s', It is not he;559
6: 6 the Lord of hosts s', Hew ye down "
16 they s', We will not walk therein. "
17 But they s', We will not hearken. "
10:19 but I s', Truly this is a grief, and I "
11: 5 answered I, and s', So be it, O Lord. "
6 Lord s' unto me, Proclaim all these "
9 the Lord s' unto me, A conspiracy "
12: 4 they s', He shall not see our last "
13: 6 the Lord s' unto me, Arise, go to "
14:11 s' the Lord unto me, Pray not for "
13 Then s' I, Ah, Lord God! behold, "
14 the Lord s' unto me, The prophets "
15: 1 s' the Lord unto me, Though Moses "
11 Lord s', Verily it shall be well with "
16:14 shall no more be s', The Lord liveth, "
17:19 s' the Lord unto me, Go, and stand "
18:10 wherewith I s' I would benefit them. "
12 And they s', There is no hope: but "
18 Then s' they, Come, and let us "
19:14 house; and s' to all the people, "
20: 3 s' Jeremiah unto him, The Lord "
9 Then I s', I will not make mention "
21: 3 s' Jeremiah unto them, Thus shall "
23:17 Lord hath s', Ye shall have peace;1696
25 I have heard what the prophets s', 559
24: 3 s' the Lord unto me, What seest "
3 And I s', Figs; the good figs, very "
25: 5 They s', Turn ye again now every * "
26:16 Then s' the princes and all the people "
28: 5 Then the prophet Jeremiah s' unto "
6 Even the prophet Jeremiah s', "
15 Then s' the prophet Jeremiah unto "
29:15 ye have s', The Lord hath raised us "
32: 6 Jeremiah s', The word of the Lord "
8 s' unto me, Buy my field, I pray "
25 thou hast s' unto me, O Lord God, "
35: 5 and I s' unto them, Drink ye wine. "
6 But they s', We will drink no wine: "
11 that we s', Come, and let us go to "
18 Jeremiah s' unto the house of the "
36:15 And they s' unto him, Sit down now, "
16 s' unto Baruch, We will surely tell "
19 Then s' the princes unto Baruch, "
37:14 Then s' Jeremiah, It is false; I fall "
17 s', Is there any word from the Lord? "
17 Lord? And Jeremiah s', There is: "
17 for, s' he, thou shalt be delivered "
18 Jeremiah s' unto king Zedekiah, "
38: 4 the princes s' unto the king, We "
5 Then Zedekiah the king s', Behold, "
12 Ebed-melech...s' unto Jeremiah, "
14 and the king s' unto Jeremiah, I "
15 Then Jeremiah s' unto Zedekiah, If "
17 Then s' Jeremiah unto Zedekiah, "
19 Zedekiah the king s' unto Jeremiah, "
20 But Jeremiah s', They shall not "
24 Then s' Zedekiah unto Jeremiah, "
25 what thou hast s' unto the king, 1696
25 also what the king s' unto thee: "
40: 2 took Jeremiah, and s' unto him, 559
3 and done according as he hath s': 1696
5 he s', Go back also to Gedaliah the
14 s' unto him, Dost thou certainly 559
16 the son of Ahikam s' unto "
41: 6 he s' unto them, Come to Gedaliah "
8 among them that s' unto Ishmael, "
42: 2 s' unto Jeremiah the prophet, Let, "
4 Jeremiah the prophet s' unto them, "
5 Then they s' to Jeremiah, The Lord "
9 s' unto them, Thus saith the Lord, "
19 The Lord hath s' concerning you, 1696
44:20, 24 Jeremiah s' unto all the people, 559
46:16 they s', Arise, and let us go against "
50: 7 their adversaries s', We offend not, "
51:61 Jeremiah s' to Seraiah, When thou "
La 3:18 And I s', My strength and my hope "
54 mine head; then I s', I am cut off. "
4:15 they s' among the heathen, They "
20 of whom we s', Under his shadow "
Eze 2: 1 he s' unto me, Son of man, stand "
3 he s' unto me, Son of man, I send "
3: 1 Moreover he s' unto me, Son of man, "
3 s' unto me, Son of man, cause thy "
4 And he s' unto me, Son of man, go, "
10 Moreover he s' unto me, Son of man, "
22 he s' unto me, Arise, go forth into "
24 me, and s' unto me, Go, shut thyself "
4:13 And the Lord s', Even thus shall the "
14 Then s' I, Ah Lord God! behold, my "
15 Then he s' unto me, Lo, I have "
16 Moreover he s' unto me, Son of man, "
6:10 I have not s' in vain that I would 1696
8: 5 s' he unto me, Son of man, lift up 559
6 He s' furthermore unto me, Son of "
8 Then s' he unto me, Son of man, "
9 he s' unto me, Go in, and behold the "
12 Then s' he unto me, Son of man, "
13 He s' also unto me, Turn thee yet "
15 s' he unto me, Hast thou seen this, "
17 he s' unto me, Hast thou seen this, "
9: 4 Lord s' unto him, Go through the "
5 to the others he s' in mine hearing, "
7 he s' unto them, Defile the house, "
8 face, and cried, and s', Ah Lord God! "
9 Then s' he unto me, The iniquity of "
10: 2 and s', Go in between the wheels, "
11: 2 Then s' he unto me, Son of man, "
5 fell upon me, and s' unto me, Speak; "
5 Thus have ye s', O house of Israel: "
13 a loud voice, and s', Ah Lord God! "
15 inhabitants of Jerusalem have s', "
12: 9 the rebellious house, s' unto thee, "
13:12 shall it not be s' unto you, Where "
16: 6, 6 I s' unto thee when thou wast in "
20: 7 s' I unto them, Cast ye away every "

Eze 20: 8 then I s', I will pour out my fury 559
13 then I s', I would pour out my fury "
18 But I s' unto their children in the "
21 then I s', I would pour out my fury "
29 Then I s' unto them, What is the "
49 Then s' I, Ah Lord God! they say of "
21:17 fury to rest: I the Lord have s' it.*1696
23:36 Lord s' moreover unto me; Son of 559
43 Then s' I unto her that was old in "
24:19 the people s' unto me, Wilt thou "
26: 2 Tyrus hath s' against Jerusalem, "
27: 3 thou hast s', I am of perfect beauty. "
28: 2 thou hast s', I am a God, I sit in the "
29: 3 hath s', My river is mine own, and "
9 he hath s', The river is mine, and I "
35:10 Because thou hast s', These two "
36: 2 the enemy hath s' against you, Aha, "
20 when they s' to them, These are the "
37: 3 And he s' unto me, Son of man, can "
4 Again he s' unto me, Prophesy upon "
9 Then s' he unto me, Prophesy unto "
11 Then he s' unto me, Son of man, "
40: 4 the man s' unto me, Son of man, 1696
45 he s' unto me, This chamber, whose "
41: 4 and he s' unto me, This is the most 559
22 he s' unto me, This is the table 1696
42:13 Then s' he unto me, The north 559
43: 7 And he s' unto me, Son of man, the "
18 And he s' unto me, Son of man, thus "
44: 2 Then s' the Lord unto me; This gate "
5 the Lord s' unto me, Son of man, "
46:20 Then s' he unto me, This is the place "
24 s' he unto me, These are the places "
47: 6 And he s' unto me, Son of man, hast "
8 s' he unto me, These waters issue "
Da 1:10 prince of the eunuchs s' unto Daniel, "
11 Then s' Daniel to Melzar, whom the "
18 king had s' he should bring them* "
2: 3 king s' unto them, I have dreamed "
5 the king answered and s' to the 560
7 They answered again and s', Let "
8 The king answered and s', I know "
10 and s', There is not a man upon the "
15 and s' to Arioch the king's captain, "
20 Daniel answered and s', Blessed be "
24 he went and s' thus unto him; "
25 and s' thus unto him, I have found a "
26 The king answered and s' to Daniel, "
27 and s', The secret which the king "
47 king answered unto Daniel, and s', "
3: 9 and s' to the king, Nebuchadnezzar, "
14 Nebuchadnezzar spake and s' unto "
16 s' to the king, O Nebuchadnezzar, "
24 spake, and s' unto his counsellors, "
24 They answered and s' unto the king, "
25 He answered and s', Lo, I see four "
26 and s', Shadrach, Meshach, and "
28 Nebuchadnezzar spake, and s', "
4:14 cried aloud, and s' thus, Hew down "
19 king spake, and s', Belteshazzar, "
19 Belteshazzar answered and s', My "
30 The king spake and s', Is not this "
5: 7 and s' to the wise men of Babylon, "
10 the queen spake and s', O king, live "
13 king spake and s' unto Daniel, Art "
17 Then Daniel answered and s' before "
6: 5 Then s' these men, We shall not "
6 and s' thus unto him, King Darius "
12 The king answered and s', the "
13 answered they and s' before the "
15 and s' unto the king, Know, O king, "
16 spake and s' unto Daniel, Thy God "
20 spake and s' to Daniel, O Daniel, "
21 Then s' Daniel unto the king, O 4449
7: 2 Daniel spake and s', I saw in my 560
5 they s' thus unto it, Arise, devour "
23 Thus he s', The fourth beast shall "
8:13 saint s' unto that certain saint 559
14 he s' unto me, Unto two thousand "
16 and s', Gabriel, make this man to "
17 but he s' unto me, Understand, O "
19 And he s', Behold, I will make thee "
9: 4 s', O Lord, the great and dreadful "
22 s', O Daniel, I am now come forth to "
10:11 And he s' unto me, O Daniel, a man "
12 s' he unto me, Fear not, Daniel: for "
16 s' unto him that stood before me, "
19 s', O man greatly beloved, fear not: "
19 and s', Let my Lord speak; for "
20 s' he, Knowest thou wherefore I "
12: 6 one s' to the man clothed in linen, "
8 then s' I, O my Lord, what shall be "
9 And he s', Go thy way, Daniel: for "
Ho 1: 2 Lord s' to Hosea, Go, take unto thee "
4 the Lord s' unto him, Call his name "
6 And God s' unto him, Call her name "
9 s' God, Call his name Lo-ammi: "
10 where it was s' unto them, Ye are "
10 there it shall be s' unto them, Ye "
2: 5 she s', I will go after my lovers, that "
12 she hath s', These are my rewards "
3: 1 Then s' the Lord unto me, Go yet, "
3 And I s' unto her, Thou shalt abide "
12: 8 Ephraim s', Yet I am become rich, "
Joe 2:32 be deliverance, as the Lord hath s', "
Am 1: 2 he s', The Lord will roar from Zion, "
7: 2 then I s', O Lord God, forgive, I "
5 Then s' I, O Lord God, cease, I "
8 Lord s' unto me, Amos, what seest "
8 seest thou? And I s', A plumbline. "
8 Then s' the Lord, Behold, I will set "
12 Also Amaziah s' unto Amos, O thou "
14 and s' to Amaziah, I was no prophet, "
15 the Lord s' unto me, Go, prophesy, "
8: 2 And he s', Amos, what seest thou? "
2 And I s', A basket of summer fruit. "

Am 8: 2 s' the Lord unto me, The end is 559
9: 1 he s', Smite the lintel of the door, "
Jon 1: 6 s' unto him, What meanest thou, O "
7 And they s' every one to his fellow, "
8 Then s' they unto him, Tell us, we "
9 he s' unto them, I am an Hebrew; "
10 s' unto him, Why hast thou done "
11 Then s' they unto him, What shall "
12 he s' unto them, Take me up, and "
14 and s', We beseech thee, O Lord, we "
2: 2 And s', I cried by reason of mine "
4 Then I s', I am cast out of thy sight; "
3: 4 and he cried, and s', Yet forty days, "
10 he had · that he would do unto 1696
4: 2 and s', I pray thee, O Lord, was not 559
4 Then s' the Lord, Doest thou well to "
8 and s', It is better for me to die than "
9 God s' to Jonah, Doest thou well "
9 he s', I do well to be angry, even "
10 Then s' the Lord, Thou hast had "
Mic 3: 1 And I s', Hear, I pray you, O heads "
7:10 shall cover her which s' unto me, "
Hab 2: 2 Lord answered me, and s', Write "
Zep 2:15 that s' in her heart, I am, and there "
3: 7 I s', Surely thou wilt fear me, thou "
16 that day it shall be s' to Jerusalem, "
Hag 2:12 And the priests answered and s', No. "
13 Then s' Haggai, If one that is "
13 priests answered and s', It shall be "
14 Haggai, and s', So is this people, "
Zec 1: 6 they returned and s', Like as the "
9 Then s' I, O my lord, what are "
9 angel that talked with me s' unto "
10 the myrtle trees answered and s', "
11 stood among the myrtle trees, and s', "
12 angel of the Lord answered and s', "
14 that communed with me s' unto me, "
19 I s' unto the angel that talked with "
21 Then s' I, What come these to do? "
2: 2 Then s' I, Whither goest thou? And "
2 And he s' unto me, To measure "
4 And s' unto him, Run, speak to this "
3: 2 And the Lord s' unto Satan, The "
4 And unto him he s', Behold, I have "
5 And I s', Let them set a fair mitre "
4: 2 And s' unto me, What seest thou? "
2 And I s', I have looked, and behold "
5 with me answered and s' unto me, "
5 these be? And I s', No, my lord. "
11 Then answered I, and s' unto him, "
12 I answered again, and s' unto him, "
13 he answered me and s', Knowest "
13 these be? And I s', No, my lord. "
14 Then s' he, These are the two "
5: 2 he s' unto me, What seest thou? "
3 s' he unto me, This is the curse "
5 s' unto me, Lift up now thine eyes, "
6 And I s', What is it? And he s', "
6 He s' moreover, This is their "
8 And he s', This is wickedness. And "
10 s' I to the angel that talked with "
11 And he s' unto me, To build it an "
6: 4 I answered and s' unto the angel "
5 the angel answered and s' unto me, "
7 and he s', Get you hence, walk to "
11: 9 Then s' I, I will not feed you: that "
12 And I s' unto them, if ye think good, "
13 the Lord s' unto me, Cast it unto "
15 And the Lord s' unto me, Take unto "
Mal 1:13 Ye s' also, Behold, what a weariness* "
3: 7 But ye s', Wherein shall we return? "
14 Ye have s', It is vain to serve God: "
M't 2: 5 they s' unto him, In Bethlehem of 2036
8 and s', Go and search diligently "
3: 7 he s' unto them, O generation of "
15 s' unto him, Suffer it to be so now: "
4: 3 he s', If thou be the Son of God, "
4 Jesus answered and s', It is written, "
7 Jesus s' unto him, It is written 5346
5:21, 27 it was s' by them of old time, 2046
31 It hath been s', Whosoever shall put "
33 it hath been s' by them of old time, "
38 it hath been s', An eye for an eye, "
43 it hath been s', Thou shalt love thy "
8: 8 centurion answered and s', Lord, I 5346
10 s' to them that followed, Verily I 4483
13 Jesus s' unto the centurion, Go thy "
19 s' unto him, Master, I will follow "
21 another of his disciples s' unto him, "
22 But Jesus s' unto him, Follow me;* "
32 And he s' unto them, Go. And when "
9: 2 s' unto the sick of the palsy; Son, "
3 of the scribes s' within themselves, "
4 Jesus knowing their thoughts s', "
11 s' unto his disciples, Why eateth "
12 he s' unto them, They that be whole "
15 Jesus s' unto them, Can the children "
21 For she s' within herself, If I may 3004
22 he s', Daughter, be of good comfort; 2036
24 He s' unto them, Give place: for 3004
28 this? They s' unto him, Yea, Lord.* "
34 Pharisees s', He casteth out devils "
11: 3 And s' unto him, Art thou he that 2036
4 s' unto them, Go and shew John "
25 and s', I thank thee, O Father, Lord "
12: 2 Pharisees saw it, they s' unto him, "
3 he s' unto them, Have ye not read "
11 he s' unto them, What man shall "
23 and s', Is not this the son of David? 3004
24 they s', This fellow doth not cast 2036
25 and s' unto them, Every kingdom "
39 answered and s' unto them, An evil "
47 one s' unto him, Behold, thy mother "
48 s' unto him that told him, Who is "
49 and s', Behold my mother and my "
13:10 and s' unto him, Why speakest thou "

M't 13:11 and s' unto them, Because it is given 2068
27 s' unto him, Sir, didst not thou sow "
28 He s' unto them, An enemy hath "
28 The servants s' unto him, Wilt *5346
29 But he s', Nay; lest while ye gather*"
37 and s' unto them, He that soweth 2036
52 s' he unto them, Therefore every "
54 and s', Whence hath this man this 3004
57 s' unto them, A prophet is not 2036
14: 2 s' unto his servants, This is John "
4 John s' unto him, It is not lawful 3004
8 s', Give me here John Baptist's *5346
16 Jesus s' unto them, They need not 2036
18 He s', Bring them hither to me. "
28 Peter...s', Lord, if it be thou, bid "
29 And he s', Come. And when Peter "
31 and s' unto him, O thou of little *3004
15: 3 and s' unto them, Why do ye also 2036
10 s' unto them, Hear, and understand:"
12 disciples, and s' unto him, Knowest"
13 But he answered and s', Every plant,"
15 answered Peter and s' unto him, "
16 Jesus s', Are ye also yet without "
24 answered and s', I am not sent but "
26 and s', It is not meet to take the "
27 she s', Truth, Lord: yet the dogs "
28 answered and s' unto her, O woman,"
32 and s', I have compassion on the "
34 And they s', Seven, and a few little "
16: 2 and s' unto them, When it is evening,"
6 Jesus s' unto them, Take heed and "
8 he s' unto them, O ye of little faith, "
14 they s', Some say that thou art John"
16 Peter answered and s', Thou art "
17 Jesus...s' unto him, Blessed art thou,"
23 and s' unto Peter, Get thee behind "
24 s' Jesus unto his disciples, If any "
17: 4 and s' unto Jesus, Lord, it is good "
5 a voice out of the cloud, which s', *3004
7 and s', Arise, and be not afraid. 2036
11 Jesus...s' unto them, Elias truly "
17 Jesus answered and s', O faithless "
19 s', Why could not we cast him out? "
20 And Jesus s' unto them, Because * "
22 Jesus s' unto them, The Son of man"
24 and s', Doth not your master pay "
18: 3 And s', Verily I say unto you, Except"
21 Peter to him, and s', Lord, how oft "
32 him, s' unto him, O thou wicked *3004
19: 4 and s' unto them, Have ye not read, 2036
5 And s', For this cause shall a man "
11 But he s' unto them, All men cannot"
14 But Jesus s', Suffer little children, "
16 one came and s' unto him, Good "
17 he s' unto him, Why callest thou me"
18 Jesus s', Thou shalt do no murder, "
21 Jesus s' unto him, If thou wilt be 5346
23 s' Jesus unto his disciples, Verily 2036
26 and s' unto them, With men this is "
27 answered Peter and s' unto him, "
28 Jesus s' unto them, Verily I say "
20: 4 And s' unto them; Go ye also into "
13 and s', Friend, I do thee no wrong: "
17 apart in the way, and s' unto them,"
21 And he s' unto her, What wilt thou?"
22 Jesus answered and s', Ye know not"
25 Jesus called them unto him, and s',"
32 stood still, and called them, and s', "
21: 11 the multitude s', This is Jesus the 3004
13 And s' unto them, It is written, My*"
16 s' unto him, Hearest thou what 2036
19 and s' unto it, Let no fruit grow on*3004
21 Jesus answered and s' unto them, 2036
23 and s', By what authority doest 3004
24 Jesus...s' unto them, I also will ask 2036
27 Jesus, and s', We cannot tell. "
27 he s' unto them, Neither tell I you 5346
28 and s', Son, go work to day in my 2036
29 He answered and s', I will not: but "
30 came to the second, and s' likewise."
30 And he answered and s', I go, sir: "
38 they s' among themselves, This is "
22: 1 them again by parables, and s', *3004
13 s' the king to the servants, Bind 2036
18 s', Why tempt ye me, ye hypocrites?"
24 Moses s', If a man die, having no "
29 Jesus...s' unto them, Ye do err, "
37 Jesus s' unto him, Thou shalt love "
44 Lord s' unto my Lord, Sit thou on "
24: 2 Jesus s' unto them, See ye not all "
4 Jesus...s' unto them, Take heed "
25: 8 foolish s' unto the wise, Give us of "
12 and s', Verily I say unto you, I know"
21 His lord s' unto him, Well done, 5346
22 and s', Lord, thou deliveredst unto 2036
23 His lord s' unto him, Well done, 5346
24 and s', Lord, I knew thee that thou 2036
26 His lord...s' unto him, Thou wicked"
26: 1 sayings, he s' unto his disciples, "
5 But they s', Not on the feast day, 3004
10 he s' unto them, Why trouble ye 2036
15 s' unto them, What will ye give me,"
18 he s', Go into the city to such a man,"
21 as they did eat, he s', Verily I say "
23 answered and s', He that dippeth "
25 Then Judas...answered and s', "
25 Master, is it I? He s' unto him, 3004
25 unto him, Thou hast s'. 2036
26 and s', Take, eat; this is my body. "
33 Peter...s' unto him, Though all men"
34 Jesus s' unto him, Verily I say 5346
35 Peter s' unto him, Though I...die 3004
35 Likewise also s' all the disciples. 2036
49 and s', Hail, master; and kissed "
50 And Jesus s' unto him, Friend, "
52 s' Jesus unto him, Put up again *3004

M't 26: 55 hour s' Jesus to the multitudes, 2036
61 And s', This fellow "
61 This fellow s', I am able to 5346
62 and s' unto him, Answerest thou 2036
63 high priest...s' unto him, I adjure "
64 Jesus saith unto him, Thou hast s':"
66 and s', He is guilty of death. "
71 maid saw him, and s' unto them *3004
73 and s' to Peter, Surely thou also 2036
75 word of Jesus, which s' unto him, 2046
27: 4 And they s', What is that to us? 2036
6 took the silver pieces, and s', It is "
11 Jesus s' unto him, Thou sayest. 5346
13 s' Pilate unto him, Hearest thou *3004
17 Pilate s' unto them, Whom will ye 2036
21 governor...s' unto them, Whether "
21 unto you? They s', Barabbas. "
23 the governor s', Why, what evil 5346
25 and s', His blood be on us, and on 2036
41 with the scribes and elders, s', 3004
43 for he s', I am the Son of God. 2036
47 s', This man calleth for Elias. 3004
49 The rest s', Let be, let us see "
63 we remember that that deceiver s', 2036
65 Pilate s' unto them, Ye have a 5346
28: 5 angel...s' unto the women, Fear not 2036
6 is not here: for he is risen, as he s'. "
10 Then s' Jesus unto them, Be not *3004
M'r 1: 17 Jesus s' unto them, Come ye after 2036
37 they s' unto him, All men seek for*3004
38 he s' unto them, Let us go into the*"
2: 5 he s' unto the sick of the palsy, Son,*"
8 he s' unto them, Why reason ye *2036
14 and s' unto him, Follow me. And*3004
16 they s' unto his disciples, How is it "
19 And Jesus s'...Can the children 2036
24 the Pharisees s' unto him, Behold, 3004
25 he s' unto them, Have ye never read"
27 s' unto them, The sabbath was made"
3: 21 for they s', He is beside himself. "
22 scribes...s', He hath Beelzebub, "
23 and s' unto them in parables, How "
30 Because they s', He hath an unclean"
32 s' unto him, Behold, thy mother *2036
34 and s', Behold my mother and my*3004
4: 2 and s' unto them in his doctrine, "
9 he s' unto them, He that hath ears "
11 he s' unto them, Unto you it is given"
13 he s' unto them, Know ye not this* "
21 he s' unto them, Is a candle brought"
24 he s' unto them, Take heed what "
26 And he s', So is the kingdom of God,"
30 And he s', Whereunto shall we liken"
39 and s' unto the sea, Peace, be still. 2036
40 s' unto them, Why are ye so fearful?"
41 s' one to another, What manner of 3004
5: 7 and s', What have I to do with *2036
8 s' unto him, Come out of the man, 3004
28 For she s', If I may touch but his "
30 and s', Who touched my clothes? "
31 disciples s' unto him, Thou seest "
34 he s' unto her, Daughter, thy faith 2036
35 certain which s', Thy daughter is *3004
41 and s' unto her, Talitha cumi; * "
6: 4 Jesus s' unto them, A prophet is not"
10 s' unto them, In what place soever "
14 s', That John the Baptist was risen "
15 Others s', That it is Elias. And "
15 And others s', That it is a prophet, "
16 he s', It is John, whom I beheaded: 2036
18 John had s' unto Herod, It is not 3004
22 the daughter of the s' Herodias * 846
22 king s' unto the damsel, Ask of me 2036
24 and s' unto her mother, What shall I"
24 she s', The head of John the Baptist."
31 he s' unto them, Come ye yourselves*"
35 and s', This is a desert place, and 3004
37 and s' unto them, Give ye them to 2036
7: 6 and s' unto them, Well hath Esaias "
9 he s' unto them, Full well ye reject 3004
10 For Moses s', Honour thy father 2036
14 he s' unto them, Hearken unto me 3004
20 he s', That which cometh out of the"
27 Jesus s' unto her, Let the children 2036
28 and s' unto him, Yes, Lord: yet the*3004
29 s' unto her, For this saying go thy 2036
8: 5 loaves have ye? And they s', Seven."
20 took ye up? And they s', Seven. * "
21 he s' unto them, How is it that ye 3004
24 and s', I see men as trees, walking. "
34 he s' unto them, Whosoever will 2036
9: 1 he s' unto them,...there be some 3004
5 and s' to Jesus, Master, it is good * "
17 and s', Master, I have brought *2036
21 unto him? And he s', Of a child. "
23 Jesus s' unto him, If thou canst "
24 and s' with tears, Lord, I believe; 3004
26 insomuch that many s', He is dead. "
29 And he s' unto them, This kind 2036
31 and s' unto them, The Son of man 3004
36 him in his arms, he s' unto them, 2036
39 But Jesus s', Forbid him not: for "
10: 3 and s' unto them, What did Moses "
4 And they s', Moses suffered to write"
5 Jesus answered and s' unto them, "
14 and s' unto them, Suffer the little "
18 Jesus s' unto him, Why callest thou"
20 and s' unto him, Master, all these "
21 s' unto him, One thing thou lackest:"
29 And Jesus answered and s', Verily "
36 And he s' unto them, What would "
37 They s' unto him, Grant unto us "
38 But Jesus s' unto them, Ye know "
39 And they s' unto him, We can. "
39 And Jesus s' unto them, Ye shall "
51 Jesus answered and s' unto him, 3004

M'r 10: 51 The blind man s' unto him, Lord, 2036
52 And Jesus s' unto him, Go thy way: "
11: 5 them that stood there s' unto them, 3004
6 s' unto them even as Jesus had 2036
14 Jesus answered and s' unto it, No "
29 Jesus answered and s' unto them, "
33 they answered and s' unto Jesus, *3004
12: 7 husbandmen s' among themselves, 2036
15 s' unto them, Why tempt ye me? "
16 And they s' unto him, Cæsar's. "
17, 24 Jesus answering s' unto them, "
32 scribe s' unto him, Well, Master, "
32 thou hast s' the truth: for there is "
34 he s' unto him, Thou art not far "
35 Jesus answered and s', while he 3004
36 David...s' by the Holy Ghost, The 2036
36 The Lord s' to my Lord, Sit thou on"
38 And he s' unto them in his doctrine, 3004
13: 2 Jesus answering s' unto him, Seest 2036
14: 2 But they s', Not on the feast day, 3004
4 and s', Why was this waste of the* "
6 And Jesus s', Let her alone; why 2036
12 his disciples s' unto him, Where *3004
16 and found as he had s' unto them: 2036
18 Jesus s', Verily I say unto you, One"
19 one, Is it I? and another s', Is it I?* "
20 he answered and s' unto them, It 2036
22 gave to them, and s', Take, eat: "
24 he s' unto them, This is my blood "
29 But Peter s' unto him, Although 5346
31 wise. Likewise also s' they all. 3004
36 And he s', Abba, Father, all things "
48 Jesus answered and s' unto them, 2036
61 s' unto him, Art thou the Christ, *3004
62 And Jesus s', I am: and ye shall 2036
67 and s', And thou also wast with *3004
70 they that stood by s' again to Peter,"
72 the word that Jesus s' unto him, 2036
15: 2 he answering s' unto him, Thou * "
12 s' again unto them, What will ye "
14 Pilate s' unto them, Why, what evil 3004
31 chief priests mocking s' among "
35 heard it, s', Behold, he calleth Elias."
39 he s', Truly this man was the Son 2036
16: 3 s' among themselves, Who shall *3004
7 ye see him, as he s' unto you. 2036
8 neither s' they any thing to any "
15 he s' unto them, Go ye into all the "
Lu 1: 13 the angel s' unto him, Fear not, "
18 And Zacharias s' unto the angel, "
19 angel...s' unto him, I am Gabriel, "
28 angel came in unto her, and s', Hail,"
30 And the angel s' unto her, Fear not,"
34 s' Mary unto the angel, How shall "
35 angel...s' unto her, The Holy Ghost "
38 Mary s', Behold the handmaid of "
42 s', Blessed art thou among women, "
46 Mary s', My soul doth magnify the "
60 his mother answered and s', Not so;"
61 they s' unto her, There is none of "
2: 10 the angel s' unto them, Fear not: "
15 shepherds s' one to another, Let us "
24 which is s' in the law of the Lord, 2046
28 his arms, and blessed God, and s', 2036
34 s' unto Mary his mother, Behold, "
48 his mother s' unto him, Son, why "
49 he s' unto them, How is it that ye "
3: 7 Then s' he to the multitude that 3004
12 s' unto him, Master, what shall we 2036
13 he s' unto them, Exact no more "
14 he s' unto them, Do violence to no "
22 voice came from heaven, which s',*3004
4: 3 the devil s' unto him, If thou be the 2036
6 the devil s' unto him, All this power"
8 Jesus answered and s' unto him, "
9 s' unto him, If thou be the Son of "
12 Jesus answering s' unto him, It is "
12 It is s', Thou shalt not tempt the 2046
22 they s', Is not this Joseph's son? 3004
23 he s' unto them, Ye will surely say 2036
24 And he s', Verily I say unto you, "
43 he s' unto them, I must preach the "
5: 4 he s' unto Simon, Launch out into "
5 And Simon answering s' unto him, "
10 And Jesus s' unto Simon, Fear not;"
20 he s' unto him, Man, thy sins are "
22 s' unto them, What reason ye in "
24 (he s' unto the sick of the palsy,) I "
27 and he s' unto him, Follow me. "
31 And Jesus answering s' unto them, "
33 s' unto him, Why do the disciples "
34 he s' unto them, Can ye make the "
6: 2 Pharisees s' unto them, Why do ye "
3 Jesus answering them s', Have ye "
5 he s' unto them, That the Son of 3004
8 and s' to the man which had the 2036
9 s' Jesus unto them, I will ask you "
10 he s' unto the man, Stretch forth "
20 and s', Blessed be ye poor: for 3004
7: 9 s' unto the people that followed 2036
13 on her, and s' unto her, Weep not. "
14 he s', Young man, I say unto thee, "
20 they s', John Baptist hath sent us "
22 Jesus answering s' unto them, Go "
31 the Lord s', Whereunto then shall* "
40 And Jesus answering s' unto him, "
43 Simon answered and s', I suppose "
43 he s' unto him, Thou hast rightly "
44 and s' unto Simon, Seest thou this 5346
48 s' unto her, Thy sins are forgiven. 2036
50 he s' to the woman, Thy faith hath "
8: 8 when he had s' these things, he 3004
10 And he s', Unto you it is given to 2036
20 was told him by certain which s', *3004
21 and s' unto them, My mother and 2036
22 and he s' unto them, Let us go over"

Lu 8:25 s' unto them, Where is your faith? 2036
28 and with a loud voice s', What have "
30 And he s', Legion: because many "
45 And Jesus s', Who touched me? "
45 they that were with him s', Master, "
46 Jesus s', Somebody hath touched "
48 he s' unto her, Daughter, be of good "
52 he s', Weep not; she is not dead, "
9: 3 And he s' unto them, Take nothing "
7 because that it was s' of some, that 3004
9 Herod s', John have I beheaded: 2036
12 came the twelve, and s' unto him, "
13 But he s' unto them, Give ye them "
13 And they s', We have no more but "
14 he s' to his disciples, Make them "
19 answering s', John the Baptist; "
20 He s' unto them, But whom say ye "
20 Peter answering s', The Christ of "
23 And he s' to them all, If any man 3004
33 Peter s' unto Jesus, Master, it is 2036
33 for Elias: not knowing what he s'. 3004
41 Jesus answering s', O faithless 2036
43 Jesus did, he s' unto his disciples, "
48 And s' unto them, Whosoever shall "
49 John answered and s', Master, we "
50 Jesus s' unto him, Forbid him not: "
54 they s', Lord, wilt thou that we "
55 s', Ye know not what manner of * "
57 a certain man s' unto him, Lord, I "
58 And Jesus s' unto him, Foxes have "
59 And he s' unto another, Follow me. "
59 But he s', Lord, suffer me first to "
60 Jesus s' unto him, Let the dead "
61 another also s', Lord, I will follow "
62 Jesus s' unto him, No man, having "
10: 2 Therefore s' he unto them, The 3004
18 he s' unto them, I beheld Satan 2036
21 s', I thank thee, O Father, Lord of "
23 s' privately, Blessed are the eyes "
26 He s' unto him, What is written in "
27 he answering s', Thou shalt love "
28 And he s' unto him, Thou hast "
29 to justify himself, s' unto Jesus, "
30 Jesus answering s', A certain man "
35 and s' unto him, Take care of him; "
37 And he s', He that shewed mercy on "
37 Then s' Jesus unto him, Go, and "
40 came to him, and s', Lord, dost thou "
41 And Jesus answered and s' unto her, "
11: 1 one of his disciples s' unto him, "
2 he s' unto them, When ye pray, say "
5 And he s' unto them, Which of you "
15 But some of them s', He casteth out "
17 s' unto them, Every kingdom "
27 s' unto him, Blessed is the womb "
28 But he s', Yea rather, blessed are "
39 And the Lord s' unto him, Now do "
45 lawyers, and s' unto him, Master, *3004
46 And he s', Woe unto you also, ye 2036
49 also s' the wisdom of God, I will "
53 as he s' these things unto them, *3004
12: 13 one of the company s' unto him, 2036
14 he s' unto him, Man, who made me "
15 And he s' unto them, Take heed, "
18 And he s', This will I do: I will pull "
20 God s' unto him, Thou fool, this "
22 he s' unto his disciples, Therefore "
41 Peter s' unto him, Lord, speakest "
42 And the Lord s', Who then is that "
54 he s' also to the people, When ye 3004
13: 2 And Jesus answering s' unto them, 2036
7 Then s' he unto the dresser of his "
8 s' unto him, Lord, let it alone this *3004
12 and s' unto her, Woman, thou art 2036
14 s' unto the people, There are six 3004
15 s', Thou hypocrite, doth not each 2036
17 when he had s' these things, all 3004
18 s' he, Unto what is the kingdom of "
20 And again he s', Whereunto shall 2036
23 s' one unto him, Lord, are there few "
23 that be saved? And he s' unto them, "
32 he s' unto them, Go ye, and tell that "
14: 12 s' he also to him that bade him, 3004
15 he s' unto him, Blessed is he that 2036
16 s' he unto him, A certain man made "
18 s' unto him, I have bought a piece "
19 another s', I have bought five yoke "
20 another s', I have married a wife, "
21 s' to his servant, Go out quickly "
22 servant s', Lord, it is done as thou "
23 lord s' unto the servant, Go out into "
25 and he turned, and s' unto them, "
15: 11 he s', A certain man had two sons: "
12 the younger of them s' to his father, "
17 he s', How many hired servants of "
21 the son s' unto him, Father, I have "
22 the father s' to his servants, Bring "
27 And he s' unto him, Thy brother is "
29 s' to his father, Lo, these many "
31 he s' unto him, Son, thou art ever "
16: 1 s' also unto his disciples, There 3004
2 s' unto him, How is it that I hear 2036
3 steward s' within himself, What "
5 s' unto the first, How much owest 3004
6 he s', An hundred measures of oil. 2036
6 And he s' unto him, Take thy bill, "
7 Then s' he to another, And how "
7 And he s', An hundred measures of "
7 he s' unto him, Take thy bill, and 3004
15 s' unto them, Ye are they which 2036
24 he cried and s', Father Abraham, "
25 But Abraham s', Son, remember "
27 he s', I pray thee therefore, father, "
30 And he s', Nay, father Abraham: "
31 And he s' unto him, If they hear not "
17: 1 Then s' he unto the disciples, It is "

Lu 17: 5 apostles s' unto the Lord, Increase 2036
6 Lord s', If ye had faith as a grain "
13 s', Jesus, Master, have mercy on *3004
14 s' unto them, Go shew yourselves 2036
17 Jesus answering s', Were there not "
19 he s' unto him, Arise, go thy way: "
20 come, he answered them and s', "
22 And he s' unto the disciples, The "
37 they answered and s' unto him, *3004
37 he s' unto them, Wheresoever the 2036
18: 4 afterward he s' within himself, "
6 the Lord s', Hear what the unjust "
16 s', Suffer little children to come * "
19 Jesus s' unto him, Why callest thou "
21 he s', All these have I kept from my "
22 he s' unto him, yet lackest thou one "
24 he s', How hardly shall they that "
26 they that heard it s', Who then can "
27 s', The things which are impossible "
28 Then Peter s', Lo, we have left all, "
29 And he s' unto them, Verily I say "
31 s' unto them, Behold, we go up to "
41 And he s', Lord, that I may receive "
42 And Jesus s' unto him, Receive thy "
19: 5 and s' unto him, Zacchæus, make "
8 and s' unto the Lord; Behold, Lord, "
9 and Jesus s' unto him, This day is "
12 He s' therefore, A certain nobleman "
13 s' unto them, Occupy till I come. "
17 And he s' unto him, Well, thou good "
19 he s' likewise to him, Be thou also "
24 he s' unto them that stood by, Take "
25 they s' unto him, Lord, he hath "
32 found even as he had s' unto them. "
33 the owners thereof s' unto them, "
34 And they s', The Lord hath need of "
39 the multitude s' unto him, Master, "
40 he answered and s' unto them, I tell "
20: 3 he answered and s' unto them, I will "
8 Jesus s' unto them, Neither tell "
13 Then s' the lord of the vineyard, "
16 when they heard it, they s', God "
17 s', What is this then that is written, "
23 s' unto them, Why tempt ye me? "
24 it? They answered and s', Cæsar's. "
25 he s' unto them, Render therefore "
34 Jesus answering s' unto them, The "
39 certain of the scribes answering s', "
39 Master, thou hast well s'. "
41 And he s' unto them, How say they "
42 The Lord s' unto my Lord, Sit thou "
45 the people he s' unto his disciples, "
21: 3 And he s', Of a truth I say unto you, "
5 with goodly stones and gifts, he s', "
8 And he s', Take heed that ye be not "
10 Then s' he unto them, Nation 3004
22: 9 And they s' unto him, Where wilt 2036
10 And he s' unto them, Behold, when "
13 and found as he had s' unto them: 2046
15 And he s' unto them, With desire 2036
17 the cup, and gave thanks, and s', "
25 And he s' unto them, The kings of "
31 And the Lord s', Simon, Simon, * "
33 he s' unto him, Lord, I am ready "
34 And he s', I tell thee, Peter, the 3004
35 And he s' unto them, When I sent 2036
35 any thing? And they s', Nothing. "
36 Then s' he unto them, But now, he "
38 And they s', Lord, behold, here are "
38 And he s' unto them, It is enough. "
40 he s' unto them, Pray that ye enter "
46 And s' unto them, Why sleep ye? "
48 But Jesus s' unto him, Judas, "
49 they s' unto him, Lord, shall we "
51 Jesus answered and s', Suffer ye "
52 Jesus s' unto the chief priests, and "
56 s', This man was also with him. "
58 and s', Thou art also of them. 5346
58 And Peter s', Man, I am not. 2036
60 And Peter s', Man, I know not what "
61 how he had s' unto him, Before the "
67 And he s' unto them, If I tell you, "
70 s' they all, Art thou then the Son 5346
70 he s' unto them, Ye say that I am. 2036
71 they s', What need we any further "
23: 3 he answered him and s', Thou 5346
4 Then s' Pilate to the chief priests 2036
14 S' unto them, Ye have brought this "
22 And he s' unto them the third time, "
28 s', Daughters of Jerusalem, weep "
34 Then s' Jesus, Father, forgive 3004
42 he s' unto Jesus, Lord, remember "
43 Jesus s' unto him, Verily I say 2036
46 had cried with a loud voice, he s', "
46 having s' thus, he gave up the ghost. "
24: 5 they s' unto them, Why seek ye the "
17 he s' unto them, What manner of "
18 Cleopas, answering s' unto him, Art "
19 And he s' unto them, What things? "
19 they s' unto him, concerning Jesus "
23 angels, which s' that he was alive. 3004
24 it even so as the women had s': 2036
25 he s' unto them, O fools, and slow "
32 they s' one to another, Did not our "
38 s' unto them, Why are ye troubled? "
41 he s' unto them, Have ye here any "
44 he s' unto them, These are the "
46 s' unto them, Thus it is written, "
Joh 1: 22 s' they unto him, Who art thou? "
23 He s', I am the voice of one crying 5346
23 the Lord, as s' the prophet Esaias. 2036
25 s' unto him, Why baptizest thou "
30 This is he of whom I s', After me "
33 the same s' unto me, Upon whom "
38 They s' unto him, Rabbi, (which is "
42 he s', Thou art Simon the son of "

Joh 1: 46 Nathanael s' unto him, Can there 2036
48, 50 Jesus answered and s' unto him "
50 Because I s' unto thee, I saw thee "
2: 16 And s' unto them that sold doves, "
18 answered the Jews and s' unto him, "
19 Jesus answered and s' unto them, "
20 Then s' the Jews, Forty and six "
22 that he had s' this unto them; *3004
22 and the word which Jesus had s'. 2036
3: 2 s' unto him, Rabbi, we know that "
3 Jesus answered and s' unto him, "
7 s' unto thee, Ye must be born again. "
9 Nicodemus answered and s' unto "
10 Jesus answered and s' unto him, "
26 came unto John, and s' unto him, "
27 John answered and s', A man can "
28 that I s', I am not the Christ, but "
4: 10, 13 Jesus answered and s' unto her, "
17 The woman answered and s', I "
17 Jesus s' unto her, Thou hast well *3004
17 Thou hast well s', I have no *2036
27 yet no man s', What seekest thou? "
32 But he s' unto them, I have meat to "
33 s' the disciples one to another, 3004
42 s' unto the woman, Now we believe, "
48 Then s' Jesus unto him, Except ye 2036
52 they s' unto him, Yesterday at the "
53 in the which Jesus s' unto him, Thy "
5: 10 The Jews therefore s' unto him 3004
11 the same s' unto me, Take up thy 2036
12 that which s' unto thee, Take up "
14 s' unto him,...thou art made whole: "
18 s' also that God was his Father, *3004
19 answered Jesus and s' unto them, 2036
6: 6 And this he s' to prove him: for he 3004
10 Jesus s', Make the men sit down. 2036
12 he s' unto his disciples, Gather up *3004
14 s', This is of a truth that prophet "
25 they s' unto him, Rabbi, when 2036
26 Jesus answered them and s', Verily, "
28 s' they unto him, What shall we do, "
29 Jesus answered and s' unto them, "
30 s' therefore unto him, What sign "
32 Then Jesus s' unto them, Verily, "
34 s' they unto him, Lord, evermore "
35 Jesus s' unto them, I am the bread "
36 But I s' unto you, That ye also have "
41 because he s', I am the bread which "
42 they s', Is not this Jesus, the son 3004
43 s' unto them, Murmur not among 2036
53 Jesus s' unto them, Verily, verily, I "
59 These things s' he in the synagogue, "
60 had heard this, s', This is an hard "
61 s' unto them, Doth this offend you? "
65 And he s',...that no man can come 3004
65 Therefore s' I unto you, that no 2046
67 s' Jesus unto the twelve, Will ye 2036
7: 3 His brethren therefore s' unto him, "
6 Then Jesus s' unto them, My time *3004
9 he had s' these words unto them, 2036
11 at the feast, and s', Where is he? 3004
12 him: for some s', He is a good man: "
12 others s', Nay; but he deceiveth the "
16 and s', My doctrine is not mine, but 2036
20 The people...s', Thou hast a devil: * "
21 s' unto them, I have done one work, "
25 Then s' some of them of Jerusalem, 3004
31 and s', When Christ cometh, will he "
33 s' Jesus unto them, Yet a little 2036
35 s' the Jews among themselves, "
36 manner of saying is this that he s', "
38 as the scripture hath s', out of his "
40 s', Of a truth this is the Prophet. 3004
41 Others s', This is the Christ. But "
41 some s', Shall Christ come out of "
42 scripture s', That Christ cometh 2036
45 and they s' unto them, Why have ye "
52 and s' unto him, Art thou also of "
8: 6 This they s', tempting him, that 3004
7 up himself, and s' unto them, 2036
10 he s' unto her, Woman, where are "
11 She s', No man, Lord. And "
11 Jesus s'...Neither do I condemn "
13 Pharisees therefore s' unto him, "
14 s' unto them, Though I bear record "
19 s' they unto him, Where is thy 3004
21 s' Jesus again unto them, I go my 2036
22 s' the Jews, Will he kill himself? 3004
23 s' unto them, Ye are from beneath; 2036
24 I s' therefore unto you, that ye "
25 s' they unto him, Who art thou? 3004
25 Even the same that I s' unto you *2980
28 s' Jesus unto them, When ye have 2036
31 Then s' Jesus to those Jews which 3004
39 and s' unto him, Abraham is our 2036
41 s' they to him, We be not born of "
42 Jesus s' unto them, If God were "
48 s' unto him, Say we not well that "
52 s' the Jews unto him, Now we know "
57 s' the Jews unto him, Thou art not "
58 Jesus s' unto them, Verily, verily, I "
9: 7 s' unto him, Go, wash in the pool of "
8 s', Is not this he that sat and 3004
9 Some s', This is he: others "
9 others s', He is like him: "
9 He is like him: but he s', I am he. 3004
10 s' they unto him, How were thine "
11 and s', A man that is called Jesus *2036
11 and s' unto me, Go to the pool of "
12 Then s' they unto him, Where is he? "
12 Where is he? He s', I know not. *3004
15 He s' unto them, He put clay upon 2036
16 s' some of the Pharisees, This man 3004
16 Others s', How can a man that is a "
17 eyes? He s', He is a prophet. 2036
20 s', We know that this is our son, "

Joh 9:23 Therefore s' his parents, He is of 2036
24 s' unto him, Give God the praise: "
25 and s', Whether he be a sinner or * "
26 s' they to him again, What did he "
28 him, and s', Thou art his disciple; "
30 man answered and s' unto them, "
34 They...s' unto him, Thou wast "
35 s' unto him, Dost thou believe on "
36 answered and s', Who is he, Lord, "
37 Jesus s' unto him, Thou hast both "
38 And he s', Lord, I believe. And he5346
39 Jesus s', For judgment I am come 2036
40 and s' unto him, Are we blind also? "
41 Jesus s' unto them, If ye were "
10: 7 s' Jesus unto them again, Verily, "
20 many of them s', He hath a devil, 3004
21 Others s', These are not the words "
24 s' unto him, How long dost thou "
26 not of my sheep, as I s' unto you. *2036
34 in your law, I s', Ye are gods? "
36 because I s', I am the Son of God? "
41 him, and s', John did no miracle: 3004
11: 4 he s', This sickness is not unto 2036
11 These things s' he: and after that* "
12 s' his disciples, Lord, if he sleep, he"
14 s' Jesus unto them plainly, Lazarus"
16 Then s' Thomas, which is called "
21 s' Martha unto Jesus, Lord, if thou "
25 s' unto her, I am the resurrection, "
28 she had so s', she went her way, "
34 And s', Where have ye laid him? "
34 s' unto him, Lord, come and see. *3004
36 s' the Jews, Behold how he loved "
37 some of them s', Could not this 2036
39 Jesus s', Take ye away the stone. 3004
40 S' I not unto thee, that, if thou 2036
41 s', Father, I thank thee that thou "
42 of the people which stand by I s' it, "
47 a council, and s', What do we? for 3004
49 s' unto them, Ye know nothing at 2036
12: 6 This he s', not that he cared for the"
7 s' Jesus, Let her alone: against "
19 Pharisees...s' among themselves, "
29 and heard it, s' that it thundered: 3004
29 others s', An angel spake to him. "
30 Jesus...s', This voice came not 2036
33 This he s', signifying what death 3004
35 Jesus s' unto them, Yet a little 2036
39 because that Esaias s' again, "
41 These things s' Esaias, when he "
44 Jesus cried and s', He that believeth"
50 even as the Father s' unto me, so I2046
13: 7 Jesus...s' unto him, What I do 2036
11 therefore s' he, Ye are not all clean."
12 s' unto them, Know ye what I have "
21 When Jesus had thus s', he was "
21 and testified, and s', Verily, verily, "
27 s' Jesus unto him, That thou *3004
29 Jesus had s' unto him, Buy those "
31 Jesus s', Now is the Son of man * "
33 and as I s' unto the Jews, Whither2036
36 Simon Peter s' unto him, Lord, *3004
37 Peter s' unto him, Lord, why * "
14:23 Jesus...s' unto him, If a man love 2036
26 whatsoever I have s' unto you. "
28 Ye have heard how I s' unto you, I "
28 because I s', I go unto the Father:* "
15:20 the word that I s' unto you, The "
16: 4 I s' not unto you at the beginning, "
6 I have s' these things unto you, *2980
15 therefore s' I, that he shall take of 2036
17 s' some of his disciples among "
18 They s' therefore, What is this 3004
19 and s' unto them, Do ye enquire 2036
19 that I s', A little while, and ye shall"
29 His disciples s' unto him, Lo, now*3004
17: 1 eyes to heaven, and s', Father, the 2036
18: 4 and s' unto them, Whom seek ye?* "
6 then as he had s' unto them, I am "
7 ye? And they s', Jesus of Nazareth."
11 s' Jesus unto Peter, Put up thy "
20 and in secret have I s' nothing. *2980
21 heard me, what I have s' unto * "
21 them: behold, they know what I s'.2036
25 They s' therefore unto him, Art not"
25 He denied it, and s', I am not. "
29 and s', What accusation bring ye* "
30 They...s' unto him, If he were not "
31 s' Pilate unto them, Take ye him, "
31 Jews...s' unto him, It is not lawful "
33 s' unto him, Art thou the King of "
37 s' unto him, Art thou a king then? "
38 when he had s' this, he went out "
19: 3 And s', Hail, King of the Jews! 3004
21 s' the chief priests of the Jews to "
21 that he s', I am king of the Jews. 2036
24 s' therefore among themselves, Let "
30 the vinegar, he s', It is finished: "
20:14 she had thus s', she turned herself "
20 he had so s', he shewed unto them "
21 s' Jesus to them again, Peace be "
22 he had s' this, he breathed on them"
25 other disciples...s' unto him, We 3004
25 he s' unto them, Except I shall see2036
26 midst, and s', Peace be unto you. "
28 Thomas...s' unto him, My Lord "
21: 6 And he s' unto them, Cast the net "
17 s' unto him the third time, Lovest "
17 he s' unto him, Lord, thou knowest"
20 s', Lord, which is he that betrayeth "
23 yet Jesus s' not unto him, He shall "
1: 7 he s' unto them, It is not for you "
11 Which also s', Ye men of Galilee, "
15 in the midst of the disciples, and s', "
24 and s', Thou, Lord, which knowest "
13 Others mocking s', These men are3004

Ac 2:14 and s' unto them, Ye men of Judæa,*669
34 The Lord s' unto my Lord, Sit thou2036
37 s' unto Peter and to the rest of the "
38 Peter s' unto them, Repent, and be5346
3: 4 him with John, s', Look on us. 2036
6 Peter s', Silver and gold have I none;"
22 Moses truly s' unto the fathers, A "
4: 8 Peter,...s' unto them, Ye rulers of "
19 s' unto them, Whether it be right "
23 priests and elders had s' unto them."
24 s', Lord, thou art God, which hast "
25 mouth of thy servant David hast s',*"
32 neither s' any of them that ought 3004
5: 3 Peter s', Ananias, why hath Satan 2036
8 And she s', Yea, for so much. "
9 Peter s' unto her, How is it that ye "
19 and brought them forth, and s', "
29 and s', We ought to obey God rather"
35 And s' unto them, Ye men of Israel,"
6: 2 s', It is not reason that we should "
11 men, which s', We have heard him3004
13 set up false witnesses, which s', "
7: 1 Then s' the high priest, Are these 2036
2 he s', Men, brethren, and fathers, 5346
3 s' unto him, Get thee out of thy 2036
7 be in bondage will I judge, s' God: "
33 Then s' the Lord to him, Put off thy"
37 which s' unto the children of Israel, "
56 And s', Behold, I see the heavens "
60 when he had s' this, he fell asleep. "
8:20 But Peter s' unto him, Thy money "
24 Simon, and s', Pray ye to the Lord "
29 the Spirit s' unto Philip, Go near, "
30 s', Understandest thou what thou "
31 And he s', How can I, except some "
34 s', I pray thee, of whom speaketh "
36 the eunuch s', See, here is water;*5346
37 Philip s', If thou believest with all*2036
37 And he answered and s', I believe* "
9: 5 And he s', Who art thou, Lord? "
5 the Lord s', I am Jesus whom thou "
6 and astonished s', Lord, what wilt* "
6 the Lord s' unto him, Arise, and go*"
10 s' the Lord in a vision, Ananias. "
10 And he s', Behold, I am here, Lord. "
11 the Lord s' unto him, Arise, and go "
15 the Lord s' unto him, Go thy way: 2036
17 his hands on him s', Brother Saul, "
21 heard him were amazed, and s'; 3004
34 Peter s' unto him, Æneas, Jesus 2036
40 him to the body s', Tabitha, arise. "
10: 4 was afraid, and s', What is it, Lord?"
4 s' unto him, Thy prayers and thine "
14 Peter s', Not so, Lord; for I have "
19 Spirit s' unto him, Behold, three "
21 s', Behold, I am he whom ye seek: "
22 And they s', Cornelius the centurion, "
28 he s' unto them, Ye know how that5346
30 Cornelius s', Four days ago I was "
31 s', Cornelius, thy prayer is heard,* "
34 s', Of a truth I perceive that God 2036
11: 8 But I s', Not so, Lord: for nothing "
13 s' unto him, Send men to Joppa, * "
16 he s', John indeed baptized with 3004
12: 8 the angel s' unto him, Gird thyself,2036
11 he s', Now I know of a surety, that "
15 And they s' unto her, Thou art mad."
15 so. Then s' they, It is his angel. 3004
17 he s', Go shew these things unto 2036
13: 2 the Holy Ghost s', Separate me "
10 And s', O full of all subtilty and all "
16 beckoning with his hand s', Men of "
22 and s', I have found David the son "
25 he s', Whom think ye that I am? 3004
34 s' on this wise, I will give you the*5346
46 s', It was necessary that the word 2036
14:10 S' with a loud voice, Stand upright "
15: 1 and s', Except ye be circumcised after*
7 Peter rose up, and s' unto them, 2036
36 Paul s' unto Barnabas, Let us go "
16:18 and s' to the spirit, I command thee"
30 and s', Sirs, what must I do to be 5346
31 they s', Believe on the Lord Jesus 2036
37 But Paul s' unto them, They have 5346
17:18 some s', What will this babbler say?3004
22 s', Ye men of Athens, I perceive 5346
28 s', For we are also his offspring. 2046
32 others s', We will hear thee again 2036
18: 6 s' unto them, Your blood be upon "
14 Gallio s' unto the Jews, If it were a "
19: 2 He s' unto them, Have ye received "
2 And they s' unto him, We have not "
3 he s' unto them, Unto what then "
3 And they s', Unto John's baptism. "
4 s' Paul, John verily baptized with "
15 evil spirit...s', Jesus I know, and "
25 s', Sirs, ye know that by this craft "
35 s', Ye men of Ephesus, what man *5346
20:10 him s', Trouble not yourselves; 2036
18 he s' unto them, Ye know, from the "
35 words of the Lord Jesus, how he s', "
21: 4 who s' to Paul through the Spirit, 3004
11 s', Thus saith the Holy Ghost, So 2036
20 s' unto him, Thou seest, brother, "
37 he s' unto the chief captain, May I3004
37 Who s', Canst thou speak Greek? 5346
39 Paul s', I am a man which am a 2036
22: 8 And he s' unto me, I am Jesus of "
10 And I s', What shall I do, Lord? "
10 the Lord s' unto me, Arise, and go "
13 s' unto me, Brother Saul, receive "
14 he s', The God of our fathers hath "
19 And I s', Lord, they know that I "
21 he s' unto me, Depart: for I will "
22 s', Away with such a fellow from 3004
25 Paul s' unto the centurion that 2036

Ac 22:27 captain came, and s' unto him, 2036
27 art thou a Roman? He s', Yea. 5346
28 And Paul s', But I was free born. "
23: 1 earnestly beholding the council, s',2036
3 Then s' Paul unto him, God shall "
4 s', Revilest thou God's high priest? "
5 s' Paul, I wist not, brethren, that 5346
7 when he had so s', there arose a 2980
11 and s', Be of good cheer, Paul: for2036
14 and s', We have bound ourselves "
17 s', Bring this young man unto the 5346
18 and s', Paul the prisoner called me*"
20 And he s', The Jews have agreed 2036
35 I will hear thee, s' he, when thine 5346
24:22 s', When Lysias the chief captain *2036
25: 5 Let them therefore, s' he, which *5346
9 Paul, and s', Wilt thou go up to 2036
10 Then s' Paul, I stand at Cæsar's "
22 Agrippa s' unto Festus, I would 5346
22 To morrow, s' he, thou shalt hear* "
24 And Festus s', King Agrippa, and* "
26: 1 Agrippa s' unto Paul, Thou art "
15 And I s', Who art thou, Lord? 2036
15 And he s', I am Jesus whom thou "
24 Festus s' with a loud voice, Paul, *5346
25 he s', I am not mad, most noble * "
28 Then Agrippa s' unto Paul, Almost "
29 Paul s', I would to God, that not 2036
32 s' Agrippa unto Festus, This man 5346
27:10 s' unto them, Sirs, I perceive that 3004
21 in the midst of them, and s', Sirs, 2036
31 Paul s' to the centurion and to the "
28: 4 s' among themselves, No doubt 3004
6 minds, and s' that he was a god. "
17 he s' unto them, Men and brethren,"
21 And they s' unto him, We neither 2036
29 he had s' these words, the Jews * "
Ro 7: 7 law had s', Thou shalt not covet. 3004
9:12 s' unto her, The elder shall serve 4483
26 s' unto them, Ye are not my people;"
29 Esaias s' before, Except the Lord 4280
1Co 11:24 he brake it, and s', Take, eat: 2036
2Co 6:16 as God hath s', I will dwell in them,"
7: 3 s' before, that ye are in our hearts 4280
9: 3 that, as I s', ye may be ready: 3004
12: 9 And he s' unto me, My grace is 2046
Ga 1: 9 As we s' before, so say I now 4280
2:14 I s' unto Peter before them all, If 2036
Tit 1:12 s', The Cretians are alway liars, "
Heb 1: 5 the angels s' he at any time, Thou "
13 angels s' he at any time, Sit on my2046
3:10 and s', They do alway err in their 2036
15 While it is s', To day if ye will hear3004
4: 3 as he s', As I have sworn in my 2046
7 as it is s', To day if ye will hear his "
5: 5 he that s' unto him, Thou art my *2980
7:21 that s' unto him, The Lord sware 3004
10: 7 Then s' I, Lo, I come (in the 2036
8 Above when he s', Sacrifice and *3004
9 Then s' he, Lo, I come to do thy 2046
15 us: for after that he had s' before, 4280
30 s', Vengeance belongeth unto me, 2036
11:18 it was s', That in Isaac shall thy 2980
12:21 Moses s', I exceedingly fear and 2036
13: 5 he hath s', I will never leave thee, 2046
Jas 2:11 that s', Do not commit adultery, 2036
11 s' also, Do not kill. Now if thou "
Jude 9 but s', The Lord rebuke thee. "
Re 4: 1 which s', Come up hither, and I *3004
5:14 And the four beasts s', Amen. "
6:11 and it was s' unto them, that they 4483
16 s' to the mountains and rocks, *3004
7:14 I s' unto him, Sir, thou knowest. *2046
14 he s' to me, These are they which 2036
10: 8 s', Go and take the little book *3004
9 and s' unto him, Give me the little* "
9 s' unto me, Take it, and eat it up;* "
11 s' unto me, Thou must prophesy * "
17: 7 angel s' unto me, Wherefore didst 2036
19: 3 And again they s', Alleluia. *2046
10 he s' unto me, See thou do it not: *3004
21: 5 he that sat upon the throne s', 2036
5 And he s' unto me, Write: for *3004
6 And he s' unto me, It is done. I 2036
22: 6 he s' unto me, These sayings are "

saidst
Ge 12:19 Why s' thou, She is my sister? so 559
26: 9 and how s' thou, She is my sister? "
32: 9 the Lord which s' unto me, Return "
12 thou s', I will surely do thee good, "
44:21 thou s' unto thy servants, Bring "
23 thou s' unto thy servants, Except "
Ex 32:13 s' unto them, I will multiply your 1696
J'g 9:38 thy mouth, wherewith thou s', 559
1Ki 2:42 and thou s' unto me, The word that "
Job 35: 2 that thou s', My righteousness is* "
3 For thou s', What advantage will* "
Ps 27: 8 When thou s', Seek ye my face; my "
89:19 s', I have laid help upon one that is "
Isa 47: 7 thou s', I shall be a lady for ever: "
57:10 yet s' thou not, There is no hope: "
Jer 2:20 thou s', I will not transgress; when "
25 thou s', There is no hope: no; for I "
22:21 but thou s', I will not hear. "
La 3:57 called upon thee: thou s', Fear not. "
Eze 25: 3 Because thou s', Aha, against my "
Ho 13:10 whom thou s', Give me a king and "
Joh 4:18 husband: in that s' thou truly. 2046

sail See also MAINSAIL; SAILED; SAILING.
Isa 33:23 they could not spread the s': 5251
Eze 27: 7 thou spreadest forth to be thy s'; 321
Ac 20: 3 as he was about to s' into Syria, 321
16 For Paul had determined to s' by 3896
27: 1 that we should s' into Italy, they 636
2 to s' by the coasts of Asia; one 4126

Ac 27:17 strake s', and so were driven. *4632
24 thee all them that s' with thee. 4126
sailed
Lu 8:23 But as they s' he fell asleep: and 4126
Ac 13: 4 and from thence they s' to Cyprus. 636
14:26 thence s' to Antioch, from whence "
15:39 took Mark, and s' unto Cyprus; 1602
18:18 brethren, and s' thence into Syria, "
21 God will. And he s' from Ephesus.*321
20: 6 we s' away from Philippi after the 1602
13 before to ship, and s' unto Assos, * 321
15 we s' thence, and came the next * 636
21: 3 on the left hand, and s' into Syria, 4126
27: 4 we s' under Cyprus, because the 5284
5 we had s' over the sea of Cilicia 1277
7 when we had s' slowly many days, 1020
7 we s' under Crete, over against 5284
13 thence, they s' close by Crete. 3881
sailing
Ac 21: 2 a ship s' over unto Phenicia, we *1276
27: 6 a ship of Alexandria s' into Italy; 4126
9 and when s' was now dangerous, *4144
sailors
Re 18:17 s', and as many as trade by sea, *3492
saint See also SAINTS.
Ps 106:16 and Aaron the s' of the Lord. 6918
Da 8:13 Then I heard one s' speaking, * "
13 and another s' said unto that * "
13 said unto that certain s' which spake,*
Ph'p 4:21 Salute every s' in Christ Jesus. 40
saints See also SAINTS'.
De 33: 2 came with ten thousands of s': *6944
3 all his s' are in thy hand: and 6918
1Sa 2: 9 He will keep the feet of his s', *2623
2Ch 6:41 and let thy s' rejoice in goodness. "
Job 5: 1 to which of the s' wilt thou turn? *6918
15:15 he putteth no trust in his s'; yea,* "
Ps 16: 3 But to the s' that are in the earth, "
30: 4 Sing unto the Lord, O ye s' of his, 2623
31:23 O love the Lord, all ye his s': for "
34: 9 O fear the Lord, ye his s': for 6918
37:28 and forsaketh not his s'; they are 2623
50: 5 Gather my s' together unto me; "
52: 9 name; for it is good before thy s'. "
79: 2 the flesh of thy s' unto the beasts "
85: 8 peace unto his people, and to his s':"
89: 5 also in the congregation of the s'.*6918
7 be feared in the assembly of the s'.* "
97:10 he preserveth the souls of his s'; 2623
116:15 of the Lord is the death of his s'. "
132: 9 and let thy s' shout for joy. "
16 and her s' shall shout aloud for joy."
145:10 Lord; and thy s' shall bless thee. "
148:14 his people, the praise of all his s'; "
149: 1 praise in the congregation of s'. "
5 Let the s' be joyful in glory: let "
9 this honour have all his s'. Praise "
Pr 2: 8 and preserveth the way of his s'. "
Da 7:18 the s' of the most High shall take 6922
21 same horn made war with the s', "
22 judgment was given to the s' of the"
22 that the s' possessed the kingdom. "
25 wear out the s' of the most High, "
27 people of the s' of the most High, "
Ho 11:12 God, and is faithful with the s'. *6918
Zec 14: 5 shall come, and all the s' with thee.* "
M't 27:52 bodies of the s' which slept arose, 40
Ac 9:13 much evil he hath done to thy s' at "
32 also to the s' which dwelt at Lydda. "
41 he had called the s' and widows, "
26:10 many of the s' did I shut up in prison, "
Ro 1: 7 Rome, beloved of God, called to be s':"
8:27 he maketh intercession for the s' "
12:13 Distributing to the necessity of s'; "
15:25 Jerusalem to minister unto the s'. "
26 the poor s' which are at Jerusalem. "
31 Jerusalem may be accepted of the s';"
16: 2 her in the Lord, as becometh s', "
15 and all the s' which are with them. "
1Co 1: 2 in Christ Jesus, called to be s', "
6: 1 the unjust, and not before the s'? "
2 that the s' shall judge the world? "
14:33 of peace, as in all churches of the s'. "
16: 1 concerning the collection for the s', "
15 addicted...to the ministry of the s',) "
2Co 1: 1 all the s' which are in all Achaia: "
8: 4 fellowship of...ministering to the s'. "
9: 1 as touching the ministering to the s'."
12 not only supplieth the want of the s'," "
13:13 All the s' salute you. "
Eph 1: 1 to the s' which are at Ephesus, and "
15 Lord Jesus, and love unto all the s', "
18 the glory of his inheritance in the s'," "
2:19 fellowcitizens with the s', and of the "
3: 8 who am less than the least of all s', "
18 to comprehend with all s' what is the"
4:12 For the perfecting of the s', for the "
5: 3 named among you, as becometh s'; "
6:18 and supplication for all s'; "
Ph'p 1: 1 to all the s' in Christ Jesus which are"
4:22 All the s' salute you, chiefly they "
Col 1: 2 To the s' and faithful brethren in "
4 the love which ye have to all the s', "
12 of the inheritance of the s' in light: "
26 but now is made manifest to his s': "
1Th 3:13 the coming of...Christ with all his s'. "
2Th 1:10 he shall come to be glorified in his s'," "
Ph'm 5 the Lord Jesus, and toward all s'; "
7 the bowels of the s' are refreshed by"
Heb 6:10 in that ye have ministered to the s', "
13:24 have the rule over you, and all the s'. "
Jude 3 faith...once delivered unto the s'. "
14 cometh with ten thousands of his s',* "
Re 5: 8 odours, which are the prayers of s'. "
8: 3 offer it with the prayers of all s' 40
4 came with the prayers of the s', "
11:18 servants the prophets, and to the s', "
13: 7 unto him to make war with the s', "
10 the patience and the faith of the s'. "
14:12 Here is the patience of the s': here "
15: 3 true are thy ways, thou King of s'.* "
16: 6 shed the blood of s' and prophets, "
17: 6 drunken with the blood of the s', "
18:24 the blood of prophets, and of s', and "
19: 8 fine linen is the righteousness of s'. "
20: 9 and compassed the camp of the s' "
saints'
1Ti 5:10 if she have washed the s' feet, if she 40
saith
Ge 22:16 myself have I sworn, s' the Lord, 5002
32: 4 Thy servant Jacob s' thus, I have 559
41:55 unto Joseph; what he s' to you, do. "
44: 7 Wherefore s' my lord these words?*1696
45: 9 Thus s' thy son Joseph, God hath 559
Ex 4:22 Thus s' the Lord, Israel is my son, "
5: 1 s' the Lord God of Israel, Let my "
10 s' Pharaoh, I will not give you straw."
7:17 s' the Lord, In this thou shalt know "
8: 1, 20 s' the Lord, Let my people go, "
9: 1, 13 s' the Lord God of the Hebrews, "
10: 3 s' the Lord God of the Hebrews, "
11: 4 s' the Lord, About midnight will I "
32:27 s' the Lord God of Israel, Put every "
Nu 14:28 As truly as I live, s' the Lord, as ye "
20:14 s' thy brother Israel, Thou knowest "
22:16 Thus s' Balak the son of Zippor, Let"
24:13 but what the Lord s', that will I *1696
32:27 the Lord to battle, as my lord s'. "
Jos 5:14 What s' my lord unto his servant? "
7:13 s' the Lord God of Israel, There is 559
22:16 Thus s' the whole congregation of "
24: 2 Thus s' the Lord God of Israel, Your"
J'g 6: 8 s' the Lord God of Israel, I brought "
11:15 s' Jephthah, Israel took not away "
1Sa 2:27 s' the Lord, Did I plainly appear "
30 Wherefore...Lord God of Israel s', 5002
30 now the Lord s', Be it far from me; "
9: 6 all that he s' cometh...to pass: 1696
10:18 s' the Lord God of Israel, I brought559
15: 2 s' the Lord of hosts, I remember "
20: 3 he s', Let not Jonathan know this, "
24:13 As s' the proverb of the ancients, "
2Sa 7: 5 Thus s' the Lord, Shalt thou build "
8 s' the Lord of hosts, I took thee "
12: 7 Thus s' the Lord...I anointed thee "
11 s' the Lord, Behold, I will raise up "
14:10 Whosoever s' ought unto thee, 1696
17: 5 and let us hear likewise what he s'.6310
24:12 Thus s' the Lord, I offer thee three1696
1Ki 2:30 him, Thus s' the king, Come forth. 559
3:23 one s', This is my son that liveth, "
23 and the other s', Nay; but thy son is"
11:31 thus s' the Lord, the God of Israel, "
12:24 Thus the Lord, Ye shall not go up, "
13: 2 said, O altar, altar, thus s' the Lord;"
21 Thus s' the Lord, Forasmuch as "
14: 7 Thus s' the Lord God of Israel, "
17:14 For thus s' the Lord God of Israel, "
20: 2 said unto him, Thus s' Ben-hadad, "
13 Thus s' the Lord, Hast thou seen all"
14 Thus s' the Lord, Even by the young"
28 s' the Lord, Because the Syrians "
32 Thy servant Ben-hadad s', I pray "
42 s' the Lord, Because thou hast let go"
21:19 Thus s' the Lord, Hast thou killed, "
19 s' the Lord, In the place where dogs "
22:11 s' the Lord, With these shalt thou "
14 what the Lord s' unto me, that will "
27 Thus s' the king, Put this fellow in "
2Ki 1: 4 s' the Lord, Thou shalt not come "
6 Thus s' the Lord, Is it not because "
16 s' the Lord, Forasmuch as thou "
2:21 s' the Lord, I have healed these "
3:16 s' the Lord, Make this valley full of "
17 s' the Lord, Ye shall not see wind, "
4:43 for thus s' the Lord, They shall eat, "
5:13 he s' to thee, Wash, and be clean? "
7: 1 s' the Lord, To morrow about this "
9: 3 s' the Lord, I have anointed thee "
6 s' the Lord...I have anointed thee "
12 s' the Lord, I have anointed thee "
18, 19 Thus s' the king, Is it peace? "
26 the blood of his sons, s' the Lord; "
26 requite...in this plat, s' the Lord. 5002
18:19 Thus s' the great king, the king of 559
29 Thus s' the king, Let not Hezekiah "
31 thus s' the king of Assyria, Make an"
19: 3 Thus s' Hezekiah, This day is a day "
6 Thus s' the Lord, Be not afraid of "
20 Thus s' the Lord God of Israel, That"
32 s' the Lord concerning the king "
33 come into this city, s' the Lord. 5002
20: 1 Thus s' the Lord, Set thine house 559
5 Thus s' the Lord, the God of David "
17 nothing shall be left, s' the Lord. "
21:12 s' the Lord God of Israel, Behold, "
22:15 s' the Lord God of Israel, Tell the "
16 s' the Lord, Behold, I will bring evil "
18 Thus s' the Lord God of Israel, As "
19 also have heard thee, s' the Lord. 5002
1Ch 17: 4 Thus s' the Lord, Thou shalt not 559
7 s' the Lord of hosts, I took thee "
21:10 s' the Lord, I offer thee three things:"
11 him, Thus s' the Lord, Choose thee "
2Ch 11: 4 Thus s' the Lord, Ye shall not go up,"
12: 5 s' the Lord, Ye have forsaken me, "
18:10 s' the Lord, With these thou shalt "
13 what my God s', that will I speak. "
26 Thus s' the king Put this fellow in "
2Ch 20:15 s' the Lord unto you, Be not afraid 559
21:12 s' the Lord God of David thy father, "
24:20 Thus s' God, Why transgress ye the "
32:10 s' Sennacherib king of Assyria, "
34:23 Thus s' the Lord God of Israel, Tell "
24 Thus s' the Lord,...I will bring evil "
26 Thus s' the Lord God of Israel "
27 even heard thee also, s' the Lord. 5002
36:23 Thus s' Cyrus king of Persia, All 559
Ezr 1: 2 Thus s' Cyrus king of Persia, The "
Ne 6: 6 and Gashmu s' it, that thou and the "
Job 28:14 The depth s', It is not in me: and "
14 and the sea s', It is not in me. "
33:24 and s', Deliver him from going "
35:10 But none s', Where is God my maker,"
37: 6 For he s' to the snow, Be thou on "
39:25 He s' among the trumpets, Ha, ha; "
Ps 12: 5 needy, now will I arise, s' the Lord; "
36: 1 The transgression of the wicked s'5002
50:16 unto the wicked God s', What hast 559
Pr 9: 4, 16 understanding, she s' to him, "
20:14 is naught, it is naught, s' the buyer: "
22:13 The slothful man s', There is a lion "
23: 7 Eat and drink, s' he to thee; but his "
24:24 He that s' unto the wicked, Thou "
26:13 The slothful man s', There is a lion "
19 neighbour, and s', Am not I in sport?"
28:24 and s', It is no transgression; "
30:16 the fire that s' not, It is enough. "
20 and s', I have done no wickedness. "
Ec 1: 2 Vanity of vanities, s' the Preacher, "
4: 8 neither s' he, For whom do I labour, "
7:27 this have I found, s' the preacher, 559
10: 3 he s' to every one that he is a fool. "
12: 8 Vanity of vanities, s' the preacher; "
Isa 1:11 sacrifices unto me? s' the Lord: "
18 let us reason together, s' the Lord: "
24 s' the Lord, the Lord of hosts, 5002
3:15 the poor? s' the Lord God of hosts. "
16 Moreover the Lord s', Because the 559
7: 7 s' the Lord God, It shall not stand, "
10: 8 For he s', Are not my princes "
13 he s', By the strength of my hand, "
24 thus s' the Lord God of hosts, O "
14:22 against them, s' the Lord of hosts,5002
22 and son, and nephew, s' the Lord. "
23 destruction, s' the Lord of hosts. "
17: 3 the glory...of Israel, s' the Lord "
6 thereof, s' the Lord God of Israel. "
19: 4 shall rule over them, s' the Lord, "
22:14 ye die, s' the Lord God of hosts, 559
15 s' the Lord God of hosts, Go, get "
25 In that day, s' the Lord of hosts, 5002
28:16 s' the Lord God,...I lay in Zion 559
29:11 and he s', I cannot; for it is sealed: "
12 thee: and he s', I am not learned. "
22 thus s' the Lord, who redeemed "
30: 1 rebellious children, s' the Lord, 5002
12 s' the Holy One of Israel, Because 559
15 s' the Lord God, the Holy One of "
31: 9 afraid of the ensign, s' the Lord, 5002
33:10 Now will I rise, s' the Lord; now 559
36: 4 Thus s' the great king, the king of "
14 Thus s' the king, Let not Hezekiah "
16 thus s' the king of Assyria, Make an "
37: 3 Thus s' Hezekiah, This day is a day "
6 Thus s' the Lord, Be not afraid of "
21 s' the Lord God of Israel, Whereas "
33 thus s' the Lord concerning the king"
34 not come into this city, s' the Lord.5002
38: 1 Thus s' the Lord, Set thine house in559
5 say to Hezekiah, Thus s' the Lord, "
39: 6 nothing shall be left, s' the Lord. "
40: 1 comfort ye my people, s' your God. "
25 or shall I be equal? s' the Holy One. "
41:14 I will help thee, s' the Lord, and 5002
21 Produce your cause, s' the Lord; 559
21 strong reasons, s' the King of Jacob."
42: 5 s' God the Lord, he that created the "
22 for a spoil, and none s', Restore. "
43: 1 thus s' the Lord that created thee, "
10 Ye are my witnesses, s' the Lord, 5002
12 ye are my witnesses, s' the Lord, "
14 Thus s' the Lord, your redeemer, 559
16 s' the Lord, which maketh a way in "
44: 2 Thus s' the Lord that made thee, "
6 Thus s' the Lord the king of Israel, "
16 s', Aha, I am warm, I have seen the "
17 s', Deliver me; for thou art my god. "
24 Thus s' the Lord, thy redeemer, "
26 that s' to Jerusalem, Thou shalt be "
27 That s' to the deep, Be dry, and I "
28 That s' of Cyrus, He is my shepherd,"
45: 1 Thus s' the Lord to his anointed, "
10 Woe...him that s' unto his father, "
11 Thus s' the Lord, the Holy One of "
13 nor reward, s' the Lord of hosts. "
14 Thus s' the Lord, The labour of "
18 thus s' the Lord that created the "
48:17 Thus s' the Lord, thy Redeemer, "
22 There is no peace, s' the Lord, unto "
49: 5 s' the Lord that formed me from "
7 Thus s' the Lord, the Redeemer of "
8 Thus s' the Lord, In an acceptable "
18 As I live, s' the Lord, thou shalt 5002
22 Thus s' the Lord God, Behold, I 559
25 thus s' the Lord, Even the captives "
50: 1 Thus s' the Lord, Where is the bill "
51:22 Thus s' thy Lord the Lord, and thy "
52: 3 For thus s' the Lord, Ye have sold "
4 For thus s' the Lord God, My people"
5 what have I here, s' the Lord, 5002
5 make them to howl, s' the Lord; "
7 that s' unto Zion, Thy God reigneth!559
54: 1 of the married wife, s' the Lord. "
6 when thou wast refused, s' thy God. "

Isa 54: 8 on thee, s' the Lord thy Redeemer. 559
10 s' the Lord that hath mercy on thee. "
17 righteousness is of me, s' the Lord.5002
55: 8 are your ways my ways, s' the Lord. "
56: 1 s' the Lord, Keep ye judgment, 559
4 thus s' the Lord unto the eunuchs "
8 gathereth the outcasts of Israel s',5002
57: 15 For thus s' the high and lofty One 559
19 to him that is near, s' the Lord; "
21 no peace, s' my God, to the wicked. "
59: 20 from transgression...s' the Lord. 5002
21 covenant with them, s' the Lord; 559
21 mouth of thy seed's seed, s' the Lord,"
65: 7 of your fathers together, s' the Lord,"
8 Thus s' the Lord, As the new wine is"
8 cluster, and one s', Destroy it not; "
13 thus s' the Lord God, Behold, my "
25 all my holy mountain, s' the Lord. "
66: 1 Thus s' the Lord, The heaven is my "
2 things have been, s' the Lord: 5002
9 cause to bring forth? s' the Lord: 559
9 and shut the womb? s' thy God. "
12 s' the Lord,...I will extend peace to "
17 consumed together, s' the Lord. 5002
20 mountain Jerusalem, s' the Lord. 559
21 priests and for Levites, s' the Lord. "
22 remain before me, s' the Lord, 5002
23 to worship before me, s' the Lord. 559
Jer 1: 8 thee to deliver thee, s' the Lord. 5002
15 kingdoms of the north, s' the Lord;"
19 thee, s' the Lord, to deliver thee. "
2: 2 Thus s' the Lord; I remember thee,559
3 shall come upon them, s' the Lord.5002
5 s' the Lord, What iniquity have 559
9 yet plead with you, s' the Lord, 5002
12 be ye very desolate, s' the Lord. "
19 my fear is not in thee, s' the Lord "
22 marked before me, s' the Lord God."
29 all have transgressed...s' the Lord. "
3: 1 yet return again to me, s' the Lord."
10 heart, but feignedly, s' the Lord. "
12 thou backsliding Israel, s' the Lord;"
12 for I am merciful, s' the Lord, and I"
13 not obeyed my voice, s' the Lord. "
14 backsliding children, s' the Lord; "
16 s' the Lord, they shall say no more, "
20 me, O house of Israel, s' the Lord. "
4: 1 wilt return, O Israel, s' the Lord, "
3 For thus s' the Lord to the men of 559
9 to pass at that day, s' the Lord, 5002
17 rebellious against me, s' the Lord. "
5: 9 visit for these things? s' the Lord: "
11 dealt...treacherously...s' the Lord. "
14 s' the Lord God of hosts, Because 559
15 far, O house of Israel, s' the Lord:5002
18 s' the Lord, I will not make a full "
22 Fear ye not me? s' the Lord: will "
29 visit for these things? s' the Lord: "
6: 9 s' the Lord of hosts, They shall 559
12 inhabitants of the land, s' the Lord.5002
15 shall be cast down, s' the Lord. 559
16 Thus s' the Lord, Stand ye in the "
21 thus s' the Lord, Behold, I will lay "
22 Thus s' the Lord, Behold, a people "
7: 3 Thus s' the Lord of hosts, the God "
11 even I have seen it, s' the Lord. 5002
13 done all these works, s' the Lord, "
19 provoke me to anger? s' the Lord: "
20 thus s' the Lord God; Behold, mine559
21 s' the Lord of hosts, the God of "
30 done evil in my sight, s' the Lord:5002
32 behold, the days come, s' the Lord, "
8: 1 At that time, s' the Lord, they shall"
3 I have driven them, s' the Lord of "
4 Thus s' the Lord; Shall they fall, 559
12 they shall be cast down, s' the Lord. "
13 surely consume them, s' the Lord:5002
17 and they shall bite you, s' the Lord."
9: 3 and they know not me, s' the Lord. "
6 refuse to know me, s' the Lord. "
7 thus s' the Lord of hosts, Behold, 559
9 them for these things? s' the Lord:5002
13 the Lord s', Because they have 559
15 thus s' the Lord of hosts, the God of "
17 Thus s' the Lord of hosts, Consider "
22 s' the Lord, Even the carcases 5002
23 Thus s' the Lord, Let not the wise 559
24 these things I delight, s' the Lord.5002
25 the days come, s' the Lord, that I "
10: 2 Thus s' the Lord, Learn not the 559
18 thus s' the Lord, Behold, I will sling"
11: 3 s' the Lord God of Israel; Cursed be"
11 s' the Lord, Behold, I will bring evil "
21 s' the Lord of the men of Anathoth, "
22 thus s' the Lord of hosts, Behold, I "
12: 14 Thus s' the Lord against all mine "
17 destroy that nation, s' the Lord. 5002
13: 1 Thus s' the Lord unto me, Go and 559
9 s' the Lord, After this manner will "
11 whole house of Judah, s' the Lord;5002
12 s' the Lord God of Israel, Every 559
13 s' the Lord, Behold, I will fill all the"
14 and the sons together, s' the Lord:5002
25 thy measures from me, s' the Lord;"
14: 10 Thus s' the Lord unto this people, 559
15 s' the Lord concerning the prophets "
15: 2 s' the Lord; Such as are for death, "
3 over them four kinds, s' the Lord:5002
6 Thou hast forsaken me, s' the Lord,"
9 before their enemies, s' the Lord. "
19 Therefore thus s' the Lord, If thou 559
20 and to deliver thee, s' the Lord. 5002
16: 3 s' the Lord concerning the sons and559
5 s' the Lord, Enter not into the house"
5 from this people, s' the Lord, 5002
9 thus s' the Lord of hosts, the God 559

Jer 16: 11 and have forsaken me, s' the Lord,5002
14 s' the Lord, that it shall no more "
16 send for many fishers, s' the Lord, "
17: 5 Thus s' the Lord; Cursed be the 559
21 Thus s' the Lord; Take heed to "
24 hearken unto me, s' the Lord, to 5002
18: 6 with you as this potter? s' the Lord."
11 s' the Lord; Behold, I frame evil 559
13 Therefore thus s' the Lord; Ask ye "
19: 1 s' the Lord, Go and get a potter's * "
3 Thus s' the Lord of hosts, the God "
6 days come, s' the Lord, that this 5002
11 Thus s' the Lord of hosts; Even 559
12 I do unto this place, s' the Lord, 5002
15 Thus s' the Lord of hosts, the God 559
20: 4 s' the Lord, Behold, I will make "
21: 4 s' the Lord God of Israel; Behold, I "
7 s' the Lord, I will deliver Zedekiah5002
8 s' the Lord; Behold, I set before 559
10 evil, and not for good, s' the Lord:5002
12 s' the Lord; Execute judgment in 559
13 and rock of the plain, s' the Lord; 5002
14 fruit of your doings, s' the Lord: "
22: 1 s' the Lord; Go down to the house*559
3 s' the Lord; Execute ye judgment "
5 I swear by myself, s' the Lord, 5002
6 thus s' the Lord unto the king's 559
11 thus s' the Lord touching Shallum "
14 s', I will build me a wide house and "
16 not this to know me? s' the Lord. 5002
18 s' the Lord concerning Jehoiakim 559
24 s' the Lord, though Coniah the 5002
30 Thus s' the Lord, Write ye this man559
23: 1 sheep of my pasture! s' the Lord. 5002
2 s' the Lord God of Israel against 559
2 evil of your doings, s' the Lord. 5002
4 shall they be lacking, s' the Lord. "
5 Behold, the days come, s' the Lord, "
7 days come, s' the Lord, that they "
11 their wickedness, s' the Lord. "
12 year of their visitation, s' the Lord."
15 s' the Lord of hosts concerning the559
16 Thus s' the Lord of hosts, Hearken "
23 Am I a God at hand, s' the Lord, 5002
24 I shall not see him? s' the Lord. "
24 I fill heaven and earth? s' the Lord."
28 the chaff to the wheat? s' the Lord. "
29 my word like as a fire? s' the Lord; "
30, 31 against the prophets, s' the Lord,"
31 use their tongues, and say, He s'. "
32 prophesy false dreams, s' the Lord,"
32 profit this people at all, s' the Lord. "
33 I will even forsake you, s' the Lord."
38 thus s' the Lord; Because ye say 559
24: 5 Thus s' the Lord, the God of Israel; "
8 surely thus s' the Lord, So will I "
25: 7 hearkened unto me, s' the Lord; 5002
8 thus s' the Lord of hosts; Because 559
9 families of the north, s' the Lord, 5002
12 and that nation, s' the Lord, for "
15 s' the Lord God of Israel unto me; 559
27 Thus s' the Lord of hosts, the God of"
28 Thus s' the Lord of hosts; Ye shall "
29 of the earth, s' the Lord of hosts. 5002
31 wicked to the sword, s' the Lord. "
32 s' the Lord of hosts, Behold, evil 559
26: 2 s' the Lord; Stand in the court of the"
4 s' the Lord; If ye will not hearken "
18 s' the Lord of hosts; Zion shall be "
27: 2 s' the Lord to me; Make thee bonds "
4 Thus s' the Lord of hosts, the God "
8 nation will I punish, s' the Lord, 5002
11 still in their own land, s' the Lord; "
15 I have not sent them, s' the Lord, "
16 Thus s' the Lord; Hearken not to 559
19 thus s' the Lord of hosts concerning"
21 thus s' the Lord of hosts, the God of "
22 day that I visit them, s' the Lord; 5002
28: 4 that went into Babylon, s' the Lord:"
11 s' the Lord; Even so will I break 559
13 Thus s' the Lord; Thou hast broken"
14 thus s' the Lord of hosts, the God of "
16 thus s' the Lord; Behold, I will cast "
29: 4 Thus s' the Lord of hosts, the God of"
8 thus s' the Lord of hosts, the God of "
9 I have not sent them, s' the Lord. 5002
10 For thus s' the Lord, That after 559
11 I think toward you, s' the Lord, 5002
14 will be found of you, s' the Lord: "
14 I have driven you, s' the Lord; and "
16 that thus s' the Lord of the king 559
17 Thus s' the Lord of hosts; Behold, "
19 to my words, s' the Lord, which 5002
19 but ye would not hear, s' the Lord. "
21 Thus s' the Lord of hosts, the God 559
23 and am a witness, s' the Lord. 5002
31 s' the Lord concerning Shemaiah 559
32 thus s' the Lord; Behold, I will "
32 will do for my people, s' the Lord;5002
30: 3 For, lo, the days come, s' the Lord, "
3 Israel and Judah, s' the Lord: 559
5 thus s' the Lord; We have heard a "
8 in that day, s' the Lord of hosts, 5002
10 O my servant Jacob, s' the Lord; "
11 I am with thee, s' the Lord, to save "
12 For thus s' the Lord, Thy bruise is "
17 heal thee of thy wounds, s' the Lord; "
18 Thus s' the Lord; Behold, I will 559
21 approach unto me? s' the Lord. 5002
31: 1 time, s' the Lord, will I be the God "
2 Thus s' the Lord, the people which 559
7 For thus s' the Lord; Sing with "
14 with my goodness, s' the Lord. 5002
15 s' the Lord; A voice was heard in 559
16 s' the Lord; Refrain thy voice from "
16 work...be rewarded, s' the Lord; 5002

Jer 31: 17 is hope in thine end, s' the Lord, 5002
20 have mercy upon him, s' the Lord. "
23 s' the Lord of hosts, the God of 559
27 the days come, s' the Lord, that I 5002
28 to build, and to plant, s' the Lord. "
31 the days come, s' the Lord, that I "
32 an husband unto them, s' the Lord:"
33 s' the Lord, I will put my law in "
34 the greatest of them, s' the Lord: "
35 s' the Lord, which giveth the sun 559
36 depart from...me, s' the Lord, 5002
37 s' the Lord; If heaven above can 559
37 that they have done, s' the Lord. 5002
38 Behold, the days come, s' the Lord."
32: 3 s' the Lord,...I will give this city 559
5 be until I visit him, s' the Lord: 5002
14, 15 s' the Lord of hosts, the God of 559
28 s' the Lord;...I will give this city "
30 work of their hands, s' the Lord. 5002
36 thus s' the Lord, the God of Israel, 559
42 thus s' the Lord; Like as I have "
44 captivity to return, s' the Lord. 5002
33: 2 s' the Lord the maker thereof, the 559
4 thus s' the Lord, the God of Israel, "
10 Thus s' the Lord; Again there shall "
11 the land, as at the first, s' the Lord. "
12 Thus s' the Lord of hosts; Again in "
13 him that telleth them, s' the Lord. "
14 the days come, s' the Lord, that I 5002
17 thus s' the Lord; David shall never559
20 Thus s' the Lord; If ye can break "
25 Thus s' the Lord; If my covenant "
34: 2 Thus s' the Lord, the God of Israel; "
2 s' the Lord;...I will give this city "
4 Thus s' the Lord of thee, Thou shalt"
5 pronounced the word, s' the Lord.5002
13 Thus s' the Lord, the God of Israel;559
17 s' the Lord; Ye have not hearkened "
17 a liberty for you, s' the Lord, to 5002
22 I will command, s' the Lord, and "
35: 13 Thus s' the Lord of hosts, the God 559
13 hearken to my words, s' the Lord.5002
17 thus s' the Lord God of hosts, the 559
18 Thus s' the Lord of hosts, the God "
19 thus s' the Lord of hosts, the God "
36: 29 Thus s' the Lord; Thou hast burned"
30 thus s' the Lord of Jehoiakim king "
37: 7 Thus s' the Lord, the God of Israel; "
9 s' the Lord; Deceive not yourselves,"
38: 2 Thus s' the Lord, He that remaineth"
3 Thus s' the Lord, This city shall "
17 Thus s' the Lord, the God of hosts, "
39: 16 Thus s' the Lord of hosts, the God "
17 deliver...in that day, s' the Lord: 5002
18 put thy trust in me, s' the Lord. "
42: 9 Thus s' the Lord, the God of Israel,559
11 be not afraid of him, s' the Lord: 5002
15, 18 s' the Lord of hosts, the God of 559
43: 10 s' the Lord of hosts, the God of "
44: 2 s' the Lord of hosts, the God of "
7 thus s' the Lord, the God of hosts, "
11 thus s' the Lord of hosts, the God of"
25 s' the Lord of hosts, the God of "
26 sworn by my great name, s' the Lord,"
29 be a sign unto you, s' the Lord, 5002
30 s' the Lord; Behold, I will give 559
45: 2 Thus s' the Lord, the God of Israel, "
4 The Lord s' thus; Behold, that "
5 evil upon all flesh, s' the Lord: 5002
46: 5 fear was round about, s' the Lord. "
8 he s', I will go up, and will cover 559
18 As I live, s' the King, whose name5002
23 cut down her forest, s' the Lord, "
25 the God of Israel, s'; Behold, I 559
26 as in the days of old, s' the Lord. 5002
28 Fear not, O Jacob...s' the Lord: "
47: 2 s' the Lord; Behold, waters rise 559
48: 1 Against Moab...s' the Lord of hosts, "
12 the days come, s' the Lord, that 5002
15 s' the King, whose name is the "
25 and his arm is broken, s' the Lord. "
30 I know his wrath, s' the Lord; but "
35 cause to cease in Moab, s' the Lord,"
38 wherein is no pleasure, s' the Lord."
40 For thus s' the Lord; Behold, he 559
43 inhabitant of Moab, s' the Lord. 5002
44 year of their visitation, s' the Lord."
47 Moab in the latter days, s' the Lord."
49: 1 s' the Lord; Hath Israel no sons? 559
2 days come, s' the Lord, that I will "
2 that were his heirs, s' the Lord. 5002
5 thee, s' the Lord God of hosts, "
6 children of Ammon, s' the Lord. "
7 s' the Lord of hosts; Is wisdom no 559
12 s' the Lord; Behold, they whose "
13 have sworn by myself, s' the Lord,5002
16 down from thence, s' the Lord. "
18 s' the Lord, no man shall abide 559
26 cut off in that day, s' the Lord of 5002
28 thus s' the Lord; Arise ye, go up 559
30 inhabitants of Hazor, s' the Lord;5002
31 dwelleth without care, s' the Lord, "
32 from all sides thereof, s' the Lord. "
35 Thus s' the Lord of hosts; Behold, 559
37 even my fierce anger, s' the Lord; 5002
38 king and the princes, s' the Lord. "
39 the captivity of Elam, s' the Lord. "
50: 4 s' the Lord, the children of Israel "
10 spoil her...be satisfied, s' the Lord. "
18 thus s' the Lord of hosts, the God 559
20 s' the Lord, the iniquity of Israel 5002
21 destroy after them, s' the Lord, "
30 be cut off in that day, s' the Lord. "
31 proud, s' the Lord God of hosts: "
33 Thus s' the Lord of hosts; The 559
35 is upon the Chaldeans, s' the Lord,5002

Jer 50:40 neighbour cities...s' the Lord; 5002
51: 1 s' the Lord; Behold, I will raise 559
24 in Zion in your sight, s' the Lord. 5002
25 O destroying mountain, s' the Lord."
26 be desolate for ever, s' the Lord. "
33 thus s' the Lord of hosts, the God 559
36 s' the Lord; Behold, I will plead "
39 sleep, and not wake, s' the Lord. 5002
48 unto her from the north, s' the Lord."
52 days come, s' the Lord, that I will "
53 spoilers come unto her, s' the Lord."
57 not wake, s' the King, whose name "
58 Thus s' the Lord of hosts; The 559
La 3:24 Lord is my portion, s' my soul; "
37 Who is he that s', and it cometh to "
Eze 2: 4 unto them, Thus s' the Lord God. "
3:11 tell them, Thus s' the Lord God; "
27 unto them, Thus s' the Lord God; "
5: 5 s' the Lord God; This is Jerusalem:"
7 thus s' the Lord God; Because ye "
8 s' the Lord God; Behold, I, even I, "
11 as I live, s' the Lord God; Surely, 5002
6: 3 s' the Lord God to the mountains, 559
11 s' the Lord God; Smite with thine "
7: 2 s' the Lord God unto the land of "
5 s' the Lord God; An evil, an only "
11: 5 s' the Lord; Thus have ye said, O "
7 Therefore thus s' the Lord God; "
8 sword upon you, s' the Lord God. 5002
16, 17 say, Thus s' the Lord God; 559
21 upon their own heads, s' the Lord 5002
12:10 Thus s' the Lord God; This burden 559
19 s' the Lord God of the inhabitants "
23 s' the Lord God; I will make this "
25 will perform it, s' the Lord God. 5002
28 Thus s' the Lord God; There shall 559
28 shall be done, s' the Lord God. 5002
13: 3 s' the Lord God; Woe unto the 559
6 divination, saying, The Lord s': 5002
7 The Lord s' it; albeit I have not "
8 s' the Lord God; Because ye have 559
8 am against you, s' the Lord God. 5002
13 thus s' the Lord God; I will even 559
16 there is no peace, s' the Lord God. 5002
18 And say, Thus s' the Lord God; 559
20 Wherefore thus s' the Lord God; "
14: 4 unto them, Thus s' the Lord God; "
6 s' the Lord God; Repent, and turn "
11 may be their God, s' the Lord God. 5002
14 righteousness, s' the Lord God. "
16, 18, 20 as I live, s' the Lord God, "
21 s' the Lord God; How much more 559
23 I have done in it, s' the Lord God. 5002
15: 6 s' the Lord God; As the vine tree 559
8 committed a trespass, s' the Lord 5002
16: 3 s' the Lord God unto Jerusalem; 559
8 a covenant with thee, s' the Lord 5002
14 had put upon thee, s' the Lord God."
19 and thus it was, s' the Lord God. "
23 woe unto thee! s' the Lord God;) "
30 weak is thine heart, s' the Lord "
36 Thus s' the Lord God; Because thy 559
43 way upon thine head, s' the Lord 5002
48 s' the Lord God, Sodom thy sister "
58 thine abominations, s' the Lord. "
59 thus s' the Lord God; I will even 559
63 that thou hast done, s' the Lord 5002
17: 3 s' the Lord God; A great eagle with 559
9 s' the Lord God; Shall it prosper? "
16 As I live, s' the Lord God, Surely 5002
19 thus s' the Lord God; As I live, 559
22 Thus s' the Lord God; I will also "
18: 3 As I live, s' the Lord God, Ye shall 5002
9 he shall surely live, s' the Lord God."
23 wicked should die? s' the Lord God:"
29 Yet s' the house of Israel, The way 559
30 to his ways, s' the Lord God. 5002
32 of him that dieth, s' the Lord God: "
20: 3 Thus s' the Lord God; Are ye come 559
3 As I live, s' the Lord God, I will 5002
5 Thus s' the Lord God; In the day 559
27 say unto them, Thus s' the Lord "
30 s' the Lord God; Are ye polluted "
31 As I live, s' the Lord God, I will 5002
33 As I live, s' the Lord God, surely "
36 I plead with you, s' the Lord God, "
39 thus s' the Lord God; Go ye, serve 559
40 s' the Lord God, there shall all 5002
44 ye house of Israel, s' the Lord God."
47 Thus s' the Lord God; Behold, I 559
21: 3 land of Israel, Thus s' the Lord; "
7 brought to pass, s' the Lord God. 5002
9 prophesy,...say, Thus s' the Lord; 559
13 shall be no more, s' the Lord God. 5002
24 thus s' the Lord God; Because ye 559
26 Thus s' the Lord God; Remove the "
28 Thus s' the Lord God concerning "
22: 3 s' the Lord God, The city sheddeth "
12 forgotten me, s' the Lord God. 5002
19 thus s' the Lord God; Because ye 559
28 s' the Lord God, when the Lord "
31 upon their heads, s' the Lord God. 5002
23:22 Aholibah, thus s' the Lord God; 559
28 For thus s' the Lord God; Behold, I "
32 Thus s' the Lord God; Thou shalt "
34 I have spoken it, s' the Lord God. "
35 thus s' the Lord God; Because thou "
46 thus s' the Lord God; I will bring "
24: 3 Thus s' the Lord God; Set on a pot, "
6, 9 thus s' the Lord God; Woe to the "
14 they judge thee, s' the Lord God. 5002
21 Thus s' the Lord God; Behold, I 559
25: 3 Thus s' the Lord God; Because "
6 For thus s' the Lord God; Because "
8, 12 Thus s' the Lord God; Because "
13 thus s' the Lord God; I will also "

Eze 25:14 my vengeance, s' the Lord God. 5002
15 Thus s' the Lord God; Because the 559
16 thus s' the Lord God; Behold, I will "
26: 3 thus s' the Lord God; Behold, I am "
5 I have spoken it, s' the Lord God: 5002
7 thus s' the Lord God; Behold, I will 559
14 have spoken it, s' the Lord God. 5002
15 s' the Lord God to Tyrus; Shall not 559
19 thus s' the Lord God; When I shall "
21 be found again, s' the Lord God. 5001
27: 3 s' the Lord God; O Tyrus, thou 559
28: 2 s' the Lord God; Because thine heart"
6 s' the Lord God; Because thou hast"
10 I have spoken it, s' the Lord God. 5002
12 s' the Lord God; Thou sealest up 559
22 say, Thus s' the Lord God; Behold, "
25 s' the Lord God; When I shall have "
29: 3 Thus s' the Lord God; Behold, I am"
8 thus s' the Lord God; Behold, I will"
13 thus s' the Lord God; At the end of "
19 thus s' the Lord God; Behold, I will"
20 wrought for me, s' the Lord God. 5002
30: 2 s' the Lord God; Howl ye, Woe 559
6 s' the Lord; They also that uphold "
6 it by the sword, s' the Lord God. 5002
10, 13 s' the Lord God; I will also 559
22 thus s' the Lord God; Behold, I am "
31:10 s' the Lord God; Because thou hast*"
15 s' the Lord God; In the day when "
18 all his multitude, s' the Lord God. 5002
32: 3 s' the Lord God; I will therefore 559
8 upon thy land, s' the Lord God. 5002
11 s' the Lord God; The sword of the 559
14 to run like oil, s' the Lord God. 5002
16 all her multitude, s' the Lord God. "
31 slain by the sword, s' the Lord God."
32 all his multitude, s' the Lord God. "
33:11 s' the Lord God, I have no pleasure "
25 Thus s' the Lord God; Ye eat with 559
27 Thus s' the Lord God; As I live, "
34: 2 s' the Lord God unto the shepherds;"
8 s' the Lord God, surely because 5002
10 Thus s' the Lord God; Behold, I am 559
11 s' the Lord God; Behold, I, even I, "
15 them to lie down, s' the Lord God. 5002
17 O my flock, thus s' the Lord God; 559
20 thus s' the Lord God unto them; "
30 are my people, s' the Lord God. 5002
31 I am your God, s' the Lord God. "
35: 3 s' the Lord God; Behold, O mount 559
6 s' the Lord God, I will prepare 5002
11 s' the Lord God, I will even do "
14 Thus s' the Lord God; When the 559
36: 2 s' the Lord God; Because the enemy"
3 Thus s' the Lord God; Because they"
4 s' the Lord God to the mountains, "
5 thus s' the Lord God; Surely in the "
6 Thus s' the Lord God; Behold, I "
7 thus s' the Lord God; I have lifted "
13 s' the Lord God; Because they say "
14 nations any more, s' the Lord God. 5002
15 to fall any more, s' the Lord God. "
22 Thus s' the Lord God; I do not this 559
23 I am the Lord, s' the Lord God, 5002
32 s' the Lord God, be it known unto "
33 Thus s' the Lord God; In the day 559
37 Thus s' the Lord God; I will yet for "
37: 5 s' the Lord God unto these bones; "
9 Thus s' the Lord God; Come from "
12 Thus s' the Lord God; Behold, O my"
14 it, and performed it, s' the Lord. 5002
19, 21 Thus s' the Lord God; Behold, I 559
38: 3 Thus s' the Lord God; Behold, I am"
10 Thus s' the Lord God; It shall also "
14 Thus s' the Lord God; In that day "
17 s' the Lord God; Art thou he of "
18 the land of Israel, s' the Lord God, 5002
21 my mountains, s' the Lord God: "
39: 1 Thus s' the Lord God; Behold, I am 559
5 I have spoken it, s' the Lord God. 5002
8 and it is done, s' the Lord God; "
10 that robbed them, s' the Lord God. "
13 I shall be glorified, s' the Lord God."
17 thus s' the Lord God; Speak unto 559
20 all men of war, s' the Lord God. 5002
25 s' the Lord God; Now will I bring 559
29 house of Israel, s' the Lord God. 5002
43:18 Son of man, thus s' the Lord God; 559
19 unto me, s' the Lord God, a young 5002
27 I will accept you, s' the Lord God. "
44: 6 Thus s' the Lord God; O ye house 559
9 Thus s' the Lord God; No stranger,"
12 against them, s' the Lord God, 5002
15 fat and the blood, s' the Lord God; "
27 his sin offering, s' the Lord God. "
45: 9 s' the Lord God; Let it suffice you, "
9 from my people, s' the Lord God. 559
15 reconciliation for them, s' the Lord 5002
18 Thus s' the Lord God; In the first 559
46: 1 s' the Lord God; The gate of the "
16 s' the Lord God; If the prince give "
47:13 s' the Lord God; This shall be the "
23 his inheritance, s' the Lord God. 5002
48:29 are their portions, s' the Lord God. "
Ho 2:13 lovers, and forgat me, s' the Lord. "
16 it shall be at that day, s' the Lord, "
21 I will hear, s' the Lord, I will hear "
11:11 them in their houses, s' the Lord. "
Joe 2:12 Therefore also now, s' the Lord, "
Am 1: 3 Thus s' the Lord; For three 559
5 into captivity unto Kir, s' the Lord. "
6 Thus s' the Lord; For three "
8 shall perish, s' the Lord God. "
9, 11, 13 Thus s' the Lord; For three "
15 his princes together, s' the Lord. "
2: 1 Thus s' the Lord; For three "

Am 2: 3 the princes...with him, s' the Lord. 559
4, 6 Thus s' the Lord; For three "
11 ye children of Israel? s' the Lord. 5002
16 away naked in that day, s' the Lord."
3:10 know not to do right, s' the Lord, "
11 thus s' the Lord God; An adversary 559
12 s' the Lord; As the shepherd taketh "
13 s' the Lord God, the God of hosts, 5001
15 shall have an end, s' the Lord. "
4: 3 them into the palace, s' the Lord. "
5 ye children of Israel, s' the Lord "
6, 8, 9, 10, 11 unto me, s' the Lord. "
5: 3 For thus s' the Lord God; The city 559
4 thus s' the Lord unto the house of "
16 the Lord, s' thus; Wailing shall be "
17 will pass through thee, s' the Lord. "
27 beyond Damascus, s' the Lord, "
6: 8 s' the Lord the God of hosts, I 5002
14 Israel, s' the Lord the God of hosts;"
7: 3 this: It shall not be, s' the Lord. 559
6 also shall not be, s' the Lord God. "
11 For thus Amos s', Jeroboam shall "
17 thus s' the Lord; Thy wife shall be "
8: 3 howlings in that day, s' the Lord 5002
9 s' the Lord God, that I will cause "
11 s' the Lord God, that I will send a "
9: 7 O children of Israel? s' the Lord. "
8 the house of Jacob, s' the Lord. "
12 name, s' the Lord that doeth this. "
13 come, s' the Lord, that the plowman"
15 given them, s' the Lord thy God. 559
Ob 1 s' the Lord God concerning Edom; "
3 that s' in his heart, Who shall bring "
4 will I bring thee down, s' the Lord. 5002
8 Shall I not in that day, s' the Lord, "
Mic 2: 3 Therefore thus s' the Lord; Behold, 559
3: 5 Thus s' the Lord concerning the "
4: 6 s' the Lord, will I assemble her 5002
5:10 to pass in that day, s' the Lord, "
6: 1 Hear ye now what the Lord s': 559
Na 1:12 s' the Lord; Though they be quiet, "
2:13 against thee, s' the Lord of hosts, 5002
3: 5 against thee, s' the Lord of hosts; "
Hab 2:19 Woe unto him that s' to the wood, 559
Zep 1: 2 from off the land, s' the Lord. 5002
3 man from off the land, s' the Lord. "
10 to pass in that day, s' the Lord, "
2: 9 as I live, s' the Lord of hosts, the "
3: 8 wait ye upon me, s' the Lord, until "
20 back your captivity...s' the Lord. 559
Hag 1: 5, 7 thus s' the Lord of hosts; Consider"
8 it, and I will be glorified, s' the Lord."
9 Why? s' the Lord of hosts. Because 5002
13 saying, I am with you, s' the Lord. "
2: 4 strong, O Zerubbabel, s' the Lord; "
4 ye people of the land, s' the Lord, "
4 I am with you, s' the Lord of hosts:"
6 thus s' the Lord of hosts; Yet once, 559
7 fill this house with glory, s' the Lord"
8 gold is mine, s' the Lord of hosts. 5002
9 of the former, s' the Lord of hosts: "
9 I give peace, s' the Lord of hosts. 559
11 Thus s' the Lord of hosts; Ask now "
14 this nation before me, s' the Lord; 5002
17 yet ye turned not to me, s' the Lord."
23 day, s' the Lord of hosts, will I take"
23 s' the Lord, and will make thee as "
23 chosen thee, s' the Lord of hosts. "
Zec 1: 3 Thus s' the Lord of hosts; Turn 559
3 ye unto me, s' the Lord of hosts, 5002
3 unto you, s' the Lord of hosts. 559
4 Thus s' the Lord of hosts; Turn ye "
4 nor hearken unto me, s' the Lord. 5002
14 s' the Lord of hosts; I am jealous "
16 thus s' the Lord; I am returned to 559
16 be built in it, s' the Lord of hosts, 5002
17 Thus s' the Lord of hosts; My cities 559
2: 5 s' the Lord, will be unto her a wall 5002
6 the land of the north, s' the Lord: "
6 winds of the heaven, s' the Lord. "
8 s' the Lord of hosts; After the glory 559
10 in the midst of thee, s' the Lord. 5002
3: 7 s' the Lord of hosts; If thou wilt 559
9 the graving...s' the Lord of hosts, 5002
10 s' the Lord of hosts, shall ye call "
4: 6 by my spirit, s' the Lord of hosts. 559
5: 4 bring it forth, s' the Lord of hosts, 5002
7:13 not hear, s' the Lord of hosts: 559
8: 2 s' the Lord of hosts; I was jealous "
3 s' the Lord; I am returned unto "
4 s' the Lord of hosts; There shall "
6 Thus s' the Lord of hosts; If it be "
6 mine eyes? s' the Lord of hosts. 5002
7 s' the Lord of hosts; Behold, I will 559
9 Thus s' the Lord of hosts; Let your "
11 former days, s' the Lord of hosts. 5002
14 s' the Lord of hosts; As I thought 559
14 provoked me to wrath, s' the Lord "
17 are things that I hate, s' the Lord. 5002
19 Thus s' the Lord of hosts; The fast 559
20 Thus s' the Lord of hosts; It shall "
23 s' the Lord of hosts; In those days "
10:12 down in his name, s' the Lord. 5002
11: 4 s' the Lord my God; Feed the flock 559
6 inhabitants of...land, s' the Lord: 5002
12: 1 s' the Lord, which stretcheth forth "
4 day, s' the Lord, I will smite every "
13: 2 in that day, s' the Lord of hosts, "
7 is my fellow, s' the Lord of hosts: "
8 s' the Lord, two parts therein shall "
Mal 1: 2 I have loved you, s' the Lord. Yet "
2 Esau Jacob's brother? s' the Lord: 559
4 Edom s', We are impoverished, but "
4 thus s' the Lord of hosts, They shall"
6 s' the Lord of hosts unto you, O "
8 thy person? s' the Lord of hosts. "

Mal 1: 9 he regard your persons? s' the Lord 559
10 no pleasure in you, s' the Lord of "
11 among the heathen, s' the Lord of "
13 ye have snuffed at it, s' the Lord "
13 this of your hand? s' the Lord. "
14 a great King, s' the Lord of hosts, "
2: 2 give glory unto my name, s' the Lord "
4 might be with Levi, s' the Lord of "
8 covenant of Levi, s' the Lord of "
16 s' that he hateth putting away: "
16 his garment, s' the Lord of hosts: "
3: 1 he shall come, s' the Lord of hosts. "
5 fear not me, s' the Lord of hosts. "
7 I will return unto you, s' the Lord "
10 prove me now herewith, s' the Lord "
11 the time in the field, s' the Lord of "
12 be a delightsome land, s' the Lord "
13 been stout against me, s' the Lord. "
17 shall be mine, s' the Lord of hosts, "
4: 1 burn them up, s' the Lord of hosts, "
3 I shall do this, s' the Lord of hosts. "
M't 4: 6 s' unto him, If thou be the Son of 3004
9 And s' unto him, All these things * "
10 s' Jesus unto him, Get thee hence, "
19 And he s' unto them, Follow me, "
7: 21 Not every one that s' unto me, Lord, "
8: 4 Jesus s' unto him, See thou tell "
7 Jesus s' unto him, I will come and "
20 Jesus s' unto him, The foxes have "
26 And he s' unto them, Why are ye "
9: 6 (then s' he to the sick of the palsy,) "
9 and he s' unto him, Follow me. "
28 Jesus s' unto them, Believe ye that "
37 Then s' he unto his disciples, The "
12: 13 Then s' he to the man, Stretch forth "
44 Then he s', I will return into my "
13: 14 which s', By hearing ye shall hear, "
51 Jesus s' unto them, Have ye * "
15: 34 And Jesus s' unto them, How many "
16: 15 He s' unto them, But whom say ye "
17: 25 He s', Yes. And when he was come "
26 Peter s' unto him, Of strangers. * "
26 Jesus s' unto him, Then are the *5346
18: 22 Jesus s' unto him, I say not unto 3004
19: 8 He s' unto them, Moses because of "
18 He s' unto him, Which? Jesus said, "
20 The young man s' unto him, All "
20: 6 s' unto them, Why stand ye here "
7 s' unto them, Go ye also into the "
8 lord of the vineyard s' unto his "
21 She s' unto him, Grant that these "
23 he s' unto them, Ye shall drink "
21: 16 Jesus s' unto them, Yea; have ye "
31 Jesus s' unto them, Verily I say "
42 Jesus s' unto them, Did ye never "
22: 8 Then s' he to his servants, The "
12 he s' unto him, Friend, how camest "
20 he s' unto them, Whose is this "
21 Then s' he unto them, Render "
43 He s' unto them, How then doth "
26: 18 The Master s', My time is at hand; "
31 s' Jesus unto them, All ye shall be "
36 s' unto the disciples, Sit ye here, "
38 Then s' he unto them, My soul is "
40 s' unto Peter, What, could ye not "
45 s' unto them, Sleep on now, and "
64 Jesus s' unto him, Thou hast said: "
27: 22 Pilate s' unto them, What shall I "
M'r 1: 41 s' unto him, I will; be thou clean. "
44 s' unto him, See thou say nothing "
2: 10 (he s' to the sick of the palsy,) "
17 Jesus heard it, he s' unto them, "
3: 3 he s' unto the man which had the "
4 he s' unto them, Is it lawful to do "
5 s' unto the man, Stretch forth thine "
4: 35 he s' unto them, Let us pass over "
5: 19 s' unto him, Go home to thy friends, "
36 s' unto the ruler of the synagogue, "
39 he s' unto them, What make ye this "
6: 38 He s' unto them, How many loaves "
50 s' unto them, Be of good cheer: it "
7: 18 And he s' unto them, Are ye so "
34 s' unto him, Ephphatha, that is, "
8: 1 his disciples unto him, and s' unto "
12 s', Why doth this generation seek "
17 he s' unto them, Why reason ye, "
29 he s' unto them, But whom say ye* "
29 Peter answereth and s' unto him, "
9: 19 and s', O faithless generation, how "
35 called the twelve, and s' unto them, "
10: 11 s' unto them, Whosoever shall put "
23 s' unto his disciples, How hardly "
24 answereth again, and s' unto them, "
27 Jesus looking upon them s', With "
42 s' unto them, Ye know that they "
11: 2 s' unto them, Go your way into the "
21 s' unto him, Master, behold, the "
22 s' unto them, Have faith in God. "
23 things which he s' shall come to "
23 he shall have whatsoever he s'. * "
33 And Jesus answering s' unto them, "
12: 16 And he s' unto them, Whose is this "
43 him his disciples, and s' unto them, "
13: 1 one of his disciples s' unto him, "
14: 13 s' unto them, Go ye into the city, "
14 s', Where is the guestchamber, "
27 Jesus s' unto them, All ye shall be "
30 And Jesus s' unto him, Verily I say "
32 he s' to his disciples, Sit ye here, "
34 s' unto them, My soul is exceeding "
37 s' unto Peter, Simon, sleepest thou? "
41 and s' unto them, Sleep on now, "
45 and s', Master, master: and kissed "
63 and s', What need we any further "
15: 28 the scripture was fulfilled, which s',* "
16: 6 he s' unto them, Be not affrighted: "

Lu 3: 11 and s' unto them, He that hath two *3004
5: 39 new: for he s', This old is better. "
7: 40 thee. And he s', Master, say on. 5346
11: 24 he s', I will return unto my house 3004
16: 29 Abraham s' unto him, They have "
18: 6 Hear what the unjust judge s'. "
19: 22 s' unto him, Out of thine own mouth "
20: 42 And David himself s' in the book of "
22: 11 The Master s' unto thee, Where is "
24: 36 and s' unto them, Peace be unto "
Joh 1: 21 Art thou Elias? And he s', I am not. "
29 s', Behold the Lamb of God, which "
36 he s', Behold the Lamb of God! "
38 and s' unto them, What seek ye? "
39 He s' unto them, Come and see. "
41 and s' unto him, We have found the "
43 Philip, and s' unto him, Follow me. "
45 and s' unto him, We have found him, "
46 Philip s' unto him, Come and see. "
47 and s' of him, Behold an Israelite "
48 Nathanael s' unto him, Whence "
49 Nathanael answered and s' unto * "
51 he s' unto him, Verily, verily, I say "
2: 3 the mother of Jesus s' unto him, "
4 Jesus s' unto her, Woman, what "
5 His mother s' unto the servants, "
5 Whatsoever he s' unto you, do it. "
7 Jesus s' unto them, Fill the "
8 he s' unto them, Draw out now, and "
10 And s' unto him, Every man at the "
3: 4 Nicodemus s' unto him, How can a "
4: 7 Jesus s' unto her, Give me to drink. "
9 s' the woman of Samaria unto him, "
10 who it is that s' to thee, Give me to "
11 The woman s' unto him, Sir, thou "
15 woman s' unto him, Sir, give me "
16 Jesus s' unto her, Go, call thy "
19 woman s' unto him, Sir, I perceive "
21 Jesus s' unto her, Woman, believe "
25 woman s' unto him, I know that "
26 Jesus s' unto her, I that speak unto "
28 way into the city, and s' to the men, "
34 Jesus s' unto them, My meat is to "
49 nobleman s' unto him, Sir, come "
50 Jesus s' unto him, Go thy way; thy "
5: 6 he s' unto him, Wilt thou be made "
8 Jesus s' unto him, Rise, take up thy "
6: 5 he s' unto Philip, Whence shall we "
8 Simon Peter's brother, s' unto him, "
20 But he s' unto them, It is I; be not "
42 then that he s', I came down from * "
7: 50 Nicodemus s' unto them, (he that "
8: 22 because he s', Whither I go, ye "
25 Jesus s' unto them, Even the same* "
39 Jesus s' unto them, If ye were "
11: 7 after that s' he to his disciples, Let "
11 and after that he s' unto them, Our "
23 Jesus s' unto her, Thy brother "
24 Martha s' unto him, I know that he "
27 She s' unto him, Yea, Lord: I "
39 s' unto him, Lord, by this time he "
40 Jesus s' unto her, Said I not unto "
44 Jesus s' unto them, Loose him, and "
12: 4 Then s' one of his disciples, Judas "
13: 6 Peter s' unto him, Lord, dost thou "
8 Peter s' unto him, Thou shalt never "
9 Simon Peter s' unto him, Lord, not "
10 Jesus s' to him, He that is washed "
25 breast s' unto him, Lord, who is it? "
14: 5 Thomas s' unto him, Lord, we "
6 Jesus s' unto him, I am the way, "
8 Philip s' unto him, Lord, shew us "
9 Jesus s' unto him, Have I been so "
22 Judas s' unto him, not Iscariot, "
16: 17 What is this that he s' unto us, A "
18 What is this that he s', A little "
18 while? we cannot tell what he s'. 2980
18: 5 Jesus s' unto them, I am he. And 3004
17 s' the damsel that kept the door "
17 man's disciples? He s', I am not. "
26 s', Did not I see thee in the garden "
38 Pilate s' unto him, What is truth? "
38 s' unto them, I find in him no fault "
19: 4 s' unto them, Behold, I bring him "
5 Pilate s' unto them, Behold the man! "
6 Pilate s' unto them, Take ye him, "
9 s' unto Jesus, Whence art thou? "
10 s' Pilate unto him, Speakest thou "
14 he s' unto the Jews, Behold your "
15 Pilate s' unto them, Shall I crucify "
24 which s', They parted my raiment "
26 s' unto his mother, Woman, behold "
27 s' he to the disciple, Behold thy "
28 scripture might be fulfilled, s', I "
35 and he knoweth that he s' true, that "
37 scripture s', They shall look on him "
20: 2 and s' unto them, They have taken "
13 She s' unto them, Because they "
15 Jesus s' unto her, Woman, why weepest "
15 s' unto him, Sir, if thou have borne "
16 Jesus s' unto her, Mary. She "
16 and s' unto him, Rabboni; which is "
17 Jesus s' unto her, Touch me not; "
19 s' unto them, Peace be unto you. "
22 s' unto them, Receive ye the Holy "
27 s' he to Thomas, Reach hither thy "
29 Jesus s' unto him, Thomas, because "
21: 3 Simon Peter s' unto them, I go a "
5 Jesus s' unto them, Children, have "
7 loved s' unto Peter, It is the Lord. "
10 Jesus s' unto them, Bring of the "
12 Jesus s' unto them, Come and dine. "
15 Jesus s' to Simon Peter, Simon, son "
15 He s' unto him, Yea, Lord; thou "
15 He s' unto him, Feed my lambs. "
16 He s' to him again the second time, "

Joh 21: 16 He s' unto him, Yea, Lord; thou 3004
16 He s' unto him, Feed my sheep. "
17 He s' unto him the third time, "
17 Jesus s' unto him, Feed my sheep. "
19 this, he s' unto him, Follow me. "
21 s' to Jesus, Lord, and what shall "
22 Jesus s' unto him, If I will that he "
Ac 1: 4 which, s' he, ye have heard of me.* "
2: 17 to pass in the last days, s' God, 3004
34 he s' himself, The Lord said unto "
7: 48 with hands; as s' the prophet, "
49 house will ye build me? s' the Lord: "
12: 8 he s' unto him, Cast thy garment "
13: 35 he s' also in another psalm, Thou "
15: 17 s' the Lord, who doeth all these "
21: 11 Thus s' the Holy Ghost, So shall "
22: 2 kept the more silence: and he s',) 5346
Ro 3: 19 that what things soever the law s', 3004
19 s' to them who are under the law:*2980
4: 3 what s' the Scripture? Abraham 3004
9: 15 he s' to Moses, I will have mercy on "
17 For the scripture s' unto Pharaoh, "
25 he s' also in Osee, I will call them "
10: 8 But what s' it? The word is nigh "
11 For the scripture s', Whosoever "
16 Esaias s', Lord, who hath believed "
19 First Moses s', I will provoke you to "
20 Esaias is very bold, and s', I was "
21 to Israel he s', All day long I have "
11: 2 ye not what the scripture s' of Elias? "
4 But what s' the answer of God unto "
9 David s', Let their table be made a "
12: 19 is mine; I will repay, s' the Lord. "
14: 11 As I live, s' the Lord, every knee "
15: 10 again he s', Rejoice, ye Gentiles, "
12 Esaias s', There shall be a root of "
1Co 1: 12 every one of you s', I am of Paul; "
3: 4 For while one s', I am of Paul; and "
6: 16 for two, s' he, shall be one flesh. 5346
9: 8 or s' not the law the same also? 3004
10 Or s' he it altogether for our sakes? "
14: 21 will they not hear me, s' the Lord. "
34 under obedience, as also s' the law. "
15: 27 But when he s' all things are put 2036
2Co 6: 2 (For he s', I have heard thee in a 3004
17 and be ye separate, s' the Lord, and "
18 daughters, s' the Lord Almighty. "
Ga 3: 16 He s' not, And to seeds, as of many; "
4: 30 Nevertheless what s' the scripture? "
Eph 4: 8 Wherefore he s', When he ascended "
5: 14 Wherefore he s', Awake thou that "
1Ti 5: 18 For the scripture s', Thou shalt not "
Heb 1: 6 he s', And let all the angels of God "
7 of the angels he s', Who maketh his "
8 But unto the Son he s', Thy throne, O "
3: 7 (as the Holy Ghost s', To day if ye 3004
5: 6 s' also in another place, Thou art a "
8: 5 for, See, s' he, that thou make all 5346
8 For finding fault with them, he s', 3004
8 days come, s' the Lord, when I will "
9 I regarded them not, s' the Lord. "
10 Israel after those days, s' the Lord; "
13 In that he s', A new covenant, he "
10: 5 he s', Sacrifice and offering thou "
16 s' the Lord, I will put my laws into "
30 me, I will recompense, s' the Lord.* "
Jas 2: 23 the scripture was fulfilled which s', "
4: 5 the scripture s' in vain, The spirit* "
6 Wherefore he s', God resisteth the "
1Jo 2: 4 He that s', I know him, and keepeth "
6 He that s' he abideth in him ought "
9 He that s' he is in the light, and "
Re 1: 8 s' the Lord, which is, and which was, "
2: 1 s' he that holdeth the seven stars in "
7 him hear what the Spirit s' unto the "
8 things s' the first and the last, "
11 him hear what the Spirit s' unto the "
12 These things s' he which hath the "
17 him hear what the Spirit s' unto the "
18 These things s' the Son of God, who "
29 him hear what the Spirit s' unto the "
3: 1 s' he that hath the seven Spirits "
6 him hear what the Spirit s' unto the "
7 These things s' he that is holy, he "
13 him hear what the Spirit s' unto the "
14 These things s' the Amen, the "
22 him hear what the Spirit s' unto the "
5: 5 of the elders s' unto me, Weep not: "
14: 13 Yea, s' the Spirit, that they may rest "
17: 15 he s' unto me, The waters which "
18: 7 for she s' in her heart, I sit a queen, "
19: 9 he s' unto me, Write, Blessed are "
9 he s' unto me, These are the true "
22: 9 s' he unto me, See thou do it not: "
10 he s' unto me, Seal not the sayings "
20 He which testifieth these things s', "

sake See also SAKES.
Ge 3: 17 cursed is the ground for thy s'; 5668
8: 21 the ground any more for man's s'; "
12: 13 it may be well with me for thy s'; "
16 he entreated Abram well for her s': "
18: 29 he said, I will not do it for forty's s'. "
31 I will not destroy it for twenty's s'. "
32 I will not destroy it for ten's s'. "
20: 11 they will slay me for my wife's s'. 1697
26: 24 seed for my servant Abraham's s'. 5668
30: 27 Lord hath blessed me for thy s'. 1558
39: 5 Egyptian's house for Joseph's s'; "
Ex 18: 8 and to the Egyptians for Israel's s', 182
21: 26 let him go free for his eye's s'. 8478
27 shall let him go free for his tooth's s'. "
Nu 11: 29 said unto him, Enviest thou for my s'? "
25: 11 zealous for my s' among them, *7068
18 day of the plague for Peor's s'. *1697
1Sa 12: 22 his people for his great name's s': 5668
23: 10 to destroy the city for my s'.

2Sa 5:12 kingdom for his people Israel's s'.5668
7:21 For thy word's s', and according to "
9: 1 him kindness for Jonathan's s'? "
7 for Jonathan thy father's s', "
18: 5 gently for my s' with the young man,
1Ki 8:41 of a far country for thy name's s'; 4616
11:12 not do it for David thy father's s': "
13 thy son for David my servant's s', "
13 Jerusalem's s' which I have chosen. "
32 one tribe for my servant David's s'."
32 for Jerusalem's s', the city which I "
34 of his life for David my servant's s',"
15: 4 for David's s' did the Lord his God "
2Ki 8:19 Judah for David his servant's s', "
19:34 this city, to save it, for mine own s'."
34 and for my servant David's s'. "
20: 6 defend this city for mine own s', "
6 and for my servant David's s'. "
Ne 9:31 for thy great mercies' s' thou didst*
Job 19:17 for the children's s' of my own body.*
Ps 23: 3 of righteousness for his name's s'.4616
25: 7 me for thy goodness s', O Lord. "
11 For thy name's s', O Lord, pardon "
31: 3 for thy name's s' lead me, and "
16 servant: save me for thy mercies' s'.*
44:22 for thy s' are we killed all the day
26 redeem us for thy mercies' s'. 4616
69: 6 God of hosts, be ashamed for my s':*
6 seek thee be confounded for my s',*
106: 8 he saved them for his name's s', 4616
109:21 God the Lord, for thy name's s': "
115: 1 for thy mercy, and for thy truth's s'.
132:10 servant David's s' turn not away 5668
143:11 me, O Lord, for thy name's s':
11 righteousness' s' bring my soul out*
Isa 37:35 this city to save it for mine own s',
35 and for my servant David's s'. 4616
42:21 pleased for his righteousness' s'; "
43:14 For your s' I have sent to Babylon, "
25 thy transgressions for mine own s'. "
48: 9 name's s' will I defer mine anger, "
11 mine own s', even for mine own s'. "
62: 1 Zion's s' will I not hold my peace, "
63:17 Return for thy servants' s', the "
Jer 14: 7 us, do thou it for thy name's s': "
21 Do not abhor us, for thy name's s', "
15:15 for thy s' I have suffered rebuke. "
Eze 20: 9, 14 I wrought for my name's s', 4616
22 and wrought for my name's s', that"
36:22 but for mine holy name's s', which *
Da 9:17 that is desolate, for the Lord's s'. 4616
19 not, for thine own s', O my God: "
Jon 1:12 for my s' this great tempest is 7945
Mic 3:12 shall Zion for your s' be plowed as1558
M't 5:10 persecuted for righteousness' s': 1752
11 evil against you falsely, for my s'. "
10:18 governors and kings for my s', for "
22 hated of all men for my name's s': "
39 that loseth his life for my s' shall 1752
14: 3 put him in prison for Herodias' s', "
9 nevertheless for the oath's s', and "
16:25 will lose his life for my s' shall 1752
19:12 for the kingdom of heaven's s'. "
29 or lands, for my name's s', shall 1752
24: 9 of all nations for my name's s'. "
22 the elect's s' those days shall be "
M'r 4:17 persecution ariseth for the word's s', "
6:17 him in prison for Herodias' s', "
26 yet for his oath's s', and for their "
8:35 shall lose his life for my s' and 1752
10:29 lands, for my s', and the gospel's, "
13: 9 before rulers and kings for my s', "
13 hated of all men for my name's s': "
20 for the elect's s', whom he hath "
Lu 6:22 as evil, for the Son of man's s'. 1752
9:24 will lose his life for my s', the "
18:29 for the kingdom of God's s'. "
21:12 kings and rulers for my name's s'. "
17 hated of all men for my name's s'. "
Joh 12: 9 they came not for Jesus' s' only, "
13:37 I will lay down my life for thy s'. *
38 thou lay down thy life for my s'? *
14:11 believe me for the very works' s'. "
15:21 they do unto you for my name's s', "
Ac 9:16 he must suffer for my name's s'. "
26: 7 For which hope's s', king Agrippa,*
Ro 4:23 was not written for his s' alone, "
8:36 For thy s' we are killed all the day1752
13: 5 wrath, but also for conscience s'. "
15:30 for the Lord Jesus Christ's s', and "
1Co 4:10 We are fools for Christ's s', but ye "
9:23 this I do for the gospel's s', that I "
10:25, 27 no question for conscience s': "
28 eat not for his s' that shewed it, "
28 for conscience s': for the earth "
2Co 4: 5 your servants for Jesus' s'. "
11 delivered unto death for Jesus' s', "
12:10 in distresses for Christ's s': for "
Eph 4:32 for Christ's s' hath forgiven you. *1722
Ph'p 1:29 him, but also to suffer for his s'; "
Col 1:24 Christ in my flesh for his body's s', "
3: 6 For which things' s' the wrath of "
1Th 1: 5 we were among you for your s'. "
5:13 highly in love for their work's s'. "
1Ti 5:23 a little wine for thy stomach's s', "
Tit 1:11 they ought not, for filthy lucre's s'. "
Ph'm 9 Yet for love's s' I rather beseech "
1Pe 2:13 ordinance of man for the Lord's s': "
3:14 if ye suffer for righteousness' s', "
1Jo 2:12 are forgiven you for his name's s'. "
2Jo 2 For the truth's s', which dwelleth "
3Jo 7 for his name's s' they went forth, "
Re 2: 3 and for my name's s' hast laboured, "

sakes
Ge 18:26 will spare all the place for their s'.*5668
Le 26:45 for their s' remember the covenant "
De 1:37 was angry with me for your s', 1558
3:26 was wroth with me for your s', 6616
4:21 was angry with me for your s', 1697
J'g 21:22 Be favourable unto them for our s':*
Ru 1:13 it grieveth me much for your s' that
1Ch 16:21 he reproved kings for their s', 5921
Ps 7: 7 for their s' therefore return thou * "
105:14 yea, he reproved kings for their s', "
122: 8 my brethren and companions' s', 6616
Isa 65: 8 so will I do for my servants' s', that"
Eze 36:22 I do not this for your s', O house of*"
32 Not for your s' do I this, saith the* "
Da 2:30 for their s' that shall make known*1701
Mal 3:11 I will rebuke the devourer for your s',
M'r 6:26 and for their s' which sat with him,*
Joh 11:15 glad for your s' that I was not there,
12:30 because of me, but for your s'.
17:19 And for their s' I sanctify myself,
Ro 11:28 they are enemies for your s': *
28 are beloved for the fathers' s'. *
1Co 4: 6 and to Apollos for your s'; *
9:10 saith he it altogether for our s'? *
10 For our s', no doubt, this is *
2Co 2:10 for your s' forgave I it in the
4:15 all things are for your s', that
8: 9 yet for your s' he became poor,
1Th 3: 9 joy for your s' before our God;
2Ti 2:10 endure all things for the elect's s',*

Sala (*sa'-lah*) See also SALAH.
Lu 3:35 of Heber, which was the son of S', 4527

Salah (*sa'-lah*) See also SALA.
Ge 10:24 Arphaxad begat S'; and S' begat*7974
11:12 five and thirty years, and begat S':*"
13 Arphaxad lived after he begat S' * "
14 S' lived thirty years, and begat * "
15 S' lived after he begat Eber four * "

Salamis (*sal'-a-mis*)
Ac 13: 5 And when they were at S', they 4529

Salathiel (*sa-la'-the-el*) See also SHEALTIEL.
1Ch 3:17 sons of Jeconiah; Assir, S' his *7597
M't 1:12 to Babylon, Jechonias begat S'; *4528
12 and S' begat Zorobabel; * "
Lu 3:27 which was the son of S', which * "

Salcah (*sal'-kah*) See also SALCHAH.
Jos 12: 5 in mount Hermon, and in S', *5548
13:11 Hermon, and all Bashan unto S';* "
1Ch 5:11 in the land of Bashan unto S': "

Salchah (*sal'-kah*) See also SALCAH.
De 3:10 all Bashan, unto S' and Edrei, *5548

sale
Le 25:27 count the years of the s' thereof, 4465
50 price of his s' shall be according "
De 18: 8 cometh of the s' of his patrimony. "

Salem (*sa'-lem*) See also JERUSALEM.
Ge 14:18 Melchizedek king of S' brought 8004
Ps 76: 2 In S' also is his tabernacle, and his"
Heb 7: 1 For this Melchisedec king of S', 4532
2 after that also King of S', which is,"

Salim (*sa'-lim*)
Joh 3:23 was baptizing in Ænon near to S',4530

Sallai (*sal'-lahee*) See also SALLU.
Ne 11: 8 And after him Gabbai, S', nine 5543
12:20 Of S', Kallai; of Amok, Eber; "

Sallu (*sal'-lu*) See also SALLAI.
1Ch 9: 7 S' the son of Meshullam, the son 5543
Ne 11: 7 S' the son of Meshullam, the son "
12: 7 S', Amok, Hilkiah, Jedaiah. These"

Salma (*sal'-mah*) See also SALMON; ZALMA.
1Ch 2:11 begat S', and S' begat Boaz, 8007
51 S' the father of Beth-lehem, "
54 The sons of S'; Beth-lehem, and "

Salmon (*sal'-mon*) See also SALMA.
Ru 4:20 Nahshon, and Nahshon begat S', 8009
21 And S' begat Boaz, and Boaz 8012
Ps 68:14 in it, it was white as snow in S'. *6756
M't 1: 4 Naasson; and Naasson begat S'; 4533
5 S' begat Booz of Rachab; and Booz"
Lu 3:32 of Booz, which was the son of S', "

Salmone (*sal-mo'-ne*)
Ac 27: 7 under Crete, over against S'; 4534

Salome (*sa-lo'-me*)
M'r 15:40 the less and of Joses, and S'; 4539
16: 1 Mary the mother of James, and S', "

salt See also SALTED; SALTPITS.
Ge 14: 3 vale of Siddim, which is the s' sea.4417
19:26 him, and she became a pillar of s'. "
Le 2:13 offering shalt thou season with s'; "
13 the s' of the covenant of thy God "
13 thine offerings thou shalt offer s'. "
Nu 18:19 it is a covenant of s' for ever before "
34: 3 coast of the s' sea eastward: "
12 out of it shall be at the s' sea: "
De 3:17 the sea of the plain, even the s' sea, "
29:23 land thereof is brimstone, and s', "
Jos 3:16 the sea of the plain, even the s' sea, "
12: 3 the sea of the plain, even the s' sea "
15: 2 was from the shore of the s' sea, "
5 And the east border was the s' sea, "
62 and the city of S', and En-gedi; 5898
18:19 were at the north bay of the s' sea 4417
J'g 9:45 down the city, and sowed it with s'. "
2Sa 8:13 of the Syrians in the valley of s', "
2Ki 2:20 Bring me a new cruse, and put s' "
21 the waters, and cast the s' in there, "
14: 7 He slew of Edom in the valley of s' "
1Ch 18:12 slew...Edomites in the valley of s' "
2Ch 13: 5 and to his sons by a covenant of s'? "
25:11 went to the valley of s', and smote "
Ezr 6: 9 wheat, s', wine, and oil, according 4416
7:22 s' without prescribing how much. "
Job 6: 6 is unsavoury be eaten without s'? 4417
Ps 60: *title* smote of Edom in the valley of s' "
Jer 17: 6 in a s' land and not inhabited. 4420
Eze 43:24 priests shall cast s' upon them, 4417
47:11 be healed; they shall be given to s'. "
M't 5:13 Ye are the s' of the earth: but if the 217
13 but if the s' have lost his savour, "
M'r 9:49 sacrifice shall be salted with s'. * 251
50 S' is good: but if the s' have lost 217
50 Have s' in yourselves, and have "
Lu 14:34 S' is good: but if the s' have lost "
Col 4: 6 alway with grace, seasoned with s', "
Jas 3:12 both yield s' water and fresh. 252

salted
Eze 16: 4 not s' at all, nor swaddled at all. 4414
M't 5:13 savour, wherewith shall it be s'? 233
M'r 9:49 For every one shall be s' with fire, "
49 every sacrifice shall be s' with salt.* "

saltness
M'r 9:50 but if the salt have lost his s', 1096,358

saltpits
Zep 2: 9 the breeding of nettles, and s', and4417

salt-sea See SALT and SEA.

Salu (*sa'-lu*)
Nu 25:14 was Zimri, the son of S', a prince 5543

salutation See also SALUTATIONS.
Lu 1:29 what manner of s' this should be. 783
41 when Elisabeth heard the s' of Mary, "
44 voice of thy s' sounded in mine ears, "
1Co 16:21 s' of me Paul with mine own hand. "
Col 4:18 The s' by the hand of me Paul. "
2Th 3:17 The s' of Paul with mine own hand, "

salutations
M'r 12:38 and love s' in the marketplaces, 783

salute See also SALUTED; SALUTETH.
1Sa 10: 4 And they will s' thee, and give 7965
13:10 to meet him, that he might s' him.1288
25:14 of the wilderness to s' our master; "
2Sa 8:10 son unto king David, to s' him,7592,7965
2Ki 4:29 if thou meet any man, s' him not; 1288
29 and if any s' thee, answer him not "
10:13 to s' the children of the king and 7965
M't 5:47 And if ye s' your brethren only, 782
10:12 when ye come into an house, s' it. "
M'r 15:18 began to s' him, Hail, King of the "
Lu 10: 4 shoes: and s' no man by the way. "
Ac 25:13 came unto Cæsarea to s' Festus. * "
Ro 16: 5 S' my wellbeloved Epænetus, who "
7 S' Andronicus and Junia, my "
9 S' Urbane, our helper in Christ, "
10 S' Apelles approved in Christ. "
10 S' them which are of Aristobulus' "
11 S' Herodion my kinsman. Greet "
12 S' Tryphena and Tryphosa, who "
12 S' the beloved Persis, which "
13 S' Rufus chosen in the Lord, and "
14 S' Asyncritus, Phlegon, Hermas, "
15 S' Philologus, and Julia, Nereus, "
16 S' one another with an holy kiss. "
16 The churches of Christ s' you. "
21 and Sosipater, my kinsmen, s' you.* "
22 who wrote this epistle, s' you in the "
1Co 16:19 The churches of Asia s' you. "
19 Aquila and Priscilla s' you much in "
2Co 13:13 All the saints s' you. "
Ph'p 4:21 S' every saint in Christ Jesus. "
22 All the saints s' you, chiefly they "
Col 4:15 S' the brethren...in Laodicea, "
2Ti 4:19 S' Prisca and Aquila, and the "
Tit 3:15 All that are with me s' thee. Greet "
Ph'm 23 There s' thee Epaphras, my * "
Heb 13:24 S' all them that have the rule over "
24 all the saints. They of Italy s' you. "
3Jo 14 Peace be to thee. Our friends s' thee."

saluted
J'g 18:15 house of Micah, and s' him. *7592,7965
1Sa 17:22 and came and s' his brethren. " "
30:21 near to the people, he s' them. " "
2Ki 10:15 he s' him, and said to him, Is thine1288
M'r 9:15 amazed, and running to him s' him.782
Lu 1:40 house of Zacharias, and s' Elisabeth."
Ac 18:22 and gone up, and s' the church, he "
21: 7 and s' the brethren, and abode with "
19 when he had s' them, he declared "

saluteth
Ro 16:23 and of the whole church, s' you. 782
23 the chamberlain of the city s' you, "
Col 4:10 Aristarchus...s' you, and Marcus, "
12 Epaphras, who is one of you,...s' you,"
1Pe 5:13 church that is at Babylon, s'...you; "

salvation
Ge 49:18 I have waited for thy s', O Lord. 3444
Ex 14:13 still, and see the s' of the Lord, "
15: 2 and song, and he is become my s': "
De 32:15 lightly esteemed the Rock of his s'. "
1Sa 2: 1 enemies; because I rejoice in thy s'. "
11:13 Lord hath wrought s' in Israel. *8668
14:45 wrought this great s' in Israel? 3444
19: 5 Lord wrought a great s' for all *8668
2Sa 22: 3 my shield, and the horn of my s', 3468
36 also given me the shield of thy s': "
47 be the God of the rock of my s'. "
51 He is the tower of s' for his king:*3444
23: 5 this is all my s', and all my desire,3468
1Ch 16:23 shew forth from day to day his s'. 3444
35 Save us, O God of our s', and 3468
2Ch 6:41 thy priests,...be clothed with s', 8666
20:17 see the s' of the Lord with you, 3444
Job 13:16 He also shall be my s': for an "
Ps 3: 8 S' belongeth unto the Lord: thy "

Ps 9:14 of Zion: I will rejoice in thy s'. 3444
13: 5 my heart shall rejoice in thy s'.
14: 7 Oh that the s' of Israel were come "
18: 2 buckler, and the horn of my s', 3468
35 also given me the shield of thy s': "
46 and let the God of my s' be exalted. "
20: 5 We will rejoice in thy s', and in the3444
21: 1 and in thy s' how...shall he rejoice! "
5 His glory is great in thy s': honour "
24: 5 righteousness from...God of his s'.3468
25: 5 for thou art the God of my s'; "
27: 1 Lord is my light and my s'; whom "
9 neither forsake me, O God of my s'."
35: 3 me: say unto my soul, I am thy s'.3444
9 the Lord: it shall rejoice in his s'. "
37: 39 s' of the righteous is of the Lord: 8668
38: 22 haste to help me, O Lord my s'. "
40: 10 declared thy faithfulness and thy s':"
16 let such as love...s' say continually."
50: 23 aright will I shew the s' of God. 3468
51: 12 Restore unto me the joy of thy s'; "
14 O God, thou God of my s': 8668
53: 6 Oh that the s' of Israel were come 3444
62: 1 upon God: from him cometh my s'. "
2, 6 He only is my rock and my s'; he"
7 In God is my s' and my glory: 3468
65: 5 thou answer us, O God of our s'; "
68: 19 benefits, even the God of our s'. 3444
20 that is our God is the God of s'; *4190
69: 13 hear me, in the truth of thy s'. 3468
29 let thy s', O God, set me up on high.3444
70: 4 let such as love...s' say continually."
71: 15 thy righteousness and thy s' all 8668
74: 12 working s' in the midst of the 3444
78: 22 in God, and trusted not in his s': "
79: 9 Help us, O God of our s', for the 3468
85: 4 Turn us, O God of our s', and cause"
7 mercy, O Lord, and grant us thy s'."
9 his s' is nigh them that fear him; "
88: 1 O Lord God of my s', I have cried 3444
89: 26 my God, and the rock of my s'. "
91: 16 I satisfy him, and shew him my s'. "
95: 1 joyful noise to the rock of our s'. 3468
96: 2 shew forth his s' from day to day. 3444
98: 2 The Lord hath made known his s': "
3 earth have seen the s' of our God. "
106: 4 thy people: O visit me with thy s'; "
116: 13 I will take the cup of s', and call "
118: 14 and song, and is become my s'. "
15 The voice of rejoicing and s' is in "
21 heard me, and art become my s'. "
119: 41 O Lord, even thy s', according to 8668
81 My soul fainteth for thy s': but I "
123 Mine eyes fail for thy s', and for 3444
155 S' is far from the wicked: for they "
166 Lord, I have hoped for thy s', and "
174 I have longed for thy s', O Lord; "
132: 16 also clothe her priests with s': 3468
140: 7 the Lord, the strength of my s', 3444
144: 10 It is he that giveth s' unto kings: 8668
149: 4 he will beautify the meek with s'. 3444
Isa 12: 2 Behold, God is my s'; I will trust, "
2 my song; he also is become my s'. "
3 ye draw water out of the wells of s'."
17: 10 hast forgotten the God of thy s', 3468
25: 9 will be glad and rejoice in his s'. 3444
26: 1 s' will God appoint for walls and "
33: 2 our s' also in the time of trouble. "
6 of thy times, and strength of s': "
45: 8 and let them bring forth s', and let3468
17 in the Lord with an everlasting s':8668
46: 13 be far off, and my s' shall not tarry:"
13 I will place s' in Zion for Israel my "
49: 6 my s' unto the end of the earth. 3444
8 in a day of s' have I helped thee: "
51: 5 my s' is gone forth, and mine arms3468
6 but my s' shall be for ever, and my3444
8 and my s' from generation to "
52: 7 tidings of good, that publisheth s'; "
10 earth shall see the s' of our God. "
56: 1 for my s' is near to come, and my "
59: 11 for s', but it is far off from us. "
16 his arm brought s' unto him; and3467
17 and an helmet of s' upon his head;3444
60: 18 but thou shalt call thy walls S', and"
61: 10 me with the garments of s', 3468
62: 1 s' thereof as a lamp that burneth. 3444
11 of Zion, Behold, thy s' cometh; 3468
63: 5 mine own arm brought s' unto me;3467
Jer 3: 23 Truly in vain is s' hoped for from the*
23 Lord our God is the s' of Israel. 8668
La 3: 26 quietly wait for the s' of the Lord. "
Jon 2: 9 I have vowed. S' is of the Lord. 3444
Mic 7: 7 I will wait for the God of my s': 3468
Hab 3: 8 thine horses and thy chariots of s'?3444
13 forth for the s' of thy people, 3468
13 even for s' with thine anointed; "
18 Lord, I will joy in the God of my s'. "
Zec 9: 9 he is just, and having s'; lowly, 3467
Lu 1: 69 hath raised up an horn of s' for us 4991
77 knowledge of s' unto his people by "
2: 30 For mine eyes have seen thy s', 4992
3: 6 And all flesh shall see the s' of God."
19: 9 This day is s' come to this house, 4991
Joh 4: 22 we worship: for s' is of the Jews. "
Ac 4: 12 Neither is there s' in any other: for "
13: 26 to you is the word of this s' sent. "
47 be for s' unto the ends of the earth."
16: 17 which shew unto us the way of s'. "
28: 28 s' of God is sent unto the Gentiles,4992
Ro 1: 16 power of God unto s' to every one 4991
10: 10 mouth confession is made unto s'. "
11: 11 fall s' is come unto the Gentiles, "
13: 11 s' nearer than when we believed. "
2Co 1: 6 it is for your consolation and s', "
6 it is for your consolation and s'. * "
2Co 6: 2 in the day of s' have I succoured 4991
2 time; behold, now is the day of s'.) "
7: 10 sorrow worketh repentance to s' "
Eph 1: 13 of truth, the gospel of your s': "
6: 17 And take the helmet of s', and the 4992
Ph'p 1: 19 turn to my s' through your prayer,4991
28 but to you of s', and that of God. "
2: 12 work out your own s' with fear and "
1Th 5: 8 and for an helmet, the hope of s'. "
9 but to obtain s' by our Lord Jesus "
2Th 2: 13 you to s' through sanctification of "
2Ti 2: 10 also obtain the s' which is in Christ "
3: 15 are able to make thee wise unto s' "
Tit 2: 11 the grace of God that bringeth s' 4992
Heb 1: 14 for them who shall be heirs of s'? 4991
2: 3 we escape, if we neglect so great s'; "
10 make the captain of their s' perfect "
5: 9 author of eternal s' unto all them "
6: 9 you, and things that accompany s', "
9: 28 the second time without sin unto s'. "
1Pe 1: 5 power of God through faith unto s' "
9 your faith, even the s' of your souls."
10 Of which s' the prophets have "
2Pe 3 15 the longsuffering of our Lord is s'; "
Jude 3 to write unto you of the common s', "
Re 7: 10 S' to our God which sitteth upon "
12: 10 Now is come s', and strength, and "
19: 1 saying, Alleluia; S', and glory, "

Samaria (*sa-ma'-re-ah*) See also SAMARITAN.
1Ki 13: 32 places which are in the cities of S',8111
16: 24 he bought the hill S' of Shemer for "
24 of Shemer, owner of the hill, S'. "
28 his fathers, and was buried in S': "
29 Ahab...reigned over Israel in S' "
32 of Baal, which he had built in S'. "
18: 2 And there was a sore famine in S'. "
20: 1 and he went up and besieged S', "
10 if the dust of S' shall suffice for "
17 There are men come out of S'. "
34 Damascus, as my father made in S'."
43 and displeased, and came to S'. "
21: 1 by the palace of Ahab king of S'. "
18 Ahab king of Israel, which is in S': "
22: 10 in the entrance of the gate of S'; "
37 king died, and was brought to S'; "
37 and they buried the king in S'. "
38 washed the chariot in the pool of S';"
51 began to reign over Israel in S' the "
2Ki 1: 2 his upper chamber that was in S', "
3 the messengers of the king of S', "
2: 25 and from thence he returned to S'. "
3: 1 began to reign over Israel in S' the"
6 king Jehoram went out of S' the "
5: 3 were with the prophet that is in S'! "
6: 19 ye seek. But he led them to S'. "
20 pass, when they were come into S'."
20 behold, they were in the midst of S'."
24 host, and went up, and besieged S'."
25 And there was a great famine in S':"
7: 1 barley for a shekel, in the gate of S'."
18 about this time in the gate of S': "
10: 1 And Ahab had seventy sons in S'. "
1 Jehu wrote letters, and sent to S', "
12 arose and departed, and came to S'."
17 And when he came to S', he slew "
17 all that remained unto Ahab in S', "
35 fathers: and they buried him in S'."
36 that Jehu reigned over Israel in S' "
13: 1 began to reign over Israel in S', "
6 there remained the grove also in S'.)"
9 fathers; and they buried him in S':"
10 Jehoahaz to reign over Israel in S'. "
13 Joash was buried in S' with the "
14: 14 and hostages, and returned to S'. "
16 was buried in S' with the kings of "
23 king of Israel began to reign in S'. "
15: 8 of Jeroboam reign over Israel in S' "
13 and he reigned a full month in S'. "
14 up from Tirzah, and came to S', "
14 Shallum the son of Jabesh in S', "
17 Israel, and reigned ten years in S'. "
23 began to reign over Israel in S', "
25 smote him in S', in the palace "
27 began to reign over Israel in S', "
17: 1 the son of Elah to reign in S' over "
5 and went up to S', and besieged it "
6 the king of Assyria took S', and "
24 and placed them in the cities of S' "
24 and they possessed S', and dwelt in"
26 and placed in the cities of S', know "
28 whom they had carried...from S' "
18: 9 king of Assyria came up against S',"
10 king of Israel, S' was taken. "
34 they delivered S' out of mine hand?"
21: 13 over Jerusalem the line of S', and "
23: 18 of the prophet that came out of S'. "
19 places that were in the cities of S', "
2Ch 18: 2 years he went down to Ahab to S'. "
9 at the entering in of the gate of S'; "
22: 9 caught him, (for he was hid in S',) "
25: 13 Judah, from S'...unto Beth-horon, "
24 hostages also, and returned to S'. "
28: 8 them, and brought the spoil to S'. "
9 out before the host that came to S'."
15 brethren: then they returned to S'."
Ezr 4: 10 and set in the cities of S', and the 8115
17 their companions that dwell in S', "
Ne 4: 2 his brethren and the army of S', 8111
Isa 7: 9 And the head of Ephraim is S', and "
9 the head of S' is Remaliah's son. "
8: 4 the spoil of S' shall be taken away "
9: 9 Ephraim and the inhabitant of S', "
10: 9 as Arpad? is not S' as Damascus? "
10 excel them of Jerusalem and of S'; "
11 I have done unto S' and her idols, "
36: 19 they delivered S' out of my hand? "
Jer 23: 13 seen folly in the prophets of S'; 8111
31: 5 vines upon the mountains of S': "
41: 5 and from S', even fourscore men, "
Eze 16: 46 thine elder sister is S', she and her "
51 Neither hath S' committed half of "
53 captivity of S' and her daughters, "
55 S' and her daughters shall return "
23: 4 S' is Aholah, and Jerusalem "
33 with the cup of thy sister S'. "
Ho 7: 1 and the wickedness of S': for they "
8: 5 Thy calf, O S', hath cast thee off; "
6 calf of S' shall be broken in pieces. "
10: 5 inhabitants of S' shall fear because"
7 As for S', her king is cut off as the "
13: 16 S' shall become desolate; for she "
Am 3: 9 upon the mountains of S', and "
12 Israel be taken out that dwell in S' "
4: 1 that are in the mountain of S', "
6: 1 and trust in the mountain of S', "
8: 14 that sware by the sin of S', and say,"
Ob 19 of Ephraim, and the fields of S': "
Mic 1: 1 saw concerning S' and Jerusalem. "
5 transgression of Jacob? is it not S'?"
6 will make S' as an heap of the field,"
Lu 17: 11 he passed through the midst of S' 4540
Joh 4: 4 And he must needs go through S'. "
5 cometh he to a city of S', which "
7 a woman of S' to draw water: "
9 saith the woman of S' unto him, * "
9 of me, which am a woman of S'? * "
Ac 1: 8 and in S', and unto the uttermost "
8: 1 the regions of Judæa and S', except"
5 Philip went down to the city of S', "
9 and bewitched the people of S', "
14 S' had received the word of God, "
9: 31 all Judæa and Galilee and S', and "
15: 3 passed through Phenice and S', "

Samaritan (*sa-mar'-i-tun*) See also SAMARITANS.
Lu 10: 33 But a certain S', as he journeyed, 4541
17: 16 him thanks: and he was a S'. "
Joh 8: 48 Say we not well that thou art a S', "

Samaritans (*sa-mar'-i-tuns*)
2Ki 17: 29 places which the S' had made, 8118
M't 10: 5 into any city of the S' enter...not: 4541
Lu 9: 52 and entered into a village of the S'."
Joh 4: 9 Jews have no dealings with the S'.)"
39 many of the S' of that city believed"
40 when the S' were come unto him, "
Ac 8: 25 gospel in many villages of the S'. "

same See also SELFSAME.
Ge 2: 13 the s' is it that compasseth the 1931
5: 29 This s' shall comfort us concerning
6: 4 the s' became mighty men which 1992
7: 11 the s' day were all the fountains 2088
10: 12 and Calah: the s' is a great city. 1931
14: 8 the king of Bela (the s' is Zoar;) "
15: 18 s' day the Lord made a covenant * "
19: 37 the s' is the father of the Moabites "
38 the s' is the father of the children "
21: 8 feast the s' day...Isaac was weaned.*
25: 30 thee, with that s' red pottage; 2088
26: 12 and received in the s' year an 1931
24 appeared unto him the s' night, "
32: 13 And he lodged there that s' night;* "
41: 48 about every city, laid he up in the s'.
44: 6 he spake unto them these s' words.
48: 7 of Ephrath; the s' is Beth-lehem. 1931
Ex 5: 6 Pharaoh commanded the s' day the "
12: 6 fourteenth day of the s' month: 2088
25: 31 and his flowers, shall be of the s'.*
35, 35, 35 under two branches of the s',*
36 and their branches shall be of the s':*
28: 8 which is upon it, shall be of the s',
30: 2 the horns thereof shall be of the s'.*
37: 17 knops, and his flowers, were of the s':*
21, 21, 21 under two branches of the s',*
22 and their branches were of the s':*
25 of it; the horns thereof were of the s'.*
38: 2 of it; the horns thereof were of the s':*
39: 5 ephod, that was upon it, was of the s',
Le 7: 15 be eaten the s' day that it is offered;*
16 be eaten the s' day that he offereth*
19: 6 be eaten the s' day ye offer it, and on
22: 30 the s' day it shall be eaten up; ye 1931
23: 6 fifteenth day of the s' month is the2088
28 ye shall do no work in that s' day:6106
29 shall not be afflicted in that s' day, "
30 doeth any work in that s' day, "
30 s' soul will I destroy from among* "
Nu 6: 11 shall hallow his head that s' day. 1931
9: 13 s' soul shall be cut off from among*"
10: 32 do unto us, the s' will we do unto thee.
15: 30 the s' reproacheth the Lord; and 1931
32: 10 anger was kindled the s' time, and* "
De 9: 20 I prayed for Aaron also the s' time. "
14: 28 tithe of thine increase the s' year, "
27: 11 Moses charged the people the s' day,"
31: 22 Moses...wrote this song the s' day, "
Jos 6: 15 the city after the s' manner seven 2088
11: 16 of Israel, and the valley of the s'; "
15: 8 the Jebusite; the s' is Jerusalem: 1931
J'g 6: 25 it came to pass the s' night, that the"
7: 4 with thee, the s' shall go with thee; "
4 not go with thee, the s' shall not go."
9 it came to pass the s' night, that "
1Sa 4: 12 came to Shiloh the s' day with his "
6: 15 sacrificed sacrifices the s' day unto "
16 they returned to Ekron the s' day. "
9: 17 this s' shall reign over my people. 2088
10: 12 one of the s' place answered and said,
14: 35 the s' was the first altar that he built
17: 23 and spake according to the s' words:428
30 and spake after the s' manner: 2088
31: 6 all his men, that s' day together. 1931

2Sa 2:23 there, and died in the s' place: 8478
5: 7 of Zion: the s' is the city of David.1931
23: 7 burned with fire in the s' place. *
8 the s' was Adino the Eznite: he 1931
1Ki 7:35 and the borders thereof were of the s'.
8:64 The s' day did the king hallow the1931
13: 3 he gave a sign the s' day, saying, "
9 again by the s' way that thou camest.*
2Ki 3: 6 went out of Samaria the s' time, *1931
8:22 Libnah revolted at the s' time. "
19:29 year that which springeth of the s';
33 that he came, by the s' shall he return,
1Ch 1:27 Abram; the s' is Abraham. 1931
4:33 that were round about the s' cities,
16:17 confirmed the s' to Jacob for a law,
17: 3 And it came to pass the s' night, 1931
2Ch 7: 8 the s' time Solomon kept the feast "
13: 9 s' may be a priest of them that are no
15:11 offered unto the Lord the s' time,*1931
16:10 some of the people the s' time. "
21:10 s' time also did Libnah revolt from "
27: 5 of Ammon gave him the s' year an "
32:12 Hath not the s' Hezekiah taken "
30 This s' Hezekiah also stopped the "
34:28 and upon the inhabitants of the s'.*
35:16 service...was prepared the s' day, 1931
Ezr 4:15 sedition within the s' of old time: 1459
5: 3 At the s' time came to them Tatnai,
13 s' king Cyrus made a decree to build*
16 Then came the s' Sheshbazzar, 1791
6: 3 the s' Cyrus the king made a decree*
10:23 and Kelaiah, (the s' is Kelita,) 1933
Ne 4:22 the s' time said I unto the people, 1931
6: 4 answered...after the s' manner. 2088
10:37 that the s' Levites might have the*1992
Es 9: 1 Adar, on the thirteenth day of the s',
17 fourteenth day of the s' rested they,
18 the fifteenth day of the s' they rested,
21 and the fifteenth day of the s', yearly,
Job 4: 8 and sow wickedness, reap the s'.
13: 2 What ye know, the s' do I know also:
Ps 68:23 the tongue of thy dogs in the s'.*
75: 8 and he poureth out the s': but the 2088
102:27 But thou art the s', and thy years 1931
105:10 confirmed the s' unto Jacob for a law,
113: 3 the sun unto the going down of the s'
Pr 28:24 s' is the companion of a destroyer.1931
Ec 9:15 man remembered that s' poor man."
Isa 7:20 In the s' day shall the Lord shave* "
37:30 year that which springeth of the s':
34 he came, by the s' shall he return,
Jer 27: 8 will not serve the s' Nebuchadnezzar
28: 1 And it came to pass the s' year, in 1931
17 the prophet died the s' year in the "
31: 1 At the s' time, saith the Lord, will* "
39:10 vineyards and fields at the s' time. "
Eze 3:18 the s' wicked man shall die in his "
10:16 the s' wheels also turned not from*1992
22 s' faces which I saw by the river of*
21:26 the crown: this shall not be the s':2063
23:38 defiled my sanctuary in the s' day,1931
39 came the s' day into my sanctuary "
24: 2 of the day, even of this s' day: *6106
2 against Jerusalem this s' day. * "
38:10 at the s' time shall things come *1931
18 the s' time when Gog shall come * "
44: 3 and shall go out by the way of the s'.
Da 3: 6 the s' hour be cast into the midst of
15 be cast the s' hour into the midst of
4:33 s' hour was the thing fulfilled upon
36 the s' time my reason returned unto
5: 5 s' hour came forth fingers of a man's
12 were found in the s' Daniel, whom
7:21 s' horn made war with the saints, 1797
12: 1 was a nation even to that s' time: 1931
Am 2: 7 his father will go in unto the s' maid,
Zep 1: 9 s' day also will I punish all those *1931
Zec 6:10 and come thou the s' day, and go into"
Mal 1:11 even unto the going down of the s'
M't 3: 4 s' John had his raiment of camel's*846
5:19 the s' shall be called great in the *3778
46 do not even the publicans the s'? 846
10:19 that s' hour what ye shall speak. *1565
12:50 the s' is my brother, and sister, and*846
13: 1 s' day went Jesus out of the house,*1565
20 the s' is he that heareth the word,*3778
15:22 woman...came out of the s' coasts,*1565
18: 1 the s' time came the disciples unto*"
4 the s' is greatest in the kingdom 3778
28 the s' servant went out, and found*1565
21:42 s' is become the head of the corner:3778
22:23 s' day came to him the Sadducees,*1565
24:13 unto the end, the s' shall be saved. 3778
25:16 talents went and traded with the s',*846
26:23 in the dish, the s' shall betray me. 3778
44 the third time, saying the s' words. 846
48 Whomsoever I...kiss, that s' is he:* "
55 In that s' hour said Jesus to the *1565
27:44 with him, cast the s' in his teeth. 846
M'r 3:35 the s' is my brother, and my sister,3778
4:35 s' day, when the even was come, *1565
8:35 the gospel's, the s' shall save it. *3778
9:35 to be first, the s' shall be last of all,*
10:10 asked him again of the s' matter. * 846
13:13 unto the end, the s' shall be saved.3778
14:39 and prayed, and spake the s' words.846
44 Whomsoever I...kiss, that s' is he;* "
Lu 2: 8 were in the s' country shepherds "
25 the s' man was just and devout, *3778
6:33 ye? for sinners also do even the s'. 846
38 s' measure that ye mete withal it * "
7:21 that s' hour he cured many of their*"
47 little is forgiven, the s' loveth little.
9:24 for my sake, the s' shall save it. 3778
48 among you all, the s' shall be great."
10: 7 And in the s' house remain, eating 846
Lu 10:10 ways out into the streets of the s',* 846
12:12 in the s' hour what ye ought to say.* "
13:31 The s' day there came certain of the*"
16: 1 s' was accused unto him that he 3778
17:29 s' day that Lot went out of Sodom it*
20:17 s' is become...head of the corner? 3778
19 s' hour sought to lay hands on him:*846
47 s'...receive greater damnation. *3778
23:40 thou art in the s' condemnation? 846
51 (The s' had not consented to the *3778
24:13 went that s' day to a village called* 846
33 And they rose up the s' hour, and * "
Joh 1: 2 s' was in the beginning with God. 3778
7 The s' came for a witness, to bear "
33 s' said unto me, Upon whom thou*1565
33 s' is he which baptizeth with the 3778
3: 2 The s' came to Jesus by night, and "
26 the s' baptizeth, and all men come "
4:53 knew that it was at the s' hour, *1565
5: 9 and on the s' day was the sabbath.*"
11 s' said unto me, Take up thy bed, "
36 s' works that I do, bear witness of *846
7:18 s' is true, and no unrighteousness3778
8:25 Even the s' that I said unto you, *3748
10: 1 way, the s' is a thief and a robber. 1565
11: 6 abode two days still in the s' place *
49 being the high priest that s' year, *1565
12:21 s' came therefore to Philip, which*3778
48 s' shall judge him in the last day. 1565
15: 5 the s' bringeth forth much fruit: 3778
18:13 was the high priest that s' year. *1565
20:19 s' day at evening, being the first * "
Ac 1:11 s' Jesus, which is taken up from *3778
22 s' day that he was taken up from us,*
2:36 that God hath made that s' Jesus,*5126
41 s' day there were added unto them*1565
7:19 s' dealt subtilly with our kindred, 3778
35 s' did God send to be a ruler and a*5126
8: 9 beforetime in the s' city used sorcery,*
35 and began at the s' scripture, and*5026
12: 6 the s' night Peter was sleeping 1565
13:33 hath fulfilled the s' unto us their 5026
14: 9 The s' heard Paul speak: who 3778
15:27 also tell you the s' things by mouth.846
16:17 s' followed Paul and us, and cried,3778
18 her. And he came out the s' hour.*846
33 took them the s' hour of the night,1565
18: 3 because he was of the s' craft, he 3673
19:23 s' time there arose no small stir *1565
21: 9 the s' man had four daughters, *5129
22:13 the s' hour I looked up upon him.* 846
24:20 Or else let these s' here say, if *3778
28: 7 s' quarters were possessions of *1565
Ro 1:32 not only do the s', but have pleasure846
2: 1 that judgest doest the s' things. "
3 and doest the s', that thou shalt "
8:20 who hath subjected the s' in hope,*
9:17 s' purpose have I raised thee up, * 846
21 the s' lump to make one vessel unto "
10:12 for the s' Lord over all is rich unto "
12: 4 all members have not the s' office: "
16 Be of the s' mind one toward another."
13: 3 and thou shalt have praise of the s': "
1Co 1:10 that ye all speak the s' thing, and "
10 the s' mind and in the s' judgment. "
7:20 every man abide in the s' calling 5026
8: 3 love God, the s' is known of him. 5778
9: 8 or saith not the law the s' also? 5023
10: 3 did all eat the s' spiritual meat; 846
4 did all drink the s' spiritual drink: "
11:23 s' night in which he was betrayed* "
25 s' manner also he took the cup, *5615
12: 4 diversities of gifts, but the s' Spirit. "
5 of administrations, but the s' Lord. "
6 it is the s' God which worketh all "
8 word of knowledge by the s' Spirit; "
9 To another faith by the s' Spirit; to "
9 the gifts of healing by the s' Spirit;*"
25 have the s' care one for another. "
15:39 All flesh is not the s' flesh: but "
2Co 1: 6 in the enduring of the s' sufferings "
2: 2 the s' which is made sorry by me?* "
3 And I wrote this s' unto you, lest,* 846
3:14 day remaineth the s' vail untaken "
18 are changed into the s' image from "
4:13 We having the s' spirit of faith, "
6:13 Now for a recompence in the s', (I * "
7: 8 the s' epistle hath made you sorry,*1565
8: 6 also finish in you the s' grace also.*846
16 put the s' earnest care into the "
19 by us to the glory of the s' Lord, *3778
9: 4 in this s' confident boasting. *5026
5 that the s' might be ready, as a "
12:18 walked we not in the s' spirit? 846
18 walked we not in the s' steps? "
Ga 2: 8 s' was mighty in me toward the *2532
10 the s' which I also was forward*846,5124
3: 7 the s' are the children of Abraham.3778
Eph 3: 6 be fellowheirs, and of the s' body, *4954
6: 8 the s' shall he receive of the Lord, 3778
9 ye masters, do the s' things unto 846
22 sent unto you for the s' purpose, * "
Ph'p 1:30 Having the s' conflict which ye saw "
2:18 For the s' cause also do ye joy, and "
3: 1 To write the s' things to you, to me "
16 let us walk by the s' rule, let us "
16 rule, let us mind the s' thing. * "
4: 2 they be of the s' mind in the Lord. "
Col 4: 2 watch in the s' with thanksgiving;* "
8 sent unto you for the s' purpose, * "
2Ti 2: 2 s' commit thou to faithful men, 5023
Heb 1:12 but thou art the s', and thy years 846
2:14 himself likewise took part of the s'; "
4:11 fall after the s' example of unbelief. "
6:11 one of you do shew the s' diligence "
10:11 offering oftentimes the s' sacrifices, "
Heb11: 9 the heirs with him of the s' promise:
13: 8 Jesus Christ the s' yesterday, and 846
Jas 3: 2 in word, the s' is a perfect man, 3778
10 Out of the s' mouth proceedeth 846
11 the s' place sweet water and bitter? "
1Pe 2: 7 s' is made the head of the corner, 3778
4: 1 likewise with the s' mind: for he 846
4 with them to the s' excess of riot, "
10 so minister the s' one to another, * "
5: 9 the s' afflictions are accomplished "
2Pe 2:19 the s' is he brought in bondage. 3778
3: 7 by the s' word are kept in store, 846
1Jo 2:23 Son, the s' hath not the Father: 3761
27 as the s' anointing teacheth you * 846
Re 3: 5 the s' shall be clothed in white *3778
11:13 s' hour was...a great earthquake, *1565
14:10 The s' shall drink of the wine of * 846

Samgar-nebo (*sam''-gar-ne'-bo*)
Jer 39: 3 Nergal-sharezer, S', Sarsechim, 5562

Samlah (*sam'-lah*)
Ge 36:36 S' of Masrekah reigned in his 8072
37 S' died, and Saul of Rehoboth by "
1Ch 1:47 S' of Masrekah reigned in his "
48 S' was dead, Shaul of Rehoboth "

Samos (*sa'-mos*)
Ac 20:15 and the next day we arrived at S'.4544

Samothracia (*sam-o-thra'-she-ah*)
Ac 16:11 came with a straight course to S',*4543

Samson (*sam'-sun*) See also SAMSON'S.
J'g 13:24 a son, and called his name S': 8123
14: 1 And S' went down to Timnath, and"
3 S' said unto his father, Get her for "
5 Then went S' down, and his father "
7 woman; and she pleased S' well. "
10 and S' made there a feast; for so "
12 S' said unto them, I will now put "
15: 1 that S' visited his wife with a kid; "
3 And S' said concerning them, "
4 S' went and caught three hundred "
6 S', the son in law of the Timnite, "
7 S' said unto them, Though ye have"
10 To bind S' are we come up, to do "
11 said to S', Knowest thou not that "
12 S' said unto them, Sware unto me, "
16 S' said, With the jawbone of an ass,"
16: 1 Then went S' to Gaza, and saw "
2 Gazites, saying, S' is come hither. "
3 And S' lay till midnight, and arose "
6 And Delilah said to S', Tell me, I "
7 S' said unto her, If they bind me "
9 The Philistines be upon thee, S'. "
10 And Delilah said unto S', Behold, "
12 The Philistines be upon thee, S'. "
13 And Delilah said unto S', Hitherto "
14,20 The Philistines be upon thee, S'. "
23 delivered S' our enemy into our "
25 Call for S', that he may make us "
25 they called for S' out of the prison "
26 S' said unto the lad that held him "
27 that beheld while S' made sport. "
28 S' called unto the Lord, and said, "
29 And S' took hold of the two middle "
30 And S' said, Let me die with the "
Heb11:32 Barak, and of S', and of Jephthae;4546

Samson's (*sam'-suns*)
J'g 14:15 they said unto S' wife, Entice thy 8123
16 S' wife wept before him, and said, "
20 S' wife was given to his companion,"

Samuel (*sam'-u-el*) See also SHEMUEL.
1Sa 1:20 a son, and called his name S', 8050
2:18 But S' ministered before the Lord, "
21 the child S' grew before the Lord. "
26 the child S' grew on, and was in "
3: 1 child S' ministered unto the Lord "
3 was, and S' was laid down to sleep;"
4 That the Lord called S': and he "
6 And the Lord called yet again, S'. "
6 S' arose and went to Eli, and said, "
7 Now S' did not yet know the Lord, "
8 the Lord called S' again the third "
9 Eli said unto S', Go, lie down: and "
9 S' went and lay down in his place. "
10 and called as at other times, S', S'. "
10 Then S' answered, Speak; for thy "
11 the Lord said to S', Behold, I will "
15 And S' lay until the morning, and "
15 S' feared to show Eli the vision. "
16 Eli called S', and said, S', my son. "
18 S' told him every whit, and hid "
19 S' grew, and the Lord was with "
20 knew that S' was established to be"
21 for the Lord revealed himself to S' "
4: 1 the word of S' came to all Israel. "
7: 3 S' spake unto all the house of "
5 And S' said, Gather all Israel to "
6 S' judged the children of Israel in "
8 the children of Israel said to S', "
9 And S' took a sucking lamb, and "
9 S' cried unto the Lord for Israel; "
10 as S' was offering up the burnt "
12 Then S' took a stone, and set it "
13 the Philistines all the days of S'. "
15 S' judged Israel all the days of his "
8: 1 when S' was old, that he made his "
4 and came to S' unto Ramah, "
6 But the thing displeased S', when "
6 us. And S' prayed unto the Lord. "
7 the Lord said unto S', Hearken "
10 S' told all the words of the Lord "
19 refused to obey the voice of S'; "
21 And S' heard all the words of the "
22 the Lord said to S', Hearken unto "
22 And S' said unto the men of Israel."

1Sa 9:14 behold, S· came out against them :8050
15 Now the Lord had told S· in his ear "
17 when S· saw Saul, the Lord said "
18 Saul drew near to S· in the gate, "
19 S· answered Saul,...I am the seer: "
22 And S· took Saul and his servant, "
23 And S· said unto the cook, Bring "
24 S· said, Behold that which is left! "
24 So Saul did eat with S· that day. 8050
25 S· communed with Saul upon the top*
26 S· called Saul to the top of the 8050
26 went out both of them, he and S·, "
27 S· said to Saul, Bid the servant pass"
10: 1 S· took a vial of oil, and poured it "
9 had turned his back to go from S·, "
14 they were no where, we came to S·. "
15 Tell me,...what S· said unto you. "
16 of the kingdom, whereof S· spake, "
17 And S· called the people together "
20 when S· had caused all the tribes of"
24 S· said to all the people, See ye him"
25 S· told the people the manner of "
25 And S· sent all the people away, "
11: 7 not forth after Saul and after S·, "
12 the people said unto S·, Who is he "
14 Then said S· to the people, Come, "
12: 1 And S· said unto all Israel, Behold, "
6 S· said unto...people, It is the Lord"
11 Lord sent...Jephthah, and S·, and "
18 So S· called unto the Lord; and the"
18 greatly feared the Lord and S·. "
19 people said unto S·, Pray for thy "
20 S· said unto the people, Fear not: "
13: 8 the set time that S· had appointed: "
8 but S· came not to Gilgal; and the "
10 S· came; and Saul went out to meet"
11 And S· said, What hast thou done? "
13 And S· said to Saul, Thou hast done"
15 And S· arose, and gat him up from "
15: 1 S·...said unto Saul, The Lord sent "
10 came the word of the Lord unto S·, "
11 And it grieved S·; and he cried unto"
12 when S· rose early to meet Saul in "
12 it was told S·, saying, Saul came "
13 And S· came to Saul: and Saul said"
14 S· said, What meaneth then this "
16 S· said unto Saul, Stay, and I will "
17 And S· said, When thou wast little "
20 And Saul said unto S·, Yea, I have "
22 And S· said, Hath the Lord as great"
24 Saul said unto S·, I have sinned: "
26 S· said unto Saul, I will not return "
27 And as S· turned about to go away, "
28 And S· said...The Lord hath rent "
31 So S· turned again after Saul; and "
32 Then said S·, Bring ye hither to me"
33 S· said, As thy sword hath made "
33 S· hewed Agag in pieces before the"
34 Then S· went to Ramah; and Saul "
35 S· came no more to see Saul until "
35 nevertheless S· mourned for Saul: "
16: 1 the Lord said unto S·, How long "
2 And S· said, How can I go? if Saul "
4 S· did that which the Lord spake, "
7 Lord said unto S·, Look not on his "
8 and made him pass before S·. "
10 seven of his sons to pass before S·. "
10 S· said unto Jesse, The Lord hath "
11 S· said unto Jesse, Are here all thy "
11 S· said unto Jesse, Send and fetch "
13 Then S· took the horn of oil, and "
13 So S· rose up, and went to Ramah. "
19:18 escaped, and came to S· to Ramah, "
18 he and S· went and dwelt in Naioth."
20 S· standing as appointed over them,"
22 and said, Where are S· and David? "
24 and prophesied before S· in like "
25: 1 And S· died; and all the Israelites "
28: 3 Now S· was dead, and all Israel had"
11 thee? And he said, Bring me up S·. "
12 when the woman saw S·, she cried "
14 And Saul perceived that it was S·, "
15 And S· said to Saul, Why hast thou"
16 Then said S·, Wherefore then dost "
20 afraid, because of the words of S·: "
1Ch 6:28 the sons of S·; the firstborn Vashni, "
9:22 David and S· the seer did ordain "
11: 3 to the word of the Lord by S·. "
26:28 And all that S· the seer, and Saul "
29:29 written in the book of S· the seer, "
2Ch 35:18 from the days of S· the prophet; "
Ps 99: 6 and S· among them that call upon "
Jer 15: 1 Though Moses and S· stood before "
Ac 3:24 Yea, and all the prophets from S· 4545
13:20 and fifty years, until S· the prophet."
Heb 11:32 of David also, and S·, and of the "

Sanballat *(san-bal'-lat)*
Ne 2:10 When S· the Horonite, and Tobiah 5571
19 when S· the Horonite, and Tobiah "
4: 1 when S· heard that we builded the "
7 to pass, that when S·, and Tobiah, "
6: 1 came to pass, when S·, and Tobiah, "
2 That S· and Geshem sent unto me, "
5 Then sent S· his servant unto me "
12 for Tobiah and S· had hired him. "
14 God, think thou upon Tobiah and S·"
13:28 was son in law to S· the Horonite: "

sanctification
1Co 1:30 righteousness,...s·, and redemption: 38
1Th 4: 3 this is the will of God, even your s·, "
4 possess his vessel in s· and honour; "
2Th 2:13 to salvation through s· of the Spirit "
1Pe 1: 2 Father, through s· of the Spirit, unto"

sanctified
Ge 2: 3 blessed the seventh day, and s· it:*6942
Ex 19:14 unto the people, and s· the people;6942
29:43 tabernacle shall be s· by my glory. "
Le 8:10 all that was therein, and s· them. "
15 at the bottom of the altar, and s· it, "
30 and s· Aaron, and his garments, "
10: 3 I will be s· in them that come nigh "
27:15 if he that s· it will redeem his house, "
19 if he that s· the field will in any wise"
Nu 7: 1 and had anointed it, and s· it, and "
1 had anointed them, and s· them; "
8:17 land of Egypt I s· them for myself. "
20:13 the Lord, and he was s· in them. "
De 32:51 because ye s· me not in the midst "
1Sa 7: 1 s· Eleazar his son to keep the ark "
16: 5 And he s· Jesse and his sons, and "
21: 5 it were s· this day in the vessel. "
1Ch 15:14 priests and...Levites s· themselves "
2Ch 5:11 priests that were present were s·, "
7:16 have I chosen and s· this house, * "
20 house, which I have s· for my name,* "
29:15 their brethren, and s· themselves, "
17 so they s· the house of the Lord in "
19 vessels,...have we prepared and s·, "
34 the other priests had s· themselves: "
30: 3 had not s· themselves sufficiently, "
8 sanctuary, which he hath s· for ever: "
15 were ashamed, and s· themselves, "
17 the congregation that were not s·: "
24 number of priests s· themselves. "
31:18 they s· themselves in holiness: "
Ne 3: 1 they s· it, and set up the doors of it; "
1 unto the tower of Meah they s· it, "
12:47 they s· holy things unto the Levites; "
47 s· them unto the children of Aaron. "
Job 1: 5 about that Job sent and s· them, and "
Isa 5:16 is holy shall be s· in righteousness. "
13: 3 I have commanded my s· ones, I * "
Jer 1: 5 camest...out of the womb I s· thee, "
Eze 20:41 will be s· in you before the heathen. "
28:22 in her, and shall be s· in her. "
25 be s·...in the sight of the heathen, "
36:23 shall be s· in you before their eyes. "
38:16 when I shall be s· in thee, O Gog, "
39:27 am s· in them in the sight of many "
48:11 the priests that are s· of the sons of "
Joh 10:36 whom the Father hath s·, and sent 37
17:19 also might be s· through the truth. "
Ac 20:32 among all them which are s·. "
26:18 among them which are s· by faith "
Ro 15:16 being s· by the Holy Ghost. "
1Co 1: 2 to them that are s· in Christ Jesus, "
6:11 but ye are washed, but ye are s·, but "
7:14 unbelieving husband is s· by the wife, "
14 unbelieving wife is s· by the husband: "
1Ti 4: 5 For it is s· by the word of God and "
2Ti 2:21 s·, and meet for the master's use, and "
Heb 2:11 that sanctifieth and they who are s· "
10:10 By the which will we are s· through "
14 perfected for ever them that are s·. "
29 of the covenant, wherewith he was s·, "
Jude 1 them that are s· by God the Father, "

sanctifieth
M't 23:17 gold, or the temple that s· the gold?*37
19 the gift, or the altar that s· the gift? "
Heb 2:11 that s· and they who are sanctified "
9:13 s· to the purifying of the flesh: * "

sanctify See also SANCTIFIED; SANCTIFIETH.
Ex 13: 2 S· unto me all the firstborn, 6942
19:10 and s· them to day and to morrow, "
22 let the priests...s· themselves, "
23 bounds about the mount, and s· it. "
28:41 and consecrate them, and s· them, "
29:27 s· the breast of the wave offering, "
33 made, to consecrate and to s· them: "
36 it, and thou shalt anoint it, to s· it. "
37 atonement for the altar, and s· it; "
44 And I will s· the tabernacle of the "
44 I will s· also both Aaron and his sons, "
30:29 And thou shalt s· them, that they "
31:13 that I am the Lord that doth s· you. "
40:10 and all his vessels, and s· the altar: "
11 shall anoint the laver...and s· it. "
13 and anoint him, and s· him; "
Le 8:11 the laver and his foot, to s· them. "
12 head, and anointed him, to s· him. "
11:44 ye shall therefore s· yourselves, "
20: 7 S· yourselves therefore, and be ye "
8 them: I am the Lord which s· you. "
21: 8 Thou shalt s· him therefore; for he "
8 I the Lord, which s· you, am holy. "
15 his people: for I the Lord do s· him. "
23 for I the Lord do s· them. "
22: 9 profane it: I the Lord do s· them. "
16 things: for I the Lord do s· them. "
27:14 when a man shall s· his house to "
16 a man shall s· unto the Lord some "
17 If he s· his field from the year of "
18 if he s· his field after the jubile, "
22 if a man s· unto the Lord a field "
26 Lord's firstling, no man shall s· it; "
Nu 11:18 S· yourselves against to morrow, "
20:12 s· me in the eyes of the children of "
27:14 s· me at the water before their eyes: "
De 5:12 Keep the sabbath day to s· it, as the* "
15:19 shalt s· unto the Lord thy God: "
Jos 3: 5 said unto the people, S· yourselves: "
7:13 Up, s· the people, and say, "
13 S· yourselves against to morrow: "
1Sa 16: 5 s· yourselves, and come with me to "
1Ch 15:12 s· yourselves, both ye and your "
23:13 he should s· the most holy things, "
2Ch 29: 5 me, ye Levites, s· now yourselves, "
5 and s· the house of the Lord God of "
17 first day of the first month to s·, "
34 upright in heart to s· themselves "
2Ch 30:17 not clean, to s· them unto the Lord 6942
35: 6 kill the passover, and s· yourselves, "
Ne 13:22 the gates, to s· the sabbath day. "
Isa 8:13 S· the Lord of hosts himself; and "
29:23 of him, they shall s· my name, "
23 and s· the Holy One of Jacob, and "
66:17 They that s· themselves, and purify "
Eze 20:12 that I am the Lord that s· them. "
36:23 And I will s· my great name, which "
37:28 know that I the Lord do s· Israel, "
38:23 I magnify myself, and s· myself; "
44:19 shall not s· the people with their "
46:20 the utter court, to s· the people. "
Joe 1:14 S· ye a fast, call a solemn assembly, "
2:15 s· a fast, call a solemn assembly: "
16 s· the congregation, assemble the "
Joh 17:17 S· them through thy truth: thy 37
19 for their sakes I s· myself, that they "
Eph 5:26 he might s· and cleanse it with the "
1Th 5:23 the very God of peace s· you wholly; "
Heb 13:12 he might s· the people with his own "
1Pe 3:15 But s· the Lord God in your hearts: "

sanctuaries
Le 21:23 that he profane not my s·: for I 4720
26:31 and bring your s· unto desolation, "
Jer 51:51 strangers are come into the s· of "
Eze 28:18 Thou hast defiled thy s· by the "
Am 7: 9 the s· of Israel shall be laid waste; "

sanctuary See also SANCTUARIES.
Ex 15:17 S·, O Lord, which thy hands have 4720
25: 8 let them make me a s·; that I may "
30:13 shekel after the shekel of the s·: 6944
24 after the shekel of the s·, and of "
36: 1 of work for the service of the s·, "
3 the work of the service of the s·, "
4 that wrought all the work of the s·, "
6 work for the offering of the s·. "
38:24 shekels, after the shekel of the s·, "
25 shekels, after the shekel of the s·: "
26 shekel, after the shekel of the s·, "
27 were cast the sockets of the s·, and "
Le 4: 6 the Lord, before the vail of the s·. "
5:15 of silver, after the shekel of the s·, "
10: 4 from before the s· out of the camp. "
12: 4 nor come into the s·, until the 4720
16:33 make an atonement for the holy s·, "
19:30 my sabbaths, and reverence my s·: "
20: 3 to defile my s·, and to profane my "
21:12 Neither shall he go out of the s·, "
12 nor profane the s· of his God; for "
26: 2 my sabbaths, and reverence my s·: "
27: 3 silver, after the shekel of the s·. 6944
25 according to the shekel of the s·: "
Nu 3:28 keeping the charge of the s·. "
31 vessels of the s· wherewith they "
32 them that keep the charge of the s·. "
38 keeping the charge of the s· for 4720
47 shekel of the s· shalt thou take 6944
50 shekels, after the shekel of the s·: "
4:12 wherewith they minister in the s·, "
15 made an end of covering the s·, "
15 and all the vessels of the s·, as the "
16 and of all that therein is, in the s·, "
7: 9 the service of the s· belonging unto "
13, 19, 25, 31, 37, 43, 49, 55, 61, 67, 73, 79,
85 shekels, after the shekel of the s·; "
86 apiece, after the shekel of the s·: "
8:19 of Israel come nigh unto the s·. "
10:21 set forward, bearing the s·: and 4720
18: 1 shall bear the iniquity of the s·: "
3 not come nigh the vessels of the s· 6944
5 ye shall keep the charge of the s·, "
16 shekels, after the shekel of the s·, "
19:20 hath defiled the s· of the Lord: 4720
Jos 24:26 oak, that was by the s· of the Lord. "
1Ch 9:29 and all the instruments of the s·, 6944
22:19 build ye the s· of the Lord God, 4720
24: 5 for the governors of the s·, and 6944
28:10 thee to build an house for the s·: 4720
2Ch 20: 8 built thee a s· therein for thy name, "
26:18 go out of the s·; for thou hast "
29:21 kingdom, for the s·, and for Judah. "
30: 8 unto the Lord, and enter into his s·, "
19 to the purification of the s·. 6944
36:17 the sword in the house of their s·, 4720
Ne 10:39 where are the vessels of the s·, and "
Ps 20: 2 Send thee help from the s·, and 6944
63: 2 so as I have seen thee in the s·. "
68:24 of my God, my King, in the s·. "
73:17 Until I went into the s· of God; 4720
74: 3 hath done wickedly in the s·. 6944
7 They have cast fire into thy s·, they 4720
77:13 Thy way, O God, is in the s·: who is 6944
78:54 them to the border of his s·, even "
69 built his s· like high palaces, like 4720
96: 6 strength and beauty are in his s·. "
102:19 down from the height of his s·; 6944
114: 2 Judah was his s·, and Israel his "
134: 2 Lift up your hands in the s·, and "
150: 1 Praise God in his s·: praise him "
Isa 8:14 he shall be for a s·; but for a stone 4720
16:12 that he shall come to his s· to pray; "
43:28 profaned the princes of the s·, 6944
60:13 to beautify the place of my s·; 4720
63:18 adversaries...trodden down thy s·. "
Jer 17:12 beginning is the place of our s·. "
La 1:10 the heathen entered into her s·, "
2: 7 he hath abhorred his s·, he hath "
20 prophet be slain in...s· of the Lord? "
4: 1 stones of the s· are poured out in 6944
Eze 5:11 because thou hast defiled my s· 4720
8: 6 that I should go far off from my s·? "
9: 6 is the mark; and begin at my s·. "
11:16 yet will I be to them as a little s· in "
38 have defiled my s· in the same day. "

Eze 23:39 same day into my s· to profane it; 4720
24:21 Behold, I will profane my s·, the "
25: 3 thou saidst, Aha, against my s·, "
37:26 will set my s· in the midst of them "
28 my s· shall be in the midst of them "
41:21 squared, and the face of the s·; 6944
23 temple and the s· had two doors. "
42:20 make a separation between the s·* "
43:21 place of the house, without the s·. 4720
44: 1 the gate of the outward s· which "
5 with every going forth of the s·. "
7 have brought into my s· strangers,* "
7 to be in my s·, to pollute it, even 4720
8 set keepers of my charge in my s· "
9 in flesh, shall enter into my s·, "
11 they shall be ministers in my s·, "
15 kept the charge of my s· when the "
16 They shall enter into my s·, and "
27 the day that he goeth into the s·, 6944
27 inner court, to minister in the s·, "
45: 2 for the s· five hundred in length * "
3 the s· and the most holy place. 4720
4 the priests the ministers of the s·, "
4 houses, and an holy place for the s·. "
18 without blemish, and cleanse the s·: "
47:12 waters they issued out of the s·: "
48: 8 the s· shall be in the midst of it. "
10 s· of the Lord shall be in the midst "
21 s· of the house shall be in the midst "
Da 8:11 the place of his s· was cast down. "
13 to give both the s· and the host to 6944
14 days; then shall the s· be cleansed. "
9:17 cause thy face to shine upon thy s· 4720
26 shall destroy the city and the s·; 6944
11:31 shall pollute the s· of strength, and 4720
Zep 3: 4 her priests have polluted the s·, 6944
Heb 8: 2 A minister of the s·, and of the true *39*
9: 1 of divine service, and a worldly s·. "
2 shewbread; which is called the s·.* "
13:11 whose blood is brought into the s·* "

sand See also QUICKSANDS.
Ge 22:17 s· which is upon the sea shore; 2344
32:12 make thy seed as the s· of the sea, "
41:49 gathered corn as the s· of the sea, "
Ex 2:12 the Egyptian, and hid him in the s·. "
De 33:19 seas, and of treasures hid in the s·. "
Jos 11: 4 as the s· that is upon the sea shore "
J'g 7:12 the s· by the sea side for multitude. "
1Sa 13: 5 as the s· which is on the sea shore "
2Sa 17:11 as the s· that is by the sea for "
1Ki 4:20 many, as the s· which is by the sea "
29 as the s· that is on the sea shore. "
Job 6: 3 be heavier than the s· of the sea: "
29:18 I shall multiply my days as the s·. "
Ps 78:27 fowls like as the s· of the sea: "
139:18 are more in number than the s·: "
Pr 27: 3 stone is heavy, and the s· weighty; "
Isa 10:22 people Israel be as the s· of the sea, "
48:19 Thy seed also had been as the s·, "
Jer 5:22 have placed the s· for the bound of "
15: 8 to me above the s· of the seas: "
33:22 neither the s· of the sea measured: "
Ho 1:10 Israel shall be as the s· of the sea, "
Hab 1: 9 shall gather the captivity as the s·. "
M't 7:26 which built his house upon the s·: *285*
Ro 9:27 of Israel be as the s· of the sea, "
Heb11:12 as the s· which is by the sea shore "
Re 13: 1 And I stood upon the s· of the sea, "
20: 8 the number...is as the s· of the sea. "

sandals
M'r 6: 9 But be shod with s·; and not put *4547*
Ac 12: 8 Gird thyself, and bind on thy s·. "

sang
Ex 15: 1 Then s· Moses and the children of 7891
Nu 21:17 Then Israel s· this song, Spring up, "
J'g 5: 1 Then s· Deborah and Barak the "
1Sa 29: 5 Is not this David, of whom they s· 6030
2Ch 29:28 the singers s·, and the trumpeters 7891
30 they s· praises with gladness, and "
Ezr 3:11 And they s· together by course in 6030
Ne 12:42 the singers s· loud, with Jezrahiah 7891
Job 38: 7 the morning stars s· together, and 7442
Ps 7: *title* David, which he s· unto the Lord, 7891
106:12 they his words; they s· his praise. "
Ac 16:25 prayed, and s· praises unto God: *5214*

sank
Ex 15: 5 they s· into the bottom as a stone.*3381
10 s· as lead in the mighty waters. 6749

Sansannah (*san-san'-nah*) See also KIRJATH-SANNAH.
Jos 15:31 Ziklag, and Madmannah, and *S*·, 5578

sap
Ps 104:16 The trees of the Lord are full of s·;††

Saph (*saf*) See also SIPHAI.
2Sa 21:18 Sibbechai the Hushathite slew *S*·, 5593

Saphir (*sa'-fur*)
Mic 1:11 ye away, thou inhabitant of *S*·, *8208

Sapphira (*saf-fi'-rah*)
Ac 5: 1 named Ananias, with *S*· his wife, *4551*

sapphire See also SAPPHIRES.
Ex 24:10 were a paved work of a s· stone, 5601
28:18 row shall be an emerald, a s·, and "
39:11 the second row, an emerald, a s·, "
Job 28:16 with the precious onyx, or the s·. "
La 4: 7 rubies, their polishing was of s·: "
Eze 1:26 as the appearance of a s· stone: "
10: 1 over them as it were a s· stone, as "
28:13 and the jasper, the s·, the emerald, "
Re 21:19 was jasper; the second, s·; the *4552*

sapphires
Job 28: 6 stones of it are the place of s·: and 5601
Ca 5:14 is as bright ivory overlaid with s·. "
Isa 54:11 and lay thy foundations with s·. "

Sara (*sa'-rah*) See also SARAH.
Heb11:11 *S*· herself received strength to *4564*
1Pe 3: 6 as *S*· obeyed Abraham, calling him* "

Sarah (*sa'-rah*) See also SARA; SARAH'S; SARAI; SERAH.
Ge 17:15 Sarai, but *S*· shall her name be. 8283
17 shall *S*·, that is ninety years old, "
19 *S*· thy wife shall bare thee a son "
21 which *S*· shall bare unto thee at "
18: 6 hastened into the tent unto *S*·, and "
9 unto him, Where is *S*· thy wife? "
10 lo, *S*· thy wife shall have a son. "
10 *S*· heard it in the tent door, which "
11 Abraham and *S*· were old and well "
11 with *S*· after the manner of women. "
12 *S*· laughed within herself, saying, "
13 Wherefore did *S*· laugh, saying, "
14 of life, and *S*· shall have a son. "
15 *S*· denied, saying, I laughed not; "
20: 2 Abraham said of *S*· his wife, She is "
2 king of Gerar sent, and took *S*·. "
14 and restored him *S*· his wife. "
16 And unto *S*· he said, Behold, I have "
18 because of *S*· Abraham's wife. "
21: 1 the Lord visited *S*· as he had said, "
1 Lord did unto *S*· as he had spoken. "
2 *S*· conceived, and bare Abraham a "
3 him, whom *S*· bare to him, Isaac. "
6 And *S*· said, God hath made me to "
7 *S*· should have given children suck? "
9 And *S*· saw the son of Hagar the "
12 in all that *S*· hath said unto thee, "
23: 1 *S*· was an hundred and seven and "
1 were the years of the life of *S*·. "
2 *S*· died in Kirjath-arba; the same "
2 and Abraham came to mourn for *S*·, "
19 Abraham buried *S*· his wife in the "
24:36 *S*· my master's wife bare a son to "
25:10 Abraham buried, and *S*· his wife. "
49:31 buried Abraham and *S*· his wife; "
Nu 26:46 of the daughter of Asher was *S*·. 8294
Isa 51: 2 father, and unto *S*· that bare you: 8283
Ro 9: 9 I come, and *S*· shall have a son. *4564*

Sarah's (*sa'-rahs*)
Ge 24:67 her into his mother *S*· tent, and 8283
25:12 *S*· handmaid, bare unto Abraham: "
Ro 4:19 yet the deadness of *S*· womb: *4564*

Sarai (*sa'-rahee*) See also SARAH; SARAI'S.
Ge 11:29 the name of Abram's wife was *S*·; 8297
30 *S*· was barren; she had no child. "
31 and *S*· his daughter in law, his son "
12: 5 Abram took *S*· his wife, and Lot "
11 he said unto *S*· his wife, Behold "
17 with great plagues because of *S*· "
16: 1 Now *S*· Abram's wife bare him no "
2 *S*· said unto Abram, Behold now, "
2 Abram hearkened to the voice of *S*·. "
3 *S*· Abram's wife took Hagar her "
5 *S*· said unto Abram, My wrong be "
6 Abram said unto *S*·, Behold, thy "
6 when *S*· dealt hardly with her, she "
8 from the face of my mistress *S*·. "
17:15 As for *S*· thy wife, thou shalt not "
15 thou shalt not call her name *S*·, but "

Sarai's (*sa'-rahees*)
Ge 16: 8 he said, Hagar, *S*· maid, whence 8297

Saraph (*sa'-raf*)
1Ch 4:22 *S*·, who had the dominion in Moab, 8315

sardine
Re 4: 3 upon like a jasper and a s· stone: *4555

Sardis (*sar'-dis*)
Re 1:11 and unto Thyatira, and unto *S*·, *4554*
3: 1 the angel of the church in *S*· write; "
4 Thou hast a few names even in *S*· "

Sardites (*sar'-dites*)
Nu 26:26 of Sered, the family of the *S*·: of *5625

sardius (*sar'-de-us*)
Ex 28:17 the first row shall be a s·, a topaz, 124
39:10 the first row was a s·, a topaz, and "
Eze 28:13 thy covering, the s·, and the diamond, "
Re 21:20 The fifth, sardonyx; the sixth, s·; *4556*

sardonyx (*sar'-do-nix*)
Re 21:20 The fifth, s·; the sixth, sardius; *4557*

Sarepta (*sa-rep'-tah*) See also ZAREPHATH.
Lu 4:26 save unto *S*·, a city of Sidon, unto *4558*

Sargon (*sar'-gon*)
Isa 20: 1 *S*· the king of Assyria sent him,) 5623

Sarid (*sa'-rid*)
Jos 19:10 of their inheritance was unto *S*·: 8301
12 And turned from *S*· eastward "

Saron (*sa'-ron*) See also SHARON.
Ac 9:35 all that dwelt at Lydda and *S*· saw *4565*

Sarsechim (*sar'-se-kim*)
Jer 39: 3 Nergal-sharezer, Samgar-nebo, *S*·, 8310

Saruch (*sa'-ruk*) See also SERUG.
Lu 3:35 Which was the son of *S*·, which *4562*

sat See also SATEST.
Ge 18: 1 he s· in the tent door in the heat 3427
19: 1 and Lot s· in the gate of Sodom: "
21:16 and s· her down over against him a "
16 And she s· over against him, and "
31:34 the images,...and s· upon them. "
37:25 And they s· down to eat bread: and "
38:14 and s· in an open place, which is by "
43:33 they s· before him, the firstborn 3427
48: 2 himself, and s· upon the bed. "
Ex 2:15 Midian: and he s· down by a well. "
12:29 of Pharaoh that s· on his throne "
16: 3 when we s· by the flesh pots, and "
17:12 put it under him, and he s· thereon; "
18:13 that Moses s· to judge the people: "
32: 6 people s· down to eat and to drink, "
Le 15: 6 whereon he s· that hath the issue "
22 toucheth any thing that she s· upon* "
De 33: 3 and they s· down at thy feet; 8497
J'g 6:11 and s· under an oak which was in 3427
13: 9 the woman as she s· in the field: "
19: 6 And they s· down, and did eat and "
15 s· him down in a street of the city: "
20:26 wept, and s· there before the Lord, "
Ru 2:14 And she s· beside the reapers: and "
4: 1 to the gate, and s· him down there: "
1 And he turned aside, and s· down. "
2 ye down here. And they s· down. "
1Sa 1: 9 Eli the priest s· upon a seat by a "
4:13 Eli s· upon a seat by the wayside "
19: 9 as he s· in his house with his javelin "
20:24 the king s· him down to eat meat. "
25 king s· upon his seat, as at other "
25 Abner s· by Saul's side, and David's "
28:23 from the earth, and s· upon the bed. "
2Sa 2:13 they s· down, the one on the one side "
7: 1 pass, when the king s· in his house,* "
18 David in, and s· before the Lord, "
18:24 And David s· between the two gates: "
19: 8 the king arose, and s· in the gate. "
23: 8 The Tachmonite that s· in the seat,* "
1Ki 2:12 s· Solomon upon the throne of David "
19 and s· down on his throne, and "
19 and she s· on his right hand. "
13:20 came to pass, as they s· at the table, "
16:11 reign, as soon as he s· on his throne, "
19: 4 and s· down under a juniper tree: "
21:13 children of Belial, and s· before him: "
22:10 king of Judah s· each on his throne, "
2Ki 1: 9 behold, he s· on the top of an hill. "
4:20 mother, he s· on her knees till noon, "
6:32 But Elisha s· in his house, and the "
32 house, and the elders s· with him; "
11:19 he s· on the throne of the kings. "
13:13 and Jeroboam s· upon his throne: "
1Ch 17: 1 to pass, as David s· in his house, * "
16 king came and s· before the Lord, "
29:23 Solomon s· on the throne of the Lord "
2Ch 18: 9 s· either of them on his throne, "
9 and they s· in a void place at the "
Ezr 9: 3 of my beard, and s· down astonied. "
4 and I s· astonied until the evening "
10: 9 s· in the street of the house of God, "
16 s· down in the first day of the tenth "
Ne 1: 4 I s· down and wept, and mourned "
8:17 booths, and s· under the booths: * "
Es 1: 2 king Ahasuerus s· on the throne "
14 which s· the first in the kingdom;) "
2:19 then Mordecai s· in the king's gate. "
21 while Mordecai s· in the king's gate, "
3:15 king and Haman s· down to drink; "
5: 1 the king s· upon his royal throne "
Job 2: 8 and he s· down among the ashes. "
13 s· down with him upon the ground "
29:25 I chose out their way, and s· chief, "
Ps 26: 4 I have not s· with vain persons, "
137: 1 rivers of Babylon, there we s· down, "
Ca 2: 3 I s· down under his shadow with "
Jer 3: 2 In the ways hast thou s· for them, "
15:17 I s· not in the assembly of the "
17 I s· alone because of thy hand: for "
26:10 s· down in the entry of the new gate "
32:12 that s· in the court of the prison. "
36:12 and, lo, all the princes s· there, "
22 Now the king s· in the winterhouse "
39: 3 came in, and s· in the middle gate, "
Eze 3:15 of Chebar, and I s· where they s·, * "
8: 1 of the month, as I s· in mine house, "
1 the elders of Judah s· before me, "
14 s· women weeping for Tammuz. "
14: 1 elders...unto me, and s· before me. "
20: 1 elders of Israel...and s· before me. "
Da 2:49 but Daniel s· in the gate of the king.* "
Jon 3: 6 with sackcloth, and s· in ashes. 3427
4: 5 and s· on the east side of the city, "
5 booth, and s· under it in the shadow, "
M't 4:16 The people which s· in darkness *2521*
16 which s· in the region and shadow "
9:10 as Jesus s· at meat in the house, *345*
10 and s· down with him and his *4873*
13: 1 the house, and s· by the sea side. *2521*
2 that he went into a ship, and s·; "
48 they drew to shore, and s· down, *2523*
14: 9 them which s· with him at meat, *4873*
15:29 a mountain, and s· down there. *2521*
24: 3 as he s· upon the mount of Olives, "
26: 7 it on his head, as he s· at meat. *345*
20 come, he s· down with the twelve.* "
55 I s· daily with you teaching in the *2516*
58 went in, and s· with the servants, *2521*
69 Now Peter s· without in the palace:* "
28: 2 stone from the door, and s· upon it. "
M'r 2:15 as Jesus s· at meat in his house, *2621
15 sinners s· also together with Jesus *4873*
3:32 And the multitude s· about him, *2521
34 looked...on them which s· about him, "
4: 1 into a ship, and s· in the sea; "
6:22 Herod and them that s· with him, *4873*
26 for their sakes which s· with him, "
40 they s· down in ranks, by hundreds, *377*
9:35 he s· down, and called the twelve, *2523*
10:46 s· by the highway side begging. *2521
11: 2 colt tied, whereon never man s·; *2523*
7 on him; and he s· upon him. "

M'r 12: 41 Jesus s' over against the treasury, 2523
13: 3 as he s' upon the mount of Olives 2521
14: 3 as he s' at meat,...came a woman 2621
18 as they s' and did eat, Jesus said, 345
54 and he s' with the servants, and *4775
16: 14 unto the eleven as they s' at meat, 345
19 and s' on the right hand of God. 2523
Lu 4: 20 again to the minister, and s' down. "
5: 3 s' down, and taught the people out "
29 of others that s' down with them. *2621
7: 15 he that was dead s' up, and began 339
36 house, and s' down to meat. 347
37 knew that Jesus s' at meat in the* 345
49 And they that s' at meat with him 4873
10: 39 Mary which also s' at Jesus' feet, 3869
11: 37 he went in, and s' down to meat. 377
14: 15 one of them that s' at meat with 4873
18: 35 blind man s' by the way side 2521
19: 30 tied, whereon never yet man s': 2523
22: 14 the hour was come, he s' down, and 377
55 Peter s' down among them. 2521
56 maid beheld him as he s' by the "
24: 30 as he s' at meat with them, he took 2625
Joh 4: 6 his journey, s' thus on the well: 2516
6: 3 and there he s' with his disciples. 2521
10 So the men s' down, in number 377
8: 2 and he s' down, and taught them. 2523
9: 8 Is not this he that s' and begged? 2521
11: 20 him: but Mary s' still in the house. 2516
12: 2 them that s' at the table with him. 4873
14 had found a young ass, s' thereon; 2523
19: 13 s' down in the judgment seat in a "
Ac 2: 3 of fire, and it s' upon each of them. "
3: 10 it was he which s' for alms at the 2521
6: 15 all that s' in the council, looking 2516
9: 40 and when she saw Peter, she s' up. 339
12: 21 s' upon his throne, and made an 2523
13: 14 on the sabbath day, and s' down. "
14: 8 there s' a certain man at Lystra, 2521
16: 13 and we s' down, and spake unto 2523
20: 9 And there s' in a window a certain 2521
25: 17 I s' on the judgment seat, and 2523
26: 30 Bernice,...they that s' with them: 4775
1Co 10: 7 people s' down to eat and drink, 2523
Heb 1: 3 s' down on the right hand of the "
10: 12 s' down on the right hand of God; "
Re 4: 2 heaven, and one s' on the throne. *2521
3 he that s' was to look upon like a "
9 thanks to him that s' on the throne,*"
10 before him that s' on the throne, * "
5: 1 hand of him that s' on the throne "
7 hand of him that s' upon the throne."
6: 2 he that s' on him had a bow; and a "
4 was given to him that s' thereon to "
5 s' on him had a pair of balances "
8 his name that s' on him was Death,"
9: 17 and them that s' on them, having "
11: 16 which s' before God on their seats,*"
14: 14 one s' like unto the Son of man, * "
15 voice to him that s' on the cloud, "
16 s' on the cloud thrust in his sickle "
19: 4 God that s' on the throne, saying,* "
11 s' upon him was called Faithful "
19 against him that s' on the horse, "
21 sword of him that s' upon the horse,"
20: 4 thrones, and they s' upon them, 2523
11 white throne, and him that s' on 2521
21: 5 he that s' upon the throne said, * "

Satan (*sa'-tun*) See also SATAN'S.
1Ch 21: 1 S' stood up against Israel, and 7854
Job 1: 6 and S' came also among them. "
7 Lord said unto S', Whence comest "
7 S' answered the Lord, and said, "
8 the Lord said unto S', Hast thou "
9 S' answered the Lord, and said, "
12 Lord said unto S', Behold, all that "
12 S' went forth from the presence of "
2: 1 and S' came also among them to "
2 Lord said unto S', From whence "
2 S' answered the Lord, and said, "
3 the Lord said unto S', Hast thou "
4 S' answered the Lord, and said, "
6 Lord said unto S', Behold, he is in "
7 went S' forth from the presence of "
Ps 109: 6 and let S' stand at his right hand.* "
Zec 3: 1 S' standing at his right hand to "
2 the Lord said unto S', The Lord "
2 Lord rebuke thee, O S'; even the "
M't 4: 10 unto him, Get thee hence, S': 4567
12: 26 And if S' cast out S', he is divided "
16: 23 Get thee behind me, S': thou art "
M'r 1: 13 forty days, tempted of S'; and was "
3: 23 parables, How can S' cast out S'? "
26 S' rise up against himself, and be "
4: 15 S' cometh immediately, and taketh"
8: 33 saying, Get thee behind me, S': "
Lu 4: 8 unto him, Get thee behind me, S':* "
10: 18 I beheld S' as lightning fall from "
11: 18 S' also be divided against himself, "
13: 16 of Abraham, whom S' hath bound, "
22: 3 Then entered S' into Judas "
31 S' hath desired to have you, that "
Joh 13: 27 after the sop S' entered into him. "
Ac 5: 3 why hath S' filled thine heart to lie "
26: 18 from the power of S' unto God, that"
Ro 16: 20 bruise S' under your feet shortly. "
1Co 5: 5 To deliver such an one unto S' "
7: 5 that S' tempt you not for your "
2Co 2: 11 S' should get an advantage of us: "
11: 14 S' himself is transformed into an "
12: 7 the messenger of S' to buffet me, "
1Th 2: 18 and again; but S' hindered us. "
2Th 2: 9 is after the working of S' with all "
1Ti 1: 20 whom I have delivered unto S', "
5: 15 are already turned aside after S'. "
Re 2: 9 not, but are the synagogue of S'. "
2: 13 slain among you, where S' dwelleth. 4567
24 have not known the depths of S', "
3: 9 make them of the synagogue of S', "
12: 9 serpent, called the Devil, and S', "
20: 2 serpent, which is the Devil, and S', "
7 S' shall be loosed out of his prison,"

Satan's (*sa'-tuns*)
Re 2: 13 dwellest, even where S' seat is: 4567

satest
Ps 9: 4 s' in the throne judging right. 3427
Eze 23: 41 s' upon a stately bed, and a table "

satiate See also SATIATED; UNSATIABLE.
Jer 31: 14 And I will s' the soul of the priests 7301
46: 10 and it shall be s' and made drunk 7646

satiated
Jer 31: 25 I have s' the weary soul, and I 7301

satisfaction
Nu 35: 31 no s' for the life of a murderer, *3724
32 no s' for him that is fled to the city*"

satisfied
Ex 15: 9 my lust shall be s' upon them; I 4390
Le 26: 26 and ye shall eat, and not be s'. 7646
De 14: 29 shall come, and shall eat and be s'; "
33: 23 O Naphtali, s' with favour, and 7649
Job 19: 22 God, and are not s' with my flesh? 7646
27: 14 offspring shall not be s' with bread."
31: 31 had of his flesh! we cannot be s'. ‡ "
Ps 17: 15 I shall be s', when I awake, with "
22: 26 The meek shall eat and be s': they "
36: 8 They shall be abundantly s' with 7301
37: 19 days of famine they shall be s'. 7646
59: 15 meat, and grudge if they be not s'. "
63: 5 My soul shall be s' as with marrow "
65: 4 we shall be s' with the goodness of "
81: 16 of the rock should I have s' thee. *7649
104: 13 earth is s' with the fruit of thy ‡7646
105: 40 s' them with the bread of heaven. 7649
Pr 12: 11 He that tilleth his land shall be s'*7646
14 A man shall be s' with good by the "
14: 14 a good man shall be s' from himself. "
18: 20 A man's belly shall be s' with the*7646
19: 23 he that hath it shall abide s'; he 7649
20: 13 and thou shalt be s' with bread. 7646
27: 20 so the eyes of man are never s'. "
30: 15 are three things that are never s', "
Ec 1: 8 the eye is not s' with seeing, nor "
4: 8 neither is his eye s' with riches; "
5: 10 He that loveth silver shall not be s' "
Isa 9: 20 left hand, and they shall not be s': "
44: 16 flesh; he roasteth roast, and is s': "
53: 11 travail of his soul, and shall be s': "
66: 11 suck, and be s' with the breasts "
Jer 31: 14 and my people shall be s' with my "
50: 10 all that spoil her shall be s', saith "
19 and his soul shall be s' upon mount"
La 5: 6 the Assyrians, to be s' with bread. "
Eze 16: 28 them, and yet couldest not be s'. "
29 and yet thou wast not s' herewith. "
Joe 2: 19 oil, and ye shall be s' therewith: "
26 ye shall eat in plenty, and be s', "
Am 4: 8 drink water; but they were not s': "
Mic 6: 14 Thou shalt eat, but not be s'; and "
Hab 2: 5 and is as death, and cannot be s', "

satisfiest
Ps 145: 16 s' the desire of every living thing. 7646

satisfieth
Ps 103: 5 s' thy mouth with good things; 7646
107: 9 he s' the longing soul, and filleth "
Isa 55: 2 your labour for that which s' not? 7654

satisfy See also SATISFIED; SATISFIEST; SATISFIETH; SATISFYING.
Job 38: 27 s' the desolate and waste ground; 7646
Ps 90: 14 O s' us early with thy mercy; that "
91: 16 With long life will I s' him, and "
132: 15 I will s' her poor with bread. "
Pr 5: 19 let her breasts s' thee at all times; 7301
6: 30 if he steal to s' his soul when he 4390
Isa 58: 10 hungry, and s' the afflicted soul; 7646
11 s' thy soul in drought, and make "
Eze 7: 19 they shall not s' their souls, "
M'r 8: 4 can a man s' these men with bread 5526

satisfying
Pr 13: 25 eateth to the s' of his soul: but 7648
Col 2: 23 any honour to the s' of the flesh. *4140

satyr (*sa'-tur*) See also SATYRS.
Isa 34: 14 and the s' shall cry to his fellow; ‡8163

satyrs (*sa'-turs*)
Isa 13: 21 there, and s' shall dance there. ‡8163

Saul (*sawl*) See also PAUL; SAUL'S; SHAUL.
Ge 36: 37 and S' of Rehoboth by the river *7586
38 And S' died, and Baal-hanan the * "
1Sa 9: 2 he had a son, whose name was S', "
3 Kish said to S' his son, Take now "
5 S' said to his servant that was with"
7 said S' to his servant, But, behold, "
8 the servant answered S' again, and "
10 said S' to his servant, Well said; "
15 told Samuel...a day before S' came, "
17 when Samuel saw S', the Lord said"
18 S' drew near to Samuel in the gate, "
19 Samuel answered S', and said, I am"
21 S' answered and said, Am not I a "
22 Samuel took S' and his servant, "
24 was upon it, and set it before S'. "
24 So S' did eat with Samuel that day."
25 communed with S' upon the top of "
26 Samuel called S' to the top of the "
26 S' arose, and they went out both of "
27 Samuel said to S', Bid the servant "
10: 11, 12 Is S' also among the prophets? "
1Sa 10: 16 S' said unto his uncle, He told us 7586
21 and S' the son of Kish was taken: "
26 S' also went home to Gibeah; and "
11: 4 the messengers to Gibeah of S', "
5 S' came after the herd out of the "
5 S' said, What aileth the people that "
6 And the Spirit of God came upon S' "
7 cometh not forth after S' and after "
11 that S' put the people in three "
12 he that said, Shall S' reign over us?"
13 S' said, There shalt not a man be "
15 made S' king before the Lord in "
15 there S' and all the men of Israel "
13: 1 S' reigned one year; and when he "
2 S' chose him three thousand men "
2 two thousand were with S' in "
3 S' blew the trumpet throughout all"
4 S' had smitten a garrison of the "
4 called together after S' to Gilgal. "
7 As for S', he was yet in Gilgal, and "
9 And S' said, Bring hither a burnt "
10 and S' went out to meet him, that "
11 And S' said, Because I saw that the "
13 Samuel said to S', Thou hast done "
15 S' numbered the people that were "
16 S', and Jonathan his son, and the "
22 of the people that were with S' and "
22 with S' and with Jonathan his son "
14: 1 that Jonathan the son of S' said "
2 S' tarried in the uttermost part of "
16 the watchmen of S' in Gibeah of "
17 said S' unto the people that were "
18 S' said unto Ahiah, Bring hither "
19 while S' talked unto the priest, that"
19 S' said unto the priest, Withdraw "
20 And S' and all the people that were"
21 Israelites that were with S' and "
24 S' had adjured the people, saying, "
33 Then they told S', saying, Behold, "
34 S' said, Disperse yourselves among"
35 S' built an altar unto the Lord: the"
36 S' said, Let us go down after the "
37 S' asked counsel of God, Shall I go "
38 S' said, Draw ye near hither, all the"
40 the people said unto S', Do what "
41 S' said unto the Lord God of Israel,"
41 S' and Jonathan were taken: but "
42 And S' said, Cast lots between me "
43 S' said to Jonathan, Tell me what "
44 S' answered, God do so and more "
45 people said unto S', Shall Jonathan"
46 Then S' went up from following "
47 S' took the kingdom over Israel, "
49 the sons of S' were Jonathan, and "
51 And Kish was the father of S'; and"
52 the Philistines all the days of S': "
52 when S' saw any strong man, or any"
15: 1 Samuel also said unto S', The Lord "
4 S' gathered the people together, "
5 S' came to a city of Amalek, and "
6 And S' said unto the Kenites, Go, "
7 And S' smote the Amalekites from "
9 S' and the people spared Agag, and"
11 repenteth me that I have set up S' "
12 Samuel rose early to meet S' in "
12 Samuel, saying, S' came to Carmel,"
13 Samuel came to S': and S' said "
15 S' said, They have brought them "
16 Samuel said unto S', Stay, and I "
20 S' said unto Samuel, Yea, I have "
24 S' said unto Samuel, I have sinned:"
26 And Samuel said unto S', I will not"
31 So Samuel turned again after S'; "
31 and S' worshipped the Lord. "
34 and S' went up to his house "
34 up to his house to Gibeah of S'. "
35 And Samuel came no more to see S'"
35 Samuel mourned for S': and the "
35 repented that he had made S' king "
16: 1 How long wilt thou mourn for S', "
2 I go? if S' hear it, he will kill me. "
14 Spirit of the Lord departed from S',"
17 S' said unto his servants, Provide "
19 S' sent messengers unto Jesse, and"
20 sent them by David his son unto S'."
21 And David came to S', and stood "
22 S' sent to Jesse, saying, Let David, "
23 evil spirit from God was upon S', "
23 so S' was refreshed, and was well, "
17: 2 And S' and the men of Israel were "
8 a Philistine, and ye servants to S'? "
11 When S' and all Israel heard those "
12 for an old man in the days of S'. "
13 sons of Jesse went and followed S' "
14 and the three eldest followed S'. "
15 David went and returned from S' "
19 S', and they, and all the men of "
31 they rehearsed them before S': "
32 And David said to S', Let no man's"
33 S' said to David, Thou art not able "
34 David said unto S', Thy servant "
37 S' said unto David, Go, and the "
38 S' armed David with his armour, "
39 And David said unto S', I cannot go"
55 S' saw David go forth against the "
57 S' with the head of the Philistine "
58 S' said unto him, Whose son art "
18: 1 made an end of speaking unto S', "
2 S' took him that day, and would let"
5 David went...whithersoever S' sent"
5 S' set him over the men of war, "
6 singing...dancing, to meet king S', "
7 said, S' has slain his thousands, "
8 S' was very wroth, and the saying "
9 S' eyed David from that day and "
10 evil spirit from God came upon S', "

1Sa 18:11 S· cast the javelin; for he said, I 7586
12 S· was afraid of David, because the "
12 him, and was departed from S·. "
13 S· removed him from him, and "
15 S· saw that he behaved himself very "
17 S· said to David, Behold my elder "
17 S· said, Let not my hand be upon "
18 And David said unto S·, Who am I? "
20 they told S·, and the thing pleased "
21 S· said, I will give him her, that she "
21 S· said to David, Thou shalt this "
22 And S· commanded his servants, "
24 the servants of S· told him, saying, "
25 S· said, Thus shall ye say to David, "
25 S· thought to make David fall by "
27 S· gave him Michal his daughter to "
28 S· saw and knew that the Lord was "
29 S· was yet the more afraid of David; "
29 and S· became David's enemy "
30 wisely than all the servants of S·; "
19: 1 S· spake to Jonathan his son, and "
2 S· my father seeketh to kill thee: "
4 spake good of David unto S· his "
6 S· hearkened unto the voice of "
6 S· sware, As the Lord liveth, he "
7 Jonathan brought David to S·, and "
9 spirit from the Lord was upon S·, "
10 S· sought to smite David even to "
11 S·...sent messengers unto David's "
14 S· sent messengers to take David, "
15 S· sent the messengers again to "
17 S· said unto Michal, Why hast thou "
17 Michal answered S·, He said unto "
18 and told him all that S· had done to "
19 And it was told S·, saying, Behold, "
20 S· sent messengers to take David: "
20 was upon the messengers of S·, "
21 told S·, he sent other messengers, "
21 S· sent messengers...the third "
24 Is S· also among the prophets? "
20:26 S· spake not any thing that day: "
27 and S· said unto Jonathan his son, "
28 And Jonathan answered S·, David "
32 Jonathan answered S· his father, "
33 S· cast a javelin at him to smite "
21: 7 a certain man of the servants of S· "
7 of the herdmen that belonged to S·. "
10 and fled that day for fear of S·, and "
11 S. hath slain his thousands, and "
22: 6 S· heard that David was discovered, "
6 S· abode in Gibeah under a tree in "
7 S· said unto his servants that stood "
9 was set over the servants of S·, and "
12 And S· said, Hear now, thou son of "
13 And S· said unto him, Why have ye "
21 that S· had slain the Lord's priests. "
22 there, that he would surely tell S·: "
23: 7 told S· that David was come to "
7 S· said, God hath delivered him "
8 S· called all the people...to war, "
9 that S· secretly practised mischief "
10 that S· seeketh to come to Keilah, "
11 will S· come down, as thy servant "
12 and my men into the hand of S·? "
13 told S· that David was escaped "
14 S· sought him every day, but God "
15 that S· was come...to seek his life: "
17 hand of S· my father shall not find "
17 that also S· my father knoweth. "
19 Then came up the Ziphites to S· to "
21 S· said, Blessed be ye of the Lord; "
24 arose, and went to Ziph before S·: "
25 S·...and his men went to seek him. "
25 when S· heard that, he pursued "
26 And S· went on this side of the "
26 haste to get away for fear of S·; "
26 S· and his men compassed David "
27 there came a messenger unto S·, "
28 S· returned from pursuing after "
24: 1 S· was returned from following the "
2 S· took three thousand chosen men "
3 and S· went in to cover his feet: "
7 suffered them not to rise against S·. "
7 But S· rose up out of the cave, and "
8 cried after S·, saying, My lord the "
8 when S· looked behind him, David "
9 And David said to S·, Wherefore "
16 of speaking these words unto S·, "
16 S· said, Is this thy voice, my son "
16 S· lifted up his voice, and wept. "
22 sware unto S·. And S· went home; "
25:44 S· had given Michal his daughter, "
26: 1 Ziphites came unto S· to Gibeah, "
2 S· arose, and went down to the "
3 S· pitched in the hill of Hachilah, "
3 saw that S· came after him in the "
4 understood that S· was come in "
5 to the place where S· had pitched: "
5 and David beheld...where S· lay, "
5 S· lay in the trench, and the people "
6 go down with me to S· to the camp? "
7 S· lay sleeping within the trench, "
17 S· knew David's voice, and said, Is "
21 Then said S·, I have sinned: "
25 S· said to David, Blessed be thou, "
25 way, and S· returned to his place. "
27: 1 perish one day by the hand of S·: "
1 S· shall despair of me, to seek me "
4 was told S· that David was fled to "
28: 3 And S· had put away those that had "
4 and S· gathered all Israel together, "
5 S· saw the host of the Philistines, "
6 S· enquired of the Lord, the Lord "
7 Then said S· unto his servants, "
8 S· disguised himself, and put on "
9 thou knowest what S· hath done, "

1Sa 28:10 S· sware to her by the Lord, saying, 7586
12 the woman spake to S·, saying, "
12 thou deceived me? for thou art S·. "
13 woman said unto S·, I saw gods "
14 S· perceived that it was Samuel, "
15 Samuel said to S·, Why hast thou "
15 S· answered, I am sore distressed; "
20 S· fell straightway all along on the "
21 the woman came unto S·, and saw "
25 And she brought it before S·, and "
29: 3 Is not this David, the servant of S· "
5 S· slew his thousands, and David "
31: 2 Philistines followed hard upon S· "
3 the battle went sore against S·, "
4 said S· unto his armourbearer, "
4 S· took a sword, and fell upon it. "
5 armourbearer saw...S· was dead, "
6 So S· died, and his three sons, and "
7 and that S· and his sons were dead, "
8 found S· and his three sons fallen "
11 the Philistines had done to S·; "
12 took the body of S· and the bodies "
2Sa 1: 1 came to pass after the death of S·, "
2 a man came out of the camp from S· "
4 S· and Jonathan his son are dead "
5 S· and Jonathan his son be dead? "
6 behold, S· leaned upon his spear; "
12 fasted until even, for S·, and for "
17 with this lamentation over S· and "
21 is vilely cast away, the shield of S·, "
22 sword of S· returned not empty. "
23 S· and Jonathan were lovely and "
24 daughters of Israel, weep over S·, "
2: 4 were they that buried S·. "
5 shewed this kindness...unto S·, "
7 for your master S· is dead, and also "
8 took Ish-bosheth the son of S·, "
12 servants of Ish-bosheth...son of S·, "
15 pertained to Ish-bosheth...son of S·, "
3: 1 long war between the house of S· "
1 the house of S· waxed weaker and "
6 was war between the house of S· "
6 himself strong for the house of S·. "
7 S· had a concubine, whose name "
8 kindness...unto the house of S· "
10 the kingdom from the house of S·, "
4: 4 tidings came of S· and Jonathan "
8 head of Ish-bosheth the son of S· "
8 avenged my lord...this day of S·, "
10 told me, saying, Behold, S· is dead, "
5: 2 past, when S· was king over us, "
6:20 the daughter of S· came out to meet "
23 the daughter of S· had no child "
7:15 as I took it from S·, whom I put "
9: 1 any that is left of the house of S·, "
2 was of the house of S· a servant "
3 there not yet any of the house of S·, "
6 the son of Jonathan, the son of S·, "
7 restore thee all the land of S· thy "
9 master's son all that pertained to S· "
12: 7 delivered thee out of the hand of S·; "
16: 5 man of the family of the house of S·, "
8 all the blood of the house of S·, "
19:17 Ziba the servant of the house of S·, "
24 Mephibosheth son of S· came "
21: 1 It is for S·, and for his bloody house "
2 S· sought to slay them in his zeal "
4 will have no silver nor gold of S·, "
6 will hang them up in Gibeah of S·, "
7 the son of Jonathan the son of S·, "
7 David and Jonathan the son of S·. "
8 two sons...whom she bare unto S·, "
8 sons of Michal the daughter of S·, "
11 what Rizpah...the concubine of S·, "
12 David went and took the bones of S· "
12 Philistines had slain S· in Gilboa: "
13 up from thence the bones of S· and "
14 bones of S· and Jonathan his son "
22: 1 enemies, and out of the hand of S·: "
1Ch 5:10 in the days of S· they made war "
8:33 Ner begat Kish, and Kish begat S·, "
33 and S· begat Jonathan, and "
9:39 Ner begat Kish; and Kish begat S·; "
39 and S· begat Jonathan, and "
10: 2 Philistines followed hard after S·, "
2 and Malchi-shua, the sons of S·. "
3 And the battle went sore against S·, "
4 Then said S· to his armourbearer, "
4 So S· took a sword, and fell upon it. "
5 his armourbearer saw that S· was "
6 So S· died, and his three sons, and "
7 and that S· and his sons were dead, "
8 they found S· and his sons fallen "
11 that the Philistines had done to S·, "
12 men, and took away the body of S·, "
13 So S· died for his transgression "
11: 2 time past, even when S· was king, "
12: 1 kept himself close because of S· "
19 came with the Philistines against S· "
19 He will fall to his master S· to the "
23 to turn the kingdom of S· to him, "
29 of Benjamin, the kindred of S·, "
29 kept the ward of the house of S·. "
13: 3 enquired not at it in the days of S·. "
15:29 Michal the daughter of S· looking "
26:28 the seer, and S· the son of Kish, "
Ps 18: *title* enemies, and from the hand of S·: "
52: *title* the Edomite came and told S·, "
54: *title* the Ziphims came and said to S·, "
57: *title* when he fled from S· in the cave. "
59: *title* when S· sent, and they watched "
Isa 10:29 is afraid; Gibeah of S· is fled. "
Ac 7:58 man's feet, whose name was S·. *4569*
8: 1 S· was consenting unto his death. "
3 As for S·, he made havock of the "
9: 1 S·, yet breathing out threatenings "

Ac 9: 4 S·, S·, why persecutest thou me? *4569*
8 And S· arose from the earth; and "
11 house of Judas for one called S·, "
17 Brother S·, the Lord, even Jesus, "
19 S· certain days with the disciples* "
22 S· increased the more in strength, "
24 their laying await was known of S·. "
26 when S· was come to Jerusalem, * "
11:25 Barnabas to Tarsus, for to seek S·: "
30 by the hands of Barnabas and S·. "
12:25 and S· returned from Jerusalem, "
13: 1 up with Herod the tetrarch, and S·. "
2 Separate me Barnabas and S· for "
7 who called for Barnabas and S·, "
9 Then S·, (who also is called Paul,) "
21 gave unto them S· the son of Cis, "
22: 7 S·, S·, why persecutest thou me? "
13 me, Brother S·, receive thy sight. "
26:14 S·, S·, why persecutest thou me? "

Saul's (*sawls*)
1Sa 9: 3 asses of Kish S· father were lost. 7586
10:14 S· uncle said unto him and to his "
15 S· uncle said, Tell me, I pray thee, "
14:50 the name of S· wife was Ahinoam, "
50 was Abner, the son of Ner, S· uncle. "
16:15 S· servants said unto him, Behold "
18: 5 and also in the sight of S· servants. "
10 and there was a javelin in S· hand.* "
19 S· daughter should have been given "
20 Michal S· daughter loved David: "
23 S· servants spake those words in "
28 that Michal S· daughter loved him. "
19: 2 Jonathan S· son delighted much in "
10 he slipped away out of S· presence, "
20:25 and Abner sat by S· side, and "
30 Then S· anger was kindled against "
23:16 Jonathan S· son arose, and went to "
24: 4 and cut off the skirt of S· robe "
5 because he had cut off S· skirt. "
26:12 the cruse of water from S· bolster; "
31: 2 and Melchi-shua, S· sons. * "
2Sa 2: 8 But Abner...captain of S· host, "
10 Ish-bosheth S· son was forty years "
3:13 thou first bring Michal S· daughter, "
14 messengers to Ish-bosheth S· son, "
4: 1 S· son heard that Abner was dead "
2 And S· son had two men that were "
4 Jonathan, S· son, had a son...lame "
6:16 Michal S· daughter looked through* "
9: 9 the king called to Ziba, S· servant, "
1Ch 12: 2 even of S· brethren of Benjamin. "

save See also SAVED; SAVEST; SAVETH; SAVING.
Ge 12:12 kill me, but they will s· thee alive. 2421
14:24 S· only that which the young men 1107
39: 6 s· the bread which he did eat. 3588,518
45: 7 and to s· your lives by a great 2421
50:20 is this day, to s· much people alive. "
Ex 1:22 and every daughter ye shall s· alive. "
12:16 s· that which every man must eat, 389
22:20 any god, s· unto the Lord only, 1115
Nu 14:30 s· Caleb the son of Jephunneh, 3588,518
26:65 s· Caleb the son of Jephunneh, " "
32:12 S· Caleb the son of Jephunneh " "
De 1:36 S· Caleb the son of Jephunneh; 2108
15: 4 S· when there shall be no poor * 657
20: 4 against your enemies, to s· you. 3467
16 s· alive nothing that breatheth: 2421
22:27 cried, and there was none to s· her. 3467
28:29 evermore, and no man shall s· thee. "
Jos 2:13 that ye will s· alive my father, 2421
10: 6 come up to us quickly, and s· us, 3467
11:13 burned none of them, s· Hazor 2108
19 s· the Hivites the inhabitants of 1115
14: 4 in the land, s· cities to dwell in, 3588,518
22:22 the Lord, (s· us not this day,) 3467
J'g 6:14 shalt s· Israel from the hand of the "
15 Lord, wherewith shall I s· Israel? "
31 ye plead for Baal? will ye s· him? "
36, 37 thou wilt s· Israel by mine hand, "
7: 7 men that lapped will I s· you, and "
14 else s· the sword of Gideon 1115,518
1Sa 4: 3 it may s· us out of the hand of our 3467
7: 8 that he will s· us out of the hand of "
9:16 he may s· my people out of the hand "
10:24 shouted, and said, God s· the king. 2421
27 said, How shall this man s· us? 3467
11: 3 and then, if there be no man to s· us, "
14: 6 is no restraint to the Lord to s· by "
19:11 If thou s· not thy life to night, 4422
21: 9 for there is no other s· that here. 2108
23: 2 smite...Philistines, and s· Keilah. 3467
30:17 s· four hundred young men, 3588,518
22 s· to every man his wife and his " "
2Sa 3:18 servant David I will s· my people 3467
12: 3 nothing, s· one little ewe lamb, 3588,518
16:16 God s· the king, God s· the king. ‡2421
22:28 the afflicted people thou wilt s·: 3467
32 For who is God, s· the Lord? and 1107
32 and who is a rock, s· our God? "
42 looked, but there was none to s·; 3467
1Ki 1:12 thou mayest s· thine own life, and 4422
25 and say, God s· king Adonijah. ‡2421
34 and say, God s· king Solomon. ‡ "
39 people said, God s· king Solomon. ‡ "
3:18 the house, s· we two in the house. 2108
8: 9 the ark s· the two tables of stone, 7535
15: 5 s· only in the matter of Uriah the
18: 5 to s· the horses and mules alive, 2421
20:31 peradventure he will s· thy life. "
22:31 s· only with the king of Israel. 3588,518
2Ki 7: 4 if they s· us alive, we shall live; 2421
11:12 hands, and said, God s· the king. ‡ "
15: 4 S· that the high places were not *7535
16: 7 s· me out of the hand of the king 3467
19:19 s· thou us out of his hand, that all "

2Ki 19:34 I will defend this city, to s· it, for 3467
24:14 s· the poorest sort of the people of 2108
1Ch 16:35 ye, S· us, O God of our salvation, 3467
2Ch 2: 6 s· only to burn sacrifice before him? 518
5:10 nothing in the ark s· the two tables 7535
18:30 s· only with the king of Israel. 3588, 518
23: 6 house of the Lord, s· the priests, "
11 him, and said, God s· the king. ‡2421
Ne 2:12 s· the beast that I rode upon. 3588, 518
6:11 go into the temple to s· his life? 2425
Job 2: 6 he is in thine hand; but s· his life.*8104
20:20 not s· of that which he desired. 4422
22:29 and he shall s· the humble person. 3467
40:14 thine own right hand can s· thee. "
Ps 3: 7 s· me, O my God: for thou hast "
6: 4 soul: oh s· me for thy mercies' sake. "
7: 1 s· me from all them that persecute "
18:27 thou wilt s· the afflicted people; but "
31 For who is God s· the Lord? 1107
31 or who is a rock s· our God? *2108
41 but there was none to s· them: 3467
20: 9 S·, Lord: let the king hear us when "
22:21 S· me from the lion's mouth: for "
28: 9 S· thy people, and bless thine "
31: 2 for an house of defence to s· me. "
16 s· me for thy mercies' sake. "
37:40 them from the wicked, and s· them,* "
44: 3 neither did their own arm s· them: "
6 bow, neither shall my sword s· me. "
54: 1 S· me, O God, by thy name, and "
55:16 upon God; and the Lord shall s· me. "
57: 3 and s· me from the reproach of him "
59: 2 and s· me from bloody men. "
60: 5 s· with thy right hand, and hear "
69: 1 S· me, O God; for the waters are "
35 For God will s· Zion, and will build "
71: 2 thine ear unto me, and s· me. "
3 hast given commandment to s· me; "
72: 4 he shall s· the children of the needy, "
13 and shall s· the souls of the needy. "
76: 9 to s· all the meek of the earth. "
80: 2 thy strength, and come and s· us. 3444
86: 2 s· thy servant that trusteth in 3467
16 and s· the son of thine handmaid. "
106:47 S· us, O Lord our God, and gather "
108: 6 s· with thy right hand, and answer "
109:26 O s· me according to thy mercy: "
31 to s· him from those that condemn "
118:25 S· now, I beseech thee, O Lord: "
119:94 I am thine, s· me; for I have "
146 cried unto thee; s· me, and I shall "
138: 7 and thy right hand shall s· me. "
145:19 hear their cry, and will s· them. "
Pr 20:22 on the Lord, and he shall s· thee. "
Isa 25: 9 waited for him, and he will s· us: "
33:22 the Lord is our king; he will s· us. "
35: 4 your God...will come and s· you. "
37:20 Lord our God, s· us from his hand, "
35 For I will defend this city to s· it "
38:20 The Lord was ready to s· me: "
45:20 and pray unto a god that cannot s·. "
46: 7 nor s· him out of his trouble. "
47:13 s· thee from these things that shall "
15 to his quarter; none shall s· thee. "
49:25 with thee, and I will s· thy children. "
59: 1 is not shortened, that it cannot s·; "
63: 1 in righteousness, mighty to s·. "
Jer 2:27 they will say, Arise, and s· us. "
28 s· thee in the time of thy trouble: "
11:12 shall not s· them at all in the time "
14: 9 as a mighty man that cannot s·? "
15:20 for I am with thee to s· thee and to "
17:14 s· me, and I shall be saved: for thou "
30:10 for, lo, I will s· thee from afar, and "
11 with thee, saith the Lord, to s· thee: "
31: 7 s· thy people, the remnant of Israel. "
42:11 for I am with you to s· you, and to "
46:27 I will s· thee from afar off, and thy "
48: 6 Flee, s· your lives, and be like the 4422
La 4:17 for a nation that could not s· us. 3467
Eze 3:18 from his wicked way, to s· his life; 2421
13:18 will ye s· the souls alive that come "
19 to s· the souls alive that should not "
18:27 and right, he shall s· his soul alive. "
34:22 Therefore will I s· my flock, and 3467
36:29 I will also s· you from all your "
37:23 but I will s· them out of all their "
Da 6: 7 s· of thee, O king, he shall be cast 3861
12 s· of thee, O king, shall be cast "
Ho 1: 7 will s· them by the Lord their God, 3467
7 and will not s· them by bow, nor by "
13:10 that may s· thee in all thy cities? "
14: 3 Asshur shall not s· us; we will not "
Hab 1: 2 of violence, and thou wilt not s·! "
Zep 3:17 he will s·, he will rejoice over thee "
19 and I will s· her that halteth, and "
Zec 8: 7 I will s· my people from the east "
13 so will I s· you, and ye shall be a "
9:16 the Lord their God shall s· them in "
10: 6 I will s· the house of Joseph, and I "
12: 7 Lord also shall s· the tents of Judah "
M't 1:21 shall s· his people from their sins. 4982
8:25 him, saying, Lord, s· us: we perish. "
11:27 any man the Father, s· the Son, 1508
13:57 honour, s· in his own country, and "
14:30 sink, he cried, saying, Lord, s· me. 4982
16:25 whosoever will s· his life shall lose "
17: 8 they saw no man, s· Jesus only. 1508
18:11 is come to s· that which was lost. *4982
19:11 saying, s· they to whom it is given.*235
27:40 buildest it in three days, s· thyself. 4982
42 saved others; himself he cannot s·. "
49 whether Elias will come to s· him. "
M'r 3: 4 or to do evil? to s· life, or to kill? "
5:37 no man to follow him, s· Peter, and 1508
6: 5 s· that he laid his hands upon a few "
M'r 6: 8 for their journey, s· a staff only; 1508
8:35 whosoever will s· his life shall lose 4982
35 the gospel's, the same shall s· it. "
9: 8 saw no man any more, s· Jesus only 235
15:30 S· thyself, and come down from 4982
31 saved others; himself he cannot s·. "
Lu 4:26 s· unto Sarepta, a city of Sidon, *1508
6: 9 do evil? to s· life, or to destroy it? 4982
8:51 suffered no man to go in, s· Peter, 1508
9:24 whosoever will s· his life shall lose 4982
24 for my sake, the same shall s· it. "
56 destroy men's lives, but to s· them. "
17:18 give glory to God, s· this stranger. 1508
33 shall seek to s· his life shall lose it;*4982
18:19 none is good, s· one, that is, God. 1508
19:10 seek and to s· that which was lost. 4982
23:35 let him s· himself, if he be Christ, "
37 be the king of the Jews, s· thyself. "
39 If thou be Christ, s· thyself and us. "
Joh 6:22 s· that one whereinto his disciples 1508
46 s· he which is of God, he hath seen "
12:27 Father, s· me from this hour: but 4982
47 judge the world, but to s· the world. "
13:10 needeth not s· to wash his feet, but 2228
Ac 2:40 S· yourselves from this untoward 4982
20:23 S· that the Holy Ghost witnesseth 4133
21:25 s· only that they keep themselves*1508
27:43 the centurion, willing to s· Paul, 1295
Ro 11:14 flesh, and might s· some of them. 4982
1Co 1:21 preaching to s· them that believe. "
2: 2 s· Jesus Christ, and him crucified. 1508
11 s· the spirit of man which is in him? "
7:16 whether thou shalt s· thy husband? 4982
16 whether thou shalt s· thy wife? "
9:22 that I might by all means s· some. "
2Co 11:24 received I forty stripes s· one. 3844
Ga 1:19 none, s· James the Lord's brother. 1508
6:14 s· in the cross of our Lord Jesus "
1Ti 1:15 came into the world to s· sinners; 4982
4:16 thou shalt both s· thyself, and them "
Heb 5: 7 that was able to s· him from death, "
7:25 also to s· them to the uttermost "
Jas 1:21 word, which is able to s· your souls. "
2:14 have not works? can faith s· him? "
4:12 who is able to s· and to destroy: who "
5:15 the prayer of faith shall s· the sick, "
20 his way shall s· a soul from death, "
1Pe 3:21 even baptism doth also now s· us "
Jude 23 others s· with fear, pulling them "
Re 13:17 or sell, s· he that had the mark, 1508

saved
Ge 47:25 Thou hast s· our lives: let us find "
Ex 1:17 but s· the men children alive. 2421
18 and have s· the men children alive? "
14:30 the Lord s· Israel that day out of 3467
Nu 10: 9 ye shall be s· from your enemies. "
22:33 I had slain thee, and s· her alive. 2421
31:15 Have ye s· all the women alive? "
De 33:29 O people s· by the Lord, the shield 3467
Jos 6:25 Joshua s· Rahab the harlot alive, *2421
J'g 7: 2 saying, Mine own hand hath s· me. 3467
8:19 if ye had s· them alive, I would not 2421
21:14 them wives which they had s· alive "
1Sa 10:19 s· you out of all your adversities *3467
14:23 So the Lord s· Israel that day: and "
23: 5 David s· the inhabitants of Keilah. "
27:11 David s· neither man nor woman 2421
2Sa 19: 5 which this day have s· thy life, 4422
9 king s· us out of the hand of our *5337
22: 4 shall I be s· from mine enemies. 3467
2Ki 6:10 and s· himself there, not once nor 8104
14:27 s· them by the hand of Jeroboam 3467
1Ch 11:14 s· them by a great deliverance. "
2Ch 32:22 Thus the Lord s· Hezekiah and the "
Ne 9:27 who s· them out of the hand of their "
Ps 18: 3 shall I be s· from mine enemies. "
33:16 is no king s· by the multitude of "
34: 6 and s· him out of all his troubles. "
44: 7 thou hast s· us from our enemies, "
80: 3 face to shine; and we shall be s·. "
7, 19 to shine; and we shall be s·. "
106: 8 he s· them for his name's sake, "
10 he s· them from the hand of him "
107:13 he s· them out of their distresses. "
Pr 28:18 walketh uprightly shall be s·: but* "
Isa 30:15 returning and rest shall ye be s·; "
43:12 I have declared, and have s·, and "
45:17 But Israel shall be s· in the Lord "
22 Look unto me, and be ye s·, all the "
63: 9 the angel of his presence s· them: "
64: 5 is continuance, and we shall be s·. "
Jer 4:14 wickedness, that thou mayest be s·. "
8:20 summer is ended, and we are not s·. "
17:14 save me, and I shall be s·: for thou "
23: 6 In his days Judah shall be s·, and "
30: 7 trouble; but he shall be s· out of it. "
33:16 In those days shall Judah be s·, "
M't 10:22 endureth to the end shall be s·. 4982
19:25 amazed, saying, Who then can be s·? "
24:13 unto the end, the same shall be s·. "
22 there should no flesh be s·: but for "
27:42 He s· others; himself he cannot "
M'r 10:26 themselves, Who then can be s·? "
13:13 unto the end, the same shall be s·. "
20 those days, no flesh should be s·: "
15:31 He s· others; himself he cannot "
16:16 believeth and is baptized shall be s·; "
Lu 1:71 we should be s· from our enemies,*4991
7:50 Thy faith hath s· thee; go in peace. 4982
8:12 lest they should believe and be s·. "
13:23 him, Lord, are there few that be s·? "
18:26 heard it said, Who then can be s·? "
42 thy sight: thy faith hath s· thee. * "
23:35 He s· others; let him save himself, "
Joh 3:17 the world through him might be s·. "
5:34 things I say, that ye might be s·. "
Joh 10: 9 if any man enter in, he shall be s·, 4982
Ac 2:21 on the name of the Lord shall be s·. "
47 church daily such as should be s·. "
4:12 among men, whereby we must be s·. "
11:14 thou and all thy house shall be s·. "
15: 1 manner of Moses, ye cannot be s·. "
11 the grace of...Christ we shall be s·, "
16:30 said, Sirs, what must I do to be s·? "
31 thou shalt be s·, and thy house. "
27:20 all hope that we should be s· was "
31 abide in the ship, ye cannot be s·. "
Ro 5: 9 shall be s· from wrath through him. "
10 reconciled, we shall be s· by his life. "
8:24 For we are s· by hope: but hope "
9:27 of the sea, a remnant shall be s·: "
10: 1 Israel is, that they might be s·. 4991
9 from the dead, thou shalt be s·. 4982
13 the name of the Lord shall be s·. "
11:26 And so all Israel shall be s·: as it "
1Co 1:18 unto us which are s· it is the power "
3:15 but he himself shall be s·; yet so "
5: 5 the spirit may be s· in the day of "
10:33 profit of many, that they may be s·. "
15: 2 By which also ye are s·, if ye keep "
2Co 2:15 in them that are s·, and in them "
Eph 2: 5 with Christ, (by grace ye are s·;) "
8 by grace are ye s· through faith; "
1Th 2:16 the Gentiles that they might be s·, "
2Th 2:10 of the truth, that they might be s·. "
1Ti 2: 4 Who will have all men to be s·, and "
15 she shall be s· in childbearing, if "
2Ti 1: 9 Who hath s· us, and called us with "
Tit 3: 5 but according to his mercy he s· us, "
1Pe 3:20 is, eight souls were s· by water. 1295
4:18 And if the righteous scarcely be s·, 4982
2Pe 2: 5 but s· Noah the eighth person, a *5442
Jude 5 s· the people out of the land of 4982
Re 21:24 which are s· shall walk in the light* "

savest
2Sa 22: 3 saviour; thou s· me from violence. 3467
Job 26: 2 how s· thou the arm that hath no * "
Ps 17: 7 O thou that s· by thy right hand "

saveth
1Sa 14:39 the Lord liveth, which s· Israel, 3467
17:47 Lord s· not with sword and spear: "
Job 5:15 he s· the poor from the sword, from "
Ps 7:10 God, which s· the upright in heart. "
20: 6 I that the Lord s· his anointed; "
34:18 s· such as be of a contrite spirit. "
107:19 he s· them out of their distresses. "

saving
Ge 19:19 hast shewed unto me in s· my life; 2421
Ne 4:23 s· that every one put them off for *
Ps 20: 6 the s· strength of his right hand. 3468
28: 8 the s· strength of his anointed. 3444
67: 2 the s· health among all nations. * "
Ec 5:11 s· the beholding of them with their 518
Am 9: 8 s· that I will not utterly destroy 657
M't 5:32 s· for the cause of fornication, 3924
Lu 4:27 cleansed, s· Naaman the Syrian. *1508
Heb 10:39 that believe to the s· of the soul. 4047
11: 7 an ark to the s· of his house; by 4991
Re 2:17 knoweth s· he that receiveth it. 1508

saviour See also SAVIOURS.
2Sa 22: 3 tower, and my refuge, my s·; 3467
2Ki 13: 5 (And the Lord gave Israel a s·, so "
Ps 106:21 They forgat God their s·, which had "
Isa 19:20 he shall send them a s·, and a great "
43: 3 God, the Holy One of Israel, thy S·: "
11 Lord; and beside me there is no s·. "
45:15 thyself, O God of Israel, the S·. "
21 a just God and a S·; there is none "
49:26 know that I the Lord am thy S· and "
60:16 know that I the Lord am thy S· and "
63: 8 that will not lie: so he was their S·. "
Jer 14: 8 the s· thereof in time of trouble, "
Ho 13: 4 me: for there is no s· beside me. "
Lu 1:47 spirit hath rejoiced in God my S·. 4990
2:11 this day in the city of David a S·, "
Joh 4:42 the Christ, the S· of the world. "
Ac 5:31 right hand to be a Prince and a S·, "
13:23 his promise raised unto Israel a S·, "
Eph 5:23 church: and he is the s· of the body. "
Ph'p 3:20 we look for the S·, the Lord Jesus "
1Ti 1: 1 the commandment of God our S·, "
2: 3 acceptable in the sight of...our S·; "
4:10 God, who is the S· of all men, "
2Ti 1:10 appearing of our S· Jesus Christ, "
Tit 1: 3 the commandment of God our S·; "
4 and the Lord Jesus Christ our S·. "
2:10 the doctrine of God our S· in all "
13 great God and our S· Jesus Christ, "
3: 4 and love of God our S· toward man "
6 through Jesus Christ our S·; "
2Pe 1: 1 righteousness of God and our S· "
11 kingdom of our Lord and S· Jesus "
2:20 the knowledge of the Lord and S· "
3: 2 us the apostles of the Lord and S·: "
18 the knowledge of our Lord and S· "
1Jo 4:14 Father sent the Son to be the S· of "
Jude 25 To the only wise God our S·, be "

saviours
Ne 9:27 mercies thou gavest them s·, who 3467
Ob 21 s· shall come up on mount Zion to "

savour See also SAVOUREST; SAVOURS.
Ge 8:21 And the Lord smelled a sweet s·; 7381
Ex 5:21 ye have made our s· to be abhorred "
29:18 it is a sweet s·, an offering made by "
25 for a sweet s· before the Lord: "
41 for a sweet s·, an offering made by "
Le 1: 9, 13, 17 of a sweet s· unto the Lord. "
2: 2 by fire, of a sweet s· unto the Lord: "
9 by fire, of a sweet s· unto the Lord. "

Le 2:12 be burnt on the altar for a sweet s'.7381
3: 5 by fire, of a sweet s' unto the Lord. "
16 offering made by fire for a sweet s': "
4:31 altar for a sweet s' unto the Lord; "
6:15 burn it upon the altar for a sweet s', "
21 offer for a sweet s' unto the Lord. "
8:21 was a burnt sacrifice for a sweet s', "
28 were consecrations for a sweet s': "
17: 6 the fat for a sweet s' unto the Lord. "
23:13 by fire unto the Lord for a sweet s': "
18 by fire, of sweet s' unto the Lord. "
26:31 smell the s' of your sweet odours. "
Nu 15: 3 to make a sweet s' unto the Lord, "
7 wine, for a sweet s' unto the Lord. "
10, 13 fire, of a sweet s' unto the Lord. "
14 by fire, of a sweet s' unto the Lord; "
24 for a sweet s' unto the Lord, with "
18:17 by fire, for a sweet s' unto the Lord. "
28: 2 made by fire, for a sweet s' unto me. "
6 in mount Sinai for a sweet s', "
8 by fire, of a sweet s' unto the Lord. "
13 for a burnt offering of a sweet s', a "
24 by fire, of a sweet s' unto the Lord: "
27 offering for a sweet s' unto the Lord; "
29: 2 offering for a sweet s' unto the Lord; "
6 for a sweet s', a sacrifice made by "
8 offering unto the Lord for a sweet s'; "
13 by fire, of a sweet s' unto the Lord; "
36 by fire, of a sweet s' unto the Lord: "
Ec 10: 1 apothecary to send...a stinking s': * "
Ca 1: 3 of the s' of thy good ointments * "
Eze 6:13 did offer sweet s' to all their idols. "
16:19 set it before them for a sweet s': "
20:28 there also they made their sweet s', "
41 I will accept you with your sweet s', "
Joe 2:20 and his ill s' shall come up, 6709
M't 5:13 but if the salt have lost his s', 3471
Lu 14:34 but if the salt have lost his s', "
2Co 2:14 manifest the s' of his knowledge 3744
15 are unto God a sweet s' of Christ, 2175
16 we are the s' of death unto death; 3744
16 to the other the s' of life unto life. "
Eph 5: 2 to God for a sweetsmelling s'. * "

savourest
M't 16:23 s' not the things that be of God, *5426
M'r 8:33 s' not the things that be of God. * "

savours
Ezr 6:10 sweet s' unto the God of heaven, *5208

savoury See also UNSAVOURY.
Ge 27: 4 make me s' meat, such as I love, 4303
7 me venison, and make me s' meat, "
9 I will make...s' meat for thy father, "
14 his mother made s' meat, such as "
17 she gave the s' meat and the bread, "
31 And he also had made s' meat, and "

saw See also FORESAW; SAWED; SAWEST; SAWN; SAWS.
Ge 1: 4 God s' the light, that it was good: 7200
10, 12, 18, 21, 25 God s' that it was good. "
31 God s' every thing that he had made, "
3: 6 woman s' that the tree was good "
6: 2 the sons of God s' the daughters of "
5 God s' that the wickedness of man "
9:22 s' the nakedness of his father, "
23 they s' not their father's nakedness. "
12:15 The princes also of Pharaoh s' her, "
16: 4, 5 she s' that she had conceived, "
18: 2 and when he s' them, he ran to meet "
21: 9 And Sarah s' the son of Hagar the "
19 her eyes, and she s' a well of water; "
22: 4 up his eyes, and s' the place afar off. "
24:30 when he s' the earring and bracelets "
63 and he lifted up his eyes, and s', "
64 when she s' Isaac, she lighted off "
26: 8 looked out at a window, and s', and "
28 We s' certainly...the Lord was with "
28: 6 When Esau s' that Isaac had blessed "
29:10 when Jacob s' Rachel the daughter "
31 the Lord s' that Leah was hated, "
30: 1 Rachel s' that she bare Jacob no "
9 Leah s' that she had left bearing, "
31:10 up mine eyes, and s' in a dream, "
32: 2 And when Jacob s' them, he said, "
25 he s' that he prevailed not against "
33: 5 and s' the women and the children; "
34: 2 Shechem...s' her, he took her, and "
37: 4 s' that their father loved him more "
18 And when they s' him afar off, even "
38: 2 Judah s'...a daughter of a certain "
14 for she s' that Shelah was grown, "
15 When Judah s' her, he thought her "
39: 3 his master s' that the Lord was with "
13 she s' that he had left his garment "
40:16 chief baker s' that the interpretation "
41:19 as I never s' in all the land of Egypt "
22 And I s' in my dream, and, behold, "
42: 1 when Jacob s' that there was corn "
7 And Joseph s' his brethren, and he "
21 in that we s' the anguish of his soul, "
35 their father s' the bundles of money, "
43:16 when Joseph s' Benjamin with them, "
29 eyes, and s' his brother Benjamin, "
44:28 in pieces; and I s' him not since: * "
45:27 he s' the wagons which Joseph had "
48:17 when Joseph s' that his father laid "
49:15 And he s' that rest was good, and "
50:11 s' the mourning in the floor of Atad, "
15 s' that their father was dead, they "
23 And Joseph s' Ephraim's children "
Ex 2: 2 when she s' him that he was a goodly "
5 when she s' the ark among the flags, "
6 she had opened it, she s' the child: "
12 when he s' that there was no man, "
3: 4 Lord s' that he turned aside to see, "

Ex 8:15 Pharaoh s' that there was respite, 7200
9:34 when Pharaoh s' that the rain and "
10:23 They s' not one another, neither "
14:30 and Israel s' the Egyptians dead "
31 And Israel s' that great work which "
16:15 when the children of Israel s' it, "
18:14 And when Moses' father in law s' all "
20:18 all the people s' the thunderings, "
18 when the people s' it, they removed, "
24:10 And they s' the God of Israel: and "
11 they s' God, and did eat and drink.2372
32: 1 the people s' that Moses delayed 7200
5 when Aaron s' it, he built an altar "
19 that he s' the calf, and the dancing: "
25 Moses s' that the people were naked; "
33:10 all the people s' the cloudy pillar "
34:30 all the children of Israel s' Moses, "
35 children of Israel s'...face of Moses, "
Le 9:24 when all the people s', they shouted, "
Nu 13:28 we s' the children of Anak there. "
32 people that we s' in it are men of a "
33 we s' the giants, the sons of Anak, "
20:29 congregation s'...Aaron was dead, "
22: 2 Balak...s' all that Israel had done "
23 And the ass s' the angel of the Lord "
25, 27 the ass s' the angel of the Lord, "
31 and he s' the angel of the Lord "
33 And the ass s' me, and turned from "
24: 1 Balaam s' that it pleased the Lord "
2 and he s' Israel abiding in his tents "
4, 16 s' the vision of the Almighty, *2372
25: 7 the son of Aaron the priest, s' it, 7200
32: 1 and when they s' the land of Jazer, "
9 valley of Eshcol, and s' the land, "
De 1:19 terrible wilderness, which ye s' by "
4:12 of the words, but s' no similitude; "
15 for ye s' no manner of similitude on "
7:19 temptations which thine eyes s', "
32:19 when the Lord s' it, he abhorred "
Jos 7:21 I s' among the spoils a goodly "
8:14 when the king of Ai s' it, that they "
20 they s', and, behold, the smoke of "
21 Israel s' that the ambush had taken "
J'g 1:24 the spies s' a man come forth out of "
3:24 when they s' that, behold, the doors "
9:36 when Gaal s' the people, he said to "
55 the men of Israel s' that Abimelech "
11:35 when he s' her, that he rent his "
12: 3 when I s' that ye delivered me not, "
14: 1 and s' a woman in Timnath of the "
11 when they s' him, that they brought "
16: 1 to Gaza, and s' there an harlot, and "
18 when Delilah s' that he had told all "
24 And when the people s' him, they "
18: 7 s' the people that were therein, how "
26 Micah s' that they were too strong "
19: 3 the father of the damsel s' him, he "
17 he s' a wayfaring man in the street "
30 all that s' it said, There was no "
20:36 of Benjamin s'...they were smitten: "
41 s' that evil was come upon them. "
Ru 1:18 s' that she was stedfastly minded "
2:18 mother in law s' what she...gleaned: "
1Sa 5: 7 the men of Ashdod s' that it was so, "
6:13 lifted up their eyes, and s' the ark, "
9:17 And when Samuel s' Saul, the Lord "
10:11 that knew him beforetime s' that, "
14 when we s' that they were no where, "
12:12 when ye s' that Nahash the king of "
13: 6 men of Israel s' that they were in a "
11 I s' that the people were scattered "
14:52 and when Saul s' any strong man, "
17:24 when they s' the man, fled from "
42 Philistine looked about,...s' David, "
51 Philistines s' their champion was "
55 Saul s' David go forth against the "
18:15 Saul s' that he behaved himself "
28 Saul s' and knew that the Lord was "
19:20 they s' the company of the prophets "
22: 9 s' the son of Jesse coming to Nob, "
23:15 David s' that Saul was come out to "
25:23 when Abigail s' David, she hasted, "
25 I thine handmaid s' not the young "
26: 3 he s' that Saul came after him into "
12 no man s' it, or knew it, neither "
28: 5 Saul s' the host of the Philistines, "
12 when the woman s' Samuel, she "
13 I s' gods ascending out of the * "
21 and s' that he was sore troubled, "
31: 5 armourbearer s'...Saul was dead, "
7 s' that the men of Israel fled, and "
2Sa 1: 7 he looked behind him, he s' me, "
6:16 s' king David leaping and dancing "
10: 6 s' that they stank before David, "
9 Joab s' that the front of the battle "
14 Ammon s'...the Syrians were fled, "
15 Syrians s' that they were smitten "
19 servants to Hadarezer s' that they "
11: 2 he s' a woman washing herself; "
12:19 when David s' that his servants "
14:24, 28 and s' not the king's face. "
17:18 Nevertheless a lad s' them, and told "
23 s' that his counsel was not followed, "
18:10 a certain man s' it, and told Joab, "
10 I s' Absalom hanged in an oak. "
26 watchman s' another man running: "
29 I s' a great tumult, but I knew not "
20:12 when the man s' that all the people "
12 s' that every one that came by him "
24:17 s' the angel that smote the people, "
20 the king and his servants coming "
1Ki 3:28 s' that the wisdom of God was in "
12:16 Israel s' that the king hearkened "
13:25 and s' the carcase cast in the way, "
16:18 Zimri s' that the city was taken, "
18:17 when Ahab s' Elijah, that Ahab "

1Ki 18:39 when all the people s' it, they fell 7200
19: 3 when he s' that, he arose, and went "
22:17 I s' all Israel scattered upon the "
19 I s' the Lord sitting on his throne, "
32 the captains of the chariots s' "
2Ki 2:12 And Elisha s' it, and he cried, My "
12 he s' him no more: and he took "
15 were to view at Jericho s' him, "
3:22 s' the water on the other side as red "
26 of Moab s' that the battle was too "
4:25 when the man of God s' her afar off, "
5:21 Naaman s' him running after him, "
6:17 eyes of the young man; and he s': "
20 Lord opened their eyes, and they s'; "
21 said unto Elisha, when he s' them, "
9:22 when Joram s' Jehu, that he said, "
27 Ahaziah the king of Judah s' this, "
11: 1 s' that her son was dead, she arose "
12:10 they s' that there was much money "
13: 4 for he s' the oppression of Israel, "
14:26 the Lord s' the affliction of Israel, "
16:10 s' an altar that was at Damascus: "
12 Damascus, the king s' the altar: "
1Ch 10: 5 armourbearer s'...Saul was dead, "
7 were in the valley s' that they fled, "
15:29 window s' king David dancing and "
19: 6 the children of Ammon s' that they "
10 Now when Joab s' that the battle "
15 Ammon s'...the Syrians were fled, "
16 Syrians s' that they were put to the "
19 servants of Hadarezer s' that they "
21:16 and s' the angel of the Lord stand "
20 Ornan turned back, and s' the angel; "
21 Ornan, Ornan looked and s' David, "
28 when David s' that the Lord had "
2Ch 7: 3 children of Israel s' how the fire * "
10:16 s' that the king would not hearken "
12: 7 the Lord s' that they humbled "
15: 9 s' that the Lord his God was with "
18:18 s' the Lord sitting upon his throne, "
31 of the chariots s' Jehoshaphat, "
22:10 Ahaziah s' that her son was dead, "
24:11 they s' that there was much money, "
25:21 they s' one another in the face, * "
31: 8 the princes came and s' the heaps, "
32: 2 Hezekiah s' that Sennacherib was "
Ne 6:16 heathen that were about us s' these* "
13:15 days s' I in Judah some treading "
23 s' I Jews that had married wives of "
Es 1:14 the king's face, and which sat "
3: 5 Haman s' that Mordecai bowed not, "
5: 2 when the king s' Esther the queen "
9 Haman s' Mordecai in the king's "
7: 7 s' that there was evil determined "
Job 2:13 s' that his grief was very great. "
3:16 as infants which never s' light. "
20: 9 eye...which s' him shall see him 7805
29: 8 The young men s' me, and hid 7200
11 when the eye s' me, it gave witness "
31:21 when I s' my help in the gate: "
32: 5 Elihu s' that there was no answer "
42:16 s' his sons, and his sons' sons, even "
Ps 48: 5 They s' it, and so they marvelled; "
73: 3 I s' the prosperity of the wicked. "
77:16 s' thee, O God, the waters s' thee; "
95: 9 me, proved me, and s' my work. "
97: 4 world: the earth s', and trembled. "
114: 3 The sea s' it, and fled: Jordan was "
Pr 24:32 Then I s', and considered it well: *2372
Ec 2:13 I s' that wisdom excelleth folly, as7200
24 This also I s', that it was from the "
3:16 I s' under the sun the place of "
4: 7 and I s' vanity under the sun. "
8:10 And so I s' the wicked buried, who "
9:11 I returned, and s' under the sun, "
Ca 3: 3 S' ye him whom my soul loveth? "
6: 9 daughters s' her, and blessed her; "
Isa 1: 1 which he s' concerning Judah and2372
2: 1 son of Amoz s' concerning Judah "
6: 1 I s' also the Lord sitting upon a 7200
10:15 the s' magnify itself against him 4883
21: 7 he s' a chariot with a couple of *7200
41: 5 The isles s' it, and feared; the ends "
59:15 the Lord s' it, and it displeased him "
16 And he s' that there was no man, "
Jer 3: 7 her treacherous sister Judah s' it. "
8 And I s', when for all the causes "
39: 4 Zedekiah the king of Judah s' them, "
41:13 people...with Ishmael s' Johanan "
44:17 and were well, and s' no evil. "
La 1: 7 adversaries s' her, and did mock at "
Eze 1: 1 opened, and I s' visions of God. "
27 And I s' as the colour of amber, as "
27 s' as it were the appearance of fire, "
28 when I s' it, I fell upon my face, and "
3:23 which I s' by the river of Chebar: "
8: 4 to the vision that I s' in the plain. "
10 I went in and s'; and behold every "
10:15 that I s' by the river of Chebar. "
20 creature that I s' under the God of "
22 which I s' by the river of Chebar, "
11: 1 I s' Jaazaniah the son of Azur, and "
16: 6 s' thee polluted in thine own blood, "
50 I took them away as I s' good. "
19: 5 when she s' that she had waited, and "
20:28 then they s' every high hill, and all "
23:11 when her sister Aholibah s' this, "
13 Then I s' that she was defiled, that "
14 when she s' men pourtrayed upon "
16 as soon as she s' them with her eyes, "
41: 8 I s' also the height of the house 7200
43: 3 appearance of the vision which I s', "
3 even according to the vision that I s' "
3 like the vision that I s' by the river "
Da 3:27 s' these men, upon whose bodies 2370
4: 5 I s' a dream which made me afraid, "

Da 4:10 I s', and behold a tree in the midst 2370
13 I s' in the visions of my head upon "
23 whereas the king s' a watcher and "
5: 5 s' the part of the hand that wrote. "
7: 2 and said, I s' in my vision by night, "
7 After this I s' in the night visions, "
13 I s' in the night visions, and, "
8: 2 And I s' in a vision; and it came to 7200
2 when I s', that I was at Shushan "
2 and I s' in a vision, and I was by "
3 Then I lifted up mine eyes, and s', "
4 I s' the ram pushing westward, and "
7 I s' him come close unto the ram, "
10: 7 And I Daniel alone s' the vision: "
7 men...with me s' not the vision; "
8 left alone, and s' this great vision, "
Ho 5:13 When Ephraim s' his sickness, and "
13 and Judah s' his wound, then went "
9:10 I s' your fathers as the firstripe in 7200
13 Ephraim, as I s' Tyrus, is planted* "
Am 1: 1 which he s' concerning Israel in 2372
9: 1 I s' the Lord standing upon the 7200
Jon 3:10 And God s' their works, that they "
Mic 1: 1 which he s' concerning Samaria 2372
Hab 3: 7 I s'...tents of Cushan in affliction: 7200
10 The mountains s' thee, and they "
Hag 2: 3 that s' this house in her first glory? "
Zec 1: 8 I s' by night, and behold a man "
18 Then lifted I up mine eyes, and s', "
M't 2: 9 the star, which they s' in the east, 1492
10 When they s' the star, they rejoiced "
11 s' the young child with Mary his 2147
16 when he s' that he was mocked of 1492
3: 7 when he s' many of the Pharisees "
16 he s' the Spirit of God descending "
4:16 which sat in darkness s' great light; "
18 s' two brethren, Simon called Peter, "
21 thence, he s' other two brethren, "
8:14 he s' his wife's mother laid, and "
18 Now when Jesus s' great multitudes "
34 when they s' him, they besought "
9: 8 But when the multitudes s' it, they "
9 he s' a man, named Matthew, "
11 when the Pharisees s' it, they said "
22 when he s' her, he said, Daughter,* "
23 and s' the minstrels and the people "
36 But when he s' the multitudes, he "
12: 2 But when the Pharisees s' it, they "
22 blind and dumb both spake and s'. 991
14:14 forth, and s' a great multitude, 1492
26 disciples s' him walking on the sea, "
30 when he s' the wind boisterous, he 991
15:31 when they s' the dumb to speak, "
17: 8 they s' no man, save Jesus only. 1492
18:31 fellowservants s' what was done, "
20: 3 and s' others standing idle in the "
21:15 scribes s' the wonderful things that "
19 when he s' a fig tree in the way, he* "
20 the disciples s' it, they marvelled, "
38 when the husbandmen s' the son, "
22:11 s' there a man which had not on a "
25:37 Lord, when s' we thee an hungred, "
38 When s' we thee a stranger, and "
39 when s' we thee sick, or in prison, "
44 Lord, when s' we thee an hungred, "
26: 8 But when his disciples s' it, they "
71 another maid s' him, and said unto "
27: 3 when he s' that he was condemned, "
24 When Pilate s' that he could prevail "
54 s' the earthquake, and those "
28:17 when they s' him, they worshipped "
M'r 1:10 he s' the heavens opened, and the "
16 he s' Simon and Andrew his brother "
19 he s' James the son of Zebedee, and "
2: 5 When Jesus s' their faith, he said* "
12 We never s' it on this fashion. "
14 he s' Levi the son of Alphæus "
16 Pharisees s' him eat with publicans "
3:11 unclean spirits, when they s' him,*2334
5: 6 when he s' Jesus afar off, he ran 1492
16 And they that s' it told them how it "
22 when he s' him, he fell at his feet,* "
6:33 And the people s' them departing, "
34 when he came out, s' much people, "
48 And he s' them toiling in rowing; * "
49 they s' him walking upon the sea, "
50 they all s' him, and were troubled. "
7: 2 they s' some of his disciples eat * "
8:23 him, he asked him if he s' ought. * 991
25 restored, and s' every man clearly. 1689
9: 8 s' no man any more, save Jesus 1492
14 he s' a great multitude about them, "
20 when he s' him, straightway the "
25 When Jesus s' that the people came "
38 we s' one casting out devils in thy "
10:14 But when Jesus s' it, he was much "
11:20 they s' the fig tree dried up from the "
12:34 s' that he answered discreetly, he "
14:67 when she s' Peter warming himself,* "
69 a maid s' him again, and began to "
15:39 s' that he so cried out, and gave up "
16: 4 s' that the stone was rolled away:*2334
5 s' a young man sitting on the right 1492
Lu 1:12 And when Zacharias s' him, he was "
29 when she s' him, she was troubled* "
2:48 And when they s' him, they were "
5: 2 s' two ships standing by the lake: "
8 When Simon Peter s' it, he fell down "
20 when he s' their faith, he said unto* "
27 s' a publican, named Levi, sitting*2300
7:13 And when the Lord s' her, he had 1492
39 Pharisee which had bidden him s' it, "
8:28 When he s' Jesus, he cried out, and "
34 When they that fed them s' what "
36 They also which s' it told them by "
47 the woman s' that she was not hid, "

Lu 9:32 they were awake, they s' his glory, 1492
49 we s' one casting out devils in thy "
54 disciples James and John s' this, "
10:31 when he s' him, he passed by on the "
33 when he s' him, he had compassion "
11:38 And when the Pharisee s' it, he "
13:12 when Jesus s' her, he called her to "
15:20 father s' him, and had compassion, "
17:14 And when he s' them, he said unto "
15 when he s' that he was healed, "
18:15 but when his disciples s' it, they "
24 Jesus s'...he was very sorrowful, * "
43 all the people, when they s' it, gave "
19: 5 he looked up, and s' him, and said* "
7 when they s' it, they all murmured, "
20:14 when the husbandmen s' him, they "
21: 1 s' the rich men casting their gifts "
2 s' also a certain poor widow casting "
22:49 they which were about him s' what "
58 after a little while another s' him, "
23: 8 And when Herod s' Jesus, he was "
47 the centurion s' what was done, "
24:24 had said: but him they s' not. "
Joh 1:32 I s' the Spirit descending from *2300
34 I s', and bare record that this is *3708
38 turned, and s' them following, and*2300
39 They came and s' where he dwelt, 1492
47 Jesus s' Nathanael coming to him, "
48 wast under the fig tree, I s' thee. "
50 thee, I s' thee under the fig tree, "
2:23 they s' the miracles which he did.*2334
5: 6 When Jesus s' him lie, and knew 1492
6: 2 they s' his miracles which he did *3708
5 s' a great company come unto him,*2300
22 s' that there was none other boat 1492
24 people...s' that Jesus was not there, "
26 me, not because ye s' the miracles, "
8:10 and s' none but the woman, he said 2300
56 my day: and he s' it, and was glad. 1492
9: 1 s' a man which was blind from his "
11:31 when they s' Mary, that she rose up, "
32 come where Jesus was, and s' him, "
33 Jesus therefore s' her weeping, "
12:41 said Esaias, when he s' his glory, "
19: 6 chief priests...and officers s' him, "
26 When Jesus therefore s' his mother, "
33 and s' that he was dead already, "
35 And he that s' it bare record, and *3708
20: 5 in, s' the linen clothes lying, yet * 991
8 sepulchre, and he s', and believed. 1492
14 s' Jesus standing, and knew not *2334
20 glad, when they s' the Lord. 1492
21: 9 land, they s' a fire of coals there, * 991
Ac 3: 9 all the people s' him walking and 1492
12 when Peter s' it, he answered unto "
4:13 s' the boldness of Peter and John,*2334
6:15 s' his face as it had been the face 1492
7:31 When Moses s' it, he wondered at "
55 and s' the glory of God, and Jesus "
8:18 Simon s' that through laying on of 2300
39 that the eunuch s' him no more: 1492
9: 8 eyes were opened, he s' no man: 991
35 dwelt at Lydda and Saron s' him, 1492
40 and when she s' Peter, she sat up. "
10: 3 He s' in a vision evidently about "
11 s' heaven opened, and a certain *2334
11: 5 in a trance I s' a vision, A certain 1492
6 s' fourfooted beasts of the earth, "
12: 3 because he s' it pleased the Jews, "
9 angel; but thought he s' a vision. 991
16 had opened the door, and s' him, 1492
13:12 deputy, when he s' what was done, "
36 unto his fathers, and s' corruption: "
37 God raised again, s' no corruption. "
45 when the Jews s' the multitudes, "
14:11 the people s' what Paul had done, "
16:19 her masters s' that the hope of their "
17:16 when he s' the city wholly given *2334
21:27 when they s' him in the temple, 2300
32 when they s' the chief captain and 1492
22: 9 were with me s' indeed the light, *2300
18 And s' him saying unto me, Make 1492
26:13 I s' in the way a light from heaven, "
28: 4 barbarians s' the venomous beast "
6 and s' no harm come to him, they*2334
15 whom when Paul s', he thanked 1492
Ga 1:19 other of the apostles s' I none, save "
2: 7 when they s' that the gospel of the "
14 I s' that they walked not uprightly "
Ph'p 1:30 the same conflict which ye s' in me, "
Heb 3: 9 me, and s' my works forty years. "
11:23 they s' he was a proper child; and "
Re 1: 2 Christ, and of all things that he s'. "
12 I s' seven golden candlesticks; "
17 when I s' him, I fell at his feet as "
4: 4 I s' four and twenty elders sitting, "
5: 1 s' in the right hand of him that sat "
2 s' a strong angel proclaiming with "
6: 1 I s' when the Lamb opened one of "
2 And I s', and behold a white horse: "
9 s' under the altar the souls of them "
7: 1 s' four angels standing on the four "
2 I s' another angel ascending from "
8: 2 I s' the seven angels which stood "
9: 1 I s' a star fall from heaven unto the "
17 thus I s' the horses in the vision, "
10: 1 s' another mighty angel come down "
5 angel which I s' stand upon the sea "
11:11 fear fell upon them which s' them.*2334
12:13 dragon s' that he was cast unto 1492
13: 1 and s' a beast rise up out of the sea, "
2 which I s' was like unto a leopard, "
3 And I s' one of his heads as it were "
14: 6 s' another angel fly in the midst of "
15: 1 I s' another sign in heaven, great "
2 s' as it were a sea of glass mingled "

Re 16:13 I s' three unclean spirits like frogs 1492
17: 3 and I s' a woman sit upon a scarlet "
6 I s' the woman drunken with the "
6 and when I s' her, I wondered with "
18: 1 these things I s' another angel come "
18 they s' the smoke of her burning,*3708
19:11 I s' heaven opened, and behold a 1492
17 I s' an angel standing in the sun; "
19 I s' the beast, and the kings of the "
20: 1 And I s' an angel come down from "
4 s' thrones, and they sat upon them, "
4 and I s' the souls of them that were "
11 I s' a great white throne, and him 1492
12 And I s' the dead, small and great, "
21: 1 I s' a new heaven and a new earth: "
2 And I John s' the holy city, new "
22 I s' no temple therein: for the Lord "
22: 8 I John s' these things, and heard 991

sawed
1Ki 7: 9 s' with saws, within and without, 1641

sawest
Ge 20:10 What s' thou, that thou hast done 7200
1Sa 19: 5 Israel: thou s' it, and didst rejoice: "
28:13 Be not afraid: for what s' thou? * "
2Sa 18:11 behold, thou s' him, and why didst "
Ps 50:18 When thou s' a thief, then thou "
Isa 57: 8 lovedst their bed where thou s' it. 2372
Da 2:31 king, s', and behold a great image. 2370
34 Thou s' till that a stone was cut out "
41 whereas thou s' the feet and toes, "
41 as thou s' the iron mixed with miry "
43 thou s' iron mixed with miry clay, "
45 thou s' that the stone was cut of the "
4:20 The tree that thou s', which grew, "
8:20 The ram which thou s' having two 7200
Re 1:20 of the seven stars which thou s' in 1492
20 candlesticks which thou s' are the* "
17: 8 The beast that thou s' was, and is "
12 the ten horns which thou s' are ten "
15 The waters which thou s', where "
16 the ten horns which thou s' upon "
18 woman which thou s' is that great "

sawn
Heb 11:37 were stoned, they were s' asunder, 4249

saws
2Sa 12:31 and put them under s', and under 4050
1Ki 7: 9 sawed with s', within and without, "
1Ch 20: 3 cut them with s', and with harrows "

say See also GAINSAY; SAID; SAITH; SAYING.
Ge 12:12 that they shall s', This is his wife: 559
13 S', I pray thee, thou art my sister: "
14:23 thou...s', I have made Abram rich: "
20:13 come, s' of me, He is my brother. "
24:14 damsel to whom I shall s', Let down "
14 she shall s', Drink, and I will give "
43 and I s' to her, Give me, I pray thee, "
44 And she s' to me, Both drink thou, "
26: 7 for he feared to s', She is my wife; "
32:18 Then thou shalt s', They be thy "
20 s' ye...Behold, thy servant Jacob "
34:11 what ye shall s' unto me I will give. "
12 according as ye shall s' unto me: "
37:17 I heard them s', Let us go to Dothan. "
20 and we will s', Some evil beast hath "
41:15 I have heard s' of thee, that thou "
43: 7 he would s', Bring your brother down? "
44: 4 s' unto them, Wherefore have ye "
16 said, What shall we s' unto my lord? "
45: 9 and s' unto him, Thus saith thy son "
17 S' unto thy brethren, This do ye; "
46:31 and shew Pharaoh, and s' unto him, "
33 shall s', What is your occupation? "
34 That ye shall s', Thy servants' trade "
50:17 So shall ye s' unto Joseph, Forgive, "
Ex 3:13 and shall s' unto them, The God of "
13 and they shall s' to me, What is his "
13 name? what shall I s' unto them? "
14,15 thou s' unto the children of Israel, "
16 s' unto them, The Lord God of your "
18 ye shall s' unto him, The Lord God "
4: 1 for they will s', The Lord hath not "
12 and teach thee what thou shalt s'.*1696
22 thou shalt s' unto Pharaoh, Thus 559
23 I s' unto thee, Let my son go, that* "
5:16 and they s' to us, Make brick: and, "
17 ye s', Let us go and do sacrifice to "
6: 6 s' unto the children of Israel, I am "
29 of Egypt all that I s' unto thee. *1696
7: 9 then thou shalt s' unto Aaron, Take 559
16 thou shalt s' unto him, The Lord "
19 S' unto Aaron, Take thy rod, and "
8: 1 Go unto Pharaoh, and s' unto him, "
5 S' unto Aaron, Stretch forth thine "
16 S' unto Aaron, Stretch out thy rod, "
20 s' unto him, Thus saith the Lord, "
9:13 before Pharaoh, and s' unto him, "
12:26 your children shall s' unto you, "
27 ye shall s', It is the sacrifice of the "
13:14 thou shalt s' unto him, By strength "
14: 3 Pharaoh will s' of the children of "
16: 9 S' unto all the congregation of the "
19: 3 shalt thou s' to the house of Jacob, "
20:22 shalt s' unto the children of Israel, "
21: 5 if the servant shall plainly s', I love "
32:12 and s', For mischief did he bring * "
33: 5 S' unto the children of Israel, Ye are "
Le 1: 2 and s' unto them, If any man of you "
15: 2 and s' unto them, When any man "
17: 2 and s' unto them; This is the thing "
8 shalt s' unto them, Whatsoever man "
18: 2 and s' unto them, I am the Lord your "
19: 2 and s' unto them, Ye shall be holy: "
20: 2 thou shalt s' to the children of Israel, "
21: 1 and s' unto them, There shall none "

Le 22: 3 S' unto them, Whosoever he be of 559
18 and s' unto them, Whatsoever he be "
23: 2 and s'...Concerning the feasts of "
10 and s' unto them, When ye be come "
25: 2 and s' unto them, When ye come into "
20 And if ye shall s', What shall we eat "
27: 2 and s'...When a man shall make a "
Nu 5: 12 s' unto them, If any man's wife go "
19 and s' unto the woman, If no man "
21 the priest shall say unto the woman, "
22 the woman shall s', Amen, amen. "
6: 2 and s' unto them, When either man "
8: 2 and s' unto him, When thou lightest "
11: 12 shouldest s' unto me, Carry them "
18 s' thou unto the people, Sanctify "
14: 28 S' unto them, As truly as I live, "
15: 2 and s' unto them, When ye be come "
18 and s' unto them, When ye come into "
18: 26 and s' unto them, When ye take of "
30 s' unto them, When ye have heaved "
21: 27 that speak in proverbs s', Come into "
22: 19 the Lord will s' unto me more. *1696
20 word which I shall s' unto thee, * "
38 any power at all to s' any thing? * "
23: 16 Go again unto Balak, and s' thus.* "
25: 12 Wherefore s', Behold, I give unto 559
28: 2 and s' unto them, My offering, and "
3 s' unto them, This is the offering "
33: 51 s' unto them, When ye are passed "
34: 2 and s' unto them, When ye come into "
35: 10 s' unto them, When ye be come over "
De 1: 42 S' unto them, Go not up, neither "
4: 6 and s', Surely this great nation is a "
5: 27 all that the Lord our God shall s': "
30 Go s' to them, Get you into your tents "
6: 21 thou shalt s' unto thy son, We were "
7: 17 shalt s' in thine heart, These nations "
8: 17 And thou s' in thine heart, My power "
9: 2 and of whom thou hast heard s', Who "
28 s', Because the Lord was not able 559
12: 20 and thou shalt s', I will eat flesh, "
13: 12 thou shalt hear s' in one of thy cities,*
15: 16 if he s' unto thee, I will not go 559
17: 14 shalt s', I will set a king over me, "
18: 21 s' in thine heart, How shall we know "
20: 3 shall s' unto them, Hear, O Israel, "
8 and they shall s', What man is there "
21: 7 and s', Our hands have not shed this "
20 shall s' unto the elders of his city, "
22: 14 and s', I took this woman, and when "
16 father shall s' unto the elders, I gave "
25: 7 s', My husband's brother refuseth to "
8 to it, and s', I like not to take her; "
9 answer and s', So shall it be done "
26: 3 and s' unto him, I profess this day "
5 s' before the Lord thy God, A Syrian "
13 shalt s' before the Lord thy God, "
27: 14 and s' unto all the men of Israel with "
15 people shall answer and s', Amen. "
16, 17, 18, 19, 20, 21, 22, 23, 24, 25, 26
And all the people shall s', Amen. "
28: 67 morning thou shalt s', Would God "
67 and at even thou shalt s', Would God "
29: 22 shall s', when they see the plagues "
24 Even all nations shall s', Wherefore "
25 shall s', Because they have forsaken "
30: 12, 13 thou shouldest s', Who shall go "
31: 17 s' in that day, Are not these evils "
32: 27 lest they should s', Our hand is high, "
37 he shall s', Where are their gods, "
40 hand to heaven, and s', I live for ever. "
33: 27 thee; and shall s', Destroy them. * "
Jos 7: 8 O Lord, what shall I s', when Israel "
13 and s', Sanctify yourselves against "
8: 6 for they will s', They flee before us, "
9: 11 s' unto them, We are your servants: "
22: 11 And the children of Israel heard s', "
27 children may not s' to our children "
28 when they should so s' to us or to "
28 we may s' again, Behold the pattern "
J'g 4: 20 enquire of thee, and s', Is there any "
20 man here? that thou shalt s', No. "
7: 4 of whom I s' unto thee, This shall go "
4 of whomsoever I s'...This shall not "
11 And thou shalt hear what they s'; 1696
18 and s', The sword of the Lord, and 559
9: 54 that men s' not of me, A woman slew "
12: 6 they unto him, S' now Shibboleth: "
16: 15 How canst thou s', I love thee, when "
18: 8 brethren said unto them, What s' ye? "
24 and what is this that ye s' unto me, "
21: 22 we will s' unto them, Be favourable "
Ru 1: 12 If I should s', I have hope, if I "
1Sa 2: 36 and shall s', Put me, I pray thee, into "
3: 9 that thou shalt s', Speak, Lord; for "
8: 7 people in all that they s' unto thee: "
10: 2 and they will s' unto thee, The asses "
11: 9 s' unto the men of Jabesh-gilead, "
13: 4 Israel heard s' that Saul had smitten "
14: 9 If they s' thus unto us, Tarry until "
10 if they s' thus, Come up unto us; "
34 and s' unto them, Bring me hither "
15: 16 And he said unto him, S' on. 1696
16: 2 and s', I am come to sacrifice to the 559
18: 22 and s', Behold, the king hath delight "
25 Thus shall ye s' to David, The king "
19: 24 Wherefore they s', Is Saul also among "
20: 6 then s', David earnestly asked leave "
7 If he s' thus, It is well; thy servant "
21 If I expressly s' unto the lad, Behold, "
22 But if I s' thus unto the young man, "
25: 6 s' to him that liveth in prosperity, "
2Sa 7: 8 thou s' unto my servant David, "
20 And what can David s' more unto 1696
11: 20 and he s' unto thee, Wherefore 559
21 then s' thou, Thy servant Uriah the "

2Sa 11: 25 thou s' unto Joab, Let not this thing 559
13: 5 s' unto him, I pray thee, let my sister "
28 when I s' unto you, Smite Amnon; "
14: 12 lord the king. And he said, S' on. 1696
32 to s', Wherefore am I come from 559
15: 10 then ye shall s', Absalom reigneth "
26 But if he thus s', I have no delight "
34 and s' unto Absalom, I will be thy "
16: 10 Who shall then s', Wherefore hast "
17: 9 whosoever heareth it will s', There "
19: 2 the people heard s' that day how the "
13 And s' ye to Amasa, Art thou not of "
20: 16 s', I pray you, unto Joab, Come near "
21: 4 What ye shall s', that will I do for "
24: 1 moved David against them to s', Go, "
12 Go and s' unto David, Thus saith * "
1Ki 1: 13 s' unto him, Didst not thou, my lord, "
25 him, and s', God save king Adonijah. "
34 and s', God save king Solomon. "
36 God of my lord the king s' so too. "
2: 14 I have somewhat to s' unto thee. 1697
14 unto thee. And she said, S' on. 1696
16 not. And she said unto him, S' on. "
17 king, (for he will not s' thee nay,) 7725
20 thee; I pray thee, s' me not nay. * "
20 mother: for I will not s' thee nay.* "
9: 8 they shall s', Why hath the Lord "
12: 10 thus shalt thou s' unto them, My *1696
13: 22 of the which the Lord did s' to thee,* "
14: 5 thus shalt thou s' unto her: for it "
16: 16 people that were encamped heard s', 559
18: 44 Go up, s' unto Ahab, Prepare thy "
22: 8 said, Let not the king s' so. "
27 And s', Thus saith the king, Put this "
2Ki 1: 3 s' unto them, Is it not because 1696
6 s' unto him, Thus saith the Lord, "
2: 18 them, Did I not s' unto you, Go not? 559
4: 13 S' now unto her, Behold, thou hast "
26 and s' unto her, Is it well with thee? "
28 did I not s', Do not deceive me? "
7: 4 If we s', We will enter into the city, "
13 behold, I s', they are even as all the*
8: 10 him, Go, s' unto him, Thou mayest 559
9: 3 and s', Thus saith the Lord, I have "
17 them, and let him s', Is it peace? "
37 they shall not s', This is Jezebel. "
18: 22 But if ye s' unto me, We trust in the "
19: 6 Thus shall ye s' to your master, Thus "
9 when he heard s' of Tirhakah king "
22: 18 thus shall ye s' to him, Thus saith "
1Ch 5: 3 sons, I s', of Reuben the firstborn of*
16: 31 and let men s' among the nations, 559
35 And s' ye, Save us, O God of our "
17: 7 shalt thou s' unto my servant David, "
21: 18 Lord commanded Gad to s' to David, "
2Ch 7: 21 that he shall s', Why hath the Lord "
10: 10 thus shalt thou s' unto them, My "
18: 7 said, Let not the king s' so. "
15 thou s' nothing but the truth to me* "
26 And s', Thus saith the king, Put this "
20: 11 Behold, I s', how they reward us, to*
21 and to s', Praise the Lord; for his 559
34: 26 so shall ye s' unto him, Thus saith "
Ezr 8: 17 what they should s' unto Iddo, 1696
9: 10 God, what shall we s' after this? 559
Ne 7: 7 I s', of the men of the people of Israel*
9: 8 to give it, I s', to his seed, and hast*
Es 1: 18 s' this day unto all the king's 559
Job 6: 22 Did I s', Bring unto me? or, Give a "
7: 4 I lie down, I s', When shall I arise, "
13 I s', My bed shall comfort me, my "
9: 12 will s' unto him, What doest thou? "
20 if I s', I am perfect, it shall also prove*
27 If I s', I will forget my complaint, 559
10: 2 s' unto God, Do not condemn me; "
19: 28 ye should s', Why persecute we him, "
20: 7 they which have seen him shall s', "
21: 14 they s' unto God, Depart from us; † "
28 For ye s', Where is the house of the "
22: 29 thou shalt s', There is lifting up; "
23: 5 understand what he would s' unto "
28: 22 Destruction and death s', We have "
32: 11 whilst ye searched out what to s'. 4405
13 Lest ye should s', We have found 559
33: 27 men, and if any s', I have sinned, * "
32 If thou hast anything to s', answer 4405
34: 18 Is it fit to s' to a king, Thou art 559
36: 23 or who can s', Thou hast wrought "
37: 19 Teach us what we shall s' unto him; "
38: 35 go, and s' unto thee, Here we are? "
Ps 3: 2 Many there be which s' of my soul, "
4: 6 There be many that s', Who will "
11: 1 how s' ye to my soul, Flee as a bird to "
13: 4 Lest mine enemy s', I have prevailed "
27: 14 thine heart: wait, I s', on the Lord.*
35: 3 s' unto my soul, I am thy salvation. 559
10 All my bones shall s', Lord, who is "
25 Let them not s' in their hearts, Ah, "
25 let them not s', We have swallowed "
27 yea, let them s' continually, Let the "
40: 15 shame that s' unto me, Aha, aha. "
16 as love thy salvation s' continually, "
41: 8 An evil disease, s' they, cleaveth fast "
42: 3 they continually s' unto me, Where 559
9 I will s' unto God my rock, Why hast "
10 while they s' daily unto me, Where "
58: 11 So that a man shall s', Verily there "
59: 7 their lips: for who, s' they, doth hear? "
64: 5 they s', Who shall see them? 559
66: 3 S' unto God, How terrible art thou "
70: 3 a reward of their shame that s', Aha, "
4 as love thy salvation s' continually, "
73: 11 And they s', How doth God know? "
15 If I s', I will speak thus; behold, I * "
79: 10 Wherefore should the heathen s', "
91: 2 I will s' of the Lord, He is my refuge "

Ps 94: 7 Yet they s', The Lord shall not see, 559
96: 10 S' among the heathen that the Lord "
106: 48 and let all the people s', Amen. "
107: 2 Let the redeemed of the Lord s' so, "
115: 2 Wherefore should the heathen s', "
118: 2 Let Israel now s', that his mercy "
3 Let the house of Aaron now s', that "
4 Let them now that fear the Lord s', "
122: 8 I will now s', Peace be within thee. 1696
124: 1 was on our side, now may Israel s'; 559
129: 1 from my youth, may Israel now s': "
8 Neither do they which go by s', The "
130: 6 I s', more than they that watch for the*
139: 11 If I s', Surely the darkness shall 559
Pr 1: 11 If they s', Come with us, let us lay "
3: 28 S' not unto thy neighbour, Go, and "
5: 12 s', How have I hated instruction, "
7: 4 S' unto wisdom, Thou art my sister; "
20: 9 Who can s', I have made my heart "
22 S' not thou, I will recompense evil; "
24: 29 S' not, I will do so to him as he hath "
30: 9 deny thee, and s', Who is the Lord? "
15 yea, four things s' not, It is enough: "
Ec 5: 6 neither s' thou before the angel, "
6: 3 I s', that an untimely birth is better "
7: 10 S' not thou, What is the cause that "
8: 4 who may s' unto him, What doest "
12: 1 nigh, when thou shalt s', I have no "
Isa 2: 3 many people shall go and s', Come "
3: 10 S' ye to the righteous, that it shall "
5: 19 That s', Let him make speed, and "
7: 4 And s' unto him, Take heed, and be "
8: 12 S' ye not, A confederacy, to all them "
12 them to whom this people shall s', A "
19 when they shall s' unto you, Seek "
9: 9 that s' in the pride and stoutness of "
12: 1 in that day thou shalt s', O Lord, "
4 that day shall ye s', Praise the Lord, "
14: 4 s', How hath the oppressor ceased! "
10 they shall speak and s' unto thee, "
19: 11 how s' ye unto Pharaoh, I am the son "
20: 6 of this isle shall s' in that day, "
22: 15 which is over the house, and s', "
29: 15 dark, and they s', Who seeth us? "
16 the work s' of him that made it, "
16 thing framed s' of him that framed "
30: 10 Which s' to the seers, See not; and "
22 thou shalt s' unto it, Get thee hence. "
33: 24 inhabitant shall not s', I am sick: "
35: 4 S' to them that are of a fearful "
36: 4 S' ye now to Hezekiah, Thus saith "
5 I s', sayest thou,...I have counsel "
7 thou s' to me, We trust in the Lord "
37: 6 Thus shall ye s' unto your master, "
9 heard s' concerning Tirhakah king "
38: 5 Go, and s' to Hezekiah, Thus saith "
15 What shall I s'? he hath both 1696
40: 9 s' unto the cities of Judah, Behold 559
41: 26 that we may s', He is righteous? "
27 The first shall s' to Zion, Behold, ‡
42: 17 s' to the molten images, Ye are our 559
43: 6 I will s' to the north, Give up; and "
9 or let them hear, and s', It is truth. "
44: 5 One shall s', I am the Lord's; and "
19 knowledge nor understanding to s', "
20 nor s', Is there not a lie in my right "
45: 9 the clay s' to him that fashioneth it, "
24 shall one s', in the Lord have I "
48: 5 shouldest s', Mine idol hath done "
7 thou...s', Behold, I knew them. "
20 s' ye, The Lord hath redeemed his "
49: 9 thou mayest s' to the prisoners, Go* "
20 s' again in thine ears, The place is "
21 Then shalt thou s' in thine heart, "
51: 16 s' unto Zion, Thou art my people. "
56: 3 eunuch s', Behold, I am a dry tree. "
12 Come ye, s' they, I will fetch wine, "
57: 14 And shall s', Cast ye up, cast ye up, 559
58: 3 we fasted, s' they, and thou seest not? "
9 cry, and he shall s', Here I am. 559
62: 11 world, S' ye to the daughter of Zion, "
65: 5 Which s', Stand by thyself, come not "
Jer 1: 7 said unto me, s' not, I am a child: "
2: 23 canst thou s', I am not polluted, I "
27 time of their trouble they will s', "
31 wherefore s' my people, We are "
3: 1 They s', If a man put away his wife, "
12 and s', Return, thou backsliding "
16 s' no more, The ark of the covenant "
4: 5 s', Blow ye the trumpet in the land: "
5 and s', Assemble yourselves, and let "
5: 2 though they s', The Lord liveth; "
15 understandest what they s'. 1696
19 shall come to pass, when ye shall s', 559
24 Neither s' they in their heart, Let us "
7: 2 s', Hear the word of the Lord, all ye "
10 s', We are delivered to do all these "
28 shalt s' unto them, This is a nation "
8: 4 Moreover thou shalt s' unto them, "
8 How do ye s', We are wise, and the "
10: 11 Thus shall ye s' unto them, The 560
11: 3 And s' thou unto them, Thus saith 559
13: 12 they shall s' unto thee, Do we not "
13 Then shalt thou s' unto them, Thus "
18 S' unto the king and to the queen, "
21 thou s' when he shall punish thee? "
22 if thou s' in thine heart, Wherefore "
14: 13 the prophets s' unto them, Ye shall "
15 yet they s', Sword and famine shall "
17 thou shalt s' this word unto them; "
15: 2 if they s' unto thee, Whither shall "
16: 10 they shall s' unto thee, Wherefore "
11 shalt thou s' unto them, Because "
19 and shall s', Surely our fathers have "
17: 15 they s' unto me, Where is the word "
20 s' unto them, Hear ye the word of "

Jer 19: 3 And s', Hear ye the word of the Lord, 559
11 shalt s' unto them, Thus saith the "
20:10 Report, s' they, and we will report it. "
21: 3 them, Thus shall ye s' to Zedekiah: 559
8 And unto this people thou shalt s', "
11 s', Hear ye the word of the Lord; *
13 which s', Who shall come down 559
22: 2 And s', Hear the word of the Lord, O "
8 shall s' every man to his neighbour, "
23: 7 shall no more s', The Lord liveth, "
17 s' still unto them that despise me, "
17 s'...No evil shall come upon you. "
31 use their tongues, and s', He saith. "
33 then s' unto them, What burden? 559
34 shall s', The burden of the Lord, "
35 ye s' every one to his neighbour, "
37 Thus shalt thou s' to the prophet, "
38 since ye s', The burden of the Lord; "
38 Because ye s' this word, The burden "
38 shall not s', The burden of the Lord; "
25:27 Therefore thou shalt s' unto them, "
28 then shalt thou s' unto them, Thus "
30 s' unto them, The Lord shall roar "
26: 4 And thou shalt s' unto them, Thus "
27: 4 them to s' unto their masters, Thus *
4 Thus shall ye s' unto your masters; "
31: 7 ye, and s', O Lord, save thy people, "
10 and s', He that scattered Israel will "
29 In those days they shall s' no more, "
32: 3 and s', Thus saith the Lord, Behold, "
36 concerning this city, whereof ye s', "
43 whereof ye s', It is desolate without "
33:10 which ye s' shall be desolate without "
11 voice of them that shall s', Praise "
36:29 shalt s' to Jehoiakim king of Judah, "
37: 7 shall ye s' to the king of Judah, "
38:22 those women shall s', Thy friends "
25 s' unto thee, Declare unto us now "
26 thou shalt s' unto them, I presented "
39:12 him even as he shall s' unto thee. 1696
42:13 But if ye s', We will not dwell in 559
20 all that the Lord our God shall s', "
43: 2 not sent thee to s', Go not into Egypt "
10 s' unto them, Thus saith the Lord "
45: 3 Thou didst s', Woe is me now! for "
4 Thus shalt thou s' unto him, The "
46:14 s' ye, Stand fast, and prepare thee; "
48:14 How s' ye, We are mighty and strong "
17 s', How is the strong staff broken, "
19 that escapeth, and s', What is done? "
50: 2 conceal not: s', Babylon is taken, "
51:35 shall the inhabitant of Zion s'; and "
35 of Chaldea, shall Jerusalem s'. "
62 Then shalt thou s', O Lord, thou "
64 thou shalt s', Thus shall Babylon "
La 2:12 They s' to their mothers, Where is "
16 they s', We have swallowed her up: "
Eze 2: 4 thou shalt s' unto them, Thus saith "
8 of man, hear what I s' unto thee; 1696
3:18 When I s' unto the wicked, Thou 559
27 thou shalt s' unto them, Thus saith "
6: 3 s', Ye mountains of Israel, hear the "
11 s', Alas for all the evil abominations "
8:12 for they s', The Lord seeth us not; "
9: 9 they s', The Lord hath forsaken the "
11: 3 Which s', It is not near; let us build "
16, 17 Therefore s', Thus saith the Lord "
12:10 S' thou unto them, Thus saith the "
11 S', I am your sign: like as I have "
19 s' unto the people of the land, Thus "
23 but s' unto them, The days are at 1696
25 I s' the word, and will perform it, * "
27 house of Israel s', The vision that 559
28 Therefore s' unto them, Thus saith "
13: 2 and s' thou unto them that prophesy "
7 whereas ye s', The Lord saith it; "
11 S' unto them which daub it with "
15 s' unto you, The wall is no more, "
18 s', Thus saith the Lord God; Woe to "
14: 4 s' unto them, Thus saith the Lord "
6 s' unto the house of Israel, Thus "
17 and s', Sword, go through the land; "
16: 3 s', Thus saith the Lord God unto "
17: 3 And s', Thus saith the Lord God; A "
9 S' thou, Thus saith the Lord God; "
12 S' now to the rebellious house, Know "
18:19 Yet s' ye, Why? doth not the son "
25 Yet ye s', The way of the Lord is not "
19: 2 s', What is thy mother? A lioness: "
20: 3 the elders of Israel, and s' unto them, "
5, 27 s' unto them, Thus saith the Lord "
30 s' unto the house of Israel, Thus "
32 ye s', We will be as the heathen, as "
47 s' to the forest of the south, Hear the "
49 they s' of me, Doth he not speak "
21: 3 s' to the land of Israel, Thus saith "
7 when they s' unto thee, Wherefore "
9 and s', Thus saith the Lord; "
9 S', A sword, a sword is sharpened, "
24 I s', that ye are come to remembrance, *
28 and s', Thus saith the Lord God 559
28 even s' thou, The sword, the sword "
22: 3 s' thou, Thus saith the Lord God, "
24 s' unto her, Thou art the land that "
24: 3 s' unto them, Thus saith the Lord "
25: 3 s' unto the Ammonites, Hear the "
8 Because that Moab and Seir do s', "
26:17 s' to thee, How art thou destroyed, "
27: 3 And s' unto Tyrus, O thou that art "
28: 2 s' unto the prince of Tyrus, Thus "
9 yet s' before him that slayeth thee, "
12 the king of Tyrus, and s' unto him, "
22 and s', Thus saith the Lord God, "
29: 3 and s', Thus saith the Lord God; "
30: 2 and s', Thus saith the Lord God; "
32: 2 s' unto him, Thou art like a young "

Eze 33: 2 and s' unto them, When I bring the 559
8 When I s' unto the wicked, O wicked "
11 S' unto them, As I live, saith the "
12 s' unto the children of thy people, "
13 When I shall s' to the righteous, "
14 I s' unto the wicked, Thou shalt "
17 Yet the children of thy people s', The "
20 Yet ye s', The way of the Lord is not "
25 Wherefore s' unto them, Thus saith "
27 S' thou thus unto them, Thus saith "
34: 2 s' unto them, Thus saith the Lord "
35: 3 s' unto it, Thus saith the Lord God; "
36: 1 s', Ye mountains of Israel, hear the "
3 prophesy and s', Thus saith the "
6 s' unto the mountains, and to the "
13 s' unto you, Thou land devourest up "
22 s' unto the house of Israel, Thus "
35 And they shall s', This land that was "
37: 4 s' unto them, O ye dry bones, hear "
9 and s' to the wind, Thus saith the "
11 they s', Our bones are dried, and our "
12 s' unto them, Thus saith the Lord "
19 S' unto them, Thus saith the Lord 1696
21 s' unto them, Thus saith the Lord "
38: 3 And s', Thus saith the Lord God; 559
11 And thou shalt s', I will go up to the "
13 s' unto thee, Art thou come to take "
14 prophesy and s' unto Gog, Thus "
39: 1 prophesy against Gog, and s', Thus "
44: 5 all that I s' unto thee concerning 1696
6 thou shalt s' to the rebellious, even 559
Da 4:35 or s' unto him, What doest thou? 560
5:11 king, I s', thy father made master of
Ho 2: 1 S' ye unto your brethren, Ammi; 559
7 shall she s', I will go and return to "
23 I will s' to them which were not my "
23 and they shall s', Thou art my God. "
10: 3 now they shall s', We have no king, "
8 shall s' to the mountains, Cover us; "
13: 2 they s' of them, Let the men that "
14: 2 s' unto him, Take away all iniquity, "
3 will we s' any more to the work of "
8 Ephraim shall s', What have I to do "
Joe 2:17 and let them s', Spare thy people, O 559
17 should they s' among the people, "
19 Lord will answer and s' unto his "
3:10 spears: let the weak s', I am strong. "
Am 3: 9 s', Assemble yourselves upon the "
4: 1 s' to their masters, Bring, and let us "
5:16 s' in all the highways, Alas! alas! "
6:10 s' unto him that is by the sides of "
10 any with thee? and he shall s', No. "
10 Then shall he s', Hold thy tongue: "
13 which s', Have we not taken to us "
8:14 and s', Thy god, O Dan, liveth; and, "
9:10 which s', The evil shall not overtake "
Mic 2: 4 and s', We be utterly spoiled: he "
6 ye not, s' they to them that prophesy: *
3:11 and s', Is not the Lord among us? 559
4: 2 s', Come, and let us go up to the "
11 thee, that s', Let her be defiled, and "
Na 3: 7 thee, and s', Nineveh is laid waste: "
Hab 2: 1 to see what he will s' unto me, *1696
6 against him, and s', Woe to him 559
Zep 1:12 s' in their heart, The Lord will not "
Hag 1: 2 This people s', The time is not come, "
Zec 1: 3 s' thou unto them, Thus saith the "
11: 5 they that sell them s', Blessed be the "
12: 5 governors of Judah shall s' in their "
13: 3 s' unto him, Thou shalt not live; "
5 he shall s', I am no prophet, I am an "
6 s' unto him, What are these wounds "
9 hear them: I will s', It is my people: "
9 they shall s', The Lord is my God. "
Mal 1: 2 Yet ye s', Wherein hast thou loved "
5 and ye shall s', The Lord will be "
6 ye s', Wherein have we despised thy "
7 and ye s', Wherein have we polluted "
7 In that ye s', The table of the Lord "
12 But ye have profaned it, in that ye s', "
2:14 Yet ye s', Wherefore? Because the "
17 Yet ye s', Wherein have we wearied "
17 When ye s', Every one that doeth "
3: 8 But ye s', Wherein have we robbed "
13 ye s', What have we spoken so much "
M't 3: 9 think not to s' within yourselves, 3004
9 I s' unto you, that God is able of "
4:17 and to s', Repent: for the kingdom "
5:11 s' all manner of evil against you 2036
18 I s' unto you, Till heaven and earth 3004
20 For I s' unto you, That except your "
22 But I s' unto you, That whosoever "
22 whosoever shall s' to his brother, 2036
22 but whosoever shall s', Thou fool, "
26 I s' unto thee, Thou shalt by no 3004
28, 32 I s' unto you, That whosoever "
34 But I s' unto you, Swear not at all; "
39 But I s' unto you, That ye resist not "
44 I s' unto you, Love your enemies, "
6: 2, 5, 16 I s' unto you, They have their "
25 I s' unto you, Take no thought for "
29 I s' unto you, That even Solomon "
7: 4 Or how wilt thou s' to thy brother, 2046
22 Many will s' to me in that day, Lord, "
8: 9 I s' to this man, Go, and he goeth; 3004
10 I s' unto you, I have not found so "
11 I s' unto you, That many shall come "
9: 5 easier, to s', Thy sins be forgiven 2036
5 thee; or to s', Arise, and walk? "
10:15 I s'...It shall be more tolerable 3004
23 I s' unto you, Ye shall not have gone "
42 I s' unto you, he shall in no wise lose "
11: 7 to s' unto the multitudes concerning "
9 yea, I s' unto you, and more than a "
11 I s' unto you, Among them that are "
18 and they s', He hath a devil. "

M't 11:19 they s', Behold a man gluttonous, 3004
22 But I s'...It shall be more tolerable "
24 But I s'...it shall be more tolerable "
12: 6 But I s' unto you, That in this place "
31 I s' unto you, All manner of sin and "
36 I s' unto you, That every idle word "
13:17 I s' unto you, That many prophets "
30 I will s' to the reapers, Gather 2046
51 They s' unto him, Yea, Lord. 3004
14:17 s' unto him, We have...five loaves, "
15: 5 But ye s', Whosoever shall "
5 s' to his father or his mother, It is 2036
33 his disciples s' unto him, Whence 3004
16: 2 it is evening, ye s', It will be fair "
13 men s' that I the Son of man am? "
14 Some s' that thou art John the "
15 them, But whom s' ye that I am? 3004
18 And I s' also...That thou art Peter, "
28 Verily I s'...There be some standing "
17:10 Why then s' the scribes that Elias "
12 I s' unto you, That Elias is come "
20 verily I s' unto you, If ye have faith "
20 ye shall s' unto this mountain, 2046
18: 3 Verily I s'...Except ye be converted, 3004
10 for I s' unto you, That in heaven "
13 I s' unto you, he rejoiceth more "
18 I s'...Whatsoever ye shall bind on "
19 I s' unto you, That if two of you "
22 I s' not unto thee, Until seven times: "
19: 7 They s' unto him, Why did Moses "
9 I s' unto you, Whosoever shall put "
10 His disciples s' unto him, If the case "
23 Verily I s' unto you, That a rich man "
24 again I s'...It is easier for a camel "
28 I s'...That ye which have followed "
20: 7 They s' unto him, Because no man "
22 They s' unto him, We are able. "
33 s' unto him, Lord, that our eyes "
21: 3 And if any man s' ought unto you, 2036
3 ye shall s', The Lord hath need of 2046
16 him, Hearest thou what these s'? *3004
21 I s' unto you, If ye have faith, and "
21 if ye shall s' unto this mountain, 2036
25 If we shall s', From heaven; "
25 he will s' unto us, Why did ye not 2046
26 But if we shall s', Of men; we fear 2036
31 They s' unto him, The first. Jesus 3004
31 I s' unto you, That the publicans "
41 They s' unto him, He will miserably "
43 s' I unto you, The kingdom of God "
22:21 They s' unto him, Cæsar's. Then "
23 which s'...there is no resurrection, "
42 They s' unto him, The son of David. "
23: 3 their works: for they s', and do not. "
16 ye blind guides, which s', Whosoever "
30 And s', If we had been in the days "
36 Verily I s' unto you, All these things "
39 I s' unto you, Ye shall not see me "
39 till ye shall s', Blessed is he that 2036
24: 2 I s'...There shall not be left one 3004
23 if any man shall s'...Lo, here is 2036
26 shall s'...Behold, he is in the desert; "
34 I s' unto you, This generation 3004
47 I s'...That he shall make him ruler "
48 evil servant shall s' in his heart, 2036
25:12 I s' unto you, I know you not. 3004
34 King s' unto them on his right 2046
40 King shall answer and s' unto them, "
40 Verily I s' unto you, Inasmuch as 3004
41 he s' also unto them on the left 2046
45 Verily I s' unto you, Inasmuch as 3004
26:13 Verily I s' unto you, Wheresoever "
18 and s' unto him, The Master saith, 2036
21 Verily I s' unto you, that one of you 3004
22 them to s' unto him, Lord, is it I? "
29 But I s' unto you, I will not drink "
34 I s' unto thee, That this night, 3346
64 I s' unto you, Hereafter shall ye 3004
27:22 They all s'...Let him be crucified. "
33 that is to s', a place of a skull, "
46 that is to s', My God, my God, why *
64 and s' unto the people, He is risen 2036
28:13 S' ye, His disciples came by night, "
M'r 1:44 See thou s' nothing to any man: "
2: 9 s' to the sick of the palsy, Thy sins "
9 or to s', Arise, and take up thy bed, "
11 I s' unto thee, Arise, and take up 3004
18 come and s'...Why do the disciples "
3:28 Verily I s' unto you, All sins shall "
4:38 and s' unto him, Master, carest thou "
5:41 Damsel, I s' unto thee, arise. "
6:11 I s'...It shall be more tolerable * "
37 And they s'...Shall we go and buy "
38 knew, they s', Five, and two fishes. "
7: 2 that is to s', with unwashen, hands, * "
11 But ye s', If a man shall "
11 shall s' to his father or mother, 2036
11 It is Corban, that is to s', a gift, by
8:12 I s' unto you, There shall no sign 3004
19 ye up? They s' unto him, Twelve. "
27 them, Whom do men s' that I am? "
28 John the Baptist: but some s', Elias; *
29 them, But whom s' ye that I am? 3004
9: 1 I s' unto you, That there be some "
6 For he wist not what to s'; for *2980
11 Why s' the scribes that Elias must 3004
13 I s' unto you, That Elias is indeed "
41 I s' unto you, he shall not lose his "
10:15 I s' unto you, Whosoever shall not "
28 Peter began to s'...Lo, we have left "
29 Verily I s' unto you, There is no man "
47 and s', Jesus, thou son of David, "
11: 3 man s' unto you, Why do ye this? 2036
3 s' ye that the Lord hath need of "
23 I s' unto you, That whosoever 3004
23 shall s' unto this mountain, Be thou 2036

M'r 11:24 I s· unto you, What things soever 3004
28 And s· unto him, By what authority* "
31 If we shall s·, From heaven; 2036
31 he will s·, Why...did ye not believe 2046
32 But if we shall s·, Of men; they 2036
12:14 they s· unto him, Master, we know 3004
18 which s· there is no resurrection; "
35 How s· the scribes that Christ is the "
13: 5 began to s·, Take heed that no man "
21 if any man shall s· to you, Lo, here 2036
30 Verily I s·...that this generation 3004
37 And what I s· unto you I s· unto all, "
14: 9 Verily I s· unto you, Wheresoever "
14 s· ye to the goodman of the house, 2036
18 Verily I s· unto you, One of you 3004
19 to s· unto him one by one, Is it I? "
25 I s· unto you, I will drink no more "
30 Verily I s· unto thee, That this day, "
58 We heard him s·, I will destroy this "
65 him, and to s· unto him, Prophesy: "
69 began to s·...This is one of them. "
Lu 3: 8 begin not to s· within yourselves, "
8 for I s· unto you, That God is able "
4:21 he began to s· unto them, This day "
23 surely s· unto me this proverb, 2046
24 Verily I s· unto you, No prophet is 3004
5:23 easier, to s·, Thy sins be forgiven 2036
23 thee; or to s·, Rise up and walk? "
24 I s· unto thee, Arise, and take up 3004
6:27 But I s· unto you which hear, Love "
42 how canst thou s· to thy brother, "
46 and do not the things which I s·? "
7: 7 but s· in a word, and my servant 2036
8 I s· unto one, Go, and he goeth; 3004
9 I s· unto you, I have not found so "
14 Young man, I s· unto thee, Arise. "
26 Yea, I s· unto you, and much more "
28 I s· unto you, Among those that are "
33 wine; and ye s·, He hath a devil. "
34 and ye s·, Behold a gluttonous man, "
40 I have somewhat to s· unto thee. 2036
40 thee. And he saith, Master, s· on. "
47 I s· unto thee, Her sins, which are 3004
49 s· within themselves, Who is this "
9:18 Whom s· the people that I am? "
19 John the Baptist;...some s·, Elias; 2036
19 others s·,...one of the old prophets*
20 But whom s· ye that I am? Peter 3004
10: 5 first s·, Peace be to this house. "
9 s· unto them, The kingdom of God "
10 into the streets of the same, and s·, 2036
12 I s·...that it shall be more tolerable 3004
11: 2 When ye pray, s·, Our Father which "
5 s· unto him, Friend, lend me three 2036
7 answer and s·, Trouble me not: "
8 I s· unto you, Though he will not 3004
9 I s· unto you, Ask, and it shall be "
18 because ye s· that I cast out devils "
29 to s·, This is an evil generation: "
51 I s· unto you, It shall be required "
12: 1 he began to s· unto his disciples "
4 I s· unto you my friends, Be not "
5 hell; yea, I s· unto you, Fear him. "
8 Also I s·...Whosoever shall confess "
11 shall answer, or what ye shall s·: 2036
12 the same hour what ye ought to s·. "
19 And I will s· to my soul, Soul, thou 2046
22 I s· unto you, Take no thought 3004
27 I s· unto you, that Solomon in all "
37 I s· unto you, that he shall gird "
44 I s·...that he will make him ruler "
45 and if that servant s· in his heart, 2036
54 ye s·, There cometh a shower; 3004
55 wind blow, ye s·, There will be heat; "
13:24 for many, I s·...will seek to enter "
25 and s· unto you, I know you not 2046
26 shall ye begin to s·, We have eaten 3004
27 shall s·, I tell you, I know you not 2046
35 I s· unto you, Ye shall not see me, 3004
35 when ye shall s·, Blessed is he 2036
14: 9 s· to thee, Give this man place; 2046
10 he may s· unto thee, Friend, go 2036
17 to s· to them that were bidden, "
24 I s· unto you, That none of those 3004
15: 7 I s· unto you, that likewise joy "
10 I s· unto you, there is joy in the "
18 will s· unto him, Father, I have 2046
16: 9 I s· unto you, Make to yourselves 3004
17: 6 ye might s· unto this sycamine "
7 will s· unto him by and by, when 2046
8 will no rather s· unto him, Make "
10 s·, We are unprofitable servants: 3004
21 Neither shall they s·, Lo here! or, 2046
23 they shall s· to you, See here; or, "
18:17 Verily I s· unto you, Whosoever 3004
29 Verily I s· unto you, There is no "
19:26 I s· unto you, That unto every one "
31 thus shall ye s· unto him, Because 2046
20: 5 If we shall s·, From heaven; 2036
5 he will s·, Why then believed ye 2046
6 if we s·, Of men; all the people 2036
41 How s· they that Christ is David's "
21: 3 Of a truth I s· unto you, that this 3004
32 Verily I s· unto you, This generation "
22:11 ye shall s· unto the goodman of 2046
16 For I s· unto you, I will not any 3004
18 For I s· unto you, I will not drink "
37 For I s· unto you, that this that is "
70 said unto them, Ye s· that I am. "
23:29 in the which they shall s·, Blessed 2046
30 they begin to s· to the mountains, 3004
43 Verily I s· unto thee, To day shalt "
Joh 1:38 (which is to s·, being interpreted, "
51 I s· unto you, Hereafter ye shall "
3: 3, 5 verily, I s· unto thee, Except a "
11 Verily, verily, I s· unto thee, We "
Joh 4:20 and ye s·, that in Jerusalem is the 3004
35 S· not ye, There are yet four months, "
35 behold, I s· unto you, Lift up your "
5:19 verily, I s· unto you, The Son can "
24 I s· unto you, He that heareth my "
25 I s· unto you, The hour is coming, "
34 these things I s·, that ye might be "
6:26 verily, I s· unto you, Ye seek me, "
32 I s· unto you, Moses gave you not "
47 I s· unto you, He that believeth on "
53 I s· unto you, Except ye eat the "
7:26 and they s· nothing unto him. Do "
8: 4 s· unto him, Master, this woman "
26 things to s· and to judge of you: *2980
34 verily, I s· unto you, Whosoever 3004
46 And if I s· the truth, why do ye not "
48 S· we not well that thou art a "
51 I s· unto you, If a man keep my "
54 of whom ye s·, that he is your God: "
55 and if I should s·, I know him not, "
58 I s· unto you, Before Abraham was, "
9:17 They s· unto the blind man again, "
19 your son, who ye s· was born blind? "
41 but now ye s·, We see; therefore "
10: 1 Verily, verily, I s· unto you, He that "
7 I s· unto you, I am the door of the "
36 S· ye of him, whom the Father "
11: 8 His disciples s· unto him, Master, "
12:24 verily, I s· unto you, Except a corn "
27 what shall I s·? Father, save me 2036
49 should s·, and what I should speak. "
13:13 Master and Lord: and ye s· well; 3004
16 I s· unto you, The servant is not "
20 I s· unto you, He that receiveth "
21 I s· unto you, that one of you shall "
33 ye cannot come; so now I s· to you. "
38 I s· unto thee, The cock shall not "
14:12 I s· unto you, He that believeth on "
16:12 yet many things to s· unto you, but "
20 I s· unto you, That ye shall weep "
23 verily, I s· unto you, Whatsoever ye "
26 I s· not unto you, that I will pray "
20:13 s· unto her, Woman, why weepest "
16 Rabboni; which is to s·, Master. "
17 s· unto them, I ascend unto my 2036
21: 3 They s· unto him, We also go with 3004
18 I s· unto thee, When thou wast "
Ac 1:19 Aceldama, that is to s·, The field of*
3:22 whatsoever he shall s· unto you. *2980
4:14 they could s· nothing against it. 471
5:38 now I s· unto you, Refrain from 3004
6:14 For we have heard him s·, that "
10:37 That word, I s·, ye know which was*
13:15 exhortation for the people, s· on. 3004
17:18 said, What will this babbler s·? "
21:23 therefore this that we s· to thee: "
23: 8 s· that there is no resurrection, "
18 hath something to s· unto thee. 2980
30 to s· before thee what they had *3004
24:20 else let these same here s·, if they 2036
26:22 which...Moses did s· should come: 2980
28:26 and s·, Hearing ye shall hear, 2036
Ro 3: 5 of God, what shall we s·? Is God 2046
8 as some affirm that we s·,) Let us 3004
26 I s·, at this time his righteousness: "
4: 1 s· then that Abraham our father, 2046
9 we s· that faith was reckoned to 3004
6: 1 What shall we s· then? Shall we 2046
7: 7 What shall we s· then? Is the law "
8:31 shall we then s· to these things? "
9: 1 I s· the truth in Christ, I lie not, 3004
14 What shall we s· then? Is there 2046
19 Thou wilt s· then unto me, Why "
20 Shall the thing formed s· to him "
30 What shall we s· then? That the "
10: 6 S· not in thine heart, Who shall 2036
18 I s·, Have they not heard? Yes 3004
19 But I s·, Did not Israel know? Yes "
11: 1 I s· then, Hath God cast away his 2046
11 I s· then, Have they stumbled that "
19 Thou wilt s· then, The branches "
12: 3 For I s·, through the grace given 3004
15: 8 s· that Jesus Christ was a minister "
1Co 1:12 Now this I s·, that every one of you* "
15 s· that I had baptized in mine 2036
7: 8 I s· therefore to the unmarried 3004
26 I s·, that it is good for a man so to be.*
29 I s·, brethren, the time is short: 5346
9: 8 S· I these things as a man? or *2980
10:15 to wise men; judge ye what I s·. 5346
19 What s· I then? that the idol is any "
20 But I s·, that the things which the "
28 But if any man s· unto you, This 2036
29 Conscience, I s·, not thine own, 3004
11:22 What shall I s· to you? shall I 2036
12: 3 no man can s·...Jesus is the Lord, "
15 If the foot shall s·, Because I am "
16 if the ear shall s·, Because I am "
21 the eye cannot s· unto the hand, I "
14:16 s· Amen at thy giving of thanks, 2046
23 will they not s· that ye are mad? "
15:12 how s· some among you that there 3004
35 But some man will s·, How are the 2046
50 Now this I s·, brethren, that flesh 5346
2Co 5: 8 We are confident, I s·, and willing
9: 4 we (that we s· not, ye) should be 3004
6 thus I s·, He which soweth sparingly,
10:10 For his letters, s· they, are weighty 5346
11:16 I s· again, Let no man think me a 3004
12: 6 for I will s· the truth: but now I *2046
Ga 1: 9 so s· I...again, If any man preach 3004
3:17 this I s·, that the covenant that "
4: 1 Now I s·, That the heir, as long as "
5: 2 I Paul s· unto you, that if ye be "
16 I s· then, Walk in the Spirit, and ye "
Eph 4:17 This I s·...and testify in the Lord, "
Ph'p 4: 4 alway: and again I s·, Rejoice. 2046
Col 1:20 by him, I s·, whether they be things
2: 4 And this I s·, lest any man should 3004
4:17 s· to Archippus, Take heed to the 2036
1Th 4:15 this we s· unto you by the word 3004
5: 3 For when they shall s·, Peace and* "
1Ti 1: 7 understanding neither what they s·, "
2Ti 2: 7 Consider what I s·; and the Lord "
Tit 2: 8 having no evil thing to s· of you. "
Ph'm 19 I do not s· to thee how thou owest "
21 thou wilt also do more than I s·. "
Heb 5:11 whom we have many things to s·, 3056
7: 9 And as I may so s·, Levi also, 2031, 2036
9:11 that is to s·, not of this building;
10:20 through the veil, that is to s·, his flesh;
11:14 they that s· such things declare 3004
32 what shall I more s·? for the time "
13: 6 So that we may boldly s·, The Lord "
Jas 1:13 Let no man s· when he is tempted, "
2: 3 and s· unto him, Sit thou here in a 2036
3 s· to the poor, Stand thou there, or "
14 though a man s· he hath faith, and 3004
16 one of you s· unto them, Depart 2036
18 a man may s·, Thou hast faith, 2046
4:13 Go to now, ye that s·, To day or 3004
15 that ye ought to s·, If the Lord will. "
1Jo 1: 6 If we s· that we have fellowship 2036
8 If we s· that we have no sin, we "
10 If we s· that we have not sinned, "
4:20 If a man s·, I love God, and hateth "
5:16 do not s· that he shall pray for it. 3004
Re 2: 2 them which s· they are apostles, *5335
9 of them which s· they are Jews, 3004
24 unto you I s·, and unto the rest "
3: 9 which s· they are Jews, and are "
6: 3 the second beast s·, Come and see.* "
5 the third beast s·, Come and see. * "
6 in the midst of the four beasts s·, * "
7 the fourth beast s·, Come and see.* "
16: 5 heard the angel of the waters s·, * "
7 heard another out of the altar s·, * "
22:17 the Spirit and the bride s·, Come.* "
17 And let him that heareth s·, Come. 2036

sayers See GAINSAYERS; SOOTHSAYERS.

sayest
Ex 33:12 s· unto me, Bring up this people: 559
Nu 22:17 I will do whatsoever thou s· unto "
Ru 3: 5 All that thou s· unto me I will do. "
1Ki 18:11, 14 And now thou s·, Go, tell thy lord, "
2Ki 18:20 Thou s·,...I have counsel and "
2Ch 25:19 Thou s·, Lo, thou hast smitten the "
Ne 5:12 of them; so will we do as thou s·. "
6: 8 are no such things done as thou s·. "
Job 22:13 And thou s·, How doth God know? "
35:14 thou s· thou shalt not see him, yet "
Ps 90: 3 and s·, Return, ye children of men. "
Pr 24:12 If thou s·, Behold, we knew it not; "
Isa 36: 5 I say, s· thou, (but they are but vain*
40:27 Why s· thou, O Jacob,...speakest, 559
47: 8 that s· in thine heart, I am, and none "
Jer 2:35 Yet thou s·, Because I am innocent,* "
35 because thou s·, I have not sinned. "
Am 7:16 Thou s·, Prophesy not against Israel, "
M't 26:70 saying, I know not what thou s·. 3004
27:11 And Jesus said unto him, Thou s·. "
M'r 5:31 thee, and s· thou, Who touched me? "
14:68 neither understand I what thou s·. "
15: 2 answering said unto him, Thou s· it. "
Lu 8:45 and s· thou, Who touched me? *2036
20:21 that thou s· and teachest rightly, 3004
22:60 said, Man, I know not what thou s·. "
23: 3 answered him and said, Thou s· it. "
Joh 1:22 sent us. What s· thou of thyself? "
8: 5 should be stoned: but what s· thou? "
33 how s· thou, Ye shall be made free? "
52 thou s·, If a man keep my saying, "
9:17 What s· thou of him, that he hath "
12:34 how s· thou, The Son of man must "
14: 9 and how s· thou then, Shew us the "
18:34 S· thou this thing of thyself, or did "
37 answered, Thou s· that I am a king. "
Ro 2:22 that s· a man should not commit "
1Co 14:16 he understandeth not what thou s·? "
Re 3:17 thou s·, I am rich, and increased "

saying See also GAINSAYING; SAYINGS; SOOTHSAYING.
Ge 1:22 God blessed them, s·, Be fruitful, 559
2:16 s·, Of every tree of the garden thou "
3:17 s·, Thou shalt not eat of it: cursed "
5:29 called his name Noah, s·, This same "
8:15 And God spake unto Noah, s·, "
9: 8 Noah, and to his sons with him, s·, "
15: 1 s·, Fear not, Abram: I am thy shield, "
4 him, s·, This shall not be thine heir; "
18 s·, Unto thy seed have I given this "
17: 3 face: and God talked with him, s·, "
18:12 Sarah laughed within herself, s·, "
13 Wherefore did Sarah laugh, s·, Shall "
15 Sarah denied, s·, I laughed not; for "
19:15 Lot, s·, Arise, take thy wife, and thy "
21:22 spake unto Abraham, s·, God is with "
22:20 that it was told Abraham, s·, Behold, "
23: 3 and spake unto the sons of Heth, s·, "
5 answered Abraham, s· unto him, "
8 he communed with them, s·, If it be "
10 went in at the gate of his city, s·, "
13 s·, But if thou wilt give it, I pray "
14 answered Abraham, s· unto him, "
24: 7 and that sware unto me, s·, Unto thy "
30 the words of Rebekah his sister, s·, "
37 my master made me swear, s·, Thou "
26:11 Abimelech charged all his people, s·, "
20 herdmen, s·, The water is ours: and "
27: 6 spake unto Jacob her son, s·, Behold, "
6 speak unto Esau thy brother, s·, "

Ge 28: 6 s', Thou shalt not take a wife of the559
20 Jacob vowed a vow, s', If God will be"
31: 1 heard the words of Laban's sons, s', "
11 spake unto me in a dream, s', Jacob:*
29 spake unto me yesternight, s', Take 559
32: 4 he commanded them, s', Thus shall "
6 the messengers returned to Jacob, s',"
17 commanded the foremost, s', When "
17 and asketh thee, s', Whose art thou?"
19 s', On this manner shall ye speak "
34: 4 s', Get me this damsel to wife. "
8 with them, s', The soul of my son "
20 with the men of their city, s', "
37: 11 but his father observed the s'. 1697
15 asked him, s', What seekest thou? 559
38: 13 Tamar, s', Behold thy father in law "
21 s', Where is the harlot, that was "
24 s', Tamar thy daughter in law hath "
25 s', By the man, whose these are, am "
28 thread, s', This came out first. "
39: 12 him by his garment, s', Lie with me:"
14 and spake unto them, s', See, he hath"
17 s', The Hebrew servant, which thou "
19 unto him, s', After this manner did "
40: 7 s', Wherefore look ye so sadly to day?"
41: 9 s', I do remember my faults this day:"
16 Pharaoh, s', It is not in me: God "
42: 14 I spake unto you, s', Ye are spies: "
22 them, s', Spake I not unto you, s', Do"
28 s' one to another, What is this that "
29 told him all that befell unto them; s',"
37 Reuben spake unto his father, s', "
43: 3 Judah spake unto him, s', The man "
3 protest unto us, s', Ye shall not see "
7 kindred, s', Is your father yet alive? "
44: 1 s', Fill the men's sacks with food, as "
19 My lord asked his servants, s', Have"
32 unto my father, s', If I bring him not"
45: 16 s', Joseph's brethren are come: and "
26 told him, s', Joseph is yet alive, and "
47: 5 unto Joseph, s', Thy father and thy "
48: 20 day, s', In thee shall Israel bless, "
20 s', God make thee as Ephraim and as"
50: 4 s', If now I have found grace in "
4 pray you, in the ears of Pharaoh, s', "
5 My father made me swear, s', Lo, I "
16 sent a messenger unto Joseph, s', "
16 did command before he died, s', "
25 s', God will surely visit you, and ye "
Ex 1: 22 his people, s', Every son that is born"
3: 16 unto me, s', I have surely visited you,"
5: 6 of the people, and their officers, s', "
8 s', Let us go and sacrifice to our God."
10 s', Thus saith Pharaoh, I will not "
13 taskmasters hasted them, s', Fulfil "
15 cried unto Pharaoh, s', Wherefore "
6: 10 And the Lord spake unto Moses, s', "
12 And Moses spake before the Lord, s',"
29 spake unto Moses, s', I am the Lord:"
7: 8 unto Moses and unto Aaron, s', "
9 unto you, s', Shew a miracle for you:"
16 s', Let my people go, that they may "
9: 5 s', To morrow the Lord shall do this"
11: 8 themselves unto me, s', Get thee out,"
12: 1 and Aaron in the land of Egypt, s', "
3 s', In the tenth day of this month "
13: 1 And the Lord spake unto Moses, s', "
8 shew thy son in that day, s', This is "
14 in time to come, s', What is this? "
19 Israel, s', God will surely visit you; "
14: 1 And the Lord spake unto Moses, s', "
12 we did tell thee in Egypt, s', Let us "
15: 1 and spake, s', I will sing unto the "
24 Moses, s', What shall we drink? "
16: 11 And the Lord spake unto Moses, s', "
12 them, s', At even ye shall eat flesh, "
17: 4 Moses cried unto the Lord, s', What "
7 s', Is the Lord among us, or not? "
19: 3 s', Thus shalt thou say to the house "
12 s', Take heed to yourselves, that ye "
23 s', Set bounds about the mount, and"
20: 1 And God spake all these words, s', "
25: 1 And the Lord spake unto Moses, s', "
30: 11, 17, 22 the Lord spake unto Moses, s',"
31 speak unto the children of Israel, s',"
31: 1, 12 the Lord spake unto Moses, s', "
13 s', Verily my sabbaths ye shall keep:"
33: 1 Jacob, s', Unto thy seed will I give it:"
35: 4 of Israel, s', This is the thing which "
4 thing which the Lord commanded, s',"
36: 5 spake unto Moses, s', The people "
6 s', Let neither man nor woman make"
40: 1 And the Lord spake unto Moses, s', "
Le 1: 1 tabernacle of the congregation, s', "
4: 1 And the Lord spake unto Moses, s', "
2 Israel, s', If a soul shall sin through"
5: 14 And the Lord spake unto Moses, s', "
6: 1, 8 the Lord spake unto Moses, s', "
9 Command Aaron and his sons, s', "
19, 24 the Lord spake unto Moses, s', "
25 s', This is the law of the sin offering:"
7: 22 And the Lord spake unto Moses, s', "
23 s', Ye shall eat no manner of fat, of "
28 And the Lord spake unto Moses, s', "
29 of Israel, s', He that offereth the "
8: 1 And the Lord spake unto Moses, s', "
31 s', Aaron and his sons shall eat it. "
9: 3 s', Take ye a kid of the goats for a "
10: 3 s', I will be sanctified in them that "
8 And the Lord spake unto Aaron, s', "
16 of Aaron which were left alive, s', "
11: 1 Moses and to Aaron, s' unto them, "
2 s', These are the beasts which ye "
12: 1 And the Lord spake unto Moses, s', "
2 s', If a woman have conceived seed, "
13: 1 Lord spake unto Moses and Aaron, s',"

Le 14: 1 And the Lord spake unto Moses, s',559
33 spake unto Moses and unto Aaron, s',"
35 tell the priest, s', It seemeth to me "
15: 1 spake unto Moses and to Aaron, s', "
17: 1 And the Lord spake unto Moses, s', "
2 which the Lord hath commanded, s',"
18: 1 And the Lord spake unto Moses, s', "
19: 1 And the Lord spake unto Moses, s', "
20: 1 And the Lord spake unto Moses, s', "
21: 16 And the Lord spake unto Moses, s', "
17 Speak unto Aaron, s', Whosoever he "
22: 1, 17, 26 the Lord spake unto Moses, s',"
23: 1, 9, 23 the Lord spake unto Moses, s',"
24 s', In the seventh month, in the first "
26, 33 the Lord spake unto Moses, s', "
34 s', The fifteenth day of this seventh "
24: 1, 13 the Lord spake unto Moses, s', "
15 s', Whosoever curseth his God shall "
25: 1 spake unto Moses in mount Sinai, s', "
27: 1 And the Lord spake unto Moses, s', "
Nu 1: 1 come out of the land of Egypt, s', "
48 the Lord had spoken unto Moses, s', "
2: 1 spake unto Moses and unto Aaron, s',"
3: 5, 11 the Lord spake unto Moses, s', "
14 Moses in the wilderness of Sinai, s', "
44 And the Lord spake unto Moses, s', "
4: 1, 17 unto Moses and unto Aaron, s', "
21 And the Lord spake unto Moses, s', "
5: 1, 5, 11 the Lord spake unto Moses, s', "
6: 1, 22 the Lord spake unto Moses, s', "
23 s', On this wise ye shall bless "
23 ye shall bless...Israel, s' unto them* "
7: 4 And the Lord spake unto Moses, s', "
8: 1, 5, 23 the Lord spake unto Moses, s', "
9: 1 come out of the land of Egypt, s', "
9 And the Lord spake unto Moses, s', "
10 s', If any man of you or of your "
10: 1 And the Lord spake unto Moses, s', "
11: 13 s', Give us flesh, that we may eat. "
18 s', Who shall give us flesh to eat? "
20 s', Why came we forth out of Egypt?"
12: 13 s', Heal her now, O God, I beseech "
13: 1 And the Lord spake unto Moses, s', "
32 s', The land, through which we have"
14: 7 s', The land, which we passed "
15 heard the fame of thee will speak, s',"
17 according as thou hast spoken, s', "
26 spake unto Moses and unto Aaron, s',"
40 s', Lo, we be here, and will go up "
15: 1, 17, 37 Lord spake unto Moses, s', "
16: 5 s', Even to morrow the Lord will "
20 spake unto Moses and unto Aaron, s',"
23 And the Lord spake unto Moses, s', "
24 s', Get you up from about the "
26 s', Depart, I pray you, from the tents"
36 And the Lord spake unto Moses, s', "
41 s', Ye have killed the people of the "
44 And the Lord spake unto Moses, s', "
17: 1 And the Lord spake unto Moses, s', "
12 Moses, s', Behold, we die, we perish,"
18: 25 And the Lord spake unto Moses, s', "
19: 1 spake unto Moses and unto Aaron, s',"
2 s', Speak unto the children of Israel, "
20: 3 s', Would God that we had died when"
7 And the Lord spake unto Moses, s', "
23 by the coast of the land of Edom, s', "
21: 21 unto Sihon king of the Amorites, s', "
22: 5 s', Behold, there is a people come "
10 king of Moab, hath sent unto me, s', "
23: 7 s', Come, curse me Jacob, and come, "
26 s', All that the Lord speaketh, that 559
24: 12 which thou sentest unto me, s', "
25: 10, 16 the Lord spake unto Moses, s', "
26: 1 and unto Eleazar...the priest, s', "
3 of Moab by Jordan near Jericho, s', "
52 And the Lord spake unto Moses, s', "
27: 2 tabernacle of the congregation, s', "
6 And the Lord spake unto Moses, s', "
8 s', If a man die, and have no son, "
15 And Moses spake unto the Lord, s', "
28: 1 And the Lord spake unto Moses, s', "
30: 1 s', This is the thing which the "
31: 1 And the Lord spake unto Moses, s', "
3 s', Arm some of yourselves unto the "
25 And the Lord spake unto Moses, s', "
32: 2 the princes of the congregation, s', "
10 the same time, and he sware, s', "
25 of Reuben spake unto Moses, s', Thy"
31 children of Reuben answered, s', As "
33: 50 of Moab by Jordan near Jericho, s', "
34: 1 And the Lord spake unto Moses, s', "
13 children of Israel, s', This is the "
16 And the Lord spake unto Moses, s', "
35: 1 of Moab by Jordan near Jericho, s', "
9 And the Lord spake unto Moses, s', "
36: 5 word of the Lord, s', The tribe of "
6 s', Let them marry to whom they "
De 1: 5 began Moses to declare this law, s', "
6 s', Ye have dwelt long enough in this"
9 s', I am not able to bear you myself "
16 s', Hear the causes between your "
23 the s' pleased me well: and I took*1697
28 s', The people is greater and taller 559
34 words, and was wroth, and sware, s',"
37 s', Thou also shalt not go in thither."
2: 2 And the Lord spake unto me, s', "
4 s', Ye are to pass through the coast "
17 That the Lord spake unto me, s', "
26 of Heshbon with words of peace, s', "
3: 18 s', The Lord your God hath given "
21 s', Thine eyes have seen all that "
23 I besought the Lord at that time, s',"
5: 5 and went not up into the mount;) s',"
6: 20 s', What mean the testimonies, and "
9: 4 s', For my righteousness the Lord "
13 me, s', I have seen this people, and, "

De 9: 23 s', Go up and possess the land which559
12: 30 s', How did these nations serve their"
13: 2 s', Let us go after other gods, which "
6 s', Let us go and serve other gods, "
12 hath given thee to dwell there, s', "
13 s', Let us go and serve other gods, "
15: 9 s', The seventh year, the year of "
11 s', Thou shalt open thine hand wide "
18: 16 s', Let me not hear again the voice "
19: 7 s', Thou shalt separate three cities "
20: 5 s', What man...hath built a new "
22: 17 s', I found not thy daughter a maid;"
27: 1 s', Keep all the commandments "
9 s', Take heed, and hearken, O Israel;"
11 charged the people the same day, s',"
29: 19 s', I shall have peace, though I walk "
31: 10 s', At the end of every seven years, "
25 ark of the covenant of the Lord, s', "
32: 48 unto Moses that selfsame day, s', "
34: 4 s', I will give it unto thy seed: I have"
Jos 1: 1 the son of Nun, Moses' minister, s', "
10 Joshua commanded the officers...s', "
11 s', Prepare you victuals; for within "
12 tribe of Manasseh, spake Joshua, s', "
13 s', The Lord your God hath given "
16 s', All that thou commandest us we "
2: 1 s', Go view the land, even Jericho. "
2 s', Behold, there came men in hither"
3 s', Bring forth the men that are come"
3: 3 s', When ye see the ark of the "
6 s', Take up the ark of the covenant, "
8 s', When ye are come to the brink of"
4: 1 that the Lord spake unto Joshua, s', "
3 s', Take you hence out of the midst "
6 s', What mean ye by these stones? "
15 And the Lord spake unto Joshua, s',"
17 priests, s', Come ye up out of Jordan."
21 s', When your children shall ask "
21 come, s', What mean these stones? "
22 s', Israel came over this Jordan on "
6: 10 s', Ye shall not shout, nor make any "
26 s', Cursed be the man before the "
7: 2 them, s', Go up and view the country."
8: 4 them, s', Behold, ye shall lie in wait "
9: 11 s', Take victuals with you for the "
22 s', Wherefore have ye beguiled us, "
22 s', We are very far from you; when "
10: 3 and unto Debir king of Eglon, s', "
6 s', Slack not thy hand from thy "
17 s', The five kings are found hid in a "
14: 9 s', Surely the land whereon thy feet "
17: 4 s', The Lord commanded Moses to "
14 s', Why hast thou given me but one "
17 s', Thou art a great people, and hast"
18: 8 s', Go and walk through the land, "
20: 1 The Lord also spake unto Joshua, s',"
2 s', Appoint out for you cities of "
21: 2 s', The Lord commanded by the hand"
22: 8 s', Return with much riches unto "
15 Gilead, and they spake with them, s',"
24 s', In time to come your children "
24 s', What have ye to do with the "
J'g 1: 1 s', Who shall go up for us against "
4: 6 s', Go and draw toward mount Tabor, "
5: 1 the son of Abinoam on that day, s', 559
6: 13 s', Did not the Lord bring us up from"
32 s', Let Baal plead against him, "
7: 2 s', Mine own hand hath saved me. "
3 s', Whosoever is fearful and afraid, "
24 s', Come down against...Midianites, "
8: 9 s', When I come again in peace, I will"
15 s', Are the hands of Zebah and "
9: 1 the house of his mother's father, s', "
31 s', Behold, Gaal the son of Ebed and "
10: 10 s', We have sinned against thee, both"
11: 12 s', What hast thou to do with me, "
17 s', Let me, I pray thee, pass through"
13: 6 s', A man of God came unto me, and "
15: 13 s', No; but we will bind thee fast, "
16: 2 Gazites, s', Samson is come hither. "
2 s', In the morning, when it is day, "
18 s', Come up this once, for he hath "
19: 22 s', Bring forth the man that came "
20: 8 s', We will not any of us go to his "
12 s', What wickedness is this that is "
23 s', Shall I go up again to battle "
28 s', Shall I yet again go out to battle "
21: 1 s', There shall not any of us give his"
5 s', He shall surely be put to death. "
10 s', Go and smite the inhabitants "
18 s', Cursed be he that giveth a wife to"
20 s', Go...lie in wait in the vineyards; "
Ru 2: 15 s', Let her glean even among the "
4: 4 s', Buy it before the inhabitants, and"
17 s', There is a son born to Naomi; and"
1Sa 1: 20 s', Because I have asked him of the "
4: 21 s', The glory is departed from 559
5: 10 s', They have brought about the ark"
6: 2 s', What shall we do to the ark of the"
21 s', The Philistines have brought "
7: 3 s', If ye do return unto the Lord "
12 s', Hitherto hath the Lord helped us."
9: 15 Lord had told Samuel in his ear...s', "
26 s', Up, that I may send thee away. "
10: 2 you, s', What shall I do for my son? "
11: 7 s', Whosoever cometh not forth after"
13: 3 the land, s', Let the Hebrews hear. "
14: 24, 28 s', Cursed be the man that "
33 told Saul, s', Behold, the people sin "
15: 10 word of the Lord unto Samuel, s', "
12 Samuel, s', Saul came to Carmel, "
16: 22 s', Let David...stand before me; "
17: 26 s', What shall be done to the man "
27 s', So shall it be done to the man "
18: 8 wroth, and the s' displeased him; 1697
22 s', Commune with David secretly, "

1Sa 18: 24 s', On this manner spake David. 559
19: 2 s', Saul my father seeketh to kill "
11 s', If thou save not thy life to night, "
15 s', Bring him up to me in the bed, "
19 s',...David is at Naioth in Ramah. "
20: 16 s', Let the Lord even require it at
21 send a lad, s', Go, find out the arrows.
42 s', The Lord be between me and 559
21: 11 s', Saul hath slain his thousands, "
23: 1 s',...the Philistines fight against "
2 David enquired of the Lord, s', Shall "
19 s', Doth not David hide himself with "
27 unto Saul, s', Haste thee, and come; "
24: 1 s', Behold, David is in the wilderness "
8 cried after Saul, s', My lord the king. "
9 s', Behold, David seeketh thy hurt? "
25: 14 Nabal's wife, s', Behold, David sent "
40 unto her, s', David sent us unto thee, "
26: 1 s', Doth not David hide himself in "
6 s', Who will go down with me to "
14 Ner, s', Answerest thou not, Abner? "
19 the Lord, s', Go, serve other gods. "
27: 11 Gath, s', Lest they should tell on us, "
11 s', So did David, and so will be his "
12 s', He hath made his people Israel "
28: 10 s', As the Lord liveth, there shall no "
12 s', Why hast thou deceived me? for "
29: 5 s', Saul slew his thousands, and "
30: 8 s', Shall I pursue after this troop? "
26 s', Behold a present for you of the "
2Sa 1: 16 s', I have slain the Lord's anointed. "
2: 1 enquired of the Lord, s', Shall I go "
4 s', That the men of Jabesh-gilead "
3: 12 on his behalf, s', Whose is the land? "
12 s' also, Make thy league with me, "
14 Saul's son, s', Deliver me my wife "
17 s', Ye sought for David in times "
18 s', By the hand of my servant David "
23 told Joab, s', Abner the son of Ner "
35 David sware, s', So do God to me, "
4: 10 told me, s', Behold, Saul is dead, "
5: 1 s',...we are thy bone and thy flesh. "
6 s', Except thou take away the blind "
19 s', Shall I go up to the Philistines? "
6: 12 s', The Lord hath blessed the house "
7: 4 of the Lord came unto Nathan, s', "
7 s', Why build ye not me an house of "
26 s', The Lord of hosts is the God "
27 s', I will build thee an house: "
11: 6 Joab, s', Send me Uriah the Hittite. "
10 s', Uriah went not down unto his "
15 s', Set ye Uriah in the forefront "
19 s', When thou hast made an end of "
13: 7 s', Go not to thy brother Amnon's "
28 s', Mark ye now when Amnon's "
30 s', Absalom hath slain all the king's "
14: 32 I sent unto thee, s', Come hither, "
15: 8 s', If the Lord shall bring me again "
10 s', As soon as ye hear the sound of "
13 s', The hearts of the men of Israel "
31 David, s', Ahithophel is among the "
17: 4 the s' pleased Absalom well, and 1697
6 s', Ahithophel hath spoken after 559
6 shall we do after his s'? if not; 1697
16 s', Lodge not this night in the 559
18: 5 s', Deal gently for my sake with the "
12 s', Beware that none touch the "
19: 8 s',...the king doth sit in the gate. "
9 s', The king saved us out of the "
11 s', Speak unto the elders of Judah, "
11 s', Why are ye the last to bring the "
20: 18 s', They were wont to speak in old "
18 s', They shall surely ask counsel at "
21: 17 s', Thou shalt go no more out with "
24: 11 the prophet Gad, David's seer, s', "
19 David, according to the s' of Gad, 1697
1Ki 1: 5 exalted himself, s', I will be king: 559
6 time in s', Why hast thou done so? "
11 s', Hast thou not heard that "
13 s', Assuredly Solomon thy son shall "
17 s', Assuredly Solomon thy son shall "
23 s', Behold Nathan the prophet. 559
30 s', Assuredly Solomon thy son shall "
47 s', God make the name of Solomon "
51 s',...Adonijah feareth king Solomon: "
51 s', Let king Solomon swear unto me "
2: 1 and he charged Solomon his son, s', "
4 s', If thy children take heed to their "
8 s', I will not put thee to death "
23 king Solomon sware by the Lord, s', "
29 of Jehoiada, s', Go, fall upon him. "
30 s', Thus said Joab, and thus he "
38 said unto the king, The s' is good: 1697
39 s', Behold, thy servants be in Gath. 559
42 s', Know for a certain, on the day "
5: 2 And Solomon sent to Hiram, s', "
5 s', Thy son, whom I will set upon "
8 s', I have considered the things "
6: 11 of the Lord came to Solomon, s', "
8: 15 hath with his hand fulfilled it, s', "
25 s', There shall not fail thee a man "
47 s', We have sinned, and have done "
55 of Israel with a loud voice, s', "
9: 5 s', There shall not fail thee a man "
12: 3 came, and spake unto Rehoboam, s', "
7 s', If thou wilt be a servant unto "
9 s', Make the yoke which thy father "
10 s', Thus shalt thou speak unto this "
10 s', Thy father made our yoke heavy, "
12 s', Come to me again the third day. "
14 s', My father made your yoke heavy, "
15 that he might perform his s', *1697
16 s', What portion have we in David? 559
22 unto Shemaiah the man of God, s', "
23 and to the remnant of the people, s', "
13: 3 s', This is the sign which the Lord "

1Ki 13: 4 Jeroboam heard the s' of the man 1697
4 from the altar, s', Lay hold on him. 559
9 s', Eat no bread, nor drink water, "
18 s', Bring him back with thee into "
21 Judah, s', Thus saith the Lord, "
27 to his sons, s', Saddle me the ass. "
30 over him, s', Alas, my brother.
31 s', When I am dead, then bury me 559
32 the s' which he cried by the word 1697
15: 18 Syria, that dwelt at Damascus, s', 559
29 according unto the s' of the Lord, 1697
16: 1 son of Hanani against Baasha, s', 559
17: 2, 8 of the Lord came unto him, s', "
15 did according to the s' of Elijah: 1697
18: 1 s', Go, shew thyself unto Ahab; 559
26 until noon, s', O Baal, hear us. "
31 came, s', Israel shall be thy name; "
19: 2 s', So let the gods do to me, and "
20: 4 according to thy s', I am thine, 1697
5 s', Although I have sent unto thee, 559
5 s', Thou shalt deliver me thy "
13 s', Thus saith the Lord, Hast thou* "
17 s', There are men come out of "
21: 2 s', Give me thy vineyard, that I may "
9 s', Proclaim a fast, and set Naboth "
10 s', Thou didst blaspheme God and "
14 sent to Jezebel, s', Naboth is stoned, "
17 Lord came to Elijah the Tishbite, s', "
19 s', Thus saith the Lord, Hast "
19 s', Thus saith the Lord, In the "
23 s', The dogs shall eat Jezebel by "
28 Lord came to Elijah the Tishbite, s', "
22: 12 s', Go up to Ramoth-gilead, and "
13 s', Behold now, the words of the "
31 s', Fight neither with small nor "
36 s', Every man to his city, and every "
2Ki 2: 22 according to the s' of Elisha which 1697
3: 7 s', The king of Moab hath rebelled 559
4: 1 s', Thy servant my husband is dead; "
31 told him, s', The child is not awaked. "
5: 4 s', Thus and thus said the maid "
6 s', Now when this letter is come "
8 s', Wherefore hast thou rent thy "
10 s', Go and wash in Jordan seven "
14 to the s' of the man of God: and 1697
22 s',...even now there be come to 559
6: 8 s', In such and such a place shall be "
9 s', Beware that thou pass not "
13 told him, s', Behold he is in Dothan. "
26 unto him, s', Help, my lord, O king. "
7: 10 s', We came to the camp of the "
12 s', When they come out of the city, "
14 host of the Syrians, s', Go and see. "
18 s', Two measures of barley for a "
8: 1 s', Arise, and go thou and thine "
2 after the s' of the man of God: *1697
4 s', Tell me, I pray thee, all the 559
6 s', Restore all that was hers, and all "
7 s', The man of God is come hither. "
8, 9 s', Shall I recover of this disease? "
9: 12 s', Thus saith the Lord, I have "
13 blew with trumpets, s', Jehu is king. "
18 s', The messenger came to them, "
20 s', He came even unto them, and "
36 s', In the portion of Jezreel shall "
10: 1 that brought up Ahab's children, s', "
5 sent to Jehu, s', We are thy servants, "
6 s', If ye be mine, and if ye will "
8 s', They have brought the heads of "
17 according to the s' of the Lord, *1697
11: 5 s', This is the thing that ye shall 559
14: 6 s', The fathers shall not be put to "
8 s', Come, let us look one another in "
9 Judah, s', The thistle that was in "
9 s', Give thy daughter to my son to "
15: 12 s', Thy sons shall sit on the throne of "
16: 7 s', I am thy servant and thy son: "
15 s', Upon the great altar burn "
17: 13 s', Turn ye from your evil ways, "
26 s', The nations which thou hast "
27 s', Carry thither one of the priests "
35 s', Ye shall not fear other gods, nor "
18: 14 s', I have offended; return from me "
28 s', Hear the word of the great king, "
30 s', The Lord will surely deliver us, "
32 you, s', The Lord will deliver us. "
36 commandment...s', Answer him not. "
19: 9 messengers again unto Hezekiah, s', "
10 s', Let not thy God in whom thou "
10 s', Jerusalem shall not be delivered "
20 s', Thus saith the Lord God of Israel, "
20: 2 wall, and prayed unto the Lord, s', "
4 word of the Lord came to him, s', "
21: 10 by his servants the prophets, s', "
22: 3 scribe, to the house of the Lord, s', "
10 s', Hilkiah the priest hath delivered "
12 Asahiah a servant of the king's, s', "
23: 21 s', Keep the passover unto the Lord "
1Ch 4: 9 s', Because I bare him with sorrow. "
10 Jabez called on the God of Israel, s', "
11: 1 s', Behold, we are thy bone and thy "
12: 19 s', He will fall to his master Saul to "
13: 12 s', How shall I bring the ark of God "
14: 10 David enquired of God, s', Shall I go "
16: 18 S', Unto thee will I give the land of "
22 S', Touch not mine anointed, and do "
17: 3 the word of God came to Nathan, s', 559
6 s', Why have ye not built me an "
24 s', The Lord of hosts is the God of "
21: 9 spake unto Gad, David's seer, s', "
10 Go and tell David, s', Thus saith the "
19 David went up at the s' of Gad, 1697
22: 8 s', Thou hast shed blood abundantly, 559
17 of Israel to help Solomon his son, s', "
2Ch 2: 3 s', As thou didst deal with David my 559
5: 13 praised the Lord, s', For he is good:

2Ch 6: 4 his mouth to my father David, s', 559
16 s', There shall not fail thee a man "
37 s', We have sinned, we have done "
7: 3 praised the Lord, s', For he is good:
18 s', There shall not fail thee a man 559
10: 3 came and spake to Rehoboam, s', "
6 s', What counsel give ye me to return "
7 s', If thou be kind to this people, "
9 s', Ease somewhat the yoke that thy "
10 s', Thus shalt thou answer the people "
10 s', Thy father made our yoke heavy, "
12 s', Come again to me on the third "
14 s', My father made your yoke heavy, "
16 s', What portion have we in David? "
11: 2 to Shemaiah the man of God, s', "
3 all Israel in Judah and Benjamin, s', "
12: 7 s', They have humbled themselves; "
16: 2 of Syria, that dwelt at Damascus, s', "
18: 11 s', Go up to Ramoth-gilead, and "
12 s', Behold, the words of the prophets "
19 And one spake s' after this manner, "
19 and another s' after that manner. "
30 s', Fight ye not with small or great, "
19: 9 s', Thus shall ye do in the fear of the "
20: 2 s', There cometh a great multitude "
8 a sanctuary therein for thy name, s', "
37 s', Because thou hast joined thyself "
21: 12 s', Thus saith the Lord God of David "
25: 4 s', The fathers shall not die for the "
7 s', O king, let not the army of Israel "
17 s', Come, let us see one another in "
18 s', The thistle that was in Lebanon "
18 s', Give thy daughter to my son to "
30: 6 s', Ye children of Israel, turn again "
18 s', The good Lord pardon every one "
32: 4 s', Why should the kings of Assyria "
6 and spake comfortably to them, s', "
9 all Judah that were at Jerusalem, s', "
11 s', The Lord our God shall deliver "
12 s', Ye shall worship before one altar, "
17 s', As the gods of the nations of other "
34: 16 s', All that was committed to thy "
18 s', Hilkiah the priest hath given me "
20 Asaiah a servant of the king's, s', "
35: 21 s', What have I to do with thee, thou "
36: 22 and put it also in writing, s', "
Ezr 1: 1 and put it also in writing, s', "
5: 11 s', We are the servants of the God 560
8: 22 s', The hand of our God is upon all 559
9: 1 s', The people of Israel, and the "
11 s', The land, unto which ye go to "
Ne 1: 8 s', If ye transgress, I will scatter you "
6: 2 s', Come, let us meet together in "
3 s', I am doing a great work, so that "
7 s', There is a king in Judah: and "
8 s', There are no such things done "
9 s', Their hands shall be weakened "
8: 11 s', Hold your peace, for the day is "
15 s', Go forth unto the mount, and "
13: 25 s', Ye shall not give your daughters
Es 1: 21 the s' pleased the king and the 1697
Job 4: 16 was silence, and I heard a voice, s',
8: 18 deny him, s', I have not seen thee.
15: 23 abroad for bread, s', Where is it?
24: 15 twilight, s', No eye shall see me: 559
33: 8 I have heard the voice of thy words, s',
Ps 2: 2 the Lord, and against his anointed, s',
22: 7 out the lip, they shake the head, s',
49: 4 open my dark s' upon the harp. 2420
71: 11 S', God hath forsaken him: 559
105: 11 S', Unto thee will I give the land of "
15 S', Touch not mine anointed, and do
119: 82 s', When wilt thou comfort me? * 559
137: 3 s', Sing us one of the songs of Zion.
Pr 1: 21 in the city she uttereth her words, s',*
Ec 1: 16 s', Lo, I am come to great estate, 559
Ca 5: 2 s', Open to me, my sister, my love,
Isa 3: 6 s', Thou hast clothing, be thou our
7 swear, s', I will not be an healer; 559
4: 1 s', We will eat our own bread, and "
6: 8 s', Whom shall I send, and who will "
7: 2 s', Syria is confederate with "
5 taken evil counsel against thee, s', "
10 the Lord spake again unto Ahaz, s', "
8: 5 Lord spake also unto me again, s', "
11 not walk in the way of this people, s', "
14: 8 s', Since thou art laid down, no feller
16 s', Is this the man that made the earth
24 s', Surely as I have thought, so 559
16: 14 s', Within three years, as the years "
18: 2 s', Go, ye swift messengers, to a nation
19: 25 s', Blessed be Egypt my people, 559
20: 2 s', Go and loose the sackcloth from "
23: 4 s', I travail not, nor bring forth "
29: 11, 12 learned, s', Read this, I pray thee: "
30: 21 s', This is the way, walk ye in it, "
36: 15 s', The Lord will surely deliver us: "
18 you, s', The Lord will deliver us. "
21 commandment...s', Answer him not. "
37: 9 he sent messengers to Hezekiah, s', "
10 s', Let not thy God in whom thou "
10 s', Jerusalem shall not be given into "
15 Hezekiah prayed unto the Lord, s', "
21 s', Thus saith the Lord God of "
38: 4 the word of the Lord to Isaiah, s', "
41: 7 s', It is ready for the sodering: and "
13 s' unto thee, Fear not; I will help "
44: 28 even s' to Jerusalem, Thou shalt be "
45: 14 s', Surely God is in thee; and there "
46: 10 s', My counsel shall stand, and I 559
56: 3 s', The Lord hath utterly separated "
63: 11 s', Where is he that brought them up
Jer 1: 4 word of the Lord came unto me, s', 559
11 me, s', Jeremiah, What seest thou? "
13 second time, s', What seest thou? "
2: 1 the word of the Lord came to me, s', "

Jer 2: 2 s', Thus saith the Lord; I remember 559
27 S' to a stock, Thou art my father;* "
4:10 s', Ye shall have peace; whereas the "
31 s', Woe is me now! for my soul is "
5:20 Jacob, and publish it in Judah, s', 559
6:14 s', Peace, peace; when there is no "
17 s', Hearken to the sound of the "
7: 1 came to Jeremiah from the Lord, s', 559
4 s', The temple of the Lord, The "
23 s', Obey my voice, and I will be your "
8: 6 wickedness, s', What have I done? "
11 s', Peace, peace; when there is no "
11: 1 came to Jeremiah from the Lord, s', "
4 s', Obey my voice, and do them, "
6 s', Hear ye...words of this covenant, "
7 and protesting, s', Obey my voice, "
19 s', Let us destroy the tree with the "
21 s', Prophesy not in the name of the 559
13: 3 came unto me the second time, s', "
8 word of the Lord came unto me, s', "
16: 1 of the Lord came also unto me, s', "
18: 1 came to Jeremiah from the Lord, s', 559
5 word of the Lord came to me, s', "
11 Jerusalem, s', Thus saith the Lord; "
20:10 s', Peradventure he will be enticed,* "
15 s', A man child is born unto thee; 559
21: 1 the son of Maaseiah the priest, s', "
22:18 s', Ah my brother! or, Ah sister! "
18 s', Ah lord! or, Ah his glory! "
23:25 s', I have dreamed, I have dreamed. 559
33 s', What is the burden of the Lord? "
38 s', Ye shall not say, The burden of "
24: 4 word of the Lord came unto me, s', "
25: 2 all the inhabitants of Jerusalem, s', "
26: 1 came this word from the Lord, s', "
8 took him, s', Thou shalt surely die. "
9 s', This house shall be like Shiloh, "
11 s', This man is worthy to die; for "
12 s', The Lord sent me to prophesy "
17 to all the assembly of the people, s', "
18 s', Thus saith the Lord of hosts; "
27: 1 unto Jeremiah from the Lord, s', "
9 s', Ye shall not serve the king of "
12 s', Bring your necks under the yoke "
14 s', Ye shall not serve the king of "
16 people, s', Thus saith the Lord; "
16 you, s',...the vessels of the Lord's "
28: 1 the priests and of all the people, s', "
2 s', I have broken the yoke of the "
11 the people, s', Thus saith the Lord; "
12 the neck of the prophet Jeremiah, s', "
13 Go and tell Hananiah, s', Thus "
29: 3 Nebuchadnezzar king of Babylon,) s', "
22 s',...Lord make thee like Zedekiah "
24 to Shemaiah the Nehelamite, s', "
25 s', Because thou hast sent letters "
25 priest, and to all the priests, s', "
28 Babylon, s', This captivity is long: "
30 word of the Lord unto Jeremiah, s', "
31 s', Thus saith the Lord concerning "
30: 1 came to Jeremiah from the Lord, s', "
2 s', Write thee all the words that I "
17 Outcast, s', This is Zion, whom no man "
31: 3 me, s', Yea, I have loved thee with an "
34 his brother, s', Know the Lord: 559
32: 3 s', Wherefore dost thou prophesy, "
6 word of the Lord came unto me, s', "
7 s', Buy thee my field that is in "
13 I charged Baruch before them, s', "
16 Neriah, I prayed unto the Lord, s', "
26 word of the Lord unto Jeremiah, s', "
33: 1 shut up in the court of the prison, s', "
19 of the Lord came unto Jeremiah, s', "
23 of the Lord came to Jeremiah, s', "
24 s', The two families which the Lord "
34: 1 and against all the cities thereof, s', "
5 s', Ah lord! for I have pronounced "
12 to Jeremiah from the Lord, s', 559
13 out of the house of bondmen, s', "
35: 1 the son of Josiah king of Judah, s', "
6 s', Ye shall drink no wine, neither "
12 word of the Lord unto Jeremiah, s', "
15 s', Return ye now every man from "
36: 1 unto Jeremiah from the Lord, s', "
5 s', I am shut up; I cannot go into "
14 s', Take in thine hand the roll "
17 they asked Baruch, s', Tell us now, "
27 wrote at the mouth of Jeremiah, s', "
29 s', Why hast thou written therein, "
29 s', The king of Babylon shall "
37: 3 s', Pray now unto the Lord our "
6 Lord unto the prophet Jeremiah, s', "
9 s', The Chaldeans shall surely "
13 prophet, s', Thou fallest away to the "
19 s', The king of Babylon shall not "
38: 1 had spoken unto all the people, s', "
8 house, and spake to the king, s', "
10 s', Take from hence thirty men with "
16 s', As the Lord liveth, that made "
39:11 the captain of the guard, s', "
15 shut up in the court of the prison, s', "
16 s', Thus saith the Lord of hosts, "
40: 9 s', Fear not to serve the Chaldeans: "
15 s', Let me go, I pray thee, and I "
42:14 S', No; but we will go into the land "
20 s', Pray for us unto the Lord our "
43: 2 s' unto Jeremiah, Thou speakest "
8 unto Jeremiah in Tahpanhes, s', "
44: 1 and in the country of Pathros, s', "
4 s', Oh, do not this abominable thing "
15 in Pathros, answered Jeremiah, s', "
20 which had given him that answer, s', "
25 s'; Ye and your wives have both "
25 s', We will surely perform our vows "
26 of Egypt, s', The Lord God liveth. "
45: 1 the son of Josiah king of Judah, s', "

Jer 48:39 shall howl, s', How is it broken down!* "
49: 4 s', Who shall come unto me? *
14 s', Gather ye together, and come
34 of Zedekiah king of Judah, s', 559
50: 5 s', Come, and let us join ourselves
51:14 s', Surely I will fill thee with men, as
La 2:15 s', Is this the city that men call The
Eze 3:12 s', Blessed be the glory of the Lord
16 word of the Lord came unto me, s', 559
6: 1 word of the Lord came unto me, s', "
7: 1 word of the Lord came unto me, s', "
9: 1 s', Cause them that have charge "
11 s', I have done as thou...commanded "
10: 6 s', Take fire from between the "
11:14 word of the Lord came unto me, s', "
12: 1 of the Lord also came unto me, s', "
8 the word of the Lord unto me, s', "
17 the word of the Lord came to me, s', "
21 word of the Lord came unto me, s', "
22 s', The days are prolonged, and "
26 the word of the Lord came to me, s', "
13: 1 word of the Lord came unto me, s', "
6 lying divination, s', The Lord saith:* "
10 have seduced my people, s', Peace; "
14: 2 word of the Lord came unto me, s', "
12 of the Lord came again to me, s', "
15: 1 word of the Lord came unto me, s', "
16: 1 word of the Lord came unto me, s', "
44 s', As...the mother, so...her daughter. "
17: 1, 11 of the Lord came unto me, s', "
18: 1 of the Lord came unto me again, s', "
2 s', The fathers have eaten sour "
20: 2 the word of the Lord unto me, s', "
5 them, s', I am the Lord your God; "
45 word of the Lord came unto me, s', "
21: 1, 8 word of the Lord came unto me, s', "
18 of the Lord came unto me again, s', "
22: 1, 17, 23 of the Lord came unto me, s', "
28 s', Thus saith the Lord God, when "
23: 1 the Lord came again unto me, s', "
24: 1, 15, 20 of the Lord came unto me, s', "
25: 1 of the Lord came again unto me, s', "
26: 1 word of the Lord came unto me, s', "
27: 1 of the Lord came again unto me, s', "
32 s', What city is like Tyrus, like the "
28: 1 of the Lord came again unto me, s', 559
11, 20 of the Lord came unto me, s', "
29: 1, 17 of the Lord came unto me, s', "
30: 1 the Lord came again unto me, s', "
20 word of the Lord came unto me, s', "
31: 1 word of the Lord came unto me, s', "
32: 1, 17 of the Lord came unto me, s', "
33: 1 word of the Lord came unto me, s', "
10 s', If our transgressions and our "
21 unto me, s', The city is smitten. "
23 word of the Lord came unto me, s', "
24 speak, s', Abraham was one, and he "
30 s', Come, I pray you, and hear what "
34: 1 word of the Lord came unto me, s', "
35: 1 word of the Lord came unto me, s', "
12 s', They are laid desolate, they are "
36:16 word of the Lord came unto me, s', "
37:15 of the Lord came again unto me, s', "
18 s', Wilt thou not shew us what thou "
38: 1 word of the Lord came unto me, s', "
Da 4: 8 and before him I told the dream, s', "
23 s', Hew the tree down, and destroy 560
31 s', O king Nebuchadnezzar, to thee "
Am 2:12 the prophets, s', Prophesy not. 559
3: 1 up from the land of Egypt, s', "
7:10 s', Amos hath conspired against the "
8: 5 S', When will the new moon be gone, "
Jon 1: 1 unto Jonah the son of Amittai, s', "
3: 1 unto Jonah the second time, s', "
7 s', Let neither man nor beast, herd "
4: 2 was not this my s', when I was 1697
Mic 2:11 s', I will prophesy unto thee of wine
Hag 1: 1 son of Josedech, the high priest, s', 559
2 s', This people say, The time is not "
3 the Lord by Haggai the prophet, s', "
13 s', I am with you, saith the Lord. "
2: 1 the Lord by the prophet Haggai, s', "
2 and to the residue of the people, s', "
10 the Lord by Haggai the prophet, s', "
11 the priests concerning the law, s', "
20 and twentieth day of the month, s', "
21 s', I will shake the heavens and the "
Zec 1: 1 the son of Iddo the prophet, s', The "
4 s', Thus saith the Lord of hosts; "
7 the son of Iddo the prophet, s', "
14 Cry thou, s', Thus saith the Lord of "
17 Cry yet, s', Thus saith the Lord of "
21 s', These are the horns which have "
2: 4 s', Jerusalem shall be inhabited as "
3: 4 s', Take away the filthy garments "
6 the Lord protested unto Joshua, s', "
4: 4 me, s', What are these, my lord? "
6 s', This is the word of the Lord unto "
6 s', Not by might, nor by power, but "
8 word of the Lord came unto me, s', "
6: 8 s',...these that go toward the north "
9 word of the Lord came unto me, s', "
12 s', Thus speaketh the Lord of hosts, "
12 s', Behold the man whose name is "
7: 3 s', Should I weep in the fifth month, "
4 of the Lord of hosts unto me, s', "
5 s', When ye fasted and mourned in "
8 of the Lord came unto Zechariah, s', "
9 s', Execute true judgment, and shew "
8: 1 the Lord of hosts came to me, s', "
18 the Lord of hosts came unto me, s', "
21 s', Let us go speedily to pray before "
23 s', We will go with you: for we have "
M't 1:20 s', Joseph, thou son of David, fear 3004
22 of the Lord by the prophet, s', "
2: 2 S', Where is he that is born King "

M't 2:13 s', Arise, and take the young child 3004
15 s', Out of Egypt have I called my "
17 spoken by Jeremy the prophet, s', "
20 S', Arise, and take the young child "
3: 2 And s', Repent ye: for the kingdom "
3 s', The voice of one crying in the "
14 s', I have need to be baptized of "
17 s', This is my beloved Son, in whom "
4:14 spoken by Esaias the prophet, s', "
5: 2 his mouth, and taught them, s', "
6:31 no thought, s', What shall we eat? "
8: 2 s', Lord, if thou wilt, thou canst "
3 him, s', I will; be thou clean. "
6 s', Lord, my servant lieth at home "
17 s', Himself took our infirmities, and "
25 him, s', Lord, save us: we perish. "
27 s', What manner of man is this, that "
29 s', What have we to do with thee, "
31 s', If thou cast us out, suffer us to "
9:14 s', Why do we and the Pharisees "
18 s', My daughter is even now dead: "
27 s', Thou son of David, have mercy "
29 s', According to your faith be it unto "
30 them, s', See that no man know it. "
33 s', It was never so seen in Israel. "
10: 5 s', Go not into the way of...Gentiles, "
11:17 s', We have piped unto you, and ye* "
12:10 s', Is it lawful to heal on...sabbath "
17 spoken by Esaias the prophet, s', "
38 s', Master, we would see a sign from "
13: 3 s', Behold, a sower went forth to "
24 them s', The kingdom of heaven is "
31 s', The kingdom of heaven is like to "
35 s', I open my mouth in parables; "
36 s', Declare unto us the parable of "
14:15 s', This is a desert place, and the "
26 s', It is a spirit; and they cried out "
27 s', Be of good cheer; it is I; be not "
30 to sink, he cried, s', Lord, save me. "
33 s', Of a truth thou art the Son of "
15: 1 and Pharisees,...of Jerusalem, s', "
4 s', Honour thy father and mother:* "
7 well did Esaias prophesy of you, s', "
12 offended, after they heard this s'? 3056
22 s', Have mercy on me, O Lord, 3004
23 s', Send her away; for she crieth "
25 worshipped him, s', Lord, help me. "
16: 7 s', It is because we have taken no "
13 s', Whom do men say that I the Son "
22 him, s', Be it far from thee, Lord: "
17: 9 s', Tell the vision to no man, until "
10 s', Why then say the scribes that "
14 man, kneeling down to him, and s', "
25 him, s', What thinkest thou, Simon? "
18: 1 Jesus, s', Who is the greatest in the "
26 s', Lord, have patience with me, "
28 throat, s', Pay me that thou owest. "
29 s', Have patience with me, and I "
19: 3 tempting him, and s' unto him, Is "
11 All men cannot receive this s', 3056
22 when the young man heard that s', "
25 s', Who then can be saved? 3004
20:12 S', These last have wrought but "
30, 31 s', Have mercy on us, O Lord, "
21: 2 S' unto them, Go into the village "
4 was spoken by the prophet, s', "
9 s', Hosanna to the son of David: "
10 the city was moved, s', Who is this? "
15 s', Hosanna to the son of David; "
20 s', How soon is the fig tree "
25 s', If we shall say, From heaven; he "
37 son, s', They will reverence my son. "
22: 4 s', Tell them which are bidden, "
16 s', Master, we know that thou art "
24 S', Master, Moses said, If a man "
31 was spoken unto you by God, s', "
35 a question, tempting him, and s', * "
42 S', What think ye of Christ? whose "
43 David in spirit call him Lord, s', "
23: 2 S', The scribes and the Pharisees "
24: 3 s', Tell us, when shall these things "
5 come in my name, s', I am Christ; "
25: 9 s', Not so; lest there be not enough "
11 virgins, s', Lord, Lord, open to us. "
20 and brought other five talents, s', "
37, 44 s', Lord, when saw we thee an "
45 s', Verily I say unto you, Inasmuch "
26: 8 s', To what purpose is this waste? "
17 s' unto him, Where wilt thou that "
27 it to them, s', Drink ye all of it; "
39 s', O my Father, if it be possible, let "
42 prayed, s', O my Father, if this cup "
44 the third time, s' the same words. 2036
48 s', Whomsoever I shall kiss, that 3004
65 s', He hath spoken blasphemy; "
68 S', Prophesy unto us, thou Christ, "
69 s', Thou also wast with Jesus of "
70 s', I know not what thou sayest. "
74 and to swear, s', I know not the man.*
27: 4 S', I have sinned in that I have 3004
9 s', And they took the thirty pieces "
11 s', Art thou the King of the Jews? "
19 s', Have thou nothing to do with "
23 the more, s', Let him be crucified.* "
24 s', I am innocent of the blood of "
29 him, s', Hail, King of the Jews! "
40 And s', Thou that destroyest the "
46 voice, s', Eli, Eli, lama sabachthani? "
54 s', Truly this was the Son of God. "
63 S', Sir, we remember that that "
28: 9 behold, Jesus met them, s', All hail. "
13 S', Say ye, His disciples came by "
15 and this s' is commonly reported 3056
18 s', All power is given unto me in 3004
M'r 1: 7 s', There cometh one mightier than "
11 heaven, s', Thou art my beloved Son,*

M'r 1:15 s', The time is fulfilled, and the 3004
24 S', Let us alone; what have we to "
25 s', Hold thy peace, and come out of "
27 themselves, s', What thing is this? "
40 and s' unto him, If thou wilt, thou "
2:12 s', We never saw it on this fashion. "
3:11 cried, s', Thou art the Son of God. "
33 them, s', Who is my mother, or my* "
5: 9 answered, s', My name is Legion:* "
12 s', Send us into the swine, that we "
23 s', My little daughter lieth at the "
6: 2 s', From whence hath this man "
25 s', I will that thou give me by and "
7:29 unto her, For this s' go thy way; 3056
37 s', He hath done all things well: 3004
8:15 he charged them, s', Take heed, "
16 s', It is because we have no bread. "
26 s', Neither go into the town, nor "
27 s' unto them, Whom do men say "
32 And he spake that s' openly. And 3056
33 s', Get thee behind me, Satan: *3004
9: 7 s', This is my beloved Son: hear "
10 they kept that s' with themselves, 3056
11 s', Why say the scribes that Elias 3004
25 s' unto him, Thou dumb and deaf "
32 But they understood not that s', 4487
38 s', Master, we saw one casting out*3004
10:22 he was sad at that s', and went 3056
26 s' among themselves, Who then 3004
33 S', Behold, we go up to Jerusalem; "
35 s', Master, we would that thou 3004
49 s' unto him, Be of good comfort, "
11: 9 s', Hosanna; Blessed is he that "
17 s' unto them, Is it not written, My "
31 s', If we shall say, From heaven; "
12: 6 s', They will reverence my son. "
18 and they asked him, s', "
26 s', I am the God of Abraham, and "
13: 6 s', I am Christ; and shall deceive "
14:44 s', Whomsoever I shall kiss, that "
57 bare false witness against him, s', "
60 s', Answerest thou nothing? what "
68 he denied, s', I know not, neither "
71 s', I know not this man of whom ye*
15: 4 again, s', Answerest thou nothing?3004
9 s', Will ye that I release unto you "
29 and s', Ah, thou that destroyest the"
34 s', Eloi, Eloi, lama sabachthani? * "
36 gave him to drink, s', Let alone; "
u 1:24 and hid herself five months, s', "
29 him, she was troubled at his s', 3056
63 and wrote, s', His name is John. 3004
66 s', What manner of child shall this "
67 the Holy Ghost, and prophesied, s', "
2:13 heavenly host praising God, and s', "
17 abroad the s' which was told 4487
50 the s' which he spake unto them. "
3: 4 s', The voice of one crying in the *3004
10 him, s', What shall we do then? "
14 him, s', And what shall we do? "
16 John answered, s' unto them all, "
4: 4 s', It is written, That man shall "
34 S', Let us alone; what have we to* "
35 rebuked him, s', Hold thy peace, "
36 themselves, s', What a word is this!"
41 s', Thou art Christ the Son of God. "
5: 8 s', Depart from me; for I am a "
12 s', Lord, if thou wilt, thou canst "
13 him, s', I will: be thou clean. 2036
21 s', Who is this which speaketh 3004
26 s', We have seen strange things to "
30 s', Why do ye eat and drink, with "
7: 4 s', That he was worthy for whom "
6 s' unto him, Lord, trouble not "
16 s', That a great prophet is risen up "
19, 20 s', Art thou he that should "
32 s', We have piped unto you, and ye "
39 s', This man, if he were a prophet, "
8: 9 s', What might this parable be? * "
24 him, s', Master, master, we perish. "
25 s' one to another, What manner of "
30 s', What is thy name? And he "
38 him: but Jesus sent him away, s', "
49 s' to him, Thy daughter is dead; "
50 s', Fear not: believe only, and* "
54 hand, and called, s', Maid, arise. "
9:18 s', Whom say the people that I am? "
22 S', The Son of man must suffer 2036
35 s', This is my beloved Son: hear 3004
38 s', Master, I beseech thee, look "
45 But they understood not this s', 4487
45 they feared to ask him of that s'. 4487
10:17 s', Lord, even the devils are subject3004
25 s',...what shall I do to inherit "
11:45 thus s' thou reproachest us also. "
12:16 s', The ground of a certain rich man"
17 And he thought within himself, s', "
13:25 s', Lord, Lord, open unto us; and "
31 s' unto him, Get thee out, and "
14: 3 s', Is it lawful to heal on the "
5 s', Which of you shall have an ass*2036
7 the chief rooms; s' unto them, 3004
30 S', This man began to build, and "
15: 2 s', This man receiveth sinners, and "
3 spake this parable unto them, s', "
6 s' unto them, Rejoice with me; for "
9 s', Rejoice with me; for I have "
17: 4 s', I repent; thou shalt forgive him."
18: 2 S', There was in a city a judge, "
3 s', Avenge me of mine adversary. "
13 s', God be merciful to me a sinner. "
18 s', Good Master, what shall I do to "
34 this s' was hid from them, neither 4487
38 cried, s', Jesus, thou son of David, 3004
41 S', What wilt thou that I shall do * "
19: 7 s', That he was gone to be guest "
Lu 19:14 s', We will not have this man to 3004
16, 18 s', Lord, thy pound hath gained "
20 s', Lord, behold, here is thy pound, "
30 S', Go ye into the village over 2036
38 S', Blessed be the King that 3004
42 S', If thou hadst known, even thou, "
46 S' unto them, It is written, My "
20: 2 s', Tell us, by what authority doest "
5 s', If we shall say, From heaven; "
14 s', This is the heir: come, let us "
21 s', Master, we know...thou sayest "
28 S', Master, Moses wrote unto us, "
21: 7 s', Master,...when shall these things"
8 s', I am Christ; and the time "
22: 8 s', Go and prepare us the passover,2036
19 s', This is my body which is given 3004
20 s', This cup is the new testament "
42 S', Father, if thou be willing, "
57 him, s', Woman, I know him not. "
59 s', Of a truth this fellow also was "
64 s', Prophesy, who is it that smote "
66 and led him into their council, s', "
23: 2 s', We found this fellow perverting "
2 s' that he himself is Christ a King. "
3 s', Art thou the King of the Jews? "
5 fierce, s', He stirreth up the people,"
18 s', Away with this man, and release"
21 cried, s', Crucify him, crucify him. "
35 s', He saved others; let him save "
37 s', If thou be the king of the Jews, "
39 s', If thou be Christ, save thyself "
40 s', Dost not thou fear God, seeing* "
47 s', Certainly this was a righteous "
24: 7 S', The Son of man must be "
23 s', that they had also seen a vision "
29 constrained him, s', Abide with us: "
34 S', The Lord is risen indeed, and "
Joh 1:15 s', This was he of whom I spake, "
26 s', I baptize with water: but there "
32 s', I saw the Spirit descending "
4:31 prayed him, s', Master, eat. "
37 herein is that s' true, One soweth, 3056
39 on him for the s' of the woman, * "
42 we believe, not because of thy s': *2981
51 and told him, s', Thy son liveth. 3004
6:52 s', How can this man give us his "
60 This is an hard s'; who can hear it?3056
7:15 s', How knoweth this man letters, 3004
28 s', Ye both know me, and ye know "
36 manner of s' is this that he said, *3056
37 s', if any man thirst, let him come 3004
40 when they heard this s', said, Of a*3056
8:12 s', I am the light of the world: he 3004
51, 52 If a man keep my s', he shall *3056
55 but I know him, and keep his s', * "
9: 2 s', Master, who did sin, this man, 3004
19 s', Is this your son, who ye say was "
10:33 s', For a good work we stone thee* "
11: 3 s', Lord,...he whom thou lovest is "
28 s', The Master is come, and calleth2036
31 s', She goeth unto the grave to *3004
32 s' unto him, Lord, if thou hadst "
12:21 him, s', Sir, we would see Jesus. "
23 s', The hour is come, that the Son "
28 s', I have both glorified it, and will "
12:38 That the s' of Esaias the prophet *3056
15:20 if they have kept my s', they will * "
18: 9 That the s' might be fulfilled, * "
22 s', Answerest thou the high priest 2036
32 s' of Jesus might be fulfilled, *3056
40 s', Not this man, but Barabbas. 3004
19: 6 out, s', Crucify him, crucify him. "
8 Pilate therefore heard that s', he *3056
12 s', If thou let this man go, thou 3004
13 Pilate therefore heard that s', he 3056
21:23 this s' abroad among the brethren, "
Ac 1: 6 s', Lord, wilt thou at this time 3004
2: 7 s' one to another, Behold, are not "
12 s' one to another, What meaneth "
40 s', Save yourselves from this "
3:25 s' unto Abraham, And in thy seed "
4:16 S', What shall we do to these men? "
5:23 S', The prison truly found we shut "
25 s', Behold, the men whom ye put* "
28 S', Did not we straitly command "
6: 5 s' pleased the whole multitude: 3056
7:26 s', Sirs, ye are brethren; why do 2036
27 s', Who made thee a ruler and a "
29 Then fled Moses at this s', and 3056
32 S', I am the God of thy fathers, the*
35 s', Who made thee a ruler and a 2036
40 S' unto Aaron, Make us gods to go "
59 s', Lord Jesus, receive my spirit. 3007
8:10 s', This man is the great power of "
19 S', Give me also this power, that on"
26 s', Arise and go toward the south "
9: 4 a voice s' unto him, Saul, Saul, why"
10: 3 him, and s' unto him, Cornelius. 2036
26 Peter took him up, s', Stand up; 3004
11: 3 S', Thou wentest in to men "
4 expounded it by order unto them, s',"
7 I heard a voice s' unto me, Arise, "
18 s', Then hath God also to the "
12: 7 raised him up, s', Rise up quickly. "
22 s', It is the voice of a god, and not "
13:15 s', Ye men and brethren, if ye have3004
47 s', I have set thee to be a light of the "
14:11 s' in the speech of Lycaonia, The 3004
15 s', Sirs, why do ye these things? "
15: 5 s',...it was needful to circumcise "
13 s', Men and brethren, hearken unto"
24 s', Ye must be circumcised, and * "
16: 9 s', Come over into Macedonia, and "
15 s', If ye have judged me to be "
17 s', These men are the servants of "
20 s', These men, being Jews, do *2036
Ac 16:28 s', Do thyself no harm: for we 3004
35 serjeants, s', Let those men go. "
36 of the prison told this s' to Paul, 3056
17: 7 s' that there is another king, one 3004
19 s', May we know what this new "
18:13 S', This fellow persuadeth men to "
21 s', I must by all means keep this 2036
19: 4 s' unto the people, that they should3004
13 s', We adjure you by Jesus whom "
21 s', After I have been there, I must 2036
26 s' that they be no gods, which are 3004
28 s', Great is Diana of the Ephesians. "
20:23 s' that the bonds and afflictions "
21:14 S', The will of the Lord be done. 2036
21 s'...they ought not to circumcise *3004
40 unto them in the Hebrew tongue, s',"
22: 7 heard a voice s' unto me, Saul, Saul,"
18 saw him s' unto me, Make haste, "
26 s', Take heed what thou doest: "
23: 9 s', We find no evil in this man: "
12 s' that they would neither eat nor "
23 s', Make ready two hundred *2036
24: 2 s', Seeing that by thee we enjoy 3004
9 s' that these things were so. *5335
25:14 s', There is a certain man left in 3004
26:14 s' in the Hebrew tongue, Saul, Saul,"
22 s' none other things than those "
31 s', This man doeth nothing worthy "
27:24 S', Fear not, Paul; thou must be "
33 s', This day is the fourteenth day "
28:26 S', Go unto this people, and say, "
Ro 4: 7 S', Blessed are they whose iniquities
11: 2 intercession...against Israel, s', *3004
13: 9 is briefly comprehended in this s',*3056
1Co 11:25 s', This cup is the new testament 3004
15:54 then shall be brought to pass the s'3056
Ga 3: 8 s', In thee shall all nations be blessed.
1Ti 1:15 This is a faithful s', and worthy of 3056
3: 1 This is a true s', If a man desire the"
4: 9 This is a faithful s' and worthy of "
2Ti 2:11 It is a faithful s': For if we be dead "
18 s' that the resurrection is past 3004
Tit 3: 8 This is a faithful s', and these 3056
Heb 2: 6 s', What is man, that thou art 3004
12 S', I will declare thy name unto my"
4: 7 s' in David, To day, after so long a "
6:14 S', Surely blessing I will bless thee"
8:11 man his brother, s', Know the Lord:"
9:20 S', This is the blood of the testament"
12:26 s',...I shake not the earth only, "
2Pe 3: 4 And s', Where is the promise of his "
Jude 14 s', Behold, the Lord cometh with "
Re 1:11 S', I am Alpha and Omega, the first"
17 hand upon me, s' unto me, Fear not;"
4: 8 day and night, s', Holy, holy, holy, "
10 their crowns before the throne, s', "
5: 9 a new song, s', Thou art worthy "
12 S' with a loud voice, Worthy is the "
13 heard I s', Blessing, and honour, "
6: 1 of the four beasts s', Come and see. "
10 s', How long, O Lord, holy and true, "
7: 3 S', Hurt not the earth, neither the "
10 s', Salvation to our God which "
12 S', Amen: Blessing, and glory, and"
13 s' unto me, What are these which "
8:13 s' with a loud voice, Woe, woe, woe, "
9:14 S' to the sixth angel which had the"
10: 4 voice from heaven s' unto me, Seal "
11: 1 s', Rise, and measure the temple of*"
12 s' unto them, Come up hither. "
15 s', The kingdoms of this world are*"
17 S', We give thee thanks, O Lord God"
12:10 s' in heaven, Now is come salvation, "
13: 4 s', Who is like unto the beast? who "
14 s' to them that dwell on the earth, "
14: 7 S' with a loud voice, Fear God, and*"
8 s', Babylon is fallen, is fallen, that "
9 s' with a loud voice, If any man "
13 s' unto me, Write, Blessed are the "
18 s', Thrust in thy sharp sickle, and "
15: 3 s', Great and marvellous are thy "
16: 1 s' to the seven angels, Go your ways,"
17 from the throne, s', It is done. "
17: 1 with me, s' unto me, Come hither; "
18: 2 s', Babylon the great is fallen, is "
4 s', Come out of her, my people, that"
10 s', Alas, alas that great city Babylon,"
16 And s', Alas, alas that great city, "
18 s', What city is like unto this great "
19 s', Alas, alas that great city, "
21 s', Thus...shall that great city be "
19: 1 much people in heaven, s', Alleluia;"
4 on the throne, s', Amen; Alleluia. "
5 throne, s', Praise our God, all ye his"
6 of mighty thunderings, s', Alleluia:"
17 s' to all the fowls that fly in the "
21: 3 s', Behold, the tabernacle of God is "
9 s', Come hither, I will shew thee the"

sayings

Nu 14:39 Moses told these s' unto all the *1697
J'g 13:17 that when thy s' come to pass we* "
1Sa 25:12 and came and told him all those s'.*"
2Ch 13:22 Abijah, and his ways, and his s', "
33:19 written among the s' of the seers.* "
Ps 49:13 their posterity approve their s'. 6310
78: 2 parable: I will utter dark s' of old:2420
Pr 1: 6 words of the wise, and their dark s'."
4:10 Hear, O my son, and receive my s'; 561
20 words; incline thine ear unto my s'. "
M't 7:24 whosoever heareth these s' of *3056
26 one that heareth these s' of mine,* "
28 when Jesus had ended these s', the*"
19: 1 when Jesus had finished these s',* "
26: 1 when Jesus...finished all these s',* "
Lu 1:65 all these s' were noised abroad 4487
2:51 but his mother kept all these s' in "

Lu 6:47 heareth my s', and doeth them, *3056
7: 1 ended all his s' in the audience of 4487
9:28 about an eight days after these s', 3056
44 Let these s' sink...into your ears: * "
Joh 10:19 again among the Jews for these s'.* "
14:24 loveth me not keepeth not my s': * "
Ac 14:18 with these s' scarce restrained 3004
19:28 when they heard these s', they were* "
Ro 3: 4 mightest be justified in thy s', *3056
Re 19: 9 me, These are the true s' of God. * "
22: 6 me, These s' are faithful and true:* "
7 that keepeth the s' of the prophecy:* "
9 them which keep the s' of this book:* "
10 Seal not the s' of the prophecy of * "

scab See also SCABBED.
Le 13: 2 a rising, a s', or bright spot, and it 5597
6 pronounce him clean: it is but a s': 4556
7 s' spread much abroad in the skin, "
8 behold, the s' spreadeth in the skin, "
14:56 and for a s', and for a bright spot: 5597
De 28:27 and with the s', and with the itch, *1618
Isa 3:17 will smite with a s' the crown of 5596

scabbard
Jer 47: 6 put up thyself into thy s', rest, and 8593

scabbed
Le 21:20 or s', or hath his stones broken; 3217
22:22 scurvy, or s', ye shall not offer these "

scaffold
2Ch 6:13 Solomon had made a brasen s', of 3595

scales
Le 11: 9 whatsoever hath fins and s' in the 7193
10 that have not fins and s' in the seas, "
12 Whatsoever hath no fins nor s' in "
De 14: 9 all that have fins and s' shall ye eat: "
10 hath not fins and s' ye may not eat; "
Job 41:15 His s' are his pride, shut up 650,4043
Isa 40:12 and weighed the mountains in s', 6425
Eze 29: 4 cause the fish...to stick unto thy s', 7193
4 all the fish...shall stick unto thy s'. "
Ac 9:18 fell from his eyes as it had been s': 3013

scaleth
Pr 21:22 wise man s' the city of the mighty, 5927

scall
Le 13:30 it is a dry s', even a leprosy upon 5424
31 priest look on the plague of the s', "
31 shall shut up him that hath...the s' "
32 and behold, if the s' spread not, "
32 the s' be not in sight deeper than "
33 but the s' shall he not shave; "
33 shall shut up him that hath the s' "
34 day the priest shall look on the s': "
34 if the s' be not spread in the skin, "
35 if the s' spread much in the skin "
36 if the s' be spread in the skin, "
37 But if the s' be in his sight at a stay, "
37 the s' is healed, he is clean: and "
14:54 manner of plague of leprosy, and s', "

scalp
Ps 68:21 hairy s' of such an one as goeth *6936

scant
Mic 6:10 the s' measure that is abominable? 7332

scapegoat
Le 16: 8 Lord, and the other lot for the s'. *5799
10 on which the lot fell to be the s', * "
10 him go for a s' into the wilderness.* "
26 goat for the s' shall wash his * "

scarce See also SCARCELY.
Ge 27:30 Jacob was yet s' gone out from the
Ac 14:18 s' restrained they the people, 3433
27: 7 s' were come over against Cnidus.* "

scarcely See also SCARCE.
Ro 5: 7 s' for a righteous man will one die: 3433
1Pe 4:18 if the righteous s' be saved, where "

scarceness
De 8: 9 thou shalt eat bread without s', 4544

scarest
Job 7:14 Then thou s' me with dreams, 2865

scarlet
Ge 38:28 bound upon his hand a s' thread, 8144
30 had the s' thread upon his hand:
Ex 25: 4 purple, and s', and fine linen, 8144,8438
26: 1 and blue, and purple, and s': " "
31 vail of blue, and purple, and s', " "
36 of blue, and purple, and s', and " "
27:16 of blue, and purple, and s', and " "
28: 5 purple, and s', and fine linen. " "
6 of blue, and of purple, of s', and " "
8 gold, of blue, and purple, and s', " "
15, 33 blue, and of purple, and of s', " "
35: 6 And blue, and purple, and s', " "
23 found blue, and purple, and s', " "
25 of blue, and of purple, and of s', " "
35 in blue, and in purple, in s', and " "
36: 8 and blue, and purple, and s': " "
35 vail of blue, and purple, and s', " "
37 door of blue, and purple, and s', " "
38:18 of blue, and purple, and s', and " "
23 purple, and in s', and fine linen. " "
39: 1 of the blue, and purple, and s', " "
2 gold, blue, and purple, and s', " "
3 in the purple, and in the s', " "
5, 8 gold, blue, and purple, and s', " "
24 of blue, and purple, and s', and " "
29 purple, and s', of needlework; " "
Le 14: 4 cedar wood, and s', and hyssop: " "
6 and the cedar wood, and the s', " "
49 cedar wood, and s', and hyssop: " "
51 and the hyssop, and the s', and " "
52 with the hyssop, and with the s': " "
Nu 4: 8 spread upon them a cloth of s', " "
Nu 19: 6 cedarwood, and hyssop, and s', 8144,8438
Jos 2:18 shalt bind this line of s' thread in 8144
21 bound the s' line in the window. "
2Sa 1:24 over Saul, who clothed you in s', "
Pr 31:21 household are clothed with s'. "
Ca 4: 3 Thy lips are like a thread of s', "
Isa 1:18 though your sins be as s', they "
La 4: 5 they that were brought up in s' "
Da 5: 7 shall be clothed with s', and have* 711
16 thou shalt be clothed with s', and* "
29 they clothed Daniel with s', and put* "
Na 2: 3 red, the valiant men are in s': 8529
M't 27:28 him, and put on him a s' robe. 2847
Heb 9:19 water, and s' wool, and hyssop, "
Re 17: 3 woman sit upon a s' coloured beast, "
4 arrayed in purple and s' colour, "
18:12 and purple, and silk, and s', and all "
16 in fine linen, and purple, and s', "

scarlet-coloured See SCARLET and COLOURED.

scatter See also SCATTERED; SCATTERETH; SCATTERING.
Ge 11: 9 did the Lord s' them abroad upon 6327
49: 7 in Jacob, and s' them in Israel.
Le 26:33 I will s' you among the heathen, 2210
Nu 16:37 and s' thou the fire yonder; for 2219
De 4:27 shall s' you among the nations, 6327
28:64 Lord shall s' thee among all people, "
32:26 said, I would s' them into corners, 6284
1Ki 14:15 and shall s' them beyond the river, 2219
Ne 1: 8 s' you abroad among the nations: 6327
Ps 59:11 s' them by thy power; and bring 5128
68:30 s' thou the people that delight in * 967
106:27 and to s' them in the lands. 2219
144: 6 Cast forth lightning, and s' them: 6327
Isa 28:25 the fitches, and s' the cummin, 2236
41:16 and the whirlwind shall s' them: 6327
Jer 9:16 s' them also among the heathen, "
13:24 will I s' them as the stubble that "
18:17 I will s' them as with an east wind "
23: 1 that destroy and s' the sheep of my "
49:32 I will s' into all winds them that 2219
36 will s' them toward all those winds; "
Eze 5: 2 third part thou shalt s' in the wind; "
10 remnant...will I s' into all the winds. "
12 and I will s' a third part into all the "
6: 5 s' your bones...about your altars. "
10: 2 coals...and s' them over the city. 2236
12:14 I will s' toward every wind all that 2219
15 shall s' them among the nations, *6327
20:23 would s' them among the heathen, "
22:15 I will s' thee among the heathen, "
29:12 I will s' the Egyptians among the "
30:23, 26 will s' the Egyptians among the "
Da 4:14 off his leaves, and s' his fruit: 921
11:24 he shall s' among them the prey, 967
12: 7 to s' the power of the holy people, *5310
Hab 3:14 came out as a whirlwind to s' me: 6327
Zec 1:21 over the land of Judah to s' it. 2219

scattered
Ge 11: 4 we be s' abroad upon the face of 6327
8 So the Lord s' them abroad from "
Ex 5:12 people were s' abroad throughout "
Nu 10:35 Lord, and let thine enemies be s'; "
De 30: 3 the Lord thy God hath s' thee. "
1Sa 11:11 that they which remained were s', "
13: 8 and the people were s' from him. "
11 that the people were s' from me, 5310
2Sa 18: 8 the battle was there s' over the 6327
22:15 he sent out arrows, and s' them; "
1Ki 22:17 I saw all Israel s' upon the hills, as "
2Ki 25: 5 and all his army were s' from him. "
2Ch 18:16 all Israel s' upon the mountains, "
Es 3: 8 is a certain people s' abroad and 6340
Job 4:11 stout lion's whelps are s' abroad. 6504
18:15 brimstone shall be s' upon his 2219
Ps 18:14 sent out his arrows, and s' them; 6327
44:11 and hast s' us among the heathen. 2219
53: 5 God hath s' the bones of him that 6340
60: 1 hast cast us off, thou hast s' us, 6555
68: 1 God arise, let his enemies be s': 6327
14 When the Almighty s' kings in it, 6566
89:10 thou hast s' thine enemies with 6340
92: 9 the workers of iniquity shall be s'. 6504
141: 7 Our bones are s' at the grave's 6340
Isa 18: 2 to a nation s' and peeled, to a *4900
7 present...of a people s' and peeled, "
33: 3 up of thyself the nations were s'. 5310
Jer 3:13 hast s' thy ways to the strangers 6340
10:21 and all their flocks shall be s'. 6327
23: 2 Ye have s' my flock, and driven "
30:11 all nations whither I have s' thee, "
31:10 He that s' Israel will gather him, 2219
40:15 gathered unto thee should be s', 6327
50:17 Israel is a s' sheep; the lions have 6340
52: 8 and all his army was s' from him. 6327
Eze 6: 8 shall be s' through the countries. 2219
11:16 have s' them among the countries, 6327
17 the countries where ye have been s', "
17:21 shall be s' toward all winds: 6566
20:34 of the countries wherein ye are s', 6327
41 countries wherein ye have been s'; "
28:25 the people among whom they are s', "
29:13 the people whither they were s': "
34: 5 And they were s', because there is "
5 of the field, when they were s'. "
6 was s' upon all the face of the earth, "
12 he is among his sheep that are s'; 6566
12 all places where they have been s' 6327
21 horns, till ye have s' them abroad; "
36:19 And I s' them among the heathen, "
46:18 s' every man from his possession.
Joe 3: 2 they have s' among the nations, 6327
Na 3:18 people is s' upon the mountains, 6340
Hab 3: 6 the everlasting mountains were s', 6327
Zec 1:19, 21 the horns which have s' Judah, 2219
Zec 7:14 I s' them with a whirlwind among*
13: 7 and the sheep shall be s': and I 6327
M't 9:36 were s' abroad, as sheep having 4496
26:31 of the flock shall be s' abroad. 1287
M'r 14:27 shepherd, and the sheep shall be s'. "
Lu 1:51 s' the proud in the imagination of "
Joh 11:52 children of God that were s' abroad. "
16:32 is now come, that ye shall be s', 4650
Ac 5:36 were s', and brought to nought. 1262
8: 1 they were all s' abroad throughout 1289
4 they that were s' abroad went "
11:19 they which were s' abroad upon the "
Jas 1: 1 twelve tribes which are s' abroad, 1290
1Pe 1: 1 strangers s' throughout Pontus, * "

scattereth
Job 37:11 cloud: he s' his bright cloud: *6327
38:24 s' the east wind upon the earth? * "
Ps 147:16 he s' the hoarfrost like ashes. 6340
Pr 11:24 There is that s', and yet increaseth; "
20: 8 s' away all evil with his eyes. 2219
26 A wise king s' the wicked, and * "
Isa 24: 1 s' abroad the inhabitants thereof. 6327
M't 12:30 gathereth not with me s' abroad. 4650
Lu 11:23 he that gathereth not with me s'. "
Joh 10:12 catcheth them, and s' the sheep. "

scattering
Isa 30:30 s', and tempest, and hailstones. *5311

scent
Job 14: 9 through the s' of water it will bud, 7381
Jer 48:11 in him, and his s' is not changed. "
Ho 14: 7 s' thereof shall be as the wine of 2143

sceptre See also SCEPTRES.
Ge 49:10 s' shall not depart from Judah, 7626
Nu 24:17 and a *S'* shall rise out of Israel, "
Es 4:11 king shall hold out the golden s', 8275
5: 2 held out to Esther the golden s'. "
2 near, and touched the top of the s'. "
8: 4 out the golden s' toward Esther. "
Ps 45: 6 and ever: the s' of thy kingdom 7626
6 of thy kingdom is a right s'. "
Isa 14: 5 the wicked, and the s' of the rulers. "
Eze 19:14 she hath no strong rod to be a s' to "
Am 1: 5 him that holdeth the s' from the "
8 that holdeth the s' from Ashkelon, "
Zec 10:11 the s' of Egypt shall depart away. "
Heb 1: 8 a s' of righteousness is the s' of 4464

sceptres
Eze 19:11 she had strong rods for the s' of 7626

Sceva (*see'-vah*)
Ac 19:14 there were seven sons of one *S'*. 4630

schism
1Co 12:25 there should be no s' in the body; 4978

scholar
1Ch 25: 8 the great, the teacher as the s'. 8527
Mal 2:12 the master and the s', out of the* 6030

school See also SCHOOLMASTER.
Ac 19: 9 daily in the s' of one Tyrannus. 4981

schoolmaster
Ga 3:24 law was our s' to bring us unto *3807
25 we are no longer under a s'. * "

science
Da 1: 4 knowledge, and understanding s', 4093
1Ti 6:20 oppositions of s' falsely so called: *1108

scoff
Hab 1:10 And they shall s' at the kings, *7046

scoffers
2Pe 3: 3 shall come in the last days s', *1703

scorch See also SCORCHED.
Re 16: 8 unto him to s' men with fire. *2739

scorched
M't 13: 6 the sun was up, they were s'; *2739
M'r 4: 6 when the sun was up, it was s'; "
Re 16: 9 And men were s' with great heat, "

score See FOURSCORE; SIXSCORE; THREESCORE.

scorn See also SCORNEST; SCORNETH; SCORNFUL; SCORNING.
2Ki 19:21 thee, and laughed thee to s';
2Ch 30:10 but they laughed them to s', and
Ne 2:19 heard it, they laughed us to s',
Es 3: 6 s' to lay hands on Mordecai alone; 959
Job 12: 4 the just upright man is laughed to s'.*
16:20 My friends s' me: but mine eye 3887
22:19 and the innocent laugh them to s'.
Ps 22: 7 they that see me laugh me to s':
44:13 a s' and a derision to them that 3933
79: 4 a s' and derision to them that are "
Isa 37:22 thee, and laughed thee to s';
Eze 23:32 thou shalt be laughed to s' and
Hab 1:10 princes shall be a s' unto them: *4890
M't 9:24 sleepeth...they laughed him to s'. 2606
M'r 5:40 And they laughed him to s'. But "
Lu 8:53 they laughed him to s', knowing "

scorner See also SCORNERS.
Pr 9: 7 He that reproveth a s' getteth to ‡3887
8 Reprove not a s', lest he hate thee: ‡ "
13: 1 but a s' heareth not rebuke. ‡ "
14: 6 A s' seeketh wisdom, and findeth ‡ "
15:12 A s' loveth not one that reproveth ‡ "
19:25 Smite a s', and the simple will ‡ "
21:11 When the s' is punished, the simple ‡ "
24 Proud and haughty s' is his name, ‡ "
22:10 Cast out the s', and contention ‡ "
24: 9 the s' is an abomination to men. ‡ "
Isa 29:20 the s' is consumed, and all that ‡ "

scorners
Pr 1:22 the s' delight in their scorning, ‡3887
3:34 Surely he scorneth the s': but he ‡ "
19:29 Judgments are prepared for s', ‡ "
Ho 7: 5 he stretched out his hand with s'. ‡3945

scornest
Pr 9:12 if thou s', thou alone shalt bear 3887
Eze 16:31 as an harlot, in that thou s' hire; 7046

scorneth
Job 39: 7 He s' the multitude of the city, 7832
18 high, she s' the horse and his rider. "
Pr 3:34 Surely he s' the scorners: but he 3887
19:28 An ungodly witness s' judgment: * "

scornful
Ps 1: 1 nor sitteth in the seat of the s'. ‡3887
Pr 29: 8 S' men bring a city into a snare: ‡3944
Isa 28:14 the word of the Lord, ye s' men, ‡ "

scorning
Job 34: 7 who drinketh up s' like water? ‡3933
Ps 123: 4 the s' of those that are at ease, ‡ "
Pr 1:22 the scorners delight in their s', ‡3944

scorpion See also SCORPIONS.
Lu 11:12 ask an egg, will he offer him a s'? 4651
Re 9: 5 torment was as the torment of a s', "

scorpions
De 8:15 were fiery serpents, and s', and 6137
1Ki 12:11, 14 but I will chastise you with s'. "
2Ch 10:11, 14 but I will chastise you with s'. "
Eze 2: 6 thee, and thou dost dwell among s': "
Lu 10:19 power to tread on serpents and s', 4651
Re 9: 3 as the s' of the earth have power. "
10 And they had tails like unto s', and "

scoured
Le 6:28 pot, it shall be both s', and rinsed 4838

scourge See also SCOURGED; SCOURGES; SCOURGETH; SCOURGING.
Job 5:21 be hid from the s' of the tongue: 7752
9:23 If the s' slay suddenly, he will "
Isa 10:26 the Lord of hosts shall stir up a s' "
28:15 overflowing s' shall pass through, 7885
18 overflowing s' shall pass through, 7752
M't 10:17 will s' you in their synagogues; 3164
20:19 to mock, and to s', and to crucify "
23:34 some of them shall ye s' in your "
M'r 10:34 shall s' him, and shall spit upon "
Lu 18:33 they shall s' him, and put him to "
Joh 2:15 he had made a s' of small cords, 5416
Ac 22:25 Is it lawful for you to s' a man 3147

scourged
Le 19:20 she shall be s'; they shall not be *1244
M't 27:26 and when he had s' Jesus, he *5417
M'r 15:15 when he had s' him, to be crucified. "
Joh 19: 1 therefore took Jesus, and s' him. 3146

scourges
Jos 23:13 s' in your sides, and thorns in your *7850

scourgeth
Heb 12: 6 s' every son whom he receiveth. 3146

scourging See also SCOURGINGS.
Ac 22:24 that he should be examined by s'; 3148

scourgings
Heb 11:36 trial of cruel mockings and s', 3148

scouring See OFFSCOURING.

scrabbled
1Sa 21:13 and s' on the doors of the gate, 8427

scrape See also SCRAPED.
Le 14:41 the dust that they s' off without 7096
Job 2: 8 a potsherd to s' himself withal; 1623
Eze 26: 4 I will also s' her dust from her, 5500

scraped
Le 14:41 cause the house to be s' within 7106
43 and after he hath s' the house, 7096

screech
Isa 34:14 the s' owl also shall rest there, *3917

scribe See also ASCRIBE; DESCRIBE; PRESCRIBED; SCRIBE'S; SCRIBES.
2Sa 8:17 priests; and Seraiah was the s'; 5608
20:25 And Sheva was s': and Zadok and "
2Ki 12:10 the king's s' and the high priest "
18:18, 37 Shebna the s', and Joah the son "
19: 2 Shebna the s', and the elder of the "
22: 3 the son of Meshullam, the s', to the "
8 priest said unto Shaphan the s', "
9 Shaphan the s' came to the king, "
10 Shaphan the s' shewed the king, "
12 And Shaphan the s', and Asahiah a "
25:19 and the principal s' of the host, "
1Ch 18:16 the priests; and Shavsha was s'; "
24: 6 Shemaiah...son of Nethaneel the s', "
27:32 a counseller, a wise man, and a s': "
2Ch 24:11 king's s' and...high priest's officer "
26:11 Jeiel the s' and Maaseiah the ruler, "
34:15 Hilkiah...said to Shaphan the s', "
18 Then Shaphan the s' told the king, "
20 and Shaphan the s', and Asaiah a "
Ezr 4: 8 and Shimshai the s' wrote a letter 5613
9 the chancellor, and Shimshai the s', "
17 chancellor, and to Shimshai the s', "
23 before Rehum, and Shimshai the s', "
7: 6 a ready s' in the law of Moses, 5608
11 gave unto Ezra the priest, the s', "
11 even a s' of the...commandments "
12, 21 s' of the law of...God of heaven, 5613
Ne 8: 1 and they spake unto Ezra the s' 5608
4 And Ezra the s' stood upon a pulpit "
9 and Ezra the priest the s', and the "
13 were gathered...unto Ezra the s', "
12:26 and of Ezra the priest, the s'. "
36 of God, and Ezra the s' before them. "
13:13 Shelemiah...and Zadok the s', "
Isa 33:18 Where is the s'? where is the * "
36: 3 Shebna the s', and Joah, Asaph's "
22 Shebna the s', and Joah, the son of "
37: 2 and Shebna the s', and the elders of "
Jer 36:10 Gemariah...son of Shaphan the s', 5608
12 sat there, even Elishama the s', and "
20 in the chamber of Elishama the s', "
26 to take Baruch the s' and Jeremiah "
32 roll, and gave it to Baruch the s', "
37:15 in the house of Jonathan the s': "
20 to the house of Jonathan the s', "
52:25 and the principal s' of the host, who "
M't 8:19 And a certain s' came, and said 1122
13:52 every s' which is instructed unto "
M'r 12:32 the s' said unto him, Well, Master, "
1Co 1:20 Where is the wise? where is the s'? "

scribe's
Jer 36:12 king's house, into the s' chamber: 5608
21 it out of Elishama the s' chamber. "

scribes
1Ki 4: 3 and Ahiah, the sons of Shisha, s'; 5608
1Ch 2:55 the families of the s' which dwelt at "
2Ch 34:13 and of the Levites there were s', "
Es 3:12 Then were the king's s' called on "
8: 9 Then were the king's s' called at "
Jer 8: 8 he it; the pen of the s' is in vain. "
M't 2: 4 chief priests and s' of the people 1122
5:20 exceed the righteousness of the s' "
7:29 having authority, and not as the s'. "
9: 3 behold, certain of the s' said within "
12:38 certain of the s' and of the Pharisees "
15: 1 came to Jesus s' and Pharisees, "
16:21 the elders and chief priests and s', "
17:10 Why then say the s' that Elias must "
20:18 the chief priests and unto the s', "
21:15 when the chief priests and s' saw "
23: 2 s' and the Pharisees sit in Moses' "
13 But woe unto you, s' and Pharisees, "
14 Woe unto you, s' and Pharisees, * "
15, 23, 25, 27, 29 Woe unto you, s' and "
34 prophets, and wise men, and s': "
26: 3 the chief priests, and the s', and the* "
57 s' and the elders were assembled. "
27:41 mocking him, with the s' and elders, "
M'r 1:22 had authority, and not as the s'. "
2: 6 were certain of the s' sitting there, "
16 the s' and Pharisees saw him eat "
3:22 s' which came down from Jerusalem "
7: 1 Pharisees, and certain of the s', "
5 the Pharisees and s' asked him, "
8:31 and of the chief priests, and s', "
9:11 Why say the s' that Elias must first "
14 and the s' questioning with them. "
16 he asked the s', What question ye* "
10:33 the chief priests, and unto the s'; "
11:18 And the s' and chief priests heard it, "
27 the chief priests, and the s', and the "
12:28 And one of the s' came, and having "
35 How say the s' that Christ is the son "
38 Beware of the s', which love to go "
14: 1 chief priests and the s' sought how "
43 from the chief priests and the s' and "
53 priests and the elders and the s'. "
15: 1 consultation with the elders and s' "
31 said among themselves with the s', "
Lu 5:21 s' and...Pharisees began to reason, "
30 their s' and Pharisees murmured "
6: 7 the s' and Pharisees watched him, "
9:22 the elders and chief priests and s', "
11:44 Woe unto you, s' and Pharisees, * "
53 s' and the Pharisees began to urge "
15: 2 Pharisees and s' murmured, saying, "
19:47 the chief priests and the s' and the "
20: 1 priests and the s' came upon him "
19 chief priests and...s' the same hour "
39 certain of the s' answering said, "
46 Beware of the s', which desire to "
22: 2 the chief priests and s' sought how "
66 priests and the s' came together, "
23:10 And the chief priests and s' stood "
Joh 8: 3 s' and Pharisees brought unto him "
Ac 4: 5 that their rulers, and elders, and s', "
6:12 the people, and the elders, and the s', "
23: 9 s' that were of the Pharisees' part "

scrip
1Sa 17:40 bag which he had, even in a s'; 3219
M't 10:10 Nor s' for your journey, neither *4082
M'r 6: 8 no s', no bread, no money in their* "
Lu 9: 3 neither staves, nor s', neither * "
10: 4 Carry neither purse, nor s', nor * "
22:35 sent you without purse, and s', and* "
36 let him take it, and likewise his s': * "

scripture See also SCRIPTURES.
Da 10:21 which is noted in the s' of truth: *3791
M'r 12:10 have ye not read this s'; The stone 1124
15:28 the s' was fulfilled, which saith, * "
Lu 4:21 This day is this s' fulfilled in your "
Joh 2:22 they believed the s', and the word "
7:38 as the s' hath said, out of his belly "
42 Hath not the s' said, That Christ "
10:35 came, and the s' cannot be broken; "
13:18 that the s' may be fulfilled, He that "
17:12 that the s' might be fulfilled. "
19:24 that the s' might be fulfilled, which "
28 that the s' might be fulfilled, saith, "
36 s' should be fulfilled, A bone of him "
37 again another s' saith, They shall "
20: 9 For as yet they knew not the s', "
Ac 1:16 s' must needs have been fulfilled, "
8:32 The place of the s' which he read "
35 began at the same s', and preached "
Ro 4: 3 For what saith the s'? Abraham "
9:17 the s' saith unto Pharaoh, Even for "
10:11 the s' saith, Whosoever believeth "
11: 2 Wot ye not what the s' saith of Elias? "
Ga 3: 8 the s', foreseeing that God would "
22 the s' hath concluded all under sin, "
4:30 Nevertheless what saith the s'? "
1Ti 5:18 the s' saith, Thou shalt not muzzle "
2Ti 3:16 All s' is given by inspiration of God, 1124
Jas 2: 8 the royal law according to the s', "
23 And the s' was fulfilled which saith, "
4: 5 ye think that the s' saith in vain, "
1Pe 2: 6 Wherefore...it is contained in the s', "
2Pe 1:20 no prophecy of the s' is of...private "

scriptures
M't 21:42 Did ye never read in the s', The 1124
22:29 Ye do err, not knowing the s', nor "
26:54 how then shall the s' be fulfilled, "
56 s' of the prophets might be fulfilled, "
M'r 12:24 err, because ye know not the s', "
14:49 me not: but the s' must be fulfilled. "
Lu 24:27 expounded unto them in all the s' "
32 and while he opened to us the s'? "
45 that they might understand the s', "
Joh 5:39 Search the s'; for in them ye think "
Ac 17: 2 reasoned with them out of the s', "
11 and searched the s' daily, whether "
18:24 eloquent man, and mighty in the s', "
28 shewing by the s' that Jesus was "
Ro 1: 2 afore by his prophets in the holy s',) "
15: 4 patience and comfort of the s' we "
16:26 by the s' of the prophets, according "
1Co 15: 3 died for our sins according to the s'; "
4 the third day according to the s': "
2Ti 3:15 child thou hast known the holy s', *1121
2Pe 3:16 wrest, as they do also the other s', 1124

scroll
Isa 34: 4 shall be rolled together as a s': 5612
Re 6:14 And the heaven departed as a s' 975

scull See SKULL.

scum
Eze 24: 6 to the pot whose s' is therein, *2457
6 and whose s' is not gone out of it! * "
11 that the s' of it may be consumed. * "
12 great s' went not forth out of her: * "
12 her s' shall be in the fire. * "

scurvy
Le 21:20 hath a blemish in his eye, or be s', 1618
22:22 or maimed, or having a wen, or s', "

Scythian (*sith'-e-un*)
Col 3:11 Barbarian, S', bond nor free: 4658

sea See also SEAFARING; SEAS.
Ge 1:26, 28 dominion over the fish of the s', 3220
9: 2 and upon all the fishes of the s'; "
14: 3 vale of Siddim, which is the salt s'. "
22:17 sand which is upon the s' shore; "
32:12 make thy seed as the sand of the s', "
41:49 gathered corn as the sand of the s', "
49:13 shall dwell at the haven of the s'; "
Ex 10:19 and cast them into the Red s'; "
13:18 way of the wilderness of the Red s': "
14: 2 between Migdol and the s', over "
2 before it shall ye encamp by the s'. "
9 overtook them encamping by the s', "
16 stretch out thine hand over the s', "
16 ground through the midst of the s'. "
21 stretched out his hand over the s'; "
21 s' to go back by a strong east wind "
21 and made the s' dry land, and the "
22 midst of the s' upon the dry ground: "
23 in after them to the midst of the s', "
26 Stretch out thine hand over the s', "
27 stretched forth his hand over the s', "
27 and the s' returned to his strength "
27 Egyptians in the midst of the s'. "
28 that came into the s' after them; "
29 upon dry land in the midst of the s'; "
30 Egyptians dead upon the s' shore. "
15: 1 rider hath he thrown into the s'. "
4 his host hath he cast into the s': "
4 also are drowned in the Red s'. "
8 congealed in the heart of the s'. "
10 with thy wind, the s' covered them: "
19 and with his horsemen into the s', "
19 the waters of the s' upon them; "
19 on dry land in the midst of the s'. "
21 rider hath he thrown into the s'. "
22 brought Israel from the Red s', "
20:11 the s', and all that in them is, and "
23:31 will set thy bounds from the Red s' "
31 even unto the s' of the Philistines, "
Nu 11:22 fish of the s' be gathered together "
31 and brought quails from the s', and "
13:29 and the Canaanites dwell by the s', "
14:25 wilderness by the way of the Red s': "
21: 4 Hor by the way of the Red s', "
14 What he did in the Red s', and in the* "
33: 8 midst of the s' into the wilderness, 3220
10 Elim, and encamped by the Red s'. "
11 And they removed from the Red s', "
34: 3 coast of the salt s' eastward: "
5 goings out of it shall be at the s'. "
6 even have the great s' for a border: "
7 great s' ye shall point out for you "
11 the side of the s' of Chinnereth "
12 out of it shall be at the salt s': "
De 1: 1 in the plain over against the Red s',* "
7 in the south, and by the s' side, 3220
40 wilderness by the way of the Red s'. "
2: 1 wilderness by the way of the Red s', "
3:17 the s' of the plain, even the salt s', "
4:49 even unto the s' of the plain, under "
11: 4 the Red s' to overflow them as they "
24 uttermost s' shall your coast be. "
30:13 Neither is it beyond the s', that "
13 Who shall go over the s' for us, and "
34: 2 land of Judah, unto the utmost s', "
Jos 1: 4 unto the great s' toward the going "
2:10 up the water of the Red s' for you, "
3:16 the s' of the plain, even the salt s', "
4:23 Lord your God did to the Red s', "

Jos 5: 1 Canaanites, which were by the s', 3220
9: 1 all the coasts of the great s' over "
11: 4 the sand that is upon the s' shore "
12: 3 the plain to the s' of Chinneroth on "
3 east, and unto the s' of the plain, "
3 plain, even the salt s' on the east, "
13: 27 the edge of the s' of Chinnereth on "
15: 2 was from the shore of the salt s', "
4 out of that coast were at the s': "
5 And the east border was the salt s', "
5 s' at the uttermost part of Jordan: "
11 out of the border were at the s'. "
12 the west border was to the great s', "
46 From Ekron even unto the s', all "
47 great s', and the border thereof: "
16: 3 the goings out thereof are at the s'. "
6 toward the s' to Michmethah on * "
8 goings out thereof were at the s'. "
17: 9 the outgoings of it were at the s': "
10 Manasseh's,...the s' is his border; "
18: 14 and compassed the corner of the s'* "
19 were at the north bay of the salt s' "
19: 11 their border went up toward the s',* "
29 at the s' from the coast to Achzib: "
23: 4 even unto the great s' westward. "
24: 6 of Egypt: and ye came unto the s'; "
6 and horsemen unto the Red s'. "
7 and brought the s' upon them, and "
J'g 5: 17 Asher continued on the s' shore, "
7: 12 sand by the s' side for multitude. "
11: 16 the wilderness unto the Red s', "
1Sa 13: 5 as the sand which is on the s' shore "
2Sa 17: 11 as the sand that is by the s' for "
22: 16 the channels of the s' appeared, the "
1Ki 4: 20 as the sand which is by the s' in "
29 as the sand that is on the s' shore. "
5: 9 down from Lebanon unto the s': "
9 I will convey them by s' in floats "
7: 23 And he made a molten s', ten cubits "
24 compassing the s' round about: "
25 the s' was set above upon them, "
39 he set the s' on the right side of "
44 s', and twelve oxen under the s'; "
9: 26 Eloth, on the shore of the Red s', "
27 that had knowledge of the s', with "
10: 22 king had at s' a navy of Tharshish "
18: 43 Go up now, look toward the s'. And "
44 ariseth a little cloud out of the s', "
2Ki 14: 25 Hamath unto the s' of the plain, "
16: 17 down the s' from off the brasen "
25: 13 the brasen s' that was in the house "
16 The two pillars, one s', and the "
1Ch 16: 32 Let the s' roar, and the fulness "
18: 8 Solomon made the brasen s', and "
2Ch 2: 16 it to thee in floats by s' to Joppa; "
4: 2 he made a molten s' of ten cubits "
3 compassing the s' round about. "
4 and the s' was set above upon them, "
6 s' was for the priests to wash in. "
10 he set the s' on the right side of the "
15 One s', and twelve oxen under it. "
8: 17 at the s' side in the land of Edom. "
18 that had knowledge of the s'; and "
20: 2 beyond the s' on this side Syria; "
Ezr 3: 7 from Lebanon to the s' of Joppa, "
Ne 9: 9 heardest their cry by the Red s'; "
11 And thou didst divide the s' before "
11 through the midst of the s' on...dry "
Es 10: 1 land, and upon the isles of the s'. "
Job 6: 3 be heavier than the sand of the s':* "
7: 12 Am I a s', or a whale, that thou "
9: 8 treadeth upon the waves of the s'. "
11: 9 the earth, and broader than the s'. "
12: 8 the fishes of the s' shall declare "
14: 11 As the waters fail from the s', and "
26: 12 He divideth the s' with his power, "
28: 14 and the s' saith, It is not with me. "
36: 30 and covereth the bottom of the s'. "
38: 8 Or who shut up the s' with doors, "
16 entered into the springs of the s'? "
41: 31 he maketh the s' like a pot of "
Ps 8: 8 the fish of the s', and whatsoever "
33: 7 He gathereth the waters of the s' "
46: 2 be carried into the midst of the s':* "
65: 5 them that are afar off upon the s': "
66: 6 He turned the s' into dry land: they "
68: 22 again from the depths of the s': "
72: 8 have dominion also from s' to s', "
74: 13 didst divide the s' by the strength: "
77: 19 Thy way is in the s', and thy path "
78: 13 He divided the s', and caused them "
27 fowls like as the sand of the s': * "
53 the s' overwhelmed their enemies. "
80: 11 sent out her boughs unto the s', "
89: 9 Thou rulest the raging of the s': "
25 I will set his hand also in the s', "
93: 4 than the mighty waves of the s'. "
95: 5 The s' is his, and he made it: and "
96: 11 let the s' roar, and the fulness "
98: 7 Let the s' roar, and the fulness "
104: 25 So is this great and wide s', wherein "
106: 7 him at the s', even at the Red s'. "
9 He rebuked the Red s' also, and it "
22 and terrible things by the Red s'. "
107: 23 that go down to the s' in ships, that "
114: 3 The s' saw it, and fled: Jordan was "
5 What ailed thee, O thou s', that "
136: 13 which divided the Red s' into parts: "
15 Pharaoh and his host in the Red s': "
139: 9 in the uttermost parts of the s'; "
146: 6 the s', and all that therein is: "
Pr 8: 29 When he gave to the s' his decree, "
23: 34 lieth down in the midst of the s', "
30: 19 way of a ship in the midst of the s'; "
Ec 1: 7 into the s'; yet the s' is not full; "
Isa 5: 30 them like the roaring of the s': "

Isa 9: 1 afflict her by the way of the s', 3220
10: 22 Israel be as the sand of the s', "
26 as his rod was upon the s', so shall "
11: 9 the Lord, as the waters cover the s'. "
11 and from the islands of the s'. "
15 the tongue of the Egyptian s'; "
16: 8 out, they are gone over the s'. "
18: 2 sendeth ambassadors by the s', "
19: 5 the waters shall fail from the s', "
21: 1 The burden of the desert of the s'. "
23: 2 of Zidon, that pass over the s', have "
4 for the s' hath spoken, even the "
4 even the strength of the s', saying, "
11 stretched out his hand over the s', "
24: 14 they shall cry aloud from the s'. "
15 God of Israel in the isles of the s'. "
27: 1 slay the dragon that is in the s'. "
42: 10 ye that go down to the s', and all "
43: 16 which maketh a way in the s', and "
48: 18 righteousness as the waves of the s'. "
50: 2 at my rebuke I dry up the s', I "
51: 10 not it which hath dried the s', the "
10 made the depths of the s' a way for "
15 Lord thy God that divided the s', "
57: 20 the wicked are like the troubled s', "
60: 5 the abundance of the s' shall be "
63: 11 that brought them up out of the s' "
Jer 5: 22 the sand for the bound of the s' "
6: 23 their voice roareth like the s'; and "
25: 22 the isles which are beyond the s', "
27: 19 concerning the s', and concerning "
31: 35 which divideth the s' when the "
33: 22 the sand of the s' measured: so "
46: 18 and as Carmel by the s', so shall he "
47: 7 Ashkelon, and against the s' shore? "
48: 32 thy plants are gone over the s', they "
32 they reach even to the s' of Jazer: "
49: 21 thereof was heard in the Red s'. "
23 there is sorrow on the s'; it cannot "
50: 42 their voice shall roar like the s', "
51: 36 I will dry up her s', and make her "
42 The s' is come up upon Babylon: "
52: 17 the brasen s' that was in the house "
20 The two pillars, one s', and twelve "
La 2: 13 for thy breach is great like the s': "
4: 3 Even the s' monsters draw out *
Eze 25: 16 destroy...remnant of the s' coast. 3220
26: 3 s' causeth his waves to come up. "
5 of nets in the midst of the s': for "
16 all the princes of the s' shall come "
17 which wast strong in the s', she and "
18 that are in the s' shall be troubled "
27: 3 art situate at the entry of the s', "
9 ships of the s' with their mariners "
29 all the pilots of the s', shall come "
32 the destroyed in the midst of the s'? "
38: 20 So that the fishes of the s', and the "
39: 11 the passengers on the east of the s': "
47: 8 into the desert, and go into the s': "
8 being brought forth into the s', "
10 as the fish of the great s', exceeding "
15 the north side from the great s', "
17 And the border from the s' shall be "
18 from the border unto the east s'. "
19 in Kadesh, the river to the great s'. "
20 west side also shall be the great s'. "
48: 28 and to the river toward the great s'. "
Da 7: 2 heaven strove upon the great s'. 3221
3 great beasts came up from the s', "
Ho 1: 10 Israel shall be as...sand of the s', 3220
4: 3 fishes of the s' also shall be taken "
Joe 2: 20 with his face toward the east s', and "
20 hinder part toward the utmost s', "
Am 5: 8 that calleth for the waters of the s', "
8: 12 And they shall wander from s' to s', "
9: 3 my sight in the bottom of the s', "
6 that calleth for the waters of the s', "
Jon 1: 4 sent out a great wind into the s', "
4 was a mighty tempest in the s', so "
5 that were in the ship into the s', "
9 which hath made the s' and the dry "
11 that the s' may be calm unto us? "
11 unto us? for the s' wrought, and was "
12 up, and cast me forth into the s'; "
12 so shall the s' be calm unto "
13 s' wrought, and was tempestuous. "
15 Jonah, and cast him forth into the s': "
15 and the s' ceased from her raging. "
Mic 7: 12 from s' to s', and from mountain "
19 their sins into the depths of the s'. "
Na 1: 4 He rebuketh the s', and maketh it "
3: 8 about it, whose rampart was the s', "
8 and her wall was from the s'? "
Hab 1: 14 makest men as the fishes of the s', "
2: 14 the Lord, as the waters cover the s'. "
3: 8 was thy wrath against the s', that "
15 walk through the s' with thine "
Zep 1: 3 the heaven, and the fishes of the s', "
2: 5 unto the inhabitants of the s' coast, "
6 the s' coast shall be dwellings and "
Hag 2: 6 heavens, and the earth, and the s', "
Zec 9: 4 he will smite her power in the s'; "
10 dominion shall be from s' even to s', "
10: 11 pass through the s' with affliction, "
11 and shall smite the waves in the s', "
14: 8 half of them toward the former s', "
8 half of them toward the hinder s': "
M't 4: 13 which is upon the s' coast, in the 3864
15 by the way of the s', beyond Jordan, 2281
18 Jesus, walking by the s' of Galilee, "
18 brother, casting a net into the s': "
8: 24 arose a great tempest in the s', "
26 and rebuked the winds and the s'; "
27 even the winds and the s' obey him! "
32 down a steep place into the s', and "
13: 1 of the house, and sat by the s' side. "

M't 13: 47 unto a net, that was cast into the s', 2281
14: 24 ship was now in the midst of the s', "
25 went unto them, walking on the s'. "
26 disciples saw him walking on the s', "
15: 29 came nigh unto the s' of Galilee; "
17: 27 go thou to the s', and cast an hook, "
18: 6 were drowned in the depth of the s'. "
21: 21 and be thou cast into the s'; "
23: 15 ye compass s' and land to make one "
M'r 1: 16 as he walked by the s' of Galilee, he "
16 brother casting a net into the s': "
2: 13 he went forth again by the s' side; "
3: 7 himself with his disciples to the s': "
4: 1 began again to teach by the s' side: "
1 entered into a ship, and sat in the s'; "
1 whole multitude was by the s' on "
39 and said unto the s', Peace, be still. "
41 even the wind and the s' obey him? "
5: 1 over unto the other side of the s', "
13 down a steep place into the s', "
13 thousand;) and...choked in the s'. "
21 him: and he was nigh unto the s'. "
6: 47 the ship was in the midst of the s', "
48 unto them, walking upon the s', "
49 they saw him walking upon the s', "
7: 31 he came unto the s' of Galilee, "
9: 42 neck, and he were cast into the s'. "
11: 23 and be thou cast into the s'; "
Lu 6: 17 from the s' coast of Tyre and Sidon, 3882
17: 2 his neck, and he cast into the s', 2281
6 root, and be thou planted in the s'; "
21: 25 the s' and the waves roaring; "
Joh 6: 1 Jesus went over the s' of Galilee, "
1 Galilee, which is the s' of Tiberias. "
16 his disciples went down unto the s', "
17 went over the s' toward Capernaum. "
18 s' arose by reason of a great wind "
19 they see Jesus walking on the s', "
22 stood on the other side of the s' saw "
25 him on the other side of the s', "
21: 1 the disciples at the s' of Tiberias; "
7 and did cast himself into the s'. "
Ac 4: 24 made heaven, and earth, and the s', "
7: 36 in the Red s', and in the wilderness "
10: 6 whose house is by the s' side: "
32 one Simon a tanner by the s' side: "
14: 15 made heaven, and earth, and the s', "
17: 14 away Paul to go as it were to the s': "
27: 5 we had sailed over the s' of Cilicia 3989
30 had let down the boat into the s', 2281
38 and cast out the wheat into the s'. "
40 committed themselves unto the s', "
43 should cast themselves first into the s'. *
28: 4 though he hath escaped the s', yet 2281
Ro 9: 27 of Israel be as the sand of the s', "
1Co 10: 1 cloud, and all passed through the s'; "
2 Moses in the cloud and in the s'; "
2Co 11: 26 in perils in the s', in perils among "
Heb 11: 12 is by the s' shore innumerable. "
29 passed through the Red s' as by dry "
Jas 1: 6 that wavereth is like a wave of the s' "
3: 7 and of things in the s', is tamed, 1724
Jude 13 Raging waves of the s', foaming 2281
Re 4: 6 was a s' of glass like unto crystal: "
5: 13 such as are in the s', and all that "
7: 1 not blow on the earth, nor on the s', "
2 given to hurt the earth and the s', "
3 Hurt not the earth, neither the s', "
8: 8 with fire was cast into the s': and "
8 third part of the s' became blood; "
9 the creatures which were in the s', "
10: 2 and he set his right foot upon the s', "
5 angel which I saw stand upon the s' "
6 s', and the things which are therein, "
8 the angel which standeth upon the s' "
12: 12 inhabiters of the earth and of the s'! "
13: 1 And I stood upon the sand of the s', "
1 and saw a beast rise up out of the s', "
14: 7 the s', and the fountains of waters. "
15: 2 were a s' of glass mingled with fire: "
2 stand on the s' of glass, having the "
16: 3 poured out his vial upon the s'; and "
3 and every living soul died in the s'. "
18: 17 sailors, and as many as trade by s', "
19 made rich all that had ships in the s' "
21 millstone, and cast it into the s', "
20: 8 of whom is as the sand of the s'. "
13 s' gave up the dead which were in it; "
21: 1 away; and there was no more s'. "

seafaring
Eze 26: 17 that wast inhabited of s' men, the 3220

seal See also SEALED; SEALEST; SEALETH; SEALING; SEALS.
1Ki 21: 8 name, and sealed them with his s'. 2368
Ne 9: 38 Levites, and priests, s' unto it. 2856
Es 8: 8 name, and s' it with the king's ring: "
Job 38: 14 It is turned as clay to the s'; and 2368
41: 15 shut up together as with a close s'. "
Ca 8: 6 Set me as a s' upon thine heart, "
6 as a s' upon thine arm: for love is "
Isa 8: 16 s' the law among my disciples. 2856
Jer 32: 44 subscribe evidences, and s' them, "
Da 9: 24 to s' up the vision and prophecy, "
12: 4 shut up the words, and s' the book, "
Joh 3: 33 hath set to his s' that God is true. 4972
Ro 4: 11 s' of the righteousness of the faith 4973
1Co 9: 2 s' of mine apostleship are ye in the "
2Ti 2: 19 of God standeth sure, having this s', "
Re 6: 3 when he had opened the second s', "
5 when he had opened the third s', "
7 when he had opened the fourth s', "
9 And when he had opened the fifth s', "
12 when he had opened the sixth s', "
7: 2 east, having the s' of the living God: "
8: 1 when he had opened the seventh s', "

Re 9: 4 not the s' of God in their foreheads.4973
10: 4 S' up those things which the seven4972
20: 3 shut him up, and set a s' upon him,*"
22:10 S' not the sayings of the prophecy "

sealed
De 32:34 and s' up among my treasures? 2856
1Ki 21: 8 name, and s' them with his seal, "
Ne 10: 1 Now those that s' were, Nehemiah, "
Es 3:12 written, and s' with the king's ring."
8: 8 name, and s' with the king's ring, "
10 s' it with the king's ring, and sent "
Job 14:17 My transgression is s' up in a bag, "
Ca 4:12 a spring shut up, a fountain s'. "
Isa 29:11 as the words of a book that is s', "
11 and he saith, I cannot; for it is s': "
Jer 32:10 subscribed the evidence, and s' it, "
11 which was s' according to the law "
14 both which is s', and this evidence "
Da 6:17 the king s' it with his own signet, 2857
12: 9 up and s' till the time of the end. 2856
Joh 6:27 for him hath God the Father s'. 4972
Ro 15:28 this, and have s' to them this fruit, "
2Co 1:22 Who hath also s' us, and given the "
Eph 1:13 s' with that holy Spirit of promise, "
4:30 are s' unto the day of redemption. "
Re 5: 1 the backside, s' with seven seals. 2696
7: 3 we have s' the servants of our God4972
4 the number of them which were s': "
4 there were s' an hundred and forty "
5 of Juda were s' twelve thousand. "
5 Reuben were s' twelve thousand. * "
5 of Gad were s' twelve thousand. * "
6 of Aser were s' twelve thousand. * "
6 Nepthalim were s' twelve thousand.*"
6 Manasses were s' twelve thousand.*"
7 of Simeon were s' twelve thousand.*"
7 of Levi were s' twelve thousand. * "
7 Issachar were s' twelve thousand.* "
8 Zabulon were s' twelve thousand.* "
8 Joseph were s' twelve thousand. * "
8 Benjamin were s' twelve thousand.*"

sealest
Eze 28:12 Thou s' up the sum, full of 2856

sealeth
Job 9: 7 riseth not; and s' up the stars. 2856
33:16 of men, and s' their instruction, "
37: 7 He s' up the hand of every man; "

sealing
M't 27:66 s' the stone, and setting a watch. 4972

seals
Re 5: 1 the backside, sealed with seven s'.4973
2 book, and to loose the s' thereof? "
5 and to loose the seven s' thereof. "
9 the book, and to open the s' thereof:"
6: 1 when the Lamb opened one of the s'."

seam
Joh 19:23 now the coat was without s', woven 729

sea-monster See SEA and MONSTER.

search See also SEARCHED; SEARCHEST; SEARCHETH; SEARCHING; UNSEARCHABLE.
Le 27:33 He shall not s' whether it be good 1239
Nu 10:33 to s' out a resting place for them.*8446
13: 2 men, that they may s' the land of * "
32 through which we have gone to s' * "
14: 7 which we passed through to s' it, * "
36 which Moses sent to s' the land, * "
38 the men that went to s' the land, * "
De 1:22 and they shall s' us out the land, 2658
33 to s' you out a place to pitch your*8446
13:14 shalt thou enquire, and make s', 2713
Jos 2: 2 of Israel to s' out the country. 2658
3 be come to s' out all the country. "
J'g 18: 2 to spy out the land, and to s' it; 2713
2 said unto them, Go, s' the land: "
1Sa 23:23 that I will s' him out throughout 2664
2Sa 10: 3 to s' the city, and to spy it out, 2713
1Ki 20: 6 and they shall s' thine house, and 2664
2Ki 10:23 S', and look that there be here "
1Ch 19: 3 servants come unto thee for to s', 2713
Ezr 4:15 s' may be made in the book of the 1240
19 and s' hath been made, and it is "
5:17 be s' made in the king's treasure "
6: 1 s' was made in the house of the "
Job 8: 8 thyself to the s' of their fathers: *2714
13: 9 Is it good that he should s' you 2713
38:16 walked in the s' of the depth? *2714
Ps 44:21 Shall not God s' this out? for he 2713
64: 6 They s' out iniquities; they 2664
6 they accomplish a diligent s': 2665
77: 6 and my spirit made diligent s'. 2664
139:23 S' me,...and know my heart: 2713
Pr 25: 2 of kings is to s' out a matter. "
27 to s' their own glory is not glory. 2714
Ec 1:13 to seek and s' out by wisdom 8446
7:25 and to s', and to seek out wisdom, "
Jer 2:34 I have not found it by secret s', *4290
17:10 I the Lord s' the heart, I try the 2713
29:13 shall s' for me with all your heart. 1875
La 3:40 Let us s' and try our ways, and 2664
Eze 34: 6 none did s' or seek after them. 1875
8 did my shepherds s' for my flock, "
11 I, will both s' my sheep, and seek "
39:14 end of seven months shall they s'. 2713
Am 9: 3 will s' and take them out thence; 2664
Zep 1:12 I will s' Jerusalem with candles, "
M't 2: 8 s' diligently for the young child; 1833
Joh 5:39 S' the scriptures; for in them ye 2045
7:52 S', and look: for out of Galilee "

searched
Ge 31:34 Laban s' all the tent, but found *4959
35 he s', but found not the images. 2664
37 whereas thou hast s' all my stuff,*4959
44:12 he s', and began at the eldest, 2664
Nu 13:21 s' the land from the wilderness *8446
32 of the land which they had s' unto* "
14: 6 were of them that s' the land, rent* "
34 of the days in which ye s' the land,* "
De 1:24 the valley of Eshcol, and s' it out.*7270
Job 5:27 Lo this, we have s' it, so it is; 2713
28:27 it; he prepared it, yea, and s' it out."
29:16 the cause which I knew not I s' out."
32:11 whilst ye s' out what to say. "
36:26 the number of his years be s' out.*2714
Ps 139: 1 O Lord, thou hast s' me, and 2713
Jer 31:37 the foundations of the earth s' out "
46:23 though it cannot be s'; because "
Ob 6 How are the things of Esau s' out!2664
Ac 17:11 s' the scriptures daily, whether *350
1Pe 1:10 have enquired and s' diligently, 1830

searchest
Job 10: 6 mine iniquity, and s' after my sin?1875
Pr 2: 4 and s' for her as for hid treasures;*2664

searcheth
1Ch 28: 9 for the Lord s' all hearts, and 1875
Job 28: 3 and s' out all perfection: the 2713
39: 8 and he s' after every green thing. 1875
Pr 18:17 his neighbour cometh and s' him. 2713
28:11 hath understanding s' him out. "
Ro 8:27 And he that s' the hearts knoweth 2045
1Co 2:10 for the Spirit s' all things, yea, the "
Re 2:23 he which s' the reins and hearts: "

searching See also SEARCHINGS.
Nu 13:25 they returned from s' of the land *8446
Job 11: 7 Canst thou by s' find out God? 2714
Pr 20:27 s' all the inward parts of the belly.2664
Isa 40:28 is no s' of his understanding. 2714
1Pe 1:11 S' what, or what manner of time 2045

searchings
J'g 5:16 there were great s' of heart. *2714

seared
1Ti 4: 2 conscience s' with a hot iron; *2743

seas
Ge 1:10 of the waters called he S': and 3220
22 and fill the waters in the s', and "
Le 11: 9 and scales in the waters, in the s', "
10 have not fins and scales in the s', "
De 33:19 suck of the abundance of the s', "
Ne 9: 6 the s', and all that is therein, and "
Ps 8: 8 passeth through the paths of the s'."
24: 2 For he hath founded it upon the s', "
65: 7 Which stilleth the noise of the s', "
69:34 the s', and every thing that moveth "
135: 6 earth, in the s', and all deep places."
Isa 17:12 a noise like the noise of the s'; "
Jer 15: 8 to me above the sand of the s': "
Eze 27: 4 borders are in the midst of the s', "
25 very glorious in the midst of the s'. "
26 broken thee in the midst of the s'. "
27 shall fall into the midst of the s' in "
33 thy wares went forth out of the s', "
34 thou shalt be broken by the s' in "
28: 2 seat of God, in the midst of the s'; "
8 that are slain in the midst of the s'. "
32: 2 and thou art as a whale in the s': "
Da 11:45 of his palace between the s' in the "
Jon 2: 3 the deep, in the midst of the s'; "
Ac 27:41 into a place where two s' met, 1337

sea-shore See SEA and SHORE.

sea-side See SEA and SIDE.

season See also SEASONED; SEASONS.
Ge 40: 4 and they continued a s' in ward. 3117
Ex 13:10 keep this ordinance in his s' from 4150
Le 2:13 offering shalt thou s' with salt; 4414
26: 4 I will give you rain in due s', and 6256
Nu 9: 2 the passover at his appointed s'. 4150
3 ye shall keep it in his appointed s':"
7 of the Lord in his appointed s', "
13 of the Lord in his appointed s', "
28: 2 to offer unto me in their due s'. "
De 11:14 the rain of your land in his due s',6256
16: 6 the s' that thou camest forth out 4150
28:12 the rain unto thy land in his s', 6256
Jos 24: 7 dwelt in the wilderness a long s'. *3117
2Ki 4:16 About this s', according to the 4150
17 bare a son at that s' that Elisha had"
2Ch 15: 3 a long s' Israel hath been without*3117
Job 5:26 shock of corn cometh in in his s'. 6256
30:17 are pierced in me in the night s': "
38:32 bring forth Mazzaroth in his s'? 6256
Ps 1: 3 bringeth forth his fruit in his s'; "
22: 2 in the night s', and am not silent. "
104:27 give them their meat in due s'. 6256
145:15 givest them their meat in due s'. "
Pr 15:23 a word spoken in due s', how good "
Ec 3: 1 To every thing there is a s', and a 2165
10:17 and thy princes eat in due s', for 6256
Isa 50: 4 know how to speak a word in s' to* "
Jer 5:24 the former and the latter, in his s':6256
33:20 not be day and night in their s'; "
Eze 34:26 the shower to come down in his s'; "
Da 7:12 their lives were prolonged for a s' 2166
Ho 2: 9 and my wine in the s' thereof, and 4150
M't 24:45 to give them meat in due s'? 2540
M'r 9:50 saltness, wherewith will ye s' it? 741
12: 2 the s' he sent to the husbandmen 2540
Lu 1:20 which shall be fulfilled in their s'. "
4:13 he departed from him for a s'. "
12:42 them their portion of meat in due s'?"
13: 1 were present at that s' some that "
20:10 at the s' he sent a servant to the "
23: 8 he was desirous to see him of a long s',*
Joh 5: 4 down at a certain s' into the pool,*2540
35 ye were willing for a s' to rejoice 5610
Ac 13:11 blind, not seeing the sun for a s'. 2540
19:22 he himself stayed in Asia for a s'. *5550
24:25 when I have a convenient s', I will 2540
2Co 7: 8 sorry, though it were but for a s'. 5610
Ga 6: 9 for in due s' we shall reap, if we 2540
2Ti 4: 2 Preach the word; be instant in s', 2121
2 be instant...out of s'; reprove, 171
Ph'm 15 he therefore departed for a s', that5610
Heb 11:25 enjoy the pleasures of sin for a s'; 4340
1Pe 1: 6 rejoice, though now for a s', if 3641
Re 6:11 they should rest yet for a little s',*5550
20: 3 that he must be loosed a little s'.* "

seasoned
Lu 14:34 his savour, wherewith shall it be s'? 741
Col 4: 6 be alway with grace, s' with salt, "

seasons
Ge 1:14 let them be for signs, and for s', 4150
Ex 18:22 them judge the people at all s': 6256
26 they judged the people at all s': "
Le 23: 4 which ye shall proclaim in their s'.*4150
Ps 16: 7 reins also instruct me in the night s'.
104:19 He appointed the moon for s': 4150
Da 2:21 he changeth the times and the s': 2166
M't 21:41 render him the fruits in their s'. 2540
Ac 1: 7 for you to know the times or the s', "
14:17 us rain from heaven, and fruitful s',"
20:18 I have been with you at all s', *5550
1Th 5: 1 of the times and the s', brethren, 2540

seat See also MERCYSEAT; SEATED; SEATS; SEATWARD.
Ex 25:17 shalt make a mercy s' of pure gold:
18 in the two ends of the mercy s'.
19 even of the mercy s' shall ye make the
20 the mercy s' with their wings, and
20 toward the mercy s' shall the faces
21 put the mercy s' above upon the ark;
22 with thee from above the mercy s',
26:34 put the mercy s' upon the ark of the
30: 6 before the mercy s' that is over the
31: 7 and the mercy s' that is thereupon,
35:12 staves thereof, with the mercy s',
37: 6 he made the mercy s' of pure gold:
7 on the two ends of the mercy s',
8 out of the mercy s' made he the
9 with their wings over the mercy s',
39:35 the staves thereof, and the mercy s',
40:20 and put the mercy s' above upon the
Le 16: 2 within the vail before the mercy s',
2 in the cloud upon the mercy s'.
13 the incense may cover the mercy s'
14 finger upon the mercy s' eastward;
14 and before the mercy s' shall he
15 and sprinkle it upon the mercy s',
15 and before the mercy s':
Nu 7:89 unto him from off the mercy s' that
J'g 3:20 thee. And he arose out of his s'. 3678
1Sa 1: 9 Eli the priest sat upon a s' by a post"
4:13 lo, Eli sat upon a s' by the wayside "
18 he fell from off the s' backward by "
20:18 because thy s' will be empty. 4186
25 And the king sat upon his s', as at "
25 times, even upon a s' by the wall: "
2Sa 23: 8 The Tachmonite that sat in the s',*7674
1Ki 2:19 s' to be set for the king's mother;*3678
10:19 either side on the place of the s', 7675
1Ch 28:11 and of the place of the mercy s', "
Es 3: 1 and set his s' above all the princes3678
Job 23: 3 that I might come even to his s'! 8499
29: 7 I prepared my s' in the street! 4186
Ps 1: 1 nor sitteth in the s' of the scornful. "
Pr 9:14 on a s' in the high places of the 3678
Eze 8: 3 the s' of the image of jealousy, 4186
28: 2 I am a God, I sit in the s' of God, "
Am 6: 3 cause the s' of violence to come 7675
M't 23: 2 and the Pharisees sit in Moses' s': 2515
27:19 he was set down on the judgment s',968
Joh 19:13 and sat down in the judgment s' in a"
Ac 18:12 and brought him to the judgment s',"
16 he drave them from the judgment s'."
17 and beat him before the judgment s'."
25: 6 next day sitting on the judgment s' "
10 Paul, I stand at Cæsar's judgment s',"
17 the morrow I sat on the judgment s',"
Ro 14:10 before the judgment s' of Christ. "
2Co 5:10 before the judgment s' of Christ; "
Re 2:13 dwellest, even where Satan's s' is:*2362
13: 2 and his s', and great authority. * "
16:10 out his vial upon the s' of the beast;*"

seated See also SET.
De 33:21 portion of the lawgiver, was he s';*5603

seats
M't 21:12 and the s' of them that sold doves, 2515
23: 6 and the chief s' in the synagogues,4410
M'r 11:15 and the s' of them that sold doves; 2515
12:39 the chief s' in the synagogues, and4410
Lu 1:52 put down the mighty from their s',*2362
11:43 uppermost s' in the synagogues, 4410
20:46 the highest s' in the synagogues, "
Jas 2: 6 draw you before the judgment s'?
Re 4: 4 throne were four and twenty s': *2362
4 upon the s' I saw four and twenty* "
11:16 which sat before God on their s', * "

seatward
Ex 37: 9 to the mercy s' were the faces of the*

Seba (*se'-bah*) See also SABEANS; SHEBA.
Ge 10: 7 S', and Havilah, and Sabtah, and 5434
1Ch 1: 9 S', and Havilah, and Sabta, and "
Ps 72:10 of Sheba and S' shall offer gifts. "
Isa 43: 3 ransom, Ethiopia and S' for thee. "

Sebat (*se'-bat*)
Zec 1: 7 month, which is the month S'. *7627

Secacah (*se-ca'-cah*)
Jos 15:61 Beth-arabah, Middin, and S'. 5527

Sechu (*se'-ku*)
1Sa 19:22 came to a great well that is in *S*:*7906
second
Ge 1: 8 and the morning were the s' day. 8145
2:13 the name of the s' river is Gihon: "
6:16 with lower, s', and third stories "
7:11 in the s' month, the seventeenth "
8:14 in the s' month, on the seven and "
22:15 Abraham out of heaven the s' time, "
30: 7 again, and bare Jacob a s' son. "
12 Leah's maid bare Jacob a s' son. "
32:19 And so commanded he the s', and "
41: 5 he slept and dreamed the s' time: "
43 made him to ride in the s' chariot 4932
52 name of the s' called he Ephraim: 8145
43:10 now we had returned this s' time. "
47:18 they came unto him the s' year, 8145
Ex 2:13 And when he went out the s' day, "
16: 1 on the fifteenth day of the s' month "
26: 4 curtain, in the coupling of the s'. "
5 that is in the coupling of the s'; "
10 the curtain which coupleth the s'. "
20 And for the s' side of the tabernacle "
28:18 And the s' row shall be an emerald, "
36:11 curtain, in the coupling of the s'. "
12 which was in the coupling of the s': "
17 the curtain which coupleth the s'. "
39:11 the s' row, an emerald, a sapphire, "
40:17 in the first month in the s' year, "
Le 5:10 offer the s' for a burnt offering, "
13:58 then it shall be washed the s' time, "
Nu 1: 1 on the first day of the s' month, "
1 s' year after they were come out of "
18 on the first day of the s' month, "
2:16 they shall set forth in the s' rank. "
7:18 s' day Nethaneel the son of Zuar, "
9: 1 in the first month of the s' year "
11 fourteenth day of the s' month at "
10: 6 When ye blow an alarm the s' time, "
11 twentieth day of the s' month, in "
11 the s' year,...the cloud was taken "
29:17 on the s' day ye shall offer twelve "
Jos 5: 2 circumcise...of Israel the s' time. "
6:14 s' day they compassed the city once, "
10:32 took it on the s' day, and smote it "
19: 1 And the s' lot came forth to Simeon, "
J'g 6:25 the s' bullock of seven years old, "
26 and take the s' bullock, and offer a "
28 the s' bullock was offered upon the "
20:24 children of Benjamin the s' day. "
25 them out of Gibeah the s' day, and "
1Sa 8: 2 and the name of his s', Abiah: 4932
20:27 which was the s' day of the month, 8145
34 eat no meat the s' day of the month: "
26: 8 I will not smite him the s' time. 8138
2Sa 3: 3 And his s', Chileab, of Abigail the 4932
14:29 when he sent again the s' time, 8145
1Ki 6: 1 month Zif, which is the s' month, "
9: 2 appeared to Solomon the s' time, "
15:25 the s' year of Asa king of Judah, 8147
18:34 And he said, Do it the s' time. 8138
34 And they did it the s' time. "
19: 7 angel...came again the s' time, 8145
2Ki 1:17 in the s' year of Jehoram the son 8147
9:19 Then he sent out a s' on horseback, 8145
10: 6 Then he wrote a letter the s' time "
14: 1 s' year of Joash son of Jehoahaz 8147
15:32 In the s' year of Pekah the son of "
19:29 in the s' year that which springeth 8145
23: 4 the priests of the s' order, and the 4932
25:17 like unto these had the s' pillar 8145
18 and Zephaniah the s' priest, and 4932
1Ch 2:13 Abinadab the s', and Shimma the 8145
3: 1 the s', Daniel, of Abigail the "
15 s' Jehoiakim, the third Zedekiah, "
7:15 the name of the s' was Zelophehad: "
8: 1 Ashbel the s', and Aharah the third, "
39 Jehush the s', and Eliphelet the "
12: 9 Ezer the first, Obadiah the s', Eliab "
15:18 their brethren of the s' degree, 4932
23:11 was the chief, and Zizah the s': 8145
19 Amariah the s', Jahaziel the third, "
20 Micah the first, and Jesiah the s'. "
24: 7 forth to Jehoiarib, the s' to Jedaiah, "
23 Jeriah the first, Amariah the s', "
25: 9 the s' to Gedaliah, who with his "
26: 2 Jediael the s', Zebadiah the third, "
4 Jehozabad the s', Joah the third, "
11 Hilkiah the s', Tebaliah the third, "
27: 4 And over the course of the s' month "
29:22 made Solomon...king the s' time, "
2Ch 3: 2 build in the s' day of the s' month, "
27: 5 him, both the s' year, and the third. "
30: 2 keep the passover in the s' month. "
13 unleavened bread in the s' month, "
15 the fourteenth day of the s' month: "
35:24 and put him in the s' chariot that 4932
Ezr 1:10 silver basons of a s' sort four "
3: 8 Now in the s' year of their coming 8145
8 in the s' month, began Zerubbabel "
4:24 the s' year of the reign of Darius 8648
Ne 8:13 the s' day were gathered together 8145
11: 9 son of Senuah was s' over the city. 4932
17 and Bakbukiah the s' among his "
Es 2:14 she returned into the s' house of 8145
19 were gathered together the s' time, "
7: 2 said again unto Esther on the s' day "
9:29 to confirm this s' letter of Purim. "
Job 42:14 and the name of the s', Kezia; "
Ec 4: 8 is one alone, and there is not a s'; "
15 with the s' child that shall stand "
Isa 11:11 shall set his hand again the s' time "
37:30 the s' year that which springeth of "
Jer 1:13 the Lord came unto me the s' time, "
13: 3 the Lord came unto me the s' time, "
33: 1 came unto Jeremiah the s' time, "
41: 4 s' day after he had slain Gedaliah, 8145
52:22 s' pillar also and the pomegranates "
24 and Zephaniah the s' priest, and 4932
Eze 10:14 the s' face was the face of a man, 8145
43:22 on the s' day thou shalt offer a kid "
Da 2: 1 in the s' year of...Nebuchadnezzar 8147
7: 5 another beast, a s', like to a bear, 8578
Jon 3: 1 Lord came unto Jonah the s' time, 8145
Na 1: 9 affliction shall not rise up the s' time. "
Zep 1:10 and an howling from the s', and 4932
Hag 1: 1 In the s' year of Darius the king, 8147
15 in the s' year of Darius the king. "
2:10 month, in the s' year of Darius, "
Zec 1: 1 month, in the s' year of Darius, "
7 Sebat, in the s' year of Darius, "
6: 2 and in the s' chariot black horses; 8145
M't 21:30 came to the s', and said likewise. *1208*
22:26 Likewise the s' also, and the third, "
39 s' is like unto it, Thou shalt love "
26:42 He went away again the s' time, "
M'r 12:21 the s' took her, and died, neither "
31 the s' is like,...Thou shalt love "
14:72 And the s' time the cock crew. "
Lu 6: 1 it came to pass on the s' sabbath *1207*
12:38 if he shall come in the s' watch, or *1208*
19:18 s' came, saying, Lord, thy pound "
20:30 the s' took her to wife, and he died "
Joh 3: 4 the s' time into his mother's womb, "
4:54 again the s' miracle that Jesus did, "
21:16 He saith to him again the s' time, "
Ac 7:13 the s' time Joseph was made known "
10:15 spake unto him again the s' time, "
12:10 were past the first and the s' ward, "
13:33 as it is also written in the s' psalm, "
1Co 15:47 the s' man is the Lord from heaven. "
2Co 1:15 that ye might have a s' benefit; "
13: 2 as if I were present, the s' time; "
subscr. The s' epistle to the Corinthians* "
2Th *subscr*. The s' epistle to...Thessalonians* "
2Ti *subscr*. The s' epistle unto Timotheus, * "
subscr. brought before Nero the s' time.* "
Tit 3:10 after the first and s' admonition "
Heb 8: 7 no place have been sought for the s'. "
9: 3 And after the s' veil, the tabernacle "
7 into the s' went the high priest "
28 he appear the s' time without sin "
10: 9 first, that he may establish the s'. "
2Pe 3: 1 This s' epistle, beloved, I now write "
Re 2:11 shall not be hurt of the s' death. "
4: 7 a lion, and the s' beast like a calf, "
6: 3 and when he had opened the s' seal, "
3 I heard the s' beast say, Come and "
8: 8 And the s' angel sounded, and as it "
11:14 The s' woe is past; and, behold, the "
16: 3 And the s' angel poured out his vial "
20: 6 on such the s' death hath no power, "
14 lake of fire. This is the s' death. "
21: 8 brimstone: which is the s' death. "
19 was jasper; the s', sapphire; the "

secondarily
1Co 12:28 first apostles, s' prophets, thirdly *1208*

secret See also SECRETS.
Ge 49: 6 soul, come not thou into their s': *5475
De 27:15 and putteth it in a s' place. 5643
29:29 s' things belong unto the Lord 5641
J'g 3:19 I have a s' errand unto thee, O 5643
13:18 after my name, seeing it is s'? *6383
1Sa 5: 9 had emerods in their s' parts. *8368
19: 2 and abide in a s' place, and hide 5643
Job 14:13 that thou wouldest keep me s', 5641
15: 8 Hast thou heard the s' of God? 5475
11 is there any s' thing with thee? * 328
20:26 darkness...be hid in his s' places: *6845
29: 4 s' of God was upon my tabernacle; 5475
40:13 and bind their faces in s'. *2934
Ps 10: 8 in the s' places doth he murder *4565
17:12 a young lion lurking in s' places. "
18:11 He made darkness his s' place; *5643
19:12 cleanse thou me from s' faults. *5641
25:14 The s' of the Lord is with them 5475
27: 5 in the s' of his tabernacle shall he *5643
31:20 hide them in the s' of thy presence "
64: 2 Hide me from the s' counsel of the 5475
4 may shoot in s' at the perfect: 4565
81: 7 thee in the s' place of thunder: 5643
90: 8 thee, our s' sins in the light of thy 5956
91: 1 dwelleth in the s' place of the most 5643
139:15 from thee, when I was made in s', "
Pr 3:32 but his s' is with the righteous. 5475
9:17 and bread eaten in s' is pleasant. 5643
21:14 A gift in s' pacifieth anger: and a "
25: 9 and discover not a s' to another: 5475
27: 5 rebuke is better than s' love. *5641
Ec 12:14 judgment, with every s' thing, *5956
Ca 2:14 in the s' places of the stairs, let *5643
Isa 3:17 Lord will discover their s' parts. 6596
45: 3 hidden riches of s' places, that 4565
19 I have not spoken in s', in a dark 5643
48:16 I have not spoken in s' from the "
Jer 2:34 I have not found it by s' search, but
13:17 weep in s' places for your pride; 4565
23:24 Can any hide himself in s' places "
49:10 I have uncovered his s' places, and "
La 3:10 in wait, and as a lion in s' places. "
Eze 7:22 and they shall pollute my s' place: 6845
28: 3 is no s' that they can hide from 5640
Da 2:18 God of heaven concerning this s'; 7328
19 s' revealed unto Daniel in a night "
22 revealeth the deep and s' things: 5642
27 s' which the king hath demanded 7328
30 this s' is not revealed to me for "
47 seeing thou couldest reveal this s'. "
4: 9 and no s' troubleth me, tell me the "
Am 3: 7 revealeth his s' unto his servants 5475
M't 6: 4 That thine alms may be in s': and *2927*
6: 4 and thy Father which seeth in s' *2927*
6 pray to thy Father which is in s'; "
6 thy Father which seeth in s' shall "
18 but unto thy Father which is in s': "
18 thy Father, which seeth in s', shall "
13:35 things which have been kept s' *2928*
24:26 behold, he is in the s' chambers; **5009*
M'r 4:22 neither was any thing kept s', but *614*
Lu 8:17 For nothing is s', that shall not *2927*
11:33 a candle, putteth it in a s' place, **2926*
Joh 7: 4 no man that doeth any thing in s', *2927*
10 not openly, but as it were in s'. "
18:20 and in s' have I said nothing. "
Ro 16:25 was kept s' since the world began, **4601*
Eph 5:12 which are done of them in s'. *2931*

secretly
Ge 31:27 didst thou flee away s', and steal 2244
De 13: 6 entice thee s', saying, Let us go 5643
27:24 he that smiteth his neighbour s'. "
28:57 eat them for want of all things s' in "
Jos 2: 1 out of Shittim two men to spy s', 2791
1Sa 18:22 Commune with David s', and say, 3909
23: 9 Saul s' practised mischief against *2790
2Sa 12:12 For thou didst it s': but I will do 5643
2Ki 17: 9 the children of Israel did s' those 2644
Job 4:12 a thing was s' brought to me, 1589
13:10 you, if ye do s' accept persons. 5643
31:27 my heart hath been s' enticed, or "
Ps 10: 9 He lieth in wait s' as a lion in his *4565
31:20 shalt keep them s' in a pavilion *6845
Jer 37:17 king asked him s' in his house, 5643
38:16 the king sware s' unto Jeremiah, "
40:15 spake to Gedaliah in Mizpah s', "
Hab 3:14 was as to devour the poor s'. 4565
Joh 11:28 way, and called Mary her sister s', *2977*
19:38 Jesus, but s' for fear of the Jews, *2928*

secrets
De 25:11 hand, and taketh him by the s': 4016
Job 11: 6 shew thee the s' of wisdom, that 8587
Ps 44:21 for he knoweth the s' of the heart. "
Pr 11:13 A talebearer revealeth s': but he 5475
20:19 about as a talebearer revealeth s': "
Da 2:28 a God in heaven that revealeth s', 7328
29 and he that revealeth s' maketh "
47 lord of kings, and a revealer of s', "
Ro 2:16 God shall judge the s' of men *2927*
1Co 14:25 the s' of his heart made manifest; "

sect
Ac 5:17 (which is the s' of the Sadducees,) *139*
15: 5 up certain of the s' of the Pharisees "
24: 5 ringleader of the s' of the Nazarenes: "
26: 5 the most straitest s' of our religion "
28:22 for as concerning this s', we know "

Secundus *se-cun'-dus*)
Ac 20: 4 Aristarchus and *S*'; and Gaius *4580*

secure
J'g 8:11 the host: for the host was s'. 983
18: 7 of the Zidonians, quiet and s'; 982
10 ye shall come unto a people s', and "
27 a people that were at quiet and s': "
Job 11:18 thou shalt be s', because there is "
12: 6 and they that provoke God are s'; 987
M't 28:14 will persuade him, and s' you. **4160,275*

securely
Pr 3:29 seeing he dwelleth s' by thee. 983
Mic 2: 8 pass by s' as men averse from war. "

security
Ac 17: 9 when they had taken s' of Jason, *2425*

sedition See also SEDITIONS.
Ezr 4:15 that they have moved s' within 849
19 rebellion and s' have been made "
Lu 23:19 for a certain s' made in the city, **4714*
25 for s' and murder was cast into "
Ac 24: 5 a mover of s' among all the Jews * "

seditions
Ga 5:20 emulations, wrath, strife, s', **1370*

seduce See also SEDUCED; SEDUCETH; SEDUCING.
M'r 13:22 to s', if it were possible, even the * *635*
1Jo 2:26 you, concerning them that s' you. **4105*
Re 2:20 to teach and to s' my servants to * "

seduced
2Ki 21: 9 Manasseh s' them to do more evil 8582
Isa 19:13 they have also s' Egypt, even they* "
Eze 13:10 they have s' my people, saying, 2937

seducers
2Ti 3:13 and s' shall wax worse and worse, **1114*

seduceth
Pr 12:26 the way of the wicked s' them. *8582

seducing
1Ti 4: 1 giving heed to s' spirits, and *4108*

see See also OVERSEE; SAW; SEEING; SEEN; SEEST; SEETH.
Ge 2:19 to s' what he would call them: 7200
8: 8 to s' if the waters were abated "
11: 5 Lord came down to s' the city and "
12:12 when the Egyptians shall s' thee, "
18:21 and s' whether they have done "
19:21 unto him, *S*, I have accepted thee 2009
21:16 me not s' the death of the child. *7200
27: 1 were dim, so that he could not s', "
27 *S*, the smell of my son is as the "
31: 5 I s' your father's countenance, that "
12 s', all the rams which leap upon the "
50 s', God is witness betwixt me and "
32:20 me, and afterward I will s' his face; "
34: 1 out to s' the daughters of the land. "
37:14 s' whether it be well with thy "
20 s' what will become of his dreams. "
39:14 *S*, he hath brought in an Hebrew "
41:41 *S*, I have set thee over all the land "

Ge 42: 9, 12 to s· the nakedness of the land7200
43: 3, 5 Ye shall not s· my face, except "
44: 23 you, ye shall s· my face no more. "
26 for we may not s· the man's face, "
34 lest peradventure I s· the evil that "
45: 12 behold, your eyes s·, and the eyes "
24 S· that ye fall not out by the way. "
28 I will go and s· him before I die. 7200
48: 10 dim for age, so that he could not s·."
11 I had not thought to s· thy face: "
Ex 1: 16 women, and s· them upon the stools;"
3: 3 turn aside, and s· this great sight, "
4 Lord saw that he turned aside to s·,"
4: 18 and s· whether they be yet alive. "
21 s· that thou do all those wonders "
5: 19 did s· that they were in evil case, "
6: 1 thou s· what I will do to Pharaoh: "
7: 1 S·, I have made thee a god to "
10: 5 one cannot be able to s· the earth: "
28 heed to thyself, s· my face no more;"
29 I will s· thy face again no more. "
12: 13 when I s· the blood, I will pass over"
13: 17 the people repent when they s· war, "
14: 13 and s· the salvation of the Lord, "
13 s· them again no more for ever. "
16: 7 ye shall s· the glory of the Lord; for"
29 S·, for that the Lord hath given you"
32 they may s· the bread wherewith I "
22: 8 to s· whether he have put his hand "
23: 5 s· the ass of him that hateth thee 7200
31: 2 S·, I have called by name Bezaleel "
33: 12 S·, thou sayest unto me, Bring up "
20 he said, Thou canst not s· my face: "
20 there shall no man s· me, and live. "
23 and thou shalt s· my back parts: "
34: 10 art shall s· the work of the Lord: "
35: 30 S·, the Lord hath called by name "
Le 13: 8 if the priest s· that, behold, the scab"
10 And the priest shall s· him: and, * "
15 And the priest shall s· the raw flesh,*"
17 And the priest shall s· him: and, * "
30 Then the priest shall s· the plague:*"
14: 36 priest go into it to s· the plague, "
36 priest shall go in to s· the house: "
20: 17 and s· her nakedness, and she s· his"
Nu 4: 20 not go in to s· when the holy things "
11: 15 and let me not s· my wretchedness. "
23 thou shalt s· now whether my word"
13: 18 And s· the land, what it is; and the "
14: 23 they shall not s· the land which I "
23 any of them that provoked me s· it:"
22: 41 that thence he might s· the utmost*"
23: 9 from the top of the rocks I s· him, "
13 from whence thou mayest s· them: "
13 thou shalt s· but the utmost part of"
13 of them, and shalt not s· them all: "
24: 17 I shall s· him, but not now: I shall "
27: 12 and s· the land which I have given* "
32: 8 from Kadesh-barnea to s· the land. "
11 shall s· the land which I swear unto"
De 1: 35 evil generation s· that good land, "
36 son of Jephunneh; he shall s· it, and"
3: 25 and s· the good land that is beyond "
28 inherit the land...thou shalt s·. "
4: 28 which neither s·, nor hear, nor eat, "
18: 16 neither let me s· this great fire any "
22: 1 Thou shalt not s· thy brother's ox "
4 Thou shalt not s· thy brother's ass "
23: 14 that he s· no unclean thing in thee, "
28: 10 s· that thou art called by the name "
34, 67 thine eyes which thou shalt s·. "
68 Thou shalt s· it no more again: and"
29: 4 eyes to s·, and ears to hear, unto "
22 they s· the plagues of that land, "
30: 15 S·, I have set before thee this day "
32: 20 I will s· what their end shall be: for"
39 S· now that I, even I, am he, and "
52 thou shalt s· the land before thee; "
34: 4 caused thee to s· it with thine eyes, "
Jos 3: 3 ye s· the ark of the covenant of the "
6: 2 S·, I have given into thine hand "
8: 1 s·, I have given into thine hand the "
8 ye do. S·, I have commanded you. "
22: 10 by Jordan, a great altar to s· to. ‡4758
J'g 9: 37 said, S· there come people down 2009
14: 8 aside to s· the carcase of the lion: 7200
16: 5 s· wherein his great strength lieth, "
21: 21 s·, and, behold, if the daughters of "
1Sa 2: 32 s· an enemy in my habitation, in *5027
3: 2 to wax dim, that he could not s·; 7200
4: 15 eyes were dim, that he could not s·. "
6: 9 s·, if it goeth up by the way of his "
13 saw the ark, and rejoiced to s· it. "
10: 24 S· ye him whom the Lord hath "
12: 16 stand and s· this great thing, which"
17 and s· that your wickedness is great,"
14: 17 now, and s· who is gone from us. "
29 s·, I pray you, how mine eyes have "
38 s· wherein this sin hath been this "
15: 35 Samuel came no more to s· Saul "
17: 28 that thou mightest s· the battle. "
19: 3 and what I s·, that I will tell thee. "
15 the messengers again to s· David, "
20: 29 I pray thee, and s· my brethren. "
21: 14 servants, Lo, ye s· the man is mad: "
23: 22 and s· his place where his haunt is, "
23 S· therefore, and take knowledge of"
24: 11 s·, yea, s· the skirt of thy robe in my"
11 and s· that their is neither evil nor "
15 s·, and plead my cause, and deliver "
25: 35 s·, I have hearkened to thy voice, "
26: 16 s· where the king's spear is, and the"
2Sa 3: 13 Thou shalt not s· my face, except "
13 when thou comest to s· my face. "
7: 2 S· now, I dwell in an house of "
13: 5 when thy father cometh to s· thee, "

2Sa 13: 5 I may s· it, and eat it at her hand. 7200
6 when the king was come to s· him, "
14: 24 house, and let him not s· my face. "
30 S·, Joab's field is near mine, and he"
32 let me s· the king's face; and if "
15: 3 S·, thy matters are good and right;"
28 S·, I will tarry in the plain of the "
24: 3 eyes of my lord the king may s· it: "
13 s· what answer I shall return to him*"
1Ki 9: 12 came out from Tyre to s· the cities "
12: 16 now s· to thine own house, David. "
14: 4 Ahijah could not s·; for his eyes "
17: 23 and Elijah said, S·, thy son liveth. "
20: 7 s· how this man seeketh mischief: "
22 and mark, and s· what thou doest: "
22: 25 Behold, thou shalt s· in that day, "
2Ki 2: 10 s· me when I am taken from thee, "
3: 14 not look toward thee, nor s· thee. "
17 not s· wind, neither shall ye s· rain;"
6: 17 thee, open his eyes, that he may s·."
20 eyes of these men, that they may s·."
32 S· ye how this son of a murderer "
7: 2 thou shalt s· it with thine eyes, but"
13 consumed:) and let us send and s·. "
14 of the Syrians, saying, Go and s·. "
19 shalt s· it with thine eyes, but shalt"
8: 29 Ahaziah...went down to s· Joram "
9: 16 Judah was come down to s· Joram. "
17 he came, and said, I s· a company. "
34 Go, s· now this cursed woman, and "
10: 16 me, and s· my zeal for the Lord. 7200
19: 16 open, Lord, thine eyes, and s·: and "
22: 20 thine eyes shall not s· all the evil "
23: 17 he said, What title is that that I s·? "
10: 16 now, David, s· to thine own house. "
2Ch 18: 16 did s· all Israel scattered upon the* "
24 Behold, thou shalt s· on that day "
20: 17 and s· the salvation of the Lord with"
22: 6 Ahaziah...went down to s· Jehoram "
24: 5 and s· that ye hasten the matter. "
25: 17 let us s· one another in the face. *7200
29: 8 to hissing, as ye s· with your eyes. "
30: 7 gave them up to desolation, as ye s·."
34: 28 thine eyes s· all the evil that I will "
Ezr 4: 14 for us to s· the king's dishonour, 2370
Ne 2: 17 Ye s· the distress that we are in, 7200
4: 11 They shall not know, neither s·, till"
9: 9 didst s· the affliction of our fathers*"
Es 3: 4 to s· whether Mordecai's matters "
5: 13 as I s· Mordecai the Jew sitting at "
8: 6 For how can I endure to s· the evil "
6 to s· the destruction of my kindred?"
Job 3: 9 let it s· the dawning of the day: * "
6: 21 ye s· my casting down, and are "
7: 7 mine eye shall no more s· good. "
8 hath seen me shall s· me no more: 7789
9: 11 he goeth by me, and I s· him not: 7200
25 they flee away, they s· no good. "
10: 15 therefore s· thou mine affliction; * "
17: 15 as for my hope, who shall s· it? 7789
19: 26 body, yet in my flesh shall I s· God: 2372
27 Whom I shall s· for myself, and "
20: 9 which saw him shall s· him no more; "
17 He shall not s· the rivers, the *7200
21: 20 His eyes shall s· his destruction, "
22: 11 Or darkness, that thou canst not s·;"
19 The righteous s· it, and are glad: "
23: 9 the right hand, that I cannot s· him:"
24: 1 that know him not s· his days? 2372
15 saying, No eye shall s· me: 7789
28: 27 Then did he s· it, and declare it; 7200
31: 4 Doth not he s· my ways, and count "
33: 26 and he shall s· his face with joy: * "
28 pit, and his life shall s· the light. * "
34: 32 That which I s· not teach thou me: 2372
35: 5 Look unto the heavens, and s·; 7200
14 thou sayest thou shalt not s· him,*7789
36: 25 Every man may s· it; man may *2372
37: 21 now men s· not the bright light 7200
Ps 10: 11 hideth his face; he will never s· it. "
14: 2 to s· if...any that did understand, "
16: 10 thine Holy One to s· corruption. "
22: 7 they that s· me laugh me to scorn: "
27: 13 to s· the goodness of the Lord in the"
31: 11 that did s· me without fled from me."
34: 8 taste and s· that the Lord is good: "
12 many days, that he may s· good? "
36: 9 life: in thy light shall we s· light. "
37: 34 wicked are cut off, thou shalt s· it. "
40: 3 many shall s· it, and fear, and shall"
41: 6 if he come to s· me, he speaketh "
49: 9 live for ever, and not s· corruption. "
19 fathers; they shall never s· light. "
52: 6 The righteous also shall s·, and fear,"
53: 2 to s· if...any that did understand, "
58: 8 that they may not s· the sun. *2372
59: 10 God shall let me s· my desire upon7200
63: 2 To s· thy power and thy glory, so as"
64: 5 they say, Who shall s· them? "
8 all that s· them shall flee away. "
66: 5 Come and s· the works of God: he "
69: 23 eyes be darkened, that they s· not; "
32 humble shall s· this, and be glad:* "
74: 9 We s· not our signs: there is no "
86: 17 that they which hate me may s· it, "
89: 48 that liveth, and shall not s· death? "
91: 8 and s· the reward of the wicked. "
92: 11 s· my desire on mine enemies, *5027
94: 7 The Lord shall not s·, neither shall7200
9 formed the eye, shall he not s·? 5027
97: 6 and all the people s· his glory. *7200
106: 5 That I may s· the good of thy chosen,"
107: 24 These s· the works of the Lord, and"
42 righteous shall s· it, and rejoice: "
112: 8 he s· his desire upon his enemies. "
10 wicked shall s· it, and be grieved; "

Ps 115: 5 eyes have they, but they s· not: 7200
118: 7 I s· my desire upon them that hate "
119: 74 thee will be glad when they s· me; "
128: 5 thou shalt s· the good of Jerusalem"
6 thou shalt s· thy children's children,"
135: 16 eyes have they, but they s· not; "
139: 16 Thine eyes did s· my substance, "
24 s· if there be any wicked way in me,"
Pr 24: 18 Lest the Lord s· it, and it displease "
29: 16 but the righteous shall s· their fall.*"
Ec 1: 10 it may be said, S·, this is new? "
2: 3 till I might s· what was that good "
3: 18 s· that they themselves are beasts. "
22 him to s· what shall be after him? "
7: 11 is profit to them that s· the sun. "
8: 16 and to s· the business that is done "
Ca 2: 14 let me s· thy countenance, let me "
6: 11 of nuts to s· the fruits of the valley, "
11 to s· whether the vine flourished, "
13 What will ye s· in the Shulamite?*2372
7: 12 let us s· if the vine flourish, 7200
Isa 5: 19 hasten his work, that we may s· it: "
6: 9 and s· ye indeed, but perceive not. "
10 lest they s· with their eyes, and hear"
13: 1 Isaiah the son of Amoz did s·. 2372
14: 16 that s· thee shall narrowly look 7200
18: 3 s· ye, when he lifteth up an ensign "
26: 11 hand is lifted up, they will not s·: 2372
11 but they shall s·, and be ashamed "
29: 18 the blind shall s· out of obscurity, 7200
30: 10 Which say to the seers, S· not; "
20 but thine eyes shall s· thy teachers:"
32: 3 eyes of them that s· shall not be dim,"
33: 17 eyes shall s· the king in his beauty: 2372
19 Thou shalt not s· a fierce people, 7200
20 s· Jerusalem a quiet habitation, "
35: 2 they shall s· the glory of the Lord, "
37: 17 open thine eyes, O Lord, and s·: "
38: 11 I said, I shall not s· the Lord, even "
40: 5 and all flesh shall s· it together: "
41: 20 That they may s·, and know, and "
42: 18 and look, ye blind, that ye may s·. "
44: 9 they s· not, nor know; that they "
18 shut their eyes, that they cannot s·;"
48: 6 Thou hast heard, s· all this; and *2372
49: 7 Kings shall s· and arise, princes 7200
52: 8 for they shall s· eye to eye, when "
10 shall s· the salvation of our God. "
15 had not been told them shall they s·;"
53: 2 when we...s· him, there is no beauty"
10 he shall s· his seed, he shall prolong"
11 He shall s· of the travail of his soul,"
60: 4 up thine eyes round about, and s·: "
5 Then thou shalt s·, and flow 3372, "
61: 9 all that s· them shall acknowledge "
62: 2 Gentiles shall s· thy righteousness, "
64: 9 s·, we beseech thee, we are all thy*5027
66: 14 when ye s· this, your heart shall 7200
18 they shall come, and s· my glory. "
Jer 1: 10 S·, I have this day set thee over the"
11 I said, I s· a rod of an almond tree. "
13 And I said, I s· a seething pot; and "
2: 10 over the isles of Chittim, and s·; "
10 and s· if there be such a thing. "
19 s· that it is an evil thing and bitter, "
23 s· thy way in the valley, know what"
31 O generation, s· ye the word of the "
3: 2 and s· where thou hast not been lien"
4: 21 How long shall I s· the standard, "
5: 1 s· now, and know, and seek in the "
12 shall we s· sword nor famine: "
21 which have eyes, and s· not; which "
6: 16 Stand ye in the ways, and s·, and "
7: 12 s· what I did to it for the wickedness"
11: 20 let me s· thy vengeance on them: "
12: 4 said, He shall not s· our last end. "
14: 13 Ye shall not s· the sword, neither "
17: 6 and shall not s· when good cometh; "
8 and shall not s· when heat cometh,*"
20: 12 let me s· thy vengeance on them: "
18 the womb to s· labour and sorrow, "
22: 10 no more, nor s· his native country. "
12 and shall s· this land no more. "
23: 24 secret places that I shall not s· him?"
30: 6 and s· whether a man doth travail "
6 do I s· every man with his hands "
42: 14 Egypt, where we shall s· no war, "
18 and ye shall s· this place no more. "
51: 61 and shalt s·, and shalt read all these"
La 1: 11 s·, O Lord, and consider; for I am "
12 s· if there be any sorrow like unto "
Eze 8: 6 thou shalt s· greater abominations. "
13, 15 shalt s· greater abominations "
12: 2 which have eyes to s·, and s· not; "
6 face, that thou s· not the ground: "
12 he s· not the ground with his eyes. "
13 shall he not s· it, though he...die "
13: 9 upon the prophets that s· vanity, 2374
16 which s· visions of peace for her, "
23 ye shall s· no more vanity, nor 2372
14: 22 s· their way and their doings: 7200
23 ye s· their ways and their doings: "
16: 37 they may s· all thy nakedness. "
20: 48 flesh shall s· that I the Lord have "
21: 29 Whiles they s· vanity unto thee, 2372
32: 31 Pharaoh shall s· them, and shall 7200
33: 6 the watchman s· the sword come, "
39: 21 heathen shall s· my judgment that "
Da 1: 10 should he s· your faces worse liking"
2: 8 ye s· the thing is gone from me. 2370
3: 25 Lo, I s· four men loose, walking in "
5: 23 which s· not, nor hear, nor know: "
Joe 2: 28 your young men shall s· visions: 7200
Am 6: 2 Pass ye unto Calneh, and s·; and "
Jon 4: 5 s· what would become of the city. "
Mic 6: 9 man of wisdom shall s· thy name: "

Mic 7:10 she that is mine enemy shall s' it, 7200
16 nations shall s' and be confounded "
Hab 1: 1 Habakkuk the prophet did s'. 2372
2: 1 to s' what he will say unto me, 7200
Zep 3:15 thou shalt not s' evil any more. * "
Hag 2: 3 how do ye s' it now? is it not in "
Zec 2: 2 s' what is the breadth thereof, and "
4:10 shall s' the plummet in the hand of "
5: 2 And I answered, I s' a flying roll; "
5 s' what is this that goeth forth. "
9: 5 Askelon shall s' it, and fear; "
5 Gaza also shall s' it, and be very *
10: 7 yea, their children shall s' it, and 7200
Mal 1: 5 your eyes shall s', and ye shall say,"
M't 5: 8 in heart: for they shall s' God. 3700
16 that they may s' your good works,1492
7: 5 then shalt thou s' clearly to cast 1227
8: 4 unto him, S' thou tell no man; 3708
9:30 saying, S' that no man know it. "
11: 4 things which ye do hear and s': 991
7 ye out into the wilderness to s'? *2300
8, 9 But what went ye out for to s'? 1492
12:38 we would s' a sign from thee. "
13:13 because they seeing s' not; and 991
14 and seeing ye shall s', and shall not "
15 they should s' with their eyes, *1492
16 blessed are your eyes, for they s': 991
17 have desired to s' those things 1492
17 those things which ye s', and have 991
15:31 lame to walk, and the blind to s': * "
16:28 till they s' the Son of man coming 1492
22:11 the king came in to s' the guests,*2300
23:39 Ye shall not s' me henceforth, till 1492
24: 2 them, S' ye not all these things? 991
6 s' that ye be not troubled: for all 3708
15 s' the abomination of desolation, 1492
30 shall s' the Son of man coming in 3700
33 when ye shall s' all these things, 1492
26:58 sat with the servants, to s' the end."
64 s' the Son of man sitting on the 3700
27: 4 What is that to us? s' thou to that. "
24 blood of this just person: s' ye to it."
49 s' whether Elias will come to save 1492
28: 1 the other Mary to s' the sepulchre.2334
6 s' the place where the Lord lay. 1492
7 there shall ye s' him: lo, I have 3700
10 Galilee, and there shall they s' me. "
M'r 1:44 S' thou say nothing to any man: 3708
4:12 That seeing they may s', and not 991
5:14 to s' what it was that was done. 1492
15 s' him that was possessed with *2334
32 to s' her that had done this thing. 1492
6:38 many loaves have ye? go and s'. "
8:18 Having eyes, s' ye not? and having 991
24 and said, I s' men as trees, walking. "
12:15 bring me a penny, that I may s' it. 1492
13: 1 s' what manner of stones and *2396
14 s' the abomination of desolation, 1492
26 shall they s'...Son of man coming 3700
29 shall s' these things come to pass, 1492
14:62 s' the Son of man sitting on the 3700
15:32 cross, that we may s' and believe. 1492
36 s' whether Elias will come to take "
16: 7 there shall ye s' him, as he said 3700
Lu 2:15 and s' this thing which is come to 1492
26 that he should not s' death, before "
3: 6 flesh shall s' the salvation of God. 3700
6:42 thou s' clearly to pull out the mote1227
7:22 that the blind s', the lame walk, 308
24 out into the wilderness for to s'? *2300
25, 26 But what went ye out to s'? 1492
8:10 that seeing they might not s', and 991
16 they which enter in may s' the light."
20 stand without, desiring to s' thee. 1492
35 they went out to s' what was done; "
9: 9 things? And he desired to s' him. "
27 till they s' the kingdom of God. "
10:23 eyes which s' the things that ye s': 991
24 have desired to s' those things 1492
24 those things which ye s', and have 991
11:33 they which come in may s' the light. "
12:54 ye s' a cloud rise out of the west, 1492
55 when ye s' the south wind blow, ye
13:28 ye shall s' Abraham, and Isaac, 3700
35 Ye shall not s' me, until the time 1492
14:18 and I must needs go and s' it: "
17:22 desire to s' one of the days of the "
22 Son of man, and ye shall not s' it. 3700
23 they shall say to you, S' here; or,*2400
23 s' there: go not after them, nor * "
19: 3 he sought to s' Jesus who he was; 1492
4 up into a sycomore tree to s' him: "
20:13 reverence him when they s' him. * "
21:20 shall s' Jerusalem compassed with "
27 shall they s'...Son of man coming 3700
30 ye s' and know of your own selves 991
31 ye s' these things come to pass, 1492
23: 8 desirous to s' him of a long season, "
24:39 it is I myself: handle me, and s'; "
39 flesh and bones, as ye s' me have.*2334
Joh 1:33 thou shalt s' the Spirit descending,1492
39 He saith unto them, Come and s'. "
46 Philip saith unto him, Come and s'. "
50 shalt s' greater things than these. 3700
51 Hereafter ye shall s' heaven open, "
3: 3 he cannot s' the kingdom of God. 1492
36 not the Son shall not s' life; but 3700
4:29 s' a man, which told me all things 1492
48 Except ye s' signs and wonders, ye "
6:19 they s' Jesus walking on the sea, *2334
30 that we may s', and believe thee? 1492
62 ye shall s' the Son of man ascend *2334
7: 3 thy disciples also may s' the works*"
8:51 my saying, he shall never s' death. "
56 Abraham rejoiced to s' my day: 1492
9:15 mine eyes, and I washed, and do s'.991
Joh 9:19 blind? how then doth he now s'? 991
25 that, whereas I was blind, now I s'. "
39 that they which s' not might s'; and"
39 they which s' might be made blind. "
41 but now ye say, We s'; therefore "
11:34 said unto him, Lord, come and s'. 1492
40 thou shouldest s' the glory of God?3700
12: 9 that they might s' Lazarus also, 1492
21 him, saying, Sir, we would s' Jesus."
40 they should not s' with their eyes, "
14:19 seeth me no more; but ye s' me: *2334
16:10 my Father, and ye s' me no more;* "
16 little while, and ye shall not s' me:*"
16 a little while, and ye shall s' me. 3700
17 while, and ye shall not s' me: and*2334
17 a little while, and ye shall s' me: 3700
19 while, and ye shall not s' me: and*2334
19 a little while, and ye shall s' me? 3700
22 but I will s' you again, and your "
18:26 Did not I s' thee in the garden with1492
20:25 I shall s' in his hands the print of "
Ac 2:17 your young men shall s' visions, 3070
27 thine Holy One to s' corruption. 1492
31 neither his flesh did s' corruption. "
33 this, which ye now s' and hear. 991
3:16 strong, whom ye s' and know: *2334
7:56 I s' the heavens opened, and the "
8:36 eunuch said, S', here is water; *2400
13:35 thine Holy One to s' corruption. 1492
15:36 word of the Lord, and s' how they do.
19:21 been there, I must also s' Rome. 1492
26 Moreover ye s' and hear, that not 2334
20:25 of God, shall s' my face no more. 3700
38 they should s' his face no more. *2334
22:11 I could not s' for the glory of that 1689
14 his will, and s' that Just One, 1492
23:22 S' thou tell no man that thou hast*
25:24 ye s' this man, about whom all the*2334
28:20 have I called for you, to s' you, and1492
26 and seeing ye shall s', and not 991
27 lest they should s' with their eyes,*1492
Ro 1:11 I long to s' you, that I may impart "
7:23 I s' another law in my members, 991
8:25 But if we hope for that we s' not, "
11: 8 eyes that they should not s', and ears"
10 be darkened, that they may not s', "
15:21 he was not spoken of, they shall s':3700
24 for I trust to s' you in my journey, 2300
1Co 1:26 For ye s' your calling, brethren, * 991
8:10 For if any man s' thee which hast 1492
13:12 now we s' through a glass, darkly; 991
16: 7 I will not s' you now by the way; 1492
10 s' that he may be...without fear: 991
2Co 8: 7 s' that ye abound in this grace also.
Ga 1:18 went up to Jerusalem to s' Peter, *2477
6:11 Ye s' how large a letter I have 1492
Eph 3: 9 all men s' what is the fellowship 5461
5:15 S' then that ye walk circumspectly,*991
Ph'p 1:27 whether I come and s' you, or else 1492
2:23 as I shall s' how it will go with me. 542
28 that, when ye s' him again, ye may1492
1Th 2:17 more abundantly to s' your face "
3: 6 always, desiring greatly to s' us, "
6 us, as we also to s' you:
10 praying...that we might s' your face,1492
5:15 S' that none render evil for evil 3708
1Ti 6:16 whom no man hath seen, nor can s':1492
2Ti 1: 4 Greatly desiring to s' thee, being "
Heb 2: 8 s' not yet all things put under him.3708
9 we s' Jesus, who was made a little*991
3:19 So we s' that they could not enter in "
8: 5 S', saith he, that thou make all 3708
10:25 more, as ye s' the day approaching.991
11: 5 that he should not s' death; 1492
12:14 which no man shall s' the Lord: 3700
25 S'...ye refuse not him that speaketh.991
13:23 if he come shortly, I will s' you. 3700
Jas 2:24 Ye s' then how that by works a 3708
1Pe 1: 8 in whom, though now ye s' him not,"
22 s' that ye love one another with a*
3:10 that will love life, and s' good days,1492
2Pe 1: 9 is blind, and cannot s' afar off, *3467
1Jo 3: 2 him; for we shall s' him as he is. 3700
5:16 If any man s' his brother sin a sin 1492
3Jo 14 But I trust I shall shortly s' thee, "
Re 1: 7 and every eye shall s' him, and 3700
12 to s' the voice that spake with me. 991
3:18 with eyesalve, that thou mayest s'. "
6: 1 the four beasts saying, Come and s'.*"
3 the second beast say, Come and s'.* "
5 the third beast say, Come and s'. "
6 s' thou hurt not the oil and the wine.*
7 the fourth beast say, Come and s'.* 991
9:20 which neither can s', nor hear, nor "
11: 9 shall s' their dead bodies three days*"
16:15 walk naked, and they s' his shame. "
18: 7 no widow, and shall s' no sorrow. 1492
9 shall s' the smoke of her burning, *991
19:10 he said unto me, S' thou do it not:3708
22: 4 And they shall s' his face; and his3708
9 saith he unto me, S' thou do it not:"

seed See also SEED'S; SEEDS; SEEDTIME.
Ge 1:11 the herb yielding s', and the fruit 2233
11 after his kind, whose s' is in itself, "
12 and herb yielding s' after his kind, "
12 yielding fruit, whose s' was in itself,"
29 given you every herb bearing s', "
29 is the fruit of a tree yielding s'; "
3:15 and between thy s' and her s'; "
4:25 appointed me another s' instead of "
7: 3 to keep s' alive upon the face of all "
9: 9 with you, and with your s' after you;"
12: 7 Unto thy s' will I give this land: "
13:15 will I give it, and to thy s' for ever. "
16 I will make thy s' as the dust of the"
16 then shall thy s' also be numbered. "
Ge 15: 3 Behold, to me thou hast given no s':2233
5 said unto him, So shall thy s' be. "
13 thy s' shall be a stranger in a land "
18 Unto thy s' have I given this land, "
16:10 I will multiply thy s' exceedingly, "
17: 7 between me and thee and thy s' "
7 unto thee, and to thy s' after thee. "
8 unto thee, and to thy s' after thee, "
9 thou, and thy s' after thee in their "
10 between me and you and thy s' "
12 any stranger, which is not of thy s'."
19 covenant, and with his s' after him."
19:32, 34 may preserve s' of our father. "
21:12 for in Isaac shall thy s' be called. "
13 make a nation, because he is thy s'."
22:17 I will multiply thy s' as the stars of"
17 thy s' shall possess the gate of his "
18 And in thy s' shall all the nations of"
24: 7 Unto thy s' will I give this land; "
60 let thy s' possess the gate of those "
26: 3 for unto thee, and unto thy s', I will"
4 make thy s' to multiply as the stars"
4 give unto thy s' all these countries;"
4 and in thy s' shall all the nations of"
24 and multiply thy s' for my servant "
28: 4 to thee, and to thy s' with thee; "
13 to thee will I give it, and to thy s'; "
14 And thy s' shall be as the dust of "
14 and in thy s' shall all the families "
32:12 make thy s' as the sand of the sea, "
35:12 to thy s' after thee will I give the "
38: 8 her, and raise up s' to thy brother. "
9 knew that the s' should not be his; "
9 that he should give s' to his brother."
46: 6 Jacob, and all his s' with him: "
7 all his s' brought he with him into "
47:19 give us s', that we may live, and not"
23 here is s' for you, and ye shall sow "
24 for s' of the field, and for your food,"
48: 4 and will give this land to thy s' after"
11 lo, God hath shewed me also thy s' "
19 his s' shall become a multitude of "
Ex 16:31 and it was like coriander s', white; "
28:43 statute for ever unto him and his s' "
30:21 to him and to his s' throughout "
32:13 I will multiply your s' as the stars "
13 spoken of will I give unto your s', "
33: 1 saying, Unto thy s' will I give it: "
Le 11:37 carcase fall upon any sowing s' "
38 But if any water be put upon the s',"
12: 2 If a woman have conceived s', and "
15:16 any man's s' of copulation go out "
17 whereon is the s' of copulation, "
18 man shall lie with s' of copulation, "
32 him whose s' goeth from him,7902, "
18:21 any of thy s' pass through the fire "
19:19 not sow thy field with mingled s': "
20: 2 giveth any of his s' unto Molech; 2233
3 he hath given of his s' unto Molech,"
4 he giveth of his s' unto Molech, "
21:15 Neither shall he profane his s' "
17 saying, Whosoever he be of thy s' "
21 hath a blemish of the s' of Aaron "
22: 3 Whosoever he be of all your s' "
4 What man soever of the s' of Aaron"
4 man whose s' goeth from him;7902,"
26:16 and ye shall sow your s' in vain, for"
27:16 estimation...be according to the s'*"
16 homer of barley s' shall be valued*"
30 whether of the s' of the land, or of "
Nu 5:28 shall be free, and shall conceive s'. "
11: 7 And the manna was as coriander s'. "
14:24 he went; and his s' shall possess it."
16:40 which is not of the s' of Aaron, "
18:19 unto thee and to thy s' with thee. "
20: 5 it is no place of s', or of figs, or of "
24: 7 and his s' shall be in many waters, "
25:13 shall have it, and his s' after him, "
De 1: 8 unto them and to their s' after them."
4:37 he chose their s' after them, and "
10:15 and he chose their s' after them, "
11: 9 to give unto them and to their s', a "
10 where thou sowedst thy s', and "
14:22 truly tithe all the increase of thy s',"
22: 9 fruit of thy s' which thou hast sown,"
28:38 carry much s' out into the field, "
46 a wonder, and upon thy s' for ever. "
59 the plagues of thy s', even great "
30: 6 thine heart, and the heart of thy s',"
19 that both thou and thy s' may live: "
31:21 out of the mouths of their s': "
34: 4 saying, I will give it unto thy s': "
Jos 24: 3 of Canaan, and multiplied his s', "
Ru 4:12 s' which the Lord shall give thee "
1Sa 2:20 The Lord give thee s' of this woman"
8:15 he will take the tenth of your s', "
20:42 between my s' and thy s' for ever. "
24:21 thou wilt not cut off my s' after me,"
2Sa 4: 8 king this day of Saul, and of his s'. "
7:12 I will set up thy s' after thee, which"
22:51 David, and to his s' for evermore. "
1Ki 2:33 and upon the head of his s' for ever:"
33 but upon David, and upon his s', "
11:14 he was of the king's s' in Edom. "
39 I will for this afflict the s' of David,"
18:32 would contain two measures of s'. "
2Ki 5:27 unto thee, and unto thy s' for ever. "
11: 1 arose and destroyed all the s' royal."
17:20 the Lord rejected all the s' of Israel."
25:25 the son of Elishama, of the s' royal,"
1Ch 16:13 O ye s' of Israel his servant, ye "
17:11 that I will raise up thy s' after thee,"
2Ch 20: 7 gavest it to the s' of Abraham thy "
22:10 arose and destroyed all the s' royal "
Ezr 2:59 their father's house, and their s', "
9: 2 holy s' have mingled themselves "

Ne 7:31 their father's house, nor their s' 2233
9: 2 s' of Israel separated themselves "
8 to give it, I say, to his s', and hast "
Es 6:13 If Mordecai be of the s' of the Jews, "
9:27 took upon them, and upon their s', "
28 memorial...perish from their s'. "
31 for themselves and for their s', "
10: 3 and speaking peace to all his s'. "
Job 5:25 know also that thy s' shall be great, "
21: 8 Their s' is established in their sight "
39:12 that he will bring home thy s', and "
Ps 18:50 David, and to his s' for evermore. "
21:10 s' from among the children of men. "
22:23 all ye the s' of Jacob, glorify him; "
23 and fear him, all ye the s' of Israel. "
30 A s' shall serve him; it shall be "
25:13 and his s' shall inherit the earth. "
37:25 forsaken, nor his s' begging bread. "
26 and lendeth; and his s' is blessed. "
28 the s' of the wicked shall be cut off. "
69:36 s' also of his servants shall inherit "
89: 4 Thy s' will I establish for ever, and "
29 His s' also will I make to endure for "
36 His s' shall endure for ever, and his "
102:28 their s' shall be established before "
105: 6 O ye s' of Abraham his servant, ye "
106:27 overthrow their s' also among the "
112: 2 His s' shall be mighty upon earth; "
126: 6 and weepeth, bearing precious s', "
Pr 11:21 but the s' of the righteous shall be "
Ec 11: 6 In the morning sow thy s', and in "
Isa 1: 4 a s' of evildoers, children that are "
5:10 s' of an homer shall yield an ephah. "
6:13 so the holy s' shall be the substance "
14:20 the s' of evildoers shall never be "
17:11 shalt thou make thy s' to flourish: "
23: 3 by great waters the s' of Sihor, the "
30:23 shall he give the rain of thy s', that "
41: 8 the s' of Abraham my friend. "
43: 5 I will bring thy s' from the east, "
44: 3 I will pour my spirit upon thy s', "
45:19 I said not unto the s' of Jacob, Seek "
25 In the Lord shall all the s' of Israel "
48:19 Thy s' also had been as the sand, "
53:10 he shall see his s', he shall prolong "
54: 3 thy s' shall inherit the Gentiles, "
55:10 that it may give s' to the sower, "
57: 3 s' of the adulterer and the whore. "
4 of transgression, a s' of falsehood, "
59:21 nor out of the mouth of thy s', "
21 nor of the mouth of thy seed's s', "
61: 9 their s' shall be known among the "
9 the s' which the Lord hath blessed. "
65: 9 I will bring forth a s' out of Jacob, "
23 are the s' of the blessed of the Lord, "
66:22 your s' and your name remain. "
Jer 2:21 thee a noble vine, wholly a right s': "
7:15 even the whole s' of Ephraim. "
22:28 are they cast out, he and his s', and "
30 for no man of his s' shall prosper, "
23: 8 led the s' of the house of Israel out "
29:32 Shemaiah the Nehelamite,...his s': "
30:10 s' from the land of their captivity; "
31:27 s' of man, and with the s' of beast. "
36 s' of Israel also shall cease from "
37 cast off all the s' of Israel for all "
33:22 will I multiply the s' of David my "
26 will I cast away the s' of Jacob, "
26 I will not take any of his s' to be "
26 to be rulers over the s' of Abraham, "
35: 7 nor sow s', nor plant vineyard, "
9 have we vineyard, nor field, nor s': "
36:31 I will punish him and his s' and his "
41: 1 the son of Elishama, of the s' royal, "
46:27 s' from the land of their captivity; "
49:10 his s' is spoiled, and his brethren, "
Eze 17: 5 He took also of the s' of the land, "
13 And hath taken of the king's s', and "
20: 5 unto the s' of the house of Jacob, "
43:19 Levites that be of the s' of Zadok, "
44:22 of the s' of the house of Israel, "
Da 1: 3 of the king's s', and of the princes; "
2:43 themselves with the s' of men: 2234
9: 1 Ahasuerus, of the s' of the Medes, 2233
Joe 1:17 The s' is rotten under their clods, *6507
Am 9:13 of grapes him that soweth s'; 2233
Hag 2:19 Is the s' yet in the barn? yea, as "
Zec 8:12 For the s' shall be prosperous; the "
Mal 2: 3 I will corrupt your s', and spread "
15 one? That he might seek a godly s'. "
M't 13:19 which received s' by the way side. *4687
20 received the s' into stony places, * "
22 that received s' among the thorns* "
23 received s' into the good ground * "
24 which sowed good s' in his field: 4690
27 not thou sow good s' in thy field? "
31 heaven is like to a grain of mustard s', "
37 the good s' is the Son of man; 4690
38 the good s' are the children of the "
17:20 ye have faith as a grain of mustard s', "
22:24 and raise up s' unto his brother. 4690
M'r 4:26 should cast s' into the ground; 4703
27 the s' should spring and grow up, "
31 It is like a grain of mustard s', 4690
12:19 and raise up s' unto his brother. "
20 took a wife, and dying left no s'. "
21 her, and died, neither left he any s': "
22 the seven had her, and left no s': "
Lu 1:55 to Abraham, and to his s' for ever. "
8: 5 A sower went out to sow his s': 4703
11 is this: The s' is the word of God. "
13:19 It is like a grain of mustard s', which "
17: 6 ye had faith as a grain of mustard s', "
20:28 and raise up s' unto his brother. 4690
Joh 7:42 Christ cometh of the s' of David, "
8:33 We be Abraham's s', and were "

Joh 8:37 I know that ye are Abraham's s'; 4690
Ac 3:25 in thy s' shall all the kindreds of "
7: 5 possession, and to his s' after him, "
6 his s' should sojourn in a strange "
13:23 Of this man's s' hath God according "
Ro 1: 3 which was made of the s' of David "
4:13 was not to Abraham, or to his s', "
16 promise might be sure to all the s' "
18 was spoken, So shall thy s' be. "
9: 7 because they are the s' of Abraham, "
7 but, In Isaac shall thy s' be called. "
8 the promise are counted for the s'. "
29 the Lord of Sabaoth had left us a s', "
11: 1 an Israelite, of the s' of Abraham, "
1Co 15:38 him, and to every s' his own body. "
2Co 9:10 he that ministereth s' to the sower "
10 food, and multiply your s' sown, 4703
11:22 Are they the s' of Abraham? so am 4690
Ga 3:16 and his s' were the promises made. "
16 one, And to thy s', which is Christ. "
19 till the s' should come to whom the "
29 Christ's, then are ye Abraham's s', "
2Ti 2: 8 Jesus Christ of the s' of David was "
Heb 2:16 he took on him the s' of Abraham. "
11:11 received strength to conceive s', "
18 That in Isaac shall thy s' be called: "
1Pe 1:23 born again, not of corruptible s', 4701
1Jo 3: 9 for his s' remaineth in him: and 4690
Re 12:17 war with the remnant of her s', "

seed's
Isa 59:21 out of the mouth of thy s' seed, 2233

seeds
De 22: 9 not sow thy vineyard with divers s':*
M't 13: 4 some s' fell by the way side, and the
32 which indeed is the least of all s': 4690
M'r 4:31 is less than all the s' that be in the "
Ga 3:16 He saith not, And to s', as of many; "

seedtime
Ge 8:22 s' and harvest, and cold and heat, 2233

seeing See also FORESEEING.
Ge 15: 2 wilt thou give me, s' I go childless,
18:18 s' that Abraham shall surely become a
19: 1 Lot s' them rose up to meet them; *7200
24:56 s' the Lord hath prospered my way;
28: 8 And Esau s' that the daughters of *7200
44:30 s' that his life is bound up in the lad's
Ex 4:11 the dumb, or the deaf, or the s', 6493
21: 8 s' he hath dealt deceitfully with her.
22:10 hurt, or driven away, no man s' it: 7200
23: 9 s' ye were strangers in the land of 3588
Le 10:17 in the holy place, s' it is most holy, "
Nu 15:26 s' all the people were in ignorance. "
16: 3 you, s' all the congregation are holy, "
35:23 s' him not, and cast it upon him, 7200
Jos 17:14 to inherit, s' I am a great people,
22:18 s' ye rebel to day against the Lord,
J'g 13:18 thus after my name, s' it is secret?
17:13 s' I have a Levite to my priest. 3588
19:23 s' that this man is come into mine 310
21: 7 s' we have sworn by the Lord that
16 s' the women are destroyed out of 3588
Ru 1:21 s' the Lord hath testified against me,
2:10 knowledge of me, s' I am a stranger?
1Sa 16: 1 s' I have rejected him from reigning
17:36 s' he hath defied the armies of the 3588
18:23 s' that I am a poor man, and lightly
24: 6 him, s' he is the anointed of the Lord.
25:26 s' the Lord hath withholden thee from
28:16 s' the Lord is departed from thee, and
2Sa 13:39 concerning Amnon, s' he was dead.
15:20 s' I go whither I may, return thou,
18:22 s' that thou hast no tidings ready?
19:11 s' the speech of all Israel is come to
1Ki 1:48 this day, mine eyes even s' it. 7200
11:28 Solomon s' the young man that * "
2Ki 10: 2 s' your master's sons are with you,
1Ch 12:17 s' there is no wrong in my hands, the
2Ch 2: 6 s' the heaven and heaven of heavens
Ezr 9:13 s' that thou our God hast punished 3588
Ne 2: 2 countenance sad, s' thou art not sick?
Job 14: 5 S' his days are determined, the 518
19:28 s' the root of the matter is found in‡
21:22 s' he judgeth those that are high.
34 s' in your answers there remaineth
28:21 S' it is hid from the eyes of all living,
Ps 22: 8 deliver him, s' he delighted in him.
50:17 S' thou hatest instruction, and castest
Pr 17:16 get wisdom, s' he hath no heart to it?
20:12 The hearing ear, and the s' eye, 7200
Ec 1: 8 the eye is not satisfied with s', nor "
2:16 s' that which now is in the days to
6:11 S' there be many things that 3588
Isa 21: 3 it; I was dismayed at the s' of it. *7200
33:15 and shutteth his eyes from s' evil;* "
42:20 S' many things, but thou observest* "
49:21 s' I have lost my children, and am
Jer 11:15 s' she hath wrought lewdness with
47: 7 s' the Lord hath given it a charge
Eze 16:30 s' thou doest all these things, the
17:18 S' he despised the oath by breaking*
21: 4 S' then that I will cut off from 3282
22:28 s' vanity, and divining lies unto
Da 2:47 s' thou couldest reveal this secret. 1768
Ho 4: 6 s' thou hast forgotten the law of thy
M't 5: 1 s' the multitudes, he went up into 1492
9: 2 Jesus s' their faith said unto the "
13:13 parables: because they s' see not; 991
14 s' ye shall see, and shall not perceive: "
M'r 4:12 s' they may see, and not perceive; "
11:13 s' a fig tree afar off having leaves, 1492
Lu 1:34 shall this be, s' I know not a man? 1893
5:12 who s' Jesus fell on his face, and *1492
8:10 s' they might not see, and hearing 991
23:40 s' thou art in the...condemnation? 3754

Joh 2:18 us, s' that thou doest these things?
9: 7 therefore, and washed, and came s'. 991
21:21 Peter s' him saith to Jesus, Lord, 1492
Ac 2:15 s' it is but the third hour of the day. 1063
31 He s' this before spake of the *4275
3: 3 Who s' Peter and John about to go 1492
7:24 And s' one of them suffer wrong, he "
8: 6 and s' the miracles which he did. * 991
9: 7 hearing a voice, but s' no man. *2334
13:11 blind, not s' the sun for a season. 991
46 but s' ye put it from you, and judge 1894
16:27 s' the prison doors open, he drew 1492
17:24 s' that he is Lord of heaven and *
25 s' he giveth to all life, and breath,
19:36 S' then that these things cannot be
24: 2 S' that by thee we enjoy great
28:26 and s' ye shall see, and not perceive: 991
Ro 3:30 S' it is one God, which shall justify *1897
1Co 14:16 s' he understandeth not what thou 1894
2Co 3:12 S' then that we have such hope, we*
4: 1 s' we have this ministry, as we have
11:18 S' that many glory after the flesh, 1893
19 gladly, s' ye yourselves are wise. *
Col 3: 9 s' that ye have put off the old man
2Th 1: 6 S' it is a righteous thing with God *1512
Heb 4: 6 S' therefore it remaineth that some 1893
14 S' then that we have a great high*
5:11 uttered, s' ye are dull of hearing. 1893
6: 6 s' they crucify to themselves the Son
7:25 s' he ever liveth to make intercession
8: 4 s' that there are priests that offer
11:27 endured, as s' him who is invisible. 3708
12: 1 s' we also are compassed about
1Pe 1:22 S' ye have purified your souls in
2Pe 2: 8 among them, in s' and hearing, 990
3:11 S' then that all these things shall be
14 s' that ye look for such things, be
17 s' ye know these things before, *

seek See also SEEKEST; SEEKETH; SEEKING; SOUGHT.
Ge 37:16 I s' my brethren: tell me, I pray 1245
43:18 that he may s' occasion against us, 1556
Le 13:36 priest shall not s' for yellow hair; 1239
19:31 neither s' after wizards, to be 1245
Nu 15:39 ye s' not after your own heart and *8446
16:10 thee: and s' ye the priesthood also? 1245
24: 1 times, to s' for enchantments, *7125
De 4:29 thou shalt s' the Lord thy God, 1245
29 if thou s' him with all thy heart 1875
12: 5 even unto his habitation shall ye s', "
22: 2 thee until thy brother s' after it, "
23: 6 Thou shalt not s' their peace nor "
Ru 3: 1 shall I not s' rest for thee, that it 1245
1Sa 9: 3 with thee, and arise, go s' the asses. "
10: 2 which thou wentest to s' are found: "
14 And he said, To s' the asses: and "
16:16 to s' out a man, who is a cunning "
23:15 Saul was come out to s' his life: "
25 Saul...and his men went to s' him. "
24: 2 went to s' David and his men upon "
25:26 they that s' evil to my lord, be as "
29 to pursue thee, and to s' thy soul: "
26: 2 s' David in the wilderness of Ziph. "
20 of Israel is come out to s' a flea, as "
27: 1 to s' me any more in any coast of "
28: 7 S' me a woman that hath a "
2Sa 5:17 the Philistines came up to s' David; "
1Ki 2:40 Gath to Achish to s' his servants: "
18:10 my lord hath not sent to s' thee: "
19:10, 14 they s' my life, to take it away. "
2Ki 2:16 go, we pray thee, and s' thy master: "
6:19 bring you to the man whom ye s'. "
1Ch 4:39 valley, to s' pasture for their flocks. "
14: 8 the Philistines went up to s' David. "
16:10 of them rejoice that s' the Lord. "
11 S' the Lord and his strength, 1875
11 strength, s' his face continually. 1245
22:19 your soul to s' the Lord your God; 1875
28: 8 s' for all the commandments of the "
9 if thou s' him, he will be found of "
2Ch 7:14 s' my face, and turn from their 1245
11:16 set their hearts to s' the Lord God "
12:14 prepared not his heart to s' the 1875
14: 4 commanded Judah to s' the Lord "
15: 2 if ye s' him, he will be found of you; "
12 into a covenant to s' the Lord God "
13 whosoever would not s' the Lord "
19: 3 hast prepared thine heart to s' God. "
20: 3 and set himself to s' the Lord, and "
4 of Judah they came to s' the Lord. 1245
30:19 prepareth his heart to s' God, the 1875
31:21 the commandments, to s' his God, "
34: 3 began to s' after the God of David "
Ezr 4: 2 for we s' your God, as ye do; and we "
6:21 land, to s' the Lord God of Israel, "
7:10 his heart to s' the law of the Lord, "
8:21 to s' of him a right way for us, and 1245
22 upon all them for good that s' him; "
9:12 nor s' their peace or their wealth 1875
Ne 2:10 to s' the welfare of the children of 1245
Job 5: 8 I would s' unto God, and unto God 1875
7:21 thou shalt s' me in the morning, 7836
8: 5 If thou wouldest s' unto God "
20:10 children shall s' to please the poor, "
Ps 4: 2 love vanity, and s' after leasing? 1245
9:10 not forsaken them that s' thee. 1875
10: 4 countenance, will not s' after God:* "
15 s' out his wickedness till thou find "
14: 2 that did understand, and s' God. "
22:26 shall praise the Lord that s' him: "
24: 6 the generation of them that s' him, "
6 him, that s' thy face, O Jacob. 1245
27: 4 of the Lord, that will I s' after; "
8 When thou saidst, S' ye my face; "
8 unto thee, Thy face, Lord, will I s'. "
34:10 that s' the Lord shall not want 1875

Ps 34:14 do good; s' peace, and pursue it. 1245
35: 4 put to shame that s' after my soul: "
38:12 s' after my life lay snares for me: "
12 that s' my hurt speak mischievous 1875
40:14 that s' after my soul to destroy it; 1245
16 Let all those that s' thee rejoice "
53: 2 did understand, that did s' God. 1875
54: 3 and oppressors s' after my soul: 1245
63: 1 art my God; early will I s' thee: 7836
9 those that s' my soul, to destroy 1245
69: 6 those that s' thee be confounded "
32 your heart shall live that s' God. 1875
70: 2 confounded that s' after my soul: 1245
4 all those that s' thee rejoice and be "
71:13 and dishonour that s' my hurt. "
24 unto shame, that s' my hurt. "
83:16 that they may s' thy name, O Lord. "
104:21 prey, and s' their meat from God. "
105: 3 of them rejoice that s' the Lord. "
4 S' the Lord, and his strength: 1875
4 strength: s' his face evermore. 1245
109:10 let them s' their bread also out of 1875
119: 2 that s' him with the whole heart. "
45 at liberty: for I s' thy precepts. * "
155 wicked: for they s' not thy statutes. "
176 s' thy servant; for I do not forget 1245
122: 9 the Lord our God I will s' thy good. "
Pr 1:28 they shall s' me early, but they 7836
7:15 diligently to s' thy face, and I have "
8:17 those that s' me early shall find me. "
21: 6 to and fro of them that s' death. 1245
23:30 they that go to s' mixed wine. 2713
35 shall I awake? I will s' it yet again. 1245
28: 5 they that s' the Lord understand "
29:10 the upright: but the just s' his soul. "
26 Many s' the ruler's favour; but "
Ec 1:13 my heart to s' and search out by 1875
7:25 to search, and to s' out wisdom, 1245
8:17 though a man labour to s' it out, "
Ca 3: 2 will s' him whom my soul loveth: "
6: 1 that we may s' him with thee. "
Isa 1:17 s' judgment, relieve the oppressed, 1875
8:19 S' unto them that have familiar "
19 not a people s' unto their God? for "
9:13 them, neither do they s' the Lord * "
11:10 to it shall the Gentiles s': and his "
19: 3 and they shall s' to the idols, and to "
26: 9 within me will I s' thee early: 7836
29:15 Woe unto them that s' deep to hide "
31: 1 of Israel, neither s' the Lord! 1875
34:16 S' ye out of the book of the Lord, "
41:12 Thou shalt s' them, and shalt not 1245
17 When the poor and needy s' water, "
45:19 the seed of Jacob, S' ye me in vain: "
51: 1 righteousness, ye that s' the Lord: "
55: 6 S' ye the Lord while he may be 1875
58: 2 Yet they s' me daily, and delight "
Jer 2:24 all they that s' her will not weary 1245
33 trimmest thou thy way to s' love? "
4:30 despise thee, they will s' thy life. "
5: 1 and s' in the broad places thereof, "
11:21 that s' thy life, saying, Prophesy "
19: 7 hands of them that s' their lives: "
9 and they that s' their lives, shall "
21: 7 the hand of those that s' their life: "
22:25 the hand of them that s' thy life, "
29: 7 s' the peace of the city whither I 1875
13 ye shall s' me, and find me, when 1245
30:14 forgotten thee; they s' thee not; 1875
34:20 the hand of them that s' their life: 1245
21 the hand of them that s' their life, "
38:16 hand of these men that s' thy life. "
44:30 the hand of them that s' his life; "
45: 5 things for thyself? s' them not: "
46:26 hand of those that s' their lives, "
49:37 and before them that s' their life: "
50: 4 shall go, and s' the Lord their God. "
La 1:11 All her people sigh, they s' bread; "
Eze 7:25 they shall s' peace, and there shall "
26 shall they s' a vision of the prophet; "
34: 6 none did search or s' after them. "
11 search my sheep, and s' them out. 1239
12 so will I s' out my sheep, and will "
16 I will s' that which was lost, and 1245
Da 9: 3 to s' by prayer and supplications, "
Ho 2: 7 she shall s' them, but shall not "
3: 5 s' the Lord their God, and David "
5: 6 and with their herds to s' the Lord; "
15 their offence, and s' my face: in "
15 affliction they will s' me early. 7836
7:10 their God, nor s' him for all this. *1245
10:12 for it is time to s' the Lord, till he 1875
Am 5: 4 Israel, S' ye me, and ye shall live: "
5 But s' not Beth-el, nor enter into "
6 S' the Lord, and ye shall live; lest "
8 S' him that maketh the seven stars "
14 S' good, and not evil, that ye may 1875
8:12 and fro to s' the word of the Lord, 1245
Na 3: 7 shall I s' comforters for thee? "
11 s' strength because of the enemy. "
Zep 2: 3 S' ye the Lord, all ye meek of the "
3 s' righteousness, s' meekness: it "
Zec 8:21 Lord, and to s' the Lord of hosts: "
22 shall come to s' the Lord of hosts "
11:16 neither shall s' the young one, nor "
12: 9 I will s' to destroy all the nations "
Mal 2: 7 should s' the law at his mouth: "
15 That he might s' a godly seed. "
3: 1 and the Lord, whom ye s', shall "
M't 2:13 s' the young child to destroy him. 2212
6:32 all these things do the Gentiles s':) 1934
33 But s' ye first the kingdom of God, 2212
7: 7 s', and ye shall find; knock, and it "
28: 5 ye s' Jesus, which was crucified. "
M'r 1:37 said unto him, All men s' for thee. * "
3:32 thy brethren without s' for thee. "

M'r 8:12 this generation s' after a sign? 1934
16: 6 Ye s' Jesus of Nazareth, which was 2212
Lu 11: 9 s', and ye shall find; knock, and it "
29 they s' a sign; and there shall no *1934
12:29 And s' not ye what ye shall eat, or 2212
30 the nations of the world s' after: 1934
31 rather s' ye the kingdom of God; 2212
13:24 for many,...will s' to enter in, and "
15: 8 and s' diligently till she find it? "
17:33 shall s' to save his life shall lose it; "
19:10 s' and to save that which was lost. "
24: 5 s' ye the living among the dead? "
Joh 1:38 and saith unto them, What s' ye? "
5:30 because I s' not mine own will, but "
44 s' not the honour that cometh "
6:26 Ye s' me, not because ye saw the "
7:25 not this he, whom they s' to kill? "
34, 36 Ye shall s' me, and shall not "
8:21 ye shall s' me, and shall die in your "
37 ye s' to kill me, because my word "
40 But now ye s' to kill me, a man "
50 And I s' not mine own glory: there "
13:33 Ye shall s' me: and as I said unto "
18: 4 and said unto them, Whom s' ye? "
7 asked he them again, Whom s' ye? "
8 if therefore ye s' me, let these go "
Ac 10:19 him, Behold, three men s' thee. "
21 said, Behold, I am he whom ye s': "
11:25 Barnabas to Tarsus, for to s' Saul: 327
15:17 of men might s' after the Lord, 1567
17:27 That they should s' the Lord, if 2212
Ro 2: 7 in well doing s' for glory and "
11: 3 am left alone, and they s' my life. "
1Co 1:22 and the Greeks s' after wisdom: "
7:27 unto a wife? s' not to be loosed. "
27 loosed from a wife? s' not a wife. "
10:24 Let no man s' his own, but every "
14:12 s' that ye may excel to the edifying "
2Co 12:14 for I s' not yours, but you: for the "
13: 3 ye s' a proof of Christ speaking in "
Ga 1:10 or do I s' to please men? for if I †‡ "
2:17 while we s' to be justified by Christ, * "
Ph'p 2:21 For all s' their own, not the things "
Col 3: 1 s' those things which are above, "
Heb 11: 6 of them that diligently s' him. 1567
14 plainly that they s' a country. *1934
13:14 city, but we s' one to come. "
1Pe 3:11 let him s' peace, and ensue it. 2212
Re 9: 6 in those days shall men s' death, "

seekest

Ge 37:15 asked him, saying, What s' thou? 1245
J'g 4:22 shew thee the man whom thou s'. "
2Sa 17: 3 the man whom thou s' is as if all "
20:19 thou s' to destroy a city and a "
1Ki 11:22 thou s' to go to thine own country? "
Pr 2: 4 If thou s' her as silver, and * "
Jer 45: 5 s' thou great things for thyself? "
Joh 4:27 yet no man said, What s' thou? 2212
20:15 why weepest thou? whom s' thou? "

seeketh

1Sa 19: 2 Saul my father s' to kill thee: now 1245
20: 1 thy father, that he s' my life? "
22:23 for he that s' my life s' thy life: "
23:10 that Saul s' to come to Keilah, to "
24: 9 saying, Behold, David s' thy hurt? "
2Sa 16:11 forth of my bowels, s' my life: "
1Ki 20: 7 and see how this man s' mischief: "
2Ki 5: 7 see how he s' a quarrel against me. 579
Job 39:29 From thence she s' the prey, and *2658
Ps 37:32 the righteous, and s' to slay him. 1245
Pr 11:27 s' good procureth favour: but 7836
27 he that s' mischief, it shall come *1875
14: 6 A scorner s' wisdom, and findeth 1245
15:14 hath understanding s' knowledge: "
17: 9 covereth a transgression s' love; "
11 an evil man s' only rebellion: "
19 exalteth his gate s' destruction. "
18: 1 s' and intermeddleth with all "
15 the ear of the wise s' knowledge. "
31:13 She s' wool, and flax, and 1875
Ec 7:28 Which yet my soul s', but I find 1245
Isa 40:20 s' unto him a cunning workman "
Jer 5: 1 executeth judgment,...s' the truth; "
30:17 is Zion, whom no man s' after. 1875
38: 4 s' not the welfare of this people, "
La 3:25 wait for him, to the soul that s' him. "
Eze 14:10 punishment of him that s' unto "
34:12 As a shepherd s' out his flock in 1243
M't 7: 8 receiveth; and he that s' findeth; 2212
12:39 evil...generation s' after a sign; 1934
16: 4 wicked...generation s' after a sign; "
18:12 and s' that which is gone astray? *2212
Lu 11:10 receiveth; and he that s' findeth; "
Joh 4:23 the Father s' such to worship him. * "
7: 4 he himself s' to be known openly. "
18 speaketh of himself s' his own glory: "
18 he that s' his glory that sent him, "
8:50 there is one that s' and judgeth. "
Ro 3:11 there is none that s' after God. 1567
11: 7 not obtained that which he s' for; 1934
1Co 13: 5 itself unseemly, s' not her own, 2212

seeking

Es 10: 3 s' the wealth of his people, and 1875
Isa 16: 5 judging, and s' judgment, and "
M't 12:43 places, s' rest, and findeth none. 2212
13:45 a merchant man, s' goodly pearls: "
M'r 8:11 him, s' of him a sign from heaven, "
Lu 2:45 back again to Jerusalem, s' him. "
11:24 walketh through dry places, s' rest; "
54 and s' to catch something out of his * "
13: 7 three years I come s' fruit on this "
Joh 6:24 came to Capernaum, s' for Jesus. "
Ac 13: 8 s' to turn away the deputy from the "
11 s' some to lead him by the hand. "

1Co 10:33 not s' mine own profit, but the 2212
1Pe 5: 8 about, s' whom he may devour: "

seem See also SEEMED; SEEMETH.

Ge 27:12 shall s' to him as a deceiver; 1961, 5869
De 15:18 It shall not s' hard unto thee, 7185
25: 3 brother should s' vile unto thee. 7034
Jos 24:15 s' evil unto you to serve the 1961, 5869
1Sa 24: 4 as it shall s' good unto thee. " "
2Sa 19:37 what shall s' good unto thee. " "
38 which shall s' good unto thee: " "
1Ki 21: 2 if it s' good to thee, I will give " "
1Ch 13: 2 If it s' good unto you, and that it
Ezr 5:17 if it s' good to the king, let there be
7:18 whatsoever shall s' good to thee, 3191
Ne 9:32 let not all the trouble s' little 4591
Es 5: 4 If it s' good unto the king, let the
8: 5 the thing s' right before the king,
Jer 40: 4 If it s' good unto thee to come 5869
4 but if it s' ill unto thee to come "
Na 2: 4 they shall s' like torches, they *4758
1Co 11:16 if any man s' to be contentious, *1380
12:22 body, which s' to be more feeble, "
2Co 10: 9 I may not s' as if I would terrify "
Heb 4: 1 of you should s' to come short of it. "
Jas 1:26 man among you s' to be religious, * "

seemed

Ge 19:14 he s' as one that mocked unto 1961, 5869
29:20 s' unto him but a few days, " "
2Sa 3:19 all that s' good to Israel, and
19 that s' good to the whole house of * "
Ec 9:13 the sun, and it s' great unto me:
Jer 18: 4 as s' good to the potter to make it. 5869
27: 5 have given it unto whom it s' meet "
M't 11:26 for so it s' good in thy sight. *1096, 2107
Lu 1: 3 It s' good to me also, having had 1380
10:21 for so it s' good in thy sight. *1096, 2107
24:11 words s' to them as idle tales, and 5316
Ac 15:25 s' good unto us, being assembled 1380
28 For it s' good to the Holy Ghost, "
Ga 2: 6 But of these who s' to be somewhat, * "
6 s' to be somewhat in conference * "
9 and John, who s' to be pillars * "

seemeth

Le 14:35 It s' to me there is as it were a 7200
Nu 16: 9 S' it but a small thing unto you,
Jos 9:25 as it s' good and right unto thee 5869
J'g 10:15 us whatsoever s' good unto thee; "
19:24 unto them what s' good unto you: "
1Sa 1:23 Do what s' thee good; tarry until "
3:18 let him do what s' him good. "
11:10 with us all that s' good unto you. "
14:36 Do whatsoever s' good unto thee. "
40 Do what s' good unto thee. "
18:23 S' it to you a light thing to be a "
2Sa 10:12 Lord do that which s' him good. "
15:26 him do to me as s' good unto him. "
18: 4 What s' you best I will do. "
24:22 offer up what s' good unto him: "
Es 3:11 with them as it s' good to thee. "
Pr 14:12 a way which s' right unto a man, 6440
16:25 is a way that s' right unto a man, "
18:17 that is first in his own cause s' just;
Jer 26:14 do with me as s' good and meet *5869
40: 4 it s' good and convenient for thee "
5 wheresoever it s' convenient unto "
Eze 34:18 S' it a small thing unto you to have
Lu 8:18 even that which he s' to have. *1380
Ac 17:18 He s' to be a setter forth of strange "
25:27 it s' to me unreasonable to send a "
1Co 3:18 you s' to be wise in this world, * "
Heb 12:11 for the present s' to be joyous, but "

seemly See also UNSEEMLY.

Pr 19:10 Delight is not s' for a fool; much 5000
26: 1 so honour is not s' for a fool. "

seen

Ge 7: 1 thee have I s' righteous before me 7200
8: 5 were the tops of the mountains s'. "
9:14 the bow shall be s' in the cloud: "
22:14 the mount of the Lord it shall be s'. * "
31:12 I have s' all that Laban doeth unto "
42 God hath s' mine affliction and the "
32:30 I have s' God face to face, and my "
33:10 for therefore I have s' thy face, "
10 as though I had s' the face of God, "
45:13 Egypt, and of all that ye have s'; "
46:30 let me die, since I have s' thy face, "
Ex 3: 7 I have surely s' the affliction of my "
9 and I have also s' the oppression "
16 s' that which is done to you in Egypt:
10: 6 nor thy fathers' fathers have s', 7200
13: 7 no leavened bread be s' with thee, "
7 shall there be leaven s' with thee "
14:13 for the Egyptians whom ye have s' "
19: 4 Ye have s' what I did unto the "
20:22 Ye have s' that I have talked with "
32: 9 unto Moses, I have s' this people, "
33:23 parts: but my face shall not be s'. "
34: 3 any man be s' throughout all the "
Le 5: 1 whether he hath s' or known of it; "
13: 7 that he hath been s' of the priest * "
7 he shall be s' of the priest again: * "
Nu 14:14 that thou Lord art s' face to face, "
22 those men which have s' my glory, "
23:21 neither hath he s' perverseness in "
27:13 And when thou hast s' it, thou also "
De 1:28 we have s' the sons of the Anakims "
31 s' how that the Lord thy God bare "
3:21 eyes have s' all that the Lord your "
4: 3 Your eyes have s' what the Lord did "
9 the things which thine eyes have s', * "
5:24 s' this day that God doth talk with "
9:13 I have s' this people, and, behold, "
10:21 things, which thine eyes have s'. "
11: 2 have not s' the chastisement of the "

De 11: 7 your eyes have s' all the great acts 7200
16: 4 shall be no leavened bread s' with "
21: 7 blood, neither have our eyes s' it. "
29: 2 Ye have s' all that the Lord did "
3 temptations...thine eyes have s', * "
17 And ye have s' their abominations, "
33: 9 and to his mother, I have not s' him; "
Jos 23: 3 have s' all that the Lord your God "
24: 7 your eyes have s' what I have done* "
J'g 2: 7 who had s' all the great works of "
5: 8 was there a shield or spear s' among "
6: 22 I have s' an angel of the Lord face "
9: 48 What ye have s' me do, make haste, "
13: 22 surely die, because we have s' God. "
14: 2 I have s' a woman in Timnath of the "
18: 9 we have s' the land, and, behold, "
19: 30 was no such deed done nor s' from "
1Sa 6: 16 lords of the Philistines had s' it, "
16: 18 Behold, I have s' a son of Jesse the "
17: 25 Have ye s' this man that is come "
23: 22 haunt is, and who hath s' him there: "
24: 10 eyes have s' how that the Lord had "
2Sa 17: 17 not be s' to come into the city: "
18: 21 Go tell the king what thou hast s'. "
22: 11 was s' upon the wings of the wind. "
1Ki 6: 18 was cedar; there was no stone s'. "
8: 8 that the ends of the staves were s' "
8 and they were not s' without: and "
10: 4 when the queen of Sheba had s' all "
7 I came, and mine eyes had s' it: "
12 trees, nor were s' unto this day. "
13: 12 s' what way the man of God went, "
20: 13 thou s' all this great multitude? "
2Ki 9: 26 s' yesterday the blood of Naboth, "
20: 5 thy prayer, I have s' thy tears: "
15 What have they s' in thine house? "
15 that are in mine house have they s': "
23: 29 at Megiddo, when he had s' him. "
1Ch 29: 17 now have I s' with joy thy people, "
2Ch 5: 9 ends of...staves were s' from the ark "
9 but they were not s' without. "
9: 3 queen of Sheba had s' the wisdom "
6 I came, and mine eyes had s' it: "
11 none such s' before in the land of "
Ezr 3: 12 men, that had s' the first house, "
Es 9: 26 they had s' concerning this matter, "
Job 4: 8 as I have s', they that plow iniquity, "
5: 3 I have s' the foolish taking root: "
7: 8 The eye of him that hath s' me *7210
8: 18 him, saying, I have not s' thee. 7200
10: 18 up the ghost, and no eye had s' me! "
13: 1 mine eye hath s' all this, mine ear "
15: 17 that which I have s' I will declare; 2372
20: 7 they which have s' him shall say, 7200
27: 12 all ye yourselves have s' it; why 2372
28: 7 which the vulture's eye hath not s': 7805
31: 19 If I have s' any perish for want of 7200
33: 21 consumed...that it cannot be s'; 7210
21 bones that were not s' stick out. 7200
38: 17 s' the doors of the shadow of death? "
22 hast thou s' the treasures of the hail, "
Ps 10: 14 Thou hast s' it; for thou beholdest "
18: 15 the channels of waters were s', * "
35: 21 said, Aha, aha, our eye hath s' it. "
22 This thou hast s', O Lord: keep not "
37: 25 have I not s' the righteous forsaken, "
35 I have s' the wicked in great power, "
48: 8 s' in the city of the Lord of hosts, "
54: 7 mine eye hath s' his desire upon "
55: 9 s' violence and strife in the city. "
63: 2 as I have s' thee in the sanctuary. *2372
68: 24 They have s' thy goings, O God; 7200
90: 15 the years wherein we have s' evil. "
98: 3 have s' the salvation of our God. "
119: 96 I have s' an end of all perfection: "
Pr 25: 7 the prince whom thine eyes have s'. "
Ec 1: 14 I have s' all the works that are done "
3: 10 I have s' the travail, which God hath "
4: 3 who hath not s' the evil work that "
5: 13 evil which I have s' under the sun, "
18 Behold that which I have s': it is "
6: 1 evil which I have s' under the sun, "
5 Moreover he hath not s' the sun, "
6 twice told, yet hath he s' no good: * "
7: 15 have I s' in the days of my vanity: "
8: 9 All this have I s', and applied my "
9: 13 This wisdom have I s' also under "
10: 5 evil which I have s' under the sun, "
7 I have s' servants upon horses, and "
Isa 6: 5 for mine eyes have s' the King, the "
9: 2 in darkness have s' a great light: "
16: 12 when it is s' that Moab is weary * "
22: 9 s' also the breaches of the city "
38: 5 heard thy prayer, I have s' thy tears: "
39: 4 What have they s' in thine house? "
4 that is in mine house have they s': "
44: 16 Aha, I am warm, I have s' the fire: "
47: 3 uncovered...thy shame shall be s': "
57: 18 I have s' his ways, and will heal him: "
60: 2 and his glory shall be s' upon thee. "
64: 4 by the ear, neither hath the eye s', "
66: 8 a thing? who hath s' such things? "
19 my fame, neither have s' my glory; "
Jer 1: 12 Thou hast well s': for I will hasten "
3: 6 s' that which backsliding Israel "
7: 11 even I have s' it, saith the Lord. "
12: 3 hast s' me, and tried mine heart * "
13: 27 I have s' thine adulteries, and thy "
23: 13 s' folly in the prophets of Samaria, "
14 s' also in the prophets of Jerusalem "
44: 2 Ye have s' all the evil that I have "
46: 5 Wherefore have I s' them dismayed "
La 1: 8 they have s' her nakedness: "
10 hath s' that the heathen entered "
2: 14 have s' vain and foolish things 2372
14 but have s' for thee false burdens "

La 2: 16 for; we have found, we have s' it. 7200
3: 1 I am the man that hath s' affliction "
59 O Lord, thou hath s' my wrong: "
60 Thou hast s' all their vengeance "
Eze 8: 12 hast thou s' what the ancients of "
15, 17 Hast thou s' this, O son of man? "
11: 24 So the vision that I had s' went up "
13: 3 own spirit, and have s' nothing! "
6 s' vanity and lying divination, 2372
7 Have ye not s' a vain vision, and "
8 ye have spoken vanity, and s' lies, "
47: 6 me, Son of man, hast thou s' this? 7200
Da 2: 26 me the dream which I have s', 2370
4: 9 visions of my dream that I have s', "
18 I king Nebuchadnezzar have s'. "
8: 6 I had s' standing before the river, *7200
15 I, even I Daniel, had s' the vision, "
9: 21 Gabriel, whom I had s' in the vision "
Ho 6: 10 I have s' an horrible thing in the "
Zec 9: 8 for now have I s' with mine eyes. "
14 And the Lord shall be s' over them, "
10: 2 and the diviners have s' a lie, and 2372
M't 2: 2 for we have s' his star in the east, *1492
6: 1 alms before men, to be s' of them: 2300
5 that they may be s' of men. 5316
9: 33 saying, It was never so s' in Israel. "
13: 17 ye see, and have not s' them; *1492
21: 32 ye, when ye had s' it, repented not* "
23: 5 works they do for to be s' of men: 2300
M'r 9: 1 they have s' the kingdom of God *1492
9 no man what things they had s', "
16: 11 was alive, and had been s' of her, 2300
14 believed not them which had s' him "
Lu 1: 22 perceived that he had s' a vision in 3708
2: 17 they had s' it, they made known *1492
20 things that they had heard and s', "
26 before he had s' the Lord's Christ. "
30 For mine eyes have s' thy salvation, "
5: 26 We have s' strange things to day. "
7: 22 tell John what things ye have s' and "
9: 36 of those things which they had s'. 3708
10: 24 ye see, and have not s' them; *1492
19: 37 the mighty works that they had s'; "
23: 8 he hoped to have s' some miracle* "
24: 23 they had also s' a vision of angels, 3708
37 supposed that they had s' a spirit. *2334
Joh 1: 18 No man hath s' God at any time; 3708
3: 11 know, and testify that we have s'; "
32 what he hath s' and heard, that he "
4: 45 having s' all the things that he did "
5: 37 voice at any time, nor s' his shape. "
6: 14 had s' the miracle that Jesus did, *1492
36 ye also have s' me, and believe 3708
46 that any man hath s' the Father, "
46 is of God, he hath s' the Father. "
8: 38 which I have s' with my Father: "
38 which ye have s' with your father.* "
57 old, and hast thou s' Abraham? "
9: 8 had s' him that he was blind, *2334
37 Thou hast both s' him, and it is he 3708
11: 45 had s' the things which Jesus did, *2300
14: 7 ye know him, and have s' him. 3708
9 that hath s' me hath s' the Father; "
15: 24 now have they both s' and hated me "
20: 18 disciples that she had s' the Lord, "
25 said unto him, We have s' the Lord. "
29 because thou hast s' me, thou hast "
29 blessed are they that have not s', *1492
Ac 1: 3 being s' of them forty days, and 3700
11 as ye have s' him go into heaven. *2300
4: 20 which we have s' and heard. *1492
7: 34 I have s',...the affliction of my * "
34 I have s' the affliction of my people, "
44 to the fashion that he had s'. 3708
9: 12 hath s' in a vision a man named 1492
27 how he had s' the Lord in the way, "
10: 17 vision which he had s' should mean, "
11: 13 how he had s' an angel in his house, "
23 came, and had s' the grace of God, "
13: 31 And he was s' many days of them 3700
16: 10 And after he had s' the vision, 1492
40 and when they had s' the brethren, "
21: 29 (For they had s' before with him 4308
22: 15 of what thou hast s' and heard. 3708
26: 16 of these things which thou hast s', "
Ro 1: 20 creation of the world are clearly s', 2529
8: 24 but hope that is s' is not hope: for 991
1Co 2: 9 Eye hath not s', nor ear heard, *1492
9: 1 have I not s' Jesus Christ our 3708
15: 5 And that he was s' of Cephas, *3700
6 he was s' of above five hundred * "
7 After that, he was s' of James; * "
8 And last of all he was s' of me also,* "
2Co 4: 18 look not at the things which are s', 991
18 but at the things which are not s': "
18 things which are s' are temporal; "
18 things which are not s' are eternal. "
Ph'p 4: 9 and heard, and s' in me, do; *1492
Col 2: 1 as have not s' my face in the flesh 3708
18 those things which he hath not s', "
1Ti 3: 16 justified in the Spirit, s' of angels, 3700
6: 16 whom no man hath s', nor can see: 1492
Heb 11: 1 for, the evidence of things not s'. 991
3 things which are s' were not made "
7 warned of God of things not s' as yet, "
13 but having s' them afar off, and 1492
Jas 5: 11 and have s' the end of the Lord; "
1Pe 1: 8 Whom having not s', ye love; in "
1Jo 1: 1 which we have s' with our eyes, 3708
2 and we have s' it, and bear witness, "
3 That which we have s' and heard "
3: 6 whosoever sinneth hath not s' him, "
4: 12 No man hath s' God at any time. *2300
14 And we have s' and do testify that* "
20 not his brother whom he hath s', 3708
20 he love God whom he hath not s'? "

3Jo 11 he that doeth evil hath not s' God. 3780
Re 1: 19 Write the things...thou hast s', *1492
11: 19 there was s' in his temple the ark 3700
22: 8 And when I had heard and s', I fell *991

seer See also OVERSEER; SEER'S; SEERS.
1Sa 9: 9 Come, and let us go to the s': for 7200
9 Prophet was beforetime called a S'.) "
11 and said unto them, Is the s' here? "
19 answered Saul, and said, I am the s': "
2Sa 15: 27 Zadok the priest, Art not thou a s'? "
24: 11 unto the prophet Gad, David's s', 2374
1Ch 9: 22 David and Samuel the s' did ordain 7200
21: 9 Lord spake unto Gad, David's s', 2374
25: 5 the sons of Heman the king's s' in "
26: 28 all that Samuel the s', and Saul 7200
29: 29 in the book of Samuel the s', "
29 and in the book of Gad the s', 2374
2Ch 9: 29 and in the visions Iddo the s' "
12: 15 Iddo the s' concerning genealogies? "
16: 7 Hanani the s' came to Asa king 7200
10 Then Asa was wroth with the s', "
19: 2 of Hanani the s' went out to meet 2374
29: 25 of David, and of Gad the king's s', "
30 of David, and of Asaph the s'. "
35: 15 Heman, and Jeduthun the king's s'; "
Am 7: 12 O thou s', go, flee thee away into "

seer's
1Sa 9: 18 Tell me,...where the s' house is. 7200

seers See also OVERSEERS.
2Ki 17: 13 all the prophets, and by all the s', *2374
2Ch 33: 18 words of the s' that spake to him "
19 written among the sayings of the s'.* "
Isa 29: 10 your rulers, the s' hath he covered. "
30: 10 Which say to the s', See not; and 7200
Mic 3: 7 Then shall the s' be ashamed, and 2374

seest
Ge 13: 15 For all the land which thou s', to 7200
16: 13 spake unto her, Thou God s' me; *7210
31: 43 and all that thou s' is mine: and 7200
Ex 10: 28 day thou s' my face thou shalt die, "
De 4: 19 and when thou s' the sun, and the "
12: 13 offerings in every place...thou s': "
20: 1 and s' horses, and chariots, and a "
21: 11 s' among the captives a beautiful "
J'g 9: 36 s' the shadow of the mountains as "
1Ki 21: 29 S' thou how Ahab humbleth "
Job 10: 4 of flesh? or s' thou as man seeth? "
Pr 22: 29 S' thou a man diligent in his 2372
26: 12 S' thou a man wise in his own 7200
29: 20 S' thou a man that is hasty in his 2372
Ec 5: 8 thou s' the oppression of the poor, 7200
Isa 58: 3 fasted, say they, and thou s' not? "
7 when thou s' the naked, that thou "
Jer 1: 11 saying, Jeremiah, what s' thou? "
13 second time, saying, What s' thou? "
7: 17 S' thou not what they do in the "
20: 12 and s' the reins and the heart, let "
24: 3 unto me, What s' thou, Jeremiah? "
32: 24 to pass; and, behold, thou s' it. "
Eze 8: 6 Son of man, s' thou what they do? "
40: 4 declare all that thou s' to the house "
Da 1: 13 as thou s', deal with thy servants "
Am 7: 8 said unto me, Amos, what s' thou? "
8: 2 And he said, Amos, what s' thou? "
Zec 4: 2 And said unto me, What s' thou? "
5: 2 he said unto me, What s' thou? "
M'r 5: 31 s' the multitude thronging thee, 991
13: 2 him, S' thou these great buildings? "
Lu 7: 44 unto Simon, S' thou this woman? "
Ac 21: 20 him, Thou s', brother, how many 2334
Jas 2: 22 S' thou how faith wrought with his 991
Re 1: 11 What thou s', write in a book, and "

seeth See also FORSEETH.
Ge 16: 13 here looked after him that s' me? 7210
44: 31 when he s' that the lad is not with 7200
Ex 4: 14 when he s' thee, he will be glad in "
12: 23 he s' the blood upon the lintel, and "
Le 13: 20 when the priest s' it, behold, it be* "
De 32: 36 he s' that their power is gone, and "
1Sa 16: 7 him: for the Lord s' not as man "
7 not as man s'; for man looketh 7200
2Ki 2: 19 this city is pleasant, as my lord s': *2372
Job 8: 17 heap, and s' the place of stones. *2372
10: 4 of flesh? or seest thou as man s'? 7200
11: 11 he s' wickedness also; will he not "
22: 14 a covering to him, that he s' not; "
28: 10 his eye s' every precious thing. "
24 and s' under the whole heaven; "
34: 21 of man, and he s' all his goings. "
42: 5 the ear: but now mine eye s' thee. "
Ps 37: 13 for he s' that his day is coming. "
49: 10 he s' that wise men die, likewise "
58: 10 rejoice when he s' the vengeance: 2372
Ec 8: 16 neither day nor night s' sleep with 7200
Isa 21: 6 let him declare what he s'. "
28: 4 he that looketh upon it s', while it "
29: 15 the dark, and they say, Who s' us? "
23 when he s' his children, the work "
47: 10 thou hast said, None s' me. Thy "
Eze 8: 12 The Lord s' us not; the Lord hath "
9: 9 the earth, and the Lord s' not. "
12: 27 vision that he s' is for many days 2372
18: 14 s' all his father's sins which he 7200
33: 3 s' the sword come upon the land, "
39: 15 when any s' a man's bone, then "
M't 6: 4 and thy Father which s' in secret 991
6 thy Father which s' in secret shall "
18 which s' in secret, shall reward thee "
M'r 5: 38 s' the tumult, and them that wept *2334
Lu 16: 23 s' Abraham afar off, and Lazarus 3708
Joh 1: 29 John s' Jesus coming unto him, 991
5: 19 but what he s' the Father do: for "
6: 40 that every one which s' the Son, *2334
9: 21 means he now s', we know not; or 991

Joh 10: 12 s· the wolf coming, and leaveth *2334
11: 9 he s· the light of this world. * 991
12: 45 that s· me s· him that sent me. *2334
14: 17 it s· him not, neither knoweth him:* "
19 and the world s· me no more; but* "
20: 1 s· the stone taken away from the 991
6 sepulchre, and s· the linen clothes*2334
12 s· two angels in white sitting, the * "
21: 20 s· the disciple whom Jesus loved 991
Ro 8: 24 for what a man s·, why doth he "
2Co 12: 6 me above that which he s· me to be, "
1Jo 3: 17 and s· his brother have need. *2334

seethe See also SEETHING; SOD.
Ex 16: 23 to day, and s· that ye will s·; ‡1310
23: 19 not s· a kid in his mother's milk. ‡ "
29: 31 and s· his flesh in the holy place. ‡ "
34: 26 not s· a kid in his mother's milk. ‡ "
De 14: 21 not s· a kid in his mother's milk. ‡ "
2Ki 4: 38 and s· pottage for the sons of the ‡ "
Eze 24: 5 let them s· the bones of it therein.‡ "
Zec 14: 21 and take of them, and s· therein: ‡ "

seethed See SOD.

seething
1Sa 2: 13 came while the flesh was in s·, ‡1310
Job 41: 20 as out of a s· pot or caldron. ‡5301
Jer 1: 13 I see a s· pot; and the face thereof‡ "

Segub (*se'-gub*)
1Ki 16: 34 thereof in his youngest son S·. 7687
1Ch 2: 21 years old; and she bare him S·. "
22 And S· begat Jair, who had three "

Seir (*se'-ur*)
Ge 14: 6 And the Horites in their mount S·,8165
32: 3 his brother unto the land of S·, the "
33: 14 until I come unto my lord unto S·. "
16 that day on his way unto S·. "
36: 8 Thus dwelt Esau in mount S·: Esau "
9 father of the Edomites in mount S·: "
20 These are the sons of S· the Horite, "
21 children of S· in the land of Edom. "
30 among their dukes in the land of S·. "
Nu 24: 18 S· also shall be a possession for his "
De 1: 2 from Horeb by the way of mount S· "
44 as bees do, and destroyed you in S·, "
2: 1 we compassed mount S· many days. "
4 children of Esau, which dwell in S·; "
5 I have given mount S· unto Esau "
8 children of Esau, which dwelt in S·, "
12 Horims also dwelt in S· beforetime; "
22 children of Esau, which dwelt in S·, "
29 children of Esau which dwelt in S·, "
33: 2 and rose up from S· unto them; "
Jos 11: 17 mount Halak, that goeth up to S·, "
12: 7 mount Halak, that goeth up to S·; "
15: 10 Baalah westward unto mount S·, "
24: 4 and I gave unto Esau mount S·, to "
J'g 5: 4 Lord, when thou wentest out of S·, "
1Ch 1: 38 the sons of S·; Lotan, and Shobal, "
4: 42 five hundred men, went to mount S·, "
2Ch 20: 10 of Ammon and Moab and mount S·, "
22 of Ammon, Moab, and mount S·, "
23 the inhabitants of mount S·, "
23 an end of the inhabitants of S·, "
25: 11 of the children of S· ten thousand. "
14 the gods of the children of S·, "
Isa 21: 11 Dumah. He calleth to me out of S·, "
Eze 25: 8 Because that Moab and S· do say, "
35: 2 set thy face against mount S·, and "
3 Behold, O mount S·, I am against "
7 I make mount S· most desolate, "
15 thou shalt be desolate, O mount S·, "

Seirath (*se'-ur-ath*)
J'g 3: 26 the quarries, and escaped unto S·.*8167

seize See also SEIZED.
Jos 8: 7 the ambush, and s· upon the city: *3423
Job 3: 6 that night, let darkness s· upon it: 3947
Ps 55: 15 Let death s· upon them, and let *3451
M't 21: 38 and let us s· on his inheritance. *2722

seized
Jer 49: 24 to flee, and fear hath s· on her: 2388

Sela (*se'-lah*) See also SELAH; SELA-HAMMAH-LEKOTH.
Isa 16: 1 the land from S· to the wilderness,5554

Selah (*se'-lah*) See also JOKTHEEL; SELA.
2Ki 14: 7 and took S· by war, and called the*5554
Ps 3: 2 is no help for him in God. S·. 5542
4 heard me out of his holy hill. S·. "
8 blessing is upon thy people. S·. "
4: 2 vanity, and seek after leasing? S·. "
4 upon your bed, and be still. S·. "
7: 5 lay mine honour in the dust. S·. "
9: 16 of his own hands. Higgaion. S·. "
20 know themselves to be but men. S·. "
20: 3 and accept thy burnt sacrifice; S·. "
21: 2 the request of his lips. S·. "
24: 6 that seek thy face, O Jacob. S·. "
10 hosts, he is the King of glory. S·. "
32: 4 into the drought of summer. S·. "
5 forgavest the iniquity of my sin. S·. "
7 with songs of deliverance. S·. "
39: 5 best state is altogether vanity. S·. "
11 surely every man is vanity. S·. "
44: 8 and praise thy name for ever. S·. "
46: 3 shake with the swelling thereof. S·. "
7, 11 God of Jacob is our refuge. S·. "
47: 4 of Jacob whom he loved. S·. "
48: 8 God will establish it for ever. S·. "
49: 13 approve their sayings. S·. "
15 grave: for he shall receive me. S·. "
50: 6 for God is judge himself. S·. "
52: 3 than to speak righteousness. S·. "
5 out of the land of the living. S·. "
54: 3 have not set God before them. S·. "
Ps 55: 7 and remain in the wilderness. S· 5542
19 even he that abideth of old. S·. "
57: 3 him that would swallow me up. S·. "
6 they are fallen themselves. S·. "
59: 5 to any wicked transgressors. S·. "
13 unto the ends of the earth. S·. "
60: 4 displayed because of the truth. S·. "
61: 4 trust in the covert of thy wings. S·. "
62: 4 mouth, but they curse inwardly. S·. "
8 him: God is a refuge for us. S·. "
66: 4 they shall sing to thy name. S·. "
7 the rebellious exalt themselves. S·. "
15 I will offer bullocks with goats. S·. "
67: 1 cause his face to shine upon us; S·. "
4 govern the nations upon earth. S·. "
68: 7 march through the wilderness; S·: "
19 even the God of our salvation. S·. "
32 O sing praises unto the Lord; S·: "
75: 3 I bear up the pillars of it. S·. "
76: 3 and the sword, and the battle. S·. "
9 save all the meek of the earth. S·. "
77: 3 my spirit was overwhelmed. S·. "
9 shut up his tender mercies? S·. "
15 the sons of Jacob and Joseph. S·. "
81: 7 thee at the waters of Meribah. S·. "
82: 2 the persons of the wicked? S·. "
83: 8 holpen the children of Lot. S·. "
84: 4 they will be still praising thee. S·. "
8 give ear, O God of Jacob. S·. "
85: 2 thou hast covered all their sin. S·. "
87: 3 spoken of thee, O city of God. S·. "
6 that this man was born there. S·. "
88: 7 afflicted me with all thy waves. S·. "
10 the dead arise and praise thee? S·. "
89: 4 thy throne to all generations. S·. "
37 as a faithful witness in heaven. S·. "
45 hast covered him with shame. S·. "
48 from the hand of the grave? S·. "
140: 3 poison is under their lips. S·. "
5 they have set gins for me. S·. "
8 lest they exalt themselves. S·. "
143: 6 after thee, as a thirsty land. S·. "
Hab 3: 3 Holy One from mount Paran. S·. "
9 of the tribes, even thy word. S·. "
13 the foundation unto the neck. S·. "

Sela-hammahlekoth (*se''-lah-ham-mah'-le-koth*)
1Sa 23: 28 therefore they called that place S·.5555

Seled (*se'-led*)
1Ch 2: 30 sons of Nadab; S·, and Appaim: 5540
30 but S· died without children. "

Seleucia (*sel-u-si'-ah*)
Ac 13: 4 the Holy Ghost, departed unto S·; 4581

self See also HERSELF; HIMSELF; ITSELF; MYSELF; SELFSAME; SELFWILL; SELVEDGE; SELVES; THYSELF.
Ex 32: 13 to whom thou swarest by thine own s·,
Joh 5: 30 I can of mine own s· do nothing: 1683
17: 5 glorify thou me with thine own s· 4572
1Co 4: 3 yea, I judge not mine own s·. 1683
Ph'm 19 owest unto me even thine own s· 4572
1Pe 2: 24 Who his own s· bare our sins in his 846

selfsame
Ge 7: 13 In the s· day entered Noah, 2088,6106
17: 23 of their foreskin in the s· day, " "
26 in the s· day was Abraham " "
Ex 12: 17 this s· day have I brought your " "
41 even the s· day it came to pass, " "
51 And it came to pass the s· day, " "
Le 23: 14 s· day that ye have brought " "
21 ye shall proclaim on the s· day, " "
De 32: 48 spake unto Moses that s· day, " "
Jos 5: 11 and parched corn in the s· day. " "
Eze 40: 1 the s· day the hand of the Lord " "
M't 8: 13 servant was healed in the s· hour.*1565
1Co 12: 11 worketh that one and the s· Spirit,*846
2Co 5: 5 wrought us for the s· thing is *846,5124
7: 11 For behold this s· thing, that ye *846

selfwill See also SELFWILLED.
Ge 49: 6 their s· they digged down a wall. 7522

selfwilled
Tit 1: 7 not s·, not soon angry, not given to 829
2Pe 2: 10 Presumptuous are they, s·, they "

sell See also SELLEST; SELLETH; SOLD.
Ge 25: 31 said, S· me this day thy birthright.4376
37: 27 and let us s· him to the Ishmeelites, "
Ex 21: 7 s· his daughter to be a maidservant, "
8 to s· her unto a strange nation he "
35 then they shall s· the live ox, and "
22: 1 ox, or a sheep, and kill it, or s· it; "
Le 25: 14 thou s· ought unto thy neighbour, "
15 of the fruits he shall s· unto thee: "
16 of the fruits doth he s· unto thee. "
29 s· a dwelling house in a walled city, "
47 and s· himself unto the stranger or "
De 2: 28 Thou shalt s· me meat for money, 7666
14: 21 thou mayest s· it unto an alien: 4376
21: 14 shalt not s· her at all for money, "
J'g 4: 9 the Lord shall s· Sisera into the "
1Ki 21: 25 did s· himself to work wickedness "
2Ki 4: 7 Go, s· the oil, and pay thy debt, and "
Ne 5: 8 and will ye even s· your brethren? "
10: 31 victuals on the sabbath day to s·, "
Pr 23: 23 Buy the truth, and s· it not; also "
Eze 30: 12 s· the land into the hand of the "
48: 14 And they shall not s· of it, neither "
Joe 3: 8 And I will s· your sons and your "
8 they shall s· them to the Sabeans, "
Am 8: 5 be gone, that we may s· corn? 7666
6 yea, and s· the refuse of the wheat?"
Zec 11: 5 they that s· them say, Blessed be 4376
M't 19: 21 go and s· that thou hast, and give 4453
25: 9 go ye rather to them that s·, and "
M'r 10: 21 s· whatsoever thou hast, and give "
Lu 12: 33 S· that ye have, and give alms; 4453
18: 22 s· all that thou hast, and distribute "
22: 36 no sword, let him s· his garment, "
Jas 4: 13 and buy and s·, and get gain: *1710
Re 13: 17 that no man might buy or s·, save 4453

seller See also SELLERS.
Isa 24: 2 as with the buyer, so with the s·; 4376
Eze 7: 12 buyer rejoice, nor the s· mourn: "
13 For the s· shall not return to that "
Ac 16: 14 named Lydia, a s· of purple, 4211

sellers
Ne 13: 20 merchants and s· of all kinds of 4376

sellest
Ps 44: 12 Thou s· thy people for nought, 4376

selleth
Ex 21: 16 that stealeth a man, and s· him, 4376
De 24: 7 merchandise of him, or s· him; * "
Ru 4: 3 s· a parcel of land, which was our "
Pr 11: 26 upon the head of him that s· it. 7666
31: 24 She maketh fine linen, and s· it; 4376
Na 3: 4 s· nations through her whoredoms, "
M't 13: 44 goeth and s· all that he hath, and 4453

selvedge
Ex 26: 4 from the s· in the coupling; and 7098
36: 11 from the s· in the coupling: "

selves See also OURSELVES; THEMSELVES; YOURSELVES.
Lu 21: 30 own s· that summer is now nigh 1438
Ac 20: 30 Also of your own s· shall men arise,846
2Co 8: 5 first gave their own s· to the Lord, 1438
13: 5 be in the faith; prove your own s·. "
5 Know ye not your own s·, how that "
2Ti 3: 2 men shall be lovers of their own s·,*5367
Jas 1: 22 hearers only, deceiving...own s·. 846

Sem (*sem*) See also SHEM.
Lu 3: 36 which was the son of S·, which *4590

Semachiah (*sem-a-ki'-ah*)
1Ch 26: 7 were strong men, Elihu, and S·. 5565

semblance See RESEMBLANCE.

Semei (*sem'-e-i*) See also SHEMAIAH.
Lu 3: 26 which was the son of S·, which *4584

Senaah (*sen'-a-ah*) See also HASSENAAH.
Ezr 2: 35 The children of S·, three thousand5570
Ne 7: 38 The children of S·, three thousand "

senate
Ac 5: 21 all the s· of the children of Israel, 1087

senators
Ps 105: 22 pleasure; and teach his s· wisdom.2205

send See also SENDEST; SENDETH; SENDING; SENT.
Ge 24: 7 he shall s· his angel before thee, 7971
12 thee, s· me good speed this day, 7136
40 will s· his angel with thee, and 7971
54 said, S· me away unto my master. "
56 s· me away that I may go to my "
27: 45 then I will s·, and fetch thee from "
30: 25 s· me away, that I may go unto "
37: 13 come, and I will s· thee unto them. "
38: 17 I will s· thee a kid from the flock. "
17 thou give me a pledge, till thou s· it? "
42: 16 S· one of you, and let him fetch "
43: 4 If thou wilt s· our brother with us, "
5 But if thou wilt not s· him, we will "
8 S· the lad with me, and we will "
14 he may s· away your other brother,* "
45: 5 For God did s· me before you to "
Ex 3: 10 I will s· thee unto Pharaoh, that "
4: 13 he said, O my Lord, s·, I pray thee, "
13 the hand of him whom thou wilt s·. "
7: 2 that he s· the children of Israel out* "
8: 21 I will s· swarms of flies upon thee, "
9: 14 will at this time s· all my plagues "
19 S· therefore now, and gather thy "
12: 33 they might s· them out of the land "
23: 20 I s· an Angel before thee, to keep "
27 I will s· my fear before thee, and "
28 And I will s· hornets before thee, "
33: 2 And I will s· an angel before thee; "
12 know whom thou wilt s· with me. "
Le 16: 21 shall s· him away by the hand of a "
26: 22 will also s· wild beasts among you, "
25 I will s· the pestilence among you; "
36 I will s· a faintness into their 935
Nu 13: 2 S· thou men, that may search the 7971
2 of their fathers shall ye s· a man, "
22: 37 earnestly s· unto thee to call thee? "
31: 4 of Israel, shall ye s· to the war. "
De 1: 22 We will s· men before us, and they "
7: 20 the Lord thy God will s· the hornet "
11: 15 I will s· grass in thy fields for thy 5414
19: 12 elders...shall s· and fetch him 7971
24: 1 hand, and s· her out of his house, "
28: 20 The Lord shall s· upon the cursing, "
48 which the Lord shall s· against thee, "
32: 24 s· the teeth of beasts upon them, "
Jos 18: 4 I will s· them, and they shall rise, "
J'g 13: 8 thou didst s· come again unto us, "
1Sa 5: 11 S· away the ark of the God of Israel, "
6: 2 wherewith we shall s· it to his place, "
3 s· away the ark of the God of Israel, "
3 s· it not empty; but in any wise "
8 and s· it away, that it may go. "
9: 16 I will s· thee a man out of the land "
26 saying, Up, that I may s· thee away. "
11: 3 we may s· messengers unto all the "
12: 17 and he shall s· thunder and rain; 5414
16: 1 s· thee to Jesse the Beth-lehemite: 7971
11 said unto Jesse, S· and fetch him: "
19 S· me David thy son, which is with "
20: 12 I then s· not unto thee, and shew

1Sa 20: 13 will shew it thee, and s' thee away,7971
21 I will s' a lad, saying, Go, find out. "
31 now s' and fetch him unto me, for "
21: 2 the business whereabout I s' thee, "
25: 25 men of my lord, whom thou didst s'." "
2Sa 11: 6 saying, S' me Uriah the Hittite. "
14: 32 that I may s' thee to the king, to "
15: 36 by them ye shall s' unto me every "
17: 16 Now therefore s' quickly, and tell "
1Ki 8: 44 whithersoever thou shalt s' them, "
18: 1 and I will s' rain upon the earth. 5414
19 s', and gather to me all Israel unto7971
20: 6 Yet I will s' my servants unto thee "
9 that thou didst s' for to thy servant "
34 s' thee away with this covenant. * "
2Ki 2: 16 valley. And he said, Ye shall not s'." "
17 till he was ashamed, he said, S'. "
4: 22 S' me, I pray thee, one of the young "
5: 5 s' a letter unto the king of Israel. "
7 doth s' unto me to recover a man "
6: 13 he is, that I may s' and fetch him. "
7: 13 consumed:) and let us s' and see. "
9: 17 an horseman, and s' to meet them, "
15: 37 the Lord began to s' against Judah "
19: 7 I will s' a blast upon him, and he *5414
1Ch 13: 2 let us s' abroad unto our brethren 7971
2Ch 2: 3 and didst s' him cedars to build him "
7 S' me now therefore a man cunning "
8 S' me also cedar trees, fir trees, "
15 of, let him s' unto his servants: "
6: 27 s' rain upon thy land, which thou 5414
34 the way that thou shalt s' them, 7971
7: 13 if I s' pestilence among my people; "
28: 16 Ahaz s' unto the kings of Assyria "
32: 9 king of Assyria s' his servants to "
Ezr 5: 17 let the king s' his pleasure to us 7972
Ne 2: 5 thou wouldest s' me unto Judah, 7971
6 So it pleased the king to s' me; "
8: 10 s' portions unto them for whom "
12 and to drink, and to s' portions, "
Job 21: 11 They s' forth their little ones like "
38: 35 Canst thou s' lightnings, that they "
Ps 20: 2 S' thee help from the sanctuary, "
43: 3 O s' out thy light and thy truth: "
57: 3 He shall s' from heaven, and save "
3 God shall s' forth his mercy and his "
68: 9 O God, didst s' a plentiful rain, 5130
33 lo, he doth s' out his voice, and *5414
110: 2 shall s' the rod of thy strength 7971
118: 25 I beseech thee, s' now prosperity. "
144: 7 S' thine hand from above; rid me,*7971
Pr 10: 26 is the sluggard to them that s' him. "
22: 21 of truth to them that s' unto thee? "
25: 13 messenger to them that s' him: "
Ec 10: 1 to s' forth a stinking savour: 5042
Isa 6: 8 Whom shall I s', and who will go 7971
8 Then said I, Here am I; s' me. "
10: 6 I will s' him against an hypocritical "
16 s' among his fat ones leanness; "
16: 1 S' ye the lamb to the ruler of the "
19: 20 and he shall s' them a saviour, and "
32: 20 s' forth thither the feet of the ox "
37: 7 I will s' a blast upon him, and he * "
57: 9 and didst s' thy messengers far off, "
66: 19 I will s' those that escape of them "
Jer 1: 7 shalt go to all that I shall s' thee, "
2: 10 and s' unto Kedar, and consider "
8: 17 I will s' serpents, cockatrices, "
9: 16 and I will s' a sword after them, till "
17 and s' for cunning women, that they "
16: 16 I will s' for many fishers, saith the "
16 and after will I s' for many hunters, "
24: 10 I will s' the sword, the famine, and "
25: 9 I will s' and take all the families of "
15 all the nations, to whom I s' thee, "
16 sword that I will s' among them. "
27 sword which I will s' among you. "
27: 3 And s' them to the king of Edom, "
29: 17 I will s' upon them the sword, the "
31 S' to all them of the captivity, "
42: 5 the Lord thy God shall s' thee to us. "
6 Lord our God, to whom we s' thee; "
43: 10 I will s' and take Nebuchadrezzar "
48: 12 that I will s' unto him wanderers, "
49: 37 and I will s' the sword after them, "
51: 2 And will s' unto Babylon fanners, "
Eze 2: 3 I s' thee to the children of Israel, "
4 I do s' thee unto them; and thou "
5: 16 shall s' upon them the evil arrows "
16 and which I will s' to destroy you: "
17 So will I s' upon you famine and "
7: 3 and I will s' mine anger upon thee, "
14: 13 and will s' famine upon it, and will "
19 Or if I s' a pestilence into that land, "
21 When I s' my four sore judgments "
28: 23 For I will s' into her pestilence, and "
39: 6 And I will s' a fire on Magog, and "
Ho 8: 14 but I will s' a fire upon his cities, "
Joe 2: 19 I will s' you corn, and wine, and oil, "
Am 1: 4 s' a fire into the house of Hazael, "
7 I will s' a fire on the wall of Gaza, "
10 I will s' a fire on the wall of Tyrus, "
12 But I will s' a fire upon Teman, "
2: 2 But I will s' a fire upon Moab, and "
5 But I will s' a fire upon Judah, and "
8: 11 that I will s' a famine in the land, "
Mal 2: 2 I will even s' a curse upon you, and "
3: 1 Behold, I will s' my messenger, "
4: 5 I will s' you Elijah the prophet "
M't 9: 38 s' forth labourers into his harvest. 1544
10: 16 I s' you forth as sheep in the midst 649
34 I am come to s' peace on earth: 906
34 I come not to s' peace, but a sword. "
11: 10 I s' my messenger before thy face, 649
12: 20 he s' forth judgment unto victory. 1544
13: 41 Son of man shall s' forth his angels, 649
M't 14: 15 s' the multitude away, that they 630
15: 23 S' her away; for she crieth after us. "
32 I will not s' them away fasting, lest "
21: 3 and straightway he will s' them. 649
23: 34 behold, I s' unto you prophets, and "
24: 31 he shall s' his angels with a great "
M'r 1: 2 I s' my messenger before thy face, "
3: 14 he might s' them forth to preach, "
5: 10 that he would not s' them away out "
12 S' us into the swine, that we may 3992
6: 7 to s' them forth by two and two; 649
36 S' them away, that they may go 630
8: 3 if I s' them away fasting to their "
11: 3 straightway he will s' him hither. 649
12: 13 s' unto him certain of the Pharisees "
13: 27 then shall he s' his angels, and shall "
Lu 7: 27 I s' my messenger before thy face, "
9: 12 S' the multitude away, that they 630
10: 2 s' forth labourers into his harvest. 1544
3 s' you forth as lambs among wolves. 649
11: 49 I will s' them prophets and apostles, "
12: 49 I am come to s' fire on the earth; *906
16: 24 s' Lazarus, that he may dip the tip 3992
27 s' him to my father's house: "
20: 13 I will s' my beloved son: it may be "
24: 49 I s' the promise of my Father upon 649
Joh 13: 20 whomsoever I s' receiveth me; 3992
14: 26 whom the Father will s' in my name, "
15: 26 I will s' unto you from the Father, "
16: 7 but if I depart, I will s' him unto you. "
17: 8 have believed that thou didst s' me. 649
20: 21 hath sent me, even so s' I you. 3992
Ac 3: 20 And he shall s' Jesus Christ, which 649
7: 34 now come, I will s' thee into Egypt. "
35 the same did God s' to be a ruler * "
10: 5 s' men to Joppa, and call for one 3992
22 angel to s' for thee into his house, 3343
32 S' therefore to Joppa, and call "
11: 13 S' men to Joppa, and call for Simon, 649
29 s' relief unto the brethren which 3992
15: 22 s' chosen men of their own company "
23 and elders and brethren s' greeting* "
25 to s' chosen men unto you with our 3992
22: 21 for I will s' thee far hence unto the 1821
25: 3 he would s' for him to Jerusalem, 3343
21 be kept till I might s' him to Cæsar. 3992
25 Augustus, I...determined to s' him. "
27 to me unreasonable to s' a prisoner,*"
26: 17 Gentiles, unto whom now I s' thee, 649
1Co 16: 3 will I s' to bring your liberality 3992
Ph'p 2: 19 to s' Timotheus shortly unto you, "
23 Him...I hope to s' presently, so "
25 necessary to s' to you Epaphroditus, "
2Th 2: 11 God shall s' them strong delusion,* "
Tit 3: 12 When I shall s' Artemas unto thee, "
Jas 3: 11 fountain s' forth at the same time 1032
Re 1: 11 s' it unto the seven churches 3992
11: 10 and shall s' gifts one to another; "

sendest
De 15: 13 thou s' him out free from thee, *7971
18 thou s' him away free from thee; * "
Jos 1: 16 whithersoever thou s' us, we will "
2Ki 1: 6 thou s' to enquire of Baal-zebub "
Job 14: 20 his continuance, and s' him away. "
Ps 104: 30 Thou s' forth thy spirit, they are "

sendeth
De 24: 3 hand, and s' her out of his house;*7971
1Ki 17: 14 until the day that the Lord s' rain5414
Job 5: 10 and s' waters upon the fields: 7971
12: 15 he s' them out, and they overturn "
Ps 104: 10 He s' the springs into the valleys, "
147: 15 He s' forth his commandment upon "
18 He s' out his word, and melteth "
Pr 26: 6 s' a message by the hand of a fool "
Ca 1: 12 my spikenard s' forth the smell *5414
Isa 18: 2 That s' ambassadors by the sea, 7971
M't 5: 45 and s' rain on the just and on the 1026
M'r 11: 1 he s' forth two of his disciples, 649
14: 13 And he s' forth two of his disciples, "
Lu 14: 32 he s' an ambassage, and desireth "
Ac 23: 26 excellent governor Felix s' greeting.*

sending
2Sa 13: 16 this evil in s' me away is greater *7971
2Ch 36: 15 rising up betimes, and s'; because "
Es 9: 19 and of s' portions one to another. 4916
22 and of s' portions one to another, "
Ps 78: 49 by s' evil angels among them. *4917
Isa 7: 25 it shall be for the s' forth of oxen, 4916
Jer 7: 25 daily rising up early and s' them: 7971
25: 4 prophets, rising early and s' them; "
26: 5 both rising up early, and s' them, "
29: 19 rising up early and s' them; "
35: 15 rising up early and s' them, "
44: 4 prophets, rising early and s' them, "
Eze 17: 15 in s' his ambassadors into Egypt, "
Ro 8: 3 God s' his own Son in the likeness 3992

Seneh (*se'-neh*)
1Sa 14: 4 and the name of the other S'. 5573

Senir (*se'-nur*) See also SHENIR.
1Ch 5: 23 Bashan unto Baal-hermon and S', 8149
Eze 27: 5 thy ship boards of fir trees of S': "

Sennacherib (*sen-nak'-er-ib*)
2Ki 18: 13 did S' king of Assyria come up 5576
19: 16 and hear the words of S', which "
20 thou hast prayed to me against S' "
36 So S' king of Assyria departed, "
2Ch 32: 1 S' king of Assyria came, and "
2 Hezekiah saw that S' was come, "
9 this did S' king of Assyria send his "
10 Thus saith S' king of Assyria, "
22 the hand of S' the king of Assyria, "
Isa 36: 1 that S' king of Assyria came up "
Isa 37: 17 and hear all the words of S', which 5576
21 thou hast prayed to me against S' "
37 So S' king of Assyria departed, "

sense See also SENSES.
Ne 8: 8 of God distinctly, and gave the s', 7922

senses
Heb 5: 14 have their s' exercised to discern 145

sensual
Jas 3: 15 above, but is earthly, s', devilish. 5591
Jude 19 s', having not the Spirit.

sent See also ASSENT; CONSENT; PRESENT-SENTEST.
Ge 3: 23 the Lord God s' him forth from 7971
8: 7 And he s' forth a raven, which went "
8 And he s' forth a dove from him, to "
10 again he s' forth the dove out of the "
12 s' forth the dove; which returned "
12: 20 and they s' him away, and his wife,* "
19: 13 the Lord hath s' us to destroy it. "
29 and s' Lot out of the midst of the "
20: 2 and Abimelech king of Gerar s', and "
21: 14 the child, and s' her away: and she "
24: 59 they s' away Rebekah their sister, "
25: 6 s' them away from Isaac his son, "
26: 27 me, and have s' me away from you? "
29 and have s' thee away in peace: "
31 and Isaac s' them away, and they "
27: 42 she s' and called Jacob her younger "
28: 5 And Isaac s' away Jacob: and he "
6 and s' him away to Padan-aram, "
31: 4 And Jacob s' and called Rachel and "
27 might have s' thee away with mirth, "
42 thou hadst s' me away now empty. "
32: 3 Jacob s' messengers before him to "
5 and I have s' to tell my lord, that I "
18 is a present s' unto my lord Esau: "
23 he took them, and s' them over 5674
23 brook, and s' over all that he had. "
37: 14 s' him out of the vale of Hebron, 7971
32 they s' the coat of many colours, "
38: 20 Judah s' the kid by the hand of his "
23 I s' this kid, and thou hast not found "
25 she s' to her father in law, saying, "
41: 8 s' and called for all the magicians "
14 then Pharaoh s' and called Joseph, "
42: 4 Jacob s' not with his brethren; "
43: 34 he took and s' messes unto them "
44: 3 was light, the men were s' away, "
45: 7 God s' me before you to preserve "
8 it was not you that s' me hither, "
23 And to his father he s' after this "
24 So he s' his brethren away, and "
27 the wagons which Joseph had s' to "
46: 5 the wagons which Pharaoh had s' "
28 s' Judah before him unto Joseph, "
50: 16 they s' a messenger unto Joseph, "
Ex 2: 5 flags, she s' her maid to fetch it. 7971
3: 12 token unto thee, that I have s' thee: "
13 God of your fathers hath s' me "
14 of Israel, I Am hath s' me unto you. "
15 God of Jacob, hath s' me unto you: "
4: 28 words of the Lord who had s' him, "
5: 22 why is it that thou hast s' me? "
7: 16 Lord God of the Hebrews hath s' me "
9: 7 And Pharaoh s', and, behold, there "
23 and the Lord s' thunder and hail, 5414
27 Pharaoh s', and called for Moses 7971
18: 2 wife, after he had s' her back, 7964
24: 5 he s' young men of the children of7971
Nu 13: 3 s' them from the wilderness of "
16 which Moses s' to spy out the land. "
17 Moses s' them to spy out the land "
14: 36 which Moses s' to search the land, "
16: 12 And Moses s' to call Dathan and "
28 shall know that the Lord hath s' me "
29 men; then the Lord hath not s' me. "
20: 14 Moses s' messengers from Kadesh "
16 he heard our voice, and s' an angel, "
21: 6 Lord s' fiery serpents among the "
21 Israel s' messengers unto Sihon "
32 And Moses s' to spy out Jaazer, "
22: 5 He s' messengers...unto Balaam "
10 king of Moab, hath s' unto me, "
15 And Balak s' yet again princes, "
40 oxen and sheep, and s' to Balaam, "
31: 6 And Moses s' them to the war, a "
32: 8 s' them from Kadesh-barnea to see "
De 2: 26 s' messengers out of the wilderness "
9: 23 Lord s' you from Kadesh-barnea, "
24: 4 former husband, which s' her away, "
34: 11 which the Lord s' him to do in the "
Jos 2: 1 s' out of Shittim two men to spy "
3 the king of Jericho s' unto Rahab, "
21 And she s' them away, and they "
6: 17 she hid the messengers that we s'. "
25 which Joshua s' to spy out Jericho. "
7: 2 Joshua s' men from Jericho to Ai, "
22 So Joshua s' messengers, and they "
8: 3 valour, and s' them away by night. "
9 Joshua therefore s' them forth: "
10: 3 king of Jerusalem s' unto Hoham "
6 the men of Gibeon s' unto Joshua "
11: 1 that he s' to Jobab king of Madon, "
14: 7 s' me from Kadesh-barnea to espy "
11 I was in the day that Moses s' me: "
22: 6 blessed them, and s' them away: "
7 And when Joshua s' them away also "
13 s' unto the children of Reuben, "
24: 5 I s' Moses also and Aaron, and I "
9 and s' and called Balaam the son "
12 And I s' the hornet before you, "
J'g 1: 23 of Joseph s' to descry Beth-el.
3: 15 Israel s' a present unto Eglon 7971
18 he s' away the people that bare the "

J'g 4: 6 she s' and called Barak the son of 7971
5: 15 he was s' on foot into the valley. * "
6: 8 Lord s' a prophet unto the children "
14 the Midianites: have not I s' thee? "
35 he s' messengers throughout all "
35 he s' messengers unto Asher, and "
7: 8 he s' all the rest of Israel every "
24 Gideon s' messengers throughout "
9: 23 Then God s' an evil spirit between "
31 he s' messengers unto Abimelech "
11: 12 Jephthah s' messengers unto the "
14 Jephthah s' messengers again unto "
17 Israel s' messengers unto the king "
17 they s' unto the king of Moab: but "
19 Israel s' messengers unto Sihon "
28 words of Jephthah which he s' him. "
38 And he s' her away for two months: "
12: 9 daughters, whom he s' abroad, "
16: 18 she s' and called for the lords of "
18: 2 children of Dan s' of their family "
19: 29 s' her into all the coast of Israel. "
20: 6 s' her throughout all the country "
12 tribes of Israel s' men through all "
21: 10 the congregation s' thither twelve "
13 congregation s' some to speak to "
1Sa 4: 4 So the people s' to Shiloh, that "
5: 8 s' therefore and gathered all the "
10 they s' the ark of God to Ekron. "
11 s' and gathered together all...lords "
6: 21 s' messengers to the inhabitants "
10: 25 And Samuel s' all the people away. "
11: 7 s' them throughout all the coasts of "
12: 8 then the Lord s' Moses and Aaron, "
11 the Lord s' Jerubbaal, and Bedan, "
18 Lord s' thunder and rain that day: 5414
13: 2 people he s' every man to his tent. 7971
15: 1 The Lord s' me to anoint thee to be "
18 the Lord s' thee on a journey, and "
20 gone the way which the Lord s' me, "
16: 12 he s', and brought him in. Now he "
19 Saul s' messengers unto Jesse, and "
20 s' them by David his son unto Saul. "
22 Saul s' to Jesse, saying, Let David, "
17: 31 before Saul: and he s' for him. 3947
18: 5 out whithersoever Saul s' him, 7971
19: 11 s' messengers unto David's house, "
14 Saul s' messengers to take David, "
15 Saul s' the messengers again to "
17 s' away mine enemy, that he is * "
20 Saul s' messengers to take David: "
21 told Saul, he s' other messengers, "
21 Saul s' messengers again the third "
20: 22 for the Lord hath s' thee away. "
22: 11 the king s' to call Ahimelech the "
25: 5 And David s' out ten young men, "
14 David s' messengers out of the "
32 which s' thee this day to meet me: "
39 And David s' and communed with "
40 David s' us unto thee, to take thee "
26: 4 David therefore s' out spies, and "
30: 26 he s' of the spoil unto the elders of "
31: 9 s' into the land of the Philistines "
2Sa 2: 5 David s' messengers unto the men "
3: 12 Abner s' messengers to David on "
14 David s' messengers to Ish-bosheth "
15 Ish-bosheth s', and took her from "
21 David s' Abner away; and he went "
22 for he had s' him away, and he was "
23 to the king, and he hath s' him away, "
24 is it that thou hast s' him away, "
26 he s' messengers after Abner, "
5: 11 Hiram king of Tyre s' messengers "
8: 10 Toi s' Joram...unto king David, "
9: 5 Then king David s', and fetched "
10: 2 And David s' to comfort him by the "
3 he hath s' comforters unto thee? "
3 not David rather s' his servants "
4 to their buttocks, and s' them away. "
5 he s' to meet them, because the "
6 children of Ammon s' and hired "
7 when David heard of it, he s' Joab. "
16 Hadarezer s', and brought out the "
11: 1 that David s' Joab, and his servants "
3 And David s' and enquired after the "
4 David s' messengers, and took her; "
5 s' and told David, and said, I am "
6 David s' to Joab, saying, Send me "
6 And Joab s' Uriah to David. "
14 and s' it by the hand of Uriah. "
18 Then Joab s' and told David all the "
22 David all that Joab had s' him for. "
27 David s' and fetched her to his "
12: 1 the Lord s' Nathan unto David. "
25 he s' by the hand of Nathan the "
27 And Joab s' messengers to David, "
13: 7 David s' home to Tamar, saying, "
14: 2 And Joab s' to Tekoah, and fetched "
29 Therefore Absalom s' for Joab, to "
29 when he s' again the second time, "
32 I s' unto thee, saying, Come hither, "
15: 10 Absalom s' spies throughout all "
12 And Absalom s' for Ahithophel the "
18: 2 David s' forth a third part of the "
29 When Joab s' the king's servant, "
19: 11 And king David s' to Zadok and to "
14 they s' this word unto the king, "
22: 15 he s' out arrows, and scattered "
17 He s' from above, he took me; he "
24: 13 I shall return to him that s' me. "
15 So the Lord s' a pestilence upon 5414
1Ki 1: 44 the king hath s' with him Zadok 7971
53 So king Solomon s', and they "
2: 25 Solomon s' by the hand of Benaiah "
29 Then Solomon s' Benaiah the son of "
36, 42 king s' and called for Shimei, "
5: 1 Hiram king of Tyre s' his servants "

1Ki 5: 2 And Solomon s' to Hiram, saying, 7971
8 Hiram s' to Solomon, saying, I have "
14 And he s' them to Lebanon, ten "
7: 13 And king Solomon s' and fetched "
8: 66 eighth day he s' the people away: "
9: 14 And Hiram s' to the king sixscore "
27 Hiram s' in the navy his servants, "
12: 3 That they s' and called him. And "
18 Then king Rehoboam s' Adoram, "
20 they s' and called him unto the "
14: 6 am s' to thee with heavy tidings. "
15: 18 king Asa s' them to Ben-hadad, the "
19 have s' unto thee a present of silver "
20 s' the captains of the hosts which "
18: 10 my lord hath not s' to seek thee: "
20 Ahab s' unto all the children of "
19: 2 Jezebel s' a messenger unto Elijah, "
20: 2 he s' messengers to Ahab king of "
5 Although I have s' unto thee, "
7 for he s' unto me for my wives, and "
10 Ben-hadad s' unto him, and said, "
17 Ben-hadad s' out, and they told "
34 with him, and s' him away. * "
21: 8 s' the letters unto the elders and to "
11 did as Jezebel had s' unto them, "
11 letters which she had s' unto them. "
14 Then they s' to Jezebel, saying, "
2Ki 1: 2 he s' messengers, and said unto "
6 again unto the king that s' you, "
9 the king s' unto him a captain of "
11 he s' unto him another captain of "
13 he s' again a captain of the third "
16 thou has s' messengers to enquire "
2: 2 for the Lord hath s' me to Beth-el. "
4 for the Lord hath s' me to Jericho. "
6 for the Lord hath s' me to Jordan. "
17 They s' therefore fifty men; and "
3: 7 he went and s' to Jehoshaphat the "
5: 6 therewith s' Naaman my servant "
8 his clothes, that he s' to the king, "
10 Elisha s' a messenger unto him, "
22 My master hath s' me, saying, "
6: 9 the man of God s' unto the king of "
10 the king of Israel s' to the place "
14 Therefore s' he thither horses, and "
23 eaten and drunk, he s' them away, "
32 the king s' a man from before him: "
32 how this son of a murderer hath s' "
7: 14 king s' after the host of the Syrians, "
8: 9 king of Syria hath s' me to thee, "
9: 19 he s' out a second on horseback, "
10: 1 wrote letters, and s' to Samaria, "
5 elders also,...s' to Jehu, saying, "
7 baskets, and s' him them to Jezreel. "
21 Jehu s' through all Israel: and all "
11: 4 Jehoiada s' and fetched the rulers "
12: 18 and s' it to Hazael king of Syria: "
14: 8 Amaziah s' messengers to Jehoash, "
9 the king of Israel s' to Amaziah "
9 s' to the cedar that was in Lebanon, "
19 but they s' after him to Lachish, "
16: 7 So Ahaz s' messengers to "
8 and s' it for a present to the king of "
10 king Ahaz s' to Urijah the priest "
11 king Ahaz had s' from Damascus: "
17: 4 he had s' messengers to So king of "
13 which I s' to you by my servants "
25 Lord s' lions among them, which "
26 he hath s' lions among them, and, "
18: 14 king of Judah s' to the king of "
17 the king of Assyria s' Tartan and "
27 my master s' me to thy master, and "
27 hath he not s' me to the men which "
19: 2 he s' Eliakim, which was over the 7971
4 hath s' to reproach the living God; "
9 s' messengers again unto Hezekiah, "
16 s' him to reproach the living God. "
20 the son of Amoz s' to Hezekiah, "
20: 12 Babylon, s' letters and a present "
22: 3 that the king s' Shaphan the son of "
15 Tell the man that s' you to me, "
18 which s' you to enquire of the Lord, "
23: 1 And the king s', and they gathered "
16 and s', and took the bones out of "
24: 2 Lord s' against him bands of the "
2 s' them against Judah to destroy it, "
1Ch 8: 8 Moab, after he had s' them away; "
10: 9 s' into the land of the Philistines "
12: 19 upon advisement s' him away, "
14: 1 Hiram king of Tyre s' messengers "
18: 10 s' Hadoram his son to king David, "
19: 2 David s' messengers to comfort him "
3 he hath s' comforters unto thee? "
4 their buttocks, and s' them away. "
5 he s' to meet them: for the men "
6 s' a thousand talents of silver to "
8 when David heard of it, he s' Joab, "
16 they s' messengers, and drew forth "
21: 12 shall bring again to him that s' me. "
14 Lord s' pestilence upon Israel: 5414
15 God s' an angel unto Jerusalem to 7971
2Ch 2: 3 Solomon s' to Huram the king of "
11 in writing, which he s' to Solomon, "
13 And now I have s' a cunning man, "
7: 10 s' the people away into their tents, "
8: 18 Huram s' him by the hands of his "
10: 3 And they s' and called him. So "
18 Then king Rehoboam s' Hadoram "
16: 2 and s' to Ben-hadad king of Syria, "
3 I have s' thee silver and gold; go, "
4 s' the captains of his armies against "
17: 7 year of his reign he s' to his princes, "
8 And with them he s' Levites, even* "
24: 19 he s' prophets to them, to bring 7971
23 and s' all the spoil of them unto the "
25: 13 the army which Amaziah s' back, 7725

2Ch 25: 15 he s' unto him a prophet, which 7971
17 s' to Joash, the son of Jehoahaz, "
18 Joash king of Israel s' to Amaziah "
18 s' to the cedar that was in Lebanon, "
27 but they s' to Lachish after him, "
30: 1 And Hezekiah s' to all Israel and "
32: 21 the Lord s' an angel, which cut off "
31 who s' unto him to enquire of the "
34: 8 he s' Shaphan the son of Azaliah, "
23 Tell ye the man that s' you to me, "
26 who s' you to enquire of the Lord, "
29 the king s' and gathered together "
35: 21 he s' ambassadors to him, saying, "
36: 10 Nebuchadnezzar s', and brought "
15 God of their fathers s' to them by "
Ezr 4: 11 copy of the letter that they s' unto 7972
14 have we s' and certified the king; "
17 s' the king an answer unto Rehum "
18 The letter which ye s' unto us hath "
5: 6 the river, s' unto Darius the king: "
7 They s' a letter unto him, wherein "
6: 13 that which Darius the king had s', "
7: 14 as thou art s' of the king, and of "
8: 16 Then s' I for Eliezer, for Ariel, for 7971
17 I s' them with commandment unto 6680
Ne 2: 9 Now the king had s' captains of 7971
6: 2 Sanballat and Geshem s' unto me, "
3 I s' messengers unto them, saying, "
4 they s' unto me four times after "
5 Then s' Sanballat his servant unto "
8 Then I s' unto him, saying, There "
12 I perceived that God had not s' him; "
17 nobles of Judah s' many letters 1980
19 And Tobiah s' letters to put me in 7971
Es 1: 22 For he s' letters into all the king's "
3: 13 letters were s' by posts into all the "
4: 4 she s' raiment to clothe Mordecai, "
5: 10 he s' and called for his friends, and "
8: 10 and s' letters by posts on horseback, "
9: 20 and s' letters unto all the Jews that "
30 he s' the letters unto all the Jews, "
Job 1: 4 s' and called for their three sisters "
5 that Job s' and sanctified them, "
22: 9 Thou hast s' widows away empty, "
39: 5 Who hath s' out the wild ass free? "
Ps 18: 14 Yea, he s' out his arrows, and "
16 He s' from above, he took me, he "
59: *title* when Saul s', and they watched "
77: 17 the skies s' out a sound: thine 5414
78: 25 food: he s' them meat to the full. 7971
45 s' divers sorts of flies among them, "
80: 11 She s' out her boughs unto the sea, "
105: 17 He s' a man before them, even "
20 The king s' and loosed him; even "
26 He s' Moses his servant; and Aaron "
28 He s' darkness, and made it dark; "
106: 15 but s' leanness into their soul. "
107: 20 He s' his word, and healed them, * "
111: 9 He s' redemption unto his people: "
135: 9 Who s' tokens and wonders into the "
Pr 9: 3 She hath s' forth her maidens: she "
17: 11 messenger shall be s' against him. "
Isa 9: 8 The Lord s' a word into Jacob, and "
20: 1 Sargon the king of Assyria s' him,) "
36: 2 king of Assyria s' Rabshakeh from "
12 my master s' me to thy master "
12 hath he not s' me to the men that "
37: 2 And he s' Eliakim, who was over 7971
4 hath s' to reproach the living God, "
9 it, he s' messengers to Hezekiah, "
17 hath s' to reproach the living God. "
21 the son of Amoz s' unto Hezekiah, "
39: 1 s' letters and a present to Hezekiah: "
42: 19 or deaf, as my messenger that I s'? "
43: 14 For your sake I have s' to Babylon, "
48: 16 God, and his Spirit, hath s' me. "
55: 11 prosper in the thing whereto I s' it. "
61: 1 s' me to bind up the brokenhearted, "
Jer 7: 25 even s' unto you all my servants the "
14: 3 their nobles have s' their little ones* "
14 I s' them not, neither have I "
15 I s' them not, yet they say, Sword "
19: 14 the Lord had s' him to prophesy; "
21: 1 king Zedekiah s' unto him Pashur "
23: 21 I have not s' these prophets, yet "
32 yet I s' them not, nor commanded "
38 I have s' unto you, saying, Ye shall "
24: 5 whom I have s' out of this place "
25: 4 hath s' unto you all his servants the "
17 unto whom the Lord had s' me: "
26: 5 the prophets, whom I s' unto you,* "
12 The Lord s' me to prophesy against "
15 Lord hath s' me unto you to speak "
22 king s' men into Egypt, namely, "
27: 15 I have not s' them, saith the Lord, "
28: 9 that the Lord hath truly s' him. "
15 The Lord hath not s' thee; but thou "
29: 1 the prophet s' from Jerusalem unto "
3 king of Judah s' unto Babylon to "
9 I have not s' them, saith the Lord. "
19 I s' unto them by my servants the "
20 whom I have s' from Jerusalem to "
25 Because thou hast s' letters in thy "
28 therefore he s' unto us in Babylon, "
31 I s' him not, and he caused you to "
35: 15 s' also unto you all my servants the "
36: 14 all the princes s' Jehudi the son "
21 the king s' Jehudi to fetch the roll: "
37: 3 Zedekiah the king s' Jehucal the "
7 s' you unto me to enquire of me; "
17 Zedekiah the king s', and took him "
38: 14 Then Zedekiah the king s', and took "
39: 13 the captain of the guard s', and "
14 Even they s', and took Jeremiah "
40: 14 s' Ishmael the son of Nethaniah to "
42: 9 s' me to present your supplication "

Jer 42: 20 ye s' me unto the Lord your God, 7971
21 the which he hath s' me unto you. "
43: 1 Lord their God had s' him to them, "
2 Lord our God hath not s' thee to "
44: 4 I s' unto you all my servants the "
49: 14 ambassador is s' unto the heathen, "
La 1: 13 From above hath he s' fire into my "
Eze 2: 9 behold, an hand was s' unto me; * "
3: 5 For thou art not s' to a people of a "
6 Surely, had I s' thee to them, they "
13: 6 and the Lord hath not s' them: and "
23: 16 and s' messengers unto them into "
40 that ye have s' for men to come "
40 unto whom a messenger was s'; "
31: 4 s' out her little rivers unto all the "
Da 3: 2 the king s' to gather together the 7972
28 the God...who hath s' his angel, "
5: 24 the part of the hand s' from him; "
6: 22 My God hath s' his angel, and hath "
10: 11 upright: for unto thee am I now s'. 7971
Ho 5: 13 the Assyrian, and s' to king Jareb: "
Joe 2: 25 great army which I s' among you. "
Am 4: 10 I have s' among you the pestilence "
7: 10 priest of Beth-el s' to Jeroboam "
Ob 1 and an ambassador is s' among the "
Jon 1: 4 the Lord s' out a great wind into 2904
Mic 6: 4 I s' before thee Moses, Aaron, and 7971
Hag 1: 12 as the Lord their God had s' him, "
Zec 1: 10 the Lord hath s' to walk to and fro "
2: 8 he s' me unto the nations which "
9 that the Lord of hosts hath s' me. "
11 Lord of hosts hath s' me unto thee. "
4: 9 Lord of hosts hath s' me unto you. "
6: 15 Lord of hosts hath s' me unto you. "
7: 2 they had s' unto the house of God "
12 Lord of hosts hath s' in his spirit "
9: 11 I have s' forth thy prisoners out of "
Mal 2: 4 that I have s' this commandment "
M't 2: 8 And he s' them to Bethlehem, and 3992
16 s' forth, and slew all the children 649
10: 5 These twelve Jesus s' forth, and "
40 receive me receiveth him that s' me. "
11: 2 of Christ, he s' two of his disciples, 3992
13: 36 Then Jesus s' the multitude away, 863
14: 10 he s', and beheaded John in the 3992
22 while he s' the multitudes away. * 630
23 when he had s' the multitudes away, "
35 they s' out into all that country 649
15: 24 I am not s' but unto the lost sheep "
39 he s' away the multitude, and took 630
20: 2 a day, he s' them into his vineyard. 649
21: 1 of Olives, then s' Jesus two disciples, "
34 s' his servants to the husbandmen, "
36 he s' other servants more than the "
37 last of all he s' unto them his son, "
22: 3 s' forth his servants to call them "
4 he s' forth other servants, saying, "
7 s' forth his armies, and destroyed 3992
16 they s' out unto him their disciples* 649
23: 37 stonest them which are s' unto thee, "
27: 19 his wife s' unto him, saying, Have "
M'r 1: 43 him, and forthwith s' him away; 1544
3: 31 standing without, s' unto him, 649
4: 36 they had s' away the multitude, * 863
6: 17 s' forth and laid hold upon John, 649
27 the king s' an executioner, and "
45 while he s' away the people. * 628
46 And when he had s' them away, he* 657
8: 9 thousand: and he s' them away. 630
26 he s' him away to his house, saying, 649
9: 37 receiveth not me, but him that s' me. "
12: 2 he s' to the husbandmen a servant, "
3 beat him, and s' him away empty. "
4 he s' unto them another servant; "
4 s' him away shamefully handled. * "
5 again he s' another; and him they "
6 he s' him also last unto them, "
Lu 1: 19 am s' to speak unto thee, and to "
26 the angel Gabriel was s' from God "
53 the rich he hath s' empty away. 1821
4: 18 s' me to heal the brokenhearted, to 649
26 But unto none of them was Elias s', 3992
43 cities also: for therefore am I s'. 649
7: 3 s' unto him the elders of the Jews, "
6 the centurion s' friends to him, 3992
10 they that were s', returning to the "
19 of his disciples, s' them to Jesus, "
20 John Baptist hath s' us unto thee, 649
8: 38 with him: but Jesus s' him away, 630
9: 2 he s' them to preach the kingdom 649
48 receive me receiveth him that s' me: "
52 And s' messengers before his face: "
10: 1 s' them two and two before his face "
16 me, despiseth him that s' me. "
13: 34 stonest them that are s' unto thee; "
14: 17 s' his servant at supper time to say "
15: 15 s' him into his fields to feed swine. 3992
19: 14 and s' a message after him, saying, 649
29 of Olives, he s' two of his disciples, "
32 they that were s' went their way, "
20: 10 he s' a servant to the husbandmen. 640
10 beat him, and s' him away empty. 1821
11 And again he s' another servant: 3992
11 shamefully,...s' him away empty. 1821
12 And again he s' a third: and they 3992
20 s' forth spies, which should feign 649
22: 8 he s' Peter and John, saying, Go and "
35 When I s' you without purse, and "
23: 7 he s' him to Herod, who himself 375
11 robe, and s' him again to Pilate. "
15 nor yet Herod: for I s' you to him; "
Joh 1: 6 There was a man s' from God, 649
8 was s' to bear witness of that Light.* "
19 Jews s' priests and Levites from 649
22 give an answer to them that s' us. 3992
24 which were s' were of the Pharisees. 649

Joh 1: 33 that s' me to baptize with water, 3992
3: 17 God s' not his Son into the world to 649
28 Christ, but that I am s' before him. "
34 God hath s' speaketh the words of "
4: 34 is to do the will of him that s' me, 3992
38 I s' you to reap that whereon ye 649
5: 23 not the Father which hath s' him. 3992
24 believeth on him that s' me, hath "
30 will of the Father which hath s' me. "
33 Ye s' unto John, and he bare 649
36 of me, that the Father hath s' me. "
37 Father himself, which hath s' me, 3992
38 for whom he hath s', him ye believe 649
6: 29 ye believe on him whom he hath s'. "
38 will, but the will of him that s' me. 3992
39 the Father's will which hath s' me, "
40 this is the will of him that s' me, "
44 Father which hath s' me draw him: "
57 As the living Father hath s' me, 649
7: 16 is not mine, but his that s' me. 3992
18 that seeketh his glory that s' him, "
28 he that s' me is true, whom ye know "
29 am from him, and he hath s' me. 649
32 chief priests s' officers to take him. "
33 and then I go unto him that s' me. 3992
8: 16 but I and the Father that s' me. "
18 Father that s' me beareth witness of "
26 he that s' me is true; and I speak "
29 he that s' me is with me: the Father "
42 came I of myself, but he s' me. 649
9: 4 work the works of him that s' me, 3992
7 (which is by interpretation, S'.) 649
10: 36 sanctified, and s' into the world, "
11: 3 Therefore his sisters s' unto him, "
42 may believe that thou hast s' me. * "
12: 44 not on me, but on him that s' me. 3992
45 that seeth me seeth him that s' me. "
49 but the Father which s' me, he gave "
13: 16 is s' greater than he that s' him. 652
20 me receiveth him that s' me. 3992
14: 24 mine, but the Father's which s' me. "
15: 21 they know not him that s' me. "
16: 5 now I go my way to him that s' me; "
17: 3 Jesus Christ, whom thou hast s'. * 649
18 As thou hast s' me into the world,* "
18 have I also s' them into the world. "
21 may believe that thou hast s' me. * "
23 may know that thou hast s' me, * "
25 have known that thou hast s' me.* "
18: 24 had s' him bound unto Caiaphas "
20: 21 as my Father hath s' me, even so "
Ac 3: 26 his Son Jesus, s' him to bless you, "
5: 21 and s' to the prison to have them "
7: 12 Egypt, he s' out our fathers first. 1821
14 Then s' Joseph,...called his father 649
8: 14 they s' unto them Peter and John: "
9: 17 hath s' me, that thou mightest "
30 and s' him forth to Tarsus. 1821
38 they s' unto him two men, desiring 649
10: 8 unto them, he s' them to Joppa. "
17 the men which were s' from "
20 doubting nothing:...I have s' them. "
21 to the men which were s' unto him* "
29 gainsaying, as soon as I was s' for: 3343
29 for what intent ye have s' for me? "
33 Immediately therefore I s' to thee; 3992
36 God s' unto the children of Israel, 649
11: 11 I was, s' from Cæsarea unto me. "
22 and they s' forth Barnabas, that he 1821
30 s' it to the elders by the hands of * 649
12: 11 that the Lord hath s' his angel, 1821
13: 3 hands on them, they s' them away. 630
4 being s' forth by the Holy Ghost, 1599
15 of the synagogue s' unto them, 649
26 you is the word of this salvation s'. "
15: 27 s' therefore Judas and Silas, who "
16: 35 magistrates s' the serjeants, saying, "
36 magistrates have s' to let you go: "
17: 10 s' away Paul and Silas by night 1599
14 the brethren s' away Paul to go as 1821
19: 22 he s' into Macedonia two of them 649
31 s' unto him, desiring him that he 3992
20: 17 s' to Ephesus, and called the elders "
23: 30 I s' straightway to thee, and gave "
24: 24 he s' for Paul, and heard him 3343
26 wherefore he s' for him the oftener, "
28: 28 salvation...is s' unto the Gentiles, 649
Ro 10: 15 shall they preach, except they be s'? "
subscr. s' by Phebe servant of the church*
1Co 1: 17 For Christ s' me not to baptize, but 649
4: 17 cause have I s' unto you Timotheus, "
2Co 8: 18 we have s' with him the brother, 4842
22 we have s' with them our brother, "
9: 3 Yet have I s' the brethren, lest our 3992
12: 17 any of them whom I s' unto you? 649
18 Titus, and with him I s' a brother. 4882
Gal 4: 4 God s' forth his Son, made of a 1821
6 God hath s' forth the Spirit of his "
Eph 6: 22 Whom I have s' unto you for the 3992
Ph'p 2: 28 s' him therefore the more carefully, "
4: 16 ye s' once and again unto my "
18 the things which were s' from you,* "
Col 4: 8 Whom I have s' unto you for the 3992
1Th 3: 2 And s' Timotheus, our brother, and "
5 I s' to know your faith, lest by some 375
2Ti 4: 12 And Tychicus have I s' to Ephesus. 649
Ph'm 12 Whom I have s' again: thou 628
Heb 1: 14 s' forth to minister for them who 649
Jas 2: 25 and had s' them out another way? 1524
1Pe 1: 12 Holy Ghost s' down from heaven; 649
2: 14 unto them that are s' by him for 3992
1Jo 4: 9 God s' his only begotten Son into 649
10 and s' his Son to be the propitiation "
14 Father s' the Son to be the Saviour "
Re 1: 1 he s' and signified it by his angel "
5: 6 of God s' forth into all the earth. "

Re 22: 6 God of the holy prophets s' his angel 649
16 Jesus have s' mine angel to testify 3992

sentence See also SENTENCES.
De 17: 9 shall shew thee the s' of judgment: 1697
10 thou shalt do according to the s', "
11 According to the s' of the law *6310
11 from the s' which they shall shew 1697
Ps 17: 2 Let my s' come forth from thy 4941
Pr 16: 10 divine s' is in the lips of the king: 7081
Ec 8: 11 s' against an evil work is not 6599
Jer 4: 12 also will I give s' against them. *4941
Lu 23: 24 Pilate gave s' that it should be 1948
Ac 15: 19 my s' is, that we trouble not them, *2919
2Co 1: 9 we had the s' of death in ourselves, †610

sentences
Da 5: 12 shewing of hard s', and dissolving 280
8: 23 understanding dark s', shall stand 2420

sentest
Ex 15: 7 thou s' forth thy wrath, which *7971
Nu 13: 27 unto the land whither thou s' us, "
24: 12 messengers which thou s' unto me, "
1Ki 5: 8 the things which thou s' to me for: * "

Senuah (*sen'-u-ah*) See also HASSENUAH.
Ne 11: 9 son of S' was second over the city. *5574

Seorim (*se-o'-rim*)
1Ch 24: 8 third to Harim, the fourth to S', 8188

separate See also SEPARATED; SEPARATETH; SEPARATING.
Ge 13: 9 s' thyself, I pray thee, from me: 6504
30: 40 And Jacob did s' the lambs, and * "
49: 26 him that was s' from his brethren. 5139
Le 15: 31 shall ye s' the children of Israel 5144
22: 2 s' themselves from the holy things "
Nu 6: 2 s' themselves to vow a vow of a *6381
2 to s' themselves unto the Lord: 5144
3 He shall s' himself from wine and "
8: 14 thou s' the Levites from among the 914
16: 21 S' yourselves from among this "
De 19: 2 Thou shalt s' three cities for thee "
7 Thou shalt s' three cities for thee. "
29: 21 s' him unto evil out of all the tribes "
Jos 16: 9 the s' cities for the children of *3995
1Ki 8: 53 s' them from among all the people 914
Ezr 10: 11 s' yourselves from the people of the "
Jer 37: 12 to s' himself thence in the midst *2505
Eze 41: 12 was before the s' place at the end 1508
13 the s' place, and the building, with "
14 and of the s' place toward the east, "
15 the s' place which was behind it, "
42: 1 that was over against the s' place, "
10 the east, over against the s' place, "
13 which are before the s' place, they "
M't 25: 32 he shall s' them one from another, 873
Lu 6: 22 shall s' you from their company, "
Ac 13: 2 S' me Barnabas and Saul for the "
Ro 8: 35 shall s' us from the love of Christ? 5562
39 able to s' us from the love of God, "
2Co 6: 17 them, and be ye s', saith the Lord, 873
Heb 7: 26 undefiled, s' from sinners, and *5562

separated
Ge 13: 11 they s' themselves the one from 6504
14 after that Lot was s' from him, "
25: 23 two manner of people shall be s' "
Ex 33: 16 so shall we be s', I and thy people, 6395
Le 20: 24 have s' you from other people. 914
25 I have s' from you as unclean. "
Nu 16: 9 God of Israel hath s' you from the "
De 10: 8 time the Lord s' the tribe of Levi, "
32: 8 when he s' the sons of Adam, he 6504
33: 16 him that was s' from his brethren. *5139
1Ch 12: 8 there s' themselves unto David into 914
23: 13 and Aaron was s', that he should "
25: 1 s' to the service of the sons of Asaph, "
2Ch 25: 10 Then Amaziah s' them, to wit, the "
Ezr 6: 21 s' themselves unto them from the 6395
8: 24 Then I s' twelve of the chief of the 914
9: 1 not s' themselves from the people of "
10: 8 himself s' from the congregation of "
16 all of them by their names, were s', "
Ne 4: 19 we are s' upon the wall, one far 6504
9: 2 seed of Israel s' themselves from 914
10: 28 all they that had s' themselves from "
13: 3 they s' from Israel all the mixed "
Pr 18: 1 desire a man, having s' himself, *6504
19: 4 the poor is s' from his neighbour. "
Isa 56: 3 Lord hath utterly s' me from his * 914
59: 2 your iniquities have s' between you "
Hos 4: 14 themselves are s' with whores, *6504
9: 10 s' themselves unto that shame; *5144
Ac 19: 9 from them, and s' the disciples, 873
Ro 1: 1 apostle, s' unto the gospel of God, "
Ga 1: 15 who s' me from my mother's womb, "
2: 12 he withdrew and s' himself, fearing "

separateth
Nu 6: 5 which he s' himself unto the Lord, 5144
6 that he s' himself unto the Lord "
Pr 16: 28 and a whisperer s' chief friends. 6504
17: 9 repeateth a matter s' very friends. "
Eze 14: 7 which s' himself from me, and 5144

separating
Zec 7: 3 s' myself, as I have done these so 5144

separation
Le 12: 2 according to the days of the s' for *5079
5 be unclean two weeks, as in her s': * "
15: 20 she lieth upon in her s' shall be * "
25 many days out of the time of her s', * "
25 if it run beyond the time of her s'; * "
25 shall be as the days of her s': she * "
26 be unto her as the bed of her s': * "
26 as the uncleanness of her s'. "
Nu 6: 4 All the days of his s' shall he eat 5145
5 days of the vow of his s' there shall "

Nu 6: 8 the days of his s' he is holy unto 5145
12 unto the Lord the days of his s'. "
12 be lost, because his s' was defiled. "
13 when the days of his s' are fulfilled: "
18 shave the head of his s' at the door "
18 take the hair of the head of his s'. "
19 after the hair of his s' is shaven: "
21 his offering unto the Lord for his s'. "
21 he must do after the law of his s'. "
19: 9 children of Israel for a water of s': 5079
13 the water of s' was not sprinkled * "
20 water of s' hath not been sprinkled* "
21 he that sprinkleth the water of s' "
21 he that toucheth water of s' * "
31: 23 be purified with the water of s': * "
Eze 42: 20 to make a s' between the sanctuary 914

Sephar (*se'-far*)
Ge 10: 30 as thou goest unto S' a mount of 5611

Sepharad (*sef'-a-rad*)
Ob 20 the captivity...which is in S'. 5614

Sepharvaim (*sef-ar-va'-im*) See also SEPHARVITES.
2Ki 17: 24 and from Hamath, and from S'. 5617
31 and Anammelech, the gods of S'. "
18: 34 where are the gods of S', Hena, "
19: 13 the king of the city of S', of Hena, "
Isa 36: 19 Arphad? where are the gods of S'? "
37: 13 and the king of the city of S', Hena. "

Sepharvites (*sef'-ar-vites*)
2Ki 17: 31 the S' burnt their children in fire 5616

sepulchre See also SEPULCHRES.
Ge 23: 6 shall withhold from thee his s'. 6913
De 34: 6 but no man knoweth of his s' 6900
J'g 8: 32 and was buried in the s' of Joash 6913
1Sa 10: 2 shalt find two men by Rachel's s' 6900
2Sa 2: 32 buried him in the s' of his father, 6913
4: 12 and buried it in the s' of Abner in* "
17: 23 was buried in the s' of his father. "
21: 14 Zelah, in the s' of Kish his father: "
1Ki 13: 22 not come unto the s' of thy fathers. "
31 s' wherein the man of God is buried; "
2Ki 9: 28 him in his s' with his fathers 6900
13: 21 cast the man into the s' of Elisha: 6913
21: 26 in his s' in the garden of Uzza: 6900
23: 17 It is the s' of the man of God, 6913
30 and buried him in his own s'. 6900
Ps 5: 9 their throat is an open s'; they 6913
Isa 22: 16 thou hast hewed thee out a s' here, "
16 that heweth him out a s' on high, "
Jer 5: 16 Their quiver is as an open s', they "
M't 27: 60 a great stone to the door of the s', *3419
61 Mary, sitting over against the s'. 5028
64 s' be made sure until the third day, "
66 So they went, and made the s' sure, "
28: 1 and the other Mary to see the s'. "
8 they departed quickly from the s' *3419
M'r 15: 46 laid him in a s' which was hewn * "
46 a stone unto the door of the s'. * "
16: 2 they came unto the s' at the rising* "
3 the stone from the door of the s'? * "
5 And entering into the s', they saw* "
8 out quickly, and fled from the s'; * "
Lu 23: 53 and laid it in a s' that was hewn *3418
55 beheld the s', and how his body *3419
24: 1 morning, they came unto the s', *3418
2 the stone rolled away from the s'. *3419
9 returned from the s', and told all * "
12 arose Peter, and ran unto the s'; * "
22 which were early at the s'; * "
24 which were with us went to the s', * "
Joh 19: 41 in the garden a new s', wherein * "
42 day; for the s' was nigh at hand. * "
20: 1 when it was yet dark, unto the s', * "
1 the stone taken away from the s'. * "
2 taken away the Lord out of the s', * "
3 other disciple, and came to the s'. * "
4 outrun Peter, and came...to the s'. * "
6 and went into the s', and seeth the* "
8 disciple, which came first to the s', * "
11 But Mary stood without at the s' * "
11 stooped down, and looked in the s', * "
Ac 2: 29 his s' is with us unto this day. *3418
7: 16 and laid in the s' that Abraham * "
13: 29 from the tree, and laid him in a s'. *3419
Ro 3: 13 Their throat is an open s'; with 5028

sepulchres
Ge 23: 6 in the choice of our s' bury thy 6913
2Ki 23: 16 he spied the s' that were there in "
16 and took the bones out of the s', and "
2Ch 16: 14 And they buried him in his own s', "
21: 20 David, but not in the s' of the kings. "
24: 25 buried him not in the s' of the kings. "
28: 27 him not into the s' of the kings of "
32: 33 in the chiefest of the s' of the sons "
35: 24 buried in one of the s' of his fathers. "
Ne 2: 3 the city, the place of my fathers' s', "
5 unto the city of my fathers' s', that "
3: 16 place over against the s' of David, "
M't 23: 27 ye are like unto whited s', which 5028
29 garnish the s' of the righteous, *3419
Lu 11: 47 for ye build the s' of the prophets, * "
48 killed them, and ye build their s'. * "

Serah (*se'-rah*) See also SARAH; TIMNATH-SERAH.
Ge 46: 17 and Beriah, and S' their sister: 8294
1Ch 7: 30 and Beriah, and S' their sister. "

Seraiah (*se-ra-i'-ah*) See also SHAVSHA.
2Sa 8: 17 priests; and S' was the scribe; 8304
2Ki 25: 18 the guard took S' the chief priest, "
23 and S' the son of Tanhumeth the "
1Ch 4: 13 the sons of Kenaz; Othniel, and S': "
14 and S' begat Joab, the father of "
35 the son of Josibiah, the son of S', "
1Ch 6: 14 begat S', and S' begat Jehozadak, 8304
Ezr 2: 2 Jeshua, Nehemiah, S', Reelaiah, "
7: 1 Ezra the son of S', the son of "
Ne 10: 2 S', Azariah, Jeremiah, "
11: 11 S' the son of Hilkiah, the son of "
12: 1 and Jeshua: S', Jeremiah, Ezra, "
12 chief of the fathers: of S', Meraiah; "
Jer 36: 26 S' the son of Azriel, and Shelemiah "
40: 8 and S' the son of Tanhumeth, and "
51: 59 commanded S' the son of Neriah, "
59 And this S' was a quiet prince. "
61 Jeremiah said to S', When thou "
52: 24 the guard took S' the chief priest, "

seraphims (*ser'-a-fims*)
Isa 6: 2 Above it stood the s': each one *8314
6 Then flew one of the s' unto me, * "

Sered (*se'-red*) See also SARDITES.
Ge 46: 14 sons of Zebulun; S', and Elon, 5624
Nu 26: 26 of S', the family of the Sardites: "

Sergius (*sur'-je-us*)
Ac 13: 7 S' Paulus, a prudent man; who 4588

serjeants
Ac 16: 35 the magistrates sent the s', saying, 4465
38 the s' told these words unto the "

serpent See also SERPENT'S; SERPENTS.
Ge 3: 1 s' was more subtil than any beast 5175
2 woman said unto the s', We may eat "
4 s' said unto the woman, Ye shall not "
13 The s' beguiled me, and I did eat. "
14 Lord God said unto the s', Because "
49: 17 Dan shall be a s' by the way, an "
Ex 4: 3 on the ground, and it became a s'; "
7: 9 Pharaoh, and it shall become a s'. 8577
10 his servants, and it became a s'. "
15 the rod which was turned to a s' 5175
Nu 21: 8 Make thee a fiery s', and set it 8314
9 Moses made a s' of brass, and put 5175
9 that if a s' had bitten any man, "
9 when he beheld the s' of brass, he "
2Ki 18: 4 the brasen s' that Moses had made: "
Job 26: 13 hand hath formed the crooked s'. "
Ps 58: 4 poison is like the poison of a s': "
140: 3 sharpened their tongues like a s'; "
Pr 23: 32 At the last it biteth like a s', and "
30: 19 the way of a s' upon a rock; the way "
Ec 10: 8 breaketh an hedge, a s' shall bite "
11 s' will bite without enchantment; "
Isa 14: 29 his fruit shall be a fiery flying s'. 8314
27: 1 punish leviathan the piercing s', 5175
1 even leviathan that crooked s'; and "
30: 6 lion, the viper and fiery flying s', 8314
Jer 46: 22 voice thereof shall go like a s'; 5175
Am 5: 19 hand on the wall, and a s' bit him. "
9: 3 sea, thence will I command the s', "
Mic 7: 17 They shall lick the dust like a s', "
M't 7: 10 ask a fish, will he give him a s'? 3789
Lu 11: 11 fish, will he for a fish give him a s'? "
Joh 3: 14 And as Moses lifted up the s' in the "
2Co 11: 3 as the s' beguiled Eve through his "
Re 12: 9 old s', called the Devil, and Satan, "
14 half a time, from the face of the s'. "
15 the s' cast out of his mouth water "
20: 2 old s', which is the Devil, and Satan, "

serpent's
Isa 14: 29 out of the s' root shall come forth 5175
65: 25 and dust shall be the s' meat. "

serpents
Ex 7: 12 man his rod, and they became s': 8577
Nu 21: 6 the Lord sent fiery s' among the 5175
7 that he take away the s' from us. "
De 8: 15 wilderness, wherein were fiery s', "
32: 24 with the poison of s' of the dust. *2119
Jer 8: 17 I will send s', cockatrices, among 5175
M't 10: 16 be ye therefore wise as s', and 3789
23: 33 Ye s', ye generation of vipers, how "
M'r 16: 18 They shall take up s'; and if they "
Lu 10: 19 power to tread on s' and scorpions, "
1Co 10: 9 tempted, and were destroyed of s'. "
Jas 3: 7 of s', and of things in the sea, is *2062
Re 9: 19 for their tails were like unto s', 3789

Serug (*se'-rug*) See also SARUCH.
Ge 11: 20 and thirty years, and begat S': 8286
21 Reu lived after he begat S' two "
22 S' lived thirty years, and begat "
23 S' lived after he begat Nahor two "
1Ch 1: 26 S', Nahor, Terah, "

servant See also BONDSERVANT; MAIDSERVANT; SERVANT'S; SERVANTS; SERVITOR.
Ge 9: 25 a s' of servants shall he be unto 5650
26, 27 Shem;...Canaan shall be his s'. "
18: 3 not away, I pray thee, from thy s': "
5 therefore are ye come to your s'. "
19: 19 thy s' hath found grace in thy sight, "
24: 2 Abraham said unto his eldest s' "
5 s' said unto him, Peradventure "
9 the s' put his hand under the thigh "
10 And the s' took ten camels of the "
14 that thou hast appointed for thy s' "
17 the s' ran to meet her, and said, "
34 And he said, I am Abraham's s'. "
52 Abraham's s' heard their words, "
53 And the s' brought forth jewels of "
59 and Abraham's s', and his men. "
61 the s' took Rebekah, and went his "
65 she had said unto the s', What man "
65 the s' had said, It is my master: "
66 the s' told Isaac all things that "
26: 24 thy seed for my s' Abraham's sake. "
32: 4 Thy s' Jacob saith thus, I have "
10 thou hast shewed unto thy s'; for "
18 shalt say, They be thy s' Jacob's; "
Ge 33: 20 Behold, thy s' Jacob is behind us. 5650
5 God hath graciously given thy s'. "
14 I pray thee, pass over before his s': "
39: 17 Hebrew s', which thou hast brought "
19 After this manner did thy s' to me; "
41: 12 s' to the captain of the guard; and "
43: 28 Thy s' our father is in good health, "
44: 10 whom it is found shall be my s'; * "
17 the cup is found, he shall be my s': * "
18 let thy s', I pray thee, speak a word "
18 not thine anger burn against thy s': "
24 we came up unto thy s' my father, "
27 thy s' my father said unto us, Ye "
30 when I come to thy s' my father, "
31 bring down the gray hairs of thy s' "
32 thy s' became surety for the lad "
33 let thy s' abide instead of the lad a "
49: 15 and became a s' unto tribute. 5647
Ex 4: 10 thou hast spoken unto thy s': but 5650
12: 44 every man's s' that is bought for "
45 an hired s' shall not eat thereof. 7916
14: 31 the Lord, and his s' Moses. 5650
21: 2 If thou buy an Hebrew s', six years "
5 If the s' shall plainly say, I love my "
20 if a man smite his s', or his maid, "
26 And if a man smite the eye of his s', "
33: 11 but his s' Joshua, the son of Nun, *8334
Le 22: 10 hired s', shall not eat of the holy 7916
25: 6 and for thy s', and for thy maid, 5650
6 and for thy hired s', and for thy 7916
40 as an hired s', and as a sojourner, "
50 according to the time of an hired s' "
53 a yearly hired s' shall he be with "
Nu 11: 11 hast thou afflicted thy s'? and 5650
28 the son of Nun, the s' of Moses, *8334
12: 7 My s' Moses is not so, who is 5650
8 to speak against my s' Moses? "
14: 24 But my s' Caleb, because he had "
De 3: 24 begun to shew thy s' thy greatness, "
5: 15 thou wast a s' in the land of Egypt, "
15: 17 door, and he shall be thy s' for ever. "
18 hath been worth a double hired s' *7916
23: 15 not deliver unto his master the s' 5650
24: 14 shalt not oppress an hired s' that 7916
34: 5 So Moses the s' of the Lord died 5650
Jos 1: 1 death of Moses the s' of the Lord "
2 Moses my s' is dead; now therefore "
7 Moses my s' commanded thee: "
13 which Moses the s' of the Lord "
15 which Moses the Lord's s' gave you "
5: 14 What saith my lord unto his s'? "
8: 31 As Moses the s' of the Lord "
33 As Moses the s' of the Lord had "
9: 24 commanded his s' Moses to give "
11: 12 them, as Moses the s' of the Lord "
15 the Lord commanded Moses his s', "
12: 6 Them did Moses the s' of the Lord "
6 Moses the s' of the Lord gave it "
13: 8 Moses the s' of the Lord gave them; "
14: 7 Moses the s' of the Lord sent me "
18: 7 Moses the s' of the Lord gave them. "
22: 2 Moses...s' of the Lord commanded "
4 Moses the s' of the Lord gave you "
5 Moses the s' of the Lord charged "
24: 29 the son of Nun, the s' of the Lord, "
J'g 2: 8 the son of Nun, the s' of the Lord, "
7: 10 with Phurah thy s' down to the 5288
11 went he down with Phurah his s' "
15: 18 deliverance into the hand of thy s': 5650
19: 3 having his s' with him, and a 5288
9 he, and his concubine, and his s', "
11 the s' said unto his master, Come, "
13 he said unto his s', Come, and let "
Ru 2: 5 Boaz unto his s' that was set over "
6 the s' that was set over the reapers "
1Sa 2: 13 the priest's s' came, while the flesh "
15 the priest's s' came, and said to the "
3: 9 Speak, Lord; for thy s' heareth. 5650
10 answered, Speak; for thy s' heareth. "
9: 5 Saul said to his s' that was with 5288
7 said Saul to his s', But, behold, if "
8 And the s' answered Saul again, "
10 Then said Saul to his s', Well said; "
22 And Samuel took Saul and his s', "
27 Saul, Bid the s' pass on before us, "
10: 14 uncle said unto him and to his s', "
17: 32 thy s' will go and fight with this 5650
34 Thy s' kept his father's sheep, and "
36 Thy s' slew both the lion and the "
58 I am the son of thy s' Jesse the "
19: 4 Let not the king sin against his s', "
20: 7 It is well; thy s' shall have peace: "
8 thou shalt deal kindly with thy s'; "
8 hast brought thy s' into a covenant "
22: 8 hath stirred up my s' against me, "
15 king impute any thing unto his s', "
15 for thy s' knew nothing of all this, "
23: 10 s' hath certainly heard that Saul "
11 come down, as thy s' hath heard? "
11 of Israel I beseech thee, tell thy s'. "
25: 39 and hath kept his s' from evil: for "
41 handmaid be a s' to wash the feet "
26: 18 my lord thus pursue after his s'? "
19 the king hear the words of his s'. "
27: 5 why should thy s' dwell in the royal "
12 therefore he shall be my s' for ever. "
28: 2 thou shalt know what thy s' can do. "
29: 3 Is not this David, the s' of Saul the "
8 what hast thou found in thy s' so "
30: 13 man of Egypt, s' to an Amalekite; "
2Sa 3: 18 By the hand of my s' David I will "
7: 5 Go and tell my s' David, Thus saith "
8 so shalt thou say unto my s' David, "
20 for thou, Lord God, knowest thy s'. "
21 things, to make thy s' know them. "
25 thou hast spoken concerning thy s', "

2Sa 7:26 and let the house of thy s· David be 5650
27 of Israel, hast revealed to thy s·, “
27 hath thy s· found in his heart to “
28 promised this goodness unto thy s·: “
29 thee to bless the house of thy s·, “
29 let the house of thy s· be blessed “
9: 2 there was of the house of Saul a s· “
2 Ziba? And he said, Thy s· is he. “
6 and he answered, Behold thy s·! “
8 What is thy s·, that thou shouldest “
9 the king called to Ziba, Saul's s·, 5288
11 commanded his s·, so shall thy s· 5650
11:21 Thy s· Uriah the Hittite is dead. “
24 and thy s· Uriah the Hittite is dead “
13:17 called his s· that ministered unto 5288
18 Then his s· brought her out, and 8334
24 now, thy s· hath sheepshearers; 5650
24 and his servants go with thy s·. “
35 sons come: as thy s· said, so it is. “
14:19 thy s· Jacob, he bade me, and he “
20 hath thy s· Joab done this thing: “
22 To day thy s· knoweth that I have “
22 hath fulfilled the request of his s·. “
15: 2 Thy s· is of one of the tribes of “
8 thy s· vowed a vow while I abode “
21 life, even there also will thy s· be. “
34 Absalom, I will be thy s·, O king; “
34 have been thy father's s· hitherto, “
34 so will I now also be thy s·: then “
16: 1 Ziba the s· of Mephibosheth met 5288
18:29 sent the king's s·, and me thy s·, 5650
19:17 Ziba the s· of the house of Saul, 5288
19 remember that which thy s· did 5650
20 thy s· doth know...I have sinned: “
26 My lord, O king, my s· deceived me: “
26 for thy s· said, I will saddle me an “
26 to the king; because thy s· is lame. “
27 he hath slandered thy s· unto my “
28 didst thou set thy s· among them “
35 can thy s· taste what I eat or what “
35 then should thy s· be yet a burden “
36 Thy s· will go a little way over “
37 Let thy s·, I pray thee, turn back “
37 But behold thy s· Chimham; let “
24:10 take away the iniquity of thy s·; “
21 is my lord the king come to his s·? “
1Ki 1:19 Solomon thy s· hath he not called. “
26 But me, even me thy s·, and Zadok “
26 thy s· Solomon, hath he not called. “
27 thou hast not shewed it unto thy s·;* “
51 to day that he will not slay his s· “
2:38 the king hath said, so will thy s· do. “
3: 6 shewed unto thy s· David my father “
7 made thy s· king instead of David “
8 thy s· is in the midst of thy people “
9 Give...thy s· an understanding “
8:24 Who hast kept with thy s· David “
25 keep with thy s· David my father “
26 thou spakest unto thy s· David my “
28 respect unto the prayer of thy s·, “
28 which thy s· prayeth before thee “
29 the prayer which thy s· shall make “
30 thou to the supplication of thy s·, “
52 unto the supplication of thy s·, “
53 spakest by the hand of Moses thy s·, “
56 promised by...hand of Moses his s·. “
59 that he maintain the cause of his s·, “
66 the Lord had done for David his s·, “
11:11 from thee, and will give it to thy s·. “
26 Ephrathite of Zereda, Solomon's s·, “
32 one tribe for my s· David's sake, “
36 that David my s· may have a light “
38 commandments, as David my s· did; “
12: 7 If thou wilt be a s· unto this people “
14: 8 thou hast not been as my s· David, “
18 spake by the hand of his s· Ahijah “
15:29 which he spake by his s· Ahijah the “
16: 9 And his s· Zimri, captain of half his “
18: 9 deliver thy s· into the hand of Ahab, “
12 but I thy s· fear the Lord from my “
36 that I am thy s·, and that I have “
43 And said to his s·, Go up now, 5288
19: 3 to Judah, and left his s· there. “
20: 9 that thou didst send for to thy s· 5650
32 Thy s· Ben-hadad saith, I pray thee, “
39 Thy s· went out into the midst of “
40 as thy s· was busy here and there, “
2Ki 4: 1 saying, Thy s· my husband is dead; “
1 that thy s· did fear the Lord: and “
12 he said to Gehazi his s·, Call this 5288
24 and said to her s·, Drive, and go “
25 he said to Gehazi his s·, Behold, “
38 he said unto his s·, Set on the great “
5: 6 sent Naaman my s· to thee, that 5650
15 pray thee, take a blessing of thy s·. “
17 given to thy s· two mules' burden “
17 thy s· will henceforth offer neither “
18 this thing the Lord pardon thy s·, “
18 the Lord pardon thy s· in this thing. “
20 the s· of Elisha the man of God, 5288
25 he said, Thy s· went no whither. 5650
6:15 the s· of the man of God was risen 8334
15 And his s· said unto him, Alas, my 5288
8: 4 Gehazi the s· of the man of God, “
13 said, But what, is thy s· a dog, 5650
9:36 spake by his s· Elijah the Tishbite, “
10:10 which he spake by his s· Elijah. “
14:25 spake by the hand of his s· Jonah, “
16: 7 saying, I am thy s· and thy son: “
17: 3 and Hoshea became his s·, and gave “
18:12 Moses...s· of the Lord commanded, “
19:34 sake, and for my s· David's sake. “
20: 6 sake, and for my s· David's sake. “
21: 8 my s· Moses commanded them. “
22:12 and Asahiah a s· of the king's, “
24: 1 and Jehoiakim became his s· three “

2Ki 25: 8 guard, a s· of the king of Babylon, 5650
1Ch 2:34 And Sheshan had a s·, an Egyptian, “
35 his daughter to Jarha his s· to wife; “
6:49 all that Moses the s· of God had “
16:13 O ye seed of Israel his s·, ye children “
17: 4 Go and tell David my s·, Thus saith “
7 shalt thou say unto my s· David, “
18 to thee for the honour of thy s·? “
18 for thou knowest thy s·. “
23 concerning thy s· and concerning “
24 house of David thy s· be established “
25 s· that thou wilt build him...house: “
25 s· hath found in his heart to pray “
26 promised this goodness unto thy s·: “
27 thee to bless the house of thy s·, “
21: 8 thee, do away the iniquity of thy s·; “
2Ch 1: 3 Moses the s· of the Lord had made “
6:15 which hast kept with thy s· David “
16 keep with thy s· David my father “
17 thou hast spoken unto thy s· David. “
19 therefore to the prayer of thy s·, “
19 which thy s· prayeth before thee: “
20 thy s· prayeth toward this place. “
21 unto the supplications of thy s·, “
42 the mercies of David thy s·. “
13: 6 the s· of Solomon the son of David, “
24: 6 of Moses the s· of the Lord, and of “
9 that Moses the s· of God laid upon “
32:16 God, and against his s· Hezekiah. “
34:20 scribe, and Asaiah a s· of the king's, “
Ne 1: 6 mayest hear the prayer of thy s·, “
7 thou commandedst thy s· Moses. “
8 thou commandedst thy s· Moses, “
11 be attentive to the prayer of thy s·, “
11 prosper, I pray thee, thy s· this day, “
2: 5 and if thy s· have found favour in “
10 and Tobiah the s·, the Ammonite, “
19 Tobiah the s·, the Ammonite, and “
4:22 with his s· lodge within Jerusalem, 5288
6: 5 sent Sanballat his s· unto me in “
9:14 laws, by the hand of Moses thy s·: 5650
10:29 was given by Moses the s· of God, “
Job 1: 8 Hast thou considered my s· Job, “
2: 3 Hast thou considered my s· Job, “
3:19 and the s· is free from his master. “
7: 2 a s· earnestly desireth the shadow, “
19:16 I called my s·, and he gave me no “
41: 4 wilt thou take him for a s· for ever? “
42: 7 that is right, as my s· Job hath. “
8 and go to my s· Job, and offer up “
8 and my s· Job shall pray for you: “
8 thing which is right, like my s· Job. “
Ps 18: *title* of David, the s· of the Lord, who “
19:11 by them is thy s· warned: and in “
13 thy s· also from presumptuous “
27: 9 me; put not thy s· away in anger: “
31:16 Make thy face to shine upon thy s·: “
35:27 pleasure in the prosperity of his s·. “
36: *title* of David the s· of the Lord. “
69:17 And hide not thy face from thy s·; “
78:70 He chose David also his s·, and took “
86: 2 save thy s· that trusteth in thee. “
4 Rejoice the soul of thy s·: for unto “
16 give thy strength unto thy s·, and “
89: 3 I have sworn unto David my s·, “
20 I have found David my s·; with my “
39 made void the covenant of thy s·: “
105: 6 O ye seed of Abraham his s·, ye “
17 even Joseph, who was sold for a s·: “
26 He sent Moses his s·; and Aaron “
42 holy promise, and Abraham his s·. “
109:28 be ashamed; but let thy s· rejoice. “
116:16 O Lord, truly I am thy s·; “
16 I am thy s·, and the son of thine “
119:17 Deal bountifully with thy s·, that I “
23 thy s· did meditate in thy statutes. “
38 Stablish thy word unto thy s·, who “
49 Remember the word unto thy s·, “
65 Thou hast dealt well with thy s·, O “
76 according to thy word unto thy s·. “
84 How many are the days of thy s·? “
122 Be surety for thy s· for good: let not “
124 thy s· according unto thy mercy, “
125 am thy s·; give me understanding, “
135 Make thy face to shine upon thy s·; “
140 very pure: therefore thy s· loveth it. “
176 astray like a lost sheep; seek thy s·; “
132:10 thy s· David's sake turn not away “
136:22 Even an heritage unto Israel his s·: “
143: 2 enter not into judgment with thy s· “
12 that afflict my soul: for I am thy s·. “
144:10 who delivereth David his s· from the “
Pr 11:29 and the fool shall be s· to the wise “
12: 9 He that is despised, and hath a s·, “
14:35 king's favour is toward a wise s·: “
17: 2 A wise s· shall have rule over a son “
19:10 much less for a s· to have rule over “
22: 7 and the borrower is s· to the lender. “
29:19 A s· will not be corrected by words: “
21 He that delicately bringeth up his s· “
30:10 Accuse not a s· unto his master, “
22 For a s· when he reigneth; and a “
Ec 7:21 lest thou hear thy s· curse thee: “
Isa 20: 3 Like as my s· Isaiah hath walked “
22:20 I will call my s· Eliakim the son of “
24: 2 as with the s·, so with his master; “
37:35 sake, and for my s· David's sake. “
41: 8 But thou, Israel, art my s·, Jacob “
9 and said unto thee, Thou art my s·; “
42: 1 Behold my s·, whom I uphold; mine “
19 Who is blind, but my s·? or deaf, as “
19 perfect, and blind as the Lord's s·? “
43:10 and my s· whom I have chosen: “
44: 1 Yet now hear, O Jacob my s·; and “
2 Fear not, O Jacob, my s·; and thou, “
21 for thou art my s·: I have formed “

Isa 44:21 thou art my s·: O Israel, thou shalt 5650
26 That confirmeth the word of his s·, “
48:20 Lord hath redeemed his s· Jacob. “
49: 3 Thou art my s·, O Israel, in whom “
5 me from the womb to be his s·, “
6 thing that thou shouldest be my s· “
7 nation abhorreth, to a s· of rulers, “
50:10 that obeyeth the voice of his s·, that “
52:13 Behold, my s· shall deal prudently, “
53:11 shall my righteous s· justify many; “
Jer 2:14 Is Israel a s·? is he a homeborn “
25: 9 and...the king of Babylon, my s·, “
27: 6 hand of...the king of Babylon, my s·; “
30:10 fear thou not, O my s· Jacob, saith “
33:21 covenant be broken with David my s·, “
22 I multiply the seed of David my s·, “
26 the seed of Jacob, and David my s·, “
34:16 and caused every man his s·, and “
43:10 take...the king of Babylon, my s·, “
46:27 But fear not thou, O my s· Jacob, “
28 Fear thou not, O Jacob my s·, saith “
Eze 28:25 land...I have given to my s· Jacob. “
34:23 shall feed them, even my s· David; “
24 my s· David a prince among them; “
37:24 David my s· shall be king over them; “
25 that I have given unto Jacob my s·, “
25 my s· David shall be their prince “
Da 6:20 O Daniel, s· of the living God, is 5649
9:11 in the law of Moses the s· of God, 5650
17 O our God, hear the prayer of thy s·, “
10:17 how can the s· of this my lord talk “
Hag 2:23 I take thee, O Zerubbabel, my s·, “
Zec 3: 8 I will bring forth my s· the Branch. “
Mal 1: 6 son...his father, and a s· his master: “
4: 4 Remember ye the law of Moses my s·, “
M't 8: 6 s· lieth at home sick of the palsy, 3816
8 only, and my s· shall be healed. “
9 to my s·, Do this, and he doeth it. 1401
13 his s· was healed in the selfsame 3816
10:24 master, nor the s· above his lord. 1401
25 as his master, and the s· as his lord. “
12:18 Behold my s·, whom I have chosen; 3816
18:26 The s· therefore fell down, and 1401
27 the lord of that s· was moved with “
28 But the same s· went out, and found “
32 O thou wicked s·, I forgave thee all “
20:27 chief among you, let him be your s· “
23:11 greatest among you shall be your s·. 1249
24:45 Who then is a faithful and wise s·, 1401
46 Blessed is that s·, whom his lord “
48 if that evil s· shall say in his heart, “
50 lord of that s· shall come in a day “
25:21 Well done, thou good and faithful s·: “
23 Well done, good and faithful s·; “
26 Thou wicked and slothful s·, thou “
30 unprofitable s· into outer darkness: “
26:51 and struck a s· of the high priest's, “
M'r 9:35 shall be last of all, and s· of all. *1249
10:44 be the chiefest, shall be s· of all. *1401
12: 2 he sent to the husbandmen a s·, “
4 again he sent unto them another s·; “
14:47 and smote a s· of the high priest, “
Lu 1:54 He hath holpen his s· Israel, in 3816
69 for us in the house of his s· David; “
2:29 lettest thou thy s· depart in peace, 1401
7: 2 a certain centurion's s·, who was “
3 that he would come and heal his s·. “
7 a word, and my s· shall be healed. 3816
8 to my s·, Do this, and he doeth it. 1401
10 the s· whole that had been sick. “
12:43 Blessed is that s·, whom his lord “
45 But and if that s· say in his heart, “
46 lord of that s· will come in a day “
47 that s·, which knew his lord's will, “
14:17 And sent his s· at supper time to say “
21 So that s· came, and shewed his lord “
21 angry said to his s·, Go out quickly “
22 the s· said, Lord, it is done as thou “
23 lord said unto his s·, Go out into “
16:13 No s· can serve two masters: for 3610
17: 7 having a s· plowing or feeding 1401
9 Doth he thank that s· because he “
19:17 said unto him, Well, thou good s·: “
22 will I judge thee, thou wicked s·. “
20:10 he sent a s· to the husbandmen, “
11 And again he sent another s·: and “
22:50 them smote the s· of the high priest, “
Joh 8:34 committeth sin is the s· of sin. * “
35 the s· abideth not in the house for* “
12:26 I am, there shall also my s· be: 1249
13:16 The s· is not greater than his lord; 1401
15:15 s· knoweth not what his lord doeth: “
20 The s· is not greater than his lord. “
18:10 and smote the high priest's s·, and “
Ac 4:25 Who by the mouth of thy s· David 3816
Ro 1: 1 Paul, a s· of Jesus Christ, called 1401
14: 4 that judgest another man's s·? 3610
16: 1 sister, which is a s· of the church 1249
subscr. sent by Phebe s· of the church “
1Co 7:21 Art thou called being a s·? care *1401
22 being a s·, is the Lord's freeman: * “
22 is called, being free, is Christ's s·. * “
9:19 yet have I made myself s· unto all, *1402
Ga 1:10 I should not be the s· of Christ. 1401
4: 1 a child, differeth nothing from a s·, * “
7 Wherefore thou art no more a s·, * “
Ph'p 2: 7 and took upon him the form of a s·, “
Col 4:12 who is one of you, a s· of Christ, “
2Ti 2:24 the s· of the Lord must not strive; “
Tit 1: 1 Paul, a s· of God, and an apostle of “
Ph'm 16 Not now as a s·, but above a s·, “
subscr. Philemon, by Onesimus a s·. *3610
Heb 3: 5 faithful in all his house, as a s·, 2324
Jas 1: 1 James, a s· of God and of the Lord 1401
2Pe 1: 1 Simon Peter, a s· and an apostle of “
Jude 1 Jude, the s· of Jesus Christ, and “

Re 1: 1 it by his angel unto his s' John: 1401
15: 3 sing the song of Moses the s' of God,"

servant's
Ge 19: 2 in, I pray you, into your s' house, 5650
2Sa 7:19 hast spoken also of thy s' house "
1Ki 11:13 to thy son for David my s' sake, "
34 days of his life for David my s' sake,"
2Ki 8:19 destroy Judah for David his s' sake,"
1Ch 17:17 hast also spoken of thy s' house "
19 Lord, for thy s' sake, and according"
Isa 45: 4 For Jacob my s' sake, and Israel "
Joh 18:10 ear. The s' name was Malchus. 1401

servants See also SERVANTS'; MAIDSERVANTS; MENSERVANTS; WOMENSERVANTS.
Ge 9:25 a servant of s' shall he be unto his5650
14:14 he armed his trained s', born in his*
15 he and his s', by night, and smote 5650
20: 8 Abimelech...called all his s', and told"
21:25 Abimelech's s' had violently taken "
26:14 of herds, and great store of s': *5657
15 which his father's s' had digged 5650
19 And Isaac's s' digged in the valley, "
25 and there Isaac's s' digged a well. "
32 that Isaac's s' came, and told him "
27:37 brethren have I given to him for s';"
32:16 delivered...into the hand of his s', "
16 said unto his s', Pass over before "
40:20 that he made a feast unto all his s':"
20 and of the chief baker among his s'."
41:10 Pharaoh was wroth with his s', and "
37 Pharaoh, and in the eyes of all his s'."
38 Pharaoh said unto his s', Can we "
42:10 but to buy food are thy s' come. "
11 we are true men, thy s' are no spies."
13 Thy s' are twelve brethren, the sons"
44: 7 God forbid that thy s' should do "
9 whomsoever of thy s' it be found, "
16 found out the iniquity of thy s': "
16 behold, we are my lord's s', both * "
19 My lord asked his s', saying, Have "
21 thou saidst unto thy s', Bring him "
23 And thou saidst unto thy s', Except"
31 and thy s' shall bring down the gray"
45:16 it pleased Pharaoh well, and his s'. "
47: 3 Thy s' are shepherds, both we, and "
4 thy s' have no pasture for their * "
4 thy s' dwell in the land of Goshen. "
19 and we and our land will be s' unto "
25 lord, and we will be Pharaoh's s'. "
50: 2 commanded his s' the physicians "
7 him went up all the s' of Pharaoh, "
17 trespass of the s' of the God of thy "
18 and they said, Behold, we be thy s'. "
Ex 5:15 dealest thou thus with thy s'? "
16 There is no straw given unto thy s'."
16 and, behold, thy s' are beaten; but "
21 Pharaoh, and in the eyes of his s', "
7:10 before Pharaoh, and before his s', "
20 Pharaoh, and in the sight of his s'; "
8: 3 bed, and into the house of thy s', "
4 thy people, and upon all thy s'. "
9 I intreat for thee, and for thy s', "
11 from thy houses, and from thy s', "
21 of flies upon thee, and upon thy s', "
29, 31 from Pharaoh, from his s', and "
9:14 upon thine heart, and upon thy s', "
20 feared...among the s' of Pharaoh "
20 made his s' and his cattle flee into "
21 left his s' and his cattle in the field. "
30 But as for thee and thy s', I know "
34 hardened his heart, he and his s'. "
10: 1 his heart, and the heart of his s', "
6 houses, and the houses of all thy s',"
7 And Pharaoh's s' said unto him, "
11: 3 in the sight of Pharaoh's s', and in "
8 all these thy s' shall come down "
12:30 up in the night, he, and all his s', "
14: 5 the heart of Pharaoh and of his s' "
32:13 Abraham, Isaac, and Israel, thy s', "
Le 25:42 For they are my s', which I brought"
55 unto me the children of Israel are s';"
55 they are my s' whom I brought "
Nu 22:18 and said unto the s' of Balak, "
22 ass, and his two s' were with him. 5288
31:49 Thy s' have taken the sum of the 5650
32: 4 for cattle, and thy s' have cattle: "
5 let this land be given unto thy s' "
25 s' will do as my lord commandeth. "
27 But thy s' will pass over, every man"
31 As the Lord hath said unto thy s', "
De 9:27 Remember thy s', Abraham, Isaac, "
29: 2 unto Pharaoh, and unto all his s', "
32:36 and repent himself for his s', when "
43 he will avenge the blood of his s', "
34:11 to Pharaoh, and to all his s', and to "
Jos 9: 8 said unto Joshua, We are thy s'. "
9 a very far country thy s' are come "
11 and say unto them, We are your s': "
24 Because it was certainly told thy s',"
10: 6 Slack not thy hand from thy s'; "
J'g 3:24 When he was gone out, his s' came;"
6:27 Then Gideon took ten men of his s',"
19:19 the young man which is with thy s':"
1Sa 4: 9 ye be not s' unto the Hebrews, as 5647
8:14 of them, and give them to his s'. 5650
15 and give to his officers, and to his s'."
17 your sheep: and ye shall be his s'. "
9: 3 Take now one of the s' with thee, "
12:19 Pray for thy s' unto the Lord thy "
16:15 And Saul's s' said unto him, Behold"
16 Let our lord now command thy s', "
17 And Saul said unto his s', Provide "
18 Then answered one of the s', and*5288
17: 8 I a Philistine, and ye s' to Saul? 5650
9 to kill me, then will we be your s': "

1Sa 17: 9 kill him, then shall ye be our s', 5650
18: 5 and also in the sight of Saul's s'. "
22 And Saul commanded his s', saying,"
22 in thee, and all his s' love thee: "
23 And Saul's s' spake those words in "
24 And the s' of Saul told him, saying,"
26 And when his s' told David these "
30 more wisely than all the s' of Saul; "
19: 1 Jonathan his son, and to all his s', "
21: 2 I have appointed my s' to such *5288
7 man of the s' of Saul was there 5650
11 the s' of Achish said unto him, Is "
14 Then said Achish unto his s', Lo, ye"
22: 6 all his s' were standing about him;)"
7 Saul said unto his s' that stood "
9 which was set over the s' of Saul, "
14 faithful among all thy s' as David, "
17 But the s' of the king would not put"
24: 7 So David stayed his s' with these *582
25: 8 cometh to thine hand unto thy s', 5650
10 Nabal answered David's s', and "
10 be many s' now a days that break "
19 she said unto her s', Go on before*5288
40 when the s' of David were come to5650
41 wash the feet of the s' of my lord. "
28: 7 Then said Saul unto his s', Seek "
7 his s' said to him, Behold, there is "
23 his s', together with the woman, "
25 it before Saul, and before his s'; "
29:10 in the morning with thy master's s'"
2Sa 2:12 and the s' of Ish-bosheth the son of"
13 the s' of David, went out, and met "
15 Saul, and twelve of the s' of David. "
17 men of Israel, before the s' of David."
30 there lacked of David's s' nineteen "
31 But the s' of David had smitten of "
3:22 the s' of David and Joab came from"
38 king said unto his s', Know ye not "
6:20 the eyes of the handmaids of his s',"
8: 2 so the Moabites became David's s', "
6 the Syrians became s' to David, "
7 shields of gold that were on the s' "
14 they of Edom became David's s'. "
9:10 thy sons, and thy s', shall till the "
10 Ziba had fifteen sons and twenty s'."
12 Ziba were s' unto Mephibosheth. "
10: 2 comfort him by the hand of his s' "
2 David's s' came into the land of the"
3 David rather sent his s' unto thee, "
4 Hanun took David's s', and shaved "
19 the kings that were s' to Hadarezer"
11: 1 sent Joab, and his s' with him, and "
9 house with all the s' of his lord, "
11 my lord Joab, and the s' of my lord,"
13 to lie on his bed with the s' of his "
17 of the people of the s' of David; "
24 shot from off the wall upon thy s'; "
24 and some of the king's s' be dead, "
12:18 s' of David feared to tell him that "
19 David saw that his s' whispered, "
19 David said unto his s', Is the child "
21 Then said his s' unto him, What "
13:24 thee, and his s' go with thy servant."
28 Absalom had commanded his s', 5288
29 s' of Absalom did unto Amnon as "
31 s' stood by with their clothes rent.5650
36 also and all his s' wept very sore. "
14:30 Therefore he said unto his s', See, "
30 Absalom's s' set the field on fire. "
31 have thy s' set my field on fire? "
15:14 David said unto all his s' that were "
15 the king's s' said unto the king, "
15 thy s' are ready to do whatsoever "
18 And all his s' passed on beside him;"
16: 6 and at all the s' of King David: and"
11 said to Abishai, and to all his s', "
17:20 Absalom's s' came to the woman to "
18: 7 were slain before the s' of David, "
9 And Absalom met the s' of David. "
19: 5 this day the face of all thy s', "
6 regardest neither princes nor s': "
7 and speak comfortably unto thy s':"
14 king, Return thou, and all thy s'. "
17 sons and his twenty s' with him; "
20: 6 take thou thy lord's s', and pursue "
21:15 went down, and his s' with him, "
22 of David, and by the hand of his s'. "
24:20 and his s' coming on toward him: "
1Ki 1: 2 Wherefore his s' said unto him, Let"
9 all the men of Judah the king's s': "
33 Take with you the s' of your lord, "
47 the king's s' came to bless our lord "
2:39 s' of Shimei ran away unto Achish "
39 saying, Behold, thy s' be in Gath. "
40 to Gath to Achish to seek his s': "
40 went, and brought his s' from Gath."
3:15 and made a feast to all his s'. "
5: 1 Hiram...sent his s' unto Solomon; "
6 my s' shall be with thy s': and unto"
6 will I give hire for thy s' according "
9 My s' shall bring them down from "
8:23 covenant and mercy with thy s' "
32 heaven, and do, and judge thy s', "
36 forgive the sin of thy s', and of thy "
9:22 they were men of war, and his s', "
27 And Hiram sent in the navy his s', "
27 of the sea, with the s' of Solomon. "
10: 5 his table, and the sitting of his s', "
8 happy are these thy s', which stand"
13 to her own country, she and her s'. "
11:17 certain Edomites of his father's s' "
12: 7 then they will be thy s' for ever. "
15:18 them into the hand of his s': and "
20: 6 Yet I will send my s' unto thee to "
6 house, and the houses of thy s'; "
12 he said unto his s', Set yourselves "

1Ki 20:23 the s' of the king of Syria said unto5650
31 his s' said unto him, Behold now, "
22: 3 the king of Israel said unto his s', "
49 Let my s' go with thy s' in the "
2Ki 1:13 and the life of these fifty thy s', be "
2:16 be with thy s' fifty strong men; "
3:11 of the king of Israel's s' answered "
5:13 his s' came near, and spake unto "
23 and laid them upon two of his s'; 5288
6: 3 I pray thee, and go with thy s', 5650
8 took counsel with his s', saying, "
11 and he called his s', and said unto "
12 one of his s' said, None, my lord, "
7:12 in the night, and said unto his s', "
13 one of his s' answered and said, "
9: 7 I may avenge the blood of my s' "
7 the blood of all the s' of the Lord, "
11 came forth to the s' of his lord: and"
28 And his s' carried him in a chariot "
10: 5 sent to Jehu, saying, We are thy s', "
19 Baal, all his s', and all his priests;*5647
23 with you none of the s' of the Lord,5650
12:20 his s' arose, and made a conspiracy,"
21 his s', smote him, and he died; "
14: 5 slew his s' which had slain the king"
17:13 I sent to you by my s' the prophets."
23 had said by all his s' the prophets. "
18:24 of the least of my master's s', and "
26 Speak,...to thy s' in the Syrian "
19: 5 So the s' of king Hezekiah came to "
6 the s' of the king of Assyria have 5288
21:10 Lord spake by his s' the prophets,5650
23 the s' of Amon conspired against "
22: 9 Thy s' have gathered the money "
23:30 his s' carried him in a chariot dead "
24: 2 he spake by his s' the prophets. "
10 the s' of Nebuchadnezzar king of "
11 the city, and his s' did besiege it. "
12 he, and his mother, and his s', and "
25:24 Fear not to be the s' of the Chaldees:"
1Ch 18: 2 the Moabites became David's s', "
6 and the Syrians became David's s', "
7 shields of gold that were on the s' "
13 all the Edomites became David's s'. "
19: 2 the s' of David came into the land "
3 are not his s' come unto thee for to "
4 Wherefore Hanun took David's s', "
19 the s' of Hadarezer saw that they "
19 with David, and became his s': *5647
20: 8 David, and by the hand of his s'. 5650
21: 3 king, are they not all my lord's s'? "
2Ch 2: 8 that thy s' can skill to cut timber "
8 behold, my s' shall be with thy s', "
10 I will give to thy s', the hewers "
15 spoken of, let him send unto his s': "
6:14 and shewest mercy unto thy s', that"
23 and judge thy s', by requiting the "
27 forgive the sin of thy s', and of thy "
8: 9 Solomon make no s' for his work; "
18 sent him by the hands of his s' "
18 s' that had knowledge of the sea; "
18 they went with the s' of Solomon "
9: 4 his table, and the sitting of his s', "
7 happy are these thy s', which stand"
10 And the s' also of Huram, and the "
10 s' of Solomon, which brought gold "
12 to her own land, she and her s'. "
21 to Tarshish with the s' of Huram: "
10: 7 to them, they will be thy s' for ever."
12: 8 Nevertheless they shall be his s'; "
24:25 his own s' conspired against him "
25: 3 slew his s' that had killed the king "
32: 9 of Assyria send his s' to Jerusalem,"
16 his s' spake yet more against the "
33:24 And his s' conspired against him, "
34:16 that was committed to thy s', they "
35:23 king said to his s', Have me away; "
24 His s' therefore took him out of the"
36:20 where they were s' to him and his "
Ezr 2:55 The children of Solomon's s': the "
58 and the children of Solomon's s', "
65 Beside their s' and their maids, of* "
4:11 Thy s' the men on this side the 5649
5:11 We are the s' of the God of heaven "
9:11 commanded by thy s' the prophets,5650
Ne 1: 6 for the children of Israel thy s', and"
10 these are thy s' and thy people, "
11 to the prayer of thy s', who desire "
2:20 we his s' will arise and build: but "
4:16 half of my s' wrought in the work,5288
23 I, nor my brethren, nor my s', nor "
5: 5 sons and our daughters to be s', 5650
10 my s', might exact of them money5288
15 their s' bare rule over the people: "
16 my s' were gathered thither unto "
7:57 The children of Solomon's s': the 5650
60 and the children of Solomon's s', "
9:10 upon Pharaoh, and on all his s', and"
36 Behold, we are s' this day, and for "
36 good thereof, behold, we are s' in it:"
11: 3 and the children of Solomon's s'. "
13:19 some of my s' set I at the gates, 5288
Es 1: 3 unto all his princes and his s'; 5650
2: 2 Then said the king's s' that 5288
18 unto all his princes and his s', 5650
3: 2 all the king's s', that were in the "
3 Then the king's s', which were in "
4:11 All the king's s', and the people of "
5:11 above the princes and s' of the king."
6: 3 Then said the king's s' that 5288
5 the king's s' said unto him, Behold, "
Job 1:15 have slain the s' with the edge of the"
16 burned up the sheep, and the s', and"
17 and slain the s' with the edge of the"
4:18 Behold, he put no trust in his s'; 5650
Ps 34:22 Lord redeemeth the soul of his s': "

Ps 69:36 The seed also of his s' shall inherit 5650
79: 2 The dead bodies of thy s' have they "
10 the revenging of the blood of thy s' "
89:50 Remember,...the reproach of thy s'; "
90:13 let it repent thee concerning thy s'. "
16 Let thy work appear unto thy s', "
102:14 thy s' take pleasure in her stones, "
28 children of thy s' shall continue, "
105:25 people, to deal subtilly with his s'. "
113: 1 Praise, O ye s' of the Lord, praise "
119:91 thine ordinances: for all are thy s'. "
123: 2 as the eyes of s' look unto the hand "
134: 1 ye the Lord, all ye s' of the Lord, "
135: 1 praise him, O ye s' of the Lord. "
9 upon Pharaoh, and upon all his s'. "
14 repent himself concerning his s'. "
Pr 29:12 to lies, all his s' are wicked. 8334
Ec 2: 7 I got me s' and maidens, and had *5650
7 and had s' born in my house; also "
10: 7 I have seen s' upon horses, and 5650
7 and princes walking as s' upon the "
Isa 14: 2 of the Lord for s' and handmaids: "
36: 9 of the least of my master's s', "
11 Speak,...unto thy s' in the Syrian "
37: 5 s' of king Hezekiah came to Isaiah. "
6 the s' of the king of Assyria have 5288
24 By thy s'...reproached the Lord, 5650
54:17 the heritage of the s' of the Lord, "
56: 6 the name of the Lord, to be his s', "
65: 9 it, and my s' shall dwell there. "
13 s' shall eat, but ye shall be hungry: "
13 my s' shall drink, but ye shall be "
13 my s' shall rejoice, but ye shall be "
14 my s' shall sing for joy of heart, but "
15 and call his s' by another name: "
66:14 Lord shall be known toward his s', "
Jer 7:25 even sent unto you all my s' the "
21: 7 Zedekiah king of Judah, and his s', "
22: 2 throne of David, thou, and thy s', "
4 and on horses, he, and his s', and "
25: 4 hath sent unto you all his s' the "
19 king of Egypt, and his s', and his "
26: 5 hearken to the words of my s' the "
29:19 unto them by my s' the prophets, "
34:11 caused the s' and the handmaids, "
11 them into subjection for s' and for "
16 unto you for s' and for handmaids. "
35:15 I have sent also unto you all my s' "
36:24 nor any of his s' that heard all these "
31 punish him and his seed and his s' "
37: 2 But neither he, nor his s', nor the "
18 against thee, or against thy s', or "
44: 4 Howbeit I sent unto you all my s' "
46:26 and into the hands of his s': and "
La 5: 8 S' have ruled over us: there is none "
Eze 38:17 I have spoken in old time by my s' "
46:17 of his inheritance to one of his s', "
Da 1:12 Prove thy s', I beseech thee, ten "
13 and as thou seest, deal with thy s'. "
2: 4 tell thy s' the dream, and we will 5649
7 Let the king tell his s' the dream, "
3:26 ye s' of the most high God, come "
28 delivered his s' that trusted in him, "
9: 6 have we hearkened unto thy s' the 5650
10 which he set before us by his s' the "
Joe 2:29 And also upon the s' and upon the "
Am 3: 7 revealeth his secret unto his s' the "
Mic 6: 4 redeemed thee out of...house of s';* "
Zec 1: 6 I commanded my s' the prophets, "
2: 9 they shall be a spoil to their s': *5647
M't 13:27 the s' of the householder came and 1401
28 s' said unto him, Wilt thou then "
14: 2 And said unto his s', This is John 3816
18:23 which would take account of his s'. 1401
21:34 he sent his s' to the husbandmen, "
35 husbandmen took his s', and beat "
36 he sent other s' more than the first: "
22: 3 sent forth his s' to call them that "
4 he sent forth other s', saying, Tell "
6 And the remnant took his s', and "
8 saith he to his s', The wedding is "
10 s' went out into the highways, and "
13 said the king to the s', Bind him 1249
25:14 who called his own s', and delivered 1401
19 time the lord of those s' cometh, "
26:58 and sat with the s', to see the end.*5257
M'r 1:20 in the ship with the hired s', 3411
13:34 and gave authority to his s', and to 1401
14:54 he sat with the s', and warmed 5257
65 s' did strike him with the palms of* "
Lu 12:37 Blessed are those s', whom the 1401
38 find them so, blessed are those s'. "
15:17 many hired s' of my father's have 3407
19 son: make me as one of thy hired s'. "
22 But the father said to his s', Bring 1401
26 he called one of the s', and asked 3816
17:10 say, We are unprofitable s': we 1401
19:13 he called his ten s', and delivered "
15 he commanded these s' to be called "
Joh 2: 5 His mother saith unto the s', 1249
9 the s' which drew the water knew;) "
4:51 going down, his s' met him, and 1401
15:15 Henceforth I call you not s'; "
18:18 the s' and officers stood there, who "
26 One of the s' of the high priest, "
36 this world, then would my s' fight, 5257
Ac 2:18 on my s' and on my handmaidens 1401
4:29 and grant unto thy s', that with all "
10: 7 he called two of his household s', and "
16:17 are the s' of the most high God, 1401
Ro 6:16 whom ye yield yourselves s' to obey, "
16 his s' ye are to whom ye obey; "
17 thanked, that ye were the s' of sin, "
18 ye became the s' of righteousness. 1402
19 your members s' to uncleanness 1401
19 your members s' to righteousness "

Ro 6:20 when ye were the s' of sin, ye were 1401
22 and become s' to God, ye have your 1402
1Co 7:23 a price; be not ye the s' of men. *1401
2Co 4: 5 ourselves your s' for Jesus' sake. "
Eph 6: 5 S', be obedient to them that are "
6 but as the s' of Christ, doing the "
Ph'p 1: 1 s' of Jesus Christ, to all the saints "
Col 3:22 S', obey in all things your masters "
4: 1 give unto your s' that which is just "
1Ti 6: 1 as many s' as are under the yoke "
Tit 2: 9 Exhort s' to be obedient unto their "
1Pe 2:16 maliciousness, but as the s' of God.* "
18 S', be subject to your masters 3610
2Pe 2:19 they...are the s' of corruption: *1401
Re 1: 1 to shew unto his s' things which "
2:20 to teach and to seduce my s' to "
7: 3 we have sealed the s' of our God in "
10: 7 hath declared to his s' the prophets. "
11:18 reward unto thy s' the prophets, "
19: 2 hath avenged the blood of his s' at "
5 Praise our God, all ye his s', and ye "
22: 3 in it; and his s' shall serve him: "
6 sent his angel to shew unto his s' "

servants'
Ge 46:34 s' trade hath been about cattle *5650
Ex 8:24 of Pharaoh, and into his s' houses, "
Isa 63:17 Return, for thy s' sake, the tribes of "
65: 8 so will I do for my s' sake, that I "

serve See also OBSERVE; PRESERVE; RESERVE; SERVED; SERVEST; SERVETH; SERVING.
Ge 15:13 is not theirs, and shall s' them; 5647
14 that nation, whom they shall s', also, "
25:23 and the elder shall s' the younger. "
27:29 Let people s' thee, and nations bow "
40 thou live, and shalt s' thy brother; "
29:15 thou therefore s' me for nought? "
18 I will s' thee seven years for Rachel "
25 did not I s' with thee for Rachel? "
27 s' with me yet seven other years. "
Ex 1:13 children of Israel to s' with rigour: "
14 they made them s', was with rigour. "
3:12 ye shall s' God upon this mountain. "
4:23 Let my son go, that he may s' me: "
7:16 they may s' me in the wilderness: "
8: 1, 20 people go, that they may s' me. "
9: 1 my people go, that they may s' me. "
10: 3 my people go, that they may s' me. "
8 them, Go, s' the Lord your God: "
11 ye that are men, and s' the Lord; "
24 Moses, and said, Go ye, s' the Lord; "
26 we take to s' the Lord our God; "
26 not with what we must s' the Lord, "
12:31 and go, s' the Lord, as ye have said. "
14:12 that we may s' the Egyptians? "
12 better for us to s' the Egyptians, "
20: 5 down thyself to them, nor s' them: "
21: 2 servant, six years he shall s': and "
6 aul; and he shall s' him for ever. "
23:24 down to their gods, nor s' them, "
25 And ye shall s' the Lord your God, "
33 if thou s' their gods, it will surely "
Le 25:39 compel him to s' as a bondservant: 5656
40 and shall s' thee unto the year of 5647
Nu 4:24 families of the Gershonites, to s', * "
26 is made for them: so shall they s'. "
8:25 thereof, and shall s' no more: "
18: 7 and within the vail; and ye shall s': "
21 for their service which they s', even "
De 4:19 to worship them, and s' them, for "
28 there ye shall s' gods, the work of "
5: 9 thyself unto them, nor s' them: "
6:13 fear the Lord thy God, and s' him, "
7: 4 me, that they may s' other gods: "
16 neither shalt thou s' their gods; "
8:19 walk after other gods, and s' them, "
10:12 to s' the Lord thy God with all thy "
20 him shalt thou s', and to him shalt "
11:13 and to s' him with all your heart "
16 ye turn aside, and s' other gods, "
12:30 How did these nations s' their gods? "
13: 2 hast not known, and let us s' them; "
4 and ye shall s' him, and cleave unto "
6, 13 Let us go and s' other gods, "
15:12 unto thee, and s' thee six years; "
20:11 unto thee, and they shall s' thee. "
28:14 to go after other gods to s' them. "
36 and there shalt thou s' other gods, "
48 shalt thou s' thine enemies which "
64 and there thou shalt s' other gods, "
29:18 and s' the gods of these nations; "
30:17 worship other gods, and s' them; "
31:20 turn unto other gods, and s' them, "
Jos 16:10 unto this day, and s' under tribute.* "
22: 5 and to s' him with all your heart "
23: 7 neither s' them, nor bow yourselves "
24:14 and s' him in sincerity and in truth: "
14 and in Egypt; and s' ye the Lord. "
15 it seem evil unto you to s' the Lord, "
15 choose you this day whom ye will s'; "
15 and my house, we will s' the Lord. "
16 forsake the Lord, to s' other gods; "
18 therefore will we also s' the Lord; "
19 Ye cannot s' the Lord: for he is an "
20 the Lord, and s' strange gods, then "
21 Nay; but we will s' the Lord. "
22 have chosen you the Lord, to s' him. "
24 The Lord our God will we s', and "
J'g 2:19 in following other gods to s' them, "
9:28 is Shechem, that we should s' him? "
28 s' the men of Hamor the father of "
28 Shechem: for why should we s' him? "
38 Abimelech, that we should s' him? "
1Sa 7: 3 unto the Lord, and s' him only: "
10: 7 that thou do as occasion s' thee; "
11: 1 covenant with us,...we will s' thee. "

1Sa 12:10 of our enemies, and we will s' thee. 5647
14 If ye will fear the Lord, and s' him, "
20 but s' the Lord with all your heart; "
24 s' him in truth with all your heart: "
17: 9 shall ye be our servants, and s' us. "
26:19 the Lord, saying, Go, s' other gods. "
2Sa 15: 8 Jerusalem, then I will s' the Lord. "
16:19 And again, whom should I s'? "
19 should I not s' in the presence of "
22:44 which I knew not shall s' me. "
1Ki 9: 6 go and s' other gods, and worship "
12: 4 upon us, lighter,...we will s' thee. "
7 and wilt s' them, and answer them, "
2Ki 10:18 little; but Jehu shall s' him much. "
17:35 nor s' them, nor sacrifice to them: "
25:24 land, and s' the king of Babylon; "
1Ch 28: 9 s' him with a perfect heart and with "
2Ch 7:19 and shall go and s' other gods, and "
10: 4 he put upon us, and we will s' thee. "
29:11 to stand before him, to s' him, *8334
30: 8 and s' the Lord your God, that the 5647
33:16 commanded Judah to s' the Lord "
34:33 all that were present in Israel to s', "
33 even to s' the Lord their God. And "
35: 3 s' now the Lord your God, and his "
Job 21:15 Almighty, that we should s' him? "
36:11 If they obey and s' him, they shall "
39: 9 the unicorn be willing to s' thee, "
Ps 2:11 S' the Lord with fear, and rejoice "
18:43 whom I have not known shall s' me. "
22:30 A seed shall s' him; it shall be "
72:11 before him: all nations shall s' him. "
97: 7 be all they that s' graven images, "
100: 2 S' the Lord with gladness: come "
101: 6 in a perfect way, he shall s' me. *8334
102:22 and the kingdoms, to s' the Lord. 5647
Isa 14: 3 wherein thou wast made to s', "
19:23 and the Egyptians shall s' with the* "
43:23 caused thee to s' with an offering,‡ "
24 hast made me to s' with thy sins,‡ "
56: 6 themselves to the Lord, to s' him, 8334
60:12 that will not s' thee shall perish; 5647
Jer 5:19 so shall ye s' strangers in a land "
11:10 went after other gods to s' them: "
13:10 walk after other gods, to s' them, "
16:13 ye s' other gods day and night; "
17: 4 will cause thee to s' thine enemies "
25: 6 go not after other gods to s' them, "
11 nations shall s' the king of Babylon "
14 kings shall s' themselves of them "
27: 6 have I given him also to s' him. "
7 And all nations shall s' him, and "
7 kings shall s' themselves of him. "
8 not s' the same Nebuchadnezzar "
9 Ye shall not s' the king of Babylon: "
11 of the king of Babylon, and s' him, "
12 and s' him and his people, and live. "
13 that will not s' the king of Babylon? "
14 Ye shall not s' the king of Babylon: "
17 s' the king of Babylon, and live: "
28:14 that they may s' Nebuchadnezzar "
14 and they shall s' him: and I have "
30: 8 shall no more s' themselves of him: "
9 they shall s' the Lord their God, "
34: 9 none should s' himself of them, to "
10 none should s' themselves of them "
35:15 go not after other gods to s' them, "
40: 9 Fear not to s' the Chaldeans: dwell "
9 land, and s' the king of Babylon, "
10 s' the Chaldeans, which will 5975,6440
44: 3 to s' other gods, whom they knew 5647
Eze 20:32 countries, to s' wood and stone. 8334
39 Go ye, s' ye every one his idols, 5647
40 all of them in the land, s' me: "
29:18 caused his army to s' a great service "
48:18 for food unto them that s' the city.* "
19 And they that s' the city shall s' * "
19 s' it out of all the tribes of Israel. * "
Da 3:12 they s' not thy gods, nor worship 6399
14 do not ye s' my gods, nor worship "
17 God whom we s' is able to deliver "
18 we will not s' thy gods, nor worship "
28 might not s' nor worship any god, "
7:14 and languages, should s' him: "
27 dominions shall s' and obey him. "
Zep 3: 9 Lord, to s' him with one consent. 5647
Mal 3:14 Ye have said, It is vain to s' God: "
M't 4:10 God, and him only shalt thou s'. 3000
6:24 No man can s' two masters: for 1398
24 Ye cannot s' God and mammon. "
Lu 1:74 might s' him without fear, 3000
4: 8 thy God, and him only shalt thou s'. "
10:40 my sister hath left me to s' alone? 1247
12:37 and will come forth and s' them. "
15:29 Lo, these many years do I s' thee, 1398
16:13 No servant can s' two masters: for "
13 Ye cannot s' God and mammon. "
17: 8 sup, and gird thyself, and s' me. 1247
22:26 he that is chief, as he that doth s'. "
Joh 12:26 If any man s' me, let him follow "
26 if any man s' me, him will my "
Ac 6: 2 leave the word of God, and s' tables. "
7: 7 come forth, and s' me in this place. 3000
27:23 of God, whose I am, and whom I s', "
Ro 1: 9 whom I s' with my spirit in the "
6: 6 henceforth we should not s' sin. *1398
7: 6 we should s' in newness of spirit, "
25 mind I myself s' the law of God; "
9:12 her, The elder shall s' the younger. "
16:18 such s' not our Lord Jesus Christ, "
Ga 5:13 flesh, but by love s' one another. * "
Col 3:24 for ye s' the Lord Christ. "
1Th 1: 9 idols to s' the living and true God; "
2Ti 1: 3 whom I s' from my forefathers 3000
Heb 8: 5 Who s' unto the example and "
9:14 dead works to s' the living God? "

Heb12: 28 we may s· God acceptably with *3000
13: 10 right to eat which s· the tabernacle."
Re 7: 15 s· him day and night in his temple: "
22: 3 it; and his servants shall s· him: ‡ "

served See also OBSERVED; PRESERVED; RESERVED; SERVEDST.
Ge 14: 4 years they s· Chedorlaomer, and 5647
29: 20 Jacob s· seven years for Rachel; "
30 s· with him yet seven other years. "
30: 26 children, for whom I have s· thee, "
29 Thou knowest how I have s· thee, "
31: 6 all my power have I s· your father. "
41 I s· thee fourteen years for thy two "
39: 4 grace in his sight, and he s· him: *8334
40: 4 Joseph with them, and he s· them:*"
De 12: 2 ye shall possess s· their gods, 5647
17: 3 And hath gone and s· other gods, "
29: 26 For they went and s· other gods, "
Jos 23: 16 and have gone and s· other gods, * "
24: 2 of Nachor: and they s· other gods. "
14, 15 the gods which your fathers s· "
31 Israel s· the Lord all the days of "
J'g 2: 7 people s· the Lord all the days of "
11 sight of the Lord, and s· Baalim: "
13 Lord, and s· Baal and Ashtaroth. "
3: 6 to their sons, and s· their gods. "
7 God, and s· Baalim and the groves. "
8 Israel s· Cushan-rishathaim eight "
14 Israel s· Eglon the king of Moab "
8: 1 him, Why hast thou s· us thus, 6213
10: 6 and s· Baalim, and Ashtaroth, and5647
6 forsook the Lord, and s· not him. "
10 forsaken our God, and...s· Baalim. "
13 forsaken me, and s· other gods: "
16 from among them, and s· the Lord:"
1Sa 7: 4 and Ashtaroth, and s· the Lord only."
8: 8 forsaken me, and s· other gods, "
12: 10 and have s· Baalim and Ashtaroth: "
2Sa 10: 19 made peace with Israel, and s· them."
16: 19 as I have s· in thy father's presence,"
1Ki 4: 21 s· Solomon all the days of his life. "
9: 9 have worshipped them, and s· them:"
16: 31 went and s· Baal, and worshipped "
22: 53 For he s· Baal, and worshipped him,"
2Ki 10: 18 unto them, Ahab s· Baal a little; "
17: 12 For they s· idols, whereof the Lord "
16 all the host of heaven, and s· Baal. "
33 the Lord, and s· their own gods, "
41 Lord, and s· their graven images, "
18: 7 the king of Assyria, and s· him not. "
21: 3 all the host of heaven, and s· them. "
21 and s· the idols that his father s·, "
1Ch 27: 1 and their officers that s· the king 8334
2Ch 7: 22 worshipped them, and s· them: 5647
24: 18 fathers, and s· groves and idols: "
33: 3 all the host of heaven, and s· them. "
22 his father had made, and s· them; "
Ne 9: 35 have not s· thee in their kingdom, "
Es 1: 10 s· in the presence of Ahasuerus *8334
Ps 106: 36 And they s· their idols: which 5647
137: 8 rewardeth thee as thou hast s· us. 1580
Ec 5: 9 the king himself is s· by the field. 5647
Jer 5: 19 and s· strange gods in your land, so"
8: 2 have loved, and whom they have s·, "
16: 11 after other gods, and have s· them, "
22: 9 worshipped other gods, and s· them."
34: 14 and when he hath s· thee six years, "
52: 12 which s· the king of Babylon,*5975,6440
Eze 29: 18 service that he had s· against it: 5647
20 labour wherewith he s· against it, "
34: 27 of those that s· themselves of them."
Ho 12: 12 Israel s· for a wife, and for a wife "
Lu 2: 37 s· God with fastings and prayers *3000
Joh 12: 2 made him a supper; and Martha s·: 1247
Ac 13: 36 after he had s· his own generation 5256
Ro 1: 25 and s· the creature more than the 3000
Ph'p 2: 22 he hath s· with me in the gospel. 1398

servedst
De 28: 47 s· not the Lord...with joyfulness, 5647

servest See also PRESERVEST.
Da 6: 16 Thy God whom thou s· continually,6399
20 thy God, whom thou s· continually, "

serveth See also PRESERVETH.
Nu 3: 36 thereof, and all that s· thereto, *5656
Mal 3: 17 spareth his own son that s· him. 5647
18 that s· God and him that s· him not."
Lu 22: 27 that sitteth at meat, or he that s·? 1247
27 but I am among you as he that s·. "
Ro 14: 18 he that in these things s· Christ is 1398
1Co 14: 22 but prophesying s·, not for them that*
Ga 3: 19 Wherefore then s· the law? It was*

service See also BONDSERVICE; EYESERVICE.
Ge 29: 27 for the s· which thou shalt serve 5656
30: 26 knowest my s· which I have done "
Ex 1: 14 and in all manner of s· in the field: "
14 all their s·,...was with rigour. "
12: 25 promised, that ye shall keep this s·. "
26 unto you, What mean ye by this s·? "
13: 5 thou shalt keep this s· in this month."
27: 19 the tabernacle in all the s· thereof, "
30: 16 it for the s· of the tabernacle of the "
31: 10 And the cloths of s·, and the holy *8278
35: 19 The cloths of s·, to do * "
19 to do s· in the holy place, *8334
21 and for all his s·, and for the holy 5656
24 shittim wood for any work of the s·,"
36: 1 of work for the s· of the sanctuary, "
3 the work of the s· of the sanctuary, "
5 than enough for the s· of the work, "
38: 21 for the s· of the Levites, by the hand"
39: 1 scarlet, they made cloths of s·, *8278
1 do s· in the holy place, and made *8334
40 vessels of the s· of the tabernacle, 5656
41 The cloths of s· to do *8278
Ex 39: 41 to do s· in the holy place, *8334
Nu 3: 7, 8 to do the s· of the tabernacle. 5656
26 the cords of it for all the s· thereof. "
31 the hanging, and all the s· thereof. "
4: 4 shall be the s· of the sons of Kohath"
19 and appoint them every one to his s·"
23 all that enter in to perform the s·, "
24 s· of the families of the Gershonites,"
26 and all the instruments of their s·, "
27 s· of the sons of the Gershonites, "
27 their burdens, and in all their s·: "
28 is the s· of the families...of Gershon"
30 every one that entereth into the s·,6635
31 according to all their s· in the 5656
32 instruments, and with all their s·: "
33 s· of the families...of Merari, "
33 according to all their s·, in the "
35 every one that entereth into the s·,6635
37 that might do s· in the tabernacle*5647
39 every one that entereth into the s·,6635
41 that might do s· in the tabernacle*5647
43 every one that entereth into the s·,6635
47 came to do the s· of the ministry, *5656
47 s· of the burden in the tabernacle* "
49 every one according to his s·, and "
7: 5 may be to do the s· of the tabernacle"
5 to every man according to his s·. "
7 of Gershon, according unto their s·: "
8 of Merari, according unto their s·, "
9 s· of the sanctuary belonging unto "
8: 11 they may execute the s· of the Lord."
15 go in to do the s· of the tabernacle5647
19 do the s· of the children of Israel 5656
22 went the Levites in to do their s· "
24 wait upon the s· of the tabernacle "
25 cease waiting upon the s· thereof,* "
26 keep the charge, and shall do no s·. "
16: 9 to do the s· of the tabernacle of the "
18: 4 for all the s· of the tabernacle: "
6 to do the s· of the tabernacle of the "
7 priest's office unto you as a s· of gift:"
21 for their s· which they serve, "
21 even the s· of the tabernacle of the "
23 shall do the s· of the tabernacle of "
31 reward for your s· in the tabernacle"
Jos 22: 27 that we might do the s· of the Lord "
1Ki 12: 4 thou the grievous s· of thy father, "
1Ch 6: 31 whom David set over the s· of song3027
48 all manner of s· of the tabernacle 5656
9: 13 work of the s· of the house of God. "
19 were over the work of the s·, keepers"
23: 24 work for the s· of the house of the "
26 any vessels of it for the s· thereof. "
28 for the s· of the house of the Lord, "
28 work of the s· of the house of God; "
32 in the s· of the house of the Lord. "
24: 3 according to their offices in their s·."
19 the orderings of them in their s· "
25: 1 separated to the s· of the sons of "
1 workmen according to their s· was:"
6 harps, for the s· of the house of God,"
26: 8 able men for strength for the s·, "
30 the Lord, and in the s· of the king. "
28: 13 work of the s· of the house of the "
13 the vessels of s· in the house of the "
14 all instruments of all manner of s·:"
14 all instruments of every kind of s·: "
20 finished all the work for the s· of the"
21 for all the s· of the house of God: "
21 skilful man, for any manner of s·: "
29: 5 is willing to consecrate his s· this 3027
7 gave for the s· of the house of God 5656
2Ch 8: 14 the courses of the priests to their s·,"
12: 8 that they may know my s·, and "
8 s· of the kingdoms of the countries."
24: 12 to such as did the work of the s· of "
29: 35 So the s· of the house of the Lord "
31: 2 every man according to his s·, the "
16 daily portion for their s· in their "
21 began in the s· of the house of God,"
34: 13 the work in any manner of s·: "
35: 2 and encouraged them to the s· of the"
10 So the s· was prepared, and the "
15 they might not depart from their s·;"
16 all the s· of the Lord was prepared "
Ezr 6: 18 their courses, for the s· of God, 5673
7: 19 given thee for the s· of the house 6402
8: 20 had appointed for the s· of the 5656
Ne 10: 32 the third part of a shekel for the s· "
Ps 104: 14 cattle, and herb for the s· of man: "
Jer 22: 13 useth his neighbour's s· without 5647
Eze 29: 18 caused his army to serve a great s·5656
18 the s· that he had served against it:"
44: 14 of the house, for all the s· thereof, "
Joh 16: 2 will think that he doeth God s·. 2999
Ro 9: 4 and the s· of God, and the promises;"
12: 1 God, which is your reasonable s·. "
15: 31 s· which I have for Jerusalem may*1248
2Co 9: 12 administration of this s· not only 3009
11: 8 taking wages of them, to do you s·.*1248
Ga 4: 8 did s· unto them which by nature *1398
Eph 6: 7 With good will doing s·, as to the "
Ph'p 2: 17 the sacrifice and s· of your faith, 3009
30 to supply your lack of s· toward me "
1Ti 6: 2 but rather do them s·, because *1398
Heb 9: 1 had also ordinances of divine s·. 2999
6 accomplishing the s· of God. * "
9 make him that did the s· perfect, *3000
Re 2: 19 thy works, and charity, and s·, *1248

servile
Le 23: 7, 8 ye shall do no s· work therein. 5656
21 ye shall do no s· work therein: it "
25 Ye shall do no s· work therein: but "
35, 36 ye shall do no s· work therein. "
Nu 28: 18 do no manner of s· work therein: "
25 convocation; ye shall do no s· work. "
Nu 28: 26 convocation; ye shall do no s· work:5656
29: 1 convocation; ye shall do no s· work: "
12 convocation: ye shall do no s· work,"
35 ye shall do no s· work therein: "

serving
Ex 14: 5 we have let Israel go from s· us? 5647
De 15: 18 to thee, in s· thee six years: * "
Lu 10: 40 was cumbered about much s·, and 1248
Ac 20: 19 S· the Lord with all humility of 1398
26: 7 instantly s· God day and night, 3000
Ro 12: 11 fervent in spirit; s· the Lord; 1398
Tit 3: 3 s· divers lusts and pleasures, living "

servitor
2Ki 4: 43 And his s· said, What, should I *8334

servitude
2Ch 10: 4 thou somewhat the grievous s· of *5656
La 1: 3 affliction, and because of great s·: "

set See also BESET; SEATED; SETTEST; SETTETH; SETTING.
Ge 1: 17 God s· them in the firmament of 5414
4: 15 And the Lord s· a mark upon Cain,*7760
6: 16 of the ark shalt thou s· in the side "
9: 13 I do s· my bow in the cloud, and it 5414
17: 21 shall bear unto thee at this s· time4150
18: 8 had dressed, and s· it before them;5414
19: 16 forth, and s· him without the city. 3240
21: 2 s· time of which God had spoken 4150
28 Abraham s· seven ewe lambs of 5324
29 which thou hast s· by themselves? "
24: 33 And there was s· meat before him 7760
28: 11 all night, because the sun was s·; 935
12 behold a ladder s· up on the earth,5324
18 pillows, and s· it up for a pillar, 7760
22 stone, which I have s· for a pillar, "
30: 36 he s· three days' journey betwixt "
38 he s· the rods which he had pilled 3322
40 s· the faces of the flocks toward 5414
31: 17 and s· his sons and his wives upon5375
21 and s· his face toward the mount 7760
37 s· it here before my brethren and "
45 Jacob took a stone, and s· it up for7311
35: 14 Jacob s· up a pillar in the place 5324
20 Jacob s· a pillar upon her grave: "
41: 33 and s· him over the land of Egypt.7896
41 s· thee over all the land of Egypt. 5414
43: 9 unto thee, and s· him before thee, 3322
31 himself, and said, S· on bread. 7760
32 And they s· on for him by himself, "
44: 21 that I may s· mine eyes upon him. "
47: 7 father, and s· him before Pharaoh:5975
48: 20 he s· Ephraim before Manasseh. 7760
Ex 1: 11 they did s· over them taskmasters "
4: 20 his sons, and s· them upon an ass,7392
5: 14 taskmasters had s· over them, 7760
7: 23 did he s· his heart to this also. *7896
9: 5 And the Lord appointed a s· time, 4150
13: 12 thou shalt s· apart unto the Lord all
19: 12 thou shalt s· bounds unto the people
23 S· bounds about the mount, and
21: 1 which thou shalt s· before them. 7760
23: 31 s· thy bounds from the Red sea 7896
25: 7 and stones to be s· in the ephod, 4394
30 shalt s· upon the table shewbread 5414
26: 17 s· in order one against another: *7947
35 shalt s· the table without the vail, 7760
28: 11 them to be s· in ouches of gold. *4142
17 shalt s· in it settings of stones, 4390
20 be s· in gold in their inclosings. *7660
31: 5 in cutting of stones, to s· them, *4390
32: 22 people, that they are s· on mischief.
35: 9 and stones to be s· for the ephod, 4394
27 and stones to be s·, for the ephod, "
33 the cutting of stones, to s· them, *4390
37: 3 to be s· by the four corners of it; *
39: 10 they s· in it four rows of stones: 4390
37 even with the lamps to be s· in order,
40: 2 first month shalt thou s· up the *6965
4 table, and s· in order the things
4 that are to be s· in order upon it; *
5 And thou shalt s· the altar of gold5414
6 thou shalt s· the altar of the burnt "
7 And thou shalt s· the laver between "
8 thou shalt s· up the court round 7760
18 s· up the boards thereof, and put in"
20 and s· the staves on the ark, and put"
21 and s· up the vail of the covering, "
23 he s· the bread in order upon it 6186
28 he s· up the hanging at the door *7760
30 he s· the laver between the tent of "
33 s· up the hanging of the court gate.5414
Le 17: 10 even s· my face against that soul "
20: 3 I will s· my face against that man, "
5 I will s· my face against that man,7760
6 even s· my face against that soul, 5414
24: 6 thou shalt s· them in two rows, 7760
8 he shall s· it in order before the
26: 1 neither shall ye s· up any image *5414
11 I will s· my tabernacle among you: "
17 And I will s· my face against you, "
Nu 1: 51 pitched, the Levites shall s· it up: 6965
2: 9 armies. These shall first s· forth. 5265
16 shall s· forth in the second rank. "
17 congregation shall s· forward with "
17 encamp, so shall they s· forward, "
34 so they s· forward, every one after "
4: 15 as the camp is to s· forward; after "
5: 16 near, and s· her before the Lord: 5975
18, 30 s· the woman before the Lord, "
7: 1 had fully s· up the tabernacle, *6965
8: 13 thou shalt s· the Levites before 5975
10: 17 and the sons of Merari s· forward, 5265
18 of the camp of Reuben s· forward "
21 And the Kohathites s· forward, "
21 the other did s· up the tabernacle 6965

Nu 10:22 children of Ephraim s· forward 5265
25 of the children of Dan s· forward, "
28 their armies, when they s· forward. "
35 to pass, when the ark s· forward, "
11:24 and s· them round about the 5975
21: 8 fiery serpent, and s· it upon a pole:7760
10 the children of Israel s· forward, *5265
22: 1 the children of Israel s· forward, * "
24: 1 s· his face toward the wilderness. 7896
27:16 s· a man over the congregation, *6485
19, 22 s· him before Eleazar the 5975
29:39 do unto the Lord in your s· feasts. 4150
De 1: 8 I have s· the land before you: go 5414
21 God hath s· the land before thee: "
4: 8 law, which I s· before you this day? "
44 law...Moses s· before the children 7760
7: 7 Lord did not s· his love upon you,
11:26 I s· before you this day a blessing 5414
32 which I s· before you this day.
14:24 God shall choose to s· his name 7760
16:22 shalt thou s· thee up any image; 6965
17:14 I will s· a king over me, like as all 7760
15 in any wise s· him king over thee, "
15 brethren shalt thou s· king over "
15 mayest not s· a stranger over thee,*5414
19:14 time have s· in thine inheritance, 1379
26: 4 s· it down before the altar of the 3240
10 shalt s· it before the Lord thy God, "
27: 2 thou shalt s· thee up great stones, 6965
4 ye shall s· up these stones, which I "
28: 1 God will s· thee on high above all 5414
36 king which thou shalt s· over thee,6965
56 to s· the sole of her foot upon the 3322
30: 1 curse, which I have s· before thee,5414
15 I have s· before thee this day life "
19 I have s· before you life and death, "
32: 8 he s· the bounds of the people 5324
22 s· on fire the foundations of the
46 *S·* your hearts unto all the words 7760
Jos 4: 9 Joshua s· up twelve stones in the 6965
6:26 son shall he s· up the gates of it. 5324
8: 8 that ye shall s· the city on fire: 3341
12 s· them to lie in ambush between 7760
13 when they had s· the people, even "
19 and hasted and s· the city on fire.
10:18 and s· men by it for to keep them: 6485
18: 1 and s· up the tabernacle of the 7931
24:25 s· them a statute and an ordinance7760
26 and s· it up there under an oak, 6965
J'g 1: 8 the sword, and s· the city on fire. 7971
6:18 my present, and s· it before thee. *3240
7: 5 him shalt thou s· by himself; 3322
19 they had but newly s· the watch: 6965
22 Lord s· every man's sword against7760
9:25 men of Shechem s· liers in wait for "
33 rise early, and s· upon the city: ‡6584
49 and s· the hold on fire upon them;
15: 5 when he had s· the brands on fire,
16:25 they s· him between the pillars. 5975
18:30 children of Dan s· up the graven 6965
31 s· them up Micah's graven image, 7760
20:22 s· their battle again in array in
29 And Israel s· liers in wait round 7760
36 which they had s· beside Gibeah. "
48 s· on fire all the cities that they 7971
Ru 2: 5, 6 his servant that was s· over the 5324
1Sa 2: 8 to s· them among princes, and to *3427
8 he hath s· the world upon them. 7896
5: 2 of Dagon, and s· it by Dagon. 3322
3 and s· him in his place again. 7725
6:18 they s· down the ark of the Lord: 3240
7:12 s· it between Mizpeh and Shen, 7760
9:20 days ago, s· not thy mind on them; "
23 I said unto thee, *S·* it by thee. "
24 was upon it, and s· it before Saul. "
24 is left! s· it before thee, and eat: "
10:19 him, Nay, but s· a king over us. "
12:13 the Lord hath s· a king over you. 5414
13: 8 s· time that Samuel had appointed:4150
15:11 that I have s· up Saul to be king: 4427
12 he s· him up a place, and is gone 5324
17: 2 s· the battle in array against the
8 come out to s· your battle in array?
18: 5 Saul s· him over the men of war, 7760
30 so that his name was much s· by. 3335
22: 9 was s· over the servants of Saul, *5324
26:24 thy life was much s· by this day 1431
24 much s· by in the eyes of the Lord, "
28:22 s· a morsel of bread before thee; 7760
2Sa 3:10 to s· up the throne of David over 6965
6: 3 s· the ark of God upon a new cart,7392
17 of the Lord, and s· it in his place, 3322
7:12 I will s· up thy seed after thee, 6965
10:17 the Syrians s· themselves in array
11:15 *S·* ye Uriah in the forefront of the 3051
12:20 they s· bread before him, and he 7760
30 stones: and it was s· on David's head.
14:30 barley there; go and s· it on fire.
30 servants s· the field on fire.
31 thy servants s· my field on fire?
15:24 and they s· down the ark of God; 3332
18: 1 and s· captains of thousands and 7760
13 wouldest have s· thyself against *3320
19:28 thou s· thy servant among them 7896
20: 5 he tarried longer than the s· time 4150
23:23 And David s· him over his guard. 7760
1Ki 2:15 that all Israel s· their faces on me, "
19 seat to be s· for the king's mother; "
24 s· me on the throne of David my 3427
5: 5 whom I will s· upon thy throne in 5414
6:19 to s· there the ark of the covenant "
27 And he s· the cherubims within the "
7:16 to s· upon the tops of the pillars: "
21 he s· up the pillars in the porch of6965
21 and he s· up the right pillar, and "
21 he s· up the left pillar, and called "

1Ki 7:25 and the sea was s· above upon them,
39 he s· the sea on the right side of 5414
8:21 I have s· there a place for the ark,7760
9: 6 my statutes which I have s· before5414
10: 9 to s· thee on the throne of Israel: "
12:29 And he s· the one in Beth-el, and 7760
14: 4 eyes were s· by reason of his age. 6965
15: 4 to s· up his son after him, and to "
16:34 and s· up the gates thereof in his 5324
20:12 servants, *S·* yourselves in array. 7760
12 they s· themselves in array against "
21: 9 and s· Naboth on high among the 3427
10 s· two men, sons of Belial, before "
12 and s· Naboth on high among the "
2Ki 4: 4 shalt s· aside that which is full. 5265
10 and let us s· for him there a bed, 7760
38 *S·* on the great pot, and seethe 8239
43 should I s· this before an hundred5414
44 So he s· it before them, and they "
6:22 s· bread and water before them, 7760
8:12 strong holds wilt thou s· on fire, 7971
10: 3 and s· him on his father's throne, 7760
12: 4 money that every man is s· at, *6187
9 s· it beside the altar, on the right 5414
17 and Hazael s· his face to go up to 7760
17:10 s· them up images and groves in 5324
18:23 on thy part to s· riders upon them.5414
20: 1 *S·* thine house in order; for thou
21: 7 he s· a graven image of the grove 7760
25:19 an officer that was s· over the men6496
28 s· his throne above the throne of 5414
1Ch 6:31 David s· over the service of song 5975
9:22 seer did ordain in their s· office. 530
26 chief porters, were in their s· office, "
31 s· office over the things that were "
11:14 s· themselves in the midst of that*3320
25 and David s· him over his guard. 7760
16: 1 s· it in the midst of the tent that 3322
19:10 that the battle was s· against him
11 and they s· themselves in array
17 s· the battle in array against them.
21:18 s· up an altar unto the Lord in *6965
22: 2 s· masons to hew wrought stones 5975
19 s· your heart and your soul to seek5414
23: 4 s· forward the work of the house *5329
31 new moons, and on the s· feasts, 4150
29: 2 onyx stones, and stones to be s·, 4394
3 I have s· my affection to the house of
2Ch 2:18 he s· threescore and ten thousand 6213
18 overseers to s· the people a work.
3: 5 s· thereon palm trees and chains. *5927
4: 7 and s· them in the temple, five on 5414
10 he s· the sea on the right side of the"
19 tables whereon the shewbread was s·;*
6:10 and am s· on the throne of Israel,*3427
13 had s· it in the midst of the court: 5414
7:19 statutes...which I have s· before you,"
9: 8 in thee to s· thee on his throne, "
11:16 as s· their hearts to seek the Lord "
13: 3 And Abijah s· the battle in array * 631
3 Jeroboam also s· the battle in array
11 the shewbread also s· they in order
14:10 s· the battle in array in the valley
17: 2 s· garrisons in the land of Judah, 5414
19: 5 he s· judges in the land throughout5975
8 did Jehoshaphat s· of the Levites, "
20: 3 and s· himself to seek the Lord, 5414
17 s· yourselves, stand ye still, and 3320
22 the Lord s· ambushments against 5414
23:10 And he s· all the people, every man5975
14 that were s· over the host, 6485
19 And he s· the porters at the gates 5975
20 and s· the king upon the throne of 3427
24: 8 and s· it without at the gate of the 5414
13 s· the house of God in his state, 5975
25:14 Seir, and s· them up to be his gods, "
29:25 he s· the Levites in the house of the"
35 house of the Lord was s· in order. 3559
31: 3 new moons, and for the s· feasts, 4150
15 of the priests, in their s· office, to 530
18 for in their s· office they sanctified "
32: 6 s· captains of war over the people,5414
33: 7 And he s· a carved image, the idol 7760
19 s· up groves and graven images, 5975
34:12 of the Kohathites, to s· it forward;5329
35: 2 he s· the priests in their charges, 5975
Ezr 2:68 house of God to s· it up in his place:"
3: 3 they s· the altar upon his bases; 3559
5 and of all the s· feasts of the Lord 4150
8 s· forward the work of the house *5329
9 to s· forward the workmen in the* "
10 they s· the priests in their apparel5975
4:10 and s· in the cities of Samaria, 3488
12 and have s· up the walls thereof, *3635
13 be builded, the walls s· up again, * "
16 again, and the walls thereof s· up,* "
5:11 king of Israel builded and s· up. * "
6:11 being s· up, let him be hanged *2211
18 s· the priests in their divisions, 6966
7:25 s· magistrates and judges, which *4483
9: 9 to s· up the house of our God, and7311
Ne 1: 9 I have chosen to s· my name there.*7931
2: 6 to send me; and I s· him a time. 5414
3: 1 sanctified it, and s· up the doors of5975
3, 6, 13, 14, 15 s· up the doors thereof, "
4: 9 s· a watch against them day and "
13 Therefore s· I in the lower places "
13 s· the people after their families "
5: 7 s· a great assembly against them.*5414
6: 1 s· up the doors upon the gates;) 5975
7: 1 was built, and I had s· up the doors,"
9:37 kings whom thou hast s· over us 5414
10:33 the new moons, for the s· feasts, 4150
13:11 together,...s· them in their place. 5975
19 some of my servants s· I at the gates,"
Es 2:17 s· the royal crown upon her head, 7760

Es 3: 1 and s· his seat above all the princes7760
6: 8 royal which is s· upon his head: 5414
8: 2 Esther s· Mordecai over the house7760
Job 5:11 To s· up on high those that be low;*"
6: 4 terrors of God do s· themselves in
7:17 shouldest s· thine heart upon him?7896
20 thou s· me as a mark against thee,7760
9:19 who shall s· me a time to plead? 3259
14:13 wouldest appoint me a s· time, 2706
16:12 pieces, and s· me up for his mark.6965
19: 8 he hath s· darkness in my paths. 7760
30: 1 have s· with the dogs of my flock. 7896
13 path, they s· forward my calamity,
33: 5 s· thy words in order before me,
34:14 If he s· his heart upon man, if he 7760
24 and s· others in their stead. *5975
36:16 that which should be s· on thy table5183
38:10 place, and s· bars and doors, 7760
33 s· the dominion...in the earth? * "
Ps 2: 2 kings of the earth s· themselves, 3320
6 Yet have I s· my king upon my 5258
3: 6 have s· themselves against me 7896
4: 3 the Lord hath s· apart him that is 6395
8: 1 s· thy glory above the heavens. 5414
10: 8 are privily s· against the poor. 6845
12: 5 I will s· him in safety from him 7896
16: 8 have s· the Lord always before me:7737
17:11 s· their eyes bowing down to the 7896
19: 4 hath he s· a tabernacle for the sun,7760
20: 5 of our God we will s· up our banners:
27: 5 he shall s· me up upon a rock. 7311
31: 8 hast s· my feet in a large room. 5975
40: 2 clay, and s· my feet upon a rock, 6965
50:21 s· them in order before thine eyes.
54: 3 they have not s· God before them. 7760
57: 4 even among them that are s· on fire,
62:10 s· not your heart upon them. 7896
69:29 salvation, O God, s· me up on high.
73: 9 They s· their mouth against the 8371
18 didst s· them in slippery places: *7896
74: 4 they s· up their ensigns for signs. 7760
17 hast s· all the borders of the earth:5324
78: 7 they might s· their hope in God, 7760
8 that s· not their heart aright, and 3559
85:13 shall s· us in the way of his steps.*7760
86:14 and have not s· thee before them. "
89:25 I will s· his hand also in the sea, "
42 hast s· up the right hand of his 7311
90: 8 Thou hast s· our iniquities before 7896
91:14 Because he hath s· his love upon me,
14 I will s· him on high, because he hath
101: 3 I will s· no wicked thing before 7896
102:13 to favour her, yea, the s· time, is come.
104: 9 Thou hast s· a bound that they 7760
109: 6 *S·* thou a wicked man over him: 6485
113: 8 That he may s· him with princes, 3427
118: 5 me, and s· me in a large place.
122: 5 there are s· thrones of judgment, 3427
132:11 thy body will I s· upon thy throne.7896
140: 5 wayside; they have s· gins for me. "
141: 2 be s· forth before thee as incense; 3559
3 *S·* a watch, O Lord, before my 7896
Pr 1:25 have s· at nought all my counsel,
8:23 I was s· up from everlasting, from5258
27 he s· a compass upon the face of 2710
22:28 landmark,...thy fathers have s·. 6213
23: 5 Wilt thou s· thine eyes upon that 5774
Ec 3:11 he hath s· the world in their heart,5414
7:14 God also hath s· the one over *6213
8:11 of men is fully s· in them to do evil.
10: 6 Folly is s· in great dignity, and 5414
12: 9 and s· in order many proverbs.
Ca 5:12 washed with milk, and fitly s·. 3427
14 are as gold rings s· with the beryl:4390
15 s· upon sockets of fine gold: his 3245
7: 2 heap of wheat s· about with lilies. 5473
8: 6 *S·* me as a seal upon thine heart, 7760
Isa 3:24 and instead of well s· hair baldness;
7: 6 and s· a king in the midst of it, even
9:11 Lord shall s· up the adversaries 7682
11:11 the Lord shall s· his hand again the
12 s· up an ensign for the nations, 5375
14: 1 and s· them in their own land: and3240
17:10 and shalt s· it with strange slips:*2232
19: 2 I will s· the Egyptians against *5526
21: 6 Go, s· a watchman, let him declare5975
8 I am s· in my ward whole nights: 5324
22: 7 horsemen shall s· themselves in 7896
23:13 they s· up the towers thereof, they6965
27: 4 s· the briers and thorns against *5414
11 women come, and s· them on fire:
36: 8 thy part to s· riders upon them. 5414
38: 1 *S·* thine house in order: for thou
41:19 I will s· in the desert the fir tree, 7760
42: 4 he have s· judgment in the earth: "
25 it hath s· him on fire round about,
44: 7 declare it,...s· it in order for me,
45:20 that s· up the wood of their graven*5375
46: 7 him, and s· him in his place, and 3240
49:22 s· up my standard to the people: 7311
50: 7 have I s· my face like a flint, and 7760
57: 7 mountain hast thou s· thy bed: "
8 hast thou s· up thy remembrance: "
62: 6 s· watchmen upon thy walls, O 6485
66:19 I will s· a sign among them, and I 7760
Jer 1:10 this day s· thee over the nations 6485
15 they shall s· every one his throne 5414
4: 6 *S·* up the standard toward Zion: 5375
5:26 they s· a trap, they catch men. 5324
6: 1 Tekoa, and s· up a sign of fire in *5375
17 Also I s· watchmen over you, 6965
23 s· in array as men for war against
27 I have s· thee for a tower and a *5414
7:12 where I s· my name at the first, *7931
30 they have s· their abominations in7760
9:13 my law which I s· before them, 5414

Jer 10:20 more, and to s· up my curtains. 6965
11:13 ye s· up altars to that shameful 7760
21: 8 I s· before you the way of life, and 5414
10 I have s· my face against this city 7760
23: 4 I will s· up shepherds over them 6965
24: 1 of figs were s· before the temple 3259
6 s· mine eyes upon them for good, 7760
26: 4 law, which I have s· before you, 5414
31:21 S· thee up waymarks, make thee 5324
21 s· thine heart toward the highway, 7896
29 the children's teeth are s· on edge.
30 grape, his teeth shall be s· on edge.
32:20 s· signs and wonders in the land 7760
29 shall come and s· fire on this city,
34 they s· their abominations in the 7760
34:16 had s· at liberty at their pleasure, *7971
35: 5 I s· before the sons of the house 5414
38:22 Thy friends have s· thee on, and 5496
40:11 s· over them Gedaliah the son of 6485
42:15 s· your faces to enter into Egypt, 7760
17 that s· their faces to go into Egypt "
43:10 will s· his throne upon these stones "
44:10 I s· before you and before your 5414
11 I will s· my face against you for 7760
12 s· their faces to go into the land of "
49:38 And I will s· my throne in Elam,
50: 2 and publish, and s· up a standard; 5375
9 s· themselves in array against her;
51:12 S· up the standard upon the walls 5375
12 s· up the watchmen, prepare the 6965
27 S· ye up a standard in the land, 5375
52:32 s· his throne above the throne of 5414
La 2:17 he hath s· up the horn of thine *7311
3: 6 He hath s· me in dark places, as *3427
12 and s· me as a mark for the arrow. 5324
Eze 2: 2 s· me upon my feet, that I heard 5975
3:24 s· me upon my feet, and speak with "
4: 2 it; s· the camp also against it, and 5414
2 s· battering rams against it round *7760
3 and s· it for a wall of iron between 5414
3 s· thy face against it, and it shall 3559
7 shalt s· thy face toward the siege of "
5: 5 s· it in the midst of the nations 7760
6: 2 s· thy face toward the mountains "
7:20 his ornament, he s· it in majesty: "
20 have I s· it far from them. *5414
9: 4 s· a mark upon the foreheads of 8427
12: 6 I have s· thee for a sign unto the 5414
13:17 s· thy face against the daughters 7760
14: 3 men have s· up their idols in their *5927
8 will s· my face against that man, 5414
15: 7 And I will s· my face against them; "
7 when I s· my face against them. 7760
16:18 hast s· mine oil and mine incense 5414
19 even s· it before them for a sweet "
17: 4 he s· it in a city of merchants. 7760
5 waters, and s· it as a willow tree. "
22 of the high cedar, and will s· it; 5414
18: 2 the children's teeth are s· on edge?
19: 8 nations s· against him on every 5414
20:46 s· thy face toward the south, and 7760
21: 2 s· thy face toward Jerusalem, and "
15 I have s· the point of the sword 5414
16 left, whithersoever thy face is s·. 3259
22: 7 they s· light by father and mother:
10 her that was s· apart for pollution. *5079
23:24 s· against thee buckler and shield 7760
24 I will s· judgment before them, 5414
25 I will s· my jealousy against thee, "
41 hast s· mine incense and mine oil. 7760
24: 2 king of Babylon s· himself against *5564
3 S· on a pot, s· it on, and also pour 8239
7 she s· it upon the top of a rock; 7760
8 I have s· her blood upon the top of 5414
11 s· it empty upon the coals thereof, 5975
25 whereupon they s· their minds, 4853
25: 2 Son of man, s· thy face against 7760
4 they shall s· their palaces in thee, 3427
26: 9 shall s· engines of war against thy 5414
20 s· thee in the low parts of the *3427
20 s· glory in the land of the living; 5414
27:10 thee; they s· forth thy comeliness. "
28: 2, 6 s· thine heart as the heart of "
14 I have s· thee so: thou wast upon "
21 of man, s· thy face against Zidon, 7760
29: 2 s· thy face against Pharaoh king "
30: 8 when I have s· a fire in Egypt, and 5414
14 and will s· fire in Zoan, and will "
16 And I will s· fire in Egypt: Sin shall "
31: 4 the deep s· him up on high with *7311
32: 8 and s· darkness upon thy land, 5414
23 graves are s· in the sides of the pit, "
25 They have s· her a bed in the midst "
33: 2 and s· for him their watchman: "
7 I have s· thee a watchman unto the "
34:23 And I will s· up one shepherd over 6965
35: 2 s· thy face against mount Seir, and 7760
37: 1 and s· me down in the midst of the 5117
26 will s· my sanctuary in the midst 5414
38: 2 s· thy face against Gog, the land of 7760
39: 9 and shall s· on fire and burn the *1197
15 then shall he s· up a sign by it, 1129
21 s· my glory among the heathen, 5414
40: 2 s· me upon a very high mountain, 5117
4 s· thine heart upon all that I shall 7760
44: 8 ye have s· keepers of my charge in "
Da 1:11 the eunuchs had s· over Daniel, *4487
2:44 God of heaven s· up a kingdom, 6966
49 and he s· Shadrach, Meshach, and *4483
3: 1 he s· it up in the plain of Dura, in 6966
2 Nebuchadnezzar the king had s· up. "
3 Nebuchadnezzar the king had s· up; "
3 that Nebuchadnezzar had s· up. "
5 Nebuchadnezzar the king hath s· up: "
7 Nebuchadnezzar the king had s· up. "
12 whom thou hast s· over the affairs *4483

Da 3:12 image which thou hast s· up. 6966
14 golden image which I have s· up? "
18 golden image which thou hast s· up. "
5:19 and whom he would he s· up; and *7313
6: 1 It pleased Darius to s· over the 6966
3 to s· him over the whole realm. "
14 s· his heart on Daniel to deliver 7761
7:10 judgment was s·, and the books 3488
8:18 he touched me, and s· me upright. 5975
9: 3 I s· my face unto the Lord God, to 5414
10 he s· before us by his servants the "
10:10 which s· me upon my knees and 5128
12 didst s· thine heart to understand, 5414
15 I s· my face toward the ground, "
11:11 shall s· forth a great multitude; 5975
13 shall s· forth a multitude greater "
17 He shall also s· his face to enter 7760
12:11 that maketh desolate s· up, there 5414
Ho 2: 3 s· her as in the day that she was 3322
3 s· her like a dry land, and slay 7896
4: 8 s· their heart on their iniquity. 5375
6:11 he hath s· an harvest for thee, *7896
8: 1 S· the trumpet to thy mouth. He
4 They have s· up kings, but not by
11: 8 how shall I s· thee as Zeboim? 7761
Joe 2: 5 a strong people s· in battle array.
Am 7: 8 s· a plumbline in the midst of my 7760
8: 5 we may s· forth wheat, making the 6605
9: 4 s· mine eyes upon them for evil, 7760
Ob 4 thou s· thy nest among the stars, "
Na 3: 6 and will s· thee as a gazingstock. "
13 gates of thy land shall be s· wide
Hab 2: 1 and s· me upon the tower, and 3320
9 that he may s· his nest on high, 7760
Zec 3: 5 them s· a fair mitre upon his head. "
5 they s· a fair mitre upon his head, "
5:11 and s· there upon her own base. 3240
6:11 s· them upon the head of Joshua 7760
8:10 I s· all men every one against his 7971
Mal 3:15 that work wickedness are s· up; *1129
M't 5: 1 and when he was s·, his disciples *2523
14 that is s· on an hill cannot be hid. 2749
10:35 to s· a man at variance against his 1369
18: 2 and s· him in the midst of them, 2476
21: 7 clothes, and they s· him thereon. *1940
25:33 s· the sheep on his right hand, but 2476
27:19 was s· down on the judgment seat, *2521
37 s· up over his head his accusation 2007
M'r 1:32 at even, when the sun did s·, they 1416
4:21 and not to be s· on a candlestick? *2007
6:41 to his disciples to s· before them; 3908
8: 6 to his disciples to s· before them; "
6 they did s· them before the people. "
7 to s· them also before them. "
9:12 many things, and be s· at nought. 1847
36 and s· him in the midst of them: 2476
12: 1 s· an hedge about it, and digged a 4060
Lu 1: 1 to s· forth in order a declaration of *392
2:34 child is s· for the fall and rising 2749
4: 9 s· him on a pinnacle of the temple, 2476
18 s· at liberty them that are bruised, 649
7: 8 also am a man s· under authority, 5021
9:16 disciples to s· before the multitude. 3908
47 took a child, and s· him by him, 2476
51 s· his face to go to Jerusalem, 4741
10: 8 such things as are s· before you: 3908
34 wine, and s· him on his own beast, 1913
11: 6 I have nothing to s· before him? 3908
19:35 the colt, and they s· Jesus thereon. 1913
22:55 and were s· down together, Peter *4776
23:11 his men of war s· him at nought, 1848
Joh 2: 6 there were s· there six waterpots 2749
10 beginning doth s· forth good wine; *5087
3:33 hath s· to his seal that God is true. 4972
6:11 disciples to them that were s· down; 345
8: 3 when they had s· her in the midst, 2476
13:12 garments, and was s· down again, *377
19:29 was s· a vessel full of vinegar: 2749
Ac 4: 7 when they had s· them in the midst, 2476
11 the stone which was s· at nought 1848
5:27 they s· them before the council: 2476
6: 6 Whom they s· before the apostles: "
13 And s· up false witnesses, which "
7: 5 not so much as to s· his foot on: 968
26 would have s· them at one again, 4900
12:21 upon a s· day Herod, arrayed in 5002
13: 9 the Holy Ghost, s· his eyes on him, *816
47 I have s· thee to be a light of the 5087
15:16 ruins thereof, and I will s· it up: 461
16:34 his house, he s· meat before them, 3908
17: 5 and s· all the city on an uproar, 2350
18:10 and no man shall s· on thee to hurt 2007
19:27 is in danger to be s· at nought; *2064
21: 2 we went abroad, and s· forth. 321
22:30 down, and s· him before them. 2476
23:24 beasts, that they may s· Paul on, 1913
26:32 man might have been s· at liberty, 630
Ro 3:25 hath s· forth to be a propitiation 4388
14:10 dost thou s· at nought thy brother? 1848
1Co 4: 9 God hath s· forth us the apostles 584
6: 4 s· them to judge who are least 2523
10:27 whatsoever is s· before you, eat, 3908
11:34 rest will I s· in order when I come. 1299
12:18 But now hath God s· the members 5087
28 And God hath s· some in the church, "
Ga 3: 1 Christ hath been evidently s· forth, 4270
Eph 1:20 s· him at his own right hand in *2523
Ph'p 1:17 s· for the defence of the gospel. 2749
Col 3: 2 S· your affection on things above. 5426
Tit 1: 5 shouldest s· in order the things 1930
Heb 2: 7 didst s· him over the works of thy 2525
6:18 hold upon the hope s· before us: 4295
8: 1 who is s· on the right hand of the *2523
12: 1 the race that is s· before us, 4295
2 for the joy that was s· before him "
2 is s· down at the right hand of the *2523

Heb 13:23 our brother Timothy is s· at liberty; 630
Jas 3: 6 nature; and it is s· on fire of hell. 5394
Jude 7 flesh, are s· forth for an example, 4295
Re 3: 8 I have s· before thee an open door, 1325
21 am s· down with my Father in his *2523
4: 2 behold, a throne was s· in heaven, 2749
10: 2 he s· his right foot upon the sea, 5087
20: 3 him up, and s· a seal upon him, *4972

Seth (*seth*) See also SHETH.
Ge 4:25 a son, and called his name S·: 8352
26 to S·, to him also there was born a "
5: 3 his image; and called his name S·: "
4 of Adam after he had begotten S· "
6 S· lived an hundred and five years, "
7 S· lived after he begat Enos eight "
8 And all the days of S· were nine "
Lu 3:38 Enos, which was the son of S·, 4589

Sethur (*se'-thur*)
Nu 13:13 of Asher, S· the son of Michael. 5639

setter See also UNDERSETTERS.
Ac 17:18 to be a s· forth of strange gods: 2604

settest
De 23:20 in all that thou s· thine hand to *4916
28: 8 in all that thou s· thine hand unto; *"
20 in all that thou s· thine hand unto *"
Job 7:12 that thou s· a watch over me? 7760
13:27 s· a print upon the heels of my feet. †
Ps 21: 3 thou s· a crown of pure gold on 7896
41:12 and s· me before thy face for ever. 5324

setteth
Nu 1:51 when the tabernacle s· forward, 5265
4: 5 And when the camp s· forward, "
De 24:15 is poor, and s· his heart upon it: 5375
27:16 that s· light by his father or his 7034
2Sa 22:34 and s· me upon my high places. 5975
Job 28: 3 He s· an end to darkness, and 7760
Ps 18:33 and s· me upon my high places. 5975
36: 4 he s· himself in a way that is not 3320
65: 6 his strength s· fast the mountains; 3559
68: 6 God s· the solitary in families: he 3427
75: 7 down one, and s· up another. *7311
83:14 flame s· the mountains on fire; 3857
107:41 s· he the poor on high from affliction,
Jer 5:26 they lay wait, as he that s· snares; *7918
43: 3 of Neriah s· thee on against us, 5496
Eze 14: 4 that s· up his idols in his heart, *5927
7 and s· up his idols in his heart, * "
Da 2:21 removeth kings, and s· up kings: 6966
4:17 and s· up over it the basest of men. "
M't 4: 5 and s· him on the pinnacle of the *2476
Lu 8:16 s· it on a candlestick, that they *2007
Jas 3: 6 s· on fire the course of nature; 5394

setting See also SETTINGS.
Eze 43: 8 In their s· of their threshold by 5414
M't 27:66 sealing the stone, and s· a watch. *3326
Lu 4:40 Now when the sun was s·, all they 1416

settings
Ex 28:17 thou shalt set in it s· of stones, 4396

settle See also SETTLED; SETTLEST.
1Ch 17:14 I will s· him in mine house and 5975
Eze 36:11 will s· you after your old estates, *3427
43:14 the lower s· shall be two cubits, 5835
14 the lesser s· even to the greater "
14 greater s· shall be four cubits, ‡ "
17 the s· shall be fourteen cubits long ‡ "
20 and on the four corners of the s·, ‡ "
45:19 upon the four corners of the s· of ‡ "
Lu 21:14 S· it therefore in your hearts, not 5087
1Pe 5:10 stablish, strengthen, s· you. * 2311

settled
1Ki 8:13 a s· place for thee to abide in for *4349
2Ki 8:11 he s· his countenance stedfastly, 5975
Ps 119:89 O Lord, thy word is s· in heaven. 5324
Pr 8:25 Before the mountains were s·, 2883
Jer 48:11 he hath s· on his lees, and hath 8252
Zep 1:12 the men that are s· on their lees: 7087
Col 1:23 in the faith grounded and s·, and *1476

settlest
Ps 65:10 thou s· the furrows thereof: thou 5181

seven See also SEVENFOLD; SEVENS; SEVENTEEN.
Ge 5: 7 Enos eight hundred and s· years, 7651
25 an hundred eighty and s· years, "
26 Lamech s· hundred eighty and "
31 days of Lamech were s· hundred "
31 seventy and s· years: and he died. "
7: 4 s· days, and I will cause it to rain "
10 it came to pass after s· days, that "
8:10, 12 And he stayed yet other s· days; "
12 he stayed yet other s· days, and "
14 s· and twentieth day of the month, "
11:21 Serug two hundred and s· years, "
21:28 Abraham set s· ewe lambs of the "
29 What mean these s· ewe lambs "
30 these s· ewe lambs shalt thou take "
23: 1 Sarah was an hundred and s· and "
25:17 hundred and thirty and s· years: "
29:18 will serve thee s· years for Rachel "
20 Jacob served s· years for Rachel; "
27 serve with me yet s· other years. "
30 served with him yet s· other years. "
31:23 pursued after him s· days' journey; "
33: 3 himself to the ground s· times, "
41: 2 of the river s· well favoured kine "
3 s· other kine came up after them "
4 eat up the s· well favoured and fat "
5 s· ears of corn came up upon one "
6 s· thin ears and blasted with the "
7 And the s· thin ears devoured the* "
7 devoured the s· rank and full ears. 7651
18 came up out of the river s· kine, "

Ge 41:19 s' other kine came up after them, 7651
20 kine did eat up the first s' fat kine: "
22 s' ears came up in one stalk, full "
23 s' ears, withered, thin, and blasted "
24 ears devoured the s' good ears: "
26 The s' good kine are s' years; and "
26 and the s' good ears are s' years: "
27 the s' thin and ill favoured kine "
27 came up after them are s' years; "
27 the s' empty ears blasted with the "
27 eas win shall be s' years of famine. "
29 there come s' years of great plenty "
30 arise after them s' years of famine; "
34 of Egypt in the plenteous years. "
36 land against the years of famine. "
47 in the s' plenteous years the earth "
48 up all the food of he s' years, "
53 the s' years of plenteousness, that "
54 s' years of dearth began to come, "
46:25 unto Jacob: all the souls were s'. "
47:28 was an hundred forty and s' years. "
50:10 a mourning for his father s' days. "
Ex 2:16 priest of Midian had s' daughters: "
6:16 an hundred thirty and s' years. "
20 hundred and thirty and s' years. "
7:25 s' days were fulfilled, after that "
12:15 S' days shall ye eat unleavened "
19 S' days shall there be no leaven "
13: 6 S' days thou shalt eat unleavened "
7 bread shall be eaten s' days; and "
22:30 s' days it shall be with his dam; on "
23:15 shalt eat unleavened bread s' days, "
25:37 shalt make the s' lamps thereof: "
29:30 his stead shall put them on s' days, "
35 s' days shalt thou consecrate them. "
37 S' days thou shalt make an "
34:18 S' days thou shalt eat unleavened "
37:23 And he made his s' lamps, and his "
38:24 and s' hundred and thirty shekels, "
25 thousand s' hundred and threescore "
28 thousand s' hundred seventy and "
Le 4: 6 and sprinkle of the blood s' times "
17 sprinkle it s' times before the Lord, "
8:11 thereof upon the altar s' times, "
33 of the congregation in s' days, "
33 for s' days shall he consecrate you. "
35 congregation day and night s' days, "
12: 2 then she shall be unclean s' days; "
13: 4 him that hath the plague s' days: "
5 shall shut him up s' days more: "
21, 26 priest shall shut him up s' days: "
31 hath the plague of the scall s' days: "
33 that hath the scall s' days more: "
50 up it that hath the plague s' days: "
54 he shall shut it up s' days more: "
14: 7 cleansed from the leprosy s' times, "
8 tarry abroad out of his tent s' days. "
16 of the oil with his fingers s' times "
27 is in his left hand s' times before "
38 and shut up the house s' days: "
51 and sprinkle the house s' times: "
15:13 he shall number to himself s' days "
19 she shall be put apart s' days: and "
24 him, he shall be unclean s' days; "
28 she shall number to herself s' days, "
16:14 of the blood with his finger s' times. "
19 upon it with his finger s' times, "
22:27 it shall be s' days under the dam; "
23: 6 s' days ye must eat unleavened "
8 made by fire unto the Lord s' days: "
15 s' sabbaths shall be complete: "
18 s' lambs without blemish of the "
34 feast of tabernacles for s' days unto "
36 S' days ye shall offer an offering "
39 keep a feast unto the Lord s' days: "
40 before the Lord your God s' days. "
41 keep a feast unto the Lord s' days "
42 Ye shall dwell in booths s' days; all "
25: 8 shalt number s' sabbaths of years "
8 years unto thee, s' times s' years; "
8 space of the s' sabbaths of years "
26:18 I will punish you s' times more "
21 I will bring s' times more plagues "
24 and will punish you yet s' times "
28 chastise you s' times for your sins. "
Nu 1:31 were fifty and s' thousand and four "
39 and two thousand and s' hundred. "
2: 8 were fifty and s' thousand and four "
26 and two thousand and s' hundred. "
31 thousand and fifty and s' thousand "
3:22 numbered of them were s' thousand "
4:36 were two thousand s' hundred and "
8: 2 the s' lamps shall give light over "
12:14 should she not be ashamed s' days? "
14 be shut out from the camp s' days, "
15 was shut out from the camp s' days: "
13:22 Hebron was built s' years before "
16:49 fourteen thousand and s' hundred, "
19: 4 of the congregation s' times: "
11 any man shall be unclean s' days. "
14 the tent, shall be unclean s' days. "
16 or a grave, shall be unclean s' days. "
23: 1 unto Balak, Build me here s' altars, "
1 me here s' oxen and s' rams. "
4 I have prepared s' altars, and I "
14 built s' altars, and offered a bullock "
29 unto Balak, Build me here s' altars, "
29 me here s' bullocks and s' rams. "
26: 7 and three thousand and s' hundred "
34 and two thousand and s' hundred. "
51 a thousand s' hundred and thirty. "
28:11 s' lambs of the first year without "
17 s' days shall unleavened bread be "
19 ram, and s' lambs of the first year: "
21 lamb, throughout the s' lambs: "
24 offer daily, throughout the s' days, "

Nu 28:27 one ram, s' lambs of the first year; 7651
29 one lamb, throughout the s' lambs; "
29: 2 s' lambs of the first year without "
4 one lamb, throughout the s' lambs: "
8 ram, and s' lambs of the first year; "
10 one lamb, throughout the s' lambs: "
12 keep a feast unto the Lord s' days: "
32 on the seventh day s' bullocks, two "
36 s' lambs of the first year without "
31:19 ye abide without the camp s' days: "
36 three hundred thousand and s' and "
43 thirty thousand and s' thousand "
52 sixteen thousand s' hundred and "
De 7: 1 s' nations greater and mightier "
15: 1 s' years thou shalt make a release. "
16: 3 s' days shalt thou eat unleavened "
4 with thee in all thy coast s' days; "
9 S' weeks shalt thou number unto "
9 begin to number the s' weeks from "
13 the feast of tabernacles s' days, "
15 S' days shalt thou keep a solemn "
28: 7 way, and flee before thee s' ways. "
25 them, and flee s' ways before them: "
31:10 At the end of every s' years, in the "
Jos 6: 4 s' priests shall bear before the ark "
4 ye shall compass the city s' times, "
4 s' trumpets of rams' horns: and "
6 let s' priests bear s' trumpets of "
8 s' priests bearing the s' trumpets "
13 And s' priests bearing s' trumpets "
15 after the same manner s' times: "
15 they compassed the city s' times. "
18: 2 the children of Israel s' tribes, "
5 they shall divide it into s' parts: "
6 describe the land into s' parts, and "
9 described it by cities into s' parts "
J'g 6: 1 into the hand of Midian s' years. "
25 the second bullock of s' years old, "
8:26 a thousand and s' hundred shekels "
12: 9 And he judged Israel s' years. "
14:12 me within the s' days of the feast, "
17 she wept before him the s' days, "
16: 7 If they bind me with s' green withs "
8 brought up to her s' green withs "
13 weavest the s' locks of my head "
19 to shave off the s' locks of his head; "
20:15 numbered s' hundred chosen men. "
16 s' hundred chosen men lefthanded; "
Ru 4:15 which is better to thee than s' sons, "
1Sa 2: 5 so that the barren hath born s'; "
6: 1 country of the Philistines s' months. "
10: 8 s' days shalt thou tarry, till I come "
11: 3 Give us s' days' respite, that we "
13: 8 And he tarried s' days, according to "
16:10 Jesse made s' of his sons to pass "
31:13 a tree at Jabesh, and fasted s' days. "
2Sa 2:11 the house of Judah was s' years "
5: 5 over Judah s' years and six months: "
8: 4 chariots, and s' hundred horsemen, "
10:18 slew the men of s' hundred chariots "
21: 6 s' men of his sons be delivered unto "
9 they fell all s' together, and were "
23:39 the Hittite: thirty and s' in all. "
24:13 s' years of famine come unto thee "
1Ki 2:11 s' years reigned he in Hebron, and "
6: 6 and the third was s' cubits broad: "
38 it. So was he s' years in building it. "
7:17 s' for the one chapiter, and s' for the "
8:65 s' days and s' days, even fourteen "
11: 3 he had s' hundred wives, princesses, "
16:15 did Zimri reign s' days in Tirzah. "
18:43 And he said, Go again s' times. "
19:18 I have left me s' thousand in Israel, "
20:15 children of Israel, being s' thousand. "
29 one over against the other s' days. "
30 fell upon twenty and s' thousand of "
2Ki 3: 9 a compass of s' days' journey: "
26 took with him s' hundred men that "
4:35 the child sneezed s' times, and the "
5:10 Go and wash in Jordan s' times, "
14 dipped himself s' times in Jordan, "
8: 1 also come upon the land s' years. "
2 the land of the Philistines s' years. "
3 it came to pass at the s' years' end, "
11:21 S' years old was Jehoash when he "
24:16 the men of might, even s' thousand, "
25:27 pass in the s' and thirtieth year of "
27 on the s' and twentieth day of the "
1Ch 3: 4 he reigned s' years and six months: "
24 and Dalaiah, and Anani, s'. "
5:13 and Jachan, and Zia, and Heber, s'. "
18 four and forty thousand s' hundred "
7: 5 fourscore and s' thousand. "
9:13 and s' hundred and threescore; "
25 to come after s' days from time to "
10:12 oak in Jabesh, and fasted s' days. "
12:25 war, s' thousand and one hundred. "
27 three thousand and s' hundred; "
34 and spear thirty and s' thousand. "
15:26 they offered s' bullocks and s' rams. "
18: 4 s' thousand horsemen, and twenty "
19:18 slew of the Syrians s' thousand men "
26:30 a thousand and s' hundred, were "
32 and s' hundred chief fathers, whom "
29: 4 s' thousand talents of refined silver, "
27 s' years reigned he in Hebron, and "
2Ch 7: 8 Solomon kept the feast s' days, "
9 the dedication of the altar s' days, "
9 and the feast s' days. "
13: 9 with a young bullock and s' rams, "
15:11 s' hundred oxen and s' thousand "
17:11 s' thousand and s' hundred rams, "
11 and s' thousand and s' hundred "
24: 1 Joash was s' years old when he "
26:13 and s' thousand and five hundred, "
29:21 brought s' bullocks, and s' rams, "

2Ch 29:21 and s' lambs, and s' he goats, for a 7651
30:21 feast of unleavened bread s' days "
22 eat throughout the feast s' days, "
23 took counsel to keep other s' days: "
23 kept other s' days with gladness. "
24 bullocks and s' thousand sheep; "
35:17 feast of unleavened bread s' days. "
Ezr 2: 5 Arah, s' hundred seventy and five. "
9 Zaccai, s' hundred and threescore. "
25 s' hundred and forty and three. "
33 Ono, s' hundred twenty and five. "
38 thousand two hundred forty and s'. "
65 there were s' thousand three "
65 three hundred thirty and s' "
66 Their horses were s' hundred thirty "
67 thousand s' hundred and twenty. "
6:22 unleavened bread s' days with joy: "
7:14 king, and of his s' counsellors, 7655
8:35 seventy and s' lambs, twelve he 7651
Ne 7:14 Zaccai, s' hundred and threescore. "
18 six hundred threescore and s'. "
19 two thousand threescore and s'. "
29 Beeroth, s' hundred forty and three. "
37 Ono, s' hundred twenty and one. "
41 thousand two hundred forty and s'. "
67 maidservants, of whom there were s' "
67 three hundred thirty and s': and "
68 horses, s' hundred thirty and six: "
69 s' hundred and twenty asses. "
72 threescore and s' priests' garments. "
8:18 they kept the feast s' days; and on "
Es 1: 1 over an hundred and s' and twenty "
5 both unto great and small, s' days, "
10 s' chamberlains that served in the "
14 the s' princes of Persia and Media, "
2: 9 s' maidens, which were meet to be "
8: 9 hundred twenty and s' provinces, "
9:30 hundred twenty and s' provinces "
Job 1: 2 there were born unto him s' sons "
3 also was s' thousand sheep, and "
2:13 the ground s' days and s' nights, "
5:19 in s' there shall no evil touch thee. "
42: 8 you now s' bullocks and s' rams, "
13 also s' sons and three daughters. 7658
Ps 12: 6 furnace of earth, purified s' times. 7659
119:164 S' times a day do I praise thee 7651
Pr 6:16 s' are an abomination unto him: "
9: 1 she hath hewn out her s' pillars: "
24:16 For a just man falleth s' times, and "
26:16 s' men that can render a reason. "
25 are s' abominations in his heart. "
Ec 11: 2 Give a portion to s', and also to "
Isa 4: 1 s' women shall take hold of one "
11:15 shall smite it in the s' streams, "
30:26 sevenfold, as the light of s' days, "
Jer 15: 9 that hath borne s' languisheth: "
34:14 end of s' years let ye go every man "
52:25 s' men of them that were near the "
30 captive of the Jews s' hundred "
31 s' and thirtieth year of the captivity "
Eze 3:15 astonished among them s' days. "
16 came to pass at the end of s' days, "
29:17 pass in the s' and twentieth year, "
39: 9 shall burn them with fire s' years: "
12 s' months shall the house of Israel "
14 end of s' months shall they search. "
40:22 they went up into it by s' steps; "
26 there were s' steps to go up to it, "
41: 3 the breadth of the door, s' cubits. "
43:25 S' days shalt thou prepare every "
26 S' days shall they purge the altar "
44:26 they shall reckon unto him s' days. "
45:21 the passover, a feast of s' days; "
23 s' days of the feast he shall prepare "
23 s' bullocks and s' rams without "
23 without blemish daily the s' days; "
25 the like in the feast of the s' days, "
Da 3:19 the furnace one s' times more 7655
4:16 and let s' times pass over him. "
23 field, till s' times pass over him; "
25, 32 and s' times shall pass over thee, "
9:25 the Prince shall be s' weeks, and 7651
Am 5: 8 Seek him that maketh the s' stars*3598
Mic 5: 5 we raise against him s' shepherds, 7651
Zec 3: 9 upon one stone shall be s' eyes: "
4: 2 top of it, and his s' lamps thereon, "
2 and s' pipes to the...lamps, which "
2 pipes to the s' lamps, which are * "
10 hand of Zerubbabel with those s'; "
M't 12:45 s' other spirits more wicked than 2033
15:34 they said, S', and a few little fishes. "
36 And he took the s' loaves and the "
37 meat that was left s' baskets full. "
16:10 Neither the s' loaves of the four "
18:21 and I forgive him? till s' times? 2034
22 say not unto thee, Until s' times: "
22 but, Until seventy times s'. 2033
22:25 Now there were with us s' brethren: "
28 whose wife shall she be of the s'? "
M'r 8: 5 loaves have ye? And they said, S'. "
6 and he took the s' loaves, and gave "
8 meat that was left s' baskets. "
20 when the s' among four thousand, "
20 took ye up? And they said, S'. "
12:20 Now there were s' brethren: and "
22 And the s' had her, and left no seed. "
23 them? for the s' had her to wife. "
16: 9 out of whom he had cast s' devils. "
Lu 2:36 had lived with an husband s' years "
8: 2 out of whom went s' devils, "
11:26 him s' other spirits more wicked "
17: 4 against thee s' times in a day, 2034
4 and s' times in a day turn again to "
20:29 There were therefore s' brethren: 2033
31 and in like manner the s' also: and "
33 them is she? for s' had her to wife. "

Ac 6: 3 among you s' men of honest report,2033
13:19 destroyed s' nations in the land of "
19:14 there were s' sons of one Sceva, a "
20: 6 five days; where we abode s' days. "
21: 4 disciples, we tarried there s' days: "
8 which was one of the s'; and abode "
27 And when the s' days were almost "
28:14 desired to tarry with them s' days: "
Ro 11: 4 to myself s' thousand men, who 2035
Heb 11:30 were compassed about s' days. 2033
Re 1: 4 John to the s' churches which are "
4 and from the s' Spirits which are "
11 the s' churches which are in Asia; "
12 I saw s' golden candlesticks; "
13 in the midst of the s' candlesticks* "
16 he had in his right hand s' stars: "
20 The mystery of the s' stars which "
20 and the s' golden candlesticks. "
20 The s' stars are the angels of the s' "
20 and the s' candlesticks which thou "
20 thou sawest are the s' churches. "
2: 1 he that holdeth the s' stars in his "
1 midst of the s' golden candlesticks; "
3: 1 s' Spirits of God, and the s' stars; "
4: 5 there were s' lamps of fire burning "
5 which are the s' Spirits of God. "
5: 1 the backside, sealed with s' seals. "
5 and to loose the s' seals thereof. "
6 slain, having s' horns and s' eyes, "
6 which are the s' Spirits of God "
8: 2 And I saw the s' angels which stood "
2 to them were given s' trumpets. "
6 s' angels which had the s' trumpets "
10: 3 s' thunders uttered their voices. "
4 s' thunders had uttered their voices, "
4 which the s' thunders uttered, and "
11:13 were slain of men s' thousand: and "
12: 3 having s' heads and ten horns, and "
3 and s' crowns upon his heads. "
13: 1 having s' heads and ten horns, and "
15: 1 s' angels having the s' last plagues; "
6 s' angels came out of the temple, "
6 having the s' plagues, clothed in "
7 unto the s' angels s' golden vials "
8 the s' plagues of the s' angels were "
16: 1 saying to the s' angels, Go your "
17: 1 the s' angels which had the s' vials, "
3 having s' heads and ten horns. "
7 hath the s' heads and ten horns. "
9 The s' heads are s' mountains, on "
10 there are s' kings: five are fallen, "
11 and is of the s', and goeth into "
21: 9 came unto me one of the s' angels "
9 s' vials full of the s' last plagues, "

sevenfold
Ge 4:15 vengeance...be taken on him s'. 7659
24 If Cain shall be avenged s', truly "
24 truly Lamech seventy and s'. "
Ps 79:12 render unto our neighbours s' into "
Pr 6:31 if he be found, he shall restore s'; "
Isa 30:26 and the light of the sun shall be s'. "

seven-hundred See SEVEN and HUNDRED.

sevens
Ge 7: 2 beast thou shalt take to thee by s',*7651
3 Of fowls also of the air by s', the * "

seventeen
Ge 37: 2 Joseph, being s' years old, 7651,6240
47:28 in the land of Egypt s' years: " "
J'g 8:14 even threescore and s' men. *7657,7651
1Ki 14:21 reigned s' years in Jerusalem, 7651,6240
2Ki 13: 1 Samaria, and reigned s' years. " "
1Ch 7:11 s' thousand and two hundred " "
2Ch 12:13 he reigned s' years in Jerusalem, " "
Ezr 2:39 of Harim, a thousand and s'. " "
Ne 7:42 of Harim, a thousand and s'. " "
Jer 32: 9 the money, even s' shekels of " "

seventeenth
Ge 7:11 month, the s' day of the month, 7651,6240
8: 4 on the s' day of the month, " "
1Ki 22:51 Israel in Samaria the s' year " "
2Ki 16: 1 the s' year of Pekah the son of " "
1Ch 24:15 The s' to Hezir, the eighteenth " "
25:24 The s' to Joshbekashah, he, " "

seventh
Ge 2: 2 s' day God ended his work which 7637
2 rested on the s' day from all his "
3 And God blessed the s' day, and "
8: 4 the ark rested in the s' month, on "
Ex 12:15 from the first day until the s' day, "
16 in the s' day there shall be an holy "
13: 6 s' day shall be a feast to the Lord. "
16:26 but on the s' day, which is the "
27 people on the s' day for to gather, "
29 go out of his place on the s' day. "
30 So the people rested on the s' day. "
20:10 s' day is the sabbath of the Lord "
11 in them is, and rested the s' day: "
21: 2 and in the s' he shall go out free "
23:11 s' year thou shalt let it rest and lie "
12 and on the s' day thou shalt rest: "
24:16 s' day he called unto Moses out of "
31:15 in the s' is the sabbath of rest, holy "
17 on the s' day he rested, and was "
34:21 but on the s' day thou shalt rest: "
35: 2 s' day there shall be to you an holy "
Le 13: 5 priest shall look on him the s' day: "
6 shall look on him again the s' day: "
27 shall look upon him the s' day: "
32, 34 s' day the priest shall look on "
51 look on the plague on the s' day: "
14: 9 But it shall be on the s' day, that "
39 priest shall come again the s' day, "
16:29 that in the s' month, on the tenth "
23: 3 the s' day is the sabbath of rest, a "

Le 23: 8 the s' day is an holy convocation: 7637
16 s' sabbath shall ye number fifty "
24 the s' month, in the first day of the "
27 on the tenth day of this s' month "
34 The fifteenth day of this s' month "
39 in the fifteenth day of the s' month, "
41 ye shall celebrate it in the s' month. "
25: 4 But in the s' year shall be a sabbath "
9 on the tenth day of the s' month, "
20 say, What shall we eat the s' year? "
Nu 6: 9 on the s' day shall he shave it. "
7:48 On the s' day Elishama the son of "
19:12 and on the s' day he shall be clean: "
12 the s' day he shall not be clean. "
19 on the third day, and on the s' day: "
19 and on the s' day he shall purify "
28:25 on the s' day ye shall have an holy "
29: 1 in the s' month, on the first day of "
7 on the tenth day of this s' month "
12 on the fifteenth day of the s' month "
32 And on the s' day seven bullocks, "
31:19 on the third day, and on the s' day. "
24 wash your clothes on the s' day, "
De 5:14 But the s' day is the sabbath of the "
15: 9 The s' year, the year of release, is "
12 s' year thou shalt let him go free "
16: 8 s' day shall be a solemn assembly "
Jos 6: 4 the s' day ye shall compass the city "
15 And it came to pass on the s' day, "
16 And it came to pass at the s' time, "
19:40 the s' lot came out for the tribe of "
J'g 14:15 And it came to pass on the s' day, "
17 on the s' day, that he told her, "
18 s' day before the sun went down, "
2Sa 12:18 on the s' day, that the child died. "
1Ki 8: 2 Ethanim, which is the s' month. "
16:10, 15 in the twenty and s' year of Asa 7651
18:44 And it came to pass at the s' time, 7637
20:29 in the s' day the battle was joined: "
2Ki 11: 4 s' year Jehoiada sent and fetched "
12: 1 the s' year of Jehu Jehoash began 7651
13:10 In the thirty and s' year of Joash "
15: 1 the twenty and s' year of Jeroboam "
18: 9 which was the s' year of Hoshea "
25: 8 month, on the s' day of the month, 7651
25 in the s' month, that Ishmael 7637
1Ch 2:15 Ozem the sixth, David the s': "
12:11 Attai the sixth, Eliel the s', "
24:10 s' to Hakkoz, the eighth to Abijah, "
25:14 The s' to Jesharelah, he, his sons, "
26: 3 Jehohanan the sixth, Elioenai the s'. "
5 Ammiel the sixth, Issachar the s', "
27:10 The s' captain for the s' month was "
2Ch 5: 3 feast which was in the s' month. "
7:10 and twentieth day of the s' month "
23: 1 in the s' year Jehoiada strengthened "
31: 7 and finished them in the s' month. "
Ezr 3: 1 And when the s' month was come, "
6 From the first day of the s' month "
7: 7 the s' year of Artaxerxes the king. 7651
8 was in the s' year of the king. 7637
Ne 7:73 and when the s' month came, the "
8: 2 upon the first day of the s' month. "
14 booths in the feast of the s' month: "
10:31 and that we would leave the s' year, "
Es 1:10 s' day, when the heart of the king "
2:16 Tebeth, in the s' year of his reign. 7651
Jer 28:17 died the same year in the s' month. 7637
41: 1 in the s' month, that Ishmael "
52:28 in the s' year three thousand Jews 7651
Eze 20: 1 And it came to pass in the s' year, 7637
30:20 month, in the s' day of the month, 7651
45:20 shalt do the s' day of the month "
25 In the s' month, in the fifteenth day "
Hag 2: 1 In the s' month, in the one and 7637
Zec 7: 5 mourned in the fifth and s' month, "
8:19 the fast of the s', and the fast of the "
M't 22:26 also, and the third, unto the s'. 2035
Joh 4:52 at the s' hour the fever left him. 1442
Heb 4: 4 spake...of the s' day on this wise, "
4 rest the s' day from all his works. "
Jude 14 And Enoch also, the s' from Adam, "
Re 8: 1 when he had opened the s' seal, "
10: 7 the days of the voice of the s' angel, "
11:15 And the s' angel sounded; and "
16:17 And the s' angel poured out his vial "
21:20 the s', chrysolite; the eighth, beryl; "

seven-thousand See SEVEN and THOUSAND.

seventy
Ge 4:24 truly Lamech s' and sevenfold. 7657
5:12 And Cainan lived s' years, and begat "
31 seven hundred s' and seven years: "
11:26 And Terah lived s' years, and begat "
12: 4 and Abram was s' and five years old "
Ex 1: 5 of the loins of Jacob were s' souls: "
24: 1 Abihu, and s' of the elders of Israel; "
9 Abihu, and s' of the elders of Israel: "
38:28 seven hundred s' and five shekels "
29 brass of the offering was s' talents, "
Nu 7:13, 19, 25, 31, 37 bowl of s' shekels, "
43 a silver bowl of s' shekels, after "
49, 55, 61, 67 73, 79 bowl of s' shekels, "
85 and thirty shekels, each bowl s': "
11:16 me s' men of the elders of Israel, "
24 s' men of the elders of the people, "
25 him, and gave it unto the s' elders: "
31:32 and s' thousand and five thousand "
J'g 9:56 father, in slaying his s' brethren: "
2Sa 24:15 to Beer-sheba s' thousand men. "
2Ki 10: 1 And Ahab had s' sons in Samaria. "
6 the king's sons, being s' persons, "
7 the king's sons, and slew s' persons, "
1Ch 21:14 there fell of Israel s' thousand men. "
Ezr 2: 3 thousand an hundred s' and two. "
4 three hundred s' and two. "

Ezr 2: 5 of Arah, seven hundred s' and five. 7657
36 Jeshua, nine hundred s' and three. "
40 children of Hodaviah, s' and four. "
8: 7 of Athaliah, and with him s' males. "
14 Zabbud, and with them s' males. "
35 s' and seven lambs, twelve he goats "
Ne 7: 8 thousand an hundred s' and two. "
9 three hundred s' and two. "
39 Jeshua, nine hundred s' and three. "
43 children of Hodevah, s' and four. "
11:19 gates, were an hundred s' and two. "
Es 9:16 of their foes s' and five thousand, "
Isa 23:15 Tyre shall be forgotten s' years, "
15 end of s' years shall Tyre sing as an "
17 to pass after the end of s' years, "
Jer 25:11 serve the king of Babylon s' years. "
12 when s' years are accomplished, "
29:10 after s' years be accomplished at "
Eze 8:11 before them s' men of the ancients "
41:12 toward the west was s' cubits broad; "
Da 9: 2 that he would accomplish s' years "
24 S' weeks are determined upon thy "
Zec 7: 5 even those s' years, did ye at all fast "
M't 18:22 times: but, Until s' times seven. 1441
Lu 10: 1 the Lord appointed other s' also, 1440
17 And the s' returned again with joy, "

seventy-thousand See SEVENTY and THOUSAND.

sever See also SEVERED.
Ex 8:22 s' in that day the land of Goshen, 6395
9: 4 shall s' between the cattle of Israel "
Eze 39:14 they shall s' out men of continual 914
M't 13:49 s' the wicked from among the just, 873

several
Nu 28:13 a s' tenth deal of flour mingled with
21 A s' tenth deal shalt thou offer for
29 A s' tenth deal unto one lamb,
29:10 A s' tenth deal for one lamb,
15 And a s' tenth deal to each lamb of the
2Ki 15: 5 death, and dwelt in a s' house. ‡2669
2Ch 11:12 And in every s' city he put shields and
26:21 death, and dwelt in a s' house. ‡2669
28:25 in every s' city of Judah he made high
31:19 suburbs of their cities, in every s' city,
M't 25:15 man according to his s' ability; 2398
Re 21:21 every s' gate was of one pearl: 303,1520

severally
1Co 12:11 dividing to every man s' as he will. 2398

severed
Le 20:26 and have s' you from other people, *914
De 4:41 s' three cities on this side Jordan* "
J'g 4:11 had s' himself from the Kenites, 6504

severity
Ro 11:22 Behold...the goodness and s' of God: 663
22 on them which fell, s'; but toward "

sew See also SEWED; SEWEST; SEWETH.
Ec 3: 7 A time to rend, and a time to s'; 8609
Eze 13:18 Woe to the women that s' pillows "

sewed
Ge 3: 7 they s' fig leaves together, and 8609
Job 16:15 I have s' sackcloth upon my skin, "

sewest
Job 14:17 and thou s' up mine iniquity. *2950

seweth
M'r 2:21 No man...s' a piece of new cloth 1976

Shaalabbin (*sha-al-ab'-bin*) See also SHAALBIM.
Jos 19:42 And S', and Ajalon, and Jethlah, 8169

Shaalbim (*sha-al'-bim*) See also SHAALABBIN; SHAALBONITE.
J'g 1:35 mount Heres in Aijalon, and in S': 8169
1Ki 4: 9 son of Dekar, in Makaz, and in S', "

Shaalbonite (*sha-al'-bo-nite*)
2Sa 23:32 Eliahba the S', of the sons of 8170
1Ch 11:33 the Baharumite, Eliahba the S', "

Shaaph (*sha'-af*)
1Ch 2:47 and Pelet, and Ephah, and S'. 8174
49 She bare also S' the father of "

Shaaraim (*sha-a-ra'-im*) See also SHARAIM; SHARUHEN.
1Sa 17:52 fell down by the way to S', even 8189
1Ch 4:31 and at Beth-birei, and at S'. "

Shaashgaz (*sha-ash'-gaz*)
Es 2:14 to the custody of S', the king's 8190

Shabbethai (*shab'-be-thahee*)
Ezr 10:15 and S' the Levite helped them. 7678
Ne 8: 7 S', Hodijah, Maaseiah, Kelita, "
11:16 And S' and Jozabad, of the chief of "

Shachia (*sha-ki'-ah*)
1Ch 8:10 And Jeuz, and S', and Mirma. 7634

shade See also SHADOW.
Ps 121: 5 Lord is thy s' upon thy right hand. 6738

shadow See also OVERSHADOW; SHADE; SHADOWING; SHADOWS.
Ge 19: 8 come they under the s' of my roof. 6738
J'g 9:15 come and put your trust in my s': "
36 Thou seest the s' of the mountains "
2Ki 20: 9 shall the s' go forward ten degrees, "
10 for the s' to go down ten degrees: "
10 the s' return backward ten degrees. "
11 the s' ten degrees backward, by "
1Ch 29:15 our days on the earth are as a s', "
Job 3: 5 and the s' of death stain it; let a 6757
7: 2 servant earnestly desireth the s', 6738
8: 9 our days upon earth are a s':) "
10:21 of darkness and the s' of death: 6757
22 and of the s' of death, without any "
12:22 bringeth out to light the s' of death. "
14: 2 is cut down: he fleeth also as a s', 6738
16:16 on my eyelids is the s' of death; 6757

Job 17: 7 and all my members are as a s'. 6738
24:17 is to them even as the s' of death: 6757
17 are in the terrors of the s' of death. "
28: 3 of darkness, and the s' of death. "
34:22 is no darkness, nor s' of death, "
38:17 seen the doors of the s' of death? "
40:22 trees cover him with their s'; the ‡6752
Ps 17: 8 hide me under the s' of thy wings, 6738
23: 4 the valley of the s' of death, 6757
36: 7 trust under the s' of thy wings. 6738
44:19 and covered us with the s' of death. 6757
57: 1 in the s' of thy wings will I make 6738
63: 7 in the s' of thy wings will I rejoice. "
80:10 hills were covered with the s' of it, "
91: 1 abide under the s' of the Almighty. "
102:11 days are like a s' that declineth; "
107:10 in darkness and in the s' of death, 6757
14 out of darkness and the s' of death, "
109:23 I am gone like the s' when it 6738
144: 4 days are as a s' that passeth away. "
Ec 6:12 vain life which he spendeth as a s'? "
8:13 prolong his days, which are as a s'; "
Ca 2: 3 I sat down under his s' with great "
Isa 4: 6 tabernacle for a s' in the daytime‡ "
9: 2 dwell in the land of the s' of death, 6757
16: 3 make thy s' as the night in the ‡6738
25: 4 a s' from the heat, when the blast‡ "
5 even the heat with the s' of a cloud:‡ "
30: 2 and to trust in the s' of Egypt! "
3 the trust in the s' of Egypt your "
32: 2 s' of a great rock in a weary land. ‡ "
34:15 and hatch, and gather under her s':‡ "
38: 8 bring again the s' of the degrees, "
49: 2 in the s' of his hand hath he hid me, "
51:16 thee in the s' of mine hand, "
Jer 2: 6 of drought, and of the s' of death, 6757
13:16 light, he turn it into the s' of death, "
48:45 fled stood under the s' of Heshbon 6738
La 4:20 Under his s' we shall live among "
Eze 17:23 the s' of the branches thereof shall‡ "
31: 6 under his s' dwelt all great nations. "
12 the earth are gone down from his s', "
17 dwelt under his s' in the midst of "
Da 4:12 beasts of the field had s' under it, 2927
Ho 4:13 because the s' thereof is good: 6738
14: 7 dwell under his s' shall return; "
Am 5: 8 the s' of death into the morning, 6757
Jon 4: 5 sat under it in the s', till he might‡6738
6 that it might be a s' over his head,‡ "
M't 4:16 sat in the region and s' of death 4639
M'r 4:32 the air may lodge under the s' of it. "
Lu 1:79 in darkness and in the s' of death, "
Ac 5:15 the s' of Peter passing by might "
Col 2:17 Which are a s' of things to come; "
Heb 8: 5 example and s' of heavenly things, "
10: 1 the law having a s' of good things "
Jas 1:17 variableness, neither s' of turning. 644

shadowing
Isa 18: 1 Woe to the land s' with wings, *6767
Eze 31: 3 with a s' shroud, and of an high 6751
Heb 9: 5 of glory s' the mercyseat; *2683

shadows
Ca 2:17 day break, and the s' flee away, 6752
4: 6 the day break, and the s' flee away, "
Jer 6: 4 s' of the evening are stretched out. "

Shadrach (*sha'-drak*) See also HANANIAH.
Da 1: 7 and to Hananiah, of S'; and to 7714
2:49 set S', Meshach, and Abed-nego, 7715
3:12 of the province of Babylon, S', "
13 and fury commanded to bring S', "
14 them, Is it true, O S', Meshach, and "
16 S', Meshach, and Abed-nego, "
19 his visage was changed against S', "
20 that were in his army to bind S', "
22 slew those men that took up S', "
23 S', Meshach, Abed-nego, fell down "
26 said, S', Meshach, and Abed-nego, "
26 Then S', Meshach, and Abed-nego, "
28 Blessed be the God of S', Meshach, "
29 thing amiss against the God of S', "
30 the king promoted S', Meshach, and "

shady
Job 40:21 He lieth under the s' trees, in the *6628
22 The s' trees cover him with their * "

shaft
Ex 25:31 his s', and his branches, his bowls, 3409
37:17 his s', and his branch, his bowls, "
Nu 8: 4 beaten gold, unto the s' thereof, * "
Isa 49: 2 me, and made me a polished s'; 2671

Shage (*sha'-ghe*)
1Ch 11:34 the son of S' the Hararite, 7681

Shahar (*sha'-har*) See also ZARETH-SHAHAR.
Ps 22: *title* chief Musician upon Aijeleth S', 7837

Shaharaim (*sha-ha-ra'-im*)
1Ch 8: 8 S' begat children in the country 7842

Shahazimah (*sha-haz'-i-mah*)
Jos 19:22 coast reacheth to Tabor, and S', *7831

shake See also SHAKED; SHAKEN; SHAKETH; SHAKING; SHOOK.
J'g 16:20 times before, and s' myself. 5287
Ne 5:13 So God s' out every man from his "
Job 4:14 which made all my bones to s'. 6342
15:33 s' off his unripe grape as the vine. 2554
16: 4 you, and s' mine head at you. 5128
Ps 22: 7 shoot out the lip, they s' the head, "
46: 3 mountains s' with the swelling 7493
69:23 make their loins continually to s'. 4571
72:16 fruit thereof shall s' like Lebanon: 7493
Isa 2:19, 21 ariseth to s' terribly the earth. 6206
10:15 if the rod should s' itself against ‡5130
32 he shall s' his hand against the * "
11:15 shall he s' his hand over the river. ‡ "
Isa 13: 2 s' the hand, that they may go into *5130
13 I will s' the heavens, and the *7264
14:16 to tremble, that did s' kingdoms; 7493
24:18 the foundations of the earth do s'. "
33: 9 and Carmel s' off their fruits. 5287
52: 2 S' thyself from the dust; arise, and "
Jer 23: 9 all my bones s'; I am like a 7363
Eze 26:10 thy walls shall s' at the noise of 7493
15 the isles s' at the sound of thy fall, "
27:28 suburbs shall s' at the sound of the "
31:16 nations to s' at the sound of his fall, "
38:20 of the earth, shall s' at my presence, "
Da 4:14 s' off his leaves, and scatter his 5426
Joe 3:16 the heavens and the earth shall s': 7493
Am 9: 1 of the door, that the posts may s': "
Hag 2: 6 while, and I will s' the heavens, "
7 I will s' all nations, and the desire "
21 I will s' the heavens and the earth; "
Zec 2: 9 I will s' mine hand upon them, and 5130
M't 10:14 or city, s' off the dust of your feet. 1621
28: 4 for fear of him the keepers did s', *4579
M'r 6:11 s' off the dust under your feet for 1621
Lu 6:48 that house, and could not s' it: for 4531
9: 5 s' off the very dust from your feet 660
Heb 12:26 once more I s' not the earth only, *4579

shaked See also SHAKEN; SHOOK.
Ps 109:25 upon me they s' their heads. *5128

Shakeh See RAB-SHAKEH.

shaken See also SHAKED.
Le 26:36 the sound of a s' leaf chase them; *5086
1Ki 14:15 Israel, as a reed is s' in the water, 5110
2Ki 19:21 of Jerusalem hath s' her head at 5128
Ne 5:13 even thus be he s' out, and 5287
Job 16:12 by my neck, and s' me to pieces, *6327
38:13 the wicked might be s' out of it? 5287
Ps 18: 7 of the hills moved and were s', 1607
Isa 37:22 of Jerusalem hath s' her head at 5128
Na 2: 3 the fir trees shall be terribly s'. 7477
3:12 if they be s', they shall even fall 5128
M't 11: 7 to see? A reed s' with the wind? 4531
24:29 powers of the heavens shall be s': "
M'r 13:25 that are in heaven shall be s'. "
Lu 6:38 measure, pressed down, s' together, "
7:24 to see? A reed s' with the wind? "
21:26 the powers of heaven shall be s'. "
Ac 4:31 the place was s' where they were "
16:26 foundations of the prison were s': "
2Th 2: 2 That ye be not soon s' in mind, or "
Heb 12:27 removing of those things that are s', "
27 which cannot be s' may remain. "
Re 6:13 when she is s' of a mighty wind. 4579

shaketh
Job 9: 6 s' the earth out of her place, and 7264
Ps 29: 8 of the Lord s' the wilderness; 2342
8 Lord s' the wilderness of Kadesh. "
60: 2 the breaches thereof; for it s'. 4131
Isa 10:15 itself against him that s' it? as 5130
19:16 Lord of hosts, which he s' over it. "
33:15 that s' his hands from holding of 5287

shaking
Job 41:29 he laugheth at the s' of a spear. *7494
Ps 44:14 a s' of the head among the people. 4493
Isa 17: 6 left in it, as the s' of an olive tree, 5363
19:16 the s' of the hand of the Lord of 8573
24:13 shall be as the s' of an olive tree, 5363
30:32 battles of s' will he fight with it. 8573
Eze 37: 7 was a noise, and behold a s', and *7494
38:19 be a great s' in the land of Israel; "

Shalal See MAHER-SHALAL-HASH-BAZ.

Shalem (*sha'-lem*)
Ge 33:18 And Jacob came to S', a city of *8003

Shalim (*sha'-lim*)
1Sa 9: 4 passed through the land of S', *8171

Shalisha (*shal'-i-shah*) See also BAAL-SHALISHA.
1Sa 9: 4 passed through the land of S', *8031

shall See in the APPENDIX; also SHALT; SHOULD.

Shallecheth (*shal'-le-keth*)
1Ch 26:16 westward, with the gate S', by the 7996

Shallum (*shal'-lum*) See also JEHOAHAZ; MESHELEMIAH; SHILLEM.
2Ki 15:10 S' the son of Jabesh conspired 7967
13 S' the son of Jabesh began to "
14 and smote S' the son of Jabesh in "
15 And the rest of the acts of S', and "
22:14 the wife of S' the son of Tikvah, "
1Ch 2:40 Sisamai, and Sisamai begat S', "
41 S' begat Jekamiah, and Jekamiah "
3:15 the third Zedekiah, the fourth S'. "
4:25 S' his son, Mibsam his son, "
6:12 begat Zadok, and Zadok begat S', "
13 S' begat Hilkiah, and Hilkiah "
7:13 Jezer, and S', the sons of Bilhah. "
9:17 the porters were, S', and Akkub, "
17 their brethren: S' was the chief; "
19 And S' the son of Kore, the son of "
31 the firstborn of S' the Korahite, "
2Ch 28:12 Jehizkiah the son of S', and Amasa "
34:22 the wife of S' the son of Tikvath, "
Ezr 2:42 The children of S', the children of "
7: 2 The son of S', the son of Zadok, "
10:24 porters; S', and Telem, and Uri. "
42 S', Amariah, and Joseph. "
Ne 3:12 repaired S' the son of Halohesh, "
7:45 The porters: the children of S', "
Jer 22:11 saith the Lord touching S' the son "
32: 7 Hanameel the son of S' thine uncle "
35: 4 chamber of Maaseiah the son of S', "

Shallun (*shal'-lun*)
Ne 3:15 gate of the fountain repaired S' 7968

Shalmai (*shal'-mahee*)
Ezr 2:46 the children of S', the children of *8073
Ne 7:48 of Hagaba, the children of S', *8014

Shalman (*shal'-man*) See also SHALMANESER.
Ho 10:14 as S' spoiled Beth-arbel in the day 8020

Shalmaneser (*shal-man-e'-zer*) See also SHALMAN.
2Ki 17: 3 him came up S' king of Assyria; 8022
18: 9 that S' king of Assyria came up "

Shalom See JEHOVAH-SHALOM.

shalt See in the APPENDIX.

Shama (*sha'-mah*)
1Ch 11:44 S' and Jehiel the sons of Hothan 8091

shambles
1Co 10:25 Whatsoever is sold in the s', that 3111

shame See also ASHAMED; SHAMED; SHAMEFACEDNESS; SHAMEFUL; SHAMELESSLY; SHAMETH.
Ex 32:25 made them naked unto their s' *8103
J'g 18: 7 that might put them to s' in any 3637
1Sa 20:34 because his father had done him s'. "
2Sa 13:13 whither shall I cause my s' to go? 2781
2Ch 32:21 with s' of face to his own land. 1322
Job 8:22 hate thee shall be clothed with s'; "
Ps 4: 2 long will ye turn my glory into s'? *3639
35: 4 put to s' that seek after my soul: 3637
26 let them be clothed with s' and 1322
40:14 and put to s' that wish me evil. *3637
15 for a reward of their s' that say 1322
44: 7 hast put them to s' that hated us. 954
9 hast cast off, and put us to s'; *3637
15 the s' of my face hath covered me, 1322
53: 5 thou hast put them to s', because 954
69: 7 reproach; s' hath covered my face. 3639
19 known my reproach, and my s', 1322
70: 3 for a reward of their s' that say, "
71:24 for they are brought unto s', that 2659
83:16 Fill their faces with s'; that they *7036
17 let them be put to s', and perish: *2659
89:45 thou hast covered him with s'. 955
109:29 adversaries be clothed with s', *3639
119:31 O Lord, put me not to s'. 954
132:18 His enemies will I clothe with s': 1322
Pr 3:35 s' shall be the promotion of fools. 7036
9: 7 a scorner getteth to himself s': ‡ "
10: 5 in harvest is a son that causeth s'. 954
11: 2 pride cometh, then cometh s': but 7036
12:16 but a prudent man covereth s'. "
13: 5 is loathsome, and cometh to s'. 2659
18 Poverty and s' shall be to him 7036
14:35 is against him that causeth s'. 954
17: 2 have rule over a son that causeth s', "
18:13 it, it is folly and s' unto him. 3639
19:26 mother, is a son that causeth s', 954
25: 8 thy neighbour hath put thee to s'. 3637
10 he that heareth it put thee to s', *2616
29:15 himself bringeth his mother to s'. 954
Isa 20: 4 uncovered, to the s' of Egypt. 6172
22:18 shall be the s' of thy lord's house. 7036
30: 3 strength of Pharaoh be your s', 1322
5 profit, but a s', and also a reproach. "
47: 3 yea, thy s' shall be seen: 2781
50: 6 not my face from s' and spitting. 3639
54: 4 for thou shalt not be put to s': 2659
4 shalt forget the s' of thy youth, 1322
61: 7 For your s' ye shall have double; "
Jer 3:24 s' hath devoured the labour of our* "
25 We lie down in our s', and our "
13:26 thy face, that thy s' may appear. 7036
20:18 days should be consumed with s'? 1322
23:40 a perpetual s', which shall not be 3640
46:12 The nations have heard of thy s', 7036
48:39 hath Moab turned the back with s'! 954
51:51 s' hath covered our faces: for *3639
Eze 7:18 and s' shall be upon all faces, and 955
16:52 bear thine own s' for thy sins that 3639
52 confounded also, and bear thy s', "
54 That thou mayest bear thine own s', "
63 mouth any more because of thy s', "
32:24, 25 yet have they borne their s' "
30 and bear their s' with them that go "
34:29 neither bear the s' of the heathen "
36: 6 yet have borne the s' of the heathen: "
7 about you, they shall bear their s'. "
15 bear in thee the s' of the heathen "
39:26 After that they have borne their s', "
44:13 but they shall bear their s', and "
Da 12: 2 to s' and everlasting contempt. 2781
Ho 4: 7 will I change their glory into s'. 7036
18 her rulers with s' do love, Give ye. "
9:10 separated themselves...that s'; *1322
10: 6 Ephraim shall receive s', and 1317
Ob 10 brother Jacob s' shall cover thee, 955
Mic 1:11 of Saphir, having thy s' naked: 1322
2: 6 them, that they shall not take s'. 3639
7:10 s' shall cover her which said unto* 955
Na 3: 5 and the kingdoms thy s'. 7036
Hab 2:10 hast consulted s' to thy house by 1322
16 Thou art filled with s' for glory: 7036
Zep 3: 5 but the unjust knoweth no s'. 1322
19 land where they have been put to s'. "
Lu 14: 9 begin with s' to take the lowest 152
Ac 5:41 worthy to suffer s' for his name. *818
1Co 4:14 I write not these things to s' you, 1788
6: 5 I speak to your s'. Is it so, that 1791
11: 6 it be a s' for a woman to be shorn 149
14 have long hair, it is a s' unto him? *819
22 of God, and s' them who have not? 2617
14:35 s' for women to speak in...church.* 149
15:34 of God: I speak this to your s'. 1791
Eph 5:12 a s' even to speak of those things 149
Ph'p 3:19 and whose glory is in their s', who 152
Heb 6: 6 afresh, and put him to an open s'. 3856

Heb12: 2 endured the cross, despising the s', 152
Jude 13 the sea, foaming out their own s': "
Re 3:18 s' of thy nakedness do not appear; "
16:15 he walk naked, and they see his s'. 808

shamed See also ASHAMED.
Ge 38:23 Let her take it to her, lest we be s':*937
2Sa 19: 5 hast s' this day the faces of all thy3001
Ps 14: 6 Ye have s' the counsel of the poor, *954

Shamed (*sha'-med*)
1Ch 8:12 and S' who built Ono, and Lod, *8106

shamefacedness
1Ti 2: 9 apparel, with s' and sobriety ; * 127

shameful
Jer 11:13 have ye...altars to that s' thing, 1322
Hab 2:16 s' spewing shall be on thy glory. *7022

shamefully
Ho 2: 5 that conceived them hath done s': 3001
M'r 12: 4 head, and sent him away s' handled.821
Lu 20:11 beat him also, and entreated him s', 818
1Th 2: 2 and were s' entreated, as ye know, 5195

shamelessly
2Sa 6:20 vain fellows s' uncovereth himself!1540

Shamer (*sha'-mur*) See also SHOMER.
1Ch 6:46 the son of Bani, the son of S', *8106
7:34 the sons of S'; Ahi, and Rohgah, * "

shameth
Pr 28: 7 of riotous men s' his father. 3637

Shamgar (*sham'-gar*)
J'g 3:31 him was S' the son of Anath, 8044
5: 6 In the days of S' the son of Anath, "

Shamhuth (*sham'-huth*) See also SHAMMOTH.
1Ch27: 8 fifth month was S' the Izrahite: 8049

Shamir (*sha'-mur*)
Jos 15:48 And in the mountains, S', and 8069
J'g 10: 1 he dwelt in S' in mount Ephraim. "
2 and died, and was buried in S'. "
1Ch24:24 Michah: of the sons of Michah; S'.8053

Shamma (*sham'-mah*) See also SHAMMAH.
1Ch 7:37 and Hod, and S', and Shilshah, 8037

Shammah (*sham'-mah*) See also SHAMMA; SHAMMOTH; SHIMEA; SHIMMA.
Ge 36:13 and Zerah, S', and Mizzah: 8048
17 duke Zerah, duke S', duke Mizzah: "
1Sa 16: 9 Then Jesse made S' to pass by. "
17:13 him Abinadab, and the third S'. "
2Sa 23:11 after him was S' the son of Agee "
25 S' the Harodite, Elika the Harodite, "
33 S' the Hararite, Ahiam the son of "
1Ch 1:37 Nahath, Zerah, S', and Mizzah. "

Shammai (*sham'-mahee*)
1Ch 2:28 sons of Onam were, S', and Jada. 8060
28 And the sons of S'; Nadab, and "
32 the sons of Jada the brother of S': "
44 Jorkoam: and Rekem begat S'. "
45 And the son of S' was Maon: and "
4:17 and she bare Miriam, and S', and "

Shammoth (*sham'-moth*) See also SHAMMAH; SHAMHUTH.
1Ch11:27 S' the Harorite, Helez the 8054

Shammua (*sham-mu'-ah*) See also SHAMMUAH; SHEMAIAH; SHIMEA.
Nu 13: 4 of Reuben, S' the son of Zaccur. 8051
1Ch14: 4 S', and Shobab, Nathan, and "
Ne 11:17 and Abda the son of S', the son of "
12:18 Of Bilgah, S'; of Shemaiah, "

Shammuah (*sham-mu'-ah*) See also SHAMMUA.
2Sa 5:14 S', and Shobab, and Nathan, and*8051

Shamsherai (*sham'-she-rahee*)
1Ch 8:26 S', and Shehariah, and Athaliah, 8125

Shan See BETH-SHAN.

shape See also SHAPEN; SHAPES.
Lu 3:22 a bodily s' like a dove upon him, *1491
Joh 5:37 voice at any time, nor seen his s'.* "

shapen
Ps 51: 5 I was s' in iniquity; and in sin 2342

shapes
Re 9: 7 s' of the locusts were like unto 3667

Shapham (*sha'-fam*)
1Ch 5:12 Joel the chief, and S' the next, 8223

Shaphan (*sha'-fan*)
2Ki 22: 3 the king sent S' the son of Azaliah,8227
8 high priest said unto S' the scribe, "
8 And Hilkiah gave the book to S', "
9 And S' the scribe came to the king, "
10 And S' the scribe shewed the king, "
10 And S' read it before the king. "
12 Ahikam the son of S', and Achbor "
12 and S' the scribe, and Asahiah a "
14 S', and Asahiah, went unto Huldah "
25:22 son of Ahikam, the son of S', ruler. "
2Ch 34: 8 he sent S' the son of Azaliah, and "
15 answered and said to S' the scribe, "
15 Hilkiah delivered the book to S'. "
16 And S' carried the book to the king, "
18 Then S' the scribe told the king, "
18 And S' read it before the king. "
20 Hilkiah, and Ahikam the son of S', "
20 the son of Micah, and S' the scribe, "
Jer 26:24 the hand of Ahikam the son of S', "
29: 3 By the hand of Elasah the son of S', "
36:10 Gemariah the son of S' the scribe, "
11 the son of Gemariah, the son of S', "
12 and Gemariah the son of S', and "
39:14 the son of Ahikam the son of S', "
40: 5 the son of Ahikam the son of S', "
9 son of Ahikam the son of S' sware "
Jer 40:11 the son of Ahikam the son of S'; 8227
41: 2 son of Ahikam the son of S' with "
43: 6 the son of Ahikam the son of S', "
Eze 8:11 stood Jaazaniah the son of S', with "

Shaphat (*sha'-fat*)
Nu 13: 5 of Simeon, S' the son of Hori. 8202
1Ki 19:16 son of S' of Abel-meholah shalt "
19 found Elisha the son of S', who was "
2Ki 3:11 Here is Elisha the son of S', which "
6:31 if the head of Elisha the son of S' "
1Ch 3:22 Bariah, and Neariah, and S', six. "
5:12 next, and Jaanai, and S' in Bashan. "
27:29 in the valleys was S' the son of "

Shapher (*sha'-fur*)
Nu 33:23 and pitched in mount S'. *8234
24 And they removed from mount S'.* "

Sharai (*sha'-rahee*)
Ezr 10:40 Machnadebai, Shashai, S', 8298

Sharaim (*sha-ra'-im*) See also SHAARAIM.
Jos 15:36 S', and Adithaim, and Gederah, *8189

Sharar (*sha'-rar*) See also SARAR.
2Sa 23:33 Ahiam the son of S' the Hararite, 8325

share See also PLOWSHARES.
1Sa 13:20 to sharpen every man his s', and 4282

Sharezer (*sha-re'-zur*) See also SHEREZER.
2Ki 19:37 and S' his son smote him with the8272
Isa 37:38 and S' his son smote him with the "

Sharon (*sha'-run*) See also SARON; SHARONITE.
1Ch 5:16 and in all the suburbs of S', upon8289
27:29 over the herds that fed in S' was "
Ca 2: 1 I am the rose of S', and the lily of "
Isa 33: 9 S' is like a wilderness; and Bashan "
35: 2 the excellency of Carmel and S', "
65:10 And S' shall be a fold of flocks, and "

Sharonite (*sha'-run-ite*)
1Ch 27:29 fed in Sharon was Shitrai the S': 8290

sharp See also SHARPER.
Ex 4:25 Then Zipporah took a s' stone, *6864
Jos 5: 2 unto Joshua, Make thee s' knives,*6697
3 Joshua made him s' knives, and * "
1Sa 14: 4 was a s' rock on the one side, *8127
4 and a s' rock on the other side: * "
Job 41:30 S' stones are under him: he 2303
30 s' pointed things upon the mire. *2742
Ps 45: 5 Thine arrows are s' in the heart 8150
52: 2 mischiefs; like a s' rasor, working3913
57: 4 and their tongue a s' sword. 2299
120: 4 S' arrows of the mighty, with 8150
Pr 5: 4 s' as a twoedged sword. 2299
25:18 maul, and a sword, and a s' arrow.8150
Isa 5:28 Whose arrows are s', and all their "
41:15 a new s' threshing instrument 2742
49: 2 made my mouth like a s' sword; 2299
Eze 5: 1 take thee a s' knife, take thee a "
Ac 15:39 contention was so s' between them,
Re 1:16 mouth went a s' twoedged sword: 3691
2:12 hath the s' sword with two edges; "
14:14 crown, and in his hand a s' sickle. "
17 heaven, he also having a s' sickle. "
18 cry to him that had the s' sickle, "
18 Thrust in thy s' sickle, and gather "
19:15 out of his mouth goeth a s' sword, "

sharpen See also SHARPENED; SHARPENETH.
1Sa 13:20 to s' every man his share, and his 3913
21 for the axes, and to s' the goads. *5324

sharpened
Ps 140: 3 They have s' their tongues like a 8150
Eze 21: 9 A sword, a sword is s', and also 2300
10 It is s' to make a sore slaughter; "
11 this sword is s', and it is furbished, "

sharpeneth
Job 16: 9 mine enemy s' his eyes upon me. 3913
Pr 27:17 Iron s' iron; so a man s' the 2300

sharper
Mic 7: 4 the most upright is s' than a thorn*
Heb 4:12 and s' than any twoedged sword, 5114

sharply
J'g 8: 1 And they did chide with him s'. 2394
Tit 1:13 Wherefore rebuke them s', that 664

sharpness
2Co 13:10 lest being present I should use s'.* 664

Sharuhen (*sha-ru'-hen*) See also SHAARAIM; SHILHIM.
Jos 19: 6 And Beth-lebaoth, and S'; 8287

Shashai (*sha'-shahee*)
Ezr 10:40 Machnadebai, S', Sharai, 8343

Shashak (*sha'-shak*)
1Ch 8:14 And Ahio, S', and Jeremoth, 8349
25 and Penuel, the sons of S'; "

Shaul (*sha'-ul*) See also SAUL, SHAULITES.
Ge 46:10 and S' the son of a Canaanitish 7586
Ex 6:15 S' the son of a Canaanitish woman: "
Nu 26:13 of S', the family of the Shaulites. "
1Ch 1:48 S' of Rehoboth by the river reigned "
49 when S' was dead, Baal-hanan the "
4:24 and Jamin, Jarib, Zerah, and S': "
6:24 son, Uzziah his son, and S' his son. "

Shaulites (*sha'-ul-ites*)
Nu 26:13 of Shaul, the family of the S'. 7587

shave See also SHAVED; SHAVEN.
Le 13:33 but the scall shall he not s'; 1548
14: 8 s' off all his hair, and wash himself "
9 s' all his hair off his head and his "
9 even all his hair he shall s' off: and "
21: 5 they s' off the corner of their beard, "
Nu 6: 9 shall s' his head in the day of his "
Nu 6: 9 on the seventh day shall he s' it. 1548
18 shall s' the head of his separation "
8: 7 let them s' all their flesh, and*5674,8593
De 21:12 she shall s' her head, and pare 1548
J'g 16:19 to s' off the seven locks of his head:* "
Isa 7:20 Lord s' with a rasor that is hired, "
Eze 44:20 Neither shall they s' their heads, "
Ac 21:24 them, that they may s' their heads:3587

shaved See also SHAVEN.
Ge 41:14 and he s' himself, and changed his1548
2Sa 10: 4 s' off the one half of their beards, "
1Ch 19: 4 s' them, and cut off their garments "
Job 1:20 s' his head, and fell down upon 1494

Shaveh (*sha'-veh*)
Ge 14: 5 and the Emims in S' Kiriathaim, 7741
17 at the valley of S', which is the 7740

Shaveh-kiriathaim See SHAVEH and KIRIATHAIM.

shaven See also SHAVED.
Le 13:33 He shall be s', but the scall shall 1548
Nu 6:19 the hair of his separation is s': "
J'g 16:17 if I be s', then my strength will go "
22 hair...grow again after he was s'. "
Jer 41: 5 men, having their beards s', and "
1Co 11: 5 is even all one as if she were s'. 3587
6 for a woman to be shorn or s', let "

Shavsha (*shav'-shah*) See also SERAIAH; SHEVA; SHISHA.
1Ch 18:16 the priests; and S' was scribe; 7798

she See in the APPENDIX; also HER.

sheaf See also SHEAVES.
Ge 37: 7 and, lo, my s' arose, and also stood 485
7 about, and made obeisance to my s'. "
Le 23:10 shall bring a s' of the firstfruits 6016
11 shall wave the s' before the Lord, "
12 ye wave the s' an he lamb without "
15 brought the s' of the wave offering; "
De 24:19 and hast forgot a s' in the field, "
Job 24:10 take away the s' from the hungry,* "
Zec 12: 6 and like a torch of fire in a s'; *5995

Sheal (*she'-al*)
Ezr 10:29 Jashub, and S', and Ramoth. 7594

Shealtiel (*she-al'-te-el*) See also SALATHIEL.
Ezr 3: 2 and Zerubbabel the son of S', and 7597
8 began Zerubbabel the son of S', "
5: 2 rose up Zerubbabel the son of S', "
Ne 12: 1 up with Zerubbabel the son of S'. "
Hag 1: 1 unto Zerubbabel the son of S', "
12 Then Zerubbabel the son of S', and "
14 spirit of Zerubbabel the son of S', "
2: 2 now to Zerubbabel the son of S', "
23 my servant, the son of S', saith "

Shean See BETH-SHEAN.

shear See also SHEARER; SHEARING; SHORN.
Ge 31:19 And Laban went to s' his sheep: 1494
38:13 up to Timnath to s' his sheep. "
De 15:19 nor s' the firstling of thy sheep. "
1Sa 25: 4 that Nabal did s' his sheep. "

Shear See SHEAR-JASHUB.

shearer See also SHEARERS.
Ac 8:32 like a lamb dumb before his s', 2751

shearers See also SHEEPSHEARERS.
1Sa 25: 7 I have heard that thou hast s': 1494
11 flesh that I have killed for my s', "
Isa 53: 7 as a sheep before her s' is dumb, so "

Sheariah (*she-a-ri'-ah*,
1Ch 8:38 Ishmael, and S', and Obadiah, 8187
9:44 Ishmael, and S', and Obadiah, "

shearing
1Sa 25: 2 he was s' his sheep in Carmel. 1494
2Ki 10:12 at the s' house in the way, 1044,7462
14 at the pit of the s' house, even 1044

shearing-house See SHEARING and HOUSE.

Shear-jashub (*she'-ar-ja'-shub*)
Isa 7: 3 meet Ahaz, thou, and S' thy son, 7610

sheath
1Sa 17:51 and drew it out of his s' thereof, 8593
2Sa 20: 8 upon his loins in the s' thereof; "
1Ch 21:27 put his sword again into the s' 5084
Eze 21: 3 forth my sword out of his s', 8593
4 my sword go forth out of his s' "
5 drew forth my sword out of his s': "
30 cause it to return into his s'? I will "
Joh 18:11 Put up thy sword into the s': 2336

sheaves
Ge 37: 7 we were binding s' in the fields, 485
7 behold, your s' stood round about, "
Ru 2: 7 after the reapers among the s': 6016
15 Let her glean even among the s', "
Ne 13:15 bringing in s', and lading asses; 6194
Ps 126: 6 rejoicing, bringing his s' with him. 485
129: 7 nor he that bindeth s' his bosom. "
Am 2:13 a cart is pressed that is full of s'. 5995
Mic 4:12 gather them as the s' into the floor. "

Sheba (*she'-bah*) See also BATH-SHEBA; BEER-SHEBA; SHEBAH.
Ge 10: 7 sons of Raamah; S', and Dedan. 7614
28 And Obal, and Abimael, and S', "
25: 3 And Jokshan begat S', and Dedan. "
Jos 19: 2 inheritance Beer-sheba, and S', 7652
2Sa 20: 1 man of Belial, whose name was S', "
2 and followed S' the son of Bichri: "
6 S' the son of Bichri do us more "
7 pursue after S' the son of Bichri. "
10 pursued after S' the son of Bichri. "
13 pursue after S' the son of Bichri. "
21 S' the son of Bichri by name, "
22 the head of S' the son of Bichri, "

1Ki 10: 1 queen of S' heard of the fame of 7614
4 queen of S' had seen all Solomon's "
10 queen of S' gave to king Solomon. "
13 unto the queen of S' all her desire, "
1Ch 1: 9 sons of Raamah; S', and Dedan. "
22 And Ebal, and Abimael, and S', "
32 sons of Jokshan; S', and Dedan. "
5:13 Meshullam; and S', and Jorai, 7652
2Ch 9: 1 queen of S' heard of the fame of 7614
3 queen of S' had seen the wisdom "
9 spice as the queen of S' gave king "
12 to the queen of S' all her desire, "
Job 6:19 companies of S' waited for them. "
Ps 72:10 kings of S' and Seba shall offer "
15 shall be given of the gold of S': "
Isa 60: 6 all they from S' shall come: they "
Jer 6:20 there to me incense from S', and "
Eze 27:22 The merchants of S' and Raamah, "
23 the merchants of S', Asshur, and "
38:13 S', and Dedan, and the merchants "

Shebah (*she'-bah*) See also SHEBA.
Ge 26:33 And he called it S': therefore the*7656

Shebam (*she'-bam*) See also SHIBMAH.
Nu 32: 3 Elealeh, and S', and Nebo, and *7643

Shebaniah (*sheb-a-ni'-ah*) See also SHECHANIAH.
1Ch 15:24 And S', and Jehoshaphat, and 7645
Ne 9: 4 Kadmiel, S', Bunni, Sherebiah, "
5 Hodijah, S', and Pethahiah, said, "
10: 4 Hattush, S', Malluch, "
10 their brethren, S', Hodijah, Kelita, "
12 Zaccur, Sherebiah, S', "
12:14 Melicu, Jonathan; of S', Joseph; "

Shebarim (*sheb'-a-rim*)
Jos 7: 5 from before the gate even unto S',7671

Sheber (*she'-bur*)
1Ch 2:48 Caleb's concubine, bare S', and 7669

Shebna (*sheb'-nah*)
2Ki 18:18 S' the scribe, and Joah the son of*7644
26 S', and Joah, unto Rab-shakeh, * "
37 S' the scribe, and Joah the son of "
19: 2 the household, and S' the scribe, "
Isa 22:15 unto this treasurer, even unto S', "
36: 3 over the house, and S' the scribe, "
11 Then said Eliakim and S' and "
22 S' the scribe, and Joah, the son of "
37: 2 S' the scribe, and the elders of the "

Shebuel (*she-bu'-el*) See also SHUBAEL.
1Ch 23:16 of Gershom, S' was the chief. 7619
25: 4 Uzziel, S', and Jerimoth, "
26:24 And S' the son of Gershom, the son "

Shecaniah (*shek-a-ni'-ah*) See also SHEBANIAH; SHECHANIAH.
1Ch 24:11 ninth to Jeshuah, the tenth to S', 7935
2Ch 31:15 and Shemaiah, Amariah, and S', "

Shechaniah (*shek-a-ni'-ah*) See also SHEBANIAH; SHECANIAH.
1Ch 3:21 sons of Obadiah, the sons of S'. *7935
22 the sons of S'; Shemaiah: and the* "
Ezr 8: 3 Of the sons of S', of the sons of * "
5 Of the sons of S'; the son of * "
10: 2 And S' the son of Jehiel, one of * "
Ne 3:29 also Shemaiah the son of S', the * "
6:18 son in law of S' the son of Arah; * "
12: 3 S', Rehum, Meremoth, * "

Shechem (*she' kem*) See also SHECHEMITES; SHECHEM'S; SICHEM; SYCHEM.
Ge 33:18 came to Shalem, a city of S', 7927
34: 2 S' the son of Hamor the Hivite, "
4 S' spake unto his father Hamor, "
6 father of S' went out unto Jacob "
8 son S' longeth for your daughter: "
11 S' said unto her father and unto "
13 And the sons of Jacob answered S' "
18 their words pleased Hamor, and S' "
20 Hamor and S' his son came unto "
24 unto S' his son hearkened all that "
26 they slew Hamor and S' his son "
35: 4 under the oak which was by S'. "
37:12 to feed their father's flock in S'. "
13 thy brethren feed the flock in S'? "
14 vale of Hebron, and he came to S'. "
Nu 26:31 S', the family of the Shechemites: 7928
Jos 17: 2 and for the children of S', and for "
7 Michmethah, that lieth before S'; 7927
20: 7 and S' in mount Ephraim, and "
21:21 gave them S' with her suburbs in "
24: 1 all the tribes of Israel to S', and "
25 a statute and an ordinance in S'. "
32 up out of Egypt, buried they in S', "
32 the father of S' for an hundred "
J'g 8:31 And his concubine that was in S', "
9: 1 son of Jerubbaal went to S' unto "
2 in the ears of all the men of S', "
3 in the ears of all the men of S' all "
6 the men of S' gathered together, "
6 plain of the pillar that was in S'. "
7 Hearken unto me, ye men of S', "
18 king over the men of S', because "
20 and devour the men of S', and the "
20 fire come out from the men of S', "
23 Abimelech and the men of S'; and "
23 the men of S' dealt treacherously "
24 upon the men of S', which aided "
25 And the men of S' set liers in wait "
26 his brethren, and went over to S': "
26 men of S' put their confidence in "
28 Who is Abimelech, and who is S', "
28 the men of Hamor the father of S': "
31 and his brethren be come to S'; "
34 they laid wait against S' in four "
39 went out before the men of S', and "
J'g 9:41 that they should not dwell in S'. 7927
46 men of the tower of S' heard that, "
47 the men of the tower of S' were "
49 men of the tower of S' died also, "
57 And all the evil of the men of S' "
21:19 that goeth up from Beth-el to S', "
1Ki 12: 1 And Rehoboam went to S': for all "
1 were come to S' to make him king. "
25 Then Jeroboam built S' in mount "
1Ch 6:67 S' in mount Ephraim with her "
7:19 of Shemidah were, Ahain, and S', 7928
28 S' also and the towns thereof, 7927
2Ch 10: 1 And Rehoboam went to S': for to "
1 S' were all Israel come to make "
Ps 60: 6 I will divide S', and mete out the "
108: 7 I will rejoice, I will divide S', and "
Jer 41: 5 That there came certain from S', "

Shechemites (*she'-kem-ites*)
Nu 26:31 of Shechem, the family of the S': 7930

Shechem's (*she'-kems*)
Ge 33:19 the children of Hamor, S' father, 7927
34:26 and took Dinah out of S' house, "

shed See also SHEDDETH; SHEDDING.
Ge 9: 6 by man shall his blood be s': for 8210
37:22 S' no blood, but cast him into "
Ex 22: 2 die, there shall no blood be s' for him.*
3 him, there shall be blood s' for him;*
Le 17: 4 he hath s' blood; and that man 8210
Nu 35:33 be cleansed of the blood that is s' "
33 but by the blood of him that s' it. "
De 19:10 That innocent blood be not s' in "
21: 7 Our hands have not s' this blood, "
1Sa 25:26 thee from coming to s' blood, *
31 thou hast s' blood causeless, or 8210
33 me this day from coming to s' blood,*
2Sa 20:10 s' out his bowels to the ground, 8210
1Ki 2: 5 and s' the blood of war in peace, 7760
31 the innocent blood, which Joab s',8210
2Ki 21:16 Manasseh s' innocent blood very "
24: 4 for the innocent blood that he s': "
1Ch 22: 8 Thou hast s' blood abundantly, and "
8 thou hast s' much blood upon the "
28: 3 a man of war, and hast s' blood. "
Ps 79: 3 Their blood have they s' like water "
10 blood of thy servants which is s'. "
106:38 s' innocent blood, even the blood "
Pr 1:16 to evil, and make haste to s' blood. "
6:17 and hands that s' innocent blood, "
Isa 59: 7 make haste to s' innocent blood: "
Jer 7: 6 s' not innocent blood in this place, "
22: 3 s' innocent blood in this place. "
17 and for to s' innocent blood, and ‡ "
La 4:13 s' the blood of the just in the midst "
Eze 16:38 wedlock and s' blood are judged; "
22: 4 in thy blood that thou hast s'; and "
6 in thee to their power to s' blood. "
9 are men that carry tales to s' blood: "
12 have they taken gifts to s' blood; "
27 ravening the prey, to s' blood, and "
23:45 manner of women that s' blood; "
33:25 toward your idols, and s' blood: "
35: 5 hast s' the blood of the children *5064
36:18 that they had s' upon the land, *8210
Joe 3:19 s' innocent blood in their land. "
M't 23:35 righteous blood s' upon the earth, 1632
26:28 s' for many for the remission of sins. "
M'r 14:24 testament, which is s' for many. "
Lu 11:50 which was s' from the foundation "
22:20 in my blood, which is s' for you. * "
Ac 2:33 he hath s' forth this, which ye now* "
22:20 blood of thy martyr Stephen was s', "
Ro 3:15 Their feet are swift to s' blood: "
5: 5 the love of God is s' abroad in our "
Tit 3: 6 s' on us abundantly through Jesus* "
Re 16: 6 For they have s' the blood of saints* "

shedder
Eze 18:10 son that is a robber, a s' of blood, 8210

sheddeth
Ge 9: 6 Whoso s' man's blood, by man 8210
Eze 22: 3 The city s' blood in the midst of it, "

shedding
Heb 9:22 and without s' of blood is no 130

Shedeur (*shed'-e-ur*)
Nu 1: 5 of Reuben; Elizur the son of S'. 7707
2:10 Reuben shall be Elizur the son of S'. "
7:30 the fourth day Elizur the son of S', "
35 the offering of Elizur the son of S'. "
10:18 his host was Elizur the son of S'. "

sheep See also SHEEPCOTE; SHEEPFOLD; SHEEPMASTER; SHEEP'S; SHEEPSHEARERS; SHEEPSKINS; SHEPHERD.
Ge 4: 2 Abel was a keeper of s', but Cain 6629
12:16 he had s', and oxen, and he asses, "
20:14 And Abimelech took s', and oxen, "
21:27 And Abraham took s' and oxen, and "
29: 2 were three flocks of s' lying by it; "
3 watered the s', and put the stone "
6 his daughter cometh with the s'. "
7 water ye the s', and go and feed "
8 well's mouth; then we water the s'. "
9 Rachel came with her father's s': "
10 s' of Laban his mother's brother, "
30:32 all the brown cattle among the s', 3775
33 the goats, and brown among the s', "
35 and all the brown among the s', "
31:19 And Laban went to shear his s': 6629
34:28 They took their s', and their oxen, "
38:13 goeth up to Timnath to shear his s'. "
Ex 9: 3 upon the oxen, and upon the s': * "
12: 5 ye shall take it out from the s', or 3532
20:24 offerings, thy s', and thine oxen: 6629
22: 1 If a man shall steal an ox, or a s', 7716
Ex 22: 1 oxen for an ox, and four s' for a 6629
1 for an ox, and four...for a s'. 7716
4 whether it be ox, or ass, or s'; he "
9 whether it be for ox, for ass, for s', "
10 an ass, or an ox, or a s', or any "
30 with thine oxen, and with thy s': 6629
34:19 whether ox or s', that is male. 7716
Le 1:10 of the s', or of the goats, for a 3775
7:23 of fat, of ox, or of s', or of goat. "
22:19 the beeves, of the s', or of the goats.*6629
21 a freewill offering in beeves or s', "
27 When a bullock, or a s', or a goat, 3775
27:26 whether it be ox, or s': it is the 7716
Nu 18:17 the firstling of a s', or the firstling3775
22:40 And Balak offered oxen and s', and6629
27:17 not as s' which have no shepherd. "
31:28 and of the asses, and of the s': * "
32 thousand and five thousand s', "
36 thousand and five hundred s': "
37 And the Lord's tribute of the s' was "
43 seven thousand and five hundred s', "
32:24 little ones, and folds for your s'; 6792
36 fenced cities: and folds for s'. 6629
De 7:13 and the flocks of thy s', in the land* "
14: 4 eat: the ox, the s', and the goat, 3775
26 for oxen, or for s', or for wine, or 6629
15:19 nor shear the firstling of thy s'. * "
17: 1 bullock, or s', wherein is blemish, 7716
18: 3 sacrifice, whether it be ox or s'; "
4 and the first of the fleece of thy s',6629
22: 1 brother's ox or his s' go astray, 7716
28: 4, 18 kine, and the flocks of thy s'. *6629
31 s' shall be given unto thine enemies, "
51 of thy kine, or flocks of thy s', * "
32:14 Butter of kine, and milk of s', with "
Jos 6:21 and s', and ass, with the edge of 7716
7:24 his asses, and his s', and his tent, 6629
J'g 6: 4 Israel, neither s', nor ox, nor ass. 7716
1Sa 8:17 He will take the tenth of your s':*6629
14:32 and took s', and oxen, and calves, "
34 every man his s', and slay them 7716
15: 3 infant and suckling, ox and s', "
9 the best of the s', and of the oxen, 6629
14 meaneth then this bleating of the s' "
15 the people spared the best of the s' "
21 people took of the spoil, s' and oxen, "
16:11 and, behold, he keepeth the s'. "
19 David thy son, which is with the s'. "
17:15 from Saul to feed his father's s' at "
20 left the s' with a keeper, and took, "
28 whom hast thou left those few s' "
34 Thy servant kept his father's s', "
22:19 and s', with the edge of the sword.7716
25: 2 he had three thousand s', and a 6629
2 he was shearing his s' in Carmel. "
4 that Nabal did shear his s'. "
16 we were with them keeping the s'. "
18 of wine, and five s' ready dressed, "
27: 9 took away the s', and the oxen, and "
2Sa 7: 8 sheepcote, from following the s', "
17:29 And honey, and butter, and s', and "
24:17 but these s', what have they done? "
1Ki 1: 9 Adonijah slew s' and oxen and fat "
19 hath slain oxen and fat cattle and s' "
25 and fat cattle and s' in abundance, "
4:23 an hundred s', beside harts, and "
8: 5 sacrificing s' and oxen, that could "
63 hundred and twenty thousand s'. "
22:17 as s' that have not a shepherd: "
2Ki 5:26 and vineyards, and s', and oxen, "
1Ch 5:21 s' two hundred and fifty thousand, "
12:40 oil, and oxen, and s' abundantly: "
17: 7 even from following the s', that thou "
21:17 for these s', what have they done? "
2Ch 5: 6 sacrificed s' and oxen, which could "
7: 5 hundred and twenty thousand s': "
14:15 away s' and camels in abundance, "
15:11 oxen and seven thousand s'. "
18: 2 Ahab killed s' and oxen for him in "
16 as s' that have no shepherd: and "
29:33 oxen and three thousand s'. "
30:24 bullocks and seven thousand s'; "
24 bullocks and ten thousand s': and "
31: 6 brought in the tithe of oxen and s', "
Ne 3: 1 priests, and they builded the s' gate; "
32 corner unto the s' gate repaired "
5:18 daily was one ox and six choice s'; "
12:39 tower of Meah, even unto the s' gate: "
Job 1: 3 substance...was seven thousand s', "
16 hath burned up the s', and the "
31:20 warmed with the fleece of my s'; 3532
42:12 for he had fourteen thousand s', 6629
Ps 8: 7 All s' and oxen, yea, and the 6792
44:11 us like s' appointed for meat; 6629
22 are counted as s' for the slaughter. "
49:14 Like s' they are laid in the grave;* "
74: 1 smoke against the s' of thy pasture? "
78:52 his own people to go forth like s', "
79:13 we thy people and s' of thy pasture "
95: 7 his pasture, and the s' of his hand. "
100: 3 his people, and the s' of his pasture. "
119:176 I have gone astray like a lost s'; 7716
144:13 our s' may bring forth thousands 6629
Ca 4: 2 Thy teeth are like a flock of s' that*
6: 6 Thy teeth are as a flock of s' which*7353
Isa 7:21 nourish a young cow, and two s'; 6629
13:14 and as a s' that no man taketh up: "
22:13 slaying oxen, and killing s', eating "
53: 6 All we like s' have gone astray; we "
7 and as a s' before her shearers is 7353
Jer 12: 3 them out like s' for the slaughter, 6629
23: 1 and scatter the s' of my pasture! "
50: 6 My people hath been lost s': their "
17 Israel is a scattered s'; the lions 7716
Eze 34: 6 My s' wandered through all the 6629
11 even I, will both search my s', and "

Eze 34:12 in the day that he is among his s' 6629
12 so will I seek out my s', and will "
Ho 12:12 for a wife, and for a wife he kept s'.
Joe 1:18 the flocks of s' are made desolate. 6629
Mic 2:12 them together as the s' of Bozrah, "
5: 8 a young lion among the flocks of s': "
Zec 13: 7 and the s' shall be scattered: and I "
M't 9:36 abroad, as s' having no shepherd. 4263
10: 6 go rather to the lost s' of the house "
16 I send you forth as s' in the midst "
12:11 that shall have one s', and if it fall "
12 then is a man better than a s'? "
15:24 but unto the lost s' of the house of "
18:12 if a man have an hundred s', and "
13 he rejoiceth more of that s', than of*
25:32 divideth his s' from the goats: 4263
33 he shall set the s' on his right hand, "
26:31 the s' of the flock shall be scattered "
M'r 6:34 were as s' not having a shepherd: "
14:27 and the s' shall be scattered. "
Lu 15: 4 man of you, having an hundred s', "
6 I have found my s' which was lost. "
Joh 2:14 that sold oxen and s' and doves, "
15 temple, and the s', and the oxen; "
5: 2 Jerusalem by the s' market a pool, 4262
10: 2 the door is the shepherd of the s'. 4263
3 openeth; and the s' hear his voice: "
3 and he calleth his own s' by name, "
4 when he putteth forth his own s',* "
4 before them, and the s' follow him: "
7 unto you, I am the door of the s'. "
8 but the s' did not hear them. "
11 shepherd giveth his life for the s'. "
12 shepherd, whose own the s' are not, "
12 and leaveth the s', and fleeth: and "
12 them, and scattereth the s'. * "
13 hireling, and careth not for the s'. "
14 know my s', and am known of mine.*
15 and I lay down my life for the s'. 4263
16 And other s' I have, which are not "
26 ye are not of my s', as I said unto "
27 My s' hear my voice, and I know "
21:16 He saith unto him, Feed my s'. "
17 Jesus saith unto him, Feed my s'. "
Ac 8:32 He was led as a s' to the slaughter; "
Ro 8:36 accounted as s' for the slaughter. "
Heb13:20 Jesus, that great shepherd of the s', "
1Pe 2:25 For ye were as s' going astray; but "
Re 18:13 and beasts, and s', and horses, and "

sheepcote See also SHEEPCOTES.
2Sa 7: 8 I took thee from the s', from 5116
1Ch 17: 7 I took thee from the s', even from "

sheepcotes
1Sa 24: 3 he came to the s' by the way, 1448,6629

sheepfold See also SHEEPFOLDS.
Joh 10: 1 not by the door into the s', but*833,4263

sheepfolds
Nu 32:16 build s' here for our cattle, 1488,6629
J'g 5:16 Why abodest thou among the s', 4942
Ps 78:70 and took him from the s': 4356,6629

sheep-gate See SHEEP and GATE.

sheep-market See SHEEP and MARKET.

sheepmaster
2Ki 3: 4 And Mesha king of Moab was a s',5349

sheep's
M't 7:15 which come to you in s' clothing, 4263

sheepshearers
Ge 38:12 went...unto his s' to Timnath, 1494,6629
2Sa 13:23 Absalom had s' in Baal-hazor, 1494
24 Behold now, thy servant hath s'; "

sheepskins
Heb11:37 they wandered about in s' and 3374

sheet See also SHEETS.
Ac 10:11 great s' knit at the four corners, 3607
11: 5 as it had been a great s', let down "

sheets
J'g 14:12 will give you thirty s' and thirty *5466
13 then shall ye give me thirty s' and* "

Shehariah (*she-ha-ri'-ah*)
1Ch 8:26 Shamsherai, and S', and Athaliah,7841

shekel (*shek'-ul*) See also SHEKELS.
Ge 24:22 golden earring of half a s' weight,1235
Ex 30:13 half a s' after the s' of the 8255
13 sanctuary: (a s' is twenty gerahs:) "
13 an half s' shall be the offering of "
15 shall not give less than half a s', "
24 after the s' of the sanctuary, "
38:24 after the s' of the sanctuary. "
25 after the s' of the sanctuary: "
26 for every man, that is, half a s', "
26 after the s' of the sanctuary, "
Le 5:15 after the s' of the sanctuary, "
27: 3 silver, after the s' of the sanctuary. "
25 according to the s' of the sanctuary: "
25 twenty gerahs shall be the s'. "
Nu 3:47 after the s' of the sanctuary shalt "
47 (the s' is twenty gerahs:) "
50 after the s' of the sanctuary: "
7:13, 19, 25, 31, 37, 43, 49, 55, 61, 67, 73,
79 after the s' of the sanctuary: "
85 after the s' of the sanctuary: "
86 apiece, after the s' of the sanctuary: "
18:16 after the s' of the sanctuary, "
1Sa 9: 8 the fourth part of a s' of silver: "
2Ki 7: 1 of fine flour be sold for a s', and "
1 and two measures of barley for a s', "
16 of fine flour was sold for a s', and "
16 and two measures of barley for a s', "
18 Two measures of barley for a s', "
18 and a measure of fine flour for a s', "
Ne 10:32 the third part of a s' for the service8255
Eze 45:12 And the s' shall be twenty gerahs: "
Am 8: 5 the ephah small, and the s' great, "

shekels
Ge 23:15 worth four hundred s' of silver; 8255
16 four hundred s' of silver, current "
Ex 21:32 unto their master thirty s' of silver, "
30:23 spices, of pure myrrh five hundred s', "
23 much, even two hundred and fifty s',*
23 calamus two hundred and fifty s',*
24 And of cassia five hundred s', *
38:24 and seven hundred and thirty s', 8255
25 and threescore and fifteen s', "
28 seven hundred seventy and five s' "
29 two thousand and four hundred s'.8255
Le 5:15 with thy estimation by s' of silver, "
27: 3 estimation shall be fifty s' of silver, "
4 thy estimation shall be thirty s' "
5 shall be of the male twenty s', "
5 and for the female ten s'. "
6 be of the male five s' of silver, "
6 estimation shall be three s' of silver. "
7 thy estimation shall be fifteen s', "
7 and for the female ten s'. "
16 shall be valued at fifty s' of silver. "
Nu 3:47 even take five s' apiece by the poll, "
50 hundred and threescore and five s', "
7:13 was an hundred and thirty s', "
13 one silver bowl of seventy s', after 8255
14 One spoon of ten s' of gold, full of "
19 was an hundred and thirty s', "
19 one silver bowl of seventy s', after8255
20 One spoon of gold of ten s', full of "
25 was an hundred and thirty s', "
25 one silver bowl of seventy s', after8255
26 One golden spoon of ten s', full of "
31 of an hundred and thirty s', "
31 one silver bowl of seventy s', after8255
32 One golden spoon of ten s', full of "
37 was an hundred and thirty s', "
37 one silver bowl of seventy s', after8255
38 One golden spoon of ten s', full of "
43 of an hundred and thirty s', "
43 a silver bowl of seventy s', after 8255
44 One golden spoon of ten s', full of "
49 was an hundred and thirty s', "
49 one silver bowl of seventy s', after8255
50 One golden spoon of ten s', full of "
55 of an hundred and thirty s', "
55 one silver bowl of seventy s', after8255
56 One golden spoon of ten s', full of "
61 was an hundred and thirty s', "
61 one silver bowl of seventy s', after8255
62 One golden spoon of ten s', full of "
67 was an hundred and thirty s', "
67 one silver bowl of seventy s', after8255
68 One golden spoon of ten s', full of "
73 was an hundred and thirty s', "
73 one silver bowl of seventy s', after8255
74 One golden spoon of ten s', full of "
79 was an hundred and thirty s', "
79 one silver bowl of seventy s', after8255
80 One golden spoon of ten s', full of "
85 weighing an hundred and thirty s', "
85 two thousand and four hundred s', "
86 full of incense, weighing ten s' apiece, "
86 spoons was an hundred and twenty s'. "
18:16 estimation, for the money of five s',8255
31:52 thousand seven hundred and fifty s'. "
De 22:19 amerce him in an hundred s' of silver, "
29 the damsel's father fifty s' of silver, "
Jos 7:21 and two hundred s' of silver, and 8255
21 a wedge of gold of fifty s' weight, "
J'g 8:26 thousand and seven hundred s' of gold; "
17: 2 The eleven hundred s' of silver that* "
3 had restored the eleven hundred s' of* "
4 mother took two hundred s' of silver,* "
10 and I will give thee ten s' of silver by* "
1Sa 17: 5 coat was five thousand s' of brass.8255
7 weighed six hundred s' of iron: "
2Sa 14:26 hair of his head two hundred s' "
18:11 would have given thee ten s' of silver,* "
12 a thousand s' of silver in mine hand,* "
21:16 weighed three hundred s' of brass in "
24:24 and the oxen for fifty s' of silver. 8255
1Ki 10:16 hundred s' of gold went to one target. "
29 of Egypt for six hundred s' of silver, "
2Ki 15:20 of each man fifty s' of silver, to 8255
1Ch 21:25 for the place six hundred s' of gold "
2Ch 1:17 a chariot for six hundred s' of silver, "
3: 9 of the nails was fifty s' of gold. 8255
9:15 hundred s' of beaten gold went to one "
16 hundred s' of gold went to one shield. "
Ne 5:15 and wine, beside forty s' of silver; 8255
Jer 32: 9 money, even seventeen s' of silver. "
Eze 4:10 shall be by weight, twenty s' a day: "
45:12 twenty s', five and twenty s', "
12 fifteen s', shall be your maneh. "

Shelah (*she'-lah*) See also SALAH; SHELANITES.
Ge 38: 5 a son; and called his name S': 7956
11 house, till S' my son be grown: "
14 for she saw that S' was grown, "
26 that I gave her not to S' my son. "
46:12 of Judah; Er, and Onan, and S', "
Nu 26:20 of S', the family of the Shelanites: "
1Ch 1:18 Arphaxad begat S', and S' begat 7974
24 Shem, Arphaxad, S', 7956
2: 3 of Judah; Er, and Onan, and S': "
4:21 The sons of S' the son of Judah "

Shelanites (*she'-lan-ites*)
Nu 26:20 S', the family of the Shelanites: 8024

Shelemiah (*shel-e-mi'-ah*) See also MESHELEMIAH; SHALLUM.
1Ch 26:14 And the lot eastward fell to S'. 8018
Ezr 10:39 And S', and Nathan, and Adaiah, 8018
41 Azareel, and S', Shemariah, "
Ne 3:30 repaired Hananiah the son of S', "
13:13 over the treasuries, S' the priest, "
Jer 36:14 the son of S', the son of Cushi, "
26 Azriel, and S' the son of Abdeel, to "
37: 3 the king sent Jehucal the son of S' "
13 name was Irijah, the son of S', "
38: 1 and Jucal the son of S', and Pashur "

Sheleph (*she'-lef*)
Ge 10:26 Joktan begat Almodad, and S', 8026
1Ch 1:20 Joktan begat Almodad, and S', "

Shelesh (*she'-lesh*)
1Ch 7:35 and Imna, and S', and Amal. 8028

Shelomi (*shel'-o-mi*)
Nu 34:27 of Asher, Ahihud the son of S'. 8015

Shelomith (*shel'-o-mith*) See also SHELOMOTH.
Le 24:11 his mother's name was S', the 8019
1Ch 3:19 and Hananiah, and S' their sister: "
23: 9 S', and Haziel, and Haran, three.*8013
18 Of the sons of Izhar; S' their chief.9019
26:25 and Zichri his son, and S' his son.*8013
26 Which S' and his brethren were * "
28 thing, it was under the hand of S',*8019
2Ch 11:20 Abijah, and Attai, and Ziza, and S'. "
Ezr 8:10 And of the sons of S'; the son of "

Shelomoth (*shel'-o-moth*) See also SHELOMITH.
1Ch 24:22 S': of the sons of S'; Jahath. 8013

shelter
Job 24: 8 embrace the rock for want of a s'. 4268
Ps 61: 3 thou hast been a s' for me, and a "

Shelumiel (*she-lu'-me-el*)
Nu 1: 6 S' the son of Zurishaddai. 8017
2:12 shall be S' the son of Zurishaddai. "
7:36 fifth day S' the son of Zurishaddai, "
41 of S' the son of Zurishaddai. "
10:19 was S' the son of Zurishaddai. "

Shem (*shem*) See also SEM.
Ge 5:32 Noah begat S', Ham, and Japheth.8035
6:10 Noah begat three sons, S', Ham, "
7:13 same day entered Noah, and S', "
9:18 that went forth of the ark, were S', "
23 S' and Japheth took a garment, "
26 Blessed be the Lord God of S'; "
27 he shall dwell in the tents of S'; "
10: 1 the sons of Noah; S', Ham, and "
21 Unto S' also, the father of all the "
22 children of S'; Elam, and Asshur, "
31 the sons of S', after their families, "
11:10 These are the generations of S': "
10 S' was an hundred years old, and "
11 S' lived after he begat Arphaxad "
1Ch 1: 4 Noah, S', Ham, and Japheth. "
17 The sons of S'; Elam, and Asshur, "
24 S', Arphaxad, Shelah,

Shema (*she'-mah*) See also SHEMAIAH; SHIMHI.
Jos 15:26 Amam, and S', and Moladah, 8087
1Ch 2:43 and Tappuah, and Rekem, and S'. "
44 And S' begat Raham, the father of "
5: 8 Bela the son of Azaz, the son of S', "
8:13 Beriah also, and S', who were "
Ne 8: 4 him stood Mattithiah, and S', and "

Shemaah (*shem'-a-ah*)
1Ch 12: 3 the sons of S' the Gebeathite; 8093

Shemaiah (*shem-a-i'-ah*) See also SHAMMUA; SHEMA; SHIMEI; SIMEI.
1Ki 12:22 word of God came unto S' the 8098
1Ch 3:22 And the sons of Shechaniah; S': "
22 and the sons of S'; Hattush, and "
4:37 the son of Shimri, the son of S', "
5: 4 S' his son, Gog his son, Shimei his "
9:14 S' the son of Hasshub, the son of "
16 And Obadiah the son of S', the son "
15: 8 S' the chief, and his brethren two "
11 S', and Eliel, and Amminadab, "
24: 6 And S' the son of Nethaneel the "
26: 4 S' the firstborn, Jehozabad the "
6 Also unto S' his son were sons "
7 The sons of S'; Othni, and Rephael, "
2Ch 11: 2 the word of the Lord came to S' "
12: 5 came S' the prophet to Rehoboam, "
7 the word of the Lord came to S', "
15 they not written in the book of S' "
17: 8 with them he sent Levites, even S', "
29:14 sons of Jeduthun; S', and Uzziel. "
31:15 and S', Amariah, and Shecaniah, "
35: 9 also, and S' and Nethaneel, his "
Ezr 8:13 are these, Eliphelet, Jeiel, and S', "
16 sent I for Eliezer, for Ariel, for S', "
10:21 and Elijah, and S', and Jehiel, and "
31 Ishijah, Malchiah, S', Shimeon, "
Ne 3:29 After him repaired also S' the son "
6:10 I came unto the house of S' the "
10: 8 Bilgai, S'; these were the priests. "
11:15 the Levites: S' the son of Hashub, "
12: 6 S', and Joiarib, Jedaiah, "
18 Shammua; of S', Jehonathan; "
34 Benjamin, and S', and Jeremiah, "
35 the son of S', the son of Mattaniah, "
36 And his brethren, S', and Azarael, "
42 And Maaseiah, and S', and Eleazar, "
Jer 26:20 the son of S' of Kirjath-jearim, "
29:24 Thus shalt thou also speak to S' "
31 Thus saith the Lord concerning S' "
31 that S' hath prophesied unto you, "
32 I will punish S' the Nehelamite, "
36:12 and Delaiah the son of S', and "

Shemariah (*shem-a-ri'-ah*)
1Ch 12: 5 Bealiah, and S', and Shephatiah 8114
2Ch 11:19 Jeush, and S', and Zaham. "

Ezr 10:32 Benjamin, Malluch, and S·. 8114
41 Azareel, and Shelemiah, S·. "

Shemeber (*shem-e'-bur*)
Ge 14: 2 S· king of Zeboiim, and the king 8038

Shemer (*she'-mur*)
1Ki 16:24 bought the hill Samaria of S· for 8106
24 after the name of S·, owner of the "

Shemesh See BETH-SHEMESH; EN-SHEMESH; IR-SHEMESH.

Shemida (*shem-i'-dah*) See also SHEMIDAH.
Nu 26:32 S·, the family of the Shemidaites: 8061
Jos 17: 2 Hepher, and for the children of S·: "

Shemidah (*shem-i'-dah*) See also SHEMIDA; SHEMIDAITES.
1Ch 7:19 And the sons of S· were, Ahian, 8061

Shemidaites (*shem'-i-dah-ites*)
Nu 26:32 of Shemida, the family of the S·: 8062

Sheminith (*shem'-i-nith*)
1Ch 15:21 with harps on the S· to excel. 8067
Ps 6: *title* Musician on Neginoth upon S·, "
12: *title* To the chief Musician upon S·, "

Shemiramoth (*she-mir'-a-moth*)
1Ch 15:18 and Jaaziel, and S·, and Jehiel, 8070
20 and Aziel, and S·, and Jehiel, and "
16: 5 to him Zachariah, Jeiel, and S·, "
2Ch 17: 8 Asahel, and S·, and Jehonathan, "

Shemite See BETH-SHEMITE.

Shemuel (*shem-u'-el*) See also SAMUEL.
Nu 34:20 Simeon, S· the son of Ammihud. 8050
1Ch 6:33 the son of Joel, the son of S·, * "
7: 2 S·, heads of their father's house, "

Shen (*shen*)
1Sa 7:12 and set it between Mizpeh and S·,8129

Shenazar (*she-na'-zar*)
1Ch 3:18 also, and Pedaiah, and S·, 8137

Shenir (*she'-nur*) See also SENIR; SION.
De 3: 9 and the Amorites call it S·;) *8149
Ca 4: 8 from the top of S· and Hermon, * "

Shepham (*she'-fam*) See also SHIPHMITE.
Nu 34:10 border from Hazar-enan to S·: 8221
11 shall go down from S· to Riblah, "

Shephatiah (*shef-a-ti'-ah*)
2Sa 3: 4 and the fifth, S· the son of Abital; 8203
1Ch 3: 3 The fifth, S· of Abital: the sixth, "
9: 8 and Meshullam the son of S·, the "
12: 5 Shemariah, and S· the Haruphite, "
27:16 Simeonites, S· the son of Maachah: "
2Ch 21: 2 and Azariah, and Michael, and S·: "
Ezr 2: 4 The children of S·, three hundred "
57 The children of S·, the children of "
8: 8 And of the sons of S·; Zebadiah the "
Ne 7: 9 The children of S·, three hundred "
59 The children of S·, the children of "
11: 4 the son of S·, the son of Mahalaleel, "
Jer 38: 1 Then S· the son of Mattan, and "

shepherd See also SHEPHERD'S; SHEPHERDS.
Ge 46:34 every s· is an abomination 7462,6629
49:24 (from thence is the s·, the stone of 7462
Nu 27:17 be not as sheep which have no s·. "
1Ki 22:17 hills, as sheep that have not a s·: "
2Ch 18:16 as sheep that have no s·; and the "
Ps 23: 1 The Lord is my s·; I shall not want. "
80: 1 Give ear, O S· of Israel, thou that "
Ec 12:11 which are given from one s·. "
Isa 40:11 He shall feed his flock like a s·: he "
44:28 That saith of Cyrus, He is my s·, "
63:11 of the sea with the s· of his flock? * "
Jer 31:10 and keep him, as a s· doth his flock. "
43:12 as a s· putteth on his garment; "
49:19 and who is that s· that will stand "
50:44 and who is that s· that will stand "
51:23 in pieces...the s· and his flock; "
Eze 34: 5 scattered, because there is no s·: "
8 because there was no s·, neither did "
12 As a s· seeketh out his flock in the "
23 And I will set up one s· over them, "
23 feed them, and he shall be their s·. "
37:24 and they all shall have one s·: they "
Am 3:12 As the s· taketh out of the mouth of "
Zec 10: 2 troubled, because there was no s·. "
11:15 yet the instruments of a foolish s·. "
16 lo, I will raise up a s· in the land, "
17 Woe to the idol s· that leaveth the 7473
13: 7 Awake, O sword, against my s·, 7462
7 smite the s·, and the sheep shall be "
M't 9:36 abroad, as sheep having no s·. 4166
25:32 as a s· divideth his sheep from the "
26:31 I will smite the s·, and the sheep of "
M'r 6:34 they were as sheep not having a s·: "
14:27 I will smite the s·, and the sheep "
Joh 10: 2 in by the door is the s· of the sheep. "
11 I am the good s·: the good s· giveth "
12 that is an hireling, and not the s·, "
14 I am the good s·, and know my "
16 there shall be one fold, and one s·. "
Heb 13:20 Jesus, that great s· of the sheep, "
1Pe 2:25 returned unto the S· and Bishop of "
5: 4 And when the chief S· shall appear, 750

shepherd's
1Sa 17:40 put them in a s· bag which he had, 7462
Isa 38:12 is removed from me as a s· tent: 7473

shepherds See also SHEPHERDS'.
Ge 46:32 the men are s·, for their trade 7462,6629
47: 3 Thy servants are s·, both we, "
Ex 2:17 And the s· came and drove them 7462
19 us out of the hand of the s·, and "
1Sa 25: 7 now thy s· which were with us, we "
Isa 13:20 neither shall the s· make their fold "
31: 4 when a multitude of s· is called forth "
Isa 56:11 they are s· that cannot understand: 7462
Jer 6: 3 The s· with their flocks shall come "
23: 4 And I will set up s· over them which "
25:34 Howl, ye s·, and cry; and wallow "
35 And the s· shall have no way to flee, "
36 A voice of the cry of the s·, and an "
33:12 an habitation of s· causing their "
50: 6 their s· have caused them to go "
Eze 34: 2 prophesy against the s· of Israel, "
2 saith the Lord God unto the s·; Woe "
2 Woe be to the s· of Israel that do "
2 should not the s· feed the flocks? "
7 ye s·, hear the word of the Lord; "
8 did my s· search for my flock, "
8 but the s· fed themselves, and fed "
9 O ye s·, hear the word of the Lord; "
10 Behold, I am against the s·; and I "
10 neither shall the s· feed themselves "
Am 1: 2 habitations of the s· shall mourn, "
Mic 5: 5 shall we raise against him seven s·, "
Na 3:18 Thy s· slumber, O king of Assyria: "
Zep 2: 6 be dwellings and cottages for s·, and "
Zec 10: 3 anger was kindled against the s·, "
11: 3 is a voice of the howling of the s·; "
5 and their own s· pity them not. "
8 Three s· also I cut off in one month; "
Lu 2: 8 country s· abiding in the field, 4166
15 the s· said one to another, Let us "
18 which were told them by the s·. "
20 And the s· returned, glorifying and "

shepherds'
Ca 1: 8 feed thy kids beside the s· tents. 7462

Shephi (*she'-fi*) See also SHEPHO.
1Ch 1:40 and Ebal, S·, and Onam. 8195

Shepho (*she'-fo*) See also SHEPHI.
Ge 36:23 and Ebal, S·, and Onam. 8195

Shephuphan (*shef'-u-fan*) See also SHUPHAM; SHUPPIM.
1Ch 8: 5 And Gera, and S·, and Huram. 8197

Sherah (*she'-rah*) See also UZZEN-SHERAH.
1Ch 7:24 his daughter was S·, who built *7609

sherd See also POTSHERD; SHERDS; SHRED.
Isa 30:14 be found in the bursting of it a s· 2789

sherds See also POTSHERDS.
Eze 23:34 thou shalt break the s· thereof, 2789

Sherebiah (*sher-e-bi'-ah*)
Ezr 8:18 and S·, with his sons and his 8274
24 S·, Hashabiah, and ten of their "
Ne 8: 7 and Bani, and S·, Jamin, Akkub, "
9: 4 Bunni, S·, Bani, and Chenani, and "
5 Bani, Hashabniah, S·, Hodijah, "
10:12 Zaccur, S·, Shebaniah, "
12: 8 Binnui, Kadmiel, S·, Judah, and "
24 Hashabiah, S·, and Jeshua the son "

Sheresh (*she'-resh*)
1Ch 7:16 the name of his brother was S·; 8329

Sherezer (*she-re'-zur*) See also SHAREZER.
Zec 7: 2 S· and Regem-melech, and their *8272

sheriffs
Da 3: 2, 3 the s·, and all the rulers of the 8614

Sheshach (*she'-shak*) See also BABYLON.
Jer 25:26 king of S· shall drink after them. 8347
51:41 How is S· taken! and how is the "

Sheshai (*she'-shahee*)
Nu 13:22 S·, and Talmai, the children of 8344
Jos 15:14 sons of Anak, S·, and Ahiman, and "
J'g 1:10 and they slew S·, and Ahiman, and "

Sheshan (*she'-shan*)
1Ch 2:31 And the sons of Ishi; S·. 8348
31 And the children of S·; Ahlai. "
34 S· had no sons, but daughters, "
34 And S· had a servant, an Egyptian, "
35 S· gave his daughter to Jarha his "

Sheshbazzar (*shesh-baz'-zur*) See also ZERUBBABEL.
Ezr 1: 8 and numbered them unto S·, the 8339
11 All these did S· bring up with them "
5:14 unto one, whose name was S·, whom "
16 Then came the same S·, and laid "

Sheth (*sheth*) See also SETH.
Nu 24:17 and destroy all the children of S·. *8352
1Ch 1: 1 Adam, S·, Enosh, * "

Shethar (*she'-thar*) See also SHETHAR-BOZNAI.
Es 1:14 Carshena, S·, Admatha, Tarshish, 8369

Shethar-boznai (*she''-thar-boz'-nahee*)
Ezr 5: 3 and S·, and their companions, and *8370
6 and S·, and his companions the * "
6: 6 S·, and your companions the * "
13 S·,...their companions, according * "

Sheva (*she'-vah*) See also SHAVSHA.
2Sa 20:25 And S· was scribe: and Zadok and 7724
1Ch 2:49 S· the father of Machbenah, and "

shew See also SHEWBREAD; SHEWED; SHEWEST; SHEWETH; SHEWING.
Ge 12: 1 unto a land that I will s· thee: 7200
20:13 thy kindness which thou shalt s· 6213
24:12 and s· kindness unto my master "
40:14 s· kindness, I pray thee, unto me, "
46:31 I will go up, and s· Pharaoh, and *5046
Ex 7: 9 you, saying, S· a miracle for you: 5414
9:16 up, for to s· in thee my power; 7200
10: 1 that I might s· these my signs 7896
13: 8 thou shalt s· thy son in that day, *5046
14:13 which he will s· to you to day: for *6213
18:20 shalt s· them the way wherein 3045
25: 9 According to all that I s· thee, 7200
33:13 s· me now thy way, that I may 3045
Ex 33:18 I beseech thee, s· me thy glory. 7200
19 will s· mercy on whom I will s· mercy. "
Nu 16: 5 the Lord will s· who are his, and 3045
De 1:33 to s· you by what way ye should go, 7200
3:24 to s· thy servants thy greatness, "
5: 5 to s· you the word of the Lord: 5046
7: 2 with them, nor s· mercy unto them: "
13:17 of his anger, and s· thee mercy, 5414
17: 9 they shall s· thee the sentence of 5046
10 the Lord shall choose shall s· thee; "
11 sentence which they shall s· thee, "
28:50 of the old, nor s· favour to the young: "
32: 7 ask thy father, and he will s· thee; 5046
Jos 2:12 ye will also s· kindness unto my *6213
5: 6 he would not s· them the land, *7200
J'g 1:24 S· us, we pray thee, the entrance "
24 the city, and we will s· thee mercy. *6213
4:22 will s· thee the man...thou seekest. 7200
6:17 s· me a sign that thou talkest with 6213
1Sa 3:15 Samuel feared to s· Eli the vision. 5046
8: 9 and s· them the manner of the king" "
9: 6 peradventure he can s· us our way * "
27 I may s· thee the word of God. *8085
10: 8 and s· thee what thou shalt do. 3045
14:12 up to us, and we will s· you a thing. "
16: 3 I will s· thee what thou shalt do: "
20: 2 or small, but that he will s· it me: *1540
12 send not unto thee, and s· it thee; * "
13 then I will s· it thee, and send thee * "
14 s· me the kindness of the Lord, 6213
22:17 he fled, and did not s· it to me. *1540
25: 8 young men, and they will s· thee. *5046
2Sa 2: 6 s· kindness and truth unto you: 6213
3: 8 s· kindness this day unto the house "
9: 1 may s· him kindness for Jonathan's "
3 that I may s· the kindness of God "
7 surely s· thee kindness for Jonathan "
10: 2 I will s· kindness unto Hanun the "
15:25 s· me both it, and his habitation: 7200
22:26 merciful thou wilt s· thyself merciful, "
26 man thou wilt s· thyself upright. "
27 the pure thou wilt s· thyself pure; "
27 froward thou wilt s· thyself unsavoury. "
1Ki 1:52 If he will s· himself a worthy man, "
2: 2 therefore, and s· thyself a man; "
7 s· kindness unto...sons of Barzillai 6213
18: 1 saying, Go, s· thyself unto Ahab; 7200
2 Elijah went to s· himself unto Ahab. "
15 I will surely s· myself unto him "
2Ki 6:11 s· me which of us is for the king 5046
7:12 s· you what the Syrians have done "
1Ch 16:23 s·...from day to day his salvation. 1319
19: 2 I will s· kindness unto Hanun the 6213
2Ch 16: 9 to s· himself strong in the behalf of "
Ezr 2:59 could not s· their father's house, 5046
Ne 7:61 could not s· their father's house, "
9:19 of fire by night, to s· them light, "
Es 1:11 to s· the people...her beauty: 7200
2:10 charged her...she should not s· it. 5046
4: 8 to s· it unto Esther, and to declare 7200
Job 10: 2 s· me wherefore thou contendest 3045
11: 6 s· thee the secrets of wisdom, 5046
15:17 I will s· thee, hear me; and that 2331
32: 6 and durst not s· you mine opinion. "
10 to me; I also will s· mine opinion. "
17 my part, I also will s· mine opinion. "
33:23 to s· unto man his uprightness: 5046
36: 2 Suffer me a little, and I will s· 2331
Ps 4: 6 that say, Who will s· us any good? 7200
9: 1 s· forth all thy marvellous works. 5608
14 That I may s· forth all thy praise "
16:11 Thou wilt s· me the path of life: 3045
17: 7 S· thy marvellous lovingkindness, "
18:25 merciful thou wilt s· thyself merciful; "
25 man thou wilt s· thyself upright; "
26 the pure thou wilt s· thyself pure; "
26 froward thou wilt s· thyself froward. "
25: 4 S· me thy ways, O Lord; teach me 3045
14 and he will s· them his covenant. "
39: 6 every man walketh in a vain s·: 6754
50:23 will I s· the salvation of God. 7200
51:15 my mouth shall s· forth thy praise. 5046
71:15 shall s· forth thy righteousness *5608
79:13 s· forth thy praise to all generations. "
85: 7 S· us thy mercy, O Lord, and 7200
86:17 S· me a token for good; that they 6213
88:10 Wilt thou s· wonders to the dead? "
91:16 him, and s· him my salvation. 7200
92: 2 To s· forth thy lovingkindness in 5046
15 To s· that the Lord is upright: he "
94: 1 vengeance belongeth, s· thyself. *3313
96: 2 s·...his salvation from day to day. 1319
106: 2 who can s· forth all his praise? 8085
109:16 he remembered not to s· mercy, 6213
Pr 18:24 hath friends must s· himself friendly: *
Isa 3: 9 The s· of their countenance doth 1971
27:11 formed them will s· them no favour. "
30:30 s· the lighting down of his arm, 7200
41:22 and s· us what shall happen: *5046
22 let them s· the former things, what * "
23 S· the things that are to come * "
43: 9 this, and s· us former things? 8085
21 they shall s· forth my praise. *5608
44: 7 shall come, let them s· unto them. *5046
46: 8 Remember this, and s· yourselves men: "
47: 6 thou didst s· them no mercy; 7760
49: 9 are in darkness, S· yourselves. 1540
58: 1 s· my people their transgression, *5046
60: 6 s· forth the praises of the Lord. *1319
Jer 16:10 shalt s· this people all these words, 5046
13 where I will not s· you favour. 5414
18:17 I will s· them the back, and not †7200
33: 3 s· thee great and mighty things, 5046
42: 3 the Lord thy God may s· us the way "
12 And I will s· mercies unto you, *5414
50:42 they are cruel, and will not s· mercy: *

Jer 51: 31 to s' the king of Babylon...his city 5046
22: 2 shalt s' her all her abominations. *3045
Eze 33: 31 their mouth they s' much love, 6213
37: 18 thou not s' us what thou meanest 5046
40: 4 heart upon all that I shall s' thee; 7200
4 that I might s' them unto thee art "
43: 10 s' the house to the house of Israel, 5046
11 s' them the form of the house, *3045
Da 2: 2 for to s' the king his dreams. *5046
4 and we will s' the interpretation. 2324
6 But if ye s' the dream, and the "
6 therefore s' me the dream, and the "
7 we will s' the interpretation of it. "
9 that ye can s' me the interpretation "
10 earth that can s' the king's matter: "
11 there is none other that can s' it "
16 s' the king the interpretation. "
24 s' unto the king the interpretation. "
27 the soothsayers, s' unto the king; "
4: 2 I thought it good to s' the signs "
5: 7 s' me the interpretation thereof, "
12 and he will s' the interpretation. "
15 they could not s' the interpretation "
9: 23 forth, and I am come to s' thee; *5046
10: 21 I will s' thee that which is noted * "
11: 2 And now will I s' thee the truth. "
Joe 2: 30 I will s' wonders in the heavens 5414
Mic 7: 15 I s' unto him marvellous things. 7200
Na 3: 5 I will s' the nations thy nakedness, "
Hab 1: 3 Why dost thou s' me iniquity, and "
Zec 1: 9 unto me, I will s' thee what these be. "
7: 9 and s' mercy and compassions 6213
M't 8: 4 thy way, s' thyself to the priest, 1166
11: 4 Go and s' John again those things *518
12: 18 shall s' judgment to the Gentiles. * "
14: 2 mighty works do s'...themselves *1754
16: 1 would s' them a sign from heaven. 1925
21 began Jesus to s' unto his disciples, 1166
22: 19 S' me the tribute money. And 1925
24: 1 s' him the buildings of the temple. "
24 shall s' great signs and wonders; 1325
M'r 1: 44 thy way, s' thyself to the priest, 1166
6: 14 mighty works do s'...themselves *1754
13: 22 and shall s' signs and wonders, to 1325
14: 15 he will s' you a large upper room 1166
Lu 1: 19 and to s' thee these glad tidings. *2097
5: 14 but go, and s' thyself to the priest, 1166
6: 47 I will s' you to whom he is like: 5263
8: 39 s' how great things God hath done *1334
17: 14 Go s' yourselves unto the priests. 1925
20: 24 S' me a penny. Whose image and "
47 and for a s' make long prayers: *4392
22: 12 he shall s' you a large upper room 1166
Joh 5: 20 s' him greater works than these, "
7: 4 things, s' thyself to the world. *5319
11: 57 knew where he was, he should s' it, 3377
14: 8 s' us the Father, and it sufficeth 1166
9 sayest thou then, S' us the Father? "
16: 13 and he will s' you things to come. * 312
14, 15 of mine, and shall s' it unto you. * "
25 I shall s' you plainly of the Father. * "
Ac 1: 24 s' whether of these two thou hast 322
2: 19 I will s' wonders in heaven above, 1325
7: 3 into the land which I shall s' thee. 1166
9: 16 For I will s' him how great things 5263
12: 17 Go s' these things unto James, and *518
16: 17 s' unto us the way of salvation. *2605
24: 27 willing to s' the Jews a pleasure, *2698
26: 23 should s' light unto the people, *2605
Ro 2: 15 s' the work of the law written in 1731
9: 17 that I might s' my power in thee, "
22 What if God, willing to s' his wrath, "
1Co 11: 26 ye do s' the Lord's death till he *2605
12: 31 s' I unto you a more excellent way. 1166
15: 51 I s' you a mystery; We shall not 3004
2Co 8: 24 Wherefore s' ye to them, and before 1731
Ga 6: 12 desire to make a fair s' in the flesh, 2146
Eph 2: 7 he might s' the exceeding riches 1731
Col 2: 15 he made a s' of them openly, 1165
23 things have indeed a s' of wisdom 3056
1Th 1: 9 s' of us what manner of entering * 518
1Ti 1: 16 might s' forth all longsuffering, 1731
5: 4 learn first to s' piety at home, and 2151
6: 15 Which in his times he shall s', 1166
2Ti 2: 15 Study to s' thyself approved unto *3936
Heb 6: 11 one of you do s' the same diligence 1731
17 to s' unto the heirs of promise the 1925
Jas 2: 18 s' me thy faith without thy works, 1166
18 I will s' thee my faith by my works. "
3: 13 let him s' out of a good conversation "
1Pe 2: 9 should s' forth the praises of him 1804
1Jo 1: 2 and s' unto you that eternal life, * 518
Re 1: 1 to s' unto his servants things which 1166
4: 1 I will s' thee things which must be "
17: 1 I will s' unto thee the judgment of "
21: 9 I will s' thee the bride, the Lamb's "
22: 6 to s' unto his servants the things "

shewbread
Ex 25: 30 shalt set upon the table s' 3899, 6440
35: 13 and all his vessels, and the s', " "
39: 36 the vessels thereof, and the s'; " "
Nu 4: 7 upon the table of s' they shall spread "
1Sa 21: 6 was no bread there but the s', 3899, "
1Ki 7: 48 of gold, whereupon the s' was, " "
1Ch 9: 32 were over the s', to prepare it 4635
23: 29 Both for the s', and for the fine "
28: 16 he gave gold for the tables of s', "
2Ch 2: 4 incense, and for the continual s', "
4: 19 tables whereon the s' was set; 3899, 6440
13: 11 the s' also set they in order 4635
29: 18 and the s' table, with all the vessels "
Ne 10: 33 For the s', and...the continual 3899, "
M't 12: 4 eat the s', which was not lawful 740, 4286
M'r 2: 26 eat the s', which is not lawful " "
Lu 6: 4 and did take and eat the s', and " "
Heb 9: 2 and the table, and the s'; 4286, 740

shewed See also SHEWEDST.
Ge 19: 19 thou hast s' unto me in saving my 6213
24: 14 hast s' kindness unto my master. "
32: 10 which thou hast s' unto thy servant; "
39: 21 with Joseph, and s' him mercy, 5186
41: 25 God hath s' Pharaoh what he is *5046
39 Forasmuch as God hath s' thee all 3045
48: 11 lo, God hath s' me also thy seed. *7200
Ex 15: 25 and the Lord s' him a tree, which 3384
25: 40 which was s' thee in the mount. 7200
26: 30 which was s' thee in the mount. "
27: 8 as it was s' thee in the mount, so "
Le 13: 19 reddish, and it be s' to the priest; "
49 and shall be s' unto the priest: "
24: 12 mind of the Lord might be s' them. *6567
Nu 8: 4 pattern...the Lord had s' Moses, 7200
13: 26 and s' them the fruit of the land. "
14: 11 signs...I have s' among them? *6213
De 4: 35 Unto thee it was s', that thou 7200
36 upon earth he s' thee his great fire; "
5: 24 Lord our God hath s' us his glory "
6: 22 the Lord s' signs and wonders, 5414
34: 1 Lord s' him all the land of Gilead, 7200
12 terror which Moses s' in the sight *6213
Jos 2: 12 since I have s' you kindness, that * "
J'g 1: 25 when he s' them the entrance into 7200
4: 12 And they s' Sisera that Barak *5046
8: 35 s' they kindness to the house of 6213
35 to all the goodness which he had s' "
13: 10 and ran, and s' her husband, and *5046
23 neither would he have s' us all 7200
16: 18 for he hath s' me all his heart. *5046
Ru 2: 11 It hath fully been s' me, all that thou "
19 she s' her mother in law with whom "
3: 10 s' more kindness in the latter 3190
1Sa 11: 9 messengers...s' it to the men of *5046
15: 6 s' kindness to all the children of 6213
19: 7 Jonathan s' him all those things. 5046
22: 21 Abiathar s' David...Saul had slain* "
24: 18 s' this day how...thou hast dealt * "
2Sa 2: 5 s' this kindness unto your lord, 6213
10: 2 as his father s' kindness unto me. "
11: 22 s' David all that Joab had sent him 5046
1Ki 1: 27 hast not s' it unto thy servant, 3045
3: 6 hast s' unto thy servant David my 6213
16: 27 he did, and his might that he s', "
22: 45 and his might that he s', and how "
2Ki 6: 6 fell it? And he s' him the place. 7200
8: 10 Lord hath s' me that he shall...die. "
13 Lord hath s' me thou shalt be king "
11: 4 Lord, and s' them the king's son. "
20: 13 s' them...the house of his precious "
13 nothing...that Hezekiah s' them not. "
15 treasures that I have not s' them. "
22: 10 Shaphan the scribe s' the king, * "
1Ch 19: 2 his father s' kindness to me. 6213
2Ch 1: 8 hast s' great mercy unto David my "
7: 10 the Lord had s' unto David, and to "
Ezr 9: 8 grace hath been s' from the Lord "
Es 1: 4 he s' the riches of his glorious 7200
2: 10 Esther had not s' her people nor 5046
20 Esther had not yet s' her kindred "
3: 6 had s' him the people of Mordecai: "
Job 6: 14 pity should be s' from his friend; "
Ps 31: 21 he hath s' me his marvellous kindness "
60: 3 Thou hast s' thy people hard things: "
71: 18 I have s' thy strength unto this *5046
20 hast s' me great and sore troubles, 7200
78: 11 his wonders that he had s' them. "
98: 2 righteousness hath he openly s' in 1540
105: 27 They s' his signs among them, and *7760
111: 6 hath s' his people the power of his 5046
118: 27 is the Lord, which hath s' us light: *
142: 2 him; I s' before him my trouble. *5046
Pr 26: 26 wickedness shall be s' before the 1540
Ec 2: 19 I have s' myself wise under the sun.
Isa 26: 10 Let favour be s' to the wicked, yet
39: 2 s' them the house of his precious 7200
2 dominion, that Hezekiah s' them not, "
4 treasures that I have not s' them. "
40: 14 s'...him the way of understanding? 3045
43: 12 have saved, and I have s', when 8085
48: 3 out of my mouth, and I s' them; "
5 before it came to pass I s' it thee: "
6 s' thee new things from this time, "
Jer 24: 1 The Lord s' me, and, behold, two 7200
38: 21 the word that the Lord hath s' me: "
Eze 11: 25 the things that the Lord had s' me. "
20: 11 and s' them my judgments, which 3045
22: 26 neither have they s' difference
Am 7: 1 hath the Lord God s' unto me; 7200
4 Thus hath the Lord God s' unto me: "
7 Thus he s' me: and, behold, the "
8: 1 Thus hath the Lord God s' unto me: "
Mic 6: 8 He hath s' thee, O man, what is 5046
Zec 1: 20 the Lord s' me four carpenters. 7200
3: 1 And he s' me Joshua the high priest "
M't 28: 11 and s' unto the chief priests all the *518
Lu 1: 51 He hath s' strength with his arm; 4160
58 Lord had s' great mercy upon her; *3170
4: 5 s' unto him all the kingdoms of the 1166
7: 18 of John s' him of all these things. * 518
10: 37 he said, He that s' mercy on him. 4160
14: 21 came, and s' his lord these things. * 518
20: 37 even Moses s' at the bush, when 3377
24: 40 he s' them his hands and his 1925
Joh 10: 32 good works have I s' you from my 1166
20: 20 he s' unto them his hands and his "
21: 1 Jesus s' himself again to the *5319
1 and on this wise s' he himself. * "
14 third time that Jesus s' himself to * "
Ac 1: 3 To whom also he s' himself alive 3936
3: 18 s' by...mouth of all his prophets, *4293
4: 22 this miracle of healing was s'. *1096
7: 26 he s' himself unto them as they *3700
36 s' wonders and signs in the land *4160
Ac 7: 52 slain them which s' before of the 4293
10: 28 God hath s' me that I should not 1166
40 day, and s' him openly; *1325, 1717, 1096
11: 13 he s' us how he had seen an angel * 518
19: 18 and confessed, and s' their deeds. * 312
20: 20 but have s' you, and have taught * "
35 I have s' you all things, how that *5263
23: 22 thou hast s' these things to me. *1718
26: 20 s' first unto them of Damascus, and *518
28: 2 people s' us no little kindness: 3930
21 came or spake any harm of thee. 518
Ro 1: 19 for God hath s' it unto them. *5319
1Co 10: 28 eat not for his sake that s' it, and 3377
Heb 6: 10 which ye have s' toward his name, 1731
8: 5 the pattern s' to thee in the mount. 1166
Jas 2: 13 mercy, that hath s' no mercy; 4160
2Pe 1: 14 our Lord Jesus Christ hath s' me. *1213
Re 21: 10 and s' me that great city, the holy 1166
22: 1 he s' me a pure river of water of "
8 the angel which s' me these things. "

shewedst
Ne 9: 10 And s' signs and wonders upon 5414
Jer 11: 18 it: then thou s' me their doings. 7200

shewest
2Ch 6: 14 s' mercy unto thy servants, that walk*
Job 10: 16 thou s' thyself marvellous upon me.
Jer 32: 18 Thou s' lovingkindness unto 6213
Joh 2: 18 What sign s' thou unto us, seeing 1166
6: 30 What sign s' thou then, that we *4160

sheweth
Ge 41: 28 about to do he s' unto Pharaoh. *7200
Nu 23: 3 and whatsoever he s' me I will tell "
1Sa 22: 8 is none that s' me that my son 1540, 241
8 or s' unto me that my son hath * "
2Sa 22: 51 and s' mercy to his anointed, unto 6213
Job 36: 9 Then he s' them their work, and 5046
33 The noise thereof s' concerning it, * "
Ps 18: 50 and s' mercy to his anointed, to 6213
19: 1 the firmament s' his handywork. 5046
2 night unto night s' knowledge. 2331
37: 21 righteous s' mercy, and giveth. *
112: 5 A good man s' favour, and lendeth: *
147: 19 He s' his word unto Jacob, his 5046
Pr 12: 17 He that speaketh truth s' forth "
27: 25 tender grass s' itself, and herbs 7200
Isa 41: 26 there is none that s', yea, there is 5046
M't 4: 8 and s' him all the kingdoms of the 1166
Joh 5: 20 s' him all things that himself doeth: "
Ro 9: 16 runneth, but of God that s' mercy. *1653
12: 8 he that s' mercy, with cheerfulness. "

shewing
Ex 20: 6 s' mercy unto thousands of them 6213
De 5: 10 s' mercy unto thousands of them "
Ps 78: 4 s' to the generation to come the *5608
Ca 2: 9 s' himself through the lattice. *6692
Da 4: 27 iniquities by s' mercy to the poor;
5: 12 s' of hard sentences, and dissolving 263
Lu 1: 80 till the day of his s' unto Israel. 323
8: 1 preaching and s' the glad tidings *
Ac 9: 39 s' the coats and garments which 1925
18: 28 s' by the scriptures that Jesus was "
2Th 2: 4 of God, s' himself that he is God. * 584
Tit 2: 7 s' thyself a pattern of good works: 3930
7 in doctrine s' uncorruptness, gravity,
10 but s' all good fidelity; that 1731
3: 2 gentle, s' all meekness unto all men. "

Shibboleth (*shib'-bo-leth*) See also SIBBOLETH.
J'g 12: 6 said they unto him, Say now S': 7641

Shibmah (*shib'-mah*) See also SHEBAM; SIBMAH.
Nu 32: 38 names being changed,) and S': *7643

Shicron (*shi'-cron*)
Jos 15: 11 and the border was drawn to S', *7942

shield See also SHIELDS.
Ge 15: 1 Fear not, Abram: I am thy s', and 4043
De 33: 29 by the Lord, the s' of thy help, "
J'g 5: 8 was there a s' or spear seen among "
1Sa 17: 7 one bearing a s' went before him. 6793
41 man that bare the s' went before "
45 and with a spear, and with a s': *3591
2Sa 1: 21 s' of the mighty is vilely cast away, 4043
21 the s' of Saul, as though he had not "
22: 3 he is my s', and the horn of my "
36 given me the s' of thy salvation: "
1Ki 10: 17 three pound of gold went to one s': "
2Ki 19: 32 nor come before it with s', nor cast "
1Ch 12: 8 that could handle s' and buckler, 6793
24 The children of Judah that bare s' "
34 with s' and spear thirty and seven "
2Ch 9: 16 shekels of gold went to one s'. 4043
17: 17 him armed men with bow and s' "
25: 5 that could handle spear and s'. 6793
Job 39: 23 the glittering spear and the s'. *3591
Ps 3: 3 But thou, O Lord, art a s' for me; 4043
5: 12 thou compass him as with a s'. 6793
18: 35 given me the s' of thy salvation: 4043
28: 7 The Lord is my strength and my s'; "
33: 20 the Lord: he is our help and our s'. "
35: 2 Take hold of s' and buckler, and "
59: 11 bring them down, O Lord our s'. "
76: 3 he the arrows of the bow, the s', "
84: 9 Behold, O God our s', and look "
11 For the Lord God is a sun and s': "
91: 4 his truth shall be thy s' and 6793
115: 9, 10, 11 he is their help and their s'. 4043
119: 114 art my hiding place and my s': "
144: 2 my s', and he in whom I trust; "
Pr 30: 5 he is a s' unto them that put their "
Isa 21: 5 arise, ye princes, and anoint the s'. "
22: 6 and Kir uncovered the s'. "
Jer 46: 3 Order ye the buckler and s', and 6793
9 the Libyans, that handle the s'; 4043
Eze 23: 24 buckler and s' and helmet round "
27: 10 hanged the s' and helmet in thee; "

Eze 38: 5 all of them with s· and helmet: 4043
Na 2: 3 s· of his mighty men is made red, "
Eph 6: 16 taking the s· of faith, wherewith *2375*

shields
2Sa 8: 7 David took the s· of gold that were 7982
1Ki 10: 17 three hundred s· of beaten gold; 4043
14: 26 took away all the s· of gold which "
27 made in their stead brasen s·, and "
2Ki 11: 10 give king David's spears and s·, 7982
1Ch 18: 7 David took the s· of gold that were "
2Ch 9: 16 three hundred s· made of beaten 4043
11: 12 every several city he puts s· and 6793
12: 9 he carried away also the s· of gold 4043
10 king Rehoboam made s· of brass, "
14: 8 that bare s· and drew bows, two "
23: 9 spears, and bucklers, and s·, that 7982
26: 14 them throughout all the host s·, 4043
32: 5 and darts and s· in abundance. "
27 and for s·, and for all manner of "
Ne 4: 16 the spears, the s·, and the bows, "
Ps 47: 9 the s· of the earth belong unto God:"
Ca 4: 4 bucklers, all s· of mighty men. 7982
Isa 37: 33 nor come before it with s·, nor 4043
Jer 51: 11 bright the arrows; gather the s·: 7982
Eze 27: 11 hanged their s· upon thy walls "
38: 4 company with bucklers and s·, *4043
39: 9 both the s· and the bucklers, the "

Shiggaion (*shig-gah'-yon*) See also SHIGIONOTH.
Ps 7: *title* S· of David, which he sang unto 7692

Shigionoth (*shig-i'-o-noth*) See also SHIGGAION.
Hab 3: 1 Habakkuk the prophet upon S·. 7692

Shihon (*shi'-hon*)
Jos 19: 19 And Haphraim, and S·, and *7866

Shihor (*shi'-hor*) See also SHIHOR-LIBNATH; SIHOR.
1Ch 13: 5 from S· of Egypt even unto the 7883

Shihor-libnath (*shi''-hor-lib'-nath*)
Jos 19: 26 to Carmel westward, and to S·; 7884

Shilhi (*shil'-hi*)
1Ki 22: 42 was Azubah the daughter of S·. 7977
2Ch 20: 31 was Azubah the daughter of S·. "

Shilhim (*shil'-him*) See also SHAARAIM; SHARUHEN.
Jos 15: 32 Lebaoth, and S·, and Ain, and 7978

Shillem (*shil'-lem*) See also SHALLUM; SHILLEMITES.
Ge 46: 24 and Guni, and Jezer, and S·. 8006
Nu 26: 49 of S·, the family of the Shillemites. "

Shillemites (*shil'-lem-ites*)
Nu 26: 49 of Shillem, the family of the S·. 8016

Shiloah (*shi-lo'-ah*) See also SILOAH; SILOAM.
Isa 8: 6 people refuseth the waters of S· 7975

Shiloh (*shi'-loh*) See also SHILONITE; TAANATH-SHILOH.
Ge 49: 10 between his feet, until S· come; 7886
Jos 18: 1 of Israel assembled together at S·,7887
8 lots for you before the Lord in S·. "
9 again to Joshua to the host at S·. "
10 Joshua cast lots for them in S· "
19: 51 an inheritance by lot in S· before "
21: 2 spake unto them at S· in the land "
22: 9 the children of Israel out of S·, "
12 together at S·, to go up to war "
J'g 18: 31 that the house of God was in S·. "
21: 12 brought them unto the camp to S·, "
19 is a feast of the Lord in S· yearly "
21 daughters of S· come out to dance "
21 his wife of the daughters of S·, "
1Sa 1: 3 sacrifice unto the Lord...in S·. "
9 rose up after they had eaten in S·, "
24 unto the house of the Lord in S·: "
2: 14 they did in S· unto all the Israelites"
3: 21 the Lord appeared again in S·: "
21 revealed himself to Samuel in S· "
4: 3 the covenant of the Lord out of S· "
4 So the people sent to S·, that they "
12 came to S· the same day with his "
14: 3 the Lord's priest in S·, wearing an "
1Ki 2: 27 concerning the house of Eli in S·. "
14: 2 and get thee to S·: behold, there is "
4 did so, and arose, and went to S·, "
Ps 78: 60 he forsook the tabernacle of S·, "
Jer 7: 12 unto my place which was in S·, "
14 your fathers, as I have done to S·. "
26: 6 will I make this house like S·, and "
9 This house shall be like S·, and "
41: 5 certain from Shechem, from S·, "

Shiloni (*shi-lo'-ni*) See also SHILONITE.
Ne 11: 5 son of Zechariah, the son of S·. *8023

Shilonite (*shi'-lon-ite*) See also SHILONI; SHILONITES.
1Ki 11: 29 the S· found him in the way; 7888
12: 15 the Lord spake by Ahijah the S· "
15: 29 spake by his servant Ahijah the S·: "
2Ch 9: 29 in the prophecy of Ahijah the S·, "
10: 15 spake by the hand of Ahijah the S· "

Shilonites (*shi'-lon-ites*)
1Ch 9: 5 And of the S·; Asaiah the firstborn,7888

Shilshah (*shil'-shah*)
1Ch 7: 37 Shamma, and S·, and Ithran, and8030

Shimea (*shim'-e-ah*) See also SHAMMAH; SHAMMUA; SHAMMUAH; SHIMEAH; SHIMEATHITES; SHIMMA.
1Ch 3: 5 S·, and Shobab, and Nathan, and 8092
6: 30 S· his son, Haggiah his son, Asaiah"
39 son of Berachiah, the son of S·, "
20: 7 Jonathan the son of S· David's "

Shimeah (*shim'-e-ah*) See also SHIMEA; SHIMEAM.
2Sa 13: 3 the son of S· David's brother: 8093
32 the son of S· David's brother, "
21: 21 Jonathan the son of S· the *8096
1Ch 8: 32 And Mikloth begat S·. And these 8039

Shimeam (*shim'-e-am*) See also SHIMEA.
1Ch 9: 38 And Mikloth begat S·. And they 8043

Shimeath (*shim'-e-ath*)
2Ki 12: 21 For Jozachar the son of S·, and 8100
2Ch 24: 26 the son of S· an Ammonitess, and "

Shimeathites (*shim'-e-ath-ites*)
1Ch 2: 55 the Tirathites, the S·, and 8101

Shimei (*shim'-e-i*) See also SHEMAIAH; SHIMHI; SHIMI; SHIMITES.
Nu 3: 18 by their families; Libni, and S·. 8096
2Sa 16: 5 whose name was S·, the son of "
7 And thus said S· when he cursed, "
13 S· went along on the hill's side over"
19: 16 S· the son of Gera, a Benjamite, "
18 S· the son of Gera fell down before "
21 Shall not S· be put to death for this,"
23 the king said unto S·, Thou shalt "
1Ki 1: 8 Nathan the prophet, and S·, and "
2: 8 hast with thee S· the son of Gera, "
36 And the king sent and called for S·,"
38 S· said unto the king, The saying "
38 S· dwelt in Jerusalem many days. "
39 two of the servants of S· ran away "
39 And they told S·, saying, Behold, "
40 And S· arose, and saddled his ass, "
40 S· went, and brought his servants "
41 was told Solomon that S· had gone "
42 And the king sent and called for S·,"
44 The king said moreover to S·, Thou"
4: 18 S· the son of Elah, in Benjamin: "
1Ch 3: 19 Pedaiah were, Zerubbabel, and S·: "
4: 26 son, Zacchur his son, S· his son. "
27 And S· had sixteen sons and six "
5: 4 his son, Gog his son, S· his son, "
6: 17 sons of Gershom; Libni, and S·. "
29 Libni his son, S· his son, Uzza his "
42 the son of Zimmah, the son of S·, "
23: 7 Gershonites were, Laadan, and S·. "
9 The sons of S·; Shelomith, and "
10 And the sons of S· were, Jahath, "
10 These four were the sons of S·. "
25: 17 The tenth to S·, he, his sons, and "
27: 27 over the vineyards was S· the "
2Ch 29: 14 the sons of Heman; Jehiel, and S·: "
31: 12 and S· his brother was the next. "
13 the hand of Cononiah and S· his "
Ezr 10: 23 of the Levites; Jozabad, and S·, "
33 Jeremai, Manasseh, and S·. "
38 And Bani, and Binnui, S·, "
Es 2: 5 the son of Jair, the son of S·, the "
Zec 12: 13 the family of S· a part, and their *8097

Shimeon (*shim'-e-on*) See also SIMEON.
Ezr 10: 31 Ishijah, Malchiah, Shemaiah, S·, 8095

Shimhi (*shim'-hi*) See also SHEMA; SHIMEI.
1Ch 8: 21 and Shimrath, the sons of S·; *8096

Shimi (*shi'-mi*) See also SHIMEI; SHIMITES.
Ex 6: 17 S·, according to their families. *8096

Shimites (*shi'-mites*)
Nu 3: 21 Libnites, and the family of the S·:*8097

Shimma (*shim'-mah*) See also SHAMMAH.
1Ch 2: 13 the second, and S· the third, *8092

Shimon (*shi'-mon*)
1Ch 4: 20 the sons of S· were, Amnon, and 7889

Shimrath (*shim'-rath*)
1Ch 8: 21 and S·, the sons of Shimhi; 8119

Shimri (*shim'-ri*) See also SIMRI.
1Ch 4: 37 the son of Jedaiah, the son of S·, 8113
11: 45 Jediael the son of S·, and Joha his "
2Ch 29: 13 sons of Elizaphan; S·, and Jeiel: "

Shimrith (*shim'-rith*) See also SHOMER.
2Ch 24: 26 and Jehozabad the son of S· a 8116

Shimrom (*shim'-rom*) See also SHIMRON.
1Ch 7: 1 and Puah, Jashub, and S·, four. *8110

Shimron (*shim'-ron*) See also SHIMROM; SHIMRONITES; SHIMRON-MERON.
Ge 46: 13 and Phuvah, and Job, and S·. 8110
Nu 26: 24 of S·, the family of the Shimronites."
Jos 11: 1 and to the king of S·, and to the "
19: 15 Kattath, and Nahallal, and S·, and "

Shimronites (*shim'-ron-ites*)
Nu 26: 24 of Shimron, the family of the S·. 8117

Shimron-meron (*shim''-ron-me'-ron*) See also SHIMRON.
Jos 12: 20 The king of S·, one; the king of 8112

Shimshai (*shim'-shahee*)
Ezr 4: 8 S· the scribe wrote a letter 8124
9 and S· the scribe, and the rest "
17 to S· the scribe, and to the rest of "
23 S· the scribe, and their companions,"

Shinab (*shi'-nab*)
Ge 14: 2 S· king of Admah, and Shemeber 8134

Shinar (*shi'-nar*)
Ge 10: 10 and Calneh, in the land of S·. 8152
11: 2 found a plain in the land of S·; "
14: 1 in the days of Amraphel king of S·,"
9 Amraphel king of S·, and Arioch "
Isa 11: 11 and from S·, and from Hamath, "
Da 1: 2 land of S· to the house of his god; "
Zec 5: 11 build it an house in the land of S·: "

shine See also SHINED; SHINETH; SHINING; SHONE.
Nu 6: 25 Lord make his face s· upon thee, 215
Job 3: 4 neither let the light s· upon it. 3313
10: 3 s· upon the counsel of the wicked? "
11: 17 thou shalt s· forth, thou shalt be *5774
18: 5 the spark of his fire shall not s·. 5050
22: 28 the light shall s· upon thy ways. "
36: 32 commandeth it not to s· by the cloud*
37: 15 caused the light of his cloud to s·? 3313
41: 18 By his neesings a light doth s·, *1984
32 He maketh a path to s· after him: 215
Ps 31: 16 thy face to s· upon thy servant: "
67: 1 and cause his face to s· upon us. "
80: 1 between the cherubims, s· forth. 3313
3 and cause thy face to s·; and we 215
7, 19 cause thy face to s·; and we "
104: 15 oil to make his face to s·, and 6670
119: 135 thy face to s· upon thy servant; 215
Ec 8: 1 man's wisdom maketh his face to s·,"
Isa 13: 10 shall not cause her light to s·. 5050
60: 1 Arise, s·; for thy light is come, 215
Jer 5: 28 They are waxen fat, they s·: yea, 6245
Da 9: 17 thy face to s· upon thy sanctuary 215
12: 3 they that be wise shall s· as the 2094
M't 5: 16 Let your light so s· before men, *2989*
13: 43 Then shall the righteous s· forth *1584*
17: 2 his face did s· as the sun, and his *2989*
2Co 4: 4 image of God, should s· unto them.* *826*
6 who commanded the light to s· *2989*
Ph'p 2: 15 among whom ye s· as lights in *5316*
Re 18: 23 light of a candle shall s· no more "
21: 23 neither of the moon, to s· in it: "

shined See also SHONE.
De 33: 2 he s· forth from mount Paran, and3313
Job 29: 3 When his candle s· upon my head,1984
31: 26 If I beheld the sun when it s·, or "
Ps 50: 2 perfection of beauty, God hath s·. 3313
Isa 9: 2 upon them hath the light s·. 5050
Eze 43: 2 and the earth s· with his glory. 215
Ac 9: 3 s· round about him a light from *4015*
12: 7 him, and a light s· in the prison: *2989*
2Co 4: 6 of darkness, hath s· in our hearts, "

shineth
Job 25: 5 even to the moon, and it s· not; *166
Ps 139: 12 but the night s· as the day: the 215
Pr 4: 18 s· more and more unto the perfect "
M't 24: 27 east, and s· even unto the west; *5316*
Lu 17: 24 s· unto the other part under *2989*
Joh 1: 5 And the light s· in darkness; and *5316*
2Pe 1: 19 unto a light that s· in a dark place,*"
1Jo 2: 8 is past, and the true light now s·. "
Re 1: 16 was as the sun s· in his strength. "

shining
2Sa 23: 4 of the earth by clear s· after rain. 5051
Pr 4: 18 path of the just is as the s· light, ‡ "
Isa 4: 5 the s· of a flaming fire by night: "
Joe 2: 10 the stars shall withdraw their s·: "
3: 15 the stars shall withdraw their s·. "
Hab 3: 11 at the s· of thy glittering spear. "
M'r 9: 3 And his raiment became s·, *4744*
Lu 11: 36 bright s· of a candle doth give thee *796*
24: 4 men stood by them in s· garments:**797*
Joh 5: 35 He was a burning and a s· light: **5316*
Ac 26: 13 s· round about me and them *4084*

ship See also FORESHIP; SHIPMASTER; SHIPMEN; SHIPPING; SHIPS; SHIPWRECK.
Pr 30: 19 way of a s· in the midst of the sea; 591
Isa 33: 21 oars, neither shall gallant s· pass 6716
Eze 27: 5 made all thy s· boards of fir trees *
Jon 1: 3 he found a s· going to Tarshish: 591
4 that the s· was like to be broken. "
5 the wares that were in the s· into "
5 gone down into the sides of the s·:5600
M't 4: 21 in a s· with Zebedee their father, *4143*
22 they immediately left the s· and * "
8: 23 when he was entered into a s·, his* "
24 the s· was covered with the waves:* "
9: 1 he entered into a s·, and passed * "
13: 2 so that he went into a s·, and sat; * "
14: 13 he departed thence by s· into a * "
22 his disciples to get into a s·, and * "
24 s· was now in the midst of the sea,* "
29 Peter was come down out of the s·,* "
32 when they were come into the s·, * "
33 they that were in the s· came and* "
15: 39 took s·, and came into the coasts * "
M'r 1: 19 were in the s· mending their nets.* "
20 left their father Zebedee in the s· * "
3: 9 that a small s· should wait on him*4142*
4: 1 so that he entered into a s·, and *4143*
36 took him even as he was in the s·.* "
37 and the waves beat into the s·, so * "
38 he was in the hinder part of the s·.*
5: 2 when he was come out of the s·, *4143*
18 And when he was come into the s·,* "
21 again by s· unto the other side, * "
6: 32 into a desert place by s· privately.* "
45 his disciples to get into the s·, * "
47 the s· was in the midst of the sea, * "
51 he went up unto them into the s·;* "
54 when they were come out of the s·,* "
8: 10 straightway he entered into a s· * "
13 and entering into the s· again * "
14 had they in the s· with them more* "
Lu 5: 3 and taught the people out of the s·.* "
7 which were in the other s·, that * "
8: 22 that he went into a s· with his * "
37 and he went up into the s·, and * "
Joh 6: 17 entered into a s·, and went over the* "
19 sea, and drawing nigh unto the s·:* "
21 willingly received him into the s·:* "
21 and immediately the s· was at the* "
21: 3 and entered into a s· immediately;* "

Joh 21: 6 the net on the right side of the s'. *4143
8 other disciples came in a little s'; *4142
Ac 20: 13 we went before to s', and sailed 4143
38 they accompanied him unto the s'. "
21: 2 And finding a s' sailing over unto "
3 the s' was to unlade her burden. "
6 leave one of another, we took s'; "
27: 2 entering into a s' of Adramyttium, "
6 centurion found a s' of Alexandria "
10 not only of the lading and s', but "
11 the master and the owner of the s',3490
15 And when the s' was caught, and 4143
17 used helps, undergirding the s'; "
18 the next day they lightened the s';*
19 own hands the tackling of the s'. 4143
22 man's life among you, but of the s'. "
30 were about to flee out of the s', "
31 Except these abide in the s', ye "
37 were in all in the s' two hundred "
38 they lightened the s', and cast out "
39 it were possible, to thrust in the s'. "
41 seas met, they ran the s' aground;*3491
44 some on broken pieces of the s'. 4143
28: 11 we departed in a s' of Alexandria, "

Shiphi (*shi'-fi*)
1Ch 4: 37 And Ziza the son of S', the son of 8230

Shiphmite (*shif'-mite*)
1Ch 27: 27 wine cellars was Zabdi the S': 8225

Shiphrah (*shif'-rah*)
Ex 1: 15 which the name of the one was S', 8236

Shiphtan (*shif'-tan*)
Nu 34: 24 Ephraim, Kemuel the son of S'. 8204

shipmaster
Jon 1: 6 So the s' came to him, and 7227,2259
Re 18: 17 every s', and all the company in 2942

shipmen
1Ki 9: 27 s' that had knowledge of the 582,591
Ac 27: 27 s' deemed that they drew near to *3492
30 the s' were about to flee out of the "

shipping
Joh 6: 24 they also took s', and came to *4143

ships
Ge 49: 13 and he shall be for an haven of s'; 591
Nu 24: 24 s' shall come from the coast of 6716
De 28: 68 bring thee into Egypt again with s',591
J'g 5: 17 and why did Dan remain in s'? "
1Ki 9: 26 made a navy of s' in Ezion-geber, "
22: 48 Jehoshaphat made s' of Tharshish 591
48 the s' were broken at Ezion-geber. "
49 go with thy servants in the s'. "
2Ch 8: 18 him by the hands of his servants s', "
9: 21 the king's s' went to Tarshish with "
21 the s' of Tarshish bringing gold, "
20: 36 him to make s' to go to Tarshish: "
36 they made the s' in Ezion-gaber. "
37 the s' were broken, that they were "
Job 9: 26 are passed away as the swift s': "
Ps 48: 7 Thou breakest the s' of Tarshish "
104: 26 There go the s': there is that "
107: 23 They that go down to the sea in s', "
Pr 31: 14 She is like the merchants' s'; she "
Isa 2: 16 And upon all the s' of Tarshish, "
23: 1 Howl, ye s' of Tarshish; for it is "
14 Howl, ye s' of Tarshish: for your "
43: 14 Chaldeans, whose cry is in the s'. "
60: 9 for me, and the s' of Tarshish first, "
Eze 27: 9 s' of the sea with their mariners "
25 The s' of Tarshish did sing of thee "
29 shall come down from their s', "
30: 9 messengers go forth from me in s' 6716
Da 11: 30 s' of Chittim shall come against "
40 with horsemen, and with many s'; 591
M'r 4: 36 were also with him other little s'. *4142
Lu 5: 2 saw two s' standing by the lake: *4143
3 And he entered into one of the s', * "
7 they came, and filled both the s', * "
11 they had brought their s' to land, * "
Jas 3: 4 Behold also the s', which though "
Re 8: 9 third part of the s' were destroyed. "
18: 17 all the company in s', and sailors,* "
19 made rich all that had s' in the sea "

shipwreck
2Co 11: 25 thrice I suffered s', a night and a 3489
1Ti 1: 19 concerning faith have made s': "

Shisha (*shi'-shah*) See also SHAVSHA.
1Ki 4: 3 and Ahiah, the sons of S', scribes; 7894

Shishak (*shi'-shak*)
1Ki 11: 40 into Egypt, unto S' king of Egypt, 7895
14: 25 S' king of Egypt came up against "
2Ch 12: 2 S' king of Egypt came up against "
5 together to Jerusalem because of S', "
5 I also left you in the hand of S'. "
7 upon Jerusalem by the hand of S'. "
9 S' king of Egypt came up against "

Shitrai (*shit'-ra-i*)
1Ch 27: 29 in Sharon was S' the Sharonite: 7861

shittah (*shit'-tah*) See also BETH-SHITTAH; SHITTIM.
Isa 41: 19 cedar, the s' tree, and the myrtle,*7848

shittah-tree See SHITTAH and TREE.

shittim See also SHITTAH; SHITTIM.
Ex 25: 5 and badgers' skins, and s' wood, *7848
10 they shall make an ark of s' wood:* "
13 thou shalt make staves of s' wood,* "
23 shalt also make a table of s' wood:* "
28 shalt make the staves of s' wood, * "
26: 15 boards for the tabernacle of s' wood* "
26 thou shalt make bars of s' wood; * "
32 hang it upon four pillars of s' wood* "
Ex 26: 37 the hanging five pillars of s' wood,*7848
27: 1 thou shalt make an altar of s' wood,* "
6 for the altar, staves of s' wood, and* "
30: 1 of s' wood shalt thou make it. * "
5 shalt make the staves of s' wood, * "
35: 7 and badgers' skins, and s' wood, * "
24 with whom was found s' wood for* "
36: 20 for the tabernacle of s' wood, * "
31 And he made bars of s' wood; five* "
36 thereunto four pillars of s' wood, * "
37: 1 Bezaleel made the ark of s' wood:* "
4 and he made staves of s' wood, and* "
10 And he made the table of s' wood:* "
15 And he made the staves of s' wood,* "
25 made the incense altar of s' wood:* "
28 And he made the staves of s' wood,* "
38: 1 altar of burnt offering of s' wood: * "
6 And he made the staves of s' wood,* "
De 10: 3 And I made an ark of s' wood, and* "

Shittim (*shit'-tim*) See also ABEL-SHITTIM.
Nu 25: 1 And Israel abode in S', and the 7851
Jos 2: 1 son of Nun sent out of S' two men "
3: 1 they removed from S', and came "
Joe 3: 18 and shall water the valley of S'. "
Mic 6: 5 answered him from S' unto Gilgal; "

shittim-wood See SHITTIM and WOOD.

shivers
Re 2: 27 potter shall they be broken to s': 4937

Shiza (*shi'-zah*)
1Ch 11: 42 Adina the son of S' the Reubenite, 7877

Shoa (*sho'-ah*)
Eze 23: 23 all the Chaldeans, Pekod, and S', 7772

Shobab (*sho'-bab*)
2Sa 5: 14 Shammuah, and S', and Nathan, 7727
1Ch 2: 18 sons are these; Jesher, and S', "
3: 5 Shimea, and S', and Nathan, and "
14: 4 and S', Nathan, and Solomon, "

Shobach (*sho'-bak*) See also SHOPHACH.
2Sa 10: 16 and S' the captain of the host of 7731
18 smote S' the captain of their host, "

Shobai (*sho'-bahee*)
Ezr 2: 42 the children of S', in all an 7630
Ne 7: 45 of Hatita, the children of S', an "

Shobal (*sho'-bal*)
Ge 36: 20 Lotan, and S', and Zibeon, and 7732
23 And the children of S' were these; "
29 duke Lotan, duke S', duke Zibeon, "
1Ch 1: 38 the sons of Seir, and Lotan, and S', "
40 The sons of S'; Alion, and "
2: 50, 52 S' the father of Kirjath-jearim, "
4: 1 and Carmi, and Hur, and S'. "
2 And Reaiah the son of S' begat "

Shobek (*sho'-bek*)
Ne 10: 24 Hallohesh, Pileha, S', 7733

Shobi (*sho'-bi*)
2Sa 17: 27 S' the son of Nahash of Rabbah of 7629

Shocho (*sho'-ko*) See also SHOCHOH.
2Ch 28: 18 and S' with the villages thereof, *7755

Shochoh (*sho'-ko*) See also SHOCHO; SHOCO; SOCHOH; SOCO; SOCOH.
1Sa 17: 1 and were gathered together at S',*7755
1 pitched between S' and Azekah, * "

shock See also SHOCKS.
Job 5: 26 s' of corn cometh in in his season. 1430

shocks
J'g 15: 5 and burnt up both the s', and also 1430

Shoco (*sho'-co*) See also SHOCHOH.
2Ch 11: 7 Beth-zur, and S', and Adullam, *7755

shod See also DRYSHOD; UNSHOD.
2Ch 28: 15 arrayed them, and s' them, and 5274
Eze 16: 10 and s' thee with badgers' skin, and "
M'r 6: 9 But be s' with sandals; and not 5265
Eph 6: 15 your feet s' with the preparation "

shoe See also SHOD; SHOELATCHET; SHOE'S; SHOES.
De 25: 9 and loose his s' from off his foot, 5275
10 of him that hath his s' loosed. "
29: 5 s' is not waxen old upon thy foot. "
Jos 5: 15 Loose thy s' from off thy foot; for "
Ru 4: 7 a man plucked off his s', and gave "
8 it for thee. So he drew off his s'. "
Ps 60: 8 over Edom will I cast out my s': "
108: 9 over Edom will I cast out my s'; "
Isa 20: 2 and put off thy s' from thy foot. "

shoelatchet
Ge 14: 23 from a thread even to a s', 8288,5275

shoe's
Joh 1: 27 s' latchet I am not worthy to *5266

shoes
Ex 3: 5 put off thy s' from off thy feet, 5275
12: 11 your s' on your feet, and your staff "
De 33: 25 Thy s' shall be iron and brass; *4515
Jos 9: 5 old s' and clouted upon their feet, 5275
13 our s' are become old by reason of "
1Ki 2: 5 and in his s' that were on his feet. "
Ca 7: 1 How beautiful are thy feet with s',* "
Isa 5: 27 the latchet of their s' be broken: "
Eze 24: 17 and put on thy s' upon thy feet, "
23 heads, and your s' upon your feet: "
Am 2: 6 and the poor for a pair of s'; "
8: 6 and the needy for a pair of s'; "
M't 3: 11 whose s' I am not worthy to bear: 5266
10: 10 neither two coats, neither s', nor "
M'r 1: 7 the latchet of whose s' I am not "
Lu 3: 16 the latchet of whose s' I am not "
10: 4 neither purse, nor scrip, nor s': "
15: 22 on his hand, and s' on his feet: "
Lu 22: 35 without purse, and scrip, and s', 5266
Ac 7: 33 Put off thy s' from thy feet: for the "
13: 25 s' of his feet I am not worthy to "

Shoham (*sho'-ham*)
1Ch 24: 27 Beno, and S', and Zaccur, and 7719

Shomer (*sho'-mur*) See also SHAMER; SHIMRITH.
2Ki 12: 21 and Jehozabad the son of S', his 7763
1Ch 7: 32 And Heber begat Japhlet, and S', "

shone See also SHINED.
Ex 34: 29 wist not that the skin of his face s' 7160
30 behold, the skin of his face s'; and "
35 that the skin of Moses' face s': and "
2Ki 3: 22 and the sun s' upon the water, and 2224
Lu 2: 9 and the glory of the Lord s' round 4034
Ac 22: 6 s' from heaven a great light round 4015
Re 8: 12 the day s' not for a third part of it,*5316

shook See also SHAKED.
2Sa 6: 6 took hold of it; for the oxen s' it. *8058
22: 8 Then the earth s' and trembled; 1607
8 foundations of heaven moved and s'. "
Ne 5: 13 Also I s' my lap, and said, So God 5287
Ps 18: 7 Then the earth s' and trembled; 1607
68: 8 The earth s', the heavens also *7493
77: 18 world: the earth trembled and s'. "
Isa 23: 11 over the sea, he s' the kingdoms: *7264
Ac 13: 51 s' off the dust of their feet against 1621
18: 6 he s' his raiment, and said unto "
28: 5 he s' off the beast into the fire, and 660
Heb 12: 26 Whose voice then s' the earth: but 4531

shoot See also SHOOTETH; SHOOTING; SHOT.
Ex 36: 33 the middle bar to s' through the *1272
1Sa 20: 20 s' three arrows on the side thereof, 3384
36 find out now the arrows which I s'. "
2Sa 11: 20 that they would s' from the wall? "
2Ki 13: 17 Then Elisha said, S'. And he shot. "
19: 32 into this city, nor s' an arrow there, "
1Ch 5: 18 and sword, and to s' with bow, 1869
2Ch 26: 15 s' arrows and great stones withal. 3384
Ps 11: 2 privily s' at the upright in heart. "
22: 7 they s' out the lip, they shake the 6362
58: 7 he bendeth his bow to s' his arrows,*
64: 3 bend their bows to s' their arrows,*
4 may s' in secret at the perfect: 3384
4 suddenly do they s' at him, and "
7 God shall s' at them with an arrow; "
144: 6 s' out thine arrows, and destroy *7971
Isa 37: 33 into this city, nor s' an arrow there, "
Jer 50: 14 bow, s' at her, spare no arrows: 3034
Eze 31: 14 s' up their top among the thick *5414
36: 8 ye shall s' forth your branches, and "
Lu 21: 30 When they now s' forth, ye see 4261

shooters
2Sa 11: 24 s' shot from off the wall upon thy 3384

shooteth
Job 8: 16 his branch s' forth in his garden. *3318
Isa 27: 8 In measure, when it s' forth, thou*7971
M'r 4: 32 s' out great branches; so that *4160

shooting
1Ch 12: 2 the left in hurling stones and s' arrows
Am 7: 1 of the s' up of the latter growth; 5927

Shophach (*sho'-fak*) See also SHOBACH.
1Ch 19: 16 and S' the captain of the host of 7780
18 Killed S' the captain of the host. "

Shophan (*sho'-fan*) See also ZAPHON.
Nu 32: 35 S', and Jaazer, and Jogbehah, 5855

shore
Ge 22: 17 the sand which is upon the sea s'; 8193
Ex 14: 30 the Egyptians dead upon the sea s'. "
Jos 11: 4 that is upon the sea s' in multitude, "
15: 2 was from the s' of the salt sea, *7097
J'g 5: 17 Asher continued on the sea s', *2348
1Sa 13: 5 as the sand which is on the sea s' 8193
1Ki 4: 29 as the sand that is on the sea s'. "
9: 26 on the s' of the Red sea, in the "
Jer 47: 7 Ashkelon, and against the sea s'? 2348
M't 13: 2 whole multitude stood on the s'. * 123
48 when it was full, they drew to s', * "
M'r 6: 53 of Gennesaret, and drew to the s'. 4358
Joh 21: 4 now come, Jesus stood on the s': * 123
Ac 21: 5 and we kneeled down on the s', and* "
27: 39 discovered a certain creek with a s',* "
40 to the wind, and made toward s'. * "
Heb 11: 12 as the sand which is by the sea s' 5491

shorn
Ca 4: 2 a flock of sheep that are even s', 7094
Ac 18: 18 having s' his head in Cenchrea: 2751
1Co 11: 6 be not covered, let her also be s': "
6 it be a shame for a woman to be s' "

short See also SHORTER.
Nu 11: 23 Is the Lord's hand waxed s'? 7114
2Ki 10: 32 days the Lord began to cut Israel s':
Job 17: 12 the light is s' because of darkness.*7138
20: 5 the triumphing of the wicked is s', "
Ps 89: 47 Remember how s' my time is: 2465
Ro 3: 23 and come s' of the glory of God; 5302
9: 28 and cut it s' in righteousness: 4932
28 a s' work will the Lord make upon* "
1Co 7: 29 this I say, brethren, the time is s';*4958
1Th 2: 17 being taken from you for a s' time 5610
Heb 4: 1 of you should seem to come s' of it. 5302
Re 12: 12 knoweth that he hath but a s' time. 3641
17: 10 he must continue a s' space. * "

shortened
Ps 89: 45 The days of his youth hast thou s': 7114
102: 23 strength in the way; he s' my days. "
Pr 10: 27 the years of the wicked shall be s'. "
Isa 50: 2 Is my hand s' at all, that it cannot "
59: 1 Behold, the Lord's hand is not s', "
M't 24: 22 except those days should be s', 2856

M't 24:22 elect's sake those days shall be s'. 2856
M'r 13:20 that the Lord had s' those days, "
20 he hath chosen, he hath s' the days."

shorter
Isa 28:20 the bed is s' than that a man can 7114
Eze 42: 5 Now the upper chambers were s': "

shortly
Ge 41:32 and God will s' bring it to pass. 4116
Jer 27:16 s' be brought again from Babylon: 4120
Eze 7: 8 I s' pour out my fury upon thee, 7138
Ac 25: 4 himself...depart s' thither. 1722,5034
Ro 16:20 bruise Satan under your feet s'. " "
1Co 4:19 I will come to you s', if the Lord 5030
Ph'p 2:19 to send Timotheus s' unto you, "
24 that I also myself shall come s'. "
1Ti 3:14 thee, hoping to come unto thee s': 5032
2Ti 4: 9 thy diligence to come s' unto me: 5030
Heb 13:23 with whom, if he come s', I will see 5032
2Pe 1:14 that s' I must put off this my *5031
3Jo 14 But I trust I shall s' see thee, and 2112
Re 1: 1 which must s' come to pass; 1722,5034
22: 6 things which must s' be done. " "

Shoshannim (*sho-shan'-nim*) See also SHOSHANNIM-EDUTH.
Ps 45: *title* To the chief Musician upon S', 7799
69: *title* To the chief Musician upon S'. "

Shoshannim-Eduth (*sho-shan''-nim-e'-duth*)
Ps 80: *title* To the chief Musician upon S', 7802

shot See also BOWSHOT.
Ge 40:10 budded, and her blossoms s' forth: 5927
49:23 and s' at him, and hated him: 7232
Ex 19:13 surely be stoned, or s' through; 3384
Nu 21:30 We have s' at them; Heshbon is "
1Sa 20:20 thereof, as though I s' at a mark. 7971
36 ran, he s' an arrow beyond him. 3384
37 the arrow which Jonathan had s', "
2Sa 11:24 And the shooters s' from off the wall "
2Ki 13:17 Then Elisha said, Shoot. And he s'. "
2Ch 35:23 And the archers s' at king Josiah; "
Ps 18:14 and he s' out lightnings, and *7232
Jer 9: 8 tongue is as an arrow s' out; it *7819
Eze 17: 6 forth branches, and s' forth sprigs. 7971
7 s' forth her branches toward him, "
31: 5 multitude of waters,...he s' forth. "
10 he hath s' up his top among the * "

should See also SHOULDEST.
Ge 2:18 is not good that the man s' be alone;
4:15 Cain, lest any finding him s' kill him.
18:25 that the righteous s' be as the wicked,
21: 7 that Sarah s' have given children suck!
23: 8 it be your mind that I s' bury my dead
26: 7 men of the place s' kill me for Rebekah;
27:45 why s' I be deprived also of you both
29: 7 is it time that the cattle s' be gathered
19 than that I s' give her to another man:
30:38 s' conceive when they came to drink.*
33:13 and if men s' overdrive them one day,*
34:31 S' he deal with our sister as with an
38: 9 Onan knew that the seed s' not be his;
9 that he s' give seed to his brother.
40:15 that they s' put me into the dungeon.
43:25 heard that they s' eat bread there.
44: 7 God forbid that thy servants s' do
8 how then s' we steal out of thy lord's
17 he said, God forbid that I s' do so:
22 for if he s' leave his father, his father
47:15 for why s' we die in thy presence? for
26 that Pharaoh s' have the fifth part;
Ex 3:11 Who am I, that I s' go unto Pharaoh,
11 and that I s' bring forth the children
5: 2 I s' obey his voice to let Israel go?
14:12 than that we s' die in the wilderness?
22: 3 him; for he s' make full restitution;
32:12 Wherefore s' the Egyptians speak,
35: 1 hath commanded, that ye s' do them.
39: 7 that they s' be stones for a memorial*
23 about the hole, that it s' not rend.
Le 4:13, 22 things which s' not be done. *
9: 6 the Lord commanded that ye s' do:
10:18 ye s' indeed have eaten it in the holy
19 s' it have been accepted in the sight*
20:26 from other people, that ye s' be mine.
24:23 s' bring forth him that had cursed *
26:13 that ye s' not be their bondmen;
27:26 beasts, which s' be the Lord's firstling,*
Nu 7: 9 that they s' bear upon their shoulders.*
9: 4 Israel, that they s' keep the passover.
11:13 Whence s' I have flesh to give unto all
12:14 s' she not be ashamed seven days?
14: 3 wives and our children s' be a prey?*
31 little ones, which ye said s' be a prey,
15:34 not declared what s' be done to him.
20: 4 that we and our cattle s' die there?
23:19 God is not a man, that he s' lie; neither
19 the son of man, that he s' repent:
27: 4 Why s' the name of our father be done
32: 9 that they s' not go into the land which
35:28 Because he s' have remained in the city
32 he s' come again to dwell in the land,
De 1:18 that time all the things which ye s' do.
33 to shew you by what way ye s' go, and
39 little ones, which ye said s' be a prey,
4: 5 that ye s' do so in the land whither ye
21 and sware that I s' not go over Jordan,
21 that I s' not go in unto that good land,
42 which s' kill his neighbour unawares,*
5:25 Now therefore why s' we die? for this
17:16 to the end that he s' multiply horses:
20:18 so s' ye sin against the Lord your God.
25: 3 if he s' exceed, and beat him above
3 then thy brother s' seem vile unto thee.
29:18 Lest there s' be among you a man, or
18 lest there s' be among you a root that
De 32:27 adversaries s' behave themselves
27 and lest they s' say, Our hand is high,
30 How s' one chase a thousand, and two
Jos 8:29 that they s' take his carcase down*
33 that they s' bless the people of Israel.
9:27 day, in the place which he s' choose.
11:20 they s' come against Israel in battle,*
22:28 s' so say to us or to our generations*
29 that we s' rebel against the Lord,
24:16 God forbid that we s' forsake the Lord,
J'g 8: 6 that we s' give bread unto thine army?
15 that we s' give bread unto thy men
9: 9 S' I leave my fatness, wherewith by
11 S' I forsake my sweetness, and my
13 S' I leave my wine, which cheereth
28 who is Shechem, that we s' serve him?
28 of Shechem: for why s' we serve him?
38 is Abimelech, that we s' serve him?
41 that they s' not dwell in Shechem.
20:38 they s' make a great flame with smoke
21: 3 s' be to day one tribe lacking in Israel?
22 them at this time, that ye s' be guilty.*
Ru 1:12 If I s' say, I have hope,
12 if I s' have an husband also to night,
12 also to night, and s' also bear sons;
1Sa 2:30 thy father, s' walk before me for ever:
8: 7 me, that I s' not reign over them.
9: 6 he can shew us our way that we s' go.*
10:22 further, if the man s' yet come thither.*
12:21 for then s' ye go after vain things,
23 forbid that I s' sin against the Lord
15:21 which s' have been utterly destroyed,*
29 for he is not a man, that he s' repent.
17:26 he s' defy the armies of the living God?
18:18 that I s' be son in law to the king?
19 daughter s' have been given to David,
19: 1 his servants, that they s' kill David.
17 me, Let me go; why s' I kill thee?
20: 2 s' my father hide this thing from me?
5 s' not fail to sit with the king at meat:
22:13 that he s' rise against me, to lie in
24: 6 The Lord forbid that I s' do this thing
26:11 forbid that I s' stretch forth mine hand
27: 1 that I s' speedily escape into the land
5 s' thy servant dwell in the royal city
11 Lest they s' tell on us, saying, So did
29: 4 for wherewith s' he reconcile himself
4 s' it not be with the heads of these men?
2Sa 2:22 s' I smite thee to the ground?
22 how then s' I hold up my face to Joab
12:23 now he is dead, wherefore s' I fast?
13:26 unto him, Why s' he go with thee?
15:20 s' I this day make thee go up and down
16: 9 Why s' this dead dog curse my lord
19 And again, whom s' I serve?
19 s' I not serve in...presence of his son?
18:12 Though I s' receive a thousand shekels
13 I s' have wrought falsehood against*
19:19 that the king s' take it to his heart.
22 ye s' this day be adversaries unto me?
34 that I s' go up with the king unto
35 s' thy servant be yet a burden unto
36 why s' the king recompense it me
43 advice s' not be first had in bringing
20:20 me, that I s' swallow up or destroy.
21: 5 we s' be destroyed from remaining in
23:17 far from me, O Lord, that I s' do this:
1Ki 1:27 who s' sit on the throne of my lord
2: 1 of David drew nigh that he s' die;
15 set their faces on me, that I s' reign:
6: 6 beams s' not be fastened in the walls
8:36 the good way wherein they s' walk,
11:10 that he s' not go after other gods:
14: 2 me that I s' be king over this people.
21: 3 I s' give the inheritance of my fathers
2Ki 3:27 son that s' have reigned in his stead,
4:43 s' I set this before an hundred men?
6:33 what s' I wait for the Lord any longer?
7:19 the Lord s' make windows in heaven,
8:13 a dog, that he s' do this great thing?
11: 9 them that s' go out on the sabbath,*
17 that they s' be the Lord's people;
17:15 them, that they s' not do like them.
28 taught them how they s' fear the Lord.
18:35 s' deliver Jerusalem out of mine hand?
22:19 s' become a desolation and a curse,
1Ch 9:28 they s' bring them in and out by tale.*
11:19 forbid it me, that I s' do this thing:
16:42 for those that s' make a sound,
21:17 on thy people, that they s' be plagued.
18 David s' go up, and set up an altar
23:13 he s' sanctify the most holy things,
32 s' keep the charge of the tabernacle
25: 1 who s' prophesy with harps, with
29:14 that we s' be able to offer so willingly
2Ch 2: 6 am I then, that I s' build him an house,
4:20 they s' burn after the manner before
6:27 the good way, wherein they s' walk;
15:13 Lord God of Israel s' be put to death,
20:21 that s' praise the beauty of holiness,
23:16 king, that they s' be the Lord's people.
19 was unclean in any thing s' enter in.
25:13 that they s' not go with him to battle,
29:11 that ye s' minister unto him, and burn
24 sin offering s' be made for all Israel.
30: 1 they s' come to the house of the Lord
5 that they s' come to keep the passover
32: 4 Why s' the kings of Assyria come, and
14 your God s' be able to deliver you
Ezr 2:63 they s' not eat of the most holy things,
4:22 why s' damage grow to the hurt of the
7:23 s' there be wrath against the realm
8:17 told them what they s' say unto Iddo,
17 that s' bring unto us ministers
9:14 S' we...break thy commandments,*
14 there s' be no remnant nor escaping?
Ezr 10: 5 that they s' do according to this word.*
7 they s' gather themselves together
8 all his substance s' be forfeited, and
Ne 2: 3 why s' not my countenance be sad,
5:12 they s' do according to this promise.
6: 3 why s' the work cease, whilst I leave
11 And I said, S' such a man as I flee?
13 that I s' be afraid, and do so, and sin,
7:65 they s' not eat of the most holy things,
8:14 children of Israel s' dwell in booths
15 s' publish and proclaim in all their
9:12 light in the way wherein they s' go.
15 that they s' go in to possess the land.
19 light, and the way wherein they s' go.
23 fathers, that they s' go in to possess it.
10:37 s' bring the firstfruits of our dough,
11:23 a certain portion s' be for the singers,*
13: 1 s' not come into the congregation of
2 Balaam against them, that he s' curse*
19 I commanded that the gates s' be shut,
19 s' not be opened till after the sabbath:
19 there s' no burden be brought in on
22 that they s' cleanse themselves, and
22 that they s' come and keep the gates,
Es 1: 8 they s' do...to every man's pleasure.
22 that every man s' bear rule in his own
22 that it s' be published according to
2:10 charged her that she s' not shew it.
11 Esther did, and what s' become of her.
3:14 that they s' be ready against that day.
4: 8 her that she s' go in unto the king,
8:13 the Jews s' be ready against that day
9:21 they s' keep the fourteenth day of the
22 they s' make them days of feasting
25 s' return upon his own head, and that
25 his sons s' be hanged on the gallows.
27 so as it s' not fail, that they would keep
28 these days s' be remembered and kept
28 days of Purim s' not fail from among
Job 3:12 me? or why the breasts that I s' suck?
13 now s' I have lain still and been quiet,
13 still and been quiet, I s' have slept:
6:10 Then s' I yet have comfort; yea, I*
11 What is my strength, that I s' hope?
11 is mine end, that I s' prolong my life?
14 pity s' be shewed from his friend;
8: 7 yet thy latter end s' greatly increase.
9: 2 but how s' man be just with God? *
32 a man, as I am, that I s' answer him,
32 we s' come together in judgment.
10:19 I s' have been as though I had not
19 I s' have been carried from the womb
11: 2 S' not the multitude of words be
2 and s' a man full of talk be justified?
3 S' thy lies make men hold their peace?
13: 5 your peace! and it s' be your wisdom.
9 Is it good that he s' search you out?
15: 2 S' a wise man utter vain knowledge,
3 S' he reason with unprofitable talk?
14 What is man, that he s' be clean? and
14 of a woman, that he s' be righteous?
16: 5 of my lips s' asswage your grief.
19:28 But ye s' say, Why persecute we him,*
21: 4 so, why s' not my spirit be troubled?
15 is the Almighty, that we s' serve him?
15 what profit s' we have, if we pray unto
23: 7 so s' I be delivered for ever from my
27: 5 God forbid that I s' justify you: till I
31: 1 why then s' I think upon a maid?
28 I s' have denied the God that is above.
32: 7 I said, Days s' speak, and
7 multitude of years s' teach wisdom.
13 Lest ye s' say, We have found out*
34: 6 S' I lie against my right? my wound*
9 that he s' delight himself with God.
10 it from God that he s' do wickedness;
10 Almighty, that he s' commit iniquity.
23 he s' enter into judgment with God.
33 S' it be according to thy mind? he will*
36:16 and that which s' be set on thy table*
16 be set on thy table s' be full of fatness.
41:11 prevented me, that I s' repay him?
Ps 27: 3 Though an host s' encamp against me,
3 though war s' rise against me, in this
30: 3 alive, that I s' not go down to the pit.
38:16 lest otherwise they s' rejoice over me:*
49: 5 Wherefore s' I fear in the days of evil,
9 That he s' still live for ever, and not
69:22 which s' have been for their welfare,*
73:15 I s' offend against the generation of*
78: 5 s' make them known to their children:
6 even the children which s' be born;
6 who s' arise and declare them to their
79:10 Wherefore s' the heathen say, Where
81:14 I s' soon have subdued their enemies,
15 haters of the Lord s' have submitted
15 their time s' have endured for ever.
16 s' have fed them also with the finest
16 of the rock s' I have satisfied thee.
95:11 that they s' not enter into my rest.
104: 5 that it s' not be removed for ever.
106:23 his wrath, lest he s' destroy them.
115: 2 Wherefore s' the heathen say, Where
119:92 I s'...have perished in mine affliction.
139:18 If I s' count them, they are more in
143: 8 to know the way wherein I s' walk;
Pr 8:29 waters s' not pass his commandment:
22: 6 Train up a child in the way he s' go:
27 s' he take away thy bed from under
Ec 2: 3 which they s' do under the heaven all
18 I s' leave it unto the man that shall*
24 a man, than that he s' eat and drink,
24 that he s' make his soul enjoy good*
3:13 also that every man s' eat and drink,
14 doeth it, that men s' fear before him.
22 a man s' rejoice in his own works;

Ec 5: 6 wherefore s' God be angry at thy voice,
7:14 that man s' find nothing after him.*
Ca 1: 7 why s' I be as one that turneth aside
8: 1 when I s' find thee without, I would
1 kiss thee; yea, I s' not be despised.
3 His left hand s' be under my head,
3 and his right hand s' embrace me.
Isa 1: 5 Why s' ye be stricken any more? ye*
9 remnant, we s' have been as Sodom,
9 we s' have been like unto Gomorrah.
5: 2 he looked that it s' bring forth grapes,
4 I looked that it s' bring forth grapes,
8:11 I s' not walk in the way of this people,
19 s' not a people seek unto their God?
10:15 if the rod s' shake itself against them
15 or as if the staff s' lift up itself, as if it
36:20 Lord s' deliver Jerusalem out of my
41: 7 it with nails, that it s' not be moved.
48:11 for how s' my name be polluted? and I
19 his name s' not have been cut off nor
49:15 she s' not have compassion on the son
50: 4 that I s' know how to speak a word in
51:14 and that he s' not die in the pit, nor
14 in the pit, nor that his bread s' fail.*
53: 2 is no beauty that we s' desire him.
54: 9 waters of Noah s' no more go over the
57: 6 offering. S' I receive comfort in these?*
16 for the spirit s' fail before me, and the
63:13 wilderness, that they s' not stumble?
Jer 5:17 thy sons and thy daughters s' eat:
20:18 my days s' be consumed with shame?
23:22 s' have turned them from their evil*
25:29 name, and s' ye be utterly unpunished?
26:24 that they s' not give him into the hand
27:10 I s' drive you out, and ye s' perish.
17 wherefore s' this city be laid waste?
29:26 that ye s' be officers in the house of
32:31 I s' remove it from before my face,
35 they s' do this abomination, to cause
33:20 and that there s' not be day and night
21 that he s' not have a son to reign upon
24 they s' be no more a nation before
34: 9 That every man s' let his manservant,
9 that none s' serve himself of them,
10 that every one s' let his manservant,
10 that none s' serve themselves of them
37:10 yet s' they rise up every man in his
21 s' commit Jeremiah into the court*
21 they s' give him daily a piece of bread*
39:14 Shaphan, that he s' carry him home:
40:14 wherefore s' he slay thee, that all the
15 are gathered unto thee s' be scattered,
44:14 they s' return into the land of Judah,
46:13 king of Babylon s' come and smite the
51:53 Babylon s' mount up to heaven,
53 and though she s' fortify the height
60 all the evil that s' come upon Babylon,
La 1:10 they s' not enter thy congregation.
16 comforter that s' relieve my soul is far
17 his adversaries s' be round about him:
3:26 It is good that a man s' both hope and
44 that our prayer s' not pass through.
4:12 enemy s' have entered into the gates
Eze 8: 6 that I s' go far off from my sanctuary?
13:19 bread, to slay the souls that s' not die,
19 to save the souls alive that s' not live,
22 he s' not return from his wicked way,
14: 3 s' I be enquired of at all by them?
14 they s' deliver but their own souls by
18:23 any pleasure...that the wicked s' die?*
23 not that he s' return from his ways,
19: 9 his voice s' no more be heard upon the
20: 9, 14 that it s' not be polluted before the
26 it s' not be polluted in the sight of the
25 judgments whereby they s' not live;
21:10 s' we then make mirth? it contemneth*
22:30 s' make up the hedge, and stand in
30 for the land, that I s' not destroy it:
24: 8 top of a rock, that it s' not be covered.
33:10 away in them, how s' we then live?
34: 2 s' not the shepherds feed the flocks?
Da 1: 3 he s' bring certain of the children of
10 why s' he see your faces worse liking
16 meat, and the wine that they s' drink;
18 the king had said he s' bring them in,*
2:13 forth that the wise men s' be slain;*
18 Daniel and his fellows s' not perish
29 bed, what s' come to pass hereafter:
46 they s' offer an oblation and sweet
3:11 s' be cast into the midst of a burning*
19 they s' heat the furnace one seven
5:15 that they s' read this writing, and
29 s' be the third ruler in the kingdom.
6: 1 which s' be over the whole kingdom.
2 and the king s' have no damage.
23 they s' take Daniel up out of the den.
7:14 nations, and languages, s' serve him:
Ho 10: 3 Lord; what then s' a king do to us?*
10 in my desire that I s' chastise them;*
13:13 he s' not stay long in the place of the
Joe 2:17 that the heathen s' rule over them:
17 s' they say among the people, Where
Jon 4:11 s' not I spare Nineveh, that great city,
Mic 6:16 that I s' make thee a desolation, and
Zep 3: 7 so their dwelling s' not be cut off,
Hag 1: 2 time that the Lord's house s' be built.*
Zec 7: 3 saying, S' I weep in the fifth month,
7 S' ye not hear the words which the
11 their ears, that they s' not hear.
12 lest they s' hear the law, and the
8: 6 s' it also be marvellous in mine eyes?
Mal 1:13 s' I accept this of your hand? saith the
2: 7 the priest's lips s' keep knowledge,
7 and they s' seek the law at his mouth:
M't 2: 4 of them where Christ s' be born.
12 that they s' not return to Herod,

M't 5:29 that one of thy members s' perish,
29 thy whole body s' be cast into hell.*
30 that one of thy members s' perish,
30 thy whole body s' be cast into hell.*
7:12 ye would that men s' do to you,
11: 3 Art thou he that s' come, or do we*
12:16 that they s' not make him known:
13:15 any time they s' see with their eyes,
15 and s' understand with their heart,*
15 s' be converted, and I s' heal them.
15:33 Whence s' we have so much bread in
16:11 that ye s' beware of the leaven of the*
20 s' tell no man that he was Jesus the
17:27 lest we s' offend them, go thou to the*
18:14 that one of these little ones s' perish.
30 into prison, till he s' pay the debt.
34 he s' pay all that was due unto him.
19:13 he s' put his hands on them, and pray:
20:10 that they s' have received more; *
31 because they s' hold their peace:
24:22 except those days s' be shortened,*
22 there s' no flesh be saved: but for the*
25:27 coming I s' have received mine own
26:35 Though I s' die with thee, yet will*1163
27:20 multitude that they s' ask Barabbas,
M'r 3: 9 a small ship s' wait on him because of
9 multitude, lest they s' throng him.
12 that they s' not make him known.
14 twelve, that they s' be with him, *
4:12 at any time they s' be converted,
12 and their sins s' be forgiven them.
22 secret, but that it s' come abroad.
26 a man s' cast seed into the ground;
27 And s' sleep, and rise night and day,
27 and the seed s' spring and grow up,*
5:43 them straitly that no man s' know it;
43 that something s' be given her to eat.
6: 8 they s' take nothing for their journey,
12 and preached that men s' repent.
7:36 them that they s' tell no man:
8:30 them that they s' tell no man of him.
9: 9 s' tell no man what things they had
10 the rising from the dead s' mean.
18 disciples that they s' cast him out;
30 would not that any man s' know it.
34 themselves, who s' be the greatest.*
10:13 to him, that he s' touch them: and
32 what things s' happen unto him, *3195
36 What would ye that I s' do for you?
48 him that he s' hold his peace:
51 What wilt thou that I s' do unto thee?
11:16 that any man s' carry any vessel
12:19 that his brother s' take his wife, and
13:20 those days, no flesh s' be saved: *
14:31 If I s' die with thee, I will not *1163
15:11 that he s' rather release Barabbas
24 upon them, what every man s' take.
Lu 1:29 what manner of salutation this s' be.*
43 mother of my Lord s' come to me?
57 time came that she s' be delivered;
71 we s' be saved from our enemies, and*
2: 1 that all the world s' be taxed.
6 accomplished that she s' be delivered.
26 that he s' not see death, before he had
4:42 him, that he s' not depart from them.
5: 7 that they s' come and help them.
6:31 as ye would that men s' do to you,
7: 4 was worthy for whom he s' do this:*
19, 20 Art thou he that s' come? or look*
8:12 lest they s' believe and be saved. *
56 they s' tell no man what was done.*
9:13 except we s' go and buy meat for all
31 he s' accomplish at Jerusalem. *3195
46 them, which of them s' be greatest.‡
51 was come that he s' be received up,
15:32 It was meet that we s' make merry,*
17: 2 he s' offend one of these little ones.
6 planted in the sea; and it s' obey *
20 when the kingdom of God s' come,*
18:39 him, that he s' hold his peace: but he
19:11 of God s' immediately appear. *3195
27 would not that I s' reign over them,
40 if these s' hold their peace, the stones*
20:10 s' give him of the fruit of the vineyard:
20 which s' feign themselves just men,*
28 his brother s' take his wife, and raise
22:23 them it was that s' do this thing. 3195
24 of them s' be accounted the greatest.*
23:24 that it s' be as they required.
24:16 holden that they s' not know him.
21 he which s' have redeemed Israel: 3195
47 remission of sins s' be preached in his
Joh 1:31 that he s' be made manifest to Israel,
2:25 needed not that any s' testify of man:
3:15 believeth in him s' not perish, *
16 believeth in him s' not perish,
20 light, lest his deeds s' be reproved.
5:23 That all men s' honour the Son, even*
6:14 prophet that s' come into the world.*
39 he hath given me I s' lose nothing,
39 s' raise it up again at the last day.
64 believed not, and who s' betray him.
71 for he it was that s' betray him, 3195
7:23 the law of Moses s' not be broken;*
39 that believe on him s' receive: *3195
8: 5 us, that such s' be stoned: *
19 ye s' have known my Father also.*
55 and if I s' say, I know him not, I
9: 3 of God s' be made manifest in him.
22 he s' be put out of the synagogue.
41 If ye were blind, ye s' have no sin:*
11:27 of God, which s' come into the world.*
37 even this man s' not have died?
50 that one man s' die for the people,
51 that Jesus s' die for that nation; 3195
52 he s' gather together in one the *

Joh 11:57 he s' shew it, that they might take
12: 4 Simon's son, which s' betray him, 3195
23 that the Son of man s' be glorified.
33 signifying what death he s' die. 3195
40 that they s' not see with their eyes,
40 and be converted, and I s' heal them.
42 they s' be put out of the synagogue:
46 on me s' not abide in darkness. *
49 what I s' say, and what I s' speak.
13: 1 hour was come that he s' depart out
11 For he knew who s' betray him;
15 that ye s' do as I have done to you.
24 that he s' ask who it s' be of whom*
29 that he s' give something to the poor.
14: 7 me, ye s' have known my Father also:*
15:16 that ye s' go and bring forth fruit,
16 fruit, and that your fruit s' remain;
16: 1 unto you, that ye s' not be offended.
30 needest not that any man s' ask thee:
17: 2 s' give eternal life to as many as thou
18: 4 all things that s' come upon him, *
14 that one man s' die for the people.
28 judgment hall, lest they s' be defiled;*
32 signifying what death he s' die. 3195
36 I s' not be delivered to the Jews:
37 that I s' bear witness unto the truth.
39 that I s' release unto you one at the
19:31 bodies s' not remain upon the cross on
36 done, that the scripture s' be fulfilled.*
21:19 by what death he s' glorify God.
23 brethren, that that disciple s' not die:
25 which, if they s' be written every one,
25 contain the books that s' be written.
Ac 1: 4 they s' not depart from Jerusalem,*
2:24 not possible that he s' be holden of
25 right hand, that I s' not be moved:
47 the church daily such as s' be saved.*
3:18 his prophets, that Christ s' suffer,
5:26 people, lest they s' have been stoned.
28 you that ye s' not teach in this name?*
40 they s' not speak in...name of Jesus.*
6: 2 that we s' leave the word of God, and
7: 6 his seed s' sojourn in a strange land;
6 that they s' bring them into bondage,
44 he s' make it according to the fashion
8:31 can I, except some man s' guide me?
10:17 vision which he hath seen s' mean,*
28 that I s' not call any man common
47 water, that these s' not be baptized,
11:22 that he s' go as far as Antioch. *
28 s' be great dearth throughout all 3195
12:19 commanded...they s' be put to death.
13:28 desired they Pilate that he s' be slain.
46 word of God s' first have been spoken
14:15 that ye s' turn from these vanities
15: 2 s' go up to Jerusalem unto the apostles
7 Gentiles by my mouth s' hear the word
17:27 That they s' seek the Lord, if haply
18:14 reason would that I s' bear with you:
19: 4 people, that they s' believe on him
4 on him which s' come after him, that
27 great goddess Diana s' be despised,
27 her magnificence s' be destroyed, 3195
20:38 that they s' see his face no more.
21: 4 that he s' not go up to Jerusalem.
16 an old disciple, with whom we s' lodge.
26 an offering s' be offered for every one*
22:22 earth: for it is not fit that he s' live.
24 that he s' be examined by scourging;
29 him which s' have examined him: 3195
23:10 Paul s' have been pulled in pieces of
27 and s' have been killed of them: *3195
24:23 he s' forbid none of his acquaintance
26 that money s' have been given him of*
25: 4 that Paul s' be kept at Cæsarea, and*
26: 8 s' it be thought a thing incredible*
8 with you, that God s' raise the dead?*
20 that they s' repent and turn to God,
22 prophets and Moses...say s' come: 3195
23 That Christ s' suffer, and that he*
23 suffer, and that he s' be the first that*
23 be the first that s' rise from the dead,*
23 s' shew light unto the people, and 3195
27: 1 determined that we s' sail into Italy,
17 lest they s' fall into the quicksands,
20 all hope that we s' be saved was then
21 ye s' have hearkened unto me, and 1163
29 lest we s' have fallen upon rocks,
42 lest any of them s' swim out, and
43 s' cast themselves first into the sea,
28: 6 looked when he s' have swollen, *3195
27 lest they s' see with their eyes, and
27 with their heart, and s' be converted,
27 be converted, and I s' heal them.
Ro 2:21 that preachest a man s' not steal,
22 sayest a man s' not commit adultery,
4:13 that he s' be the heir of the world,
6: 4 so we also s' walk in newness of life.*
6 that henceforth we s' not serve sin.
12 that ye s' obey it in the lusts thereof.
7: 4 that ye s' be married to another,
4 that we s' bring forth fruit unto God.*
6 that we s' serve in newness of spirit,*
8:26 know not what we s' pray for as we*
11: 8 eyes that they s' not see, and ears
8 and ears that they s' not hear;) unto
11 Have they stumbled that they s' fall?*
25 that ye s' be ignorant of this mystery,*
25 ye s' be wise in your own conceits;*
15:16 I s' be the minister of Jesus Christ to
20 lest I s' build upon another man's*
1Co 1:15 s' say that I had baptized in mine own
17 the cross of Christ s' be made of none
29 That no flesh s' glory in his presence.
2: 5 your faith s' not stand in the wisdom
4: 3 small thing that I s' be judged of you.

1Co 5: 1 that one s· have his father's wife.*
9: 10 he that ploweth s· plow in hope; *3784
10 in hope s· be partaker of his hope.*
12 lest we s· hinder the gospel of Christ.*
14 preach the gospel s· live of the gospel.
15 things, that it s· be so done unto me:*
15 any man s· make my glorying void.
27 to others, I myself s· be a castaway.
10: 1 I would not that ye s· be ignorant,*
6 intent we s· not lust after evil things,
20 that ye s· have fellowship with devils.
11: 31 judge ourselves, we s· not be judged.
32 s· not be condemned with the world.*
12: 25 there s· be no schism in the body;
25 s· have the same care one for another.
2Co 1: 9 that we s· not trust in ourselves, but
17 that with me there s· be yea yea, and
2: 3 I s· have sorrow from them of whom I
4 not that ye s· be grieved, but that ye
7 such a one s· be swallowed up with
11 Lest Satan s· get an advantage of us:*
4: 4 the image of God, s· shine unto them.
5: 15 s· not henceforth live unto themselves,
8: 20 no man s· blame us in this abundance
9: 3 lest our boasting of you s· be in vain*
4 s· be ashamed in this same confident
10: 8 though I s· boast somewhat more of
8 destruction, I s· not be ashamed:*
11: 3 so your minds s· be corrupted from
12: 6 lest any man s· think of me above
7 lest I s· be exalted above measure*
7 me, lest I s· be exalted above measure.
13: 7 evil; not that we s· appear approved,*
7 that ye s· do that which is honest,*
10 lest being present I s· use sharpness,*
Ga 1: 10 men, I s· not be the servant of Christ.
2: 2 lest by any means I s· run, or had run,
9 that we s· go unto the heathen, and
10 would that we s· remember the poor;
3: 1 that ye s· not obey the truth, before*
17 it s· make the promise of none effect.*
19 the seed s· come to whom the promise
21 verily righteousness s· have been by*
23 the faith which s· afterwards be *3195*
5: 7 you that ye s· not obey the truth?
6: 12 s· suffer persecution for the cross of*
14 God forbid that I s· glory, save in the*
Eph 1: 4 s· be holy and without blame before
12 s· be to the praise of his glory, who
2: 9 Not of works, lest any man s· boast.
10 ordained that we s· walk in them.
3: 6 That the Gentiles s· be fellowheirs,*
8 I s· preach among the Gentiles the*
5: 27 it s· be holy and without blemish.
Ph'p 1: 12 But I would ye s· understand, *
2: 10 the name of Jesus every knee s· bow,
11 every tongue s· confess that Jesus
27 lest I s· have sorrow upon sorrow.*
Col 1: 19 that in him s· all fulness dwell;
2: 4 lest any man s· beguile you with *
1Th 3: 3 That no man s· be moved by these*
4 that we s· suffer tribulation; *3195*
4: 3 that ye s· abstain from fornication:*
4 one of you s· know how to possess his*
5: 4 that day s· overtake you as a thief.
10 or sleep, we s· live together with him.
2Th 2: 11 delusion, that they s· believe a lie;
3: 10 any would not work, neither s· he eat.*
1Ti 1: 16 them which s· hereafter believe *3195*
Tit 2: 12 we s· live soberly, righteously, and
3: 7 we s· be made heirs according to the
Ph'm 14 that thy benefit s· not be as it were
Heb 2: 1 lest at any time we s· let them slip.*
9 he by the grace of God s· taste death
3: 18 whom sware he that they s· not enter
4: 1 any of you s· seem to come short of it.
7: 11 was there that another priest s· rise
8: 4 were on earth, he s· not be a priest,*
7 then s· no place have been sought for*
9: 23 of things in the heaven s· be purified
25 Nor yet that he s· offer himself often,
10: 2 purged s· have no more conscience*
4 of bulls and of goats s· take away sins.
11: 5 translated that he s· not see death;
8 a place which he s· after receive *3195
28 destroyed the firstborn s· touch them.
40 without us s· not be made perfect.
12: 19 that the word s· not be spoken to them
Jas 1: 18 that we s· be a kind of firstfruits of his
1Pe 1: 10 of the grace that s· come unto you:
11 Christ, and the glory that s· follow.
2: 9 that ye s· shew forth the praises of*
21 example, that ye s· follow his steps:
24 to sins, s· live unto righteousness:*
3: 9 called, that ye s· inherit the blessing.
4: 2 That he no longer s· live the rest of
2Pe 2: 6 those that after s· live ungodly; *3195*
3: 9 not willing that any s· perish, but
9 but that all s· come to repentance.
1Jo 3: 1 that we s· be called the sons of God:
11 beginning, that we s· love one another.
23 we s· believe on the name of his Son
4: 3 ye have heard that it s· come; and*
2Jo 6 from the beginning, ye s· walk in it.
Jude 3 ye s· earnestly contend for the faith*
18 they told you there s· be mockers*
18 s· walk after their own ungodly lusts.*
Re 6: 4 earth, and that they s· kill one another:
11 they s· rest yet for a little season,
11 that s· be killed as they were, *3195*
11 be killed as they were, s· be fulfilled.
7: 1 the wind s· not blow on the earth, nor
8: 3 that he s· offer it with the prayers of
9: 4 that they s· not hurt the grass of the
5 it was given that they s· not kill them,
5 that they s· be tormented five months:
Re 9: 20 that they s· not worship devils, and
10: 6 that there s· be time no longer: *
7 the mystery of God s· be finished, as*
11: 18 that they s· be judged, and that thou*
12: 6 they s· feed her there a thousand two*
13: 14 they s· make an image to the beast,
15 the image of the beast s· both speak,
15 the image of the beast s· be killed,
19: 8 that she s· be arrayed in fine linen,
15 that with it he s· smite the nations:
20: 3 that he s· deceive the nations no more,
3 till the thousand years s· be fulfilled:

shoulder See also SHOULDERPIECES; SHOULDERS.
Ge 21: 14 unto Hagar, putting it on her s·, 7926
24: 15 brother, with her pitcher upon her s·. "
45 forth with her pitcher on her s·; "
49: 15 bowed his s· to bear, and became "
Ex 29: 22 is upon them, and the right s·; *7785
27 the s· of the heave offering, which* "
Le 7: 32 the right s· shall ye give unto the* "
33 shall have the right s· for his part.* "
34 and the heave s· have I taken of * "
8: 25 and their fat, and the right s·: * "
26 on the fat, and upon the right s·: * "
9: 21 and the right s· Aaron waved * "
10: 14 and heave s· shall ye eat in a clean* "
15 heave s· and the wave breast shall* "
Nu 6: 19 take the sodden s· of the ram, 2220
20 with the wave breast and heave s·:*7785
18: 18 breast and as the right s· are thine.* "
De 18: 3 shall give unto the priest the s·, 2220
Jos 4: 5 man of you a stone upon his s·, 7926
J'g 9: 48 and took it, and laid it on his s·, "
1Sa 9: 24 And the cook took up the s·, and *7785
Ne 9: 29 withdrew the s·, and hardened 3802
Job 31: 22 mine arm fall from my s· blade, 7929
36 Surely I would take it upon my s·,7926
Ps 81: 6 I removed his s· from the burden: "
Isa 9: 4 and the staff of his s·, the rod of his "
6 government shall be upon his s·: "
10: 27 shall be taken away from off thy s·. "
22: 22 house of David will I lay upon his s·; "
46: 7 They bear him upon the s·, they 3802
Eze 12: 7 I bear it upon my s· in their sight. "
12 bear upon his s· in the twilight, "
24: 4 good piece, the thigh, and the s·; "
29: 7 didst break, and rend all their s·: * "
18 bald, and every s· was peeled: "
34: 21 have thrust with side and with s·, "
Zec 7: 11 to hearken, and pulled away the s·, "

shoulder-blade See SHOULDER and BLADE.

shoulderpieces
Ex 28: 7 It shall have the two s· thereof 3802
25 on the s· of the ephod before it. "
39: 4 They made s· for it, to couple it "
18 and put them on the s· of the ephod. "

shoulders
Ge 9: 23 and laid it upon both their s·, and7926
Ex 12: 34 up in their clothes upon their s·. "
28: 12 stones upon the s· of the ephod *3802
12 upon his two s· for a memorial. "
39: 7 he put them on the s· of the ephod.* "
Nu 7: 9 that they should bear upon their s·. "
De 33: 12 and he shall dwell between his s·. "
J'g 16: 3 put them upon his s·, and carried "
1Sa 9: 2 from his s· and upward he was 7926
10: 23 the people from his s· and upward. "
17: 6 a target of brass between his s·. 3802
1Ch 15: 15 bare the ark of God upon their s· "
2Ch 35: 3 shall not be a burden upon your s·: "
Isa 11: 14 fly upon the s· of the Philistines "
14: 25 burden depart from off their s·. *7926
30: 6 riches upon the s· of young asses, 3802
49: 22 shall be carried upon their s·. "
Eze 12: 6 sight shalt thou bear it upon thy s·,* "
M't 23: 4 borne, and lay them on men's s·; *5606*
Lu 15: 5 hath found it, he layeth it on his s·, "

shouldest
Ge 3: 11 commanded thee that thou s· not eat?
14: 23 lest thou s· say, I have made Abram
26: 10 thou s· have brought guiltiness upon
29: 15 s· thou therefore serve me for nought?
Nu 11: 12 that thou s· say unto me, Carry them
De 4: 19 s· be driven to worship them, and*
26: 18 thou s· keep all his commandments;
29: 12 That thou s· enter into covenant
30: 12 It is not in heaven, that thou s· say,
13 is it beyond the sea, that thou s· say,
J'g 11: 23 people Israel, and s· thou possess it?
Ru 2: 10 that thou s· take knowledge of me,
1Sa 20: 8 why s· thou bring me to thy father?
2Sa 9: 8 thou s· look upon such a dead dog
1Ki 1: 20 that thou s· tell them who shall sit
2Ki 8: 14 told me that thou s· surely recover.
13: 19 Thou s· have smitten five or six
14: 10 for why s· thou meddle to thy hurt,
10 that thou s· fall, even thou, and
19: 25 thou s· be to lay waste fenced cities
1Ch 17: 7 s· be ruler over my people Israel:
2Ch 19: 2 S· thou help the ungodly, and love
25: 16 forbear; why s· thou be smitten?
19 why s· thou meddle to thine hurt,
19 that thou s· fall, even thou, and
Job 7: 17 is man, that thou s· magnify him?
17 thou s· set thine heart upon him?
18 that thou s· visit him every morning,
10: 3 it good unto thee that thou s· oppress,
3 thou s· despise the work of thine
38: 20 thou s· take it to the bound thereof,
20 thou s· know the paths to the house
Ps 50: 16 s· take my covenant in thy mouth?*
130: 3 If thou, Lord, s· mark iniquities, O
Pr 5: 6 Lest thou s· ponder the path of life,*
Pr 25: 7 than that thou s· be put lower in the
27: 22 thou s· bray a fool in a mortar among
Ec 5: 5 Better is it that thou s· not vow,
5 than that thou s· vow and not pay.
7: 16 wise: why s· thou destroy thyself?
17 why s· thou die before thy time?
18 is good that thou s· take hold of this;
Isa 37: 26 that thou s· be to lay waste defenced
48: 5 lest thou s· say, Mine idol hath done
7 lest thou s· say, Behold, I knew them.
17 thee by the way that thou s· go.
49: 6 light thing that thou s· be my servant
51: 12 s· be afraid of a man that shall die,*
Jer 14: 8 why s· thou be as a stranger in the
9 Why s· thou be as a man astonied,
29: 26 that thou s· put him in prison, and in
49: 16 s· make thy nest as high as the eagle,
Ob 12 thou s· not have looked on the day of*
12 neither s· thou have rejoiced over*
12 neither s· thou have spoken proudly*
13 Thou s· not have entered into the*
13 thou s· not have looked on their *
14 s· thou have stood in the crossway,*
14 neither s· thou have delivered up*
M't 8: 8 that thou s· come under my roof:
18: 33 S· not thou also have had compassion
M'r 10: 35 thou s· do for us whatsoever we shall
Lu 7: 6 that thou s· enter under my roof:
Joh 11: 40 believe, thou s· see the glory of God?
17: 15 thou s· take them out of the world,
15 that thou s· keep them from the evil.
Ac 13: 47 that thou s· be for salvation unto the
22: 14 that thou s· know his will, and see*
14 and s· hear the voice of his mouth.*
Tit 1: 5 that thou s· set in order the things
Ph'm 15 that thou s· receive him for ever;
Re 11: 18 thou s· give reward unto thy servants*
18 s· destroy them which destroy the*

shout See also SHOUTED; SHOUTETH; SHOUTING.
Ex 32: 18 voice of them that s· for mastery, 6030
Nu 23: 21 the s· of a king is among them. 8643
Jos 6: 5 the trumpet, all the people shall s·7321
5 with a great s·; and the wall of 8643
10 shall not s·, nor make any noise 7321
10 day I bid you s·; then shall ye s·. "
16 Joshua said unto the people, S·; for "
20 the people shouted with a great s·,8643
1Sa 4: 5 all Israel shouted with a great s·, "
6 Philistines heard the noise of the s·, "
6 noise of this great s· in the camp "
2Ch 13: 15 Then the men of Judah gave a s·: 7321
Ezr 3: 11 the people shouted with a great s·,8643
13 not discern the noise of the s· of joy "
13 the people shouted with a loud s·, "
Ps 5: 11 let them ever s· for joy, because 7442
32: 11 s· for joy, all ye that are upright in "
35: 27 Let them s· for joy, and be glad, "
47: 1 s· unto God with the voice of 7321
5 God is gone up with a s·, the Lord8643
65: 13 they s· for joy, they also sing. 7321
132: 9 and let thy saints s· for joy. 7442
16 her saints shall s· aloud for joy. "
Isa 12: 6 Cry out and s·, thou inhabitant of "
42: 11 s· from the top of the mountains. 6681
44: 23 s·, ye lower parts of the earth: 7321
Jer 25: 30 he shall give a s·, as they that6030,1959
31: 7 s· among the chief of the nations: 6670
50: 15 S· against her round about: she 7321
51: 14 they shall lift up a s· against thee.1959
La 3: 8 when I cry and s·, he shutteth out*7768
Zep 3: 14 s·, O Israel; be glad and rejoice 7321
Zec 9: 9 Zion; s·, O daughter of Jerusalem: "
Ac 12: 22 And the people gave a s·, saying, *2019*
1Th 4: 16 descend from heaven with a s·, *2752*

shouted
Ex 32: 17 the noise of the people as they s·, 7452
Le 9: 24 when all the people saw, they s·, 7442
Jos 6: 20 people s· when the priests blew 7321
20 the people s· with a great shout, "
J'g 15: 14 Lehi, the Philistines s· against him: "
1Sa 4: 5 all Israel s· with a great shout, so "
10: 24 the people s·, and said, God save the "
17: 20 to the fight, and s· for the battle. "
52 of Israel and of Judah arose, and s·, "
2Ch 13: 15 as the men of Judah s·, it came to "
Ezr 3: 11 all the people s· with a great shout, "
12 voice; and many s· aloud for joy: 8643
13 for the people s· with a loud shout,7321
Job 38: 7 and all the sons of God s· for joy? "

shouteth
Ps 78: 65 man that s· by reason of wine. 7442

shouting See also SHOUTINGS.
2Sa 6: 15 up the ark of the Lord with s·, 8643
1Ch 15: 28 up the ark...of the Lord with s·, "
2Ch 15: 14 with a loud voice, and with s·, and "
Job 39: 25 thunder of the captains, and the s·. "
Pr 11: 10 when the wicked perish, there is s·.7440
Isa 16: 9 for the s· for thy summer fruits *1959
10 singing, neither shall there be s·:*7321
10 made their vintage s· to cease. *1959
Jer 20: 16 morning, and the s· at noontide; 8643
48: 33 none shall tread with s·; 1959
33 their s· shall be no s·. "
Eze 21: 22 to lift up the voice with s·, 8643
Am 1: 14 thereof, with s· in the day of battle, "
2: 2 Moab shall die with tumult, with s·, "

shoutings
Zec 4: 7 the headstone thereof with s·, 8663

shovel See also SHOVELS.
Isa 30: 24 hath been winnowed with the s· 7371

shovels
Ex 27: 3 and his s·, and his basons, and his3257
38: 3 pots, and the s·, and the basons, "

Nu 4:14 the fleshhooks, and the s', and the 3257
1Ki 7:40 Hiram made the lavers, and the s', "
45 pots, and the s', and the basons: "
2Ki 25:14 pots, and the s', and the snuffers, "
2Ch 4:11 Huram made the pots, and the s', "
16 The pots also, and the s', and the "
Jer 52:18 The caldrons also, and the s', and "

show See SHEW.

shower See also SHOWERS.
Eze 13:11 there shall be an overflowing s'; 1653
13 and there shall be an overflowing s' "
34:26 I will cause the s' to come down in "
Lu 12:54 ye say, There cometh a s'; and so *3655*

showers
De 32: 2 and as the s' upon the grass: 7241
Job 24: 8 wet with the s' of the mountains, 2230
Ps 65:10 thou makest it soft with s': thou 7241
72: 6 grass: as s' that water the earth. "
Jer 3: 3 the s' have been withholden, and "
14:22 rain? or can the heavens give s'? "
Eze 34:26 there shall be s' of blessing. 1653
Mic 5: 7 the Lord, as the s' upon the grass, 7241
Zec 10: 1 clouds, and give them s' of rain, 1653

shrank
Ge 32:32 eat not of the sinew which s', *5384
32 Jacob's thigh in the sinew that s'.* "

shred See also SHERD.
2Ki 4:39 s' them into the pot of pottage: 6398

shrines
Ac 19:24 which made silver s' for Diana, *3485*

shrink See SHRANK.

shroud
Eze 31: 3 and with a shadowing s', and of an 2793

shrubs
Ge 21:15 cast the child under one of the s'. 7880

Shua (*shu'-ah*) See also BATH-SHUA; SHUAH.
1Ch 2: 3 daughter of S' the Canaanitess. 7770
7:32 and Hotham, and S' their sister. 7774

Shuah (*shu'-ah*) See also SHUA; SHUHITE.
Ge 25: 2 and Midian, and Ishbak, and S'. 7744
38: 2 Canaanite, whose name was S'; 7770
12 daughter of S' Judah's wife died;* "
1Ch 1:32 and Midian, and Ishbak, and S'. 7744
4:11 the brother of S' begat Mehir, *7746

Shual (*shu'-al*) See also HAZAR-SHUAL.
1Sa 13:17 to Ophrah, unto the land of S': 7777
1Ch 7:36 and Harnepher, and S', and Beri, "

Shubael (*shu'-ba-el*) See also SHEBUEL.
1Ch 24:20 Of the sons of Amram; S': of the 2619
25:20 thirteenth to S', he, his sons, and "

Shuham (*shu'-ham*) See also HUSHIM; SHUHAMITES.
Nu 26:42 S', the family of the Shuhamites. 7748

Shuhamites (*shu'-ham-ites*)
Nu 26:42 of Shuham, the family of the S'. 7749
43 the families of the S', according "

Shuhite (*shu'-hite*)
Job 2:11 the Temanites, and Bildad the S', 7747
8: 1 Then answered Bildad the S', and "
18: 1 Then answered Bildad the S', and "
25: 1 Then answered Bildad the S', and "
42: 9 the Temanite and Bildad the S' "

Shulamite (*shu'-lam-ite*)
Ca 6:13 Return, return, O S'; return, *7759
13 What will ye see in the S'? As it* "

Shumathites (*shu'-math-ites*)
1Ch 2:53 the Puhites, and the S', and the 8126

shun See also SHUNNED.
2Ti 2:16 But s' profane and vain babblings: *4026*

Shunammite (*shu'-nam-mite*)
1Ki 1: 3 and found Abishag a S', and 7767
15 Abishag the S' ministered unto "
2:17 he give me Abishag the S' to wife. "
21 Abishag the S' be given to Adonijah "
22 ask Abishag the S' for Adonijah? "
2Ki 4:12 to Gehazi his servant, Call this S'. "
25 servant, Behold, yonder is that S': "
36 called Gehazi, and said, Call this S'. "

Shunem (*shu'-nem*) See also SHUNAMMITE.
Jos 19:18 Jezreel, and Chesulloth, and S', 7766
1Sa 28: 4 and came and pitched in S': "
2Ki 4: 8 on a day, that Elisha passed to S', "

Shuni (*shu'-ni*) See also SHUNITES.
Ge 46:16 and Haggi, S', and Ezbon, Eri, 7764
Nu 26:15 of S', the family of the Shunites: "

Shunites (*shu'-nites*)
Nu 26:15 of Shuni, the family of the S': 7765

shunned
Ac 20:27 I have not s' to declare unto you *5288*

Shupham (*shu'-fam*) See also SHEPHUPHAN; SHUPHAMITES.
Nu 26:39 S', the family of the Shuphamites: *8197

Shuphamites (*shu'-fam-ites*)
Nu 26:39 Of Shupham, the family of the S': 7781

Shuppim (*shup'-pim*) See also MUPPIM; SHEPHUPHAN.
1Ch 7:12 S' also, and Huppim, the children 8206
15 to wife the sister of Huppim and S', "
26:16 To S' and Hosah the lot came forth "

Shur (*shur*)
Ge 16: 7 by the fountain in the way to S'. 7793
20: 1 dwelled between Kadesh and S', "
25:18 they dwelt from Havilah unto S', "
Ex 15:22 went out into the wilderness of S'; "
1Sa 15: 7 Havilah until thou comest to S', 7793
27: 8 as thou goest to S', even unto the "

Shushan (*shu'-shan*) See also SHOSHANNIM; SHUSHAN-EDUTH.
Ne 1: 1 year, as I was in S' the palace, 7800
Es 1: 2 throne...which was in S' the palace, "
5 the people that were present in S' "
2: 3 all the fair young virgins unto S' "
5 in S' the palace...was a certain Jew, "
8 were gathered together unto S' "
3:15 decree was given in S' the palace. "
15 but the city S' was perplexed. "
4: 8 of the decree that was given at S' "
16 all the Jews that are present in S', "
8:14 decree was given at S' the palace. "
15 the city of S' rejoiced and was glad. "
9: 6 in S' the palace the Jews slew and "
11 the number of those...slain in S' "
12 destroyed five hundred men in S' "
13 granted to the Jews which are in S' "
14 and the decree was given at S'; "
15 the Jews that were in S' gathered "
15 and slew three hundred men at S'; "
18 the Jews that were at S' assembled "
Da 8: 2 saw, that I was at S' in the palace, "

Shushan-eduth (*shu''-shan-e'-duth*)
Ps 60: *title* To the chief Musician upon S', 7802

shut See also SHUTTETH; SHUTTING.
Ge 7:16 him: and the Lord s' him in. 5462
19: 6 unto them, and s' the door after him, "
10 house to them, and s' to the door. "
Ex 14: 3 the wilderness hath s' them in. "
Le 13: 4 priest shall s' up him that hath the "
5 priest shall s' him up seven days "
11 unclean, and shall not s' him up: "
21, 26 priest shall s' him up seven days: "
31, 33 priest shall s' up him that hath "
50 s' up it that hath the plague seven "
54 he shall s' it up seven days more: "
14:38 and s' up the house seven days: "
46 into the house...while that it is s' "
Nu 12:14 let her be s' out from the camp "
15 Miriam was s' out from the camp "
De 11:17 s' up the heaven, that there be no 6113
15: 7 nor s' thine hand from thy poor 7092
32:30 and the Lord had s' them up? *5462
36 and there is none s' up, or left. 6113
Jos 2: 7 were gone out, they s' the gate. 5462
6: 1 Jericho was straitly s' up because "
J'g 3:23 and s' the doors of the parlour upon "
9:51 they of the city, and s' it to them, "
1Sa 1: 5 but the Lord had s' up her womb. "
6 the Lord had s' up her womb. "
6:10 and s' up their calves at home: 3607
23: 7 for he is s' in, by entering into a 5462
2Sa 20: 3 s' up unto the day of their death, 6887
1Ki 8:35 When heaven is s' up, and there is 6113
14:10 him that is s' up and left in Israel, "
21:21 him that is s' up and left in Israel, "
2Ki 4: 4 thou shalt s' the door upon thee 5462
5 and s' the door upon her and upon "
21 s' the door upon him, and went out. "
33 and s' the door upon them twain, "
6:32 s' the door, and hold him fast at the "
9: 8 him that is s' up and left in Israel. 6113
14:26 for there was not any s' up, nor any "
17: 4 the king of Assyria s' him up, and "
2Ch 6:26 When the heaven is s' up, and there "
7:13 I s' up heaven that there be no rain, "
28:24 s' up the doors of the house of the 5462
29: 7 have s' up the doors of the porch, "
Ne 6:10 son of Mehetabeel, who was s' up; 6113
10 let us s' the doors of the temple: 5462
7: 3 let them s' the doors, and bar them: 1479
13:19 that the gates should be s', and 5462
Job 3:10 s' not up the doors of my mother's "
11:10 If he cut off, and s' up, or gather "
38: 8 Or who s' up the sea with doors, 5526
41:15 s' up together as with a close seal. 5462
Ps 31: 8 s' me up into the hand of the enemy; "
69:15 not the pit s' her mouth upon me. 332
77: 9 in anger s' up his tender mercies? 7092
88: 8 I am s' up, and I cannot come 3607
Ec 12: 4 the doors shall be s' in the streets, 5462
Ca 4:12 a spring s' up, a fountain sealed. 5274
Isa 6:10 their ears heavy, and s' their eyes; 8173
22:22 he shall open, and none shall s'; 5462
22 and he shall s', and none shall open. "
24:10 every house is s' up, that no man "
22 and shall be s' up in the prison, "
26:20 and s' thy doors about thee: "
44:18 for he hath s' their eyes, that they 2902
45: 1 and the gates shall not be s'; 5462
52:15 kings shall s' their mouths at him: 7092
60:11 they shall not be s' day nor night; 5462
66: 9 to bring forth, and s' the womb? 6113
Jer 13:19 cities of the south shall be s' up, 5462
20: 9 a burning fire s' up in my bones, 6113
32: 2 Jeremiah...was s' up in the court 3607
3 For Zedekiah...had s' him up, "
33: 1 while he was yet s' up in the court 6113
36: 5 saying, I am s' up; I cannot go "
39:15 while he was s' up in the court of "
Eze 3:24 Go, s' thyself within thine house. 5462
44: 1 toward the east; and it was s'. "
2 This gate shall be s', it shall not be "
2 entered in...therefore it shall be s'. "
46: 1 shall be s' the six working days; "
2 gate shall not be s' until...evening. "
12 going forth one shall s' the gate. "
Da 6:22 and hath s' the lions' mouths, that 5463
8:26 wherefore s' thou up the vision; 5640
12: 4 But thou, O Daniel, s' up the words, "
Mal 1:10 would s' the doors for nought? 5462
M't 6: 6 and when thou hast s' thy door. *2808*
23:13 for ye s' up the kingdom of heaven *2808*
25:10 the marriage: and the door was s'. "
Lu 3:20 all, that he s' up John in prison. *2623*
4:25 heaven was s' up three years and *2808*
11: 7 the door is now s', and my children "
13:25 is risen up, and hath s' to the door, *608*
Joh 20:19 doors were s' where the disciples *2808*
26 then came Jesus, the doors being s', "
Ac 5:23 The prison truly found we s' with "
21:30 and forthwith the doors were s'. "
26:10 of the saints did I s' up in prison, *2623*
Ga 3:23 s' up unto the faith which should *4788*
Re 3: 8 open door, and no man can s' it: *2808*
11: 6 These have power to s' heaven, that "
20: 3 the bottomless pit, and s' him up, "
21:25 the gates of it shall not be s' at all "

Shuthalhites (*shu'-thal-hites*)
Nu 26:35 Shuthelah, the family of the S': *8364

Shuthelah (*shu'-the-lah*) See also SHUTHALHITES.
Nu 26:35 of S' the family of...Shuthalhites: 7803
36 And these are the sons of S': "
1Ch 7:20 sons of Ephraim; S', and Bered "
21 And Zabad his son, and S' his son, "

shutteth
Job 12:14 he s' up a man, and there can be 5462
Pr 16:30 He s' his eyes to devise froward 6095
17:28 that s' his lips is esteemed a man 331
Isa 33:15 and s' his eyes from seeing evil; 6105
La 3: 8 and shout, he s' out my prayer. 5640
1Jo 3:17 s' up his bowels of compassion *2808*
Re 3: 7 he that openeth, and no man s'; * "
7 and s', and no man openeth; "

shutting
Jos 2: 5 about the time of s' of the gate, 5462

shuttle
Job 7: 6 days are swifter than a weaver's s'. 708

Sia (*si'-ah*) See also SIAHA.
Ne 7:47 children of S', the children of 5517

Siaha (*si'-a-hah*) See also SIA.
Ezr 2:44 children of S', the children of 5517

Sibbecai (*sib'-be-cahee*) See also SIBBECHAI.
1Ch 11:29 S' the Hushathite, Ilai the Ahohite, 5444
27:11 was S' the Hushathite, of the sons "

Sibbechai (*sib'-be-kahee*) See also SIBBECAI.
2Sa 21:18 S' the Hushathite slew Saph, *5444
1Ch 20: 4 S' the Hushathite slew Sippai, * "

Sibboleth (*sib'-bo-leth*) See also SHIBBOLETH.
J'g 12: 6 and he said S': for he could not 5451

Sibmah (*sib'-mah*)
Jos 13:19 S', and Zareth-shahar in the 7643
Isa 16: 8 languish, and the vine of S': the "
9 weeping of Jazer the vine of S': "
Jer 48:32 O vine of S', I will weep for thee "

Sibraim (*sib'-ra-im*)
Eze 47:16 S', which is between the border of 5453

Sichem (*si'-kem*) See also SHECHEM; SYCHEM.
Ge 12: 6 the land unto the place of S', *7927

sick
Ge 48: 1 Joseph, Behold, thy father is s': 2470
Le 15:33 of her that is s' of her flowers, and 1739
1Sa 19:14 to take David, she said, He is s'. 2470
30:13 because three days agone I fell s'. "
2Sa 12:15 bare unto David, and it was very s'. 605
13: 2 that he fell s' for his sister Tamar; 2470
5 on thy bed, and make thyself s': "
6 lay down, and made himself s': "
1Ki 14: 1 Abijah the son of Jeroboam fell s'. "
5 of thee for her son; for he is s': "
17:17 the mistress of the house, fell s'; "
2Ki 1: 2 that was in Samaria, and was s': "
8: 7 the king of Syria was s'; and it "
29 Ahab in Jezreel, because he was s'. "
13:14 Elisha was fallen s' of his sickness "
20: 1 days was Hezekiah s' unto death. "
12 heard that Hezekiah had been s'. "
2Ch 22: 6 Ahab at Jezreel, because he was s'. "
32:24 days Hezekiah was s' to the death, "
Ne 2: 2 sad, seeing thou art not s'? this "
Ps 35:13 when they were s', my clothing "
Pr 13:12 Hope deferred maketh the heart s': "
23:35 shalt thou say, and I was not s'; * "
Ca 2: 5 me with apples: for I am s' of love. "
5: 8 that ye tell him, I am s' of love. "
Isa 1: 5 the whole head is s', and the whole 2483
33:24 inhabitant shall not say, I am s': 2470
38: 1 days was Hezekiah s' unto death. "
9 king of Judah, when he had been s', "
39: 1 he had heard that he had been s', "
Jer 14:18 them that are s' with famine! 8463
Eze 34: 4 have ye healed that which was s', 2470
16 will strengthen that which was s': "
Da 8:27 fainted, and was s' certain days; "
Ho 7: 5 king the princes have made him s' "
Mic 6:13 will I make thee s' in smiting thee, * "
Mal 1: 8 if ye offer the lame and s', is it not "
13 was torn, and the lame, and the s'; "
M't 4:24 brought unto him all s' people *2192,2560*
8: 6 servant...at home s' of the palsy, *3885*
14 wife's mother laid,...s' of a fever. *4445*
16 and healed all that were s': *2192,2560*
9: 2 brought...a man s' of the palsy, *3885*
2 faith said unto the s' of the palsy; "
6 (then saith he to the s' of the palsy,) "
12 physician, but they that are s'. *2192,2560*
10: 8 Heal the s', cleanse the lepers, *770*
14:14 toward them, and he healed their s'. *732*
25:36 I was s', and ye visited me: I was *770*
39 when saw we thee s', or in prison, *772*
43 s', and in prison, and ye visited me "
44 naked, or s', or in prison, and did "

M'r 1:30 Simon's wife's mother lay s· of a 4445
34 he healed many that were s· 2192,2560
2: 3 him, bringing one s· of the palsy, 3885
4 bed wherein the s· of the palsy lay. "
5 he said unto the s· of the palsy, Son,"
9 it easier to say to the s· of the palsy,"
10 sins, (he saith to the s· of the palsy,)"
17 physician, but they that are s·:2192,2560
6: 5 laid his hands upon a few s· folks, 732
13 anointed with oil many that were s·,"
55 in beds those that were s·, 2192,2560
56 they laid the s· in the streets, and 770
16:18 they shall lay hands on the s·, and 732
Lu 4:40 all they that had any s· with divers 770
5:24 (he said unto the s· of the palsy,) *3885
31 physician; but they that are s·.2192,2560
7: 2 him, was s·, and ready to die. " "
10 the servant whole that had been s·.*770
9: 2 kingdom of God, and to heal the s·. "
10: 9 And heal the s· that are therein, 772
Joh 4:46 whose son was s· at Capernaum. 770
11: 1 Now a certain man was s·, named "
2 hair, whose brother Lazarus was s·.)"
3 behold, he whom thou lovest is s·. "
6 had heard therefore that he was s·, "
Ac 5:15 they brought forth the s· into the 772
16 bringing s· folks, and them which "
9:33 years, and was s· of the palsy. *3885
37 days, that she was s·, and died: 770
19:12 brought unto the s· handkerchiefs "
28: 8 father of Publius lay s· of a fever and
Ph'p 2:26 ye had heard that he had been s·. 770
27 indeed he was s· nigh unto death: "
2Ti 4:20 Trophimus have I left at Miletum s·."
Jas 5:14 Is any s· among you? let him call "
15 prayer of faith shall save the s·, 2577

sickle
De 16: 9 beginnest to put the s· to the corn.2770
23:25 not move a s· unto thy neighbour's "
Jer 50:16 that handleth the s· in the time of 4038
Joe 3:13 Put ye in the s·, for the harvest is "
M'r 4:29 immediately he putteth in the s·, 1407
Re 14:14 crown, and in his hand a sharp s·. "
15 cloud, Thrust in thy s·, and reap: "
16 cloud thrust in his s· on the earth; "
17 heaven, he also having a sharp s·. "
18 cry to him that had the sharp s·, "
18 Thrust in thy sharp s·, and gather "
19 angel thrust in his s· into the earth,"

sickly
1Co 11:30 many are weak and s· among you. 732

sickness See also SICKNESSES.
Ex 23:25 I will take s· away from the midst4245
Le 20:18 lie with a woman having her s·, 1739
De 7:15 will take away from thee all s·, 2483
28:61 Also every s·, and every plague, "
1Ki 8:37 plague, whatsoever s· there be; 4245
17:17 his s· was so sore, that there was 2483
2Ki 13:14 Now Elisha was fallen sick of his s· "
2Ch 6:28 sore or whatsoever s· there be: 4245
21:15 shalt have great s· by disease of 2483
15 bowels fall out by reason of the s· "
19 bowels fell out by reason of his s·: "
Ps 41: 3 wilt make all his bed in his s·. "
Ec 5:17 sorrow and wrath with his s·. "
Isa 38: 9 sick, and was recovered of his s·: "
12 he will cut me off with pining s·, *
Ho 5:13 When Ephraim saw his s·, and 2483
M't 4:23 healing all manner of s· and all 3554
9:35 healing every s· and every disease* "
10: 1 to heal all manner of s· and all * "
Joh 11: 4 This s· is not unto death, but for 769

sicknesses
De 28:59 sore s·, and of long continuance. 2483
29:22 s· which the Lord hath laid upon 8463
M't 8:17 our infirmities, and bare our s·. *3554
M'r 3:15 to have power to heal s·, and to * "

Siddim (*sid'-dim*)
Ge 14: 3 joined together in the vale of *S*·. 7708
8 battle with them in the vale of *S*·; "
10 the vale of *S*· was full of slimepits; "

side See also ASIDE; BACKSIDE; BESIDE; INSIDE; OUTSIDE; SIDES; UPSIDE.
Ge 6:16 ark shalt thou set in the s· thereof;6654
38:21 harlot, that was openly by the way s·?
Ex 2: 5 walked along by the river's s·; and3027
12: 7 strike it on the two s· posts and on
22 strike the lintel and the two s· posts
23 upon the lintel, and on the two s· posts,
17:12 one s·, and the other on the other s·;
25:12 rings shall be in the one s· of it, 6763
12 and two rings in the other s· of it. "
32 of the candlestick out of the one s·,6654
32 the candlestick out of the other s·: "
26:13 a cubit on the one s·, and a cubit on
13 the other s· of that which remaineth
13 on this s· and on that s·, to cover
18 boards on the south s· southward. 6285
20 the second s· of the tabernacle on 6763
20 the north s· there shall be twenty 6285
26 of the one s· of the tabernacle, 6763
27 of the other s· of the tabernacle, and"
27 boards of the s· of the tabernacle, "
35 the s· of the tabernacle toward the "
35 shalt put the table on the north s·. "
27: 9 for the south s· southward there 6285
9 an hundred cubits long for one s·: "
11 likewise for the north s· in length "
12 the west s· shall be hangings of fifty"
13 breadth of the court on the east s· "
14 The hangings of one s· of the gate3802
15 on the other s· shall be hangings "
28:26 is in the s· of the ephod inward. 5676
32:15 on the one s· and on the other were

Ex 32:26 said, Who is on the Lord's s·? let him
27 Put every man his sword by his s·,*3409
36:11 uttermost s· of another curtain, *8193
23 boards for the south s· southward:6285
25 for the other s· of the tabernacle, 6763
31 of the one s· of the tabernacle, "
32 of the other s· of the tabernacle, "
37: 3 even two rings upon the one s· of it,"
3 and two rings upon the other s· of it."
8 One cherub on the end on this s·,*
8 cherub on the other end on that s·:*
18 out of the one s· thereof, and 6654
18 out of the other s· thereof: "
38: 9 south s· southward the hangings 6285
11 for the north s· the hangings were "
12 for the west s· were hangings of "
13 for the east s· eastward fifty cubits."
14 hangings of the one s· of the gate 3802
15 for the other s· of the court gate, "
39:19 was on the s· of the ephod inward.5676
40:22 the s· of the tabernacle northward,3409
24 the s· of the tabernacle southward. "
Le 1:11 shall kill it on the s· of the altar "
15 be wrung out at the s· of the altar:7023
5: 9 sin offering upon the s· of the altar;"
Nu 2: 3 the east s· toward the rising of the6924
10 On the south s· shall be the standard
18 On the west s· shall be the standard
25 camp of Dan shall be on the north s·
3:29 the s· of the tabernacle southward.3409
35 the s· of the tabernacle northward. "
10: 6 the camps that lie on the south s·
11:31 it were a day's journey on this s·, 3541
31 a day's journey on the other s·, "
16:27 Dathan, and Abiram, on every s·: 5439
21:13 pitched on the other s· of Arnon, 5676
22: 1 Moab on this s· Jordan by Jericho.* "
24 being on this s·, and a wall on that s·.
24: 6 as gardens by the river's s·, as the
32:19 not inherit...on yonder s· Jordan, 5676
19 is fallen to us on this s· Jordan "
32 inheritance on this s· Jordan may* "
34:11 to Riblah, on the east s· of Ain; 6924
11 unto the s· of the sea of Chinnereth3802
15 their inheritance on this s· Jordan*5676
35: 5 on the east s· two thousand cubits,6285
5 on the south s· two thousand cubits,"
5 on the west s· two thousand cubits,"
5 on the north s· two thousand cubits;"
14 give three cities on this s· Jordan,*5676
De 1: 1 unto all Israel on this s· Jordan in* "
5 On this s· Jordan, in the land of * "
7 in the south, and by the sea s·, *2348
3: 8 land that was on this s· Jordan, *5676
4:32 one s· of heaven unto the other, *7097
41 cities on this s· Jordan toward the*5676
46 On this s· Jordan, in the valley over*"
47 were on this s· Jordan toward the* "
49 plain on this s· Jordan eastward, * "
11:30 Are they not on the other s· Jordan,*"
31:26 in the s· of the ark of the covenant6654
Jos 1:14 Moses gave you on this s· Jordan;*5676
15 gave you on this s· Jordan toward* "
2:10 that were on the other s· Jordan, * "
5: 1 were on the s· of Jordan westward,*"
7: 2 Beth-aven, on the east s· of Beth-el,
7 and dwelt on the other s· Jordan!*5676
8: 9 Beth-el and Ai, on the west s· of Ai:
11 and pitched on the north s· of Ai:
12 and Ai, on the west s· of the city.
22 in the midst of Israel, some on this s·,
22 and some on that s·: and they smote
33 their judges, stood on this s· the ark
33 that s· before the priests the Levites,
9: 1 which were on this s· Jordan, in *5676
12: 1 other s· Jordan toward the rising* "
7 Israel smote on this s· Jordan on* "
13:27 on the other s· Jordan eastward. * "
32 of Moab, on the other s· Jordan, by*"
14: 3 half tribe on the other s· Jordan: * "
15: 3 to the south s· to Maaleh-acrabbim,*
3 on the south s· unto Kadesh-barnea,*
7 which is on the s· side of the river:
8 unto the south s· of the Jebusite; 3802
10 along unto the s· of mount Jearim, "
10 which is Chesalon, on the north s·,*
11 unto the s· of Ekron northward: 3802
16: 5 inheritance on the east s· was *
6 to Michmethah on the north s·; *
17: 5 which were on the other s· Jordan;*5676
9 was on the north s· of the river,
18:12 border on the north s· was from 6285
12 border went up to the s· of Jericho3802
12 of Jericho on the north s·, and went*
13 to the s· of Luz, which is Beth-el, 3802
13 the south s· of the nether Beth-horon.*
16 to the s· of Jebusi on the south, 3802
18 toward the s· over against Arabah "
19 the s· of Beth-hoglah northward: "
20 was the border of it on the east s·.*6285
19:14 it on the north s· to Hannathon: *
27 toward the north s· of Beth-emek,*
34 reacheth to Zebulun on the south s·,*
34 and reacheth to Asher on the west s·,*
20: 8 on the other s· Jordan by Jericho*5676
22: 4 gave you on the other s· Jordan. * "
7 their brethren on this s· Jordan * "
24: 2 Your fathers dwelt on the other s'* "
3 from the other s· of the flood, and* "
8 which dwelt on the other s· Jordan;*"
14 fathers served on the other s· of * "
15 were on the other s· of the flood, * "
30 the north s· of the hill of Gaash. *
J'g 2: 9 on the north s· of the hill Gaash. *
7: 1 Midianites were on the north s·
12 sand by the sea s· for multitude. *8193

J'g 7:18 also on every s· of all the camp, 5439
25 to Gideon on the other s· Jordan.*5676
8:34 of all their enemies on every s·: 5439
10: 8 that were on the other s· Jordan *5676
11:18 by the east s· of the land of Moab,
18 pitched on the other s· of Arnon, 5676
19: 1 on the s· of mount Ephraim, who 3411
18 toward the s· of mount Ephraim; "
21:19 which is on the north s· of Beth-el,*
19 on the east s· of the highway that
1Sa 4:18 backward by the s· of the gate, 3027
6: 8 in a coffer by the s· thereof; and 6654
12:11 hand of your enemies on every s·, 5439
14: 1 garrison, that is on the other s·. 5676
4 was a sharp rock on the one s·, "
4 and a sharp rock on the other s·: "
40 he unto all Israel, Be ye on one s·, "
40 my son will be on the other s·. "
47 against all his enemies on every s·,5439
17: 3 stood on a mountain on the one s·,
3 stood on a mountain on the other s·:
20:20 I will shoot three arrows on the s·6654
21 the arrows are on this s· of thee,
25 and Abner sat by Saul's s·, and 6654
23:26 went on this s· of the mountain,
26 his men on that s· of the mountain:"
26:13 David went over to the other s·, 5676
31: 7 Israel that were on the other s· of "
7 that were on the other s· Jordan, * "
2Sa 2:13 the one on the one s· of the pool,
13 the other on the other s· of the pool.
16 thrust his sword in his fellow's s·;6654
13:34 by the way of the hill s· behind "
16:13 Shimei went along on the hill's s· 6763
18: 4 And the king stood by the gate s·, 3027
24: 5 on the right s· of the city that lieth3225
1Ki 4:24 all the region on this s· the river, 5676
24 all the kings on this s· the river: "
5: 3 which were about him on every s·,
4 hath given me rest on every s·, 5439
6: 8 was in the right s· of the house: 3802
31 lintel and s· posts were a fifth part *
7: 7 cedar from one s· of the floor to the*
30 molten, at the s· of every addition.5676
39 bases on the right s· of the house, 3802
39 and five on the left s· of the house: "
39 the sea on the right s· of the house "
49 of pure gold, five on the right s·, and
10:19 were stays on either s· on the place of
20 twelve lions stood there on the one s·
2Ki 3:22 the water on the other s· as red *5048
12: 9 it beside the altar, on the right s· 3225
16:14 put it on the north s· of the altar. 3409
1Ch 4:39 even unto the east s· of the valley, 4217
6:78 on the other s· Jordan by Jericho,*5676
78 on the east s· of Jordan, were 4217
12:18 Thine are we, David, and on thy s·,
37 on the other s· of Jordan, of the 5676
22:18 he not given you rest on every s·? 5439
26:30 them of Israel on this s· Jordan *5676
2Ch 4: 8 five on the right s·, and five on the
10 he set the sea on the right s· of the3802
8:17 at the sea s· in the land of Edom.*8193
9:18 stays on each s· of the sitting place,
19 lions stood there on the one s·, and
14: 7 he hath given us rest on every s·. 5439
20: 2 beyond the sea on this s· Syria; *
23:10 from the right s· of the temple to 3802
10 to the left s· of the temple, along by"
32:22 and guided them on every s·. 5439
30 to the west s· of the city of David.
33:14 on the west s· of Gihon, in the valley,
Ezr 4:10 rest that are on this s· the river, *5675
11 the men on this s· the river, and at*"
16 have no portion on this s· the river.*"
5: 3, 6 Tatnai, governor on this s· the * "
6 which were on this s· the river, * "
6:13 Tatnai, governor on this s· the river,*"
8:36 the governors on this s· the river: *5676
Ne 3: 7 of the governor on this s· the river.*"
4:18 had his sword girded by his s·, 4975
Job 1:10 about all that he hath on every s·? 5439
18:11 shall make him afraid on every s·, "
12 destruction...be ready at his s·. †6763
19:10 He hath destroyed me on every s·,5439
Ps 12: 8 The wicked walk on every s·, when "
31:13 fear was on every s·: while they "
65:12 the little hills rejoice on every s·. *2296
71:21 and comfort me on every s·. *5437
91: 7 A thousand shall fall at thy s·, and6654
118: 6 Lord is on my s·; I will not fear:
124: 1, 2 been the Lord who was on our s·,
Ec 4: 1 s· of their oppressors there was 3027
Isa 60: 4 daughters...be nursed at thy s·. *6654
Jer 6:25 the enemy and fear is on every s·. 5439
20:10 defaming of many, fear on every s·. "
49:29 cry unto them, Fear is on every s·. "
52:23 and six pomegranates on a s·; *7307
Eze 1:10 the face of a lion, on the right s·: 3225
10 had the face of an ox on the left s·; 8040
23 had two, which covered on this s·,
23 had two, which covered on that s·,
4: 4 Lie thou also upon thy left s·, and 6654
6 lie again on thy right s·, and thou "
8 turn thee from one s· to another, "
9 days that thou shalt lie upon thy s·,"
9: 2 with a writer's inkhorn by his s·: 4975
3 had the writer's inkhorn by his s·; "
11 which had the inkhorn by his s·, "
10: 3 cherubims stood on the right s· of 3225
11:23 mountain which is on the east s· of6924
16:33 come unto thee on every s· for thy5439
19: 8 nations set against him on every s· "
23:22 bring them against thee on every s·;"
25: 9 I will open the s· of Moab from the3802
28:23 by the sword upon her on every s·;5439

Eze 34: 21 thrust with s' and with shoulder, 6654
36: 3 and swallowed you up on every s', 5439
37: 21 and will gather them on every s', "
39: 17 gather yourselves on every s' to my"
40: 10 on this s', and three on that s'; 6311
10 measure on this s' and on that s'.
12 chambers was one cubit on this s',
12 the space was one cubit on that s':
12 on this s', and six cubits on that s'.
18 pavement by the s' of the gates 3802
21 three on this s' and three on that s';
26 on this s', and another on that s',
34, 37 thereof, on this s', and on that s':
39 on this s', and two tables on that s',
40 at the s' without, as one goeth up 3802
40 and on the other s', which was at "
41 on this s', and four tables on that s',"
41 by the s' of the gate; eight tables, "
44 was at the s' of the north gate; "
44 one at the s' of the east gate having"
48 on this s', and five cubits on that s': "
48 on this s', and three cubits on that s'.
49 one on this s', and another on that s'.
41: 1 six cubits broad on the one s', 6311
1 six cubits broad on the other s',
2 were five cubits on the one s',
2 and five cubits on the other s':
5 the breadth of every s' chamber, 6763
5 round about the house on every s'.5439
6 And the s' chambers were three, 6763
6 of the house for the s' chambers "
7 still upward to the s' chambers: "
8 the foundations of the s' chambers "
9 was for the s' chamber without, "
9 was the place of the s' chambers "
10 about the house on every s'. 5439
11 the doors of the s' chambers were 6763
15 galleries thereof on the one s' and
15 on the other s', an hundred cubits,
19 toward the palm tree on the one s',
19 toward the palm tree on the other s':
26 palm trees on the one s' and on
26 and on the other s', on the sides of
26 upon the s' chambers of the house,6763
42: 9 was the entry on the east s', as 6921
16 east s' with the measuring reed, 7307
17 the north s', five hundred reeds, "
18 the south s', five hundred reeds, "
19 He turned about to the west s', and"
45: 7 shall be for the prince on the one s'
7 other s' of the oblation of the holy
7 city, from the west s' westward, 6285
7 and from the east s' eastward:
46: 19 which was at the s' of the gate,
47: 1 from the right s' of the house,
1 house, at the south s' of the altar.*
2 there ran out waters on...right s'. 3802
7 many trees on the one s' and on the
12 upon the bank thereof, on this s' and
12 on that s', shall grow all trees for
15 of the land toward the north s', 6285
17 Hamath. And this is the north s'. "
18 the east s' ye shall measure from "
18 east sea. And this is the east s'. "
19 And the south s' southward, from "
19 And this is the south s' southward. "
20 The west s' also shall be the great "
20 Hamath. This is the west s'. "
48: 2 the border of Dan, from the east s' "
2 the west s', a portion for Asher. "
3 the east s' even unto the west s', "
4, 5 from the east s' unto the west s', "
6 the east s' even unto the west s', "
7, 8 from the east s' unto the west s', "
8 from the east s' unto the west s': "
16 the north s' four thousand and five "
16 the south s' four thousand and five "
16 the east s' four thousand and five "
16 the west s' four thousand and five "
21 on the one s' and on the other of the"
23, 24, 25, 26, 27 east s' unto the west s',"
28 of Gad, at the south s' southward, "
30 out of the city on the north s', "
32 at the east s' four thousand and "
33 the south s' four thousand and five "
34 the west s' four thousand and five "
Da 7: 5 and it raised up itself on one s', 7859
10: 4 I was by the s' of the great river, 3027
11: 17 but she shall not stand on his s', *
12: 5 on this s' of the bank of the river,
5 the other on that s' of the bank of
Ob 11 that thou stoodest on the other s', 5048
Jon 4: 5 and sat on the east s' of the city, 6924
Zec 4: 3 one upon the right s' of the bowl,
3 and the other upon the left s' thereof.
11 upon the right s' of the candlestick
11 and upon the left s' thereof?
5: 3 shall be cut off as on this s' according
3 shall be cut off as on that s' according
M't 8: 18 to depart unto the other s'. *4008*
28 when he was come to the other s' "
13: 1 of the house, and sat by the sea s'.*3844*
4 some seeds fell by the way s', and "
19 which received seed by the way s'. "
14: 22 to go before him unto the other s',*4008*
16: 5 disciples were come to the other s', "
20: 30 blind men sitting by the way s', *3844*
M'r 2: 13 he went forth again by the sea s'; "
4: 1 began again to teach by the sea s': "
4 as he sowed, some fell by the way s'."
15 And these are they by the way s', "
35 Let us pass over unto the other s'.*4008*
5: 1 over unto the other s' of the sea, "
21 again by ship unto the other s', "
6: 45 the other s' before unto Bethsaida, "
8: 13 ship again departed to the other s'. "
M'r 10: 1 Judæa by the farther s' of Jordan: *4008*
46 sat by the highway s' begging. *3844*
16: 5 young man sitting on the right s', *1188*
Lu 1: 11 standing on the right s' of the altar "
8: 5 he sowed, some fell by the way s'; *3844*
12 Those by the way s' are they that "
22 over unto the other s' of the lake. *4008*
10: 31 him, he passed by on the other s'. *492*
32 him, and passed by on the other s'. "
18: 35 man sat by the way s' begging: *3844*
19: 43 round, and keep thee in on every s',*3840*
Joh 6: 22 stood on the other s' of the sea *4008*
25 found him on the other s' of the "
19: 18 other with him, on either s' one, *1782*
34 with a spear pierced his s', and *4125*
20: 20 unto them his hands and his s'. "
25 and thrust my hand into his s', I "
27 thy hand, and thrust it into my s': "
21: 6 Cast the net on the right s' of the *3313*
Ac 10: 6 he whose house is by the sea s': *3844*
32 one Simon a tanner by the sea s': "
12: 7 smote Peter on the s', and raised *4125*
16: 13 went out of the city by a river s', *3844*
2Co 4: 8 We are troubled on every s', yet not
7: 5 but we were troubled on every s';
Re 22: 2 on either s' of the river, was there *1782*

side-chamber See SIDE and CHAMBER.

side-posts See SIDE and POSTS.

sides
Ex 25: 14 into the rings by the s' of the ark, 6763
32 shall come out of the s' of it; 6654
26: 13 hang over the s' of the tabernacle "
22 the s' of the tabernacle westward*3411
23 of the tabernacle in the two s'. * "
27 tabernacle, for the two s' westward.*"
27: 7 be upon the two s' of the altar, 6763
28: 27 two s' of the ephod underneath, *3802
30: 3 and the s' thereof round about, 7023
4 the two s' of it shalt thou make it; 6654
32: 15 were written on both their s'; 5676
36: 27 the s' of the tabernacle westward*3411
28 of the tabernacle in the two s'. * "
32 the tabernacle for the s' westward.*"
37: 5 into the rings by the s' of the ark, 6763
18 going out of the s' thereof; 6654
26 and the s' thereof round about, 7023
27 upon the two s' thereof, to be 6654
38: 7 the rings on the s' of the altar, 6763
39: 20 two s' of the ephod underneath, *3802
Nu 33: 55 your eyes, and thorns in your s', 6654
Jos 23: 13 and scourges in your s', and thorns"
J'g 2: 3 they shall be as thorns in your s', "
5: 30 colours of needlework on both s',
1Sa 24: 3 remained in the s' of the cave. *3411
1Ki 4: 24 and he had peace on all s' round 5676
6: 16 cubits on the s' of the house, *3411
2Ki 19: 23 mountains, to the s' of Lebanon, * "
Ps 48: 2 mount Zion, on the s' of the north, "
128: 3 vine by the s' of thine house: * "
Isa 14: 13 congregation, in the s' of the north:*"
15 down to hell, to the s' of the pit. * "
37: 24 mountains, to the s' of Lebanon; * "
66: 12 ye shall be borne upon her s', and 6654
Jer 6: 22 be raised from the s' of the earth.*3411
48: 28 nest in the s' of the hole's mouth.‡5676
49: 32 their calamity from all s' thereof,* "
Eze 1: 8 under their wings on their four s';7253
17 went, they went upon their four s';"
10: 11 went, they went upon their four s';"
32: 23 graves are set in the s' of the pit, *3411
41: 2 the s' of the door were five cubits 3802
26 on the s' of the porch, and upon "
42: 20 He measured it by the four s': it 7307
46: 19 a place on the two s' westward. *3411
48: 1 for these are his s' east and west; 6285
Am 6: 10 him that is by the s' of the house,*3411
Jon 1: 5 gone down into the s' of the ship;* "

Sidon (*si'-don*) See also SIDONIANS; ZIDON.
Ge 10: 15 And Canaan begat *S'* his firstborn,*6721
19 of the Canaanites was from *S'*. "
M't 11: 21 had been done in Tyre and *S'*, *4605*
22 be more tolerable for Tyre and *S'* "
15: 21 into the coasts of Tyre and *S'*. "
M'r 3: 8 and they about Tyre and *S'*, a great"
7: 24 into the borders of Tyre and *S'*, "
31 from the coasts of Tyre and *S'*, "
Lu 4: 26 save unto Sarepta, a city of *S'*, unto"
6: 17 from the sea coast of Tyre and *S'*, "
10: 13 had been done in Tyre and *S'*, "
14 be more tolerable for Tyre and *S'* "
Ac 12: 20 displeased with them of Tyre and *S'*:"
27: 3 And the next day we touched at *S'*."

Sidonians (*si-do'-ne-uns*) See also ZIDONIANS.
De 3: 9 Which Hermon the *S'* call Sirion; 6722
Jos 13: 4 and Mearah that is beside the *S'*,* "
6 and all the *S'*, them will I drive out*"
J'g 3: 3 and all the Canaanites, and the *S'*,*"
1Ki 5: 6 skill to hew timber like unto the *S'*.*"

siege See also BESIEGE.
De 20: 19 down...to employ them in the s': *4692
28: 53 in the s', and in the straitness, "
55 he hath nothing left in the s', and "
57 secretly in the s' and straitness, "
1Ki 15: 27 and all Israel laid s' to Gibbethon.6696
2Ch 32: 9 but he himself laid s' against Lachish,*
10 ye abide in the s' in Jerusalem? 4692
Isa 29: 3 and will lay s' against thee with a 6696
Jer 19: 9 eat the flesh of his friend in the s' 4692
Eze 4: 2 And lay s' against it, and build a "
3 and thou shalt lay s' against it. 6696
7 face toward the s' of Jerusalem, 4692
8 thou hast ended the days of thy s'. "
5: 2 when the days of the s' are fulfilled:"
Mic 5: 1 troops: he hath laid s' against us:4692
Na 3: 14 Draw thee waters for the s', fortify "
Zec 12: 2 shall be in the s' both against Judah"

sieve
Isa 30: 28 the nations with the s' of vanity: 5299
Am 9: 9 nations, like as corn is sifted in a s',3531

sift See also SIFTED.
Isa 30: 28 to s' the nations with the sieve of 5130
Am 9: 9 I will s' the house of Israel among5128
Lu 22: 31 you, that he may s' you as wheat: *4617*

sifted
Am 9: 9 nations, like as corn is s' in a sieve,5128

sigh See also SIGHED; SIGHEST; SIGHETH; SIGHING; SIGHS.
Isa 24: 7 all the merryhearted do s'. 584
La 1: 4 priests s', her virgins are afflicted, "
11 All her people s', they seek bread; "
21 They have heard that I s': there is "
Eze 9: 4 upon the foreheads of the men that s'"
21: 6 *S'* therefore, thou son of man, with "
6 with bitterness s' before their eyes. "

sighed
Ex 2: 23 children of Israel s' by reason of 584
M'r 7: 34 And looking up to heaven, he s', *4727*
8: 12 he s' deeply in his spirit, and saith, *389*

sighest
Eze 21: 7 say unto thee, Wherefore s' thou? 584

sigheth
La 1: 8 yea, she s', and turneth backward. 584

sighing
Job 3: 24 For my s' cometh before I eat, and 585
Ps 12: 5 of the poor, for the s' of the needy, 603
31: 10 with grief, and my years with s': 585
79: 11 the s' of the prisoner come before 603
Isa 21: 2 the s' thereof have I made to cease.585
35: 10 and sorrow and s' shall flee away. "
Jer 45: 3 fainted in my s', and I find no rest.* "

sighs
La 1: 22 for my s' are many, and my heart is585

sight See also OVERSIGHT; SIGHTS.
Ge 2: 9 every tree that is pleasant to the s',4758
18: 3 now I have found favour in thy s', 5869
19: 19 servant hath found grace in thy s', "
21: 11 was very grievous in Abraham's s' "
12 Let it not be grievous in thy s' "
23: 4 may bury my dead out of my s'. 6440
8 should bury my dead out of my s'; "
32: 5 lord,...I may find grace in thy s'. 5869
33: 8 to find grace in the s' of my lord. "
10 if now I have found grace in thy s', "
15 me find grace in the s' of my lord. "
38: 7 was wicked in the s' of the Lord; "
39: 4 And Joseph found grace in his s', "
21 him favour in the s' of the keeper "
47: 18 not ought left in the s' of my lord, 6440
25 us find grace in the s' of my lord. 5869
29 If now I have found grace in thy s', "
Ex 3: 3 turn aside, and see this great s', 4758
21 favour in the s' of the Egyptians: 5869
4: 30 did the signs in the s' of the people. "
7: 20 in the river, in the s' of Pharaoh, "
20 and in the s' of his servants; and "
9: 8 the heaven in the s' of Pharaoh. "
11: 3 favour in the s' of the Egyptians. "
3 in the s' of Pharaoh's servants, and"
3 and in the s' of the people. "
12: 36 favour in the s' of the Egyptians, "
15: 26 wilt do that which is right in his s',*"
17: 6 Moses did so in the s' of the elders "
19: 11 down in the s' of all the people upon"
24: 17 the s' of the glory of the Lord *4758
33: 12 hast also found grace in my s'. 5869
13 if I have found grace in thy s', "
13 that I may find grace in thy s': and "
16 people have found grace in thy s'? "
17 for thou hast found grace in my s'. "
34: 9 If now I have found grace in thy s', "
40: 38 in the s' of all the house of Israel, "
Le 10: 19 been accepted in the s' of the Lord?"
13: 3 the plague in s' be deeper than the*4758
4 in s' be not deeper than the skin, * "
5 if the plague in his s' be at a stay,*5869
20 it be in s' lower than the skin, *4758
25, 30 it be in s' deeper than the skin;*"
31 it be not in s' deeper than the skin,*"
32 be not in s' deeper than the skin;* "
34 nor be in s' deeper than the skin;* "
37 if the scall be in his s' at a stay, *5869
14: 37 which in s' are lower than the *4758
20: 17 be cut off in the s' of their people: 5869
25: 53 rule with rigour over him in thy s'. "
26: 45 of Egypt in the s' of the heathen, "
Nu 3: 4 in the s' of Aaron their father. *6440
11: 11 have I not found favour in thy s', 5869
15 If I have found favour in thy s'; "
13: 33 were in our own s' as grasshoppers, "
33 and so we were in their s'. "
19: 5 one shall burn the heifer in his s'; "
20: 27 Hor in the s' of all the congregation."
25: 6 woman in the s' of Moses, and in "
6 the s' of all the congregation of the "
27: 19 and give him a charge in their s'. "
32: 5 if we have found grace in thy s', let "
13 had done evil in the s' of the Lord, "
33: 3 hand in the s' of all the Egyptians. "
De 4: 6 wisdom...in the s' of the nations, "
25 shall do evil in the s' of the Lord "
37 brought thee out in his s' with his*6440
6: 18 and good in the s' of the Lord: 5869
9: 18 wickedly in the s' of the Lord, to "
12: 25 which is right in the s' of the Lord.*"
28 good and right in the s' of the Lord*"

De 17: 2 wickedness in the s' of the Lord 5869
21: 9 which is right in the s' of the Lord.*"
28: 34 mad for the s' of thine eyes which 4758
67 for the s' of thine eyes which thou "
31: 7 unto him in the s' of all Israel, 5869
29 ye will do evil in the s' of the Lord, "
34: 12 Moses shewed in the s' of all Israel. "
Jos 3: 7 magnify thee in the s' of all Israel, "
4: 14 Joshua in the s' of all Israel; and "
10: 12 and he said in the s' of Israel, Sun, "
23: 5 and drive them from out of your s';6440
24: 17 did those great signs in our s', and5869
J'g 2: 11 Israel did evil in the s' of the Lord, "
3: 7 Israel did evil in the s' of the Lord, "
12 did evil again in the s' of the Lord: "
12 had done evil in the s' of the Lord. "
4: 1 again did evil in the s' of the Lord, "
6: 1 Israel did evil in the s' of the Lord: "
17 If now I have found grace in thy s', "
21 of the Lord departed out of his s'. "
10: 6 did evil again in the s' of the Lord, "
13: 1 did evil again in the s' of the Lord; "
Ru 2: 2 him in whose s' I shall find grace. "
13 Let me find favour in thy s', my "
1Sa 1: 18 handmaid find grace in thy s'. "
12: 17 ye have done in the s' of the Lord, "
15: 17 thou wast little in thine own s', "
19 and didst evil in the s' of the Lord? "
16: 22 for he hath found favour in my s'. "
18: 5 was accepted in the s' of all the "
5 also in the s' of Saul's servants. "
29: 6 me in the host is good in my s': "
9 know that thou art good in my s', "
2Sa 6: 22 and will be base in mine own s': "
7: 9 off all thine enemies out of thy s',*6440
19 was yet a small thing in thy s', *5869
12: 9 of the Lord, to do evil in his s'? "
11 with thy wives in the s' of this sun. "
13: 5 dress the meat in my s', that I "
6 make me a couple of cakes in my s', "
8 made cakes in his s', and did bake "
14: 22 that I have found grace in thy s', "
16: 4 thee that I may find grace in thy s', "
22 concubines in the s' of all Israel. "
22: 25 to my cleanness in his eye s'. "
1Ki 8: 25 shall not fail thee a man in my s' 6440
9: 7 my name, will I cast out of my s'; "
11: 6 did evil in the s' of the Lord, and 5869
19 great favour in the s' of Pharaoh, "
38 do that is right in my s', to keep * "
14: 22 Judah did evil in the s' of the Lord, "
15: 26, 34 he did evil in the s' of the Lord, "
16: 7 evil...he did in the s' of the Lord, "
19 in doing evil in the s' of the Lord, "
30 Omri did evil in the s' of the Lord "
21: 20 to work evil in the s' of the Lord. "
25 wickedness in the s' of the Lord, "
22: 52 he did evil in the s' of the Lord, and"
2Ki 1: 13 thy servants, be precious in thy s'. "
14 my life now be precious in thy s'. "
3: 2 wrought evil in the s' of the Lord; "
18 a light thing in the s' of the Lord: "
8: 18 and he did evil in the s' of the Lord. "
27 and did evil in the s' of the Lord, "
12: 2 was right in the s' of the Lord all * "
13: 2 which was evil in the s' of the Lord, "
11 which was evil in the s' of the Lord; "
14: 3 was right in the s' of the Lord, * "
24 which was evil in the s' of the Lord: "
15: 3 was right in the s' of the Lord, * "
9 which was evil in the s' of the Lord, "
18, 24, 28 was evil in the s' of the Lord: "
34 was right in the s' of the Lord: he "
16: 2 was right in the s' of the Lord his* "
17: 2 which was evil in the s' of the Lord, "
17 to do evil in the s' of the Lord, to "
18 and removed them out of his s': 6440
20 until he had cast them out of his s'. "
23 Lord removed Israel out of his s', "
18: 3 was right in the s' of the Lord, *5869
20: 3 done that which was good in thy s'. "
21: 2 which was evil in the s' of the Lord, "
6 wickedness in the s' of the Lord, "
15 done that which was evil in my s', "
16 which was evil in the s' of the Lord. "
20 which was evil in the s' of the Lord, "
22: 2 was right in the s' of the Lord, * "
23: 27 remove Judah also out of my s', 6440
32, 37 was evil in the s' of the Lord, 5869
24: 3 to remove them out of his s', for 6440
9, 19 was evil in the s' of the Lord, 5869
1Ch 2: 3 was evil in the s' of the Lord; and "
19: 13 do that which is good in his s'. * "
22: 8 blood upon the earth in my s'. 6440
28: 8 therefore in the s' of all Israel the 5869
29: 25 exceedingly in the s' of all Israel, "
2Ch 6: 16 shall not fail thee a man in my s' 6440
7: 20 will I cast out of my s', and will "
20: 32 was right in the s' of the Lord. *5869
22: 4 he did evil in the s' of the Lord like "
24: 2 was right in the s' of the Lord all* "
25: 2 was right in the s' of the Lord, * "
26: 4 was right in the s' of the Lord, * "
27: 2 was right in the s' of the Lord, * "
28: 1 was right in the s' of the Lord, * "
29: 2 was right in the s' of the Lord, * "
32: 23 magnified in the s' of all nations "
33: 2 which was evil in the s' of the Lord, "
6 much evil in the s' of the Lord, "
22 which was evil in the s' of the Lord, "
34: 2 was right in the s' of the Lord, * "
36: 5 evil in the s' of the Lord his God. "
9 which was evil in the s' of the Lord. "
12 evil in the s' of the Lord his God. "
Ezr 9: 9 us in the s' of the kings of Persia, 6440
Ne 1: 11 him mercy in the s' of this man. "

Ne 2: 5 servant have found favour in thy s',6440
8: 5 book in the s' of all the people; 5869
Es 2: 15 in the s' of all them that looked "
17 obtained grace and favour in his s'6440
5: 2 that she obtained favour in his s': 5869
8 found favour in the s' of the king, "
7: 3 have found favour in thy s', O king, "
8: 5 and if I have found favour in his s', "
Job 15: 15 the heavens are not clean in his s'. "
18: 3 beasts, and reputed vile in your s'? "
19: 15 stranger: I am an alien in their s'. "
21: 8 established in their s' with them, 6440
25: 5 the stars are not pure in his s'. 5869
34: 26 wicked men in...open s' of others; 7200
41: 9 be cast down even at the s' of him?4758
Ps 5: 5 foolish shall not stand in thy s': 5869
9: 19 the heathen be judged in thy s'. 6440
10: 5 are far above out of his s': as for 5048
19: 14 be acceptable in thy s', O Lord, 6440
51: 4 sinned and done this evil in thy s': 5869
72: 14 precious...their blood be in his s'. "
76: 7 who may stand in thy s' when once 6440
78: 12 did he in the s' of their fathers, 5048
79: 10 known among the heathen in our s'5869
90: 4 For a thousand years in thy s' are "
98: 2 shewed in the s' of the heathen. "
101: 7 telleth lies shall not tarry in my s'.* "
116: 15 Precious in the s' of the Lord is the "
143: 2 in thy s' shall no man living be 6440
Pr 1: 17 net is spread in the s' of any bird.*5869
3: 4 understanding in the s' of God and "
4: 3 beloved in the s' of my mother. 6440
Ec 2: 26 man that is good in his s' wisdom,* "
6: 9 Better is the s' of the eyes than 4758
8: 3 Be not hasty to go out of his s': *6440
11: 9 heart, and in the s' of thine eyes: 4758
Isa 5: 21 eyes, and prudent in their own s'! 6440
11: 3 not judge after the s' of his eyes, 4758
26: 17 so have we been in thy s', O Lord.*6440
38: 3 done that which is good in thy s'. 5869
43: 4 Since thou wast precious in my s', "
Jer 4: 1 thine abominations out of my s', 6440
7: 15 And I will cast you out of my s', as "
30 of Judah have done evil in my s', 5869
15: 1 cast them out of my s', and let 6440
18: 10 If it do evil in my s', that it obey not5869
23 neither blot...their sin from thy s', 6440
19: 10 break the bottle in...s' of the men 5869
32: 12 in the s' of Hanameel mine uncle's* "
34: 15 and had done right in my s', * "
43: 9 in the s' of the men of Judah; "
51: 24 they have done in Zion in your s', "
Eze 4: 12 that cometh out of man, in their s'. "
5: 8 of thee in the s' of the nations. "
14 thee, in the s' of all that pass by. "
10: 2 the city. And he went in in my s'. "
19 mounted up from the earth in my s': "
12: 3 and remove by day in their s'; "
3 place to another place in their s': "
4 forth thy stuff by day in their s', "
4 shalt go forth at even in their s', "
5 Dig...through the wall in their s', "
6 In their s' shalt thou bear it upon "
7 bare it upon my shoulder in their s'. "
16: 41 upon thee in the s' of many women: "
20: 9 in whose s' I made myself known "
14 in whose s' I brought them out. "
22 be polluted in the s' of the heathen, "
22 in whose s' I brought them forth. "
43 lothe yourselves in your own s' 6440
21: 23 as a false divination in their s', 5869
22: 16 in thyself in the s' of the heathen, "
28: 18 the s' of all them that behold thee. "
25 in them in the s' of the heathen, "
36: 31 lothe yourselves in your own s' 6440
34 in the s' of all that passed by. 5869
39: 27 in them in the s' of many nations; "
43: 11 and write it in their s', that they "
Da 4: 11 and the s' thereof to the end of all 2379
20 and the s' thereof to all the earth; "
Ho 2: 2 her whoredoms out of her s', *6440
10 lewdness in the s' of her lovers, 5869
6: 2 us up, and we shall live in his s'. *6440
Am 9: 3 though they be hid from my s' in 5869
Jon 2: 4 Then I said, I am cast out of thy s';* "
Mal 2: 17 evil is good in the s' of the Lord, "
M't 11: 5 The blind receive their s', and the 308
26 for so it seemed good in thy s'. 1715
20: 34 immediately their eyes received s', 308
M'r 10: 51 Lord, that I might receive my s'. "
52 And immediately he received his s', "
Lu 1: 15 shall be great in the s' of the Lord,1799
4: 18 and recovering of s' to the blind, 309
7: 21 many that were blind he gave s'. 991
10: 21 for so it seemed good in thy s'. 1715
15: 21 against heaven, and in thy s', 1799
16: 15 is abomination in the s' of God. "
18: 41 Lord, that I may receive my s'. 308
42 Jesus said unto him, Receive thy s': "
43 And immediately he received his s', "
23: 48 that came together to that s', 2335
24: 31 him; and he vanished out of their s'. "
Joh 9: 11 went and washed, and I received s'.308
15 him how he had received his s'. "
18 had been blind, and received his s', "
18 parents of him that...received his s'. "
Ac 1: 9 cloud received him out of their s'. 5788
4: 19 Whether it be right in...s' of God 1799
7: 10 and wisdom in the s' of Pharaoh *1726
31 saw it, he wondered at the s': 3705
8: 21 heart is not right in the s' of God.*1799
9: 9 And he was three days without s', 991
12 him, that he might receive his s'. 308
17 that thou mightest receive thy s', "
18 he received s' forthwith, and arose, "
10: 31 in remembrance in the s' of God. 1799

Ac 22: 13 me, Brother Saul, receive thy s'. 308
Ro 3: 20 shall no flesh be justified in his s':1799
12: 17 things honest in the s' of all men. "
2Co 2: 17 the s' of God speak we in Christ. 2714
4: 2 man's conscience in the s' of God. 1799
5: 7 (For we walk by faith, not by s':) 1491
7: 12 care for you in the s' of God might1799
8: 21 not only in the s' of the Lord, but "
21 Lord, but also in the s' of men. "
Ga 3: 11 by the law in the s' of God, it is 3844
Col 1: 22 and unreproveable in his s': * 2714
1Th 1: 3 in the s' of God and our Father *1715
1Ti 2: 3 in the s' of God our Saviour; 1799
6: 13 I give thee charge in the s' of God, "
Heb 4: 13 that is not manifest in his s': "
12: 21 And so terrible was the s', that * 5324
13: 21 that which is wellpleasing in his s',1799
Jas 4: 10 yourselves in the s' of the Lord, "
1Pe 3: 4 is in the s' of God of great price. "
1Jo 3: 22 things that are pleasing in his s'. "
Re 4: 3 throne, in s' like unto an emerald.*3706
13: 13 on the earth in the s' of men, 1799
14 power to do in the s' of the beast; "

sights
Lu 21: 11 fearful s' and great signs shall *5400

sign See also ENSIGN; SIGNED; SIGNS.
Ex 4: 8 hearken to the voice of the first s', 226
8 will believe the voice of the latter s'. "
8: 23 people: to morrow shall this s' be. "
13: 9 for a s' unto thee upon thine hand, "
31: 13 for it is a s' between me and you "
17 a s' between me and the children of "
Nu 16: 38 they shall be a s' unto the children "
26: 10 fifty men: and they became a s'. 5251
De 6: 8 bind them for a s' upon thine hand,226
11: 18 bind them for a s' upon your hand, "
13: 1 and giveth thee a s' or a wonder, "
2 the s' or the wonder come to pass, "
28: 46 they shall be upon thee for a s' and "
Jos 4: 6 That this may be a s' among you, "
J'g 6: 17 me a s' that thou talkest with me. "
20: 38 there was an appointed s' between "
1Sa 2: 34 this shall be a s' unto thee, that 226
14: 10 hand: and this shall be a s' unto us. "
1Ki 13: 3 he gave a s' the same day, saying, 4159
3 the s' which the Lord hath spoken; "
5 according to the s' which the man of "
2Ki 19: 29 And this shall be a s' unto thee, Ye 226
20: 8 What shall be the s' that the Lord "
9 This s' shalt thou have of the Lord, "
2Ch 32: 24 unto him, and he gave him a s'. 4159
Isa 7: 11 Ask thee a s' of the Lord thy God; 226
14 the Lord himself shall give you a s'; "
19: 20 it shall be for a s' and for a witness "
20: 3 s' and wonder upon Egypt and upon "
37: 30 this shall be a s' unto thee, Ye shall "
38: 7 this shall be a s' unto thee from the "
22 What is the s' that I shall go up to "
55: 13 for an everlasting s' that shall not be "
66: 19 I will set a s' among them, and I "
Jer 6: 1 up a s' of fire in Beth-haccerem: *4864
44: 29 And this shall be a s' unto you, 226
Eze 4: 3 shall be a s' to the house of Israel. "
12: 6 for a s' unto the house of Israel. 4159
11 Say, I am your s': like as I have "
14: 8 will make him a s' and a proverb, 226
20: 12 to be a s' between me and them, "
20 shall be a s' between me and you, "
24: 24 Thus Ezekiel is unto you a s': 4159
27 and thou shalt be a s' unto them; "
39: 15 then shall he set up a s' by it, till 6725
Da 6: 8 and s' the writing, that it be not 7560
M't 12: 38 we would see a s' from thee. 4592
39 generation seeketh after a s'; "
39 and there shall no s' be given to it, "
39 but the s' of the prophet Jonas: "
16: 1 would shew them a s' from heaven. "
4 generation seeketh after a s'; "
4 and there...no s' be given unto it, "
4 but the s' of the prophet Jonas. "
24: 3 what shall be the s' of thy coming, "
30 appear the s' of the Son of man in "
26: 48 that betrayed him gave them a s', "
M'r 8: 11 seeking of him a s' from heaven, "
12 doth this generation seek after a s'? "
12 no s' be given unto this generation. "
13: 4 what shall be the s' when all these "
Lu 2: 12 And this shall be a s' unto you; Ye "
34 and for a s' which shall be spoken "
11: 16 sought of him a s' from heaven. "
29 an evil generation: they seek a s'; "
29 and there shall no s' be given it, "
29 but the s' of Jonas the prophet. "
30 Jonas was a s' unto the Ninevites, "
21: 7 what s' will there be when these "
Joh 2: 18 him, What s' shewest thou unto us, "
6: 30 What s' shewest thou then, that we "
Ac 28: 11 whose s' was Castor and Pollux. 3902
Ro 4: 11 he received the s' of circumcision, 4592
1Co 1: 22 For the Jews require a s', and the* "
14: 22 Wherefore tongues are for a s', "
Re 15: 1 I saw another s' in heaven, great "

signed See also ASSIGNED.
Da 6: 9 king Darius s' the writing and the7560
10 Daniel knew that the writing was s', "
12 Hast thou not s' a decree, that "
13 nor the decree that thou hast s', but "

signet See also SIGNETS.
Ge 38: 18 Thy s', and thy bracelets, and thy 2368
25 the s', and bracelets, and staff. 2858
Ex 28: 11 stone, like the engravings of a s', 2368
21 names, like the engravings of a s'; "
36 upon it, like the engravings of a s', "
39: 14 names, like the engravings of a s', "
30 like to the engravings of a s'. "

Jer 22:24 were the *s'* upon my right hand. 2368
Da 6:17 the king sealed it with his own *s'*. 5824
17 and with the *s'* of his lords; that the"
Hag 2:23 Lord, and will make thee as a *s'*: 2368

signets
Ex 39: 6 of gold, graven, as *s'* are graven. 2368

signification
1Co 14:10 and none of them is without *s'*. *880*

signified
Ac 11:28 *s'* by the spirit that there should be *4591*
Re 1: 1 *s'* it by his angel unto his servant "

signifieth
Heb 12:27 *s'* the removing of those things *1213*

signify See also SIGNIFIED; SIGNIFIETH; SIGNIFYING.
Ac 21:26 to *s'* the accomplishment of the **1229*
23:15 the council *s'* to the chief captain *1718*
25:27 to *s'* the crimes laid against him. *4591*
1Pe 1:11 of Christ which was in them did *s'*.**1213*

signifying
Joh 12:33 said, *s'* what death he should die. *4591*
18:32 spake, *s'* what death he should die. "
21:19 *s'* by what death he should glorify "
Heb 9: 8 The Holy Ghost this *s'*, that the *1213*

signs See also ENSIGNS.
Ge 1:14 let them be for *s'*, and for seasons, 226
Ex 4: 9 will not believe also these two *s'*, "
17 hand, wherewith thou shalt do *s'*. "
28 all the *s'* which he had commanded "
30 did the *s'* in the sight of the people. "
7: 3 my *s'* and my wonders in the land of "
10: 1 might shew these my *s'* before him: "
2 and my *s'* which I have done among "
Nu 14:11 for all the *s'* which I have shewed "
De 4:34 by *s'*, and by wonders, and by war, "
6:22 the Lord shewed *s'* and wonders, "
7:19 and the *s'*, and the wonders, and the "
26: 8 and with *s'*, and with wonders: "
29: 3 the *s'*, and those great miracles: "
34:11 In all the *s'* and the wonders, which "
Jos 24:17 which did those great *s'* in our sight, "
1Sa 10: 7 when these *s'* are come unto thee, "
9 all those *s'* came to pass that day. "
Ne 9:10 *s'* and wonders upon Pharaoh, and "
Ps 74: 4 they set up their ensigns for *s'*. "
9 We see not our *s'*: there is no more "
78:43 How he had wrought his *s'* in Egypt, "
105:27 shewed his *s'* among them, 1697. "
Isa 8:18 are for *s'* and for wonders in Israel "
Jer 10: 2 not dismayed at the *s'* of heaven; "
32:20 hast set *s'* and wonders in the land "
21 out of the land of Egypt with *s'*, and "
Da 4: 2 I thought it good to shew the *s'* and 852
3 How great are his *s'*! and how "
6:27 and he worketh *s'* and wonders in "
M't 16: 3 ye not discern the *s'* of the times? *4592*
24:24 shall shew great *s'* and wonders; "
M'r 13:22 and shall shew *s'* and wonders, to "
16:17 And these *s'* shall follow them that "
20 and confirming the word with *s'* "
Lu 1:62 they made *s'* to his father, how he *1770*
21:11 *s'* shall there be from heaven. *4592*
25 And there shall be *s'* in the sun, "
Joh 4:48 Except ye see *s'* and wonders, ye "
20:30 many other *s'* truly did Jesus in the "
Ac 2:19 above, and *s'* in the earth beneath; "
22 by miracles and wonders and *s'*, "
43 wonders and *s'* were done by the "
4:30 that *s'* and wonders may be done by "
5:12 were many *s'* and wonders wrought "
7:36 shewed wonders and *s'* in the land "
8:13 miracles and *s'* which were done. "
14: 3 granted *s'* and wonders to be done "
Ro 15:19 Through mighty *s'* and wonders, by "
2Co 12:12 Truly the *s'* of an apostle were "
12 in *s'*, and wonders, and mighty "
2Th 2: 9 of Satan with all power and *s'* and "
Heb 2: 4 witness, both with *s'* and wonders, "

Sihon (*si'-hon*)
Nu 21:21 Israel sent messengers unto *S'*, 5511
23 *S'* would not suffer Israel to pass "
23 but *S'* gathered all his people "
26 For Heshbon was the city of *S'* the "
27 city of *S'* be built and prepared: "
28 a flame from the city of *S'*: it hath "
29 into captivity unto *S'* king of the "
34 him as thou didst unto *S'* king of "
32:33 kingdom of *S'* king of the Amorites, "
De 1: 4 After he had slain *S'* the king of "
2:24 into thine hand *S'* the Amorite, "
26 wilderness of Kedemoth unto *S'* "
30 *S'* king of Heshbon would not let us "
31 have begun to give *S'* and his land "
32 Then *S'* came out against us, he "
3: 2 as thou didst unto *S'* king of the "
6 as we did unto *S'* king of Heshbon, "
4:46 land of *S'* king of the Amorites, "
29: 7 this place, *S'* the king of Heshbon, "
31: 4 shall do unto them as he did to *S'* "
Jos 2:10 the other side Jordan, *S'* and Og, "
9:10 to *S'* king of Heshbon, and to Og "
12: 2 *S'* king of the Amorites, who dwelt "
5 the border of *S'* king of Heshbon. "
13:10 cities of *S'* king of the Amorites, "
21 all the kingdom of *S'* king of the "
21 which were dukes of *S'*, dwelling "
27 kingdom of *S'* king of Heshbon, "
J'g 11:19 Israel sent messengers unto *S'* "
20 But *S'* trusted not Israel to pass "
20 *S'* gathered all his people together, "
21 Lord God of Israel delivered *S'* and "
1Ki 4:19 country of *S'* king of the Amorites, "

Ne 9:22 So they possessed the land of *S'*, 5511
Ps 135:11 *S'* king of the Amorites, and Og "
136:19 *S'* king of the Amorites: for his "
Jer 48:45 and a flame from the midst of *S'*, "

Sihor (*si'-hor*) See also SHIHOR.
Jos 13: 3 From *S'*, which is before Egypt, *7883
Isa 23: 3 And by great waters the seed of *S'*,* "
Jer 2:18 Egypt, to drink the waters of *S'*?* "

Silas (*si'-las*) See also SILVANUS.
Ac 15:22 Barsabas,...*S'*, chief men among *4609*
27 have sent therefore Judas and *S'*, "
32 Judas and *S'*, being prophets also "
34 it pleased *S'* to abide there still. * "
40 And Paul chose *S'*, and departed, "
16:19 they caught Paul and *S'*, and drew "
25 at midnight Paul and *S'* prayed, "
29 and fell down before Paul and *S'*, "
17: 4 and consorted with Paul and *S'*; "
10 sent away Paul and *S'* by night "
14 but *S'* and Timotheus abode there "
15 receiving a commandment unto *S'* "
18: 5 when *S'* and Timotheus were come "

silence
J'g 3:19 thee, O king: who said, Keep *s'*. 2013
Job 4:16 there was *s'*, and I heard a voice, 1827
29:21 waited, and kept *s'* at my counsel. 1826
31:34 that I kept *s'*, and went not out of "
Ps 31:18 Let the lying lips be put to *s'*: * 481
32: 3 When I kept *s'*, my bones waxed 2790
35:22 keep not *s'*: O Lord, be not far "
39: 2 I was dumb with *s'*, I held my 1747
50: 3 shall come, and shall not keep *s'*: 2790
21 hast thou done, and I kept *s'*; "
83: 1 Keep not thou *s'*, O God: hold not 1824
94:17 my soul had almost dwelt in *s'*. 1745
115:17 neither any that go down into *s'*. "
Ec 3: 7 a time to keep *s'*, and a time to 2814
Isa 15: 1 is laid waste, and brought to *s'*; *1820
41: 1 Keep *s'* before me, O islands; and 2790
62: 6 mention of the Lord, keep not *s'*, *1824
65: 6 I will not keep *s'*, but will 2814
Jer 8:14 the Lord our God hath put us to *s'*, 1826
La 2:10 sit upon the ground, and keep *s'*: "
3:28 He sitteth alone and keepeth *s'*, "
Am 5:13 Therefore the prudent shall keep *s'* "
8: 3 shall cast them forth with *s'*. 2013
Hab 2:20 temple: let all the earth keep *s'* "
M't 22:34 he had put the Sadducees to *s'*, *5392*
Ac 15:12 Then all the multitude kept *s'*, *4601*
21:40 when there was made a great *s'*, *4602*
22: 2 to them, they kept the more *s'*: **2271*
1Co 14:28 let him keep *s'* in the church; and *4601*
34 Let your women keep *s'* in the "
1Ti 2:11 Let the woman learn in *s'* with all **2271*
12 over the man, but to be in *s'*. * "
1Pe 2:15 put to *s'* the ignorance of foolish *5392*
Re 8: 1 there was *s'* in heaven about the *4602*

silent
1Sa 2: 9 the wicked shall be *s'* in darkness; 1826
Ps 22: 2 in the night season, and am not *s'*. 1747
28: 1 O Lord my rock; be not *s'* to me: *2790
1 lest, if thou be *s'* to me, I become "
30:12 sing praise to thee, and not be *s'*. 1826
31:17 and let them be *s'* in the grave. "
Isa 47: 5 Sit thou *s'*, and get thee into 1748
Jer 8:14 cities, and let us be *s'* there: for 1826
Zec 2:13 Be *s'*, O all flesh, before the Lord: 2013

silk
Pr 31:22 her clothing is *s'* and purple. *8336
Eze 16:10 linen, and I covered thee with *s'*. 4897
13 raiment was of fine linen, and *s'*, "
Re 18:12 and purple, and *s'*, and scarlet, *2596*

Silla (*sil'-lah*)
2Ki 12:20 Millo, which goeth down to *S'*. 5538

silly
Job 5: 2 man, and envy slayeth the *s'* one. 6601
Ho 7:11 Ephraim also is like a *s'* dove "
2Ti 3: 6 lead captive *s'* women laden with *1133*

Siloah (*si-lo'-ah*) See also SHILOAH; SILOAM.
Ne 3:15 the wall of the pool of *S'* by the *7975

Siloam (*si-lo'-am*) See also SILOAH.
Lu 13: 4 upon whom the tower in *S'* fell, *4611*
Joh 9: 7 him, Go, wash in the pool of *S'*, "
11 said unto me, Go to the pool of *S'*, "

Silvanus (*sil-va'-nus*) See also SILAS.
2Co 1:19 even by me and *S'* and Timotheus, *4610*
1Th 1: 1 Paul, and *S'*, and Timotheus, unto "
2Th 1: 1 Paul, and *S'*, and Timotheus, unto "
1Pe 5:12 By *S'*, a faithful brother unto you, "

silver See also SILVERLINGS; SILVERSMITH.
Ge 13: 2 was very rich in cattle, in *s'*, and 3701
20:16 thy brother a thousand pieces of *s'*: "
23:15 worth four hundred shekels of *s'*; "
16 Abraham weighed to Ephron the *s'*, "
16 four hundred shekels of *s'*, current "
24:35 given him flocks, and herds, and *s'*, "
53 servants brought forth jewels of *s'*, "
37:28 Ishmeelites for twenty pieces of *s'*: "
44: 2 the *s'* cup, in the sack's mouth of "
8 we steal out of thy lord's house *s'* or "
45:22 he gave three hundred pieces of *s'*, "
Ex 3:22 in her house, jewels of *s'*, and "
11: 2 of her neighbour, jewels of *s'*, and "
12:35 of the Egyptians jewels of *s'*, and "
20:23 shall not make with me gods of *s'*, "
21:32 their master thirty shekels of *s'*, "
25: 3 of them; gold, and *s'*, and brass, "
26:19 forty sockets of *s'* under the twenty "
21 And their forty sockets of *s'*; two "
25 boards, and their sockets of *s'*, "
32 gold, upon the four sockets of *s'*. "

Ex 27:10 pillars and their fillets shall be of *s'*.3701
11 the pillars and their fillets of *s'*. "
17 the court shall be filleted with *s'*; "
17 their hooks shall be of *s'*, and their "
31: 4 to work in gold, and in *s'*, and in "
35: 5 the Lord; gold, and *s'*, and brass, "
24 offer an offering of *s'* and brass "
32 to work in gold, and in *s'*, and in "
36:24 forty sockets of *s'* he made under "
26 And their forty sockets of *s'*; two "
30 sockets were sixteen sockets of *s'*, "
36 he cast for them four sockets of *s'*. "
38:10 pillars and their fillets were of *s'*. "
11, 12 pillars and their fillets of *s'*. "
17 the pillars and their fillets of *s'*; "
17 overlaying of their chapiters of *s'*; "
17 of the court were filleted with *s'*. "
19 their hooks of *s'*, and the overlaying "
19 their chapiters and their fillets of *s'*. "
25 the *s'* of them that were numbered "
27 the hundred talents of *s'* were cast "
Le 5:15 with thy estimation by shekels of *s'*, "
27: 3 estimation shall be fifty shekels of *s'*, "
6 be of the male five shekels of *s'*, "
6 for the female...three shekels of *s'*. "
16 be valued at fifty shekels of *s'*. "
Nu 7:13 And his offering was one *s'* charger, "
13 one *s'* bowl of seventy shekels, "
19 for his offering one *s'* charger, "
19 one *s'* bowl of seventy shekels, "
25 His offering was one *s'* charger, "
25 one *s'* bowl of seventy shekels, "
31 His offering was one *s'* charger of "
31 one *s'* bowl of seventy shekels, "
37 His offering was one *s'* charger, "
37 one *s'* bowl of seventy shekels, "
43 His offering was one *s'* charger of "
43 a *s'* bowl of seventy shekels, after "
49 His offering was one *s'* charger "
49 one *s'* bowl of seventy shekels, "
55 His offering was one *s'* charger of "
55 one *s'* bowl of seventy shekels, "
61 His offering was one *s'* charger, "
61 one *s'* bowl of seventy shekels, "
67 His offering was one *s'* charger, "
67 one *s'* bowl of seventy shekels, "
73 His offering was one *s'* charger, "
73 one *s'* bowl of seventy shekels, "
79 His offering was one *s'* charger, "
79 one *s'* bowl of seventy shekels, "
84 chargers of *s'*, twelve *s'* bowls, "
85 Each charger of *s'* weighing an "
85 *s'* vessels weighed two thousand "
10: 2 Make thee two trumpets of *s'*; of a "
22:18 give me his house full of *s'* and gold, "
24:13 give me his house full of *s'* and gold, "
31:22 Only the gold, and the *s'*, the brass, "
De 7:25 thou shalt not desire the *s'* or gold "
8:13 thy *s'* and thy gold is multiplied, "
17:17 multiply to himself *s'* and gold. "
22:19 him in an hundred shekels of *s'*, "
29 damsel's father fifty shekels of *s'*, "
29:17 idols, wood and stone, *s'* and gold, "
Jos 6:19 But all the *s'*, and gold, and vessels "
24 only the *s'*, and the gold, and the "
7:21 and two hundred shekels of *s'*, and "
21 midst of my tent, and the *s'* under it. "
22 hid in his tent, and the *s'* under it. "
24 and the *s'*, and the garment, and the "
22: 8 with *s'*, and with gold, and with "
24:32 for an hundred pieces of *s'*: *7192
J'g 9: 4 him threescore and ten pieces of *s'* 3701
16: 5 of us eleven hundred pieces of *s'*. "
17: 2 The eleven hundred shekels of *s'* "
2 mine ears, behold, the *s'* is with me; "
3 the eleven hundred shekels of *s'* "
3 dedicated the *s'* unto the Lord "
4 took two hundred shekels of *s'*, "
10 and I will give thee ten shekels of *s'* "
1Sa 2:36 and crouch to him for a piece of *s'* "
9: 8 the fourth part of a shekel of *s'*: "
2Sa 8:10 brought with him vessels of *s'*, "
11 *s'* and gold that he had dedicated "
18:11 have given thee ten shekels of *s'*, "
12 receive a thousand shekels of *s'* in "
21: 4 We will have no *s'* nor gold of Saul, "
24:24 and the oxen for fifty shekels of *s'*. "
1Ki 7:51 even the *s'*, and the gold, and the "
10:21 were of pure gold; none were of *s'*: "
22 bringing gold, and *s'*, ivory, and "
25 vessels of *s'*, and vessels of gold, "
27 *s'* to be in Jerusalem as stones, "
29 for six hundred shekels of *s'*, and "
15:15 into the house of the Lord, *s'*, and "
18 Asa took all the *s'* and the gold "
19 unto thee a present of *s'* and gold; "
16:24 of Shemer for two talents of *s'*, "
20: 3 Thy *s'* and thy gold is mine; thy "
5 Thou shalt deliver me thy *s'*, and "
7 and for my *s'*, and for my gold; "
39 or else thou shalt pay a talent of *s'*. "
2Ki 5: 5 and took with him ten talents of *s'*, "
22 give them, I pray thee, a talent of *s'*, "
23 bound two talents of *s'* in two bags, "
6:25 was sold for fourscore pieces of *s'*, "
25 of dove's dung for five pieces of *s'*. "
7: 8 and carried thence *s'*, and gold, and "
12:13 the house of the Lord bowls of *s'*, "
13 any vessels of gold, or vessels of *s'*, "
14:14 And he took all the gold and *s'*, and "
15:19 gave Pul a thousand talents of *s'*, "
20 of each man fifty shekels of *s'*, to "
16: 8 Ahaz took the *s'* and gold that was "
18:14 Judah three hundred talents of *s'* "
15 Hezekiah gave him all the *s'* that "
20:13 the *s'*, and the gold, and the spices, "

2Ki 22: 4 may sum the s' which is brought *3701
23: 33 tribute of an hundred talents of s', "
35 Jehoiakim gave the s' and the gold "
35 he exacted the s' and the gold of the "
25: 15 were of gold, in gold, and of s', in s'; "
1Ch 18: 10 all manner of vessels of gold and s' "
11 s' and the gold that he brought "
19: 6 sent a thousand talents of s' to hire "
22: 14 a thousand thousand talents of s'; "
16 Of the gold, the s', and the brass, "
28: 14 of all manner of service; s' also "
14 for all instruments of s' by weight 3701
15 for the candlesticks of s' by weight, "
16 and likewise s' for the tables of s': "
17 for every bason; and likewise s' *
17 by weight for every bason of s': 3701
29: 2 of gold, and the s' for things of s', "
3 own proper good, of gold and s', "
4 seven thousand talents of refined s', "
5 of gold, and the s' for things of s', "
7 and of s' ten thousand talents, and "
2Ch 1: 15 made s' and gold...as plenteous "
17 for six hundred shekels of s', and "
2: 7 cunning to work in gold, and in s', "
14 skilful to work in gold, and in s', "
5: 1 and the s', and the gold, and all the "
9: 14 brought gold and s' to Solomon. "
20 were of pure gold: none were of s'; "
21 bringing gold, and s', ivory, and "
24 vessels of s', and vessels of gold, "
27 made s' in Jerusalem as stones, "
15: 18 dedicated, s', and gold, and vessels. "
16: 2 Asa brought out s' and gold out of "
3 behold, I have sent thee s' and gold; "
17: 11 brought...presents, and tribute s'; "
21: 3 father gave them great gifts of s', "
24: 14 spoons, and vessels of gold and s'. "
25: 6 Israel for an hundred talents of s'. "
24 And he took all the gold and the s', "
27: 5 same year an hundred talents of s', "
32: 27 he made himself treasuries for s', "
36: 3 the land in an hundred talents of s' "
Ezr 1: 4 men of his place help him with s' "
6 hands with vessels of s', with gold, "
9 of gold, a thousand chargers of s', "
10 s' basons of a second sort four "
11 All the vessels of gold and of s' "
2: 69 and five thousand pound of s', "
5: 14 And the vessels also of gold and s' 3702
6: 5 also let the golden and s' vessels "
7: 15 And to carry the s' and gold, which "
16 all the s' and gold that thou canst "
18 with the rest of the s' and the gold, "
22 Unto an hundred talents of s', and "
8: 25 And weighed unto them the s', 3701
26 six hundred and fifty talents of s', "
26 and s' vessels an hundred talents, "
28 and the s' and the gold are a freewill "
30 the weight of the s', and the gold, "
33 was the s' and the gold...weighed "
Ne 5: 15 and wine, beside forty shekels of s'; "
7: 71 and two hundred pound of s'. "
72 gold, and two thousand pound of s', "
Es 1: 6 to s' rings and pillars of marble: "
6 the beds were of gold and s', upon "
3: 9 I will pay ten thousand talents of s' "
11 s' is given to thee, the people also, "
Job 3: 15 who filled their houses with s': "
22: 25 and thou shalt have plenty of s'. "
27: 16 Though he heap up s' as the dust, "
17 and the innocent shall divide the s'. "
28: 1 Surely there is a vein for the s', "
15 s' be weighed for the price thereof. "
Ps 12: 6 as s' tried in a furnace of earth, "
66: 10 thou hast tried us, as s' is tried. "
68: 13 the wings of a dove covered with s', "
30 submit himself with pieces of s': "
105: 37 He brought them forth also with s' "
115: 4 Their idols are s' and gold, the work "
119: 72 me than thousands of gold and s'. "
135: 15 idols of the heathen are s' and gold, "
Pr 2: 4 If thou seekest her as s', and "
3: 14 is better than the merchandise of s', "
8: 10 Receive my instruction, and not s'; "
19 and my revenue than choice s'. "
10: 20 tongue of the just is as choice s': "
16: 16 rather to be chosen than s'! "
17: 3 fining pot is for s', and the furnace "
22: 1 and loving favour rather than s' and "
25: 4 Take away the dross from the s', "
11 like apples of gold in pictures of s'. "
26: 23 a potsherd covered with s' dross. "
27: 21 fining pot for s', and the furnace "
Ec 2: 8 I gathered me also s' and gold, and "
5: 10 He that loveth s' shall not be "
10 shall not be satisfied with s': "
12: 6 Or ever the s' cord be loosed, or the "
Ca 1: 11 borders of gold with studs of s'. "
3: 10 He made the pillars thereof of s', "
8: 9 will build upon her a palace of s': "
11 was to bring a thousand pieces of s'. "
Isa 1: 22 Thy s' is become dross, thy wine "
2: 7 Their land also is full of s' and gold, "
20 day a man shall cast his idols of s', "
13: 17 Medes...which shall not regard s'; "
30: 22 covering of thy graven images of s', "
31: 7 man shall cast away his idols of s', "
39: 2 the s', and the gold, and the spices, "
40: 19 with gold, and casteth s' chains. "
46: 6 and weigh s' in the balance, and "
48: 10 I have refined thee, but not with s'; "
60: 9 their s' and their gold with them, "
17 and for iron I will bring s', and for "
Jer 6: 30 Reprobate s' shall men call them, "
10: 4 They deck it with s' and with gold; "
9 S' spread into plates is brought "

Jer 32: 9 even seventeen shekels of s'. 3701
52: 19 gold, and that which was of s' in s', "
Eze 7: 19 shall cast their s' in the streets, "
19 their s' and their gold shall not be "
16: 13 wast thou decked with gold and s'; "
17 fair jewels of my gold and of my s', "
22: 18 they are even the dross of s'. "
20 they gather s', and brass, and iron, "
22 As s' is melted in the midst of the "
27: 12 with s', iron, tin, and lead, they "
28: 4 gold and s' into thy treasures: "
38: 13 to carry away s' and gold, to take "
Da 2: 32 gold, his breast and his arms of s', 3702
35 clay, the brass, the s', and the gold, "
45 brass, the clay, the s', and the gold; "
5: 2 to bring the golden and s' vessels "
4 praised the gods of gold, and of s', "
23 thou hast praised the gods of s', "
11: 8 with their precious vessels of s' 3701
38 shall he honour with gold, and s', "
43 the treasures of gold and of s', and "
Ho 2: 8 and multiplied her s' and gold, "
3: 2 her to me for fifteen pieces of s', "
8: 4 of their s' and their gold have they "
9: 6 pleasant places for their s', nettles "
13: 2 them molten images of their s', and "
Joe 3: 5 ye have taken my s' and my gold, "
Am 2: 6 they sold the righteous for s', and "
8: 6 That we may buy the poor for s', "
Na 2: 9 Take ye the spoil of s', take the "
Hab 2: 19 it is laid over with gold and s', and "
Zep 1: 11 all they that bear s' are cut off: "
18 Neither their s' nor their gold shall "
Hag 2: 8 s' is mine, and the gold is mine, "
Zec 6: 11 Then take s' and gold, and make "
9: 3 heaped up s' as the dust, and fine "
11: 12 for my price thirty pieces of s'. "
13 I took the thirty pieces of s', and "
13: 9 and will refine them as s' is refined, "
14: 14 together, gold, and s', and apparel, "
Mal 3: 3 sit as a refiner and purifier of s': "
3 and purge them as gold and s', "
M't 10: 9 neither gold, nor s', nor brass in *696*
26: 15 with him for thirty pieces of s'. *694*
27: 3 the thirty pieces of s' to the chief "
5 he cast down the pieces of s' in the "
6 the chief priests took the s' pieces, "
9 took the thirty pieces of s', the price "
Lu 15: 8 what woman having ten pieces...s', *1406*
Ac 3: 6 said, S' and gold have I none; but *694*
17: 29 the Godhead is like unto gold, or s', *696*
19: 19 found it fifty thousand pieces of s'. *694*
24 which make s' shrines for Diana, *693*
20: 33 I have coveted no man's s', or gold, *694*
1Co 3: 12 this foundation gold, s', precious *696*
2Ti 2: 20 not only vessels of gold and of s', *693*
Jas 5: 3 Your gold and s' is cankered; and *696*
1Pe 1: 18 corruptible things, as s' and gold, *694*
Re 9: 20 devils, and idols of gold, and s', and *693*
18: 12 The merchandise of gold, and s', *696*

silverlings
Isa 7: 23 a thousand vines at a thousand s', 3701

silversmith
Ac 19: 24 certain man named Demetrius, a s', *695*

Simeon (*sim'-e-un*) See also SHIMEON; SIMEONITES; SIMON.
Ge 29: 33 also: and she called his name S'. 8095
34: 25 of the sons of Jacob, S' and Levi, "
30 And Jacob said to S' and Levi, Ye "
35: 23 and S', and Levi, and Judah, and "
42: 24 and took from them S', and bound "
36 Joseph is not, and S' is not, and ye "
43: 23 And he brought S' out unto them. "
46: 10 And the sons of S'; Jemuel, and "
48: 5 as Reuben and S', they shall be "
49: 5 S' and Levi are brethren; "
Ex 1: 2 Reuben, S', Levi, and Judah, "
6: 15 And the sons of S'; Jemuel, and "
15 woman: these are the families of S'. "
Nu 1: 6 Of S'; Shelumiel the son of "
22 Of the children of S', by their "
23 even of the tribe of S', were fifty "
2: 12 by him shall be the tribe of S': "
12 captain of the children of S' shall "
7: 36 prince of the children of S', did "
10: 19 of the tribe of the children of S' "
13: 5 Of the tribe of S', Shaphat the son "
26: 12 The sons of S' after their families: "
34: 20 of the tribe of the children of S', "
De 27: 12 S', and Levi, and Judah, and "
Jos 19: 1 the second lot came forth to S', "
1, 8 children of S' according to their "
9 inheritance of the children of S': "
9 children of S' had their inheritance "
21: 4 and out of the tribe of S', and out *8099
9 of the tribe of the children of S', 8095
J'g 1: 3 Judah said unto S' his brother, "
3 into thy lot. So S' went with him. "
17 Judah went with S' his brother, "
1Ch 2: 1 Reuben, S', Levi, and Judah, "
4: 24 The sons of S' were, Nemuel, and "
42 even of the sons of S', five hundred "
6: 65 of the tribe of the children of S', "
12: 25 Of the children of S', mighty men "
2Ch 15: 9 Ephraim and Manasseh,...out of S': "
34: 6 and S', even unto Naphtali, with "
Eze 48: 24 west side, S' shall have a portion. "
25 by the border of S', from the east "
33 one gate of S', one gate of "
Lu 2: 25 Jerusalem, whose name was S'; *4826*
34 And S' blessed them, and said unto "
3: 30 Which was the son of S', which was* "
Ac 13: 1 and S' that was called Niger, and* "
15: 14 S' hath declared how God at the * "
Re 7: 7 the tribe of S' were sealed twelve "

Simeonites (*sim'-e-un-ites*)
Nu 25: 14 of a chief house among the S'. 8099
26: 14 These are the families of the S', "
1Ch 27: 16 of the S', Shephatiah the son of "

similitude See also SIMILITUDES.
Nu 12: 8 the s' of the Lord shall he behold: *8544
De 4: 12 voice of the words, but saw no s'; * "
15 ye saw no manner of s' on the day * "
16 the s' of any figure, the likeness of * "
2Ch 4: 3 under it was the s' of oxen, which 1823
Ps 106: 20 their glory into the s' of an ox *8403
144: 12 polished after the s' of a palace: * "
Da 10: 16 s' of the sons of men touched my 1823
Ro 5: 14 the s' of Adam's transgression, *3667*
Heb 7: 15 the s' of Melchisedec there ariseth *3665*
Jas 3: 9 are made after the s' of God. *3669*

similitudes
Ho 12: 10 and used s', by the ministry of the 1819

Simon (*si'-mun*) See also BAR-JONA; NIGER; PETER; SIMEON; SIMON'S; ZELOTES.
M't 4: 18 S' called Peter, and Andrew his *4613*
10: 2 The first, S', who is called Peter, "
4 S' the Canaanite, and Judas "
13: 55 and Joses, and S', and Judas? "
16: 16 S' Peter answered and said, Thou "
17 Blessed art thou, S' Bar-jona: for "
17: 25 What thinkest thou, S'? of whom "
26: 6 in the house of S' the leper, "
27: 32 a man of Cyrene, S' by name: him "
M'r 1: 16 he saw S' and Andrew his brother "
29 entered into the house of S' and "
36 S' and they that were with him "
3: 16 And S' he surnamed Peter; "
18 Thaddæus, and S' the Canaanite, "
6: 3 and Joses, and of Juda, and S'? "
14: 3 in the house of S' the leper, as he "
37 saith unto Peter, S', sleepest thou? "
15: 21 they compel one S' a Cyrenian, who "
Lu 5: 4 he said unto S', Launch out into "
5 And S' answering said unto him, "
8 When S' Peter saw it, he fell down "
10 which were partners with S'. "
10 Jesus said unto S', Fear not; from "
6: 14 S', (whom he also named Peter,) "
15 of Alphæus, and S' called Zelotes, "
7: 40 S', I have somewhat to say unto "
43 S' answered and said, I suppose "
44 unto S', Seest thou this woman? "
22: 31 S', S', behold, Satan hath desired "
23: 26 away, they laid hold upon one S', "
24: 34 indeed, and hath appeared to S'. "
Joh 1: 40 was Andrew, S' Peter's brother. "
41 He first findeth his own brother S', "
42 Thou art S' the son of Jona: thou "
6: 8 Andrew, S' Peter's brother, saith "
68 Then S' Peter answered him, Lord, "
71 of Judas Iscariot the son of S': for "
13: 6 Then cometh he to S' Peter: and "
9 S' Peter saith unto him, Lord, not "
24 S' Peter therefore beckoned to him, "
26 it to Judas Iscariot, the son of S'. "
36 S' Peter said unto him, Lord, "
18: 10 S' Peter having a sword drew it, "
15 S' Peter followed Jesus, and so did "
25 S' Peter stood and warmed himself. "
20: 2 runneth, and cometh to S' Peter, "
6 cometh S' Peter following him, and "
21: 2 There were together S' Peter, and "
3 S' Peter saith unto them, I go a "
7 when S' Peter heard that it was "
11 S' Peter went up, and drew the net "
15 Jesus saith to S' Peter, S', son of "
16, 17 S', son of Jonas, lovest thou me? "
Ac 1: 13 S' Zelotes, and Judas the brother "
8: 9 there was a certain man, called S', "
13 Then S' himself believed also: and "
18 when S' saw that through laying "
24 Then answered S', and said, Pray "
9: 43 days in Joppa with one S' a tanner. "
10: 5 for one S', whose surname is Peter: "
6 He lodgeth with one S' a tanner, "
18 S', which was surnamed Peter, "
32 call hither S', whose surname is "
32 in the house of one S' a tanner by "
11: 13 call for S', whose surname is Peter; "
2Pe 1: 1 S' Peter, a servant and an apostle "

Simon's (*si'-muns*)
M'r 1: 30 But S' wife's mother lay sick of a *4613*
Lu 4: 38 and entered into S' house. And * "
38 S' wife's mother was taken with a * "
5: 3 into one of the ships, which was S', "
Joh 12: 4 disciples, Judas Iscariot, S' son, * "
13: 2 the heart of Judas Iscariot, S' son, "
Ac 10: 17 had made enquiry for S' house, "

simple
Ps 19: 7 Lord is sure, making wise the s'. 6612
116: 6 The Lord preserveth the s': I was "
119: 130 giveth understanding unto the s'. "
Pr 1: 4 To give subtilty to the s', to the "
22 How long, ye s' ones, will ye love "
32 the turning away of the s' shall "
7: 7 And beheld among the s' ones, I "
8: 5 O ye s', understand wisdom: and, "
9: 4 Whoso is s', let him turn in hither: "
13 she is s', and knoweth nothing. 6615
16 Whoso is s', let him turn in hither: 6612
14: 15 The s' believeth every word: but "
18 s' inherit folly: but the prudent "
19: 25 a scorner, and the s' will beware: "
21: 11 is punished, the s' is made wise: "
22: 3 the s' pass on, and are punished. "
27: 12 the s' pass on, and are punished. "
Eze 45: 20 that erreth, and for him that is s': "

Ro 16:18 deceive the hearts of the s'. * 172
19 is good, and s' concerning evil. 185

simplicity
2Sa 15:11 and they went in their s', and they 8537
Pr 1:22 ye simple ones, will ye love s'? 6612
Ro 12: 8 that giveth, let him do it with s'; * 572
2Co 1:12 that in s' and godly sincerity, not * "
11: 3 from the s' that is in Christ. "

Simri (*sim'-ri*) See also SHIMRI.
1Ch 26:10 Hosah,...had sons; S' the chief, *8113

sin See also SINFUL; SINNED; SINNEST; SINNETH; SINNING; SINS.
Ge 4: 7 doest not well, s' lieth at the door. 2403
18:20 because their s' is very grievous; "
20: 9 me and on my kingdom a great s'? 2401
31:36 what is my s', that thou hast so 2403
39: 9 wickedness, and s' against God? 2398
42:22 saying, Do not s' against the child; "
50:17 of thy brethren, and their s'; 2403
Ex 10:17 forgive,...my s' only this once, "
20:20 before your faces, that ye s' not. 2398
23:33 lest they make thee s' against me: "
29:14 the camp: it is a s' offering. 2403
36 every day a bullock for a s' offering "
30:10 of the s' offering of atonements: "
32:21 brought so great a s' upon them? 2401
30 people, Ye have sinned a great s': "
30 make an atonement for your s'. 2403
31 this people have sinned a great s'. 2401
32 now, if thou wilt forgive their s'—; 2403
34 visit I will visit their s' upon them. "
34: 7 iniquity and transgression and s', 2402
9 pardon our iniquity and our s', 2403
Le 4: 2 a soul shall s' through ignorance 2398
3 If the priest that is anointed do s' "
3 according to the s' of the people; * 819
3 then let him bring for his s', 2403
3 unto the Lord for a s' offering. "
8 fat of the bullock for the s' offering; "
13 of Israel s' through ignorance, *7686
14 When the s', which they have 2403
14 offer a young bullock for the s', "
20 with the bullock for a s' offering, "
21 a s' offering for the congregation. "
23 if his s', wherein he hath sinned, "
24 before the Lord: it is a s' offering. "
25 take of the blood of the s' offering "
26 for him as concerning his s', "
27 any one of the common people s' 2398
28 Or if his s', which he hath sinned, 2403
28 for his s' which he hath sinned. "
29 upon the head of the s' offering, "
29 slay the s' offering in the place of "
32 if he bring a lamb for a s' offering, "
33 upon the head of the s' offering, "
33 slay it for a s' offering in the place "
34 take of the blood of the s' offering "
35 make an atonement for his s' that "
5: 1 if a soul s', and hear the voice of 2398
6 for his s' which he hath sinned, 2403
6 a kid of the goats, for a s' offering; "
6 for him concerning his s'. "
7 one for a s' offering, and the other "
8 which is for the s' offering first, "
9 the blood of the s' offering upon the "
9 of the altar: it is a s' offering. "
10 him for his s' which he hath sinned, "
11 ephah of fine flour for a s' offering; "
11 thereon: for it is a s' offering. "
12 unto the Lord: it is a s' offering. "
13 touching his s' that he hath sinned "
15 s' through ignorance, in the holy 2398
17 And if a soul s', and commit any of "
6: 2 If a soul s', and commit a trespass "
17 is most holy, as is the s' offering, 2403
25 This is the law of the s' offering: "
25 shall the s' offering be killed before "
26 that offereth it for s' shall eat it: 2398
30 no s' offering, whereof any of the 2403
7: 7 As the s' offering is, so is the "
37 and of the s' offering, and of the "
8: 2 and a bullock for the s' offering, "
14 the bullock for the s' offering: "
14 of the bullock for the s' offering. "
9: 2 thee a young calf for a s' offering, "
3 a kid of the goats for a s' offering; "
7 the altar, and offer thy s' offering, "
8 and slew the calf of the s' offering, "
10 above the liver of the s' offering, "
15 was the s' offering for the people, "
15 slew it, and offered it for s', as the "
22 from offering of the s' offering, "
10:16 sought the goat of the s' offering, "
17 have ye not eaten the s' offering in "
19 have they offered their s' offering "
19 I had eaten the s' offering to day, "
12: 6 or a turtledove, for a s' offering, "
8 and the other for a s' offering: "
14:13 where he shall kill the s' offering "
13 as the s' offering is the priest's, so "
19 the priest shall offer the s' offering, "
22 and the one shall be a s' offering, "
31 able to get, the one for a s' offering, "
15:15 the one for a s' offering, and the "
30 shall offer the one for a s' offering, "
16: 3 a young bullock for a s' offering, "
5 kids of the goats for a s' offering, "
6 offer his bullock of the s' offering, "
9 fell, and offer him for a s' offering. "
11 bring the bullock of the s' offering, "
11 kill the bullock of the s' offering, "
15 he kill the goat of the s' offering, "
25 fat of the s' offering shall he burn "
27 And the bullock for the s' offering, "

Le 16:27 and the goat for the s' offering, 2403
19:17 and not suffer s' upon him. 2399
22 for his s' which he hath done: 2403
22 the s' which he hath done shall be "
20:20 they shall bear their s'; they shall 2399
22: 9 lest they bear s' for it, and die "
23:19 kid of the goats for a s' offering, 2403
24:15 curseth his God shall bear his s'. 2399
Nu 5: 6 commit any s' that men commit, 2403
7 Then they shall confess their s' "
6:11 offer the one for a s' offering, and "
14 without blemish for a s' offering, "
16 shall offer his s' offering, and his "
7:16, 22, 28, 34, 40, 46, 52, 58, 64, 70,
76, 82 of the goats for a s' offering: "
87 the kids of the goats for s' offering "
8: 8 shalt thou take for a s' offering. "
12 shalt offer the one for a s' offering, "
9:13 that man shall bear his s'. 2399
12:11 lay not the s' upon us, wherein 2403
15:24 kid of the goats for a s' offering. "
25 their s' offering before the Lord, "
27 if any soul s' through ignorance, 2398
27 of the first year for a s' offering. 2403
16:22 shall one man s', and wilt thou be 2398
18: 9 and every s' offering of theirs, and 2403
22 lest they bear s', and die. 2399
32 ye shall bear no s' by reason of it, "
19: 9 separation: it is a purification for s'. 2403
17 burnt heifer of purification for s', "
27: 3 but died in his own s', and had no 2399
28:15 kid of the goats for a s' offering 2403
22 one goat for a s' offering, to make "
29: 5 kid of the goats for a s' offering, "
11 kid of the goats for a s' offering; "
11 beside the s' offering of atonement, "
16, 19 kid of the goats for a s' offering; "
22 one goat for a s' offering; beside "
25 kid of the goats for a s' offering; "
28, 31, 34, 38 one goat for a s' offering; "
32:23 be sure your s' will find you out. "
De 9:21 I took your s', the calf which ye had "
27 to their wickedness, nor to their s': "
15: 9 thee, and it be s' unto thee. 2399
19:15 for any iniquity, or for any s', 2403
15 in any s' that he sinneth: at the 2399
20:18 so should ye s' against the Lord 2398
21:22 And if a man have committed a s' 2399
22:26 the damsel no s' worthy of death: "
23:21 thee; and it would be s' in thee. "
22 to vow, it shall be no s' in thee. "
24: 4 thou shalt not cause the land to s', 2398
15 the Lord, and it be s' unto thee. 2399
16 shall be put to death for his own s'. "
1Sa 2:17 the s' of the young men was very 2403
25 If one man s' against another, the 2398
25 but if a man s' against the Lord, "
12:23 God forbid that I should s' against "
14:33 people s' against the Lord, in that "
34 s' not against the Lord in eating "
38 see wherein this s' hath been this 2403
15:23 rebellion is as the s' of witchcraft, "
25 I pray thee, pardon my s', and turn "
19: 4 Let not the king s' against his 2398
5 wilt thou s' against innocent blood, "
20: 1 what is my s' before thy father, 2403
2Sa 12:13 Lord also hath put away thy s'; "
1Ki 8:34 forgive the s' of thy people Israel, "
35 thy name, and turn from their s', "
36 and forgive the s' of thy servants, "
46 If they s' against thee, (for there 2398
12:30 And this thing became a s': for 2403
13:34 became s' unto...house of Jeroboam, "
14:16 the sins of Jeroboam, who did s', *2398
16 and who made Israel to s'. "
15:26 way of his father, and in his s'. 2403
26 wherewith he made Israel to s'. 2398
30 sinned, and which he made Israel s'. "
34 the way of Jeroboam, and in his s' 2403
34 wherewith he made Israel to s'. 2398
16: 2 hast made my people Israel to s', "
13 by which they made Israel to s', "
19 the way of Jeroboam, and in his s' 2403
19 which he did, to make Israel to s'. 2398
26 way of Jeroboam...and in his s' 2403
26 wherewith he made Israel to s', 2398
17:18 me to call my s' to remembrance, 5771
21:22 me to anger, and made Israel to s'. 2398
22:52 Jeroboam...who made Israel to s': "
2Ki 3: 3 Jeroboam...which made Israel to s'; "
10:29 Jeroboam...who made Israel to s', "
31 Jeroboam, which made Israel to s'. "
12:16 s' money was not brought into the
13: 2 of Nebat, which made Israel to s'; 2398
6 of Jeroboam, who made Israel s', "
11 Jeroboam...who made Israel s': "
14: 6 shall be put to death for his own s'. 2399
24 Jeroboam...who made Israel to s'. 2398
15: 9, 18, 24, 28 who made Israel to s'. "
17:21 and made them s' [2398] a great s'. 2401
21:11 and hath made Judah also to s' 2398
16 beside his s' wherewith he made 2403
16 wherewith he made Judah to s', 2398
17 he did, and his s' that he sinned, 2403
23:15 Jeroboam...who made Israel to s', 2398
2Ch 6:22 If a man s' against his neighbour, "
25 forgive the s' of thy people Israel, 2403
26 thy name, and turn from their s', "
27 and forgive the s' of thy servants, "
36 If they s' against thee, (for there 2398
7:14 heaven, and will forgive their s', 2403
25: 4 every man shall die for his own s'. 2399
29:21 for a s' offering for the kingdom, 2403
23 for the s' offering before the king "
24 s' offering should be made for all "
Ezr 6:17 and for a s' offering for all Israel, 2409

Ezr 8:35 twelve he goats for a s' offering: 2403
Ne 4: 5 and let not their s' be blotted out "
6:13 should be afraid, and do so, and s', 2398
10:33 s' offerings to make an atonement 2403
13:26 Did not Solomon king of Israel s' 2398
26 did outlandish women cause to s'. "
Job 2:10 all this did not Job s' with his lips. "
5:24 thy habitation, and shalt not s'. * "
10: 6 and searchest after my s'? 2403
14 If I s', then thou markest me, and 2398
13:23 know my transgression and my s'. 2403
14:16 dost thou not watch over my s'? "
20:11 bones are full of the s' of his youth,*
31:30 have I suffered my mouth to s' 2398
34:37 he addeth rebellion unto his s', 2403
35: 3 I have, if I be cleansed from my s'?*"
Ps 4: 4 Stand in awe, and s' not: commune 2398
32: 1 is forgiven, whose s' is covered. 2401
5 I acknowledged my s' unto thee, 2403
5 thou forgavest the iniquity of my s'. "
38: 3 rest in my bones because of my s'. "
18 iniquity; I will be sorry for my s'. "
39: 1 ways, that I s' not with my tongue: 2398
40: 6 s' offering hast thou not required. 2401
51: 2 and cleanse me from my s'. 2403
3 and my s' is ever before me. "
5 in s' did my mother conceive me. 2399
59: 3 my transgression, nor for my s', 2403
12 the s' of their mouth and the words "
85: 2 thou hast covered all their s'. "
109: 7 and let his prayer become s'. 2401
14 and let not the s' of his mother be 2403
119:11 that I might not s' against thee. 2398
Pr 10:16 to life: the fruit of the wicked to s'. *2403
19 of words there wanteth not s': *6588
14: 9 Fools make a mock at s': but * 817
34 but s' is a reproach to any people. 2403
20: 9 heart clean, I am pure from my s'? "
21: 4 and the plowing of the wicked, is s'. "
24: 9 The thought of foolishness is s': "
Ec 5: 6 thy mouth to cause thy flesh to s'; 2398
Isa 3: 9 they declare their s' as Sodom, 2403
5:18 and s' as it were with a cart rope: 2402
6: 7 is taken away, and thy s' purged. 2403
27: 9 is all the fruit to take away his s'; "
30: 1 spirit, that they may add s' to s': "
31: 7 hands have made unto you for a s'. 2399
53:10 make his soul an offering for s', 817
12 he bare the s' of many, and made 2399
Jer 16:10 or what is our s' that we have 2403
18 their iniquity and their s' double; "
17: 1 s' of Judah is written with a pen of "
3 spoil, and thy high places for s', "
18:23 neither blot out their s' from thy "
31:34 I will remember their s' no more. "
32:35 abomination, to cause Judah to s'. 2398
36: 3 forgive their iniquity and their s'. 2403
51: 5 was filled with s' against the Holy* 817
La 4: 6 the punishment of the s' of Sodom, 2403
Eze 3:20 warning, he shall die in his s', 2403
21 man, that the righteous s' not, 2398
21 and he doth not s', he shall surely "
18:24 and in his s' that he hath sinned, 2403
33:14 if he turn from his s', and do that "
40:39 burnt offering and the s' offering "
42:13 meat offering, and the s' offering, "
43:19 a young bullock for a s' offering. "
21 the bullock also of the s' offering, "
22 without blemish for a s' offering; "
25 every day a goat for a s' offering: "
44:27 he shall offer his s' offering, saith "
29 meat offering, and the s' offering, "
45:17 he shall prepare the s' offering, and "
19 take of the blood of the s' offering, "
22 the land a bullock for a s' offering. "
23 of the goats daily for a s' offering. "
25 days, according to the s' offering, "
46:20 trespass offering and the s' offering "
Da 9:20 my s' and the s' of my people Israel "
Ho 4: 8 They eat up the s' of my people, "
8:11 hath made many altars to s', ‡2398
11 altars shall be unto him to s'. ‡ "
10: 8 places also of Aven, the s' of Israel, 2403
12: 8 none iniquity in me that were s'. 2399
13: 2 And now they s' more and more, 2398
12 Ephraim is bound up; his s' is hid. 2403
Am 8:14 that swear by the s' of Samaria, 819
Mic 1:13 she is the beginning of the s' to 2403
3: 8 transgression, and to Israel his s'. "
6: 7 of my body for the s' of my soul? "
Zec 13: 1 fountain...for s' and...uncleanness. "
M't 12:31 All manner of s' and blasphemy 266
18:21 oft shall my brother s' against me, 264
Joh 1:29 taketh away the s' of the world. 266
5:14 s' no more, lest a worse thing 264
8: 7 He that is without s' among you, 361
11 condemn thee: go, and s' no more. 264
34 committeth s' is the servant of s'. 266
46 Which of you convinceth me of s'? "
9: 2 Master, who did s', this man, or his 264
41 ye were blind, ye should have no s': 266
41 We see; therefore your s' remaineth. "
15:22 unto them, they had not had s': but "
22 now they have no cloke for their s'. "
24 other man did, they had not had s': "
16: 8 he will reprove the world of s', and "
9 Of s', because they believe not on me; "
19:11 delivered me...hath the greater s'. "
Ac 7:60 Lord, lay not this s' to their charge. "
Ro 3: 9 Gentiles, that they are all under s'; "
20 for by the law is the knowledge of s'. "
4: 8 whom the Lord will not impute s'. "
5:12 by one man s' entered into the world, "
12 into the world, and death by s'; "
13 until the law s' was in the world: "
13 s' is not imputed when there is no "

Ro 5:20 But where s· abounded, grace did 266
21 That as s· hath reigned unto death, "
6: 1 Shall we continue in s·, that grace "
2 How shall we that are dead to s·, live"
6 the body of s· might be destroyed, "
6 henceforth we should not serve s·. "
7 For he that is dead is freed from s·. "
10 in that he died, he died unto s· once:"
11 ye also...to be dead indeed unto s·, "
12 Let not s· therefore reign in your "
13 of unrighteousness unto s·: "
14 s· shall not have dominion over you:"
15 shall we s·, because we are not under264
16 whether of s· unto death, or of 266
17 that ye were the servants of s·, but "
18 Being then made free from s·, ye "
20 For when ye were the servants of s·, "
22 But now being made free from s·, "
23 For the wages of s· is death; but the "
7: 7 Is the law s·? God forbid. Nay, "
7 I had not known s·, but by the law: "
8 But s·, taking occasion by the "
8 For without the law s· was dead. "
9 the commandment came, s· revived, "
11 For s·, taking occasion by the "
13 But s·, that it might appear s·, "
13 that s· by the commandment might "
14 but I am carnal, sold under s·. "
17, 20 it, but s· that dwelleth in me. "
23 me into captivity to the law of s· "
25 God; but with the flesh the law of s·."
8: 2 me free from the law of s· and death."
3 likeness for sinful flesh, and for s·, "
3 condemned s· in the flesh: "
10 you, the body is dead because of s·; "
14:23 for whatsoever is not of faith is s·. "
1Co 6:18 Every s· that a man doeth is without265
8:12 when ye s· so against the brethren,*264
12 weak conscience, ye s· against Christ."
15:34 Awake to righteousness, and s· not; "
56 The sting of death is s·; and the 266
56 and the strength of s· is the law. "
2Co 5:21 him to be s· for us, who knew no s·; "
Ga 2:17 is therefore Christ the minister of s·?"
3:22 hath concluded all under s·, that "
Eph 4:26 Be ye angry, and s· not: let not the264
2Th 2: 3 that man of s· be revealed, the son 266
1Ti 5:20 Them that s· rebuke before all, 264
Heb 3:13 through the deceitfulness of s· 266
4:15 like as we are, yet without s·. "
9:26 hath he appeared to put away s· "
28 appear...without s· unto salvation. "
10: 6 burnt offerings and sacrifices for s· "
8 burnt offerings and offering for s· "
18 is, there is no more offering for s·. "
26 if we s· wilfully after that we have 264
11:25 than to enjoy the pleasures of s· for266
12: 1 s· which doth so easily beset us, "
4 unto blood, striving against s·. "
13:11 sanctuary by the high priest for s·, "
Jas 1:15 it bringeth forth s·: and s·, when it "
2: 9 respect of persons, ye commit s·, "
4:17 and doeth it not, to him it is s·. "
1Pe 2:22 Who did no s·, neither was guile "
4: 1 in the flesh hath ceased from s·; "
2Pe 2:14 and that cannot cease from s·; "
1Jo 1: 7 his Son cleanseth us from all s·. "
8 If we say that we have no s·, we "
2: 1 write I unto you, that ye s· not. 264
1 if any man s·, we have an advocate "
3: 4 committeth s· transgresseth also 266
4 for s· is the transgression of the law."
5 away our sins; and in him is no s·. "
8 He that committeth s· is of the devil;"
9 is born of God doth not commit s·; "
9 he cannot s·, because he is born of 264
5:16 If any man see his brother s· * "
16 a s· which is not unto death, he 266
16 for them that s· not unto death. 264
16 There is a s· unto death: I do not 266
17 All unrighteousness is s·: and there "
17 and there is a s· not unto death. "

Sin (*sin*)
Ex 16: 1 came unto the wilderness of S·, 5512
17: 1 journeyed from the wilderness of S·,"
Nu 33:11 encamped in the wilderness of S·. "
12 journey out of the wilderness of S·, "
Eze 30:15 And I will pour my fury upon S·, "
16 S· shall have great pain, and No "

Sina (*si'-nah*) See also SINAI.
Ac 7:30 him in the wilderness of mount S·*4614
38 which spake to him in the mount S·,*"

Sinai (*si'-nahee*) See also HOREB; SINA.
Ex 16: 1 which is between Elim and S·, on 5514
19: 1 came they into the wilderness of S·. "
2 were come to the desert of S·, and "
11 of all the people upon mount S·. "
18 And mount S· was altogether on a "
20 Lord came down upon mount S·, "
23 cannot come up to mount S·: for "
24:16 of the Lord abode upon mount S·, "
31:18 him upon mount S·, two tables "
34: 2 up in the morning unto mount S·, "
4 and went up unto mount S·, as the "
29 Moses came down from mount S· "
32 had spoken with him in mount S·. "
Le 7:38 commanded Moses in mount S·, in "
38 the Lord, in the wilderness of S·. "
25: 1 spake unto Moses in mount S·, "
26:46 children of Israel in mount S· by "
27:34 the children of Israel in mount S·. "
Nu 1: 1 unto Moses in the wilderness of S·, "
19 them in the wilderness of S·. "
3: 1 spake with Moses in mount S·. "
4 the Lord, in the wilderness of S·. "
3:14 unto Moses in the wilderness of S·, 5514
9: 1 unto Moses in the wilderness of S·, "
5 at even in the wilderness of S·: "
10:12 journeys out of...wilderness of S·; "
26:64 of Israel in the wilderness of S·. "
28: 6 which was ordained in mount S· "
33:15 and pitched in the wilderness of S·. "
16 removed from the desert of S·, "
De 33: 2 The Lord came from S·, and rose "
J'g 5: 5 even that S· from before the Lord "
Ne 9:13 camest down also upon mount S·, "
Ps 68: 8 even S· itself was moved at the "
17 the Lord is among them, as in S·, "
Ga 4:24 the one from the mount S·, which 4614
25 this Agar is mount S· in Arabia, "

since See also SITH.
Ge 30:30 Lord hath blessed thee s· my coming:*
44:28 in pieces; and I saw him not s·: 2008
46:30 let me die, s· I have seen thy face, 310
Ex 4:10 nor s· thou hast spoken unto thy 227
5:23 s· I came to Pharaoh to speak in 4480
9:18 in Egypt s· the foundation thereof "
10: 6 s· the day that they were upon the "
Nu 22:30 hast ridden ever s· I was thine *5750
De 4:32 s· the day that God created man 4480
34:10 a prophet s· in Israel like unto 5750
Jos 2:12 s· I have shewed you kindness, 3588
14:10 s· the Lord spake this word unto* 227
Ru 2:11 law s· the death of thine husband: 310
1Sa 8: 8 works which they have done s· the day
9:24 hath it been kept for thee s· I said,*
21: 5 about these three days, s· I came out,*
29: 3 him s· he fell unto me unto this day?
8 s· the day of thy coming unto me unto
2Sa 7: 6 s· the time that I brought up the
11 as s· the time that I commanded *4480
1Ki 8:16 S· the day that I brought forth my "
2Ki 8: 6 field s· the day that she left the land,
21:15 s· the day their fathers came forth4480
1Ch 17: 5 s· the day that I brought up Israel "
10 s· the time that I commanded judges*
2Ch 6: 5 S· the day that I brought forth my4480
30:26 s· the time of Solomon the son of
31:10 S· the people began to bring the
Ezr 4: 2 unto him s· the days of Esar-haddon
5:16 s· that time even until now hath 4481
9: 7 s· the days of our fathers have we been
Ne 8:17 s· the days of Jeshua the son of Nun
9:32 s· the time of the kings of Assyria
Job 20: 4 s· man was placed upon earth, 4480
38:12 commanded the morning s· thy days;
Isa 14: 8 S· thou art laid down, no feller is 227
16:13 spoken concerning Moab s· that time.*
43: 4 S· thou wast precious in my sight,
44: 7 me, s· I appointed the ancient people?
64: 4 s· the beginning of the world men*
Jer 7:25 S· the day that your fathers came 4480
15: 7 s· they return not from their ways.*
20: 8 For s· I spake, I cried out, I cried*1767
23:38 s· ye say, The burden of the Lord;*518
31:20 for s· I spake against him, I do * 1767
44:18 s· we left off to burn incense 4480,227
48:27 for s· thou spakest of him, thou *1767
Da 12: 1 as never was s· there was a nation
Hag 2:16 S· those days were, when one came*
M't 24:21 not s· the beginning of the world to*575
M'r 9:21 How long is it ago s· this came 5613
Lu 1:70 have been s· the world began: ‡ 575
7:45 but this woman s· the time I came in"
16:16 s· that time the kingdom of God is* "
24:21 third day s· these things were done. "
Joh 9:32 S· the world began was it not 1537
Ac 3:21 holy prophets s· the world began.‡ 575
19: 2 the Holy Ghost s· ye believed? *
24:11 but twelve days s· I went up to575,3739
Ro 16:25 was kept secret s· the world began,*
1Co 15:21 For s· by man came death, by man1894
2Co 13: 3 S· ye seek a proof of Christ *1893
Col 1: 4 S· we heard of your faith in Christ*
6 also in you, s· the day ye heard of it,575
9 s· the day we heard it, do not cease "
Heb 7:28 of the oath, which was s· the law,*3326
9:26 s· the foundation of the world: 575
2Pe 3: 4 s· the fathers fell asleep, all *575,3739
Re 16:18 such as was not s· men were " "

sincere
Ph'p 1:10 ye may be s· and without offence 1506
1Pe 2: 2 desire the s· milk of the word, that* 97

sincerely
J'g 9:16 if ye have done truly and s·, in *8549
19 If ye then have dealt truly and s· * "
Ph'p 1:16 preach Christ of contention, not s·, 55

sincerity
Jos 24:14 and serve him in s· and in truth: 8549
1Co 5: 8 with the unleavened bread of s·and1505
2Co 1:12 that in simplicity and godly s·, not "
2:17 but as of s·, but as of God, in the "
8: 8 and to prove the s· of your love. 1103
Eph 6:24 love our Lord Jesus Christ in s·. * 861
Tit 2: 7 shewing uncorruptness, gravity, s·,*"

sinew See also SINEWS.
Ge 32:32 eat not of the s· which shrank, 1517
32 Jacob's thigh in the s· that shrank. "
Isa 48: 4 and thy neck is an iron s·, and thy "

sinews
Job 10:11 hast fenced me with bones and s·. 1517
30:17 season: and my s· take no rest. *6207
40:17 the s· of his stones are wrapped 1517
Eze 37: 6 And I will lay s· upon you, and will "
8 s· and the flesh came up upon them, "

sinful
Nu 32:14 an increase of s· men, to augment 2400
Isa 1: 4 Ah s· nation, a people laden with 2398
Am 9: 8 Lord God are upon the s· kingdom,2401
M'r 8:38 this adulterous and s· generation; 268
Lu 5: 8 from me; for I am a s· man, O Lord."
24: 7 delivered into the hands of s· men, "
Ro 7:13 sin...might become exceeding s·. "
8: 3 own Son in the likeness of s· flesh, 266

sing See also SANG; SINGETH; SINGING; SUNG.
Ex 15: 1 I will s· unto the Lord, for he hath7891
21 S· ye to the Lord, for he hath "
32:18 the noise of them that s· do I hear.6031
Nu 21:17 Spring up, O well; s· ye unto it: 6030
J'g 5: 3 I, even I, will s· unto the Lord; 7891
3 will s· praise to the Lord of Israel.2167
1Sa 21:11 s· one to another of him in dances,6030
2Sa 22:50 I will s· praises unto thy name. 2167
1Ch 16: 9 S· unto him,...talk ye of all his 7891
9 s· psalms unto him, talk ye of all
23 S· unto the Lord, all the earth; 7891
33 shall the trees of the wood s· out 7442
2Ch 20:22 they began to s· and to praise, 7440
23:13 and such as taught to s· praise. *1984
29:30 to s· praise unto the Lord with the "
Job 29:13 the widow's heart to s· for joy. 7442
Ps 7:17 will s· praise to the name of the Lord
9: 2 I will s· praise to thy name, O thou
11 S· praises to the Lord, which
13: 6 I will s· unto the Lord, because he7891
18:49 and s· praises unto thy name.
21:13 so will we s· and praise thy power.7891
27: 6 sacrifice of joy; I will s·, yea,
6 I will s· praises unto the Lord. 2167
30: 4 S· unto the Lord, O ye saints of his,"
12 that my glory may s· praise to thee."
33: 2 s· unto him with the psaltery and 2167
3 S· unto him a new song; play 7891
47: 6 S· praises to God, s· praises: 2167
6 s· praises unto our King, s· praises."
7 s· ye praises with understanding. "
51:14 shall s· aloud of thy righteousness.7442
57: 7 is fixed: I will s· and give praise. 7891
9 s· unto thee among the nations. 2167
59:16 But I will s· of thy power; yea, I 7891
16 I will s· aloud of thy mercy in the 7442
17 Unto thee, O my strength, will I s·:2167
61: 8 So will I s· praise unto thy name for"
65:13 they shout for joy, they also s·. 7891
66: 2 S· forth the honour of his name: 2167
4 worship thee, and...s· unto thee; "
4 they shall s· to thy name. Selah. "
67: 4 the nations be glad and s· for joy: 7442
68: 4 S· unto God,...extol him that rideth7891
4 s· praises to his name: extol him 2167
32 S· unto God, ye kingdoms of the 7891
32 O s· praises unto the Lord; Selah:2167
71:22 unto thee will I s· with the harp, "
23 greatly rejoice when I s· unto thee;"
75: 9 I will s· praises to the God of Jacob.
81: 1 S· aloud unto God our strength: 7442
89: 1 I will s· of the mercies of the Lord7891
92: 1 and to s· praises unto thy name, O 2167
95: 1 O come, let us s· unto the Lord: 7442
96: 1 O s· unto the Lord a new song: 7891
1 s· unto the Lord, all the earth. "
2 S· unto the Lord, bless his name; "
98: 1 O s· unto the Lord a new song; for "
4 noise, and rejoice, and s· praise. 2167
5 S· unto the Lord with the harp; "
101: 1 I will s· of mercy and judgment: 7891
1 unto thee, O Lord, will I s·. 2167
104:12 which s· among the branches.5414,6963
33 s· unto the Lord as long as I live: 7891
33 s· praise to my God while I have 2167
105: 2 S· unto him,...talk ye of all his 7891
2 s· psalms unto him: talk ye of 2167
108: 1 I will s· and give praise, even with7891
3 I will s· praises unto thee among 2167
135: 3 s· praises unto his name; for it is "
137: 3 S· us one of the songs of Zion. 7891
4 s· the Lord's song in a strange "
138: 1 the gods will I s· praise unto thee.2167
5 shall s· in the ways of the Lord: 7891
144: 9 I will s· a new song unto thee, O "
9 ten strings will I s· praises unto 2167
145: 7 and shall s· of thy righteousness. 7442
146: 2 I will s· praises unto...God while I 2167
147: 1 is good to s· praises unto our God; "
7 S· unto...Lord with thanksgiving;6030
7 s· praise upon the harp unto our 2167
149: 1 S· unto the Lord a new song, and 7891
3 s· praises unto him with...timbrel 2167
5 let them s· aloud upon their beds. 7442
Pr 29: 6 the righteous doth s· and rejoice. "
Isa 5: 1 will I s· to my wellbeloved a song 7891
12: 5 S· unto the Lord; for he hath 2167
23:15 years shall Tyre s· as an harlot. *7892
16 make sweet melody, s· many songs, "
24:14 shall s· for the majesty of the *7442
26:19 Awake and s·, ye that dwell in "
27: 2 In that day s· ye unto her, A 6031
35: 6 and the tongue of the dumb s·: 7442
42:10 S· unto the Lord a new song, and 7891
11 let the inhabitants of the rock s·, 7442
44:23 S·, O ye heavens; for the Lord "
49:13 S·, O heavens; and be joyful, O "
52: 8 the voice together shall they s·: "
9 joy, s· together, ye waste places of "
54: 1 S·, O barren, thou that didst not "
65:14 servants shall s· for joy of heart, "
Jer 20:13 S· unto the Lord, praise ye the 7891
31: 7 S· with gladness for Jacob, and 7442
12 come and s· in the height of Zion, "
51:48 that is therein, shall s· for Babylon:"
Eze 27:25 ships of Tarshish did s· of thee in*7788
Ho 2:15 she shall s· there, as in the days *6030
Zep 2:14 voice shall s· in the windows; 7891
3:14 S·, O daughter of Zion; shout, O 7442
Zec 2:10 S· and rejoice, O daughter of Zion: "

Ro 15: 9 Gentiles, and s· unto thy name. 5567
1Co 14: 15 also: I will s· with the spirit, and "
15 will s· with the understanding also." "
Heb 2: 12 the church will I s· praise unto thee. 5214
Jas 5: 13 is any merry? let him s· psalms. 5567
Re 15: 3 And they s· the song of Moses the 103

singed
Da 3: 27 nor was an hair of their head s·, 2761

singer See also SINGERS.
1Ch 6: 33 Heman a s·, the son of Joel, the 7891
Hab 3: 19 To the chief s· on my stringed *5329

singers
1Ki 10: 12 harps also and psalteries for s·: 7891
1Ch 9: 33 these are the s·, chief of the fathers "
15: 16 the s· with instruments of musick, "
19 So the s·, Heman, Asaph, and "
27 that bare the ark and the s·, and "
27 the master of the song with the s·: "
2Ch 5: 12 the Levites which were the s·, all of "
13 the trumpeters and s· were as one, "
9: 11 and harps and psalteries for s·: "
20: 21 he appointed s· unto the Lord, and* "
23: 13 the s· with instruments of musick, "
29: 28 and the s· sang, and the trumpets 7892
35: 15 And the s· the sons of Asaph were 7891
Ezr 2: 41 The s·: the children of Asaph, an "
70 people, and the s·, and the porters, "
7: 7 priests, and the Levites, and the s·, "
24 Levites, s·, porters, Nethinims, 2171
10: 24 Of the s· also; Eliashib: and of 7891
Ne 7: 1 and the s· and the Levites were "
44 The s·: the children of Asaph, an "
73 Levites, and the porters, and the s·, "
10: 28 the Levites, the porters, the s·, the "
39 minister,...the porters, and the s·: "
11: 22 the s· were over the business of the "
23 certain portion should be for the s·, "
12: 28 And the sons of the s· gathered "
29 s· had builded them villages round "
42 the s· sang loud, with Jezrahiah "
45 both the s· and the porters kept "
46 of old th( ) were chief of the s·, "
47 gave the portions of the s· and the "
13: 5 be given to the Levites, and the s·, "
10 the Levites, and the s·, that did the "
Ps 68: 25 The s· went before, the players on "
87: 7 As well the s· as the players on * "
Ec 2: 8 I gat me men s· and women s·, and "
Eze 40: 44 the chambers of the s· in the inner "

singeth
Pr 25: 20 so is he that s· songs to an heavy 7891

singing
1Sa 18: 6 cities of Israel, s· and dancing, 7891
2Sa 19: 35 the voice of s· men and s· women? "
1Ch 6: 32 of the congregation with s·, until *7892
13: 8 with s·, and with harps, and with* "
2Ch 23: 18 Moses, with rejoicing and with s·, "
30: 21 s· with loud instruments unto the "
35: 25 all the s· men and the s· women 7891
Ezr 2: 65 two hundred s· men and s· women. "
Ne 7: 67 and five s· men and s· women. "
12: 27 with thanksgivings, and with s·, 7892
Ps 100: 2 come before his presence with s·. 7445
126: 2 laughter, and our tongue with s·: 7440
Ca 2: 12 time of the s· of birds is come, 2158
Isa 14: 7 is quiet: they break forth into s·. 7440
16: 10 the vineyards there shall be no s·, 7442
35: 2 and rej ice even with joy and s·: "
44: 23 break forth into s·, ye mountains, 7440
48: 20 with a voice of s· declare ye, tell "
49: 13 break forth into s·, O mountains: "
51: 11 return, and come with s· unto Zion; "
54: 1 break forth into s·, and cry al( )d, "
55: 12 shall break forth before you into s·, "
Zep 3: 17 love, he will joy over thee with s·. 7440
Eph 5: 19 s· and making melody in your 103
Col 3: 16 s· with grace in your hearts to the "

single
M't 6: 22 if therefore thine eye be s·, thy 573
Lu 11: 34 therefore when thine eye is s·, thy "

singleness
Ac 2: 46 with gladness and s· of heart, 858
Eph 6: 5 in s· of your heart, as unto Christ; 572
Col 3: 22 but in s· of heart, fearing God: "

singular
Le 27: 2 when a man shall make a s· vow, *6381

Sinim (*si'-nim*)
Isa 49: 12 and these from the land of *S*·. 5515

Sinite (*si'-nite*)
Ge 10: 17 Hivite, and the Arkite, and the *S*·, 5513
1Ch 1: 15 Hivite, and the Arkite, and the *S*·, "

sink See also SANK; SUNK.
Ps 69: 2 I s· in deep mire, where there is 2883
14 out of the mire, and let me not s·: "
Jer 51: 64 Thus shall Babylon s·, and shall 8257
M't 14: 30 beginning to s·, he cried, saying, 2670
Lu 5: 7 the ships, so that they began to s·. 1036
9: 44 sayings s· down into your ears: 5087

sinned
Ex 9: 27 unto them, I have s· this time: 2398
34 he s· yet more, and hardened his "
10: 16 I have s· against the Lord your God, "
32: 30 the people, Ye have s· a great sin: "
31 Oh, this people have s· a great sin, "
33 Whosoever hath s· against me, him "
Le 4: 3 bring for his sin, which he hath s·, "
14 sin, which they have s· against it, is "
22 When a ruler hath s·, and done * "
23 if his sin, wherein he hath s·, come "
28 if his sin, which he hath s·, come to "
Le 4: 28 for his sin which he hath s·. 2398
5: 5 that he shall confess that he hath s· "
6 Lord for his sin which he hath s·, "
10 for him for his sin which he hath s·, "
11 that s· shall bring for his offering "
13 as touching his sin that he hath s· "
6: 4 because he hath s·, and is guilty, "
Nu 6: 11 for him, for that he s· by the dead, "
12: 11 foolishly, and wherein we have s·. "
14: 40 Lord hath promised: for we have s·. "
21: 7 We have s·, for we have spoken "
22: 34 I have s·; for I knew not that thou "
32: 23 behold, ye have s· against the Lord: "
De 1: 41 We have s· against the Lord, we "
9: 16 ye had s· against the Lord your God, "
18 because of all your sins which ye s·, "
Jos 7: 11 Israel hath s·, and they have also "
20 Indeed I have s· against the Lord "
J'g 10: 10 saying, We have s· against thee, "
15 We have s·: do thou unto us "
11: 27 I have not s· against thee, but thou "
1Sa 7: 6 We have s· against the Lord. "
12: 10 unto the Lord, and said, We have s·, "
15: 24 Saul said unto Samuel, I have s·: "
30 Then he said, I have s·: yet honour "
19: 4 because he hath not s· against thee, "
24: 11 and I have not s· against thee; "
26: 21 Then said Saul, I have s·: return, "
2Sa 12: 13 Nathan, I have s· against the Lord. "
19: 20 servant doth know that I have s·: "
24: 10 I have s· greatly in that I have done: "
17 Lo, I have s·, and I have done "
1Ki 8: 33 because they have s· against thee, "
35 because they have s· against thee; "
47 saying, We have s·, and have done "
50 And forgive thy people that have s· "
15: 30 the sins of Jeroboam which he s·, "
16: 13 of Elah his son, by which they s·, "
19 his sins which he s· in doing evil "
18: 9 What have I s·, that thou wouldest "
2Ki 17: 7 Israel had s· against the Lord their "
21: 17 that he did, and his sin that he s·, "
1Ch 21: 8 said unto God, I have s· greatly, "
17 even I it is that have s· and done "
2Ch 6: 24, 26 because they have s· against "
37 We have s·, we have done amiss, "
39 forgive thy people which have s· "
Ne 1: 6 which we have s· against thee: "
6 I and my father's house have s·. "
9: 29 but s· against thy judgments, "
Job 1: 5 It may be tha( ) my sons have s·, "
22 In all this Job ( ) no( ), nor charged "
7: 20 I have s·; wha( ) sha( ) I do unto thee, "
8: 4 If thy childre( ) have s· against him, "
24: 19 doth the grave those which have s·. "
33: 27 if any say, I have s·, and perverted "
Ps 41: 4 my soul; for I have s· against thee. "
51: 4 Against thee, ( )e only, have I s·, "
78: 17 And they s· y( ) more against him* "
32 For all this they s· still, and believed "
106: 6 We have s· with our fathers, we "
Isa 42: 24 Lord, he against whom we have s·? "
43: 27 Thy first father hath s·, and thy "
64: 5 thou art wroth; f( )r we have s·: "
Jer 2: 35 because thou sayest, I have not s·. "
3: 25 for we have s· ag( )inst the Lord our "
8: 14 because we have s· against the Lord. "
14: 7 are ( )any; we h( )ve s· against thee. "
20 fa( )rs: for we have s· against thee. "
33: 8 whe( )eby they have s· against me; "
8 iniq( )ities, whereby they have s·, "
40: 3 because ye have s· against the Lord, "
44: 23 because ye have s· against the Lord, "
50: 7 they have s· against the Lord, "
14 for she hath s· against the Lord. "
La 1: 8 Jerusalem hath grievously s·; "
5: 7 Our fathers have s·, and are not; "
16 head: wo( ) unto us, that we have s·! "
Eze 18: 24 and in his sin that he hath s·, in "
28: 16 thee with violence, and thou hast s·: "
37: 23 dwellingplaces, wherein they...s·, "
Da 9: 5 We have s·, and have committed "
8 because we have s· against thee. "
11 because we have s· against him. "
15 we have s·, we have done wickedly. "
Ho 4: 7 increased, so they s· against me: "
10: 9 thou hast s· from the days of Gibeah: "
Mic 7: 9 Lord, because I have s· against him, "
Hab 2: 10 people, and hath s· against thy soul. "
Zep 1: 17 they have s· against the Lord: "
M't 27: 4 I have s· in that I have betrayed 264
Lu 15: 18, 21 Father, I have s· against heaven, "
Joh 9: 3 Neither hath this man s·, nor his * "
Ro 2: 12 For as many as have s· without law "
12 and as many as have s· in the law "
3: 23 For all have s·, and come short of "
5: 12 upon all men, for that all have s·: "
14 that had not s· after the similitude "
16 And not as it was by one that s·, so "
1Co 7: 28 and if thou marry, thou hast not s·; "
28 if a virgin marry, she hath not s·. "
2Co 12: 21 many which have s· already, 4258
13: 2 to them which heretofore have s·, "
Heb 3: 17 was it not with them that had s·, 264
2 Pe 2: 4 God spared not the angels that s·, "
1Jo 1: 10 If we say that we have not s·, we "

sinner See also SINNERS.
Pr 11: 31 much more the wicked and the s·. 2398
13: 6 wickedness overthroweth the s·. 2403
22 the wealth of the s· is laid up for 2398
Ec 2: 26 but to the s· he giveth travail, to "
7: 26 but the s· shall be taken by her. "
8: 12 Though a s· do evil an hundred "
9: 2 as is the good, so is the s·; and he "
18 but one s· destroyeth much good. "
Isa 65: 20 the s· being an hundred years old "
Lu 7: 37 woman in the city, which was a s·, 268
39 that toucheth him: for she is a s·. "
15: 7 heaven over one s· that repenteth, "
10 of God over one s· that repenteth. "
18: 13 saying, God be merciful to me a s·. "
19: 7 to be guest with a man that is a s·. "
Joh 9: 16 man that is a s· do such miracles? "
24 we know that this man is a s·. "
25 Whether he be a s· or no, I know not: "
Ro 3: 7 why yet am I also judged as a s·? "
Jas 5: 20 converteth the s· from the error of "
1Pe 4: 18 shall the ungodly and the s· appear? "

sinners
Ge 13: 13 men of Sodom were wicked and s· 2400
Nu 16: 38 The censers of these s· against "
1Sa 15: 18 destroy the s· the Amalekites, "
Ps 1: 1 nor standeth in the way of s·, nor "
5 nor s· in the congregation of the "
25: 8 therefore will he teach s· in the way. "
26: 9 Gather not my soul with s·, nor my "
51: 13 s· shall be converted unto thee. "
104: 35 s· be consumed out of the earth, "
Pr 1: 10 if s· entice thee, consent thou not. "
13: 21 Evil pursueth s·: but to the "
23: 17 Let not thine heart envy s·: but be "
Isa 1: 28 of the transgressors and of the s· "
13: 9 and he shall destroy the s· thereof "
33: 14 The s· in Zion are afraid; fearfulness "
Am 9: 10 All the s· of my people shall die by "
M't 9: 10 many publicans and s· came and 268
11 your Master with publicans and s·? "
13 the righteous, but s· to repentance. "
11: 19 a friend of publicans and s·. "
26: 45 is betrayed into the hands of s·. "
M'r 2: 15 publicans and s· sat also together "
16 saw him eat with publicans and s·, "
16 and drinketh with publicans and s·? "
17 the righteous, but s· to repentance. "
14: 41 is betrayed into the hands of s·. "
Lu 5: 30 eat and drink with publicans and s·? "
32 the righteous, but s· to repentance. "
6: 32 for s· also love those that love them. "
33 ye? for s· also do even the same. "
34 s· also lend to s·, to receive as much "
7: 34 a friend of publicans and s·! "
13: 2 were s· above all the Galilæans, "
4 were s· above all men that dwelt in 3781
15: 1 publicans and s· for to hear him. 268
2 This man receiveth s·, and eateth "
Joh 9: 31 we know that God heareth not s·: "
Ro 5: 8 while we were yet s·, Christ died for "
19 disobedience many were made s·, "
Ga 2: 15 by nature, and not s· of the Gentiles, "
17 we ourselves also are found s·, is "
1Ti 1: 9 for the ungodly and for s·, for unholy "
15 Jesus came into the world to save s·; "
Heb 7: 26 undefiled, separate from s·, and "
12: 3 contradiction of s· against himself, "
Jas 4: 8 Cleanse your hands, ye s·; and "
Jude 15 ungodly s· have spoken against him. "

sinnest
Job 35: 6 If thou s·, what doest thou against *2398

sinneth
Nu 15: 28 for the soul that s· ignorantly, *7683
28 s· by ignorance before the Lord, 2398
29 for him that s· through ignorance, *6213
De 19: 15 for any sin, in any sin that he s·: 2398
1Ki 8: 46 (for there is no man that s· not,) "
2Ch 6: 36 (for there is no man which s· not,) "
Pr 8: 36 s· against me wrongeth his own "
14: 21 He that despiseth his neighbour s·: "
19: 2 and he that hasteth with his feet s·. "
20: 2 whoso provoketh him to anger s· "
Ec 7: 20 earth, that doeth good, and s· not. "
Eze 14: 13 when the land s· against me by "
18: 4 mine: the soul that s·, it shall die. "
20 The soul that s·, it shall die. The "
33: 12 righteousness in the day that he s·. "
1Co 6: 18 fornication s· against his own body. 264
7: 36 let him do what he will, he s· not: "
Tit 3: 11 he that is such is subverted, and s·, "
1Jo 3: 6 Whosoever abideth in him s· not: "
6 whosoever s· hath not seen him, "
8 for the devil s· from the beginning. "
5: 18 whosoever is born of God s· not; "

sinning
Ge 20: 6 for I also withheld thee from s· 2398
Le 6: 3 these that a man doeth, s· therein: "

sin-offering See SIN and OFFERING.

sins
Le 16: 16 their transgressions in all their s·: 2403
21 their transgressions in all their s·, "
30 from all your s· before the Lord. "
34 of Israel for all their s· once a year. "
26: 18 you seven times more for your s·. "
21 upon you according to your s·. "
24 you yet seven times for your s·. "
28 chastise you seven times for your s·. "
Nu 16: 26 lest ye be consumed in all their s·. "
De 9: 18 because of all your s· which ye * "
Jos 24: 19 your transgressions nor your s·. "
1Sa 12: 19 added unto all our s· this evil, "
1Ki 14: 16 up because of the s· of Jeroboam, "
22 their s· which they had committed, "
15: 3 he walked in all the s· of his father, "
30 the s· of Jeroboam which he sinned, "
16: 2 provoke me to anger with their s·; "
13 For all the s· of Baasha, and the "
13 and the s· of Elah his son, by which "
19 his s· which he sinned in doing evil "
31 him to walk in the s· of Jeroboam "
2Ki 3: 3 he cleaved unto the s· of Jeroboam "
10: 29 s· of Jeroboam the son of Nebat, 2399

2Ki 10: 31 not from the s' of Jeroboam, 2403
13: 2 and followed the s' of Jeroboam "
6 the s' of the house of Jeroboam, "
11 from all the s' of Jeroboam the son "
14: 24 from all the s' of Jeroboam the son "
15: 9, 18, 24, 28 s' of Jeroboam the son of "
17: 22 walked in all the s' of Jeroboam "
24: 3 for the s' of Manasseh, according to "
2Ch 28: 10 you, s' against the Lord your God?*819
13 ye intend to add more to our s' 2403
33: 19 and all his s', and his trespass, and*"
Ne 1: 6 and confess the s' of the children of "
9: 2 and stood and confessed their s', "
37 hast set over us because of our s': "
Job 13: 23 many are mine iniquities and s'? "
Ps 19: 13 servant also from presumptuous s'; "
25: 7 Remember not the s' of my youth, 2403
18 and my pain; and forgive all my s'. "
51: 9 Hide thy face from my s', and blot 2399
69: 5 and my s' are not hid from thee. 819
79: 9 deliver us, and purge away our s', 2403
90: 8 our secret s' in the light of thy "
103: 10 hath not dealt with us after our s': 2399
Pr 5: 22 be holden with the cords of his s'.*2403
10: 12 up strifes: but love covereth all s'.*6588
28: 13 covereth his s' shall not prosper: * "
Isa 1: 18 though your s' be as scarlet, they 2399
38: 17 hast cast all my s' behind thy back. "
40: 2 Lord's hand double for all her s'. 2403
43: 24 hast made me to serve with thy s', "
25 sake, and will not remember thy s'. "
44: 22 as a cloud, thy s': return unto me; "
58: 1 and the house of Jacob their s'. "
59: 2 your s' have hid his face from you, "
12 thee, and our s' testify against us: "
Jer 5: 25 and your s' have withholden good "
14: 10 their iniquity, and visit their s'. "
15: 13 and that for all thy s', even in all "
30: 14 because thy s' were increased. "
15 because thy s' were increased, I "
50: 20 the s' of Judah, and they shall not "
La 3: 39 man for the punishment of his s'? 2399
4: 13 For the s' of her prophets, and the 2403
22 of Edom; he will discover thy s'. "
Eze 16: 51 Samaria committed half of thy s'; "
52 for thy s' that thou hast committed "
18: 14 that seeth all his father's s' which "
21 all his s' that he hath committed, "
21: 24 all your doings your s' do appear; "
23: 49 ye shall bear the s' of your idols: 2399
33: 10 If our transgressions and our s' be 2403
16 of his s' that he hath committed "
Da 4: 27 break off thy s' by righteousness, 2408
9: 16 for our s', and for the iniquities 2399
24 to make an end of s', and to make 2403
Ho 8: 13 their iniquity, and visit their s': "
9: 9 their iniquity, he will visit their s'. "
Am 5: 12 transgressions and your mighty s': "
Mic 1: 5 and for the s' of the house of Israel. "
6: 13 thee desolate because of thy s'. "
7: 19 their s' into the depths of the sea. "
M't 1: 21 shall save his people from their s'. 266
3: 6 of him in Jordan, confessing their s'. "
9: 2 good cheer; thy s' be forgiven thee. "
5 to say, Thy s' be forgiven thee; or "
6 hath power on earth to forgive s', "
26: 28 shed for many for the remission of s'. "
M'r 1: 4 of repentance for the remission of s'. "
5 river of Jordan, confessing their s'. "
2: 5 palsy, Son, thy s' be forgiven thee. "
7 who can forgive s' but God only? "
9 the palsy, Thy s' be forgiven thee; "
10 hath power on earth to forgive s', "
3: 28 s' shall be forgiven unto the sons of 265
4: 12 their s' should be forgiven them. * "
Lu 1: 77 people by the remission of their s', 266
3: 3 repentance for the remission of s'; "
5: 20 him, Man, thy s' are forgiven thee. "
21 Who can forgive s', but God alone? "
23 to say, Thy s' be forgiven thee; or to "
24 hath power upon earth to forgive s', "
7: 47 Her s', which are many, are forgiven; "
48 he said unto her, Thy s' are forgiven. "
49 Who is this that forgiveth s' also? "
11: 4 forgive us our s'; for we also forgive "
24: 47 remission of s' should be preached "
Joh 8: 21 seek me, and shall die in your s': * "
24 unto you, that ye shall die in your s': "
24 that I am he, ye shall die in your s'. "
9: 34 Thou wast altogether born in s', "
20: 23 Whose soever s' ye remit, they are "
23 whose soever s' ye retain, they are "
Ac 2: 38 Jesus Christ for the remission of s', 266
3: 19 that your s' may be blotted out, "
5: 31 to Israel, and forgiveness of s'. "
10: 43 in him receive shall remission of s'. "
13: 38 unto you the forgiveness of s': "
22: 16 be baptized, and wash away thy s', "
26: 18 they may receive forgiveness of s', "
Ro 3: 25 for the remission of s' that are past, 265
4: 7 forgiven, and whose s' are covered. 266
7: 5 the motions of s', which were by the*"
11: 27 when I shall take away their s'. "
1Co 15: 3 how that Christ died for our s' "
17 faith is vain; ye are yet in your s'. "
Ga 1: 4 Who gave himself for our s', that he "
Eph 1: 7 the forgiveness of s', according to *3900
2: 1 who were dead in trespasses and s': 266
5 Even when we were dead in s', *3900
Col 1: 14 blood, even the forgiveness of s': 266
2: 11 off the body of the s' of the flesh by* "
13 And you, being dead in your s' *3900
1Th 2: 16 be saved, to fill up their s' alway: 266
1Ti 5: 22 be partaker of other men's s': "
24 Some men's s' are open beforehand, "
2Ti 3: 6 captive silly women laden with s', "
Heb 1: 3 he had by himself purged our s', sat 266
2: 17 reconciliation for the s' of the people. "
5: 1 offer both gifts and sacrifices for s': "
3 so also for himself, to offer for s'. "
7: 27 first for his own s', and then for the "
8: 12 and their s' and their iniquities will I "
9: 28 once offered to bear the s' of many; "
10: 2 have had no more conscience of s'. "
3 is a remembrance again made of s' "
4 and of goats should take away s'. "
11 which can never take away s': "
12 he had offered one sacrifice for s' "
17 s' and iniquities will I remember "
26 remaineth no more sacrifice for s', "
Jas 5: 15 if he have committed s', they shall "
20 and shall hide a multitude of s'. "
1Pe 2: 24 own self bare our s' in his own body "
24 that we, being dead to s', should live "
3: 18 Christ also hath once suffered for s', "
4: 8 shall cover the multitude of s'. "
2Pe 1: 9 that he was purged from his old s'. "
1Jo 1: 9 If we confess our s', he is faithful and "
9 faithful and just to forgive us our s', "
2: 2 And he is the propitiation for our s': "
2 but also for the s' of the whole world.*
12 because your s' are forgiven you for 266
3: 5 was manifested to take away our s'; "
4: 10 Son to be the propitiation for our s'. "
Re 1: 5 and washed us from our s' in his own "
18: 4 that ye be not partakers of her s', "
5 her s' have reached unto heaven, "

Sion (*si'-on*) See also SHENIR; SIRION; ZION.
De 4: 48 unto mount S', which is Hermon. 7865
Ps 65: 1 waiteth for thee, O God, in S': *6726
M't 21: 5 Tell ye the daughter of S', Behold,*4622
Joh 12: 15 Fear not, daughter of S': behold, * "
Ro 9: 33 I lay in S' a stumblingstone and * "
11: 26 shall come out of S' the Deliverer,*"
Heb 12: 22 But ye are come unto mount S', * "
1Pe 2: 6 I lay in S' a chief corner stone, * "
Re 14: 1 lo, a Lamb stood on the mount S',* "

Siphmoth (*sif'-moth*)
1Sa 30: 28 and to them which were in S', 8224

Sippai (*sip'-pahee*) See also SAPH.
1Ch 20: 4 Sibbechai the Hushathite slew S', 5598

sir See also SIRS.
Ge 43: 20 O s', we came indeed down at the* 113
M't 13: 27 S', didst not thou sow good seed in 2962
21: 30 and said, I go, s'; and went not. "
27: 63 S', we remember that that deceiver "
Joh 4: 11 S', thou hast nothing to draw with, "
15 S', give me this water, that I thirst "
19 S', I perceive...thou art a prophet. "
49 S', come down ere my child die. "
5: 7 S', I have no man, when the water "
12: 21 saying, S', we would see Jesus. "
20: 15 S', if thou have borne him hence, "
Re 7: 14 I said unto him, S', thou knowest.*"

Sirah (*si'-rah*)
2Sa 3: 26 him again from the well of S': 5626

Sirion (*sir'-e-on*) See also HERMON.
De 3: 9 Hermon the Sidonians call S'; 8303
Ps 29: 6 Lebanon and S' like a...unicorn "

sirs
Ac 7: 26 S', ye are brethren; why do ye 435
14: 15 saying, S', why do ye these things? "
16: 30 S', what must I do to be saved? 2962
19: 25 S', ye know that by this craft we 435
27: 10 S', I perceive that this voyage will "
21 S', ye should have hearkened unto "
25 Wherefore, s', be of good cheer: for "

Sisamai (*sis'-a-mahee*)
1Ch 2: 40 Eleasah begat S', and S' begat 5581

Sisera (*sis'-e-rah*)
J'g 4: 2 the captain of whose host was S', 5516
7 S' the captain of Jabin's army, with "
9 the Lord shall sell S' into the hand "
12 And they shewed S' that Barak the "
13 And S' gathered together all his "
14 Lord hath delivered S' into thine "
15 And the Lord discomfited S', and "
15 that S' lighted down off his chariot, "
16 host of S' fell upon the edge of the "
17 S' fled away on his feet to the tent "
18 And Jael went out to meet S', and "
22 as Barak pursued S', Jael came out "
22 S' lay dead, and the nail was in his "
5: 20 in their courses fought against S'. "
26 and with the hammer she smote S', "
28 The mother of S' looked out at a "
30 to S' a prey of divers colours, a "
1Sa 12: 9 he sold them into the hand of S', "
Ezr 2: 53 the children of S', the children of "
Ne 7: 55 the children of S', the children of "
Ps 83: 9 as to S', as to Jabin, at the brook "

sister See also SISTER'S; SISTERS.
Ge 4: 22 the s' of Tubal-cain was Naamah. 269
12: 13 Say, I pray thee, thou art my s': "
19 Why saidst thou, She is my s'? so I "
20: 2 said of Sarah his wife, She is my s': "
5 Said he not unto me, She is my s'? "
12 And yet indeed she is my s'; she is "
24: 30 heard the words of Rebekah his s', "
59 they sent away Rebekah their s', "
60 and said unto her, Thou art our s', "
25: 20 the s' to Laban the Syrian. "
26: 7 said, She is my s': for he feared "
9 and how saidst thou, She is my s'? "
28: 9 the s' of Nebajoth, to be his wife. "
30: 1 no children, Rachel envied her s'; "
8 have I wrestled with my s', and I "
Ge 34: 13 he had defiled Dinah their s': 269
14 our s' to one that is uncircumcised; "
27 because they had defiled their s'. "
31 deal with our s' as with an harlot? "
36: 3 Ishmael's daughter, s' of Nebajoth. "
22 Heman; and Lotan's s' was Timna. "
46: 17 Isui, and Beriah, and Serah their s': "
Ex 2: 4 And his s' stood afar off, to wit what "
7 said his s' to Pharaoh's daughter, "
6: 20 Jochebed his father's s' to wife: 1733
23 Amminadab s' of Naashon, to wife; 269
15: 20 the prophetess, the s' of Aaron, "
Le 18: 9 nakedness of thy s' the daughter "
11 begotten of thy father, she is thy s'. "
12 the nakedness of thy father's s': "
13 the nakedness of thy mother's s': "
18 shalt thou take a wife to her s', "
20: 17 And if a man shall take his s', his "
19 the nakedness of thy mother's s', nor "
19 of thy father's s': for he uncovereth "
21: 3 And for his s' a virgin, that is nigh "
Nu 6: 7 mother, for his brother, or for his s', "
25: 18 of a prince of Midian, their s', "
26: 59 and Moses, and Miriam their s'. "
De 27: 22 Cursed be he that lieth with his s', "
J'g 15: 2 not her younger s' fairer than she? "
Ru 1: 15 thy s' in law is gone back unto her 2994
15 gods: return thou after thy s' in law. "
2Sa 13: 1 the son of David had a fair s', 269
2 that he fell sick for his s' Tamar; "
4 Tamar, my brother Absalom's s'. "
5 let my s' Tamar come, and give me "
6 let Tamar my s' come, and make me "
11 unto her, Come lie with me, my s'. "
20 thee? but hold now thy peace, my s': "
22 because he had forced his s' Tamar. "
32 the day that he forced his s' Tamar. "
17: 25 Nahash, s' to Zeruiah Joab's mother. "
1Ki 11: 19 him to wife the s' of his own wife, "
19 wife, the s' of Tahpenes the queen. "
20 s' of Tahpenes bare him Genubath "
2Ki 11: 2 But Jehosheba, ...s' of Ahaziah, "
1Ch 1: 39 Homam: and Timna was Lotan's s'. "
3: 9 the concubines, and Tamar their s'. "
19 Hananiah, and Shelomith their s': "
4: 3 name of their s' was Hazelelponi: "
19 of his wife Hodiah the s' of Naham, "
7: 15 took to wife the s' of Huppim and* "
18 And his s' Hammoleketh bare Ishod, "
30 and Beriah, and Serah their s'. "
32 and Hotham, and Shua their s'. "
2Ch 22: 11 (for she was the s' of Ahaziah,) hid "
Job 17: 14 Thou art my mother, and my s'. "
Pr 7: 4 Say unto wisdom, Thou art my s'; "
Ca 4: 9 Thou hast ravished my heart, my s', "
10 How fair is thy love, my s', my "
12 A garden inclosed is my s', my "
5: 1 I am come into my garden, my s', my "
2 knocketh, saying, Open to me, my s', "
8: 8 We have a little s', and she hath no "
8 what shall we do for our s' in the day "
Jer 3: 7 her treacherous s' Judah saw it. "
8 her treacherous s' Judah feared not, "
10 her treacherous s' Judah hath not "
22: 18 Ah my brother! or, Ah s'! they shall "
Eze 16: 45 and thou art the s' of thy sisters, "
46 And thine elder s' is Samaria, she "
46 thy younger s', that dwelleth at thy "
48 Sodom thy s' hath not done, she nor "
49 was the iniquity of thy s' Sodom, "
56 For thy s' Sodom was not mentioned "
22: 11 another in thee hath humbled his s', "
23: 4 the elder, and Aholibah her s': "
11 when her s' Aholibah saw this, she "
11 more than her s' in her whoredoms. "
18 my mind was alienated from her s'. "
31 hast walked in the way of thy s'; "
33 with the cup of thy s' Samaria. "
44: 25 or for s' that hath had no husband, "
M't 12: 50 the same is my brother, and s', and 79
M'r 3: 35 the same is my brother, and my s', "
Lu 10: 39 And she had a s' called Mary, which "
40 not care that my s' hath left me to "
Joh 11: 1 the town of Mary and her s' Martha. "
5 Now Jesus loved Martha, and her s', "
28 called Mary her s' secretly, saying, "
39 Martha, the s' of him that was dead, "
19: 25 his mother, and his mother's s', "
Ro 16: 1 I commend unto you Phebe our s', "
15 and Julia, Nereus, and his s', and "
1Co 7: 15 A brother or a s' is not under "
9: 5 we not power to lead about a s', a * "
Jas 2: 15 If a brother or s' be naked, and "
2Jo 13 The children of thy elect s' greet "

sister-in-law See SISTER and LAW.

sister's
Ge 24: 30 and bracelets upon his s' hands, 269
29: 13 heard the tidings of Jacob his s' son, "
Le 20: 17 he hath uncovered his s' nakedness; "
1Ch 7: 15 whose s' name was Maachah;) and "
Eze 23: 32 shalt drink of thy s' cup deep and "
Ac 23: 16 when Paul's s' son heard of their 79
Col 4: 10 and Marcus, s' son to Barnabas, * 431

sisters
Jos 2: 13 and my brethren, and my s', and all 269
1Ch 2: 16 Whose s' were Zeruiah, and Abigail. "
Job 1: 4 called for their three s' to eat and to "
42: 11 him all his brethren, and all his s', "
Eze 16: 45 thou art the sister of thy s', which "
51 hast justified thy s' in all thine "
52 Thou also, which hast judged thy s', "
52 in that thou hast justified thy s'. "
55 thy s', Sodom and her daughters, "
61 when thou shalt receive thy s', thine "
Ho 2: 1 Ammi; and to your s', Ruhamah. "

M't 13:56 And his s', are they not all with us? 79
19:29 forsaken houses, or brethren, or s', "
M'r 6: 3 and are not his s' here with us? "
10:29 hath left house, or brethren, or s', "
30 houses, and brethren, and s', and "
Lu 14:26 and children, and brethren, and s', "
Joh 11: 3 Therefore his s' sent unto him, "
1Ti 5: 2 the younger as s', with all purity. "
sit See also SAT; SITTEST; SITTETH; SITTING.
Ge 27:19 s' and eat of my venison, that thy 3427
Nu 32: 6 go to war, and shall ye s' here? "
J'g 5:10 ye that s' in judgment, and walk by "
Ru 3:18 S' still, my daughter, until thou "
4: 1 a one! turn aside, s' down here. "
2 the city, and said, S' ye down here. "
1Sa 9:22 made them s' in the chiefest place 5414
16:11 for we will not s' down till he come 5437
20: 5 fail to s' with the king at meat: 3427
2Sa 19: 8 Behold, the king doth s' in the gate. "
1Ki 1:13 and he shall s' upon my throne? "
17 and he shall s' upon my throne. "
20 shall s' on the throne of my lord "
24 and he shall s' upon my throne? "
27 should s' on the throne of my lord "
30 he shall s' upon my throne in my "
35 may come and s' upon my throne; "
48 hath given one to s' on my throne "
3: 6 him a son to s' on his throne, as it "
8:20 s' on the throne of Israel, as the "
25 sight to s' on the throne of Israel; "
2Ki 7: 3 Why s' we here until we die? "
4 and if we s' still here, we die also. "
10:30 shall s' on the throne of Israel. "
15:12 Thy sons shall s' on the throne of "
18:27 me to the men which s' on the wall, "
1Ch 28: 5 Solomon...to s' upon the throne of "
2Ch 6:16 to s' upon the throne of Israel; "
Ps 26: 5 and will not s' with the wicked. "
69:12 They that s' in the gate speak "
107:10 Such as s' in darkness and in the* "
110: 1 S' thou at my right hand, until I "
119:23 Princes also did s' and speak * "
127: 2 you to rise up early, to s' up late, * "
132:12 shall also s' upon thy throne for "
Ec 10: 6 dignity, and the rich s' in low place. "
Isa 3:26 desolate shall s' upon the ground. "
14:13 I will s' also upon the mount of the "
16: 5 he shall s' upon it in truth in the "
30: 7 this, Their strength is to s' still. *7674
36:12 to the men that s' upon the wall, 3427
42: 7 s' in darkness out of the prison "
47: 1 Come down, and s' in the dust, O "
1 of Babylon, s' on the ground: "
5 S' thou silent, and get thee into "
8 I shall not s' as a widow, neither "
14 to warm at, nor fire to s' before it. "
52: 2 arise, and s' down; O Jerusalem: "
Jer 8:14 Why do we s' still? assemble "
13:13 kings that s' upon David's throne, "
18 queen, humble yourselves, s' down: "
16: 8 to s' with them to eat and to drink. "
33:17 want a man to s' upon the throne of "
36:15 S' down now, and read it in our "
30 have none to s' upon the throne of "
48:18 from thy glory, and s' in thirst; for "
La 1: 1 How doth the city s' solitary, that "
2:10 the daughter of Zion s' upon the "
Eze 26:16 they shall s' upon the ground, and "
28: 2 I s' in the seat of God, in the midst "
33:31 they s' before thee as my people, "
44: 3 he shall s' in it to eat bread before "
Da 7: 9 the Ancient of days did s', whose 3488
26 But the judgment shall s', and they "
Joe 3:12 will I s' to judge all the heathen 3427
Mic 4: 4 shall s' every man under his vine "
7: 8 when I s' in darkness, the Lord "
Zec 3: 8 and thy fellows that s' before thee: "
6:13 shall s' and rule upon his throne; "
Mal 3: 3 he shall s' as a refiner and purifier "
M't 8:11 shall s' down with Abraham, and 347
14:19 multitude to s' down on the grass, "
15:35 multitude to s' down on the ground. 377
19:28 Son of man shall s' in the throne 2523
28 ye also shall s' upon twelve thrones, "
20:21 that these my two sons may s', the "
23 to s' on my right hand, and on my "
22:44 S' thou on my right hand, till I 2521
23: 2 the Pharisees s' in Moses' seat: 2523
25:31 then shall he s' upon the throne of "
26:36 S' ye here, while I go and pray "
M'r 6:39 to make all s' down by companies 347
8: 6 people to s' down on the ground: 377
10:37 Grant unto us that we may s', one 2523
40 But to s' on my right hand and on "
12:36 S' thou on my right hand, till I 2521
14:32 S' ye here, while I shall pray. 2523
Lu 1:79 light to them that s' in darkness 2521
9:14 Make them s' down by fifties in a 2625
15 did so, and made them all s' down. 347
12:37 and make them to s' down to meat, "
13:29 s' down in the kingdom of God. "
14: 8 s' not down in the highest room; 2625
10 go and s' down in the lowest room; 377
10 of them that s' at meat with thee. 4873
16: 6 s' down quickly, and write fifty. 2523
17: 7 the field, Go and s' down to meat? 377
20:42 Lord, S' thou on my right hand, 2521
22:30 s' on thrones judging the twelve 2523
69 Son of man s' on the right hand *2521
Joh 6:10 Jesus said, Make the men s' down. 377
Ac 2:30 raise up Christ to s' on his throne;*2523
34 Lord, S' thou on my right hand, 2521
8:31 he would come up and s' with him. 2523
1Co 8:10 s' at meat in the idol's temple, *2621
Eph 2: 6 made us s' together in heavenly 4776
Heb 1:13 S' on my right hand, until I make 2521
Jas 2: 3 him, S' thou here in a good place; 2521
3 or s' here under my footstool: "
Re 3:21 grant to s' with me in my throne, 2523
17: 3 woman s' upon a scarlet coloured *2521
18: 7 I s' a queen, and am no widow, and "
19:18 of them that s' on them, and the "
sith See also SINCE.
Eze 35: 6 s' thou hast not hated blood, even‡ 518
Sitnah (*sit'-nah*)
Ge 26:21 and he called the name of it S'. 7856
sittest
Ex 18:14 why s' thou thyself alone, and all 3427
De 6: 7 them when thou s' in thine house, "
11:19 them when thou s' in thine house, "
Ps 50:20 Thou s' and speakest against thy "
Pr 23: 1 When thou s' to eat with a ruler, "
Jer 22: 2 that s' upon the throne of David, "
Ac 23: 3 s' thou to judge me after the law, 2521
sitteth
Ex 11: 5 Pharaoh that s' upon his throne, 3427
Le 15: 4 every thing, whereon he s', shall be "
6 he that s' on any thing whereon he "
20 every thing also that she s' upon "
23 bed, or on any thing whereon she s', "
26 and whatsoever she s' upon shall be "
De 17:18 when he s' upon the throne of his "
1Ki 1:46 Solomon s' on the throne of the "
Es 6:10 the Jew, that s' at the king's gate: "
Ps 1: 1 nor s' in the seat of the scornful. "
2: 4 that s' in the heavens shall laugh: "
10: 8 He s' in the lurking places of the "
29:10 The Lord s' upon the flood; * "
10 yea, the Lord s' King for ever. "
47: 8 s' upon the throne of his holiness. "
99: 1 he s' between the cherubims; let "
Pr 9:14 For she s' at the door of her house, "
20: 8 that s' in the throne of judgment "
31:23 when he s' among the elders of the "
Ca 1:12 While the king s' at his table, my* "
Isa 28: 6 to him that s' in judgment, 3427
40:22 that s' upon the circle of the earth, "
Jer 17:11 As the partridge s' on eggs, and †1716
29:16 that s' upon the throne of David, 3427
La 3:28 He s' alone and keepeth silence, * "
Zec 1:11 all the earth s' still, and is at rest. "
5: 7 that s' in the midst of the ephah. * "
M't 23:22 of God, and by him that s' thereon. 2521
Lu 14:28 s' not down first, and counteth *2523
31 s' not down first, and consulteth * "
22:27 is greater, he that s' at meat, or he 345
27 is not he that s' at meat? but I am "
1Co 14:30 be revealed to another that s' by, *2521
Col 3: 1 Christ s' on the right hand of God.* "
2Th 2: 4 he as God s' in the temple of God, 2523
Re 5:13 unto him that s' upon the throne, 2521
6:16 face of him that s' on the throne, "
7:10 our God which s' upon the throne, "
15 he that s' on the throne shall dwell "
17: 1 whore that s' upon many waters: "
9 mountains, on which the woman s'. "
15 where the whore s', are peoples, "
sitting See also DOWNSITTING.
De 22: 6 and the dam s' upon the young, or 7257
J'g 3:20 and he was s' in a summer parlour, 3427
1Ki 10: 5 table, and the s' of his servants, 4186
13:14 and found him s' under an oak: 3427
22:19 I saw the Lord s' on his throne, and "
2Ki 4:38 of the prophets were s' before him: "
9: 5 the captains of the host were s'; 3427
2Ch 9: 4 table, and the s' of his servants, 4186
18 stays on each side of the s' place, *3427
18:18 I saw the Lord s' upon his throne, "
Ne 2: 6 unto me, (the queen also s' by him,) "
Es 5:13 Mordecai...s' at the king's gate. "
Isa 6: 1 I saw also the Lord s' upon a throne, "
Jer 17:25 princes s' upon the throne of David, "
22: 4 kings s' upon the throne of David, "
30 s' upon the throne of David, and "
38: 7 then s' in the gate of Benjamin; "
La 3:63 Behold their s' down, and their "
M't 9: 9 s' at the receipt of custom: 2521
11:16 unto children s' in the markets, "
20:30 two blind men s' by the way side, "
21: 5 thee, meek, and s' upon an ass, *1910
26:64 Son of man s' on the right hand 2521
27:36 s' down they watched him there; * "
61 Mary, s' over against the sepulchre. "
M'r 2: 6 were certain of the scribes s' there, "
14 Alphæus s' at the receipt of custom, "
5:15 had the legion, s', and clothed, and "
14:62 Son of man s' on the right hand of "
16: 5 a young man s' on the right side, "
Lu 2:46 s' in the midst of the doctors, both 2516
5:17 and doctors of the law s' by, which 2521
27 Levi, s' at the receipt of custom: "
7:32 unto children s' in the marketplace, * "
8:35 s' at the feet of Jesus, clothed, and "
10:13 repented, s' in sackcloth and ashes. "
Joh 2:14 and the changers of money s': "
12:15 King cometh, s' on an ass's colt. "
20:12 And seeth two angels in white s', 2516
Ac 2: 2 all the house where they were s'. 2521
8:28 s' in his chariot read Esaias the "
25: 6 next day s' on the judgment seat *2523
Re 4: 4 I saw four and twenty elders s', 2521
sitting-place See SITTING and PLACE.
situate
1Sa 14: 5 one was s' northward over against *4690
Eze 27: 3 that art s' at the entry of the sea, *3427
Na 3: 8 No, that was s' among the rivers, "
situation
2Ki 2:19 the s' of this city is pleasant, as 4186
Ps 48: 2 Beautiful for s', the joy of the *5131
Sivan (*siv'-an*)
Es 8: 9 third month, that is, the month S', 5510
six See also SIXSCORE; SIXTEEN.
Ge 7: 6 Noah was s' hundred years old 8337
11 the s' hundredth year of Noah's life, "
8:13 in the s' hundredth and first year, "
16:16 Abram was fourscore and s' years "
30:20 because I have born him s' sons: "
31:41 and s' years for thy cattle: "
46:26 the souls were threescore and s'; "
Ex 12:37 s' hundred thousand on foot that "
14: 7 he took s' hundred chosen chariots, "
16:26 S' days ye shall gather it; but on "
20: 9 S' days shalt thou labour, and do "
11 s' days the Lord made heaven and "
21: 2 servant, s' years he shall serve: "
23:10 s' years thou shalt sow thy land, "
12 S' days thou shalt do thy work, and "
24:16 and the cloud covered it s' days: "
25:32 s' branches shall come out of the "
33 the s' branches that come out of the "
35 the s' branches that proceed out of "
26: 9 and s' curtains by themselves, and "
22 westward thou shalt make s' boards. "
28:10 S' of their names on one stone, and "
10 s' names of the rest on the other "
31:15 S' days may work be done; but in "
17 s' days the Lord made heaven and "
34:21 S' days thou shalt work, but on the "
35: 2 S' days shall work be done, but on "
36:16 and s' curtains by themselves. "
27 westward he made s' boards. "
37:18 s' branches going out of the sides "
19 the s' branches going out of the "
21 to the s' branches going out of it. "
38:26 for s' hundred thousand and three "
Le 12: 5 purifying threescore and s' days. "
23: 3 S' days shall work be done: but "
24: 6 set them in two rows, s' on a row, "
25: 3 S' years thou shalt sow thy field, "
3 and s' years thou shalt prune thy "
Nu 1:21 and s' thousand and five hundred. "
25 five thousand s' hundred and fifty. "
27 fourteen thousand and s' hundred. "
46 s' hundred thousand and three "
2: 4 fourteen thousand and s' hundred. "
9 and s' thousand and four hundred, "
11 and s' thousand and five hundred. "
15 thousand and s' hundred and fifty. "
31 seven thousand and s' hundred. "
32 s' hundred thousand and three "
3:28 eight thousand and s' hundred, "
34 were s' thousand and two hundred. "
4:40 two thousand and s' hundred and "
7: 3 s' covered wagons, and twelve oxen; "
11:21 are s' hundred thousand footmen; "
26:41 and five thousand and s' hundred. "
51 of Israel, s' hundred thousand and "
31:32 s' hundred thousand and seventy "
37 was s' hundred and threescore and "
38 beeves were thirty and s' thousand; "
44 And thirty and s' thousand beeves, "
35: 6 there shall be s' cities for refuge, "
13 s' cities shall ye have for refuge. "
15 These s' cities shall be a refuge, "
De 5:13 S' days thou shalt labour, and do "
15:12 unto thee, and serve thee s' years; "
18 to thee, in serving thee s' years: "
16: 8 S' days thou shalt eat unleavened "
Jos 6: 3 once. Thus shalt thou do s' days. "
14 into the camp: so they did s' days. "
7: 5 smote...about thirty and s' men: "
15:59, 62 s' cities with their villages. "
J'g 3:31 slew of the Philistines s' hundred "
12: 7 Jephthah judged Israel s' years. "
18:11, 16 s' hundred men appointed with "
17 s' hundred men that were appointed "
20:15 cities twenty and s' thousand men "
47 s' hundred men turned and fled to "
Ru 3:15 he measured s' measures of barley, "
17 s' measures of barley gave he me; "
1Sa 13: 5 chariots, and s' thousand horsemen, "
15 with him, about s' hundred men. "
14: 2 him were about s' hundred men; "
17: 4 height was s' cubits and a span. "
7 spear's head weighed s' hundred "
23:13 men, which were about s' hundred, "
27: 2 passed over with the s' hundred men "
30: 9 s' hundred men that were with "
2Sa 2:11 was seven years and s' months. "
5: 5 Judah seven years and s' months: "
6:13 ark of the Lord had gone s' paces, "
15:18 s' hundred men which came after "
21:20 that had on every hand s' fingers, "
20 and on every foot s' toes, four and "
1Ki 6: 6 and the middle was s' cubits broad, "
10:14 Solomon in one year was s' hundred "
14 threescore and s' talents of gold, "
16 s' hundred shekels of gold went to "
19 The throne had s' steps, and the "
20 and on the other upon the s' steps: "
29 for s' hundred shekels of silver, "
11:16 s' months did Joab remain there "
16:23 s' years reigned he in Tirzah. "
2Ki 5: 5 and s' thousand pieces of gold, and "
11: 3 in the house of the Lord s' years. "
13:19 have smitten five or s' times; "
15: 8 over Israel in Samaria s' months. "
1Ch 3: 4 s' were born unto him in Hebron; "
4 reigned seven years and s' months: "
22 and Neariah, and Shaphat, s'. "
4:27 had sixteen sons and s' daughters; "
7: 2 twenty thousand and s' hundred. "
4 for war, s' and thirty thousand men: "
40 was twenty and s' thousand men. "
8:38 And Azel had s' sons, whose names "

1Ch 9: 6 brethren, s' hundred and ninety. 8337
9 nine hundred and fifty and s'. "
44 And Azel had s' sons, whose names "
12:24 s' thousand and eight hundred, "
26 Levi four thousand and s' hundred. "
35 and eight thousand and s' hundred. "
20: 6 s' on each hand, and s' on each foot: "
21:25 s' hundred shekels of gold by "
23: 4 and s' thousand were officers and "
25: 3 Hashabiah, and Mattithiah, s', "
26:17 Eastward were s' Levites, "
2Ch 1:17 a chariot for s' hundred shekels of "
2: 2 and s' hundred to oversee them. "
17 three thousand and s' hundred. "
18 thousand and s' hundred overseers "
3: 8 amounting to s' hundred talents. "
9:13 Solomon in one year was s' hundred "
13 threescore and s' talents of gold; "
15 s' hundred shekels of beaten gold "
18 there were s' steps to the throne, "
19 and on the other upon the s' steps. "
16: 1 s' and thirtieth year of the reign "
22:12 hid in the house of God s' years: "
26:12 were two thousand and s' hundred. "
29:33 were s' hundred oxen and three "
35: 8 and s' hundred small cattle, and "
Ezr 2:10 of Bani, s' hundred forty and two. "
11 of Bebai, s' hundred twenty and "
13 Adonikam, s' hundred sixty and s'. "
14 Bigvai, two thousand fifty and s'. "
22 The men of Netophah, fifty and s'. "
26 Gaba, s' hundred twenty and one. "
30 Magbish, an hundred fifty and s'. "
35 three thousand and s' hundred "
60 Nekoda, s' hundred fifty and two. "
66 were seven hundred thirty and s'; "
67 s' thousand seven hundred and "
8:26 s' hundred and fifty talents of "
35 for all Israel, ninety and s' rams, "
Ne 5:18 was one ox and s' choice sheep; "
7:10 of Arah, s' hundred fifty and two. "
15 Binnui, s' hundred forty and eight. "
16 of Bebai, s' hundred twenty and "
18 Adonikam, s' hundred threescore "
20 of Adin, s' hundred fifty and five. "
30 Gaba, s' hundred twenty and one. "
62 Nekoda, s' hundred forty and two. "
68 horses, seven hundred thirty and s': "
69 s' thousand seven hundred and "
Es 2:12 to wit, s' months with oil of myrrh, "
12 and s' months with sweet odours, "
Job 5:19 He shall deliver thee in s' troubles: "
42:12 s' thousand camels, and a thousand "
Pr 6:16 These s' things doth the Lord hate: "
Isa 6: 2 seraphims: each one had s' wings; "
Jer 34:14 when he hath served thee s' years, "
52:23 were ninety and s' pomegranates "
30 were four thousand and s' hundred. "
Eze 9: 2 s' men came from the way of the "
40: 5 a measuring reed of s' cubits long "
12 s' cubits on this side, and s' cubits "
41: 1 s' cubits broad on the one side, and "
1 s' cubits broad on the other side, "
3 two cubits; and the door, s' cubits; "
5 the wall of the house, s' cubits; "
8 were a full reed of s' great cubits. "
46: 1 shall be shut the s' working days; "
4 shall be s' lambs without blemish, "
6 blemish, and s' lambs, and a ram: "
Da 3: 1 and the breadth thereof s' cubits: 8353
M't 17: 1 after s' days Jesus taketh Peter, 1803
M'r 9: 2 after s' days Jesus taketh with him "
Lu 4:25 shut up three years and s' months, "
13:14 are s' days in which men ought to "
Joh 2: 6 were set there s' waterpots of stone, "
20 Forty and s' years was this temple "
12: 1 s' days before the passover came to "
Ac 11:12 these s' brethren accompanied me, "
18:11 there a year and s' months, "
Jas 5:17 space of three years and s' months. "
Re 4: 8 each of them s' wings about him; "
13:18 is S' hundred threescore and s'. 5516
14:20 thousand and s' hundred furlongs. 1812

six-hundred See SIX and HUNDRED.

sixscore
1Ki 9:14 to the king s' talents of gold. 3967,6242
Jon 4:11 more than s' thousand 8147,6240,7239

sixteen
Ge 46:18 she bare unto Jacob, even s' 8337,6240
Ex 26:25 sockets of silver, s' sockets; "
36:30 their sockets were s' sockets of "
Nu 26:22 s' thousand and five hundred. "
31:40 the persons were s' thousand; "
46 And s' thousand persons;) "
52 s' thousand seven hundred and "
Jos 15:41 s' cities with their villages. "
19:22 s' cities with their villages. "
2Ki 13:10 Samaria, and reigned s' years. "
14:21 which was s' years old, and "
15: 2 S' years old was he when he "
33 reigned s' years in Jerusalem. "
16: 2 reigned s' years in Jerusalem, "
1Ch 4:27 Shimei had s' sons and six "
24: 4 of Eleazar there were s' chief "
2Ch 13:21 two sons, and s' daughters. "
26: 1 Uzziah, who was s' years old, "
3 S' years old was Uzziah when "
27: 1 reigned s' years in Jerusalem. "
8 reigned s' years in Jerusalem. "
28: 1 reigned s' years in Jerusalem: "
Ac 27:37 threescore and s' souls. 1440,1803

sixteenth
1Ch 24:14 to Bilgah, the s' to Immer, 8337,6240
25:23 The s' to Hananiah, he, his "
2Ch 29:17 in the s' day of the first month "

sixth
Ge 1:31 and the morning were the s' day. 8345
30:19 again, and bare Jacob the s' son. "
Ex 16: 5 on the s' day they shall prepare "
22 on the s' day they gathered twice "
29 on the s' day the bread of two days; "
26: 9 shalt double the s' curtain in the "
Le 25:21 blessing upon you in the s' year, "
Nu 7:42 On the s' day Eliasaph the son of "
29:29 on the s' day eight bullocks, two "
Jos 19:32 The s' lot came out to the children "
2Sa 3: 5 the s', Ithream, by Eglah David's "
1Ki 16: 8 In the twenty and s' year of Asa 8337
2Ki 18:10 even in the s' year of Hezekiah, "
1Ch 2:15 Ozem the s', David the seventh: 8345
3: 3 s', Ithream by Eglah his wife. "
12:11 Attai the s', Eliel the seventh, "
24: 9 to Malchijah, the s' to Mijamin, "
25:13 The s' to Bukkiah, he, his sons, and "
26: 3 Elam the fifth, Jehohanan the s', "
5 Ammiel the s', Issachar the "
27: 9 The s' captain for the s' month was "
Ezr 6:15 was in the s' year of the reign of 8353
Ne 3:30 and Hanun the s' son of Zalaph, 8345
Eze 4:11 by measure, the s' part of an hin: "
8: 1 pass in the s' year, in the s' month, "
39: 2 and leave but the s' part of thee. *8338
45:13 offer; the s' part of an ephah of an 8345
13 give the s' part of an ephah of an 8341
46:14 the s' part of an ephah, and the 8345
Hag 1: 1 of Darius the king, in the s' month, "
15 and twentieth day of the s' month, "
M't 20: 5 out about the s' and ninth hour, 1623
27:45 the s' hour there was darkness "
M'r 15:33 when the s' hour was come, there "
Lu 1:26 the s' month the angel Gabriel was "
36 this is the s' month with her, who "
23:44 it was about the s' hour, and there "
Joh 4: 6 well: and it was about the s' hour. "
19:14 passover, and about the s' hour: "
Ac 10: 9 housetop to pray about the s' hour: "
Re 6:12 when he had opened the s' seal, "
9:13 the s' angel sounded, and I heard a "
14 Saying to the s' angel which had "
16:12 And the s' angel poured out his vial "
21:20 The fifth, sardonyx; the s', sardius; "

six-thousand See SIX and THOUSAND.

sixty See also SIXTYFOLD.
Ge 5:15 Mahalaleel lived s' and five years, 8346
18 Jared lived an hundred s' and two "
20 Jared were nine hundred s' and two "
21 And Enoch lived s' and five years, "
23 of Enoch were three hundred s' and "
27 Methuselah were nine hundred s' "
Le 27: 3 from twenty years old even unto s' "
7 if it be from s' years old and above; "
Nu 7:88 the rams s', the he goats s', "
88 the lambs of the first year s'. This "
Ezr 2:13 Adonikam, six hundred s' and six. "
M't 13:23 some an hundredfold, some s', 1835
M'r 4: 8 some thirty, and some s', and some* "
20 some thirtyfold, some s', and some* "

sixtyfold
M't 13: 8 some s', some thirtyfold. *1835

size
Ex 36: 9 the curtains were all of one s'. *4060
15 the eleven curtains were of one s'.* "
1Ki 6:25 were of one measure and one s'. *7095
7:37 casting, one measure, and one s'.* "
1Ch 23:29 for all manner of measure and s'; 4060

skies
2Sa 22:12 waters, and thick clouds of the s'. 7834
Ps 18:11 waters and thick clouds of the s'. "
77:17 out water: the s' sent out a sound: "
Isa 45: 8 let the s' pour down righteousness: "
Jer 51: 9 and is lifted up even to the s'. "

skilful See also UNSKILFUL.
1Ch 5:18 and s' in war, were four and forty 3925
15:22 about the song, because he was s'. 995
28:21 every willing s' man, for any *2451
2Ch 2:14 s' to work in gold, and in silver, in 3045
Eze 21:31 of brutish men, and s' to destroy. 2796
Da 1: 4 favoured, and s' in all wisdom, 7919
Am 5:16 such as are s' of lamentation to 3045

skilfully
Ps 33: 3 song; play s' with a loud noise. 3190

skilfulness
Ps 78:72 them by the s' of his hands. 8394

skill See also SKILFUL.
1Ki 5: 6 can s' to hew timber like unto the ‡3045
2Ch 2: 7 s' to grave with the cunning men ‡ "
8 thy servants can s' to cut timber ‡ "
34:12 could s' of instruments of musick. ‡ 995
Ec 9:11 nor yet favour to men of s'; but 3045
Da 1:17 and s' in all learning and wisdom: 7919
9:22 to give thee s' and understanding.* "

skin See also FORESKIN; SKINS.
Ex 22:27 only, it is his raiment for his s': 5785
29:14 the flesh of the bullock, and his s', "
34:29 wist not that the s' of his face shone "
30 behold, the s' of his face shone; "
35 that the s' of Moses' face shone: "
Le 4:11 And the s' of the bullock, and all "
7: 8 himself the s' of the burnt offering "
11:32 vessel of wood, or raiment, or s', or "
13: 2 have in the s' of his flesh a rising, "
2 it be in the s' of his flesh like the "
3 on the plague in the s' of the flesh: "
3 be deeper than the s' of his flesh, "
4 spot be white in the s' of his flesh, "
4 in sight be not deeper than the s', "
5 and the plague spread not in the s'; "
Le 13: 6 the plague spread not in the s', the 5785
7 scab spread much abroad in the s', "
8 the scab spreadeth in the s', then "
10 if the rising be white in the s', and "
11 an old leprosy in the s' of his flesh, "
12 leprosy break out abroad in the s', "
12 leprosy cover all the s' of him that "
18 in the s' thereof, was a boil, and is "
20 it be in sight lower than the s', and "
21 and if it be not lower than the s', "
22 if it spread much abroad in the s', "
24 s' whereof there is a hot burning, "
25 it be in sight deeper than the s'; "
26 it be no lower than the other s', "
27 it be spread much abroad in the s', "
28 his place, and spread not in the s', "
30 if it be in sight deeper than the s'; "
31 it be not in sight deeper than the s', "
32 be not in s' deeper then the s'; "
34 if the scall be not spread in the s', "
34 nor be in sight deeper than the s', "
35 if the scall spread much in the s' "
36 if the scall be spread in the s', the "
38 in the s' of their flesh bright spots, "
39 bright spots in the s' of their flesh "
39 spot that groweth in the s'; he is "
43 appeareth in the s' of the flesh; "
48 in a s', or in any thing made of s'; "
49 reddish in the garment, or in the s', "
49 in the woof, or in any thing of s'; "
51 the warp, or in the woof, or in a s', "
51 or in any work that is made of s'; "
52 or any thing of s', wherein the "
53 or in the woof, or in any thing of s'; "
56 out of the garment, or out of the s', "
57 or in the woof, or in any thing of s'; "
58 or whatsoever thing of s' it be, "
15:17 And every garment, and every s', "
Nu 19: 5 burn the heifer in his sight; her s', "
Job 2: 4 S' for s', yea, all that a man "
7: 5 my s' is broken, and become "
10:11 hast clothed me with s' and flesh, "
16:15 have sewed sackcloth upon my s', 1539
18:13 shall devour the strength of his s': *5785
19:20 My bone cleaveth to my s' and to "
20 and I am escaped with the s' of my "
26 though after my s' worms destroy "
30:30 My s' is black upon me, and my "
41: 7 thou fill his s' with barbed irons? "
Ps 102: 5 my bones cleave to my s'. *1320
Jer 13:23 Can the Ethiopian change his s', 5785
La 3: 4 flesh and my s' hath he made old; "
4: 8 their s' cleaveth to their bones; it "
5:10 Our s' was black like an oven "
Eze 16:10 and shod thee with badgers' s', and*
37: 6 upon you, and cover you with s', 5785
8 and the s' covered them above: but "
Mic 3: 2 pluck off their s' from off them, "
3 and flay their s' from off them; and "
M'r 1: 6 a girdle of a s' about his loins; *1193

skins See also FORESKINS; GOATSKINS; SHEEPSKINS.
Ge 3:21 did the Lord God make coats of s', 5785
27:16 she put the s' of the kids of the "
Ex 25: 5 rams' s' dyed red, and badgers' s', "
26:14 for the tent of rams' s' dyed red, "
14 and a covering above of badgers' s'. "
35: 7 rams' s' dyed red, and badgers' s', "
23 and red s' of rams, and badgers' s', "
36:19 for the tent of rams' s' dyed red, "
19 and a covering of badgers' s' above "
39:34 the covering of rams' s' dyed red, "
34 the covering of badgers' s', and the "
Le 13:59 warp, or woof, or any thing of s', * "
16:27 they shall burn in the fire their s', "
Nu 4: 6 thereon the covering of badgers' s',* "
8 same with a covering of badgers' s',* "
10 within a covering of badgers' s', * "
11 it with a covering of badgers' s', * "
12 them with a covering of badgers' s',* "
14 upon it a covering of badgers' s', * "
25 covering of the badgers' s' that is* "
31:20 all that is made of s', and all work *5785

skip See also SKIPPED; SKIPPING.
Ps 29: 6 them also to s' like a calf; 7540

skipped See also SKIPPEDST.
Ps 114: 4 The mountains s' like rams, and 7540
6 mountains, that ye s' like rams; * "

skippedst
Jer 48:27 spakest of him, thou s' for joy. *5110

skipping
Ca 2: 8 the mountains, s' upon the hills. 7092

skirt See also SKIRTS.
De 22:30 wife, nor discover his father's s'. 3671
27:20 he uncovereth his father's s'. "
Ru 3: 9 spread therefore thy s' over thine "
1Sa 15:27 laid hold upon the s' of his mantle, "
24: 4 cut off the s' of Saul's robe privily. "
5 because he had cut off Saul's s'. "
11 see the s' of thy robe in my hand: "
11 in that I cut off the s' of thy robe, "
Eze 16: 8 and I spread my s' over thee, and "
Hag 2:12 holy flesh in the s' of his garment, "
12 and with his s' do touch bread, or "
Zec 8:23 hold of the s' of him that is a Jew, "

skirts
Ps 133: 2 down to the s' of his garments; *6310
Jer 2:34 Also in thy s' is found the blood of 3671
13:22 iniquity are thy s' discovered, and 7757
26 I discover thy s' upon thy face, "
La 1: 9 Her filthiness is in her s'; she "
Eze 5: 3 number, and bind them in thy s'. 3671
Na 3: 5 will discover thy s' upon thy face. 7757

skull
J'g 9:53 head, and all to brake his s'. 1538
2Ki 9:35 found no more of her than the s', "
M't 27:33 that is to say, a place of a s', *2898*
M'r 15:22 being interpreted, The place of a s'. "
Joh 19:17 into a place called the place of a s', "

sky See also SKIES.
De 33:26 and in his excellency on the s'. *7834
Job 37:18 thou with him spread out the s', "
M't 16: 2 be fair weather: for the s' is red. **3772*
3 day: for the s' is red and lowering. "
3 ye can discern the face of the s'; * "
Lu 12:56 ye can discern the face of the s' * "
Heb11:12 so many as the stars of the s' in * "

slack See also SLACKED.
De 7:10 not be s' to him that hateth him, 309
23:21 thy God, thou shalt not s' to pay it: "
Jos 10: 6 S' not thy hand from thy servants;7503
18: 3 How long are ye s' to go to possess "
2Ki 4:24 s' not thy riding for me, except I *6113
Pr 10: 4 poor that dealeth with a s' hand: 7423
Zep 3:16 Zion, Let not thine hands be s'. 7503
2Pe 3: 9 The Lord is not s' concerning his *1019*

slacked
Hab 1: 4 the law is s', and judgment doth 6313

slackness
2Pe 3: 9 promise, as some men count s'; *1022*

slain
Ge 4:23 I have s' a man to my wounding, 2026
34:27 sons of Jacob came upon the s', 2491
Le 14:51 them in the blood of the s' bird, 7819
26:17 shall be s' before your enemies: *5062
Nu 11:22 flocks of the herds be s' for 7819
14:16 hath s' them in the wilderness. "
19:16 one that is s' with a sword in 2491
18 a bone, or one s', or one dead, or a "
22:33 surely now also I had s' thee, and 2026
23:24 and drink the blood of the s'. 2491
25:14 name of the Israelite that was s', 5221
14 was s' with the Midianitish woman, "
15 Midianitish woman that was s' was "
18 was s' in the day of the plague for "
31: 8 the rest of them that were s'; 2491
19 and whosoever hath touched any s', "
De 1: 4 he had s' Sihon the king of the *5221
21: 1 be found s' in the land which the 2491
1 it be not known who hath s' him: "
2 are round about him that is s': "
3 city which is next unto the s' man, "
6 that are next unto the s' man, shall "
28:31 Thine ox shall be s' before thine 2873
32:42 with the blood of the s' and of the 2491
Jos 11: 6 deliver them up all s' before Israel: "
13:22 among them that were s' by them. "
J'g 9:18 and have s' his sons, threescore 2026
15:16 an ass have I s' a thousand men. *5221
20: 4 husband of the woman that was s',*7523
5 night, and thought to have s' me: 2026
1Sa 4:11 Hophni and Phinehas, were s'. 4191
18: 7 Saul hath s' his thousands, and 5221
19: 6 the Lord liveth, he shall not be s'.*4191
11 to morrow thou shalt be s'. "
20:32 Wherefore shall he be s'? what "
21:11 Saul hath s' his thousands, and 5221
22:21 Saul had s' the Lord's priests. 2026
31: 1 and fell down s' in mount Gilboa. 2491
8 the Philistines came to strip the s', "
2Sa 1:16 I have s' the Lord's anointed. 4191
19 The beauty of Israel is s' upon thy 2491
22 From the blood of the s', from the "
25 thou wast s' in thine high places. "
3:30 he had s' their brother Asahel at *4191
4:11 men have s' a righteous person in 2026
12: 9 and hast s' him with the sword of "
13:30 Absalom hath s' all the king's 5221
32 s' all the young men the king's *4191
18: 7 people of Israel were s' before the*5062
21:12 Philistines had s' Saul in Gilboa: *5221
16 sword, thought to have s' David. "
1Ki 1:19, 25 oxen and fat cattle and sheep2076
9:16 s' the Canaanites that dwelt in the 2026
11:15 host was gone up to bury the s', 2491
13:26 which hath torn him, and s' him, 4191
16:16 and hath also s' the king: *5221
19: 1 how he had s' all the prophets 2026
10, 14 s' thy prophets with the sword; "
2Ki 3:23 the kings are surely s', and they *2717
11: 2 the king's sons which were s'; 4191
2 from Athaliah, so that he was not s'. "
8 within the ranges, let him be s': "
15 Let her not be s' in the house of the "
16 king's house: and there was she s'. "
14: 5 his servants which had s' the king5221
1Ch 5:22 there fell down many s', because 2491
10: 1 and fell down s' in mount Gilboa. "
8 the Philistines came to strip the s', "
11:11 hundred s' by him at one time. * "
2Ch 13:17 fell down s' of Israel five hundred "
21:13 also hast s' thy brethren of thy 2026
22: 1 to the camp had s' all the eldest. "
9 and when they had s' him, they *4191
11 among the king's sons that were s', "
23:14 her, let him be s' with the sword. "
21 they had s' Athaliah with the sword.* "
28: 9 and ye have s' them in a rage that 2026
Es 7: 4 my people, to be destroyed, to be s', "
9:11 of those that were s' in Shushan "
12 The Jews have s' and destroyed "
Job 1:15, 17 s' the servants with the edge of5221
39:30 and where the s' are, there is she. 2491
Ps 62: 3 ye shall be s' all of you: as a *7523
88: 5 like the s' that lie in the grave, 2491
89:10 Rahab in pieces, as one that is s'; "
Pr 7:26 strong men have been s' by her. 2026
Pr 22:13 without, I shall be s' in the streets.†7523
24:11 and those that are ready to be s'; 2027
Isa 10: 4 and they shall fall under the s'. 2026
14:19 as the raiment of those that are s', "
20 thy land, and s' thy people: "
22: 2 s' men are not s' with the sword, 2491
26:21 and shall no more cover her s'. 2026
27: 7 he s' according to the slaughter of "
7 of them that are s' by him? "
34: 3 Their s' also shall be cast out, and 2491
66:16 the s' of the Lord shall be many. "
Jer 9: 1 the s' of the daughter of my people! "
14:18 then behold the s' with the sword! "
18:21 young men be s' by the sword in *5221
25:33 s' of the Lord shall be at that day 2491
33: 5 whom I have s' in mine anger 5221
41: 4 day after he had s' Gedaliah, 4191
9 he had s' because of Gedaliah, 5221
9 filled it with them that were s'. 2491
16 s' Gedaliah the son of Ahikam, 5221
18 son of Nethaniah had s' Gedaliah "
51: 4 the s' shall fall in the land of the 2491
47 her s' shall fall in the midst of her. "
49 hath caused the s' of Israel to fall, "
49 shall fall the s' of all the earth. "
La 2:20 the priest and the prophet be s' in 2026
21 s' them in the day of thine anger; "
3:43 thou hast s', thou hast not pitied. "
4: 9 They that be s' with the sword are2491
9 than they that be s' with hunger: "
Eze 6: 4 down your s' men before your idols. "
7 the s' shall fall in the midst of you, "
13 when their s' men shall be among "
9: 7 house, and fill the courts with the s': "
11: 6 have multiplied your s' in this city, "
6 filled the streets thereof with the s'. "
7 Your s' whom ye have laid in the "
16:21 That thou hast s' my children, and7819
21:14 the third time, the sword of the s': *2491
14 sword of the great men that are s',* "
29 upon the necks of them that are s',* "
23:39 when they had s' their children to7819
26: 6 the field shall be s' by the sword; 2026
28: 8 are s' in the midst of the seas. 2491
30: 4 when the s' shall fall in Egypt, and "
11 Egypt, and fill the land with the s'. "
31:17 them that be s' with the sword; "
18 with them that be s' by the sword. "
32:20 of them that are s' by the sword: "
21 lie uncircumcised, s' by the sword. "
22 all of them s', fallen by the sword: "
23, 24 all of them s', fallen by the sword, "
25 set her a bed in the midst of the s' "
25 uncircumcised, s' by the sword: "
25 put in the midst of them that be s'. "
26 uncircumcised, s' by the sword, 2490
28 them that are s' with the sword. 2491
29 by them that were s' by the sword: "
30 which are gone down with the s'; "
30 with them that be s' by the sword, "
31 Pharaoh and all his army s' by the "
32 them that are s' with the sword, "
35: 8 fill his mountains with his s' men: "
8 they fall that are s' with the sword. "
37: 9 breathe upon these s', that they 2026
Da 2:13 that the wise men should be s'; 6992
13 Daniel and his fellows to be s'. "
5:30 was...the king of the Chaldeans s'. "
7:11 I beheld even till the beast was s', "
11:26 and many shall fall down s'. 2491
Ho 6: 5 s' them by the words of my mouth: 2026
Am 4:10 young men have I s' with the sword, "
Na 3: 3 and there is a multitude of s', and 2491
Zep 2:12 also, ye shall be s' by my sword. "
Lu 9:22 be s', and be raised the third day. * *615*
Ac 2:23 wicked hands have crucified and s':* *337*
5:36 who was s'; and all, as many as "
7:42 have ye offered to me s' beasts and*4968*
52 they have s' them which shewed *615*
13:28 they Pilate that he should be s'. *337*
23:14 eat nothing until we have s' Paul.* *615*
Eph 2:16 cross, having s' the enmity thereby: "
Heb11:37 were s' with the sword: *1722,5408,599*
Re 2:13 martyr, who was s' among you, * *615*
5: 6 stood a Lamb as it had been s', *4969*
9 thou wast s', and hast redeemed "
12 Worthy is the Lamb that was s' to "
6: 9 that were s' for the word of God, "
11:13 were s' of men seven thousand: * *615*
13: 8 the Lamb s' from the foundation *4969*
18:24 of all that were s' upon the earth. "
19:21 remnant were s' with the sword of **615*

slander See also SLANDERED; SLANDEREST; SLANDERETH; SLANDERS.
Nu 14:36 by bringing up a s' upon the land,*1681
Ps 31:13 For I have heard the s' of many: * "
Pr 10:18 and he that uttereth a s', is a fool. "

slandered
2Sa 19:27 hath s' thy servant unto my lord 7270

slanderest
Ps 50:20 s' thine own mother's son. 5414,1848

slandereth
Ps 101: 5 Whoso privily s' his neighbour, 3960

slanderously
Ro 3: 8 (as we be s' reported, and as some *987*

slanders
Jer 6:28 revolters, walking with s': 7400
9: 4 every neighbour will walk with s'. "

slanderers
1Ti 3:11 must their wives be grave, not s', *1228*

slang
1Sa 17:49 and took thence a stone, and s' it, 7049

slaughter
Ge 14:17 from the s' of Chedorlaomer, 5221
Jos 10:10 and slew them with a great s' at 4347
20 slaying them with a very great s', "
J'g 11:33 the vineyards, with a very great s'. "
15: 8 them hip and thigh with a great s': "
1Sa 4:10 and there was a very great s'; for "
17 there hath been also a great s' 4046
6:19 many of the people with a great s'.4347
14:14 And that first s', which Jonathan "
30 not been now a much greater s' "
17:57 David returned from the s' of the 5221
18: 6 David was returned from the s' of "
19: 8 and slew them with a great s'; 4347
23: 5 and smote them with a great s'. "
2Sa 1: 1 David was returned from the s' of 5221
17: 9 s' among the people that follow 4046
18: 7 there was there a great s' that day "
1Ki 20:21 slew the Syrians with a great s'. 4347
2Ch 13:17 people slew them with a great s': "
25:14 come from the s' of the Edomites, 5221
28: 5 who smote him with a great s'. 4347
Es 9: 5 the sword, and s', and destruction,2027
Ps 44:22 we are counted as sheep for the s'.2878
Pr 7:22 as an ox goeth to the s', or as a 2875
Isa 10:26 according to the s' of Midian at 4347
14:21 Prepare s' for his children for the 4293
27: 7 according to the s' of them that 2027
30:25 of waters in the day of the great s', "
34: 2 he hath delivered them to the s'. 2875
6 a great s' in the land of Idumea. "
53: 7 he is brought as a lamb to the s', "
65:12 and ye shall all bow down to the s': "
Jer 7:32 of Hinnom, but the valley of s': 2028
11:19 or an ox that is brought to the s'; 2873
12: 3 pull them out like sheep for the s', "
3 and prepare them for the day of s'.2028
19: 6 of Hinnom, but The valley of s'. "
25:34 for the days of your s' and of your 2873
48:15 young men are gone...to the s', 2875
50:27 let them go down to the s': woe "
51:40 them down like lambs to the s', 2873
Eze 9: 2 every man a s' weapon in his hand;4660
21:10 It is sharpened to make a sore s'; 2873
15 bright, it is wrapped up for the s'. 2875
22 to open the mouth in the s', to lift 7524
28 is drawn: for the s' it is furbished,2875
26:15 when the s' is made in the midst 2027
Ho 5: 2 revolters are profound to make s', 7819
Ob 9 mount of Esau may be cut off by s'.6993
Zec 11: 4 my God; Feed the flock of the s'; 2028
7 And I will feed the flock of s', even "
Ac 8:32 He was led as a sheep to the s'; *4967*
9: 1 s' against the disciples of the Lord,*5408*
Ro 8:36 are accounted as sheep for the s'. *4967*
Heb 7: 1 returning from the s' of the kings.*2871*
Jas 5: 5 your hearts, as in a day of s'. *4967*

slave See also SLAVES.
Jer 2:14 Israel a servant? is he a homeborn s'?

slaves
Re 18:13 chariots, and s', and souls of men. *4983*

slay See also SLAIN; SLAYETH; SLAYING; SLEW.
Ge 4:14 one that findeth me shall s' me. 2026
18:25 s' the righteous with the wicked: 4191
20: 4 thou s' also a righteous nation? 2026
11 they will s' me for my wife's sake. "
22:10 and took the knife to s' his son. 7819
27:41 then will I s' my brother Jacob. 2026
34:30 together against me, and s' me; *5221
37:18 conspired against him to s' him. 4191
20 let us s' him, and cast him into 2026
26 What profit is it if we s' our brother, "
42:37 S' my two sons, if I bring him not 4191
43:16 Bring these men home, and s', 2875
Ex 2:15 this thing, he sought to s' Moses. 2026
4:23 I will s' thy son, even thy firstborn. "
5:21 put a sword in their hand to s' us. "
21:14 his neighbour, to s' him with guile; "
23: 7 innocent and righteous s' thou not: "
29:16 And thou shalt s' the ram, and 7819
32:12 out, to s' them in the mountains, 2026
27 s' every man his brother, and every "
Le 4:29 s' the sin offering in the place of *7819
33 s' it for a sin offering in the place* "
14:13 he shall s' the lamb in the place * "
20:15 death; and ye shall s' the beast. 2026
Nu 19: 3 one shall s' her before his face: 7819
25: 5 S' ye every one his men that were 2026
35:19 himself shall s' the murderer: *4191
19 he meeteth him, he shall s' him. * "
21 of blood shall s' the murderer, * "
De 9:28 out to s' them in the wilderness. * "
19: 6 the way is long, and s' him; *5221
27:25 reward to s' an innocent person: "
Jos 13:22 children of Israel s' with the sword2026
J'g 8:19 saved them alive, I would not s' you. "
20 his firstborn, Up, and s' them. "
9:54 Draw thy sword, and s' me, that *4191
1Sa 2:25 because the Lord would s' them. "
5:10 ark...to us, to s' us and our people. "
11 that it s' us not, and our people: "
14:34 sheep, and s' them here, and eat; 7819
15: 3 but s' both man and woman, 4191
19: 5 blood, to s' David without a cause? "
11 him, and to s' him in the morning: "
15 to me in the bed, that I may s' him. "
20: 8 be in me iniquity, s' me thyself; "
33 determined of his father to s' David.* "
22:17 Turn, and s' the priests of the Lord; "
2Sa 1: 9 Stand...upon me, and s' me: for "
3:37 it was not of the king to s' Abner "
21: 2 Saul sought to s' them in his zeal 5221
1Ki 1:51 not s' his servant with the sword. 4191
3:26 the living child, and in no wise s' it. "
27 the living child, and in no wise s' it: "

1Ki 15:28 did Baasha s· him, and reigned in 4191
17:18 to remembrance, and to s· my son? "
18: 9 into the hand of Ahab, to s· me? "
12 he cannot find thee, he shall s· me:2026
14 Elijah is here: and he shall s· me. "
19:17 the sword of Hazael shall Jehu s· 4191
17 the sword of Jehu shall Elisha s·. "
20:36 from me, a lion shall s· thee. 5221
2Ki 8:12 young men wilt thou s· with the 2026
10:25 the captains, Go in, and s· them; 5221
17:26 s· them, because they know not 4191
2Ch 20:23 utterly to s· and destroy them: 2763
23:14 S· her not in the house of the Lord,4191
Ne 4:11 and s· them, and cause the work to2026
6:10 for they will come to s· thee; "
10 the night will they come to s· thee. "
Es 8:11 to s·, and to cause to perish, all the "
Job 9:23 If the scourge s· suddenly, he will 4191
13:15 Though he s· me, yet will I trust 6991
20:16 the viper's tongue shall s· him. 2026
Ps 34:21 Evil shall s· the wicked: and they 4191
37:14 and to s· such as be of upright 2873
32 righteous, and seeketh to s· him. 4191
59:11 S· them not, lest my people forget:2026
94: 6 s· the widow and the stranger, and "
109:16 might even s· the broken in heart. 4191
139:19 Surely thou wilt s· the wicked, 6991
Pr 1:32 away of the simple shall s· them, 2026
Isa 11: 4 of his lips shall he s· the wicked. 4191
14:30 and he shall s· thy remnant. *2026
27: 1 he shall s· the dragon that is in the "
65:15 for the Lord God shall s· thee, and4191
Jer 5: 6 lion out of the forest shall s· them,5221
15: 3 sword to s·, and the dogs to tear, 2026
18:23 their counsel against me to s· me:1194
20: 4 and shall s· them with the sword. 5221
29:21 he shall s· them before your eyes; "
40:14 son of Nethaniah to s· thee? *5221,5315
15 and I will s· Ishmael the son of 5221
15 wherefore should he s· thee, that * "
41: 8 that said unto Ishmael, S· us not:4191
50:27 S· all her bullocks; let them go 2717
Eze 9: 6 S· utterly old and young, both 2026
13:19 to s· the souls that should not die,4191
23:47 they shall s· their sons and their "
26: 8 s· with the sword thy daughters in "
11 he shall s· thy people by the sword, "
40:39 to s· thereon the burnt offering 7819
44:11 they shall s· the burnt offering and "
Da 2:14 was gone forth to s· the wise men 6992
Ho 2: 3 a dry land, and s· her with thirst. 4191
9:16 I s· even the beloved fruit of their "
Am 2: 3 will s· all the princes thereof with 2026
9: 1 s· the last of them with the sword: "
4 the sword, and it shall s· them: "
Hab 1:17 spare continually to s· the nations? "
Zec 11: 5 Whose possessors s· them, and hold "
Lu 11:49 and some of them they shall s· and*615
19:27 hither, and s· them before me. 2695
Joh 5:16 Jesus, and sought to s· him, * 615
Ac 5:33 heart, and took counsel to s· them. 337
9:29 but they went about to s· him. "
10:13 unto me, Arise, Peter; s· and eat. *2380
Re 9:15 year, for to s· the third part of men.*615

slayer See also MANSLAYER.
Nu 35:11 that the s· may flee thither, which*7523
24 between the s· and the revenger *5221
25 congregation shall deliver the s· *7523
26 But if the s· shall at any time come* "
27 the revenger of blood kill the s·; * "
28 s· shall return into the land of his* "
De 4:42 That the s· might flee thither, * "
19: 3 that every s· may flee thither. * "
4 this is the case of the s·, which * "
6 avenger of the blood pursue the s·,* "
Jos 20: 3 That the s· that killeth any person* "
5 they shall not deliver the s· up into* "
6 then shall the s· return, and come* "
21:13, 21, 27, 32, 38 city of refuge for...s·;* "
Eze 21:11 to give it into the hand of the s·. 2026

slayeth
Ge 4:15 him, Therefore whosoever s· Cain,2026
De 22:26 his neighbour, and s· him, 7523,5315
Job 5: 2 man, and envy s· the silly one. 4191
Eze 28: 9 before him that s· thee, I am God?2026
9 in the hand of him that s· thee. *2490

slaying
Jos 8:24 end of s· all the inhabitants of Ai 2026
10:20 had made an end of s· them with 5221
J'g 9:56 father, in s· his seventy brethren: 2026
1Ki 17:20 whom I sojourn, by s· her son? 4191
Isa 22:13 s· oxen, and killing sheep, eating 2026
57: 5 s· the children in the valleys *7819
Eze 9: 8 to pass, while they were s· them, *5221

sleep See also ASLEEP; SLEEPEST; SLEEPETH; SLEEPING; SLEPT.
Ge 2:21 a deep s· to fall upon Adam, and 3462
15:12 down, a deep s· fell upon Abram; 8639
28:11 and lay down in that place to s·. 7901
16 And Jacob awaked out of his s·, 8142
31:40 and my s· departed from mine eyes." "
Ex 22:27 for his skin: wherein shall he s·? 7901
De 24:12 poor, shall not s· with his pledge: "
13 that he may s· in his own raiment, "
31:16 thou shalt s· with thy fathers; and "
J'g 16:14 And he awaked out of s·, and went8142
19 she made him s· upon her knees; 3462
20 he awoke out of his s·, and said, 8142
1Sa 3: 3 was, and Samuel was laid down to s·; "
26:12 a deep s· from the Lord was fallen8639
2Sa 7:12 and thou shalt s· with thy fathers,7901
1Ki 1:21 the king shall s· with his fathers, "
Es 6: 1 that night could not the king s·, 8142
Job 4:13 when deep s· falleth on men, 8639
7:21 for now shall I s· in the dust; and*7901
14:12 awake, nor be raised out of their s·.8142
33:15 when deep s· falleth upon men, in "
Ps 4: 8 both lay me down in peace, and s·:3462
13: 3 God: lighten mine eyes, lest I s· "
3 lest I...the s· of death; "
76: 5 spoiled, they have slept their s·: 8142
6 and horse is cast into a dead s·. 7290
78:65 the Lord awaked as one out of s·, 3463
90: 5 as with a flood; they are as a s·: 8142
121: 4 Israel shall neither slumber nor s·.3462
127: 2 for so he giveth his beloved s·. 8142
132: 4 I will not give s· to mine eyes, or "
Pr 3:24 down, and thy s· shall be sweet, "
4:16 For they s· not, except they have 3462
16 and their s· is taken away, unless 8142
6: 4 Give not s· to thine eyes, nor "
9 How long wilt thou s·, O sluggard?7901
9 when wilt thou arise out of thy s·?8142
10 Yet a little s·, a little slumber, a "
10 a little folding of the hands to s·: 7901
19:15 Slothfulness casteth into a deep s·;3462
20:13 Love not s·, lest thou come to 8142
24:33 Yet a little s·, a little slumber, a "
33 a little folding of the hands to s·: 7901
Ec 5:12 s· of a labouring man is sweet, 8142
12 of the rich will not suffer him to s·.3462
8:16 nor night seeth s· with his eyes:) 8142
Ca 5: 2 I s·, but my heart waketh: it is the*3463
Isa 5:27 none shall slumber nor s·; neither "
29:10 out upon you the spirit of deep s·, 8639
Jer 31:26 and my s· was sweet unto me. 8142
51:39 that they may rejoice, and s· 3462
39 a perpetual s·, and not wake, 8142
57 mighty men: and they shall s· 3462
57 a perpetual s·, and not wake 8142
Eze 34:25 wilderness, and s· in the woods. 3462
Da 2: 1 and his s· brake from him. 8142
6:18 him: and his s· went from him. 8139
8:18 I was in a deep s· on my face 7290
10: 9 then was I in a deep s· on my face, "
12: 2 many of them that s· in the dust 3463
Zec 4: 1 man that is wakened out of his s·, 8142
M't 1:24 Joseph being raised from s· did as 5258
26:45 S· on now, and take your rest: 2518
M'r 4:27 And should s·, and rise night and "
14:41 S· on now, and take your rest: "
Lu 9:32 were with him were heavy with s·: 5258
22:46 Why s· ye? rise and pray, lest ye 2518
Joh 11:11 that I may awake him out of s·. 1852
12 Lord, if he s·, he shall do well. *2837
13 had spoken of taking of rest in s·. 5258
Ac 13:36 fell on s·, and was laid unto his 2837
16:27 of the prison awaking out of his s·,1853
20: 9 being fallen into a deep s·: 5258
9 he sunk down with s·, and fell "
Ro 13:11 it is high time to awake out of s·: "
1Co 11:30 sickly among you, and many s·. 2837
15:51 We shall not all s·, but we shall all * "
1Th 4:14 so them also which s· in Jesus * "
5: 6 let us not s·, as do others; but let 2518
7 For they that s· s· in the night; "
10 for us, that, whether we wake or s·," "

sleeper
Jon 1: 6 What meanest thou, O s·? arise, 7290

sleepest
Ps 44:23 why s· thou, O Lord? arise, cast 3462
Pr 6:22 when thou s·, it shall keep thee; 7901
M'r 14:37 saith unto Peter, Simon, s· thou? 2518
Eph 5:14 Awake thou that s·, and arise from "

sleepeth
1Ki 18:27 peradventure he s·, and must be 3463
Pr 10: 5 s· in harvest is a son that causeth 7290
Ho 7: 6 wait: their baker s· all the night; 3463
M't 9:24 for the maid is not dead, but s·. 2518
M'r 5:39 the damsel is not dead, but s·. "
Lu 8:52 Weep not; she is not dead, but s·. "
Joh 11:11 unto them, Our friend Lazarus s·; 2837

sleeping
1Sa 26: 7 Saul lay s· within the trench, and 3463
Isa 56:10 s·, lying down, loving to slumber.*1957
M'r 13:36 coming suddenly he find you s·. 2518
14:37 he cometh, and findeth them s·, "
Lu 22:45 he found them s· for sorrow, 2837
Ac 12: 6 Peter was s· between two soldiers, "

sleight
Eph 4:14 by the s· of men, and cunning 2940

slept
Ge 2:21 to fall upon Adam, and he s·: and 3462
41: 5 And he s· and dreamed the second "
2Sa 11: 9 Uriah s· at the door of the king's 7901
1Ki 2:10 David s· with his fathers, and was "
3:20 while thine handmaid s·, and laid 3463
11:21 that David s· with his fathers, and7901
43 And Solomon s· with his fathers, "
14:20 he s· with his fathers, and Nadab "
31 And Rehoboam s· with his fathers, "
15: 8 And Abijam s· with his fathers; and "
24 Asa s· with his fathers, and was "
16: 6 So Baasha s· with his fathers, and "
28 So Omri s· with his fathers, and "
19: 5 he lay and s· under a juniper tree, 3462
22:40 So Ahab s· with his fathers; and 7901
50 Jehoshaphat s· with his fathers, "
2Ki 8:24 And Joram s· with his fathers, and "
10:35 And Jehu s· with his fathers: and "
13: 9 And Jehoahaz s· with his fathers; "
13 And Joash s· with his fathers; and "
14:16 And Jehoash s· with his fathers, "
22 that the king s· with his fathers. "
29 And Jeroboam s· with his fathers, "
15: 7 So Azariah s· with his fathers; and "
22 And Menahem s· with his fathers; "
38 Jotham s· with his fathers, and was "
2Ki 16:20 Ahaz s· with his fathers, and was 7901
20:21 And Hezekiah s· with his fathers: "
21:18 And Manasseh s· with his fathers, "
24: 6 So Jehoiakim s· with his fathers: "
2Ch 9:31 Solomon s· with his fathers, and he "
12:16 And Rehoboam s· with his fathers, "
14: 1 So Abijah s· with his fathers, and "
16:13 Asa s· with his fathers, and died in "
21: 1 Jehoshaphat s· with his fathers, "
26: 2 that the king s· with his fathers. "
23 So Uzziah s· with his fathers, and "
27: 9 Jotham s· with his fathers, and they "
28:27 And Ahaz s· with his fathers, and "
32:33 And Hezekiah s· with his fathers, "
33:20 So Manasseh s· with his fathers, and "
Job 3:13 and been quiet, I should have s·: 3462
Ps 3: 5 I laid me down and s·; I awaked; "
76: 5 spoiled, they have s· their sleep: 5123
M't 13:25 But while men s·, his enemy came 2518
25: 5 tarried, they all slumbered and s·. "
27:52 bodies of the saints which s· arose,*2837
28:13 and stole him away while we s·. * "
1Co 15:20 the firstfruits of them that s·. * "

slew See also SLEWEST.
Ge 4: 8 Abel his brother, and s· him. 2026
25 seed instead of Abel, whom Cain s·. "
34:25 the city boldly, and s· all the males. "
26 they s· Hamor and Shechem his son "
38: 7 of the Lord; and the Lord s· him. 4191
10 the Lord: wherefore he s· him also. "
49: 6 for in their anger they s· a man, 2026
Ex 2:12 he s· the Egyptian, and hid him in*5221
13:15 the Lord s· all the firstborn in the 2026
Le 8:15 And he s· it; and Moses took the 7819
23 And he s· it; and Moses took of the "
9: 8 s· the calf of the sin offering, which "
12 And he s· the burnt offering; and "
15 s· it, and offered it for sin, as the "
18 He s· also the bullock and the ram7819
Nu 31: 7 Moses; and they s· all the males. 2026
8 they s· the kings of Midian, beside "
8 son of Beor they s· with the sword. "
Jos 8:21 again, and s· the men of Ai. 5221
9:26 of Israel, that they s· them not. 2026
10:10 s· them with a great slaughter at 5221
11 children of Israel s· with...sword. 2026
26 Joshua smote them, and s· them, *4191
11:17 took, and smote them, and s· them.* "
J'g 1: 4 s· of them in Bezek ten thousand *5221
5 and they s· the Canaanites and the* "
10 and they s· Sheshai, and Ahiman, * "
17 s· the Canaanites that inhabited * "
3:29 they s· of Moab at that time about* "
31 s· of the Philistines six hundred * "
7:25 they s· Oreb upon the rock Oreb, *2026
25 and Zeeb they s· at the winepress of "
8:17 Penuel, and s· the men of the city. "
18 were they whom ye s· at Tabor? "
21 arose, and s· Zebah and Zalmunna, "
9: 5 s· his brethren...sons of Jerubbaal, "
24 their brother, which s· them; and "
44 were in the fields, and s· them. *5221
45 s· the people that was therein, 2026
54 say not of me, A woman s· him. "
12: 6 s· him at the passages of Jordan: 7819
14:19 s· thirty men of them, and took *5221
15:15 s· a thousand men therewith.* "
16:24 our country, which s· many of us.*2491
30 the dead which he s· at his death 4191
30 than they which he s· in his life. "
20:45 and s· two thousand men of them.*5221
1Sa 1:25 they s· a bullock, and brought the 7819
4: 2 and they s· of the army in the field5221
11:11 s· the Ammonites until the heat of* "
14:13 and his armourbearer s· after him.4191
32 calves, and s· them on the ground:7819
34 him that night, and s· them there. "
17:35 beard, and smote him, and s· him.4191
36 Thy servant s· both the lion and 5221
50 smote the Philistine, and s· him; 4191
51 and s· him, and cut off his head "
18:27 s· of the Philistines two hundred 5221
19: 5 in his hand, and s· the Philistine, * "
8 and s· them with a great slaughter;" "
22:18 s· on that day fourscore and five 4191
29: 5 Saul s· his thousands, and David *5221
30: 2 they s· not any, either great or 4191
31: 2 and the Philistines s· Jonathan, 5221
2Sa 1:10 So I stood upon him, and s· him, 4191
3:30 and Abishai his brother s· Abner, 2026
4: 7 and they smote him, and s· him, 4191
10 hold of him, and s· him in Ziklag, 2026
12 and they s· them, and cut off their "
8: 5 David s· of the Syrians two and *5221
10:18 David s· the men of seven hundred2126
14: 6 one smote the other, and s· him. *4191
7 the life of his brother whom he s·;2026
18:15 and smote Absalom, and s· him. 4191
21: 1 house, because he s· the Gibeonites.* "
18 Sibbechai the Hushathite s· Saph, 5221
19 s· the brother of Goliath the Gittite," "
21 the brother of David s· him. "
23: 8 hundred, whom he s· at one time.*2491
12 defended it, and s· the Philistines: 5221
18 three hundred, and s· them, and 2491
20 he s· two lionlike men of Moab: 5221
20 and s· a lion in the midst of a pit "
21 And he s· an Egyptian, a goodly 2026
21 and s· him with his own spear. 5221
1Ki 1: 9 Adonijah s· sheep and oxen and 2076
2: 5 and unto Amasa...whom he s·, 2026
32 than he, and s· them with the sword," "
34 up, and fell upon him, and s· him: 4191
11:24 when David s· them of Zobah: 2026
13:24 met him by the way, and s· him: 4191
16:11 that he s· all the house of Baasha: *5221

1Ki 18:13 I did when Jezebel s· the prophets 2026
40 brook Kishon, and s· them there. 7819
19:21 took a yoke of oxen, and s· them, 2076
20:20 And they s· every one his man: 5221
21 and s· the Syrians with a great "
29 Israel s· of the Syrians an hundred "
36 him, a lion found him, and s· him. "
2Ki 9:31 Zimri peace, who s· his master? *2026
10: 7 king's sons, and s· seventy persons, 7819
9 against my master, and s· him: 2026
9 but who s· all these? *5221
11 So Jehu s· all that remained of the* "
14 s· them at the pit of the shearing 7819
17 he s· all that remained unto Ahab *5221
11:18 and s· Mattan the priest of Baal 2026
20 they s· Athaliah with the sword "
12:20 and s· Joash in the house of Millo, *5221
14: 5 s· his servants which had slain the "
6 children of...murderers he s· not: *4191
7 s· of Edom in the valley of salt ten 5221
19 him to Lachish, and s· him there. 4191
15:10, 14 s· him, and reigned in his stead. "
30 s· him, and reigned in his stead. "
16: 9 of it captive to Kir, and s· Rezin. 4191
17:25 them, which s· some of them. *2026
21:23 and s· the king in his own house. *4191
24 s· all them that had conspired 5221
23:20 he s· all the priests of the high 2076
29 he s· him at Megiddo, when he had 4191
25: 7 And they s· the sons of Zedekiah 7819
21 s· them at Riblah in the land *4191
1Ch 2: 3 sight of the Lord; and he s· him. "
7:21 that were born in that land s·, 2026
10: 2 and the Philistines s· Jonathan, 5221
14 s· him, and turned the kingdom 4191
11:14 delivered it, and s· the Philistines; 5221
20 against three hundred, he s· them, 2490
22 he s· two lionlike men of Moab: 5221
22 s· a lion in a pit in a snowy day. "
23 he s· an Egyptian, a man of great "
23 and s· him with his own spear. 2026
18: 5 David s· of the Syrians two and *5221
12 s· of the Edomites in the valley of* "
19:18 and David s· of the Syrians seven 2026
20: 4 Sibbechai the Hushathite s· Sippai, 5221
5 Elhanan the son of Jair s· Lahmi "
7 of Shimea David's brother s· him. "
2Ch 13:17 And Abijah and his people s· them "
21: 4 s· all his brethren with the sword, 2026
22: 8 ministered to Ahaziah, he s· them. "
11 Athaliah, so that she s· him not. 4191
23:15 the king's house, they s· her there. "
17 and s· Mattan the priest of Baal 2026
24:22 not the kindness...but s· his son. "
25 and s· him on his bed, and he died: "
25: 3 he s· his servants that had killed "
4 But he s· not their children, but *4191
27 to Lachish after him, and s· him "
28: 6 s· in Judah an hundred and 2026
7 s· Maaseiah the king's son, and "
32:21 s· him there with the sword. 5307
33:24 and s· him in his own house. *4191
25 s· all them that had conspired 5221
36:17 who s· their young men with the 2026
Ne 9:26 and s· thy prophets which testified "
Es 9: 6 Jews s· and destroyed five hundred "
10 the enemy of the Jews, s· they "
15 s· three hundred men at Shushan; "
16 and s· of their foes seventy and five "
Ps 78:31 s· the fattest of them, and smote "
34 When he s· them, then they sought "
105:29 waters into blood, and s· their fish. 4191
135:10 great nations, and s· mighty kings; 2026
136:18 And s· famous kings: for his mercy "
Isa 66: 3 killeth an ox as if he s· a man; *5221
Jer 20:17 he s· me not from the womb; or 4191
26:23 king; who s· him with the sword, 5221
39: 6 Babylon s· the sons of Zedekiah 7819
6 Babylon s· all the nobles of Judah. "
41: 2 s· him, whom the king of Babylon 4191
3 Ishmael also s· all the Jews that 5221
7 the son of Nethaniah s· them, and 7819
8 s· them not among their brethren. 4191
52:10 Babylon s· the sons of Zedekiah 7819
10 he s· also all the princes of Judah "
La 2: 4 s· all that were pleasant to the eye *2026
Eze 9: 7 they went forth, and s· in the city. *5221
23:10 daughters, and s· her with the sword: "
40:41 whereupon they s·...sacrifices. 7819
42 they s· the burnt offering and the "
Da 3:22 the flame of the fire s· those men 6992
5:19 whom he would he s·; and whom he "
M't 2:16 s· all the children...in Bethlehem, 337
21:39 out of the vineyard, and s· him. * 615
22: 6 them spitefully, and s· them. * "
23:35 s· between the temple and...altar. 5407
Lu 13: 4 tower in Siloam fell, and s· them, * 615
Ac 5:30 raised up Jesus, whom ye s· and 1315
10:39 whom they s· and hanged on a tree: 337
22:20 kept the raiment of them that s· him. "
Ro 7:11 deceived me, and by it s· me. 615
1Jo 3:12 wicked one, and s· his brother. 4969
12 And wherefore s· he him? Because "

slewest
1Sa 21: 9 whom thou s· in the valley of Elah, 5221

slidden
Jer 8: 5 this people of Jerusalem s· back 7725

slide See also BACKSLIDING; SLIDDEN; SLIDETH.
De 32:35 their foot shall s· in due time: 4131
Ps 26: 1 the Lord; therefore I shall not s·. *4571
37:31 his heart; none of his steps shall s·. "

slideth
Ho 4:16 s· back as a backsliding heifer: *5637

slight See SLEIGHT.

slightly
Jer 6:14 of the daughter of my people s·, †7043
8:11 of the daughter of my people s·, † "

slime See also SLIMEPITS.
Ge 11: 3 stone, and s· had they for morter. 2564
Ex 2: 3 daubed it with s· and with pitch, "

slimepits
Ge 14:10 the vale of Siddim was full of s·; 2564

sling See also SLANG; SLINGS; SLINGSTONES.
J'g 20:16 could s· stones at an hair breadth, 7049
1Sa 17:40 and his s· was in his hand: and he 7050
50 with a s· and with a stone, "
25:29 enemies, them shall he s· out, as 7049
29 as out of the middle of a s·. 7050
Pr 26: 8 As he that bindeth a stone in a s·, †4773
Jer 10:18 s· out the inhabitants of the land 7049
Zec 9:15 devour, and subdue with s· stones; 7050

slingers
2Ki 3:25 the s· went about it, and smote it. 7051

slings
2Ch 26:14 and bows, and s· to cast stones. *7050

slingstones See also SLING and STONES.
Job 41:28 s· are turned with him into 68,7050

slip See also SLIPPED; SLIPPETH; SLIPS.
2Sa 22:37 me; so that my feet did not s·. *4571
Job 12: 5 He that is ready to s· with his feet* "
Ps 17: 5 thy paths, that my footsteps s· not. *4131
18:36 under me, that my feet did not s·. *4571
Heb 2: 1 at any time we should let them s·. *3901

slipped
1Sa 19:10 he s· away out of Saul's presence, 6362
Ps 73: 2 gone; my steps had well nigh s·. 8210

slippery
Ps 35: 6 Let their way be dark and s: and 2519
73:18 thou didst set them in s· places: 2513
Jer 23:12 way shall be unto them as s· ways 2519

slippeth
De 19: 5 and the head s· from the helve, 5394
Ps 38:16 when my foot s·, they magnify 4131
94:18 When I said, My foot s·; thy mercy, "

slips
Isa 17:10 and shalt set it with strange s·: 2156

slothful
J'g 18: 9 be not s· to go, and to enter to 6101
Pr 12:24 but the s· shall be under tribute. 7423
27 The s· man roasteth not that which "
15:19 way of the s· man is as an hedge *6102
18: 9 He also that is s· in his work is *7503
19:24 A s· man hideth his hand in his *6102
21:25 The desire of the s· killeth him; * "
22:13 The s· man saith, There is a lion * "
24:30 I went by the field of the s·, and "
26:13 The s· man saith, There is a lion in* "
14 hinges, so doth the s· upon his bed.* "
15 s· hideth his hand in his bosom; * "
M't 25:26 Thou wicked and s· servant, thou 3636
Ro 12:11 Not s· in business; fervent in spirit; "
Heb 6:12 That ye be not s·, but followers of *3576

slothfulness
Pr 19:15 S· casteth into a deep sleep; and 6103
Ec 10:18 By much s· the building decayeth; "

slow
Ex 4:10 s· of speech, and of a s· tongue. 3515
Ne 9:17 s· to anger, and of great kindness, 750
Ps 103: 8 s· to anger, and plenteous in mercy. "
145: 8 s· to anger, and of great mercy. "
Pr 14:29 He that is s· to wrath is of great "
15:18 that is s· to anger appeaseth strife. "
16:32 He that is s· to anger is better than "
Joe 2:13 s· to anger, and of great kindness, "
Jon 4: 2 s· to anger, and of great kindness, "
Na 1: 3 The Lord is s· to anger, and great in "
Lu 24:25 O fools, and s· of heart to believe 1021
Tit 1:12 alway liars, evil beasts, s· bellies. * 692
Jas 1:19 to hear, s· to speak, s· to wrath: 1021

slowly
Ac 27: 7 when we had sailed s· many days, 1020

sluggard
Pr 6: 6 Go to the ant, thou s·; consider 6102
9 How long wilt thou sleep, O s·? "
10:26 so is the s· to them that send him. "
13: 4 The soul of the s· desireth, and "
20: 4 The s· will not plow by reason of * "
26:16 The s· is wiser in his own conceit "

sluices
Isa 19:10 that make s· and ponds for fish. *7938

slumber See also SLUMBERED; SLUMBERETH; SLUMBERING.
Ps 121: 3 he that keepeth thee will not s·. 5123
4 Israel shall neither s· nor sleep. "
132: 4 to my eyes, or s· to mine eyelids, 8572
Pr 6: 4 thine eyes, nor s· to thine eyelids. "
10 Yet a little sleep, a little s·, a little "
24:33 Yet a little sleep, a little s·, a little "
Isa 5:27 none shall s· nor sleep; neither 5123
56:10 sleeping, lying down, loving to s·. "
Na 3:18 Thy shepherds s·, O king of "
Ro 11: 8 hath given them the spirit of s·, *2659

slumbered
M't 25: 5 tarried, they all s· and slept. 3573

slumbereth
2Pe 2: 3 not, and their damnation s· not. 3573

slumberings
Job 33:15 upon men, in s· upon the bed; 8572

small See also SMALLEST.
Ge 19:11 with blindness, both s· and great: 6996
30:15 a s· matter that thou hast taken 4592
Ex 9: 9 shall become s· dust in all the land
16:14 wilderness...lay a s· round thing, 1851
14 as s· as the hoar frost on the ground. "
18:22 every s· matter they shall judge: 6996
26 s· matter they judged themselves. "
30:36 thou shalt beat some of it very s·, 1854
Le 16:12 full of sweet incense beaten s·, 1851
Nu 16: 9 it but a s· thing unto you, that 4592
13 s· thing that thou hast brought us "
32:41 and took the s· towns thereof, *
De 1:17 hear the s· as well as the great; 6996
9:21 stamped it, and ground it very s·, 3190
21 even until it was as s· as dust: *1854
25:13 divers weights, a great and a s·. 6996
14 divers measures, a great and a s·. "
32: 2 as the s· rain upon the tender herb,
1Sa 5: 9 men of the city, both s· and great, 6996
20: 2 will do nothing either great or s·, "
30: 2 slew not any, either great or s·, "
19 to them, neither s· nor great, "
2Sa 7:19 this was yet a s· thing in thy sight, 6994
17:13 be not one s· stone found there. 1571
22:43 I beat them as s· as the dust of the
1Ki 2:20 I desire one s· petition of thee; 6996
19:12 and after the fire a still s· voice. 1851
22:31 Fight neither with s· nor great, 6996
2Ki 19:26 their inhabitants were of s· power, 7116
23: 2 all the people, both s· and great: 6996
6, 15 and stamped it s· to powder, 1854
25:26 all the people, both s· and great, 6996
1Ch 17:17 this was a s· thing in thine eyes, 6994
25: 8 ward, as well the s· as the great, 6996
26:13 lots, as well the s· as the great, "
2Ch 15:13 put to death, whether s· or great, "
18:30 Fight ye not with s· or great, save "
24:24 came with a s· company of men, 4705
31:15 as well to the great as to the s·: 6996
34:30 and all the people, great and s·: "
35: 8 thousand and six hundred s· cattle,
9 offerings five thousand s· cattle,
36:18 of the house of God, great and s·, 6996
Es 1: 5 both unto great and s·, seven days, "
20 honour, both to great and s·. "
Job 3:19 The s· and great are there; and the "
8: 7 Though thy beginning was s·, yet 4705
15:11 consolations of God s· with thee? 4592
36:27 he maketh s· the drops of water: *1639
37: 6 likewise to the s· rain, and to the *
Ps 18:42 did I beat them s· as the dust before
104:25 both s· and great beasts. 6996
115:13 fear the Lord, both s· and great. "
119:141 I am s· and despised: yet do not 6810
Pr 24:10 day of adversity, thy strength is s·. 6862
Ec 2: 7 possessions of great and s· cattle *
Isa 1: 9 left unto us a very s· remnant, 4592
7:13 Is it a s· thing for you to weary men, "
16:14 the remnant shall be very s· and 4213
22:24 all vessels of s· quantity, from the 6996
29: 5 thy strangers shall be like s· dust, 1851
37:27 their inhabitants were of s· power, 7116
40:15 counted as the s· dust of the balance:
41:15 the mountains, and beat them s·, 1854
43:23 me the s· cattle of thy burnt offerings;
54: 7 For a s· moment have I forsaken 6996
60:22 and a s· one a strong nation: 6810
Jer 16: 6 Both the great and the s· shall die 6996
30:19 them, and they shall not be s·. 6819
44:28 Yet a s· number that escape the *4962
49:15 I will make thee s· among the 6996
Eze 16:20 of thy whoredoms a s· matter, 4592
34:18 Seemeth it a s· thing unto you to "
Da 11:23 become strong with a s· people. "
Am 7: 2, 5 shall Jacob arise? for he is s·. 6996
8: 5 forth wheat, making the ephah s·, 6694
Ob 2 made thee s· among the heathen: 6996
Zec 4:10 hath despised the day of s· things? "
M'r 3: 9 that a s· ship should wait on him *4142
8: 7 And they had a few s· fishes: and 2485
Joh 2:15 he had made a scourge of s· cords, *4979
6: 9 five barley loaves,...two s· fishes: *3795
Ac 12:18 was no s· stir among the soldiers, 3641
15: 2 no s· dissension and disputation "
19:23 arose no s· stir about that way. "
24 no s· gain unto the craftsman; * "
26:22 witnessing both to s· and great, 3398
27:20 and no s· tempest lay on us, all 3641
1Co 4: 3 with me it is a very s· thing that 1646
Jas 3: 4 turned about with a very s· helm, "
Re 11:18 that fear thy name, s· and great; 3398
13:16 both s· and great, rich and poor, "
19: 5 that fear him, both s· and great. "
18 free and bond, both s· and great. "
20:12 And I saw the dead, s· and great, "

smallest
1Sa 9:21 of the s· of the tribes of Israel? 6996
1Co 6: 2 unworthy to judge the s· matters? 1646

smart
Pr 11:15 for a stranger shall s· for it: 7321,7451

smell See also SMELLED; SMELLETH; SMELLING.
Ge 27:27 he smelled the s· of his raiment, 7381
27 s· of my son is as the s· of a field "
Ex 30:38 make like unto that, to s· thereto, 7306
Le 26:31 will not s· the savour of your sweet "
De 4:28 see, nor hear, nor eat, nor s·. "
Ps 45: 8 All thy garments s· of myrrh, and
115: 6 noses have they, but they s· not: 7306
Ca 1:12 my spikenard sendeth forth the s· *7381
2:13 the tender grape give a good s·. * "
4:10 and the s· of thine ointments than "
11 the s· of thy garments is like the "
11 garments is like the s· of Lebanon. "
7: 8 and the s· of thy nose like apples; "
13 The mandrakes give a s·, and at * "
Isa 3:24 instead of sweet s· there shall be *1314
Da 3:27 nor the s· of fire had passed on 7382

Hos 14: 6 olive tree, and his s' as Lebanon. 7381
Am 5: 21 not s' in your solemn assemblies.*7306
Ph'p 4: 18 an odour of a sweet s', a sacrifice 2175

smelled
Ge 8: 21 And the Lord s' a sweet savour: *7306
27: 27 and he s' the smell of his raiment, "

smelleth
Job 39: 25 and he s' the battle afar off, the 7306

smelling See also SWEETSMELLING.
Ca 5: 5 my fingers with sweet s' myrrh, *5674
13 lilies, dropping sweet s' myrrh. * "
1Co 12: 17 were hearing, where were the s'? 3750

smite See also SMITEST; SMITETH; SMITING; SMITTEN; SMOTE.
Ge 8: 21 neither will I again s' any more 5221
32: 8 come to the one company, and s' it, "
11 him, lest he will come and s' me, "
Ex 3: 20 s' Egypt with all my wonders which"
7: 17 I will s' with the rod that is in mine"
8: 2 I will s' all thy borders with frogs:5062
16 and s' the dust of the land, that it 5221
9: 15 I may s' thee and thy people with * "
12: 12 will s' all the firstborn in the land of"
13 you, when I s' the land of Egypt. "
23 pass through to s' the Egyptians; 5062
23 come in unto your houses to s' you."
17: 6 thou shalt s' the rock, and there 5221
21: 18 and one s' another with a stone, or*"
20 And if a man s' his servant, or his "
26 if a man s' the eye of his servant, "
27 he s' out his manservant's tooth, 5307
Nu 14: 12 I will s' them with the pestilence, 5221
22: 6 that we may s' them, and that I may"
24: 17 and shall s' the corners of Moab, 4272
25: 17 Vex the Midianites, and s' them: 5221
35: 16 if he s' him with an instrument of* "
17 if he s' him with throwing a stone,* "
18 if he s' him with an hand weapon * "
21 Or in enmity s' him with his hand,* "
De 7: 2 thou shalt s' them, and utterly "
13: 15 Thou shalt surely s' the inhabitants"
19: 11 and s' him mortally that he die, and"
20: 13 thou shalt s' every male thereof "
28: 22 shall s' thee with a consumption, "
27 s' thee with the botch of Egypt, "
28 Lord shall s' thee with madness, "
35 The Lord shall s' thee in the knees,"
33: 11 s' through the loins of them that 4272
Jos 7: 3 thousand men go up and s' Ai; 5221
10: 4 help me, that we may s' Gibeon: "
19 and s' the hindmost of them; "
12: 6 Lord and the children of Israel s':*5221
13: 12 these did Moses s', and cast them "
J'g 6: 16 shalt s' the Midianites as one man. "
20: 31 and they began to s' of the people, "
39 Benjamin began to s' and kill of the"
21: 10 saying, Go and s' the inhabitants of"
1Sa 15: 3 Now go and s' Amalek, and utterly "
17: 46 I will s' thee, and take thine head "
18: 11 I will s' David even to the wall with "
19: 10 Saul sought to s' David even to the "
20: 33 Saul cast a javelin at him to s' him: "
23: 2 Shall I go and s' these Philistines? "
2 Go, and s' the Philistines, and save"
26: 8 therefore let me s' him, I pray thee,"
8 and I will not s' him the second time.
10 Lord liveth, the Lord shall s' him;5062
2Sa 2: 22 should I s' thee to the ground? 5221
5: 24 to s' the host of the Philistines. "
13: 28 when I say unto you, S' Amnon; "
15: 14 and s' the city with the edge of the "
17: 2 flee; and I will s' the king only: "
18: 11 thou not s' him there to the ground?"
1Ki 14: 15 the Lord shall s' Israel, as a reed "
20: 35 word of the Lord, S' me, I pray thee."
35 And the man refused to s' him.
37 man, and said, S' me, I pray thee.
2Ki 3: 19 And ye shall s' every fenced city, "
6: 18 S' this people, I pray thee, with "
21 shall I s' them? shall I s' them? "
22 answered, Thou shalt not s' them: "
22 thou s' those whom thou hast taken"
9: 7 thou shalt s' the house of Ahab thy "
27 and said, S' him also in the chariot."
13: 17 thou shalt s' the Syrians in Aphek, "
18 king of Israel, S' upon the ground. "
19 now thou shalt s' Syria but thrice. "
1Ch 14: 15 to s' the host of the Philistines. "
2Ch 21: 14 plague will the Lord s' thy people,5062
Ps 121: 6 The sun shall not s' thee by day, 5221
141: 5 Let the righteous s' me; it shall be1986
Pr 19: 25 S' a scorner, and the simple will 5221
Isa 3: 17 Lord will s' with a scab the crown 5596
10: 24 he shall s' thee with a rod, and 5221
11: 4 he shall s' the earth with the rod of"
15 and shall s' it in the seven streams, "
19: 22 And the Lord shall s' Egypt: he 5062
22 he shall s' and heal it: and they * "
49: 10 shall the heat nor sun s' them: 5221
58: 4 and to s' with the fist of wickedness:"
Jer 18: 18 and let us s' him with the tongue, "
21: 6 And I will s' the inhabitants of this "
7 he shall s' them with the edge of the"
43: 11 he shall s' the land of Egypt, and "
46: 13 come and s' the land of Egypt. "
49: 28 which Nebuchadrezzar...shall s', * "
Eze 5: 2 part, and s' about it with a knife: "
6: 11 S' with thine hand, and stamp with"
9: 5 after him through the city, and s': "
21: 12 s' therefore upon thy thigh. 5606
14 and s' thine hands together, and 5221
17 I will also s' mine hands together, "
32: 15 when I shall s' all them that dwell "
39: 3 And I will s' thy bow out of thy left "
Am 3: 15 I will s' the winter house with the 5221
6: 11 and he will s' the great house with* "
9: 1 S' the lintel of the door, that the "
Mic 5: 1 s' the judge of Israel with a rod "
Na 2: 10 the knees s' together, and much 6375
Zec 9: 4 and he will s' her power in the sea,5221
10: 11 and shall s' the waves in the sea, "
11: 6 they shall s' the land, and out of 3807
12: 4 s' every horse with astonishment, 5221
4 s' every horse of the people with "
13: 7 s' the shepherd, and the sheep shall"
14: 12 the Lord will s' all the people that5062
18 the Lord will s' the heathen that "
Mal 4: 6 come and s' the earth with a curse.5221
M't 5: 39 shall s' thee on thy right cheek, *4474
24: 49 begin to s' his fellowservants, *5180
26: 31 I will s' the shepherd, and the 3960
M'r 14: 27 I will s' the shepherd, and the "
Lu 22: 49 Lord, shall we s' with the sword? "
Ac 23: 2 by him to s' him on the mouth. 5180
3 God shall s' thee, thou whited wall:"
2Co 11: 20 if a man s' you on the face. *1194
Re 11: 6 to s' the earth with all plagues, 3960
19: 15 with it he should s' the nations: "

smiters
Isa 50: 6 I gave my back to the s', and my 5221

smitest
Ex 2: 13 Wherefore s' thou thy fellow? 5221
Joh 18: 23 evil: but if well, why s' thou me? 1194

smiteth
Ex 21: 12 He that s' a man, so that he die, 5221
15 he that s' his father, or his mother, "
De 25: 11 out of the hand of him that s' him, "
27: 24 he that s' his neighbour secretly. "
Jos 15: 16 He that s' Kirjath-sepher, and "
J'g 1: 12 He that s' Kirjath-sepher, and "
2Sa 5: 8 and s' the Jebusites, and the lame* "
1Ch 11: 6 Whosoever s' the Jebusites first "
Job 26: 12 he s' through the proud. 4272
Isa 9: 13 turneth not unto him that s' them,*5221
La 3: 30 giveth his cheek to him that s' him: "
Eze 7: 9 know that I am the Lord that s'. * "
Lu 6: 29 him that s' thee on the one cheek 5180

smith See also COPPERSMITH; SMITHS.
1Sa 13: 19 no s' found throughout all the 2796
Isa 44: 12 The s' with the tongs both 2796,1270
54: 16 created the s' that bloweth the 2796

smiths
2Ki 24: 14 and all the craftsmen and s': 4525
16 craftsmen and s' a thousand, all "
Jer 24: 1 with the carpenters and s', from "
29: 2 and the carpenters, and the s', were"

smiting
Ex 2: 11 he spied an Egyptian s' an Hebrew,5221
2Sa 8: 13 he returned from s' of the Syrians "
1Ki 20: 37 him, so that in s' he wounded him. "
2Ki 3: 24 they went forward s' the Moabites, "
Mic 6: 13 will I make thee sick in s' thee, * "

smitten
Ex 7: 25 that the Lord had s' the river. 5221
9: 31 And the flax and the barley was s': "
32 the wheat and the rie were not s': "
22: 2 breaking up, and be s' that he die, "
Nu 14: 42 ye be not s' before your enemies. 5062
22: 28 thou hast s' me these three times?5221
32 thou s' thine ass these three times? "
33: 4 which the Lord had s' among them:"
De 1: 42 lest ye be s' before your enemies. 5062
28: 7 thee to be s' before thy face: they "
25 thee to be s' before thine enemies: "
J'g 1: 8 s' it with the edge of the sword, *5221
20: 32 They are s' down before us, as at 5062
36 of Benjamin saw that they were s': "
39 Surely they are s' down before us, "
1Sa 4: 2 Israel was s' before the Philistines:"
3 Wherefore hath the Lord s' us to "
10 Philistines fought, and Israel was s',"
5: 12 died not were s' with the emerods:5221
6: 19 the Lord had s' many of the people "
7: 10 and they were s' before Israel. 5062
13: 4 that Saul had s' a garrison of the 5221
30: 1 s' Ziklag, and burned it with fire; "
2Sa 2: 31 servants of David...s' of Benjamin, "
8: 9 that David had s' all the host of "
10 against Hadadezer, and s' him: "
10: 15, 19 that they were s' before Israel.*5062
15 ye from him, that he may be s'. 5221
1Ki 8: 33 When thy people Israel be s' down5062
11: 15 he had s' every male in Edom; 5221
2Ki 2: 14 when he also had s' the waters, "
3: 23 and they have s' one another: now "
13: 19 shouldest have s' five or six times; "
19 s' Syria till thou hadst consumed it:"
14: 10 Thou hast indeed s' Edom, and "
1Ch 18: 9 how David had s' all the host of "
10 against Hadarezer, and s' him; "
2Ch 20: 22 against Judah; and they were s'. 5062
25: 16 forbear; why shouldest thou be s'?5221
19 Lo, thou hast s' the Edomites; "
26: 20 out, because the Lord had s' him. 5060
28: 17 Edomites had come and s' Judah, 5221
Job 16: 10 they have s' me upon the cheek "
Ps 3: 7 s' all mine enemies upon the cheek "
69: 26 persecute him whom thou hast s'; "
102: 4 My heart is s', and withered like "
143: 3 he hath s' my life down to the 1792
Isa 5: 25 against them, and hath s' them: 5221
24: 12 and the gate is s' with destruction.3807
27: 7 Hath he s' him, as he smote those 5221
53: 4 stricken, s' of God, and afflicted. "
Jer 2: 30 In vain have I s' your children; "
14: 19 why hast thou s' us, and there is no"
37: 10 ye had s' the whole army of the "
Eze 22: 13 have s' mine hand at thy dishonest 5221
33: 21 unto me, saying, The city is s'. "
40: 1 year after that the city was s', in "
Ho 6: 1 he hath s', and he will bind us up. "
9: 16 Ephraim is s', their root is dried "
Am 4: 9 I have s' you with blasting and "
Ac 23: 3 me to be s' contrary to the law? 5180
Re 8: 12 the third part of the sun was s', 4141

smoke See also SMOKING.
Ge 19: 28 the s' of the country went up as 7008
28 went up as the s' of a furnace.
Ex 19: 18 Sinai was altogether on a s', 6225
18 fire: and the s' thereof ascended 6227
18 ascended as the s' of a furnace, "
De 29: 20 jealousy shall s' against that man,6225
Jos 8: 20 the s' of the city ascended up to 6227
21 and that the s' of the city ascended,"
J'g 20: 38 great flame with s' rise up out of "
40 up out of the city with a pillar of s',"
2Sa 22: 9 went up a s' out of his nostrils, and"
Job 41: 20 Out of his nostrils goeth s', as out "
Ps 18: 8 went up a s' out of his nostrils, and "
37: 20 into s' shall they consume away. "
68: 2 As s' is driven away, so drive them "
74: 1 thine anger s' against the sheep 6225
102: 3 my days are consumed like s', and6227
104: 32 toucheth the hills, and they s'. 6225
119: 83 am become like a bottle in the s'; 7008
144: 5 the mountains, and they shall s'. 6225
Pr 10: 26 to the teeth, and as s' to the eyes, 6227
Ca 3: 6 of the wilderness like pillars of s'. "
Isa 4: 5 assemblies, a cloud and s' by day, "
6: 4 and the house was filled with s'. "
9: 18 mount up like the lifting up of s'. "
14: 31 there shall come from the north a s',"
34: 10 the s' thereof shall go up for ever: "
51: 6 heavens shall vanish away like s', "
65: 5 These are a s' in my nose, a fire that"
Hos 13: 3 and as the s' out of the chimney. "
Joe 2: 30 blood, and fire, and pillars of s'. "
Na 2: 13 I will burn her chariots in the s', "
Ac 2: 19 blood, and fire, and vapour of s': 2586
Re 8: 4 And the s' of the incense, which "
9: 2 and there arose a s' out of the pit, "
2 as the s' of a great furnace; and the"
2 was darkened by reason of the s' "
3 there came out of the s' locusts "
17 issued fire and s' and brimstone. "
18 killed, by the fire, and by the s', "
14: 11 the s' of their torment ascendeth "
15: 8 filled with s' from the glory of God, "
18: 9 they shall see the s' of her burning,"
18 when they saw the s' of her burning,"
19: 3 And her s' rose up for ever and ever."

smoking
Ge 15: 17 behold a s' furnace, and a burning 6227
Ex 20: 18 the trumpet, and the mountain s':6226
Isa 7: 4 the two tails of these s' firebrands, "
42: 3 the s' flax shall he not quench: 3544
M't 12: 20 and s' flax shall he not quench. 5187

smooth See also SMOOTHER; SMOOTHETH.
Ge 27: 11 a hairy man, and I am a s' man: 2509
16 hands, and upon the s' of his neck:2513
1Sa 17: 40 chose him five s' stones out of the 2512
Isa 30: 10 speak unto us s' things, prophesy 2513
57: 6 Among the s' stones of the stream 2511
Lu 3: 5 the rough ways shall be made s'; 3006

smoother
Ps 55: 21 of his mouth were s' than butter, *2505
Pr 5: 3 and her mouth is s' than oil: 2513

smootheth
Isa 41: 7 and he that s' with the hammer 2505

smote See also SMOTEST.
Ge 14: 5 and s' the Rephaims in Ashteroth 5221
7 s' all the country of the Amalekites,"
15 by night, and s' them, and pursued "
19: 11 s' the men that were at the door of "
36: 35 who s' Midian in the field of Moab, "
Ex 7: 20 s' the waters that were in the river, "
8: 17 his rod, and s' the dust of the earth,"
9: 25 the hail s' throughout the land of "
25 the hail s' every herb of the field, "
12: 27 Egypt, when he s' the Egyptians, 5062
29 the Lord s' all the firstborn in the 5221
21: 19 then shall he that s' him be quit: "
Nu 3: 13 that I s' all the firstborn in the land"
8: 17 that I s' every firstborn in the land "
11: 33 Lord s' the people with a very great"
14: 45 and s' them, and discomfited them, "
20: 11 with his rod he s' the rock twice: "
21: 24 Israel s' him with the edge of the "
35 So they s' him, and his sons, and "
22: 23 Balaam s' the ass, to turn her into "
25 the wall: and he s' her again. "
27 and he s' the ass with a staff. "
24: 10 and he s' his hands together: 5606
32: 4 the country which the Lord s' 5221
35: 21 he that s' him shall surely be put to"
De 2: 33 we s' him, and his sons, and all his "
3: 3 we s' him until none was left to him"
4: 46 Moses and the children of Israel s',"
25: 18 the way, and s' the hindmost of thee,
29: 7 us unto battle, and we s' them: 5221
Jos 7: 5 men of Ai s' of them about thirty "
5 and s' them in the going down: "
8: 22 they s' them, so that they let none "
24 unto Ai, and s' it with the edge of "
9: 18 the children of Israel s' them not, "
10: 10 and s' them to Azekah, and unto "
26 afterward Joshua s' them, and slew"
28 and s' it with the edge of the sword,"
30 he s' it with the edge of the sword, "
32 and s' it with the edge of the sword,"
33 and Joshua s' him and his people,

Jos 10: 35, 37 s' it with the edge of the sword,5221
39 s' them with the edge of the sword, "
40 Joshua s'...the country of the hills, "
41 s' them from Kadesh-barnea even "
11: 8 who s' them, and chased them unto "
8 s' them, until they left them none "
10 s' the king thereof with the sword: "
11 s' all the souls that were therein "
12 s' them with the edge of the sword, "
14 every man they s' with the edge of "
17 their kings he took, and s' them, "
12: 1 land, which the children of Israel s', "
7 Joshua and the children of Israel s' "
13: 21 whom Moses s' with the princes of "
19: 47 and s' it with the edge of the sword, "
20: 5 he s' his neighbour unwittingly, "
J'g 1: 25 they s' the city with the edge of the "
3: 13 and Amalek, and went and s' Israel, "
4: 21 and s' the nail into his temples, 8628
5: 26 with the hammer she s' Sisera, 1986
26 she s' off his head, when she had 4277
7: 13 unto a tent, and s' it that it fell, 5221
8: 11 Gideon went up...and s' the host: "
9: 43 rose up against them, and s' them. "
11: 21 hand of Israel, and they s' them: "
33 And he s' them from Aroer, even "
12: 4 and the men of Gilead s' Ephraim, "
15: 8 s' them hip and thigh with a great "
18: 27 s' them with the edge of the sword, "
20: 35 Lord s' Benjamin before Israel: 5062
37 s' all the city with the edge of the 5221
48 s' them with the edge of the sword, "
1Sa 4: 8 are the Gods that s' the Egyptians "
5: 6 s' them with emerods, even Ashdod "
9 s' the men of the city, both small "
6: 9 that it is not his hand that s' us; 5060
19 he s' the men of Beth-shemesh, 5221
7: 11 pursued the Philistines, and s' them, "
13: 3 s' the garrison of the Philistines "
14: 31 And they s' the Philistines that day "
48 an host, and s' the Amalekites, and "
15: 7 And Saul s' the Amalekites from "
17: 35 I went out after him, and s' him, "
35 caught him by his beard, and s' him, "
49 and s' the Philistine in his forehead, "
50 with a stone, and s' the Philistine, "
19: 10 and he s' the javelin into the wall: "
22: 19 s' he with the edge of the sword, "
23: 5 and s' them with a great slaughter.* "
24: 5 afterward, that David's heart s' him, "
25: 38 the Lord s' Nabal, that he died. 5062
27: 9 David s' the land, and left neither 5221
30: 17 David s' them from the twilight "
2Sa 1: 15 him. And he s' him that he died. "
2: 23 spear s' him under the fifth rib, "
3: 27 and s' him there under the fifth rib, "
4: 6 and they s' him under the fifth rib: "
7 and they s' him, and slew him, and "
5: 20 and David s' them there, and said, "
25 s' the Philistines from Geba until "
6: 7 and God s' him there for his error; "
8: 1 that David s' the Philistines, and "
2 he s' Moab, and measured them "
3 David s' also Hadadezer, the son of "
10: 18 s' Shobach...captain of their host, "
11: 21 Who s' Abimelech the son of "
14: 6 the one s' the other, and slew him. "
7 Deliver him that s' his brother, that "
18: 15 and s' Absalom, and slew him. "
20: 10 he s' him therewith in the fifth rib, "
21: 17 and s' the Philistine, and killed him. "
23: 10 s' the Philistines until his hand was "
24: 10 David's heart s' him after that he "
17 he saw the angel that s' the people, "
1Ki 15: 20 the cities of Israel, and s' Ijon, and "
27 and Baasha s' him at Gibbethon, "
29 he s' all the house of Jeroboam; "
16: 10 Zimri went in and s' him, and killed "
20: 21 s' the horses and chariots, and slew "
37 the man s' him, so that in smiting "
22: 24 near, and s' Micaiah on the cheek, "
34 s' the king of Israel between the "
2Ki 2: 8 his mantle,...and s' the waters, "
14 the mantle... and s' the waters, "
3: 24 rose up and s' the Moabites, "
25 the slingers went about it, and s' it. "
6: 18 s' them with blindness according "
8: 21 rose by night, and s' the Edomites "
9: 24 and s' Jehoram between his arms, "
10: 25 s' them with the edge of the sword; "
32 Hazael s' them in all the coasts of "
12: 21 his servants, s' him, and he died; "
13: 18 And he s' thrice, and stayed. "
15: 5 And the Lord s' the king, so that he "
10 s' him before the people, and slew "
14 and s' Shallum the son of Jabesh in "
16 Then Menahem s' Tiphsah, and all "
16 not to him, therefore he s' it; "
25 against him, and s' him in Samaria, "
30 s' him, and slew him, and reigned "
18: 8 s' the Philistines, even unto Gaza, "
19: 35 s' in the camp of the Assyrians an "
37 his sons s' him with the sword: "
25: 21 And the king of Babylon s' them, "
25 ten men with him, and s' Gedaliah, "
1Ch 1: 46 which s' Midian in the field of Moab, "
4: 41 s' their tents, and the habitations, "
43 they s' the rest of the Amalekites "
13: 10 kindled against Uzza, and he s' him, "
14: 11 and David s' them there. "
16 s' the hosts of the Philistines from "
18: 1 that David s' the Philistines, and "
2 And he s' Moab; and the Moabites "
3 David s' Hadarezer king of Zobah "
20: 1 Joab s' Rabbah, and destroyed it. "
21: 7 this thing; therefore he s' Israel. "
2Ch 13: 15 God s' Jeroboam and all Israel 5062
14: 12 Lord s' the Ethiopians before Asa, "
14 they s' all the cities round about 5221
15 They s' also the tents of cattle, and "
16: 4 and they s' Ijon, and Dan, and "
18: 23 and s' Micaiah upon the cheek, and "
33 s' the king of Israel between the "
21: 9 up by night, and s' the Edomites "
18 the Lord s' him in his bowels with 5062
22: 5 and the Syrians s' Joram. *5221
25: 11 and s' of the children of Seir ten "
13 and s' three thousand of them, and "
28: 5 and they s' him, and carried away "
5 who s' him with a great slaughter. "
23 gods of Damascus, which s' him: "
Ne 13: 25 s' certain of them, and plucked off "
Es 9: 5 the Jews s' all their enemies with "
Job 1: 19 s' the four corners of the house, 5060
2: 7 s' Job with sore boils from the 5221
Ps 60: *title* and s' of Edom in the valley of "
78: 20 he s' the rock, that the waters "
31 s' down the chosen men of Israel. 3766
51 And s' all the firstborn in Egypt; 5221
66 And he s' his enemies in the hinder "
105: 33 He s' their vines also and their fig "
36 He s' also all the firstborn in their "
135: 8 Who s' the firstborn of Egypt, both "
10 Who s' great nations, and slew "
136: 10 him that s' Egypt in their firstborn: "
17 To him which s' great kings: for "
Ca 5: 7 me, they s' me, they wounded me; "
Isa 10: 20 again stay upon him that s' them; "
14: 6 He who s' the people in wrath with "
29 rod of him that s' thee is broken: "
27: 7 Hath he smitten him, as he s' 4347
7 those that s' him? or is he slain 5221
30: 31 beaten down, which s' with a rod. "
37: 36 and s' in the camp of the Assyrians "
38 his sons s' him with the sword; "
41: 7 the hammer him that s' the anvil,*1986
57: 17 was I wroth, and s' him: I hid me,5221
60: 10 for in my wrath I s' thee, but in my "
Jer 20: 2 Pashur s' Jeremiah the prophet, "
31: 19 was instructed, I s' upon my thigh: 5606
37: 15 wroth with Jeremiah, and s' him, 5221
41: 2 s' Gedaliah the son of Ahikam the "
46: 2 Nebuchadrezzar king of Babylon s' "
47: 1 before that Pharaoh s' Gaza. "
52: 27 And the king of Babylon s' them, "
Da 2: 34 s' the image upon his feet that were 4223
35 the stone that s' the image became "
5: 6 his knees s' one against another. 5368
8: 7 and s' the ram, and brake his two 5221
Jon 4: 7 and it s' the gourd that it withered. "
Hag 2: 17 I s' you with blasting and with "
M't 26: 51 the high priest's, and s' off his ear.*851
67 others s' him with the palms of 4474
68 thou Christ, Who is he that s' thee?*3817
27: 30 the reed, and s' him on the head. 5180
M'r 14: 47 and s' a servant of the high priest, 3817
15: 19 s' him on the head with a reed, 5180
Lu 18: 13 s' upon his breast, saying, God be "
22: 50 s' the servant of the high priest, 3960
63 held Jesus mocked him,...s' him. *1194
64 Prophesy, who is it that s' thee? *3817
23: 48 s' their breasts, and returned. *5180
Joh 18: 10 and s' the high priest's servant, *3817
19: 3 they s' him with their hands. *1325,4475
Ac 7: 24 oppressed, and s' the Egyptian: *3960
12: 7 he s' Peter on the side, and raised "
23 angel of the Lord s' him, because "

smotest
Ex 17: 5 rod, wherewith thou s' the river, 5221

Smyrna (*smir'-na*)
Re 1: 11 unto S', and unto Pergamos, and 4667
2: 8 unto the angel of the church in S' 4668

snail
Le 11: 30 and the lizard, and the s', and the*2546
Ps 58: 8 As a s' which melteth, let every 7642

snare See also SNARED; SNARES.
Ex 10: 7 shall this man be a s' unto us? 4170
23: 33 it will surely be a s' unto thee. "
34: 12 it be for a s' in the midst of thee: "
De 7: 16 for that will be a s' unto thee. "
J'g 2: 3 their gods shall be a s' unto you. "
8: 27 thing became a s' unto Gideon, "
1Sa 18: 21 that she may be a s' to him, and "
28: 9 then layest thou a s' for my life, 5367
Job 18: 8 feet, and he walketh upon a s'. *7639
10 s' is laid for him in the ground, *2256
Ps 69: 22 Let their table become a s' before 6341
91: 3 thee from the s' of the fowler, and "
106: 36 idols: which were a s' unto them. 4170
119: 110 The wicked have laid a s' for me: 6341
124: 7 bird out of the s' of the fowlers: "
7 s' is broken, and we are escaped. "
140: 5 The proud have hid a s' for me, and "
142: 3 have they privily laid a s' for me. "
Pr 7: 23 as a bird hasteth to the s', and "
18: 7 and his lips are the s' of his soul. 4170
20: 25 It is a s' to the man who devoureth "
22: 25 his ways, and get a s' to thy soul. "
29: 6 of an evil man there is a s': but the "
8 Scornful men bring a city into a s': *6315
25 The fear of man bringeth a s': 4170
Ec 9: 12 birds that are caught in the s'; 6341
Isa 8: 14 and for a s' to the inhabitants of 4170
24: 17 the pit, and the s', are upon thee, 6341
18 of the pit shall be taken in the s': "
29: 21 lay a s' for him that reproveth in 6983
Jer 48: 43 the pit, and the s', shall be upon 6341
44 of the pit shall be taken in the s': "
50: 24 I have laid a s' for thee, and thou 3369
La 3: 47 Fear and a s' is come upon us, *6354
Eze 12: 13 and he shall be taken in my s': 4686
17: 20 him, and he shall be taken in my s', "
Ho 5: 1 ye have been a s' on Mizpah, and 6341
9: 8 the prophet is a s' of a fowler in all "
Am 3: 5 a bird fall in a s' upon the earth, "
5 shall one take up a s' from the "
Lu 21: 35 as a s' shall it come on all them *3803
Ro 11: 9 Let their table be made a s', and a "
1Co 7: 35 not that I may cast a s' upon you, 1029
1Ti 3: 7 reproach and the s' of the devil. 3803
6: 9 rich fall into temptation and a s', "
2Ti 2: 26 themselves out of the s' of the devil. "

snared See also ENSNARED.
De 7: 25 unto thee, lest thou be s' therein: 3369
12: 30 thou be not s' by following them.*5367
Ps 9: 16 wicked is s' in the work of his own "
Pr 6: 2 s' with the words of thy mouth, 3369
12: 13 wicked is s' by the transgression 4170
Ec 9: 12 the sons of men s' in an evil time, 3369
Isa 8: 15 be broken, and be s', and be taken. "
28: 13 and be broken, and s', and taken. "
42: 22 they are all of them s' in holes, 6351

snares
Jos 23: 13 shall be s' and traps unto you, *6341
2Sa 22: 6 the s' of death prevented me; 4170
Job 22: 10 Therefore s' are round about thee, 6341
40: 24 eyes: his nose pierceth through s'.*4170
Ps 11: 6 Upon the wicked he shall rain s', 6341
18: 5 the s' of death prevented me. 4170
38: 12 seek after my life lay s' for me: 5367
64: 5 they commune of laying s' privily; 4170
141: 9 me from the s' which they have 6341
Pr 13: 14 life, to depart from the s' of death. 4170
14: 27 life, to depart from the s' of death. "
22: 5 Thorns and s' are in the way of 6341
Ec 7: 26 whose heart is s' and nets, and 4685
Jer 5: 26 lay wait, as he that setteth s'; *3353
18: 22 to take me, and hid s' for my feet. 6341

snatch
Isa 9: 20 And he shall s' on the right hand, 1504

sneezed
2Ki 4: 35 and the child s' seven times, and 2237

sneezings See NEESINGS.

snorting
Jer 8: 16 The s' of his horses was heard 5170

snout
Pr 11: 22 As a jewel of gold in a swine's s', 639

snow
Ex 4: 6 behold, his hand was leprous as s'. 7950
Nu 12: 10 became leprous, white as s': and "
2Sa 23: 20 in the midst of a pit in time of s': "
2Ki 5: 27 his presence a leper as white as s'. "
Job 6: 16 the ice, and wherein the s' is hid: "
9: 30 If I wash myself with s' water, and "
24: 19 and heat consume the s' waters: "
37: 6 For he saith to the s', Be thou on "
38: 22 entered into the treasures of the s'? "
Ps 51: 7 me, and I shall be whiter than s'. "
68: 14 in it, it was white as s' in Salmon.*7949
147: 16 He giveth s' like wool: he 7950
148: 8 Fire, and hail; s', and vapours; "
Pr 25: 13 As the cold of s' in the time of "
26: 1 As s' in summer, and as rain in "
31: 21 She is not afraid of the s' for her "
Isa 1: 18 scarlet, they shall be as white as s'; "
55: 10 down, and the s' from heaven, and "
Jer 18: 14 Will a man leave the s' of Lebanon "
La 4: 7 Her Nazarites were purer than s', "
Da 7: 9 whose garment was white as s', 8517
M't 28: 3 and his raiment white as s': 5510
M'r 9: 3 shining, exceeding white as s'; * "
Re 1: 14 were white like wool, as white as s'; "

snowy
1Ch 11: 22 slew a lion in a pit in a s' day. *7950

snuff See SNUFFDISHES; SNUFFED; SNUFFETH.

snuffdishes
Ex 25: 38 the s' thereof, shall be of pure 4289
37: 23 his snuffers, and his s', of pure gold. "
Nu 4: 9 lamps, and his tongs, and his s', "

snuffed
Jer 14: 6 they s' up the winds like dragons;*7602
Mal 1: 13 ye have s' at it, saith the Lord of 5301

snuffers
Ex 37: 23 made his seven lamps, and his s', †4457
1Ki 7: 50 the bowls, and the s', and the 4212
2Ki 12: 13 of the Lord bowls of silver, s', "
25: 14 pots, and the shovels, and the s', "
2Ch 4: 22 And the s', and the basons, and the "
Jer 52: 18 and the s', and the bowls, and the "

snuffeth
Jer 2: 24 s' up the wind at her pleasure; 7602

so See also ALSO; INSOMUCH; SOEVER.
Ge 1: 7 the firmament: and it was s'. 3651
9 the dry land appear: and it was s'. "
11 itself, upon the earth: and it was s'. "
15 light upon the earth: and it was s'. "
24 earth after his kind: and it was s'. "
27 S' God created man in his own image,*
30 green herb for meat: and it was s'. 3651
3: 24 S' he drove out the man; and he
6: 22 God commanded him, s' did he. 3651
11: 8 S' the Lord scattered them abroad
12: 4 S' Abram departed, as the Lord had
19 s' I might have taken her to me to
13: 6 s' that they could not dwell together.
16 s' that if a man can number the 834
15: 5 unto him, S' shall thy seed be. 3541
18: 5 they said, S' do, as thou hast said. 3651
19: 7 pray you, brethren, do not s' wickedly,
11 s' that they wearied themselves to find

Ge 19:18 said unto them, Oh, not s·, my Lord:*
20:17 S· Abraham prayed unto God: and*
21: 6 s· that all that hear will laugh with me.*
25:22 she said, If it be s·, why am I thus?3651
27:20 is it that thou hast found it s· quickly,
23 Esau's hands: s· he blessed him.
28:21 S· that I come again to my father's
29:26 not be s· done in our country, 3651
28 And Jacob did s·, and fulfilled her "
30:33 S· shall my righteousness answer for
42 s· the feebler were Laban's, and the
31:21 S· he fled with all that he had; and he
28 hast now done foolishly in s· doing.*
36 thou hast s· hotly pursued after me?*
32:19 s· commanded he the second, and*1571
21 S· went the present over before him:
33:16 S· Esau returned that day on his way
34:12 Ask me never s· much dowry and gift,
35: 6 S· Jacob came to Luz, which is in the
37:14 S· he sent him out of the vale of
40: 7 Wherefore look ye s· sadly to day?
41: 4 and fat kine. S· Pharaoh awoke.
13 as he interpreted to us, s· it was; 3651
21 as at the beginning. S· I awoke.
39 there is none s· discreet and wise as
57 the famine was s· sore in all lands.*
42:20 s· shall your words be verified,
20 ye shall not die. And they did s·. 3651
34 s· will I deliver you your brother, and
43: 6 Wherefore dealt ye s· ill with me, as to
11 If it must be s· now, do this; take 3651
34 mess was five times s· much as
44: 5 ye have done evil in s· doing. 834
17 God forbid that I should do s·: 2063
45: 8 S· now it was not you that sent me
21 And the children of Israel did s·: 3651
24 S· he sent his brethren away, and
47:13 s· that the land of Egypt and all the
20 them: s· the land became Pharaoh's.*
28 s· the whole age of Jacob was an
48:10 dim for age, s· that he could not see.
18 Not s·, my father: for this is the 3651
49:17 s· that his rider shall fall backward.
50: 3 for s· are fulfilled the days of 3651
17 S· shall ye say unto Joseph, 3541
26 S· Joseph died, being an hundred and
Ex 1:10 us, and s· get them up out of the land.*
2:18 that ye are come s· soon to day?
4:26 S· he let him go: then she said, A
5:12 S· the people were scattered abroad
22 thou s· evil entreated this people?*
6: 9 Moses spake s· unto the children 3651
7: 6 Lord commanded them, s· did they."
10 did s· as the Lord had commanded:"
20 And Moses and Aaron did s·, as the"
22 did s· with their enchantments: * "
8:24 the Lord did s·; and there came a "
9:24 S· there was hail, and fire mingled
10:10 Let the Lord be s· with you, as I 3651
11 Not s·: go now ye that are men, "
15 earth, s· that the land was darkened;
20 s· that he would not let the children*
11:10 s· that he would not let the children*
12:28 Moses and Aaron, s· did they. 3651
36 s· that they lent unto them such
50 Moses and Aaron, s· did they. 3651
14: 4 I am the Lord. And they did s·. "
20 s· that the one came not near the*
25 s· that the Egyptians said, Let us flee
28 remained not s· much as one of 5704
15:22 S· Moses brought Israel from the*
16:30 S· the people rested on the seventh
34 Moses, s· Aaron laid it up before the
17: 6 And Moses did s· in the sight of 3651
10 S· Joshua did as Moses had said to
18:22 s· shall it be easier for thyself, and
23 God commanded thee s·, then thou
24 S· Moses hearkened to the voice of
19:16 s· that all the people that was in the*
25 S· Moses went down unto the people,
21:12 that smiteth a man, s· that he die,
22 s· that her fruit depart from her, and
22: 6 s· that the stacks of corn, or the
25: 9 thereof, even s· shall ye make it. 3651
33 s· in the six branches that come
27: 8 in the mount, s· shall they make it. "
28: 7 and s· it shall be joined together.*
30:21 S· they shall wash their hands and
23 of sweet cinnamon half s· much, even
32:21 hast brought s· great a sin upon *
24 S· they gave it me: then I cast it into
33:16 s· shall we be separated, I and thy
36:13 taches: s· it became one tabernacle.
37:19 s· throughout the six branches 3651
39:32 commanded Moses, s· did they. "
42 s· the children of Israel made all "
43 even s· had they done it: and Moses"
40:16 Lord commanded him, s· did he. "
33 gate. S· Moses finished the work.
Le 4:20 offering, s· shall he do with this: 3651
7: 7 offering is, s· is the trespass offering:
8:34 s· the Lord hath commanded to do, to
35 die not: for s· I am commanded: 3651
36 S· Aaron and his sons did all things*
10: 5 S· they went near, and carried them
13 made by fire: for s· I commanded.3651
11:32 until the even; s· it shall be cleansed.*
14:13 the priest's, s· is the trespass offering:
21 if he be poor, and cannot get s· much;
16: 4 flesh in water, and s· put them on.*
16 s· shall he do for the tabernacle of3651
24:19 done, s· shall it be done to him; "
20 s· shall it be done to him again. "
26:15 s· that ye will not do all my
27:12 it, who art the priest, s· shall it be.3651
14 shall estimate it, s· shall it stand. "

Nu 1:19 commanded Moses, s· he numbered
45 S· were all those that were numbered
54 commanded Moses, s· did they. 3651
2:17 s· shall they set forward, every man"
34 s· they pitched by their standards, "
34 s· they set forward, every one after "
4:26 made for them: s· shall they serve.*
5: 4 the children of Israel did s·, and 3651
4 Moses, s· did the children of Israel. "
6:21 s· he must do after the law of his "
8: 4 Moses, s· he made the candlestick. "
7 clothes, and s· make themselves clean.*
20 s· did the children of Israel unto 3651
22 the Levites, s· did they unto them. "
9: 5 Moses, s· did the children of Israel. "
14 the manner thereof, s· shall he do: "
16 S· it was alway: the cloud covered "
20 s· it was, when the cloud was a few*
21 s· it was, when the cloud abode from*
12: 7 My servant Moses is not s·, who is 3651
13:21 S· they went up, and searched the
33 and s· we were in their sight.
14:28 in mine ears, s· will I do to you: 3651
15:12 prepare, s· shall ye do to every one3602
14 the Lord; as ye do, s· he shall do. 3651
15 s· shall the stranger be before the
20 threshingfloor, s· shall ye heave it.3651
16:27 S· they gat up from the tabernacle
17:11 And Moses did s·: as the Lord
11 Lord commanded him, s· did he. 3651
20: 8 s· thou shalt give the congregation
21:35 S· they smote him, and his sons, and
22:35 S· Balaam went with the princes of
25: 8 S· the plague was stayed from the
31: 5 S· there were delivered out of the
32:23 if ye will not do s·, behold, ye have3651
28 S· concerning them Moses
31 unto thy servants, s· will we do. 3651
35: 7 S· all the cities which ye shall give*
16 an instrument of iron, s· that he die,
33 S· ye shall not pollute the land
36: 3 s· shall it be taken from the lot of our
4 s· shall their inheritance be taken
7 S· shall not the inheritance of the
10 Moses, s· did the daughters of 3651
De 1:11 you a thousand times s· many more
15 S· I took the chief of your tribes, wise
43 S· I spake unto you; and ye would
46 S· ye abode in Kadesh many days,
2: 5 no, not s· much as a foot breadth;
16 S· it came to pass, when all the men
3: 3 S· the Lord our God delivered into
21 s· shall the Lord do unto all the 3651
29 S· we abode in the valley over against
4: 5 that ye should do s· in the land 3651
7 For what nation is there s· great,*
7 who hath God s· nigh unto them, as
8 And what nation is there s· great, that*
8 and judgments s· righteous as all this
7: 4 s· will the anger of the Lord be
19 s· shall the Lord thy God do unto 3651
8: 5 s· the Lord thy God chasteneth thee.
20 before your face, s· shall ye perish;3651
9: 3 s· shalt thou drive them out, and
8 s· that the Lord was angry with you*
15 S· I turned and came down from the
12: 4 shall not do s· unto the Lord your 3651
10 round about, s· that ye dwell in safety;
22 is eaten, s· thou shalt eat them: 3651
30 gods? even s· will I do likewise. "
31 shalt not do s· unto the Lord thy "
13: 5 S· shalt thou put the evil away from
14:24 s· that thou art not able to carry
17: 7 S· thou shalt put the evil away from
18:14 hath not suffered thee s· to do. 3651
19:10 inheritance, and s· blood be upon thee.
19 s· shalt thou put the evil away from
20:18 s· should ye sin against the Lord your
21: 9 S· shalt thou put away the guilt of
21 s· shalt thou put evil away from
22: 3 s· shalt thou do with his raiment; 3651
5 all that do s· are abomination unto*428
21 s· shalt thou put evil away from
22 s· shalt thou put away evil from Israel.
24 s· thou shalt put away evil from
26 slayeth him, even s· is this matter:3651
24: 8 them, s· ye shall observe to do.
25: 9 S· shall it be done unto that man 3602
28:34 S· that thou shalt be mad for the
54 S· that the man that is tender among*
55 S· that he will not give to any of them
63 s· the Lord will rejoice over you 3651
29:22 S· that the generation to come of*
30:17 turn away, s· that thou wilt not hear,*
31:17 s· that they will say in that day, Are
33:25 as thy days, s· shall thy strength be.
34: 5 S· Moses the servant of the Lord died
8 s· the days of weeping and mourning
Jos 1: 5 was with Moses, s· I will be with thee:
17 s· will we hearken unto thee: 3651
2:21 According unto your words, s· be it."
23 S· the two men returned, and *
3: 7 was with Moses, s· I will be with thee.
4: 8 did s· as Joshua commanded, 3651
5:15 standest is holy. And Joshua did s·."
6:11 S· the ark of the Lord compassed the
14 the camp: s· they did six days. 3541
20 S· the people shouted when the
20 s· that the people went up into the
27 S· the Lord was with Joshua; and his
7: 4 S· there went up thither of the people
16 S· Joshua rose up early in the morning,
22 S· Joshua sent messengers, and they
26 S· the Lord turned from...fierceness*
8: 3 S· Joshua arose, and all the people of
22 s· they were in the midst of Israel,

Jos 8:22 s· that they let none of them 5704
25 s· it was, that all that fell that day,*
9:26 s· did he unto them, and delivered 3651
10: 1 s· he had done to Ai and her king; "
7 S· Joshua ascended from Gilgal, he,
23 And they did s·, and brought forth3651
39 s· he did to Debir, and to the king "
40 S· Joshua smote all the country of the
11: 7 S· Joshua came, and all the people of
15 s· did Moses command Joshua, 3651
15 command Joshua,...s· did Joshua; "
16 S· Joshua took all that land, the hills,
23 S· Joshua took the whole land,
14: 5 s· the children of Israel did, and 3651
11 even s· is my strength now, for war,
12 if s· be the Lord will be with me, *
15: 7 s· northward, looking toward Gilgal,
16: 4 S· the children of Joseph, Manasseh*
19:51 S· they made an end of dividing the
21:40 S· all the cities for the children of*
22: 6 S· Joshua blessed them, and sent
25 s· shall your children make our
28 they should s· say to us or to our
23:15 s· shall the Lord bring upon you 3651
24:10 still: s· I delivered you out of his hand.
25 S· Joshua made a covenant with the
28 S· Joshua let the people depart, every
J'g 1: 3 thy lot. S· Simeon went with him.
7 done, s· God hath requited me. 3651
35 prevailed, s·...they became tributaries.
2:14 s· that they could not any longer
17 of the Lord; but they did not s·. 3651
3:14 S· the children of Israel served Eglon*
22 s·...he could not draw the dagger *3588
30 S· Moab subdued that day under the
4:14 S· Barak went down from mount
15 s· that Sisera lighted down off his*
21 fast asleep and weary. S· he died.
23 S· God subdued on that day Jabin the
5:28 Why is his chariot s· long in coming?
31 S· let all thine enemies perish, O 3651
6: 3 And s· it was, when Israel had sown,
20 pour out the broth. And he did s·.3651
27 s· it was, because he feared his father's*
38 it was s·: for he rose up early on 3651
40 God did s· that night: for it was "
7: 1 s·...the host of the Midianites were*
5 S· he brought down the people unto
8 S· the people took victuals in their
15 it was s·, when Gideon heard the
17 be that, as I do, s· shall ye do. 3651
19 S· Gideon, and the hundred men that
8:18 As thou art, s· were they; each 1992
21 for as the man is, s· is his strength.
28 s· that they lifted up their heads no*
9:49 s· that all the men of the tower of
10: 9 s· that Israel was sore distressed.
11: 5 And it was s·, that when the children
10 if we do not s· according to thy 3651
21 s· Israel possessed all the land of the
23 S· now the Lord God of Israel hath
24 S· whomsoever the Lord our God
32 S· Jephthah passed over unto the
12: 5 and it was s·, that when those
13:19 S· Manoah took a kid with a meat
14:10 S· his father went down unto the*
10 for s· used the young men to do. 3651
15 us to take that we have? is it not s·?
15:11 me, s· have I done unto them. 3651
16: 9 fire. S· his strength was not known.
16 s· that his soul was vexed unto death;*
30 S· the dead which he slew at his
17:10 thy victuals. S· the Levite went in.
18:21 S· they turned and departed, and put
19: 4 s· they did eat and drink, and lodged
21 S· he brought him into his house, and
23 nay, I pray you, do not s· wickedly;
24 this man do not s· vile a thing. *2063
25 s· the man took his concubine, and
30 And it was s·, that all that saw it said,
20:11 S· all the men of Israel were gathered
36 S· the children of Benjamin saw that
46 S· that all which fell that day of
21:14 and yet s· they sufficed them not. 3651
23 And the children of Benjamin did s·,"
Ru 1:17 Lord do s· to me, and more also, if 3541
19 S· they two went out until they
22 S· Naomi returned, and Ruth the
2: 7 s· she came, and hath continued even
17 S· she gleaned in the field until even,
23 S· she kept fast by the maidens of
4: 8 it for thee. S· he drew off his shoe.*
13 S· Boaz took Ruth, and she was his
1Sa 1: 7 as he did s· year by year, when she3651
7 s· she provoked her; therefore she "
9 S· Hannah rose up after they had
18 S· the woman went her way, and did
23 S· the woman abode, and gave her son
2: 3 Talk no more s· exceeding proudly;
5 s· that the barren hath born seven;*5704
14 S· they did in Shiloh unto all the 3602
21 visited Hannah, s· that she conceived,*
3: 9 S· Samuel went and lay down in his
17 God do s· to thee, and more also, if3541
4: 4 S· the people sent to Shiloh, that they
5 shout, s· that the earth rang again.
5: 7 men of Ashdod saw that it was s·, 3651
9 it was s·, that, after they had carried
11 S· they sent and gathered together*
6:10 And the men did s·; and took two 3651
7:13 S· the Philistines were subdued, and
8: 8 gods, s· do they also unto thee. 3651
9:10 S· they went unto the city where the
21 then speakest thou s· to me? 1697
24 S· Saul did eat with Samuel that day.
10: 9 it was s·, that, when he had turned his

1Sa 11: 7 s' shall it be done unto his oxen. 3541
11 it was s' on the morrow, that Saul
11 s' that two of them were not left
12: 18 S' Samuel called unto the Lord; and
13: 22 S' it came to pass in the day of
14: 15 s' it was a very great trembling.
23 S' the Lord saved Israel that day: and
24 S' none of the people tasted any food.
44 God do s' and more also: for thou 3541
45 S' the people rescued Jonathan, that
47 S' Saul took the kingdom over Israel,*
15: 6 S' the Kenites departed from among
31 S' Samuel turned again after Saul;
33 s' shall thy mother be childless 3651
16: 13 S' Samuel rose up, and went to
23 s' Saul was refreshed, and was well,
17: 27 s' shall it be done to the man that 3541
50 S' David prevailed over the Philistine
18: 30 s' that his name was much set by.
19: 12 S' Michal let David down through a
17 Why hast thou deceived me s', and*3602
18 S' David fled, and escaped, and came*
20: 2 this thing from me? it is not s'.
13 The Lord do s' and much more to 3541
16 S' Jonathan made a covenant with the
24 S' David hid himself in the field: and
34 S' Jonathan arose from the table in
21: 6 S' the priest gave him hallowed bread:
22: 14 And who is s' faithful among all thy
23: 5 S' David and his men went to Keilah,*
5 S' David saved the inhabitants of
24: 7 S' David stayed his servants with
25: 12 S' David's young men turned their
20 it was s', as she rode on the ass, that
21 s' that nothing was missed of all that
22 S' and more also do God unto the 3541
25 for as his name is, s' is he; Nabal 3651
35 S' David received of her hand that
26: 7 S' David and Abishai came to the
12 S' David took the spear and the cruse
24 s' let my life be much set by in the3651
25 S' David went on his way, and Saul
27: 1 s' shall I escape out of his hand.
11 s' did David, and s' will be his 3541
28: 23 S' he arose from the earth, and sat
29: 8 thy servant s' long as I have been with
11 S' David and his men rose up early to
30: 3 S' David and his men came to the*
9 S' David went, he and the six hundred
10 were s' faint that they could not go
21 were s' faint that they could not follow
23 Ye shall not do s', my brethren, 3651
24 s' shall his part be that tarrieth by the
25 And it was s' from that day forward,
31: 6 S' Saul died, and his three sons, and
2Sa 1: 2 and s' it was, when he came to David,
10 S' I stood upon him, and slew him,
2: 2 S' David went up thither, and his two
16 side; s' they fell down together:
28 S' Joab blew a trumpet, and all the
31 s' that three hundred and threescore
3: 9 S' do God to Abner, and more also, 3541
9 to David, even s' I do to him; 3651
20 S' Abner came to David to Hebron,
30 S' Joab and Abishai his brother slew
34 before wicked men, s' fellest thou.
35 S' do God to me, and more also, if3541
5: 3 S' all the elders of Israel came to the
9 S' David dwelt in the fort, and called*
25 And David did s', as the Lord had 3651
6: 10 S' David would not remove the ark of
12 S' David went and brought up the ark*
13 it was s', that when they that bare the
15 S' David and all the house of Israel
19 S' all the people departed every one to
7: 8 s' shalt thou say unto my servant*
17 s' did Nathan speak unto David. 3651
8: 2 And s' the Moabites became David's*
9: 11 his servant, s' shall thy servant do.3651
13 S' Mephibosheth dwelt in Jerusalem:
10: 14 S' Joab returned from the children of*
19 S' the Syrians feared to help the
11: 12 S' Uriah abode in Jerusalem that day,
20 if s' be that the king's wrath arise,*
20 approached ye s' nigh unto the city
22 S' the messenger went, and came and
12: 31 S' David and all the people returned*
13: 2 And Amnon was s' vexed, that he fell
6 S' Amnon lay down, and made
8 S' Tamar went to her brother
15 s' that the hatred wherewith he hated*
20 S' Tamar remained desolate in her
35 come: as thy servant said, s' it is. 3651
38 S' Absalom fled, and went to Geshur,
14: 3 S' Joab put the words in her mouth.
7 s' they shall quench my coal which is*
17 s' is my lord the king to discern 3651
23 S' Joab arose and went to Geshur,
24 S' Absalom returned to his own house,
25 be s' much praised as Absalom for
28 S' Absalom dwelt two full years in*
33 S' Joab came to the king, and told
15: 2 it was s', that when any man that had
5 it was s', that when any man came
6 s' Absalom stole the hearts of the men
9 S' he arose, and went to Hebron.
34 s' will I now also be thy servant:
37 S' Hushai David's friend came into
16: 10 s' let him curse, because the *3588
10 say, Wherefore hast thou done s'? 3651
19 presence, s' will I be in thy presence."
22 S' they spread Absalom a tent upon
23 s' was...the counsel of Ahithophel 3651
17: 3 s' all the people shall be in peace.
12 S' shall we come upon him in some
12 shall not be left s' much as one. 1571

2Sa 17: 26 S' Israel and Absalom pitched in the*
18: 6 S' the people went out into the field
19: 13 God do s' to me, and more also, if 3541
14 s' that they sent this word unto the
15 S' the king returned, and came to
20: 2 S' every man of Israel went up from
3 S' they were shut up unto the day of
5 S' Amasa went to assemble the men
10 s' he smote him therewith in the fifth
10 S' Joab and Abishai his brother *
18 and s' they ended the matter. 3651
21 The matter is not s': but a man of "
22: 4 s' shall I be saved from mine enemies.
35 s' that a bow of steel is broken by
37 under me; s' that my feet did not slip.*
23: 5 my house be not s' with God; yet 3651
24: 8 S' when they had gone through all
13 S' Gad came to David, and told him,
15 S' the Lord sent a pestilence upon
24 S' David bought the threshingfloor
25 S' the Lord was intreated for the
1Ki 1: 3 S' they sought for a fair damsel
6 in saying, Why hast thou done s'? 3602
30 even s' will I certainly do this day.3651
36 God of my lord the king say s' too. "
37 king, even s' be he with Solomon, "
38 S' Zadok the priest, and Nathan the
40 s' that the earth rent with the sound
45 rejoicing, s' that the city rang again.
53 S' king Solomon sent, and they
2: 7 for s' they came to me when I fled3651
10 S' David slept with his fathers, and*
27 S' Solomon thrust out Abiathar from
34 S' Benaiah the son of Jehoiada went*
38 hath said, s' will thy servant do. 3651
46 S' the king commanded Benaiah the
3: 9 judge this thy s' great a people? *
12 s' that there was none like thee before
13 s' that there shall not be any among
4: 1 S' king Solomon was king over all*
5: 4 s' that there is neither adversary nor*
10 S' Hiram gave Solomon cedar trees
18 s' they prepared timber and stones to*
6: 7 s' that there was neither hammer nor*
9 S' he built the house, and finished it;
14 S' Solomon built the house, and
20 and s' covered the altar which was of*
21 S' Solomon overlaid the house within
26 and s' was it of the other cherub. 3651
27 s' that the wing of the one touched the
33 S' also made he for the door of the3651
38 S' was he seven years in building it.
7: 9 s' on the outside toward the great
18 and s' did he for the other chapiter.3651
22 s' was the work of the pillars finished.
40 S' Hiram made an end of doing all
51 S' was ended all the work that king*
8: 11 S' that the priests could not stand to
25 s' that thy children take heed *7535
46 s' that they carry them away captives
48 And s' return unto thee with all their*
54 And it was s', that when Solomon had
63 S' the king and all the children of
9: 25 the Lord. S' he finished the house.
10: 13 S' she turned and went to her own
23 S' king Solomon exceeded all the
29 and s' for all the kings of the Hittites,
11: 19 s' that he gave him to wife the sister
12: 12 S' Jeroboam and all the people came
16 S' when all Israel saw that the king*
16 S' Israel departed unto their tents.
19 S' Israel rebelled against the house
32 S' did he in Beth-el, sacrificing 3651
33 S' he offered upon the altar which he*
13: 4 s' that he could not pull it in again to
9 s' was it charged me by the word 3651
10 S' he went another way, and returned
13 S' they saddled him the ass: and he
19 S' he went back with him, and did
14: 4 Jeroboam's wife did s', and arose, 3651
6 And it was s', when Ahijah heard the
28 And it was s', when the king went into
15: 20 S' Ben-hadad hearkened unto...Asa,*
16: 6 S' Baasha slept with his fathers, and*
22 s' Tibni died, and Omri reigned.
28 S' Omri slept with his fathers, and
17: 5 S' he went and did according unto the
10 S' he arose and went to Zarephath.
17 and his sickness was s' sore, that 3966
18: 4 For it was s', when Jezebel cut off the
6 S' they divided the land between them
12 s' when I come and tell Ahab, and he
16 S' Obadiah went to meet Ahab, and
20 S' Ahab sent unto all the children of
42 S' Ahab went up to eat and to drink.
19: 2 S' let the gods do to me, and more3541
13 And it was s', when Elijah heard it,
19 S' he departed thence, and found
20: 10 The gods do s' unto me, and more3541
19 S' these young men of the princes of
25 unto their voice, and did s'. 3651
29 And s' it was, that in the seventh day
32 S' they girded sackcloth on their
34 S' he made a covenant with him, and
37 s' that in smiting he wounded him.*
38 S' the prophet departed, and waited
40 him, S' shall thy judgment be; 3651
21: 8 S' she wrote letters in Ahab's name,
22: 8 said, Let not the king say s'. 3651
15 S' he came to the king. And the king*
22 prevail also: go forth, and do s'. 3651
29 S' the king of Israel and Jehoshaphat
37 S' the king died, and was brought to
40 S' Ahab slept with his fathers; and
2Ki 1: 17 S' he died according to the word of
2: 2 thee. S' they went down to Beth-el.

2Ki 2: 4 leave thee. S' they came to Jericho.
8 s' that they two went over on dry
10 from thee, it shall be s' unto thee; 3651
10 but if not, it shall not be s'.
22 S' the waters were healed unto this
3: 9 S' the king of Israel went, and the
12 S' the king of Israel and Jehoshaphat
24 s' that they fled before them: but
4: 5 S' she went from him, and shut the
8 s' it was, that as oft as he passed by,
25 S' she went and came unto the man of
40 S' they poured out for the men to eat.
44 S' he set it before them, and they did
5: 8 And it was s', when Elisha the man of
9 S' Naaman came with his horses and
12 S' he turned and went away in a rage.
19 S' he departed from him a little way.
21 S' Gehazi followed after Naaman.
6: 4 S' he went with them. And when
23 S' the bands of Syria came no more*
29 S' we boiled my son, and did eat him:
31 God do s' and more also to me, if 3541
7: 10 S' they came and called unto the
16 S' a measure of fine flour was sold for
20 And s' it fell out unto him: for the3651
8: 6 S' the king appointed unto her a
9 S' Hazael went to meet him, and took
14 S' he departed from Elisha, and came*
15 spread it on his face, s' that he died:
21 S' Joram went over to Zair, and all the*
9: 4 S' the young man, even the young
14 S' Jehu the son of Jehoshaphat the
16 S' Jehu rode in a chariot, and went to
18 S' there went one on horseback to
22 s' long as the whoredoms of thy
22 and her witchcrafts are s' many?
27 And they did s' at the going up to Gur,*
33 S' they threw her down: and some of
37 s' that they shall not say, This is
10: 11 S' Jehu slew all that remained of the
16 S' they made him ride in his chariot
21 s' that there was not a man left that
11: 2 Athaliah, s' that he was not slain.
6 s' shall ye keep the watch of the
12: 6 But it was s', that in the three and
10 And it was s', when they saw that
13: 24 S' Hazael king of Syria died; and*
15: 5 s' that he was a leper unto the day of
7 S' Azariah slept with his fathers;*
12 And s' it came to pass. 3651
20 S' the king of Assyria turned back,
16: 7 S' Ahaz sent messengers to
11 s' Urijah the priest made it 3651
17: 7 For s' it was, that the children of
23 S' was Israel carried away out of
25 And s' it was at the beginning of their
32 S' they feared the Lord, and made
41 S' these nations feared the Lord, and
41 their fathers, s' do they unto this day.
18: 5 s' that after him was none like him
21 s' is Pharaoh king of Egypt unto 3651
19: 5 S' the servants of king Hezekiah
8 S' Rab-shakeh returned, and found
36 S' Sennacherib king of Assyria
22: 14 S' Hilkiah the priest, and Ahikam,
23: 18 S' they let his bones alone, with the
24: 6 S' Jehoiakim slept with his fathers:
25: 6 S' they took the king, and brought*
21 S' Judah was carried away out of
1Ch 9: 1 S' all Israel were reckoned by
23 S' they and their children had the
10: 4 S' Saul took a sword, and fell upon it.*
6 S' Saul died, and his three sons, and
13 S' Saul died for his transgression
11: 6 S' Joab the son of Zeruiah went first*
9 S' David waxed greater and greater:*
13: 4 said that they would do s': for 3651
5 S' David gathered all Israel together,
13 S' David brought not the ark home to
14: 11 S' they came up to Baal-perazim; and
15: 14 S' the priests and...Levites sanctified
17 S' the Levites appointed Heman the
19 S' the singers, Heman, Asaph, and
25 S' David, and the elders of Israel, and
16: 1 S' they brought the ark of God, and*
37 S' he left there before the ark of the
18: 14 S' David reigned over all Israel, and*
19: 2 S' the servants of David came into the*
7 S' they hired thirty and two thousand
14 S' Joab and the people that were with
17 S' when David had put the battle in
20: 3 s' dealt David with all the cities *3651
21: 3 an hundred times s' many more 1992
11 S' Gad came to David, and said unto
14 S' the Lord sent pestilence upon
25 S' David gave to Ornan for the place
22: 5 S' David prepared abundantly before
23: 1 S' when David was old and full of*
25: 7 S' the number of them, with their*
29: 14 able to offer s' willingly after this sort?
2Ch 1: 3 S' Solomon, and all the congregation
10 judge this thy people, that is s' great?
17 s' brought they out horses for all the
2: 3 dwell therein, even s' deal with me.
5: 14 S' that the priests could not stand to
6: 16 yet s' that thy children take heed to*
31 s' long as they live in the land 3605
7: 5 s' the king and all the people dedicated
21 s' that he shall say, Why hath the*
8: 14 for s' had David the man of God 3651
16 S' the house of the Lord was
9: 12 S' she turned, and went away to her
10: 3 S' Jeroboam and all Israel came and*
12 S' Jeroboam and all the people came
15 S' the king hearkened not unto the
16 S' all Israel went to their tents.

2Ch 11:17 S· they strengthened the kingdom of
12: 9 S· Shishak king of Egypt came up
13 S· king Rehoboam strengthened
13: 9 s·...whosoever cometh to consecrate
13 s· they were before Judah, and the
17 s· there fell down slain of Israel five
14: 1 S· Abijah slept with his fathers, and
7 side. S· they built and prospered.
12 S· the Lord smote the Ethiopians
15:10 S· they gathered themselves together
17:10 s· that they made no war against
18: 7 said, Let not the king say s·. 3651
11 And all the prophets prophesied s·, "
21 also prevail: go out, and do even s·."
28 S· the king of Israel and Jehoshaphat
29 S· the king of Israel disguised
19:10 s· wrath come upon you, and upon
20: 6 s· that none is able to withstand thee?
20 your God, s· shall ye be established;
20 his prophets, s· shall ye prosper.
25 gathering of the spoil, it was s· much.
30 S· the realm of Jehoshaphat was
21:10 S· the Edomites revolted from under
17 s· that there was never a son left him,
19 sickness: s· he died of sore diseases.*
22: 1 S· Ahaziah the son of Jehoram king
9 S· the house of Ahaziah had no power*
11 S· Jehoshabeath, the daughter of the
11 Athaliah, s· that she slew him not.
23: 8 S· the Levites and all Judah did
15 S· they laid hands on her; and when
24:13 S· the workmen wrought, and the
24 S· they executed judgment against
25:21 S· Joash the king of Israel went up;
26:23 S· Uzziah slept with his fathers, and
27: 5 S· much did the children of 2063
6 S· Jotham became mighty, because
28:14 S· the armed men left the captives
29:17 s· they sanctified the house of the*
22 S· they killed the bullocks, and the
25 s· was the commandment of the Lord*
34 s· that they could not flay all the
35 S· the service of the house of the
30: 5 S· they established a decree to make
6 S· the posts went with the letters
9 s· that they should come again into*
10 S· the posts passed from city to city
26 S· there was great joy in Jerusalem:
32: 4 S· there was gathered much people
17 s· shall not the God of Hezekiah 3651
21 S· he returned with shame of face to
23 s· that he was magnified in the sight
26 s· that the wrath of the Lord came not
33: 8 s· that they will take heed to do all*
9 S· Manasseh made Judah and the*
20 S· Manasseh slept with his fathers,
34: 6 s· did he in the cities of Manasseh,
26 s· shall ye say unto him, Thus saith*
28 S· they brought the king word again.*
35: 6 S· kill the passover, and sanctify *
10 S· the service was prepared, and the
12 And s· did they with the oxen. 3651
16 S· all the service of the Lord was
Ezr 2:70 S· the priests, and the Levites, and
3:13 S· that the people could not discern
4:15 s· shalt thou find in the book of the
24 S· it ceased unto the second year of*
5:17 whether it be s·, that a decree was
6:13 king had sent, s· they did speedily.*3660
8:23 S· we fasted and besought our God
30 S· took the priests and the Levites the
9: 2 s· that the holy seed have mingled
14 s· that there should be no remnant
10:12 As thou hast said, s· must we do. 3651
16 the children of the captivity did s·. "
Ne 2: 4 S· I prayed to the God of heaven.
6 S· it pleased the king to send me; and
11 S· I came to Jerusalem, and was there
15 the gate of the valley, and s· returned.
18 S· they strengthened their hands for
4: 6 S· built we the wall; and all the wall
10 s· that we are not able to build the
18 girded by his side, and s· builded.
21 S· we laboured in the work: and half
23 S· neither I, nor my brethren, nor my
5:12 them; s· will we do as thou sayest.3651
13 S· God shake out every man from 3602
15 s· did not I, because of the fear of 3651
6: 3 work, s· that I cannot come down:
13 be afraid, and do s·, and sin, and 3651
15 S· the wall was finished in the twenty
7:73 S· the priests, and the Levites, and the
8: 8 S· they read in the book in the law of*
11 S· the Levites stilled all the people,
16 S· the people went forth, and brought
17 not the children of Israel done s·. 3651
9:10 S· didst thou get thee a name, as it*
11 s· that they went through the midst of
21 wilderness, s·...they lacked nothing;*
22 s· they possessed the land of Sihon,
24 S· the children went in and possessed
25 s· they did eat, and were filled, and
28 s· that they had the dominion over
12:40 S· stood the two companies of them
43 s· that the joy of Jerusalem was heard
13:20 S· the merchants and sellers of all
21 if ye do s· again, I will lay hands on
Es 1: 8 for s· the king had appointed to all3651
13 (for s· was the king's manner "
17 s·...they shall despise their husbands*
2: 4 pleased the king; and he did s·. 3651
8 S· it came to pass, when the king's
12 (for s· were the days of their 3651
16 S· Esther was taken unto king
17 s· that he set the royal crown upon her
3: 2 for the king had s· commanded 3651
Es 4: 4 S· Esther's maids and her *
6 S· Hatach went forth to Mordecai
16 s· will I go in unto the king, which3651
17 S· Mordecai went his way, and did
5: 2 it was s·, when the king saw Esther
2 S· Esther drew near, and touched the
5 S· the king and Haman came to the
13 s· long as I see Mordecai the Jew 6256
6: 6 S· Haman came in. And the king
10 do even s· to Mordecai the Jew, 3651
7: 1 S· the king and Haman came to
5 presume in his heart to do s·? 3651
10 S· they hanged Haman on the gallows
8: 4 S· Esther arose, and stood before the
14 S· the posts that rode upon mules and
9:14 king commanded it s· to be done: 3651
27 s· as it should not fail, that they would
Job 1: 3 s· that this man was the greatest of
5 And it was s·, when the days of their
12 S· Satan went forth from the presence
2: 7 S· went Satan forth from the presence
13 S· they sat down with him upon the
5:12 s· that their hands cannot perform
16 S· the poor hath hope, and iniquity
27 Lo this, we have searched it, s· it is;3651
7: 3 S· am I made to possess months of "
9 s· he that goeth down to the grave "
15 S· that my soul chooseth strangling,
20 thee, s· that I am a burden to myself?
8:13 S· are the paths of all that forget 3651
9: 2 I know it is s· of a truth: but how "
30 and make my hands never s· clean;
35 fear him; but it is not s· with me. 3651
13: 9 mocketh another, do ye s· mock him?*
14:12 S· man lieth down, and riseth not:
23: 7 s· should I be delivered for ever from
24:19 s· doth the grave those which have
25 And if it be not s· now, who will make
27: 6 reproach me s· long as I live. 3605
32: 1 S· these three men ceased to answer
22 in s· doing my maker would soon take*
33:20 S· that his life abhorreth bread, and
34:25 the night, s· that they are destroyed.
28 S· that they cause the cry of the poor
35:15 because it was not s·, he hath visited*
36:16 Even s· would he have removed thee*
41:10 None is s· fierce that dare stir him up:
16 One is s· near to another, that no air
42: 7 And it was s·, that after the Lord had
9 S· Eliphaz the Temanite and Bildad
12 S· the Lord blessed the latter end of
15 were no women found s· fair as the
17 S· Job died, being old and full of days.
Ps 1: 4 The ungodly are not s·: but are 3651
7: 7 S· shall the congregation of the people*
18: 3 s· shall I be saved from mine enemies.
34 s· that a bow of steel is broken by
21:13 s· will we sing and praise thy power.
22: 1 why art thou s· far from helping me,
26: 6 s· will I compass thine altar, O Lord:
35:25 their hearts, Ah, s· would we have it:
37: 3 s· shalt thou dwell in the land, and
40:12 me, s· that I am not able to look up;
42: 1 s· panteth my soul after thee, O 3651
45:11 S· shall the king greatly desire thy
48: 5 They saw it, and s· they marvelled;*3651
8 s· have we seen in the city of the "
10 s· is thy praise unto the ends of the "
58: 5 charmers, charming never s· wisely.
11 S· that a man shall say, Verily there
61: 8 S· will I sing praise unto thy name 3651
63: 2 s· as I have seen thee in the
64: 8 S· they shall make their own tongue
65: 9 when thou hast s· provided for it. 3651
68: 2 s· let the wicked perish at the presence
72: 7 s· long as the moon endureth. 5704
73:20 s·, O Lord, when thou awakest, thou
22 S· foolish was I, and ignorant: I was
77: 4 I am s· troubled that I cannot speak.
13 who is s· great a God as our God?*
78:21 s· a fire was kindled against Jacob,*
29 S· they did eat, and were well filled:
53 them on safely s· that they feared not:
60 S· that he forsook the tabernacle of
72 S· he fed them according to the
79:13 S· we thy people and sheep of thy
80:12 s· that all they which pass by the way
18 S· will not we go back from thee:
81:12 S· I gave them up unto their own
83:15 S· persecute them with thy 3651
90:11 according to thy fear, s· is thy wrath.*
12 S· teach us to number our days, 3651
102: 4 grass; s· that I forget to eat my bread.*
15 S· the heathen shall fear the name of
103: 5 s· that thy youth is renewed like the
11 s· great is his mercy toward them that
12 s· far hath he removed our
13 s· the Lord pitieth them that fear him.
104:25 S· is this great and wide sea, wherein*
106: 9 s· he led them through the depths, as
30 and s· the plague was stayed.
32 s· that it went ill with Moses for their
33 s· that he spake unadvisedly with his*
107: 2 Let the redeemed of the Lord say s·,
29 s· that the waves thereof are still.
30 s· he bringeth them unto their desired
38 s· that they are multiplied greatly;
109:17 loved cursing, s· let it come unto him:*
17 in blessing, s· let it be far from him.*
18 s· let it come into his bowels like *
115: 8 s· is every one that trusteth in them.*
119:27 s· shall I talk of thy wondrous works.
42 S· shall I have wherewith to answer
44 S· shall I keep thy law continually
88 s· shall I keep the testimony of thy
123: 2 s· our eyes wait upon the Lord 3651
Ps 125: 2 s· the Lord is round about his people
127: 2 for s· he giveth his beloved sleep. 3651
4 man; s· are children of the youth. "
135:18 s· is every one that trusteth in them.*
147:20 hath not dealt s· with any nation: 3651
Pr 1:19 S· are the ways of every one that is "
2: 2 S· that thou incline thine ear unto
3: 4 S· shalt thou find favour and good
10 S· thy barns be filled with plenty,
22 S· shall they be life unto thy soul, and
6:11 S· shall thy poverty come as one that
29 S· he that goeth in to his 3651
7:13 S· she caught him, and kissed him,
10:25 passeth, s· is the wicked no more:*
26 s· is the sluggard to them that send
11:19 s· he that pursueth evil pursueth it to*
22 s· is a fair woman which is without
15: 7 heart of the foolish doeth not s·. 3651
19:24 not s· much as bring it to his mouth
20:30 s· do stripes the inward parts of the*
23: 7 he thinketh in his heart, s· is he: 3651
24:14 S· shall the knowledge of wisdom "
29 I will do s· to him as he hath done "
34 S· shall thy poverty come as one that
25:12 s· is a wise reprover upon an obedient
13 s· is a faithful messenger to them that
16 eat s· much as is sufficient for thee,
17 he be weary of thee, and s· hate thee.*
20 s· is he that singeth songs to an heavy
23 s· doth an angry countenance a
25 s· is good news from a far country.
27 s· for men to search their own glory is
26: 1 s· honour is not seemly for a fool. 3651
2 s· the curse causeless shall not "
7 s· is a parable in the mouth of fools.
8 s· is he that giveth honour to a 3651
9 s· is a parable in the mouth of fools.
11 vomit, s· a fool returneth to his folly.
14 s· doth the slothful upon his bed.
19 S· is the man that deceiveth his 3651
20 s· where there is no talebearer, the*
21 s· is a contentious man to kindle
27: 8 s· is a man that wandereth from 3651
9 s· doth the sweetness of a man's
17 s· a man sharpeneth the countenance
18 s· he that waiteth on his master shall*
19 face, s· the heart of man to man. 3651
20 s· the eyes of man are never satisfied.*
21 for gold; s· is a man to his praise.*
28:15 s· is a wicked ruler over the poor
30:33 s· the forcing of wrath bringeth forth
31:11 s· that he shall have no need of spoil.*
Ec 2: 9 S· I was great, and increased more
15 the fool, s· it happeneth even to me;
3:11 s· that no man can find out the
19 the one dieth, s· dieth the other; 3651
19 s· that a man hath no preeminence*
4: 1 S· I returned, and considered all the*
5:16 points as he came, s· shall he go: 3651
6: 2 s· that he wanteth nothing for his soul
3 s· that the days of his years be many,
7: 6 pot, s· is the laughter of the fool: 3651
8:10 And s· I saw the wicked buried, * "
10 in the city where they had s· done:*"
9: 2 as is the good, s· is the sinner; and he
12 s· are the sons of men snared in 1992
10: 1 s· doth a little folly him that is in
Ca 2: 2 s· is my love among the daughters.3651
3 s· is my beloved among the sons. "
5: 9 that thou dost s· charge us? 3602
Isa 6:13 s· the holy seed shall be the substance
10: 7 Howbeit he meaneth not s·, 3651
7 neither doth his heart think s·; but"
11 s· do to Jerusalem and her idols? "
26 s· shall he lift it up after the manner*
14:24 I have purposed, s· shall it stand: 3651
16: 2 s· the daughters of Moab shall be at
6 wrath: but his lies shall not be s·.*3651
18: 4 For s· the Lord said unto me, I will*3541
20: 2 And he did s·, walking naked and 3651
4 S· shall the king of Assyria lead "
21: 1 s· it cometh from the desert, from a*
22:22 s· he shall open, and none shall shut;*
23: 1 s· that there is no house, no entering
5 s· shall they be sorely pained at the*
24: 2 with the people, s· with the priest;
2 with the servant, s· with his master;
2 with the maid, s· with her mistress;
2 as with the buyer, s· with the seller;
2 with the lender, s· with the borrower;
2 s· with the giver of usury to him.
26:17 s· have we been in thy sight, O 3651
28: 8 s· that there is no place clean.
30:14 s· that there shall not be found in the
31: 4 s· shall the Lord of hosts come 3651
36: 6 s· is Pharaoh king of Egypt to all "
37: 5 S· the servants of king Hezekiah
8 S· Rabshakeh returned, and found the
37 S· Sennacherib king of Assyria
38: 8 S· the sun returned ten degrees, by
13 s· will he break all my bones: 3651
14 crane or a swallow, s· did I chatter:"
16 s· wilt thou recover me, and make me*
40:20 He that is s· impoverished that he*
41: 7 S· the carpenter encouraged the
47: 7 s· that thou didst not lay these 5704
12 if s· be thou shalt be able to profit,
12 if s· be thou mayest prevail.
52:15 S· shall he sprinkle many nations;3651
53: 7 dumb, s· he openeth not his mouth.†
54: 9 s· have I sworn that I would not be3651
55: 9 s· are my ways higher than your "
11 S· shall my word be that goeth "
59:19 S· shall they fear the name of the
60:15 s· that no man went through thee,
61:11 s· the Lord God will cause 3651

Isa 62: 5 a virgin, s' shall thy sons marry thee:
5 s' shall thy God rejoice over thee.
63: 8 will not lie: s' he was their Saviour.
14 s' didst thou lead thy people, to 3651
65: 8 s' will I do for my servants' sakes, "
66: 13 comforteth, s' will I comfort you; "
22 s' shall your seed and your name "
Jer 2: 26 s' is the house of Israel ashamed; "
36 Why gaddest thou about s' much
3: 20 s' have ye dealt treacherously with 3651
5: 19 s' shall ye serve strangers in a land "
27 s' are their houses full of deceit: "
31 and my people love to have it s': "
6: 7 s' she casteth out her wickedness: "
9: 10 s' that none can pass through
10: 18 them, that they may find it s'. *
11: 4 s' shall ye be my people, and I will be
5 and said, S' be it, O Lord. * 543
13: 2 S' I got a girdle according to the
5 S' I went, and hid it by Euphrates,
11 s' have I caused to cleave unto me 3651
17: 11 s' he that getteth riches, and not by
18: 4 s' he made it again another vessel,*
6 s' are ye in mine hand, O house of 3651
19: 11 Even s' will I break this people 3602
21: 2 if s' be that the Lord will deal with us*
24: 2 not be eaten, they were s' bad.
3 cannot be eaten, they are s' evil.
5 s' will I acknowledge them that 3651
8 cannot be eaten, they are s' evil;
8 S' will I give Zedekiah the king of 3651
26: 3 If s' be they will hearken, and turn*
7 S' the priests and the prophets and*
28: 6 Amen: the Lord do s': the Lord 3651
11 Even s' will I break the yoke of 3602
17 S' Hananiah the prophet died the
29: 17 cannot be eaten, they are s' evil.
30: 7 day is great, s' that none is like it:
31: 28 s' will I watch over them, to build, 3651
32: 8 S' Hanameel mine uncle's son came
11 S' I took the evidence of the
42 s' will I bring upon them all the 3651
33: 22 s' will I multiply the seed of David "
26 s' that I will not take any of his seed
34: 5 s' shall they burn odours for thee; 3651
36: 14 S' Baruch the son of Neriah took the
15 ears. S' Baruch read it in their ears.
21 S' the king sent Jehudi to fetch the
37: 14 S' Irijah took Jeremiah, and brought
38: 6 mire: s' Jeremiah sunk in the mire.*
11 S' Ebed-melech took the men with
12 the cords. And Jeremiah did s'. 3651
13 S' they drew up Jeremiah with cords,
16 S' Zedekiah the king sware secretly
20 s' it shall be well unto thee, and thy
23 S' they shall bring out all thy wives*
27 S' they left off speaking with him;
28 S' Jeremiah abode in the court of the
39: 13 S' Nebuzar-adan the captain of the
14 home: s' he dwelt among the people.
40: 5 S' the captain of the guard gave him
41: 7 it was s', when they came into the
8 S' he forbare, and slew them not
14 S' all the people that Ishmael had
42: 17 S' shall it be with all the men that set
18 s' shall my fury be poured forth 3651
20 s' declare unto us, and we will do it."
43: 4 S' Johanan the son of Kareah, and all
7 S' they came into the land of Egypt:*
44: 14 S' that none of the remnant of Judah,
22 S' that the Lord could no longer bear,
46: 18 Carmel by the sea, s' shall he come.
48: 30 the Lord; but it shall not be s'; *3651
30 his lies shall not s' effect it. * "
50: 40 s' shall no man abide there, neither
51: 8 her pain, if s' be she may be healed.
49 s' at Babylon shall fall the slain of all
60 S' Jeremiah wrote in a book all the*
52: 5 S' the city was besieged unto the
6 s' that there was no bread for the
26 S' Nebuzar-adan the captain of the*
La 2: 22 s' that in the day of the Lord's anger*
3: 29 the dust; if s' be there may be hope.
4: 14 s' that men could not touch their
5: 20 for ever, and forsake us s' long time?
Eze 1: 18 were s' high that they were dreadful;*
28 s' was the appearance of the 3651
3: 2 S' I opened my mouth, and he caused
4: 5 s' shalt thou bear the iniquity of the
5: 15 S' it shall be a reproach and a taunt,
17 S' will I send upon you famine and*
6: 14 S' will I stretch out my hand upon*
8: 5 S' I lifted up mine eyes the way
10 S' I went in and saw; and behold
11: 24 S' the vision that I had seen went up
12: 7 And I did s' as I was commanded: 3651
11 done, s' shall it be done unto them:"
13: 14 S' will I break down the wall that ye
14 s' that the foundation thereof shall
14: 15 s' that it be desolate, that no man
17 s' that I cut off man and beast from it:
15: 6 s' will I give the inhabitants of 3651
16: 16 shall not come, neither shall it be s'.
42 S' will I make my fury toward thee
44 As is the mother, s' is her daughter.
17: 6 s' it became a vine, and brought forth
18: 4 s' also the soul of the son is mine:
30 s' iniquity shall not be your ruin.
20: 36 s' will I plead with you, saith the 3651
22: 20 s' will I gather you in mine anger "
22 s' shall ye be melted in the midst* "
23: 18 S' she discovered her whoredoms,
27 s' that thou shalt not lift up thine
44 s' went they in unto Aholah and 3651
24: 18 S' I spake unto the people in the
19 things are to us, that thou doest s'?

Eze 28: 14 and I have set thee s': thou wast upon
31: 9 s' that all the trees of Eden, that
33: 7 S' thou, O son of man, I have set thee
34: 12 s' will I seek out my sheep, and 3651
35: 15 desolate, s' will I do unto thee: "
36: 38 s' shall the waste cities be filled "
37: 7 S' I prophesied as I was commanded:
10 S' I prophesied as he commanded me,
23 s' shall they be my people, and I will
38: 20 S' that the fishes of the sea, and the
39: 7 S' will I make my holy name known*
10 S' that they shall take no wood out of
22 S' the house of Israel shall know that
23 enemies; s' fell they all by the sword.*
40: 5 s' he measured the breadth of the
47 S' he measured the court, an hundred*
41: 4 S' he measured the length thereof,*
7 s' increased from the lowest chamber
13 S' he measured the house, an hundred
18 s' that a palm tree was between a*
19 S' that the face of a man was toward
43: 5 S' the spirit took me up, and brought*
15 S' the altar shall be four cubits; and*
27 and s' forward, the priests shall make*
45: 20 s' thou shalt do the seventh day 3651
20 simple: s' shall ye reconcile the house.
47: 21 S' shall ye divide this land unto you
Da 1: 5 s' nourishing them three years, that*
14 S' he consented to them in this
2: 2 S' they came and stood before the
15 is the decree s' hasty from the king?
42 s' the kingdom shall be partly strong,
3: 17 If it be s', our God whom we serve is
5: 6 s' that the joints of his loins were*
6: 23 S' Daniel was taken up out of the den,
28 S' this Daniel prospered in the reign
8: 4 s' that no beasts might stand before*
17 S' he came near where I stood: and
10: 7 s' that they fled to hide themselves.*
11: 9 S' the king of the south shall come*
15 S' the king of the north shall come,
30 s' shall he do; he shall even return.*
Ho 1: 3 S' he went and took Gomer the
3: 2 S' I bought her to me for fifteen pieces
3 man: s' will I also be for thee. 1571
4: 7 s' they sinned against me: 3651
6: 9 s' the company of priests murder in
8: 7 if s' be it yield, the strangers shall
10: 15 S' shall Beth-el do unto you 3602
11: 2 them, s' they went from them: "
14: 2 s' will we render the calves of our
Joe 2: 4 as horsemen, s' shall they run. 3651
3: 17 S' shall ye know that I am the Lord
Am 3: 12 s' shall the children of Israel be 3651
4: 8 S' two or three cities wandered unto
5: 9 s' that the spoiled shall come against
14 and s' the Lord, the God of hosts, 3651
Ob 16 s' shall all the heathen drink
Jon 1: 3 s' he paid the fare thereof, and went
4 s' that the ship was like to be broken.
6 S' the shipmaster came to him, and
7 S' they cast lots, and the lot fell upon
12 s' shall the sea be calm unto you: for
15 S' they took up Jonah, and cast him
3: 3 S' Jonah arose, and went unto
5 S' the people of Nineveh believed God,*
4: 5 S' Jonah went out of the city, and sat*
6 S' Jonah was exceeding glad of the
Mic 2: 2 s' they oppress a man and his house,*
5: 14 of thee: s' will I destroy thy cities.*
7: 3 mischievous desire: s' they wrap it up.*
Zep 3: 6 s' that there is no man, that there
7 s' their dwelling should not be cut off,
Hag 2: 5 s' my spirit remaineth among you:*
14 S' is this people, and s' is this 3651
14 s' is every work of their hands; "
Zec 1: 6 doings, s' hath he dealt with us. "
14 S' the angel that communed with me
21 s' that no man did lift up his head:
3: 5 S' they set a fair mitre upon his head,
6: 7 S' they walked to and fro through the
7: 3 as I have done these s' many years?
13 s' they cried, and I would not hear; 3651
8: 15 S' again have I thought in these "
10: 1 s' the Lord shall make bright clouds,*
11: 11 s' the poor of the flock that waited* 3651
12 S' they weighed for my price thirty
14: 15 And s' shall be the plague of the 3651
Mal 3: 13 have we spoken s' much against thee?*
M't 1: 17 S' all the generations from 3767
3: 15 said unto him, Suffer it to be s' now:*
5: 12 s' persecuted they the prophets 3779
16 Let your light s' shine before men, "
19 and shall teach men s', he shall be "
47 do not even the publicans s'? * "
6: 30 if God s' clothe the grass of the "
7: 12 do to you, do ye even s' to them: *3779
17 Even s' every good tree bringeth "
8: 10 I have not found s' great faith, no, 5118
13 hast believed, s' be it done unto thee.
28 s' that no man might pass by that 5620
31 S' the devils besought him, saying,* 1161
9: 19 followed him, and s' did his disciples.
33 It was never s' seen in Israel. 3779
11: 26 Even s', Father: for...it seemed * "
26 for s' it seemed good in thy sight. "
12: 40 s' shall the Son of man be three "
45 Even s' shall it be also unto this 3779
13: 2 s' that he went into a ship, and 5620
27 S' the servants of the householder* 1161
32 s' that the birds of the air come 5620
40 s' shall it be in the end of this 3779
49 S' shall it be at the end of the "
15: 33 s' much bread in the wilderness, 5118
33 as to fill s' great a multitude? "
18: 13 if s' be that he find it, verily I say 1437

M't 18: 14 Even s' it is not the will of your 3779
31 S' when his fellowservants saw 1161
35 S' likewise shall my heavenly 3779
19: 8 from the beginning it was not s'. "
10 of the man be s' with his wife, "
12 s' born from their mother's womb: "
20: 8 S' when even was come, the lord *1161
16 S' the last shall be first, and the 3779
26 But it shall not be s' among you: "
34 S' Jesus had compassion on them,*1161
22: 10 S' those servants went out into *2532
23: 28 Even s' ye also outwardly appear 3779
24: 27 s' shall also the coming of the "
33 S' likewise ye, when ye shall see "
37, 39 s' shall also the coming of the "
46 when he cometh shall find s' doing. "
25: 9 Not s'; lest there be not enough for*
20 s' he that had received five talents*2532
27: 64 s' the last error shall be worse * "
28: 15 S' they took the money, and did as*1161
M'r 2: 2 not s' much as about the door: *3366
8 s' reasoned within themselves, 3779
3: 20 again, s' that they could not 5620
20 could not s' much as eat bread. 3383
4: 1 s' that he entered into a ship, and 5620
17 and s' endured but for a time: *
26 said, S' is the kingdom of God, 3779
32 s' that the fowls of the air may 5620
37 the ship, s' that it was now full. * "
40 unto them, Why are ye s' fearful? *3779
6: 31 they had no leisure s' much as to 3761
7: 18 Are ye s' without understanding 3779
36 s' much the more a great deal
8: 8 S' they did eat, and were filled: *1161
9: 3 s' as no fuller on earth can white 3634
10: 8 s' then they are no more twain, 5620
43 But s' shall it not be among you: 3779
13: 29 S' ye in like manner, when ye shall 2532
14: 59 neither s' did their witness agree 3779
15: 5 nothing; s' that Pilate marvelled.*5620
15 s' Pilate, willing to content the people,*
39 saw that he s' cried out, and gave 3779
16: 19 S' then after the Lord had 3303
Lu 1: 21 that he tarried s' long in the temple.*
60 Not s'; but he shall be called John.
2: 6 s' it was, that, while they were there,*
21 which was s' named of the angel
5: 7 ships, s' that they began to sink. 5620
10 And s' was also James and John, 3668
15 s' much the more went there a
6: 3 Have ye not read s' much as this, *3761
10 And he did s': and his hand was 3779
26 s' did their fathers to the false*2596,5623
7: 9 I have not found s' great faith, 5118
9: 15 they did s', and made them all sit 3779
10: 21 them unto babes: even s', Father;*3483
21 for s' it seemed good in thy sight. 3779
11: 2 be done, as in heaven, s' in earth. *2532
30 s' shall also the Son of man be to 3779
12: 21 S' is he that layeth up treasure for "
28 If then God s' clothe the grass, "
38 and find them s', blessed are those "
43 when he cometh shall find s' doing. "
54 There cometh a shower; and s' it is. "
14: 21 S' that servant came, and shewed*2532
33 S' likewise, whosoever he be of 3767
16: 5 S' he called every one of his lord's*2532
26 s' that they which would pass *3704
17: 10 S' likewise ye, when ye shall have 3779
24 s' shall also the Son of man be in "
26 s' shall it be also in the days of the "
18: 13 would not lift up s' much as his eyes 3761
39 cried s' much the more, Thou son* 3123
20: 15 S'...cast him out of the vineyard, *2532
20 that s' they might deliver him unto 1519
21: 31 S' likewise ye, when ye see these 3779
34 s' that day come upon you unawares.*
22: 26 But ye shall not be s': but he that 3779
24: 24 found it even s' as the women had "
Joh 3: 8 s' is every one that is born of the "
14 s' must the Son of man be lifted up:"
16 For God s' loved the world, that "
4: 40 S' when the Samaritans were 3767
46 S' Jesus came again into Cana of* "
53 S' the father knew that it was at "
5: 21 even s' the Son quickeneth whom 3779
26 s' hath he given to the Son to have "
6: 9 but what are they among s' many? 5118
10 S' the men sat down, in number 3767
19 S' when they had rowed about five* "
57 s' he that eateth me, even he shall 2532
7: 43 S' there was a division among the 3767
8: 7 S' when they continued asking *1161
59 midst of them, and s' passed by. *3779
10: 15 me, even s' know I the Father: *
11: 28 And when she had s' said, she *5023
12: 37 done s' many miracles before them, 5118
50 Father said unto me, s' I speak. 3779
13: 12 S' after he had washed their feet, 3767
13 Lord: and ye say well; for s' I am.
33 ye cannot come; s' now I say to you. 2532
14: 2 if it were not s', I would have told you.
9 Have I been s' long time with you, 5118
31 gave me commandment, even s' I 3779
15: 8 fruit; s' shall ye be my disciples. 2532
9 loved me, s' have I loved you: *2504
17: 18 even s' have I also sent them into the
18: 15 Jesus, and s' did another disciple:
22 Answereth thou the high priest s'? 3779
20: 4 S' they ran both together: and the* 1161
20 And when he had s' said, he shewed 5124
21 hath sent me, even s' send I you.
21: 11 and for all there were s' many, yet 5118
15 S' when they had dined, Jesus 3767
Ac 1: 11 shall s' come in like manner as ye 3779
3: 12 or why look ye s' earnestly on us, as*

Ac 3:18 should suffer, he hath s· fulfilled. *3779
4:21 S· when they...further threatened* 1161
5: 8 ye sold the land for s· much? 5118
8 And she said, Yea, for s· much. "
32 s· is also the Holy Ghost, whom God
7: 1 high priest, Are these things s·? 3779
5 no, not s· much as to set his foot on:
8 and s· Abraham begat Isaac, and 3779
15 S· Jacob went down into Egypt, *1161
19 s· that they cast out their young *
51 as your fathers did, s· do ye. 2532
8:32 s· opened he not his mouth: 3779
10:14 Peter said, Not s·, Lord; for I have 3365
11: 8 But I said, Not s·, Lord: for nothing "
12: 8 bind on thy sandals. And s· he did. 3779
15 constantly affirmed...it was even s·. "
13: 4 S· they, being sent forth by the 3767
8 s· is his name by interpretation) 3779
47 s· hath the Lord commanded us, "
14: 1 and s· spake, that a great multitude "
15:30 S· when they were dismissed, they 3767
39 contention was s· sharp between 5620
39 s· Barnabas took Mark, and sailed* 5037
16: 5 s· were the churches established in 3767
26 s· that the foundations of the 5620
17:11 whether those things were s·. 3779
33 S· Paul departed from among * "
19: 2 have not s· much as heard whether 3761
10 s· that all they which dwelt in Asia 5620
12 S· that from his body were brought* "
14 chief of the priests, which did s·. *5124
16 s· that they fled out of that house 5620
20 S· mightily grew the word of God 3779
22 S· he sent into Macedonia two of them*
27 S· that not only this our craft is in*
20:11 till break of day, s· he departed. 3779
13 for s· had he appointed, minding "
24 s· that I might finish my course 5613
35 s· labouring ye ought to support 3779
21:11 S· shall the Jews at Jerusalem bind "
35 s· it was, that he was borne of the 4819
22:24 wherefore they cried s· against 3779
23: 7 And when he had s· said, there 5124
11 s· must thou bear witness also at 3779
18 S· he took him, and brought him 3767
22 S· the chief captain then let the
24: 9 saying that these things were s·. 3779
14 s· worship I the God of my fathers, "
27:17 strake sail, and s· were driven. "
44 s· it came to pass, that they escaped "
28: 9 S· when this was done, others *3767
14 and s· we went toward Rome. 3779
Ro 1:15 S·, as much as in me is, I am ready "
20 s· that they are without excuse: *1519
4:18 was spoken, S· shall thy seed be. 3779
5: 3 And not only s·, but we glory in
11 And not only s·, but we also joy in God
12 s· death passed upon all men, for 3779
15 the offence, s· also is the free gift. "
16 was by one that sinned, s· is the gift:
18 even s· by the righteousness of one 3779
19 s· by the obedience of one shall "
21 even s· might grace reign through "
6: 3 s· many of us as were baptized *3745
4 s· we also should walk in newness 3779
19 even s· now yield your members "
7: 2 to her husband s· long as he liveth;*
3 S· then if, while her husband 686
3 s· that she is no adulteress, though
25 S· then with the mind I myself 686
8: 8 S· then they that are in the flesh *
9 if s· be that the Spirit of God dwell in
17 if s· be that we suffer with him, that
9:16 S· then it is not of him that willeth, 686
10:17 S· then faith cometh by hearing, "
11: 5 Even s· then at this present time 3779
16 root be holy, s· are the branches. 2532
26 And s· all Israel shall be saved: as it 3779
31 s· have these also now not believed, "
12: 5 S· we, being many, are one body "
20 in s· doing thou shalt heap coals 5124
14:12 S· then every one of us shall give 686
15:19 s· that from Jerusalem, and 5620
20 Yea, s· have I strived to preach the 3779
1Co 1: 7 S· that ye come behind in no gift: 5620
2:11 even s· the things of God knoweth 3779
3: 7 S· then neither is he that planteth 5620
15 shall be saved; yet s· as by fire. 3779
4: 1 Let a man s· account of us, as of "
5: 1 not s· much as named among the *3761
3 him that hath s· done this deed, 3779
6: 5 Is it s·, that there is not a wise man "
7:17 called every one, s· let him walk. "
17 And s· ordain I in all churches. "
26 that it is good for a man s· to be. * "
36 need s· require, let him do what he "
37 hath s· decreed in his heart that *5124
38 S· then he that giveth her in 5620
40 But she is happier if she s· abide, *3779
8:12 when ye sin s· against the brethren,* "
9:14 Even s· hath the Lord ordained "
15 that it should be s· done unto me: "
24 prize? S· run, that ye may obtain. "
26 therefore s· run, not as uncertainly; "
26 s· fight I, not as one that beateth "
11:12 s· is the man also by the woman; "
28 and s· let him eat of that bread, "
12:12 are one body: s· also is Christ. "
13: 2 s· that I could remove mountains, 5620
14: 9 S· likewise ye, except ye utter by 3779
10 s· many kinds of voices in the 5118
12 Even s· ye, forasmuch as ye are 3779
25 s· falling down on his face he will "
15:11 s· we preach, and s· ye believed. "
15 up, if s· be that the dead rise not. 686
22 s· in Christ shall be all made alive 3779

1Co 15:42 S· also is the resurrection of the 3779
45 s· it is written, The first man Adam "
54 S· when this corruptible shall *1161
16: 1 churches of Galatia, even s· do ye. 3779
2Co 1: 5 s· our consolation also aboundeth "
7 s· shall ye be also of the consolation. "
10 delivered us from s· great a death, 5082
2: 7 S· that contrariwise ye ought 5620
3: 7 s· that the children of Israel could "
4:12 S· then death worketh in us, but "
5: 3 If s· be that being clothed we shall
7: 7 me; s· that I rejoiced the more. 5620
14 even s· our boasting, which I made 3779
8: 6 s· he would also finish in you the "
11 s· there may be a performance also "
9: 7 purposeth in his heart, s· let him give;*
10: 7 is Christ's, even s· are we Christ's. 3779
11: 3 s· your minds should be corrupted* "
9 unto you, and s· will I keep myself.
22 Are they Hebrews? s· am I. 2504
22 Are they Israelites? s· am I. "
22 they the seed of Abraham? s· am I. "
12:16 But be it s·, I did not burden you:
Ga 1: 6 that ye are s· soon removed from 3779
9 we said before, s· say I now again, 2532
3: 3 Are ye s· foolish? having begun in 3779
4 suffered s· many things in vain? 5118
9 S· then they which be of faith are 5620
4: 3 Even s· we, when we were children, 3779
29 after the Spirit, even s· it is now. "
31 S· then, brethren, we are not * 686
5:17 s· that ye cannot do the things *2443
6: 2 and s· fulfil the law of Christ. 3779
Eph 2:15 twain one new man, s· making peace;
4:20 But ye have not s· learned Christ; 3779
21 If s· be that ye have heard him, and "
5:24 s· let the wives be to their own "
28 S· ought men to love their wives as "
33 s· love his wife even as himself; * "
Ph'p 1:13 S· that my bonds in Christ are 5620
20 s· now also Christ shall be magnified
2:23 s· soon as I shall see how it will go 5613
3:17 s· as ye have us for an ensample. 3779
4: 1 s· stand fast in the Lord, my dearly "
Col 2: 6 Jesus the Lord, s· walk ye in him:
3:13 Christ forgave you, s· also do ye. 3779
1Th 1: 7 S· that ye were ensamples to all 5620
8 s· that we need not to speak any "
2: 4 with the gospel, even s· we speak; 3779
8 S· being affectionately desirous of "
4: 1 s· ye would abound more and more.*
14 even s· them also which sleep in 3779
17 s· shall we ever be with the Lord. "
5: 2 s· cometh as a thief in the night. "
2Th 1: 4 S· that we ourselves glory in you 5620
2: 4 s· that he as God sitteth in the "
3:17 token in every epistle: s· I write. 3779
1Ti 1: 4 godly edifying which is in faith: s· do.
3:11 Even s· must their wives be grave, *5615
6:20 oppositions of science falsely s· called:
2Ti 3: 8 s· do these also resist the truth: 3779
Heb 1: 4 s· much better than the angels, 5118
2: 3 if we neglect s· great salvation; 5082
3:11 S· I sware in my wrath, They *5613
19 S· we see that they could not enter 2532
4: 7 To day, after s· long a time; as it 5118
5: 3 s· also for himself, to offer for sins. 3779
5 S· also Christ glorified not himself "
6:15 And s·, after he had patiently * "
7: 9 And as I may s· say, Levi also, who 5613
22 By s· much was Jesus made a 5118
9:28 S· Christ was once offered to bear 3779
10:25 s· much the more, as ye see the 5118
33 of them that were s· used. 3779
11: 3 s· that things which are seen were 1519
12 s· many as the stars of the sky in
12: 1 with s· great a cloud of witnesses, 5118
1 the sin which doth s· easily beset us,
20 And if s· much as a beast touch the*
21 And s· terrible was the sight, that 3779
13: 6 S· that we may boldly say, The 5620
Jas 1:11 s· also shall the rich man fade 3779
2:12 S· speak ye, and s· do, as they that "
17 Even s· faith, if it hath not works, "
26 s· faith without works is dead also. "
3: 4 which though they be s· great, 5082
5 s· the tongue is a little member, 3779
6 s· is the tongue among our * "
10 these things ought not s· to be. "
12 s· can no fountain both yield salt * "
1Pe 1:15 s· be ye holy in all manner of *2532
2: 3 If s· be ye have tasted that the Lord*
15 For s· is the will of God, that with 3779
3:17 if the will of God be s·, that ye suffer
4:10 s· minister the same one to another,*
2Pe 1:11 s· an entrance shall be ministered* 3779
1Jo 2: 6 him ought himself also s· to walk,* "
4:11 Beloved, if God s· loved us, we ought* "
17 as he is, s· are we in this world. 2532
Re 1: 7 because of him. Even s·, Amen. 3483
2:15 S· hast thou also them that hold 3779
3:16 S· then because thou art lukewarm, "
8:12 s· as the third part of them was *2443
13:13 s· that he maketh fire come down * "
16: 7 Even s·, Lord God Almighty, true *3483
18 the earth, s· mighty an earthquake, 5082
18 an earthquake, and s· great. 3779
18: 7 s· much torment and sorrow give 5118
17 s· great riches is come to nought. "
22:20 Amen. Even s·, come, Lord Jesus. *3483

So (*so*)
2Ki 17: 4 messengers to S· king of Egypt, 5471

soaked
Isa 34: 7 their land shall be s· with blood, *7301

soap See SOPE.

so-be-it See SO.

sober
2Co 5:13 or whether we be s·, it is for your 4993
1Th 5: 6 others; but let us watch and be s·. 3525
8 But let us, who are of the day, be s·, "
1Ti 3: 2 husband of one wife, vigilant, s·, *4998
11 wives be grave, not slanderers, s·, *3524
Tit 1: 8 a lover of good men, s·, just, *4998
2: 2 That the aged men be s·, grave, *3524
4 teach the young women to be s·, *4994
6 likewise exhort to be s· minded. 4993
1Pe 1:13 be s·, and hope to the end for the 3525
4: 7 be ye therefore s·, and watch unto *4993
5: 8 Be s·, be vigilant; because your 3525

soberly
Ro 12: 3 but to think s·, according as 1519,4993
Tit 2:12 we should live s·, righteously, and 4996

sober-minded See SOBER and MINDED.

soberness
Ac 26:25 forth the words of truth and s·. 4997

sobriety
1Ti 2: 9 with shamefacedness and s·; not 4997
15 and charity and holiness with s·. "

Socho (*so'-ko*) See also SOCHOH.
1Ch 4:18 and Heber the father of S·, and *7755

Sochoh (*so'-ko*) See also SHOCHOH; SOCHO; SOCOH.
1Ki 4:10 to him pertained S·, and all the *7755

socket See also SOCKETS.
Ex 38:27 hundred talents, a talent for a s·. 134

sockets
Ex 26:19 forty s· of silver under the twenty 134
19 two s· under one board for his two "
19 and two s· under another board for "
21 And their forty s· of silver; "
21 two s· under one board, "
21 and two s· under another board. "
25 and their s· of silver, sixteen s·; "
25 two s· under one board, "
25 and two s· under another board. "
32 be of gold, upon the four s· of silver. "
37 shalt cast five s· of brass for them. "
27:10 their twenty s· shall be of brass; "
11 pillars and their twenty s· of brass; "
12 their pillars ten, and their s· ten. "
14, 15 pillars three, and their s· three. "
16 shall be four, and their s· four. "
17 be of silver, and their s· of brass. "
18 twined linen, and their s· of brass. "
35:11 his bars, his pillars, and his s·, "
17 his pillars, and their s·, and the "
36:24 forty s· of silver he made under the "
24 two s· under one board for his two "
24 two s· under another board for his "
26 And their forty s· of silver; "
26 two s· under one board, "
26 and two s· under another board. "
30 and their s· were sixteen s· of silver, "
30 under every board two s·. "
36 he cast for them four s· of silver. "
38 but their five s· were of brass. "
38:10 twenty, and their brasen s· twenty; "
11 and their s· of brass twenty; "
12 their pillars ten, and their s· ten; "
14 pillars three, and their s· three. "
15 pillars three, and their s· three. "
17 the s· for the pillars were of brass; "
19 were four, and their s· of brass four; "
27 were cast the s· of the sanctuary, "
27 sanctuary, and the s· of the vail; "
27 hundred s· of the hundred talents, "
30 s· to the door of the tabernacle "
31 And the s· of the court round about, "
31 and the s· of the court gate, and all "
39:33 his bars, and his pillars, and his s·, "
40 of the court, his pillars, and his s·, "
40:18 fastened his s·, and set up the boards "
Nu 3:36 the pillars thereof, and the s· thereof, "
37 their s·, and their pins, and their "
4:31 the pillars thereof, and s· thereof, "
32 their s·, and their pins, and their "
Ca 5:15 of marble, set upon s· of fine gold: "

Socoh (*so'-ko*) See also SOCHOH.
Jos 15:35 and Adullam, S·, and Azekah, 7755
48 Shamir, and Jattir, and S·, "

sod See also SEETHE; SODDEN.
Ge 25:29 And Jacob s· pottage: and Esau ‡2102
2Ch 35:13 other holy offerings s· they in pots, ‡1310

sodden
Ex 12: 9 it raw, nor s· at all with water, ‡1310
Le 6:28 the earthen vessel wherein it is s‡ "
28 and if it be s· in a brasen pot, it ‡ "
Nu 6:19 priest shall take the s· shoulder ‡1311
1Sa 2:15 he will not have s· flesh of thee, ‡1310
La 4:10 women have s· their own children: ‡ "

sodering
Isa 41: 7 saying, It is ready for the s·: 1694

Sodi (*so'-di*)
Nu 13:10 Zebulun, Gaddiel the son of S·. 5476

Sodom (*sod'-om*) See also SODOMA; SODOMITE.
Ge 10:19 goest, unto S·, and Gomorrah, 5467
13:10 before the Lord destroyed S· and "
12 and pitched his tent toward S·. "
13 men of S· were wicked and sinners "
14: 2 made war with Bera king of S·, "
8 there went out the king of S·, and "
10 kings of S· and Gomorrah fled, "
11 they took all the goods of S· and "
12 brother's son, who dwelt in S·, and "

Ge 14:17 the king of S· went out to meet 5467
21 And the king of S· said unto Abram, "
22 And Abram said to the king of S·, I "
18:16 from thence, and looked toward S·: "
20 cry of S· and Gomorrah is great, "
22 from thence, and went toward S·: "
26 said, If I find in S· fifty righteous "
19: 1 And there came two angels to S· at "
1 even; and Lot sat in the gate of S·: "
4 the men of S·, compassed the house "
24 rained upon S· and upon Gomorrah "
28 he looked toward S· and Gomorrah, "
De 29:23 like the overthrow of S·, and "
32:32 For their vine is of the vine of S·, "
Isa 1: 9 we should have been as S·, and we "
10 word of the Lord, ye rulers of S·; "
3: 9 and they declare their sin as S·, "
13:19 as when God overthrew S· and "
Jer 23:14 they are all of them unto me as S·, "
49:18 the overthrow of S· and Gomorrah "
50:40 As God overthrew S· and Gomorrah "
La 4: 6 the punishment of the sin of S·, "
Eze16:46 right hand, is S· and her daughters. "
48 S· thy sister hath not done, she nor "
49 this was the iniquity of thy sister S·, "
53 captivity of S· and her daughters, "
55 thy sisters, S· and her daughters, "
56 thy sister S· was not mentioned by "
Am 4:11 God overthrew S· and Gomorrah, "
Zep 2: 9 Surely Moab shall be as S·, and the "
M't 10:15 more tolerable for the land of S· 4670
11:23 done in thee, had been done in S·, "
24 more tolerable for the land of S· "
M'r 6:11 shall be more tolerable for S· and * "
Lu 10:12 more tolerable in that day for S·, "
17:29 same day that Lot went out of S· "
2Pe 2: 6 And turning the cities of S· and "
Jude 7 Even as S· and Gomorrha, and the "
Re 11: 8 city, which spiritually is called S· "

Sodoma (*sod'-o-mah*) See also SODOM.
Ro 9:29 we had been as S·, and been made*4670

sodomite (*sod'-om-ite*) See also SODOMITES.
De 23:17 nor a s· of the sons of Israel. 6945

sodomites (*sod'-om-ites*)
1Ki 14:24 there were also s· in the land: 6945
15:12 took away the s· out of the land, "
22:46 And the remnant of the s·, which "
2Ki 23: 7 he brake down the houses of the s·, "

soever See also WHATSOEVER; WHENSOEVER; WHERESOEVER; WHITHERSOEVER; WHOMSOEVER; WHOSESOEVER; WHOSOEVER.
Le 15: 9 what saddle s· he rideth upon that 834
17: 3 man s· there be of the house of Israel, "
22: 4 What man s· of the seed of Aaron is a "
De 12:32 What thing s· I command you, 834
2Sa 15:35 that what thing s· thou shalt hear out "
24: 3 unto the people, how many s· they be, "
1Ki 8:38 What prayer and supplication s· 834
2Ch 6:29 what prayer or what supplication s· "
19:10 And what cause s· shall come to you* "
M'r 3:28 blasphemies wherewith s· they 3745,302
6:10 what place s· ye enter into an *1437
11:24 What things s· ye desire, when*3745,302
Joh 5:19 for what things s· he doeth, these "
20:23 Whose s· sins ye remit, they are "
23 and whose s· sins ye retain, they are "
Ro 3:19 that what things s· the law saith, 1437

soft See also SOFTER.
Job 23:16 For God maketh my heart s·, and *7401
41: 3 will he speak s· words unto thee? 7390
Ps 65:10 thou makest it s· with showers: 4127
Pr 15: 1 A s· answer turneth away wrath: 7390
25:15 and a s· tongue breaketh the bone. "
M't 11: 8 A man clothed in s· raiment? 3120
8 behold, they that wear s· clothing "
Lu 7:25 A man clothed in s· raiment? "

softer
Ps 55:21 his words were s· than oil, yet 7401

softly
Ge 33:14 I will lead on s·, according as the 328
J'g 4:21 and went s· unto him, and smote 3814
Ru 3: 7 came s· and uncovered his feet, 3909
1Ki 21:27 and lay in sackcloth, and went s·. 328
Isa 8: 6 the waters of Shiloah that go s·, "
38:15 I shall go s· all my years in the "
Ac 27:13 And when the south wind blew s·, 5285

soil
Eze 17: 8 It was planted in a good s· by 7704

sojourn See also SOJOURNED; SOJOURNER; SOJOURNETH; SOJOURNING.
Ge 12:10 went down into Egypt to s· there; 1481
19: 9 This one fellow came in to s·, and "
26: 3 S· in this land, and I will be with "
47: 4 For to s· in the land are we come; "
Ex 12:48 when a stranger shall s· with thee, "
Le 17: 8 the strangers which s· among you, "
10, 13 the strangers that s· among you, "
19:33 And if a stranger s· with thee in "
20: 2 or of the strangers that s· in Israel, "
25:45 the strangers that do s· among you, "
Nu 9:14 if a stranger shall s· among you, "
15:14 And if a stranger s· with you, or "
J'g 17: 8 to s· where he could find a place: "
9 I go to s· where I may find a place. "
Ru 1: 1 went to s· in the country of Moab. "
1Ki 17:20 evil upon the widow with whom I s·, "
2Ki 8: 1 and s· wheresoever thou canst s·: "
Ps 120: 5 Woe is me, that I s· in Mesech, that "
Isa 23: 7 feet shall carry her afar off to s·. "
52: 4 aforetime into Egypt to s· there; "
Jer 42:15 enter into Egypt, and go to s· there; "
17 faces to go into Egypt to s· there; "

Jer 42:22 whither ye desire to go and to s·. 1481
43: 2 say, Go not into Egypt to s· there: "
44:12, 14, 28 the land of Egypt to s· there, "
La 4:15 They shall no more s· there. "
Eze 20:38 out of the country where they s·, 4033
47:22 to the strangers that s· among you, 1481
Ac 7: 6 should s· in a strange land; 1510,3941

sojourned
Ge 20: 1 Kadesh and Shur, and s· in Gerar. 1481
21:23 to the land wherein thou hast s·. "
34 And Abraham s· in the Philistines' "
32: 4 I have s· with Laban, and stayed "
35:27 where Abraham and Isaac s·. "
De 18: 6 gates out of all Israel, where he s·* "
26: 5 Egypt, and s· there with a few, "
J'g 17: 7 who was a Levite, and he s· there. "
19:16 and he s· in Gibeah: but the men "
2Ki 8: 2 and s· in the land of the Philistines "
Ps 105:23 and Jacob s· in the land of Ham. "
Heb 11: 9 faith he s· in the land of promise, *3939

sojourner See also SOJOURNERS.
Ge 23: 4 I am a stranger and a s· with you: 8453
Le 22:10 a s· of the priest, or an hired "
25:35 though he be a stranger, or a s·; "
40 But as an hired servant, and as a s·, "
47 a s· or stranger wax rich by thee, *1616
47 sell himself unto the stranger or s· 8453
Nu 35:15 and for the s· among them: that "
Ps 39:12 and a s·, as all my fathers were. "

sojourners
Le 25:23 ye are strangers and s· with me. 8453
2Sa 4: 3 and were s· there until this day.) 1481
1Ch 29:15 are strangers before thee, and s·, 8453

sojourneth
Ex 3:22 of her that s· in her house, jewels 1481
12:49 unto the stranger that s· among "
Le 16:29 or a stranger that s· among you: "
17:12 any stranger that s· among you eat "
18:26 nor any stranger that s· among you: "
25: 6 for thy stranger that s· with thee, *"
Nu 15:15 for the stranger that s· with you, "
16 for the stranger that s· with you. "
26 the stranger that s· among them; "
29 the stranger that s· among them. "
19:10 the stranger that s· among them, "
Jos 20: 9 the stranger that s· among them, "
Ezr 1: 4 remaineth in any place where he s·, "
Eze 14: 7 or of the stranger that s· in Israel, *"
47:23 that in what tribe the stranger s·, "

sojourning
Ex 12:40 the s· of the children of Israel, 4186
J'g 19: 1 a certain Levite s· on the side of 1481
1Pe 1:17 the time of your s· here in fear: 3940

solace
Pr 7:18 let us s· ourselves with loves. 5965

sold
Ge 25:33 he s· his birthright unto Jacob. 4376
31:15 for he hath s· us, and hath quite "
37:28 and s· Joseph to the Ishmeelites for "
36 Midianites s· him into Egypt unto "
41:56 and s· unto the Egyptians; and 7666
42: 6 he it was that s· to all the people "
45: 4 brother, whom ye s· into Egypt. 4376
5 yourselves, that ye s· me hither: "
47:20 Egyptians s· every man his field, "
22 wherefore they s· not their lands. "
Ex 22: 3 then he shall be s· for his theft. "
Le 25:23 The land shall not be s· for ever: "
25 hath s· away...of his possession, * "
25 redeem that which his brother s·. 4465
27 unto the man to whom he s· it; 4376
28 that which is s· shall remain in 4465
29 within a whole year after it is s·; "
33 then the house that was s·, and the "
34 of their cities may not be s·; 4376
39 waxen poor, and be s· unto thee; *"
42 they shall not be s· as bondmen. "
48 After...he is s· he may be redeemed "
50 from the year that he was s· to him "
27:20 he have s· the field to another man, "
27 be s· according to thy estimation. "
28 possession, shall be s· or redeemed: "
De 15:12 Hebrew woman, be s· unto thee, "
28:68 ye shall be s· unto your enemies * "
32:30 except their Rock had s· them, and "
J'g 2:14 he s· them into the hands of their "
3: 8 and he s· them into the hand of "
4: 2 Lord s· them into the hand of Jabin "
10: 7 and he s· them into the hands of the "
1Sa 12: 9 he s· them into the hand of Sisera, "
1Ki 21:20 hast s· thyself to work evil in the "
2Ki 6:25 ass's head was s· for fourscore pieces "
7: 1 of fine flour be s· for a shekel, "
16 of fine flour was s· for a shekel, "
17:17 and s· themselves to do evil in the 4376
Ne 5: 8 which were s· unto the heathen; "
8 or shall they be s· unto us? "
13:15 in the day wherein they s· victuals. "
16 s· on the sabbath unto the children "
Es 7: 4 For we are s·, I and my people, to "
4 if we had been s· for bondmen and "
Ps 105:17 Joseph, who was s· for a servant: "
Isa 50: 1 creditors is it to whom I have s· you? "
1 iniquities have ye s· yourselves, "
52: 3 Ye have s· yourselves for nought; "
Jer 34:14 which hath been s· unto thee; "
La 5: 4 money; our wood is s· unto us. 935,4242
Eze 7:13 shall not return to that which is s·, 4465
Joe 3: 3 s· a girl for wine, that they might 4376
6 have ye s· unto the Grecians, "
7 the place whither ye have s· them, "
Am 2: 6 they s· the righteous for silver, and "
M't 10:29 not two sparrows s· for a farthing? 4453

M't 13:46 went and s· all that he had, and 4097
18:25 his lord commanded him to be s·, "
21:12 that s· and bought in the temple, 4453
12 the seats of them that s· doves, "
26: 9 ointment might have been s· for 4097
M'r 11:15 that s· and bought in the temple, 4453
15 and the seats of them that s· doves; "
14: 5 s· for more than three hundred 4097
Lu 12: 6 five sparrows s· for two farthings, 4453
17:28 they bought, they s·, they planted, "
19:45 to cast out them that s· therein, and "
Joh 2:14 in the temple those that s· oxen and "
16 said unto them that s· doves, Take "
12: 5 this ointment s· for three hundred 4097
Ac 2:45 And s· their possessions and goods, "
4:34 of lands or houses s· them, and 4453
34 prices of the things that were s·, 4097
37 Having land, s· it, and brought the 4453
5: 1 Sapphira his wife, s· a possession, "
4 and after it was s·, was it not in 4097
8 whether ye s· the land for so much? 591
7: 9 with envy, s· Joseph into Egypt: "
Ro 7:14 but I am carnal, s· under sin. 4097
1Co 10:25 Whatsoever is s· in the shambles, 4453
Heb 12:16 morsel of meat s· his birthright. 591

soldering See SODERING.

soldier See also SOLDIERS.
Joh 19:23 made four parts, to every s· a part; 4757
Ac 10: 7 a devout s· of them that waited on "
28:16 by himself with a s· that kept him. "
2Ti 2: 3 as a good s· of Jesus Christ. "
4 who hath chosen him to be a s·. 4758

soldiers See also FELLOWSOLDIERS; SOLDIERS'.
1Ch 7: 4 fathers, were bands of s· for war, *6635
11 thousand and two hundred s·, * "
2Ch 25:13 the s· of the army which Amaziah *1121
Ezr 8:22 to require of the king a band of s· 2428
Isa 15: 4 the armed s· of Moab...cry out; *2502
M't 8: 9 authority, having s· under me: 4757
27:27 the s· of the governor took Jesus "
27 unto him the whole band of s·. * "
28:12 they gave large money unto the s·, 4757
M'r 15:16 the s· led him away into the hall, "
Lu 3:14 the s· likewise demanded of him, 4754
7: 8 authority, having under me s·, 4757
23:36 the s· also mocked him, coming to "
Joh 19: 2 the s· platted a crown of thorns, "
23 s·, when they had crucified Jesus, "
24 These things therefore the s· did. "
32 Then came the s·, and brake the "
34 one of the s· with a spear pierced "
Ac 12: 4 him to four quaternions of s· to "
6 Peter was sleeping between two s·, "
18 was no small stir among the s·, "
21:32 Who immediately took s· and "
32 saw the chief captain and the s·, "
35 that he was borne of the s· for the "
23:10 commanded the s· to go down, and 4758
23 Make ready two hundred s· to go to 4757
31 the s·, as it was commanded them, "
27:31 said to the centurion and to the s·, "
32 Then the s· cut off the ropes of the "

soldiers'
Ac 27:42 And the s· counsel was to kill the 4757

sole See also SOLES.
Ge 8: 9 no rest for the s· of her foot, 3709
De 28:35 from the s· of thy foot unto the top "
56 to set the s· of her foot upon the "
65 shall the s· of thy foot have rest: "
Jos 1: 3 the s· of your foot shall tread upon, "
2Sa 14:25 from the s· of his foot even to the "
2Ki 19:24 with the s· of my feet have I dried "
Job 2: 7 the s· of his foot unto his crown. "
Isa 1: 6 s· of the foot even unto the head "
37:25 with the s· of my feet have I dried "
Eze 1: 7 s· of their feet was like the s· of a "

solemn
Le 23:36 it is a s· assembly; and ye shall 6116
Nu 10:10 gladness, and in your s· days, *4150
15: 3 in your s· feasts, to make a sweet* "
29:35 day ye shall have a s· assembly: 6116
De 16: 8 seventh day shall be a s· assembly "
15 thou keep a s· feast unto the Lord *2287
2Ki 10:20 Proclaim a s· assembly for Baal. 6116
2Ch 2: 4 on the s· feasts of the Lord your *4150
7: 9 day they made a s· assembly: 6116
8:13 new moons, and on the s· feasts, *4150
Ne 8:18 the eighth day was a s· assembly, 6116
Ps 81: 3 appointed, on our s· feast day. 2282
92: 3 upon the harp with a s· sound.
Isa 1:13 it is iniquity, even the s· meeting. 6116
La 1: 4 because none come to the s· feasts: 4150
2: 6 Lord hath caused the s· feasts and "
7 Lord, as in the day of a s· feast. "
22 called as in a s· day my terrors "
Eze 36:38 of Jerusalem in her s· feasts; so * "
46: 9 before the Lord in the s· feasts, * "
Ho 2:11 her sabbaths, and all her s· feasts. "
9: 5 What will ye do in the s· day, and "
12: 9 as in the days of the s· feast. "
Joe 1:14 ye a fast, call a s· assembly, 6116
2:15 sanctify a fast, call a s· assembly: "
Am 5:21 not smell in your s· assemblies. "
Na 1:15 keep thy s· feasts, perform thy *2282
Zep 3:18 are sorrowful for the s· assembly, 4150
Mal 2: 3 even the dung of your s· feasts; †2282

solemnities
Isa 33:20 Look upon Zion, the city of our s·: 4150
Eze 45:17 in all s· of the house of Israel: * "
46:11 in the s· the meat offering shall be "

solemnity See also SOLEMNITIES.
De 31:10 in the s· of the year of release, *4150
Isa 30:29 the night when a holy s· is kept; *2282

solemnly
Ge 43: 3 The man did s· protest unto us, 5749
1Sa 8: 9 howbeit yet protest s· unto them, "

soles
De 11: 24 s· of your feet shall tread shall be*3709
Jos 3: 13 the s· of the feet of the priests that "
4: 18 s· of the priests' feet were lifted "
1Ki 5: 3 put them under the s· of his feet. "
Isa 60: 14 down at the s· of thy feet; and "
Eze 43: 7 and the place of the s· of my feet, "
Mal 4: 3 be ashes under the s· of your feet "

solitarily
Mic 7: 14 which dwell s· in the wood, in the 910

solitary
Job 3: 7 Lo, let that night be s·, let no *1565
30: 3 For want and famine they were s·:* "
Ps 68: 6 God setteth the s· in families: he 3173
107: 4 in the wilderness in a s· way; *3452
Isa 35: 1 s· place shall be glad for them; 6723
La 1: 1 How doth the city sit s·, that was 910
M'r 1: 35 out, and departed into a s· place, *2048

Solomon (*sol'-o-mun*) See also JEDIDIAH; SOLOMON'S.
2Sa 5: 14 Shobab, and Nathan, and S·, 8010
12: 24 a son, and he called his name S·: "
1Ki 1: 10 and S· his brother, he called not. "
11 unto Bath-sheba the mother of S·, "
12 own life, and the life of thy son S·. "
13, 17 S· thy son shall reign after me, "
19 S· thy servant hath he not called. "
21 I and my son S· shall be counted "
26 thy servant S·, hath he not called. "
30 S· thy son shall reign after me, "
33 S· my son to ride upon mine own "
34 and say, God save king S·. "
37 even so be he with S·, and make "
38 and caused S· to ride upon king "
39 of the tabernacle, and anointed S·. "
39 the people said, God save king S·. "
43 king David hath made S· king. "
46 also S· sitteth on the throne of the "
47 name of S· better than thy name, "
50 And Adonijah feared because of S·, "
51 And it was told S·, saying, Behold, "
51 Adonijah feareth king S·: for, lo, "
51 Let king S· swear unto me to day "
52 S· said, If he will shew himself a "
53 So king S· sent, and they brought "
53 and bowed himself to king S·: "
53 and S· said unto him, Go to thine "
2: 1 and he charged S· his son, saying, "
12 sat S· upon the throne of David "
13 to Bath-sheba the mother of S·. "
17 Speak, I pray thee, unto S· the king, "
19 Bath-sheba...went unto king S·, "
22 king S· answered and said unto his "
23 Then king S· sware by the Lord, "
25 And king S· sent by the hand of "
27 S· thrust out Abiathar from being "
29 it was told king S· that Joab was "
29 Then S· sent Benaiah the son of "
41 And it was told S· that Shimei had "
45 king S· shall be blessed, and the "
46 was established in the hand of S·. "
3: 1 And S· made affinity with Pharaoh "
3 S· loved the Lord, walking in the "
4 burnt offerings, did S· offer upon "
5 Lord appeared to S· in a dream by "
6 S· said, Thou hast shewed unto "
10 Lord, that S· had asked this thing. "
15 And S· awoke, and behold, it was a "
4: 1 king S· was king over all Israel. "
7 And S· had twelve officers over all "
11 had Taphath the daughter of S· to "
15 Basmath the daughter of S· to "
21 S· reigned over all kingdoms from "
21 served S· all the days of his life. "
25 to Beer-sheba, all the days of S·. "
26 S· had forty thousand stalls of "
27 provided victual for king S·, and "
29 S· wisdom and understanding "
34 all people to hear the wisdom of S·, "
5: 1 of Tyre sent his servants unto S·; "
2 And S· sent to Hiram, saying, "
7 when Hiram heard the words of S·, "
8 Hiram sent to S·, saying, I have "
10 So Hiram gave S· cedar trees and "
11 S· gave Hiram twenty thousand "
11 gave S· to Hiram year by year. "
12 the Lord gave S· wisdom, as he "
12 was peace between Hiram and S·; "
13 S· raised a levy out of all Israel; "
15 And S· had threescore and ten "
6: 2 house which king S· built for the "
11 the word of the Lord came to S·, "
14 So S· built the house, and finished "
21 S· overlaid the house within with "
7: 1 But S· was building his own house "
8 S· made also an house for Pharaoh's* "
13 king S· sent and fetched Hiram out "
14 he came to king S·, and wrought all "
40 work that he made king S· for the "
45 which Hiram made to king S· for "
47 S· left all the vessels unweighed, "
48 And S· made all the vessels that "
51 all the work that king S· made for "
51 And S· brought in the things which "
8: 1 S· assembled the elders of Israel, "
1 Israel, unto king S· in Jerusalem, "
2 assembled themselves unto king S· "
5 king S·, and all the congregation of "
12 Then spake S·, The Lord said that "
22 S· stood before the altar of the Lord "
54 S· had made an end of praying all "
1Ki 8: 63 And S· offered a sacrifice of peace 8010
65 at that time S· held a feast, and all "
9: 1 when S· had finished the building "
2 appeared to S· the second time, "
10 when S· had built the two houses, "
11 king of Tyre had furnished S· with "
11 king S· gave Hiram twenty cities "
12 the cities which S· had given him; "
15 of the levy which king S· raised; "
17 S· built Gezer, and Beth-horon the "
19 all the cities of store that S· had, "
19 and that which S· desired to build "
21 upon those did S· levy a tribute of "
22 of Israel did S· make no bondmen: "
24 house which S· had built for her: "
25 a year did S· offer burnt offerings 8010
26 king S· made a navy of ships in "
27 of the sea, with the servants of S·. "
28 talents, and brought it to king S·. "
10: 1 of Sheba heard of the fame of S· "
2 and when she was come to S·, she "
3 S· told her all her questions: there "
10 the queen of Sheba gave to king S·. "
13 S· gave unto the queen of Sheba all "
13 S· gave her of his royal bounty. "
14 of gold that came to S· in one year "
16 king S· made two hundred targets "
21 accounted of in the days of S·. "
23 So king S· exceeded all the kings "
24 all the earth sought to S·, to hear "
26 S· gathered together chariots and "
28 S· had horses brought out of Egypt, "
11: 1 king S· loved many strange women, "
2 gods: S· clave unto these in love. "
4 when S· was old, that his wives "
5 S· went after Ashtoreth the goddess "
6 S· did evil in the sight of the Lord, "
7 S· build an high place for Chemosh, "
9 Lord was angry with S·, because "
11 the Lord said unto S·, Forasmuch "
14 stirred up an adversary unto S·, "
25 to Israel all the days of S·, "
27 S· built Millo, and repaired the "
28 S· seeing the young man that he "
31 the kingdom out of the hand of S·, "
40 S· sought...to kill Jeroboam. And "
40 was in Egypt until the death of S·. "
41 And the rest of the acts of S·, and "
41 in the book of the acts of S·? "
42 time that S· reigned in Jerusalem "
43 S· slept with his fathers, and was "
12: 2 fled from the presence of king S·, "
6 men, that stood before S· his father "
21 again to Rehoboam the son of S·. "
23 unto Rehoboam, the son of S·, "
14: 21 Rehoboam the son of S· reigned in "
26 shields of gold which S· had made. "
2Ki 21: 7 said to David, and to S· his son, "
23: 13 S· the king of Israel had builded "
24: 13 the vessels of gold which S· king of "
25: 16 bases which S· had made for the "
1Ch 3: 5 Shobab, and Nathan, and S·, four, "
6: 10 temple that S· built in Jerusalem.) "
32 S· had built the house of the Lord "
14: 4 and Shobab, Nathan, and S·, "
18: 8 wherewith S· made the brasen sea, "
22: 5 S· my son is young and tender, and "
6 Then he called for S· his son, and "
7 David said to S·, My son, as for me, "
9 for his name shall be S·, and I will "
17 princes of Israel to help S· his son, "
23: 1 made S· his son king over Israel. "
28: 5 chosen S· my son to sit upon the "
6 S· thy son, he shall build my house "
9 S· my son, know thou the God of "
11 Then David gave to S· his son the "
20 David said to S· his son, Be strong "
29: 1 S· my son, whom alone God hath "
19 give unto S· my son a perfect heart, "
22 they made S· the son of David king "
23 S· sat on the throne of the Lord as "
24 submitted themselves unto S· the "
25 the Lord magnified S· exceedingly "
28 and S· his son reigned in his stead. "
2Ch 1: 1 And S·...was strengthened in his "
2 Then S· spake unto all Israel, to the "
3 So S·, and all the congregation "
5 and S· and the congregation sought "
6 S· went up thither to the brasen "
7 that night did God appear unto S·, "
8 And S· said unto God, Thou hast "
11 And God said to S·, Because this "
13 Then S· came from his journey to "
14 And S· gathered chariots and "
16 S· had horses brought out of Egypt, "
2: 1 S· determined to build an house for "
2 And S· told out threescore and ten "
3 S· sent to Huram the king of Tyre, "
11 in writing, which he sent to S·, "
17 S· numbered all the strangers that "
3: 1 S· began to build the house of the "
3 things wherein S· was instructed "
4: 11 that he was to make for king S· for "
16 Huram his father make to king S· "
18 S· made all these vessels in great "
19 S· made all the vessels that were "
5: 1 all the work that S· made for the "
1 and S· brought in all the things that "
2 S· assembled the elders of Israel, "
6 king S·, and all the congregation "
6: 1 Then said S·, The Lord hath said "
13 For S· had made a brasen scaffold, "
7: 1 S· had made an end of praying, "
5 S· offered a sacrifice of twenty and "
7 Moreover S· hallowed the middle of "
7 the brasen altar which S· had made "
2Ch 7: 8 time S· kept the feast seven days 8010
10 had shewed unto David, and to S·, "
11 S· finished the house of the Lord, "
12 the Lord appeared to S· by night, "
8: 1 wherein S· had built the house of "
2 which Huram had restored to S·, "
2 S· built them, and caused the "
3 And S· went to Hamath-zobah, and "
6 and all the store cities that S· had, "
6 and all that S· desired to build in "
8 them did S· make to pay tribute "
9 of Israel did S· make no servants "
11 And S· brought up the daughter of "
12 S· offered burnt offerings unto the "
16 work of S· was prepared unto the "
17 Then went S· to Ezion-geber, and "
18 with the servants of S· to Ophir, "
18 gold, and brought them to king S·. "
9: 1 of Sheba heard of the fame of S·, "
1 she came to prove S· with hard "
1 and when she was come to S·, she "
2 And S· told her all her questions: "
2 nothing hid from S· which he told "
3 of Sheba had seen the wisdom of S·, "
9 as the queen of Sheba gave king S·. "
10 servants of S·, which brought gold "
12 S· gave to the queen of Sheba all "
13 weight of gold that came to S· in "
14 brought gold and silver to S·. "
15 king S· made two hundred targets "
20 drinking vessels of king S· were of "
20 accounted of in the days of S·. "
22 S· passed all the kings of the earth "
23 kings...sought the presence of S·, "
25 And S· had four thousand stalls for "
28 they brought unto S· horses out of "
29 Now the rest of the acts of S·, first "
30 S· reigned in Jerusalem over all "
31 And S· slept with his fathers, and "
10: 2 he had fled from the presence of S· "
6 stood before S· his father while he "
11: 3 unto Rehoboam the son of S·, king "
17 Rehoboam the son of S· strong, "
17 walked in the way of David and S·. "
12: 9 shields of gold which S· had made. "
13: 6 the servant of S· the son of David, "
7 against Rehoboam the son of S·, "
30: 26 for since the time of S· the son of "
33: 7 had said to David and to S· his son, "
35: 3 house which S· the son of David "
4 to the writing of S· his son. "
Ne 12: 45 commandment of David, and of S· "
13: 26 Did not S· king of Israel sin by "
Ps 72: *title* A Psalm for S·. "
127: *title* A Song of degrees for S·. "
Pr 1: 1 The proverbs of S· the son of David, "
10: 1 proverbs of S·. A wise son maketh "
25: 1 These are also proverbs of S·, which "
Ca 1: 5 of Kedar, as the curtains of S·. "
3: 9 King S· made himself a chariot of "
11 and behold king S· with the crown "
8: 11 S· had a vineyard at Baal-hamon; "
12 thou, O S·, must have a thousand, "
Jer 52: 20 king S· had made in the house of "
M't 1: 6 and David the king begat S· of her *4672*
7 S· begat Roboam; and Roboam "
6: 29 S· in all his glory was not arrayed "
12: 42 the earth to hear the wisdom of S·; "
42 behold, a greater than S· is here. "
Lu 11: 31 the earth to hear the wisdom of S·; "
31 behold, a greater than S· is here. "
12: 27 S· in all his glory was not arrayed "
Ac 7: 47 But S· built him an house. "

Solomon's (*sol'-o-muns*)
1Ki 4: 22 And S· provision for one day was 8010
27 all that came unto king S· table, "
30 S· wisdom excelled the wisdom of "
5: 16 Beside the chief of S· officers which "
18 S· builders, and Hiram's builders "
6: 1 fourth year of S· reign over Israel, "
9: 1 S· desire which he was pleased to "
16 present unto his daughter, S· wife. "
23 the officers that were over S· work, "
10: 4 of Sheba had seen all S· wisdom, * "
21 all king S· drinking vessels were of "
11: 26 S· servant, whose mother's name* "
1Ch 3: 10 S· son was Rehoboam, Abia his son, "
2Ch 7: 11 all that came into S· heart to make "
8: 10 were the chief of king S· officers,* "
Ezr 2: 55 The children of S· servants: the "
58 and the children of S· servants, "
Ne 7: 57 The children of S· servants: the "
60 and the children of S· servants, "
11: 3 and the children of S· servants. "
Ca 1: 1 The song of songs, which is S·. "
3: 7 Behold his bed, which is S·; * "
Joh 10: 23 walked in the temple in S· porch. *4672*
Ac 3: 11 them in the porch that is called S·, "
5: 12 all with one accord in S· porch. "

solve See DISSOLVE; RESOLVED.

some See also BURDENSOME; DELIGHTSOME; LOATHSOME; NOISOME; SOMEBODY; SOMETHING; SOMETIME; SOMEWHAT; WEARISOME; WHOLESOME.
Ge 19: 19 lest s· evil take me, and I die: *
30: 35 and every one that had s· white in it,*
37: 20 slay him, and cast him into s· pit,* 259
20 S· evil beast hath devoured him:*
42: 6 he took s· of his brethren, even *7097
Ex 16: 17 did so, and gathered, s· more, s· less.
20 but s· of them left of it until the 582
27 went out s· of the people on the
30: 36 thou shalt beat s· of it very small,
Le 4: 7 the priest shall put s· of the blood*
17 shall dip his finger in s· of the blood,*

Le 4:18 put s· of the blood upon the horns*
14:14 take s· of the blood of the trespass*
15 the priest shall take s· of the log of oil,*
27 with his right finger s· of the oil that
25:25 hath sold away s· of his possession,
27:16 s· part of a field of his possession.*
Nu 5:20 s· man have lain with thee beside
21: 1 Israel, and took s· of them prisoners.
27:20 shalt put s· of thine honour upon him,*
31: 3 Arm s· of yourselves unto the war,*582
De 24: 1 hath found s· uncleanness in her: 1697
Jos 8:22 s· on this side, and s· on that side: 428
J'g 21:13 whole congregation sent s· to speak*
Ru 2:16 let fall also s· of the handfuls of
1Sa 8:11 and s· shall run before his chariots.*
13: 7 s· of the Hebrews went over Jordan to
24:10 and s· bade me kill thee: but mine eye
27: 5 let them give me a place in s· town*259
2Sa 11:17 and there fell s· of the people of the
24 and s· of the king's servants be dead,
17: 9 he is hid now in s· pit, or in s· other259
9 s· of them be overthrown at the first,"
12 shall we come upon him in s· place "
1Ki 14:13 in him there is found s· good thing
2Ki 2:16 and cast him upon s· mountain, 259
16 mountain, or unto s· valley. "
5:13 had bid thee do s· great thing,
7: 9 light, s· mischief will come upon us:*
13 Let s· take, I pray thee, five of the
9:33 s· of her blood was sprinkled on the
17:25 among them, which slew s· of them.
1Ch 4:42 s· of them, even of the sons of Simeon,
9:29 S· of them also were appointed to
30 And s· of the sons of the priests made
12:19 And there fell s· of Manasseh to David,
2Ch 12: 7 I will grant them s· deliverance; 4592
16:10 And Asa oppressed s· of the people
17:11 Also s· of the Philistines brought
20: 2 there came s· that told Jehoshaphat,
Ezr 2:68 And s· of the chief of the fathers, when
70 s· of the people, and the singers, and
7: 7 there went up s· of the children of
10:44 s· of them had wives by whom they
Ne 2:12 night, I and s· few men with me; 4592
5: 3 S· also there were that said, We have
5 s· of our daughters are brought unto
6: 2 in s· one of the villages in the plain of*
7:70 s· of the chief of the fathers gave 7097
71 s· of the chief of the fathers gave to
73 and the singers and s· of the people,
11:25 s· of the children of Judah dwelt at
12:44 s· appointed over the chambers for*582
13:15 in Judah s· treading wine presses on
19 s· of my servants set I at the gates,
Job 24: 2 S· remove the landmarks; they *
Ps 20: 7 S· trust in chariots, and s· in 428
69:20 and I looked for s· to take pity, but
Pr 4:16 away, unless they cause s· to fall.
Jer 49: 9 they not leave s· gleaning grapes?
Eze 6: 8 have s· that shall escape the sword
Da 8:10 it cast down s· of the host and of the
11:35 s· of them of understanding shall fall,
12: 2 shall awake, s· to everlasting life, 428
2 s· to shame...everlasting contempt. "
Am 4:11 I have overthrown s· of you, as God
Ob 5 thee, would they not leave s· grapes?
M't 13: 4 s· seeds fell by the way side, 3588,3303
5 S· fell...stony places, where * " 243
7 s· fell among thorns; and the " "
8 forth fruit, s· an hundredfold, " 3303
8 s· sixtyfold, s· thirtyfold. " 1161
23 bringeth forth, s·...hundredfold," 3303
24 hundredfold, s· sixty, s· thirty. " 1161
16:14 S· say...thou art John the Baptist:" 3303
14 s·, Elias; and others, Jeremias," "
28 There be s· standing here, which 5100
19:12 For there are s· eunuchs, which were*
12 and there are s· eunuchs, which were*
23:34 s· of them ye shall kill and crucify;
34 s· of them shall ye scourge in your
27:47 S· of them that stood there, when 5100
28:11 s· of the watch came into the city, "
17 worshipped him: but s· doubted. 3588
M'r 2: 1 entered into Capernaum after s· days;
4: 4 he sowed, s· fell by...way side, 3588,3303
5 s· fell on stony ground, where it * 243
7 and s· fell among thorns, and the "
8 and brought forth, s· thirty, *1520
8 and s· sixty, and s· an hundred. "
20 and bring forth fruit, s· thirtyfold,* "
20 s· sixty, and s· an hundred. "
7: 2 saw s· of his disciples eat bread 5100
8:28 s· say, Elias; and others, One of * 243
9: 1 be s· of them that stand here, 5100
12: 5 many others; beating s·, and 3588,3303
5 others; beating...and killing s· 3588
14: 4 were s· that had indignation 5100
65 And s· began to spit on him, and to "
15:35 And s· of them that stood by, when "
Lu 8: 5 sowed, s· fell by the way side;3588,3303
6 s· fell upon a rock; and as soon as*2087
7 And s· fell among thorns; and the "
9: 7 because that it was said of s·, that5100
8 And of s·, that Elias had appeared; "
19 but s· say, Elias; and others say, * 243
27 there be s· standing here, which 5100
11:15 But s· of them said, He casteth out "
49 and s· of them they shall slay and
13: 1 s· that told him of the Galilæans, 5100
19:39 s· of the Pharisees from among the "
21: 5 And as s· spake of the temple, how "
16 s· of you shall they cause to be put to
23: 8 have seen s· miracle done by him. 5100
Joh 3:25 between s· of John's disciples and*
6:64 are s· of you that believe not. 5100
7:12 for s· said, He is a good man: 3588,3303

Joh 7:25 Then said s· of them of Jerusalem,5100
41 s· said, Shall Christ come out of 243
44 s· of them would have taken him; 5100
9: 9 S· said, This is he: others said, He*243
16 said s· of the Pharisees, This man 5100
40 s· of the Pharisees which were with*
10: 1 but climbeth up s· other way, the
11:37 s· of them said, Could not this 5100
46 s· of them went their ways to the "
13:29 s· of them thought, because Judas "
16:17 Then said s· of his disciples among
Ac 5:15 by might overshadow s· of them. 5100
8: 9 out that himself was s· great one: "
31 I, except s· man should guide me? "
34 this? of himself, or of s· other man?" "
11:20 s· of them were men of Cyprus and "
13:11 seeking s· to lead him by the hand.
15:36 And s· days after Paul said unto 5100
17: 4 s· of them believed, and consorted "
18 s· said, What will this babbler say? "
18 s·, He seemeth to be a setter forth 3588
21 to tell, or to hear s· new thing.) 5100
32 the resurrection...s· mocked: 3588,3303
18:23 after he had spent s· time there, 5100
19:32 S·...cried one thing, and s· another:243
21:34 And s· cried one thing, s· another,
27:27 that they drew near to s· country; 5100
34 I pray you to take s· meat: for this is
36 good cheer, and they also took s· meat.*
44 And the rest, s· on boards, 3588,3303
44 on boards, and s· on broken pieces1161
28:24 s· believed the things which 3588,3303
24 were spoken, and s· believed not. 3588
Ro 1:11 impart unto you s· spiritual gift, 5100
13 I might have s· fruit among you "
3: 3 For what if s· did not believe? shall"
8 and as s· affirm that we say,) Let "
5: 7 good man s· would even dare to die."
11:14 flesh, and might save s· of them. "
17 if s· of the branches be broken off, "
15:15 more boldly unto you in s· sort,575,3313
1Co 4:18 Now s· are puffed up, as though I 5100
6:11 And such were s· of you: but ye are"
8: 7 for s· with conscience of the idol "
9:22 that I might by all means save s·. "
10: 7 be ye idolaters, as were s· of them; "
8 fornication,...s· of them committed,"
9 Christ, as s· of them also tempted, "
10 ye, as s· of them also murmured, "
12:28 God hath set s· in the church,3588,3303
15: 6 present, but s· are fallen asleep. 5100
12 say s· among you that there is no "
34 s· have not the knowledge of God: "
35 s· man will say, How are the dead "
37 of wheat, or of s· other grain: "
2Co 3: 1 or need we, as s· others, epistles of "
10: 2 bold against s·, which think of us "
12 or compare ourselves with s· that* "
Ga 1: 7 but there be s· that trouble you,
Eph 4:11 And he gave s·, apostles; 3588,3303
11 apostles; and s·, prophets; and 3588
11 and s·, evangelists; and s·, pastors "
Ph'p 1:15 S· indeed preach Christ even of 5100
15 and strife; and s· also of good will:"
Col 3: 7 the which ye also walked s· time, *4218
1Th 3: 5 lest by s· means the tempter have *3381
2Th 3:11 are s· which walk among you 5100
1Ti 1: 3 s· that they teach no other doctrine,*"
6 s· having swerved have turned "
19 s· having put away concerning faith"
4: 1 times s· shall depart from the faith,"
5:15 s· are already turned aside after "
24 S· men's sins are open beforehand, "
24 and s· men they follow after. "
25 also the good works of s· are manifest*
6:10 which while s· coveted after, they 5100
21 s· professing have erred concerning"
2Ti 2:18 and overthrow the faith of s·. "
20 and of earth; s· to honour, 3588,3303
20 to honour, and s· to dishonour. 3588
Heb 3: 4 For every house is builded by s· 5100
16 For s·, when they had heard, did * "
4: 6 it remaineth that s· must enter "
10:25 together, as the manner of s· is; "
11:40 provided s· better thing for us, "
13: 2 thereby s· have entertained angels "
1Pe 4:12 though s· strange thing happened*
2Pe 3: 9 as s· men count slackness; but 5100
16 s· things hard to be understood, "
Jude 22 s· have compassion, making 3588,3303

somebody
Lu 8:46 Jesus said, S· hath touched me: *5100
Ac 5:36 Theudas, boasting himself to be s·;"

something
1Sa 20:26 S· hath befallen him, he is not 4745
M'r 5:43 that s· should be given her to eat.
Lu 11:54 to catch s· out of his mouth, that 5100
Joh 13:29 that he should give s· to the poor. "
Ac 3: 5 expecting to receive s· of them. "
23:15 s· more perfectly concerning him: *
18 thee, who hath s· to say unto thee.5100
Ga 6: 3 a man think himself to be s·, when "

sometime See also SOME and TIME; SOMETIMES.
Col 1:21 you, that were s· alienated and *4218
1Pe 3:20 Which s· were disobedient, when * "

sometimes See also SOMETIME.
Eph 2:13 ye who s· were far off are made *4218
5: 8 For ye were s· darkness, but now * "
Tit 3: 3 we ourselves also were s· foolish, * "

somewhat
Le 4:13 they have done s· against any of the*
22 done s· through ignorance against*
27 while he doeth s· against any of the*
13: 6 behold, if the plague be s· dark, *3544

Le 13:19 bright spot, white, and s· reddish,*
21 than the skin, but be s· dark; *3544
24 bright spot, s· reddish, or white; *
26 the other skin, but be s· dark; *3544
28 not in the skin, but it be s· dark; * "
56 be s· dark after the washing of it; * "
1Ki 2:14 I have s· to say unto thee. And
2Ki 5:20 run after him, and take s· of him. 3972
2Ch 10: 4 ease thou s· the grievous servitude*
9 Ease s· the yoke that thy father did*
10 but make thou it s· lighter for us;*
Lu 7:40 Simon, I have s· to say unto thee. 5100
Ac 23:20 enquire s· of him more perfectly. "
25:26 had, I might have s· to write. "
Ro 15:24 I be s· filled with your company. *3313
2Co 5:12 that ye may have s· to answer them*
10: 8 boast s· more of our authority, 5100
Ga 2: 6 But of these who seemed to be s·. "
6 who seemed to be s· in conference*
Heb 8: 3 that this man have s· also to offer. 5100
Re 2: 4 Nevertheless I have s· against thee,*

son See also SON'S; SONS.
Ge 4:17 after the name of his s·, Enoch. 1121
25 she bare a s·, and called his name "
26 to him also there was born a s·; "
5: 3 begat a s· in his own likeness, after
28 and two years, and begat a s·: 1121
9:24 his younger s· had done unto him. "
11:31 Terah took Abram his s·, and Lot "
31 Lot the s· of Haran his son's s·, and
31 daughter in law, his s· Abram's wife;
12: 5 and Lot his brother's s·, and all 1121
14:12 took Lot, Abram's brother's s·, who"
16:11 art with child, and shalt bear a s·, "
15 Hagar bare Abram a s·: and Abram"
17:16 her, and give thee a s· also of her: "
19 thy wife shall bear thee a s· indeed;"
23 And Abraham took Ishmael his s·, "
25 Ishmael his s· was thirteen years "
26 circumcised, and Ishmael his s·. "
18:10 lo, Sarah thy wife shall have a s·. "
14 of life, and Sarah shall have a s·. "
19:12 s· in law, and thy sons, and thy "
37 the firstborn bare a s·, and called "
38 she also bare a s·, and called his "
21: 2 bare Abraham a s· in his old age. "
3 Abraham called the name of his s· "
4 Abraham circumcised his s· Isaac "
5 his s· Isaac was born unto him. "
7 I have born him a s· in his old age. "
9 And Sarah saw the s· of Hagar the "
10 out this bondwoman and her s·: "
10 for the s· of this bondwoman shall "
10 shall not be heir with my s·, even "
11 Abraham's sight because of his s·.1121
13 s· of the bondwoman will I make a "
23 with my s·, nor with my son's s·: 5220
22: 2 And he said, Take now thy s·, 1121
2 thine only s· Isaac, whom thou "
3 men with him, and Isaac his s·, 1121
6 and laid it upon Isaac his s·; and "
7 and he said, Here am I, my s·. "
8 My s·, God will provide himself a "
9 and bound Isaac his s·, and laid "
10 and took the knife to slay his s·. "
12 seeing thou hast not withheld thy s·."
12 withheld...thine only s· from me. "
13 burnt offering in the stead of his s·.1121
16 thing, and hast not withheld thy s·, "
16 withheld...thine only s·: "
23: 8 for me to Ephron the s· of Zohar, 1121
24: 3 shalt not take a wife unto my s· of "
4 and take a wife unto my s· Isaac. "
5 must I needs bring thy s· again "
6 that thou bring not my s· thither "
7 thou shalt take a wife unto my s· "
8 only bring not my s· thither again. "
15 was born to Bethuel, s· of Milcah, "
24 daughter of Bethuel the s· of Milcah,"
36 master's wife bare a s· to my master"
37 shalt not take a wife to my s· of the "
38 kindred, and take a wife unto my s·."
40 take a wife for my s· of my kindred,"
44 appointed out for my master's s·. "
47 daughter of Bethuel, Nahor's s·, "
48 brother's daughter unto his s·. "
25: 6 sent them away from Isaac his s·, "
9 the field of Ephron the s· of Zohar "
11 that God blessed his s· Isaac; "
12 of Ishmael, Abraham's s·, "
19 generations of Isaac, Abraham's s·:"
27: 1 he called Esau his eldest s·, and "
1 and said unto him, My s·: and he "
5 when Isaac spake to Esau his s·. "
6 Rebekah spake unto Jacob her s·, "
8 therefore, my s·, obey my voice "
13 Upon me be thy curse, my s·: only "
15 raiment of her eldest s· Esau, "
15 them upon Jacob her youngest s·: "
17 into the hand of her s· Jacob. "
18 Here am I; who art thou, my s·? "
20 Isaac said unto his s·, How is it "
20 thou hast found it so quickly, my s·?"
21 that I may feel thee, my s·, whether"
21 thou be my very s· Esau or not. "
24 he said, Art thou my very s· Esau? "
26 Come near now, and kiss me, my s·."
27 the smell of my s· is as the smell of "
32 I am thy s·, thy firstborn Esau. "
37 shall I do now unto thee, my s·? "
42 these words of Esau her elder s· "
42 and called Jacob her younger s·, "
43 therefore, my s·, obey my voice; "
28: 5 Laban, s· of Bethuel the Syrian, "
9 daughter of Ishmael Abraham's s·, "
29: 5 Know ye Laban the s· of Nahor? "

Ge 29:12 and that he was Rebekah's s': 1121
13 the tidings of Jacob his sister's s', "
32 And Leah conceived, and bare a s', "
33 she conceived again, and bare a s'; "
33 hath therefore given me this s' also: "
34 she conceived again, and bare a s';1121
35 she conceived again, and bare a s': "
30: 5 conceived, and bare Jacob a s'. "
6 my voice, and hath given me a s': "
7 again, and bare Jacob a second s'. "
10 Zilpah Leah's maid bare Jacob a s'. "
12 Leah's maid bare Jacob a second s'. "
17 and bare Jacob the fifth s'. "
19 again, and bare Jacob the sixth s'. "
23 And she conceived, and bare a s'; "
24 Lord shall add to me another s'. "
34: 2 And when Shechem the s' of Hamor "
8 soul of my s' Shechem longeth for "
18 Hamor, and Shechem Hamor's s'. "
20 Hamor and Shechem his s' came "
24 Hamor and unto Shechem his s' "
26 slew Hamor and Shechem his s' "
35:17 not; thou shalt have this s' also. "
36:10 Eliphaz the s' of Adah the wife of "
10 Reuel the s' of Bashemath the wife "
12 concubine to Eliphaz Esau's s'; "
15 of Eliphaz the firstborn s' of Esau;*
17 are the sons of Reuel Esau's s'; 1121
32 Bela the s' of Beor reigned in Edom: "
33 Jobab the s' of Zerah of Bozrah "
35 Hadad the s' of Bedad, who smote "
38 Baal-hanan the s' of Achbor reigned "
39 Baal-hanan the s' of Achbor died, "
37: 3 because he was the s' of his old age: "
34 and mourned for his s' many days. "
35 go down into the grave unto my s' "
38: 3 And she conceived, and bare a s'; "
4 she conceived again, and bare a s'; "
5 yet again conceived, and bare a s'; "
11 house, till Shelah my s' be grown: "
26 that I gave her not to Shelah my s'. "
42:38 My s' shall not go down with you; "
43:29 brother Benjamin, his mother's s', "
29 God be gracious unto thee, my s'. "
45: 9 Thus saith thy s' Joseph, God hath "
28 enough; Joseph my s' is yet alive: "
46:10 and Shaul the s' of a Canaanitish "
47:29 die: and he called his s' Joseph, and "
48: 2 Behold, thy s' Joseph cometh unto "
19 said, I know it, my s', I know it: "
49: 9 the prey, my s', thou art gone up: "
50:23 also of Machir the s' of Manasseh "
Ex 1:16 if it be a s', then ye shall kill him: "
22 Every s' that is born ye shall cast "
2: 2 woman conceived, and bare a s': "
10 daughter, and he became her s'. "
22 she bare him a s', and he called "
4:22 Thus saith the Lord, Israel is my s', "
23 Let my s' go, that he may serve me: "
23 behold, I will slay thy s', even thy "
25 and cut off the foreskin of her s', "
6:15 and Shaul the s' of a Canaanitish "
25 Eleazar Aaron's s' took him one of "
10: 2 ears of thy s', and of thy son's s', "
13: 8 thou shalt shew thy s' in that day, "
14 be when thy s' asketh thee in time "
20:10 not do any work, thou, nor thy s', "
21: 9 if he have betrothed her unto his s', "
31 Whether he have gored a s', or have "
23:12 and the s' of thy handmaid, and the "
29:30 that s' that is priest in his stead "
31: 2 Bezaleel the s' of Uri, the s' of Hur, "
6 Aholiab, the s' of Ahisamach, of the "
32:29 every man upon his s', and upon "
33:11 Joshua, the s' of Nun, a young man, "
35:30 Bezaleel the s' of Uri, the s' of Hur, "
34 Aholiab, the s' of Ahisamach, of the "
38:21 of Ithamar, s' to Aaron the priest. "
22 Bezaleel the s' of Uri, the s' of Hur, "
23 him was Aholiab, s' of Ahisamach, "
Le 12: 6 her purifying are fulfilled, for a s', "
21: 2 and for his s', and for his daughter, "
24:10 the s' of an Israelitish woman, "
10 this s' of the Israelitish woman "
11 Israelitish woman's s' blasphemed "
25:49 Either his uncle, or his uncle's s', "
Nu 1: 5 Reuben; Elizur the s' of Shedeur. "
6 Shelumiel the s' of Zurishaddai. "
7 Nahshon the s' of Amminadab. "
8 Issachar; Nethaneel the s' of Zuar. "
9 Of Zebulun; Eliab the s' of Helon. "
10 Elishama the s' of Ammihud: "
10 Gamaliel the s' of Pedahzur. "
11 Benjamin; Abidan the s' of Gideoni. "
12 Ahiezer the s' of Ammishaddai. "
13 Of Asher; Pagiel the s' of Ocran. "
14 Of Gad; Eliasaph the s' of Deuel. "
15 Of Naphtali; Ahira the s' of Enan. "
20 children of Reuben, Israel's eldest s',*
2: 3 Nahshon the s' of Amminadab 1121
5 Nethaneel the s' of Zuar shall be "
7 and Eliab the s' of Helon shall be "
10 shall be Elizur the s' of Shedeur. "
12 be Shelumiel the s' of Zurishaddai. "
14 shall be Eliasaph the s' of Reuel. "
18 be Elishama the s' of Ammihud. "
20 be Gamaliel the s' of Pedahzur. "
22 shall be Abidan the s' of Gideoni. "
25 be Ahiezer the s' of Ammishaddai. "
27 shall be Pagiel the s' of Ocran. "
29 shall be Ahira the s' of Enan. "
3:24 shall be Eliasaph the s' of Lael. "
30 shall be Elizaphan the s' of Uzziel. "
32 Eleazar the s' of Aaron the priest "
35 was Zuriel the s' of Abihail: "
4:16 Eleazar the s' of Aaron the priest "

Nu 4:28, 33 Ithamar...s' of Aaron the priest.1121
7: 8 Ithamar the s' of Aaron the priest. "
12 was Nahshon the s' of Amminadab, "
17 of Nahshon the s' of Amminadab. "
18 Nethaneel the s' of Zuar, prince of "
23 offering of Nethaneel the s' of Zuar. "
24 Eliab the s' of Helon, prince of the "
29 the offering of Eliab the s' of Helon. "
30 Elizur the s' of Shedeur, prince of "
35 offering of Elizur the s' of Shedeur. "
36 Shelumiel the s' of Zurishaddai, "
41 of Shelumiel the s' of Zurishaddai. "
42 Eliasaph the s' of Deuel, prince of "
47 offering of Eliasaph the s' of Deuel. "
48 day Elishama the s' of Ammihud, "
53 of Elishama the s' of Ammihud. "
54 offered Gamaliel the s' of Pedahzur, "
59 of Gamaliel the s' of Pedahzur. "
60 Abidan the s' of Gideoni, prince of "
65 offering of Abidan the s' of Gideoni. "
66 day Ahiezer the s' of Ammishaddai, "
71 of Ahiezer the s' of Ammishaddai. "
72 Pagiel the s' of Ocran, prince of the "
77 offering of Pagiel the s' of Ocran. "
78 Ahira the s' of Enan, prince of "
83 the offering of Ahira the s' of Enan. "
10:14 was Nahshon the s' of Amminadab. "
15 was Nethaneel the s' of Zuar. "
16 Zebulun was Eliab the s' of Helon. "
18 host was Elizur the s' of Shedeur. "
19 Shelumiel the s' of Zurishaddai. "
20 of Gad was Eliasaph the s' of Deuel. "
22 was Elishama the s' of Ammihud. "
23 was Gamaliel the s' of Pedahzur. "
24 was Abidan the s' of Gideoni. "
25 was Ahiezer the s' of Ammishaddai. "
26 of Asher was Pagiel the s' of Ocran. "
27 Naphtali was Ahira the s' of Enan. "
29 said unto Hobab, the s' of Raguel "
11:28 Joshua the s' of Nun, the servant of "
13: 4 Reuben, Shammua the s' of Zaccur. "
5 of Simeon, Shaphat the s' of Hori. "
6 Judah, Caleb the s' of Jephunneh. "
7 of Issachar, Igal the s' of Joseph. "
8 of Ephraim, Oshea the s' of Nun. "
9 of Benjamin, Palti the s' of Raphu. "
10 of Zebulun, Gaddiel the s' of Sodi. "
11 of Manasseh, Gaddi the s' of Susi. "
12 of Dan, Ammiel the s' of Gemalli. "
13 of Asher, Sethur the s' of Michael. "
14 of Naphtali, Nahbi the s' of Vophsi. "
15 tribe of Gad, Geuel the s' of Machi. "
16 called Oshea...s' of Nun Jehoshua. "
14: 6 And Joshua the s' of Nun, and "
6 and Caleb the s' of Jephunneh, "
30 save Caleb the s' of Jephunneh, "
30 and Joshua the s' of Nun. "
38 But Joshua the s' of Nun, and Caleb "
38 and Caleb the s' of Jephunneh, "
16: 1 Now Korah, the s' of Izhar, "
1 the s' of Kohath, the s' of Levi, and "
1 of Eliab, and On, the s' of Peleth, "
37 Eleazar the s' of Aaron the priest, "
20:25 Take Aaron and Eleazar his s', and "
26 and put them upon Eleazar his s': "
28 and put them upon Eleazar his s'; "
22: 2 Balak the s' of Zippor saw all that "
4 Balak the s' of Zippor was king of "
5 Balaam the s' of Beor to Pethor, "
10 Balak...s' of Zippor, king of Moab, "
16 Thus saith Balak the s' of Zippor, "
23:18 hearken unto me, thou s' of Zippor: "
19 s' of man, that he should repent: "
24: 3, 15 Balaam the s' of Beor hath said, "
25: 7 when Phinehas, the s' of Eleazar, "
7 the s' of Aaron the priest, saw it, he "
11 Phinehas, the s' of Eleazar, the "
11 the s' of Aaron the priest, hath "
14 Zimri, the s' of Salu, a prince of a "
26: 1 Eleazar the s' of Aaron the priest, "
5 Reuben, the eldest s' of Israel: the*
33 Zelophehad the s' of Hepher had 1121
65 save Caleb the s' of Jephunneh, "
65 and Joshua the s' of Nun. "
27: 1 of Zelophehad, the s' of Hepher, "
1 the s' of Gilead, the s' of Machir, "
1 the s' of Manasseh, of the families "
1 of Manasseh the s' of Joseph: "
4 his family, because he hath no s'? "
8 If a man die, and have no s', then "
18 Take thee Joshua the s' of Nun, a "
31: 6 Phinehas...s' of Eleazar the priest, "
8 Balaam also the s' of Beor they slew "
32:12 Save Caleb the s' of Jephunneh the "
12 and Joshua the s' of Nun: for they "
28 Joshua the s' of Nun, and the chief "
33 tribe of Manasseh the s' of Joseph, "
39 children of Machir...s' of Manasseh "
40 unto Machir the s' of Manasseh; "
41 Jair the s' of Manasseh went and "
34:17 the priest, and Joshua the s' of Nun. "
19 Judah, Caleb the s' of Jephunneh. "
20 Shemuel the s' of Ammihud. "
21 Benjamin, Elidad the s' of Chislon. "
22 of Dan, Bukki the s' of Jogli. "
23 Manasseh, Hanniel the s' of Ephod. "
24 Kemuel the s' of Shiphtan. "
25 Elizaphan the s' of Parnach. "
26 of Issachar, Paltiel the s' of Azzan. "
27 of Asher, Ahihud the s' of Shelomi. "
28 Pedahel the s' of Ammihud. "
36: 1 the s' of Machir, the s' of Manasseh, "
12 sons of Manasseh the s' of Joseph, "
De 1:31 bare thee, as a man doth bear his s', "
36 Save Caleb the s' of Jephunneh; he "
38 But Joshua the s' of Nun, which "

De 3:14 Jair the s' of Manasseh took all the 1121
5:14 not do any work, thou, nor thy s', "
6: 2 thou, and thy s', and thy son's s', "
20 when thy s' asketh thee in time to "
21 Then thou shalt say unto thy s', We "
7: 3 thou shalt not give unto his s', "
3 nor his daughter...unto thy s'. "
4 turn away thy s' from following me, "
8: 5 as a man chasteneth his s', so the "
10: 6 Eleazar his s' ministered in the "
11: 6 the sons of Eliab, the s' of Reuben: "
12:18 thou, and thy s', and thy daughter, "
13: 6 the s' of thy mother, or thy s', or thy "
16:11, 14 and thy s', and thy daughter, "
18:10 maketh his s' or...daughter to pass "
21:15 if the firstborn s' be hers that was "
16 may not make the s' of the beloved "
16 firstborn before the s' of the hated, "
17 acknowledge the s' of the hated for "
18 have a stubborn and rebellious s', "
20 our s' is stubborn and rebellious, "
23: 4 Balaam the s' of Beor of Pethor of "
28:56 and toward her s', and toward her "
31:23 gave Joshua the s' of Nun a charge, "
32:44 he, and Hoshea the s' of Nun. "
34: 9 Joshua the s' of Nun was full of "
Jos 1: 1 spake unto Joshua the s' of Nun, "
2: 1 And Joshua the s' of Nun sent out of "
23 and came to Joshua the s' of Nun, "
6: 6 And Joshua the s' of Nun called the "
26 in his youngest s' shall he set up the "
7: 1 for Achan, the s' of Carmi, 1121
1 the s' of Zabdi, the s' of Zerah, of "
18 man; and Achan, the s' of Carmi, "
18 the s' of Zabdi, the s' of Zerah, of the "
19 And Joshua said unto Achan, My s', "
24 took Achan the s' of Zerah, and the "
13:22 Balaam also the s' of Beor, the "
31 of Machir the s' of Manasseh, "
14: 1 the priest, and Joshua the s' of Nun, "
6, 13, 14 Caleb the s' of Jephunneh "
15: 6 the stone of Bohan the s' of Reuben: "
8 by the valley of the s' of Hinnom "
13 unto Caleb the s' of Jephunneh he "
17 Othniel the s' of Kenaz, the brother "
17: 2 of Manasseh the s' of Joseph by "
3 But Zelophehad, the s' of Hepher, "
3 the s' of Gilead, the s' of Machir, "
3 the s' of Manasseh, had no sons, but "
4 and before Joshua the s' of Nun, "
18:16 the valley of the s' of Hinnom, "
17 the stone of Bohan the s' of Reuben, "
19:49 Joshua the s' of Nun among them: "
51 the priest, and Joshua the s' of Nun, "
21: 1 and unto Joshua the s' of Nun, and "
12 they to Caleb the s' of Jephunneh "
22:13 Phinehas...s' of Eleazar the priest, "
20 not Achan the s' of Zerah commit "
31 Phinehas the s' of Eleazar the priest "
32 Phinehas...s' of Eleazar the priest, "
24: 9 Then Balak the s' of Zippor, king "
9 and called Balaam the s' of Beor "
29 Joshua the s' of Nun, the servant "
33 And Eleazar the s' of Aaron died; "
33 that pertained to Phinehas his s', "
J'g 1:13 Othniel the s' of Kenaz, Caleb's "
2: 8 Joshua the s' of Nun, the servant "
3: 9 Othniel the s' of Kenaz, Caleb's "
11 and Othniel the s' of Kenaz died. "
15 Ehud the s' of Gera, a Benjamite, "
31 him was Shamgar the s' of Anath, "
4: 6 called Barak the s' of Abinoam out "
12 Barak the s' of Abinoam was gone "
5: 1 Barak the s' of Abinoam on that "
6 days of Shamgar the s' of Anath, "
12 captive, thou s' of Abinoam. "
6:11 his s' Gideon threshed wheat by "
29 Gideon the s' of Joash hath done "
30 Joash, Bring out thy s', that he "
7:14 sword of Gideon the s' of Joash, "
8:13 Gideon the s' of Joash returned "
22 and thy s', and thy son's s' also: "
23 neither shall my s' rule over you: "
29 Jerubbaal the s' of Joash went and "
31 she also bare him a s', whose name "
32 Gideon the s' of Joash died in a "
9: 1 Abimelech the s' of Jerubbaal went "
5 Jotham...youngest s' of Jerubbaal "
18 Abimelech,...s' of his maidservant, "
26 Gaal the s' of Ebed came with his "
28 Gaal the s' of Ebed said, Who is "
28 is not he the s' of Jerubbaal? and "
30 the words of Gaal the s' of Ebed, "
31 Behold, Gaal the s' of Ebed and his "
35 And Gaal the s' of Ebed went out, "
57 curse of Jotham...s' of Jerubbaal. "
10: 1 Tola the s' of Puah, the s' of Dodo, "
11: 1 and he was the s' of an harlot: and "
2 thou art the s' of a strange woman. "
25 better than Balak the s' of Zippor, "
34 her he had neither s' nor daughter. "
12:13 after him Abdon the s' of Hillel, a "
15 And Abdon the s' of Hillel, the "
13: 3 thou shalt conceive, and bear a s'. "
5, 7 shalt conceive, and bear a s'; "
24 the woman bare a s', and called "
15: 6 Samson,...s' in law of the Timnite, 2860
17: 2 be thou of the Lord, my s'. 1121
3 the Lord from my hand for my s', "
18:30 Jonathan, the s' of Gershom, "
30 the s' of Manasseh, he and his "
19: 5 father said unto his s' in law, 2860
20:28 And Phinehas, the s' of Eleazar, 1121
28 the s' of Aaron, stood before it "
Ru 4:13 her conception, and she bare a s'. "
17 There is a s' born to Naomi; and "

1Sa 1: 1 was Elkanah, the s' of Jeroham, 1121
1 the s' of Elihu, the s' of Tohu, "
1 the s' of Zuph, an Ephrathite: "
20 that she bare a s', and called his "
23 gave her s' suck until she weaned "
3: 6 I called not, my s'; lie down again. "
16 Samuel, and said, Samuel, my s'. "
4: 16 said, What is there done, my s'? "
20 Fear not; for thou hast born a s'. "
7: 1 Eleazar his s' to keep the ark of "
9: 1 Kish, the s' of Abiel, the s' of Zeror, "
1 s' of Bechorath, the s' of Aphiah, "
2 he had a s', whose name was Saul, "
3 Kish said to Saul his s', Take now "
10: 2 saying, What shall I do for my s'? "
11 that is come unto the s' of Kish? "
21 and Saul the s' of Kish was taken: "
13: 16 Saul, and Jonathan his s', and the "
22 Saul and with Jonathan his s' was "
14: 1 that Jonathan the s' of Saul said "
3 Ahiah, the s' of Ahitub, I-chabod's "
3 brother, the s' of Phinehas, the "
3 the s' of Eli, the Lord's priest "
39 though it be in Jonathan my s', he "
40 I and Jonathan my s' will be on "
42 between me and Jonathan my s'. "
50 Abner, the s' of Ner, Saul's uncle. "
51 father of Abner was the s' of Abiel. "
16: 18 a s' of Jesse the Beth-lehemite, "
19 Send me David thy s', which is "
20 them by David his s' unto Saul. "
17: 12 David was the s' of that Ephrathite "
17 Jesse said unto David his s', Take "
55 Abner, whose s' is this youth? And "
56 thou whose s' the stripling is. "
58 Whose s' art thou, thou young man? "
58 I am the s' of thy servant Jesse the "
18: 18 I should be s' in law to the king? 2860
21 shalt this day be my s' in law in 2859
22 therefore be the king's s' in law. "
23 light thing to be a king's s' in law, "
26 well to be the king's s' in law: "
27 he might be the king's s' in law. "
19: 1 Saul spake to Jonathan his s', 1121
2 Jonathan Saul's s' delighted much "
20: 27 and Saul said unto Jonathan his s', "
27 cometh not the s' of Jesse to meat, "
30 Thou s' of the perverse rebellious "
30 thou hast chosen the s' of Jesse "
31 For as long as the s' of Jesse liveth "
22: 7 the s' of Jesse give every one of you "
8 sheweth me that my s' hath made "
8 a league with the s' of Jesse, "
8 my s' hath stirred up my servant "
9 I saw the s' of Jesse coming to Nob, "
9 Nob, to Ahimelech the s' of Ahitub. "
11 call Ahimelech...the s' of Ahitub, "
12 said, Hear now, thou s' of Ahitub. "
13 me, thou and the s' of Jesse, "
14 as David,...the king's s' in law, 2860
20 of Ahimelech the s' of Ahitub, 1121
23: 6 Abiathar the s' of Ahimelech fled "
16 Jonathan Saul's s' arose, and went "
24: 16 said, Is this thy voice, my s' David? "
25: 8 thy servants, and to thy s' David. "
10 David? and who is the s' of Jesse? "
17 for he is such a s' of Belial, that a "
44 to Phalti the s' of Laish, which was "
26: 5 Abner the s' of Ner, the captain of "
6 and to Abishai the s' of Zeruiah, "
14 and to Abner the s' of Ner, saying, "
17 said, Is this thy voice, my s' David? "
21 I have sinned: return, my s' David: "
25 Blessed be thou, my s' David: "
27: 2 unto Achish, the s' of Maoch, king "
30: 7 Abiathar the priest, Ahimelech's s', "
2Sa 1: 4 Saul and Jonathan his s' are dead "
5 Saul and Jonathan his s' be dead? "
12 for Saul, and for Jonathan his s', "
13 I am the s' of a stranger, an "
17 over Saul and over Jonathan his s': "
2: 8 But Abner the s' of Ner, captain of "
8 took Ish-bosheth the s' of Saul, "
10 Ish-bosheth Saul's s' was forty "
12 Abner...s' of Ner, and the servants "
12 of Ish-bosheth the s' of Saul, went "
13 And Joab the s' of Zeruiah, and the "
15 to Ish-bosheth the s' of Saul, and "
3: 3 Absalom the s' of Maacah the "
4 fourth, Adonijah the s' of Haggith; "
4 fifth, Shephatiah the s' of Abital; "
14 to Ish-bosheth Saul's s', saying, "
15 even from Phaltiel the s' of Laish. "
23 Abner the s' of Ner came to the "
25 Thou knowest Abner the s' of Ner, "
28 the blood of Abner the s' of Ner: "
37 king to slay Abner the s' of Ner. "
4: 1 Saul's s' heard that Abner was "
2 Saul's s' had two men that were "
4 Saul's s', had a s' that was lame "
8 head of Ish-bosheth the s' of Saul "
7: 14 his father, and he shall be my s'. "
8: 3 also Hadadezer, the s' of Rehob, "
10 Toi sent Joram his s' unto king "
12 spoil of Hadadezer, s' of Rehob, "
16 Joab the s' of Zeruiah was over the "
16 Jehoshaphat the s' of Ahilud was "
17 And Zadok the s' of Ahitub, and "
17 and Ahimelech, the s' of Abiathar, "
18 Benaiah the s' of Jehoiada was "
9: 3 Jonathan hath yet a s', which is "
4, 5 in Machir, the s' of Ammiel, "
6 Mephibosheth, the s' of Jonathan, "
6 the s' of Saul, was come unto David, "
9 I have given unto thy master's s' "
10 master's s' may have food to eat: "

2Sa 9: 10 thy master's s' shall eat bread 1121
12 And Mephibosheth had a young s'. "
10: 1 Hanun his s' reigned in his stead. "
2 unto Hanun the s' of Nahash, as "
11: 21 Abimelech the s' of Jerubbesheth? "
27 became his wife, and bare him a s'. "
12: 24 and she bare a s', and he called his "
13: 1 Absalom the s' of David had a fair "
1 Amnon the s' of David loved her. "
3 Jonadab, the s' of Shimeah David's "
4 art thou, being the king's s', lean "
25 Nay, my s', let us not all now go, "
32 Jonadab, the s' of Shimeah David's "
37 went to Talmai, the s' of Ammihud, "
37 David mourned for his s' every day. "
14: 1 Joab the s' of Zeruiah perceived "
11 any more, lest they destroy my s'. "
11 there shall not one hair of thy s' fall "
16 destroy me and my s' together "
15: 27 two sons with you, Ahimaaz thy s', "
27 and Jonathan the s' of Abiathar. "
36 their two sons, Ahimaaz Zadok's s', "
36 and Jonathan Abiathar's s'; "
16: 3 said, And where is thy master's s'? 1121
5 name was Shimei, the s' of Gera: "
8 into the hand of Absalom thy s': "
9 Then said Abishai the s' of Zeruiah "
11 Behold, my s', which came forth of "
19 I not serve in the presence of his s'? "
17: 25 Amasa was a man's s', whose name "
27 Shobi the s' of Nahash of Rabbah, "
27 and Machir the s' of Ammiel of "
18: 2 hand of Abishai the s' of Zeruiah, "
12 mine hand against the king's s': "
18 said, I have no s' to keep my name "
19 Then said Ahimaaz the s' of Zadok, "
20 because the king's s' is dead. "
22 Then said Ahimaaz the s' of Zadok "
22 Wherefore wilt thou run, my s', "
27 running of Ahimaaz the s' of Zadok. "
33 said, O my s' Absalom, my s', my s' "
33 for thee, O Absalom, my s', my s'! "
19: 2 how the king was grieved for his s'. "
4 with a loud voice, O my s' Absalom, "
4 Absalom, O Absalom, my s', my s'! "
16 Shimei the s' of Gera, a Benjamite, "
18 Shimei the s' of Gera fell down "
21 Abishai the s' of Zeruiah answered "
24 Mephibosheth the s' of Saul came "
20: 1 name was Sheba, the s' of Bichri, "
1 we inheritance in the s' of Jesse: "
2 and followed Sheba the s' of Bichri: "
6 Sheba the s' of Bichri do us more "
7 pursue after Sheba the s' of Bichri. "
10 pursued after Sheba the s' of Bichri. "
13 pursue after Sheba the s' of Bichri. "
21 Sheba the s' of Bichri by name, "
22 the head of Sheba the s' of Bichri. "
23 Benaiah the s' of Jehoiada was over "
24 Jehoshaphat the s' of Ahilud was "
21: 7 Mephibosheth, the s' of Jonathan "
7 of Jonathan the s' of Saul, "
7 David and Jonathan the s' of Saul. "
8 up for Adriel the s' of Barzillai the "
12 and the bones of Jonathan his s' "
13 and the bones of Jonathan his s'; "
14 bones of Saul and Jonathan his s' "
17 Abishai the s' of Zeruiah succoured "
19 Elhanan the s' of Jaare-oregim, "
21 Jonathan the s' of Shimeah the "
23: 1 David the s' of Jesse said, and the "
9 Eleazar the s' of Dodo the Ahohite, "
11 was Shammah the s' of Agee the "
18 And Abishai,...the s' of Zeruiah, "
20 And Benaiah the s' of Jehoiada, the "
20 the s' of a valiant man, of Kabzeel, "
22 did Benaiah the s' of Jehoiada, "
24 Elhanan the s' of Dodo of "
26 Ira the s' of Ikkesh the Tekoite, "
29 Heleb the s' of Baanah, a "
29 Ittai the s' of Ribai out of Gibeah "
33 Ahiam the s' of Sharar the Hararite, "
34 Eliphelet the s' of Ahasbai, "
34 the s' of the Maachathite, "
34 Eliam the s' of Ahithophel the "
36 Igal the s' of Nathan of Zobah, "
37 to Joab the s' of Zeruiah, and "
1Ki 1: 5 Adonijah the s' of Haggith exalted "
7 with Joab the s' of Zeruiah, and "
8 and Benaiah the s' of Jehoiada, "
11 Adonijah the s' of Haggith doth "
12 life, and the life of thy s' Solomon. "
13, 17 Solomon thy s' shall reign after "
21 I and my s' Solomon...be counted "
26 and Benaiah the s' of Jehoiada, "
30 Solomon thy s' shall reign after me, "
32 and Benaiah the s' of Jehoiada. "
33 cause Solomon my s' to ride upon "
36 Benaiah the s' of Jehoiada answered "
38 and Benaiah the s' of Jehoiada, "
42 Jonathan...s' of Abiathar the priest "
44 and Benaiah the s' of Jehoiada, "
2: 1 he charged Solomon his s', saying, "
5 what Joab the s' of Zeruiah did to "
5 Israel, unto Abner the s' of Ner, "
5 and unto Amasa the s' of Jether, "
8 with thee Shimei the s' of Gera, "
13 Adonijah the s' of Haggith came to "
22 and for Joab the s' of Zeruiah. "
25 hand of Benaiah the s' of Jehoiada; "
29 sent Benaiah the s' of Jehoiada, "
32 Abner the s' of Ner, captain of the "
32 Amasa the s' of Jether, captain of "
34 Benaiah the s' of Jehoiada went up, "
35 king put Benaiah the s' of Jehoiada "
39 Achish s' of Maachah king of Gath. "

1Ki 2: 46 Benaiah the s' of Jehoiada; 1121
3: 6 given him a s' to sit on his throne, "
20 and took my s' from beside me, "
21 it was not my s', which I did bear. "
22 living is my s',...the dead is thy s'. "
22 dead is thy s',...the living is my s'. "
23 my s'...liveth, and thy s' is the dead: "
23 thy s' is dead, and my s' is...living. "
26 for her bowels yearned upon her s', "
4: 2 Azariah the s' of Zadok the priest, "
3 Jehoshaphat the s' of Ahilud, the "
4 Benaiah the s' of Jehoiada was over "
5 Azariah the s' of Nathan was over "
5 Zabud...s' of Nathan was principal "
6 Adoniram the s' of Abda was over "
8 The s' of Hur, in mount Ephraim: *1133
9 The s' of Dekar, in Makaz, and in *1128
10 The s' of Hesed, in Aruboth; to *1136
11 The s' of Abinadab, in all the *1125
12 Baana the s' of Ahilud; to him *1121
13 The s' of Geber, in Ramoth-gilead; *1127
13 towns of Jair the s' of Manasseh, 1121
14 Ahinadab the s' of Iddo had "
16 Baanah the s' of Hushai was in "
17 Jehoshaphat the s' of Paruah, in "
18 Shimei the s' of Elah, in Benjamin: "
19 Geber the s' of Uri was in the "
5: 5 Thy s', whom I will set upon thy "
7 hath given unto David a wise s' "
7: 14 He was a widow's s' of the tribe of "
8: 19 thy s' that shall come forth out of "
11: 12 rend it out of the hand of thy s'. "
13 but will give one tribe to thy s' for "
20 bare him Genubath his s', whom "
23 adversary, Rezon the s' of Eliadah, "
26 And Jeroboam the s' of Nebat, an "
36 And unto his s' will I give one tribe, "
43 and Rehoboam his s' reigned in his "
12: 2 when Jeroboam the s' of Nebat, "
15 unto Jeroboam the s' of Nebat. "
16 we inheritance in the s' of Jesse: "
21 to Rehoboam the s' of Solomon. "
23 unto Rehoboam, the s' of Solomon, "
14: 1 Abijah the s' of Jeroboam fell sick. "
5 to ask a thing of thee for her s'; "
20 Nadab his s' reigned in his stead. "
21 Rehoboam...s' of Solomon reigned "
31 Abijam his s' reigned in his stead. "
15: 1 of king Jeroboam the s' of Nebat "
4 to set up his s' after him, and to "
8 and Asa his s' reigned in his stead. "
18 Ben-hadad, the s' of Tabrimon, "
18 the s' of Hezion, king of Syria, "
24 Jehoshaphat his s' reigned in his "
25 Nadab the s' of Jeroboam began to "
27 And Baasha the s' of Ahijah, of the "
33 began Baasha the s' of Ahijah to "
16: 1 came to Jehu the s' of Hanani "
3 house of Jeroboam the s' of Nebat. "
6 Elah his s' reigned in his stead. "
7 the prophet Jehu the s' of Hanani "
8 began Elah the s' of Baasha to reign "
13 Baasha, and the sins of Elah his s', "
21 followed Tibni the s' of Ginath, "
22 that followed Tibni the s' of Ginath: "
26 way of Jeroboam the s' of Nebat, "
28 Ahab his s' reigned in his stead. "
29 began Ahab the s' of Omri to reign "
29 Ahab the s' of Omri reigned over "
30 Ahab the s' of Omri did evil in the "
31 sins of Jeroboam the s' of Nebat, "
34 thereof in his youngest s' Segub, "
34 he spake by Joshua the s' of Nun. 1121
17: 12 go in and dress it for me and my s', "
13 after make for thee and for thy s'. "
17 the s' of the woman, the mistress of "
18 to remembrance, and to slay my s'? "
19 he said unto her, Give me thy s'. "
20 whom I sojourn, by slaying her s'? "
23 and Elijah said, See, thy s' liveth. "
19: 16 Jehu the s' of Nimshi shalt thou "
16 and Elisha the s' of Shaphat of "
19 found Elisha the s' of Shaphat, who "
21: 22 house of Jeroboam the s' of Nebat, "
22 house of Baasha the s' of Ahijah, "
22: 8 one man, Micaiah the s' of Imlah, "
9 hither Micaiah the s' of Imlah. "
11 And Zedekiah the s' of Chenaanah "
24 Zedekiah the s' of Chenaanah went "
26 the city, and to Joash the king's s'; "
40 Ahaziah his s' reigned in his stead. "
41 Jehoshaphat the s' of Asa began to "
49 said Ahaziah the s' of Ahab unto "
50 Jehoram his s' reigned in his stead. "
51 Ahaziah...s' of Ahab began to reign "
52 way of Jeroboam the s' of Nebat, "
2Ki 1: 17 of Jehoram the s' of Jehoshaphat "
17 of Judah; because he had no s'. "
3: 1 Now Jehoram the s' of Ahab began "
3 sins of Jeroboam the s' of Nebat, "
11 Here is Elisha the s' of Shaphat, "
27 took his eldest s' that should have "
4: 6 that she said unto her s', Bring me "
16 time of life, thou shalt embrace a s'. "
17 and bare a s' at that season that "
28 said, Did I desire a s' of my lord? "
36 unto him, he said, Take up thy s'. "
37 and took up her s', and went out. "
6: 28 Give thy s', that we may eat him "
28 and we will eat my s' to morrow. "
29 So we boiled my s', and did eat him: "
29 Give thy s', that we may eat him: "
29 eat him: and she hath hid her s'. "
31 head of Elisha the s' of Shaphat "
32 See ye how this s' of a murderer "
8: 1, 5 whose s' he had restored to life, "

2Ki 8: 5 and this is her s', whom Elisha 1121
9 Thy s' Ben-hadad king of Syria "
16 Joram the s' of Ahab king of Israel. "
16 Jehoram the s' of Jehoshaphat king "
24 Ahaziah his s' reigned in his stead. "
25 Joram the s' of Ahab king of Israel "
25 Ahaziah the s' of Jehoram king of "
27 the s' in law of the house of Ahab. 2860
28 he went with Joram the s' of Ahab 1121
29 Ahaziah the s' of Jehoram king of "
29 down to see Joram the s' of Ahab "
9: 2 look out there Jehu the s' of "
2 Jehoshaphat the s' of Nimshi, "
9 house of Jeroboam the s' of Nebat, "
9 house of Baasha the s' of Ahijah: "
14 So Jehu the s' of Jehoshaphat the "
14 the s' of Nimshi conspired "
20 driving of Jehu the s' of Nimshi; "
29 of Joram the s' of Ahab began "
10: 15 on Jehonadab the s' of Rechab "
23 and Jehonadab the s' of Rechab, "
29 sins of Jeroboam the s' of Nebat, "
35 And Jehoahaz his s' reigned in his "
11: 1 Athaliah...saw that her s' was dead, "
2 took Joash the s' of Ahaziah, and "
4 and shewed them the king's s'. "
12 And he brought forth the king's s', "
12: 21 For Jozachar the s' of Shimeath, "
21 and Jehozabad the s' of Shomer, "
21 Amaziah his s' reigned in his stead. "
13: 1 of Joash the s' of Ahaziah king of "
1 Jehoahaz the s' of Jehu began to "
2 sins of Jeroboam the s' of Nebat, "
3 hand of Ben-hadad the s' of Hazael, "
9 Joash his s' reigned in his stead. "
10 Jehoash the s' of Jehoahaz to reign "
11 sins of Jeroboam the s' of Nebat, "
24 and Ben-hadad his s' reigned in his "
25 Jehoash the s' of Jehoahaz took "
25 hand of Ben-hadad the s' of Hazael "
14: 1 year of Joash s' of Jehoahaz king "
1 Amaziah the s' of Joash king of "
8 to Jehoash, the s' of Jehoahaz "
8 s' of Jehu, king of Israel, saying, "
9 Give thy daughter to my s' to wife: "
13 the s' of Jehoash the s' of Ahaziah, "
16 Jeroboam his s' reigned in his stead. "
17 Amaziah the s' of Joash king of "
17 the death of Jehoash s' of Jehoahaz "
23 Amaziah the s' of Joash king of "
23 Jeroboam the s' of Joash king of "
24 sins of Jeroboam the s' of Nebat, "
25 servant Jonah, the s' of Amittai, "
27 hand of Jeroboam the s' of Joash. "
29 Zachariah his s' reigned in his "
15: 1 began Azariah s' of Amaziah king "
5 Jotham the king's s' was over the "
7 Jotham his s' reigned in his stead. "
8 did Zachariah the s' of Jeroboam "
9 sins of Jeroboam the s' of Nebat. "
10 Shallum the s' of Jabesh conspired "
13 Shallum the s' of Jabesh began to "
14 Menahem the s' of Gadi went up "
14 smote Shallum the s' of Jabesh "
17 Menahem the s' of Gadi to reign "
18 sins of Jeroboam the s' of Nebat. "
22 Pekahiah his s' reigned in his "
23 Pekahiah the s' of Menahem began "
24 sins of Jeroboam the s' of Nebat. "
25 But Pekah the s' of Remaliah, a "
27 Pekah the s' of Remaliah began to "
28 sins of Jeroboam the s' of Nebat. "
30 Hoshea the s' of Elah made a "
30 against Pekah the s' of Remaliah, "
30 year of Jotham the s' of Uzziah. "
32 Pekah the s' of Remaliah king of "
32 Jotham the s' of Uzziah king of "
37 and Pekah the s' of Remaliah. "
38 and Ahaz his s' reigned in his stead. "
16: 1 year of Pekah the s' of Remaliah "
1 Ahaz the s' of Jotham king of Judah "
3 made his s' to pass through the fire, "
5 Pekah s' of Remaliah king of Israel "
7 I am thy servant and thy s': come "
20 Hezekiah his s' reigned in his stead. "
17: 1 began Hoshea the s' of Elah to reign "
21 Jeroboam the s' of Nebat king: "
18: 1 of Hoshea s' of Elah king of Israel, "
1 that Hezekiah the s' of Ahaz king "
9 of Hoshea s' of Elah king of Israel, "
18 to them Eliakim the s' of Hilkiah, "
18 Joah the s' of Asaph the recorder. "
26 Then said Eliakim the s' of Hilkiah, "
37 came Eliakim the s' of Hilkiah, "
37 Joah the s' of Asaph the recorder, "
19: 2 to Isaiah the prophet the s' of Amoz. "
20 Isaiah the s' of Amoz sent to "
37 Esarhaddon his s' reigned in his "
20: 1 prophet Isaiah the s' of Amoz came "
12 Berodach-baladan,...s' of Baladan, "
21 Manasseh his s' reigned in his stead. "
21: 6 made his s' pass through the fire, "
7 said to David, and to Solomon his s', "
18 Amon his s' reigned in his stead. "
24 made Josiah his s' king in his stead. "
26 Josiah his s' reigned in his stead. "
22: 3 sent Shaphan the s' of Azaliah, "
3 the s' of Meshullam, the scribe, to "
12 and Ahikam the s' of Shaphan, "
12 and Achbor the s' of Michaiah, and "
14 the wife of Shallum the s' of Tikvah, "
14 the s' of Harhas, keeper of the "
23: 10 make his s' or his daughter to pass "
15 which Jeroboam the s' of Nebat, "
30 took Jehoahaz the s' of Josiah, "
34 made Eliakim the s' of Josiah king "

2Ki 24: 6 Jehoiachin his s' reigned in his 1121
25: 22 made Gedaliah the s' of Ahikam, "
22 the s' of Shaphan, ruler. "
23 even Ishmael the s' of Nethaniah, "
23 and Johanan the s' of Careah, and "
23 Seraiah the s' of Tanhumeth the "
23 Jaazaniah the s' of a Maachathite, "
25 that Ishmael the s' of Nethaniah, "
25 the s' of Elishama, of the seed royal, "
1Ch 1: 43 of Israel; Bela the s' of Beor: "
44 Jobab the s' of Zerah of Bozrah "
46 Hadad the s' of Bedad, which "
49 Baal-hanan the s' of Achbor reigned "
2: 18 And Caleb the s' of Hezron begat "
45 And the s' of Shammai was Maon: "
50 the sons of Caleb the s' of Hur, "
3: 2 Absalom the s' of Maachah the "
2 fourth, Adonijah the s' of Haggith: "
10 And Solomon's s' was Rehoboam, "
10 Abia his s', Asa his s', "
10 Jehoshaphat his s', "
11 Joram his s', Ahaziah his s', "
11 Joash his s', "
12 Amaziah his s', "
12 Azariah his s', Jotham his s', "
13 Ahaz his s', Hezekiah his s', "
13 Manasseh his s', "
14 Amon his s', Josiah his s'. "
16 Jeconiah his s', Zedekiah his s'. "
17 of Jeconiah; Assir, Salathiel his s', "
4: 2 And Reaiah the s' of Shobal begat "
8 of Aharhel the s' of Harum. "
15 sons of Caleb the s' of Jephunneh; "
21 The sons of Shelah the s' of Judah "
25 Shallum his s', "
25 Mibsam his s', Mishma his s'. "
26 Hamuel his s', Zacchur his s', "
26 Shimei his s'. "
34 and Joshah the s' of Amaziah, "
35 Joel, and Jehu the s' of Josibiah, "
35 the s' of Seraiah, the s' of Asiel, "
37 Ziza the s' of Shiphi, the s' of Allon, "
37 the s' of Jedaiah, the s' of Shimri, "
37 the s' of Shemaiah; "
5: 1 the sons of Joseph the s' of Israel: "
4 sons of Joel; Shemaiah his s', "
4 Gog his s', Shimei his s', "
5 Micah his s', "
5 Reaia his s', Baal his s', "
6 Beerah his s', whom "
8 And Bela the s' of Azaz, "
8 the s' of Shema, the s' of Joel, who "
14 children of Abihail the s' of Huri, "
14 the s' of Jaroah, the s' of Gilead, "
14 s' of Michael, the s' of Jeshishai, "
14 the s' of Jahdo, the s' of Buz; "
15 Ahi the s' of Abdiel, the s' of Guni, "
6: 20 Of Gershom; Libni his s', "
20 Jahath his s', Zimmah his s', "
21 Joah his s', Iddo his s', "
21 Zerah his s', Jeaterai his s'. "
22 sons of Kohath; Amminadab his s', "
22 Korah his s', Assir his s', "
23 Elkanah his s', and Ebiasaph "
23 Ebiasaph his s', and Assir his s', "
24 Tahath his s', Uriel his s', "
24 Uzziah his s', and Shaul his s'. "
26 Zophai his s', and Nahath his s', "
27 Eliab his s', Jeroham his s', "
27 Elkanah his s'. "
29 sons of Merari; Mahli, Libni his s', "
29 Shimei his s', Uzza his s', "
30 Shimea his s', Haggiah his s', "
30 Asaiah his s'. "
33 Heman a singer, the s' of Joel, "
33 the s' of Shemuel, "
34 s' of Elkanah, the s' of Jeroham, "
34 the s' of Eliel, the s' of Toah, "
35 The s' of Zuph, the s' of Elkanah, "
35 the s' of Mahath, the s' of Amasai, "
36 The s' of Elkanah, the s' of Joel, "
36 s' of Azariah, the s' of Zephaniah, "
37 The s' of Tahath, the s' of Assir, "
37 the s' of Ebiasaph, the s' of Korah, "
38 The s' of Izhar, the s' of Kohath, "
38 the s' of Levi, the s' of Israel. "
39 even Asaph the s' of Berachiah, "
39 the s' of Shimea, "
40 s' of Michael, the s' of Baaseiah, "
40 of Baaseiah, the s' of Malchiah, "
41 The s' of Ethni, the s' of Zerah, "
41 of Zerah, the s' of Adaiah, "
42 The s' of Ethan, the s' of Zimmah, "
42 of Zimmah, the s' of Shimei, "
43 The s' of Jahath, the s' of Gershom, "
43 of Gershom, the s' of Levi. "
44 left hand: Ethan the s' of Kishi, "
44 the s' of Abdi, the s' of Malluch, "
45 s' of Hashabiah, the s' of Amaziah, "
45 of Amaziah, the s' of Hilkiah, "
46 The s' of Amzi, the s' of Bani, the "
46 of Bani, the s' of Shamer, "
47 The s' of Mahli, the s' of Mushi, "
47 the s' of Merari, the s' of Levi. "
50 the sons of Aaron; Eleazar his s', "
50 Phinehas his s', Abishua his s', "
51 Bukki his s', Uzzi his s', "
51 Zerahiah his s', "
52 Meraioth his s', "
52 Amariah his s', Ahitub his s', "
53 Zadok his s', Ahimaaz his s'. "
56 gave to Caleb the s' of Jephunneh. "
7: 16 the wife of Machir bare a s', and "
17 sons of Gilead, the s' of Machir, "
17 the s' of Manasseh. "
20 Shuthelah, and Bered his s', and "

1Ch 7: 20 and Tahath his s', 1121
20 Eladah his s', and Tahath his s', "
21 Zabad his s', and Shuthelah his s', "
23 she conceived, and bare a s', and he "
25 Rephah was his s', also Resheph, "
25 and Telah his s', and Tahan his s', "
26 Laadan his s', Ammihud his s', "
26 Elishama his s', "
27 Non his s', Jehoshuah his s'. "
29 children of Joseph the s' of Israel. "
8: 30 his firstborn s' Abdon, and Zur, and "
34 the s' of Jonathan was Merib-baal; "
37 begat Binea: Rapha was his s', "
37 Eleasah his s', Azel his s': "
9: 4 Uthai the s' of Ammihud, "
4 the s' of Omri, the s' of Imri, "
4 s' of Bani, of the children of Pharez "
4 children of Pharez the s' of Judah. "
7 Sallu the s' of Meshullam, "
7 s' of Hodaviah, the s' of Hasenuah, "
8 And Ibneiah the s' of Jeroham, "
8 Elah the s' of Uzzi, the s' of Michri, "
8 Meshullam the s' of Shephathiah, "
8 the s' of Reuel, the s' of Ibnijah; "
11 And Azariah the s' of Hilkiah, "
11 the s' of Meshullam, "
11 the s' of Zadok, the s' of Meraioth, "
11 s' of Ahitub, the ruler of the house "
12 And Adaiah the s' of Jeroham, "
12 s' of Pashur, the s' of Malchijah, "
12 and Maasiai the s' of Adiel, "
12 s' of Jahzerah, the s' of Meshullam, "
12 s' of Meshillemith, the s' of Immer; "
14 Shemaiah the s' of Hasshub, the "
14 the s' of Azrikam, "
14 the s' of Hashabiah, of the sons of "
15 and Mattaniah the s' of Micah, "
15 the s' of Zichri, the s' of Asaph; "
16 And Obadiah the s' of Shemaiah, "
16 the s' of Galal, the s' of Jeduthun, "
16 and Berechiah the s' of Asa, "
16 the s' of Elkanah, that dwelt in "
19 And Shallum the s' of Kore, "
19 the s' of Ebiasaph, the s' of Korah, "
20 Phinehas the s' of Eleazar was the "
21 Zechariah the s' of Meshelemiah "
36 And his firstborn s' Abdon, then "
40 the s' of Jonathan was Merib-baal: "
43 begat Binea; and Rephaiah his s', "
43 Eleasah his s', Azel his s'. "
10: 14 kingdom unto David the s' of Jesse. "
11: 6 So Joab the s' of Zeruiah went first "
12 him was Eleazar the s' of Dodo, "
22 Benaiah the s' of Jehoiada, the "
22 the s' of a valiant man of Kabzeel, "
24 did Benaiah the s' of Jehoiada, "
26 of Joab, Elhanan the s' of Dodo of "
28 Ira the s' of Ikkesh the Tekoite, "
30 Heled the s' of Baanah the "
31 Ithai the s' of Ribai of Gibeah, that "
34 Jonathan the s' of Shage the "
35 Ahiam the s' of Sacar the Hararite, "
35 the Hararite, Eliphal the s' of Ur, "
37 Carmelite, Naarai the s' of Ezbai, "
38 Nathan, Mibhar the s' of Haggeri, "
39 of Joab the s' of Zeruiah, "
41 the Hittite, Zabad the s' of Ahlai, "
42 Adina the s' of Shiza the "
43 Hanan the s' of Maachah, and "
45 Jediael the s' of Shimri, and Joha "
12: 1 close because of Saul the s' of Kish: "
18 and on thy side, thou s' of Jesse: "
15: 17 appointed Heman the s' of Joel; "
17 brethren, Asaph the s' of Berechiah; "
17 Ethan the s' of Kushaiah; "
16: 38 Obed-edom also the s' of Jeduthun "
17: 13 his father, and he shall be my s': "
18: 10 sent Hadoram his s' to king David, "
12 Abishai the s' of Zeruiah slew of "
15 Joab the s' of Zeruiah was over the "
15 and Jehoshaphat the s' of Ahilud, "
16 And Zadok the s' of Ahitub, and "
16 Abimelech the s' of Abiathar, were "
17 Benaiah the s' of Jehoiada was "
19: 1 and his s' reigned in his stead. "
2 unto Hanun the s' of Nahash, "
20: 5 Elhanan the s' of Jair slew Lahmi "
6 he also was the s' of the giant. *3205
7 Jonathan the s' of Shimea David's 1121
22: 5 said, Solomon my s' is younger and "
6 Then he called for Solomon his s', "
7 David said to Solomon, My s', as "
9 a s' shall be born to thee, who shall "
10 he shall be my s', and I will be his "
11 Now, my s', the Lord be with thee; "
17 of Israel to help Solomon his s', "
23: 1 he made Solomon his s' king over "
24: 6 Shemaiah the s' of Nethaneel the "
6 and Ahimelech the s' of Abiathar, "
29 Kish: the s' of Kish was Jerahmeel. "
26: 1 was Meshelemiah the s' of Kore, of "
6 Shemaiah his s' were sons born, "
14 Then for Zechariah his s', a wise "
24 And Shebuel the s' of Gershom, "
24 the s' of Moses, was ruler over "
25 by Eliezer; Rehabiah his s', and "
25 Jeshaiah his s', and Joram his s', "
25 Zichri his s', and Shelomith his s'. "
28 the seer, and Saul the s' of Kish, "
28 and Abner the s' of Ner, "
28 and Joab the s' of Zeruiah, had "
27: 2 was Jashobeam the s' of Zabdiel: "
5 was Benaiah the s' of Jehoiada, "
6 his course was Ammizabad his s'. "
7 and Zebadiah his s' after him: "
9 Ira the s' of Ikkesh the Tekoite: "

1Ch 27: 16 was Eliezer the s' of Zichri: 1121
16 Shephatiah the s' of Maachah: "
17 Hashabiah the s' of Kemuel: "
18 Issachar, Omri the s' of Michael: "
19 Zebulun, Ishmaiah the s' of Obadiah: "
19 Naphtali, Jerimoth the s' of Azriel: "
20 Hoshea the s' of Azaziah: "
20 Manasseh, Joel the s' of Pedaiah: "
21 in Gilead, Iddo the s' of Zechariah: "
21 Benjamin, Jaasiel the s' of Abner: "
22 Of Dan, Azareel the s' of Jeroham. "
24 Joab the s' of Zeruiah began to "
25 was Azmaveth the s' of Adiel: "
25 was Jehonathan the s' of Uzziah: "
26 ground was Ezri the s' of Chelub: "
29 was Shaphat the s' of Adlai: "
32 Jehiel the s' of Hachmoni was with "
34 was Jehoiada the s' of Benaiah, "
28: 5 chosen Solomon my s' to sit upon "
6 Solomon thy s', he shall build "
6 for I have chosen him to be my s', "
9 Solomon my s', know thou the God "
11 gave to Solomon his s' the pattern "
20 And David said to Solomon his s', "
29: 1 Solomon my s', whom alone God "
19 unto Solomon my s' a perfect heart, "
22 made Solomon the s' of David king "
26 David the s' of Jesse reigned over "
28 Solomon his s' reigned in his stead. "
2Ch 1: 1 And Solomon the s' of David was "
5 Bezaleel the s' of Uri, the s' of Hur, "
2: 12 given to David the king a wise s', "
14 The s' of a woman of the daughters "
6: 9 thy s' which shall come forth out of "
9: 29 against Jeroboam the s' of Nebat? "
31 and Rehoboam his s' reigned in his "
10: 2 when Jeroboam the s' of Nebat, "
15 to Jeroboam the s' of Nebat. "
16 none inheritance in the s' of Jesse: "
11: 3 unto Rehoboam the s' of Solomon, "
17 Rehoboam the s' of Solomon strong, "
18 of Jerimoth the s' of David to wife, "
18 daughter of Eliab the s' of Jesse; "
22 Abijah the s' of Maachah the chief, "
12: 16 Abijah his s' reigned in his stead. "
13: 6 Yet Jeroboam the s' of Nebat, the "
6 servant of Solomon the s' of David, "
7 against Rehoboam...s' of Solomon, "
14: 1 and Asa his s' reigned in his stead. "
15: 1 came upon Azariah the s' of Oded: "
17: 1 Jehoshaphat his s' reigned in his "
16 him was Amasiah the s' of Zichri, "
18: 7 the same is Micaiah the s' of Imla. "
8 Fetch quickly Micaiah the s' of Imla. "
10 And Zedekiah the s' of Chenaanah "
23 Zedekiah the s' of Chenaanah came "
25 the city, and to Joash the king's s'; "
19: 2 Jehu the s' of Hanani the seer went "
11 and Zebadiah the s' of Ishmael, the "
20: 14 upon Jahaziel the s' of Zechariah, "
14 the s' of Benaiah, the s' of Jeiel, the "
14 the s' of Mattaniah, a Levite of the "
34 in the book of Jehu the s' of Hanani, "
37 Then Eliezer the s' of Dodavah of "
21: 1 Jehoram his s' reigned in his stead. "
17 there was never a s' left him, save "
22: 1 made Ahaziah his youngest s' king "
1 So Ahaziah the s' of Jehoram king "
5 went with Jehoram the s' of Ahab "
6 And Azariah the s' of Jehoram king "
6 down to see Jehoram the s' of Ahab "
7 against Jehu the s' of Nimshi, "
9 they, he is the s' of Jehoshaphat, "
10 Athaliah...saw that her s' was dead, "
11 took Joash the s' of Ahaziah, and "
23: 1 Azariah the s' of Jeroham, and "
1 and Ishmael the s' of Jehohanan, "
1 and Azariah the s' of Obed, and "
1 and Maaseiah the s' of Adaiah, and "
1 and Elishaphat the s' of Zichri, "
3 Behold, the king's s' shall reign, "
11 they brought out the king's s', and "
24: 20 Zechariah...s' of Jehoiada the priest, "
22 had done to him, but slew his s'. "
26 Zabad the s' of Shimeath an "
26 Jehozabad the s' of Shimrith a "
27 Amaziah his s' reigned in his stead. "
25: 17 sent to Joash, the s' of Jehoahaz, "
17 the s' of Jehu, king of Israel, "
18 Give thy daughter to my s' to wife: "
23 took Amaziah...the s' of Joash, "
23 of Joash, the s' of Jehoahaz, "
25 And Amaziah the s' of Joash king of "
25 death of Joash s' of Jehoahaz king "
26: 21 Jotham his s' was over the king's "
22 Isaiah the prophet, the s' of Amoz, "
23 Jotham his s' reigned in his stead. "
27: 9 Ahaz his s' reigned in his stead. "
28: 3 in the valley of the s' of Hinnom, "
6 Pekah the s' of Remaliah slew in "
7 slew Maaseiah the king's s', and "
12 Azariah the s' of Johanan, "
12 Berechiah the s' of Meshillemoth, "
12 and Jehizkiah the s' of Shallum, "
12 and Amasa the s' of Hadlai, stood "
27 and Hezekiah his s' reigned in his "
29: 12 arose, Mahath the s' of Amasai, "
12 and Joel the s' of Azariah, of the "
12 sons of Merari, Kish the s' of Abdi, "
12 and Azariah the s' of Jehalelel: "
12 Joah the s' of Zimmah, "
12 and Eden the s' of Joah: "
30: 26 time of Solomon the s' of David "
31: 14 Kore the s' of Imnah the Levite, the "
32: 20 the prophet Isaiah the s' of Amoz, "
32 Isaiah the prophet, the s' of Amoz, "

2Ch 32: 33 And Manasseh his s' reigned in his 1121
33: 6 in the valley of the s' of Hinnom: "
7 said to David and to Solomon his s', "
20 Amon his s' reigned in his stead. "
25 made Josiah his s' king in his stead. "
34: 8 he sent Shaphan the s' of Azaliah, "
8 Joah the s' of Joahaz the recorder, "
20 and Ahikam the s' of Shaphan, "
20 and Abdon the s' of Micah, and "
22 wife of Shallum the s' of Tikvath, "
22 Tikvath, the s' of Hasrah, keeper of "
35: 3 which Solomon the s' of David king "
4 to the writing of Solomon his s'. "
36: 1 land took Jehoahaz the s' of Josiah, "
8 and Jehoiachin his s' reigned in his "
Ezr 3: 2 stood up Jeshua the s' of Jozadak, "
2, 8 Zerubbabel the s' of Shealtiel, "
8 and Jeshua the s' of Jozadak, and "
5: 1 and Zechariah the s' of Iddo, 1247
2 up Zerubbabel the s' of Shealtiel, "
2 and Jeshua the s' of Jozadak, and "
6: 14 and Zechariah the s' of Iddo. "
7: 1 of Persia, Ezra the s' of Seraiah, 1121
1 the s' of Azariah, the s' of Hilkiah, "
2 The s' of Shallum, the s' of Zadok, "
2 of Zadok, the s' of Ahitub, "
3 s' of Amariah, the s' of Azariah, "
3 of Azariah, the s' of Meraioth, "
4 The s' of Zerahiah, the s' of Uzzi, "
4 of Uzzi, the s' of Bukki, "
5 s' of Abishua, the s' of Phinehas, "
5 the s' of Eleazar, the s' of Aaron the "
8: 4 Elihoenai the s' of Zerahiah, and "
5 the s' of Jahaziel, and with him "
6 Ebed the s' of Jonathan, and with "
7 Jeshaiah the s' of Athaliah, and "
8 Zebadiah the s' of Michael, and "
9 Obadiah the s' of Jehiel, and with "
10 the s' of Josiphiah, and with him "
11 Zechariah the s' of Bebai, and with "
12 Johanan the s' of Hakkatan, and "
18 Mahli,...s' of Levi, the s' of Israel; "
33 hand of Meremoth the s' of Uriah "
33 was Eleazar the s' of Phinehas; "
33 was Jozabad the s' of Jeshua, and "
33 Noadiah the s' of Binnui, Levites; "
10: 2 And Shechaniah the s' of Jehiel, "
6 of Johanan the s' of Eliashib: "
15 Only Jonathan the s' of Asahel and "
15 Jahaziah the s' of Tikvah were "
18 sons of Jeshua the s' of Jozadak, "
Ne 1: 1 of Nehemiah the s' of Hachaliah. "
3: 2 them builded Zaccur the s' of Imri. "
4 Meremoth...s' of Urijah,...s' of Koz. "
4 Meshullam the s' of Berechiah, "
4 Berechiah, the s' of Meshezabeel. "
4 repaired Zadok the s' of Baana. "
6 repaired Jehoiada the s' of Paseah, "
6 and Meshullam the s' of Besodeiah; "
8 repaired Uzziel the s' of Harhaiah, "
8 the s' of one of the apothecaries, *
9 repaired Rephaiah the s' of Hur, "
10 Jedaiah the s' of Harumaph, even "
10 Hattush the s' of Hashabniah. "
11 Malchijah the s' of Harim, and "
11 Hashub the s' of Pahath-moab, "
12 repaired Shallum the s' of Halohesh, "
14 repaired Malchiah the s' of Rechab, "
15 repaired Shallun the s' of Col-hozeh, "
16 repaired Nehemiah the s' of Azbuk, "
17 repaired...Rehum the s' of Bani. "
18 brethren, Bavai the s' of Henadad, "
19 him repaired Ezer the s' of Jeshua, "
20 Baruch the s' of Zabbai earnestly "
21 Meremoth...s' of Urijah...s' of Koz "
23 Azariah the s' of Maaseiah "
23 the s' of Ananiah by his house. "
24 repaired Binnui the s' of Henadad "
25 Palal the s' of Uzai, over against "
25 After him Pedaiah the s' of Parosh. "
29 repaired Zadok the s' of Immer "
29 Shemaiah the s' of Shechaniah, "
30 Hananiah the s' of Shelemiah, "
30 and Hanun the sixth s' of Zalaph, "
30 Meshullam the s' of Berechiah "
31 Malchiah the goldsmith's s' "
6: 10 house of Shemaiah the s' of Delaiah "
10 the s' of Mehetabeel, who was shut "
18 he was the s' in law of Shechaniah 2860
18 of Shechaniah the s' of Arah; 1121
18 and his s' Johanan had taken the "
18 of Meshullam the s' of Berechiah. "
8: 17 days of Jeshua the s' of Nun unto "
10: 1 Nehemiah,...the s' of Hachaliah, "
9 both Jeshua the s' of Azaniah, "
38 priest the s' of Aaron shall be with "
11: 4 Judah; Athaiah the s' of Uzziah, "
4 s' of Zechariah, the s' of Amariah, "
4 the s' of Shephatiah, "
4 the s' of Mahalaleel, "
5 And Maaseiah the s' of Baruch, "
5 the s' of Col-hozeh, "
5 s' of Hazaiah, the s' of Adaiah, "
5 s' of Joiarib, the s' of Zechariah, "
5 of Zechariah, the s' of Shiloni. "
7 Sallu the s' of Meshullam, "
7 the s' of Joed, the s' of Pedaiah, "
7 s' of Kolaiah, the s' of Maaseiah, "
7 the s' of Ithiel, the s' of Jesaiah. "
9 And Joel the s' of Zichri was their "
9 Judah the s' of Senuah was second "
10 Jedaiah the s' of Joiarib, Jachin. "
11 Seraiah the s' of Hilkiah, "
11 the s' of Meshullam, "
11 the s' of Zadok, the s' of Meraioth, "
11 the s' of Ahitub, was the ruler of "

Ne 11: 12 and Adaiah the s' of Jeroham, 1121
12 the s' of Pelaliah, "
12 the s' of Amzi, the s' of Zechariah, "
12 the s' of Pashur, the s' of Malchiah, "
13 and Amashai the the s' of Azareel, "
13 s' of Ahasai, the s' of Meshillemoth, "
13 the s' of Immer, "
14 Zabdiel, the s' of one of the great "
15 Shemaiah the s' of Hashub, "
15 the s' of Azrikam, "
15 s' of Hashabiah, the s' of Bunni; "
17 And Mattaniah the s' of Micha, "
17 the s' of Zabdi, the s' of Asaph, was "
17 and Abda the s' of Shammua, "
17 the s' of Galal, the s' of Jeduthun. "
22 was Uzzi the s' of Bani, the "
22 the s' of Hashabiah, "
22 the s' of Mattaniah, the s' of Micha. "
24 Pethahiah the s' of Meshezabeel, of "
24 children of Zerah the s' of Judah, "
12: 1 Zerubbabel the s' of Shealtiel, and "
23 days of Johanan the s' of Eliashib. "
24 Jeshua the s' of Kadmiel, with their "
26 days of Joiakim the s' of Jeshua, "
26 the s' of Jozadak, and in the days "
35 Zechariah the s' of Jonathan, "
35 the s' of Shemaiah, "
35 s' of Mattaniah, the s' of Michaiah, "
35 the s' of Zaccur, the s' of Asaph: "
45 of David, and of Solomon his s'. "
13: 13 them was Hanan the s' of Zaccur, "
13 the s' of Mattaniah: for they were "
28 Joiada, the s' of Eliashib the high "
28 was s' in law to Sanballat the 2860
Es 2: 5 name was Mordecai, the s' of Jair, 1121
5 the s' of Shimei, the s' of Kish, a "
3: 1, 10 Haman the s' of Hammedatha "
8: 5 by Haman the s' of Hammedatha "
9: 10, 24 Haman the s' of Hammedatha, "
Job 18: 19 shall neither have s' nor nephew 5209
25: 6 the s' of man, which is a worm? 1121
32: 2 wrath of Elihu the s' of Barachel "
6 Elihu the s' of Barachel the Buzite "
35: 8 may profit the s' of man. "
Ps 2: 7 hath said unto me, Thou art my *S'*; "
12 Kiss the *S'*, lest he be angry, and 1248
3: *title* when he fled from Absalom his s'. 1121
8: 4 s' of man, that thou visitest him? "
50: 20 slanderest thine own mother's s'. "
72: 1 righteousness unto the king's s'. "
20 prayers of David the s' of Jesse are "
80: 17 upon the s' of man whom thou "
86: 16 and save the s' of thine handmaid. "
89: 22 nor the s' of wickedness afflict him. "
116: 16 and the s' of thine handmaid: "
144: 3 or the s' of man, that thou makest "
146: 3 nor in the s' of man, in whom there "
Pr 1: 1 of Solomon the s' of David, king "
8 My s', hear the instruction of thy "
10 My s', if sinners entice thee, "
15 My s', walk not thou in the way "
2: 1 My s', if thou wilt receive my "
3: 1 My s', forget not my law; but let "
11 My s', despise not the chastening "
12 even as a father the s' in whom he "
21 My s', let not them depart from "
4: 3 For I was my father's s', tender "
10 Hear, O my s', and receive my "
20 My s', attend to my words; incline "
5: 1 My s', attend unto my wisdom, and "
20 why wilt thou, my s', be ravished "
6: 1 My s', if thou be surety for thy "
3 Do this now, my s', and deliver "
20 My s', keep thy father's "
7: 1 My s', keep my words, and lay up "
10: 1 A wise s' maketh a glad father: "
1 but a foolish s' is the heaviness of "
5 gathereth in summer is a wise s': "
5 harvest is a s' that causeth shame. "
13: 1 A wise s' heareth his father's "
24 that spareth his rod hateth his s': "
15: 20 A wise s' maketh a glad father: but "
17: 2 servant shall have rule over a s' "
25 A foolish s' is a grief to his father, "
19: 13 A foolish s' is the calamity of his "
18 Chasten thy s' while there is hope, "
26 is a s' that causeth shame, and "
27 Cease, my s', to hear the "
23: 15 My s', if thine heart be wise, my "
19 Hear thou, my s', and be wise, and "
26 My s', give me thine heart, and let "
24: 13 My s', eat thou honey, because it is "
21 My s', fear thou the Lord and the "
27: 11 My s', be wise, and make my heart "
28: 7 Whoso keepeth the law is a wise s': "
29: 17 Correct thy s', and he shall give "
21 shall have him become his s' at 4497
30: 1 The words of Agur the s' of Jakeh, 1121
31: 2 my s'?...what, the s' of my womb? 1248
2 and what, the s' of my vows? "
Ec 1: 1 of the Preacher, the s' of David, 1121
5: 14 and he begetteth a s', and there is "
10: 17 when thy king is the s' of nobles, "
12: 12 And further, by these, my s', be "
Isa 1: 1 The vision of Isaiah the s' of Amoz, "
2: 1 word that Isaiah the s' of Amoz "
7: 1 the days of Ahaz the s' of Jotham, "
1 the s' of Uzziah, the king of Judah, "
1 and Pekah the s' of Remaliah, king "
3 thou, and Shear-jashub thy s', at "
4 Syria, and of the s' of Remaliah, "
5 Ephraim, and the s' of Remaliah, "
6 midst of it, even the s' of Tabeal: "
9 head of Samaria is Remaliah's s'. "
14 virgin shall conceive, and bare a s', "
8: 2 Zechariah the s' of Jeberechiah. "

Isa 8: 3 and she conceived, and bare a s'. 1121
6 rejoice in Rezin and Remaliah's s'; "
9: 6 child is born, unto us a s' is given: "
13: 1 Isaiah the s' of Amoz did see. "
14: 12 O Lucifer, s' of the morning! how "
22 and remnant, and s', and nephew. 5209
19: 11 Pharaoh, I am the s' of the wise. 1121
11 the s' of ancient kings? "
20: 2 the Lord by Isaiah the s' of Amoz, "
22: 20 servant Eliakim the s' of Hilkiah: "
36: 3 unto him Eliakim, Hilkiah's s', "
3 and Joah, Asaph's s', the recorder. "
22 came Eliakim, the s' of Hilkiah, "
22 Joah, the s' of Asaph, the recorder, "
37: 2 Isaiah the prophet the s' of Amoz. "
21 Isaiah the s' of Amoz sent unto "
38 Esar-haddon his s' reigned in his "
38: 1 Isaiah the prophet the s' of Amoz "
39: 1 Merodach-baladan,...s' of Baladan, "
49: 15 compassion on the s' of her womb? "
51: 12 and of the s' of man which shall be "
56: 2 and the s' of man that layeth hold "
3 Neither let the s' of the stranger, * "
Jer 1: 1 of Jeremiah the s' of Hilkiah, "
2 days of Josiah the s' of Amon king "
3 days of Jehoiakim the s' of Josiah "
3 year of Zedekiah the s' of Josiah "
6: 26 thee mourning, as for an only s', 3173
7: 31 in the valley of the s' of Hinnom, 1121
32 nor the valley of the s' of Hinnom, "
15: 4 of Manasseh the s' of Hezekiah "
19: 2 unto the valley of the s' of Hinnom, "
6 nor The valley of the s' of Hinnom, "
20: 1 Pashur the s' of Immer the priest, "
21: 1 unto him Pashur the s' of Melchiah, "
1 and Zephaniah the s' of Maaseiah "
22: 11 touching Shallum the s' of Josiah "
18 Jehoiakim the s' of Josiah king of "
24 Coniah the s' of Jehoiakim king of "
24: 1 Jeconiah the s' of Jehoiakim king "
25: 1 year of Jehoiakim the s' of Josiah "
3 year of Josiah the s' of Amon king "
26: 1 reign of Jehoiakim the s' of Josiah "
20 Urijah the s' of Shemaiah of "
22 Elnathan the s' of Achbor, and "
24 hand of Ahikam the s' of Shaphan "
27: 1 reign of Jehoiakim the s' of Josiah "
7 him, and his s', and his son's s', "
20 Jeconiah the s' of Jehoiakim king "
28: 1 that Hananiah the s' of Azur the "
4 Jeconiah the s' of Jehoiakim king "
29: 3 hand of Elasah the s' of Shaphan, "
3 and Gemariah the s' of Hilkiah, "
21 of Israel, of Ahab the s' of Kolaiah, "
21 of Zedekiah the s' of Maaseiah, "
25 Zephaniah the s' of Maaseiah the "
31: 20 Is Ephraim my dear s'? is he a "
32: 7 Hanameel the s' of Shallum thine "
8 So Hanameel mine uncle's s' came "
9 the field of Hanameel my uncle's s', "
12 unto Baruch the s' of Neriah, "
12 the s' of Maaseiah, "
12 sight of Hanameel mine uncle's s', "
16 unto Baruch the s' of Neriah, 1121
35 in the valley of the s' of Hinnom, "
33: 21 should not have a s' to reign upon "
35: 1 of Jehoiakim the s' of Josiah king "
3 took Jaazaniah the s' of Jeremiah, "
3 the s' of Habaziniah, and his "
4 Hanan, the s' of Igdaliah, a man of "
4 of Maaseiah the s' of Shallum, the "
6 for Jonadab the s' of Rechab our "
8 voice of Jonadab the s' of Rechab "
14 words of Jonadab the s' of Rechab, "
16 sons of Jonadab the s' of Rechab "
19 Jonadab the s' of Rechab shall not "
36: 1 Jehoiakim the s' of Josiah king of "
4 called Baruch the s' of Neriah: and "
8 And Baruch the s' of Neriah did "
9 Jehoiakim the s' of Josiah king of "
10 of Gemariah the s' of Shaphan the "
11 When Michaiah the s' of Gemariah, "
11 s' of Shaphan, had heard out of the "
12 and Delaiah the s' of Shemaiah, "
12 and Elnathan the s' of Achbor, "
12 and Gemariah the s' of Shaphan, "
12 and Zedekiah the s' of Hananiah, "
14 sent Jehudi the s' of Nethaniah, "
14 the s' of Shelemiah, the s' of Cushi, "
14 Baruch the s' of Neriah took the roll "
26 Jerahmeel the s' of Hammelech, "
26 and Seraiah the s' of Azriel, and "
26 and Shelemiah the s' of Abdeel, "
32 Baruch the scribe, the s' of Neriah; "
37: 1 Zedekiah the s' of Josiah reigned "
1 instead of Coniah...s' of Jehoiakim, "
3 sent Jehucal the s' of Selemiah "
3 and Zephaniah the s' of Maaseiah "
13 was Irijah, the s' of Shelemiah, the "
13 the s' of Hananiah; and he took "
38: 1 Then Shephatiah the s' of Mattan, "
1 and Gedaliah the s' of Pashur, "
1 and Jucal the s' of Shelemiah, "
1 and Pashur the s' of Malchiah, "
6 of Malchiah the s' of Hammelech, "
39: 14 unto Gedaliah the s' of Ahikam "
14 the s' of Shaphan, that he should "
40: 5 also to Gedaliah the s' of Ahikam "
5 the s' of Shaphan, whom the king "
6 unto Gedaliah the s' of Ahikam to "
7 made Gedaliah the s' of Ahikam "
8 even Ishmael the s' of Nethaniah, "
8 and Seraiah the s' of Tanhumeth, "
8 Jezaniah the s' of a Maachathite, "
9 And Gedaliah the s' of Ahikam "
9 the s' of Shaphan sware unto them "

Jer 40: 11 them Gedaliah the s' of Ahikam 1121
11 the s' of Shaphan; "
13 Johanan the s' of Kareah, and all "
14 sent Ishmael the s' of Nethaniah "
14 Gedaliah the s' of Ahikam believed "
15 Johanan the s' of Kareah spake to "
15 slay Ishmael the s' of Nethaniah, "
16 Gedaliah the s' of Ahikam said unto "
16 said unto Johanan the s' of Kareah, "
41: 1 that Ishmael the s' of Nethaniah "
1 s' of Elishama, of the seed royal, "
1 unto Gedaliah the s' of Ahikam to "
2 arose Ishmael the s' of Nethaniah, "
2 smote Gedaliah the s' of Ahikam "
2 the s' of Shaphan with the sword, "
6 Ishmael the s' of Nethaniah went "
6 Come to Gedaliah the s' of Ahikam. "
7 Ishmael the s' of Nethaniah slew "
9 Ishmael the s' of Nethaniah filled "
10 to Gedaliah the s' of Ahikam: "
10 and Ishmael the s' of Nethaniah "
11 when Johanan the s' of Kareah, and "
11 that Ishmael the s' of Nethaniah "
12 with Ishmael the s' of Nethaniah, "
13 saw Johanan the s' of Kareah, and "
14 went unto Johanan the s' of Kareah. "
15 But Ishmael the s' of Nethaniah "
16 took Johanan the s' of Kareah, and "
16 from Ishmael the s' of Nethaniah, "
16 had slain Gedaliah the s' of Ahikam, "
18 Ishmael the s' of Nethaniah had "
18 slain Gedaliah the s' of Ahikam, "
42: 1 and Johanan the s' of Kareah, "
1 and Jezaniah the s' of Hoshaiah, "
8 called he Johanan the s' of Kareah, "
43: 2 spake Azariah the s' of Hoshaiah, "
2 and Johanan the s' of Kareah, and "
3 Baruch the s' of Neriah setteth the "
4 So Johanan the s' of Kareah, and "
5 But Johanan the s' of Kareah, and "
6 with Gedaliah the s' of Ahikam the "
6 the s' of Shaphan, and Jeremiah "
6 and Baruch the s' of Neriah. "
45: 1 spake unto Baruch the s' of Neriah, "
1 Jehoiakim the s' of Josiah king of "
46: 2 Jehoiakim the s' of Josiah king of "
49: 18 neither shall a s' of man dwell in it. "
33 there, nor any s' of man dwell in it. "
50: 40 shall any s' of man dwell therein. "
51: 43 doth any s' of man pass thereby. "
59 Seraiah the s' of Neriah, "
59 the s' of Maaseiah, when he went "
Eze 1: 3 Ezekiel the priest, the s' of Buzi, "
2: 1 S' of man, stand upon thy feet, and "
3 S' of man, I send thee to the "
6 s' of man, be not afraid of them, "
8 s' of man, hear what I say unto "
3: 1 S' of man, eat that thou findest; "
3 S' of man, cause thy belly to eat, "
4 S' of man, go, get thee unto the "
10 S' of man, all my words that I shall "
17 S' of man, I have made thee a "
25 O s' of man, behold, they shall put "
4: 1 s' of man, take thee a tile, and lay "
16 S' of man, behold, I will break the "
5: 1 s' of man, take thee a sharp knife, "
6: 2 S' of man, set thy face toward the "
7: 2 thou s' of man, thus saith the Lord "
8: 5 S' of man, lift up thine eyes now "
6 S' of man, seest thou what they do? "
8 S' of man, dig now in the wall: and "
11 stood Jaazaniah the s' of Shaphan, "
12 S' of man, hast thou seen what the "
15, 17 Hast thou seen this, O s' of man? "
11: 1 I saw Jaazaniah the s' of Azur, "
1 and Pelatiah the s' of Benaiah, "
2 S' of man, these are the men that "
4 them, prophesy, O s' of man. "
13 that Pelatiah the s' of Benaiah died. "
15 S' of man, thy brethren, even thy "
12: 2 S' of man, thou dwellest in the "
3 thou s' of man, prepare thee stuff "
9 S' of man, hath not the house of "
18 S' of man, eat thy bread with "
22 S' of man, what is that proverb that "
27 S' of man, behold, they of the house "
13: 2 S' of man, prophesy against the "
17 thou s' of man, set thy face against "
14: 3 S' of man, these men have set up "
13 S' of man, when the land sinneth "
20 deliver neither s' nor daughter; "
15: 2 S' of man, What is the vine tree "
16: 2 S' of man, cause Jerusalem to know "
17: 2 S' of man, put forth a riddle, and "
18: 4 so also the soul of the s' is mine: "
10 If he beget a s' that is a robber, a "
14 Now, lo, if he beget a s', that seeth "
19 the s' bear the iniquity of the father? "
19 s' hath done that which is lawful "
20 s' shall not bear the iniquity of the "
20 father bear the iniquity of the s': "
20: 3 S' of man, speak unto the elders of "
4 s' of man, wilt thou judge them? "
27 s' of man, speak unto the house of "
46 S' of man, set thy face toward the "
21: 2 S' of man, set thy face toward "
6 Sigh therefore, thou s' of man, with "
9 S' of man, prophesy, and say, Thus "
10 it contemneth the rod of my s', as "
12 Cry and howl, s' of man: for it shall "
14 s' of man, prophesy, and smite "
19 s' of man, appoint thee two ways, "
28 thou, s' of man, prophesy and say, "
22: 2 Now, thou s' of man, wilt thou judge, "
18 s' of man, the house of Israel is to "
24 S' of man, say unto her, Thou art "

Eze 23: 2 S' of man, there were two women, 1121
36 S' of man, wilt thou judge Aholah "
24: 2 S' of man, write thee the name of "
16 S' of man, behold, I take away "
25 s' of man, shall it not be in the day "
25: 2 S' of man, set thy face against the "
26: 2 S' of man, because that Tyrus hath "
27: 2 s' of man, take up a lamentation "
28: 2 S' of man, say unto the prince of "
12 S' of man, take up a lamentation "
21 S' of man, set thy face against "
29: 2 S' of man, set thy face against "
18 S' of man, Nebuchadrezzar king of "
30: 2 S' of man, prophesy and say, Thus "
21 S' of man, I have broken the arm "
31: 2 S' of man, speak unto Pharaoh "
32: 2 S' of man, take up a lamentation "
18 S' of man, wail for the multitude "
33: 2 S' of man, speak to the children of "
7 So thou, O s' of man, I have set thee "
10 s' of man, speak unto the house of "
12 s' of man, say unto the children of "
24 S' of man, they that inhabit those "
30 thou s' of man, the children of thy "
34: 2 S' of man, prophesy against the "
35: 2 S' of man, set thy face against "
36: 1 Also, thou s' of man, prophesy unto "
17 S' of man, when the house of Israel "
37: 3 me, S' of man, can these bones live? "
9 prophesy, s' of man, and say to the "
11 S' of man, these bones are the "
16 thou s' of man, take thee one stick, "
38: 2 S' of man, set thy face against Gog, "
14 s' of man, prophesy and say unto "
39: 1 s' of man, prophesy against Gog, "
17 s' of man, thus saith the Lord God; "
40: 4 S' of man, behold with thine eyes, "
43: 7 S' of man, the place of my throne, "
10 Thou s' of man, shew the house to "
18 S' of man, thus saith the Lord "
44: 5 S' of man, mark well, and behold "
25 mother, or for s', or for daughter, "
47: 6 me, S' of man, hast thou seen this? "
Da 3: 25 of the fourth is like the S' of God. 1247
5: 22 And thou his s', O Belshazzar, hast "
7: 13 one like the S' of man came with "
8: 17 unto me, Understand, O s' of man: 1121
9: 1 year of Darius the s' of Ahasuerus, "
Ho 1: 1 came unto Hosea, the s' of Beeri, "
1 days of Jeroboam the s' of Joash, "
3 which conceived, and bare him a s'. "
8 she conceived, and bare a s'. "
11: 1 him, and called my s' out of Egypt. "
13: 13 he is an unwise s'; for he should "
Joe 1: 1 that came to Joel the s' of Pethuel. "
Am 1: 1 days of Jeroboam the s' of Joash "
7: 14 neither was I a prophet's s'; "
8: 10 make it as the mourning of an only s'. "
Jon 1: 1 came unto Jonah the s' of Amittai, 1121
Mic 6: 5 Balaam the s' of Beor answered "
7: 6 For the s' dishonoureth the father, "
Zep 1: 1 unto Zephaniah the s' of Cushi, "
1 s' of Gedaliah, the s' of Amariah, "
1 of Amariah, the s' of Hizkiah, in "
1 the days of Josiah the s' of Amon, "
Hag 1: 1 unto Zerubbabel the s' of Shealtiel, "
1 and to Joshua the s' of Josedech, "
12 Then Zerubbabel the s' of Shealtiel, "
12 and Joshua the s' of Josedech, the "
14 of Zerubbabel the s' of Shealtiel, "
14 spirit of Joshua the s' of Josedech, "
2: 2 to Zerubbabel the s' of Shealtiel, "
2 and to Joshua the s' of Josedech, "
4 be strong, O Joshua, s' of Josedech, "
23 my servant, the s' of Shealtiel, "
Zec 1: 1 unto Zechariah, s' of Berechiah, "
1 the s' of Iddo the prophet, "
7 Zechariah, the s' of Berechiah, "
7 the s' of Iddo the prophet, "
6: 10 house of Josiah the s' of Zephaniah; "
11 head of Joshua the s' of Josedech, "
14 and to Hen the s' of Zephaniah, for "
12: 10 as one mourneth for his only s', "
Mal 1: 6 A s' honoureth his father, and a 1121
3: 17 as a man spareth his own s' that "
M't 1: 1 of Jesus Christ, the s' of David, 5207
1 of David, the s' of Abraham. "
20 Joseph, thou s' of David, fear not to "
21 she shall bring forth a s', and thou "
23 child, and shall bring forth a s', "
25 had brought forth her firstborn s': "
2: 15 Out of Egypt have I called my s'. "
3: 17 This is my beloved S', in whom I "
4: 3 If thou be the S' of God, command "
6 If thou be the S' of God, cast "
21 James the s' of Zebedee, and John his "
7: 9 if his s' ask bread, will he give him 5207
8: 20 S' of man hath not where to lay his "
29 do with thee, Jesus, thou S' of God? "
9: 2 S', be of good cheer; thy sins be 5043
6 S' of man hath power on earth to 5207
27 Thou s' of David, have mercy on us. "
10: 2 James the s' of Zebedee, and John his "
3 James the s' of Alphæus, and "
23 Israel, till the S' of man be come. 5207
37 loveth s' or daughter more than me "
11: 19 The S' of man came eating and "
27 and no man knoweth the S', but the "
27 any man the Father, save the S', "
27 whomsoever the S' will reveal him. "
12: 8 S' of man is Lord...of the sabbath "
23 and said, Is not this the S' of David? "
32 a word against the S' of man, "
40 shall the S' of man be three days "
13: 37 the good seed is the S' of man; "
41 The S' of man shall send forth his "

M't 13:55 Is not this the carpenter's s'? is not 5207
14:33 Of a truth thou art the S' of God. "
15:22 on me, O Lord, thou s' of David; "
16:13 men say that I the S' of man am? "
16 the Christ, the S' of the living God. "
27 S' of man shall come in the glory "
28 till they see the S' of man coming "
17: 5 This is my beloved S', in whom I "
9 until the S' of man be risen again "
12 shall...the S' of man suffer of them. "
15 Lord, have mercy on my s': for he "
22 S' of man shall be betrayed into "
18:11 For the S' of man is come to save* "
19:28 S' of man shall sit in the throne of "
20:18 S' of man shall be betrayed unto "
28 S' of man came not to be ministered "
30, 31 on us, O Lord, thou s' of David. "
21: 9 saying, Hosanna to the s' of David: "
15 saying, Hosanna to the s' of David; "
28 S', go work to day in my vineyard. 5043
37 last of all he sent unto them his s', 5207
37 saying, They will reverence my s'. "
38 when the husbandmen saw the s', "
22: 2 which made a marriage for his s', "
42 think ye of Christ? whose s' is he? "
42 They say unto him, The s' of David.
45 call him Lord, how is he his s'? 5207
23:35 blood of Zacharias s' of Barachias, "
24:27 also the coming of the S' of man be. "
30 sign of the S' of man in heaven: "
30 the S' of man coming in the clouds "
37, 39 the coming of the S' of man be. "
44 ye think not the S' of man cometh. "
25:13 wherein the S' of man cometh. * "
31 S' of man shall come in his glory, "
26: 2 and the S' of man is betrayed to be "
24 the S' of man goeth as it is written "
24 by whom the S' of man is betrayed! "
45 S' of man is betrayed into the hands "
63 thou be the Christ, the S' of God. "
64 the S' of man sitting on the right "
27:40 If thou be the S' of God, come down "
43 for he said, I am the S' of God. "
54 Truly this was the S' of God. "
28:19 name of the Father, and of the S', "
M'r 1: 1 of Jesus Christ, the S' of God; "
11 Thou art my beloved S', in whom I "
19 he saw James the s' of Zebedee, and
2: 5 S', thy sins be forgiven thee. 5043
10 the S' of man hath power on earth 5207
14 he saw Levi the s' of Alphæus sitting
28 S' of man is Lord...of the sabbath. 5207
3:11 saying, Thou art the S' of God. "
17 And James the s' of Zebedee, and
18 and James the s' of Alphæus, and
5: 7 thou S' of the most high God? 5207
6: 3 this the carpenter, the s' of Mary, "
8:31 S' of man must suffer many things, "
38 shall the S' of man be ashamed, "
9: 7 This is my beloved S': hear him. "
9 S' of man were risen from the dead. "
12 how it is written of the S' of man, "
17 I have brought unto thee my s', "
31 The S' of man is delivered into the "
10:33 S' of man shall be delivered unto "
45 For...the S' of man came not to be "
46 blind Bartimæus, the s' of Timæus, "
47 Jesus, thou s' of David, have mercy "
48 Thou s' of David, have mercy on me. "
12: 6 Having yet therefore one s', his "
6 saying, They will reverence my s'. "
35 that Christ is the s' of David? "
37 Lord; and whence is he then his s'? "
13:12 to death, and the father the s'; *5043
26 see the S' of man coming in the 5207
32 neither the S', but the Father. "
34 For the S' of man is as a man taking*
14:21 S' of man indeed goeth, as it is 5207
21 by whom the S' of man is betrayed! "
41 S' of man is betrayed into the hands "
61 the Christ, the S' of the Blessed? "
62 S' of man sitting on the right hand "
15:39 Truly this man was the S' of God. "
Lu 1:13 wife Elisabeth shall bear thee a s', "
31 bring forth a s', and shalt call his "
32 shall be called the S' of the Highest: "
35 thee shall be called the S' of God, "
36 also conceived a s' in her old age: "
57 and she brought forth a s'. "
2: 7 she brought forth her firstborn s', "
48 S', why hast thou thus dealt with 5043
3: 2 came unto John the s' of Zacharias 5207
22 Thou art my beloved S'; in thee "
23 (as was supposed) the s' of Joseph, "
23 which was the s' of Heli,
24 Which was the s' of Matthat,
24 which was the s' of Levi,
24 which was the s' of Melchi,
24 which was the s' of Janna,
24 which was the s' of Joseph,
25 Which was the s' of Mattathias,
25 which was the s' of Amos,
25 which was the s' of Naum,
25 which was the s' of Esli,
25 which was the s' of Nagge,
26 Which was the s' of Maath,
26 which was the s' of Mattathias,
26 which was the s' of Semei,
26 which was the s' of Joseph,
26 which was the s' of Juda,
27 Which was the s' of Joanna,
27 which was the s' of Rhesa,
27 which was the s' of Zorobabel,
27 which was the s' of Salathiel,
27 which was the s' of Neri,
28 Which was the s' of Melchi,

Lu 3:28 which was the s' of Addi,
28 which was the s' of Cosam,
28 which was the s' of Elmodam,
28 which was the s' of Er,
29 Which was the s' of Jose,
29 which was the s' of Eliezer,
29 which was the s' of Jorim,
29 which was the s' of Matthat,
29 which was the s' of Levi,
30 Which was the s' of Simeon,
30 which was the s' of Juda,
30 which was the s' of Joseph,
30 which was the s' of Jonan,
30 which was the s' of Eliakim,
31 Which was the s' of Melea,
31 which was the s' of Menan,
31 which was the s' of Mattatha,
31 which was the s' of Nathan,
31 which was the s' of David,
32 Which was the s' of Jesse,
32 which was the s' of Obed,
32 which was the s' of Booz,
32 which was the s' of Salmon,
32 which was the s' of Naasson,
33 Which was the s' of Aminadab,
33 which was the s' of Aram,
33 which was the s' of Esrom,
33 which was the s' of Phares,
33 which was the s' of Juda,
34 Which was the s' of Jacob,
34 which was the s' of Isaac,
34 which was the s' of Abraham,
34 which was the s' of Thara,
34 which was the s' of Nachor,
35 Which was the s' of Saruch,
35 which was the s' of Ragau,
35 which was the s' of Phalec,
35 which was the s' of Heber,
35 which was the s' of Sala,
36 Which was the s' of Cainan,
36 which was the s' of Arphaxad,
36 which was the s' of Sem,
36 which was the s' of Noe,
36 which was the s' of Lamech,
37 Which was the s' of Mathusala,
37 which was the s' of Enoch,
37 which was the s' of Jared,
37 which was the s' of Maleleel,
37 which was the s' of Cainan,
38 Which was the s' of Enos,
38 which was the s' of Seth,
38 which was the s' of Adam,
38 which was the s' of God.
4: 3 If thou be the S' of God, command 5207
9 If thou be the S' of God, cast "
22 they said, Is not this Joseph's s'? "
41 Thou art Christ the S' of God. "
5:24 S' of man hath power upon earth "
6: 5 S' of man is Lord...of the sabbath. "
15 James the s' of Alphæus, and Simon
22 as evil, for the S' of man's sake. 5207
7:12 the only s' of his mother, and she "
34 The S' of man is come eating and "
8:28 Jesus, thou S' of God most high? "
9:22 S' of man must suffer many things, "
26 shall the S' of man be ashamed, "
35 This is my beloved S': hear him. "
38 I beseech thee, look upon my s': "
41 suffer you? Bring thy s' hither. "
44 S' of man shall be delivered into "
56 S' of man is not come to destroy * "
58 the S' of man hath not where to lay "
10: 6 and if the s' of peace be there, your "
22 no man knoweth who the S' is, but "
22 and who the Father is, but the S', "
22 and he to whom the S' will reveal "
11:11 If a s' shall ask bread of any of you "
30 the S' of man be to this generation. "
12: 8 shall the S' of man also confess "
10 speak a word against the S' of man, "
40 S' of man cometh at an hour when "
53 shall be divided against the s', "
53 and the s' against the father; the "
15:13 younger s' gathered all together, "
19 no more worthy to be called thy s': "
21 And the s' said unto him, Father, I "
21 no more worthy to be called thy s'. "
24 For this my s' was dead, and is "
25 Now his elder s' was in the field: "
30 But as soon as this thy s' was come, "
31 S', thou art ever with me, and all 5043
16:25 S', remember that thou in thy "
17:22 one of the days of the S' of man, 5207
24 also the S' of man be in his day. "
26 be also in the days of the S' of man. "
30 day when the S' of man is revealed. "
18: 8 when the S' of man cometh, shall he "
31 prophets concerning the S' of man "
38, 39 s' of David, have mercy on me. "
19: 9 as he also is a s' of Abraham. "
10 For the S' of man is come to seek "
20:13 I will send my beloved s': it may be "
41 say they that Christ is David's s'? "
44 him Lord, how is he then his s'? "
21:27 see the S' of man coming in a cloud "
36 and to stand before the S' of man. "
22:22 And truly the S' of man goeth, as it "
48 betrayest thou the S' of man with a "
69 the S' of man sit on the right hand "
70 all, Art thou then the S' of God? "
24: 7 S' of man must be delivered into "
Joh 1:18 the only begotten S', which is in "
34 record that this is the S' of God. "
42 Thou art Simon the s' of Jona: "
45 Jesus of Nazareth, the s' of Joseph. "
49 Rabbi, thou art the S' of God; "

Joh 1:51 descending upon the S' of man. 5207
3:13 the S' of man which is in heaven. "
14 so must the S' of man be lifted up: "
16 that he gave his only begotten S', "
17 God sent not his S' into the world "
18 name of the only begotten S' of God. "
35 The Father loveth the S', and hath "
36 He that believeth on the S' hath "
36 and he that believeth not the S' "
4: 5 that Jacob gave to his s' Joseph. "
46 whose s' was sick at Capernaum. "
47 would come down, and heal his s': "
50 unto him, Go thy way; thy s' liveth. "
51 told him, saying, Thy s' liveth. 3816
53 Jesus said unto him, Thy s' liveth: 5207
5:19 The S' can do nothing of himself, "
19 these also doeth the S' likewise. "
20 For the Father loveth the S', and "
21 so the S' quickeneth whom he will. "
22 committed all judgment unto the S': "
23 That all men should honour the S', "
23 He that honoureth not the S' "
25 shall hear the voice of the S' of God: "
26 hath he given to the S' to have life "
27 also, because he is the S' of man. "
6:27 which the S' of man shall give unto "
40 that every one which seeth the S', "
42 Is not this Jesus, the s' of Joseph, "
53 ye eat the flesh of the S' of man, "
62 shall see the S' of man ascend up "
69 art that Christ, the S' of the living* "
71 of Judas Iscariot the s' of Simon: "
8:28 ye have lifted up the S' of man, 5207
35 for ever: but the S' abideth ever. "
36 S' therefore shall make you free, ye "
9:19 Is this your s', who ye say was born "
20 We know that this is our s', and "
35 Dost thou believe on the S' of God? "
10:36 because I said, I am the S' of God? "
11: 4 the S' of God might be glorified "
27 thou art the Christ, the S' of God, "
12: 4 Simon's s', which should betray him,*
23 the S' of man should be glorified. 5207
34 The S' of man must be lifted up? "
34 lifted up? who is this S' of man? "
13: 2 Iscariot, Simon's s', to betray him;
26 it to Judas Iscariot, the s' of Simon.
31 Now is the S' of man glorified, 5207
14:13 Father may be glorified in the S'. "
17: 1 the hour is come; glorify thy S', "
1 that thy S' also may glorify thee: "
12 them is lost, but the s' of perdition; "
19: 7 he made himself the S' of God. "
26 his mother, Woman, behold thy s'! "
20:31 Jesus is the Christ, the S' of God; "
21:15 s' of Jonas, lovest thou me more than
16, 17 Simon, s' of Jonas, lovest thou me?
Ac 1:13 James the s' of Alphæus, and Simon
3:13 fathers,...glorified his S' Jesus; *3816
26 having raised up his S' Jesus, sent* "
4:36 interpreted, The s' of consolation, 5207
7:21 and nourished him for her own s'. "
56 the S' of man standing on the right "
8:37 that Jesus Christ is the S' of God.* "
9:20 that he is the S' of God. "
13:21 gave unto them Saul the s' of Cis, "
22 I have found David the s' of Jesse,
33 Thou art my S', this day have I 5207
16: 1 Timotheus,...s' of a certain woman, "
23: 6 am a Pharisee, the s' of a Pharisee: "
16 And when Paul's sister's s' heard of "
Ro 1: 3 his S' Jesus Christ our Lord, "
4 declared to be the S' of God with "
9 my spirit in the gospel of his S', "
5:10 reconciled...by the death of his S', "
8: 3 sending his own S' in the likeness "
29 be conformed to the image of his S', "
32 He that spared not his own S', but "
9: 9 I come, and Sarah shall have a s'. "
1Co 1: 9 of his S' Jesus Christ our Lord. "
4:17 Timotheus, who is my beloved s',*5043
15:28 the S' also himself be subject unto 5207
2Co 1:19 For the S' of God, Jesus Christ, "
Ga 1:16 To reveal his S' in me, that I might "
2:20 I live by the faith of the S' of God, "
4: 4 God sent forth his S', made of a "
6 the Spirit of his S' into your hearts, "
7 art no more a servant, but a s'; "
7 if a s', then an heir of God through "
30 Cast out the bondwoman and her s': "
30 s' of the bondwoman shall not be "
30 heir with the s' of the freewoman. "
Eph 4:13 of the knowledge of the S' of God, "
Ph'p 2:22 him, that, as a s' with the father, *5043
Col 1:13 into the kingdom of his dear S': 5207
4:10 Marcus, sister's s' to Barnabas, * 431
1Th 1:10 to wait for his S' from heaven, 5207
2Th 2: 3 be revealed, the s' of perdition; "
1Ti 1: 2 Timothy, my own s' in the faith: *5043
18 I commit unto thee, s' Timothy, * "
2Ti 1: 2 To Timothy, my dearly beloved s':* "
2: 1 my s', be strong in the grace that * "
Tit 1: 4 To Titus, mine own s' after the * "
Ph'm 10 I beseech thee for my s' Onesimus,* "
Heb 1: 2 last days spoken unto us by his S', 5207
5 Thou art my S', this day have I "
5 Father, and he shall be to me a S'? "
8 unto the S' he saith, Thy throne, "
2: 6 the s' of man, that thou visitest him? "
3: 6 Christ as a s' over his own house; "
4:14 the heavens, Jesus the S' of God, "
5: 5 him, Thou art my S', to day have I "
8 Though he were a S', yet learned he "
6: 6 they crucify...the S' of God afresh, "
7: 3 but made like unto the S' of God; "
28 maketh the S', who is consecrated "

Heb10: 29 trodden under foot the *S*· of God. 5207
11: 17 offered up his only begotten *s*·. "
24 the *s*· of Pharaoh's daughter; 5207
12: 5 My *s*·, despise not...the chastening "
6 and scourgeth every *s*· whom he "
7 *s*· is he whom the father chasteneth "
Jas 2: 21 offered Isaac his *s*· upon the altar? "
1Pe 5: 13 you; and so doth Marcus my *s*·. "
2Pe 1: 17 This is my beloved *S*·, in whom I am "
2: 15 the way of Balaam the *s*· of Bosor, "
1Jo 1: 3 and with his *S*· Jesus Christ. 5207
7 the blood of Jesus Christ his *S*· "
2: 22 that denieth the Father and the *S*·. "
23 Whosoever denieth the *S*·, the same "
23 he that acknowledgeth the *S*· hath "
24 ye also shall continue in the *S*·. 5207
3: 8 For this purpose the *S*· of God was "
23 believe on the name of his *S*· Jesus "
4: 9 God sent his only begotten *S*· into "
10 his *S*· to be the propitiation for our "
14 *S*· to be the Saviour of the world. "
15 confess that Jesus is the *S*· of God. "
5: 5 believeth that Jesus is the *S*· of God? "
9 which he hath testified of his *S*·. "
10 He that believeth on the *S*· of God "
10 the record that God gave of his *S*·. "
11 life, and this life is in his *S*·. "
12 He that hath the *S*· hath life; and "
12 hath not the *S*· of God hath not life. "
13 on the name of the *S*· of God; * "
13 on the name of the *S*· of God. "
20 we know that the *S*· of God is come, "
20 is true, even in his *S*· Jesus Christ. "
2Jo 3 Jesus Christ, the *S*· of the Father, "
9 he hath both the Father and the *S*·. "
Re 1: 13 one like unto the *S*· of man, "
2: 18 These things saith the *S*· of God, "
14: 14 one sat like unto the *S*· of man, "
21: 7 be his God, and he shall be my *s*·. "

song See also SONGS.
Ex 15: 1 of Israel this *s*· unto the Lord, 7892
2 The Lord is my strength and *s*·, 2176
Nu 21: 17 Israel sang this *s*·, Spring up, O 7892
De 31: 19 therefore write ye this *s*· for you, "
19 that this *s*· may be a witness for me "
21 this *s*· shall testify against them as "
22 Moses therefore wrote this *s*· the "
30 of Israel the words of this *s*·, "
32: 44 and spake all the words of this *s*· in "
J'g 5: 12 Deborah: awake, awake, utter a *s*·: "
2Sa 22: 1 unto the Lord the words of this *s*· "
1Ch 6: 31 David set over the service of *s*· "
15: 22 chief of the Levites, was for *s*·: 4853
22 he instructed about the *s*·, because "
27 Chenaniah the master of the *s*· with "
25: 6 the hands of their father for *s*· in 7892
2Ch 29: 27 *s*· of the Lord began also with the "
Job 30: 9 And now am I their *s*·, yea, I am 5058
Ps 18: *title* unto the Lord...words of this *s*· 7892
28: 7 and with my *s*· will I praise him. "
30: *title* A Psalm and *S*· at the dedication "
33: 3 Sing unto him a new *s*·; play "
40: 3 he hath put a new *s*· in my mouth, "
42: 8 in the night his *s*· shall be with me. "
45: *title* of Korah, Maschil, A *S*· of loves. "
46: *title* of Korah, A *S*· upon Alamoth. "
48: *title* A *S*· and Psalm for the sons of "
65: *title* A Psalm and *S*· of David. "
66: *title* the chief Musician, A *S*· or Psalm. "
67: *title* on Neginoth, A Psalm or *S*·. "
68: *title* Musician, A Psalm or *S*· of David. "
69: 12 and I was the *s*· of the drunkards. 5058
30 praise the name of God with a *s*·, 7892
75: *title* A Psalm or *S*· of Asaph. "
76: *title* A Psalm or *S*· of Asaph. "
77: 6 I call to remembrance my *s*· in the 5058
83: *title* A *S*· or Psalm of Asaph. 7892
87: *title* Psalm or *S*· for the sons of Korah. "
88: *title* *S*· or Psalm for the sons of Korah. "
92: *title* A Psalm or *S*· for the sabbath day. "
96: 1 O sing unto the Lord a new *s*·: "
98: 1 O sing unto the Lord a new *s*·; for "
108: *title* A *S*· or Psalm of David. "
118: 14 The Lord is my strength and *s*·, 2176
120: *title* A *S*· of degrees. 7892
121: *title* A *S*· of degrees. "
122: *title* A *S*· of degrees of David. "
123: *title* A *S*· of degrees. "
124: *title* A *S*· of degrees of David. "
125: *title* A *S*· of degrees. "
126: *title* A *S*· of degrees. "
127: *title* A *S*· of degrees for Solomon. "
128: *title* A *S*· of degrees. "
129: *title* A *S*· of degrees. "
130: *title* A *S*· of degrees. "
131: *title* A *S*· of degrees of David. "
132: *title* A *S*· of degrees. "
133: *title* A *S*· of degrees of David. "
134: *title* A *S*· of degrees. "
137: 3 captive required of us a *s*·; *1697
4 How shall we sing the Lord's *s*· in a "
144: 9 I will sing a new *s*· unto thee, O "
149: 1 Sing unto the Lord a new *s*·, and "
Ec 7: 5 for a man to hear the *s*· of fools. "
Ca 1: 1 The *s*· of songs, which is Solomon's. "
Isa 5: 1 will sing to my wellbeloved a *s*· "
12: 2 Jehovah is my strength and my *s*·; 2176
24: 9 shall not drink wine with a *s*·; 7892
26: 1 this *s*· be sung in the land of Judah; "
30: 29 Ye shall have a *s*·, as in the night "
42: 10 Sing unto the Lord a new *s*·, and "
La 3: 14 my people; and their *s*· all the day. 5058
Eze 33: 32 art unto them as a very lovely *s*· 7892
Re 5: 9 And they sung a new *s*·, saying, 5603
14: 3 And they sung as it were a new *s*· "
3 no man could learn that *s*· but the "
15: 3 And they sing the *s*· of Moses the 5603
3 and the *s*· of the Lamb, saying, "

songs
Ge 31: 27 thee away with mirth, and with *s*·, 7892
1Ki 4: 32 and his *s*· were a thousand and five. "
1Ch 25: 7 instructed in the *s*· of the Lord, * "
Ne 12: 46 *s*· of praise and thanksgiving unto "
Job 35: 10 maker, who giveth *s*· in the night; 2158
Ps 32: 7 me about with *s*· of deliverance. 7438
119: 54 Thy statutes have been my *s*· in 2158
137: 3 Sing us one of the *s*· of Zion. 7892
Pr 25: 20 he that singeth *s*· to an heavy heart. "
Ca 1: 1 The song of *s*·, which is Solomon's. "
Isa 23: 16 make sweet melody, sing many *s*·, "
24: 16 part of the earth have we heard *s*·, 2158
35: 10 to Zion with *s*· and everlasting *7440
38: 20 we will sing my *s*· to the stringed 5058
Eze 26: 13 cause the noise of thy *s*· to cease; 7892
Am 5: 23 away from me the noise of thy *s*·; "
8: 3 And the *s*· of the temple shall be "
10 and all your *s*· into lamentation; "
Eph 5: 19 psalms and hymns and spiritual *s*·, 5603
Col 3: 16 psalms and hymns and spiritual *s*·, "

son-in-law See SON and LAW.

son's
Ge 11: 31 Lot the son of Haran his *s*· son, 1121
16: 15 Abram called his *s*· name, which * "
21: 23 with my son, nor with my *s*· son: 5220
24: 51 let her be thy master's *s*· wife, as 1121
27: 25 me, and I will eat of my *s*· venison, "
31 arise, and eat of his *s*· venison, "
30: 14 Give me,...of thy *s*· mandrakes. "
15 take away my *s*· mandrakes also? "
15 thee to night for thy *s*· mandrakes. "
16 hired thee with my *s*· mandrakes. "
37: 32 now whether it be thy *s*· coat or no. "
33 knew it, and said, It is my *s*· coat; "
Ex 10: 2 ears of thy son, and of thy *s*· son, "
Le 18: 10 The nakedness of thy *s*· daughter, "
15 she is thy *s*· wife; thou shalt not "
17 shalt thou take her *s*· daughter, "
De 6: 2 thou, and thy son, and thy *s*· son, "
J'g 8: 22 and thy son, and thy *s*· son also: "
1Ki 11: 35 the kingdom out of his *s*· hand, "
21: 29 in his *s*· days will I bring the evil "
Pr 30: 4 his name, and what is his *s*· name, "
Jer 27: 7 him, and his son, and his *s*· son, "

sons See also SONS'.
Ge 5: 4, 7, 10, 13, 16, 19, 22, 26, 30 begat *s*· and 1121
6: 2 the *s*· of God saw the daughters of "
4 the *s*· of God came in unto the "
10 Noah begat three *s*·, Shem, Ham, "
18 come into the ark, thou, and thy *s*·, "
7: 7 Noah went in, and his *s*·, and his "
13 Ham, and Japheth, the *s*· of Noah, "
13 three wives of his *s*· with them, "
8: 16 ark, thou, and thy wife, and thy *s*·, "
18 Noah went forth, and his *s*·, and his "
9: 1 God blessed Noah and his *s*·, and "
8 unto Noah, and to his *s*· with him, "
18 the *s*· of Noah, that went forth of "
19 These are the three *s*· of Noah: and "
10: 1 the generations of the *s*· of Noah; "
1 unto them were *s*· born after the "
2 The *s*· of Japheth; Gomer, and "
3 the *s*· of Gomer; Ashkenaz, and "
4 And the *s*· of Javan; Elishah, and "
6 the *s*· of Ham; Cush, and Mizraim, "
7 the *s*· of Cush; Seba, and Havilah, "
7 and the *s*· of Raamah; Sheba, and "
20 These are the *s*· of Ham, after their "
25 unto Eber were born two *s*·: the "
29 all these were the *s*· of Joktan. "
31 These are the *s*· of Shem, after "
32 are the families of the *s*· of Noah, "
11: 11, 13, 15, 17, 19, 21, 23, 25 begat *s*· and "
19: 12 son in law, and thy *s*·, and thy "
14 out, and spake unto his *s*· in law, 2860
14 one that mocked unto his *s*· in law. "
23: 3 and spake unto the *s*· of Heth, *1121
11 the presence of the *s*· of my people * "
16 in the audience of the *s*· of Heth, * "
20 of a buryingplace by the *s*· of Heth. * "
25: 3 the *s*· of Dedan were Asshurim, and "
4 And the *s*· of Midian; Ephah, and "
6 But unto the *s*· of the concubines, "
9 his *s*· Isaac and Ishmael buried "
10 purchased of the *s*· of Heth: there * "
13 are the names of the *s*· of Ishmael, "
16 These are the *s*· of Ishmael, and "
27: 29 thy mother's *s*· bow down to thee: "
29: 34 because I have born him three *s*·: "
30: 20 me, because I have born him six *s*·: "
35 gave them into the hand of his *s*·. "
31: 1 he heard the word's of Laban's *s*·, "
17 his *s*· and his wives upon camels; "
28 not suffered me to kiss my *s*· and "
55 kissed his *s*· and his daughters, "
32: 22 womenservants, and his eleven *s*·, *3206
34: 5 now his *s*· were with his cattle in 1121
7 *s*· of Jacob came out of the field "
13 *s*· of Jacob answered Shechem and "
25 two of the *s*· of Jacob, Simeon and "
27 *s*· of Jacob came upon the slain, "
35: 5 did not pursue after the *s*· of Jacob. "
22 Now the *s*· of Jacob were twelve: "
23 The *s*· of Leah; Reuben, Jacob's "
24 And the *s*· of Rachel; Joseph and "
25 *s*· of Bilhah, Rachel's handmaid; "
26 the *s*· of Zilpah, Leah's handmaid; "
26 these are the *s*· of Jacob, which "
29 his *s*· Esau and Jacob buried him. "
36: 5 these are the *s*· of Esau, which were "
6 Esau took his wives, and his *s*·, and "
Ge 36: 10 These are the names of Esau's *s*·; 1121
11 *s*· of Eliphaz were Teman, Omar, "
12 were the *s*· of Adah Esau's wife. "
13 are the *s*· of Reuel; Nahath, and "
13 the *s*· of Bashemath Esau's wife. "
14 the *s*· of Aholibamah, the daughter "
15 These were dukes of the *s*· of Esau: "
15 *s*· of Eliphaz the firstborn son of "
16 Edom; these were the *s*· of Adah. "
17 are the *s*· of Reuel Esau's son; "
17 the *s*· of Bashemath Esau's wife. "
18 the *s*· of Aholibamah Esau's wife; "
19 the *s*· of Esau, who is Edom, and "
20 These are the *s*· of Seir the Horite, "
37: 2 the lad was with the *s*· of Bilhah, "
2 with the *s*· of Zilpah, his father's "
35 his *s*· and all his daughters rose up "
41: 50 And unto Joseph were born two *s*· "
42: 1 Jacob said unto his *s*·, Why do ye "
5 the *s*· of Israel came to buy corn "
11 We are all one man's *s*·; we are "
13 the *s*· of one man in the land of "
32 twelve brethren, *s*· of our father; "
37 Slay my two *s*·, if I bring him not "
44: 27 know that my wife bare me two *s*·: "
46: 5 *s*· of Israel carried Jacob their 1121
7 His *s*·, and his sons' *s*· with him, "
8 came into Egypt, Jacob and his *s*·: "
9 *s*· of Reuben; Hanoch, and Phallu, "
10 *s*· of Simeon; Jemuel, and Jamin, "
11 the *s*· of Levi; Gershon, Kohath, "
12 the *s*· of Judah; Er, and Onan, "
12 the *s*· of Pharez were Hezron and "
13 And the *s*· of Issachar; Tolah, and "
14 the *s*· of Zebulun; Sered, and Elon, "
15 These be the *s*· of Leah, which she "
15 the souls of his *s*· and his daughters "
16 the *s*· of Gad; Ziphion, and Haggi, "
17 And the *s*· of Asher; Jimnah, and "
17 and the *s*· of Beriah; Heber, and "
18 These are the *s*· of Zilpah, whom "
19 The *s*· of Rachel Jacob's wife; "
21 And the *s*· of Benjamin were Belah, "
22 These are the *s*· of Rachel, which "
23 And the *s*· of Dan; Hushim. "
24 *s*· of Naphtali; Jahzeel, and Guni, "
25 These are the *s*· of Bilhah, which "
27 the *s*· of Joseph, which were born "
48: 1 and he took with him his two *s*·, "
5 thy two *s*·, Ephraim and Manasseh, "
8 Israel beheld Joseph's *s*·, and said, "
9 They are my *s*·, whom God hath "
49: 1 Jacob called unto his *s*·, and said, "
2 together, and hear, ye *s*· of Jacob; "
33 made an end of commanding his *s*·, "
50: 12 his *s*· did unto him according as he "
13 his *s*· carried him into the land of "
Ex 3: 22 and ye shall put them upon your *s*·, "
4: 20 And Moses took his wife and his *s*·, "
6: 14 The *s*· of Reuben the firstborn of "
15 And the *s*· of Simeon; Jemuel, and "
16 are the names of the *s*· of Levi "
17 *s*· of Gershon; Libni, and Shimi, "
18 And the *s*· of Kohath; Amram, and "
19 And the *s*· of Merari; Mahali, and "
21 And the *s*· of Izhar; Korah, and "
22 And the *s*· of Uzziel; Mishael, and "
24 And the *s*· of Korah; Assir, and "
10: 9 with our *s*· and with our daughters, "
12: 24 to thee and to thy *s*· for ever. "
18: 3 her two *s*·; of which the name of "
5 came with his *s*· and his wife unto "
6 thy wife, and her two *s*· with her. "
21: 4 she have born him *s*· or daughters; "
22: 29 firstborn of thy *s*· shalt thou give "
27: 21 Aaron and his *s*· shall order it "
28: 1 thy brother, and his *s*· with him, "
1 Eleazar and Ithamar, Aaron's *s*·. "
4 for Aaron thy brother, and his *s*·, "
40 Aaron's *s*· thou shalt make coats, "
41 thy brother, and his *s*· with him; "
43 be upon Aaron, and upon his *s*·, "
29: 4 Aaron and his *s*· thou shalt bring "
8 shalt bring his *s*·, and put coats "
9 with girdles, Aaron and his *s*·, and "
9 shalt consecrate Aaron and his *s*·. "
10, 15, 19 Aaron and his *s*· shall put "
20 the tip of the right ear of his *s*·, "
21 upon his garments, and upon his *s*·, "
21 upon the garments of his *s*· with "
21 and his garments and his *s*·, and "
24 Aaron, and in the hands of his *s*·; "
27 and of that which is for his *s*·: "
32 Aaron and his *s*· shall eat the flesh "
35 thou do unto Aaron, and to his *s*·, "
44 sanctify also both Aaron and his *s*·, "
30: 19 Aaron and his *s*· shall wash their "
30 thou shalt anoint Aaron and his *s*·, "
31: 10 the garments of his *s*·, to minister "
32: 2 the ears of your wives, of your *s*·, "
26 the *s*· of Levi gathered themselves "
34: 16 take of their daughters unto thy *s*·, "
16 and make thy *s*· go a whoring after "
20 All the firstborn of thy *s*· thou "
35: 19 the garments of his *s*·, to minister "
39: 27 work for Aaron, and for his *s*·, "
40: 12 thou shalt bring Aaron and his *s*· "
14 thou shalt bring his *s*·, and clothe "
31 Moses and Aaron and his *s*· washed "
Le 1: 5 Aaron's *s*·, shall bring the blood, "
7 *s*· of Aaron the priest shall put fire "
8 Aaron's *s*·, shall lay the parts, the "
11 Aaron's *s*·, shall sprinkle his blood "
2: 2 And he shall bring it to Aaron's *s*· "
3: 2 Aaron's *s*· the priests shall sprinkle "
5 And Aaron's *s*· shall burn it on the

Le 3: 8 Aaron's s· shall sprinkle the blood 1121
13 and the s· of Aaron shall sprinkle "
6: 9 Command Aaron and his s·, saying, "
14 the s· of Aaron shall offer it before "
16 thereof shall Aaron and his s· eat: "
20 the offering of Aaron and of his s·, "
22 priest of his s· that is anointed in "
25 Speak unto Aaron and to his s·, "
7: 10 shall all the s· of Aaron have, one "
33 He among the s· of Aaron, that "
34 Aaron the priest and unto his s· by "
35 of the anointing of his s·, out of "
8: 2 Take Aaron and his s· with him, "
6 Moses brought Aaron and his s·, "
13 Moses brought Aaron's s·, and put "
14, 18, 22 Aaron and his s· laid their "
24 he brought Aaron's s·, and Moses "
30 his garments, and upon his s·, and "
30 and his s·, and his sons' garments "
31 said unto Aaron and to his s·, "
31 saying, Aaron and his s· shall eat it. "
36 So Aaron and his s· did all things "
9: 1 that Moses called Aaron and his s·, "
9 the s· of Aaron brought the blood "
12, 18 Aaron's s· presented unto him "
10: 1 Nadab and Abihu, the s· of Aaron, "
4 the s· of Uzziel the uncle of Aaron, "
6 Eleazar and unto Ithamar, his s·, "
9 drink, thou, nor thy s· with thee, "
12 unto Ithamar, his s· that were left, "
14 thy s·, and thy daughters with thee: "
16 the s· of Aaron which were left "
13: 2 or unto one of his s· the priests: "
16: 1 the death of the two s· of Aaron, "
17: 2 Speak unto Aaron, and unto his s·, "
21: 1 unto the priests the s· of Aaron, "
24 told it unto Aaron, and to his s·, "
22: 2 Speak unto Aaron, and to his s·, "
18 Speak unto Aaron, and to his s·, "
26: 29 And ye shall eat the flesh of your s·, "
Nu 2: 14 and the captain of the s· of Gad *
18 the captain of the s· of Ephraim *
22 the captain of the s· of Benjamin *
3: 2 are the names of the s· of Aaron; "
3 are the names of the s· of Aaron, "
9 the Levites unto Aaron and to his s·: "
10 thou shalt appoint Aaron and his s·, "
17 were the s· of Levi by their names; "
18 are the names of the s· of Gershon "
19 the s· of Kohath by their families; "
20 the s· of Merari by their families; "
25 the charge of the s· of Gershon in "
29 The families of the s· of Kohath "
36 charge of the s· of Merari shall be "
38 and Aaron and his s·, keeping the "
48 redeemed, unto Aaron and to his s·, "
51 redeemed unto Aaron and to his s·, "
4: 2 Take the sum of the s· of Kohath "
2 from among the s· of Levi, after "
4 be the service of the s· of Kohath "
5 Aaron shall come, and his s·, and "
15 when Aaron and his s· have made "
15 s· of Kohath shall come to bear it: "
15 are the burden of the s· of Kohath "
19 Aaron and his s· shall go in, and "
22 also the sum of the s· of Gershon, "
27 appointment of Aaron and his s· "
27 service of the s· of the Gershonites, "
28 the families of the s· of Gershon "
29 As for the s· of Merari, thou shalt "
31 of the families of the s· of Merari, "
34 numbered the s· of the Kohathites "
38 numbered of the s· of Gershon, "
41 the families of the s· of Gershon, "
42, 45 the families of the s· of Merari, "
6: 23 Speak unto Aaron and unto his s·, "
7: 7 he gave unto the s· of Gershon, "
8 oxen he gave unto the s· of Merari, "
9 unto the s· of Kohath he gave none: "
8: 13 before Aaron, and before his s·, "
19 as a gift to Aaron and to his s· "
22 before Aaron, and before his s·: as "
10: 8 And the s· of Aaron, the priests, "
17 s· of Gershon and the s· of Merari "
13: 33 we saw the giants, the s· of Anak, "
16: 1 and Abiram, the s· of Eliab, "
1 of Peleth, s· of Reuben, took men: "
7 too much upon you, ye s· of Levi. "
8 Hear, I pray you, ye s· of Levi: "
10 all thy brethren the s· of Levi with "
12 and Abiram, the s· of Eliab: which "
27 wives, and their s·, and their little "
18: 1 Thou and thy s· and thy father's "
1 s· with thee shall bear the iniquity "
2 and thy s· with thee shall minister "
7 thy s· with thee shall keep your "
8 to thy s·, by an ordinance for ever. "
9 most holy for thee and for thy s·. "
11 to thy s· and to thy daughters with "
19 thy s· and thy daughters with thee, "
21: 29 he hath given his s· that escaped, "
35 So they smote him, and his s·, and "
26: 8 And the s· of Pallu; Eliab. "
9 the s· of Eliab; Nemuel and Dathan, "
12 s· of Simeon after their families: "
19 The s· of Judah were Er and Onan: "
20 the s· of Judah after their families "
21 the s· of Pharez were; of Hezron, "
23 s· of Issachar after their families: "
26 s· of Zebulun after their families: "
28 The s· of Joseph after their families "
29 Of the s· of Manasseh: of Machir, "
30 These are the s· of Gilead: of "
33 the son of Hepher had no s·, but "
35 s· of Ephraim after their families: "
36 And these are the s· of Shuthelah: "

Nu 26: 37 the families of the s· of Ephraim 1121
37 the s· of Joseph after their families. "
38 s· of Benjamin after their families: "
40 s· of Bela were Ard and Naaman: "
41 s· of Benjamin after their families: "
42 the s· of Dan after their families: "
45 Of the s· of Beriah: of Heber, the "
47 are the families of the s· of Asher "
48 s· of Naphtali after their families: "
27: 3 died in his own sin, and had no s·. "
36: 1 of the families of the s· of Joseph, "
3 to any of the s· of the other tribes "
5 tribe of the s· of Joseph hath said "
11 unto their father's brothers' s·: "
12 the families of the s· of Manasseh "
De 1: 28 we have seen the s· of the Anakims "
2: 33 we smote him, and his s·, and all "
4: 9 teach them thy s·, and thy sons' s·;* "
11: 6 Dathan and Abiram, the s· of Eliab, "
12: 12 ye, and your s·, and your daughters, "
31 even their s· and their daughters "
18: 5 of the Lord, him and his s· for ever. "
21: 5 the priests the s· of Levi shall come "
16 maketh his s· to inherit that which "
23: 17 nor a sodomite of the s· of Israel. "
28: 32 s· and thy daughters shall be given "
53 flesh of thy s· and of thy daughters, "
31: 9 it unto the priests the s· of Levi, "
32: 8 when he separated the s· of Adam,* "
19 because of the provoking of his s·, "
Jos 7: 24 wedge of gold, and his s·, and his "
15: 14 drove thence the three s· of Anak, "
17: 3 the son of Manasseh, had no s·, but "
6 had an inheritance among his s·: "
6 rest of Manasseh's s· had the land "
24: 32 Jacob bought of the s· of Hamor "
J'g 1: 20 expelled thence...three s· of Anak. "
3: 6 gave their daughters to their s·, "
8: 19 brethren, even the s· of my mother: "
30 Gideon had threescore and ten s· "
9: 2 either that all the s· of Jerubbaal, "
5 his brethren the s· of Jerubbaal, "
18 have slain his s·, threescore and ten "
24 threescore and ten s· of Jerubbaal "
10: 4 he had thirty s· that rode on thirty "
11: 2 Gilead's wife bare him s·; and his "
2 wife's s· grew up, and they thrust "
12: 9 had thirty s·, and thirty daughters, "
9 daughters from abroad for his s·. "
14 he had forty s· and thirty nephews, "
17: 5 and consecrated one of his s·, who "
11 man was unto him as one of his s·. "
18: 30 he and his s· were priests to the "
19: 22 certain s· of Belial, beset the house "
Ru 1: 1 Moab, he, and his wife, and his two s·. "
2 the name of his two s· Mahlon and "
3 and she was left, and her two s·. "
5 left of her two s· and her husband. *3206
11 there yet any more s· in my womb, 1121
12 to night, and should also bear s·; "
4: 15 which is better to thee than seven s·, "
1Sa 1: 3 two s· of Eli, Hophni and Phinehas, "
4 her s· and her daughters, portions: "
8 am not I better to thee than ten s·? "
2: 12 Now the s· of Eli were s· of Belial; "
21 she conceived, and bare three s· and "
22 all that his s· did unto all Israel; "
24 Nay, my s·; for it is no good report "
29 and honourest thy s· above me, to "
34 thy two s·, Hophni and Phinehas, "
3: 13 because his s· made themselves vile, "
4: 4, 11 s· of Eli, Hophni and Phinehas, "
17 two s· also, Hophni and Phinehas, "
8: 1 he made his s· judges over Israel. "
3 his s· walked not in his ways, but "
5 and thy s· walk not in thy ways: "
11 He will take your s·, and appoint "
12: 2 and, behold, my s· are with you: "
14: 49 s· of Saul were Jonathan, and Ishui, "
16: 1 provided me a king among his s·. "
5 And he sanctified Jesse and his s·, "
10 Jesse made seven of his s· to pass "
17: 12 was Jesse; and he had eight s·: "
13 eldest s· of Jesse...followed Saul "
13 names of his three s· that went to "
22: 20 one of the s· of Ahimelech the son "
28: 19 shalt thou and thy s· be with me: "
30: 3 and their s· and their daughters, "
6 every man for his s· and for his "
19 nor great, neither s· nor daughters, "
31: 2 hard upon Saul and upon his s·; "
2 and Melchi-shua, Saul's s·. "
6 So Saul died, and his three s·, and "
7 and that Saul and his s· were dead, "
8 found Saul and his three s· fallen in "
12 body of Saul and the bodies of his s· "
2Sa 2: 18 there were three s· of Zeruiah there, "
3: 2 unto David were s· born in Hebron: "
39 s· of Zeruiah be too hard for me: "
4: 2 the s· of Rimmon a Beerothite, "
5 the s· of Rimmon the Beerothite, "
5: 13 yet s· and daughters born to David. "
6: 3 Uzzah and Ahio, the s· of Abinadab, "
8: 18 and David's s· were chief rulers. "
9: 10 Thou...and thy s·, and thy servants, "
10 had fifteen s· and twenty servants. "
11 at my table, as one of the king's s·. "
13: 23 Absalom invited all the king's s·. "
27 and all the king's s· go with him. "
29 Then all the king's s· arose, and "
30 Absalom hath slain all the king's s·, "
32 slain...the young men the king's s·; "
33 think that all the king's s· are dead: "
35 king, Behold, the king's s· come: "
36 the king's s· came, and lifted up "
14: 6 thy handmaid had two s·, and they "

2Sa 14: 27 Absalom there were born three s·, 1121
15: 27 in peace, and your two s· with you, "
36 have there with them their two s·, "
16: 10 I to do with you, ye s· of Zeruiah? "
19: 5 lives of thy s· and of thy daughters, "
17 fifteen s· and his twenty servants "
22 I to do with you, ye s· of Zeruiah, "
21: 6 Let seven men of his s· be delivered "
8 the king took the two s· of Rizpah "
8 five s· of Michal...daughter of Saul, "
16 which was of the s· of the giant, 3211
18 which was of the s· of the giant. "
23: 6 the s· of Belial shall be all of them as *
32 of the s· of Jashen, Jonathan, 1121
1Ki 1: 9 called all his brethren the king's s·, "
19 and hath called all the s· of the king, "
25 and hath called all the king's s·, "
2: 7 kindness unto the s· of Barzillai "
4: 3 Ahiah, the s· of Shisha, scribes; "
31 and Darda, the s· of Mahol: and "
11: 20 household among the s· of Pharaoh. "
12: 31 which were not of the s· of Levi. "
13: 11 and his s· came and told him all "
12 his s· had seen what way the man "
13 And he said unto his s·, saddle me "
27 he spake to his s·, saying, Saddle "
31 he spake to his s·, saying, When I "
18: 31 of the tribes of the s· of Jacob, "
20: 35 man of the s· of the prophets said "
21: 10 set two men, s· of Belial, before ‡ "
2Ki 2: 3, 5 the s· of the prophets that were "
7 men of the s· of the prophets went, "
15 when the s· of the prophets which "
4: 1 wives of the s· of the prophets unto "
1 come to take unto him my two s· *3206
4 door upon thee and upon thy s·, 1121
5 the door upon her and upon her s·, "
38 the s· of the prophets were sitting "
38 pottage for the s· of the prophets. "
5: 22 men of the s· of the prophets: give "
6: 1 s· of the prophets said unto Elisha, "
9: 26 of Naboth, and the blood of his s·, "
10: 1 Ahab had seventy s· in Samaria. "
2 seeing your master's s· are with "
3 and meetest of your master's s·, "
6 heads of the men your master's s·, "
6 Now the king's s·, being seventy "
7 that they took the king's s·, and "
8 brought the heads of the king's s·. "
11: 2 and stole from among the king's s· "
15: 12 Thy s· shall sit on the throne of "
17: 17 caused their s· and their daughters "
19: 37 and Sharezer his s· smote him with* "
20: 18 of thy s· that shall issue from thee, "
25: 7 they slew the s· of Zedekiah before "
1Ch 1: 5 s· of Japheth; Gomer, and Magog, "
6 the s· of Gomer; Ashchenaz, and "
7 s· of Javan; Elishah, and Tarshish, "
8 The s· of Ham; Cush, and Mizraim, "
9 s· of Cush; Seba, and Havilah, and "
9 And the s· of Raamah; Sheba, and "
17 s· of Shem; Elam, and Asshur, and "
19 And unto Eber were born two s·: "
23 All these were the s· of Joktan. "
28 The s· of Abraham; Isaac, and "
31 These are the s· of Ishmael. "
32 Now the s· of Keturah, Abraham's "
32 s· of Jokshan; Sheba, and Dedan. "
33 s· of Midian; Ephah, and Epher, "
33 All these are the s· of Keturah. "
34 The s· of Isaac; Esau and Israel. "
35 The s· of Esau; Eliphaz, Reuel, and "
36 s· of Eliphaz; Teman, and Omar, "
37 The s· of Reuel; Nahath, Zerah, "
38 s· of Seir; Lotan, and Shobal, and "
39 the s· of Lotan; Hori, and Homam: "
40 s· of Shobal; Alian, and Manahath, "
40 the s· of Zibeon; Aiah, and Anah. "
41 The s· of Anah; Dishon. And the "
41 s· of Dishon; Amram, and Eshban, "
42 The s· of Ezer; Bilhan, and Zavan, "
42 The s· of Dishan; Uz, and Aran. "
2: 1 These are the s· of Israel; Reuben, "
3 The s· of Judah; Er, and Onan, "
4 Zerah. All the s· of Judah were five. "
5 s· of Pharez; Hezron, and Hamul. "
6 the s· of Zerah; Timri, and Ethan; "
7 s· of Carmi; Achar, the troubler of "
8 And the s· of Ethan; Azariah. "
9 s· also of Hezron, that were born "
16 s· of Zeruiah; Abishai, and Joab, "
18 her s· are these; Jesher, and "
23 these belonged to the s· of Machir "
25 the s· of Jerahmeel the firstborn of "
27 And the s· of Ram the firstborn of "
28 s· of Onam were, Shammai, and "
28 the s· of Shammai; Nadab, and "
30 s· of Nadab; Seled, and Appaim: "
31 And the s· of Appaim; Ishi. "
31 the s· of Ishi; Sheshan. And the "
32 s· of Jada the brother of Shammai; "
33 s· of Jonathan; Peleth, and Zaza. "
33 These were the s· of Jerahmeel. "
34 Sheshan had no s·, but daughters. "
42 Now the s· of Caleb the brother of "
42 the s· of Mareshah the father of "
43 s· of Hebron; Korah, and Tappuah, "
47 s· of Jahdai; Regem, and Jotham, "
50 These were the s· of Caleb the son "
52 the father of Kirjath-jearim had s·; "
54 The s· of Salma; Beth-lehem, and "
3: 1 Now these were the s· of David, "
9 These were all the s· of David, "
9 beside the s· of the concubines, and "
15 the s· of Josiah were, the firstborn "
16 s· of Jehoiakim; Jeconiah his son, "

1Ch 3:17 s' of Jeconiah; Assir, Salathiel his 1121
19 the s' of Pedaiah were, Zerubbabel, “
19 s' of Zerubbabel; Meshullam, and “
21 the s' of Hananiah; Pelatiah, and “
21 the s' of Rephaiah, the s' of Arnan, “
21 s' of Obadiah, the s' of Shechaniah. “
22 the s' of Shechaniah; Shemaiah: “
22 s' of Shemaiah; Hattush, and Igeal, “
23 the s' of Neariah; Elioenai, and “
24 s' of Elioenai were, Hodaiah, and “
4: 1 s' of Judah; Pharez, Hezron, and “
4 are the s' of Hur, the firstborn “
6 These were the s' of Naarah. “
7 And the s' of Helah were, Zereth, “
13 s' of Kenaz; Othniel, and Seraiah: “
13 and the s' of Othniel; Hathath. “
15 s' of Caleb the son of Jephunneh; “
15 and the s' of Elah, even Kenaz. “
16 s' of Jehaleleel; Ziph, and Ziphah, “
17 And the s' of Ezra were, Jether, and “
18 And these are the s' of Bithiah the “
19 And the s' of his wife Hodiah the “
20 And the s' of Shimon were, Amnon, “
20 And the s' of Ishi were, Zoheth, and “
21 s' of Shelah the son of Judah were, “
24 The s' of Simeon were, Nemuel, and “
26 the s' of Mishma; Hamuel his son, “
27 And Shimei had sixteen s' and six “
42 of them, even of the s' of Simeon, “
42 Rephaiah, and Uzziel, the s' of Ishi. “
5: 1 s' of Reuben the firstborn of Israel, “
1 the s' of Joseph the son of Israel: “
3 The s',...of Reuben the firstborn “
4 The s' of Joel; Shemaiah his son, “
18 The s' of Reuben, and the Gadites, “
6: 1 s' of Levi; Gershon, Kohath, and “
2 s' of Kohath; Amram, Izhar, and “
3 s' also of Aaron; Nadab and Abihu, “
16 s' of Levi; Gershom, Kohath, and “
17 be the names of the s' of Gershom; “
18 the s' of Kohath were, Amram, and “
19 The s' of Merari; Mahli, and Mushi. “
22 s' of Kohath; Amminadab his son, “
25 And the s' of Elkanah; Amasai, and “
26 the s' of Elkanah; Zophai his son, “
28 s' of Samuel; the firstborn Vashni, “
29 s' of Merari; Mahli, Libni his son, “
33 Of the s' of the Kohathites: Heman “
44 And their brethren the s' of Merari “
49 But Aaron and his s' offered upon “
50 And these are the s' of Aaron; “
54 in their coasts, of the s' of Aaron, “
57 to the s' of Aaron they gave the “
61 And unto the s' of Kohath, which “
62 to the s' of Gershom throughout “
63 Unto the s' of Merari were given by “
66 of the families of the s' of Kohath “
70 of the remnant of the s' of Kohath. “
71 Unto the s' of Gershom were given “
7: 1 Now the s' of Issachar were, Tola, “
2 the s' of Tola; Uzzi, and Rephaiah, “
3 And the s' of Uzzi; Izrahiah: and “
3 the s' of Izrahiah; Michael, and “
4 for they had many wives and s'. “
6 s' of Benjamin; Bela, and Becher, and “
7 And the s' of Bela; Ezbon, and 1121
8 And the s' of Becher; Zemira, and “
8 All these are the s' of Becher. “
10 The s' also of Jediael; Bilhan: and “
10 s' of Bilhan; Jeush, and Benjamin, “
11 All these are the s' of Jediael, by “
12 of Ir, and Hushim, the s' of Aher. “
13 s' of Naphtali; Jahziel, and Guni, “
13 and Shallum, the s' of Bilhah. “
14 s' of Manasseh; Ashriel, whom she “
16 and his s' were Ulam and Rakem. “
17 And the s' of Ulam; Bedan. These “
17 the s' of Gilead, the son of Machir, “
19 the s' of Shemidah were, Ahian, “
20 the s' of Ephraim; Shuthelah, and “
30 The s' of Asher; Imnah, and Isuah, “
31 And the s' of Beriah; Heber, and “
33 And the s' of Japhlet; Pasach, and “
34 And the s' of Shamer; Ahi, and “
35 And the s' of his brother Helem; “
36 The s' of Zophah; Suah, and “
38 And the s' of Jether; Jephunneh, “
39 the s' of Ulla; Arah, and Haniel, “
8: 3 And the s' of Bela were, Addar, and “
6 And these are the s' of Ehud: these “
10 These were his s', heads of the “
12 s' of Elpaal; Eber, and Misham, “
16 Ispah, and Joha, the s' of Beriah. “
18 and Jobab, the s' of Elpaal; “
21 and Shimrath, the s' of Shimhi; “
25 and Penuel, the s' of Shashak; “
27 and Zichri, the s' of Jeroham. “
35 And the s' of Micah were, Pithon, “
38 And Azel had six s', whose names “
38 All these were the s' of Azel. “
39 the s' of Eshek his brother were, “
40 the s' of Ulam were mighty men of “
40 and had many s', and sons' s', an “
40 All these are of the s' of Benjamin. “
9: 5 Asaiah the firstborn, and his s'. “
6 of the s' of Zerah; Jeuel, and their “
7 of the s' of Benjamin; Sallu the “
30 of the s' of the priests made the “
32 the s' of the Kohathites, were over “
41 And the s' of Micah were, Pithon, “
44 Azel had six s', whose names are “
44 Hanan: these were the s' of Azel. “
10: 2 hard after Saul, and after his s'; “
2 and Malchi-shua, the s' of Saul. “
6 So Saul died, and his three s', and “
7 and that Saul and his s' were dead, “

1Ch 10: 8 they found Saul and his s' fallen in 1121
12 of Saul, and the bodies of his s', “
11:34 The s' of Hashem the Gizonite, “
44 Shama and Jehiel the s' of Hothan “
46 and Joshaviah the s' of Elnaam, “
12: 3 the s' of Shemaah the Gibeathite; “
3 and Pelet, the s' of Azmaveth; “
7 the s' of Jeroham of Gedor. “
14 These were of the s' of Gad, “
14: 3 David begat more s' and daughters. “
15: 5 Of the s' of Kohath; Uriel the chief, “
6 the s' of Merari; Asaiah the chief, “
7 the s' of Gershom; Joel the chief, “
8 Of the s' of Elizaphan; Shemaiah “
9 Of the s' of Hebron; Eliel the chief, “
10 Of the s' of Uzziel; Amminadab the “
17 of the s' of Merari their brethren, “
16:42 the s' of Jeduthun were porters. “
17:11 after thee, which shall be of thy s'; “
18:17 s' of David were chief about the “
21:20 four s' with him hid themselves. “
23: 6 into courses among the s' of Levi, “
8 s' of Laadan; the chief was Jehiel, “
9 s' of Shimei; Shelomith, and Haziel, “
10 s' of Shimei were, Jahath, Zina, and “
10 These four were the s' of Shimei. “
11 Jeush and Beriah had not many s'; “
12 The s' of Kohath; Amram, Izhar, “
13 The s' of Amram; Aaron and Moses: “
13 holy things, he and his s' for ever, “
14 s' were named of the tribe of Levi “
15 The s' of Moses were, Gershom, and “
16 Of the s' of Gershom, Shebuel was “
17 the s' of Eliezer were, Rehabiah the “
17 And Eliezer had none other s'; but “
17 the s' of Rehabiah were very many. “
18 the s' of Izhar; Shelomith the chief. “
19 the s' of Hebron; Jeriah the first, “
20 Of the s' of Uzziel; Micah the first, “
21 The s' of Merari; Mahli, and Mushi. “
21 The s' of Mahli; Eleazar, and Kish. “
22 Eleazar died, and had no s', but “
22 brethren the s' of Kish took them. “
23 The s' of Mushi; Mahli, and Eder, “
24 These were the s' of Levi after the “
28 to wait on the s' of Aaron for the “
32 the charge of the s' of Aaron their “
24: 1 are the divisions of the s' of Aaron. “
1 The s' of Aaron; Nadab, and Abihu, “
3 both Zadok of the s' of Eleazar, and “
3 and Ahimelech of the s' of Ithamar, “
4 men found of the s' of Eleazar “
4 than of the s' of Ithamar; and thus “
4 Among the s' of Eleazar there were “
4 and eight among the s' of Ithamar “
5 of God, were of the s' of Eleazar, “
5 and of the s' of Ithamar. “
20 And the rest of the s' of Levi were “
20 Of the s' of Amram; Shubael: of “
20 of the s' of Shubael; Jehdeiah. “
21 of the s' of Rehabiah, the first was “
22 of the s' of Shelomoth; Jahath. “
23 the s' of Hebron; Jeriah the first, “
24 Of the s' of Uzziel; Michah: “
24 of the s' of Michah; Shamir. “
25 of the s' of Isshiah; Zechariah. “
26 s' of Merari were Mahli and Mushi: “
26 Mushi: the s' of Jaaziah; Beno. “
27 The s' of Merari by Jaaziah; Beno, “
28 Mahli came Eleazar, who had no s'. “
30 s' also of Mushi; Mahli, and Eder, “
30 were the s' of the Levites after the “
31 their brethren the s' of Aaron “
25: 1 of the s' of Asaph, and of Heman, “
2 the s' of Asaph; Zaccur, and Joseph, “
2 the s' of Asaph under the hands of “
3 the s' of Jeduthun; Gedaliah, and “
4 s' of Heman; Bukkiah, Mattaniah, “
5 All these were the s' of Heman the “
5 God gave to Heman fourteen s' and “
9 who with his brethren and s' were “
10 Zaccur, he, his s', and his brethren, “
11 to Izri, he, his s', and his brethren, “
12 to Nethaniah, he, his s', and his “
13 to Bukkiah, he, his s', and his “
14 to Jesharelah, he, his s', and his “
15 to Jeshaiah, he, his s', and his “
16 to Mattaniah, he, his s', and his “
17 Shimei, he, his s', and his brethren, “
18 Azareel, he, his s', and his brethren, “
19 to Hashabiah, he, his s', and his “
20 Shubael, he, his s', and his brethren, “
21 to Mattithiah, he, his s', and his “
22 to Jeremoth, he, his s', and his “
23 to Hananiah, he, his s', and his “
24 Joshbekashah, he, his s', and his “
25 Hanani, he, his s', and his brethren, “
26 to Mallothi, he, his s', and his “
27 to Eliathah, he, his s', and his “
28 Hothir, he, his s', and his brethren, “
29 to Giddalti, he, his s', and his “
30 to Mahazioth, he, his s', and his “
31 Romamti-ezer, he, his s', and his “
26: 1 the son of Kore, of the s' of Asaph. “
2 And the s' of Meshelemiah were, “
4 Moreover the s' of Obed-edom were, “
6 unto Shemaiah his son were s' born, “
7 The s' of Shemaiah; Othni, and “
8 All these of the s' of Obed-edom: “
8 they and their s' and their brethren, “
9 Meshelemiah had s' and brethren, “
10 of the children of Merari, had s'; “
11 all the s' and brethren of Hosah “
15 and to his s' the house of Asuppim. “
19 of the porters among the s' of Kore, “
19 and among the s' of Merari.

1Ch 26:21 As concerning the s' of Laadan; 1121
21 the s' of the Gershonite Laadan, “
22 The s' of Jehieli; Zetham, and Joel “
29 Chenaniah and his s' were for the “
27:32 Hachmoni was with the king's s': “
28: 1 possession of the king, and of his s', “
4 among the s' of my father he liked “
5 And of all my s', (for the Lord hath “
5 hath given me many s',) he hath “
29:24 and all the s' likewise of king David, “
2Ch 5:12 with their s' and their brethren, “
11:14 Jeroboam and his s' had cast them “
21 and begat twenty and eight s', and “
13: 5 to him and to his s' by a covenant “
8 Lord in the hand of the s' of David; “
9 the s' of Aaron, and the Levites, “
10 unto the Lord, are the s' of Aaron, “
21 and begat twenty and two s', and “
20:14 a Levite of the s' of Asaph, “
21: 2 had brethren the s' of Jehoshaphat, “
2 these were the s' of Jehoshaphat “
7 a light to him and to his s' for ever.* “
17 in the king's house, and his s' also. “
17 Jehoahaz, the youngest of his s'. “
22: 8 the s' of the brethren of Ahaziah, “
11 among the king's s' that were slain, “
23: 3 Lord hath said of the s' of David. “
11 Jehoiada and his s' anointed him, “
24: 3 and he begat s' and daughters. “
7 For the s' of Athaliah, that wicked “
25 for the blood of the s' of Jehoiada “
27 Now concerning his s', and the “
26:18 but to the priests the s' of Aaron, “
28: 8 women, s', and daughters, and took “
29: 9 our s' and our daughters and our “
11 My s', be not now negligent: for the “
12 Azariah, of the s' of the Kohathites: “
12 of the s' of Merari, Kish the son of “
13 And of the s' of Elizaphan; Shimri, “
13 and of the s' of Asaph; Zechariah, “
14 And of the s' of Heman; Jehiel, and “
14 of the s' of Jeduthun; Shemaiah, “
21 the s' of Aaron to offer them on the “
31:18 their wives, and their s', and their “
19 Also of the s' of Aaron the priests, “
32:33 of the sepulchres of the s' of David: “
34:12 the Levites, of the s' of Merari; “
12 of the s' of the Kohathites, “
35:14 priests the s' of Aaron were busied “
14 and for the priests the s' of Aaron. “
15 the singers the s' of Asaph were in “
36:20 servants to him and his s' until “
Ezr 3: 9 stood Jeshua with his s' and his “
9 Kadmiel and his s', the s' of Judah, “
9 the s' of Henadad, with their s' and “
10 and the Levites the s' of Asaph with “
6:10 the life of the king, and of his s'. 1123
7:23 the realm of the king and his s'? “
8: 2 Of the s' of Phinehas; Gershom: 1121
2 of the s' of Ithamar; Daniel: of the “
2 Daniel: of the s' of David; Hattush. “
3 Of the s' of Shechaniah, of the “
3 of the s' of Pharosh; Zechariah: “
4 s' of Pahath-moab; Elihoenai “
5 Of the s' of Shechaniah; the son of “
6 Of the s' also of Adin; Ebed the son “
7 And of the s' of Elam; Jeshaiah the “
8 of the s' of Shephatiah; Zebadiah “
9 Of the s' of Joab; Obadiah the son “
10 And of the s' of Shelomith; the son “
11 And of the s' of Bebai; Zechariah “
12 And of the s' of Azgad; Johanan the “
13 of the last s' of Adonikam, whose “
14 Of the s' also of Bigvai; Uthai, and “
15 found there none of the s' of Levi. “
18 of the s' of Mahli, the son of Levi, “
18 his s' and his brethren, eighteen; “
19 him Jeshaiah of the s' of Merari, “
19 his brethren and their s', twenty; “
9: 2 for themselves, and for their s': “
12 not your daughters unto their s', “
12 take their daughters unto your s', “
10: 2 one of the s' of Elam, answered and “
18 among the s' of the priests there “
18 of the s' of Jeshua the son of “
20 of the s' of Immer; Hanani, and “
21 of the s' of Harim; Maaseiah, and “
22 And of the s' of Pashur; Elioenai, “
25 of the s' of Parosh; Ramiah, and “
26 And of the s' of Elam; Mattaniah, “
27 And of the s' of Zattu; Elioenai, “
28 Of the s' also of Bebai; Jehohanan, “
29 And of the s' of Bani; Meshullam, “
30 of the s' of Pahath-moab; Adna, “
31 And of the s' of Harim; Eliezer, “
33 Of the s' of Hashum; Mattenai, “
34 Of the s' of Bani; Maadai, Amram, “
43 Of the s' of Nebo; Jeiel, Mattithiah, “
Ne 3: 3 gate did the s' of Hassenaah build, “
4:14 and fight for your brethren, your s', “
5: 2 We, our s', and our daughters, are “
5 we bring into bondage our s' and “
10: 9 Binnui of the s' of Henadad, “
28 their s', and their daughters, every “
30 nor take their daughters for our s': “
36 Also the firstborn of our s', and of “
11: 6 All the s' of Perez that dwelt at “
7 these are the s' of Benjamin; Sallu “
22 Of the s' of Asaph, the singers were “
12:23 The s' of Levi, the chief of the “
28 And the s' of the singers gathered “
35 of the priests' s' with trumpets; “
13:25 give your daughters unto their s', “
25 take their daughters unto your s', “
28 one of the s' of Joiada, the son of “
10 The ten s' of Haman the son of, “

Es 9:12 palace, and the ten s' of Haman; 1121
13 let Haman's ten s' be hanged upon "
14 and they hanged Haman's ten s'. "
25 he and his s' should be hanged on "
Job 1: 2 him seven s' and three daughters. "
4 his s' went and feasted in their "
5 It may be that my s' have sinned, "
6 when the s' of God came to present "
13 when his s' and his daughters were "
18 Thy s' and thy daughters were "
2: 1 when the s' of God came to present "
14:21 His s' came to honour, and he "
38: 7 all the s' of God shouted for joy? "
32 thou guide Arcturus with his s'? *
42:13 also seven s' and three daughters "
16 saw his s', and his sons' s', even "
Ps 4: 2 O ye s' of men, how long will ye "
31:19 trust in thee before the s' of men! "
33:13 he beholdeth all the s' of men. "
42: *title* Maschil, for the s' of Korah. "
44: *title* Musician for the s' of Korah, "
45: *title* Shoshannim, for the s' of Korah, "
46: *title* chief Musician for the s' of Korah, "
47: *title* A Psalm for the s' of Korah. "
48: *title* and Psalm for the s' of Korah "
49: *title* A Psalm for the s' of Korah. "
57: 4 even the s' of men, whose teeth are "
58: 1 judge uprightly, O ye s' of men? "
77:15 people, the s' of Jacob and Joseph "
84: *title* A Psalm for the s' of Korah. "
85: *title* A Psalm for the s' of Korah. "
87: *title* Psalm or Song for the s' of Korah. "
88: *title* Psalm for the s' of Korah, to the "
89: 6 who among the s' of the mighty can "
106:37 they sacrificed their s' and their "
38 even the blood of their s' and of "
144:12 That our s' may be as plants grown "
145:12 To make known to the s' of men "
Pr 8: 4 and my voice is to the s' of man. "
31 delights were with the s' of men. "
Ec 1:13 hath God given to the s' of man to "
2: 3 was that good for the s' of men, "
8 and the delights of the s' of men, "
3:10 God hath given to the s' of men "
18 concerning...estate of the s' of men, "
19 that which befalleth the s' of men "
8:11 heart of the s' of men is fully set in "
9: 3 heart of the s' of men is full of evil, "
12 so are the s' of men snared in an "
Ca 2: 3 so is my beloved among the s'. "
Isa 37:38 Adrammelech and Sharezer his s "
39: 7 thy s' that shall issue from thee. "
43: 6 bring my s' from far, and my "
45:11 things to come concerning my s', "
49:22 shall bring thy s' in their arms, "
51:18 none to guide her among all the s' "
18 taketh her by the hand of all the s' "
20 Thy s' have fainted, they lie at the "
52:14 his form more than the s' of men: "
56: 5 and a name better than of s' and "
6 Also the s' of the stranger, that * "
57: 3 ye s' of the sorceress, the seed of "
60: 4 thy s' shall come from far, and thy "
9 to bring thy s' from far, their silver "
10 the s' of strangers shall build up * "
14 s' also of them that afflicted thee "
61: 5 the s' of the alien shall be your * "
62: 5 virgin, so shall thy s' marry thee: "
8 s' of the stranger shall not drink * "
Jer 3:24 herds, their s' and their daughters. "
5:17 s' and thy daughters should eat: "
6:21 fathers and...s' together shall fall "
7:31 burn their s' and their daughters in "
11:22 s' and their daughters shall die by "
13:14 the fathers and the s' together, "
14:16 nor their s', nor their daughters: "
16: 2 shalt thou have s' or daughters in "
3 saith the Lord concerning the s' "
19: 5 to burn their s' with fire for burnt "
9 them to eat the flesh of their s' and "
29: 6 wives, and beget s' and daughters; "
6 and take wives for your s', and give "
6 they may bear s' and daughters, "
32:19 upon all the ways of the s' of men: "
35 their s' and their daughters to pass "
35: 3 his brethren, and all his s', and the "
4 the chamber of the s' of Hanan, the "
5 I set before the s' of the house of "
6 neither ye, nor your s' for ever: "
8 wives, our s', nor our daughters; "
14 commanded his s' not to drink wine, "
16 Because the s' of Jonadab the son "
39: 6 of Babylon slew the s' of Zedekiah "
40: 8 and Jonathan the s' of Kareah, "
8 the s' of Ephai the Netophathite, "
48:46 for thy s' are taken captives, and "
49: 1 Hath Israel no s'? hath he no heir? "
52:10 of Babylon slew the s' of Zedekiah "
La 4: 2 precious s' of Zion, comparable to "
Eze 5:10 the fathers shall eat the s' in the "
10 and the s' shall eat their fathers; "
14:16 deliver neither s' nor daughters; "
18 deliver neither s' nor daughters, "
22 forth, both s' and daughters: "
16:20 thou hast taken thy s' and thy "
20:31 your s' to pass through the fire, "
23: 4 and they bare s' and daughters. "
10 they took her s' and her daughters, "
25 shall take thy s' and thy daughters; "
37 have also caused their s', whom "
47 they shall slay their s' and their "
24:21 your s' and your daughters whom "
25 minds, their s' and their daughters, "
40:46 altar: these are the s' of Zadok "
46 among the s' of Levi, which come "
44:15 priests the Levites, the s' of Zadok, "
Eze 46:16 prince give a gift unto any of his s, 1121
18 he shall give his s' inheritance out "
48:11 are sanctified of the s' of Zadok; "
Da 5:21 he was driven from the s' of men, 1123
10:16 like the similitude of the s' of men 1121
11:10 But his s' shall be stirred up, and "
Ho 1:10 Ye are the s' of the living God. "
Joe 1:12 withered away from the s' of men. "
2:28 your s' and your daughters shall "
3: 8 will sell your s' and your daughters "
Am 2:11 I raised up of your s' for prophets, "
7:17 thy s' and thy daughters shall fall "
Mic 5: 7 man, nor waiteth for the s' of men "
Zec 9:13 and raised up thy s', O Zion, "
13 against thy s', O Greece, and made "
Mal 3: 3 and he shall purify the s' of Levi, "
6 ye s' of Jacob are not consumed. "
M't 20:20 of Zebedee's children with her s' 5207
21 Grant that these my two s' may sit, "
21:28 A certain man had two s'; and he 5043
26:37 Peter and the two s' of Zebedee, 5207
M'r 3:17 which is, The s' of thunder: "
28 shall be forgiven unto the s' of men, "
10:35 James and John, the s' of Zebedee, "
Lu 5:10 James, and John, the s' of Zebedee, "
11:19 by whom do your s' cast them out? "
15:11 he said, A certain man had two s': "
Joh 1:12 he power to become the s' of God, 5043
21: 2 the s' of Zebedee, and two other "
Ac 2:17 your s' and your daughters shall 5207
7:16 sum of money of the s' of Emmor "
29 of Madian, where he begat two s'. "
19:14 there were seven s' of one Sceva, "
Ro 8:14 Spirit of God, they are the s' of God. "
19 the manifestation of the s' of God. "
1 Co 4:14 but as my beloved s' I warn you. *5043
2 Co 6:18 ye shall be my s' and daughters, 5207
Ga 4: 5 might receive the adoption of s' 5206
6 because ye are s', God hath sent 5207
22 Abraham had two s', the one by a "
Eph 3: 5 not made known unto the s' of men, "
Ph'p 2:15 the s' of God, without rebuke, *5043
Heb 2:10 in bringing many s' unto glory, 5207
7: 5 they that are of the s' of Levi, who "
11:21 blessed both the s' of Joseph; and "
12: 7 God dealeth with you as with s'; "
8 then are ye bastards, and not s'. "
1 Jo 3: 1 we should be called the s' of God: *5043
2 Beloved, now are we the s' of God, * "

sons'
Ge 6:18 wife, and thy s' wives with thee. 1121
7: 7 his wife, and his s' wives with him. "
8:16 sons, and thy s' wives with thee. "
18 his wife, and his s' wives with him: "
46: 7 His sons, and his s' sons with him, "
7 his daughters, and his s' daughters, "
26 besides Jacob's s' wives, all the "
Ex 29:21 sons, and his s' garments with him. "
28 it shall be Aaron's and his s' by a * "
29 of Aaron shall be his s' after him, * "
39:41 and his s' garments, to minister in * "
Le 2: 3, 10 shall be Aaron's and his s': "
7:31 breast shall be Aaron's and his s'. "
8:27 hands, and upon his s' hands, * "
30 and upon his s' garments with him; "
30 sons, and his s' garments with him. "
10:13 it is thy due, and thy s' due, of the "
14 for they be thy due, and thy s' due, "
15 shall be thine, and thy s' with thee, "
24: 9 And it shall be Aaron's and his s'; * "
De 4: 9 them thy sons, and thy s' sons; * "
1Ch 8:40 and s' sons, an hundred and fifty. "
Job 42:16 his s' sons, even four generations. "
Eze 46:16 inheritance thereof shall be his s'; * "
17 but his inheritance shall be his s' * "

soon see also SOONER.
Ge 18:33 as s' as he had left communing 834
27:30 as s' as Isaac had made an end of "
44: 3 As s' as the morning was light, the "
Ex 2:18 How is it that ye are come so s' 4116
9:29 As s' as I am gone out of the city, I "
32:19 as s' as he came nigh unto the camp, 834
De 4:26 ye shall s' utterly perish from off 4116
Jos 2: 7 as s' as they which pursued after 834
11 And as s' as we had heard these "
3:13 as s' as the soles of the feet of the * "
8:19 as s' as he had stretched out his hand: "
29 and as s' as the sun was down, Joshua * "
J'g 8:33 to pass, as s' as Gideon was dead, 834
9:33 as s' as the sun is up, thou shalt rise "
1Sa 9:13 As s' as ye be come into the city, ye "
13:10 that as s' as he had made an end of "
20:41 And as s' as the lad was gone, David "
29:10 and as s' as ye be up early in the "
2Sa 6:18 And as s' as David had made an end * "
13:36 as s' as he had made an end of "
15:10 As s' as ye hear the sound of the "
22:45 as s' as they hear, they shall be "
1Ki 16:11 as s' as he sat on his throne, that he "
18:12 pass, as s' as I am gone up from thee, "
20:36 as s' as thou art departed from me, "
36 as s' as he was departed from him, "
2Ki 10: 2 Now as s' as this letter cometh to you, "
25 as s' as he had made an end of offering "
14: 5 as s' as the kingdom was confirmed 834
2Ch 31: 5 as s' as the commandment came "
Job 32:22 my maker would s' take me away. 4592
Ps 18:44 s' as they hear of me, they shall obey "
37: 2 shall s' be cut down like the grass, 4120
58: 3 go astray as s' as they be born, "
68:31 Ethiopia shall s' stretch out her *7323
81:14 s' have subdued their enemies, 4592
90:10 for it is s' cut off, and we fly away. 2440
106:13 They s' forgat his works; they 4116
Pr 14:17 that is s' angry dealeth foolishly: 7116
Isa 66: 8 s' as Zion travailed, she brought 1571
Eze 23:16 s' as she saw them with her eyes, 4758
M't 21:20 How s' is the fig tree withered *3916
M'r 1:42 And as s' as he had spoken, *
5:36 As s' as Jesus heard the word that *2112
11: 2 and as s' as ye be entered into it, ye * "
14:45 And as s' as he was come, he goeth * "
Lu 1:23 s' as the days of his ministration *
44 as s' as the voice of thy salutation *
8: 6 s' as it was sprung up, it withered
15:30 as s' as this thy son was come, *3753
22:66 And as s' as it was day, the elders
23: 7 And as s' as he knew that he belonged *
Joh 11:20 as s' as she heard that Jesus was *
29 As s' as she heard that, she arose *
16:21 but as s' as she is delivered of the 3752
18: 6 As s' then as he had said unto *
21: 9 As s' then as they were come to *
Ac 10:29 gainsaying, as s' as I was sent for: *
12:18 as s' as it was day, there was no 1096
Ga 1: 6 ye are so s' removed from him 5030
Ph'p 2:23 so s' as I shall see how it will go
2Th 2: 2 That ye be not s' shaken in mind, *5030
Tit 1: 7 not s' angry, not given to wine, no 3711
Re 10:10 as s' as I had eaten it, my belly *3753
12: 4 for to devour her child as s' as it *3752

sooner
Heb 13:19 I may be restored to you the s'. 5032

sooth See FORSOOTH; SOOTHSAYER.

soothsayer See also SOOTHSAYERS.
Jos 13:22 Balaam also the son of Beor, the s'. 7080

soothsayers
Isa 2: 6 and are s' like the Philistines, and 6049
Da 2:27 the s', shew unto the king; 1505
4: 7 the Chaldeans, and the s': and I "
5: 7 the Chaldeans, and the s'. "
11 astrologers, Chaldeans, and s'; "
Mic 5:12 and thou shalt have no more s': 6049

soothsaying
Ac 16:16 her masters much gain by s': 3132

sop
Joh 13:26 He it is, to whom I shall give a s', 5596
26 when he had dipped the s', he gave "
27 after the s' Satan entered into him. "
30 He then having received the s' "

Sopater (*so'-pa-tur*) See also SOSIPATER.
Ac 20: 4 accompanied him into Asia S' of 4986

sope
Jer 2:22 and take thee much s', yet thine 1287
Mal 3: 2 refiner's fire, and like fullers' s': "

Sophereth (*so-fe'-reth*)
Ezr 2:55 of Sotai, the children of S', the *5618
Ne 7:57 of Sotai, the children of S', the "

sorcerer See also SORCERERS; SORCERESS.
Ac 13: 6 they found a certain s', a false 3097
8 But Elymas the s' (for so is his "

sorcerers
Ex 7:11 called the wise men and the s': 3784
Jer 27: 9 nor to your s', which speak unto 3786
Da 2: 2 and the s', and the Chaldeans, for 3784
Mal 3: 5 be a swift witness against the s', "
Re 21: 8 and whoremongers, and s', and 5332
22:15 For without are dogs, and s', and 5333

sorceress
Isa 57: 3 near hither, ye sons of the s', 6049

sorceries
Isa 47: 9 for the multitude of thy s', and 3785
12 and with the multitude of thy s', "
Ac 8:11 he had bewitched them with s'. 3095
Re 9:21 of their murders, nor of their s', 5331
18:23 by thy s' were all nations deceived. * "

sorcery See also SORCERIES.
Ac 8: 9 beforetime in the same city used s', 3096

sore See also SORER; SORES.
Ge 19: 9 And they pressed s' upon the man, 3966
20: 8 ears: and the men were s' afraid. "
31:30 thou s' longedst after thy father's "
34:25 when they were s', that two of 3510
41:56 the famine waxed s' in the land of 2388
57 the famine was so s' in all lands. "
43: 1 And the famine was s' in the land. 3515
47: 4 famine is s' in the land of Canaan: "
13 the famine was very s', so that the "
50:10 a great and very s' lamentation: "
Ex 14:10 them; and they were s' afraid: 3966
Le 13:42 bald forehead, a white reddish s'; *5061
43 rising of the s' be white reddish * "
Nu 22: 3 Moab was s' afraid of the people, 3966
De 6:22 signs and wonders, great and s', 7451
28:35 a s' botch that cannot be healed, "
59 and s' sicknesses, and of long "
Jos 9:24 we were s' afraid of our lives 3966
J'g 10: 9 so that Israel was s' distressed. "
14:17 her, because she lay s' upon him: "
15:18 And he was s' athirst, and called 3966
20:34 all Israel, and the battle was s': 3513
21: 2 up their voices, and wept s'; 1065, 1419
1Sa 1: 6 adversary also provoked her s', 3708
10 prayed unto the Lord, and wept s'. "
5: 7 his hand is s' upon us, and upon 7185
14:52 was s' war against the Philistines 2389
17:24 fled from him, and were s' afraid. 3966
21:12 was s' afraid of Achish the king of "
28:15 Saul answered, I am s' distressed; "
20 on the earth, and was s' afraid, "
21 and saw that he was s' troubled, "
31: 3 the battle went s' against Saul, 3513
3 he was s' wounded of the archers. *3966
4 would not; for he was s' afraid. "

2Sa 2:17 there was a very s· battle that day; 7188
13:36 and all his servants wept very s·. 1419
1Ki 17:17 and his sickness was so s·, that 2389
18: 2 there was a s· famine in Samaria. "
2Ki 3:26 that the battle was too s· for him, 2388
6:11 king of Syria was s· troubled for this
20: 3 thy sight. And Hezekiah wept s·. 1419
1Ch 10: 3 the battle went s· against Saul, 3513
4 would not; for he was s· afraid. 3966
2Ch 6:28 whatsoever s· or whatsoever *5061
29 one shall know his own s· and his* "
21:19 so he died of s· diseases. And his 7451
28:19 and transgressed s· against the Lord.
35:23 me away; for I am s· wounded. 3966
Ezr 10: 1 for the people wept very s·.
Ne 2: 2 of heart. Then I was very s· afraid, 7235
13: 8 it grieved me s·: therefore I cast 3966
Job 2: 7 smote Job with s· boils from the 7451
5:18 For he maketh s·, and bindeth up: 3510
Ps 2: 5 and vex them in his s· displeasure.
6: 3 My soul is also s· vexed: but thou, 3966
10 enemies be ashamed and s· vexed: "
38: 2 in me, and thy hand presseth me s·.
8 I am feeble and s· broken: I 5704, 3966
11 friends stand aloof from my s·; *5061
44:19 s· broken us in the place of dragons,
55: 4 My heart is s· pained within me: and
71:20 shewed me great and s· troubles, 7451
77: 2 my s· ran in the night, and ceased *3027
118:13 Thou hast thrust s· at me that I might
18 The Lord hath chastened me s·: but
Ec 1:13 this s· travail hath God given to 7451
4: 8 is also vanity, yea, it is a s· travail. "
5:13 a s· evil which I have seen under *2470
16 this also is a s· evil, that in all * "
Isa 27: 1 his s· and great and strong sword 7186
38: 3 sight. And Hezekiah wept s·. 1419
59:11 like bears, and mourn s· like doves:
64: 9 Be not wroth very s·, O Lord, 3966
12 thy peace, and afflict us very s·?
Jer 13:17 and mine eye shall weep s·, and run
22:10 but weep s· for him that goeth away:
50:12 mother shall be s· confounded; ‡3966
52: 6 the famine was s· in the city, so 2388
La 1: 2 She weepeth s· in the night, and her
3:52 Mine enemies chased me s·, like a
Eze 14:21 I send my four s· judgments upon 7451
21:10 sharpened to make a s· slaughter;*
27:35 and their kings shall be s· afraid, *8178
Da 6:14 was s· displeased with himself, 7690
Mic 2:10 you, even with a s· destruction. *4834
Zec 1: 2 s· displeased with your fathers.
15 very s· displeased with the heathen
M't 17: 6 on their face, and were s· afraid. 4970
15 for he is lunatick, and s· vexed: *2560
21:15 of David; they were s· displeased,* 23
M'r 6:51 were s· amazed in themselves 3029
9: 6 to say; for they were s· afraid. 1630
26 the spirit cried, and rent him s·, *4183
14:33 began to be s· amazed, and to be *1568
Lu 2: 9 them: and they were s· afraid. 3173
Ac 20:37 they all wept s·, and fell on Paul's 2425
Re 16: 2 fell a noisome and grievous s· upon 1668

Sorek (*so'-rek*)
J'g 16: 4 loved a woman in the valley of S·, 7796

sorely
Ge 49:23 The archers have s· grieved him, 4843
Isa 23: 5 they be s· pained at the report of Tyre.

sorer
Heb 10:29 Of how much s· punishment, 5501

sores
Isa 1: 6 and bruises, and putrifying s·: 4347
Lu 16:20 was laid at his gate, full of s·, 1669
21 the dogs came and licked his s·. 1668
Re 16:11 because of their pains and their s·, "

sorrow See also SORROWED; SORROWETH; SORROWFUL; SORROWING; SORROWS.
Ge 3:16 said, I will greatly multiply thy s· 6093
16 in s· shalt thou bring forth 6089
17 in s· shalt thou eat of it all the 6093
42:38 my gray hairs with s· to the grave. 3015
44:29 my gray hairs with s· to the grave. 7451
31 our father with s· to the grave. 3015
Ex 15:14 s·...take hold on the inhabitants *2427
Le 26:16 the eyes, and cause s· of heart: *1727
De 28:65 failing of eyes, and s· of mind: *1671
1Ch 4: 9 Because I bare him with s·. 6090
Ne 2: 2 this is nothing else but s· of heart. 7455
Es 9:22 turned unto them from s· to joy, 3015
Job 3:10 womb, nor hid s· from mine eyes. *5999
6:10 yea, I would harden myself in s·: *2427
17: 7 eye also is dim by reason of s·, 3708
41:22 s· is turned into joy before him. *1670
Ps 13: 2 soul, having s· in my heart daily? 3015
38:17 my s· is continually before me. 4341
39: 2 from good; and my s· was stirred. 3511
55:10 mischief...and s· are in the midst *5999
90:10 yet is their strength labour and s·; 205
107:39 oppression, affliction, and s·. 3015
116: 3 upon me: I found trouble and s·. "
Pr 10:10 winketh with the eye causeth s·: 6094
22 rich, and he addeth no s· with it. 6089
15:13 but by s· of the heart the spirit is 6094
17:21 begetteth a fool doeth it to his s·: 8424
23:29 Who hath woe? who hath s·? who 17
Ec 1:18 knowledge increaseth s·. 4341
5:17 s· and wrath with his sickness. *3708
7: 3 S· is better than laughter: for by "
11:10 Therefore remove s· from thy heart, "
Isa 5:30 the land, behold darkness and s·, *6862
14: 3 shall give thee rest from thy s·, 6090
17:11 day of grief and of desperate s·. 3511
29: 2 there shall be heaviness and s·: * 592
35:10 and s· and sighing shall flee away. 3015
50:11 mine hand; ye shall lie down in s·. 4620
51:11 s· and mourning shall flee away. 3015
65:14 but ye shall cry for s· of heart, and 3511
Jer 8:18 I would comfort myself against s·, 3015
20:18 of the womb to see labour and s·, "
30:15 s· is incurable for the multitude *4341
31:12 they shall not s· any more at all. 1669
13 make them rejoice from their s·. 3015
45: 3 Lord hath added grief to my s·; *4341
49:23 there is s· on the sea; it cannot be 1674
51:29 And the land shall tremble and s·: *2342
La 1:12 if there be any s· like unto my s·, 4341
18 you, all people, and behold my s·: "
3:65 Give them s· of heart, thy curse *4044
Eze 23:33 be filled with drunkenness and s·, 3015
Ho 8:10 they shall s· a little for the burden *2490
Lu 22:45 he found them sleeping for s·, 3077
Joh 16: 6 unto you, s· hath filled your heart. "
20 but your s· shall be turned into joy. "
21 when she is in travail hath s·, "
22 And ye now therefore have s·: but I "
Ro 9: 2 and continual s· in my heart. *3601
2Co 2: 3 s· from them of whom I ought to 3077
7 be swallowed up with overmuch s·. "
7:10 For godly s· worketh repentance to "
10 the s· of the world worketh death. "
Ph'p 2:27 also, lest I should have s· upon s·. "
1Th 4:13 that ye s· not, even as others which 3076
Re 18: 7 so much torment and s· give her: *3997
7 am no widow, and shall see no s·.* "
21: 4 neither s·, nor crying, neither shall* "

sorrowed
2Co 7: 9 sorry, but that ye s· to repentance: *3076
11 thing, that ye s· after a godly sort, * "

sorroweth
1Sa 10: 2 s· for you, saying, What shall I ††1672

sorrowful
1Sa 1:15 lord, I am a woman of a s· spirit: 7186
Job 6: 7 refused to touch are as my s· meat. *1741
Ps 69:29 But I am poor and s·: let thy 3510
Pr 14:13 Even in laughter the heart is s·; "
Jer 31:25 I have replenished every s· soul. 1669
Zep 3:18 are s· for the solemn assembly, *3013
Zec 9: 5 also shall see it, and be very s·, *2342
M't 19:22 that saying, he went away s·: for 3076
26:22 they were exceeding s·, and began "
37 and began to be s· and very heavy. "
38 My soul is exceeding s·, even unto 4036
M'r 14:19 And they began to be s·, and to say 3076
34 My soul is exceeding s· unto death: 4036
Lu 18:23 when he heard this, he was very s·: "
24 when Jesus saw that he was very s·, * "
Joh 16:20 and ye shall be s·, but your sorrow 3076
2Co 6:10 As s·, yet alway rejoicing; as poor, "
Ph'p 2:28 and that I may be the less s·. 253

sorrowing
Lu 2:48 father and I have sought thee s·. 3600
Ac 20:38 S· most of all for the words which "

sorrows
Ex 3: 7 taskmasters; for I know their s·; 4341
2Sa 22: 6 s· of hell compassed me about; *2256
Job 9:28 I am afraid of all my s·, I know 6094
21:17 God distributeth s· in his anger. 2256
39: 3 young ones, they cast out their s·. "
Ps 16: 4 Their s· shall be multiplied that 6094
18: 4 The s· of death compassed me, *2256
5 s· of hell compassed me about: * "
32:10 Many s· shall be to the wicked: but 4341
116: 3 The s· of death compassed me, *2256
127: 2 sit up late, to eat the bread of s·: *6089
Ec 2:23 all his days are s·, and his travail 4341
Isa 13: 8 and s· shall take hold of them; 2256
53: 3 a man of s·, and acquainted with 4341
4 our griefs, and carried our s·: "
Jer 13:21 shall not s· take thee, as a woman 2256
49:24 anguish and s· have taken her, as a "
Da 10:16 vision my s· are turned upon me, 6735
Ho 13:13 The s· of a travailing woman shall 2256
M't 24: 8 All these are the beginning of s·. *5604
M'r 13: 8 these are the beginnings of s·. * "
1Ti 6:10 themselves through with many s·. 3601

sorry
1Sa 22: 8 is none of you that is s· for me, 2470
Ne 8:10 neither be ye s·; for the joy of the *6087
Ps 38:18 iniquity; I will be s· for my sin. 1672
Isa 51:19 thee; who shall be s· for thee? *5110
M't 14: 9 And the king was s·: nevertheless *3076
17:23 again. And they were exceeding s·. "
18:31 what was done, they were very s·, "
M'r 6:26 And the king was exceeding s·; 4036
2Co 2: 2 For if I make you s·, who is he 3076
2 the same which is made s· by me? "
7: 8 though I made you s· with a letter, "
8 the same epistle hath made you s·, "
9 rejoice, not that ye were made s·, "
9 were made s· after a godly manner, "

sort See also CONSORTED; RESORT; SORTS.
Ge 6:19 two of every s· shalt thou bring into
20 two of every s· shall come unto thee,
7:14 his kind, every bird of every s·. 3671
2Ki 24:14 save the poorest s· of the people
1Ch 24: 5 were divided by lot, one s· with another;
29:14 able to offer so willingly after this s·?
2Ch 30: 5 long time in such s· as it was written.
Ezr 1:10 silver basons of a second s· four
4: 8 to Artaxerxes the king in this s·: 3660
Ne 6: 4 unto me four times after this s·; 1697
Eze 39: 4 unto the ravenous birds of every s·, 3671
44:30 of every s· of your oblations, shall be* "
Da 1:10 children which are of your s·? *1524
3:29 God that can deliver after this s·.
Ac 17: 5 certain lewd fellows of the baser s·, *
Ro 15:15 more boldly unto you in some s·, *3313
1Co 3:13 every man's work of what s· it is. 3697
2Co 7:11 that ye sorrowed after a godly s·, what
2Ti 3: 6 For of this s· are they which creep into*
3Jo 6 on their journey after a godly s·, * 516

sorts
De 22:11 shalt not wear a garment of divers s·, *
Ne 5:18 in ten days store of all s· of wine:
Ps 78:45 He sent divers s· of flies among them, *
105:31 spake, and there came divers s· of flies, *
Ec 2: 8 musical instruments, and that of all s·. *
Eze 27:24 thy merchants in all s· of things, *4360
38: 4 clothed with all s· of armour, *4358

Sosipater (*so-sip'-a-tur*) See also SOPATER.
Ro 16:21 and S·, my kinsmen, salute you. 4989

Sosthenes (*sos'-the-neze*)
Ac 18:17 Greeks took S·, the chief ruler 4988
1Co 1: 1 will of God, and S· our brother, "

Sotai (*so'-tahee*)
Ezr 2:55 the children of S·, the children of 5479
Ne 7:57 the children of S·, the children of "

sottish
Jer 4:22 they are s· children, and they 5530

sought See also BESOUGHT.
Ge 43:30 and he s· where to weep; and he 1245
Ex 2:15 this thing, he s· to slay Moses. "
4:19 the men are dead which s· thy life. "
24 Lord met him, and s· to kill him. "
33: 7 every one which s· the Lord went "
Le 10:16 Moses diligently s· the goat of the 1875
Nu 35:23 his enemy, neither s· his harm: 1245
De 13:10 he hath s· to thrust thee away from "
Jos 2:22 the pursuers s· them throughout "
J'g 14: 4 that he s· an occasion against the "
18: 1 the Danites s· them an inheritance "
1Sa 10:21 when they s· him, he could not be "
13:14 Lord hath s· him a man after his "
14: 4 by which Jonathan s· to go over "
19:10 Saul s· to smite David even to the "
23:14 And Saul s· him every day, but God "
27: 4 and he s· no more again for him. "
2Sa 3:17 Ye s· for David in times past to be "
4: 8 Saul thine enemy, which s· thy life; "
17:20 they had s· and could not find them, "
21: 2 and Saul s· to slay them in his zeal "
1Ki 1: 2 Let there be s· for my lord the king "
3 So they s· for a fair damsel "
10:24 And all the earth s· to Solomon, "
11:40 Solomon s·...to kill Jeroboam. "
2Ki 2:17 s· three days, but found him not. "
1Ch 15:13 we s· him not after the due order. 1875
26:31 the reign of David they were s· for, "
2Ch 1: 5 and the congregation s· unto it. "
9:23 earth s· the presence of Solomon, 1245
14: 7 we have s· the Lord our God, 1875
7 we have s· him, and he hath given "
15: 4 and s· him, he was found of them. 1245
15 and s· him with their whole desire; "
16:12 his disease he s· not to the Lord, 1875
17: 3 David, and s· not unto Baalim; "
4 s· to the Lord God of his father, "
22: 9 he s· Ahaziah: and they caught 1245
9 who s· the Lord with all his heart. 1875
25:15 s· after the gods of the people, "
20 they s· after the gods of Edom. "
26: 5 he s· God in the days of Zechariah, * "
5 as long as he s· the Lord, God made "
Ezr 2:62 These s· their register among 1245
Ne 7:64 These s· their register among those "
12:27 they s· the Levites out of all their "
Es 2: 2 fair young virgins s· for the king, "
21 s· to lay hand on...king Ahasuerus. "
3: 6 Haman s· to destroy all the Jews "
6: 2 s· to lay hand on...king Ahasuerus. "
9: 2 lay hand on such as s· their hurt: "
Ps 34: 4 I s· the Lord, and he heard me, 1875
37:36 I s· him, but he could not be found. 1245
77: 2 day of my trouble I s· the Lord: 1875
78:34 he slew them, then they s· him: * "
86:14 violent men have s· after my soul; 1245
111: 2 s· out of all...that have pleasure 1875
119:10 my whole heart have I s· thee: "
94 save me; for I have s· thy precepts. "
Ec 2: 3 I s· in mine heart to give myself *8446
7:29 they have s· out many inventions. 1245
12: 9 and s· out, and set in order many 2713
10 s· to find out acceptable words: 1245
Ca 3: 1 bed I s· him whom my soul loveth: "
1 I s· him, but I found him not. "
5: 6 I s· him, but I could not find him; "
Isa 62:12 called, S· out, A city not forsaken. 1875
65: 1 I am s· of them that asked not for * "
1 am found of them that s· me not: 1245
10 in, for my people that have s· me. 1875
Jer 8: 2 whom they have s·, and whom they "
10:21 brutish, and have not s· the Lord: * "
26:21 the king s· to put him to death: 1245
44:30 his enemy, and that s· his life. "
50:20 iniquity of Israel shall be s· for, "
La 1:19 while they s· their meat to relieve "
Eze 22:30 And I s· for a man among them, "
26:21 though thou be s· for, yet shalt "
34: 4 neither have ye s· that which was "
Da 2:13 they s· Daniel and his fellows to 1158
4:36 and my lords s· unto me; and I was "
6: 4 s· to find occasion against Daniel "
8:15 the vision, and s· for the meaning, 1245
Ob 6 how are his hidden things s· up! 1156
Zep 1: 6 those that have not s· the Lord, 1245
Zec 6: 7 and s· to go that they might walk "
M't 2:20 which s· the young child's life. 2212
21:46 when they s· to lay hands on him, "
26:16 he s· opportunity to betray him. "

M't 26: 59 s· false witness against Jesus, to 2212
M'r 11: 18 and s· how they might destroy him: "
12: 12 And they s· to lay hold on him, but "
14: 1 scribes s· how they might take him "
11 he s· how he might conveniently "
55 council s· for witness against Jesus "
Lu 2: 44 they s· him among their kinsfolk 327
48 and I have s· thee sorrowing. 2212
49 unto them, How is it that ye s· me? "
4: 42 the people s· him, and came unto "
5: 18 and they s· means to bring him in, "
6: 19 whole multitude s· to touch him: "
11: 16 him, s· of him a sign from heaven. "
13: 6 and he came and s· fruit thereon, "
19: 3 And he s· to see Jesus who he was; "
47 of the people s· to destroy him, "
20: 19 same hour s· to lay hands on him; "
22: 2 scribes s· how they might kill him; "
6 s· opportunity to betray him unto "
Joh 5: 16 persecute Jesus, and s· to slay him,* "
18 the Jews s· the more to kill him, "
7: 1 because the Jews s· to kill him. "
11 Then the Jews s· him at the feast, "
30 Then they s· to take him: but no "
10: 39 they s· again to take him: but he "
11: 8 the Jews of late s· to stone thee; * "
56 Then s· they for Jesus, and spake "
19: 12 thenceforth Pilate s· to release him: "
Ac 12: 19 And when Herod had s· for him, 1934
17: 5 s· to bring them out to the people. 2212
Ro 9: 32 Because they s· it not by faith, but "
10: 20 I was found of them that s· me not; "
1Th 2: 6 Nor of men s· we glory, neither of* "
2Ti 1: 17 he s· me out very diligently, and "
Heb 8: 7 then should no place have been s· "
12: 17 though he s· it carefully with tears. 1567
soul See also SOUL'S; SOULS.
Ge 2: 7 life; and man became a living s·. 5315
12: 13 and my s· shall live because of thee. "
17: 14 that s· shall be cut off from his "
19: 20 a little one?) and my s· shall live. "
27: 4 my s· may bless thee before I die. "
19 venison, that thy s· may bless me. "
25 venison, that my s· may bless thee. "
31 venison, that thy s· may bless me. "
34: 3 And his s· clave unto Dinah the "
8 The s· of my son Shechem longeth "
35: 18 as her s· was in departing, (for she "
42: 21 that we saw the anguish of his s·, "
49: 6 O my s·, come not thou into their "
Ex 12: 15 that s· shall be cut off from Israel. "
19 even that s· shall be cut off from the "
30: 12 give every man a ransom for his s· "
31: 14 that s· shall be cut off from among "
Le 4: 2 If a s· shall sin through ignorance* "
5: 1 And if a s· sin, and hear the voice* "
2 Or if a s· touch any unclean thing,* "
4 Or if a s· swear, pronouncing with* "
15 If a s· commit a trespass, and sin* "
17 And if a s· sin, and commit any of* "
6: 2 If a s· sin, and commit a trespass* "
7: 18 the s· that eateth of it shall bear his "
20 the s· that eateth of the flesh of the "
20 even that s· shall be cut off from "
21 the s· that shall touch any unclean* "
21 even that s· shall be cut off from his "
25 the s· that eateth it shall be cut off "
27 Whatsoever s· it be that eateth any* "
27 even that s· shall be cut off from his "
17: 10 will even set my face against that s· "
11 maketh an atonement for the s·. * "
12 No s· of you shall eat blood, neither "
15 every s· that eateth that which died "
19: 8 that s· shall be cut off from among "
20: 6 the s· that turneth after such as "
6 even set my face against that s·, "
22: 3 that s· shall be cut off from my "
6 The s· which hath touched any such "
11 But if the priest buy any s· with his "
23: 29 whatsoever s· it be that shall not be "
30 whatsoever s· it be that doeth any "
30 same s· will I destroy from among "
26: 11 and my s· shall not abhor you. "
15 or if your s· abhor my judgments, "
30 idols, and my s· shall abhor you. "
43 their s· abhorred my statutes. "
Nu 9: 13 same s· shall be cut off from among "
11: 6 But now our s· is dried away: there "
15: 27 if any s· sin through ignorance, * "
28 make an atonement for the s· that "
30 But the s· that doeth ought "
30 that s· shall be cut off from among "
31 that s· shall utterly be cut off; "
19: 13 that s· shall be cut off from Israel: "
20 that s· shall be cut off from among "
22 s· that toucheth it shall be unclean "
21: 4 and the s· of the people was much "
5 and our s· loatheth this light bread. "
30: 2 an oath to bind his s· with a bond; "
4 wherewith she hath bound her s·, "
4 wherewith she hath bound her s· "
5 wherewith she hath bound her s·, "
6 lips, wherewith she bound her s·, "
7 bonds wherewith she bound her s· "
8 lips, wherewith she bound her s·, "
10 bound her s· by a bond with an oath; "
11 bond wherewith she bound her s· "
12 or concerning the bond of her s·, "
13 every binding oath to afflict the s·, "
31: 28 one s· of five hundred, both of the "
De 4: 9 and keep thy s· diligently, lest thou "
29 with all thy heart and with all thy s·. "
6: 5 all thine heart, and with all thy s·, "
10: 12 with all thy heart and with all thy s·, "
11: 13 all your heart and with all your s·, "
18 words in your heart and in your s·, "
De 12: 15 whatsoever thy s· lusteth after, 5315
20 because thy s· longeth to eat flesh; "
20, 21 whatsoever thy s· lusteth after. "
13: 3 all your heart and with all your s·. "
6 friend, which is as thine own s·, "
14: 26 for whatsoever thy s· lusteth after, "
26 or for whatsoever thy s· desireth: "
26: 16 all thine heart, and with all thy s·. "
30: 2 all thine heart, and with all thy s·; "
6 all thine heart, and with all thy s·, "
10 all thine heart, and with all thy s·. "
Jos 22: 5 all your heart and with all your s·. "
J'g 5: 21 O my s·, thou hast trodden down "
10: 16 his s· was grieved for the misery of "
16: 16 so that his s· was vexed unto death; "
1Sa 1: 10 And she was in bitterness of s·, and "
15 poured out my s· before the Lord. "
26 as thy s· liveth, my lord, I am the "
2: 16 take as much as thy s· desireth; "
17: 55 As thy s· liveth, O king, I cannot "
18: 1 that the s· of Jonathan was knit "
1 was knit with the s· of David, "
1 Jonathan loved him as his own s·. "
3 because he loved him as his own s·. "
20: 3 as thy s· liveth, there is but a step "
4 Whatsoever thy s· desireth, I will "
17 he loved him as he loved his own s·. "
23: 20 according to all the desire of thy s· "
24: 11 yet thou huntest my s· to take it. ‡ "
25: 26 and as thy s· liveth, seeing the Lord "
29 to pursue thee, and to seek thy s·: "
29 s· of my lord shall be bound in the "
26: 21 my s· was precious in thine eyes * "
30: 6 the s· of all the people was grieved, "
2Sa 4: 9 who hath redeemed my s· out of all "
5: 8 blind, that are hated of David's s·, "
11: 11 as thy s· liveth, I will not do this "
13: 39 the s· of king David longed to go forth
14: 19 As thy s· liveth, my lord the king, 5315
1Ki 1: 29 redeemed my s· out of all distress, "
2: 4 all their heart and with all their s·, "
8: 48 all their heart, and with all their s·, "
11: 37 according to all that thy s· desireth, "
17: 21 let this child's s· come into him "
22 the s· of the child came into him, "
2Ki 2: 2, 4, 6 Lord liveth, and as thy s· liveth, "
4: 27 for her s· is vexed within her: "
30 Lord liveth, and as thy s· liveth, "
23: 3 with all their heart and all their s·, "
25 all his heart, and with all his s·, "
1Ch 22: 19 set your heart and your s· to seek "
2Ch 6: 38 all their heart and with all their s· "
15: 12 all their heart and with all their s·; "
34: 31 all his heart, and with all his s·, "
Job 3: 20 and life unto the bitter in s·; "
6: 7 things that my s· refused to touch "
7: 11 complain in the bitterness of my s·. "
15 So that my s· chooseth strangling, "
9: 21 yet would I not know my s·: "
10: 1 My s· is weary of my life; I will "
1 speak in the bitterness of my s·. "
12: 10 hand is the s· of every living thing, "
14: 22 and his s· within him shall mourn. "
16: 4 if your s· were in my soul's stead, I "
19: 2 How long will ye vex my s·, and "
21: 25 dieth in the bitterness of his s·, and "
23: 13 and what his s· desireth, even that "
24: 12 the s· of the wounded crieth out: "
27: 2 Almighty, who hath vexed my s·; "
8 when God taketh away his s·? "
30: 15 they pursue my s· as the wind: *5082
16 now my s· is poured out upon me; 5315
25 was not my s· grieved for the poor? "
31: 30 to sin by wishing a curse to his s·.* "
33: 18 keepeth back his s· from the pit, "
20 bread, and his s· dainty meat. "
22 his s· draweth near unto the grave, "
28 He will deliver his s· from going "
30 To bring back his s· from the pit, "
Ps 3: 2 Many there be which say of my s·, "
6: 3 My s· is also sore vexed: but thou, "
4 Return, O Lord, deliver my s·: O "
7: 2 Lest he tear my s· like a lion, "
5 Let the enemy persecute my s·, "
11: 1 how say ye to my s·, Flee as a bird "
5 that loveth violence his s· hateth. "
13: 2 long shall I take counsel in my s·, "
16: 2 O my s·, thou hast said unto the Lord,*
10 thou wilt not leave my s· in hell; 5315
17: 13 deliver my s· from the wicked, "
19: 7 Lord is perfect, converting the s·: "
22: 20 Deliver my s· from the sword; my "
29 and none can keep alive his own s·. "
23: 3 He restoreth my s·: he leadeth me "
24: 4 not lifted up his s· unto vanity, "
25: 1 thee, O Lord, do I lift up my s·. "
13 His s· shall dwell at ease; and his "
20 O keep my s·, and deliver me: let "
26: 9 Gather not my s· with sinners, nor "
30: 3 brought up my s· from the grave: "
31: 7 hast known my s· in adversities; "
9 with grief, yea, my s· and my belly. "
33: 19 To deliver their s· from death, and "
20 Our s· waiteth for the Lord: he is "
34: 2 My s· shall make her boast in the "
22 The Lord redeemeth the s· of his "
35: 3 say unto my s·, I am thy salvation. "
4 put to shame that seek after my s·: "
7 cause they have digged for my s·. "
9 my s· shall be joyful in the Lord: "
12 evil for good to the spoiling of my s·. "
13 I humbled my s· with fasting; and "
17 rescue my s· from...destructions, "
40: 14 that seek after my s· to destroy it; "
41: 4 heal my s·; for I have sinned "
42: 1 so panteth my s· after thee, O God. "
Ps 42: 2 My s· thirsteth for God, for the 5315
4 things, I pour out my s· in me: "
5 Why art thou cast down, O my s·? "
6 God, my s· is cast down within me: "
11 Why art thou cast down, O my s·? "
43: 5 Why art thou cast down, O my s·? "
44: 25 For our s· is bowed down to the "
49: 8 redemption of their s· is precious,‡ "
15 But God will redeem my s· from the "
18 while he lived he blessed his s·: "
54: 3 and oppressors seek after my s·: "
4 is with them that uphold my s·. "
55: 18 He hath delivered my s· in peace "
56: 6 my steps, when they wait for my s·. "
13 hast delivered my s· from death: "
57: 1 for my s· trusteth in thee: yea, in "
4 My s· is among lions: and I lie even "
6 for my steps; my s· is bowed down: "
59: 3 For, lo, they lie in wait for my s·: "
62: 1 Truly my s· waiteth upon God: "
5 My s·, wait thou only upon God; "
63: 1 my s· thirsteth for thee, my flesh "
5 My s· shall be satisfied as with "
8 My s· followeth hard after thee: "
9 those that seek my s·, to destroy "
66: 9 Which holdeth our s· in life, and "
16 declare what he hath done for my s·. "
69: 1 the waters are come in unto my s·. "
10 and chastened my s· with fasting, "
18 Draw nigh unto my s·, and redeem "
70: 2 confounded that seek after my s·: "
71: 10 they that lay wait for my s· take "
13 that are adversaries to my s·; "
23 my s·, which thou hast redeemed. "
72: 14 shall redeem their s· from deceit "
74: 19 deliver not the s· of thy turtledove "
77: 2 my s· refused to be comforted. "
78: 50 he spared not their s· from death, "
84: 2 My s· longeth, yea, even fainteth "
86: 2 Preserve my s·; for I am holy: O "
4 Rejoice the s· of thy servant: for "
4 unto thee, O Lord, do I lift up my s·. "
13 delivered my s· from the lowest "
14 violent men...sought after my s·; and "
88: 3 For my s· is full of troubles: and "
14 Lord, why castest thou off my s·? "
89: 48 shall he deliver his s· from the hand "
94: 17 my s· had almost dwelt in silence. "
19 thy comforts delight my s·. "
21 against the s· of the righteous, "
103: 1 Bless the Lord, O my s·: and all "
2 Bless the Lord, O my s·, and forget "
22 dominion: bless the Lord, O my s·. "
104: 1 Bless the Lord, O my s·. O Lord "
35 Bless thou the Lord, O my s·. "
106: 15 but sent leanness into their s·. "
107: 5 and thirsty, their s· fainted in them. "
9 For he satisfieth the longing s·, and "
9 filleth the hungry s· with goodness. "
18 s· abhorreth all manner of meat; "
26 their s· is melted because of trouble. "
109: 20 them that speak evil against my s·. "
31 him from those that condemn his s·. "
116: 4 Lord, I beseech thee, deliver my s·. "
7 Return unto thy rest, O my s·; for "
8 hast delivered my s· from death, "
119: 20 My s· breaketh for the longing that "
25 My s· cleaveth unto the dust: "
28 My s· melteth for heaviness: "
81 My s· fainteth for thy salvation: "
109 My s· is continually in my hand: "
129 therefore doth my s· keep them. "
167 My s· hath kept thy testimonies; "
175 Let my s· live, and it shall praise "
120: 2 Deliver my s·, O Lord, from lying "
6 My s· hath long dwelt with him "
121: 7 all evil: he shall preserve thy s·. "
123: 4 Our s· is exceedingly filled with the "
124: 4 us, the stream had gone over our s·: "
5 proud waters had gone over our s·. "
7 Our s· is escaped as a bird out of "
130: 5 I wait for the Lord, my s· doth wait, "
6 My s· waiteth for the Lord more "
131: 2 my s· is even as a weaned child. "
138: 3 me with strength in my s·. "
139: 14 and that my s· knoweth right well. "
141: 8 my trust; leave not my s· destitute. "
142: 4 failed me; no man cared for my s·. "
7 Bring my s· out of prison, that I "
143: 3 the enemy hath persecuted my s·; "
6 my s· thirsteth after thee, as a "
8 walk; for I lift up my s· unto thee. "
11 sake bring my s· out of trouble. "
12 destroy all them that afflict my s·: "
146: 1 Lord. Praise the Lord, O my s·. "
Pr 2: 10 knowledge is pleasant unto thy s·; "
3: 22 So shall they be life unto thy s·, "
6: 30 a thief, if he steal to satisfy his s· "
32 that doeth it destroyeth his own s·. "
8: 36 against me wrongeth his own s·: "
10: 3 not suffer the s· of the righteous to "
11: 17 man doeth good to his own s·: "
25 The liberal s· shall be made fat: "
13: 2 the s· of the transgressors shall eat "
4 The s· of the sluggard desireth, and "
4 s· of the diligent shall be made fat. "
19 accomplished is sweet to the s·: "
25 eateth to the satisfying of his s·: "
15: 32 instruction despiseth his own s·: "
16: 17 keepeth his way preserveth his s·. "
24 as an honeycomb, sweet to the s·, "
18: 7 and his lips are the snare of his s·. "
19: 2 that the s· be without knowledge, "
8 getteth wisdom loveth his own s·: "
15 and an idle s· shall suffer hunger. "
16 commandment keepeth his own s·; "

Pr 19:18 let not thy s' spare for his crying.*5315
20: 2 anger sinneth against his own s'.* "
21:10 The s' of the wicked desireth evil: "
23 tongue keepeth his s' from troubles. "
22: 5 he that doth keep his s' shall be far "
23 spoil the s' of those that spoiled * "
25 his ways, and get a snare to thy s'. "
23:14 and shalt deliver his s' from hell. "
24:12 he that keepeth thy s', doth not he "
14 knowledge of wisdom be unto thy s': "
25:13 he refresheth the s' of his masters. "
25 As cold waters to a thirsty s', so is "
27: 7 The full s' loatheth an honeycomb; "
7 to the hungry s' every bitter thing "
29:10 upright: but the just seek his s'. * "
17 he shall give delight unto thy s'. "
24 with a thief hateth his own s': "
Ec 2:24 he should make his s' enjoy good "
4: 8 labour, and bereave my s' of good? "
6: 2 he wanteth nothing for his s' of all "
3 and his s' be not filled with good, "
7:28 Which yet my s' seeketh, but I find "
Ca 1: 7 Tell me, O thou whom my s' loveth, "
3: 1 I sought him whom my s' loveth: "
2 I will seek him whom my s' loveth: "
3 Saw ye him whom my s' loveth? "
4 I found him whom my s' loveth: "
5: 6 gone: my s' failed when he spake: "
6:12 my s' made me like the chariots of "
Isa 1:14 your appointed feasts my s' hateth: "
3: 9 Woe unto their s'! for they have "
10:18 his fruitful field, both s' and body: "
26: 8 the desire of our s' is to thy name, "
9 With my s' have I desired thee in "
29: 8 he awaketh, and his s' is empty: "
8 he is faint, and his s' hath appetite: "
32: 6 to make empty the s' of the hungry, "
38:15 my years in the bitterness of my s'. "
17 thou hast in love to my s' delivered "
42: 1 elect, in whom my s' delighteth; "
44:20 aside, that he cannot deliver his s', "
51:23 which have said to thy s', Bow down, "
53:10 thou shalt make his s' an offering "
11 He shall see of the travail of his s', "
12 hath poured out his s' unto death: "
55: 2 let your s' delight itself in fatness. "
3 me: hear, and your s' shall live; "
58: 3 wherefore have we afflicted our s', "
5 a day for a man to afflict his s'? is it "
10 thou draw out thy s' to the hungry, "
10 hungry, and satisfy the afflicted s'; "
11 and satisfy thy s' in drought, and "
61:10 my s' shall be joyful in my God; "
66: 3 s' delighteth in their abominations. "
Jer 4:10 the sword reacheth unto the s'. ‡ "
19 O my s', the sound of the trumpet, "
31 s' is wearied because of murderers. "
5: 9, 29 s' be avenged on such a nation "
6: 8 lest my s' depart from thee; lest "
9: 9 shall not my s' be avenged on such "
12: 7 the dearly beloved of my s' into the "
13:17 my s' shall weep in secret places "
14:19 Judah? hath thy s' lothed Zion? "
18:20 for they have digged a pit for my s'. "
20:13 he hath delivered the s' of the poor "
31:12 and their s' shall be as a watered "
14 I will satiate the s' of the priests "
25 I have satiated the weary s', and I "
25 replenished every sorrowful s'. "
32:41 whole heart and with my whole s'. "
38:16 Lord liveth, that made us this s', "
17 then thy s' shall live, and this city "
20 well unto thee, and thy s' shall live. "
50:19 his s' shall be satisfied upon mount "
51: 6 and deliver every man his s': be * "
45 deliver ye every man his s' from * "
La 1:11 things for meat to relieve the s': "
16 comforter that should relieve my s' "
2:12 when their s' was poured out into "
3:17 thou hast removed my s' far off "
20 My s' hath them...in remembrance, "
24 Lord is my portion, saith my s'; "
25 for him, to the s' that seeketh him, "
58 hast pleaded the causes of my s'; "
Eze 3:19 but thou hast delivered thy s'. "
21 also thou hast delivered thy s'. "
4:14 my s' hath not been polluted: "
18: 4 are mine; as the s' of thine father, "
4 so also the s' of the son is mine: "
4 the s' that sinneth, it shall die. "
20 The s' that sinneth, it shall die. "
27 and right, he shall save his s' alive. "
24:21 and that which your s' pitieth; "
33: 5 taketh warning shall deliver his s'. "
9 but thou hast delivered thy s'. "
Ho 9: 4 bread for their s' shall not come "
Jon 2: 5 me about, even to the s': the "
7 When my s' fainted within me I "
Mic 6: 7 of my body for the sin of my s'? "
7: 1 my s' desired the firstripe fruit. "
Hab 2: 4 his s' which is lifted up is not "
10 and hast sinned against thy s'. "
Zec 11: 8 one month; and my s' lothed them, "
8 and their s' also abhorred me. "
M't 10:28 but are not able to kill the s': 5590
28 to destroy both s' and body in hell. "
12:18 in whom my s' is well pleased: "
16:26 whole world, and lose his own s'?* "
26 a man give in exchange for his s'?* "
22:37 all thy heart, and with all thy s', "
26:38 My s' is exceeding sorrowful, even "
M'r 8:36 whole world, and lose his own s'?* "
37 a man give in exchange for his s'?* "
12:30 all thy heart, and with all thy s', "
33 understanding, and with all the s',* "
14:34 My s' is exceeding sorrowful unto "

Lu 1:46 said, My s' doth magnify the Lord, 5590
2:35 shall pierce through thy own s' "
10:27 all thy heart, and with all thy s', "
12:19 say to my s', S', thou hast much "
20 this night thy s' shall be required "
Joh 12:27 Now is my s' troubled; and what "
Ac 2:27 thou wilt not leave my s' in hell, "
31 that his s' was not left in hell, * "
43 And fear came upon every s': and "
3:23 every s', which will not hear that "
4:32 were of one heart and of one s': "
Ro 2: 9 every s' of man that doeth evil; "
13: 1 Let every s' be subject unto the "
1Co 15:45 man Adam was made a living s'; "
2Co 1:23 call God for a record upon my s', "
1Th 5:23 your whole spirit and s' and body "
Heb 4:12 dividing asunder of s' and spirit, "
6:19 we have as an anchor of the s', "
10:38 my s' shall have no pleasure in "
39 that believe to the saving of the s'. "
Jas 5:20 his way shall save a s' from death, "
1Pe 2:11 lusts, which war against the s'; "
2Pe 2: 8 vexed his righteous s' from day to "
3Jo 2 in health, even as thy s' prospereth. "
Re 16: 3 and every living s' died in the sea. "
18:14 fruits that thy s' lusted after are "

soul's
Job 16: 4 if your soul were in my s' stead, 5315

souls
Ge 12: 5 and the s' that they had gotten in 5315
46:15 the s' of his sons and his daughters "
18 bare unto Jacob, even sixteen s'. "
22 to Jacob: all the s' were fourteen. "
25 unto Jacob: all the s' were seven. "
26 All the s' that came with Jacob "
26 all the s' were threescore and six; "
27 born him in Egypt, were two s': "
27 all the s' of the house of Jacob, "
Ex 1: 5 all the s' that came out of the loins "
5 the loins of Jacob were seventy s': "
12: 4 according to the number of the s'; "
30:15, 16 make an atonement for your s'. "
Le 16:29 ye shall afflict your s', and do no "
31 ye shall afflict your s', by a statute "
17:11 to make an atonement for your s': "
18:29 the s' that commit them shall be "
20:25 make your s' abominable by beast, "
23:27 ye shall afflict your s', and offer an "
32 of rest, and ye shall afflict your s': "
Nu 16:38 these sinners against their own s',* "
29: 7 ye shall afflict your s': ye shall not "
30: 9 they have bound their s', shall * "
31:50 to make an atonement for our s' "
Jos 10:28, 30 and all the s' that were therein; "
32 and all the s' that were therein, "
35 and all the s' that were therein he "
37 and all the s' that were therein; "
37 and all the s' that were therein. "
39 all the s' that were therein; he left "
11:11 smote all the s' that were therein "
23:14 all your hearts and in all your s', "
1Sa 25:29 the s' of thine enemies, them shall "
Ps 72:13 and shall save the s' of the needy. "
97:10 preserveth the s' of his saints; he "
Pr 11:30 life; and he that winneth s' is wise. "
14:25 A true witness delivereth s': but a "
Isa 57:16 and the s' which I have made. 5397
Jer 2:34 the blood of the s' of the poor 5315
6:16 and ye shall find rest for your s'. "
26:19 procure great evil against our s'. "
44: 7 ye this great evil against your s', "
La 1:19 sought their meat to relieve their s'. "
Eze 7:19 they shall not satisfy their s', "
13:18 the head of every stature to hunt s'! "
18 Will ye hunt the s' of my people, "
18 will ye save the s' alive that come "
19 to slay the s' that should not die, "
19 to save the s' alive that should not "
20 there hunt the s' to make them fly, "
20 your arms, and will let the s' go, "
20 s' that ye hunt to make them fly. "
14:14 they should deliver but their own s' "
20 they shall but deliver their own s' "
18: 4 Behold, all s' are mine; as the soul "
22:25 they have devoured s'; they have "
27 to shed blood, and to destroy s', to "
M't 11:29 and ye shall find rest unto your s'. 5590
Lu 21:19 your patience possess ye your s'. "
Ac 2:41 unto them about three thousand s'. "
7:14 kindred, threescore and fifteen s'. "
14:22 Confirming the s' of the disciples, "
15:24 with words, subverting your s', "
27:37 hundred threescore and sixteen s'. "
1Th 2: 8 of God only, but also our own s', "
Heb 13:17 for they watch for your s', as they "
Jas 1:21 word, which is able to save your s'. "
1Pe 1: 9 faith, even the salvation of your s'. "
22 have purified your s' in obeying the "
2:25 Shepherd and Bishop of your s'. "
3:20 is, eight s' were saved by water. "
4:19 commit the keeping of their s' to "
2Pe 2:14 from sin; beguiling unstable s': "
Re 6: 9 under the altar the s' of them that "
18:13 chariots, and slaves, and s' of men. "
20: 4 the s' of them that were beheaded "

sound See also SOUNDED; SOUNDETH; SOUNDING; SOUNDS.
Ex 28:35 and his s' shall be heard when he 6963
Le 25: 9 trumpet of the jubile to s' on the *5674
9 the trumpet s' throughout all your* "
26:36 the s' of a shaken leaf shall chase 6963
Nu 10: 7 blow, but ye shall not s' an alarm. 7321
Jos 6: 5 when ye hear the s' of the trumpet, 6963
20 people heard the s' of the trumpet, "
2Sa 5:24 the s' of a going in the tops of the "

2Sa 6:15 and with the s' of the trumpet. 6963
15:10 as ye hear the s' of the trumpet, "
1Ki 1:40 the earth rent with the s' of them. "
41 Joab heard the s' of the trumpet, "
14: 6 when Ahijah heard the s' of her feet, "
18:41 there is a s' of abundance of rain. "
2Ki 6:32 s' of his master's feet behind him? "
1Ch 14:15 hear a s' of going in the tops of the "
15:19 to s' with cymbals of brass; 8085
28 and with s' of the cornet, and with 6963
16: 5 but Asaph made a s' with cymbals;*8085
42 for those that should make a s', "
2Ch 5:13 one s' to be heard in praising and 6963
Ne 4:20 ye hear the s' of the trumpet, "
Job 15:21 A dreadful s' is in his ears: in "
21:12 and rejoice at the s' of the organ. "
37: 2 the s' that goeth out of his mouth. 1899
39:24 he that it is the s' of the trumpet.*6963
Ps 47: 5 the Lord with the s' of a trumpet. "
77:17 out water: the skies sent out a s': "
89:15 the people that know the joyful s': 8643
92: 3 upon the harp with a solemn s'. 1902
98: 6 With trumpets and s' of cornet 6963
119:80 Let my heart be s' in thy statutes;*8549
150: 3 him with the s' of the trumpet: 8629
Pr 2: 7 He layeth up s' wisdom for the 8454
3:21 keep s' wisdom and discretion: "
8:14 Counsel is mine, and s' wisdom: I "
14:30 A s' heart is the life of the flesh: 4832
Ec 12: 4 when the s' of the grinding is low, 6963
Isa 16:11 my bowels shall s' like an harp for 1993
Jer 4:19 the s' of the trumpet, the alarm of 6963
21 and hear the s' of the trumpet? "
6:17 Hearken to the s' of the trumpet. "
8:16 trembled at the s' of the neighing "
25:10 s' of the millstones, and the light "
42:14 nor hear the s' of the trumpet, "
48:36 mine heart shall s' for Moab like *1993
36 mine heart shall s' like pipes for * "
50:22 A s' of battle is in the land, and of 6963
51:54 A s' of a cry cometh from Babylon, "
Eze 10: 5 the s' of the cherubims' wings was "
26:13 the s' of thy harps shall be no more "
15 the isles shake at the s' of thy fall, "
27:28 shake at the s' of the cry of thy "
31:16 nations to shake at the s' of his fall, "
33: 4 whosoever heareth the s' of the "
5 He heard the s' of the trumpet, and "
Da 3: 5 ye hear the s' of the cornet, flute, 7032
7 people heard the s' of the cornet, "
10 that shall hear the s' of the cornet, "
15 ye hear the s' of the cornet, flute, "
Joe 2: 1 s' an alarm in my holy mountain: 7321
Am 2: 2 and with the s' of the trumpet: 6963
6: 5 That chant to the s' of the viol, and 6310
M't 6: 2 do not s' a trumpet before thee, as 4537
24:31 angels with a great s' of a trumpet, 5456
Lu 15:27 he hath received him safe and s' 5198
Joh 3: 8 thou hearest the s' thereof, but *5456
Ac 2: 2 there came a s' from heaven as of 2279
Ro 10:18 their s' went into all the earth, 5353
1Co 14: 7 even things without life giving s',*5456
8 if the trumpet give an uncertain s',* "
15:52 the trumpet shall s', and the dead 4537
1Ti 1:10 that is contrary to s' doctrine; 5198
2Ti 1: 7 and of love, and of a s' mind. *4995
13 Hold fast the form of s' words, 5198
4: 3 they will not endure s' doctrine; "
Tit 1: 9 he may be able by s' doctrine both "
13 that they may be s' in the faith; "
2: 1 things which become s' doctrine: "
2 s' in faith, in charity, in patience. "
8 S' speech, that cannot be 5199
Heb 12:19 And the s' of a trumpet, and the 2279
Re 1:15 his voice as the s' of many waters.*5456
8: 6 angels...prepared themselves to s'.4537
13 the three angels, which are yet to s'! "
9: 9 and the s' of their wings was as the 5456
9 as the s' of chariots of many horses "
10: 7 angel, when he shall begin to s', 4537
18:22 s' of a millstone shall be heard no 5456

sounded
1Sa 20:12 when I have s' my father about 2713
2Ch 7: 6 priests s' trumpets before them, 2690
13:14 the priests s' with the trumpets. "
23:13 rejoiced, and s' with trumpets, *8628
29:28 sang, and the trumpeters s': 2690
Ne 4:18 he that s' the trumpet was by me. 8628
Lu 1:44 of thy salutation s' in mine ears, *1096
Ac 27:28 s', and found it twenty fathoms: 1001
28 they s' again, and found it fifteen "
1Th 1: 8 you s' out the word of the Lord 1837
Re 8: 7 The first angel s', and there 4537
8 the second angel s', and as it were "
10 the third angel s', and there fell a "
12 the fourth angel s', and the third "
9: 1 the fifth angel s', and I saw a star "
13 the sixth angel s', and I heard a "
11:15 And the seventh angel s'; and there "

soundeth
Ex 19:13 when the trumpet s' long, they shall

sounding
1Ch 15:16 harps and cymbals, s', by lifting 8085
2Ch 5:12 twenty priests s' with trumpets:) 2690
13:12 with s' trumpets to cry alarm *8643
Ps 150: 5 him upon the high s' cymbals. *1995
Isa 63:15 the s' of thy bowels and of thy *1995
Eze 7: 7 not the s' again of the mountains.*1906
1Co 13: 1 I am become as s' brass, or a 2278

soundness
Ps 38: 3 no s' in my flesh because of thine 4974
7 and there is no s' in my flesh. "
Isa 1: 6 unto the head there is no s' in it; "
Ac 3:16 him hath given him this perfect s' 3647

sounds
1Co 14: 7 they give a distinction in the s·, 5353
sour
Isa 18: 5 and the s· grape is ripening in the*1155
Jer 31: 29 The fathers have eaten a s· grape, "
30 every man that eateth the s· grape, "
Eze 18: 2 The fathers have eaten s· grapes, "
Ho 4: 18 Their drink is s·: they have 5493
south See also SOUTHWARD.
Ge 12: 9 going on still toward the s·. 5045
13: 1 had, and Lot with him, into the s·. "
3 journey from the s·...to Beth-el, "
20: 1 from thence toward the s· country, "
24: 62 for he dwelt in the s· country. "
28: 14 east, and to the north, and to the s·: "
Ex 26: 18 boards on the s· side southward. "
35 of the tabernacle toward the s·: 8486
27: 9 s· side southward there shall be 5045
36: 23 boards for the s· side southward: "
38: 9 s· side southward the hangings of "
Nu 2: 10 the s· side shall be the standard 8486
10: 6 camps that lie on the s· side shall "
13: 22 And they ascended by the s·, and 5045
29 Amalekites dwell in...the s·: "
21: 1 Canaanite, which dwelt in the s·, "
33: 40 which dwelt in the s· in the land of "
34: 3 your s· quarter shall be from the "
3 your s· border shall be the outmost "
4 turn from the s· to the ascent of * "
4 be from the s· to Kadesh-barnea, * "
35: 5 on the s· side two thousand cubits, "
De 1: 7 in the vale, and in the s·, and by the "
33: 23 possess thou the west and the s·. 1864
34: 3 the s·, and the plain of the valley of 5045
Jos 10: 40 country of the hills, and of the s·, "
11: 2 and of the plains s· of Chinneroth, "
16 all the s· country, and all the land "
12: 3 the s·, under Ashdoth-pisgah: 8486
8 wilderness, and in the s· country; 5045
13: 4 From the s·, all the land of the 8486
15: 1 the uttermost part of the s· coast. 5045
2 their s· border was from the shore "
3 to the s· side to Maaleh-acrabbim,* "
3 on the s· side unto Kadesh-barnea, "
4 the sea: this shall be your s· coast. "
7 which is on the s· side of the river: "
8 unto the s· side of the Jebusite; * "
19 for thou hast given me a s· land; "
18: 5 shall abide in their coast on the s·, "
13 hill that lieth on the s· side of the "
15 the s· quarter was from the end of "
16 to the side of Jebusi on the s·, and* "
19 the salt sea at the s· end of Jordan: "
19 of Jordan: this was the s· coast. "
19: 8 to Baalath-beer, Ramath of the s·. "
34 reacheth to Zebulun on the s· side, "
J'g 1: 9 in the mountain, and in the s·, and "
15 for thou hast given me a s· land; "
16 which lieth in the s· of Arad; "
21: 19 Shechem, and on the s· of Lebonah. "
1Sa 20: 41 arose out of a place toward the s·, "
23: 19 which is on the s· of Jeshimon? 3225
24 in the plain on the s· of Jeshimon. "
27: 10 said, Against the s· of Judah, and 5045
10 against the s· of the Jerahmeelites, "
10 and against the s· of the Kenites. "
30: 1 the Amalekites had invaded the s·, "
14 upon the s· of the Cherethites, "
14 to Judah, and upon the s· of Caleb; "
27 to them which were in s· Ramoth,* "
2Sa 24: 7 they went out to the s· of Judah, "
1Ki 7: 25 and three looking toward the s·, "
39 house eastward over against the s·. "
1Ch 9: 24 toward the east, west, north, and s·. "
2Ch 4: 4 and three looking toward the s·, "
10 of the east end, over against the s·. "
28: 18 low country, and of the s· of Judah, "
Job 9: 9 and the chambers of the s·. 8486
37: 9 Out of the s· cometh...whirlwind: 2315
17 quieteth the earth by the s· wind? 1864
39: 26 stretch her wings toward the s·? 8486
Ps 75: 6 from the west, nor from the s·. 4057
78: 26 power he brought in the s· wind. 8486
89: 12 north and the s· thou hast created 3225
107: 3 from the north, and from the s·. 3220
126: 4 O Lord, as the streams in the s·. 5045
Ec 1: 6 The wind goeth toward the s·, 1864
11: 3 and if the tree fall toward the s·, "
Ca 4: 16 O north wind; and come, thou s·; 8486
Isa 21: 1 As whirlwinds in the s· pass 5045
30: 6 The burden of the beasts of the s·: "
43: 6 up; and to the s·, Keep not back: 8486
Jer 13: 19 The cities of the s· shall be shut 5045
17: 26 the mountains, and from the s·, "
32: 44 valley, and in the cities of the s·, "
33: 13 the vale, and in the cities of the s·, "
Eze 20: 46 man, set thy face toward the s·, 8486
46 and drop thy word toward the s·, 1864
46 against the forest of the s· field; 5045
47 say to the forest of the s·, Hear the "
47 all faces from the s· to the north "
21: 4 all flesh from the s· to the north: "
40: 2 was as the frame of a city on the s·. "
24 that he brought me toward the s·, 1864
24 and behold a gate toward the s·: "
27 in the inner court toward the s·: "
27 from gate to gate toward the s·: "
28 to the inner court by the s· gate: "
28 he measured the s· gate according "
44 their prospect was toward the s·: "
45 whose prospect is toward the s·, "
41: 11 and another door toward the s·: "
42: 12 chambers that were toward the s· "
13 chambers and the s· chambers, "
18 measured the s· side, five hundred "
Eze 46: 9 go out by the way of the s· gate; 5045
9 entereth by the way of the s· gate "
47: 1 the house, at the s· side of the altar. "
19 And the s· side southward, from "
19 And this is the s· side southward. 8486
48: 10 and toward the s· five and twenty 5045
16 the s· side four thousand and five "
17 and toward the s· two hundred and "
28 of Gad, at the s· side southward, "
33 at the s· side four thousand and "
Da 8: 9 toward the s·, and toward the east, "
11: 5 the king of the s· shall be strong, "
6 for the king's daughter of the s· "
9 So the king of the s· shall come "
11 the king of the s· shall be moved "
14 stand up against the king of the s·: "
15 arms of the s· shall not withstand, "
25 courage against the king of the s· "
25 king of the s· shall be stirred up to "
29 return, and come toward the s·; "
40 shall the king of the s· push at "
Ob 19 And they of the s· shall possess the "
20 shall possess the cities of the s·. "
Zec 6: 6 go forth toward the s· country. 8486
7: 7 inhabited the s· and the plain? 5045
9: 14 shall go with whirlwinds of the s·. 8486
14: 4 north, and half of it toward the s·. 5045
10 Geba to Rimmon s· of Jerusalem: "
M't 12: 42 queen of the s· shall rise up in the 3558
Lu 11: 31 queen of the s· shall rise up in the "
12: 55 And when ye see the s· wind blow, "
13: 29 and from the s·, and shall sit down "
Ac 8: 26 Arise, and go toward the s· unto 3314
27: 12 toward the s· west and north west. 3047
13 And when the s· wind blew softly,*3558
28: 13 and after one day the s· wind blew, "
Re 21: 13 three gates; on the s· three gates; "
south-country See SOUTH and COUNTRY.
south-quarter See SOUTH and QUARTER.
south-side See SOUTH and SIDE.
southward
Ge 13: 14 s·, and eastward, and westward: 5045
Ex 26: 18 twenty boards on the south side s·. 8486
27: 9 south side s· there shall be hangings "
36: 23 twenty boards for the south side s·: "
38: 9 on the south side s· the hangings "
40: 24 the south side of the tabernacle s·. 5045
Nu 3: 29 on the side of the tabernacle s·. 8486
13: 17 Get you up this way s·, and go up*5045
De 3: 27 northward, and s·, and eastward, 8486
Jos 15: 1 the wilderness of Zin s· was the "
2 sea, from the bay that looketh s·: 5045
21 Judah toward the coast of Edom s· "
17: 9 unto the river Kanah, s· of the river: "
10 S· it was Ephraim's, and northward "
18: 13 side of Luz, which is Beth-el, s·; "
14 compassed the corner of the sea s·, "
14 hill that lieth before Beth-horon s·; "
1Sa 14: 5 the other s· over against Gibeah. * "
1Ch 26: 15 To Obed-edom s·; and to his sons "
17 northward four a day, s· four a day, "
Eze 47: 19 And the south side s·, from Tamar "
19 sea. And this is the south side s·. "
48: 28 border of Gad, at the south side s·, "
Da 8: 4 westward, and northward, and s·; "
south-west See SOUTH and WEST.
south-wind See SOUTH and WIND.
sow See also SOWED; SOWEST; SOWETH; SOWING; SOWN.
Ge 47: 23 for you, and ye shall s· the land. 2232
Ex 23: 10 six years thou shalt s· thy land, "
Le 19: 19 shalt not s· thy field with mingled "
25: 3 Six years thou shalt s· thy field, "
4 thou shalt neither s· thy field, nor "
11 ye shall not s·, neither reap that "
20 we shall not s·, nor gather in our "
22 And ye shall s· the eighth year, and "
26: 16 and ye shall s· your seed in vain, "
De 22: 9 shalt not s· thy vineyard with divers "
2Ki 19: 29 in the third year s· ye, and reap, "
Job 4: 8 plow iniquity, and s· wickedness, "
31: 8 Then let me s·, and let another eat; "
Ps 107: 37 s· the fields, and plant vineyards, "
126: 5 that s· in tears shall reap in joy. "
Ec 11: 4 observeth the wind shall not s·; "
6 In the morning s· thy seed, and in "
Isa 28: 24 the plowman plow all day to s·? "
30: 23 seed, that thou shalt s· the ground "
32: 20 Blessed are ye that s· beside all "
37: 30 in the third year s· ye, and reap, "
Jer 4: 3 ground, and s· not among thorns. "
31: 27 that I will s· the house of Israel and "
35: 7 shall ye build house, nor s· seed, "
Ho 2: 23 I will s· her unto me in the earth; "
10: 12 S· to yourselves in righteousness, "
Mic 6: 15 Thou shalt s·, but thou shalt not "
Zec 10: 9 I will s· them among the people: "
M't 6: 26 the fowls of the air: for they s· not, 4687
13: 3 Behold, a sower went forth to s·; "
27 Sir, didst thou not s· good seed in "
M'r 4: 3 there went out a sower to s·: "
Lu 8: 5 A sower went out to s· his seed: "
12: 24 for they neither s· nor reap; which "
19: 21 and reapest that thou didst not s·. "
22 down, and reaping that I did not s·: "
2Pe 2: 22 and the s· that was washed to her 5300
sowed
Ge 26: 12 Then Isaac s· in that land, and 2232
J'g 9: 45 down the city, and s· it with salt. "
M't 13: 4 when he s·, some seeds fell by the 4687
24 unto a man which s· good seed in "
25 came and s· tares among the wheat, "
31 which a man took, and s· in his field: "
M't 13: 39 The enemy that s· them is the devil; 4687
25: 26 knewest that I reap where I s· not, "
M'r 4: 4 as he s·, some fell by the way side, "
Lu 8: 5 as he s·, some fell by the way side; "
sowedst
De 11: 10 where thou s· thy seed, and 2232
sower
Isa 55: 10 that it may give seed to the s·, 2232
Jer 50: 16 Cut off the s· from Babylon, and "
M't 13: 3 Behold, a s· went forth to sow; 4687
18 Hear ye...the parable of the s·. "
M'r 4: 3 Behold, there went out a s· to sow: "
14 The s· soweth the word. "
Lu 8: 5 A s· went out to sow his seed: and "
2Co 9: 10 he that ministereth seed to the s· "
sowest
1Co 15: 36 which thou s· is not quickened, 4687
37 And that which thou s·, "
37 thou s· not that body that shall be "
soweth
Pr 6: 14 continually; he s· discord. 7971
19 that s· discord among brethren. "
11: 18 but to him that s· righteousness 2232
16: 28 A froward man s· strife: and a *7971
22: 8 He that s· iniquity shall reap 2232
Am 9: 13 treader of grapes him that s· seed: 4900
M't 13: 37 He that s· the good seed is the Son 4687
M'r 4: 14 The sower s· the word. "
Joh 4: 36 that both he that s· and he that "
37 true, One s·, and another reapeth. "
2Co 9: 6 He which s· sparingly shall reap "
6 he which s· bountifully shall reap "
Ga 6: 7 whatsoever a man s·, that shall he "
8 For he that s· to his flesh shall of "
8 but he that s· to the Spirit shall of "
sowing
Le 11: 37 their carcase fall upon any s· seed 2221
26: 5 shall reach unto the s· time: 2233
sowing-time See SOWING and TIME.
sown
Ex 23: 16 which thou hast s· in the field: *2232
Le 11: 37 any sowing seed which is to be s·, "
De 21: 4 which is neither eared nor s·, "
22: 9 fruit of thy seed which thou hast s·, "
29: 23 and burning, that it is not s·, nor "
J'g 6: 3 And so it was when Israel had s·, "
Ps 97: 11 Light is s· for the righteous, and "
Isa 19: 7 every thing s· by the brooks, shall 4218
40: 24 yea, they shall not be s·: yea, 2232
61: 11 things that are s· in it to spring 2221
Jer 2: 2 in a land that was not s·. 2232
12: 13 They have s· wheat, but shall reap "
Eze 36: 9 you, and ye shall be tilled and s·: "
Ho 8: 7 For they have s· the wind, and they* "
Na 1: 14 that no more of thy name be s·: "
Hag 1: 6 Ye have s· much, and bring in "
M't 13: 19 that which was s· in his heart. 4687
25: 24 reaping where thou hast not s·, * "
M'r 4: 15 the way side, where the word is s·; "
15 the word that was s· in their hearts. "
16 which are s· on stony ground; who, "
18 they which are s· among thorns; "
20 they which are s· on good ground; "
31 when it is s· in the earth, is less "
32 But when it is s·, it groweth up, and "
1Co 9: 11 have s· unto you spiritual things,* "
15: 42 It is s· in corruption; it is raised in "
43 It is s· in dishonour; it is raised in "
43 it is s· in weakness; it is raised in "
44 It is s· a natural body; it is raised "
2Co 9: 10 multiply your seed s·, and increase* "
Jas 3: 18 fruit of righteousness is s· in peace 4687
space
Ge 29: 14 abode with him the s· of a month. 3117
32: 16 put a s· betwixt drove and drove. 7305
Le 25: 8 the s· of the seven sabbaths of *3117
30 within the s· of a full year, then 4390
De 2: 14 And the s· in which we came from *3117
Jos 3: 4 shall be a s· between you and it, 7350
1Sa 26: 13 a great s· being between them: 4725
Ezr 9: 8 a little s· grace hath been shewed*7281
Jer 28: 11 within the s· of two full years. *5750
Eze 40: 12 s· also before the little chambers *1366
12 the s· was one cubit on that side: * "
Lu 22: 59 And about the s· of one hour after 1339
Ac 5: 7 it was about the s· of three hours 1292
34 to put the apostles forth a little s·; *1024
13: 20 the s· of four hundred and fifty years,* "
21 of Benjamin, but the s· of forty years. "
15: 33 after they had tarried there a s·, *5550
19: 8 boldly for the s· of three months, 1909
10 continued by the s· of two years; "
34 about the s· of two hours cried out, "
20: 31 the s· of three years I ceased not 4158
Jas 5: 17 the s· of three years and six months.* "
Re 2: 21 And I gave her s· to repent of her *5550
8: 1 in heaven about the s· of half an hour. "
14: 20 s· of a thousand and six hundred * 575
17: 10 cometh, he must continue a short s·.* "
Spain (*spane*)
Ro 15: 24 I take my journey into S·, I will 4681
28 fruit, I will come by you into S·. "
spake See also SPAKEST.
Ge 8: 15 And God s· unto Noah, saying, 1696
9: 8 And God s· unto Noah, and to his 559
16: 13 name of the Lord that s· unto her, 1696
18: 29 And he s· unto him yet again, and "
19: 14 out, and s· unto his sons in law, "
21: 22 chief captain...s· unto Abraham, 559
22: 7 Isaac s· unto Abraham his father, "
23: 3 s· unto the sons of Heth, saying, 1696
13 he s· unto Ephron in the audience "

Ge 24: 7 which s· unto me, and that sware 1696
30 Thus s· the man unto me; that he "
27: 5 when Isaac s· to Esau his son. "
6 Rebekah s· unto Jacob her son, 559
29: 9 And while he yet s· with them, 1696
31: 11 angel of God s· unto me in a dream,559
29 the God of your father s· unto me "
34: 3 and s· kindly unto the damsel. 1696
4 And Shechem s· unto his father 559
35: 15 the place where God s· with him, 1696
39: 10 as she s· to Joseph day by day, "
14 house, and s· unto them, saying, 559
17 And she s· unto him according to 1696
19 of his wife, which she s· unto him, "
41: 9 s· the chief butler unto Pharaoh, "
42: 7 them, and s· roughly unto them; "
14 That is it that I s· unto you, saying," "
22 S· I not unto you, saying, Do not 559
23 he s· unto them by an interpreter.* "
30 lord of the land, s· roughly to us, 1696
37 Reuben s· unto his father, saying, 559
43: 3 And Judah s· unto him, saying, The "
27 well, the old man of whom ye s·? "
29 brother, of whom ye s· unto me? "
44: 6 and he s· unto them these same 1696
46: 2 God s· unto Israel in the visions of 559
47: 5 Pharaoh s· unto Joseph, saying, Thy "
49: 28 it that their fathers s· unto them, 1696
50: 4 were past, Joseph s· unto the house "
17 And Joseph wept when they s· unto "
21 them, and s· kindly unto them. "
Ex 1: 15 s· to the Hebrew midwives, 559
4: 30 Aaron s· all the words which the 1696
5: 10 and they s· to the people, saying, 559
6: 2 And God s· unto Moses, and said 1696
9 And Moses s· so unto the children "
10 And the Lord s· unto Moses, saying, "
12 And Moses s· before the Lord, "
13 Lord s· unto Moses and unto Aaron, "
27 These are they which s· to Pharaoh "
28 day when the Lord s· unto Moses "
29 That the Lord s· unto Moses, saying, "
7: 7 old, when they s· unto Pharaoh. "
8 Lord s· unto Moses and unto Aaron,559
19 Lord s· unto Moses, Say unto Aaron,* "
8: 1 And the Lord s· unto Moses, Go unto "
5 Lord s· unto Moses, Say unto Aaron,* "
12: 1 the Lord s· unto Moses and Aaron "
13: 1 the Lord s· unto Moses, saying, 1696
14: 1 And the Lord s· unto Moses, saying, "
15: 1 this song unto the Lord, and s·, 559
16: 9 Moses s· unto Aaron, Say unto all* "
10 Aaron s· unto the...congregation 1696
11 And the Lord s· unto Moses, saying, "
19: 19 Moses s·, and God answered him by "
25 unto the people, and s· unto them.*559
20: 1 And God s· all these words, saying,1696
25: 1 And the Lord s· unto Moses, saying, "
30: 11, 17 the Lord s· unto Moses, saying, "
22 Moreover the Lord s· unto Moses, "
31: 1 And the Lord s· unto Moses, saying, "
12 And the Lord s· unto Moses, saying,559
33: 11 Lord s· unto Moses face to face, 1696
34: 34 and s· unto the children of Israel "
35: 4 Moses s· unto all the congregation 559
36: 5 And they s· unto Moses, saying, The "
40: 1 the Lord s· unto Moses, saying, 1696
Le 1: 1 s· unto him out of the tabernacle of "
4: 1 And the Lord s· unto Moses, saying, "
5: 14 And the Lord s· unto Moses, saying, "
6: 1, 8, 19, 24 Lord s· unto Moses, saying, "
7: 22, 28 the Lord s· unto Moses, saying, "
8: 1 And the Lord s· unto Moses, saying, "
10: 3 This is it that the Lord s·, saying, I "
8 And the Lord s· unto Aaron, saying, "
12 And Moses s· unto Aaron, and unto "
11: 1 Lord s· unto Moses and to Aaron, "
12: 1 And the Lord s· unto Moses, saying, "
13: 1 the Lord s· unto Moses and Aaron, "
14: 1 And the Lord s· unto Moses, saying, "
33 Lord s· unto Moses and unto Aaron, "
15: 1 Lord s· unto Moses and to Aaron, "
16: 1 Lord s· unto Moses after the death "
17: 1 And the Lord s· unto Moses, saying, "
18: 1 And the Lord s· unto Moses, saying, "
19: 1 And the Lord s· unto Moses, saying, "
20: 1 And the Lord s· unto Moses, saying, "
21: 16 And the Lord s· unto Moses, saying, "
22: 1, 17, 26 Lord s· unto Moses, saying, "
23: 1, 9, 23, 26, 33 Lord s· unto Moses, "
24: 1, 13 the Lord s· unto Moses, saying, "
23 Moses s· to the children of Israel, "
25: 1 Lord s· unto Moses in mount Sinai, "
27: 1 And the Lord s· unto Moses, saying, "
Nu 1: 1 And the Lord s· unto Moses in the "
2: 1 Lord s· unto Moses and unto Aaron, "
3: 1 Lord s· with Moses in mount Sinai. "
5, 11 the Lord s· unto Moses, saying, "
14 And the Lord s· unto Moses in the "
44 And the Lord s· unto Moses, saying, "
4: 1, 17 Lord s· unto Moses and...Aaron, "
21 And the Lord s· unto Moses, saying, "
5: 1 And the Lord s· unto Moses, saying, "
4 as the Lord s· unto Moses, so did "
5, 11 the Lord s· unto Moses, saying, "
6: 1, 22 the Lord s· unto Moses, saying, "
7: 4 And the Lord s· unto Moses, saying,559
89 cherubims: and he s· unto him. 1696
8: 1, 5, 23 Lord s· unto Moses, saying, "
9: 1 And the Lord s· unto Moses in the "
4 And Moses s· unto the children of "
9 And the Lord s· unto Moses, saying, "
10: 1 And the Lord s· unto Moses, saying, "
11: 25 down in a cloud, and s· unto him, "
12: 1 Miriam and Aaron s· against Moses "
4 the Lord s· suddenly unto Moses, 559

Nu 13: 1 the Lord s· unto Moses, saying, 1696
14: 7 they s· unto all the company of the 559
26 Lord s· unto Moses and...Aaron, 1696
15: 1, 17 And the Lord s· unto Moses, "
37 And the Lord s· unto Moses, saying,559
16: 5 he s· unto Korah and unto all his 1696
20 Lord s· unto Moses and unto Aaron, "
23 And the Lord s· unto Moses, saying, "
26 And he s· unto the congregation, "
36, 44 the Lord s· unto Moses, saying, "
17: 1 And the Lord s· unto Moses, saying, "
6 And Moses s· unto the children of "
12 children of Israel s· unto Moses, 559
18: 8 And the Lord s· unto Aaron, 1696
20 And the Lord s· unto Aaron, * 559
25 the Lord s· unto Moses, saying, 1696
19: 1 Lord s· unto Moses and unto Aaron, "
20: 3 people chode with Moses, and s·, 559
7 the Lord s· unto Moses, saying, 1696
12 Lord s· unto Moses and Aaron, * 559
23 the Lord s· unto Moses and Aaron "
21: 5 And the people s· against God, 1696
22: 7 and s· unto him the words of Balak. "
24: 12 S· I not also to thy messengers "
25: 10, 16 the Lord s· unto Moses, saying, "
26: 1 Lord s· unto Moses and...Eleazar 559
3 Moses and Eleazar the priest s· 1696
52 And the Lord s· unto Moses, saying, "
27: 6 And the Lord s· unto Moses, saying,559
15 Moses s· unto the Lord, saying, 1696
28: 1 And the Lord s· unto Moses, saying, "
30: 1 And Moses s· unto the heads of the "
31: 1 And the Lord s· unto Moses, saying, "
3 And Moses s· unto the people, "
25 And the Lord s· unto Moses, saying,559
32: 2 Reuben came and s· unto Moses, "
25 children of Reuben s· unto Moses, "
33: 50 Lord s· unto Moses in the plains 1696
34: 1, 16 the Lord s· unto Moses, saying, "
35: 1 Lord s· unto Moses in the plains "
9 And the Lord s· unto Moses, saying, "
36: 1 came near, and s· before Moses, "
De 1: 1 which Moses s· unto all Israel "
3 Moses s· unto the children of Israel, "
6 Lord our God s· unto us in Horeb, "
9 I s· unto you at that time, saying, I 559
43 So I s· unto you; and ye would not1696
2: 1 Red sea, as the Lord s· unto me: "
2 And the Lord s· unto me, saying, 559
17 That the Lord s· unto me, saying, 1696
4: 12 Lord s· unto you out of the midst "
15 that the Lord s· unto you in Horeb "
45 Moses s· unto the children of Israel, "
5: 22 the Lord s· unto all your assembly "
28 of your words, when ye s· unto me; "
9: 10 the Lord s· with you in the mount "
13 Furthermore the Lord s· unto me, 559
10: 4 the Lord s· unto you in the mount 1696
13: 2 to pass, whereof he s· unto thee, "
27: 9 the Levites s· unto all Israel, saying, "
28: 68 by the way whereof I s· unto thee,* 559
31: 1 Moses went and s· these words 1696
30 And Moses s· in the ears of all the "
32: 44 and s· all the words of this song "
48 Lord s· unto Moses that selfsame "
Jos 1: 1 the Lord s· unto Joshua the son of 559
12 the tribe of Manasseh, s· Joshua, "
3: 6 Joshua s· unto the priests, saying, "
4: 1 that the Lord s· unto Joshua, saying, "
8 as the Lord s· unto Joshua, 1696
12 of Israel, as Moses s· unto them: "
15 the Lord s· unto Joshua, saying, 559
21 And he s· unto the children of Israel, "
7: 2 and s· unto them, saying, Go up and "
9: 11 inhabitants of our country s· to us, "
22 them, and he s· unto them, saying,1696
10: 12 Then s· Joshua to the Lord in the "
14: 10 the Lord s· this word unto Moses, "
12 whereof the Lord s· in that day; "
17: 14 children of Joseph s· unto Joshua, "
17 Joshua s· unto the house of Joseph,559
20: 1 Lord also s· unto Joshua, saying, 1696
2 I s· unto you by the hand of Moses: "
21: 2 they s· unto them at Shiloh in the "
22: 8 he s· unto them, saying, Return 559
15 and they s· with them, saying, 1696
30 and the children of Manasseh s·, "
23: 14 things which the Lord your God s· "
24: 27 the words of the Lord which he s· "
J'g 2: 4 the angel of the Lord s· these words "
8: 8 Penuel, and s· unto them likewise: "
9 he s· also unto the men of Penuel, 559
9: 3 his mother's brethren s· of him in 1696
37 Gaal s· again and said, See there "
15: 13 And they s· unto him, saying, No; 559
19: 22 and s· to the master of the house, "
Ru 4: 1 kinsman of whom Boaz s· came 1696
1Sa 1: 13 Now Hannah, she s· in her heart; "
7: 3 And Samuel s· unto all the house of559
9: 9 went to enquire of God, thus he s·,* "
17 the man whom I s· to thee of! this "
10: 16 the kingdom, whereof Samuel s·, he "
16: 4 Samuel did that which the Lord s·,1696
17: 23 s· according to the same words: "
26 David s· to the men that stood by 559
28 heard when he s· unto the men; 1696
30 and s· after the same manner: 559
31 words were heard which David s·, 1696
18: 23 Saul's servants s· those words in the "
24 saying, On this manner s· David. "
19: 1 And Saul s· to Jonathan his son, and "
4 And Jonathan s· good of David unto "
20: 26 Saul s· not any thing that day: for "
25: 9 s· to Nabal according to all those "
40 they s· unto her, saying, David sent "
28: 12 and the woman s· to Saul, saying, 559

1Sa 28: 17 hath done to him, as he s· by me: 1696
30: 6 for the people s· of stoning him, 559
2Sa 3: 19 And Abner also s· in the ears of 1696
5: 1 s·, saying, Behold, we are thy bone 559
6 which s· unto David, saying, Except "
7: 7 s· I a word with any of the tribes 1696
12: 18 child was yet alive, we s· unto him, "
13: 22 And Absalom s· unto his brother "
14: 4 the woman of Tekoah s· to the king,559
17: 6 Absalom s· unto him, saying, "
20: 18 Then she s·, saying, They were wont "
22: 1 David s· unto the Lord the words 1696
23: 2 The Spirit of the Lord s· by me, and "
3 the Rock of Israel s· to me, He that "
24: 17 David s· unto the Lord when he saw 559
1Ki 1: 11 Nathan s· unto Bath-sheba the "
42 while he yet s·, behold, Jonathan 1696
2: 4 word which he s· concerning me, "
27 he s· concerning the house of Eli in "
3: 22 son. Thus they s· before the king. "
26 Then s· the woman whose the living 559
4: 32 he s· three thousand proverbs: 1696
33 he s· of trees, from the cedar tree "
33 he s· also of beasts, and of fowl, and "
5: 5 the Lord s· unto David my father, "
6: 12 which I s· unto David thy father: "
8: 12 Then s· Solomon, The Lord said 559
15 s· with his mouth unto David 1696
20 hath performed his word that he s·, "
12: 3 Israel came, and s· unto Rehoboam, "
7 they s· unto him, saying, If thou "
10 grown up with him s· unto him, "
10 unto this people that s· unto thee, "
14 s· to them after the counsel of the "
15 which the Lord s· by Ahijah the "
13: 18 an angel s· unto me by the word of "
26 of the Lord, which he s· unto him. "
27 he s· to his sons, saying, Saddle me "
31 him, that he s· to his sons, saying, 559
14: 18 he s· by the hand of his servant 1696
15: 29 which he s· by his servant Ahijah "
16: 12 which he s· against Baasha by Jehu "
34 which he s· by Joshua the son of "
17: 16 of the Lord, which he s· by Elijah. "
20: 28 God, and s· unto the king of Israel, 559
21: 2 Ahab s· unto Naboth, saying, Give 1696
6 I s· unto Naboth the Jezreelite, and "
23 of Jezebel also s· the Lord, saying, "
22: 13 gone to call Micaiah s· unto him, "
38 the word of the Lord which he s·. "
2Ki 1: 9 he s· unto him, Thou man of God, "
2: 22 to the saying of Elisha which he s·. "
5: 13 s· unto him, and said, My father, if "
7: 17 who s· when the king came down "
8: 1 Then s· Elisha unto the woman, * "
9: 12 Thus and thus s· he to me, saying, 559
36 which he s· by his servant Elijah 1696
10: 10 the Lord s· concerning the house of "
10 which he s· by his servant Elijah. "
17 of the Lord, which he s· to Elijah. "
14: 25 he s· by the hand of his servant "
15: 12 of the Lord which he s· unto Jehu, "
17: 26 they s· to the king of Assyria, 559
18: 28 in the Jews' language, and s·, 1696
21: 10 And the Lord s· by his servants the "
22: 19 heardest what I s· against this place, "
24: 2 he s· by his servants the prophets. "
25: 28 And he s· kindly to him, and set his "
1Ch 15: 16 David s· to the chief of the Levites 559
17: 6 s· I a word to any of the judges of 1696
21: 9 And the Lord s· unto Gad, David's "
19 which he s· in the name of the Lord. "
2Ch 1: 2 Then Solomon s· unto all Israel, to 559
6: 4 that which he s· with his mouth 1696
10: 3 all Israel came and s· to Rehoboam, "
7 they s· unto him, saying, If thou be "
10 brought up with him s· unto him, "
10 answer the people that s· unto thee, "
15 which he s· by the hand of Ahijah "
18: 12 that went to call Micaiah s· to him, "
19 one s· saying after this manner, 559
30: 22 Hezekiah s· comfortably unto all 1696
32: 6 s· comfortably to them, saying, "
16 his servants s· yet more against the "
19 s· against the God of Jerusalem, "
24 he s· unto him, and he gave him a 559
33: 10 And the Lord s· to Manasseh, and 1696
18 words of the seers that s· to him in "
34: 22 and they s· to her to that effect. "
35: 25 the singing women s· of Josiah in 559
Ne 4: 2 he s· before his brethren and the "
8: 1 and they s· unto Ezra the scribe to "
13: 24 their children s· half in the speech 1696
Es 3: 4 pass, when they s· daily unto him, 559
4: 10 Again Esther s· unto Hatach, and "
8: 3 And Esther s· yet again before the 1696
Job 2: 13 and none s· a word unto him: for "
3: 2 And Job s·, and said, *6030
19: 18 I arose, and they s· against me. *1696
29: 22 After my words they s· not again; and
32: 16 (for they s· not, but stood still, and*1696
35: 1 Elihu s· moreover, and said, *6030
Ps 18: *title* who s· unto the Lord the words 1696
33: 9 For he s·, and it was done; he 559
39: 3 burned: then s· I with my tongue, 1696
78: 19 Yea, they s· against God; they said, "
99: 7 He s· unto them in the cloudy pillar: "
105: 31 He s·, and there came divers sorts 559
34 He s·, and the locusts came, and "
106: 33 so that he s· unadvisedly with his 981
Pr 30: 1 the man s· unto Ithiel, even unto *5002
Ca 2: 10 My beloved s·, and said unto me, 6030
5: 6 gone: my soul failed when he s·: 1696
Isa 7: 10 Lord s· again unto Ahaz, saying, "
8: 5 The Lord s· also unto me again, "
11 For the Lord s· thus to me with a 559

Isa 20: 2 At the same time s· the Lord by 1696
65: 12 when I s·, ye did not hear; but did "
66: 4 when I s·, they did not hear: but "
Jer 7: 13 I s· unto you, rising up early and "
22 For I s· not unto your fathers, nor "
8: 6 and heard, but they s· not aright: "
14: 14 them, neither s· unto them: "
19: 5 which I commanded not, nor s· it, "
20: 8 For since I s·, I cried out, I cried* "
22: 21 I s· unto thee in thy prosperity; but "
25: 2 the prophet s· unto all the people of "
26: 11 s· the priests and the prophets unto 559
12 s· Jeremiah unto all the princes "
17 s· to all the assembly of the people, "
18 s· to all the people of Judah, saying, "
27: 12 I s· also to Zedekiah king of Judah 1696
16 Also I s· to the priests and to all "
28: 1 s· unto me in the house of the Lord, 559
11 And Hananiah s· in the presence of "
30: 4 that the Lord s· concerning Israel 1696
31: 20 for since I s· against him, I do "
34: 6 Jeremiah the prophet s· all these "
36: 2 nations, from the day I s· unto thee, "
37: 2 he s· by the prophet Jeremiah. "
38: 8 the king's house, and s· to the king, "
40: 15 the son of Kareah s· to Gedaliah in 559
43: 2 s· Azariah the son of Hoshaiah, and "
45: 1 that Jeremiah the prophet s· unto 1696
46: 13 word that the Lord s· to Jeremiah "
50: 1 that the Lord s· against Babylon "
51: 12 done that which he s· against the "
52: 32 And s· kindly unto him, and set his "
Eze 1: 28 and I heard a voice of one that s·. "
2: 2 spirit entered into me when he s· "
2 that I heard him that s· unto me. "
3: 24 me upon my feet, and s· with me, "
10: 2 he s· unto the man clothed with 559
11: 25 I s· unto them of the captivity 1696
24: 18 So I s· unto the people in the "
Da 1: 3 And the king s· unto Ashpenaz the 559
2: 4 Then s· the Chaldeans to the king 1696
3: 9 They s· and said to the king *6032
14 Nebuchadnezzar s· and said unto* "
19 therefore he s·, and commanded "
24 rose up in haste, and s·, and said "
26 s·, and said, Shadrach, Meshach, "
28 Then Nebuchadnezzar s·, and said, "
4: 19 The king s·, and said, Belteshazzar,* "
30 The king s·, and said, Is not this "
5: 7 king s·, and said to the wise men "
10 and the queen s· and said, O king, "
13 the king s· and said unto Daniel, "
6: 12 and s· before the king concerning 560
16 the king s· and said unto Daniel, 6032
20 and the king s· and said to Daniel, "
7: 2 Daniel s· and said, I saw in my "
11 the great words which the horn s·: 4449
20 a mouth that s· very great things, "
8: 13 unto that certain saint which s·, 1696
9: 6 which s· in thy name to our kings, "
12 which he s· against us, and against "
10: 16 then I opened my mouth, and s·, "
Ho 12: 4 in Beth-el, and there he s· with us; "
13: 1 When Ephraim s· trembling, he "
Jon 2: 10 And the Lord s· unto the fish, and 559
Hag 1: 13 s· Haggai the Lord's messenger "
Zec 1: 21 he s·, saying, These are the horns "
3: 4 And he answered and s· unto those "
4: 4 So I answered and s· to the angel "
6 Then he answered and s· unto me, "
6: 8 he upon me, and s· unto me, 1696
Mal 3: 16 the Lord s· often one to another: "
M't 9: 18 While he s· these things unto them, 2980
33 the devil was cast out, the dumb s·: "
12: 22 blind and dumb both s· and saw. "
13: 3 he s· many things...in parables, "
33 Another parable s· he unto them; "
34 these things s· Jesus...in parables; "
34 and without a parable s· he not "
14: 27 straightway Jesus s· unto them, "
16: 11 I s· it not to you concerning bread, 2036
17: 5 While he yet s·, behold, a bright *2980
13 s· unto them of John the Baptist. 3004
21: 45 they perceived that he s· of them. 3004
22: 1 s· unto them again by parables, 2036
23: 1 Then s· Jesus to the multitude, 2980
26: 47 And while he yet s·, lo, Judas, one "
28: 18 And Jesus came and s· unto them, "
M'r 3: 9 he s· to his disciples, that a small 2036
4: 33 many such parables s· he the word 2980
34 But without a parable s· he not "
5: 35 While he yet s·, there came from "
7: 35 tongue was loosed, and he s· plain. "
8: 32 And he s· that saying openly. And "
9: 18 and I s· to thy disciples that they 2036
12: 26 how in the bush God s· unto him, "
14: 31 But he s· the more vehemently, 3004
39 prayed, and s· the same words. *2036
43 while he yet s·, cometh Judas, one 2980
Lu 1: 42 And she s· out with a loud voice, * 400
55 As he s· to our fathers, to Abraham, 2980
64 and his tongue loosed, and he s·, "
70 As he s· by the mouth of his holy "
2: 38 s· of him to all them that looked "
50 the saying which he s· unto them. "
4: 36 amazed, and s· among themselves, 4814
5: 36 he s· also a parable unto them; 3004
6: 39 And he s· a parable unto them, 2036
7: 39 he s· within himself, saying, This "
8: 4 out of every city, he s· by a parable: "
49 While he yet s·, there cometh one 2980
9: 11 and s· unto them of the kingdom "
31 s· of his decease which he should 3004
34 While he thus s·, there came a * "
11: 14 devil was gone out, the dumb s·; 2980
27 as he s· these things, a certain *3004

Lu 11: 37 And as he s·, a certain Pharisee 2980
12: 16 he s· a parable unto them, saying, 2036
13: 6 He s· also this parable; A certain 3004
14: 3 s· unto the lawyers and Pharisees, 2036
15: 3 And he s· this parable unto them, "
18: 1 he s· a parable unto them to this 3004
9 he s· this parable unto certain 2036
19: 11 he added and s· a parable, because "
20: 2 And s· unto him, saying, Tell us, "
21: 5 And as some s· of the temple, how 3004
29 he s· to them a parable; Behold 2036
22: 47 And while he yet s·, behold a 2980
60 while he yet s·, the cock crew. "
65 blasphemously s· they against him. 3004
23: 20 to release Jesus, s· again to them. 4377
24: 6 remember how he s· unto you 2980
36 And as they thus s·, Jesus himself "
44 are the words which I s· unto you, "
Joh 1: 15 This was he of whom I s·, He that* 2036
2: 21 he s· of the temple of his body. 3004
6: 71 He s· of Judas Iscariot the son of "
7: 13 Howbeit no man s· openly of him 2980
39 (But this s· he of the Spirit, which 2036
46 Never man s· like this man. 2980
8: 12 Then s· Jesus again unto them, "
20 words s· Jesus in the treasury, "
27 that he s· to them of the Father. 3004
30 As he s· these words, many 2980
9: 22 These words s· his parents, *2036
29 We know that God s· unto Moses: *2980
10: 6 This parable s· Jesus unto them: 2036
6 what things they were which he s· 2980
41 things that John s· of this man 2036
11: 13 Howbeit Jesus s· of his death: *2046
51 And this s· he not of himself: *2036
56 and s· among themselves, as they 3004
12: 29 others said, An angel s· to him. *2980
36 These things s· Jesus, and "
38 might be fulfilled, which he s·, 2036
41 he saw his glory, and s· of him. 2980
13: 22 another, doubting of whom he s·. 3004
24 who it should be of whom he s·. * "
28 knew for what intent he s· this 2036
17: 1 These words s· Jesus, and lifted 2980
18: 9 might be fulfilled, which he s·, 2036
16 and s· unto her that kept the door, "
20 I s· openly to the world; I ever *2980
32 he s·, signifying what death he 2036
21: 19 s· he, signifying by what death he "
Ac 1: 16 David s· before concerning Judas, 4277
2: 31 s· of the resurrection of Christ, 2980
4: 1 And as they s· unto the people, "
31 s· the word of God with boldness. "
6: 10 wisdom and...spirit by which he s·. "
7: 6 And God s· on this wise, That his "
38 angel which s· to him in the mount "
8: 6 unto those things which Philip s·, *3004
26 angel of the Lord s· unto Philip, 2980
9: 29 s· boldly in the name of the Lord * "
10: 7 the angel which s· unto Cornelius "
15 voice s· unto him again the second* "
44 While Peter yet s· these words, 2980
11: 20 s· unto the Grecians, preaching the "
13: 45 s· against those things which were* 483
14: 1 and so s·, that a great multitude 2980
16: 13 s· unto the women which resorted "
32 s· unto him the word of the Lord, "
18: 9 s· the Lord to Paul in the night by* 2036
25 s· and taught diligently the things 2980
19: 6 and s· with tongues, and prophesied. "
8 s· boldly for the space of three "
9 but s· evil of that way before the *2551
20: 38 of all for the words which he s·, *2046
21: 40 he s· unto them in the Hebrew 4377
22: 2 he s· in the Hebrew tongue to them, "
9 heard not the voice of him that s· 2980
26: 24 And as he thus s· for himself, * 626
28: 19 But when the Jews s· against it, 483
21 shewed or s· any harm of thee. *2980
25 Well s· the Holy Ghost by Esaias "
1Co 13: 11 When I was a child, I s· as a child, "
14: 5 I would that ye all s· with tongues, * "
2Co 7: 14 as we s· all things to you in truth, "
Ga 4: 15 Where is then the blessedness ye s· of?* "
Heb 1: 1 s· in time past unto the fathers *2980
4: 4 For he s· in a certain place of the *2046
7: 14 of which tribe Moses s· nothing 2980
12: 25 refused him that s· on earth, who *5537
2Pe 1: 21 men of God s· as they were moved 2980
Re 1: 12 And I turned to see the voice that s· "
10: 8 from heaven s· unto me again, * "
13: 11 like a lamb, and he s· as a dragon. "

spakest
J'g 13: 11 the man that s· unto the woman? 1696
17: 2 cursedst, and s· of also in mine ears, *559
1Sa 28: 21 thy words which thou s· unto me. 1696
1Ki 8: 24 thou s· also with thy mouth, and "
26 thou s· unto thy servant David my "
53 as thou s· by the hand of Moses thy "
2Ch 6: 15 s· with thy mouth, and hast fulfilled "
Ne 9: 13 and s· with them from heaven, and "
Ps 89: 19 Then thou s· in vision to thy holy "
Jer 48: 27 for since thou s· of him, thou *1697

span. See also SPANNED.
Ex 28: 16 a s· shall be the length thereof, 2239
16 a s· shall be the breadth thereof. "
39: 9 a s· was the length thereof, and a "
9 and a s· the breadth thereof, being "
1Sa 17: 4 whose height was six cubits and a s·. "
Isa 40: 12 and meted out heaven with the s·, "
La 2: 20 fruit, and children of a s· long? *2949
Eze 43: 13 thereof round about shall be a s·: 2239

spanned
Isa 48: 13 right hand hath s· the heavens: *2946

spare See also SPARED; SPARETH; SPARING.
Ge 18: 24 also destroy and not s· the place 5375
26 will s· all the place for their sakes. "
De 13: 8 eye pity him, neither shalt thou s·, 2550
29: 20 The Lord will not s· him, but then *5545
1Sa 15: 3 that they have, and s· them not; 2550
Ne 13: 22 s· me according to the greatness 2347
Job 6: 10 let him not s·; for I have not *2550
16: 13 my reins asunder, and doth not s·; "
20: 13 Though he s· it, and forsake it not; "
27: 22 shall cast upon him, and not s·: "
30: 10 me, and s· not to spit in my face. 2820
Ps 39: 13 O s· me, that I may recover 8159
72: 13 He shall s· the poor and needy, *2347
Pr 6: 34 will not s· in the day of vengeance. 2550
19: 18 let not thy soul s· for his crying. *5375
Isa 9: 19 fire: no man shall s· his brother. *2550
13: 18 their eye shall not s· children. 2347
30: 14 broken in pieces; he shall not s·: *2550
54: 2 s· not, lengthen thy cords, and 2820
58: 1 Cry aloud, s· not, lift up thy voice "
Jer 13: 14 I will not pity, nor s·, nor have 2347
21: 7 he shall not s· them, neither have "
50: 14 bow, shoot at her, s· no arrows: 2550
51: 3 s· ye not her young men; destroy "
Eze 5: 11 neither shall mine eye s·, neither 2347
7: 4 mine eye shall not s· thee, neither "
9 And mine eye shall not s·, neither "
8: 18 mine eye shall not s·, neither will I "
9: 5 let not your eye s·, neither have ye "
10 mine eye shall not s·, neither will I "
24: 14 I will not go back, neither will I s·, "
Joe 2: 17 S· thy people, O Lord, and give not "
Jon 4: 11 should not I s· Nineveh, that great* "
Hab 1: 17 and not s· continually to slay the 2550
Mal 3: 17 I will s· them, as a man spareth "
Lu 15: 17 have bread enough and to s·, 4052
Ro 11: 21 take heed lest he also s· not thee. 5339
1Co 7: 28 trouble in the flesh: but I s· you. "
2Co 1: 23 to s· you I came not as yet unto "
13: 2 that, if I come again, I will not s·: "

spared
1Sa 15: 9 But Saul and the people s· Agag, 2550
15 people s· the best of the sheep and "
24: 10 but mine eye s· thee; and I said, 2347
2Sa 12: 4 he s· to take of his own flock and 2550
21: 7 But the king s· Mephibosheth, the "
2Ki 5: 20 my master hath s· Naaman this 2820
Ps 78: 50 he s· not their soul from death, "
Eze 20: 17 mine eye s· them from destroying 2347
Ro 8: 32 He that s· not his own Son, but 5339
11: 21 if God s· not the natural branches, "
2Pe 2: 4 if God s· not the angels that sinned, "
5 And s· not the old world, but saved "

spareth
Pr 13: 24 He that s· his rod hateth his son: 2820
17: 27 that hath knowledge s· his words: "
21: 26 but the righteous giveth and s· not.* "
Mal 3: 17 man s· his own son that serveth 2550

sparing
Ac 20: 29 wolves enter...not s· the flock. 5339

sparingly
2Co 9: 6 which soweth s· shall reap also s·; 5340

spark See also SPARKS.
Job 18: 5 the s· of his fire shall not shine. 7632
Isa 1: 31 as tow, and the maker of it as a s·, 5213

sparkled
Eze 1: 7 s· like the colour of burnished 5340

sparks
Job 5: 7 trouble, as the s· fly upward. 1121, 7565
41: 19 lamps, and s· of fire leap out. 3590
Isa 50: 11 compass yourselves about with s·: *2131
11 and in the s· that ye have kindled.* "

sparrow See also SPARROWS.
Ps 84: 3 Yea, the s· hath found an house, 6833
102: 7 am as a s· alone upon the house "

sparrows
M't 10: 29 Are not two s· sold for a farthing? 4765
31 ye are of more value than many s·. "
Lu 12: 6 not five s· sold for two farthings, "
7 ye are of more value than many s·. "

spat See also SPITTED.
Joh 9: 6 he s· on the ground, and made 4429

speak See also SPAKE; SPEAKEST; SPEAKETH; SPEAKING; SPOKEN; UNSPEAKABLE.
Ge 18: 27 taken upon me to s· unto the Lord, 1696
30 not the Lord be angry, and I will s·: "
31 taken upon me to s· unto the Lord: "
32 and I will s· yet but this once: "
24: 33 mine errand. And he said, S· on. "
50 we cannot s· unto thee bad or good. "
27: 6 I heard thy father s· unto Esau thy "
31: 24 Take heed that thou s· not to Jacob "
29 thou heed that thou s· not to Jacob "
32: 4 Thus shall ye s· unto my lord Esau; *559
19 this manner shall ye s· unto Esau, 1696
37: 4 could not s· peaceably unto him. "
44: 16 say unto my lord? what shall we s·? "
18 thee, s· a word in my lord's ears, "
50: 4 s·,...in the ears of Pharaoh, saying, "
Ex 4: 14 brother? I know that he can s· well. "
15 And thou shalt s· unto him, and put "
5: 23 came to Pharaoh to s· in thy name, "
6: 11 s· unto Pharaoh king of Egypt, that "
29 s· thou unto Pharaoh king of Egypt "
7: 2 shalt s· all that I command thee: "
2 thy brother shall s· unto Pharaoh, "
9 When Pharaoh shall s· unto you, "
11: 2 S· now in the ears of the people, "
12: 3 S· ye unto all the congregation of "

Ex 14: 2 S' unto the children of Israel, that 1696
15 s' unto the children of Israel, that "
16: 12 s' unto them, saying, At even ye "
19: 6 shalt s' unto the children of Israel. "
9 may hear when I s' with thee, and "
20: 19 said unto Moses, S' thou with us, "
19 let not God s' with us, lest we die. "
23: 2 neither shalt thou s' in a cause to 6030
22 obey his voice, and do all that I s'; 1696
25: 2 S' unto the children of Israel, that "
28: 3 s' unto all that are wise hearted, "
29: 42 will meet you, to s' there unto thee. "
30: 31 shalt s' unto the children of Israel, "
31: 13 S' thou...unto the children of Israel, "
32: 12 Wherefore should the Egyptians s', 559
34: 34 in before the Lord to s' with him, 1696
35 until he went in to s' with him. "
Le 1: 2 S' unto the children of Israel, and "
4: 2 S' unto the children of Israel, "
6: 25 S' unto Aaron and to his sons, "
7: 23, 29 S' unto the children of Israel, "
9: 3 the children of Israel thou shalt s', "
11: 2 S' unto the children of Israel, "
12: 2 S' unto the children of Israel, "
15: 2 S' unto the children of Israel, and "
16: 2 S' unto Aaron thy brother, that he "
17: 2 S' unto Aaron, and unto his sons, "
18: 2 S' unto the children of Israel, and "
19: 2 S' unto all the congregation of the "
21: 1 S' unto the priests the sons of 559
17 S' unto Aaron, saying, Whosoever 1696
22: 2 S' unto Aaron and to his sons, that "
18 S' unto Aaron, and to his sons, and "
23: 2, 10, 24, 34 S' unto...children of Israel, "
24: 15 shalt s' unto the children of Israel, "
25: 2 S' unto the children of Israel, and "
27: 2 S' unto the children of Israel, and "
Nu 5: 6, 12 S' unto the children of Israel, "
6: 2 S' unto the children of Israel, and "
23 S' unto Aaron and unto his sons, "
7: 89 Moses was gone...to s' with him, "
8: 2 S' unto Aaron, and say unto him, "
9: 10 S' unto the children of Israel, "
12: 6 and will s' unto him in a dream. "
8 With him will I s' mouth to mouth, "
8 afraid to s' against my servant "
14: 15 have heard the fame of thee will s', 559
15: 2, 18, 38 S' unto...children of Israel, 1696
16: 24 S' unto the congregation, saying, "
37 S' unto Eleazar the son of Aaron 559
17: 2 S' unto the children of Israel, and 1696
18: 26 Thus s' unto the Levites, and say "
19: 2 S' unto the children of Israel, that "
20: 8 s' ye unto the rock before their eyes; "
21: 27 they that s' in proverbs say, Come "
22: 8 as the Lord shall s' unto me: 1696
35 I...s' unto thee, that thou shalt s'. "
38 putteth in my mouth, that shall I s'. "
23: 5 unto Balak, and thus thou shalt s'. "
12 to s' that which the Lord hath put "
24: 13 what the Lord saith, that will I s'? "
27: 7 daughters of Zelophehad s' right: "
8 shalt s' unto the children of Israel, "
33: 51 S' unto the children of Israel, and "
35: 10 S' unto the children of Israel, and "
De 3: 26 s' no more unto me of this matter. "
5: 1 judgments which I s' in your ears "
27 s' thou unto us all that the Lord "
27 the Lord our God shall s' unto thee; "
31 s' unto thee all the commandments, "
9: 4 S' not thou in thine heart, after 559
11: 2 for I s' not with your children which "
18: 18 s' unto them all that I...command 1696
19 words which he shall s' in my name, "
20 presume to s' a word in my name, "
20 I have not commanded him to s', "
20 shall s' in the name of other gods, "
20: 2 approach and s' unto the people, "
5 the officers shall s' unto the people, "
8 the officers shall s' further unto the "
25: 8 city shall call him, and s' unto him: "
26: 5 shalt s' and say before the Lord *6030
27: 14 And the Levites shall s', and say "
31: 28 I may s' these words in their ears, 1696
32: 1 Give ear, O ye heavens, and I will s'; "
Jos 4: 10 Lord commanded Joshua to s' unto "
20: 2 S' to the children of Israel, saying, "
22: 24 children might s' unto our children, 559
J'g 5: 10 S', ye that ride on white asses, *7878
6: 39 me, and I will s' but this once: 1696
9: 2 S', I pray you, in the ears of all the "
19: 3 to s' friendly unto her, and to bring "
30 it, take advice, and s' your minds. "
21: 13 to s' to the children of Benjamin * "
1Sa 3: 9 S', Lord; for thy servant heareth. "
10 S'; for thy servant heareth. "
25: 17 Belial, that a man cannot s' to him. "
24 handmaid,...s' in thine audience, "
2Sa 3: 19 went also to s' in the ears of David* "
27 in the gate to s' with him quietly, "
7: 17 vision, so did Nathan s' unto David. "
13: 13 Now...I pray thee, s' unto the king; "
14: 3 and s' on this manner unto him. "
12 s' one word unto my lord the king. "
13 the king doth s' this thing as one * "
15 to s' of this thing unto my lord the "
15 said, I will now s' unto the king; "
18 said, Let my lord the king now s'. "
17: 6 do after his saying? if not; s' thou. "
19: 7 s' comfortably unto thy servants: "
10 why s' ye not a word of bringing 2790
11 S' unto the elders of Judah, 1696
20: 16 Come near...that I may s' with thee. "
18 They were wont to s' in old time, "
1Ki 2: 17 said, S', I pray thee, unto Solomon 559
18 I will s' for thee unto the king. 1696

1Ki 2: 19 to s' unto him for Adonijah. 1696
12: 7 and s' good words to them, then "
10 Thus shalt thou s' unto this people. *559
23 S' unto Rehoboam, the son of "
21: 19, 19 And thou shalt s' unto him, 1696
22: 13 of them, and s' that which is good. "
14 Lord saith unto me, that will I s'. "
24 Spirit...from me to s' unto thee? "
2Ki 18: 19 S' ye now to Hezekiah, Thus saith *559
26 S',...to thy servants in the Syrian 1696
27 and to thee, to s' these words? "
19: 10 Thus shall ye s' to Hezekiah king 559
1Ch 17: 15 so did Nathan s' unto David. 1696
18 What can David s' more to thee for the*
2Ch 10: 7 them, and s' good words to them, 1696
11: 3 S' unto Rehoboam the son of 559
18: 12 one of theirs, and s' thou good. 1696
13 what my God saith, that will I s'. "
23 Spirit...from me to s' unto thee? "
32: 17 God of Israel, and to s' against him 559
Ne 13: 24 could not s' in the Jews' language, 1696
Es 5: 14 to morrow s' thou unto the king 559
6: 4 to s' unto the king to hang Mordecai "
Job 7: 11 will s' in the anguish of my spirit; 1696
8: 2 How long wilt thou s' these 4448
9: 19 If I s' of strength, lo, he is strong: and
35 Then would I s', and not fear him; 1696
10: 1 I will s' in the bitterness of my soul. "
11: 5 But oh that God would s', and open "
12: 8 s' to the earth, and it shall teach 7878
13: 3 Surely I would s' to the Almighty, 1696
7 Will ye s' wickedly for God? and "
13 peace, let me alone, that I may s', "
22 or let me s', and answer thou me. "
16: 4 I also could s' as ye do: if your soul "
6 Though I s', my grief is not "
18: 2 mark, and afterwards we will s'. "
21: 3 Suffer me that I may s'; and after "
27: 4 My lips shall not s' wickedness, nor "
32: 7 Days should s', and multitude of "
20 I will s', that I may be refreshed: "
33: 31 me: hold thy peace, and I will s'. "
32 me: s', for I desire to justify thee. "
34: 33 I: therefore s' what thou knowest. "
36: 2 I have yet to s' on God's behalf. *4405
37: 20 Shall it be told him that I s'? 1696
20 if a man s',...he shall be swallowed *559
41: 3 will he s' soft words unto thee? 1696
42: 4 Hear, I beseech thee, and I will s': "
Ps 2: 5 shall he s' unto them in his wrath, "
5: 6 shalt destroy them that s' leasing: "
12: 2 They s' vanity every one with his "
2 and with a double heart do they s'. "
17: 10 with their mouth they s' proudly. "
28: 3 which s' peace to their neighbours, "
29: 9 doth every one s' of his glory. * 559
31: 18 which s' grievous things proudly 1696
35: 20 For they s' not peace: but they "
28 shall s' of thy righteousness and *1897
38: 12 that seek my hurt s' mischievous 1696
40: 5 if I would declare and s' of them, "
41: 5 Mine enemies s' evil of me, When 559
45: 1 I s' of the things which I have made "
49: 3 My mouth shall s' of wisdom; and 1696
50: 7 Hear, O my people, and I will s'; O "
52: 3 rather than to s' righteousness. "
58: 1 Do ye indeed s' righteousness, O "
59: 12 cursing and lying which they s'. 5608
63: 11 mouth of them that s' lies shall be 1696
69: 12 that sit in the gate s' against me; *7878
71: 10 For mine enemies s' against me; 559
73: 8 They are corrupt, and s' wickedly *1696
8 oppression: they s' loftily. "
15 If I say, I will s' thus; behold, I 5608
75: 5 on high: s' not with a stiff neck. 1696
77: 4 I am so troubled that I cannot s'. "
85: 8 will hear what God the Lord will s': "
8 he will s' peace unto his people, "
94: 4 shall they utter and s' hard things? "
109: 20 them that s' evil against my soul. "
115: 5 They have mouths, but they s' not: "
7 s' they through their throat. 1897
119: 23 Princes...did sit and s' against me: *1696
46 I will s' of thy testimonies also "
172 My tongue shall s' of thy word: *6030
120: 7 but when I s', they are for war. 1696
127: 5 but they shall s' with the enemies "
135: 16 They have mouths, but they s' not; "
139: 20 For they s' against thee wickedly, 559
145: 5 I will s' of the glorious honour of *7878
6 men shall s' of the might of thy 559
11 They shall s' of the glory of thy "
21 My mouth shall s' the praise of the 1696
Pr 8: 6 for I will s' of excellent things; "
7 For my mouth shall s' truth; and *1897
23: 9 S' not in the ears of a fool: for he 1696
16 when thy lips s' right things. "
Ec 3: 7 to keep silence, and a time to s'; "
Ca 7: 9 lips of those that are asleep to s'. *1680
Isa 8: 10 s' the word, and it shall not stand: 1696
20 they s' not according to this word, 559
14: 10 they shall s' and say unto thee, *6030
19: 18 Egypt s' the language of Canaan, 1696
28: 11 another tongue will he s' to this "
29: 4 and shalt s' out of the ground, and "
30: 10 s' unto us smooth things, prophesy "
32: 4 the stammerers shall be ready to s' "
6 the vile person will s' villany, and "
36: 11 S', I pray thee, unto thy servants "
11 s' not to us in the Jews' language, "
12 and to thee to s' these words? "
37: 10 Thus shall ye s' to Hezekiah king 559
40: 2 S' ye comfortably to Jerusalem, 1696
41: 1 them come near; then let them s': "
45: 19 I the Lord s' righteousness, I "
50: 4 know how to s' a word in season *5790

Isa 52: 6 that day that I am he that doth s': 1696
56: 3 hath joined himself to the Lord, s', 559
59: 4 they trust in vanity, and s' lies; 1696
63: 1 I that s' in righteousness, mighty "
Jer 1: 6 Ah, Lord God! behold, I cannot s': "
7 I command thee thou shalt s'. "
17 s' unto them all that I command "
5: 5 great men, and will s' unto them; "
14 Because ye s' this word, behold, I "
6: 10 To whom shall I s', and give "
7: 27 shalt s' all these words unto them; "
9: 5 neighbour, and will not s' the truth: "
5 have taught their tongue to s' lies, "
22 S', Thus saith the Lord, Even the "
10: 5 as the palm tree, but s' not: they "
11: 2 and s' unto the men of Judah, and "
12: 6 though they s' fair words unto thee. "
13: 12 thou shalt s' unto them this word; 559
18: 7, 9 I shall s' concerning a nation, 1696
11 go to, s' to the men of Judah, and 559
20 before thee to s' good for them, 1696
20: 9 him, nor s' any more in his name. "
22: 1 of Judah, and s' there this word, "
23: 16 they s' a vision of their own heart, "
28 word, let him s' my word faithfully. "
26: 2 and s' unto all the cities of Judah, "
2 I command thee to s' unto them; "
8 commanded him to s' unto all the "
15 s' all these words in your ears. "
27: 9 your sorcerers, which s' unto you, 559
14 of the prophets that s' unto you, "
28: 7 this word that I s' in thine ears, 1696
29: 24 shalt thou also s' to Shemaiah the 559
32: 4 shall s' with him mouth to mouth, 1696
34: 2 Go and s' to Zedekiah king of 559
3 he shall s' with thee mouth to 1696
35: 2 the Rechabites, and s' unto them, "
38: 20 of the Lord, which I s' unto thee: "
39: 16 Go and s' to Ebed-melech the 559
Eze 2: 1 thy feet, and I will s' unto thee. 1696
7 thou shalt s' my words unto them, "
3: 1 and go s' unto the house of Israel. "
4 and s' with my words unto them. "
10 all my words that I shall s' unto "
11 and s' unto them, and tell them, "
27 when I s' with thee, I will open thy "
11: 5 upon me, and said unto me, S'; 559
12: 25 For I am the Lord: I will s', and 1696
25 word that I shall s' shall come to "
14: 4 Therefore s' unto them, and say "
17: 2 and s' a parable unto the house of 4911
20: 3 man, s' unto the elders of Israel, 1696
27 man, s' unto the house of Israel, "
49 of me, Doth he not s' parables? *4911
24: 21 S' unto the house of Israel, Thus 559
27 and thou shalt s', and be no more 1696
29: 3 S', and say, Thus saith the Lord "
31: 2 s' unto Pharaoh king of Egypt, * 559
32: 21 strong among the mighty shall s' 1696
33: 2 s' to the children of thy people, and "
8 dost not s' to warn the wicked from "
10 man, s' unto the house of Israel; * 559
10 ye s', saying, If our transgressions "
24 those wastes of the land of Israel s', "
30 s' one to another, every one to his 1696
37: 18 of thy people shall s' unto thee, 559
39: 17 S' unto every feathered fowl, and "
Da 2: 9 and corrupt words to s' before me, 560
3: 29 which s' any thing amiss against "
7: 25 he shall s' great words against 4449
10: 11 understand the words that I s' 1696
19 said, Let my lord s'; for thou hast "
11: 27 and they shall s' lies at one table; "
36 shall s' marvellous things against "
Ho 2: 14 and s' comfortably unto her. "
Hab 2: 3 but at the end it shall s', and not *6315
Zep 3: 13 shall not do iniquity, nor s' lies; 1696
Hag 2: 2 S' now to Zerubbabel the son of 559
21 S' to Zerubbabel, governor of "
Zec 2: 4 Run, s' to this young man, saying, 1696
6: 12 And s' unto him, saying, Thus 559
7: 3 to s' unto the priests which were "
5 S' unto all the people of the land, "
8: 16 S' ye every man the truth to his 1696
9: 10 he shall s' peace unto the heathen: "
M't 8: 8 s' the word only, and my servant *2036
10: 19 thought how or what ye shall s': 2980
19 in that same hour what ye shall s'. "
20 For it is not ye that s', but the "
27 in darkness, that s' ye in light: 2036
12: 34 can ye, being evil, s' good things? 2980
36 every idle word that men shall s', "
46 without, desiring to s' with him. "
47 without, desiring to s' with thee. "
13: 13 Therefore s' I to them in parables: "
15: 31 when they saw the dumb to s', the* "
M'r 1: 34 and suffered not the devils to s', "
2: 7 doth this man thus s' blasphemies? "
7: 37 the deaf to hear, and the dumb to s'. "
9: 39 name, that can lightly s' evil of me. 2551
12: 1 began to s' unto them by parables. 3004
13: 11 beforehand what ye shall s', 2980
11 given you in that hour, that s' ye: "
11 for it is not ye that s', but the Holy "
14: 71 know not this man of whom ye s'. 3004
16: 17 they shall s' with new tongues; 2980
Lu 1: 19 and am sent to s' unto thee, and to "
20 shalt be dumb, and not able to s', "
22 out, he could not s' unto them: "
4: 41 them suffered them not to s': "
6: 26 when all men shall s' well of you! 2036
7: 15 was dead sat up, and began to s'. 2980
24 s' unto...people concerning John, *3004
11: 53 provoke him to s' of many things: 658
12: 10 s' a word against the Son of man, 2046
13 Master, s' to my brother, that he *2036

Lu 20: 9 he to s' to the people this parable;3004
Joh 1: 37 the two disciples heard him s', and 2980
40 One of the two which heard John s',
3: 11 We s' that we do know, and testify 2980
4: 26 unto her, I that s' unto thee am he. "
6: 63 the words that I s' unto you, they* "
7: 17 be of God, or whether I s' of myself. "
8: 26 and I s' to the world those things 3004
28 hath taught me, I s' these things. 2980
38 I s' that which I have seen with my "
9: 21 ask him: he shall s' for himself. "
12: 49 I should say, and what I should s'. "
50 whatsoever I s' therefore, even as "
50 as the Father said unto me, so I s'. "
13: 18 I s' not of you all: I know whom I 3004
14: 10 the words that I s' unto you *2980
10 I s' not of myself: but the Father "
16: 13 for he shall not s' of himself; but "
13 he shall hear, that shall he s': "
25 no more s' unto you in proverbs, "
17: 13 these things I s' in the world, that "
Ac 2: 4 they began to s' with other tongues, "
6 heard them s' in his own language.* "
7 are not all these which s' Galilæans? "
11 we do hear them s' in our tongues* "
29 let me freely s'...of the patriarch *2036
4: 17 they s' henceforth to no man in 2980
18 commanded them not to s' at all 5350
20 s' the things which we have seen 2980
29 all boldness they may s' thy word, "
5: 20 Go, stand and s' in the temple to the "
40 should not s' in the name of Jesus, "
6: 11 heard him s' blasphemous words "
13 man ceaseth not to s' blasphemous "
10: 32 when he cometh, shall s' unto thee.* "
46 they heard them s' with tongues, "
11: 15 as I began to s', the Holy Ghost fell "
14: 9 The same heard Paul s': who * "
18: 9 Be not afraid, but s', and hold not "
26 began to s' boldly in the synagogue: "
21: 37 chief captain, May I s' unto thee?*2036
37 Who said, Canst thou s' Greek? *1097
39 suffer me to s' unto the people. 2980
23: 5 shalt not s' evil of the ruler of thy 2046
24: 10 had beckoned unto him to s', 3004
26: 1 Thou art permitted to s' for thyself. "
25 but s' forth the words of truth and 669
26 things, before whom...I s' freely: 2980
28: 20 you, to see you, and to s' with you: 4354
Ro 3: 5 taketh vengeance? (I s' as a man) 3004
6: 19 I s' after the manner of men "
7: 1 (for I s' to them that know the law,)2980
11: 13 For I s' to you Gentiles, inasmuch 3004
15: 18 I will not dare to s' of any of those 2980
1Co 1: 10 that ye all s' the same thing, and 3004
2: 6 we s' wisdom among them that 2980
7 But we s' the wisdom of God in a "
13 Which things also we s', not in the "
3: 1 not s' unto you as unto spiritual, "
6: 5 I s' to your shame. Is it so, that *3004
7: 6 I s' this by permission, and not of* "
12 But to the rest s' I, not the Lord: * "
35 And this I s' for your own profit; * "
10: 15 I s' as to wise men; judge ye what I "
12: 30 do all s' with tongues? do all 2980
13: 1 I s' with the tongues of men and of "
14: 6 except I shall s' to you either by "
9 spoken? for ye shall s' into the air.* "
18 I s' with tongues more than ye all: "
19 I had rather s' five words with my "
21 other lips will I s' unto this people; "
23 one place, and all s' with tongues, "
27 any man s' in an unknown tongue,* "
28 let him s' to himself, and to God. "
29 Let the prophets s' two or three, "
34 it is not permitted unto them to s'; "
35 is a shame for women to s' in the "
39 and forbid not to s' with tongues. "
15: 34 of God: I s' this to your shame. 3004
2Co 2: 17 in the sight of God s' we in Christ. 2980
4: 13 we also believe, and therefore s'; "
6: 13 (I s' as unto my children,) be ye also3004
7: 3 I s' not this to condemn you: for I* "
8: 8 I s' not by commandment, but by "
11: 17 That which I s', I s' it not after the 2980
21 I s' as concerning reproach, as 3004
21 bold, (I s' foolishly,) I am bold also. "
23 Christ? (I s' as a fool) I am more; 2980
12: 19 we s' before God in Christ: but we "
Ga 3: 15 I s' after the manner of men; 3004
Eph 4: 25 s' every man truth with his 2980
5: 12 a shame even to s' of those things 3004
32 but I s' concerning Christ and the "
6: 20 that therein I may s' boldly, as I ought
20 boldly, as I ought to s'. 2980
Ph'p 1: 14 are much more bold to s' the word "
4: 11 Not that I s' in respect of want: 3004
Col 4: 3 to s' the mystery of Christ, for 2980
4 make it manifest, as I ought to s'. "
1Th 1: 8 so that we need not to s' any thing. "
2: 2 bold in our God to s' unto you the "
4 trust with the gospel, even so we s'; "
16 Forbidding us to s' to the Gentiles "
1Ti 2: 7 s' the truth in Christ, and lie not;) 3004
5: 14 to the adversary to s' reproachfully.*
Tit 2: 1 s' thou the things which become 2980
15 These things s', and exhort, and "
3: 2 To s' evil of no man, to be no 987
Heb 2: 5 the world to come, whereof we s'. 2980
6: 9 salvation, though we thus s'. "
9: 5 we cannot now s' particularly. 3004
Jas 1: 19 to hear, slow to s', slow to wrath: 2980
2: 12 So s' ye, and so do, as they that "
4: 11 S' not evil one of another, 2635
1Pe 2: 12 they s' against you as evildoers, "
3: 10 and his lips that they s' no guile: 2980
1Pe 3: 16 whereas they s' evil of you, as of 2635
4: 11 If any man s', let him *2980
11 him s' as the oracles of God; * "
2Pe 2: 10 are not afraid to s' evil of dignities.*987
12 s' evil of the things that they * "
18 when they s' great swelling words*5350
1Jo 4: 5 therefore s' they of the world, and 2980
2Jo 12 s' face to face, that our joy may be "
3Jo 14 thee, and we shall s' face to face. "
Jude 8 dominion, and s' evil of dignities. *987
10 these s' evil of those things which* "
Re 2: 24 the depths of Satan, as they s'; *3004
13: 15 image of the beast should both s', 2980

speaker
Ps 140: 11 not an evil s' be established 376,3956
Ac 14: 12 because he was the chief s'. 3056

speakest
1Sa 9: 21 wherefore then s' thou so to me? 1696
2Sa 19: 29 him, Why s' thou any more of thy "
2Ki 6: 12 words...thou s' in thy bedchamber. "
Job 2: 10 Thou s' as one of the foolish women "
Ps 50: 20 sittest and s' against thy brother; "
51: 4 mightest be justified when thou s', "
Isa 40: 27 Why sayest thou, O Jacob, and s', O "
Jer 40: 16 for thou s' falsely of Ishmael. "
43: 2 unto Jeremiah, Thou s' falsely: "
Eze 3: 18 nor s' to warn the wicked from his "
Zec 13: 3 thou s' lies in the name of the Lord: "
M't 13: 10 Why s'...unto them in parables? 2980
Lu 12: 41 Lord, s' thou this parable unto us,3004
Joh 16: 29 unto him, Lo, now s' thou plainly, 2980
29 thou plainly, and s' no proverb. 3004
19: 10 unto him, S' thou not unto me? 2980
Ac 17: 19 new doctrine, whereof thou s', is?* "

speaketh
Ge 45: 12 it is my mouth that s' unto you. 1696
Ex 33: 11 to face, as a man s' unto his friend. "
Nu 23: 26 All that the Lord s', that I must do? "
De 18: 22 When a prophet s' in the name of "
1Ki 20: 5 said, Thus s' Ben-hadad, saying, 559
Job 2: 10 as one of the foolish women s'. 1696
17: 5 He that s' flattery to his friends, *5046
33: 14 God s' once, yea twice, yet man 1696
Ps 12: 3 the tongue that s' proud things: "
15: 2 and s' the truth in his heart. "
37: 30 mouth of the righteous s' wisdom.*1897
41: 6 if he come to see me, he s' vanity: 1696
144: 8 Whose mouth s' vanity, and their "
11 children, whose mouth s' vanity, "
Pr 2: 12 the man that s' froward things; * "
6: 13 he s' with his feet, he teacheth 4448
19 A false witness that s' lies, and he*6315
10: 32 mouth of the wicked s' frowardness.
12: 17 He that s' truth showeth forth *6315
18 s' like the piercings of a sword: 981
14: 25 but a deceitful witness s' lies. *6315
16: 13 and they love him that s' right. 1696
19: 5 he that s' lies shall not escape. *6315
9 and he that s' lies shall perish. "
21: 28 man that heareth s' constantly. *1696
26: 25 When he s' fair, believe him not: 6963
Isa 9: 17 and every mouth s' folly. 1696
32: 7 words, even when the needy s' right. "
33: 15 righteously, and s' uprightly; "
Jer 9: 8 as an arrow shot out; it s' deceit: "
8 one s' peaceably to his neighbour "
10: 1 word which the Lord s' unto you, "
28: 2 Thus s' the Lord of hosts, the God 559
29: 25 Thus s' the Lord of hosts, the God "
30: 2 Thus s' the Lord God of Israel, "
Eze 10: 5 of the Almighty God when he s'. 1696
Am 5: 10 they abhor him that s' uprightly. "
Hag 1: 2 Thus s' the Lord of hosts, saying, 559
Zec 6: 12 Thus s' the Lord of hosts, saying, "
7: 9 Thus s' the Lord of hosts, saying, "
M't 10: 20 of your Father which s' in you. 2980
12: 32 whosoever s' a word against the *2036
32 whosoever s' against the Holy "
34 out...of the heart the mouth s'. 2980
Lu 5: 21 Who is this which s' blasphemies? "
6: 45 of the heart his mouth s'. "
Joh 3: 31 earth is earthly, and s' of the earth: "
34 God hath sent s' the words of God: "
7: 18 He that s' of himself seeketh his "
26 But, lo, he s' boldly, and they say "
8: 44 When he s' a lie, he s' of his own: "
19: 12 himself a king s' against Cæsar. 483
Ac 2: 25 For David s' concerning him, I *3004
8: 34 thee, of whom s' the prophet this? "
Ro 10: 6 which is of faith s' on this wise, * "
1Co 14: 2 he that s' in an unknown tongue 2980
2 s' not unto men, but unto God: for "
2 in the spirit he s' mysteries. "
3 he that prophesieth s' unto men "
4 s' in an unknown tongue edifieth "
5 than he that s' with tongues, "
11 be unto him that s' a barbarian, "
11 and he that s' shall be a barbarian "
13 let him that s' in an unknown "
1Ti 4: 1 the Spirit s' expressly, that in the *3004
Heb 11: 4 and by it he being dead yet s'. 2980
12: 5 which s' unto you as unto children,*1256
24 that s' better things than that of 2980
25 See that ye refuse not him that s'. "
25 away from him that s' from heaven: "
Jas 4: 11 He that s' evil of his brother, and 2635
11 s' evil of the law, and judgeth the "
Jude 16 mouth s' great swelling words, 2980

speaking See also SPEAKINGS.
Ge 24: 15 to pass, before he had done s', 1696
45 before I had done s' in mine heart, "
Ex 34: 33 till Moses had done s' with them, "
Nu 7: 89 heard the voice of one s' unto him "
Nu 16: 31 made an end of s' all these words, 1696
De 4: 33 God s' out of the midst of the fire, "
5: 26 God s' out of the midst of the fire, "
11: 19 s' of them when thou sittest in * "
20: 9 made an end of s' unto the people, * "
32: 45 Moses made an end of s' all these "
J'g 15: 17 when he had made an end of s', "
Ru 1: 18 with her, then she left s' unto her. "
1Sa 18: 1 had made an end of s' unto Saul, "
24: 16 an end of s' these words unto Saul, "
2Sa 13: 36 soon as he had made an end of s', "
2Ch 36: 12 the prophet s' from the mouth of the "
Es 10: 3 people, and s' peace to all his seed.1696
Job 1: 16, 17, 18 While he was yet s', there "
4: 2 who can withhold himself from s'?4405
32: 15 answered no more: they left off s'.* "
Ps 34: 13 evil, and thy lips from s' guile. 1696
58: 3 as soon as they be born, s' lies. "
Isa 58: 9 forth of the finger, and s' vanity; "
13 pleasure, nor s' thine own words: "
59: 13 s' oppression and revolt, conceiving "
65: 24 while they are yet s', I will hear. "
Jer 7: 13 rising up early and s', but ye heard "
25: 3 rising early and s'; but ye have "
26: 7 heard Jeremiah s' these words in "
8 Jeremiah had made an end of s' all "
35: 14 unto you, rising early and s'; but "
38: 4 people, in s' such words unto them: "
27 So they left off s' with him; for the2790
43: 1 had made an end of s' unto all the1696
Eze 43: 6 I heard him s' unto me out of the "
Da 7: 8 man, and a mouth s' great things.4449
8: 13 Then I heard one saint s', and 1696
18 Now as he was s' with me, I was in "
9: 20 And whiles I was s', and praying, "
21 whiles I was s' in prayer, even the "
M't 6: 7 shall be heard for their much s'. 4180
Lu 5: 4 Now when he had left s', he said 2980
Ac 1: 3 s' of the things pertaining to the 3004
7: 44 s' unto Moses, that he should *2980
13: 43 who, s' to them, persuaded them 4354
14: 3 abode they s' boldly in the Lord, "
20: 30 s' perverse things, to draw away 2980
26: 14 I heard a voice s' unto me, and * "
1Co 12: 3 that no man s' by the Spirit of God "
14: 6 I come unto you s' with tongues, "
2Co 13: 3 ye seek a proof of Christ s' in me, * "
Eph 4: 15 s' the truth in love, may grow up 226
31 and evil s', be put away from you,* 988
5: 19 S' to yourselves in psalms and 2980
1Ti 4: 2 S' lies in hypocrisy; having their*5573
5: 13 s' things which they ought not. 2980
1Pe 4: 4 same excess of riot, s' evil of you: 987
2Pe 2: 16 the dumb ass s' with man's voice *5350
3: 16 epistles, s' in them of these things;2980
Re 13: 5 him a mouth s' great things and "

speakings
1Pe 2: 1 and envies, and all evil s', 2636

spear See also SPEARMEN; SPEAR'S; SPEARS.
Jos 8: 18 Stretch out the s' that is in thy *3591
18 Joshua stretched out the s' that * "
26 wherewith he stretched out the s',* "
J'g 5: 8 a shield or s' seen among forty 7420
1Sa 13: 22 neither sword nor s' found in the 2595
17: 7 staff of his s' was like a weaver's "
45 to me with a sword, and with a s', "
47 Lord saveth not with sword and s': "
21: 8 here under thine hand s' or sword? "
22: 6 having his s' in his hand, and all "
26: 7 his s' stuck in the ground at his "
8 with the s' even to the earth at "
11 now the s' that is at his bolster, "
12 So David took the s' and the cruse "
16 now see where the king's s' is, and "
22 and said, Behold the king's s'! and "
2Sa 1: 6 behold, Saul leaned upon his s'; "
2: 23 end of the s' smote him under the "
23 that the s' came out behind him; "
21: 16 s' weighed three hundred shekels 7013
19 of whose s' was like a weaver's 2595
23: 7 with iron and the staff of a s'; and "
8 lift up his s' against eight hundred.*
18 up his s' against three hundred, 2595
21 the Egyptian had a s' in his hand; "
21 the s' out of the Egyptian's hand, "
21 hand, and slew him with his own s'. "
1Ch 11: 11 up his s' against three hundred "
20 up his s' against three hundred, "
23 was a s' like a weaver's beam; and "
23 the s' out of the Egyptian's hand, "
23 hand, and slew him with his own s'. "
12: 24 of Judah that bare shield and s' 7420
34 them with shield and s' thirty and2595
20: 5 whose s' staff was like a weaver's "
2Ch 25: 5 that could handle s' and shield. 7420
Job 39: 23 the glittering s' and the shield. 2595
41: 26 the s', the dart, nor the habergeon. "
29 he laugheth at the shaking of a s'.*3591
Ps 35: 3 Draw out also the s', and stop the 2595
46: 9 bow, and cutteth the s' in sunder; "
Jer 6: 23 They shall lay hold on bow and s':3591
Na 3: 3 bright sword and the glittering s':2595
Hab 3: 11 at the shining of thy glittering s'. "
Joh 19: 34 soldiers with a s' pierced his side, 3057

spearmen
Ps 68: 30 Rebuke the company of s', the *7070
Ac 23: 23 s' two hundred, at the third hour 1187

spear's
1Sa 17: 7 his s' head weighed six hundred 2595

spears
1Sa 13: 19 Hebrews make them swords or s':2595
2Ki 11: 10 give king David's s' and shields, "
2Ch 11: 12 several city he put shields and s'. 7420

2Ch 14: 8 of men that bare targets and s', 7420
23: 9 to the captains of hundreds s', 2595
26:14 all the host shields, and s', and 7420
Ne 4:13 their swords, their s', and their "
16 half of them held both the s', and "
21 half of them held the s' from the "
Job 41: 7 irons? or his head with fish s'? 6767
Ps 57: 4 whose teeth are s' and arrows, 2595
Isa 2: 4 and their s' into pruninghooks: "
Jer 46: 4 furbish the s', and put on the 7420
Eze 39: 9 and the handstaves, and the s', and "
Joe 3:10 and your pruninghooks into s': "
Mic 4: 3 and their s' into pruninghooks: 2595

special
De 7: 6 to be a s' people unto himself, †‡5459
Ac 19:11 God wrought s' miracles *3756,3858,5177*

specially See also ESPECIALLY.
De 4:10 S' the day that thou stoodest before*
Ac 25:26 and s' before thee, O king Agrippa, *3122*
1Ti 4:10 of all men, s' of those that believe. "
5: 8 and s' for those of his own house, "
Tit 1:10 s' they of the circumcision: "
Ph'm 16 servant, a brother beloved, s' to me,"

speckled
Ge 30:32 thence all the s' and spotted cattle,5348
32 the spotted and s' among the goats:"
33 not s' and spotted among the goats,"
35 she goats that were s' and spotted, "
39 cattle ringstraked, s', and spotted. "
31: 8 said thus, The s' shall be thy wages;"
8 wages; then all the cattle bare s': "
10 were ringstraked, s', and grisled. "
12 are ringstraked, s', and grisled: "
Jer 12: 9 heritage is unto me as a s' bird, 6641
Zec 1: 8 there red horses, s', and white. *8320

spectacle
1Co 4: 9 we are made a s' unto the world, *2302*

sped
J'g 5:30 Have they not s'? have they not *4672

speech See also SPEECHES; SPEECHLESS.
Ge 4:23 of Lamech, hearken unto my s': 565
11: 1 was of one language, and of one s'.1697
7 not understand one another's s'. 8193
Ex 4:10 but I am slow of s', and of a slow 6310
De 22:14 give occasions of s' against her, *1697
17 given occasions of s' against her, * "
32: 2 my s' shall distil as the dew, as the 565
2Sa 14:20 To fetch about this form of s' hath*1697
19:11 s' of all Israel is come to the king, "
1Ki 3:10 s' pleased the Lord, that Solomon "
2Ch 32:18 with a loud voice in the Jews' s', *3066
Ne 13:24 spake half in the s' of Ashdod, and "
Job 12:20 removeth away the s' of the trusty,8193
13:17 Hear diligently my s', and my 4405
21: 2 Hear diligently my s', and let this be"
24:25 and make my s' nothing worth? "
29:22 and my s' dropped upon them. "
37:19 we cannot order our s' by reason of "
Ps 17: 6 thine ear to me, and hear my s'. 565
19: 2 Day unto day uttereth s', and night 562
3 There is no s' nor language, where "
Pr 7:21 With her much fair s' she caused 3948
17: 7 Excellent s' becometh not a fool: 8193
Ca 4: 3 of scarlet, and thy s' is comely: *4057
Isa 28:23 my voice; hearken, and hear my s'. 565
29: 4 thy s' shall be low out of the dust, "
4 thy s' shall whisper out of the dust. "
32: 9 daughters; give ear unto my s'. "
33:19 a people of a deeper s' than thou 8193
Jer 31:23 use this s' in the land of Judah, 1697
Eze 1:24 the voice of s', as the noise of an *1999
3: 5 not sent to a people of a strange s' 8193
6 to many a people of a strange s' and"
Hab 3: 2 O Lord, I have heard thy s', and *8088
M't 26:73 them; for thy s' bewrayeth thee. *2981*
M'r 7:32 and had an impediment in his s'; *3424*
14:70 and thy s' agreeth thereto. **2981*
Joh 8:43 Why do ye not understand my s'? "
Ac 14:11 saying in the s' of Lycaonia, *3072*
20: 7 continued his s' until midnight. *3056*
1Co 2: 1 with excellency of s' or of wisdom, "
4 my s' and my preaching was not "
4:19 not the s' of them which are puffed*"
2Co 3:12 hope, we use great plainness of s': "
7: 4 Great is my boldness of s' toward "
10:10 is weak, and his s' contemptible. *3056*
11: 6 But though I be rude in s', yet not "
Col 4: 6 Let your s' be always with grace, "
Tit 2: 8 Sound s', that cannot be condemned;"

speeches
Nu 12: 8 apparently, and not in dark s'; 2420
Job 6:26 and the s' of one that is desperate, 561
15: 3 s' wherewith he can do no good? 4405
32:14 will I answer him with your s'. 561
33: 1 Job, I pray thee, hear my s', and *4405
Ro 16:18 fair s' deceive the hearts of the **2129*
Jude 15 hard s' which ungodly sinners have*

speechless
M't 22:12 wedding garment? And he was s'. *5392*
Lu 1:22 unto them, and remained s'. **2974*
Ac 9: 7 which journeyed with him stood s',*1769*

speed See also SPED.
Ge 24:12 send me good s' this day, and shew7136
1Sa 20:38 the lad, Make s', haste, stay not. 4120
2Sa 15:14 make s' to depart, lest he overtake4116
1Ki 12:18 Rehoboam made s' to get him up to553
2Ch 10:18 Rehoboam made s' to get him up to "
Ezr 6:12 a decree; let it be done with s'. *629
Isa 5:19 Let him make s', and hasten his 4116
26 they shall come with s' swiftly: 4120
Ac 17:15 for to come to him with all s', *5613,5033*

2Jo 10 house, neither bid him God s': **5463*
11 For he that biddeth him God s' is* "

speedily
Ge 44:11 they s' took down every man his *4116
1Sa 27: 1 I should s' escape into the land of*4422
2Sa 17:16 the wilderness, but s' pass over; *5674
2Ch 35:13 divided them s' among all the people.*
Ezr 6:13 the king had sent, so they did s'. * 629
7:17 thou mayest buy s' with this money*"
21 shall require of you, it be done s'.* "
26 judgment be executed s' upon him,* "
Es 2: 9 and he s' gave her her things for 926
Ps 31: 2 thine ear to me; deliver me s': 4120
69:17 for I am in trouble: hear me s'. 4118
79: 8 thy tender mercies s' prevent us: "
102: 2 in the day when I call answer me s'."
143: 7 Hear me s', O Lord: my spirit * "
Ec 8:11 an evil work is not executed s', 4120
Isa 58: 8 thine health shall spring forth s': "
Joe 3: 4 s' will I return your recompence "
Zec 8:21 us go s' to pray before the Lord, 1980
Lu 18: 8 that he will avenge them s'. *1722,5034*

speedy
Zep 1:18 a s' riddance of all them that dwell*926

spend See also SPENDEST; SPENDETH; SPENT.
De 32:23 I will s' mine arrows upon them. 3615
Job 21:13 They s' their days in wealth, 1086, "
36:11 shall s' their days in prosperity, "
Ps 90: 9 we s' our years as a tale that is told.*"
Isa 55: 2 do ye s' money for that which is 8254
Ac 20:16 he would not s' the time in Asia: *5551*
2Co 12:15 I will very gladly s' and be spent *1159*

spendest
Lu 10:35 whatsoever thou s' more, when I *4325*

spendeth
Pr 21:20 wise; but a foolish man s' it up. *1104
29: 3 with harlots s' his substance. * 6
Ec 6:12 vain life which he s' as a shadow? 6213

spent
Ge 21:15 And the water was s' in the bottle,3615
47:18 my lord, how that our money is s';8552
Le 26:20 your strength shall be s' in vain: "
J'g 19:11 were by Jebus, the day was far s'; 7286
1Sa 9: 7 for the bread is s' in our vessels, 235
Job 7: 6 shuttle, and are s' without hope. 3615
Ps 31:10 For my life is s' with grief, and "
Isa 49: 4 I have s' my strength for nought, "
Jer 37:21 all the bread in the city were s'. 8552
M'r 5:26 had s' all that she had, and was *1159*
6:35 when the day was now far s', his
Lu 8:43 which had s' all her living upon *4321*
15:14 when he had s' all, there arose a *1159*
24:29 evening, and the day is far s'. *2827*
Ac 17:21 there s' their time in nothing else, *2119*
18:23 after he had s' some time there, *4160*
27: 9 Now when much time was s', and *1230*
Ro 13:12 The night is far s', the day is at *4298*
2Co 12:15 gladly spend and be s' for you; *1550*

spewing See also SPUE.
Hab 2:16 shameful s' shall be on thy glory.*7022

spice See also SPICED; SPICES.
Ex 35:28 s', and oil for the light, and for 1314
1Ki 10:15 of the traffick of the s' merchants,*7402
2Ch 9: 9 there any such s' as the queen of 1314
Ca 5: 1 gathered my myrrh with my s'; 1313
Eze 24:10 consume the flesh, and s' it well, *7543

spiced
Ca 8: 2 cause thee to drink of s' wine of 7544

spice-merchants See SPICE and MERCHANTS.

spicery
Ge 37:25 bearing s' and balm and myrrh, 5219

spices
Ge 43:11 s', and myrrh, nuts, and almonds:*5219
Ex 25: 6 s' for anointing oil, and for sweet 1314
30:23 also unto thee principal s', of pure "
34 Take unto thee sweet s', stacte, 5561
34 sweet s' with pure frankincense: "
35: 8 s' for anointing oil, and for the 1314
37:29 and the pure incense of sweet s', 5561
1Ki 10: 2 with camels that bare s', and very 1314
10 of gold, and of s' very great store, "
10 no more such abundance of s' as "
25 garments, and armour, and s', and "
2Ki 20:13 gold, and the s', and the precious "
1Ch 9:29 and the frankincense, and the s'. "
30 priests made the ointment of the s'. "
2Ch 9: 1 and camels that bare s', and gold in "
9 of gold, and of s' great abundance, "
24 raiment, harness, and s', horses, "
16:14 sweet odours and divers kinds of s' "
32:27 precious stones, and for s', and 1314
Ca 4:10 smell of thine ointments than all s'! "
14 and aloes, with all the chief s': "
16 that the s' thereof may flow out. "
5:13 His cheeks are as a bed of s', as "
6: 2 into his garden, to the beds of s', "
8:14 hart upon the mountains of s'. "
Isa 39: 2 and the gold, and the s', and the "
Eze 27:22 in thy fairs with chief of all s', "
M'r 16: 1 and Salome, had bought sweet s', *759*
Lu 23:56 and prepared s' and ointments; "
24: 1 bringing the s' which they had "
Joh 19:40 wound it in linen clothes with the s'."

spider See also SPIDER'S.
Pr 30:28 The s' taketh hold with her hands,*8079

spider's
Job 8:14 and whose trust shall be a s' web. 5908
Isa 59: 5 eggs, and weave the s' web: "

spied See also ESPIED.
Ex 2:11 And he s' an Egyptian smiting an*7200
Jos 6:22 men that had s' out the country, 7270
2Ki 9:17 he s' the company of Jehu as he 7200
13:21 that, behold, they s' a band of men;"
23:16 he s' the sepulchres that were there"
24 abominations that were s' in the "

spies
Ge 42: 9 and said unto them, Ye are s'; 7270
11 true men, thy servants are no s'. "
14 spake unto you, saying, Ye are s': "
16 the life of Pharaoh surely ye are s'. "
30 and took us for s' of the country. "
31 We are true men; we are no s': "
34 I know that ye are no s', but that "
Nu 21: 1 Israel came by the way of the s'; * 871
Jos 6:23 young men that were s' went in, 7270
J'g 1:24 the s' saw a man come forth out of8104
1Sa 26: 4 David therefore sent out s', and 7270
2Sa 15:10 Absalom sent s' throughout all the "
Lu 20:20 watched him, and sent forth s', *1455*
Heb 11:31 when she had received the s' with *2685*

spikenard
Ca 1:12 my s' sendeth forth the smell 5373
4:13 pleasant fruits; camphire, with s', "
14 S' and saffron; calamus and "
M'r 14: 3 box of ointment of s' very ‡*3487,4101*
Joh 12: 3 Mary a pound of ointment of s'‡ "

spilled See also SPILT.
Ge 38: 9 that he s' it on the ground, lest 7843
M'r 2:22 the bottles, and the wine is s', **1632*
Lu 5:37 will burst the bottles, and be s', "

spilt See also SPILLED.
2Sa 14:14 and are as water s' on the ground,5064

spin See also SPUN.
Ex 35:25 that were wise hearted did s' 2901
M't 6:28 they toil not, neither do they s': *3514*
Lu 12:27 grow: they toil not, they s' not; "

spindle
Pr 31:19 She layeth her hands to the s', *3601

spirit (or Spirit) See also SPIRITS.
Ge 1: 2 S' of God moved upon the face of 7307
6: 3 My s' shall not always strive with "
41: 8 morning that his s' was troubled; "
38 is, a man in whom the S' of God is? "
45:27 the s' of Jacob their father revived: "
Ex 6: 9 not unto Moses for anguish of s', "
28: 3 I have filled with the s' of wisdom, "
31: 3 I have filled him with the s' of God, "
35:21 one whom his s' made willing, "
31 hath filled him with the s' of God, "
Le 20:27 or woman that hath a familiar s', 178
Nu 5:14, 14 s' of jealousy came upon him, 7307
30 the s' of jealousy cometh upon him, "
11:17 take of the s' which is upon thee, "
25 took of the s' that was upon him, "
25 when the s' rested upon them, they "
26 and the s' rested upon them; and "
29 Lord would put his s' upon them! "
14:24 he had another s' with him, and "
24: 2 and the s' of God came upon him. "
27:18 of Nun, a man in whom is the s', "
De 2:30 the Lord thy God hardened his s', "
34: 9 of Nun was full of the s' of wisdom; "
Jos 5: 1 was there s' in them any more, "
J'g 3:10 the S' of the Lord came upon him, "
6:34 S' of the Lord came upon Gideon, "
9:23 Then God sent an evil s' between "
11:29 Then the S' of the Lord came upon "
13:25 S' of the Lord began to move him "
14: 6 S' of the Lord came mightily upon "
19 the S' of the Lord came upon him, "
15:14 S' of the Lord came mightily upon "
19 his s' came again, and he revived: "
1Sa 1:15 I am a woman of a sorrowful s': "
10: 6 S' of the Lord will come upon thee, "
10 and the S' of God came upon him, "
11: 6 And the S' of God came upon Saul "
16:13 S' of the Lord came upon David "
14 S' of the Lord departed from Saul, "
14 evil s' from the Lord troubled him. "
15 an evil s' from God troubleth thee. "
16 the evil s' from God is upon thee, "
23 the evil s' from God was upon Saul, "
23 and the evil s' departed from him. "
18:10 evil s' from God came upon Saul, "
19: 9 evil s' from the Lord was upon Saul, "
20 S' of God was upon the messengers "
23 the S' of God was upon him also, "
28: 7 a woman that hath a familiar s', 178
7 is a woman that hath a familiar s'. "
8 divine unto me by the familiar s', "
30:12 eaten, his s' came again to him: 7307
2Sa 23: 2 The S' of the Lord spake by me, "
1Ki 10: 5 Lord; there was no more s' in her. "
18:12 the S' of the Lord shall carry thee "
21: 5 Why is thy s' so sad, that thou "
22:21 And there came forth a s', and stood "
22 I will be a lying s' in the mouth of "
23 hath put a lying s' in the mouth of "
24 Which way went the S' of the Lord "
2Ki 2: 9 double portion of thy s' be upon me. "
15 The s' of Elijah doth rest on Elisha. "
16 S' of the Lord hath taken him up, "
1Ch 5:26 up the s' of Pul king of Assyria, "
26 and the s' of Tilgath-pilneser king "
10:13 of one that had a familiar s', 178
12:18 Then the s' came upon Amasai, 7307
28:12 pattern of all that he had by the s', "
2Ch 9: 4 Lord; there was no more s' in her. "
15: 1 the S' of God came upon Azariah "
18:20 Then there came out a s', and stood "

2Ch 18:21 be a lying *s'* in the mouth of all his 7307
22 hath put a lying *s'* in the mouth of "
23 Which way went the *S'* of the Lord "
20:14 came the *S'* of the Lord in the midst "
21:16 Jehoram the *s'* of the Philistines, "
24:20 the *S'* of God came upon Zechariah "
33:6 and dealt with a familiar *s'*, and * 178
36:22 up the *s'* of Cyrus king of Persia, 7307
Ezr 1:1 up the *s'* of Cyrus king of Persia, "
5 all them whose *s'* God had raised, "
Ne 9:20 gavest also thy good *s'* to instruct "
30 testifiedst against them by thy *s'* in "
Job 4:15 Then a *s'* passed before my face; "
6:4 poison whereof drinketh up my *s'*: "
7:11 I will speak in the anguish of my *s'*; "
10:12 visitation hath preserved my *s'*. "
15:13 that turnest thy *s'* against God, "
20:3 and the *s'* of my understanding "
21:4 why should not my *s'* be troubled?* "
26:4 and whose *s'* came from thee? 5397
13 By his *s'* he hath garnished the 7307
27:3 and the *s'* of God is in my nostrils; "
32:8 But there is a *s'* in man: and the "
18 the *s'* within me constraineth me. "
33:4 The *S'* of God hath made me, and "
34:14 if he gather unto himself his *s'* and "
Ps 31:5 Into thine hand I commit my *s'*: "
32:2 and in whose *s'* there is no guile. "
34:18 saveth such as be of a contrite *s'*. "
51:10 and renew a right *s'* within me. "
11 and take not thy holy *s'* from me. "
12 and uphold me with thy free *s'*. "
17 sacrifices of God are a broken *s'*: "
76:12 He shall cut off the *s'* of princes: "
77:3 and my *s'* was overwhelmed. "
6 and my *s'* made diligent search. "
78:8 whose *s'* was not stedfast with God. "
104:30 Thou sendest forth thy *s'*, they are "
106:33 Because they provoked his *s'*, so "
139:7 Whither shall I go from thy *s'*? or "
142:3 When my *s'* was overwhelmed "
143:4 is my *s'* overwhelmed within me; "
7 speedily, O Lord: my *s'* faileth: "
10 thou art my God: thy *s'* is good; "
Pr 1:23 I will pour out my *s'* unto you, I "
11:13 he that is of a faithful *s'* concealeth "
14:29 he that is hasty of *s'* exalteth folly. "
15:4 perverseness...is a breach in the *s'*. "
13 sorrow of the heart the *s'* is broken. "
16:18 and an haughty *s'* before a fall. "
19 be of an humble *s'* with the lowly, "
32 and he that ruleth his *s'* than he "
17:22 but a broken *s'* drieth the bones. "
27 understanding is of an excellent *s'*. "
18:14 The *s'* of a man will sustain his "
14 but a wounded *s'* who can bear? "
20:27 The *s'* of man is the candle of the 5397
25:28 that hath no rule over his own *s'* 7307
29:23 shall uphold the humble in *s'*. "
Ec 1:14 all is vanity and vexation of *s'*. * "
17 that this also is vexation of *s'*. * "
2:11 all was vanity and vexation of *s'*, * "
17 all is vanity and vexation of *s'*. * "
26 also is vanity and vexation of *s'*. * "
3:21 the *s'* of man that goeth upward, "
21 *s'* of the beast that goeth downward "
4:4 is also vanity and vexation of *s'*. * "
6 full with travail and vexation of *s'*.* "
16 also is vanity and vexation of *s'*. * "
6:9 is also vanity and vexation of *s'*. * "
7:8 and the patient in *s'* is better "
8 is better than the proud in *s'*. "
9 Be not hasty in thy *s'* to be angry: "
8:8 power over the *s'* to retain the *s'*; "
10:4 If the *s'* of the ruler rise up against "
11:5 knowest not...the way of the *s'*, * "
12:7 and the *s'* shall return unto God "
Isa 4:4 midst thereof by the *s'* of judgment, "
4 judgment, and by the *s'* of burning. "
11:2 *s'* of the Lord shall rest upon him, "
2 the *s'* of wisdom and understanding, "
2 the *s'* of counsel and might, "
2 the *s'* of knowledge and of the fear "
19:3 *s'* of Egypt shall fail in the midst "
14 Lord hath mingled a perverse *s'* "
26:9 with my *s'* within me will I seek "
28:6 a *s'* of judgment to him that sitteth "
29:4 be, as of one that hath a familiar *s'*, 178
10 out upon you the *s'* of deep sleep, 7307
24 They also that erred in *s'* shall "
30:1 with a covering, but not of my *s'*, "
31:3 and their horses flesh, and not *s'*. "
32:15 Until the *s'* be poured upon us from "
34:16 and his *s'* it hath gathered them. "
38:16 all these things is the life of my *s'*: "
40:7 the *s'* of the Lord bloweth upon it:* "
13 hath directed the *S'* of the Lord, "
42:1 I have put my *s'* upon him: he shall "
5 and *s'* to them that walk therein: "
44:3 I will pour my *s'* upon thy seed, "
48:16 Lord God, and his *S'*, hath sent me. "
54:6 a woman forsaken and grieved in *s'*, "
57:15 that is of a contrite and humble *s'*, "
15 to revive the *s'* of the humble and "
16 for the *s'* should fail before me, and "
59:19 *S'* of the Lord...lift up a standard* "
21 My *s'* that is upon thee, and my "
61:1 The *S'* of the Lord God is upon me; "
3 of praise for the *s'* of heaviness; "
63:10 rebelled, and vexed his holy *S'*: "
11 he that put his holy *S'* within him? "
14 *S'* of the Lord caused him to rest: "
65:14 and shall howl for vexation of *s'*. "
66:2 him that is poor and of a contrite *s'*, "
Jer 51:11 up the *s'* of the kings of the Medes: "
Eze 1:12 whither the *s'* was to go, they went; "

Eze 1:20 Whithersoever the *s'* was to go 7307
20 went, thither was their *s'* to go; "
20, 21 *s'* of the living creature was in "
2:2 *s'* entered into me when he spake "
3:12 Then the *s'* took me up, and I heard "
14 So the *s'* lifted me up, and took me "
14 in bitterness, in the heat of my *s'*; "
24 Then the *s'* entered into me, and "
8:3 *s'* lifted me up between the earth "
10:17 the *s'* of the living creature was in "
11:1 Moreover the *s'* lifted me up, and "
5 the *S'* of the Lord fell upon me, "
19 and I will put a new *s'* within you; "
24 Afterwards the *s'* took me up, and "
24 brought me...by the *S'* of God into "
13:3 prophets, that follow their own *s'*, "
18:31 make you a new heart and a new *s'*: "
21:7 be feeble, and every *s'* shall faint, "
36:26 and a new *s'* will I put within you: "
27 And I will put my *s'* within you, "
37:1 carried me out in the *s'* of the Lord, "
14 And shall put my *s'* in you, and ye "
39:29 poured out my *s'* upon the house of "
43:5 So the *s'* took me up, and brought "
Da 2:1 wherewith his *s'* was troubled, "
3 *s'* was troubled to know the dream. "
4:8 in whom is the *s'* of the holy gods: 7308
9 the *s'* of the holy gods is in thee, "
18 for the *s'* of the holy gods is in thee. "
5:11 in whom is the *s'* of the holy gods; "
12 Forasmuch as an excellent *s'*, and "
14 that the *s'* of the gods is in thee, "
6:3 because an excellent *s'* was in him; "
7:15 I Daniel was grieved in my *s'* in the "
Ho 4:12 *s'* of whoredoms hath caused them 7307
5:4 *s'* of whoredoms is in the midst of "
Joe 2:28 I will pour out my *s'* upon all flesh; "
29 in those days will I pour out my *s'*. "
Mic 2:7 is the *s'* of the Lord straitened? "
11 If a man walking in the *s'* and †
3:8 full of power by the *s'* of the Lord, "
Hag 1:14 stirred up the *s'* of Zerubbabel the "
14 *s'* of Joshua the son of Josedech, "
14 *s'* of all the remnant of the people; "
2:5 so my *s'* remaineth among you: "
Zec 4:6 might, nor by power, but by my *s'*, "
6:8 quieted my *s'* in the north country. "
7:12 the Lord of hosts hath sent in his *s'* "
12:1 formeth the *s'* of man within him. "
10 the *s'* of grace and of supplications: "
13:2 prophets and the unclean *s'* to pass "
Mal 2:15 Yet had he the residue of the *s'*. "
15 Therefore take heed to your *s'*. "
16 therefore take heed to your *s'*. "
M't 3:16 he saw the *S'* of God descending 4151
4:1 led up of the *s'* into the wilderness "
5:3 Blessed are the poor in *s'*: for "
10:20 *S'* of your Father which speaketh "
12:18 I will put my *s'* upon him, and he "
28 I cast out devils by the *S'* of God, "
43 When the unclean *s'* is gone out of "
14:26 were troubled, saying, It is a *s'*; *5326
22:43 doth David in *s'* call him Lord, 4151
26:41 the *s'* indeed is willing, but the "
M'r 1:10 and the *S'* like a dove descending "
12 immediately the *s'* driveth him "
23 a man with an unclean *s'*; and he "
26 when the unclean *s'* had torn him, "
2:8 Jesus perceived in his *s'* that they "
3:30 they said, He hath an unclean *s'*. "
5:2 tombs a man with an unclean *s'*, "
8 out of the man, thou unclean *s'*. "
6:49 they supposed it had been a *s'*, *5326
7:25 daughter had an unclean *s'*, 4151
8:12 And he sighed deeply in his *s'*, and "
9:17 thee my son, which hath a dumb *s'*; "
20 him, straightway the *s'* tare him; "
25 he rebuked the foul *s'*, saying unto "
25 Thou dumb and deaf *s'*, I charge "
26 And the *s'* cried, and rent him sore,* "
14:38 The *s'* truly is ready, but the flesh 4151
Lu 1:17 him in the *s'* and power of Elias, "
47 And my *s'* hath rejoiced in God my "
80 child grew, and waxed strong in *s'*, "
2:27 came by the *S'* into the temple: "
40 child grew, and waxed strong in *s'*,* "
4:1 led by the *S'* into the wilderness, "
14 in the power of the *S'* into Galilee: "
18 The *S'* of the Lord is upon me, "
33 which had a *s'* of an unclean devil, "
8:29 unclean *s'* to come out of the man. "
55 her *s'* came again, and she arose "
9:39 And, lo, a *s'* taketh him, and he "
42 And Jesus rebuked the unclean *s'*, "
55 not what manner of *s'* ye are of. * "
10:21 In that hour Jesus rejoiced in *s'*, "
11:13 Father give the Holy *S'* to them "
24 When the unclean *s'* is gone out of "
13:11 woman which had a *s'* of infirmity "
23:46 into thy hands I commend my *s'*: "
24:37 supposed that they had seen a *s'*. "
39 for a *s'* hath not flesh and bones, as "
Joh 1:32 I saw the *S'* descending from "
33 thou shalt see the *S'* descending, "
3:5 be born of water and of the *S'*, "
6 that which is born of the *S'* is *s'*. "
8 is every one that is born of the *S'*. "
34 God giveth not the *S'* by measure "
4:23 shall worship the Father in *s'* and "
24 God is a *S'*: and they that worship "
24 him must worship him in *s'* and in "
6:63 It is the *s'* that quickeneth; the "
63 you, they are *s'*, and they are life. "
7:39 (But this spake he of the *S'*, which "
11:33 her, he groaned in the *s'*, and was "
13:21 thus said, he was troubled in *s'*, "

Joh 14:17 Even the *S'* of truth; whom the 4151
15:26 the *S'* of truth, which proceedeth "
16:13 when he, the *S'* of truth, is come, "
Ac 2:4 as the *S'* gave them utterance. "
17 God, I will pour out of my *S'* upon "
18 pour out in those days of my *S'*; "
5:9 to tempt the *S'* of the Lord? "
6:10 the wisdom and the *s'* by which he "
7:59 saying, Lord Jesus, receive my *s'*. "
8:29 Then the *S'* said unto Philip, Go "
39 *S'* of the Lord caught away Philip, "
10:19 *S'* said unto him, Behold, three "
11:12 And the *S'* bade me go with them, "
28 and signified by the *s'* that there "
16:7 but the *S'* suffered them not. "
16 with a *s'* of divination met us, "
18 grieved, turned and said to the *s'*, "
17:16 his *s'* was stirred in him, when he "
18:5 Paul was pressed in the *s'*, and *
25 being fervent in the *s'*, he spake "
19:15 And the evil *s'* answered and said, "
16 the man in whom the evil *s'* was "
21 Paul purposed in the *s'*, when he "
20:22 go bound in the *s'* unto Jerusalem, "
21:4 who said to Paul through the *S'*, "
23:8 resurrection, neither angel, nor *s'*: "
9 but if a *s'* or an angel hath spoken "
Ro 1:4 according to the *s'* of holiness, by "
9 I serve with my *s'* in the gospel of "
2:29 in the *s'*, and not in the letter; "
7:6 we should serve in newness of *s'*, "
8:1 not after the flesh, but after the *S'*.* "
2 the law of the *S'* of life in Christ "
4 not after the flesh, but after the *S'*. "
5 after the *S'* the things of the *S'*. "
9 are not in the flesh, but in the *S'*, "
9 be that the *S'* of God dwell in you. "
9 any man have not the *S'* of Christ, "
10 *S'* is life because of righteousness. "
11 the *S'* of him that raised up Jesus "
11 by his *S'* that dwelleth in you. "
13 if ye through the *S'* do mortify the "
14 many as are led by the *S'* of God, "
15 have not received the *s'* of bondage "
15 have received the *S'* of adoption, "
16 *S'* itself beareth witness with our "
16 beareth witness with our *s'*, that "
23 which have the firstfruits of the *S'*, "
26 Likewise the *S'* also helpeth our "
26 *S'* itself maketh intercession for us "
27 knoweth what is the mind of the *S'*, "
11:8 hath given them the *s'* of slumber, "
12:11 fervent in *s'*; serving the Lord; "
15:19 by the power of the *S'* of God; *
30 and for the love of the *S'*, that ye "
1Co 2:4 but in demonstration of the *S'* and "
10 revealed them unto us by his *S'*: "
10 for the *S'* searcheth all things, yea, "
11 save the *s'* of man which is in him? "
11 knoweth no man, but the *S'* of God. "
12 received, not the *s'* of the world, "
12 world, but the *s'* which is of God; "
14 not the things of the *S'* of God: "
3:16 that the *S'* of God dwelleth in you? "
4:21 in love, and in the *s'* of meekness? "
5:3 absent in body, but present in *s'*, "
4 my *s'*, with the power of our Lord "
5 that the *s'* may be saved in the day "
6:11 Jesus, and by the *S'* of our God. "
17 is joined unto the Lord is one *s'*. "
20 and in your *s'*, which are God's. * "
7:34 may be holy both in body and in *s'*: "
40 also that I have the *S'* of God. "
12:3 no man speaking by the *S'* of God "
4 diversities of gifts, but the same *S'*. "
7 of the *S'* is given to every man to "
8 one is given by the *S'* the word of "
8 word of knowledge by the same *S'*; "
9 To another faith by the same *S'*; "
9 the gifts of healing by the same *S'*; "
11 that one and the selfsame *S'*, "
13 by one *S'* are we all baptized into "
13 been all made to drink into one *S'*. "
14:2 in the *s'* he speaketh mysteries. "
14 an unknown tongue, my *s'* prayeth, "
15 I will pray with the *s'*, and I will "
15 I will sing with the *s'*, and I will "
16 when thou shalt bless with the *S'*, "
15:45 Adam was made a quickening *s'*. "
16:18 For they have refreshed my *s'* and "
2Co 1:22 and given the earnest of the *S'* in "
2:13 I had no rest in my *s'*, because I "
3:3 but with the *S'* of the living God; "
6 not of the letter, but of the *s'*: for "
6 letter killeth, but the *s'* giveth life. "
8 the ministration of the *s'* be rather "
17 Now the Lord is that *S'*: and where "
17 where the *S'* of the Lord is, there is "
18 glory, even as by the *S'* of the Lord. "
4:13 We having the same *s'* of faith, "
5:5 given unto us the earnest of the *S'*. "
7:1 all filthiness of the flesh and *s'*, "
13 because his *s'* was refreshed by you "
11:4 or if ye receive another *s'*, which ye "
12:18 walked we not in the same *s'*? "
Ga 3:2 Received ye the *S'* by the works of "
3 having begun in the *S'*, are ye now "
5 that ministereth to you the *S'*, and "
14 might receive the promise of the *S'* "
4:6 sent forth the *S'* of his Son into "
29 him that was born after the *S'*, "
5:5 we through the *S'* wait for the hope "
16 Walk in the *S'*, and ye shall not "
17 For the flesh lusteth against the *S'*, "
17 and the *S'* against the flesh: and "
18 But if ye be led of the *S'*, ye are not "

Ga 5:22 fruit of the S' is love, joy, peace, 4151
25 If we live in the S', let us also walk "
25 let us also walk in the S'. "
6: 1 such an one in the s' of meekness; "
8 soweth to the S' shall of the S' reap "
18 Lord Jesus Christ be with your s'. "
Eph 1:13 sealed with that holy S' of promise, "
17 may give unto you the s' of wisdom "
2: 2 the s' that now worketh in the "
18 access by one S' unto the Father. "
22 habitation of God through the S'. "
3: 5 apostles and prophets by the S'; "
16 strengthened with might by his S' "
4: 3 to keep the unity of the S' in the "
4 There is one body, and one S', "
23 be renewed in the s' of your mind; "
30 And grieve not the holy S' of God, "
5: 9 (For the fruit of the S' is in all *
18 excess; but be filled with the S'; "
6:17 the sword of the S', which is the "
18 prayer and supplication in the S', "
Ph'p 1:19 supply of the S' of Jesus Christ, "
27 that ye stand fast in one s', with "
2: 1 of love, if any fellowship of the S', "
3: 3 which worship God in the s', and "
Col 1: 8 unto us your love in the S'. "
2: 5 yet am I with you in the s', joying "
1Th 4: 8 hath also given unto us his holy S'. "
5:19 Quench not the S'. "
23 your whole s' and soul and body be "
2Th 2: 2 neither by s', nor by word, nor by "
8 consume with the s' of his mouth,* "
13 through sanctification of the S' "
1Ti 3:16 justified in the S', seen of angels, "
4: 1 Now the S' speaketh expressly, "
12 in charity, in s', in faith, in purity.* "
2Ti 1: 7 hath not given us the s' of fear; "
4:22 Lord Jesus Christ be with thy s'. "
Ph'm 25 Lord Jesus Christ be with your s'. "
Heb 4:12 the dividing asunder of soul and s', "
9:14 who through the eternal s' offered "
10:29 done despite unto the S' of grace? "
Jas 2:26 as the body without the s' is dead, "
4: 5 The s' that dwelleth in us lusteth "
1Pe 1: 2 through sanctification of the S', "
11 S' of Christ which was in them did "
22 obeying the truth through the S'* "
3: 4 ornament of a meek and quiet s', "
18 the flesh, but quickened by the S': "
4: 6 but live according to God in the s'. "
14 s' of glory and of God resteth upon "
1Jo 3:24 by the S' which he hath given us. "
4: 1 Beloved, believe not every s', but "
2 Hereby know ye the S' of God: "
2 Every s' that confesseth that Jesus "
3 every s' that confesseth not that "
3 this is that s' of antichrist, whereof "
6 the s' of truth, and the s' of error. 4151
13 because he hath given us of his S'. "
5: 6 it is the S' that beareth witness, "
6 witness, because the S' is truth. "
8 s', and the water, and the blood: "
Jude 19 sensual, having not the S'. "
Re 1:10 I was in the S' on the Lord's day, "
2: 7, 11, 17 S' saith unto the churches; "
29 the S' saith unto the churches. "
3: 6, 13, 22 S' saith unto the churches. "
4: 2 And immediately I was in the s': "
11:11 the S' of life from God entered into* "
14:13 Yea, saith the S', that they may "
17: 3 So he carried me away in the s' "
18: 2 devils, and the hold of every foul s', "
19:10 of Jesus is the s' of prophecy. "
21:10 And he carried me away in the s' to "
22:17 the S' and the bride say, Come. "

spirits
Le 19:31 Regard not...that have familiar s', 178
20: 6 turneth after such as have familiar s', "
Nu 16:22 God, the God of the s' of all flesh, 7307
27:16 Lord, the God of the s' of all flesh, "
De 18:11 or a consulter with familiar s', or 178
1Sa 28: 3 put away those that had familiar s', "
9 cut off those that have familiar s', "
2Ki 21: 6 dealt with familiar s' and wizards: "
23:24 Moreover...workers with familiar s', "
Ps 104: 4 Who maketh his angels s'; his *7307
Pr 16: 2 eyes; but the Lord weigheth the s'. "
Isa 8:19 Seek...them that have familiar s', 178
19: 3 and to them that have familiar s', "
Zec 6: 5 are the four s' of the heavens, *7307
M't 8:16 he cast out the s' with his word, 4151
10: 1 gave them power against unclean s', "
12:45 seven other s' more wicked than "
M'r 1:27 commandeth he even the unclean s', "
3:11 unclean s', when they saw him, fell "
5:13 And the unclean s' went out, and "
6: 7 gave them power over unclean s'; "
Lu 4:36 he commandeth the unclean s', "
6:18 that were vexed with unclean s': "
7:21 and plagues, and of evil s'; and "
8: 2 which had been healed of evil s' "
10:20 that the s' are subject unto you; "
11:26 seven other s' more wicked than "
Ac 5:16 which were vexed with unclean s': "
8: 7 unclean s', crying with loud voice, "
19:12 and the evil s' went out of them. "
13 call over them which had evil s' "
1Co 12:10 to another discerning of s'; to "
14:32 s' of the prophets are subject to the "
1Ti 4: 1 giving heed to seducing s', and "
Heb 1: 7 Who maketh his angels s', and his* "
14 Are they not all ministering s', sent "
12: 9 in subjection unto the Father of s', "
23 to the s' of just men made perfect, "
1Pe 3:19 and preached unto the s' in prison; "
1Jo 4: 1 try the s' whether they are of God: 4151
Re 1: 4 the seven S' which are before his "
3: 1 he that hath the seven S' of God, "
4: 5 which are the seven S' of God. "
5: 6 which are the seven S' of God sent "
16:13 three unclean s' like frogs come out "
14 they are the s' of devils, working "

spiritual
Ho 9: 7 is a fool, the s' man is mad, *7307
Ro 1:11 may impart unto you some s' gift, 4152
7:14 For we know that the law is s': but "
15:27 made partakers of their s' things, "
1Co 2:13 comparing s' things with s'. "
15 But he that is s' judgeth all things, "
3: 1 not speak unto you as unto s', "
9:11 If we have sown unto you s' things, "
10: 3 And did all eat the same s' meat; "
4 And did all drink the same s' drink: "
4 drank of that s' Rock that followed "
12: 1 Now concerning s' gifts, brethren, I "
14: 1 after charity, and desire s' gifts, "
12 as ye are zealous of s' gifts, seek 4151
37 himself to be a prophet, or s', 4152
15:44 natural body; it is raised a s' body. "
44 natural body, and there is a s' body. "
46 that was not first which is s', but "
46 and afterward that which is s'. "
Ga 6: 1 ye which are s', restore such an one "
Eph 1: 3 blessed us with all s' blessings in "
5:19 in psalms and hymns and s' songs, "
6:12 against s' wickedness in high "
Col 1: 9 all wisdom and s' understanding; "
3:16 in psalms and hymns and s' songs, "
1Pe 2: 5 stones, are built up a s' house, "
5 priesthood, to offer up s' sacrifices, "

spiritually
Ro 8: 6 but to be s' minded is life and*3588,4151
1Co 2:14 because they are s' discerned. 4153
Re 11: 8 which s' is called Sodom and Egypt, "

spit See also SPAT; SPITTED; SPITTING.
Le 15: 8 he that hath the issue s' upon him 7556
Nu 12:14 her father had but s' in her face, 3417
De 25: 9 and s' in his face, and shall answer "
Job 30:10 me, and spare not to s' in my face. 7536
M't 26:67 Then did they s' in his face, and 1716
27:30 And they s' upon him, and took the* "
M'r 7:33 and he s', and touched his tongue;*4429
8:23 when he had s' on his eyes, and put "
10:34 and shall s' upon him, and shall *1716
14:65 And some began to s' on him, and to "
15:19 did s' upon him, and bowing their "

spite See also DESPITE; SPITEFULLY.
Ps 10:14 thou beholdest mischief and s', to 3708

spitefully
M't 22: 6 servants, and entreated them s', *5195
Lu 18:32 shall be mocked, and s' entreated,* "

spitted See also SPAT.
Lu 18:32 spitefully entreated, and s' on: *1716

spitting
Isa 50: 6 hid not my face from shame and s'. 7536

spittle
1Sa 21:13 let his s' fall down upon his beard. 7388
Job 7:19 alone till I swallow down my s'? 7536
Joh 9: 6 ground, and made clay of the s', 4427

spoil See also SPOILED; SPOILEST; SPOILETH; SPOILING; SPOILS.
Ge 49:27 and at night he shall divide the s'. 7998
Ex 3:22 and ye shall s' the Egyptians. 5337
15: 9 will overtake, I will divide the s'; 7998
Nu 31: 9 and took the s' of all their cattle, * 962
11 And they took all the s', and all the 7998
12 and the s', unto Moses, and Eleazer "
53 (For the men of war had taken s',* 962
De 2:35 the s' of the cities which we took. 7998
3: 7 the cattle, and the s' of the cities, "
13:16 thou shalt gather all the s' of it into "
16 and all the s' thereof every whit, "
20:14 all the s' thereof, shalt thou take "
14 shalt eat the s' of thine enemies, "
Jos 8: 2 only the s' thereof, and the cattle "
27 s' of that city Israel took for a prey "
11:14 the s' of these cities, and the cattle, "
22: 8 divide the s' of your enemies with "
J'g 5:30 the necks of them that take the s'? "
14:19 men of them, and took their s', 2488
1Sa 14:30 had eaten freely to day of the s' of 7998
32 And the people flew upon the s', "
36 and s' them until the morning light, 962
15:19 but didst fly upon the s', and didst 7998
21 But the people took of the s', sheep "
30:16 because of all the great s' that they "
19 neither s', nor any thing that they "
20 cattle, and said, This is David's s'. "
22 will not give them ought of the s' "
26 of the s' unto the elders of Judah, "
26 a present for you of the s' of the "
2Sa 3:22 and brought in a great s' with them: "
8:12 and of the s' of Hadadezer, son of "
12:30 he brought forth the s' of the city "
23:10 returned after him only to s'. 6584
2Ki 3:23 now therefore, Moab, to the s'. 7998
21:14 prey and a s' to all their enemies; 4933
1Ch 20: 2 he brought also exceeding much s' 7998
2Ch 14:13 they carried away very much s'. * "
14 was exceeding much s' in them. 961
15:11 of the s' which they had brought, 7998
20:25 came to take away the s' of them, "
25 three days in gathering of the s', "
24:23 sent all the s' of them unto the king "
25:13 thousand of them, and took much s'. 961
2Ch 28: 8 took also away much s' from them, 7998
8 and brought the s' to Samaria. "
14 the s' before the princes and all the 961
15 with the s' clothed all that were 7998
Ezr 9: 7 to a s', and to confusion of face, as*961
Es 3:13 to take the s' of them for a prey. 7998
8:11 to take the s' of them for a prey, "
9:10 on the s' laid they not their hand. 961
Job 29:17 and plucked the s' out of his teeth.*2964
Ps 44:10 which hate us s' for themselves. 8154
68:12 that tarried at home divided the s'. 7998
89:41 All that pass by the way s' him: 8155
109:11 and let the strangers s' his labour. 962
119:162 word, as one that findeth great s'. 7998
Pr 1:13 we shall fill our houses with s': "
16:19 than to divide the s' with the proud. "
22:23 and s' the soul of those that spoiled*6906
24:15 righteous; s' not his resting place:‡7703
31:11 so that he shall have no need of s'.*7998
Ca 2:15 the little foxes, that s' the vines: 2254
Isa 3:14 the s' of the poor is in your houses. 1500
8: 4 the s' of Samaria shall be taken 7998
9: 3 men rejoice when they divide the s'. "
10: 6 to take the s', and to take the prey, "
11:14 they shall s' them of the east 962
17:14 is the portion of them that s' us, 8154
33: 1 when thou shalt cease to s', thou 7703
4 your s' shall be gathered like the 7998
23 is the prey of a great s' divided; "
42:22 for a s', and none saith, Restore. 4933
24 Who gave Jacob for a s', and 4882
53:12 divide the s' with the strong; 7998
Jer 5: 6 wolf of the evenings shall s' them, 7703
6: 7 violence and s' is heard in her; 7701
15:13 thy treasures will I give to the s' 957
17: 3 and all thy treasures to the s', and "
20: 5 which shall s' them, and take them,‡962
8 cried out, I cried violence and s'; 7701
30:16 and they that s' thee shall be a "
16 shall be a s', and all that prey 4933
47: 4 cometh to s' all the Philistines, ‡7703
4 for the Lord will s' the Philistines, "
49:28 to Kedar, and s' the men of the east. "
32 the multitude of their cattle a s': 7998
50:10 And Chaldea shall be a s': all that‡ "
10 all that s' her shall be satisfied, ‡ "
Eze 7:21 to the wicked of the earth for a s'; "
14:15 they s' it, so that it be desolate, 7921
25: 7 will deliver thee for a s' to the 957
26: 5 it shall become a s' to the nations. "
12 they shall make a s' of thy riches, 7997
29:19 and take her s', and take her prey; "
32:12 they shall s' the pomp of Egypt, 7703
38:12 To take a s', and to take a prey; 7998
13 thee, Art thou come to take a s'? "
13 cattle and goods, to take a great s'? "
39:10 and they shall s' those that spoiled 7997
45: 9 remove violence and s', and 7701
Da 11:24 among them the prey, and s', and 7998
33 by captivity, and by s', many days. 961
Ho 10: 2 altars, he shall s' their images. 7703
13:15 he shall s' the treasure of all 8154
Na 2: 9 the s' of silver, take the s' of gold: 962
Hab 2: 8 of the people shall s' thee; 7997
17 and the s' of beasts, which made *7701
Zep 2: 9 residue of my people shall s' them, 962
Zec 2: 9 shall be a s' to their servants: 7998
14: 1 thy s' shall be divided in the midst "
M't 12:29 man's house, and s' his goods, 1283
29 man? and then he will s' his house. "
M'r 3:27 man's house, and s' his goods, "
27 man; and then he will s' his house. "
Col 2: 8 Beware lest any man s' you 4812

spoiled
Ge 34:27 came upon the slain, and s' the city, 962
29 s' even all that was in the house. "
Ex 12:36 And they s' the Egyptians. 5337
De 28:29 be only oppressed and s' evermore, 1497
J'g 2:14 the hands of spoilers that s' them, 8155
16 of the hand of those that s' them. 8154
1Sa 14:48 of the hands of them that s' them. "
17:53 Philistines, and they s' their tents. 8155
2Ki 7:16 out, and s' the tents of the Syrians. 962
2Ch 14:14 and they s' all the cities; for there‡ "
Job 12:17 He leadeth counsellers away s', 7758
19 He leadeth princes away s', and "
Ps 76: 5 The stouthearted are s', they have‡7997
Pr 22:23 the soul of those that s' them. *6906
Isa 13:16 their houses shall be s', and their 8155
18: 2 whose land the rivers have s'! *958
7 whose land the rivers have s', to the* "
24: 3 be utterly emptied, and utterly s': 962
33: 1 that spoilest, and thou wast not s'; 7703
1 cease to spoil, thou shalt be s'. "
42:22 But this is a people robbed and s'; 8154
Jer 2:14 he a homeborn slave? why is he s'?*957
4:13 Woe unto us! for we are s'. ‡7703
20 is cried; for the whole land is s': ‡ "
20 suddenly are my tents s', and my‡ "
30 when thou art s', what wilt thou do?‡ "
9:19 heard out of Zion, How are we s'! ‡ "
10:20 My tabernacle is s', and all my ‡ "
21:12 deliver him that is s' out of the 1497
22: 3 deliver the s' out of the hand of the "
25:36 for the Lord hath s' their pasture.*7703
48: 1 Woe unto Nebo! for it is s': * "
15 Moab is s', and gone up out of her* "
20 tell ye it in Arnon, that Moab is s',* "
49: 3 Howl, O Heshbon, for Ai is s': cry,‡ "
10 his seed is s', and his brethren, and‡ "
51:55 Because the Lord hath s' Babylon,‡ "
Eze 18: 7 hath s' none by violence, hath 1497
12 hath s' by violence, hath not "
18 s' his brother by violence, and did "
23:46 give them to be removed and s'. 957

Eze 39:10 they shall spoil those that s' them. 7997
Ho 10:14 and all thy fortresses shall be s'. 7703
14 as Shalman s' Beth-arbel in the 7701
Am 3:11 thee, and thy palaces shall be s'. 962
5: 9 strengtheneth the s' against the *7701
9 that the s' shall come against the* "
Mic 2: 4 and say, We be utterly s': he hath 7703
Hab 2: 8 thou hast s' many nations, all the 7997
Zec 2: 8 me unto the nations which s' you:‡ "
11: 2 fallen; because the mighty are s':‡ 7703
3 for their glory is s': a voice of the* "
3 lions; for the pride of Jordan is s'.‡ "
Col 2:15 having s' principalities...powers, †‡554

spoiler See also SPOILERS.
Isa 16: 4 to them from the face of the s': 7703
4 the s' ceaseth, the oppressors are *7701
21: 2 treacherously, and the s' spoileth. 7703
Jer 6:26 the s' shall suddenly come upon us. "
15: 8 of the young men a s' at noonday: "
48: 8 the s' shall come upon every city, "
18 s' of Moab shall come upon thee, "
32 s' is fallen upon thy summer fruits "
51:56 Because the s' is come upon her, "

spoilers
J'g 2:14 the hands of s' that spoiled them, 8154
1Sa 13:17 the s' came out of the camp of the 7843
14:15 and the s', they also trembled, and "
2Ki 17:20 them into the hand of s', until 8154
Jer 12:12 s' are come upon all high places 7703
51:48 the s' shall come unto her from the "
53 yet from me shall s' come unto her, "

spoilest
Isa 33: 1 Woe to thee that s', and thou wast 7703

spoileth
Ps 35:10 the needy from him that s' him? 1497
Isa 21: 2 treacherously, and the spoiler s'. 7703
Ho 7: 1 the troop of robbers s' without. 6584
Na 3:16 the cankerworm s', and fleeth away. "

spoiling
Ps 35:12 evil for good to the s' of my soul. *7908
Isa 22: 4 because of the s' of the daughter 7701
Jer 48: 3 s' and great destruction. ‡ "
Hab 1: 3 for s' and violence are before me: "
Heb 10:34 took joyfully the s' of your goods, 724

spoils
Jos 7:21 among the s' a goodly Babylonish *7998
1Ch 26:27 Out of the s' won in battles did * "
Isa 25:11 together with the s' of their hands. *698
Lu 11:22 he trusted, and divideth his s'. 4661
Heb 7: 4 Abraham gave the tenth of the s'. 205

spoke See SPAKE; SPOKEN; SPOKES; SPOKESMAN.

spoken
Ge 12: 4 as the Lord had s' unto him; 1696
18:19 that which he had s' of him. "
19:21 this city, for the which thou hast s'. "
21: 1 Lord did unto Sarah as he had s'. "
2 time of which God had s' to him. "
24:51 son's wife, as the Lord hath s'. "
28:15 done that which I have s' to thee of. "
41:28 thing...I have s' unto Pharaoh: * "
44: 2 to the word that Joseph had s'. "
Ex 4:10 nor since thou hast s' unto thy "
30 which the Lord had s' unto Moses, "
9:12 as the Lord had s' unto Moses. "
35 go; as the Lord had s' by Moses. "
10:29 Thou hast s' well, I will see thy "
19: 8 All that the Lord hath s' we will do. "
32:13 all this land that I have s' of will I 559
34 place of which I have s' unto thee: 1696
33:17 do this thing also that thou hast s': "
34:32 all that the Lord had s' with him in "
Le 10:11 which the Lord hath s' unto them "
Nu 1:48 the Lord had s' unto Moses, saying,* "
10:29 the Lord hath s' good concerning "
12: 2 the Lord indeed s' only by Moses? "
2 hath he not s' also by us? And the "
14:17 be great, according as thou hast s', "
28 as ye have s' in mine ears, so will I "
15:22 which the Lord hath s' unto Moses, "
21: 7 for we have s' against the Lord, "
23: 2 And Balak did as Balaam had s'; "
17 unto him, What hath the Lord s'? "
19 or hath he s', and shall he not make "
De 1:14 thing which thou hast s' is good for "
5:28 which they have s' unto thee: "
28 have well said all that they have s'. "
6:19 before thee, as the Lord hath s'. "
13: 5 he hath s' to turn you away from "
18:17 Lord said unto me, They have well s'* "
17 that which they have s'. 1696
21 word which the Lord hath not s'? "
22 thing which the Lord hath not s', "
22 prophet hath s' it presumptuously: "
26:19 the Lord thy God, as he hath s'. "
Jos 6: 8 when Joshua had s' unto the people, 559
21:45 the Lord had s' unto the house of 1696
Ru 2:13 for thou hast s' friendly unto thine "
1Sa 1:16 and grief have I s' hitherto. "
3:12 things which I have s' concerning "
20:23 matter which thou and I have s' of, "
25:30 the good that he hath s' concerning "
2Sa 2:27 unless thou hadst s', surely then in "
3:18 the Lord hath s' of David, saying, 559
6:22 maidservants which thou hast s' of, "
7:19 hast s' also of thy servant's house 1696
25 word that thou hast s' concerning "
29 for thou, O Lord God, hast s' it: "
14:19 ought that my lord the king hath s': "
17: 6 Ahithophel hath s' after this "
1Ki 2:23 if Adonijah have not s' this word "
12: 9 this people, who have s' to me, "

1Ki 13: 3 is the sign which the Lord hath s'; 1696
11 words which he had s' unto the king, "
14:11 the air eat: for the Lord hath s' it. "
18:24 answered and said, It is well s'. 1697
21: 4 the Jezreelite had s' to him: for 1696
22:23 Lord hath s' evil concerning thee. "
28 peace, the Lord hath not s' by me. "
2Ki 1:17 of the Lord which Elijah had s'. "
4:13 wouldest thou be s' for to the king, "
7:18 the man of God had s' to the king, 1696
19:21 the Lord hath s' concerning him; "
20: 9 will do the thing that he hath s': "
19 word of the Lord which thou hast s'. "
1Ch 17:17 hast also s' of thy servant's house "
23 thou hast s' concerning thy servant "
2Ch 2:15 the wine, which my lord hath s' of, 559
6:10 his word that he hath s': *1696
17 thou hast s' unto thy servant David.* "
10: 9 people, which have s' to me, saying, "
18:22 the Lord hath s' evil against thee. "
27 then hath not the Lord s' by me. "
36:22 word...s' by the mouth of Jeremiah* "
Ezr 8:22 we had s' unto the king, saying, 559
Ne 2:18 king's words that he had s' unto me. "
Es 6:10 nothing fail of all...thou hast s'. 1696
7: 9 who had s' good for the king, "
Job 21: 3 and after that I have s', mock on. "
32: 4 Elihu had waited till Job had s'. *1697
33: 2 my tongue hath s' in my mouth. 1696
8 Surely thou hast s' in mine hearing, 559
34:35 Job hath s' without knowledge, *1696
40: 5 Once have I s'; but I will not "
42: 7 Lord had s' these words unto Job, "
7 for ye have not s' of me the thing "
8 that ye have not s' of me the thing "
Ps 50: 1 God, even the Lord, hath s', and "
60: 6 God hath s' in his holiness; I will "
62:11 God hath s' once; twice have I "
66:14 and my mouth hath s', when I was "
87: 3 Glorious things are s' of thee, O "
108: 7 God hath s' in his holiness; I will "
109: 2 s' against me with a lying tongue. "
116:10 believed, therefore have I s': I was* "
Pr 15:23 a word s' in due season, how good* "
25:11 word fitly s' is like apples of gold 1696
Ec 7:21 no heed unto all words that are s'; "
Ca 8: 8 the day when she shall be s' for? "
Isa 1: 2 ear, O earth: for the Lord hath s', "
20 for the mouth of the Lord hath s' it. "
16:13 the word that the Lord hath s' "
14 But now the Lord hath s', saying, "
21:17 the Lord God of Israel hath s' it. "
22:25 be cut off: for the Lord hath s' it. "
23: 4 O Zidon: for the sea hath s', even 559
24: 3 for the Lord hath s' this word. 1696
25: 8 the earth: for the Lord hath s' it. "
31: 4 For thus hath the Lord s' unto me, *559
37:22 the word which the Lord hath s' 1696
38: 7 will do this thing that he hath s'; "
15 hath both s' unto me, and himself 559
39: 8 is the word...which thou hast s'. 1696
40: 5 for the mouth of the Lord hath s' it. "
45:19 I have not s' in secret, in a dark "
46:11 I have s' it, I will also bring it to "
48:15 I, even I, have s'; yea, I have "
16 I have not s' in secret from the "
58:14 for the mouth of the Lord hath s' it. "
59: 3 your lips have s' lies, your tongue "
Jer 3: 5 thou hast s' and done evil things as "
4:28 because I have s' it, I have purposed "
9:12 the mouth of the Lord hath s', "
13:15 be not proud: for the Lord hath s'. "
23:21 I have not s' to them, yet they * "
35, 37 and, What hath the Lord s'? "
25: 3 and I have s' unto you, rising early "
26:16 he hath s' to us in the name of the "
27:13 the Lord hath s' against the nation "
29:23 have s' lying words in my name, "
30: 2 Write...all the words that I have s' "
32:24 what thou hast s' is come to pass; "
33:24 not what this people have s', saying, "
35:14 I have s' unto you, rising early "
17 because I have s' unto them, but "
36: 2 write...all the words that I have s' "
4 which he had s' unto him, upon a "
38: 1 words that Jeremiah had s' unto "
44:16 the word that thou hast s' unto us "
25 your wives have both s' with your "
48: 8 be destroyed, as the Lord hath s'. 559
51:62 thou hast s' against this place, to 1696
Eze 5:13 I the Lord have s' it in my zeal, "
15 rebukes. I the Lord have s' it. "
17 upon thee. I the Lord have s' it. "
12:28 word which I have s' shall be done,* "
13: 7 have ye not s' a lying divination, "
7 Lord saith it; albeit I have not s'? 559
8 Because ye have s' vanity, and 1696
14: 9 deceived when he hath s' a thing,* "
17:21 know that I the Lord have s' it. "
24 I the Lord have s' and have done it. "
21:32 for I the Lord have s' it. "
22:14 I the Lord have s' it, and will do it. "
28 God, when the Lord hath not s'. "
23:34 I have s' it, saith the Lord God. "
24:14 I the Lord have s' it: it shall come "
26: 5 for I have s' it, saith the Lord God: "
14 for I the Lord have s' it, saith the "
28:10 for I have s' it, saith the Lord God. "
30:12 of strangers: I the Lord have s' it. "
34:24 among them; I the Lord have s' it. "
35:12 thy blasphemies which thou hast s' 559
36: 5 in the fire of my jealousy have I s' 1696
6 I have s' in my jealousy and in my "
36 I the Lord have s' it, and I will do it. "
37:14 ye know that I the Lord have s' it, "
38:17 he of whom I have s' in old time * "

Eze 38:19 and in the fire of my wrath have I s'. 1696
39: 5 for I have s' it, saith the Lord God. "
8 this is the day whereof I have s'. "
Da 4:31 Nebuchadnezzar, to thee it is s'; 560
10:11 when he had s' this word unto me, 1696
15 when he had s' such words unto "
19 And when he had s' unto me, I was* "
Ho 7:13 yet they have s' lies against me. "
10: 4 They have s' words, swearing * "
12:10 I have also s' by the prophets, and "
Joe 3: 8 far off: for the Lord hath s' it. "
Am 3: 1 word that the Lord hath s' against "
8 the Lord hath s', who can but "
5:14 shall be with you, as ye have s'. * 559
Ob 12 shouldest thou have s' proudly in *6310
18 of Esau; for the Lord hath s' it. 1696
Mic 4: 4 mouth of the Lord of hosts hath s' "
6:12 the inhabitants thereof have s' lies, "
Zec 10: 2 For the idols have s' vanity, and the "
Mal 3:13 What have we s' so much against "
M't 1:22 which was s' of the Lord by the 4483
2:15 which was s' of the Lord by the "
17 which was s' by Jeremy the prophet, "
23 which was s' by the prophets, "
3: 3 that was s' of by the prophet Esaias, "
4:14 which was s' by Esaias the prophet, "
8:17 which was s' by Esaias the prophet, "
12:17 which was s' by Esaias the prophet, "
13:35 which was s' by the prophet, "
21: 4 which was s' by the prophet, "
22:31 that which was s' unto you by God, "
24:15 s' of by Daniel the prophet, stand "
26:65 saying, He hath s' blasphemy; 987
27: 9 was s' by Jeremy the prophet, 4483
35 which was s' by the prophet, * "
M'r 1:42 And as soon as he had s', *2036
5:36 Jesus heard the word that was s', 2980
12:12 had s' the parable against them: *2036
13:14 s' of by Daniel the prophet, 4483
14: 9 be s' of for a memorial of her. 2980
16:19 after the Lord had s' unto them, "
Lu 2:33 those things which were s' of him. "
34 for a sign which shall be s' against; 483
12: 3 whatsoever ye have s' in darkness *2036
3 ye have s' in the ear in closets 2980
18:34 they the things which were s'. *3004
19:28 And when he had thus s', he went 2036
20:19 had s' this parable against them.* "
24:25 all that the prophets have s': 2980
40 when he had thus s', he shewed *2036
Joh 4:50 word that Jesus had s' unto him, * "
9: 6 When he had thus s', he spat on the "
11:13 had s' of taking of rest in sleep. *3004
43 And when he thus had s', he cried 2036
12:48 the word that I have s', the same *2980
49 For I have not s' of myself; but * "
14:25 These things have I s' unto you, "
15: 3 the word which I have s' unto you. "
11 These things have I s' unto you, "
22 if I had not come and s' unto them, "
16: 1 These things have I s' unto you, "
25 have I s' unto you in proverbs: "
33 These things I have s' unto you, "
18: 1 When Jesus had s' these words, 2036
22 when he had thus s', one of the * "
23 If I have s' evil, bear witness of 2980
20:18 he had s' these things unto her. *2036
21:19 And when he had s' this, he saith "
Ac 1: 9 when he had s' these things, while* "
2:16 which was s' by the prophet Joel; 2046
3:21 God hath s' by the mouth of all *2980
24 as many as have s', have likewise "
8:24 none of these things...ye have s' 2046
9:27 way, and that he had s' to him, 2980
13:40 you, which is s' of in the prophets: 2046
45 things which were s' by Paul, 3004
46 should first have been s' to you. 2980
16:14 the things which were s' of Paul. "
19:36 these things cannot be s' against, * 369
41 when he had thus s', he dismissed 2036
20:36 when he had thus s', he kneeled "
23: 9 a spirit or an angel hath s' to him, 2980
26:30 And when he had thus s', the king *2036
27:11 things which were s' by Paul. 3004
35 he had thus s', he took bread, *2036
28:22 that every where it is s' against. 483
24 believed the things which were s', 3004
25 after that Paul had s' one word, 2036
Ro 1: 8 that your faith is s' of throughout 2605
4:18 according to that which was s', So 2046
14:16 Let not then your good be evil s' of: 987
15:21 To whom he was not s' of, they * 312
1Co 10:30 why am I evil s' of for that for 987
14: 9 how shall it be known what is s'? 2980
2Co 4:13 believed, and therefore have I s'; * "
Heb 1: 2 last days s' unto us by his Son, "
2: 2 word s' by angels was stedfast, "
3 the first began to be s' by the Lord, "
3: 5 things which were to be s' after; "
4: 8 afterward have s' of another day. "
7:13 he of whom these things are s' *3004
8: 1 things...we have s' this is the sum.* "
9:19 when Moses had s' every precept 2980
12:19 should not be s' to them any more: 4369
13: 7 who have s' unto you the word of *2980
Jas 5:10 who have s' in the name of the * "
1Pe 4:14 on their part he is evil s' of, but on* 987
2Pe 2: 2 the way of truth shall be evil s' of. "
3: 2 s' before by the holy prophets, 4280
Jude 15 which ungodly sinners have s' 2980
17 were s' before of the apostles 4280

spokes
1Ki 7:33 their felloes, and their s', were all 2840

spokesman
Ex 4:16 he shall be thy s' unto the people: 1696

sponge See SPUNGE.

spoon See also SPOONS.
Nu 7:14 One s' of ten shekels of gold, full 3709
20 One s' of gold of ten shekels, full of "
26, 32, 38, 44, 50, 56, 62, 68, 74, 80 One golden s' of ten shekels, full of 3709

spoons
Ex 25:29 the dishes thereof, and s' thereof, 3709
37:16 the table, his dishes, and his s', "
Nu 4: 7 thereon the dishes, and the s', and "
7:84 silver bowls, twelve s' of gold: "
86 The golden s' were twelve, full of "
86 the gold of the s' was an hundred "
1Ki 7:50 and the s', and the censers of pure "
2Ki 25:14 the snuffers, and the s', and all the "
2Ch 4:22 and the s', and the censers, of pure "
24:14 s', and vessels of gold and silver. "
Jer 52:18 the bowls, and the s', and all the "
19 the candlesticks, and the s', and "

sport See also SPORTING.
J'g 16:25 Samson, that he may make us s'. 7832
25 house; and he made them s': 6711
27 that beheld while Samson made s'. 7832
Pr 10:23 It is as s' to a fool to do mischief: 7814
26:19 neighbour, and saith, Am...I in s'? 7832
Isa 57: 4 Against whom do ye s' yourselves? 6026

sporting
Ge 26: 8 behold, Isaac was s' with Rebekah 6711
2Pe 2:13 s' themselves with their own *1792

spot See also SPOTS; SPOTTED.
Le 13: 2 flesh a rising, a scab, or bright s', 934
4 If the bright s' be white in the skin "
19 be a white rising, or a bright s', "
23 But if the bright s' stay in his place, "
24 that burneth have a white bright s', "
25 the hair in the bright s' be turned "
26 be no white hair in the bright s', "
28 And if the bright s' stay in his place, "
39 it is a freckled s' that groweth in * 933
14:56 and for a scab, and for a bright s': 934
Nu 19: 2 bring thee a red heifer without s', 8549
28: 3 lambs of the first year without s' * "
9 lambs of the first year without s', * "
11 lambs of the first year without s'; * "
29:17, 26 of the first year without s': * "
De 32: 5 their s' is not...of his children: *3971
5 is not the s' of his children: they * "
Job 11:15 thou lift up thy face without s'; 3971
Ca 4: 7 fair, my love; there is no s' in thee. "
Eph 5:27 not having s', or wrinkle, or any 4696
1Ti 6:14 keep this commandment without s', 784
Heb 9:14 offered himself without s' to God, * 299
1Pe 1:19 without blemish and without s': 784
2Pe 3:14 found of him in peace, without s', "

spots
Le 13:38 bright s', even white bright s'; 934
39 if the bright s' in the skin of their "
Jer 13:23 his skin, or the leopard his s'? 2272
2Pe 2:13 S' they are and blemishes, 4696
Jude 12 These are s' in your feasts of *4694

spotted See also UNSPOTTED.
Ge 30:32 all the speckled and s' cattle, and 2921
32 s' and speckled among the goats: "
33 is not speckled and s' among the "
35 goats that were ringstraked and s', "
35 goats that were speckled and s'. "
39 ringstraked, speckled, and s'. "
Jude 23 even the garment s' by the flesh. 4695

spouse See also ESPOUSED; SPOUSES.
Ca 4: 8 with me from Lebanon, my s', *3618
9 my heart, my sister, my s'; thou * "
10 fair is thy love, my sister, my s'! * "
11 Thy lips, O my s', drop as the * "
12 garden inclosed is my sister, my s'; * "
5: 1 into my garden, my sister, my s': * "

spouses
Ho 4:13 and your s' shall commit adultery. *3618
14 your s' when they commit adultery: * "

spouts See WATERSPOUTS.

sprang See also SPRUNG.
M'r 4: 5 and immediately it s' up, because 1816
8 yield fruit that s' up and increased, *305
Lu 8: 7 and the thorns s' up with it, and *4855
8 fell on good ground, and s' up, *5453
Ac 16:29 he called for a light, and s' in, and 1530
Heb 7:14 that our Lord s' out of Juda; of * 393
11:12 Therefore s' there even of one, and 1080

spread See also OVERSPREAD; SPREADEST; SPREADETH; SPREADING.
Ge 10:18 of the Canaanites s' abroad. 6327
28:14 thou shalt s' abroad to the west, 6555
33:19 a field, where he had s' his tent, 5186
35:21 and s' his tent beyond the tower of "
Ex 9:29 I will s' abroad my hands unto the 6566
33 and s' abroad his hands unto the "
37: 9 the cherubims s' out their wings on "
40:19 And he s' abroad the tent over the "
Le 13: 5 and the plague s' not in the skin; 6581
6 and the plague s' not in the skin, "
7 if the scab s' much abroad in the "
22 if it s' much abroad in the skin, "
23 spot stay in his place, and s' not, "
27 if it be s' much abroad in the skin, "
28 his place, and s' not in the skin, "
32 if the scall s' not, and there be in it "
34 if the scall be not s' in the skin, "
35 But if the scall s' much in the skin "
36 behold, if the scall be s' in the skin, "
51 if the plague be s' in the garment, "
53 the plague be not s' in the garment, "
Le 13:55 colour, and the plague be not s'; 6581
14:39 if the plague be s' in the walls of "
44 if the plague be s' in the house, it "
48 the plague hath not s' in the house, "
Nu 4: 6 shall s' over it a cloth wholly of 6566
7 they shall s' a cloth of blue, and "
8 shall s' upon them a cloth of scarlet, "
11 altar they shall s' a cloth of blue, "
13 altar, and s' a purple cloth thereon: "
14 they shall s' upon it a covering of "
11:32 and they s' them all abroad for 7849
24: 6 As the valleys are they s' forth, as 5186
De 22:17 shall s' the cloth before the elders 6566
J'g 8:25 And they s' a garment, and did cast "
15: 9 Judah, and s' themselves in Lehi. 5203
Ru 3: 9 s' therefore thy skirt over thine 6566
1Sa 30:16 were s' abroad upon all the earth, 5203
2Sa 5:18, 22 and s' themselves in the valley "
16:22 So they s' Absalom a tent upon 5186
17:19 s' a covering over the well's mouth, 6566
19 and s' ground corn thereon; and *7849
21:10 and s' it for her upon the rock, 5186
22:43 the street, and did s' them abroad. 7554
1Ki 6:32 and s' gold upon the cherubims, 7286
8: 7 the cherubims s' forth their two 6566
22 s' forth his hands toward heaven: "
38 and s' forth his hands toward this "
54 with his hands s' up to heaven. "
2Ki 8:15 and s' it on his face, so...he died: "
19:14 the Lord, and s' it before the Lord. "
1Ch 14: 9 Philistines came...s' themselves *6584
13 Philistines yet again s' themselves* "
28:18 cherubims, that s' out their wings, 6566
2Ch 3:13 wings of...cherubims s' themselves "
5: 8 the cherubims s' forth their wings "
6:12 of Israel, and s' forth his hands: "
13 s' forth his hands toward heaven, "
29 s' forth his hands in this house: "
26: 8 and his name s' abroad even to the 3212
15 And his name s' far abroad; for he 3318
Ezr 9: 5 s' out my hands unto the Lord my 6566
Job 29:19 My root was s' out by the waters, 6605
37:18 thou with him s' out the sky, 7554
Ps 105:39 He s' a cloud for a covering; and 6566
140: 5 they have s' a net by the wayside; "
Pr 1:17 Surely in vain the net is s' in the 2219
Isa 1:15 And when ye s' forth your hands, 6566
14:11 the worm is s' under thee, and the 3331
19: 8 they that s' nets upon the waters 6566
25: 7 the vail that is s' over all nations. 5259
11 And he shall s' forth his hands in 6566
33:23 mast, they could not s' the sail: "
37:14 the Lord, and s' it before the Lord. "
42: 5 he that s' forth the earth, and that 7554
58: 5 to s' sackcloth and ashes under 3331
65: 2 I have s' out my hands all the day 6566
Jer 8: 2 they shall s' them before the sun, 7849
10: 9 Silver s' into plates is brought *7554
43:10 he shall s' his royal pavilion over 5186
48:40 and shall s' his wings over Moab. 6566
49:22 and s' his wings over Bozrah: and "
La 1:10 The adversary hath s' out his hand "
13 he hath s' a net for my feet, he hath "
Eze 2:10 And he s' it before me; and it was "
12:13 My net also will I s' upon him, and "
16: 8 I s' my skirt over thee, and covered "
17:20 And I will s' my net upon him, and "
19: 8 and s' their net over him: "
26:14 shalt be a place to s' nets upon; *4894
32: 3 I will therefore s' out my net over 6566
47:10 shall be a place to s' forth nets; *4894
Ho 5: 1 Mizpah, and a net s' upon Tabor. 6566
7:12 go, I will s' my net upon them; "
14: 6 His branches shall s', and his 3212
Joe 2: 2 morning s' upon the mountains: 6566
Hab 1: 8 horsemen shall s' themselves, 6335
Zec 1:17 prosperity shall yet be s' abroad; 6327
2: 6 s' you abroad as the four winds 6566
Mal 2: 3 seed, and s' dung upon your faces, 2219
M't 9:31 s' abroad his fame in all that 1310
21: 8 s' their garments in the way; 4766
M'r 1:28 immediately his fame s' abroad *1831
11: 8 many s' their garments in the way 4766
Lu 19:36 they s' their clothes in the way. 5291
Ac 4:17 it s' no further among the people, 1268
1Th 1: 8 faith to God-ward is s' abroad; *1831

spreadest
Eze 27: 7 which thou s' forth to be thy sail; *4666

spreadeth
Le 13: 8 the scab s' in the skin, then the *6581
De 32:11 As an eagle...s' abroad her wings, *6566
Job 9: 8 Which alone s' out the heavens, *5186
26: 9 throne, and s' his cloud upon it. 6576
36:30 Behold, he s' his light upon it, 6566
41:30 he s' sharp pointed things upon 7502
Pr 29: 5 his neighbour s' a net for his feet. 6566
Isa 25:11 that swimmeth s' forth his hands "
40:19 the goldsmith s' it over with gold, 7554
22 s' them out as a tent to dwell in: 4969
44:24 s' abroad the earth by myself; 7554
Jer 4:31 that s' her hands, saying, Woe is 6566
17: 8 that s' out her roots by the river, 7971
La 1:17 Zion s' forth her hands, and there 6566

spreading See also OVERSPREADING; SPREADINGS.
Le 13:57 thing of skin; it is a s' plague: *6524
Ps 37:35 s' himself like a green bay tree. 6168
Eze 17: 6 became a s' vine of low stature, 5628
26: 5 be a place for the s' of nets in the 4894

spreadings
Job 36:29 understand the s' of the clouds, 4666

sprigs
Isa 18: 5 cut off the s' with pruning hooks, 2150
Eze 17: 6 forth branches, and shot forth s'. 6288

spring See also DAYSPRING; OFFSPRING; SPRANG; SPRINGETH; SPRINGING; SPRINGS; SPRUNG.
Nu 21:17 sang this song, S' up, O well; 5927
De 8: 7 and depths that s' out of valleys *3318
J'g 19:25 when the day began to s', they let 5927
1Sa 9:26 to pass about the s' of the day, "
2Ki 2:21 forth unto the s' of the waters, 4161
Job 5: 6 neither doth trouble s' out of the 6779
38:27 bud of the tender herb to s' forth? "
Ps 85:11 Truth shall s' out of the earth; and* "
92: 7 When the wicked s' as the grass, 6524
Pr 25:26 fountain, and a corrupt s'. 4726
Ca 4:12 a s' shut up, a fountain sealed. 1530
Isa 42: 9 before they s' forth I tell you of 6779
43:19 now it shall s' forth; shall ye not "
44: 4 they shall s' up as among the grass, "
45: 8 let righteousness s' up together; "
58: 8 thine health shall s' forth speedily: "
11 like a s' of water, whose waters 4161
61:11 that are sown in it to s' forth; 6779
11 and praise to s' forth before all the "
Eze 17: 9 wither in all the leaves of her s', *6780
Ho 13:15 and his s' shall become dry, and 4726
Joe 2:22 pastures of the wilderness do s', 1876
M'r 4:27 and the seed should s' and grow up, 985

springeth
1Ki 4:33 the hyssop that s' out of the wall: 3318
2Ki 19:29 year that which s' of the same; 7823
Isa 37:30 year that which s' of the same: "
Ho 10: 4 thus judgment s' up as hemlock 6524

springing
Ge 26:19 and found there a well of s' water. 2416
2Sa 23: 4 as the tender grass s' out of the earth*
Ps 65:10 thou blessest the s' thereof. 6780
Joh 4:14 of water s' up into everlasting life. 242
Heb 12:15 lest any root of bitterness s' up 5453

springs
De 4:49 the plain, under the s' of Pisgah. * 794
Jos 10:40 and of the s', and all their kings; * "
12: 8 and in the s', and in the wilderness, * "
15:19 land; give me also s' of water. 1543
19 her the upper s', and the nether s'. "
J'g 1:15 land; give me also s' of water. "
15 her the upper s' and the nether s'. "
Job 38:16 entered into the s' of the sea? 5033
Ps 87: 7 be there: all my s' are in thee. *4599
104:10 He sendeth the s' into the valleys, "
Isa 35: 7 and the thirsty land s' of water: 4002
41:18 and the dry land s' of water. 4161
49:10 s' of water shall he guide them. 4002
Jer 51:36 up her sea, and make her s' dry. *4726

sprinkle See also SPRINKLED; SPRINKLETH; SPRINKLING.
Ex 9: 8 let Moses s' it toward the heaven 2236
29:16 and s' it round about the altar. "
20 s' the blood upon the altar round "
21 s' it upon Aaron, and upon his 5137
Le 1: 5 s' the blood round about upon the 2236
11 s' his blood round about upon the "
3: 2 shall s' the blood upon the altar "
8 s' the blood thereof round about "
13 s' the blood thereof upon the altar "
4: 6 s' of the blood seven times before 5137
17 s' it seven times before the Lord, "
5: 9 s' of the blood of the sin offering "
7: 2 he s' round about upon the altar. 2236
14: 7 s' upon him that is to be cleansed 5137
16 shall s' of the oil with his finger "
27 shall s' with his right finger some "
51 water, and s' the house seven times: "
16:14 and s' it with his finger upon the "
14 he s' of the blood with his finger "
15 and s' it upon the mercy seat, and "
19 he shall s' of the blood upon it with "
17: 6 priest shall s' the blood upon the 2236
Nu 8: 7 S' water of purifying upon them, 5137
18:17 shalt s' their blood upon the altar, 2236
19: 4 s' of her blood directly before the 5137
18 s' it upon the tent, and upon all the "
19 the clean person shall s' upon the "
2Ki 16:15 and s' upon it all the blood of the 2236
Isa 52:15 So shall he s' many nations; the 5137
Eze 36:25 will I s' clean water upon you, and 2236
43:18 thereon, and to s' blood thereon. "

sprinkled
Ex 9:10 Moses s' it up toward heaven; 2236
24: 6 half of the blood he s' on the altar. "
8 the blood, and s' it on the people, "
Le 6:27 when there is s' of the blood 5137
27 whereon it was s' in the holy place. "
8:11 he s'...upon the altar seven times, "
19, 24 and Moses s' the blood upon 2236
30 s' it upon Aaron, and upon his 5137
9:12 he s' round about upon the altar. 2236
18 which he s' upon the altar round "
Nu 19:13 water of separation was not s' upon "
20 water...hath not been s' upon him; "
2Ki 9:33 of her blood was s' on the wall, 5137
16:13 s' the blood of his peace offerings, 2236
2Ch 29:22 the blood, and s' it on the altar: "
22 they s' the blood upon the altar: "
22 they s' the blood upon the altar. "
30:16 the priests s' the blood, which they "
35:11 the priests s' the blood from their "
Job 2:12 s' dust upon their heads toward "
Isa 63: 3 blood...be s' upon my garments, 5137
Heb 9:19 and s' both the book, and all the 4472
21 s' with blood both the tabernacle, "
10:22 hearts s' from an evil conscience, "

sprinkleth
Le 7:14 be the priest's that s' the blood 2236
Nu 19:21 he that s' the water of separation 5137

sprinkling
Heb 9:13 ashes of an heifer s· the unclean, *4472*
11:28 the passover, and the s· of blood, *4378*
12:24 to the blood of s·, that speaketh *4473*
1Pe 1: 2 and s· of the blood of Jesus Christ: "

sprout
Job 14: 7 be cut down, that it will s· again, 2498

sprung See also SPRANG.
Ge 41: 6 the east wind s· up after them. 6779
23 the east wind, s· up after them: "
Le 13:42 a leprosy s· up in his bald head, 6524
M't 4:16 and shadow of death light is s· up.* *393*
13: 5 and forthwith they s· up, because* *1816*
7 the thorns s· up, and choked them:* *305*
26 But when the blade was s· up, and* *985*
Lu 8: 6 soon as it was s· up, it withered *5453*

spue See also SPEWING; SPUED.
Le 18:28 That the land s· not you out also, *6958
20:22 to dwell therein, s· you not out. * "
Jer 25:27 be drunken, and s·, and fall, and 7006
Re 3:16 I will s· thee out of my mouth. *1692*

spued
Le 18:28 as it s· out the nations that were *6958

spun
Ex 35:25 brought that which they had s·, 4299
26 them up in wisdom s· goats' hair. 2901

spunge
M't 27:48 a s·, and filled it with vinegar, **4699*
M'r 15:36 ran and filled a s· full of vinegar. * "
Joh 19:29 and they filled a s· with vinegar, * "

spy See also ESPY; SPIED; SPIES.
Nu 13:16 Moses sent to s· out the land. 8446
17 Moses sent them to s· out the land "
21:32 And Moses sent to s· out Jaazer, 7270
Jos 2: 1 of Shittim two men to s· secretly, "
6:25 Joshua sent to s· out Jericho. "
J'g 18: 2 to s· out the land, and to search it; "
14 went to s· out the country of Laish, "
17 men that went to s· out the land "
2Sa 10: 3 to search the city, and to s· it out, "
2Ki 6:13 Go and s· where he is, that I may* 7200
1Ch 19: 3 overthrow, and to s· out the land? "
Ga 2: 4 came in privily to s· out our liberty *2684*

square See also FOURSQUARE; SQUARED; SQUARES; STONESQUARERS.
1Ki 7: 5 all the doors and posts were s·, 7251
Eze 43:16 s· in the four squares thereof. "
45: 2 hundred in breadth, s· round about;"

squared
Eze 41:21 The posts of the temple were s·, 7251

squares
Eze 43:16 square in the four s· thereof. *7253
17 and fourteen broad in the four s· * "

stability
Isa 33: 6 shall be the s· of thy times, 530

stable See also UNSTABLE.
1Ch 16:30 the world also shall be s·, that it *3559
Eze 25: 5 will make Rabbah a s· for camels, 5116

stablish See also ESTABLISH; STABLISHED; STABLISHETH.
2Sa 7:13 I will s· the throne of his kingdom*3559
1Ch 17:12 and I will s· his throne for ever. * "
18: 3 to s· his dominion by the river ‡5324
2Ch 7:18 Then will I s· the throne of thy *6965
Es 9:21 To s· this among them, that they * "
Ps 119:38 S· thy word unto thy servant, who* "
Ro 16:25 to s· you according to my gospel, *4741*
1Th 3:13 To the end he may s· your hearts "
2Th 2:17 and s· you in every good word and "
3: 3 who shall s· you, and keep you "
Jas 5: 8 Be ye also patient; s· your hearts: "
1Pe 5:10 make you perfect, s·, strengthen, "

stablished See also ESTABLISHED.
2Ch 17: 5 the Lord s· the kingdom in his ‡3559
Ps 93: 1 the world also is s·, that it cannot‡ "
148: 6 He hath also s· them for ever and‡5975
Col 2: 7 and s· in the faith, as ye have been *950*

stablisheth See also ESTABLISHETH.
Hab 2:12 blood, and s· a city by iniquity! ‡3559
2Co 1:21 he which s· us with you in Christ, *950*

Stachys (*sta'-kis*)
Ro 16: 9 in Christ, and S· my beloved. *4720*

stacks
Ex 22: 6 in thorns, so that the s· of corn, *1430

stacte (*stac'-te*)
Ex 30:34 Take unto thee sweet spices, s·, 5198

staff See also STAVES.
Ge 32:10 for with my s· I passed over this 4731
38:18 and thy s· that is in thine hand. 4294
25 the signet, and bracelets, and s·. "
Ex 12:11 feet, and your s· in your hand; 4731
21:19 and walk abroad upon his s·, then 4938
Le 26:26 have broken the s· of your bread, 4294
Nu 13:23 bare it between two upon a s·; 4132
22:27 and he smote the ass with a s·. 4731
J'g 6:21 put forth the end of the s· that was4938
1Sa 17: 7 And the s· of his spear was like a 2671
40 And he took his s· in his hand, and4731
2Sa 3:29 is a leper, or that leaneth on a s', 6418
21:19 the s· of whose spear was like a 6086
23: 7 with iron and the s· of a spear; "
21 but he went down to him with a s·,7626
2Ki 4:29 and take my s· in thine hand, and 4938
29 lay my s· upon the face of the child "
31 and laid the s· upon the face of the "
18:21 thou trustest upon the s· of this "
1Ch 11:23 he went down to him with a s·, 7626
20: 5 spear s· was like a weaver's beam.6086
Ps 23: 4 rod and thy s· they comfort me. 4938
105:16 he brake the whole s· of bread. 4294
Isa 3: 1 from Judah the stay and the s·, 4938
9: 4 the s· of his shoulder, the rod of 4294
10: 5 and the s· in their hand is mine "
15 or as if the s· should lift up itself, "
24 and shall lift up his s· against thee,"
14: 5 hath broken the s· of the wicked, "
28:27 the fitches are beaten out with a s·, "
30:32 where the grounded s· shall pass, "
36: 6 Lo, thou trustest in the s· of this 4938
Jer 48:17 How is the strong s· broken, and 4294
Eze 4:16 I will break the s· of bread in "
5:16 and will break your s· of bread: "
14:13 and will break the s· of the bread "
29: 6 they have been a s· of reed to the 4938
Ho 4:12 and their s· declareth unto them: 4731
Zec 8: 4 every man with his s· in his hand 4938
11:10 And I took my s·, even Beauty, 4731
14 Then I cut asunder mine other s·, "
M'r 6: 8 for their journey, save a s· only; *4464*
Heb11:21 leaning upon the top of his s·. "

stagger See also STAGGERED; STAGGERETH.
Job 12:25 them to s· like a drunken man. 8582
Ps 107:27 fro, and s· like a drunken man, 5128
Isa 29: 9 they s·, but not with strong drink. "

staggered
Ro 4:20 He s· not at the promise of God **1252*

staggereth
Isa 19:14 as a drunken man s· in his vomit. 8582

staid See STAYED.

stain
Job 3: 5 and the shadow of death s· it; *1350
Isa 23: 9 to s· the pride of all glory, and to 2490
63: 3 and I will s· all my raiment. *1351

stairs
1Ki 6: 8 with winding s· into the middle 3883
2Ki 9:13 it under him on the top of the s·, 4609
Ne 3:15 the s· that go down from the city "
9: 4 up upon the s·, of the Levites, 4608
12:37 up by the s· of the city of David, 4609
Ca 2:14 rock, in the secret places of the s·,*4095
Eze 40: 6 east, and went up the s· thereof, *4609
43:17 his s· shall look toward the east. * "
Ac 21:35 And when he came upon the s·, so *304*
40 Paul stood on the s·, and beckoned "

stakes
Isa 33:20 not one of the s· thereof shall ever3489
54: 2 thy cords, and strengthen thy s·; "

stalk See also STALKS.
Ge 41: 5 ears of corn came up upon one s·, 7070
22 seven ears came up in one s·, full "
Ho 8: 7 reap the whirlwind: it hath no s·:*7054

stalks
Jos 2: 6 and hid them with the s· of flax, 6086

stall See also STALLED; STALLS.
Am 6: 4 calves out of the midst of the s·; 4770
Mal 4: 2 and grow up as calves of the s·. "
Lu 13:15 loose his ox or his ass from the s·, *5336*

stalled
Pr 15:17 than a s· ox and hatred therewith. 75

stalls
1Ki 4:26 had forty thousand s· of horses 723
2Ch 9:25 had four thousand s· for horses "
32:28 and s· for all manner of beasts, and "
Hab 3:17 there shall be no herd in the s·: 7517

stammerers
Isa 32: 4 s· shall be ready to speak plainly. 5926

stammering
Isa 28:11 with s· lips and another tongue *3934
33:19 of a s· tongue, that thou canst not*3932

stamp See also STAMPED; STAMPING.
2Sa 22:43 I did s· them as the mire of the 1854
Eze 6:11 thine hand, and s· with thy foot, 7554

stamped
De 9:21 and burnt it with fire, and s· it, 3807
2Ki 23: 6 s· it small to powder, and cast the 1854
15 s· it small to powder, and burned "
2Ch 15:16 Asa cut down her idol, and s· it, * "
Eze 25: 6 and s· with the feet, and rejoiced 7554
Da 7: 7 s· the residue with the feet of it: 7512
19 and s· the residue with his feet; "
8: 7 to the ground, and s· upon him: *7429
10 to the ground, and s· upon them. "

stamping
Jer 47: 3 noise of the s· of the hoofs of his 8161

stanched
Lu 8:44 immediately her issue of blood s·. *2476*

stand See also STANDEST; STANDETH; STANDING; STOOD; WITHSTAND.
Ge 19: 9 And they said, S· back. And they 5066
24:13 I s· here by the well of water; and 5324
43 Behold, I s· by the well of water; "
Ex 7:15 thou shalt s· by the river's brink "
8:20 morning, and s· before Pharaoh; 3320
9:11 the magicians could not s· before 5975
13 morning, and s· before Pharaoh, 3320
14:13 Fear ye not, s· still, and see the "
17: 6 I will s· before thee there upon the5975
9 I will s· on the top of the hill with 5324
18:14 and all the people s· by thee from "
33:10 cloudy pillar s· at the tabernacle 5975
21 me, and thou shalt s· upon a rock:5324
Le 18:23 shall any woman s· before a beast 5975
19:16 shalt thou s· against the blood of "
Le 26:37 power to s· before your enemies. 8617
27:14 shall estimate it, so shall it s·. 6965
17 to thy estimation it shall s·. "
Nu 1: 5 of the men that shall s· with you: 5975
9: 8 S· still, and I will hear what the * "
11:16 that they may s· there with thee. 3320
16: 9 and to s· before the congregation 5975
23: 3 S· by thy burnt offering, and I 3320
15 S· here by thy burnt offering, while"
27:21 shall s· before Eleazar the priest, 5975
30: 4 then all her vows shall s·, and 6965
4 she hath bound her soul shall s·. "
5 she hath bound her soul, shall s·: "
7 then her vows shall s·, and her "
7 she bound her soul, shall s·. "
9 have bound their souls, shall s· "
11 then all her vows shall s·, and every "
11 wherewith...bound her soul shall s·."
12 the bond of her soul, shall not s·: "
35:12 until he s· before the congregation5975
De 5:31 But as for thee, s· thou here by me, "
7:24 no man be able to s· before thee, 3320
9: 2 can s· before the children of Anak! "
10: 8 to s· before the Lord to minister 5975
11:25 no man be able to s· before you: 3320
18: 5 to s· to minister in the name of 5975
7 do, which s· there before the Lord. "
19:17 shall s· before the Lord, before the "
24:11 Thou shalt s· abroad, and the man "
25: 8 if he s· to it, and say, I like not to "
27:12 These shall s· upon mount Gerizim "
13 shall s· upon mount Ebal to curse; "
29:10 Ye s· this day all of you before the 5324
Jos 1: 5 not any man be able to s· before 3320
3: 8 Jordan, ye shall s· still in Jordan. 5975
13 and they shall s· upon an heap. "
7:12 could not s· before their enemies, 6965
13 canst not s· before thine enemies, "
10: 8 not a man of them s· before thee. 5975
12 Sun, s· thou still upon Gibeon; 1826
20: 4 shall s· at the entering of the gate 5975
6 until he s· before the congregation "
23: 9 man hath been able to s· before you*"
J'g 2:14 could not...s· before their enemies. "
4:20 S· in the door of the tent, and it "
1Sa 6:20 Who is able to s· before this holy "
9:27 but s· thou still a while, that I may "
12: 7 Now therefore s· still, that I may 3320
16 Now...s· and see this great thing, "
14: 9 then we will s· still in our place, 5975
16:22 Let David, I pray thee, s· before me; "
19: 3 And I will go out and s· beside my "
2Sa 1: 9 S·, I pray thee, upon me, and slay "
18:30 unto him, Turn aside, and s· here.3320
1Ki 1: 2 and let her s· before the king, and 5975
8:11 the priests could not s· to minister "
10: 8 thy servants, which s· continually "
17: 1 of Israel liveth, before whom I s·, "
18:15 of hosts liveth, before whom I s·, "
19:11 s· upon the mount before the Lord. "
2Ki 3:14 Lord...liveth, before whom I s·, "
5:11 will surely come out to me, and s·, "
16 the Lord liveth, before whom I s·, I "
6:31 if the head of Elisha...s· on him "
10: 4 before him: how then shall we s·? "
1Ch 21:16 angel of the Lord s· between the "
23:30 to s· every morning to thank and "
2Ch 5:14 the priests could not s· to minister "
9: 7 which s· continually before thee, "
20: 9 we s· before this house, and in thy "
17 s· ye still, and see the salvation of "
29:11 Lord hath chosen you to s· before "
34:32 Jerusalem and Benjamin to s· to it. "
35: 5 s· in the holy place according to the"
Ezr 9:15 we cannot s· before thee because of "
10:13 and we are not able to s· without, "
14 our rulers of all the congregation s·,*"
Ne 7: 3 while they s· by, let them shut the "
9: 5 S· up and bless the Lord your God6965
Es 3: 4 Mordecai's matters would s·: 5975
8:11 and to s· for their life, to destroy, "
Job 8:15 upon his house, but it shall not s·: "
19:25 he shall s· at the latter day upon 6965
30:20 I s· up, and thou regardest me 5975
33: 5 thy words in order before me, s· up.3320
37:14 Hearken unto this, O Job: s· still, 5975
38:14 the seal; and they s· as a garment.3320
41:10 who then is able to s· before me? "
Ps 1: 5 the ungodly shall not s· in the 6965
4: 4 S· in awe, and sin not: commune "
5: 5 foolish shall not s· in thy sight: 3320
20: 8 but we are risen, and s· upright. 5749
24: 3 or who shall s· in his holy place? 6965
30: 7 made my mountain to s· strong: 5975
33: 8 inhabitants of the world s· in awe 1481
35: 2 buckler, and s· up for mine help. 6965
38:11 My lovers and my friends s· aloof 5975
11 my sore; and my kinsmen s· afar off."
45: 9 thy right hand did s· the queen in 5324
73: 7 Their eyes s· out with fatness: 3318
76: 7 and who may s· in thy sight when 5975
78:13 made the waters to s· as an heap. 5324
89:28 my covenant shall s· fast with him. 539
43 not made him to s· in the battle. 6965
94:16 who will s· up for me against the 3320
109: 6 and let Satan s· at his right hand. 5975
31 he shall s· at the right hand of the "
111: 8 They s· fast for ever and ever, and*5564
122: 2 Our feet shall s· within thy gates,*5975
130: 3 iniquities, O Lord, who shall s'? "
134: 1 which by night s· in the house of the"
135: 2 Ye that s· in the house of the Lord, "
147:17 morsels: who can s· before his cold?"
Pr 12: 7 the house of the righteous shall s·. "
19:21 counsel of the Lord, that shall s·. 6965
22:29 business? he shall s· before kings; 3320

Pr 22:29 he shall not s' before mean men. 3320
25: 6 s' not in the place of great men: 5975
27: 4 but who is able to s' before envy? "
Ec 4:15 second child that shall s' up in his* "
8: 3 of his sight: s' not in an evil thing;*"
Isa 7: 7 It shall not s', neither shall it 6965
8:10 speak the word, and it shall not s': "
11:10 s' for an ensign of the people; *5975
14:24 as I have purposed, so shall it s': 6965
21: 8 I s'...upon the watchtower 5975
27: 9 groves and images shall not s' up.*6965
28:18 agreement with hell shall not s'; "
32: 8 and by liberal things shall he s'. "
40: 8 word of our God shall s' for ever. "
44:11 gathered together, let them s' up; 5975
46:10 My counsel shall s', and I will do 6965
47:12 S' now with thine enchantments, 5975
13 the monthly prognosticators, s' up, "
48:13 call unto them, they s' up together. "
50: 8 let us s' together: who is mine "
51:17 awake, s' up, O Jerusalem, which 6965
61: 5 strangers shall s' and feed your 5975
65: 5 Which say, S' by thyself, come not7126
Jer 6:16 S' ye in the ways, and see, and 5975
7: 2 S' in the gate of the Lord's house, "
10 come and s' before me in this house,"
14: 6 wild asses did s' in the high places, "
15:19 again, and thou shalt s' before me: "
17:19 Go and s' in the gate of the children"
26: 2 S' in the court of the Lord's house, "
35:19 want a man to s' before me for ever."
44:28 shall know whose words shall s', 6965
29 words shall surely s' against you "
46: 4 and s' forth with your helmets; 3320
14 S' fast, and prepare thee; for the "
21 they did not s', because the day of 5975
48:19 inhabitant of Aroer, s' by the way, "
49:19 who is that shepherd that will s' "
50:44 who is that shepherd that will s' "
51:50 the sword, go away, s' not still: "
Eze 2: 1 Son of man, s' upon thy feet, and I "
13: 5 to s' in the battle in the day of the "
17:14 keeping of his covenant it might s'. "
22:30 s' in the gap before me for the land,"
27:29 ships, they shall s' upon the land; "
29: 7 madest all their loins to be at a s'.5976
31:14 their trees s' up in their height, 5975
33:26 Ye s' upon your sword, ye work "
44:11 shall s' before them to minister unto"
15 and they shall s' before me to offer "
24 they shall s' in judgment; and "
46: 2 and shall s' by the post of the gate, "
47:10 that the fishers shall s' upon it from"
Da 1: 4 in them to s' in the king's palace, "
5 they might s' before the king. "
2:44 kingdoms, and it shall s' for ever. 6966
7: 4 and made s' upon the feet as a man,"
8: 4 that no beasts might s' before him,5975
7 there was no power in the ram to s'"
22 four kingdoms shall s' up out of the"
23 dark sentences, shall s' up. "
25 shall also s' up against the Prince "
10:11 I speak unto thee, and s' upright: "
11: 2 there shall s' up yet three kings in "
3 And a mighty king shall s' up, that "
4 when he shall s' up, his kingdom "
6 neither shall he s', nor his arm: "
7 branch of her roots shall one s' up "
14 many s' up against the king of the "
16 will, and none shall s' before him: "
16 and he shall s' in the glorious land, "
17 she shall not s' on his side, neither "
20 s' up in his estate a raiser of taxes "
21 his estate shall s' up a vile person, "
25 mighty army; but he shall not s': "
31 And arms shall s' on his part, and "
12: 1 And at that time shall Michael s' up,"
13 s' in thy lot at the end of the days. "
Am 2:15 shall he s' that handleth the bow; "
Mic 5: 4 he shall s' and feed in the strength "
Na 1: 6 Who can s' before his indignation? "
2: 8 S', s', shall they cry; but none shall"
Hab 2: 1 I will s' upon my watch, and set me"
Zec 3: 7 to walk among these that s' by. "
4:14 s' by the Lord of the whole earth. "
14: 4 his feet shall s' in that day upon "
12 away while they s' upon their feet, "
Mal 3: 2 who shall s' when he appeareth? "
M't 12:25 divided against itself shall not s': 2476
26 how shall then his kingdom s'? "
47 mother and thy brethren s' without,*"
20: 6 them, Why s' ye here all the day idle?"
24:15 the prophet, s' in the holy place, * "
M'r 3: 3 had the withered hand, S' forth. 1453
24 itself, that kingdom cannot s'. 2476
25 against itself, that house cannot s'. "
26 and be divided, he cannot s', but "
9: 1 there be some of them that s' here, "
11:25 And when ye s' praying, forgive, 4739
Lu 1:19 that s' in the presence of God; 3936
6: 8 Rise up, and s' forth in the midst. 2476
8:20 mother and thy brethren s' without,"
11:18 himself, how shall his kingdom s'? "
13:25 and ye begin to s' without, and to "
21:36 and to s' before the Son of man. "
Joh 11:42 of the people which s' by I said it,*4026
Ac 1:11 why s' ye gazing up into heaven? 2476
4:10 this man s' here before you whole.3936
5:20 Go, s' and speak in the temple to 2476
8:38 commanded the chariot to s' still: "
10:26 S' up; I myself also am a man. 450
10:30 a loud voice, S' upright on thy feet. "
25:10 I s' at Cæsar's judgment seat, *2476
26: 6 I s' and am judged for the hope of "
16 But rise, and s' upon thy feet: for "
Ro 5: 2 faith into this grace wherein we s'. "
Ro 9:11 God according to election might s',3306
14: 4 up: for God is able to make him s'.2476
10 we shall all s' before the judgment3936
1Co 2: 5 should not s' in the wisdom of men,1510
15: 1 I have received, and wherein ye s'; 2476
30 why s' we in jeopardy every hour? "
16:13 s' fast in the faith, quit you like 4739
2Co 1:24 of your joy: for by faith ye s'. 2476
Ga 4:20 my voice; for I s' in doubt of you.* 639
5: 1 S' fast therefore in the liberty 4739
Eph 6:11 may be able to s' against the wiles2476
13 evil day, and having done all, to s'. "
14 S' therefore, having your loins girt "
Ph'p 1:27 that ye s' fast in one spirit, with 4739
4: 1 so s' fast in the Lord, my dearly "
Col 4:12 ye may s' perfect and complete in 2476
1Th 3: 8 we live, if ye s' fast in the Lord. 4739
2Th 2:15 s' fast, and hold the traditions "
Jas 2: 3 S' thou there, or sit here under 2476
1Pe 5:12 the true grace of God wherein ye s'."
Re 3:20 Behold, I s' at the door, and knock: "
6:17 come; and who shall be able to s'? "
10: 5 angel which I saw s' upon the sea* "
15: 2 s' on the sea of glass, having the * "
18:15 shall s' afar off for the fear of her "
20:12 I saw the dead,...s' before God; * "

standard See also STANDARDBEARER; STANDARDS.
Nu 1:52 and every man by his own s', 1714
2: 2 of Israel shall pitch by his own s', "
3 they of the s' of the camp of Judah "
10 be the s' of the camp of Reuben "
18 be the s' of the camp of Ephraim "
25 The s' of the camp of Dan shall be "
10:14 went the s' of the camp...of Judah "
18 And the s' of the camp of Reuben "
22 the s' of the camp...of Ephraim "
25 And the s' of the camp...of Dan "
Isa 49:22 and set up my s' to the people: *5251
59:19 Spirit of the Lord shall lift up a s'*5127
62:10 stones; lift up a s' for the people.*5251
Jer 4: 6 Set up the s' toward Zion: retire, "
21 How long shall I see the s', and "
50: 2 and publish, and set up a s'; "
51:12 Set...s' upon the walls of Babylon, "
27 Set ye up a s' in the land, blow the "

standardbearer
Isa 10:18 shall be as when a s' fainteth. 5264

standards
Nu 2:17 every man in his place by their s'.1714
31 shall go hindmost with their s'. "
34 so they pitched by their s', and so "

standest See also UNDERSTANDEST.
Ge 24:31 wherefore s' thou without? for I 5975
Ex 3: 5 the place whereon thou s' is holy "
Jos 5:15 the place whereon thou s' is holy. "
Ps 10: 1 Why s' thou afar off, O Lord? why "
Ac 7:33 for the place where thou s' is holy 2476
Ro 11:20 broken off, and thou s' by faith. "

standeth See also UNDERSTANDETH.
Nu 14:14 and that thy cloud s' over them, 5975
De 1:38 son of Nun, which s' before thee, "
17:12 that s' to minister there before the "
29:15 him that s' here with us this day "
J'g 16:26 pillars whereupon the house s', *3559
Es 6: 5 Behold, Haman s' in the court. 5975
7: 9 gallows...s' in the house of Haman. "
Ps 1: 1 nor s' in the way of sinners, nor "
26:12 My foot s' in an even place: in the "
33:11 The counsel of the Lord s' for ever,"
82: 1 God s' in the congregation of the 5324
119:161 but my heart s' in awe of thy word.
Pr 8: 2 She s' in the top of high places, by5324
Ca 2: 9 he s' behind our wall, he looketh 5975
Isa 3:13 The Lord s' up to plead, 5324
13 and s' to judge the people. 5975
46: 7 and set him in his place, and he s'; "
59:14 backward, and justice s' afar off: "
Da 12: 1 prince which s' for the children of "
Zec 11:16 broken, nor feed that that s' still:*5324
Joh 1:26 but there s' one among you, whom2476
3:29 which s' and heareth him, "
Ro 14: 4 to his own master he s' or falleth. 4739
1Co 7:37 he that s' stedfast in his heart, 2476
8:13 I will eat no flesh while the world s',*
10:12 let him that thinketh he s' take 2476
2Ti 2:19 the foundation of God s' sure, "
Heb 10:11 every priest s' daily ministering "
Jas 5: 9 behold, the judge s' before the door."
Re 10: 8 the angel which s' upon the sea and"

standing See also UNDERSTANDING.
Ex 22: 6 stacks of corn, or the s' corn, 7054
26:15 tabernacle of shittim wood s' up. 5975
36:20 tabernacle of shittim wood, s' up. "
Le 26: 1 neither rear you up a s' image, *4676
Nu 22:23, 31 angel of the Lord s' in the way,5324
De 23:25 When thou comest into the s' corn7054
25 sickle unto thy neighbour's s' corn."
J'g 15: 5 into the s' corn of the Philistines, "
5 the shocks, and also the s' corn, "
1Sa 19:20 Samuel s' as appointed over them,5975
22: 6 his servants were s' about him;) 5324
1Ki 13:25 and the lion s' by the carcase: 5975
28 ass and the lion s' by the carcase: "
22:19 and all the host of heaven s' by him"
2Ch 9:18 place, and two lions s' by the stays:"
18:18 the host of heaven s' on his right "
Es 5: 2 Esther the queen s' in the court, "
Ps 69: 2 deep mire, where there is no s': *4613
107:35 the wilderness into a s' water, * 98
114: 8 turned the rock into a s' water, * "
Da 8: 6 I had seen s' before the river, 5975
Am 9: 1 I saw the Lord s' upon the altar: 5324
Mic 1:11 he shall receive of you his s'. *5979
Mic 5:13 thy s' images out of the midst of *4676
Zec 3: 1 the high priest s' before the angel 5975
1 Satan s' at his right hand to resist "
6: 5 from s' before the Lord of all the 3320
M't 6: 5 to pray s' in the synagogues *2476
16:28 There be some s' here, which shall "
20: 3 others s' idle in the marketplace, "
6 went out, and found others s' idle, "
M'r 3:31 and, s' without, sent unto him, "
13:14 desolation,...s' where it ought not, "
Lu 1:11 s' on the right side of the altar of "
5: 2 And saw two ships s' by the lake: "
9:27 there be some s' here, which shall* "
18:13 publican, s' afar off, would not lift "
Joh 8: 9 and the woman s' in the midst. * "
19:26 disciple s' by, whom he loved, 3936
20:14 herself back, and saw Jesus s', 2476
Ac 2:14 Peter, s' up with the eleven, lifted "
4:14 the man which was healed s' with "
5:23 keepers s' without before the doors:"
25 put in prison are s' in the temple, "
7:55 Jesus s' on the right hand of God. "
56 Son of man s' on the right hand of "
22:20 I also was s' by, and consenting 2186
24:21 voice, that I cried s' among them, 2476
Heb 9: 8 the first tabernacle was yet s':2192,4714
2Pe 3: 5 earth s' out of the water and in *4921
Re 7: 1 four angels s' on the four corners 2476
11: 4 two candlesticks s' before the God "
18:10 S' afar off for...fear of her torment, "
19:17 And I saw an angel s' in the sun; "

stank
Ex 7:21 and the river s', and the Egyptians 887
8:14 upon heaps: and the land s'. "
16:20 morning, and it bred worms, and s': "
2Sa 10: 6 saw that they s' before David, the* "

star See also STARGAZERS; STARS.
Nu 24:17 shall come a S' out of Jacob, and 3556
Am 5:26 your images, the s' of your god, "
M't 2: 2 for we have seen his s' in the east, 792
7 what time the s' appeared. "
9 the s', which they saw in the east, "
10 When they saw the s', they rejoiced "
Ac 7:43 and the s' of your god Remphan, 798
1Co 15:41 for one s' differeth from another 792
41 differeth from another s' in glory. "
2Pe 1:19 the day s' arise in your hearts: 5459
Re 2:28 And I will give him the morning s'.792
8:10 there fell a great s' from heaven, "
11 name of the s' is called Wormwood: "
9: 1 I saw a s' fall from heaven unto the "
22:16 and the bright and morning s'. "

stare
Ps 22:17 bones: they look and s' upon me. 7200

stargazers
Isa 47:13 now the astrologers, the s', 2374,3556

stars
Ge 1:16 the night: he made the s' also. 3556
15: 5 now toward heaven, and tell the s', "
22:17 thy seed as the s' of the heaven, "
26: 4 seed to multiply as the s' of heaven,"
37: 9 eleven s' made obeisance to me. "
Ex 32:13 your seed as the s' of heaven, and "
De 1:10 as the s' of heaven for multitude. "
4:19 the sun, and the moon, and the s', "
10:22 made thee as the s' of heaven for "
28:62 ye were as the s' of heaven for "
J'g 5:20 the s' in their courses fought "
1Ch 27:23 Israel like to the s' of the heavens. "
Ne 4:21 the morning till the s' appeared. "
9:23 thou as the s' of heaven, and "
Job 3: 9 Let the s' of the twilight...be dark; "
9: 7 it riseth not; and sealeth up the s'. "
22:12 and behold the height of the s', how"
25: 5 yea, the s' are not pure in his sight,"
38: 7 When the morning s' sang together,"
Ps 8: 3 the moon and the s', which thou "
136: 9 The moon and s' to rule by night: "
147: 4 He telleth the number of the s'; "
148: 3 moon: praise him, all ye s' of light."
Ec 12: 2 moon, or the s', be not darkened, "
Isa 13:10 For the s' of heaven and the "
14:13 will exalt my throne above the s' "
Jer 31:35 and of the s' for a light by night, "
Eze 32: 7 and make the s' thereof dark; "
Da 8:10 host and of the s' to the ground, "
12: 3 as the s' for ever and ever. "
Joe 2:10 the s' shall withdraw their shining:"
3:15 the s' shall withdraw their shining. "
Am 5: 8 Seek him that maketh the seven s'*3598
Ob 4 thou set thy nest among the s', 3556
Na 3:16 merchants above the s' of heaven: "
M't 24:29 and the s' shall fall from heaven, 792
M'r 13:25 And the s' of heaven shall fall, and "
Lu 21:25 sun, and in the moon, and in the s';798
Ac 27:20 sun nor s' in many days appeared, "
1Co 15:41 moon, and another glory of the s': 792
Heb 11:12 as the s' of the sky in multitude, 798
Jude 13 wandering s', to whom is reserved 792
Re 1:16 he had in his right hand seven s': "
20 The mystery of the seven s' which "
20 seven s' are the angels of the seven "
2: 1 he that holdeth the seven s' in his "
3: 1 Spirits of God, and the seven s'; "
6:13 the s' of heaven fell unto the earth, "
8:12 moon, and the third part of the s'; "
12: 1 upon her head a crown of twelve s': "
4 the third part of the s' of heaven, "

state See also ESTATE.
Ge 43: 7 The man asked us straitly of our s',*
2Ch 24:13 they set the house of God in his s',4971
Es 1: 7 according to the s' of the king. *3027
2:18 according to the s' of the king. * "
Ps 39: 5 at his best s' is altogether vanity.*5324

Pr 27:23 to know the s· of thy flocks, and 6440
28: 2 the s· thereof shall be prolonged. 3651
Isa 22:19 and from thy s· shall he pull thee *4612
M't 12:45 the last s· of that man is worse than
Lu 11:26 the last s· of that man is worse than
Ph'p 2:19 comfort, when I know your s·. *3588,4012*
20 will naturally care for your s·. "
4:11 in whatsoever s· I am, therewith to
Col 4: 7 my s· shall Tychicus declare *3588,2596*

stately
Eze 23:41 satest upon a s· bed, and a table 3520

station
Isa 22:19 And I will drive thee from thy s·, *4673

stature
Nu 13:32 we saw in it are men of a great s·. 4060
1Sa 16: 7 or on the height of his s·; because 6967
2Sa 21:20 where was a man of great s·, that 4055
1Ch 11:23 an Egyptian, a man of great s·, 4060
20: 6 Gath, where was a man of great s·, "
Ca 7: 7 This thy s· is like to a palm tree, 6967
Isa 10:33 high ones of s· shall be hewn down, "
45:14 and of the Sabeans, men of s·, 4060
Eze 13:18 the head of every s· to hunt souls! 6967
17: 6 became a spreading vine of low s·, "
19:11 her s· was exalted among the thick "
31: 3 shadowing shroud,...of an high s·; "
M't 6:27 can add one cubit unto his s·? ‡2244
Lu 2:52 Jesus increased in wisdom and s·, "
12:25 thought can add to his s· one cubit?‡"
19: 3 press, because he was little of s·. "
Eph 4:13 unto the measure of the s· of the "

statute See also STATUTES.
Ex 15:25 there he made for them a s· and 2706
27:21 it shall be a s· for ever unto their 2708
28:43 it shall be a s· for ever unto him "
29: 9 shall be theirs for a perpetual s·: "
28 and his sons' by a s· for ever from 2706
30:21 and it shall be a s· for ever to them."
Le 3:17 It shall be a perpetual s· for your 2708
6:18 It shall be a s· for ever in your *2706
22 it is a s· for ever unto the Lord; it "
7:34 and unto his sons by a s· for ever* "
36 by a s· for ever throughout their *2708
10: 9 be a s· for ever throughout your "
15 sons' with thee, by a s· for ever; *2706
16:29 this shall be a s· for ever unto you:2708
31 afflict your souls, by a s· for ever. "
34 shall be an everlasting s· unto you, "
17: 7 This shall be a s· for ever unto "
23:14 be a s· for ever throughout your "
21 it shall be a s· for ever in all your "
31 be a s· for ever throughout your "
41 It shall be a s· for ever in your "
24: 3 it shall be a s· for ever in your "
9 made by fire by a perpetual s·. 2706
Nu 18:11, 19 with thee, by a s· for ever: * "
23 be a s· for ever throughout your 2708
19:10 among them, for a s· for ever. "
21 it shall be a perpetual s· unto them,"
27:11 children of Israel a s· of judgment, "
35:29 things shall be for a s· of judgment "
Jos 24:25 set them a s· and an ordinance in 2706
1Sa 30:25 he made it a s· and an ordinance "
Ps 81: 4 For this was a s· for Israel, and a "
Da 6: 7 together to establish a royal s·, 7010
15 no decree nor s· which the king "

statutes
Ge 26: 5 my commandments, my s·, and my 2708
Ex 15:26 commandments, and keep...his s·, 2706
18:16 do make them know the s· of God, "
Le 10:11 all the s· which the Lord hath "
18: 5 Ye shall therefore keep my s·, and 2708
26 Ye shall therefore keep my s· and "
19:19 Ye shall keep my s·. Thou shalt "
37 Therefore shall ye observe all my s·,"
20: 8 ye shall keep my s·, and do them: "
22 Ye shall therefore keep all my s·, "
25:18 Wherefore ye shall do my s·, and "
26: 3 If ye walk in my s·, and keep my "
15 And if ye shall despise my s·, or if "
43 because their soul abhorred my s·. "
46 These are the s· and judgments and"
Nu 30:16 These are the s·, which the Lord 2706
De 4: 1 unto the s· and unto the judgments,"
5 I have taught you s· and judgments,"
6 which shall hear all these s·, and "
8 that hath s· and judgments so "
14 me at that time to teach you s· and "
40 Thou shalt keep therefore his s·, "
45 are the testimonies, and the s·, and "
5: 1 the s· and judgments which I speak "
31 all the commandments, and the s·, "
6: 1 are the commandments, the s·, and "
2 all his s· and his commandments, 2708
17 his s·, which he hath commanded 2706
20 mean the testimonies, and the s·, "
24 commanded us to do all these s·, "
7:11 keep the commandments, and the s·,"
8:11 his s·, which I command thee this 2708
10:13 his s·, which I command thee this "
11: 1 and keep his charge, and his s·, "
32 ye shall observe to do all the s· 2706
12: 1 These are the s· and judgments, "
16:12 thou shalt observe and do these s·. "
17:19 the words of this law and these s·, "
26:16 hath commanded thee to do these s·"
17 to keep his s·, and...commandments,"
27:10 do his commandments and his s·, "
28:15 his s· which I command thee this 2708
45 keep his commandments and his s· "
30:10, 16 his commandments and his s· "
2Sa 22:23 as for his s·, I did not depart from "
1Ki 2: 3 to walk in his ways, to keep his s·, "
3: 3 walking in the s· of David his "

1Ki 3:14 keep my s· and...commandments, 2706
6:12 if thou wilt walk in my s·, and 2708
8:58 his commandments, and his s·, 2706
61 to walk in his s·, and to keep his "
9: 4 wilt keep my s· and my judgments: "
6 keep my commandments and...s· 2708
11:11 not kept my covenant and my s·, "
33 to keep my s· and my judgments, "
34 kept my commandments and my s·:"
38 keep my s· and my commandments,"
2Ki 17: 8 And walked in the s· of the heathen,"
13 keep my commandments and my s·,"
15 And they rejected his s·, and his 2706
19 walked in the s· of Israel which 2708
34 neither do they after their s·, or "
37 And the s·, and the ordinances, 2706
23: 3 his testimonies and his s· with all 2708
1Ch 22:13 heed to fulfil the s· and judgments2706
29:19 thy testimonies, and thy s·, and to "
2Ch 7:17 observe my s· and my judgments; "
19 if ye turn away, and forsake my s·2708
19:10 s· and judgments, ye shall even 2706
33: 8 to the whole law and the s· and "
34:31 his testimonies, and his s·, with all "
Ezr 7:10 to teach in Israel s· and judgments."
11 of the Lord, and of his s· to Israel. "
Ne 1: 7 kept the commandments, nor the s·, "
9:13 laws, good s· and commandments: "
14 s·, and laws, by the hand of Moses "
10:29 Lord, and his judgments and his s·; "
Ps 18:22 I did not put away his s· from me. 2708
19: 8 The s· of the Lord are right, *6490
50:16 hast thou to do to declare my s·, 2706
89:31 If they break my s·, and keep not 2708
105:45 That they might observe his s·, 2706
119: 5 ways were directed to keep thy s·! "
8 I will keep thy s·: O forsake me not "
12 art thou, O Lord: teach me thy s·. "
16 I will delight myself in thy s·: I 2708
23 thy servant did meditate in thy s·. 2706
26 thou heardest me: teach me thy s·. "
33 me, O Lord, the way of thy s·; and "
48 loved; and I will meditate in thy s·. "
54 Thy s· have been my songs in the "
64 full of thy mercy: teach me thy s·. "
68 and doest good; teach me thy s·. "
71 afflicted; that I might learn thy s·. "
80 Let my heart be sound in thy s·; "
83 smoke; yet do I not forget thy s·. "
112 mine heart to perform thy s· alway, "
117 and I will have respect unto thy s· "
118 down all them that err from thy s·: "
124 unto thy mercy, and teach me thy s·. "
135 thy servant; and teach me thy s·. "
145 hear me, O Lord: I will keep thy s·. "
155 wicked: for they seek not thy s·. "
171 when thou hast taught me thy s·. "
147:19 his s· and...judgments unto Israel. "
Jer 44:10 nor in my s·, that I set before you 2708
23 nor in his s·, nor in his testimonies; "
Eze 5: 6 my s· more than the countries that "
6 refused my judgments and my s·, "
7 have not walked in my s·, neither "
11:12 for ye have not walked in my s·, 2706
20 That they may walk in my s·, and 2708
18: 9 Hath walked in my s·, and hath "
17 judgments, hath walked in my s·; "
19 hath kept all my s·, and hath done "
21 keep all my s·, and do that which is "
20:11 And I gave them my s·, and shewed "
13 they walked not in my s·, and they "
16 walked not in my s·, but polluted "
18 Walk...not in the s· of your fathers,2706
19 Lord your God; walk in my s·, 2708
21 they walked not in my s·, neither "
24 but had despised my s·, and had "
25 gave them...s· that were not good, 2706
33:15 walk in the s· of life, without 2708
36:27 cause you to walk in my s·, and ye 2706
37:24 and observe my s·, and do them. 2708
44:24 they shall keep my laws and my s· "
Mic 6:16 For the s· of Omri are kept, and all "
Zec 1: 6 But my words and my s·, which I 2706
Mal 4: 4 Israel, with the s· and judgments. "

staunched See STANCHED.

staves See also HANDSTAVES.
Ex 25:13 thou shalt make s· of shittim wood, 905
14 thou shalt put the s· into the rings "
15 The s· shall be in the rings of the "
27 shall the rings be for places of the s·."
28 shalt make the s· of shittim wood, "
27: 6 And thou shalt make s· for the altar,"
6 s· of shittim wood, and overlay them"
7 the s· shall be put into the rings, "
7 the s· shall be upon the two sides of "
30: 4 for places for the s· to bear it withal."
5 shalt make the s· of shittim wood, "
35:12 The ark, and the s· thereof, with the "
13 The table, and his s·, and all his "
15 And the incense altar, and his s·, "
16 grate, his s·, and all his vessels, the "
37: 4 And he made s· of shittim wood, and"
5 he put the s· into the rings by the "
14 places for the s· to bear the table. "
15 And he made the s· of shittim wood, "
27 to be places for the s· to bear it "
28 And he made the s· of shittim wood, "
38: 5 grate of brass, to be places for the s·."
6 And he made the s· of shittim wood, "
7 he put the s· into the rings on the "
39:35 of the testimony, and the s· thereof, "
39 grate...his s·, and all his vessels, "
40:20 the ark, and set the s· on the ark, "
Nu 4: 6 blue, and shall put in the s· thereof. "
8 and shall put in the s· thereof. "

Nu 4:11 and shall put to the s· thereof: 905
14 badgers' skins, and put to the s· of it."
21:18 of the lawgiver, with their s·. 4938
1Sa 17:43 that thou comest to me with s·? 4731
1Ki 8: 7 covered the ark and the s· thereof 905
8 they drew out the s·, that the ends "
8 s· were seen out in the holy place "
1Ch 15:15 upon their shoulders with the s· 4133
2Ch 5: 8 covered the ark and the s· thereof 905
9 And they drew out the s· of the ark, "
9 ends of the s· were seen from the ark"
Hab 3:14 didst strike through with his s· 4294
Zec 11: 7 I took unto me two s·; the one I 4731
M't 10:10 coats, neither shoes, nor yet s·: *4464*
26:47 great multitude with swords and s·, *3586*
55 against a thief with swords and s· "
M'r 14:43 great multitude with swords and s·,"
48 with swords and with s· to take me?"
Lu 9: 3 your journey, neither s·, nor scrip,*4464*
22:52 against a thief, with swords and s·?*3586*

stay See also STAYED; STAYETH; STAYS.
Ge 19:17 neither s· thou in all the plain; 5975
Ex 9:28 let you go, and ye shall s· no longer."
Le 13: 5 the plague in his sight be at a s·, "
23, 28 if the bright spot s· in his place, "
37 if the scall be in his sight at a s·, "
Jos 10:19 And s· ye not, but pursue after your"
Ru 1:13 would ye s· for them from having 5702
1Sa 15:16 S·, and I will tell thee what the 7503
20:38 the lad, Make speed, haste, s· not. 5975
2Sa 22:19 calamity: but the Lord was my s·. 4937
24:16 It is enough: s· now thine hand. 7503
1Ch 21:15 It is enough, s· now thine hand. "
Job 37: 4 will not s· them when his voice *6117
38:37 who can s· the bottles of heaven, *7901
Ps 18:18 calamity: but the Lord was my s·. 4937
Pr 28:17 flee to the pit; let no man s· him. 8551
Ca 2: 5 S· me with flagons, comfort me 5564
Isa 3: 1 from Judah the s· and the staff, 4937
1 the staff, the whole s· of bread, 8172
1 bread, and the whole s· of water, 4937
10:20 no more...s· upon him that smote‡ "
20 shall s· upon the Lord, the Holy ‡8172
19:13 are the s· of the tribes thereof. *6438
29: 9 S· yourselves, and wonder; cry *4102
30:12 and perverseness, and s· thereon:‡8172
31: 1 s· on horses, and trust in chariots,‡ "
48: 2 and s·...upon the God of Israel; 5564
50:10 of the Lord, and s· upon his God. ‡8172
Jer 4: 6 toward Zion: retire, s· not: 5975
20: 9 with forbearing, and I could not s·.* "
Da 4:35 none can s· his hand, or say unto 4223
Ho 13:13 he should not s· long in the place *5975

stayed
Ge 8:10 And he s· yet other seven days; 2342
12 And he s· yet other seven days; 3176
32: 4 with Laban, and s· there until now:309
Ex 10:24 your flocks and your herds be s·: 3322
17:12 Aaron and Hur s· up his hands, 8551
Nu 16:48, 50 and the plague was s·. 6113
25: 8 plague was s· from the children of "
De 10:10 I s· in the mount, according to the5975
Jos 10:13 the sun stood still, and the moon s·,"
1Sa 20:19 And when thou hast s· three days, "
24: 7 David s· his servants with these *8156
30: 9 those that were left behind s·. 5975
2Sa 17:17 and Ahimaaz s· by En-rogel; for "
24:21 plague may be s· from the people. 6113
25 and the plague was s· from Israel. "
1Ki 22:35 the king was s· up in his chariot 5975
2Ki 4: 6 not a vessel more. And the oil s·. "
13:18 And he smote thrice, and s·. "
15:20 back, and s· not there in the land. "
1Ch 21:22 plague may be s· from the people. 6113
2Ch 18:34 king...s· himself up in his chariot 5975
Job 38:11 here shall thy proud waves be s·? 7896
Ps 106:30 and so the plague was s·. 6113
Isa 26: 3 peace, whose mind is s· on thee: 5564
La 4: 6 moment, and no hands s· on her. *2342
Eze 31:15 and the great waters were s·: 3607
Hag 1:10 the heaven over you is s· from dew, "
10 and the earth is s· from her fruit. "
Lu 4:42 s· him, that he should not depart *2722*
Ac 19:22 he himself s· in Asia for a season. *1907*

stayeth
Isa 27: 8 he s· his rough wind in the day of *1898

stays
1Ki 10:19 there were s· on either side on 3027
19 and two lions stood beside the s·. "
2Ch 9:18 s· on each side of the sitting place, "
18 and two lions standing by the s·: "

stead See also BESTEAD; INSTEAD; STEADS; STEDFAST.
Ge 22:13 burnt offering in the s· of his son. 8478
30: 2 Am I in God's s·, who hath withheld"
36:33 died, and Jobab...reigned in his s·. "
34 and Husham...reigned in his s·. "
35 died, and Hadad...reigned in his s·. "
36 and Samlah...reigned in his s·. "
37 died, and Saul...reigned in his s·. "
38 Baal-hanan...reigned in his s·. "
39 died, and Hadar reigned in his s·: "
Ex 29:30 And that son that is priest in his s· "
Le 6:22 his sons that is anointed in his s· "
16:32 the priest's office in his father's s·, "
Nu 32:14 ye are risen up in your fathers' s·, "
De 2:12 before them, and dwelt in their s·; "
22 and dwelt in their s· even unto this "
23 them, and dwelt in their s·. "
10: 6 in the priest's office in his s·. "
Jos 5: 7 whom he raised up in their s·, "
2Sa 10: 1 Hanun his son reigned in his s·. "
16: 8 Saul, in whose s· thou hast reigned; "
1Ki 1:30 shall sit upon my throne in my s·; "

1Ki 1:35 for he shall be king in my s·: 8478
11:43 Rehoboam his son reigned in his s·. "
14:27 Rehoboam made in their s· brasen "
31 Abijam his son reigned in his s·. "
15: 8 and Asa his son reigned in his s·. "
24 Jehoshaphat...reigned in his s·. "
28 Baasha...reigned in his s·. "
16: 6 and Elah his son reigned in his s·. "
10 And Zimri...and reigned in his s·. "
22:40 Ahaziah his son reigned in his s·. "
50 Jehoram his son reigned in his s·. "
2Ki 1:17 And Jehoram reigned in his s· in "
3:27 that should have reigned in his s·. "
8:15 died: and Hazael reigned in his s·. "
24 Ahaziah his son reigned in his s·. "
10:35 Jehoahaz his son reigned in his s·. "
12:21 Amaziah his son reigned in his s·. "
13: 9 and Joash his son reigned in his s·. "
24 Ben-hadad his son reigned in his s·. "
14:16 Jeroboam his son reigned in his s·. "
29 Zachariah his son reigned in his s·. "
15: 7 Jotham his son reigned in his s·. "
10 And Shallum...reigned in his s·. "
14 Menahem...reigned in his s·. "
22 Pekahiah his son reigned in his s·. "
30 And Hoshea...reigned in his s·. "
38 and Ahaz his son reigned in his s·. "
16:20 Hezekiah his son reigned in his s·. "
19:37 Esarhaddon...reigned in his s·. "
20:21 Manasseh his son reigned in his s·. "
21:18 and Amon his son reigned in his s·. "
24 made Josiah his son king in his s·. "
26 Josiah his son reigned in his s·. "
23:30 made him king in his father's s·. "
24: 6 Jehoiachin his son reigned in his s·. "
17 his father's brother king in his s·. "
1Ch 1:44 dead, Jobab...reigned in his s·. "
45 dead, Husham...reigned in his s·. "
46 dead, Hadad...reigned in his s·: "
47 dead, Samlah...reigned in his s·. "
48 dead, Shaul...reigned in his s·. "
49 Baal-hanan...reigned in his s·. "
50 was dead, Hadad reigned in his s·. "
19: 1 died, and his son reigned in his s·. "
2Ch 1: 8 and hast made me to reign in his s·. "
12:16 and Abijah his son reigned in his s·. "
14: 1 and Asa his son reigned in his s·. "
17: 1 Jehoshaphat...reigned in his s·. "
21: 1 Jehoram his son reigned in his s·. "
22: 1 made Ahaziah...king in his s·: "
24:27 Amaziah his son reigned in his s·. "
27: 9 And Ahaz his son reigned in his s·. "
28:27 Hezekiah his son reigned in his s·. "
32:33 Manasseh his son reigned in his s·. "
33:20 and Amon his son reigned in his s·. "
25 made Josiah his son king in his s·. "
36: 1 Jehoahaz...king in his father's s· "
8 Jehoiachin his son reigned in his s·. "
Job 16: 4 if your soul were in my soul's s·, I "
33: 6 according to thy wish in God's s·:* "
34:24 number, and set others in their s·. 8478
Pr 11: 8 and the wicked cometh in his s·. "
Isa 37:38 Esar-haddon...reigned in his s·. "
Jer 29:26 thee priest in the s· of Jehoiada "
2Co 5:20 we pray you in Christ's s·, be ye *5228
Ph'm 13 in thy s· he might have ministered* "

steadfast See STEDFAST.

steads
1Ch 5:22 dwelt in their s· until the captivity.*8478

steady
Ex 17:12 his hands were s· until the going 530

steal See also STEALETH; STEALING; STOLE; STOLEN.
Ge 31:27 secretly, and s· away from me; 1589
44: 8 should we s· out of thy lord's house "
Ex 20:15 Thou shalt not s·. "
22: 1 If a man shall s· an ox, or a sheep, "
Le 19:11 Ye shall not s·, neither deal falsely, "
De 5:19 Neither shalt thou s·. "
2Sa 19: 3 as people being ashamed s· away "
Pr 6:30 if he s· to satisfy his soul when he "
30: 9 or lest I be poor, and s·, and take "
Jer 7: 9 Will ye s·, murder, and commit "
23:30 that s· my words every one from his "
M't 6:19 thieves break through and s·: 2813
20 thieves do not break through nor s·: "
19:18 Thou shalt not s·, Thou shalt not "
27:64 come by night, and s· him away, "
M'r 10:19 Do not kill, Do not s·, Do not bear "
Lu 18:20 Do not kill, Do not s·, Do not bear "
Joh 10:10 The thief cometh not, but for to s·, "
Ro 2:21 a man should not s·, dost thou s·? "
13: 9 shalt not kill, Thou shalt not s·, "
Eph 4:28 Let him that stole s· no more: but "

stealers See MENSTEALERS.

stealeth
Ex 21:16 he that s· a man, and selleth him, 1589
Job 27:20 tempest s· him away in the night. "
Zec 5: 3 for every one that s· shall be cut off "

stealing
De 24: 7 If a man be found s· any of his 1589
Ho 4: 2 and lying, and killing, and s·, and "

stealth
2Sa 19: 3 them by s· that day into the city, 1589

stedfast
Job 11:15 yea, thou shalt be s·, and shalt not 3332
Ps 78: 8 whose spirit was not s· with God. 539
37 neither were they s· in his covenant.* "
Da 6:26 is the living God, and s· for ever, 7011
1Co 7:37 he that standeth s· in his heart, *1476*
15:58 my beloved brethren, be ye s·, "
2Co 1: 7 And our hope of you is s·, knowing, *949*
Heb 2: 2 if the word spoken by angels was s·, *949*
3:14 of our confidence s· unto the end; * "
6:19 anchor of the soul, both sure and s·, "
1Pe 5: 9 Whom resist s· in the faith, *4731*

stedfastly
Ru 1:18 she was s· minded to go with her, 553
2Ki 8:11 he settled his countenance s·, 7760
Lu 9:51 s· set his face to go to Jerusalem, *4741*
Ac 1:10 they looked s· toward heaven as *816*
2:42 they continued s· in the apostles' *4342*
6:15 looking s· on him, saw his face as* *816*
7:55 looked up s· into heaven, and saw "
14: 9 Paul speak: who s· beholding him,* "
2Co 3: 7 could not s· behold the face of "
13 could not s· look to the end of that "

stedfastness
Col 2: 5 and the s· of your faith in Christ. *4733*
2Pe 3:17 the wicked, fall from your own s·. *4740*

steel
2Sa 22:35 bow of s· is broken by mine arms.*5154
Job 20:24 and the bow of s· shall strike him* "
Ps 18:34 bow of s· is broken by mine arms.* "
Jer 15:12 the northern iron and the s·? *5178

steep
Eze 38:20 s· places shall fall, and every wall 4095
Mic 1: 4 that are poured down a s· place. 4174
M't 8:32 ran violently down a s· place into *2911*
M'r 5:13 herd ran violently down a s· place "
Lu 8:33 herd ran violently down a s· place "

stem
Isa 11: 1 forth a rod out of the s· of Jesse, *1503

step See also STEPPED; STEPPETH; STEPS.
1Sa 20: 3 is but a s· between me and death. 6587
Job 31: 7 If my s· hath turned out of the way, 838

Stephanas (*stef'-a-nas*)
1Co 1:16 baptized also the household of *S*·: *4734*
16:15 brethren, (ye know the house of *S*·, "
17 I am glad of the coming of *S*· and "
subscr. was written from Philippi by *S*·,* "

Stephen (*ste'-ven*)
Ac 6: 5 they chose *S*·, a man full of faith *4736*
8 And *S*·, full of faith and power, did "
9 and of Asia, disputing with *S*·. "
7:59 they stoned *S*·, calling upon God, "
8: 2 devout men carried *S*· to his burial, "
11:19 the persecution that arose about *S*· "
22:20 blood of thy martyr *S*· was shed, "

stepped
Joh 5: 4 the troubling of the water s· in **1684*

steppeth
Joh 5: 7 coming, another s· down before *2597*

steps See also FOOTSTEPS.
Ex 20:26 thou go up by s· unto mine altar, 4609
2Sa 22:37 hast enlarged my s· under me; 6806
1Ki 10:19 The throne had six s·, and the top 4609
20 and on the other upon the six s·: "
2Ch 9:18 And there were six s· to the throne, "
19 and on the other upon the six s·. "
Job 14:16 For now thou numberest my s·: 6806
18: 7 s· of his strength shall be straitened, "
23:11 My foot hath held his s·, his way 838
29: 6 When I washed my s· with butter, 1978
31: 4 see my ways, and count all my s·? 6806
37 unto him the number of my s·; "
Ps 17:11 have now compassed us in our s·: 838
18:36 hast enlarged my s· under me, 6806
37:23 The s· of a good man are ordered*4703
31 his heart; none of his s· shall slide. 838
44:18 have our s· declined from thy way; "
56: 6 they mark my s·, when they wait 6119
57: 6 have prepared a net for my s·; 6471
73: 2 gone; my s· had well nigh slipped. 838
85:13 shall set us in the way of his s·. *6471
119:133 Order my s· in thy word: and let* "
Pr 4:12 thy s· shall not be straitened; 6806
5: 5 to death; her s· take hold on hell. "
16: 9 way: but the Lord directeth his s·. "
Isa 26: 6 the poor, and the s· of the needy. 6471
Jer 10:23 man that walketh to direct his s·. 6806
La 4:18 They hunt our s·, that we cannot "
Eze 40:22 they went up unto it by seven s·; 4609
26 there were seven s· to go up to it, "
31, 34, 37 going up to it had eight s·. "
49 he brought me by the s· whereby "
Da 11:43 the Ethiopians shall be at his s·. 4703
Ro 4:12 walk in the s· of that faith of our *2487*
2Co 12:18 spirit? walked we not in the same s·? "
1Pe 2:21 that ye should follow his s·: "

stern
Ac 27:29 cast four anchors out of the s·, *4403*

steward See also STEWARDS.
Ge 15: 2 the s· of my house is this *1121,4943
43:19 to the s· of Joseph's house, 376,834,5921
44: 1 commanded the s· of his house, " "
4 far off, Joseph said unto his s·, " "
1Ki 16: 9 Arza s· of his house in Tirzah. * "
M't 20: 8 of the vineyard saith unto his s·, *2012*
Lu 8: 3 the wife of Chuza Herod's s·, and "
12:42 then is that faithful and wise s·, *3623*
16: 1 a certain rich man, which had a s·; "
2 for thou mayest be no longer s·. *3621*
3 Then the s· said within himself, *3622*
8 the lord commended the unjust s·, "
Tit 1: 7 must be blameless, as the s· of God;"

stewards
1Ch 28: 1 the s· over all the substance and *8269
1Co 4: 1 and s· of the mysteries of God. *3623*
2 Moreover it is required in s·, that a "
1Pe 4:10 s· of the manifold grace of God. "

stewardship
Lu 16: 2 give an account of thy s·; for thou *3622*
3 lord taketh away from me the s·: "
4 when I am put out of the s·, they "

stick See also CANDLESTICK; STICKETH; STICKS, STUCK.
2Ki 6: 6 And he cut down a s·, and cast it 6086
Job 33:21 bones that were not seen s· out. 8205
41:17 they s· together, that they cannot 3920
Ps 38: 2 For thine arrows s· fast in me, and5181
La 4: 8 is withered, it is become like a s·. 6086
Eze 29: 4 the fish of thy rivers to s· unto thy1692
4 the fish of thy rivers shall s· unto "
37:16 thou son of man, take thee one s·, 6086
16 then take another s·, and write upon "
16 For Joseph, the s· of Ephraim, and "
17 them one to another into one s·; "
19 Behold, I will take the s· of Joseph, "
19 with him, even with the s· of Judah, "
19 and make them one s·, and they "

sticketh
Pr 18:24 is a friend that s· closer than a 1695

sticks
Nu 15:32 they found a man that gathered s· 6086
33 they that found him gathering s· "
1Ki 17:10 woman was there gathering of s·: "
12 behold, I am gathering two s·, that "
Eze 37:20 the s· whereon thou writest shall "
Ac 28: 3 Paul had gathered a bundle of s·, *5434*

stiff See also STIFFHEARTED; STIFFNECKED.
De 31:27 thy rebellion, and thy s· neck: 7186
Ps 75: 5 on high: speak not with a s· neck. 6277
Jer 17:23 but made their neck s·, that they 7185

stiffened
2Ch 36:13 but he s· his neck, and hardened 7185

stiffhearted
Eze 2: 4 are impudent children and s·. 2389,3820

stiffnecked
Ex 32: 9 and, behold, it is a s· people: 7186,6203
33: 3 thee; for thou art a s· people: " "
5 Ye are a s· people: I will come " "
34: 9 among us; for it is a s· people; " "
De 9: 6 for thou art a s· people. " "
13 and, behold, it is a s· people: " "
10:16 your heart, and be no more s·. 7185, "
2Ch 30: 8 be ye not s·, as your fathers "
Ac 7:51 Ye s· and uncircumcised in heart *4644*

still See also STILLED; STILLEST; STILLETH.
Ge 12: 9 going on s· toward the south. 5265
41:21 but they were s· ill favoured, as at the
Ex 14:13 not stand s·, and see the salvation of
15:16 arm they shall be as s· as a stone; 1826
23:11 thou shalt let it rest and lie s·; *
Le 13:57 And if it appear s· in the garment, 5750
Nu 9: 8 them, Stand s·, and I will hear what
14:38 that went to search the land, lived s·.*
Jos 3: 8 Jordan, ye shall stand s· in Jordan.
10:12 Sun, stand thou s· upon Gibeon; 1826
13 And the sun stood s·, and the moon "
13 So the sun stood s· in the midst of*
11:13 cities that stood s· in their strength,*
24:10 Balaam; therefore he blessed you s·:
J'g 18: 9 it is very good: and are ye s·? 2814
1Sa 9:27 but stand thou s· a while, that I may
12: 7 Now therefore stand s·, that I may
25 But if ye shall s· do wickedly, ye shall
14: 9 then we will stand s· in our place,
26:25 great things, and also shalt s· prevail.*
2Sa 2:23 Asahel fell down and died stood s·.
28 and all the people stood s·, and
11: 1 But David tarried s· at Jerusalem.*
16: 5 came forth, and cursed s· as he came.
18:30 And he turned aside, and stood s·.
20:12 saw that all the people stood s·,
12 every one that came by him stood s·.
1Ki 19:12 and after the fire a s· small voice. 1827
22: 3 Gilead is ours, and we be s·, and
2Ki 2:11 And it came to pass, as they s· went on,
7: 4 and if we sit s· here, we die also.
12: 3 the people s· sacrificed and burnt 5750
15: 4 burnt incense s· on the high places."
35 and burned incense s· in the high "
2Ch 20:17 stand ye s·, and see the salvation of
22: 9 no power to keep s· the kingdom.*
33:17 did sacrifice s· in the high places, 5750
Ne 12:39 they stood s· in the prison gate.
Job 2: 3 s· he holdeth fast his integrity, 5750
9 Dost thou s· retain thine integrity?"
3:13 For now should I have lain s· and*
4:16 It stood s·, but I could not discern
20:13 but keep it s· within his mouth:
32:16 they spake not, but stood s·, and 5975
37:14 stand s·, and consider the wondrous"
Ps 4: 4 heart upon your bed, and be s·. 1826
8: 2 thou mightest s· the enemy and 7673
23: 2 leadeth me beside the s· waters. 4496
46:10 Be s·, and know that I am God: I 7503
49: 9 That he should s· live for ever, and5750
68:21 one as goeth on s· in his trespasses.
76: 8 the earth feared, and was s·, 8252
78:32 For all this they sinned s·, and 5750
83: 1 thy peace, and be not s·, O God. 8252
84: 4 they will be s· praising thee. 5750
92:14 They shall s· bring forth fruit in old"
107:29 so that the waves thereof are s·. 2814
139:18 when I awake, I am s· with thee. 5750
Ec 12: 9 he s· taught the people knowledge;"
Isa 5:25 but his hand is stretched out s·. "
9:17, 21 but his hand is stretched out s·. "
10: 4 but his hand is stretched out s·. "
23: 2 Be s·, ye inhabitants of the isle; 1826
30: 7 this, Their strength is to sit s·. 7673

Isa 42:14 I have been s·, and refrained 2790
Jer 8:14 Why do we sit s·? assemble
23:17 They say s· unto them that despise me,*
27:11 I let remain s· in their own land,*
31:20 I do earnestly remember him s·: 5750
42:10 If ye will s· abide in this land, then
47: 6 into thy scabbard, rest, and be s·. 1826
51:50 the sword, go away, stand not s·: 5975
La 3:20 soul hath them s· in remembrance,
Eze 33:30 thy people s· are talking against thee*
41: 7 a winding about s· upward to the side*
7 about the house went s· upward *
7 breadth of the house was s· upward,*
Hab 3:11 The sun and moon stood s· in
Zec 1:11 all the earth sitteth s·, and is at
11:16 nor feed that that standeth s·: *
M't 20:32 Jesus stood s·, and called them, *2476*
M'r 4:39 said unto the sea, Peace, be s·. *5392*
10:49 Jesus stood s·, and commanded *2476*
Lu 7:14 and they that bare him stood s·.
Joh 7: 9 unto them, he abode s· in Galilee.
11: 6 abode two days s· in the same place*
20 him: but Mary sat s· in the house.
Ac 8:38 commanded the chariot to stand s·:*2476*
15:34 it pleased Silas to abide there s·. *
17:14 Silas and Timotheus abode there s·.
Ro 11:23 also, if they abide not s· in unbelief,*
1Ti 1: 3 thee to abide s· at Ephesus, when **4357*
Re 22:11 is unjust, let him be unjust s·: *2089*
11 which is filthy, let him be filthy s·: "
11 righteous, let him be righteous s·: "
11 he that is holy, let him be holy s·. "

stilled
Nu 13:30 Caleb s· the people before Moses, 2013
Ne 8:11 So the Levites s· all the people, 2814

stillest
Ps 89: 9 waves thereof arise, thou s· them. 7623

stilleth
Ps 65: 7 Which s· the noise of the seas, 7623

sting See also STINGETH; STINGS.
1Co 15:55 O death, where is thy s·? O grave, *2759*
56 The s· of death is sin; and the "

stingeth
Pr 23:32 a serpent, and s· like an adder. 6567

stings
Re 9:10 and there were s· in their tails: *2759*

stink See STANK; STINKETH.
Ge 34:30 have troubled me to make me to s·‡887
Ex 7:18 shall die, and the river shall s·; "
16:24 it did not s·, neither was there any "
Ps 38: 5 My wounds s· and are corrupt "
Isa 3:24 of sweet smell there shall be s·; *4716
34: 3 their s· shall come up out of their‡ 889
Joe 2:20 his s· shall come up, and his ill ‡ "
Am 4:10 made the s· of your camps to come‡ "

stinketh
Isa 50: 2 their fish s·, because there is no 887
Joh 11:39 him, Lord, by this time he s·: *3605*

stinking
Ec 10: 1 to send forth a s· savour: so ‡ 887

stir See also BESTIR; STIRRED; STIRRETH; STIRS.
Nu 24: 9 a great lion: who shall s· him up?*6965
Job 17: 8 the innocent shall s· up himself 5782
41:10 is so fierce that dare s· him up: "
Ps 35:23 S· up thyself, and awake to my "
78:38 and did not s· up all his wrath. "
80: 2 and Manasseh s· up thy strength, "
Pr 15: 1 but grievous words s· up anger. *5927
Ca 2: 7 ye s· not up, nor awake my love, 5782
3: 5 ye s· not up, nor awake my love, "
8: 4 ye s· not up, nor awake my love. "
Isa 10:26 Lord of hosts shall s· up a scourge "
13:17 I will s· up the Medes against them, "
42:13 he shall s· up jealousy like a man "
Da 11: 2 shall s· up all against the realm of "
25 And he shall s· up his power and "
Ac 12:18 no small s· among the soldiers, *5017*
19:23 there arose no small s· about that "
2Ti 1: 6 that thou s· up the gift of God, *329*
2Pe 1:13 to s· you up by putting you in *1326*
3: 1 I s· up your pure minds by way of "

stirred
Ex 35:21 every one whose heart s· him up, 5375
26 women whose heart s· them up in "
36: 2 one whose heart s· him up to come "
1Sa 22: 8 son hath s· up my servant against 6965
26:19 Lord have s· thee up against me, 5496
1Ki 11:14 the Lord s· up an adversary unto *6965
23 God s· him up another adversary,* "
21:25 whom Jezebel his wife s· up. 5496
1Ch 5:26 the God of Israel s· up the spirit 5782
2Ch 21:16 the Lord s· up against Jehoram the "
36:22 Lord s· up the spirit of Cyrus king "
Ezr 1: 1 Lord s· up the spirit of Cyrus king "
Ps 39: 2 good; and my sorrow was s·. 5916
Da 11:10 But his sons shall be s· up, and *1624
10 then shall he return, and be s· up,* "
25 king of the south shall be s· up to* "
Hag 1:14 And the Lord s· up the spirit of 5782
Ac 6:12 And they s· up the people, and the *4787*
13:50 the Jews s· up the devout and **3951*
14: 2 Jews s· up the Gentiles, and *1892*
17:13 thither also, and s· up the people. *4531*
16 his spirit was s· in him, when **3947*
21:27 s· up all the people, and laid *4797*

stirreth
De 32:11 As an eagle s· up her nest, 5782
Pr 10:12 Hatred s· up strifes: but love "
15:18 A wrathful man s· up strife: but 1624
28:25 is of a proud heart s· up strife: "
29:22 An angry man s· up strife, and a 1624
Isa 14: 9 it s· up the dead for thee, even all 5782
64: 7 that s· up himself to take hold of "
Lu 23: 5 He s· up the people, teaching *383*

stirs
Isa 22: 2 Thou that art full of s·, a *8663

stock See also GAZINGSTOCK; STOCKS.
Le 25:47 to the s· of the stranger's family: 6133
Job 14: 8 the s· thereof die in the ground; 1503
Isa 40:24 their s· shall not take root in the "
44:19 shall I fall down to the s· of a tree? 944
Jer 2:27 Saying to a s·, Thou art my father; 6086
10: 8 the s· is a doctrine of vanities. "
Ac 13:26 children of the s· of Abraham, and *1085*
Ph'p 3: 5 the eighth day, of the s· of Israel, "

stocks
Job 13:27 puttest my feet also in the s·, and 5465
33:11 He putteth my feet in the s·, he "
Pr 7:22 a fool to the correction of the s·; *5914
Jer 3: 9 adultery with stones and with s·. 6086
20: 2 put him in the s· that were in the 4115
3 forth Jeremiah out of the s·. "
29:26 put him in prison, and in the s·. 6729
Ho 4:12 My people ask counsel at their s·,*6086
Ac 16:24 and made their feet fast in the s·. *3586*

Stoicks (*sto'-ics*)
Ac 17:18 and of the S·, encountered him. *4770*

stole See also STOLEN.
Ge 31:20 Jacob s· away unawares to Laban 1589
2Sa 15: 6 Absalom s· the hearts of the men "
2Ki 11: 2 s· him from among the king's sons "
2Ch 22:11 s· him from among the king's sons "
M't 28:13 and s· him away while we slept. *2813*
Eph 4:28 Let him that s· steal no more: but "

stolen
Ge 30:33 that shall be counted s· with me. 1589
31:19 Rachel had s· the images that were* "
26 thou hast s· away unawares to me, "
30 wherefore hast thou s· my gods? "
32 knew not that Rachel had s· them. "
39 whether s· by day, or s· by night. "
40:15 I was s· away out of the land of the "
Ex 22: 7 and it be s· out of the man's house; "
12 if it be s· from him, he shall make "
Jos 7:11 have also s·, and dissembled also, "
2Sa 19:41 the men of Judah s· thee away, "
21:12 had s· them from the street of "
Pr 9:17 S· waters are sweet, and bread "
Ob 5 not have s· till they have enough?* "

stomacher
Isa 3:24 of a s· a girding of sackcloth; ‡6614

stomach's
1Ti 5:23 a little wine for thy s· sake and *4751*

stone See also BRIMSTONE; HEADSTONE; MILLSTONE; STONED; STONE'S; STONES; STONESQUARERS; STONEST; STONING; STUMBLINGSTONE.
Ge 2:12 there is bdellium and the onyx s·. 68
11: 3 And they had brick for s·, and slime "
28:18 the s· that he had put for his pillows, "
22 this s·, which I have set for a pillar, "
29: 2 a great s· was upon the well's mouth. "
3 rolled the s· from the well's mouth, "
3 put the s· again upon the well's "
8 roll the s· from the well's mouth; "
10 rolled the s· from the well's mouth, "
31:45 And Jacob took a s·, and set it up for "
35:14 talked with him, even a pillar of s·: "
49:24 is the shepherd, the s· of Israel:) "
Ex 4:25 Zipporah took a sharp s·, and cut *6697
7:19 vessels of wood, and in vessels of s·. 68
8:26 their eyes, and will they not s· us? 5619
15: 5 they sank into the bottom as a s·. 68
16 arm they shall be as still as a s·; "
17: 4 they be almost ready to s· me. 5619
12 they took a s·, and put it under him, 68
20:25 if thou wilt make me an altar of s·, "
25 thou shalt not build it of hewn s·: *
21:18 and one smite another with a s·, 68
24:10 it were a paved work of a sapphire s·, "
12 and I will give thee tables of s·, and 68
28:10 Six of their names on one s·, and the "
10 six names of the rest on the other s·, "
11 With the work of an engraver in s·, "
31:18 two tables of testimony, tables of s·, "
34: 1 Hew thee two tables of s· like unto "
4 he hewed two tables of s· like unto "
4 took in his hand the two tables of s·. "
Le 20: 2 of the land shall s· him with stones. 7275
27 they shall s· them with stones: "
24:14 and let all the congregation s· him. "
16 congregation shall certainly s· him: "
23 the camp, and s· him with stones. "
26: 1 neither shall ye set up any image of s·68
Nu 14:10 all the congregation bade s· them 7275
15:35 congregation...s· him with stones* "
35:17 if he smite him with throwing a s·, 68
23 Or with any s·, wherewith a man "
De 4:13 he wrote them upon two tables of s·. "
28 work of men's hands, wood and s·, "
5:22 he wrote them in two tables of s·, "
9: 9 the mount to receive the tables of s·, "
10 delivered unto me two tables of s·, "
11 Lord gave me the two tables of s·, "
10: 1 Hew thee two tables of s· like unto "
3 and hewed two tables of s· like unto "
13:10 thou shalt s· him with stones, that 5619
17: 5 and shalt s· them with stones, till "
21:21 all the men of his city shall s· him 7275
22:21 the men of her city shall s· her with 5619
24 ye shall s· them with stones that "
28:36 thou serve other gods, wood and s·. 68
De 28:64 have known, even wood and s·. 68
29:17 and their idols, wood and s·, silver "
Jos 4: 5 take ye up every man of you a s·, "
15: 6 border went up to the s· of Bohan "
18:17 descended to the s· of Bohan the son "
24:26 took a great s·, and set it up there "
27 this s· shall be a witness unto us; "
J'g 9: 5 and ten persons, upon one s·: "
18 and ten persons, upon one s·, and "
1Sa 6:14 there, where there was a great s·: "
15 were, and put them on the great s·: "
18 even unto the great s· of Abel, whereon
18 which s· remaineth unto this day in
7:12 Then Samuel took a s·, and set it 68
14:33 roll a great s· unto me this day. "
17:49 and took thence a s·, and slang it, "
49 that the s· sunk into his forehead; "
50 Philistine with a sling and with a s·, "
20:19 and shalt remain by the s· Ezel. "
25:37 within him, and he became as a s·. "
2Sa 17:13 be not one small s· found there. 6872
20: 8 at the great s· which is in Gibeon, 68
1Ki 1: 9 and fat cattle by the s· of Zoheleth, "
6: 7 built of s· made ready before it was "
18 all was cedar; there was no s· seen. "
36 court with three rows of hewed s·, 1496
8: 9 in the ark save the two tables of s·, 68
21:10 carry him out, and s· him, that he 5619
2Ki 3:25 piece of land cast every man his s·, 68
12:12 And to masons, and hewers of s·, "
12 buy timber and hewed s· to repair "
19:18 work of men's hands, wood and s·: "
22: 6 to buy timber and hewn s· to repair "
1Ch 22:14 timber also and s· have I prepared; "
15 hewers and workers of s· and "
2Ch 2:14 brass, in iron, in s·, and in timber, "
34:11 to buy hewn s·, and timber for "
Ne 4: 3 shall even break down their s· wall. "
9:11 as a s· into the mighty waters. "
Job 28: 2 and brass is molten out of the s·. "
38: 6 or who laid the corner s· thereof; "
30 The waters are hid as with a s·, and "
41:24 His heart is as firm as a s·; yea, as "
Ps 91:12 lest thou dash thy foot against a s·. "
118:22 The s· which the builders refused "
22 is become the head s· of the corner.* "
Pr 17: 8 A gift is as a precious s· in the eyes 68
24:31 the s· wall thereof was broken down. "
26: 8 As he that bindeth a s· in a sling, ‡
27 and he that rolleth a s·, it will return "
27: 3 A s· is heavy, and the sand weighty; "
Isa 8:14 but for a s· of stumbling and for a "
28:16 Zion for a foundation a s·, a tried s·, "
16 a precious corner s·, a sure "
37:19 work of men's hands, wood and s·: 68
Jer 2:27 and to a s·, Thou hast brought me "
51:26 not take of thee a s· for a corner, "
26 nor a s· for foundations; but thou "
63 that thou shalt bind a s· to it, and "
La 3: 9 inclosed my ways with hewn s·, 1496
53 the dungeon, and cast a s· upon me. 68
Eze 1:26 as the appearance of a sapphire s·: "
10: 1 over them as it were a sapphire s·, "
9 was as the colour of a beryl s·. "
16:40 and they shall s· thee with stones, 7275
20:32 the countries, to serve wood and s·. 68
23:47 company shall s· them with stones, 7275
28:13 every precious s· was thy covering, 68
40:42 four tables were of hewn s· for the "
Da 2:34 that a s· was cut out without hands, 69
35 the s· that smote the image became "
45 the s· was cut out of the mountain "
5: 4 of brass, of iron, of wood, and of s·. "
23 of brass, iron, wood, and s·, which "
6:17 And a s· was brought, and laid upon "
Am 5:11 ye have built houses of hewn s·, 1496
Hab 2:11 For the s· shall cry out of the wall, 68
19 to the dumb s·, Arise, it shall teach! "
Hag 2:15 a s· was laid upon a s· in the temple "
Zec 3: 9 behold the s· that I have laid before "
9 upon one s· shall be seven eyes: "
7:12 their hearts as an adamant s·, 8068
12: 3 make Jerusalem a burdensome s· 68
M't 4: 6 thou dash thy foot against a s·. *3037*
7: 9 ask bread, will he give him a s·? "
21:42 The s· which the builders rejected, "
44 shall fall on this s· shall be broken: "
24: 2 not be left here one s· upon another. "
27:60 rolled a great s· to the door of the "
66 sealing the s·, and setting a watch. "
28: 2 came and rolled back the s· from "
M'r 12:10 The s· which the builders rejected "
13: 2 not be left one s· upon another, "
15:46 and rolled a s· unto the door of the "
16: 3 roll us away the s· from the door "
4 they saw that the s· was rolled "
Lu 4: 3 command this s· that it be made "
11 thou dash thy foot against a s·. "
11:11 is a father, will he give him a s·? "
19:44 leave in thee one s· upon another; "
20: 6 all the people will s· us: for they *2642*
17 The s· which the builders rejected, *3037*
18 shall fall upon that s· be broken; "
21: 6 not be left one s· upon another, "
23:53 in a sepulchre that was hewn in s·, *2991*
24: 2 they found the s· rolled away from *3037*
Joh 1:42 which is by interpretation, A s·. **4074*
2: 6 were set there six waterpots of s·, *3035*
8: 7 you, let him first cast a s· at her. *3037*
10:31 Jews took...stones again to s· him. *3034*
32 which of those works do ye s· me? "
33 For a good work we s· thee not; "
11: 8 the Jews of late sought to s· thee; "
38 It was a cave, and a s· lay upon it. *3037*
39 Jesus said, Take ye away the s·. "
41 they took away the s· from the "

Joh 20: 1 seeth the s' taken away from the 3037
Ac 4:11 This is the s' which was set at "
14: 5 them despitefully, and to s' them, 3036
17:29 is like unto gold, or silver, or s', 3037
2Co 3: 3 not in tables of s', but in fleshy 3035
Eph 2:20 himself being the chief corner s';
1Pe 2: 4 whom coming, as unto a living s', 3037
6 I lay in Sion a chief corner s', elect, "
7 s' which the builders disallowed, "
8 And a s' of stumbling, and a rock of "
Re 2:17 and will give him a white s', 5586
17 and in the s' a new name written, "
4: 3 like a jasper and a sardine s': 3037
9:20 gold, and silver, and brass, and s', 3035
16:21 every s' about the weight of a talent:
18:21 mighty angel took up a s' like a 3037
21:11 was like unto a s' most precious, "
11 like a jasper s', clear as crystal; "

stoned
Ex 19:13 but he shall surely be s', or shot 5619
21:28 then the ox shall be surely s', and "
29 the ox shall be s', and his owner "
32 of silver, and the ox shall be s'. "
Nu 15:36 s' him with stones, and he died; 7275
Jos 7:25 And all Israel s' him with stones, 5619
25 after they had s' them with stones.7275
1Ki 12:18 and all Israel s' him with stones,
21:13 s' him with stones, that he died. 5619
14 saying, Naboth is s', and is dead. "
15 Jezebel heard that Naboth was s', "
2Ch 10:18 children of Israel s' him with 7275
24:21 and s' him with stones at the "
M't 21:35 and killed another, and s' another.3036
Joh 8: 5 commanded us, that such...be s': "
Ac 5:26 lest they should have been s'. 3034
7:58 him out of the city, and s' him: 3036
59 they s' Stephen, calling upon God, "
14:19 having s' Paul, drew him out of 3034
2Co 11:25 once was I s', thrice I suffered "
Heb 11:37 They were s', they were sawn "
12:20 it shall be s', or thrust through 3036

stone's
Lu 22:41 from them about a s' cast, 3037

stones See also CHALKSTONES; HAILSTONES; MILLSTONES; SLINGSTONES.
Ge 28:11 and he took of the s' of that place, 68
31:46 said unto his brethren, Gather s'; "
46 and they took s', and made an heap:"
Ex 25: 7 Onyx s', and s' to be set in the ephod, "
28: 9 And thou shalt take two onyx s', and"
11 shalt thou engrave the two s' with "
12 put the two s' upon the shoulders of "
12 for s' of memorial unto the children "
17 And thou shalt set in it settings of s',"
17 even four rows of s': the first row "
21 the s' shall be with the names of the "
31: 5 And in cutting of s', to set them, and"
35: 9 onyx s', and s' to be set for the ephod,"
27 And the rulers brought onyx s', and "
27 and s' to be set, for the ephod, and "
33 And in the cutting of s', to set them, "
39: 6 wrought onyx s' inclosed in ouches "
7 be s' for a memorial to the children "
10 And they set in it four rows of s': the"
14 the s' were according to the names "
Le 14:40 take away the s' in which the plague"
42 And they shall take other s', and put"
42 and put them in the place of those s';"
43 after that he hath taken away the s',"
45 break down the house, the s' of it, "
20: 2 of the land shall stone him with s'. "
27 death: they shall stone them with s':"
21:20 or scabbed, or hath his s' broken; 810
24:23 of the camp, and stone him with s'. 68
Nu 14:10 bade stone them with s'. "
15:35 congregation shall stone him with s'"
36 and stoned him with s', and he died;"
De 8: 9 a land whose s' are iron, and out of "
13:10 thou shalt stone him with s', that he "
17: 5 shalt stone them with s', till they die."
21:21 of his city shall stone him with s', "
22:21 shall stone her with s' that she die: "
24 ye shall stone them with s' that they"
23: 1 He that is wounded in the s', or hath "
27: 2 that thou shalt set thee up great s', 68
4 that ye shall set up these s', which I "
5 unto the Lord thy God, an altar of s':"
6 altar of the Lord thy God of whole s':"
8 write upon the s' all the words of "
Jos 4: 3 the priests' feet stood firm, twelve s', "
6 saying, What mean ye by these s'? "
7 these s' shall be for a memorial unto"
8 took up twelve s' out of the midst of "
9 Joshua set up twelve s' in the midst "
20 those twelve s', which they took out "
21 come, saying, What mean these s'? "
7:25 And all Israel stoned him with s', "
25 after they had stoned them with s'. "
26 raised over him a great heap of s' "
8:29 and raise thereon a great heap of s', "
31 an altar of whole s', over which no "
32 he wrote there upon the s' a copy of "
10:11 Lord cast down great s' from heaven"
18 Roll great s' upon the mouth of the "
27 and laid great s' in the cave's mouth,"
J'g 20:16 could sling s' at an hair breadth, "
1Sa 17:40 chose him five smooth s' out of the "
2Sa 12:30 a talent of gold with the precious s':"
16: 6 And he cast s' at David, and at all "
13 and threw s' at him, and cast dust. "
18:17 and laid a very great heap of s' upon "
1Ki 5:17 and they brought great s', costly s', "
17 hewed s', to lay the foundation of * "
18 prepared timber and s' to build the "
7: 9 All these were of costly s', according "
1Ki 7: 9 to the measures of hewed s', *1496
10 was of costly s', even great s', 68
10 s' of ten cubits, and s' of eight cubits. "
11 And above were costly s', after the "
11 after the measures of hewed s', *1496
12 was with three rows of hewed s', * "
10: 2 and very much gold, and precious s':68
10 very great store, and precious s': "
11 of almug trees, and precious s'. "
27 made silver to be in Jerusalem as s', "
12:18 all Israel stoned him with s', that he "
15:22 and they took away the s' of Ramah, "
18:31 Elijah took twelve s', according to "
32 with the s' he built an altar in the "
38 the wood, and the s', and the dust, "
21:13 and stoned him with s', that he died."
2Ki 3:19 mar every good piece of land with s'."
25 Kir-haraseth left they the s' thereof;"
16:17 and put it upon a pavement of s'. * "
1Ch 12: 2 right hand and the left in hurling s' "
20: 2 and there were precious s' in it; and "
22: 2 he set masons to hew wrought s' to "
29: 2 wood for things of wood; onyx s', "
2 and s' to be set, glistering
2 glistering s', and of divers colours, 68
2 manner of precious s', and marble s'"
8 with whom precious s' were found "
2Ch 1:15 gold at Jerusalem as plenteous as s',"
3: 6 garnished the house with precious s'"
9: 1 gold in abundance, and precious s': "
9 great abundance, and precious s': "
10 brought algum trees and precious s':"
27 king made silver in Jerusalem as s', "
10:18 children of Israel stoned him with s', "
16: 6 they carried away the s' of Ramah, "
24:21 stoned him with s' at...commandment"
26:14 and bows, and slings to cast s'. "
15 to shoot arrows and great s' withal. "
32:27 and for gold, and for precious s', "
Ezr 5: 8 which is builded with great s', and 69
6: 4 With three rows of great s', and a "
Ne 4: 2 they revive the s' out of the heaps 68
Job 5:23 be in league with the s' of the field: "
6:12 Is my strength the strength of s'? or"
8:17 the heap, and seeth the place of s'. "
14:19 waters wear the s': thou washest "
22:24 the gold of Ophir as the s' of the 6697
28: 3 the s' of darkness, and the shadow of68
6 s' of it are the place of sapphires: "
40:17 the sinews of his s' are wrapped *6344
41:30 Sharp s' are under him: he *2789
Ps 18:12 clouds passed, hail s' and coals of fire.
13 gave his voice; hail s' and coals of fire.
102:14 thy servants take pleasure in her s', 68
137: 9 thy little ones against the s'. *5553
144:12 our daughters may be as corner s',2106
Ec 3: 5 A time to cast away s', and a time to68
5 a time to gather s' together; a time "
10: 9 Whoso removeth s' shall be hurt "
Isa 5: 2 it, and gathered out the s' thereof,5619
9:10 but we will build with hewn s': *1496
14:19 that go down to the s' of the pit; 68
27: 9 when he maketh all the s' of the altar"
34:11 of confusion, and the s' of emptiness.*"
54:11 I will lay thy s' with fair colours, and"
12 and all thy borders of pleasant s'. "
57: 6 Among the smooth s' of the stream is
60:17 and for wood brass, and for s' iron: 68
62:10 up the highway; gather out the s'; "
Jer 3: 9 committed adultery with s' and with "
43: 9 Take great s' in thine hand, and hide"
10 set his throne upon these s' that I "
La 3:16 broken my teeth with gravel s', 2687
4: 1 s' of the sanctuary are poured out in68
Eze 16:40 and they shall stone thee with s', "
23:47 company shall stone them with s', "
26:12 they shall lay thy s' and thy timber "
27:22 and with all precious s', and gold. "
28:14 down in the midst of the s' of fire. "
16 from the midst of the s' of fire. "
Da 11:38 and with precious s', and pleasant "
Mic 1: 6 I will pour down the s' thereof into "
Zec 5: 4 the timber thereof and the s' thereof."
9:15 devour, and subdue with sling s'; "
16 for they shall be as the s' of a crown,"
M't 3: 9 able of these s' to raise up children 3037
4: 3 that these s' be made bread. "
M'r 5: 5 crying, and cutting himself with s'. "
12: 4 and at him they cast s', and *3036
13: 1 see what manner of s' and what 3037
Lu 3: 8 able of these s' to raise up children "
19:40 the s' would immediately cry out. "
21: 5 adorned with goodly s' and gifts, "
Joh 8:59 Then took they up s' to cast at him: "
10:31 the Jews took up s' again to stone "
1Co 3:12 gold, silver, precious s', wood, hay, "
2Co 3: 7 death, written and engraven in s', "
1Pe 2: 5 Ye also, as lively s', are built up a "
Re 17: 4 decked with gold and precious s' * "
18:12 gold, and silver, and precious s', "
16 decked with gold, and precious s',* "
21:19 with all manner of precious s'.

stonesquarers
1Ki 5:18 builders did hew them, and the s':*1382

stonest
M't 23:37 s' them which are sent unto thee,*3036
Lu 13:34 s' them that are sent unto thee; * "

stoning
1Sa 30: 6 for the people spake of s' him, 5619

stony
Ps 141: 6 are overthrown in s' places, *5553
Eze 11:19 take the s' heart out of their flesh, 68
36:26 away the s' heart out of your flesh, "
M't 13: 5 Some fell upon s' places, where *4075
13:20 received the seed into s' places, *4075
M'r 4: 5 And some fell on s' ground, where* "
16 which are sown on s' ground; * "

stood See also STOODEST; UNDERSTOOD; WITHSTOOD.
Ge 18: 2 and, lo, three men s' by him: 5324
8 and he s' by them under the tree, 5975
22 Abraham s' yet before the Lord. "
19:27 place where he s' before the Lord: "
23: 3 Abraham s' up...before his dead, *6965
7 And Abraham s' up, and bowed * "
24:30 he s' by the camels at the well. 5975
28:13 And, behold, the Lord s' above it, 5324
37: 7 my sheaf arose, and also s' upright;"
7 your sheaves s' round about, and *
41: 1 and, behold, he s' by the river. 5975
3 s' by the other kine upon the brink "
17 I s' upon the bank of the river: "
46 years old when he s' before Pharaoh"
43:15 to Egypt, and s' before Joseph. "
45: 1 before all them that s' by him; 5324
1 And there s' no man with him, 5975
Ex 2: 4 his sister s' afar off, to wit what 3320
17 but Moses s' up and helped them, 6965
5:20 met Moses...who s' in the way, 5324
9:10 furnace, and s' before Pharaoh; 5975
14:19 their face, and s' behind them: "
15: 8 the floods s' upright as an heap, 5324
18:13 and the people s' by Moses from 5975
19:17 and they s' at the nether part of 3320
20:18 it, they removed, and s' afar off. 5975
21 And the people s' afar off, and "
32:26 Moses s' in the gate of the camp, "
33: 8 and s' every man at his tent door, 5324
9 s' at the door of the tabernacle, 5975
34: 5 the cloud, and s' with him there, 3320
Le 9: 5 drew near and s' before the Lord. 5975
Nu 11:32 And the people s' up all that day, *6965
12: 5 s' in the door of the tabernacle, 5975
16:18 and s' in the door of the tabernacle "
27 and s' in the door of their tents, 5324
48 s' between the dead and the living;5975
22:22 angel of the Lord s' in the way *3320
24 angel of the Lord s' in a path of 5975
26 further, and s' in a narrow place, "
23: 6 lo, he s' by his burnt sacrifice, he, 5324
17 behold, he s' by his burnt offering, "
27: 2 And they s' before Moses, and 5975
De 4:11 near and s' under the mountain; "
5: 5 (I s' between the Lord and you at "
31:15 pillar of the cloud s' over the door "
Jos 3:16 waters which came...from above s' "
17 priests...s' firm on dry ground "
4: 3 where the priests' feet s' firm, 4673
9 bare the ark of the covenant s': "
10 which bare the ark s' in the midst 5975
5:13 there s' a man over against him with"
8:33 s' on this side the ark and on that "
10:13 And the sun s' still, and the moon 1826
13 So the sun s' still in the midst of *5975
11:13 cities that s' still in their strength, "
20: 9 until he s' before the congregation. "
21:44 s' not a man of all their enemies "
J'g 3:19 all that s' by him went out from "
6:31 Joash said unto all that s' against "
7:21 And they s' every man in his place "
9: 7 he went and s' in the top of mount "
35, 44 s' in the entering of the gate of "
16:29 pillars upon which the house s', *3559
18:16 Dan, s' by the entering of the gate.5324
17 priest s' in the entering of the gate "
20:28 Aaron, s' before it in those days,) 5975
1Sa 1:26 I am the woman that s' by thee 5324
3:10 the Lord came, and s', and called 3320
4:20 women that s' by her said unto her,5324
6:14 s' there, where there was a great 5975
10:23 and when he s' among the people, 3320
16:21 came to Saul, and s' before him: 5975
17: 3 the Philistines s' on a mountain "
3 Israel s' on a mountain on the other"
8 he s' and cried unto the armies of "
26 David spake to the men that s' by "
51 David...s' upon the Philistine, and "
22: 7 his servants that s' about him, *5324
17 unto the footmen that s' about him,"
26:13 and s' on the top of an hill afar off;5975
2Sa 1:10 So I s' upon him, and slew him, "
2:23 where Asahel fell down...s' still. "
25 troop, and s' on the top of an hill. "
28 trumpet, and all the people s' still, "
13:31 s' by with their clothes rent. 5324
15: 2 and s' beside the way of the gate: "
18: 4 And the king s' by the gate side, 5975
30 And he turned aside, and s' still. "
20:11 And one of Joab's men s' by him, "
12 man saw that all the people s' still, "
12 every one that came by him s' still. "
15 the city, and it s' in the trench: "
23:12 he s' in the midst of the ground, 3320
1Ki 1:28 presence, and s' before the king. 5975
3:15 s' before the ark of the covenant of "
16 unto the king, and s' before him. "
7:25 It s' upon twelve oxen, three looking"
8:14 all the congregation of Israel s';) "
22 Solomon s' before the altar of the "
55 And he s', and blessed all the "
10:19 and two lions s' beside the stays. * "
20 twelve lions s' there on the one side"
12: 6 that s' before Solomon his father "
8 with him, and which s' before him: "
13: 1 Jeroboam s' by the altar to burn * "
24 cast in the way, and the ass s' by it,"
24 the lion also s' by the carcase. "
19:13 and s' in the entering in of the cave."
22:21 a spirit, and s' before the Lord, "
2Ki 2: 7 went, and s' to view afar off: "

2Ki 2: 7 afar off: and they two s' by Jordan. 5975
13 back, and s' by the bank of Jordan; "
3: 21 and upward, and s' in the border. "
4: 12 had called her, she s' before him. "
15 had called her, she s' in the door. "
5: 9 s' at the door of the house of Elisha. "
15 and came, and s' before him: "
25 went in, and s' before his master. "
8: 9 and came and s' before him, and "
9: 17 there s' a watchman on the tower "
10: 4 Behold, two kings s' not before him: "
9 went out, and s', and said to all the "
11: 11 And the guard s', every man with "
14 behold, the king s' by a pillar, as "
13: 21 he revived, and s' up on his feet. 6965
18: 17 and s' by the conduit of the upper 5975
28 Then Rab-shakeh s' and cried with "
23: 3 the king s' by a pillar, and made a "
3 all the people s' to the covenant. "
1Ch 6: 39 Asaph, who s' on his right hand, "
44 the sons of Merari s' on the left hand:*
21: 1 And Satan s' up against Israel, 5975
15 angel...s' by the threshingfloor "
28: 2 David the king s' up upon his feet, 6965
2Ch 3: 13 and they s' on their feet, and their 5975
4: 4 It s' upon twelve oxen, three looking "
5: 12 harps, s' at the east end of the altar, "
6: 3 all the congregation of Israel s'. "
12 he s' before the altar of the Lord "
13 upon it he s', and kneeled down "
7: 6 before them, and all Israel s'. "
9: 19 twelve lions s' there on the one side "
10: 6 old men that had s' before Solomon "
8 young men...that s' before him. "
13: 4 And Abijah s' up upon mount 6965
18: 20 a spirit, and s' before the Lord, 5975
20: 5 Jehoshaphat s' in the congregation "
13 And all Judah s' before the Lord, "
19 s' up to praise the Lord God of 6965
20 Jehoshaphat s' and said, Hear me, 5975
23 Moab s' up against the inhabitants "
23: 13 king s' at his pillar at the entering "
24: 20 priest, which s' above the people, "
28: 12 s' up against them that came from 6965
29: 26 Levites s' with the instruments of 5975
30: 16 they s' in their place after their "
34: 31 the king s' in his place, and made "
35: 10 and the priests s' in their place, "
Ezr 2: 63 till there s' up a priest with Urim "
3: 2 s' up Jeshua the son of Jozadak, 6965
9 Then s' Jeshua with his sons and 5975
10: 10 Ezra the priest s' up, and said unto 6965
Ne 7: 65 till there s' up a priest with Urim 5975
8: 4 Ezra the scribe s' upon a pulpit of "
4 and beside him s' Mattithiah, and "
5 he opened it, all the people s' up: "
7 law: and the people s' in their place. "
9: 2 and s' and confessed their sins, 5975
3 they s' up in their place, and read 6965
4 Then s' up upon the stairs, of the "
12: 39 and they s' still in the prison gate. 5975
40 So s' the two companies of them "
Es 5: 1 s' in the inner court of the king's "
9 the king's gate, that he s' not up, 6965
7: 7 Haman s' up to make request for 5975
8: 4 Esther arose, and s' before the king, "
9: 16 together, and s' for their lives, "
Job 4: 15 face; the hair of my flesh s' up: 5568
16 It s' still, but I could not discern 5975
29: 8 and the aged arose, and s' up. "
30: 28 the sun: I s' up, and I cried in the *6965
32: 16 (for they spake not, but s' still, *5975
Ps 33: 9 done; he commanded, and it s' fast. "
104: 6 the waters s' above the mountains. "
106: 23 not Moses his chosen s' before him "
30 Then s' up Phinehas, and executed "
Isa 6: 2 Above it s' the seraphims: each one "
36: 2 he s' by the conduit of the upper "
13 Then Rabshakeh s', and cried with "
Jer 15: 1 Moses and Samuel s' before me, yet "
18: 20 I s' before thee to speak good for "
19: 14 and he s' in the court of the Lord's "
23: 18 hath s' in the counsel of the Lord, "
22 But if they had s' in my counsel, "
28: 5 all the people that s' in the house of "
36: 21 princes which s' beside the king. "
44: 15 all the women that s' by, a great "
46: 15 they s' not, because the Lord did "
48: 45 They that fled s' under the shadow*"
La 2: 4 he s' with his right hand as an 5324
Eze 1: 21 and when those s', these s'; and 5975
24 when they s', they let down their "
25 when they s', and had let down "
3: 23 the glory of the Lord s' there, as "
8: 11 there s' before them seventy men "
11 in the midst of them s' Jaazaniah "
9: 2 in, and s' beside the brasen altar. "
10: 3 the cherubims s' on the right side "
4 and s' over the threshold of the house; "
6 went in, and s' beside the wheels. 5975
17 When they stood, these s'; and "
18 house, and s' over the cherubims. "
19 every one s' at the door of the east "
11: 23 s' upon the mountain which is on "
21: 21 king of Babylon s' at the parting "
37: 10 lived, and s' up upon their feet, "
40: 3 reed; and he s' in the gate. "
43: 6 the house; and the man s' by me. "
47: 1 of the house s' toward the east,*
Da 1: 19 therefore s' they before the king. 5975
2: 2 they came and s' before the king. "
31 was excellent, s' before thee; 6966
3: 3 and they s' before the image that "
7: 10 times ten thousand s' before him: "
16 near unto one of them that s' by, "
8: 3 there s' before the river a ram 5975
Da 8: 15 s' before me as the appearance of 5975
17 So he came near where I s': and 5977
22 whereas four s' up for it, four 5975
10: 11 this word unto me, I s' trembling. "
16 said unto him that s' before me, "
11: 1 s' to confirm and to strengthen "
12: 5 behold, there s' other two, the one "
Ho 10: 9 there they s': the battle in Gibeah "
Am 7: 7 the Lord s' upon a wall made by a 5324
Ob 14 thou have s' in the crossway, to *5975
Hab 3: 6 He s', and measured the earth: he "
11 The sun and moon s' still in their "
Zec 1: 8 he s' among the myrtle trees that "
10 man that s' among the myrtle trees "
11 angel...s' among the myrtle trees, "
3: 3 garments, and s' before the angel. "
4 unto those that s' before him, "
5 And the angel of the Lord s' by. "
M't 2: 9 s' over where the young child was. 2476
12: 46 mother and his brethren s' without, "
13: 2 the whole multitude s' on the shore. "
20: 32 And Jesus s' still, and called them, "
26: 73 while came unto him they that s' by, "
27: 11 And Jesus s' before the governor: "
47 Some of them that s' there, when "
M'r 10: 49 Jesus s' still, and commanded him "
11: 5 certain of them that s' there said "
14: 47 of them that s' by drew a sword, 3936
60 the high priest s' up in the midst, 450
69 began to say to them that s' by, 3936
70 they that s' by said again to Peter, "
15: 35 And some of them that s' by, when "
39 centurion, which s' over against "
Lu 4: 16 sabbath day, and s' up for to read. 450
39 And he s' over her, and rebuked 2186
5: 1 he s' by the lake of Gennesaret, *2476
6: 8 midst. And he arose and s' forth. "
17 down with them, and s' in the plain, "
7: 14 and they that bare him s' still. "
38 s' at his feet behind him weeping,* "
9: 32 and the two men that s' with him. 4921
10: 25 behold, a certain lawyer s' up, and 450
17: 12 that were lepers, which s' afar off: 2476
18: 11 Pharisee s' and prayed thus with "
40 And Jesus s', and commanded him "
19: 8 And Zacchæus s', and said unto the "
24 And he said unto them that s' by, 3936
23: 10 scribes s' and vehemently accused 2476
35 And the people s' beholding. And "
49 s' afar off, beholding these things. "
24: 4 two men s' by them in shining 2186
36 Jesus...s' in the midst of them, 2476
Joh 1: 35 Again the next day after John s',* "
6: 22 people which s' on the other side of "
7: 37 Jesus s' and cried, saying, If any "
11: 56 themselves, as they s' in the temple, "
12: 29 The people therefore, that s' by, "
18: 5 which betrayed him, s' with them.* "
16 But Peter s' at the door without. * "
18 the servants and officers s' there, * "
18 Peter s' with them, and warmed * "
22 officers which s' by struck Jesus *3936
25 Peter s' and warmed himself. *2476
19: 25 s' by the cross of Jesus his mother,* "
20: 11 Mary s' without at the sepulchre * "
19 came Jesus and s' in the midst, and "
26 s' in the midst, and said, Peace be "
21: 4 now come, Jesus s' on the shore: "
Ac 1: 10 men s' by them in white apparel; 3936
15 days Peter s' up in the midst of the 450
3: 8 And he leaping up s', and walked, 2476
4: 26 The kings of the earth s' up, and *3936
5: 34 Then s' there up one in the council, 450
9: 7 journeyed with him s' speechless, 2476
39 all the widows s' by him weeping, 3936
10: 17 house, and s' before the gate, 2186
30 s' before me in bright clothing, 2476
11: 13 which s' and said unto him, Send* "
28 And there s' up one of them named 450
12: 14 told how Peter s' before the gate. 2476
13: 16 Then Paul s' up, and beckoning 450
14: 20 the disciples s' round about him, 2944
16: 9 There s' a man of Macedonia, and *2476
17: 22 Paul s' in the midst of Mars' hill, "
21: 40 Paul s' on the stairs, and beckoned* "
22: 13 Came unto me, and s', and said *2186
25 said unto the centurion that s' by, 2476
23: 2 them that s' by him to smite him 3936
4 And they that s' by said, Revilest "
11 night following the Lord s' by him, 2186
24: 20 in me, while I s' before the council, 2476
25: 7 Jews...from Jerusalem s' round 4026
18 whom when the accusers s' up, they 2476
27: 21 Paul s' forth in the midst of them, "
23 For there s' by me this night the 3936
2Ti 4: 16 first answer no man s' with me, *4836
17 Lord s' with me, and strengthened 3936
Heb 9: 10 Which s' only in meats and drinks,*
Re 5: 6 s' a Lamb as it had been slain, *2476
7: 9 s' before the throne, and before the* "
11 angels s' round about the throne,* "
8: 2 seven angels which s' before God;* "
3 angel came and s' at the altar, "
11: 1 and the angel s', saying, Rise, and* "
11 them, and they s' upon their feet; "
12: 4 and the dragon s' before the woman‡ "
13: 1 And I s' upon the sand of the sea, "
14: 1 lo, a Lamb s' on the mount Sion, * "
18: 17 as many as trade by sea, s' afar off, "

stoodest
Nu 22: 34 I knew not that thou s' in the way 5324
De 4: 10 day that thou s' before the Lord 5975
Ob 11 day that thou s' on the other side, "

stool See also FOOTSTOOL; STOOLS.
2Ki 4: 10 there a bed, and a table, and a s', 3678

stools
Ex 1: 16 women, and see them upon the s'; 70

stoop See also STOOPED; STOOPETH; STOOPING.
Job 9: 13 proud helpers do s' under him. 7817
Pr 12: 25 in the heart of man maketh it s': 7812
Isa 46: 2 They s', they bow down together; 7164
M'r 1: 7 I am not worthy to s' down and 2955

stooped
Ge 49: 9 he s' down, he couched as a lion, 3766
1Sa 24: 8 David s' with his face to the earth,*6915
28: 14 he s' with his face to the ground, * "
2Ch 36: 17 old man, or him that s' for age: *3486
Joh 8: 6 But Jesus s' down, and with his 2955
8 again he s' down, and wrote on the "
20: 11 she s' down, and looked into the 3879

stoopeth
Isa 46: 1 Bel boweth down, Nebo s', their 7164

stooping
Lu 24: 12 and s' down, he beheld the linen 3879
Joh 20: 5 And he s' down, and looking in, saw "

stop See also STOPPED; STOPPETH.
1Ki 18: 44 down, that the rain s' thee not. 6113
2Ki 3: 19 s' all wells of water, and mar every 5640
2Ch 32: 3 to s' the waters of the fountains "
Ps 35: 3 and s' the way against them that 5462
107: 42 and all iniquity shall s' her mouth. 7092
Eze 39: 11 and it shall s' the noses of the 2629
2Co 11: 10 no man shall s' me of this boasting 5420

stopped See also UNSTOPPED.
Ge 8: 2 the windows of heaven were s', 5534
26: 15 the Philistines had s' them, and 5640
18 for the Philistines had s' them after "
Le 15: 3 or his flesh be s' from his issue, it 2856
2Ki 3: 25 and they s' all the wells of water, 5640
2Ch 32: 4 who s' all the fountains, and the "
30 s' the upper watercourse of Gihon, "
Ne 4: 7 that the breaches began to be s', "
Ps 63: 11 of them that speak lies shall be s'. 5534
Jer 51: 32 that the passages are s', and the *8610
Zec 7: 11 s' their ears, that they should not 3513
Ac 7: 57 s' their ears, and ran upon him 4912
Ro 3: 19 that every mouth may be s', and all 5420
Tit 1: 11 Whose mouths must be s', who 1993
Heb 11: 33 promises, s' the mouths of lions, 5420

stoppeth
Job 5: 16 hope, and iniquity s' her mouth. 7092
Ps 58: 4 like the deaf adder that s' her ear; 331
Pr 21: 13 Whoso s' his ears at the cry of the "
Isa 33: 15 that s' his ears from hearing of blood, "

store See also RESTORE; STOREHOUSE.
Ge 26: 14 of herds, and great s' of servants:*
41: 36 that food shall be for s' to the land 6487
Le 25: 22 fruits come in ye shall eat of the old s'.
26: 10 And ye shall eat old s', and bring 3462
De 28: 5, 17 shall be thy basket and thy s'. *4863
32: 34 Is not this laid up in s' with me, and
1Ki 9: 19 the cities of s' that Solomon had, 4543
10: 10 and of spices very great s', and
2Ki 20: 17 which thy fathers have laid up in s' 686
1Ch 29: 16 all this s' that we have prepared 1995
2Ch 8: 4 all the s' cities, which he built in 4543
6 all the s' cities that Solomon had, "
11: 11 s' of victual, and of oil and wine. 214
16: 4 and all the s' cities of Naphtali. 4543
17: 12 in Judah castles, and cities of s'. "
31: 10 that which is left is this great s'. 1995
Ne 5: 18 in ten days s' of all sorts of wine: 7235
Ps 144: 13 be full, affording all manner of s':
Isa 39: 6 which thy fathers have laid up in s' 686
Am 3: 10 who s' up violence and robbery in
Na 2: 9 for there is none end of the s' and 8498
1Co 16: 2 every one of you lay by him in s', 2343
1Ti 6: 19 Laying up in s' for themselves a 597
2Pe 3: 7 by the same word are kept in s', *2343

store-cities See STORE and CITIES.

storehouse See also STOREHOUSES.
Mal 3: 10 Bring ye all the tithes into the s', 214
Lu 12: 24 which neither have s' nor barn; *5009

storehouses
Ge 41: 56 And Joseph opened all the s', and 834
De 28: 8 the blessing upon thee in thy s', * 618
1Ch 27: 25 and over the s' in the fields, in the *214
2Ch 32: 28 S' also for the increase of corn, 4543
Ps 33: 7 heap: he layeth up the depth in s'. 214
Jer 50: 26 the utmost border, open her s': 3965

stories
Ge 6: 16 second, and third s' shalt thou make it.
Eze 42: 3 was gallery against gallery in three s'.*
6 For they were in three s', but had not
Am 9: 6 that buildeth his s' in the heaven, *4609

stork
Le 11: 19 the s', the heron after her kind, 2624
De 14: 18 And the s', and the heron after her "
Ps 104: 17 as for the s', the fir trees are her "
Jer 8: 7 the s' in the heaven knoweth her "
Zec 5: 9 had wings like the wings of a s': "

storm
Job 21: 18 chaff that the s' carrieth away. 5492
27: 21 as a s' hurleth him out of his place.*
Ps 55: 8 my escape from the windy s' and *5584
83: 15 and make them afraid with thy s'. 5492
107: 29 He maketh the s' a calm, so that 5591
Isa 4: 6 for a covert from s' and from rain, 2230
25: 4 a refuge from the s', a shadow from "
4 blast...is as a s' against the wall. "
28: 2 tempest of hail and a destroying s', 8178
29: 6 great noise, with s' and tempest, *5492
Eze 38: 9 shalt ascend and come like a s', 7722

Na 1: 3 in the whirlwind and in the s', 8183
M'r 4: 37 there arose a great s' of wind, and 2978
Lu 8: 23 there came down a s' of wind on "

stormy
Ps 107: 25 raiseth the s' wind, which lifteth 5591
148: 8 vapours; s' wind fulfilling his word: "
Eze 13: 11 fall; and a s' wind shall rend it. "
13 even rend it with a s' wind in my "

story See also STORIES.
2Ch 13: 22 in the s' of the prophet of Iddo. *4097
24: 27 in the s' of the book of the kings. * "

stout See also STOUTHEARTED.
Job 4: 11 the s' lion's whelps are scattered *
Isa 10: 12 punish the fruit of the s' heart of 1433
Da 7: 20 look was more s' than his fellows. 7229
Mal 3: 13 words have been s' against me, 2388

stouthearted
Ps 76: 5 The s' are spoiled, they have 47,3820
Isa 46: 12 Hearken unto me, ye s', that " "

stoutness
Isa 9: 9 say in the pride and s' of heart, 1433

straight See also STRAIGHTWAY; STRAIT.
Jos 6: 5 ascend up every man s' before him.
20 the city, every man s' before him,
1Sa 6: 12 the kine took the s' way to the 3474
2Ch 32: 30 brought it s' down to the west side "
Ps 5: 8 make thy way s' before my face. † "
Pr 4: 25 let thine eyelids look s' before thee. "
Ec 1: 15 is crooked cannot be made s': 8626
7: 13 for who can make that s', which he "
Isa 40: 3 make s' in the desert a highway 3474
4 the crooked shall be made s', and 4334
42: 16 before them, and crooked things s'. "
45: 2 and make the crooked places s': *3474
Jer 31: 9 by the river of waters in a s' way, "
Eze 1: 7 their feet were s' feet; and the sole "
9 they went every one s' forward. 5676
12 they went every one s' forward:
23 the firmament were their wings s',3474
10: 22 they went every one s' forward. 5676
M't 3: 3 of the Lord, make his paths s'. 2117
M'r 1: 3 way of the Lord, make his paths s'. "
Lu 3: 4 way of the Lord, make his paths s'. "
5 and the crooked shall be made s', "
13: 13 and immediately she was made s', 461
Joh 1: 23 Make s' the way of the Lord, as 2116
Ac 9: 11 into the street which is called S', 2117
16: 11 with a s' course to Samothracia, 2113
21: 1 came with a s' course unto Coos, "
Heb 12: 13 And make s' paths for your feet, 3717

straightly See STRAITLY.

straightway
1Sa 9: 13 into the city, ye shall s' find him, 3651
28: 20 Saul fell s' all along on the earth, 4116
Pr 7: 22 He goeth after her s', as an ox 6597
Da 10: 17 s' there remained no strength in 6258
M't 3: 16 went up s' out of the water: and, 2117
4: 20 they s' left their nets, and followed 2112
14: 22 s' Jesus constrained his disciples "
27 But s' Jesus spake unto them, "
21: 2 s' ye shall find an ass tied, and a "
3 of them; and s' he will send them. "
25: 15 ability; and s' took his journey. * "
27: 48 And s' one of them ran, and took a "
M'r 1: 10 And s' coming up out of the water, "
18 And s' they forsook their nets, and "
20 And s' he called them: and they "
21 s' on the sabbath day he entered "
2: 2 s' many were gathered together, * "
3: 6 s' took counsel with the Herodians "
5: 29 s' the fountain of her blood was "
42 s' the damsel arose, and walked; "
6: 25 And she came in s' with haste unto "
45 And s' he constrained his disciples "
54 out of the ship, s' they knew him, "
7: 35 And s' his ears were opened, and * "
8: 10 s' he entered into a ship with his "
9: 15 s' all the people, when they beheld "
20 he saw him, s' the spirit tare him; "
24 s' the father of the child cried out, "
11: 3 and s' he will send him hither. "
14: 45 he was come, he goeth s' to him, "
15: 1 s' in the morning the chief priests "
Lu 5: 39 drunk old wine s' desireth new: * "
8: 55 came again, and she arose s': *3916
12: 54 s' ye say, There cometh a shower; 2112
14: 5 not s' pull him out on the sabbath "
Joh 13: 32 himself, and shall s' glorify him. 2117
Ac 5: 10 Then fell she down s' at his feet, *3916
9: 20 And s' he preached Christ in the 2112
16: 33 was baptized, he and all his, s'. 3916
22: 29 Then s' they departed from him 2112
23: 30 man, I sent s' to thee, and gave *1824
Jas 1: 24 s' forgetteth what manner of man 2112

strain See also RESTRAIN.
M't 23: 24 blind guides, which s' at a gnat, 1368

strait See also STRAIGHT; STRAITEST; STRAITS.
1Sa 13: 6 Israel saw that they were in a s', 6887
2Sa 24: 14 said unto Gad, I am in a great s': "
2Ki 6: 1 dwell with thee is too s' for us. 6862
1Ch 21: 13 said unto Gad, I am in a great s': 6887
Job 36: 16 remove thee out of the s' into a *6862
Isa 49: 20 ears, The place is too s' for me: "
M't 7: 13 Enter ye in at the s' gate: for wide*4728
14 s' is the gate, and narrow is the * "
Lu 13: 24 Strive to enter in at the s' gate: * "
Ph'p 1: 23 For I am in a s' betwixt two, 4912

straiten See also STRAITENED; STRAITENETH.
Jer 19: 9 that seek their lives, shall s' them.‡6693

straitened
Job 18: 7 steps of his strength shall be s', 3334
37: 10 the breadth of the waters is s'. 4164
Pr 4: 12 goest, thy steps shall not be s'; 3334
Eze 42: 6 the building was s' more than the 680
Mic 2: 7 Jacob, is the spirit of the Lord s'? 7114
Lu 12: 50 am I s' till it be accomplished! 4912
2Co 6: 12 Ye are not s' in us, but ye are 4729
12 but ye are s' in your own bowels. "

straiteneth
Job 12: 23 the nations, and s' them again. †‡5148

straitest
Ac 26: 5 that after the most s' sect of our 196

straitly
Ge 43: 7 The man asked us s' of our state,
Ex 13: 19 had s' sworn the children of Israel,
Jos 6: 1 Jericho was s' shut up because
1Sa 14: 28 Thy father s' charged the people
M't 9: 30 Jesus s' charged them, saying, See*
M'r 1: 43 he s' charged him, and forthwith sent*
3: 12 And he s' charged them that they*4183
5: 43 he charged them s' that no man * "
Lu 9: 21 he s' charged them, and commanded*
Ac 4: 17 let us s' threaten them, that they * 547
5: 28 Did not we s' command you that ye

straitness
De 28: 53, 55 in the siege, and in the s', ‡4689
57 things secretly in the siege and s',‡ "
Job 36: 16 broad place, where there is no s'; 4164
Jer 19: 9 of his friend in the siege and s', ‡4689

straits
Job 20: 22 of his sufficiency he shall be in s': 3334
La 1: 3 overtook her between the s'. 4712

strake See also STRAKES; STRUCK.
Ac 27: 17 s' sail, and so were driven. *5465

strakes
Ge 30: 37 and pilled white s' in them, and 6479
Le 14: 37 walls of the house with hollow s', 8258

strange See also ESTRANGED; STRANGER.
Ge 35: 2 Put away the s' gods...among you,5236
4 gave unto Jacob all the s' gods "
42: 7 but made himself s' unto them, 5234
Ex 2: 22 I have been a stranger in a s' land.5237
18: 3 I have been an alien in a s' land: "
21: 8 to sell her unto a s' nation he shall "
30: 9 Ye shall offer no s' incense 2114
Le 10: 1 and offered s' fire before the Lord, "
Nu 3: 4 they offered s' fire before the Lord, "
26: 61 they offered s' fire before the Lord. "
De 32: 12 and there was no s' god with him. 5236
16 him to jealousy with s' gods, 2114
Jos 24: 20 the Lord, and serve s' gods, then 5236
23 the s' gods which are among you, "
J'g 10: 16 put away the s' gods from among "
11: 2 thou art the son of a s' woman. * 312
1Sa 7: 3 then put away the s' gods and 5236
1Ki 11: 1 Solomon loved many s' women, 5237
8 likewise did he for all his s' wives, "
2Ki 19: 24 have digged and drunk s' waters, 2114
2Ch 14: 3 away the altars of the s' gods, 5236
33: 15 he took away the s' gods, and the "
Ezr 10: 2 have taken s' wives of the people 5237
10 and have taken s' wives, to increase "
11 of the land, and from the s' wives. "
14 all them which have taken s' wives "
17 all the men that had taken s' wives "
18 found that had taken s' wives: "
44 All these had taken s' wives: and "
Ne 13: 27 transgress...in marrying s' wives? "
Job 19: 3 that ye make yourselves s' to me.*1970
17 My breath is s' to my wife, 2114
31: 3 a s' punishment to the workers *5235
Ps 44: 20 stretched out...hands to a s' god; 2114
81: 9 There shall no s' god be in thee; "
9 shalt thou worship any s' god. 5236
114: 1 Jacob from a people of s' language;3937
137: 4 sing the Lord's song in a s' land? 5236
144: 7 from the hand of s' children; †‡ "
Pr 2: 16 deliver thee from the s' woman, 2114
5: 3 the lips of a s' woman drop as an "
20 son, be ravished with a s' woman, "
6: 24 of the tongue of a s' woman. *5237
7: 5 keep thee from the s' woman, 2114
20: 16 a pledge of him for a s' woman. *5237
21: 8 way of man is froward and s': *2114
22: 14 mouth of s' women is a deep pit: "
23: 27 and a s' woman is a narrow pit. 5237
33 Thine eyes shall behold s' women,2114
27: 13 a pledge of him for a s' woman. 5237
Isa 17: 10 and shalt set it with s' slips: 2114
28: 21 he may do his work, his s' work; "
21 bring to pass his act, his s' act. 5237
43: 12 there was no s' god among you: 2114
Jer 2: 21 the degenerate plant of a s' vine 5237
5: 19 and served s' gods in your land, 5236
8: 19 images, and with s' vanities? "
Eze 3: 5 not sent to a people of a s' speech 6012
6 Not to many people of a s' speech "
Da 11: 39 most strong holds with a s' god, 5236
Ho 5: 7 they have begotten s' children: 2114
8: 12 they were counted as a s' thing. "
Zep 1: 8 as are clothed with s' apparel. *5237
Mal 2: 11 married the daughter of a s' god. 5236
Lu 5: 26 We have seen s' things to day. 3861
Ac 7: 6 seed should sojourn in a s' land; 245
17: 18 to be a setter forth of s' gods: 3581
20 certain s' things to our ears: 3579
26: 11 I persecuted them...unto s' cities. *1854
Heb 11: 9 land of promise, as in a s' country,*245
13: 9 about with divers and s' doctrines.3581
1Pe 4: 4 think it s'...ye run not with them 3579
12 think it not s' concerning the fiery "
1Pe 4: 12 some s' thing happened unto you: 3581
Jude 7 and going after s' flesh, are set 2087

strangely
De 32: 27 should behave themselves s', †‡5234

stranger See also STRANGER'S; STRANGERS.
Ge 15: 13 be a s' in a land that is not theirs, 1616
17: 8 the land wherein thou art a s', *4033
12 bought with money of any s',1121,5235
27 bought with money of the s', * "
23: 4 I am a s' and a sojourner with you: 1616
28: 4 the land wherein thou art a s', *4033
37: 1 land wherein his father was a s', * "
Ex 2: 22 I have been a s' in a strange land.*1616
12: 19 whether he be a s', or born in the * "
43 There shall no s' eat thereof:*1121,5235
48 when a s' shall sojourn with thee, 1616
49 the s' that sojourneth among you. "
20: 10 nor thy s' that is within thy gates: "
22: 21 Thou shalt neither vex a s', nor "
23: 9 Also thou shalt not oppress a s': "
9 for ye know the heart of a s', seeing "
12 son of thy handmaid, and the s', "
29: 33 but a s' shall not eat thereof, 2114
30: 33 putteth any of it upon a s', "
Le 16: 29 a s' that sojourneth among you: 1616
17: 12 any s' that sojourneth among you "
15 be one of your own country, or a s', "
18: 26 any s' that sojourneth among you: "
19: 10 shalt leave them for the poor and s': "
33 if a s' sojourn with thee in your land, "
34 But the s' that dwelleth with you "
22: 10 There shall no s' eat of the holy 2114
12 daughter...married unto a s', 376, "
13 but there shall no s' eat thereof. 2114
23: 22 them unto the poor, and the s': 1616
24: 16 as well the s', as he that is born in "
22 as well for the s', as for one of your "
25: 6 thy s' that sojourneth with thee, 8453
35 though he be a s', or a sojourner; 1616
47 sojourner or s' wax rich by thee, *8453
47 and sell himself unto the s' or 1616
Nu 1: 51 s' that cometh nigh shall be put 2114
3: 10, 38 s' that cometh nigh shall be put "
9: 14 if a s' shall sojourn among you, 1616
14 for the s', and for him that was born "
15: 14 And if a s' sojourn with you, or "
15 for the s' that sojourneth with you, "
15 so shall the s' be before the Lord. "
16 for the s' that sojourneth with you. "
26 the s' that sojourneth among them; "
29 the s' that sojourneth among them. "
30 he be born in the land, or a s', "
16: 40 no s', which is not of the seed 376,2114
18: 4 a s' shall not come nigh unto you. "
7 the s' that cometh nigh shall be put "
19: 10 s' that sojourneth among them, 1616
35: 15 children of Israel, and for the s', "
De 1: 16 brother, and the s' that is with him. "
5: 14 nor thy s' that is within thy gates; "
10: 18 and loveth the s', in giving him food "
19 Love ye therefore the s': for ye "
14: 21 shalt give it unto the s' that is in thy "
29 and the s', and the fatherless, and "
16: 11, 14 the s', and the fatherless, and "
17: 15 mayest not set a s' over thee, *376,5237
23: 7 because thou wast a s' in his land. 1616
20 Unto a s' thou mayest lend upon 5237
24: 17 not pervert the judgment of the s',1616
19, 20, 21 it shall be for the s', for the "
25: 5 not marry without unto a s': 376,2114
26: 11 and the s' that is among you. 1616
12 s', the fatherless, and the widow, "
13 unto the s', to the fatherless, and to "
27: 19 perverteth the judgment of the s', "
28: 43 The s' that is within thee shall get "
29: 11 and thy s' that is in thy camp, "
22 the s' that shall come from a far *5237
31: 12 and thy s' that is within thy gates, 1616
Jos 8: 33 as well the s', as he that was born "
20: 9 for the s' that sojourneth among "
J'g 19: 12 aside hither into the city of a s', 5237
Ru 2: 10 knowledge of me, seeing I am a s'?‡ "
2Sa 1: 13 answered, I am the son of a s', 376,1616
15: 19 thou art a s', and also an exile. ‡5237
1Ki 3: 18 was no s' with us in the house, 2114
8: 41 Moreover concerning a s', that is 5237
43 all that the s' calleth to thee for: "
2Ch 6: 32 Moreover concerning the s', which "
33 to all that the s' calleth to thee for; "
Job 15: 19 and no s' passed among them. 2114
19: 15 and my maids, count me for a s': "
31: 32 The s' did not lodge in the street: 1616
Ps 39: 12 I am a s' with thee, and a sojourner "
69: 8 I am...a s' unto my brethren, 2114
94: 6 They slay the widow and the s', 1616
119: 19 I am a s' in the earth: hide not thy* "
Pr 2: 16 from the s' which flattereth with 5237
5: 10 thy labours be in the house of a s';* "
20 and embrace the bosom of a s'? "
6: 1 hast stricken thy hand with a s', 2114
7: 5 from the s' which flattereth with 5237
11: 15 that is surety for a s' shall smart 2114
14: 10 a s' doth not intermeddle with his "
20: 16 his garment that is surety for a s': "
27: 2 a s', and not thine own lips. 5237
13 his garment that is surety for a s'.2114
Ec 6: 2 eat thereof, but a s' eateth it: 376,5237
Isa 56: 3 Neither let the son of the s', that 5236
6 Also the sons of the s', that join * "
62: 8 the sons of the s' shall not drink * "
Jer 7: 6 If ye oppress not the s', the 1616
14: 8 thou be as a s' in the land, and * "
22: 3 no wrong, do no violence to the s', "
Eze 14: 7 the s' that sojourneth in Israel, * "

Eze 22: 7 dealt by oppression with the s': 1616
29 have oppressed the s' wrongfully. "
44: 9 s', uncircumcised in heart, *1121,5236
9 of any s' that is among the * "
47:23 in what tribe the s' sojourneth, 1616
Ob 12 in the day that he became a s'; *5235
Zec 7:10 widow, nor the fatherless, the s', 1616
Mal 3: 5 turn aside the s' from his right, "
M't 25:35 I was a s', and ye took me in: 3581
38 When saw we thee a s', and took "
43 I was a s', and ye took me not in: "
44 or a s', or naked, or sick, or in "
Lu 17:18 to give glory to God, save this s'. 241
24:18 Art thou only a s' in Jerusalem, *3939
Joh 10: 5 And a s' will they not follow, but 245
Ac 7:29 was a s' in the land of Madian, *3941

stranger's
Le 22:25 Neither from a s' hand shall *1121,5236
25:47 or to the stock of the s' family: 1616

strangers See also STRANGERS'.
Ge 31:15 Are we not counted of him s'? for 5237
36: 7 and the land wherein they were s'*4033
Ex 6: 4 pilgrimage, wherein they were s'.*1481
22:21 for ye were s' in the land of Egypt.1616
23: 9 ye were s' in the land of Egypt. "
Le 17: 8, 10, 13 s' which sojourn among you, "
19:34 for ye were s' in the land of Egypt: "
20: 2 of the s' that sojourn in Israel, that"
22:18 house of Israel, or of the s' in Israel,"
25:23 ye are s' and sojourners with me. "
45 the s' that do sojourn among you, 8453
De 10:19 ye were s' in the land of Egypt. 1616
24:14 thy s' that are in thy land within "
31:16 after the gods of the s' of the land,*5236
Jos 8:35 s' that were conversant among 1616
2Sa 22:45 S' shall submit themselves 1121,5236
46 S' shall fade away, and they "
1Ch 16:19 but few, even a few, and s' in it. *1481
22: 2 to gather together the s' that 1616
29:15 For we are s' before thee, and "
2Ch 2:17 Solomon numbered all the s' 582, "
15: 9 the s' with them out of Ephraim *1481
30:25 the s' that came out of the land of 1616
Ne 9: 2 Israel separated...from all s', 1121,5236
13:30 Thus cleansed I them from all s', "
Ps 18:44 s' shall submit themselves 1121, "
45 The s' shall fade away, and be " "
54: 3 For s' are risen up against me, 2114
105:12 yea, very few, and s' in it. *1481
109:11 and let the s' spoil his labour. 2114
146: 9 The Lord preserveth the s'; he 1616
Pr 5:10 Lest s' be filled with thy wealth; 2114
Isa 1: 7 land, s' devour it in your presence, "
7 it is desolate, as overthrown by s'. "
2: 6 themselves in the children of s'. 5237
5:17 places of the fat ones shall s' eat.*1481
14: 1 the s' shall be joined with them, *1616
25: 2 a palace of s' to be no city; it 2114
5 shalt bring down the noise of s', as "
29: 5 multitude of thy s'...be like...dust,* "
60:10 sons of s' shall build up thy walls, 5236
61: 5 s' shall stand and feed your flocks,2114
Jer 2:25 for I have loved s', and after them "
3:13 hast scattered thy ways to the s' "
5:19 so shall ye serve s' in a land that "
30: 8 s' shall no more serve themselves "
35: 7 days in the land where ye be s'. *1481
51:51 s' are come into the sanctuaries 2114
La 5: 2 Our inheritance is turned to s', our "
Eze 7:21 into the hands of the s' for a prey, "
11: 9 and deliver you into the hands of s', "
16:32 taketh s' instead of her husband! "
28: 7 therefore I will bring s' upon thee, "
10 uncircumcised by the hand of s': "
30:12 that is therein, by the hand of s': "
31:12 And s', the terrible of the nations, "
44: 7 brought into my sanctuary s',*1121,5236
47:22 to the s' that sojourn among you, 1616
Hos 7: 9 S' have devoured his strength, 2114
8: 7 it yield, the s' shall swallow it up. "
Joe 3:17 shall no s' pass through her any "
Ob 11 s' carried away captive his forces, "
M't 17:25 of their own children, or of s'? 245
26 Peter saith unto him, Of s'. Jesus "
27: 7 the potter's field, to bury s' in. 3581
Joh 10: 5 for they know not the voice of s'. 245
Ac 2:10 s' of Rome, Jews and proselytes, 1927
13:17 dwelt as s' in...land of Egypt,*1722,3940
17:21 s' which were there spent their 3581
Eph 2:12 s' from the covenants of promise, "
19 ye are no more s' and foreigners, "
1Ti 5:10 up children, if she have lodged s', 3580
Heb 11:13 confessed that they were s' and 3581
13: 2 Be not forgetful to entertain s': 5381
1Pe 1: 1 to the s' scattered throughout *3927
2:11 I beseech you as s' and pilgrims, *3941
3Jo 5 doest to the brethren, and to s'; 3581

strangers'
Pr 5:17 thine own, and not s' with thee. 2114

strangled
Na 2:12 whelps, and s' for his lionesses, 2614
Ac 15:20 fornication, and from things s', 4156
29 and from blood, and from things s', "
21:25 and from s', and from fornication. "

strangling
Job 7:15 So that my soul chooseth s', and 4267

straw See also STRAWED.
Ge 24:25 We have both s' and provender 8401
32 s' and provender for the camels, "
Ex 5: 7 give the people s' to make brick, "
7 go and gather s' for themselves. "
10 Pharaoh, I will not give you s'. "
Ex 5:11 get you s' where ye can find it: yet8401
12 to gather stubble instead of s'. "
13 daily tasks, as when there was s'. "
16 is no s' given unto thy servants, "
18 for there shall no s' be given you, "
J'g 19:19 Yet there is both s' and provender "
1Ki 4:28 Barley also and s' for the horses "
Job 41:27 He esteemeth iron as s', and brass "
Isa 11: 7 and the lion shall eat s' like the ox. "
25:10 even as s' is trodden down for the 4963
65:25 lion shall eat s' like the bullock: 8401

strawed See also STROWED.
Ex 32:20 powder, and s' it upon the water, *2219
M't 21: 8 the trees, and s' them in the way. *4766
25:24 gathering where thou hast not s':*1287
26 and gather where I have not s': * "
M'r 11: 8 the trees, and s' them in the way.*4766

stray See ASTRAY.

streaked See STRAKED.

streaks See STRAKES.

stream See also STREAMS.
Nu 21:15 at the s' of the brooks that goeth * 793
Job 6:15 as the s' of brooks they pass away;*650
Ps 124: 4 us, the s' had gone over our soul: 5158
Isa 27:12 of the river unto the s' of Egypt, * "
30:28 his breath, as an overflowing s', "
33 like a s' of brimstone, doth kindle "
57: 6 Among the smooth stones of the s'* "
66:12 of the Gentiles like a flowing s': "
Da 7:10 A fiery s' issued and came forth 5103
Am 5:24 and righteousness as a mighty s'. 5158
Lu 6:48 the s' beat vehemently upon that 4215
49 against which the s' did beat "

streams
Ex 7:19 the waters of Egypt, upon their s',*5104
8: 5 thine hand with thy rod over the s',*"
Ps 46: 4 the s' whereof shall make glad the6388
78:16 He brought s' also out of the rock,5140
20 gushed out, and the s' overflowed;5158
126: 4 O Lord, as the s' in the south. 650
Ca 4:15 waters, and s' from Lebanon. 5140
Isa 11:15 and shall smite it in the seven s', 5158
30:25 rivers and s' of waters in the day 2988
33:21 us a place of broad rivers and s'; 2975
34: 9 the s' thereof shall be turned into 5158
35: 6 break out, and s' in the desert. "

street See also STREETS.
Ge 19: 2 we will abide in the s' all night. 7339
De 13:16 of it into the midst of the s' thereof, "
Jos 2:19 the doors of thy house into the s', 2351
J'g 19:15 he sat him down in a s' of the city:7339
17 wayfaring man in the s' of the city: "
20 upon me; only lodge not in the s'. "
2Sa 21:12 them from the s' of Beth-shan, "
22:43 stamp them as the mire of the s', *2351
2Ch 29: 4 them together into the east s', *7339
32: 6 him in the s' of the gate of the city,*"
Ezr 10: 9 sat in the s' of the house of God, * "
Ne 8: 1 s' that was before the water gate;* "
3 s' that was before the water gate* "
16 and in the s' of the water gate, and*"
16 in the s' of the gate of Ephraim. * "
Es 4: 6 to Mordecai unto the s' of the city,* "
6: 9, 11 horseback through the s' of the "
Job 18:17 shall have no name in the s'. 2351,6440
29: 7 when I prepared my seat in the s'!7339
31:32 stranger did not lodge in the s': 2351
Pr 7: 8 through the s' near her corner; 7784
Isa 42: 2 his voice to be heard in the s'. 2351
51:23 as the s', to them that went over. "
59:14 truth is fallen in the s', and equity7339
Jer 37:21 piece of bread out of the bakers' s',2351
La 2:19 for hunger in the top of every s'. "
4: 1 poured out in the top of every s'. "
Eze 16:24 thee an high place in every s'. 7339
31 makest thine high place in every s'; "
Da 9:25 the s' shall be built again, and the "
Ac 9:11 the s' which is called Straight, 4505
12:10 out, and passed on through one s'; "
Re 11: 8 dead bodies shall lie in the s' of 4113
21:21 the s' of the city was pure gold, as it "
22: 2 In the midst of the s' of it, and on "

streets
2Sa 1:20 publish it not in the s' of Askelon;2351
1Ki 20:34 shalt make s' for thee in Damascus,"
Ps 18:42 cast them out as the dirt in the s'. "
55:11 and guile depart not from her s'. 7339
144:13 and ten thousands in our s': *2351
14 there be no complaining in our s'. 7339
Pr 1:20 she uttereth her voice in the s': * "
5:16 abroad, and rivers of waters in the s'."
7:12 Now is she without, now in the s',* "
22:13 without, I shall be slain in the s'. "
26:13 a lion in the way; a lion is in the s'."
Ec 12: 4 the doors shall be shut in the s', *7784
5 and the mourners go about the s': "
Ca 3: 2 now, and go about the city in the s'," "
Isa 5:25 were torn in the midst of the s'. 2351
10: 6 them down like the mire of the s'. "
15: 3 In their s' they shall gird themselves"
3 in their s', every one shall howl, *7339
24:11 is a crying for wine in the s'; all 2351
51:20 they lie at the head of all the s', as "
Jer 5: 1 and fro through the s' of Jerusalem, "
7:17 of Judah and in the s' of Jerusalem?"
34 from the s' of Jerusalem, the voice "
9:21 and the young men from the s'. 7339
11: 6 Judah, and in the s' of Jerusalem, 2351
13 the number of the s' of Jerusalem "
14:16 be cast out in the s' of Jerusalem "
33:10 Judah, and in the s' of Jerusalem, "
44: 6 of Judah and in the s' of Jerusalem; "
9 Judah, and in the s' of Jerusalem? "
Jer 44:17 Judah, and in the s' of Jerusalem:2351
21 Judah, and in the s' of Jerusalem, "
48:38 of Moab, and in the s' thereof: 7339
49:26 her young men shall fall in her s', "
50:30 shall her young men fall in the s', "
51: 4 that are thrust through in her s'. 2351
La 2:11 and the sucklings swoon in the s' 7339
12 swooned as the wounded in the s' "
21 the old lie on the ground in the s':2351
4: 5 delicately are desolate in the s': "
8 they are not known in the s': "
14 wandered as blind men in the s', "
18 steps, that we cannot go in our s':7339
Eze 7:19 shall cast their silver in the s', 2351
11: 6 filled the s' thereof with the slain. "
26:11 shall he tread down all thy s': "
28:23 pestilence, and blood into her s'; "
Am 5:16 Wailing shall be in all the s'; *7339
Mic 7:10 trodden down as the mire of the s'.2351
Na 2: 4 The chariots shall rage in the s', "
3:10 dashed in pieces at...top of...the s': "
Zep 3: 6 I made their s' waste, that none "
Zec 8: 4 and old women dwell in the s' of 7339
5 s' of the city shall be full of boys "
5 and girls playing in the s' thereof. "
9: 3 and fine gold as the mire of the s'.2351
10: 5 in the mire of the s' in the battle: "
M't 6: 2 in the synagogues and in the s', 4505
5 and in the corners of the s', 4113
12:19 any man hear his voice in the s'. "
M'r 6:56 they laid the sick in the s', and * 58
Lu 10:10 go your ways out into the s' of 4113
13:26 and thou hast taught in our s'. "
14:21 Go out quickly into the s' and lanes"
Ac 5:15 brought forth the sick into the s', "

strength
Ge 4:12 shall not...yield unto thee her s'; 3581
49: 3 might, and the beginning of my s', 202
24 But his bow abode in s', and the 386
Ex 13: 3 by s' of hand the Lord brought you2392
14 By s' of hand the Lord brought us "
16 by s' of hand the Lord brought us "
14:27 sea returned to his s' when the 386
15: 2 The Lord is my s' and song, and 5797
13 thou hast guided them in thy s' "
Le 26:20 And your s' shall be spent in vain: 3581
Nu 23:22 hath as it were the s' of an unicorn.8443
24: 8 hath as it were the s' of an unicorn:"
De 21:17 for he is the beginning of his s'; 202
33:25 and as thy days, so shall thy s' be.1679
Jos 11:13 cities that stood still in their s', *8510
14:11 s' was then, even so is my s' now, 3581
J'g 5:21 soul, thou hast trodden down s'. 5797
8:21 for as the man is, so is his s'. 1369
16: 5 and see wherein his great s' lieth, 3581
6 Tell me,...wherein thy great s' lieth,"
9 the fire. So his s' was not known. "
15 told me wherein thy great s' lieth. "
17 shaven, then my s' will go from me,"
19 him, and his s' went from him. "
1Sa 2: 4 that stumbled are girded with s'. 2428
9 for by s' shall no man prevail. 3581
10 and he shall give s' unto his king, 5797
15:29 the S' of Israel will not lie nor 5331
28:20 and there was no s' in him; for he 3581
22 and eat, that thou mayest have s', "
2Sa 22:33 God is my s' and power: and he *4581
40 hast girded me with s' to battle: 2428
1Ki 19: 8 and went in the s' of that meat 3581
2Ki 9:24 Jehu drew a bow with his full s', 3027
18:20 I have counsel and s' for the war. 1369
19: 3 and there is not s' to bring forth. 3581
1Ch 16:11 Seek the Lord and his s', seek his 5797
27 s' and gladness are in his place. "
28 give unto the Lord glory and s'. "
26: 8 able men for s' for the service, 3581
29:12 make great, and to give s' unto all.2388
2Ch 6:41 place, thou, and the ark of thy s': 5797
13:20 Neither did Jeroboam recover s' 3581
Ne 4:10 The s' of the bearers of burdens "
8:10 for the joy of the Lord is your s'. 4581
Job 6:11 What is my s', that I should hope? 3581
12 Is my s' the s' of stones? or is my "
9: 4 is wise in heart, and mighty in s': "
19 If I speak of s', lo, he is strong: "
12:13 With him is wisdom and s', he *1369
16 With him is s' and wisdom: the 5797
21 weakeneth the s' of the mighty. *4206
18: 7 steps of his s' shall be straitened, 202
12 His s' shall be hungerbitten, and "
13 It shall devour the s' of his skin: * 905
13 firstborn of death shall devour his s'.*"
21:23 One dieth in his full s', being 6106
23: 6 power? No; but he would put s' in me.*
26: 2 savest...the arm that hath no s'? 5797
30: 2 the s' of their hands profit me, 3581
36: 5 he is mighty in s' and wisdom. "
19 no, not gold, nor all the forces of s'."
37: 6 and to the great rain of his s'. 5797
39:11 trust him, because his s' is great? 3581
19 Hast thou given the horse s'? *1369
21 the valley, and rejoiceth in his s': 3581
40:16 his s' is in his loins, and his force "
41:22 In his neck remaineth s', and 5797
Ps 8: 2 sucklings hast thou ordained s' "
18: 1 I will love thee, O Lord, my s'. 2391
2 my God, my s', in whom I will *6697
32 It is God that girded me with s', 2428
39 For thou hast girded me with s' "
19:14 O Lord, my s', and my redeemer. *6697
20: 6 with...saving s' of his right hand. 1369
21: 1 king shall joy in thy s', O Lord; 5797
13 Be...exalted, Lord, in thine own s': "
22:15 My s' is dried up like a potsherd; 3581
19 O my s', haste thee to help me. * 360

Ps 27: 1 Lord is the s' of my life; of whom 4581
28: 7 The Lord is my s' and my shield; 5797
8 The Lord is their s', and he is the "
8 is the saving s' of his anointed. *4581
29: 1 give unto the Lord glory and s'. 5797
11 Lord will give s' unto his people; "
31: 4 privily for me: for thou art my s'.*4581
10 my s' faileth because of mine 3581
33:16 man is not delivered by much s'. "
17 he deliver any by his great s'. *2428
37:39 is their s' in the time of trouble. *4581
38:10 heart panteth, my s' faileth me: 3581
39:13 O spare me, that I may recover s',1082
43: 2 For thou art the God of my s': 4581
46: 1 God is our refuge and s', a very 5797
52: 7 the man that made not God his s':4581
54: 1 thy name, and judge me by thy s'.*1369
59: 9 Because of his s' will I wait upon 5797
17 Unto thee, O my s', will I sing: for "
60: 7 Ephraim...is the s' of mine head; *4581
62: 7 the rock of my s', and my refuge, 5797
65: 6 by...s' setteth fast the mountains; 3581
68:28 Thy God hath commanded thy s': 5797
34 Ascribe ye s' unto God: his "
34 Israel, and his s' is in the clouds. "
35 that giveth s'...unto his people. "
71: 9 forsake me not when my s' faileth.3581
16 I will go in the s' of the Lord God:*1369
18 I have shewed thy s' unto this 2220
73: 4 in their death: but their s' is firm. 193
26 but God is the s' of my heart, and 6697
74:13 Thou didst divide the sea by thy s':5797
77:14 declared thy s' among the people. "
78: 4 the praises of the Lord, and his s',5807
51 chief of their s' in the tabernacles 202
61 And delivered his s' into captivity,5797
80: 2 and Manasseh stir up my s', *1369
81: 1 Sing aloud unto God our s': make5797
84: 5 is the man whose s' is in thee; "
7 They go from s' to s', every one of2428
86:16 give thy s' unto thy servant, and 5797
88: 4 pit: I am as a man that hath no s':*353
89:17 For thou art the glory of their s': 5797
90:10 by reason of s' they be fourscore 1369
10 yet is their s' labour and sorrow;*7296
93: 1 the Lord is clothed with s', 5797
95: 4 the s' of the hills is his also. *8443
96: 6 s' and beauty are in his sanctuary.5797
7 give unto the Lord glory and s'. "
99: 4 The king's s' also loveth judgment;"
102:23 He weakened my s' in the way; he3581
103:20 ye his angels, that excel in s', that "
105: 4 Seek the Lord, and his s': seek his5797
36 their land, the chief of all their s'. 202
108: 8 Ephraim...is the s' of mine head; *4581
110: 2 send the rod of thy s' out of Zion: 5797
118:14 The Lord is my s' and song, and is "
132: 8 thy rest; thou, and the ark of thy s'. "
138: 3 strengthenedst...with s' in my soul. "
140: 7 the Lord, the s' of my salvation, "
144: 1 Blessed be the Lord my s', which *6697
147:10 delighteth not in...s' of the horse: 1369
Pr 8:14 I am understanding; I have s'. * "
10:29 The way of the Lord is s' to the *4581
14: 4 increase is by the s' of the ox. 3581
20:29 glory of young men is their s': "
21:22 and casteth down the s' of the 5797
24: 5 a man of knowledge increaseth s'.*3581
10 day of adversity, thy s' is small. "
31: 3 Give not thy s' unto women, nor 2428
17 She girdeth her loins with s', and 5797
25 S' and honour are her clothing; "
Ec 9:16 said I, Wisdom is better than s': 1369
10:10 edge, then must he put to more s':2428
17 princes eat in due season, for s', 1369
Isa 5:22 men of s' to mingle strong drink: 2428
10:13 By the s' of my hand I have done 3581
12: 2 Jehovah is my s' and my song; 5797
17:10 been mindful of the rock of thy s',4581
23: 4 hath spoken, even the s' of the sea,*"
10 of Tarshish: there is no more s'.†‡4206
14 Tarshish: for your s' is laid waste.*4581
25: 4 For thou hast been a s' to the poor,* "
4 a s' to the needy in his distress, "
26: 4 Lord Jehovah is everlasting s': *6697
27: 5 Or let him take hold of my s', 4581
28: 6 for s' to them that turn the battle 1369
30: 2 themselves in the s' of Pharaoh, 4581
3 the s' of Pharaoh be your shame, "
7 I cried...Their s' is to sit still. *7293
15 and in confidence shall be your s':1369
33: 6 of thy times, and s' of salvation: *2633
36: 5 I have counsel and s' for war: 1369
37: 3 and there is not s' to bring forth. 3581
40: 9 tidings, lift up thy voice with s'; "
29 have no might he increaseth s'. 6109
31 the Lord shall renew their s'; 3581
41: 1 and let the people renew their s': "
42:25 of his anger, and the s' of battle: 5807
44:12 worketh it with the s' of his arms:*3581
12 yea, he is hungry, and his s' faileth:"
45:24 Lord have I righteousness and s':5797
49: 4 I have spent my s' for nought, and3581
5 Lord, and my God shall be my s'. 5797
51: 9 awake, put on s', O arm of the Lord;"
52: 1 awake; put on thy s', O Zion; "
62: 8 hand, and by the arm of his s', "
63: 1 travelling in...greatness of his s'? 3581
6 bring down their s' to the earth. *5332
15 where is thy zeal and thy s', the *1369
Jer 16:19 O Lord, my s', and my fortress, 5797
20: 5 I will deliver all the s' of this city,*2633
51:53 should fortify the height of her s',5797
La 1: 6 they are gone without s' before 3581
14 he hath made my s' to fall, the "
3:18 My s' and my hope is perished 5331
Eze 24:21 excellency of your s', the desire *5797
25 when I take from them their s', 4581
30:15 my fury upon Sin, the s' of Egypt;* "
18 pomp of her s' shall cease in her: *5797
33:28 and the pomp of her s' shall cease;*"
Da 2:37 thee a kingdom, power, and s', 8632
41 shall be in it of the s' of the iron, 5326
10: 8 and there remained no s' in me: 3581
8 corruption, and I retained no s'. "
16 upon me, and I have retained no s'."
17 there remained no s' in me, neither"
11: 2 by his s' through his riches he *2394
15 neither shall there be any s' to 3581
17 to enter with the s' of his whole 8633
31 shall pollute the sanctuary of s', *4581
Ho 7: 9 Strangers have devoured his s', 3581
12: 3 by his s' he had power with God: * 202
Joe 2:22 tree and the vine do yield their s'. 2428
3:16 the s' of the children of Israel. *4581
Am 3:11 shall bring down thy s' from thee,5797
6:13 taken to us horns by our own s'? 2392
Mic 5: 4 and feed in the s' of the Lord, 5797
Na 3: 9 Ethiopia and Egypt were her s', 6109
11 seek s' because of the enemy. *4581
Hab 3:19 The Lord God is my s', and he will2428
Hag 2:22 destroy the s' of the kingdoms of 2392
Zec 12: 5 shall be my s' in the Lord of hosts 556
M'r 12:30 all thy mind, and with all thy s': 2479
33 all the soul, and with all the s', "
Lu 1:51 He hath shewed s' with his arm; 2904
10:27 all thy soul, and with all thy s', 2479
Ac 3: 7 feet and ancle bones received s'. 4732
9:22 But Saul increased the more in s',1743
Ro 5: 6 For when we were yet without s', * 772
1Co 15:56 is sin; and the s' of sin is the law.*1411
2Co 1: 8 pressed out of measure, above s',* "
12: 9 s' is made perfect in weakness. "
Heb 9:17 of no s' at all while the testator *2480
11:11 Sara...received s' to conceive seed,*1411
Re 1:16 was as the sun shineth in his s'. "
3: 8 thou hast a little s', and hast kept* "
5:12 and riches, and wisdom, and s', *2479
12:10 Now is come salvation, and s', and*1411
17:13 their power and s' unto the beast.*1849

strengthen See also STRENGTHENED; STRENGTHENETH; STRENGTHENING.
De 3:28 and encourage him, and s' him: 553
J'g 16:28 s' me, I pray thee, only this once, 2388
1Ki 20:22 Go, s' thyself, and mark, and see "
Ezr 6:22 to s' their hands in the work of the "
Ne 6: 9 therefore, O God, s' my hands. "
Job 16: 5 I would s' you with my mouth, and553
Ps 20: 2 sanctuary, and s' thee out of Zion;5582
27:14 and he shall s' thine heart: * 553
31:24 courage, and he shall s' your heart,* "
41: 3 Lord will s' him upon the bed of *5582
68:28 s', O God, that which thou hast 5810
89:21 mine arm also shall s' him. 553
119:28 s'...me according unto thy word. 6965
Isa 22:21 robe, and s' him with thy girdle, 2388
30: 2 to s'...in the strength of Pharaoh, 5810
33:23 they could not well s' their mast, 2388
35: 3 S' ye the weak hands, and confirm "
41:10 I will s' thee; yea, I will help thee; 553
54: 2 thy cords, and s' thy stakes; 2388
Jer 23:14 they s' also the hands of evildoers, "
Eze 7:13 s' himself in the iniquity of his life. "
16:49 s' the hand of the poor and needy. "
30:24 s' the arms of the king of Babylon, "
25 s' the arms of the king of Babylon,*"
34:16 and will s' that which was sick: "
Da 11: 1 I, stood to confirm and to s' him. 4581
Am 2:14 and the strong shall not s' his force,553
Zec 10: 6 And I will s' the house of Judah, 1396
12 And I will s' them in the Lord; "
Lu 22:32 art converted, s' thy brethren. *4741
1Pe 5:10 perfect, stablish, s', settle you. 4599
Re 3: 2 and s' the things which remain, *4741

strengthened See also STRENGTHENEDST.
Ge 48: 2 Israel s' himself, and sat upon 2388
J'g 3:12 Lord s' Eglon the king of Moab "
7:11 shall thine hands be s' to go down "
1Sa 23:16 the wood, and s' his hand in God. "
2Sa 2: 7 Therefore now let your hands be s',*"
1Ch 11:10 s' themselves...in his kingdom, * "
2Ch 1: 1 Solomon...was s' in his kingdom, "
11:17 So they s' the kingdom of Judah, "
12: 1 the kingdom, and had s' himself, *2394
13 So king Rehoboam s' himself in 2388
13: 7 s' themselves against Rehoboam 553
17: 1 and s' himself against Israel. 2388
21: 4 s' himself, and slew all his brethren"
23: 1 seventh year Jehoiada s' himself, "
24:13 house of God in his state, and s' it. 553
25:11 Amaziah s' himself, and led forth*2388
26: 8 for he s' himself exceedingly. * "
28:20 and distressed him, but s' him not. "
32: 5 Also he s' himself, and built up all* "
Ezr 1: 6 s' their hands with vessels of silver,"
7:28 I was s' as the hand of the Lord my"
Ne 2:18 s' their hands for this good work. "
Job 4: 3 and thou hast s' the weak hands. "
4 and thou hast s' the feeble knees.†‡553
Ps 52: 7 and s' himself in his wickedness. 5810
147:13 he hath s' the bars of thy gates; 2388
Pr 8:28 he s' the fountains of the deep: *5810
Eze 13:22 and s' the hands of the wicked, 2388
34: 4 The diseased have ye not s', neither"
Da 10:18 appearance of a man, and he s' me,"
19 he had spoken unto me, I was s'. "
19 my lord speak; for thou hast s' me."
11: 6 and he that s' her in these times. "
12 but he shall not be s' by it. *5810
Ho 7:15 I have bound and s' their arms, 2388
Ac 9:19 he had received meat, he was s'. 1765
Eph 3:16 to be s' with might by his Spirit 2901
Col 1:11 S' with all might, according to his 1412
2Ti 4:17 Lord stood with me, and s' me; 1743

strengthenedst
Ps 138: 3 s' me with strength in my soul. *7292

strengtheneth
Job 15:25 s' himself against the Almighty. *1396
Ps 104:15 and bread which s' man's heart. 5582
Pr 31:17 with strength, and s' her arms. * 553
Ec 7:19 Wisdom s' the wise more than ten*5810
Isa 44:14 the oak, which he s' for himself 553
Am 5: 9 s' the spoiled against the strong,*1082
Ph'p 4:13 things through Christ which s' me. 1743

strengthening
Lu 22:43 an angel...from heaven, s' him. 1765
Ac 18:23 in order, s' all the disciples. *1991

stress See DISTRESS.

stretch See also STRETCHED; STRETCHEST; STRETCHETH; STRETCHING.
Ex 3:20 s' out my hand, and smite Egypt *7971
7: 5 I s' forth mine hand upon Egypt, 5186
19 s' out thine hand upon the waters "
8: 5 S' forth thine hand with thy rod "
16 S' out thy rod, and smite the dust "
9:15 For now I will s' out my hand, that*7971
22 S'...thine hand toward heaven, 5186
10:12 S' out thine hand over...Egypt "
21 S' out thine hand toward heaven, "
14:16 and s' out thine hand over the sea, "
26 S' out thine hand over the sea, that"
25:20 cherubims...s' forth their wings *6566
Jos 8:18 S' out the spear that is in thy 5186
1Sa 24: 6 to s' forth mine hand against him,*7971
26: 9 s' forth his hand against the Lord's*"
11, 23 s'...mine hand against the Lord's*"
2Sa 1:14 not afraid to s' forth thine hand * "
2Ki 21:13 I will s' over Jerusalem the line 5186
Job 11:13 s' out thine hands toward him; 6566
30:24 not s' out his hand to the grave, *7971
39:26 s' her wings toward the south? 6566
Ps 68:31 Ethiopia shall soon s' out her 7323
138: 7 s'...thine hand against the wrath 7971
143: 6 I s' forth my hands unto thee: *6566
Isa 28:20 than that a man can s' himself 8311
31: 3 the Lord shall s' out his hand, 5186
34:11 s' out upon it the line of confusion,"
54: 2 and let them s' forth the curtains "
Jer 6:12 s'...my hand upon the inhabitants "
10:20 none to s' forth my tent any more, "
15: 6 will I s' out my hand against thee,* "
51:25 I will s' out mine hand upon thee, "
Eze 6:14 So will I s' out my hand upon them,"
14: 9 and I will s' out my hand upon him,"
13 then will I s' out mine hand upon it,"
25: 7 I will s' out mine hand upon thee,* "
13 also s' out mine hand upon Edom, "
16 s'...mine hand upon the Philistines,"
30:25 s' it out upon the land of Egypt. "
35: 3 I will s' out mine hand against thee,"
Da 11:42 He shall s' forth his hand also 7971
Am 6: 4 s' themselves upon their couches.5628
Zep 1: 4 also s' out mine hand upon Judah,5186
2:13 s' out his hand against the north, "
M't 12:13 he to the man, S' forth thine hand.1614
M'r 3: 5 unto the man, S' forth thine hand. "
Lu 6:10 unto the man, S' forth thy hand. "
Joh 21:18 old, thou shalt s' forth thy hands, "
2Co 10:14 we s' not ourselves beyond our 5239

stretched See also OUTSTRETCHED; STRETCHEDST.
Ge 22:10 And Abraham s' forth his hand, 7971
48:14 And Israel s' out his right hand, "
Ex 6: 6 will redeem you with a s' out arm,5186
8: 6 Aaron s'...his hand over the waters "
17 Aaron s' out his hand with his rod, "
9:23 Moses s'...his rod toward heaven: "
10:13 Moses s' forth his rod over...Egypt, "
22 Moses s'...his hand toward heaven; "
14:21 Moses s' out his hand over the sea; "
27 Moses s' forth his hand over the sea,"
De 4:34 a mighty hand, and by a s' out arm, "
5:15 a mighty hand and by a s' out arm: "
7:19 mighty hand, and the s' out arm, "
9:29 mighty power and by thy s' out arm. "
11: 2 mighty hand, and his s' out arm, "
Jos 8:18 Joshua s' out the spear that he had "
19 as soon as he had s' out his hand: "
26 back, wherewith he s' out the spear,"
2Sa 24:16 when the angel s' out his hand 7971
1Ki 6:27 s'...the wings of the cherubims, 6566
8:42 hand, and of thy s' out arm;) 5186
17:21 he s' himself upon the child three 4058
2Ki 4:34 and he s' himself upon the child; 1457
35 went up, and s' himself upon him: "
17:36 with great power and a s' out arm,5186
1Ch 21:16 sword...s' out over Jerusalem. "
2Ch 6:32 mighty hand, and thy s' out arm; "
Job 38: 5 or who hath s' the line upon it? "
Ps 44:20 s'...our hands to a strange god; *6566
88: 9 I have s' out my hands unto thee.*7849
136: 6 To him that s' out the earth above*7554
12 strong hand, and...a s' out arm: 5186
Pr 1:24 I have s' out my hand, and no man "
Isa 3:16 and walk with s' forth necks and "
5:25 s' forth his hand against them, "
25 away, but his hand is s' out still. "
9:12, 17, 21 but his hand is s' out still. "
10: 4 away, but his hand is s' out still. "
14:26 hand...s' out upon all the nations. "
27 his hand is s' out, and who shall "
16: 8 her branches are s' out, they are *5203
23:11 He s' out his hand over the sea, he5186
42: 5 the heavens, and s' them out; "

Isa 45:12 my hands, have s' out the heavens.5186
51:13 that hath s' forth the heavens, and "
Jer 6: 4 shadows of the evening are s' out. "
10:12 s' out the heavens by his discretion."
32:17 by thy great power and s' out arm, "
21 strong hand, and with a s' out arm, "
51:15 and hath s' out the heaven by his "
La 2: 8 he hath s' out a line, he hath not "
Eze 1:11 and their wings were s' upward; *6504
22 s' forth over their heads above. 5186
10: 7 And one cherub s' forth his hand 7971
16:27 I have s' out my hand over thee, 5186
20:33 and with a s' out arm, and with fury"
34 mighty hand, and with a s' out arm, "
Ho 7: 5 he s' out his hand with scorners. 4900
Am 6: 7 and the banquet of them that s' 5628
Zec 1:16 shall be s' forth upon Jerusalem. 5186
M't 12:13 he s' it forth; and it was restored 1614
49 And he s' forth his hand toward his"
14:31 Jesus s' forth his hand, and caught "
26:51 s' out his hand, and drew his sword,"
M'r 3: 5 And he s' it out: and his hand was "
Lu 22:53 ye s' forth no hands against me: "
Ac 12: 1 Herod the king s' forth his hands *1911
26: 1 Then Paul s' forth the hand, and 1614
Ro 10:21 I have s' forth my hands unto a *1600

stretchedst
Ex 15:12 Thou s' out thy right hand, the 5186

stretchest
Ps 104: 2 s' out the heavens like a curtain: 5186

stretcheth
Job 15:25 he s' out his hand against God, *5186
26: 7 He s' out the north over the empty "
Pr 31:20 She s' out her hand to the poor; *6566
Isa 40:22 s' out the heavens as a curtain, 5186
44:13 The carpenter s' out his rule; he "
24 that s' forth the heavens alone; "
Zec 12: 1 Lord, which s' forth the heavens, "

stretching
Isa 8: 8 the s' out of his wings shall fill the4298
Ac 4:30 By s' forth thine hand to heal; and*1614

strewed See STRAWED.

stricken See also STRUCK.
Ge 18:11 Sarah were old and well s' in age; 935
24: 1 Abraham was old, and well s' in age:"
Jos 13: 1 Now Joshua was old and s' in years;"
1 Thou art old and s' in years, and "
23: 1 that Joshua waxed old and s' in age."
2 unto them, I am old and s' in age: "
J'g 5:26 and s' through his temples. *2498
1Ki 1: 1 king David was old and s' in years; 935
Pr 6: 1 hast s' thy hand with a stranger, 8628
23:35 They have s' me, shalt thou say, 5221
Isa 1: 5 Why should ye be s' any more? "
16: 7 shall ye mourn; surely they are s'.5218
53: 4 yet we did esteem him s', smitten 5060
8 transgression of my people...he s'.5061
Jer 5: 3 thou hast s' them, but they have 5221
La 4: 9 s' through for want of the fruits of 1856
Lu 1: 7 both were now well s' in years. 4260
18 man, and my wife well s' in years. "

strife See also STRIFES.
Ge 13: 7 was a s' between the herdmen of 7379
8 said unto Lot, Let there be no s', 4808
Nu 27:14 of Zin, in the s' of the congregation,"
De 1:12 and your burden, and your s'? 7379
J'g 12: 2 I and my people were at great s' "
2Sa 19: 9 the people were at s' throughout 1777
Ps 31:20 a pavilion from the s' of tongues. 7379
55: 9 have seen violence and s' in the city."
80: 6 us a s' unto our neighbours: 4066
106:32 angered him...at the waters of s', *4808
Pr 15:18 A wrathful man stirreth up s': *4066
18 that is slow to anger appeaseth s'.7379
16:28 A froward man soweth s': and a 4066
17: 1 an house full of sacrifices with s'. 7379
14 The beginning of s' is as when one4066
19 loveth transgression that loveth s':4683
20: 3 honour for a man to cease from s':7379
22:10 yea, s' and reproach shall cease. 1779
26:17 meddleth with s' belonging not 7379
20 is no talebearer, the s' ceaseth. *4066
21 is a contentious man to kindle s'. 7379
28:25 is of a proud heart stirreth up s': 4066
29:22 An angry man stirreth up s', and a "
30:33 forcing of wrath bringeth forth s'. 7379
Isa 58: 4 Behold, ye fast for s' and debate, "
Jer 15:10 a man of s' and a man of contention"
Eze 47:19 even to the waters of s' in Kadesh,*4808
48:28 unto the waters of s' in Kadesh, * "
Hab 1: 3 and there are that raise up s' and 7379
Lu 22:24 there was also a s' among them. *5379
Ro 13:13 wantonness, not in s' and envying.2054
1Co 3: 3 you envying, and s', and divisions, "
Ga 5:20 emulations, wrath, s', seditions, *2052
Ph'p 1:15 preach Christ even of envy and s'; 2054
2: 3 Let nothing be done through s' or*2052
1Ti 6: 4 whereof cometh envy, s', railings, 2054
Heb 6:16 oath...is to them an end of all s'. *485
Jas 3:14 envying and s' in your hearts, *2052
16 For where envying and s' is, there* "

strifes
Pr 10:12 Hatred stirreth up s': but love 4090
2Co 12:20 envyings, wraths, s', backbitings,*2052
1Ti 6: 4 about questions and s' of words, *3055
2Ti 2:23 knowing that they do gender s'. 3163

strike See also STRAKE; STRICKEN; STRIKETH; STRUCK.
Ex 12: 7 and s' it on the two side posts *5414
22 s' the lintel and the two side posts 5060
De 21: 4 and shall s' off the heifer's neck *
2Ki 5:11 and s' his hand over the place, *5130
Job 17: 3 is he that will s' hands with me? 8628
20:24 bow of steel shall s' him through. 2498
Ps 110: 5 The Lord...shall s' through kings 4272
Pr 7:23 Till a dart s' through his liver; as 6398
17:26 good, nor to s' princes for equity. *5221
22:26 Be not...one of them that s' hands,8628
Hab 3:14 didst s' through with his staves *5344
M'r 14:65 did s' him with the palms of their* 906

striker
1Ti 3: 3 Not given to wine, no s', not greedy4131
Tit 1: 7 not given to wine, no s', not given to"

striketh
Job 34:26 He s' them as wicked men in the 5606
Pr 17:18 void of understanding s' hands, 8628
Re 9: 5 a scorpion, when he s' a man. 3817

string See also STRINGED; STRINGS.
Ps 11: 2 ready their arrow upon the s', 3499
M'r 7:35 the s' of his tongue was loosed, *1199

stringed
Ps 150: 4 praise him with s' instruments 4482
Isa 38:20 my songs to the s' instrument 5058
Hab 3:19 chief singer on my s' instruments. "

strings
Ps 21:12 arrows upon thy s' against the *4340
33: 2 and an instrument of ten s'. "
92: 3 Upon an instrument of ten s', and "
144: 9 and an instrument of ten s' will I "

strip See also STRIPPED.
Nu 20:26 s' Aaron of his garments, and put 6584
1Sa 31: 8 the Philistines came to s' the slain, "
1Ch 10: 8 the Philistines came to s' the slain, "
Isa 32:11 s' you, and make you bare, and "
Eze 16:39 shall s' thee also of thy clothes, "
23:26 shall also s' thee out of thy clothes,"
Ho 2: 3 Lest I s' her naked, and set her as "

stripe See also STRIPES.
Ex 21:25 wound for wound, s' for s'. 2250

stripes
De 25: 3 Forty s' he may give him, and 5221
3 him above these with many s', 4347
2Sa 7:14 with the s' of the children of men:5061
Ps 89:32 rod, and their iniquity with s'. "
Pr 17:10 than an hundred s' into a fool. 5221
19:29 and s' for the back of fools. 4112
20:30 so do s' the inward parts of the *4347
Isa 53: 5 and with his s' we are healed. 2250
Lu 12:47 will, shall be beaten with many s'.
48 commit things worthy of s', shall 4127
48 shall be beaten with few s'. For "
Ac 16:23 they had laid many s' upon them, "
33 of the night, and washed their s'; "
2Co 6: 5 In s', in imprisonments, in tumults,"
11:23 in s' above measure, in prisons "
24 times received I forty s' save one. "
1Pe 2:24 by whose s' ye were healed. 3468

stripling
1Sa 17:56 Enquire...whose son this s' is. 5958

stripped See also STRIPT.
Ex 33: 6 children of Israel s' themselves 5337
Nu 20:28 Moses s' Aaron of his garments, 6584
1Sa 18: 4 Jonathan s' himself of the robe "
19:24 And he s' off his clothes also, and "
31: 9 off his head, and s' off his armour, "
1Ch 10: 9 when they had s' him, they took "
2Ch 20:25 which they s' off for themselves, 5337
Job 19: 9 He hath s' me of my glory, and 6584
22: 6 and s' the naked of their clothing. "
Mic 1: 8 and howl, I will go s' and naked: 7758
M't 27:28 And they s' him, and put on him a 1562
Lu 10:30 which s' him of his raiment, and "

stript See also STRIPPED.
Ge 37:23 they s' Joseph out of his coat, his 6584

strive See also STRIVED; STRIVETH; STRIVING.
Ge 6: 3 My spirit shall not...s' with man, 1777
26:20 did s' with Isaac's herdmen, *7378
Ex 21:18 if men s' together, and one smite* "
22 If men s', and hurt a woman with 5327
De 25:11 men s' together one with another, "
33: 8 whom thou didst s' at the waters 7378
J'g 11:25 did he ever s' against Israel, or did "
Job 33:13 Why dost thou s' against him? for "
Ps 35: 1 Lord, with them that s' with me: 3401
Pr 3:30 S' not with a man without cause, 7378
25: 8 Go not forth hastily to s', lest thou "
Isa 41:11 they that s' with thee shall perish.7379
45: 9 the potsherd s' with the potsherds "
Ho 4: 4 no man s', nor reprove another: 7378
4 are as they that s' with the priest. "
M't 12:19 He shall not s', nor cry; neither 2051
Lu 13:24 S' to enter in at the strait gate: 75
Ro 15:30 ye s' together with me in your 4865
2Ti 2: 5 if a man also s' for masteries, yet * 118
5 not crowned, except he s' lawfully.* "
14 s' not about words to no profit, 3054
24 servant of the Lord must not s'; 3164

strived See also STRIVEN; STROVE.
Ro 15:20 so have I s' to preach the gospel, *5389

striven See also STRIVED.
Jer 50:24 thou hast s' against the Lord. 1624

striveth
Isa 45: 9 unto him that s' with his Maker! 7378
1Co 9:25 every man that s' for the mastery 75

striving See also STRIVINGS.
Ph'p 1:27 one mind s' together for the faith 4866
Col 1:29 s' according to his working, which 75
Heb 12: 4 resisted unto blood, s' against sin. 464

strivings
2Sa 22:44 delivered me from the s' of my 7379
Ps 18:43 delivered me from the s' of the "
Tit 3: 9 contentions, and s' about the law;*3163

stroke See also STROKES.
De 17: 8 between s' and s', being matters 5061
19: 5 his hand fetcheth a s' with the axe
21: 5 controversy and every s' be tried: 5061
Es 9: 5 enemies with the s' of the sword, 4347
Job 23: 2 s' is heavier than my groaning. 3027
36:18 he take thee away with his s': †‡5607
Ps 39:10 Remove thy s' away from me: I 5061
Isa 14: 6 the people...with a continual s', 4347
30:26 and healeth the s' of their wound. 4273
Eze 24:16 the desire of thine eyes with a s': 4046

strokes
Pr 18: 6 and his mouth calleth for s'. *4112

strong See also STRONGER; STRONGEST.
Ge 49:14 Issachar is a s' ass couching 1634
24 were made s' by the hands of the 6339
Ex 6: 1 a s' hand shall he let them go, 2389
1 a s' hand shall he drive them out "
10:19 Lord turned a mighty s' west wind, "
13: 9 for with a s' hand hath the Lord "
14:21 sea to go back by a s' east wind 5794
Le 10: 9 Do not drink wine nor s' drink, thou,
Nu 6: 3 himself from wine and s' drink, and
3 or vinegar of s' drink, neither shall he
13:18 whether they be s' or weak, few 2389
19 whether in tents, or in s' holds; 4013
28 people be s' that dwell in the land,5794
20:20 much people, and with a s' hand. 2389
21:24 the children of Ammon was s'. 5794
24:21 S' is thy dwellingplace, and thou 386
28: 7 thou cause the s' wine to be poured
De 2:36 was not one city too s' for us: 7682
11: 8 that ye may be s', and go in and 2388
14:26 for sheep, or for wine, or for s' drink,
29: 6 have ye drunk wine or s' drink:
31: 6 Be s' and of a good courage, fear 2388
7, 23 Be s' and of a good courage, for "
Jos 1: 6 Be s' and of a good courage: for "
7 be thou s' and very courageous, "
9 Be s' and of a good courage; be "
18 only be s' and of a good courage. "
10:25 be s' and of good courage: for "
14:11 As yet I am as s' this day as I was 2389
17:13 children of Israel were waxen s', 2388
18 chariots, and though they be s'. 2389
19:29 to Ramah, and to the s' city Tyre;*4013
23: 9 before you great nations and s': 6099
J'g 1:28 came to pass, when Israel was s', 2388
6: 2 mountains,...caves, and s' holds. 4679
9:51 was a s' tower within the city, 5797
13: 4 and drink not wine nor s' drink, and
7 and now drink no wine nor s' drink,
14 neither let her drink wine or s' drink,
14:14 out of the s' came forth sweetness. 5794
18:26 Micah saw that they were too s' 2389
1Sa 1:15 have drunk neither wine nor s' drink,
4: 9 Be s', and quit yourselves like 2388
14:52 when Saul saw any s' man, or any*1368
23:14 abode in the wilderness in s' holds,4679
19 not David hide...with us in s' holds "
29 and dwelt in s' holds at En-gedi. "
2Sa 3: 6 Abner made himself s' for the 2388
5: 7 David took the s' hold of Zion: 4686
10:11 If the Syrians be too s' for me, 2388
11 if the children of Ammon be too s' "
11:25 thy battle more s' against the city, "
15:12 And the conspiracy was s'; for the 533
16:21 the hands of all...with thee be s'. 2388
22:18 delivered me from my s' enemy, 5794
18 me: for they were too s' for me. * 553
24: 7 And came to the s' hold of Tyre, 4013
1Ki 2: 2 be thou s' therefore, and shew 2388
8:42 great name, and of thy s' hand, *2389
19:11 and s' wind rent the mountains, "
2Ki 2:16 be with thy servants fifty s' men; 2428
8:12 their s' holds wilt thou set on fire,4013
24:16 all that were s' and apt for war, 1368
1Ch 19:12 If the Syrians be too s' for me, 2388
12 children of Ammon be too s' "
22:13 be s', and of good courage; dread "
26: 7 whose brethren were s' men, *2428
9 had sons and brethren, s' men, * "
28:10 the sanctuary: be s', and do it. 2388
20 his son, be s' and of good courage, "
2Ch 11:11 he fortified the s' holds, and put 4694
12 and made them exceeding s', 2388
17 Rehoboam the son of Solomon s', 553
15: 7 Be ye s' therefore, and let not your2388
16: 9 shew himself s' in...behalf of them "
25: 8 wilt go, do it, be s' for the battle: "
26:15 marvellously helped, till he was s'. "
16 But when he was s', his heart was 2394
32: 7 Be s' and courageous, be not 2388
Ezr 9:12 that ye may be s', and eat the good "
Ne 1:10 great power, and by thy s' hand. 2389
9:25 they took s' cities, and a fat land,*1219
Job 8: 2 of thy mouth be like a s' wind? *3524
9:19 If I speak of strength, lo, he is s':* 533
30:21 with thy s' hand thou opposest *6108
33:19 multitude of his bones with s' pain:*386
37:18 spread out the sky, which is s', 2389
39:28 crag of the rock, and the s' place. 4686
40:18 His bones are as s' pieces of brass;*650
Ps 10:10 the poor may fall by his s' ones. 6099
18:17 delivered me from my s' enemy, 5794
17 me: for they were too s' for me. * 553
19: 5 and rejoiceth as a s' man to run a 1368
22:12 s' bulls of Bashan have beset me 47
24: 8 The Lord s' and mighty, the Lord 5808
30: 7 made my mountain to stand s': 5797

Ps 31: 2 be thou my s' rock, for an house 4581
21 marvellous kindness in a s' city. 4692
35: 10 the poor from him that is too s' 2389
38: 19 are lively, and they are s': and 6105
60: 9 Who will bring me into the s' city?4692
61: 3 and a s' tower from the enemy. 5797
71: 3 Be thou my s' habitation, 6697
7 many; but thou art my s' refuge. 5797
80: 15 that thou madest s' for thyself. 553
17 whom thou madest s' for thyself. "
89: 8 who is a s' Lord like unto thee? *2626
10 thine enemies with thy s' arm. *5797
13 s' is thy hand, and high is thy 5810
40 hast brought his s' holds to ruin. 4013
108: 10 Who will bring me into the s' city?*"
136: 12 With a s' hand, and with a 2389
144: 14 That our oxen may be s' to labour;*
Pr 7: 26 many s' men have been slain by *6099
10: 15 rich man's wealth is his s' city: 5797
11: 16 honour: and s' men retain riches.*6184
14: 26 fear of the Lord is s' confidence: 5797
18: 10 The name of the Lord is a s' tower:"
11 The rich man's wealth is his s' city,"
19 is harder to be won than a s' city: "
20: 1 Wine is a mocker, s' drink is raging:
21: 14 a reward in the bosom s' wrath. 5794
24: 5 A wise man is s'; yea, a man of 5797
30: 25 The ants are a people not s', yet 5794
31: 4 to drink wine; nor for princes s' drink:
6 Give s' drink unto him that is ready to
Ec 9: 11 nor the battle to the s', neither yet1368
12: 3 the s' men shall bow themselves, 2428
Ca 8: 6 for love is s' as death; jealousy is 5794
Isa 1: 31 And the s' shall be as tow, and the2634
5: 11 that they may follow s' drink; that
22 men of strength to mingle s' drink:
8: 7 waters of the river, s' and many, 6099
11 spake thus to me with a s' hand, 2393
17: 9 shall his s' cities be as a forsaken 4581
23: 11 city, to destroy the s' holds thereof. "
24: 9 s' drink shall be bitter to them that
25: 3 shall the s' people glorify thee, 5794
26: 1 We have a s' city; salvation will 5797
27: 1 great and s' sword shall punish 2389
28: 2 the Lord hath a mighty and s' one, 533
7 through s' drink are out of the way;
7 prophet have erred through s' drink,
7 are out of the way through s' drink;
22 lest your bands be made s': for I 2388
29: 9 they stagger, but not with s' drink.
31: 1 in horsemen,...they are very s'; 6105
9 and shall pass over to his s' hold *5553
35: 4 of a fearful heart, be s', fear not: 2388
40: 10 Lord God will come with s' hand, *2389
26 might, for that he is s' in power; 533
41: 21 bring forth your s' reasons, saith 6110
53: 12 shall divide the spoil with the s'; 6099
56: 12 we will fill ourselves with s' drink;
60: 22 and a small one a s' nation: 6099
Jer 8: 16 sound of the neighing of his s' ones;47
21: 5 outstretched hand and...a s' arm, 2389
32: 21 with wonders, and with a s' hand,
47: 3 of the hoofs of his s' horses, at the 47
48: 14 mighty and s' men for the war? *2428
17 How is the s' staff broken, and the5797
18 and he shall destroy thy s' holds. 4013
41 the s' holds are surprised, and the 4679
49: 19 against the habitation of the s': 386
50: 34 Their Redeemer is s'; the Lord of 2389
44 Jordan unto the habitation of the s': 386
51: 12 make the watch s', set up the 2388
La 2: 2 s' holds of the daughter of Judah;4013
5 he hath destroyed his s' holds, and "
Eze 3: 8 thy face s' against their faces, *2389
8 forehead s' against their foreheads.*"
14 hand of the Lord was s' upon me. 2388
7: 24 make the pomp of the s' to cease; 5794
19: 11 she had s' rods for the sceptres of 5797
12 s' rods were broken and withered; "
14 she hath no s' rod to be a sceptre "
22: 14 endure, or can thine hands be s', 2388
26: 11 s' garrisons shall go down to the *5797
17 city, which wast s' in the sea, 2389
30: 21 to make it s' to hold the sword. 2388
22 the s', and that which was broken;2389
32: 21 s' among the mighty shall speak 410
34: 16 I will destroy the fat and the s'; 2389
Da 2: 40 fourth kingdom shall be s' as iron:8624
42 the kingdom shall be partly s', and "
4: 11 The tree grew, and was s', and the8631
20 The tree...which grew, and was s', "
22 king, that art grown and become s':"
7: 7 and terrible, and s' exceedingly; 8624
8: 8 when he was s', the great horn 6105
10: 19 be unto thee, be s', yea, be s'. 2388
11: 5 the king of the south shall be s', "
5 and he shall be s' above him, and "
23 become s' with a small people. 6105
24 his devices against the s' holds, 4013
32 that do know their God shall be s',2388
39 shall he do in the most s' holds *4581
Joe 1: 6 is come up upon my land, s', 6099
2: 2 a great people and a s'; there hath "
5 as a s' people set in battle array. "
11 for he is s' that executeth his word:"
3: 10 spears: let the weak say, I am s'. 1368
Am 2: 9 cedars, and he was s' as the oaks;2634
14 s' shall not strengthen his force, 2389
5: 9 the spoiled against the s', 5794
Mic 2: 11 unto thee of wine and of s' drink; 7941
4: 3 and rebuke s' nations afar off; 6099
7 her that was cast far off a s' nation:"
8 s' hold of the daughter of Zion, *6076
5: 11 and throw down all thy s' holds: 4013
6: 2 and ye s' foundations of the earth:*386
Na 1: 7 a s' hold in the day of trouble; 4581

Na 2: 1 make thy loins s', fortify thy power2388
3: 12 s' holds shall be like fig trees with*4013
14 for the siege, fortify thy s' holds: * "
14 the morter, make s' the brickkiln. 2388
Hab 1: 10 they shall deride every s' hold; 4013
Hag 2: 4 Yet now be s', O Zerubbabel, saith2388
4 be s', O Joshua, son of Josedech, "
4 and be s', all ye people of the land, "
Zec 8: 9 Let your hands be s', ye that hear "
13 fear not, but let your hands be s'. "
22 s' nations shall come to seek the 6099
9: 3 Tyrus did build herself a s' hold, 4692
12 Turn you to the s' hold, ye 1225
M't 12: 29 one enter into a s' man's house, *2478*
29 except he first bind the s' man? "
M'r 3: 27 can enter into a s' man's house, "
27 except he will first bind the s' man;"
Lu 1: 15 drink neither wine nor s' drink; *4608*
80 child grew, and waxed s' in spirit, *2901*
2: 40 child grew, and waxed s' in spirit, "
11: 21 s' man armed keepeth his palace, *2478*
Ac 3: 16 his name hath made this man s', *4732*
Ro 4: 20 was s' in faith, giving glory to God;*1743*
15: 1 We...that are s' ought to bear the *1415*
1Co 4: 10 we are weak, but ye are s'; *2478*
16: 13 the faith, quit you like men, be s'. *2901*
2Co 10: 4 to the pulling down of s' holds;) *3794*
12: 10 for when I am weak, then am I s'. *1415*
13: 9 when we are weak, and ye are s': "
Eph 6: 10 my brethren, be s' in the Lord, *1743*
2Th 2: 11 God shall send them s' delusion, *1753*
2Ti 2: 1 my son, be s' in the grace that is *1743*
Heb 5: 7 with s' crying and tears unto him *2478*
12 need of milk, and not of s' meat. *4731*
14 But s' meat belongeth to them that*"
6: 18 we might have a s' consolation, *2478*
11: 34 out of weakness were made s', *1743*
1Jo 2: 14 young men, because ye are s', and*2478*
Re 5: 2 I saw a s' angel proclaiming with "
18: 2 he cried mightily with a s' voice, **3173*
8 s' is the Lord God who judgeth *2478*

strong-drink See STRONG and DRINK.

stronger
Ge 25: 23 shall be s' than the other people; 553
30: 41 the s' cattle did conceive, 7194
42 were Laban's, and the s' Jacob's. "
Nu 13: 31 people; for they are s' than we. 2389
J'g 14: 18 honey? and what is s' than a lion?5794
2Sa 1: 23 eagles, they were s' than lions. 1396
3: 1 but David waxed s'...and the 2390
1 but David waxed...s', and the
13: 14 but, being s' than she, forced her. 2388
1Ki 20: 23 therefore they were s' than we; "
23, 25 surely we shall be s' than they. "
Job 17: 9 that hath clean hands shall be s' 555
9 that hath clean hands shall be...s',
Ps 105: 24 made them s' than their enemies. 6105
142: 6 persecutors; for they are s' than I.553
Jer 20: 7 thou art s' than I, and hast 2388
31: 11 hand of him that was s' than he. "
Lu 11: 22 when a s' than he shall come upon*2478*
1Co 1: 25 the weakness of God is s' than men." "
10: 22 to jealousy? are we s' than he? "

strongest
Pr 30: 30 A lion which is s' among beasts, *1368

strong-hold See STRONG and HOLD.

strongly
Ezr 6: 3 the foundations thereof be s' laid;

strove See also STRIVED.
Ge 26: 20 Esek; because they s' with him. *6229
21 another well, and s' for that also: 7378
22 another well;...for that they s' not: "
Ex 2: 13 men of the Hebrews s' together: 5327
Le 24: 10 of Israel s' together in the camp; "
Nu 20: 13 children of Israel s' with the Lord,7378
26: 9 who s' against Moses and against 5327
9 when they s' against the Lord: "
2Sa 14: 6 they two s' together in the field, "
Ps 60: *title* when he s' with Aram-naharaim "
Da 7: 2 four winds of the heaven s' upon *1519
Joh 6: 52 Jews...s' among themselves, *3164*
Ac 7: 26 he shewed himself...as they s', "
23: 9 the Pharisees' part arose, and s', *1264*

strowed See also STRAWED.
2Ch 34: 4 s' it upon the graves of them that 2236

struck See also STRAKE; STRICKEN.
1Sa 2: 14 And he s' it into the pan, or kettle,5221
2Sa 12: 15 the Lord s' the child that Uriah's 5062
20: 10 the ground, and s' him not again; 8138
2Ch 13: 20 and the Lord s' him, and he died.*5062
M't 26: 51 s' a servant of the high priest's, **3960*
Lu 22: 64 him, they s' him on the face, **5180*
Joh 18: 22 s' Jesus with the palm of his *1325,4475*

struggled
Ge 25: 22 children s' together within her; 7533

stubble
Ex 5: 12 to gather s' instead of straw. 7179
15: 7 wrath, which consumed them as s'. "
Job 13: 25 and wilt thou pursue the dry s'? "
21: 18 They are as s' before the wind, 8401
41: 28 slingstones are turned...into s'. 7179
29 Darts are counted as s': he "
Ps 83: 13 wheel; as the s' before the wind. "
Isa 5: 24 as the fire devoureth the s', and "
33: 11 chaff, ye shall bring forth s': "
40: 24 shall take them away as s'. "
41: 2 sword, and as driven s' to his bow. "
47: 14 Behold, they shall be as s'; the fire "
Jer 13: 24 scatter them as the s' that passeth "
Joe 2: 5 flame of fire that devoureth the s', "

Ob 18 flame, and the house of Esau for s',7179
Na 1: 10 they shall be devoured as s' "
Mal 4: 1 all that do wickedly, shall be s': "
1Co 3: 12 precious stones, wood, hay, s'; *2562*

stubborn
De 21: 18 man have a s' and rebellious son, 5637
20 This our son is s' and rebellious, "
J'g 2: 19 doings, nor from their s' way. 7186
Ps 78: 8 a s' and rebellious generation; 5637
Pr 7: 11 (She is loud and s'; her feet abide "

stubbornness
De 9: 27 look not unto the s' of this people, 7190
1Sa 15: 23 and s' is as iniquity and idolatry. 6484

stuck
1Sa 26: 7 his spear s' in the ground at his 4600
Ps 119: 31 I have s' unto thy testimonies: *1692
Ac 27: 41 the forepart s' fast, and remained**2043*

studs
Ca 1: 11 borders of gold with s' of silver. 5351

studieth
Pr 15: 28 of the righteous s' to answer: 1897
24: 2 For their heart s' destruction, and "

study See also STUDIETH.
Ec 12: 12 much s' is a weariness of the flesh.3854
1Th 4: 11 that ye s' to be quiet, and to do *5389*
2Ti 2: 15 *S'* to shew thyself approved unto **4704*

stuff
Ge 31: 37 thou hast searched all my s', 3627
37 thou found of all thy household s'? "
45: 20 Also regard not your s'; for the "
Ex 22: 7 his neighbour money or s' to keep, "
36: 7 s' they had was sufficient for all 4399
Jos 7: 11 put it even among their own s'. 3627
1Sa 10: 22 he hath hid himself among the s'.‡ "
25: 13 and two hundred abode by the s'.‡ "
30: 24 his part be that tarrieth by the s':‡ "
Ne 13: 8 forth all the household s' of Tobiah "
Eze 12: 3 prepare thee s' for removing, "
4 shalt thou bring forth thy s' by day "
4 in their sight, as s' for removing: "
7 I brought forth my s' by day, "
7 as s' for captivity, and in the even "
Lu 17: 31 housetop, and his s' in the house,**4632*

stumble See also STUMBLED; STUMBLETH; STUMBLING.
Pr 3: 23 safely, and thy foot shall not s'. 5062
4: 12 thou runnest, thou shalt not s'. 3782
19 they know not at what they s'. "
Isa 5: 27 shall be weary nor s' among them; "
8: 15 And many among them shall s', "
28: 7 err in vision, they s' in judgment. 6328
59: 10 we s' at noon day as in the night; 3782
63: 13 wilderness, that they should not s'?*"
Jer 13: 16 feet s' upon the dark mountains, 5062
18: 15 caused them to s' in their ways 3782
20: 11 therefore my persecutors shall s', "
31: 9 way, wherein they shall not s': "
46: 6 shall s', and fall toward the north* "
50: 32 the most proud shall s' and fall, "
Da 11: 19 shall s' and fall, and not be found "
Na 2: 5 they shall s' in their walk; they "
3: 3 corpses; they s' upon their corpses:"
Mal 2: 8 have caused many to s' at the law; "
1Pe 2: 8 even to them which s' at the word, *4350*

stumbled
1Sa 2: 4 that s' are girded with strength. 3782
1Ch 13: 9 to hold the ark; for the oxen s'. 8058
Ps 27: 2 eat up my flesh, they s' and fell. 3782
Jer 46: 12 man hath s' against the mighty, "
Ro 9: 32 they s' at that stumblingstone; *4350*
11: 11 Have they s' that they should fall?*4417*

stumbleth
Pr 24: 17 thine heart be glad when he s': *3782
Joh 11: 9 man walk in the day, he s' not, *4350*
10 if a man walk in the night, he s', "
Ro 14: 21 any thing whereby thy brother s', "

stumbling See also STUMBLINGBLOCK; STUMBLINGSTONE.
Isa 8: 14 for a stone of s' and for a rock of 5063
57: 14 take up the s' block out of the way4383
1Pe 2: 8 And a stone of s', and a rock of *4348*
1Jo 2: 10 there is none occasion of s' in him.*4625*

stumblingblock See also STUMBLINGBLOCKS.
Le 19: 14 deaf, nor put a s' before the blind, 4383
Isa 57: 14 [*in some editions*] s' out of the way "
Eze 3: 20 iniquity, and I lay a s' before him, "
7: 19 because it is the s' of their iniquity. "
14: 3 put the s' of their iniquity before "
4, 7 and putteth the s' of his iniquity "
Ro 11: 9 made a snare, and a trap, and a s',*4625*
14: 13 no man put a s' or an occasion to *4348*
1Co 1: 23 unto the Jews a s', and unto the *4625*
8: 9 become a s' to them that are weak.*4348*
Re 2: 14 to cast a s' before the children of *4625*

stumblingblocks
Jer 6: 21 I will lay s' before this people, 4383
Zep 1: 3 sea, and the s' with the wicked; 4384

stumblingstone
Ro 9: 32 For they stumbled at that s';**3037,4348*
33 I lay in Zion a s' and rock of "

stump
1Sa 5: 4 only the s' of Dagon was left to him.
Da 4: 15 leave the s' of his roots in the 6136
23 yet leave the s' of the roots thereof "
26 to leave the s' of the tree roots; "

Suah (*su'-ah*)
1Ch 7: 36 *S'*, and Harnepher, and Shual, 5477

subdue See also SUBDUED; SUBDUETH.
Ge 1:28 and replenish the earth, and s' it: 3533
1Ch 17:10 Moreover I will s'...thine enemies. 3665
Ps 47: 3 He shall s' the people under us, 1696
Isa 45: 1 holden, to s' nations before him; 7286
Da 7:24 first, and he shall s' three kings. *8214
Mic 7:19 he will s' our iniquities; and thou*3533
Zec 9:15 devour, and s' with sling stones; * "
Ph'p 3:21 to s' all things unto himself. *5293

subdued See also SUBDUEDST.
Nu 32:22 the land be s' before the Lord: 3533
29 and the land shall be s' before you;"
De 20:20 war with thee, until it be s'. *3381
Jos 18: 1 And the land was s' before them. 3533
J'g 3:30 So Moab was s' that day under the3665
4:23 So God s' on that day Jabin the "
8:28 was Midian s' before the children "
11:33 the children of Ammon were s' "
1Sa 7:13 So the Philistines were s', and they "
2Sa 8: 1 smote the Philistines, and s' them: "
11 of all nations which he s'; 3533
22:40 against me hast thou s' under me. 3766
1Ch 18: 1 smote the Philistines, and s' them, 3665
20: 4 of the giant: and they were s'. "
22:18 and the land is s' before the Lord, 3533
Ps 18:39 thou hast s' under me those that 3766
81:14 should soon have s' their enemies,*3665
1Co 15:28 all things shall be s' unto him, *5293
Heb 11:33 Who through faith s' kingdoms, 2610

subduedst
Ne 9:24 and thou s' before them the 3665

subdueth
Ps 18:47 me, and s' the people under me. 1696
144: 2 trust; who s' my people under me.7286
Da 2:40 in pieces and s' all things: and as 2827

subject See also SUBJECTED.
Lu 2:51 Nazareth, and was s' unto them: 5293
10:17 devils are s' unto us through thy "
20 not, that the spirits are s' unto you;"
Ro 8: 7 for it is not s' to the law of God, "
20 the creature was made s' to vanity,*"
13: 1 every soul be s' unto the higher * "
5 Wherefore ye must needs be s', not*"
1Co 14:32 the prophets are s' to the prophets. "
15:28 the Son also himself be s' unto him*"
Eph 5:24 as the church is s' unto Christ, "
Col 2:20 the world, are ye s' to ordinances, 1379
Tit 3: 1 in mind to be s' to principalities *5293
Heb 2:15 all their lifetime s' to bondage. 1777
Jas 5:17 Elias...a man s' to like passions *3663
1Pe 2:18 Servants, be s' to your masters *5293
3:22 powers being made s' unto him. "
5: 5 all of you be s' one to another, and*"

subjected
Ro 8:20 who hath s' the same in hope, 5293

subjection
Ps 106:42 brought into s' under their hand. 3665
Jer 34:11 brought them into s' for servants 3533
16 to return, and brought them into s'."
1Co 9:27 my body, and bring it into s': *1396
2Co 9:13 your professed s' unto the gospel *5292
Ga 2: 5 To whom we gave place by s', no, "
1Ti 2:11 woman learn in silence with all s'. "
3: 4 his children in s' with all gravity; "
Heb 2: 5 not put in s' the world to come, *5293
8 Thou hast put all things in s' under"
8 in that he put all in s' under him,* "
12: 9 rather be in s' unto the Father of "
1Pe 3: 1 be in s' to your own husbands; "
5 in s' unto their own husbands: "

submit See also SUBMITTED; SUBMITTING.
Ge 16: 9 and s' thyself under her hands. 6031
2Sa 22:45 Strangers shall s' themselves unto3584
Ps 18:44 strangers shall s' themselves unto "
66: 3 shall thine enemies s' themselves "
68:30 s' himself with pieces of silver: *7511
1Co 16:16 That ye s' yourselves unto such, *5293
Eph 5:22 Wives, s' yourselves unto your own*"
Col 3:18 Wives, s' yourselves unto your own*"
Heb 13:17 rule over you, and s' yourselves: 5226
Jas 4: 7 S' yourselves therefore to God. *5293
1Pe 2:13 S' yourselves to every ordinance * "
5: 5 s' yourselves unto the elder. * "

submitted
1Ch 29:24 s' themselves unto Solomon 5414,3027
Ps 81:15 should have s' themselves unto *3584
Ro 10: 3 have not s' themselves unto the *5293

submitting
Eph 5:21 S' yourselves one to another in *5293

suborned
Ac 6:11 Then they s' men, which said, 5260

subscribe See also SUBSCRIBED.
Isa 44: 5 s' with his hand unto the Lord, 3789
Jer 32:44 and s' evidences, and seal them, * "

subscribed
Jer 32:10 I s' the evidence, and sealed it, 3789
12 witnesses that s' the book of the "

substance
Ge 7: 4 living s' that I have made will I *3351
23 And every living s' was destroyed "
12: 5 all their s' that they had gathered,7399
13: 6 for their s' was great, so that they "
15:14 shall they come out with great s'. "
34:23 shall not their cattle and their s' 7075
36: 6 all his s', which he had got in the * "
De 11: 6 s' that was in their possession, *3351
33:11 Bless, Lord, his s', and accept the 2428
Jos 14: 4 for their cattle and for their s'. 7075
1Ch 27:31 rulers of the s' which was king 7399
28: 1 the stewards over all the s' and "
2Ch 21:17 away all the s' that was found in 7399
31: 3 portion of his s' for the burnt "
32:29 God had given him s' very much. "
35: 7 these were of the king's s'. "
Ezr 8:21 for our little ones, and for all our s'."
10: 8 elders, all his s' should be forfeited,"
Job 1: 3 His s' also was seven thousand 4735
10 and his s' is increased in the land. "
5: 5 the robber swalloweth up their s'. 2428
6:22 Give a reward for me of your s'? 3581
15:29 rich, neither shall his s' continue, 2428
20:18 according to his s' shall the "
22:20 Whereas our s' is not cut down, *7009
30:22 upon it, and dissolvest my s'. *7738
Ps 17:14 leave the rest of their s' to their babes. "
105:21 his house, and ruler of all his s': 7075
139:15 My s' was not hid from thee, *6108
16 Thine eyes did see my s', yet 1564
Pr 1:13 We shall find all precious s', we 1952
3: 9 Honour the Lord with thy s', and "
6:31 he shall give all the s' of his house. "
8:21 those that love me to inherit s'; 3426
10: 3 casteth away the s' of the wicked.*1942
12:27 the s' of a diligent man is precious.1952
28: 8 and unjust gain increaseth his s', "
29: 3 with harlots spendeth his s'. "
Ca 8: 7 give all the s' of his house for love, "
Isa 6:13 as an oak, whose s' is in them, *4678
13 the holy seed shall be the s' thereof.*"
Jer 15:13 Thy s' and thy treasures will I 2428
17: 3 I will give thy s' and all thy "
Hos 12: 8 rich, I have found me out s': * 202
Ob 13 laid hands on their s' in the day of2428
Mic 4:13 their s' unto the Lord of the whole "
Lu 8: 3 ministered unto him of their s'. 5224
15:13 wasted his s' with riotous living. 3776
Heb 10:34 a better and an enduring s'. *5223
11: 1 faith is the s' of things hoped for, *5287

subtil
Ge 3: 1 the serpent was more s' than any 6175
2Sa 13: 3 and Jonadab was a very s' man. 2450
Pr 7:10 attire of an harlot, and s' of heart.*5341

subtilly
1Sa 23:22 told me that he dealeth very s'. 6191
Ps 105:25 to deal s' with his servants. 5230
Ac 7:19 The same dealt s' with our kindred,2686

subtilty
Ge 27:35 The brother came with s', and *4820
2Ki 10:19 But Jehu did it in s', to the intent 6122
Pr 1: 4 To give s' to the simple, to the 6195
M't 26: 4 that they might take Jesus by s', 1388
Ac 13:10 O full of all s' and all mischief, * "
2Co 11: 3 beguiled Eve through his s', *3834

subtle See SUBTIL.

suburbs
Le 25:34 field of the s' of their cities may 4054
Nu 35: 2 unto the Levites s' for the cities "
3 and the s' of them shall be for their"
4 the s' of the cities, which ye shall "
5 shall be to them the s' of the cities. "
7 them shall ye give with their s'. "
Jos 14: 4 their s' for their cattle and for their"
21: 2 with the s' thereof for our cattle. "
3 the Lord, these cities and their s'. "
8 Levites these cities with their s', "
11 with the s' thereof round about it. "
13 the priest Hebron with her s', "
13 the slayer; and Libnah with her s', "
14 And Jattir with her s', "
14 and Eshtemoa with her s', "
15 And Holon with her s', "
15 and Debir with her s', "
16 And Ain with her s', "
16 and Juttah with her s', "
16 and Beth-shemesh with her s'; "
17 of Benjamin, Gibeon with her s', "
17 Geba with her s', "
18 Anathoth with her s', "
18 and Almon with her s'; four cities. "
19 were thirteen cities with their s'. "
21 gave them Shechem with her s' in "
21 the slayer; and Gezer with her s', "
22 And Kibzaim with her s', "
22 and Beth-horon with her s'; "
23 tribe of Dan, Eltekeh with her s', "
23 Gibbethon with her s', "
24 Aijalon with her s', "
24 Gath-rimmon with her s'; "
25 of Manasseh, Tanach with her s', "
25 and Gath-rimmon with her s'; "
26 All the cities were ten with their s' "
27 gave Golan in Bashan with her s', "
27 and Beesh-terah with her s'; "
28 of Issachar, Kishon with her s', "
28 Dabareh with her s', "
29 Jarmuth with her s', "
29 En-gannim with her s'; four cities. "
30 tribe of Asher, Mishal with her s', "
30 Abdon with her s', "
31 Helkath with her s', "
31 and Rehob with her s'; four cities. "
32 Kedesh in Galilee with her s', "
32 and Hammoth-dor with her s', "
32 and Kartan with her s', "
33 were thirteen cities with their s'. "
34 of Zebulun, Jokneam with her s', "
34 and Kartah with her s', "
35 Dimnah with her s', "
35 Nahalal with her s'; four cities. "
36 tribe of Reuben, Bezer with her s', "
36 and Jahazah with her s', "
37 Kedemoth with her s', "
37 and Mephaath with her s'; "
38 Ramoth in Gilead with her s', 4054
Jos 21:38 slayer; and Mahanaim with her s',4054
39 Heshbon with her s', "
39 Jazer with her s'; four cities in all. "
41 forty and eight cities with their s'. "
42 cities were every one with their s' "
2Ki 23:11 chamberlain, which was in the s',*6503
1Ch 5:16 towns, and in all the s' of Sharon, 4054
6:55 and the s' thereof round about it. "
57 Hebron,...and Libnah with her s', "
57 Jattir, and Eshtemoa, with their s', "
58 And Hilen with her s', "
58 Debir with her s', "
59 And Ashan with her s', "
59 and Beth-shemesh with her s': "
60 of Benjamin; Geba with her s', "
60 and Alemeth with her s', "
60 and Anathoth with her s'. "
64 Levites these cities with their s'. "
67 Shechem...with her s'; "
67 they gave also Gezer with her s', "
68 And Jokmeam with her s', "
68 and Beth-horon with her s', "
69 And Aijalon with her s', "
69 and Gath-rimmon with her s': "
70 of Manasseh; Aner with her s', "
70 and Bileam with her s', "
71 Golan in Bashan with her s', "
71 and Ashtaroth with her s': "
72 of Issachar; Kedesh with her s', "
72 Daberath with her s', "
73 And Ramoth with her s', "
73 and Anem with her s': "
74 tribe of Asher; Mashal with her s', "
74 and Abdon with her s', "
75 And Hukok with her s', "
75 and Rehob with her s': "
76 Kedesh in Galilee with her s', "
76 and Hammon with her s', "
76 and Kirjathaim with her s'. "
77 of Zebulun, Rimmon with her s', "
77 Tabor with her s': "
78 Bezer in the wilderness with her s', "
78 and Jahzah with her s', "
79 Kedemoth also with her s', "
79 and Mephaath with her s': "
80 Ramoth in Gilead with her s', "
80 and Mahanaim with her s', "
81 And Heshbon with her s', "
81 and Jazer with her s'. "
13: 2 which are in their cities and s', "
2Ch 11:14 left their s' and their possession, "
31:19 in the fields of the s' of their cities, "
Eze 27:28 The s' shall shake at the sound of "
45: 2 round about for the s' thereof. "
48:15 for the city, for dwelling, and for s':"
17 the s' of the city shall be toward "

subvert See also SUBVERTED; SUBVERTING.
La 3:36 To s' a man in his cause, the Lord5791
Tit 1:11 who s' whole houses, teaching * 396

subverted
Tit 3:11 Knowing that he that is such is s',*1612

subverting
Ac 15:24 you with words, s' your souls, 384
2Ti 2:14 profit, but to the s' of the hearers. 2692

succeed See also SUCCEEDED; SUCCEEDEST.
De 25: 6 shall s' in the name of his brother 6965

succeeded
De 2:12 but the children of Esau s' them, 3423
21, 22 they s' them, and dwelt in their "

succeedest
De 12:29 and thou s' them, and dwellest in*3423
19: 1 and thou s' them, and dwellest in "

success
Jos 1: 8 and then thou shalt have good s'. 7919

succor See SUCCOUR.

Succoth (*suc'-coth*) See also SUCCOTH-BENOTH.
Ge 33:17 Jacob journeyed to S', and built 5523
17 the name of the place is called S'. "
Ex 12:37 journeyed from Rameses to S', "
13:20 they took their journey from S', "
Nu 33: 5 from Rameses, and pitched in S'. "
6 they departed from S', and pitched"
Jos 13:27 Beth-nimrah, and S', and Zaphon, "
J'g 8: 5 men of S', Give, I pray you, loaves "
6 And the princes of S' said, Are the "
8 as the men of S' had answered him. "
14 a young man of the men of S', "
14 he described...the princes of S', "
15 And he came unto the men of S', "
16 with them he taught the men of S'. "
1Ki 7:46 ground between S' and Zarthan. "
2Ch 4:17 ground between S' and Zeredathah. "
Ps 60: 6 and mete out the valley of S'. "
108: 7 and mete out the valley of S'. "

Succoth-benoth (*suc''-coth-be'-noth*)
2Ki 17:30 And the men of Babylon made S',5524

succour See also SUCCOURED.
2Sa 8: 5 Syrians of Damascus came to s' 5826
18: 3 that thou s' us out of the city. "
Heb 2:18 is able to s' them that are tempted. 997

succoured
2Sa 21:17 Abishai the son of Zeruiah s' him,5826
2Co 6: 2 the day of salvation have I s' thee: *997

succourer
Ro 16: 2 for she hath been a s' of many, 4368

such
Ge 4:20 was the father of s' as dwell in tents,
20 and of s' as have cattle. *
21 the father of all s' as handle the harp
27: 4 make me savoury meat, s' as I love,

Ge 27:46 the daughters of Heth, s· as these
30:32 the goats: and of s· shall be my hire.
41:19 s· as I never saw in all the land of 2007
38 Can we find s· a one as this is, a
44:15 wot ye not that s· a man as I can
Ex 10:14 there were no s· locusts as they, 3651
14 neither after them shall be s·.
12:36 they lent unto them s· things as they*
18:21 s· as fear God, men of truth, hating
21 and place s· over them, to be rulers of
34:10 s· as have not been done in all the
Le 10:19 and s· things have befallen me: 428
11:34 that on which s· water cometh shall*
34 be drunk in every s· vessel shall be
14:22 young pigeons, s· as he is able to get;
30 young pigeons, s· as he can get;
31 Even s· as he is able to get, the one
20: 6 that turneth after s· as have familiar*
22: 6 touched any s· shall be unclean until
27: 9 man giveth of s· unto the Lord shall
Nu 8:16 instead of s· as open every womb,*
De 4:32 hath been any s· thing as this great
5:29 O that there were s· an heart in 2888
13:11 shall do no more any s· wickedness
14 s· abomination is wrought among 2063
16: 9 from s· time as thou beginnest to put*
17: 4 that s· abomination is wrought in 2063
19:20 commit no more any s· evil among
25:16 For all that do s· things, and all 428
J'g 3: 2 s· as before knew nothing thereof;
13:23 have told us s· things as these.
18:23 that thou comest with s· a company?
19:30 was no s· deed done nor seen from2063
Ru 4: 1 Ho, s· a one! turn aside, sit down 6423
1Sa 2:23 unto them, Why do ye s· things? 428
4: 7 not been s· a thing heretofore. 2063
21: 2 servants to s· [6423] and s· a place. 492
25:17 for he is s· a son of Belial, that a man
2Sa 9: 8 look upon s· a dead dog as I am?
12: 8 given unto thee s· and s· things. 2007
13:12 no s· thing ought to be done in 3651
18 for with s· robes were the king's "
14:13 then hast thou thought s· a thing 2063
16: 2 that s· as be faint in the wilderness
19:36 recompense...with s· a reward? 2063
1Ki 10:10 no more s· abundance of spices 1931
12 there came no s· almug trees, nor 3651
2Ki 6: 8 In s·... a place shall be my camp. 6423
8 and s· a place shall be my camp. 492
9 Beware...thou pass not s· a place; 2088
7:19 in heaven, might s· a thing be?
19:29 year s· things as grow of themselves,*
21:12 I am bringing s· evil upon Jerusalem
23:22 there was not holden s· a passover 2088
25:15 bowls, and s· things as were of gold,*
1Ch 12:33, 36 s· as went forth to battle, expert in
29:25 bestowed upon him s· royal majesty
2Ch 1:12 s· as none of the kings have had 834
4: 6 s· things as they offered for the burnt
9: 9 s· spice as the queen of Sheba gave1932
11 there were none s· seen before in 1992
11:16 s· as set their hearts to seek the Lord
23:13 and s· as taught to sing praise. *
24:12 Jehoiada gave it to s· as did the work
12 and also s· as wrought iron and brass
30: 5 long time in s· sort as it was written.
35:18 keep s· a passover as Josiah kept,
Ezr 4:10, 11 side the river, and at s· a time.*3706
17 the river, Peace, and at s· a time.* "
6:21 all s· as had separated themselves
7:12 perfect peace, and at s· a time. *3706
25 all s· as know the laws of thy God;
27 put s· a thing as this in the king's
8:31 and of s· as lay in wait by the way.*
9:13 hast given us s· deliverance as this;
10: 3 the wives, and s· as are born of them,
Ne 6: 8 are no s· things done as thou sayest,428
11 I said, Should s· a man as I flee? 3644
Es 2: 9 with s· things as belonged to her, and*
4:11 s· to whom the king shall hold out 834
14 the kingdom for s· a time as this?
9: 2 lay hand on s· as sought their hurt:
27 upon all s· as joined themselves unto
Job 12: 3 knoweth not s· things as these? 3644
14: 3 open thine eyes upon s· an one, 2088
15:13 lettest s· words go out of thy mouth?
16: 2 I have heard many s· things: 428
18:21 s· are the dwellings of the wicked, "
23:14 and many s· things are with him. 2007
Ps 25:10 and truth unto s· as keep his covenant
27:12 me, and s· as breathe out cruelty.
34:18 saveth s· as be of a contrite spirit.
37:14 slay s· as be of upright conversation.
22 s· as be blessed of him shall inherit
40: 4 proud, nor s· as turn aside to lies.
16 let s· as love thy salvation say
50:21 I was altogether s· an one as thyself:
55:20 against s· as be at peace with him:
68:21 scalp of s· an one as goeth on still
70: 4 let s· as love thy salvation say
73: 1 even to s· as are of a clean heart.
103:18 To s· as keep his covenant, and to
107:10 S· as sit in darkness and in the
125: 5 for s· as turn aside unto their crooked
139: 6 S· knowledge is too wonderful for me;
144:15 is that people, that is in s· a case: 3602
Pr 11:20 s· as are upright in their way are his
28: 4 s· as keep the law contend with them.
30:20 S· is the way of an adulterous *3651
31: 8 all s· as are appointed to destruction.
Ec 4: 1 the tears of s· as were oppressed,
Isa 9: 1 dimness shall not be s· as was in her*
10:20 s· as are escaped of the house of *
20: 6 Behold, s· is our expectation, 3541
37:30 eat this year s· as groweth of itself;*
58: 5 Is it s· a fast that I have chosen? 2088

Isa 66: 8 Who hath heard s· a thing? 2063
8 who hath seen s· things? 428
Jer 2:10 and see if there be s· a thing. 2063
5: 9, 29 avenged on s· a nation as this? 834
9: 9 soul be avenged on s· a nation as "
15: 2 Lord; S· as are for death, to death;
2 and s· as for the sword, to the sword;
2 and s· as are for the famine, to the
2 and s· as are for the captivity, to the
18:13 heathen, who hath heard s· things:428
21: 7 and s· as are left in this city from the
38: 4 in speaking s· words unto them: 428
43:11 deliver s· as are for death to death;
11 and s· as are for captivity to captivity;
11 s· as are for the sword to the sword.
44:14 shall return but s· as shall escape.
Eze 17:15 he escape that doeth s· things? 428
18:14 considereth, and doeth not s· like,2007
Da 1: 4 s· as had ability in them to stand in
2:10 asked s· things at any magician, 1836
10:15 he had spoken s· words unto me, * 428
11:32 And s· as do wickedly against the
12: 1 trouble, s· as never was since there 834
Am 5:16 and s· as are skilful of lamentation to
Mic 5:15 heathen, s· as they have not heard.*
Zep 1: 8 and all s· as are clothed with strange
M't 9: 8 had given s· power unto men. 5108
18: 5 shall receive one s· little child in my "
19:14 for of s· is the kingdom of heaven. "
24:21 s· as was not since the beginning 3634
44 in s· an hour as ye think not the Son*
26:18 Go into the city to s· a man, and 1170
M'r 4:18 thorns; s· as hear the word, *3778
20 s· as hear the word, and receive it,3748
33 with many s· parables spake he 5108
6: 2 even s· mighty works are wrought "
7: 8 many other s· like things ye do. * "
13 and many s· like things do ye. "
9:37 receive one of s· children in my "
10:14 not; for of s· is the kingdom of God. "
13: 7 for s· things must needs be; but the*
19 s· as was not from the beginning 3634
Lu 9: 9 is this, of whom I hear s· things?
10: 7 and drinking s· things as they give:
8 eat s· things as are set before you:
11:41 give alms of s· things as ye have; *
13: 2 because they suffered s· things? *5108
18:16 not: for of s· is the kingdom of God. "
Joh 4:23 Father seeketh s· to worship him. "
7:32 the people murmured s· things *5023
8: 5 us, that s· should be stoned: 5108
9:16 man that is a sinner do s· miracles? "
Ac 2:47 church daily s· as should be saved.*
3: 6 I none; but s· as I have give I thee:*
15:24 whom we gave no s· commandment:*
16:24 Who, having received s· a charge, 5108
18:15 I will be no judge of s· matters. *5130
21:25 that they observe no s· thing, *5108
22:22 with s· a fellow from the earth:
25:18 accusation of s· things as I supposed:
20 I doubted of s· manner of questions,*
26:29 and altogether s· as I am, except 5108
28:10 they laded us with s· things as were
Ro 1:32 s· things are worthy of death, 5108
2: 2 them which commit s· things. "
3 judgest them which do s· things, "
16:18 they that are s· serve not our Lord "
1Co 5: 1 s· fornication as is not so much as "
5 To deliver s· an one unto Satan for "
11 with s· an one no not to eat. "
6:11 And s· were some of you: but ye 5023
7:15 is not under bondage in s· cases: 5108
28 s· shall have trouble in the flesh: "
10:13 taken you but s· as is common to man:
11:16 we have no s· custom, neither the 5108
15:48 s· are they also that are earthy: "
48 s· are they also that are heavenly. "
16:16 that ye submit yourselves unto s·, "
18 acknowledge ye them that are s·. "
2Co 2: 6 Sufficient to s· a man is this "
7 s· a one should be swallowed up "
3: 4 s· trust have we through Christ "
12 Seeing then that we have s· hope, "
10:11 Let s· an one think this, that, 3634
11 s· as we are in word by letters *5108
11 s· will we be also in deed when we "
11:13 For s· are false apostles, deceitful "
12: 2 s· an one caught up to the third "
3 And I knew s· a man, (whether in "
5 Of s· an one will I glory: yet of "
20 I shall not find you s· as I would, 3634
20 found unto you s· as ye would not: "
Ga 5:21 revellings, and s· like: 5125
21 which do s· things shall not inherit5108
23 against s· there is no law. "
6: 1 restore s· an one in the spirit of "
Eph 5:27 spot, or wrinkle, or any s· thing; "
Ph'p 2:29 gladness; and hold s· in reputation: "
1Th 4: 6 the Lord is the avenger of all s·, *5130
2Th 3:12 them that are s· we command and 5108
1Ti 6: 5 godliness: from s· withdraw thyself.*
2Ti 3: 5 power thereof: from s· turn away.*5128
Tit 3:11 that he that is s· is subverted, and 5108
Ph'm 9 being s· an one as Paul the aged,
Heb 5:12 are become s· as have need of milk,
7:26 s· an high priest became us, who 5108
8: 1 We have s· an high priest, who is "
11:14 For they that say s· things declare "
12: 3 him that endured s· contradiction "
13: 5 content with s· things as ye have: 3588
16 s· sacrifices God is well pleased. 5108
Jas 4:13 to morrow we will go into s· a city,*3592
16 boastings: all s· rejoicing is evil. 5108
2Pe 1:17 there came s· a voice to him from 5107
3:14 seeing that ye look for s· things, *5023
3Jo 8 We therefore ought to receive s·, 5108

Re 5:13 and s· as are in the sea, and all that*
16:18 s· as was not since men were upon 3634
20: 6 on s· the second death hath no *5130

Suchathites (*soo'-kath-ites*)
1Ch 2:55 the Shimeathites, and S·. 7756

suck See also SUCKED; SUCKING.
Ge 21: 7 should have given children s·? 3243
De 32:13 him to s· honey out of the rock, "
33:19 s· of the abundance of the seas, "
1Sa 1:23 gave her son s· until she weaned "
1Ki 3:21 in the morning to give my child s·, "
Job 3:12 why the breasts that I should s·? "
20:16 He shall s· the poison of asps: "
39:30 Her young ones also s· up blood: 5966
Isa 60:16 also s· the milk of the Gentiles, 3243
16 and shalt s· the breast of kings: "
66:11 That ye may s·, and be satisfied "
12 then shall ye s·, ye shall be borne "
La 4: 3 they give s· to their young ones: "
Eze 23:34 shalt even drink it and s· it out, *4680
Joe 2:16 and those that s· the breasts: 3243
M't 24:19 and to them that give s· in those 2337
M'r 13:17 to them that give s· in those days! "
Lu 21:23 to them that give s·, in those days! "
23:29 and the paps which never gave s·. "

sucked
Ca 8: 1 that s· the breasts of my mother! 3243
Lu 11:27 and the paps which thou hast s·. *2337

sucking
Nu 11:12 nursing father beareth the s· child,3243
1Sa 7: 9 Samuel took a s· lamb, and offered2461
Isa 11: 8 the s· child shall play on the hole 3243
49:15 Can a woman forget her s· child, 5764
La 4: 4 The tongue of the s· child cleaveth3243

suckling See also SUCKLINGS.
De 32:25 the s· also with the man of gray 3243
1Sa 15: 3 infant and s·, ox and sheep, camel "
Jer 44: 7 you man and woman, child and s·, "

sucklings
1Sa 22:19 men and women, children and s·, 3243
Ps 8: 2 Out of the mouth of babes and s· "
La 2:11 and the s· swoon in the streets "
M't 21:16 Out of the mouth of babes and s· 2337

sudden
Job 22:10 thee, and s· fear troubleth thee; 6597
Pr 3:25 Be not afraid of s· fear, neither of "
1Th 5: 3 then s· destruction cometh upon 160

suddenly
Nu 6: 9 if any man die very s· by him, 6597
12: 4 And the Lord spake s· unto Moses, "
35:22 if he thrust him s· without enmity,6621
De 7: 4 against you, and destroy thee s·. *4118
Jos 10: 9 therefore came unto them s·, and 6597
11: 7 them by the waters of Merom s·; "
2Sa 15:14 lest he overtake us s·, and bring *4116
2Ch 29:36 people: for the thing was done s·.6597
Job 5: 3 root: but s· I cursed his habitation."
9:23 If the scourge slay s·, he will laugh "
Ps 6:10 them return and be ashamed s·. 7281
64: 4 s· do they shoot at him, and fear 6597
7 arrow; s· shall they be wounded. "
Pr 6:15 shall his calamity come s·; "
15 s· shall he be broken without *6621
24:22 For their calamity shall rise s·; 6597
29: 1 shall s· be destroyed, and that 6621
Ec 9:12 time, when it falleth s· upon them.6597
Isa 29: 5 yea, it shall be at an instant s·. "
30:13 breaking cometh s· at an instant. "
47:11 desolation shall come upon thee s·, "
48: 3 them; I did them s·, and they came "
Jer 4:20 s· are my tents spoiled, and my "
6:26 the spoiler shall s· come upon us. "
15: 8 I have caused him to fall upon it s·, "
18:22 shalt bring a troop s· upon them: "
49:19 s· make him run away from her: 7280
50:44 make them s· run away from her: "
51: 8 Babylon is s· fallen and destroyed:6597
Hab 2: 7 Shall they not rise up s· that shall 6621
Mal 3: 1 seek, shall s· come to his temple, 6597
M'r 9: 8 s·, when they had looked round 1819
13:36 coming s· he find you sleeping. 1810
Lu 2:13 And s· there was with the angel a "
9:39 taketh him, and he s· crieth out; "
Ac 2: 2 s· there came a sound from heaven 869
9: 3 s· there shined round about him a 1810
16:26 s· there was a great earthquake, 869
22: 6 s· there shone from heaven a great1810
28: 6 swollen, or fallen down dead s·: 869
1Ti 5:22 Lay hands s· on no man, neither *5030

sue
M't 5:40 If any man will s· thee at the law,*2919

suffer See also SUFFERED; SUFFEREST; SUFFERETH; SUFFERING.
Ex 12:23 will not s· the destroyer to come 5414
22:18 Thou shalt not s· a witch to live.
Le 2:13 shalt thou s· the salt...to be lacking
19:17 neighbour,...not s· sin upon him. *5375
22:16 Or s· them to bear the iniquity of * "
Nu 21:23 Sihon would not s· Israel to pass 5414
Jos 10:19 s· them not to enter into their cities: "
J'g 1:34 would not s· them to come down to "
15: 1 father would not s· him to go in. "
16:26 S· me that I may feel the pillars 3240
2Sa 14:11 not s· the revengers of blood to *
1Ki 15:17 that he might not s· any to go out 5414
Es 3: 8 not for the king's profit to s· them.3240
Job 9:18 will not s· me to take my breath, 5414
21: 3 S· me that I may speak; and after 5375
24:11 tread their winepresses, and s· thirst.
36: 2 S· me a little, and I will shew thee 3803
Ps 9:13 consider my trouble which I s· of them
16:10 wilt thou s· thine Holy One to see 5414

Ps 34:10 young lions do lack, and s' hunger:
55:22 he shall never s' the righteous to 5414
88:15 I s' thy terrors I am distracted. 5375
89:33 from him, nor s' my faithfulness to fail.
101: 5 and a proud heart will not I s'. 3201
121: 3 will not s' thy foot to be moved: 5414
Pr 10: 3 will not s' the...righteous to famish:
19:15 sleep; and an idle soul shall s' hunger.
19 great wrath shall s' punishment: 5375
Ec 5: 6 S' not thy mouth to cause thy flesh5414
12 the rich will not s' him to sleep. 3240
Eze 44:20 heads, nor s' their locks to grow long;
M't 3:15 said unto him, S' it to be so now: 863
8:21 s' me first to go and bury my 2010
31 s' us to go away into the herd of * "
16:21 s' many things of the elders and 3958
17:12 also the Son of man s' of them. "
17 with you? how long shall I s' you?*430
19:14 S' little children, and forbid them 863
23:13 neither s' ye them that are entering "
M'r 7:12 ye s' him no more to do ought for "
8:31 Son of man must s' many things, 3958
9:12 man, that he must s' many things, "
19 with you? how long shall I s' you?*430
10:14 S' the little children to come unto 863
11:16 would not s' that any man should "
Lu 8:32 would s' them to enter into them.*2010
9:22 Son of man must s' many things, 3958
41 shall I be with you, and s' you? * 430
59 Lord, s' me first to go and bury my2010
17:25 But first must he s' many things, 3958
18:16 S' little children to come unto me, 863
22:15 this passover with you before I s': 3958
51 answered and said, S' ye thus far. 1439
24:46 and thus it behoved Christ to s', 3958
Ac 2:27 wilt thou s' thine Holy One to see*1325
3:18 prophets, that Christ should s', 3958
5:41 counted worthy to s' shame for his 818
7:24 seeing one of them s' wrong, he
9:16 him how great things he must s' 3958
13:35 shalt not s' thine Holy One to see *1325
21:39 s' me to speak unto the people. *2010
26:23 That Christ should s', and that he 3805
Ro 8:17 If so be that we s' with him, that 4841
1Co 3:15 shall be burned, he shall s' loss: 2210
4:12 bless; being persecuted, we s' it: * 430
6: 7 rather s' yourselves to be defrauded?*
9:12 but s' all things, lest we should *4722
10:13 will not s' you to be tempted above1439
12:26 whether one member s', all the *3958
26 all the members s' with it; or one 4841
2Co 1: 6 same sufferings which we also s': 3958
11:19 For ye s' fools gladly, seeing ye * 430
20 For ye s', if a man bring you into * "
Ga 5:11 why do I yet s' persecution? then*1377
6:12 should s' persecution for the cross* "
Ph'p 1:29 on him, but also to s' for his sake; 3958
4:12 both to abound and to s' need. *5302
1Th 3: 4 before that we should s' tribulation;
2Th 1: 5 kingdom of God, for which ye also s':
1Ti 2:12 I s' not a woman to teach, nor to *2010
4:10 we both labour and s' reproach, *
2Ti 1:12 which cause I also s' these things: 3958
2: 9 Wherein I s' trouble, as an evil doer,2553
12 If we s', we shall also reign with *5278
3:12 Christ Jesus shall s' persecution. 1377
Heb 11:25 Choosing rather to s' affliction *4778
13: 3 and them which s' adversity, as *2558
22 s' the word of exhortation: for * 430
1Pe 2:20 when ye do well, and s' for it, ye 3958
3:14 if ye s' for righteousness' sake, "
17 that ye s' for well doing, than for "
4:15 let none of you s' as a murderer, or "
16 if any man s' as a Christian, let him
19 let them that s' according to the 3958
Re 2:10 of those things which thou shalt s': "
11: 9 not s' their dead bodies to be put in 863

suffered
Ge 20: 6 s' I thee not to touch her. 5414
31: 7 but God s' him not to hurt me. "
28 not s' me to kiss my sons and my 5203
De 8: 3 and s' thee to hunger, and fed thee
18:14 thy God hath not s' thee so to do. 5414
J'g 3:28 Moab, and s' not a man to pass over."
1Sa 24: 7 and s' them not to rise against Saul."
2Sa 21:10 and s' neither the birds of the air "
1Ch 16:21 He s' no man to do them wrong: 3240
Job 31:30 Neither have I s' my mouth to sin 5414
Ps 105:14 He s' no man to do them wrong: 3240
Jer 15:15 that for thy sake I have s' rebuke.5375
M't 3:15 all righteousness. Then he s' him.*863
19: 8 s' you to put away your wives: 2010
24:43 have s' his house to be broken up. 1439
27:19 for I have s' many things this day 3958
M'r 1:34 and s' not the devils to speak, 863
5:19 Howbeit Jesus s' him not, but saith "
26 s' many things of many physicians,3958
37 And he s' no man to follow him, 863
10: 4 s' to write a bill of divorcement, 2010
Lu 4:41 rebuking...s' them not to speak: 1439
8:32 enter into them. And he s' them.*2010
51 he s' no man to go in, save Peter, 863
12:39 s' his house to be broken through. * "
13: 2 because they s' such things? 3958
24:26 not Christ to have s' these things,* "
Ac 13:18 s' he their manners in the ‡5159
14:16 s' all nations to walk in their own 1439
16: 7 but the Spirit s' them not. "
17: 3 that Christ must needs have s', *3958
19:30 people, the disciples s' him not. 1439
28:16 Paul was s' to dwell by himself 2010
2Co 7:12 nor for his cause that s' wrong, but
11:25 was I stoned, thrice I s' shipwreck,
Ga 3: 4 Have ye s' so many things in vain?*3958
Ph'p 3: 8 I have s' the loss of all things, 2210
1Th 2: 2 even after that we had s' before, 4310
1Th 2:14 s' like things of your...countrymen,3958
Heb 2:18 he himself hath s' being tempted, "
5: 8 he obedience by the things...he s'; "
7:23 were not s' to continue by reason *2967
9:26 For then must he often have s' 3958
13:12 his own blood, s' without the gate. "
1Pe 2:21 because Christ also s' for us, "
23 when he s', he threatened not; but "
3:18 Christ also hath once s' for sins, "
4: 1 as Christ hath s' for us in the flesh "
1 for he that hath s' in the flesh hath "
5:10 after that ye have s' a while, make "

sufferest
Re 2:20 thou s' that woman Jezebel, 1439

suffereth
Ps 66: 9 and s' not our feet to be moved. 5414
107:38 and s' not their cattle to decrease.
M't 11:12 the kingdom of heaven s' violence, 971
Ac 28: 4 sea, yet vengeance s' not to live. *1439
1Co 13: 4 Charity s' long, and is kind; 3114

suffering See also LONGSUFFERING; SUFFERINGS.
Ac 27: 7 the wind not s' us, we sailed under4330
Heb 2: 9 than the angels for the s' of death,3804
Jas 5:10 for an example of s' affliction, 2552
1Pe 2:19 God endure grief, s' wrongfully. 3958
Jude 7 s' the vengeance of eternal fire. 5254

sufferings
Ro 8:18 I reckon that the s' of this present3804
2Co 1: 5 as the s' of Christ abound in us, "
6 enduring of the same s' which we "
7 that as ye are partakers of the s', "
Ph'p 3:10 and the fellowship of his s', "
Col 1:24 Who now rejoice in my s' for you, "
Heb 2:10 their salvation perfect through s'. "
1Pe 1:11 testified beforehand the s' of Christ,"
4:13 as ye are partakers of Christ's s'; "
5: 1 and a witness of the s' of Christ, "

suffice See also SUFFICED; SUFFICETH.
Nu 11:22 herds be slain for them, to s' them?4672
22 gathered...for them, to s' them? "
De 3:26 Lord said unto me, Let it s' thee; 7227
1Ki 20:10 dust of Samaria...s' for handfuls 5606
Eze 44: 6 it s' you of all your abominations, 7227
45: 9 Let it s' you, O princes of Israel: "
1Pe 4: 3 the time past of our life may s' us 713

sufficed
J'g 21:14 and yet so they s' them not. 4672
Ru 2:14 corn, and she did eat, and was s', 7646
18 she had reserved after she was s'. 7648

sufficeth
Joh 14: 8 shew us the Father, and it s' us. 714

sufficiency
Job 20:22 In the fulness of his s' he shall be 5607
2Co 3: 5 of ourselves; but our s' is of God; 2426
9: 8 always having all s' in all things, 841

sufficient
Ex 36: 7 stuff they had was s' for all the 1767
De 15: 8 surely lend him s' for his need, "
33: 7 let his hands be s' for him; and *7227
Pr 25:16 eat so much as is s' for thee, lest 1767
Isa 40:16 And Lebanon is not s' to burn, nor "
16 the beasts thereof s' for a burnt "
M't 6:34 S' unto the day is the evil thereof. 713
Lu 14:28 cost, whether he have s' to finish it?*
Joh 6: 7 pennyworth of bread is not s' for 714
2Co 2: 6 S' to such...is this punishment, 2425
16 And who is s' for these things? "
3: 5 Not that we are s' of ourselves to "
12: 9 unto me, My grace is s' for thee: 714

sufficiently
2Ch 30: 3 had not sanctified themselves s', *4078
Isa 23:18 eat s', and for durable clothing. 7654

suit See also SUITS.
J'g 17:10 a s' of apparel, and thy victuals. 6187
2Sa 15: 4 that every man which has any s' 7379
Job 11:19 many shall make s' unto thee. 2470

suits
Isa 3:22 The changeable s' of apparel, and the*

Sukkiims (*suk'-ke-ims*)
2Ch 12: 3 the Lubims, the S', and the *5525

sum
Ex 21:30 be laid on him a s' of money, *3724
30:12 takest the s' of the children of 7218
38:21 This is the s' of the tabernacle, 6485
Nu 1: 2 Take ye the s' of the congregation7218
49 Levi, neither take the s' of them "
4: 2 Take the s' of the sons of Kohath "
22 Take...the s' of the sons of Gershon,"
26: 2 Take the s' of all the congregation "
4 Take the s' of the people, from twenty
31:26 Take the s' of the prey that was 7218
49 have taken the s' of the men of war"
2Sa 24: 9 the s' of the number of the people 4557
2Ki 22: 4 that he may s' the silver which is 8552
1Ch 21: 5 the s' of the number of the people 4557
Es 4: 7 the s' of the money that Haman 6575
Ps 139:17 God! how great is the s' of them! 7218
Eze 28:12 Thou sealest up the s', full of 8508
Da 7: 1 and told the s' of the matters. 7217
Ac 7:16 Abraham bought for a s' of money*5092
22:28 a great s' obtained I this freedom.2774
Heb 8: 1 we have spoken this is the s': * "

summer
Ge 8:22 cold and heat, and s' and winter, 7019
J'g 3:20 and he was sitting in a s' parlour,‡4747
24 covereth his feet in his s' chamber.‡"
2Sa 16: 1 and an hundred of s' fruits, and a 7019
2 s' fruit for the young men to eat; "
Ps 32: 4 is turned into the drought of s'. "
Ps 74:17 thou hast made s' and winter. 7019
Pr 6: 8 Provideth her meat in the s', and "
10: 5 that gathereth in s' is a wise son: "
26: 1 As snow in s', and as rain in "
30:25 they prepare their meat in the s'; "
Isa 16: 9 for the shouting for thy s' fruits "
18: 6 and the fowls shall s' upon them, 6972
28: 4 as the hasty fruit before the s'; 7019
Jer 8:20 The harvest is past, the s' is ended,"
40:10 gather ye wine, and s' fruits, and "
12 gathered wine and s' fruits very "
48:32 spoiler is fallen upon thy s' fruits "
Da 2:35 the chaff of the s' threshingfloors;7007
Am 3:15 winter house with the s' house; 7019
8: 1 me: and behold a basket of s' fruit. "
2 And I said, A basket of s' fruit. "
Mic 7: 1 they have gathered the s' fruits, "
Zec 14: 8 sea: in s' and in winter shall it be. "
M't 24:32 leaves, ye know that s' is nigh: 2330
M'r 13:28 leaves, ye know that s' is near: "
Lu 21:30 selves that s' is now nigh at hand. "

sumptuously See also PRESUMPTUOUSLY.
Lu 16:19 fine linen, and fared s' every day: 2988

sun See also SUNRISING.
Ge 15:12 And when the s' was going down, 8121
17 when the s' went down, and it was "
19:23 The s' was risen upon the earth "
28:11 all night, because the s' was set; "
32:31 as he passed over Penuel the s' rose"
37: 9 the s' and the moon and the eleven "
Ex 16:21 when the s' waxed hot, it melted. "
17:12 until the going down of the s'. "
22: 3 If the s' be risen upon him, there "
26 unto him by that the s' goeth down:"
Le 22: 7 And when the s' is down, he shall be"
Nu 2: 3 toward the rising of the s' shall they*
25: 4 up before the Lord against the s', 8121
De 4:19 and when thou seest the s', and the"
11:30 the way where the s' goeth down, "
16: 6 at the going down of the s', at the "
17: 3 either the s', or moon, or any of the"
23:11 when the s' is down, he shall come "
24:13 again when the s' goeth down, "
15 neither shall the s' go down upon it;"
33:14 fruits brought forth by the s', "
Jos 1: 4 sea toward the going down of the s',"
8:29 and as soon as the s' was down, "
10:12 S', stand thou still upon Gibeon; "
13 And the s' stood still, and the moon "
13 s' stood still in the midst of heaven,"
27 the time of the going down of the s',"
12: 1 Jordan toward the rising of the s',* "
J'g 5:31 as the s' when he goeth forth in his "
8:13 from battle before the s' was up, *2775
9:33 as soon as the s' is up, thou shalt 8121
14:18 day before the s' went down, 2775
19:14 and the s' went down upon them 8121
1Sa 11: 9 by that time the s' be hot, ye shall "
2Sa 2:24 the s' went down when they were "
3:35 or ought else, till the s' be down. "
12:11 with thy wives in the sight of this s'."
12 before all Israel, and before the s'. "
23: 4 of the morning, when the s' riseth, "
1Ki 22:36 host about the going down of the s',"
2Ki 3:22 and the s' shone upon the water, "
23: 5 burned incense unto Baal, to the s',"
11 kings of Judah had given to the s', "
11 and burned the chariots of the s' "
2Ch 18:34 time of the s' going down he died. "
Ne 7: 3 be opened until the s' be hot; "
Job 8:16 He is green before the s', and his "
9: 7 Which commandeth the s', and it 2775
30:28 I went mourning without the s': 2535
31:26 If I beheld the s' when it shined, 216
Ps 19: 4 hath he set a tabernacle for the s',8121
50: 1 the earth from the rising of the s' "
58: 8 that they may not see the s'. "
72: 5 as long as the s' and moon endure, "
17 be continued as long as the s': "
74:16 hast prepared the light and the s'. "
84:11 For the Lord God is a s' and shield:"
89:36 and his throne as the s' before me. "
104:19 the s' knoweth his going down. "
22 The s' ariseth, they gather "
113: 3 From the rising of the s' unto the "
121: 6 The s' shall not smite thee by day, "
136: 8 The s' to rule by day: for his mercy"
148: 3 Praise ye him, s' and moon: praise "
Ec 1: 3 labour...he taketh under the s'? "
5 The s' also ariseth, and the s' goeth "
9 there is no new thing under the s'. "
14 works that are done under the s'; "
2:11 and there was no profit under the s'."
17 work that is wrought under the s': "
18 labour...I had taken under the s': "
19 shewed myself wise under the s'. "
20 labour which I took under the s'. "
22 he hath laboured under the s'? "
3:16 under the s' the place of judgment,"
4: 1 the oppressions...done under the s':"
3 evil work that is done under the s'. "
7 and I saw vanity under the s'. "
15 the living which walk under the s'. "
5:13 sore evil...I have seen under the s', "
18 labour that he taketh under the s' "
6: 1 evil which I have seen under the s', "
5 Moreover he hath not seen the s', "
12 shall be after him under the s'? "
7:11 is profit to them that see the s'. "
8: 9 work that is done under the s': "
15 hath no better thing under the s', "
15 which God giveth him under the s'. "
17 the work that is done under the s': "
9: 3 things that are done under the s', "
6 any thing that is done under the s'."

Ec 9: 9 he hath given thee under the s'. 8121
9 labour...thou takest under the s'. "
11 I returned, and saw under the s', "
13 wisdom have I seen...under the s', "
10: 5 evil which I have seen under the s', "
11: 7 it is for the eyes to behold the s': "
12: 2 While the s', or the light, or the "
Ca 1: 6 because the s' hath looked upon me: "
6: 10 fair as the moon, clear as the s', 2535
Isa 13: 10 s' shall be darkened in his going 8121
24: 23 confounded, and the s' ashamed, 2535
30: 26 moon shall be as the light of the s', "
26 light of the s' shall be sevenfold, 8121
38: 8 is gone down in the s' dial of Ahaz, "
8 So the s' returned ten degrees, by "
41: 25 from the rising of the s' shall he "
45: 6 may know from the rising of the s', "
49: 10 shall the heat nor s' smite them: "
59: 19 his glory from the rising of the s'. "
60: 19 The s' shall be no more thy light by "
20 Thy s' shall no more go down; "
Jer 8: 2 they shall spread them before the s', "
15: 9 her s' is gone down while it was yet "
31: 35 giveth the s' for a light by day, "
Eze 8: 16 they worshipped the s' toward the "
32: 7 I will cover the s' with a cloud, and "
Da 6: 14 laboured till...going down of the s' 8122
Joel 2: 10 the s' and the moon shall be dark, 8121
31 s' shall be turned into darkness, "
3: 15 s' and the moon shall be darkened, "
Am 8: 9 cause the s' to go down at noon, "
Jon 4: 8 came to pass, when the s' did arise, "
8 the s' beat upon the head of Jonah, "
Mic 3: 6 and the s' shall go down over the "
Na 3: 17 when the s' ariseth they flee away, "
Hab 3: 11 The s' and moon stood still in their "
Mal 1: 11 from the rising of the s' even unto "
4: 2 the S' of righteousness arise with "
M't 5: 45 for he maketh his s' to rise on the 2246
13: 6 And when the s' was up, they were "
43 the righteous shine forth as the s' "
17: 2 his face did shine as the s', and his "
24: 29 days shall the s' be darkened, "
M'r 1: 32 when the s' did set, they brought "
4: 6 But when the s' was up, it was "
13: 24 the s' shall be darkened, and the "
16: 2 the sepulchre at the rising of the s'. "
Lu 4: 40 Now when the s' was setting, all they "
21: 25 And there shall be signs in the s', "
23: 45 And the s' was darkened, and the* "
Ac 2: 20 s' shall be turned into darkness, "
13: 11 blind, not seeing the s' for a season. "
26: 13 above the brightness of the s', "
27: 20 when neither s' nor stars in many "
1Co 15: 41 There is one glory of the s', and "
Eph 4: 26 not the s' go down upon your wrath: "
Jas 1: 11 For the s' is no sooner risen with a "
Re 1: 16 as the s' shineth in his strength. "
6: 12 the s' became black as sackcloth of "
7: 16 neither shall the s' light on them, "
8: 12 the third part of the s' was smitten, "
9: 2 the s' and the air were darkened by "
10: 1 and his face was as it were the s', "
12: 1 a woman clothed with the s', and "
16: 8 poured out his vial upon the s'; "
19: 17 I saw an angel standing in the s'; "
21: 23 And the city had no need of the s', "
22: 5 no candle, neither light of the s'; "

sunder See also ASUNDER; SUNDERED.
Ps 46: 9 bow, and cutteth the spear in s'; "
107: 14 death, and break their bands in s'. "
16 of brass, and cut the bars of iron in s'. "
Isa 27: 9 as chalkstones that are beaten in s', "
Na 1: 13 thee, and will burst thy bonds in s'. "
Lu 12: 46 he is not aware, and will cut him in s',*

sundered
Job 41: 17 together, that they cannot be s'. 6504

sundry
Heb 1: 1 at s' times and in divers manners*4181

sung See also SANG.
Isa 26: 1 In that day shall this song be s' in 7891
M't 26: 30 when they had s' an hymn, they 5214
M'r 14: 26 when they had s' an hymn, they "
Re 5: 9 they s' a new song, saying, Thou * 103
14: 3 s' as it were a new song before the* "

sunk See also SANK.
1Sa 17: 49 the stone s' into his forehead; *2883
2Ki 9: 24 and he s' down in his chariot. 3766
Ps 9: 15 heathen are s' down in the pit 2883
Jer 38: 6 mire: so Jeremiah s' in the mire.* "
22 thy feet are s' in the mire, and they "
La 2: 9 Her gates are s' into the ground; "
Ac 20: 9 preaching, he s' down with sleep,*2702

sunrising
Nu 21: 11 is before Moab, toward the s'.4217,8121
34: 15 Jericho eastward, toward the s'. 4217
De 4: 41, 47 side Jordan toward the s';4217,8121
Jos 1: 15 this side Jordan toward the s'. " "
13: 5 and all Lebanon, toward the s', " "
19: 12 Sarid eastward toward the s' " "
27 And turneth toward the s' to " "
34 upon Jordan toward the s'. " "
J'g 20: 43 against Gibeah toward the s'. " "

sup See also SUPPED.
Hab 1: 9 faces shall s' up as the east wind,*4041
Lu 17: 8 Make ready wherewith I may s', 1172
Re 3: 20 in to him, and will s' with him, "

superfluity
Jas 1: 21 filthiness and s' of naughtiness, *4050

superfluous
Le 21: 18 hath a flat nose, or any thing s', 8311
22: 23 any thing s' or lacking in his parts, "
2Co 9: 1 it is s' for me to write to you: 4053

superscription
M't 22: 20 them, Whose is this image and s'? 1923
M'r 12: 16 them, Whose is this image and s'? "
15: 26 the s' of his accusation was written "
Lu 20: 24 Whose image and s' hath it? They "
23: 38 And a s' also was written over him "

superstition
Ac 25: 19 against him of their own s', and *1175

superstitious
Ac 17: 22 that in all things ye are too s'. ‡1174

supped
1Co 11: 25 he took the cup, when he had s', *1172

supper
M'r 6: 21 birthday made a s' to his lords, 1173
Lu 14: 12 When thou makest a dinner or a s', "
16 A certain man made a great s', and "
17 sent his servant at s' time to say to "
24 were bidden shall taste of my s'. "
22: 20 Likewise also the cup after s', 1172
Joh 12: 2 There they made him a s'; and 1173
13: 2 s' being ended, the devil having "
4 He riseth from s', and laid aside "
21: 20 also leaned on his breast at s', and "
1Co 11: 20 this is not to eat the Lord's s'. "
21 one taketh before other his own s': "
Re 19: 9 unto the marriage s' of the Lamb. "
17 unto the s' of the great God; "

supplant See also SUPPLANTED.
Jer 9: 4 for every brother will utterly s', 6117

supplanted
Ge 27: 36 for he hath s' me these two times:6117

supple
Eze 16: 4 thou washed in water to s' thee; *4935

suppliants
Zep 3: 10 the rivers of Ethiopia my s', 6282

supplication See also SUPPLICATIONS.
1Sa 13: 12 I have not made s' unto the Lord:2470
1Ki 8: 28 prayer of thy servant, and to his s',8467
30 And hearken thou to the s' of thy "
33 make s' unto thee in this house: 2603
38 prayer and s' soever be made by 8467
45 in heaven their prayer and their s', "
47 and make s' unto thee in the land 2603
49 their prayer and their s' in heaven 8467
52 be open unto the s' of thy servant, "
52 and unto the s' of thy people Israel, "
54 all this prayer and s' unto the Lord, "
59 I have made s' before the Lord, 2603
9: 3 have heard thy prayer and thy s', 8467
2Ch 6: 19 prayer of thy servant, and to his s', "
24 make s' before thee in this house; 2603
29 what s' soever shall be made of 8467
35 heavens their prayer and their s', "
33: 13 and heard his s', and brought him "
Es 4: 8 the king, to make s' unto him, 2603
Job 8: 5 and make thy s' to the Almighty; "
9: 15 but I would make s' to my judge. "
Ps 6: 9 The Lord hath heard my s'; the 8467
30: 8 and unto the Lord I made s'. 2603
55: 1 and hide not thyself from my s'. 8467
119: 170 Let my s' come before thee: "
142: 1 unto the Lord did I make my s'. 2603
Isa 45: 14 they shall make s' unto thee, 6419
Jer 36: 7 present their s' before the Lord, 8467
37: 20 let my s', I pray thee, be accepted "
38: 26 I presented my s' before the king, "
42: 2 our s' be accepted before thee, and "
9 me to present your s' before him; "
Da 6: 11 and making s' before his God. 2604
9: 20 presenting my s' before the Lord 8467
Ho 12: 4 he wept, and made s' unto him: 2603
Ac 1: 14 with one accord in prayer and s', *1162
Eph 6: 18 with all prayer and s' in the Spirit, "
18 perseverance and s' for all saints; "
Ph'p 4: 6 by prayer and s' with thanksgiving "

supplications
2Ch 6: 21 unto the s' of thy servant, and 8469
39 their prayer and their s', and 8467
Job 41: 3 Will he make many s' unto thee? 8469
Ps 28: 2 Hear the voice of my s', when I cry "
6 he hath heard the voice of my s'. "
31: 22 heardest the voice of my s' when I "
86: 6 and attend to the voice of my s'. "
116: 1 he hath heard my voice and my s'. "
130: 2 be attentive to the voice of my s'. "
140: 6 hear the voice of my s', O Lord. "
143: 1 prayer, O Lord, give ear to my s': "
Jer 3: 21 weeping and s' of the children of "
31: 9 and with s' will I lead them: "
Da 9: 3 Lord God, to seek by prayer and s', "
17 prayer of thy servant, and his s', "
18 for we do not present our s' before "
23 At the beginning of thy s' the "
Zec 12: 10 the spirit of grace and of s': and "
1Ti 2: 1 that, first of all, s', prayers, 1162
5: 5 continueth in s' and prayers night "
Heb 5: 7 he had offered up prayers and s' 2428

supplied
1Co 16: 17 lacking on your part they have s'. 378
2Co 11: 9 which came from Macedonia s': 4322

supplieth
2Co 9: 12 not only s' the want of the saints, *4322
Eph 4: 16 by that which every joint s', 2024

supply See also SUPPLIED; SUPPLIETH.
2Co 8: 14 abundance...be a s' for their want,
14 also may be a s' for your want:
Ph'p 1: 19 the s' of the Spirit of Jesus Christ, 2024
2: 30 to s' your lack of service toward 378
4: 19 But my God shall s' all your need†4137

support
Ac 20: 35 labouring ye ought to s' the weak,*482
1Th 5: 14 s' the weak, be patient toward all 472

suppose See also SUPPOSED; SUPPOSING.
2Sa 13: 32 not my lord s' that they have slain 559
Lu 7: 43 I s' that he, to whom he forgave 5274
12: 51 S' ye that I am come to give peace*1380
13: 2 S' ye that these Galilæans were * "
Joh 21: 25 I s' that even the world itself 3633
Ac 2: 15 these are not drunken, as ye s', 5274
1Co 7: 26 I s' therefore that this is good for*3543
2Co 11: 5 I s' I was not a whit behind the *3049
Heb 10: 29 much sorer punishment, s' ye, *1380
1Pe 5: 12 a faithful brother...as I s', *3049

supposed
M't 20: 10 s' that they should have received 3543
M'r 6: 49 sea, they s' it had been a spirit, 1380
Lu 3: 23 being (as was s') the son of Joseph,3543
24: 37 and s' that they had seen a spirit. 1380
Ac 7: 25 For he s' his brethren would have 3543
21: 29 whom they s'...Paul had brought "
25: 18 accusation of such things as I s': 5282
Ph'p 2: 25 I s' it necessary to send to you *2233

supposing
Lu 2: 44 they, s' him...in the company, 3543
Joh 20: 15 She, s' him to be the gardener, 1380
Ac 14: 19 out of the city, s' he had been dead.3543
16: 27 s' that the prisoners had been fled. "
27: 13 s' that they had obtained their 1380
Ph'p 1: 16 s' to add affliction to my bonds: *3633
1Ti 6: 5 truth, s' that gain is godliness: 3543

supreme
1Pe 2: 13 whether it be to the king, as s'; 5242

Sur (*sur*)
2Ki 11: 6 part shall be at the gate of S'; 5495

sure See also ASSURE.
Ge 23: 17 borders round about, were made s'6965
20 were made s' unto Abraham for a "
Ex 3: 19 I am s'...the king of Egypt will not*3045
Nu 32: 23 and be s' your sin will find you out." "
De 12: 23 be s' that thou eat not the blood: 2388
1Sa 2: 35 and I will build him a s' house; 539
20: 7 be s'...evil is determined by him. *3045
25: 28 certainly make my lord a s' house; 539
2Sa 1: 10 I was s' that he could not live 3045
23: 5 ordered in all things, and s': 8104
1Ki 11: 38 and build thee a s' house, as I built 539
Ne 9: 38 we make a s' covenant, and write 548
Job 24: 22 riseth up, and no man is s' of life. 539
Ps 19: 7 the testimony of the Lord is s', "
93: 5 Thy testimonies are very s': "
111: 7 all his commandments are s'. "
Pr 6: 3 thyself, and make s' thy friend. *7292
11: 15 and he that hateth suretiship is s'. 982
18 righteousness shall be a s' reward. 571
Isa 22: 23 fasten him as a nail in a s' place; 539
25 nail that is fastened in the s' place "
28: 16 corner stone, a s' foundation: 3245
32: 18 and in s' dwellings, and in quiet 4009
33: 16 given him; his waters shall be s'. 539
55: 3 you, even the s' mercies of David. "
Da 2: 45 and the interpretation thereof s'. 546
4: 26 thy kingdom shall be s' unto thee,7011
M't 27: 64 sepulchre be made s' until the third 805
65 your way, make it as s' as ye can. "
66 went, and made the sepulchre s', "
Lu 10: 11 be ye s' of this, that the kingdom *1097
Joh 6: 69 are s' that thou art that Christ, * "
16: 30 Now are we s' that thou knowest *1492
Ac 13: 34 give you the s' mercies of David. 4103
Ro 2: 2 we are s' that the judgment of God*1492
4: 16 might be s' to all the seed; 949
15: 29 And I am s' that, when I come *1492
2Ti 2: 19 the foundation of God standeth s',*4731
Heb 6: 19 of the soul, both s' and stedfast, 804
2Pe 1: 10 make your calling and election s': 949
19 also a more s' word of prophecy; "

surely
Ge 2: 17 thou eatest thereof thou shalt s' die.
3: 4 unto the woman, Ye shall not s' die:
9: 5 s' your blood...will I require; 389
18: 18 Abraham shall s' become a great and
20: 7 know thou that thou shalt s' die, 3588
11 S' the fear of God is not in this 7535
26: 11 or his wife shall s' be put to death.
28: 16 said, S' the Lord is in this place; 403
22 me I will s' give the tenth unto thee.
29: 14 S' thou art my bone and my flesh. 389
32 S' the Lord hath looked upon my*3588
30: 16 s' I have hired thee with my son's
31: 42 s' thou hadst sent me away now 3588
32: 12 I will s' do thee good, and make thy
42: 16 by the life of Pharaoh s' ye are spies.
43: 10 s'...we had returned this second 3588
44: 28 S' he is torn in pieces; and I saw 389
46: 4 and I will also s' bring thee up again:
50: 24 God will s' visit you, and bring you
25 God will s' visit you, and ye shall
Ex 2: 14 and said, S' this thing is known. 403
3: 7 I have s' seen the affliction of my
16 I have s' visited you, and seen that
4: 25 S' a bloody husband art thou to 3588
11: 1 he shall s' thrust you out hence
13: 19 of Israel, saying, God will s' visit you;
18: 18 Thou wilt s' wear away, both thou,
19: 12 the mount shall be s' put to death:
13 touch it, but he shall s' be stoned,3588
21: 12 so that he die, shall be s' put to death.
15 or his mother, shall be s' put to death.
16 in his hand, he shall s' be put to death.
17 or his mother, shall s' be put to death.
20 his hand; he shall be s' punished.

Ex 21: 22 he shall be s· punished, according as
28 then the ox shall be s· stoned, and his
36 he shall s· pay ox for ox; and the dead
22: 6 the fire shall s· make restitution.
14 not with it, he shall s· make it good.
16 he shall s· endow her to be his wife.
19 with a beast shall s· be put to death.
23 at all unto me, I will s· hear their cry;
23: 4 shalt s· bring it back to him again.
5 help him, thou shalt s· help with him.
33 it will s· be a snare unto thee. 3588
31: 14 that defileth it shall s· be put to death:
15 day, he shall s· be put to death.
40: 15 anointing shall s· be an everlasting*
Le 20: 2 Molech; he shall s· be put to death:
9 or his mother shall be s· put to death:
10 the adulteress shall s· be put to death.
11 both of them shall s· be put to death;
12 both of them shall s· be put to death:
13 they shall s· be put to death; their
15 a beast, he shall s· be put to death:
16 beast: they shall s· be put to death;
27 a wizard, shall s· be put to death:
24: 16 the Lord, he shall s· be put to death,
17 any man shall s· be put to death.
27: 29 redeemed; but shall s· be put to death.
Nu 13: 27 and s· it floweth with milk and honey;
14: 23 S· they shall not see the land 518
35 I will s· do it unto all this evil "
15: 35 The man shall be s· put to death:
18: 15 firstborn of man shalt thou s· redeem.
22: 33 s· now also I had slain thee, and 3588
23: 23 S· there is no enchantment against
26: 65 They shall s· die in the wilderness.
27: 7 thou shalt s· give them a possession of
32: 11 S· none of the men that came up 518
35: 16, 17, 18 shall s· be put to death.
21 smote him shall s· be put to death;
31 death: but he shall be s· put to death.
De 1: 35 S· there shall not one of these men518
4: 6 S· this great nation is a wise and
8: 19 this day that ye shall s· perish. 3588
13: 9 But thou shalt s· kill him; thine "
15 s· smite the inhabitants of that city
15: 8 shalt s· lend him sufficient for his need,
10 Thou shalt s· give him, and thine
16: 15 therefore thou shalt s· rejoice. * 389
22: 4 s· help him to lift them up again.
23: 21 thy God will s· require it of thee;
30: 18 that ye shall s· perish, and that 3588
31: 18 And I will s· hide my face in that day
Jos 14: 9 S· the land whereon thy feet have 518
J'g 3: 24 said, S· he covereth his feet in his 389
4: 9 And she said, I will s· go with thee:
6: 16 S· I will be with thee, and thou 3588
11: 31 of Ammon, shall s· be the Lord's, *
13: 22 We shall s· die, because we have seen
15: 13 hand: but s· we will not kill thee.
20: 39 S· they are smitten down before 389
21: 5 saying, He shall s· be put to death.
Ru 1: 10 S· we will return with thee unto *3588
1Sa 9: 6 all that he saith cometh s· to pass:
14: 39 Jonathan my son, he shall s· die. 3588
44 for thou shalt s· die, Jonathan.
15: 32 S· the bitterness of death is past. 403
16: 6 S· the Lord's anointed is before 389
17: 25 s· to defy Israel is he come up: 3588
20: 26 he is not clean; s· he is not clean. "
31 him unto me, for he shall s· die.
22: 16 Thou shalt s· die, Ahimelech, thou,
22 there, that he would s· tell Saul:
24: 20 well that thou shalt s· be king,
25: 21 S· in vain have I kept all that this 389
34 s· there had not been left unto 3588,518
28: 2 S· thou shalt know what thy *3651
29: 6 S·, as the Lord liveth, thou hast been*
30: 8 for thou shalt s· overtake them,
2Sa 2: 27 s· then in the meaning the people 3588
9: 7 s· shew thee kindness for Jonathan "
11: 23 S· the men prevailed against us, * "
12: 5 hath done this thing shall s· die: *
14 that is born unto thee shall s· die.
15: 21 s· in what place my lord the king 3588
18: 2 I will s· go forth with you myself also.
20: 18 They shall s· ask counsel at Abel:
24: 24 will s· buy it of thee at a price:*3588,518
1Ki 2: 37 for certain that thou shalt s· die:
42 any whither, that thou shalt s· die?
8: 13 I have s· built thee an house to 403
11: 2 for s· they will turn away your heart"
11 I will s· rend the kingdom from thee,
13: 32 of Samaria, shall s· come to pass. 3588
18: 15 I will s· shew myself unto him to "
20: 23, 25 s· we shall be stronger than 518
22: 32 they said, S· it is the king of Israel.389
2Ki 1: 4, 6, 16 art gone up, but shalt s· die. 3588
3: 14 s·, were it not that I regard the "
23 the kings are s· slain, and they have
5: 11 He will s· come out to me, and stand,
8: 10 shewed me that he shall s· die.
14 me that thou shouldest s· recover.
9: 26 S· I have seen yesterday the blood of
18: 30 The Lord will s· deliver us, and this
23: 22 S· there was not holden such a 3588
24: 3 S· at the commandment of the 389
Es 6: 13 him, but shalt s· fall before him. 3588
Job 8: 6 s· now he would awake for thee,
13: 3 S· I would speak to the Almighty, 199
10 He will s· reprove you, if ye do
14: 18 And s· the mountain falling cometh199
18: 21 S· such are the dwellings of the 389
20: 20 S· he shall not feel quietness in *3588
28: 1 S· there is a vein for the silver, and"
31: 36 S· I would take it upon my 518,3808
33: 8 S·...hast spoken in mine hearing, 389
34: 12 Yea, s· God will not do wickedly,* 551
Job 34: 31 S· it is meet to be said unto God, *3588
35: 13 S· God will not hear vanity, neither389
37: 20 s· he shall be swallowed up. *3588
40: 20 S· the mountains bring him forth "
Ps 23: 6 S· goodness and mercy shall 389
32: 6 s· in the floods of great waters 7535
39: 6 S· every man walketh in a vain 389
6 s· they are disquieted in vain: he "
11 like a moth: s· every man is vanity. "
62: 9 S· men of low degree are vanity, "
73: 18 S· thou didst set them in slippery "
76: 10 S· the wrath of man shall praise 3588
77: 11 s· I will remember thy wonders of old.*
85: 9 S· his salvation is nigh them that 389
91: 3 S· he shall deliver thee from the *3588
112: 6 S· he shall not be moved for ever:* "
131: 2 S· I have behaved and quieted518,3808
132: 3 S· I will not come into...tabernacle 518
139: 11 S· the darkness shall cover me; 389
19 S· thou wilt slay the wicked, O God :518
Pr 1: 17 S· in vain the net is spread in the*3588
3: 34 S· he scorneth the scorners: but 518
10: 9 that walketh uprightly walketh s·: 983
22: 16 to the rich, shall s· come to want.* 389
23: 18 For s· there is an end; and thine
30: 2 S· I am...brutish than any man, 3588
33 S· the churning of milk bringeth * "
Ec 4: 16 S· this also is vanity and vexation "
7: 7 S· oppression maketh a wise man "
8: 12 s· I know it shall be well with them "
10: 11 S· the serpent will bite without * 518
Isa 7: 9 s· ye shall not be established. 3588
14: 24 S· as I have thought, so shall 518,3808
16: 7 ye mourn; s· they are stricken. * 389
19: 11 S· the princes of Zoan are fools, * "
22: 14 S· this iniquity shall not be purged518
17 mighty captivity, and will s· cover thee.
18 He will s· violently turn and toss thee
29: 16 S· your turning of things upside * 518
36: 15 saying, The Lord will s· deliver us:
40: 7 upon it: s· the people is grass. 403
45: 14 S· God is in thee; and there is none389
49: 4 s· my judgment is with the Lord, 403
18 shalt s· clothe thee with them all. 3588
53: 4 S· he hath borne our griefs, and 403
54: 15 they shall s· gather together, but not
60: 9 S· the isles shall wait for me, and 3588
62: 8 S· I will no more give thy corn to 518
63: 8 For he said, S· they are my people, 389
Jer 2: 35 s· his anger shall turn from me.
3: 20 S· as a wife treacherously 403
4: 10 s· thou hast greatly deceived this "
5: 2 Lord liveth; s· they swear falsely. "
4 S· these are poor; they are foolish :389
8: 13 I will s· consume them, saith the *
16: 19 S· our fathers have inherited lies,* 389
22: 6 s· I...make thee a wilderness, 518,3808
22 s· then shalt thou be ashamed and3588
24: 8 s· thus saith the Lord, So will I give"
26: 8 took him, saying, Thou shalt s· die.
15 ye shall s· bring innocent blood *3588
31: 18 I have s· heard Ephraim bemoaning
19 S· after...I was turned, I repented :3588
20 I will s· have mercy upon him, saith
32: 4 shall s· be delivered into the hand of
34: 3 not escape...but shalt s· be taken. 3588
36: 16 will s· tell the king of all these words.
37: 9 The Chaldeans shall s· depart from us:
38: 3 This city shall s· be given into the
15 thee, wilt thou not s· put me to death?
39: 18 For I will s· deliver thee, and thou
44: 25 We will s· perform our vows that we
25 ye will s· accomplish your vows, and*
25 your vows, and s· perform your vows.*
29 my words shall s· stand against
46: 18 S· as Tabor is among...mountains,3588
49: 12 but thou shalt s· drink of it.
20 S· the least of the flock shall 518,3808
20 s· he...make their habitations " "
50: 45 S· the least of the flock shall " "
45 s· he shall make their habitation" "
51: 14 S· I will fill thee with men, as 3588,518
56 God of recompences shall s· requite.
La 3: 3 S· against me is he turned; he 389
Eze 3: 6 S·, had I sent thee to them, 518,3808
18 say unto the wicked, Thou shalt s· die;
21 and he doth not sin, he shall s· live,
5: 11 S·, because thou hast defiled 518,3808
17: 16 s· in the place where the king " "
19 s· mine oath that he hath " "
18: 9 he is just, he shall s· live, saith the
13 he shall s· die; his blood shall be upon
17 iniquity of his father, he shall s· live.
19 and hath done them, he shall s· live.
21, 28 he shall s· live, he shall not die.
20: 33 s· with a mighty hand, and 518,3808
31: 11 heathen; he shall s· deal with him:
33: 8 O wicked man, thou shalt s· die;
13 to the righteous, that he shall s· live;
14 unto the wicked, Thou shalt s· die;
15 he shall s· live, he shall not die.
16 is lawful and right; he shall s· live.
27 s· they that are in the wastes 518,3808
34: 8 s· because my flock became a " "
36: 5 S· in the fire of my jealousy " "
7 S· the heathen that are about " "
38: 19 S· in that day there shall be a " "
Ho 5: 9 made known that which shall s· be. 539
12: 11 s· they are vanity: they sacrifice * 389
Am 3: 7 S· the Lord God will do nothing, 3588
5: 5 for Gilgal shall s· go into captivity,
7: 11 Israel shall s· be led away captive out
17 Israel shall s· go into captivity forth
Mic 2: 12 I will s· assemble, O Jacob, all of thee;
Hab 2: 3 it will s· come, it will not tarry.
Zep 2: 9 S· Moab shall be as Sodom, and 3588
M't 26: 73 S· thou also art one of them; * 230
M'r 14: 70 to Peter, S· thou art one of them:* "
Lu 1: 1 things which are most s· believed*4135
4: 23 will s· say unto me this proverb, 3843
Joh 17: 8 known s· that I came out from * 230
Heb 6: 14 S· blessing I will bless thee, and 2229
Re 22: 20 things saith, S· I come quickly. *3483

sureties
Pr 22: 26 or of them that are s· for debts. 6148

suretiship
Pr 11: 15 it: and he that hateth s· is sure. 8628

surety See also SURETIES.
Ge 15: 13 Know of a s· that thy seed shall be 3045
18: 13 Shall I of a s· bear a child, which 552
26: 9 said, Behold, of a s· she is thy wife:389
43: 9 I will be s· for him; of my hand 6148
44: 32 servant became s· for the lad unto "
Job 17: 3 down now, put me in a s· with thee;"
Ps 119: 122 Be s· for thy servant for good: let "
Pr 6: 1 My son, if thou be s· for thy friend, "
11: 15 He that is s· for a stranger shall "
17: 18 becometh s· in the presence of his 6161
20: 16 garment that is s· for a stranger: 6148
27: 13 garment that is s· for a stranger, "
Ac 12: 11 Now I know of a s·, that the Lord * 230
Heb 7: 22 made a s· of a better testament. 1450

surfeiting
Lu 21: 34 hearts be overcharged with s·, 2897

surmisings
1Ti 6: 4 cometh envy, strife, railings, evil s·,5283

surname See also SURNAMED.
Isa 44: 5 s· himself by the name of Israel. 3655
M't 10: 3 whose s· was Thaddæus; *1941
Ac 10: 5 for one Simon, whose s· is Peter: * "
32 hither Simon, whose s· is Peter; "
11: 13 call for Simon, whose s· is Peter; "
12: 12 of John, whose s· was Mark; "
25 them John, whose s· was Mark. "
15: 37 them John, whose s· was Mark. *2564

surnamed
Isa 45: 4 I have s· thee, though thou hast 3655
M'r 3: 16 And Simon he s· Peter; 2007,3686
17 he s· them Boanerges, which " "
Lu 22: 3 Satan into Judas s· Iscariot, *1941
Ac 1: 23 Barsabas, who was s· Justus, and "
4: 36 by the apostles was s· Barnabas, "
10: 18 whether Simon, which was s· Peter, "
15: 22 Judas s· Barsabas, and Silas, chief* "

surprised
Isa 33: 14 fearfulness hath s· the hypocrites.‡270
Jer 48: 41 taken, and the strong holds are s·,8610
51: 41 is the praise of the whole earth s·! "

Susah See HAZAR-SUSAH.

Susanchites (*su'-san-kites*)
Ezr 4: 9 the S·, the Dehavites, and the *7801

Susanna (*su-zan'-nah*)
Lu 8: 3 wife of...Herod's steward, and S·, 4677

Susi (*su'-si*)
Nu 13: 11 of Manasseh, Gaddi the son of S·. 5485

Susim See HAZAR-SUSIM.

sustain See also SUSTAINED.
1Ki 17: 9 a widow woman there to s· thee. 3557
Ne 9: 21 Yea, forty years didst thou s· them "
Ps 55: 22 upon the Lord, and he shall s· thee:"
Pr 18: 14 spirit of a man will s· his infirmity; "

sustained
Ge 27: 37 with corn and wine have I s· him: 5564
Ps 3: 5 I awaked; for the Lord s· me. * "
Isa 59: 16 and his righteousness, it s· him. * "

sustenance
J'g 6: 4 left no s· for Israel, neither sheep, 4241
2Sa 19: 32 and he had provided the king of s·3557
Ac 7: 11 and our fathers found no s·. 5527

swaddled
La 2: 22 those...I have s· and brought up *2946
Eze 16: 4 wast not salted at all, nor s· at all.2853

swaddling See also SWADDLINGBAND.
Lu 2: 7 and wrapped him in s· clothes, 4683
12 find the babe wrapped in s· clothes," "

swaddlingband
Job 38: 9 and thick darkness a s· for it, 2854

swaddling-clothes See SWADDLING and CLOTHES.

swallow See also SWALLOWED; SWALLOWETH.
Nu 16: 30 open her mouth, and s· them up, 1104
34 said, Lest the earth s· us up also. "
2Sa 20: 19 why wilt thou s· up the inheritance "
20 me, that I should s· up or destroy. "
Job 7: 19 me alone till I s· down my spittle? "
20: 18 he restore, and shall not s· it down:"
Ps 21: 9 Lord shall s· them up in his wrath, "
56: 1 O God: for man would s· me up; 7602
2 Mine enemies would daily s· me up:"
57: 3 reproach of him that would s· me "
69: 15 neither let the deep s· me up, and 1104
84: 3 house, and the s· a nest for herself,1866
Pr 1: 12 us s· them up alive as the grave; 1104
26: 2 by wandering, as the s· by flying, 1866
Ec 10: 12 the lips of a fool will s· up himself.1104
Isa 25: 8 He will s· up death in victory; and*"
38: 14 Like a crane or a s·, so did I *5693
Jer 8: 7 s· observe the time of their coming;*"
Ho 8: 7 yield, the strangers shall s· it up. 1104
Am 8: 4 this, O ye that s· up the needy, 7602
Ob 16 drink, and they shall s· down, 3886
Jon 1: 17 a great fish to s· up Jonah. 1104
M't 23: 24 strain at a gnat, and s· a camel. 2666

swallowed
Ex 7:12 but Aaron's rod s' up their rods. 1104
15:12 thy right hand, the earth s' them. "
Nu 16:32 and s' them up, and their houses, "
26:10 and s' them up together with Korah, "
De 11: 6 s' them up, and their households, "
2Sa 17:16 lest the king be s' up, and all the "
Job 6: 3 sea: therefore my words are s' up.*3886
20:15 He hath s' down riches, and he 1104
37:20 man speak, surely he shall be s' up. "
Ps 35:25 them not say, We have s' him up. "
106:17 The earth opened and s' up Dathan, "
124: 3 Then they had s' us up quick, when "
Isa 28: 7 they are s' up of wine, they are out "
49:19 that s' thee up shall be far away. "
Jer 51:34 he hath s' me up like a dragon, he "
44 mouth that which he hath s' up: 1105
La 2: 2 Lord hath s' up all the habitations 1104
5 as an enemy: he hath s' up Israel, "
5 he hath s' up all her palaces: he "
16 We have s' her up: certainly this is "
Eze 36: 3 and s' you up on every side, that 7602
Ho 8: 8 Israel is s' up: now shall they be 1104
1Co 15:54 written, Death is s' up in victory. *2666*
2Co 2: 7 be s' up with overmuch sorrow. "
5: 4 that mortality might be s' up of life. "
Re 12:16 s' up the flood which the dragon "

swalloweth
Job 5: 5 the robber s' up their substance. *7602
39:24 He s' the ground with fierceness 1572

swan
Le 11:18 And the s', and the pelican, and *8580
De 14:16 owl, and the great owl, and the s',* "

sware See also SWAREST.
Ge 21:31 because there they s' both of them.7650
24: 7 me, and that s' unto me, saying, "
9 s' to him concerning that matter. "
25:33 me this day; and he s' unto him: "
26: 3 oath which I s' unto Abraham thy "
31 the morning, and s' one to another: "
31:53 Jacob s' by the fear of his father "
47:31 unto me. And he s' unto him. "
50:24 the land which he s' to Abraham, "
Ex 13: 5 he s' unto thy fathers to give thee, "
11 he s' unto thee and to thy fathers, "
33: 1 the land which I s' unto Abraham, "
Nu 14:16 the land which he s' unto them, "
23 land which I s' unto their fathers, "
30 I s' to make you dwell therein, *5375
32:10 kindled the same time, and he s', 7650
11 the land which I s' unto Abraham, "
De 1: 8 land which the Lord s' unto your "
34 your words, and was wroth, and s', "
35 land, which I s' to give unto your "
2:14 the host, as the Lord s' unto them. "
4:21 s' that I should not go over Jordan, "
31 covenant...which he s' unto them. "
6:10 land which he s' unto thy fathers, "
18 which the Lord s' unto thy fathers, "
23 land which he s' unto our fathers. "
7:12 which he s' unto thy fathers: "
13 land which he s' unto thy fathers "
8: 1 the Lord s' unto your fathers. "
18 his covenant which he s' unto thy "
9: 5 which the Lord s' unto thy fathers, "
10:11 which I s' unto their fathers to give "
11: 9, 21 the Lord s' unto your fathers "
26: 3 which the Lord s' unto your fathers "
28:11 which the Lord s' unto thy fathers "
30:20 which the Lord s' unto thy fathers, "
31:20 land which I s' unto their fathers, "
21 them into the land which I s'. "
23 into the land which I s' unto them: "
34: 4 the land which I s' unto Abraham, "
Jos 1: 6 which I s' unto their fathers to give "
5: 6 the Lord s' that he would not shew "
6 land, which the Lord s' unto their "
6:22 all that she hath, as ye s' unto her. "
9:15 princes of the congregation s' unto "
20 of the oath which we s' unto them. "
14: 9 And Moses s' on that day, saying, "
21:43 he s' to give unto their fathers; "
44 to all that he s' unto their fathers: "
J'g 2: 1 land which I s' unto your fathers; "
1Sa 19: 6 and Saul s', As the Lord liveth, he "
20: 3 And David s' moreover, and said, "
24:22 And David s' unto Saul. And Saul "
28:10 Saul s' to her by the Lord, saying, "
2Sa 3:35 while it was yet day, David s', "
19:23 not die. And the king s' unto him. "
21:17 Then the men of David s' unto him, "
1Ki 1:29 the king s', and said, As the Lord "
30 Even as I s' unto thee by the Lord "
2: 8 and I s' to him by the Lord, saying, "
2Ki 25:24 Gedaliah s' to them, and to their "
2Ch 15:14 s' unto the Lord with a loud voice, "
Ezr 10: 5 according to this word. And they s'. "
Ps 95:11 Unto whom I s' in my wrath that "
132: 2 he s' unto the Lord, and vowed "
Jer 38:16 So Zedekiah the king s' secretly "
40: 9 son of Shaphan s' unto them and to "
Eze 16: 8 I s' unto thee, and entered into a "
Da 12: 7 and s' by him that liveth for ever "
M'r 6:23 he s' unto her, Whatsoever thou *3660*
Lu 1:73 The oath which he s' to our father "
Heb 3:11 So I s' in my wrath, They shall not "
18 to whom s' he that they should not "
6:13 by no greater, he s' by himself, "
7:21 The Lord s' and will not repent, "
Re 10: 6 s' by him that liveth for ever and "

swarest
Ex 32:13 to whom thou s' by thine own self.7650
Nu 11:12 the land which thou s' unto their "
De 26:15 as thou s' unto our fathers, a land "
1Ki 1:17 thou s' by the Lord thy God unto 7650
Ps 89:49 thou s' unto David in thy truth? "

swarm See also SWARMS.
Ex 8:24 there came a grievous s' of flies *6157
24 by reason of the s' of flies. * "
J'g 14: 8 was a s' of bees and honey in the 5712

swarms
Ex 8:21 I will send s' of flies upon thee, 6157
21 Egyptians shall be full of s' of flies, "
22 that no s' of flies shall be there; "
29 that the s' of flies may depart from "
31 and he removed the s' of flies from "

swear See also FORSWEAR; SWARE; SWEARETH; SWEARING; SWORN.
Ge 21:23 therefore s' unto me here by God 7650
24 And Abraham said, I will s'. "
24: 3 I will make thee s' by the Lord, the "
37 And my master made me s', saying, "
25:33 And Jacob said, *S'* to me this day; "
47:31 And he said, *S'* unto me. And he "
50: 5 My father made me s', saying, Lo, I "
6 according as he made thee s'. "
Ex 6: 8 I did s' to give it to Abraham, *5375
Le 5: 4 Or if a soul s', pronouncing with 7650
19:12 ye shall not s' by my name falsely, "
Nu 30: 2 or s' an oath to bind his soul with* "
De 6:13 him, and shalt s' by his name. "
10:20 thou cleave, and s' by his name. "
Jos 2:12 s' unto me by the Lord, since I "
17 oath which thou hast made us s'. "
20 oath which thou hast made us to s'. "
23: 7 nor cause to s' by them, neither "
J'g 15:12 said unto them, *S'* unto me, that "
1Sa 20:17 Jonathan caused David to s' again, "
24:21 *S'* now...unto me by the Lord, "
30:15 *S'* unto me by God, that thou wilt "
2Sa 19: 7 for I s' by the Lord, if thou go not "
1Ki 1:13 O king, s' unto thine handmaid, "
51 Let king Solomon s' unto me to "
2:42 I not make thee to s' by the Lord, "
8:31 laid upon him to cause him to s', 422
2Ch 6:22 be laid upon him to make him s', "
36:13 who had made him s' by God: 7650
Ezr 10: 5 to s' that they should do according "
Ne 13:25 and made them s' by God, saying, "
Isa 3: 7 In that day shall he s', saying, I *5375
19:18 and s' to the Lord of hosts; one 7650
45:23 shall bow, every tongue shall s'. "
48: 1 which s' by the name of the Lord, "
65:16 earth shall s' by the God of truth; "
Jer 4: 2 And thou shalt s', The Lord liveth, "
5: 2 Lord liveth; surely they s' falsely. "
7: 9 commit adultery, and s' falsely, "
12:16 to s' by my name, The Lord liveth; "
16 taught my people to s' by Baal; "
22: 5 I s' by myself, saith the Lord, that "
32:22 thou didst s' to their fathers to give "
Hos 4:15 Beth-aven, nor s', The Lord liveth. "
Am 8:14 They that s' by the sin of Samaria, "
Zep 1: 5 worship and that s' by the Lord, "
5 and that s' by Malcham; "
M't 5:34 *S'* not at all; neither by heaven; *3660*
36 Neither shalt thou s' by thy head, "
23:16 Whosoever shall s' by the temple, "
16 shall s' by the gold of the temple, "
18 Whosoever shall s' by the altar, it "
20 therefore shall s' by the altar, * "
21 And whoso shall s' by the temple, * "
22 And he that shall s' by heaven, * "
26:74 Then began he to curse and to s', "
M'r 14:71 But he began to curse and to s', "
Heb 6:13 because he could s' by no greater, "
16 For men verily s' by the greater: "
Jas 5:12 all things, my brethren, s' not, "

swearers
Mal 3: 5 and against false s', and against 7650

sweareth
Le 6: 3 lieth concerning it, and s' falsely;*7650
Ps 15: 4 He that s' to his own hurt, and "
63:11 one that s' by him shall glory: "
Ec 9: 2 he that s', as he that feareth an "
Isa 65:16 he that s' in the earth shall swear "
Zec 5: 3 every one that s' shall be cut off as "
4 of him that s' falsely by my name: "
M't 23:18 whosoever s' by the gift that is *3660*
20 s' by it, and by all things thereon. "
21 s' by it, and by him that dwelleth "
22 by heaven, s' by the throne of God, "

swearing
Le 5: 1 soul sin, and hear the voice of s',* 423
Jer 23:10 because of s' the land mourneth; "
Ho 4: 2 By s', and lying, and killing, and 422
10: 4 s' falsely in making a covenant: "

sweat
Ge 3:19 In the s' of thy face shalt thou eat 2188
Eze 44:18 with any thing that causeth s'. 3154
Lu 22:44 his s' was as it were great drops of *2402*

sweep See also SWEEPING; SWEPT.
Isa 14:23 and I will s' it with the besom of 2894
28:17 hail shall s' away the refuge of lies, 3261
Lu 15: 8 light a candle, and s' the house, *4563*

sweeping
Pr 28: 3 is like a s' rain that leaveth no 5502

sweet See also SWEETER; SWEETSMELLING.
Ge 8:21 And the Lord smelled a s' savour; 5207
Ex 15:25 waters, the waters were made s': 4985
25: 6 anointing oil, and for s' incense, 5561
29:18 it is a s' savour, an offering made 5207
25 for a s' savour before the Lord: "
41 for a s' savour, an offering made "
30: 7 burn thereon s' incense every 5561
23 and of s' cinnamon half so much, 1314
Ex 30:23 of s' calamus two hundred and fifty 1314
34 Take unto thee s' spices, stacte, 5561
34 s' spices with pure frankincense: "
31:11 and s' incense for the holy place: "
35: 8 anointing oil,...for the s' incense, 5561
15 anointing oil, and the s' incense, "
28 anointing oil, and for the s' incense. "
37:29 and the pure incense of s' spices, "
39:38 anointing oil, and the s' incense, "
40:27 And he burnt s' incense thereon; as "
Le 1: 9, 13, 17 of a s' savour unto the Lord. 5207
2: 2 by fire, of a s' savour unto the Lord: "
9 by fire, of a s' savour unto the Lord. "
12 burnt on the altar for a s' savour. "
3: 5 by fire, of a s' savour unto the Lord. "
16 made by fire for a s' savour: "
4: 7 the horns of the altar of s' incense 5561
31 for a s' savour unto the Lord; 5207
6:15 it upon the altar for a s' savour, "
21 offer for a s' savour unto the Lord. "
8:21 a burnt sacrifice for a s' savour, "
28 were consecrations for a s' savour: "
16:12 his hands full of s' incense beaten 5561
17: 6 fat for a s' savour unto the Lord. 5207
23:13 fire unto the Lord for a s' savour: "
18 by fire, of s' savour unto the Lord. "
26:31 smell the savour of your s' odours. "
Nu 4:16 for the light, and the s' incense, 5561
15: 3 to make a s' savour unto the Lord. 5207
7 wine, for a s' savour unto the Lord. "
10, 13 fire, of a s' savour unto the Lord. "
14 by fire, of a s' savour unto the Lord; "
24 for a s' savour unto the Lord, "
18:17 fire, for a s' savour unto the Lord. "
28: 2 by fire, for a s' savour unto me, "
6 in mount Sinai for a s' savour, "
8 by fire, of a s' savour unto the Lord. "
13 for a burnt offering of a s' savour, "
24 fire, of a s' savour unto the Lord: "
27 for a s' savour unto the Lord; "
29: 2 for a s' savour unto the Lord; "
6 for a s' savour, a sacrifice made by "
8 unto the Lord for a s' savour; "
13 fire, of a s' savour unto the Lord; "
36 fire, of a s' savour unto the Lord: "
2Sa 23: 1 and the s' psalmist of Israel, said, 5273
2Ch 2: 4 and to burn before him s' incense, 5561
13:11 burnt sacrifices and s' incense: "
16:14 in the bed...filled with s' odours 1314
Ezr 6:10 s' savours unto the God of heaven, 5208
Ne 8:10 way, eat the fat, and drink the s', 4477
Es 2:12 and six months with s' odours, 1314
Job 20:12 wickedness be s' in his mouth, 4985
21:33 The clods of the valley shall be s' "
38:31 bind the s' influences of Pleiades, *4575
Ps 55:14 We took s' counsel together, and 4985
104:34 My meditation of him shall be s': 6148
119:103 How s' are thy words unto my 4452
141: 6 hear my words; for they are s'. 5276
Pr 3:24 lie down, and thy sleep shall be s'. 6148
9:17 Stolen waters are s', and bread 4985
13:19 desire accomplished is s' to the 6148
16:24 as an honeycomb, s' to the soul, 4966
20:17 Bread of deceit is s' to a man; but 6149
23: 8 vomit up, and lose thy s' words. 5273
24:13 the honeycomb, which is s' to thy 4966
27: 7 hungry soul every bitter thing is s'. "
Ec 5:12 The sleep of a labouring man is s', "
11: 7 Truly the light is s', and a pleasant "
Ca 2: 3 and his fruit was s' to my taste. "
14 s' is thy voice, and thy countenance 6149
5: 5 fingers with s' smelling myrrh, *5674
13 as a bed of spices, as s' flowers: 4840
13 lilies, dropping s' smelling myrrh. *5674
16 His mouth is most s': yea, he is 4477
Isa 3:24 instead of s' smell...shall be stink; 1314
5:20 put bitter for s', and s' for bitter! 4966
23:16 make s' melody, sing many songs, 3190
43:24 hast bought me no s' cane with money, "
49:26 their own blood, as with s' wine: 6071
Jer 6:20 the s' cane from a far country? 2896
20 nor your sacrifices s' unto me. *6148
31:26 and my sleep was s' unto me. "
Eze 6:13 offer s' savour to all their idols. 5207
16:19 set it before them for a s' savour: "
20:28 there also they made their s' savour, "
41 will accept you with your s' savour, "
Da 2:46 an oblation and s' odours unto him. 5208
Am 9:13 the mountains shall drop s' wine, *6071
Mic 6:15 and s' wine, but shalt not drink *8492
M'r 16: 1 and Salome, had bought s' spices, *
2Co 2:15 are unto God a s' savour of Christ, *2175*
Ph'p 4:18 an odour of a s' smell, a sacrifice "
Jas 3:11 same place s' water and bitter? *1099*
Re 10: 9 it shall be in thy mouth s' as honey. "
10 and it was in my mouth s' as honey: "

sweeter
J'g 14:18 What is s' than honey? and what 4966
Ps 19:10 s'...than honey and the honeycomb. "
119:103 yea, s' than honey to my mouth! "

sweetly
Job 24:20 the worm shall feed s' on him; he 4988
Ca 7: 9 that goeth down s', causing the *4339

sweetness
J'g 9:11 Should I forsake my s', and my 4987
14:14 and out of the strong came forth s'. 4966
Pr 16:21 s' of the lips increaseth learning. 4986
27: 9 so doth the s' of a man's friend by "
Eze 3: 3 was in my mouth as honey for s'. 4966

sweetsmelling See also SWEET and SMELLING.
Eph 5: 2 a sacrifice to God for a s' savour. *2175*

swell See also SWELLED; SWELLING; SWOLLEN.
Nu 5:21 thigh to rot, and thy belly to s', 6639
22 to make thy belly to s', and thy 6638

Nu 5:27 and her belly shall s·, and her thigh 6638
De 8: 4 neither did thy foot s·, these forty 1216

swelled See also SWOLLEN.
Ne 9:21 waxed not old, and their feet s· not. 1216

swelling See also SWELLINGS.
Ps 46: 3 the mountains shake with the s· 1346
Isa 30:13 s· out in a high wall, whose 1158
Jer 12: 5 wilt thou do in the s· of Jordan? *1347
49:19 up like a lion from the s· of Jordan* "
50:44 up like a lion from the s· of Jordan* "
2Pe 2:18 speak great s· words of vanity, 5246
Jude 16 mouth speaketh great s· words, "

swellings
2Co 12:20 backbitings, whisperings, s·, 5450

swept
J'g 5:21 The river of Kishon s· them away, 1640
Jer 46:15 Why are thy valiant men s· away? 5502
M't 12:44 findeth it empty, s·, and garnished. 4563
Lu 11:25 he findeth it s· and garnished. "

swerved
1Ti 1: 6 From which some having s· have 795

swift See also SWIFTER.
De 28:49 of the earth, as s· as the eagle flieth; *
1Ch 12: 8 were as s· as the roes upon the 4116
Job 9:26 are passed away as the s· ships: 16
24:18 He is s· as the waters; their 7031
Pr 6:18 feet...be s· in running to mischief, 4116
Ec 9:11 that the race is not to the s·, nor 7031
Isa 18: 2 Go, ye s· messengers, to a nation "
19: 1 the Lord rideth upon a s· cloud, "
30:16 flee: and, We will ride upon the s·; "
16 shall they that pursue you be s·. 7043
66:20 upon mules, and upon s· beasts, 3753
Jer 2:23 thou art a s· dromedary traversing 7031
46: 6 Let not the s· flee away, nor the "
Am 2:14 the flight shall perish from the s·, "
15 and he that is s· of foot shall not "
Mic 1:13 bind the chariot to the s· beast: 7409
Mal 3: 5 I will be a s· witness against the 4116
Ro 3:15 Their feet are s· to shed blood: 3691
Jas 1:19 let every man be s· to hear, slow 5036
2Pe 2: 1 upon themselves s· destruction. 5031

swifter
2Sa 1:23 they were s· than eagles, they 7043
Job 7: 6 My days are s· than a weaver's "
9:25 Now my days are s· than a post: "
Jer 4:13 his horses are s· than eagles. "
La 4:19 persecutors are s· than the eagles 7031
Hab 1: 8 horses...are s· than the leopards, 7043

swiftly
Ps 147:15 earth: his word runneth very s·. 4120
Isa 5:26 they shall come with speed s·: 7031
Da 9:21 being caused to fly s·, touched me 3288
Joe 3: 4 s· and speedily will I return your 7031

swim See also SWIMMEST; SWIMMETH.
2Ki 6: 6 it in thither; and the iron did s·. 6687
Ps 6: 6 all the night make I my bed to s·; 7811
Isa 25:11 spreadeth forth his hands to s·: "
Eze 47: 5 waters were risen, waters to s· in, 7813
Ac 27:42 lest any of them should s· out, 1579
43 they which could s· should cast 2860

swimmest
Eze 32: 6 thy blood the land wherein thou s·, 6824

swimmeth
Isa 25:11 that s· spreadeth forth his hands 7811

swine See also SWINE'S.
Le 11: 7 the s·, though he divide the hoof, 2386
De 14: 8 the s·, because it divideth the hoof, "
M't 7: 6 neither cast ye...pearls before s·, 5519
8:30 them an herd of many s· feeding. "
31 us to go away into the herd of s·. "
32 out, they went into the herd of s·: "
32 whole herd of s· ran violently down* "
M'r 5:11 a great herd of s· feeding. "
12 Send us into the s·, that we may "
13 went out, and entered into the s·: "
14 they that fed the s· fled, and told "
16 the devil, and also concerning the s·. "
Lu 8:32 an herd of many s· feeding on the "
33 of the man, and entered into the s·: "
15:15 he sent him into his fields to feed s·. "
16 with the husks that the s· did eat: "

swine's
Pr 11:22 As a jewel of gold in a s· snout, so 2386
Isa 65: 4 which eat s· flesh, and broth of "
66: 3 oblation, as if he offered s· blood; "
17 tree in the midst, eating s· flesh, "

swollen See also SWELLED.
Ac 28: 6 looked when he should have s·, 4092

swoon See also SWOONED.
La 2:11 the sucklings s· in the streets of 5848

swooned
La 2:12 when they s· as the wounded in *5848

sword See also SWORDS.
Ge 3:24 a flaming s· which turned every 2719
27:40 And by thy s· shalt thou live, and "
31:26 as captives taken with the s·? "
34:25 brethren, took each man his s·, "
26 his son with the edge of the s·, "
48:22 hand of the Amorite with my s· "
Ex 5: 3 us with pestilence, or with the s·. "
21 to put a s· in their hand to slay us. "
15: 9 I will draw my s·, my hand shall "
17:13 his people with the edge of the s·. "
18: 4 delivered me from the s· of Pharaoh: "
22:24 hot, and I will kill you with the s·; "
32:27 Put every man his s· by his side, "
Le 26: 6 shall the s· go through your land. "
Le 26: 7 they shall fall before you by the s·. 2719
8 enemies...fall before you by the s·. "
25 And I will bring a s· upon you, that "
33 and will draw out a s· after you: "
36 they shall flee, as fleeing from a s·; "
37 as it were before a s·, when none "
Nu 14: 3 us unto this land, to fall by the s·, "
43 you, and ye shall fall by the s·: "
19:16 is slain with a s· in the open fields, "
20:18 I come out against thee with the s·. "
21:24 smote him with the edge of the s·, "
22:23 way, and his s· drawn in his hand: "
29 would there were a s· in mine hand, "
31 way, and his s· drawn in his hand: "
31: 8 son of Beor they slew with the s·. "
De 13:15 of that city with the edge of the s·, "
15 cattle thereof, with...edge of the s·. "
20:13 male thereof with the edge of the s·: "
28:22 and with the s·, and with blasting, "
32:25 The s· without, and terror within, "
41 If I whet my glittering s·, and mine "
42 blood, and my s· shall devour flesh; "
33:29 and who is the s· of thy excellency! "
Jos 5:13 him with his s· drawn in his hand: "
6:21 and ass, with the edge of the s·. "
8:24 were all fallen on the edge of the s·, "
24 and smote it with the edge of the s·. "
10:11 children of Israel slew with the s·. "
28, 30, 32, 35, 37, 39 the edge of the s·. "
11:10 smote the king thereof with the s·: "
11 souls...therein with...edge of the s·, "
12 smote them with the edge of the s·, "
14 they smote with the edge of the s·, "
13:22 children of Israel slay with the s·. "
19:47 and smote it with the edge of the s·, "
24:12 not with thy s·, nor with thy bow. "
J'g 1: 8 smitten it with the edge of the s·, "
25 smote the city with...edge of the s·; "
4:15 the edge of the s· before Barak; "
16 Sisera fell upon the edge of the s·; "
7:14 nothing else save the s· of Gideon "
18 The s· of the Lord, and of Gideon.*
20 The s· of the Lord, and of Gideon. 2719
22 every man's s· against his fellow, "
8:10 twenty thousand men that drew s·. "
20 But the youth drew not his s·: for "
9:54 Draw thy s·, and slay me, that men "
18:27 smote them with the edge of the s·, "
20: 2 thousand footmen that drew s·. "
15 and six thousand men that drew s·. "
17 hundred thousand men that drew s·: "
25 thousand men; all these drew the s·. "
35 hundred men: all these drew the s·. "
37 all the city with the edge of the s·. "
46 five thousand men that drew the s·; "
48 smote them with the edge of the s·, "
21:10 Jabesh-gilead with the edge of the s·. "
1Sa 13:22 was neither s· nor spear found in "
14:20 every man's s· was against his "
15: 8 the people with the edge of the s·. "
33 thy s· hath made women childless, "
17:39 girded his s· upon his armour, "
45 Thou comest to me with a s·, and "
47 that the Lord saveth not with s· and "
50 was no s· in the hand of David. "
51 upon the Philistine, and took his s·, "
18: 4 and his garments, even to his s·, "
21: 8 here under thine hand spear or s·? "
8 have neither brought my s· nor my "
9 The s· of Goliath the Philistine, "
22:10 and gave him the s· of Goliath the "
13 thou hast given him bread, and a s·, "
19 smote he with the edge of the s·, "
19 and sheep, with the edge of the s·. "
25:13 men, Gird ye on every man his s·. "
13 they girded on every man his s·; "
13 and David also girded on his s·: "
31: 4 Draw thy s·, and thrust me through "
4 Saul took a s·, and fell upon it. "
5 dead, he fell likewise upon his s·, "
2Sa 1:12 because they were fallen by the s·. "
22 the s· of Saul returned not empty. "
2:16 thrust his s· in his fellow's side; "
26 said, Shall the s· devour for ever? "
3:29 or that falleth on the s·, or that "
11:25 for the s· devoureth one as well as "
12: 9 killed Uriah the Hittite with the s·, "
9 hast slain him with the s· of the "
10 the s· shall never depart from thine "
15:14 the city with the edge of the s·. "
18: 8 more people that day than the s· "
20: 8 upon it a girdle with a s· fastened "
10 Amasa took no heed to the s· that "
21:16 he being girded with a new s·, "
23:10 and his hand clave unto the s·: 2719
24: 9 valiant men that drew the s·; "
1Ki 1:51 will not slay his servant with the s·. "
2: 8 not put thee to death with the s·. "
32 than he, and slew them with the s·, "
3:24 And the king said, Bring me a s·. "
24 they brought a s· before the king. "
19: 1 slain all the prophets with the s·. "
10, 14 slain thy prophets with the s·; "
17 him that escapeth the s· of Hazael "
17 that escapeth from the s· of Jehu "
2Ki 6:22 thou hast taken captive with thy s· "
8:12 men wilt thou slay with the s·, and "
10:25 smote them with the edge of the s·; "
11:15 that followeth her kill with the s·. "
20 slew Athaliah with the s· beside the "
19: 7 to fall by the s· in his own land. "
37 his sons smote him with the s·: "
1Ch 5:18 men able to bear buckler and s·, "
10: 4 Draw thy s·, and thrust me through "
4 So Saul took a s·, and fell upon it. "
5 he fell likewise on the s·, and died. "
1Ch 21: 5 hundred thousand men...drew s·: 2719
5 and ten thousand men that drew s·. "
12 the s· of thine enemies overtaketh "
12 else three days the s· of the Lord, "
16 having a drawn s· in his hand "
27 put up his s· again into the sheath "
30 afraid because of the s· of the angel "
2Ch 20: 9 evil cometh upon us, as the s·, "
21: 4 slew all his brethren with the s·, "
23:14 her, let him be slain with the s·. "
21 they had slain Athaliah with the s·. "
29: 9 our fathers have fallen by the s·, "
32:21 bowels slew him there with the s·. "
36:17 slew their young men with the s· in "
20 them that had escaped from the s· "
Ezr 9: 7 to the s·, to captivity, and to a spoil, "
Ne 4:18 every one had his s· girded by his "
Es 9: 5 enemies with the stroke of the s·, "
Job 1:15, 17 servants with the edge of the s·; "
5:15 But he saveth the poor from the s·, "
20 and in war from the power of the s·. "
15:22 and he is waited for of the s·. "
19:29 Be ye afraid of the s·: for wrath "
29 bringeth the punishment of the s·, "
20:25 the glittering s· cometh out of his *1300
27:14 be multiplied, it is for the s·: 2719
33:18 his life from perishing by the s·. 7973
36:12 not, they shall perish by the s·, "
39:22 neither turneth...back from the s·. 2719
40:19 he that made him can make his s· "
41:26 s· of him that layeth at him cannot "
Ps 7:12 If he turn not, he will whet his s·; "
17:13 from the wicked, which is thy s·: "
22:20 Deliver my soul from the s·; my "
37:14 The wicked have drawn out the s·, "
15 s· shall enter into their own heart, "
42:10 As with a s· in my bones, mine 7524
44: 3 land in possession by their own s·, 2719
6 bow, neither shall my s· save me. "
45: 3 Gird thy s· upon thy thigh, O most "
57: 4 arrows, and their tongue a sharp s·. "
63:10 They shall fall by the s·: they shall "
64: 3 Who whet their tongue like a s·, "
76: 3 bow, the shield, and the s·, and the "
78:62 his people over also unto the s·; "
64 Their priests fell by the s·; and "
89:43 hast also turned the edge of his s·, "
144:10 his servant from the hurtful s·. "
149: 6 and a twoedged s· in their hand; "
Pr 5: 4 wormwood, sharp as a twoedged s·. "
12:18 speaketh like the piercings of a s·: "
25:18 his neighbour is a maul, and a s·, "
Ca 3: 8 every man...his s· upon his thigh "
Isa 1:20 ye shall be devoured with the s·: "
2: 4 shall not lift up s· against nation, "
3:25 Thy men shall fall by the s·, and "
13:15 joined unto them shall fall by the s·. "
14:19 are slain, thrust through with a s·, "
21:15 from the drawn s·, and from the "
22: 2 slain men are not slain with the s·, "
27: 1 great and strong s· shall punish "
31: 8 shall the Assyrian fall with the s·, "
8 and the s·, not of a mean man, shall "
8 but he shall flee from the s·, and "
34: 5 my s· shall be bathed in heaven: "
6 s· of the Lord is filled with blood, "
37: 7 him to fall by the s· in his own land. "
38 his sons smote him with the s·; "
41: 2 he gave them as the dust to his s·, "
49: 2 made my mouth like a sharp s·; "
51:19 and the famine, and the s·: by "
65:12 will I number you to the s·, and "
66:16 by his s· will the Lord plead with "
Jer 2:30 your own s· hath devoured your "
4:10 the s· reacheth unto the soul. "
5:12 neither shall we see s· nor famine: "
17 wherein thou trustedst, with the s·. "
6:25 for the s· of the enemy and fear is "
9:16 and I will send a s· after them, till I "
11:22 the young men shall die by the s·; "
12:12 for the s· of the Lord shall devour "
14:12 but I will consume them by the s·, "
13 Ye shall not see the s·, neither shall "
15 S· and famine shall not be in this "
15 By s· and famine shall those "
16 because of the famine and the s·; "
18 then behold the slain with the s·! "
15: 2 such as are for the s·, to the s·; "
3 the s· to slay, and the dogs to tear, "
9 will I deliver to the s· before their "
16: 4 they shall be consumed by the s·, "
18:21 their blood by the force of the s·; "
21 their young men be slain by the s· "
19: 7 I will cause them to fall by the s· "
20: 4 shall fall by the s· of their enemies, "
4 and shall slay them with the s·. "
21: 7 from the s·, and from the famine, "
7 smite them with the edge of the s·; "
9 in this city shall die by the s·, and "
24:10 And I will send the s·, the famine, "
25:16 the s· that I will send among them. "
27 the s· which I will send among you. "
29 for I will call for a s· upon all the "
31 give them that are wicked to the s·, "
26:23 who slew him with the s·, and cast "
27: 8 punish, saith the Lord, with the s·, "
13 die, thou and thy people, by the s·, "
29:17 I will send upon them the s·, the "
18 I will persecute them with the s·, "
31: 2 The people which were left of the s· "
32:24 because of the s·, and of the famine, "
36 of the king of Babylon by the s·, "
33: 4 down by the mounts, and by the s·; "
34: 4 thee, Thou shalt not die by the s·: "
17 to the s·, to the pestilence, and "
38: 2 in this city shall die by the s·, by "

Jer 39:18 and thou shalt not fall by the s·, 2719
41: 2 the son of Shaphan with the s·, "
42:16 that the s·, which ye feared, shall "
17 they shall die by the s·, by the "
22 that ye shall die by the s·, by the "
43:11 and such as are for the s· to the s·. "
44:12, 12 by the s· and by the famine: "
13 have punished Jerusalem, by the s·, "
18 and have been consumed by the s· "
27 shall be consumed by the s· and "
28 a small number that escape the s· "
46:10 and the s· shall devour, and it shall "
14 for the s· shall devour round about "
16 our nativity, from the oppressing s·. "
47: 6 O thou s· of the Lord, how long will "
48: 2 Madmen; the s· shall pursue thee. "
10 that keepeth back his s· from blood. "
49:37 and I will send the s· after them. "
50:16 for fear of the oppressing s· they "
35 A s· is upon the Chaldeans, saith "
36 A s· is upon the liars; and they "
36 a s· is upon her mighty men; and "
37 A s· is upon their horses, and upon "
37 a s· is upon her treasures; and they "
51:50 that have escaped the s·, go away, "
La 1:20 abroad the s· bereaveth, at home "
2:21 my young men are fallen by the s·; "
4: 9 that be slain with the s· are better "
5: 9 because of the s· of the wilderness. "
Eze 5: 2 and I will draw out a s· after them. "
12 and a third part shall fall by the s· "
12 and I will draw out a s· after them. "
17 and I will bring the s· upon thee. "
6: 3 I, even I, will bring a s· upon you, "
8 escape the s· among the nations, "
11 shall fall by the s·, by the famine, "
12 he that is near shall fall by the s·; "
7:15 The s· is without, and the pestilence "
15 is in the field shall die with the s·; "
11: 8 Ye have feared the s·; and I will "
8 bring a s· upon you, saith the Lord "
10 Ye shall fall by the s·; I will judge "
12:14 I will draw out the s· after them. "
16 leave a few men of them from the s·, "
14:17 Or if I bring a s· upon that land, "
17 and say, S·, go through the land; "
21 Jerusalem, the s·, and the famine, "
17:21 all his bands shall fall by the s·, "
21: 3 draw forth my s· out of his sheath "
4 my s· go forth out of his sheath "
5 drawn forth my s· out of his sheath: "
9 Say, A s·, a s· is sharpened, and "
11 s· is sharpened, and it is furbished, "
12 terrors by reason of the s· shall be "
13 what if the s· contemn even the rod?* "
14 and let the s· be doubled the third 2719
14 time, the s· of the slain: it is the "
14 s· of the great men that are slain, "
15 I have set the point of the s· against "
19 s· of the king of Babylon may come: "
20 the s· may come to Rabbath of the "
28 say thou, The s·, the s· is drawn: "
23:10 daughters, and slew her with the s·: "
25 and thy remnant shall fall by the s·: "
24:21 whom ye have left shall fall by the s·. "
25:13 they of Dedan shall fall by the s·. "
26: 6 in the field shall be slain by the s·: "
8 shall slay with the s· thy daughters "
11 he shall slay thy people by the s·, "
28:23 judged in the midst of her by the s· "
29: 8 I will bring a s· upon thee, and cut "
30: 4 And the s· shall come upon Egypt, "
5 shall fall with them by the s·. "
6 Syene shall they fall in it by the s·, "
17 and of Pi-beseth shall fall by the s·: "
21 it, to make it strong to hold the s·. "
22 cause the s· to fall out of his hand. "
24 Babylon, and put my s· in his hand: "
25 put my s· into the hand of the king "
31:17 unto them that be slain with the s·; "
18 with them that be slain by the s·. "
32:10 I shall brandish my s· before them; "
11 s· of the king of Babylon shall come "
20 of them that are slain by the s·: "
20 she is delivered to the s·: draw her "
21 lie uncircumcised, slain by the s·. "
22 all of them slain, fallen by the s·: "
23, 24 all of them slain, fallen by the s·, "
25 them uncircumcised, slain by the s·: "
26 them uncircumcised, slain by the s·, "
28 with them that are slain with the s·. "
29 by them that were slain by the s·: "
30 with them that be slain by the s·, "
31 and all his army slain by the s·, "
32 with them that are slain with the s·, "
33: 2 When I bring the s· upon a land, if "
3 he seeth the s· come upon the land, "
4 if the s· come, and take him away, "
6 if the watchman see the s· come, "
6 if the s· come, and take any person "
26 Ye stand upon your s·, ye work "
27 are in the wastes shall fall by the s·, "
35: 5 blood...of Israel by the force of the s· "
8 they fall that are slain with the s·. "
38: 8 that is brought back from the s·, "
21 And I will call for a s· against him "
21 every man's s· shall be against his "
39:23 enemies: so fell they all by the s·. "
Da 11:33 yet they shall fall by the s·, and by "
Ho 1: 7 not save them by bow, nor by s·, "
2:18 and I will break the bow and the s· "
7:16 their princes shall fall by the s· "
11: 6 And the s· shall abide on his cities, "
13:16 they shall fall by the s·: their "
Joe 2: 8 and when they fall upon the s·, *7973
Am 1:11 did pursue his brother with the s·, 2719
4:10 young men have I slain with the s·, 2719
7: 9 the house of Jeroboam with the s·. "
11 saith, Jeroboam shall die by the s·, "
17 thy daughters shall fall by the s·, "
9: 1 slay the last of them with the s·: "
4 thence will I command the s·, and "
10 sinners of my people...die by the s·, "
Mic 4: 3 shall not lift up a s· against nation, "
5: 6 waste...land of Assyria with the s·, "
6:14 deliverest will I give up to the s·. "
Na 2:13 the s· shall devour thy young lions: "
3: 3 horseman lifteth up...the bright s· "
15 the s· shall cut thee off, it shall eat "
Zep 2:12 also, ye shall be slain by my s·. "
Hag 2:22 every one by the s· of his brother. "
Zec 9:13 made thee as the s· of a mighty man. "
11:17 the s· shall be upon his arm, and "
13: 7 Awake, O s·, against my shepherd, "
M't 10:34 I came not to send peace, but a s·. 3162
26:51 drew his s·, and struck a servant "
52 Put up again thy s· into his place: "
52 for all they that take the s· "
52 shall perish with the s·. "
M'r 14:47 one of them that stood by drew a s·, "
Lu 2:35 a s·...pierce through thy own soul 4501
21:24 they shall fall by the edge of the s·, 3162
22:36 he that hath no s·, let him sell his* "
49 Lord, shall we smite with the s·? "
Joh 18:10 Simon Peter having a s· drew it, "
11 Peter, Put up thy s· into the sheath: "
Ac 12: 2 And he killed James...with the s·. "
16:27 doors open, he drew out his s·, and "
Ro 8:35 or nakedness, or peril, or s·? "
13: 4 for he beareth not the s· in vain: "
Eph 6:17 s· of the Spirit, which is the word "
Heb 4:12 and sharper than any twoedged s·, "
11:34 escaped the edge of the s·, out of "
37 tempted, were slain with the s·: "
Re 1:16 mouth went a sharp twoedged s·: 4501
2:12 hath the sharp s· with two edges; "
16 them with the s· of my mouth. "
6: 4 was given unto him a great s·. 3162
8 to kill with s·, and with hunger, 4501
13:10 he that killeth with the s· 3162
10 must be killed with the s·. "
14 beast, which had the wound by a s·, "
19:15 out of his mouth goeth a sharp s·, 4501
21 the remnant were slain with the s· "
21 which s· proceeded out of his mouth:

swords
1Sa 13:19 Lest the Hebrews make them s· 2719
2Ki 3:26 seven hundred men that drew s·, * "
Ne 4:13 after their families with their s·, "
Ps 55:21 than oil, yet were they drawn s·. 6609
59: 7 their mouths: s· are in their lips: 2719
Pr 30:14 a generation, whose teeth are as s·, "
Ca 3: 8 all hold s·, being expert in war: "
Isa 2: 4 shall beat their s· into plowshares, "
21:15 For they fled from the s·, from the "
Eze 16:40 thrust thee through with their s·. "
23:47 and dispatch them with their s·; "
28: 7 draw their s· against the beauty of "
30:11 shall draw their s· against Egypt, "
32:12 By the s· of the mighty will I cause "
27 have laid their s· under their heads, "
38: 4 and shields, all of them handling s·: "
Joe 3:10 Beat your plowshares into s·, and "
Mic 4: 3 shall beat their s· into plowshares, "
M't 26:47 with him a great multitude with s· 3162
55 come out as against a thief with s· "
M'r 14:43 with him a great multitude with s· "
48 come out, as against a thief, with s· "
Lu 22:38 said, Lord, behold, here are two s·. "
52 come out, as against a thief, with s· "

swore See SWARE.

sworn
Ge 22:16 By myself have I s·, saith the Lord, 7650
Ex 13:19 straitly s· the children of Israel, "
17:16 Lord hath s· that the 3027,5920,3676
Le 6: 5 about which he hath s· falsely; 7650
De 7: 8 keep the oath which he hath s· * "
13:17 thee, as he hath s· unto thy fathers; "
19: 8 as he hath s· unto thy fathers, "
28: 9 himself, as he hath s· unto thee, "
29:13 and as he hath s· unto thy fathers,* "
31: 7 Lord hath s· unto their fathers to "
Jos 9:18 the princes...had s· unto them by "
19 We have s· unto them by the Lord "
J'g 2:15 and as the Lord had s· unto them: "
21: 1 the men of Israel had s· in Mizpeh, "
7 seeing we have s· by the Lord that "
18 for the children of Israel have s· "
1Sa 3:14 I have s· unto the house of Eli, "
20:42 we have s· both of us in the name of "
2Sa 3: 9 as the Lord hath s· to David, even "
21: 2 children of Israel had s· unto them: "
2Ch 15:15 for they had s· with all their heart, "
Ne 6:18 many in Judah s· unto him, 1167,7621
9:15 which thou hadst s· to give them.*5375
Ps 24: 4 unto vanity, nor s· deceitfully. 7650
89: 3 I have s· unto David my servant, "
35 Once have I s· by my holiness that "
102: 8 mad against me are s· against me. "
110: 4 Lord hath s·, and will not repent, "
119:106 I have s·, and I will perform it, "
132:11 Lord hath s· in truth unto David; "
Isa 14:24 The Lord of hosts hath s·, saying, "
45:23 I have s· by myself, the word is "
54: 9 I have s· that the waters of Noah "
9 so have I s· that I would not be "
62: 8 Lord hath s· by his right hand, and "
Jer 5: 7 and s· by them that are no gods: "
11: 5 the oath which I have s· unto your* "
44:26 I have s· by my great name, saith "
49:13 I have s· by myself, saith the Lord, "
51:14 Lord of hosts hath s· by himself, 7650
Eze 21:23 sight, to them that have s· oaths: "
Am 4: 2 Lord God hath s· by his holiness, "
6: 8 The Lord God hath s· by himself, "
8: 7 hath s· by the excellency of Jacob, "
Mic 7:20 which thou hast s· unto our fathers "
Ac 2:30 God had s· with an oath to him, 3660
7:17 which God had s· to Abraham, the* "
Heb 4: 3 As I have s· in my wrath, if they * "

sycamine
Lu 17: 6 ye might say unto the s· tree, Be 4807

sycamore See SYCOMORE.

Sychar (*si'-kar*) See also SHECHEM.
Joh 4: 5 city of Samaria, which is called S·, 4965

Sychem (*si'-kem*) See also SHECHEM.
Ac 7:16 And were carried over into S·, *4966
16 sons of Emmor the father of S·. * "

sycomore See also SYCOMORES.
1Ki 10:27 as the s· trees that are in the vale, 8256
1Ch 27:28 s· trees that were in the low plains "
2Ch 1:15 cedar trees made he as the s· trees "
9:27 cedar trees made he as the s· trees "
Ps 78:47 hail, and their s· trees with frost. "
Am 7:14 herdman, and a gatherer of s· fruit: "
Lu 19: 4 climbed up into a s· tree to see 4809

sycomores
Isa 9:10 the s· are cut down, but we will 8256

sycomore-trees See SYCOMORE and TREES.

Syene (*si-e'-ne*)
Eze 29:10 from the tower of S· even unto *5482
30: 6 from the tower of S· shall they fall* "

synagogue See also SYNAGOGUE'S; SYNAGOGUES.
M't 12: 9 thence, he went into their s·: 4864
13:54 country, he taught them in their s·, "
M'r 1:21 sabbath day he entered into the s·, "
23 in their s· a man with an unclean "
29 when they were come out of the s·, "
3: 1 And he entered again into the s·; "
5:22 cometh one of the rulers of the s·, 752
36 unto the ruler of the s·, Be not "
38 to the house of the ruler of the s·, "
6: 2 come, he began to teach in the s·: 4864
Lu 4:16 he went into the s· on the sabbath "
20 eyes of all them that were in the s· "
28 And all they in the s·, when they "
33 in the s· there was a man, which "
38 he arose out of the s·, and entered "
6: 6 he entered into the s· and taught: "
7: 5 nation, and he hath built us a s·. "
8:41 and he was a ruler of the s·: and "
13:14 the ruler of the s· answered with 752
Joh 6:59 These things said he in the s·, as 4864
9:22 he should be put out of the s·. 656
12:42 lest they should be put out of the s·: "
18:20 I ever taught in the s·, and in the *4864
Ac 6: 9 Then there arose certain of the s·, "
9 is called the s· of the Libertines, "
13:14 and went into the s· on the sabbath "
15 the rulers of the s· sent unto them, 752
42 the Jews were gone out of the s·, *4864
14: 1 both together into the s· of the "
17: 1 where was a s· of the Jews: "
10 thither went into the s· of the Jews. "
17 disputed he in the s· with the Jews, "
18: 4 reasoned in the s· every sabbath, "
7 whose house joined hard to the s·. "
8 Crispus, the chief ruler of the s·, 752
17 Sosthenes, the chief ruler of the s·, "
19 but he himself entered into the s·, 4864
26 he began to speak boldly in the s·: "
19: 8 And he went into the s·, and spake "
22:19 and beat in every s· them that "
26:11 I punished them oft in every s·, * "
Re 2: 9 and are not, but are the s· of Satan. "
3: 9 I will make them of the s· of Satan, "

synagogue's
M'r 5:35 came from the ruler of the s· house 752
Lu 8:49 one from the ruler of the s· house, "

synagogues
Ps 74: 8 have burned up all the s· of God 4150
M't 4:23 teaching in their s·, and preaching 4864
6: 2 as the hypocrites do in the s· and "
5 they love to pray standing in the s· "
9:35 teaching in their s·, and preaching "
10:17 they will scourge you in their s·; "
23: 6 feasts, and the chief seats in the s·, "
34 of them shall ye scourge in your s·, "
M'r 1:39 he preached in their s· throughout "
12:39 And the chief seats in the s·, and "
13: 9 and in the s· ye shall be beaten: "
Lu 4:15 And he taught in their s·, being "
44 he preached in the s· of Galilee. "
11:43 love the uppermost seats in the s·, "
12:11 when they bring you unto the s·, "
13:10 he was teaching in one of the s· "
20:46 and the highest seats in the s·, and "
21:12 delivering you up to the s·, and into "
Joh 16: 2 They shall put you out of the s·: 656
Ac 9: 2 him letters to Damascus to the s·, 4864
20 he preached Christ in the s·, that "
13: 5 preached the word of God in the s· "
15:21 being read in the s· every sabbath "
24:12 neither in the s·, nor in the city: "

Syntyche (*sin'-ti-ke*)
Ph'p 4: 2 I beseech Euodias, and beseech S·, 4941

Syracuse (*sir'-a-cuse*)
Ac 28:12 landing at S·, we tarried there 4946

Syria (*sir'-e-ah*) See also ARAM; SYRIA-DAMASCUS; SYRIA-MAACHAH; SYRIAN.
J'g 10: 6 and the gods of S', and the gods of 758
2Sa 8: 6 put garrisons in S' of Damascus: "
12 Of S', and of Moab, and of the "
15: 8 vow while I abode at Geshur in S', "
1Ki 10:29 Hittites, and for the kings of S'. "
11:25 Israel, and reigned over S'. "
15:18 the son of Hezion, king of S', that "
19:15 anoint Hazael to be king over S': "
20: 1 Ben-hadad the king of S' gathered "
20 the king of S' escaped on an horse "
22 king of S' will come up against thee."
23 servants of the king of S' said unto "
22: 1 without war between S' and Israel. "
3 not out of the hand of the king of S'?"
31 king of S' commanded his thirty "
2Ki 5: 1 captain of the host of the king of S', "
1 Lord had given deliverance unto S': "
5 the king of S' said, Go to, go, and I "
6: 8 king of S' warred against Israel, "
11 the heart of the king of S' was sore "
23 the bands of S' came no more into "
24 Ben-hadad king of S' gathered all "
7: 5 uttermost part of the camp of S', * "
8: 7 Ben-hadad the king of S' was sick; "
9 Ben-hadad king of S' hath sent me "
13 that thou shalt be king over S'. "
28 the war against Hazael king of S' "
29 he fought against Hazael king of S'. "
9:14 Israel, because of Hazael king of S'. "
15 he fought with Hazael king of S'.) "
12:17 Then Hazael king of S' went up, and "
18 and sent it to Hazael king of S': "
13: 3 into the hand of Hazael king of S', "
4 the king of S' oppressed them. "
7 the king of S' had destroyed them, "
17 the arrow of deliverance from S': "
19 then hadst thou smitten S' till thou "
19 now thou shalt smite S' but thrice. "
22 Hazael king of S' oppressed Israel "
24 So Hazael king of S' died; and "
15:37 against Judah Rezin the king of S', "
16: 5 Then Rezin king of S' and Pekah "
6 Rezin king of S' recovered Elath "
6 recovered Elath to S', and drave the"
7 me out of the hand of the king of S', "
2Ch 1:17 for the kings of S', by their means. "
16: 2 and sent to Ben-hadad king of S', "
7 thou hast relied on the king of S', "
7 king of S' escaped out of thine hand."
18:10 With these thou shalt push S' until*"
30 the king of S' had commanded the "
20: 2 from beyond the sea on this side S'; "
22: 5 to war against Hazael king of S' at "
2Ch 22: 6 he fought with Hazael king of S'. 758
24:23 the host of S' came up against him:* "
28: 5 him into the hand of the king of S'; "
23 gods of the kings of S' help them, "
Isa 7: 1 Rezin the king of S', and Pekah the "
2 S' is confederate with Ephraim. "
4 for the fierce anger of Rezin with S',"
5 Because S', Ephraim, and the son "
8 For the head of S' is Damascus, and"
17: 3 Damascus, and the remnant of S': "
Eze 16:57 thy reproach of the daughters of S', "
27:16 S' was thy merchant by reason of "
Ho 12:12 Jacob fled into the country of S', * "
Am 1: 5 people of S' shall go into captivity "
M't 4:24 his fame went throughout all S': 4947
Lu 2: 2 when Cyrenius was governor of S'.)"
Ac 15:23 of the Gentiles in Antioch and S' "
41 he went through S' and Cilicia, "
18:18 brethren, and sailed thence into S',"
20: 3 as he was about to sail into S', he "
21: 3 sailed into S', and landed at Tyre: "
Gal 1:21 I came into the regions of S' and "

Syriack (*sir'-e-ak*) See also SYRIAN.
Da 2: 4 the Chaldeans to the king in S', * 762

Syria-damascus (*sir''-e-ah-da-mas'-cus*) See also SYRIA and DAMASCUS.
1Ch 18: 6 David put garrisons in S'; *758,1834

Syria-maachah (*sir''-e-ah-ma'-a-kah*)
1Ch 19: 6 and out of S', and out of Zobah. * 758

Syrian (*sir'-e-un*) See also ARAMITES; SYRIANS; SYROPHENICIAN.
Ge 25:20 of Bethuel the S' of Padan-aram, 761
20 the sister to Laban the S'. "
28: 5 unto Laban, son of Bethuel the S', "
31:20 away unawares to Laban the S', "
24 And God came to Laban the S' in a "
De 26: 5 A S' ready to perish was my father, "
2Ki 5:20 master hath spared Naaman this S'. "
18:26 to thy servants in the S' language;762
Ezr 4: 7 letter was written in the S' tongue, "
7 and interpreted in the S' tongue. "
Isa 36:11 thy servant in the S' language; "
Lu 4:27 cleansed, saving Naaman the S'. 4948

Syrians (*sir'-e-uns*)
2Sa 8: 5 S' of Damascus came to succour 758
5 David slew of the S' two and twenty"
6 the S' became servants to David, "
13 from smiting of the S' in the valley "
10: 6 and hired the S' of Beth-rehob, "
6 and the S' of Zoba, twenty thousand"
8 the S' of Zoba, and of Rehob, and "
9 put them in array against the S': "
11 If the S' be too strong for me, then "
2Sa 10:13 him, unto the battle against the S':758
14 of Ammon saw that the S' were fled, "
15 the S' saw that they were smitten "
16 the S' that were beyond the river: "
17 S' set themselves in array against "
18 And the S' fled before Israel; and "
18 of seven hundred chariots of the S', "
19 the S' feared to help the children of "
1Ki 20:20 S' fled; and Israel pursued them: "
21 slew the S' with a great slaughter. "
26 that Ben-hadad numbered the S', "
27 kids; but the S' filled the country. "
28 Because the S' have said, The Lord"
29 the children of Israel slew of the S' "
22:11 With these shalt thou push the S', "
35 up in his chariot against the S', "
2Ki 5: 2 the S' had gone out by companies, "
6: 9 for thither the S' are come down. "
7: 4 let us fall unto the host of the S': "
5 to go unto the camp of the S': "
6 made...host of the S' to hear a noise"
10 We came to the camp of the S', and."
12 you what the S' have done to us. "
14 the king sent after the host of the S',"
15 which the S' had cast away in their "
16 out, and spoiled the tents of the S'. "
8:28 and the S' wounded Joram. 761
29 wounds which the S' had given him"
9:15 wounds which the S' had given him,"
13: 5 out from under the hand of the S':758
17 for thou shalt smite the S' in Aphek."
16: 6 and the S' came to Elath, and dwelt "
24: 2 bands of the S', and bands of the "
1Ch 18: 5 the S' of Damascus came to help "
5 David slew of the S' two and twenty"
6 and the S' became David's servants, "
19:10 and put them in array against the S'."
12 If the S' be too strong for me, then "
14 nigh before the S' unto the battle; "
15 Ammon saw that the S' were fled, "
16 the S' saw that they were put to the "
16 the S' that were beyond the river: "
17 the battle in array against the S'. "
18 But the S' fled before Israel; and "
18 David slew of the S' seven thousand"
19 the S' help the children of Ammon "
2Ch 18:34 in his chariot against the S' until "
22: 5 and the S' smote Joram. 761
24:24 army of the S' came with a small 758
Isa 9:12 The S' before, and the Philistines "
Jer 35:11 and for fear of the army of the S': "
Am 9: 7 from Caphtor, and the S' from Kir? "

Syrophenician (*sy''-ro-fe-ne'-she-un*)
M'r 7:26 The woman was a Greek, a S' by *4949

T.

Taanach (*ta'-a-nak*) See also TANACH.
Jos 12:21 The king of T', one; the king of 8590
17:11 the inhabitants of T' and her towns."
J'g 1:27 nor T' and her towns, nor the "
5:19 fought the kings of Canaan in T' "
1Ki 4:12 to him pertained T' and Megiddo, "
1Ch 7:29 T' and her towns, Megiddo and her"

Taanath-shiloh (*ta''-a-nath-shi'-lo*)
Jos 16: 6 went about eastward unto T'. 8387

Tabbaoth (*tab'-ba-oth*)
Ezr 2:43 of Hasupha, the children of T', 2884
Ne 7:46 of Hashupha, the children of T'. "

Tabbath (*tab'-bath*)
J'g 7:22 border of Abel-meholah, unto T'. 2888

Tabeal (*tab'-e-al*) See also TABEEL.
Isa 7: 6 the midst of it, even the son of T':*2870

Tabeel (*tab'-e-el*) See also TABEAL.
Ezr 4: 7 wrote Bishlam, Mithredath, T', 2870

taber See TABERING.

Taberah (*tab'-e-rah*)
Nu 11: 3 called the name of the place T': 8404
De 9:22 And at T', and at Massah, and at "

tabering
Na 2: 7 of doves, t' upon their breasts. ‡8608

tabernacle See also TABERNACLES.
Ex 25: 9 thee, after the pattern of the t', 4908
26: 1 shalt make the t' with ten curtains "
6 the taches: and it shall be one t'. "
7 hair to be a covering upon the t': "
9 curtain in the forefront of the t'. * 168
12 hang over the backside of the t'. 4908
13 it shall hang over the sides of the t',"
15 boards for the t' of shittim wood "
17 make for all the boards of the t'. "
18 shalt make the boards for the t', "
20 second side of the t' on the north "
22 And for the sides of the t' westward"
23 thou make for the corners of the t' "
26 the boards of the one side of the t', "
27 boards of the other side of the t', "
27 for the boards of the side of the t', "
30 shalt rear up the t' according to the"
35 the side of the t' toward the south: "
27: 9 thou shalt make the court of the t' "
19 vessels of the t' in all the service "
21 In the t' of...congregation without* 168
28:43 come in unto...t' of...congregation,* "
29: 4 door of the t' of the congregation, * "
10 before the t' of the congregation, * "
11 door of the t' of the congregation:* "
30 into the t' of the congregation * "
Ex 29:32 door of the t' of the congregation.* 168
42 door of the t' of the congregation* "
43 the t' shall be sanctified by my glory.*
44 sanctify the t' of the congregation,*168
30:16 service of the t' of the congregation;*"
18 between the t' of the congregation* "
20 go into the t' of the congregation,* "
26 anoint the t' of the congregation * "
36 testimony in...t' of...congregation,* "
31: 7 t' of the congregation, and the ark* "
7 and all the furniture of the t', * "
33: 7 And Moses took the t', and pitched it*"
7 called it...T' of the congregation.* "
7 out unto the t' of the congregation,* "
8 when Moses went out unto the t',* "
8 Moses, until he was gone into the t'.*"
9 pass, as Moses entered into the t',* "
9 pillar...stood at the door of the t',* "
10 cloudy pillar stand at the t' door:* "
11 Joshua,...departed not out of the t'.* "
35:11 The t', his tent, and his covering, 4908
15 the door at the entering in of the t', "
18 The pins of the t', and the pins of "
21 work of the t' of the congregation,* 168
36: 8 that wrought the work of the t' 4908
13 with the taches: so it became one t'. "
14 goats' hair for the tent over the t': "
20 boards for the t' of shittim wood, "
22 he make for all the boards of the t'. "
23 And he made boards for the t'; "
25 And for the other side of the t', "
27 And for the sides of the t' westward"
28 made he for the corners of the t' "
31 the boards of the one side of the t', "
32 boards of the other side of the t', "
32 and five bars for the boards of the t'"
37 made an hanging for the t' door. * 168
38: 8 door of the t' of the congregation.* "
20 And all the pins of the t', and of 4908
21 This is the sum of the t', even of "
21 even of the t' of testimony, as it was"
30 door of the t' of the congregation,* 168
31 and all the pins of the t', and all 4908
39:32 t' of the tent of the congregation "
33 And they brought the t' unto Moses, "
38 and the hanging for the t' door, * 168
40 the vessels of the service of the t', 4908
40: 2 t' of the tent of the congregation. "
5 put the hanging of the door to the t'. "
6 t' of the tent of the congregation. "
9 anoint the t', and all that is therein,"
12 door of the t' of the congregation,* 168
17 month, that the t' was reared up. 4908
18 And Moses reared up the t', and "
19 spread abroad the tent over the t', "
Ex 40:21 And he brought the ark into the t', 4908
22 upon the side of the t' northward, "
24 on the side of the t' southward. "
28 up the hanging at the door of the t'. "
29 t' of the tent of the congregation, "
33 round about the t' and the altar, "
34, 35 the glory of the Lord filled the t'."
36 cloud was taken up from over the t',"
38 cloud of the Lord was upon the t' "
Le 1: 1 out of the t' of the congregation, * 168
3 door of the t' of the congregation.* "
5 door of the t' of the congregation.* "
3: 2 door of the t' of the congregation:* "
8, 13 before the t' of the congregation:*"
4: 4 door of the t' of the congregation * "
5 bring it to the t' of...congregation:* "
7 is in the t' of the congregation; * "
7 door of the t' of the congregation.* "
14 before the t' of the congregation. * "
16 blood to the t' of the congregation:* "
18 that is in the t' of the congregation,*"
18 door of the t' of the congregation.* "
6:16 court of the t' of the congregation* "
26 court of the t' of the congregation.* "
30 into the t' of the congregation * "
8: 3, 4 door of the t' of the congregation. "
10 anointed the t' and all...therein, 4908
31 door of the t' of the congregation:* 168
35 door of the t' of the congregation * "
9: 5 before the t' of the congregation:* "
23 went into the t' of the congregation,*"
10: 7 door of the t' of the congregation.* "
9 go into the t' of the congregation,* "
12: 6 door of the t' of the congregation,* "
14:11 door of the t' of the congregation:* "
23 door of the t' of the congregation.* "
15:14 door of the t' of the congregation,* "
29 door of the t' of the congregation.* "
31 defile my t' that is among them. 4908
16: 7 door of the t' of the congregation.* 168
16 he do for the t' of the congregation,*"
17 no man in the t' of the congregation*"
20 place, and the t' of...congregation,* "
23 come into the t' of...congregation,* "
33 atonement for...t' of...congregation,*"
17: 4 door of the t' of the congregation,* "
4 the Lord before the t' of the Lord;4908
5, 6, 9 door of the t' of...congregation,*168
19:21 door of the t' of the congregation,* "
24: 3 in the t' of the congregation, "
26:11 And I will set my t' among you: 4908
Nu 1: 1 Sinai, in the t' of the congregation,*168
50 Levites over the t' of testimony, 4908
50 shall bear the t', and all the vessels "
50 shall encamp round about the t'. "

Nu 1:51 And when the t' setteth forward, 4908
51 and when the t' is to be pitched, the "
53 round about the t' of testimony, "
53 the charge of the t' of testimony. "
2: 2 about the t' of the congregation * 168
17 the t' of the congregation shall set* "
3: 7 before the t' of the congregation,* "
7 to do the service of the t'. 4908
8 of the t' of the congregation, * 168
8 Israel, to do the service of the t'. 4908
23 shall pitch behind the t' westward. "
25 in the t' of the congregation * 168
25 shall be the t', and the tent, 4908
25 door of the t' of the congregation,* 168
26 of the court, which is by the t', 4908
29 on the side of the t' southward. "
35 on the side of the t' northward. "
36 shall be the boards of the t', and "
38 before the t' toward the east, even "
38 before the t' of the congregation * 168
4: 3 work in the t' of the congregation* "
4 Kohath in the t' of...congregation,* "
15 Kohath in the t' of...congregation.* "
16 and the oversight of all the t', and 4908
23 work in the t' of the congregation.* 168
25 shall bear the curtains of the t', 4908
25 and the t' of the congregation, his* 168
25 door of the t' of the congregation,* "
26 which is by the t' and by the altar 4908
28 Gershon in the t' of...congregation:* 168
30 work of the t' of the congregation.* "
31 service in the t' of...congregation;* "
31 the boards of the t', and the bars 4908
33 service, in the t' of...congregation,* 168
35 work in the t' of the congregation:* "
37 service in the t' of the congregation,* "
39 work in the t' of the congregation,* "
41 service in the t' of the congregation,* "
43 work in the t' of the congregation,* "
47 burden in the t' of the congregation,* "
5:17 dust that is in the floor of the t' 4908
6:10, 13 door of the t' of...congregation:* 168
18 door of the t' of the congregation,* "
7: 1 that Moses had fully set up the t', 4908
3 they brought them before the t'. "
5 service of the t' of...congregation;* 168
89 gone into the t' of the congregation* "
8: 9 before the t' of the congregation:* "
15 service of the t' of the congregation:* "
19 Israel in the t' of the congregation,* "
22 service in the t' of the congregation* "
24 service of the t' of the congregation:* "
26 brethren in the t' of...congregation,* "
9:15 And on the day that the t' was 4908
15 reared up the cloud covered the t', "
15 at even there was upon the t' as it "
17 the cloud was taken up from the t',* 168
18 as the cloud abode upon the t' 4908
19 the cloud tarried long upon the t' "
20 cloud was a few days upon the t'; "
22 that the cloud tarried upon the t', "
10: 3 door of the t' of the congregation.* 168
11 was taken up from off the t' of the 4908
17 And the t' was taken down; and the "
17 Merari set forward, bearing the t'. "
21 the other did set up the t' against "
11:16 them unto the t' of...congregation,* 168
24 and set them round about the t'. "
26 but went not out unto the t': and* "
12: 4 three unto the t' of...congregation.* "
5 and stood in the door of the t', and* "
10 the cloud departed from off the t';* "
14:10 appeared in the t' of...congregation* "
16: 9 do the service of the t' of the Lord, 4908
18 door of the t' of the congregation* 168
19 door of the t' of the congregation:* "
24 you up from about the t' of Korah, 4908
27 they gat up from the t' of Korah, "
42 toward the t' of the congregation:* 168
43 before the t' of the congregation. * "
50 door of the t' of the congregation:* "
17: 4 them up in the t' of...congregation* "
7 before the Lord in the t' of witness.* "
8 Moses went into the t' of witness;* "
13 near unto the t' of the Lord shall 4908
18: 2 minister before the t' of witness. * 168
3 charge, and the charge of all the t':* "
4 charge of the t' of the congregation,* "
4 for all the service of the t': and a* "
6 service of the t' of the congregation.* "
21 service of the t' of the congregation.* "
22 come nigh the t' of...congregation,* "
23 service of the t' of the congregation,* "
31 service in the t' of the congregation.* "
19: 4 before the t' of the congregation * "
13 himself, defileth the t' of the Lord; 4908
20: 6 door of the t' of the congregation,* 168
25: 6 door of the t' of the congregation.* "
27: 2 door of the t' of the congregation,* "
31:30 the charge of the t' of the Lord. 4908
47 the charge of the t' of the Lord; "
54 it into the t' of the congregation, * 168
De 31:14 yourselves in...t' of...congregation,* "
14 in the t' of the congregation. * "
15 Lord appeared in the t' in a pillar of "
15 cloud stood over the door of the t'.* "
Jos 18: 1 set up the t' of the congregation * "
19:51 door of the t' of the congregation.* "
22:19 wherein the Lord's t' dwelleth, 4908
29 Lord our God that is before his t'. "
1Sa 2:22 door of the t' of the congregation.* 168
2Sa 6:17 t' that David had pitched for it: * "
7: 6 have walked in a tent and in a t'. 4908
1Ki 1:39 took an horn of oil out of the t', * 168
2:28 Joab fled unto the t' of the Lord, * "
29 was fled unto the t' of the Lord; * "
1Ki 2:30 Benaiah came to the t' of the Lord,* 168
8: 4 and the t' of the congregation, and* "
4 the holy vessels that were in the t',* "
1Ch 6:32 place of the t' of the congregation* "
48 of the t' of the house of God. 4908
9:19 keepers of the gates of the t': ‡ 168
21 door of the t' of the congregation.* "
23 the house of the t', by wards. ‡ "
16:39 priests, before the t' of the Lord 4908
17: 5 to tent, and from one t' to another. "
21:29 For the t' of the Lord, which Moses "
23:26 they shall no more carry the t', nor "
32 charge of the t' of...congregation,* 168
2Ch 1: 3 there was the t' of the congregation* "
5 he put before the t' of the Lord: 4908
6 was at the t' of the congregation,* 168
13 before the t' of the congregation, * "
5: 5 and the t' of the congregation, * "
5 the holy vessels that were in the t',* "
24: 6 of Israel, for the t' of witness? * "
Job 5:24 know that thy t' shall be in peace;* "
18: 6 The light shall be dark in his t', and* "
14 confidence...be rooted out of his t',* "
15 It shall dwell in his t', because it is* "
19:12 me, and encamp round about my t'.* "
20:26 go ill with him that is left in his t'.* "
29: 4 the secret of God was upon my t';* "
31:31 If the men of my t' said not, Oh * "
36:29 the clouds, or the noise of his t'? *5521
Ps 15: 1 Lord, who shall abide in thy t'? 168
19: 4 In them hath he set a t' for the sun, "
27: 5 In the secret of his t' shall he hide "
6 will I offer in his t' sacrifices of joy; "
61: 4 I will abide in thy t' for ever: I will "
76: 2 In Salem also is his t', and his 5520
78:60 So that he forsook the t' of Shiloh, 4908
67 he refused the t' of Joseph, and * 168
132: 3 not come into the t' of my house, "
Pr 14:11 the t' of the upright shall flourish.* "
Isa 4: 6 a t' for a shadow in the daytime *5521
16: 5 upon it in truth in the t' of David,* 168
33:20 a t' that shall not be taken down;* "
Jer 10:20 My t' is spoiled, and all my cords * "
La 2: 4 in the t' of the daughter of Zion: * "
6 he hath violently taken away his t', 7900
Eze 37:27 My t' also shall be with them: 4908
41: 1 which was the breadth of the t'. 168
Am 5:26 the t' of your Moloch and Chiun *5522
9:11 day will I raise up the t' of David 5521
Ac 7:43 ye took up the t' of Moloch, and 4633
44 Our fathers had the t' of witness in "
46 to find a t' for the God of Jacob. *4633
15:16 will build again the t' of David, 4633
2Co 5: 1 our earthly house of this t' were 4636
4 For we that are in this t' do groan, "
Heb 8: 2 and of the true t', which the Lord 4633
5 when he was about to make the t'. "
9: 2 For there was a t' made; the first, "
3 t' which is called the Holiest of all; "
6 priests went always into the first t', "
8 as the first t' was yet standing: "
11 by a greater and more perfect t', "
21 he sprinkled with blood both the t', "
13:10 no right to eat which serve the t'. "
2Pe 1:13 as long as I am in this t', to stir 4638
14 shortly I must put off this my t', "
Re 13: 6 to blaspheme his name, and his t', 4633
15: 5 temple of the t' of the testimony "
21: 3 the t' of God is with men, and he "

tabernacles
Le 23:34 be the feast of t' for seven days 5521
Nu 24: 5 tents, O Jacob, and thy t', O Israel! 4908
De 16:13 observe the feast of t' seven days, 5521
16 feast of weeks, and in the feast of t': "
31:10 the year of release, in the feast of t', "
2Ch 8:13 feast of weeks, and in the feast of t'. "
Ezr 3: 4 They kept also the feast of t', as it is "
Job 11:14 let not wickedness dwell in thy t'.* 168
12: 6 The t' of robbers prosper, and they* "
15:34 fire shall consume the t' of bribery.* "
22:23 put away iniquity far from thy t'. * "
Ps 43: 3 me unto thy holy hill, and to thy t'. 4908
46: 4 place of the t' of the most High. "
78:51 of their strength in the t' of Ham:* 168
83: 6 t' of Edom, and the Ishmaelites; * "
84: 1 How amiable are thy t', O Lord of 4908
118:15 is in the t' of the righteous: *168
132: 7 We will go into his t': we will 4908
Da 11:45 he shall plant the t' of his palace * 168
Ho 9: 6 them: thorns shall be in their t'. * "
12: 9 will yet make thee to dwell in t', * "
Zec 14:16 of hosts, and to keep the feast of t'. 5521
18, 19 not up to keep the feast of t'. "
Mal 2:12 the scholar, out of the t' of Jacob,* 168
M't 17: 4 let us make here three t'; one for 4633
M'r 9: 5 let us make three t'; one for thee, "
Lu 9:33 let us make three t'; one for thee, "
Joh 7: 2 the Jews' feast of t' was at hand. 4634
Heb 11: 9 dwelling in t' with Isaac...Jacob, *4633

Tabitha (*tab'-ith-ah*)
Ac 9:36 a certain disciple named T', 5000
40 him to the body said, T', arise. "

table See also TABLES.
Ex 25:23 also make a t' of shittim wood: 7979
27 places of the staves to bear the t'. "
28 that the t' may be borne with them. "
30 thou shalt set upon the t' shewbread "
26:35 thou shalt set the t' without the vail, "
35 the candlestick over against the t' "
35 shalt put the t' on the north side. "
30:27 And the t' and all his vessels, and "
31: 8 And the t' and his furniture, and the "
35:13 The t', and his staves, and all his "
37:10 And he made the t' of shittim wood: "
Ex 37:14 places for the staves to bear the t'. 7979
15 them with gold, to bear the t'. "
16 the vessels which were upon the t', "
39:36 The t', and all the vessels thereof, "
40: 4 And thou shalt bring in the t', and "
22 And he put the t' in the tent of the "
24 over against the t', on the side of "
Le 24: 6 upon the pure t' before the Lord. "
Nu 3:31 charge shall be the ark, and the t', "
4: 7 upon the t' of shewbread they shall "
J'g 1: 7 gathered their meat under my t': "
1Sa 20:29 he cometh not unto the king's t'. "
34 Jonathan arose from the t' in fierce "
2Sa 9: 7 and thou shalt eat bread at my t' "
10 son shall eat bread alway at my t'. "
11 he shall eat at my t', as one of the "
13 did eat continually at the king's t'; "
19:28 them that did eat at thine own t'. "
1Ki 2: 7 them be of those that eat at thy t': "
4:27 that came unto king Solomon's t', "
7:48 the altar of gold, and the t' of gold, "
10: 5 the meat of his t', and the sitting "
13:20 it came to pass, as they sat at the t', "
18:19 hundred, which eat at Jezebel's t'. "
2Ki 4:10 us set for him there a bed, and a t', "
1Ch 28:16 tables of shewbread, for every t'; "
2Ch 9: 4 the meat of his t', and the sitting "
13:11 set they in order upon the pure t'; "
29:18 and the shewbread t', with all the "
Ne 5:17 there were at my t' an hundred and "
Job 36:16 that which should be set on thy t' "
Ps 23: 5 Thou preparest a t' before me in the "
69:22 Let their t' become a snare before "
78:19 God furnish a t' in the wilderness? "
128: 3 like olive plants round about thy t'. "
Pr 3: 3 them upon the t' of thine heart: 3871
7: 3 write them upon the t' of thine heart. "
9: 2 she hath also furnished her t'. 7979
Ca 1:12 While the king sitteth at his t', my 4524
Isa 21: 5 Prepare the t', watch in the 7979
30: 8 Now go, write it before them in a t',* 3871
65:11 that prepare a t' for that troop, 7979
Jer 17: 1 graven upon the t' of their heart, 3871
Eze 23:41 bed, and a t' prepared before it, 7979
39:20 Thus ye shall be filled at my t' with "
41:22 This is the t' that is before the Lord. "
44:16 and they shall come near to my t', "
Da 11:27 and they shall speak lies at one t'; "
Mal 1: 7 The t' of the Lord is contemptible. "
12 say, The t' of the Lord is polluted; "
M't 15:27 which fall from their masters' t'. 5132
M'r 7:28 yet the dogs under the t' eat of the "
Lu 1:63 And he asked for a writing t', and* 4093
16:21 which fell from the rich man's t': 5132
22:21 betrayeth me is with me on the t'. "
30 ye may eat and drink at my t' in my "
Joh 12: 2 of them that sat at the t' with him.*
13:28 Now no man at the t' knew for what 345
Ro 11: 9 saith, Let their t' be made a snare, 5132
1Co 10:21 cannot be partakers of the Lord's t', "
21 and of the t' of devils. "
Heb 9: 2 and the t', and the shewbread; "

tables
Ex 24:12 and I will give thee t' of stone, 3871
31:18 two t' of testimony, t' of stone, "
32:15 two t' of the testimony were in his "
15 t' were written on both their sides; "
16 And the t' were the work of God, "
16 writing of God, graven upon the t'. "
19 and he cast the t' out of his hands, "
34: 1 two t' of stone like unto the first: "
1 I will write upon these t' the words "
1 in the first t', which thou brakest. "
4 two t' of stone like unto the first; "
4 took in his hand the two t' of stone. "
28 wrote upon the t' the words of the "
29 two t' of testimony in Moses' hand, "
De 4:13 he wrote them upon two t' of stone. "
5:22 he wrote them in two t' of stone, "
9: 9 the mount to receive the t' of stone, "
9 t' of the covenant which the Lord "
10 delivered unto me two t' of stone "
11 Lord gave me the two t' of stone, "
11 stone, even the t' of the covenant. "
15 two t' of the covenant were in my "
17 I took the two t', and cast them out "
10: 1 two t' of stone like unto the first, "
2 I will write on the t' the words that "
2 in the first t' which thou brakest, "
3 two t' of stone like unto the first, "
3 having the two t' in mine hand. "
4 he wrote on the t', according to the "
5 and put the t' in the ark which I had "
1Ki 8: 9 in the ark save the two t' of stone, "
1Ch 28:16 gave gold for the t' of shewbread, 7979
16 likewise silver for the t' of silver: "
2Ch 4: 8 He made also ten t', and placed "
19 t' whereon the shewbread was set; "
5:10 nothing in the ark save the two t' 3871
Isa 28: 8 For all t' are full of vomit and 7979
Eze 40:39 in the porch of the gate were two t' "
39 this side, and two t' on that side, "
40 entry of the north gate, were two t'; "
40 the porch of the gate, were two t'. "
41 Four t' were on this side, and four "
41 and four t' on that side, by the side "
41 eight t', whereupon they slew their "
42 four t' were of hewn stone for the "
43 and upon the t' was the flesh of the "
Hab 2: 2 vision, and make it plain upon t', 3871
M't 21:12 the t' of the moneychangers, and 5132
M'r 7: 4 and pots, brasen vessels, and of t'.* 2825
11:15 the t' of the moneychangers, 5132
Joh 2:15 money, and overthrew the t'; "
Ac 6: 2 leave the word of God, and serve t', "
2Co 3: 3 living God; not in t' of stone. 4109

2Co 3: 3 but in fleshy t· of the heart. 4109
Heb 9: 4 budded, and the t· of the covenant; "
tablets
Ex 35: 22 and earrings, and rings, and t·, all*3558
Nu 31: 50 bracelets, rings, earrings, and t·, * "
Isa 3: 20 headbands, and the t·, and *1004,5315
Tabor (*ta'-bor*) See also AZNOTH-TABOR; CHISLOTH-TABOR.
Jos 19: 22 And the coast reacheth to T·, and 8396
J'g 4: 6 Go and draw toward mount T·, and "
12 Barak...was gone up to mount T·. "
14 Barak went down from mount T·, "
8: 18 men were they whom ye slew at T·? "
1Sa 10: 3 thou shalt come to the plain of T·, "
1Ch 6: 77 her suburbs, T· with her suburbs: "
Ps 89: 12 T· and Hermon shall rejoice in thy "
Jer 46: 18 as T· is among the mountains, and "
Ho 5: 1 Mizpah, and a net spread upon T·. "
tabret See also TABRETS.
Ge 31: 27 with songs, with t·, and with harp?8596
1Sa 10: 5 and a t·, and a pipe, and a harp, * "
Job 17: 6 and aforetime I was as a t·. †‡8611
Isa 5: 12 the t·, and pipe, and wine, are in 8596
tabrets
1Sa 18: 6 to meet king Saul, with t·, with *8596
Isa 24: 8 The mirth of t· ceaseth, the noise of "
30: 32 him, it shall be with t· and harps: "
Jer 31: 4 shalt again be adorned with thy t·, "
Eze 28: 13 the workmanship of thy t· and of "
Tabrimon (*tab'-rim-on*)
1Ki 15: 18 them to Ben-hadad,...son of T·, *2886
taches (*tatch'-ez*)
Ex 26: 6 thou shalt make fifty t· of gold, *7165
6 the curtains together with the t·: * "
11 thou shalt make fifty t· of brass, * "
11 and put the t· into the loops, and * "
33 shalt hang up the vail under the t·,*"
35: 11 his covering, his t·, and his boards,*"
36: 13 And he made fifty t· of gold, and * "
13 one unto another with the t·: so * "
18 made fifty t· of brass to couple the* "
39: 33 all his furniture, his t·, his boards,* "
Tachmonite (*tak'-mun-ite*) See also HACHMONITE.
2Sa 23: 8 The T· that sat in the seat, chief *8461
tackling See also TACKLINGS.
Ac 27: 19 our own hands the t· of the ship. 4631
tacklings
Isa 33: 23 Thy t· are loosed; they could not 2256
Tadmor (*tad'-mor*)
1Ki 9: 18 Baalath, and T· in the wilderness,*8412
2Ch 8: 4 he built T· in the wilderness, and "
Tahan (*ta'-han*) See also TAHANITES.
Nu 26: 35 T·, the family of the Tahanites. 8465
1Ch 7: 25 and Telah his son, and T· his son, "
Tahanites (*ta'-han-ites*)
Nu 26: 35 of Tahan, the family of the T·. 8470
Tahapanes (*ta-hap'-a-neze*) See also TAHPANHES; TAHPENES.
Jer 2: 16 the children of Noph and T· have*8471
Tahath (*ta'-hath*)
Nu 33: 26 Makheloth, and encamped at T·. 8480
27 they departed from T·, and pitched "
1Ch 6: 24 T· his son, Uriel his son, Uzziah "
37 The son of T·, the son of Assir, "
7: 20 Bered his son, and T· his son, "
20 Eladah his son, and T· his son, "
Tahpanhes (*tah'-pan-heze*) See also TAHAPANES; TAHPENES; TEHAPHNEHES.
Jer 43: 7 Lord: thus came they even to T·. 8471
8 of the Lord unto Jeremiah in T·, "
9 the entry of Pharaoh's house in T·, "
44: 1 which dwell at Migdol, and at T·, "
46: 14 and publish in Noph and in T·: "
Tahpenes (*tah'-pe-neze*) See also TAHPANHES.
1Ki 11: 19 wife, the sister of T· the queen. 8472
20 sister of T· bare him Genubath "
20 T· weaned in Pharaoh's house: "
Tahrea (*tah'-re-ah*) See also TAREA.
1Ch 9: 41 and Melech, and T·, and Ahaz. 8475
Tahtim-hodshi (*tah''-tim-hod'-shi*)
2Sa 24: 6 to Gilead, and to the land of T·; 8483
tail See also TAILS.
Ex 4: 4 thine hand, and take it by the t·. 2180
De 28: 13 thee the head, and not the t·; "
44 the head, and thou shalt be the t·. "
J'g 15: 4 turned t· to t·, and put a firebrand "
Job 40: 17 He moveth his t· like a cedar: the "
Isa 9: 14 cut off from Israel head and t·, "
15 that teacheth lies, he is the t·. "
19: 15 which the head or t·, branch or "
Re 12: 4 his t· drew the third part of the 3769
tails
J'g 15: 4 in the midst between two t·. 2180
Isa 7: 4 two t· of these smoking firebrands, "
Re 9: 10 they had t· like unto scorpions, 3769
10 and there were stings in their t·: "
19 is in their mouth, and in their t·: "
19 their t· were like unto serpents, "
take See also OVERTAKE; TAKEN; TAKEST; TAKETH; TAKING; TOOK; UNDERTAKE.
Ge 3: 22 t· also of the tree of life, and eat, 3947
6: 21 t· thou unto thee of all food that is "
7: 2 clean beast thou shalt t· to thee by "
12: 19 behold thy wife, t· her, and go thy "
14: 21 persons, and t· the goods to thyself."
23 I will not t· from a thread even to a "
Ge 14: 23 I will not t· any thing that is thine,*3947
24 Mamre; let them t· their portion. "
15: 9 T· me an heifer of three years old, "
19: 15 t· thy wife, and thy two daughters, "
19 lest some evil t· me, and I die: *1692
21: 30 lambs shalt thou t· of my hand, 3947
22: 2 T· now thy son, thine only son "
23: 13 t· it of me, and I will bury my dead "
24: 3 shalt not t· a wife unto my son of "
4 and t· a wife unto my son Isaac. "
7 and thou shalt t· a wife unto my son "
37 shalt not t· a wife to my son of the "
38 kindred, and t· a wife unto my son. "
40 thou shalt t· a wife for my son of "
48 to t· my master's brother's daughter "
51 Rebekah is before thee, t· her, and "
27: 3 t·, I pray thee, thy weapons, thy 5375
3 the field, and t· me some venison; 6679
46 if Jacob t· a wife of the daughters 3947
28: 1 shalt not t· a wife of the daughters "
2 t· thee a wife from thence of the "
6 to t· him a wife from thence; and "
6 shalt not t· a wife of the daughters "
30: 15 t· away my son's mandrakes also? "
31: 24 T· heed that thou speak not to "
29 T· thou heed that thou speak not "
31 t· by force thy daughters from 1497
32 is thine with me, and t· it to thee. 3947
50 if thou shalt t· other wives beside "
33: 11 T·, I pray thee, my blessing that is "
12 Let us t· our journey, and let us go,
34: 9 and t· our daughters unto you. 3947
16 we will t· your daughters to us, "
17 then will we t· our daughter, and "
21 let us t· their daughters to us for "
38: 23 Let her t· it to her, lest we be "
41: 34 t· up the fifth part of the land of "
42: 33 and t· food for the famine of your 3947
36 not, and ye will t· Benjamin away: "
43: 11 t· of the best fruits in the land in "
12 t· double money in your hand; and "
13 T· also your brother, and arise, go "
18 t· us for bondmen, and our asses. "
44: 29 And if ye t· this also from me, and "
45: 18 t· your father and your households, "
19 t· your wagons out of the land of "
Ex 2: 9 T· this child away, and nurse it 3212
4: 4 thine hand, and t· it by the tail. 270
9 shalt t· of the water of the river, 3947
17 shalt t· this rod in thine hand, "
6: 7 I will t· you to me for a people, and "
7: 9 T· thy rod, and cast it before "
15 serpent shalt thou t· in thine hand. "
19 T· thy rod, and stretch out thine "
8: 8 that he may t· away the frogs from5493
9: 8 T· to you handfuls of ashes of the 3947
10: 17 t· away from me this death only. 5493
26 we t· to serve the Lord our God; 3947
28 t· heed to thyself, see my face no "
12: 3 t· to them every man a lamb, 3947
4 t· it according to the number of the "
5 ye shall t· it out from the sheep, "
7 And they shall t· of the blood, and "
21 t· you a lamb according to your "
22 And ye shall t· a bunch of hyssop, "
32 Also t· your flocks and your herds, "
15: 14 shall t· hold on the inhabitants of* 270
15 trembling shall t· hold upon them;* "
16: 16 t· ye every man for them which 3947
33 T· a pot, and put an omer full of "
17: 5 t· with thee of the elders of Israel; "
5 the river, t· in thine hand, and go. "
19: 12 T· heed to yourselves, that ye go "
20: 7 shalt not t· the name of the Lord 5375
21: 10 If he t· him another wife; her 3947
14 thou shalt t· him from mine altar, "
22: 26 at all t· thy neighbour's raiment 2254
23: 8 And thou shalt t· no gift: for the 3947
25 t· sickness away from the midst 5493
25: 2 his heart ye shall t· my offering. 3947
3 offering which ye shall t· of them; "
26: 5 loops may t· hold one of another. *6901
28: 1 And t· thou unto thee Aaron thy *7126
5 And they shall t· gold, and blue, 3947
9 And thou shalt t· two onyx stones, "
29: 1 T· one young bullock, and two "
5 And thou shalt t· the garments, "
7 Then shalt thou t· the anointing oil, "
12 shalt t· of the blood of the bullock, "
13 thou shalt t· all the fat that covereth "
15 Thou shalt also t· one ram; and "
16 ram, and thou shalt t· his blood, "
19 And thou shalt t· the other ram; "
20 kill the ram, and t· of his blood, "
21 t· of the blood that is upon the altar, "
22 t· of the ram the fat and the rump, "
26 thou shalt t· the breast of the ram "
31 shalt t· the ram of the consecration, "
30: 16 thou shalt t· the atonement money "
23 T· thou also unto thee principal "
34 T· unto thee sweet spices, stacte, "
33: 23 And I will t· away mine hand, 5493
34: 9 sin, and t· us for thine inheritance.
12 T· heed to thyself, lest thou make
16 t· of their daughters unto thy sons,3947
35: 5 T· ye from among you an offering "
40: 9 And thou shalt t· the anointing oil, "
Le 2: 2 t· thereout his handful of the flour7061
9 shall t· from the meat offering 7311
3: 4 and the fat...it shall he t· away. 5493
9 shall he t· off hard by the backbone; "
10, 15 and the fat...it shall he t· away. "
4: 5 shall t· of the bullock's blood, 3947
8 he shall t· off from it all the fat of 3318
9 and the fat...it shall he t· away, 5493
19 he shall t· all his fat from him, 7311
Le 4: 25 t· of the blood of the sin offering 3947
30 And the priest shall t· of the blood "
31 he shall t· away all the fat thereof,5493
34 t· of the blood of the sin offering 3947
35 he shall t· away all the fat thereof,5493
5: 12 the priest shall t· his handful of it,7061
6: 10 t· up the ashes which the fire hath7311
15 And he shall t· of it his handful, "
7: 4 and the fat...it shall he t· away: 5493
8: 2 T· Aaron and his sons with him, 3947
9: 2 T·...a young calf for a sin offering, "
3 T· ye a kid of the goats for a sin "
10: 12 T· the meat offering that remaineth "
14: 4 to t· for him that is to be cleansed "
6 As for the living bird, he shall t· it, "
10 t· two he lambs without blemish, "
12 And the priest shall t· one he lamb, "
14 the priest shall t· some of the blood "
15 priest shall t· some of the log of oil, "
21 t· one lamb for a trespass offering "
24 t· the lamb of the trespass offering, "
25 the priest shall t· some of the blood "
40 t·...the stones in which the plague 2502
42 And they shall t· other stones, and3947
42 he shall t· other morter, and shall "
49 And he shall t· to cleanse the house "
51 he shall t· the cedar wood, and the "
15: 14 he shall t· to him two turtledoves, "
29 she shall t· unto her two turtles, "
16: 5 And he shall t· of the congregation "
7 And he shall t· the two goats, and "
12 t· a censer full of burning coals of "
14, 18 t· of the blood of the bullock, "
18: 17 shalt thou t· her son's daughter, "
18 shalt thou t· a wife to her sister, "
20: 14 if a man t· a wife and her mother, "
17 And if a man shall t· his sister, his "
21 if a man shall t· his brother's wife, "
21: 7 shall not t· a wife that is a whore, "
7 shall they t· a woman put away from "
13 he shall t· a wife in her virginity. "
14 or an harlot, these shall he not t·: "
14 he shall t· a virgin of his own people "
22: 5 a man of whom he may t· uncleanness,
23: 40 t· you on the first day the boughs 3947
24: 5 thou shalt t· fine flour, and bake "
25: 36 T· thou no usury of him, or "
46 t· them as an inheritance for your*
Nu 1: 2 T· ye the sum of...congregation 5375
49 Levi, neither t· the sum of them "
51 the Levites shall t· it down: 3381
3: 40 and t· the number of their names. 5375
41 thou shalt t· the Levites from me 3947
45 T· the Levites instead of all the "
47 shalt even t· five shekels apiece "
47 of the sanctuary shalt thou t· them: "
4: 2 T· the sum of the sons of Kohath 5375
5 they shall t· down the covering vail,3381
9 And they shall t· a cloth of blue, 3947
12 t· all the instruments of ministry, "
13 shall t· away the ashes from the altar, "
22 T·...sum of the sons of Gershon, 5375
5: 17 And the priest shall t· holy water 3947
17 and of the dust...the priest shall t·, "
25 priest shall t· the jealousy offering "
26 shall t· an handful of the offering, 7061
6: 18 shall t· the hair of the head of his 3947
19 priest shall t· the sodden shoulder "
7: 5 T· it of them, that they may be to "
8: 6 T· the Levites from among the "
8 Then let them t· a young bullock "
8 shalt thou t· for a sin offering. "
10: 6 the south side shall t· their journey:
11: 17 t· of the spirit which is upon thee, 680
16: 3 Ye t· too much upon you, seeing all
6 T· you censers, Korah, and all his 3947
7 ye t· too much upon you, ye sons of
17 And t· every man his censer, and 3947
37 that he t· up the censers out of the7311
46 T· a censer, and put fire therein 3947
17: 2 and t· of every one of them a rod "
10 quite t· away their murmurings *3615
18: 26 t· of the children of Israel the tithes3947
19: 4 Eleazar...shall t· of her blood "
6 And the priest shall t· cedar wood, "
17 t· of the ashes of the burnt heifer "
18 And a clean person shall t· hyssop, "
20: 8 T· the rod, and gather thou the "
25 T· Aaron and Eleazar his son, and "
21: 7 he t· away the serpents from us. 5493
23: 12 Must I not t· heed to speak that
25: 4 T· all the heads of the people, and3947
26: 2 T· the sum of all the congregation5375
4 T· the sum of the people, from twenty
27: 18 T· thee Joshua the son of Nun, 3947
31: 26 T· the sum of the prey that was 5375
29 T· it of their half, and give it unto3947
30 thou shalt t· one portion of fifty, of "
34: 18 ye shall t· one prince of every tribe, "
35: 31 t· no satisfaction for the life of a "
32 t· no satisfaction for him that is fled "
De 1: 7 Turn you, and t· your journey, and go
13 T· you wise men, and 3051
40 t· your journey into the wilderness
2: 4 t· ye good heed unto yourselves
24 Rise ye up, t· your journey, and pass
4: 9 Only t· heed to thyself, and keep
15 T· ye...good heed unto yourselves;
23 T· heed unto yourselves, lest ye
34 assayed to go and t· him a nation 3947
5: 11 shalt not t· the name of the Lord 5375
7: 3 his daughter...t· unto thy son. 3947
15 t· away from thee all sickness, 5493
25 silver or gold...nor t· it unto thee, 3947
10: 11 Arise, t· thy journey before the people,
11: 16 T· heed to yourselves, that your

De 12:13 T' heed to thyself that thou offer
19 T' heed to thyself that thou forsake
26 and thy vows, thou shalt t', and go5375
30 T' heed to thyself that thou be
15:17 Then thou shalt t' an aul, and 3947
16:19 respect persons, neither t' a gift: "
20: 7 the battle, and another man t' her. "
14 thereof, shalt thou t' unto thyself; 962
19 in making war against it to t' it, 8610
21: 3 elders of that city...t' an heifer, 3947
22: 6 shalt not t' the dam with the young: "
7 dam go, and t' the young to thee; "
13 If any man t' a wife, and go in unto "
15 t' and bring forth the tokens of the "
18 elders of that city shall t' that man "
30 man shall not t' his father's wife, "
24: 4 may not t' her again to be his wife, "
6 shall t' the nether or the upper 2254
8 T' heed in the plague of leprosy,
17 t' a widow's raiment to pledge: 2254
25: 5 unto her, and t' her to him to wife,3947
7 man like not to t' his brother's wife, "
8 to it, and say, I like not to t' her; "
26: 2 shalt t' of the first of all the fruit of "
4 t' the basket out of thine hand, "
27: 9 T' heed, and hearken, O Israel; *5535
31:26 T' this book of the law, and put 3947
32:41 mine hand t' hold on judgment; 270
Jos 3: 6 T' up the ark of the covenant, and5375
12 t' you twelve men out of the tribes3947
4: 2 T' you twelve men...of the people, "
3 T' you hence out of the midst of 5375
5 t' ye up every man of you a stone 7311
6: 6 T' up the ark of the covenant, and5375
18 when ye t' of the accursed thing, 3947
7:13 t' away the accursed thing from 5493
14 the family which the Lord shall t' 3920
14 household which the Lord shall t' "
8: 1 t' all the people of war with thee, 3947
2 shall ye t' for a prey unto yourselves: "
29 t' his carcase down from a tree, *3381
9:11 T' victuals...for the journey, 3947
10:42 their land...Joshua t' at one time, 3920
11:12 all the kings of them, did Joshua t', "
20: 4 shall t' him into the city unto them,622
22: 5 t'...heed to do the commandment
19 and t' possession among us: but 270
23:11 T' good heed therefore unto your
J'g 4: 6 t' with thee ten thousand men of 3947
5:30 the necks of them that t' the spoil?*
6:20 T' the flesh and the unleavened 3947
25 T' thy father's young bullock, even "
26 t' the second bullock, and offer a "
7:24 t' before them the waters unto 3920
14: 3 to t' a wife of the uncircumcised 3947
8 after a time he returned to t' her, "
15 ye called us to t' that we have? *3423
15: 2 sister fairer than she? t' her, 1961
19:30 consider of it, t' advice, and speak
20:10 we will t' ten men of an hundred 3947
Ru 2:10 thou shouldest t' knowledge of me,
19 be he that did t' knowledge of thee.
1Sa 2:16 and then t' as much as thy soul 3947
16 now: and if not, I will t' it by force."
6: 7 t' two milch kine, on which there * "
8 t' the ark of the Lord, and lay it "
8:11 He will t' your sons, and appoint "
13 And he will t' your daughters to be "
14 And he will t' your fields, and your "
15 And he will t' the tenth of your seed,
16 And he will t' your menservants, 3947
17 He will t' the tenth of your sheep:
9: 3 T' now one of the servants with 3947
5 for the asses, and t' thought for us.‡
16: 2 T' an heifer with thee, and say, I 3947
17:17 T' now for thy brethren an ephah "
18 brethren fare, and t' their pledge.
46 thee, and t' thine head from thee; 5493
19: 2 t' heed to thyself until...morning,
14 Saul sent messengers to t' David, 3947
20 Saul sent messengers to t' David: "
20:21 are on this side of thee, t' them; "
21: 9 if thou wilt t' that, t' it: for there "
23:23 t' knowledge of all the lurking places
26 his men round about to t' them. 8610
24:11 yet thou huntest my soul to t' it. 3947
25:11 Shall I then t' my bread, and my "
39 Abigail, to t' her to him to wife. "
40 unto thee, to t' thee to him to wife. "
26:11 t' thou now the spear that is at his "
2Sa 2:21 young men, and t' thee his armour. "
4:11 and t' you away from the earth? 1197
5: 6 t' away the blind and the lame, 5493
12: 4 he spared to t' of his own flock 3947
11 I will t' thy wives before thine eyes,"
28 encamp against the city, and t' it:3920
28 lest I t' the city, and it be called "
13:33 the king t' the thing to his heart, 7760
15:20 return thou, and t' back thy brethren:
16: 9 me go over,...and t' off his head. 5493
19:19 the king should t' it to his heart. 7760
30 Yea, let him t' all, forasmuch as 3947
20: 6 t' thou thy lord's servants, and "
24:10 t' away the iniquity of thy servant;*5674
22 t' and offer up what seemeth good3947
1Ki 1:33 T' with you the servants of your "
2: 4 thy children t' heed to their way,
31 mayest t' away the innocent blood,5493
8:25 thy children t' heed to their way,
11:31 to Jeroboam, T' thee ten pieces: 3947
34 will not t' the whole kingdom out "
35 I will t' the kingdom out of his "
37 I will t' thee, and thou shalt reign "
14: 3 And t' with thee ten loaves, and "
10 t' away the remnant of the house *1197
16: 3 t' away the posterity of Baasha, * "

1Ki 18:40 them, T' the prophets of Baal; 8610
19: 4 now, O Lord, t' away my life; for 3947
10, 14 they seek my life, to t' it away. "
20: 6 put it in their hand, and t' it away. "
18 come out for peace, t' them alive; 8610
18 be come out for war, t' them alive. "
24 T' the kings away, every man out5493
21:15 t' possession of the vineyard of 3423
16 the Jezreelite, to t' possession of it. "
21 and will t' away thy posterity, *1197
22: 3 t' it not out of the hand of the king3947
26 T' Micaiah, and carry him back "
2Ki 2: 1 when the Lord would t' up Elijah 5927
3, 5 Lord will t' away thy master 3947
4: 1 creditor is come to t' unto him my "
29 loins, and t' my staff in thine hand,"
36 unto him, he said, T' up thy son. 5375
5:15 thee, t' a blessing of thy servant. 3947
16 And he urged him to t' it; but he "
20 after him, and t' somewhat of him. "
23 said, Be content, t' two talents. "
6: 2 and t' thence every man a beam, "
7 Therefore said he, T' it up to thee.7311
32 hath sent to t' away mine head? 5493
7:13 Let some t',...five of the horses 3947
8: 8 T' a present in thine hand, and go, "
9: 1 and t' this box of oil in thine hand, "
3 t' the box of oil, and pour it on his "
17 T' an horseman, and send to meet "
25 T' up, and cast him in the portion5375
26 t' and cast him into the plat of "
10: 6 t' ye the heads of the men your 3947
14 And he said, T' them alive. 8610
12: 5 Let the priests t' it to them, 3947
13:15 said unto him, T' bow and arrows. "
18 And he said, T' the arrows. And he"
18:32 Until I come and t' you...to a land "
20: 7 And Isaiah said, T' a lump of figs. "
18 of thy sons...shall they t' away; "
1Ch 7:21 came down to t' away their cattle. "
17:13 not t' my mercy away from him, 5493
21:23 said unto David, T' it to thee, and 3947
24 I will not t' that which is thine for5375
28:10 T' heed now; for the Lord hath 7200
2Ch 6:16 t' heed to their way to walk in my
18:25 T' ye Micaiah, and carry him back3947
19: 6 to the judges, T' heed what ye do:*7200
7 be upon you; t' heed and do it:
20:25 his people came to t' away the spoil962
32:18 them; that they might t' the city. 3920
33: 8 they will t' heed to do all that I *
Ezr 4:22 T' heed now that ye fail not to do 2095
5:14 Cyrus the king t' out of the temple5312
15 T' these vessels, go, carry them 5376
9:12 t' their daughters unto your sons, 5375
Ne 5: 2 therefore we t' up corn for them, *3947
6: 7 and let us t' counsel together.
10:30 nor t' their daughters for our sons:3947
38 Levites, when the Levites t' tithes:
13:25 t' their daughters unto your sons, 5375
Es 4: 4 to t' away his sackcloth from him:5493
6:10 and t' the apparel and the horse, 3947
11 and to t' the spoil of them for a prey,
Job 7:21 and t' away mine iniquity? 5674
9:18 He will not suffer me to t' my breath,
34 Let him t' his rod away from me, 5493
10:20 alone, that I may t' comfort a little,
11:18 and thou shalt t' thy rest in safety.7901
13:14 do I t' my flesh in my teeth, and 5375
18: 9 The gin shall t' him by the heel, 270
21:12 They t' the timbrel and harp, and*5375
23:10 But he knoweth the way that I t': 5978
24: 2 they violently t' away flocks, and 1497
3 they t' the widow's ox for a pledge.2254
9 breast, and t' a pledge of the poor. "
10 they t' away the sheaf from the *5375
27:20 Terrors t' hold on him as waters, *5381
30:17 season: and my sinews t' no rest. 7901
31:36 I would t' it upon my shoulder, *5375
32:22 my maker would soon t' me away. "
36:17 judgment and justice t' hold on 8551
18 he t' thee away with his stroke: †‡5496
21 T' heed, regard not iniquity: for
38:13 it might t' hold of the ends of the 270
20 thou shouldest t' it to the bound 3947
41: 4 thou t' him for a servant for ever? "
42: 8 t' unto you now seven bullocks and "
Ps 2: 2 and the rulers t' counsel together,
7: 5 persecute my soul, and t' it; *5381
13: 2 long shall I t' counsel in my soul, 7896
16: 4 nor t' up their names into my lips.5375
27:10 me, then the Lord will t' me up. 622
31:13 they devised to t' away my life. 3947
35: 2 T' hold of shield and buckler, and2388
39: 1 I will t' heed to my ways, that I
50: 9 will t' no bullock out of thy house,3947
16 or thou shouldest t' my covenant*5375
51:11 and t' not thy holy spirit from me.3947
52: 5 he shall t' thee away, and pluck 2846
58: 9 t' them away as with a whirlwind, 8175
69:20 I looked for some to t' pity, but there
24 wrathful anger t' hold of them. *5381
71:10 that lay wait for my soul t' counsel
11 persecute and t' him; for there is 8610
80: 9 and didst cause it to t' deep root, *
81: 2 T' a psalm, and bring hither the 5375
83:12 t'...the houses of God in possession.
89:33 will I not utterly t' from him, 6331
102:14 thy servants t' pleasure in her stones,
24 t' me not away in the midst of my 5927
109: 8 few; and let another t' his office. 3947
116:13 I will t' the cup of salvation, and 5375
119:43 t' not the word of truth utterly out5337
139: 9 If I t' the wings of the morning, 5375
20 thine enemies t' thy name in vain. "
Pr 2:19 t' they hold of the paths of life. *5381

Pr 4:13 T' fast hold of instruction; let her2388
5: 5 to death; her steps t' hold on hell.8551
22 own iniquities shall t' the wicked 3920
6:25 let her t' thee with her eyelids. 3947
27 Can a man t' fire in his bosom, and2846
7:18 let us t' our fill of love until the
20:16 T' his garment that is surety for 3947
16 t' a pledge of him for a strange *2254
22:27 why should he t' away thy bed 3947
25: 4 T' away the dross from the silver,1898
5 T' away the wicked from before "
27:13 T' his garment that is surety for 3947
13 t' a pledge of him for a strange *2254
30: 9 and t' the name of my God in vain.*8610
Ec 5:15 and shall t' nothing of his labour, 5375
19 t' his portion, and to rejoice in his "
7:18 that thou shouldest t' hold of this; 270
21 t' no heed unto all words that are 5414
Ca 2:15 T' us the foxes, the little foxes, 270
7: 8 I will t' hold of the boughs thereof: "
Isa 1:25 thy dross, and t' away all thy tin: 5493
3: 1 t' away from Jerusalem and from "
6 a man shall t' hold of his brother 8610
18 Lord will t' away the bravery of 5493
4: 1 seven women shall t' hold of one 2388
1 thy name, to t' away our reproach. 622
5: 5 I will t' away the hedge thereof, 5493
23 and t' away the righteousness of the"
7: 4 unto him, T' heed, and be quiet;
8: 1 T' thee a great roll, and write in 3947
10 T' counsel together, and it shall
10: 2 to t' away the right from the poor 1497
6 give him a charge, to t' the spoil, 7997
6 to t' the prey, and to tread them 962
13: 8 and sorrows shall t' hold of them; 270
14: 2 And the people shall t' them, and 3947
2 they shall t' them captives, whose
4 shalt t' up this proverb against 5375
16: 3 T' counsel, execute judgment; * 935
18: 4 I will t' my rest, and I will consider*
5 t' away and cut down the branches.5493
23:16 T' an harp, go about the city, 3947
25: 8 the rebuke of his people...t' away 5493
27: 5 Or let him t' hold of my strength, 2388
6 them that come of Jacob to t' root: "
9 is all the fruit to t' away his sin; *5493
28:19 that it goeth forth it shall t' you: 3947
30: 1 that t' counsel, but not of me; 6213
14 a sherd to t' fire from the hearth, 2846
14 or to t' water withal out of the pit. 2834
33:23 spoil divided; the lame t' the prey.*962
36:17 Until I come and t' you away to a 3947
37:31 of Judah shall...t' root downward,
38:21 Let them t' a lump of figs, and lay 5375
39: 7 shalt beget, shall they t' away; 3947
40:24 their stock shall not t' root in the "
24 the whirlwind shall t' them away 5375
44:15 for he will t' thereof, and warm *3947
45:21 yea, let them t' counsel together:
47: 2 T' the millstones, and grind meal:3947
3 I will t' vengeance, and I will not "
56: 4 me, and t' hold of my covenant; *2388
57:13 all away; vanity shall t' them: *3947
14 t' up the stumbling block out of 7311
58: 2 they t' delight in approaching to God.*
9 t' away from the midst of thee the5493
64: 7 up himself to t' hold of thee: for 2388
66:21 I will also t' of them for priests 3947
Jer 2:22 with nitre, and t' thee much sope,
3:14 and I will t' you one of a city, 3947
4: 4 and t' away the foreskins of your 5493
5:10 t' away her battlements; for they "
7:29 and t' up a lamentation on high 5375
9: 4 T' ye heed every one of his
10 mountains will I t' up a weeping 5375
18 and t' up a wailing for us, that our "
13: 4 T' the girdle that thou hast got, 3947
6 t' the girdle from thence, which "
21 shall not sorrows t' thee, as a 270
15:15 O Lord,...t' me not away in thy 3947
19 if thou t' forth the precious from 3318
16: 2 Thou shalt not t' thee a wife, 3947
17:21 T' heed to yourselves, and bear
18:22 they have digged a pit to t' me, 3920
19: 1 and t' of the ancients of the people,
20: 5 shall spoil them, and t' them, 3947
10 and we shall t' our revenge on him. "
25: 9 and t' all the families of the north, "
10 will t' from them the voice of mirth, 6
15 T' the wine cup of this fury at my3947
28 if they refuse to t' the cup at thine "
29: 6 T' ye wives, and beget sons and "
6 and t' wives for your sons, and give"
32: 3 king of Babylon, and he shall t' it;3920
14 T' these evidences, this evidence 3947
24 are come unto the city to t' it; 3920
25 field for money, and t' witnesses;*5749
28 king of Babylon, and he shall t' it:3920
44 t' witnesses in...land of Benjamin, 5749
33:26 not t' any of his seed to be rulers 3947
34:22 shall fight against it, and t' it, 3920
36: 2 T' thee a roll of a book, and write 3947
14 T' in thine hand the roll wherein "
26 to t' Baruch the scribe and "
28 T' thee again another roll, and "
37: 8 fight against this city, and t' it, 3920
38: 3 Babylon's army, which shall t' it. "
10 T' from hence thirty men with 3947
10 t' up Jeremiah the prophet out of "
39:12 T' him, and look well to him, and "
43: 9 T' great stones in thine hand, and "
10 will send and t' Nebuchadrezzar "
44:12 I will t' the remnant of Judah, "
46:11 Go up into Gilead, and t' balm, "
49:29 and their flocks shall they t' away: "
29 they shall t' to themselves their *5375

Jer 50:15 t' vengeance upon her; as she hath
51: 8 t' balm for her pain, if so be she 3947
26 not t' of thee a stone for a corner,
36 cause, and t' vengeance for thee;
La 2:13 thing shall I t' to witness for thee?*
Eze 4: 1 t' thee a tile, and lay it before 3947
3 t' thou unto thee an iron pan, and "
9 T' thou also unto thee wheat, and "
5: 1 son of man, t' thee a sharp knife, "
1 t' thee a barber's rasor, and cause "
1 then t' thee balances to weigh, and "
2 and thou shalt t' a third part, and "
3 shalt...t' thereof a few in number, "
4 Then t' of them again, and cast "
10: 6 T' fire from between the wheels, "
11:18 t' away all the detestable things 5493
19 t' the stony heart out of their flesh, "
14: 5 That I may t' the house of Israel 8610
15: 3 will men t' a pin of it to hang any 3947
16:16 And of thy garments thou didst t', "
39 and shall t' thy fair jewels, and "
17:22 I will also t' of the highest branch "
19: 1 t' thou up a lamentation for the 5375
21:26 the diadem, and t' off the crown: 7311
22:16 thou shalt t' thine inheritance *
23:25 t' away thy nose and thine ears; 5493
25 t' thy sons and thy daughters; 3947
26 and t' away thy fair jewels. "
29 and shall t' away all thy labour, "
24: 5 T' the choice of the flock, and "
8 fury to come up to t' vengeance;
16 I t' away from thee the desire of 3947
25 when I t' from them their strength, "
26:17 shall t' up a lamentation for thee, 5375
27: 2 t' up a lamentation for Tyrus; "
32 shall t' up a lamentation for thee, "
28:12 t' up a lamentation upon the king "
29:19 and he shall t' her multitude, * "
19 t' [7997] her spoil, and t' her prey; 962
30: 4 they shall t' away her multitude, 3947
32: 2 t' up a lamentation for Pharaoh 5375
33: 2 people...t' a man of their coasts, 3947
4 the sword come, and t' him away, "
6 t' any person from among them, "
36:24 t' you from among the heathen, "
26 I will t' away the stony heart out 5493
37:16 t' thee one stick, and write upon 3947
16 then t' another stick, and write "
19 I will t' the stick of Joseph, which "
21 I will t' the children of Israel from "
38:12 To t' [7997] a spoil, and to t' a prey; 962
13 thee, Art thou come to t' a spoil? 7997
13 gathered thy company to t' a prey? 962
13 gold, to t' away cattle and goods, 3947
13 and goods, to t' a great spoil? "
39:10 shall t' no wood out of the field, 5375
43:20 thou shalt t' of the blood thereof, 3947
21 shalt t' the bullock also of the sin "
44:22 they t' for their wives a widow, "
22 t' maidens of the seed of the house "
45: 9 t' away your exactions from my 7311
18 thou shalt t' a young bullock 3947
19 t' of the blood of the sin offering, "
46:18 prince shall not t' of the people's "
Da 6:23 should t' Daniel up out of the den.5267
7:18 most High shall t' the kingdom, *6902
26 they shall t' away his dominion, 5709
11:15 and t' the most fenced cities: 3920
18 unto the isles, and shall t' many: "
31 shall t' away the daily sacrifice, 5493
Ho 1: 2 to Hosea, Go, t' unto thee a wife of3947
6 but I will utterly t' them away. *5375
2: 9 and t' away my corn in the time 3947
17 will t' away the names of Baalim 5493
4:10 have left off to t' heed to the Lord.
11 and new wine t' away the heart. 3947
5:14 I will t' away, and none shall *5375
11: 4 as they that t' off the yoke on their7311
14: 2 T' with you words, and turn to the3947
2 T' away all iniquity, and receive 5375
Am 3: 5 one t' up a snare from the earth, *5927
4: 2 he will t' you away with hooks, 5375
5: 1 this word which I t' up against you, "
11 ye t' from him burdens of wheat: 3947
12 they afflict the just, they t' a bribe, "
23 T' thou away from me the noise of5493
6:10 And a man's uncle shall t' him up,5375
9: 2 thence shall mine hand t' them; 3947
3 I will search and t' them out thence;"
Jon 1:12 T' me up, and cast me forth into 5375
4: 3 O Lord, t', I beseech thee, my life 3947
Mic 2: 2 fields, and t' them by violence; *5375
2 and houses, and t' them away: so "
4 one t' up a parable against you, "
6 them, that they shall not t' shame.*5253
6:14 and thou shalt t' hold, but shalt not*"
Na 1: 2 will t' vengeance on his adversaries,*
2: 9 T' ye the spoil of silver, 962
9 t' the spoil of gold: for there is none"
Hab 1:10 for they shall heap dust, and t' it.*3920
15 They t' up all of them with the *5927
2: 6 not all these t' up a parable against5375
Zep 3:11 I will t' away out of the midst of 5493
Hag 1: 8 I will t' pleasure in it, and I will be
2:23 will I t' thee, O Zerubbabel, my 3947
Zec 1: 6 they not t' hold of your fathers? *5381
3: 4 T' away the filthy garments from 5493
6:10 T' of them of the captivity, even 3947
11 Then t' silver and gold, and make "
8:23 that ten men shall t' hold out of all2388
23 t' hold of the skirt of him that is a "
9: 7 I will t' away his blood out of his 5493
11:15 T' unto thee yet the instruments 3947
14:21 sacrifice shall come and t' of them, "
Mal 2: 3 and one shall t' you away with it.*5375
15 Therefore t' heed to your spirit,

Mal 2:16 therefore t' heed to your spirit,
M't 1:20 fear not to t' unto thee Mary thy 3880
2:13, 20 t' the young child and his mother,"
5:40 at the law, and t' away thy coat, 2983
6: 1 T' heed that ye do not your alms
25 T' no thought for your life, what *
28 And why t' ye thought for raiment?*
31 t' no thought, saying, What shall *
34 T' therefore no thought for the *
34 shall t' thought for the things of itself.*
9: 6 t' up thy bed, and go unto thine 142
10:19 t' no thought how or what ye shall*
11:12 and the violent t' it by force. 726
29 T' my yoke upon you, and learn of 142
15:26 not meet to t' the children's bread,2983
16: 5 side, they had forgotten to t' bread. "
6 T' heed and beware of the leaven
24 and t' up his cross, and follow me. 142
17:25 do the kings of the earth t' custom 2983
27 t' up the fish that first cometh up; 142
27 that t', and give unto them for me 2983
18:10 T' heed that ye despise not one of*
16 then t' with thee one or two more, 3880
23 would t' account of his servants. *4868
20:14 T' that thine is, and go thy way: I 142
22:13 him hand and foot, and t' him away,*"
24: 4 T' heed that no man deceive you.
17 to t' any thing out of his house: 142
18 the field return back to t' his clothes."
25:28 T' therefore the talent from him,
26: 4 they might t' Jesus by subtilty, 2902
26 and said, T', eat; this is my body. 2983
45 Sleep on now, and t' your rest:
52 they that t' the sword shall perish 2983
55 swords and staves for to t' me? *4815
M'r 2: 9 or to say, Arise, and t' up thy bed, 142
11 unto thee, Arise, and t' up thy bed, "
4:24 unto them, T' heed what ye hear:
6: 8 should t' nothing for their journey, 142
7:27 not meet to t' the children's bread,2983
8:14 disciples had forgotten to t' bread, "
15 T' heed, beware of the leaven of
34 deny himself, and t' up his cross, 142
10:21 come, t' up the cross, and follow me.*"
12:19 that his brother should t' his wife, 2983
13: 5 T' heed lest any man deceive you:
9 t' heed to yourselves: for they shall
11 t' no thought beforehand what ye shall*
15 to t' any thing out of his house: 142
16 back again for to t' up his garment. "
23 But t' ye heed: behold, I have foretold
33 T' ye heed, watch and pray: for ye
14: 1 how they might t' him by craft, 2902
22 and said, T', eat: this is my body. 2983
36 to thee; t' away this cup from me:*3911
41 Sleep on now, and t' your rest: it is
44 t' him, and lead him away safely. 2902
48 swords and with staves to t' me? *4815
15:24 them, what every man should t'. 142
36 Elias will come to t' him down. 2507
16:18 They shall t' up serpents; and if 142
Lu 1:25 to t' away my reproach among men.851
5:24 t' up thy couch, and go into thine 142
6: 4 and did t' and eat the shewbread, 2983
29 thy cloke forbid not to t' thy coat also.*
8:18 T' heed therefore how ye hear: for
9: 3 them, T' nothing for your journey, 142
23 himself, and t' up his cross daily, "
10:35 and said unto him, T' care of him;
11:35 T' heed therefore that the light *4648
12:11 t' ye no thought how or what thing*
15 T' heed, and beware of covetousness:
19 t' thine ease, eat, drink, and be merry.
22 T' no thought for your life, what *
26 why t' ye thought for the rest? *
14: 9 with shame to t' the lowest room. 2722
16: 6 T' thy bill, and sit down quickly, 1209
7 him, T' thy bill, and write fourscore."
17: 3 T' heed to yourselves: If thy
31 let him not come down to t' it away:142
19:24 T' from him the pound, and give it "
20:20 that they might t' hold of his words,1949
26 they could not t' hold of his words "
28 that his brother should t' his wife, 2983
21: 8 T' heed that ye be not deceived:
34 t' heed to yourselves, lest at any
22:17 said, T' this, and divide it among 2983
36 he that hath a purse, let him t' it, 142
Joh 2:16 sold doves, T' these things hence; "
5: 8 him, Rise, t' up thy bed, and walk. "
11 unto me, T' up thy bed, and walk. "
12 unto thee, T' up thy bed, and walk? "
6: 7 every one of them may t' a little. 2983
15 would come and t' him by force, 726
7:30 Then they sought to t' him: but no4084
32 chief priests sent officers to t' him. "
10:17 my life, that I might t' it again. 2983
18 and I have power to t' it again. "
39 they sought again to t' him; but he4084
11:39 Jesus said, T' ye away the stone. 142
48 t' away both our place and nation. "
57 shew it, that they might t' him. 4084
16:15 he shall t' of mine, and shall shew*2983
17:15 shouldest t' them out of the world, 142
18:31 said Pilate unto them, T' ye him, 2983
19: 6 them, T' ye him, and crucify him: "
38 he might t' away the body of Jesus:142
20:15 hast laid him, and I will t' him away."
Ac 1:20 and his bishoprick let another t'. 2983
25 he may t' part of this ministry and "
5:35 t' heed to yourselves what ye
12: 3 he proceeded further to t' Peter *4815
15:14 to t' out of them a people for his 2983
37 determined to t' with them John, 4838
38 not good to t' him with them, who "
20:13 Assos, there intending to t' in Paul: 353

Ac 20:26 I t' you to record this day, that *
28 T' heed therefore unto yourselves, and
21:24 Them t', and purify thyself with 3880
22:26 T' heed what thou doest: for this*
23:10 t' him by force from among them, 726
24: 8 t' knowledge of all these things,
27:33 Paul besought them all to t' meat, 3335
34 I pray you to t' some meat: for 4355
Ro 11:21 t' heed lest he also spare not thee.*
27 when I shall t' away their sins. 851
15:24 I t' my journey into Spain, I will *
1Co 3:10 let every man t' heed how he buildeth
6: 7 Why do ye not rather t' wrong? Why
15 then t' the members of Christ, and 142
8: 9 But t' heed lest by any means this
9: 9 corn. Doth God t' care for oxen? *
10:12 he standeth t' heed lest he fall.
11:24 T', eat: this is my body, which is*2983
2Co 8: 4 t' upon us the fellowship of the *
11:20 if a man t' of you, if a man exalt *2983
12:10 I t' pleasure in infirmities, in
Ga 5:15 t' heed that ye be not consumed one
Eph 6:13 t' unto you the whole armour of 353
17 t' the helmet of salvation, and the 1209
Col 4:17 T' heed to the ministry which thou
1Ti 3: 5 shall he t' care of the church of God?)
4:16 T' heed unto thyself, and unto the
2Ti 4:11 T' Mark, and bring him with thee: 353
Heb 3:12 T' heed, brethren, lest there be in
7: 5 t' tithes of the people according to the
10: 4 and of goats should t' away sins. 851
11 which can never t' away sins: 4014
Jas 5:10 T', my brethren, the prophets, who2983
1Pe 2:20 your faults, ye shall t' it patiently?
20 ye t' it patiently, this is acceptable
2Pe 1:19 whereunto ye do well that ye t' heed, as
1Jo 3: 5 manifested to t' away our sins; 142
Re 3:11 hast, that no man t' thy crown. 2983
5: 9 Thou art worthy to t' the book, and "
6: 4 thereon to t' peace from the earth, "
10: 8 Go and t' the little book which is "
9 said unto me, T' it, and eat it up; "
22:17 let him t' the water of life freely. 2902
19 if any man shall t' away from the 851
19 God shall t' away his part out of the "

taken See also OVERTAKEN; UNTAKEN.
Ge 2:22 rib,...the Lord God had t' from man,3947
23 because she was t' out of Man. "
3:19 ground; for out of it wast thou t': "
23 the ground from whence he was t'. "
4:15 vengeance shall be t' on him sevenfold.
12:15 the woman was t' into Pharaoh's 3947
19 I might have t' her to me to wife: * "
14:14 that his brother was t' captive,
18:27, 31 I have t' upon me to speak unto2974
20: 3 for the woman which thou hast t';3947
21:25 servants had violently t' away. 1497
27:33 where is he that hath t' venison, 6679
35 and hath t' away thy blessing. 3947
36 now he hath t' away my blessing. "
30:15 that thou hast t' my husband?
23 God hath t' away my reproach: 622
31: 1 Jacob hath t' away all that was 3947
9 God hath t' away the cattle of your5337
16 which God hath t' from our father, "
26 as captives t' with the sword? *
34 Rachel had t' the images, and put 3947
Ex 14:11 hast thou t' us away to die in the "
25:15 ark: they shall not be t' from it. 5493
40:36 the cloud was t' up from over the 5927
37 if the cloud were not t' up, then "
37 not till the day that it was t' up. "
Le 4:10 As it was t' off from the bullock 7311
31 fat is t' away from off the sacrifice "
35 as the fat of the lamb is t' away from"
6: 2 or in a thing t' away by violence, *1497
7:34 and the heave shoulder have I t' 3947
14:43 that he hath t' away the stones, 2502
24: 8 being t' from the children of Israel by*
Nu 3:12 I have t' the Levites from among 3947
5:13 neither she be t' with the manner;8610
8:16 of Israel, have I t' them unto me. 3947
18 And I have t' the Levites for all the "
9:17 when the cloud was t' up from the5927
21 the cloud was t' up in the morning, "
21 by night that the cloud was t' up, "
22 when it was t' up, they journeyed. "
10:11 the cloud was t' up from off the "
17 the tabernacle was t' down; and 3381
16:15 I have not t' one ass from them, 5375
18: 6 I have t' your brethren the Levites3947
21:26 and t' all his land out of his hand, "
31:26 the sum of the prey that was t', 7628
49 servants have t' the sum of...men 5375
53 (For the men of war had t' spoil, every
36: 3 be t' from the inheritance of our 1639
3 t' from the lot of our inheritance. "
4 shall their inheritance be t' away "
De 4:20 the Lord hath t' you, and brought 3947
20: 7 a wife, and hath not t' her? "
21:10 and thou hast t' them captive, *
24: 1 When a man hath t' a wife, and *3947
5 When a man hath t' a new wife, he*"
5 cheer up his wife which he hath t'. "
26:14 neither have I t' away ought *1197
28:31 thine ass shall be violently t' away1497
Jos 7:11 have even t' of the accursed thing,3947
15 that is t' with the accursed thing 3920
16 and the tribe of Judah was t': "
17 man by man; and Zabdi was t': "
18 Zerah, of the tribe of Judah, was t'. "
8: 8 shall be, when ye have t' the city *8610
21 that the ambush had t' the city, 3920
10: 1 had heard how Joshua had t' Ai, "
J'g 1: 8 against Jerusalem, and had t' it, * "
11:36 Lord hath t' vengeance for thee 6213

J'g 14: 9 had t' the honey out of the carcase7287
15: 6 because he had t' his wife, and 3947
17: 2 shekels of silver...t' from thee, "
18: 24 Ye have t' away my gods which I "
1Sa 4: 11 the ark of God was t'; and the two "
17 are dead, and the ark of God is t'. "
19 tidings that the ark of God was t', "
21 because the ark of God was t', and "
22 from Israel: for the ark of God is t'. "
7: 14 cities which the Philistines had t' "
10: 20 near, the tribe of Benjamin was t'.3920
21 the family of Matri was t', and Saul "
21 and Saul the son of Kish was t': "
12: 3 his anointed: whose ox have I t'? 3947
3 or whose ass have I t'? or whom "
4 neither hast thou t' ought of any "
14: 41 And Saul and Jonathan were t': 3920
42 my son. And Jonathan was t'. "
21: 6 that was t' from before the Lord, 5493
6 in the day when it was t' away. 3947
30: 2 And had t' the women captives,
3 their daughters, were t' captives.
5 David's two wives were t' captives.
16 all the great spoil that they had t' 3947
19 any thing that they had t' to them: "
2Sa 12: 9 and hast t' his wife to be thy wife, "
10 hast t' the wife of Uriah the Hittite "
27 and have t' the city of waters. 3920
16: 8 behold, thou art t' in thy mischief,
18: 9 t' up between the heaven and the 5414
18 had t' and reared up...a pillar, 3947
23: 6 they cannot be t' with hands:
1Ki 7: 8 daughter, whom he had t' to wife, "
9: 9 and have t' hold upon other gods,*2388
16 Egypt had gone up, and t' Gezer, 3920
16: 18 when Zimri saw that the city was t', "
21: 19 thou killed, and also t' possession?
22: 43 the high places were not t' away; 5493
2Ki 2: 9 before I be t' away from thee. 3947
10 thou see me when I am t' from thee, "
16 Spirit of the Lord hath t' him up, 5375
4: 20 when he had t' him, and brought "
6: 22 thou hast t' captive with thy sword
12: 3 But...high places were not t' away:5493
13: 25 the cities, which he had t' out of 3947
14: 4 the high places were not t' away: 5493
18: 10 king of Israel, Samaria was t'. 3920
22 altars Hezekiah hath t' away, 5493
24: 7 king of Babylon had t' from the 3947
1Ch 24: 6 one principal household being t' 270
6 for Eleazer, and one t' for Ithamar. "
2Ch 15: 8 cities which he had t' from mount 3920
17 the high places were not t' away 5493
17: 2 which Asa his father had t'. 3920
19: 3 hast t' away the groves out of the*1197
20: 33 the high places were not t' away: 5493
28: 11 have t' captive of your brethren:
18 had t' Beth-shemesh, and Ajalon, 3920
30: 2 For the king had t' counsel, and
32: 12 Hezekiah t' away his high places 5493
Ezr 9: 2 t' of their daughters...themselves, 5375
10: 2 t' strange wives of the people of *3427
10 and have t' strange wives, * "
14 them which have t' strange wives* "
17 the men that had t' strange wives* "
18 found that had t' strange wives: * "
44 All these had t' strange wives: 5375
Ne 5: 15 had t' of them bread and wine, *3947
6: 18 son Johanan had t' the daughter of "
Es 2: 15 who had t' her for his daughter, "
16 Esther was t' unto king Ahasuerus "
8: 2 ring, which he had t' from Haman,5674
Job 1: 21 gave, and the Lord hath t' away; 3947
16: 12 he hath also t' me by my neck, and 247
19: 9 and t' the crown from my head. 5493
20: 19 hath violently t' away an house 1497
22: 6 hast t' a pledge from thy brother 2254
24: 24 are t' out of the way as all other, 7092
27: 2 who hath t' away my judgment; 5493
28: 2 Iron is t' out of the earth, and 3947
30: 16 of affliction have t' hold upon me. 270
34: 5 God hath t' away my judgment. 5493
20 and the mighty shall be t' away
Ps 9: 15 which they hid is their own foot t'.3920
10: 2 let them be t' in the devices that 8610
40: 12 iniquities have t' hold upon me, *5381
59: 12 let them even be t' in their pride: 3920
83: 3 They have t' crafty counsel against*
85: 3 Thou hast t' away all thy wrath: 5375
119: 53 Horror hath t' hold upon me 270
111 testimonies have I t' as an heritage
143 and anguish have t' hold on me: 4672
Pr 3: 26 shall keep thy foot from being t'. 3921
4: 16 and their sleep is t' away, unless 1497
6: 2 t' with the words of thy mouth. 3920
7: 20 hath t' a bag of money with him, 3947
11: 6 transgressors shall be t' in their 3920
Ec 2: 18 labour which I had t' under the 6001
3: 14 put to it, nor any thing t' from it: 1639
7: 26 but the sinner shall be t' by her. 3920
9: 12 the fishes that are t' in an evil net, 270
Isa 6: 6 he had t' with the tongs from off 3947
7 thine iniquity is t' away, and thy 5493
7: 5 have t' evil counsel against thee, *
8: 4 spoil of Samaria shall be t' away *5375
15 broken, and be snared, and be t'. 3920
10: 27 that his burden shall be t' away *5493
29 have t' up their lodging at Geba; 3885
16: 10 And gladness is t' away, and joy out622
17: 1 Damascus is t' away from being a 5493
21: 3 pangs have t' hold upon me, as the 270
23: 8 hath t' this counsel against Tyre,*
24: 18 of the pit shall be t' in the snare: 3920
28: 13 and be broken, and snared, and t'. "
33: 20 tabernacle...shall not be t' down; *6813
36: 7 altars Hezekiah hath t' away, 5493

Isa 41: 9 have t' from the ends of the earth, 2388
49: 24 the prey be t' from the mighty, or 3947
25 captives of the mighty shall be t' "
51: 22 have t' out of thine hand the cup of "
52: 5 my people is t' away for nought? "
53: 8 He was t' from prison and from "
57: 1 and merciful men are t' away, none622
1 righteous is t' away from the evil to "
64: 6 like the wind, have t' us away. *5375
Jer 6: 11 husband with the wife shall be t', 3920
24 anguish hath t' hold of us, and 2388
8: 9 ashamed,...are dismayed and t':
21 astonishment hath t' hold on me. 2388
12: 2 planted them, yea, they have t' root:
16: 5 t' away my peace from this people, 622
29: 22 And of them shall be t' up a curse 3947
34: 3 shalt surely be t', and delivered 8610
38: 23 shalt be t' by...the king of Babylon: "
28 until the day...Jerusalem was t': 3920
28 was there when Jerusalem was t'. "
39: 5 and when they had t' him, they 3947
40: 1 when he had t' him being bound in "
10 dwell in your cities that ye have t'.8610
48: 1 Kiriathaim is confounded and t': 3920
7 thy treasures, thou shalt also be t': "
33 joy...is t' from the plentiful field, 622
41 Kerioth is t', and the strong holds 3920
44 out of the pit shall be t' in the snare: "
46 for thy sons are t' captives, and thy3947
49: 20 Lord, that he hath t' against Edom;3289
24 anguish and sorrows have t' her, 270
30 king of Babylon hath t' counsel
50: 2 Babylon is t', Bel is confounded, 3920
9 from thence she shall be t': their "
24 thou art also t', O Babylon, and thou "
45 that he hath t' against Babylon; 3289
51: 31 king of Babylon that his city is t' 3920
41 How is Sheshach t'! and how is the "
56 Babylon, and her mighty men are t', "
La 2: 6 hath violently t' away his tabernacle,
4: 20 of the Lord, was t' in their pits, 3920
Eze 12: 13 and he shall be t' in my snare: 8610
15: 3 wood be t' thereof to do any work?3947
16: 17 Thou hast also t' thy fair jewels of* "
20 t' thy sons and thy daughters,
37 with whom thou hast t' pleasure,
17: 12 and hath t' the king thereof, and *3947
13 And hath t' of the king's seed, and* "
13 him, and hath t' an oath of him: * 935
13 hath also t' the mighty of the land:*3947
20 and he shall be t' in my snare, and8610
18: 8 neither hath t' any increase, that 3947
13 upon usury, and hath t' increase: "
17 hath t' off his hand from the poor,*7725
19: 4 he was t' in their pit, and they 8610
8 net over him: he was t' in their pit. "
21: 23 the iniquity, that they may be t'. "
24 ye shall be t' with the hand.
22: 12 have they t' gifts to shed blood; 3947
12 thou hast t' usury and increase, "
25 have t' the treasure and precious * "
25: 15 t' vengeance with a despiteful heart,
27: 5 they have t' cedars from Lebanon 3947
33: 6 he is t' away in his iniquity; but "
36: 3 ye are t' up in the lips of talkers, 5927
Da 5: 2 had t' out of the temple which 5312
3 the golden vessels that were t' out "
6: 23 So Daniel was t' up out of the den,5267
7: 12 they had their dominion t' away: 5709
8: 11 the daily sacrifice was t' away, *7311
11: 12 he hath t' away the multitude, 5375
12: 11 the daily sacrifice shall be t' away,5493
Ho 4: 3 the fishes...also shall be t' away. 622
Joe 3: 5 ye have t' my silver and my gold, 3947
Am 3: 4 of his den, if he have t' nothing? 3920
5 earth, and have t' nothing at all? 3947
12 children of Israel be t' out that *5337
4: 10 and have t' away your horses; 7628
6: 13 Have we not t' to us horns by our 3947
Mic 2: 9 have ye t' away my glory for ever.* "
4: 9 pangs have t' thee as a woman in 2388
Zep 3: 15 Lord hath t' away thy judgments, 5493
Zec 14: 2 the city shall be t', and the houses 3947
M't 4: 24 that were t' with divers diseases *4912
9: 15 bridegroom shall be t' from them, 522
13: 12 from him shall be t' away even that 142
16: 7 It is because we have t' no bread. *2983
21: 43 kingdom of God shall be t' from you,142
24: 40, 41 one shall be t', and the other 3880
25: 29 be t' away even that which he hath. 142
27: 59 And when Joseph had t' the body,*2983
28: 12 with the elders, and had t' counsel, "
M'r 2: 20 bridegroom shall be t' away from 522
4: 25 shall be t' even that which he hath. 142
6: 41 when he had t' the five loaves and*2983
9: 36 when he had t' him in his arms, he*1723
Lu 1: 1 as many have t' in hand to set 2021
4: 38 mother was t' with a great fever; *4912
5: 5 all the night, and have t' nothing:*2983
9 of the fishes which they had t': 4815
18 bed a man which was t' with a palsy:*
35 bridegroom shall be t' away from 522
36 the piece that was t' out of the new*
8: 18 from him shall be t' even that which142
37 for they were t' with great fear: *4912
9: 17 there was t' up of fragments that 142
10: 42 which shall not be t' away from her.851
11: 52 have t' away the key of knowledge:*142
17: 34, 35 the one shall be t', and the other3880
36 one shall be t', and the other left. *
19: 8 t' any thing...by false accusation, *
26 he hath shall be t' away from him. 142
Joh 7: 44 some of them would have t' him; 4084
8: 3 unto him a woman t' in adultery; 2638
4 this woman was t' in adultery, in "
13: 12 had t' his garments, and was set 2983

Joh 19: 31 and that they might be t' away. 142
20: 1 and seeth the stone t' away from the "
2 They have t' away the Lord out of "
13 they have t' away my Lord, and I "
Ac 1: 2 Until the day in which he was t' up,*353
9 while they beheld, he was t' up; 1869
11 Jesus, which is t' up from you into*353
22 same day that he was t' up from us,*"
2: 23 ye have t', and by wicked hands *2983
8: 7 and many t' with palsies, and that*
33 his judgment was t' away: 142
33 for his life is t' from the earth. "
17: 9 when they had t' security of Jason,2983
20: 9 the third loft, and was t' up dead. 142
21: 6 And when we had t' our leave one of*782
23: 27 This man was t' of the Jews, and *4815
27: 17 Which when they had t' up, they * 142
20 should be saved was then t' away. 4014
33 fasting, having t' nothing. 4355
40 when they had t' up the anchors, *4014
Ro 9: 6 the word of God hath t' none effect.*
1Co 5: 2 done this deed might be t' away 1808
10: 13 There hath no temptation t' you 2983
2Co 3: 16 the Lord, the vail shall be t' away. 4014
1Th 2: 17 being t' from you for a short time * 642
2Th 2: 7 let, until he be t' out of the way. 1096
1Ti 5: 9 not a widow be t' into the number*2639
2Ti 2: 26 who are t' captive by him at his will.2221
Heb 5: 1 every high priest t' from among 2983
2Pe 2: 12 beasts, made to be t' and destroyed,259
Re 5: 8 when he had t' the book, the four 2983
11: 17 thou hast t' to thee thy great power,"
19: 20 the beast was t', and with him the 4084

taker See also PARTAKER.
Isa 24: 2 as with the t' of usury, so with the

takest See also PARTAKEST.
Ex 4: 9 the water which thou t' out of the 3947
30: 12 thou t' the sum of the children 5375
J'g 4: 9 the journey that thou t' shall not be1980
1Ch 22: 13 if thou t' heed to fulfil the statutes*8104
Ps 104: 29 thou t' away their breath, they die, 622
Ec 9: 9 labour...thou t' under the sun. *6001
Isa 58: 3 our soul, and thou t' no knowledge?
Lu 19: 21 t' up that thou layedst not down, 142

taketh See also OVERTAKETH.
Ex 20: 7 guiltless that t' his name in vain. 5375
De 5: 11 guiltless that t' his name in vain. "
10: 17 not persons, nor t' reward: 3947
24: 6 for he t' a man's life to pledge. 2254
25: 11 hand, and t' him by the secrets: 2388
27: 25 that t' reward to slay an innocent 3947
32: 11 t' them, beareth them on her wings:*"
Jos 7: 14 tribe which the Lord t' shall come 3920
15: 16 smiteth Kirjath-sepher, and t' it, "
J'g 1: 12 smiteth Kirjath-sepher, and t' it, "
1Sa 17: 26 t' away the reproach from Israel? 5493
1Ki 14: 10 as a man t' away dung, till it be *1197
Job 5: 5 and t' it even out of the thorns, 3947
13 He t' the wise in their...craftiness:3920
9: 12 he t' away, who can hinder him? 2862
12: 20 t' away the understanding of the 3947
24 He t' away the heart of the chief 5493
21: 6 and trembling t' hold on my flesh. 270
27: 8 gained, when God t' away his soul?7953
40: 24 He t' it with his eyes: his nose *3947
Ps 15: 3 nor t' up a reproach against his 5375
5 nor t' reward against the innocent.3947
118: 7 Lord t' my part with them that help*
137: 9 that t' and dasheth thy little ones 270
147: 10 t' not pleasure in the legs of a man.
11 Lord t' pleasure in them that fear
149: 4 the Lord t' pleasure in his people:
Pr 1: 19 which t' away the life of the owners3947
16: 32 his spirit than he that t' a city. 3920
17: 23 man t' a gift out of the bosom 3947
25: 20 As he that t' away a garment in 5710
26: 17 like one that t' a dog by the ears. 2388
30: 28 The spider t' hold with her hands, 8610
Ec 1: 3 labour which he t' under the sun?*5998
2: 23 yea, his heart t' not rest in the night.
5: 18 his labour that he t' under the sun*5998
Isa 13: 14 and as a sheep that no man t' up:*6908
40: 15 he t' up the isles as a very little 5190
44: 14 and t' the cypress and the oak, 3947
51: 18 there any that t' her by the hand 2388
56: 6 polluting it,...t' hold of my covenant;*"
Eze 16: 32 which t' strangers instead of her 3947
33: 4 of the trumpet, and t' not warning;
5 that t' warning shall deliver his soul.*
Am 3: 12 t' out of the mouth of the lion *5337
M't 4: 5 devil t' him up into the holy city, 3880
8 devil t' him up into an exceeding "
9: 16 in to fill it up t' from the garment, 142
10: 38 And he that t' not his cross, and *2983
12: 45 t' with himself seven other spirits 3880
17: 1 after six days Jesus t' Peter, James,"
M'r 2: 21 that filled it up t' away from the old,142
4: 15 and t' away the word that was sown "
5: 40 he t' the father and the mother of 3880
9: 2 six days Jesus t' with him Peter, "
18 wheresoever he t' him, he teareth 2638
14: 33 he t' with him Peter and James and3880
Lu 6: 29 him that t' away thy cloke forbid 142
30 of him that t' away thy goods ask "
8: 12 t' away the word out of their hearts, "
9: 39 lo, a spirit t' him, and he suddenly2983
11: 22 he t' from him all his armour 142
26 and t' to him seven other spirits 3880
16: 3 t' away from me the stewardship: 851
Joh 1: 29 which t' away the sin of the world. 142
10: 18 No man t' it from me, but I lay it "
15: 2 me that beareth not fruit he t' away:"
16: 22 and your joy no man t' from you. "
21: 13 and t' bread, and giveth them, 2983
Ro 3: 5 unrighteous who t' vengeance? *2018

1Co 3:19 t' the wise in their own craftiness. 1405
11:21 t' before other his own supper: 4301
Heb 5: 4 no man t' this honour unto himself, 2983
10: 9 He t' away the first, that he may 337

taking
2Ch 19: 7 respect of persons, nor t' of gifts. 4727
Job 5: 3 I have seen the foolish t' root: but
Ps 119: 9 by t' heed thereto according to thy
Jer 50:46 At the noise of the t' of Babylon the 8610
Eze 25:12 the house of Judah by t' vengeance,
Ho 11: 3 also to go, t' them by their arms; *3947
M't 6:27 Which of you by t' thought can *
M'r 13:34 of man is as a man t' a far journey,*
Lu 4: 5 t' him up into an high mountain, * 321
12:25 And which of you with t' thought*
19:22 man, t' up that I laid not down, 142
Joh 11:13 he had spoken of t' of rest in sleep.
Ro 7: 8 But sin, t' occasion by the *2983
11 For sin, t' occasion by the * "
2Co 2:13 t' my leave of them, I went from
11: 8 other churches, t' wages of them, 2983
Eph 6:16 Above all, t' the shield of faith, 353
2Th 1: 8 t' vengeance on them that know *1325
1Pe 5: 2 flock...t' the oversight thereof, not by*
3Jo 7 forth, t' nothing of the Gentiles. 2983

tale See also TALEBEARER; TALES.
Ex 5: 8 And the t' of the bricks, which 4971
18 yet shall ye deliver the t' of bricks. 8506
1Sa 18:27 they gave them in full t' to the king,
1Ch 9:28 bring them in and out by t'. *4557
Ps 90: 9 spend our years as a t' that is told. 1899

talebearer
Le 19:16 down as a t' among thy people: 7400
Pr 11:13 A t' revealeth secrets: but he 1980. "
18: 8 The words of a t' are as wounds, *5372
20:19 about as a t' revealeth secrets: 7400
26:20 there is no t', the strife ceaseth. *5372
22 The words of a t' are as wounds, * "

talent See also TALENTS.
Ex 25:39 Of a t' of pure gold shall he make 3603
37:24 Of a t' of pure gold made he it, and "
38:27 hundred talents, a t' for a socket. "
2Sa 12:30 a t' of gold with the precious stones: "
1Ki 20:39 or else thou shalt pay a t' of silver. "
2Ki 5:22 give them, I pray thee, a t' of silver. "
23:33 talents of silver, and a t' of gold. "
1Ch 20: 2 and found it to weigh a t' of gold, "
2Ch 36: 3 talents of silver and a t' of gold. "
Zec 5: 7 there was lifted up a t' of lead: "
M't 25:24 he which had received the one t' 5007
25 went and hid thy t' in the earth: "
28 Take therefore the t' from him, and "
Re 16:21 stone about the weight of a t': 5006

talents
Ex 38:24 offering, was twenty and nine t', 3603
25 the silver...was an hundred t', "
27 of the hundred t' of silver were cast "
27 hundred sockets of the hundred t', "
29 brass of the offering was seventy t', "
1Ki 9:14 sent to the king sixscore t' of gold. "
28 gold, four hundred and twenty t', "
10:10 an hundred and twenty t' of gold, "
14 threescore and six t' of gold. "
16:24 of Shemer for two t' of silver, "
2Ki 5: 5 and took with him ten t' of silver, "
23 said, Be content, take two t'. "
23 bound two t' of silver in two bags, "
15:19 gave Pul a thousand t' of silver, "
18:14 unto Hezekiah...three hundred t' "
14 of silver and thirty t' of gold. "
23:33 tribute of an hundred t' of silver, "
1Ch 19: 6 Ammon sent a thousand t' of silver "
22:14 an hundred thousand t' of gold, "
14 a thousand thousand t' of silver; "
29: 4 Even three thousand t' of gold, of "
4 seven thousand t' of refined silver, "
7 of gold five thousand t' and ten "
7 and of silver ten thousand t', "
7 and of brass eighteen thousand t', "
7 one hundred thousand t' of iron. "
2Ch 3: 8 gold, amounting to six hundred t'. "
8:18 four hundred and fifty t' of gold, "
9: 9 an hundred and twenty t' of gold, "
13 and threescore and six t' of gold; "
25: 6 Israel for an hundred t' of silver. "
9 the hundred t' which I have given "
27: 5 same year an hundred t' of silver, "
36: 3 the land in an hundred t' of silver "
Ezr 7:22 Unto an hundred t' of silver, and 3604
8:26 six hundred and fifty t' of silver, 3603
26 and silver vessels an hundred t', "
26 and of gold an hundred t'; "
Es 3: 9 I will pay ten thousand t' of silver "
M't 18:24 which owed him ten thousand t'. 5007
25:15 And unto one he gave five t', and to "
16 he that had received the five t' went "
16 same, and made them other five t'. "
20 And so he that had received five t' "
20 came and brought other five t', "
20 thou deliveredst unto me five t': "
20 gained beside them five t' more. "
22 He also that had received two t' "
22 thou deliveredst unto me two t': "
22 gained two other t' beside them. "
28 give it unto him which hath ten t'. "

tales
Eze 22: 9 men that carry t' to shed blood: *7400
Lu 24:11 words seemed to them as idle t', *3026

Talitha (*tal'-ith-ah*)
M'r 5:41 hand, and said unto her, T' cumi; 5008

talk See also TALKED; TALKEST; TALKETH; TALKING.
Nu 11:17 come down and t' with thee there: 1696
De 5:24 this day that God doth t' with man. "
6: 7 t' of them when thou sittest in thine 1696
1Sa 2: 3 T' no more so exceeding proudly; "
2Ki 18:26 and t' not...in the Jews' language * "
1Ch 16: 9 t' ye of all his wondrous works. 7878
Job 11: 2 should a man full of t' be justified? 8193
13: 7 God? and t' deceitfully for him? 1696
15: 3 he reason with unprofitable t'? 1697
Ps 69:26 they t' to the grief of those whom *5608
71:24 also shall t' of thy righteousness 1897
77:12 all thy work, and t' of thy doings. *7878
105: 2 t' ye of all his wondrous works. "
119:27 so shall I t' of thy wondrous works: * "
145:11 thy kingdom, and t' of thy power; 1696
Pr 6:22 thou awakest, it shall t' with thee. 7878
14:23 but the t' of the lips tendeth only 1697
24: 2 and their lips t' of mischief. 1696
Ec 10:13 the end of his t' is mischievous 6310
Jer 12: 1 t' with thee of thy judgments: *1696
Eze 3:22 plain, and I will there t' with thee. "
Da 10:17 the servant...t' with this my lord? "
M't 22:15 they might entangle him in his t'. 3056
Joh 14:30 Hereafter I will not t' much with *2980

talked
Ge 4: 8 And Cain t' with Abel his brother: *559
17: 3 on his face: and God t' with him, 1696
35:13 in the place where he t' with him. * "
14 in the place where he t' with him, * "
45:15 after that his brethren t' with him. "
Ex 20:22 that I have t' with you from heaven. "
33: 9 and the Lord t' with Moses. * "
34:29 his face shone while he t' with him. * "
31 unto him: and Moses t' with them. * "
De 5: 4 The Lord t' with you face to face * "
J'g 14: 7 went down, and t' with the woman; "
1Sa 14:19 pass, while Saul t' unto the priest, "
17:23 And as he t' with them, behold, "
1Ki 1:22 lo, while she yet t' with the king, "
2Ki 2:11 to pass, as they still went on, and t', "
6:33 And while he yet t' with them, "
8: 4 the king t' with Gehazi the servant * "
2Ch 25:16 as he t' with him, that the king said "
Jer 38:25 princes hear...I have t' with thee, "
Da 9:22 informed me, and t' with me, and "
Zec 1: 9 And the angel that t' with me said "
13 answered the angel that t' with me "
19 said unto the angel that t' with me, "
2: 3 angel that t' with me went forth, "
4: 1 angel that t' with me came again, "
4 spake to the angel that t' with me, "
5 the angel that t' with me answered "
5: 5 angel that t' with me went forth, "
10 said I to the angel that t' with me, "
6: 4 said unto the angel that t' with me, "
M't 12:46 While he yet t' to the people, *2980
M'r 6:50 And immediately t' with them, * "
Lu 9:30 there t' with him two men, which 4814
24:14 they t' together of all these things *3656
32 while he t' with us by the way, *2980
Joh 4:27 marvelled...he t' with the woman: * "
Ac 10:27 as he t' with him, he went in, and 4926
20:11 and t' a long while, even till break 3656
26:31 aside, they t' between themselves, *2980
Re 17: 1 t' with me, saying unto me, Come * "
21: 9 t' with me, saying, Come hither, * "
15 that t' with me had a golden reed * "

talkers
Eze 36: 3 ye are taken up in the lips of t', 3956
Tit 1:10 unruly and vain t' and deceivers, 3151

talkest
J'g 6:17 me a sign that thou t' with me. 1696
1Ki 1:14 while thou...t' there with the king, "
Joh 4:27 thou? or, Why t' thou with her? *2980

talketh
Ps 37:30 and his tongue t' of judgment. *1696
Joh 9:37 him, and it is he that t' with thee. *2980

talking
Ge 17:22 And he left off t' with him, and 1696
1Ki 18:27 either he is t', or he is pursuing, *7879
Es 6:14 while they were yet t' with him, 1696
Job 29: 9 The princes refrained t', and laid 4405
Eze 33:30 people still are t' against thee *1696
M't 17: 3 them Moses and Elias t' with him. 4814
M'r 9: 4 Moses: and they were t' with Jesus. "
Eph 5: 4 nor foolish t', nor jesting, 3473
Re 4: 1 it were of a trumpet t' with me; *2980

tall See also TALLER.
De 2:10 a people great, and many, and t', 7311
21 A people great, and many, and t', "
9: 2 A people great and t', the children "
2Ki 19:23 will cut down the t' cedar trees 6967
Isa 37:24 I will cut down the t' cedars thereof, "

taller
De 1:28 people is greater and t' than we; 7311

Talmai (*tal'-mahee*)
Nu 13:22 where Ahiman, Sheshai, and T', 8526
Jos 15:14 Sheshai, and Ahiman, and T', "
J'g 1:10 slew Sheshai, and Ahiman, and T'. "
2Sa 3: 3 the daughter of T' king of Geshur; "
13:37 But Absalom fled, and went to T', "
1Ch 3: 2 the daughter of T' king of Geshur: "

Talmon (*tal'-mon*)
1Ch 9:17 Shallum, and Akkub, and T', 2929
Ezr 2:42 children of Ater, the children of T', "
Ne 7:45 children of Ater, the children of T', "
11:19 the porters, Akkub, T', and their "
12:25 Meshullam, T', Akkub, were porters "

Tamah (*ta'-mah*) See also THAMAH.
Ne 7:55 of Sisera, the children of T', *8547

Tamar (*ta'-mar*) See also BAAL-TAMAR; HAZAZON-TAMAR; THAMAR.
Ge 38: 6 his firstborn, whose name was T'. 8559
11 Judah to T' his daughter in law. "
11 T' went and dwelt in her father's 8559
13 And it was told T', saying, Behold "
24 T' thy daughter in law hath played "
Ru 4:12 Pharez, whom T' bare unto Judah. "
2Sa 13: 1 a fair sister, whose name was T'; "
2 that he fell sick for his sister T'; "
4 I love T', my brother Absalom's "
5 let my sister T' come, and give me "
6 let T' my sister come, and make me "
7 David sent home to T', saying, Go "
8 So T' went to her brother Amnon's "
10 And Amnon said unto T', Bring the "
10 T' took the cakes which she had "
19 T' put ashes on her head, and rent "
20 So T' remained desolate in her "
22 because he had forced his sister T'. "
32 the day that he forced his sister T'. "
14:27 one daughter, whose name was T': "
1Ch 2: 4 T' his daughter in law bare him "
3: 9 the concubines, and T' their sister. "
Eze 47:19 from T' even to the waters of strife "
48:28 from T' unto the waters of strife in "

tame See also TAMED.
M'r 5: 4 neither could any man t' him. 1150
Jas 3: 8 But the tongue can no man t'; it is "

tamed
Jas 3: 7 and of things in the sea, is t', 1150
7 and hath been t' of mankind: "

Tammuz (*tam'-muz*)
Eze 8:14 there sat women weeping for T'. 8542

Tanach (*ta'-nak*) See also TAANACH.
Jos 21:25 Manasseh, T' with her suburbs, *8590

tangle See ENTANGLE.

Tanhumeth (*tan'-hu-meth*)
2Ki 25:23 the son of T' the Netophathite, 8576
Jer 40: 8 Kareah, and Seraiah the son of T', "

tanner
Ac 9:43 days in Joppa with one Simon a t'. 1038
10: 6 He lodgeth with one Simon a t', "
32 in the house of one Simon a t' by the "

tapestry
Pr 7:16 decked my bed with coverings of t',
31:22 She maketh herself coverings of t';

Taphath (*ta'-fath*)
1Ki 4:11 T'...daughter of Solomon to wife: 2955

Tappuah (*tap'-pu-ah*) See also BETH-TAPPUAH; EN-TAPPUAH.
Jos 12:17 The king of T', one; the king of 8599
15:34 and En-gannim, T', and Enam, "
16: 8 from T' westward unto the river "
17: 8 Now Manasseh had the land of T': "
8 but T' on the border of Manasseh "
1Ch 2:43 the sons of Hebron; Korah, and T'. "

Tarah (*ta'-rah*)
Nu 33:27 from Tahath, and pitched at T'. *8646
28 they removed from T', and pitched * "

Taralah (*tar'-a-lah*)
Jos 18:27 And Rekem, and Irpeel, and T', 8634

tare See also TARES.
2Sa 13:31 king arose, and t' his garments, *7167
2Ki 2:24 t' forty and two children of them. 1234
M'r 9:20 him, straightway the spirit t' him; 4682
Lu 9:42 devil threw him down, and t' him. 4952

Tarea (*ta'-re-ah*) See also TAHREA.
1Ch 8:35 and Melech, and T', and Ahaz. 8390

tares
M't 13:25 and sowed t' among the wheat, 2215
26 fruit, then appeared the t' also. "
27 field? from whence then hath it t'? "
29 Nay; lest while ye gather up the t', "
30 Gather ye together first the t', and "
36 us the parable of the t' of the field. "
38 the t' are the children of the wicked "
40 the t' are gathered and burned in the "

target See also TARGETS.
1Sa 17: 6 t' of brass between his shoulders. *3591
1Ki 10:16 shekels of gold went to one t'. ‡6793
2Ch 9:15 of beaten gold went to one t'. ‡ "

targets
1Ki 10:16 two hundred t' of beaten gold: ‡6793
2Ch 9:15 two hundred t' of beaten gold: ‡ "
14: 8 had an army of men that bare t' and * "

Tarpelites (*tar'-pel-ites*)
Ezr 4: 9 the Apharsathchites, the T', the 2967

tarried
Ge 24:54 were with him, and t' all night; 3885
28:11 certain place, and t' there all night, "
31:54 bread, and t' all night in the mount. "
Nu 9:19 cloud t' long upon the tabernacle 748
22 the cloud t' upon the tabernacle, "
J'g 3:25 they t' till they were ashamed: 2342
26 And Ehud escaped while they t', 4102
19: 8 And they t' until afternoon, and "
Ru 2: 7 that she t' a little in the house. 3427
1Sa 13: 8 he t' seven days, according to the 3176
14: 2 Saul t' in the uttermost part of *3427
2Sa 11: 1 But David t' still at Jerusalem. "
15:17 and t' in a place that was far off. 5975
29 to Jerusalem: and they t' there. *3427
20: 5 but he t' longer than the set time 3186
2Ki 2:18 again to him, (for he t' at Jericho,) 3427
1Ch 20: 1 Rabbah. But David t' at Jerusalem. "
Ps 68:12 and she that t' at home divided the *5116
M't 25: 5 While the bridegroom t', they all 5549
Lu 1:21 that he t' so long in the temple.
2:43 child Jesus t' behind in Jerusalem; 5278
Joh 3:22 and there he t' with them, and 1304

Ac 9:43 he t' many days in Joppa with one*3306
15:33 after they had t' there a space, *4160
18:18 Paul after this t' there yet a good 4357
20: 5 These going before t'...at Troas. *3306
15 at Samos, and t' at Trogyllium; * "
21: 4 disciples, we t' there seven days: 1961
10 And as we t' there many days, "
25: 6 he had t' among them more than 1304
27:33 the fourteenth day that ye have t'*4328
28:12 at Syracuse, we t' there three days.1961

tarriest
Ac 22:16 And now why t' thou? arise, and be3195

tarrieth
1Sa 30:24 his part be that t' by the stuff: 3427
Mic 5: 7 upon the grass, that t' not for man,6960

tarry See also TARRIED; TARRIEST; TARRIETH; TARRYING.
Ge 19: 2 t' all night, and wash your feet, 3885
27:44 And t' with him a few days, until 3427
30:27 I have found favour in thine eyes, t': "
45: 9 Egypt: come down unto me, t' not:5975
Ex 12:39 out of Egypt, and could not t', 4102
24:14 T' ye here for us, until we come 3427
Le 14: 8 t' abroad out of his tent seven days.*"
Nu 22:19 t' ye also here this night, that I may"
J'g 5:28 why t' the wheels of his chariots? 309
6:18 I will t' until thou come again. 3427
19: 6 and t' all night, and let thine 3885
9 evening, I pray you t' all night: "
10 But the man would not t' that night."
Ru 1:13 t' for them till they were grown? 7663
3:13 T' this night, and it shall be in the3885
1Sa 1:23 t' until thou have weaned him; 3427
10: 8 seven days shalt thou t', till I come3176
14: 9 T' until we come to you; then we 1826
2Sa 10: 5 T' at Jericho until your beards be 3427
11:12 T' here to day also, and to morrow "
15:28 t' in the plain of the wilderness, 4102
18:14 Joab, I may not t' thus with thee. 3176
19: 7 there will not t' one with thee this 3885
2Ki 2: 2 unto Elisha, T' here, I pray thee; 3427
4 him, Elisha, t' here, I pray thee; "
6 unto him, T', I pray thee, here; "
7: 9 if we t' till the morning light, some2442
9: 3 open the door, and flee, and t' not. "
14:10 glory of this, and t' at home: for *3427
1Ch 19: 5 T' at Jericho until your beards be "
Ps 101: 7 he that telleth lies shall not t' in *3559
Pr 23:30 They that t' long at the wine; they 309
Isa 46:13 off, and my salvation shall not t': "
Jer 14: 8 that turneth aside to t' for a night?3885
Hab 2: 3 not lie: though it t', wait for it; 4102
3 it will surely come, it will not t'. * 309
M't 26:38 t' ye here, and watch with me. *3306
M'r 14:34 unto death: t' ye here, and watch.* "
Lu 24:29 And he went in to t' with them. "
49 but t' ye in the city of Jerusalem, 2523
Joh 4:40 him that he would t' with them: *3306
21:22, 23 If I will that he t' till I come, "
Ac 10:48 prayed they him to t' certain days.1961
18:20 they desired him to t' longer time*3306
28:14 desired to t' with them seven days:1961
1Co 11:33 together to eat, t' one for another.*1551
16: 7 I trust to t' a while with you, if the1961
8 will t' at Ephesus until Pentecost. "
1Ti 3:15 But if I t' long, that thou mayest 1019
Heb10:37 come will come, and will not t'. 5549

tarrying
Ps 40:17 deliverer; make no t', O my God. 309
70: 5 my deliverer; O Lord, make no t'. "

Tarshish (*tar'-shish*) See also THARSHISH.
Ge 10: 4 sons of Javan; Elishah, and T'. 8659
1Ch 1: 7 the sons of Javan; Elishah and T'. "
2Ch 9:21 For the king's ships went to T' "
21 came the ships of T' bringing gold."
20:36 him to make ships to go to T': "
37 they were not able to go to T'. "
Es 1:14 Admatha, T', Meres, Marsena, "
Ps 48: 7 Thou breakest the ships of T' "
72:10 The kings of T' and of the isles "
Isa 2:16 And upon all the ships of T', and "
23: 1 Howl, ye ships of T': for it is laid "
6 Pass ye over to T': howl, ye "
10 land as a river, O daughter of T': "
14 Howl, ye ships of T': for your "
60: 9 for me, and the ships of T' first, * "
66:19 them unto the nations, to T', Pul, "
Jer 10: 9 into plates is brought from T', "
Eze 27:12 T' was thy merchant by reason of "
25 The ships of T' did sing of thee "
38:13 Dedan, and the merchants of T', "
Jon 1: 3 But Jonah rose up to flee unto T' "
3 and he found a ship going to T': "
3 unto it, to go with them unto T' "
4: 2 Therefore I fled before unto T': "

Tarsus (*tar'-sus*)
Ac 9:11 Judas for one called Saul, of T': 5018
30 Cæsarea, and sent him forth to T'.5019
11:25 Then departed Barnabas to T', "
21:39 I am a man which am a Jew of T',5018
22: 3 man which am a Jew, born in T', 5019

Tartak (*tar'-tak*)
2Ki 17:31 the Avites made Nibhaz and T', 8662

Tartan (*tar'-tan*)
2Ki 18:17 And the king of Assyria sent T' 8661
Isa 20: 1 year that T' came unto Ashdod, "

Taschith See AL-TASCHITH.

task See also TASKMASTERS; TASKS.
Ex 5:14 fulfilled your t' in making brick 2706
19 from your bricks of your daily t'. *1697

taskmasters
Ex 1:11 they did set over them t' 8269,4522
3: 7 their cry by reason of their t'; 5065
5: 6 And Pharaoh commanded...the t' "
10 And the t' of the people went out, "
13 And the t' hasted them, saying, "
14 Pharaoh's t' had set over them, "

tasks
Ex 5:13 Fulfil your works, your daily t'. 1697

taste See also TASTED; TASTETH.
Ex 16:31 t' of it was like wafers made with 2940
Nu 11: 8 the t' of it was as the t' of fresh oil. "
1Sa 14:43 I did but t' a little honey with the 2938
2Sa 3:35 to me, and more also, if I t' bread, "
19:35 t' what I eat or what I drink? "
Job 6: 6 there any t' in the white of an egg?2940
30 my t' discern perverse things? 2441
12:11 and the mouth t' his meat? *2938
Ps 34: 8 O t' and see that the Lord is good: "
119:103 sweet are thy words unto my t'! 2441
Pr 24:13 honeycomb, which is sweet to thy t':"
Ca 2: 3 and his fruit was sweet to my t'. "
Jer 48:11 therefore his t' remained in him, 2940
Jon 3: 7 beast, herd nor flock, t' any thing: 2938
M't 16:28 here, which shall not t' of death, 1089
M'r 9: 1 here, which shall not t' of death, "
Lu 9:27 here, which shall not t' of death, "
14:24 were bidden shall t' of my supper. "
Joh 8:52 saying, he shall never t' of death. "
Col 2:21 (Touch not; t' not; handle not; * "
Heb 2: 9 should t' death for every man. "

tasted
1Sa 14:24 So none of the people t' any food. 2938
29 because I t' a little of this honey. "
Da 5: 2 Belshazzar, whiles he t' the wine, 2942
M't 27:34 had t' thereof, he would not drink.1089
Joh 2: 9 t' the water that was made wine, "
Heb 6: 4 and have t' of the heavenly gift, and "
5 And have t' the good word of God, "
1Pe 2: 3 ye have t' that the Lord is gracious."

tasteth
Job 34: 3 words, as the mouth t' meat. 2938

Tatnai (*tat'-nahee*)
Ezr 5: 3, 6 T', governor on this side the *8674
6: 6 T', governor beyond the river, * "
13 T', governor on this side the river,*"

tattlers
1Ti 5:13 idle, but t' also and busybodies, 5397

taught
De 4: 5 Behold, I have t' you statutes and 3925
31:22 day, and t' it the children of Israel. "
J'g 8:16 them he t' the men of Succoth. 3045
2Ki 17:28 t' them how they should fear the 3384
2Ch 6:27 thou hast t' them the good way, * "
17: 9 they t' in Judah, and had the book3925
9 cities of Judah, and t' the people. "
23:13 and such as t' to sing praise. *3045
30:22 t' the good knowledge of the Lord:*7919
35: 3 unto the Levites that t' all Israel, 4000
Ne 8: 9 and the Levites that t' the people, 995
Ps 71:17 thou hast t' me from my youth: 3925
119:102 judgments: for thou hast t' me. 3384
171 when thou hast t' me thy statutes.*3925
Pr 4: 4 He t' me also, and said unto me, 3384
11 I have t' thee in the way of wisdom;"
31: 1 prophecy that his mother t' him. 3256
Ec 12: 9 he still t' the people knowledge; 3925
Isa 29:13 fear toward me is t' by the precept*"
40:13 being his counsellor hath t' him? 3045
14 t' him in the path of judgment, 3925
14 and t' him knowledge, and shewed "
54:13 children shall be t' of the Lord; 3928
Jer 2:33 hast thou also t' the wicked ones 3925
9: 5 have t' their tongue to speak lies, "
14 Baalim, which their fathers t' them:"
12:16 they t' my people to swear by Baal;"
13:21 thou hast t' them to be captains, † "
28:16 hast t' rebellion against the Lord.*1696
29:32 hath t' rebellion against the Lord.* "
32:33 though I t' them, rising up early 3925
Eze 23:48 be t' not to do after your lewdness.3256
Ho 10:11 Ephraim is as an heifer that is t', 3925
11: 3 I t' Ephraim also to go, taking 8637
Zec 13: 5 t' me to keep cattle from my youth.*
M't 5: 2 he opened his mouth, and t' them, 1321
7:29 he t' them as one having 2258, "
13:54 he t' them in their synagogue, "
28:15 the money, and did as they were t': "
M'r 1:21 entered into the synagogue, and t'. "
22 for he t' them as one that had 2258, "
2:13 resorted unto him, and he t' them. "
4: 2 he t' them many things by parables,"
6:30 they had done, and what they had t'."
9:31 For he t' his disciples, and said unto"
10: 1 as he was wont, he t' them again. "
11:17 he t', saying unto them, Is it not "
12:35 and said, while he t' in the temple, "
Lu 4:15 And he t' in their synagogues, being"
31 t' them on the sabbath days. *2258, "
5: 3 and t' the people out of the ship. "
6: 6 entered into the synagogue and t': "
11: 1 pray, as John also t' his disciples. "
13:26 and thou hast t' in our streets. "
19:47 And he t' daily in the temple. *2258, "
20: 1 as he t' the people in the temple. * "
Joh 6:45 And they shall be all t' of God. 1318
59 synagogue, as he t' in Capernaum.1321
7:14 went up into the temple, and t'. "
28 cried Jesus in the temple as he t',* "
8: 2 and he sat down, and t' them. "
20 treasury, as he t' in the temple: "
28 as my Father hath t' me, I speak "
18:20 I ever t' in the synagogue, and in "
Ac 4: 2 grieved that they t' the people, "
5:21 temple early in the morning, and t'.1321
11:26 the church, and t' much people. "
14:21 to that city, and had t' many, *3100
15: 1 down from Judæa t' the brethren, 1321
18:25 t' diligently the things of the Lord, "
20:20 you, and have t' you publickly, * "
22: 3 t' according to the perfect manner*3811
Ga 1:12 it of man, neither was I t' it, 1321
6: 6 Let him that is t' in the word 2727
Eph 4:21 heard him, and...been t' by him, 1321
Col 2: 7 in the faith, as ye have been t', "
1Th 4: 9 are t' of God to love one another. 2312
2Th 2:15 traditions which ye have been t', 1321
Tit 1: 9 faithful word as he hath been t', *1322
1Joh 2:27 no lie, and even as it hath t' you, 1321
Re 2:14 t' Balac to cast a stumblingblock "

taunt See also TAUNTING.
Jer 24: 9 and a proverb, a t' and a curse, 8148
Eze 5:15 So it shall be a reproach and a t', 1422

taunting
Hab 2: 6 and a t' proverb against him, and 4426

taverns
Ac 28:15 far as Appii forum,...The three t': 4999

taxation
2Ki 23:35 of every one according to his t', to 6187

taxed
2Ki 23:35 he t' the land to give the money 6186
Lu 2: 1 that all the world should be t'. * 582
3 all went to be t', every one into his* "
5 be t' with Mary his espoused wife.* "

taxes
Da 11:20 a raiser of t' in the glory of the *5065

taxing
Lu 2: 2 And this t' was first made when * 583
Ac 5:37 Judas of Galilee in the days of the t'."

teach See also TAUGHT; TEACHER; TEACHEST; TEACHETH; TEACHING.
Ex 4:12 and t' thee what thou shalt say. 3384
15 and will t' you what ye shall do. "
18:20 thou shalt t' them ordinances and 2094
24:12 written; that thou mayest t' them.3384
35:34 hath put in his heart that he may t',"
Le 10:11 may t' the children of Israel all the "
14:57 t' when it is unclean, and when it is"
De 4: 1 the judgments, which I t' you, for 3925
9 but t' them thy sons, and thy sons'*3045
10 and that they may t' their children.3925
14 me at that time to t' you statutes "
5:31 judgments, which thou shalt t' them, "
6: 1 your God commanded to t' you, "
7 shalt t' them diligently unto thy 8150
11:19 And ye shall t' them your children,3925
17:11 of the law which they shall t' thee,3384
20:18 they t' you not to do after all their3925
24: 8 the priests the Levites shall t' you:3384
31:19 you, and t' it the children of Israel:3925
33:10 They shall t' Jacob thy judgments,3384
J'g 3: 2 Israel might know, to t' them war,3925
13: 8 and t' us what we shall do unto the3384
1Sa 12:23 I will t' you the good and the right*"
2Sa 1:18 bade them t' the children of Judah3925
1Ki 8:36 that thou t' them the good way *3384
2Ki 17:27 t' them the manner of the God of "
2Ch 17: 7 to t' in the cities of Judah. 3925
Ezr 7:10 and to t' in Israel statutes and "
25 and t' ye them that know them not.3045
Job 6:24 T' me, and I will hold my tongue:3384
10 Shall not they t' thee, and tell thee, "
12: 7 the beasts, and they shall t' thee; "
8 to the earth, and it shall t' thee: "
21:22 Shall any t' God knowledge? seeing3925
27:11 I will t' you by the hand of God: 3384
32: 7 multitude of years...t' wisdom. 3045
33:33 peace, and I shall t' thee wisdom. 502
34:32 That which I see not t' thou me: 3384
37:19 T' us what we shall say unto him;3045
Ps 25: 4 thy ways, O Lord; t' me thy paths.3925
5 Lead me in thy truth, and t' me: "
8 will he t' sinners in the way. *3384
9 and the meek will he t' his way. 3925
12 him shall he t' in the way that he*3384
27:11 T' me thy way, O Lord, and lead "
32: 8 I will instruct thee and t' thee in the"
34:11 I will t' you the fear of the Lord. 3925
45: 4 thy right hand shall t' thee terrible3384
51:13 will I t' transgressors thy ways; 3925
60: *title* Michtam of David, to t'; when "
86:11 T' me thy way, O Lord; I will 3384
90:12 t' us to number our days, that we 3045
105:22 pleasure; and t' his senators wisdom. "
119:12 thou, O Lord: t' me thy statutes. 3925
26 heardest me: t' me thy statutes. "
33 T' me, O Lord, the way of thy 3384
64 of thy mercy: t' me thy statutes. 3925
66 T' me...judgment and knowledge; "
68 and doest good; t' me thy statutes. "
108 O Lord, and t' me thy judgments. "
124 thy mercy, and t' me thy statutes. "
135 thy servant; and t' me thy statutes."
132:12 my testimony that I shall t' them, "
143:10 T' me to do thy will; for thou art "
Pr 9: 9 t' a just man, and he will increase 3045
Isa 2: 3 he will t' us of his ways, and we 3384
28: 9 Whom shall he t' knowledge? and "
26 him to discretion, and doth t' him. "
Jer 9:20 and t' your daughters wailing, and3925
31:34 t' no more every man his neighbour,"
Eze 44:23 shall t' my people the difference 3384
Da 1: 4 whom they might t' the learning 3925
Mic 3:11 and the priests thereof t' for hire, 3384
4: 2 and he will t' us of his ways, and we"
Hab 2:19 Arise, it shall t'! Behold, it is laid "
M't 5:19 and shall t' men so, he shall be 1321

M't 5:19 but whosoever shall do and t' them, 1321
11: 1 to t' and to preach in their cities. "
28:19 Go ye therefore, and t' all nations, *3100
M'r 4: 1 began again to t' by the sea side: 1321
6: 2 he began to t' in the synagogue: "
34 he began to t' them many things. "
8:31 he began to t' them, that the Son of "
Lu 11: 1 said unto him, Lord, t' us to pray, "
12:12 Holy Ghost shall t' you in the same "
Joh 7:35 the Gentiles, and t' the Gentiles? "
9:34 born in sins, and dost thou t' us? "
14:26 he shall t' you all things, and bring* "
Ac 1: 1 that Jesus began both to do and t', "
4:18 at all nor t' in the name of Jesus. "
5:28 that ye should not t' in this name? "
42 ceased not to t' and preach Jesus "
16:21 t' customs, which are not lawful *3605
1Co 4:17 I t' every where in every church. 1321
11:14 Doth not even nature itself t' you, "
14:19 by my voice I might t' others also, *2727
1Ti 1: 3 some that they t' no other doctrine, 2085
2:12 But I suffer not a woman to t', nor 1321
3: 2 given to hospitality, apt to t'; 1317
4:11 These things command and t'. 1321
6: 2 benefit. These things t' and exhort. "
3 If any man t' otherwise, and *2085
2Ti 2: 2 who shall be able to t' others also. 1321
24 but be gentle unto all men, apt to t', 1317
Tit 2: 4 t' the young women to be sober, *4994
Heb 5:12 ye have need that one t' you again 1321
8:11 not t' every man his neighbour, "
1Jo 2:27 ye need not that any man t' you: "
Re 2:20 to t' and to seduce my servants to * "

teacher See also TEACHERS.
1Ch 25: 8 as the great, the t' as the scholar. 995
Hab 2:18 the molten image, and a t' of lies, 3384
Joh 3: 2 that thou art a t' come from God: 1320
Ro 2:20 a t' of babes, which hast the form "
1Ti 2: 7 a t' of the Gentiles in faith and "
2Ti 1:11 an apostle, and a t' of the Gentiles. "

teachers
Ps 119:99 understanding than all my t': 3925
Pr 5:13 have not obeyed the voice of my t', 3384
Isa 30:20 not thy t' be removed into a corner "
20 but thine eyes shall see thy t': "
43:27 t' have transgressed against me. *3887
Ac 13: 1 at Antioch certain prophets and t'; 1320
1Co 12:28 secondarily prophets, thirdly t', "
29 are all prophets? are all t'? are all "
Eph 4:11 and some, pastors and t'; "
1Ti 1: 7 Desiring to be t' of the law; 3547
2Ti 4: 3 shall they heap to themselves t', 1320
Tit 2: 3 to much wine, t' of good things; 2567
Heb 5:12 when for the time ye ought to be t', 1320
2Pe 2: 1 there shall be false t' among you, 5572

teachest
Ps 94:12 O Lord, and t' him out of thy law; 3925
M't 22:16 true, and t' the way of God in truth, 1321
M'r 12:14 men, but t' the way of God in truth: "
Lu 20:21 know that thou sayest and t' rightly, "
21 of any, but t' the way of God truly: "
Ac 21:21 that thou t' all the Jews which are "
Ro 2:21 Thou therefore which t' another, "
21 t' thou not thyself? thou that "

teacheth
2Sa 22:35 He t' my hands to war; so that a 3925
Job 35:11 Who t' us more than the beasts of 502
36:22 by his power: who t' like him? *3384
Ps 18:34 He t' my hands to war, so that a 3925
94:10 he that t' man knowledge, shall not "
144: 1 which t' my hands to war, and my "
Pr 6:13 his feet, he t' with his fingers; *3384
16:23 The heart of the wise t' his mouth, *7919
Isa 9:15 prophet that t' lies, he is the tail. 3384
48:17 thy God which t' thee to profit, 3925
Ac 21:28 man, that t' all men every where 1321
Ro 12: 7 or he that t', on teaching; "
1Co 2:13 the words which man's wisdom t', 1318
13 but which the Holy Ghost t'; "
Gal 6: 6 unto him that t' in all good things. 2727
1Jo 2:27 as the same anointing t' you of all 1321

teaching
2Ch 15: 3 without a t' priest, and without 3384
Jer 32:33 them, rising up early and t' them, 3925
M't 4:23 all Galilee, t' in their synagogues, 1321
9:35 and villages, t' in their synagogues, "
15: 9 t' for doctrines the commandments "
21:23 people came unto him as he was t', "
26:55 sat daily with you t' in the temple, "
28:20 T' them to observe all things "
M'r 6: 6 he went round about the villages, t'. "
7: 7 t' for doctrines the commandments "
14:49 was daily with you in the temple t', "
Lu 5:17 pass on a certain day, as he was t', "
13:10 he was t' in one of the synagogues "
22 through the cities and villages, t', "
21:37 day time he was t' in the temple; "
23: 5 the people, t' throughout all Jewry, "
Ac 5:25 in the temple, and t' the people. "
15:35 t' and preaching the word of the "
18:11 t' the word of God among them. "
28:31 t' those things which concern the "
Ro 12: 7 or he that teacheth, on t'; 1319
Col 1:28 and t' every man in all wisdom; 1321
3:16 t' and admonishing one another "
Tit 1:11 t' things which they ought not, for "
2:12 T' us that, denying ungodliness *3811

tear See also TARE; TEARETH; TEARS; TORN.
J'g 8: 7 I will t' your flesh with the thorns 1758
Ps 7: 2 Lest he t' my soul like a lion, 2963
35:15 they did t' me, and ceased not: 7167
50:22 lest I t' you in pieces, and there be 2963
Jer 15: 3 sword to slay, and the dogs to t', 5498
16: 7 shall men t' themselves for them *6536
Eze 13:20 and I will t' them from your arms, 7167
21 Your kerchiefs also will I t', and "
Ho 5:14 I, even I, will t' and go away; I will 2963
13: 8 lion: the wild beast shall t' them. 1234
Am 1:11 and his anger did t' perpetually, 2963
Na 2:12 The lion did t' in pieces enough for "
Zec 11:16 the fat, and t' their claws in pieces. 6561

teareth
De 33:20 t' the arm with the crown of the 2963
Job 16: 9 He t' me in his wrath, who hateth* "
18: 4 He t' himself in his anger: shall * "
Mic 5: 8 both treadeth down, and t' in pieces, "
M'r 9:18 he taketh him, he t' him: and he *4486
Lu 9:39 and it t' him that he foameth again, 4682

tears
2Ki 20: 5 thy prayer, I have seen thy t': 1832
Es 8: 3 besought him with t' to put away 1058
Job 16:20 but mine eye poureth out t' unto God.
Ps 6: 6 to swim; I water my couch with t'. 1832
39:12 my cry; hold not thy peace at my t': "
42: 3 My t' have been my meat day and "
56: 8 put thou my t' into thy bottle: are "
80: 5 feedest them with the bread of t'; "
5 them t' to drink in great measure. "
116: 8 mine eyes from t', and my feet from "
126: 5 They that sow in t' shall reap in joy. "
Ec 4: 1 the t' of such as were oppressed, "
Isa 16: 9 I will water thee with my t', O "
25: 8 Lord God will wipe away t' from off "
38: 5 heard thy prayer, I have seen thy t': "
Jer 9: 1 and mine eyes a fountain of t', that "
18 that our eyes may run down with t', "
13:17 weep sore, and run down with t', "
14:17 Let mine eyes run down with t' "
31:16 weeping, and thine eyes from t': "
La 1: 2 night, and her t' are on her cheeks: "
2:11 Mine eyes do fail with t', my "
18 let t' run down like a river day and "
Eze 24:16 weep, neither shall thy t' run down. "
Mal 2:13 covering...altar of the Lord with t', "
M'r 9:24 and said with t', Lord, I believe; *1144
Lu 7:38 and began to wash his feet with t', "
44 she hath washed my feet with t', "
Ac 20:19 humility of mind, and with many t', "
31 every one night and day with t'. "
2Co 2: 4 I wrote unto you with many t'; not "
2Ti 1: 4 to see thee, being mindful of thy t', "
Heb 5: 7 with strong crying and t' unto him "
12:17 he sought it carefully with t'. "
Re 7:17 and God shall wipe away all t' from* "
21: 4 and God shall wipe away all t' from* "

teats
Isa 32:12 They shall lament for the t', for *7699
Eze 23: 3 bruised the t' of their virginity. ‡1717
21 in bruising thy t' by the Egyptians‡ "

Tebah (te'-bah)
Ge 22:24 was Reumah, she bare also T', 2875

Tebaliah (teb-a-li'-ah)
1Ch 26:11 Hilkiah the second, T' the third, 2882

Tebeth (te'-beth)
Es 2:16 month, which is the month T', 2887

tedious
Ac 24: 4 that I be not further t' unto thee. 1465

teeth
Ge 49:12 wine, and his t' white with milk. 8127
Nu 11:33 the flesh was yet between their t', "
De 32:24 also send the t' of beasts upon them, "
1Sa 2:13 a fleshhook of three t' in his hand; "
Job 4:10 lions, and the t' of the young lions, "
13:14 do I take my flesh in my t', and put "
16: 9 he gnasheth upon me with his t'; "
19:20 I am escaped with the skin of my t'. "
29:17 and plucked the spoil out of his t'. "
41:14 his t' are terrible round about. "
Ps 3: 7 hast broken the t' of the ungodly. "
35:16 they gnashed upon me with their t'. "
37:12 and gnasheth upon him with his t'. "
57: 4 whose t' are spears and arrows, "
58: 6 Break their t', O God, in their "
6 break out the great t' of the young 4973
112:10 he shall gnash with his t', and 8127
124: 6 not given us as a prey to their t'. "
Pr 10:26 As vinegar to the t', and as smoke "
30:14 generation, whose t' are as swords, "
14 their jaw t' as knives, to devour 4973
Ca 4: 2 Thy t' are like a flock of sheep 8127
6: 6 Thy t' are as a flock of sheep which "
Isa 41:15 threshing instrument having t': 6374
Jer 31:29 the children's t' are set on edge. 8127
30 grape, his t' shall be set on edge. "
La 2:16 thee: they hiss and gnash the t': "
3:16 broken my t' with gravel stones, "
Eze 18: 2 the children's t' are set on edge? "
Da 7: 5 mouth of it between the t' of it: 8128
7 it had great iron t': it devoured "
19 whose t' were of iron, and his nails "
Joe 1: 6 whose t' are the t' of a lion, and 8127
6 hath the cheek t' of a great lion. 4973
Am 4: 6 have given you cleanness of t' 8127
Mic 3: 5 people err, that bite with their t', "
Zec 9: 7 abominations from between his t': "
M't 8:12 be weeping and gnashing of t'. 3599
13:42, 50 be wailing and gnashing of t'. "
22:13 be weeping and gnashing of t'. "
24:51 be weeping and gnashing of t'. "
25:30 be weeping and gnashing of t'. "
27:44 with him, cast the same in his t'. *3679
M'r 9:18 foameth, and gnasheth with his t', 3599
Lu 13:28 be weeping and gnashing of t', "
Ac 7:54 they gnashed on him with their t'. "
Re 9: 8 and their t' were as...of lions. "
8 were as the t' of lions. *

Tehaphnehes (te-haf'-ne-heze) See also TAHAPANES.
Eze 30:18 At T'...the day shall be darkened, 8471

Tehinnah (te-hin'-nah)
1Ch 4:12 and T' the father of Ir-nahash. 8468

teil (teel)
Isa 6:13 as a t' tree, and as an oak, whose * 424

Tekel (te'-kel)
Da 5:25 Mene, Mene, T', Upharsin. 8625
27 T'; Thou art weighed in the "

Tekoa (te-ko'-ah) See also TEKOAH; TEKOITE.
1Ch 2:24 bare him Ashur the father of T'. 8620
4: 5 Ashur the father of T' had two "
2Ch 11: 6 even Beth-lehem, and Etam, and T'. "
20:20 went forth into the wilderness of T': "
Jer 6: 1 and blow the trumpet in T', and "
Am 1: 1 who was among the herdmen of T', "

Tekoah (te-ko'-ah) See also TEKOA.
2Sa 14: 2 And Joab sent to T', and fetched *8620
4 woman of T' spake to the king, *8621
9 woman of T' said unto the king, * "

Tekoite (te-ko'-ite) See also TEKOITES.
2Sa 23:26 Ira the son of Ikkesh the T', 8621
1Ch 11:28 Ira the son of Ikkesh the T', "
27: 9 was Ira the son of Ikkesh the T': "

Tekoites (te-ko'-ites)
Ne 3: 5 next unto them the T' repaired; 8621
27 the T' repaired another piece, "

Tel See TEL-ABIB; TEL-HARESHA; TEL-MELAH.

Tel-abib (tel-a'-bib)
Eze 3:15 to them of the captivity at T', 8512

Telah (te'-lah)
1Ch 7:25 and T' his son, and Tahan his son, 8520

Telaim (tel'-a-im) See also TELEM.
1Sa 15: 4 and numbered them in T', 2923

Telassar (te-las'-sar) See also THELASSAR.
Isa 37:12 children of Eden which were in T'? 8515

Telem (te'-lem) See also TELAIM.
Jos 15:24 Ziph, and T', and Bealoth, 2928
Ezr 10:24 porters; Shallum, and T', and Uri. "

Tel-haresha (tel-ha-re'-shah) See also TEL-HARSA.
Ne 7:61 Tel-melah, T', Cherub, Addon, *8521

Tel-harsa (tel-har'-sah) See also TEL-HARESHA.
Ezr 2:59 Tel-melah, T', Cherub, Addan, *8521

tell See also FORETELL; TELLEST; TELLETH; TELLING; TOLD.
Ge 12:18 not t' me that she was thy wife? 5046
15: 5 toward heaven, and t' the stars, ‡5608
21:26 neither didst thou t' me, neither 5046
22: 2 mountains which I will t' thee of. 559
24:23 daughter art thou? t' me, I pray 5046
49 and truly with my master, t' me: "
49 and if not, t' me; that I may turn "
26: 2 in the land which I shall t' thee of: 559
29:15 t' me, what shall thy wages be? 5046
31:27 and didst not t' me, that I might "
32: 5 I have sent to t' my lord, that I may "
29 said, T' me, I pray thee, thy name. "
37:16 t' me, I pray thee, where they feed "
40: 8 to God? t' me them, I pray you. 5608
43: 6 to t' the man whether ye had yet 5046
22 we cannot t' who put our money *3045
45:13 shall t' my father of all my glory 5046
49: 1 t' you that which shall befall you "
Ex 9: 1 Go in unto Pharaoh, and t' him, 1696
10: 2 mayest t' in the ears of thy son, 5608
14:12 this the word that we did t' thee *1696
19: 3 and t' the children of Israel; 5046
Le 14:35 house shall come and t' the priest, "
Nu 14:14 t' it to the inhabitants of this land: 559
21: 1 heard t' that Israel came by the way
23: 3 he sheweth me I will t' thee. 5046
De 17:11 judgment which they shall t' thee, 559
32: 7 thy elders, and they will t' thee. "
Jos 7:19 t' me now what thou hast done; 5046
J'g 14:16 my mother, and shall I t' it thee? "
16: 6 T' me, I pray thee, wherein thy "
10 t' me, I pray thee, wherewith thou "
13 t' me wherewith thou mightest be "
20: 3 T' us, how was this wickedness? 1696
Ru 3: 4 he will t' thee what thou shalt do. 5046
4: 4 it, then t' me, that I may know: "
1Sa 6: 2 t' us wherewith we shall send it *3045
9: 8 the man of God, to t' us our way. 5046
18 T' me,...where the seer's house is. "
19 will t' thee all that is in thine heart. "
10:15 T' me, I pray thee, what Samuel "
14:43 T' me what thou hast done. "
15:16 will t' thee what the Lord hath said "
17:55 thy soul liveth, O king, I cannot t'. 3045
19: 3 and what I see, that I will t' thee. 5046
20: 9 thee, then would not I t' to thee? "
10 to Jonathan, Who shall t' me? or "
22:22 there, that he would surely t' Saul: "
23:11 Israel, I beseech thee, t' thy servant. "
27:11 Lest they should t' on us, saying, "
2Sa 1: 4 went the matter? I pray thee, t' me. "
20 T' it not in Gath, publish it not in "
7: 5 Go and t' my servant David, Thus 559
12:18 feared to t' him that the child was 5046
18 if we t' him that the child is dead? 559
22 Who can t' whether God will be *3045
13: 4 day to day? wilt thou not t' me? 5046
15:35 shalt t' it to Zadok and Abiathar the "
17:16 send quickly, and t' David, saying, "
18:21 Go t' the king what thou hast seen. "
1Ki 1:20 t' them who shall sit on the throne "
14: 3 he shall t' thee what shall become "
7 t' Jeroboam, Thus saith the Lord 559
18: 8, 11 t' thy lord, Behold, Elijah is here. "

1Ki 18:12 and so when I come and t' Ahab, 5046
14 t' thy lord, Behold, Elijah is here: 559
20: 9 T' my lord the king, All that thou "
11 T' him, Let not him that girdeth 1696
22:16 t' me nothing but that which is true*"
18 Did I not t' thee that he would 559
2Ki 4: 2 t' me, what hast thou in the house?5046
7: 9 may go and t' the king's household."
8: 4 T' me, I pray thee, all the great 5608
9:12 they said, It is false; t' us now. 5046
15 of the city to go to t' it in Jezreel. "
20: 5 and t' Hezekiah the captain of my* 559
22:15 T' the man that sent you to me, "
1Ch 17: 4 Go and t' David my servant, Thus "
10 I t' thee that the Lord will build 5046
21:10 Go and t' David, saying, Thus 1696
2Ch 18:17 Did I not t' thee that he would not 559
34:23 T' ye the man that sent you to me, "
Job 1:15, 16, 17, 19 escaped alone to t' thee. 5046
8:10 not they teach thee, and t' thee, 559
12: 7 of the air, and they shall t' thee: 5046
34:34 Let men of understanding t' me, * 559
Ps 22:17 I may t' all my bones: they look 5608
26: 7 and t' of all thy wondrous works. "
48:12 about her: t' the towers thereof. ‡ "
13 that ye may t' it to the generation "
50:12 I were hungry, I would not t' thee: 559
Pr 30: 4 is his son's name, if thou canst t'?*3045
Ec 6:12 for who can t' a man what shall be5046
8: 7 for who can t' him when it shall be?"
10:14 a man cannot t' what shall be; and*"
14 shall be after him, who can t' him? "
20 hath wings shall t' the matter. "
Ca 1: 7 T' me, O thou whom my soul loveth,"
5: 8 ye t' him, that I am sick of love. "
Isa 5: 5 I will t' you what I will do to my 3045
6: 9 and t' this people, Hear ye indeed, 559
19:12 let them t' thee now, and let them 5046
42: 9 they spring forth I t' you of them. 8085
45:21 T' ye, and bring them near; yea, *5046
48:20 t' this, utter it even to the end of 8085
Jer 15: 2 shalt t' them, Thus saith the Lord; 559
19: 2 the words that I shall t' thee, 1696
23:27 they t' every man to his neighbour,5608
28 hath a dream, let him t' a dream; "
32 do t' them, and cause my people "
28:13 Go and t' Hananiah, saying, Thus 559
34: 2 Zedekiah king of Judah, and t' him, "
35:13 Go and t' the men of Judah and the*"
36:16 We will surely t' the king of all 5046
17 T' us now, How didst thou write all"
48:20 t' ye it in Arnon,...Moab is spoiled, "
Eze 3:11 and speak unto them, and t' them, 559
12:23 T' them therefore, Thus saith the "
17:12 t' them, Behold, the king of Babylon"
24:19 t' us what these things are to us, 5046
Da 2: 4 t' thy servants the dream, and we 560
7 the king t' his servants the dream, "
9 t' me the dream, and I shall know "
36 and we will t' the interpretation "
4: 9 t' me the visions of my dream that I "
Joe 1: 3 T' ye your children of it, and let 5608
3 and let your children t' their children, "
Jon 1: 8 T' us,...for whose cause this 5046
3: 9 Who can t' if God will turn and *3045
M't 8: 4 saith unto him, See thou t' no man;2036
10:27 What I t' you in darkness, that 3004
16:20 should t' no man that he was Jesus2036
17: 9 T' the vision to no man, until the "
18:15 t' him his fault between thee and *1650
17 hear them, t' it unto the church: 2036
21: 5 T' ye the daughter of Sion, Behold,"
24 ask you one thing, which if ye t' me,"
24 will t' you by what authority I do 2046
27 Jesus, and said, We cannot t'. *1492
27 Neither t' I you by what authority 3004
22: 4 T' them which are bidden, Behold,2036
17 T' us therefore, What thinkest thou?"
24: 3 T' us, when shall these things be? "
26:63 t' us whether thou be the Christ, "
28: 7 t' his disciples that he is risen from "
9 And as they went to t' his disciples,*518
10 go t' my brethren that they go into "
M'r 1:30 fever, and anon they t' him of her. 3004
5:19 t' them how great things the Lord 312
7:36 them that they should t' no man: 2036
8:26 town, nor t' it to any in the town. * "
30 that they should t' no man of him. 3004
9: 9 t' no man what things they had 1334
10:32 and began to t' them what things 3004
11:29 will t' you by what authority I do 2046
33 and said unto Jesus, We cannot t'.*1492
33 them, Neither do I t' you by what 3004
13: 4 T' us, when shall these things be?2036
16: 7 t' his disciples and Peter that he "
Lu 4:25 I t' you of a truth, many widows *3004
5:14 And he charged him to t' no man: 2036
7:22 t' John what things ye have seen 518
42 T' me...which of them will love *2036
8:56 should t' no man what was done. "
9:21 them to t' no man that thing; "
27 I t' you of a truth, there be some 3004
10:24 For I t' you, that many prophets * "
12:51 I t' you, Nay; but rather division: "
59 I t' thee, thou shalt not depart * "
13: 3, 5 I t' you, Nay: but, except ye "
27 I t' you, I know you not whence ye "
32 Go ye, and t' that fox, Behold, I *2036
17:34 I t' you, in that night there shall *3004
18: 8 I t' you that he will avenge them * "
14 I t' you, this man went down to his*"
19:40 I t' you that, if these should hold "
20: 2 T' us, by what authority doest 2036
7 they could not t' whence it was. *1492
8 Neither t' I you by what authority 3004
22:34 I t' thee, Peter, the cock shall not "
22:67 Art thou the Christ? t' us. And he2036
67 them, If I t' you, ye will not believe:"
Joh 3: 8 but canst not t' whence it cometh,*1492
12 if I t' you of heavenly things? 2036
4:25 he is come, he will t' us all things.*312
8:14 but ye cannot t' whence I come, *1492
45 And because I t' you the truth, ye*3004
10:24 If thou be the Christ, t' us plainly. 2036
12:22 again Andrew and Philip t' Jesus. 3004
13:19 Now I t' you before it come, that, "
16: 7 Nevertheless I t' you the truth; It is"
18 while? we cannot t' what he saith.*1492
18:34 or did others t' it thee of me? 2036
20:15 t' me where thou hast laid him, and"
Ac 5: 8 T' me whether ye sold the land for "
10: 6 t' thee what thou oughtest to do. *2980
11:14 Who shall t' thee words, whereby * "
15:27 t' you the same things by mouth. 518
17:21 either to t', or to hear some new 3004
22:27 him, T' me, art thou a Roman? "
23:17 he hath a certain thing to t' him. 518
19 him, What is that thou hast to t' me?"
22 t' no man that thou hast shewed 1583
2Co 12: 2 (whether in the body, I cannot t';*1492
2 whether out of the body, I cannot t':*"
3 or out of the body, I cannot t': * "
Ga 4:16 enemy, because I t' you the truth?‡ 226
21 T' me, ye that desire to be under 3004
5:21 of the which I t' you before, as I *4302
Ph'p 3:18 and now t' you even weeping, that3004
Heb11:32 time would fail me to t' of Gedeon,1334
Re 17: 7 t' thee the mystery of the woman, 2046

tellest
Ps 56: 8 Thou t' my wanderings: put thou‡5608

telleth
2Sa 7:11 Also the Lord t' thee that he will 5046
2Ki 6:12 t' the king of Israel the words that "
Ps 41: 6 when he goeth abroad, he t' it. 1696
101: 7 he that t' lies shall not tarry in my*"
147: 4 He t' the number of the stars; he‡4487
Jer 33:13 the hands of him that t' them, ‡ "
Joh 12:22 Philip cometh and t' Andrew: and3004

telling
J'g 7:15 Gideon heard the t' of the dream, 4557
2Sa 11:19 an end of t' the matters of the war1696
2Ki 8: 5 as he was t' the king how he had 5608

Tel-melah (*tel-me'-lah*)
Ezr 2:59 were they which went up from T',8528
Ne 7:61 they which went up also from T', "

Tema (*te'-mah*)
Ge 25:15 Hadar, and T', Jetur, Naphish, 8485
1Ch 1:30 and Dumah, Massa, Hadad, and T', "
Job 6:19 The troops of T' looked, the "
Isa 21:14 inhabitants...of T' brought water "
Jer 25:23 Dedan, and T', and Buz, and all "

Teman (*te'-man*) See also TEMANITE.
Ge 36:11 And the sons of Eliphaz were T', 8487
15 duke T', duke Omar, duke Zepho, "
42 Duke Kenaz, duke T', duke Mibzar,"
1Ch 1:36 The sons of Eliphaz; T', and Omar, "
53 Duke Kenaz, duke T', duke Mibzar,"
Jer 49: 7 Is wisdom no more in T'? is counsel"
20 against the inhabitants of T': "
Eze 25:13 I will make it desolate from T'; "
Am 1:12 But I will send a fire upon T', which"
Ob 9 And thy mighty men, O T', shall be"
Hab 3: 3 God came from T', and the Holy "

Temani (*te'-ma-ni*) See also TEMANITE.
Ge 36:34 Husham of the land of T' reigned*8489

Temanite (*te'-man-ite*) See also TEMANI; TEMANITES.
Job 2:11 Eliphaz the T', and Bildad the 8489
4: 1 Eliphaz the T' answered and said, "
15: 1 Then answered Eliphaz the T', and"
22: 1 Eliphaz the T' answered and said, "
42: 7 the Lord said to Eliphaz the T', My"
9 So Eliphaz the T' and Bildad the "

Temanites (*te'-man-ites*)
1Ch 1:45 Husham of the land of the T' 8489

Temeni (*tem'-e-ni*)
1Ch 4: 6 Hepher, and T', and Haahashtari. 8488

temper See also TEMPERED.
Eze 46:14 hin of oil, to t' with the fine flour;*7450

temperance
Ac 24:25 as he reasoned of righteousness, t',1466
Ga 5:23 Meekness, t': against such there is "
2Pe 1: 6 And to knowledge t'; and to "
6 and to t' patience; and to patience "

temperate
1Co 9:25 for the mastery is t' in all things. 1467
Tit 1: 8 of good men, sober, just, holy, t'; 1468
2: 2 the aged men be sober, grave, t', *4998

tempered See also UNTEMPERED.
Ex 29: 2 and cakes unleavened t' with oil, *1101
30:35 t' together, pure and holy: *4414
1Co 12:24 but God hath t' the body together, 4786

tempest
Job 9:17 For he breaketh me with a t', and 8183
27:20 t' stealeth him away in the night. 5492
Ps 11: 6 and brimstone, and an horrible t':*7307
55: 8 from the windy storm and t'. 5591
83:15 So persecute them with thy t', and "
Isa 28: 2 strong one, which as a t' of hail 2230
29: 6 and great noise, with storm and t',5591
30:30 scattering, and t', and hailstones. 2230
32: 2 the wind, and a covert from the t'; "
54:11 O thou afflicted, tossed with t', and5590
Am 1:14 a t' in the day of the whirlwind: 5591
Jon 1: 4 there was a mighty t' in the sea, "
12 my sake this great t' is upon you. 5591
M't 8:24 there arose a great t' in the sea, 4578
Ac 27:18 being exceedingly tossed with a t',*5492
20 and no small t' lay on us, all hope 5494
Heb12:18 blackness, and darkness, and t', 2366
2Pe 2:17 clouds that are carried with a t'; *2978

tempestuous
Ps 50: 3 it shall be very t' round about him.8175
Jon 1:11 for the sea wrought, and was t'. 5490
13 wrought, and was t' against them. "
Ac 27:14 there arose against it a t' wind, 5189

temple See also TEMPLES.
1Sa 1: 9 seat by a post of the t' of the Lord.1964
3: 3 lamp...went out in the t' of the Lord,"
2Sa 22: 7 he did hear my voice out of his t', "
1Ki 6: 3 the porch before the t' of the house,"
5 both of the t' and of the oracle: "
17 the t' before it, was forty cubits "
33 for the door of the t' posts of olive "
7:21 up the pillars in the porch of the t':"
50 doors of the house, to wit, of the t'. "
2Ki 11:10 that were in the t' of the Lord. *1004
11 king, from the right corner of the t'*"
11 to the left corner of the t', along by*"
11 along by the altar and the t'. "
13 she came to the people into the t' * "
18:16 gold from the doors of the t' of the1964
23: 4 bring forth out of the t' of the Lord "
24:13 had made in the t' of the Lord, "
1Ch 6:10 office in the t' that Solomon built 1004
10:10 fastened his head in...t' of Dagon.* "
2Ch 3:17 reared up the pillars before the t',1964
4: 7 set them in the t', five on the right "
8 and placed them in the t', five on the"
22 doors of the house of the t', were of "
23:10 hand, from the right side of the t'*1004
10 to the left side of the t', along by * "
10 along by the altar and the t', by the*"
26:16 went into the t' of the Lord to burn1964
27: 2 entered not into the t' of the Lord. "
29:16 that they found in the t' of the Lord"
35:20 when Josiah had prepared the t', 1004
36: 7 and put them in his t' at Babylon. 1964
Ezr 3: 6 the foundation of the t' of the Lord "
10 the foundation of the t' of the Lord,"
4: 1 builded the t' unto the Lord God "
5:14 out of the t' that was in Jerusalem,1965
14 brought them into the t' of Babylon,"
14 king take out of the t' of Babylon, "
15 them into the t' that is in Jerusalem,"
6: 5 out of the t' which is at Jerusalem, "
5 unto the t' which is at Jerusalem, "
Ne 6:10 in the house of God, within the t', 1964
10 and let us shut the doors of the t': "
11 go into the t' to save his life? "
Ps 5: 7 will I worship toward thy holy t'. "
11: 4 The Lord is in his holy t', the Lord's"
18: 6 he heard my voice out of his t', and "
27: 4 of the Lord, and to enquire in his t'."
29: 9 in his t' doth every one speak of his"
48: 9 O God, in the midst of thy t'. "
65: 4 of thy house, even of thy holy t'. "
68:29 Because of thy t' at Jerusalem shall"
79: 1 thy holy t' have they defiled; they "
138: 2 I will worship toward thy holy t', "
Isa 6: 1 lifted up, and his train filled the t'. "
44:28 and to the t', Thy foundation shall "
66: 6 a voice from the t', a voice of the "
Jer 7: 4 words, saying, The t' of the Lord, "
4 t' of the Lord, The t' of the Lord, "
24: 1 were set before the t' of the Lord, "
50:28 our God, the vengeance of his t', "
51:11 the Lord, the vengeance of his t'. "
Eze 8:16 at the door of the t' of the Lord, "
16 backs toward the t' of the Lord, "
41: 1 Afterward he brought me to the t', "
4 breadth, twenty cubits, before the t':"
15 with the inner t', and the porches of"
20 trees made, and on the wall of the t'."
21 The posts of the t' were squared, "
23 t' and the sanctuary had two doors."
25 made on them, on the doors of the t',"
42: 8 the t' were an hundred cubits. "
Da 5: 2 of the t' which was in Jerusalem; 1965
3 out of the t' of the house of God "
Am 8: 3 songs of the t' shall be howlings 1964
Jon 2: 4 I will look again toward thy holy t'."
7 came in unto thee, into thine holy t'."
Mic 1: 2 you, the Lord from his holy t'. "
Hab 2:20 But the Lord is in his holy t': let all"
Hag 2:15 upon a stone in the t' of the Lord: "
18 foundation of the Lord's t' was laid,"
Zec 6:12 he shall build the t' of the Lord: "
13 he shall build the t' of the Lord; "
14 for a memorial in the t' of the Lord."
15 come and build in the t' of the Lord,"
8: 9 was laid, that the t' might be built. "
Mal 3: 1 seek, shall suddenly come to his t', "
M't 4: 5 setteth him on a pinnacle of the t',2411
12: 5 priests in the t' profane...sabbath, "
6 this place is one greater than the t'. "
21:12 And Jesus went into the t' of God, "
12 them that sold and bought in the t',"
14 and the lame came to him in the t'; "
15 and the children crying in the t', "
23 And when he was come into the t', "
23:16 Whosoever shall swear by the t', 3485
16 shall swear by the gold of the t', "
17 or the t' that sanctifieth the gold? "
21 And whoso shall swear by the t', "
35 slew between the t' and the altar.* "
24: 1 out, and departed from the t': 2411
1 to shew him the buildings of the t'. "
26:55 daily with you teaching in the t', "
61 I am able to destroy the t' of God, 3485

M't 27: 5 down the pieces of silver in the t'. *3485
40 Thou that destroyest the t', and "
51 the veil of the t' was rent in twain "
M'r 11: 11 into Jerusalem, and into the t': 2411
15 Jesus went into the t', and began to"
15 them that sold and bought in the t'."
16 carry any vessel through the t'. "
27 as he was walking in the t', there "
12: 35 and said, while he taught in the t', "
13: 1 as he went out of the t', one of his "
3 mount of Olives over against the t', "
14: 49 daily with you in the t' teaching, "
58 destroy this t'...made with hands, 3485
15: 29 Ah, thou that destroyest the t', "
38 the veil of the t' was rent in twain "
Lu 1: 9 when he went into the t' of the Lord."
21 that he tarried so long in the t'. "
22 that he had seen a vision in the t': "
2: 27 he came by the Spirit into the t': 2411
37 which departed not from the t', but "
46 three days they found him in the t', "
4: 9 and set him on a pinnacle of the t', "
11: 51 between the altar and the t': *3624
18: 10 men went up into the t' to pray; 2411
19: 45 And he went into the t', and began "
47 And he taught daily in the t'. But "
20: 1 as he taught the people in the t', "
21: 5 And as some spake of the t', how "
37 day time he was teaching in the t'; "
38 in the morning to him in the t', "
22: 52 chief priests, and captains of the t'."
53 When I was daily with you in the t'."
23: 45 veil of the t' was rent in the midst. 3485
24: 53 And were continually in the t', 2411
Joh 2: 14 found in the t' those that sold oxen "
15 he drove them all out of the t', "
19 Destroy this t', and in three days 3485
20 six years was this t' in building, "
21 But he spake of the t' of his body. "
5: 14 Jesus findeth him in the t', and 2411
7: 14 the feast Jesus went up into the t', "
28 cried Jesus in the t' as he taught, "
8: 2 morning he came again into the t', "
20 the treasury, as he taught in the t': "
59 hid himself, and went out of the t', "
10: 23 Jesus walked in the t' in Solomon's "
11: 56 themselves, as they stood in the t', "
18: 20 in the synagogue, and in the t', "
Ac 2: 46 daily with one accord in the t', "
3: 1 John went up together into the t' "
2 gate of the t'...is called Beautiful, "
2 alms of them that entered...the t'; "
3 and John about to go into the t' "
8 and entered with them into the t', "
10 alms at the Beautiful gate of the t': "
4: 1 priests, and the captain of the t', "
5: 20 and speak in the t' to the people "
21 into the t' early in the morning, "
24 the captain of the t' and the chief "
25 put in prison are standing in the t', "
42 daily in the t', and in every house, "
19: 27 the t' of the great goddess Diana "
21: 26 with them entered into the t', "
27 Asia, when they saw him in the t', "
28 brought Greeks also into the t', "
29 that Paul had brought into the t'.) "
30 Paul, and drew him out of the t': "
22: 17 while I prayed in the t', I was in a "
24: 6 hath gone about to profane the t': "
12 And they neither found me in the t'"
18 Asia found me purified in the t', "
25: 8 neither against the t', nor yet "
26: 21 the Jews caught me in the t', "
1Co 3: 16 ye not that ye are the t' of God, 3485
17 If any man defile the t' of God, "
17 destroy; for the t' of God is holy, "
17 of God is holy, which t' ye are. "
6: 19 body is the t' of the Holy Ghost 3485
8: 10 knowledge sit at meat in the idol's t', "
9: 13 things live of the things of the t'? 2411
2Co 6: 16 hath the t' of God with idols? 3485
16 for ye are the t' of the living God; "
Eph 2: 21 groweth unto an holy t' in the Lord: "
2Th 2: 4 he as God sitteth in the t' of God, "
Re 3: 12 I make a pillar in the t' of my God, "
7: 15 serve him day and night in his t': "
11: 1 Rise, and measure the t' of God, "
2 the court which is without the t' "
19 the t' of God was opened in heaven, "
19 was seen in his t' the ark of his "
14: 15 another angel came out of the t', "
17 another angel came out of the t', "
15: 5 t' of the tabernacle of the testimony "
6 the seven angels came out of the t', "
8 And the t' was filled with smoke "
8 no man was able to enter into the t', "
16: 1 I heard a great voice out of the t' "
17 great voice out of the t' of heaven, "
21: 22 I saw no t' therein: for the Lord "
22 and the Lamb are the t' of it. "

temples
J'g 4: 21 and smote the nail into his t', and 7541
22 lay dead, and the nail was in his t'. "
5: 26 pierced and stricken through his t'. "
Ca 4: 3 t' are like a piece of a pomegranate "
6: 7 a piece of a pomegranate are thy t' "
Ho 8: 14 his Maker, and buildeth t'; *1964
Joe 3: 5 have carried into your t' my goodly "
Ac 7: 48 dwelleth not in t' made with *3485
17: 24 dwelleth not in t' made with hands; "

temporal
2Co 4: 18 the things which are seen are t'; 4340

tempt See also TEMPTED; TEMPTETH; TEMPTING.
Ge 22: 1 things, that God did t' Abraham, *5254
Ex 17: 2 me? wherefore do ye t' the Lord? "
De 6: 16 Ye shall not t' the Lord your God, 5254
Isa 7: 12 not ask, neither will I t' the Lord. "
Mal 3: 15 that t' God are even delivered. 974
M't 4: 7 shalt not t' the Lord thy God. ‡1598
22: 18 said, Why t' ye me, ye hypocrites? ‡3985
M'r 12: 15 said unto them, Why t' ye me? ‡ "
Lu 4: 12 shalt not t' the Lord thy God. ‡1598
20: 23 and said unto them, Why t' ye me? ‡3985
Ac 5: 9 to t' the Spirit of the Lord? ‡ "
15: 10 Now therefore why t' ye God, to ‡ "
1Co 7: 5 t' you not for your incontinency. "
10: 9 Neither let us t' Christ, as some of ‡1598

temptation See also TEMPTATIONS.
Ps 95: 8 in the day of t' in the wilderness: *4531
M't 6: 13 lead us not into t', but deliver 3986
26: 41 and pray, that ye enter not into t': "
M'r 14: 38 ye and pray, lest ye enter into t'. "
Lu 4: 13 when the devil had ended all the t'. "
8: 13 believe, and in time of t' fall away. "
11: 4 lead us not into t'; but deliver "
22: 40 Pray that ye enter not into t'. "
46 rise and pray, lest ye enter into t'. "
1Co 10: 13 There hath no t' taken you but such "
13 with the t'...make a way to escape, "
Ga 4: 14 And my t' which was in my flesh ye "
1Ti 6: 9 will be rich fall into t' and a snare, "
Heb 3: 8 in the day of t' in the wilderness: ‡ "
Jas 1: 12 is the man that endureth t': "
Re 3: 10 will keep thee from the hour of t',* "

temptations
De 4: 34 by t', by signs, and by wonders, ‡4531
7: 19 The great t' which thine eyes saw, ‡ "
29: 3 The great t' which thine eyes have ‡ "
Lu 22: 28 have continued with me in my t'. ‡3986
Ac 20: 19 and t', which befell me by the lying* "
Jas 1: 2 all joy when ye fall into divers t'; "
1Pe 1: 6 in heaviness through manifold t': ‡ "
2Pe 2: 9 how to deliver the godly out of t',* "

tempted
Ex 17: 7 because they t' the Lord, saying, 5254
Nu 14: 22 and have t' me now these ten times, "
De 6: 16 your God, as ye t' him in Massah. "
Ps 78: 18 they t' God in their heart by asking "
41 they turned back and t' God, and "
56 they t' and provoked the most high "
95: 9 When your fathers t' me, proved me, "
106: 14 wilderness, and t' God in the desert. "
M't 4: 1 wilderness to be t' of the devil. 3985
M'r 1: 13 wilderness forty days, t' of Satan; "
Lu 4: 2 Being forty days t' of the devil. "
10: 25 lawyer stood up, and t' him, ‡1598
1Co 10: 9 as some of them also t', and were ‡3985
13 not suffer you to be t' above that ye "
Ga 6: 1 thyself, lest thou also be t'. "
1Th 3: 5 means the tempter have t' you, "
Heb 2: 18 he himself hath suffered being t', "
18 is able to succour them that are t'. "
3: 9 When your fathers t' me, proved ‡ "
4: 15 was in all points t' like as we are, "
11: 37 they were sawn asunder, were t', "
Jas 1: 13 say when he is t', I am t' of God: "
13 for God cannot be t' with evil, 551
14 every man is t', when he is drawn 3985

tempter
M't 4: 3 And when the t' came to him, he 3985
1Th 3: 5 means the t' have tempted you, "

tempteth
Jas 1: 13 with evil, neither t' he any man: 3985

tempting
M't 16: 1 and t' desired him that he would ‡3985
19: 3 came unto him, t' him, and saying ‡ "
22: 35 asked him a question, t' him, ‡ "
M'r 8: 11 of him a sign from heaven, t' him. ‡ "
10: 2 a man to put away his wife? t' him. ‡ "
Lu 11: 16 others, t' him, sought of him a sign ‡ "
Joh 8: 6 This they said, t' him, that they ‡ "

ten See also EIGHTEEN; FOURTEEN; NINETEEN; SEVENTEEN; SIXTEEN; TEN'S; TENS.
Ge 5: 14 were nine hundred and t' years: 6235
16: 3 after Abram had dwelt t' years in "
18: 32 Peradventure t' shall be found "
24: 10 the servant took t' camels of the "
22 hands of t' shekels weight of gold; "
55 with us a few days, at the least t'; 6218
31: 7 and changed my wages t' times; 6235
41 hast changed my wages t' times. "
32: 15 their colts, forty kine, and t' bulls, "
15 twenty she asses, and t' foals. "
42: 3 Joseph's t' brethren went down to "
45: 23 t' asses laden with the good things "
23 t' she asses laden with corn and "
46: 27 into Egypt, were threescore and t'. "
50: 3 mourned for him threescore and t' days. "
22 Joseph lived an hundred and t' 6235
26 being an hundred and t' years old: "
Ex 15: 27 and threescore and t' palm trees: "
26: 1 with t' curtains of fine twined linen, 6235
16 T' cubits shall be the length of a "
27: 12 their pillars t', and their sockets t'. "
34: 28 the covenant, the t' commandments. "
36: 8 t' curtains of fine twined linen, "
21 The length of a board was t' cubits, "
38: 12 their pillars t', and their sockets t': "
Le 26: 8 you shall put t' thousand to flight: 7233
26 t' women shall bake your bread 6235
27: 5, 7 and for the female t' shekels. "
Nu 7: 14 One spoon of t' shekels of gold, "
20 One spoon of gold of t' shekels, "
26, 32, 38, 44, 50, 56, 62, 68, 74, 80 One
golden spoon of t' shekels, full of 6235
86 weighing t' shekels apiece, after the "
11: 19 neither t' days, nor twenty days; "
32 gathered least gathered t' homers: "
Nu 14: 22 have tempted me now these t' times 6235
29: 23 And on the fourth day t' bullocks, "
33: 9 and threescore and t' palm trees; "
De 4: 13 perform, even t' commandments; 6235
10: 4 the t' commandments, which the "
22 Egypt with threescore and t' persons; "
32: 30 and two put t' thousand to flight, 7233
33: 2 he came with t' thousands of saints: "
17 are the t' thousands of Ephraim, "
Jos 15: 57 t' cities with their villages. 6235
17: 5 there fell t' portions to Manasseh, "
21: 5 the half tribe of Manasseh, t' cities. "
26 the cities were t' with their suburbs "
22: 14 with him t' princes, of each chief "
24: 29 being an hundred and t' years old. "
J'g 1: 4 of them in Bezek t' thousand men. "
7 Threescore and t' kings, having their
2: 8 being an hundred and t' years old. 6235
3: 29 that time about t' thousand men, "
4: 6 and take with thee t' thousand men "
10 he went up with t' thousand men "
14 and t' thousand men after him. "
6: 27 Gideon took t' men of his servants, "
7: 3 and there remained t' thousand. "
8: 30 Gideon had threescore and t' sons "
9: 2 which are threescore and t' persons, "
4 him threescore and t' pieces of silver
5 being threescore and t' persons,
18 his sons, threescore and t' persons,
24 done to the threescore and t' sons of
12: 11 and he judged Israel t' years. 6235
14 rode on threescore and t' ass colts: "
17: 10 I will give thee t' shekels of silver 6235
20: 10 we will take t' men of an hundred "
10 and a thousand out of t' thousand, 7233
34 came against Gibeah t' thousand 6235
Ru 1: 4 they dwelled there about t' years. "
4: 2 he took t' men of the elders of the "
1Sa 1: 8 am not I better to thee than t' sons? "
6: 19 thousand and threescore and t' men: *
15: 4 and t' thousand men of Judah. 6235
17: 17 these t' loaves, and run to the camp "
18 these t' cheeses unto the captain of "
18: 7 and David his t' thousands. 7233
8 ascribed unto David t' thousands, "
21: 11 and David his t' thousands? "
25: 5 And David sent out t' young men, 6235
38 it came to pass about t' days after, "
29: 5 and David his t' thousands? 7233
2Sa 15: 16 And the king left t' women, which 6235
18: 3 thou art worth t' thousand of us: "
11 have given thee t' shekels of silver, "
15 And t' young men that bare Joab's "
19: 43 We have t' parts in the king, and "
20: 3 and the king took the t' women his "
1Ki 4: 23 T' fat oxen, and twenty oxen out of "
5: 14 t' thousand a month by courses: "
15 and t' thousand that bare burdens, "
6: 3 t' cubits was the breadth thereof 6235
23 cherubims...each t' cubits high. "
24 part of the other were t' cubits. "
25 And the other cherub was t' cubits: "
26 of the one cherub was t' cubits, "
7: 10 great stones, stones of t' cubits, "
23 t' cubits from the one brim to the "
24 t' in a cubit, compassing the sea "
27 And he made t' bases of brass; four "
37 this manner he made the t' bases: "
38 Then made he t' lavers of brass: "
38 upon every one of the t' bases one "
43 t' bases, and t' lavers on the bases; "
11: 31 to Jeroboam, Take thee t' pieces: "
31 and will give t' tribes to thee: "
35 will give it unto thee, even t' tribes. "
14: 3 And take with thee t' loaves and "
2Ki 5: 5 took with him t' talents of silver, "
5 of gold, and t' changes of raiment. "
13: 7 but fifty horsemen, and t' chariots, "
7 and t' thousand footmen; "
14: 7 in the valley of salt t' thousand, "
15: 17 and reigned t' years in Samaria. "
20: 9 the shadow go forward t' degrees, "
9 degrees, or go back t' degrees? "
10 the shadow to go down t' degrees: "
10 shadow return backward t' degrees. "
11 the shadow t' degrees backward, "
24: 14 valour, even t' thousand captives, "
25: 25 and t' men with him, and smote "
1Ch 6: 61 tribe of Manasseh, by lot, t' cities. "
21: 5 t' thousand men that drew sword: "
29: 7 talents and t' thousand drams, 7239
7 and of silver t' thousand talents, 6235
2Ch 2: 2 t' thousand men to bear burdens,
18 t' thousand of them to be bearers of
4: 1 and t' cubits the height thereof. 6235
2 a molten sea of t' cubits from brim "
3 t' in a cubit, compassing the sea "
6 He made also t' lavers, and put five "
7 And he made t' candlesticks of gold "
8 He made also t' tables, and placed "
14: 1 his days the land was quiet t' years. "
25: 11 of the children of Seir t' thousand. "
12 And other t' thousand left alive did "
27: 5 and t' thousand measures of wheat, "
5 of wheat, and t' thousand of barley. "
29: 32 was threescore and t' bullocks, an "
30: 24 bullocks and t' thousand sheep: 6235
36: 9 reigned three months and t' days in "
21 to fulfil threescore and t' years. "
Ezr 1: 10 a second sort four hundred and t', 6235
8: 12 with him an hundred and t' males. "
24 and t' of their brethren with them, "
Ne 4: 12 they said unto us t' times, From all "
5: 18 once in t' days store of all sorts of "
11: 1 bring one of t' to dwell in Jerusalem "
Es 3: 9 will pay t' thousand talents of silver "

Es 9:10 The t' sons of Haman the son of 6235
12 palace, and the t' sons of Haman; "
13 let Haman's t' sons be hanged upon"
14 and they hanged Haman's t' sons. "
Job 19: 3 t' times have ye reproached me: ye "
Ps 3: 6 be afraid of t' thousands of people,7233
33: 2 and an instrument of t' strings. 6218
90:10 our years are threescore years and t'; "
91: 7 and t' thousand at thy right hand;7233
92: 3 Upon an instrument of t' strings, 6218
144: 9 instrument of t' strings will I sing "
13 and t' thousands in our streets: 7231
Ec 7:19 the wise more than t' mighty men 6235
Ca 5:10 the chiefest among t' thousand. 7233
Isa 5:10 t' acres of vineyard shall yield one6235
38: 8 dial of Ahaz, t' degrees backward. "
8 So the sun returned t' degrees, by "
Jer 41: 1 even t' men with him, came unto "
2 and the t' men that were with him, "
8 But t' men were found among them"
42: 7 And it came to pass after t' days, "
Eze 40:11 of the entry of the gate, t' cubits; "
41: 2 breadth of the door was t' cubits; "
42: 4 chambers was a walk of t' cubits "
45: 1 the breadth shall be t' thousand. "
3 and the breadth of t' thousand: "
5 and the t' thousand of breadth, "
14 cor, which is an homer of t' baths; "
14 for t' baths are an homer: "
48: 9 and of t' thousand in breadth. "
10 the west t' thousand in breadth, "
10 the east t' thousand in breadth, "
13 length, and t' thousand in breadth: "
13 and the breadth t' thousand. "
18 shall be t' thousand eastward, "
18 and t' thousand westward: "
Da 1:12 Prove thy servants,...t' days; "
14 matter, and proved them t' days. "
15 end of t' days their countenances "
20 he found them t' times better than "
7: 7 before it; and it had t' horns. 6236
10 t' thousand times t' thousand 7240
20 the t' horns that were in his head, 6236
24 And the t' horns out of this kingdom"
24 are t' kings that shall arise: "
11:12 cast down many t' thousands: 7239
Am 5: 3 forth by an hundred shall leave t', 6235
6: 9 there remain t' men in one house, "
Mic 6: 7 with t' thousands of rivers of oil? 7233
Hag 2:16 twenty measures, there were...t': 6235
Zec 1:12 these threescore and t' years? "
5: 2 and the breadth thereof t' cubits. 6235
8:23 t' men shall take hold out of all "
M't 18:24 owed him t' thousand talents. 3463
20:24 the t' heard it, they were moved 1176
25: 1 of heaven be likened unto t' virgins,"
28 it unto him which hath t' talents. "
M'r 10:41 when the t' heard it, they began to "
Lu 14:31 able with t' thousand to meet him "
15: 8 woman having t' pieces of silver, "
17:12 met him t' men that were lepers, "
17 said, Were there not t' cleansed? "
19:13 And he called his t' servants, and "
13 and delivered them t' pounds, and "
16 thy pound hath gained t' pounds. "
17 have thou authority over t' cities. "
24 give it to him that hath t' pounds. "
25 unto him, Lord, he hath t' pounds.) "
Ac 23:23 and horsemen threescore and t', "
25: 6 among them more than t' days, 1176
1Co 4:15 ye have t' thousand instructers in 3463
14:19 t' thousand words in an unknown "
Jude 14 with t' thousands of his saints, 3461
Re 2:10 ye shall have tribulation t' days: 1176
5:11 was t' thousand times t' thousand, 3461
12: 3 having seven heads and t' horns, 1176
13: 1 having seven heads and t' horns, "
1 and upon his horns t' crowns, and "
17: 3 having seven heads and t' horns. "
7 hath the seven heads and t' horns. "
12 t' horns...thou sawest are t' kings, "
16 the t' horns which thou sawest "

tend See also ATTEND; CONTEND; EXTEND; INTEND; TENDETH.
Pr 21: 5 the diligent t' only to plenteousness;

tender See also TENDERHEARTED.
Ge 18: 7 and fetcht a calf t' and good, and 7390
29:17 Leah was t' eyed; but Rachel was "
33:13 knoweth that the children are t', "
De 28:54 that the man that is t' among you, "
56 The t' and delicate woman among "
32: 2 as the small rain upon the t' herb, and
2Sa 23: 4 t' grass springing out of the earth
2Ki 22:19 Because thine heart was t', and 7401
1Ch 22: 5 Solomon my son is young and t', 7390
29: 1 Solomon...is yet young and t', "
2Ch 34:27 Because thine heart was t', and 7401
Job 14: 7 t' branch thereof will not cease. 3127
38:27 the bud of the t' herb to spring forth?
Ps 25: 6 Remember, O Lord, thy t' mercies
40:11 Withhold not thou thy t' mercies from
51: 1 unto the multitude of thy t' mercies
69:16 to the multitude of thy t' mercies.
77: 9 he in anger shut up his t' mercies?
79: 8 let thy t' mercies speedily prevent us:
103: 4 with lovingkindness and t' mercies;
119:77 Let thy t' mercies come unto me, that
156 Great are thy t' mercies, O Lord:
145: 9 his t' mercies are over all his works.
Pr 4: 3 t' and only beloved in the sight of 7390
12:10 the t' mercies of the wicked are cruel.
27:25 and the t' grass sheweth itself, and
Ca 2:13 with the t' grape give a good smell.*
15 vines: for our vines have t' grapes.*
7:12 whether the t' grape appear. *
Isa 47: 1 thou shalt no more be called t' and7390
53: 2 grow up before him as a t' plant, 3126
Eze 17:22 the top of his young twigs a t' one,7390
Da 1: 9 Daniel into favour and t' love *
4:15, 23 brass, in the t' grass of the field;
M't 24:32 When his branch is yet t', and 527
M'r 13:28 When her branch is yet t', and "
Lu 1:78 Through the t' mercy of our God; 4698
Jas 5:11 is very pitiful, and of t' mercy. *3629

tender-eyed See TENDER and EYED.

tenderhearted
2Ch 13: 7 Rehoboam was young and t', 7390,3824
Eph 4:32 t', forgiving one another, even as 2155

tenderness
De 28:56 ground for delicateness and t', 7391

tendeth
Pr 10:16 The labour of the righteous t' to life:
11:19 As righteousness t' to life: so he that*
24 more than is meet, but it t' to poverty.
14:23 the talk of the lips t' only to penury.
19:23 The fear of the Lord t' to life: and he

tenons
Ex 26:17 Two t' shall there be in one board,3027
19 under one board for his two t', "
19 under another board for his two t'. "
36:22 One board had two t', equally "
24 under one board for his two t', "
24 under another board for his two t'. "

tenor
Ge 43: 7 according to the t' of these words:6310
Ex 34:27 for after the t' of these words I have"

ten's
Ge 18:32 I will not destroy it for t' sake. 6235

tens
Ex 18:21 rulers of fifties, and rulers of t': 6235
25 rulers of fifties, and rulers of t'. "
De 1:15 over fifties, and captains over t', "

tent See also TENTMAKERS; TENTS.
Ge 9:21 and he was uncovered within his t'.168
12: 8 pitched his t', having Beth-el on the "
13: 3 place where his t' had been at the "
12 and pitched his t' toward Sodom. 167
18 Then Abram removed his t', and
18: 1 he sat in the t' door in the heat of 168
2 he ran to meet them from the t' door,"
6 Abraham hastened into the t' unto "
9 wife? And he said, Behold, in the t'."
10 And Sarah heard it in the t' door, "
24:67 her into his mother Sarah's t', "
26:17 pitched his t' in the valley of Gerar,*
25 the Lord, and pitched his t' there: 168
31:25 Now Jacob had pitched his t' in the "
33 into Jacob's t', and into Leah's t', "
33 Then went he out of Leah's t', "
33 and entered into Rachel's t'. "
34 And Laban searched all the t', but "
33:18 and pitched his t' before the city.*
19 a field, where he had spread his t', 168
35:21 and spread his t' beyond the tower of"
Ex 18: 7 welfare; and they came into the t'. "
26:11 couple the t' together, that it may be"
12 remaineth of the curtains of the t', "
13 in the length of the curtains of the t',"
14 a covering for the t' of rams' skins "
36 an hanging for the door of the t', "
33: 8 and stood every man at his t' door, "
10 worshipped, every man in his t' door."
35:11 The tabernacle, his t', and his "
36:14 made curtains of goats' hair for the t'"
18 of brass to couple the t' together, "
19 a covering for the t' of rams' skins "
39:32 the t' of the congregation finished: "
33 the tabernacle unto Moses, the t', and"
40 for the t' of the congregation, "
40: 2, 6 of the t' of the congregation. "
7 between the t' of the congregation "
19 abroad the t' over the tabernacle, "
19 and put the covering of the t' above "
22 table in the t' of the congregation, "
24 candlestick in...t' of...congregation, "
26 altar in the t' of the congregation "
29 of the t' of the congregation, "
30 between the t' of the congregation "
32 went into the t' of the congregation, "
34 covered the t' of the congregation, "
35 enter into the t' of the congregation,"
Le 14: 8 tarry abroad out of his t' seven days."
Nu 3:25 shall be the tabernacle, and the t', "
9:15 namely, the t' of the testimony: "
11:10 every man in the door of his t': "
19:14 is the law, when a man dieth in a t': "
14 into the t', and all that is in the t', "
18 the water, and sprinkle it upon the t',"
25: 8 after the man of Israel into the t',*6898
Jos 7:21 in the earth in the midst of my t', 168
22 they ran unto the t'; and, behold, "
22 it was hid in his t', and the silver "
23 took them out of the midst of the t', "
24 and his t', and all that he had: "
J'g 4:11 his t' unto the plain of Zaanaim, "
17 Sisera fled away on his feet to the t' "
18 he had turned in unto her into the t',"
20 Stand in the door of the t', and it "
21 Heber's wife took a nail of the t', * "
22 And when he came into her t', behold,"
5:24 shall she be above women in the t'.168
7: 8 rest of Israel every man unto his t', "
13 host of Midian, and came unto a t', "
13 overturned it, that the t' lay along. "
20: 8 We will not any of us go to his t', "
1Sa 4:10 and they fled every man into his t': "
13: 2 people he sent every man to his t'. "
1Sa 17:54 but he put his armour in his t'. 168
2Sa 7: 6 walked in a t' and in a tabernacle. "
16:22 So they spread Absalom a t' upon "
18:17 all Israel fled every one to his t'. "
19: 8 Israel had fled every man to his t'. "
20:22 from the city, every man to his t'. "
2Ki 7: 8 they went into one t', and did eat "
8 again, and entered into another t', "
1Ch 15: 1 ark of God, and pitched for it a t'. "
16: 1 and set it in the midst of the t' that "
17: 5 but have gone from t' to t', and "
2Ch 1: 4 had pitched a t' for it at Jerusalem. "
25:22 and they fled every man to his t'. "
Ps 78:60 the t' which he placed among men; "
Isa 13:20 shall the Arabian pitch t' there; 167
38:12 from me as a shepherd's t': 168
40:22 them out as a t' to dwell in: "
54: 2 Enlarge the place of thy t', and let "
Jer 10:20 none to stretch forth my t' any more,"
37:10 they rise up every man in his t', "

tent-door See TENT and DOOR.

tenth
Ge 8: 5 continually until the t' month: 6224
5 in the t' month, on the first day of "
28:22 I will surely give the t' unto thee. 6237
Ex 12: 3 In the t' day of this month they 6218
16:36 an omer is the t' part of an ephah. 6224
29:40 with the one lamb a t' deal of flour6241
Le 5:11 t' part of an ephah of fine flour 6224
6:20 the t' part of an ephah of fine flour "
14:10 three t' deals of fine flour for a 6241
21 one t' deal of fine flour mingled "
16:29 month, on the t' day of the month, 6218
23:13 two t' deals of fine flour mingled 6241
17 two wave loaves of two t' deals: "
27 Also on the t' day of this seventh 6218
24: 5 two t' deals shall be in one cake. 6241
25: 9 the t' day of the seventh month, 6218
27:32 the t' shall be holy unto the Lord. 6224
Nu 5:15 the t' part of an ephah of barley "
7:66 On the t' day Ahiezer the son of "
15: 4 meat offering of a t' deal of flour 6241
6 meat offering two t' deals of flour "
9 offering of three t' deals of flour "
18:21 children of Levi...the t' in Israel *4643
26 Lord, even a t' part of the tithe. * "
28: 5 a t' part of an ephah of flour for a 6224
9 two t' deals of flour for a meat 6241
12 three t' deals of flour for a meat "
12 and two t' deals of flour for a meat "
13 a several t' deal of flour mingled "
20 three t' deals shall ye offer for a "
20 and two t' deals for a ram; "
21 A several t' deal shalt thou offer "
28 oil, three t' deals unto one bullock, "
28 bullock, two t' deals unto one ram, "
29 A several t' deal unto one lamb, "
29: 3 oil, three t' deals for a bullock, "
3 bullock, and two t' deals for a ram, "
4 And one t' deal for one lamb, "
7 on the t' day of this seventh month6218
9 oil, three t' deals to a bullock, 6241
9 and two t' deals to one ram, "
10 A several t' deal for one lamb, "
14 three t' deals unto every bullock of "
14 two t' deals to each ram of the two "
15 a several t' deal to each lamb of "
De 23: 2 even to his t' generation shall he 6224
3 even to their t' generation shall "
Jos 4:19 on the t' day of the first month, 6218
1Sa 8:15 he will take the t' of your seed, 6237
17 He will take the t' of your sheep: "
2Ki 25: 1 year of his reign, in the t' month, 6218
1 in the t' day of the month, that "
1Ch 12:13 Jeremiah the t', Machbanai the 6224
24:11 to Jeshuah, the t' to Shecaniah, "
25:17 t' to Shimei, he, his sons, and his "
27:13 The t' captain for the t' month was "
Ezr 10:16 down in the first day of the t' month"
Es 2:16 into his house royal in the t' month,"
Isa 6:13 But yet in it shall be a t', and it "
Jer 32: 1 t' year of Zedekiah king of Judah, "
39: 1 t' month, came Nebuchadrezzar "
52: 4 year of his reign, in the t' month, "
4 in the t' day of the month, that 6218
12 month, in the t' day of the month, "
Eze 20: 1 month, the t' day of the month, that"
24: 1 in the ninth year, in the t' month, 6224
1 in the t' day of the month, the 6218
29: 1 In the t' year, in the t' month, 6224
33:21 in the t' month, in the fifth day of "
40: 1 year, in the t' day of the month, 6218
45:11 contain the t' part of an homer, 4643
11 the ephah the t' part of an homer: 6224
14 the t' part of a bath out of the cor. 4643
Zec 8:19 and the fast of the t', shall be to 6224
Joh 1:39 day: for it was about the t' hour. 1182
Heb 7: 2 also Abraham gave a t' part of all; 1181
4 Abraham gave the t' of the spoils. "
Re 11:13 and the t' part of the city fell, and 1182
21:20 a topaz; the t', a chrysoprasus; "

tenth-deal See TENTH and DEAL.

ten-thousand See TEN and THOUSAND.

tentmakers
Ac 18: 3 by their occupation they were t'. 4635

tents
Ge 4:20 the father of such as dwell in t', 168
9:27 and he shall dwell in the t' of Shem; "
13: 5 Abram, had flocks, and herds, and t'. "
25:27 was a plain man, dwelling in t', "
31:33 and into the two maidservants' t'; * "
Ex 16:16 man for them which are in his t'. * "
Nu 1:52 children of Israel shall pitch their t',
9:17 the children of Israel pitched their t'.*

Nu 9:18 tabernacle they rested in their t'.*
20 of the Lord they abode in their t',*
22 children of Israel abode in their t',*
23 of the Lord they rested in the t', *
13:19 whether in t', or in strong holds; *4264
16:26 from the t' of these wicked men, 168
27 out, and stood in the door of their t', "
24: 2 saw Israel abiding in his t' according* "
5 How goodly are thy t', O Jacob, 168
De 1:27 And ye murmured in your t', and "
33 you out a place to pitch your t' in, "
5:30 to them, Get you into your t' again. 168
11: 6 their households, and their t', and "
16: 7 in the morning, and go unto thy t'. "
33:18 going out; and, Issachar, in thy t'. "
Jos 3:14 the people removed from their t', "
22: 4 return ye, and get you unto your t', "
6 away: and they went unto their t'. "
7 sent them away also unto their t', "
8 with much riches unto your t', and "
J'g 6: 5 came up with their cattle and their t', "
8:11 by the way of them that dwelt in t' "
1Sa 17:53 Philistines, and...spoiled their t'. *4264
2Sa 11:11 Israel, and Judah, abide in t'; *5521
20: 1 every man to his t', O Israel. 168
1Ki 8:66 went unto their t' joyful and glad "
12:16 to your t', O Israel: now see to thine "
16 So Israel departed unto their t'. "
2Ki 7: 7 left their t', and their horses, and "
10 asses tied, and the t' as they were. "
16 and spoiled the t' of the Syrians. *4264
8:21 and the people fled into their t'. 168
13: 5 children of Israel dwelt in their t', "
14:12 and they fled every man to their t'.* "
1Ch 4:41 smote their t', and the habitations "
5:10 they dwelt in their t' throughout all "
2Ch 7:10 he sent the people away into their t'. "
10:16 every man to your t', O Israel: "
16 So all Israel went to their t'. "
14:15 They smote also the t' of cattle, and "
31: 2 in the gates of the t' of the Lord. *4264
Ezr 8:15 there abode we in t' three days: *2583
Ps 69:25 and let none dwell in their t'. 168
78:55 tribes of Israel to dwell in their t'. "
84:10 than to dwell in the t' of wickedness. "
106:25 But murmured in their t', and "
120: 5 that I dwell in the t' of Kedar! "
Ca 1: 5 as the t' of Kedar, as the curtains of "
8 thy kids beside the shepherds' t'. 4908
Jer 4:20 suddenly are my t' spoiled, and my 168
6: 3 they shall pitch their t' against her "
30:18 again the captivity of Jacob's t', "
35: 7 but all your days ye shall dwell in t'; "
10 But we have dwelt in t', and have "
49:29 Their t' and their flocks shall they "
Hab 3: 7 I saw the t' of Cushan in affliction: "
Zec 12: 7 also shall save the t' of Judah first, "
14:15 the beasts that shall be in these t',*4264

Terah (*te'-rah*) See also THARA.
Ge 11:24 and twenty years, and begat T': 8646
25 And Nahor lived after he begat T' "
26 T' lived seventy years, and begat "
27 these are the generations of T': "
27 T' begat Abram, Nahor, and Haran; "
28 Haran died before his father T' in "
31 T' took Abram his son, and Lot "
32 days of T' were two hundred and "
32 five years: and T' died in Haran. "
Jos 24: 2 even T', the father of Abraham, "
1Ch 1:26 Serug, Nahor, T', "

teraphim (*ter'-af-im*)
J'g 17: 5 and made an ephod, and t', and 8655
18:14 is in these houses an ephod, and t', "
17 image, and the ephod, and the t', "
18 carved image, the ephod, and the t', "
20 and he took the ephod, and the t', "
Hos 3: 4 without an ephod, and without t': "

Teresh (*te'-resh*)
Es 2:21 chamberlains, Bigthan and T', 8657
6: 2 had told of Bigthana and T', "

termed
Isa 62: 4 Thou shalt no more be t' Forsaken :559
4 thy land any more be t' Desolate: "

terraces
2Ch 9:11 king made of the algum trees t' 4546

terrestrial
1Co 15:40 also celestial bodies, and bodies t':1919
40 and the glory of the t' is another. "

terrible
Ex 34:10 for it is a t' thing that I will do 3372
De 1:19 all that great and t' wilderness, "
7:21 is among you, a mighty God and t'. "
8:15 through...great and t' wilderness, "
10:17 a great God, a mighty, and a t', "
21 for thee these great and t' things, "
J'g 13: 6 of an angel of God, very t': "
2Sa 7:23 to do for you great things and t', "
Ne 1: 5 of heaven, the great and t' God, "
4:14 the Lord, which is great and t', "
9:32 great, the mighty, and the t' God, "
Job 37:22 the north: with God is t' majesty. "
39:20 the glory of his nostrils is t'. 367
41:14 face? his teeth are t' round about.* "
Ps 45: 4 hand shall teach thee t' things. 3372
47: 2 For the Lord most high is t'; he is "
65: 5 By t' things in righteousness wilt "
66: 3 God, How t' art thou in thy works! "
5 he is t' in his doing toward the "
68:35 O God, thou art t' out of thy holy "
76:12 he is t' to the kings of the earth. "
99: 3 them praise thy great and t' name; "
106:22 Ham, and t' things by the Red sea. "
145: 6 speak of the might of thy t' acts: "
Ca 6: 4 t' as an army with banners. ‡ 366
Ca 6:10 and t' as an army with banners? ‡ 366
Isa 13:11 lay low the haughtiness of the t'. 6184
18: 2 to a people t' from their beginning3372
7 to a people t' from their beginning "
21: 1 from the desert, from a t' land. "
25: 3 the city of the t' nations shall fear 6184
4 the blast of the t' ones is as a storm "
5 the branch of the t' ones shall be "
29: 5 multitude of the t' ones shall be as "
20 For the t' one is brought to nought, "
49:25 the prey of the t' shall be delivered: "
64: 3 When thou didst t' things which we3372
Jer 15:21 thee out of the hand of the t'. 6184
20:11 Lord is with me as a mighty t' one: "
La 5:10 an oven because of the t' famine. *2152
Eze 1:22 was as the colour of the t' crystal, 3372
28: 7 upon thee, the t' of the nations: 6184
30:11 with him, the t' of the nations, "
31:12 the t' of the nations, have cut him "
32:12 the t' of the nations, all of them: "
Da 2:31 thee; and the form thereof was t'.1763
7: 7 a fourth beast, dreadful and t', * 574
Joe 2:11 day of the Lord is great and very t';3372
31 the great and the t' day of the Lord "
Hab 1: 7 They are t' and dreadful: their 366
Zep 2:11 The Lord will be t' unto them: 3372
Heb 12:21 so t' was the sight, that Moses *5398

terribleness
De 26: 8 and with great t', and with signs, 4172
1Ch 17:21 thee a name of greatness and t', *3372
Jer 49:16 Thy t' hath deceived thee, and the 8606

terribly
Isa 2:19, 21 he ariseth to shake t' the earth.*6206
Na 2: 3 and the fir trees shall be t' shaken.

terrified
De 20: 3 neither be ye t' because of them; *6206
Lu 21: 9 of wars and commotions, be not t':4422
24:37 But they were t' and affrighted, "
Ph'p 1:28 in nothing t' by your adversaries:*4426

terrifiest
Job 7:14 dreams, and t' me through visions:1204

terrify See also TERRIFIED; TERRIFIEST.
Job 3: 5 let the blackness of the day t' it. 1204
9:34 from me, and let not his fear t' me:* "
31:34 the contempt of families t' me, *2865
2Co 10: 9 seem as if I would t' you by letters.1629

terror See also TERRORS.
Ge 35: 5 the t' of God was upon the cities 2847
Le 26:16 I will even appoint over you t', 928
De 32:25 The sword without, and t' within, 367
34:12 the great t' which Moses shewed 4172
Jos 2: 9 and that your t' is fallen upon us,‡ 367
Job 31:23 destruction from God was a t' to 6343
33: 7 my t' shall not make thee afraid, 367
Ps 91: 5 not be afraid for the t' by night; 6343
Isa 10:33 hosts, shall lop the bough with t': 4637
19:17 of Judah shall be a t' unto Egypt, 2283
33:18 Thine heart shall meditate t'. 367
54:14 and from t'; for it shall not come 4288
Jer 17:17 Be not a t' unto me: thou art my "
20: 4 I will make thee a t' to thyself, 4032
32:21 strong hand,...and with great t'; 4172
Eze 26:17 which cause their t' to be on all 2851
21 I will make thee a t', and thou 1091
27:36 thou shalt be a t', and never shalt "
28:19 thou shalt be a t', and never shalt "
32:23 which caused t' in the land of the 2851
24 which caused their t' in the land of "
25 their t' was caused in the land of "
26 they caused their t' in the land of "
27 the t' of the mighty in the land of "
30 with their t' they are ashamed of "
32 I have caused my t' in the land of "
Ro 13: 3 rulers are not a t' to good works, 5401
2Co 5:11 Knowing...the t' of the Lord, we * "
1Pe 3:14 be not afraid of their t', neither be* "

terrors
De 4:34 stretched out arm, and by great t',4172
Job 6: 4 t' of God do set themselves in 1161
18:11 T' shall make him afraid on every1091
14 shall bring him to the king of t'. "
20:25 out of his gall: t' are upon him. 367
24:17 in the t' of the shadow of death. 1091
27:20 T' take hold on him as waters, a "
30:15 T' are turned upon me: they "
Ps 55: 4 the t' of death are fallen upon me. 367
73:19 they are utterly consumed with t'.1091
88:15 while I suffer thy t' I am distracted.367
16 over me; thy t' have cut me off. 1161
Jer 15: 8 it suddenly, and t' upon the city. 928
La 2:22 a solemn day my t' round about, 4032
Eze 21:12 t' by reason of the sword shall be *4048

Tertius (*tur'-she-us*)
Ro 16:22 I T', who wrote this epistle, 5060

Tertullus (*tur-tul'-lus*)
Ac 24: 1 with a certain orator named T'. *5061
2 T' began to accuse him, saying, "

testament
M't 26:28 For this is my blood of the new t', 1242
M'r 14:24 This is my blood of the new t', * "
Lu 22:20 This cup is the new t' in my blood,* "
1Co 11:25 This cup is the new t' in my blood:* "
2Co 3: 6 us able ministers of the new t'; * "
14 away in the reading of the old t'; * "
Heb 7:22 Jesus made a surety of a better t'.* "
9:15 he is the mediator of the new t', * "
15 that were under the first t', * "
16 For where a t' is, there must also of "
17 For a t' is of force after men are "
18 Whereupon neither the first t' was* "
20 This is the blood of the t' which *1242
Re 11:19 seen in his temple the ark of his t':* "

testator
Heb 9:16 necessity be the death of the t'. *1303
17 strength at all while the t' liveth.* "

testified See also TESTIFIEDST.
Ex 21:29 and it hath been t' to his owner, 5749
De 19:18 hath t' falsely against his brother;6030
Ru 1:21 seeing the Lord hath t' against me, "
2Sa 1:16 for thy mouth hath t' against thee, "
2Ki 17:13 Yet the Lord t' against Israel, and 5749
15 his testimonies which he t' against "
2Ch 24:19 Lord; and they t' against them: "
Ne 9:26 slew thy prophets which t' against "
13:15 and I t' against them in the day "
21 Then I t' against them, and said "
Joh 4:39 the saying of the woman, which t', 3140
44 For Jesus himself t', that a prophet "
13:21 he was troubled in spirit, and t', "
Ac 8:25 they had t' and preached the word 1263
18: 5 t' to the Jews that Jesus was * "
23:11 as thou hast t' of me in Jerusalem, "
28:23 and t' the kingdom of God, * "
1Co 15:15 we have t' of God that he raised *3140
1Th 4: 6 also have forewarned you and t'. 1263
1Ti 2: 6 ransom for all, to be t' in due time.*3142
Heb 2: 6 But one in a certain place t', 1263
1Pe 1:11 it t' beforehand the sufferings of 4303
1Jo 5: 9 God which he hath t' of his Son. *3140
3Jo 3 and t' of the truth that is in thee,* "

testifiedst
Ne 9:29 And t' against them, that thou 5749
30 t' against them by thy spirit in thy "

testifieth
Ho 7:10 the pride of Israel t' to his face: *6030
Joh 3:32 hath seen and heard, that he t'; *3140
21:24 disciple which t' of these things, * "
Heb 7:17 For he t', Thou art a priest for ever* "
Re 22:20 He which t' these things saith, "

testify See also TESTIFIED; TESTIFIETH; TESTIFYING.
Nu 35:30 one witness shall not t' against *6030
De 8:19 I t' against you this day that ye *5749
19:16 to t' against him that which is *6030
31:21 this song shall t' against them as a* "
32:46 words which I t' among you this 5749
Ne 9:34 thou didst t' against them. "
Job 15: 6 yea, thine own lips t' against thee.6030
Ps 50: 7 Israel, and I will t' against thee: 5749
81: 8 my people, and I will t' unto thee: "
Isa 59:12 thee, and our sins t' against us: 6030
Jer 14: 7 though our iniquities t' against us, "
Ho 5: 5 pride of Israel doth t' to his face: "
Am 3:13 and t' in the house of Jacob, saith 5749
Mic 6: 3 I wearied thee? t' against me. 6030
Lu 16:28 that he may t' unto them, lest 1263
Joh 2:25 not that any should t' of man; *3140
3:11 know, and t' that we have seen; * "
5:39 and they are they which t' of me.* "
7: 7 me it hateth, because I t' of it, "
15:26 from the Father, he shall t' of me:* "
Ac 2:40 other words did he t' and exhort, *1263
10:42 to t' that it is he which was "
20:24 to t' the gospel of the grace of God. "
26: 5 if they would t', that after the 3140
Ga 5: 3 For I t' again to every man that is 3143
Eph 4:17 t' in the Lord, that ye henceforth "
1Jo 4:14 and do t' that the Father sent the *3140
Re 22:16 sent mine angel to t' unto you "
18 I t' unto every man that heareth 4828

testifying
Ac 20:21 T' both to the Jews, and also to 1263
Heb 11: 4 was righteous, God t' of his gifts:*3140
1Pe 5:12 and t' that this is the true grace 1957

testimonies
De 4:45 These are the t', and the statutes,5713
6:17 his t', and his statutes, which he "
20 What mean the t', and the statutes, "
1Ki 2: 3 his judgments, and his t', as it is 5715
2Ki 17:15 his t' which he testified against "
23: 3 keep his commandments and his t' "
1Ch 29:19 keep thy commandments, thy t', "
2Ch 34:31 keep his commandments, and his t'. "
Ne 9:34 thy commandments and thy t', "
Ps 25:10 as keep his covenant and his t'. 5713
78:56 high God, and kept not his t': "
93: 5 Thy t' are very sure: holiness "
99: 7 they kept his t', and the ordinance "
119: 2 Blessed are they that keep his t', "
14 have rejoiced in the way of thy t', 5715
22 contempt; for I have kept thy t'. 5713
24 Thy t' also are my delight and my "
31 I have stuck unto thy t': O Lord, 5715
36 Incline my heart unto thy t', and "
46 I will speak of thy t' also before 5713
59 and turned my feet unto thy t'. "
79 and those that have known thy t'. "
95 me: but I will consider thy t'. 5715
99 for thy t' are my meditation. "
111 Thy t' have I taken as an heritage "
119 dross: therefore I love thy t'. 5713
125 that I may know thy t'. "
129 Thy t' are wonderful: therefore 5715
138 Thy t' that thou hast commanded 5713
144 The righteousness of thy t' is 5715
146 save me, and I shall keep thy t'. 5713
152 Concerning thy t', I have known of "
157 yet do I not decline from thy t'. 5715
167 My soul hath kept thy t'; and I 5713
168 I have kept thy precepts and thy t': "
Jer 44:23 no in his statutes, nor in his t'; 5715

testimony See also TESTIMONIES.
Ex 16:34 so Aaron laid it up before the T'. 5715
25:16 thou shalt put into the ark the t' "
21 in the ark thou shalt put the t' "

Ex 25:22 which are upon the ark of the t'. 5715
26:33 within the vail the ark of the t': "
34 mercy seat upon the ark of the t' "
27:21 the vail, which is before the t', "
30: 6 the vail that is by the ark of the t', "
6 the mercy seat that is over the t', "
26 therewith, and the ark of the t', "
36 of it before the t' in the tabernacle "
31: 7 the ark of the t', and the mercy seat "
18 two tables of t', tables of stone, "
32:15 the two tables of the t' were in his "
34:29 the two tables of t' in Moses' hand, "
38:21 even of the tabernacle of t', as it "
39:35 The ark of the t', and the staves "
40: 3 shalt put therein the ark of the t', "
5 the incense before the ark of the t', "
20 he took and put the t' into the ark, "
21 and covered the ark of the t': "
Le 16:13 the mercy seat that is upon the t', "
24: 3 Without the vail of the t', in the "
Nu 1:50 Levites over the tabernacle of t', "
53 round about the tabernacle of t', "
53 the charge of the tabernacle of t'. "
4: 5 vail, and cover the ark of t' with it: "
7:89 seat that was upon the ark of t', "
9:15 namely, the tent of the t': "
10:11 up from off the tabernacle of the t'. "
17: 4 of the congregation before the t', "
10 Bring Aaron's rod again before...t', "
Jos 4:16 priests that bear the ark of the t', "
Ru 4: 7 and this was a t' in Israel. *8584
2Ki 11:12 upon him, and gave him the t'; 5715
2Ch 23:11 him the crown, and gave him the t', "
Ps 19: 7 the t' of the Lord is sure, making "
78: 5 he established a t' in Jacob, and "
81: 5 he ordained in Joseph for a t', "
119:88 so shall I keep the t' of thy mouth. "
122: 4 unto the t' of Israel, to give thanks "
132:12 and my t' that I shall teach them, 5713
Isa 8:16 Bind up the t', seal the law among 8584
20 To the law and to the t': if they "
M't 8: 4 commanded, for a t' unto them. 3142
10:18 a t' against them and the Gentiles. "
M'r 1:44 commanded, for a t' unto them. "
6:11 your feet for a t' against them. "
13: 9 for my sake, for a t' against them. "
Lu 5:14 commanded, for a t' unto them. "
9: 5 your feet for a t' against them. "
21:13 And it shall turn to you for a t'. "
Joh 3:32 and no man receiveth his t'. *3141
33 He that hath received his t' hath * "
5:34 But I receive not t' from man: but* "
8:17 law, that the t' of two men is true.* "
21:24 and we know that his t' is true. "
Ac 13:22 to whom also he gave t', and said,*3140
14: 3 which gave t' unto the word of his* "
22:18 not receive thy t' concerning me. 3141
1Co 1: 6 Even as the t' of Christ was 3142
2: 1 declaring unto you the t' of God. * "
2Co 1:12 is this, the t' of our conscience, "
2Th 1:10 our t' among you was believed) "
2Ti 1: 8 ashamed of the t' of our Lord, "
Heb 3: 5 a t' of those things which were to be "
11: 5 had this t', that he pleased God. *3140
Re 1: 2 God, and of the t' of Jesus Christ, 3141
9 God, and for the t' of Jesus Christ. "
6: 9 God, and for the t' which they held: "
11: 7 they shall have finished their t', "
12:11 Lamb, and by the word of their t'; "
17 God, and have the t' of Jesus Christ. "
15: 5 the tabernacle of the t' in heaven 3142
19:10 brethren that have the t' of Jesus: 3141
10 t' of Jesus is the spirit of prophecy. "

tetrarch
M't 14: 1 Herod the t' heard of the fame of 5076
Lu 3: 1 and Herod being t' of Galilee, and 5075
1 his brother Philip t' of Ituræa and "
1 and Lysanias the t' of Abilene, "
19 Herod the t', being reproved by 5076
9: 7 Herod the t' heard of all that was "
Ac 13: 1 been brought up with Herod the t'. "

Thaddæus (*thad-de'-us*) See also JUDE; LEBBÆUS.
M't 10: 3 Lebbæus, whose surname was T': 2280
M'r 3:18 the son of Alphæus, and T', and

Thahash (*tha'-hash*)
Ge 22:24 Gaham, and T', and Maachah. *8477

Thamah (*tha'-mah*) See also TAMAH.
Ezr 2:53 of Sisera, the children of T' *8547

Thamar (*tha'-mar*) See also TAMAR.
M't 1: 3 begat Phares and Zara of T': *2283

than
Ge 3: 1 more subtle t' any beast of the field
4:13 My punishment is greater t' I can bear.
19: 9 we deal worse with thee, t' with them.
25:23 shall be stronger t' the other people;
26:16 us; for thou art much mightier t' we.
29:19 t' that I should give her to another
30 and he loved also Rachel more t' Leah,
34:19 more honourable t' all the house of*
36: 7 riches were more t' that they might*
37: 3 loved Joseph more t' all his children,
4 their father loved him more t' all his
38:26 She hath been more righteous t' I;
41:40 in the throne will I be greater t' thou.
48:19 younger brother shall be greater t' he,
Ex 1: 9 of Israel are more and mightier t' we:
14:12 t' that we should die in the wilderness.
18:11 that the Lord is greater t' all gods:
30:15 poor shall not give less t' half a shekel,
36: 5 much more t' enough for the service
Le 13: 3 sight be deeper t' the skin of his flesh,
4 and in sight be not deeper t' the skin,
21 if it be not lower t' the skin, and be 4480
Le 13:25 it be in sight deeper t' the skin; 4480
26 and it be no lower t' the other skin, "
30 be in sight deeper t' the skin; and "
31 it be not in sight deeper t' the skin, "
32 be not in sight deeper t' the skin; "
34 nor be in sight deeper t' the skin; "
14:37 which in sight are lower t' the wall; "
27: 8 But if he be poorer t' thy estimation,
Nu 3:46 which are more t' the Levites; *5921
22:15 more, and more honourable t' they.
24: 7 and his king shall be higher t' Agag.
De 1:28 The people is greater and taller t' we;
4:38 thee greater and mightier t' thou art,
7: 1 nations greater and mightier t' thou;
7 ye were more in number t' any people;
17 heart, These nations are more t' I;
9: 1 nations greater and mightier t' thyself,
14 a nation mightier and greater t' they.
11:23 nations and mightier t' yourselves.
20: 1 and a people more t' thou, be not
Jos 10: 2 and because it was greater t' Ai, 4480
11 t' they whom the children of Israel
J'g 2:19 themselves more t' their fathers,
8: 2 better t' the vintage of Abiezer?
11:25 art thou any thing better t' Balak the
14:18 went down, What is sweeter t' honey?
18 and what is stronger t' a lion? And he
15: 2 is not her younger sister fairer t' she?
3 be more blameless t' the Philistines,*
16:30 more t' they which he slew in his life.
Ru 3:10 the latter end t' at the beginning, 4480
12 howbeit there is a kinsman nearer t' I.
4:15 which is better to thee t' seven sons,
1Sa 1: 8 am not I better to thee t' ten sons?
9: 2 of Israel a goodlier person t' he:
2 he was higher t' any of the people.
10:23 he was higher t' any of the people
15:22 Behold, to obey is better t' sacrifice,
22 and to hearken t' the fat of rams.
28 of thine, that is better t' thou.
18:30 wisely t' all the servants of Saul;
24:17 to David, Thou art more righteous t' I:
27: 1 me t' that I should speedily escape 3588
2Sa 1:23 divided: they were swifter t' eagles,
23 eagles, they were stronger t' lions.
6:22 And I will yet be more vile t' thus, and
13:14 but, being stronger t' she, forced her,
15 he hated her was greater t' the love
16 greater t' the other that thou didst
17:14 is better t' the counsel of Ahithophel.
19: 7 worse unto thee t' all the evil that
43 have also more right in David t' ye:
43 fiercer t' the words of the men of Israel.
20: 5 he tarried longer t' the set time 4480
6 do us more harm t' did Absalom: "
23:23 was more honourable t' the thirty, "
1Ki 1:37 greater t' the throne of my lord king
47 name of Solomon better t' thy name,
47 make his throne greater t' thy throne.
2:32 men more righteous and better t' he,
4:31 For he was wiser t' all men;
31 t' Ethan the Ezrahite, and Heman, and
12:10 shall be thicker t' my father's loins.
19: 4 life; for I am not better t' my fathers.
20:23 therefore they were stronger t' we;
23, 25 we shall be stronger t' they.
21: 2 give thee for it a better vineyard t' it;
2Ki 5:12 better t' all the waters of Israel?
9:35 no more of her t' the skull, 3588,518
21: 9 to do more evil t' did the nations 4480
1Ch 4: 9 was more honourable t' his brethren:
11:21 he was more honourable t' the two;
24: 4 Eleazar t' of the sons of Ithamar; 4480
2Ch 10:10 shall be thicker t' my father's loins.
21:13 house, which were better t' thyself:
25: 9 is able to give thee much more t' this.
29:34 to sanctify themselves t' the priests.
32: 7 for there be more with us t' with him:
33: 9 and to do worse t' the heathen, 4480
Es 1:19 unto another that is better t' she.
2:17 favour in his sight more t' all the
4:13 the king's house, more t' all the Jews.
6: 6 delight to do honour more t' to myself?
Job 3:21 dig for it more t' for hid treasures;
4:17 Shall mortal man be more just t' God?
17 shall a man be more pure t' his maker?
6: 3 be heavier t' the sand of the sea:
7: 6 My days are swifter t' a weaver's
15 strangling, and death rather t' my life.
9:25 Now my days are swifter t' a post: 4480
11: 6 God exacteth of thee less t' thine
9 thereof is longer t' the earth, 4480
9 the earth, and broader t' the sea.
17 age shall be clearer t' the noonday;
15:10 aged men, much elder t' thy father.
23: 2 stroke is heavier t' my groaning. 5921
12 his mouth more t' my necessary food.
30: 1 are younger t' I have me in derision,
8 men: they were viler t' the earth. *4480
32: 4 spoken, because they were elder t' he.
33:12 thee, that God is greater t' man.
25 His flesh shall be fresher t' a child's:
34:19 regardeth the rich more t'...poor? 6440
23 will not lay upon man more t' right;*
35: 2 My righteousness is more t' God's?
5 the clouds which are higher t' thou.
11 Who teacheth us more t' the beasts of
11 and maketh us wiser t' the fowls of
36:21 hast thou chosen rather t' affliction.
42:12 latter end of Job more t' his beginning:
Ps 4: 7 more t' in the time that their corn and
19:10 are they t' gold, yea, t' much fine gold:
10 sweeter also t' honey and...honeycomb.
37:16 is better t' the riches of many wicked.
40: 5 they are more t' can be numbered.
12 are more t' the hairs of mine head:
Ps 52: 3 Thou lovest evil more t' good; and
3 lying rather t' to speak righteousness.
55:21 of his mouth were smoother t' butter.*
21 his words were softer t' oil, yet were
63: 3 thy lovingkindness is better t' life,
69: 4 are more t' the hairs of mine head:
31 please the Lord better t' an ox or
73: 7 they have more t' heart could wish.
84:10 in thy courts is better t' a thousand.
10 t' to dwell in the tents of wickedness.
87: 2 Zion more t' all the dwellings of Jacob.
93: 4 mightier t' the noise of many waters,*
4 yea, t' the mighty waves of the sea.*
105:24 made them stronger t' their enemies.
118: 9 Lord t' to put confidence in princes.
119:72 unto me t' thousands of gold and
98 hast made me wiser t' mine enemies:
99 understanding t' all my teachers:
100 I understand more t' the ancients,
130: 6 Lord more t' they that watch for the
6 I say, more t' they that watch for the
139:18 they are more in number t' the sand:
142: 6 persecutors; for they are stronger t' I.
Pr 3:14 it is better t' the merchandise of silver,
14 silver, and the gain thereof t' fine gold.
15 She is more precious t' rubies: and all
5: 3 and her mouth is smoother t' oil:
8:10 and knowledge rather t' choice gold.
11 For wisdom is better t' rubies; and all
19 is better t' gold, yea, t' fine gold;
11:24 is that withholdeth more t' is meet,
12: 9 is better t' he that honoureth himself,
26 is more excellent t' his neighbour:
15:16 t' great treasure and trouble therewith.
17 is, t' a stalled ox and hatred therewith.
16: 8 t' great revenues without right.
16 much better is it to get wisdom t' gold!
16 rather to be chosen t' silver!
19 t' to divide the spoil with the proud.
32 his spirit t' he that taketh a city.
17: 1 t' an house full of sacrifices with
10 wise man t' an hundred stripes into a
12 meet a man, rather t' a fool in his folly.
18:19 is harder to be won t' a strong city:
24 friend that sticketh closer t' a brother.
19: 1 t' he that is perverse in his lips, and is
22 and a poor man is better t' a liar.
21: 3 acceptable to the Lord t' sacrifice.
9 t' with a brawling woman in a wide
19 t' with a contentious and an angry
22: 1 is rather to be chosen t' great riches,
1 loving favour rather t' silver and gold.
25: 7 t' that thou shouldest be put lower in
24 t' with a brawling woman and in a
27: 3 a fool's wrath is heavier t' them both.
5 Open rebuke is better t' secret love.
10 that is near t' a brother far off.
28: 6 t' he that is perverse in his ways,
23 favour t' he that flattereth with the
29:20 there is more hope of a fool t' of him.
30: 2 Surely I am more brutish t' any man,
Ec 1:16 wisdom t' all they that have been *5921
2: 9 increased more t' all that were before
16 wise more t' of the fool for ever; *5973
24 a man, t' that he should eat and drink,
25 else can hasten hereunto, more t' I?
3:22 t' that a man should rejoice in his own
4: 2 t' the living which are yet alive. 4480
3 Yea, better is he t' both they, which
5: 1 to hear, t' to give the sacrifice of fools:
5 t' that thou shouldest vow and not pay.
8 for he that is higher t' the highest 5921
8 and there be higher t' they. "
6: 3 that an untimely birth is better t' he.
5 this hath more rest t' the other.
8 hath the wise more t' the fool? 4480
9 sight of the eyes t' the wandering
10 with him that is mightier t' he.
7: 1 A good name is better t' precious
1 day of death t' the day of one's birth.
2 t' to go to the house of feasting:
3 Sorrow is better t' laughter: for by
5 t' for a man to hear the song of fools.
8 is the end of a thing t' the beginning
8 in spirit is better t' the proud in spirit.
10 the former days were better t' these?
19 the wise more t' mighty men which
26 I find more bitter t' death the woman,
8:15 thing under the sun, t' to eat, 3588,518
9: 4 living dog is better t' a dead lion. 4480
16 said I, Wisdom is better t' strength:
17 more t' the cry of him that ruleth
18 Wisdom is better t' weapons of war:
Ca 4:10 how much better is thy love t' wine!
10 smell of thine ointments t' all spices!
5: 9, 9 thy beloved more t' another beloved,
Isa 13:12 a man more precious t' fine gold;
12 a man t' the golden wedge of Ophir.
28:20 is shorter t' that a man can stretch
20 narrower t' that he can wrap himself
33:19 deeper speech t' thou canst perceive;*
40:17 to him less t' nothing, and vanity.
52:14 visage was so marred more t' any man,
14 and his form more t' the sons of men:
54: 1 t' the children of the married wife,
55: 9 as the heavens are higher t' the earth,
9 so are my ways higher t' your ways,
9 and my thoughts t' your thoughts.
56: 5 better t' of sons and of daughters:
65: 5 near to me; for I am holier t' thou.
Jer 4:13 his horses are swifter t' eagles.
5: 3 have made their faces harder t' a rock;
7:26 neck: they did worse t' their fathers.
8: 3 death shall be chosen rather t' life by
16:12 ye have done worse t' your fathers;
20: 7 thou art stronger t' I, and hast

Jer 31:11 hand of him that was stronger t' he.
La 4: 7 Her Nazarites were purer t' snow, they
7 they were whiter t' milk, they were
7 were more ruddy in body t' rubies,
8 Their visage is blacker t' a coal; they
9 t' they that be slain with hunger:
19 are swifter t' the eagles of the heaven:
Eze 3: 9 As an adamant harder t' flint have I
5: 6 wickedness more t' the nations, 4480
6 statutes more t' the countries that "
7 multiplied more t' the nations that "
6:14 more desolate t' the wilderness *
8:15 see greater abominations t' these.
15: 2 What is the vine tree more t' any tree,
2 or t' a branch which is among the*
16:47 wast corrupted more t' they in all thy
51 thine abominations more t' they,
52 committed more abominable t' they:
52 they are more righteous t' thou: yea,
23:11 corrupt in her inordinate love t' she,
11 more t' her sister in her whoredoms.
28: 3 thou art wiser t' Daniel; there is no
42: 5 for the galleries were higher t' these,*
5 t' the lower, and
5 t' the middlemost of the building.*
6 straitened more t' the lowest and the
Da 1:10 faces worse liking t' the children 4480
15 fatter in flesh t' all the children "
20 better t' all the magicians and 5921
2:30 that I have more t' any living, 4481
3:19 seven times more t' it was wont 1768
7:20 was more stout t' his fellows. 4481
8: 3 one was higher t' the other, and 4480
11: 2 fourth shall be far richer t' they all:
8 more years t' the king of the north.*
13 multitude greater t' the former, 4480
Ho 2: 7 then was it better with me t' now.
6: 6 of God more t' burnt offerings.
Am 6: 2 be they better t' these kingdoms? 4480
2 or their border greater t' your border?
Jon 4: 3 for it is better for me to die t' to live.
8 said, It is better for me to die t' to live.
11 are more t' sixscore thousand persons
Mic 7: 4 upright is sharper t' a thorn hedge:
Na 3: 8 Art thou better t' populous No, that
Hab 1: 8 horses also are swifter t' the leopards,
8 are more fierce t' the evening wolves:
13 art of purer eyes t' to behold evil, and
13 the man that is more righteous t' he?
Hag 2: 9 shall be greater t' of the former,
M't 3:11 that cometh after me is mightier t' I,
5:37 is more t' these cometh of evil.
47 only, what do ye more t' others?
6:25 Is not the life more t' meat, and the
25 meat, and the body t' raiment?
26 them. Are ye not much better t' they?
10:15 day of judgment, t' for that city. 2228
31 are of more value t' many sparrows.
37 loveth father or mother more t' me5228
37 loveth son or daughter more t' me "
11: 9 unto you, and more t' a prophet.
11 hath not risen a greater t' John the
11 the kingdom of heaven is greater t' he.
22 at the day of judgment, t' for you. 2228
24 in the day of judgment, t' for thee. "
12: 6 place is one greater t' the temple.
12 much then is a man better t' a sheep?
41 behold, a greater t' Jonas is here.
42 behold, a greater t' Solomon is here.
45 other spirits more wicked t' himself,
45 state of that man is worse t' the first.
18: 8 t' having two hands or two feet 2228
9 t' having two eyes to be cast into "
13 t' of the ninety and nine which "
19:24 t' for a rich man to enter into the "
21:36 sent other servants more t' the first:
23:15 more the child of hell t' yourselves.
26:53 more t' twelve legions of angels? 2228
27:64 last error shall be worse t' the first:
M'r 1: 7 cometh one mightier t' I after me,
4:31 is less t' all the seeds that be in the
32 and becometh greater t' all herbs,
6:11 day of judgment, t' for that city. *2228
8:14 ship with them more t' one loaf. 1508
9:43 t' having two hands to go into hell,2228
45 t' having two feet to be cast into "
47 t' having two eyes to be cast into "
10:25 t' for a rich man to enter into the "
12:31 other commandment greater t' these.
33 is more t' all whole burnt offerings
43 t' all they which have cast into the
14: 5 for more t' three hundred pence, 1883
Lu 3:13 no more t' that which is appointed 3844
16 one mightier t' I cometh, the latchet
7:26 you, and much more t' a prophet.
28 a greater prophet t' John the Baptist:
28 in the kingdom of God is greater t' he.
10:12 day for Sodom, t' for that city. 2228
14 Sidon at the judgment, t' for you. "
11:26 other spirits more wicked t' himself;
26 of that man is worse t' the first.
31 behold, a greater t' Solomon is here.
32 behold, a greater t' Jonas is here.
12: 7 ye are of more value t' many sparrows.
23 The life is more t' meat,
23 and the body is more t' raiment.
24 much more are ye better t' the fowls?
14: 8 a more honourable man t' thou be
15: 7 more t' over ninety and nine just 2228
16: 8 wiser t' the children of light. 5228
17 t' one tittle of the law to fail. 2228
17: 2 t' that he should offend one of "
18:14 house justified rather t' the other: "
25 t' for a rich man to enter into the "
21: 3 widow hath cast in more t' they all:
Joh 1:50 thou shalt see greater things t' these.
Joh 3:19 loved darkness rather t' light, 2228
4: 1 and baptized more disciples t' John, "
12 Art thou greater t' our father Jacob, "
5:20 shew him greater works t' these, that
36 I have greater witness t' that of John:
7:31 he do more miracles t' these which
8:53 thou greater t' our father Abraham,
10:29 which gave them me, is greater t' all;
12:43 of men more t' the praise of God. 2260
13:16 The servant is not greater t' his lord;
16 is sent greater t' he that sent him.
14:12 and greater works t' these shall he do;
28 Father: for my Father is greater t' I.
15:13 Greater love hath no man t' this, that
20 The servant is not greater t' his lord.
21:15 Jonas, lovest thou me more t' these?
Ac 4:19 unto you more t' unto God, judge 2228
5:29 ought to obey God rather t' men. "
15:28 you no greater burden t' these 4133
20:35 is more blessed to give t' to receive.
23:13 more t' forty which had made this
21 for him of them more t' forty men,
25: 6 among them more t' ten days, 2228
26:22 saying none other things t' those *
27:11 t' those things which were spoken 2228
Ro 1:25 the creature more t' the Creator, 3844
3: 9 are we better t' they? No, in no wise:
8:37 more t' conquerors through him 5245
12: 3 more highly t' he ought to think;
13:11 nearer t' when we believed. 2228
1Co 1:25 foolishness of God is wiser t' men;
25 weakness of God is stronger t' men.
3:11 can no man lay t' that is laid, 3844
7: 9 for it is better to marry t' to burn. 2228
9:15 t' that any man should make my "
10:22 to jealousy? are we stronger t' he?
14: 5 t' he that speaketh with tongues, 2228
18 speak with tongues more t' ye all:
19 t' ten thousand words in an 2228
15:10 laboured more abundantly t' they all:
2Co 1:13 t' what ye read or acknowledge; 2228
Ga 1: 8 t' that which we have preached 3844
9 you t' that ye have received, "
4:27 more children t' she which hath a 2228
Eph 3: 8 who am less t' the least of all saints,
Ph'p 2: 3 esteem other better t' themselves.
1Ti 1: 4 rather t' godly edifying which is 2228
2Ti 3: 4 pleasures more t' lovers of God; "
Ph'm 21 thou wilt also do more t' I say. *5228
Heb 1: 4 Being made so much better t' angels,
4 a more excellent name t' they. 3844
2: 7 him a little lower t' the angels; "
9 was made a little lower t' the angels"
3: 3 worthy of more glory t' Moses, "
3 house hath more honour t' the house.
4:12 sharper t' any twoedged sword, 5228
7:26 and made higher t' the heavens;
9:23 with better sacrifices t' these. 3844
11: 4 a more excellent sacrifice t' Cain, "
25 t' to enjoy the pleasures of sin 2228
26 greater riches t' the treasures in
12:24 better things t' that of Abel. 3844
1Pe 1: 7 more precious t' of gold that perisheth,
3:17 for well doing, t' for evil doing. 2228
2Pe 2:20 worse with them t' the beginning.
21 t', after they have known it, to 2228
1Jo 3:20 God is greater t' our heart, and
4: 4 in you, t' he that is in the world. 2228
3Jo 4 no greater joy t' to hear that my
Re 2:19 and the last to be more t' the first.

thank See also THANKED; THANKFUL; THANKING; THANKS; THANKWORTHY.
1Ch 16: 4 to t' and praise the Lord God of 3034
7 first this psalm to t' the Lord * "
23:30 morning to t' and praise the Lord, "
29:13 our God, we t' thee, and praise thy "
2Ch 29:31 t' offerings into the house of the 8426
31 brought...sacrifices and t' offerings;"
33:16 peace offerings and t' offerings, * "
Da 2:23 I t' thee, and praise thee, O thou 3029
M't 11:25 and said, I t' thee, O Father, Lord 1843
Lu 6:32 which love you, what t' have ye? 5485
33 do good to you, what t' have ye? "
34 ye hope to receive, what t' have ye? "
10:21 and said, I t' thee, O Father, Lord 1843
17: 9 he t' that servant because 2192,5485
18:11 God, I t' thee, that I am not as 2168
Joh 11:41 I t' thee that thou hast heard me. "
Ro 1: 8 I t' my God through Jesus Christ "
7:25 I t' God through Jesus Christ our "
1Co 1: 4 I t' my God always on your behalf, "
14 I t' God that I baptized none of you,"
14:18 I t' my God, I speak with tongues "
Ph'p 1: 3 I t' my God upon every remembrance"
1Th 2:13 this cause also t' we God without "
2Th 1: 3 We are bound to t' God always for* "
1Ti 1:12 And I t' Christ Jesus our Lord,2192,5485
2Ti 1: 3 I t' God, whom I serve from my " "
Ph'm 4 I t' my God, making mention of 2168

thanked
2Sa 14:22 bowed himself, and t' the king: *1288
Ac 28:15 saw, he t' God, and took courage. 2168
Ro 6:17 But, God be t', that ye were the *5485

thankful See also UNTHANKFUL.
Ps 100: 4 be t' unto him, and bless his name.*3034
Ro 1:21 him not as God, neither were t'; *2168
Col 3:15 called in one body; and be ye t'. 2170

thankfulness
Ac 24: 3 most noble Felix, with all t'. 2169

thanking
2Ch 5:13 heard in praising and t' the Lord; 3034

thank-offerings See THANK and OFFERINGS.

thanks See also THANKSGIVING.
2Sa 22:50 Therefore I will give t' unto thee, 3034
1Ch 16: 8 Give t' unto the Lord, call upon his "
34 O give t' unto the Lord; for he is "
35 we may give t' to thy holy name, "
41 by name, to give t' to the Lord, "
25: 3 to give t' and to praise the Lord. "
2Ch 31: 2 to minister, and to give t', and to "
Ezr 3:11 and giving t' unto the Lord; "
Ne 12:24 to praise and to give t', according "
31 companies of them that gave t', 8426
38 other company of them that gave t' "
40 companies of them that gave t' "
Ps 6: 5 in the grave who shall give thee t'?3034
18:49 will I give t' unto thee, O Lord, "
30: 4 give t' at the remembrance of his "
12 I will give t' unto thee for ever. "
35:18 thee t' in the great congregation: "
75: 1 Unto thee, O God, do we give t', "
1 unto thee do we give t': for that "
79:13 we thy people...give thee t' for ever:"
92: 1 good thing to give t' unto the Lord, "
97:12 give t' at the remembrance of his "
105: 1 O give t' unto the Lord; call upon "
106: 1 O give t' unto the Lord; for he is "
47 to give t' unto thy holy name, and "
107: 1 O give t' unto the Lord, for he is "
118: 1, 29 O give t' unto the Lord: for he is"
119:62 At midnight I will rise to give t' "
122: 4 give t' unto the name of the Lord. "
136: 1 O give t' unto the Lord; for he is "
2 O give t' unto the God of gods: for "
3 O give t' to the Lord of lords: for "
26 O give t' unto the God of heaven: "
140:13 the righteous shall give t' unto thy "
Da 6:10 prayed, and gave t' before his God,3029
M't 15:36 and gave t', and brake them, 2168
26:27 And he took the cup, and gave t', "
M'r 8: 6 took the seven loaves, and gave t', "
14:23 when he had given t', he gave it to "
Lu 2:38 gave t' likewise unto the Lord, 437
17:16 his face at his feet, giving him t': 2168
22:17 And he took the cup, and gave t', "
19 And he took bread, and gave t', "
Joh 6:11 when he had given t', he distributed"
23 after that the Lord had given t':) "
Ac 27:35 gave t' to God in presence of them "
Ro 14: 6 to the Lord, for he giveth God t'; "
6 he eateth not, and giveth God t'. "
16: 4 unto whom not only I give t', but "
1Co 10:30 of for that for which I give t'? "
11:24 when he had given t', he brake it, "
14:16 say Amen at thy giving of t', 2169
17 thou verily givest t' well, but the 2168
15:57 But t' be to God, which giveth us 5485
2Co 1:11 t' may be given by many on our 2168
2:14 Now t' be unto God, which always 5485
8:16 But t' be to God, which put the "
9:15 T' be unto God for his unspeakable"
Eph 1:16 Cease not to give t' for you, 2168
5: 4 convenient: but rather giving of t'.2169
20 Giving t' always for all things 2168
Col 1: 3 We give t' to God and the Father "
12 Giving t' unto the Father, which "
3:17 giving t' to God and the Father by "
1Th 1: 2 We give t' to God always for you "
3: 9 For what t' can we render to God *2169
5:18 In every thing give t': for this is 2168
2Th 2:13 are bound to give t' alway to God "
1Ti 2: 1 intercessions, and giving of t', *2169
Heb 13:15 of our lips giving t' to his name. *3670
Re 4: 9 t' to him that sat on the throne, 2169
11:17 We give thee t', O Lord God 2168

thanksgiving See also THANKSGIVINGS.
Le 7:12 If he offer it for a t', then he shall 8426
12 with the sacrifice of t' unleavened "
13 bread with the sacrifice of t' of his "
15 his peace offerings for t' shall be "
22:29 offer a sacrifice of t' unto the Lord, "
Ne 11:17 principal to begin the t' in prayer:3034
12: 8 Mattaniah, which was over the t', 1960
46 songs of praise and t' unto God. 3034
Ps 26: 7 may publish with the voice of t', 8426
50:14 Offer unto God t'; and pay thy vows"
69:30 song, and will magnify him with t'. "
95: 2 us come before his presence with t', "
100: 4 Enter into his gates with t', and "
107:22 them sacrifice the sacrifices of t', "
116:17 I will offer to thee the sacrifice of t', "
147: 7 Sing unto the Lord with t'; sing "
Isa 51: 3 gladness shall be found therein, t', "
Jer 30:19 out of them shall proceed t' and the"
Am 4: 5 offer a sacrifice of t' with leaven, "
Jon 2: 9 unto thee with the voice of t'; "
2Co 4:15 through the t' of many redound to2169
9:11 which causeth through us t' to God."
Ph'p 4: 6 by prayer and supplication with t' "
Col 2: 7 taught, abounding therein with t'. "
4: 2 and watch in the same with t'; "
1Ti 4: 3 to be received with t' of them which"
4 be refused, if it be received with t': "
Re 7:12 and wisdom, and t', and honour, "

thanksgivings
Ne 12:27 both with t', and with singing, 8426
2Co 9:12 also by many t' unto God; 2169

thankworthy
1Pe 2:19 this is t', if a man for conscience *5485

Thara (*tha'-rah*) See also TERAH.
Lu 3:34 which was the son of T', which *2291

Tharshish (*thar'-shish*) See also TARSHISH.
1Ki 10:22 the king had at sea a navy of T' *8659
22 in three years came the navy of T'.* "

1Ki 22:48 Jehoshaphat made ships of T· to *8659
1Ch 7:10 Zethan, and T·, and Ahishahar. * "

that See in the APPENDIX.

the See in the APPENDIX; also NEVERTHELESS.

theatre
Ac 19:29 rushed with one accord into the t·.2302
31 not adventure himself into the t·. "

Thebez (*the'-bez*)
J'g 9:50 Then went Abimelech to T·, and 8405
50 encamped against T·, and took it. "
2Sa 11:21 from the wall, that he died in T·? "

thee See in the APPENDIX; also THEE-WARD.

thee-ward
1Sa 19: 4 his works have been to t· very good:

theft See also THEFTS.
Ex 22: 3 then he shall be sold for his t·. 1591
4 If the t· be certainly found in his "

thefts
M't 15:19 fornications, t·, false witness, 2829
M'r 7:22 T·, covetousness, wickedness, "
Re 9:21 of their fornication, nor of their t·.2809

their See in the APPENDIX; also THEIRS.

theirs
Ge 15:13 a stranger in a land that is not t·, 1992
34:23 and every beast of t· be ours?
43:34 was five times so much as any of t·.
Ex 29: 9 the priest's office shall be t· for a *1992
Le 18:10 for t· is thine own nakedness. 2007
Nu 16:26 and touch nothing of t·, lest ye be 1992
18: 9 from the fire: every oblation of t·,
9 every meat offering of t·, and every
9 and every sin offering of t·, and
9 every trespass offering of t·, which
Jos 21:10 Levi, had: for t· was the first lot. "
1Ch 6:54 the Kohathites: for t· was the lot. "
2Ch 18:12 I pray thee, be like one of t·, and "
Jer 44:28 whose words shall stand, mine, or t·."
Eze 7:11 of their multitude, nor of any of t·:*"
44:29 dedicated thing in Israel shall be t·."
Hab 1: 6 the dwellingplaces that are not t·.
M't 5: 3, 10 for t· is the kingdom of heaven. 846
1Co 1: 2 Christ our Lord, both t· and ours:*
2Ti 3: 9 manifest unto...men, as t· also3588,1565

Thelasar (*the-la'-sar*) See also TELASSAR.
2Ki 19:12 of Eden which were in T·? *8515

them See in the APPENDIX; also THEMSELVES.

themselves
Ge 3: 7 together, and made t· aprons. 1992
8 hid t· from the presence of the Lord
13:11 they separated t· the one from the
19:11 that they wearied t· to find the door.
30:40 and he put his own flocks by t·. * 905
32:16 of his servants, every drove by t·;* "
33: 6 their children, and they bowed t·.
7 children came near, and bowed t·:
7 near and Rachel, and they bowed t·.
34:30 they shall gather t· together against
42: 6 and bowed down t· before him with
43:26 and bowed t· to him to the earth.
32 him by himself, and for them by t·. 905
32 which did eat with him, by t·: "
Ex 5: 7 let them go and gather straw for t·.1992
11: 8 and bow down t· unto me, saying,
12:39 they prepared for t· any victual. 1992
18:26 every small matter they judged t·. "
19:22 sanctify t·, lest the Lord break forth
26: 9 thou shalt couple five curtains by t·,905
9 and six curtains by t·, and shalt "
32: 1 the people gathered t· together unto
7 the land of Egypt, have corrupted t·:
26 sons of Levi gathered t· together unto
33: 6 of Israel stripped t· of their ornaments
36:16 And he coupled five curtains by t·, 905
16 and six curtains by t·. "
Le 15:18 they shall both bathe t· in water, and
22: 2 that they separate t· from the holy
Nu 6: 2 shall separate t· to vow a vow of a*
2 Nazarite, to separate t· unto the Lord:*
8: 7 clothes, and so make t· clean. 1992
10: 3 shall assemble t· to thee at the door
4 of Israel, shall gather t· unto thee.
11:32 them all abroad for t· round about1992
16: 3 gathered t· together against Moses
20: 2 gathered t· together against Moses
27: 3 gathered t· together against the Lord
De 7:20 that are left, and hide t· from thee,
9:12 forth out of Egypt have corrupted t·;
31:14 and presented t· in the tabernacle of
20 they shall have eaten and filled t·,
32: 5 They have corrupted t·, their spot is*
27 adversaries...behave t· strangely,†‡
31 even our enemies t· being judges.
Jos 8:27 city Israel took for a prey unto t·. 1992
9: 2 That they gathered t· together, to
10: 5 king of Eglon, gathered t· together,
13 had avenged t· upon their enemies.
16 fled, and hid t· in a cave at Makkedah.
11:14 of Israel took for a prey unto t·; 1992
22:12 children of Israel gathered t· together
24: 1 and they presented t· before God.
J'g 2:12 about them, and bowed t· unto them,
17 other gods, and bowed t· unto them:
19 corrupted t· more than their fathers,*
5: 2 when the people willingly offered t·.
9 offered t· willingly among the people.
7: 2 lest Israel vaunt t· against me, saying,
23 gathered t· together out of Naphtali,*
24 men of Ephraim gathered t· together,*
10:17 of Israel assembled t· together,
12: 1 men of Ephraim gathered t· together,*
J'g 15: 9 in Judah, and spread t· in Lehi.
20: 2 presented t· in the assembly of the
14 of Benjamin gathered t· together out
20 men of Israel put t· in array to fight*
22 the men of Israel encouraged t·,
22 where they put t· in array the first
30 and put t· in array against Gibeah,
33 and put t· in array at Baal-tamar:
37 and the liers in wait drew t· along,
1Sa 2: 5 were full have hired out t· for bread;
3:13 because his sons made t· vile, and 1992
4: 2 the Philistines put t· in array against
8: 4 elders of Israel gathered t· together,
13: 5 Philistines gathered t· together to
6 then the people did hide t· in caves,
11 Philistines gathered t· together at
14:11 discovered t· unto the garrison of the
11 out of the holes where they had hid t·.
20 that were with him assembled t·, *
22 which had hid t· in mount Ephraim,
21: 4 have kept t· at least from women.
22: 2 discontented, gathered t· unto him;
28: 4 the Philistines gathered t· together,
2Sa 2:25 of Benjamin gathered t· together
5:18, 22 and spread t· in the valley of
10: 8 and Maacah, were by t· in the field. 905
15 Israel, they gathered t· together.
17 the Syrians set t· in array against
16:14 came weary, and refreshed t· there.*
22:45 Strangers shall submit t· unto me:
1Ki 8: 2 all the men of Israel assembled t·
47 they shall bethink t· in the land
18:23 let them choose one bullock for t·, 1992
28 and cut t· after their manner with
20:12 they set t· in array against the city.
2Ki 2:15 bowed t· to the ground before him.
7:12 out of the camp to hide t· in the field,
8:20 of Judah, and made a king over t·.1992
17:17 sold t· to do evil in the sight of the
19:29 eat this year such things as grow of t·,*
1Ch 11: 1 Then all Israel gathered t· to David
10 who strengthened t· with him in his
14 they set t· in the midst of that parcel,*
12: 8 Gadites there separated t· unto David
13: 2 that they may gather t· unto us:
14: 9 spread t· in the valley of Rephaim.*
13 spread t· abroad in the valley. *
15:14 sanctified t· to bring up the ark of the
19: 6 that they had made t· odious to David,
7 gathered t· together from their cities,
9 were come were by t· in the field. 905
11 they set t· in array against the children
21:20 and his four sons with him hid t·.
29:24 submitted t· unto Solomon the king.
2Ch 3:13 spread t· forth twenty cubits:
5: 3 all the men of Israel assembled t·
6:37 Yet if they bethink t· in the land
7: 3 bowed t· with their faces to the
14 shall humble t·, and pray, and seek
12: 6 Israel and the king humbled t·;
7 the Lord saw that they humbled t·,
7 They have humbled t·; therefore
13: 7 strengthened t· against Rehoboam
14:13 that they could not recover t·; 1992
15:10 gathered t· together at Jerusalem
20: 4 And Judah gathered t· together, to
25 jewels, which they stripped off for t·,
26 assembled t· in the valley of Berachah;
21: 8 of Judah, and made t· a king.
29:15 their brethren, and sanctified t·,
29 that were present with him bowed t·,
34 the other priests had sanctified t·:
34 more upright in heart to sanctify t·
30: 3 had not sanctified t· sufficiently,
3 had the people gathered t· together
11 Manasseh and of Zebulun humbled t·,
15 were ashamed, and sanctified t·,
18 and Zebulun, had not cleansed t·,
24 great number of priests sanctified t·.
31:18 for in their set office they sanctified t·
32: 8 rested t· upon the words of Hezekiah
35:14 afterward they made ready for t·, 1992
14 the Levites prepared for t·, and "
Ezr 3: 1 people gathered t· together as one
6:20 brethren the priests, and for t·. 1992
21 such as had separated t· unto them
9: 1 have not separated t· from the people
2 taken of their daughters for t·, 1992
2 mingled t· with the people of those
10: 7 that they should gather t· together
9 gathered t· together unto Jerusalem
Ne 4: 2 feeble Jews? will they fortify t·? 1992
8: 1 people gathered t· together as one
16 and made t· booths, every one 1992
9: 2 Israel separated t· from all strangers,
25 and delighted t· in thy great goodness.
10:28 that had separated t· from the people
11: 2 that willingly offered t· to dwell at
12:28 of the singers gathered t· together,
30 the priests and the Levites purified t·,
13:22 Levites, that they should cleanse t·,
Es 8:11 in every city to gather t· together,
13 that day to avenge t· on their enemies.
9: 2 Jews gathered t· together in their
15 gathered t· together on the fourteenth
16 king's provinces gathered t· together,
27 upon all such as joined t· unto them,
31 had decreed for t· and for their 5315
Job 1: 6 came to present t· before the Lord,
2: 1 came to present t· before the Lord,
3:14 which built desolate places for t·;
6: 4 terrors of God do set t· in array
16:10 have gathered t· together against me.
24: 4 the poor of the earth hide t· together.
16 had marked for t· in the daytime:
29: 8 The young men saw me, and hid t·:
Job 30:14 the desolation they rolled t· upon me.
34:22 the workers of iniquity may hide t·.
41:23 they are firm in t·; they cannot be*
25 by reason of breakings they purify t·.
Ps 2: 2 The kings of the earth set t·, and the
3: 6 have set t· against me round about.
9:20 nations may know t· to be but men.
18:44 strangers shall submit t· unto me.
35:15 rejoiced, and gathered t· together:
15 gathered t· together against me,
26 dishonour that magnify t· against me.
37:11 delight t· in the abundance of peace.
38:16 slippeth, they magnify t· against me.
44:10 and they which hate us spoil for t·.
49: 6 boast t· in the multitude of their
56: 6 They gathered t· together, they hide
6 they hide t·, they mark my steps,
57: 6 the midst whereof they are fallen t·.
59: 4 They run and prepared t· without my
64: 5 They encourage t· in an evil matter:
8 their own tongue to fall upon t·: *
66: 3 thine enemies submit t· unto thee.
7 nations: let not the rebellious exalt t·.
80: 6 and our enemies laugh among t·.
81:15 should have submitted t· unto him:
94: 4 all the workers of iniquity boast t·?
21 They gather t· together against the
97: 7 graven images, that boast t· of idols:
104:22 sun ariseth, they gather t· together,*
106:28 They joined t· also unto Baal-peor,
109:29 cover t· with their own confusion,
140: 8 his wicked device; lest they exalt t·.
Pr 23: 5 for riches certainly make t· wings;
28:28 When the wicked rise, men hide t·:
Ec 3:18 might see that they t· are beasts. 1992
11: 3 of rain, they empty t· upon the earth:
12: 3 and the strong men shall bow t·, and
Isa 2: 6 please t· in the children of strangers.*
3: 9 they have rewarded evil unto t·. 1992
8:21 they shall be hungry, they shall fret t·,
10:31 inhabitants of Gebim gather t· to flee.‡
15: 3 they shall gird t· with sackcloth:
22: 7 and the horsemen shall set t· in array
30: 2 strengthen t· in the strength of
46: 2 but t· are gone into captivity. 5315
47:14 deliver t· from the power of the
48: 2 For they call t· of the holy city, and
2 and stay t· upon the God of Israel;
49:18 all these gather t· together, and
56: 6 that join t· to the Lord, to serve him,
59: 6 shall they cover t· with their works:
60: 4 all they gather t· together, they come
14 bow t· down at the soles of thy feet;
66:17 They that sanctify t·, and purify
17 and purify t· in the gardens behind
Jer 2:24 that seek her will not weary t·;
4: 2 and the nations shall bless t· in him,
5: 7 assembled t· by troops in the harlot's
22 and though the waves thereof toss t·,
7:19 do they not provoke t· to the
9: 5 and weary t· to commit iniquity.
11:17 done against t· to provoke me 1992
12:13 they have put t· to pain, but shall not
16: 6 shall men lament for them, nor cut t·,
6 nor make t· bald for them:
7 Neither shall men tear t· for them in*
25:14 great kings shall serve t· of them also:
27: 7 and great kings shall serve t· of him.
30: 8 shall no more serve t· of him:
21 And their nobles shall be of t·, and
34:10 none should serve t· of them any
41: 5 their clothes rent, and having cut t·,
49:29 they shall take to t· their curtains,1992
50: 9 shall set t· in array against her;
La 2:10 they have girded t· with sackcloth:
4:14 they have polluted t· with blood, so*
Eze 6: 9 and they shall lothe t· for the evils6440
7:18 They shall also gird t· with sackcloth,
10:17 lifted up, these lifted up t· also: *
22 of Chebar, their appearances and t·:*
14:18 but they only shall be delivered t·.
26:16 they shall clothe t· with trembling;
27:30 they shall wallow t· in the ashes:
31 shall make t· utterly bald for thee,
31:14 by the waters exalt t· for their height,
34: 2 shepherds of Israel that do feed t·!
8 the shepherds fed t·, and fed not my
10 the shepherds feed t· any more; 853
27 hand of those that served t· of them.
37:23 defile t· any more with their idols,
43:26 it; and they shall consecrate t·. *3027
44:18 gird t· with any thing that causeth
25 come at no dead person to defile t·:
25 had no husband, they may defile t·.
45: 5 ministers of the house, have for t·,1992
Da 2:43 shall mingle t· with the seed of men:
10: 7 upon them, so that they fled to hide t·.
11: 6 end of years they shall join t· together;
14 shall exalt t· to establish the vision;
Hos 1:11 together, and appoint t· one head, 1992
4:14 for t· are separated with whores, "
7:14 they assemble t· for corn and wine,
9: 9 They have deeply corrupted t·, as in
10 and separated t· unto that shame;
10:10 they shall bind t· in their furrows.*
Am 2: 8 And they lay t· down upon clothes
6: 4 and stretch t· upon their couches, and
5 invent to t· instruments of 1992
6 anoint t· with the chief ointments:
7 that stretched t· shall be removed.
9: 3 they hide t· in the top of Carmel,
Mic 3: 4 have behaved t· ill in their doings.*
Hab 1: 7 and their dignity shall proceed of t·.
8 and their horsemen shall spread t·,
Zep 2: 8 and magnified t· against thier border.
10 magnified t· against the people of

Zec 4:12 pipes empty the golden oil out of t'?
11: 5 slay them, and hold t' not guilty: and
12: 3 burden t' with it shall be cut in pieces,
7 do not magnify t' against Judah. *
M't 9: 3 of the scribes said within t', 1438
14: 2 works do shew forth t' in him. *
15 the villages, and buy t' victuals. 1438
16: 7 they reasoned among t', saying, "
19:12 made t' eunuchs for the kingdom "
21:25 And they reasoned with t', saying, "
38 they said among t', This is the "
23: 4 but they t' will not move them with
M'r 1:27 they questioned among t', saying, 848
2: 8 that they so reasoned within t', 1438
4:17 have no root in t', and so endure "
6:14 mighty works do shew forth t' in him.*
30 apostles gathered t' together unto
36 into the villages, and buy t' bread: 1438
51 they were sore amazed in t' beyond "
8:16 they reasoned among t', saying, * 240
9: 2 into an high mountain apart by t': 3441
8 any more, save Jesus only with t'. 1438
10 they kept that saying with t', "
34 way they had disputed among t', * 240
10:26 saying among t', Who then can be* 1438
11:31 they reasoned with t', saying, If we "
12: 7 those husbandmen said among t', "
14: 4 some that had indignation within t', "
15:31 priests mocking said among t' 240
16: 3 they said among t', Who shall roll 1438
Lu 4:36 all amazed, and spake among t', * 240
7:30 the counsel of God against t', 1438
49 with him began to say within t', "
18: 9 unto certain which trusted in t' "
20: 5 they reasoned with t', saying, If we "
14 they reasoned among t', saying, * "
20 which should feign t' just men, "
22:23 they began to enquire among t', "
23:12 they were at enmity between t'. "
24:12 beheld the linen clothes laid by t', 3441
Joh 6:52 Jews therefore strove among t', * 240
7:35 Then said the Jews among t', 1438
11:55 before the passover, to purify t'. "
56 spake among t', as they stood in * 240
12:19 Pharisees therefore said among t', 1438
16:17 said some of his disciples among t',* 240
17:13 might have my joy fulfilled in t'. 848
18:18 it was cold: and they warmed t': "
28 they t' went not into the judgment 846
19:24 They said therefore among t', Let* 240
Ac 4:15 the council, they conferred among t', "
5:36 of men, about four hundred, joined t':
11:26 they assembled t' with the church,*
15:32 and Silas, being prophets also t', 846
16:37 let them come t' and fetch us out. "
18: 6 when they opposed t', and blasphemed,
21:25 keep t' from things offered to idols,
23:12 and bound t' under a curse, 1438
21 which have bound t' with an oath, "
24:15 which they t' also allow, that there 846
26:31 gone aside, they talked between t',* 240
27:40 they committed t' unto the sea, and*
43 swim should cast t' first into the sea,
28: 4 they said among t', No doubt this* 846
25 And when they agreed not among t', "
29 had great reasoning among t'. * 1438
Ro 1:22 Professing t' to be wise, they became
24 their own bodies between t': 1438
27 receiving in t' that recompence of "
2:14 not the law, are a law unto t': "
10: 3 submitted t' unto the righteousness of
13: 2 resist shall receive to t' damnation. 1438
1Co 6: 9 nor abusers of t' with mankind,
16:15 have addicted t' to the ministry 1438
2Co 5:15 should not henceforth live unto t', "
8: 3 their power they were willing of t';* 830
10:12 with some that commend t': 1438
12 but they measuring t' by t', "
12 and comparing t' among t', "
11:13 transforming t' into the apostles of
Ga 6:13 neither they t' who are circumcised 846
Eph 4:19 given t' over unto lasciviousness, 1438
Ph'p 2: 3 let each esteem other better than t'.* "
1Th 1: 9 For they t' shew of us what manner 846
1Ti 1:10 for them that defile t' with mankind,
2: 9 that women adorn t' in modest 1438
3:13 well purchase to t' a good degree, "
6:10 pierced t' through with many "
19 Laying up...for t' a good foundation "
2Ti 2:25 instructing those that oppose t';
26 recover t' out of the snare of the devil,
4: 3 lusts shall they heap to t' teachers, 1438
Tit 1:12 One of t', even a prophet of their 846
Heb 6: 6 they crucify to t' the Son of God 1438
9:23 the heavenly things t' with better 846
1Pe 1:12 that not unto t', but unto us they 1438
3: 5 adorned t', being in subjection unto "
2Pe 2: 1 and bring upon t' swift destruction. "
19 t' are the servants of corruption: 846
Jude 7 manner, giving t' over to fornication,
10 in those things they corrupt t'. *
12 with you, feeding t' without fear: 1438
19 These be they who separate t', "
Re 6:15 hid t' in the dens and in the rocks "
8: 6 trumpets prepared t' to sound. "

then

Ge 3: 5 thereof, t' your eyes shall be opened,
4:26 t' began men to call upon the name 227
8: 9 T' he put forth his hand, and took her,
12: 6 the Canaanite was t' in the land. 227
13: 7 the Perizzite dwelled t' in the land. "
9 the left hand, t' I will go to the right;
9 the right hand, t' I will go to the left.
11 T' Lot chose him all the plain of *
16 t' shall thy seed also be numbered.
18 T' Abram removed his tent, and *
Ge 17:17 T' Abraham fell upon his face, and
18:15 T' Sarah denied, saying, I laughed
26 t' I will spare all the place for their
19:15 arose, t' the angels hastened Lot,
24 T' the Lord rained upon Sodom and
20: 9 T' Abimelech called Abraham, and
21:32 t' Abimelech rose up, and Phichol the
22: 4 T' on the third day Abraham lifted up*
24: 8 t' thou shalt be clear from this my
41 T' shalt thou be clear from this my 227
50 T' Laban and Bethuel answered and
25: 1 T' again Abraham took a wife, and*
8 T' Abraham gave up the ghost, and*
34 T' Jacob gave Esau bread and *
26:12 T' Isaac sowed in that land, and *
26 T' Abimelech went to him from Gerar,
27:41 hand; t' will I slay my brother Jacob.
45 t' I will send, and fetch thee from
28: 9 T' went Esau unto Ishmael, and took*
21 in peace; t' shall the Lord be my God:
29: 1 T' Jacob went on his journey, and
8 well's mouth; t' we water the sheep.
25 wherefore t' hast thou beguiled me?
30:14 T' Rachel said to Leah, Give me, I
31: 8 wages; t' all the cattle bare speckled:
8 t' bare all the cattle ringstraked.
16 now t', whatsoever God hath said unto
17 T' Jacob rose up, and set his sons and
25 T' Laban overtook Jacob. Now Jacob*
33 T' went he out of Leah's tent, and*
54 T' Jacob offered sacrifice upon the*
32: 7 T' Jacob was greatly afraid and
8 t' the other company which is left
18 T' thou shalt say, They be thy servant
33: 6 T' the handmaidens came near, they
10 t' receive my present at my hand:
34:16 T' will we give our daughters unto you,
17 t' will we take our daughter, and we
35: 2 T' Jacob said unto his household, and
37:28 T' there passed by Midianites *
38:11 T' said Judah to Tamar his daughter
21 T' he asked the men of that place,
39: 9 how t' can I do this great wickedness,
41: 9 T' spake the chief butler unto Pharaoh,
14 T' Pharaoh sent and called Joseph,
42:25 T' Joseph commanded to fill their
34 t' shall I know that ye are no spies,
38 t' shall ye bring down my gray hairs
43: 9 thee, t' let me bear the blame for ever:
44: 8 t' should we steal out of thy lord's
11 T' they speedily took down every man
13 T' they rent their clothes, and laded
18 T' Judah came near unto him, and
26 brother be with us, t' will we go down:
32 t' I shall bear the blame to my father
45: 1 T' Joseph could not refrain himself
47: 1 T' Joseph came and told Pharaoh, and
6 t' make them rulers over my cattle.
23 T' Joseph said unto the people, Behold,
49: 4 father's bed; t' defiledst thou it: 227
Ex 1:16 stools; if it be a son, t' ye shall kill him:
16 but if it be a daughter, t' she shall live.
2: 7 T' said his sister to Pharaoh's
4:25 T' Zipporah took a sharp stone, and
26 t' she said, A bloody husband thou 227
31 t' they bowed their heads and
5:15 T' the officers of the children of Israel
6: 1 T' the Lord said unto Moses, Now*
12 how t' shall Pharaoh hear me, who am
7: 9 t' thou shalt say unto Aaron, Take thy
11 T' Pharaoh also called the wise men
8: 8 T' Pharaoh called for Moses and
19 T' the magicians said unto Pharaoh,
10:16 T' Pharaoh called for Moses and
12:21 T' Moses called for all the elders of
44 him, t' shall he eat thereof. 227
48 t' let him come near and keep it: "
13:13 redeem it, t' thou shalt break his neck: "
15: 1 T' sang Moses and the children of 227
15 T' the dukes of Edom shall be "
16: 4 T' said the Lord unto Moses, Behold,
6 t' ye shall know that the Lord hath
7 t' ye shall see the glory of the Lord;
17: 8 T' came Amalek, and fought with
18:23 t' thou shalt be able to endure, and all
19: 5 t' ye shall be a peculiar treasure unto
21: 3 t' his wife shall go out with him.
6 T' his master shall bring him unto
8 t' shall he let her be redeemed:
11 t' shall she go out free without money.
13 t' I will appoint thee a place whither
19 t' shall he that smote him be quit:
23 follow, t' thou shalt give life for life,
28 t' the ox shall be surely stoned, and*
30 t' he shall give for the ransom of his
35 t' they shall sell the live ox, and divide
22: 3 t' he shall be sold for his theft.
8 t' the master of the house shall be
11 T' shall an oath of the Lord be *
13 pieces, t' let him bring it for witness,*
23:22 t' I will be an enemy unto thine
24: 9 T' went up Moses, and Aaron, Nadab,
29: 7 T' shalt thou take the anointing oil,
20 T' shalt thou kill the ram, and take of
34 t' thou shalt burn the remainder with
30:12 t' shall they give every man a ransom
32:24 t' I cast it into the fire, and there came*
26 T' Moses stood in the gate of the
34:20 him not, t' shalt thou break his neck.
36: 1 T' wrought Bezaleel and Aholiab, and*
40:34 T' a cloud covered the tent of the
37 t' they journeyed not till the day that
Le 1:14 t' he shall bring his offering of
3: 7 t' shall he offer it before the Lord.
12 t' he shall offer it before the Lord.
4: 3 t' let him bring for his sin, which he
Le 4:14 t' the congregation shall offer a young
28 t' he shall bring his offering, a kid of
5: 1 utter it, t' he shall bear his iniquity.
3 knoweth of it, t' he shall be guilty.
4 t' he shall be guilty in one of these.
7 t' he shall bring for his trespass, which
11 t' he that sinned shall bring for his
12 T' shall he bring it to the priest, and*
15 t' he shall bring for his trespass unto
6: 4 T' it shall be, because he hath sinned,
7:12 t' he shall offer with the sacrifice of
10: 3 T' Moses said unto Aaron, This is it
12: 2 t' she shall be unclean seven days;
4 shall t' continue in the blood of her*
5 t' she shall be unclean two weeks,
8 t' she shall bring two turtles, or two
13: 2 t' he shall be brought unto Aaron the
4 t' the priest shall shut him up that
5 t' the priest shall shut him up seven
8 t' the priest shall pronounce him
9 t' he shall be brought unto the priest;
13 T' the priest shall consider: and,
17 t' the priest shall pronounce him
21 t' the priest shall shut him up seven
22 t' the priest shall pronounce him
25 T' the priest shall look upon it: and,
26 t' the priest shall shut him up seven
27 t' the priest shall pronounce him
30 T' the priest shall see the plague:
30 t' the priest shall pronounce him
31 t' the priest shall shut up him that
34 t' the priest shall pronounce him
36 T' the priest shall look on him: and,
39 T' the priest shall look: and, behold,
43 T' the priest shall look upon it: and,
54 T' the priest shall command that they
56 t' he shall rend it out of the garment,
58 t' it shall be washed the second time,
14: 4 T' shall the priest command to take
21 t' he shall take one lamb for a trespass
36 T' the priest shall command that they
38 T' the priest shall go out of the house
40 T' the priest shall command that they
44 T' the priest shall come and look, and,
48 t' the priest shall pronounce the house
15: 8 t' he shall wash his clothes, and bathe
13 t' he shall number to himself seven
16 t' he shall wash all his flesh in water,
28 t' she shall number to herself seven
16:15 T' shall he kill the goat of the sin
17:15 until the even: t' shall he be clean.
16 his flesh; t' he shall bear his iniquity.
19:23 t' ye shall count the fruit thereof as
20: 5 T' I will set my face against that man,
22:14 t' he shall put the fifth part thereof
27 t' it shall be seven days under the dam:
23:10 t' ye shall bring a sheaf of the
19 T' ye shall sacrifice one kid of the*
25: 2 t' shall the land keep a sabbath unto
9 T' shalt thou cause the trumpet of the
21 T' I will command my blessing upon
25 t' shall he redeem that which his *
27 T' let him count the years of the sale
28 t' that which is sold shall remain in
29 t' he may redeem it within a whole
30 t' the house that is in the walled city
33 t' the house that was sold, and the city
35 with thee; t' thou shalt relieve him:
41 t' shall he depart from thee, both he
52 t' he shall count with him, and
54 t' he shall go out in the year of jubilee.
26: 4 T' I will give you rain in due season,
18 t' I will punish you seven times more
24 T' will I also walk contrary unto you,
28 T' I will walk contrary unto you also
34 T' shall the land enjoy...sabbaths, 227
34 t' shall the land rest, and enjoy her "
41 if t' their uncircumcised hearts be "
41 they t' accept of the punishment of "
42 T' will I remember my covenant with
27: 4 t' thy estimation shall be thirty
5, 6 t' thy estimation shall be of the
7 t' thy estimation shall be fifteen
8 t' he shall present himself before the
10 t' it and the exchange thereof shall be
11 t' he shall present the beast before the
13 t' he shall add a fifth part thereof unto
14 t' the priest shall estimate it, whether
15 t' he shall add the fifth part of the
16 t' thy estimation shall be according to
18 t' the priest shall reckon unto him the
19 t' he shall add the fifth part of the
23 T' the priest shall reckon unto him the
27 t' he shall redeem it according to
27 t' it shall be sold according to thy
33 t' both it and the change thereof shall
Nu 2: 7 T' the tribe of Zebulun: and Eliab the*
14 T' the tribe of Gad: and the captain of*
17 T' the tabernacle of the congregation
22 T' the tribe of Benjamin: and the*
29 T' the tribe of Naphtali: and the *
5: 7 T' they shall confess their sin which
15 T' shall the man bring his wife unto
21 T' the priest shall charge the woman
25 T' the priest shall take the jealousy*
27 t' it shall come to pass, that, if she be
28 t' she shall be free, and shall conceive
31 T' shall the man be guiltless from*
6: 9 t' he shall shave his head in the day of
7:89 t' he heard the voice of one speaking
8: 8 T' let him take a young bullock with
9:17 t' after that the children of Israel
19 t' the children of Israel kept the
21 in the morning, t' they journeyed:*
10: 4 t' the princes, which are heads of
5 t' the camps that lie on the east parts*

Nu 10: 6 t' the camps that lie on the south side*
9 t' ye shall blow an alarm with the
11:10 T' Moses heard the people weep *
12: 8 wherefore t' were ye not afraid to speak
14: 5 T' Moses and Aaron fell on their faces
8 in us, t' he will bring us into this land,
13 T' the Egyptians shall hear it, (for
15 t' the nations which have heard the
45 T' the Amalekites came down, and the
15: 4 T' shall he that offereth his offering
9 T' shall he bring with a bullock a
24 T' it shall be, if ought be committed
27 t' he shall bring a she goat of the first
16: 3 wherefore t' lift ye up yourselves
29 all men; t' the Lord hath not sent me.
30 t' ye shall understand that these men
18:26 t' ye shall offer up an heave offering of
30 t' it shall be counted unto the Levites
19: 7 T' the priest shall wash his clothes,
12 t' the seventh day he shall not be
20: 1 T' came the children of Israel, even*
19 drink of thy water, t' I will pay for it:
21: 1 t' he fought against Israel, and took*
2 t' I will utterly destroy their cities.
17 T' Israel sang this song, Spring up,227
22:31 T' the Lord opened the eyes of
27: 1 T' came the daughters of Zelophehad,
8 t' ye shall cause his inheritance to
9,10,11 t' ye shall give...inheritance unto
30: 4 t' all her vows shall stand, and every
7 t' her vows shall stand, and her bonds
11 t' all her vows shall stand, and every
12 t' whatsoever proceedeth out of her
14 t' he establisheth all her vows, or all
15 them; t' he shall bear her iniquity.
32:22 t' afterward ye shall return, and be
33:52 T' ye shall drive out all the inhabitants
55 t' it shall come to pass, that those
34: 3 T' your south quarter shall be from
35:11 T' ye shall appoint you cities to be
24 T' the congregation shall judge
36: 3 t' shall their inheritance be taken from
4 t' shall their inheritance be put unto
De 1:29 T' I said unto you, Dread not, neither
41 T' ye answered and said unto me, We
2: 1 T' we turned, and took our journey
32 T' Sihon came out against us, he and
3: 1 T' we turned, and went up the way to
20 t' shall ye return every man unto his
4:41 T' Moses severed three cities on 227
5:25 Lord our God any more, t' we shall die.
6:12 T' beware lest thou forget the Lord,
21 T' thou shalt say unto thy son, We
8:10 t' thou shalt bless the Lord thy God*
14 T' thine heart be lifted up, and thou
9: 9 t' I abode in the mount forty days and
23 t' ye rebelled against...commandment
11:17 t' the Lord's wrath be kindled against*
23 T' will the Lord drive out all these
12:11 T' there shall be a place which the
21 t' thou shalt kill of thy herd and of thy
13:14 T' shalt thou enquire, and make
14:25 T' shalt thou turn it into money, and
15:12 t' in the seventh year thou shalt let
17 T' thou shalt take an aul, and thrust
17: 5 T' shalt thou bring forth that man or
8 t' shalt thou arise, and get thee up
18: 7 T' he shall minister in the name of the
19: 9 t' shalt thou add three cities more for
12 T' the elders of his city shall send and
17 T' both the men, between whom the
19 T' shall ye do unto him, as he had
20:10 against it, t' proclaim peace unto it.
12 against thee, t' thou shalt besiege it:
21: 2 T' thy elders and thy judges shall
12 T' thou shalt bring her home to thine
14 t' thou shalt let her go whither she
16 T' it shall be, when he maketh his
19 T' shall his father and his mother lay
22: 2 t' thou shalt bring it unto thine own
8 t' thou shalt make a battlement for
15 T' shall the father of the damsel, and
21 T' they shall bring out the damsel to
22 t' they shall both of them die, both the
24 T' ye shall bring them both out unto
25 t' the man only that lay with her shall
29 T' the man that lay with her shall
23: 9 t' keep thee from every wicked thing.
10 t' shall he go abroad out of the camp,
24: 1 t' let him write her a bill of *
7 or selleth him; t' that thief shall die;
25: 1 t' they shall justify the righteous, and
3 t' thy brother should seem vile unto
7 t' let his brother's wife go up to the
8 T' the elders of his city shall call him,
9 T' shall his brother's wife come unto
12 T' thou shalt cut off her hand, thine
26:13 T' thou shalt say before the Lord thy*
28:59 T' the Lord will make thy plagues
29:20 but t' the anger of the Lord and his227
25 T' men shall say, Because they have
30: 3 That t' the Lord thy God will turn thy
31:17 T' my anger shall be kindled against
20 t' will they turn unto other gods, and
32:15 t' he forsook God which made him,
33:28 Israel t' shall dwell in safety alone:*
Jos 1: 8 for t' thou shalt make thy way 227
8 and t' thou shalt have good success. "
10 T' Joshua commanded the officers of
15 t' ye shall return unto the land of your
2:15 T' she let them down by a cord
20 t' we will be quit of thine oath which
3: 3 t' ye shall remove from your place,
4: 4 T' Joshua called the twelve men,
7 T' ye shall answer them, That the
22 T' ye shall let your children know,

Jos 6:10 day I bid you shout; t' shall ye shout.
7:21 t' I coveted them, and took them; and,
8: 7 T' ye shall rise up from the ambush,*
21 t' they turned again, and slew the men
30 T' Joshua built an altar unto the 227
10:12 T' spake Joshua to the Lord in the "
22 T' said Joshua, Open the mouth of the
29 T' Joshua passed from Makkedah,*
33 T' Horam king of Gezer came up 227
14: 6 T' the children of Judah came unto
11 as my strength was t', even so is 227
12 t' I shall be able to drive them out,*
15: 1 This t' was the lot of the tribe of the*
17:15 t' get thee up to the wood country, and*
19:12 t' goeth out to Daberath, and goeth up*
29 t' the coast turneth to Ramah, and to*
34 And t' the coast turneth westward to*
20: 5 t' they shall not deliver the slayer up
6 t' shall the slayer return, and come227
21: 1 T' came near the heads of the fathers
22: 1 T' Joshua called the Reubenites, 227
7 unto their tents, t' he blessed them,*
19 t' pass ye over unto the land of the
21 T' the children of Reuben and the
23:16 t' shall the anger of the Lord be
24: 9 T' Balak the son of Zippor, king of
20 t' he will turn and do you hurt, and
J'g 2:18 judges, t' the Lord was with the judge,
3:23 T' Ehud went forth through the porch,
4: 8 If thou wilt go with me, t' I will go:
8 wilt not go with me, t' I will not go.*
21 T' Jael Heber's wife took a nail of the
5: 1 T' sang Deborah and Barak the son
8 new gods; t' was war in the gates: 227
11 t' shall the people of the Lord go down
13 T' he made him that remaineth 227
19 t' fought the kings of Canaan in "
22 T' were the horsehoofs broken by "
6:13 with us, why t' is all this befallen us?
17 t' shew me a sign that thou talkest
21 T' the angel of the Lord put forth the
21 T' the angel of the Lord departed out*
24 T' Gideon built an altar there unto
27 T' Gideon took ten men of his
30 T' the men of the city said unto Joash,
33 T' all the Midianites and the
37 t' shall I know that thou wilt save
7: 1 T' Jerubbaal, who is Gideon, and all
11 T' went he down with Phurah his
18 t' blow ye the trumpets also on every
24 T' all the men of Ephraim gathered*
8: 3 T' their anger was abated toward 227
7 t' I will tear your flesh with the thorns
18 T' said he unto Zebah and Zalmunna,
21 T' Zebah and Zalmunna said, Rise
22 T' the men of Israel said unto
9:12 T' said the trees unto the vine, Come*
14 T' said all the trees unto the bramble,
15 you, t' come and put your trust in my
19 If ye t' have dealt truly and sincerely
19 t' rejoice ye in Abimelech, and let
23 T' God sent an evil spirit between*
29 hand! T' would I remove Abimelech.
33 t' mayest thou do to them as thou
38 T' said Zebul unto him, Where is now
50 T' went Abimelech to Thebez, and
54 T' he called hastily unto the young
10:17 T' the children of Ammon were
11: 3 T' Jephthah fled from his brethren,
11 T' Jephthah went with the elders of
17 T' Israel sent messengers unto the
18 T' they went along through the
29 T' the Spirit of the Lord came upon
31 T' it shall be, that whatsoever
12: 3 t' are ye come up unto me this day,
4 T' Jephthah gathered together all the
6 T' said they unto him, Say now
6 T' they took him, and slew him at the
7 T' died Jephthah the Gileadite, and
10 T' died Ibzan, and was buried at*
13: 6 T' the woman came and told her
8 T' Manoah intreated the Lord, and
21 T' Manoah knew that he was an 227
14: 3 T' his father and his mother said
5 T' went Samson down, and his
12 t' I will give you thirty sheets and
13 t' shall ye give me thirty sheets and
15: 6 T' the Philistines said, Who hath
9 T' the Philistines went up, and
11 T' three thousand men of Judah went
16: 1 T' went Samson to Gaza, and saw*
7 t' shall I be weak, and be as another
8 T' the lords of the Philistines brought
11 t' shall I be weak, and be as another
17 t' my strength will go from me,
18 T' the lords of the Philistines came up
23 T' the lords of the Philistines *
31 T' his brethren and all the house of
17:13 T' said Micah, Now know I that the
18: 7 T' the five men departed, and came
14 T' answered the five men that went
18 T' said the priest unto them, What do*
19:26 T' came the woman in the dawning of
28 T' the man took her up upon an ass,
20: 1 T' all the children of Israel went out,
3 T' said the children of Israel, Tell us,*
26 T' all the children of Israel, and all
21:16 T' the elders of the congregation said,
19 T' they said, Behold, there is a feast*
21 t' come ye out of the vineyards,
Ru 1: 6 T' she arose with her daughters in
9 T' she kissed them; and they lifted
18 her, t' she left speaking unto her.*
21 why t' call ye me Naomi, seeing the*
2: 5 T' said Boaz unto his servant that
8 T' said Boaz unto Ruth, Hearest thou

Ru 2:10 T' she fell on her face, and bowed
13 T' she said, Let me find favour in thy
3: 1 T' Naomi her mother in law said unto*
13 t' will I do the part of a kinsman to
18 T' said she, Sit still, my daughter,
4: 1 T' went Boaz up to the gate, and sat*
4 redeem it, t' tell me, that I may know:
5 T' said Boaz, What day thou buyest
1Sa 1: 8 T' said Elkanah her husband to her,*
11 t' I will give him unto the Lord all the
17 T' Eli answered and said, Go in peace:
22 be weaned, and t' I will bring him,
2:16 t' take as much as thy soul desireth;
16 t' he would answer him, Nay; but
3:10 T' Samuel answered, Speak; for thy
16 T' Eli called Samuel, and said,
6: 3 t' ye shall be healed, and it shall be227
4 T' said they, What shall be the
6 t' do ye harden your hearts, as the
9 t' he hath done us this great evil:
9 t' we shall know that it is not his
7: 3 t' put away the strange gods and
4 T' the children of Israel did put away
12 T' Samuel took a stone, and set it
8: 4 T' all the elders of Israel gathered
9: 4 t' they passed through the land of
7 T' said Saul to his servant, But,
10 T' said Saul to his servant, Well said;
18 T' Saul drew near to Samuel in the
21 wherefore t' speakest thou so to me?
10: 1 T' Samuel took a vial of oil, and
2 t' thou shalt find two men by Rachel's
3 T' shalt thou go on forward from
11 t' the people said one to another,
25 T' Samuel told the people the manner
11: 1 T' Nahash the Ammonite came up,
3 t', if there be no man to save us, we
4 T' came the messengers to Gibeah of
14 T' said Samuel to the people, Come,
12: 8 t' the Lord sent Moses and Aaron,
14 t' shall both ye and also the king that*
15 t' shall the hand of the Lord be
21 t' should ye go after vain things,
13: 6 t' the people did hide themselves in
14: 8 T' said Jonathan, Behold, we will
10 Come up unto us; t' we will go up:
17 T' said Saul unto the people that were
28 T' answered one of the people, and
29 T' said Jonathan, My father hath
33 T' they told Saul, saying, Behold, the
36 T' said the priest, Let us draw near
40 T' said he unto all Israel, Be ye on
43 T' Saul said to Jonathan, Tell me
46 T' Saul went up from following the
15:10 T' came the word of the Lord unto
14 What meaneth t' this bleating of the
16 T' Samuel said unto Saul, Stay, and
19 Wherefore t' didst thou not obey the
30 T' he said, I have sinned: yet honour
32 T' said Samuel, Bring ye hither to
34 T' Samuel went to Ramah; and Saul
16: 8 T' Jesse called Abinadab, and made
9 T' Jesse made Shammah to pass by.
13 T' Samuel took the horn of oil, and
18 T' answered one of the servants, and
17: 9 kill me, t' will we be your servants:
9 t' shall ye be our servants, and serve
45 T' said David to the Philistine, Thou
18: 3 T' Jonathan and David made a
30 T' the princes of the Philistines went
19: 5 wherefore t' wilt thou sin against
22 T' went he also to Ramah, and came
20: 4 T' said Jonathan unto David,
6 t' say, David earnestly asked leave of
7 t' be sure that evil is determined by
9 upon thee, t' would not I tell it thee?
10 T' said David to Jonathan, Who
12 I t' send not unto thee, and shew it 227
13 t' I will shew it thee, and send thee*
18 T' Jonathan said to David, To
19 t' thou shalt go down quickly, and*
21 t' come thou: for there is peace to*
30 T' Saul's anger was kindled against
21: 1 T' came David to Nob to Ahimelech
14 T' said Achish unto his servants, Lo,
14 wherefore t' have ye brought him to
22: 5 T' David departed, and came into the
7 T' Saul said unto his servants that*
9 T' answered Doeg the Edomite,
11 T' the king sent to call Ahimelech the
14 T' Ahimelech answered the king, and
15 I t' begin to enquire of God for 3117
23: 1 T' they told David, saying, Behold,*
3 how much more t' if we come to 3588
4 T' David enquired of the Lord yet
10 T' said David, O Lord God of Israel,
12 T' said David, Will the men of Keilah
13 T' David and his men, which were
19 T' came up the Ziphites to Saul to
24: 2 T' Saul took three thousand chosen
4 T' David arose, and cut off the skirt
25:11 Shall I t' take my bread, and my
18 T' Abigail made haste, and took two
31 my lord, t' remember thine handmaid.
26: 2 T' Saul arose, and went down to the
6 T' answered David and said to
8 T' said Abishai to David, God hath
13 T' David went over to the other side,
14 T' Abner answered and said, Who art
15 wherefore t' hast thou not kept thy
21 T' said Saul, I have sinned: return,
25 T' Saul said to David, Blessed be
27: 6 T' Achish gave him Ziklag that day:
28: 7 T' said Saul unto his servants, Seek
9 wherefore t' layest thou a snare for
11 T' said the woman, Whom shall I

1Sa 28:16 T· said Samuel, Wherefore *
16 Wherefore t· dost thou ask of me,
20 T· Saul fell straightway all along on
25 T· they rose up, and went away that
29: 3 T· said the princes of the Philistines,
6 T· Achish called David, and said unto
30: 4 T· David and the people that were
22 T· answered all the wicked men and
23 T· said David, Ye shall not do so, my
31: 4 T· said Saul unto his armourbearer,
2Sa 1:11 T· David took hold on his clothes,
2:15 T· there arose and went over by
20 T· Abner looked behind him, and
22 how t· should I hold up my face to
26 T· Abner called to Joab, and said,
27 surely t· in the morning the people
3: 8 T· was Abner very wroth for the
16 T· said Abner unto him, Go, return,
18 Now t· do it: for the Lord hath
24 T· Joab came to the king, and said,
5: 1 T· came all the tribes of Israel to
24 that t· thou shalt bestir thyself: 227
24 t· shall the Lord go out before thee, "
6:20 T· David returned to bless his
7:18 T· went king David in, and sat before
8: 6 T· David put garrisons in Syria of
10 T· Toi sent Joram his son unto king
9: 5 T· king David sent, and fetched him
9 T· the king called to Ziba, Saul's
11 T· said Ziba unto the king, According
10: 2 T· said David, I will shew kindness*
5 your beards be grown, and t· return,
11 strong for me, t· thou shalt help me:
11 for thee, t· I will come and help thee.
14 t· fled they also before Abishai, and*
11:10 why t· didst thou not go down unto*
11 shall I t· go into mine house, to eat
18 T· Joab sent and told David all the
21 t· say thou, Thy servant Uriah the
25 T· David said unto the messenger,
12:18 how will he t· vex himself, if we tell
20 T· David arose from the earth, and
20 t· he came to his own house; and
21 T· said his servants unto him, What
13: 7 T· David sent home to Tamar, saying,
15 T· Amnon hated her exceedingly: so
17 T· he called his servant that
18 T· his servant brought her out, and
26 T· said Absalom, If not, I pray thee,
28 Smite Amnon; t· kill him, fear not:
29 T· all the king's sons arose, and
31 T· the king arose, and tare his
14:11 T· said she, I pray thee, let the king
12 T· the woman said, Let thine
13 Wherefore t· hast thou thought
17 T· thine handmaid said, The word of
18 T· the king answered and said unto
31 T· Joab arose, and came to Absalom
15: 2 t· Absalom called unto him, and said,
8 to Jerusalem, t· I will serve the Lord.
10 t· ye shall say, Absalom reigneth in
19 T· said the king to Ittai the Gittite,
34 t· mayest thou for me defeat the
16: 4 T· said the king to Ziba, Behold,
9 T· said Abishai the son of Zeruiah,
10 Who shall t· say, Wherefore hast thou
20 T· said Absalom to Ahithophel, Give
21 t· shall the hands of all that are with
17: 5 T· said Absalom, Call now Hushai the
13 t· shall all Israel bring ropes to that
15 T· said Hushai unto Zadok and to
22 T· David arose, and all the people that
24 T· David came to Mahanaim. And
18:14 T· said Joab, I may not tarry thus
19 T· said Ahimaaz the son of Zadok,
21 T· said Joab to Cushi, Go tell the
22 T· said Ahimaaz the son of Zadok
23 T· Ahimaaz ran by the way of the
19: 6 this day, t· it had pleased thee well.227
8 T· the king arose, and sat in the gate.
12 wherefore t· are ye the last to bring
35 wherefore t· should thy servant be
40 T· the king went on to Gilgal, and*
42 wherefore t· be ye angry for this
43 why t· did ye despise us, that our
20: 4 T· said the king to Amasa, Assemble
16 T· cried a wise woman out of the
17 T· she said unto him, Hear the words
18 T· she spake, saying, They were wont
22 T· the woman went unto all the
21: 1 T· there was a famine in the days of*
17 T· the men of David sware unto 227
18 t· Sibbechai the Hushathite slew "
22: 8 T· the earth shook and trembled; the
43 T· did I beat them as small as the
23:14 And David was t· in an hold, and 227
14 the Philistines was t· in Beth-lehem.
1Ki 1: 5 T· Adonijah the son of Haggith
13 throne? why t· doth Adonijah reign?
28 T· king David answered and said,
31 T· Bath-sheba bowed with her face to
35 T· ye shall come up after him, that he
2:12 T· sat Solomon upon the throne of*
20 T· she said, I desire one small petition
23 T· king Solomon sware by the Lord,
28 T· tidings came to Joab: for Joab had*
29 T· Solomon sent Benaiah the son of
3:14 did walk, t· I will lengthen thy days.
16 T· came there two women, that 227
23 T· said the king, The one saith, This
26 T· spake the woman whose the living
27 T· the king answered and said, Give
6:10 t· he built chambers against all the*
12 t· will I perform my word with thee,
7: 7 T· he made a porch for the throne*
38 T· made he ten lavers of brass: one*

1Ki 8: 1 T· Solomon assembled the elders 227
12 T· spake Solomon, The Lord said "
32 T· hear thou in heaven, and do, and
34, 36 T· hear thou in heaven, and
39 T· hear thou in heaven thy
45 T· hear thou in heaven their prayer
49 T· hear thou their prayer and their
9: 5 T· I will establish the throne of thy
7 T· will I cut off Israel out of the land
11 that t· king Solomon gave Hiram 227
24 built for her: t· did he build Millo. "
11: 7 T· did Solomon build an high place
22 T· Pharaoh said unto him, But what
12: 5 for three days, t· come again to me.
7 t· they will be thy servants for ever.
18 T· king Rehoboam sent Adoram, who
25 T· Jeroboam built Shechem in mount
27 t· shall the heart of this people turn
13:15 T· he said unto him, Come home with
31 t· bury me in the sepulchre wherein
15:18 T· Asa took all the silver and the gold
22 T· king Asa made a proclamation
16: 1 T· the word of the Lord came to Jehu*
21 T· were the people of Israel 227
18:21 follow him: but if Baal, t· follow him.
22 T· said Elijah unto the people, I, even
38 T· the fire of the Lord fell, and
19: 2 T· Jezebel sent a messenger unto
5 behold, t· an angel touched him, and*
20 my mother, and t· I will follow thee.
21 T· he arose, and went after Elijah,
20: 7 T· the king of Israel called all the
14 T· he said, Who shall order the
15 T· he numbered the young men of the
33 T· he said, Go ye, bring him.
33 T· Ben-hadad came forth to him; and
34 T· said Ahab, I will send thee away*
36 T· said he unto him, Because thou
37 T· he found another man, and said,
39 t· shall thy life be for his life, or else
21:10 t· carry him out, and stone him, that
13 T· they carried him forth out of the
14 T· they sent to Jezebel, saying,
22: 6 T· the king of Israel gathered the
9 T· the king of Israel called an officer,
47 There was t· no king in Edom: a *
49 T· said Ahaziah the son of Ahab 227
2Ki 1: 1 T· Moab rebelled against Israel after*
9 T· the king sent unto him a captain of
10 t· let fire come down from heaven,*
3:27 T· he took his eldest son that should
4: 3 T· he said, Go, borrow thee vessels
7 T· she came and told the man of God.
14 he said, What t· is to be done for her?
20 sat on her knees till noon, and t· died.
24 T· she saddled an ass, and said to her
28 T· she said, Did I desire a son of my
29 T· he said to Gehazi, Gird up thy
35 T· he returned, and walked in the
37 T· she went in, and fell at his feet,
41 But he said, T· bring meal. And he
5:13 how much rather t·, when he saith to
14 T· went he down, and dipped himself
17 Shall there not t·, I pray thee, be *
6: 8 T· the king of Syria warred against*
31 T· he said, God do so and more also to
7: 1 T· Elisha said, Hear ye the word of*
2 T· a lord on whose hand the king
4 t· the famine is in the city, and we
9 T· they said one to another, We do
8: 1 T· spake Elisha unto the woman,*
16 Jehoshaphat being t· king of Judah,
22 T· Libnah revolted at the same 227
9: 3 T· take the box of oil, and pour it on
3 T· open the door, and flee, and tarry
11 T· Jehu came forth to the servants of
13 T· they hasted, and took every man
15 t· let none go forth nor escape out of
19 T· he sent out a second on horseback,
25 T· said Jehu to Bidkar his captain,
10: 4 before him: how t· shall we stand?
6 T· he wrote a letter the second time
12: 7 T· king Jehoash called for Jehoiada
17 T· Hazael king of Syria went up, 227
13:17 T· Elisha said, Shoot. And he shot.
19 t· hadst thou smitten Syria till thou227
14: 8 T· Amaziah sent messengers to "
15:16 T· Menahem smote Tiphsah, and "
16: 5 T· Rezin king of Syria, and Pekah "
17: 5 T· the king of Assyria came up
27 T· the king of Assyria commanded,
28 T· one of the priests whom they had*
18:24 How t· wilt thou turn away the face of
26 T· said Eliakim the son of Hilkiah,
28 T· Rab-shakeh stood and cried with a
31 t· eat ye every man of his own vine,*
37 T· came Eliakim the son of Hilkiah,
19:20 T· Isaiah the son of Amoz sent to
20: 2 T· he turned his face to the wall, and
14 T· came Isaiah the prophet unto king
19 T· said Hezekiah unto Isaiah, Good is
23:17 T· he said, What title is that that I see?
24: 1 t· he turned and rebelled against him.
1Ch 1:29 t· Kedar, and Adbeel, and Mibsam,
2:24 t· Abiah Hezron's wife bare him
6:32 t· they waited on their office according*
9:36 And his firstborn son Abdon, t· Zur,*
10: 4 T· said Saul to his armourbearer,
7 t· they forsook their cities, and fled:*
11: 1 T· all Israel gathered themselves to
16 And David was t· in the hold, and 227
16 garrison was t· at Beth-lehem. "
12: 3 The chief was Ahiezer, t· Joash, the
18 T· the spirit came upon Amasai, who
18 T· David received them, and made
14:11 T· David said, God hath broken in*

1Ch 14:15 that t· thou shalt go out to battle: 227
15: 2 T· David said, None ought to carry "
16: 7 T· on that day David delivered first "
33 T· shall the trees of the wood sing "
17: 2 T· Nathan said unto David, Do all*
18: 6 T· David put garrisons in
19: 5 T· there went certain, and told David
5 your beards be grown, and t· return.
12 strong for me, t· thou shalt help me:
12 strong for thee, t· I will help thee.
15 city. T· Joab came to Jerusalem.
21: 3 why t· doth my lord require this *
16 T· David and the elders of Israel, who
18 T· the angel of the Lord commanded
22 T· David said to Ornan, Grant me the
28 the Jebusite, t· he sacrificed there.
22: 1 T· David said, This is the house of
6 T· he called for Solomon his son, and
13 T· shalt thou prosper, if thou 227
26:14 T· for Zechariah his son, a wise
28: 2 T· David the king stood up upon his
11 T· David gave to Solomon his son the
29: 5 And who t· is willing to consecrate his
6 T· the chief of the fathers and princes
9 T· the people rejoiced, for that they
23 T· Solomon sat on the throne of the
2Ch 1: 2 T· Solomon spake unto all Israel, to*
13 T· Solomon came from his journey to*
2: 6 who am I t·, that I should build him a
11 T· Huram the king of Tyre answered
3: 1 T· Solomon began to build the house
5: 2 T· Solomon assembled the elders 227
11 and did not t· wait by course: *
13 t· the house was filled with a cloud,
6: 1 T· said Solomon, The Lord hath 227
17 Now t·, O Lord God of Israel, let thy*
23 T· hear thou from heaven, and do,
25 T· hear thou from the heavens, and
27 T· hear thou from heaven, and forgive
29 T· what prayer or what supplication*
30 T· hear thou from heaven thy
33 T· hear thou from the heavens, even
35 T· hear thou from the heavens their
39 T· hear thou from the heavens, even
7: 4 T· the king and all the people offered
14 t· will I hear from heaven, and will
18 T· will I stablish the throne of thy
20 T· will I pluck them up by the roots
8:12 T· Solomon offered burnt offerings227
17 T· went Solomon to Ezion-geber, * "
10:18 T· king Rehoboam sent Hadoram that
12: 5 T· came Shemaiah the prophet to*
13:15 T· the men of Judah gave a shout:
14:10 T· Asa went out against him, and
16: 2 T· Asa brought out silver and gold
6 T· Asa the king took all Judah; and
10 T· Asa was wroth with the seer, and
18:16 T· he said, I did see all Israel *
20 T· there came out a spirit, and stood*
23 T· Zedekiah the son of Chenaanah
25 T· the king of Israel said, Take ye*
27 t· hath not the Lord spoken by me.*
20: 2 T· there came some that told
9 affliction, t· thou wilt hear and help.*
14 T· upon Jahaziel the son of
27 T· they returned, every man of Judah
37 T· Eliezer the son of Dodavah of
21: 9 T· Jehoram went forth with his
23:11 T· they brought out the king's son,
13 T· Athaliah rent her clothes, and said,
14 T· Jehoiada the priest brought out*
17 T· all the people went to the house of*
24:17 T· the king hearkened unto them.
25:10 T· Amaziah separated them, to wit,
16 T· the prophet forbare, and said, I
17 T· Amaziah king of Judah took
26: 1 T· all the people of Judah took *
19 T· Uzziah was wroth, and had a
28:12 T· certain of the heads of the children
15 brethren: t· they returned to Samaria.
29:12 T· the Levites arose, Mahath the son
18 T· they went in to Hezekiah the king,
20 T· Hezekiah the king rose early, and
31 T· Hezekiah answered and said, Now
30:15 T· they killed the passover on the
27 T· the priests the Levites arose and
31: 1 T· all the children of Israel returned,
9 T· Hezekiah questioned with the
11 T· Hezekiah commanded to prepare
32:18 T· they cried with a loud voice in the*
33:13 T· Manasseh knew that the Lord he
34:18 T· Shaphan the scribe told the king,*
29 T· the king sent and gathered
36: 1 T· the people of the land took
Ezr 1: 5 T· rose up the chief of the fathers of
3: 2 T· stood up Jeshua the son of
9 T· stood Jeshua with his sons and his
4: 2 T· they came to Zerubbabel, and to
4 T· the people of the land weakened
9 T· wrote Rehum the chancellor, 116
13 t· will they not pay toll, tribute, and
17 T· sent the king an answer unto
24 T· ceased the work of the house of 116
5: 1 T· the prophets, Haggai the prophet,*
2 T· rose up Zerubbabel the son of 116
4 T· said we unto them after this "
5 t· they returned answer by letter "
9 T· asked we those elders, and said "
16 T· came the same Sheshbazzar, and"
6: 1 T· Darius the king made a decree, "
13 T· Tatnai, governor on this side the "
8:16 T· sent I for Eliezer, for Ariel, for
21 T· I proclaimed a fast there, at the
24 T· I separated twelve of the chief of
31 T· we departed from the river of
9: 4 T· were assembled unto me every one

Ezr 10: 5 T' arose Ezra, and made the chief
6 T' Ezra rose up from before the
9 T' all the men of Judah and
12 T' all the congregation answered and
Ne 2: 2 of heart. T' I was very sore afraid.
4 T' the king said unto me, For what
9 T' I came to the governors beyond the
14 T' I went on to the gate of the
15 T' went I up in the night by the
17 T' said I unto them, Ye see the
18 T' I told them of the hand of my God*
20 T' answered I them, and said unto
3: 1 T' Eliashib the high priest rose up
4: 7 to be stopped, t' they were very wroth,
5: 7 T' I consulted with myself, and I
8 T' held they their peace, and found
12 T' said they, We will restore them, and
12 T' I called the priests, and took an
6: 5 T' sent Sanballat his servant unto me
8 T' I sent unto him, saying, There are
8: 10 T' he said unto them, Go your way,
9: 4 T' stood up upon the stairs, of the
5 T' the Levites, Jeshua, and Kadmiel,
12: 31 T' I brought up the princes of Judah
13: 9 T' I commanded, and they cleansed
11 T' contended I with the rulers, and
12 T' brought all Judah the tithe of the
17 T' I contended with the nobles of
21 T' I testified against them, and said
27 Shall we t' hearken unto you to do all
Es 1: 13 T' the king said to the wise men,
2: 2 T' said the king's servants that
13 T' thus came every maiden unto the
18 T' the king made a great feast unto
19 t' Mordecai sat in the king's gate.
3: 3 T' the king's servants, which were in
5 reverence, t' was Haman full of wrath.
12 T' were the king's scribes called on
4: 4 T' was the queen exceedingly grieved;*
5 T' called Esther for Hatach, one of the
13 T' Mordecai commanded to answer
14 t' shall there enlargement and
15 T' Esther bade them return Mordecai
5: 3 T' said the king unto her, What wilt
5 T' the king said, Cause Haman to
7 T' answered Esther, and said, My
9 T' went Haman forth that day joyful
14 T' said Zeresh his wife and all his
14 t' go thou in merrily with the king
6: 3 T' said the king's servants that
10 T' the king said to Haman, Make
11 T' took Haman the apparel and the
13 T' said his wise men and Zeresh his
7: 3 T' Esther the queen answered and
5 T' the king Ahasuerus answered and
6 T' Haman was afraid before the king
8 T' the king returned out of the palace
8 T' said the king, Will he force the
9 T' the king said, Hang him thereon.*
10 T' was the king's wrath pacified.
8: 4 T' the king held out the golden
7 T' the king Ahasuerus said unto
9 T' were the king's scribes called at
9: 13 T' said Esther, If it please the king,
29 T' Esther the queen, the daughter of
Job 1: 7, 9 T' Satan answered the Lord, and
20 T' Job arose, and rent his mantle, and
2: 9 T' said his wife unto him, Dost thou
3: 13 have slept: t' had I been at rest. 227
4: 1 T' Eliphaz the Temanite answered
15 T' a spirit passed before my face; the
6: 10 T' should I yet have comfort; yea, I‡
7: 14 T' thou scarest me with dreams, and
8: 1 T' answered Bildad the Shuhite, and
18 t' it shall deny him, saying, I have not
9: 1 T' Job answered and said,
29 If I be wicked, why t' labour I in vain?
35 T' would I speak, and not fear him;
10: 14 If I sin, t' thou markest me, and thou
18 Wherefore t' hast thou brought me
20 cease t', and let me alone, that I may
11: 1 T' answered Zophar the Naamathite,
10 or gather together, t' who can hinder
11 also; will he not t' consider it? *
15 For t' shalt thou lift up thy face 227
13: 20 t' will I not hide myself from thee. "
22 T' call thou, and I will answer: or let
15: 1 T' answered Eliphaz the Temanite,
16: 1 T' Job answered and said,
22 t' I shall go the way whence I shall*
18: 1 T' answered Bildad the Shuhite, and
19: 1 T' Job answered and said,
20: 1 T' answered Zophar the Naamathite,
21: 34 How t' comfort ye me in vain, seeing
22: 1 T' Eliphaz the Temanite answered
24 T' shalt thou lay up gold as dust, and*
26 For t' shalt thou have thy delight 227
29 t' thou shalt say, There is lifting up;*
23: 1 T' Job answered and said,
25: 1 T' answered Bildad the Shuhite, and
4 How t' can man be justified with God?
27: 12 it; why t' are ye thus altogether vain?
28: 20 Whence t' cometh wisdom? and where
27 T' did he see it, and declare it; he 227
29: 11 the ear heard me, t' it blessed me;
18 T' I said, I shall die in my nest, and I
30: 26 looked for good, t' evil came unto me:
31: 1 why t' should I think upon a maid?
8 T' let me sow, and let another eat;
10 T' let my wife grind unto another, and
14 What t' shall I do when God riseth up?
22 T' let mine arm fall from my shoulder
32: 2 T' was kindled the wrath of Elihu the
5 three men, t' his wrath was kindled.*
33: 16 T' he openeth the ears of men, and 227
24 T' he is gracious unto him, and saith,

Job 34: 29 quietness, who t' can make trouble?
29 hideth his face, who t' can behold him?
36: 9 T' he sheweth them their work, and
18 t' a great ransom cannot deliver thee.*
37: 8 T' the beasts go into dens, and
38: 1 T' the Lord answered Job out of the
21 thou it, because thou wast t' born? 227
40: 3 T' Job answered the Lord, and said,
6 T' answered the Lord unto Job out of
14 T' will I also confess unto thee that
41: 10 up: who t' is able to stand before me?
42: 1 T' Job answered the Lord, and said,
11 T' came there unto him all his
Ps 2: 5 T' shall he speak unto them in his 227
18: 7 T' the earth shook and trembled; the
15 T' the channels of waters were seen,
42 T' did I beat them small as the dust
19: 13 t' shall I be upright, and I shall be 227
27: 10 forsake me, t' the Lord will take me*
39: 3 burned: t' spake I with my tongue,
40: 7 T' said I, Lo, I come: in the volume 227
43: 4 T' will I go unto the altar of God,
50: 18 a thief, t' thou consentedst with him, *
51: 13 T' will I teach transgressors thy ways;
19 T' shalt thou be pleased with the 227
19 t' shall they offer bullocks upon "
55: 6 for t' would I fly away, and be at rest.
7 Lo, t' would I wander far off, and
12 me; t' I could have borne it:
12 t' I would have hid myself from him:
56: 9 t' shall mine enemies turn back: 227
67: 6 T' shall the earth yield her increase;*
69: 4 t' I restored that which I took not 227
73: 17 of God; t' understood I their end.*
78: 34 he slew them, t' they sought him: and
65 T' the Lord awaked as one out of
80: 12 Why hast thou t' broken down her*
89: 19 T' thou spakest in vision to thy 227
32 T' will I visit their transgression with
96: 12 t' shall all the trees of the wood 227
106: 12 T' believed they his words; they sang
30 T' stood up Phinehas, and executed
107: 6, 13 T' they cried unto the Lord in
19, 28 T' they cry unto the Lord in
30 T' are they glad because they be quiet;
116: 4 T' called I upon the name of the Lord;
119: 6 T' shall I not be ashamed, when I 227
92 I should t' have perished in mine
124: 3 T' they had swallowed us up quick, 233
4 T' the waters had overwhelmed us, "
5 T' the proud waters had gone over "
126: 2 T' was our mouth filled with 227
2 t' said they among the heathen,
142: 3 within me, t' thou knewest my path.*
Pr 1: 28 T' shall they call upon me, but I 227
2: 5 T' shalt thou understand the fear "
9 T' shalt thou understand "
3: 23 T' shalt thou walk in thy way safely, "
8: 30 T' I was by him, as one brought up
11: 2 When pride cometh, t' cometh shame:
15: 11 how much more t' the hearts of the
18: 3 cometh, t' cometh also contempt,*
20: 14 he is gone his way, t' he boasteth. 227
24 how can a man t' understand his own
24: 14 found it, t' there shall be a reward,
32 T' I saw, and considered it well: I
Ec 2: 11 T' I looked on all the works that my
13 T' I saw that wisdom excelleth folly,
15 T' said I in my heart, As it happeneth
15 to me; and why was I t' more wise? 227
15 T' I said in my heart, that this also is
4: 7 T' I returned, and I saw vanity under
11 if two lie together, t' they have heat:
8: 15 T' I commended mirth, because a man
17 T' I beheld all the work of God, that a
9: 16 T' said I, Wisdom is better than
10: 10 edge, t' must he put to more strength:
12: 7 T' shall the dust return to the earth*
Ca 8: 10 t' was I in his eyes as one that found 227
Isa 5: 17 T' shall the lambs feed after their
6: 5 T' said I, Woe is me! for I am undone;
6 T' flew one of the seraphims unto me,
8 us? T' said I, Here am I; send me.
11 T' said I, Lord, how long? And he
7: 3 T' said the Lord unto Isaiah, Go forth
8: 3 T' said the Lord to me, Call his name
14: 25 t' shall his yoke depart from off them,
32 shall one t' answer the messengers of
24: 23 T' the moon shall be confounded, and
28: 18 t' ye shall be trodden down by it.
30: 23 T' shall he give the rain of thy seed,*
31: 8 T' shall the Assyrian fall with the
32: 16 T' judgment shall dwell in the
33: 23 t' is the prey of a great spoil 227
35: 5 T' the eyes of the blind shall be "
6 T' shall the lame man leap as an "
36: 3 T' came forth unto him Eliakim,
9 How t' wilt thou turn away the face of
11 T' said Eliakim and Shebna and Joah
13 T' Rabshakeh stood, and cried with a
22 T' came Eliakim, the son of Hilkiah,
37: 21 T' Isaiah the son of Amoz sent unto
36 T' the angel of the Lord went forth,*
38: 2 T' Hezekiah turned his face toward
4 T' came the word of the Lord to
39: 3 T' came Isaiah the prophet unto king
4 T' said he, What have they seen in
5 T' said Isaiah to Hezekiah, Hear the
8 T' said Hezekiah to Isaiah, Good is
40: 18 To whom t' will ye liken God? or what
25 To whom t' will ye liken me, or shall I
41: 1 them come near; t' let them speak: 227
44: 15 T' shall it be for a man to burn: for he
48: 18 t' had thy peace been as a river, and
49: 4 T' I said, I have laboured in vain, I*
21 T' shalt thou say in thine heart, Who

Isa 58: 8 T' shall thy light break forth as 227
9 T' shalt thou call, and the Lord "
10 t' shall thy light rise in obscurity, and
14 T' shalt thou delight thyself in the 227
60: 5 T' thou shalt see, and flow together, "
63: 11 T' he remembered the days of old,
66: 12 t' shall ye suck, ye shall be borne*
Jer 1: 4 T' the word of the Lord came unto*
6 T' said I, Ah, Lord God! behold, I
9 T' the Lord put forth his hand, and
12 T' said the Lord unto me, Thou hast
14 T' the Lord said unto me, Out of the
2: 21 how t' art thou turned into the
4: 1 of my sight, t' shalt thou not remove.
10 T' said I, Ah, Lord God! surely thou
5: 7 to the full, they t' committed adultery,*
19 t' shalt thou answer them, Like as ye
7: 7 T' will I cause you to dwell in this
34 T' will I cause to cease from the cities
8: 5 Why t' is this people of Jerusalem
22 why t' is not the health of the 3588
11: 5 T' answered I, and said, So be it, O
6 T' the Lord said unto me, Proclaim all*
12 T' shall the cities of Judah and
15 thou doest evil, t' thou rejoicest. 227
18 t' thou shewedst me their doings. "
12: 5 t' how canst thou contend with horses?
5 t' how wilt thou do in the swelling of*
16 t' shall they be built in the midst of my
13: 7 T' I went to Euphrates, and digged,
8 T' the word of the Lord came unto
13 T' shalt thou say unto them, Thus
23 T' may ye also do good, that are
14: 11 T' said the Lord unto me, Pray not*
13 T' said I, Ah, Lord God! behold, the
14 T' the Lord said unto me, The
18 t' behold the slain with the sword!
18 t' behold them that are sick with
15: 1 T' said the Lord unto me, Though
2 t' thou shalt tell them, Thus saith the
19 thou return, t' will I bring thee again,
16: 11 T' shalt thou say unto them, Because
17: 25 T' shall there enter into the gates of
18: 3 T' I went down to the potter's house,
5 T' the word of the Lord came to me,
10 t' I will repent of the good, wherewith
18 T' said they, Come, and let us devise
19: 10 T' shalt thou break the bottle in the
14 T' came Jeremiah from Tophet,
20: 2 T' Pashur smote Jeremiah the
3 T' said Jeremiah unto him, The Lord
9 T' I said, I will not mention of him,*
21: 3 T' said Jeremiah unto them, Thus
22: 4 t' shall there enter in by the gates of
9 T' they shall answer, Because they
15 justice, and t' it was well with him? 227
16 and needy; t' it was well with him: "
22 surely t' shalt thou be ashamed and "
23: 22 t' they should have turned them from*
33 thou shalt t' say unto them, What
24: 3 T' said the Lord unto me, What seest
25: 17 T' took I the cup at the Lord's hand,
28 t' shalt thou say unto them, Thus
26: 6 T' will I make this house like Shiloh,
10 t' they came up from the king's house*
11 T' spake the priests and the prophets
12 T' spake Jeremiah unto all the
16 T' said the princes and all the people
17 T' rose up certain of the elders of the
27: 7 t' many nations and great kings shall
22 t' will I bring them up, and restore
28: 5 T' the prophet Jeremiah said unto the
9 t' shall the prophet be known, that the
10 T' Hananiah the prophet took the
12 T' the word of the Lord came unto
15 T' said the prophet Jeremiah unto
29: 12 T' shall ye call upon me, and ye shall*
30 T' came the word of the Lord unto
31: 13 T' shall the virgin rejoice in the
36 t' the seed of Israel also shall cease
32: 2 For t' the king of Babylon's army * 227
8 T' I knew that this was the word of
26 T' came the word of the Lord unto
33: 21 T' may also my covenant be broken
26 T' will I cast away the seed of 1571
34: 6 T' Jeremiah the prophet spake all
10 more, t' they obeyed, and let them go.*
35: 3 T' I took Jaazaniah the son of
12 T' came the word of the Lord unto
36: 4 T' Jeremiah called Baruch the son of
10 T' read Baruch in the book the words
12 T' he went down into the king's house,*
13 T' Michaiah declared unto them all
18 T' Baruch answered them, He
19 T' said the princes unto Baruch, Go,
27 T' the word of the Lord came to
32 T' took Jeremiah another roll, and
37: 5 T' Pharaoh's army was come forth out*
6 T' came the word of the Lord unto the
12 T' Jeremiah went forth out of
14 T' said Jeremiah, It is false; I fall not
17 T' Zedekiah the king sent, and took
21 T' Zedekiah the king commanded
38: 1 T' Shephatiah the son of Mattan, and*
5 T' Zedekiah the king said, Behold, he*
6 T' took they Jeremiah, and cast him
7 king t' sitting in the gate of Benjamin;
10 T' the king commanded Ebed-melech
14 T' Zedekiah the king sent, and took
15 T' Jeremiah said unto Zedekiah, If I
17 T' said Jeremiah unto Zedekiah, Thus
17 t' thy soul shall live, and this city shall
18 t' shall this city be given into the hand
24 T' said Zedekiah unto Jeremiah, Let
26 T' thou shalt say unto them, I
27 T' came all the princes unto Jeremiah,

Jer 39: 4 t' they fled, and went forth out of the
6 T' the king of Babylon slew the sons
9 T' Nebuzar-adan the captain of the
40: 6 T' went Jeremiah unto Gedaliah the
8 T' they came to Gedaliah to Mizpah,
15 T' Johanan the son of Kareah spake
41: 2 T' arose Ishmael the son of Nethaniah,
10 T' Ishmael carried away captive all
12 T' they took all the men, and went to
13 that were with him, t' they were glad.
16 T' took Johanan the son of Kareah,
42: 1 T' all the captains of the forces, and
4 T' Jeremiah the prophet said unto
5 T' they said to Jeremiah, The Lord
8 T' called he Johanan the son of
10 abide in this land, t' will I build you,
16 T' it shall come to pass, that the
43: 2 T' spake Azariah the son of Hoshaiah,
8 T' came the word of the Lord unto
44: 15 T' all the men which knew that their
17 t' had we plenty of victuals, and were
20 T' Jeremiah said unto all the people,
47: 2 t' the men shall cry, and all the *
49: 1 why t' doth their king inherit Gad,
2 t' shall Israel be heir unto them that
51: 48 T' the heaven and the earth, and all
62 T' shalt thou say, O Lord, thou hast*
52: 7 T' the city was broken up, and all
9 T' they took the king, and carried
11 T' he put out the eyes of Zedekiah;*
15 T' Nebuzar-adan the captain of the
La 3: 54 mine head; t' I said, I am cut off.*
Eze 3: 3 T' did I eat it; and it was in my
12 T' the spirit took me up, and I heard
15 T' I came to them of the captivity at
23 T' I arose, and went forth into the
24 T' the spirit entered into me, and set
4: 14 T' said I, Ah Lord God! behold, my
15 T' he said unto me, Lo, I have given
5: 1 t' take thee balances to weigh, and
4 T' take of them again, and cast them*
6: 13 T' shall ye know that I am the Lord.*
7: 26 t' shall they seek a vision of the *
8: 2 T' I beheld, and lo a likeness as the
5, 8, 12 T' said he unto me, Son of man,
14 T' he brought me to the door of the
15 T' said he unto me, Hast thou seen
17 T' he said unto me, Hast thou seen
9: 6 T' they began at the ancient men
9 T' said he unto me, The iniquity of
10: 1 T' I looked, and, behold, in the
4 T' the glory of the Lord went up from*
6 t' he went in, and stood beside the*
18 T' the glory of the Lord departed from*
11: 2 T' said he unto me, Son of man, these*
13 T' fell I down upon my face, and cried
22 T' did the cherubims lift up their
25 T' I spake unto them of the captivity
12: 4 T' shalt thou bring forth thy stuff by*
14: 1 T' came certain of the elders of Israel
13 t' will I stretch out mine hand upon it,*
16: 9 T' washed I thee with water; yea, I
53 t' will I bring again the captivity of*
55 t' thou and thy daughters shall return*
61 T' thou shalt remember thy ways, and
18: 13 shall he t' live? he shall not live: he
19: 5 t' she took another of her whelps, and
8 T' the nations set against him on
20: 2 T' came the word of the Lord unto*
7 T' said I unto them, Cast ye away*
8 t' I said, I will pour out my fury upon
13, 21 t' I said, I would pour out my fury
28 t' they saw every high hill, and all the
29 T' I said unto them, What is the high
49 T' said I, Ah Lord God! they say of
21: 4 Seeing t' that I will cut off from thee
10 glitter: should we t' make mirth? 176
22: 3 T' say thou, Thus saith the Lord *
23: 13 T' I saw that she was defiled, that*
18 t' my mind was alienated from her,
39 t' they came the same day into my
43 T' said I unto her that was old in
24: 11 T' set it empty upon the coals thereof,
20 T' I answered them, The word of the
26: 16 T' all the princes of the sea shall come
28: 25 t' shall they dwell in their land that I
32: 4 T' will I leave thee upon the land,*
14 T' will I make their waters deep, 227
15 t' shall they know that I am the Lord.
33: 4 T' whosoever heareth the sound of the
10 away in them, how should we t' live?
23 T' the word of the Lord came unto me,*
29 T' shall they know that I am the Lord,
33 t' shall they know that a prophet hath
36: 25 T' will I sprinkle clean water upon*
31 T' shall ye remember your own evil
36 T' the heathen that are left round
37: 9 T' said he unto me, Prophesy unto the
11 T' he said unto me, Son of man, these
14 t' shall ye know that I the Lord have*
16 t' take another stick, and write upon
39: 15 t' shall he set up a sign by it, till the
28 T' shall they know that I am the Lord*
40: 6 T' came he unto the gate which looketh
9 T' measured he the porch of the gate,
13 He measured t' the gate from the roof*
17 T' brought he me into the outward
19 T' he measured the breadth from the
41: 3 T' went he inward, and measured the
42: 1 T' he brought me forth into the utter
13 T' said he unto me, The north
14 t' shall they not go out of the holy
44: 1 T' he brought me back the way of the
2 T' said the Lord unto me; This gate*
4 T' brought he me the way of the
46: 2 t' he shall go forth; but the gate shall

Eze 46: 12 one shall t' open him the gate that*
12 t' he shall go forth; and after his
17 t' it shall be his to the year of liberty;*
20 T' said he unto me, This is the place*
21 T' he brought me forth into the utter
24 T' said he unto me, These are the
47: 2 T' brought he me out of the way of
6 T' he brought me, and caused me to
8 T' said he unto me, These waters
Da 1: 10 t' shall ye make me endanger my*
11 T' said Daniel to Melzar, whom the
13 T' let our countenances be looked
18 t' the prince of the eunuchs brought*
2: 2 T' the king commanded to call the
4 T' spake the Chaldeans to the king in
14 T' Daniel answered with counsel 116
15 T' Arioch made the thing known to "
16 T' Daniel went in, and desired of the*
17 T' Daniel went to his house, and 116
19 T' was the secret revealed unto "
19 T' Daniel blessed the God of heaven."
25 T' Arioch brought in Daniel before "
35 T' was the iron, the clay, the brass, "
46 T' the king Nebuchadnezzar fell "
48 T' the king made Daniel a great "
49 T' Daniel requested of the king, and*
3: 2 T' Nebuchadnezzar the king sent to
3 T' the princes, the governors, and 116
4 T' an herald cried aloud, To you it is
13 T' Nebuchadnezzar in his rage and 116
13 T' they brought these men before "
19 T' was Nebuchadnezzar full of fury, "
21 T' these men were bound in their "
24 T' Nebuchadnezzar the king was "
26 T' Nebuchadnezzar came near to "
26 T' Shadrach, Meshach, and "
28 T' Nebuchadnezzar spake, and said,*
30 T' the king promoted Shadrach, 116
4: 7 T' came in the magicians, the "
19 T' Daniel, whose name was "
5: 3 T' they brought the golden vessels "
6 T' the king's countenance was "
8 T' came in all the king's wise men: "
9 T' was king Belshazzar greatly "
13 T' was Daniel brought in before the "
17 T' Daniel answered and said before "
24 T' was the part of the hand sent "
29 T' commanded Belshazzar, and they "
6: 3 T' this Daniel was preferred above "
4 T' the presidents and princes "
5 T' said these men, We shall not find "
6 T' these presidents and princes "
11 T' these men assembled, and found "
12 T' they came near, and spake before "
13 T' answered they and said before "
14 T' the king, when he heard these "
15 T' these men assembled unto the "
16 T' the king commanded, and they "
18 T' the king went to his palace, and "
19 T' the king arose very early in the "
21 T' said Daniel unto the king, O king, "
23 T' was the king exceeding glad for "
25 T' king Darius wrote unto all people, "
7: 1 t' he wrote the dream, and told the "
11 I beheld t' because of the voice of* "
19 T' I would know the truth of the "
8: 3 T' I lifted up mine eyes, and saw,
13 T' I heard one saint speaking, and
14 t' shall the sanctuary be cleansed.
15 t', behold, there stood before me as*
10: 5 T' I lifted up mine eyes, and looked,*
9 t' was I in a deep sleep on my face,
12 T' said he unto me, Fear not, Daniel:
16 t' I opened my mouth, and spake, and
18 T' there came again and touched me
20 T' said he, Knowest thou wherefore I
11: 10 t' shall he return, and be stirred up,*
19 T' he shall turn his face toward the
20 T' shall stand up in his estate a
28 T' shall he return into his land with
12: 5 T' I Daniel looked, and, behold, there
8 t' said I, O my Lord, what shall be the
Ho 1: 9 T' said God, Call his name Lo-ammi:*
11 T' shall the children of Judah and the*
2: 7 t' shall she say, I will go and return to
7 t' was it better with me than now. 227
3: 1 T' said the Lord unto me, Go yet,*
5: 13 t' went Ephraim to the Assyrian,
6: 3 T' shall we know, if we follow on*
7: 1 t' the iniquity of Ephraim was
10: 3 Lord; what t' should a king do to us?*
11: 1 Israel was a child, t' I loved him, and
10 t' the children shall tremble from the*
Joe 2: 18 T' will the Lord be jealous for his
23 Be glad t', ye children of Zion, and
3: 17 t' shall Jerusalem be holy, and there
Am 6: 2 t' go down to Gath of the Philistines:
10 T' shall he say, Hold thy tongue: for
7: 2 t' I said, O Lord God, forgive, I
5 T' said I, O Lord God, cease, I
8 T' said the Lord, Behold, I will set a
10 T' Amaziah the priest of Beth-el sent
14 T' answered Amos, and said to
8: 2 T' said the Lord unto me, The end is
Jon 1: 5 T' the mariners were afraid, and cried
8 T' said they unto him, Tell us, we
10 T' were the men exceedingly afraid,
11 T' said they unto him, What shall we
16 T' the men feared the Lord
2: 1 T' Jonah prayed unto the Lord his
4 T' I said, I am cast out of thy sight;*
4: 4 T' said the Lord, Doest thou well to*
10 T' said the Lord, thou hast had pity*
Mic 3: 4 T' shall they cry unto the Lord, 227
7 T' shall the seers be ashamed, and*
5: 3 t' the remnant of his brethren shall

Mic 5: 5 t' shall we raise against him seven
7: 10 T' she that is mine enemy shall see it,
Hab 1: 11 T' shall his mind change, and he 227
Zep 3: 9 t' will I turn to the people a pure "
11 t' I will take away out of the midst "
Hag 1: 3 T' came the word of the Lord by
12 T' Zerubbabel the son of Shealtiel,
13 T' spake Haggai the Lord's
2: 13 T' said Haggai, If one that is
14 T' answered Haggai, and said, So is
Zec 1: 9 T' said I, O my lord, what are these?
12 T' the angel of the Lord answered
18 T' lifted I up mine eyes, and saw, and*
21 T' said I, What come these to do?
2: 2 T' said I, Whither goest thou? And
3: 7 t' thou shalt also judge my house,
4: 5 T' the angel that talked with me
6 T' he answered and spake unto me,
11 T' answered I, and said unto him,
14 T' said he, These are the two
5: 1 T' I turned, and lifted up mine eyes,
3 T' said he unto me, This is the curse
5 T' the angel that talked with me went
9 T' lifted I up mine eyes, and looked,
10 T' said I to the angel that talked with
6: 4 T' I answered and said unto the
8 T' cried he upon me, and spake unto
11 T' take silver and gold, and make*
7: 4 T' came the word of the Lord of hosts
11: 9 T' said I, I will not feed you: that that
14 T' I cut asunder mine other staff, even
13: 3 t' his father and his mother that begat
6 T' he shall answer, Those with which
14: 3 T' shall the Lord go forth, and fight
Mal 1: 6 if t' I be a father, where is mine
3: 4 T' shall the offering of Judah and
16 T' they that feared the Lord spake
18 T' shall ye return, and discern
M't 1: 19 T' Joseph her husband,...a just *1161
24 T' Joseph being raised from sleep* "
2: 7 T' Herod, when he had privily 5119
16 T' Herod, when he saw that he was "
17 T' was fulfilled that which was "
3: 5 T' went out to him Jerusalem, and "
13 T' cometh Jesus from Galilee to "
15 righteousness. T' he suffered him. "
4: 1 T' was Jesus led up of the spirit "
5 T' the devil taketh him up into the "
10 T' saith Jesus unto him, Get thee "
11 T' the devil leaveth him, and, "
5: 24 and t' come and offer thy gift. "
7: 5 t' shalt thou see clearly to cast out "
11 If ye t', being evil, know how to 3767
23 t' will I profess unto them, I never 5119
8: 26 T' he arose, and rebuked the winds "
9: 6 (t' saith he to the sick of the palsy,) "
14 T' came to him the disciples of "
15 from them, and t' shall they fast. "
29 T' touched he their eyes, saying, "
37 T' saith he unto his disciples, The "
11: 20 T' began he to upbraid the cities "
12: 12 How much t' is a man better than 3767
13 T' saith he to the man, Stretch 5119
14 T' the Pharisees went out,...held *1161
22 T' was brought unto him one 5119
26 how shall t' his kingdom stand? 3767
28 t' the kingdom of God is come 686
29 and t' he will spoil his house. 5119
38 T' certain of the scribes and of the "
44 T' he saith, I will return into my "
45 T' goeth he, and taketh with "
47 T' one said unto him, Behold, thy* "
13: 19 t' cometh the wicked one, and
26 fruit, t' appeared the tares also. 5119
27 from whence t' hath it tares? 3767
28 Wilt thou t' that we go and gather "
36 T' Jesus sent the multitude away, 5119
43 T' shall the righteous shine forth "
52 T' said he unto them, Therefore *1161
56 Whence t' hath this man all these 3767
14: 33 T' they that were in the ship came *1161
15: 1 T' came to Jesus scribes and 5119
12 T' came his disciples, and said unto "
15 T' answered Peter and said unto *1161
21 T' Jesus went thence, and *2532
25 T' came she and worshipped him, *1161
28 T' Jesus answered and said unto 5119
32 T' Jesus called his disciples unto *1161
16: 6 T' Jesus said unto them, Take * "
12 T' understood they how that he 5119
20 T' charged he his disciples that "
22 T' Peter took him, and began to *2532
24 T' said Jesus unto his disciples, 5119
27 and t' he shall reward every man "
17: 4 T' answered Peter, and said unto *1161
10 Why t' say the scribes that Elias 3767
13 T' the disciples understood that 5119
17 T' Jesus answered and said, O *1161
19 T' came the disciples to Jesus 5119
26 unto him, T' are the children free. *686
18: 16 t' take with thee one or two more,*
21 T' came Peter to him, and said, 5119
27 T' the lord of that servant was *1161
32 T' his lord, after that he had 5119
19: 7 did Moses t' command to give a 3767
13 T' were...brought unto him little 5119
23 T' said Jesus unto his disciples, *1161
25 saying, Who t' can be saved? 686
27 T' answered Peter and said unto 5119
20: 20 T' came to him the mother of "
21: 1 Olives, t' sent Jesus two disciples, "
25 us, Why did ye not t' believe him? 3767
22: 8 T' saith he to his servants, The 5119
13 T' said the king to the servants, "
15 T' went the Pharisees, and took "
21 T' saith he unto them, Render "

M't 22:35 T' one of them, which was a *2532
43 How t' doth David in spirit call 3767
45 If David t' call him Lord, how is he "
23: 1 T' spake Jesus to the multitude, 5119
32 Fill ye up t' the measure of your 2532
24: 9 T' shall they deliver you up to be 5119
10 t' shall many be offended, and shall "
14 nations; and t' shall the end come. "
16 T' let them which be in Judæa flee "
21 t' shall be great tribulation, such as "
23 T' if any man shall say unto you, "
30 t' shall appear the sign of the Son "
30 t' shall all the tribes of the earth "
40 T' shall two be in the field; the one "
45 t' is a faithful and wise servant, 686
25: 1 T' shall the kingdom of heaven be 5119
7 T' all those virgins arose, and "
16 T' he that had received the five *1161
24 T' he which had received the one* "
27 t' at my coming I should have received*
31 t' shall he sit upon the throne of 5119
34 T' shall the King say unto them on "
37 T' shall the righteous answer him, "
41 T' shall he say also unto them on "
44 T' shall they also answer him, "
45 T' shall he answer them, saying, "
26: 3 T' assembled together the chief "
14 T' one of the twelve, called Judas "
25 T' Judas, which betrayed him, *1161
31 T' saith Jesus unto them, All ye 5119
36 T' cometh Jesus with them unto a "
38 T' saith he unto them, My soul is "
45 T' cometh he to his disciples, and "
50 T' came they, and laid hands on "
52 T' said Jesus unto him, Put up "
54 But how t' shall the scriptures be 3767
56 T' all the disciples forsook him, 5119
65 T' the high priest rent his clothes, "
67 T' did they spit in his face, and "
74 T' began he to curse and to swear, "
27: 3 T' Judas, which had betrayed him, "
9 T' was fulfilled that which was "
13 T' said Pilate unto him, Hearest "
16 And they had t' a notable prisoner, "
22 What shall I do t' with Jesus 3767
25 T' answered all the people, and *2532
26 T' released he Barabbas unto 5119
27 T' the soldiers of the governor took "
38 T' were there two thieves crucified "
58 T' Pilate commanded the body to "
28:10 T' said Jesus unto them, Be not "
16 T' the eleven disciples went away *1161
M'r 2:20 and t' shall they fast in those days. 5119
3:27 man; and t' he will spoil his house. "
31 There came t' his brethren and his *3767
4:13 and how t' will ye know all parables? *
28 first the blade, t' the ear, after 1534
7: 1 T' came together unto him the *2532
5 T' the Pharisees and scribes *1899
10: 8 so t' they are no more twain, but one *
21 T' Jesus beholding him loved *1161
26 themselves, Who t' can be saved?
28 T' Peter began to say unto him, *2532
11:31 say, Why t' did ye not believe him? 3767
12:18 T' come unto him the Sadducees, *2532
37 him Lord; and whence is he t' his son? *
13:14 t' let them that be in Judæa flee to 5119
21 t' if any man shall say to you, Lo, "
26 t' shall they see the Son of man "
27 And t' shall he send his angels, and "
14:63 T' the high priest rent his clothes, *1161
15:12 What will ye t' that I shall do unto 3767
14 T' Pilate said unto them, Why, *1161
16:19 So t' after the Lord had spoken 3767
Lu 1:34 T' said Mary unto the angel, How *1161
2:28 T' took he him up in his arms, *2532
3: 7 T' said he to the multitude that *3767
10 him, saying, What shall we do t'? "
12 T' came also publicans to be *1161
5:35 and t' shall they fast in those days. 5119
36 t' both the new maketh a rent, *
6: 9 T' said Jesus unto them, I will *3767
42 t' shalt thou see clearly to pull out 5119
7: 6 T' Jesus went with them. And *1161
22 T' Jesus answering said unto *2532
31 Whereunto t' shall I liken the men 3767
8:12 t' cometh the devil, and taketh 1534
19 T' came to him his mother and *1161
24 T' he arose, and rebuked the wind* "
33 T' went the devils out of the man, * "
35 T' they went out to see what was "
37 T' the...multitude of the country *2532
9: 1 T' he called his twelve disciples *1161
12 t' came the twelve, and said unto * "
16 T' he took the five loaves and the* "
46 T' there arose a reasoning among* "
10:37 T' said Jesus unto him, Go, and *3767
11:13 If ye t', being evil, know how to give "
24 T' goeth he, and taketh to him 5119
45 T' answered one of the lawyers, *1161
12:20 t' whose shall those things be, * "
26 If ye t' be not able to do that thing 3767
28 If t' God so clothe the grass, which *1161
41 T' Peter said unto him, Lord, * "
42 Who t' is that faithful and wise 686
13: 7 T' said he unto the dresser of his *1161
9 t' after that thou shall cut it down. *
15 The Lord t' answered him, and *3767
18 T' said he, Unto what is the *1161
23 T' said one unto him, Lord, are * "
26 T' shall ye begin to say, We have 5119
14:10 t' shalt thou have worship in the "
12 T' said he also to him that bade *1161
16 T' said he unto him, A certain * "
21 T' the master of the house being 5119
15: 1 T' drew near...all the publicans *1161
Lu 16: 3 T' the steward said within himself, *1161
7 T' said he to another, And how 1899
27 T' he said, I pray thee, therefore, *1161
17: 1 T' said he unto the disciples, It is* "
18:26 heard it said, Who t' can be saved? *2532
28 T' Peter said, Lo, we have left all, *1161
31 T' he took unto him the twelve, * "
19:15 t' he commanded these servants to *2532
16 T' came the first, saying, Lord, *1161
23 Wherefore t' gavest not thou my 2532
20: 5 say, Why t' believe ye him not? *3767
9 T' began he to speak to the people *1161
13 T' said the lord of the vineyard, * "
17 What is this t' that is written, 3767
27 T' came to him certain of the *1161
39 T' certain of the scribes answering* "
44 calleth...Lord, how is he t' his son? *2532
45 T' in the audience of all the *1161
21:10 T' said he unto them, Nation shall 5119
20 t' know that the desolation thereof is "
21 T' let them which are in Judæa "
27 t' shall they see the Son of man "
28 t' look up, and lift up your heads; *
22: 3 T' entered Satan into Judas *1161
7 T' came the day of unleavened * "
36 T' said he unto them, But now, *3767
52 T' Jesus said unto...chief priests, *1161
54 T' took they him, and led him, * "
70 T' said they all, Art thou * "
70 all, Art thou t' the Son of God? 3767
23: 4 T' said Pilate to the chief priests *1161
9 T' he questioned...him in many * "
30 T' shall they begin to say to the 5119
34 T' said Jesus, Father, forgive *1161
24:12 T' arose Peter, and ran unto the * "
25 T' he said unto them, O fools, and* "
45 T' opened he their understanding, 5119
Joh 1:21 him, What t'? Art thou Elias? 3767
22 T' said they unto him, Who art * "
25 Why baptizest thou t', if thou be "
38 T' Jesus turned, and saw them *1161
2:10 well drunk, t' that which is worse: 5119
18 T' answered the Jews and said *3767
20 T' said the Jews, Forty and six * "
3:25 T' there arose a question between* "
4: 5 T' cometh he to a city of Samaria, * "
9 T' saith the woman of Samaria * "
11 from whence t' hast thou that "
28 The woman t' left her waterpot, * "
30 T' they went out of the city, and * "
35 four months, and t' cometh harvest?
45 T' when he was come into Galilee, *3767
48 T' said Jesus unto him, Except ye* "
52 T' enquired he of them the hour * "
5: 4 whosoever t' first after...troubling * "
12 T' asked they him, What man is * "
19 T' answered Jesus and said unto * "
6: 5 When Jesus t' lifted up his eyes, * "
14 T' those men, when they had seen* "
21 T' they willingly received him into* "
28 T' said they unto him, What shall* "
30 What sign shewest thou t', that we "
32 T' Jesus said unto them, Verily, * "
34 T' said they unto him, Lord, * "
41 The Jews t' murmured at him, * "
42 how is it t' that he saith, I came * "
53 T' Jesus said unto them, Verily, * "
67 T' said Jesus unto the twelve, Will* "
68 T' Simon Peter answered him, * "
7: 6 T' Jesus said unto them, My time* "
10 t' went he also up unto the feast, 5119
11 T' the Jews sought him at the *3767
25 T' said some of them of Jerusalem, * "
28 T' cried Jesus in the temple as he* "
30 T' they sought to take him: but no* "
33 T' said Jesus unto them, Yet a * "
33 and t' I go unto him that sent me. *
35 T' said the Jews among *3767
45 T' came the officers to the chief * "
47 T' answered them the Pharisees, * "
8:12 T' spake Jesus again unto them, * "
19 T' said they unto him, Where is * "
21 T' said Jesus again unto them, I * "
22 T' said the Jews, Will he kill * "
25 T' said they unto him, Who art * "
28 T' said Jesus unto them, When ye *5119
28 t' shall ye know that I am he, *3767
31 T' said Jesus to those Jews which* "
31 t' are ye my disciples indeed;
41 T' said they to him, We be not *3767
48 T' answered the Jews, and said * "
52 T' said the Jews unto him, Now * "
57 T' said the Jews unto him, Thou* "
59 T' took they up stones to cast at * "
9:12 T' said they unto him, Where is he? * "
15 T' again the Pharisees also asked* "
19 born blind? how t' doth he now see? "
24 T' again called they the man that* "
26 T' said they to him again, What *1161
28 T' they reviled him, and said, *3767
10: 7 T' said Jesus unto them again, * "
24 T' came the Jews round about him, * "
31 T' the Jews took up stones again* "
11: 7 T' after that saith he to his 1899
12 T' said his disciples, Lord, if he *3767
14 T' said Jesus unto them plainly, * "
16 T' said Thomas, which is called * "
17 T' when Jesus came, he found that* "
20 T' Martha, as soon as she heard * "
21 T' said Martha unto Jesus, Lord, * "
31 The Jews t' which were with her in "
32 T' when Mary was come where * "
36 T' said the Jews, Behold how he* "
41 T' they took away the stone from* "
45 T' many of the Jews which came* "
47 T' gathered the chief priests and * "
Joh 11:53 T' from that day forth they took *3767
56 T' sought they for Jesus, and * "
12: 1 T' Jesus six days before the * "
3 T' took Mary a pound of ointment* "
4 T' saith one of his disciples, Judas* "
7 T' said Jesus, Let her alone: * "
16 t' remembered they that these 5119
28 T' came there a voice from *3767
35 T' Jesus said unto them, Yet a * "
13: 6 T' cometh he to Simon Peter: and* "
14 If I t', your Lord and Master, have* "
22 T' the disciples looked one on * "
25 He t' lying on Jesus' breast saith *1161
27 T' said Jesus unto him, That thou *3767
30 He t' having received the sop went "
14: 9 and how sayest thou t', Shew us the*
16:17 T' said some of his disciples *3767
18: 3 Judas t', having received a band of "
6 As soon t' as he had said unto them, * "
7 T' asked he them again, Whom * "
10 T' Simon Peter having a sword * "
11 T' said Jesus unto Peter, Put up * "
12 T' the band and the captain and * "
16 T' went out that other disciple, * "
17 T' saith the damsel that kept the* "
19 The high priest t' asked Jesus of * "
27 Peter t' denied again: and * "
28 T' led they Jesus from Caiaphas * "
29 Pilate t' went out unto them, and* "
31 T' said Pilate unto them, Take ye* "
33 T' Pilate entered into the judgment* "
36 world, t' would my servants fight,
37 said unto him, Art thou a king t'? 3766
40 T' cried they all again, saying, *3767
19: 1 T' Pilate therefore took Jesus, 5119
5 T' came Jesus forth, wearing the *3767
10 T' saith Pilate unto him, Speakest* "
16 T' delivered he him therefore *5119
20 This title t' read many of the Jews: *3767
21 T' said the chief priests of the * "
23 T' the soldiers, when they had * "
27 T' saith he to the disciple, 1534
32 T' came the soldiers, and brake *3767
40 T' took they the body of Jesus, * "
20: 2 T' she runneth, and cometh to * "
6 T' cometh Simon Peter following* "
8 T' went in also that other disciple, 5119
10 T' the disciples went away again *3767
19 T' the same day at evening, being* "
20 T' were the disciples glad, when * "
21 T' said Jesus to them again, Peace* "
26 t' came Jesus, the doors being shut, *
27 T' said he to Thomas, Reach 1534
21: 5 T' Jesus saith unto them, *3767
9 soon t' as they were come to land, * "
13 Jesus t' cometh, and taketh bread, * "
20 T' Peter, turning about, seeth the *1161
23 T' went this saying abroad among *3767
Ac 1:12 T' returned they unto Jerusalem *5119
2:38 T' Peter said unto them, Repent, *1161
41 T' they that gladly received his 3767
3: 6 T' Peter said, Silver and gold have *1161
4: 8 T' Peter, filled with the Holy 5119
5: 9 T' Peter said unto her, How is it *1161
10 T' fell she down straightway at his* "
17 T' the high priest rose up, and all* "
25 T' came one and told them, saying, * "
26 T' went the captain with the 5119
29 T' Peter and the other apostles *1161
34 T' stood there up one in...council, * "
6: 2 T' the twelve called the multitude * "
9 T' there arose certain of the * "
11 T' they suborned men, which said, 5119
7: 1 T' said the high priest, Are these *1161
4 T' came he out of the land of the 5119
14 T' sent Joseph, and called his *1161
29 T' fled Moses at this saying, and * "
32 T' Moses trembled, and durst not* "
33 T' said the Lord to him, Put off thy* "
42 T' God turned, and gave them up* "
57 T' they cried out with a loud voice, * "
8: 5 T' Philip went down to the city of* "
13 T' Simon himself believed also: * "
17 T' laid they their hands on them, 5119
24 T' answered Simon, and said, *1161
29 T' the Spirit said unto Philip, Go* "
35 T' Philip opened his mouth, and * "
9:13 T' Ananias answered, Lord, I have* "
19 T' was Saul certain days with the* "
25 T' the disciples took him by night, * "
31 T' had the churches rest *3767
39 T' Peter arose and went with *1161
10:21 T' Peter went down to the men * "
23 T' called he them in, and lodged *3767
34 T' Peter opened his mouth, and *1161
46 magnify God. T' answered Peter, 5119
48 T' prayed they him to tarry * "
11:16 T' remembered I the word of the *1161
17 Forasmuch t' as God gave them 3767
18 T' hath God also to the Gentiles 686
22 T' tidings of these things came *1161
25 T' departed Barnabas to Tarsus, * "
29 T' the disciples, every man * "
12: 3 (T' were the days of unleavened * "
15 even so. T' said they, It is his * "
13: 9 T' Saul, (who also is called Paul,)* "
12 T' the deputy, when he saw what 5119
16 T' Paul stood up, and beckoning *1161
46 T' Paul and Barnabas waxed bold, * "
14:13 T' the priest of Jupiter, which was* "
15:12 T' all the multitude kept silence, * "
22 T' pleased it the apostles and 5119
16: 1 T' came he to Derbe and Lystra: *1161
29 T' he called for a light, and * "
17:14 t' immediately the brethren sent 5119
18 T' certain philosophers of the *1161

Ac 17:22 *T'* Paul stood in the midst of Mars'*1161
29 Forasmuch *t'* as we are the 3767
18: 9 *T'* spake the Lord to Paul in the *1161
17 *T'* all the Greeks took Sosthenes, * "
18 and *t'* took his leave of the brethren,*
19: 3 Unto what *t'* were ye baptized? 3767
4 *T'* said Paul, John verily baptized*1161
13 *T'* certain of the vagabond Jews, * "
36 Seeing *t'* that these things cannot 3767
21:13 *T'* Paul answered, What mean ye 1161
26 *T'* Paul took the men, and the 5119
33 *T'* the chief captain came near, "
22:22 and *t'* lifted up their voices, and said,*
27 *T'* the chief captain came, and *1161
29 *T'* straightway they departed from3767
23: 3 *T'* said Paul unto him, God shall 5119
5 *T'* said Paul, I wist not, brethren,*5037
17 *T'* Paul called one of...centurions*1161
19 *T'* the chief captain took him by * "
22 captain *t'* let the young man depart,*
27 *t'* came I with an army, and rescued*
31 *T'* the soldiers, as it was *3767
24:10 *T'* Paul, after that...governor had*1161
25: 2 *T'* the high priest and the chief of* "
10 *T'* said Paul, I stand at Cæsar's * "
12 *T'* Festus, when he had conferred 5119
22 *T'* Agrippa said...Festus, I would *1161
26: 1 *T'* Agrippa said unto Paul, Thou * "
1 *T'* Paul stretched forth the hand, 5119
20 of Judæa, and *t'* to the Gentiles, *
28 *T'* Agrippa said unto Paul, *1161
32 *T'* said Agrippa unto Festus, This* "
27:20 be saved was *t'* taken away. *3063
29 *T'* fearing lest we should have *5037
32 *T'* the soldiers cut off the ropes of5119
36 *T'* were they all of good cheer, and1161
28: 1 *t'* they knew that the island was 5119
Ro 3: 1 What advantage *t'* hath the Jew? 3767
6 for *t'* how shall God judge the world?
9 What *t'*? are we better than they? 3767
27 Where is boasting *t'*? It is * "
31 Do we *t'* make void the law through "
4: 1 What shall we say *t'* that Abraham "
9 Cometh this blessedness *t'* upon "
10 How was it *t'* reckoned? when he "
5: 9 Much more *t'*, being now justified "
6: 1 What shall we say *t'*? Shall we "
15 What *t'*? shall we sin, because we "
18 Being *t'* made free from sin, ye *1161
21 fruit had ye *t'* in those things 5119,3767
7: 3 So *t'* if, while her husband liveth, 686
7 What shall we say *t'*? Is the law 3767
13 *t'* that which is good made death "
16 If *t'* I do that which I would not, I*1161
17 *t'* it is no more I that do it, but sin* "
21 I find *t'* a law, that, when I would 686
25 *t'* with the mind I myself serve the "
8: 8 So *t'* they that are in...flesh cannot*1161
17 if children, *t'* heirs; heirs of God, 2535
25 *t'* do we with patience wait for it.
31 What shall we *t'* say to these 3767
9:14 What shall we say *t'*? Is there "
16 So *t'* it is not of him that willeth, 686
19 Thou wilt say *t'* unto me, Why 3767
30 What shall we say *t'*? That the "
10:14 *t'* shall they call on him in whom "
17 So *t'* faith cometh by hearing, and* 686
11: 1 I say *t'*, Hath God cast away his 3767
5 Even so *t'* at this present time also "
6 if by grace, *t'* is it no more of works:
6 it be of works, *t'* is it no more grace:*
7 What *t'*? Israel hath not obtained3767
11 I say *t'*, Have they stumbled that "
19 Thou wilt say *t'*, The branches "
12: 6 Having *t'* gifts differing according*1161
13: 3 thou *t'* not be afraid of the power?* "
14:12 So *t'* every one of us shall give an 686
16 Let not *t'* your good be evil spoken3767
15: 1 We *t'* that are strong ought to bear*1161
1Co 3: 5 Who *t'* is Paul, and who is 3767
7 So *t'* neither is he that planteth any
4: 5 *t'* shall every man have praise of 5119
5:10 *t'* must ye needs go out of the world686
6: 4 If *t'* ye have judgments of things 3767
15 I *t'* take the members of Christ, "
7:38 *t'* he that giveth her in marriage 2532
9:18 What is my reward *t'*? Verily 3767
10:19 What say I *t'*? that the idol is "
12:28 *t'* gifts of healings, helps, 1534
13:10 *t'* that which is in part shall be *5119
12 a glass, darkly; but *t'* face to face: "
12 *t'* shall I know even as also I am "
14:15 What is it *t'*? I will pray with the 3767
26 How is it *t'*, brethren? when ye "
15: 5 seen of Cephas, *t'* of the twelve: 1534
7 seen of James; *t'* of all the apostles."
13 of the dead, *t'* is Christ not risen: *3761
14 not risen, *t'* is our preaching vain, 686
16 rise not, *t'* is not Christ raised: *3761
18 *T'* they also which are fallen 686
24 *T'* cometh the end, when he shall 1534
28 *t'* shall the Son also himself be 5119
29 why are they *t'* baptized for the dead?
54 *t'* shall be brought to pass the 5119
2Co 2: 2 who is he *t'* that maketh me glad, 2532
3:12 Seeing *t'* that we have such hope,*3767
4:12 So *t'* death worketh in us, but life 3303
5:14 if one died for all, *t'* were all dead:*686
20 Now *t'* we are ambassadors for Christ,*
6: 1 We *t'*, as workers together with *3767
12:10 am weak, *t'* am I strong. *5119,1161,2532
Ga 1:18 *T'* after three years I went up to 1899
2: 1 *T'* fourteen years after I went up "
21 the law, *t'* Christ is dead in vain. 686
3: 9 So *t'* they which be of faith are
19 Wherefore *t'* serveth the law? It 3767
Ga 3:21 law *t'* against the promises of God?3767
29 Christ's, *t'* are ye Abraham's seed, 686
4: 7 *t'* an heir of God through Christ. 2532
8 Howbeit *t'*, when ye knew not *5119
15 Where is *t'* the blessedness ye 3767
29 But as *t'* he that was born after 5119
31 So *t'*, brethren, we are not * 686
5:11 *t'* is the offense of the cross ceased.
16 This I say *t'*, Walk in the Spirit, *1161
6: 4 *t'* shall he have rejoicing in 5119
Eph 5:15 See *t'* that ye walk circumspectly,*3767
Ph'p 1:18 What *t'*? notwithstanding, every 1063
Col 3: 1 If ye *t'* be risen with Christ, seek 3767
4 *t'* shall ye also appear with him in5119
1Th 4: 1 *t'* we beseech you, brethren, 3767
17 *T'* we which are alive and remain 1899
5: 3 *t'* sudden destruction cometh upon5119
2Th 2: 8 *t'* shall that Wicked be revealed, "
1Ti 2:13 For Adam was first formed, *t'* Eve.1534
3: 2 A bishop *t'* must be blameless, *3767
10 *t'* let them use the office of a 1534
Heb 2:14 Forasmuch *t'* as the children are 3767
4: 8 *t'* would he not afterward have *
14 Seeing *t'* that we have a great 3767
7:27 own sins, and *t'* for the people's: 1899
8: 7 *t'* should no place have been sought
9: 1 *T'* verily the first covenant had *3767
9 a figure for the time *t'* present, ††3588
26 For *t'* must he often have suffered*
10: 2 For *t'* would they not have ceased to*
7 *T'* said I, Lo, I come (in the 5119
9 *T'* said he, Lo, I come to do thy "
12: 8 *t'* are ye bastards, and not sons. 686
26 Whose voice *t'* shook the earth: 5119
Jas 1:15 *T'* when lust hath conceived, it 1534
2: 4 Are ye not *t'* partial in yourselves,*2532
24 Ye see *t'* how that by works a *5106
3:17 above is first pure, *t'* peaceable, 1899
4:14 a little time, and *t'* vanisheth away."
1Pe 4: 1 Forasmuch *t'* as Christ hath 3767
2Pe 3: 6 Whereby the world that *t'* was, 5119
11 Seeing *t'* that all these things *3767
1Jo 1: 5 This *t'* is the message which we *2532
3:21 *t'* have we confidence toward God.*
Re 3:16 So *t'* because thou art lukewarm, and*
22: 9 *T'* saith he unto me, See thou do *2532

thence See also THENCEFORTH.
Ge 2:10 from *t'* it was parted, and became 8033
11: 8 Lord scattered them abroad from *t'*"
9 *t'* did the Lord scatter them abroad"
12: 8 removed from *t'* unto a mountain "
18:16 And the men rose up from *t'*, and "
22 the men turned their faces from *t'*, "
20: 1 And Abraham journeyed from *t'* "
26:17 And Isaac departed *t'*, and pitched "
22 he removed from *t'*, and digged "
23 he went up from *t'* to Beer-sheba. "
27:45 I will send, and fetch thee from *t'*: "
28: 2 take thee a wife from *t'* of the "
6 to take him a wife from *t'*; "
30:32 removing from *t'* all the speckled "
42: 2 thither, and buy for us from *t'*; "
26 asses with the corn, and departed *t'*."
49:24 (from *t'* is the shepherd, the stone "
Nu 13:23 cut down from *t'* a branch with one "
24 children of Israel cut down from *t'*."
21:12, 13 From *t'* they removed, and "
22:41 *t'* he might see the utmost part of "
23:13 all: and curse me them from *t'*. "
27 mayest curse me them from *t'*. "
De 4:29 But if from *t'* thou shalt seek the "
6:23 he brought us out from *t'*, that he "
10: 7 From *t'* they journeyed unto "
19:12 his city shall send and fetch him *t'*, "
22: 8 thine house, if any man fall from *t'*. "
24:18 Lord thy God redeemed thee *t'*: 8033
30: 4 from *t'* will the Lord thy God "
4 thee, and from *t'* will he fetch thee:"
Jos 6:22 and bring out *t'* the woman, and all "
15: 4 From *t'* it passed toward Azmon, *
14 And Caleb drove *t'* the three sons 8033
15 he went up *t'* to the inhabitants "
18:13 went over from *t'* toward Luz, "
14 border was drawn *t'*, and compassed*
19:13 And from *t'* passeth on along on 8033
34 and goeth out from *t'* to Hukkok. "
J'g 1:11 And from *t'* he went against the "
20 expelled *t'* the three sons of Anak. "
8: 8 he went up *t'* to Penuel, and spake "
18:11 there went from *t'* of the family of "
13 passed *t'* unto mount Ephraim. "
19:18 from *t'* am I: and I went to "
21:24 children of Israel departed *t'* at "
24 went out from *t'* every man to his "
1Sa 4: 4 might bring from *t'* the ark of the "
10: 3 shalt thou go on forward from *t'*. "
23 And they ran and fetched him *t'*: "
17:49 took *t'* a stone, and slang it, and "
22: 1 David therefore departed *t'*, and "
3 David went *t'* to Mizpeh of Moab: "
23:29 And David went up from *t'*, and "
2Sa 6: 2 bring up from *t'* the ark of God, "
14: 2 fetched *t'* a wise woman, and said "
16: 5 *t'* came out a man of the family of "
21:13 he brought up from *t'* the bones of "
1Ki 1:45 they are come up from *t'* rejoicing, "
2:36 and go not forth *t'* any whither. "
9:28 to Ophir, and fetched from *t'* gold, "
12:25 and went out from *t'*, and built "
19:19 So he departed *t'*, and found Elisha "
2Ki 2:21 shall not be from *t'* any more death "
23 he went up from *t'* unto Beth-el: "
25 he went from *t'* to mount Carmel, "
25 and from *t'* he returned to Samaria."
6: 2 and take *t'* every man a beam, "
7: 8 and carried *t'* silver, and gold, "
2Ki 7: 8 carried *t'* also, and went and hid it.8033
10:15 when he was departed *t'*, he lighted "
17:27 priests whom ye brought from *t'*; "
33 whom they carried away from *t'*. * "
23:12 brake them down from *t'*, and cast "
24:13 he carried out *t'* all the treasures "
1Ch 13: 6 to bring up *t'* the ark of God the "
2Ch 8:18 and took *t'* four hundred and fifty "
26:20 they thrust him out from *t'*; yea, "
Ezr 6: 6 beyond the river, be ye far from *t'*:8536
Ne 1: 9 yet will I gather them from *t'*, and 8033
Job 39:29 From *t'* she seeketh the prey, and "
Isa 52:11 depart ye, go ye out from *t'*, "
65:20 be no more *t'* an infant of days, "
Jer 5: 6 one that goeth out *t'* shall be torn 2007
13: 6 and take the girdle from *t'*, 8033
36:29 cause to cease from *t'* man and beast? "
37:12 separate himself *t'* in the midst of*8033
38:11 took *t'* old cast clouts and old rotten "
43:12 he shall go forth from *t'* in peace. "
49:16 I will bring thee down from *t'*, saith"
38 will destroy from *t'* the king and "
50: 9 her; from *t'* she shall be taken: "
Eze 11:18 all the abominations thereof from *t'*. "
Ho 2:15 give her her vineyards from *t'*, 8033
Am 6: 2 from *t'* go ye to Hamath the great: "
9: 2 hell, *t'* shall mine hand take them; "
2 to heaven, *t'* will I bring them down:"
3 I will search and take them out *t'*; "
3 *t'* will I command the serpent, and "
4 *t'* will I command the sword, and it"
Ob 4 *t'* will I bring thee down, saith the "
M't 4:21 going on from *t'*, he saw other two 1564
5:26 by no means come out *t'*, till thou "
9: 9 as Jesus passed forth from *t'*, he saw"
27 when Jesus departed *t'*, two blind "
10:11 worthy; and there abide till ye go *t'*.*
11: 1 he departed *t'* to teach and to preach1564
12: 9 when he was departed *t'*, he went "
15 knew it,...withdrew himself from *t'*:"
13:53 these parables, he departed *t'*. "
14:13 he departed *t'* by ship into a desert "
15:21 Jesus went *t'*, and departed into the"
29 Jesus departed from *t'*, and came "
19:15 his hands on them, and departed *t'*. "
M'r 1:19 when he had gone a little farther *t'*,*"
6: 1 he went out from *t'*, and came into "
11 when ye depart *t'*, shake off the "
7:24 from *t'* he arose, and went into the "
9:30 they departed *t'*, and passed "
10: 1 And he arose from *t'*, and cometh "
Lu 9: 4 into, there abide, and *t'* depart. "
12:59 thou shalt not depart *t'*, till thou "
16:26 pass to us, that would come from *t'*."
Joh 4:43 Now after two days he departed *t'*, "
11:54 went *t'* unto a country near to the "
Ac 7: 4 from *t'*, when his father was dead, "
13: 4 and from *t'* they sailed to Cyprus. "
14:26 And *t'* sailed to Antioch, from "
16:12 from *t'* to Philippi, which is the chief"
18: 7 he departed *t'*, and entered into a "
18 sailed *t'* into Syria, and with him "
20:15 And we sailed *t'*, and came the 1564
21: 1 Rhodes, and from *t'* unto Patara: "
27: 4 when we had launched from *t'*, we "
12 more part advised to depart *t'* also, "
13 loosing *t'*, they sailed close by Crete.*
28:13 And from *t'* we fetched a compass, 3606
15 And from *t'*, when the brethren 1564
2Co 2:13 them, I went from *t'* into Macedonia.*

thenceforth
Le 22:27 and *t'* it shall be accepted for an 1973
2Ch 32:23 the sight of all nations from *t'*.310,3651
M't 5:13 it is *t'* good for nothing, but to be 2089
Joh 19:12 *t'* Pilate sought to release *1537,5127

Theophilus (*the-of'-il-us*)
Lu 1: 3 thee in order, most excellent *T'*, 2321
Ac 1: 1 treatise have I made, O *T'*, of all "

there See also THEREABOUT; THEREAT; THEREBY; THEREFORE; THEREFROM; THEREIN; THEREOF; THEREON; THEREOUT; THEREUNTO; THEREUPON; THEREWITH.
Ge 1: 3 Let *t'* be light: and *t'* was light.
6 Let *t'* be a firmament in the midst
14 said, Let *t'* be lights in the firmament
30 upon the earth, wherein *t'* is life,
2: 5 *t'* was not a man to till the ground.
6 But *t'* went up a mist from the earth,
8 *t'* he put the man whom he had 8033
11 land of Havilah, where *t'* is gold;
12 *t'* is bdellium and the onyx stone. 8033
20 Adam *t'* was not found an help meet
4:26 to Seth, to him also *t'* was born a son;
6: 4 *T'* were giants in the earth in those*
7: 9 *T'* went in two and two unto Noah
9:11 shall *t'* any more be a flood to destroy
11: 2 land of Shinar; and they dwelt *t'*. 8033
7 and *t'* confound their language,
9 Lord did *t'* confound the language
31 they came unto Haran, and dwelt *t'*.
12: 7 *t'* builded he an altar unto the Lord,
8 *t'* he builded an altar unto the Lord,
10 And *t'* was a famine in the land: and
10 down into Egypt to sojourn *t'*; 8033
13: 4 which he had made *t'* at the first:
7 *t'* was a strife between the herdmen
8 said unto Lot, Let *t'* be no strife,
18 built *t'* an altar unto the Lord. 8033
14: 8 And *t'* went out the king of Sodom,
10 and Gomorrah fled, and fell *t'*; 8033
13 And *t'* came one that had escaped, and
18:24 *t'* be fifty righteous within the city:
24 *t'* shall lack five of the fifty righteous:
28 If I find *t'* forty and five, I will 8033
29 *t'* shall be forty found *t'*.

Ge 18:30 *t'* shall thirty be found *t'*. 8033
30 I will not do it, if I find thirty *t'*. "
31 *t'* shall be twenty found *t'*. "
32 Peradventure ten shall be found *t'*. "
19: 1 *t'* came two angels to Sodom at even;*
31 is old, and *t'* is not a man in the earth
21:31 *t'* they sware both of them. 8033
33 called *t'* on the name of the Lord, "
22: 2 and offer him *t'* for a burnt offering "
9 Abraham built an altar *t'*, and laid "
23:13 it of me, and I will bury my dead *t'*. "
24:23 is *t'* room in thy father's house for us
33 *t'* was set meat before him to eat: but
25:10 *t'* was Abraham buried, and Sarah8033
24 behold, *t'* were twins in her womb.
26: 1 And *t'* was a famine in the land,
8 when he had been *t'* a long time, 8033
17 in the valley of Gerar, and dwelt *t'*. "
19 found *t'* a well of springing water. "
25 he builded an altar *t'*, and called "
25 the Lord, and pitched his tent *t'*: "
25 and *t'* Isaac's servants digged a well"
28 said, Let *t'* be now an oath betwixt us.
28:11 place, and tarried *t'* all night, 8033
29: 2 *t'* were three flocks of sheep lying "
31:14 Is *t'* yet any portion or inheritance for
46 and they did eat *t'* upon the heap. 8033
32: 4 with Laban, and stayed *t'* until now:*
13 And he lodged *t'* that same night; 8033
24 and *t'* wrestled a man with him until
29 my name? And he blessed him *t'*. 8033
33:20 And he erected *t'* an altar, and "
35: 1 Arise, go up to Beth-el, and dwell *t'*:"
1 and make *t'* an altar unto God, "
3 I will make *t'* an altar unto God, "
7 he built *t'* an altar, and called the "
7 because *t'* God appeared unto him, "
16 *t'* was but a little way to come to
36:31 before *t'* reigned any king over the
37:24 pit was empty, *t'* was no water in it.
28 *t'* passed by Midianites merchantmen;
38: 2 And Judah saw *t'* a daughter of a 8033
21 said, *T'* was no harlot in this place.
22 that *t'* was no harlot in this place.
39: 9 *T'* is none greater in this house than I;
11 and *t'* was none of the men of the
11 of the men of the house *t'* within. 8033
20 and he was *t'* in the prison. "
22 whatsoever they did *t'*, he was the "
40: 8 a dream, and *t'* is no interpreter of it.
17 *t'* was of all manner of bakemeats
41: 2 *t'* came up out of the river seven well
8 *t'* was none that could interpret them
12 And *t'* was...with us a young man,
12 was *t'* with us a young man, an 8033
15 and *t'* is none that can interpret it:
18 *t'* came up out of the river seven kine,
24 *t'* was none that could declare it to me.
29 *t'* come seven years of great plenty
30 *t'* shall arise after them seven years of
39 *t'* is none so discreet and wise as thou
54 in all the land of Egypt *t'* was bread.
42: 1 Jacob saw that *t'* was corn in Egypt,
2 I have heard that *t'* is corn in Egypt:
16 proved, whether *t'* be any truth in you:
43:25 heart that they should eat bread *t'*.8033
30 into his chamber, and wept *t'*. "
44:14 to Joseph's house; for he was yet *t'*:"
45: 1 And *t'* stood no man with him, while
6 and yet *t'* are five years, in the
6 which *t'* shall neither be earing nor
11 And *t'* will I nourish thee; for yet 8033
11 for yet *t'* are five years of famine,
46: 3 will *t'* make of thee a great nation:8033
47:13 *t'* was no bread in all the land; for the
18 *t'* is not ought left in the sight of my
48: 7 yet *t'* was but a little way to come
7 and I buried her *t'* in the way of 8033
49:31 *T'* they buried Abraham and Sarah "
31 *t'* they buried Isaac and Rebekah "
31 his wife; and *t'* I buried Leah. "
50: 5 of Canaan, *t'* shalt thou bury me. "
9 *t'* went up with him both chariots and
10 *t'* they mourned with a great and 8033
Ex 1: 8 *t'* arose up a new king over Egypt,
10 when *t'* falleth out any war, they join
2: 1 *t'* went a man of the house of Levi,
12 and when he saw that *t'* was no man,
5: 9 *t'* more work be laid upon the men,*
13 daily tasks, as when *t'* was straw.
16 *T'* is no straw given unto thy
18 for *t'* shall no straw be given you,
7:19 that *t'* may be blood throughout all
21 *t'* was blood throughout all the land*
8:10 *t'* is none like unto the Lord our God.
15 when Pharaoh saw that *t'* was respite,
18 so *t'* were lice upon man, and upon
24 *t'* came a grievous swarm of flies into
31 from his people; *t'* remained not one.
9: 3 *t'* shall be a very grievous murrain.
4 *t'* shall nothing die of all that is the
7 *t'* was not one of the cattle of the
14 that *t'* is none like me in all the earth.
22 that *t'* may be hail in all the land of
24 So *t'* was hail, and fire mingled with
24 such as *t'* was none like it in all the*
26 children of Israel were, was *t'* no hail.
28 *t'* be no more mighty thunderings and
29 neither shall *t'* be any more hail;
10:14 *t'* were no such locusts as they,
15 *t'* remained not any green thing in
19 *t'* remained not one locust in all the
21 that *t'* may be darkness over the land
22 *t'* was a thick darkness in all the land
26 *t'* shall not an hoof be left behind; for
11: 6 *t'* shall be a great cry throughout all

Ex 11: 6 such as *t'* was none like it, nor shall
12:16 day *t'* shall be an holy convocation,
16 day *t'* shall be an holy convocation,*
19 Seven days shall *t'* be no leaven found
30 and *t'* was a great cry in Egypt;
30 cry in Egypt; for *t'* was not a house
30 house where *t'* was not one dead.
43 *T'* shall no stranger eat thereof:
13: 3 *t'* shall no leavened bread be eaten.
7 *t'* shall no leavened bread be seen with
7 neither shall *t'* be leaven seen with
14:11 Because *t'* were no graves in Egypt,
28 *t'* remained not so much as one of
15:25 *t'* he made for them a statute and 8033
25 ordinance, and *t'* he proved them. "
27 they encamped *t'* by the waters. "
16:14 wilderness *t'* lay a small round thing,*
24 neither was *t'* any worm therein.
26 is the sabbath, in it *t'* shall be none.
27 that *t'* went out some of the people on
17: 1 *t'* was no water for the people to drink.
3 the people thirsted *t'* for water; 8033
6 I will stand before thee *t'* upon the "
6 *t'* shall come water out of it, that the
19: 2 *t'* Israel camped before the mount.8033
13 *T'* shall not an hand touch it, but he
16 that *t'* were thunders and lightnings,
21:30 If *t'* be laid on him a sum of money,
22: 2 die, *t'* shall no blood be shed for him.
23:26 *T'* shall nothing cast their young, nor
24:10 and *t'* was under his feet as it were a
12 to me into the mount, and be *t'*: 8033
25:35 *t'* shall be a knop under two branches*
26:17 Two tenons shall *t'* be in one board,
20 side *t'* shall be twenty boards: *
27: 9 *t'* shall be hangings for the court of
11 *t'* shall be hangings of an hundred
28:32 *t'* shall be an hole in the top of it,*
29:42 meet you, to speak *t'* unto thee. 8033
43 *t'* I will meet with the children of "
30:12 that *t'* be no plague among them,
34 of each shall *t'* be a like weight:
32:17 *T'* is a noise of war in the camp.
24 into the fire, and *t'* came out this calf.
28 *t'* fell of the people that day about
33:20 for *t'* shall no man see me, and live.*
21 Lord said, Behold, *t'* is a place by me,
34: 2 present thyself *t'* to me in the top 8033
5 in the cloud, and stood with him *t'*, "
28 he was *t'* with the Lord forty days "
35: 2 day *t'* shall be to you an holy day,
36:30 And *t'* were eight boards; and their
39:23 *t'* was an hole in the midst of the robe,*
40:30 put water *t'*, to wash withal. *8033
Le 6:27 when *t'* is sprinkled of the blood
7: 7 *t'* is one law for them: the priest that
8:31 *t'* eat it with the bread that is in 8033
9:24 *t'* came a fire out from before the Lord,
10: 2 *t'* went out fire from the Lord, and
13:10 *t'* be quick raw flesh in the rising;
19 place of the boil *t'* be a white rising,
21 behold, *t'* be no white hairs therein,
24 Or if *t'* be any flesh, in the *
24 in the skin whereof *t'* is a hot burning,*
26 *t'* be no white hair in the bright spot,
30 skin; and *t'* be in it a yellow thin hair;
31 skin, and that *t'* is no black hair in it;
32 not, and *t'* be in it no yellow hair,
37 *t'* is black hair grown up therein;*
42 if *t'* be in the bald head, or bald
14:35 *t'* is as it were a plague in the house:
16:17 *t'* shall be no man in the tabernacle
23 place, and shall leave them *t'*: 8033
17: 3 What man soever *t'* be of the house of
8, 10 man *t'* be of the house of Israel,
13 man *t'* be of the children of Israel,
20:14 that *t'* be no wickedness among you.
21: 1 *T'* shall none be defiled for the dead
22:10 *T'* shall no stranger eat of the holy
13 but *t'* shall no stranger eat thereof.
21 *t'* shall be no blemish therein.
23:27 seventh month *t'* shall be a day of*
25:51 If *t'* be yet many years behind,
52 *t'* remain but few years unto the year
Nu 1: 4 you *t'* shall be a man of every tribe;
53 *t'* be no wrath upon the congregation
5:13 and *t'* be no witness against her,
6: 5 *t'* shall no rasor come upon his
8:19 *t'* be no plague among the children of
9: 6 *t'* were certain men, who were defiled
15 at even *t'* was upon the tabernacle as *
17 *t'* the children of Israel pitched 8033
11: 6 *t'* is nothing at all, beside this manna,
16 that they may stand *t'* with thee. 8033
17 come down and talk with thee *t'*: "
26 But *t'* remained two of the men in the
27 *t'* ran a young man, and told Moses,
31 *t'* went forth a wind from the Lord,
34 because *t'* they buried the people 8033
12: 6 If *t'* be a prophet among you, I the
13:20 whether *t'* be wood therein, or not.
33 *t'* we saw the giants, the sons of 8033
14:35 be consumed, and *t'* they shall die. "
43 the Canaanites are *t'* before you, "
16:35 And *t'* came out a fire from the Lord,*
46 for *t'* is wrath gone out from the Lord;
18: 5 that *t'* be no wrath any more upon
19:18 and upon the persons that were *t'*,8033
20: 1 Miriam died *t'*, and was buried *t'*. "
2 *t'* was no water for the congregation:
4 we and our cattle should die *t'*? 8033
5 neither is *t'* any water to drink.
26 unto his people, and shall die *t'*. 8033
28 and Aaron died *t'* in the top of the "
21: 5 the wilderness? for *t'* is no bread,
5 neither is *t'* any water;

Nu 21:28 For *t'* is a fire gone out of Heshbon,*
32 out the Amorites that were *t'*. 8033
35 until *t'* was none left him alive:
22: 5 *t'* is a people come out from Egypt:
11 *t'* is a people come out of Egypt, *
29 I would *t'* were a sword in mine hand,
23:23 *t'* is no enchantment against Jacob,
23 is *t'* any divination against Israel:
24:17 *t'* shall come a Star out of Jacob, and a
26:62 *t'* was no inheritance given them
64 among these *t'* was not a man of them
65 And *t'* was not left a man of them,
31: 5 *t'* were delivered out of the thousands
16 *t'* was a plague among the *
49 and *t'* lacketh not one man of us.
32:26 shall be *t'* in the cities of Gilead: 8033
33: 9 ten palm trees; and they pitched *t'*."
38 and died *t'*, in the fortieth year "
35: 6 *t'* shall be six cities for refuge, *
De 1: 2 (*T'* are eleven days' journey from*
28 seen the sons of the Anakims *t'*. 8033
35 *t'* shall not one of these men of this
46 unto the days that ye abode *t'*.
2:36 *t'* was not one city too strong for us:
3: 4 *t'* was not a city which we took not
24 what God is *t'* in heaven or in earth,
4: 7 For what nation is *t'* so great, who
8 what nation is *t'* so great, that hath
28 *t'* ye shall serve gods, the work of 8033
32 whether *t'* hath been any such thing
35 he is God; *t'* is none else beside him.
39 the earth beneath: *t'* is none else.
5:26 For who is *t'* of all flesh, that hath
29 O that *t'* were such a heart in them,
7:14 *t'* shall not be male nor female barren
24 *t'* shall no man be able to stand before
8:15 and drought, where *t'* was no water;*
10: 5 *t'* they be, as the Lord commanded8033
6 *t'* Aaron died, and *t'* he was buried;"
11:17 that *t'* be no rain, and that the land
25 *T'* shall no man be able to stand before
12: 5 all your tribes to put his name *t'*, 8033
7 *t'* ye shall eat before the Lord your "
11 *t'* shall be a place which the Lord*
11 to cause his name to dwell *t'*; 8033
14 *t'* thou shalt offer thy burnt "
14 *t'* thou shalt do all that I "
21 God hath chosen to put his name *t'* "
13: 1 If *t'* arise among you a prophet, or a
17 *t'* shall cleave nought of the cursed
14:23 shall choose to place his name *t'*, 8033
24 God shall choose to set his name *t'*, "
26 shalt eat *t'* before the Lord thy God,"
15: 4 when *t'* shall be no poor among you;
7 If *t'* be among you a poor man of one
9 *t'* be not a thought in thy wicked
21 And if *t'* be any blemish therein, as if*
16: 2 shall choose to place his name *t'*. 8033
4 *t'* shall be no leavened bread seen
4 neither shall *t'* any thing of the flesh,*
6 *t'* thou shalt sacrifice the passover8033
11 hath chosen to place his name *t'*. "
17: 2 If *t'* be found among you, within
8 If *t'* arise a matter too hard for thee in
12 to minister *t'* before the Lord thy 8033
18: 7 do, which stand *t'* before the Lord. "
10 *T'* shall not be found among you any
20: 5 man is *t'* that hath built a new house,
7 man is *t'* that hath betrothed a wife,
8 What man is *t'* that is fearful and
21: 4 the heifer's neck *t'* in the valley: 8033
22:26 *t'* is in the damsel no sin worthy of
27 cried, and *t'* was none to save her.
23:10 *t'* be among you any man, that is not
17 *T'* shall be no whore of the daughters
25: 1 If *t'* be a controversy between men,
26: 2 shall choose to place his name *t'*. 8033
5 Egypt, and sojourned *t'* with a few. "
5 *t'* a nation, great, mighty, and "
27: 5 *t'* shalt thou build an altar unto the"
7 peace offerings, and shalt eat *t'*, "
28:32 and *t'* shall be no might in thine hand.
36 *t'* shalt thou serve other gods, "
64 and *t'* thou shalt serve other gods, "
65 shall give thee *t'* a trembling heart,"
68 *t'* ye shall be sold unto your enemies"
29:18 Lest *t'* should be among you man, or
18 lest *t'* should be among you a root that
31:26 it may be *t'* for a witness against 8033
32:12 and *t'* was no strange god with him.
28 is *t'* any understanding in them.
36 is gone, and *t'* is none shut up, or left.
39 I, am he, and *t'* is no god with me:
39 neither is *t'* any that can deliver out
33:19 *t'* they shall offer sacrifices of 8033
21 *t'*, in a portion of the lawgiver, was "
26 *T'* is none like unto the God of
34: 5 the servant of the Lord died *t'* in 8033
10 *t'* arose not a prophet since in Israel
Jos 1: 5 *T'* shall not any man be able to stand
2: 1 house, named Rahab, and lodged *t'*.8033
2 *t'* came men in hither to night of the
4 *T'* came men unto me, but I wist not*
11 neither did *t'* remain...more courage
16 and hide yourselves *t'* three days, 8033
22 mountain, and abode *t'* three days, "
3: 1 lodged *t'* before they passed over. "
4 Yet *t'* shall be a space between you
4: 8 lodged, and laid them down *t'*. 8033
9 stood: and they are *t'* unto this day."
5: 1 neither was *t'* spirit in them any more,
13 *t'* stood a man over against him with
7: 4 So *t'* went up thither of the people
13 *T'* is an accursed thing in the midst
8:11 *t'* was a valley between them and Ai.
14 wist not that *t'* were liers in ambush

Jos 8:17 t' was not a man left in Ai or Beth-el.
32 And he wrote t' upon the stones 8033
35 T' was not a word of all that Moses
9:23 and t' shall none of you be freed
10: 8 t' shall not a man of them stand before
14 And t' was no day like that before it
11:11 t' was not any left to breathe: and he
19 T' was not a city that made peace
22 T' was none of the Anakims left in
22 in Gath, and in Ashod, t' remained.*
13: 1 t' remaineth yet very much land to be
14:12 day how the Anakims were t'. 8033
17: 1 T' was also a lot for the tribe of *
2 T' was also a lot for the rest of the*
5 And t' fell ten portions to Manasseh,
15 cut down for thyself t' in the land 8033
18: 1 tabernacle of the congregation t'. "
2 t' remained among the children of
10 t' Joshua divided the land unto the8033
21:44 t' stood not a man of all their enemies
45 T' failed not ought of any good thing
22:10 tribe of Manasseh built t' an altar 8033
17 t' was a plague in the congregation of
24:26 and set it up t' under an oak, 8033
J'g 1: 7 him to Jerusalem, and t' he died. "
2: 5 they sacrificed t' unto the Lord. "
10 t' arose another generation after them,
3:29 of valour; and t' escaped not a man.
4:16 the sword; and t' was not a man left.
17 t' was peace between Jabin the king
20 of thee, and say, Is t' any man here?
5: 8 was t' a shield or spear seen among
11 t' shall they rehearse the righteous
14 Out of Ephraim was t' a root of them*
15 t' were great thoughts of heart.
16 t' were great searchings of heart.
27 he bowed, t' he fell down dead. 8033
6:11 t' came an angel of the Lord, and sat*
21 t' rose up fire out of the rock, and
24 Then Gideon built an altar t' unto8033
39 and upon all the ground let t' be dew.
40 only, and t' was dew on all the ground.
7: 3 t' returned of the people twenty and
3 and t' remained ten thousand.
4 and I will try them for thee t': 8033
13 t' was a man that told a dream unto
8:10 t' fell an hundred and twenty
9:21 and went to Beer, and dwelt t'. 8033
36 t' come people down from the top
37 t' come people down by the middle
51 t' was a strong tower within the city,
10: 1 t' arose to defend Israel Tola the son
11: 3 t' were gathered vain men to Jephthah,
12: 6 t' fell at that time of the Ephraimites,
13: 2 t' was a certain man of Zorah, of the
14: 3 t' never a woman among the daughters
8 t' was a swarm of bees and honey in
10 and Samson made t' a feast; 8033
15:19 the jaw, and t' came water thereout;
16: 1 to Gaza, and saw t' an harlot, 8033
9 t' were men lying in wait, abiding*
12 t' were liers in wait abiding in the*
17 T' hath not come a rasor upon mine
27 lords of the Philistines were t'; 8033
27 t' were upon the roof about three
17: 1 And t' was a man of mount Ephraim,
6 In those days t' was no king in Israel,
7 And t' was a young man out of
7 was a Levite, and he sojourned t'. 8033
18: 1 In those days t' was no king in Israel:
2 house of Micah, they lodged t'. 8033
7 t' was no magistrate in the land, that
10 where t' is no want of any thing
11 t' went from thence of the family
14 that t' is in these houses an ephod,
28 t' was no deliverer, because it was far
19: 1 days, when t' was no king in Israel,
1 t' was a certain Levite sojourning on
2 and was t' four whole months. 8033
4 did eat and drink, and lodged t'. "
7 him: therefore he lodged t' again. "
10 t' were with him two asses saddled,
15 for t' was no man that took them into
16 t' came an old man from his work
18 t' is no man that receiveth me to
19 t' is both straw and provender for our
19 and t' is bread and wine also for me,
19 servants: t' is no want of any thing.
30 T' was no such deed done, nor seen
20:16 t' were seven hundred chosen men
26 wept, and sat t' before the Lord, 8033
27 ark of the covenant of God was t' "
34 t' came against Gibeah ten thousand
38 Now t' was an appointed sign between*
44 t' fell of Benjamin eighteen thousand
21: 1 T' shall not any...give his daughter
2 and abode t' till even before God, 8033
3 t' should be to day one tribe lacking
4 rose early, and built t' an altar, 8033
5 Who is t' among all the tribes of Israel
6 T' is one tribe cut off from Israel this
8 What one is t' of the tribes of Israel
8 t' came none to the camp from
9 t' were none of the inhabitants of
9 inhabitants of Jabesh-gilead t'. 8033
17 T' must be an inheritance for them
19 t' is a feast of the Lord in Shiloh
25 In those days t' was no king in Israel:
Ru 1: 1 that t' was a famine in the land.
2 country of Moab, and continued t'. 8033
4 they dwelled t' about ten years. "
11 are t' yet any more sons in my womb,*
17 will I die, and t' will I be buried: 8033
3:12 t' is a kinsman nearer than I.
4: 1 to the gate, and sat him down t': 8033
4 for t' is none to redeem it beside thee;

Ru 4:17 saying, T' is a son born to Naomi;
1Sa 1: 1 Now t' was a certain man of
3 the priests of the Lord, were t'. 8033
11 t' shall no rasor come upon his head.
22 the Lord, and t' abide for ever. 8033
28 And he worshipped the Lord t'. "
2: 2 T' is none holy as the Lord:
2 for t' is none beside thee:
2 neither is t' any rock like our God.
27 And t' came a man of God unto Eli,
31, 32 t' shall not be an old man in thine
3: 1 in those days; t' was no open vision.
4: 4 were t' with the ark of the covenant8033
7 for t' hath not been such a thing
10 and t' was a very great slaughter;
10 for t' fell of Israel thirty thousand
12 t' ran a man of Benjamin out of the
16 And he said, What is t' done, my son?*
17 and t' hath been also a great slaughter
5:11 t' was a deadly destruction throughout
11 the hand of God was very heavy t'.
6: 7 kine, on which t' hath come no yoke,
14 the cart came...and stood t', 8033
14 where t' was a great stone:
7: 6 and said t', We have sinned against"
14 t' was peace between Israel and the
17 to Ramah; for t' was his house; 8033
17 and t' he judged Israel; and "
17 t' he built an altar unto the Lord. "
9: 1 Now t' was a man of Benjamin, whose
2 t' was not among the children of Israel
4 land of Shalim, and t' they were not:
6 now, t' is in this city a man of God,
7 t' is not a present to bring to the man
12 t' is a sacrifice of the people to day*
10: 3 and t' shall meet thee three men
24 t' is none like him among all the
26 and t' went with him a band of men,
11: 3 and then, if t' be no man to save us,
13 T' shall not a man be put to death
14 Gilgal, and renew the kingdom t'. 8033
15 t' they made Saul king before the "
15 t' they sacrificed sacrifices of peace "
15 t' Saul and all the men of Israel "
13:19 t' was no smith found throughout all
22 that t' was neither sword nor spear
22 with Jonathan his son was t' found.
14: 4 t' was a sharp rock on the one side,
6 for t' is no restraint to the Lord to
15 And t' was trembling in the host, in
17 and his armourbearer were not t'.
20 and t' was a very great discomfiture.
25 and t' was honey upon the ground.
30 for had t' not been now a much
34 him that night, and slew them t'. 8033
39 But t' was not a man among all the
45 t' shall not one hair of his head fall to
52 t' was sore war against the Philistines
16:11 said, T' remaineth yet the youngest,
17: 3 and t' was a valley between them.
4 And t' went out a champion out of the
23 behold, t' came up the champion,
29 have I now done? Is t' not a cause?
34 father's sheep, and t' came a lion,
46 may know that t' is a God in Israel.
50 t' was no sword in the hand of David.
18:10 and t' was a javelin in Saul's hand.*
19: 8 t' was war again: and David went out,
16 in, behold, t' was an image in the bed,*
20: 3 t' is but a step between me and death.
6 his city: for t' is a yearly sacrifice*
6 sacrifice t' for all the family. 8033
8 if t' be in me iniquity, slay me thyself;
12 behold, if t' be good toward David,
21 come thou: for t' is peace to thee,
29 he hath commanded me to be t':
21: 3 in mine hand, or what t' is present.
4 T' is no common bread under mine
4 mine hand, but t' is hallowed bread;
6 hallowed bread: for t' was no bread
6 was no bread t' but the shewbread,8033
7 of the servants of Saul was t' that day,
8 is t' not here under thine hand spear
9 it: for t' is no other save that here.
9 And David said, T' is none like that;
22: 2 t' were with him about four hundred
8 t' is none that sheweth me that my
8 and t' is none of you that is sorry
22 when Doeg the Edomite was t', 8033
23:22 haunt is, and who hath seen him t':"
27 But t' came a messenger unto Saul,
24:11 and see that t' is neither evil nor
25: 2 And t' was a man in Maon, whose
7 neither was t' ought missing unto
10 t' be many servants now a days that
13 t' went up after David about four
34 surely t' had not been left unto Nabal
26:15 t' came one of the people in to destroy
27: 1 t' is nothing better for me than that I
5 the country, that I may dwell t': 8033
28: 7 t' is a woman that hath a familiar
10 t' shall no punishment happen to thee
20 and t' was no strength in him; for he
30:17 and t' escaped not a man of them, save
19 And t' was nothing lacking to them,
31:12 came to Jabesh, and burnt them t'.8033
2Sa 1:21 mountains of Gilboa, let t' be no dew,
21 neither let t' be rain, upon you, nor*
21 t' the shield of the mighty is vilely8033
2: 4 t' they anointed David king over the"
15 t' arose and went over by number*
17 And t' was a very sore battle that day;*
18 And t' were three sons of Zeruiah*
18 were three sons of Zeruiah t', 8033
23 and he fell down t', and died in the "
30 t' lacked of David's servants nineteen

2Sa 3: 1 t' was long war between the house of
6 while t' was war between the house of
27 smote him t' under the fifth rib, 8033
29 let t' not fail from the house of Joab
38 Know ye not that t' is a prince and a
4: 3 were sojourners t' until this day.) 8033
5:13 t' were yet sons and daughters born to
20 David smote them t', and said, The8033
21 t' they left their images, and David "
6: 7 and God smote him t' for his error; "
7 and t' he died by the ark of God. "
7:22 O Lord God: for t' is none like thee,
22 neither is t' any God beside thee,
9: 1 Is t' yet any that is left of the house of
2 t' was of the house of Saul a servant
3 Is t' not yet any of the house of Saul,
10:18 captain of their host, who died t'. 8033
11: 8 t' followed him a mess of meat from
17 t' fell some of the people of the
12: 1 T' were two men in one city; the one
4 t' came a traveller unto the rich man,
13:16 And she said unto him, T' is no cause:*
30 sons, and t' is not one of them left.
34 t' came much people by the way of the
38 to Geshur, and was t' three years. 8033
14: 6 t' was none to part them, but the one
11 t' shall not one hair of thy son fall to
25 t' was none to be so much praised as
25 crown of his head t' was no blemish
27 unto Absalom t' were born three sons,
30 he hath barley t'; go and set it on 8033
32 good for me to have been t' still: "
32 if t' be any iniquity in me, let him kill
15: 3 t' is no man deputed of the king to
13 t' came a messenger to David, saying,
21 even t' also will thy servant be. 8033
28 until t' come word from you to certify
29 to Jerusalem: and they tarried t'. 8033
35 hast thou not t' with thee Zadok "
36 have t' with them their two sons, "
16:14 weary, and refreshed themselves t'."
17: 9 T' is a slaughter among the people
12 t' shall not be left so much as one.*
13 until t' be not one small stone found
13 be not one small stone found t'. 8033
22 by the morning light t' lacked not one
18: 7 and t' was...a great slaughter that day
7 was t' a great slaughter that day 8033
8 the battle was t' scattered over the "
11 and why didst thou not smite him t'"
13 for t' is no matter hid from the king,
19: 7 t' will not tarry one with thee this
17 t' were a thousand men of Benjamin
18 And t' went over a ferry boat to carry
22 shall t' any man be put to death this
20: 1 t' happened to be...a man of Belial,
1 happened to be t' a man of Belial, 8033
7 And t' went out after him Joab's men,
21: 1 t' was a famine in the days of David
18 t' was again a battle with the
19 t' was again a battle in Gob with the
20 And t' was yet a battle in Gath, where
22: 9 T' went up a smoke out of his nostrils,
42 They looked, but t' was none to save;
23: 9 defied the Philistines that were t' 8033
24: 9 and t' were in Israel eight hundred
15 t' died of the people from Dan even to
25 David built t' an altar unto the 8033
1Ki 1: 2 Let t' be sought for my lord the king a
14 thou yet talkest t' with the king, 8033
34 anoint him t' king over Israel: "
52 t' shall not an hair of him fall to the
2: 4 t' shall not fail thee (said he) a man on
33 shall t' be peace for ever from the
36 house in Jerusalem, and dwell t', 8033
3: 2 t' was no house built unto the name
4 king went to Gibeon to sacrifice t';8033
12 that t' was none like thee before thee,
13 t' shall not be any among the kings
18 t' was no stranger with us in the
4:34 And t' came of all people to hear the
5: 4 that t' is neither adversary nor evil
6 for thou knowest that t' is not among
9 cause them to be discharged t', 8033
12 t' was peace between Hiram and
6: 7 t' was neither hammer nor axe nor
18 all was cedar; t' was no stone seen.
19 to set t' the ark of the covenant of 8033
7: 4 And t' were windows in three rows,
24 brim of it round about t' were knops
29 upon the ledges t' was a base above:
34 t' were four undersetters to the four
35 top of the base was t' a round compass
8: 8 and t' they are unto this day. 8033
9 T' was nothing in the ark save the
9 which Moses put t' at Horeb, 8033
21 I have set t' a place for the ark,
23 t' is no God like thee, in heaven above,
25 T' shall not fail thee a man in my
29 hast said, My name shall be t': 8033
35 heaven is shut up, and t' is no rain,
37 If t' be in the land famine,
37 If t' be pestilence, blasting, mildew,
37 locust, or if t' be caterpillar; *
37 plague, whatsoever sickness t' be;
46 (for t' is no man that sinneth not,)
56 t' hath not failed one word of all his
60 Lord is God, and that t' is none else.
64 for t' he offered burnt offerings, 8033
9: 3 built, to put my name t' for ever;
3 mine heart shall be t' perpetually. "
5 T' shall not fail thee a man upon the
10: 3 t' was not any thing hid from the king,
5 the Lord; t' was no more spirit in her,
10 t' came no more such abundance of
12 t' came no such almug trees, nor were

1Ki 10:19 t' were stays on either side on the
20 And twelve lions stood t' on the 8033
20 t' was not the like made in any
11:16 six months did Joab remain t' 8033
36 have chosen me to put my name t'. "
12:20 t' was none that followed the house of
13: 1 t' came a man of God out of Judah by
11 t' dwelt an old prophet in Beth-el;
17 eat no bread nor drink water t', 8033
14: 2 t' is Ahijah the prophet, which told "
13 in him t' is found some good thing
21 tribes of Israel, to put his name t'.8033
24 t' were also Sodomites in the land:
30 t' was war between Rehoboam and
15: 6 t' was war between Rehoboam and
7 t' was war between Abijam and
16 t' was war between Asa and Baasha
19 T' is a league between me and thee,
32 t' was war between Asa and Baasha
17: 1 t' shall not be dew nor rain these
4 the ravens to feed thee t'. 8033
7 because t' had been no rain in the land.
9 belongeth to Zidon, and dwell t': 8033
9 a widow woman t' to sustain thee. "
10 the widow woman was t' gathering "
17 sore, that t' was no breath left in him.
18: 2 And t' was a sore famine in Samaria.*
10 t' is no nation or kingdom, whither my
10 when they said, He is not t'; he took*
26 But t' was no voice, nor any that
29 that t' was neither voice, nor any to
40 brook Kishon, and slew them t'. 8033
41 for t' is a sound of abundance of rain.
43 and looked, and said, T' is nothing.
44 t' ariseth a little cloud out of the sea,
45 and wind, and t' was a great rain.
19: 3 to Judah, and left his servant t'. 8033
6 t' was a cake baken on the coals,
9 thither unto a cave, and lodged t';8033
13 behold, t' came a voice unto him, and
20: 1 t' were thirty and two kings with him,
13 t' came a prophet unto Ahab king of*
17 T' are men come out of Samaria.
28 t' came a man of God, and spake unto*
30 t' a wall fell upon twenty and seven*
40 as thy servant was busy here and t',2008
21:13 t' came in two men, children of *
25 t' was none like unto Ahab, which did
22: 7 Is t' not here a prophet of the Lord
8 T' is yet one man, Micaiah the son of
21 t' came forth a spirit, and stood before
36 t' went a proclamation throughout
47 T' was then no king in Edom: a
2Ki 1: 3 it not because t' is not a God in Israel,
6 T' came a man up to meet us, and said
6 it not because t' is not a God in Israel,
10 t' came down fire from heaven, and
14 Behold, t' came fire down from heaven,
16 t' is no God in Israel to enquire of
2:11 t' appeared a chariot of fire, and
16 t' be with thy servants fifty strong
21 the waters, and cast the salt in t',*8033
21 t' shall not be from thence any more
23 t' came forth little children out of the
24 t' came forth two she bears out of the
3: 9 t' was no water for the host, and for
11 Is t' not here a prophet of the Lord,
20 t' came water by the way of Edom, and
27 t' was great indignation against Israel:
4: 1 t' cried a certain woman of the wives
6 said unto her, T' is not a vessel more.
10 and let us set for him t' a bed, and8033
11 into the chamber, and lay t'. "
31 but t' was neither voice, nor hearing.
38 t' was a dearth in the land; and the
40 thou man of God, t' is death in the pot.
41 eat. And t' was no harm in the pot.
42 t' came a man from Baal-shalisha, and
5: 8 know that t' is a prophet in Israel.
15 now I know that t' is no God in all the
17 Shall t' not then, I pray thee, be given
18 house of Rimmon to worship t', 8033
22 t' be come to me from mount Ephraim
6: 2 let us make us a place t', where 8033
10 and saved himself t', not once nor "
25 t' was a great famine in Samaria:
26 t' cried a woman unto him, saying,
7: 3 And t' were four leprous men at the
4 enter into the city,...we shall die t':8033
5 camp of Syria, behold, t' was no man
5 of Syria, behold,...was no man t'. 8033
10 Syrians, and, behold, t' was no man
10 was no man t'; neither voice of 8033
9: 2 out t' Jehu the son of Jehoshaphat "
10 and t' shall be none to bury her.
16 went to Jezreel; for Joram lay t'. 8033
17 t' stood a watchman on the tower in*
18 t' went one on horseback to meet him,
23 and said to Ahaziah, T' is treachery,
27 he fled to Megiddo, and died t'. 8033
32 t' looked out to him two or three
10: 2 t' are with you chariots and horses,
8 t' came a messenger, and told him,
10 now that t' shall fall unto the earth
21 t' was not a man left that came not.
23 and look that t' be here with you none
11:16 king's house: and t' was she slain.8033
12:10 they saw that t' was much money they
13 Howbeit t' were not made for the house
13: 6 t' remained the grove also in Samaria.
14: 9 t' passed by a wild beast that was in
19 him to Lachish, and slew him t'. 8033
26 t' was not any shut up, nor any left,
15:20 and stayed not t' in the land. 8033
16: 6 to Elath, and dwelt t' to this day. "
17:11 t' they burnt incense in all the high"

2Ki 17:18 t' was none left but the tribe of Judah
25 the beginning of their dwelling t', 8033
27 and let them go and dwell t', and "
18:18 t' came out to them Eliakim the son
19: 3 and t' is not strength to bring forth.
32 this city, nor shoot an arrow t', 8033
20:13 t' was nothing in his house, nor in all
15 t' is nothing among my treasures that
22: 7 t' was no reckoning made with them
23:16 spied the sepulchres that were t' 8033
20 upon the high places that were t' "
22 t' was not holden such a passover
25 like unto him was t' no king before
25 neither after him arose t' any like him.
27 which I said, My name shall be t'. 8033
34 and he came to Egypt, and died t'. "
25: 3 t' was no bread for the people of the
23 t' came to Gedaliah to Mizpah, *
1Ch 3: 4 t' he reigned seven years and six 8033
4:23 t' they dwelt with the king for his "
40 for they of Ham had dwelt t' of old. "
41 the habitations that were found t', "
41 in their rooms: because t' was pasture
41 was pasture t' for their flocks. 8033
43 escaped, and dwelt t' unto this day."
5:22 For t' fell down many slain, because
11:13 t' the Philistines were gathered 8033
12: 8 of the Gadites t' separated themselves
16 t' came of the children of Benjamin
17 seeing t' is no wrong in mine hands,
19 t' fell some of Manasseh to David,
20 to Ziklag, t' fell to him of Manasseh,
22 day by day t' came to David to help
39 t' they were with David three 8033
40 abundantly: for t' was joy in Israel.
13:10 ark: and t' he died before God. 8033
14:11 and David smote them t'. "
12 when they had left their gods t', "
16:37 So he left t' before the ark of the "
17:20 O Lord, t' is none like thee, neither is
20 neither is t' any God beside thee,
19: 5 Then t' went certain, and told David
20: 2 gold, and t' were precious stones in it;
4 that t' arose war at Gezer with the
5 t' was war again with the Philistines;
6 And yet again t' was war at Gath,
21:14 and t' fell of Israel seventy thousand
26 David built t' an altar unto the 8033
28 the Jebusite, then he sacrificed t'. "
22:15 Moreover t' are workmen with thee in
16 brass, and the iron, t' is no number.
24: 4 t' were more chief men found of the
4 t' were sixteen chief men of the house*
26:31 t' were found among them mighty
27:24 t' fell wrath for it against Israel;
28:21 t' shall be with thee for all manner of
29:15 as a shadow, and t' is none abiding.
2Ch 1: 3 for t' was the tabernacle of the 8033
12 neither shall t' any after thee have the
5: 9 And t' it is unto this day. 8033
10 T' was nothing in the ark save the
6: 5, 6 that my name might be t'; 8033
14 t' is no God like thee in the heaven,
16 T' shall not fail thee a man in my
20 thou wouldest put thy name t'; 8033
26 heaven is shut up, and t' is no rain,
28 If t' be dearth in the land,
28 if t' be pestilence, if t' be blasting,
28 sore or whatsoever sickness t' be:
36 (for t' is no man which sinneth not,)
7: 7 t' he offered burnt offerings, and 8033
13 If I shut up heaven that t' be no rain,
16 that my name may be t' for ever: 8033
16 mine heart shall be t' perpetually. "
18 T' shall not fail thee a man to be ruler
8: 2 the children of Israel to dwell t'. 8033
9: 2 and t' was nothing hid from Solomon
4 Lord; t' was no more spirit in her.
9 neither was t' any such spice as the
11 t' were none such seen before in the
18 And t' were six steps to the throne,
19 twelve lions stood t' on the one 8033
19 T' was not the like made in any
12:13 tribes of Israel, to put his name t'.8033
15 t' were wars between Rehoboam and
13: 2 And t' was war between Abijah and
7 t' are gathered unto him vain men,
8 t' are with you golden calves, which
17 t' fell down slain of Israel five hundred
14: 9 t' came out against them Zerah the
14 t' was exceeding much spoil in them.
15: 5 t' was no peace to him that went out,
19 t' was no more war unto the five and
16: 3 T' is a league between me and thee,
3 as t' was between my father and thy
18: 6 Is t' not here a prophet of the Lord
7 T' is yet one man, by whom we may
20 Then t' came out a spirit, and stood
19: 3 t' are good things found in thee,
7 for t' is no iniquity with the Lord our
20: 2 t' came some that told Jehoshaphat,
2 T' cometh a great multitude against
6 and in thine hand is t' not power and*
26 t' they blessed the Lord: therefore8033
21:12 t' came a writing to him from Elijah
17 so that t' was never a son left him,
23:15 king's house, they slew her t'. 8033
24:11 they saw that t' was much money,
25: 7 t' came a man of God to him, saying,
18 t' passed by a wild beast that was in
27 after him, and slew him t'. 8033
28: 9 But a prophet of the Lord was t', "
10 but are t' not with you, even with you,
13 and t' is fierce wrath against Israel.
18 villages thereof: and they dwelt t'.8033
30:13 And t' assembled at Jerusalem much

2Ch 30:17 t' were many in the congregation that
26 So t' was great joy in Jerusalem: for
26 Israel t' was not the like in Jerusalem.
32: 4 So t' was gathered much people
7 for t' be more with us than with him:
14 Who was t' among all the gods of
21 bowels slew him t' with the sword. 8033
25 therefore t' was wrath upon him, and
34:13 and of the Levites t' were scribes, and
35:18 And t' was no passover like to that
36:16 his people, till t' was no remedy.
23 Who is t' among you of all his people?
Ezr 1: 3 Who is t' among you of all his people?
2:63 till t' stood up a priest with Urim and
65 of whom t' were seven thousand three
65 and t' were among them two hundred*
4:20 T' have been mighty kings also over
5:17 let t' be search made in the king's
17 house, which is t' at Babylon, 8536
6: 2 And t' was found at Achmetha, in the
12 hath caused his name to dwell t' 8536
7: 7 t' went up some of the children of
23 should t' be wrath against the realm
8:15 t' abode we in tents three days: 8033
15 found t' none of the sons of Levi. "
21 Then I proclaimed a fast t', at the "
25 all Israel t' present, had offered:
32 and abode t' three days. 8033
9:14 t' should be no remnant nor escaping?
10: 1 t' assembled unto him out of Israel a
2 t' is hope in Israel concerning this
18 among the sons of the priests t' were
Ne 1: 3 are left of the captivity t' in the 8033
9 though t' were of you cast out unto*
9 I have chosen to set my name t'. 8033
2:10 t' was come a man to seek the welfare
11 Jerusalem, and was t' three days. 8033
12 neither was t' any beast with me,
14 t' was no place for the beast that was
4:10 t' is much rubbish; so that we are not
5: 1 t' was a great cry of the people and
2 t' were that said, We, our sons, and
3 Some also t' were that said, We have
4 T' were also that said, We have
17 t' were at my table an hundred and
6: 1 that t' was no breach left therein;
7 T' is a king in Judah: and now shall
8 T' are no such things done as thou
11 and who is t', that, being as I am,
18 t' were many in Judah sworn unto
7:65 till t' stood up a priest with Urim and
67 of whom t' were seven thousand three
8:17 so. And t' was very great gladness.
12:46 of old t' were chief of the singers,
13:16 T' dwelt men of Tyre also therein,
19 t' should no burden be brought in on
26 many nations was t' no king like him,
Es 1:18 Thus shall t' arise too much contempt
19 t' go a royal commandment from him,
2: 2 Let t' be fair young virgins sought for
5 in...the palace t' was a certain Jew,
3: 8 T' is a certain people scattered
12 t' was written according to all that
4: 3 t' was great mourning among the
11 t' is one law of his to put him to death,
14 t' enlargement and deliverance arise*
6: 3 unto him, T' is nothing done for him.
7: 7 he saw that t' was evil determined
Job 1: 1 T' was a man in the land of Uz,
2 t' were born unto him seven sons and
6 t' was a day when the sons of God‡
8 that t' is none like him in the earth,
13 t' was a day when his sons and his*
14 And t' came a messenger unto Job,
16, 17, 18 speaking, t' came also another,
19 t' came a great wind from the
2: 1 Again t' was a day when the sons of‡
3 that t' is none like him in the earth,
3: 3 was said, T' is a man child conceived.
17 T' the wicked cease from 8033
17 and t' the weary be at rest.
18 T' the prisoners rest together; they
19 The small and great are t'; and 8033
4:16 t' was silence, and I heard a voice,
5: 1 if t' be any that will answer thee;
4 gate, neither is t' any to deliver them.
19 in seven t' shall no evil touch thee.
6:30 Is t' iniquity in my tongue? cannot
7: 1 Is t' not an appointed time to man
9:33 Neither is t' any daysman betwixt us,
10: 7 t' is none that can deliver out of thine
11:18 thou shalt be secure, because t' is hope;
12:14 up a man, and t' can be no opening.
24 in a wilderness where t' is no way.
14: 7 For t' is hope of a tree, if it be cut
15:11 is t' any secret thing with thee? *
17: 2 Are t' not mockers with me? and doth
19: 7 I cry aloud, but t' is no judgment.
29 that ye may know t' is a judgment.
20:21 T' shall none of his meat be left;
21:33 him, as t' are innumerable before him.
34 your answers t' remaineth falsehood?
22:29 then thou shalt say, T' is lifting up;
23: 7 T' the righteous might dispute 8033
8 Behold, I go forward, but he is not t';
25: 3 Is t' any number of his armies? and
28: 1 Surely t' is a vein for the silver, and a
7 T' is a path which no fowl knoweth,*
30:26 I waited for light, t' came darkness.
31: 2 what portion of God is t' from above?*
32: 5 Elihu saw that t' was no answer in
8 But t' is a spirit in man: and the
12 t' was none of you that convinced Job.
33: 9 innocent; neither is t' iniquity in me.
23 If t' be a messenger with him, an
34:22 T' is no darkness, nor shadow of

Job 35:12 T' they cry, but none giveth 8033
36:16 broad place, where t' is no straitness;
18 Because t' is wrath, beware lest he‡
38:26 the wilderness, wherein t' is no man;
39:30 and where the slain are, t' is she. 8033
41:33 Upon earth t' is not his like, who is
42:11 Then came t' unto him all his
Ps 3: 2 Many t' be which say of my soul,
2 T' is no help for him in God. Selah.
4: 6 T' be many that say, Who will shew
5: 9 t' is no faithfulness in their mouth;
6: 5 For in death t' is no remembrance of
7: 2 it in pieces, while t' is none to deliver.
3 if t' be iniquity in my hands;
14: 1 hath said in his heart, T' is no God.
1 works, t' is none that doeth good.
2 if t' were any that did understand,
3 t' is none that doeth good, no, not one.
5 T' were they in great fear: for 8033
16:11 hand t' are pleasures for evermore.
18: 8 T' went up a smoke out of his nostrils,
41 cried, but t' was none to save them:
19: 3 T' is no speech nor language, where
6 t' is nothing hid from the heat thereof.
11 in keeping of them t' is great reward.
22:11 trouble is near; for t' is none to help.
30: 9 What profit is t' in my blood, when I
32: 2 and in whose spirit t' is no guile.
33:16 T' is no king saved by the multitude
34: 9 for t' is no want to them that fear him.
36: 1 t' is no fear of God before his eyes.
12 T' are the workers of iniquity 8033
38: 3 T' is no soundness in my flesh
3 neither is t' any rest in my bones
7 and t' is no soundness in my flesh.
45:12 the daughter of Tyre shall be t'
46: 4 T' is a river, the streams whereof
48: 6 Fear took hold upon them t', and 8033
50:22 in pieces, and t' be none to deliver.
53: 1 hath said in his heart, T' is no God.
1 iniquity: t' is none that doeth good.
2 if t' were any that did understand,
3 t' is none that doeth good, no, not one.
5 T' were they in great fear, where 8033
55:18 against me: for t' were many with me.*
58:11 Verily t' is a reward for the righteous:
66: 6 on foot: t' did we rejoice in him. 8033
68:27 T' is little Benjamin with their "
69: 2 in deep mire, where t' is no standing:
20 some to take pity, but t' was none;
35 that they may dwell t', and have it in
71:11 him; for t' is none to deliver him.
72:16 T' shall be an handful of corn in the
73: 4 For t' are no bands in their death:
11 and is t' knowledge in the most High?
25 t' is none upon earth that I desire
74: 9 our signs: t' is no more any prophet:
9 neither is t' among us any that
75: 8 in the hand of the Lord t' is a cup,
76: 3 T' brake he the arrows of the bow,8033
79: 3 and t' was none to bury them.
81: 9 T' shall no strange god be in thee;
86: 8 Among the gods t' is none like unto
8 are t' any works like unto thy works.
87: 4 Ethiopia; this man was born t'. 8033
6 people, that this man was born t'. "
7 the players on instruments shall be t':*
91:10 T' shall no evil befall thee, neither
92:15 and t' is no unrighteousness in him.
104:26 T' go the ships: 8033
26 t' is that leviathan, whom thou
105:31 spake, and t' came divers sorts of flies,
37 t' was not one feeble person among
106:11 enemies: t' was not one of them left.
107:12 fell down, and t' was none to help.
36 t' he maketh the hungry to dwell, 8033
40 in the wilderness, where t' is no way.
109:12 Let t' be none to extend mercy unto
12 let t' be any to favour his fatherless
112: 4 t' ariseth light in the darkness:
122: 5 For t' are set thrones of judgment,8033
130: 4 But t' is forgiveness with thee, that
7 for with the Lord t' is mercy, and with
132:17 T' will I make the horn of David 8033
133: 3 for t' the Lord commanded the "
135:17 neither is t' any breath in their
137: 1 rivers of Babylon, t' we sat down, 8033
3 For t' they that carried us away "
139: 4 For t' is not a word in my tongue, but,
8 ascend up into heaven, thou art t':8033
8 my bed in hell, behold, thou art t'.
10 Even t' shall thy hand lead me, 8033
16 when as yet t' was none of them.
24 see if t' be any wicked way in me, and
142: 4 t' was no man that would know me:
144:14 that t' be no breaking in, nor going
14 t' be no complaining in our streets.*
146: 3 the son of man, in whom t' is no help.
Pr 7:10 t' met him a woman with the attire of
8: 8 t' is nothing froward or perverse in
24 t' were no depths, I was brought forth;
24 t' were no fountains abounding with
27 prepared the heavens, I was t': 8033
9:18 he knoweth not that the dead are t';"
10:19 In the multitude of words t' wanteth
11:10 when the wicked perish, t' is shouting.
14 multitude of counsellers, t' is safety.
24 T' is that scattereth, and yet
24 t' is that withholdeth more than is
12:18 T' is that speaketh like the piercings
21 T' shall no evil happen to the just:
28 in the pathway thereof t' is no death.
13: 7 T' is that maketh himself rich, yet
7 t' is that maketh himself poor, yet
23 t' is that is destroyed for want of
14: 9 but among the righteous t' is favour.

Pr 14:12 T' is a way which seemeth right unto
23 In all labour t' is profit: but the talk
16:25 T' is a way that seemeth right unto a
27 and in his lips t' is as a burning fire.
17:16 is t' a price in the hand of a fool to
18:24 t' is a friend that sticketh closer than a
19:18 Chasten thy son while t' is hope, and
21 T' are many devices in a man's heart;
20:15 T' is gold, and a multitude of rubies:
21:20 T' is treasure to be desired and oil in
30 T' is no wisdom nor understanding
22:13 The slothful man saith, T' is a lion
23:18 For surely t' is an end; and thine
24: 6 in multitude of counsellers t' is safety.
14 found it, then t' shall be a reward,
20 t' shall be no reward to the evil man;
25: 4 and t' shall come forth a vessel for the
26:12 t' is more hope of a fool than of him.
13 man saith, T' is a lion in the way;
20 no wood is, t' the fire goeth out: so*
20 t' is no talebearer, the strife ceaseth.
25 t' are seven abominations in his heart.
28:12 men do rejoice, t' is great glory:
29: 6 of an evil man t' is a snare:
9 he rage or laugh, t' is no rest.
18 Where t' is no vision, the people
20 t' is more hope of a fool than of him.
30:11 T' is a generation that curseth their
12 T' is a generation that are pure in
13 T' is a generation, O how lofty are
14 T' is a generation, whose teeth are as
15 T' are three things that are never
18 T' be three things which are too
24 T' be four things which are little upon
29 T' be three things which go well, yea,
31 king, against whom t' is no rising up.
Ec 1: 9 t' is no new thing under the sun.
10 Is t' any thing whereof it may be said,
11 T' is no remembrance of former
11 neither shall t' be any remembrance
2:11 and t' was no profit under the sun.
16 t' is no remembrance of the wise
21 t' is a man whose labour is in wisdom,
24 T' is nothing better for a man, than
3: 1 To every thing t' is a season, and a
12 I know that t' is no good in them, but
16 judgment, that wickedness was t';8033
16 righteousness, that iniquity was t'. "
17 t' is a time...for every purpose and
17 is a time t' for every purpose and 8033
22 I perceive that t' is nothing better,
4: 1 side of their oppressors t' was power;
8 T' is one alone, and...is not a second;
8 is one alone, and t' is not a second;*
8 is t' no end of all his labour; neither
16 T' is no end of all the people, even of
5: 7 words t' are also divers vanities: †
8 regardeth; and t' be higher than they.
11 what good is t' to the owners thereof,
13 T' is a sore evil which I have seen
14 a son, and t' is nothing in his hand.
6: 1 T' is an evil which I have seen under
11 t' be many things that increase vanity,
7:11 by it t' is profit to them that see the*
15 t' is a just man that perisheth in his
15 t' is a wicked man that prolongeth his
20 For t' is not a just man upon earth,
8: 4 the word of a king is, t' is power:*
6 to every purpose t' is time and
8 T' is no man that hath power over the
8 and t' is no discharge in that war;
9 t' is a time wherein one man ruleth
14 T' is a vanity which is done upon the
14 that t' be just men, unto whom it
14 again, t' be wicked men, to whom it
16 t' is that neither day nor night seeth
9: 2 t' is one event to the righteous, and
3 the sun, that t' is one event unto all:
4 is joined to all the living t' is hope:
10 for t' is no work, nor device, nor
14 T' was a little city, and few men
14 and t' came a great king against it,
15 t' was found in it a poor wise man,
10: 5 T' is an evil which I have seen under
3 the tree falleth, t' it shall be. 8033
12:12 of making many books t' is no end;
Ca 4: 4 whereon t' hang a thousand bucklers,
7 all fair, my love; t' is no spot in thee.
6: 6 t' is not one barren among them.*
8 T' are threescore queens, and
7:12 bud forth: t' will I give thee my loves.
8: 5 t' thy mother brought thee forth:
5 t' she brought thee forth that bare
Isa 1: 6 unto the head t' is no soundness in it;
2: 7 is t' any end of their treasures;
7 neither is t' any end of their chariots:
3:24 instead of sweet smell t' shall be stink;
4: 6 t' shall be a tabernacle for a shadow
5: 6 but t' shall come up briers and thorns:
8 lay field to field, till t' be no place,
6:12 t' be a great forsaking in the midst*
7:23 where t' were a thousand vines at a
25 t' shall not come thither the fear of*
8:20 it is because t' is no light in them.
9: 7 and peace t' shall be no end,
10:14 t' was none that moved the wing, or
11: 1 t' shall come forth a rod out of the
10 in that day t' shall be a root of Jesse,*
16 t' shall be an highway for the remnant
13:20 shall the Arabian pitch tent t'; 8033
20 the shepherds make their fold t'. "
21 beasts of the desert shall lie t'; "
21 creatures; and owls shall dwell t', "
21 and satyrs shall dance t'. "
14:31 t' shall come from the north a smoke,
15: 6 the grass faileth, t' is no green thing.

Isa 16:10 in the vineyards t' shall be no singing,
10 neither shall t' be shouting: the *
17: 9 Israel: and t' shall be desolation.*
19:15 shall t' be any work for Egypt, which
19 In that day shall t' be an altar to the
23 In that day shall t' be a highway out
22:18 a large country: t' shalt thou die, 8033
18 t' the chariots of thy glory shall be "
23: 1 laid waste, so that t' is no house,
10 of Tarshish: t' is no more strength.
12 t' also shalt thou have no rest. 8033
24:11 T' is a crying for wine in the streets;
13 t' shall be as the shaking of an olive*
27:10 wilderness: t' shall the calf feed, 8033
10 t' shall he lie down, and consume "
28: 8 filthiness, so that t' is no place clean.
10 line; here a little, and t' a little: 8033
13 line; here a little, and t' a little; "
29: 2 and t' shall be heaviness and sorrow:
30:14 so that t' shall not be found in the
25 t' shall be upon every high mountain,
28 t' shall be a bridle in the jaws of the*
33:21 But t' the glorious Lord will be 8033
34:12 the kingdom, but none shall be t', "
14 the screech owl also shall rest t', "
15 T' shall the great owl make her "
15 t' shall the vultures also be "
35: 8 And an highway shall be t', and a "
9 No lion shall be t', nor any "
9 up thereon, it shall not be found t';"
9 but the redeemed shall walk t':
37: 3 and t' is not strength to bring forth.
33 this city, nor shoot an arrow t', 8033
39: 2 t' was nothing in his house, nor in all
4 t' is nothing among my treasures that
8 t' shall be peace and truth in my days.
40:28 t' is no searching of his understanding.
41:17 and needy seek water, and t' is none,
26 yea, t' is none that sheweth,
26 yea, t' is none that declareth,
26 t' is none that heareth your words.
28 For I beheld, and t' was no man; even
28 among them, and t' was no counseller,
43:10 before me t' was no God formed,
10 formed, neither shall t' be after me.
11 Lord; and beside me t' is no saviour.
12 t' was no strange god among you:
13 t' is none that can deliver out of my
44: 6 the last; and beside me t' is no God.
8 my witnesses. Is t' a God beside me?
8 Yea, t' is no God; I know not any.
19 neither is t' knowledge nor
20 say, Is t' not a lie in my right hand?
45: 5 I am the Lord, and t' is none else,
5 t' is no God beside me: I girded thee,
6 the west, that t' is none beside me.
6 I am the Lord, and t' is none else.
14 thee; and t' is none else, t' is no God.
18 I am the Lord; and t' is none else.
21 and t' is no God else beside me; a just
21 and a Saviour; t' is none beside me.
22 for I am God, and t' is none else.
46: 9 old: for I am God, and t' is none else;
9 I am God, and t' is none like me,
47: 1 t' is no throne, O daughter of the *
14 t' shall not be a coal to warm at, nor*
48:16 from the time that it was, t' am I: 8033
22 T' is no peace, saith the Lord, unto
50: 2 when I came, was t' no man?
2 when I called, was t' none to answer?
2 t' is no water, and dieth for thirst.
51:18 T' is none to guide her among all the
18 neither is t' any that taketh her by the
52: 1 for henceforth t' shall no more come
4 aforetime into Egypt to sojourn t';8033
53: 2 t' is no beauty that we should desire
57:10 yet saidst thou not, T' is no hope:
21 T' is no peace, saith my God, to the
59: 8 and t' is no judgment in their goings:
11 we look for judgment, but t' is none;
15 him that t' was no judgment.
16 and he saw that t' was no man, and
16 wondered that t' was no intercessor:
63: 3 and of the people t' was none with me:
5 And I looked, and t' was none to help;
5 and I wondered that t' was none to
64: 7 t' is none that calleth upon thy name,
65: 9 it, and my servants shall dwell t'. 8033
20 T' shall be no more thence an infant
Jer 2:10 diligently, and see if t' be such a thing.
25 T' is no hope: no; for I have loved‡
3: 3 and t' hath been no latter rain;
6 tree, and t' hath played the harlot.8033
4:25 I beheld, and, lo, t' was no man, and
5: 1 if t' be any that executeth judgment,
6:14 Peace, peace; when t' is no peace.
20 purpose cometh t' to me incense from
7: 2 house, and proclaim t' this word, 8033
32 bury in Tophet, till t' be no place.
8:11 Peace, peace; where t' is no peace.
13 t' shall be no grapes on the vine, nor
14 cities, and let us be silent t': 8033
22 Is t' no balm in Gilead; is t' no
22 is...no physician t'? why then is 8033
10: 6 as t' is none like unto thee, O Lord;
7 kingdoms, t' is none like unto thee.
13 t' is a multitude of waters in the
14 falsehood, and t' is no breath in them.
20 t' is none to stretch forth my tent any
11:23 t' shall be no remnant of them: for I
13: 4 and hide it t' in a hole of the rock. 8033
6 which I commanded thee to hide t'."
14: 4 for t' was no rain in the earth, the*
5 and forsook it, because t' was no grass.
6 eyes did fail, because t' was no grass.
19 smitten us, and t' is no healing for us?

Jer 14:19 looked for peace, and t' is no good;*
22 Are t' any among the vanities of the
16:13 t' shall ye serve other gods day 8033
19 and things wherein t' is no profit.
17:25 t' enter into the gates of this city kings
18: 2 t' I will cause thee to hear my 8033
12 And they said, T' is no hope: but we
19: 2 proclaim t' the words that I shall 8033
11 in Tophet, till t' be no place to bury.
20: 6 to Babylon, and t' thou shalt die, 8033
6 and shalt be buried t', thou, and all "
22: 1 of Judah, and speak t' this word,
4 then shall t' enter in by the gates of
26 were not born; and t' shall ye die.8033
26:20 And t' was also a man that prophesied
27:22 t' shall they be until the day that 8033
29: 6 that ye may be increased t', and "
30:13 T' is none to plead thy cause, that
31: 6 For t' shall be a day, that the
17 t' is hope in thine end, saith the Lord,
24 t' shall dwell in Judah itself, and in*
32: 5 t' shall he be until I visit him, 8033
17 and t' is nothing too hard for thee:
27 flesh: is t' any thing too hard for me?
33:10 Again t' shall be heard in this place,
20 that t' should not be day and night in
36:12 the princes sat t', even Elishama 8033
22 t' was a fire on the hearth burning
32 t' were added besides unto them many
37:10 t' remained but wounded men among
13 a captain of the ward was t', 8033
16 had remained t' many days; "
17 said, Is t' any word from the Lord?
17 And Jeremiah said, T' is: for, said he,
20 Jonathan the scribe, lest I die t'. 8033
38: 6 in the dungeon t' was no water, but
9 for t' is no more bread in the city.
26 to Jonathan's house, to die t'. 8033
28 he was t' when Jerusalem was taken.*
41: 1 t' they did eat bread together in 8033
3 the Chaldeans that were found t', "
5 That t' came certain from Shechem,
42:14 of bread; and t' will we dwell: 8033
15 into Egypt, and go to sojourn t'; "
16 shall overtake you t' in the land of "
16 follow close after you t' in Egypt; "
16 in Egypt; and t' ye shall die. "
17 faces to go into Egypt to sojourn t';"
43: 2 Go not into Egypt to sojourn t': "
44:12, 14 the land of Egypt to sojourn t', "
14 have a desire to return to dwell t': "
27 the famine, until t' be an end of them.
28 the land of Egypt to sojourn t', 8033
46:17 They did cry t', Pharaoh king of "
47: 7 sea shore? t' hath he appointed it. "
48: 2 T' shall be no more praise of Moab:*
38 T' shall be lamentation generally
49:18 the Lord, no man shall abide t', 8033
23 t' is sorrow on the sea; it cannot be
33 for ever: t' shall no man abide *
33 shall no man abide t', nor any 8033
36 and t' shall be no nation whither the
50: 3 out of the north t' cometh up a nation
20 be sought for, and t' shall be none;
39 beasts of the islands shall dwell t', "
40 so shall no man abide t', neither "
51:16 voice, t' is a multitude of waters in the
17 falsehood, and t' is no breath in them.
52: 6 so that t' was no bread for the people
23 t' were ninety and six pomegranates
34 t' was a continual diet given him of
La 1:12 see if t' be any sorrow like unto my
17 hands, and t' is none to comfort her:
20 bereaveth, at home t' is as death.
21 that I sigh: t' is none to comfort me:
3:29 in the dust; if so be t' may be hope.
4:15 They shall no more sojourn t'. *
5: 8 t' is none that doth deliver us out of
Eze 1: 3 hand of the Lord was t' upon him.8033
25 And t' was a voice from the firmament
2: 5 t' hath been a prophet among them.
10 t' was written therein lamentations,
3:15 sat, and remained t' astonished 8033
22 hand of the Lord was t' upon me; "
22 plain, and I will t' talk with thee. "
23 the glory of the Lord stood t', as "
4:14 neither came t' abominable flesh into
7:11 neither shall t' be wailing for them.
25 shall seek peace, and t' shall be none.
8: 1 hand of the Lord...fell t' upon me. 8033
4 glory of the God of Israel was t', "
11 And t' stood before them seventy men
14 t' sat women weeping for Tammuz.8033
10: 1 t' appeared over them as it were a
8 t' appeared in the cherubims the form
12:13 not see it, though he shall die t'. 8033
24 t' shall be no more any vain vision nor
28 T' shall none of my words be prolonged
13:10 saying, Peace; and t' was no peace;
11 t' shall be an overflowing shower; and
13 and t' shall be an overflowing shower
16 and t' is no peace, saith the Lord God.
20 wherewith ye t' hunt the souls to 8033
17: 7 T' was also another great eagle with
20 plead with him t' for his trespass "
20:28 and they offered t' their sacrifices, "
28 t' they presented the provocation "
28 t'...they made their sweet savour, "
28 poured out t' their drink offerings. "
35 t' will I plead with you face to face. "
40 t' shall all the house of Israel, all of "
40 serve me: t' will I accept them, "
40 and t' will I require your offerings, "
43 t' shall ye remember your ways, "
22:20 and I will leave you t', and melt you.
25 T' is a conspiracy of her prophets in
Eze 23: 2 t' were two women, the daughters of
3 t' were their breasts pressed, and 8033
3 t' they bruised the teats of their "
28: 3 t' is no secret that they can hide from
24 t' shall be no more a pricking brier
29:14 they shall be t' a base kingdom. 8033
30:13 t' shall be no more a prince of the land
18 shall break t' the yokes of Egypt: 8033
32:22 Asshur is t' and all her company: "
24 T' is Elam and all her multitude "
26 T' is Meshech, Tubal, and all her "
29 T' is Edom, her kings, and all her "
30 T' be the princes of the north, all "
34: 5 scattered, because t' is no shepherd:
8 because t' was no shepherd, neither
14 t' shall they lie in a good fold, and8033
26 season; t' shall be showers of blessing.
35:10 whereas the Lord was t': 8033
37: 2 t' were very many in the open valley;
7 t' was a noise, and behold a shaking,
8 but t' was no breath in them.
38:19 in that day t' shall be a great shaking
39:11 give unto Gog a place t' of graves*8033
11 t' shall they bury Gog and all his "
28 have left none of them any more t'. "
40: 3 t' was a man, whose appearance
16 t' were narrow windows to the little
17 court, and, lo, t' were chambers,
25 t' were windows in it and in the arches
26 And t' were seven steps to go up to it,
27 t' was a gate in the inner court toward
29 t' were windows in it and in the arches
33 t' were windows therein and in the
49 t' were pillars by the posts, one on this
41: 7 t' was an enlarging, and a winding*
25 t' were made on them, on the doors of
25 t' were thick planks upon the face of
26 t' were narrow windows and palm
42:13 t' shall they lay the most holy 8033
14 t' shall they lay their garments "
45: 2 this t' shall be for the sanctuary five
46:19 t' was a place on the two sides 8033
21 corner of the court t' was a court.
22 of the court t' were courts joined
23 t' was a row of building round about
47: 2 t' ran out waters on the right side.
9 t' shall be a very great multitude of
23 t' shall ye give him his inheritance.8033
48:35 that day shall be, The Lord is t'. "
Da 2: 9 the dream, t' is but one decree for you:
10 T' is not a man upon the earth that
10 t' is no king, lord, nor ruler, that *
11 t' is none other that can shew it before
28 t' is a God in heaven that revealeth
41 t' shall be in it of the strength of the
3:12 T' are certain Jews whom thou hast
29 t' is no other God that can deliver
4:31 mouth, t' fell a voice from heaven,
5:11 T' is a man in thy kingdom, in whom
6: 4 neither was t' any error or fault found
7: 8 t' came up among them another little
8 before whom t' were three of the *
14 And t' was given him dominion, and
8: 3 t' stood before the river a ram which
4 neither was t' any that could deliver
7 t' was no power in the ram to stand
7 t' was none that could deliver the ram
15 t' stood before me as the appearance
10: 8 and t' remained no strength in me:
13 I remained t' with the kings of 8033
17 t' remained no strength in me,
17 in me, neither is t' breath left in me.
18 t' came again and touched me one
21 t' is none that holdeth with me in these
11: 2 t' shall stand up yet three kings in
14 in those times t' shall many stand up
15 neither shall t' be any strength to
12: 1 t' shall be a time of trouble, such as
1 such as never was since t' was a nation
5 t' stood other two, the one on this side
11 t' shall be a thousand two hundred and
Ho 1:10 people, t' it shall be said unto them,
2:15 she shall sing t', as in the days of 8033
4: 1 because t' is no truth, nor mercy,
9 And t' shall be, like people, like priest:*
6: 7 t' have they dealt treacherously 8033
10 t' is the whoredom of Ephraim, "
7: 7 t' is none among them that calleth
9 gray hairs are here and t' upon him,
9:12 them, that t' shall not be a man left:
15 in Gilgal: for t' I hated them: 8033
10: 9 the days of Gibeah: t' they stood: "
12: 4 in Beth-el, and t' he spake with us; "
11 Is t' iniquity in Gilead? surely they*
13: 4 but me: for t' is no saviour beside me.
8 t' will I devour them like a lion: 8033
Joe 2: 2 t' hath not been ever the like, neither
3: 2 plead with them t' for my people 8033
12 t' will I sit to judge all the heathen "
17 t' shall no strangers pass through her
Am 3: 6 shall t' be evil in a city, and the Lord*
11 An adversary t' shall be even round
4: 7 when t' were yet three months to the
5: 2 her land; t' is none to raise her up.
6 and t' be none to quench it in Beth-el.
6: 9 if t' remain ten men in one house,
10 of the house, Is t' yet any with thee?
12 rock? will one plow t' with oxen?
7:12 and t' eat bread, and prophesy t': 8033
8: 3 t' shall be many dead bodies in every*
Ob 7 thee: t' is none understanding in him.
17 deliverance, and t' shall be holiness;*
18 and t' shall not be any remaining of
Jon 1: 4 t' was a mighty tempest in the sea,
4: 5 and t' made him a booth, and sat 8033
Mic 3: 7 their lips; for t' is no answer of God.
Mic 4: 9 is t' no king in thee? is thy counseller
10 to Babylon; t' shalt thou be delivered;
10 t' the Lord shall redeem thee from8033
6:10 Are t' yet the treasures of wickedness
7: 1 of the vintage: t' is no cluster to eat:
2 and t' is none upright among men:
Na 1:11 T' is one come out of thee, that
2: 9 for t' is none end of the store and glory
3: 3 t' is a multitude of slain, and a great*
3 and t' is none end of their corpses;
15 T' shall the fire devour thee; the 8033
19 T' is no healing of thy bruise; thy
Hab 1: 3 and t' are that raise up strife and
2:19 t' is no breath at all in the midst of it.
3: 4 and t' was the hiding of his power.8033
17 and t' shall be no herd in the stalls:
Zep 1:10 t' shall be the noise of a cry from the
14 mighty man shall cry t' bitterly. 8033
2: 5 thee, that t' shall be no inhabitant.
15 heart, I am, and t' is none beside me:
3: 6 are destroyed, so that t' is no man,
6 is no man, that t' is none inhabitant.
Hag 1: 6 ye clothe you, but t' is none warm;
2:14 that which they offer t' is unclean.8033
16 of twenty measures, t' were but ten:
16 out of the press, t' were but twenty.
Zec 1: 8 and behind him were t' red horses,
5: 7 behold, t' was lifted up a talent of lead:
9 and, behold, t' came out two women,
11 and set t' upon her own base. 8033
6: 1 behold, t' came four chariots out from
8: 4 T' shall yet old men and old women
10 these days t' was no hire for man,
10 neither was t' any peace to him that
20 to pass, that t' shall come people,
10: 2 troubled, because t' was no shepherd.
11: 3 T' is a voice of the howling of the*
12:11 that day shall t' be a great mourning
13: 1 that day t' shall be a fountain opened
14: 4 and t' shall be a very great valley;
9 that day shall t' be one Lord, and his*
11 t' shall be no more utter destruction;
18 t' shall be the plague, wherewith the
20 that day shall t' be upon the bells of
21 in that day t' shall be no more the
Mal 1:10 is t' even among you that would shut
3:10 that t' may be meat in mine house,
10 t' shall not be room enough to receive
M't 2: 1 t' came wise men from the east to*
13 be thou t' until I bring thee word: 1563
15 And was t' until the death of Herod:"
18 In Rama was t' a voice heard, *
4:25 t' followed him great multitudes of
5:23 t' rememberest that thy brother 1563
24 Leave t' thy gift before the altar, "
6:21 is, t' will your heart be also. "
7: 9 Or what man is t' of you, whom if his
13 and many t' be which go in thereat:*
14 unto life, and few t' be that find it.*
8: 2 t' came a leper and worshipped him,
5 t' came unto him a centurion,
12 t' shall be weeping and gnashing 1563
24 t' arose a great tempest in the sea,
26 and the sea; and t' was a great calm.
28 t' met him two possessed with devils,
30 And t' was a good way off from them
10:11 and t' abide till ye go thence. 1563
26 t' is nothing covered, that shall not be
11:11 t' hath not risen a greater than John
12:10 t' was a man which had his hand *
11 What man shall t' be among you, that
39 t' shall no sign be given to it, but the
45 and they enter in and dwell t': 1563
13:42, 50 t' shall be wailing and gnashing "
58 he did not many mighty works t' "
14:23 evening was come, he was t' alone. "
15:29 up into a mountain, and sat down t'."
16: 4 and t' shall no sign be given unto it,
28 T' be some standing here, which shall
17: 3 t' appeared unto them Moses and
14 t' came to him a certain man, kneeling
18:20 name, t' am I in the midst of them.1563
19: 2 him; and he healed them t'. "
12 For t' are some eunuchs, which were
12 t' are some eunuchs, which were made
12 t' be eunuchs, which have made
13 were t' brought unto him...children,
17 t' is none good but one, that is, God:
21:17 into Bethany; and he lodged t'. 1563
33 T' was a certain householder, which
22:11 saw t' a man which had not on a 1563
13 t' shall be weeping and gnashing of"
23 which say that t' is no resurrection,
25 Now t' were with us seven brethren:
24: 2 T' shall not be left here one stone
7 t' shall be famines, and pestilences,
22 shortened, t' should no flesh be saved:*
23 unto you, Lo, here is Christ, or t';*5602
24 t' shall arise false Christs, and false
28 is, t' will the eagles be gathered 1563
51 t' shall be weeping and gnashing of"
25: 6 at midnight t' was a cry made,
9 lest t' be not enough for us and you:
25 earth: lo, t' thou hast that is thine.*
30 t' shall be weeping and gnashing 1563
26: 5 lest t' be an uproar among the people.*
7 T' came unto him a woman having
13 t' shall also this, that this woman*
71 and said unto them that were t', 1563
27:36 sitting down they watched him t'; "
38 were t' two thieves crucified with him,
45 from the sixth hour t' was darkness
47 Some of them that stood t', when 1563
55 many women were t' beholding "
57 t' came a rich man of Arimathæa,
61 t' was Mary Magdalene, and the 1563

M't 28: 2 behold, t' was a great earthquake: for
7 t' shall ye see him: lo, I have told 1563
10 Galilee, and t' shall they see me. "
M'r 1: 5 t' went out unto him all the land of
7 T' cometh one mightier than I after
11 t' came a voice from heaven, saying,*
13 t' in the wilderness forty days, *1563
23 t' was in their synagogue a man with
35 into a solitary place, and t' prayed.1563
38 towns, that I may preach t' also: "
40 t' came a leper to him, beseeching
2: 2 that t' was no room to receive them,
6 t' were certain of the scribes sitting
6 scribes sitting t', and reasoning 1563
15 for t' were many, and they followed
3: 1 and t' was a man...which had a
1 a man t' which had a withered 1563
31 T' came then his brethren and his
4: 1 t' was gathered unto him a great
3 Behold, t' went out a sower to sow:*
22 For t' is nothing hid, which shall not
36 t' were also with him other little *
37 t' arose a great storm of wind, and the
39 wind ceased, and t' was a great calm.
5: 2 t' met him out of the tombs a man
11 t' was...nigh unto the mountains
11 was t' nigh unto the mountains 1563
22 t' cometh one of the rulers of the
35 t' came from the ruler of the *
6: 5 he could t' do no mighty work, 1563
10 t' abide till ye depart...that place. "
31 for t' were many coming and going,
7: 4 And many other things t' be, which
15 T' is nothing from without a man,
8: 12 T' shall no sign be given unto this
9: 1 That t' be some of them that stand
4 t' appeared unto them Elias with
7 t' was a cloud that overshadowed
39 for t' is no man which shall do a
10: 17 t' came one running, and kneeled to
18 t' is none good but one, that is, God.*
29 T' is no man that hath left house,
11: 5 certain of them that stood t' 1563
27 t' come to him the chief priests,
12: 18 which say t' is no resurrection; and
20 t' were seven brethren: and the first
31 T' is none other commandment
32 hast said the truth: for t' is one God;*
32 one God; and t' is none other but he:
42 And t' came a certain poor widow,
13: 2 t' shall not be left one stone upon
8 and t' shall be earthquakes in divers
8 and t' shall be famines and troubles:
21 here is Christ; or, lo, he is t'; 1563
14: 2 day, lest t' be an uproar of the people.
3 t' came a woman having an alabaster
4 And t' were some that had indignation
13 and t' shall meet you a man bearing a
15 prepared: t' make ready for us. 1563
51 t' followed him a certain young man,*
57 t' arose certain, and bare false witness
66 t' cometh one of the maids of the high
15: 7 And t' was one named Barabbas,
33 t' was darkness over the whole land
40 T' were also women looking on afar
16: 7 t' shall ye see him, as he said unto1563
Lu 1: 5 T' was in the days of Herod, the king
11 t' appeared unto him an angel of the
33 and of his kingdom t' shall be no end.
45 t' shall be a performance of those
61 T' is none of thy kindred that is
2: 1 that t' went out a decree from Cæsar
6 while they were t', the days were 1563
7 t' was no room for them in the inn.
8 t' were in the same country shepherds
13 And suddenly t' was with the angel a
25 t' was a man in Jerusalem, whose
36 And t' was one Anna, a prophetess, the
4: 14 t' went out a fame of him through all*
17 t' was delivered unto him the book
33 And in the synagogue t' was a man,
5: 15 much the more went t' a fame abroad*
17 that t' were Pharisees and doctors of
29 t' was a great company of publicans
6: 6 t' was a man whose right hand 1563
19 for t' went virtue out of him, and *
7: 12 behold, t' was a dead man carried out,
16 And t' came a fear on all: and they*
28 t' is not a greater prophet than
41 T' was a certain creditor which had*
8: 23 t' came down a storm of wind on the
24 and they ceased, and t' was a calm.
27 t' met him out of the city a certain
32 And t' was...an herd of many swine
32 t' an herd of many swine feeding 1563
41 behold, t' came a man named Jairus,
49 t' cometh one from the ruler of the
9: 4 house ye enter into, t' abide, and 1563
17 t' was taken up of fragments that
27 of a truth, t' be some standing here,
30 behold, t' talked with him two men,
34 While he thus spake, t' came a cloud,
35 And t' came a voice out of the cloud,*
46 t' arose a reasoning among them,
10: 6 And if the son of peace be t', your 1563
31 by chance t' came down a certain*
11: 26 they enter in, and dwell t': and 1563
29 and t' shall no sign be given it, but
12: 1 when t' were gathered together an*
2 For t' is nothing covered, that shall
18 t' will I bestow all my fruits and 1563
34 treasure is, t' will your heart be "
52 t' shall be five in one house divided,
54 T' cometh a shower; and so it is.
55 T' will be heat; and it cometh to pass.
13: 1 T' were present at that season some

Lu 13: 11 t' was a woman which had a spirit of*
14 T' are six days in which men ought
23 him, Lord, are t' few that be saved?*
28 T' shall be weeping and gnashing 1563
30 behold, t' are last which shall be first,
30 and t' are first which shall be last.
31 The same day t' came certain of the
14: 2 t' was a certain man before him
22 hast commanded, and yet t' is room.
25 t' went great multitudes with him:
15: 10 t' is joy in the presence of the angels
13 and t' wasted his substance with 1563
14 t' arose a mighty famine in that land;
16: 1 T' was a certain rich man, which had
19 T' was a certain rich man, which was
20 t' was a...beggar named Lazarus, *
26 between us and you t' is a great gulf
17: 12 t' met him ten men that were lepers,
17 Were t' not ten cleansed? but where*
18 T' are not found that returned to give
21 shall they say, Lo here! or, lo t'! 1563
23 shall say to you, See here; or, see t':"
34 night t' shall be two men in one bed;
18: 2 T' was in a city a judge, which feared
3 And t' was a widow in that city; and
29 T' is no man that hath left house, or
19: 2 behold, t' was a man named Zacchæus,*
20: 27 which deny that t' is any resurrection;
29 T' were therefore seven brethren: and
21: 6 t' shall not be left one stone upon
7 what sign will t' be when these things*
11 great signs shall t' be from heaven.
18 t' shall not an hair of your head perish.*
23 t' shall be great distress in the land,
25 t' shall be signs in the sun, and in the
22: 10 into the city, t' shall a man meet you,
12 room furnished: t' make ready. 1563
24 t' was also a strife among them,
43 t' appeared an angel unto him from
23: 27 t' followed him a great company of
32 t' were also two other, malefactors,
33 Calvary, t' they crucified him, 1563
44 t' was a darkness over all the earth*
50 behold, t' was a man named Joseph,*
24: 18 things which are come to pass t'1722,846
Joh 1: 6 T' was a man sent from God, whose
26 t' standeth one among you, whom ye*
46 Can t' any good thing come out of*
2: 1 the third day t' was a marriage in Cana
1 and the mother of Jesus was t': 1563
6 t' were set...six waterpots of stone,
6 set t' six waterpots of stone, 1563
12 they continued t' not many days. "
3: 1 T' was a man of the Pharisees, named
22 and t' he tarried with them, and 1563
23 to Salim, because t' was much water
23 because...was much water t': 1563
25 Then t' arose a question between some
4: 6 Now Jacob's well was t'. Jesus 1563
7 T' cometh a woman of Samaria to
35 T' are yet four months, and then
40 them: and he abode t' two days. 1563
46 And t' was a certain nobleman, whose
5: 1 After this t' was a feast of the Jews;
2 Now t' is at Jerusalem by the sheep
5 And a certain man was t', which 1563
32 T' is another that beareth witness of*
45 t' is one that accuseth you, even Moses,
6: 3 and t' he sat with his disciples. 1563
9 T' is a lad here, which hath five
10 Now t' was much grass in the place.
22 saw that t' was none other boat
22 saw that...was none other boat t', 1563
23 t' came other boats from Tiberias
24 therefore saw that Jesus was not t',1563
64 But t' are some of you that believe not.
7: 4 t' is no man that doeth any thing in*
12 t' was much murmuring among the
43 So t' was a division among the people
8: 44 the truth, because t' is no truth in him.
50 t' is one that seeketh and judgeth.
9: 16 And t' was a division among them.
10: 16 t' shall be one fold, and one shepherd.*
19 T' was a division therefore again
40 at first baptized; and t' he abode. 1563
42 And many believed on him t'. "
11: 9 Are t' not twelve hours in the day?
10 stumbleth, because t' is no light in him,*
15 for your sakes that I was not t', 1563
31 She goeth unto the grave to weep t'."
54 and t' continued with his disciples. "
12: 2 T' they made him a supper; and "
9 Jews therefore knew that he was t':"
20 t' were certain Greeks among them
26 I am, t' shall also my servant be: 1563
28 Then came t' a voice from heaven,
13: 23 t' was leaning on Jesus' bosom one of
14: 3 that where I am, t' ye may be also.
18: 18 And the servants and officers stood t',
19: 25 Now t' stood by the cross of Jesus his
29 Now t' was set a vessel full of vinegar:
34 and forthwith came t' out blood and
39 t' came also Nicodemus, which at the
41 where he was crucified t' was a garden;
42 T' laid they Jesus therefore 1563
21: 2 T' were together Simon Peter, and
9 they saw a fire of coals t', and fish
11 and for all t' were so many, yet was
25 t' are also many other things which
Ac 2: 2 And suddenly t' came a sound from
3 And t' appeared unto them cloven
5 t' were dwelling at Jerusalem Jews,
41 t' were added unto them about three
4: 12 Neither is t' salvation in any other:
12 t' is none other name under heaven
34 Neither was t' any among them that

Ac 5: 16 T' came also a multitude out of the
34 Then stood t' up one in the council,
6: 1 t' arose a murmuring of the Grecians
9 t' arose certain of the synagogue,
7: 11 t' came a dearth over all the land of
12 Jacob heard that t' was corn in Egypt,
30 t' appeared to him in the wilderness*
8: 1 at that time t' was a great persecution
8 And t' was great joy in that city.
9 But t' was a certain man, called Simon,
9: 3 suddenly t' shined round about him a
10 t' was a certain disciple at Damascus,
18 t' fell from his eyes as it had been
33 t' he found a certain man named 1563
36 Now t' was at Joppa a certain disciple
38 had heard that Peter was t', 1722,846
10: 1 T' was a certain man in Cæsarea
13 t' came a voice to him, Rise, Peter;
18 surnamed Peter, were lodged t'. 1759
11: 11 immediately t' were three men already*
28 And t' stood up one of them named
28 spirit that t' should be great dearth
12: 18 t' was no small stir among the soldiers,
19 from Judæa to Cæsarea, and t' abode.
13: 1 Now t' were in the church that was at
11 immediately t' fell on him a mist and a
25 t' cometh one after me, whose shoes
14: 5 And when t' was an assault made both
7 And t' they preached the gospel. 1563
8 And t' sat a certain man at Lystra,
19 t' came thither certain Jews from
28 t' they abode long time with the *1563
15: 5 t' rose up certain of the sect of the
7 And when t' had been much disputing,
33 And after they had tarried t' a space,
34 it pleased Silas to abide t' still. * 847
16: 1 a certain disciple was t', named 1563
9 T' stood a man of Macedonia, and
15 come into my house, and abide t'.
26 suddenly t' was a great earthquake, so
17: 7 that t' is another king, one Jesus.
14 Silas and Timotheus abode t' still. 1563
21 and strangers which were t' 1927
18: 11 And he continued t' a year and six
18 Paul after this tarried t' yet a good
19 came to Ephesus, and left them t': 847
23 after he had spent some time t', he
19: 2 heard whether t' be any Holy Ghost.*
14 t' were seven sons of one Sceva, a
21 After I have been t', I must also 1563
23 same time t' arose no small stir about
35 what man is t' that knoweth not how
38 the law is open, and t' are deputies:
40 this day's uproar, t' being no cause
20: 3 t' abode three months. And when the
4 And t' accompanied him into Asia
8 And t' were many lights in the upper
9 t' sat in a window a certain young
13 Assos, t' intending to take in Paul:1564
22 things that shall befall me t': 1722,846
21: 3 for t' the ship was to unlade her 1566
4 disciples, we tarried t' seven days: 847
10 And as we tarried t' many days,
10 t' came down from Judæa a certain
16 T' went with us also certain of the
20 thousands of Jews t' are which believe;
40 when t' was made a great silence, he
22: 5 were t' bound unto Jerusalem, 1566
6 t' shone from heaven a great light
10 t' it shall be told thee of all things 1563
12 report of all the Jews which dwelt t',
23: 7 he had so said, t' arose a dissension
8 say that t' is no resurrection,
9 t' arose a great cry: and the scribes
10 when t' arose a great dissension, the
21 for t' lie in wait for him of them more
24: 11 that t' are yet but twelve days since*
15 t' shall be a resurrection of the dead,
25: 5 man, if t' be any wickedness in him.
9 t' be judged of these things before 1563
11 if t' be none of these things whereof*
14 when they had been t' many days, 1563
14 T' is a certain man left in bonds by
20 and t' be judged of these matters. 1563
27: 6 And t' the centurion found a ship "
12 attain to Phenice, and t' to winter;
14 after t' arose against it a tempestuous
22 t' shall be no loss of any man's life
23 For t' stood by me this night the angel
34 for t' shall not an hair fall from the
28: 3 the fire, t' came a viper out of the heat,*
12 at Syracuse, we tarried t' three days.
18 t' was no cause of death in me.
23 t' came many to him into his lodging;*
Ro 2: 11 t' is no respect of persons with God.
3: 1 or what profit is t' of circumcision?*
10 T' is none righteous, no, not one:
11 T' is none that understandeth,
11 t' is none that seeketh after God.
12 t' is none that doeth good, no, not one.
18 T' is no fear of God before their eyes.
20 t' shall no flesh be justified in his*
22 that believe: for t' is no difference:
4: 15 where no law is, t' is no transgression.
5: 13 sin is not imputed when t' is no law.
8: 1 T' is therefore now no condemnation
9: 14 Is t' unrighteousness with God? God
26 t' shall they be called the children 1563
10: 12 t' is no difference between the Jew
11: 5 present time also t' is a remnant
26 T' shall come out of Sion the
13: 1 For t' is no power but of God: the
9 if t' be any other commandment, it is
14: 14 that t' is nothing unclean of itself:*
15: 12 saith, T' shall be a root of Jesse,
1Co 1: 10 and that t' be no divisions among you:

1Co 1:11 that t' are contentions among you.
3: 3 for whereas t' is among you envying,
5: 1 reported...that t' is fornication
6: 5 that t' is not a wise man among you?
7 t' is utterly a fault among you, *
7:34 T' is difference also between a wife
8: 4 and that t' is none other God but one.
5 For though t' be that are called gods,
5 (as t' be gods many, and lords many,)
6 But to us t' is but one God, the Father,
7 t' is not in every man that knowledge:
10:13 T' hath no temptation taken you but
11:18 I hear that t' be divisions among you;*
19 t' must be also heresies among you,
12: 4 t' are diversities of gifts, but the same
5 t' are differences of administrations,
6 t' are diversities of operations, but it
25 t' should be no schism in the body;
13: 8 but whether t' be prophecies, they
8 whether t' be tongues, they shall
8 whether t' be knowledge, it shall
14:10 T' are, it may be, so many kinds of
23 t' come in those that are unlearned, or
24 t' come in one that believeth not, or
28 But if t' be no interpreter, let him
15:12 among you that t' is no resurrection
13 if t' be no resurrection of the dead,
39 but t' is one kind of flesh of men,
40 T' are also celestial bodies, and
41 T' is one glory of the sun, and
44 T' is a natural body,
44 and t' is a spiritual body.
16: 2 that t' be no gatherings when I come.*
9 unto me, and t' are many adversaries.
2Co 1:17 that with me t' should be yea yea, and
3:17 Spirit of the Lord is, t' is liberty. 1563
8:11 that as t' was a readiness to will,
11 so t' may be a performance also out of
12 For if t' be first a willing mind, it is
14 for your want: that t' may be equality:
12: 7 t' was given to me a thorn in the flesh,
20 lest t' be debates, envyings, wraths,
Ga 1: 7 but t' be some that trouble you, and
3:21 for if t' had been a law given which
28 T' is neither Jew nor Greek,
28 t' is neither bond nor free,
28 t' is neither male nor female: for ye
5:23 temperance: against such t' is no law.
Eph 4: 4 T' is one body, and one Spirit, even as
6: 9 neither is t' respect of persons with
Ph'p 2: 1 If t' be therefore any consolation in
4: 8 if t' be any virtue,...if t' be any praise,
Col 3:11 Where t' is neither Greek nor Jew,
25 done; and t' is no respect of persons.
2Th 2: 3 except t' come a falling away first,*
3:11 t' are some which walk among you*
1Ti 1:10 if t' be any other thing that is contrary
2: 5 For t' is one God, and one mediator
2Ti 2:20 t' are not only vessels of gold and of
4: 8 t' is laid up for me a crown of
Tit 1:10 t' are many unruly and vain talkers
3:12 for I have determined t' to winter. 1563
Ph'm 23 T' salute thee Epaphras, my *
Heb 3:12 lest t' be in any of you an evil heart of
4: 9 T' remaineth therefore a rest to the
13 Neither is t' any creature that is not
7: 8 t' he receiveth them, of whom it is 1563
11 what further need was t' that another
12 t' is made of necessity a change also
15 of Melchisedec t' ariseth another
18 For t' is verily a disannulling of the
8: 4 t' are priests that offer gifts according
9: 2 For t' was a tabernacle made; the
16 t' must also of necessity be the death
10: 3 in those sacrifices t' is a remembrance
18 these is, t' is no more offering for sin.
26 t' remaineth no more sacrifice for sins,
11:12 sprang t' even of one, and he as good
12:16 Lest t' be any fornicator, or profane
Jas 2: 2 t' come unto your assembly a man
2 t' come in also a poor man in vile
3 and say to the poor, Stand thou t', 1563
19 Thou believest that t' is one God;*
3:16 t' is confusion and every evil work.1563
4:12 T' is one lawgiver, who is able to save*
13 such a city, and continue t' a year,1563
2Pe 1:17 t' came such a voice to him from the
2: 1 t' were false prophets also among the
1 t' shall be false teachers among you,
3: 3 t' shall come in the last days scoffers,*
1Jo 2:10 t' is none occasion of stumbling in
18 even now are t' many antichrists;
4:18 T' is no fear in love; but perfect love
5: 7 t' are three that bear record in heaven,*
8 t' are three that bear witness in earth,
16 T' is a sin unto death: I do not say
17 is sin: and t' is a sin not unto death.
2Jo 10 t' come any unto you, and bring not*
Jude 4 t' are certain men crept in unawares,
18 t' should be mockers in the last time,
Re 2:14 thou hast t' them that hold the 1563
4: 3 t' was a rainbow round about the
5 t' were seven lamps of fire burning
6 before the throne t' was a sea of glass*
6: 4 t' went out another horse that was*
4 t' was given unto him a great sword.
12 and, lo, t' was a great earthquake;
7: 4 t' were sealed an hundred and forty*
8: 1 t' was silence in heaven about the
3 t' was given unto him much incense,
5 and t' were voices, and thunderings,
7 t' followed hail and fire mingled with
10 and t' fell a great star from heaven,
9: 2 and t' arose a smoke out of the pit,
3 t' came out of the smoke locusts upon*
10 and t' were stings in their tails: *
Re 9:12 t' come two woes more hereafter.
10: 6 that t' should be time no longer:
11: 1 t' was given me a reed like unto a rod:
13 same hour was t' a great earthquake,
15 t' were great voices in heaven, saying,
19 t' was seen in his temple the ark of
19 and t' were lightnings, and voices,
12: 1 t' appeared a great wonder in heaven;*
3 t' appeared another wonder in heaven;
6 should feed her t' a thousand two 1563
7 t' was war in heaven: Michael and his
13: 5 And t' was given unto him a mouth
14: 8 And t' followed another angel, saying,*
16: 2 t' fell a noisome and grievous sore*
17 t' came a great voice out of the temple
18 And t' were voices, and thunders,
18 t' was a great earthquake, such as
21 t' fell upon men a great hail out of*
17: 1 t' came one of the seven angels which
10 t' are seven kings: five are fallen,*
20:11 and t' was found no place for them.
21: 1 passed away; and t' was no more sea.*
4 t' shall be no more death, neither*
4 neither shall t' be any more pain:
9 t' came unto me one of the seven
25 at all by day: for t' shall be no night
25 shall be no night t'. 1563
27 t' shall in no wise enter into it any
22: 2 of the river, was t' the tree of life,*
3 And t' shall be no more curse: but the
5 t' shall be no night...and they need
5 shall be no night t'; and they 1563

thereabout

Lu 24: 4 they were much perplexed t', 4012,5127

thereat

Ex 30:19 wash their hands and their feet t':
40:31 washed their hands and their feet t':
M't 7:13 many there be which go in t': *1223,846

thereby

Le 11:43 them, that ye should be defiled t'.
Job 22:21 peace: t' good shall come unto thee.
Pr 20: 1 whosoever is deceived t' is not wise.
Ec 10: 9 cleaveth wood shall be endangered t'.
Isa 33:21 oars, neither shall gallant ship pass t'.
Jer 18:16 that passeth t' shall be astonished,5921
19: 8 that passeth t' shall be astonished " "
51:43 doth any son of man pass t'. 2004
Eze 12: 5 wall in their sight, and carry out t'.
12 dig through the wall to carry out t':
33:12 he shall not fall t' in the day that he
18 iniquity, he shall even die t'. *
19 is lawful and right, he shall live t'.
Zec 9: 2 And Hamath also shall border t';*
Joh 11: 4 of God might be glorified t'. 1223,846
Eph 2:16 having slain the enmity t': 1722, "
Heb12:11 them which are exercised t'. 1223, "
15 you, and t' many be defiled; " 5026
13: 2 t' some have entertained angels " "
1Pe 2: 2 the word, that ye may grow t': 1722,846

therefore

Ge 2:24 T' shall a man leave...father 5921,3651
3:23 T' the Lord God sent him forth from
4:15 T' whosoever slayeth Cain, 3651
11: 9 T' is the name of it called 5921, "
12:12 T' it shall come to pass, when the*
19 t' behold thy wife, take her, and go
17: 9 Thou shalt keep my covenant t', thou*
18: 5 for t' are ye come to your *5921,3651
12 T' Sarah laughed within herself,*
19: 8 t' came they under the *5921,3651
22 T' the name of the city was " "
20: 6 t' suffered I thee not to touch
7 t' restore the man his wife; for he
8 T' Abimelech rose early in the *
21:23 Now t' swear unto me here by God
24:65 t' she took a vail, and covered herself.*
25:30 t' was his name called Edom. 5921,3651
26:33 t' the name of the city is " "
27: 3 t' take, I pray thee, thy weapons,
8 Now t', my son, obey my voice
28 T' God give thee of the dew of heaven.*
43 Now t', my son, obey my voice; and
29:15 shouldest thou t' serve me for nought?
32 now t' my husband will love me. *3588
33 he hath t' given me this son also: 1571
34 t' was his name called Levi. 5921,3651
35 t' she called his name Judah; " "
30: 6 t' called she his name Dan. " "
15 T' he shall lie with thee to night " "
31:44 t' come thou, let us make a covenant,*
48 T' was the name of it called 5921,3651
32:32 T' the children of Israel eat " "
33:10 for t' I have seen thy face, as * " "
17 t' the name of the place is " "
34:21 t' let them dwell in the land, and
37:20 Come now t', and let us slay him,
38:29 thee: t' his name was called Pharez.
41:33 t' let Pharaoh look out a man discreet
42:21 t' is this distress come upon 5921,3651
22 t', behold,...his blood is required. 1571
44:30 Now t' when I come to thy servant my
33 t', I pray thee, let thy servant abide
45: 5 Now t' be not grieved, nor angry with*
47: 4 t', we pray thee, let thy servants dwell
50: 5 t' let me go up, I pray thee, and bury
21 Now t' fear ye not: I will nourish you,
Ex 1:11 T' they did set over them taskmasters
20 T' God dealt well with the midwives:*
3: 9 Now t', behold, the cry of the children*
10 Come now t', and I will send thee
4:12 Now t' go, and I will be with thy
5: 8 t' they cry, saying, Let us go 5921,3651
17 t' ye say, Let us go and do
18 Go t' now, and work; for there shall
Ex 9:19 Send t' now, and gather thy cattle,
10:17 Now t' forgive, I pray thee, my sin
12:17 t' shall ye observe this day in your
13:10 Thou shalt t' keep this ordinance in
15 t' I sacrifice to the Lord all 5921,3651
15:23 t' the name of it was called " "
16:29 t' he giveth you on the sixth " "
19: 5 Now t', if ye will obey my voice
31:14 Ye shall keep the sabbath t'; for it is
32:10 t' let me alone, that my wrath may
34 T' now go, lead the people unto the*
33: 5 t' now put off thy ornaments from
13 Now t', I pray thee, if I have found
Le 8:35 T' shall ye abide at the door of the*
9: 8 Aaron t' went unto the altar, and *
11:44 ye shall t' sanctify yourselves, and ye
45 God: ye shall t' be holy, for I am holy.
13:52 He shall t' burn that garment, *
16: 4 t' shall he wash his flesh in water,*
17:12 T' I said unto the children of5921,3651
14 t' I said unto the children of Israel,
18: 5 Ye shall t' keep my statutes, and my
25 t' I do visit the iniquity thereof upon
26 Ye shall t' keep my statutes and my
30 T' shall ye keep mine ordinance, that
19: 8 T' every one that eateth it shall bear*
37 T' shall ye observe all my statutes,*
20: 7 Sanctify yourselves t', and be ye holy:
22 Ye shall t' keep all my statutes, and
23 these things, and t' I abhorred them.
25 Ye shall t' put difference between
21: 6 they do offer: t' they shall be holy.
8 Thou shalt sanctify him t'; for he
22: 9 They shall t' keep mine ordinance,
9 for it, and die t', if they profane it:*
31 T' shall ye keep my commandments,
25:17 Ye shall not t' oppress one another;*
Nu 3:12 Israel: t' the Levites shall be mine;*
11:18 t' the Lord will give you flesh, and ye
14:16 t' he hath slain them in the
43 Lord, t' the Lord will not be with you.
16:38 before the Lord, t' they are hallowed:
18: 7 T' thou and thy sons with thee shall*
24 t' I have said unto them, 5921,3651
30 T' thou shalt say unto them, When ye
20:12 t' ye shall not bring this 3651
21: 7 T' the people came to Moses, and*
22: 5 He sent messengers t' unto Balaam*
6 Come now t', I pray thee, curse me
17 come t', I pray thee, curse me this
19 Now t', I pray you, tarry ye also here
34 now t', if I displease thee, I will get
24:11 T' now flee thou to thy place: I
14 come t', and I will advertise thee *
27: 4 Give unto us t' a possession among*
31:17 t' kill every male among the little
50 t' brought an oblation for the Lord,*
35:34 Defile not t' the land which ye shall*
De 2: 4 take ye good heed unto yourselves t':
4: 1 Now t' hearken, O Israel, unto the*
6 Keep t' and do them; for this is your
15 Take ye t' good heed unto yourselves;
37 t' he chose their seed after them, and
39 Know t' this day, and consider it in
40 Thou shalt keep t' his statutes, and*
5:15 t' the Lord...commanded 5921,3651
25 t' why should we die? for this great
32 Ye shall observe to do t' as the Lord
6: 3 Hear t', O Israel, and observe to do it;
7: 9 Know t' that the Lord thy God, he is
11 shalt t' keep the commandments,
8: 6 T' thou shalt keep the
9: 3 Understand t' this day, that the Lord
6 Understand t', that the Lord thy God
26 I prayed t' unto the Lord, and said,*
10:16 Circumcise t' the foreskin of your
19 Love ye t' the stranger: for ye were
11: 1 T' thou shalt love the Lord thy God,
8 T' shall ye keep all the
18 T' shall ye lay up these my words in
14: 7 hoof; t' they are unclean unto you.*
15:11 t' I command thee, saying, 5921,3651
15 t' I command thee this thing to " "
16: 2 Thou shalt t' sacrifice the passover*
15 hands, t' thou shalt surely rejoice.*
18: 2 T' shall they have no inheritance*
23:14 before thee; t' shall thy camp be holy:
24:18, 22 t' I command thee to do 5921,3651
25:19 T' it shall be, when the Lord thy God
26:16 thou shalt t' keep and do them with
27: 4 T' it shall be when ye be gone over*
10 shalt t' obey the voice of the Lord
28:48 T' shalt thou serve thine enemies
29: 9 Keep t' the words of this covenant,
30:19 t' choose life, that both thou and thy
31:19 Now t' write ye this song for you, and
22 Moses t' wrote this song the same*
Jos 1: 2 now t' arise, go over this Jordan,
2:12 Now t', I pray you, swear unto me by
3:12 Now t' take you twelve men out of the
4:17 Joshua t' commanded the priests,
7:12 T' the children of Israel could not
14 In the morning t' ye shall be brought
8: 6 the first: t' we will flee before them.*
9 Joshua t' sent them forth: and they*
9: 6 now t' make ye a league with us.
11 t' now make ye a league with us.*
19 Israel: now t' we may not touch them.
23 Now t' ye are cursed, and there shall
24 t' we were sore afraid of our lives
10: 5 T' the five kings of the Amorites, the
9 Joshua t' came unto them suddenly,
13: 7 t' divide this land for an inheritance
14: 4 t' they gave no part unto the Levites*
12 Now t' give me this mountain, whereof
14 Hebron t' became the inheritance of

Jos 17: 1 of war, t' he had Gilead and Bashan.
4 T' according to the commandment of
18: 6 shall t' describe the land into seven*
19: 9 t' the children of Simeon had their
47 t' the children of Dan went up to *
22: 4 t' now return ye, and get you unto
26 T' we said, Let us now prepare to
28 T' said we, that it shall be, when they
23: 6 Be ye t' very courageous to keep and
11 Take good heed t' unto your selves,
15 T' it shall come to pass, that as all*
24: 10 t' he blessed you still: so I delivered
14 Now t' fear the Lord, and serve him in
18 t' will we also serve the Lord; for he
23 t' put away, said he, the strange gods
27 it shall be t' a witness unto you, lest
J'g 2: 23 T' the Lord left those nations, *
3: 8 T' the anger of the Lord was hot
25 t' they took a key, and opened them:
6: 32 T' on that day he called him
7: 3 t' go to, proclaim in the ears of the
8: 7 T' when the Lord hath delivered
9: 16 Now t', if ye have done truly and
32 Now t' up by night, thou and the
11: 8 T' we turn again to thee now,
13 t' restore those lands again peaceably.
26 why t' did ye not recover them within*
13: 4 t' beware, I pray thee, and drink not
14: 2 now t' get her for me to wife.
15: 2 her; t' I gave her to thy companion:
16: 12 Delilah t' took new ropes, and bound*
17: 3 now t' I will restore it unto thee.
18: 14 now t' consider what ye have to do.
19: 7 urged him: t' he lodged there again.*
20: 13 Now t' deliver us the men, the
42 T' they turned their backs before the
21: 20 T' they commanded the children of*
Ru 3: 3 Wash thyself t', and anoint thee, and
9 spread t' thy skirt over thine
4: 8 T' the kinsman said unto Boaz, Buy*
1Sa 1: 7 her; t' she wept, and did not eat.
13 t' Eli thought she had been drunken.
28 T' also I have lent him to the Lord; as
3: 9 T' Eli said unto Samuel, Go, lie down:
14 t' I have sworn unto the house of Eli,
5: 5 T' neither the priests of 5921,3651
8 They sent t' and gathered all the
10 T' they sent the ark of God to Ekron.*
6: 7 Now t' make a new cart, and take two
8: 9 Now t' hearken unto their voice:
9: 13 Now t' get you up; for about this time
10: 12 T' it became a proverb, Is 5921,3651
19 t' present yourselves before the Lord
22 T' they enquired of the Lord further,
11: 10 T' the men of Jabesh said, To
12: 7 Now t' stand still, that I may reason
13 Now t' behold the king whom ye have
16 Now t' stand and see this great 1571
13: 12 T' said I, The Philistines will come
12 I forced myself t', and offered a burnt
14: 41 T' Saul said unto the Lord God of
15: 1 now t' hearken thou unto the voice of
25 Now t', I pray thee, pardon my sin,
17: 51 T' David ran, and stood upon the*
18: 13 T' Saul removed him from him, and
22 thee: now t' be the king's son in law.
19: 2 now t', I pray thee, take heed to
20: 8 T' thou shalt deal kindly with thy
29 T' he cometh not unto the 5921,3651
21: 3 Now t' what is under thine hand? give
22: 1 David t' departed thence, and escaped
23: 2 T' David enquired of the Lord,
20 Now t', O king, come down according
23 See t', and take knowledge of all the
28 t' they called that place 5921,3651
24: 15 The Lord t' be judge, and judge
21 Swear now t' unto me by the Lord,
25: 17 t' know and consider what thou wilt
26 Now t', my lord, as the Lord liveth,
26: 4 David t' sent out spies, and
8 now t' let me smite him, I pray thee,
19 Now t', I pray thee, let my lord the
20 Now t', let not my blood fall to the
27: 12 him; t' he shall be my servant for ever.
28: 2 T' will I make thee keeper of mine
15 t' I have called thee, that thou mayest
18 t' hath the Lord done this 5921,3651
22 Now t', I pray thee, hearken thou also
31: 4 T' Saul took a sword, and fell upon it.
2Sa 2: 7 T' now let your hands be
4: 11 shall I not t' now require his blood*
5: 20 T' he called the name of that 5921,3651
6: 21 Israel: t' will I play before the Lord.
23 T' Michal the daughter of Saul had*
7: 8 Now t' so shalt thou say unto my
27 t' hath thy servant found in his heart
29 T' now let it please thee to bless the
9: 10 Thou t', and thy sons, and thy *
12: 10 Now t' the sword shall never depart
16 David t' besought God for the child;
19 t' David said unto his servants, Is the*
28 Now t' gather the rest of the people
13: 13 Now t', I pray thee, speak unto the
33 t' let not my lord the king take the
14: 15 t' that I am come to speak of this
17 t' the Lord thy God will be with thee.*
21 t', bring the young man Absalom
26 was heavy on him, t' he polled it:)
29 T' Absalom sent for Joab, to have*
30 T' he said unto his servants, See,
32 now t' let me see the king's face; and
15: 29 Zadok t' and Abiathar carried the ark
35 t' it shall be, that what thing soever
17: 11 T' I counsel that all Israel be *
16 Now t' send quickly, and tell David,
18: 3 t' now it is better that thou succour us

2Sa 19: 7 Now t' arise, go forth, and speak
10 t' why speak ye not a word of bringing
20 t', behold, I am come the first this day
23 T' the king said unto Shimei, Thou*
27 God: do t' what is good in thine eyes.
28 What right t' have I yet to cry any
22: 25 T' the Lord hath recompensed me
50 T' I will give thanks unto 5921,3651
23: 17 of their lives? t' he would not drink it.
19 of three? t' he was their captain:
1Ki 1: 12 now t' come, let me, I pray thee, give
2: 2 be thou strong t', and show thyself a
6 Do t' according to thy wisdom, and let
9 Now t' hold him not guiltless: for
19 Bath-sheba t' went unto king
24 Now t', as the Lord liveth, which hath
33 Their blood shall t' return upon the*
44 t' the Lord shall return thy wickedness
3: 9 Give t' thy servant an understanding
5: 6 Now t' command thou that they hew
8: 25 T' now, Lord God of Israel, keep
61 your heart t' be perfect with the Lord
9: 9 t' hath the Lord brought upon 5921,3651
10: 9 t' made he thee king, to do judgment
11: 40 Solomon sought t' to kill Jeroboam.
12: 4 now t' make thou the grievous service
18 t' king Rehoboam made speed to get*
24 They hearkened t' to the word of the*
13: 26 t' the Lord hath delivered him unto
14: 10 T', behold, I will bring evil upon the*
12 Arise thou t', get thee to thine own
18: 19 Now t' send, and gather to me all
23 Let them t' give us two bullocks; and
20: 23 t' they were stronger than we; 5921,3651
28 t' will I deliver all this great multitude
42 t' thy life shall go for his life, and thy
22: 19 Hear thou t' the word of the Lord: 3651
23 Now t', behold, the Lord hath put a
2Ki 1: 4 Now t' thus saith the Lord, Thou 3651
6 t' thou shalt not come down from "
14 t' let my life now be precious in thy*
16 t' thou shalt not come down off that
2: 17 They sent t' fifty men; and they
3: 23 another: now t', Moab, to the spoil.
4: 33 He went in t', and shut the door upon
5: 15 now t', I pray thee, take a blessing of
27 leprosy t' of Naaman shall cleave unto
6: 7 T' said he, Take it up to thee. And he*
11 T' the heart of the king of Syria was*
14 T' sent he thither horses, and
7: 4 Now t' come, and let us fall unto the
9 now t' come, that we may go and tell
12 t' are they gone out of the camp to
14 They took t' two chariot horses; and
9: 26 Now t' take and cast him into the plat
10: 19 Now t' call unto me all the prophets of
12: 7 now t' receive no more money of your
14: 11 T' Jehoash king of Israel went up;*
15: 16 they opened not to him, t' he smote it;
17: 4 t' the king of Assyria shut him up, and
18 T' the Lord was very angry with
25 t' the Lord sent lions among them,
26 t' he hath sent lions among them, and
18: 23 Now t', I pray thee, give pledges to my
19: 18 stone: t' they have destroyed them.
19 Now t', O Lord our God, I beseech thee,
26 T' their inhabitants were of small
28 t' I will put my hook in thy nose, and
32 T' thus saith the Lord concerning 3651
21: 12 T' thus saith the Lord God of "
22: 17 t' my wrath shall be kindled against
20 Behold t', I will gather thee unto 3651
1Ch 10: 14 t' he slew him, and turned the
11: 3 T' came all the elders of Israel to the*
7 t' they called it the city of 5921,3651
19 brought it. T' he would not drink it.
14: 11 t' they called the name of 5921,3651
14 T' David inquired again of God; and*
16 David t' did as God commanded him:*
17: 7 t' thus shalt thou say unto my servant
23 T' now, Lord, let the thing that thou*
25 t' thy servant hath found in 5921,3651
27 Now t' let it please thee to bless the*
21: 7 with this thing; t' he smote Israel.
12 t' advise thyself what word I shall
22: 5 I will t' now make preparation for it.
16 Arise t', and be doing, and the Lord be*
19 arise t', and build ye the sanctuary
23: 11 t' they were in one reckoning,
24: 2 t' Eleazar and Ithamar executed the
28: 8 Now t', in the sight of all Israel the
29: 13 Now t', our God, we thank thee, and
2Ch 2: 7 Send me now t' a man cunning to
15 Now t' the wheat, and the barley, the
6: 10 The Lord t' hath performed his word*
16 Now t', O Lord God of Israel, keep
19 Have respect t' to the prayer of thy*
21 Hearken t' unto the supplications of*
41 Now t' arise, O Lord God, into thy
7: 22 t' hath he brought all this 5921,3651
9: 8 t' made he thee king over them, to do
10: 4 now t' ease thou somewhat the
12: 5 t' have I also left you in the hand of
7 t' I will not destroy them, but I will*
14: 7 T' he saith unto Judah, Let us build*
15: 7 Be ye strong t', and let not your hands*
16: 7 t' is the host of the king of 5921,3651
9 t'...henceforth thou shalt have wars.*
17: 5 T' the Lord stablished the kingdom in
18: 5 T' the king of Israel gathered *
12 let thy word t', I pray thee, be like one
16 them return t' every man to his house*
18 T' hear the word of the Lord; 3651
22 Now t', behold, the Lord hath put a
31 T' they compassed about him to fight:
33 t' he said to his chariot man, Turn*

2Ch 19: 2 t' is wrath come upon thee from *2063
20: 26 t' the name of the same place 5921,3651
28: 11 Now hear me t', and deliver the
23 t' will I sacrifice to them, that they
30: 7 who t' gave them up to desolation, as*
17 t' the Levites had the charge of the
32: 15 Now t' let not Hezekiah deceive you,
25 t' there was wrath upon him, and
34: 25 t' my wrath shall be poured out upon
35: 14 t' the Levites prepared for themselves,
24 His servants t' took him out of that*
36: 17 T' he brought upon them the king of
Ezr 2: 62 t' were they, as polluted, put from the
4: 14 t' have we sent and certified 5921,1836
5: 17 Now t', if it seem good to the king, let
6: 6 Now t', Tatnai, governor beyond the
9: 12 t' give not your daughters unto their
10: 3 t' let us make a covenant with our God
11 Now t' make confession unto the Lord
Ne 2: 20 t' we his servants will arise and build:
4: 13 T' set I in the lower places behind the
20 In what place t' ye hear the sound of*
5: 2 t' we take up corn for them, that we*
6: 7 Come now t', and let us take counsel
9 Now t', O God, strengthen my hands.
13 T' was he hired, that I should be
7: 64 t' were they, as polluted, put from the
9: 27 T' thou deliveredst them into the
28 t' leftest thou them in the hand of
30 t' gavest thou them into the hand of
32 Now t', our God, the great, the mighty,
13: 8 t' I cast forth all the household stuff
28 Horonite: t' I chased him from me.
Es 1: 12 t' was the king very wroth, and his
2: 23 t' they were both hanged on a tree:*
3: 8 t' it is not for the king's profit to suffer
9: 19 T' the Jews of the villages, 5921,3651
26 T' for all the words of this " "
Job 5: 17 t' despise not thou the chastening of
6: 3 t' my words are swallowed up. 5921,3651
28 Now t' be content, look upon me; for
7: 11 T' I will not refrain my mouth; I 1571
9: 22 This is one thing, t' I said it, 5921,3651
10: 15 confusion; t' see thou mine affliction;*
11: 6 Know t' that God exacteth of thee less
17: 4 t' shalt thou not exalt them. 5921,3651
20: 2 T' do my thoughts cause me to "
21 t' shall no man look for his 5921, "
21: 14 T' they say unto God, Depart from†‡
22: 10 T' snares are round about 5921,3651
23: 15 T' am I troubled at his "
32: 10 T' I said, Hearken to me; I also "
34: 10 T' hearken unto me, ye men of "
25 T' he knoweth their works, and he "
33 and not I: t' speak what thou knowest.
35: 14 is before him; t' trust thou in him.*
16 T' doth Job open his mouth in vain;
37: 24 Men do t' fear him: he respecteth 3651
42: 3 t' have I uttered that I understood "
8 T' take unto you now seven bullocks
Ps 1: 5 T' the ungodly shall not 5921,3651
2: 10 Be wise now t', O ye kings: be
7: 7 for their sakes t' return thou on high.*
16: 9 T' my heart is glad, and my glory 3651
18: 24 T' hath the Lord recompensed me
49 T' will I give thanks unto 5921,3651
21: 12 T' shalt thou make them turn their*
25: 8 t' will he teach sinners in the 5921,3651
26: 1 also in the Lord; t' I shall not slide.*
27: 6 t' will I offer in his tabernacle *
28: 7 t' my heart greatly rejoiceth; and
31: 3 t' for thy name's sake lead me, and
36: 7 t' the children of men put their trust*
40: 12 of mine head: t' my heart faileth me.*
42: 6 t' will I remember thee from 5921,3651
45: 2 t' God hath blessed thee " "
7 t' God, thy God, hath anointed " "
17 t' shall the people praise thee " "
46: 2 T' will not we fear, though the* "
55: 19 have no changes, t' they fear not God.*
59: 5 Thou t', O Lord God of hosts, the God*
63: 7 t' in the shadow of thy wings will I*
73: 6 T' pride compasseth them about as a
10 T' his people return hither: and 3651
78: 21 T' the Lord heard this, and was
33 T' their days did he consume in
91: 14 his love upon me, t' will I deliver him:
106: 23 T' he said that he would destroy them,
26 T' he lifted up his hand against them,
40 T' was the wrath of the Lord kindled
107: 12 T' he brought down their heart with
110: 7 t' shall he lift up the head. 5921,3651
116: 2 t' will I call upon him as long as I live.
10 I believed, t' have I spoken: I was*3588
118: 7 t' shall I see my desire upon them that
119: 104 t' I hate every false way. 5921,3651
119 dross: t' I love thy testimonies.
127 T' I love thy commandments 5921,3651
128 T' I esteem all thy precepts " "
129 t' doth my soul keep them. " "
140 is very pure: t' thy servant loveth it.
139: 19 depart from me t', ye bloody men.
143: 4 T' is my spirit overwhelmed within
Pr 1: 31 T' shall they eat of the fruit of their
4: 7 is the principal thing; t' get wisdom:
5: 7 Hear me now t', O ye children, and
6: 15 T' shall his calamity come 5921,3651
34 t' he will not spare in the day of*
7: 15 T' came I forth to meet thee, 5921,3651
24 Hearken unto me now t', O ye
8: 32 Now t' hearken unto me, O ye
17: 11 t' a cruel messenger shall be sent
14 t' leave off contention, before it be
20: 4 t' shall he beg in harvest, and have
19 t' meddle not with him that flattereth
Ec 2: 1 thee with mirth, t' enjoy pleasure:

Ec 2:17 T' I hated life; because the work that
20 T' I went about to cause my heart to
5: 2 earth: t' let thy words be few.5921,3651
8: 6 t' the misery of man is great upon*
11 t' the heart of the sons of men5921,3651
11:10 T' remove sorrow from thy heart, and
Ca 1: 3 t' do the virgins love thee. 5921,3651
Isa 1:24 T' saith the Lord, the Lord of hosts,"
2: 6 T' thou hast forsaken thy people the*
9 humbleth himself: t' forgive them not.
3:17 T' the Lord will smite with a scab the
5:13 T' my people are gone into 3651
14 T' hell hath enlarged herself, and "
24 T' as the fire devoureth the stubble,"
25 T' is the anger of the Lord 5921, "
7:14 T' the Lord himself shall give you "
8: 7 Now t', behold, the Lord bringeth "
9:11 T' the Lord shall set up the "
14 T' the Lord will cut off from Israel
17 T' the Lord shall have no joy5921,3651
10:16 T' shall the Lord, the Lord of hosts,"
24 T' thus saith the Lord God of hosts,"
12: 3 T' with joy shall ye draw water out of
13: 7 T' shall all hands be faint, 5921,3651
13 T' I will shake the heavens, " "
15: 4 t' the armed soldiers of Moab " "
7 T' the abundance they have " "
16: 7 T' shall Moab howl for Moab, every" "
9 T' I will bewail with the 5921, "
17:10 t' shalt thou plant pleasant " "
21: 3 T' are my loins filled with " "
22: 4 T' said I, Look away fromme; " "
24: 6 T' hath the curse devoured the" "
6 t' the inhabitants of the earth " "
25: 3 T' shall the strong people " "
26:14 t' hast thou visited and destroyed "
27: 9 t' shall the iniquity of Jacob be "
11 t' he that made them will not5921, "
28:16 T' thus saith the Lord God, Behold,"
22 Now t' be ye not mockers, lest your
29:14 T', behold, I will proceed to do a 3651
22 T' thus saith the Lord, who "
30: 3 T' shall the strength of Pharaoh be
7 t' have I cried concerning this, 3651
13 T' this iniquity shall be to you as a "
16 upon horses; t' shall ye flee: 5921, "
16 t' shall they that pursue you be" "
18 t' will the Lord wait, that he may "
18 unto you, and t' will he be exalted, "
36: 8 Now t' give pledges, I pray thee, to
37:19 stone: t' they have destroyed them.
20 Now t', O Lord our God, save us from
27 T' their inhabitants were of small
29 t' will I put my hook in thy nose, and
33 T' thus saith the Lord concerning3651
38:20 t' we will sing my songs to the stringed
42:25 T' he hath poured upon him the fury
43: 4 t' will I give men for thee, and people
12 t' ye are my witnesses, saith the Lord,
28 T' I have profaned the princes of the
47: 8 T' hear now this, thou that art given
11 T' shall evil come upon thee; thou
50: 7 t' shall I not be confounded: 5921,3651
7 t' have I set my face like a "
51:11 T' the redeemed of the Lord shall*
21 T' hear now this, thou afflicted, 3651
52: 5 Now t', what have I here, saith the
6 T' my people shall know my 3651
6 t' they shall know in that day that I"
53:12 T' will I divide him a portion with "
57:10 t' thou wast not grieved. 5921, "
59: 9 T' is judgment far from us, "
16 t' his arm brought salvation unto
60:11 T' thy gates shall be open continually;*
61: 7 T' in their land they shall possess 3651
63: 5 t' mine own arm brought salvation
10 t' he was turned to be their enemy,
65: 7 t' will I measure their former work
12 T' will I number you to the sword,*
13 T' thus saith the Lord God, 3651
Jer 1:17 Thou t' gird up thy loins, and arise,
2:19 know t' and see that it is an evil thing
33 t' hast thou also taught the wicked3651
3: 3 T' the showers have been withholden,
5: 4 T' I said, Surely these are poor; they*
27 t' they are become great, and5921,3651
6:11 T' I am full of the fury of the Lord; I
15 t' they shall fall among them that3651
18 T' hear, ye nations, and know, O "
21 T' thus saith the Lord, Behold, I "
7:14 T' will I do unto this house, which is
16 T' pray not thou for this people,
20 T' thus saith the Lord God; 3651
27 T' thou shalt speak all these words*
32 T', behold, the days come, saith 3651
8:10 T' will I give their wives unto "
12 t' shall they fall among them that "
9: 7, 15 T' thus saith the Lord of hosts, "
10:21 t' they shall not prosper, and 5921, "
11: 8 t' I will bring upon them all the words
11 T' thus saith the Lord, Behold, I 3651
14 T' pray not thou for this people,
21 T' thus saith the Lord of the men3651
22 T' thus saith the Lord of hosts, "
12: 8 against me: t' have I hated it.5921, "
13:12 T' thou shalt speak unto them this
24 T' will I scatter them as the stubble
26 T' will I discover thy skirts upon thy
14:10 t' the Lord doth not accept them;
15 T' thus saith the Lord concerning3651
17 T' thou shalt say this word unto *
22 t' we will wait upon thee: for thou
15: 6 t' will I stretch out my hand against
19 T' thus saith the Lord, If thou 3651
16:13 T' will I cast you out of this land into
14 T', behold, the days come, saith 3651

Jer 16:21 T', behold, I will this once cause 3651
18:11 Now t' go to, speak to the men of
13 T' thus saith the Lord; Ask ye 3651
21 T' deliver up their children to the "
19: 6 T', behold, the days come, saith "
20:11 t' my persecutors shall 5921, "
22:18 T' thus saith the Lord concerning "
23: 2 T' thus saith the Lord God of "
7 T', behold, the days come, saith "
15 T' thus saith the Lord of hosts "
30 T', behold, I am against the "
32 t' they shall not profit this people at*
38 T' thus saith the Lord; Because 3651
39 T', behold, I, even I, will utterly "
25: 8 T' thus saith the Lord of hosts; "
27 T' thou shalt say unto them, Thus*
30 T' prophesy thou against them all
26:13 T' now amend your ways and your
27: 9 T' hearken not ye to your prophet,*
14 T' hearken not unto the words of the*
28:16 T' thus saith the Lord; Behold, I 3651
29:20 Hear ye t' the word of the Lord, all ye
27 Now t' why hast thou not reproved
28 t' he sent unto us in Babylon,*5921,3651
32 T' thus saith the Lord; Behold, I "
30:10 T' fear thou not, O my servant Jacob,
16 T' all they that devour thee shall 3651
31: 3 t' with lovingkindness have I 5921, "
12 T' they shall come and sing in the*
20 t' my bowels are troubled for 5921,3651
32:23 t' thou hast caused all this evil to
28 T' thus saith the Lord; 5921,3651
36 And now t' thus saith the Lord, the"
34:12 T' the word of the Lord came to
17 T' thus saith the Lord; Ye have 3651
35:17 T' thus saith the Lord God of hosts,"
19 T' thus saith the Lord of hosts, "
36: 6 T' go thou, and read in the roll, which
14 T' all the princes sent Jehudi the son
30 T' thus saith the Lord of 3651
37:20 T' hear now, I pray thee, O my lord*
38: 4 T' the princes said unto the king, We*
40: 3 voice, t' this thing is come upon you.
42:15 now t' hear the word of the Lord, 3651
22 t' know certainly that ye shall die
44: 7 T' now thus saith the Lord, the God
11 T' thus saith the Lord of hosts, 3651
22 t' is your land a desolation, and an
26 T' hear ye the word of the Lord, 3651
48:11 t' his taste remained in him, 5921, "
12 T', behold, the days come, saith "
31 T' will I howl for Moab, and 5921, "
36 T' mine heart shall sound for "
49: 2 T', behold, the days come, saith "
20 T' hear the counsel of the Lord, "
26 T' her young men shall fall in her "
50:18 T' thus saith the Lord of hosts, in "
30 T' shall her young men fall in the "
39 T' the wild beasts of the desert "
45 T' hear ye the counsel of the Lord, "
51: 7 wine; t' the nations are mad. 5921, "
36 T' thus saith the Lord; Behold, I "
47 T', behold, the days come, that I "
La 1: 8 sinned; t' she is removed: 5921, "
9 end; t' she came down wonderfully:
2: 8 t' he made the rampart and the wall*
3:21 to my mind, t' have I hope. 5921,3651
24 my soul; t' will I hope in him. " "
Eze 3:17 t' hear the word at my mouth, and
4: 7 T' thou shalt set thy face toward the*
5: 7, 8 T' thus saith the Lord God; 3651
10 T' the fathers shall eat the sons in "
11 t' will I also diminish thee; neither
7:20 t' have I set it far from them.5921,3651
8:18 T' will I also deal in fury: mine eye
11: 4 T' prophesy against them, 3651
7 T' thus saith the Lord God; Your "
16, 17 T' say, Thus saith the Lord God;"
12: 3 T', thou son of man, prepare thee
23 Tell them t', Thus saith the Lord 3651
28 T' say unto them, Thus saith the "
13: 8 T' thus saith the Lord God; "
8 t', behold, I am against you, saith "
13 T' thus saith the Lord God; I will "
23 T' ye shall see no more vanity, "
14: 4 T' speak unto them, and say unto "
6 T' say unto the house of Israel, "
15: 6 T' thus saith the Lord God; As the"
16:27 t' I have stretched out my hand
34 given unto thee, t' thou art contrary.
37 t' I will gather all thy lovers, with3651
43 t' I also will recompense thy way upon
50 t' I took them away as I saw good.
17:19 T' thus saith the Lord God; As I 3651
18:30 T' I will judge you, O house of "
20:27 T', son of man, speak unto the "
21: 4 t' shall my sword go forth out of his
6 Sigh t', thou son of man, with the
12 my people: smite t' upon thy thigh.
14 Thou t', son of man, prophesy, and
24 T' thus saith the Lord God; 3651
22: 4 t' have I made thee a reproach5921, "
13 t' I have smitten mine hand at thy
19 T' thus saith the Lord God; 3651
19 t' I will gather you into the midst "
31 T' have I poured out mine indignation
23:22 T', O Aholibah, thus saith the 3651
31 t' will I give her cup into thine hand.
35 T' thus saith the Lord God; 3651
35 t' bear thou also thy lewdness and thy
24: 9 T' thus saith the Lord God; Woe 3651
25: 4 t' I will deliver thee to the men of "
7 t' I will stretch out mine hand "
9 T', behold, I will open the side of "
13, 16 T' thus saith the Lord God; I "
26: 3 T' thus saith the Lord God;

Eze 28: 6 T' thus saith the Lord God; 3651
7 t' I will bring strangers upon thee, "
16 t' I will cast thee as profane out of the
18 t' will I bring forth a fire from the
29: 8 T' thus saith the Lord God; 3651
10 t' I am against thee, and against "
19 T' thus saith the Lord God; "
30:22 T' thus saith the Lord God; "
31: 5 T' his height was exalted above5921,"
10 T' thus saith the Lord God; "
11 I have t' delivered him into the hand*
32: 3 I will t' spread out my net over thee*
33: 7 t' thou shalt hear the word at my
10 T', O thou son of man, speak unto the*
12 T', thou son of man, say unto the*
34: 7 T', ye shepherds, hear the word of3651
9 T', O ye shepherds, hear the word "
20 T' thus saith the Lord God unto "
22 T' will I save my flock, and they shall
35: 6, 11 T', as I live, saith the Lord God,3651
36: 3 T' prophesy and say, Thus saith "
4 T', ye mountains of Israel, hear "
7 T' thus saith the Lord God; Surely "
6 Prophesy t' concerning the land of "
7 T' thus saith the Lord God; I have "
14 T' thou shalt devour men no more,"
22 T' say unto the house of Israel, "
37:12 T' prophesy and say unto them, "
38:14 T', son of man, prophesy and say "
39: 1 T', thou son of man, prophesy *
23 t' hid I my face from them, and gave*
25 T' thus saith the Lord God; Now 3651
41: 7 t' the breadth of the house 5921, "
42: 6 t' the building was straitened " "
44: 2 hath entered in by it, t' it shall be shut.
12 t' have I lifted up mine hand 5921,3651
Da 1: 8 t' he requested of the prince of the
19 Azariah: t' stood they before the king.
2: 6 t' shew me the dream, and the 2006
9 t' tell me the dream, and I shall "
10 t' there is no king, lord,* 3606,6903,1768
24 T' Daniel went in unto " " "
3: 7 T' at that time, when all " " 1836
19 t' he spake, and commanded that they
22 T' because the king's 3606,6903,1836
29 T' I make a decree, That every
4: 6 T' made I a decree to bring in all the
8: 8 T' the he goat waxed very great: and*
9:11 t' the curse is poured upon us, and the
14 T' hath the Lord watched upon the
17 Now t', O our God, hear the prayer of
23 t' understand the matter, and consider
25 Know t' and understand, that from the
10: 8 T' I was left alone, and saw this great*
11:30 t' he shall be grieved, and return, and
44 t' he shall go forth with great fury to*
Ho 2: 2 let her t' put away her whoredoms out*
6 T', behold, I will hedge up thy 3651
9 T' will I return, and take away my "
14 T', behold, I will allure her, and "
4: 3 T' shall the land mourn, and 5921,3651
5 T' shalt thou fall in the day, and the*
7 t' will I change their glory into shame.*
13 t' your daughters...commit 5921,3651
14 t' the people that doth not understand*
5: 5 t' shall Israel and Ephraim fall in
10 t' I will pour out my wrath upon them*
12 T' will I be unto Ephraim as a moth,
6: 5 T' have I hewed them by the 5921,3651
8: 6 workman made it; t' it is not God:*
9: 9 t' he will remember their iniquity, he*
10:14 T' shall a tumult arise among thy
12: 6 T' turn thou to thy God: keep mercy
14 t' shall he leave his blood upon him,
13: 3 T' they shall be as the morning 3651
6 t' have they forgotten me. 5921, "
7 T' I will be unto them as a lion: as a
Joe 2:12 T' also now, saith the Lord, turn *1571
Am 2:14 T' the flight shall perish from the*
3: 2 t' I will punish you for all 5921,3651
11 T' thus saith the Lord God; An "
4:12 T' thus will I do unto thee, O "
5:11 Forasmuch t' as your treading is "
13 T' the prudent shall keep silence "
16 T' the Lord, the God of hosts, the "
27 T' will I cause you to go into captivity
6: 7 T' now shall they go captive with 3651
8 t' will I deliver up the city with all
7:16 Now t' hear thou the word of the Lord:
17 T' thus saith the Lord; Thy wife 3651
Jon 4: 2 T' I fled...unto Tarshish: 5921, "
3 T' now, O Lord, take, I beseech thee,
Mic 1: 6 T' I will make Samaria as an heap of
8 T' I will wail and howl, I will go *
14 T' shalt thou give presents to 3651
2: 3 T' thus saith the Lord; Behold, "
5 T' thou shalt have none that shall "
3: 6 T' night shall be unto you, that ye "
12 T' shall Zion for your sake be "
5: 3 T' will he give them up, until the "
6:13 T' also will I make thee sick in
16 t' ye shall bear the reproach of my*
7: 7 T' I will look unto the Lord; I will*
Hab 1: 4 T' the law is slacked, and 5921,3651
4 righteous; t' wrong judgment " "
15 t' they rejoice and are glad. " "
16 T' they sacrifice unto their net, " "
17 Shall they t' empty their net, and "
Zep 1:13 T' their goods shall become a booty,*
2: 9 T' as I live, saith the Lord of 3651
3: 8 T' wait ye upon me, saith the Lord,"
Hag 1: 5 Now t' thus saith the Lord of hosts;
10 T' the heaven over you is 5921,3651
Zec 1: 3 T' say thou unto them, Thus saith the
16 T' thus saith the Lord; I am 3651
7:12 t' came a great wrath from the Lord

Zec 7:13 T' it is come to pass, that as he cried,*
8:19 feasts; t' love the truth and peace.
10: 2 t' they went their way as a 5921,3651
Mal 2: 9 T' have I also made you contemptible
15 T' take heed to your spirit, and let
16 t' take heed to your spirit, that ye deal
3: 6 t' ye sons of Jacob are not consumed.
M't 3: 8 Bring forth t' fruits meet for 3767
10 t' every tree which bringeth not "
5:19 Whosoever t' shall break one of "
23 T' if thou bring thy gift to the "
48 Be ye t' perfect, even as your Father "
6: 2 T' when thou doest thine alms, do "
8 Be not ye t' like unto them: for "
9 After this manner t' pray ye: Our "
22 if t' thine eye be single, thy whole "
23 If t' the light that is in thee be "
25 T' I say unto you, Take no 1223,5124
31 T' take no thought, saying, What 3767
34 Take t' no thought for the morrow: "
7:12 T' all things whatsoever ye would "
24 T' whosoever heareth these sayings "
9:38 Pray ye t' the Lord of the harvest, "
10:16 be ye t' wise as serpents, and "
26 Fear them not t': for there is "
31 Fear ye not t', ye are of more value "
32 Whosoever t' shall confess me before "
12:27 t' they shall be your judges. 1223,5124
13:13 T' speak I to them in parables: "
18 Hear ye t' the parable of the sower.*3767
40 As t' the tares are gathered and "
52 T' every scribe which is 1223,5124
14: 2 t' mighty works do shew forth " "
18: 4 Whosoever t' shall humble himself 3767
23 T' is the kingdom of heaven 1223,5124
26 The servant t' fell down, and 3767
19: 6 What t' God hath joined together, "
27 thee; what shall we have t'? * 686
21:40 When the lord t' of the vineyard 3767
43 T' say I unto you, The 1223,5124
22: 9 Go ye t' into the highways, and as 3767
17 Tell us t', What thinkest thou? Is it "
21 Render t' unto Cæsar the things "
28 T' in the resurrection whose wife "
23: 3 t' whatsoever they bid you observe, "
14 t' ye shall receive the greater*1223,5124
20 Whoso t' shall swear by the altar, 3767
24:15 ye t' shall see the abomination "
42 Watch t': for ye know not what "
44 T' be ye also ready: for in 1223,5124
25:13 Watch t', for ye know neither the 3767
27 Thou oughtest t' to have put my "
28 Take t' the talent from him, and "
27:17 T' when they were gathered "
64 Command t' that the sepulchre be "
28:19 Go ye t', and teach all nations, "
M'r 1:38 there also: for t' came I forth.*1519,5124
2:28 T' the Son of man is Lord also of *5620
6:14 t' mighty works do shew forth 1223,5124
19 T' Herodias had a quarrel against*
8:38 Whosoever t' shall be ashamed of*1063
10: 9 What t' God hath joined together, 3767
11:24 T' I say unto you, What 1223,5124
12: 6 Having yet t' one son, his *3767
9 What shall t' the lord of the "
23 In the resurrection t', when they * "
24 Do ye not t' err, because ye *1223,5124
27 the living: ye t' do greatly err. *3767
37 David t' himself calleth him Lord;*"
13:35 Watch ye t': for ye know not when "
Lu 1:35 t' also that holy thing which shall*1352
3: 8 Bring forth t' fruits worthy of 3767
9 every tree t' which bringeth not "
4: 7 If thou t' wilt worship me, all shall "
43 cities also: for t' am I sent. 1519,5124
6:36 Be ye t' merciful, as your Father *3767
7:42 Tell me t', which of them will love "
8:18 Take heed t' how ye hear: for "
10: 2 T' said he unto them, The harvest*"
2 pray ye t' the Lord of the harvest,
40 alone? bid her t' that she help me. 3767
11:19 t' shall they be your judges. 1223,5124
34 t' when thine eye is single, thy *3767
35 Take heed t' that the light which is "
36 If thy whole body t' be full of light, "
49 T' also said the wisdom of God, I
12: 3 T' whatsoever ye have spoken*473,5607
7 Fear not t': ye are of more value *3767
22 T' I say unto you, Take no 1223,5124
40 Be ye t' ready also: for the Son of*3767
13:14 in them t' come and be healed, and "
14:20 a wife, and t' I cannot come. 1223,5124
15:28 t' came his father out, and *3767
16:11 If t' ye have not been faithful in "
27 I pray thee t', father, that thou "
19:12 He said t', A certain nobleman "
20:15 What t' shall the lord of the "
25 Render t' unto Cæsar the things *5106
29 There were t' seven brethren: and3767
33 T' in the resurrection whose wife "
44 David t' calleth him Lord, how is he
21: 8 near: go ye not t' after them. *3767
14 Settle it t' in your hearts, not to "
36 Watch ye t', and pray always, that* "
23:16 I will t' chastise him, and release "
20 Pilate t', willing to release Jesus, * "
22 I will t' chastise him, and let him "
Joh 1:31 t' am I come baptizing with *1223,5124
2:22 When t' he was risen from the 3767
3:29 voice: this my joy t' is fulfilled. "
4: 1 When t' the Lord knew how the "
6 Jesus t', being wearied with his "
33 T' said the disciples one to * "
5:10 Jews t' said unto him that was * "
16 And t' did the Jews persecute*1223,5124
18 T' the Jews sought the more to " "

Joh 6:13 T' they gathered them together, *3767
15 When Jesus t' perceived that they "
24 When the people t' saw that Jesus "
30 They said t' unto him, What sign "
43 Jesus t' answered and said unto * "
45 Every man t' that hath heard, and* "
52 Jews t' strove among themselves, "
60 Many t' of his disciples, when they "
65 T' said I unto you, that no *1223,5124
7: 3 His brethren t' said unto him, 3767
22 Moses t' gave unto you †1223,5124
40 Many of the people t', when they 3767
8:13 The Pharisees t' said unto him, "
24 I said t' unto you, that ye shall die "
36 If the Son t' shall make you free, ye"
47 ye t' hear them not, because *1223,5124
9: 7 He went his way t', and washed, 3767
8 The neighbours t', and they which "
10 T' said they unto him, How were "
16 T' said some of the Pharisees, This"
23 T' said his parents, He is of 1223,5124
41 We see; t' your sin remaineth. *3767
10:17 T' doth my Father love me, 1223,5124
19 was a division t' again among the*3767
39 T' they sought again to take him:* "
11: 3 T' his sisters sent unto him, "
6 he had heard t' that he was sick, "
33 When Jesus t' saw her weeping, "
38 Jesus t' again groaning in himself "
54 Jesus t' walked no more openly "
12: 9 the Jews t' knew that he was there: "
17 people t' that was with him when "
19 The Pharisees t' said among "
21 The same came t' to Philip, which "
29 The people t', that stood by, and "
39 T' they could not believe, *1223,5124
50 I speak t', even as the Father, "
13:11 t' said he, Ye are not all clean.1223,5124
24 Simon Peter t' beckoned to him, 3767
31 T', when he was gone out, Jesus "
15:19 world, t' the world hateth you.1223,5124
16:15 t' said I, that he shall take of " "
18 They said t', What is this that he 3767
22 And ye now t' have sorrow: but I "
18: 4 Jesus t', knowing all things that "
8 if t' ye seek me, let these go their "
25 They said t' unto him, Art not thou "
31 The Jews t' said unto him, It is not* "
37 Pilate t' said unto him, Art thou a "
39 will ye t' that I release unto you "
19: 1 Then Pilate t' took Jesus, and "
4 Pilate t' went forth again, and * "
6 the chief priests t' and officers saw "
8 When Pilate t' heard that saying, "
11 t' he that delivered me unto 1223,5124
13 When Pilate t' heard that saying, 3767
16 Then delivered he him t' unto them "
24 They said t' among themselves, Let "
24 These things t' the soldiers did. "
26 When Jesus t' saw his mother, and "
30 When Jesus t' had received the "
31 The Jews t', because it was the "
38 He came t', and took the body of "
42 There laid they Jesus t' because of* "
20: 3 Peter t' went forth, and that other "
25 other disciples t' said unto him, "
21: 6 They cast t', and now they were not "
7 T' that disciple whom Jesus loved "
Ac 1: 6 When they t' were come together, "
2:26 T' did my heart rejoice, and 1223,5124
30 T' being a prophet, and knowing 3767
33 T' being by the right hand of God "
36 T' let all the house of Israel know "
3:19 Repent ye t', and be converted, "
8: 4 T' they that were scattered abroad "
22 Repent t' of this thy wickedness, "
10:20 Arise t', and get thee down, and go*235
29 T' came I unto you without *1352
29 I ask t' for what intent ye have 3767
32 Send t' to Joppa, and call hither "
33 Immediately t' I sent to thee; and "
33 t' are we all here present before "
12: 5 Peter t' was kept in prison: but "
13:38 Be it known unto you t', men and "
40 Beware t', lest that come upon you. "
14: 3 Long time t' abode they speaking "
15: 2 When t' Paul and Barnabas had no* "
10 Now t' why tempt ye God, to put a "
27 We have sent t' Judas and Silas, "
16:11 T' loosing from Troas, we came "
36 go: now t' depart, and go in peace. "
17:12 T' many of them believed; also of "
17 T' disputed he in the synagogue * "
20 know t' what these things mean. "
23 Whom t' ye ignorantly worship, "
19:32 Some t' cried one thing, and some "
20:11 When he t' was come up again, * "
28 Take heed t' unto yourselves, and to*
31 T' watch, and remember, that by*1352
21:22 What is it t'? the multitude must 3767
23 Do t' this that we say to thee: We "
23:15 Now t' ye with the council signify "
25: 5 Let them t', said he, which among "
17 T', when they were come hither, "
26:22 Having t' obtained help of God, I "
28:20 For this cause t' have I called for "
28 Be it known t' unto you, that the "
Ro 2: 1 T' thou art inexcusable, O man, *1352
21 Thou t' which teachest another, 3767
26 T' if the uncircumcision keep the "
3:20 T' by the deeds of the law there *1360
28 T' we conclude that a man is 3767
4:16 T' it is of faith, that it might*1223,5124
22 t' it was imputed to him for *1352
5: 1 T' being justified by faith, we 3767
18 T' as by the offence of one *686, "

Ro 6: 4 T' we are buried with him by 3767
12 Let not sin t' reign in your mortal "
8: 1 There is t' now no condemnation * 686
12 T', brethren, we are debtors, *686,3767
9:18 T' hath he mercy on whom he* " "
11:22 Behold t' the goodness...of God: * "
12: 1 I beseech you t', brethren, by the "
20 T' if thine enemy hunger, feed * "
13: 2 Whosoever t' resisteth the power, 5620
7 Render t' to all their dues: *3767
10 t' love is the fulfilling of the law. "
12 us t' cast off the works of darkness, "
14: 8 whether we live t', or die, we are "
13 Let us not t' judge one another any "
19 Let us t' follow after the things*686, "
15:17 t' whereof I may glory through "
28 When t' I have performed this, "
16:19 I am glad t' on your behalf: but yet "
1Co 3:21 T' let no man glory in men. For *5620
4: 5 T' judge nothing before the time,* "
5: 7 Purge out t' the old leaven, that *3767
8 T' let us keep the feast, not with *5620
13 T' put away from among yourselves*
6: 7 Now t' there is utterly a fault *3767
20 t' glorify God in your body, and in 1211
7: 8 I say t' to the unmarried and *1160
26 I suppose t' that this is good for 3767
8: 4 As concerning t' the eating of those "
9:26 I t' so run, not as uncertainly; so 5106
10:31 Whether t' ye eat, or drink, or 3767
11:20 ye come together t' into one place, "
12:15, 16 is it t' not of the body?3756,3844,5124
14:11 T' if I know not the meaning of *3767
23 If t' the whole church be come "
15:11 T' whether it were I or they, so we* "
58 T', my beloved brethren, be ye *5620
16:11 Let no man t' despise him: but 3767
18 t' acknowledge ye them that are "
2Co 1:17 When I t' was thus minded, did I "
4: 1 T' seeing we have this 1223,5124
13 I believed, and t' have I spoken; 1352
13 we also believe, and t' speak; "
5: 6 T' we are always confident, 3767
11 Knowing t' the terror of the Lord, "
17 T' if any man be in Christ, he is a*5620
7: 1 Having t' these promises, dearly 3767
13 T' we were comforted in your 1223,5124
16 I rejoice t' that I have confidence in*
8: 7 T', as ye abound in every thing, 235
11 Now t' perform the doing of it; *2532
9: 5 T' I thought it necessary to exhort3767
11:15 T' it is no great thing if his "
12: 9 gladly t' will I rather glory in my "
10 T' I take pleasure in infirmities, *1352
13:10 T' I write these things being*1223,5124
Ga 2:17 is t' Christ the minister of sin? * 686
3: 5 He t' that ministereth to you the 3767
7 Know ye t' that they which are of 686
4:16 Am I t' become your enemy, *5620
5: 1 Stand fast t' in the liberty 3767
6:10 As we have t' opportunity, let* 685,
Eph 2:19 Now t' ye are no more strangers * 686
4: 1 I t', the prisoner of the Lord, 3767
17 This I say t', and testify in the "
5: 1 Be ye t' followers of God, as dear *
7 Be not ye t' partakers with them. "
24 T' as the church is subject unto * 235
6:14 Stand t', having your loins girt 3767
Ph'p 2: 1 If there be t' any consolation in "
23 Him t' I hope to send presently, "
28 I sent him t' the more carefully, "
29 Receive him t' in the Lord with all "
3:15 Let us t', as many as be perfect, be "
4: 1 T', my brethren dearly beloved *5620
Col 2: 6 As ye have t' received Christ 3767
16 Let no man t' judge you in meat, "
3: 5 Mortify t' your members which are "
12 Put on t', as the elect of God, holy "
1Th 3: 7 T', brethren, we were *1223,5124
4: 8 He t' that despiseth, despiseth not 5105
5: 6 T' let us not sleep, as do * 686,3767
2Th 2:15 T', brethren, stand fast, and * "
1Ti 2: 1 I exhort t', that, first of all, "
8 I will t' that men pray every where, "
4:10 t' we both labour and suffer *1519,5124
5:14 I will t' that the younger women marry, 3767
2Ti 1: 8 Be not thou t' ashamed of the "
2: 1 Thou t', my son, be strong in the "
3 Thou t' endure hardness, as a good* "
10 T' I endure all things for the elect's "
21 If a man t' purge himself from 3767
4: 1 I charge thee t' before God, and * "
Ph'm 12 thou t' receive him, that is, mine own*
15 he t' departed for a season, 1223,5124
17 If thou count me t' a partner, *3767
Heb 1: 9 t' God, even thy God, hath 1223,5124
2: 1 T' we ought to give the more "
4: 1 Let us t' fear, lest, a promise 3767
6 Seeing t' it remaineth that some "
9 remaineth t' a rest unto the people 686
11 labour t' to enter into that rest, 3767
16 Let us t' come boldly unto the "
6: 1 T' leaving the principles of the *
7:11 If t' perfection were by the *3767
9:23 It was t' necessary that the "
10:19 Having t', brethren, boldness to "
35 Cast not away t' your confidence, "
11:12 T' sprang there even of one, and *1352
13:13 Let us go forth t' unto him without 5106
15 By him t' let us offer the sacrifice*3767
Jas 4: 4 whosoever t' will be a friend of the "
7 Submit yourselves t' to God, "
17 T' to him that knoweth to do good, "
5: 7 Be patient t', brethren, unto the "
1Pe 2: 7 Unto you t' which believe he is "
4: 7 be ye t' sober, and watch unto "

1Pe 5: 6 Humble yourselves t' under the 8767
2Pe 3:17 Ye t', beloved, seeing ye know "
1Jo 2:24 Let that t' abide in you, which ye* "
3: 1 t' the world knoweth us not, *1223,5124
4: 5 t' speak they of the world, and " "
3Jo 8 We t' ought to receive such, that 3767
Jude 5 I will t' put you in remembrance,*
Re 2: 5 Remember t' from whence thou 3767
3: 3 Remember t' how thou hast "
3 If t' thou shalt not watch, I will "
19 chasten: be zealous t', and repent. "
7:15 T' are they before the throne 1223,5124
12:12 T' rejoice, ye heavens, and ye " "
18: 8 T' shall her plagues come in one "

therefrom
Jos 23: 6 ye turn not aside t' to the right hand
2Ki 3: 3 made Israel to sin; he departed not t'.
13: 2 made Israel to sin; he departed not t'.

therein See also THEREINTO.
Ge 9: 7 in the earth, and multiply t'.
18:24 for the fifty righteous that are t'? 7130
23:11 and the cave that is t', I give it thee;
17 field, and the cave was t', and all the
20 And the field, and the cave that is t',
34:10 be before you; dwell and trade ye t',
10 and get you possessions t'.
21 dwell in the land, and trade t';
47:27 they had possessions t', and grew, and
49:32 of the cave that is t' was from the
Ex 2: 3 and with pitch, and put the child t';
5: 9 the men, that they may labour t';
16:24 stink, neither was there any worm t'.
33 and put an omer full of manna t'. 8033
21:33 cover it, and an ox or an ass fall t'; "
29:29 his sons' after him, to be anointed t',*
30:18 altar, and thou shalt put water t'. 8033
31:14 for whosoever doeth any work t', that
35: 2 doeth work t' shall be put to death.
40: 3 put t' the ark of the testimony, 8033
7 the altar, and shall put water t'. "
9 the tabernacle, and all that is t',
Le 6: 3 these that a man doeth, sinning t':2007
7 that he hath done in trespassing t'.*
8:10 the tabernacle and all that was t',
10: 1 them his censer, and put fire t', 2004
13:21 and, behold, there be no white hairs t',
37 that there is black hair grown up t';
18: 4 and keep mine ordinances, to walk t':
30 and that ye defile not yourselves t':
20:22 land, whither I bring you to dwell t',
22:21 accepted; there shall be no blemish t'.
23: 3 convocation; ye shall do no work t':*
7, 8 ye shall do no servile work t'. *
21 you: ye shall do no servile work t':*
25 Ye shall do no servile work t': but ye*
35, 36 ye shall do no servile work t'. *
25:19 eat your fill, and dwell t' in safety.5921
26:32 your enemies which dwell t' shall be
Nu 4:16 all the tabernacle, and of all that t' is,
13:18 and the people that dwelleth t', *5921
20 fat or lean, whether there be wood t',
14:30 which I sware to make you dwell t',
16: 7 And put fire t', and put incense in 2004
46 and put fire t' from off the altar, 5921
28:18 shall do no manner of servile work t':*
29: 7 your souls: ye shall not do any work t':*
35 ye shall do no servile work t': *
32:40 the son of Manasseh; and he dwelt t'.
33:53 inhabitants of the land, and dwell t':
35:33 be cleansed of the blood that is shed t',
De 2:10 The Emims dwelt t' in times past, a
20 of giants; giants dwelt t' in old time;
7:25 it unto thee, lest thou be snared t':
8:12 hast built goodly houses, and dwelt t';
10:14 God, the earth also, with all that t' is.
11:31 and ye shall possess it, and dwell t'.
13:15 destroying it utterly, and all that is t',
15:21 And if there be any blemish t', as if it*
16: 8 thy God: thou shalt do no work t'.
17:14 and shalt possess it, and shalt dwell t',
19 he shall read t' all the days of his life:
20:11 the people that is found t' shall be
26: 1 and possessest it, and dwellest t';
28:30 an house, and thou shalt not dwell t':
29:23 nor beareth, nor any grass groweth t',
Jos 1: 8 thou shalt meditate t' day and night,
8 do according to all that is written t':
6:17 even it, and all that are t', to the Lord:
24 the city with fire, and all that was t':
10:28 them, and all the souls that were t';
30 sword, and all the souls that were t';
32 sword, and all the souls that were t',
35 souls that were t' he utterly destroyed
37 thereof, and all the souls that were t';
37 utterly, and all the souls that were t'.
39 destroyed all the souls that were t';
11:11 they smote all the souls that were t'
19:47 and dwelt t', and called Leshem, Dan,
50 and he built the city, and dwelt t'.
21:43 and they possessed it, and dwelt t'.
J'g 2:22 keep the way of the Lord to walk t',
8:25 did cast t' every man the earrings 8033
9:45 and slew the people that was t', and
16:30 and upon all the people that were t'.
18: 7 and saw the people that were t', 7130
28 And they built a city, and dwelt t'.
1Sa 30: 2 the women captives, that were t':
2Sa 12:31 brought forth the people that were t',
1Ki 8:16 house, that my name might be t';*8033
11:24 they went to Damascus, and dwelt t',
12:25 in mount Ephraim, and dwelt t';
2Ki 2:20 me a new cruse, and put salt t'. 8033
12: 9 put t' all the money that was brought"
13: 6 who made Israel sin, but walked t':
11 who made Israel sin: but he walked t'.
2Ki 15:16 smote Tiphsah, and all that were t',
16 the women t' that were with child he
1Ch 16:32 let the fields rejoice, and all that is t'.
21:22 I may build an altar t' unto the Lord:*
2Ch 2: 3 cedars to build him an house to dwell t',
5:10 the two tables which Moses put t' at*
20: 8 And they dwelt t', and have built thee
8 built thee a sanctuary t' for thy name,
Ezr 4:19 and sedition have been made t'.
6: 2 and t' was a record thus written: 1459
Ne 6: 1 and that there was no breach left t';
7: 4 but the people were few t', and the
5 up at the first, and found written t',
8: 3 And he read t' before the street that
9: 6 earth, and all things that are t', *5921
6 the seas, and all that is t', and thou*
13: 1 and t' was found written, that the
16 There dwelt men of Tyre also t', which
Job 3: 7 be solitary, let no joyful voice come t'.
20:18 be, and he shall not rejoice t'. *
Ps 24: 1 the world, and they that dwell t'.
37:29 the land, and dwell t' for ever. 5921
68:10 Thy congregation hath dwelt t': thou,
69:34 seas, and every thing that moveth t'.
36 they that love his name shall dwell t'.
96:12 Let the field be joyful, and all that is t':
98: 7 the world, and they that dwell t'.
104:26 whom thou hast made to play t'.
107:34 the wickedness of them that dwell t'.
111: 2 out of all them that have pleasure t'.
119:35 thy commandments; for t' do I delight.
146: 6 and earth, the sea, and all that t' is:*
Pr 15: 4 but perverseness t' is a breach in the
22:14 abhorred of the Lord shall fall t'. 8033
26:27 Whoso diggeth a pit shall fall t': and
Ec 2:21 yet to a man that hath not laboured t'
Isa 5: 2 of it, and also made a winepress t':8432
7: 6 it, and let us make a breach t' for us,
24: 6 and they that dwell t' are desolate:
33:24 the people that dwell t' shall be
34: 1 the earth hear, and all that is t'; *4393
17 to generation shall they dwell t'.
35: 8 men, though fools, shall not err t'.
42: 5 upon it, and spirit to them that walk t':
10 down to the sea, and all that is t'; 4393
44:23 mountains, O forest, and every tree t':
51: 3 joy and gladness shall be found t',
6 and they that dwell t' shall die in like
59: 8 whosoever goeth t' shall not know
Jer 4:29 forsaken, and not a man dwell t'. 2004
6:16 where is the good way, and walk t',
16 But they said, We will not walk t'.
8:16 in it; the city, and those that dwell t'.
9:13 obeyed my voice, neither walked t';
12: 4 the wickedness of them that dwell t'?
17:24 the sabbath day, to do no work t';
23:12 they shall be driven on, and fall t':
27:11 Lord; and they shall till it, and dwell t'.
36: 2 write t' all the words that I have 413
29 Why hast thou written t', saying, 5921
32 who wrote t' from the mouth of
44: 2 a desolation, and no man dwelleth t',
47: 2 overflow the land, and all that is t';4393
2 the city, and them that dwell t':
48: 9 desolate, without any to dwell t'. 2004
50: 3 land desolate, and none shall dwell t':
39 dwell there, and the owls shall dwell t':
40 neither shall any son of man dwell t'.
51:48 all that is t', shall sing for Babylon:
Eze 2: 9 me; and, lo, a roll of a book was t';
10 there was written t' lamentations, 413
7:20 and of their detestable things t':
12:19 may be desolate from all that is t',4393
19 the violence of all them that dwell t'.
14:22 t' shall be left a remnant that shall be
20:47 south to the north shall be burned t'.*
24: 5 let them seethe the bones of it t'. *8432
6 to the pot whose scum is t', and whose
28:26 And they shall dwell safely t', and 5921
30:12 the land waste, and all that is t', 4393
32:15 I shall smite all them that dwell t',
37:25 and they shall dwell t', even they,
40:33 and there were windows t' and in the
42:14 When the priests enter t', then shall*
44:14 and for all that shall be done t'.
Da 5: 2 and his concubines, might drink t'.
Ho 4: 3 one that dwelleth t' shall languish,
14: 9 but the transgressors shall fall t'.
Am 6: 8 up the city with all that is t'. 4393
8: 8 and every one mourn that dwelleth t'?
9: 5 melt, and all that dwell t' shall mourn:
Mic 1: 2 hearken, O earth, and all that t' is:4393
7:13 desolate because of them that dwell t',
Na 1: 5 yea, the world, and all that dwell t'.
Hab 2: 8, 17 of the city, and of all that dwell t'.
18 the maker of his work trusteth t', 5921
Zec 2: 4 the multitude of men and cattle t':8432
6: 6 black horses which are t' go forth into*
13: 8 two parts t' shall be cut off and die;
8 and die; but the third shall be left t'.
14:21 come and take of them, and seethe t':
M't 23:21 by it, and by him that dwelleth t'.
M'r 10:15 child, he shall not enter t'. 1519,846
13:15 down into the house, neither enter t',*
Lu 10: 9 And heal the sick that are t', 1722,846
18:17 child shall in no wise enter t'. 1519, "
19:45 to cast out them that sold t', *1722, "
Joh 12: 6 the bag, and bare what was put t'.
Ac 1:20 and let no man dwell t': 1722,846
14:15 sea, and all things that are t': * " "
17:24 made the world and all things t', " "
27: 6 sailing into Italy; and he put us t'. "
Ro 1:17 t' is the righteousness of God 1722,846
6: 2 dead to sin, live any longer t'? " "
Co 17:24 he is called, t' abide with God. " 5129
Eph 6:20 that t' I may speak boldly, as I* " 846
Ph'p 1:18 and I t' do rejoice, yea, and will 1722,5129
Col 2: 7 abounding t'...thanksgiving. * " 846
Heb 4: 6 that some must enter t', *1519, "
10: 8 not, neither hadst pleasure t';
13: 9 that have been occupied t'. *1722,3639
Jas 1:25 law of liberty, and continueth t',*
2Pe 2:20 they are again entangled t', and 5125
3:10 the works that are t' shall be 1722,846
Re 1: 3 things which are written t': " "
10: 6, 6 and the things that t' are, " "
6 and the things which are t', " "
11: 1 altar, and them that worship t'. " "
13:12 earth and them which dwell t' " "
21:22 And I saw no temple t': for the " "

thereinto
Lu 21:21 are in the countries enter t'. *1519,846

thereof
Ge 2:19 living creature, that was the name t'.
21 ribs, and closed up the flesh instead t.;
3: 5 doth know that in the day ye eat t',
6 she took of the fruit t', and did eat,
4: 4 firstlings of his flock and of the fat t'.
6:16 of the ark shalt thou set in the side t';
9: 4 with the life t', which is the blood t',
40:10 the clusters t' brought forth ripe
18 and said, This is the interpretation t':
41: 8 of Egypt, and all the wise men t':
47:21 of Egypt even to the other end t'.
Ex 3:20 which I will do in the midst t':
5: 8 ye shall not diminish ought t':
9:18 been in Egypt since the foundation t'*
10:26 t' must we take to serve the Lord our
12: 9 his legs, and with the purtenance t'.
43 there shall no stranger eat t':
44 circumcised him, then shall he eat t'.
45 and an hired servant shall not eat t'.
46 neither shall ye break a bone t'.
48 no uncircumcised person shall eat t'.
16:31 of Israel called the name t' Manna:
19:18 the smoke t' ascended as the smoke of
22:11 and the owner of it shall accept t', and
12 make restitution unto the owner t'.
14 or die, the owner t' being not with it,
15 if the owner t' be with it, he shall not
23:10 land, and shalt gather in the fruits t':
25: 9 the pattern of all the instruments t',
10 and a half shall be the length t',
10 and a cubit and a half the breadth t',
10 and a cubit and a half the height t'.
12 it, and put them in the four corners t';
17 and a half shall be the length t',
17 and a cubit and a half the breadth t'.
19 the cherubims on the two ends t'.
23 two cubits shall be the length t',
23 and a cubit the breadth t',
23 and a cubit and a half the height t'.
25 make a golden crown to the border t'
26 corners that are on the four feet t'.
29 shalt make the dishes t', and spoons t',
29 and covers t', and bowls t', to cover
37 thou shalt make the seven lamps t':
37 and they shall light the lamps t', that
38 the tongs t', and the snuffdishes t',
26:30 to the fashion t' which was shewed
27: 1 and the height t' shall be three cubits.
2 horns of it upon the four corners t':
3 vessels t' thou shalt make of brass.
4 four brasen rings in...four corners t'.
10 the twenty pillars t' and their twenty
19 of the tabernacle in all the service t',
19 and all the pins t', and all the pins of
28: 7 It shall have the two shoulderpieces t'*
7 joined at the two edges t'; and so it
8 of the same, according to the work t';
16 doubled; a span shall be the length t',
16 and a span shall be the breadth t'.
26 of the breastplate in the border t',
27 underneath, toward the forepart t',
27 over against the other coupling t',
28 bind the breastplate by the rings t'
32 hole in the top of it, in the midst t':
33 of scarlet, round about the hem t';
29:33 but a stranger shall not eat t', because
41 according to the drink offering t', for a
30: 2 A cubit shall be the length t',
2 a cubit the breadth t': foursquare
2 and two cubits shall be the height t':
2 the horns t' shall be of the same.
3 overlay it with pure gold, the top t',
3 and the sides t' round about, and the
3 and the horns t'; and thou shalt make
4 the crown of it, by the two corners t',
37 according to the composition t':
35:12 The ark, and the staves t', with the
36:29 coupled together at the head t', to one
37: 6 two cubits and a half was the length t',
6 one cubit and a half the breadth t'.
8 he the cherubims on the two ends t'.
10 wood: two cubits was the length t',
10 and a cubit the breadth t', and a cubit
10 and a cubit and a half the height t':
12 made a crown of gold for the border t'
13 four corners that were in...four feet t'.
18 six branches going out of the sides t';
18 the candlestick out of the one side t',
18 candlestick out of the other side t':
24 gold made he it, and all the vessels t'.
25 height of it; horns t' were of the same.
26 top of it, and the sides t' round about,
27 rings of gold for it under the crown t',
27 corners of it, upon the two sides t',*
38: 1 wood: five cubits was the length t',
1 and five cubits the breadth t'; it was
1 and three cubits the height t'.
2 he made the horns t' on the four

Ex 38: 2 the horns t' were of the same: and he
3 all the vessels t' made he of brass.
4 of network under the compass t' *
39: 5 of the same, according to the work t';
9 double: a span was the length t',
9 a span the breadth t', being doubled.
20 it, over against the other coupling t',
35 ark of the testimony, and the staves t',
36 The table, and all the vessels t', and
37 pure candlestick, with the lamps t',
37 be set in order, and all the vessels t',
40: 4 the candlestick, and light the lamps t'.
9 shalt hallow it, and all the vessels t':
18 his sockets, and set up the boards t',
18 and put in the bars t', and reared up
Le 1: 15 the blood t' shall be wrung out at the
17 he shall cleave it with the wings t',
2: 2 of the flour t', and of the oil t',
2 with all the frankincense t'; and the
9 from the meat offering a memorial t',
16 beaten corn t', and part of the oil t',
16 with all the frankincense t': it is an
3: 8 Aaron's sons shall sprinkle the blood t'
9 the fat t', and the whole rump, it shall
13 Aaron shall sprinkle the blood t' upon
14 And he shall offer t' his offering, even
4: 30 the priest shall take of the blood t'
30 and shall pour out all the blood t' at
31 he shall take away all the fat t', as the
34 and shall pour out all the blood t' at
35 he shall take away all the fat t', as the
5: 12 his handful of it, even a memorial t',
6: 15 of the meat offering, and of the oil t',
16 remainder t' shall Aaron and his sons
20 it in the morning, and half t' at night.
27 shall touch the flesh t' shall be holy:
27 when there is sprinkled of the blood t'
29 males among the priests shall eat t':
7: 2 the blood t' shall he sprinkle round
3 And he shall offer of it all the fat t';
6 male among the priests shall eat t':
19 the flesh, all that be clean shall eat t'.
8: 11 he sprinkled t' upon the altar seven
9: 13 him, with the pieces t', and the head:*
17 took a handful t', and burnt it upon*
11: 39 he that toucheth the carcase t' shall*
13: 4 and the hair t' be not turned white;
18 which, even in the skin t', was a boil,
14: 45 and the timber t', and all the morter
17: 13 he shall even pour out the blood t',
14 the blood of it is for the life t':
14 for the life of all flesh is the blood t':
18: 25 I do visit the iniquity t' upon it,
19: 23 count the fruit t' as uncircumcised:
24 all the fruit t' shall be holy to praise
25 fifth year shall ye eat of the fruit t',
25 it may yield unto you the increase t':
22: 13 but there shall no stranger eat t'.
14 he shall put the fifth part t' unto it,
24 neither shall ye make any offering t'*
23: 10 and shall reap the harvest t', then ye
13 And the meat offering t' shall be two
13 drink offering t' shall be of wine,
24: 5 fine flour, and bake twelve cakes t':
25: 3 vineyard, and gather in the fruit t';
7 land, shall all the increase t' be meat.
10 all the land unto all the inhabitants t':
12 eat the increase t' out of the field.
16 years thou shalt increase the price t',
27 let him count the years of the sale t',
27: 10 it and the exchange t' shall be holy.*
13 add a fifth part t' unto thy estimation.
16 shall be according to the seed t':
21 the possession t' shall be the priest's.
31 he shall add thereto the fifth part t'.
33 it and the change t' shall be holy;*
Nu 1: 50 testimony, and over all the vessels t',
50 the tabernacle, and all the vessels t';
2: 6, 8, 11 and those that were numbered t',
3: 25 the covering t', and the hanging for
26 the cords of it for all the service t'.
31 the hanging, and all the service t'.
36 and the bars t', and the pillars t',
36 the sockets t', and all the vessels t',
4: 6 of blue, and shall put in the staves t'.
9 snuffdishes, and all the oil vessels t',
10 they shall put it and all the vessels t'
11 skins, and shall put to the staves t':
14 shall put upon it all the vessels t',
16 in the sanctuary, and in the vessels t'.
31 of the tabernacle, and the bars t',
31 and the pillars t', and sockets t',
5: 7 his trespass with the principal t',*
7 add unto it the fifth part t', and give
26 of the offering, even the memorial t',
7: 1 sanctified it, and all...instruments t',
1 both the altar and all the vessels t',
8: 3 he lighted the lamps t' over against
4 unto the shaft t', unto the flowers t',
25 shall cease waiting upon the service t',*
9: 3 and according to all the ceremonies t',
14 and according to the manner t', so
11: 7 the colour t' as the colour of bdellium.
13: 32 land that eateth up the inhabitants t';
18: 28 shall give t' the Lord's heave offering
29 offering of the Lord, of all the best t',
29 even the hallowed part t' out of it.
30 ye have heaved the best t' from it,
21: 25 in Heshbon, and in all the villages t'.
32 Jaazer, and they took the villages t',
26: 56 shall the possession t' be divided*
28: 7 drink offering t' shall be the fourth
8 and as the drink offering t', thou shalt
9 with oil, and the drink offering t':
29: 19 and the meat offering t', and their
32: 33 with the cities t' in the coasts, even

Nu 32: 41 went and took the small towns t',
42 and took Kenath, and the villages t',
34: 2 the land of Canaan with the coasts t':)
4 and the going forth t' shall be from
12 shall be you land with the coasts t'
De 3: 11 nine cubits was the length t', and
12 half mount Gilead, and the cities t',
17 plain also, and Jordan, and the coast t',
9: 21 and I cast the dust t' into the brook
12: 15 the unclean and the clean may eat t',
13: 15 all that is therein, and the cattle t',
16 of it into the midst of the street t',
16 city, and all the spoil t' every whit,
15: 23 Only thou shalt not eat the blood t';
20: 13 smite every male t' with the edge of
14 is in the city, even all the spoil t',
19 thou shalt not destroy the trees t' by
26: 14 I have not eaten t' in my mourning,
14 neither have I taken away ought t' for
14 use, nor given ought t' for the dead:
28: 30 and shalt not gather the grapes t'.
31 thine eyes, and thou shalt not eat t':
29: 23 that the whole land t' is brimstone,
33: 16 things of the earth and fulness t',
Jos 6: 2 thine hand Jericho, and the king t',
26 he shall lay the foundation t' in his
7: 14 come according to the families t';*
8: 2 only the spoil t', and the cattle t',
9: 1 and Hivite, and the Jebusite, heard t';
10: 2 Ai, and all the men t' were mighty.
28 and the king t' he utterly destroyed,
30 the king t', into the hand of Israel;
30 but did unto the king t' as he did unto
37 and the king t', and all the cities t',
39 and the king t', and all the cities t';
39 so he did to Debir, and to the king t';
11: 10 and smote the king t' with the sword:
13: 23 Reuben was Jordan, and the border t'.
23 families, the cities and the villages t'.
15: 7 and the goings out t' were at En-rogel:
12 was to the great sea, and the coast t'.
47 and the great sea, and the border t'.
16: 3 and the goings out t' are at the sea.
8 and the goings out t' were at the sea.
18: 12, 14 and the goings out t' were at
20 by the coasts t' round about,
19: 14 outgoings t' are in the valley of
29 the outgoings t' are at the sea from
33 and the outgoings t' were at Jordan:
21: 2 in, with the suburbs t' for our cattle.
11 with the suburbs t' round about it.
12 fields of the city, and the villages t',
22: 7 unto the other half t' gave Joshua*
23: 14 you, and not one thing hath failed t'.
J'g 1: 18 Judah took Gaza with the coast t',
18 and Askelon with the coast t',
18 and Ekron with the coast t'.
26 a city, and called the name t' Luz:
26 which is the name t' unto this day.
3: 2 least such as before knew nothing t';
5: 23 curse ye bitterly the inhabitants t';
7: 15 the dream, and the interpretation t',
8: 14 princes of Succoth, and the elders t',
27 And Gideon made an ephod t', and
14: 9 he took t' in his hands, and went on*
15: 19 he called the name t' En-hakkore,
17: 4 who made t' a graven image and a
1Sa 5: 6 even Ashdod and the coasts t'.
6: 8 offering, in a coffer by the side t';
7: 14 the coasts t' did Israel deliver out of
17: 51 sword, and drew it out of the sheath t',
20: 20 I will shoot three arrows on the side t',
28: 24 it, and did bake unleavened bread t':
2Sa 20: 8 upon his loins in the sheath t';
1Ki 2: 32 my father David not knowing t', to*
3: 27 in no wise slay it: she is the mother t'.
6: 2 the length t' was threescore cubits,
2 and the breadth t' twenty cubits,
2 and the height t' thirty cubits.
3 twenty cubits was the length t',
3 and ten cubits was the breadth t'
20 and twenty cubits in the height t': and
38 finished throughout all the parts t',
7: 2 the length t' was an hundred cubits,
2 and the breadth t' fifty cubits,
2 and the height t' thirty cubits,
6 pillars; the length t' was fifty cubits,
6 and the breadth t' thirty cubits: and
21 pillar, and called the name t' Jachin:
21 pillar, and called the name t' Boaz.
26 brim t' was wrought like the brim of a
27 base, and four cubits the breadth t',
30 the four corners t' had undersetters:
31 the mouth t' was round after the work
35 on the top of the base the ledges t'
35 and the borders t' were of the same.
36 For on the plates of the ledges t', and
36 and on the borders t', he graved
8: 7 covered the ark and the staves t'
13: 26 him back from the way heard t',
15: 21 when Baasha heard t', that he left off
22 stones of Ramah, and the timber t',
16: 34 he laid the foundation t' in Abiram his
34 and set up the gates t' in his youngest
17: 13 but make me t' a little cake first, 8033
2Ki 2: 12 chariot of Israel, and the horsemen t'.
3: 25 in Kir-haraseth left they the stones t';
4: 39 gathered t' wild gourds his lap full,
40 in the pot. And they could not eat t'.
42 and full ears of corn in the husk t'.*
43 They shall eat, and shall leave t'.
44 them, and they did eat, and left t',
7: 2, 19 thine eyes, but shalt not eat t'.
13: 14 chariot of Israel, and the horsemen t'.
15: 16 therein, and the coasts t' from Tirzah:
16: 10 according to all the workmanship t'.

2Ki 17: 24 Samaria, and dwelt in the cities t'.
18: 8 unto Gaza, and the borders t', from
19: 23 will cut down the tall cedar trees t',
23 and the choice fir trees t': and I will
29 plant vineyards, and eat the fruits t'.
22: 16 place, and upon the inhabitants t',
19 place, and against the inhabitants t',
23: 6 and cast the powder t' upon the graves
1Ch 2: 23 the towns t', even threescore cities.
6: 55 and the suburbs t' round about it.
56 and the villages t', they gave to Caleb
7: 28 Beth-el and the towns t', and eastward
28 westward Gezer, with the towns t';
28 Shechem also and the towns t',
28 unto Gaza and the towns t':
8: 12 built Ono, and Lod, with the towns t':
9: 27 opening t' every morning pertained to
16: 32 Let the sea roar, and the fulness t':
21: 27 up his sword again into the sheath t'.
23: 26 nor any vessels of it for the service t'.
28: 11 the houses t', and of the treasuries t',
11 and of the upper chambers t',
11 and of the inner parlours t', and of the
15 candlestick, and for the lamps t':
15 candlestick, and also for the lamps t',
2Ch 3: 7 the beams, the posts, and the walls t',
7 and the doors t', with gold;
8 and the breadth t' twenty cubits:
4: 1 of brass, twenty cubits the length t',
1 and twenty cubits the breadth t',
1 and ten cubits the height t'.
2 compass, and five cubits the height t':
22 inner doors t' for the most holy place,
5: 8 covered the ark and the staves t'
13: 11 candlestick of gold with the lamps t',
19 from him, Beth-el with the towns t',
19 and Jeshanah with the towns t',
19 and Ephrain with the towns t'.
16: 6 stones of Ramah, and the timber t',
28: 18 and Shocho with the villages t',
18 and Timnah with the villages t',
18 Gimzo also and the villages t': they
29: 18 burnt offering, with all the vessels t',
18 table, with all the vessels t'.
32: 1 things, and the establishment t', *
34: 24 place, and upon the inhabitants t',
27 place, and against the inhabitants t',
36: 19 and burnt all the palaces t' with fire,
19 and destroyed all the goodly vessels t'.
Ezr 4: 12 and have set up the walls t', and *
16 builded again, and the walls t' set up,*
6: 3 let the foundations t' be strongly laid;
3 the height t' threescore cubits,
3 and the breadth t' threescore cubits;
9: 9 to repair the desolations t', and to
10: 14 elders of every city, and the judges t',
Ne 1: 3 and the gates t' are burned with fire.
2: 3 the gates t' are consumed with fire?
13 the gates t' were consumed with fire.
17 and the gates t' are burned with fire:
3: 3 the beams t', and set up the doors t',
3 the locks t', and the bars t'.
6 the beams t', and set up the doors t',
6 and the locks t', and the bars t'.
13 they built it, and set up the doors t',
13 the locks t', and the bars t', and a
14 he built it, and set up the doors t',
14 the locks t', and the bars t'.
15 and covered it, and set up the doors t',
15 the locks t', and the bars t', and the
4: 6 was joined together unto the half t':
6: 16 that when all our enemies heard t',
9: 36 to eat the fruit t' and the good t',
11: 25 at Kirjath-arba, and in the villages t',
25 and at Dibon, and in the villages t',
25 at Jekabzeel, and in the villages t',
27 at Beer-sheba, and in the villages t',
28 and at Mekonah, and in the villages t',
30 at Lachish, and the fields t',
30 at Azekah, and in the villages t',
13: 14 house of my God, and for the offices t'.
Es 1: 22 province according to the writing t',
2: 22 Esther certified the king t' in
3: 12 province according to the writing t',
8: 9 on the three and twentieth day t';
9 province according to the writing t',
9: 18 together on the thirteenth day t',
18 and on the fourteenth t'; and on
Job 3: 9 the stars of the twilight t' be dark;
4: 12 to me, and mine ear received a little t'.
16 but I could not discern the form t':
9: 6 her place, and the pillars t' trembled.
24 he covereth the faces of the judges t';
11: 9 The measure t' is longer than the
14: 7 the tender branch t' will not cease.
8 the root t' wax old in the earth,
8 and the stock t' die in the ground;
15: 29 he prolong the perfection t' upon‡
24: 2 take away the flocks, and feed t'. *
13 the light; they know not the ways t',
13 nor abide in the paths t'.
26: 5 the waters, and the inhabitants t'.
28: 13 Man knoweth not the price t'; neither
15 shall silver be weighed for the price t'.
22 heard the fame t' with our ears.
23 God understandeth the way t',
23 and he knoweth the place t'.
31: 17 and the fatherless hath not eaten t';
38 that the furrows likewise t' complain;
39 If I have eaten the fruits t' without
39 the owners t' to lose their life:
36: 27 down rain according to the vapour t':*
33 The noise t' sheweth concerning it,
38: 5 Who hath laid the measures t', if
6 are the foundations t' fastened?
6 or who laid the corner stone t';

Job 38: 9 I made the cloud the garment t',
19 as for darkness, where is the place t',
20 thou shouldest take it to the bound t',
20 know the paths to the house t'?
33 thou set the dominion t' in the earth?
Ps 19: 6 there is nothing hid from the heat t'.
24: 1 earth is the Lord's, and the fulness t';
34: 2 the humble shall hear t', and be glad.
46: 3 Though the waters t' roar and be
3 mountains shake with the swelling t'.
48: 12 go round about her: tell the towers t'.
50: 1 of the sun unto the going down t'.
12 the world is mine, and the fulness t'.
55: 10 they go about it upon the walls t':
11 Wickedness is in the midst t': deceit
60: 2 heal the breaches t'; for it shaketh.
65: 10 waterest the ridges t' abundantly:
10 thou settlest the furrows t': thou
10 thou blessest the springing t'.
71: 15 days; for I know not the numbers t'.
72: 16 the fruit t' shall shake like Lebanon:
74: 6 they break down the carved work t' at
75: 3 all the inhabitants t' are dissolved:
8 but the dregs t', all the wicked of the
80: 10 the boughs t' were like the goodly
89: 9 when the waves t' arise, thou stillest
11 for the world and the fulness t', thou
96: 11 let the sea roar, and the fulness t'.
97: 1 let the multitude of isles be glad t'.*
98: 7 Let the sea roar, and the fulness t';
102: 14 in her stones, and favour the dust t'.*
103: 16 and the place t' shall know it no more.
107: 25 wind, which lifteth up the waves t'.
29 a calm, so that the waves t' are still.
137: 2 harps upon the willows in the midst t'.
7 it, rase it, even to the foundation t'.
Pr 1: 19 taketh away the life of the owners t'.
3: 14 silver, and the gain t' than fine gold.
12: 28 in the pathway t' there is no death.
14: 12 but the end t' are the ways of death.
16: 25 but the end t' are the ways of death.
33 the whole disposing t' is of the Lord.
18: 21 they that love it shall eat the fruit t'.
20: 21 but the end t' shall not be blessed.
21: 22 down the strength of the confidence t'.
24: 31 and nettles had covered the face t',
31 the stone wall t' was broken down.
25: 8 know not what to do in the end t',
27: 18 the fig tree shall eat the fruit t':
28: 2 of a land many are the princes t':
2 knowledge the state t' shall be
Ec 5: 11 what good is there to the owners t',
13 riches kept for the owners t' to their
19 and hath given him power to eat t',
6: 2 God giveth him not power to eat t',
7: 8 end of a thing than the beginning t':
Ca 1: 12 spikenard sendeth forth the smell t'.*
3: 10 He made the pillars t' of silver,
10 the bottom t' of gold, the covering of
10 midst t' being paved with love, for the
4: 16 that the spices t' may flow out.
7: 8 tree, I will take hold of the boughs t':
8: 6 the coals t' are coals of fire, which
11 every one for the fruit t' was to bring
12 and those that keep the fruit t' two
Isa 3: 14 of his people, and the princes t':
4: 4 blood of Jerusalem from the midst t'
5: 2 it, and gathered out the stones t',
5 I will take away the hedge t', and
5 and break down the wall t', and it
30 light is darkened in the heavens t'.
6: 13 holy seed shall be the substance t'.
13: 9 shall destroy the sinners t' out of it.
10 of heaven and the constellations t'
14: 17 wilderness, and destroyed the cities t';
15: 8 of Moab; the howling t' unto Eglaim,
8 and the howling t' unto Beer-elim.
16: 8 broken down the principal plants t',
17: 6 in the outmost fruitful branches t',*
19: 3 of Egypt shall fail in the midst t';*
3 and I will destroy the counsel t': and
10 shall be broken in the purposes t',*
13 they that are the stay of the tribes t'.*
14 a perverse spirit in the midst t': *
14 caused Egypt to err in every work t',
17 one that maketh mention t' shall
19 a pillar at the border t' to the Lord.
21: 2 all the sighing t' have I made to cease.
22: 11 have not looked unto the maker t',*
23: 11 city to destroy the strong holds t'.
13 wilderness: they set up the towers t',*
13 they raised up the palaces t'; and he
24: 1 scattereth abroad the inhabitants t'.
5 is defiled under the inhabitants t';
20 transgression t' shall be heavy upon
27: 10 down, and consume the branches t'.
11 When the boughs t' are withered,
28: 25 When he hath made plain the face t',
30: 27 his anger, and the burden t' is heavy:*
33 the pile t' is fire and much wood;
31: 4 for mount Zion, and for the hill t'.
33: 20 not one of the stakes t' shall ever be
20 shall any of the cords t' be broken.
34: 9 streams t' shall be turned into pitch,
9 and the dust t' into brimstone, and
9 land t' shall become burning pitch.
10 the smoke t' shall go up for ever:
12 call the nobles t' to the kingdom,
13 and brambles in the fortresses t':
37: 24 and I will cut down the tall cedars t',
24 and the choice fir trees t': and I will
30 plant vineyards, and eat the fruit t'.
40: 6 and all the godliness t' is as the flower
16 beasts t' sufficient for a burnt offering.
22 inhabitants t' are as grasshoppers;
41: 9 called thee from the chief men t', and

Isa 42: 10 the isles, and the inhabitants t'.
11 wilderness and the cities t' lift up
44: 15 for he will take t', and warm himself;
16 He burneth part t' in the fire; with
16 with part t' he eateth flesh; he
17 And the residue t' he maketh a god,
19 I have baked bread upon the coals t';
19 I make the residue t' an abomination?
26 I will raise up the decayed places t':
48: 19 of thy bowels like the gravel t';
62: 1 the righteousness t' go forth as *
1 and the salvation t' as a lamp that*
Jer 1: 13 and the face t' is toward the north.
15 against all the walls t' round about,
18 the princes t', against the priests t',
2: 7 to eat the fruit t' and the goodness t';
4: 26 and all the cities t' were broken down
5: 1 know, and seek in the broad places t'.
22 though the waves t' toss themselves,
31 and what will ye do in the end t'?
6: 24 We have heard the fame t': our hands
11: 19 us destroy the tree with the fruit t',
14: 2 mourneth, and the gates t' languish;
8 the saviour t' in time of trouble, why
17: 27 then will I kindle a fire in the gates t',
19: 8 and hiss because of all the plagues t'.
12 the Lord, and to the inhabitants t',
20: 5 of this city, and all the labours t',
5 and all the precious things t', and all
21: 14 I will kindle a fire in the forest t', and*
23: 14 and the inhabitants t' as Gomorrah.
25: 9 and against the inhabitants t', and
18 and the kings t', and the princes t', to
26: 15 this city, and upon the inhabitants t':
29: 7 in the peace t' shall ye have peace.
30: 18 shall remain after the manner t'.
31: 23 the land of Judah and in the cities t'.
24 itself, and in all the cities t' together,
35 the sea when the waves t' roar;
33: 2 Thus saith the Lord the maker t',*
12 and in all the cities t', shall be a
34: 1 Jerusalem, against all the cities t',
18 twain, and passed between the parts t',
46: 8 destroy the city and the inhabitants t'.
22 voice t' shall go like a serpent; for
48: 9 the cities t' shall be desolate, without*
38 of Moab, and in the streets t':
49: 13 the cities t' shall be perpetual wastes.
17 and shall hiss at all the plagues t'.
18 Gomorrah and the neighbour cities t',
21 the noise t' was heard in the Red sea.*
32 bring their calamity from all sides t',*
50: 29 it round about; let none t' escape:
40 Gomorrah and the neighbour cities t',
51: 28 the captains t', and all the rulers t',
42 with the multitude of the waves t'.
52: 21 and the thickness t' was four fingers:
La 2: 2 polluted the kingdom and the princes t'.
4: 11 it hath devoured the foundations t'.
Eze 1: 4 and out of the midst t' as the colour of
5 out of the midst t' came the likeness
4: 9 in one vessel, and make thee bread t',
9 and ninety days shalt thou eat t'.
5: 3 shalt also take t' a few in number,
4 for t' shall a fire come forth into all the*
7: 12 for wrath is upon all the multitude t'.
13 is touching the whole multitude t',
14 my wrath is upon all the multitude t'.
9: 4 that be done in the midst t'.
10: 7 and took t', and put it into the hands
11: 6 have filled the streets t' with the slain.
9 I will bring you out of the midst t', and
11 shall ye be the flesh in the midst t';
18 take away all the detestable things t'
18 all the abominations t' from thence.
13: 14 the foundation t' shall be discovered,
14 ye shall be consumed in the midst t':
14: 13 and will break the staff of the bread t',
15: 3 Shall wood be taken t' to do any work?
17: 6 him, and the roots t' were under him:
9 shall he not pull up the roots t',
9 and cut off the fruit t', that it wither?
9 people to pluck it up by the roots t'.
12 taken the king t', and the princes t',
23 in the shadow of the branches t' shall
19: 7 land was desolate, and the fulness t',
20: 29 the name t' is called Bamah unto this
22: 21 and ye shall be melted in the midst t'.
22 so shall ye be melted in the midst t';
25 of her prophets in the midst t',
25 made her many widows in the midst t'.
27 Her princes in the midst t' are like
23: 34 and thou shalt break the sherds t', and
24: 4 Gather the pieces t' into it, even every
11 Then set it empty upon the coals t',
27: 9 wise men t' were in thee thy calkers:
31: 15 and I restrained the floods t', and the
32: 7 heaven, and make the stars t' dark;
12 all the multitude t' shall be destroyed.
13 I will destroy also all the beasts t'
38: 13 Tarshish, with all the young lions t',
40: 6 the east, and went up the stairs t',
9 and the posts t', two cubits; and the
20 the length t', and the breadth t'.
21 little chambers t' were three on this
21 the posts t' and the arches t' were after
21 the length t' was fifty cubits, and the
22 and the arches t' were before them.
24 measured the posts t' and the arches t'
25 in it and in the arches t' round about,
26 it, and the arches t' were before them:
26 on that side, upon the posts t'.
29 the little chambers t', and the posts t',
29 and the arches t', according to these
29 in it and in the arches t' round about:
31 arches t' were toward the utter court;

Eze 40: 31 and palm trees were upon the posts t':
33 the little chambers t', and the posts t',
33 and the arches t', were according to
33 and in the arches t' round about:
34 the arches t' were toward the outward
34 and palm trees were upon the posts t',
36 The little chambers t', the posts t',
36 and the arches t', and the windows
37 posts t' were toward the utter court;
37 and palm trees were upon the posts t',
38 the entries t' were by the posts of the
41: 2 and he measured the length t', forty
4 he measured the length t', twenty
12 about, and the length t' ninety cubits.
13 and the building, with the walls t',
15 and the galleries t' on the one side and
22 high, and the length t' two cubits;
22 and the corners t', and the length t',
22 and the walls t', were of wood:
42: 7 chambers, the length t' was fifty cubits.
43: 11 form of the house, and the fashion t',
11 and the goings out t',
11 and the comings in t',
11 and all the forms t',
11 and all the ordinances t',
11 and all the forms t',
11 and all the laws t': and write it in
11 that they may keep the whole form t',
11 and all the ordinances t', and do them.
12 the whole limit t' round about shall
13 the breadth a cubit, and the border t'
13 by the edge t' round about shall be a
16 broad, square in the four squares t'.
17 fourteen broad in the four squares t':
17 the bottom t' shall be a cubit about;
20 And thou shalt take of the blood t', and
44: 5 house of the Lord, and all the laws t';
14 of the house, for all the service t',
45: 1 This shall be holy in all the borders t'
2 cubits round about for the suburbs t'.
11 measure t' shall be after the homer.
46: 8 and he shall go forth by the way t'.
16 the inheritance t' shall be his sons';*
47: 11 But the miry places t', and
11 the marishes t' shall not be healed;
12 And by the river upon the bank t',
12 neither shall the fruit t' be consumed:
12 and the fruit t' shall be for meat,
12 and the leaf t' for medicine.
48: 10 sanctuary...shall be in the midst t'.
15 and the city shall be in the midst t'.
16 And these shall be the measures t';
18 and the increase t' shall be for food
21 sanctuary...shall be in the midst t'.
Da 1: 5 at the end t' they might stand before
2: 5 the dream, with the interpretation t',
6 the dream, and the interpretation t',
6 the dream, and the interpretation t'.
9 ye can shew me the interpretation t'.
26 I have seen, and the interpretation t'?
31 thee; and the form t' was terrible.
36 and we will tell the interpretation t'
45 certain, and the interpretation t' sure.
3: 1 cubits, and the breadth t' six cubits:
4: 7 known unto me the interpretation t'.
9 I have seen, and the interpretation t'.
10 the earth, and the height t' was great.
11 and the height t' reached unto heaven,
11 the sight t' to the end of all the earth:
12 The leaves t' were fair, and the
12 and the fruit t' much, and in it was
12 of the heaven dwelt in the boughs t',
18 declare the interpretation t', *
19 or the interpretation t', trouble thee.*
19 the interpretation t' to thine enemies.
20 and the sight t' to all the earth;
21 and the fruit t' much, and in it was
23 yet leave the stump of the roots t' in
5: 7 and shew me the interpretation t',
8 known to the king the interpretation t'.*
15 known unto me the interpretation t':
16 known to me the interpretation t',
7: 4 I beheld till the wings t' were plucked,
9: 26 and the end t' shall be with a flood, †
Ho 2: 9 and take away my corn in the time t',
9 and my wine in the season t',
4: 13 elms, because the shadow t' is good:
8: 14 and it shall devour the palaces t'.
9: 4 all that eat t' shall be polluted:
10: 5 for the people t' shall mourn over it,
5 and the priests t' that rejoiced on it,
5 for the glory t', because it is departed
14: 7 the scent t' shall be as the wine of
Joe 1: 7 away; the branches t' are made white.
Am 1: 3, 6 not turn away the punishment t';
7 which shall devour the palaces t':
9 will not turn away the punishment t';
10 which shall devour the palaces t'.
11, 13 not turn away the punishment t';
14 and it shall devour the palaces t', with
2: 1 will not turn away the punishment t';
3 will cut off the judge from the midst t',
3 will slay all the princes t' with him,
4, 6 not turn away the punishment t';
3: 9 the great tumults in the midst t', *
9 and the oppressed in the midst t'.
8: 10 son, and the end t' as a bitter day.
9: 11 is fallen, and close up the breaches t';
14 plant vineyards, and drink the wine t';
Jon 1: 3 so he paid the fare t', and went down
Mic 1: 6 pour down the stones t' into the valley,
6 and I will discover the foundations t'.
7 the graven images t' shall be beaten*
7 and all the hires t' shall be burned*
7 and all the idols t' will I lay desolate:*
3: 11 The heads t' judge for reward,

Mic 3:11 and the priests t' teach for hire,
11 and the prophets t' divine for money:
5: 6 the land of Nimrod in the entrances t':
6:12 For the rich men t' are full of violence,
12 the inhabitants t' have spoken lies,
16 and the inhabitants t' an hissing:
Na 1: 8 will make an utter end of the place t',
2: 5 they shall make haste to the wall t',
Hab 2:18 that the maker t' hath graven it;
Zep 1:13 vineyards, but not drink the wine t'.
3: 5 The just Lord is in the midst t'; he*
Zec 2: 2 to see what is the breadth t',
2 and what is the length t'.
3: 9 I will engrave the graving t', saith
4: 2 lamps, which are upon the top t':
3 and the other upon the left side t'.
7 forth the headstone t' with shoutings,*
11 candlestick and upon the left side t'?
5: 2 roll; the length t' is twenty cubits,
2 and the breadth t' ten cubits.
4 it with the timber t' and the stones t'.
8 weight of lead upon the mouth t'.
7: 7 and the cities t' round about her, when
8: 5 boys and girls playing in the streets t'.
9: 1 and Damascus shall be the rest t':*
14: 4 of Olives shall cleave in the midst t'
Mal 1:12 and the fruit t', even his meat, is
M't 2:16 in Bethlehem, and in all the coasts t',846
6:34 Sufficient unto the day is the evil t'. "
12:36 they shall give account t' in 4012, "
13:32 come and lodge in the branches t'. "
44 for joy t' goeth and selleth all that he*"
14:13 and when the people had heard t', they
21:43 a nation bringing forth the fruits t'.846
22: 7 But when the king heard t', he was*
27:34 and when he had tasted t', he would*
M'r 6:16 But when Herod heard t', he said, It is
Lu 19:33 owners t' said unto them, Why loose
21:20 know that the desolation t' is nigh.*846
22:16 I will not any more eat t', until*1538, "
Joh 3: 8 thou hearest the sound t', but canst "
4:12 the well, and drank t' himself, 1538, "
6:50 a man may eat t', and not die. "
7: 7 of it, that the works t' are evil.*3012, "
Ac 15:16 I will build again the ruins t', and I "
Ro 6:12 that ye should obey it in the lusts t'. "
13:14 for the flesh, to fulfil the lusts t'.
1Co 9: 7 and eateth not of the fruit t'? 846
23 that I might be partaker t' with you."
10:26 earth is the Lord's, and the fulness t'."
28 earth is the Lord's, and the fulness t':*"
2Ti 3: 5 godliness, but denying the power t': "
Heb 7:18 weakness and unprofitableness t'.* "
Jas 1:11 the grass, and the flower t' falleth, "
1Pe 1:24 and the flower t' falleth away: "
5: 2 is among you, taking the oversight t'.*
1Jo 2:17 world passeth away, and the lust t':846
Re 5: 2 the book, and to loose the seals t'? "
5 book, and to loose the seven seals t'. "
9 the book, and to open the seals t': "
16:12 water t' was dried up, that the way "
21 for the plague t' was exceeding great."
21:15 city, and the gates t', and the wall t'. "
17 he measured the wall t', an hundred "
23 lighten it, and the Lamb is the light t'."

thereon See also THEREUPON.
Ge 35:14 and he poured a drink offering t', 5921
14 and he poured oil t'. "
Ex 17:12 and put it under him, and he sat t'; "
20:24 shalt sacrifice t' thy burnt offerings,"
26 thy nakedness be not discovered t'. "
30: 7 Aaron shall burn t' sweet incense "
9 Ye shall offer no strange incense t'," "
9 shall ye pour drink offering t'. "
40:27 And he burnt sweet incense t'; as "
35 because the cloud abode t', and the "
Le 2: 1 oil upon it, and put frankincense t': "
6 part it in pieces, and pour oil t': "
15 put oil upon it, lay frankincense t': "
5:11 shall he put any frankincense t': "
6:12 he shall burn t' the fat of the peace "
10: 1 put fire therein, and put incense t', "
11:38 and any part of their carcase fall t', "
Nu 4: 6 put t' the covering of badgers' skins, "
7 put t' the dishes, and the spoons, "
7 and the continual bread shall be t': "
13 altar, and spread a purple cloth t': "
5:15 oil upon it, nor put frankincense t'; "
9:22 upon the tabernacle, remaining t', "
16:18 put fire in them, and laid incense t', "
De 27: 6 thou shalt offer burnt offerings t' "
Jos 8:29 and raise t' a great heap of stones, "
31 they offered t' burnt offerings unto "
22:23 or if to offer t' burnt offering or "
23 or if to offer peace offerings t', let "
2Sa 17:19 mouth, and spread ground corn t'; "
19:26 saddle me an ass, that I may ride t'," "
1Ki 6:35 carved t' cherubims and palm trees "
13:13 him the ass: and he rode t'. 5921
2Ki 16:12 to the altar, and offered t'. "
1Ch 12:17 the God of our fathers look t', and "
15:15 their shoulders with the staves t'. 5921
2Ch 3: 5 and set t' palm trees and chains. "
14 linen, and wrought cherubims t'. "
33:16 and sacrificed t' peace offerings and"
Ezr 3: 2 to offer burnt offerings t', as it is "
3 they offered burnt offerings t' unto "
6:11 being set up, let him be hanged t'; "
Es 5:14 that Mordecai may be hanged t': "
7: 9 Then the king said, Hang him t'. "
Isa 30:12 and perverseness, and stay t': "
35: 9 nor any ravenous beast shall go up t'.
Eze 15: 3 a pin of it to hang any vessel t'? 5921
40:39 to slay t' the burnt offering and the "
43:18 make it, to offer burnt offerings t', "
18 and to sprinkle blood t'. "

Zec 4: 2 and his seven lamps t', and seven 5921
M't 21: 7 clothes, and they set him t'. 1883,846
19 found nothing t', but leaves 1722, "
23:20 by it, and by all things t'. 1883, "
22 God, and by him that sitteth t'. "
M'r 11:13 he might find any thing t': 1722, "
14:72 And when he thought t', he wept. 1911
Lu 13: 6 he came and sought fruit t', 1722,846
19:35 upon the colt, and they set Jesus t'.1913
Joh 12:14 had found a young ass, sat t'; 1909,846
21: 9 coals there, and fish laid t', and 1945
1Co 3:10 foundation, and another buildeth t'.2026
Re 5: 3 to open the book, neither to look t'. 846
4 to read the book, neither to look t'. "
6: 4 was given to him that sat t' 1909, "
21:12 and names written t', which are the1924

thereout
Le 2: 2 he shall take t' his handful of the 8033
J'g 15:19 in the jaw, and there came water t';

thereto
Ex 25:24 make t' a crown of gold round about.
29:41 shalt do t' according to the meat
30:38 shall make like unto that, to smell t',
Le 5:16 and shall add the fifth part t'. 5921
6: 5 and shall add the fifth part more t', "
18:23 stand before a beast to lie down t':
20:16 unto any beast, and lie down t',
27:27 and shall add a fifth part of it t': 5921
31 shall add t' the fifth part thereof.
Nu 3:36 vessels thereof, and all that serveth t',*
19:17 running water shall be put t' in a 5921
De 12:32 thou shalt not add t', nor diminish "
J'g 11:17 king of Edom would not hearken t'.*
1Ch 22:14 prepared; and thou mayest add t'.5921
2Ch 10:14 your yoke heavy, but I will add t': "
21:11 fornication, and compelled Judah t'.*
Ps 119: 9 taking heed t' according to thy word.
Isa 44:15 a graven image, and falleth down t'.
M'r 14:70 a Galilæan, and thy speech agreeth t'.
Ga 3:15 no man disannulleth, or addeth t'. 1928

thereunto
Ex 32: 8 worshipped it, and have sacrificed t',*
36:36 he made t' four pillars of shittim
37:11 made t' a crown of gold round about.*
12 he made t' a border of an handbreadth*
De 1: 7 and unto all the places nigh t', in the
Eph 6:18 and watching t' with all 1519,846,5124
1Th 3: 3 that we are appointed t'. *1519, "
Heb 10: 1 make the comers t' perfect. *4334
1Pe 3: 9 knowing that ye are t' called,*1519,5124

thereupon
Ex 31: 7 and the mercy seat that is t',
Eze 16:16 colours, and playedst the harlot t':*
Zep 2: 7 the house of Judah; they shall feed t':
1Co 3:10 man take heed how he buildeth t'.*2026
14 work abide which he hath built t',* "

therewith
Ex 22: 6 corn, or the field, be consumed t';*
30:26 the tabernacle of the congregation t',
38:30 t' he made the sockets to the door
Lev 7: 7 that maketh atonement t' shall have it.
8: 7 of the ephod, and bound it unto him t'.
15:32 goeth from him, and is defiled t';*
18:23 lie with any beast to defile thyself t':
22: 8 he shall not eat to defile himself t':
De 16: 3 shalt thou eat unleavened bread t',5921
23:13 thou shalt dig t', and shalt turn back
J'g 15:15 took it, and slew a thousand men t'.
16:12 took new ropes, and bound him t',
1Sa 12: 3 any bribe to blind mine eyes t'? and
17:51 and slew him, and cut off his head t'.
31: 4 thy sword, and thrust me through t';
2Sa 20:10 so he smote him t' in the fifth rib, and
2Ki 5: 6 I have t' sent Naaman my servant to*
12:14 and repaired t' the house of the Lord.
1Ch 10: 4 thy sword, and thrust me through t';
23: 5 which I made, said David, to praise t'.
2Ch 16: 6 and he built t' Geba and Mizpah.
Pr 15:16 than great treasure and trouble t'.
17 love is, than a stalled ox and hatred t'.
17: 1 is a dry morsel, and quietness t',
25:16 thee, lest thou be filled t', and vomit it.
Ec 1:13 to the sons of man to be exercised t'.
2: 6 pools of water, to water t' the wood*
10: 9 removeth stones shall be hurt t';
Isa 10:15 itself against him that heweth t'?
Eze 4:15 thou shalt prepare thy bread t'. *5921
Joe 2:19 and oil, and ye shall be satisfied t': 854
Ph'p 4:11 whatsoever state I am, t' to be content.*
1Ti 6: 8 and raiment let us be t' content. 5125
Jas 3: 9 T' bless we God, even the 1722,846
9 t' curse we men, which are
3Jo 10 not content t', neither doth 1909,5125

these
Ge 2: 4 T' are the generations of the 428
6: 9 T' are the generations of Noah: "
9:19 T' are three sons of Noah: and of "
10: 1 t' are the generations of the sons "
5 By t' were the isles of the Gentiles "
20 T' are the sons of Ham, after their "
29 all t' were the sons of Joktan. "
31 T' are the sons of Shem, after their "
32 T' are the families of the sons of "
32 by t' were the nations divided in "
11:10 T' are the generations of Shem: "
27 t' are the generations of Terah: "
14: 2 That t' made war with Bera king *
3 All t' were joined together in the 428
13 t' were confederate with Abram. 1992
15: 1 After t' things the word of the 428
10 he took unto him all t', and divided "
19: 8 only unto t' men do nothing; for "
20: 8 and told all t' things in their ears. "
25: 4 All t' were the children of Keturah. "

Ge 25: 7 And t' are the days of the years of 428
12 Now t' are the generations of "
13 And t' are the names of the sons of "
16 T' are the sons of Ishmael, and "
16 t' are their names, by their towns, "
17 And t' are the years of the life of "
19 And t' are the generations of Isaac, "
26: 3 thy seed, I will give all t' countries, 411
4 give unto thy seed all t' countries; "
27:36 hath supplanted me t' two times: 2088
42 t' words of Esau her elder son *
46 as t' which are of the daughters 428
29:13 And he told Laban all t' things. "
31:43 T' daughters are my daughters, *
43 and t' children are my children, *
43 and t' cattle are my cattle, and all that*
32:17 thou? and whose are t' before thee?428
33: 8 T' are to find grace in the sight of my*
34:21 T' men are peaceable with us; 428
35:26 t' are the sons of Jacob, which were "
36: 1 Now t' are the generations of Esau, "
5 t' are the sons of Esau, which were "
9 And t' are the generations of Esau "
10 T' are the names of Esau's sons; "
12 t' were the sons of Adah Esau's "
13 t' are the sons of Reuel; Nahath, "
13 t' were the sons of Bashemath "
14 t' were the sons of Aholibamah, the "
15 T' were the dukes of the sons of "
16 t' are the dukes that came of "
16 of Edom; t' were the sons of Adah. "
17 t' are the sons of Reuel Esau's son; "
17 t' are the dukes that came of Reuel "
17 t' are the sons of Bashemath Esau's "
18 t' are the sons of Aholibamah "
18 t' were the dukes that came of "
19 T' are the sons of Esau, who is "
19 Edom, and t' are their dukes. "
20 T' are the sons of Seir the Horite, "
21 t' are the dukes of the Horites, the "
23 And the children of Shobal were t'; "
24 t' are the children of Zibeon; both "
25 And the children of Anah were t'; "
26 And t' are the children of Dishon; "
27 The children of Ezer are t'; Bilhan, "
28 The children of Dishan are t'; Uz, "
29 T' are the dukes that came of the "
30 T' are the dukes that came of Hori, "
31 t' are the kings that reigned in the "
40 t' are the names of the dukes that "
43 t' be the dukes of Edom, according "
37: 2 T' are the generations of Jacob. "
38:25 man, whose t' are, am I with child: "
25 whose are t', the signet, and "
39: 7 it came to pass after t' things, that "
17 unto him according to t' words, "
40: 1 And it came to pass after t' things, "
42:36 away: all t' things are against me. "
43: 7 according to the tenor of t' words: 428
16 Bring t' men home, and slay, and *
16 for t' men shall dine with me at noon.*
44: 6 he spake unto them t' same words. 411
7 Wherefore saith my lord t' words? 428
45: 6 t' two years hath the famine been 2088
46: 8 t' are the names of the children of 428
15 T' be the sons of Leah, which she "
18 T' are the sons of Zilpah, whom "
18 t' she bare unto Jacob, even "
22 T' are the sons of Rachel, which "
25 T' are the sons of Bilhah, which "
25 and she bare t' unto Jacob: all the "
48: 1 And it came to pass after t' things, "
8 Joseph's sons, and said, Who are t'? "
49:28 All t' are the twelve tribes of Israel: "
Ex 1: 1 t' are the names of the children of "
4: 9 will not believe also t' two signs, "
6:14 T' be the heads of their father's "
14 Carmi: t' be the families of Reuben."
15 t' are the families of Simeon. "
16 t' are the names of the sons of Levi "
19 t' are the families of Levi according"
24 t' are the families of the Korhites. "
25 t' are the heads...of the Levites "
26 T' are that Aaron and Moses, to 1931
27 T' are they which spake to 1992
10: 1 might shew t' my signs before him:428
11: 8 all t' thy servants shall come down "
10 Moses and Aaron did all t' wonders "
14:20 them, but it gave light by night to t':*
15:26 will put none of t' diseases upon thee,*
19: 7 laid before their faces all t' words 428
20: 1 And God spake all t' words, saying, "
21: 1 Now t' are the judgments which "
11 if he do not t' three unto her, then "
24: 8 with you concerning all t' words. "
25:39 shall he make it, with all t' vessels. "
28: 4 t' are the garments which they shall "
30:34 t' sweet spices with...frankincense:*
32: 4, 8 T' be thy gods, O Israel, which 428
33: 4 the people heard t' evil tidings, they
34: 1 I will write upon t' tables the words*
27 unto Moses, Write thou t' words: 428
27 for after the tenor of t' words I have"
35: 1 T' are the words which the Lord "
Le 2: 8 is made of t' things unto the Lord: "
5: 4 then he shall be guilty in one of t'. "
5 shall be guilty in one of t' things, "
13 sin that he hath sinned in one of t', "
17 commit any of t' things which are*
6: 3 any of all t' that a man doeth, sinning
11: 2 T' are the beasts which ye shall 2063
4 t' shall ye not eat of them that 2088
9 T' shall ye eat of all that are in "
13 t' are they which ye shall have in 428
21 Yet t' may ye eat of every 2088
22 Even t' of them ye may eat; the 428

Le 11:24 And for t' ye shall be unclean: 428
29 T' also shall be unclean unto you 2088
31 T' are unclean to you among all "
16: 4 t' are holy garments; therefore *1992
18:24 ye yourselves in any of t' things: 428
24 for in all t' the nations are defiled "
26 not commit any of t' abominations; "
27 all t' abominations have the men 411
29 commit any of t' abominations, 428
30 any one of t' abominable customs,
20:23 for they committed all t' things, 428
21:14 or an harlot, t' shall he not take: "
22:22 ye shall not offer t' unto the Lord, "
25 the bread of your God of any of t'; "
23: 2 convocations, even t' are my feasts. "
4, 37 T' are the feasts of the Lord, "
25:54 he be not redeemed in t' years, then "
26:14 will not do all t' commandments; "
23 not be reformed by me by t' things, "
46 T' are the statutes and judgments "
27:34 T' are the commandments, which "
Nu 1: 5 t' are the names of the men that "
16 T' were the renowned of the "
17 And Moses and Aaron took t' men "
44 T' are those that were numbered, "
2: 9 their armies. T' shall first set forth.*
32 T' are those which were numbered 428
3: 1 T' also are the generations of "
2 t' are the names of the sons of "
3 T' are the names of the sons of "
17 t' were the sons of Levi by their "
18 t' are the names of the sons of "
20 T' are the families of the Levites "
21 t' are the families of...Gershonites. "
27 t' are the families of...Kohathites. "
33 t' are the families of Merari. "
35 t' shall pitch on the side of the *
4:15 T' things are the burden of the 428
37 T' were they that were numbered "
41 T' are they that were numbered of "
45 T' be those that were numbered of "
5:23 priest shall write t' curses in a book, "
13: 4 t' were their names: of the tribe of "
16 T' are the names of the men which "
14:22 tempted me now t' ten times, and 2088
39 Moses told t' sayings unto all the 428
15:13 shall do t' things after this manner, "
22 not observed all t' commandments, "
16:14 thou put out the eyes of t' men? 1992
26 from the tents of t' wicked men, 428
28 hath sent me to do all t' works; "
29 If t' men die the common death of "
30 that t' men have provoked the Lord.
31 an end of speaking all t' words, 428
38 censers of t' sinners against their "
21:25 And Israel took all t' cities: and "
22: 9 said, What men are t' with thee? "
28 hast smitten me t' three times? 2088
32 smitten thine ass t' three times? "
33 and turned from me t' three times: "
24:10 blessed them t' three times. "
26: 7, 14, 18 T' are the families of the 428
22 T' are the families of Judah "
25 T' are the families of Issachar "
27 T' are the families of the "
30 T' are the sons of Gilead: of Jeezer, "
34 T' are the families of Manasseh, "
35 T' are the sons of Ephraim after "
36 And t' are the sons of Shuthelah: "
37 T' are the families of the sons of "
37 T' are the sons of Joseph after their "
41 T' are the sons of Benjamin after "
42 T' are the sons of Dan after their "
42 T' are the families of Dan after "
47 T' are the families of the sons of "
50 T' are the families of Naphtali "
51 T' were the numbered of the "
53 Unto t' the land shall be divided for "
57 t' are they that were numbered of "
58 T' are the families of the Levites: "
63 T' are they that were numbered by "
64 But among t' there was not a man "
27: 1 t' are the names of his daughters: "
28:23 offer t' beside the burnt offering "
29:39 T' things ye shall do unto the Lord "
30:16 T' are the statutes, which the Lord "
31:16 t' caused the children of Israel, 2007
33: 1 T' are the journeys of the children 428
2 t' are their journeys according to "
34:17 T' are the names of the men which "
19 And the names of the men are t': Of "
29 T' are they whom the Lord "
35:13 t' cities which ye shall give six cities*
15 T' six cities shall be a refuge, both 428
24 blood according to t' judgments: "
29 So t' things shall be for a statute of "
36:13 T' are the commandments and the "
De 1: 1 T' be the words which Moses spake "
35 shall not one of t' men of this evil "
2: 7 t' forty years the Lord thy God 2088
3: 5 t' cities were fenced with high 428
21 God hath done unto t' two kings: "
4: 6 which shall hear all t' statutes, and "
30 all t' things are come upon thee, "
42 fleeing unto one of t' cities he might 411
45 T' are the testimonies, and the 428
5:22 T' words the Lord spake unto all "
6: 1 Now t' are the commandments, *2063
24 commanded us to do all t' statutes, 428
25 to do all t' commandments before *2063
7:12 if ye hearken to t' judgments, and 428
17 heart, T' nations are more than I; "
8: 2 thy God led thee t' forty years in 2088
4 did thy foot swell, t' forty years. "
9: 4, 5 for the wickedness of t' nations 428
10:21 for thee t' great and terrible things, "
De 11:18 ye lay up t' my words in your heart 428
22 keep all t' commandments which *2063
23 the Lord drive out all t' nations 428
12: 1 T' are the statutes and judgments, "
28 hear all t' words which I command "
30 How did t' nations serve their gods? "
14: 4 T' are the beasts which ye shall 2063
7 t' ye shall not eat of them that 2088
9 T' ye shall eat of all that are in "
12 t' are they of which ye shall not eat: "
15: 5 to do all t' commandments which *2063
16:12 shalt observe and do t' statutes. 428
17:19 the words of this law and t' statutes, "
18:12 that do t' things are an abomination "
12 because of t' abominations the "
14 For t' nations, which thou shalt "
19: 9 keep all t' commandments to do *2063
9 cities more for thee, beside t' three: "
11 die, and fleeth into one of t' cities: 411
20:15 not of the cities of t' nations. 428,2007
16 But of the cities of t' people, which 428
22:17 t' are the tokens of my daughter's "
23:18 even both t' are abomination unto the "
25: 3 beat him above t' with many stripes, "
26:16 commanded thee to do t' statutes 428
27: 4 that ye shall set up t' stones, which I "
12 T' shall stand upon mount Gerizim "
13 t' shall stand upon mount Ebal to "
28: 2 all t' blessings shall come on thee, "
15, 45 all t' curses shall come upon thee, "
65 among t' nations shalt thou find no 1992
29: 1 T' are the words of the covenant, 428
18 and serve the gods of t' nations; *1992
30: 1 all t' things are come upon thee, 428
7 all t' curses upon thine enemies, "
31: 1 and spake t' words unto all Israel. "
3 destroy t' nations from before thee, "
17 Are not t' evils come upon us, "
28 I may speak t' words in their ears, "
32:45 an end of speaking all t' words "
Jos 2:11 And as soon as we heard t' things, our*
4: 6 saying, What mean ye by t' stones? 428
7 t' stones shall be for a memorial "
21 come, saying, What mean t' stones? "
9:13 t' bottles of wine, which we filled, "
13 t' our garments and our shoes are "
10:16 But t' five kings fled, and hid "
24 your feet upon the necks of t' kings. "
42 t' kings and their land did Joshua "
11: 5 when all t' kings were met together, "
14 And all the spoil of t' cities, and the "
12: 1 Now t' are the kings of the land, "
7 t' are the kings of the country which "
13:12 t' did Moses smite, and cast them out.
32 T' are the countries which Moses 428
14: 1 And t' are the countries which the "
10 as he said, t' forty and five years. 2088
17: 2 t' were the male children of 428
3 t' are the names of his daughters, "
9 t' cities of Ephraim are among the "
19: 8 the villages...round about t' cities "
16, 31, 48 t' cities with their villages. "
51 T' are the inheritances, which "
20: 9 T' were the cities appointed for all "
21: 3 the Lord, t' cities and their suburbs. "
8 unto the Levites t' cities with their "
9 t' cities which are here mentioned "
42 T' cities were every one with their "
42 about them: thus were all t' cities. "
22: 3 not left your brethren t' many days "
23: 3 done unto all t' nations because of "
4 you by lot t' nations that remain, "
7 That ye come not among t' nations, "
7 t' that remain among you; neither "
12 unto the remnant of t' nations, "
12 even t' that remain among you, and "
13 no more drive out any of t' nations "
24:26 Joshua wrote t' words in the book "
29 And it came to pass after t' things, "
J'g 2: 4 the angel of the Lord spake t' words "
3: 1 Now t' are the nations which the "
9: 3 all the men of Shechem all t' words: "
13:23 he have shewed us all t' things, "
23 have told us such things as t'. 2063
16:15 hast mocked me t' three times, 2088
18:14 that there is in t' houses an ephod, 428
18 And t' went into Micah's house, and "
19:13 draw near to one of t' places to lodge "
20:17 sword: all t' were men of war. 2088
25 men; all t' drew the sword. 428
35 hundred men: all t' drew the sword. "
44 men; all t' were men of valour. "
46 sword: all t' were men of valour. "
Ru 3:17 T' six measures of barley gave he "
4:18 t' are the generations of Pharez: "
1Sa 4: 8 out of the hand of t' mighty Gods? "
8 t' are the Gods that smote the "
6:17 t' are the golden emerods which "
10: 7 when t' signs are come unto thee, "
14: 6 the garrison of t' uncircumcised: "
8 Behold, we will pass over unto t' men,*
49 names of his two daughters were t': "
16:10 Jesse, The Lord hath not chosen t'. 428
17:17 t' ten loaves, and run to the camp 2088
18 And carry t' ten cheeses unto the 428
39 said unto Saul, I cannot go with t': "
18:26 his servants told David t' words, "
21: 5 been kept from us about t' three days, "
12 David laid up t' words in his heart, 428
23: 2 Shall I go and smite t' Philistines? "
24: 7 stayed his servants with t' words, and "
16 made an end of speaking t' words 428
29: 3 What do t' Hebrews here? "
3 been with me t' days, or t' years, 2088
4 not be with the heads of t' men? 1992
31: 4 t' uncircumcised come and thrust 428
2Sa 3: 5 T' were born to David in Hebron. 428
39 t' men the sons of Zeruiah be too "
5:14 t' be the names of those that were "
7:17 According to all t' words, and "
21 hast thou done all t' great things, *2063
13:21 king David heard of all t' things, 428
14:19 he put all t' words in the mouth of "
16: 2 unto Ziba, What meanest thou by t'? "
21:22 T' four were born to the giant in "
23: 1 Now t' be the last words of David. "
8 T' be the names of the mighty men "
17 T' things did t' three mighty men. "
22 T' things did Benaiah the son of "
24:17 but t' sheep, what have they done? "
23 All t' things did Araunah, as a king,
1Ki 4: 2 t' were the princes which he had; 428
8 And t' are their names: The son of "
7: 9 All t' were of costly stones, according "
45 all t' vessels, which Hiram made "
8:59 And let t' my words, wherewith I "
9:13 What cities are t' which thou hast "
23 T' were the chief of the officers that "
10: 8 happy are t' thy servants, which "
10 abundance of spices as t' which 1931
11: 2 Solomon clave unto t' in love. 1992
17: 1 shall not be dew nor rain t' years, 428
17 And it came to pass after t' things, "
18:36 have done all t' things at thy word. "
20:19 So t' young men of the princes of "
21: 1 And it came to pass after t' things, "
22:11 With t' shalt thou push the Syrians, "
17 the Lord said, T' have no master: "
23 the mouth of all t' thy prophets, "
2Ki 1: 7 to meet you, and told you t' words? "
13 and the life of t' fifty thy servants, "
2:21 the Lord, I have healed t' waters; "
3:10, 13 called t' three kings together, "
6:20 Lord, open the eyes of t' men, that "
7: 8 And when t' lepers came to the "
10: 9 and slew him: but who slew all t'? "
17:41 So t' nations feared the Lord, and "
18:27 and to thee, to speak t' words? "
20:14 said unto him, What said t' men? "
21:11 of Judah hath done t' abominations, "
23:16 proclaimed, who proclaimed t' words, "
17 and proclaimed t' things that thou "
25:16 the brass of all t' vessels was without "
17 like unto t' had the second pillar "
25:20 captain of the guard took t', and *
1Ch 1:23 All t' were the sons of Joktan. 428
29 T' are their generations: The "
31 T' are the sons of Ishmael. 428,1992
33 All t' are the sons of Keturah. 428
43 t' are the kings that reigned in the "
54 Iram. T' are the dukes of Edom. "
2: 1 T' are the sons of Israel; Reuben, "
18 her sons are t'; Jesher, and Shobab, "
23 t' belonged to the sons of Machir "
33 Zaza. T' were the sons of Jerahmeel. "
50 T' were the sons of Caleb the son of "
55 T' are the Kenites that came of 1992
3: 1 Now t' were the sons of David, 428
4 T' six were born unto him in Hebron;*
5 And t' were born unto him in 428
9 T' were all the sons of David, beside "
4: 2 T' are the families of the 428
3 And t' were of the father of Etam; "
4 T' are the sons of Hur, the "
6 T' were the sons of Naarah. "
12 Ir-nahash. T' are the men of Rechah. "
18 And t' are the sons of Bithiah the "
22 And t' are ancient things. *
23 T' were the potters, and those 1992
31 T' were their cities unto the reign 428
33 T' were their habitations, and 2063
38 T' mentioned by their names were 428
41 t' written by name came in the days "
5:14 T' are the children of Abihail the "
17 t' were reckoned by genealogies in the "
24 t' were the heads of the house of 428
6:17 And t' be the names of the sons of "
19 t' are the families of the Levites "
31 t' are they whom David set over the "
33 t' are they that waited with their 428
50 t' are the sons of Aaron; Eleazar his "
54 Now t' are their dwelling places "
64 to the Levites t' cities with their *
65 t' cities, which are called by their "
7: 8 All t' are the sons of Becher. 428
11 All t' the sons of Jediael, by the "
17 T' were the sons of Gilead, the son "
29 In t' dwelt the children of Joseph "
33 T' are the children of Japhlet. "
40 All t' were the children of Asher, "
8: 6 And t' are the sons of Ehud: "
6 t' are the heads of the fathers 428,1992
10 T' were his sons, heads of the 428
28 T' were heads of the fathers, by "
28 chief men. T' dwelt in Jerusalem. "
32 t' also dwelt with their brethren *1992
38 sons, whose names are t', Azrikam, 428
38 Hanan. All t' were the sons of Azel. "
40 fifty. All t' are the sons of Benjamin. "
9: 9 t' men were chief of the fathers in "
22 t' which were chosen to be porters in "
22 T' were reckoned by their 1992
26 t' Levites, the four chief porters, *
33 And t' are the singers, chief of the 428
34 T' chief fathers of the Levites were "
34 generations; t' dwelt at Jerusalem. "
44 had six sons, whose names are t', "
44 Hanan: t' were the sons of Azel. "
10: 4 lest t' uncircumcised come and the "
11:10 T' also are the chief of the mighty "
19 shall I drink the blood of t' men that "
19 T' things did...three mightiest.

1Ch 11:19 things did t' three mightiest. *
24 T' things did Benaiah the son of 428
12: 1 t' are they that came to David to "
14 T' were of the sons of Gad, captains"
15 T' are they that went over 428,1992
23 t' are the numbers of the bands 428
38 t' men of war, that could keep rank, "
14: 4 Now t' are the names of his children"
17:15 According to all t' words, and "
19 in making known all t' great things. "
18:11 that he brought from all t' nations;*
20: 8 T' were born unto the giant in 411
21:17 but as for t' sheep, what have they 428
23: 9 T' were the chief of the fathers of "
10 T' four were the sons of Shimei. "
24 T' were the sons of Levi after the "
24: 1 t' are the divisions of the sons of "
19 T' were the orderings of them in * 428
20 the rest of the sons of Levi were t':*
30 T' were the sons of the Levites 428
31 T' likewise cast lots over against 1992
25: 5 All t' were the sons of Heman the 428
6 All t' were under the hands of their "
26: 8 All t' of the sons of Obed-edom: "
12 Among t' were the divisions of the "
19 T' are the divisions of the porters "
27:22 T' were the princes of the tribes of "
31 t' were the rulers of the substance "
29:17 I have willingly offered all t' things:"
19 and to do all t' things, and to build "
2Ch 3: 3 t' are the things wherein Solomon 428
13 The wings of t' cherubims spread "
4:18 Solomon made all t' vessels in great "
5: 5 t' did the priests and Levites bring "
8:10 t' were the chief of king Solomon's 428
9: 7 men, and happy are t' thy servants, "
14: 7 Let us build t' cities, and make "
8 all t' were mighty men of valour. "
15: 8 when Asa heard t' words, and the "
17:14 And t' are the numbers of them * "
19 T' waited on the king, beside those "
18:10 With t' thou shalt push Syria until "
16 the Lord said, T' have no master; "
22 in the mouth of t' thy prophets, "
21: 2 all t' were the sons of Jehoshaphat "
24:26 t' are they that conspired against "
29:32 t' were for a burnt offering to the "
32: 1 After t' things, and the "
35: 7 t' were of the king's substance. "
36:18 princes; all t' he brought to Babylon. "
Ezr 1:11 t' did Sheshbazzar bring up with them
2: 1 t' are the children of the province 428
59 t' were they which went up from "
62 T' sought their register among "
4:21 to cause t' men to cease, 479
5: 9 house, and to make up t' walls? *1836
11 that was builded t' many years ago, "
15 Take t' vessels, go, carry them into412
6: 8 ye shall do to the elders of t' Jews 479
8 expences be given unto t' men, "
7: 1 Now after t' things, in the reign of 428
8: 1 T' are now the chief of their fathers,"
13 whose names are t', Eliphelet, Jeiel, "
9: 1 Now when t' were done, the princes "
14 with the people of t' abominations? "
10:44 All t' had taken strange wives: and "
Ne 1: 4 came to pass, when I heard t' words, "
10 Now t' are thy servants and thy 1992
2: 2 and said, What do t' feeble Jews? "
5: 6 when I heard their cry and t' words.428
6: 6 be their king, according to t' words. "
7 to the king according to t' words. "
14 according to t' their works, "
16 heathen...about us saw t' things, *
7: 6 T' are the children of the province,428
61 t' were they which went up also from"
64 T' sought their register among "
10: 8 Shemaiah: t' were the priests. "
11: 3 t' are the chief of the province that "
7 t' are the sons of Benjamin; Sallu "
12: 1 t' are the priests and the Levites "
7 T' were the chief of the priests and "
26 T' were in the days of Joiakim the "
Es 1: 5 And when t' days were expired, the "
2: 1 After t' things, when the wrath of "
3: 1 After t' things did king Ahasuerus "
4:11 in unto the king t' thirty days. 2088
9:20 And Mordecai wrote t' things, and 428
26 Wherefore they called t' days Purim"
27 that they would keep t' two days "
28 that t' days should be remembered "
28 and that t' days of Purim should not"
31 To confirm t' days of Purim in their "
32 confirmed t' matters of Purim; "
Job 8: 2 How long wilt thou speak t' things? "
10:13 And t' things hast thou hid in thine "
12: 3 who knoweth not such things as t'? "
9 knoweth not in all t' that the hand "
19: 3 T' ten times have ye reproached 2088
26:14 Lo, t' are parts of his ways: but 428
32: 1 t' three men ceased to answer Job, "
5 answer in the mouth of t' three men, "
33:29 t' things worketh God oftentimes 428
42: 7 Lord had spoken t' words unto Job, "
Ps 15: 5 He that doeth t' things shall never "
42: 4 When I remember t' things, I pour "
50:21 T' things hast thou done, and I "
57: 1 refuge, until t' calamities be overpast. "
73:12 t' are the ungodly, who prosper in 428
104:27 T' wait all upon thee; that thou "
107:24 T' see the works of the Lord, and 1992
43 is wise, and will observe t' things, 428
Pr 6:16 T' six things doth the Lord hate:*2007
24:23 T' things also belong to the wise. 428
25: 1 T' are also proverbs of Solomon, "
Ec 7:10 the former days were better than t'? "
Ec 11: 9 that for all t' things God will bring 428
12:12 by t', my son, be admonished: of *1992
Isa 7: 4 two tails of t' smoking firebrands, 428
34:16 no one of t' shall fail, none shall 2007
36:12 and to thee to speak t' words? 428
20 they among all the gods of t' lands, "
38:16 O Lord, by t' things men live, 5921
16 in all t' things is the life of my spirit:*
39: 3 said unto him, What said t' men? 428
40:26 behold who hath created t' things, "
42:16 T' things will I do unto them, and "
44:21 Remember t', O Jacob and Israel; "
45: 7 evil: I the Lord do all t' things. "
47: 7 didst not lay t' things to thy heart, "
9 But t' two things shall come to thee "
13 save thee from t' things that shall*
48:14 them hath declared t' things? 428
49:12 Behold, t' shall come from far: and, "
12 t' from the north and from the west;"
12 west; and t' from the land of Sinim. "
18 all t' gather themselves together, and
21 Who hath begotten me t', seeing I 428
21 fro? and who hath brought up t'? 2004
21 left alone; t', where had they been?428
51:19 T' two things are come unto thee;2007
57: 6 Should I receive comfort in t'? 428
60: 8 Who are t' that fly as a cloud, and as"
64:12 thou refrain thyself for t' things, "
65: 5 T' are a smoke in my nose, a fire "
Jer 2:34 it by secret search, but upon all t'. "
3: 7 said after she had done all t' things, "
12 Go and proclaim t' words toward "
4:18 have procured t' things unto thee; "
5: 4 I said, Surely t' are poor; they are 1992
5 t' have altogether broken the yoke, "
9 Shall I not visit for t' things? saith 428
19 Lord our God all t' things unto us? "
25 have turned away t' things, "
29 Shall I not visit for t' things? saith "
7: 2 that enter in at t' gates to worship "
4 The temple of the Lord, are t'. 1992
10 delivered to do all t' abominations? 428
13 because ye have done all t' works, "
27 shalt speak all t' words unto them; "
9: 9 Shall I not visit them for t' things? "
24 for in t' things I delight, saith the "
26 for all t' nations are uncircumcised,*
10:11 earth, and from under t' heavens.* 429
11: 6 Proclaim all t' words in the cities of428
13:22 Wherefore come t' things upon me? "
14:22 for thou hast made all t' things. "
16:10 shalt shew this people all t' words, "
17:20 Jerusalem, that enter in by t' gates: "
20: 1 that Jeremiah prophesied t' things. "
22: 2 thy people that enter in by t' gates: "
5 if ye will not hear t' words, I swear "
23:21 I have not sent t' prophets, yet they "
24: 5 Like t' good figs, so will I 428
25: 9 against all t' nations round about, "
11 t' nations shall serve the king of "
30 thou against them all t' words, "
26: 7 heard Jeremiah speaking t' words in"
10 the princes of Judah heard t' things, "
15 to speak all t' words in your ears. "
27: 6 now have I given all t' lands into the"
12 of Judah according to all t' words, "
28:14 iron upon the neck of all t' nations, "
29: 1 Now t' are the words of the letter "
30: 4 t' are the words that the Lord spake "
15 I have done t' things unto thee. "
31:21 of Israel, turn again to t' thy cities. "
32:14 Take t' evidences, this evidence of "
34: 6 spake all t' words unto Zedekiah "
7 t' defenced cities remained of the 2007
36:16 surely tell the king of all t' words. 428
17 thou write all t' words at his mouth?"
18 He pronounced all t' words unto me "
24 his servants that heard all t' words. "
38: 9 t' men have done evil in all that they"
12 Put now t' old cast clouts and rotten "
16 hand of t' men that seek thy life. 428
24 Let no man know of t' words, and "
27 told them according to all t' words "
43: 1 sent him to them, even all t' words, "
10 set his throne upon t' stones that I "
51:60 all t' words that are written against "
61 shalt see, and shalt read all t' words;"
52:20 the brass of all t' vessels was without"
22 the pomegranates were like unto t'. "
La 1:16 For t' things I weep; mine eye, mine"
4: 9 for t' pine away, stricken through 1992
5:17 for t' things our eyes are dim. 428
Eze 1:21 When those went, t' went; and when
21 when those stood, t' stood; and when
8:15 see greater abominations than t'. 428
10:17 When they stood, t' stood; and when
17 were lifted up, t' lifted up themselves
11: 2 t' are the men that devise mischief,428
14: 3 t' men have set up their idols in "
14 Though t' three men, Noah, Daniel, "
16, 18 Though t' three men were in it, "
16: 5 to do any of t' unto thee, to have "
20 t' hast thou sacrificed unto them to be
30 seeing thou doest all t' things, the 428
43 but hast fretted me in all t' things; "
17:12 Know ye not what t' things mean? "
18 and hath done all t' things, he shall "
18:10 doeth the like to any one of t' things,"
13 he hath done all t' abominations; he"
23:10 T' discovered her nakedness: 1992
30 I will do t' things unto thee, 428
24:19 not tell us what t' things are to us, "
27:21 goats: in t' were they thy merchants. "
24 T' were thy merchants in all sorts1992
30:17 t' cities shall go into captivity. 2007
35:10 T' two nations and t' two countries
Eze 36:20 T' are the people of the Lord, and 428
37: 3 me, Son of man, can t' bones live? "
4 Prophesy upon t' bones, and say "
5 saith the Lord God unto t' bones; "
9 breathe upon t' slain, that they may "
11 man, t' bones are the whole house of"
18 shew us what thou meanest by t'? "
40:24 thereof according to t' measures. "
28 south gate according to t' measures;"
29 thereof, according to t' measures: "
32 the gate according to t' measures. "
33 were according to t' measures: "
35 it according to t' measures; "
46 t' are the sons of Zadok among the1992
42: 5 the galleries were higher than t', 2007
9 under t' chambers was the entry 428
43:13 t' are the measures of the altar after "
18 T' are the ordinances of the altar in "
27 when t' days are expired, it shall *
46:22 t' four corners were of one measure.
24 T' are the places of them that boil,428
47: 8 T' waters issue out toward the east "
9 because t' waters shall come thither:"
48: 1 Now t' are the names of the tribes. "
1 for t' are his sides east and west; a*
16 t' shall be the measures thereof; 428
29 and t' are their portions, saith the "
30 t' are the goings out of the city on "
Da 1: 6 among t' were of the children of 1992
17 As for t' four children, God gave 428
2:28 of thy head upon thy bed, are t'; 1836
40 as iron that breaketh all t', shall it 459
44 in the days of t' kings shall the * 581
44 and consume all t' kingdoms, 459
3:12 t' men, O king, have not regarded 479
13 they brought t' men before the king."
21 t' men were bound in their coats, "
23 t' three men, Shadrach, Meshach, "
27 saw t' men, upon whose bodies the "
6: 2 And over t' three presidents; of 4481
5 Then said t' men, We shall not find 479
6 Then t' presidents and princes 459
11 Then t' men assembled, and found 479
14 when he heard t' words, was sore "
15 t' men assembled unto the king, 479
7:17 T' great beasts, which are four, are459
10:21 that holdeth with me in t' things, 428
11: 6 he that strengthened her in t' times.*
27 both t' kings' hearts shall be to do
41 t' shall escape out of his hand, even428
12: 6 shall it be to the end of t' wonders?
7 all t' things shall be finished. 428
8 what shall be the end of t' things? "
Ho 2:12 T' are my rewards that my lovers 1992
14: 9 and he shall understand t' things? 428
Am 6: 2 be they better than t' kingdoms? or "
Mic 2: 7 Lord straitened? are t' his doings? "
Hab 2: 6 Shall not all t' take up a parable "
Hag 2:13 by a dead body touch any of t', "
Zec 1: 9 Then said I, O my lord, what are t'? "
9 unto me, I will shew thee what t' be. "
10 T' are they whom the Lord hath "
12 had indignation t' threescore and 2086
19 that talked with me, What be t'? 428
19 T' are the horns which have "
21 Then said I, What come t' to do? "
21 saying, T' are the horns which have"
21 but t' are come to fray them, to cast "
3: 7 to walk among t' that stand by. "
4: 4 me, saying, What are t', my lord? "
5 me, Knowest thou not what t' be? "
11 What are t' two olive trees upon the "
12 What be t' two olive branches which
13 said, Knowest thou not what t' be? 428
14 T' are the two anointed ones, that "
5:10 me, Whither do t' bear the ephah?1992
6: 4 with me, What are t', my lord? 428
5 T' are the four spirits of the "
8 t' that go toward the north country*
7: 3 as I have done t' so many years? 2088
8: 6 remnant of this people in t' days, *1992
9 ye that hear in t' days t' words by 428
10 before t' days there was no hire *1992
12 this people to possess all t' things. 428
15 have I thought in t' days to do well "
16 T' are the things that ye shall do; "
17 for all t' are things that I hate, "
13: 6 What are t' wounds in thine hands? "
14:15 the beasts that shall be in t' tents,*1992
M't 1:20 But while he thought on t' things, 5023
2: 3 Herod the king had heard t' things,*
3: 9 God is able of t' stones to raise up 5130
4: 3 command that t' stones be made 3778
9 him, All t' things will I give thee. 5023
5:19 one of t' least commandments, 5130
37 whatsoever is more than t' cometh "
6:29 glory was not arrayed like one of t'. "
32 all t' things do the Gentiles seek:) 5023
32 that ye have need of all t' things. 5130
33 t' things shall be added unto you. 5023
7:24 whosoever heareth t' sayings of 5128
26 every one that heareth t' sayings of"
28 when Jesus had ended t' sayings, "
9:18 While he spake t' things unto them,5023
10: 2 names of the twelve apostles are t'; "
5 T' twelve Jesus sent forth, and 5128
42 unto one of t' little ones a cup of 5130
11:25 hast hid t' things from the wise 5023
13:34 All t' things spake Jesus unto the "
51 Have ye understood all t' things? "
53 when Jesus...finished t' parables, 5025
54 this wisdom, and t' mighty works? 3588
56 then hath this man all t' things? 5023
15:20 T' are the things which defile a "
18: 6 shall offend one of t' little ones 5130
10 ye despise not one of t' little ones: "

M't 18:14 one of t' little ones should perish. 5130
19: 1 when Jesus had finished t' sayings, 5128
20 All t' things have I kept from my 5023
20:12 T' last have wrought but one 3778
21 Grant that t' my two sons may sit, "
21:16 unto him, Hearest thou what t' say?"
23 authority doest thou t' things? 5023
24, 27 by what authority I do t' things."
22:22 had heard t' words, they marvelled,*
40 On t' two commandments hang all 5025
23:23 t' ought ye to have done, and not 5023
36 All t' things shall come upon this "
24: 2 unto them, See ye not all t' things? "
3 Tell us, when shall t' things be? "
6 for all t' things must come to pass, "
8 All t' are the beginning of sorrows. 5023
33 ye, when ye shall see all t' things, "
34 pass, till all t' things be fulfilled. "
25:40 one of the least of t' my brethren, 5130
45 ye did it not to one of the least of t'."
46 t' shall go away into everlasting 3778
26: 1 Jesus had finished all t' sayings, 5128
62 what is it which t' witness against 3778
M'r 2: 8 reason ye t' things in your hearts? 5023
4:11 all t' things are done in parables:*3588
15 And t' are they by the way side, 3778
16 t' are they likewise which are sown "
18 t' are they which are sown among *"
20 t' are they which are sown on good*"
6: 2 whence hath this man t' things? 5023
7:23 t' evil things come from within, "
8: 4 can a man satisfy t' men with 5128
9:42 offend one of t' little ones that 3588
10:20 t' have I observed from my youth. 5023
11:28 what authority doest thou t' things?"
28 thee this authority to do t' things? "
29, 33 by what authority I do t' things."
12:31 commandment greater than t'. 5130
40 t' shall receive greater damnation. 3778
13: 2 Seest thou t' great buildings? 5025
4 Tell us, when shall t' things be? 5023
4 when all t' things shall be fulfilled?"
8 t' are the beginnings of sorrows. "
29 ye shall see t' things come to pass, "
30 not pass, till all t' things be done. "
14:60 what is it which t' witness against 3778
16:17 t' signs shall follow them that 5023
Lu 1:19 and to shew thee t' glad tidings. "
20 that t' things shall be performed, "
65 all t' sayings were noised abroad "
2:19 But Mary kept all t' things, and "
51 his mother kept all t' sayings in "
3: 8 God is able of t' stones to raise up 5130
4:28 when they heard t' things, were 5023
5:27 And after t' things he went forth, "
7: 9 When Jesus heard t' things, he "
18 John shewed him of all t' things. 5130
8: 8 And when he had said t' things, he 5023
13 and t' have no root, which for a 3778
21 are t' which hear the word of God, "
9:28 an eight days after t' sayings, 5128
44 Let t' sayings sink down into your "
10: 1 After t' things the Lord appointed 5023
21 hast hid t' things from the wise "
36 Which now of t' three, thinkest 5130
11:27 as he spake t' things, a certain 5023
42 t' ought ye to have done, and not to "
53 as he said t' things unto them, the*"
12:27 was not arrayed like one of t'. 5130
30 all t' things do the nations of the 5023
30 that ye have need of t' things. 5130
31 t' things shall be added unto you. 5023
13: 2 Suppose ye that t' Galilæans were 3778
7 t' three years I come seeking fruit on
16 hath bound, lo, t' eighteen years,
17 when he had said t' things, all his 5023
14: 6 not answer him again to t' things."
15 sat at meat with him heard t' things,"
21 came, and shewed his lord t' things."
15: 26 and asked what t' things meant. 5023
29 Lo, t' many years do I serve thee, 5118
16:14 Pharisees...heard all t' things: 5023
17: 2 should offend one of t' little ones. 5130
18:21 All t' have I kept from my youth 5023
22 Now when Jesus heard t' things, * "
34 they understood none of t' things: 5130
19:11 And as they heard t' things, he 5023
15 he commanded t' servants to be 5128
40 that, if t' should hold their peace, 3778
20: 2 authority doest thou t' things? 5023
8 by what authority I do t' things. "
16 come and destroy t' husbandmen, 5128
21: 4 all t' have of their abundance cast 3778
6 As for t' things which ye behold, 5023
7 Master, but when shall t' things be?"
7 when t' things shall come to pass? "
9 t' things must first come to pass; "
12 But before all t', they shall lay 5130
22 For t' be the days of vengeance, 3778
28 when t' things begin to come to 5130
31 when ye see t' things come to pass, 5023
36 worthy to escape all t' things "
23:31 if they do t' things in a green tree, "
49 stood afar off, beholding t' things. "
24: 9 told all t' things unto the eleven, "
10 told t' things unto the apostles. "
14 they talked together of all t' things 5130
17 of communications are t' that ye 3778
18 are come to pass there in t' days? 5025
21 day since t' things were done. 5023
26 Christ to have suffered t' things, "
44 T' are the words which I spake 3778
48 And ye are witnesses of t' things. 5130
Joh 1:28 T' things were done in Bethabara 5023
50 shalt see greater things than t'. 5130
2:16 sold doves, Take t' things hence; 5023

Joh 2:18 seeing that thou doest t' things? 5023
3: 2 for no man can do t' miracles that "
9 unto him, How can t' things be? "
10 Israel, and knowest not t' things? "
22 After t' things came Jesus and his "
5: 3 In t' lay a great multitude of 5025
16 had done t' things on the sabbath 5023
19 t' also doeth the Son likewise. "
20 shew him greater works than t', 5130
34 t' things I say, that ye might be 5023
6: 1 After t' things Jesus went over the "
5 we buy bread, that t' may eat? 3778
59 T' things said he in the synagogue, 5023
7: 1 t' things Jesus walked in Galilee: "
4 If thou do t' things, shew thyself to "
9 When he had said t' words unto "
31 will he do more miracles than t' *5130
8:20 T' words spake Jesus in the 5023
28 hath taught me, I speak t' things. "
30 As he spake t' words, many "
9:22 T' words spake his parents, "
40 were with him heard t' words, "
10:19 among the Jews for t' sayings. 5128
21 T' are not the words of him that 5023
11:11 T' things said he: and after that he"
12:16 T' things understood not his "
16 that t' things were written of him, "
16 they had done t' things unto him. "
36 T' things spake Jesus, and "
41 T' things said Esaias, when he saw"
13:17 If ye know t' things, happy are ye "
14:12 greater works than t' shall he do; 5130
25 T' things have I spoken unto you, 5023
15:11 T' things have I spoken unto you, "
17 T' things I command you, that ye "
21 all t' things will they do unto you "
16: 1 T' things have I spoken unto you, "
3 And t' things will they do unto you, "
4 t' things have I told you, that when"
4 t' things I said not unto you at the "
6 I have said t' things unto you, "
25 T' things have I spoken unto you "
33 T' things I have spoken unto you, "
17: 1 T' words spake Jesus, and lifted up"
11 but t' are in the world, and I come 3778
13 and t' things I speak in the world, 5023
20 Neither pray I for t' alone, but for 5130
25 t' have known that thou hast sent 3778
18: 1 When Jesus had spoken t' words, 5023
8 ye seek me, let t' go their way: 5128
19:24 T' things therefore the soldiers 5023
36 For t' things were done, that the "
20:18 he had spoken t' things unto her. "
31 But t' are written, that ye might "
21: 1 After t' things Jesus shewed "
15 lovest thou me more than t'? 5130
24 which testifieth of t' things, "
24 and wrote t' things: and we know 5023
Ac 1: 9 And when he had spoken t' things, "
14 T' all continued with one accord 3778
21 t' men which have companied *5130
24 whether of t' two thou hast chosen, "
2: 7 not all t' which speak Galilæans? 3778
13 said, T' men are full of new wine.*
15 For t' are not drunken, as ye 3778
22 Ye men of Israel, hear t' words; 5128
3:24 have likewise foretold of t' days. 5025
4:16 What shall we do to t' men? for 5125
5: 5 And Ananias hearing t' words fell 5128
5 on all them that heard t' things. *5023
11 upon as many as heard t' things, "
24 the chief priests heard t' things, 5128
32 we are his witnesses of t' things; 5130
35 intend to do as touching t' men. 5125
36 before t' days rose up Theudas, 5130
38 Refrain from t' men, and let them "
7: 1 the high priest, Are t' things so? 5023
50 not my hand made all t' things? "
54 they heard t' things, they were cut "
8:24 that none of t' things which ye have
10: 8 when he had declared all t' things*
44 While Peter yet spake t' words, 5023
47 that t' should not be baptized, 5128
11:12 t' six brethren accompanied me, 3778
18 When they heard t' things, they 5023
22 Then tidings of t' things came unto*846
27 in t' days came prophets from 5125
12:17 Go shew t' things unto James, and 5023
13:42 Gentiles besought that t' words "
14:15 saying, Sirs, why do ye t' things? 5130
15 turn from t' vanities unto the 5023
18 t' sayings scarce restrained they "
15:17 the Lord, who doeth all t' things. "
28 burden than t' necessary things; 5130
16:17 T' men are the servants of the most 3778
20 T' men, being Jews, do exceedingly"
38 serjeants told t' words unto the 5023
17: 6 T'...have turned the world upside 3778
7 t' all do contrary to the decrees of "
8 the city, when they heard t' things. 5023
11 T' were more noble than those in 3778
20 know...what t' things mean. 5023
18: 1 After t' things Paul departed from "
19:21 After t' things were ended, Paul "
28 And when they heard t' sayings, they*
36 that t' things cannot be spoken 5130
37 For ye have brought hither t' men, 5128
20: 5 T' going before tarried for us at 3778
24 But none of t' things move me, *
34 t' hands have ministered unto my 3778
21:12 And when we heard t' things, both 5023
38 before t' days madest an uproar, 5130
23:22 thou hast shewed t' things to me. 5023
24: 8 take knowledge of all t' things,* 5130
9 saying that t' things were so. 5023
20 Or else let t' same here say, if they 3778

Ac 24:22 And when Felix heard t' things, *5023
25: 9 be judged of t' things before me? 5130
11 if there be none of t' things *
11 whereof t' accuse me, no man may 3778
20 and there be judged of t' matters. 5130
26:16 of t' things which thou hast seen, *
21 For t' causes the Jews caught me *5130
26 For the king knoweth of t' things, "
26 that none of t' things are hidden "
29 such as I am, except t' bonds. "
27:31 Except t' abide in the ship, ye 3778
28:29 And when he had said t' words, *5023
Ro 2:14 t', having not the law, are a law 3778
8:31 What shall we then say to t' things? 5023
37 in all t' things we are more than 5125
9: 8 t' are not the children of God: *5023
11:24 how much more shall t', which be 3778
31 so have t' also now not believed, "
14:18 he that in t' things serveth Christ*5125
15:23 having no more place in t' parts, "
23 having a great desire t' many years
1Co 4: 6 And t' things, brethren, I have in 5023
14 I write not t' things to shame you, "
9: 8 Say I t' things as a man? or saith "
15 But I have used none of t' things: 5130
15 neither have I written t' things, 5023
10: 6 Now t' things were our examples, "
11 Now all t' things happened unto "
12:11 But all t' worketh that one and the "
23 upon t' we bestow more abundant 5125
13:13 faith, hope, charity, t' three; 5023
13 but the greater of t' is charity. 5130
2Co 2:16 And who is sufficient for t' things? 5023
7: 1 Having therefore t' promises, 5025
13:10 I write t' things being absent, 5023
Ga 2: 6 But of t' who seemed to be somewhat,*
4:24 for t' are the two covenants, one 3778
5:17 t' are contrary the one to the "
19 of the flesh are manifest, which are t';
Eph 5: 6 of t' things cometh the wrath of 5023
Ph'p 4: 8 be any praise, think on t' things. "
Col 3:14 above all t' things put on charity, 5125
4:11 T' only are my fellowworkers unto 3778
1Th 3: 3 should be moved by t' afflictions: 5025
4:18 comfort one another with t' words. 5125
2Th 2: 5 yet with you, I told you t' things? 5023
1Ti 3:10 And let t' also first be proved; 3778
14 T' things write I unto thee, 5023
4: 6 in remembrance of t' things, "
11 T' things command and teach. "
15 Meditate upon t' things; give "
5: 7 And t' things give in charge, that "
21 that thou observe t' things without "
6: 2 T' things teach and exhort. "
11 thou, O man of God, flee t' things; "
2Ti 1:12 which cause I also suffer t' things: "
2:14 Of t' things put them in "
21 therefore purge himself from t', 5130
3: 8 so do t' also resist the truth: 3778
Tit 2:15 T' things speak, and exhort, and 5023
3: 8 t' things I will that thou affirm 5130
8 T' things are good and profitable 5023
Heb 1: 2 in t' last days spoken unto us by 5130
7:13 he of whom t' things are spoken 5023
9: 6 t' things were thus ordained, 5130
23 should be purified with t'; 5125
23 with better sacrifices than t'. 5025
10:18 Now where remission of t' is, there 5130
11:13 T' all died in faith, not having 3778
39 And t' all, having obtained a good "
Jas 3:10 t' things ought not so to be. 5023
1Pe 1:20 manifest in t' last times for you, *3588
2Pe 1: 4 that by t' ye might be partakers of 5130
8 For if t' things be in you, and 5023
9 he that lacketh t' things is blind, "
10 for if ye do t' things, ye shall never "
12 in remembrance of t' things, 5130
15 t' things always in remembrance. "
2:12 But t', as natural brute beasts, 3778
17 T' are wells without water, clouds "
3:11 all t' things shall be dissolved, 5130
16 speaking in them of t' things; "
1Jo 1: 4 And t' things write we unto you, 5023
2: 1 t' things write I unto you, that ye "
26 T' things have I written unto you "
5: 7 Holy Ghost: and t' three are one.*3778
8 blood: and t' three agree in one. * "
13 T' things have I written unto you 5023
Jude 8 Likewise also t' filthy dreamers 3778
10 But t' speak evil of those things "
12 T' are spots in your feasts of "
14 prophesied of t', saying, Behold, 5125
16 T' are murmurers, complainers, 3778
19 T' be they who separate "
Re 2: 1 T' things saith he that holdeth 3592
8 T' things saith the first and the "
12 T' things saith he which hath the "
18 T' things saith the Son of God, "
3: 1 T' things saith he that hath the "
7 T' things saith he that is holy, he "
14 T' things saith the Amen, the "
7: 1 after t' things I saw four angels *5023
13 What are t' which are arrayed in 3778
14 T' are they which came out of "
9:18 By t' three was the third part of 5130
20 were not killed by t' plagues yet 5025
11: 4 T' are the two olive trees, and the 3778
6 T' have power to shut heaven, that"
10 t' two prophets tormented them "
14: 4 T' are they which were not defiled "
4 T' are they which follow the Lamb "
4 T' were redeemed from among "
16: 9 which hath power over t' plagues: 5025
17:13 T' have one mind, and shall give 3778
14 T' shall make war with the Lamb, "
16 t' shall hate the whore, and shall "

Re 18: 1 after t' things I saw another angel *5023*
15 The merchants of t' things, which *5130*
19: 1 after t' things I heard a great *5023*
9 T' are the true sayings of God. *3778*
20 T' both were cast alive into a lake* *3588*
21: 5 for t' words are true and faithful. *3778*
22: 6 T' sayings are faithful and true: "
8 I John saw t' things, and heard *5023*
8 angel which shewed me t' things. "
16 angel to testify unto you t' things "
18 any man shall add unto t' things, * "
20 He which testifieth t' things saith, "

Thessalonians (*thes-sa-lo'-ne-uns*)
Ac 20: 4 and of the T', Aristarchus and *2331*
1Th 1: 1 unto the church of the T' which "
1Th *subscr.* The first epistle unto the T' was "
2Th 1: 1 unto the church of the T' in God "
2Th *subscr.* The second epistle to the T' was "

Thessalonica (*thes-sa-lo-ni'-cah*) See also THESSALONIANS.
Ac 17: 1 they came to T', where was a *2332*
11 were more noble than those in T', "
13 the Jews of T' had knowledge "
27: 2 Aristarchus, a Mecedonian of T', *2331*
Ph'p 4:16 For even in T' ye sent once and *2332*
2Ti 4:10 world, and is departed into T'; "

Theudas (*thew'-das*)
Ac 5:36 For before these days rose up T'. *2333*

they See in the APPENDIX; also THEIR; THEM.

thick See also THICKER.
Ex 10:22 there was a t' darkness in all the 653
19: 9 Lo, I come unto thee in a t' cloud, 5645
16 and a t' cloud upon the mount, 3515
20:21 Moses drew near unto the t' darkness
Le 23:40 and the boughs of t' trees, and 5687
De 4:11 darkness, clouds, and t' darkness.
5:22 the cloud, and of the t' darkness,
32:15 art waxen fat, thou art grown t', 5666
2Sa 18: 9 under the t' boughs of a great oak,
22:12 waters, and t' clouds of the skies.
1Ki 7: 6 and the t' beam were before them.
26 And it was an hand breadth t', 5672
8:12 he would dwell in the t' darkness.
2Ki 8:15 he took a t' cloth, and dipped it in*
2Ch 6: 1 he would dwell in the t' darkness.
Ne 8:15 and branches of t' trees, to make 5687
Job 15:26 upon the t' bosses of his bucklers: 5672
22:14 T' clouds are a covering to him,
26: 8 up the waters in his t' clouds;
37:11 by watering he wearieth the t' cloud:
38: 9 t' darkness a swaddlingband for it,
Ps 18:11 dark waters and t' clouds of the
12 before him his t' clouds passed,
74: 5 lifted up axes upon the t' trees. *5441
Isa 44:22 blotted out, as a t' cloud, thy
Eze 6:13 green tree, and under every t' oak, 5687
8:11 and a t' cloud of incense went up. 6282
19:11 was exalted among the t' branches, 5688
20:28 high hill, and all the t' trees, 5687
31: 3 his top was among the t' boughs. 5688
10 up his top among the t' boughs, "
14 up their top among the t' boughs, "
41:12 of the building was five cubits t' 7341
25 t' planks upon the face of the 5645
26 of the house, and t' planks.
Joe 2: 2 day of clouds and of t' darkness,
Hab 2: 6 that ladeth himself with t' clay! *
Zep 1:15 a day of clouds and t' darkness,
Lu 11:29 the people were gathered t' together,*

thicker
1Ki 12:10 finger shall be t' than my father's 5666
2Ch 10:10 finger shall be t' than my father's "

thicket See also THICKETS.
Ge 22:13 a ram caught in a t' by his horns: 5442
Jer 4: 7 The lion is come up from his t', 5441

thickets
1Sa 13: 6 hide themselves in caves, and in t', 2337
Isa 9:18 shall kindle in the t' of the forests, 5442
10:34 shall cut down the t' of the forest "
Jer 4:29 they shall go into the t', and climb 5645

thickness
2Ch 4: 5 the t' of it was an handbreadth, 5672
Jer 52:21 and the t' thereof was four fingers: "
Eze 41: 9 The t' of the wall, which was for 7341
42:10 chambers were in the t' of the wall "

thief See also THIEVES.
Ex 22: 2 If a t' be found breaking up, and 1590
7 if a t' be found, let him pay double. "
8 If the t' be not found, then the "
De 24: 7 selleth him; then that t' shall die; "
Job 24:14 needy, and in the night is as a t'. "
30: 5 (they cried after them as after a t';) "
Ps 50:18 When thou sawest a t', then thou "
Pr 6:30 Men do not despise a t', if he steal "
29:24 Whoso is partner with a t' hateth "
Jer 2:26 As the t' is ashamed when he is "
Ho 7: 1 the t' cometh in, and the troop of "
Joe 2: 9 enter in at the windows like a t'. "
Zec 5: 4 shall enter into the house of the t', "
M't 24:43 in what watch the t' would come, *2812*
26:55 Are ye come out as against a t' *3027*
M'r 14:48 Are ye come out, as against a t', * "
Lu 12:33 where no t' approacheth, neither *2812*
39 what hour the t' would come,
22:52 Be ye come out, as against a t', *3027*
Joh 10: 1 way, the same is a t' and a robber. *2812*
10 The t' cometh not, but for to steal, "
12: 6 but because he was a t', and had the "
1Th 5: 2 Lord so cometh as a t' in the night. "
4 day should overtake you as a t'. "
1Pe 4:15 you suffer as a murderer, or as a t', "
2Pe 3:10 Lord will come as a t' in the night; "

Re 3: 3 watch, I will come on thee as a t', *2812*
16:15 Behold, I come as a t'. Blessed is "

thieves
Isa 1:23 rebellious, and companions of t': 1590
Jer 48:27 unto thee? was he found among t'? "
49: 9 if t' by night, they will destroy till "
Ob 5 If t' came to thee, if robbers by "
M't 6:19 where t' break through and steal: *2812*
20 where t' do not break through nor "
21:13 but ye have made it a den of t'. *3027*
27:38 there two t' crucified with him; * "
44 The t' also, which were crucified * "
M'r 11:17 but ye have made it a den of t'. "
15:27 And with him they crucify two t'; * "
Lu 10:30 to Jericho, and fell among t', * "
36 unto him that fell among the t'? * "
19:46 but ye have made it a den of t'. * "
Joh 10: 8 that ever came before me are t' *2812*
1Co 6:10 Nor t', nor covetous, nor drunkards, "

thigh See also THIGHS.
Ge 24: 2 pray thee, thy hand under my t': 3409
9 his hand under the t' of Abraham "
32:25 he touched the hollow of his t'; "
25 hollow of Jacob's t' was out of joint, "
31 him, and he halted upon his t'. "
32 which is upon the hollow of the t', "
32 touched the hollow of Jacob's t' in "
47:29 I pray thee, thy hand under my t', "
Nu 5:21 the Lord doth make thy t' to rot, "
22 thy belly to swell, and thy t' to rot: "
27 shall swell, and her t' shall rot: "
J'g 3:16 under his raiment upon his right t'. "
21 took the dagger from his right t', "
15: 8 And he smote them hip and t' with "
Ps 45: 3 Gird thy sword upon thy t', O most "
Ca 3: 8 man hath his sword upon his t' "
Isa 47: 2 bare the leg, uncover the t', *7785
Jer 31:19 instructed, I smote upon my t': 3409
Eze 21:12 smite therefore upon thy t'. "
24: 4 good piece, the t', and the shoulder; "
Re 19:16 and on his t' a name written, *3382*

thighs
Ex 28:42 the loins even unto the t' they 3409
Ca 7: 1 the joints of thy t' are like jewels. "
Da 2:32 silver, his belly and his t' of brass, 3410

Thimnathah (*thim'-nath-ah*) See also TIMNAH.
Jos 19:43 And Elon, and T', and Ekron, 8553

thin
Ge 41: 6 seven t' ears and blasted with the 1851
7 And the seven t' ears devoured the "
23 behold, seven ears, withered, t', "
24 the t' ears devoured the seven good "
27 the seven t' and ill favoured kine *7534
Ex 39: 3 they did beat the gold into t' plates,
Le 13:30 and there be in it a yellow t' hair; 1851
1Ki 7:29 certain additions made of t' work.*4174
Isa 17: 4 the glory of Jacob shall be made t', 1809

thine See also THY.
Ge 13:14 Lift up now t' eyes, and look from the
14:20 delivered t' enemies into thy hand.
23 that I will not take any thing that is t',
15: 4 him, saying, This shall not be t' heir;
4 out of t' own bowels shall be t' heir.
20: 7 surely die, thou, and all that are t'.
21:18 up the lad, and hold him in t' hand;
22: 2 Take now thy son, t' only son Isaac,
12 Lay not t' hand upon the lad, neither
12 withheld thy son, t' only son from me.
16 hast not withheld thy son, t' only son:
30:27 if I have found favour in t' eyes, tarry:
31:12 he said, Lift up now t' eyes, and see,
32 discern thou what is t' with me,
38:18 and thy staff that is in t' hand.
40:13 days shall Pharaoh lift up t' head,
44:18 not t' anger burn against thy servant:
46: 4 shall put his hand upon t' eyes.
47:19 Wherefore shall we die before t' eyes,
48: 6 thou begettest after them, shall be t',
49: 8 shall be in the neck of t' enemies;
Ex 4: 4 Put forth t' hand, and take it by the
6 him, Put now t' hand into thy bosom.
7 Put t' hand into thy bosom again.
17 And thou shalt take this rod in t' hand,
21 Pharaoh, which I have put in t' hand:
5:16 but the fault is in t' own people.
7:15 to a serpent shalt thou take in t' hand.
19 stretch out t' hand upon the waters of
8: 3 shall go up and come into t' house,
3 and upon thy people, and into t' ovens,
5 Stretch forth t' hand with thy rod over
9:14 send all my plagues upon t' heart,
22 Stretch forth t' hand toward heaven,
10:12 Stretch out t' hand over the land of
21 Stretch out t' hand toward heaven,
13: 9 be for a sign unto thee upon t' hand,
9 and for a memorial between t' eyes,
16 it shall be for a token upon t' hand,
16 and for frontlets between t' eyes:
14:16 and stretch out t' hand over the sea,
26 Stretch out t' hand over the sea, that
15: 7 in the greatness of t' excellency thou
16 by the greatness of t' arm they shall
17 them in the mountain of t' inheritance,
17: 5 thou smotest the river, take in t' hand,
20:24 offerings, thy sheep, and t' oxen:
22:30 Likewise shalt thou do with t' oxen,
23: 1 put not t' hand with the wicked to be
4 meet t' enemy's ox or his ass going
12 that t' ox and t' ass may rest, and the
22 I will be an enemy unto t' enemies,
22 and an adversary unto t' adversaries.
27 I will make all t' enemies turn their
32:13 to whom thou swarest by t' own self,
34: 9 our sin, and take us for t' inheritance.

Le 2:13 all t' offerings thou shalt offer salt.
10:15 it shall be t', and thy sons' with thee,
18:10 for theirs is t' own nakedness.
19:17 shalt not hate thy brother in t' heart:
27:23 he shall give t' estimation in that day,
27 redeem it according to t' estimation,
Nu 5:20 have lain with thee beside t' husband:
10:35 Lord, and let t' enemies be scattered;
18: 9 shall be t' of the most holy things,
11 And this is t'; the heave offering of
13 shall bring unto the Lord, shall be t';
13 every one that is clean in t' house*
14 thing devoted in Israel shall be t'.
15 it be of men or beasts, shall be t':
16 redeem, according to t' estimation,
18 And the flesh of them shall be t',
18 breast and as the right shoulder are t'.
20 I am thy part and t' inheritance
22:30 Am not I t' ass, upon which thou hast
30 ridden ever since I was t' unto this*
32 thou smitten t' ass these three times?
27:18 is the spirit, and lay t' hand upon him;
20 shalt put some of t' honour upon him,
De 2:24 I have given into t' hand Sihon the
3:21 T' eyes have seen all that the Lord
27 Pisgah, and lift up t' eyes westward,
27 eastward, and behold it with t' eyes:
4: 9 the things which t' eyes have seen,
19 lest thou lift up t' eyes unto heaven,
39 consider it in t' heart, that the Lord
6: 5 the Lord thy God with all t' heart,
6 thee this day, shall be in t' heart:
7 of them when thou sittest in t' house,
8 bind them for a sign upon t' hand,
8 shall be as frontlets between t' eyes.
19 To cast out all t' enemies from before
7:16 t' eye shall have no pity upon them:
17 say in t' heart, These nations are
19 great temptations which t' eyes saw,
24 shall deliver their kings into t' hand,
26 bring an abomination into t' house,
8: 2 thee, to know what was in t' heart,
5 Thou shalt also consider in t' heart,
14 Then t' heart be lifted up, and thou
17 And thou say in t' heart, My power
9: 4 Speak not thou in t' heart, after that
5 or for the uprightness of t' heart, dost
29 are thy people and t' inheritance,
10:21 things, which t' eyes have seen.
11:14 in thy corn, and thy wine, and t' oil.
20 them upon the door posts of t' house,
12:17 offerings, or heave offering of t' hand:
18 in all that thou puttest t' hands unto.
13: 6 thy friend, which is as t' own soul,
9 t' hand shall be first upon him to
14:23 of thy corn, of thy wine, and of t' oil,
25 and bind up the money in t' hand,
26 shalt rejoice, thou, and t' household,
28 bring forth all the tithe of t' increase
29 bless thee in all the work of t' hand
15: 3 but that which is t' with thy brother
3 with thy brother t' hand shall release,
7 thee, thou shalt not harden t' heart,
7 nor shut t' hand from thy poor brother:
8 thou shalt open t' hand wide unto
9 t' eye be evil against thy poor brother,
10 t' heart shall not be grieved when thou
10 in all that thou puttest t' hand unto.
11 open t' hand wide unto thy brother,
16 because he loveth thee and t' house,
16:10 tribute of a freewill offering of t' hand,
15 God shall bless thee in all t' increase,
15 and in all the works of t' hands,
18:21 say in t' heart, How shall we know the
19:13 T' eye shall not pity him, but thou
14 of old time have set in t' inheritance,
21 t' eye shall not pity; but life shall go
20: 1 goest out to battle against t' enemies,
13 thy God hath delivered it into t' hands,
14 thou shalt eat the spoil of t' enemies,
21:10 goest forth to war against t' enemies,
10 God hath delivered them into t' hands,
12 thou shalt bring her home to t' house,
13 shall remain in t' house, and bewail
22: 2 thou shalt bring it unto t' own house,
8 thou bring not blood upon t' house,
23: 9 host goeth forth against t' enemies,
14 and to give up t' enemies before thee;
20 thee in all that thou settest t' hand to
24 eat grapes thy fill at t' own pleasure;
25 mayest pluck the ears with t' hand;
24:19 cuttest down t' harvest in thy field,
19 bless thee in all the work of t' hands.
20 When thou beatest t' olive tree, thou
25:12 off her hand, t' eye shall not pity her.
14 have in t' house divers measures,
19 given thee rest from all t' enemies
26: 4 shall take the basket out of t' hand,
11 given unto thee, and unto t' house,
12 all the tithes of t' increase the third
16 keep and do them with all t' heart,
28: 7 The Lord shall cause t' enemies that
8 in all that thou settest t' hand unto;
12 and to bless all the work of t' hand:
20 in all that thou settest t' hand unto
25 thee to be smitten before t' enemies:
31 T' ox shall be slain before t' eyes, and
31 t' ass shall be violently taken away
31 sheep shall be given unto t' enemies,
32 t' eyes shall look, and fail with
32 there shall be no might in t' hand.
34 shalt be mad for the sight of t' eyes
40 oil; for t' olive shall cast his fruit.
48 shalt thou serve t' enemies which
53 thou shalt eat the fruit of t' own body,
53 t' enemies shall distress thee:

De 28: 55 t' enemies shall distress thee in all
57 t' enemy shall distress thee in thy
67 fear of t' heart wherewith thou shalt
67 for the sight of t' eyes which thou
29: 3 temptations which t' eyes have seen,
30: 2 with all t' heart, and with all thy soul;
4 If any of t' be driven out unto the
6 thy God will circumcise t' heart,
6 the Lord thy God with all t' heart,
7 put all these curses upon t' enemies,
9 plenteous in every work of t' hand,
10 the Lord thy God with all t' heart,
17 But if t' heart turn away, so that thou
33: 10 whole burnt sacrifice upon t' altar.
29 t' enemies shall be found liars unto
34: 4 caused thee to see it with t' eyes,
Jos 2: 3 thee, which are entered into t' house:
17 We will be blameless of this t' oath
20 then we will be quit of t' oath which
6: 2 I have given into t' hand Jericho,
7: 13 canst not stand before t' enemies,
8: 18 Ai; for I will give it into t' hand.
9: 25 And now, behold, we are in t' hand:
10: 8 I have delivered them into t' hand;
14: 9 have trodden shall be t' inheritance,*
17: 18 But the mountain shall be t'; for it is
18 and the outgoings of it shall be t':
J'g 4: 7 and I will deliver him into t' hand.
9 thou takest shall not be for t' honour;
14 hath delivered Sisera into t' hand:
5: 31 So let all t' enemies perish, O Lord:
6: 39 Let not t' anger be hot against me,
7: 7 deliver the Midianites into t' hand:
9 for I have delivered it into t' hand.
11 shall t' hands be strengthened
8: 6 Zebah and Zalmunna now in t' hand,
6 we should give bread unto t' army?
15 Zebah and Zalmunna now in t' hand,
9: 29 to Abimelech, Increase t' army, and
11: 36 vengeance for thee of t' enemies,
12: 1 burn t' house upon thee with fire.
16: 15 thee, when t' heart is not with me?
18: 19 lay t' hand upon thy mouth, and go
19: 5 Comfort t' heart with a morsel of
6 all night, and let t' heart be merry.
8 said, Comfort t' heart, I pray thee.
9 here, that t' heart may be merry;
22 forth the man that came into t' house,
20: 28 I will deliver them into t' hand.
Ru 2: 9 Let t' eyes be on the field that they do
10 Why have I found grace in t' eyes,*
11 in law since the death of t' husband:
13 spoken friendly unto t' handmaid,
13 not like unto one of t' handmaidens.
3: 9 answered, I am Ruth t' handmaid:
9 therefore thy skirt over t' handmaid;
4: 11 that is come into t' house like Rachel
15 thy life, and a nourisher of t' old age:
1Sa 1: 11 look on the affliction of t' handmaid,
11 me, and not forget t' handmaid,
11 wilt give unto t' handmaid a man
16 Count not t' handmaid for a daughter
18 Let t' handmaid find grace in thy*
2: 31 days come, that I will cut off t' arm,
31 shall not be an old man in t' house.
32 not be an old man in t' house for ever.
33 the man of t', whom I shall not cut
33 consume t' eyes, and to grieve t' heart:
33 all the increase of t' house shall die
36 every one that is left in t' house shall
9: 19 and will tell thee all that is in t' heart.
20 for t' asses that were lost three days
14: 7 unto him, Do all that is in t' heart:
19 unto the priest, Withdraw t' hand.
15: 17 When thou wast little in t' own sight,
28 and hath given it to a neighbour of t',
16: 1 fill t' horn with oil, and go, I will send
17: 28 pride, and the naughtiness of t' heart;
46 thee, and take t' head from thee;
20: 3 that I have found grace in t' eyes;
29 if I have found favour in t' eyes, let
30 the son of Jesse to t' own confusion,
21: 3 Now therefore what is under t' hand?
8 is there not here under t' hand spear
22: 14 bidding, and is honourable in t' house?
23: 4 deliver the Philistines into t' hand.
24: 4 I will deliver t' enemy into t' hand,
10 this day t' eyes have seen how that the
15 cause, and deliver me out of t' hand.
18 Lord had delivered me into t' hand,
20 Israel shall be established in t' hand.
25: 6 both to thee, and peace be to t' house,
8 the young men find favour in t' eyes:
8 whatsoever cometh to t' hand unto
24 and let t' handmaid, I pray thee,
24 speak in t' audience, and hear the
24 and hear the words of t' handmaid.
25 I t' handmaid saw not the young men
26 avenging thyself with t' own hand,
26 now let t' enemies, and they that
27 now this blessing which t' handmaid*
28 forgive the trespass of t' handmaid:
29 and the souls of t' enemies, them shall
31 my lord, then remember t' handmaid.
35 unto her, Go up in peace to t' house;
41 let t' handmaid be a servant to wash
26: 8 hath delivered t' enemy into t' hand
21 my soul was precious in t' eyes this
27: 5 If I have now found grace in t' eyes,
28: 16 from thee, and is become t' enemy?
17 hath rent the kingdom out of t' hand,
21 t' handmaid hath obeyed thy voice,
22 also unto the voice of t' handmaid,
2Sa 1: 14 not afraid to stretch forth t' hand to
25 thou wast slain in t' high places. *
3: 21 reign over all that t' heart desireth.*

2Sa 4: 8 Ish-bosheth the son of Saul t' enemy,
5: 19 deliver the Philistines into t' hand.
7: 3 the king, Go, do all that is in t' heart;
9 have cut off all t' enemies out of thy
11 thee to rest from all t' enemies.
16 t' house and thy kingdom shall be
21 according to t' own heart, hast thou
11: 10 didst thou not go down unto t' house?
12: 10 shall never depart from t' house;
11 evil against thee out of t' own house,
11 I will take thy wives before t' eyes,
13: 10 chamber, that I may eat of t' hand.
14: 7 family is risen against t' handmaid,
8 Go to t' house, and I will give charge
12 Let t' handmaid, I pray thee, speak
17 Then t' handmaid said, The word of
19 words in the mouth of t' handmaid:
16: 4 t' are all that pertained unto
17: 11 thou go to battle in t' own person.
19: 6 In that thou lovest t' enemies, and*
27 do therefore what is good in t' eyes.
28 them that did eat at t' own table.
20: 17 him, Hear the words of t' handmaid.
22: 28 t' eyes are upon the haughty, that
24: 13 flee three months before t' enemies,*
16 people, It is enough: stay now t' hand.
17 let t' hand, I pray thee, be against me,
1Ki 1: 12 that thou mayest save t' own life, and
13 O king, swear unto t' handmaid,
17 by the Lord thy God unto t' handmaid,
53 said unto him, Go to t' house.
2: 26 thee to Anathoth, unto t' own fields;
37 thy blood shall be upon t' own head.
44 wickedness which t' heart is privy to,
44 thy wickedness upon t' own head;
3: 11 nor hast asked the life of t' enemies;
20 beside me, while t' handmaid slept,
26 it be neither mine nor t', but divide it.
8: 18 it was in t' heart to build an house
18 thou didst well that it was in t' heart.
24 and hast fulfilled it with t' hand,
29 That t' eyes may be open toward this
31 the oath come before t' altar in this
51 they be thy people, and t' inheritance,
52 That t' eyes may be open unto the
53 of the earth, to be t' inheritance,
11: 22 thou seekest to go to t' own country?
12: 16 now see to t' own house, David.
13: 8 If thou wilt give me half t' house, I
18 Bring him back with thee into t' house,
14: 12 therefore, get thee to t' own house:
17: 11 thee, a morsel of bread in t' hand.
19: 10, 14 thrown down t' altars, and slain thy
20: 4 thy saying, I am t', and all that I have.
6 they shall search t' house, and the
6 that whatsoever is pleasant in t' eyes,
13 I will deliver it into t' hand this day;
28 all this great multitude into t' hand,
21: 7 eat bread, and let t' heart be merry:
19 shall dogs lick thy blood, even t'. 859
22 And will make t' house like the house
22: 34 Turn t' hand, and carry me out of the
2Ki 4: 2 T' handmaid hath not any thing in
16 of God, do not lie unto t' handmaid.
29 and take my staff in t' hand, and go
7: 2, 19 thou shalt see it with t' eyes, but
8: 1 Arise, and go thou and t' household,
8 Take a present in t' hand, and go,
9: 1 and take this box of oil in t' hand,
10: 5 do thou that which is good in t' eyes.
15 Is t' heart right, as my heart is with
13: 16 of Israel, Put t' hand upon the bow.
14: 10 and t' heart hath lifted thee up:
19: 16 Lord, bow down t' ear, and hear:
16 open, Lord, t' eyes, and see: and hear
22 voice, and lifted up t' eyes on high?
20: 1 Set t' house in order; for thou shalt
15 said, What have they seen in t' house?
17 days come, that all that is in t' house,
22: 19 Because t' heart was tender, and thou
20 t' eyes shall not see all the evil which
1Ch 4: 10 and that t' hand might be with me,
12: 18 T' are we, David, and on thy side,
18 unto thee, and peace be to t' helpers;
14: 10 for I will deliver them into t' hand.
17: 2 unto David, Do all that is in t' heart;
8 cut off all t' enemies from before thee,
10 Moreover I will subdue all t' enemies.
17 was a small thing in t' eyes, O God;
19 according to t' own heart, hast thou
22 Israel didst thou make t' own people
21: 12 sword of t' enemies overtaketh thee;
15 It is enough, stay now t' hand.
17 let t' hand, I pray thee, O Lord my
24 not take that which is t' for the Lord,
29: 11 T', O Lord, is the greatness, and the
11 is in the heaven and in the earth is t';
11 t' is the kingdom, O Lord, and thou
12 and in t' hand is power and might;
12 and in t' hand it is to make great, and
14 and of t' own have we given thee.
16 build thee an house for t' holy name
16 cometh of t' hand, and is all t' own.
2Ch 1: 11 Because this was in t' heart, and thou
11 or honour, nor the life of t' enemies,*
6: 8 as it was in t' heart to build an house
8 didst well in that it was in t' heart:
15 and hast fulfilled it with t' hand, as it
20 That t' eyes may be open upon this
22 the oath come before t' altar in this
40 Now, my God, let,...t' eyes be open,
40 let t' ears be attent unto the prayer
42 turn not away the face of t' anointed:
9: 5 I heard in mine own land of t' acts,
10: 16 and now, David, see to t' own house.
16: 7 king of Syria escaped out of t' hand.

2Ch 16: 8 Lord, he delivered them into t' hand.
18: 33 Turn t' hand, that thou mayest carry
19: 3 hast prepared t' heart to seek God.
20: 6 in t' hand is there not power and
25: 15 their own people out of t' hand?
19 and t' heart lifteth thee up to boast:
19 why shouldest thou meddle to t' hurt,*
26: 18 neither shall it be for t' honour from
34: 27 Because t' heart was tender, and thou
28 neither shall t' eyes see all the evil
Ezr 7: 14 law of thy God which is in t' hand;
25 wisdom of thy God, that is in t' hand,
Ne 1: 6 Let t' ear now be attentive, and
6 and t' eyes open, that thou mayest
11 let now t' ear be attentive to the prayer
6: 8 thou feignest them out of t' own heart.
Job 1: 11 But put forth t' hand now, and touch
12 upon himself put not forth t' hand.
2: 5 But put forth t' hand now, and touch
6 he is in t' hand; but save his life.
9 Dost thou still retain t' integrity?
5: 25 t' offspring as the grass of the earth.
7: 8 t' eyes are upon me, and I am not.
17 thou shouldest set t' heart upon him?*
10: 3 shouldest despise the work of t' hands,
7 none that can deliver out of t' hand.
8 T' hands have made me and
13 these things hast thou hid in t' heart:
17 increasest t' indignation upon me;
11: 4 is pure, and I am clean in t' eyes.
6 of thee less than t' iniquity deserveth.
13 If thou prepare t' heart, and stretch
13 and stretch out t' hands toward him;
14 If iniquity be in t' hand, put it far
17 And t' age shall be clearer than the*
13: 21 Withdraw t' hand far from me: and
24 thy face, and holdest me for t' enemy?
14: 3 thou open t' eyes upon such an one,
15 have a desire to the work of t' hands.
15: 5 For thy mouth uttereth t' iniquity,
6 T' own mouth condemneth thee, and
6 yea, t' own lips testify against thee.
12 Why doth t' heart carry thee away?
22: 5 great? and t' iniquities infinite?
22 and lay up his words in t' heart.
30 delivered by the pureness of t' hands.
35: 7 him? or what receiveth he of t' hand?
40: 14 that t' own right hand can save thee.
41: 8 Lay t' hand upon him, remember the
Ps 2: 8 thee the heathen for t' inheritance,
6: 1 O Lord, rebuke me not in t' anger,
7: 6 Arise, O Lord, in t' anger, lift up
8: 2 strength because of t' enemies,
10: 12 O God, lift up t' hand: forget not the
17 heart, thou wilt cause t' ear to near:
16: 10 wilt thou suffer t' Holy One to see
17: 2 let t' eyes behold the things that are
6 incline t' ear unto me, and hear my
20: 4 Grant thee according to t' own heart,*
21: 8 T' hand shall find out all t' enemies:
9 as a fiery oven in the time of t' anger:
12 make ready t' arrows upon thy strings*
13 thou exalted, Lord, in t' own strength:*
26: 6 so will I compass t' altar, O Lord:
8 the place where t' honour dwelleth.*
27: 14 and he shall strengthen t' heart:
28: 9 thy people, and bless t' inheritance:
31: 2 Bow down t' ear to me; deliver me
5 Into t' hand I commit my spirit: thou
22 haste, I am cut off from before t' eyes:
37: 4 he shall give thee the desire of t' heart,
38: 2 For t' arrows stick fast in me, and thy
3 in my flesh because of t' anger;
39: 10 I am consumed by the blow of t' hand.
44: 3 t' arm,...the light of thy countenance,
45: 5 T' arrows are sharp in the heart of the
10 and consider, and incline t' ear;
10 forget also t' own people, and thy
50: 20 thou slanderest t' own mother's son.
21 and set them in order before t' eyes.
51: 19 shall they offer bullocks upon t' altar.
56: 7 in t' anger cast down the people, O*
66: 3 shall t' enemies submit themselves
68: 9 thou didst confirm t' inheritance,
23 be dipped in the blood of t' enemies,*
69: 9 the zeal of t' house hath eaten me up;
24 Pour out t' indignation upon them,
71: 2 incline t' ear unto me, and save me.
16 of thy righteousness, even of t' only.
74: 1 why doth t' anger smoke against the
2 rod of t' inheritance, which thou hast
4 T' enemies roar in the midst of thy
16 The day is t', the night also is t': thou
22 Arise, O God, plead t' own cause:
23 Forget not the voice of t' enemies: the
77: 15 hast with t' arm redeemed thy people,
17 a sound: t' arrows also went abroad.
79: 1 heathen are come into t' inheritance;
83: 2 For, lo, t' enemies make a tumult:
84: 3 she may lay her young, even t' altars,
9 and look upon the face of t' anointed.
85: 3 thyself from the fierceness of t' anger.
4 and cause t' anger toward us to cease.
5 wilt thou draw out t' anger to all
86: 1 Bow down t' ear, O Lord, hear me: for
16 and save the son of t' handmaid.
88: 2 before thee: incline t' ear unto my cry;
89: 10 hast scattered t' enemies with thy
11 the heavens are t', the earth also is t':
38 thou hast been wroth with t' anointed
51 Wherewith t' enemies...reproached, O
51 reproached the footsteps of t' anointed
90: 7 For we are consumed by t' anger, and
11 Who knoweth the power of t' anger?
91: 8 Only with t' eyes shalt thou behold
92: 9 For, lo, t' enemies, O Lord, for, lo,

Ps 92: 9 t' enemies shall perish; all the
93: 5 holiness becometh t' house, O Lord,
94: 5 people, O Lord, and afflict t' heritage.
102: 2 am in trouble; incline t' ear unto me:
10 Because of t' indignation and thy
103: 3 Who forgiveth all t' iniquities; who
104: 28 thou openest t' hand, they are filled
106: 5 that I may glory with t' inheritance.
110: 1 until I make t' enemies thy footstool.
2 rule thou in the midst of t' enemies.
116: 16 servant, and the son of t' handmaid:
119: 91 this day according to t' ordinances:
94 I am t', save me; for I have sought
173 Let t' hand help me; for I have chosen
128: 2 thou shalt eat the labour of t' hands:
3 a fruitful vine by the side of t' house:
130: 2 let t' ears be attentive to the voice of
132: 10 turn not away the face of t' anointed.
138: 7 thou shalt stretch forth t' hand against
8 forsake not the works of t' own hands.
139: 5 and before, and laid t' hand upon me.
16 T' eyes did see my substance, yet
20 and t' enemies take thy name in vain.
144: 6 shoot out t' arrows, and destroy them.
7 Send t' hand from above; rid me, and
145: 16 Thou openest t' hand, and satisfiest
Pr 2: 2 that thou incline t' ear unto wisdom,
2 and apply t' heart to understanding;
10 When wisdom entereth into t' heart,
3: 1 let t' heart keep my commandments:
3 write them upon the table of t' heart:
5 Trust in the Lord with all t' heart;
5 lean not unto t' own understanding.
7 Be not wise in t' own eyes: fear the
9 with the firstfruits of all t' increase:
21 son, let not them depart from t' eyes:
27 it is in the power of t' hand to do it.
4: 4 unto me, Let t' heart retain my words:
9 give to t' head an ornament of grace:
20 words; incline t' ear unto my sayings.
21 Let them not depart from t' eyes;
21 keep them in the midst of t' heart.
25 Let t' eyes look right on, and let
25 let t' eyelids look straight before thee.
5: 1 and bow t' ear to my understanding:
9 Lest thou give t' honour unto others,
15 Drink waters out of t' own cistern, and
15 and running waters out of t' own well.
17 Let them be only t' own, and not *
6: 4 Give not sleep to t' eyes, nor slumber
4 eyes, nor slumber to t' eyelids.
21 Bind them continually upon t' heart,
25 Lust not after her beauty in t' heart;
7: 2 live; and my law as the apple of t' eye.
3 write them upon the table of t' heart.
25 Let not t' heart decline to her ways, go
20: 13 open t' eyes, and thou shalt be satisfied
22: 17 Bow down t' ear, and hear the words
17 and apply t' heart unto my knowledge.
23: 4 to be rich: cease from t' own wisdom.
5 thou set t' eyes upon that which is not?
12 Apply t' heart unto instruction, and
12 and t' ears to the words of knowledge.
15 if t' heart be wise, my heart shall
17 Let not t' heart envy sinners: but be
18 and t' expectation shall not be cut off.*
19 be wise, and guide t' heart in the way.
26 My son, give me t' heart, and let
26 heart, and let t' eyes observe my ways.
33 T' eyes shall behold strange women,
33 t' heart shall utter perverse things.
24: 17 Rejoice not when t' enemy falleth, and
17 let not t' heart be glad when he
27 field; and afterwards build t' house.
25: 7 of the prince whom t' eyes have seen.
10 shame, and t' infamy turn not away.
21 If t' enemy be hungry, give him bread
27: 2 praise thee, and not t' own mouth;
2 a stranger, and not t' own lips.
10 T' own friend, and thy father's friend,
30: 32 evil, lay t' hand upon thy mouth.
Ec 5: 2 not t' heart be hasty to utter any thing
6 and destroy the work of t' hands?
7: 18 also from this withdraw not t' hand:
22 oftentimes also t' own heart knoweth
11: 6 in the evening withhold not t' hand:
9 and walk in the ways of t' heart, and
9 and in the sight of t' eyes: but know
Ca 4: 9 ravished my heart with one of t' eyes,
10 smell of t' ointments than all spices!
6: 5 Turn away t' eyes from me, for they
7: 4 t' eyes like the fishpools in Heshbon,
5 T' head upon thee is like Carmel, and
5 and the hair of t' head like purple;
8: 6 Set me as a seal upon t' heart, as a seal
6 as a seal upon t' arm; for love is
Isa 6: 7 t' iniquity is taken away, and thy sin
12: 1 t' anger is turned away, and thou
14: 13 For thou hast said in t' heart, I will
26: 11 fire of t' enemies shall devour them.
30: 20 but t' eyes shall see thy teachers:
21 t' ears shall hear a word behind thee,
33: 17 T' eyes shall see the king in...beauty:
18 T' heart shall meditate terror. Where
20 t' eyes shall see Jerusalem a quiet
37: 17 Incline t' ear, O Lord, and hear; open
17 hear; open t' eyes, O Lord, and see:
23 thy voice, and lifted up t' eyes on high?
38: 1 Set t' house in order: for thou shalt
39: 4 he, What have they seen in t' house?
6 days come, that all that is in t' house,
42: 6 will hold t' hand, and will keep thee,
43: 24 hast wearied me with t' iniquities.
44: 3 and my blessing upon t' offspring:
45: 14 over unto thee, and they shall be t':
47: 6 and given them into t' hand:
Isa 47: 8 that sayest in t' heart, I am, and none
9 great abundance of t' enchantments.
10 and thou hast said in t' heart, I am,
12 Stand now with t' enchantments, and
48: 8 that time that t' ear was not opened:
49: 18 Lift up t' eyes round about, and
20 the other, shall say again in t' ears,
21 Then shalt thou say in t' heart, Who
51: 22 have taken out of t' hand the cup of
54: 2 forth the curtains of t' habitations:
5 For thy Maker is t' husband; the Lord
57: 10 thou hast found the life of t' hand;*
58: 7 thou hide not thyself from t' own flesh?
8 t' health shall spring forth speedily:*
13 honour him, not doing t' own ways,
13 nor finding t' own pleasure, nor
13 pleasure, nor speaking t' own words:
60: 4 Lift up t' eyes round about, and see:
5 t' heart shall fear, and be enlarged;
17 peace, and t' exactors righteousness.
20 the Lord shall be t' everlasting light,
62: 8 thy corn to be meat for t' enemies;
63: 2 Wherefore art thou red in t' apparel,
17 sake, the tribes of t' inheritance.
19 We art t': thou never barest rule*
64: 2 thy name known to t' adversaries,
Jer 2: 2 of thy youth, the love of t' espousals,
19 T' own wickedness shall correct thee,
22 yet t' iniquity is marked before me,
37 from him, and t' hands upon t' head:
3: 2 Lift up t' eyes unto the high places,
13 Only acknowledge t' iniquity, that
4: 1 put away t' abominations out of my
14 wash t' heart from wickedness,
18 because it reacheth unto t' heart.
5: 3 Lord, are not t' eyes upon the truth?
17 shall eat up t' harvest, and thy bread,
17 shall eat up thy flocks and t' herds:
6: 9 turn back t' hand as a grapegatherer
7: 29 Cut off t' hair, O Jerusalem, and cast
9: 6 T' habitation is in the midst of
10: 24 not in t' anger, lest thou bring me to
13: 22 And if thou say in t' heart, Wherefore
22 For the greatness of t' iniquity are thy
27 I have seen t' adulteries, and thy
27 and t' abominations on the hills in
15: 14 to pass with t' enemies into a land
17: 4 discontinue from t' heritage that I
4 I will cause thee to serve t' enemies in
18: 23 thus with them in the time of t' anger.
20: 4 enemies, and t' eyes shall behold it:
6 Pashur, and all that dwell in t' house
22: 17 But t' eyes and t' heart are not but for
25: 28 refuse to take the cup at t' hand to
28: 7 now this word that I speak in t' ears,
30: 14 one, for the multitude of t' iniquity;
15 Why criest thou for t' affliction? thy*
15 for the multitude of t' iniquity:
16 all t' adversaries, every one of them,
31: 16 from weeping, and t' eyes from tears:
17 And there is hope in t' end, saith the*
21 set t' heart toward the highway, even
32: 7 Hanameel the son of Shallum t' uncle
7 the right of redemption is t' to buy it.
8 for the right of inheritance is t', and
8 the redemption is t'; buy it for thyself.
19 for t' eyes are open upon all the ways*
34: 3 t' eyes shall behold the eyes of the
36: 14 Take in t' hand the roll wherein thou
38: 12 rotten rags under t' armholes under
17 fire; and thou shalt live, and t' house:
40: 4 the chains which were upon t' hand.
42: 2 few of many, as t' eyes do behold us:)
43: 9 Take great stones in t' hand, and
49: 16 and the pride of t' heart, O thou that
51: 13 abundant in treasures, t' end is come,
La 2: 14 they have not discovered t' iniquity,
16 t' enemies have opened their mouth
17 caused t' enemy to rejoice over thee,*
17 set up the horn of t' adversaries.
18 rest; let not the apple of t' eye cease.
19 pour out t' heart like water before
21 hast slain them in the day of t' anger;
3: 56 hide not t' ear at my breathing, at my
4: 22 The punishment of t' iniquity is
22 he will visit t' iniquity, O daughter of
Eze 3: 10 speak unto thee receive in t' heart,
10 heart, and hear with t' ears.
18, 20 his blood will I require at t' hand.
24 me, Go, shut thyself within t' house.
4: 7 and t' arm shall be uncovered,
5: 1 and cause it to pass upon t' head and
9 like, because of all t' abominations.
11 and with all t' abominations, therefore
6: 11 Smite with t' hand, and stamp with
7: 3 upon thee all t' abominations.
4 t' abominations shall be in the midst
8 thee for all t' abominations.
9 thy ways and t' abominations that are
8: 5 lift up t' eyes now the way toward the
10: 2 fill t' hands with coals of fire between
16: 6 saw thee polluted in t' own blood, I*
7 are fashioned, and t' hair is grown,
12 thy forehead, and earrings in t' ears,
12 and a beautiful crown upon t' head.
15 But thou didst trust in t' own beauty,
22 t' abominations and thy whoredoms
27 and have diminished t' ordinary food,
30 How weak is t' heart, saith the Lord
31 buildest t' eminent place in the head
31 makest t' high place in every street;*
39 shall throw down t' eminent place,
41 they shall burn t' houses with fire, and
43 will recompense thy way upon t' head,
43 lewdness above all t' abominations.
46 t' elder sister is Samaria, she and her
Eze 16: 51 multiplied t' abominations more than
51 thy sisters in all t' abominations
52 bear t' own shame for thy sins that
54 That thou mayest bear t' own shame,
58 thy lewdness and t' abominations,
61 thy sisters, t' elder and thy younger:
21: 14 prophesy, and smite t' hands together,
22: 4 and hast defiled thyself in t' idols
14 Can t' heart endure, or can
14 can t' hands be strong, in the days
16 shalt take t' inheritance in thyself*
23: 25 shall take away thy nose and t' ears;
27 shalt not lift up t' eyes unto them,
31 will I give her cup into t' hand.
34 thereof, and pluck off t' own breasts:*
24: 16 the desire of t' eyes with a stroke:
17 bind the tire of t' head upon thee,*
26 to cause thee to hear it with t' ears?
25: 6 Because thou hast clapped t' hands,
27: 6 of Bashan have they made t' oars;
10 of Lud and of Phut were in t' army,
11 The men of Arvad with t' army were
15 isles were the merchandise of t' hand:
28: 2 Because t' heart is lifted up, and thou
2 thou set t' heart as the heart of God:
4 thy wisdom and with t' understanding
5 t' heart is lifted up because of thy
6 hast set t' heart as the heart of God;
17 T' heart was lifted up because of thy
18 by the multitude of t' iniquities, by
33: 8 but his blood will I require at t' hand.
35: 11 I will even do according to t' anger,
11 according to t' envy which thou hast
37: 17 and they shall become one in t' hand.
20 shall be in t' hand before their eyes.
38: 4 will bring thee forth, and all t' army,
12 turn t' hand upon the desolate places
39: 3 t' arrows to fall out of thy right hand.
40: 4 me, Son of man, behold with t' eyes,
4 eyes, and hear with t' ears,
4 set t' heart upon all that I shall shew
44: 5 mark well, and behold with t' eyes,
5 hear with t' ears all that I say unto
30 cause the blessing to rest in t' house.
Da 2: 38 the heaven hath he given into t' hand,
3: 17 and he will deliver us out of t' hand, O
4: 19 interpretation thereof to t' enemies.
27 t' iniquities by shewing mercy to the
5: 22 hast not humbled t' heart, though
9: 16 t' anger and thy fury be turned away
18 O my God, incline t' ear, and hear;
18 open t' eyes, and behold our
19 defer not, for t' own sake, O my God:
10: 12 thou didst set t' heart to understand,
Ho 9: 7 mad, for the multitude of t' iniquity,
13: 9 thyself; but in me is t' help. *
14: 1 for thou hast fallen by t' iniquity.
Joe 2: 17 and give not t' heritage to reproach,
Ob 3 The pride of t' heart hath deceived
15 reward shall return upon t' own head.
Jon 1: 8 What is t' occupation? and whence
2: 7 came in unto thee, into t' holy temple.
Mic 4: 10 thee from the hand of t' enemies.
13 of Zion: for I will make t' horn iron,
5: 9 T' hand sha'l be lifted up upon
9 shall be lifted up upon t' adversaries,
9 and all t' enemies shall be cut off.
12 will cut off witchcrafts out of t' hand;
13 more worship the work of t' hands.
7: 14 the flock of t' heritage, which dwell
Na 3: 13 be set wide open unto t' enemies:
Hab 3: 8 was t' anger against the rivers? was
8 that thou didst ride upon t' horses
11 at the light of t' arrows they went,
13 even for salvation with t' anointed;
15 walk through the sea with t' horses,
Zep 3: 15 judgments, he hath cast out t' enemy:
16 and to Zion, Let not t' hands be slack.
Zec 3: 4 I have caused t' iniquity to pass from
5: 5 Lift up now t' eyes, and see what is
13: 6 What are these wounds in t' hands?
M't 5: 25 Agree with t' adversary quickly, 4675
33 perform unto the Lord t' oaths: "
43 thy neighbour, and hate t' enemy. "
6: 2 Therefore when thou doest t' alms,*
4 That t' alms may be in secret: 4675
13 t' is the kingdom, and the power,* "
17 when thou fastest, anoint t' head,* "
22 if therefore t' eye be single, thy "
23 But if t' eye be evil, thy whole body "
7: 3 not the beam that is in t' own eye? 4674
4 me pull out the mote out of t' eye; 4675
4 behold, a beam is in t' own eye? "
5 cast out the beam out of t' own eye; "
9: 6 up thy bed, and go unto t' house. * "
12: 13 to the man, Stretch forth t' hand. "
18: 9 if t' eye offend thee, pluck it out, "
20: 14 Take that t' is, and go thy way: I 4674
15 Is t' eye evil, because I am good? 4675
22: 44 till I make t' enemies thy footstool? "
25: 25 lo, there thou hast that is t'. 4674
M'r 2: 11 bed, and go thy way into t' house.* 4675
3: 5 the man, Stretch forth t' hand. * "
9: 47 if t' eye offend thee, pluck it out: "
12: 36 till I make t' enemies thy footstool. "
Lu 4: 7 wilt worship me, all shall be t'. "
5: 24 up thy couch, and go into t' house.* "
33 Pharisees; but t' eat and drink? 4674
6: 41 not the beam that is in t' own eye? 2398
42 pull out the mote that is in t' eye, 4675
42 not the beam that is in t' own eye? "
42 out first the beam out of t' own eye. "
7: 44 I entered into t' house, thou gavest "
8: 39 Return to t' own house, and shew* "
11: 34 therefore when t' eye is single, thy "
34 but when t' eye is evil, thy body also "

Lu 12:19 take t' ease, eat, drink, and be merry.
58 When thou goest with t' adversary 4675
13:12 thou art loosed from t' infirmity.
15:31 with me, and all that I have is t'. 4674
19:22 Out of t' own mouth will I judge 4675
42 but now they are hid from t' eyes. "
43 that t' enemies shall cast a trench "
20:43 I make t' enemies thy footstool. "
22:42 not my will, but t', be done. 4674
Joh 2:17 zeal of t' house hath eaten me up. 4675
8:10 where are those t' accusers? * "
9:10 unto him, How were t' eyes opened? "
17 of him, that he hath opened t' eyes? "
26 he to thee? how opened he t' eyes? "
17:5 glorify thou me with t' own self 4572
6 t' they were, and thou gavest them 4671
9 thou hast given me; for they are t'. "
10 And all mine are t', and 4674
10 and t' are mine; and I am 3588,
11 keep through t' own name those *4675
18:35 T' own nation and the chief 4674
Ac 2:27 wilt thou suffer t' Holy One to see 4675
4:30 By stretching forth t' hand to heal; * "
5:3 Satan filled t' heart to lie to the "
4 it remained, was it not t' own? 4671
4 was it not in t' own power? 3588, 4674
4 conceived this thing in t' heart? *4675
8:22 the thought of t' heart may be *4671
37 If thou believest with all t' heart, *3588
10:4 t' alms are come up for a memorial * "
31 t' alms are had in remembrance 4675
13:35 shalt not suffer t' Holy One to see * "
23:35 when t' accusers are also come. "
Ro 10:6 Say not in t' heart, Who shall * "
9 shalt believe in t' heart that God * "
11:3 and digged down t' altars; "
12:20 Therefore if t' enemy hunger, feed "
1Co 10:29 I say, not t' own, but of the other: 1438
1Ti 5:23 sake and t' often infirmities. 4675
Ph'm 19 unto me even t' own self besides. 4572
Heb 1:10 heavens are the works of t' hands: *4675
13 I make t' enemies thy footstool? "
Re 3:18 and anoint t' eyes with eyesalve, "

thing See also ANYTHING; NOTHING; SOMETHING; THINGS.
Ge 1:24 and creeping t', and beast of the earth
25 every t' that creepeth upon the earth
26 over every creeping t' that creepeth
28 every living t' that moveth upon the
30 every t' that creepeth upon the earth,
31 God saw every t' that he had made,
6:7 man, and beast, and the creeping t',
17 every t' that is in the earth shall die.
19 And of every living t' of all flesh, two
20 every creeping t' of the earth after his
7:8 every t' that creepeth upon the earth,
14, 21 every creeping t' that creepeth
8:1 and every living t', and all the cattle
17 Bring forth with thee every living t'
17 every creeping t' that creepeth upon
19 Every beast, every creeping t', and
9:3 Every moving t' that liveth shall be
18:14 Is any t' too hard for the Lord? 1697
19:21 thee concerning this t' also, "
20:10 thou, that thou hast done this t'? "
21:11 And the t' was very grievous in "
26 I wot not who hath done this t': "
22:16 for because thou hast done this t', "
24:50 The t' proceedeth from the Lord: "
30:31 Thou shalt not give me any t': * "
31 if thou wilt do this t' for me, I will "
34:7 which t' ought not to be done. 3651
14 We cannot do this t', to give our 1697
19 man deferred not to do the t', "
38:10 the t' which he did displeased the
39:9 hath he kept back any t' from me 3972
23 looked not to any t' that was under "
41:28 This is the t' which I have spoken 1697
32 because the t' is established by God, "
37 t' was good in the eyes of Pharaoh, "
44:7 should do according to this t': "
Ex 1:18 Why have ye done this t', and have "
2:14 and said, Surely this t' is known. "
15 Now when Pharaoh heard this t', "
9:5 the Lord shall do this t' in the land. "
6 the Lord did that t' on the morrow, "
10:15 remained not any green t' in the trees,
12:24 observe this t' for an ordinance 1697
16:14 there lay a small round t', as small as
16, 32 This is the t' which the Lord 1697
18:11 in the t' wherein they dealt proudly "
14 t' that thou doest to the people? "
17 The t' that thou doest is not good. "
18 for this t' is too heavy for thee; "
23 If thou shalt do this t', and God "
20:4 or any likeness of any t' that is in*
17 ass, nor any t' that is thy neighbour's.
22:9 raiment, or for any manner of lost t',
15 if it be an hired t', it came for his
29:1 this is the t' that thou shalt do 1697
33:17 this t' also that thou hast spoken: "
34:10 is a terrible t' that I will do with thee.
35:4 the t' which the Lord commanded, 1697
Le 2:3, 10 it is a t' most holy of the offerings
4:13 the t' be hid from the eyes of the 1697
5:2 Or if a soul touch any unclean t',
5 confess that he hath sinned in that t':*
16 harm that he hath done in the holy t',
6:2 or in a t' taken away by violence, or *
4 the t' which he hath deceitfully gotten,
4 to keep, or the lost t' which he found,
7 forgiven him for any t' of all that he*
7:19 flesh that toucheth any unclean t'
21 soul that shall touch any unclean t',
21 beast, or any abominable unclean t',*
Le 8:5 the t' which the Lord commanded 1697
9:6 the t' which the Lord commanded "
11:10 living t' which is in the waters, *5315
21 may ye eat of every flying creeping t'*
35 every t' whereupon any part of their
41 every creeping t' that creepeth upon
43 abominable with any creeping t' that
44 creeping t' that creepeth upon the
12:4 she shall touch no hallowed t', nor
13:48 a skin, or in any t' made of skin; 4399
49 or in the woof, or in any t' of skin; 3627
52 linen, or any t' of skin, wherein the "
53 or in the woof, or in any t' of skin; "
54 wash the t' wherein the plague is, "
57 or in the woof, or in any t' of skin; 3627
58 woof, or whatsoever t' of skin it be, "
59 warp, or woof, or any t' of skins, "
15:4 and every t', whereon he sitteth, "
6 he that sitteth on any t' whereon "
10 toucheth any t' that was under him
20 And every t' that she lieth upon in
20 every t' also that she sitteth upon
22 toucheth any t' that she sat upon 3627
23 or on any t' whereon she sitteth, "
17:2 This is the t' which the Lord hath 1697
19:8 hath profaned the hallowed t' of the
26 Ye shall not eat any t' with the blood:
20:17 it is a wicked t'; and they shall be cut
21 his brother's wife, it is an unclean t':*
25 any manner of living t' that creepeth
21:18 hath a flat nose, or any t' superfluous,
22:4 whoso toucheth any t' that is unclean
5 whosoever toucheth any creeping t',
10 shall no stranger eat of the holy t':
10 servant, shall not eat of the holy t'.
14 if a man eat of the holy t' unwittingly,
14 give it unto the priest with the holy t'.
23 lamb that hath any t' superfluous or
23:37 offerings, every t' upon his day: *1697
27:23 that day, as a holy t' unto the Lord.
28 no devoted t', that a man shall devote
28 every devoted t' is most holy unto the
Nu 4:15 but they shall not touch any holy t',*
16:9 Seemeth it but a small t' unto you,
13 it a small t' that thou hast brought us
30 But if the Lord make a new t', and the
17:13 cometh any t' near unto the tabernacle*
18:7 office for every t' of the altar, 1697
14 t' devoted in Israel shall be thine.
15 t' that openeth the matrix in all flesh,
20:19 without doing any t' else, go 1697
22:38 now any power at all to say any t'? 3972
30:1 t'...the Lord hath commanded. 1697
31:23 Every t' that may abide the fire, "
32:20 If ye will do this t', if ye will go "
35:22 him any t' without laying of wait, 3627
36:6 t' which the Lord doth command 1697
De 1:14 t' which thou hast spoken is good "
32 this t' ye did not believe the Lord "
4:18 The likeness of any t' that creepeth on
23, 25 image, or the likeness of any t',
32 there hath been any such t' as this
32 been any such...as this great t' is, 1697
5:8 likeness of any t' that is in heaven*
21 or any t' that is thy neighbour's.
7:26 house, lest thou be a cursed t' like it:
26 utterly abhor it; for it is a cursed t'.
8:9 thou shalt not lack any t' in it;
12:32 What t' soever I command you, 1697
13:14 if it be truth, and the t' certain, "
17 of the cursed t' to thine hand:
14:3 Thou shalt not eat any abominable t'.
19 every creeping t' that flieth is unclean*
21 not eat of any t' that dieth of itself:
15:10 for this t' the Lord thy God shall 1697
15 I command thee this t' to day. "
16:4 shall there any t' of the flesh,
17:4 it be true, and the t' certain, 1697
5 have committed that wicked t', "
18:22 if the t' follow not, nor come to pass, "
22 t' which the Lord hath not spoken, "
22:3 and with all lost t' of thy brother's,
20 But if this t' be true, and the tokens 1697
23:9 keep thee from every wicked t'. "
14 that he see no unclean t' in thee, "
19 usury of any t' that is lent upon "
24:10 dost lend thy brother any t', *4859
18, 22 I command thee to do this t'. 1697
26:11 thou shalt rejoice in every good t'*
31:13 children, which have not known any t',*
32:47 For it is not a vain t' for you; 1697
47 through this t' ye shall prolong "
Jos 4:10 until every t' was finished that the "
6:18 keep yourselves from the accursed t',
18 accursed, when ye take the accursed t',
7:1 a trespass in the accursed t':
1 of Judah, took of the accursed t':
11 have even taken of the accursed t',
13 is an accursed t' in the midst of thee,
13 away the cursed t' from among you.
15 he that is taken with the accursed t'
9:24 of you, and have done this t'. 1697
14:6 knowest the t' that the Lord said "
21:45 failed not ought of any good t' which "
22:20 commit a trespass in the accursed t',
24 rather done it for fear of this t', *1697
33 the t' pleased the children of Israel; "
23:14 not one t' hath failed of all the good "
14 and not one t' hath failed thereof. "
J'g 6:29 another, Who hath done this t'? "
29 the son of Joash hath done this t'. "
8:27 which t' became a snare unto Gideon,*
11:25 art thou any t' better than Balak
37 father, Let this t' be done for me: 1697
13:4 drink, and eat not any unclean t':
7 drink, neither eat any unclean t':
J'g 13:14 not eat of any t' that cometh from the
14 strong drink, nor eat any unclean t':
18:7 put them to shame in any t'; 1697
10 where there is no want of any t' "
19:19 servants: there is no want of any t'. "
24 unto this man do not so vile a t'. * "
20:9 the t' which we will do to Gibeah; "
21:11 And this is the t' that ye shall do, "
Ru 3:18 he have finished the t' this day. "
1Sa 3:11 Behold, I will do a t' in Israel, at "
17 the t' that the Lord hath said unto "
17 if thou hide any t' from me of all "
4:7 hath not been such a t' heretofore.
8:6 But the t' displeased Samuel, 1697
12:16 stand and see this great t', "
14:12 up to us, and we will shew you a t'. "
15:9 every t' that was vile and refuse, 4399
18:20 told Saul, and the t' pleased him. 1697
23 a light t' to be the king's son in law,
20:2 my father hide this t' from me? 1697
26 Saul spake not any t' that day:
39 But the lad knew not any t': only
21:2 man know any t' of the business 1697
22:15 impute any t' unto his servant, "
24:6 should do this t' unto my master, "
25:15 hurt, neither missed we any t',
26:16 t' is not good that thou hast done. 1697
28:10 happen to thee for this t'. "
18 hath the Lord done this t' unto thee "
30:19 any t' that they had taken to them:
2Sa 2:6 because ye have done this t'. 1697
3:13 but one t' I require of thee, that is, "
7:19 yet a small t' in thy sight, O Lord
11:11 soul liveth, I will not do this t'. 1697
25 Let not this t' displease thee, for "
27 But the t' that David had done "
12:5 the man that hath done this t' shall*
6 fourfold, because he did this t', 1697
12 I will do this t' before all Israel, "
21 What t' is this that thou hast done? "
13:2 hard for him to do any t' to her.
12 for no such t' ought to be done in 3651
20 thy brother; regard not this t'. 1697
33 the king take the t' to his heart, "
14:13 thought such a t' against the people of
13 speak this t' as one that is faulty, *1697
15 speak of this t' unto my lord the * "
18 thee, the t' that I shall ask thee. "
20 hath thy servant Joab done this t': "
21 Behold now, I have done this t'. "
15:11 simplicity, and they knew not any t'. "
35 that what t' soever thou shalt hear "
36 send unto me every t' that ye can "
17:19 thereon; and the t' was not known. * "
24:3 my lord the king delight in this t'? "
1Ki 1:27 Is this t' done by my lord the king, "
3:10 that Solomon had asked this t'. "
11 Because thou hast asked this t', "
10:3 was not any t' hid from the king, "
11:10 commanded him concerning this t', "
12:24 to his house; for this t' is from me. "
30 And this t' became a sin: for the "
13:33 After this t' Jeroboam returned not "
34 this t' became sin unto the house of "
14:5 wife of Jeroboam cometh to ask a t' * "
13 there is found some good t' toward "
15:5 turned not aside from any t' that he "
16:31 had been a light t' for him to walk in
20:9 I will do: but this t' I may not do. 1697
24 And do this t', Take the kings away, "
33 whether any t' would come from him,*
2Ki 2:10 And he said, Thou hast asked a hard t':
3:18 but a light t' in the sight of the Lord:
4:2 Thine handmaid hath not any t' in the
5:13 had bid thee do some great t', 1697
18 this t' the Lord pardon thy servant, "
18 Lord pardon thy servant in this t'. "
6:11 Syria was sore troubled for this t'; "
7:2 windows in heaven, might this t' be? "
19 in heaven, might such a t' be?
8:9 even of every good t' of Damascus,
13 that he should do this great t'? 1697
11:5 This is the t' that ye shall do; A "
17:12 unto them, Ye shall not do this t'. "
20:9 will do the t' that he hath spoken:
10 is a light t' for the shadow to go down
1Ch 2:7 who transgressed in the t' accursed.
11:19 forbid it me, that I should do this t':*
13:4 t' was right in the eyes of all the 1697
17:17 yet this was a small t' in thine eyes,
23 let the t' that thou hast spoken *1697
21:3 why then doth my lord require this t'? "
7 God was displeased with this t'; 1697
8 greatly, because I have done this t': "
26:28 and whosoever had dedicated any t',
2Ch 9:20 any t' accounted of in the days of*
11:4 house: for this t' is done of me. 1697
16:10 in a rage with him because of this t'.
23:4 This is the t' that ye shall do; A 1697
19 unclean in any t' should enter in.
29:36 people: for the t' was done suddenly. "
30:4 the t' pleased the king and all the "
Ezr 7:27 such a t' as this in the king's heart,
9:3 when I heard this t', I rent my 1697
10:2 is hope in Israel concerning this t'.
13 that have transgressed in this t'. 1697
Ne 2:19 What is this t' that ye do? will ye "
13:17 What evil t' is this that ye do, and "
Es 2:4 And the t' pleased the king; and he "
22 the t' was known to Mordecai, who "
5:14 And the t' pleased Haman; and he "
6:13 friends every t' that had befallen him.
8:5 the t' seem right before the king, 1697
Job 3:25 the t' which I greatly feared is come
4:12 a t' was secretly brought to me, 1697
6:8 God would grant me the t' that I long

Job 9:22 This is one t', therefore I said it, He
12:10 hand is the soul of every living t',
13:28 And he, as a rotten t', consumeth, as a
14: 4 can bring a clean t' out of an unclean?
15:11 is there any secret t' with thee? *1697
22:28 Thou shalt also decree a t', and it 562
23:14 he performeth the t' that is appointed*
26: 3 plentifully declared the t' as it is?*
28:10 and his eye seeth every precious t'.
11 the t' that is hid bringeth he forth to
33:32 [*In most editions*] If thou hast any t' to
39: 8 and he searcheth after every green t'.
42: 2 I know that thou canst do every t',*
7 not spoken of me the t' that is right,
8 not spoken of me the t' which is right,
Ps 2: 1 and the people imagine a vain t'?
27: 4 One t' have I desired of the Lord, that
33:17 An horse is a vain t' for safety:
34:10 the Lord shall not want any good t'.
38:20 because I follow the t' that good is.
69:34 seas, and every t' that moveth therein.
84:11 no good t' will he withhold from them
89:34 nor alter the t' that is gone out of my
92: 1 It is a good t' to give thanks unto the
101: 3 set no wicked t' before mine eyes: 1697
141: 4 Incline not my heart to any evil t'. "
145:16 satisfiest the desire of every living t'.
150: 6 t' that hath breath praise the Lord.
Pr 4: 7 Wisdom is the principal t'; therefore
18:22 Whoso findeth a wife findeth a good t',
22:18 For it is a pleasant t' if thou keep
25: 2 is the glory of God to conceal a t': 1697
27: 7 the hungry soul every bitter t' is sweet.
Ec 1: 9 The t' that hath been, it is that which*
9 and there is no new t' under the sun.
10 Is there any t' whereof it may be 1697
3: 1 To every t' there is a season, and a
11 He hath made every t' beautiful in his
14 be put to it, nor any t' taken from it:
19 beasts; even one t' befalleth them:
5: 2 thine heart be hasty to utter any t'1697
6: 5 not seen the sun, nor known any t':*
7: 8 end of a t' than the beginning 1697
8: 1 knoweth the interpretation of a t'? "
3 stand not in an evil t'; for he doeth "
5 commandment shall feel no evil t': "
15 a man hath no better t' under the sun,
9: 5 but the dead know not any t',
6 any more a portion forever in any t'
11: 7 A pleasant t' it is for the eyes to
12:14 with every secret t', whether it be good,
Isa 7:13 Is it a small t' for you to weary men,
15: 6 the grass faileth, there is no green t'.
17:13 like a rolling t' before the whirlwind.*
19: 7 every t' sown by the brooks, shall*
29:16 the t' framed say of him that framed it,
21 turn aside the just for a t' of nought.
38: 7 will do this t' that he hath spoken:1697
40:15 he taketh up the isles as a very little t'.
41:12 be as nothing, and as a t' of nought.
43:19 Behold, I will do a new t'; now it shall
49: 6 a light t' that thou shouldest be my
52:11 out from thence, touch no unclean t';
55:11 prosper in the t' whereto I sent it.
64: 6 But we are all as an unclean t', and*
66: 8 Who hath heard such a t'? who hath
Jer 2:10 diligently, and see if there be such a t'.
19 see that it is an evil t' and bitter,
5:30 horrible t' is committed in the land;
7:23 But this t' commanded I them, 1697
11:13 ye set up altars to that shameful t',
14:14 a t' of nought, and the deceit of their
18:13 of Israel hath done a very horrible t'.
22: 4 if ye do this t' indeed, then shall 1697
23:14 prophets of Jerusalem an horrible t':
31:22 Lord hath created a new t' in the earth,
32:27 is there any t' too hard for me? 1697
33:14 I will perform that good t' which I "
38: 5 he that can do any t' against you.
14 unto Jeremiah, I will ask thee a t'; "
40: 3 therefore this t' is come upon you. "
16 Kareah, Thou shalt not do this t': "
42: 3 walk, and the t' that we may do. "
4 that whatsoever t' the Lord shall "
21 nor any t' for the which he hath sent
44: 4 not this abominable t' that I hate. 1697
17 do whatsoever t' goeth forth out of* "
La 2:13 What t' shall I take to witness for thee?*
13 what t' shall I liken to thee, O *
Eze 8:17 Is it a light t' to the house of Judah
14: 9 deceived when he hath spoken a t',*1697
16:47 but, as if that were a very little t',
34:18 a small t' unto you to have eaten up
44:18 with any t' that causeth sweat.
29 every dedicated t' in Israel shall be
31 shall not eat of any t' that is dead of
47: 9 every t' that liveth, which moveth,*5315
9 every t' shall live whither the river
48:12 shall be unto them a t' most holy
Da 2: 5 Chaldeans, The t' is gone from me:4406
8 ye see the t' is gone from me. "
11 is a rare t' that the king requireth, "
15 Then Arioch made the t' known to "
17 made the t' known to Hananiah, "
3:29 which speak any t' amiss against the
4:33 The same hour was the t' fulfilled 4406
5:15 shew the interpretation of the t': * "
26 This is the interpretation of the t': "
6:12 answered and said, The t' is true, "
10: 1 a t' was revealed unto Daniel, 1697
1 and the t' was true, but the time "
1 was long: and he understood the t'," "
Ho 6:10 seen an horrible t' in the house of
8: 3 Israel hath cast off the t' that is good:*
12 but they were counted as a strange t'.
Am 6:13 Ye which rejoice in a t' of nought, 1697

Jon 3: 7 beast, herd nor flock, taste any t':
Mal 1:14 sacrificeth unto the Lord a corrupt t':
M't 8:33 and told every t', and what was
18:19 agree on earth as touching any t' 4229
19:16 Good Master, what good t' shall I do,
20:20 him, and desiring a certain t' of him.
21:24 I also will ask you one t', which if*3056
24:17 to take any t' out of his house: *
M'r 1:27 themselves, saying, What t' is this?*
4:22 neither was any t' kept secret, but
5:32 about to see her that had done this t'.
7:18 whatsoever t' from without entereth*
9:22 but if thou canst do any t', have
10:21 and said unto him, One t' thou lackest:
11:13 haply he might find any t' thereon:
13:15 to take any t' out of his house:
16: 8 neither said they any t' to any man;*
18 and if they drink any deadly t', it shall
Lu 1:35 also that holy t' which shall be born‡
2:15 see this t' which is come to pass, 4487
6: 9 unto them, I will ask you one t'; *
8:17 neither any t' hid, that shall not be
9:21 them to tell no man that t'; *
10:42 But one t' is needful: and Mary
12:11 how or what t' ye shall answer, *
26 not able to do that t' which is least,*
18:22 unto him, Yet lackest thou one t':
19: 8 have taken any t' from any man by*
20: 3 them, I will also ask you one t'; *3056
22:23 of them it was that should do this t'.
35 and scrip, and shoes, lacked ye any t'?
Joh 1: 3 was not any t' made that was made.
46 any good t' come out of Nazareth?
5:14 more, lest a worse t' come unto thee.
7: 4 is no man that doeth any t' in secret,
9:25 one t' I know, that, whereas I was
30 Why herein is a marvellous t', that ye*
14:14 If ye shall ask any t' in my name,
18:34 Sayest thou this t' of thyself, or did*
Ac 5: 4 conceived this t' in thine heart? 4229
10:14 never eaten any t' that is common
28 unlawful t' for a man that is a Jew to
12:12 And when he had considered the t', he
17:21 either to tell, or to hear some new t'.)
25 as though he needed any t', seeing
19:32 Some therefore cried one t', and some
39 any t' concerning other matters,
21:25 concluded that they observe no such t',*
34 And some cried one t', some another,
23:17 for he hath a certain t' to tell him.*
25: 8 Cæsar, have I offended any t' at all.*
11 committed any t' worthy of death,
26 no certain t' to write unto my lord.
26: 8 be thought a t' incredible with you,*
10 Which t' I also did in Jerusalem:*
26 this t' was not done in a corner. *
Ro 7:18 is, in my flesh,) dwelleth no good t':
8:33 Who shall lay any t' to the charge of
9:20 Shall the t' formed say to him that4110
13: 6 attending continually upon this very t'.
8 Owe no man any t', but to love one
14:14 that esteemeth any t' to be unclean,
21 nor any t' whereby thy brother
22 condemneth not himself in that t'*
1Co 1: 5 in every t' ye are enriched by him,
10 that ye all speak the same t', and that
2: 2 not to know any t' among you,
3: 7 neither is he that planteth any t',
4: 3 very small t' that I should be judged
8: 2 man think that he knoweth any t',
7 hour eat it as a t' offered unto an idol;
9:11 is it a great t' if we shall reap your*
17 For if I do this t' willingly, I have a*
10:19 say I then? that the idol is any t',
19 offered in sacrifice to idols is any t'?
14:30 If any t' be revealed to another that*
35 And if they will learn any t', let
2Co 2:10 To whom ye forgive any t', I forgive
10 for if I forgave any t', to whom I
3: 5 to think any t' as of ourselves;
5: 5 wrought us for the selfsame t' is God,
6: 3 Giving no offence in any t', that
17 Lord, and touch not the unclean t';
7:11 For behold this selfsame t', that ye
14 For if I have boasted any t' to him of
8: 7 Therefore, as ye abound in every t', in
9:11 in every t' to all bountifulness,
10: 5 every high t' that exalteth itself 5313
11:15 it is no great t' if his ministers
12: 8 For this t' I besought the Lord thrice,
Ga 4:18 affected always in a good t', *
5: 6 circumcision availeth any t', nor
6:15 neither circumcision availeth any t',
Eph 4:28 with his hands the t' which is good,
5:24 be to their own husbands in every t'.
27 spot, or wrinkle, or any such t';
6: 8 whatsoever good t' any man doeth,
Ph'p 1: 6 Being confident of this very t', that
3:13 but this one t' I do, forgetting 1520
15 if in any t' ye be otherwise minded,
16 the same rule, let us mind the same t'.*
4: 6 in every t' by prayer and supplication
1Th 1: 8 that we need not to speak any t'.
5:18 In every t' give thanks: for this is the
2Th 1: 6 righteous t' with God to recompense
1Ti 1:10 and if there be any other t' that is
2Ti 1:14 good t' which was committed unto
Tit 2: 8 having no evil t' to say of you.
Ph'm 6 by the acknowledging of every good t'
Heb10:29 an unholy t', and hath done despite
31 It is a fearful t' to fall into the hands
11:40 God having provided some better t'
13: 9 it is a good t' that the heart be *
Jas 1: 7 he shall receive any t' of the Lord.
1Pe 4:12 some strange t' happened unto you:
2Pe 3: 8 be not ignorant of this one t',

1Jo 2: 8 which t' is true in him and in you:
5:14 if we ask any t' according to his will,
Re 2:15 of the Nicolaitanes, which t' I hate.*
9: 4 neither any green t', neither any tree;
21:27 enter into it any t' that defileth,
things See also THINGS'.
Ge 7:23 and the creeping t', and the fowl of the*
9: 3 the green herb have I given you all t'.*
15: 1 After these t' the word of the Lord1697
20: 8 and told all these t' in their ears: "
22: 1, 20 And it came to pass after these t'," "
24:28 of her mother's house these t'. * "
53 brother and to her mother precious t'.
66 servant told Isaac all t' that he 1697
29:13 And he told Laban all these t'. "
39: 7 And it came to pass after these t', "
40: 1 And it came to pass after these t', "
42:36 away: all these t' are against me.
45:23 ten asses laden with the good t' of
48: 1 And it came to pass after these t', 1697
Ex 10: 2 what t' I have wrought in Egypt, and
12:36 unto them such t' as they required.*
23:13 And in all t' that I have said unto you
25:22 of all t' which I will give thee in
28:38 may bear the iniquity of the holy t',
29:33 eat those t' wherewith the atonement
35 all t' which I have commanded thee:*
40: 4 order the t' that are to be set in order
Le 2: 8 offering that is made of these t' unto
4: 2 t' which ought not to be done,
13, 22 t' which should not be done,
27 t' which ought not to be done,
5: 2 or the carcase of unclean creeping t',
5 he shall be guilty in one of these t',
15 ignorance, in the holy t' of the Lord;
17 commit any of these t' which are
8:36 Aaron and his sons did all the t' 1697
10:19 Lord; and such t' have befallen me:
11:23 But all other flying creeping t', which
29 unto you among the creeping t'
42 hath more feet among all creeping t'
14:11 that is to be made clean, and those t',
15:10 and he that beareth any of those t'
27 whosoever toucheth those t' shall be
18:24 not ye yourselves in any of these t':
20:23 for they committed all these t', and
22: 2 from the holy t' of the children of
2 name in those t' which they hallow*
3 that goeth unto the holy t', which the
4 he shall not eat of the holy t', until he
6 and shall not eat of the holy t', unless
7 and shall afterward eat of the holy t';
12 not eat of an offering of the holy t'.
15 And they shall not profane the holy t'
16 trespass, when they eat their holy t':
26:23 will not be reformed by me by these t',
Nu 1:50 and over all t' that belong to it: *
4: 4 congregation, about the most holy t':
15 t' are the burden of the sons of Kohath
19 they approach unto the most holy t':
20 in to see when the holy t' are covered,*
5: 9 And every offering of all the holy t' of
10 every man's hallowed t' shall be his:
15:13 shall do these t' after this manner, in
18: 8 hallowed t' of the children of Israel;
9 This shall be thine of the most holy t',
19 All the heave offerings of the holy t',
32 neither shall ye pollute the holy t' of
29:39 These t' ye shall do unto the Lord*
31:20 of goats' hair, and all t' made of wood.
35:29 So these t' shall be for a statute of
De 1:18 at that time all the t' which ye 1697
4: 7 God is in all t' that we call upon him*
9 the t' which thine eyes have seen, 1697
30 and all these t' are come upon thee, "
6:11 And houses full of all good t', which
10:21 for thee these great and terrible t',
12: 8 do after all the t' that we do here this
26 Only thy holy t' which thou hast, and
18:12 For all that do these t' are an
25:16 For all that do such t', and all that do
26:13 I have brought away the hallowed t'
28:47 of heart, for the abundance of all t';
48 in nakedness, and in want of all t':
57 for she shall eat them for want of all t'
29:29 secret t' belong unto the Lord our
29 t' which are revealed belong unto us
30: 1 all these t' are come upon thee, 1697
32:35 the t' that shall come upon them make
33:13 for the precious t' of heaven, for the
14 the precious t' put forth by the moon,
15 chief t' of the ancient mountains,
15 for the precious t' of the lasting hills,
16 And for the precious t' of the earth
Jos 1:17 as we hearkened unto Moses in all t',
2:11 And as soon as we had heard these t',*
23 and told him all t' that befell them:*
11: 1 king of Hazor had heard those t',* "
23:14 thing hath failed of all the good t' 1697
15 as all good t' are come upon you, "
15 the Lord bring upon you all evil t'. "
24:29 And it came to pass after these t', "
J'g 13:23 would he have shewed us all these t',
23 time have told us such t' as these.
18:27 took the t' which Micah had made,*
Ru 4: 7 changing, for to confirm all t';
1Sa 2:23 unto them, Why do ye such t'? 1697
3:12 against Eli all t' which I have spoken*
17 hide any thing from me of all the t'
12:21 for then should ye go after vain t',
24 consider how great t' he hath done for
15:21 the chief of the t' which should
19: 7 Jonathan shewed him all those t'. 1697
25:37 and his wife had told him these t', "
26:25 David: thou shalt both do great t',*
2Sa 7:21 hast thou done all these great t', to*

2Sa 7:23 and to do for you great t' and terrible.
11:18 told David all the t' concerning 1697
12: 8 have given unto thee such and such t'.
13:21 king David heard of all these t', 1697
14:20 to know all t' that are in the earth.
23: 5 covenant, ordered in all t' and sure:
17 These t' did these three mighty men.
22 These t' did Benaiah the son of
24:12 saith the Lord, I offer thee three t';
23 all these t' did Araunah, as a king*
1Ki 4:33 fowl, and of creeping t', and of fishes.
5: 8 considered the t' which thou sentest*
7:51 the t' which David his father had
15:15 brought in the t' which his father had
15 the t' which himself had dedicated,
17:17 And it came to pass after these t', 1697
18:36 I have done all these t' that thy "
21: 1 And it came to pass after these t', "
26 according to all t' as did the Amorites,*
2Ki 8: 4 the great t' that Elisha hath done.
11: 9 according to all t' that Jehoiada the*
12: 4 All the money of the dedicated t' that
18 all the hallowed t' that Jehoshaphat,
18 and his own hallowed t', and all the
14: 3 according to all t' as Joash his father*
17: 9 did secretly those t' that were not 1697
11 wrought wicked t' to provoke the "
19:29 shall eat this year such t' as grow of*
20:13 them all the house of his precious t',
15 All the t' that are in mine house have*
23:17 proclaimed these t' that thou hast 1697
25:15 and such t' as were of gold, in gold,*
1Ch 4:22 And these are ancient t'. *1697
9:31 set office over the t' that were made in
11:19 These t' did these three mightiest.
24 These t' did Benaiah the son of
17:19 in making known all these great t'.
21:10 saith the Lord, I offer thee three t':
23:13 he should sanctify the most holy t', he
28 and in the purifying of all holy t', and
26:20 over the treasures of the dedicated t'.
26 all the treasures of the dedicated t'.
28:12 of the treasuries of the dedicated t':
14 gave of gold by weight for t' of gold,*
29: 2 God the gold for t' to be made of gold,
2 and the silver for t' of silver,
2 and the brass for t' of brass,
2 the iron for t' of iron,
2 and wood for t' of wood;
5 The gold for t' of gold,
5 and the silver for t' of silver,
14 for all t' come of thee, and of thine
17 I have willingly offered all these t':
19 and to do all these t', and to build the
2Ch 3: 3 t' wherein Solomon was instructed*
4: 6 such t' as they offered for the burnt
5: 1 all the t' that David his father had
12:12 and also in Judah t' went well. 1697
15:18 of God the t' that his father had
19: 3 there are good t' found in thee, in 1697
21: 3 silver, and of gold, and of precious t',
23: 8 according to all t' that Jehoiada the*
24: 7 the dedicated t' of the house of the
29:33 consecrated t' were six hundred oxen
31: 5 the tithe of all t' brought they in
6 of holy t' which were consecrated
12 tithes and the dedicated t' faithfully:
14 of the Lord, and the most holy t'.
32: 1 After these t', and the 1697
Ezr 1: 6 with beasts, and with precious t',
2:63 should not eat of the most holy t',
7: 1 Now after these t', in the reign of 1697
9: 1 Now when these t' were done, the
Ne 6: 8 are no such t' done as thou sayest,1697
16 that were about us saw these t', *
7:65 should not eat of the most holy t',
9: 6 the earth, and all t' that are therein,
10:33 for the set feasts, and for the holy t',
12:47 sanctified holy t' unto the Levites;*
13:26 Solomon king of Israel sin by these t'?
Es 2: 1 After these t', when the wrath of 1697
3 let their t' for purification be given
9 gave her her t' for purification,
9 with such t' as belonged to her, and*
12 with other t' for the purifying of the
3: 1 After these t' did king Ahasuerus 1697
5:11 all the t' wherein the king had
9:20 And Mordecai wrote these t', 1697
Job 5: 9 doeth great t' and unsearchable;
9 marvellous t' without number:
6: 7 The t' that my soul refused to touch*
30 cannot my taste discern perverse t'?
8: 2 How long wilt thou speak these t'?
9:10 Which doeth great t' past finding out;
10:13 these t' hast thou hid in thine heart:
12: 3 yea, who knoweth not such t' as these?
22 discovereth deep t' out of darkness,
13:20 Only do not two t' unto me: then will I
26 For thou writest bitter t' against me,
14:19 thou washest away the t' which grow*
16: 2 I have heard many such t': miserable
22:18 Yet he filled their houses with good t':
23:14 me: and many such t' are with him.
26: 5 Dead t' are formed from under the*
33:29 these t' worketh God oftentimes with
37: 5 great t' doeth he, which we cannot
41:30 sharp pointed t' upon the mire. *
34 He beholdeth all high t': he is a king*
42: 3 t' too wonderful for me, which I knew
Ps 8: 6 thou hast put all t' under his feet:
12: 3 the tongue that speaketh proud t':
15: 5 He that doeth these t' shall never be
17: 2 thine eyes behold the t' that are equal.*
31:18 which speak grievous t' proudly and*
35:11 laid to my charge t' that I knew not.
38:12 seek my hurt speak mischievous t',

Ps 42: 4 When I remember these t', I pour out
45: 1 I speak of the t' which I have made
4 right hand shall teach thee terrible t'.
50:21 These t' hast thou done, and I kept
57: 2 God that performeth all t' for me.
60: 3 Thou hast shewed thy people hard t':
65: 5 By terrible t' in righteousness wilt
71:19 is very high, who hast done great t':
72:18 of Israel, who only doeth wondrous t'.
78:12 Marvellous t' did he in the sight of
86:10 thou art great, and doest wondrous t':
87: 3 Glorious t' are spoken of thee, O city
94: 4 long shall they utter and speak hard t'?*
98: 1 song; for he hath done marvellous t':
103: 5 Who satisfieth thy mouth with good t';
104:25 wherein are t' creeping innumerable,
106:21 which had done great t' in Egypt;
22 Ham, and terrible t' by the Red sea.
107:43 is wise, and will observe these t',
113: 6 to behold the t' that are in heaven,
119:18 may behold wondrous t' out of thy law.
128 thy precepts concerning all t' to be
126: 2 The Lord hath done great t' for them.
3 The Lord hath done great t' for us;
131: 1 great matters, or in t' too high for me.
148:10 all cattle; creeping t', and flying fowl:
Pr 2:12 the man that speaketh froward t';
3:15 and all the t' thou canst desire are not
6:16 These six t' doth the Lord hate: yea,
8: 6 for I will speak of excellent t'; and
6 opening of my lips shall be right t'.
11 all the t' that may be desired are not
15:28 of the wicked poureth out evil t'.
16: 4 The Lord hath made all t' for himself:*
30 shutteth his eyes to devise froward t':
22:20 Have not I written to thee excellent t'
23:16 rejoice, when thy lips speak right t'.
33 and thine heart shall utter perverse t'.
24:23 These t' also belong to the wise. It is*
26:10 The great God that formed all t' both*
28: 5 that seek the Lord understand all t'.
10 the upright shall have good t' in *
30: 7 Two t' have I required of thee; deny
15 are three t' that are never satisfied,
15 yea, four t' say not, It is enough: *
18 be three t' which are too wonderful
21 For three t' the earth is disquieted,
24 There be four t' which are little upon
29 There be three t' which go well, yea,
Ec 1: 8 All t' are full of labour; man 1697
11 is no remembrance of former t'; *
11 be any remembrance of t' that are*
13 out by wisdom concerning all t' that*
6:11 be many t' that increase vanity, 1697
7:15 All t' have I seen in the days of my*
25 seek out wisdom, and the reason of t',
9: 2 All t' come alike to all: there is one
3 is an evil among all t' that are done*
10:19 merry: but money answereth all t'.
11: 9 that for all these t' God will bring thee
Isa 12: 5 Lord; for he hath done excellent t':
25: 1 for thou hast done wonderful t'; thy
6 make unto all people a feast of fat t',
6 of fat t' full of marrow, of wines on
29:16 Surely your turning of t' upside down
30:10 Prophesy not unto us right t',
10 speak unto us smooth t', prophesy
32: 8 But the liberal deviseth liberal t';
8 and by liberal t' shall he stand.
34: 1 world, and all t' that come forth of it.
38:16 O Lord, by these t' men live,
16 in all these t' is the life of my spirit:*
39: 2 them the house of his precious t',
40:26 and behold who hath created these t',*
41:22 let them shew the former t', what they
22 of them; or declare us t' for to come.
23 Shew the t' that are to come hereafter,
42: 9 Behold, the former t' are come to pass,
9 and new t' do I declare: before they
16 them, and crooked t' straight. *
16 These t' will I do unto them, and 1697
20 Seeing many t', but thou observest
43: 9 declare this, and shew us former t'?
18 Remember ye not the former t',
18 neither consider the t' of old.
44: 7 and the t' that are coming, and shall
9 and their delectable t' shall not profit;
24 I am the Lord that maketh all t';
45: 7 create evil: I the Lord do all these t'.
11 Ask me of t' to come concerning my
19 I declare t' that are right.
46: 9 Remember the former t' of old: for I
10 from ancient times the t' that are not
47: 7 thou didst not lay these t' to thy heart,
9 these two t' shall come to thee in a
13 save thee from these t' that shall come
48: 3 I have declared the former t' from the
6 I have shewed thee new t' from this
6 even hidden t', and thou didst not
14 among them hath declared these t'?
51:19 These two t' are come unto thee; who
56: 4 choose the t' that please me, and take
61:11 garden causeth the t' that are sown
64: 3 terrible t' which we looked not for,
11 and all our pleasant t' are laid waste.‡
12 refrain thyself for these t', O Lord?
65: 4 of abominable t' is in their vessels;
66: 2 For all those t' hath mine hand made,
2 and all those t' have been, saith the
8 such a thing? who hath seen such t'?
Jer 2: 8 and walked after t' that do not profit.
3: 5 thou hast spoken and done evil t' as
7 said after she had done all these t',
4:18 have procured these t' unto thee.
5: 9 Shall I not visit for these t'? saith the
19 doeth the Lord our God all these t'

Jer 5:25 iniquities have turned away these t',
25 your sins have withholden good t'*
29 Shall I not visit for these t'? saith the
8:13 t' that I have given them shall pass
9: 9 Shall I not visit them for these t'?
24 in these t' I delight, saith the Lord.
10:16 for he is the former of all t'; and Israel
13:22 Wherefore come these t' upon me?
14:22 thee: for thou hast made all these t'.
16:18 of their detestable and abominable t'.
19 and t' wherein there is no profit.
17: 9 The heart is deceitful above all t', and
18:13 the heathen, who hath heard such t':
20: 1 that Jeremiah prophesied these t'.1697
5 and all the precious t' thereof, and all
21:14 it shall devour all t' round about it.*
26:10 princes of Judah heard these t', 1697
30:15 I have done these t' unto thee.
31: 5 and shall eat them as common t'. *
33: 3 and shew thee great and mighty t',
42: 5 according to all t' for the which *1697
44:18 we have wanted all t', and have been
45: 5 And seekest thou great t' for thyself?
51:19 them: for he is the former of all t':
La 1: 7 all her pleasant t' that she had in the
10 out his hand upon all her pleasant t':
11 have given their pleasant t' for meat
16 For these t' I weep; mine eye, mine
2:14 prophets have seen vain and foolish t'*
5:17 is faint; for these t' our eyes are dim.
Eze 5:11 sanctuary with all thy detestable t',
7:20 and of their detestable t' therein:
8:10 and behold every form of creeping t',
11: 5 for I know the t' that come into your
18 take away all the detestable t' thereof
21 after the heart of their detestable t'
25 all the t' that the Lord had shewed1697
16:16 the like t' shall not come, neither shall
30 seeing thou doest all these t', the work
43 but hast fretted me in all these t';
17:12 Know ye not what these t' mean?
15 shall he escape that doeth such t'? or
18 and hath done all these t', he shall not
18:10 doeth the like to any one of these t',
20:40 your oblations, with all your holy t'.
22: 8 Thou hast despised mine holy t', and
25 taken the treasure and precious t';
26 law, and have profaned mine holy t':
23:30 I will do these t' unto thee, because
24:19 thou not tell us what these t' are to us,
27:24 were thy merchants in all sorts of t',*
37:23 their idols, nor with their detestable t',
38:10 time shall t' come into thy mind, 1697
20 and all creeping t' that creep upon the
42:13 the Lord shall eat the most holy t':
13 there shall they lay the most holy t',
14 to those t' which are for the people.*
44: 8 not kept the charge of mine holy t':
13 nor to come near to any of my holy t',
30 the first of all the firstfruits of all t',*
Da 2:10 that asked such t' at any magician,*
22 He revealeth the deep and secret t':
40 breaketh in pieces and subdueth all t':
7: 8 man, and a mouth speaking great t'.
16 know the interpretation of the t'. 4406
20 and a mouth that spake very great t',
10:21 none that holdeth with me in these t',*
11:36 marvellous t' against the God of gods,
38 with precious stones, and pleasant t'.
43 and over all the precious t' of Egypt:
12: 7 people, all these t' shall be finished.
8 Lord, what shall be the end of these t'?
Ho 2:18 and with the creeping t' of the ground:
8:12 written to him the great t' of my law,†
9: 3 they shall eat unclean t' in Assyria.*
14: 9 and he shall understand t' things?
Joe 2:20 up, because he hath done great t'.
21 rejoice: for the Lord will do great t'.
3: 5 your temples my goodly pleasant t':
Ob 6 How are the t' of Esau searched out!
6 how are his hidden t' sought up!*
Mic 7:15 will I shew unto him marvellous t'.
Hab 1:14 as the creeping t', that have no ruler
Zep 1: 2 utterly consume all t' from off the
Zec 4:10 who hath despised the day of small t'?
8:12 of this people to possess all these t'.
16 These are the t' that ye shall do;
17 for all these are t' that I hate, saith
M't 1:20 But while he thought on these t',
2: 3 Herod the king had heard these t',*
4: 9 All these t' will I give thee, if thou
6: 8 knoweth what t' ye have need of,
32 all these t' do the Gentiles seek:)
32 that ye have need of all these t'.
33 all these t' shall be added unto you.
34 take thought for the t' of itself. *
7:11 is in heaven give good t' to them that
12 Therefore all t' whatsoever ye would
9:18 While he spake these t' unto them,
11: 4 shew John again those t' which ye do
25 hast hid these t' from the wise and
27 All t' are delivered unto me of my
12:34 can ye, being evil, speak good t'?
35 of the heart bringeth forth good t':
35 the evil treasure bringeth forth evil t
13: 3 he spake many t' unto them in
17 desired to see those t' which ye see,
17 and to hear those t' which ye hear,
34 All these t' spake Jesus unto the
35 I will utter t' which have been kept
41 out of his kingdom all t' that offend,
51 Have ye understood all these t'?
52 out of his treasure t' new and old.
56 then hath this man all these t'?
15:18 those t' which proceed out of the
20 These are the t' which defile a man:

M't 16:21 and suffer many t' of the elders and
23 savourest not the t' that be of God,
17:11 shall first come, and restore all t'
19:20 All these t' have I kept from my
26 but with God all t' are possible.
21:15 saw the wonderful t' that he did,
22 all t', whatsoever ye shall ask in
23 authority doest thou these t'?
24, 27 by what authority I do these t'.
22: 4 all t' are ready: come unto the
21 Cæsar the t' which are Cæsar's;
21 unto God the t' that are God's.
23:20 sweareth by it, and by all t' thereon.
36 All these t' shall come upon this
24: 2 unto them, See ye not all these t'?
3 Tell us, when shall these t' be?
6 for all these t' must come to pass,
33 ye, when ye shall see all these t',
34 not pass, till all these t' be fulfilled.
25:21 thou hast been faithful over a few t',
21 I will make thee ruler over many t':
23 thou hast been faithful over a few t',
23 I will make thee ruler over many t':
27:13 many t' they witness against thee?
19 I have suffered many t' this day in
54 and those t' that were done,
28:11 priests all the t' that were done.
20 to observe all t' whatsoever I have
M'r 1:44 those t' which Moses commanded,
2: 8 Why reason ye these t' in your
3: 8 they had heard what great t' he did,
4: 2 taught them many t' by parables,
11 all these t' are done in parables:
19 lusts of other t' entering in, choke
34 he expounded all t' to his disciples.
5:19 tell them how great t' the Lord hath
20 great t' Jesus had done for him:
26 And had suffered many t' of many
6: 2 whence hath this man these t'?
20 he did many t', and heard him gladly.*
30 unto Jesus, and told him all t',
34 and he began to teach them many t'.
7: 4 many other t' there be, which they
8 and many other such like t' ye do.*
13 and many such like t' do ye.
15 but the t' which come out of him,
23 All these evil t' come from within,
37 saying, He hath done all t' well: he
8:31 the Son of man must suffer many t',
33 savourest not the t' that be of God,
33 of God, but the t' that be of men.
9: 9 tell no man what t' they had seen,
12 cometh first, and restoreth all t';
12 of man, that he must suffer many t',
23 t' are possible to him that believeth.
10:27 for with God all t' are possible.
32 tell them what t' should happen
11:11 had looked round about upon all t',
23 those t' which he saith shall come*
24 What t' soever ye desire, when ye
28 what authority doest thou these t'?
28 thee this authority to do these t'?
29, 33 by what authority I do these t'.
12:17 to Cæsar the t' that are Cæsar's,
17 and to God the t' that are God's.
13: 4 Tell us, when shall these t' be?
4 when all these t' shall be fulfilled?
7 for such t' must needs be; but the
23 behold, I have foretold you all t'.
29 shall see these t' come to pass,
30 not pass, till all these t' be done.
14:36 Father, all t' are possible unto thee;
15: 3 priests accused him of many t':
4 how many t' they witness against
Lu 1: 1 in order a declaration of those t' *4229
3 had perfect understanding of all t'
4 know the certainty of those t', 3056
20 until the day that these t' shall be
45 of those t' which were told her
49 mighty hath done to me great t';
53 hath filled the hungry with good t';
2:18 wondered at those t' which were told
19 But Mary kept all these t', and 4487
20 praising God for all the t' that they
33 marvelled at those t' which were
39 had performed all t' according to the
3:18 other t' in his exhortation preached*
4:28 when they heard these t', were filled
5:26 We have seen strange t' to day.
27 And after these t' he went forth,
6:46 Lord, and do not the t' which I say?
7: 9 Jesus heard these t', he marvelled
18 John shewed him of all these t'.
22 tell John what t' ye have seen and
8: 8 when he had said these t', he cried,
39 how great t' God hath done unto
39 how great t' Jesus had done unto
9: 9 who is this, of whom I hear such t'?
22 Son of man must suffer many t',
36 any of those t' which they had seen.
43 they wondered every one at all t'
10: 1 After these t' the Lord appointed
7 and drinking such t' as they give:
8 eat such t' as are set before you:
21 hid these t' from the wise and
22 All t' are delivered to me of my
23 eyes which see the t' that ye see:
24 desired to see those t' which ye see,
24 and to hear those t' which ye hear,
41 careful and troubled about many t':
11:27 as he spake these t', a certain
41 give alms of such t' as ye have;
41 behold, all t' are clean unto you.
53 as he said these t' unto them, *
53 to provoke him to speak of many t':
12:15 of the t' which he possesseth.

Lu 12:20 then whose shall those t' be, which
30 these t' do the nations of the world
30 that ye have need of these t'.
31 all these t' shall be added unto
48 and did commit t' worthy of stripes,
13: 2 because they suffered such t'?
17 And when he had said these t',
17 glorious t' that were done by him.
14: 6 not answer him again to these t'.
15 sat at meat with him heard these t',
17 Come; for all t' are now ready.
21 came, and shewed his lord these t'.
15:26 and asked what these t' meant.
16:14 were covetous, heard all these t':
25 thy lifetime receivedst thy good t',
25 and likewise Lazarus evil t': but now
17: 9 he did the t' that were commanded
10 he shall have done all those t' which
25 But first must he suffer many t',
18:22 Now when Jesus heard these t', *
27 t' which are impossible with men are
31 t' that are written by the prophets
34 they understood none of these t':
34 neither knew they the t' which were
19:11 as they heard these t', he added
42 the t' which belong unto thy peace!
20: 2 authority doest thou these t'?
8 by what authority I do these t'.
25 Cæsar the t' which be Cæsar's,
25 and unto God the t' which be God's.
21: 6 As for these t' which ye behold,
7 Master, but when shall these t' be?
7 when these t' shall come to pass?
9 for these t' must first come to pass;
22 t' which are written may be fulfilled.
26 looking after those t' which are
28 when these t' begin to come to pass,
31 when ye see these t' come to pass,
36 these t' that shall come to pass,
22:37 the t' concerning me have an end.*
65 many other t' blasphemously spake
23: 8 because he had heard many t' of him;*
14 touching those t' whereof ye accuse
31 if they do these t' in a green tree,
48 beholding the t' which were done,
49 stood afar off, beholding these t'.
24: 9 and told all these t' unto the eleven,
10 which told these t' unto the apostles.
14 they talked together of all these t'
18 hast not known the t' which are come
19 And he said unto them, What t'? And
21 third day since these t' were done.
26 not Christ to have suffered these t',
27 scriptures the t' concerning himself.
35 they told what t' were done in the way,
44 that all t' must be fulfilled, which
48 And ye are witnesses of these t'.
Joh 1: 3 All t' were made by him; and without
28 These t' were done in Bethabara
50 thou shalt see greater t' than these.
2:16 Take these t' hence; make not
18 us, seeing that thou doest these t'?
3: 9 unto him, How can these t' be?
10 Israel, and knowest not these t'?
12 If I have told you earthly t', and ye
12 ye believe if I tell you of heavenly t'?
22 After these t' came Jesus and his
35 and hath given all t' into his hand.
4:25 when he is come, he will tell us all t'.
29 which told me all t' that ever I did:
45 seen all t' that he did at Jerusalem
5:16 done these t' on the sabbath day.
19 for what t' soever he doeth, these also
20 sheweth him all t' that himself doeth:
34 these t' I say, that ye might be saved.
6: 1 After these t' Jesus went over the
59 These t' said he in the synagogue,
7: 1 After these t' Jesus walked in
4 If thou do these t', shew thyself to
32 that the people murmured such t'
8:26 I have many t' to say and to judge of
26 world those t' which I have heard of
28 hath taught me, I speak these t'.
29 I do always those t' that please him.
10: 6 they understood not what t' they were
41 but all t' that John spake of this man
11:11 These t' said he: and after that he5023
45 and had seen the t' which Jesus did,*
46 and told them what t' Jesus had done.
12:16 These t' understood not his disciples
16 they that these t' were written of him,
16 they had done these t' unto him.
36 These t' spake Jesus, and departed,
41 These t' said Esaias, when he saw
13: 3 Father had given all t' into his hands,
17 If ye know these t', happy are ye
29 Buy those t' that we have need of
14:25 These t' have I spoken unto you,
26 he shall teach you all t', and bring all
26 and bring all t' to your remembrance,*
15:11 These t' have I spoken unto you,
15 all t' that I have heard of my Father
17 These t' I command you, that ye
21 But all these t' will they do unto
16: 1 These t' have I spoken unto you,
3 And these t' will they do unto you,
4 But these t' have I told you, that
4 these t' I said not unto you at the
6 I have said these t' unto you,
12 I have yet many t' to say unto you,
13 and he will shew you t' to come.
15 All t' that the Father hath are mine:
25 These t' have I spoken unto you
30 are we sure that thou knowest all t',
33 These t' have I spoken unto you,
17: 7 that all t' whatsoever thou hast given

Joh 17:13 and these t' I speak in the world, that
18: 4 knowing all t' should come upon him,
19:24 these t' therefore the soldiers did.
28 that all t' were now accomplished,
36 For these t' were done, that the
20:18 he had spoken these t' unto her.
21: 1 After these t' Jesus shewed himself
17 unto him, Lord, thou knowest all t';
24 disciple which testifieth of these t',
24 and wrote these t': and we know
25 also many other t' which Jesus did,
Ac 1: 3 t' pertaining to the kingdom of God:
9 And when he had spoken these t',
2:44 together, and had all t' common;
3:18 But those t', which God before had
21 the times of restitution of all t', which
22 shall ye hear in all t' whatsoever he
4:20 speak the t' which we have seen and
25 rage, and the people imagine vain t'?
32 ought of the t' which he possessed
32 his own; but they had all t' common.
34 the prices of the t' that were sold,
5: 5 on all them that heard these t'. *
11 and upon as many as heard these t'.
24 the chief priests heard these t', *3056
32 we are his witnesses of these t'; 4487
7: 1 the high priest, Are these t' so?
50 Hath not my hand made all these t'?
54 When they heard these t', they were
8: 6 gave heed unto these t' which Philip
12 Philip preaching the t' concerning*
24 none of these t' which ye have spoken
9:16 shew him how great t' he must suffer
10: 8 had declared all these t' unto them,
12 beasts, and creeping t', and fowls
33 to hear all t' that are commanded thee
39 we are witnesses of all t' which he did
11: 6 beasts, and creeping t', and fowls
18 When they heard these t', they held
22 Then tidings of these t' came unto*
12:17 said, Go shew these t' unto James,
13:39 that believe are justified from all t',
45 those t' which were spoken by Paul,
14:15 Sirs, why do ye these t'? We also
15 and the sea, and all t' that are therein:*
15: 4 and they declared all t' that God had
17 the Lord, who doeth all these t'.
20 fornication, and from t' strangled,*
27 also tell you the same t' by mouth.
28 burden than these necessary t';
29 and from blood, and from t' strangled,
16:14 unto the t' which were spoken of Paul.
17: 8 the city, when they heard these t'.
11 daily, whether those t' were so.
20 bringest certain strange t' to our ears:
20 know therefore what these t' mean.
22 that in all t' ye are too superstitious.
24 that made the world and all t' therein,
25 giveth to all life, and breath, and all t';
18: 1 After these t' Paul departed from
17 And Gallio cared for none of those t'.
25 taught diligently the t' of the Lord,
19: 8 the t' concerning the kingdom of God.
21 After these t' were ended, Paul
36 these t' cannot be spoken against,
20:22 not knowing the t' that shall befall me
24 But none of these t' move me, 3056
30 shall men arise, speaking perverse t',
35 I have shewed you all t', how that so
21:12 And when we heard these t', both
19 particularly what t' God had wrought
24 and all may know that those t',
25 themselves from t' offered to idols,
22:10 told thee of all t' which are appointed
23:22 thou hast shewed these t' to me.
24: 8 take knowledge of all these t',
9 saying that these t' were so.
13 they prove the t' whereof they now
14 all t' which are written in the law
22 when Felix heard these t', having*
25: 9 be judged of these t' before me?
11 none of these t' whereof these accuse
18 accusation of such t' as I supposed:
26: 2 touching all the t' whereof I am
9 many t' contrary to the name of Jesus
16 both of these t' which thou hast seen,
16 of those t' in the which I will appear
22 saying none other t' than those which*
26 For the king knoweth of these t',
26 that none of these t' are hidden
27:11 those t' which were spoken by Paul.
28:10 us with such t' as were necessary.
24 And some believed the t' which were
31 teaching those t' which concern the
Ro 1:20 invisible t' of him from the creation
20 understood by the t' that are made,
23 fourfooted beasts, and creeping t'.
28 do those t' which are not convenient;
30 inventors of evil t', disobedient to
32 which commit such t' are worthy of
2: 1 thou that judgest doest the same t'.
2 against them which commit such t'
3 that judgest them which do such t'.
14 nature the t' contained in the law,
18 approvest the t' that are more
3:19 that what t' soever the law saith,
4:17 those t' which be not as though they
6:21 What fruit had ye then in those t'
21 for the end of those t' is death.
8: 5 the flesh do mind the t' of the flesh;
5 after the Spirit the t' of the Spirit.
28 we know that all t' work together for
31 What shall we then say to these t'?
32 not with him also freely give us all t'?
37 in all these t' we are more than
38 nor t' present, nor t' to come,

Ro 10: 5 man which doeth those t' shall live*
15 and bring glad tidings of good t'! 18
11: 36 through him, and to him, are all t':
12: 16 Mind not high t', but condescend to
17 Provide t' honest in the sight of all
14: 2 one believeth that he may eat all t':
18 For he that in these t' serveth Christ*
19 after the t' which make for peace,
19 t' wherewith one may edify another.
20 All t' indeed are pure; but it is evil
15: 4 For whatsoever t' were written
17 in those t' which pertain to God.
18 not dare to speak of any of those t'
27 made partakers of their spiritual t',
27 to minister unto them in carnal t'.
1Co 1: 27 hath chosen the foolish t' of the world
27 hath chosen the weak t' of the world
27 to confound the t' which are mighty;
28 And base t' of the world, and
28 and t' which are despised, hath God
28 God chosen, yea, and t' which are not,
28 are not, to bring to nought t' that are:
2: 9 t' which God hath prepared for them
10 searcheth all t', yea, the deep t' of God.
11 For what man knoweth the t' of a man,
11 even so the t' of God knoweth no man,
12 know the t' that are freely given to us
13 Which t' also we speak, not in the
13 comparing spiritual t' with spiritual.
14 natural man receiveth not the t' of
15 But he that is spiritual judgeth all t',
3: 21 glory in men. For all t' are yours;
22 or death, or t' present, or t' to come;
4: 5 to light the hidden t' of darkness,
6 these t', brethren, I have in a figure
13 the offscouring of all t' unto this day.
14 I write not these t' to shame you,
6: 3 much more t' that pertain to this life?
4 judgments of t' pertaining to this life,
12 All t' are lawful unto me, but all
12 unto me, but all t' are not expedient:
12 all t' are lawful for me, but I will not
7: 1 concerning the t' whereof ye wrote
32 is unmarried careth for the t' that
33 married careth for the t' that are of
34 woman careth for the t' of the Lord,
34 married careth for the t' of the world,
8: 1 Now as touching t' offered unto idols,
4 the eating of those t' that are offered
6 God, the Father, of whom are all t',
6 Lord Jesus Christ, by whom are all t',
10 eat those t' which are offered to idols;
9: 8 Say I these t' as a man? or saith not
11 If we have sown unto you spiritual t',
11 thing if we shall reap your carnal t'?
12 but suffer all t', lest we should hinder
13 they which minister about holy t'
13 live of the t' of the temple? and they
15 But I have used none of these t':
15 neither have I written these t',
22 I am made all t' to all men, that I
25 for the mastery is temperate in all t'.
10: 6 Now these t' were our examples,
6 intent we should not lust after evil t',
11 all these t' happened unto them
20 that the t' which the Gentiles sacrifice,
23 All t' are lawful for me, but all
23 but all t' are not expedient:
23 all t' are lawful for me, but all
23 are lawful for me, but all t' edify not.
33 Even as I please all men in all t', not
11: 2 that ye remember me in all t',
12 also by the woman; but all t' of God.
13: 7 Beareth all t', believeth all t',
7 hopeth all t', endureth all t'.
11 became a man, I put away childish t'.
14: 7 And even t' without life giving sound,
26 Let all t' be done unto edifying.
37 acknowledge that the t' that I write
40 all t' be done decently and in order.
15: 27 For he hath put all t' under his feet.
27 he saith all t' are put under him,
27 which did put all t' under him.
28 when all t' shall be subdued unto him,
28 unto him that put all t' under him,
16: 14 Let all your t' be done with charity.*
2Co 1: 13 For we write none other t' unto you,
17 or the t' that I purpose, do I purpose
2: 9 you, whether ye be obedient in all t'.
16 And who is sufficient for these t'?
4: 2 have renounced the hidden t' of
15 For all t' are for your sakes, that the
18 we look not at the t' which are seen,
18 but at the t' which are not seen:
18 for the t' which are seen are temporal;
18 the t' which are not seen are eternal.
5: 10 every one may receive the t' done in
17 new creature: old t' are passed away;
17 behold, all t' are become new.
18 all t' are of God, who hath reconciled
6: 4 in all t' approving ourselves as the*
10 nothing, and yet possessing all t'.
7: 11 In all t' ye have approved yourselves*
14 but as we spake all t' to you in truth,
16 I have confidence in you in all t'. *
8: 21 Providing for honest t', not only in the
22 oftentimes proved diligent in many t',
9: 8 always having all sufficiency in all t',*
10: 7 on t' after the outward appearance?
13 not boast of t' without our measure,*
15 boasting of t' without our measure,*
16 line of t' made ready to our hand.
11: 6 made manifest among you in all t'.*
9 all t' I have kept myself from being*
28 Beside those t' that are without, that
30 glory of the t' which concern mine

2Co 12: 19 we do all t', dearly beloved, for your
13: 10 I write these t' being absent, lest
Ga 1: 20 Now the t' which I write unto you,*
2: 18 For if I build again the t' which I
3: 4 Have ye suffered so many t' in vain?
10 that continueth not in all t' which are
4: 24 Which t' are an allegory: for these are
5: 17 that ye cannot do the t' that ye would.
21 which do such t' shall not inherit the
6: 6 him that teacheth in all good t'.
Eph 1: 10 together in one all t' in Christ,
11 who worketh all t' after the counsel
22 And hath put all t' under his feet, and
22 be the head over all t' to the church,
3: 9 who created all t' by Jesus Christ:
4: 10 all heavens, that he might fill all t'.)
15 may grow up into him in all t', which
5: 6 because of these t' cometh the
12 those t' which are done of them in
13 But all t' that are reproved are made
20 Giving thanks always for all t' unto
6: 9 ye masters, do the same t' unto them,
21 Lord, shall make known to you all t':
Ph'p 1: 10 ye may approve t' that are excellent;
12 the t' which happened unto me have
2: 4 Look not every man on his own t',
4 but every man also on the t' of others.
10 knee should bow, of t' in heaven,
10 and t' in earth, and t' under the earth;
14 Do all t' without murmurings and
21 not the t' which are Jesus Christ's.
3: 1 To write the same t' to you, to me
7 But what t' were gain to me, those I
8 and I count all t' but loss for the
8 whom I have suffered the loss of all t',
13 forgetting those t' which are behind,
13 reaching forth unto those t' which
19 is in their shame, who mind earthly t'.
21 he is able even to subdue all t' unto
4: 8 brethren, whatsoever t' are true,
8 whatsoever t' are honest,
8 whatsoever t' are just,
8 whatsoever t' are pure,
8 whatsoever t' are lovely,
8 whatsoever t' are of good report; if
8 there be any praise, think on these t'.
9 Those t', which ye have both learned,
12 in all t' I am instructed both to be
13 I can do all t' through Christ which
18 the t' which were sent from you, an
Col 1: 16 For by him were all t' created, that are
16 all t' were created by him, and for
17 before all t', and by him all t' consist.
18 that in all t' he might have the
20 him to reconcile all t' unto himself;
20 they be t' in earth, or t' in heaven.
2: 17 Which are a shadow of t' to come;
18 intruding into those t' which he hath
23 t' have indeed a shew of wisdom
3: 1 Christ, seek those t' which are above,
2 Set your affection on t' above,
2 not on t' on the earth.
4 And above all these t' put on charity,
20 Children, obey your parents in all t':
22 obey in all t' your masters according
4: 9 shall make known unto you all t'
1Th 2: 14 have suffered like t' of your own
5: 21 Prove all t'; hold fast that which is
2Th 2: 5 yet with you, I told you these t'?
3: 4 will do the t' which we command you.
1Ti 3: 11 not slanderers sober, faithful in all t'.
14 These t' write I unto thee, hoping
4: 6 brethren in remembrance of these t',
8 but godliness is profitable unto all t',
11 These t' command and teach.
15 Meditate upon these t'; give thyself
5: 7 And these t' give in charge, that
13 speaking t' which they ought not.
21 observe these t' without perferring
6: 2 benefit. These t' teach and exhort.
11 thou, O man of God, flee these t';
13 sight of God, who quickeneth all t',
17 who giveth us richly all t' to enjoy;
2Ti 1: 12 which cause I also suffer these t':
18 how many t' he ministered unto me at
2: 2 t' that thou hast heard of me among
7 Lord give thee understanding in all t'.
10 I endure all t' for the elect's sake,
14 these t' put them in remembrance,
3: 14 in the t' which thou hast learned
4: 5 But watch thou in all t', endure
Tit 1: 5 set in order the t' that are wanting,
11 teaching t' which they ought not, for
15 Unto the pure all t' are pure: but unto
2: 1 t' which become sound doctrine:
3 too much wine, teachers of good t';*
7 In all t' shewing thyself a pattern of
9 and to please them well in all t';
10 doctrine of God our Saviour in all t'.
15 These t' speak, and exhort, and
3: 8 t' I will that thou affirm constantly,
8 t' are good and profitable unto
Heb 1: 2 whom he hath appointed heir of all t',
3 and upholding all t' by the word of his
2: 1 earnestly to the t' which we have
8 put all t' in subjection under his feet.
8 we see not yet all t' put under him.
10 it became him, for whom are all t',
10 and by whom are all t', in bringing
17 in all t' it behoved him to be made like
17 high priest in t' pertaining to God,
3: 4 man; but he that built all t' is God.
5 those t' which were to be spoken after;
4: 13 t' are naked and opened unto the eyes
5: 1 for men in t' pertaining to God,
8 learned he obedience by the t' which

Heb 5: 11 Of whom we have many t' to say, and
6: 9 we are persuaded better t' of you,
9 and t' that accompany salvation,
18 That by two immutable t', in
7: 13 he of whom these t' are spoken 4229
8: 1 t' which we have spoken this is the
5 example and shadow of heavenly t',
5 make all t' according to the pattern
9: 6 Now when these t' were thus
11 being come a high priest of good t'
22 all t' are by the law purged with blood
23 the patterns of t' in the heavens
23 the heavenly t' themselves with better
10: 1 having a shadow of good t' to come,
1 and not the very image of the t', 4229
11: 1 faith is the substance of t' hoped "
1 for, the evidence of t' not seen.
3 so that t' which are seen were not*
3 were not made of t' which do appear.
7 being warned of God of t' not seen as
14 they that say such t' declare plainly
20 Jacob and Esau concerning t' to come.
12: 24 speaketh better t' than that of Abel.*
27 removing of those t' that are shaken,
27 that are shaken, as of t' that are made,
27 those t' which cannot be shaken may
13: 5 and be content with such t' as ye have:
18 in all t' willing to live honestly.
Jas 2: 16 ye give them not those t' which are
3: 2 For in many t' we offend all. If any
5 little member, and boasteth great t'.
7 and of serpents, and of t' in the sea, is
10 these t' ought not so to be.
5: 12 But above all t', my brethren, swear
1Pe 1: 12 unto us they did minister the t', 846
12 which t' the angels desire to look into.
18 were not redeemed with corruptible t',
4: 7 But the end of all t' is at hand: be ye
8 And above all t' have fervent charity
11 that God in all t' may be glorified
2Pe 1: 3 given unto us all t' that pertain unto
8 For if these t' be in you, and
9 he that lacketh these t' is blind,
10 for if ye do these t', ye shall never
12 always in remembrance of these t',
15 these t' always in remembrance.
2: 12 speak evil of the t' that they *
3: 4 t' continue as they were from the
11 that all these t' shall be dissolved,
14 seeing that ye look for such t',
16 speaking in them of these t';
16 are some t' hard to be understood,
17 seeing ye know these t' before,
1Jo 1: 4 And these t' write we unto you,
2: 1 children, these t' write I unto you,
15 neither the t' that are in the world.
20 from the Holy One, and ye know all t'.
26 These t' have I written unto you
27 same anointing teacheth you of all t',
3: 20 than our heart, and knoweth all t'.
22 and do those t' that are pleasing in his
5: 13 These t' have I written unto you
2Jo 8 not those t' which we have wrought,
12 Having many t' to write unto you,
3Jo 2 above all t' that thou mayest prosper
13 I had many t' to write, but I will not
Jude 10 speak evil of those t' which they know
10 in those t' they corrupt themselves.
Re 1: 1 servants t' which must shortly come
2 Christ, and of all t' that he saw.
3 keep those t' which are written
19 Write the t' which thou hast seen, and
19 thou hast seen, and the t' which are,
19 and the t' which shall be hereafter;
2: 1 These t' saith he that holdeth the
8 These t' saith the first and the last,
10 Fear none of those t' which thou shalt
12 These t' saith he which hath the sharp
14 But I have a few t' against thee,
14 to eat t' sacrificed unto idols, and to
18 These t' saith the Son of God, who
20 I have a few t' against thee, *
20 and to eat t' sacrificed unto idols.
3: 1 These t' saith he that hath the seven
2 and strengthen the t' which remain,
7 These t' saith he that is holy, he that
14 These t' saith the Amen, the faithful
4: 1 shew these t' which must be hereafter.
11 for thou hast created all t', and for
7: 1 after these t' I saw four angels *
10: 4 t' which the seven thunders uttered,
6 heaven, and the t' that therein are,
6 the earth, and the t' that therein are,
6 the sea, and the t' which are therein,
13: 5 a mouth speaking great t' and
18: 1 And after these t' I saw another
14 and all t' which were dainty and
15 The merchants of these t', which
19: 1 after these t' I heard a great voice
20: 12 t' which were written in the books,
21: 4 for the former t' are passed away.
5 said, Behold, I will make all t' new.
7 that overcometh shall inherit all t';
22: 6 the t' which must shortly be done.
8 And I John saw these t', and
8 angel which shewed me these t'.
16 testify unto you these t' in the
18 If any man shall add unto these t',*
19 the t' which are written in this book.*
20 He which testifieth these t' saith,

things'
Col 3: 6 For which t' sake the wrath of God

think See also BETHINK; THINKEST; THINKETH; THINKING; THOUGHT.
Ge 40: 14 t' on me when it shall be well *2142

Nu 36: 6 them marry to whom they t' best; 5869
2Sa 13: 33 t' that all the king's sons are dead: 559
2Ch 13: 8 And now ye t' to withstand the "
Ne 5: 19 T' upon me, my God, for good, *2142
6: 6 that thou and the Jews t' to rebel: 2803
14 My God, t' thou upon Tobiah and *2142
Es 4: 13 T' not with thyself that thou shalt 1819
Job 31: 1 why then should I t' upon a maid?* 995
41: 32 one would t' the deep to be hoary. 2803
Ec 8: 17 though a wise man t' to know it, 559
Isa 10: 7 so, neither doth his heart t' so; 2803
Jer 23: 27 Which t' to cause my people to "
29: 11 the thoughts that I t' toward you, "
Eze 38: 10 and thou shalt t' an evil thought: * "
Da 7: 25 and t' to change times and laws: 5452
Jon 1: 6 if so be that God will t' upon us, 6245
Zec 11: 12 If ye t' good, give me my price; 5869
M't 3: 9 t' not to say within yourselves, 1380
5: 17 T' not that I am come to destroy 3543
6: 7 they t' that they shall be heard for 1380
9: 4 Wherefore t' ye evil in your hearts? 1760
10: 34 T' not that I am come to send 3543
18: 12 How t' ye? if a man have an 1380
21: 28 what t' ye? A certain man had "
22: 42 Saying, What t' ye of Christ? whose "
24: 44 in such an hour as ye t' not the Son "
26: 66 What t' ye? They answered and "
M'r 14: 64 heard the blasphemy: what t' ye? 5316
Lu 12: 40 cometh at an hour when ye t' not. 1380
13: 4 t' ye that they were sinners above "
Joh 5: 39 in them ye t' ye have eternal life: "
45 Do not t' that I will accuse you to "
11: 56 What t' ye, that he will not come to "
16: 2 will t' that he doeth God service. "
Ac 13: 25 Whom t' ye that I am? I am not *5282
17: 29 not to t' that the Godhead is like 3543
26: 2 I t' myself happy, king Agrippa, 2233
Ro 12: 3 not to t' of himself more highly 5252
3 more highly than he ought to t'; 5426
3 but to t' soberly, according as God "
1Co 4: 6 not to t' of men above that which is* "
9 For I t' that God hath set forth us 1380
7: 36 if any man t' that he behaveth *3543
40 I t' also that I have the Spirit of 1380
8: 2 if any man t' that he knoweth any* "
12: 23 which we t' to be less honourable, "
14: 37 If any man t' himself to be a * "
2Co 3: 5 to t' any thing as of ourselves; *3049
10: 2 I t' to be bold against some, which* "
2 which t' of us as if we walked * "
7 let him of himself t' this again, * "
11 Let such an one t' this, that, such* "
11: 16 say again, Let no man t' me a fool; 1380
12: 6 man should t' of me above that 3049
19 t' ye that we excuse ourselves unto 1380
Ga 6: 3 if a man t' himself to be something,* "
Eph 3: 20 above all that we ask or t', 3539
Ph'p 1: 7 is meet for me to t' this of you all,* 5426
4: 8 be any praise, t' on these things. 3049
Jas 1: 7 that man t' that he shall receive 3633
4: 5 Do ye t' that the scripture saith in 1380
1Pe 4: 4 t' it strange that ye run not with them
12 t' it not strange concerning the fiery
2Pe 1: 13 Yea, I t' it meet, as long as I am in 2233

thinkest
2Sa 10: 3 T' thou that David doth honour 5869
1Ch 19: 3 T' thou that David doth honour "
Job 35: 2 T' thou this to be right, that thou 2803
M't 17: 25 him, saying, What t' thou, Simon? 1380
22: 17 Tell us therefore, What t' thou? "
26: 53 T' thou that I cannot now pray to "
Lu 10: 36 Which now of these three, t' thou, "
Ac 28: 22 desire to hear of thee what thou t': 5426
Ro 2: 3 And t' thou this, O man, that 3049

thinketh
2Sa 18: 27 Me t' the running of the foremost‡ 7200
Ps 40: 17 needy; yet the Lord t' upon me: 2803
Pr 23: 7 For as he t' in his heart, so is he: ‡8176
1Co 10: 12 let him that t' he standeth take 1380
13: 5 is not easily provoked, t' no evil; *3049
Ph'p 3: 4 If any other man t' that he hath 1380

thinking
2Sa 4: 10 t'...have brought good tidings, 1931,1961
5: 6 t', David cannot come in hither. 559

third
Ge 1: 13 and the morning were the t' day. 7992
2: 14 name of the t' river is Hiddekel: "
6: 16 and t' stories shalt thou make it. "
22: 4 t' day Abraham lifted up his eyes, "
31: 22 told Laban on the t' day that Jacob "
32: 19 he the second, and the t', and all "
34: 25 came to pass on the t' day, when "
40: 20 came to pass the t' day, which was "
42: 18 Joseph said unto them the t' day, "
50: 23 children of the t' generation: 8029
Ex 19: 1 In the t' month, when the children 7992
11 And be ready against the t' day: "
11 t' day the Lord will come down in "
15 Be ready against the t' day: come 7969
16 it came to pass on the t' day in the 7992
20: 5 unto the t' and fourth generation. 8029
28: 19 the t' row a ligure, an agate, and 7992
34: 7 unto the t' and to the fourth 8029
39: 12 the t' row, a ligure, an agate, and 7992
Le 7: 17 flesh of the sacrifice on the t' day "
18 be eaten at all on the t' day, "
19: 6 if ought remain until the t' day, it "
7 if it be eaten at all on the t' day, it "
Nu 2: 24 they shall go forward in the t' rank. "
7: 24 On the t' day Eliab the son of Helon, "
14: 18 unto the t' and fourth generation 8029
15: 6 mingled with the t' part of an hin 7992
7 offer the t' part of an hin of wine, "
19: 12 purify himself with it on the t' day, "
Nu 19: 12 if he purify not himself the t' day, 7992
19 upon the unclean on the t' day, "
28: 14 and the t' part of an hin unto a ram, "
29: 20 on the t' day eleven bullocks, two "
31: 19 and your captives on the t' day, "
De 5: 9 unto the t' and fourth generation 8029
23: 8 of the Lord in their t' generation. 7992
26: 12 tithes of thine increase the t' year, "
Jos 9: 17 came unto their cities on the t' day. "
19: 10 the t' lot came up for the children "
J'g 20: 30 children of Benjamin on the t' day, "
1Sa 3: 8 called Samuel again the t' time. "
17: 13 Abinadab, and the t' Shammah. "
19: 21 sent messengers again the t' time, "
20: 5 myself in the field unto the t' day "
12 to morrow any time, or the t' day, "
30: 1 were come to Ziklag on the t' day, "
2Sa 1: 2 It came even to pass on the t' day, "
3: 3 the t', Absalom the son of Maacah "
18: 2 David sent forth a t' part of the "
2 a t' part under the hand of Abishai "
2 t' part under the hand of Ittai the "
1Ki 3: 18 the t' day after that I was delivered, "
6: 6 the t' was seven cubits broad: for "
8 and out of the middle into the t'. "
12: 12 came to Rehoboam the t' day, "
12 saying, Come to me again the t' day. "
15: 28 Even in the t' year of Asa king of 7969
33 t' year of Asa king of Judah began "
18: 1 Lord came to Elijah in the t' year, 7992
34 And he said, Do it the t' time. 8027
34 And they did it the t' time. "
22: 2 it come to pass in the t' year, that 7992
2Ki 1: 13 sent again a captain of the t' fifty "
13 And the t' captain of fifty went up, "
11: 5 A t' part of you that enter in on the "
6 a t' part shall be at the gate of Sur; "
6 a t' part at the gate behind the "
18: 1 to pass in the t' year of Hoshea 7969
19: 29 in the t' year sow ye, and reap, and 7992
20: 5 t' day thou shalt go up unto the "
8 the house of the Lord the t' day? "
1Ch 2: 13 the second, and Shimma the t', "
3: 2 t', Absalom the son of Maachah the "
15 t' Zedekiah, the fourth Shallum. "
8: 1 the second, and Aharah the t', "
39 the second, and Eliphelet the t'. "
12: 9 Obadiah the second, Eliab the t', "
23: 19 Jahaziel the t', and Jekameam the "
24: 8 t' to Harim, the fourth to Seorim, "
23 Jehaziel the t', Jekameam the "
25: 10 t' to Zaccur, he, his sons, and his "
26: 2 Zebadiah the t', Jathniel the fourth, "
4 Joah the t', and Sacar the fourth, "
11 Tebaliah the t', Zechariah "
27: 5 t' captain of the host for the "
5 t' month was Benaiah the son of "
2Ch 10: 12 came to Rehoboam on the t' day, "
12 Come again to me on the t' day. "
15: 10 at Jerusalem in the t' month, in "
17: 7 in the t' year of his reign he sent 7969
23: 4 A t' part of you entering on the 7992
5 t' part shall be at the king's house; "
5 t' part at the gate of the foundation: "
27: 5 both the second year, and the t'. "
31: 7 t' month they began to lay the "
Ezr 6: 15 house was finished on the t' day 8531
Ne 10: 32 t' part of a shekel for the service 7992
Es 1: 3 In the t' year of his reign, he made 7969
5: 1 Now it came to pass on the t' day, 7992
8: 9 called at that time in the t' month, "
Job 42: 14 the name of the t', Keren-happuch. "
Isa 19: 24 shall Israel be the t' with Egypt "
37: 30 in the t' year sow ye, and reap, and "
Jer 38: 14 t' entry that is in the house of the "
Eze 5: 2 Thou shalt burn with fire a t' part "
2 thou shalt take a t' part, and smite "
2 a t' part thou shalt scatter in the "
12 A t' part of thee shall die with the "
12 a t' part shall fall by the sword "
12 I will scatter a t' part into all the "
10: 14 and the t' the face of a lion, and the "
21: 14 let the sword be doubled the t' time, "
31: 1 the eleventh year, in the t' month, "
46: 14 the t' part of an hin of oil, to temper "
Da 1: 1 t' year of the reign of Jehoiakim 7969
2: 39 and another t' kingdom of brass, 8523
5: 7 shall be the t' ruler in the kingdom. "
16, 29 be the t' ruler in the kingdom. 8531
8: 1 In the t' year of the reign of king 7969
10: 1 the t' year of Cyrus king of Persia "
Ho 6: 2 t' day he will raise us up, and we 7992
Zec 6: 3 And in the t' chariot white horses; "
13: 8 die; but the t' shall be left therein. "
9 bring the t' part through the fire, "
M't 16: 21 and be raised again the t' day. 5154
17: 23 and the t' day he shall be raised "
20: 3 And he went out about the t' hour, "
19 and the t' day he shall rise again. "
22: 26 also, and the t', unto the seventh. "
26: 44 and prayed the t' time, saying the "
27: 64 be made sure until the t' day, "
M'r 9: 31 he is killed, he shall rise the t' day.* "
10: 34 and the t' day he shall rise again. * "
12: 21 he any seed: and the t' likewise. "
14: 41 he cometh the t' time, and saith "
15: 25 And it was the t' hour, and they "
Lu 9: 22 be slain, and be raised the t' day. "
12: 38 watch, or come in the t' watch, "
13: 32 and the t' day I shall be perfected. "
18: 33 and the t' day he shall rise again. "
20: 12 And again he sent a t': and they "
31 And the t' took her; and in like "
23: 22 And he said unto them the t' time, "
24: 7 crucified, and the t' day rise again. "
21 to day is the t' day since these "
Lu 24: 46 to rise from the dead the t' day: 5154
Joh 2: 1 the t' day there was a marriage "
21: 14 t' time that Jesus shewed himself "
17 He saith unto him the t' time, "
17 he said unto him the t' time, "
Ac 2: 15 it is but the t' hour of the day. "
10: 40 Him God raised up the t' day, and "
20: 9 and fell down from the t' loft, 5152
23: 23 at the t' hour of the night; 5154
27: 19 And the t' day we cast out with "
1Co 15: 4 he rose again the t' day according "
2Co 12: 2 an one caught up to the t' heaven. "
14 t' time I am ready to come to you; "
13: 1 is the t' time I am coming to you. "
Re 4: 7 and the t' beast had a face as a man, "
6: 5 when he had opened the t' seal, "
5 I heard the t' beast say, Come and "
8: 7 the t' part of trees was burnt up, "
8 the t' part of the sea became blood; "
9 the t' part of the creatures which "
9 t' part of the ships were destroyed. "
10 And the t' angel sounded, and there "
10 fell upon the t' part of the rivers, "
11 the t' part of the waters became "
12 the t' part of the sun was smitten, "
12 and the t' part of the moon, and the "
12 moon, and the t' part of the stars; "
12 t' part of them was darkened, and "
12 the day shone not for a t' part of it, "
9: 15 year, for to slay the t' part of men. "
18 three was the t' part of men killed, "
11: 14 behold, the t' woe cometh quickly. "
12: 4 tail drew the t' part of the stars of "
14: 9 And the t' angel followed them, "
16: 4 t' angel poured out his vial upon "
21: 19 the t', a chalcedony; the fourth, an "

thirdly
1Co 12: 28 secondarily prophets, t' teachers, 5154

thirst See also ATHIRST; THIRSTED; THIRSTETH.
Ex 17: 3 our children and our cattle with t'? 6772
De 28: 48 hunger, and in t', and in nakedness, "
29: 19 heart, to add drunkenness to t': *6771
J'g 15: 18 and now shall I die for t', and fall 6772
2Ch 32: 11 yourselves to die by famine and...t', "
Ne 9: 15 for them out of the rock for their t', "
20 and gavest them water for their t'. "
Job 24: 11 their winepresses, and suffer t'. 6770
Ps 69: 21 in my t' they gave me vinegar to 6772
104: 11 the wild asses quench their t'. "
Isa 5: 13 their multitude dried up with t'. "
41: 17 and their tongue faileth for t', "
49: 10 They shall not hunger nor t'; 6770
50: 2 there is no water, and dieth for t'. 6772
Jer 2: 25 unshod, and thy throat from t': 6773
48: 18 down from thy glory, and sit in t'; 6772
La 4: 4 to the roof of his mouth for t': "
Ho 2: 3 like a dry land, and slay her with t'. "
Am 8: 11 famine of bread, nor a t' for water, "
13 virgins and young men faint for t'. "
M't 5: 6 hunger and t' after righteousness: 1372
Joh 4: 13 drinketh...this water shall t' again: "
14 that I shall give him shall never t'; "
15 give me this water, that I t' not, "
6: 35 that believeth on me shall never t'. "
7: 37 If any man t', let him come unto "
19: 28 might be fulfilled, saith, I t'. "
Ro 12: 20 feed him; if he t', give him drink: "
1Co 4: 11 both hunger, and t', and are naked, "
2Co 11: 27 watchings often, in hunger and t', 1373
Re 7: 16 no more, neither t' any more; 1372

thirsted
Ex 17: 3 And the people t' there for water; 6770
Isa 48: 21 And they t' not when he led them "

thirsteth
Ps 42: 2 My soul t' for God, for the living 6770
63: 1 my soul t' for thee, my flesh longeth "
143: 6 my soul t' after thee, as a thirsty "
Isa 55: 1 Ho, every one that t', come ye to 6771

thirsty See also BLOODTHIRSTY.
J'g 4: 19 a little water to drink; for I am t'. 6770
2Sa 17: 29 is hungry, and weary, and t', 6771
Ps 63: 1 longeth for thee in a dry and t' land, "
107: 5 Hungry and t', their soul fainted 6771
143: 6 soul thirsteth after thee, as a t' land. *
Pr 25: 21 and if he be t', give him water to 6771
25 As cold waters to a t' soul, so is good "
Isa 21: 14 brought water to him that was t', 6771
29: 8 or as when a t' man dreameth, and, "
32: 6 will cause the drink of the t' to fail. "
35: 7 and the t' land springs of water: 6774
44: 3 pour water upon him that is t', 6771
65: 13 shall drink, but ye shall be t': 6770
Eze 19: 13 wilderness, in a dry and t' ground. 6772
M't 25: 35 I was t', and ye gave me drink: 1372
37 fed thee? or t', and gave thee drink?* "
42 I was t', and ye gave me no drink: "

thirteen
Ge 17: 25 his son was t' years old, 7969,6240
Nu 3: 43 hundred and threescore and t'. 7969
46 hundred and threescore and t' of "
29: 13 t' young bullocks, two rams, 7969,6240
14 every bullock of the t' bullocks, "
Jos 19: 6 t' cities and their villages: "
21: 4 the tribe of Benjamin, t' cities. "
6 Manasseh in Bashan, t' cities. "
19 t' cities with their suburbs. "
33 t' cities with their suburbs. "
1Ki 7: 1 building his own house t' years, "
1Ch 6: 60 their families were t' cities. "
62 Manasseh in Bashan, t' cities. "
26: 11 and brethren of Hosah were t'. "
Eze 40: 11 length of the gate, t' cubits. "

thirteenth
Ge 14: 4 in the t· year they rebelled. 7969,6240
1Ch 24:13 t· to Huppah, the fourteenth "
25:20 The t· to Shubael, he, his sons, " "
Es 3:12 scribes called on the t· day " "
13 upon the t· day of the twelfth " "
8:12 upon the t· day of the twelfth " "
9: 1 Adar, on the t· day of the same, " "
17 the t· day of the month Adar; " "
18 together on the t· day thereof, " "
Jer 1: 2 in the t· year of his reign. " "
25: 3 the t· year of Josiah the son of " "

thirtieth
2Ki 15:13 in the nine and t· year of Uzziah 7970
17 In the nine and t· year of Azariah "
25:27 seven and t· year of the captivity of "
2Ch 15:19 five and t· year of the reign of Asa. "
16: 1 six and t· year of the reign of Asa "
Ne 5:14 two and t· year of Artaxerxes the "
13: 6 the two and t· year of Artaxerxes "
Jer 52:31 seven and t· year of the captivity of "
Eze 1: 1 Now it came to pass in the t· year, "

thirty See also THIRTYFOLD.
Ge 5: 3 And Adam lived an hundred and t· 7970
5 were nine hundred and t· years: "
16 Jared eight hundred and t· years, "
6:15 cubits, and the height of it t· cubits. "
11:12 Arphaxad lived five and t· years, "
14 And Salah lived t· years, and begat "
16 And Eber lived four and t· years, "
17 Peleg four hundred and t· years, "
18 And Peleg lived t· years, and begat "
20 And Reu lived two and t· years, and "
22 And Serug lived t· years, and begat "
18:30 there shall t· be found there. "
30 I will not do it, if I find t· there. "
25:17 an hundred and t· and seven years: "
32:15 T· milch camels with their colts, "
41:46 And Joseph was t· years old when "
46:15 his daughters were t· and three. "
47: 9 are an hundred and t· years: "
Ex 6:16 were an hundred t· and seven years. "
18 were an hundred t· and three years. "
20 an hundred and t· and seven years. "
12:40 was four hundred and t· years. "
41 end of the four hundred and t· years, "
21:32 their masters t· shekels of silver, "
26: 8 of one curtain shall be t· cubits, "
36:15 length of one curtain was t· cubits, "
38:24 and seven hundred and t· shekels, "
Le 12: 4 of her purifying three and t· days; "
27: 4 thy estimation shall be t· shekels. "
Nu 1:35 were t· and two thousand and two "
37 were t· and five thousand and four "
2:21 were t· and two thousand and two "
23 were t· and five thousand and four "
4: 3, 23, 30, 35, 39 t· years old and upward "
40 thousand and six hundred and t·. "
43, 47 From t· years old and upward "
7:13, 19, 25, 31, 37, 43, 49, 55, 61, 67, 73,
79, 85 an hundred and t· shekels, 7970
20:29 they mourned for Aaron t· days, "
26: 7 thousand and seven hundred and t·. "
37 them, t· and two thousand and five "
51 a thousand seven hundred and t·. "
31:35 t· and two thousand persons in all, "
36 seven and t· thousand and five "
38 beeves were t· and six thousand; "
39 the asses were t· thousand and five "
40 the Lord's tribute was t· and two "
43 hundred thousand and t· thousand "
44 And t· and six thousand beeves, "
45 t· thousand asses and five hundred, "
De 2:14 brook Zered, was t· and eight years; "
34: 8 Moses in the plains of Moab t· days: "
Jos 7: 5 smote of them about t· and six men: "
8: 3 and Joshua chose out t· thousand "
12:24 one: all the kings t· and one. "
J'g 10: 4 had t· sons that rode on t· ass colts, "
4 and they had t· cities, which are "
12: 9 he had t· sons, and t· daughters, "
9 took in t· daughters from abroad "
14 he had forty sons and t· nephews, "
14:11 they brought t· companions to be "
12 t· sheets and t· change of garments: "
13 t· sheets and t· change of garments. "
19 slew t· men of them, and took their "
20:31 in the field, about t· men of Israel. "
39 and kill of the men of Israel about t· "
1Sa 4:10 fell of Israel t· thousand footmen. "
9:22 which were about t· persons. "
11: 8 and the men of Judah t· thousand. "
13: 5 t· thousand chariots, and six "
2Sa 5: 4 David was t· years old when he "
5 he reigned t· and three years over "
6: 1 chosen men of Israel, t· thousand. "
23:13 And three of the t· chief went down, "
23 He was more honourable than the t·, "
24 brother of Joab was one of the t·; "
39 the Hittite: t· and seven in all. "
1Ki 2:11 t· and three years reigned he in "
4:22 day was t· measures of fine flour, "
5:13 and the levy was t· thousand men. "
6: 2 and the height thereof t· cubits. "
7: 2 and the height thereof t· cubits, "
6 and the breadth thereof t· cubits: "
23 and a line of t· cubits did compass it "
16:23 the t· and first year of Asa king of "
29 the t· and eighth year of Asa king "
20: 1 there were t· and two kings with "
15 they were two hundred and t· two: "
16 t· and two kings that helped him. "
22:31 t· and two captains that had rule "
42 Jehoshaphat was t· and five years "
2Ki 8:17 T· and two years old was he when "
13:10 t· and seventh year of Joash king 7970
15: 8 t· and eighth year of Azariah king "
18:14 of silver and t· talents of gold. "
22: 1 and he reigned t· and one years in "
1Ch 3: 4 he reigned t· and three years. "
7: 4 for war, six and t· thousand men: "
7 and two thousand and t· and four. "
11:15 Now three of the t· captains went "
25 he was honourable among the t·, "
42 of the Reubenites, and t· with him, "
12: 4 man among the t·, and over the t·; "
34 and spear t· and seven thousand. "
15: 7 and his brethren an hundred and t·: "
19: 7 hired t· and two thousand chariots, "
23: 3 the age of t· years and upward: "
3 by man, was t· and eight thousand. "
27: 6 among the t·, and above the t·: "
29:27 t· and three years reigned he in "
2Ch 3:15 two pillars of t· and five cubits high, "
4: 2 a line of t· cubits did compass it "
16:12 Asa in the t· and ninth year of his "
20:31 he was t· and five years old when he "
21: 5 Jehoram was t· and two years old "
20 T· and two years old was he when "
24:15 an hundred and t· years old was he "
34: 1 in Jerusalem one and t· years. "
35: 7 to the number of t· thousand, and "
Ezr 1: 9 t· chargers of gold, a thousand "
10 T· basons of gold, silver basons of "
2:35 thousand and six hundred and t·. "
42 in all an hundred t· and nine. "
65 three hundred t· and seven: "
66 were seven hundred t· and six; "
67 camels, four hundred t· and five; "
Ne 7:38 three thousand nine hundred and t·. "
45 of Shobai, an hundred t· and eight. "
67 three hundred t· and seven: "
68 horses, seven hundred t· and six: "
69 camels, four hundred t· and five: "
70 hundred and t· priests' garments. "
Es 4:11 come in unto the king these t· days. "
Jer 38:10 Take from hence t· men with thee, "
52:29 eight hundred t· and two persons: "
Eze 40:17 t· chambers were upon the "
41: 6 one over another, and t· in order; "
46:22 of forty cubits long and t· broad: "
Da 6: 7 of any God or man for t· days, 8533
12 of any God or man within t· days, "
12:12 hundred and five and t· days. 7970
Zec 11:12 for my price t· pieces of silver. "
13 and I took the t· pieces of silver, "
M't 13:23 hundredfold, some sixty, some t·. 5144
26:15 with him for t· pieces of silver. "
27: 3 brought again the t· pieces of silver "
9 they took the t· pieces of silver, the "
M'r 4: 8 forth, some t·, and some sixty, and* "
Lu 3:23 began to be about t· years of age, "
Joh 5: 5 had an infirmity t· and eight years. "
6:19 about five and twenty or t· furlongs, "
Ga 3:17 four hundred and t· years after, "

thirtyfold
M't 13: 8 some sixtyfold, some t·. 5144
M'r 4:20 forth fruit, some t·, some sixty, "

thirty-thousand See THIRTY and THOUSAND.

this See also THESE.
Ge 2:23 T· is now bone of my bones, and 2063
3:13 What is t· that thou hast done? "
14 Because thou hast done t·, thou "
4:14 thou hast driven me out t· day from "
5: 1 T· is the book of the generations 2088
29 T· same shall comfort us "
6:15 t· is the fashion which thou shalt "
7: 1 before me in t· generation. "
9:12 T· is the token of the covenant 2063
11: 6 t· they begin to do: and now 2088
12: 7 Unto thy seed will I give t· land: 2063
12 that they shall say, T· is his wife: "
18 What is t· that thou hast done "
15: 2 house is t· Eliezer of Damascus? *1931
4 saying, T· shall not be thine heir; 2088
7 to give thee t· land to inherit it. 2063
18 Unto thy seed have I given t· land, "
17:10 T· is my covenant, which ye shall "
21 at t· set time in the next year. 2088
18:25 from thee to do after t· manner, "
32 and I will speak yet but t· once: 6471
19: 5 men which came in to thee t· night? "
9 T· one fellow came in to sojourn, "
12 city, bring them out of t· place: *
13 For we will destroy t· place, 2088
14 said, Up, get you out of t· place; "
14 for the Lord will destroy t· city. "
20 now, t· city is near to flee unto, 2063
21 accepted thee concerning t· thing 2088
21 that I will not overthrow t· city, "
34 make him drink wine t· night also; "
37 father of the Moabites unto t· day. "
38 the children of Ammon unto t· day. "
20: 5 of my hands have I done t·. 2063
6 thou didst t· in the integrity of thy "
10 that thou hast done t· thing? 2088
11 the fear of God is not in t· place; "
13 T· is thy kindness which thou "
21:10 Cast out t· bondwoman and her 2063
10 the son of t· bondwoman shall not "
26 I wot not who hath done t· thing: 2088
24:58 unto her, Wilt thou go with t· man? "
65 What man is t· that walketh in 1976
25:31 said, Sell me t· day thy birthright.
32 what profit shall t· birthright do *2088
33 And Jacob said, Swear to me t· day; "
26: 3 Sojourn in t· land, and I will be 2063
10 What is t· thou hast done unto us? "
11 He that toucheth t· man or his 2088
33 the city is Beer-sheba unto t· day. "
Ge 28:15 will bring thee again into t· land; 2063
16 Surely the Lord is in t· place; and 2088
17 and said, How dreadful is t· place! "
17 t· is none other but the house of "
17 God, and t· is the gate of heaven. "
20 will keep me in t· way that I go, "
22 t· stone, which I have set for a 2063
29:25 What is t· thou hast done unto me? "
27 we will give thee t· also for the * "
33 therefore given me t· son also: 2088
34 t· time will my husband be joined
30:31 if thou wilt do t· thing for me, I 2088
31: 1 father's hath he gotten all t· glory. "
13 arise, get thee out from t· land, 2063
38 T· twenty years have I been with 2088
43 what can I do t· day unto these my
48 T· heap is a witness between me 2088
48 witness between me and thee t· day.
51 said to Jacob, Behold t· heap, 2088
51 behold t· pillar, which I have
52 T· heap be witness, and 2088
52 t· pillar be witness, that I will not*
52 will not pass over t· heap to thee, 2088
52 t· heap [2088] and t· pillar unto 2063
32: 2 them, he said, T· is God's host: 2088
10 my staff I passed over t· Jordan; "
19 On t· manner shall ye speak unto "
32 hollow of the thigh, unto t· day: "
33: 8 What meanest thou by all t· drove "
34: 4 saying, Get me t· damsel to wife. 2063
14 We cannot do t· thing, to give our 2088
15 in t· will we consent unto you: 2063
35:17 thou shalt have t· son also. *2088
20 pillar of Rachel's grave unto t· day.
36:24 t· was that Anah that found the 1931
37: 6 t· dream which I have dreamed: 2088
10 t· dream that thou hast dreamed? "
19 Behold, t· dreamer cometh. 1976
22 cast him into t· pit that is in the 2088
32 and said, T· have we found: 2063
38:21 There was no harlot in t· place. *2088
22 that there was no harlot in t· place.* "
23 behold, I sent t· kid, and thou "
28 thread, saying, T· came out first. "
39: 9 is none greater in t· house than I; "
9 can I do t· great wickedness, and 2063
11 And it came to pass about t· time, 2088
19 t· manner did thy servant to me; 428
40:12 T· is the interpretation of it: 2088
14 and bring me out of t· house: "
18 T· is the interpretation thereof: "
41: 9 I do remember my faults t· day: "
24 and I told t· unto the magicians; *
34 Let Pharaoh do t·, and let him
38 Can we find such a one as t· is, 2088
39 as God hath shewed thee all t·, 2063
42:13 youngest is t· day with our father,
18 T· do, and live; for I fear God: 2063
21 is t· distress come upon us. "
28 What is t· that God hath done "
32 youngest is t· day with our father
43:10 we had returned t· second time. *2088
11 If it must be so now, do t·; 2063
29 Is t· your younger brother, of 2088
44: 5 Is not t· it in which my lord "
7 should do according to t· thing: * "
29 And if ye take t· also from me, "
45:17 Say unto thy brethren, T· do ye; 2063
19 Now thou art commanded, t· do ye; "
23 his father he sent after t· manner; "
47:23 I have bought you t· day and your
26 the land of Egypt unto t· day, 2088
48: 4 will give t· land to thy seed after 2063
9 God hath given me in t· place. *2088
18 for t· is the firstborn; put thy "
49:28 t· is it that their father spake 2063
50:11 T· is a grievous mourning to the 2088
20 as it is t· day, to save much people "
24 bring you out of t· land unto the 2063
Ex 1:18 Why have ye done t· thing, and 2088
2: 6 T· is one of the Hebrews' children. "
9 Take t· child away, and nurse it "
12 he looked t· way and that way, 3541
14 and said, Surely t· thing is known.*
15 when Pharaoh heard t· thing, 2088
3: 3 turn aside, and see t· great sight, "
15 unto you: t· is my name for ever, "
15 and t· is my memorial unto all "
4:17 shalt take t· rod in thine hand, "
5:22 thou so evil entreated t· people? "
23 he hath done evil to t· people; "
7:17 In t· thou shalt know that I am 2063
23 did he set his heart to t· also. "
8:19 Pharaoh, T· is the finger of God: 1931
23 to morrow shall t· sign be. 2088
32 hardened his heart at t· time also, 2063
9: 5 the Lord shall do t· thing in the "
14 For I will at t· time send all my 2063
16 for t· cause have I raised thee up, "
18 to morrow about t· time I will cause
27 unto them, I have sinned t· time:
10: 6 were upon the earth unto t· day. 2088
7 How long shall t· man be a snare "
17 I pray thee, my sin only t· once, "
17 take away from me t· death only. 2088
12: 2 T· month shall be unto you the "
3 In the tenth day of t· month they "
12 through the land of Egypt t· night,* "
14 t· day shall be unto you for a "
17 in t· selfsame day have I brought "
24 observe t· thing for an ordinance "
26 you, What mean ye by t· service? 2063
42 t· is that night of the Lord to be 2088
13: 3 Remember t· day, in which ye "
3 brought you out from t· place: "
4 T· day came ye out in the month

Ex 13: 5 shalt keep t' service in t' month. 2088
8 T' is done because of that which*
10 keep t' ordinance in his season 2063
14 time to come, saying, What is t? "
14: 5 Why have we done t', that we have "
12 Is not t' the word that we did tell 2088
15: 1 the children of Israel t' song unto 2063
16: 3 us forth into t' wilderness, 2088
3 to kill t' whole assembly with "
15 T' is the bread which the Lord *1931
16 T' is the thing which the Lord 2088
23 T' is that which the Lord hath 1931
32 T' is the thing which the Lord 2088
17: 3 Wherefore is t' that thou hast * "
4 What shall I do unto t' people? "
14 Write t' for a memorial in a book, 2063
18: 14 What is t' thing that thou doest 2088
18 and t' people that is with thee: "
18 for t' thing is too heavy for thee;*
23 If thou shalt do t' thing, and God 2088
23 all t' people shall also go to their "
21: 31 according to t' judgment shall it be"
25: 3 t' is the offering which ye shall 2063
26: 13 on t' side and on that side, 2088
28: 17 carbuncle: t' shall be the first row.*
29: 1 t' is the thing that thou shalt do 2088
38 t' is that which thou shalt offer "
42 T' shall be a continual burnt *
30: 13 T' they shall give, every one that 2088
31 T' shall be an holy anointing oil "
32: 1 for as for t' Moses, the man that "
9 unto Moses, I have seen t' people, "
12 repent of t' evil against thy people.
13 all t' land that I have spoken of 2063
21 What did t' people unto thee, that 2088
23 for as for t' Moses, the man that "
24 the fire, and there came out t' calf.
29 bestow upon you a blessing t' day.
31 t' people have sinned a great sin, 2088
33: 12 sayest unto me, Bring up t' people: "
17 I will do t' thing also that thou "
34: 11 that which I command thee t' day:
35: 4 T' is the thing which the Lord 2088
37: 8 One cherub on the end on t' side, * "
38: 15 on t' hand and that hand, were "
21 T' is the sum of the tabernacle, 428
39: 10 and a carbuncle: t' was the first row.*
Le 4: 20 a sin offering, so shall he do with t':
6: 9 T' is the law of the burnt offering:2063
14 t' is the law of the meat offering: "
20 T' is the offering of Aaron and of 2088
25 T' is the law of the sin offering: 2063
7: 1 t' is the law of the trespass "
11 t' is the law of the sacrifice of peace"
35 T' is the portion of the anointing "
37 T' is the law of the burnt offering, "
8: 5 T' is the thing which the Lord 2088
34 As he hath done t' day, so the Lord "
9: 6 T' is the thing which the Lord "
10: 3 T' is it that the Lord spake, 1931
19 t' day have they offered their sin
11: 46 T' is the law of the beasts, and of 2063
12: 7 T' is the law for her that hath born "
13: 59 T' is the law of the plague of "
14: 2 T' shall be the law of the leper in "
32 T' is the law of him in whom is the"
54 T' is the law for all manner of "
57 it is clean: t' is the law of leprosy. "
15: 3 t' shall be his uncleanness in his "
32 T' is the law of him that hath an "
16: 29 t' shall be a statute for ever unto you:*
34 t' shall be an everlasting statute 2063
17: 2 T' is the thing which the Lord "
7 T' shall be a statute for ever unto "
23: 27 the tenth day of t' seventh month 2088
34 fifteenth day of t' seventh month "
24: 10 t' son of the Israelitish woman and a*
25: 13 In the year of t' jubile ye shall 2063
26: 18 if ye will not yet for all t' hearken* 428
27 if ye will not for all t' hearken 2063
Nu 4: 4 T' shall be the service of the sons "
24, 28 T' is the service of the families "
31 And t' is the charge of their burden,"
33 T' is the service of the families of "
5: 19 free from t' bitter water that causeth
22 t' water that causeth the curse shall
29 T' is the law of jealousies, when 2063
30 shall execute upon her all t' law. "
31 t' woman shall bear her iniquity. *1931
6: 13 And t' is the law of the Nazarite, 2063
20 t' is holy for the priest, with the 1931
21 T' is the law of the Nazarite who 2063
23 On t' wise ye shall bless the 3541
7: 17 t' was the offering of Nahshon the 2088
23 t' was the offering of Nathaneel the"
29 t' was the offering of Eliab the son "
35 t' was the offering of Elizur the son"
41 t' was the offering of Shelumiel the "
47 t' was the offering of Eliasaph the "
53 t' was the offering of Elishama the "
59 t' was the offering of Gamaliel the "
65 t' was the offering of Abidan the "
71 t' was the offering of Ahiezer the "
77 t' was the offering of Pagiel the son"
83 t' was the offering of Ahira the son "
84, 88 T' was the dedication of the 2063
8: 4 t' work of the candlestick was of 2088
24 T' is it that belongeth unto the 2063
9: 3 In the fourteenth day of t' month, 2088
11: 6 is nothing at all, beside t' manna,
11 burden of all t' people upon me? 2088
12 Have I conceived all t' people? "
13 have flesh to give unto all t' people?"
14 not able to bear all t' people alone, "
31 it were a day's journey on t' side, 3541
13: 17 Get you up t' way southward, and 2088

Nu 13: 27 and honey; and t' is the fruit of it.2088
14: 2 God we had died in t' wilderness! "
3 the Lord brought us unto t' land, 2063
8 then he will bring us into t' land,
11 long will t' people provoke me? 2088
13 (for thou broughtest up t' people in"
14 tell it to the inhabitants of t' land:2063
14 thou Lord art among t' people, 2088
15 shalt kill all t' people as one man, "
16 was not able to bring t' people into "
19 Pardon,...the iniquity of t' people "
19 and as thou hast forgiven t' people."
27 I bear with t' evil congregation, 2063
29 carcases...fall in t' wilderness; 2088
32 they shall fall in t' wilderness. "
35 do it unto all t' evil congregation, 2063
35 in t' wilderness they shall be 2088
15: 13 shall do these things after t' manner,
16: 6 T' do; Take you censers, Korah, 2063
21 from among t' congregation,
45 you up from among t' congregation."
18: 9 T' shall be thine of the most holy 2088
11 t' is thine; the heave offering of "
27 And t' your heave offering shall be*
19: 2 T' is the ordinance of the law 2063
14 T' is the law, when a man dieth in "
20: 4 of the Lord into t' wilderness, 2088
5 to bring us in unto t' evil place? "
10 we fetch you water out of t' rock? "
12 ye shall not bring t' congregation "
13 T' is the water of Meribah; *1992
21: 2 deliver t' people into my hand, 2088
5 and our soul loatheth t' light bread.
17 Then Israel sang t' song, Spring 2088
22: 1 plains of Moab on t' side Jordan *
4 Now shall t' company lick up all that
6 I pray thee, curse me t' people; 2088
8 Lodge here t' night, and I will bring
17 I pray thee, curse me t' people. 2088
19 tarry ye also here t' night, that I may
24 a wall being on t' side, and a wall 2088
30 ever since I was thine unto t' day? "
23: 23 according to t' time it shall be said of*
24: 14 t' people shall do to thy people 2088
23 Alas, who shall live when God doeth t'!
26: 9 T' is that Dathan and Abiram, *1931
27: 12 Get thee up into t' mount Abarim, 2088
28: 10 T' is the burnt offering of every
14 t' is the burnt offering of every 2063
17 the fifteenth day of t' month is the 2088
24 After t' manner ye shall offer daily, 428
29: 7 day of t' seventh month an holy 2088
30: 1 T' is the thing which the Lord hath"
31: 21 T' is the ordinance of the law 2063
32: 5 t' land be given unto thy servants "
15 and ye shall destroy all t' people. 2088
19 is fallen to us on t' side Jordan
20 If ye will do t' thing, if ye will go 2088
22 t' land shall be your possession 2063
32 inheritance on t' side Jordan may*
34: 2 (t' is the land that shall fall unto 2063
6 t' shall be your west border. 2088
7 And t' shall be your north border: "
9 t' shall be your north border. "
12 t' shall be your land with the 2063
13 T' is the land...ye shall inherit by "
15 inheritance on t' side Jordan near*
35: 5 t' shall be to them the suburbs of 2088
14 give three cities on t' side Jordan,*
36: 6 T' is the thing which the Lord 2088
De 1: 1 unto all Israel on t' side Jordan *
5 On t' side Jordan, in the land of *
5 began Moses to declare t' law, 2063
6 dwelt long enough in t' mount: 2088
10 ye are t' day as the stars of heaven
32 Yet in t' thing ye did not believe 2088
35 of these men of t' evil generation "
2: 3 have compassed t' mountain long "
7 walking through t'...wilderness: "
18 through Ar, the coast of Moab, t' day:
22 in their stead even unto t' day: 2088
25 T' day will I begin to put the dread"
30 into thy hand, as appeareth t' day. "
3: 8 land that was on t' side Jordan, *
12 t' land, which we possessed at 2063
14 Bashan-havoth-jair, unto t' day. 2088
18 your God hath given you t' land 2063
26 no more unto me of t' matter. 2088
27 thou shalt not go over t' Jordan. "
28 he shall go over before t' people, "
4: 4 God are alive every one of you t' day.
6 for t' is your wisdom and your 1931
6 Surely t' great nation is a wise 2088
8 so righteous as all t' law, which 2063
8 law, which I set before you t' day?
20 of inheritance, as ye are t' day. 2088
22 But I must die in t' land, I must "
26 earth to witness against you t' day,
32 any such thing as t' great thing 2088
38 for an inheritance, as it is t' day. "
39 Know therefore t' day, and consider it
40 which I command thee t' day, that
41 three cities on t' side Jordan *
44 t' is the law which Moses set 2063
46 On t' side Jordan, in the valley *
47 which were on t' side Jordan *
49 plain on t' side Jordan eastward, *
5: 1 which I speak in your ears t' day,
3 Lord made not t' covenant with 2063
3 who are all of us here alive t' day.
24 seen t' day that God doth talk 2088
25 for t' great fire will consume us: 2088
28 the voice of the words of t' people,2088
6: 6 words, which I command thee t' day,
24 preserve us alive, as it is at t' day.2088
7: 11 which I command thee t' day,

De 8: 1 which I command thee t' day shall ye
11 which I command thee t' day:
17 hand hath gotten me t' wealth. 2088
18 unto thy fathers, as it is t' day. "
19 I testify against you t' day that ye
9: 1 Thou art to pass over Jordan t' day,
3 Understand therefore t' day, that the
4 brought me in to possess t' land: 2088
6 God giveth thee not t' good land 2063
7 until ye came unto t' place, ye 2088
13 me, saying, I have seen t' people, "
27 unto the stubbornness of t' people, "
10: 8 to bless in his name, unto t' day. "
13 I command thee t' day for thy good?
15 above all people, as it is t' day. 2088
11: 2 And know ye t' day: for I speak not
4 hath destroyed them unto t' day; 2088
8, 13 which I command you t' day,
26 I set before you t' day a blessing and
27 God, which I command you t' day:
28 the way which I command you t' day,
32 which I set before you t' day.
12: 8 all the things that we do here t' day,
13: 11 such wickedness as t' is among 2088
18 which I command thee t' day,
15: 2 t' is the manner of the release: 2088
5 which I command thee t' day.
10 t' thing the Lord thy God shall 2088
15 I command thee t' thing to day.
17: 18 him a copy of t' law in a book 2063
19 to keep all the words of t' law and "
18: 3 t' shall be the priest's due from 2088
16 neither let me see t' great fire 2063
19: 4 t' is the case of the slayer, which 2088
9 I command thee t' day, to love the
20: 3 ye approach t' day unto battle against
21: 7 Our hands have not shed t' blood, 2088
20 T' our son is stubborn and "
22: 14 I took t' woman, and when I came 2063
16 my daughter unto t' man to wife, 2088
20 But if t' thing be true, and the "
26 slayeth him, even so is t' matter: "
24: 18, 22 I command thee to do t' thing. "
26: 3 I profess t' day unto the Lord thy God,
9 he hath brought us into t' place, 2088
9 given us t' land, even a land that 2063
16 T' day the Lord thy God hath 2088
17 the Lord t' day to be thy God,
18 Lord hath avouched thee t' day to be
27: 1 which I command you t' day.
3 upon them all the words of t' law, 2063
4 which I command you t' day, in
8 the stones all the words of t' law 2063
9 t' day thou art become the people 2088
10 which I command thee t' day.
26 not all the words of t' law to do 2063
28: 1, 13 which I command thee t' day,
14 words which I command thee t' day,
15 which I command thee t' day;
58 to do all the words of t' law that 2063
58 that are written in t' book, that 2088
58 fear t' glorious and fearful name,
61 not written in the book of t' law, 2063
29: 4 see, and ears to hear, unto t' day. 2088
7 when ye came unto t' place, Sihon "
9 therefore the words of t' covenant,2063
10 stand t' day all of you before the Lord
12 Lord thy God maketh with thee t' day:
14 do I make t' covenant and t' oath; 2063
15 him that standeth here with us t' day
15 him that is not here with us t' day:
18 heart turneth...t' day from the Lord
19 he heareth the words of t' curse, 2063
20 curses that are written in t' book 2088
21 are written in t' book of the law: "
24 the Lord done thus unto t' land? 2063
24 the heat of t' great anger? 2088
27 Lord was kindled against t' land, 1931
27 curses that are written in t' book:2088
28 into another land, as it is t' day.
29 may do all the words of t' law. 2063
30: 2 to all that I command thee t' day,
8 which I command thee t' day.
10 are written in t' book of the law. 2088
11 For t' commandment which I 2063
11 which I command thee t' day, it is
15 set before thee t' day life and good,
16 that I command thee t' day to love
18 I denounce unto you t' day, that ye
19 earth to record t' day against you,
31: 2 hundred and twenty years old t' day;
2 Thou shalt not go over t' Jordan. 2088
7 thou must go with t' people unto "
9 Moses wrote t' law, and delivered 2063
11 read t' law before all Israel in their "
12 to do all the words of t' law: "
16 t' people will rise up, and go a 2088
19 therefore write ye t' song for you, 2063
19 t' song may be a witness for me "
21 t' song shall testify against them "
22 Moses therefore wrote t' song the "
24 writing the words of t' law in a "
26 Take t' book of the law, and put 2088
27 while I am yet alive with you t' day,
30 of Israel the words of t' song, 2063
32: 27 and the Lord hath not done all t'. "
29 were wise, that they understood t', "
34 Is not t' laid up in store with me, 1931
44 words of t' song in the ears of the 2063
46 which I testify among you t' day,
46 to do, all the words of t' law. 2063
47 through t' thing ye shall prolong 2088
49 thee up into t' mountain Abarim,
33: 1 t' is the blessing, wherewith Moses2063
7 t' is the blessing of Judah: and he "
34: 4 T' is the land which I sware unto "

De 34: 6 of his sepulchre unto t' day. 2088
Jos 1: 2 therefore arise, go over t' Jordan,
2 thou, and all t' people, unto the 2088
4 t' Lebanon even unto the great "
6 unto t' people shalt thou divide for "
8 T' book of the law shall not depart "
11 days ye shall pass over t' Jordan,
13 rest, and hath given you t' land. 2063
14 Moses gave you on t' side Jordan;*
15 servant gave you on t' side Jordan*
2:14 if ye utter not t' our business. 2088
17 will be blameless of t' thine oath "
18 shalt bind t' line of scarlet thread "
20 And if thou utter t' our business, "
3: 4 ye have not passed t' way heretofore. "
7 T' day will I begin to magnify 2088
4: 3 place, where ye shall lodge t' night. "
6 That t' may be a sign among you, 2063
9 and they are there unto t' day. "
22 Israel came over t' Jordan on dry 2088
5: 4 t' is the cause why Joshua did
9 T' day have I rolled away the
9 place is called Gilgal unto t' day. 2088
6:25 dwelleth in Israel even unto t' day;"
26 that riseth up and buildeth t' city 2063
7: 7 all brought t' people over Jordan, 2088
25 the Lord shall trouble thee t' day. "
26 a great heap of stones unto t' day. "
26 The valley of Achor, unto t' day. "
8:20 had no power to flee t' way or that 2007
22 some on t' side, and some on that 2088
28 ever, even a desolation unto t' day. "
29 stones, that remaineth unto t' day. "
33 stood on t' side the ark and on that "
9: 1 which were on t' side Jordan, *
12 T' our bread we took hot for our 2088
20 T' we will do to them; we will 2063
24 of you, and have done t' thing. 2088
27 altar of the Lord, even unto t' day, "
10:13 Is not t' written in the book of 1931
27 which remain until t' very day. 2088
11: 6 for to morrow about t' time will I 2063
12: 7 Israel smote on t' side Jordan on *
13: 2 T' is the land that yet remaineth: 2063
7 divide t' land for an inheritance
13 among the Israelites until t' day. 2088
23 T' was the inheritance of the 2063
28 T' is the inheritance of the children"
29 t' was the possession of the half tribe*
14:10 Lord spake t' word unto Moses, 2088
10 I am t' day fourscore and five years
11 I am as strong t' day as I was in the
12 therefore give me t' mountain, 2088
14 Jephunneh the Kenezite...t' day,
15: 1 T' then was the lot of the tribe of the*
4 sea: t' shall be your south coast. 2088
12 T' is the coast of the children of "
20 T' is the inheritance of the tribe 2063
63 Judah at Jerusalem unto t' day. 2088
16: 8 T' is the inheritance of the tribe 2063
10 the Ephraimites unto t' day, 2088
18:14 Judah: t' was the west quarter. 2063
19 of Jordan: t' was the south coast. 2088
20 T' was the inheritance of the 2063
28 T' is the inheritance of the children"
19: 8 T' is the inheritance of the tribe of"
16 T' is the inheritance of the children"
23, 31, 39, 48 T' is the inheritance of "
22: 3 these many days unto t' day, 2088
7 their brethren on t' side Jordan *
16 What trespass is t' that ye have 2088
16 turn away t' day from following the
16 ye might rebel t' day against the
17 we are not cleansed until t' day. 2088
18 turn away t' day from following the
22 the Lord, (save us not t' day,) 2088
24 rather done it for fear of t' thing,* 2063
29 turn t' day from following the Lord, to
31 T' day we perceive that the Lord is
31 not committed t' trespass against 2088
23: 8 God, as ye have done unto t' day. "
9 to stand before you unto t' day. "
13 perish from off t' good land which 2063
14 t' day I am going the way of all the
15 destroyed you from off t' good land 2063
24:15 choose you t' day whom ye will serve;
27 t' stone shall be a witness unto 2063
J'g 1:21 Benjamin in Jerusalem unto t' day. 2088
26 is the name thereof unto t' day. "
2: 2 with the inhabitants of t' land; 2063
2 my voice: why have ye done t'? "
20 that t' people hath transgressed 2088
4:14 t' is the day in which the Lord hath"
6:13 us, why then is all t' befallen us? 2063
14 Go in t' thy might, and thou shalt 2088
20 cakes, and lay them upon t' rock, 1975
24 t' day it is yet in Ophrah of the 2088
26 thy God upon the top of t' rock, "
29 to another, Who hath done t' thing?"
29 the son of Joash hath done t' thing."
39 me, and I will speak but t' once:
39 thee, but t' once with the fleece;
7: 4 T' shall go with thee, the same 2088
4 T' shall not go with thee, the same"
14 T' is nothing else save the sword 2063
8: 9 in peace, I will break down t' tower.
9:18 up against my father's house t' day,
19 and with his house t' day, 2088
29 to God t' people were under my "
38 t' the people...thou hast despised? "
10: 4 are called Havoth-jair unto t' day, "
15 us only, we pray thee, t' day. "
11:27 t' day between the children of Israel
37 Let t' thing be done for me: 2088
12: 3 then are ye come up unto me t' day,"
13:23 as at t' time have told us such things

J'g 15: 6 Philistines said, Who hath done t'? 2063
7 Though ye have done t', yet will "
11 what is t' that thou hast done unto "
18 hast given t' great deliverance into"
19 which is in Lehi unto t' day. "
16:18 Come up t' once, for he hath
28 I pray thee, only t' once, O God, 2088
18: 3 and what makest thou in t' place? 6311
12 place Mahaneh-dan unto t' day: 2088
24 and what is t' that ye say unto me,*"
19:11 let us turn in into t' city of the 2063
23 seeing that t' man is come into 2088
23 into mine house, do not t' folly. 2063
24 unto t' man do not so vile a thing. 2088
30 of the land of Egypt unto t' day: "
20: 3 Tell us, how was t' wickedness? 2063
9 t' shall be the thing that we will do "
12 wickedness is t' that is done among"
16 Among all t' people there were 2088
21: 3 why is t' come to pass in Israel, 2063
6 one tribe cut off from Israel t' day.
11 And t' is the thing that ye shall do, 2063
22 ye did not give unto them at t' time,*
Ru 1:19 them, and they said, Is t' Naomi? 2063
2: 5 the reapers, Whose damsel is t'? "
3:13 Tarry t' night, and it shall be in the
18 he have finished the thing t' day.
4: 7 t' was the manner in former time 2063
7 and t' was the testimony in Israel. "
9 Ye are witnesses t' day, that I have
10 of his place: ye are witnesses t' day.
12 shall give thee of t' young woman. 2063
1Sa 1: 3 t' man went up out of his city 1931
27 For t' child I prayed; and the 2088
2:20 give thee seed of t' woman for the 2063
23 your evil dealings by all t' people. 428
34 And t' shall be a sign unto thee, 2088
4: 6 meaneth the noise of t' great shout 2063
14 meaneth the noise of t' tumult? 2088
5: 5 of Dagon in Ashdod unto t' day. "
6: 9 then he hath done us t' great evil: 2063
18 stone remaineth unto t' day in the 2088
20 to stand before t' holy Lord God? "
8: 8 up out of Egypt even unto t' day, "
11 T' will be the manner of the king "
9: 6 there is in t' city a man of God, 2063
13 up; for about t' time ye shall find him.
16 To morrow about t' time I will send
17 t' same shall reign over my people. 2088
24 for unto t' time hath it been kept for*
10:11 What is t' that is come unto the 2088
19 And ye have t' day rejected your God,
27 said, How shall t' man save us? 2088
11: 2 On t' condition will I make a 2063
13 not a man be put to death t' day: 2088
12: 2 you from my childhood unto t' day."
5 and his anointed is witness t' day, "
16 stand and see t' great thing, "
19 have added unto all our sins t' evil,
20 ye have done all t' wickedness: 2063
14:10 and t' shall be a sign unto us. 2088
28 the man that eateth any food t' day.
29 because I tasted a little of t' honey. 2088
33 roll a great stone unto me t' day.
38 wherein t' sin hath been t' day. 2088
45 hath wrought t' great salvation in "
45 he hath wrought with God t' day. "
15:14 What meaneth then t' bleating of "
16 the Lord hath said to me t' night.
28 kingdom of Israel from thee t' day,
16: 8, 9 Neither hath the Lord chosen t'. 2088
12 Arise, anoint him: for t' is he. "
17:10 defy the armies of Israel t' day; "
17 an ephah of t' parched corn, "
25 Have ye seen t' man that is come "
26 the man that killeth t' Philistine, 1975
26 who is t' uncircumcised Philistine, 2088
27 answered him after t' manner, "
32 will go and fight with t' Philistine. "
33 not able to go against t' Philistine "
36 t' uncircumcised Philistine shall be"
37 me out of the hand of t' Philistine. "
46 T' day will the Lord deliver thee "
46 the Philistines t' day unto the fowls"
47 t' assembly shall know that the "
55 host, Abner, whose son is t' youth? "
18:21 Thou shalt t' day be my son in law in
24 saying, On t' manner spake David. 428
20: 2 should my father hide t' thing 2088
3 Let not Jonathan know t', lest he 2063
21 the arrows are on t' side of thee, 2007
21: 5 it were sanctified t' day in the vessel.*
11 not t' David the king of the land? 2088
15 have brought t' fellow to play the "
15 shall t' fellow come into my house?"
22: 8, 13 me, to lie in wait, as at t' day? "
15 thy servant knew nothing of all t', 2063
23:26 And Saul went on t' side of the 2088
24: 6 should do t' thing unto my master, "
16 said, Is t' thy voice, my son David? "
18 thou hast shewed t' day how that thou
19 thou hast done unto me t' day. "
25:21 have I kept all that t' fellow hath "
24 my lord, upon me let t' iniquity be:*
25 regard t' man of Belial, even 2088
27 t' blessing which thine handmaid 2063
31 That t' shall be no grief unto thee, "
32 which sent thee t' day to meet me: 2088
33 hast kept me t' day from coming to "
26: 8 enemy into thine hand t' day:
16 T' thing is not good that thou 2088
17 said, Is t' thy voice, my son David? "
19 driven me out t' day from abiding
21 was precious in thine eyes t' day: 2088
24 much set by t' day in mine eyes, "
27: 6 the kings of Judah unto t' day. "

1Sa 28:10 happen to thee for t' thing. 2088
18 Lord done t' thing unto thee t' day. "
29: 3 Is not t' David, the servant of Saul "
3 since he fell unto me unto t' day? "
4 Make t' fellow return, that he may*
5 Is not t' David, of whom they sang 2088
6 of thy coming unto me unto t' day: "
8 I have been with thee unto t' day? "
30: 8 Shall I pursue after t' troop? shall I"
15 thou bring me down to t' company? "
15 will bring thee down to t' company. "
20 cattle, and said, T' is David's spoil. "
24 will hearken unto you in t' matter? "
25 an ordinance for Israel unto t' day. "
2Sa 1:17 David lamented with t' 2063
2: 1 And it came to pass after t', that 3651
5 t' kindness unto your Lord, 2088
6 I also will requite you t' kindness, "
6 because ye have done t' thing. "
3: 8 shew kindness t' day unto the house
8 with a fault concerning t' woman?
38 great man fallen t' day in Israel? 2088
39 I am t' day weak, though anointed
4: 3 were sojourners there until t' day.) 2088
8 my lord the king t' day of Saul, "
6: 8 of the place Perez-uzzah to t' day. "
7: 6 even to t' day, but have walked in a"
17 and according to all t' vision, so did"
19 t' was yet a small thing in thy 2063
19 And is t' the manner of man, O "
27 found in his heart to pray t' prayer "
28 promised t' goodness unto thy 2088
8: 1 And after t' it came to pass, that 3651
10: 1 And it came to pass after t', that "
11: 3 Is not t' Bath-sheba, the daughter 2063
11 soul liveth, I will not do t' thing. 2088
25 Let not t' thing displease thee, for "
12: 5 hath done t' thing shall surely die: 2063
6 because he did t' thing, and 2088
11 thy wives in the sight of t' sun. 2088
12 I will do t' thing before all Israel, 2088
14 because by t' deed thou hast given "
21 What thing is t' that thou hast "
13: 1 And it came to pass after t', that 3651
12 in Israel: do not thou t' folly. 2063
16 t' evil in sending me away is "
17 Put now t' woman out from me, "
20 is thy brother; regard not t' thing. "
32 t' hath been determined from the day
14: 3 and speak on t' manner unto him. 2088
13 for the king doth speak t' thing as "
15 come to speak of t' thing unto my "
19 hand of Joab with thee in all t'? 2063
20 To fetch about t' form of speech hath*
20 thy servant Joab done t' thing: 2088
21 Behold now, I have done t' thing: "
15: 1 And it came to pass after t', that 3651
6 on t' manner did Absalom to all 2088
20 should I t' day make thee go up and
16: 9 Why should t' dead dog curse my 2088
11 more now may t' Benjamite do it?
12 me good for his cursing t' day. 2088
17 Is t' thy kindness to thy friend? "
18 but whom the Lord, and t' people, "
17: 1 arise and pursue after David t' night:
6 hath spoken after t' manner: 2088
7 hath given is not good at t' time. 2063
16 Lodge not t' night in the plains of the
18:18 it is called unto t' day, Absalom's 2088
20 Thou shalt not bear tidings t' day, "
20 t' day thou shalt bear no tidings, "
31 Lord hath avenged thee t' day of all
19: 5 hast shamed t' day the faces of all thy
5 which t' day have saved thy life,
6 thou hast declared t' day, that thou
6 t' day I perceive, that if Absalom had
6 we had died t' day, then it had pleased
7 will not tarry one with thee t' night:
14 that they sent t' word unto the king,*
20 I am come the first t' day of all the
21 not Shimei be put to death for t', 2063
22 ye should t' day be adversaries unto
22 man be put to death t' day in Israel?
22 that I am t' day king over Israel?
35 I am t' day fourscore years old: and
42 then be ye angry for t' matter? 2088
21:18 it came to pass after t', that there 3651
22: 1 unto the Lord the words of t' song 2063
23: 5 for t' is all my salvation, and all my*
17 me, O Lord, that I should do t': 2063
17 t' the blood of the men that went in*
24: 3 lord the king delight in t' thing? 2088
1Kj 1:25 For he is gone down t' day, and hath
27 t' thing done by my lord the king, 2088
30 even so will I certainly do t' day. "
41 Wherefore is t' noise of the city being
45 T' is the noise that ye have heard. 1931
48 given one to sit on my throne t' day,
2:23 spoken t' word against his own 2088
24 Adonijah shall be put to death t' day.
26 not at t' time put thee to death: 2088
3: 6 hast kept for him t' great kindness, "
6 to sit on his throne, as it is t' day. "
9 to judge t' thy so great a people? "
10 that Solomon had asked t' thing. "
11 Because thou hast asked t' thing, "
17 lord, I and t' woman dwell in one 2063
18 that t' woman was delivered also; "
19 t' woman's child died in the night; "
22 t' said, No; but the dead is thy son, "
23 one saith, T' is my son that liveth, "
4:24 all the region on t' side the river, "
24 all the kings on t' side the river: "
5: 7 Blessed be the Lord t' day, which hath
7 a wise son over t' great people. 2088
6:12 Concerning t' house which thou art"

1Ki 7: 8 taken to wife, like unto t· porch. 2088
28 of the bases was on t· manner: "
37 After t· manner he made the ten 2063
8: 8 and there they are unto t· day. 2088
24 it with thine hand, as it is t· day. "
27 less t· house that I have builded? "
29 eyes may be open toward t· house "
29 servant shall make toward t· place. "
30 they shall pray toward t· place: "
31 come before thine altar in t· house: "
33 supplication unto thee in t· house: "
35 if they pray toward t· place, and "
38 forth his hands toward t· house: "
42 come and pray toward t· house; "
43 that they may know that t· house, "
54 an end of praying all t· prayer 2063
61 his commandments, as at t· day. 2088
9: 3 have hallowed t· house, which thou "
7 t· house, which I have hallowed for
8 And at t· house, which is high, 2088
8 the Lord done thus unto t· land, 2063
9 Lord brought upon them all t· evil. "
13 the land of Cabul unto t· day. 2088
15 t· is the reason of the levy which "
21 tribute of bondservice unto t· day. "
10: 12 trees, nor were seen unto t· day. "
11: 10 had commanded him concerning t· "
11 Forasmuch as t· is done of thee, 2063
27 And t· was the cause that he lifted 2088
39 will for t· afflict the seed of David, 2063
12: 6 that I may answer t· people? 2088
7 be a servant unto t· people t· day, "
9 ye that we may answer t· people, "
10 shalt thou speak unto t· people "
19 the house of David unto t· day. "
24 his house; for t· thing is from me. "
27 If t· people go up to do sacrifice in "
27 the heart of t· people turn again "
30 And t· thing became a sin: for the "
13: 3 T· is the sign which the Lord hath "
8 bread nor drink water in t· place: "
16 drink water with thee in t· place: "
33 After t· thing Jeroboam returned "
34 t· thing became sin unto the house "
14: 2 that I should be king over t· people. "
15 root up Israel out of t· good land, 2063
17: 21 let t· child's soul come into him 2088
24 by t· I know that thou art a man of* "
18: 36 be known t· day that thou art God "
37 that t· people may know that thou "
19: 2 of them by to morrow about t· time.
20: 6 unto thee to morrow about t· time,
7 see how t· man seeketh mischief: 2088
9 will do: but t· thing I may not do. "
12 when Ben-hadad heard t· message, "
13 thou seen all t· great multitude? "
13 deliver it into thine hand t· day; "
24 And do t· thing, Take the kings 2088
28 deliver all t· great multitude into "
34 I will send thee away with t· covenant.
39 unto me, and said, Keep t· man: 2088
22: 20 And one said on t· manner, and 3541
27 Put t· fellow in the prison, and 2088
2Ki 1: 2 whether I shall recover of t· disease. "
2: 19 the situation of t· city is pleasant, "
22 the waters were healed unto t· day, 2088
3: 16 Lord, Make t· valley full of ditches. "
18 t· is but a light thing in the sight 2063
23 they said, T· is blood: the kings 2088
4: 9 that t· is an holy man of God, 1931
12 his servant, Call t· Shunammite. 2063
13 been careful for us with all t· care; "
16 About t· season, according to the 2088
36 and said, Call t· Shunammite. 2088
43 I set t· before an hundred men? 2088
5: 6 when t· letter is come unto thee, "
7 that t· man doth send unto me to "
18 In t· thing the Lord pardon thy "
18 Lord pardon thy servant in t· thing. "
20 hath spared Naaman t· Syrian, "
6: 11 was sore troubled for t· thing; "
18 Smite t· people, I pray thee, with "
19 said unto them, T· is not the way,
19 neither is t· the city: follow me, 2090
24 And it came to pass after t·, that 3651
28 T· woman said unto me, Give thy 2063
31 Shaphat shall stand on him t· day.
33 said, Behold, t· evil is of the Lord; 2063
7: 1 To morrow about t· time shall a
2 in heaven, might t· thing be? 2088
9 t· day is a day of good tidings, and 1931
18 to morrow about t· time in the gate of
8: 5 My lord, O king, t· is the woman, 2063
5 and t· is her son, whom Elisha 2088
8, 9 Shall I recover of t· disease? "
13 that he should do t· great thing? "
9: 1 and take t· box of oil in thine hand, "
11 came t· mad fellow to thee? "
25 the Lord laid t· burden upon him; "
26 and I will requite thee in t· plat, 2063
27 Ahaziah the king of Judah saw t·,
34 Go, see now t· cursed woman, and 2063
36 T· is the word of the Lord, which 1931
37 they shall not say, T· is Jezebel. 2063
10: 2 as soon as t· letter cometh to you, 2088
6 to me to Jezreel by to morrow t· time.
27 it a draught house unto t· day. 2088
11: 5 T· is the thing that ye shall do; "
14: 7 the name of it Joktheel unto t· day. "
10 up: glory of t·, and tarry at home:* "
15: 12 T· was the word of the Lord 1931
16: 6 Elath, and dwelt there unto t· day. 2088
17: 12 unto them, Ye shall not do t· thing. "
23 own land to Assyria unto t· day. "
34 t· day they do after the former "
41 their fathers, so do they unto t· day. "

2Ki 18: 19 What confidence is t· wherein thou 2088
21 upon the staff of t· bruised reed, "
22 before t· altar in Jerusalem? "
25 Lord against t· place to destroy it? "
25 Go up against t· land, and destroy 2063
30 t· city shall not be delivered into "
19: 3 T· day is a day of trouble, and of 2088
21 T· is the word that the Lord hath "
29 And t· shall be a sign unto thee, Ye "
29 shall eat t· year such things as grow of
31 of the Lord of hosts shall do t·. 2063
33 and shall not come into t· city, "
34 For I will defend t· city, to save it, "
20: 6 I will deliver thee and t· city out of "
6 defend t· city for mine own sake, "
9 T· sign shalt thou have of the 2088
17 have laid up in store unto t· day, "
21: 7 In t· house, and in Jerusalem, "
15 forth out of Egypt, even unto t· day, "
22: 13 concerning the words of t· book "
13 hearkened unto the words of t· book, "
16 I will bring evil upon t· place, and "
17 shall be kindled against t· place, "
19 what I spake against t· place, "
20 which I will bring upon t· place. "
23: 3 perform the words of t· covenant 2063
3 that were written in t· book. 2088
21 written in the book of t· covenant. "
23 wherein t· passover was holden to "
27 and will cast off t· city Jerusalem 2063
24: 3 of the Lord came t· upon Judah,
1Ch 4: 43 and dwelt there unto t· day. 2088
5: 26 and to the river Gozan, unto t· day. "
11: 11 t· is the number of the mighty men 428
19 it me, that I should do t· thing: 2063
13: 11 place is called Perez-uzza to t· day. 2088
16: 7 first t· psalm to thank the Lord *
17: 5 I brought up Israel unto t· day; 2088
15 according to all t· vision, so did "
17 t· was a small thing in thine eyes, 2063
19 hast thou done all t· greatness, "
26 hast promised t· goodness unto thy "
18: 1 Now after t· it came to pass, that 3651
19: 1 Now it came to pass after t·, that "
20: 4 And it came to pass after t·, that "
21: 3 then doth my lord require t· thing? 2063
7 God was displeased with t· thing; 2088
8 because I have done t· thing: "
22 me the place of t· threshingfloor,
22: 1 T· is the house of the Lord God, 2088
1 t· is the altar of the burnt offering "
27: 6 T· is that Benaiah, who was 1931
28: 7 and my judgments, as at t· day. 2088
8 that ye may possess t· good land, and
19 All t·, said David, the Lord made me
19 me, even all the works of t· pattern.
29: 5 consecrate his service t· day unto the
14 to offer so willingly after t· sort? 2063
16 all t· store that we have prepared 2088
18 keep t· for ever in the imagination 2063
2Ch 1: 10 out and come in before t· people: 2088
10 for who can judge t· thy people, "
11 Because t· was in thine heart, and 2063
2: 4 T· is an ordinance for ever to Israel. "
5: 9 And there it is unto t· day. 2088
6: 18 how much less t· house which I "
20 eyes may be open upon t· house "
20 thy servant prayeth toward t· place. "
21 they shall make toward t· place: "
22 come before thine altar in t· house; "
24 supplication before thee in t· house; "
26 yet if they pray toward t· place, and "
29 spread forth his hands in t· house: "
32 if they come and pray in t· house; "
33 know that t· house which I have "
34 pray unto thee toward t· city 2063
40 prayer that is made in t· place. 2088
7: 12 chosen t· place to myself for an "
15 prayer that is made in t· place. "
16 I chosen and sanctified t· house, "
20 t· house, which I have sanctified "
21 And t· house, which is high, shall "
21 the Lord done thus unto t· land, 2063
21 land, and unto t· house? 2088
22 he brought all t· evil upon them. 2063
8: 8 make to pay tribute until t· day. 2088
10: 6 me to return answer to t· people? "
7 If thou be kind to t· people, and "
9 we may return answer to t· people, "
19 the house of David unto t· day. "
11: 4 house: for t· thing is done of me. "
14: 11 name we go against t· multitude. "
16: 10 rage with him because of t· thing. 2063
18: 19 one spake saying after t· manner, 3602
26 Put t· fellow in the prison, and 2088
19: 10 t· do, and ye shall not trespass. 3541
20: 1 It came to pass after t· also, that 3651
2 from beyond the sea on t· side Syria;*
7 out the inhabitants of t· land 2063
9 we stand before t· house, and in 2088
9 (for thy name is in t· house,) and "
12 might against t· great company "
15 by reason of t· great multitude; "
17 shall not need to fight in t· battle: 2063
26 valley of Berachah, unto t· day. 2088
35 after t· did Jehoshaphat king of 3651
21: 10 the hand of Judah unto t· day. 2088
18 after all t· the Lord smote him in 2063
23: 4 T· is the thing that ye shall do; 2088
24: 4 And it came to pass after t·, that 3651
18 Jerusalem for t· their trespass. 2063
25: 9 to give thee much more than t·. 2088
16 because thou hast done t·, and 2063
28: 22 the Lord: t· is that king Ahaz. 1931
29: 9 our wives are in captivity for t·. 2088
28 t· continued until the burnt offering

2Ch 30: 9 shall come again unto t· land: 2063
31: 1 Now when all t· was finished, all
10 that which is left is t· great store. 2088
32: 9 t· did Sennacherib king of Assyria "
15 nor persuade you on t· manner, 2063
20 for t· cause Hezekiah the king, "
30 T· same Hezekiah also stopped 1931
33: 7 In t· house, and in Jerusalem, 2088
14 after t· he built a wall without 3651
34: 21 after all that is written in t· book. 2088
24 I will bring evil upon t· place, and "
25 shall be poured out upon t· place, "
27 heardest his words against t· place, "
28 evil that I will bring upon t· place, "
31 which are written in t· book. "
35: 19 of Josiah was t· passover kept. "
20 After all t·, when Josiah had 2063
21 I come not against thee t· day, but
25 in their lamentations to t· day,
Ezr 1: 9 t· is the number of them: thirty 428
3: 12 foundation of t· house was laid 2088
4: 8 to Artaxerxes the king in t· sort: 3660
10 rest that are on t· side the river, *
11 T· is the copy of the letter that 1836
11 servants the men on t· side the *
13 if t· city be builded, and the walls 1791
15 that t· city is a rebellious city,
15 which cause was t· city destroyed. "
16 if t· city be builded again, and the "
16 by t· means thou shalt have no 1836
16 have no portion on t· side the river.*
19 that t· city of old time hath made 1791
21 that t· city be not builded, until
22 heed now that ye fail not to do t·: *1836
5: 3 governor on t· side the river, *
3 commanded you to build t· house, 1836
3 and to make up t· wall? "
4 we unto them after t· manner, 3660
4 of the men that make t· building? 1836
5 by letter concerning t· matter. "
6 governor on t· side the river, *
6 which were on t· side the river, *
8 and t· work goeth fast on, and 1791
9 commanded you to build t· house, 1836
12 Chaldean, who destroyed t· house, "
13 a decree to build t· house of God. "
17 king to build t· house of God at 1791
17 to us concerning t· matter. 1836
6: 7 work of t· house of God alone; 1791
7 of the Jews build t· house of God "
8 for the building of t· house of God: "
11 that whosoever shall alter t· word, 1836
11 his house be made a dunghill for t·. "
12 to alter and to destroy t· house of 1791
13 governor on t· side the river, *
15 t· house was finished on the third 1836
16 dedication of t· house of God with "
17 dedication of t· house of God "
7: 6 T· Ezra went up from Babylon; 1931
11 t· is the copy of the letter that 2088
17 speedily with t· money bullocks, 1836
24 or ministers of t· house of God,
27 a thing as t· in the king's heart, 2063
8: 1 t· is the genealogy of them that 428
23 and besought our God for t·: 2063
35 t· was a burnt offering unto the Lord.
36 governors on t· side the river: *
9: 2 hath been chief in t· trespass. 2088
3 And when I heard t· thing, I rent "
7 in a great trespass unto t· day; "
7 confusion of face, as it is t· day. "
10 God, what shall we say after t·? 2063
13 given us such deliverance as t·; * "
15 remain yet escaped, as it is t· day: "
15 stand before thee because of t·. "
10: 2 hope in Israel concerning t· thing. "
4 t· matter belongeth unto thee: we*
5 should do according to t· word. 2088
9 God, trembling because of t· matter, "
13 neither is t· a work of one day or two:
13 that have transgressed in t· thing. 2088
14 wrath of our God for t· matter be "
15 were employed about t· matter: 2063
Ne 1: 11 I pray thee, thy servant t· day,
11 him mercy in the sight of t· man. 2088
2: 2 t· is nothing else but sorrow of
18 their hands for t· good work. *
19 What is t· thing that ye do? will 2088
3: 7 the governor on t· side the river. *
5: 10 pray you, let us leave off t· usury. 2088
11 to them, even t· day, their lands,
12 should do according to t· promise. 2088
13 that performeth not t· promise, "
13 people did according to t· promise. "
16 continued in the work of t· wall, 2063
18 for all t· required not I the bread 2088
18 bondage was heavy upon t· people. "
19 all that I have done for t· people. "
6: 4 unto me four times after t· sort; "
12 pronounced t· prophecy against me: "
16 t· work was wrought of our God. 2063
7: 7 men of the people of Israel was t·;*
8: 9 T· day is holy unto the Lord your
10 for t· day is holy unto our Lord:
9: 1 twenty and fourth day of t· month 2088
10 get thee a name, as it is t· day. "
18 T· is thy God that brought thee up "
32 of the kings of Assyria unto t· day. "
36 Behold, we are servants t· day, and
38 because of all t· we make a sure 2063
13: 4 And before t·, Eliashib the priest, 2088
6 all t· time was not I at Jerusalem: "
14 me, O my God, concerning t·, and "
17 What evil thing is t· that ye do, "
18 our God bring all t· evil upon us, "
18 upon us, and upon t· city? yet ye 2063

Ne 13:22 me, O my God, concerning t' also, 2063
27 unto you to do all t' great evil,
Es 1: 1 (t' is Ahasuerus which reigned, 1931
17 For t' deed of the queen shall come
18 of Persia and Media say t' day 2088
4:14 holdest thy peace at t' time, 2063
14 the kingdom for such a time as t'? "
15 them return Mordecai t' answer, *
5: 4 Haman come t' day unto the banquet
13 Yet all t' availeth me nothing, 2088
6: 3 hath been done to Mordecai for t'? "
9 let t' apparel and horse be delivered*
7: 6 and enemy is t' wicked Haman. 2088
9: 4 t' man Mordecai waxed greater and*
13 also according unto t' day's decree,
21 To stablish t' among them, that they*
26 had seen concerning t' matter, 3602
29 confirm t' second letter of Purim. 2063
Job 1: 3 so that t' man was the greatest 1931
22 In all t' Job sinned not, nor 2063
2:10 In all t' did not Job sin with his "
11 heard of all t' evil that was come "
3: 1 After t' opened Job his mouth, 3651
4: 6 Is not t' thy fear, thy confidence, thy*
5:27 Lo t', we have searched it, so it is;2063
8:19 t' is the joy of his way, and out of 1931
9:22 T' is one thing, therefore I said it,*"
10:13 heart: I know that t' is with thee. 2063
12: 9 hand of the Lord hath wrought t'? "
13: 1 Lo, mine eye hath seen all t', mine ear
17: 8 men shall be astonied at t', and 2063
18:21 t' is the place of him that knoweth2088
19:26 my skin worms destroy t' body, †2063
20: 4 Knowest thou not t' of old, since "
29 T' is the portion of a wicked man 2088
21: 2 and let t' be your consolations. 2063
27:13 T' is the portion of a wicked man 2088
31:11 For t' is an heinous crime; yea, it*1931
28 T' also were an iniquity to be "
33:12 Behold, in t' thou art not just: I 2063
34:16 thou hast understanding, hear t': "
35: 2 Thinkest thou t' to be right, that "
36:21 t' hast thou chosen rather than 2088
37: 1 At t' also my heart trembleth, 2063
14 Hearken unto t', O Job: stand still, "
38: 2 Who is t' that darkeneth counsel 2088
42:16 After t' lived Job an hundred and 2063
Ps 2: 7 my Son; t' day have I begotten thee.
7: 3 O Lord my God, if I have done t'; 2063
11: 6 t' shall be the portion of their cup.*
12: 7 preserve them from t' generation 2098
17:14 which have their portion in t' life,
18: *title* the words of t' song in the day 2063
22:31 shall be born, that he hath done t'.*
24: 6 T' is the generation of them that 2088
8 Who is t' King of glory? The Lord*"
10 Who is t' King of glory? The Lord "
27: 3 me, in t' will I be confident. *2063
32: 6 t' shall every one that is godly pray "
34: 6 T' poor man cried, and the Lord 2088
35:22 T' thou hast seen, O Lord: keep not*
41:11 t' I know that thou favourest me, 2063
44:17 t' is come upon us; yet have we "
21 Shall not God search t' out? for he "
48:14 For t' God is our God for ever and 2088
49: 1 Hear t', all ye people; give ear, all 2063
13 T' their way is their folly: yet 2088
50:22 Now consider t', ye that forget 2063
51: 4 I sinned, and done t' evil in thy sight:*
52: 7 t' is the man that made not God his
56: 9 back: t' I know; for God is for me.2088
62:11 twice have I heard t'; that power 2098
68:16 t' is the hill which God desireth to*
69:31 T' also shall please the Lord better*
32 The humble shall see t', and be glad:*
71:18 thy strength unto t' generation, *
73:16 When I thought to know t', it was 2063
74: 2 t' mount Zion, wherein thou hast *2088
18 Remember t', that the enemy 2063
77:10 And I said, T' is my infirmity: 1931
78:21 Therefore the Lord heard t', and was*
32 For all t' they sinned still, and 2063
54 even to t' mountain, which his 2088
59 When God heard t', he was wroth, and
80:14 and behold, and visit t' vine; 2063
81: 4 t' was a statute for Israel, and a *1931
5 T' he ordained in Joseph for a *
87: 4 Ethiopia; t' man was born there. 2088
5 T' and that man was born in her:
6 that t' man was born there. 2088
92: 6 neither doth a fool understand t'. 2063
95:10 long was I grieved with t' generation,*
102:18 T' shall be written for the 2088
104:25 So is t' great and wide sea, wherein*"
109:20 Let t' be the reward of mine 2063
27 they may know that t' is thy hand; "
113: 2 name of the Lord from t' time forth
115:18 will bless the Lord from t' time forth
118:20 T' gate of the Lord, into which 2088
23 T' is the Lord's doing; it is 2063
24 T' is the day which the Lord hath2088
119:91 continue t' day according to thine
121: 8 and thy coming in from t' time forth,
149: 9 t' honour have all his saints. 1931
Pr 6: 3 Do t' now, my son, and deliver 2063
7:14 me; t' day have I payed my vows.
22:19 I have made known to thee t' day,
Ec 1:10 it may be said, See, t' is new? 2088
13 t' sore travail hath God given to *1931
17 I perceived that t' also is vexation2088
2: 1 and, behold, t' also is vanity. 1931
10 and t' was my portion of all my 2088
15 in my heart, that t' also is vanity. "
19 under the sun. T' is also vanity. "
21 T' also is vanity and a great evil. "
23 the night. T' is also vanity. 2088.1931

Ec 2:24 T' also I saw, that it was from the2088
26 T' also is vanity and vexation of "
4: 4 that for t' a man is envied of his 1931
4 T' is also vanity and vexation of 2088
8 T' is also vanity, yea, it is a sore "
16 t' also is vanity and vexation of "
5:10 with increase: t' is also vanity. "
16 t' also is a sore evil, that in all 2090
19 in his labour; t' is the gift of God. "
6: 2 it: t' is vanity, and it is an evil 2088
5 t' hath more rest than the other. "
9 t' is also vanity and vexation of "
12 what is good for man in t' life, *
7: 6 of the fool: t' also is vanity. 2088
10 not enquire wisely concerning t'? "
18 that thou shouldest take hold of t'; "
18 from t' withdraw not thine hand: * "
23 All t' have I proved by wisdom: 2090
27 Behold, t' have I found, saith the 2088
29 t' only have I found, that God hath "
8: 9 All t' have I seen, and applied my "
10 they had so done: t' is also vanity. "
14 I said that t' also is vanity. "
9: 1 For all t' I consider in my heart "
1 even to declare all t', that the "
3 T' is an evil among all things that "
9 that is thy portion in t' life, and *
13 T' wisdom have I seen also under2090
11: 6 shall prosper, either t' or that, 2088
12:13 for t' is the whole duty of man.
Ca 3: 6 Who is t' that cometh out of the 2063
5:16 T' is my beloved, and t' is my 2088
7: 7 T' thy stature is like to a palm 2063
8: 5 Who is t' that cometh up from the "
Isa 1:12 who hath required t' at your hand, "
3: 6 and let t' ruin be under thy hand: "
5:25 For all t' his anger is not turned "
6: 7 said, Lo, t' hath touched thy lips; 2088
9 And he said, Go, and tell t' people, "
10 Make the heart of t' people fat, and "
8: 6 as t' people refuseth the waters of "
11 not walk in the way of t' people, "
12 them to whom t' people shall say, "
20 they speak not according to t' word, "
9: 7 the Lord of hosts will perform t'. 2063
12 For all t' his anger is not turned "
16 the leaders of t' people cause them2088
17, 21 all t' his anger is not turned 2063
10: 4 For all t' his anger is not turned "
12: 5 things: t' is known in all the earth. "
14: 4 take up t' proverb against the 2088
16 Is t' the man that made the earth "
26 T' is the purpose that is purposed2063
26 t' is the hand that is stretched out "
28 king Ahaz died was t' burden. 2088
16:13 T' is the word that the Lord hath "
17:14 T' is the portion of them that spoil "
20: 6 inhabitant of t' isle shall say in that"
22:14 t' iniquity shall not be purged from "
15 Go, get thee unto t' treasurer, even "
23: 7 Is t' your joyous city, whose 2088
8 hath taken t' counsel against Tyre, "
13 t' people was not, till the Assyrian2088
24: 3 for the Lord hath spoken t' word. "
25: 6 And in t' mountain shall the Lord "
7 he will destroy in t' mountain the "
9 in that day, Lo, t' is our God; "
9 t' is the Lord; we have waited for "
10 in t' mountain shall the hand of the"
26: 1 In that day shall t' song be sung "
27: 9 By t' therefore shall the iniquity 2063
9 t' is all the fruit to take away his 2088
28:11 tongue will he speak to t' people. "
12 T' is the rest wherewith ye may 2063
12 to rest; and t' is the refreshing: "
14 that rule t' people...in Jerusalem. 2088
29 T' also cometh forth from the Lord"
29:11, 12 saying, Read t', I pray thee: "
14 marvellous work among t' people, "
30: 7 have I cried concerning t', Their *2063
9 That t' is a rebellious people, lying1931
12 Because ye despise t' word, and 2088
13 t' iniquity shall be to you as a "
21 T' is the way, walk ye in it, when "
36: 4 What confidence is t' wherein thou "
6 in the staff of t' broken reed, "
7 Ye shall worship before t' altar? "
10 Lord against t' land to destroy it? 2063
10 unto me, Go up against t' land, and"
15 t' city shall not be delivered into "
37: 3 T' day is a day of trouble, and of 2088
22 T' is the word which the Lord hath"
30 And t' shall be a sign unto thee, "
30 eat t' year such as groweth of itself;
32 of the Lord of hosts shall do t'. 2063
33 He shall not come into t' city, nor "
34 and shall not come into t' city, saith"
35 For I will defend t' city to save it "
38: 6 I will deliver thee and t' city out of "
6 of Assyria: and I will defend t' city."
7 t' shall be a sign unto thee from 2088
7 Lord will do t' thing that he hath "
19 he shall praise thee, as I do t' day:
39: 6 have laid up in store until t' day, 2088
41:20 the hand of the Lord hath done t', 2063
42:22 t' is a people robbed and spoiled; 1931
23 Who among you will give ear to t'?2063
43: 9 who among them can declare t', "
21 T' people have I formed for *2098
45:21 declared t' from ancient time? 2063
46: 8 Remember t', and shew yourselves "
47: 8 Therefore hear now t', thou that art"
48: 1 Hear ye t', O house of Jacob, which "
6 Thou hast heard, see all t'; and will
6 shewed thee new things from t' time,
16 Come ye near unto me, hear ye t'; 2063

Isa 48:20 tell t', utter it even to the end of the2063
50:11 T' shall ye have of mine hand; ye "
51:21 hear now t', thou afflicted, and "
54: 9 t' is as the waters of Noah unto me:"
17 T' is the heritage of the servants of"
56: 2 Blessed is the man that doeth t', "
12 and to morrow shall be as t' day, 2088
58: 4 ye shall not fast as ye do t' day, to
5 wilt thou call t' a fast, and an 2088
6 Is not t' the fast that I have chosen?"
59:21 me, t' is my covenant with them, 2063
63: 1 Who is t' that cometh from Edom, 2088
1 t' that is glorious in his apparel, "
66: 2 but to t' man will I look, even to "
14 And when ye see t', your heart shall*
Jer 1:10 t' day set thee over the nations 2088
18 have made thee t' day a defenced city,
2:12 Be astonished, O ye heavens, at t', 2063
17 thou not procured t' unto thyself, "
3: 4 thou not from t' time cry unto me,
10 yet for all t' her treacherous sister2063
25 from our youth even unto t' day, 2088
4: 8 For t' gird you with sackcloth, 2063
10 hast greatly deceived t' people and2088
11 time shall it be said to t' people "
18 t' is thy wickedness, because it is 2063
28 For t' shall the earth mourn, and "
5: 7 How shall I pardon thee for t'? thy*"
9 be avenged on such a nation as t'?2088
14 Because ye speak t' word, behold, I "
14 t' people wood, and it shall devour "
20 Declare t' in the house of Jacob, 2063
21 Hear now t', O foolish people, and "
23 But t' people hath a revolting and 2088
6: 6 t' is the city to be visited; she is 1931
19 I will bring evil upon t' people, 2088
21 stumblingblocks before t' people, "
7: 2 house, and proclaim there t' word, "
3 I will cause you to dwell in t' place. "
6 shed not innocent blood in t' place, "
7 will I cause you to dwell in t' place, "
10 and stand before me in t' house, "
11 Is t' house, which is called by my "
14 Therefore will I do unto t' house, *
16 pray not thou for t' people, neither2088
20 shall be poured out upon t' place, "
23 But t' thing commanded I them, "
25 out of the land of Egypt unto t' day "
28 T' is a nation that obeyeth not the "
33 carcases of t' people shall be meat "
8: 3 them that remain of t' evil family, 2063
5 then is t' people of Jerusalem 2088
9: 9 be avenged on such a nation as t'? "
12 wise man, that may understand t'?2063
15 even t' people, with wormwood, 2088
24 let him that glorieth glory in t', 2063
10:18 inhabitants of the land at t' once,
19 Truly t' is a grief, and I must bear2088
11: 2 Hear ye the words of t' covenant, "
3 not the words of t' covenant, "
5 with milk and honey, as it is t' day. "
6 Hear ye the words of t' covenant, "
7 even unto t' day, rising early and "
8 them all the words of t' covenant, "
14 pray not thou for t' people, neither "
13: 9 After t' manner will I mar the pride of
10 T' evil people, which refuse to 2088
10 shall even be as t' girdle, which is "
12 thou shalt speak unto them t' word; "
13 I will fill all the inhabitants of t' land,
25 T' is thy lot, the portion of thy 2088
14:10 Thus saith the Lord unto t' people, "
11 Pray not for t' people for their good."
13 give you assured peace in t' place. "
15 and famine shall not be in t' land; 2063
17 thou shalt say t' word unto them; 2088
15: 1 mind could not be toward t' people:"
20 unto t' people a fenced brasen wall:"
16: 2 have sons or daughters in t' place. "
3 daughters that are born in t' place, "
3 fathers that begat them in t' land; "
5 away my peace from t' people, "
6 and the small shall die in t' land: 2063
9 cease out of t' place in your eyes, 2088
10 shew t' people all these words, "
10 Lord pronounced all t' great evil 2063
13 I cast you out of t' land into a land "
21 I will t' once cause them to know, "
17:24 burden through the gates of t' city2063
25 enter into the gates of t' city kings "
25 and t' city shall remain for ever. 2088
18: 6 cannot I do with you as t' potter? "
19: 3 I will bring evil upon t' place, "
4 me, and have estranged t' place, "
4 t' place with the blood of innocents;"
6 t' place shall no more be called "
7 of Judah and Jerusalem in t' place;"
8 And I will make t' city desolate, 2063
11 Even so will I break t' people and 2088
11 t' city, as one breaketh a potter's 2063
12 Thus will I do unto t' place, saith 2088
12 and even make t' city as Tophet: 2063
20: 5 deliver all the strength of t' city, "
21: 4 them into the midst of t' city. "
6 will smite the inhabitants of t' city,"
7 such as are left in t' city from the "
8 And unto t' people thou shalt say, 2088
9 abideth in t' city shall die by the 2063
10 set my face against t' city for evil. "
22: 1 of Judah, and speak there t' word, 2088
3 shed innocent blood in t' place. "
4 if ye do t' thing indeed, then shall "
4 enter in by the gates of t' house "
5 t' house shall become a desolation. "
8 many nations shall pass by t' city,2063
8 Lord done thus unto t' great city? "

Jer 22:11 which went forth out of t' place; 2088
12 and shall see t' land no more. 2063
16 was not t' to know me? saith the 1931
21 T' hath been thy manner from 2088
28 Is t' man Coniah a despised broken "
30 Write ye t' man childless, a man "
23: 6 t' is his name whereby he shall be "
26 shall t' be in the heart of the prophets
32 shall not profit t' people at all, 2088
33 when t' people, or the prophet, or a "
38 Because ye say t' word, The burden"
24: 5 whom I have sent out of t' place into"
6 I will bring them again to t' land: 2063
8 residue...that remain in t' land, "
25: 3 even unto t' day, that is the three 2088
9 will bring them against t' land, 2063
11 t' whole land shall be a desolation, "
13 even all that is written in t' book, 2088
15 Take the wine cup of t' fury at my 2063
18 and a curse; as it is t' day; 2088
26: 1 Judah came t' word from the Lord, "
6 will I make t' house like Shiloh, "
6 t' city a curse to all the nations 2063
9 T' house shall be like Shiloh, 2088
9 t' city shall be desolate without an2063
11 T' man is worthy to die; for he 2088
11 he hath prophesied against t' city, 2063
12 me to prophesy against t' house 2088
12 and against t' city all the words 2063
15 upon yourselves, and upon t' city, "
16 T' man is not worthy to die: for 2088
20 against t' city and against t' land 2063
27: 1 came t' word unto Jeremiah from 2088
16 to the priests and to all t' people, "
17 should t' city be laid waste? 2063
19 of the vessels that remain in t' city,"
22 up, and restore them to t' place. 2008
28: 3 will I bring again into t' place all "
3 Babylon took away from t' place, "
4 And I will bring again to t' place "
6 captive, from Babylon into t' place."
7 hear thou now t' word that I speak "
15 makest t' people to trust in a lie. "
16 t' year thou shalt die, because thou
29:10 causing you to return to t' place. 2088
16 the people that dwelleth in t' city, 2063
28 saying, T' captivity is long: *1931
32 a man to dwell among t' people; 2088
30:17 T' is Zion, whom no man seeketh*1931
21 who is t'...engaged his heart *1931,2088
31:23 they shall use t' speech in the land "
26 Upon t' I awaked, and beheld; 2063
33 t' shall be the covenant that I will "
32: 3 will give t' city into the hand of the"
8 that t' was the word of the Lord. 1931
14 t' evidence of the purchase, both 2088
14 and t' evidence which is open; "
15 be possessed again in t' land. 2063
20 land of Egypt, even unto t' day, 2088
20 made thee a name, as at t' day; "
22 And hast given them t' land, 2063
23 all t' evil to come upon them: "
28 give t' city into the hand of the "
29 Chaldeans, that fight against t' city,"
29 shall come and set fire on t' city, "
31 For t' city hath been to me as a "
31 that they built it even unto t' day;2088
35 they should do t' abomination, 2063
36 concerning t' city, whereof ye say; "
41 will plant them in t' land assuredly"
42 as I have brought all t' great evil "
42 evil upon t' people, so will I bring 2088
43 fields shall be bought in t' land, 2063
33: 4 concerning the houses of t' city, "
5 I have hid my face from t' city. "
10 there shall be heard in t' place, 2088
12 Again in t' place, which is desolate "
16 t' is the name wherewith she shall "
24 not what t' people have spoken, "
34: 2 give t' city into the hand of the 2063
8 T' is the word that came unto *
22 cause them to return to t' city; 2063
35:14 for unto t' day they drink none, 2088
16 t' people hath not hearkened unto "
36: 1 t' word came unto Jeremiah from "
2 days of Josiah, even unto t' day. "
7 hath pronounced against t' people."
29 Thou hast burned t' roll, saying, 2063
29 certainly come and destroy t' land, "
37: 8 and fight against t' city, and take it,"
10 his tent, and burn t' city with fire. "
18 thy servants, or against t' people, 2088
19 against you, nor against t' land? 2063
38: 2 He that remaineth in t' city shall "
3 T' city shall surely be given into "
4 thee, let t' man be put to death: 2088
4 men of war that remain in t' city, 2063
4 for t' man seeketh not the welfare 2088
4 welfare of t' people, but the hurt. "
16 Lord liveth, that made us t' soul, 2063
17 t' city shall not be burned with fire;"
18 t' city be given into the hand of the "
21 t' is the word that the Lord hath 2088
23 t' city to be burned with fire. 2063
39:16 bring my words upon t' city for evil,"
40: 2 thy God hath pronounced t' evil
2 evil upon t' place. 2088
3 t' thing is come upon you. "
4 I loose thee t' day from the chains
16 Thou shalt not do t' thing: for 2088
42: 2 thy God, even for all t' remnant; 2063
10 If ye will still abide in t' land, then "
13 say, We will not dwell in t' land, "
18 and ye shall see t' place no more. 2088
19 that I have admonished you t' day.
21 now I have t' day declared it to you:

Jer 44: 2 t' day they are a desolation, and 2088
4 do not t' abominable thing that "
6 wasted and desolate, as at t' day. "
7 Wherefore commit ye t' great evil
10 are not humbled even unto t' day, 2088
22 without an inhabitant, as at t' day. "
23 therefore t' evil is happened unto 2063
23 happened unto you, as at t' day. 2088
29 And t' shall be a sign unto you, 2063
29 that I will punish you in t' place, 2088
45: 4 I will pluck up, even t' whole land.1931
46: 7 Who is t' that cometh up as a 2088
10 t' is the day of the Lord God of *1931
50:17 and last t' Nebuchadrezzar king of2088
25 t' is the work of the Lord God of *1931
51: 6 for t' is the time of the Lord's * "
59 And t' Seraiah was a quiet prince.*
62 thou hast spoken against t' place, 2088
63 made an end of reading t' book, "
52:28 T' is the people...Nebuchadrezzar "
La 2:15 Is t' the city that men call The "
16 t' is the day that we looked for; "
20 to whom thou hast done t'. *3541
3:21 T' I recall to my mind, therefore 2063
5:17 For t' our heart is faint; for these 2088
Eze 1: 5 t' was their appearance; they had "
23 had two, which covered on t' side, 2007
28 T' was the appearance of the 1931
2: 3 against me, even unto t' very day. 2088
3: 1 eat t' roll, and go speak unto the 2063
3 fill thy bowels with t' roll that I "
4: 3 T' shall be a sign to the house of 1931
5: 5 T' is Jerusalem: I have set it in 2063
6:10 that I would do t' evil unto them. "
8: 5 t' image of jealousy in the entry. 2088
15, 17 Hast thou seen t', O son of man?
10:15, 20 T' is the living creature that I 1931
11: 2 and give wicked counsel in t' city:2063
3 t' city is the caldron, and we be 1931
6 multiplied your slain in t' city, 2063
7 flesh, and t' city is the caldron: 1931
11 T' city shall not be your caldron, "
15 unto us is t' land given in "
12:10 T' burden concerneth the prince 2088
23 I will make t' proverb to cease, and"
16:20 t' of thy whoredoms a small matter.*
43 shalt not commit t' lewdness above all
44 shall use t' proverb against thee, "
49 t' was the iniquity of thy sister 2088
17: 7 t' vine did bend her roots toward 2063
18: 2 use t' proverb concerning the land2088
3 more to use t' proverb in Israel. "
19:14 T' is a lamentation, and shall be 1931
20:27 in t' your fathers have blasphemed2063
29 is called Bamah unto t' day. 2088
31 with all your idols, even unto t' day:
21:11 t' sword is sharpened, and it is *1931
26 t' shall not be the same: exalt him*2063
23:11 And when her sister Aholibah saw t',
38 t' they have done unto me: they 2063
24: 2 of the day, even of t' same day: 2088
2 against Jerusalem t' same day. "
24 and when t' cometh, ye shall know
31:18 T' is Pharaoh and all his 1931
32:16 T' is the lamentation wherewith "
33:33 And when t' cometh to pass, (lo, it will
36:22 I do not t' for your sakes, O house of
32 Not for your sakes do I t', saith the
35 T' land that was desolate is 1977
39: 8 t' is the day whereof I have 1931
40:10 eastward were three on t' side, 6311
10 one measure on t' side and on that "
12 chambers was one cubit on t' side, "
12 were six cubits on t' side, 6311
21 three on t' side and three on that "
26 it had palm trees, one on t' side, "
34, 37 on t' side, and on that side: "
39 the gate were two tables on t' side, "
41 Four tables were on t' side, and "
45 T' chamber, whose prospect is 2090
48 five cubits on t' side, and five 6311
48 the gate was three cubits on t' side,"
49 one on t' side, and another on that "
41: 4 me, T' is the most holy place. 2088
22 T' is the table that is before the "
43:12 T' is the law of the house; Upon 2063
12 Behold, t' is the law of the house. "
13 t' shall be the higher place of the 2088
44: 2 T' gate shall be shut, it shall not "
45: 1 T' shall be holy in all the borders 1931
2 Of t' there shall be for the 2088
3 of t' measure shalt thou measure 2063
13 T' is the oblation that ye shall offer;"
16 t' oblation for the prince in Israel. "
46: 3 worship at the door of t' gate *1931
20 T' is the place where the priests 2088
47: 6 unto me, Son of man, hast thou seen t'?
12 on t' side and on that side, shall 2088
13 T' shall be the border, whereby ye "
14 t' land shall fall unto you for 2063
15 t' shall be the border of the land 2088
17 of Hamath. And t' is the north side.
18 the east sea. And t' is the east side.
19 And t' is the south side southward.
20 Hamath. T' is the west side. 2063
21 So shall ye divide t' land unto "
48:10 the priests, shall be t' holy oblation;*
12 t' oblation of the land that is offered*
29 T' is the land which ye shall 2063
Da 1:14 he consented to them in t' matter, 2088
2:12 For t' cause the king was angry 1836
18 God of heaven concerning t' secret;"
30 t' secret is not revealed to me for "
31 T' great image, whose brightness 1797
32 T' image's head was of fine gold, 1931
36 T' is the dream; and we will tell 1836

Da 2:38 them all. Thou art t' head of gold.*1931
47 thou couldest reveal t' secret. 1836
3:16 careful to answer thee in t' matter. "
29 God that can deliver after t' sort. "
4:17 T' matter is by the decree of the*
18 t' dream I king Nebuchadnezzar 1836
24 T' is the interpretation, O king, "
24 t' is the decree of the most High, *1931
28 t' came upon the king Nebuchadnezzar.
30 and said, Is not t' great Babylon, 1668
5: 7 Whosoever shall read t' writing, 1836
15 that they should read t' writing, and"
22 heart, though thou knewest all t'; "
24 him; and t' writing was written. "
25 t' is the writing that was written. "
26 T' is the interpretation of the "
6: 3 t' Daniel was preferred above the "
5 find any occasion against t' Daniel, "
28 t' Daniel prospered in the reign of "
7: 6 After t' I beheld, and lo another, "
7 After t' I saw in the night visions, "
8 in t' horn were eyes like the eyes 1668
16 and asked him the truth of all t'. 1836
24 horns out of t' kingdom are ten kings
8:16 t' man to understand the vision. 1975
9: 7 us confusion of faces, as at t' day; 2088
13 Moses, all t' evil is come upon us: 2063
15 hast gotten thee renown, as at t' day;
10: 8 was left alone, and saw t' great vision,
11 he had spoken t' word unto me, 2088
17 how can the servant of t' my lord "
17 talk with t' my lord? for as for me, "
11:18 t' shall he turn his face unto the isles,
12: 5 on t' side of the bank of the river, 2008
Ho 5: 1 Hear ye t', O priests; and hearken, 2063
7:10 their God, nor seek him for all t'. "
16 t' shall be their derision in the 2097
Joe 1: 2 Hear t', ye old men, and give ear, 2063
2 Hath t' been in your days, or even "
3: 9 Proclaim ye t' among the Gentiles; "
Am 3: 1 Hear t' word that the Lord hath 2088
4: 1 Hear t' word, ye kine of Bashan, "
5 t' liketh you, O ye children of 3651
12 because I will do t' unto thee, 2063
5: 1 Hear ye t' word which I take up 2088
7: 3 The Lord repented for t': It shall 2063
6 The Lord repented for t': "
6 T' also shall not be, saith the 1931
8: 4 Hear t', O ye that swallow up the 2063
8 Shall not the land tremble for t', "
9:12 name, saith the Lord that doeth t'. "
Ob 20 captivity of t' host of the children 2088
Jon 1: 7 for whose cause t' evil is upon us. 2063
8 for whose cause t' evil is upon us; "
10 unto him, Why hast thou done t'? "
14 let us not perish for t' man's life, 2088
4: 2 thee, O Lord, was not t' my saying, "
Mic 1: 5 transgression of Jacob is all t'. 2063
2: 3 against t' family do I devise an evil, "
3 ye go haughtily: for t' time is evil.1931
10 depart; for t' is not your rest: 2063
11 even be the prophet of t' people. 2088
3: 9 Hear t', I pray you, ye heads of the2063
5: 5 And t' man shall be the peace, 2088
Hab 1:11 imputing t' his power unto his *2098
Zep 2:10 T' shall they have for their pride, 2063
15 T' is the rejoicing city that dwelt "
Hag 1: 2 T' people say, The time is not 2088
4 houses, and t' house lie waste? "
2: 3 that saw t' house in her first glory? "
7 and I will fill t' house with glory, "
9 The glory of t' latter house shall be "
9 and in t' place will I give peace, "
14 So is t' people, and so is t' nation "
15 consider from t' day and upward, "
18 Consider now from t' day and "
19 fourth: from t' day will I bless you."
Zec 2: 4 Run, speak to t' young man, 1975
3: 2 is not t' a brand plucked out of 2088
4: 6 T' is the word of the Lord unto "
9 have laid the foundation of t' house;"
5: 3 T' is the curse that goeth forth 2063
3 shall be cut off as on t' side *2088
5 see what is t' that goeth forth. 2063
6 T' is an ephah that goeth forth. "
6 T' is their resemblance through "
7 t' is a woman that sitteth in the "
8 And he said, T' is wickedness. "
6:15 And t' shall come to pass, if ye "
8: 6 remnant of t' people in these days,2088
11 not be unto the residue of t' people "
12 remnant of t' people to possess all "
14:12 t' shall be the plague wherewith 2063
15 shall be in these tents, as t' plague. "
19 T'...be the punishment of Egypt, "
Mal 1: 9 t' hath been your means: will he "
13 should I accept t' of your hand?
2: 1 t' commandment is for you. 2063
4 sent t' commandment unto you, "
12 Lord will cut off the man that doeth t',
13 t' have ye done again, covering the
3: 9 have robbed me, even t' whole nation.
4: 3 your feet in the day that I shall do t',
M't 1:18 of Jesus Christ was on t' wise: 3779
22 Now all t' was done, that it might 5124
3: 3 t' is he that was spoken of by the 3778
17 T' is my beloved Son, in whom I "
6: 9 After t' manner therefore pray ye: 3779
11 Give us t' day our daily bread. 4594
7:12 for t' is the law and the prophets. 3778
8: 9 I say to t' man, Go, and he goeth; 5129
9 my servant, Do t', and he doeth it. 5124
27 What manner of man is t', that 3778
9: 3 themselves, T' man blasphemeth. "
28 Believe ye that I am able to do t'? 5124
10:23 when they persecute you in t' city,5026

M't 11:10 For t' is he, of whom it is written, 3778
16 shall I liken t' generation? 5026
23 would have remained until t' day. 4594
12: 6 in t' place is one greater than the 5602
7 But if ye had known what t' meaneth,
23 said, Is not t' the son of David? 3778
24 T' fellow doth not cast out devils. "
32 neither in t' world, neither in the 5129
41 in judgment with t' generation, 5026
42 in the judgment with t' generation, "
45 be also unto t' wicked generation. "
13:15 t' people's heart is waxed gross, 5127
19 T' is he which received seed by 3778
22 and the care of t' world, and the 5127
28 unto them, An enemy hath done t'. 5124
40 shall it be in the end of t' world. *5127
54 hath t' [5129] man t' wisdom, and 3778
55 Is not t' the carpenter's son? is not "
56 then hath t' man all these things? 5129
14: 2 T' is John the Baptist; he is risen 3778
15 T' is a desert place, and the time *3588
15: 8 T' people draweth nigh unto me 3778
11 out of the mouth, t' defileth a man. 5124
12 offended, after they heard t' saying? 3588
15 him, Declare unto us t' parable. 5026
16:18 upon t' rock I will build my church;"
22 Lord: t' shall not be unto thee. 5124
17: 5 T' is my beloved Son, in whom I 3778
20 ye shall say unto t' mountain, 5129
21 Howbeit t' kind goeth not out by *5124
18: 4 humble himself as t' little child, "
19: 5 t' cause shall a man leave father 5127
11 All men cannot receive t' saying, 5126
26 With men t' is impossible; but 5124
20:14 I will give unto t' last, even as unto 5129
21: 4 All t' was done, that it might be 5124
10 city was moved, saying, Who is t'? 3778
11 T' is Jesus the prophet of Nazareth"
21 only do t' which is done to the fig *3588
21 if ye shall say unto t' mountain, 5129
23 and who gave thee t' authority? 5026
38 among themselves, T' is the heir; 3778
42 t' is the Lord's doing, and it is "
44 whosoever shall fall on t' stone 5126
22:20 unto them, Whose is t' image and 3778
33 And when the multitude heard t',*
38 T' is the first and great 3778
23:36 shall come upon t' generation. 5026
24:14 t' gospel of the kingdom shall be 5124
21 beginning of the world to t' time, *3568
34 T' generation shall not pass, till 3778
43 But know t', that if the goodman 1565
26: 8 To what purpose is t' waste? 3778
9 t' ointment might have been sold 5124
12 poured t' ointment on my body, "
13 t' gospel shall be preached in the "
13 the whole world, there shall also t',*3778
13 that t' woman hath done, be told "
26 and said, Take, eat; t' is my body. 5124
28 t' is my blood of the new testament,"
29 not drink henceforth of t' fruit of 5127
31 offended because of me t' night: 5026
34 That t' night, before the cock crow,"
39 possible, let t' cup pass from me: 5124
42 if t' cup may not pass away from "
56 But all t' was done, that the "
61 T' fellow said, I am able to 3778
71 T' fellow was also with Jesus of "
27: 8 The field of blood, unto t' day. 4594
19 I have suffered many things t' day "
24 of the blood of t' just person: 5127
37 T' Is Jesus The King Of The 3778
47 that, said, T' man calleth for Elias."
54 saying, Truly t' was the Son of God."
28:14 if t' come to the governor's ears, 5124
15 t' saying is commonly reported 3778
15 among the Jews until t' day. 4594
M'r 1:27 saying, What thing is t'? what 3778
27 what new doctrine is t'? for with *5124
2: 7 Why doth t' man thus speak 3778
12 We never saw it on t' fashion. 3779
4:13 them, Know ye not t' parable? 5026
19 And the cares of t' world, and the *3588
41 What manner of man is t', that even 3778
5:32 to see her that had done t' thing. 5124
39 Why make ye t' ado, and weep? *
6: 2 whence hath t' man these things? 5129
2 what wisdom is t' which is given *3588
3 Is not t' the carpenter, the son of 3778
35 T' is a desert place, and now the *3588
7: 6 T' people honoureth me with their 3778
29 unto her, For t' saying go thy way; 5126
8:12 Why doth t' generation seek after 3778
12 sign be given unto t' generation. 5026
38 t' adulterous and sinful generation;"
9: 7 T' is my beloved Son: hear him. 3778
21 is it ago since t' came unto him? 5124
29 T' kind can come forth by nothing,"
10: 5 your heart he wrote you t' precept. 5026
7 t' cause shall a man leave his father 5127
30 an hundredfold now in t' time, 5129
11: 3 man say unto you, Why do ye t'? 5124
23 shall say unto t' mountain, Be 5129
28 who gave thee t' authority to do 5026
12: 7 among themselves, T' is the heir; 3778
10 And have ye not read t' scripture; 5026
11 T' was the Lord's doing, and it is 3778
16 is t' image and superscription? * "
30 t' is the first commandment. * "
31 the second is like, namely t', "
43 t' poor widow hath cast more in, "
13:19 which God created unto t' time, *3568
30 that t' generation shall not pass, 3778
14: 4 Why was t' waste of the ointment "
9 t' gospel shall be preached *5124
9 t' also that she hath done shall be

M'r 14:22 and said, Take, eat: t' is my body. 5124
24 T' is my blood of the new testament,"
27 offended because of me t' night: *5026
30 I say unto thee, That t' day, *4594
30 even in t' night, before the cock 5026
36 thee; take away t' cup from me: 5124
58 destroy t' temple that is made 5126
69 that stood by, T' is one of them. 3778
71 I know not t' man of whom ye 5126
15:39 Truly t' man was the Son of God. 3778
Lu 1:18 angel, Whereby shall I know t'? 5124
29 manner of salutation t' should be. 3778
34 How shall t' be, seeing I know not 5124
36 t' is the sixth month with her, who 3778
43 And whence is t' to me, that the 5124
61 kindred that is called by t' name. 5129
66 What manner of child shall t' be! 5124
2: 2 (And t' taxing was first made when 3778
11 is born t' day in the city of David a 4594
12 t' shall be a sign unto you; ye shall 5124
15 t' thing which is come to pass, "
17 was told them concerning t' child. 5127
34 t' child is set for the fall and rising 3778
3:20 Added yet t' above all, that he shut 5124
4: 3 t' stone that it be made bread. 5129
6 All t' power will I give thee, and 5026
21 T' day is...scripture fulfilled in *4594
21 is t' scripture fulfilled in your 3778
22 they said, Is not t' Joseph's son? "
23 will surely say unto me t' proverb, 5026
36 saying, What a word is t'! for 3778
5: 6 And when they had t' done, they 5124
21 saying, Who is t' which speaketh 3778
6: 3 Have ye not read so much as t', 5124
7: 4 worthy for whom he should do t': "
8 my servant, Do t', and he doeth it. "
17 t' rumour of him went forth 3778
27 T' is he, of whom it is written, "
31 I liken the men of t' generation? 5026
39 T' man, if he were a prophet, 3778
39 manner of woman t'...that toucheth 3588
44 unto Simon, Seest thou t' woman? 5026
45 t' woman since the time I came in,*3778
46 t' woman hath anointed my feet * "
49 Who is t' that forgiveth sins also? "
8: 9 saying, What might t' parable be? "
11 Now the parable is t': The seed is "
14 and riches and pleasures of t' life, 3588
25 another, What manner of man is t'! 3778
9: 9 but who is t', of whom I hear such "
13 go and buy meat for all t' people. 5126
35 T' is my beloved Son: hear him. 3778
45 they understood not t' saying, 5127
48 shall receive t' child in my name 5124
54 his disciples James and John saw t',
10: 5 first say, Peace be to t' house. 5129
11 notwithstanding be ye sure of t', 5124
20 Notwithstanding in t' rejoice not, 5129
28 right: t' do, and thou shalt live. 5124
11:29 to say, T' is an evil generation: 3778
30 the Son of man be to t' generation. 5026
31 with the men of t' generation, "
32 the judgment with t' generation, "
50 may be required of t' generation; "
51 It shall be required of t' generation."
12:18 And he said, T' will I do: I will 5124
20 t' night thy soul shall be required 5026
39 t' know, that if the goodman of the 5124
41 speakest thou t' parable unto us, 5026
56 is it that ye do not discern t' time? 5126
13: 6 He spake also t' parable; A certain 5026
7 I come seeking fruit on t' fig tree,
8 Lord, let it alone t' year also, till I 5124
16 And ought not t' woman, being a 5026
16 be loosed from t' bond on the 5127
14: 9 and say to thee, Give t' man place; 5129
30 T' man began to build, and was 3778
15: 2 T' man receiveth sinners, and "
3 And he spake t' parable unto them, 5026
24 t' my son was dead, and is alive 3778
30 as soon as t' thy son was come, "
32 t' thy brother was dead, and is alive"
16: 2 How is it that I hear t' of thee? 5124
8 children of t' world are in their 5127
24 for I am tormented in t' flame. 5026
26 beside all t', between us and you 5125
28 also come into t' place of torment. 5126
17: 6 might say unto t' sycamine tree, 5026
18 give glory to God, save t' stranger.*3778
25 and be rejected of t' generation. 5026
18: 1 a parable unto them to t' end,* 3588
5 because t' widow troubleth me, I 5026
9 he spake t' parable unto certain "
11 adulterers, or even as t' publican. 3778
14 t' man went down to his house "
23 And when he heard t', he was very*5023
30 manifold more in t' present time, 5129
34 t' saying was hid from them, 5124
19: 9 him, T' day is salvation come *4594
9 is salvation come to t' house, 5129
14 not have t' man to reign over us. 5126
42 known,...at least in t' thy day, 5026
20: 2 is he that gave thee t' authority? "
9 he to speak to the people t' parable;"
14 T' is the heir: come, let us kill 3778
17 What is t' then that is written, 5124
19 spoken t' parable against them. 5026
34 The children of t' world marry, 5126
21: 3 t' poor widow hath cast in more 3778
23 the land, and wrath upon t' people. 5129
32 T' generation shall not pass away, 3778
34 and drunkenness, and cares of t' life,
22:15 to eat t' passover with you before 5124
17 Take t', and divide it among "
19 T' is my body which is given for "
19 you: t' do in remembrance of me. "

Lu 22:20 T' cup is the new testament in my 5124
23 them it was that should do t' thing. "
34 the cock shall not crow t' day, 4594
37 that t' that is written must yet be 5124
42 be willing, remove t' cup from me: "
53 but t' is your hour, and the power of 3778
56 said, T' man was also with him. "
59 Of a truth t' fellow also was with "
23: 2 We found t' fellow perverting the 5126
4 people, I find no fault in t' man. 5129
5 beginning from Galilee to t' place. 5602
14 Ye have brought t' man unto me, 5129
14 have found no fault in t' man 5126
18 Away with t' man, and release unto"
38 T' Is The King Of The Jews. 3778
41 t' man hath done nothing amiss. "
47 Certainly t' was a righteous man. "
52 T' man went unto Pilate, and "
24:21 and beside all t', to day is the third 5125
Joh 1:15 T' was he of whom I spake, He 3778
19 t' is the record of John, when the "
30 T' is he of whom I said, After me "
34 bare record that t' is the Son of God."
2:11 T' beginning of miracles did Jesus 5026
12 After t' he went...to Capernaum, 5124
19 Destroy t' temple, and in three 5126
20 Forty and six years was t' temple 3778
22 that he had said t' unto them; 5124
3:19 And t' is the condemnation, that 3778
29 voice: t' my joy therefore is fulfilled."
4:13 drinketh of t' water shall thirst 5127
15 Sir, give me t' water, that I thirst 5124
20 fathers worshipped in t' mountain; 5129
21 ye shall neither in t' mountain, nor "
27 And upon t' came his disciples, and "
29 that ever I did: is not t' the Christ? 3778
42 know that t' is indeed the Christ, "
54 T' is again the second miracle 5124
5: 1 After t' there was a feast of the 5023
28 Marvel not at t': for the hour is 5124
6: 6 And t' he said to prove him: for he "
14 T' is of a truth that prophet that 3778
29 T' is the work of God, that ye 5124
34 Lord, evermore give us t' bread. 5126
39 t' is the Father's will which hath 5124
40 t' is the will of him that sent me, "
42 Is not t' Jesus, the son of Joseph, 3778
50 T' is the bread which cometh down"
51 if any man eat of t' bread, he shall 5127
52 How can t' man give us his flesh 3778
58 T' is that bread which came down "
58 he that eateth of t' bread shall live 5126
60 disciples, when they heard t', said,
60 T' is an hard saying; who can 3778
61 unto them, Doth t' offend you?
7: 8 Go ye up unto t' feast: I go not up*5026
8 I go not up yet unto t' feast; for "
15 How knoweth t' man letters, 3778
25 Is not t' he, whom they seek to kill?"
26 indeed that t' is the very Christ? "
27 we know t' man whence he is: but 5126
31 these which t' man hath done? 3778
36 What manner of saying is t' that he"
39 (But t' spake he of the Spirit, which 5124
40 when they heard t' saying, *3588
40 said, Of a truth t' is the Prophet. 3778
41 Others said, T' is the Christ. But "
46 Never man spake like t' man. "
49 t' people who knoweth not the law "
8: 4 t' woman was taken in adultery, "
6 T' they said, tempting him, that 5124
23 am from above: ye are of t' world; 5127
23 I am not of t' world. "
40 heard of God: t' did not Abraham. 5124
9: 2 who did sin, t' man, or his parents, 3778
3 Neither hath t' man sinned, nor his "
8 Is not t' he that sat and begged? "
9 Some said, T' is he: others said, * "
16 T' man is not of God, because he "
19 Is t' your son, who...was born blind?"
20 We know that t' is our son, and "
24 we know that t' man is a sinner. "
29 as for t' fellow, we know not from 5126
33 If t' man were not of God, he 3778
39 judgment I am come into t' world 5126
10:16 sheep I have,...are not of t' fold: 5026
18 T' commandment have I received "
41 John spake of t' man were true. 5127
11: 4 T' sickness is not unto death, but 3778
9 he seeth the light of t' world. 5127
26 shall never die. Believest thou t'? 5124
37 Could not t' man, which opened 3778
37 even t' man should not have died? "
39 him, Lord, by t' time he stinketh: 2235
47 for t' man doeth many miracles. 3778
51 And t' spake he not of himself: but 5124
12: 5 t' ointment sold for three hundred "
6 T' he said, not that he cared for the "
7 day of my burying hath she kept t'.*846
18 t' cause the people also met him, 5124
18 heard that he had done t' miracle. "
25 he that hateth his life in t' world 5129
27 say? Father, save me from t' hour: 5026
27 but for t' cause came I unto...hour. 5124
27 cause came I unto t' hour. 5026
30 T' voice came not because of me, 3778
31 Now is the judgment of t' world: 5127
31 the prince of t' world be cast out. "
33 T' he said, signifying what death 5124
34 lifted up? who is t' Son of man? 3778
13: 1 out of t' world unto the Father, 5127
28 what intent he spake t' unto him. 5124
35 t' shall all men know that ye are 5129
14:30 for the prince of t' world cometh, *5127
15:12 T' is my commandment, That ye 3778
13 Greater love hath no man than t', 5026

Joh 15:25 But t' cometh to pass, that the word
16:11 the prince of t' world is judged. 5127
17 What is t' that he saith unto us, 5124
18 What is t' that he saith, A little "
30 by t' we believe that thou camest 5129
17: 3 t' is life eternal, that they might 3778
18:17 also one of t' man's disciples? 5127
29 accusation bring ye against t' man?"
34 Sayest thou t' thing of thyself, or 5124
36 My kingdom is not of t' world: 5127
36 if my kingdom were not of t' world, "
37 I am a king. To t' end was I born, 5124
37 for t' cause came I into the world, "
38 when he had said t', he went out "
40 saying, Not t' man, but Barabbas. 5126
19:12 If thou let t' man go, thou art not "
20 T' title then read many of the Jews:"
28 After t', Jesus knowing that all 5124
38 And after t' Joseph of Arimathæa, 5023
20:22 And when he had said t', he 5124
30 which are not written in t' book: 5129
21: 1 and on t' wise shewed he himself. 3779
14 T' is now the third time that 5124
19 T' spake he, signifying by what "
19 when he had spoken t', he saith "
21 Lord, and what shall t' man do? 3778
23 Then went t' saying abroad "
24 T' is the disciple which testifieth "
Ac 1: 6 wilt thou at t' time restore again 5129
11 t' same Jesus, which is taken up 3778
16 t' scripture must needs have been*5026
17 had obtained part of t' ministry. "
18 Now t' man purchased a field 3778
25 he may take part of t' ministry 5026
2: 6 Now when t' was noised abroad, the "
12 one to another, What meaneth t'? 5124
14 t' known unto you, and hearken to "
16 t' is that which was spoken by the "
29 his sepulchre is with us unto t' day. 5026
31 seeing t' before spake of...resurrection
32 T' Jesus hath God raised up, 5126
33 he hath shed forth t', which ye 5124
37 they heard t', they were pricked in
40 Save yourselves from t' untoward 5026
3:12 men of Israel, why marvel ye at t'? 5129
12 we had made t' man to walk? * 846
16 name hath made t' man strong, 5026
16 given him t' perfect soundness 5126
4: 7 or by what name, have ye done t'? 5124
9 If we t' day be examined of the 4594
10 by him doth t' man stand here 3778
11 T' is the stone which was set at * "
17 speak...to no man in t' name. 5129
22 on whom t' miracle of healing was 5124
5: 4 conceived t' thing in thine heart? "
20 to the people all the words of t' life. 5026
24 of them whereunto t' would grow. 5124
28 ye should not teach in t' name? 5129
28 to bring t' man's blood upon us. 5127
37 After t' man rose up Judas of 5126
38 for if t' [3778] counsel or t' work 5124
6: 3 we may appoint over t' business. 5026
13 T' man ceaseth not to speak 5127
13 words against t' holy place, and 3778
14 t' Jesus of Nazareth shall destroy 5126
14 of Nazareth shall destroy t' place, 3778
7: 4 he removed him into t' land, 5026
6 And God spake on t' wise, That 3779
7 forth, and serve me in t' place. 5129
29 Then fled Moses at t' saying, and "
35 T' Moses whom they refused, 5126
37 T' is that Moses, which said unto 3778
38 T' is he, that was in the church in "
40 for as for t' Moses, which brought "
60 Lord, lay not t' sin to their charge. 5026
60 And when he had said t', he fell 5124
8:10 T' man is the great power of God. 3778
19 Give me also t' power, that on 5026
21 neither part nor lot in t' matter: 5129
22 Repent...of t' thy wickedness, 5026
29 near, and join thyself to t' chariot. 5129
32 the scripture which he read was t', 3778
34 of whom speaketh the prophet t'? 5124
9: 2 if he found any of t' way, whether *3588
13 I have heard by many of t' man, 5127
21 Is not t' he that destroyeth them 3778
21 called on t' name in Jerusalem, 5124
22 proving that t' is very Christ. 3778
36 t' woman was full of good works "
10:16 T' was done thrice: and the 5124
17 what t' vision which he had seen *3588
30 ago I was fasting until t' hour; 5026
11:10 And t' was done three times: and 5124
13:17 The God of t' people of Israel chose 5127
23 t' man's seed hath God according "
26 you is the word of t' salvation sent. 5026
33 Son, t' day have I begotten thee. 4594
34 he said on t' wise, I will give you 3779
38 through t' man is preached unto you 5127
48 when the Gentiles heard t', they were
15: 2 and elders about t' question. 5127
6 for to consider of t' matter. "
15 And to t' agree the words of the 5129
16 After t' I will return, and will *5023
23 they wrote letters by them after t' *3592
16:18 And t' did she many days. But 5124
36 the prison told t' saying to Paul, *5128
17: 3 t' Jesus, whom I preach unto you, 3778
18 said, What will t' babbler say? "
19 May we know what t' new doctrine, "
23 I found an altar with t' inscription, 3739
30 times of t' ignorance God winked *3588
32 will hear thee again of t' matter. 5127
18:10 for I have much people in t' city. 5026
13 T' fellow persuadeth men to 3778
18 Paul after t' tarried there yet a good

Ac 18:21 t' feast that cometh in Jerusalem:*3588
25 T' man was instructed in the way 3778
19: 5 When they heard t', they were baptized
10 t' continued by the space of two 5124
17 t' was known to all the Jews and "
25 by t' craft we have our wealth. 5026
26 t' Paul hath persuaded and turned 3778
27 not only t' our craft is in danger to 5124
40 in question for t' day's uproar, 4594
40 give an account of t' concourse. 5026
20:26 Wherefore I take you to record t' 4594
29 For I know t', that after my *5124
21:11 bind the man that owneth t' girdle, 3778
23 therefore t' that we say to thee: 5124
28 T' is the man, that teacheth all 3778
28 people, and the law, and t' place: 5126
28 and hath polluted t' holy place. 5127
22: 3 in t' city at the feet of Gamaliel, 5026
3 toward God, as ye all are t' day. 4594
4 I persecuted t' way unto the death, 5026
22 gave him audience unto t' word, 5127
26 thou doest: for t' man is a Roman. 3778
28 a great sum obtained I t' freedom. 5026
23: 1 conscience before God until t' day. "
9 saying, We find no evil in t' man: 5129
13 which had made t' conspiracy. 5026
17 Bring t' young man unto the chief 5126
18 to bring t' young man unto thee, "
25 he wrote a letter after t' manner: "
27 T' man was taken of the Jews, and "
24: 2 unto t' nation by thy providence, 5129
5 found t' man a pestilent fellow, 5126
10 many years a judge unto t' nation, 5129
14 But t' I confess unto thee, that 5124
21 Except it be for t' one voice, that I 5026
21 called in question by you t' day. 4594
25 Go thy way for t' time; when I 3568
25: 5 down with me, and accuse t' man,* 846
24 ye see t' man, about whom all the 5126
26: 2 I shall answer for myself t' day *4594
16 appeared unto thee for t' purpose, 5124
22 I continue unto t' day, witnessing 5026
26 t' thing was not done in a corner. 5124
29 but also all that hear me t' day, 4594
31 T' man doeth nothing worthy of 3778
32 T' man might have been set at "
27:10 I perceive that t' voyage will be *3588
21 to have gained t' harm and loss. 5026
23 stood by me t' night the angel of "
33 T' day is the fourteenth day that 4594
34 meat: for t' is for your health: 5124
28: 4 No doubt t' man is a murderer, 3778
9 So when t' was done, others also, 5127
20 For t' cause therefore have I called 5026
20 of Israel I am bound with t' chain. "
22 for as concerning t' sect, we know "
26 Go unto t' people, and say, 5126
27 heart of t' people is waxed gross, 5127
Ro 1:26 For t' cause God gave them up 5124
2: 3 And thinkest thou t', O man, that "
3:26 at t' time his righteousness: 3588,3568
4: 9 Cometh t' blessedness then upon 3778
5: 2 into t' grace wherein we stand, 5026
6: 6 Knowing t', that our old man is 5124
7:24 me from the body of t' death? 5127
8:18 sufferings of t' present time are 3588
9: 9 For t' is the word of promise, At 3778
9 At t' time will I come, and Sarah 5126
10 And not only t'; but when Rebecca* "
17 for t' same purpose...I raised thee 5124
10: 6 is of faith speaketh on t' wise, *3779
11: 5 t' present time...there is a remnant 3588
8 they should not hear;) unto t' day. 4594
25 should be ignorant of t' mystery, 5124
27 For t' is my covenant unto them, 3778
12: 2 And be not conformed to t' world: 5129
13: 6 for t' cause pay ye tribute also: 5124
6 continually upon t' very thing. "
9 For t', Thou shalt not commit 3588
9 briefly comprehended in t' saying, 5129
14: 9 For to t' end Christ both died, and 5124
13 but judge t' rather, that no man "
15: 9 For t' cause I will confess to thee * "
28 When therefore I have performed t', "
28 and have sealed to them t' fruit, 5126
16:22 I Tertius, who wrote t' epistle, *3588
1Co 1:12 Now t' I say, that every one of you 5124
20 where is the disputer of t' world? 5127
20 foolish the wisdom of t' world? * "
2: 6 yet not the wisdom of t' world, nor "
6 nor of the princes of t' world, that "
8 of the princes of t' world knew: "
3:12 man build upon t' foundation gold,*5126
18 seemeth to be wise in t' world, 5129
19 wisdom of t' world is foolishness 5127
4:11 t' present hour we both hunger, 3588
13 offscouring of all things unto t' day. 737
17 For t' cause have I sent unto you 5124
5: 2 he that hath done t' deed might be "
3 him that hath so done t' deed, "
10 with the fornicators of t' world, 5127
6: 3 more things that pertain to t' life?
4 of things pertaining to t' life,
7: 6 But I speak t' by permission, and 5124
7 one after t' manner, and another 3779
26 t' is good for the present distress, 5124
29 t' I say, brethren, the time is short:"
31 And they that use t' world, as not*5127
31 for the fashion of t' world passeth 5129
35 t' I speak for your own profit; not 5124
8: 7 conscience of the idol unto t' hour* 737
9 t' liberty of yours become a 3778
9: 3 to them that do examine me is t', "
10 For our sakes, no doubt, t' is written:*
12 If others be partakers of t' power 3588
12 we have not used t' power; 5026

1Co 9:17 if I do t' thing willingly, I have a 5124
23 t' I do for the gospel's sake, that I* "
10:28 T' is offered in sacrifice unto idols, "
11:10 For t' cause ought the woman to "
17 in t' that I declare unto you I praise"
20 t' is not to eat the Lord's supper. * "
22 to you? shall I praise you in t'? 5129
24 t' is my body, which is broken for 5124
24 you: t' do in remembrance of me. "
25 T' cup is the new testament in my "
25 t' do ye, as oft as ye drink it, in "
26 For as often as ye eat t' bread, 5126
26 and drink t' cup, ye do shew the 5124
27 whosoever shall eat t' bread, and *5126
27 and drink t' cup of the Lord, * "
30 t' cause many are weak and sickly 5124
14:21 lips will I speak unto t' people; 5129
15: 6 greater part remain unto t' present,*
19 If in t' life only we have hope in 5126
34 of God: I speak t' to your shame.
50 Now t' I say, brethren, that flesh 5124
53 For t' corruptible must put on "
53 t' mortal must put on immortality. "
54 t' corruptible shall have put on "
54 and t' mortal shall have put on "
16:12 was not at all to come at t' time; *3568
2Co 1:12 our rejoicing is t', the testimony 3778
15 in t' confidence I was minded to 5026
2: 1 But I determined t' with myself, 5124
3 And I wrote t' same unto you, lest, "
6 to such a man is t' punishment, 3778
9 For to t' end also did I write, that 5124
3:10 glorious had no glory in t' respect, 5129
14 until t' day remaineth the same 4594
15 But even unto t' day, when Moses "
4: 1 seeing we have t' ministry, 5026
4 god of t' world hath blinded the 5127
7 t' treasure in earthen vessels, 5126
5: 1 earthly house of t' tabernacle *3588
2 in t' we groan, earnestly desiring 5129
4 that are in t' tabernacle do groan, 3588
7: 3 I speak not t' to condemn you: for*
11 behold t' selfsame thing, that ye 5124
11 yourselves...be clear in t' matter. *3588
8: 5 t' they did, not as we hoped, but first
7 that ye abound in t' grace also. 5124
10 t' is expedient for you, who have "
14 at t' time your abundance may 3588,3568
19 to travel with us with t' grace, 5124
20 Avoiding t', that no man should "
20 in t' abundance which is 5026
9: 3 you should be in vain in t' behalf; 5129
4 in t' same confident boasting. 3588
6 But t' I say, He which soweth 5124
12 the administration of t' service 5026
13 the experiment of t' ministration "
10: 7 let him of himself think t' again, 5124
11 Let such an one think t', that, such "
11:10 man shall stop me of t' boasting in 3778
17 in t' confidence of boasting. 5026
12: 8 For t' thing I besought the Lord 5127
13 to you? forgive me t' wrong. 5026
13: 1 T' is the third time I am coming 5124
9 t' also we wish, even your perfection."
Ga 1: 4 deliver us from t' present evil 3588
3: 2 T' only would I learn of you, 5124
17 t' I say, that the covenant, that "
4:25 t' Agar is mount Sinai in Arabia, 3588
5: 8 T' persuasion cometh not of him "
14 is fulfilled in one word, even in t'; "
16 T' I say then, Walk in the Spirit, and*
6:16 many as walk according to t' rule, 5129
Eph 1:21 not only in t' world, but also in 3588
2: 2 according to the course of t' world, 5127
3: 1 For t' cause I Paul, the prisoner "
8 is t' grace given, that I should 3778
14 For t' cause I bow my knees unto 5127
4:17 T' I say therefore, and testify in 5124
5: 5 t' ye know, that no whoremonger, "
31 For t' cause shall a man leave his 5127
32 T' is a great mystery: but I speak 5124
6: 1 parents in the Lord: for t' is right. "
12 rulers of the darkness of t' world,*5127
Ph'p 1: 6 Being confident of t' very thing, 5124
7 meet for me to think t' of you all, * "
9 t' I pray, that your love may abound"
19 that t' shall turn to my salvation "
22 flesh, t' is the fruit of my labour: "
25 having t' confidence, I know that "
2: 5 Let t' mind be in you, which was "
3:13 t' one thing I do, forgetting those*
15 God shall reveal even t' unto you. 5124
Col 1: 9 For t' cause we also, since the day "
27 the glory of t' mystery among the 5127
2: 4 And t' I say, lest any man should 5124
3:20 t' is well pleasing unto the Lord. "
4:16 when t' epistle is read among you, 3588
1Th 2:13 t' cause also thank we God without 5124
3: 5 For t' cause, when I could no "
4: 3 For t' is the will of God, even your "
15 t' we say unto you by the word of "
5:18 t' is the will of God in Christ Jesus "
27 t' epistle be read unto all the holy *3588
2Th 1:11 count you worthy of t' calling, "
2:11 for t' cause God shall send them 5124
3:10 t' we commanded you, that if any "
14 man obey not our word by t' epistle, 3588
1Ti 1: 9 Knowing t', that the law is not 5124
15 T' is a faithful saying, and worthy *3588
16 for t' cause I obtained mercy, 5124
18 T' charge I commit unto thee, 5026
2: 3 For t' is good and acceptable in 5124
4: 9 T' is a faithful saying and worthy *3588
16 in doing t' thou shalt both save 5124
6: 7 we brought nothing into t' world, *3588
14 That thou keep t' commandment * "

1Ti 6:17 them that are rich in t' world, 3588,3568
2Ti 1:15 T' thou knowest, that all they 5124
2: 4 himself with the affairs of t' life;
19 standeth sure, having t' seal, 5026
3: 1 T' know also, that in the last days 5124
6 t' sort are they which creep into *5130
4:10 me, having loved t' present world, 3588
Tit 1: 5 For t' cause left I thee in Crete, 5127
13 T' witness is true. Wherefore 3778
2:12 and godly, in t' present world; 3588
3: 8 T' is a faithful saying, and these * "
Heb 1: 5 Son, t' day have I begotten thee? 4594
3: 3 For t' man was counted worthy of *3778
4: 4 place of the seventh day on t' wise, 3779
5 And in t' place again, If they shall 5129
5: 4 man taketh t' honour unto himself, *3588
6: 3 And t' will we do, if God permit. 5124
7: 1 t' Melchisedec, king of Salem, 3778
4 consider how great t' man was,
27 t' he did once, when he offered up 5124
8: 1 which we have spoken t' is the sum:
3 t' man have somewhat...to offer. 5126
10 t' is the covenant that I will make 3778
9: 8 The Holy Ghost t' signifying, that 5124
11 that is to say, not of t' building; 5026
15 for t' cause he is the mediator of 5124
20 T' is the blood of the testament "
27 to die, but after t' the judgment: "
10:12 t' man, after he had offered one *3778
16 T' is the covenant that I will make "
11: 5 his translation he had t' testimony,*
12:27 t' word, Yet once more, signifieth 3588
13:19 I beseech you the rather to do t', 5124
Jas 1: 3 Knowing t', that the trying of your*
25 t' man shall be blessed in his 3778
26 heart, t' man's religion is vain. 5127
27 before God and the Father is t', 3778
2: 5 the poor of t' world rich in faith, *5127
3:15 T' wisdom descendeth not from 3778
4:15 we shall live, and do t', or that. 5124
1Pe 1:25 t' is the word which by the gospel "
2:19 For t' is thankworthy, if a man for "
20 patiently, t' is acceptable with God."
3: 5 For after t' manner in the old time 3779
4: 6 t' cause was the gospel preached 5124
16 let him glorify God on t' behalf. 5129
5:12 that t' is the true grace of God 5026
2Pe 1: 5 beside t', giving all diligence, 5124
13 as long as I am in t' tabernacle, 5129
14 I must put off t' my tabernacle, *3588
17 T' is my beloved Son, in whom I 3778
18 t' voice which came from heaven 5026
20 Knowing t' first, that no prophecy 5124
3: 1 T' second epistle, beloved, I now 5026
3 Knowing t' first, that there shall 5124
5 t' they willingly are ignorant of, "
8 be not ignorant of t' one thing, "
1Jo 1: 5 T' then is the message which we 3778
2:25 And t' is the promise that he hath "
3: 3 every man that hath t' hope in him 5026
8 For t' purpose the Son of God was 5124
10 In t' the children of God are 5129
11 t' is the message that ye heard 3778
17 But whoso hath t' world's good, *3588
23 t' is his commandment, That we 3778
4: 3 t' is that spirit of antichrist, 5124
9 In t' was manifested the love of *5129
17 as he is, so are we in t' world. "
21 t' commandment have we from 5026
5: 2 By t' we know that we love the *5129
3 t' is the love of God, that we keep 3778
4 t' is the victory that overcometh "
6 T' is he that came by water and "
9 t' is the witness of God which he "
11 t' is the record, that God hath "
11 life, and t' life is in his Son. "
14 t' is the confidence that we have in "
20 T' is the true God, and eternal life. "
2Jo 6 t' is love, that we walk after his "
6 T' is the commandment, That, as "
7 T' is a deceiver and an antichrist. "
10 you, and bring not t' doctrine, 5026
Jude 4 old ordained to t' condemnation, 5124
5 though ye once knew t', how * "
Re 1: 3 that hear the words of t' prophecy,*3588
2: 6 t' thou hast, that thou hatest the 5124
24 as many as have not t' doctrine, 5026
4: 1 After t' I looked, and, behold, a *5023
7: 9 After t' I beheld, and, lo, a great * "
11: 5 he must in t' manner be killed. 3779
15 kingdoms of t' world are become *5026
20: 5 T' is the first resurrection. 3778
14 of fire. T' is the second death. "
22: 7 sayings of the prophecy of t' book. 5127
9 which keep the sayings of t' book: "
10 sayings of the prophecy of t' book: "
18 words of the prophecy of t' book, "
18 plagues that are written in t' book: 5129
19 words of the book of t' prophecy, "
19 which are written in t' book. 5026

thistle See also THISTLES.
2Ki 14: 9 The t' that was in Lebanon sent 2336
9 Lebanon, and trode down the t'. "
2Ch 25:18 The t' that was in Lebanon sent "
18 Lebanon, and trode down the t'. "
Ho 10: 8 t' shall come up on their altars; 1863

thistles
Ge 3:18 and t' shall it bring forth to thee; 1863
Job 31:40 Let t' grow instead of wheat, 2336
M't 7:16 grapes of thorns, or figs of t'? 5146

thither See also THITHERWARD.
Ge 29: 3 t' were all the flocks gathered: 8033
39: 1 which had brought him down t'. "
42: 2 get you down t', and buy for us "
Ex 10:26 serve the Lord, until we come t'. "
26:33 bring in t' within the vail the ark 8033
Nu 35: 6 manslayer, that he may flee t': "
11 that the slayer may flee t', which "
15 any person unawares may flee t'. "
De 1:37 saying, Thou also shalt not go in t'. "
38 before thee, he shall go in t': "
39 they shall go in t', and unto them "
4:42 that the slayer might flee t', which "
12: 5 ye seek, and t' thou shalt come: "
6 And t' ye shall bring your burnt "
11 t' shall ye bring all that I command"
19: 3 parts, that every slayer may flee t'. "
4 of the slayer, which shall flee t', "
32:52 thou shalt not go t' unto the land "
34: 4 but thou shalt not go over t'. "
Jos 7: 3 not all the people to labour t'; "
4 So there went up t' of the people "
20: 3 and unwittingly may flee t': "
9 person at unawares might flee t', "
J'g 8:27 Israel went t' a whoring after it: * "
9:51 and t' fled all the men and women, "
18: 3 they turned in t', and said unto "
17 came in t', and took the graven "
19:15 And they turned aside t', to go in "
21:10 sent t' twelve thousand men of the "
1Sa 2:14 unto all the Israelites that came t'. "
5: 8 the ark of the God of Israel about t'. "
10: 5 when thou art come t' to the city, 8033
10 And when they came t' to the hill, "
22 if the man should yet come t'. 1988
19:23 he went t' to Naioth in Ramah: 8033
22: 1 heard it, they went down t' to him. "
30: 7 brought t' the ephod to David. "
2Sa 2: 2 So David went up t', and his two 8033
4: 6 came t' into the midst of the house, "
1Ki 6: 7 made ready before it was brought t':*
19: 9 And he came t' unto a cave, and 8033
2Ki 2: 8 they were divided hither and t', 2008
14 waters, they parted hither and t': "
4: 8 by, he turned in t' to eat bread. 8033
10 to us, that he shall turn in t'. "
11 And it fell on a day, that he came t'," "
6: 6 cut down a stick, and cast it in t'; "
9 for t' the Syrians are come down. "
14 Therefore sent he t' horses, and "
9: 2 And when thou comest t', look out "
17:27 Carry t' one of the priests whom ye "
2Ch 1: 6 Solomon went up t' to the brasen "
Ezr 10: 6 when he came t', he did eat no bread. "
Ne 4:20 of the trumpet, resort ye t' unto us: "
5:16 were gathered t' unto the work. "
13: 9 t' brought I again the vessels of "
Job 1:21 womb, and naked shall I return t': * "
6:20 they came t', and were ashamed. 5704
Ec 1: 7 rivers come, t' they return again. 8033
Isa 7:24 and with bows shall men come t'; "
25 not come t' the fears of briers and "
32:20 that send forth t' the feet of the ox*
55:10 from heaven, and returneth not t', 8033
57: 7 t' wentest thou up to offer sacrifice. "
Jer 22:11 He shall not return t' any more: "
27 to return, t' shall they not return. "
31: 8 a great company shall return t'. 2008
40: 4 convenient for thee to go, t' go. 8033
Eze 1:20 they went, t' was their spirit to go; "
11:18 they shall come t', and they shall "
40: 1 was upon me, and brought me t'. "
3 And he brought me t', and, behold, "
M't 2:22 Herod, he was afraid to go t': 1563
M'r 6:33 and ran afoot t' out of all cities, * "
Lu 17:37 t' will the eagles be gathered "
21: 2 poor widow casting in t' two mites.*
Joh 7:34 and where I am, t' ye cannot come.*
36 and where I am, t' ye cannot come?*
11: 8 thee; and goest thou t' again? 1563
18: 2 Jesus ofttimes resorted t' with his "
3 cometh t' with lanterns and torches"
Ac 8:30 Philip ran t' to him, and heard him*4370
14:19 came t' certain Jews from Antioch 1904
16:13 unto the women which resorted t'.*
17:10 coming t' went into the synagogue 3854
13 they came t' also, and stirred up 1563
25: 4 he himself would depart shortly t'.

thitherward
J'g 18:15 And they turned t', and came to the 8033
Jer 50: 5 the way to Zion with their faces t', 2008
Ro 15:24 to be brought on my way t' by you, 1563

Thomas (*tom'-us*) See also DIDYMUS.
M't 10: 3 T', and Matthew the publican; 2381
M'r 3:18 T', and James the son of Alphæus, "
Lu 6:15 T', James the son of Alphæus, "
Joh 11:16 said T', which is called Didymus, "
14: 5 T' saith unto him, Lord, we know "
20:24 But T', one of the twelve, called "
26 were within, and T' with them: "
27 Then saith he to T', Reach hither "
28 T' answered and said unto him, "
29 T', because thou hast seen me, * "
21: 2 Peter, and T' called Didymus, "
Ac 1:13 T', Bartholomew, and Matthew, "

thongs
Ac 22:25 as they bound him with t', Paul 2438

thorn See also THORNS.
Job 41: 2 or bore his jaw through with a t'? 2336
Pr 26: 9 As a t' goeth up into the hand of a "
Isa 55:13 of the t' shall come up the fir tree, 5285
Eze 28:24 grieving t' of all that are round 6975
Ho 10: 8 the t' and the thistle shall come up "
Mic 7: 4 upright is sharper than a t' hedge: 4534
2Co 12: 7 was given to me a t' in the flesh, 4647

thorn-hedge See THORN and HEDGE.

thorns
Ge 3:18 T' also and thistles shall it bring 6975
Ex 22: 6 If fire break out, and catch in t', so "
Nu 33:55 in your eyes, and t' in your sides, 6796
Jos 23:13 in your sides, and t' in your eyes, "
J'g 2: 3 but they shall be as t' in your sides, "
8: 7 I will tear your flesh with the t' 6975
16 and t' of the wilderness and briers, "
2Sa 23: 6 be all of them as t' thrust away, "
2Ch 33:11 took Manasseh among the t', *2336
Job 5: 5 and taketh it even out of the t', 6791
Ps 58: 9 Before your pots can feel the t', he 329
118:12 they are quenched as the fire of t': 6975
Pr 15:19 slothful man is as an hedge of t': 2312
22: 5 T' and snares are in the way of 6791
24:31 all grown over with t', and nettles 7063
Ec 7: 6 as the crackling of t' under a pot, 5518
Ca 2: 2 As the lily among t', so is my love 2336
Isa 5: 6 there shall come up briers and t': 7898
7:19 upon all t', and upon all bushes. 5285
23 it shall even be for briers and t'. 7898
24 the land shall become briers and t'. "
25 thither the fear of briers and t': "
9:18 it shall devour the briers and t', "
10:17 shall burn and devour his t' and his"
27: 4 set the briers and t' against me in "
32:13 people shall come up t' and briers; 6975
33:12 t' cut up shall they be burned in the"
34:13 t' shall come up in her palaces, 5518
Jer 4: 3 ground, and sow not among t'. 6975
12:13 have sown wheat, but shall reap t': "
Eze 2: 6 though briers and t' be with thee, 5544
Ho 2: 6 I will hedge up thy way with t', 5518
9: 6 t' shall be in their tabernacles. 2336
Na 1:10 while they be folden together as t', 5518
M't 7:16 Do men gather grapes of t', or figs 173
13: 7 And some fell among t'; "
7 the t' sprung up, and choked them: "
22 also that received seed among the t' "
27:29 when they had platted a crown of t', "
M'r 4: 7 And some fell among t', "
7 and the t' grew up, and choked it, "
18 are they which are sown among t'; "
15:17 platted a crown of t', and put it 174
Lu 6:44 of t' men do not gather figs, nor of 173
8: 7 And some fell among t'; "
7 t' sprung up with it, and choked it. "
14 that which fell among t' are they, "
Joh 19: 2 the soldiers platted a crown of t', "
5 Jesus forth, wearing the crown of t', 174
Heb 6: 8 that which beareth t' and briers is 173

thoroughly See also THROUGHLY.
Ex 21:19 shall cause him to be t' healed. 7495
2Ki 11:18 his images brake they in pieces t', 3190

those
Ge 6: 4 were giants in the earth in t' days; 1992
15:17 lamp that passed between t' pieces.*428
19:25 And he overthrew t' cities, and all 411
24:60 possess the gate of t' which hate them
33: 5 and said, Who are t' with thee? * 428
41:35 gather all the food of t' good years "
42: 5 came to buy corn among t' that came: "
50: 3 the days of t' which are embalmed:*
Ex 2:11 And it came to pass in t' days, 1992
4:21 thou do all t' wonders before Pharaoh,*
29:33 they shall eat t' things wherewith the
35:35 and of t' that devise cunning work.
Le 11:27 all four, t' are unclean unto you: *1992
14:11 and t' things, before the Lord,
42 and put them in the place of t' stones;
15:10 that beareth any of t' things shall
27 whosoever toucheth t' things shall be
22: 2 t' things which they hallow unto me:
Nu 1:21 T' that were numbered of them, even
22 fathers, t' that were numbered of them,
23, 25, 27, 29, 31, 33, 35, 37, 39, 41, 43 t' that were numbered of them, even of
44 These are t' that were numbered,*
45 t' that were numbered of the children*
2: 4 t' that were numbered of them, were
5 t' that do pitch next unto him shall be
6, 8, 11 t' that were numbered thereof,
12 And t' which pitch by him shall be the
13 t' that were numbered of them, were
15, 19, 21, 23, 26 t' that were numbered of
27 t' that encamp by him shall be the
28, 30 t' that were numbered of them,
32 are t' which were numbered of the*
3:22 T' that were numbered of them,
22 t' that were numbered of them were
34 And t' that were numbered of them,
38 But t' that encamp before the
43 t' that were numbered of them, were
46 for t' that are to be redeemed of the*
4:36 t' that were numbered of them by
38 t' that were numbered of the sons of
40 Even t' that were numbered of them,
42 t' that were numbered of the families
44 t' that were numbered of them after
45 These be t' that were numbered of*
46 t' that were numbered of the Levites,
48 Even t' that were numbered of them,
9: 7 And t' men said unto him, we are 1992
14:22 t' men which have seen my glory, 582
37 t' men that did bring up the evil "
18:16 And t' that are to be redeemed from a
25: 9 t' that died in the plague were twenty
26:18, 22, 25, 27 according to t' that were numbered of them,
34 and t' that were numbered of them,*
37, 43, 47, 54 according to t' that were numbered of
62 t' that were numbered of them were*
33:55 t' which ye let remain of them shall
De 7:22 will put out t' nations before thee 411
17: 9 the judge that shall be in t' days, 1992
18: 9 the abominations of t' nations.
19: 5 he shall flee unto one of t' cities, * 428

De 19:17 judges, which shall be in t' days; 1992
20 And t' which remain shall hear, and
26: 3 the priest that shall be in t' days, 1992
29: 3 the signs, and t' great miracles: "
32:21 with t' which are not a people;
Jos 3:16 t' that came down toward the sea of
4:20 t' twelve stones, which they took 428
10:22 and bring out t' five kings unto me "
23 brought forth t' five kings unto him "
24 brought out t' kings unto Joshua, "
11: 1 king of Hazor had heard t' things,*
10 was the head of all t' kingdoms. 428
12 And all the cities of t' kings, and all "
18 war a long time with all t' kings. "
17:12 drive out the inhabitants of t' cities; "
20: 4 he that doth flee unto one of t' cities "
21:16 nine cities out of t' two tribes.
24:17 which did t' great signs in our sight."
J'g 2:16 of the hand of t' that spoiled them.
23 the Lord left t' nations, without 428
7: 8 and retained t' three hundred men:
11:13 therefore restore t' lands again
12: 5 t' Ephraimites which were escaped*
17: 6 In t' days there was no king in 1992
18: 1 In t' days there was no king in "
1 in t' days the tribe of the Danites "
19: 1 it came to pass in t' days, when "
20:27 of God was there in t' days, "
28 of Aaron, stood before it in t' days,) "
21:25 In t' days there was no king in "
1Sa 3: 1 the Lord was precious in t' days; "
7:16 and judged Israel in all t' places. 428
10: 9 all t' signs came to pass that day. "
11: 6 upon Saul when he heard t' tidings, "
17:11 Saul and all Israel heard t' words of "
28 whom hast thou left t' few sheep 2007
18:23 Saul's servants spake t' words in 428
19: 7 Jonathan shewed him all t' things. "
25: 9 according to all t' words in the "
12 came and told them all t' sayings. "
27: 8 for t' nations were of old the 2007
28: 1 And it came to pass in t' days, that1992
3 had put away t' that had familiar
9 hath cut off t' that have familiar
30: 9 where t' that were left behind stayed.
20 they drave before t' other cattle, 1931
22 of Belial, of t' that went with David,
2Sa 5:14 be the names of t' that were born unto
16:23 which he counselled in t' days, 1992
1Ki 2: 7 let them be of t' that eat at thy table:
3: 2 name of the Lord, until t' days. 1992
4:27 t' officers provided victual for 428
8: 4 t' did the priests and the Levites *
9:21 upon t' did Solomon levy a tribute of*
21:27 when Ahab heard t' words, that he 428
2Ki 4: 4 shalt pour out into all t' vessels,
6:22 wouldest thou smite t' whom thou
10:32 In t' days the Lord began to cut 1992
15:37 In t' days the Lord began to send "
17: 9 did secretly t' things that were not*
18: 4 unto t' days the children of Israel 1992
20: 1 In t' days was Hezekiah sick unto "
24:15 t' carried he into captivity from*
1Ch 4:23 and t' that dwelt among plants and*
16:42 and cymbals for t' that should make a
2Ch 14: 6 rest, and he had no war in t' years; 428
15: 5 t' times there was no peace to him 1992
17:19 t' whom the king put in the fenced
20:29 on all the kingdoms of t' countries,*
32:13 the gods of the nations of t' lands*
14 among all the gods of t' nations 428
24 In t' days Hezekiah was sick to 1992
Ezr 1: 8 Even t' did Cyrus king of Persia bring
2: 1 t' which had been carried away, whom
3: 3 because of the people of t' countries:*
5: 9 Then asked we t' elders, and said 479
14 t' did Cyrus the king take out of 1994
7:19 t' deliver thou before the God of *
8:35 children of t' that had been carried*
9: 2 themselves with the people of t' lands:*
4 transgression of t' that had been *
10: 8 and of t' that trembled at the
8 congregation of t' that had been *
Ne 4:17 that bare burdens, with t' that laded,*
5:17 beside t' that came unto us from
6:17 in t' days the nobles of Judah sent1992
7: 6 of t' that had been carried away, whom
64 register among t' that were reckoned
8: 3 women, and t' that could understand;
10: 1 Now t' that sealed were, Nehemiah,
13:15 In t' days saw I in Judah some 1992
23 In t' days also saw I Jews that had "
Es 1: 2 That in t' days, when the king "
2:21 In t' days, while Mordecai sat in "
21 of t' which kept the door, were wroth,
8: 9 the hands of t' that have the charge
9: 5 they would unto t' that hated them.*
11 the number of t' that were slain in
Job 5:11 To set up on high t' that be low; that
11 t' which mourn may be exalted to
21:22 seeing he judgeth t' that are high.
24:13 are of t' that rebel against the light;*
19 doth the grave t' which have sinned.
27:15 T' that remain of him shall be buried
Ps 5:11 t' that put their trust in thee rejoice:
13: 4 t' that trouble me rejoice when I am*
17: 7 thee from t' that rise up against them.
18:30 is a buckler to all t' that trust in him.*
39 subdued under me t' that rose up
48 liftest me up above t' that rise up*
21: 8 hand shall find out t' that hate thee.
37: 9 t' that wait upon the Lord, they shall
40:16 Let all t' that seek thee rejoice and be
50: 5 t' that have made a covenant with me
61: 5 the heritage of t' that fear thy name.
63: 9 But t' that seek my soul, to destroy it,

Ps 68: 6 he bringeth out t' which are bound*
11 the company of t' that published it.*
69: 6 let not t' that seek thee be confounded
26 they talk to the grief of t' whom thou
70: 4 Let all t' that seek thee rejoice and be
74:23 the tumult of t' that rise up against
79:11 preserve thou t' that are appointed to
92:13 T' that be planted in the house of the*
102:20 to loose t' that are appointed to death;
103:18 t' that remember his commandments
106:46 of all t' that carried them captives.
109:31 him from t' that condemn his soul.*
119:79 Let t' that fear thee turn unto me,
79 t' that have known thy testimonies.*
132 usest to do unto t' that love thy name.
123: 4 the scorning of t' that are at ease,
125: 4 Do good, O Lord, unto t' that be good,
139:21 I grieved with t' that rise up against
140: 9 As for the head of t' that compass me
143: 3 as t' that have been long dead.
145:14 raiseth up all t' that be bowed down.
147:11 fear him, in t' that hope in his mercy.
Pr 1:12 whole, as t' that go down into the pit:
4:22 they are life unto t' that find them,
8:17 t' that seek me early shall find me.
21 may cause t' that love me to inherit
22:23 spoil the soul of t' that spoiled them.
24:11 death, and t' that are ready to be slain;
26:28 A lying tongue hateth t' that are
31: 6 and wine unto t' that be of heavy*
Ec 1:11 are to come with t' that shall come
5:14 t' riches perish by evil travail: 1931
7:28 a woman among all t' have I not 428
8: 8 deliver t' that are given to it. *
12: 3 t' that look out of the windows be
Ca 7: 9 the lips of t' that are asleep to speak.
8:12 and t' that keep the fruit thereof two
Isa 14:19 as the raiment of t' that are slain,*
27: 7 him, as he smote t' that smote him?
35: 8 not pass over it; but it shall be for t':
38: 1 In t' days was Hezekiah sick unto 1992
40:11 gently lead t' that are with young.
56: 8 beside t' that are gathered unto him.*
60:12 yea, t' nations shall be utterly wasted.
64: 5 t' that remember thee in thy ways:
5 in t' is continuance, and we shall *1992
66: 2 all t' things hath mine hand made,*428
2 all t' things have been, saith the * "
19 t' that escape of them unto the *1992
Jer 3:16 in t' days, saith the Lord, they "
18 In t' days the house of Judah "
4:12 full wind from t' places shall come*428
5:18 Nevertheless in t' days, saith the 1992
8:16 it; the city, and t' that dwell therein.
14:15 and famine shall t' prophets be 1992
21: 7 the hand of t' that seek their life:
27:11 t' will I let remain still in their own*
31:29 In t' days they shall say no more, 1992
33 After t' days, saith the Lord, I will "
36 If t' ordinances depart from * 428
33:15 In t' days, and at that time, will 1992
16 In t' days shall Judah be saved, "
38:22 t' women shall say, Thy friends 2007
39: 9 and t' that fell away, that fell to him,*
46:26 the hand of t' that seek their lives,
49: 5 hosts, from all t' that be about thee;*
36 scatter them toward all t' winds; 428
50: 4, 20 In t' days, and in that time, 1992
52:15 t' that fell away, that fell to the king
La 2:22 t' that I have swaddled and brought
3:62 The lips of t' that rose up against me,
Eze 1:21 When t' went, these went; and when
21 and when t' stood, these stood; and
21 when t' were lifted up from the earth,
18:11 that doeth not any of t' duties, but 428
22: 5 T' that be near, and t' that be far
28:26 upon all t' that despise them round
33:24 that inhabit t' wastes of the land 428
34:27 hand of t' that served themselves of
38:17 prophesied in t' days many years, 1992
39:14 t' that remain on the face of the *
40:25 round about, like t' windows: 428
42:14 approach to t' things which are for*
Da 3:22 flame of the fire slew t' men that 479
4:37 t' that walk in pride he is able to 1768
6:24 t' men which had accused Daniel, 479
10: 2 In t' days I Daniel was mourning 1992
11: 4 up, even for others beside t'. * 428
14 And in t' times there shall many 1992
Joe 2:16 children, and t' that suck the breasts:
29 t' days will I pour out my spirit. 1992
3: 1 For, behold, in t' days, and in that "
Ob 14 to cut off t' of his that did escape;
14 have delivered up t' of his that did
Zep 1: 6 t' that have not sought the Lord,
9 punish all t' that leap on the
Hag 2:16 Since t' days were, when one came to*
22 chariots, and t' that ride in them;
Zec 3: 4 spake unto t' that stood before him,
4:10 hand of Zerubbabel with t' seven;* 428
7: 5 even t' seventy years, did ye at *2088
8:23 In t' days it shall come to pass, 1992
11:16 which shall not visit t' that be cut off,
13: 6 T' with which I was wounded in the
14: 3 forth, and fight against t' nations,1992
Mal 3: 5 against t' that oppress the hireling
M't 3: 1 In t' days came John the Baptist, 1565
4:24 t'...were possessed with devils, 3588
24 devils, and t' which were lunatick,*
24 lunatick, and t' that had the palsy;*
11: 4 shew John again t' things which ye
13:17 desired to see t' things which ye see,*
17 and to hear t' things which ye hear,*
15:18 t' things which proceed out of the*3588
30 with them t' that were lame, blind,*
16:23 be of God, but t' that be of men. *3588

M't 21:40 will he do unto t' husbandmen? 1565
41 miserably destroy t' wicked men, 846
22: 7 and destroyed t' murderers, and 1565
10 So t' servants went out into the "
24:19 to them that give suck in t' days! "
22 except t' days should be shortened."
22 sake t' days shall be shortened. "
29 after the tribulation of t' days "
25: 7 Then all t' virgins arose, and "
19 the lord of t' servants cometh, "
27:54 and t' things that were done, they*3588
M'r 1: 9 And it came to pass in t' days, that1565
44 cleansing t' things which Moses *
2:20 then shall they fast in t' days. *1565
6:55 about in beds t' that were sick, 3588
7:15 t' are they that defile the man. 1565
8: 1 In t' days the multitude being very "
10:13 disciples rebuked t' that brought *3588
11:23 shall believe that t' things which he*
12: 7 But t' husbandmen said among 1565
13:17 to them that give suck in t' days! "
19 For in t' days shall be affliction, "
20 the Lord had shortened t' days, *3588
24 in t' days, after that tribulation, "
Lu 1: 1 a declaration of t' things which are3588
4 know the certainty of t' things, *
24 after t' days his wife Elisabeth *5025
39 Mary arose in t' days, and went * "
45 t' things which were told her from*3588
2: 1 it came to pass in t' days, that 1565
18 wondered at t' things which were told*
33 marvelled at t' things which were *3588
4: 2 And in t' days he did eat nothing: 1565
5:35 and then shall they fast in t' days. "
6:12 And it came to pass in t' days, that*5025
32 sinners also love t' that love them.3588
7:28 Among t' that are born of women*
8:12 T' by the way side are they that 3588
9:36 close, and told no man in t' days 1565
36 any of t' things which they had seen.*
10:24 desired to see t' things which ye see,*
24 and to hear t' things which ye hear,*
12:20 then whose shall t' things be, which*
37 Blessed are t' servants, whom the 1565
38 them so, blessed are t' servants. "
13: 4 Or t' eighteen, upon whom the "
14: 7 a parable to t' which were bidden, 3588
24 t' men which were bidden shall 1565
17:10 have done all t' things which are *3588
19:27 t' mine enemies, which would not*1565
20: 1 that on one of t' days, as he taught*"
21:23 to them that give suck, in t' days! "
23:14 touching t' things whereof ye accuse
Joh 2:14 in the temple t' that sold oxen 3588
6:14 Then t' men, when they had seen * "
8:10 where are t' thine accusers? *1565
26 t' things which I have heard of *5023
29 always t' things that please him. *3588
31 said Jesus to t' Jews which believed"
10:32 which of t' works do ye stone me? 846
13:29 Buy t' things that we have need of*
17:11 name t' whom thou hast given me,*846
12 t' that thou gavest me I have kept,* "
Ac 1:15 t' days Peter stood up in the *5025
2:18 pour out in t' days of my Spirit; 1565
3:18 But t' things, which God before had*
24 Samuel and t' that follow after, *3588
6: 1 And in t' days, when the number *5025
7:41 made a calf in t' days, and offered 1565
8: 6 unto t' things which Philip spake,*3588
9:37 to pass in t' days, that she was 1565
13:45 spake against t' things which were*3588
16: 3 Jews which were in t' quarters: 1565
35 serjeants, saying, Let t' men go.
17:11 noble than t' in Thessalonica, 3588
11 daily, whether t' things were so. *5023
18:17 Gallio cared for none of t' things. *5130
20: 2 when he had gone over t' parts, 1565
21: 5 when we had accomplished t' days,3588
15 t' days we took up our carriages, *5025
24 all may know that t' things, whereof*
26:16 t' things in the which I will appear*
22 saying none other things than t' which*
27:11 t' things which were spoken by 3588
28:31 teaching t' things which concern * "
Ro 1:28 t' things which are not convenient; "
4:17 calleth t' things which be not as * "
6:13 as t' that are alive from the dead,*
21 fruit had ye then in t' things which*
21 for the end of t' things is death. 1565
10: 5 man which doeth t' things shall live*846
15:17 in t' things which pertain to God. *3588
18 t' things which Christ hath not
1Co 8: 4 eating of t' things that are offered*3588
10 eat t' things which are offered to * "
12:22 much more t' members of the body,"
23 t' members of the body, which we
14:23 there come in t' that are unlearned,*
2Co 7: 6 comforteth t' that are cast down, *3588
11:28 Beside t' things that are without, * "
Eph 5:12 t' things which are done in secret.* "
Ph'p 3: 7 me, t' I counted loss for Christ. *5023
13 forgetting t' things...are behind, *3588
13 reaching forth unto t' things which*"
4: 9 T' things, which ye have both *5023
Col 2:18 into t' things which he hath not seen,*
3: 1 Christ, seek t' things which are *3588
1Ti 4:10 all men, specially of t' that believe.*
5: 8 specially for t' of his own house, *3588
2Ti 2:25 instructing t'...oppose themselves;*"
3: 3 fierce, despisers of t' that are good,*
Heb 3: 5 testimony of t' things which were 3588
5:14 t' who by reason of use have their "
6: 4 it is impossible for t' who were once"
7:21 t' priests were made without an * "
27 needeth not daily, as t' high priests."

Heb 8:10 the house of Israel after t' days, 1565
10: 1 can never with t' sacrifices 3588,846
3 in t' sacrifices...is a remembrance "
16 will make with them after t' days, 1565
12:27 removing of t' things...are shaken,3588
27 t' things which cannot be shaken "
13:11 For the bodies of t' beasts, whose 5130
Jas 2:16 t' things which are needful to the *3588
2Pe 2: 6 ensample unto t' that after should "
18 t' that were clean escaped from "
1Jo 3:22 t' things that are pleasing in his * "
2Jo 8 lose not t' things we have wrought,*
Jude 10 t' things which they know not: *3745
10 t' things they corrupt themselves.*5125
Re 1: 3 t' things...are written therein: *3588
2:10 Fear none of t' things which thou* "
13 t' days wherein Antipas was my * "
4: 9 t' beasts give glory and honour * "
9: 4 t' men which have not the seal of * "
6 in t' days shall men seek death, 1565
10: 4 t' things which the seven thunders* "
13:14 means of t' miracles which he had*3588
20:12 t' things which were written in the*"

thou See in the APPENDIX; also THEE; THY.

though See also ALTHOUGH.

Ge 31:30 t' thou wouldest needs be gone,
33:10 t' I had seen the face of God, and *
40:10 and it was as t' it budded, and her
Le 5:17 t' he wist it not, yet is he guilty,
11: 7 And the swine, t' he divide the hoof,*
25:35 t' he be a stranger, or a sojourner;*
De 29:19 t' I walk in the imagination of 3588
Jos 17:18 t' they have iron chariots, "
18 chariots, and t' they be strong. "
J'g 13:16 T' thou detain me, I will not eat 518
15: 3 t' I do them a displeasure. *3588
7 T' ye have done this, yet will I be* 518
Ru 2:13 t' I be not like unto one of thine
1Sa 14:39 t' it be in Jonathan my son, 3588,518
20:20 side thereof, as t' I shot at a mark.
21: 5 t' it were sanctified this day in 3588
2Sa 1:21 as t' he had not anointed with oil.*
3:39 am this day weak, t' anointed king;
4: 6 as t' they would have fetched wheat;
18:12 T' I should receive a thousand 3863
1Ki 2:28 t' he turned not after Absalom.
1Ch 26:10 t' he was not the firstborn, yet his
2Ch 30:19 t' he be not cleansed according to the
Ne 1: 9 t' there were of you cast out unto 518
6: 1 (t' at that time I had not set up 1571
Es 9: 1 (t' it was turned to the contrary, *
Job 8: 7 T' thy beginning was small, yet thy
9:15 t' I were righteous, yet would I 518
21 T' I were perfect, yet would I not
10:19 have been as t' I had not been;
11:12 t' man be born like a wild ass's colt.
13:15 T' he slay me, yet will I trust in him:‡
14: 8 T' the root thereof wax old in the 518
16: 6 T' I speak, my grief is not "
6 and t' I forbear, what am I eased?
19:17 t' I entreated for the children's sake*
26 And t' after my skin worms destroy*
27 t' my reins be consumed within me.*
20: 6 T' his excellency mount up to the
12 T' wickedness be sweet in his 518
12 mouth, t' he hide it under his tongue;
13 T' he spare it, and forsake it not; but
23 T' it be given him to be in safety,*
24:23 T' it be given him to be in safety,*
27: 8 t' he hath gained, when God taketh3588
16 T' he heap up silver as the dust 518
30:24 grave, t' they cry in his destruction. "
39:16 young ones, as t' they were not hers:
Ps 23: 4 t' I walk through the valley of 3588
27: 3 T' an host should encamp against 518
3 t' war should rise against me, in "
35:14 t' he had been my friend or brother:
37:24 T' he fall, he shall not be utterly 3588
44:19 T' thou hast sore broken us in * "
46: 2 we fear, t' the earth be removed,
2 and t' the mountains be carried into
3 T' the waters thereof roar and be
3 t' the mountains shake with the
49:18 T' while he lived he blessed his 3588
68:13 T' ye have lien among the pots, * 518
78:23 T' he had commanded the clouds*
99: 8 t' thou tookest vengeance of their
138: 6 T' the Lord be high, yet hath he 3588
7 T' I walk in the midst of trouble, 518
Pr 6:35 content, t' thou givest many gifts. 3588
11:21 T' hand join in hand, the wicked shall
16: 5 t' hand join in hand, he shall not be
27:22 T' thou shouldest bray a fool in a 518
28: 6 is perverse in his ways, t' he be rich.
Ec 6: 6 t' he live a thousand years twice told,
8:12 T' a sinner do evil an hundred times,
17 because t' a man labour to seek it* 834
17 t' a wise man think to know it, 518
Isa 1:18 t' your sins be as scarlet, they shall "
18 t' they be red like crimson, they "
10:22 t' thy people Israel be as the sand "
12: 1 t' thou wast angry with me, thine 3588
30:20 And t' the Lord give you the bread
35: 8 men, t' fools, shall not err therein.*
45: 4 thee, t' thou hast not known me.
5 thee, t' thou hast not known me:
49: 5 T' Israel be not gathered, yet shall I*
63:16 t' Abraham be ignorant of us, 3588
Jer 2:22 For t' thou wash thee with nitre, 518
4:30 T' thou clothest thyself with 3588
30 t' thou deckest thee with ornaments"
30 t' thou rentest thy face with "
5: 2 t' they say, The Lord liveth; surely518
22 t' the waves thereof toss themselves,
22 t' they roar, yet can they not pass over
11:11 t' they shall cry unto me, I will not*

Jer 12: 6 t' they speak fair words unto thee.3588
14: 7 t' our iniquities testify against us, 518
15: 1 T' Moses and Samuel stood before "
22:24 t' Coniah the son of Jehoiakim3588, "
30:11 t' I make a full end of all nations *3588
32: 5 t' ye fight with the Chaldeans, ye "
33 t' I taught them, rising up early and
37:10 For t' ye had smitten the whole 518
49:16 t' thou shouldest make thy nest 3588
51: 5 t' their land was filled with sin "
53 T' Babylon should mount up to "
53 t' she should fortify the height of "
La 3:32 But t' he cause grief, yet will he 518
Eze 2: 6 t' briers and thorns be with thee, 3588
6 looks, t' they be a rebellious house. "
3: 9 looks, t' they be a rebellious house.
8:18 t' they cry in mine ears with a loud
12: 3 t' they be a rebellious house. 3518
13 shall he not see it, t' he shall die there.
14:14 T' these three men, Noah, Daniel, and
16, 18 T' these three men were in it, as I
20 T' Noah, Daniel, and Job, were in it,
26:21 t' thou be sought for, yet shalt thou
28: 2 t' thou set thine heart as the heart of
32:25 t' their terror was caused in the *3588
26 t' they caused their terror in the * "
27 t' they were the terror of the mighty*"
Da 5:22 t' thou knewest all this; 3606,6903,1768
9: 9 t' we have rebelled against him; *3588
Ho 4:15 T' thou, Israel, play the harlot, 518
5: 2 t' I have been a rebuker of them all.*
7:13 t' I have redeemed them, yet they
15 T' I have bound and strengthened
8:10 Yea, t' they have hired among the 3588
9:12 T' they bring up their 3588,518
16 yea, t' they bring forth, yet will I 3588
11: 7 t' they called them to the most High,
13:15 T' he be fruitful among his 3588
Am 5:22 T' ye offer me burnt offerings 3588,518
9: 2 T' they dig into hell, thence shall "
2 t' they climb up to heaven, thence "
3 t' they hide themselves in the top "
3 t' they be hid from my sight in the "
4 t' they go into captivity before their "
Ob 4 T' thou exalt thyself as the eagle, "
4 t' thou set thy nest among the stars,"
16 they shall be as t' they had not been.
Mic 5: 2 Beth-lehem Ephratah, t' thou be little*
Na 1:12 T' they be quiet, and likewise 518
12 T' I have afflicted thee, I will afflict
Hab 1: 5 will not believe, t' it be told you. 3588
2: 3 t' it tarry, wait for it; because it 518
Zec 9: 2 and Zidon, t' it be very wise. *3588
10: 6 be as t' I had not cast them off: 834
12: 3 t' all the people of the earth be *
M't 26:33 T' all men shall be offended *1499
35 T' I should die with thee, yet will*2579
60 t' many false witnesses came, yet found
Lu 9:53 was as t' he would go to Jerusalem.
11: 8 T' he will not rise and give him, 1499
16:31 t' one rose from the dead. *1437
18: 4 T' I fear not God, nor regard man;1499
7 him, t' he bear long with them? *2532
24:28 as t' he would have gone further.
Joh 4: 2 (T' Jesus himself baptized not, *2544
8: 6 on the ground, as t' he heard them not.*
14 T' I bear record of myself, yet my*2579
10:38 t' ye believe not me, believe the "
11:25 t' he were dead, yet shall he live: "
12:37 t' he had done so many miracles before
Ac 3:12 as t' by our own power or holiness we
13:28 t' they found no cause of death in him,
41 t' a man declare it unto you. *1437
17:25 as t' he needed any thing, seeing he
27 t' he be not far from every one of 2544
23:15 as t' ye would enquire something
20 as t' they would enquire somewhat of
27:30 as t' they would have cast anchors out
28: 4 whom, t' he hath escaped the sea,
17 t' I have committed nothing against
Ro 4:11 believe, t' they be not circumcised;1228
17 things which be not as t' they were.
7: 3 t' she be married to another man.
9: 6 Not as t' the word of God hath 3754
27 T' the number of the children of *1437
1Co 4:15 t' ye have ten thousand instructers "
18 up, as t' I would not come to you.
5: 3 judged already, as t' I were present,
7:29 that have wives be as t' they had none;
30 they that weep, as t' they wept not;
30 that rejoice, as t' they rejoiced not;
30 they that buy, as t' they possessed not;
8: 5 t' there be that are called gods, 1512
9:16 For t' I preach the gospel, I have *1437
19 For t' I be free from all men, yet
13: 1 T' I speak with the tongues of *1437
2 And t' I have the gift of prophecy,* "
2 t' I have all faith, so that I could * "
3 t' I bestow all my goods to feed * "
3 and t' I give my body to be burned,*"
2Co 4:16 t' our outward man perish, yet the1499
5:16 t' we have known Christ after the "
20 as t' God did beseech you by us:
7: 8 t' I made you sorry with a letter, 1499
8 I do not repent, t' I did repent: "
8 sorry, t' it were but for a season. "
12 Wherefore, t' I wrote unto you, I * "
8: 9 that, t' he was rich, yet for your sakes
10: 3 t' we walk in the flesh, we do not war
8 t' I should boast somewhat more 1437
14 as t' we reached not unto you:
11: 6 t' I be rude in speech, yet not in 1499
21 reproach, as t' we had been weak. 3754
12: 6 For t' I would desire to glory, I *1437
11 chiefest apostles, t' I be nothing. 1499
15 t' the more abundantly I love you,* "

2Co 13: 4 For t' he was crucified through *1487
7 is honest, t' we be as reprobates.
Ga 1: 8 But t' we, or an angel from heaven,1437
3:15 T' it be but a man's covenant, yet 3676
4: 1 from a servant, t' he be lord of all;
Ph'p 3: 4 T' I might also have confidence in2539
12 Not as t' I had already attained, *3754
Col 2: 5 t' I be absent in the flesh, yet am 1499
20 as t' living in the world, are ye subject
Ph'm 8 t' I might be much bold in Christ to
Heb 5: 8 T' he were a Son, yet learned he 2539
6: 9 salvation, t' we thus speak. 1499
7: 5 t' they come out of the loins of 2539
12:17 t' he sought it carefully with tears. "
Jas 2:14 t' a man say he hath faith, and *1437
3: 4 the ships, which t' they be so great,
1Pe 1: 6 ye greatly rejoice, t' now for a season,
7 that perisheth, t' it be tried with fire,
8 t' now ye see him not, yet believing,
4:12 t' some strange thing happened unto
2Pe 1:12 of these things, t' ye know them, 2539
2Jo 5 not as t' I wrote a new commandment
Jude 5 in remembrance, t' ye once knew this,

thought See also THOUGHTEST; THOUGHTS.

Ge 20:11 I t', Surely the fear of God is not 559
38:15 saw her, he t' her to be an harlot; 2803
48:11 I had not t' to see thy face: 6419
50:20 as for you, ye t' evil against me; *2803
Ex 32:14 the evil which he t' to do unto his *1696
Nu 24:11 I t' to promote thee unto great 559
33:56 unto you, as I t' to do unto them. *1819
De 15: 9 be not a t' in thy wicked heart, 1697
19:19 as he had t' to have done unto his 2161
J'g 15: 2 I verily t' that thou hadst utterly 559
20: 5 by night, and t' to have slain me: 1819
Ru 4: 4 I t' to advertise thee, saying, Buy 559
1Sa 1:13 Eli t' she had been drunken. 2803
9: 5 for the asses, and take t' for us. ‡1672
18:25 Saul t' to make David fall by the 2803
20:26 for he t', Something hath befallen 559
2Sa 4:10 who t' that I would have given him a*
13: 2 Amnon t' it hard for him to do *5869
14:13 hast thou t' such a thing against *2803
19:18 and to do what he t' good. 5869
21:16 new sword, t' to have slain David. 559
2Ki 5:11 I t', He will surely come out to me, "
2Ch 11:22 for he t' to make him king. *
32: 1 and t' to win them for himself. 559
Ne 6: 2 But they t' to do me mischief. 2803
Es 3: 6 t' scorn to lay hands on Mordecai 5869
6: 6 Now Haman t' in his heart, To * 559
Job 12: 5 despised in the t' of him that is at 6248
42: 2 no t' can be withholden from *4209
Ps 48: 9 We have t' of thy lovingkindness, 1819
49:11 Their inward t' is, that their houses
64: 6 the inward t' of every one of them,
73:16 When I t' to know this, it was too 2803
119:59 I t' on my ways, and turned my "
139: 2 thou understandest my t' afar off. 7454
Pr 24: 9 The t' of foolishness is sin: and 2154
30:32 or if thou hast t' evil, lay thine 2161
Ec 10:20 not the king, no not in thy t'; 4093
Isa 14:24 Surely as I have t', so shall it come1819
Jer 18: 8 the evil that I t' to do unto them. 2803
Eze 38:10 and thou shalt think an evil t': *4284
Da 4: 2 I t' it good to shew the signs*8232,6925
6: 3 king t' to set him over the whole 6246
Am 4:13 declareth unto man what is his t', 7807
Zec 1: 6 the Lord of hosts t' to do unto us, 2161
8:14 As I t' to punish you, when your "
15 again have I t' in these days to do "
Mal 3:16 Lord, and that t' upon his name. 2803
M't 1:20 But while he t' on these things, 1760
6:25 Take no t' for your life, what ye *3309
27 you by taking t' can add one cubit* "
28 And why take ye t' for raiment? * "
31 take no t', saying, What shall we * "
34 Take...no t' for the morrow: * "
34 morrow shall take t' for the things*"
10:19 take no t' how or what ye shall * "
M'r 13:11 take no t' beforehand what ye *4305
14:72 And when he t' thereon, he wept. 1911
Lu 7: 7 neither t' I myself worthy to come
9:47 perceiving the t' of their heart, *1261
12:11 take ye no t' how or what thing ye*3309
17 And he t' within himself, saying, *1260
22 Take no t' for your life, what ye *3309
25 you with taking t' can add to his * "
26 is least, why take ye t' for the rest?*"
19:11 they t' that the kingdom of God *1380
Joh 11:13 they t' that he had spoken of taking"
13:29 some of them t', because Judas had"
Ac 8:20 thou hast t' that the gift of God 3543
22 t' of thine heart may be forgiven 1963
10:19 While Peter t' on the vision, the 1760
12: 9 the angel; but t' he saw a vision. 1380
15:38 Paul t' not good to take him with
26: 8 should it be t' a thing incredible *2919
9 I verily t' with myself, that I 1380
1Co 13:11 as a child, I t' as a child: 3049
2Co 9: 5 I t' it necessary to exhort the 2233
10: 5 every t' to the obedience of Christ;3540
Ph'p 2: 6 t' it not robbery to be equal with *2233
1Th 3: 1 we t' it good to be left at Athens 2106
Heb 10:29 shall he be t' worthy, who hath *

thoughtest

Ps 50:21 thou t' that I was altogether such 1819

thoughts

Ge 6: 5 the t' of his heart was only evil 4284
J'g 5:15 there were great t' of heart. *2711
1Ch 28: 9 all the imaginations of the t': 4284
29:18 of the t' of the heart of thy people, "
Job 4:13 t' from the visions of the night, 5587
17:11 broken off, even the t' of my heart.4180

Job 20: 2 do my t' cause me to answer, 5587
21: 27 I know your t', and the devices 4284
Ps 10: 4 after God: God is not in all his t'. 4209
33: 11 t' of his heart to all generations. 4284
40: 5 and thy t' which are to us-ward: "
56: 5 all their t' are against me for evil. "
92: 5 thy works! and thy t' are very deep." "
94: 11 The Lord knoweth the t' of man, "
19 In the multitude of my t' within 8312
119: 113 I hate vain t': but thy law do I *5588
139: 17 How precious...are thy t' unto me, 7454
23 heart: try me, and know my t': 8312
146: 4 in that very day his t' perish. 6250
Pr 12: 5 The t' of the righteous are right: 4284
15: 26 t' of the wicked are an abomination*"
16: 3 and thy t' shall be established. "
21: 5 The t' of the diligent tend only to "
Isa 55: 7 and the unrighteous man his t': "
8 For my t' are not your t', neither "
9 your ways, and my t' than your t'. "
59: 7 blood: their t' are t' of iniquity; "
65: 2 was not good, after their own t'; "
66: 18 For I know their works and their t':"
Jer 4: 14 How long shall thy vain t' lodge "
6: 19 people, even the fruit of their t', "
23: 20 have performed the t' of his heart:*4209
29: 11 I know the t' that I think toward 4284
11 t' of peace, and not of evil, to "
Da 2: 29 O king, thy t' came into thy mind 7476
30 mightest know the t' of thy heart. "
4: 5 t' upon my bed and the visions 2031
19 one hour, and his t' troubled him. 7476
5: 6 changed, and his t' troubled him, "
10 let not thy t' trouble thee, nor "
Mic 4: 12 they know not the t' of the Lord, 4284
M't 9: 4 And Jesus knowing their t' said, 1761
12: 25 Jesus knew their t', and said unto "
15: 19 out of the heart proceed evil t', 1261
M'r 7: 21 the heart of men, proceed evil t', "
Lu 2: 35 t' of many hearts may be revealed. "
5: 22 But when Jesus perceived their t',* "
6: 8 he knew their t', and said to the "
11: 17 knowing their t', said unto them, 1270
24: 38 and why do t' arise in your hearts?*1261
Ro 2: 15 and their t' the mean while 3053
1Co 3: 20 Lord knoweth the t' of the wise, *1261
Heb 4: 12 a discerner of the t' and intents of 1761
Jas 2: 4 and are become judges of evil t'? 1261

thousand See also THOUSANDS.
Ge 20: 16 thy brother a t' pieces of silver: 505
Ex 12: 37 six hundred t' on foot that were "
32: 28 people that day about three t' men. "
38: 25 a t' seven hundred and threescore "
26 six hundred t' and three t' and five "
28 t' seven hundred seventy and five "
29 two t' and four hundred shekels. "
Le 26: 8 of you shall put ten t' to flight: 7233
Nu 1: 21 forty and six t' and five hundred. 505
23 fifty and nine t' and three hundred. "
25 and five t' six hundred and fifty. "
27 and fourteen t' and six hundred. "
29 fifty and four t' and four hundred. "
31 fifty and seven t' and four hundred. "
33 were forty t' and five hundred. "
35 thirty and two t' and two hundred. "
37 thirty and five t' and four hundred. "
39 and two t' and seven hundred. "
41 forty and one t' and five hundred. "
43 fifty and three t' and four hundred. "
46 numbered were six hundred t' and "
46 three t' and five hundred and fifty. "
2: 4 and fourteen t' and six hundred. "
6 fifty and four t' and four hundred. "
8 fifty and seven t' and four hundred. "
9 were an hundred t' and fourscore t' "
9 and six t' and four hundred. "
11 forty and six t' and five hundred. "
13 fifty and nine t' and three hundred. "
15 five t' and six hundred and fifty. "
16 were an hundred t' and fifty and one" "
16 one t' and four hundred and fifty. "
19 were forty t' and five hundred. "
21 thirty and two t' and two hundred. "
23 thirty and five t' and four hundred. "
24 were an hundred t' and eight t' "
26 and two t' and seven hundred. "
28 forty and one t' and five hundred. "
30 fifty and three t' and four hundred. "
31 camp of Dan were an hundred t' "
31 fifty and seven t' and six hundred. "
32 their hosts were six hundred t' "
32 three t' and five hundred and fifty. "
3: 22 were seven t' and five hundred. "
28 were eight t' and six hundred. "
34 were six t' and two hundred. "
39 upward, were twenty and two t'. "
43 two t' two hundred and threescore "
50 t' three hundred and threescore "
4: 36 two t' seven hundred and fifty. "
40 two t' and six hundred and thirty. "
44 were three t' and two hundred. "
48 were eight t' and five hundred and "
7: 85 two t' and four hundred shekels. "
11: 21 I am, are six hundred t' footmen; "
16: 49 were fourteen t' and seven hundred, "
25: 9 the plague were twenty and four t'. "
26: 7 and three t' and seven hundred and "
14 twenty and two t' and two hundred. "
18 of them, forty t' and five hundred. "
22 and sixteen t' and five hundred. "
25 and four t' and three hundred. "
27 threescore t' and five hundred. "
34 fifty and two t' and seven hundred. "
37 thirty and two t' and five hundred. "
41 forty and five t' and six hundred. "
43 and four t' and four hundred "

Nu 26: 47 fifty and three t' and four hundred. 505
50 forty and five t' and four hundred. "
51 children of Israel, six hundred t' "
51 and a t' seven hundred and thirty. "
62 of them were twenty and three t', "
31: 4 Of every tribe a t', throughout all "
5 of Israel, a t' of every tribe, "
5 every tribe, twelve t', armed for war." "
6 them to the war, a t' of every tribe, "
32 war had caught, was six hundred t' "
32 seventy t' and five t' sheep, "
33 threescore and twelve t' beeves, "
34 And threescore and one t' asses, "
35 And thirty and two t' persons in all, "
36 was in number three hundred t' "
36 thirty t' and five hundred sheep: "
38 the beeves were thirty and six t'; "
39 were thirty t' and five hundred; "
40 And the persons were sixteen t'; "
43 congregation was three hundred t' "
43 and thirty t' and seven t' and five "
44 And thirty and six t' beeves, "
45 And thirty t' asses and five hundred, "
46 And sixteen t' persons;) "
52 was sixteen t' seven hundred and "
35: 4 outward a t' cubits round about. "
5 city on the east side two t' cubits, "
5 and on the south side two t' cubits, "
5 and on the west side two t' cubits, "
5 and on the north side two t' cubits; "
De 1: 11 make you a t' times so many more "
7: 9 commandments to a t' generations; "
32: 30 How should one chase a t', and two "
30 and two put ten t' to flight, except "
Jos 3: 4 it, about two t' cubits by measure: "
4: 13 About forty t' prepared for war "
7: 3 let about two or three t' men go up "
4 of the people about three t' men: "
8: 3 chose out thirty t' mighty men of "
12 And he took about five t' men, and "
25 men and women, were twelve t', "
23: 10 One man of you shall chase a t': for "
J'g 1: 4 slew of them in Bezek ten t' men. "
3: 29 slew...at that time about ten t' men, "
4: 6 with thee ten t' men of the children "
10 went up with ten t' men at his feet: "
14 Tabor, and ten t' men after him. "
5: 8 spear seen among forty t' in Israel? "
7: 3 of the people twenty and two t'; "
3 and there remained ten t'. "
8: 10 with them, about fifteen t' men, "
10 and twenty t' men that drew sword. "
26 a t' and seven hundred shekels of "
9: 49 also, about a t' men and women. "
12: 6 the Ephraimites forty and two t'. "
15: 11 Then three t' men of Judah went to "
15 took it, and slew a t' men therewith. "
16 jaw of an ass have I slain a t' men. "
16: 27 roof about three t' men and women, "
20: 2 hundred t' footmen that drew sword." "
10 of Israel, and an hundred of a t', "
10 a t'...to fetch victual for the people, "
10 out of ten t', to fetch victual for 7233
15 and six t' men that drew sword, 505
17 four hundred t' men that drew "
21 that day twenty and two t' men. "
25 of Israel again eighteen t' men; "
34 against Gibeah ten t' chosen men "
35 twenty and five t' and an hundred "
44 fell of Benjamin eighteen t' men; "
45 them in the highways five t' men; "
45 unto Gidom, and slew two t' men of "
46 twenty and five t' men that drew the" "
21: 10 twelve t' men of the valiantest, "
1Sa 4: 2 army in the field about four t' men. "
10 there fell of Israel thirty t' footmen. "
6: 19 fifty t' and threescore and ten men: "
11: 8 of Israel were three hundred t', "
8 and the men of Judah thirty t'. "
13: 2 Saul chose him three t' men of "
2 two t' were with Saul in Michmash "
2 a t' were with Jonathan in Gibeah "
5 to fight with Israel, thirty t' chariots," "
5 six t' horsemen, and people as the "
15: 4 in Telaim, two hundred t' footmen, "
4 footmen, and ten t' men of Judah. "
17: 5 the coat was five t' shekels of brass. "
18 cheeses unto the captain of their t', "
18: 13 and made him his captain over a t'; "
24: 2 Saul took three t' chosen men out of" "
25: 2 had three t' sheep, and a t' goats: "
26: 2 three t' chosen men of Israel with "
2Sa 6: 1 the chosen men of Israel, thirty t'. "
8: 4 David took from him a t' chariots, "
4 horsemen, and twenty t' footmen: "
5 the Syrians two and twenty t' men. "
13 valley of salt, being eighteen t' men." "
10: 6 Syrians of Zoba, twenty t' footmen, "
6 and of king Maacah a t' men, "
6 and of Ish-tob twelve t' men. "
18 the Syrians, and forty t' horsemen, "
17: 1 me now choose out twelve t' men, "
18: 3 but now thou art worth ten t' of us: "
7 slaughter that day of twenty t' men." "
12 I should receive a t' shekels of silver" "
19: 17 a t' men of Benjamin with him, "
24: 9 Israel eight hundred t' valiant men "
9 of Judah were five hundred t' men. "
15 even to Beer-sheba seventy t' men. "
1Ki 3: 4 t' burnt offerings did Solomon offer "
4: 26 Solomon had forty t' stalls of horses" "
26 chariots, and twelve t' horsemen. "
32 And he spake three t' proverbs: "
32 and his songs were a t' and five. "
5: 11 gave Hiram twenty t' measures of "
13 and the levy was thirty t' men. "

1Ki 5: 14 Lebanon, ten t' a month by courses: 505
15 and ten t' that bare burdens, "
15 and fourscore t' hewers in the "
16 three t' and three hundred, which "
7: 26 of lilies: it contained three t' baths. "
8: 63 the Lord, two and twenty t' oxen, "
63 and an hundred and twenty t' sheep." "
10: 26 had a t' and four hundred chariots, "
26 and twelve t' horsemen, whom he "
12: 21 hundred and fourscore t' chosen "
19: 18 Yet I have left me seven t' in Israel, "
20: 15 the children of Israel, being seven t'." "
29 the Syrians an hundred t' footmen "
30 upon twenty and seven t' of the men" "
2Ki 3: 4 king of Israel an hundred t' lambs, "
4 an hundred t' rams, with the wool. "
5: 5 six t' pieces of gold, and ten changes "
13: 7 ten chariots, and ten t' footmen; "
14: 7 of Edom in the valley of salt ten t', "
15: 19 gave Pul a t' talents of silver, "
18: 23 and I will deliver thee two t' horses, "
19: 35 an hundred fourscore and five t': "
24: 14 men of valour, even ten t' captives, "
16 all the men of might, even seven t', "
16 and craftsmen and smiths a t', all "
1Ch 5: 18 four and forty t' seven hundred "
21 their cattle; of their camels fifty t', "
21 of sheep two hundred and fifty t', "
21 and of asses two t', "
21 and of men an hundred t'. "
7: 2 two and twenty t' and six hundred. "
4 for war, six and thirty t' men: "
5 genealogies fourscore and seven t'. "
7 twenty and two t' and thirty and "
9 was twenty t' and two hundred. "
11 were seventeen t' and two hundred "
40 battle was twenty and six t' men. "
9: 13 a t' and seven hundred and "
12: 14 hundred, and the greatest over a t'. "
24 were six t' and eight hundred, "
25 the war, seven t' and one hundred. "
26 children of Levi four t' and six "
27 were three t' and seven hundred; "
29 the kindred of Saul, three t': "
30 of Ephraim twenty t' and eight "
31 half tribe of Manasseh eighteen t', "
33 war, fifty t', which could keep rank: "
34 And of Naphtali a t' captains, and "
34 shield and spear thirty and seven t'." "
35 in war twenty and eight t' and six "
36 to battle, expert in war, forty t'. "
37 battle, an hundred and twenty t'. "
16: 15 he commanded to a t' generations; "
18: 4 David took from him a t' chariots, "
4 and seven t' horsemen, "
4 and twenty t' footmen: David also "
5 the Syrians two and twenty t' men. "
12 in the valley of salt eighteen t'. "
19: 6 Ammon sent a t' talents of silver to "
7 they hired thirty and two t' chariots," "
18 slew of the Syrians seven t' men "
18 in chariots, and forty t' footmen, "
21: 5 all they of Israel were a t' t' and "
5 an hundred t' men that drew sword: "
5 hundred threescore and ten t' men "
14 there fell of Israel seventy t' men. "
22: 14 Lord an hundred t' talents of gold, "
14 and a t' t' talents of silver; "
23: 3 man by man, was thirty and eight t'." "
4 four t' were to set forward the work "
4 and six t' were officers and judges: "
5 Moreover four t' were porters; "
5 and four t' praised the Lord with the" "
26: 30 of valour, a t' and seven hundred, "
32 were two t' and seven hundred chief "
27: 1 course were twenty and four t'. "
2 his course were twenty and four t'. "
4 likewise were twenty and four t'. "
5, 7, 8, 9, 10, 11, 12, 13, 14, 15
his course were twenty and four t'. 505
29: 4 Even three t' talents of gold, of the "
4 and seven t' talents of refined silver," "
7 of God of gold five t' talents "
7 and ten t' drams, 7239
7 and of silver ten t' talents, and of 505
7 and of brass eighteen t' talents, 7239, "
7 and one hundred t' talents of iron. "
21 even a t' bullocks, a t' rams, "
21 a t' lambs, with their drink offerings," "
2Ch 1: 6 offered a t' burnt offerings upon it. "
14 had a t' and four hundred chariots, "
14 and twelve t' horsemen, which he "
2: 2 and ten t' men to bear burdens, "
2 fourscore t' to hew in the mountain, "
2 three t' and six hundred to oversee "
10 twenty t' measures of beaten wheat, "
10 and twenty t' measures of barley, "
10 barley, and twenty t' baths of wine, "
10 wine, and twenty t' baths of oil. "
17 were found an hundred and fifty t' "
17 and three t' and six hundred. "
18 and ten t' of them to be bearers of "
18 and fourscore t' to be hewers in the "
18 three t' and six hundred overseers "
4: 5 it received and held three t' baths. "
7: 5 a sacrifice of twenty and two t' oxen, "
5 and an hundred and twenty t' sheep: "
9: 25 Solomon had four t' stalls for horses" "
25 chariots, and twelve t' horsemen; "
11: 1 and fourscore t' chosen men, "
12: 3 chariots, and threescore t' horsemen: "
13: 3 even four hundred t' chosen men: "
3 with eight hundred t' chosen men, "
17 of Israel five hundred t' chosen men. "
14: 8 out of Judah three hundred t'; "
8 bows, two hundred and fourscore t': "

2Ch 14: 9 the Ethiopian with an host of a t' t', 505
15: 11 hundred oxen and seven t' sheep. "
17: 11 seven t' and seven hundred rams, "
11 seven t' and seven hundred he goats. "
14 men of valour three hundred t'. "
15 him two hundred and fourscore t'. "
16 hundred t' mighty men of valour. "
17 with bow and shield two hundred t'. "
18 fourscore t' ready prepared for the "
25: 5 them three hundred t' choice men, "
6 hired also an hundred t' mighty men "
11 smote of the children of Seir ten t'. "
12 ten t' left alive did the children of "
13 and smote three t' of them, and took "
26: 12 valour were two t' and six hundred. "
13 was an army, three hundred t' and "
13 and seven t' and five hundred, that "
27: 5 silver, and ten t' measures of wheat, "
5 and ten t' of barley. So much did "
28: 6 an hundred and twenty t' in one day, "
8 of their brethren two hundred t', "
29: 33 six hundred oxen and three t' sheep. "
30: 24 a t' bullocks and seven t' sheep; "
24 a t' bullocks and ten t' sheep: "
35: 7 present, to the number of thirty t', "
7 and three t' bullocks: these were of "
8 two t' and six hundred small cattle, "
9 offerings five t' small cattle, "
Ezr 1: 9 of gold, a t' chargers of silver, "
10 and ten, and other vessels a t'. "
11 silver were five t' and four hundred. "
2: 3 two t' an hundred seventy and two. "
6 two t' eight hundred and twelve. "
7 a t' two hundred fifty and four. "
12 a t' two hundred twenty and two. "
14 of Bigvai, two t' fifty and six. "
31 a t' two hundred fifty and four. "
35 three t' and six hundred and thirty. "
37 children of Immer, a t' fifty and two. "
38 a t' two hundred forty and seven. "
39 of Harim, a t' and seventeen. "
64 forty and two t' three hundred and "
65 seven t' three hundred thirty and "
67 six t' seven hundred and twenty. "
69 threescore and one t' drams of gold, "
69 and five t' pound of silver, and one "
8: 27 basons of gold, of a t' drams; "
Ne 3: 13 a t' cubits on the wall unto the dung "
7: 8 two t' an hundred seventy and two. "
11 two t' and eight hundred and "
12 a t' two hundred fifty and four. "
17 two t' three hundred twenty and "
19 Bigvai, two t' threescore and seven. "
34 a t' two hundred fifty and four. "
38 three t' nine hundred and thirty. "
40 children of Immer, a t' fifty and two. "
41 a t' two hundred forty and seven. "
42 of Harim, a t' and seventeen. "
66 two t' three hundred and threescore, "
67 were seven t' three hundred thirty "
69 t' seven hundred and twenty asses. "
70 to the treasure a t' drams of gold, "
71 the work twenty t' drams of gold, 7239
71 and two t' and two hundred pound 505
72 gave was twenty t' drams of gold, "
72 and two t' pound of silver, and 7239
Es 3: 9 I will pay ten t' talents of silver to 505
9: 16 slew of their foes seventy and five t', "
Job 1: 3 substance also was seven t' sheep, "
3 three t' camels, and five hundred "
9: 3 he cannot answer him one of a t'. "
33: 23 one among a t', to shew unto man "
42: 12 for he had fourteen t' sheep, and six "
12 sheep, and six t' camels, and a "
12 and a t' yoke of oxen, and a "
12 yoke of oxen, and a t' she asses. "
Ps 50: 10 mine, and the cattle upon a t' hills. "
60: *title* Edom in the valley of salt twelve t'. "
68: 17 The chariots of God are twenty t', 7239
84: 10 a day in thy courts is better than a t'. 505
90: 4 For a t' years in thy sight are but as "
91: 7 A t' shall fall at thy side, and ten "
7 and ten t' at thy right hand; but it 7233
105: 8 he commanded to a t' generations. 505
Ec 6: 6 though he live a t' years twice told, "
7: 28 one man among a t' have I found; "
Ca 4: 4 whereon there hang a t' bucklers, "
5: 10 ruddy, the chiefest among ten t' 7233
8: 11 was to bring a t' pieces of silver. 505
12 thou, O Solomon, must have a t', "
Isa 7: 23 were a t' vines at a t' silverlings, "
30: 17 One t' shall flee at the rebuke of one; "
36: 8 and I will give thee two t' horses, "
37: 36 a hundred and fourscore and five t': "
60: 22 A little one shall become a t', and a "
Jer 52: 28 three t' Jews and three and twenty: "
30 were four t' and six hundred. "
Eze 45: 1 length of five and twenty t' reeds, "
1 and the breadth shall be ten t'. "
3 the length of five and twenty t', "
3 the breadth of ten t': and in it shall "
5 And the five and twenty t' of length, "
5 and the ten t' of breadth, shall also "
6 possession of the city five t' broad, "
6 and five and twenty t' long, over "
47: 3 eastward, he measured a t' cubits, "
4, 4 Again he measured a t', and "
5 Afterward he measured a t'; and it "
48: 8 five and twenty t' reeds in breadth, "
9 be of five and twenty t' in length, "
9 in length, and of ten t' in breadth. "
10 north five and twenty t' in length, "
10 toward the west ten t' in breadth, "
10 toward the east ten t' in breadth, "
10 south five and twenty t' in length: "
13 have five and twenty t' in length, "

Eze 48: 13 in length, and ten t' in breadth: 505
13 length shall be five and twenty t', "
13 and the breadth ten t'. "
15 five t', that are left in the breadth "
15 over against the five and twenty t', "
16 north side four t' and five hundred, "
16 south side four t' and five hundred, "
16 east side four t' and five hundred, "
16 west side four t' and five hundred. "
18 holy portion shall be ten t' eastward, "
18 and ten t' westward: and it shall be "
20 and twenty t' by five and twenty t': "
21 the five and twenty t' of the oblation "
21 over against the five and twenty t' "
30 four t' and five hundred measures. "
32 east side four t' and five hundred: "
33 four t' and five hundred measures: "
34 west side four t' and five hundred, "
35 round about eighteen t' measures: "
Da 5: 1 a great feast to a t' of his lords, 506
1 lords, and drank wine before the t'. "
7: 10 t' thousands ministered unto him, "
10 ten t' times ten t' stood before him: 7240
8: 14 Unto two t' and three hundred days: 505
12: 11 be a t' two hundred and ninety days. "
12 cometh to the t' three hundred and "
Am 5: 3 city that went out by a t' shall leave "
Jon 4: 11 sixscore t' persons that cannot 7239
M't 14: 21 had eaten were about five t' men, 4000
15: 38 they that did eat were four t' men, 5070
16: 9 the five loaves of the five t', 4000
10 the seven loaves of the four t', 5070
18: 24 which owed him ten t' talents. 3463
M'r 5: 13 (they were about two t';) and were 1367
6: 44 the loaves were about five t' men. 4000
8: 9 that had eaten were about four t': 5070
19 brake the five loaves among five t', 4000
20 And when the seven among four t', 5070
Lu 9: 14 For they were about five t' men. 4000
14: 31 be able with ten t' to meet him 3463
31 cometh against him with twenty t'?" "
Joh 6: 10 sat down, in number about five t'. 4000
Ac 2: 41 unto them about three t' souls. 5153
4: 4 of the men was about five t'. 5505
19: 19 and found it fifty t' pieces of silver. 3461
21: 38 four t' men that were murderers? 5070
Ro 11: 4 reserved to myself seven t' men, 2035
1Co 4: 15 ye have ten t' instructers in Christ, 3463
10: 8 fell in one day three and twenty t'. 5505
14: 19 ten t' words in an unknown tongue. 3463
2Pe 3: 8 day is with the Lord as a t' years, 5507
8 years, and a t' years as one day. "
Re 5: 11 of them was ten t' times ten t', 3461
7: 4 forty and four t' of all the tribes 5505
5 tribe of Juda were sealed twelve t'. "
5 of Reuben were sealed twelve t'. "
5 tribe of Gad were sealed twelve t'. "
6 tribe of Aser were sealed twelve t'. "
6 of Nepthalim were sealed twelve t'. "
6 of Manasses were sealed twelve t'. "
7 of Simeon were sealed twelve t'. "
7 tribe of Levi were sealed twelve t'. "
7 of Issachar were sealed twelve t'. "
8 of Zabulon were sealed twelve t'. "
8 of Joseph were sealed twelve t'. "
8 of Benjamin were sealed twelve t'. "
9: 16 horsemen were two hundred t' t': 3461
11: 3 a t' two hundred and threescore 5507
13 were slain of men seven t': 5505
12: 6 a t' two hundred and threescore 5507
14: 1 him an hundred forty and four t', 5505
3 the hundred and forty and four t', "
20 of a t' and six hundred furlongs. 5507
20: 2 Satan, and bound him a t' years, "
3 till the t' years should be fulfilled: "
4 and reigned with Christ a t' years. "
5 until the t' years were finished. "
6 and shall reign with him a t' years. "
7 when the t' years are expired, Satan "
21: 16 with the reed, twelve t' furlongs. 5505

thousands
Ge 24: 60 be thou the mother of t' of millions, 505
Ex 18: 21 to be rulers of t', and rulers of "
25 rulers of t', rulers of hundreds, "
20: 6 shewing mercy unto t' of them that "
34: 7 Keeping mercy for t', forgiving "
Nu 1: 16 their fathers, heads of t' in Israel. "
10: 4 which are heads of the t' of Israel, "
36 O Lord, unto the many t' of Israel. "
31: 5 were delivered out of the t' of Israel, "
14 the host, with the captains over t', "
48 which were over t' of the host, "
48 the captains of t', and captains of "
52 of the captains of t', and of the "
54 took the gold of the captains of t' "
De 1: 15 heads over you, captains over t', "
5: 10 shewing mercy unto t' of them that "
33: 2 and he came with ten t' of saints: 7233
17 and they are the ten t' of Ephraim, "
17 and they are the t' of Manasseh. 505
Jos 22: 14 fathers among the ten t' of Israel. "
21 unto the heads of the t' of Israel, "
30 the t' of Israel which were with him, "
1Sa 8: 12 he will appoint him captains over t', "
10: 19 Lord by your tribes, and by your t'. "
18: 7 Saul hath slain his t', "
7 and David his ten t'. "
8 have ascribed unto David ten t', 7233
8 to me they have ascribed but t': 505
21: 11 Saul hath slain his t', "
11 and David his ten t'? 7233
22: 7 and make you all captains of t', and 505
23: 23 out throughout all the t' of Judah. "
29: 2 passed on by hundreds, and by t': "
5 Saul slew his t', "
5 and David his ten t'? 7233

2Sa 18: 1 and set captains of t' and captains 505
4 came out by hundreds and by t'. "
1Ch 12: 20 captains of the t' that were of "
13: 1 the captains of t' and hundreds, "
15: 25 and the captains over t', went to "
26: 26 the captains over t' and hundreds, "
27: 1 and captains of t' and hundreds, "
28: 1 and the captains over the t', and "
29: 6 the captains of t' and of hundreds, "
2Ch 1: 2 to the captains of t' and of hundreds, "
17: 14 Of Judah, the captains of t'; Adnah "
25: 5 and made them captains over t', "
Ps 3: 6 not be afraid of ten t' of people, 7233
68: 17 thousand, even t' of angels; 505
119: 72 unto me than t' of gold and silver. "
144: 13 our sheep may bring forth t' 503
13 and ten t' in our streets: 7232
Jer 32: 18 shewest lovingkindness unto t', 505
Da 7: 10 thousand t' ministered unto him, 506
11: 12 he shall cast down many ten t': 7239
Mic 5: 2 thou be little among the t' of Judah, 505
6: 7 the Lord be pleased with t' of rams, "
7 or with ten t' of rivers of oil? shall 7233
Ac 21: 20 t' of Jews there are which believe; 3461
Jude 14 cometh with ten t' of his saints, "
Re 5: 11 times ten thousand, and t' of t'; 5505

thousand-thousand See THOUSAND.

thread
Ge 14: 23 take from a t' even to a shoelatchet, 2339
38: 28 bound upon his hand a scarlet t', "
30 that had the scarlet t' upon his hand: "
Jos 2: 18 shalt bind this line of scarlet t' 2339
J'g 16: 9 as a t' of tow is broken when it *6616
12 them from off his arms like a t'. 2339
Ca 4: 3 Thy lips are like a t' of scarlet, and "

threaten See also THREATENED; THREATENING.
Ac 4: 17 let us straitly t' them, that they 546

threatened
Ac 4: 21 So when they had further t' them, 4324
1Pe 2: 23 again; when he suffered, he t' not; 546

threatening See also THREATENINGS.
Eph 6: 9 things unto them, forbearing t': 547

threatenings
Ac 4: 29 And now, Lord, behold their t': and 547
9: 1 And Saul, yet breathing out t' and* "

three See also THIRTEEN; THREEFOLD; THREESCORE.
Ge 5: 22 Methuselah t' hundred years, 7969
23 Enoch was t' hundred sixty and five "
6: 10 Noah begat t' sons, Shem, Ham, "
15 the ark shall be t' hundred cubits, "
7: 13 the t' wives of his sons with them, "
9: 19 These are the t' sons of Noah: and "
28 after the flood t' hundred and fifty "
11: 13 Salah four hundred and t' years, "
15 Eber four hundred and t' years, "
14: 14 own house, t' hundred and eighteen, "
15: 9 Take me an heifer of t' years old, 8027
9 and a she goat of t' years old, and a "
9 a ram of t' years old, and a "
18: 2 and, lo, t' men stood by him: 7969
6 quickly t' measures of fine meal, "
29: 2 there were t' flocks of sheep lying "
34 because I have born him t' sons: "
30: 36 t' days' journey betwixt himself and "
38: 24 came to pass about t' months after, "
40: 10 And in the vine were t' branches: "
12 The t' branches are t' days: "
13 within t' days shall Pharaoh lift "
16 I had t' white baskets on my head: "
18 thereof: The t' baskets are t' days: "
19 within t' days shall Pharaoh lift "
42: 17 them all together into ward t' days. "
45: 22 gave t' hundred pieces of silver, "
46: 15 his daughters were thirty and t'. "
Ex 2: 2 goodly child, she hid him t' months. "
3: 18 t' days' journey into the wilderness, "
5: 3 t' days' journey into the desert, and "
6: 18 an hundred thirty and t' years. "
7: 7 Aaron fourscore and t' years old, "
8: 27 t' days' journey into the wilderness, "
10: 22 in all the land of Egypt t' days: "
23 rose any from his place for t' days: "
15: 22 they went t' days in the wilderness, "
21: 11 And if he do not these t' unto her, "
23: 14 T' times thou shalt keep a feast "
17 T' times in the year all thy males "
25: 32, 32 t' branches of the candlestick "
33 T' bowls made like unto almonds, "
33 t' bowls made like almonds in the "
27: 1 the height thereof shall be t' cubits. "
14, 15 pillars t', and their sockets t'. "
32: 28 that day about t' thousand men. "
37: 18, 18 t' branches of the candlestick "
19 T' bowls made after the fashion of "
19 and t' bowls made like almonds in "
38: 1 and t' cubits the height thereof. "
14, 15 pillars t', and their sockets t'. "
26 t' thousand and five hundred and "
Le 12: 4 of her purifying t' and thirty days; "
14: 10 t' tenth deals of fine flour for a "
19: 23 t' years shall it be as uncircumcised "
25: 21 it shall bring forth fruit for t' years. "
27: 6 estimation...be t' shekels of silver. "
Nu 1: 23 and nine thousand and t' hundred. "
43 fifty and t' thousand and four "
46 hundred thousand and t' thousand "
2: 13 and nine thousand and t' hundred. "
30 and t' thousand and four hundred. "
32 hundred thousand and t' thousand "
3: 50 t' hundred and threescore and five "
4: 44 were t' thousand and two hundred. "
10: 33 mount of the Lord t' days' journey: "

Nu 10:33 before them in the *t'* days' journey.7969
12: 4 Come out ye *t'* unto the tabernacle "
4 And they *t'* came out. "
15: 9 offering of *t'* tenth deals of flour "
22:28 hast smitten me these *t'* times? "
32 smitten thine ass these *t'* times? "
33 and turned from me these *t'* times: "
24:10 blessed them these *t'* times. "
26: 7 forty and *t'* thousand and seven "
25 and four thousand and *t'* hundred. "
47 were fifty and *t'* thousand and four "
62 twenty and *t'* thousand, all males "
28:12 *t'* tenth deals of flour for a meat "
20 *t'* tenth deals shall ye offer for a "
28 *t'* tenth deals unto one bullock, two "
29: 3 *t'* tenth deals for a bullock, and "
9 *t'* tenth deals to a bullock, and two "
14 *t'* tenth deals unto every bullock of "
31:36 *t'* hundred thousand and seven "
43 *t'* hundred thousand and thirty "
33: 8 *t'* days' journey in the wilderness "
39 hundred and twenty and *t'* years "
35:14 give *t'* cities on this side Jordan, "
14 *t'* cities shall ye give in the land of "
De 4:41 Moses severed *t'* cities on this side "
14:28 the end of *t'* years thou shalt bring "
16:16 *T'* times in a year shall all thy "
17: 6 of two witnesses, or *t'* witnesses, "
19: 2 separate *t'* cities for thee in the "
3 thee to inherit, into *t'* parts, 8027
7 shalt separate *t'* cities for thee. 7969
9 thou add *t'* cities more for thee, "
15 or at the mouth of *t'* witnesses, "
Jos 1:11 within *t'* days ye shall pass over "
2:16 and hide yourselves there *t'* days, "
22 and abode there *t'* days, until the "
3: 2 it came to pass after *t'* days, that "
7: 3 about two or *t'* thousand men go up "
4 the people about *t'* thousand men: "
9:16 came to pass at the end of *t'* days "
15:14 drove thence the *t'* sons of Anak, "
17:11 and her towns, even *t'* countries. "
18: 4 among you *t'* men for each tribe: "
21:32 Kartan with her suburbs; *t'* cities. "
J'g 1:20 thence the *t'* sons of Anak. "
7: 6 their mouth, were *t'* hundred men: "
7 By the *t'* hundred men that lapped "
8 and retained those *t'* hundred men: "
16 *t'* hundred men into *t'* companies, "
20 the *t'* companies blew the trumpets, "
22 the *t'* hundred blew the trumpets, "
8: 4 *t'* hundred men that were with him, "
9:22 had reigned *t'* years over Israel, "
43 and divided them into *t'* companies, "
10: 2 judged Israel twenty and *t'* years, "
11:26 coasts of Arnon, *t'* hundred years? "
14:14 not in *t'* days expound the riddle. "
15: 4 went and caught *t'* hundred foxes, "
11 *t'* thousand men of Judah went to "
16:15 hast mocked me these *t'* times, "
27 about *t'* thousand men and women, "
19: 4 and he abode with him *t'* days: "
1Sa 1:24 him up with her, with *t'* bullocks, "
2:13 a fleshhook of *t'* teeth in his hand; "
21 bare *t'* sons and two daughters. "
9:20 thine asses that were lost *t'* days "
10: 3 meet thee *t'* men going up to God "
3 one carrying *t'* kids, and another "
3 another carrying *t'* loaves of bread, "
11: 8 of Israel were *t'* hundred thousand, "
11 put the people in *t'* companies; "
13: 2 Saul chose him *t'* thousand men of "
17 of the Philistines in *t'* companies: "
17:13 the *t'* eldest sons of Jesse went and "
13 the names of his *t'* sons that went "
14 and the *t'* eldest followed Saul. "
20:19 when thou hast stayed *t'* days, 8027
20 I will shoot *t'* arrows on the side 7969
41 and bowed himself *t'* times: "
21: 5 kept from us about these *t'* days, 8032
24: 2 took *t'* thousand chosen men out 7969
25: 2 he had *t'* thousand sheep, and a "
26: 2 having *t'* thousand chosen men of "
30:12 any water, *t'* days and *t'* nights. "
13 because *t'* days agone I fell sick. "
31: 6 So Saul died, and his *t'* sons, and "
8 Saul and his *t'* sons fallen in mount "
2Sa 2:18 there were *t'* sons of Zeruiah there, "
31 so that *t'* hundred and threescore "
5: 5 he reigned thirty and *t'* years over "
6:11 Obed-edom the Gittite *t'* months: "
13:38 to Geshur, and was there *t'* years. "
14:27 Absalom there were born *t'* sons, "
18:14 And he took *t'* darts in his hand, "
20: 4 the men of Judah within *t'* days, "
21: 1 famine in the days of David *t'* years, "
16 spear weighed *t'* hundred shekels "
23: 9 one of the *t'* mighty men with "
13 *t'* of the thirty chief went down, 7991
16 the *t'* mighty men brake through 7969
17 things did these *t'* mighty men. "
18 son of Zeruiah, was chief among *t'*. 7992
18 up his spear against *t'* hundred, 7969
18 them, and had the name among *t'*. "
19 Was he not most honourable of *t'*? "
19 he attained not unto the first *t'*. "
22 the name among *t'* mighty men. "
23 but he attained not to the first *t'*. "
24:12 the Lord, I offer thee *t'* things; "
13 wilt thou flee *t'* months before "
13 that there be *t'* days' pestilence in "
1Ki 2:11 thirty and *t'* years reigned he in "
39 came to pass at the end of *t'* years, "
4:32 And he spake *t'* thousand proverbs: "
5:16 *t'* thousand and *t'* hundred, which "
6:36 court with *t'* rows of hewed stone, "
1Ki 7: 4 And there were windows in *t'* rows,7969
4, 5 was against light in *t'* ranks. "
12 was with *t'* rows of hewed stones, "
25 oxen, *t'* looking toward the north, "
25 and *t'* looking toward the west, "
25 and *t'* looking toward the south, "
25 and *t'* looking toward the east: "
27 and *t'* cubits the height of it. "
9:25 *t'* times in a year did Solomon offer "
10:17 *t'* hundred shields of beaten gold; "
17 *t'* pound of gold went to one shield: "
22 once in *t'* years came the navy of "
11: 3 and *t'* hundred concubines: and "
12: 5 Depart yet for *t'* days, then come "
15: 2 *T'* years reigned he in Jerusalem. "
17:21 himself upon the child *t'* times, "
22: 1 they continued *t'* years without war "
2Ki 2:17 they sought *t'* days, but found him "
3:10, 13 called these *t'* kings together, "
9:32 out to him two or *t'* eunuchs. "
12: 6 the *t'* and twentieth year of king "
13: 1 the *t'* and twentieth year of Joash "
25 *T'* times did Joash beat him, and "
17: 5 to Samaria, and besieged it *t'* years. "
18:10 at the end of *t'* years they took it: "
14 *t'* hundred talents of silver and "
23:31 Jehoahaz was twenty and *t'* years "
31 he reigned *t'* months in Jerusalem. "
24: 1 became his servant *t'* years: "
8 he reigned in Jerusalem *t'* months. "
25:17 the height of the chapiter *t'* cubits; "
18 and the *t'* keepers of the door: "
1Ch 2: 3 which *t'* were born unto him of the "
16 Abishai, and Joab, and Asahel, *t'*. "
22 who had *t'* and twenty cities in the "
3: 4 he reigned thirty and *t'* years. "
23 and Hezekiah, and Azrikam, *t'*. "
7: 6 Bela, and Becher, and Jediael, *t'*. "
10: 6 Saul died, and his *t'* sons, and all "
11:11 *t'* hundred slain by him at one time. "
12 who was one of the *t'* mighties. "
15 *t'* of the thirty captains went down "
18 the *t'* brake through the host of the "
19 These things did these *t'* mightiest. "
20 of Joab, he was chief of the *t'*: "
20 up his spear against *t'* hundred, "
20 and had a name among the *t'*. "
21 Of the *t'*, he was more honourable "
21 he attained not to the first *t'*. "
24 the name among the *t'* mighties. "
25 but attained not to the first *t'*: "
12:27 *t'* thousand and seven hundred; "
29 the kindred of Saul, *t'* thousand: "
39 there they were with David *t'* days, "
13:14 Obed-edom in his house *t'* months. "
21:10 the Lord, I offer thee *t'* things: "
12 Either *t'* years' famine; "
12 or *t'* months to be destroyed before "
12 else *t'* days the sword of the Lord, "
23: 8 Jehiel, and Zetham, and Joel, *t'*. "
9 and Haziel, and Haran, *t'*. "
23 Mahli, and Eder, and Jeremoth, *t'*. "
24:18 The *t'* and twentieth to Delaiah, "
25: 5 fourteen sons and *t'* daughters. "
30 The *t'* and twentieth to Mahazioth, "
29: 4 Even *t'* thousand talents of gold, "
27 thirty and *t'* years reigned he in "
2Ch 2: 2 *t'* thousand and six hundred to "
17 and *t'* thousand and six hundred. "
18 and *t'* thousand and six hundred "
4: 4 oxen, *t'* looking toward the north, "
4 and *t'* looking toward the west, "
4 and *t'* looking toward the south, "
4 and *t'* looking toward the east: and "
5 and held *t'* thousand baths. "
6:13 *t'* cubits high, and had set it in the "
7:10 *t'* and twentieth day of the seventh "
8:13 solemn feasts, *t'* times in the year, "
9:16 *t'* hundred shields made he of "
16 *t'* hundred shekels of gold went to "
21 every *t'* years once came the ships "
10: 5 Come again unto me after *t'* days. "
11:17 the son of Solomon strong, *t'* years: "
17 for *t'* years they walked in the way "
13: 2 He reigned *t'* years in Jerusalem. "
14: 8 out of Judah *t'* hundred thousand; "
9 thousand, and *t'* hundred chariots; "
17:14 men of valour *t'* hundred thousand. "
20:25 they were *t'* days in gathering of "
25: 5 found them *t'* hundred thousand "
13 and smote *t'* thousand of them, "
26:13 *t'* hundred thousand and seven "
29:33 oxen and *t'* thousand sheep. "
31:16 from *t'* years old and upward, "
35: 7 thousand, and *t'* thousand bullocks: "
8 small cattle, and *t'* hundred oxen. "
36: 2 was twenty and *t'* years old when "
2 he reigned *t'* months in Jerusalem. "
9 he reigned *t'* months and ten days "
Ezr 2: 4 *t'* hundred seventy and two. "
11 of Bebai, six hundred twenty and *t'*. "
17 of Bezai, *t'* hundred twenty and *t'*. "
19 two hundred twenty and *t'*. "
21 an hundred twenty and *t'*. "
25 seven hundred and forty and *t'*. "
28 and Ai, two hundred twenty and *t'*. "
32 of Harim, *t'* hundred and twenty. "
34 Jericho, *t'* hundred forty and five. "
35 *t'* thousand and six hundred and "
36 nine hundred seventy and *t'*. "
58 were *t'* hundred ninety and two. "
64 forty and two thousand *t'* hundred "
65 seven thousand *t'* hundred thirty "
6: 4 With *t'* rows of great stones, and a8532
8: 5 and with him *t'* hundred males. 7969
15 there abode we in tents *t'* days: "
Ezr 8:32 Jerusalem, and abode there *t'* days.7969
10: 8 would not come within *t'* days, "
9 unto Jerusalem within *t'* days. "
Ne 2:11 Jerusalem, and was there *t'* days. "
7: 9 *t'* hundred seventy and two. "
17 two thousand *t'* hundred twenty "
22 *t'* hundred twenty and eight. "
23 Bezai, *t'* hundred twenty and four. "
29 Beeroth, seven hundred forty and *t'*. "
32 and Ai, an hundred twenty and *t'*. "
35 of Harim, *t'* hundred and twenty. "
36 Jericho, *t'* hundred forty and five. "
38 *t'* thousand nine hundred and "
39 nine hundred seventy and *t'*. "
60 were *t'* hundred ninety and two. "
66 thousand *t'* hundred and threescore, "
67 *t'* hundred thirty and seven: "
Es 4:16 neither eat nor drink *t'* days, night "
8: 9 on the *t'* and twentieth day thereof; "
9:15 slew *t'* hundred men at Shushan; "
Job 1: 2 him seven sons and *t'* daughters. "
3 and *t'* thousand camels, and five "
4 their *t'* sisters to eat and to drink "
17 The Chaldeans made out *t'* bands, "
2:11 Job's *t'* friends heard of all this evil "
32: 1 these *t'* men ceased to answer Job, "
3 against his *t'* friends was his wrath "
5 answer in the mouth of these *t'* men, "
42:13 also seven sons and *t'* daughters. "
Pr 30:15 *t'* things that are never satisfied, "
18 *t'* things which are too wonderful "
21 For *t'* things the earth is disquieted, "
29 There be *t'* things which go well, "
Isa 15: 5 Zoar, an heifer of *t'* years old: *7992
16:14 Within *t'* years, as the years of an 7969
17: 6 two or *t'* berries in the top of the "
20: 3 walked naked and barefoot *t'* years "
Jer 25: 3 that is the *t'* and twentieth year, "
36:23 Jehudi had read *t'* or four leaves, "
48:34 as an heifer of *t'* years old: *7992
52:24 and the *t'* keepers of the door: 7969
28 *t'* thousand Jews and *t'* and twenty: "
30 In the *t'* and twentieth year of "
Eze 4: 5 days, *t'* hundred and ninety days: "
9 *t'* hundred and ninety days shalt "
14:14 Though these *t'* men, Noah, Daniel, "
16, 18 Though these *t'* men were in it, "
40:10 *t'* on this side, and *t'* on that side; "
10 side; they *t'* were of one measure: "
21 *t'* on this side and *t'* on that side; "
48 the gate was *t'* cubits on this side, "
48 this side, and *t'* cubits on that side. "
41: 6 the side chambers were *t'*, one "
16 round about on their *t'* stories, "
22 altar of wood was *t'* cubits high, "
42: 3 gallery against gallery in *t'* stories.*7992
6 For they were in *t'* stories, but had 8027
48:31 *t'* gates northward; one gate of 7969
32 *t'* gates; and one gate of Joseph, "
33 hundred measures: and *t'* gates; "
34 five hundred, with their *t'* gates; "
Da 1: 5 so nourishing them *t'* years, that at "
3:23 these *t'* men, Shadrach, Meshach, 8532
24 Did not we cast *t'* men bound into "
6: 2 And over these *t'* presidents; of "
10 upon his knees *t'* times a day, "
13 maketh his petition *t'* times a day. "
7: 5 it had *t'* ribs in the mouth of it "
8 whom there were *t'* of the first "
20 came up, and before whom *t'* fell; "
24 first, and he shall subdue *t'* kings. "
8:14 thousand and *t'* hundred days; 7969
10: 2 Daniel was mourning *t'* full weeks. "
3 till *t'* whole weeks were fulfilled. "
11: 2 shall stand up yet *t'* kings in Persia; "
12:12 thousand *t'* hundred and five and "
Am 1: 3 For *t'* transgressions of Damascus, "
6 For *t'* transgressions of Gaza, and "
9 For *t'* transgressions of Tyrus, and "
11 For *t'* transgressions of Edom, and "
13 For *t'* transgressions of the children "
2: 1 For *t'* transgressions of Moab, and "
4 For *t'* transgressions of Judah, and "
6 For *t'* transgressions of Israel, and "
4: 4 and your tithes after *t'* years: "
7 were yet *t'* months to the harvest: "
8 So two or *t'* cities wandered unto "
Jon 1:17 belly of the fish *t'* days and *t'* nights. "
3: 3 great city of *t'* days' journey. "
Zec 11: 8 *T'* shepherds also I cut off in one "
M't 12:40 as Jonas was *t'* days and *t'* nights 5140
40 *t'* days and *t'* nights in the heart of "
13:33 and hid in *t'* measures of meal, "
15:32 they continue with me now *t'* days, "
17: 4 let us make here *t'* tabernacles; "
18:16 in the mouth of two or *t'* witnesses "
20 two or *t'* are gathered together in "
26:61 of God, and to build it in *t'* days. "
27:40 and buildest it in *t'* days, save "
63 alive, After *t'* days I will rise again. "
M'r 8: 2 have now been with me *t'* days, "
31 killed, and after *t'* days rise again. "
9: 5 and let us make *t'* tabernacles; one "
14: 5 for more than *t'* hundred pence, 5145
58 within *t'* days I will build another 5140
15:29 temple, and buildest it in *t'* days, "
Lu 1:56 abode with her about *t'* months, "
2:46 after *t'* days they found him in the "
4:25 shut up *t'* years and six months, "
9:33 and let us make *t'* tabernacles; one "
10:36 Which now of these *t'*, thinkest "
11: 5 unto him, Friend, lend me *t'* loaves; "
12:52 *t'* against two, and two against *t'*. "
13: 7 these *t'* years I come seeking fruit "
21 took and hid in *t'* measures of meal, "
Joh 2: 6 containing two or *t'* firkins apiece. "

Joh 2:19 and in t' days I will raise it up. 5140
20 and wilt thou rear it up in t' days? "
12: 5 ointment sold for t' hundred pence,5145
21:11 fishes, an hundred and fifty and t':5140
Ac 2:41 them about t' thousand souls. 5158
5: 7 about the space of t' hours after, 5140
7:20 up in his father's house t' months: "
9: 9 And he was t' days without sight, "
10:19 unto him, Behold, t' men seek thee."
11:10 And this was done t' times: and all*5151
11 t' men already come unto the house5140
17: 2 t' sabbath days reasoned with them"
19: 8 boldly for the space of t' months, "
20: 3 And there abode t' months. And "
31 the space of t' years I ceased not 5148
25: 1 after t' days he ascended from 5140
28: 7 and lodged us t' days courteously. "
11 And after t' months we departed in "
12 Syracuse, we tarried there t' days. "
15 as Appii forum, and The t' taverns: "
17 after t' days Paul called the chief "
1Co 10: 8 in one day t' and twenty thousand. "
13:13 faith, hope, charity, these t'; "
14:27 let it be by two, or at the most by t',"
29 Let the prophets speak two or t', "
2Co 13: 1 mouth of two or t' witnesses shall "
Ga 1:18 Then after t' years I went up to "
1Ti 5:19 but before two or t' witnesses. "
Heb10:28 mercy under two or t' witnesses: "
11:23 was hid t' months of his parents, 5150
Jas 5:17 space of t' years and six months. 5140
1Jo 5: 7 are t' that bear record in heaven, * "
7 Holy Ghost: and these t' are one.* "
8 are t' that bear witness in earth, "
8 blood: and these t' agree in one. "
Re 6: 6 t' measures of barley for a penny; "
8:13 of the trumpet of the t' angels, "
9:18 By these t' was the third part of "
11: 9 dead bodies t' days and an half, "
11 after t' days and an half the Spirit "
16:13 I saw t' unclean spirits like frogs "
19 great city was divided into t' parts, "
21:13 On the east t' gates; "
13 on the north t' gates; "
13 on the south t' gates; "
13 and on the west t' gates. "

threefold
Ec 4:12 a t' cord is not quickly broken. 8027

three-hundred See THREE and HUNDRED.

threescore
Ge 25: 7 an hundred t' and fifteen years. 7657
26 Isaac was t' years old when she 8346
46:26 all the souls were t' and six; "
27 came into Egypt, were t' and ten. 7657
50: 3 mourned for him t' and ten days. "
Ex 15:27 water, and t' and ten palm trees: "
38:25 hundred and t' and fifteen shekels, "
Le 12: 5 of her purifying t' and six days. 8346
Nu 1:27 were t' and fourteen thousand 7657
39 were t' and two thousand and 8346
2: 4 were t' and fourteen thousand 7657
26 were t' and two thousand and 8346
3:43 two hundred and t' and thirteen. 7657
46 two hundred and t' and thirteen "
50 hundred and t' and five shekels, 8346
26:22 t' and sixteen thousand and five 7657
25 t' and four thousand and three 8346
27 them, t' thousand and five hundred."
43 were t' and four thousand and "
31:33 t' and twelve thousand beeves, 7657
34 And t' and one thousand asses, 8346
37 six hundred and t' and fifteen. 7657
38 Lord's tribute was t' and twelve. "
39 the Lord's tribute was t' and one. 8346
33: 9 water, and t' and ten palm trees; 7657
De 3: 4 t' cities, all the region of Argob, 8346
10:22 Egypt with t' and ten persons; 7657
Jos 13:30 which are in Bashan, t' cities: 8346
J'g 1: 7 T' and ten kings, having their 7657
8:14 thereof, even t' and seventeen men.*"
30 had t' and ten sons of his body "
9: 2 which are t' and ten persons, reign "
4 they gave him t' and ten pieces "
5 Jerubbaal, being t' and ten persons,"
18 slain his sons, t' and ten persons, "
24 to the t' and ten sons of Jerubbaal "
12:14 that rode on t' and ten ass colts: "
1Sa 6:19 fifty thousand and t' and ten men:* "
2Sa 2:31 three hundred and t' men died. 8346
1Ki 4:13 t' great cities with walls and "
22 fine flour, and t' measures of meal. "
5:15 had t' and ten thousand that bare 7657
6: 2 the length thereof was t' cubits, 8346
10:14 hundred t' and six talents of gold, "
2Ki 25:19 and t' men of the people of the land "
1Ch 2:21 whom he married when he was t' "
23 the towns thereof, even t' cities. "
5:18 thousand seven hundred and t', "
9:13 and seven hundred and t'; "
16:38 with their brethren, t' and eight; "
21: 5 t' and ten thousand men that drew7657
26: 8 were t' and two of Obed-edom. 8346
2Ch 2: 2 t' and ten thousand men to bear 7657
18 t' and ten thousand of them to be "
3: 3 the first measure was t' cubits, 8346
9:13 six hundred and t' and six talents "
11:21 eighteen wives, and t' concubines: "
21 and eight sons, and t' daughters.) "
12: 3 chariots, and t' thousand horsemen:"
29:32 brought, was t' and ten bullocks, 7657
36:21 sabbath, to fulfil t' and ten years. "
Ezr 2: 9 of Zaccai, seven hundred and t'. 8346
64 two thousand three hundred and t'."
69 t' and one thousand drams of gold,7239
6: 3 the height thereof t' cubits, and 8361
Ezr 6: 3 and the breadth thereof t' cubits; 8361
8:10 him an hundred and t' males. 8346
13 Shemaiah, and with them t' males. "
Ne 7:14 of Zaccai, seven hundred and t'. "
18 six hundred t' and seven. "
19 Bigvai, two thousand t' and seven. "
66 two thousand three hundred and t'."
72 and t' and seven priests' garments."
11: 6 four hundred t' and eight valiant "
Ps 90:10 of our years are t' years and ten; 7657
Ca 3: 7 t' valiant men are about it, of the "
6: 8 There are t' queens, and fourscore "
Isa 7: 8 and within t' and five years shall "
Jer 52:25 and t' men of the people of the land,"
Eze 40:14 He made also posts of t' cubits, "
Da 3: 1 gold, whose height was t' cubits, 8361
5:31 being about t' and two years old. "
9:25 weeks, and t' and two weeks: 8346
26 And after t' and two weeks shall "
Zec 1:12 indignation these t' and ten years?7657
Lu 24:13 from Jerusalem about t' furlongs. 1835
Ac 7:14 his kindred, t' and fifteen souls. 1440
23:23 and horsemen t' and ten, and "
27:37 two hundred t' and sixteen souls. "
1Ti 5: 9 the number under t' years old, 1835
Re 11: 3 thousand two hundred and t' days, "
12: 6 thousand two hundred and t' days. "
13:18 number is Six hundred t' and six. 5516

threescore-thousand See THREESCORE and THOUSAND.

three-taverns See THREE and TAVERNS.

three-thousand See THREE and THOUSAND.

thresh See also THRESHED; THRESHETH; THRESHING.
Isa 41:15 thou shalt t' the mountains, and 1758
Jer 51:33 threshingfloor, it is time to t' her:*1869
Mic 4:13 Arise and t', O daughter of Zion: 1758
Hab 3:12 thou didst t' the heathen in anger. "

threshed
J'g 6:11 Gideon t' wheat by the winepress,*2251
Isa 28:27 fitches are not t' with a threshing 1758
Am 1: 3 they have t' Gilead with threshing "

thresheth
1Co 9:10 he that t' in hope should be partaker 248

threshing See also THRESHINGFLOOR; THRESHINGPLACE.
Le 26: 5 And your t' shall reach unto the 1786
2Sa 24:22 and t' instruments and other 4173
2Ki 13: 7 had made them like the dust by t'.1758
1Ch 21:20 Now Ornan was t' wheat. "
23 and the t' instruments for wood, 4173
Isa 21:10 O my t', and the corn of my floor: 4098
28:27 not threshed with a t' instrument, 2742
28 because he will not ever be t' it, 1758
41:15 a new sharp t' instrument having 4173
Am 1: 3 Gilead with t' instruments of iron:2742

threshingfloor See also THRESHINGFLOORS.
Ge 50:10 And they came to the t' of Atad, 1637
Nu 15:20 as ye do the heave offering of the t'."
18:27 as though it were the corn of the t',"
30 Levites as the increase of the t', "
Ru 3: 2 winnoweth barley to night in the t'."
2Sa 6: 6 when they came to Nachon's t', "
24:18 unto the Lord in the t' of Araunah "
21 David said, To buy the t' of thee, "
24 David bought the t' and the oxen "
1Ch 13: 9 they came unto the t' of Chidon, "
21:15 angel of the Lord stood by the t' "
18 unto the Lord in the t' of Ornan "
21 saw David, and went out of the t', "
22 Grant me the place of this t', that "
28 answered him in the t' of Ornan "
2Ch 3: 1 had prepared in the t' of Ornan "
Jer 51:33 The daughter of Babylon is like a t',"

threshingfloors
1Sa 23: 1 Keilah, and they rob the t'. 1637
Da 2:35 like the chaff of the summer t'; 147

threshingplace
2Sa 24:16 angel of the Lord was by the t' 1637

threshold See also THRESHOLDS.
J'g 19:27 and her hands were upon the t'. 5592
1Sa 5: 4 his hands were cut off upon the t':4670
5 tread on the t' of Dagon in Ashdod "
1Ki 14:17 she came to the t' of the door, 5592
Eze 9: 3 he was, to the t' of the house. 4670
10: 4 and stood over the t' of the house; "
18 from off the t' of the house, "
40: 6 and measured the t' of the gate, 5592
6 and the other t' of the gate, which "
7 the t' of the gate by the porch of "
43: 8 setting of their t' by my thresholds, "
46: 2 shall worship at the t' of the gate: 4670
47: 1 waters issued out from under the t' "
Zep 1: 9 punish all those that leap on the t', "

thresholds
Ne 12:25 the ward at the t' of the gates. * 624
Eze 43: 8 setting of their threshold by my t',*5592
Zep 2:14 desolation shall be in the t': "

threw See also OVERTHREW; THREWEST.
2Sa 16:13 t' stones at him, and cast dust. 5619
2Ki 9:33 her down. So they t' her down: 8058
2Ch 31: 1 t' down the high places and the *5422
M'r 12:42 widow, and she t' in two mites, * 906
Lu 9:42 devil t' him down, and tare him. *4952
Ac 22:23 clothes, and t' dust into the air, * 906

threwest
Ne 9:11 persecutors thou t' into the deeps.*7993

thrice
Ex 34:23 T' in the year shall all your *7969,6471
24 Lord thy God t' in the year. * "
2Ki 13:18 And he smote t', and stayed. 7969,6471
19 thou shalt smite Syria but t'. "
M't 26:34, 75 crow, thou shalt deny me t'. 5151
M'r 14:30, 72 twice, thou shalt deny me t'. "
Lu 22:34 shalt t' deny that thou knowest "
61 cock crow, thou shalt deny me t'. "
Joh 13:38 crow, till thou hast denied me t'. "
Ac 10:16 This was done t': and the vessel "
2Co 11:25 T' was I beaten with rods, once "
25 t' I suffered shipwreck, a night "
12: 8 this thing I besought the Lord t'. "

throat
Ps 5: 9 their t' is an open sepulchre; they1627
69: 3 weary of my crying: my t' is dried: "
115: 7 neither speak they through their t'."
Pr 23: 2 And put a knife to thy t', if thou 3930
Jer 2:25 unshod, and thy t' from thirst: 1627
M't 18:28 and took him by the t', saying, 4155
Ro 3:13 Their t' is an open sepulchre; 2995

throne See also THRONES.
Ge 41:40 only in the t' will I be greater 3678
Ex 11: 5 of Pharaoh that sitteth upon his t', "
12:29 of Pharaoh that sat on his t' "
De 17:18 sitteth upon the t' of his kingdom, "
1Sa 2: 8 make them inherit the t' of glory: "
2Sa 3:10 to set up the t' of David over Israel "
7:13 will stablish the t' of his kingdom "
16 thy t' shall be established for ever. "
14: 9 the king and his t' be guiltless. "
1Ki 1:13 me, and he shall sit upon my t'? "
17 me, and he shall sit upon my t'. "
20 who shall sit on the t' of my lord "
24 me, and he shall sit upon my t'? "
27 who should sit on the t' of my lord "
30 he shall sit upon my t' in my stead;"
35 he may come and sit upon my t'; "
37 Solomon, and make his t' greater "
37 than the t' of my lord king David. "
46 Solomon sitteth on the t' of the "
47 and make his t' greater than thy t'. "
48 given one to sit on my t' this day, "
2: 4 (said he) a man on the t' of Israel. "
12 sat Solomon upon the t' of David "
19 and sat down on his t', and caused "
24 set me on the t' of David my father,"
33 upon his t', shall there be peace "
45 the t' of David shall be established "
3: 6 hast given him a son to sit on his t',"
5: 5 son, whom I will set upon thy t' in "
7: 7 he made a porch for the t' where he"
8:20 my father, and sit on the t' of Israel,"
25 in my sight to sit on the t' of Israel;"
9: 5 will establish the t' of thy kingdom "
5 thee a man upon the t' of Israel. "
10: 9 thee, to set thee on the t' of Israel: "
18 the king made a great t' of ivory, "
19 The t' had six steps, and the top of "
19 the top of the t' was round behind: "
16:11 reign, as soon as he sat on his t', "
22:10 king of Judah sat each on his t', "
19 I saw the Lord sitting on his t', "
2Ki 10: 3 sons, and set him on his father's t', "
30 shall sit on the t' of Israel. "
11:19 And he sat on the t' of the kings. "
13:13 and Jeroboam sat upon his t': "
15:12 sons shall sit on the t' of Israel "
25:28 set his t' above the t' of the kings "
1Ch 17:12 and I will stablish his t' for ever. "
14 and his t' shall be established for "
22:10 establish the t' of his kingdom over"
28: 5 to sit upon the t' of the kingdom of "
29:23 Solomon sat on the t' of the Lord "
2Ch 6:10 and am set on the t' of Israel, as "
16 sight to sit upon the t' of Israel; "
7:18 will I stablish the t' of thy kingdom,"
9: 8 in thee to set thee on his t', "
17 the king made a great t' of ivory, "
18 And there were six steps to the t', "
18 gold, which were fastened to the t', "
18: 9 Judah sat either of them on his t', "
18 I saw the Lord sitting upon his t', "
23:20 king upon the t' of the kingdom. "
Ne 3: 7 unto the t' of the governor on this "
Es 1: 2 king Ahasuerus sat on the t' of his "
5: 1 king sat upon his royal t' in the "
Job 26: 9 He holdeth back the face of his t', "
36: 7 with kings are they on the t'; yea, "
Ps 9: 4 thou satest in the t' judging right. "
7 ever: he hath prepared his t' for "
11: 4 temple, the Lord's t' is in heaven: "
45: 6 Thy t', O God, is for ever and ever: "
47: 8 God sitteth upon the t' of his "
89: 4 build up thy t' to all generations. "
14 are the habitation of thy t': "
29 and his t' as the days of heaven. "
36 and his t' as the sun before me. "
44 and cast his t' down to the ground. "
93: 2 Thy t' is established of old: thou "
94:20 the t' of iniquity have fellowship "
97: 2 are the habitation of his t'. "
103:19 hath prepared his t' in the heavens;"
132:11 of thy body will I set upon thy t'. "
12 also sit upon thy t' for evermore. "
Pr 16:12 t' is established by righteousness. "
20: 8 A king that sitteth in the t' of "
28 and his t' is upholden by mercy. "
25: 5 his t' shall be established in "
29:14 his t' shall be established for ever. "
Isa 6: 1 saw also the Lord sitting upon a t', "
9: 7 upon the t' of David, and upon his "
14:13 exalt my t' above the stars of God: "
16: 5 in mercy shall the t' be established:"
22:23 a glorious t' to his father's house. "
47: 1 there is no t', O daughter of the "
66: 1 The heaven is my t', and the earth "

Jer 1:15 set every one his t' at the entering 3678
3:17 call Jerusalem the t' of the Lord; "
13:13 the kings that sit upon David's t', "
14:21 do not disgrace the t' of thy glory: "
17:12 A glorious high t' from the "
25 princes sitting upon the t' of David, "
22: 2 that sittest upon the t' of David, "
4 kings sitting upon the t' of David, "
30 sitting upon the t' of David, "
29:16 that sitteth upon the t' of David, "
33:17 upon the t' of the house of Israel; "
21 not have a son to reign upon his t'; "
36:30 none to sit upon the t' of David: "
43:10 will set his t' upon these stones "
49:38 I will set my t' in Elam, and will "
52:32 set his t' above the t' of the kings "
La 5:19 t' from generation to generation. "
Eze 1:26 their heads was the likeness of a t', "
26 upon the likeness of the t' was the "
10: 1 appearance of the likeness of a t'. "
43: 7 the place of my t', and the place of "
Da 5:20 he was deposed from his kingly t',3764
7: 9 his t' was like the fiery flame, and "
Jon 3: 6 Nineveh, and he arose from his t', 3678
Hag 2:22 I will overthrow the t' of kingdoms, "
Zec 6:13 and shall sit and rule upon his t'; "
13 he shall be a priest upon his t': "
M't 5:34 by heaven; for it is God's t': 2362
19:28 man shall sit in the t' of his glory, "
23:22 heaven, sweareth by the t' of God, "
25:31 shall he sit upon the t' of his glory: "
Lu 1:32 unto him the t' of his father David: "
Ac 2:30 raise up Christ to sit on his t'; "
7:49 Heaven is my t', and earth is my "
12:21 in royal apparel, sat upon his t', 968
Heb 1: 8 Thy t', O God, is for ever and ever: 2362
4:16 come boldly unto the t' of grace, "
8: 1 right hand of the t' of the Majesty "
12: 2 at the right hand of the t' of God. "
Re 1: 4 Spirits which are before his t'; "
3:21 will I grant to sit with me in my t', "
21 set down with my Father in his t'. "
4: 2 and, behold, a t' was set in heaven, "
2 and one sat on the t'. "
3 was a rainbow round about the t', "
4 about the t' were four and twenty "
5 out of the t' proceeded lightnings "
5 lamps of fire burning before the t', "
6 before the t' there was a sea of "
6 and in the midst of the t', "
6 and round about the t', were four "
9 thanks to him that sat on the t', "
10 down before him that sat on the t', "
10 and cast their crowns before the t', "
5: 1 hand of him that sat on the t' a "
6 in the midst of the t' and of the "
7 hand of him that sat upon the t'. "
11 of many angels round about the t' "
13 unto him that sitteth upon the t', "
6:16 face of him that sitteth on the t', "
7: 9 stood before the t', and before the "
10 our God which sitteth upon the t', "
11 angels stood round about the t', "
11 and fell before the t' on their faces, "
15 are they before the t' of God, "
15 he that sitteth on the t' shall dwell "
17 Lamb which is in the midst of the t' "
8: 3 altar which was before the t'. "
12: 5 caught up unto God, and to his t'. "
14: 3 as it were a new song before the t', "
5 without fault before the t' of God.* "
16:17 from the t', saying, It is done. "
19: 4 worshipped God that sat on the t', "
5 a voice came out of the t', saying, "
20:11 I saw a great white t', and him that "
21: 5 he that sat upon the t' said, Behold, "
22: 1 proceeding out of the t' of God and "
3 the t' of God and of the Lamb shall "

thrones
Ps 122: 5 For there are set t' of judgment, 3678
5 the t' of the house of David. "
Isa 14: 9 raised up from their t' all the kings "
Eze 26:16 sea shall come down from their t', "
Da 7: 9 I beheld till the t' were cast down, 3764
M't 19:28 ye also shall sit upon twelve t', 2362
Lu 22:30 sit on t' judging the twelve tribes "
Col 1:16 whether they be t', or dominions, "
Re 20: 4 I saw t', and they sat upon them, "

throng See also THRONGED; THRONGING.
M'r 3: 9 multitude, lest they should t' him. 2346
Lu 8:45 the multitude t' thee and press *4912

thronged
M'r 5:24 people followed him, and t' him. 4918
Lu 8:42 But as he went the people t' him. 4846

thronging
M'r 5:31 Thou seest the multitude t' thee, 4918

through See also THROUGHOUT.
Ge 6:13 is filled with violence t' them; 6440
12: 6 Abram passed t' the land unto the
13:17 walk t' the land in the length of it and
30:32 I will pass t' all thy flock to day,
41:36 that the land perish not t' the famine.
Ex 10:15 of the field, t' all the land of Egypt.
12:12 pass t' the land of Egypt this night,
23 will pass t' to smite the Egyptians;
13:17 God led them not t' the way of the*
18 t' the way of the wilderness of the*
14:16 ground t' the midst of the sea. *8432
24 of the Egyptians t' the pillar of fire
19:13 shall surely be stoned, or shot t';
21 lest they break t' unto the Lord to
24 people break t' to come up unto the
21: 6 shall bore his ear t' with an aul;
26:33 middle bar to shoot t' the boards 8432
Le 4: 2 If a soul shall sin t' ignorance against*
13 congregation...Israel sin t' ignorance,*
22 and done somewhat t' ignorance *
27 the common people sin t' ignorance,*
5:15 a trespass, and sin t' ignorance, *
18:21 of thy seed pass t' the fire to Molech,
26: 6 neither shall the sword go t' your land.
Nu 13:32 t' which we have gone to search it,
14: 7 land, which we passed t' to search it,
15:27 And if any soul sin t' ignorance, *
29 law for him that sinneth t' ignorance,*
20:17 us pass, I pray thee, t' thy country:
17 country: we will not pass t' the fields,
17 or t' the vineyards, neither will we
19 any thing else, go t' on my feet. 5674
20 And he said, Thou shalt not go t'. "
21 to give Israel passage t' his border:
21:22 Let me pass t' thy land: we will not
23 not suffer Israel to pass t' his border:
24: 8 and pierce them t' with his arrows.
25: 8 the tent, and thrust both of them t',
8 Israel, and the woman t' her belly. 413
31:16 t' the counsel of Balaam, to commit
23 ye shall make it go t' the fire, and it
23 fire ye shall make go t' the water.
33: 8 and passed t' the midst of the sea 8432
De 1:19 t' all that great and terrible wilderness,
2: 4 are to pass t' the coast of your brethren
7 thy walking t' this great wilderness:
8 t' the way of the plain from Elath,*
18 Thou art to pass over t' Ar, the coast*
27 Let me pass t' thy land: I will go
28 drink: only I will pass t' on my feet;
5:15 thee out thence t' a mighty hand *
8:15 t' that great and terrible wilderness,
9:26 thou hast redeemed t' thy greatness,
15:17 and thrust it t' his ear unto the door,
18:10 son or his daughter to pass t' the fire,
29:16 t' the nations which ye passed by; 7130
31:29 him to anger t' the work of your hands.
32:47 t' this thing ye shall prolong your days
33:11 smite t' the loins of them that rise
Jos 1:11 Pass t' the host, and command the7130
2:15 down by a cord t' the window: 1157
3: 2 that the officers went t' the host; 7130
18: 4 and they shall rise, and go t' the land,
8 Go and walk t' the land, and describe
9 the men went and passed t' the land,
12 went up t' the mountains westward;
24:17 all the people t' whom we passed: 7130
J'g 2:22 That t' them I may prove Israel, *
3:23 Then Ehud went forth t' the porch,*
5: 6 and the travellers walked t' byways.
26 pierced and stricken t' his temples.
28 a window, and cried t' the lattice. 1157
9:54 And his young man thrust him t'.
11:16 t' the wilderness unto the Red sea,
17 Let me, I pray thee, pass t' thy land:
18 they went along t' the wilderness,
19 pray thee, t' thy land into my place.
20 trusted not Israel to pass t' his coast:
20:12 sent men t' all the tribe of Benjamin,
1Sa 9: 4 And he passed t' mount Ephraim, and
4 and passed t' the land of Shalisha,
4 then they passed t' the land of Shalim,
4 passed t' the land of the Benjamites,
19:12 Michal let David down t' a window: 1157
31: 4 sword, and thrust me t' therewith;
4 uncircumcised come and thrust me t',
2Sa 2:29 men walked all that night t' the plain,
29 over Jordan, and went t' all Bithron,
4: 7 and gat them away t' the plain all*1870
6:16 daughter looked t' a window, 1157
12:31 and made them pass t' the brickkiln:
18:14 thrust them t' the heart of Absalom,
20:14 And he went t' all the tribes of Israel
22:13 T' the brightness before him were*
30 For by thee I have run t' a troop: by*
23:16 brake t' the host of the Philistines,1234
24: 2 Go now t' all the tribes of Israel, 7751
8 So when they had gone t' all the land,
2Ki 1: 2 Ahaziah fell down t' a lattice in his1157
3: 8 The way t' the wilderness of Edom.*
26 break t'...unto the king of Edom: 1234
10:21 And Jehu sent t' all Israel: and all the
16: 3 and made his son to pass t' the fire,
17:17 and their daughters to pass t' the fire,
21: 6 And he made his son pass t' the fire,
23:10 daughter to pass t' the fire to Molech.
24:20 t' the anger of the Lord it came to 5921
1Ch 10: 4 sword, and thrust me t' therewith;
11:18 brake t' the host of the Philistines,1234
2Ch 19: 4 he went out again t' the people from*
23:20 they came t' the high gate into 8432
24: 9 made a proclamation t' Judah and
30:10 t' the country of Ephraim and
32: 4 that ran t' the midst of the land, 8432
33: 6 caused his children to pass t' the fire
Ezr 6:14 they prospered t' the prophesying of
Ne 9:11 they went t' the midst of the sea 8432
Es 6: 9 bring him on horseback t' the street
11 brought him on horseback t' the street
Job 7:14 dreams, and terrifiest me t' visions:
14: 9 Yet t' the scent of water it will bud,
20:24 the bow of steel shall strike him t'.
22:13 know? can he judge t' the dark cloud?
24:16 In the dark they dig t' houses, 2864
26:12 understanding he smiteth t' the proud.
29: 3 when by his light I walked t' darkness;
7 I went out to the gate t' the city, *5921
40:24 his eyes: his nose pierceth t' snares.
41: 2 nose? or bore his jaw t' with a thorn?
Ps 8: 8 passeth t' the paths of the seas.
10: 4 wicked, t' the pride of his countenance,*
18:29 For by thee I have run t' a troop; and*
19: 4 Their line is gone out t' all the earth,
21: 7 t' the mercy of the most High he shall
23: 4 t' the valley of the shadow of death,
32: 3 my bones waxed old t' my roaring all
44: 5 T' thee will we push down our
5 t' thy name will we tread them under
60:12 T' God we shall do valiantly: for he it
66: 3 t' the greatness of thy power shall
6 land: they went t' the flood on foot:
12 heads; we went t' fire and t' water:
68: 7 thou didst march t' the wilderness;
73: 9 their tongue walketh t' the earth.
78:13 the sea, and caused them to pass t';
81: 5 he went out t' the land of Egypt: *5921
84: 6 passing t' the valley of Baca make it a
92: 4 Lord, hast made me glad t' thy work:
106: 9 t' the depths, as t' the wilderness.
107:39 and brought low t' oppression,
108:13 T' God we shall do valiantly: for he it
109:24 My knees are weak t' fasting; and
110: 5 strike t' kings in the day of his wrath.
115: 7 not: neither speak they t' their throat.
119:98 Thou t' thy commandments hast*
104 T' thy precepts I get understanding:
136:14 Israel to pass t' the midst of it: 8432
16 which led his people t' the wilderness:
Pr 7: 6 of my house I looked t' my casement,
8 Passing t' the street near her corner;
23 Till a dart strike t' his liver; as a bird
11: 9 but t' knowledge shall the just be
18: 1 T' desire a man, having separated*
24: 3 T' wisdom is an house builded; and
Ec 5: 3 a dream cometh t' the multitude of*
10:18 t' idleness of the hands the house
18 the hands the house droppeth t'. *1811
Ca 2: 9 shewing himself t' the lattice. 4480
Isa 8: 8 And he shall pass t' Judah; he shall*
21 And they shall pass t' it, hardly
9:19 T' the wrath of the Lord of hosts is
13:15 one that is found shall be thrust t'; 1856
14:19 are slain, thrust t' with a sword, 2944
16: 8 they wandered t' the wilderness: *
21: 1 As whirlwinds in the south pass t'; so
23:10 Pass t' thy land as a river, O daughter
27: 4 I would go t' them, I would burn *
28: 7 But they also have erred t' wine, and‡
7 t' strong drink are out of the way;‡
7 have erred t' strong drink, ‡
7 are out of the way t' strong drink;‡4480
15, 18 overflowing scourge shall pass t',
30:31 For t' the voice of the Lord shall the
34:10 none shall pass t' it for ever and ever.
43: 2 When thou passest t' the waters, I will
2 t' the rivers, they shall not overflow
2 when thou walkest t' the fire, thou1119
48:21 not when he led them t' the deserts:
60:15 hated, so that no man went t' thee.5674
62:10 Go t', go t' the gates; prepare ye "
63:13 That led them t' the deep, as an horse
Jer 2: 6 of Egypt, that led us t' the wilderness,
6 t' a land of deserts and of pits,
6 t' a land of drought, and of the shadow
6 t' a land that no man passed t', and
3: 9 t' the lightness of her whoredom,
5: 1 Run ye to and fro t' the streets of
9: 6 t' deceit they refuse to know me, saith
10 up, so that none can pass t' them;
12 a wilderness, that none passeth t'?
12:12 upon all high places t' the wilderness:*
17:24 in no burden t' the gates of this city
32:35 their daughters to pass t' the fire unto
51: 4 that are thrust t' in her streets. 1856
52 t' all her land the wounded shall
52: 3 t' the anger of the Lord it came to 5921
La 3:44 that our prayer should not pass t'.
4: 9 stricken t' for want of the fruits of the
21 the cup shall also pass t' unto thee:
Eze 5:17 and blood shall pass t' thee;
6: 8 ye shall be scattered t' the countries.
9: 4 Go t' the midst of the city, 5674
4 t' the midst of Jerusalem, and set a
5 Go ye after him t' the city, and smite:
12: 5 Dig thou t' the wall in their sight, and
7 and in the even I digged t' the wall
12 they shall dig t' the wall to carry out
14: 5 all estranged from me t' their idols.
15 noisome beasts to pass t' the land,
15 no man may pass t' because of the
17 land, and say, Sword, go t' the land;
16:14 for it was perfect t' my comeliness,
21 cause them to pass t' the fire for them?
36 discovered t' thy whoredoms with thy
40 and thrust thee t' with their swords.
20:23 and disperse them t' the countries;
26 t' the fire all that openeth the womb,
31 ye make your sons to pass t' the fire,
23:37 to pass for them t' the fire, to devour
29:11 No foot of man shall pass t' it, nor
11 foot of beast shall pass t' it, neither
12 will disperse them t' the countries.
30:23 will disperse them t' the countries.
33:28 be desolate, that none shall pass t'.
34: 6 My sheep wandered t' all the
36:19 they were dispersed t' the countries:
39:14 passing t' the land to bury with the
15 the passengers that pass t' the land,
41:19 made t' all the house round about. 413
46:19 he brought me t' the entry, which was
47: 3 and he brought me t' the waters; 5674
4 and brought me t' the waters;
4 a thousand, and brought me t';
Da 8:25 And t' his policy also he shall 5921
9: 7 t' all the countries whither thou hast
11: 2 strength t' his riches he shall stir up
10 come, and overflow, and pass t':
Joe 3:17 no strangers pass t' her any more.

Am 2:10 led you forty years t' the wilderness,*
5:17 for I will pass t' thee, saith the 7130
Jon 3: 7 proclaimed and published t' Nineveh
Mic 2:13 and have passed t' the gate, and are*
5: 8 if he go t', both treadeth down, 5674
Na 1:12 be cut down, when he shall pass t'.*
15 the wicked shall no more pass t' thee;
3: 4 that selleth nations t' her whoredoms,
4 and familiar t' her witchcrafts.
Hab 1: 6 shall march t' the breadth of the land,
3:12 didst march t' the land in indignation,
14 Thou didst strike t' with his staves*
15 didst walk t' the sea with thine horses,*
15 horses, t' the heap of great waters.*
Zec 1:10 sent to walk to and fro t' the earth.
11 have walked to and fro t' the earth,
17 My cities t' prosperity shall yet be
4:10 run to and fro t' the whole earth.
12 t' the two golden pipes empty the*3027
5: 6 is their resemblance t' all the earth.*
6: 7 might walk to and fro t' the earth:
7 hence, walk to and fro t' the earth.
7 So they walked to and fro t' the earth.
7:14 that no man passed t' nor returned:
9: 8 no oppressor shall pass t' them any
15 drink, and make a noise as t' wine;
10: 7 their heart shall rejoice as t' wine:
11 he shall pass t' the sea with affliction,
13: 3 that begat him shall thrust him t'
9 I will bring the third part t' the fire,
M't 6:19 where thieves break t' and steal: 1358
20 thieves do not break t' nor steal: "
9:34 devils t' the prince of the devils. *1722
12: 1 on the sabbath day t' the corn; 1223
43 he walketh t' dry places, seeking "
19:24 camel to go t' the eye of a needle, "
M'r 2:23 t' the corn fields on the sabbath "
6:55 ran t' that whole region round *4063
7:13 God of none effect t' your tradition,*
31 t' the midst of the coast of 303
9:30 thence, and passed t' Galilee; 1223
10:25 a camel to go t' the eye of a needle, "
11:16 carry any vessel t' the temple. "
Lu 1:78 T' the tender mercy of our God; * "
2:35 sword shall pierce t' thy own soul 1330
4:14 fame of him t' all the region 2596
30 he passing t' the midst of them 1223
5:19 let him down t' the tiling with his "
6: 1 that he went t' the corn fields; "
9: 6 and went t' the towns, preaching 2596
10:17 are subject unto us t' thy name. *1722
11:15 casteth out devils t' Beelzebub the* "
18 I cast out devils t' Beelzebub. * "
24 he walketh t' dry places, seeking 1223
12:39 suffered his house to be broken t'. 1358
13:22 he went t' the cities and villages, 2596
17: 1 woe unto him, t' whom they come! 1223
11 he passed t' the midst of Samaria ‡ "
18:25 for a camel to go t' a needle's eye, "
19: 1 Jesus entered...passed t' Jericho. 1330
Joh 1: 7 that all men t' him might believe. 1223
3:17 the world t' him might be saved. "
4: 4 And he must needs go t' Samaria. "
8:59 t' the midst of them, and so passed*"
15: 3 Now ye are clean t' the word which*"
17:11 t' thine own name those whom *1722
17 Sanctify them t' thy truth: thy * "
19 might be sanctified t' the truth. "
20 shall believe on me t' their word; 1223
20:31 ye might have life t' his name. *1722
Ac 1: 2 after that he t' the Holy Ghost had 1223
3:16 his name t' faith in his name *1909
17 I wot that t' ignorance ye did it, *2596
4: 2 preached t' Jesus the resurrection*1722
8:18 that t' laying on of the apostles' 1223
40 passing t' he preached in all the "
10:43 t' his name whosoever believeth "
12:10 out, and passed on t' one street; "
13: 6 when they had gone t' the isle unto 1330
38 that t' this man is preached unto 1223
14:22 t' much tribulation enter into the "
15: 3 they passed t' Phenice and Samaria, 1330
11 we believe that t' the grace of the 1223
41 And he went t' Syria and Cilicia, 1330
16: 4 And as they went t' the cities, they 1279
17: 1 when they had passed t' Amphipolis 1653
18:27 which had believed t' grace: 1223
19: 1 having passed t' the upper coasts 1330
21 when he had passed t' Macedonia "
20: 3 purposed to return t' Macedonia. 1223
21: 4 who said to Paul t' the Spirit, that "
Ro 1: 8 I thank my God t' Jesus Christ for "
24 uncleanness t' the lusts of their *1722
2:23 t' breaking the law dishonourest 1223
24 blasphemed among the Gentiles t'* "
3: 7 abounded t' my lie unto his glory; 1722
24 t' the redemption that is in Christ 1223
25 a propitiation t' faith in his blood, "
25 past, t' the forbearance of God; *1722
30 faith, and uncircumcision t' faith. 1223
31 then make void the law t' faith? "
4:13 Abraham, or to his seed, t' the law.*"
13 but t' the righteousness of faith. "
20 not at the promise of God t' unbelief;
5: 1 peace with God t' our Lord Jesus 1223
9 shall be saved from wrath t' him. "
11 in God t' our Lord Jesus Christ, "
15 if t' the offence of one many be dead.*
21 grace reign t' righteousness 1223
6:11 alive unto God t' Jesus Christ our*1722
23 God is eternal life t' Jesus Christ * "
7:25 I thank God t' Jesus Christ our 1223
8: 3 do, in that it was weak t' the flesh, "
13 if ye t' the Spirit do mortify the deeds*
37 conquerors t' him that loved us. 1223
11:11 rather t' their fall salvation is come*

Ro 11:30 now obtained mercy t' their unbelief:*
31 t' your mercy they also may obtain*
36 and t' him, and to him, are all 1223
12: 3 For I say, t' the grace given unto me, "
15: 4 we t' patience and comfort of the "
13 t' the power of the Holy Ghost. *1722
17 I may glory t' Jesus Christ in * "
19 T' mighty signs and wonders, by* "
16:27 be glory t' Jesus Christ for ever. 1223
1Co 1: 1 Jesus Christ t' the will of God, "
4:15 I have begotten you t' the gospel. "
8:11 t' thy knowledge shall the weak 1909
10: 1 cloud, and all passed t' the sea; 1223
13:12 For now we see t' a glass, darkly;* "
15:57 the victory t' our Lord Jesus Christ."
16: 5 you, when I shall pass t' Macedonia:1330
5 for I do pass t' Macedonia. "
2Co 3: 4 such trust have we t' Christ to 1223
4:15 t' the thanksgiving of many "
8: 9 that ye t' his poverty might be rich. "
9:11 causeth t' us thanksgiving to God. 1223
10: 4 but mighty t' God to the pulling down*
11: 3 beguiled Eve t' his subtilty, *1722
33 t' a window in a basket was I let 1223
12: 7 t' the abundance of the revelations,*
13: 4 he was crucified t' weakness, 1537
Ga 2:19 I t' the law am dead to the law, 1223
3: 8 would justify the heathen t' faith,*1537
14 on the Gentiles t' Jesus Christ; *1722
14 the promise of the Spirit t' faith. 1223
4: 7 son, then an heir of God t' Christ. "
13 t' infirmity of the flesh I preached* "
5: 5 For we t' the Spirit wait for the hope
10 confidence in you t' the Lord, *1722
Eph 1: 7 we have redemption t' his blood, 1223
2: 7 toward us t' Christ Jesus. *1722
8 For by grace are ye saved t' faith; 1223
18 t' him we both have access by one "
22 an habitation of God t' the Spirit.*1722
4: 6 above all, and t' all, and in you all. 1223
18 t' the ignorance that is in them, * "
Ph'p 1:19 to my salvation t' your prayer, "
2: 3 Let nothing be done t' strife or 2596
3: 9 that which is t' the faith of Christ, 1223
4: 7 hearts and minds t' Christ Jesus. *1722
13 I can do all things t' Christ which* "
Col 1:14 we have redemption t' his blood, *1223
20 peace t' the blood of his cross, "
22 In the body of his flesh t' death, to "
2: 8 any man spoil you t' philosophy "
12 ye are risen with him t' the faith of "
2Th 2:13 you to salvation t' sanctification *1722
16 consolation and good hope t' grace, "
1Ti 6:10 pierced themselves t' with many 4044
2Ti 1:10 immortality to light t' the gospel: 1223
3:15 salvation t' faith which is in Christ "
Tit 1: 3 manifested his word t' preaching,*1722
3: 6 on us abundantly t' Jesus Christ 1223
Ph'm 22 that t' your prayers I shall be given"
Heb 2:10 their salvation perfect t' sufferings."
14 that t' death he might destroy him "
15 t' fear of death were all their lifetime
3:13 hardened t' the deceitfulness of sin.*
6:12 who t' faith and patience inherit 1223
9:14 who t' the eternal Spirit offered "
10:10 t' the offering of the body of Jesus "
20 t' the veil, that is to say, his flesh; "
11: 3 T' faith we understand that the* "
11 T' faith also Sara herself received*
28 T' faith he kept the passover, and the*
29 they passed t' the Red sea as by dry 1224
33 Who t' faith subdued kingdoms, 1223
39 obtained a good report t' faith. "
12:20 be stoned, or thrust t' with a dart:*2700
13:20 t' the blood of the everlasting *1722
21 in his sight, t' Jesus Christ; 1223
1Pe 1: 2 t' sanctification of the Spirit, unto*1722
5 of God t' faith unto salvation 1223
6 heaviness t' manifold temptations:*1722
22 in obeying the truth t' the Spirit *1223
4:11 may be glorified t' Jesus Christ, "
2Pe 1: 1 faith with us t' the righteousness*1722
2 unto you t' the knowledge of God,* "
3 t' the knowledge of him that hath 1223
4 that is in the world t' lust. *1722
2: 3 t' covetousness shall they with * "
18 they allure t' the lusts of the flesh,* "
18 t' much wantonness, those that * "
20 world t' the knowledge of the Lord 1722
1Jo 4: 9 world, that we might live t' him. 1223
Re 8:13 an angel flying t' the midst of *1722
18: 3 rich t' the abundance of her *1537
22:14 may enter in t' the gates into the city.*

throughly See also THOROUGHLY.
Ge 11: 3 us make brick, and burn them t'. ‡
Job 6: 2 Oh that my grief were t' weighed,*
Ps 51: 2 Wash me t' from mine iniquity, ‡7235
Jer 6: 9 They shall t' glean the remnant ‡
7: 5 if ye t' amend your ways and your
5 if ye t' execute judgment between
50:34 he shall t' plead their cause, that ‡
Eze 16: 9 I t' washed away thy blood from thee,
M't 3:12 he will t' purge his floor, and gather 1245
Lu 3:17 he will t' purge his floor, and will "
2Co 11: 6 been t' made manifest among*1722,3956
2Ti 3:17 t' furnished unto all good works. *1822

throughout
Ge 41:29 great plenty t' all the land of Egypt:
46 and went t' all the land of Egypt.
45: 8 and a ruler t' all the land of Egypt.*
Ex 5:12 abroad t' all the land of Egypt
7:19 may be blood t' all the land of Egypt,
21 was blood t' all the land of Egypt.
8:16 become lice t' all the land of Egypt.
17 became lice t' all the land of Egypt.

Ex 9: 9 upon beast, t' all the land of Egypt.
16 name may be declared t' all the earth.
22 herb of the field, t' the land of Egypt.
25 hail smote t' all the land of Egypt
12:14 feast to the Lord t' your generations;
29:42 burnt offering t' your generations
30: 8 before the Lord t' your generations.
10 upon it t' your generations:
21 and to his seed t' their generations.
31 oil unto me t' your generations.
31:13 me and you t' your generations;
16 the sabbath t' their generations,
32:27 and out from gate to gate t' the camp,
34: 3 let any man be seen t' all the mount;
35: 3 kindle no fire t' your habitations
36: 6 caused it to be proclaimed t' the camp,
37:19 t' the six branches going out of the*
40:15 priesthood t' their generations.
38 house of Israel, t' all their journeys.
Le 3:17 your generations t' all your dwellings,*
7:36 a statute for ever t' their generations.
10: 9 a statute for ever t' your generations:
17: 7 ever unto them t' their generations.
23:14 a statute for ever t' your generations
21 all your dwellings t' your generations
31 a statute for ever t' your generations
25: 9 the trumpet sound t' all your land.
10 proclaim liberty t' all the land unto
30 him that bought it t' his generations:
Nu 1:42 of Naphtali, t' their generations,*
52 by his own standard, t' their hosts.
2: 3 camp of Judah pitch t' their armies:*
9 and four hundred, t' their armies.*
16 hundred and fifty, t' their armies.*
24 and an hundred, t' their armies.*
32 numbered of the camps t' their hosts*
3:39 t' their families, all the males from a*
4:22 Gershon, t' the houses of their fathers,*
38 the sons of Gershon, t' their families,*
40 numbered of them, t' their families,*
42 of the sons of Merari, t' their families,*
10: 8 ordinance for ever t' your generations.
25 of all the camps t' their hosts:*
11:10 the people weep t' their families,
15:38 of their garments t' their generations,
18:23 a statute for ever t' your generations,
26: 2 and upward, t' their father's house,*
28:14 every month t' the months of the year.
21 for every lamb, t' the seven lambs:*
24 ye shall offer daily, t' the seven days,*
29 unto one lamb, t' the seven lambs;*
29: 4, 10 for one lamb, t' the seven lambs:*
31: 4 a thousand, t' all the tribes of Israel,
35:29 unto you t' your generations in all
De 16:18 thy God giveth thee, t' thy tribes:*
28:40 shalt have olive trees t' all thy coasts,
52 wherein thou trustedst, t' all thy land:
52 thee in all thy gates t' all thy land.
Jos 2:22 pursuers sought them t' all the way,
6:27 his fame was noised t' all the country.*
16: 1 up from Jericho t' mount Beth-el,*
22:14 a prince t' all the tribes of Israel;*
24: 3 and led him t' all the land of Canaan,
J'g 6:35 he sent messengers t' all Manasseh;
7:22 against his fellow, even t' the host:*
24 sent messengers t' all mount Ephraim,
20: 6 and sent her t' all the country of the
10 an hundred t' all the tribes of Israel,
1Sa 5:11 a deadly destruction t' all the city;
11: 7 sent them t' all the coasts of Israel
13: 3 Saul blew the trumpet t' all the land,
19 no smith found t' all the land of Israel:
23:23 out t' all the thousands of Judah.*
2Sa 8:14 t' all Edom put he garrisons, and all
15:10 sent spies t' all the tribes of Israel,
19: 9 were at strife t' all the tribes of Israel,
1Ki 1: 3 for a fair damsel t' all the coasts
6:38 house finished t' all the parts thereof,
15:22 made a proclamation t' all Judah;*
18: 6 the land between them to pass t' it:
22:36 there went a proclamation t' the host
2Ki 17: 5 of Assyria came up t' all the land,
1Ch 5:10 in their tents t' all the east land 5921
6:54 their dwelling places t' their castles*
60 t' their families were thirteen cities.
62 the sons of Gershom t' their families*
63 were given by lot, t' their families,*
7:40 t' the genealogy of them that were*
9:34 were chief t' their generations;
12:30 famous t' the house of their fathers.*
21: 4 Joab departed, and went t' all Israel,
12 destroying t' all the coasts of Israel.
22: 5 of fame and of glory t' all countries:
26: 6 that ruled t' the house of their father:*
27: 1 by month t' all the months of the year.
2Ch 8: 6 and t' all the land of his dominion.*
11:23 children t' all the countries of Judah
16: 9 run to and fro t' the whole earth,
17: 9 went about t' all the cities of Judah,
19 put in the fenced cities t' all Judah.
19: 5 t' all the fenced cities of Judah,
20: 3 and proclaimed a fast t' all Judah. 5921
25: 5 fathers, t' all Judah and Benjamin:*
26:14 for them t' all the host shields, *
30: 5 to make proclamation t' all Israel,
6 the king and his princes t' all Israel
22 they did eat t' the feast seven days,
31:20 And thus did Hezekiah t' all Judah,
34: 7 the idols t' all the land of Israel,
36:22 a proclamation t' all his kingdom,
Ezr 1: 1 a proclamation t' all his kingdom,
10: 7 And they made proclamation t' Judah
Es 1:20 shall be published t' all his empire,
3: 6 Jews that were t' the whole kingdom
9: 2 cities t' all the provinces of the king
4 his fame went out t' all the provinces;

Es 9:28 and kept t' every generation.
Ps 72: 5 and moon endure, t' all generations.
102:24 thy years are t' all generations.
135:13 memorial, O Lord, t' all generations.
145:13 dominion endureth t' all generations.
Jer 17: 3 high places for sin, t' all thy borders.
Eze 38:21 against him t' all my mountains, *
M't 4:24 And his fame went t' all Syria: *1519
M'r 1:28 fame spread abroad t' all the region*"
39 in their synagogues t' all Galilee, "
14: 9 be preached t' the whole world, "
Lu 1:65 t' all the hill country of Judæa. 1722
4:25 great famine was t' all the land; *1909
7:17 of him went forth t' all Judæa, *1722
17 and t' all the region round about.* "
8: 1 he went t' every city and village, *2596
39 and published t' the whole city how "
23: 5 the people, teaching t' all Jewry,
Joh 19:23 seam, woven from the top t'. 1223,3650
Ac 8: 1 scattered abroad t' the regions of 2596
9:31 had the churches rest t' all Judæa "
32 as Peter passed t' all quarters, he 1223
42 And it was known t' all Joppa; 2596
10:37 which was published t' all Judæa,
11:28 be great dearth t' all the world: *1909
13:49 was published t' all the region. 1223
14:24 after they had passed t' Pisidia, *1330
16: 6 when they had gone t' Phrygia * "
19:26 but almost t' all Asia, this Paul
24: 5 among all the Jews t' the world, 2596
26:20 and t' all the coast of Judæa, 1519
Ro 1: 8 is spoken of t' the whole world. 1722
9:17 might be declared t' all the earth.* "
2Co 8:18 is in the gospel t' all the churches;*1223
Eph 3:21 church by Christ Jesus t' all ages,*1519
1Pe 1: 1 to the strangers scattered t' Pontus,*

throw See also OVERTHROW; THREW; THROWING; THROWN.
J'g 2: 2 ye shall t' down their altars: *5422
6:25 t' down the altar of Baal that thy 2040
2Sa 20:15 battered the wall, to t' it down. 5307
2Ki 9:33 And he said, T' her down. So 8058
Jer 1:10 and to destroy, and to t' down, *2040
31:28 to t' down, and to destroy, and to * "
Eze 16:39 shall t' down thine eminent place, "
Mic 5:11 and t' down all thy strong holds: "
Mal 1: 4 They shall build, but I will t' down;"

throwing
Nu 35:17 if he smite him with t' a stone, *3027

thrown See also OVERTHROWN.
Ex 15: 1, 21 rider hath he t' into the sea. 7411
J'g 6:32 because he hath t' down his altar.*5422
2Sa 20:21 his head shall be t' to thee over 7993
1Ki 19:10, 14 covenant, t' down thine altars, 2040
Jer 31:40 nor t' down any more for ever.
33: 4 which are t' down by the mounts,*5422
50:15 are fallen, her walls are t' down: 2040
La 2: 2 he hath t' down in his wrath the "
17 hath t' down, and hath not pitied: "
Eze 29: 5 leave thee t' into the wilderness, ‡
38:20 the mountains shall be t' down, 2040
Na 1: 6 and the rocks are t' down by him.*5422
M't 24: 2 another, that shall not be t' down. 2647
M'r 13: 2 another, that shall not be t' down. "
Lu 4:35 the devil had t' him in the midst, 4496
21: 6 another, that shall not be t' down. 2647
Re 18:21 that great city Babylon be t' down,*906

thrust See also THRUSTETH.
Ex 11: 1 he shall surely t' you out hence 1644
12:39 because they were t' out of Egypt, "
Nu 22:25 she t' herself unto the wall, and 3905
25: 8 tent, and t' both of them through, 1856
35:20 But if he t' him of hatred, or hurl 1920
22 t' him suddenly without enmity, "
De 13: 5 to t' thee out of the way which *5080
10 to t' thee away from the Lord thy * "
15:17 t' it through his ear unto the door,5414
33:27 he shall t' out the enemy from 1644
J'g 3:21 right thigh, and t' it into his belly:8628
6:38 t' the fleece together, and wringed*2115
9:41 Zebul t' out Gaal and his brethren,*1644
54 his young man t' him through, 1856
11: 2 they t' out Jephthah, and said *1644
1Sa 11: 2 I may t' out all your right eyes, *5365
31: 4 and t' me through therewith; 1856
4 come and t' me through,
2Sa 2:16 and t' his sword in his fellow's side;
18:14 and t' them through the heart of 8628
23: 6 be all of them as thorns t' away, 5074
1Ki 2:27 So Solomon t' out Abiathar from 1644
2Ki 4:27 Gehazi came near to t' her away. 1920
1Ch 10: 4 and t' me through therewith; 1856
2Ch 26:20 and they t' him out from thence; 926
Ps 118:13 Thou hast t' sore at me that I 1760
Isa 13:15 that is found shall be t' through; 1856
14:19 are slain, t' through with a sword, 2944
Jer 51: 4 that are t' through in her streets. 1856
Eze 16:40 t' thee through with their swords. 1333
34:21 ye have t' with side and with 1920
46:18 to t' them out of their possession; 3238
Joe 2: 8 Neither shall one t' another; they 1766
Zec 13: 3 begat him shall t' him through 1856
Lu 4:29 rose up, and t' him out of the city,*1544
5: 3 would t' out a little from the land.*1877
10:15 heaven, shall be t' down to hell. *2601
13:28 of God, and you yourselves t' out.*1544
Joh 20:25 nails, and t' my hand into his side,* 906
27 thy hand, and t' it into my side: * "
Ac 7:27 his neighbour wrong t' him away, 683
39 not obey, but t' him from them, "
16:24 t' them into the inner prison, * 906
37 and now do they t' us out privily?*1544
27:39 it were possible, to t' in the ship. *1856
Heb 12:20 stoned, or t' through with a dart: *2700

Re 14:15 T' in thy sickle, and reap: for *3992
16 cloud t' in his sickle on the earth;* 906
18 T' in thy sharp sickle, and gather*3992
19 the angel t' in his sickle into the * 906

thrusteth
Job 32:13 God t' him down, not man. *5086

thumb See also THUMBS.
Ex 29:20 and upon the t' of their right hand, 931
Le 8:23 and upon the t' of his right hand, "
14:14, 17, 25, 28 the t' of his right hand, "

thumbs
Le 8:24 upon the t' of their right hands, * 931
J'g 1: 6 cut off his t' and his great toes. 931,3027
7 t' and their great toes cut off, " "

Thummim (*thum'-mim*)
Ex 28:30 of judgment the Urim and the T': 8550
Le 8: 8 breastplate the Urim and the T'. "
De 33: 8 Let thy T' and thy Urim be with "
Ezr 2:63 a priest with Urim and with T'. "
Ne 7:65 up a priest with Urim and T'. "

thunder See also THUNDERBOLTS; THUNDERED; THUNDERETH; THUNDERINGS; THUNDERS.
Ex 9:23 the Lord sent t' and hail, and the 6963
29 and the t' shall cease, neither shall* "
1Sa 2:10 of heaven shall he t' upon them: 7481
7:10 the Lord thundered with a great t' 6963
12:17 Lord, and he shall send t' and rain; "
18 the Lord sent t' and rain that day: "
Job 26:14 but the t' of his power who can 7482
28:26 a way for the lightning of the t': 6963
38:25 or a way for the lightning of t'; "
39:19 hast thou clothed his neck with t'?*7483
25 the t' of the captains, and the 7482
40: 9 thou t' with a voice like him? 7481
Ps 77:18 voice of thy t' was in the heaven: 7482
81: 7 thee in the secret place of t': "
104: 7 voice of thy t' they hasted away. "
Isa 29: 6 visited of the Lord of hosts with t', "
M'r 3:17 Boanerges,... The sons of t': 1027
Re 6: 1 I heard, as it were the noise of t', "
14: 2 waters, and as a voice of a great t': "

thunderbolts
Ps 78:48 the hail, and their flocks to hot t'. 7565

thundered
1Sa 7:10 the Lord t' with a great thunder 7481
2Sa 22:14 The Lord t' from heaven, and "
Ps 18:13 The Lord also t' in the heavens, "
Joh 12:29 and heard it, said that it t': 1027,1096

thundereth
Job 37: 4 t' with the voice of his excellency;7481
5 God t' marvellously with his voice;"
Ps 29: 3 the God of glory t': the Lord is "

thunderings
Ex 9:28 be no more mighty t' and hail; 6963
20:18 And all the people saw the t', and "
Re 4: 5 lightnings and t' and voices: *1027
8: 5 and there were voices, and t', and* "
11:19 were lightnings, and voices, and t',* "
19: 6 and as the voice of mighty t', * "

thunders
Ex 9:33 t' and hail ceased, and the rain 6963
34 and the hail and the t' were ceased,"
19:16 that there were t' and lightnings, "
Re 10: 3 cried, seven t' uttered their voices.1027
4 seven t' had uttered their voices, "
4 things which the seven t' uttered, "
16:18 were voices, and t', and lightnings;"

thus
Ge 2: 1 T' the heavens and the earth were*
6:22 T' did Noah; according to all that
19:36 T' were both the daughters of Lot
20:16 with all other: t' she was reproved.*
24:30 T' spake the man unto me; that 3541
25:22 she said, If it be so, why am I t'? *2088
25:34 t' Esau despised his birthright. *
31: 8 If he said t', The speckled shall 3541
8 if he said t', The ringstraked shall "
9 T' God hath taken away the cattle of
40 T' I was; in the day the drought
41 T' have I been twenty years in *2088
32: 4 T' shall ye speak unto my lord 3541
4 Thy servant Jacob saith t', I have "
36: 8 T' dwelt Esau in mount Seir: Esau*
37:35 T' his father wept for him. *
42:25 the way: and t' did he unto them. 3651
45: 9 T' saith thy son Joseph, God hath 3541
Ex 3:14 T' shalt thou say unto the "
4:22 T' saith the Lord, Israel is my son, "
5: 1 T' saith the Lord God of Israel, "
10 T' saith Pharaoh, I will not give "
15 dealest thou t' with thy servants? "
8: 1, 20 T' saith the Lord, Let my "
9: 1, 13 T' saith the Lord God of the "
10: 3 T' saith the Lord God of the "
11: 4 T' saith the Lord, About midnight "
12:11 t' shall ye eat it; with your loins 3602
50 T' did all the children of Israel; as
14:11 hast thou dealt t' with us, to carry 2063
30 T' the Lord saved Israel that day out
19: 3 T' shalt thou say to the house of 3541
20:22 T' thou shalt say unto the "
26:17 t' shalt thou make for all the 3651
24 t' shall it be for them both; they
29:35 t' shalt thou do unto Aaron, and to his
32:27 T' saith the Lord God of Israel, 3541
36:22 t' did he make for all the boards 3651
29 t' he did to both of them in both the"
39:32 T' was all the work of the tabernacle
40:16 T' did Moses: according to all that
Le 15:31 T' shall ye separate the children of
16: 3 T' shall Aaron come into the holy*2063

Nu 4:19 t' do unto them, that they may live,
49 t' were they numbered of him, as the
8: 7 t' shalt thou do unto them, to 3541
14 T' shalt thou separate the Levites
26 T' shalt thou do unto the Levites 3602
10:28 T' were the journeyings of the 428
11:15 if thou deal t' with me, kill me, 3602
15:11 T' shall it be done for one bullock, "
18:26 T' speak unto the Levites, and say*
28 T' ye also shall offer an heave 3651
20:14 T' saith thy brother Israel, Thou 3541
21 T' Edom refused to give Israel
21:31 T' Israel dwelt in the land of the
22:16 T' saith Balak the son of Zippor, 3541
23: 5 unto Balak, and t' thou shalt speak."
16 Go again unto Balak, and say t'. "
32: 8 T' did your fathers, when I sent "
De 7: 5 t' shall ye deal with them; ye shall "
9:25 T' I fell down before the Lord forty*
20:15 T' shalt thou do unto all the 3651
29:24 the Lord done t' unto this land? 3662
32: 6 Do ye t' requite the Lord, O 2063
Jos 2: 4 said t', There came men unto me,*3651
6: 3 once. T' shalt thou do six days. 3541
7:10 liest thou t' upon thy face? 2088
13 for t' saith the Lord God of Israel,3541
20 Israel, and t' and t' have I done: 2063
10:25 t' shall the Lord do to all your 3602
16: 5 according to their families was t':
21:13 T' they gave to the children of Aaron*
42 them: t' were all these cities. 3651
22:16 T' saith the whole congregation of3541
24: 2 T' saith the Lord God of Israel, "
J'g 6: 8 T' saith the Lord God of Israel, I "
8: 1 Why hast thou served us t', 1697,2007
28 T' was Midian subdued before the*
9:56 T' God rendered the wickedness of
11:15 T' saith Jephthah, Israel took not3541
33 T' the children of Ammon were *
13:18 askest thou t' after my name, *2088
18: 4 T'...dealeth Micah with me, 2090
4 and t' dealeth Micah with me, 2088
20:43 T' they inclosed the Benjamites *
1Sa 2:27 T' saith the Lord, Did I plainly 3541
9: 9 t' he spake, Come, and let us go to "
10:18 T' saith the Lord God of Israel, "
11: 9 T' shall ye say unto the men of "
14: 9 If they say t' unto us, Tarry until "
10 But if they say t', Come up unto us;"
15: 2 T' saith the Lord of hosts, I "
18:25 T' shall ye say to David, The king "
20: 7 If he say t', It is well; thy servant "
22 But if I say t' unto the young man, "
25: 6 t' shall ye say to him that liveth in "
26:18 doth my lord t' pursue after his *2088
2Sa 6:22 I will yet be more vile than t', 2063
7: 5 T' saith the Lord, Shalt thou 3541
8 T' saith the Lord of hosts, I took "
11:25 T' shalt thou say unto Joab, Let "
12: 7 T' saith the Lord God of Israel, I "
11 T' saith the Lord, Behold, I will "
31 t' did he unto all the cities of the 3651
15:26 But if he t' say, I have no delight 3541
16: 7 And t' said Shimei when he cursed, "
17:15 T' and t' did Ahithophel counsel 2063
15 and t' and t' have I counselled. "
21 for t' hath Ahithophel counselled 3602
18:14 Joab, I may not tarry t' with thee. 3651
33 t' he said, O my son Absalom, 3541
24:12 T' saith the Lord, I offer thee "
1Ki 1:48 also t' said the king, Blessed be 3602
2:30 T' saith the king, Come forth. 3541
30 T' said Joab, and t' he answered "
3:22 T' they spake before the king.
5:11 t' gave Solomon to Hiram year by 3541
9: 8 the Lord done t' unto this land, 3602
11:31 for t' saith the Lord, the God of 3541
12:10 T' shalt thou speak unto this "
10 t' shalt thou say unto them, My "
24 T' saith the Lord, Ye shall not go "
13: 2 O altar, altar, t' saith the Lord; "
21 T' saith the Lord, Forasmuch as "
14: 5 t'...shalt thou say unto her: 2090
5 and t' shalt thou say unto her: 2088
7 T' saith the Lord God of Israel, 3541
16:12 T' did Zimri destroy all the house
17:14 For t' saith the Lord God of Israel,3541
20: 2 said unto him, T' saith Ben-hadad, "
5 T' speaketh Ben-hadad, saying, "
13 T' saith the Lord, Hast thou seen "
14 T' saith the Lord, Even by the "
28 T' saith the Lord, Because the "
42 T' saith the Lord, Because thou "
21:19 T' saith the Lord, Hast thou killed,"
19 T' saith the Lord, In the place "
22:11 T' saith the Lord, With these shalt "
27 T' saith the king, Put this fellow "
2Ki 1: 4 Now therefore t' saith the Lord, "
6 T' saith the Lord, Is it not because"
11 t' hath the king said, Come down "
16 T' saith the Lord, Forasmuch as "
2:21 T' saith the Lord, I have healed "
3:16 T' saith the Lord, Make this valley "
17 t' saith the Lord, Ye shall not see "
4:43 t' saith the Lord, They shall eat, "
5: 4 T' and t' said the maid that is of 2063
7: 1 T' saith the Lord, To morrow 3541
9: 3 T' saith the Lord, I have anointed "
6 T' saith the Lord God of Israel, "
12 he said, T' and t' spake he to me. 2063
12 T' saith the Lord, I have anointed3541
18, 19 T' saith the king, Is it peace? "
10:28 T' Jehu destroyed Baal out of
16:16 T' did Urijah the priest, according
18:19 T' saith the great king, the king 3541
29 T' saith the king, Let not "

2Ki 18: 31 t' saith the king of Assyria, Make 3541
19: 3 T' saith Hezekiah, This day is a "
6 T' shall ye say to your master, "
6 T' saith the Lord, Be not afraid of "
10 T' shall ye speak to Hezekiah king "
20 T' saith the Lord God of Israel, "
32 t' saith the Lord concerning the "
20: 1 T' saith the Lord, Set thine house "
5 T' saith the Lord, the God of David "
21: 12 t' saith the Lord God of Israel, "
22: 15 T' saith the Lord God of Israel, "
16 T' saith the Lord, Behold, I will "
18 of the Lord, t' shall ye say to him, "
18 T' saith the Lord God of Israel, "
1Ch 15: 28 T' all Israel brought up the ark of
17: 4 T' saith the Lord, Thou shalt not 3541
7 t' shalt thou say unto my servant "
7 T' saith the Lord of hosts, I took "
18: 6, 13 T' the Lord preserved David *
21: 10 T' saith the Lord, I offer thee 3541
11 T' saith the Lord, Choose thee "
24: 4 Ithamar; and t' were they divided.
5 T' were they divided by lot, one sort
29: 26 T' David the son of Jesse reigned*
2Ch 4: 18 T' Solomon made all these vessels
5: 1 T' all the work that Solomon made
7: 11 T' Solomon finished the house of the
21 the Lord done t' unto this land, 3602
10: 10 T' shalt thou answer the people 3541
10 t' shalt thou say unto them, My "
11: 4 T' saith the Lord, Ye shall not go "
12: 5 T' saith the Lord, Ye have forsaken "
13: 18 T' the children of Israel were brought
18: 10 T' saith the Lord, With these thou 3541
26 T' saith the king, Put this fellow "
19: 9 T' shall ye do in the fear of the "
20: 15 T' saith the Lord unto you, Be not "
21: 12 T' saith the Lord God of David thy "
24: 11 T' they did day by day, and "
20 T' saith God, Why transgress ye "
22 T' Joash the king remembered not
31: 20 t' did Hezekiah throughout all 2063
32: 10 T' saith Sennacherib king of 3541
22 T' the Lord saved Hezekiah and
34: 23 T' saith the Lord God of Israel, 3541
24 T' saith the Lord, Behold, I will "
26 T' saith the Lord God of Israel "
36: 23 T' saith Cyrus king of Persia, All "
Ezr 1: 2 T' saith Cyrus king of Persia, The "
5: 3 and said t' unto them, Who hath 3652
7 unto him, wherein was written t'; 1836
9 and said unto them t', Who 3660
11 t' they returned us answer, saying, "
6: 2 therein was a record t' written: 3652
Ne 5: 13 even t' be he shaken out, and 3602
13: 18 Did not your fathers t', and did 3541
30 T' cleansed I them from all strangers,
Es 1: 18 T' shall there arise too much *
2: 13 t' came every maiden unto the *2088
6: 9 T' shall it be done to the man 3602
11 T' shall it be done unto the man "
9: 5 T' the Jews smote all their enemies*
Job 1: 5 hearts. T' did Job continually. 3602
27: 12 then are ye t' altogether vain? *2088
Ps 38: 14 T' I was as a man that heareth not,*
63: 4 T' will I bless thee while I live: *3651
73: 15 If I say, I will speak t'; behold, 3644
21 T' my heart was grieved, and I *3588
106: 20 T' they changed their glory into the
29 T' they provoked him to anger with
39 T' were they defiled with their own
128: 4 t' shall the man be blessed that 3651
Isa 7: 7 T' saith the Lord God, It shall 3541
8: 11 spake t' to me with a strong hand, "
10: 24 t' saith the Lord God of hosts, "
21: 6 t' hath the Lord said unto me, Go, "
16 For t' hath the Lord said unto me, "
22: 15 T' saith the Lord God of hosts, Go, "
24: 13 When t' it shall be in the midst of "
28: 16 Therefore t' saith the Lord God, "
29: 22 t' saith the Lord, who redeemed "
30: 12 t' saith the Holy One of Israel, "
15 t' saith the Lord God, the Holy One "
31: 4 t' hath the Lord spoken unto me, "
36: 4 T' saith the great king, the king of "
14 T' saith the king, Let not Hezekiah "
16 t' saith the king of Assyria, Make "
37: 3 T' saith Hezekiah, This day is a "
6 T' shall ye say unto your master, "
6 T' saith the Lord, Be not afraid of "
10 T' shall ye speak to Hezekiah king "
21 T' saith the Lord God of Israel, "
33 t' saith the Lord concerning the "
38: 1 T' saith the Lord, Set thine house "
5 T' saith the Lord, the God of David "
42: 5 T' saith God the Lord, he that "
43: 1 now t' saith the Lord that created "
14 T' saith the Lord, your redeemer, "
16 T' saith the Lord, which maketh a "
44: 2 T' saith the Lord that made thee, "
6 T' saith the Lord the King of Israel, "
24 T' saith the Lord, thy redeemer, "
45: 1 T' saith the Lord to his anointed, "
11 T' saith the Lord, the Holy One of "
14 T' saith the Lord, The labour of "
18 For t' saith the Lord that created "
47: 15 T' shall they be unto thee with 3651
48: 17 T' saith the Lord, thy Redeemer, 3541
49: 7 T' saith the Lord, the Redeemer of "
8 T' saith the Lord, In an acceptable "
22 T' saith the Lord God, Behold, I "
25 t' saith the Lord, Even the captives "
50: 1 T' saith the Lord, Where is the bill "
51: 22 T' saith thy Lord the Lord, and "
52: 3 For t' saith the Lord, Ye have sold "
4 t' saith the Lord God, My people "

Isa 56: 1 T' saith the Lord, Keep ye 3541
4 t' saith the Lord unto the eunuchs "
57: 15 For t' saith the high and lofty One "
65: 8 T' saith the Lord, As the new wine "
13 Therefore t' saith the Lord God, "
66: 1 T' saith the Lord, The heaven is "
12 For t' saith the Lord, Behold, I will "
Jer 2: 2 T' saith the Lord; I remember "
5 T' saith the Lord, What iniquity "
4: 3 For t' saith the Lord to the men of "
27 For t' hath the Lord said, The "
5: 13 them: t' shall it be done unto them. "
14 t' saith the Lord God of hosts, "
6: 6 For t' hath the Lord of hosts said, "
9 T' saith the Lord of hosts, They "
16 T' saith the Lord, Stand ye in the "
21 Therefore t' saith the Lord, Behold, "
22 T' saith the Lord, Behold, a people "
7: 3 T' saith the Lord of hosts, the God "
20 Therefore t' saith the Lord God; "
21 T' saith the Lord of hosts, the God "
8: 4 say unto them, T' saith the Lord; "
9: 7, 15 t' saith the Lord of hosts, "
17 T' saith the Lord of hosts, Consider "
22 T' saith the Lord, Even the "
23 T' saith the Lord, Let not the wise "
10: 2 T' saith the Lord, Learn not the "
11 T' shall ye say unto them, The 1836
18 For t' saith the Lord, Behold, I 3541
11: 3 T' saith the Lord God of Israel; "
11 Therefore t' saith the Lord, Behold, "
21 Therefore t' saith the Lord of the "
22 t' saith the Lord of hosts, Behold, "
12: 14 T' saith the Lord against all mine "
13: 1 T' saith the Lord unto me, Go and "
9 T' saith the Lord, After this "
12 T' saith the Lord God of Israel, "
13 T' saith the Lord, Behold, I will "
14: 10 T' saith the Lord unto this people, "
10 T' have they loved to wander, *3651
15 t' saith the Lord concerning the 3541
15: 19 t' saith the Lord, If thou return, "
16: 3 t' saith the Lord concerning the "
5 t' saith the Lord, Enter not into the "
9 t' saith the Lord of hosts, the God "
17: 5 T' saith the Lord; Cursed be the "
19 T' said the Lord unto me; Go and "
21 T' saith the Lord; Take heed to "
18: 11 saying, T' saith the Lord; Behold, "
13 Therefore t' saith the Lord; Ask ye "
23 deal t' with them in the time of thine*
19: 1 T' saith the Lord, Go and get a 3541
3 T' saith the Lord of hosts, the God "
11 them, T' saith the Lord of hosts; "
12 T' will I do unto this place, saith 3651
15 T' saith the Lord of hosts, the 3541
20: 4 t' saith the Lord, Behold, I will "
21: 3 them, T' shall ye say to Zedekiah: "
4 T' saith the Lord God of Israel; "
8 thou shalt say, T' saith the Lord; "
12 house of David, t' saith the Lord; "
22: 1 T' saith the Lord; Go down to the "
3 T' saith the Lord; Execute ye "
6 t' saith the Lord unto the king's "
8 Lord done t' unto this great city? 3602
11 For t' saith the Lord touching 3541
18 t' saith the Lord concerning "
30 T' saith the Lord, Write ye this "
23: 2 t' saith the Lord God of Israel "
15 Therefore t' saith the Lord of hosts "
16 T' saith the Lord of hosts, Hearken "
35 T' shall ye say every one to his "
37 T' shalt thou say to the prophet, "
38 therefore t' saith the Lord; "
24: 5 T' saith the Lord, the God of "
8 t' saith the Lord, So will I give "
25: 8 t' saith the Lord of hosts; Because "
15 t' saith the Lord God of Israel unto "
27 T' saith the Lord of hosts, the God "
28 T' saith the Lord of hosts; Ye shall "
32 T' saith the Lord of hosts, Behold, "
26: 2 T' saith the Lord; Stand in the "
4 T' saith the Lord; If ye will not "
18 T' saith the Lord of hosts; Zion "
19 T' might we procure great evil "
27: 2 T' saith the Lord to me; Make 3541
4 T' saith the Lord of hosts, the God "
4 T' shall ye say unto your masters; "
16 T' saith the Lord; Hearken not to "
19 For t' saith the Lord of hosts "
21 t' saith the Lord of hosts, the God "
28: 2 T' speaketh the Lord of hosts, the "
11 T' saith the Lord; Even so will I 3602
13 T' saith the Lord; Thou hast 3541
14 t' saith the Lord of hosts, the God "
16 t' saith the Lord; Behold, I will "
29: 4 T' saith the Lord of hosts, the God "
8 t' saith the Lord of hosts, the God "
10 For t' saith the Lord, That after "
16 that t' saith the Lord of the king "
17 T' saith the Lord of hosts; Behold, "
21 T' saith the Lord of hosts, the God "
24 T' shalt thou also speak to Shemaiah*
25 T' speaketh the Lord of hosts, the 3541
31 T' saith the Lord concerning "
32 Therefore t' saith the Lord; Behold, "
30: 2 T' speaketh the Lord God of Israel, "
5 t' saith the Lord; We have heard a "
12 t' saith the Lord, Thy bruise is "
18 T' saith the Lord; Behold, I will "
31: 2 T' saith the Lord, The people "
7 For t' saith the Lord; Sing with "
15 T' saith the Lord; A voice was "
16 T' saith the Lord; Refrain thy "
18 heard Ephraim bemoaning himself t'; "
23 T' saith the Lord of hosts, the 3541

Jer 31: 35 T' saith the Lord, which giveth the 3541
37 T' saith the Lord; If heaven above "
32: 3 T' saith the Lord, Behold, I will "
14 T' saith the Lord of hosts, the God "
15 t' saith the Lord of hosts, the God "
28 t' saith the Lord; Behold, I will "
36 And now therefore t' saith the Lord, "
42 t' saith the Lord; Like as I have "
33: 2 T' saith the Lord the maker "
4 For t' saith the Lord, the God of "
10 T' saith the Lord; Again there "
12 T' saith the Lord of hosts; Again "
17 t' saith the Lord; David shall never; "
20 T' saith the Lord; If ye can break "
24 t' they have despised my people, that
25 T' saith the Lord; If my covenant 3541
34: 2 T' saith the Lord, the God of Israel; "
2 T' saith the Lord; Behold, I will "
4 T' saith the Lord of thee, Thou "
13 T' saith the Lord, the God of Israel; "
17 t' saith the Lord; ye have not "
35: 8 T' have we obeyed the voice of *
13 T' saith the Lord of hosts, the 3541
17 t' saith the Lord God of hosts, the "
18 T' saith the Lord of hosts, the God "
36: 29 T' saith the Lord; Thou hast "
30 t' saith the Lord of Jehoiakim king "
37: 7 T' saith the Lord, the God of Israel; "
7 T' shall ye say to the king of Judah, "
9 T' saith the Lord; Deceive not "
21 T' Jeremiah remained in the court of
38: 2 T' saith the Lord, He that 3541
3 T' saith the Lord, This city shall "
4 t' he weakeneth the hands of *5921,3651
17 T' saith the Lord, the God of 3541
39: 16 T' saith the Lord of hosts, the God "
42: 9 T' saith the Lord, the God of Israel, "
15 T' saith the Lord of hosts, the God "
18 For t' saith the Lord of hosts, the "
43: 7 t' came they even to Tahpanhes. *
10 T' saith the Lord of hosts, the 3541
44: 2 T' saith the Lord of hosts, the God "
7 now t' saith the Lord, the God "
11 t' saith the Lord of hosts, the God "
25 T' saith the Lord of hosts, the God "
30 T' saith the Lord; Behold, I will "
45: 2 T' saith the Lord, the God of Israel, "
4 T' shalt thou say unto him, The "
4 Lord saith t'; Behold, that which "
47: 2 T' saith the Lord; Behold, waters "
48: 1 Moab t' saith the Lord of hosts, "
40 t' saith the Lord; Behold, he shall "
47 T' far is the judgment of Moab. 2008
49: 1 t' saith the Lord; Hath Israel no 3541
7 Edom, t' saith the Lord of hosts; "
12 For t' saith the Lord; Behold, they "
28 t' saith the Lord; Arise ye, go up to "
35 T' saith the Lord of hosts; Behold, "
50: 18 t' saith the Lord of hosts, the God "
33 T' saith the Lord of hosts; The "
51: 1 T' saith the Lord; Behold, I will "
4 T' the slain shall fall in the land of*
33 t' saith the Lord of hosts, the God 3541
36 t' saith the Lord; Behold, I will "
58 T' saith the Lord of hosts; The "
64 T' shall Babylon sink, and shall 3602
64 T' far are the words of Jeremiah. 2008
52: 27 T' Judah was carried away captive*
Eze 1: 11 T' were their faces: and their wings*
2: 4 unto them, T' saith the Lord God. 3541
3: 11 T' saith the Lord God; whether "
27 T' saith the Lord God; He that "
4: 13 t' shall the children of Israel eat 3602
5: 5 T' saith the Lord God; This is 3541
7 t' saith the Lord God; Because ye "
8 t' saith the Lord God; Behold, I, "
13 T' shall mine anger be accomplished,
6: 3 T' saith the Lord God to the 3541
11 T' saith the Lord God; Smite with "
12 t' will I accomplish my fury upon
7: 2 t' saith the Lord God unto the 3541
5 T' saith the Lord God; An evil, an "
11: 5 unto me, Speak; T' saith the Lord; "
5 T' have ye said, O house of Israel: 3651
7 Therefore t' saith the Lord God; 3541
16 T' saith the Lord God; Although I "
17 T' saith the Lord God; I will even "
12: 10 T' saith the Lord God; This "
19 T' saith the Lord God of the "
23 T' saith the Lord God; I will make "
28 T' saith the Lord God; There shall "
13: 3 T' saith the Lord God; Woe unto "
8, 13 Therefore t' saith the Lord God; "
15 T' will I accomplish my wrath upon
18 T' saith the Lord God; Woe to the 3541
20 Wherefore t' saith the Lord God; "
14: 4 T' saith the Lord God; Every man "
6 T' saith the Lord God; Repent, and "
15: 6 Therefore t' saith the Lord God; As "
16: 3 say, T' saith the Lord God unto "
13 T' wast thou decked with gold and
19 and t' it was, saith the Lord God.
36 T' saith the Lord God; Because 3541
59 For t' saith the Lord God; I will "
17: 3 T' saith the Lord God; A great "
9 T' saith the Lord God; Shall it "
19 Therefore t' saith the Lord God; As "
22 T' saith the Lord God; I will also "
20: 3 T' saith the Lord God; Are ye "
5 T' saith the Lord God; In the day "
27 T' saith the Lord God; Yet in this "
30 T' saith the Lord God; Are ye "
39 t' saith the Lord God; Go ye, serve "
47 T' saith the Lord God; Behold, I "
21: 3 T' saith the Lord; Behold, I am "
9 T' saith the Lord; Say, A sword, a "

Eze 21:24 t' saith the Lord God; Because ye 3541
26 T' saith the Lord God; Remove the "
28 T' saith the Lord God concerning "
22: 3 T' saith the Lord God, The city "
19 t' saith the Lord God; Because ye "
28 T' saith the Lord God, when the "
23: 4 T' were their names; Samaria is *
7 T' she committed her whoredoms*
21 T' thou calledst to remembrance the
22 t' saith the Lord God; Behold, I 3541
27 T' will I make thy lewdness to cease
28 t' saith the Lord God; Behold, I 3541
32 T' saith the Lord God; Thou shalt "
35 Therefore t' saith the Lord God; "
39 t' have they done in the midst of "
46 t' saith the Lord God; I will bring "
48 T' will I cause lewdness to cease out
24: 3 T' saith the Lord God; Set on a 3541
6 Wherefore t' saith the Lord God; "
9 Therefore t' saith the Lord God; "
21 T' saith the Lord God; Behold, I "
24 T' Ezekiel is unto you a sign according
25: 3 T' saith the Lord God; Because 3541
6 For t' saith the Lord God; Because "
8, 12 T' saith the Lord God; Because "
13 t' saith the Lord God; I will also "
15 T' saith the Lord God; Because the "
16 t' saith the Lord God; Behold, I "
26: 3 t' saith the Lord God; Behold, I am "
7 For t' saith the Lord God; Behold, "
15 T' saith the Lord God to Tyrus; "
19 t' saith the Lord God; When I shall "
27: 3 T' saith the Lord God; O Tyrus, "
28: 2 T' saith the Lord God; Because "
6 Therefore t' saith the Lord God; "
12 T' saith the Lord God; Thou "
22 T' saith the Lord God; Behold, I "
25 T' saith the Lord God; When I "
29: 3 T' saith the Lord God; Behold, I "
8 Therefore t' saith the Lord God; "
13 Yet t' saith the Lord God; At the "
19 Therefore t' saith the Lord God; "
30: 2 T' saith the Lord God; Howl ye, "
6 T' saith the Lord; They also that "
10, 13 T' saith the Lord God; I will "
19 T' will I execute judgments in Egypt:
22 Therefore t' saith the Lord God; 3541
31: 7 T' was he fair in his greatness, in the
10 Therefore t' saith the Lord God; 3541
15 T' saith the Lord God; In the day "
18 To whom art thou t' like in glory 3602
32: 3 T' saith the Lord God; I will 3541
11 For t' saith the Lord God; The "
33:10 T' ye speak, saying, If our 3651
25 T' saith the Lord God; Ye eat 3541
27 Say thou t' unto them, "
27 T' saith the Lord God; As I live, "
34: 2 T' saith the Lord God unto the "
10 T' saith the Lord God; Behold, I "
11, 17 t' saith the Lord God; Behold, "
20 t' saith the Lord God unto them; "
30 T' shall they know that I the Lord*
35: 3 T' saith the Lord God; Behold, O 3541
7 T' will I make mount Seir most
13 T' with your mouth ye have boasted*
14 T' saith the Lord God; When the 3541
36: 2, 3 T' saith the Lord God; Because "
4 T' saith the Lord God to the "
5 Therefore t' saith the Lord God; "
6 T' saith the Lord God; Behold, I "
7 t' saith the Lord God; I have lifted "
13 T' saith the Lord God; Because "
22 T' saith the Lord God; I do not "
33 T' saith the Lord God; In the day "
37 T' saith the Lord God; I will yet "
37: 5 T' saith the Lord God unto these "
12, 19, 21 T' saith the Lord God; "
38: 3 T' saith the Lord God; Behold, I "
10 T' saith the Lord God; It shall "
14 T' saith the Lord God; In that day "
17 T' saith the Lord God; Art thou he "
23 T' will I magnify myself, and sanctify*
39: 1 T' saith the Lord God; Behold, I 3541
16 T' shall they cleanse the land.
17 t' saith the Lord God; Speak unto 3541
20 T' ye shall be filled at my table with*
25 t' saith the Lord God; Now will I 3541
43:18 t' saith the Lord God; These are "
20 t' shalt thou cleanse and purge it.
44: 6 T' saith the Lord God; O ye house 3541
9 T' saith the Lord God; No stranger, "
45: 9 T' saith the Lord God; Let it "
18 T' saith the Lord God; In the first "
46: 1 T' saith the Lord God; The gate of "
15 T' shall they prepare the lamb, and
16 T' saith the Lord God; If the 3541
47:13 T' saith the Lord God; This shall "
Da 1:16 T' Melzar took away the portion of*
2:24 said t' unto him; Destroy not the 3652
25 said t' unto him; I have found a "
4:10 T' were the visions of mine head in
14 He cried aloud, and said t', Hew 3652
6: 6 and said t' unto him, King Darius, "
7: 5 they said t' unto it, Arise, devour "
23 T' he said, The fourth beast shall "
11:17 upright ones with him; t' shall he do:*
39 T' shall he do in the most strong holds*
Ho 10: 4 t' judgment springeth up as hemlock *
Am 1: 3, 6, 11, 13 T' saith the Lord; For 3541
2: 1, 4, 6 T' saith the Lord; For three "
11 Is it not even t', O ye children of 2063
3:11 Therefore t' saith the Lord God; 3541
12 T' saith the Lord; As the shepherd "
4:12 Therefore t' will I do unto thee, O "
5: 3 t' saith the Lord God; The city that "
4 t' saith the Lord unto the house of "
Am 5:16 the Lord, saith t'; Wailing shall be 3541
7: 1, 4 T' hath the Lord God shewed "
7 T' he shewed me: and, behold, the "
11 For t' Amos saith, Jeroboam shall "
17 t' saith the Lord; Thy wife shall "
8: 1 T' hath the Lord God shewed unto "
Ob 1 T' saith the Lord God concerning "
Mic 2: 3 t' saith the Lord; Behold, against "
3: 5 T' saith the Lord concerning the "
5: 6 t' shall he deliver us from the *
Na 1:12 T' saith the Lord; Though they 3541
12 yet t' shall they be cut down, *3651
Zec 1: 3, 4 T' saith the Lord of hosts; 3541
14 T' saith the Lord of hosts; I am "
16 Therefore t' saith the Lord; I am "
17 T' saith the Lord of hosts; My "
2: 8 For t' saith the Lord of hosts; After "
3: 7 T' saith the Lord of hosts; If thou "
6:12 T' speaketh the Lord of hosts, "
7: 9 T' speaketh the Lord of hosts, "
14 T' the land was desolate after them,
8: 2 T' saith the Lord of hosts; I was 3541
3 T' saith the Lord; I am returned "
4 T' saith the Lord of hosts; There "
6 T' saith the Lord of hosts; If it be "
7 T' saith the Lord of hosts; Behold, "
9 T' saith the Lord of hosts; Let "
14 For t' saith the Lord of hosts; As I "
19 T' saith the Lord of hosts; The fast "
20 T' saith the Lord of hosts; It shall "
23 T' saith the Lord of hosts; In those "
11: 4 T' saith the Lord my God; Feed "
M't 2: 5 for t' it is written by the prophet, 3779
3:15 for t' it becometh us to fulfil all "
15: 6 T' have ye...the commandment *2532
26:54 be fulfilled, that t' it must be? 3779
M'r 2: 7 this man t' speak blasphemies? "
Lu 1:25 T' hath the Lord dealt with me in "
2:48 Son, why hast thou t' dealt with us? "
9:34 While he t' spake, there came a *5023
11:45 t' saying thou reproachest us also.* "
17:30 Even t' shall it be in the day *2596, "
18:11 stood and prayed t' with himself, "
19:28 when he had t' spoken, he went "
31 t' shall ye say unto him, Because 3779
22:51 answered and said, Suffer ye t' far. 5127
23:46 and having said t', he gave up the 5023
24:36 And as they t' spake, Jesus himself* "
40 when he had t' spoken, he shewed* 5124
46 said unto them, T' it is written, 3779
46 t' it behoved Christ to suffer, * "
Joh 4: 6 with his journey, sat t' on the well: "
9: 6 When he had t' spoken, he spat on 5023
11:43 when he t' had spoken, he cried "
48 If we let him t' alone, all men will 3779
13:21 When Jesus had t' said, he was 5023
18:22 when he had t' spoken, one of the* "
20:14 when she had t' said, she turned "
Ac 19:41 And when he had t' spoken, he "
20:36 when he had t' spoken, he kneeled "
21:11 T' saith the Holy Ghost, So shall 3592
26:24 And as he t' spake for himself, 5023
30 when he had t' spoken, the king * "
27:35 when he had t' spoken, he took * "
Ro 9:20 it, Why hast thou made me t'? 3779
1Co 14:25 t' are the secrets of his heart made* "
2Co 1:17 When I therefore was t' minded, 5124
5:14 because we t' judge, that if one died "
Ph'p 3:15 as many as be perfect, be t' minded: "
Heb 6: 9 salvation, though we t' speak. 3779
9: 6 when these things were t' ordained, "
Re 9:17 t' I saw the horses in the vision, "
16: 5 be, because thou hast judged t'. 5023
18:21 T' with violence shall that great 3779

thy See in the APPENDIX; also THINE; THYSELF.

Thyatira (*thi-a-ti'-rah*)
Ac 16:14 a seller of purple, of the city of T', 2363
Re 1:11 and unto T', and unto Sardis, and "
2:18 the angel of the church in T' write; "
24 you I say, and unto the rest in T', "

thyine (*thi'-ine*)
Re 18:12 silk, and scarlet, and all t' wood, 2367

thyself
Ge 13: 9 separate t', I pray thee, from me: if
16: 9 and submit t' under her hands.
33: 9 brother; keep that thou hast unto t'.*
Ex 9:17 yet exaltest thou t' against my people,
10: 3 thou refuse to humble t' before me
28 take heed to t', see my face no more;
18:14 why sittest thou t' alone, and all the 859
18 thou art not able to perform it t' alone.
22 so shall it be easier for t', and they
20: 5 Thou shalt not bow down t' to them,
34: 2 present t' there to me in the top of the
12 Take heed to t', lest thou make a
Le 9: 7 and make an atonement for t', and for
18:20 neighbour's wife, to defile t' with her.
23 with any beast to defile t' therewith:
19:18 thou shalt love thy neighbour as t':
34 you, and thou shalt love him as t';
Nu 11:17 thee, that thou bear it not t' alone.
16:13 thou make t' altogether a prince over
De 4: 9 Only take heed to t', and keep thy
5: 9 shalt not bow down t' unto them, nor
9: 1 nations greater and mightier than t',
12:13 Take heed to t' that thou offer not thy
19 Take heed to t' that thou forsake not
30 Take heed to t' that thou be not
20:14 spoil thereof, shalt thou take unto t';
22: 1 go astray, and hide t' from them:
3 do likewise: thou mayest not hide t'.
4 by the way, and hide t' from them:
12 vesture, wherewith thou coverest t'.
De 23:13 when thou wilt ease t' abroad, thou*
28:40 thou shalt not anoint t' with the oil;
Jos 17:15 and cut down for t' there in the land
Ru 3: 3 Wash t' therefore, and anoint thee,
3 make not t' known unto the man,
4: 6 redeem thou my right to t'; for I *
1Sa 19: 2 thee, take heed to t' until the morning,
2 abide in a secret place, and hide t':
20: 8 there be in me iniquity, slay me t'; 859
19 to the place where thou didst hide t'
25:26 from avenging t' with thine own hand,
2Sa 5:24 trees, that then thou shalt bestir t':
7:24 hast confirmed to t' thy people Israel
13: 5 down on thy bed, and make t' sick:
14: 2 I pray thee, feign t' to be a mourner,
2 and anoint not t' with oil, but be as a
18:13 and thou t' wouldest have set * 859
13 wouldest have set t' against me.
22:26 merciful thou wilt shew t' merciful,
26 upright man thou wilt shew t' upright.
27 With the pure thou wilt shew t' pure;
27 froward thou wilt shew t' unsavoury.
1Ki 2: 2 strong therefore, and shew t' a man;
3 and whithersoever thou turnest t':
3:11 and hast not asked for t' long life;
11 neither hast asked riches for t', nor
11 t' understanding to discern judgment;
13: 7 Come home with me, and refresh t',
14: 2 and disguise t', that thou be not known
6 why feignest thou t' to be another?
17: 3 hide t' by the brook Cherith, that is
18: 1 year, saying, Go, shew t' unto Ahab;
20:22 Go, strengthen t', and mark, and see
40 thy judgment be; t' hast decided it.
21:20 sold t' to work evil in the sight of the
22:25 go into an inner chamber to hide t'.
2Ki 22:19 thou hast humbled t' before the Lord,
1Ch 21:12 advise t' what word I shall bring *
2Ch 1:11 asked wisdom and knowledge for t',
18:24 go into an inner chamber to hide t'.
20:37 thou hast joined t' with Ahaziah,
21:13 house, which were better than t':
34:27 and thou didst humble t' before God,
27 and humbledst t' before me, and
Es 4:13 Think not with t' that thou shalt 5315
Job 8: 8 prepare t' to the search of their
10:16 thou shewest t' marvellous upon me.
15: 8 dost thou restrain wisdom to t'? 413
22:21 Acquaint now t' with him, and be
30:21 hand thou opposest t' against me.*
40:10 Deck t' now with majesty and
10 and array t' with glory and beauty.
Ps 7: 6 lift up t' because of the rage of mine
10: 1 why hidest thou t' in times of trouble?
18:25 merciful thou wilt shew t' merciful;
25 man thou wilt shew t' upright;
26 With the pure thou wilt shew t' pure;
26 froward thou wilt shew t' froward.
35:23 Stir up t', and awake to my judgment,
37: 1 Fret not t' because of evildoers,
4 Delight t' also in the Lord; and he
7 fret not t' because of him who
8 fret not t' in any wise to do evil.
49:18 thee, when thou doest well to t'.
50:21 I was altogether such an one as t':
52: 1 Why boastest thou t' in mischief, O
55: 1 and hide not t' from my supplication.
60: 1 displeased; O turn t' to us again.*
80:15 branch that thou madest strong for t'.
17 man whom thou madest strong for t'.
85: 3 turned t' from the fierceness of thine
89:46 long, Lord? wilt thou hide t' forever?
94: 1 whom vengeance belongeth, shew t'.*
2 Lift up t', thou judge of the earth:
104: 2 Who coverest t' with light as with a
Pr 6: 3 Do this now, my son, and deliver t',
3 humble t', and make sure thy friend.
5 Deliver t' as a roe from the hand of
9:12 thou be wise, thou shalt be wise for t':
24:19 Fret not t' because of evil men,
27 and make it fit for t' in the field; *
25: 6 Put not forth t' in the presence of the
27: 1 Boast not t' of to morrow; for thou
30:32 hast done foolishly in lifting up t',
Ec 7:16 over much; neither make t' over wise:
16 wise: why shouldest thou destroy t'?
22 thou t' likewise hast cursed others. 859
Isa 26:20 hide t' as it were for a little moment,
33: 3 at the lifting up of t' the nations
45:15 Verily thou art a God that hidest t',
52: 2 Shake t' from the dust; arise, and sit
2 loose t' from the bands of thy neck,
57: 8 hast discovered t' to another than me,
9 off, and didst debase t' even unto hell.
58: 7 thou hide not t' from thine own flesh?
14 Then shalt thou delight t' in the Lord;
63:14 people, to make t' a glorious name.
64:12 Wilt thou refrain t' for these things,
65: 5 say, Stand by t', come not near to me;
Jer 2:17 Hast thou not procured this unto t',
4:30 Though thou clothest t' with crimson,
30 in vain shalt thou make t' fair;
6:26 sackcloth, and wallow t' in ashes:
17: 4 And thou, even t', shalt discontinue
20: 4 I will make thee a terror to t', and to
22:15 because thou closest t' in cedar? *
32: 8 the redemption is thine; buy it for t'.
45: 5 And seekest thou great things for t'?
46:19 Egypt, furnish t' to go into captivity:
47: 5 their valley: how long wilt thou cut t'?
6 put up t' into thy scabbard, rest, and
La 2:18 give t' no rest; let not the apple of
3:44 Thou hast covered t' with a cloud,
4:21 be drunken, and shalt make t' naked.
Eze 3:24 me, Go, shut t' within thine house.
16:17 thee, and madest to t' images of men,*

Eze 22: 4 defiled t' in thine idols which thou*
16 thou shalt take thine inheritance in t'
23: 40 for whom thou didst wash t',
40 eyes, and deckedst t' with ornaments,
31: 10 thou hast lifted up t' in height, and*
38: 7 and prepare for t', thou, and all thy
Da 5: 17 Let thy gifts be to t', and give thy
23 hast lifted up t' against the Lord of
10: 12 and to chasten t' before thy God, thy
Hos 13: 9 O Israel, thou hast destroyed t'; but*
Ob 4 Though thou exalt t' as the eagle,*
Mic 1: 10 house of Aphrah roll t' in the dust.*
5: 1 Now gather t' in troops, O daughter
Na 3: 15 make t' many as the cankerworm,
15 make t' many as the locusts.
Zec 2: 7 Deliver t', O Zion, that dwellest with*
M't 4: 6 be the Son of God, cast t' down: 4572
5: 33 Thou shalt not forswear t', but shalt "
8: 4 shew t' to the priest, and offer the 4572
19: 19 Thou shalt love thy neighbour as t'. "
22: 39 Thou shalt love thy neighbour as t'. "
27: 40 buildest it in three days, save t'. "
M'r 1: 44 shew t' to the priest, and offer for "
12: 31 Thou shalt love thy neighbour as t'. "
15: 30 Save t', and come down from the "
Lu 4: 9 of God, cast t' down from hence: "
23 me this proverb, Physician, heal t': "
5: 14 but go, and shew t' to the priest, "
6: 42 when thou t' beholdest not the beam 846
7: 6 unto him, Lord, trouble not t': for "
10: 27 thy mind; and thy neighbour as t'. 4572
17: 8 and gird t', and serve me, till I have "
23: 37 be the king of the Jews, save t'. 4572
39 If thou be Christ, save t' and us. "
Joh 1: 22 sent us. What sayest thou of t'? "
7: 4 these things, shew t' to the world. "
8: 13 him, Thou bearest record of t'; "
53 are dead: whom makest thou t'? "
10: 33 thou, being a man, makest t' God. "
14: 22 that thou wilt manifest t' unto us, "
18: 34 Sayest thou this thing of t', or did 1438
21: 18 thou wast young, thou girdedst t', 4572
Ac 8: 29 Go near, and join t' to this chariot. "
12: 8 him, Gird t', and bind on thy sandals. "
16: 28 Do t' no harm: for we are all here 4572
21: 24 take, and purify t' with them, "
24 that thou t' also walkest orderly, 846
24: 8 t' mayest take knowledge of all "
26: 1 Thou art permitted to speak for t' 4572
24 a loud voice, Paul, thou art beside t':* "
Ro 2: 1 another, thou condemnest t'; 4572
5 treasurest up unto t' wrath against "
19 thou t' art a guide of the blind, "
21 another, teachest thou not t'? "
13: 9 Thou shalt love thy neighbour as t'. 1438
14: 22 thou faith? have it to t' before God. 4572
Ga 5: 14 Thou shalt love thy neighbour as t'. 1438
6: 1 considering t', lest thou also be 4572
1Ti 3: 15 to behave t' in the house of God, *
4: 7 exercise t' rather unto godliness. 4572
15 these things; give t' wholly to them; "
16 Take heed unto t', and unto the 4572
16 doing this thou shalt both save t', "
5: 22 of other men's sins: keep t' pure. "
6: 5 godliness: from such withdraw t'.* "
2Ti 2: 15 Study to show t' approved unto 4572
Tit 2: 7 showing t' a pattern of good works: "
Jas 2: 8 Thou shalt love thy neighbour as t'. "

Tiberias (*ti-be'-re-as*)
Joh 6: 1 of Galilee, which is the sea of T'. 5085
23 there came other boats from T' "
21: 1 to the disciples at the sea of T'; "

Tiberius (*ti-be'-re-us*) See also CÆSAR.
Lu 3: 1 year of the reign of T' Cæsar, 5086

Tibhath (*tib'-hath*)
1Ch 18: 8 Likewise from T', and from Chun, 2880

Tibni (*tib'-ni*)
1Ki 16: 21 the people followed T' the son of 8402
22 people that followed T' the son of "
22 so T' died, and Omri reigned. "

Tidal (*ti'-dal*)
Ge 14: 1 of Elam, and T' king of nations; 8413
9 Elam, and with T' king of nations, "

tide See EVENINGTIDE; EVENTIDE; NOONTIDE.

tidings
Ge 29: 13 when Laban heard the t' of Jacob 8088
Ex 33: 4 when the people heard these evil t', 1697
1Sa 4: 19 heard the t' that the ark of God 8052
11: 4 and told the t' in the ears of the *1697
5 him the t' of the men of Jabesh. * "
6 upon Saul when he heard those t',* "
27: 11 nor woman alive, to bring t' to Gath,* "
2Sa 4: 4 five years old when the t' came 8052
10 thinking to have brought good t'. 1319
10 have given him a reward for his t': 1309
13: 30 that t' came to David, saying, 8052
18: 19 me now run, and bear the king t', 1319
20 Thou shalt not bear t' this day, 1309
20 but thou shalt bear t' another day: 1319
20 but this day thou shalt bear no t', "
22 seeing that thou hast no t' ready? 1309
25 be alone, there is t' in his mouth, "
26 the king said, He also bringeth t'. 1319
27 man, and cometh with good t'. 1309
31 Cushi said, T', my lord the king: 1319
1Ki 1: 42 valiant man, and bringest good t'. "
2: 28 Then t' came to Joab: for Joab 8052
14: 6 for I am sent to thee with heavy t'. "
2Ki 7: 9 this day is a day of good t', and we 1309
1Ch 10: 9 to carry t' unto their idols, and to 1319
Ps 112: 7 He shall not be afraid of evil t': 8052
Isa 40: 9 O Zion, that bringest good t', get 1319
9 O Jerusalem, that bringest good t', "
Isa 41: 27 one that bringeth good t'. 1319
52: 7 feet of him that bringeth good t', "
7 that bringeth good t' of good, that "
61: 1 to preach good t' unto the meek; "
Jer 20: 15 man who brought t' to my father, "
37: 5 Jerusalem heard t' of them, 8088
49: 23 Arpad: for they have heard evil t': 8052
Eze 21: 7 that thou shalt answer, For the t'; "
Da 11: 44 But t' out of the east and out of the "
Na 1: 15 feet of him that bringeth good t', 1319
Lu 1: 19 thee, and to shew thee these glad t'. 2097
2: 10 I bring you good t' of great joy, "
8: 1 shewing the glad t' of the kingdom "
Ac 11: 22 t' of these things came unto the *3056
13: 32 And we declare unto you glad t', 2097
21: 31 t' came unto the chief captain of 5334
Ro 10: 15 and bring glad t' of good things! 2097
1Th 3: 6 and brought us good t' of your faith "

tie See also TIED.
1Sa 6: 7 no yoke, and t' the kine to the cart, 631
Pr 6: 21 and t' them about thy neck. 6029

tied
Ex 39: 31 And they t' unto it a lace of blue, 5414
1Sa 6: 10 milch kine, and t' them to the cart, 631
2Ki 7: 10 but horses t', and asses t', and the "
M't 21: 2 straightway ye shall find an ass t', 1210
M'r 11: 2 ye shall find a colt t', whereon "
4 and found the colt t' by the door "
Lu 19: 30 your entering ye shall find a colt t', "

Tiglath-pileser (*tig''-lath-pi-le'-zur*) See also TILGATH-PILNESER.
2Ki 15: 29 Israel came T' king of Assyria, 8407
16: 7 So Ahaz sent messengers to T' "
10 Ahaz went to Damascus to meet T'" "

Tikvah (*tik'-vah*) See also TIKVATH.
2Ki 22: 14 wife of Shallum the son of T', 8616
Ezr 10: 15 and Jahaziah the son of T' were "

Tikvath (*tik'-vath*) See also TIKVAH.
2Ch 34: 22 the wife of Shallum the son of T',*8616

tile See also TILING.
Eze 4: 1 son of man, take thee a t', and lay it 3843

Tilgath-pilneser (*til''-gath-pil-ne'-zur*) See also TIGLATH-PILESER.
1Ch 5: 6 whom T' king of Assyria carried 8407
26 and the spirit of T' king of Assyria," "
2Ch 28: 20 T' king of Assyria came unto him, "

tiling
Lu 5: 19 let him down through the t' with *2766

till See also TILLED; TILLER; TILLEST; TILLETH; UNTIL.
Ge 2: 5 was not a man to t' the ground. 5647
3: 19 t' thou return unto the ground; 5704
23 to t' the ground from whence he 5647
19: 22 I cannot do any thing t' thou be 5704
29: 8 t' they roll the stone from the well's* "
38: 11 house, t' Shelah my son be grown: 5704
17 give me a pledge, t' thou send it? "
Ex 15: 16 t' thy people pass over, O Lord, "
16 t' the people pass over, which thou "
16: 19 no man leave of it t' the morning. "
24 And they laid it up t' the morning, "
34: 33 t' Moses had done speaking with them,*
40: 37 the day that it was taken up. 5704
Nu 12: 15 t' Miriam was brought in again. "
De 17: 5 stone them with stones, t' they die.*
28: 45 thee, t' thou be destroyed; 5704
Jos 5: 6 t' all the people that were men of "
8 in the camp, t' they were whole. "
8: 6 t' we have drawn them from the "
10: 20 slaughter, t' they were consumed, "
J'g 3: 25 they tarried t' they were ashamed: "
6: 4 t' thou come unto Gaza, and left no "
11: 33 even t' thou come to Minnith, * "
16: 3 Samson lay t' midnight, and arose "
19: 26 where her lord was, t' it was light. "
21: 2 and abode there t' even before God, "
Ru 1: 13 tarry for them t' they were grown? "
1Sa 10: 8 shalt thou tarry, t' I come to thee, "
16: 11 will not sit down t' he come hither. "
22: 3 t' I know what God will do for me. "
2Sa 3: 35 or ought else, t' the sun be down. 6440
9: 10 servants, shall t' the land for him. 5647
1Ki 14: 10 taketh away dung, t' it be all gone. 5704
18: 28 t' the blood gushed out upon them. "
2Ki 2: 17 they urged him t' he was ashamed, "
4: 20 he sat on her knees t' noon, and "
7: 9 if we tarry t' the morning light, "
10: 17 Samaria, t' he had destroyed him, "
21: 16 t' he had filled Jerusalem from one "
2Ch 26: 15 helped, t' he was strong. 5704, 3588
29: 34 help them, t' the work was ended, 5704
36: 16 his people, t' there was no remedy. "
Ezr 2: 63 t' there stood up a priest with Urim "
5: 5 t' the matter came to Darius: 5705
9: 14 us t' thou hadst consumed us, 5704
Ne 2: 7 me over t' I come into Judah; "
4: 11 t' we come in the midst among "
21 the morning t' the stars appeared. "
7: 65 t' there stood up a priest with Urim "
13: 19 not be opened t' after the sabbath: "
Job 7: 19 alone t' I swallow down my spittle? "
8: 21 T' he fill thy mouth with laughing,* "
14: 6 t' he shall accomplish, as an "
12 t' the heavens be no more, they "
14 will I wait, t' my change comes. "
27: 5 t' I die I will not remove mine "
32: 4 Elihu had waited t' Job had spoken,*
Ps 10: 15 out his wickedness t' thou find none.
18: 37 turn again t' they were consumed. 5704
68: 30 t' every one submit himself with *
Pr 7: 23 T' a dart strike through his liver; 5704
29: 11 a wise man keepeth it in t' afterwards.
Ec 2: 3 t' I might see what was that good 5704
Ca 2: 7 nor awake my love, t' he please. * "
3: 5 nor awake my love, t' he please. * "
Isa 5: 8 field to field, t' there be no place, "
11 until night, t' wine inflame them! "
22: 14 not be purged from you t' ye die. 5704
23: 13 t' the Assyrian founded it for them*
30: 17 t' ye be left as a beacon upon the top
38: 13 I reckoned t' morning, that, as a *5704
42: 4 t' he have set judgment in the "
62: 7 give him no rest, t' he establish, "
7 t' he make Jerusalem a praise in "
Jer 7: 32 bury in Tophet, t' there be no place.
9: 16 them, t' I have consumed them. 5704
19: 11 in Tophet, t' there be no place to bury
23: 20 t' he have performed the thoughts 5704
24: 10 t' they be consumed from off the "
27: 11 they shall t' it, and dwell therein. 5647
49: 37 them, t' I have consumed them: 5704
52: 3 t' he had cast them out from his * "
11 in prison t' the day of his death. "
La 3: 50 T' the Lord look down, and behold "
Eze 4: 8 t' thou hast ended the days of thy "
14 even t' now have I not eaten of that "
24: 13 t' I have caused my fury to rest "
28: 15 t' iniquity was found in thee. "
34: 21 t' ye have scattered them abroad; "
39: 15 t' the buriers have buried it in the "
19 And ye shall eat fat t' ye be full, and
19 and drink blood t' ye be drunken, of
47: 20 t' a man come over against *5704
Da 2: 9 before me, t' the time be changed: "
34 sawest t' that a stone was cut out "
4: 23 field, t' seven times pass over him; "
25 t' thou know that the most High "
33 t' his hairs were grown like eagles' "
5: 21 t' he knew that the most high God* "
6: 14 laboured t' the going down of the "
7: 4 t' the wings thereof were plucked, "
9 t' the thrones were cast down, "
11 beheld even t' the beast was slain, "
10: 3 t' three whole weeks were fulfilled. "
11: 36 t' the indignation be accomplished: "
12: 9 and sealed t' the time of the end. "
13 But go thou thy way t' the end be: "
Ho 5: 15 t' they acknowledge their offence, 5704
10: 12 t' he come and rain righteousness "
Ob 5 not have stolen t' they had enough? "
Jon 4: 5 t' he might see what would 5704
Zep 3: 3 gnaw not the bones t' the morrow.
M't 1: 25 not t' she had brought forth her 2193
2: 9 t' it came and stood over where the "
5: 18 T' heaven and earth pass, one jot "
18 pass from the law, t' all be fulfilled. "
26 t' thou hast paid the uttermost "
10: 11 and there abide t' ye go thence. "
23 Israel, t' the Son of man be come. "
12: 20 t' he send forth judgment unto "
13: 33 meal, t' the whole was leavened. "
16: 28 t' they see the Son of man coming "
18: 21 and I forgive him? t' seven times? "
30 prison, t' he should pay the debt. "
34 t' he should pay all that was due "
22: 44 t' I make thine enemies thy "
23: 39 t' ye shall say, Blessed is he that "
24: 34 pass, t' all these things be fulfilled. "
M'r 6: 10 abide t' ye depart from that place. "
9: 1 t' they have seen the kingdom of "
9 t' the Son of man were risen *1508, 3752
12: 36 t' I make thine enemies thy 2193
13: 30 pass, t' all these things be done. *3360
Lu 1: 80 t' the day of his shewing unto 2193
9: 27 t' they see the kingdom of God. "
12: 50 straitened t' it be accomplished! "
59 t' thou hast paid the very last mite. "
13: 8 t' I shall dig about it, and dung it: "
21 meal, t' the whole was leavened. "
15: 8 and seek diligently t' she find it? * "
17: 8 me, t' I have eaten and drunken; "
19: 13 said unto them, Occupy t' I come. "
20: 43 T' I make thine enemies thy "
21: 32 not pass away, t' all be fulfilled. "
Joh 13: 38 crow, t' thou hast denied me thrice. "
21: 22, 23 If I will that he tarry t' I come, "
Ac 7: 18 T' another king arose, which 891, 3757
8: 40 the cities, t' he came to Cæsarea. 2193
20: 11 even t' break of day, so he departed. 891
21: 5 children, t' we were out of the city: 2193
23: 12 nor drink t' they had killed Paul. "
21 nor drink t' they have killed him: "
25: 21 kept t' I might send him to Cæsar. "
28: 23 prophets, from morning t' evening. "
1Co 11: 26 the Lord's death t' he come. 891, 3757
15: 25 t' he hath put all enemies under " "
Ga 3: 19 t' the seed shall come to whom "
Eph 4: 13 T' we all come in the unity of the 3360
Ph'p 1: 10 offence t' the day of Christ; *1519
1Ti 4: 13 T' I come, give attendance to 2193
Heb 10: 13 t' his enemies be made his footstool. "
Re 2: 25 have already hold fast t' I come. 891
7: 3 t' we have sealed the servants of "
15: 8 t' the seven plagues of the seven "
20: 3 t' the thousand years shall be * "

tillage
1Ch 27: 26 the work of the field for t' of the 5656
Ne 10: 37 the tithes in all the cities of our t'. "
Pr 13: 23 Much food is in the t' of the poor: 5215

tilled
Eze 36: 9 you, and ye shall be t' and sown: 5647
34 And the desolate land shall be t', "

tiller
Ge 4: 2 but Cain was a t' of the ground. 5647

tillest
Ge 4: 12 When thou t' the ground, it shall 5647

tilleth
Pro 12:11 He that t' his land shall be 5647
28:19 He that t' his land shall have plenty"
Tilon (ti'-lon)
1Ch 4:20 and Rinnah, Ben-hanan, and T'. 8436
Timæus (ti-me'-us) See also BARTIMÆUS.
M'r 10:46 blind Bartimæus, the son of T'. 5090
timber
Ex 31: 5 and in carving of t', to work in all*6086
Le 14:45 the stones of it, and the t' thereof, "
1Ki 5: 6 that can skill to hew t' like unto the"
8 thy desire concerning t' of cedar, "
8 of cedar, and concerning t' of fir. "
18 prepared t' and stones to build the "
6:10 rested on the house with t' of cedar. "
15:22 stones of Ramah, and the t' thereof, "
2Ki 12:12 to buy t' and hewed stone to repair "
22: 6 to buy t' and hewn stone to repair "
1Ch 14: 1 and t' of cedars, with masons and* "
22:14 t' also and stone have I prepared; "
15 and workers of stone and t', and "
2Ch 2: 8 can skill to cut t' in Lebanon; "
9 to prepare me t' in abundance: "
10 thy servants, the hewers that cut t', "
14 brass, in iron, in stone, and in t', "
16: 6 stones of Ramah, and the t' thereof, "
34:11 hewn stone, and t' for couplings, "
Ezr 5: 8 stones, and t' is laid in the walls, 636
6: 4 of great stones, and a row of new t': "
11 let t' be pulled down from his house,*"
Ne 2: 8 he may give me t' to make beams 6086
Eze 26:12 thy stones and thy t' and thy dust "
Hab 2:11 beam out of the t' shall answer it. "
Zec 5: 4 the t' thereof and the stones thereof. "
timbrel See also TIMBRELS.
Ex 15:20 of Aaron, took a t' in her hand; 8596
Job 21:12 They take the t' and harp, and "
Ps 81: 2 a psalm, and bring hither the t', "
149: 3 sing praises unto him with the t' "
150: 4 Praise him with the t' and dance: "
timbrels
Ex 15:20 women went out after her with t' 8596
J'g 11:34 came out to meet him with t' and "
2Sa 6: 5 harps, and on psalteries, and on t', "
1Ch 13: 8 and with psalteries, and with t', "
Ps 68:25 were the damsels playing with t' 8608
time See also AFORETIME; BEFORETIME; DAYTIME; LIFETIME; MEALTIME; SOMETIME; TIMES; UNTIMELY.
Ge 4: 3 And in process of t' it came to pass,3117
17:21 shall bear unto thee at this set t' "
18:10 thee according to the t' of life; *6256
14 At the t' appointed I will return "
14 according to the t' of life, and *6256
21: 2 at the set t' of which God had "
22 it came to pass at that t', that 6256
22:15 out of heaven the second t', "
24:11 of water at the t' of the evening, "
11 the t' that women go out to draw "
26: 8 when he had been there a long t', 3117
29: 7 neither is it t' that the cattle 6256
34 this t' will my husband be joined 6471
30:33 answer for me in t' to come, *3117
31:10 at the t' that the cattle conceived, 6256
38: 1 came to pass at that t', that Judah "
12 in process of t' the daughter of 3117
27 to pass in the t' of her travail, 6256
39: 5 from the t' that he had made him "
11 it came to pass about this t', that 3117
41: 5 he slept and dreamed the second t': "
43:10 we had returned this second t'. 6471
18 returned in our sacks at the first t'8462
20 we came indeed down at the first t' "
47:29 the t' drew nigh that Israel must 3117
Ex 2:23 it came to pass in process of t', "
8:32 hardened his heart at this t' also, 6471
9: 5 And the Lord appointed a set t', "
14 will at this t' send all my plagues 6471
18 to morrow about this t' I will cause6256
27 unto them, I have sinned this t': 6471
13:14 thy son asketh thee in t' to come, 4279
21:19 he shall pay for the loss of his t', 7674
29 push with his horn in t' past, 8543,8032
36 hath used to push in t' past, " "
23:15 in the t' appointed of the month
34:18 thee, in the t' of the month Abib: 4150
21 in earing t' and in harvest thou shalt
Le 13:58 then it shall be washed the second t', "
15:25 out of the t' of her separation, 6256
25 run beyond the t' of her separation;"
18:18 besides the other in her life t'.
25:32 may the Levites redeem at any t'.
50 according to the t' of an hired servant
26: 5 vintage shall reach unto the sowing t':
Nu 10: 6 When ye blow an alarm the second t',
13:20 t' was the t' of the firstripe grapes.3117
20:15 we have dwelt in Egypt a long t'
22: 4 king of the Moabites at that t'. 6256
23:23 according to this t' it shall be said* "
26:10 t' the fire devoured two hundred and
32:10 anger was kindled the same t', *3117
35:26 if the slayer shall at any t' come
De 1: 9 I spake unto you at that t', saying,6256
16 I charged your judges at that t', "
18 I commanded you at that t' all the "
2:20 giants dwelt therein in old t'; and*
34 And we took all his cities at that t',6256
3: 4 And we took all his cities at that t'. "
8 we took at that t' out of the hand "
12 land, which we possessed at that t'. "
18 I commanded you at that t', saying, "
21 I commanded Joshua at that t', "
23 And I besought the Lord at that t'. "
De 4:14 the Lord commanded me at that t'6256
5: 5 between the Lord and you at that t'."
6:20 thy son asketh thee in t' to come, 4279
9:19 Lord hearkened unto me at that t'6471
20 prayed for Aaron also the same t'. 6256
10: 1 At that t' the Lord said unto me, "
8 At that t' the Lord separated the "
10 according to the first t', forty days3117
10 Lord hearkened unto me at that t'6471
19: 4 whom he hated not in t' past;8543,8032
6 as he hated him not in t' past. " "
14 which they of old t' have set in thine
20:19 thou shalt besiege a city a long t', 3117
32:35 their foot shall slide in due t': for 6256
Jos 2: 5 about the t' of shutting of the gate,
3:15 all his banks all the t' of harvest,) 3117
4: 6, 21 ask their fathers in t' to come, 4279
5: 2 At that t' the Lord said unto 6256
2 the children of Israel the second t'.
6:16 it came to pass at the seventh t', 6471
26 Joshua adjured them at that t', 6256
8:14 he and all his people, at a t' appointed,
10:27 at the t' of the going down of the 6256
42 land did Joshua take at one t', 6471
11: 6 about this t' will I deliver them 6256
10 And Joshua at that t' turned back, "
18 Joshua made war a long t' with 3117
21 And at that t' came Joshua, and 6256
22:24 In t' to come your children might 4279
27 say to our children in t' to come, "
28 to our generations in t' to come, "
23: 1 it came to pass a long t' after that*3117
24: 2 the other side of the flood in old t',5769
J'g 3:29 slew of Moab at that t' about ten 6256
4: 4 she judged Israel at that t'. "
9: 8 The trees went forth on a t' to anoint
10:14 you in the t' of your tribulation. 6256
11: 4 it came to pass in process of t', *3117
26 ye not recover them within that t'?6256
12: 6 fell at that t' of the Ephraimites "
13:23 nor would as at this t' have told us "
14: 4 for at that t' the Philistines had "
8 after a t' he returned to take her,*3117
15: 1 in the t' of wheat harvest, that
18:31 all the t' that the house of God was "
20:15 Benjamin were numbered at that t'*"
21:14 Benjamin came again at that t'; 6256
22 ye did not give unto them at this t',* "
24 of Israel departed thence at that t'. "
Ru 4: 7 the manner in former t' in Israel 6440
1Sa 1: 4 the t' was that Elkanah offered, *3117
20 when the t' was come about after
3: 2 And it came to pass at that t', when"
8 Lord called Samuel again the third t'.
4:20 And about the t' of her death the 6256
7: 2 that the t' was long; for it 3117
9:13 for about this t' ye shall find him.
16 To morrow about this t' I will 6256
24 unto this t' hath it been kept for 4150
11: 9 To morrow, by that t' the sun be hot,
13: 8 according to the set t' that Samuel
14:18 the ark of God was at that t' with 3117
21 the Philistines before that t', *8032
18:19 came to pass at the t' when Merab 6256
19:21 sent messengers again the third t'.
20:12 my father about to morrow any t',6256
35 at the t' appointed with David,
26: 8 I will not smite him the second t'.
27: 7 the t' that David dwelt in the*4557,3117
2Sa 2:11 the t' that David was king in "
5: 2 Also in t' past, when Saul was *865,8543
7: 6 since the t' that I brought up the *3117
11 as since the t' that I commanded * "
11: 1 at the t' when kings go forth to 6256
14: 2 woman that had a long t' mourned3117
29 when he sent again the second t',
17: 7 hath given is not good at this t'. 6471
20: 5 he tarried longer than the set t'
18 They were wont to speak in old t',
23: 8 hundred, whom he slew at one t'. 6471
13 came to David in the harvest t' unto
20 in the midst of a pit in t' of snow: 3117
24:15 morning even to the t' appointed: 6256
1Ki 1: 6 had not displeased him at any t' in3117
2:26 will not at this t' put thee to death, "
8:65 at that t' Solomon held a feast, 6256
9: 2 appeared to Solomon the second t',
11:29 at that t' when Jeroboam went 6256
42 And the t' that Solomon reigned in3117
14: 1 At that t' Abijah the son of 6256
15:23 in the t' of his old age he was
18:29 until the t' of the offering of the
34 And he said, Do it the second t'.
34 And they did it the second t'.
34 And he said, Do it the third t'.
34 And they did it the third t'.
36 t' of the offering of the evening
44 And it came to pass at the seventh t',
19: 2 them by to morrow about this t'. 6256
7 of the Lord came again the second t',
20: 6 unto thee to morrow about this t',6256
2Ki 3: 6 went out of Samaria the same t', 3117
4:16 according to the t' of life, thou 6256
17 unto her, according to the t' of life. "
5:26 Is it a t' to receive money, and to "
7: 1 To morrow about this t' shall a "
18 to morrow about this t' in the gate "
8:22 Libnah revolted at the same t'. "
10: 6 Then he wrote a letter the second t'
6 me to Jezreel by to morrow this t'.6256
36 t' that Jehu reigned over Israel 3117
16: 6 At that t' Rezin king of Syria 6256
18:16 At that t' did Hezekiah cut off the "
20:12 that t' Berodach-baladan, the son "
24:10 t' the servants of Nebuchadnezzar "
1Ch 9:20 was the ruler over them in t' past, 6440
1Ch 9:25 seven days from t' to t' with them. 6256
11: 2 And moreover in t' past, even *8543
11 hundred slain by him at one t'. 6471
12:22 at that t' day by day there came *6256
17:10 since the t' that I commanded *3117
20: 1 the t' that kings go out to battle, 6256
4 t' Sibbechai the Hushathite slew * 227
21:28 t' when David saw that the Lord 6256
29:22 the son of David king the second t',
27 t' that he reigned over Israel was 3117
2Ch 7: 8 at the same t' Solomon kept the 6256
13:18 were brought under at that t', "
15:11 offered unto the Lord the same t',*3117
16: 7 t' Hanani the seer came to Asa 6256
10 some of the people the same t'. "
18:34 t' of the sun going down he died. "
21:10 The same t' also did Libnah revolt "
19 came to pass, that in process of t',3117
24:11 at what t' the chest was brought 6256
25:27 after the t' that Amaziah did turn "
28:16 At that t' did king Ahaz send unto "
22 And in the t' of his distress did he "
30: 3 they could not keep it at that t', "
5 they had not done it of a long t' in*
26 since the t' of Solomon the son of 3117
35:17 kept the passover at that t', 6256
Ezr 4:10, 11 side the river, and at such a t'.*
15 sedition within the same of old t': 3118
17 the river, Peace, and at such a t'. *
19 it is found that this city of old t' 3118
5: 3 the same t' came to them Tatnai, 2166
16 and since that t' even until now 116
7:12 perfect peace, and at such a t'. *
8:34 the weight was written at that t'. 6256
10:13 many, and it is a t' of much rain, "
Ne 2: 6 to send me; and I set him a t'. 2165
4:16 it came to pass from that t' forth, 3117
22 the same t' said I unto the people,6256
5:14 from the t' that I was appointed 3117
6: 1 at that t' I had not set up the 6256
5 fifth t' with an open letter in his 6471
9:27 and in the t' of their trouble, when6256
32 since the t' of the kings of Assyria 3117
12:44 And at that t' were some appointed*"
13: 6 in all this t' was not I at Jerusalem:
21 From that t' forth came they no 6256
Es 2:19 were gathered together the second t',
4:14 holdest thy peace at this t', 6256
14 to the kingdom for such a t' as this?"
8: 9 called at that t' in the third month, "
9:27 according to their appointed t' 2165
Job 6:17 What t' they wax warm, they 6256
7: 1 appointed t' to man upon earth? *6635
9:19 who shall set me a t' to plead? ‡
14:13 thou wouldest appoint me a set t',
14 days of my appointed t' will I wait,*6635
15:32 shall be accomplished before his t',3117
22:16 Which were cut down out of t', 6256
30: 3 in former t' desolate and waste. * 570
38:23 reserved against the t' of trouble, 6256
39: 1 thou the t' when the wild goats "
2 thou the t' when they bring forth? "
18 What t' she lifteth up herself on "
Ps 4: 7 in the t' that their corn and their * "
21: 9 a fiery oven in the t' of thine anger:"
27: 5 t' of trouble he shall hide me in *3117
32: 6 pray unto thee in a t' when thou 6256
37:19 shall not be ashamed in the evil t': "
39 is their strength in the t' of trouble."
41: 1 will deliver him in t' of trouble. *3117
56: 3 What t' I am afraid, I will trust in "
69:13 thee, O Lord, in an acceptable t': 6256
71: 9 Cast me not off in the t' of old age: "
78:38 many a t' turned he his anger
81: 3 t' appointed, on our solemn feast *
15 their t' should have endured for 6256
89:47 Remember how short my t' is:
102:13 for the t' to favour her, yea, 6256
13 her, yea, the set t', is come.
105:19 Until the t' that his word came: 6256
113: 2 from this t' forth and for evermore.
115:18 bless the Lord from this t' forth 6258
119:126 It is t' for thee, Lord, to work: 6256
121: 8 and thy coming in from this t' forth,
129: 1, 2 Many a t' have they afflicted me 7227
Pr 25:13 cold of snow in the t' of harvest, 3117
19 an unfaithful man in t' of trouble
31:25 and she shall rejoice in t' to come.
Ec 1:10 it hath been already of old t', *
3: 1 a t' to every purpose under the 6256
2 A t' to be born, and a t' to die;
2 a t' to plant, and a t' to pluck up that"
3 A t' to kill, and a t' to heal; "
3 a t' to break down, and a t' to build "
4 A t' to weep, and a t' to laugh; "
4 a t' to mourn, and a t' to dance; "
5 A t' to cast away stones, and a "
5 and a t' to gather stones together; "
5 a t' to embrace, and a t' to refrain "
6 A t' to get, and a t' to lose; "
6 a t' to keep, and a t' to cast away; "
7 A t' to rend, and a t' to sew; "
7 a t' to keep silence, and a t' to speak;"
8 A t' to love, and a t' to hate; "
8 a t' of war, and a t' of peace.
11 every thing beautiful in his t': "
17 there is a t' there for every purpose "
7:17 shouldest thou die before thy t'?
8: 5 man's heart discerneth both t' and "
6 to every purpose there is t' and "
9 a t' wherein one man ruleth over "
9:11 t' and chance happeneth to them "
12 For man also knoweth not his t': "
12 sons of men snared in an evil t', "
Ca 2:12 t' of the singing of birds is come, "
Isa 11:11 shall set his hand again the second "

Isa 13:22 and her t' is near to come, and 6256
16:13 concerning Moab since that t'. * 227
18: 7 In that t' shall the present be 6256
20: 2 At the same t' spake the Lord by "
26:17 draweth near the t' of her delivery, "
28:19 From the t' that it goeth forth it 1767
30: 8 may be for the t' to come for ever 3117
33: 2 salvation also in the t' of trouble. 6256
39: 1 At that t' Merodach-baladan, the "
42:14 I have long t' holden my peace; "
23 and hear for the t' to come? 268
44: 8 have not I told thee from that t', * 227
45:21 hath declared this from ancient t'? "
21 who hath told it from that t'? have*227
48: 6 thee new things from this t', 6258
8 from that t' that thine ear was not*227
16 from the t' that it was, there am I:6256
49: 8 an acceptable t' have I heard thee, "
60:22 I the Lord will hasten it in his t'. "
Jer 1:13 Lord came unto me the second t',
2:20 For of old t' I have broken thy yoke,
27 t' of their trouble they will say, 6256
28 save thee in the t' of thy trouble: "
3: 4 thou not from this t' cry unto me, 6258
17 At that t' they shall call Jerusalem6256
4:11 At that t' shall it be said to this "
6:15 at the t' that I visit them they shall "
8: 1 At that t', saith the Lord, they "
7 crane and...swallow observe the t' "
12 t' of their visitation they shall be "
15 and for a t' of health, and behold "
10:15 t' of their visitation they shall "
11:12 at all in the t' of their trouble. "
14 hear them in the t' that they cry "
13: 3 Lord came unto me the second t',
14: 8 the saviour thereof in t' of trouble,6256
19 and for the t' of healing, and behold"
15:11 t' of evil and in the t' of affliction. "
18:23 with them in the t' of thine anger. "
27: 7 until the very t' of his land come: "
30: 7 it is even the t' of Jacob's trouble; "
31: 1 At the same t', saith the Lord, will "
33: 1 came unto Jeremiah the second t',
15 at that t', will I cause the Branch 6256
39:10 vineyards and fields at the same t'.3117
46:17 he hath passed the t' appointed.
21 them, and the t' of their visitation.6256
49: 8 him, the t' that I will visit him. "
19 and who will appoint me the t'? and
50: 4 and in that t', saith the Lord, 6256
16 the sickle in the t' of harvest: "
20 and in that t', saith the Lord, the "
27 day is come, the t' of their visitation."
31 is come, the t' that I will visit thee. "
44 and who will appoint me the t'? and
51: 6 is the t' of the Lord's vengeance; 6256
18 t' of their visitation they perish. "
33 threshingfloor, it is t' to thresh her:"
33 and the t' of her harvest is come. "
La 5:20 ever, and forsake us so long t'? 3117
Eze 4:10 from t' to t' shalt thou eat it. 6256
11 hin: from t' to t' shalt thou drink. "
7: 7 the t' is come, the day of trouble "
12 The t' is come, the day draweth "
16: 8 behold, thy t' was the t' of love; "
57 as the t' of thy reproach of the "
21:14 the sword be doubled the third t',
22: 3 midst of it, that her t' may come, 6256
26:20 with the people of old t', and
27:34 the t' when thou shalt be broken 6256
30: 3 it shall be the t' of the heathen. "
35: 5 sword in the t' of their calamity, "
5 in the t' that their iniquity had an "
38:10 same t' shall things come into thy*3117
17 of whom I have spoken in old t'
18 come to pass at the same t' when * "
Da 2: 8 certainty that ye would gain the t',5732
9 before me, till the t' be changed: "
16 king that he would give him t', 2166
3: 5 at what t' ye hear the sound of 5732
7 at that t', when all the people 2166
8 at that t' certain Chaldeans came "
15 at what t' ye hear the sound of 5732
4:36 the same t' my reason returned 2166
7:12 prolonged for a season and t'. 5732
22 t' came that the saints possessed 2166
25 given into his hand until a t' and 5732
25 and times and the dividing of t'. "
8:17 at the t' of the end shall be the 6256
19 the t' appointed the end shall be. "
23 And in the latter t' of their kingdom,
9:21 about the t' of the evening 6256
10: 1 true, but the t' appointed was long:
11:24 the strong holds, even for a t'. 6256
27 end shall be at the t' appointed. "
29 At the t' appointed he shall return,
35 white, even to the t' of the end: 6256
35 because it is yet for a t' appointed.
40 at the t' of the end shall the king 6256
12: 1 at that t' shall Michael stand up, "
1 and there shall be a t' of trouble, "
1 was a nation even to that same t': "
1 that t' thy people shall be delivered,"
4 the book, even to the t' of the end: "
7 be for a t', times, and an half; 4150
9 and sealed till the t' of the end. 6256
11 the t' that the daily sacrifice shall "
Ho 2: 9 away my corn in the t' thereof,
9:10 in the fig tree at her first t': *7225
10:12 for it is t' to seek the Lord, till he 6256
Joe 3: 1 in that t', when I shall bring again "
Am 5:13 shall keep silence in that t'; "
13 for it is an evil t'. "
Jon 3: 1 Lord came unto Jonah the second t',
Mic 2: 3 go haughtily: for this t' is evil. 6256
3: 4 hide his face from them at that t', "
Mic 5: 3 the t' that she which travaileth 6256
Na 1: 9 shall not rise up the second t'. 6471
Hab 2: 3 vision is yet for an appointed t',
Zep 1:12 it shall come to pass at that t', 6256
3:19 at that t' I will undo all that afflict "
20 At that t' will I bring you again, "
20 even in the t' that I gather you: for "
Hag 1: 2 people say, The t' is not come, "
2 the t' that the Lord's house should "
4 Is it t' for you, O ye, to dwell in "
Zec 10: 1 rain in the t' of the latter rain; "
14: 7 that at evening t' it shall be light. "
Mal 3:11 your vine cast her fruit before the t'
M't 1:11 about the t' they were carried 1909
2: 7 of them diligently what t' the star 5550
16 according to the t' which he had "
4: 6 lest at any t' thou dash thy foot *3379
17 that t' Jesus began to preach, 5119
5:21 that it was said by them of old t', 744
25 lest at any t' the adversary deliver*3379
27 that it was said by them of old t', * 744
33 it hath been said by them of old t', "
8:29 hither to torment us before the t'? 2540
11:25 At that t' Jesus answered and said,*"
12: 1 that t' Jesus went on the sabbath * "
13:15 lest at any t' they should see with the*3379
30 in the t' of harvest I will say to the2540
14: 1 At that t' Herod the tetrarch heard*"
15 place, and the t' is now past; 5610
16:21 From that t' forth began Jesus to 5119
18: 1 At the same t' came the disciples *5610
21:34 when the t' of the fruit drew near,*2540
24:21 beginning of the world to this t', * "
25:19 After a long t' the lord of those 5550
26:16 from that t' he sought opportunity 5119
18 The Master saith, My t' is at hand;2540
42 He went away again the second t',
44 away again, and prayed the third t',
M'r 1:15 The t' is fulfilled, and the kingdom2540
4:12 lest at any t' they...be converted, *3379
17 and so endure but for a t': *4340
6:35 and now the t' is far passed: *5610
10:30 an hundredfold now in this t', 2540
11:13 for the t' of figs was not yet. * "
13:19 which God created unto this t', *3568
33 for ye know not when the t' is. 2540
14:41 he cometh the third t', and saith unto
72 And the second t' the cock crew.
Lu 1:10 were praying without at the t' of *5610
57 Now Elisabeth's full t' came that 5550
4: 5 of the world in a moment of t'. "
11 lest at any t' thou dash thy foot *3379
27 were in Israel in the t' of Eliseus 1909
7:45 woman since the t' I came in hath
8:13 and in t' of temptation fall away. 2540
27 man, which had devils long t', and*5550
9:51 the t' was come that he should be *2250
12:56 is it that ye do not discern this t'? 2540
13:35 until the t' come when ye shall say,*
14:17 sent his servant at supper t' to say 5610
15:29 neither transgressed I at any t' thy *
16:16 t' the kingdom of God is preached, 5119
18:30 manifold more in this present t', 2540
19:44 knewest not the t' of thy visitation. "
20: 9 into a far country for a long t'. 5550
21: 8 Christ; and the t' draweth near: 2540
34 at any t'...hearts be overcharged *3379
37 in the day t' he was teaching in *2250
23: 7 also was at Jerusalem at that t'. * "
22 And he said unto them the third t',
Joh 1:18 No man hath seen God at any t'; 4455
3: 4 second t' into his mother's womb, 1208
5: 6 had been now a long t' in that case,5550
37 neither heard his voice at any t', 4455
6:66 From that t', many of his disciples*
7: 6 unto them, My t' is not yet come: 2540
6 come: but your t' is alway ready. "
8 feast; for my t' is not yet full come."
11:39 him, Lord, by this t' he stinketh: 2235
14: 9 Have I been so long t' with you, 5550
16: 2 yea, the t' cometh, that whosoever*5610
4 when the t' shall come, ye may * "
25 the t' cometh, when I shall no more*"
21:14 now the third t' that Jesus shewed
16 saith to him again the second t',
17 He saith unto him the third t', Simon,
17 said unto him the third t', Lovest thou
Ac 1: 6 thou at this t' restore again the 5550
21 have companied with us all the t' "
7:13 And at the second t' Joseph was made
17 the t' of the promise drew nigh, 5550
20 In which t' Moses was born, and 2540
8: 1 And at that t' there was a great *2250
11 of long t' he had bewitched them 5550
10:15 spake unto him again the second t',
11: 8 hath at any t' entered into my mouth.*
12: 1 Now about that t' Herod the king 2540
13:18 about the t' of forty years suffered 5550
14: 3 Long t'...abode they speaking "
28 abode long t' with the disciples. "
15:21 Moses of old t' hath in every city *1074
17:21 spent their t' in nothing else, but 2119
18:20 him to tarry longer t' with them, 5550
23 after he had spent some t' there, he"
19:23 same t' there arose no small stir 2540
20:16 he would not spend the t' in Asia: 5551
24:25 answered, Go thy way for this t'; 3568
27: 9 when much t' was spent, and when5550
Ro 3:26 I say, at this t' his righteousness: *2540
5: 6 in due t' Christ died for...ungodly.* "
8:18 sufferings of this present t' are not "
9: 9 At this t' will I come, and Sarah * "
11: 5 at this present t' also there is a "
13:11 And that, knowing the t', that now*"
11 it is high t' to awake out of sleep: 5610
1Co 4: 5 judge nothing before the t', until 2540
1Co 7: 5 except it be with consent for a t', *2540
29 this I say, brethren, the t' is short: "
9: 7 warfare any t' at his own charges?*4218
15: 8 me also, as of one born out of due t'.‡
16:12 was not at all to come at this t'; *3568
12 when he shall have convenient t'. *2119
2Co 6: 2 I have heard thee in a t' accepted, 2540
2 now is the accepted t'; behold, now"
8:14 this t' your abundance may be a "
12:14 the third t' I am ready to come to you
13: 1 This is the third t' I am coming to you
2 as if I were present, the second t';
Ga 1:13 heard of my conversation in t' past4218
4: 2 until...t' appointed of the father. *4287
4 the fulness of the t' was come, 5550
5:21 as I have also told you in t' past, *
Eph 2: 2 in t' past ye walked according to *4218
11 that ye being in t' past Gentiles "
12 at that t' ye were without Christ, 2540
5:16 Redeeming the t', because the days "
Col 3: 7 the which ye also walked some t',*4218
4: 5 that are without, redeeming the t'.2540
1Th 2: 5 neither at any t' used we flattering4218
17 from you for a short t' in presence,*2540
2Th 2: 6 that he might be revealed in his t'.*"
1Ti 2: 6 for all, to be testified in due t'. * "
6:19 foundation against the t' to come, 3195
2Ti 4: 3 the t' will come when they will not2540
6 the t' of my departure is at hand. "
subscr. brought before Nero the second t'.*
Ph'm 11 in t' past was to thee unprofitable,*4218
Heb 1: 1 spake in t' past unto the fathers 3819
5, 13 of the angels said he at any t', 4218
2: 1 at any t' we should let them slip. * "
4: 7 David, To day, after so long a t'; 5550
16 and find grace to help in t' of need.2121
5:12 for the t' ye ought to be teachers, 5550
9: 9 a figure for the t' then present, in 2540
10 on them until the t' of reformation. "
28 shall he appear the second t' without
11:32 t' would fail me to tell of Gibeon, 5550
Jas 4:14 that appeareth for a little t', and then
1Pe 1: 5 ready to be revealed in the last t'. 2540
11 or what manner of t' the Spirit of "
17 t' of your sojourning here in fear: 5550
2:10 Which in t' past were not a people,4218
3: 5 in the old t' the holy women also, "
4: 2 should live the rest of his t' in the 5550
3 t' past of our life may suffice us to "
17 the t' is come that judgment must 2540
5: 6 that he may exalt you in due t': "
2Pe 1:21 prophecy came not in old t' by the*4218
2: 3 whose judgment now of a long t' *1597
13 count it pleasure to riot in the day t'.
1Jo 2:18 Little children, it is the last t': *5610
18 whereby we know...it is the last t'.* "
4:12 No man hath seen God at any t'. 4455
Jude 18 should be mockers in the last t', 5550
Re 1: 3 therein: for the t' is at hand. 2540
10: 6 that there should be t' no longer: *5550
11:18 is come, and the t' of the dead, 2540
12:12 knoweth that he hath but a short t'."
14 where she is nourished for a t', "
14 and half a t', from the face of the "
14:15 for the t' is come for thee to reap; *5610
22:10 of this book: for the t' is at hand. 2540

times See also BETIMES; OFTENTIMES; OFTTIMES SOMETIMES.

Ge 27:36 hath supplanted me these two t': 6471
31: 7 me, and changed my wages ten t';4489
41 thou hast changed my wages ten t'."
33: 3 himself to the ground seven t', 6471
43:34 five t' so much as any of theirs. 3027
Ex 23:14 Three t' thou shalt keep a feast unto
17 Three t' in the year all thy males 6471
Le 4: 6 and sprinkle of the blood seven t' "
17 sprinkle it seven t' before the Lord,"
8:11 thereof upon the altar seven t', "
14: 7 cleansed from the leprosy seven t', "
16 of the oil with his finger seven t' "
27 oil that is in his left hand seven t' "
51 and sprinkle the house seven t': "
16: 2 not at all t' into the holy place 6256
14 the blood with his finger seven t'. 6471
19 upon it with his finger seven t', "
19:26 ye use enchantment, nor observe t'.*
25: 8 unto thee, seven t' seven years: 6471
26:18 punish you seven t' more for your
21 bring seven t' more plagues upon
24 punish you yet seven t' for your
28 chastise you seven t' for your sins.
Nu 14:22 have tempted me now these ten t',
19: 4 of the congregation seven t'.
22:28 thou hast smitten me these three t'?
32 these thou smitten thine ass three t'?
33 and turned from me these three t':
24: 1 he went not, as at other t', to seek6471
10 altogether blessed them these three t'
De 1:11 you a thousand t' so many more 6471
2:10 The Emims dwelt therein in t' past,*
4:42 and hated him not in t' past; *8543
16:16 Three t' in a year shall all they 6471
18:10 divination, or an observer of t', *
14 hearkened unto observers of t', and*
Jos 6: 4 ye shall compass the city seven t', 6471
15 after the same manner seven t': "
15 they compassed the city seven t'. "
J'g 13:25 began to move him at t' in the camp*
16:15 hast mocked me these three t', 6471
20 I will go out as at other t' before, "
20:30 against Gibeah, as at other t', "
31 the people, and kill, as at other t', "
1Sa 3:10 and called as other t', Samuel,
18:10 with his hand, as at other t': *3117
19: 7 in his presence, as in t' past. *865,8543
20:25 sat upon his seat, as at other t', 6471

1Sa 20: 41 ground,...bowed himself three t': 6471
2Sa 3: 17 ye sought for David in t' past 8543
1Ki 8: 59 cause of his people Israel at all t',*3117
9: 25 three t' in a year did Solomon 6471
17: 21 himself upon the child three t', "
18: 43 And he said, Go again seven t'. "
22: 16 How many t' shall I adjure thee "
2Ki 4: 35 and the child sneezed seven t', and "
5: 10 Go and wash in Jordan seven t', "
14 dipped himself seven t' in Jordan, "
13: 19 shouldest have smitten five or six t';"
25 Three t' did Joash beat him, and "
19: 25 of ancient t' that I have formed it?3117
21: 6 fire, and observed t', and used *
1Ch 12: 32 men that had understanding of the t',
21: 3 his people an hundred t' so many 6471
29: 30 and the t' that went over him, and
2Ch 8: 13 three t' in the year, even in the 6471
15: 5 in those t' there was no peace to him
18: 15 How many t' shall I adjure thee 6471
33: 6 also he observed t', and used *
Ezr 10: 14 in our cities come at appointed t', 6256
Ne 4: 12 they said unto us ten t', From all 6471
6: 4 they sent unto me four t' after "
9: 28 many t' didst thou deliver them 6256
10: 34 at t' appointed year by year, to "
13: 31 the wood offering, at t' appointed, "
Es 1: 13 to the wise men, which knew the t'."
9: 31 of Purim in their t' appointed, 2165
Job 19: 3 ten t' have ye reproached me: 6471
24: 1 seeing t' are not hidden from the 6256
Ps 9: 9 oppressed, a refuge in t' of trouble. "
10: 1 hidest thou thyself in t' of trouble? "
12: 6 in a furnace of earth, purified seven t'.
31: 15 My t' are in thy hand: deliver me 6256
34: 1 I will bless the Lord at all t': his "
44: 1 in their days, in the t' of old. *3117
62: 8 Trust in him at all t'; ye people, 6256
77: 5 days of old, the years of ancient t'.
106: 3 that doeth righteousness at all t'. 6256
43 Many t' did he deliver them; but 6471
119: 20 hath unto thy judgments at all t'. 6256
164 Seven t' a day do I praise thee because
Pr 5: 19 her breasts satisfy thee at all t'; 6256
17: 17 A friend loveth at all t', and a "
24: 16 For a just man falleth seven t', and
Ec 8: 12 a sinner do evil an hundred t',
Isa 14: 31 shall be alone in his appointed t'. 4151
33: 6 shall be the stability of thy t', 6256
37: 26 ancient t', that I have formed it? 3117
46: 10 from ancient t' the things that are not
Jer 8: 7 heaven knoweth her appointed t'; 6256
Eze 12: 27 he prophesieth of the t' that are far "
Da 1: 20 he found them ten t' better than all
2: 21 changeth the t' and the seasons: 5732
3: 19 heat the furnace one seven t' more
4: 16 and let seven t' pass over him. 5732
23 field, till seven t' pass over him; "
25, 32 and seven t' shall pass over thee,"
6: 10 upon his knees three t' a day, 2166
13 maketh his petition three t' a day. "
7: 10 ten thousand t' ten thousand stood
25 and think to change t' and laws: 2166
25 a time and t' and the dividing of 5732
9: 25 and the wall, even in troublous t'. 6256
11: 6 he that strengthened her in these t'."
14 in those t' there shall many stand "
12: 7 shall be for a time, t', and an half; 4150
M't 16: 3 can ye not discern...signs of the t'? 2540
18: 21 me, and I forgive him till seven t'? 2034
22 I say not unto thee, Until seven t': "
22 but, Until seventy t' seven. 1441
Lu 17: 4 trespass against thee seven t' in a 2034
4 seven t' in a day turn again to thee,"
21: 24 the t' of the Gentiles be fulfilled. 2540
Ac 1: 7 you to know the t' or the seasons, 5550
3: 19 when the t' of refreshing shall *2540
21 until the t' of restitution of all 5550
11: 10 And this was done three t': and *5151
14: 16 Who in t' past suffered all nations*1074
17: 26 determined...t' before appointed, *2540
30 the t' of this ignorance God winked5550
Ro 11: 30 in t' past have not believed God, *4218
2Co 11: 24 five t' received I forty stripes save 3999
Ga 1: 23 he which persecuted us in t' past *4218
4: 10 observe days, and months, and t',*2540
Eph 1: 10 the dispensation of the fulness of t' "
2: 3 our conversation in t' past in the *4218
1Th 5: 1 of the t' and the seasons, brethren, 2540
1Ti 4: 1 latter t' some shall depart from 5550
6: 15 Which in his t' he shall shew, who "
2Ti 3: 1 the last days perilous t' shall come."
Tit 1: 3 hath in due t' manifested his word*"
Heb 1: 1 who at sundry t' and in divers *
1Pe 1: 20 manifest in these last t' for you, 5550
Re 5: 11 was ten thousand t' ten thousand,
12: 14 for a time, and t', and half a time, 2540

Timna (*tim'-nah*) See also TIMNATH.
Ge 36: 12 T' was concubine to Eliphaz 8555
22 Hemam; and Lotan's sister was T'. "
1Ch 1: 36 Gatam, Kenaz, and T', and Amalek."
39 Homam: and T' was Lotan's sister."

Timnah (*tim'-nah*) See also TIMNA; TIMNATH; TIMNITE.
Ge 36: 40 duke T', duke Alvah, duke 8555
Jos 15: 10 and passed on to T': 8553
57 Gibeah, and T'; ten cities with "
1Ch 1: 51 the dukes of Edom were; duke T',*8555
2Ch 28: 18 and T' with the villages thereof, 8553

Timnath (*tim'-nath*) See also THIMNATHAH; TIMNAH; TIMNATH-HERES.
Ge 38: 12 up unto his sheepshearers to T', *8553
13 father in law goeth up to T' to * "
14 place, which is by the way to T': * "
J'g 14: 1 Samson went down to T', and *8553
1, 2 a woman in T' of the daughters* "
5 his father and his mother, to T', * "
5 and came to the vineyards of T': * "

Timnath-heres (*tim''-nath-he'-rez*) See also TIMNATH-SERAH.
J'g 2: 9 border of his inheritance in T', 8556

Timnath-serah (*tim''-nath-se'-rah*) See also TIMNATH-HERES.
Jos 19: 50 asked, even T' in mount Ephraim: 8556
24: 30 border of his inheritance in T', "

Timnite (*tim'-nite*)
J'g 15: 6 Samson, the son in law of the T', 8554

Timon (*ti'-mon*)
Ac 6: 5 T', and Parmenas, and Nicolas a 5096

Timotheus (*tim-o'-the-us*) See also TIMOTHY.
Ac 16: 1 disciple was there, named T', *5095
17: 14 but Silas and T' abode there still.* "
15 a commandment unto Silas and T'*"
18: 5 when Silas and T' were come from*"
19: 22 ministered unto him, T' and * "
20: 4 and Gaius of Derbe, and T'; * "
Ro 16: 21 T' my workfellow, and Lucius, * "
1Co 4: 17 this cause have I sent unto you T',*"
16: 10 if T' come, see that he may be with*"
subscr. Fortunatus, and Achaicus, and T'. "
2Co 1: 19 even by me and Silvanus and T', "
Ph'p 1: 1 Paul and T', the servants of Jesus*"
2: 19 Jesus to send T' shortly unto you,*"
Col 1: 1 the will of God, and T' our brother,*"
1Th 1: 1 Silvanus, and T', unto the church* "
3: 2 sent T', our brother, and minister*"
6 But now when T' came from you * "
2Th 1: 1 Silvanus, and T', unto the church* "
2Ti subscr. The second epistle unto T', * "

Timothy (*tim'-o-thy*) See also TIMOTHEUS.
2Co 1: 1 T' our brother, unto the church 5095
1Ti 1: 2 Unto T', my own son in the faith: "
18 charge I commit unto thee, son T', "
6: 20 O T', keep that which is committed"
subscr. The first to T' was written from "
2Ti 1: 2 To T', my dearly beloved son: "
Ph'm 1 and T' our brother, unto Philemon "
Heb13: 23 our brother T' is set at liberty; "
subscr. to the Hebrews from Italy by T'.* "

tin
Nu 31: 22 the brass, the iron, the t', and the 913
Isa 1: 25 away thy dross, take away all thy t':"
Eze 22: 18 all they are brass, and t', and iron, "
20 brass, and iron, and lead, and t', "
27: 12 with silver, iron, t', and lead, they "

tingle
1Sa 3: 11 every one that heareth it shall t'. 6750
2Ki 21: 12 heareth of it, both his ears shall t'. "
Jer 19: 3 whosoever heareth, his ears shall t'. "

tinkling
Isa 3: 16 and making a t' with their feet: 5913
18 of their t' ornaments about their feet;*
1Co 13: 1 as sounding brass, or a t' cymbal.* 214

tip
Ex 29: 20 the t' of the right ear of Aaron, 8571
20 the t' of the right ear of his sons, "
Le 8: 23 it upon the t' of Aaron's right ear, "
24 blood upon the t' of their right ear, "
14: 14 put it upon the t' of the right ear "
17 put upon the t' of the right ear "
25 put it upon the t' of the right ear "
28 upon the t' of the right ear of him "
Lu 16: 24 may dip the t' of his finger in water,206

Tiphsah (*tif'-sah*)
1Ki 4: 24 T' even to Azzah, over all the 8607
2Ki 15: 16 Then Menahem smote T', and all "

Tiras (*ti'-ras*)
Ge 10: 2 and Tubal, and Meshech, and T'. 8493
1Ch 1: 5 and Tubal, and Meshech, and T'. "

Tirathites (*ti'-rath-ites*)
1Ch 2: 55 the T', the Shimeathites, and 8654

tire See also ATTIRE; RETIRE; TIRED; TIRES.
Eze 24: 17 the t' of thine head upon thee, and*6287

tired See also RETIRED.
2Ki 9: 30 painted her face, and t' her head, ‡3190

tires
Isa 3: 18 and their round t' like the moon, *7720
Eze 24: 23 your t' shall be upon your heads, 6287

Tirhakah (*tur-ha'-kah*)
2Ki 19: 9 heard say of T' king of Ethiopia, 8640
Isa 37: 9 say concerning T' king of Ethiopia,"

Tirhanah (*tur-ha'-nah*)
1Ch 2: 48 concubine, bare Sheber, and T'. 8647

Tiria (*tir'-e-ah*)
1Ch 4: 16 Jehaleleel; Ziph, and Ziphah, T', 8493

Tirshatha (*tur'-sha-thah*)
Ezr 2: 63 the T' said unto them, that they 8660
Ne 7: 65 the T' said unto them, that they "
70 The T' gave to the treasure a "
8: 9 And Nehemiah, which is the T', "
10: 1 sealed were, Nehemiah, the T', "

Tirzah (*tur'-zah*)
Nu 26: 33 Noah, Hoglah, Milcah, and T'. 8656
27: 1 and Hoglah, and Milcah, and T', "
36: 11 For Mahlah, T', and Hoglah, and "
Jos 12: 24 The king of T', one: all the kings "
17: 3 and Noah, Hoglah, Milcah, and T'. "
1Ki 14: 17 and departed, and came to T': "
15: 21 building of Ramah, and dwelt in T'."
33 Ahijah to reign over all Israel in T',"
16: 6 his fathers, and was buried in T': "
1Ki 16: 8 Baasha to reign over Israel in T', 8656
9 as he was in T', drinking himself "
9 of Arza steward of his house in T'. "
15 did Zimri reign seven days in T'. "
17 with him, and they besieged T'. "
23 years: six years reigned he in T'. "
2Ki 15: 14 the son of Gadi went up from T', "
16 and the coasts thereof from T': "
Ca 6: 4 art beautiful, O my love, as T', "

Tishbite (*tish'-bite*)
1Ki 17: 1 And Elijah the T', who was of 8664
21: 17, 28 the Lord came to Elijah the T', "
2Ki 1: 3 of the Lord said to Elijah the T', "
8 And he said, It is Elijah the T'. "
9: 36 spake by his servant Elijah the T'. "

tithe See also TITHES; TITHING.
Le 27: 30 all the t' of the land, whether of 4643
32 concerning the t' of the herd, or of "
Nu 18: 26 Lord, even a tenth part of the t'. "
De 12: 17 within thy gates the t' of thy corn, "
14: 22 truly t' all the increase of thy seed,6237
23 t' of thy corn, of thy wine, and of 4643
28 forth all the t' of thine increase "
2Ch 31: 5 the t' of all things brought they in "
6 brought in the t' of oxen and sheep,"
6 the t' of holy things which were "
Ne 10: 38 the Levites shall bring up the t' of "
13: 12 brought all Judah the t' of the corn "
M't 23: 23 for ye pay t' of mint and anise 586
Lu 11: 42 ye t' mint and rue and all manner "

tithes
Ge 14: 20 hand. And he gave him t' of all. *4643
Le 27: 31 will at all redeem ought of his t', * "
Nu 18: 24 But the t' of the children of Israel,*"
26 the t' which I have given you from*"
28 offering unto the Lord of all your t',"
De 12: 6 your t', and heave offerings of your "
11 your t', and the heave offering of "
26: 12 the t' of thine increase the third * "
2Ch 31: 12 brought in the offerings and the t' "
Ne 10: 37 the t' of our ground unto the "
37 have the t' in all the cities of our 6237
38 Levites, when the Levites take t': "
38 bring up the tithe of the t' unto 4643
12: 44 for the firstfruits, and for the t', "
13: 5 the vessels, and the t' of the corn, "
Am 4: 4 and your t' after three years: "
Mal 3: 8 robbed thee? In t' and offerings. "
10 ye all the t' into the storehouse, * "
Lu 18: 12 week, I give t' of all that I possess. 586
Heb 7: 5 to take t' of the people according to "
6 from them received t' of Abraham,1183
8 And here men that die receive t'; 1181
9 receiveth t', payed t' in Abraham. 1183

tithing
De 26: 12 made an end of t' all the tithes 6237
12 third year, which is the year of t', 4643

title See also TITLES.
2Ki 23: 17 said, What t' is that that I see? *6725
Joh 19: 19 And Pilate wrote a t', and put it 5102
20 This t' then read many of the Jews: "

titles
Job 32: 21 let me give flattering t' unto man.
22 For I know not to give flattering t';

tittle
M't 5: 18 one t' shall in no wise pass from 2762
Lu 16: 17 pass, than one t' of the law to fail. "

Titus (*ti'-tus*)
2Co 2: 13 I found not T' my brother: 5103
7: 6 comforted us by the coming of T': "
13 the more joyed we for the joy of T'."
14 boasting, which I made before T', "
8: 6 Insomuch that we desired T', that "
16 care into the heart of T' for you. "
23 Whether any do enquire of T', he "
12: 18 I desired T', and with him I sent "
18 brother. Did T' make a gain of you?"
subscr. of Macedonia, by T' and Lucas. * "
Ga 2: 1 and took T' with me also. "
3 But neither T', who was with me, "
2Ti 4: 10 to Galatia, T' unto Dalmatia. "
Tit 1: 4 To T', mine own son after the "
subscr. written to T', ordained the first * "

Tizite (*ti'-zite*)
1Ch 11: 45 and Joha his brother, the T', 8491

to See in the APPENDIX; also ALLTO; HERETOFORE; HITHERTO; INTO; THERETO; TOGETHER; TOO; TOWARD; UNTO; WHERETO.

Toah (*to'-ah*) See also NAHATH; TOHU.
1Ch 6: 34 the son of Eliel, the son of T', 8430

Tob (*tob*) See also ISH-TOB; TOB-ADONIJAH.
J'g 11: 3 and dwelt in the land of T': 2897
5 Jephthah out of the land of T': "

Tob-adonijah (*tob''-ad-o-ni'-jah*)
2Ch 17: 8 and Tobijah, and T', Levites; 2899

Tobiah (*to-bi'-ah*) See also TOBIJAH.
Ezr 2: 60 of Delaiah, the children of T', 2900
Ne 2: 10, 19 Horonite, and T' the servant, "
4: 3 Now T' the Ammonite was by him, "
7 pass, that when Sanballat, and T', "
6: 1 to pass, when Sanballat, and T', "
12 for T' and Sanballat had hired him."
14 think thou upon T' and Sanballat "
17 Judah sent many letters unto T', "
17 the letters of T' came unto them. "
19 T' sent letters to put me in fear. "
7: 62 the children of T', the children of "
13: 4 of our God, was allied unto T': "
7 the evil that Eliashib did for T', "
8 forth all the household stuff of T' "

Tobijah (*to-bi'-jah*) See also TOBIAH.
2Ch 17: 8 and *T*, and Tob-adonijah, Levites; 2900
Zec 6: 10 even of Heldai, of *T*, and of "
14 shall be to Helem, and to *T*, "

Tochen (*to'-ken*)
1Ch 4: 32 and *T*, and Ashan, five cities: 8507

to-day See DAY.

toe See also TOES.
Ex 29: 20 upon the great *t* of their right foot, 931
Le 8: 23 upon the great *t* of his right foot. "
14: 14 upon the great *t* of his right foot: "
17 upon the great *t* of his right foot, "
25 upon the great *t* of his right foot: "
28 upon the great *t* of his right foot, "

toes
Le 8: 24 the great *t* of their right feet: * 931
J'g 1: 6 off his thumbs and his great *t*. 931, 7272
7 thumbs and...great *t* cut off, " "
2Sa 21: 20 fingers, and on every foot six *t*, 676
1Ch 20: 6 whose fingers and *t* were four and "
Da 2: 41 whereas thou sawest the feet and *t*, 677
42 And as the *t* of the feet were part of "

Togarmah (*to-gar'-mah*)
Ge 10: 3 Ashkenaz, and Riphath, and *T*. 8425
1Ch 1: 6 Ashchenaz, and Riphath, and *T*. "
Eze 27: 14 the house of *T* traded in thy fairs "
38: 6 house of *T* of the north quarters, "

together See also ALTOGETHER.
Ge 1: 9 heaven be gathered *t* unto one place,
10 gathering *t* of the waters called he
3: 7 and they sewed fig leaves *t*, and
13: 6 them, that they might dwell *t*: 3162
6 so that they could not dwell *t*. "
14: 3 were joined *t* in the vale of Siddim,
22: 6 and they went both of them *t*. 3162
8 so they went both of them *t*. "
19 rose up and went *t* to Beer-sheba; "
25: 22 children struggled *t* within her;
29: 7 the cattle should be gathered *t*:
8 until all the flocks be gathered *t*,
22 Laban gathered *t* all the men of
34: 30 gather themselves *t* against me,
36: 7 than that they might dwell *t*; 3162
42: 17 put them all *t* into ward three days.
49: 1 and said, Gather yourselves *t*,
2 Gather yourselves *t*, and hear, ye*
Ex 2: 13 two men of the Hebrews strove *t*:
3: 16 and gather the elders of Israel *t*,
4: 29 and gathered *t* all the elders of the
8: 14 they gathered them *t* upon heaps:
15: 8 the waters were gathered *t*, *
19: 8 And all the people answered *t*, 3162
21: 18 And if men strive *t*, and one smite *
26: 3 five curtains shall be coupled *t*
6 and couple the curtains *t* with the*
11 and couple the tent *t*, that it may be
24 they shall be coupled *t* beneath, *
24 and they shall be coupled *t* above*3162
28: 7 and so it shall be joined *t*.
30: 35 art of the apothecary, tempered *t*,*
32: 1 gathered themselves *t* unto Aaron,
26 gathered themselves *t* unto him.
35: 1 of the children of Israel *t*, *
36: 18 taches of brass to couple the tent *t*,
29 coupled *t* at the head thereof, *3162
39: 4 shoulderpieces for it, to couple it *t*:
4 by the two edges was it coupled *t*.
Le 8: 3 gather thou all the congregation *t**
4 and the assembly was gathered *t**
24: 10 a man of Israel strove *t* in the camp;
26: 25 ye are gathered *t* within your cities,
Nu 1: 18 assembled all the congregation *t*
8: 9 gather...the children of Israel *t*: *
10: 7 congregation is to be gathered *t*,
11: 22 the fish of the sea be gathered *t* for
14: 35 that are gathered *t* against me:
16: 3 And they gathered themselves *t*
11 all thy company are gathered *t*
20: 2 and they gathered themselves *t*
8 and gather thou the assembly *t*, *
10 Aaron gathered the congregation *t*
21: 16 unto Moses, Gather the people *t*,
23 but Sihon gathered all his people *t*,
26: 10 and swallowed them up *t* with Korah,
27: 3 gathered themselves *t* against
De 4: 10 unto me, Gather me the people *t*,*
22: 10 plough with an ox and an ass *t*. 3162
11 sorts, as of woollen and linen *t*. "
25: 5 If brethren dwell *t*, and one of "
11 men strive *t* one with another, "
31: 12 Gather the people *t*, men, and
33: 5 tribes of Israel were gathered *t*. 3162
17 he shall push the people *t* to the * "
Jos 8: 16 people that were in Ai were called *t*
9: 2 That they gathered themselves *t*, 3162
10: 5 gathered themselves *t*, and went
6 mountains are gathered *t* against us.
11: 5 when all these kings were met *t*, 3162
5 came and pitched *t* at the waters "
17: 10 they met *t* in Asher on the north,*
18: 1 of Israel assembled *t* at Shiloh,
22: 12 gathered themselves *t* at Shiloh,
J'g 4: 13 Sisera gathered *t* all his chariots,
6: 33 of the east were gathered *t*, 3162
38 and thrust the fleece *t*, and wringed
7: 23 of Israel gathered themselves *t*
24 of Ephraim gathered themselves *t*,
9: 6 the men of Shechem gathered *t*,
47 of Shechem were gathered *t*.
10: 17 children of Ammon were gathered *t*,
17 of Israel assembled themselves *t*,
11: 20 but Sihon gathered all his people *t*,
12: 1 Ephraim gathered themselves *t*,
4 Jephthah gathered *t* all the men

J'g 16: 23 Philistines gathered them *t* for to
18: 22 to Micah's house were gathered *t*,
19: 6 did eat and drink both of them *t*: 3162
29 and divided her, *t* with her bones,*
20: 1 was gathered *t* as one man, *
11 the city, knit *t* as one man.
14 of Benjamin gathered themselves *t*
1Sa 5: 11 gathered *t* all the lords of the
7: 6 And they gathered *t* to Mizpeh,
7 Israel were gathered *t* to Mizpeh,
8: 4 of Israel gathered themselves *t*,
10: 17 Samuel called the people *t* unto
11: 11 that two of them were not left *t*. 3162
13: 4 people were called *t* after Saul to
5 Philistines gathered...*t* to fight
11 Philistines gathered themselves *t*
15: 4 And Saul gathered the people *t*, *
17: 1 Philistines gathered *t* their armies
1 and were gathered *t* at Shochoh,
2 men of Israel were gathered *t*, 3162
10 give me a man, that we may fight *t*. "
23: 8 Saul called all the people *t* to war,* "
25: 1 all the Israelites were gathered *t*,
28: 1 Philistines gathered their armies *t*
4 Philistines gathered themselves *t*,
4 and Saul gathered all Israel *t*, and
23 But his servants, *t* with the woman,
29: 1 the Philistines gathered *t* all their
31: 6 and all his men, that same day *t*. 3162
2Sa 2: 13 and met *t* by the pool of Gibeon: * "
16 fellow's side; so they fell down *t*: "
25 Benjamin gathered themselves *t*
30 he had gathered all the people *t*,
6: 1 David gathered *t* all the chosen men
10: 15 they gathered themselves *t*. 3162
17 told David, he gathered all Israel *t*,
12: 3 it grew up *t* with him, and with 3162
28 gather the rest of the people *t*,
29 David gathered all the people *t*,
14: 6 and they two strove *t* in the field,
16 would destroy me and my son *t* 3162
20: 14 they were gathered *t*, and went also
21: 9 they fell all seven *t*, and were put 3162
23: 9 were there gathered *t* to battle,
11 Philistines were gathered *t* into a
1Ki 3: 18 we were *t*; there was no stranger 3162
5: 12 and they two made a league *t*.
10: 26 And Solomon gathered *t* chariots
11: 1 *t* with the daughter of Pharaoh,
18: 20 and gathered the prophets *t* unto
20: 1 of Syria gathered all his host *t*:
22: 6 of Israel gathered the prophets *t*,
2Ki 2: 8 took his mantle, and wrapped it *t*,
3: 10, 13 hath called these three kings *t*,
9: 25 I and thou rode *t* after Ahab his 6776
10: 18 Jehu gathered all the people *t*,
1Ch 10: 6 Saul...and all his house died *t*. 3162
11: 13 Philistines were gathered *t* to
13: 5 So David gathered all Israel *t*,
15: 3 And David gathered all Israel *t* *
16: 35 and gather us *t*, and deliver us
19: 7 of Ammon gathered themselves *t*
22: 2 David commanded to gather *t* the
23: 2 he gathered *t* all the princes of
2Ch 12: 5 that were gathered *t* to Jerusalem
15: 10 they gathered...*t* at Jerusalem
18: 5 of Israel gathered *t* of prophets
20: 4 And Judah gathered themselves *t*,
24: 5 he gathered *t* the priests and the
25: 5 Amaziah gathered Judah *t*, and
28: 24 Ahaz gathered *t* the vessels of the
29: 4 and gathered them *t* into the east
30: 3 the people gathered themselves *t*
32: 4 was gathered much people *t*,
6 gathered them *t*...in the street
34: 17 they have gathered *t* the money *
29 sent and gathered *t* all the elders
Ezr 2: 64 whole congregation *t* was forty 259
3: 1 gathered themselves *t* as one man
9 and his sons, the sons of Judah, *t*, 259
11 they sang *t* by course in praising*
4: 3 we ourselves *t* will build unto the 3162
6: 20 and the Levites were purified *t*, 259
7: 28 gathered *t* out of Israel chief men
8: 15 I gathered them *t* to the river that
10: 7 should gather...*t* unto Jerusalem;
9 Benjamin gathered themselves *t*
Ne 4: 6 all the wall was joined *t* unto the
8 conspired all of them *t* to come 3162
6: 2 Come, let us meet *t* in some one of "
7 therefore, and let us take counsel *t*. "
10 Let us meet *t* in the house of God,
7: 5 mine heart to gather *t* the nobles,
66 whole congregation *t* was forty 259
8: 1 gathered themselves *t* as one man
13 were gathered *t* the chief of the
12: 28 the singers gathered themselves *t*,
13: 11 And I gathered them *t*, and set
Es 2: 3 gather *t* all the fair young virgins
8 many maidens were gathered *t*
19 virgins were gathered *t* the second
4: 16 Go, gather *t* all the Jews that are
8: 11 every city to gather themselves *t*,
9: 2 The Jews gathered themselves *t*
15 in Shushan gathered themselves *t*
16 provinces gathered themselves *t*
18 that were at Shushan assembled *t*
Job 2: 11 they had made an appointment *t* 3162
3: 18 There the prisoners rest *t*; they "
6: 2 my calamity laid in the balances *t*!‡"
9: 32 and we should come *t* in judgment."
10: 8 have made me and fashioned me *t* "
11: 10 cut off, and shut up, or gather *t*, *
16: 10 gathered themselves *t* against me. 3162
17: 16 pit, when our rest *t* is in the dust.* "
19: 12 His troops come *t*, and raise up

Job 24: 4 the poor of the earth hide...*t*. ‡3162
30: 7 the nettles they were gathered *t*.
34: 15 All flesh shall perish *t*, and man 3162
38: 7 When the morning stars sang *t*, "
38 and the clods cleave fast *t*?
40: 13 Hide them in the dust *t*; and bind 3162
17 sinews of his stones are wrapped *t*.
41: 15 pride, shut up *t* as with a close seal.
17 they stick *t*, that they cannot be
23 flakes of his flesh are joined *t*:
Ps 2: 2 and the rulers take counsel *t*, 3162
14: 3 aside, they are all *t* become filthy: "
31: 13 they took counsel *t* against me,
33: 7 He gathereth the waters of the sea *t*
34: 3 me, and let us exalt his name *t*. 3162
35: 15 and gathered themselves *t*:
15 the abjects gathered themselves *t*
26 and brought to confusion *t* 3162
37: 38 transgressors shall be destroyed *t*: "
40: 14 be ashamed and confounded *t* "
41: 7 All that hate me whisper *t* against "
47: 9 The princes...are gathered *t*, "
48: 4 were assembled, they passed by *t*. "
49: 2 Both low and high, rich and poor, *t*."
50: 5 Gather my saints *t* unto me;
55: 14 We took sweet counsel *t*, and 3162
56: 6 They gather themselves *t*, they hide
71: 10 wait for my soul take counsel *t*, 3162
74: 8 hearts, Let us destroy them *t*: * "
83: 5 have consulted *t* with one consent: "
85: 10 Mercy and truth are met *t*;
88: 17 they compassed me about *t*. 3162
94: 21 They gather themselves *t* against
98: 8 hands: let the hills be joyful *t* 3162
102: 22 When the people are gathered *t*,
104: 22 ariseth, they gather themselves *t*,*
122: 3 as a city that is compact *t*: 3162
133: 1 is for brethren to dwell *t* in unity! "
140: 2 are they gathered *t* for war.
147: 2 gathered *t* the outcasts of Israel.
Pr 22: 2 The rich and poor meet *t*: the Lord is
29: 13 poor and the deceitful man meet *t*:
Ec 3: 5 and a time to gather stones *t*;
4: 11 if two lie *t*, then they have heat:
Isa 1: 18 Come now, and let us reason *t*, saith
28 and of the sinners shall be *t*, and 3162
31 spark, and they shall both burn *t*, "
8: 10 Take counsel *t*, and it shall come to
9: 11 him, and join his enemies *t*; *
21 they *t* shall be against Judah. 3162
11: 6 the young lion and the fatling *t*; "
7 their young ones shall lie down *t*: "
12 gather *t* the dispersed of Judah
14 shall spoil them of the east *t*: 3162
13: 4 kingdoms of nations gathered *t*:
18: 6 They shall be left *t* unto the fowls 3162
22: 3 All thy rulers are fled *t*, they are "
3 that are found in thee are bound *t*, "
9 gathered *t* the waters of the lower
24: 22 And they shall be gathered *t*, as
25: 11 and he shall bring down their pride *t*
26: 19 *t* with my dead body shall they arise.*
27: 4 them, I would burn them *t*. 3162
31: 3 fall down, and they shall fail *t*. "
34: 4 the heavens shall be rolled *t* as
40: 5 and all flesh shall see it *t*: 3162
41: 1 let us come near *t* to judgment. "
19 and the pine, and the box tree *t*: "
20 and consider, and understand *t*, "
23 may be dismayed, and behold it *t*. "
43: 9 Let all the nations be gathered *t*, "
17 they shall lie down *t*, they shall not "
26 me in remembrance: let us plead *t*: "
44: 11 let them all be gathered *t*, let
11 and they shall be ashamed *t*. 3162
45: 8 let righteousness spring up *t*; I
16 go to confusion *t* that are makers
20 draw near *t*, ye that are escaped of "
21 near; yea, let them take counsel *t*: "
46: 2 They stoop, they bow down *t*; "
48: 13 call unto them, they stand up *t*. "
49: 18 all these gather themselves *t*, and
50: 8 contend with me? let us stand *t*: 3162
52: 8 with the voice *t* shall they sing: "
9 Break forth into joy, sing *t*, ye "
54: 15 they shall surely gather *t*, but
15 whosoever shall gather *t* against
60: 4 all they gather themselves *t*, they
5 Then thou shalt see, and flow *t*,
7 shall be gathered *t* unto thee,
13 tree, the pine tree, and the box *t*. 3162
62: 9 that have brought it *t* shall drink*
65: 7 the iniquities of your fathers *t*, 3162
25 The wolf and the lamb shall feed *t*, 259
66: 17 the mouse, shall be consumed *t*, 3162
Jer 3: 18 they shall come *t* out of the land of "
4: 5 cry, gather *t*, and say, Assemble *
6: 11 the assembly of young men *t*: 3162
12 with their fields and wives *t*: "
21 the sons *t* shall fall upon them; "
13: 14 even the fathers and the sons *t*, "
31: 8 her that travaileth with child *t*:
12 shall flow *t* to the goodness of the
13 dance, both young men and old *t*: 3162
24 and in all the cities thereof *t*, "
41: 1 they did eat bread *t* in Mizpah.
46: 12 mighty, and they are fallen both *t*. "
21 turned back, and are fled away *t*: "
48: 7 with his priests and his princes *t*. "
49: 3 and his priests and his princes *t*. "
14 Gather ye *t*, and come against
50: 4 they and the children of Judah *t*, 3162
29 Call *t* the archers against
33 of Judah were oppressed *t*: 3162
51: 27 call *t* against her the kingdoms of
38 They shall roar *t* like lions: they 3162

Jer 51:44 nations shall not flow t' any more
La 2: 8 to lament; they languished t'. 3162
Eze 21:14 prophesy, and smite thine hands t'.
17 I will also smite mine hands t', and I
29: 5 thou shalt not be brought t', nor
37: 7 bones came t', bone to his bone.
Da 2:35 and the gold, broken to pieces t', 2298
3: 2 king sent to gather t' the princes,
3 gathered t' unto the dedication of
27 counsellers, being gathered t',
6: 6 presidents and princes assembled t'
7 have consulted t' to establish
11: 6 they shall join themselves t';
Ho 1:11 children of Israel be gathered t', 3162
11: 8 me, my repentings are kindled t'. "
Joe 3:11 gather yourselves t' round about:
Am 1:15 captivity, he and his princes t', 3162
3: 3 Can two walk t', except they be "
Mic 2:12 them t' as the sheep of Bozrah,
Na 1:10 while they be folden t' as thorns,†‡
2:10 melteth, and the knees smite t',
Zep 2: 1 Gather yourselves t', yea,
1 yea, gather t', O nation not desired;
Zec 10: 4 bow, out of him every oppressor t'.3162
12: 3 people of the earth be gathered t'
14:14 round about shall be gathered t',
M't 1:18 before they came t', she was found4905
2: 4 priests and scribes of the people t'.4863
13: 2 great multitudes were gathered t' "
30 Let both grow t' until the harvest:4886
30 Gather ye t' first the tares, and *4816
18:20 three are gathered t' in my name, 4863
19: 6 What therefore God hath joined t',4801
22:10 gathered t' all as many as they 4863
34 they were gathered t'. 1909,3588,846
41 the Pharisees were gathered t', 4863
23:37 I have gathered thy children t', 1996
24:28 will the eagles be gathered t'. 4863
31 gather t' his elect from the four 1996
26: 3 Then assembled t' the chief priests,4863
27:17 when they were gathered t', "
62 and Pharisees came t' unto Pilate, "
M'r 1:33 city was gathered t' at the door. 1996
2: 2 many were gathered t', 4863
15 and sinners sat also t' with Jesus *4873
3:20 the multitude cometh t' again, 4905
6:30 apostles gathered themselves t' 4863
33 them, and came t' unto him. 4905
7: 1 came t' unto him the Pharisees, 4863
9:25 that the people came running t', 1998
10: 9 What therefore God hath joined t',4801
12:28 having heard them reasoning t', 4802
13:27 gather t' his elect from the four 1996
14:56 him, but their witness agreed not t'.
59 neither so did their witness agree t'.
15:16 and they call t' the whole band. 4779
Lu 5:15 great multitudes came t' to hear, 4905
6:38 measure, pressed down, and shaken t',
8: 4 much people were gathered t', 4896
9: 1 he called his twelve disciples t', 4779
11:29 the people were gathered thick t', 1865
12: 1 were gathered t' an innumerable 1996
13:11 was bowed t', and could in no wise4794
34 I have gathered thy children t', 1996
15: 6 he calleth t' his friends and 4779
9 her friends and her neighbours t',
13 the younger son gathered all t', 4863
17:35 women...be grinding t'; 1909,3588,846
37 will the eagles be gathered t'. 4863
22:55 were set down t', Peter sat down 4776
66 priests and the scribes came t', 4863
23:12 Herod were made friends t': *3326,240
13 he had called t' the chief priests 4779
48 all the people that came t' to that 4836
24:14 they talked t' of all these *4314,240
15 they communed t' and reasoned,
33 and found the eleven gathered t', 4867
Joh 4:36 he that reapeth may rejoice t'. 3674
6:13 Therefore they gathered them t', *4863
11:52 gather t' in one the children of God"
53 they took counsel t' for to put *4858
20: 4 So they ran both t': and the 3674
7 but wrapped t' in a place by itself.*1794
21: 2 There were t' Simon Peter, and 3674
Ac 1: 4 being assembled t' with them, 4871
6 When they therefore were come t',4905
15 of names t' were about an 1909,3588,846
2: 6 abroad, the multitude came t', 4905
44 all that believed were t', 1909,3588,846
3: 1 Peter and John went up t'* "
11 all the people ran t' unto 4936,1909, "
4: 6 were gathered t' at Jerusalem. 4863
26 rulers were gathered t' 1909,3588,846
27 people of Israel, were gathered t', 4863
31 where they were assembled t';
5: 9 it that ye have agreed t' to tempt 4856
21 him, and called the council t', 4779
10:24 called t' his kinsmen and near
27 and found many that were come t'.4905
12:12 many were gathered t' praying. 4867
13:44 came almost the whole city t' to 4863
14: 1 they went both t' into the 2596,3588,846
27 and had gathered the church t', 4863
15: 6 And the apostles and elders came t'"
30 they had gathered the multitude t', "
16:22 multitude rose up t' against them:4911
19:19 arts brought their books t', 4851
25 he called t' with the workmen 4867
32 not wherefore they were come t'. 4897
20: 7 disciples came t' to break bread, 4863
8 where they were gathered t'.
21:22 multitude must needs come t': *4905
30 was moved, and the people ran t': 4890
23:12 certain of the Jews banded t', 4966
28:17 Paul called the chief of the Jews t':4779
17 and when they were come t', he 4905

Ro 1:12 I may be comforted t' with you *4837
3:12 they are t' become unprofitable; 260
6: 5 planted t' in the likeness of his *4854
8:17 that we may be also glorified t'. *4888
22 groaneth and travaileth in pain t' 4944
28 that all things work t' for good 4903
15:30 strive t' with me in your prayers 4865
1Co 1:10 that ye be perfectly joined t' in the2675
3: 9 For we are labourers t' with God: *4904
5: 4 when ye are gathered t', and my 4863
7: 5 come t' again, that Satan 1909,3588,846
11:17 that ye come t' not for the better, 4905
18 when ye come t' in the church, I "
20 When ye come t' therefore into one "
33 when ye come t' to eat, tarry one "
34 ye come not t' unto condemnation. "
12:24 but God hath tempered the body t',4786
14:23 whole church be come t' into one 4905
26 when ye come t', every one of you "
2Co 1:11 Ye also helping t' by prayer for us,4943
6: 1 We then, as workers t' with him, 4903
14 Be ye not unequally yoked t' with*2086
Eph 1:10 might gather t' in one all things * 346
2: 5 hath quickened us t' with Christ, 4806
6 And hath raised us up t', *4891
6 made us sit t' in heavenly places *4776
21 all the building fitly framed t' 4883
22 In whom ye also are builded t' for 4925
4:16 the whole body fitly joined t' and 4883
Ph'p 1:27 one mind striving t' for the faith *4866
3:17 Brethren, be followers t' of me, 4831
Col 2: 2 be comforted, being knit t' in love,4822
13 hath he quickened t' with him, 4806
19 ministered, and knit t', 4822
1Th 4:17 remain shall be caught up t' with 260
5:10 sleep, we should live t' with him. "
11 Wherefore comfort yourselves t', * 240
2Th 2: 1 and by our gathering t' unto him, 1997
Heb 10:25 the assembling of ourselves t', "
Jas 5: 3 Ye have heaped treasure t' for the*
1Pe 3: 7 being heirs t' of the grace of life; *4789
5:13 is at Babylon, elected t' with you, 4899
Re 6:14 as a scroll when it is rolled t'; *
16:16 he gathered them t' into a place 4863
19:17 Come and gather yourselves t' unto"
19 armies, gathered t' to make war "
20: 8 Magog, to gather them t' to battle: "

Tohu (*to'-hu*) See also NAHATH; TOAH.
1Sa 1: 1 the son of Elihu, the son of T'. 8459

Toi (*to'-i*) See also TOU.
2Sa 8: 9 When T' king of Hamath heard 8583
10 T' sent Joram his son unto king "
10 for Hadadezer had wars with T'. "

toil See also TOILED; TOILING.
Ge 5:29 our work and t' of our hands, 6093
41:51 hath made me forget all my t', 5999
M't 6:28 they t' not, neither do they spin: 2872
Lu 12:27 grow: they t' not, they spin not;

toiled
Lu 5: 5 Master, we have t' all the night, 2872

toiling
M'r 6:48 And he saw them t' in rowing; for* 928

token See also TOKENS.
Ge 9:12 This is the t' of the covenant which226
13 t' of a covenant between me and "
17 This is the t' of the covenant, which "
17:11 t' of the covenant betwixt me and "
Ex 3:12 this shall be a t' unto thee, that I "
12:13 the blood shall be to you for a t' "
13:16 shall be for a t' upon thine hand, * "
Nu 17:10 be kept for a t' against the rebels; "
Jos 2:12 father's house, and give me a true t':"
Ps 86:17 Shew me a t' for good; that they "
M'r 14:44 betrayed him had given them a t', 4953
Ph'p 1:28 to them an evident t' of perdition, 1732
2Th 1: 5 a manifest t' of the righteous 1730
3:17 which is the t' in every epistle: 4592

tokens
De 22:15 forth the t' of the damsel's virginity
17 are the t' of my daughter's virginity.
20 t' of virginity be not found for the
Job 21:29 way? and do ye not know their t', 226
Ps 65: 8 uttermost parts are afraid at thy t': "
135: 9 sent t' and wonders into the midst "
Isa 44:25 That frustrateth the t' of the liars, "

Tola (*to'-lah*) See also TOLAITES.
Ge 46:13 sons of Issachar; T', and Phuvah,8439
Nu 26:23 of T', the family of the Tolaites: "
J'g 10: 1 defend Israel T' the son of Puah, "
1Ch 7: 1 sons of Issachar were, T', and "
2 sons of T'; Uzzi, and Rephaiah, "
2 their father's house, to wit, of T': "

Tolad (*to'-lad*) See also EL-TOLAD.
1Ch 4:29 Bilhah, and at Ezem, and at T', 8434

Tolaites (*to'-lah-ites*)
Nu 26:23 of Tola, the family of the T': 8440

told See also FORETOLD.
Ge 3:11 Who t' thee that thou wast naked?5046
9:22 and t' his two brethren without. "
14:13 escaped, and t' Abram the Hebrew;"
20: 8 t' all these things in their ears: 1696
22: 3 the place of which God had t' him. 559
9 the place which God had t' him of; "
20 that it was t' Abraham, saying, 5046
24:28 t' them of her mother's house these "
33 eat, until I have t' mine errand. 1696
66 servant t' Isaac all things that he 5608
26:32 and t' him concerning the well 5046
27:42 her elder son were t' to Rebekah: "
29:12 Jacob t' Rachel that he was her "
12 and she ran and t' her father. "
13 And he t' Laban all these things. 5608

Ge 31:20 in that he t' him not that he fled. 5046
22 t' Laban on the third day that "
37: 5 a dream, and he t' it his brethren: "
9 dream, and t' it his brethren, and 5608
10 And he t' it to his father, and to "
38:13 was t' Tamar, saying, Behold, thy 5046
24 that it was t' Judah, saying, "
40: 9 chief butler t' his dream to Joseph,5608
41: 8 and Pharaoh t' them his dream; "
12 we t' him, and he interpreted to us "
24 and I t' this unto the magicians; 559
42:29 t' him all that befell unto them; 5046
43: 7 we t' him according to the tenor "
44:24 we t' him the words of my lord. "
45:26 t' him, saying, Joseph is yet alive, "
27 t' him all the words of Joseph, 1696
47: 1 Joseph came and t' Pharaoh, and 5046
48: 1 that one t' Joseph, Behold, thy 559
2 one t' Jacob, and said, Behold, 5046
Ex 4:28 Moses t' Aaron all the words of "
5: 1 Aaron went in, and t' Pharaoh, * 559
14: 5 it was t' the king of Egypt that the5046
16:22 congregation came and t' Moses. "
18: 8 Moses t' his father in law all that 5608
19: 9 Moses t' the words of the people 5046
24: 3 Moses came and t' the people all 5608
Le 21:24 Moses t' it unto Aaron, and to his*1696
Nu 11:24 t' the people the words of the Lord,"
27 ran a young man, and t' Moses, 5046
13:27 t' him, and said, We came unto 5608
14:39 Moses t' these sayings unto all 1696
23:26 said unto Balak, T' not I thee, "
29:40 t' the children of Israel according 559
De 17: 4 And it be t' thee, and thou hast 5046
Jos 2: 2 And it was t' the king of Jericho, 559
23 t' him all things that befell them: 5608
9:24 it was certainly t' thy servants, 5046
10:17 it was t' Joshua, saying, The five "
J'g 6:13 miracles which our fathers t' us 5608
7:13 there was a man that t' a dream "
9: 7 And when they t' it to Jotham, 5046
25 by them: and it was t' Abimelech. "
42 the field; and they t' Abimelech. "
47 it was t' Abimelech, that all the men"
13: 6 woman came and t' her husband, 559
6 was, neither t' he me his name: 5046
23 at this time have t' us such things8085
14: 2 and t' his father and his mother, 5046
6 he t' not his father or his mother "
9 he t' not them that he had taken "
16 my people, and hast not t' it me. "
16 I have not t' it my father nor my "
17 on the seventh day, that he t' her, "
17 she t' the riddle to the children of "
16: 2 it was t' the Gazites, saying, Samson
10, 13 hast mocked me, and t' me lies:1696
15 hast not t' me wherein thy great 5046
17 That he t' her all his heart, and "
18 saw that he had t' her all his heart,"
Ru 3:16 she t' her all that the man had done"
1Sa 3:13 t' him that I will judge his house "
18 Samuel t' him every whit, and hid "
4:13 man came into the city, and t' it, "
14 man came in hastily, and t' Eli. "
8:10 Samuel t' all the words of the Lord 559
9:15 Lord had t' Samuel in his ear a *1540
10:16 He t' us plainly that the asses 5046
16 Samuel spake, he t' him not. "
25 Samuel t' the people the manner 1696
11: 4 t' the tidings in the ears of the * "
5 t' him the tidings of the men of *5608
14: 1 side. But he t' not his father. 5046
33 Then they t' Saul, saying, Behold, "
43 Jonathan t' him, and said, I did but"
15:12 it was t' Samuel, saying, Saul came "
18:20 they t' Saul, and the thing pleased "
24 the servants of Saul t' him, saying, "
26 his servants t' David these words, "
19: 2 and Jonathan t' David, saying, "
11 Michal David's wife t' him, saying, "
18 and t' him all that Saul had done to"
19 t' Saul, saying, Behold, David is at "
21 when it was t' Saul, he sent other "
23: 1 they t' David, saying, Behold, the "
7 it was t' Saul that David was come "
13 was t' Saul that David was escaped "
22 t' me that he dealeth very subtilly. 559
25 they t' David: wherefore he came 5046
24: 1 that it was t' him, saying, Behold, "
25:12 came and t' him all those sayings. "
14 one of the young men t' Abigail, "
19 But she t' not her husband Nabal. "
36 she t' him nothing, less or more, "
37 his wife had t' him these things, "
27: 4 t' Saul that David was fled to Gath: "
2Sa 1: 5 unto the young man that t' him, "
6 the young man that t' him said, As "
13 said unto the young man that t' him,"
2: 4 And they t' David, saying, That the "
3:23 they t' Joab, saying, Abner the son "
4:10 When one t' me, saying, Behold, "
6:12 And it was t' king David, saying, "
10: 5 When they t' it unto David, he sent "
17 was t' David, he gathered all Israel "
11: 5 conceived, and sent and t' David, "
10 when they had t' David, saying, "
18 Then Joab sent and t' David all the "
14:33 Joab came to the king, and t' him: "
15:31 And one t' David, saying, Ahithophel"
17:17 and a wench went and t' them; * "
17 and they went and t' king David. "
18 a lad saw them, and t' Absalom; "
21 went and t' king David, and said "
18:10 a certain man saw it, and t' Joab, "
11 Joab said unto the man that t' him, "
25 watchman cried, and t' the king. "

2Sa 19: 1 And it was t' Joab, Behold, the king 5046
8 they t' unto all the people, saying, "
21: 11 it was t' David what Rizpah the "
24: 13 So Gad came to David, and t' him, "
1Ki 1: 23 they t' the king, saying, Behold "
51 And it was t' Solomon, saying, "
2: 29 t' king Solomon that Joab was fled "
39 And they t' Shimei, saying, Behold, "
41 it was t' Solomon that Shimei had "
8: 5 that could not be t' nor numbered‡5608
10: 3 Solomon t' her all her questions: 5046
3 from the king, which he t' her not. "
7 and, behold, the half was not t' me: "
13: 11 his sons came and t' him all the 5608
11 them they t' also to their father. "
25 and t' it in the city where the old 1696
14: 2 which t' me that I should be king * "
18: 13 Was it not t' my lord what I did 5046
16 went to meet Ahab, and t' him: "
19: 1 Ahab t' Jezebel all that Elijah had "
20: 17 Ben-hadad sent out, and they t' him, "
2Ki 1: 7 meet you, and t' you these words? 1696
4: 7 she came and t' the man of God. 5046
27 hid it from me, and hath not t' me. "
31 and t' him, saying, The child is not "
5: 4 one went in, and t' his lord, saying, "
6: 10 man of God t' him and warned him 559
13 was t' him, saying, Behold, he is 5046
7: 10 they t' them, saying, We came to "
11 they t' it to the king's house within. "
15 messengers returned,...t' the king. "
8: 6 king asked the woman, she t' him. 5608
7 t' him, saying, The man of God is 5046
14 He t' me that thou shouldest surely 559
9: 18 the watchman t', saying, The 5046
20 watchman t', saying, He came even "
36 they came again, and t' him. "
10: 8 there came a messenger, and t' him, "
12: 10 t' the money that was found in ‡4487
11 they gave the money, being t'. *8505
18: 37 t' him the words of Rab-shakeh. 5046
23: 17 the men of the city t' him, It is the 559
1Ch 17: 25 hast t' thy servant that thou wilt *1540
19: 5 t' David how the men were served. 5046
17 it was t' David; and he gathered "
2Ch 2: 2 Solomon t' out threescore and ten 5608
5: 6 which could not be t' nor numbered‡ "
9: 2 Solomon t' her all her questions: 5046
2 from Solomon which he t' her not. "
6 of thy wisdom was not t' me: "
20: 2 came some that t' Jehoshaphat, "
34: 18 Then Shaphan the scribe t' the king. "
Ezr 8: 17 I t' them what they should 7760,6310
Ne 2: 12 neither t' I any man what my God 5046
16 neither had I as yet t' it to the Jews, "
18 I t' them of the hand of my God "
Es 2: 22 who t' it unto Esther the queen; * "
3: 4 that they t' Haman, to see whether "
4 he had t' them that he was a Jew. "
4: 4 chamberlains came and t' it her. "
7 And Mordecai t' him of all that had "
9 And Hatach came and t' Esther the "
12 they t' to Mordecai Esther's words. "
5: 11 Haman t' them of the glory of his *5608
6: 2 that Mordecai had t' of Bigthana "
13 Haman t' Zeresh his wife and all *5608
8: 1 Esther had t' what he was unto 5046
Job 15: 18 wise men have t' from their fathers, "
37: 20 Shall it be t' him that I speak? if a 5608
Ps 44: 1 our fathers have t' us, what work "
52: *title* the Edomite came and t' Saul, 5046
78: 3 known, and our fathers have t' us. 5608
90: 9 we spend our years as a tale that is t'. "
Ec 6: 6 he live a thousand years twice t'. "
Isa 7: 2 And it was t' the house of David, 5046
36: 22 t' him the words of Rabshakeh. "
40: 21 not been t' you from the beginning? "
44: 8 have not I t' thee from that time, *8085
45: 21 who hath t' it from that time? *5046
52: 15 that which had not been t' them 5608
Jer 36: 20 and t' all the words in the ears of 5046
38: 27 he t' them according to all these "
Da 4: 7 and I t' the dream before them; 560
8 before him I t' the dream, saying, "
7: 1 and t' the sum of the matters. "
16 So he t' me, and made me know the "
8: 26 the vision...which was t' is true: "
Jon 1: 10 the Lord, because he had t' them. 5046
Hab 1: 5 not believe, though it be t' you. 5608
Zec 10: 2 a lie, and have t' false dreams; 1696
M't 8: 33 into the city, and t' every thing, *518*
12: 48 and said unto him that t' him, *2036*
14: 12 buried it, and went and t' Jesus. *518*
18: 31 t' unto their lord all that was done. *1285*
24: 25 Behold, I have t' you before. *4280*
26: 13 done, be t' for a memorial of her. **2980*
28: 7 shall ye see him: lo, I have t' you. *2036*
M'r 5: 14 t' it in the city, and in the country. *312*
16 they that saw it t' them how it *1334*
33 him, and t' him all the truth. *2036*
6: 30 t' him all things, both what they *518*
9: 12 he answered and t' them, Elias **2036*
16: 10 t' them that had been with him, *518*
13 they went and t' it unto the residue: "
Lu 1: 45 which were t' her from the Lord. **2980*
2: 17 was t' them concerning this child.* "
18 were t' them by the shepherds. * "
20 and seen, as it was t' unto them. * "
8: 20 it was t' him by certain which said, *518*
34 went and t' it in the city and in the "
36 which saw it t' them by what means "
9: 10 t' him all that they had done. **1334*
36 and t' no man in those days any of *518*
13: 1 some that t' him of the Galilæans, "
18: 37 they t' him, that Jesus of Nazareth "
24: 9 t' all these things unto the eleven, "
Lu 24: 10 t' these things unto the apostles. *3004*
35 t' what things were done in the **1834*
Joh 3: 12 If I have t' you earthly things, and *2036*
4: 29 t' me all things that ever I did: "
39 He t' me all that ever I did. "
51 and t' him, saying, Thy son liveth. **518*
5: 15 and t' the Jews that it was Jesus, *312*
8: 40 a man that hath t' you the truth, *2980*
9: 27 I have t' you already, and ye did *2036*
10: 25 them, I t' you, and ye believed not: "
11: 46 and t' them what things Jesus had "
14: 2 it were not so, I would have t' you. "
29 have t' you before it come to pass, *2046*
16: 4 But these things have I t' you, **2980*
4 remember that I t' you of them. *2036*
18: 8 I have t' you that I am he: "
20: 18 t' the disciples that she had seen * *518*
Ac 5: 22 the prison, they returned, and t' "
25 Then came one and t' them, saying, "
9: 6 be t' thee what thou must do. *2980*
12: 14 t' how Peter stood before the gate. *518*
16: 36 keeper of the prison t' this saying* "
38 serjeants t' these words unto the * *312*
22: 10 it shall be t' thee of all things *2980*
26 he went and t' the chief captain, *518*
23: 16 entered into the castle, and t' Paul. "
30 it was t' me how that the Jews **3377*
27: 25 it shall be even as it was t' me. **2980*
2Co 7: 7 when he t' us your earnest desire, *312*
13: 2 I t' you before, and foretell you, **4280*
Ga 5: 21 as I have also t' you in time past, **4277*
Ph'p 3: 18 walk of whom I have t' you often, *3004*
1Th 3: 4 we t' you before that we should *4302*
2Th 2: 5 with you, I t' you these things? *3004*
Jude 18 that they t' you there should be * "

tolerable
M't 10: 15 It shall be more t' for the land of *414*
11: 22 It shall be more t' for Tyre and "
24 it shall be more t' for the land of "
M'r 6: 11 It shall be more t' for Sodom and * "
Lu 10: 12 it shall be more t' in that day for "
14 it shall be more t' for Tyre and "

toll
Ezr 4: 13 then will they not pay t', tribute, *4061
20 t', tribute, and custom, was paid * "
7: 24 it shall not be lawful to impose t',* "

tomb See also TOMBS.
Job 21: 32 grave, and shall remain in the t'. 1430
M't 27: 60 laid it in his own new t', which he *3419*
M'r 6: 29 up his corpse, and laid it in a t'. "

tombs
M't 8: 28 with devils, coming out of the t', *3419*
23: 29 ye build the t' of the prophets, **5028*
M'r 5: 2 there met him out of the t' a man *3419*
3 had his dwelling among the t'; and "
5 and in the t', crying, and cutting *3418*
Lu 8: 27 abode in any house, but in the t'. "

to-morrow See MORROW.

tongs
Ex 25: 38 t' thereof, and the snuffdishes ‡4457
Nu 4: 9 and his t', and his snuffdishes, ‡ "
1Ki 7: 49 and the lamps, and the t' of gold, ‡ "
2Ch 4: 21 the lamps, and the t', made he of ‡ "
Isa 6: 6 which he had taken with the t' "
44: 12 smith with the t' both worketh in *4621

tongue See also DOUBLETONGUED; TONGUES.
Ge 10: 5 every one after his t', after their 3956
Ex 4: 10 slow of speech, and of a slow t'. "
11: 7 Israel shall not a dog move his t', "
De 28: 49 whose t' thou shalt not understand; "
Jos 10: 21 none moved his t' against any of "
J'g 7: 5 lappeth of the water with his t', "
2Sa 23: 2 by me, and his word was in my t'. "
Ezr 4: 7 letter was written in the Syrian t',* 762
7 and interpreted in the Syrian t'. "
Es 7: 4 bondwomen, I had held my t', *2790
Job 5: 21 be hid from the scourge of the t': 3956
6: 24 Teach me, and I will hold my t': *2790
30 Is there iniquity in my t'? cannot 3956
13: 19 if I hold my t', I shall give up the *2790
15: 5 thou choosest the t' of the crafty. 3956
20: 12 though he hide it under his t'; "
16 asps: the viper's t' shall slay him. "
27: 4 wickedness, nor my t' utter deceit. "
29: 10 their t' cleaved to the roof of their "
33: 2 my t' hath spoken in my mouth. "
41: 1 or his t' with a cord which thou "
Ps 5: 9 sepulchre; they flatter with their t'. "
10: 7 under his t' is mischief and vanity. "
12: 3 the t' that speaketh proud things: "
4 said, With our t' will we prevail; "
15: 3 He that backbiteth not with his t', "
22: 15 my t' cleaveth to my jaws; and thou "
34: 13 Keep thy t' from evil, and thy lips "
35: 28 And my t' shall speak of thy "
37: 30 and his t' talketh of judgment. "
39: 1 my ways, that I sin not with my t': "
3 burned: then spake I with my t', "
45: 1 my t' is the pen of a ready writer. "
50: 19 to evil, and thy t' frameth deceit. "
51: 14 my t' shall sing aloud of thy "
52: 2 Thy t' deviseth mischiefs; like a "
4 words, O thou deceitful t'. "
57: 4 arrows, and their t' a sharp sword. "
64: 3 Who whet their t' like a sword, and "
8 shall make their own t' to fall upon "
66: 17 and he was extolled with my t'. "
68: 23 and the t' of thy dogs in the same. "
71: 24 My t' also shall talk of thy "
73: 9 their t' walketh through the earth. "
109: 2 spoken against me with a lying t'. "
119: 172 My t' shall speak of thy word: for "
120: 2 lying lips, and from a deceitful t'. "
3 be done unto thee, thou false t'? "
126: 2 laughter, and our t' with singing: "
Ps 137: 6 let my t' cleave to the roof of my 3956
139: 4 For there is not a word in my t', "
Pr 6: 17 A proud look, a lying t', and hands "
24 of the t' of a strange woman. "
10: 20 t' of the just is as choice silver: "
31 but the froward t' shall be cut out. "
12: 18 but the t' of the wise is health. "
19 but a lying t' is but for a moment. "
15: 2 The t' of the wise useth knowledge "
4 A wholesome t' is a tree of life: but "
16: 1 answer of the t', is from the Lord. "
17: 4 a liar giveth ear to a naughty t'. "
20 a perverse t' falleth into mischief. "
18: 21 and life are in the power of the t': "
21: 6 lying t' is a vanity tossed to and fro "
23 keepeth his mouth and his t' "
25: 15 and a soft t' breaketh the bone. "
23 angry countenance a backbiting t'. "
26: 28 A lying t' hateth those that are "
28: 23 than he that flattereth with the t'. "
31: 26 and in her t' is the law of kindness. "
Ca 4: 11 honey and milk are under thy t'; "
Isa 3: 8 their t' and their doings are against "
11: 15 destroy the t' of the Egyptian sea; "
28: 11 and another t' will he speak to this "
30: 27 and his t' as a devouring fire: "
32: 4 the t' of the stammerers shall be "
33: 19 of a stammering t', that thou canst "
35: 6 hart, and the t' of the dumb sing: "
41: 17 none, and their t' faileth for thirst, "
45: 23 knee shall bow, every t' shall swear. "
50: 4 hath given me the t' of the learned, "
54: 17 every t' that shall rise against thee "
57: 4 a wide mouth, and draw out the t'? "
59: 3 your t' hath muttered perverseness. "
Jer 9: 5 have taught their t' to speak lies, "
8 Their t' is as an arrow shot out; it "
18: 18 and let us smite him with the t', "
La 4: 4 t' of the sucking child cleaveth to "
Eze 3: 26 make thy t' cleave to the roof of thy "
Da 1: 4 and the t' of the Chaldeans. "
Ho 7: 16 by the sword for the rage of their t': "
Am 6: 10 Then shall he say, Hold thy t': *2013
Mic 6: 12 their t' is deceitful in their mouth. 3956
Hab 1: 13 holdest thy t' when the wicked *2790
Zep 3: 13 shall a deceitful t' be found in 3956
Zec 14: 12 their t' shall consume away in their "
M'r 7: 33 and he spit, and touched his t'; *1100*
35 and the string of his t' was loosed, "
Lu 1: 64 and his t' loosed, and he spake, and "
16: 24 his finger in water, and cool my t'; "
Joh 5: 2 called in the Hebrew t' Bethesda, **1447*
Ac 1: 19 field is called in their proper t', **1258*
2: 8 hear we every man in our own t', * "
26 heart rejoice, and my t' was glad; *1100*
21: 40 spake unto them in the Hebrew t', **1258*
22: 2 he spake in the Hebrew t' to them, * "
26: 14 and saying in the Hebrew t', Saul, * "
Ro 14: 11 and every t' shall confess to God. *1100*
1Co 14: 2 he that speaketh in an unknown t' "
4 He that speaketh in an unknown t' "
9 except ye utter by the t' words "
13 him that speaketh in an unknown t' "
14 For if I pray in an unknown t', my "
19 thousand words in an unknown t'. "
26 a psalm, hath a doctrine, hath a t', "
27 If any man speak in an unknown t', "
Ph'p 2: 11 every t' should confess that Jesus "
Jas 1: 26 be religious, and bridleth not his t', "
3: 5 Even so the t' is a little member, "
6 the t' is a fire, a world of iniquity: "
6 so is the t' among our members, "
8 But the t' can no man tame; it is "
1Pe 3: 10 let him refrain his t' from evil, "
1Jo 3: 18 let us not love in word, neither in t'; "
Re 5: 9 out of every kindred, and t', and "
9: 11 name in the Hebrew t' is Abaddon, **1447*
11 the Greek t' hath his name Apollyon. "
14: 6 every nation, and kindred, and t', *1100*
16: 16 in the Hebrew t' Armageddon. **1447*

tongues
Ge 10: 20, 31 their families, after their t', 3956
Ps 31: 20 in a pavilion from the strife of t'. "
55: 9 Destroy, O Lord, and divide their t':* "
78: 36 they lied unto him with their t'. * "
140: 3 sharpened their t' like a serpent; * "
Isa 66: 18 that I will gather all nations and t'; "
Jer 9: 3 they bend their t' like their bow for "
23: 31 that use their t', and say, He saith. "
M'r 16: 17 they shall speak with new t'; *1100*
Ac 2: 3 there appeared unto them cloven t' "
4 began to speak with other t', as the "
11 we do hear them speak in our t' the "
10: 46 For they heard them speak with t', "
19: 6 they spake with t', and prophesied. "
Ro 3: 13 with their t' they have used deceit; "
1Co 12: 10 spirits; to another divers kinds of t'; "
10 to another the interpretation of t': "
28 governments, diversities of t'. "
30 do all speak with t'? do all "
13: 1 Though I speak with the t' of men "
8 fail; whether there be t', they shall "
14: 5 I would that ye all spake with t', "
5 than he that speaketh with t', "
6 if I come unto you speaking with t', "
18 I speak with t' more than ye all: "
21 With men of other t' and other lips *2084*
22 Wherefore t' are for a sign, not to *1100*
23 and all speak with t', and there "
39 and forbid not to speak with t'. "
Re 7: 9 kindreds, and people, and t', stood "
10: 11 many peoples, and nations, and t', "
11: 9 of the people and kindreds and t' "
13: 7 all kindreds, and t', and nations. * "
16: 10 and they gnawed their t' for pain, "
17: 15 and multitudes, and nations, and t'. "

too
Ge 18:14 Is any thing t' hard for the Lord?
Ex 12: 4 the household be t' little for the lamb,
18:18 for this thing is t' heavy for thee;
36: 7 the work to make it, and t' much. 3498
Nu 11:14 alone, because it is t' heavy for me.
16: 3 Ye take t' much upon you, seeing
7 ye take t' much upon you, ye sons
22: 6 people; for they are t' mighty for me:
De 1:17 the cause that is t' hard for you, bring
2:36 was not one city t' strong for us:
12:21 his name there be t' far from thee,7368
14:24 And if the way be t' long for thee, so
24 or if the place be t' far from thee,
17: 8 arise a matter t' hard for thee in
Jos 17:15 mount Ephraim be t' narrow for thee.
19: 9 of Judah was t' much for them:
47 of Dan went out t' little for them:*
22:17 Is the iniquity of Peor t' little for us,
J'g 18:26 saw that they were t' strong for him,
Ru 1:12 for I am t' old to have an husband.
2Sa 3:39 sons of Zeruiah be t' hard for me:
10:11 If the Syrians be t' strong for me,
11 children of Ammon be t' strong for
12: 8 and if that had been t' little, I would
22:18 me: for they were t' strong for me.
1Ki 1:36 Lord God of my lord the king say so t'.
8:64 t' little to receive the burnt offerings,
12:28 It is t' much for you to go up to
19: 7 because the journey is t' great for thee.
2Ki 3:26 saw that the battle was t' sore for him,
6: 1 we dwell with thee is t' strait for us.
1Ch 19:12 If the Syrians be t' strong for me,
12 children of Ammon be t' strong for
2Ch 29:34 But the priests were t' few, so that they
Es 1:18 shall there arise t' much contempt*1767
Job 42: 3 things t' wonderful for me, which I
Ps 18:17 me: for they were t' strong for me.
35:10 from him that is t' strong for him,
38: 4 heavy burden they are t' heavy for me.
73:16 to know this, it was t' painful for me;
131: 1 matters, or in things t' high for me.
139: 6 Such knowledge is t' wonderful for me;
Pr 24: 7 Wisdom is t' high for a fool: he
30:18 three things which are t' wonderful
Isa 49:20 ears, The place is t' strait for me:
Jer 32:17 and there is nothing t' hard for thee:
27 flesh: is there any thing t' hard for me?
Ac 17:22 all things ye are t' superstitious. †*1174*

took See also OVERTOOK; TOOKEST; UNDERTOOK.
Ge 2:15 And the Lord God t' the man, and 3947
21 and he t' one of his ribs, and "
3: 6 she t' of the fruit thereof, and did "
4:19 And Lamech t' unto him two wives: "
5:24 and he was not; for God t' him. "
6: 2 they t' them wives of all which they "
8: 9 he put forth his hand, and t' her, "
20 t' of every clean beast, and of every "
9:23 Shem and Japheth t' a garment, "
11:29 Abram and Nahor t' them wives: "
31 Terah t' Abram his son, and Lot "
12: 5 Abram t' Sarai his wife, and Lot "
14:11 And they t' all the goods of Sodom "
12 they t' Lot, Abram's brother's son, "
15:10 And he t' unto him all these, and "
16: 3 Abram's wife t' Hagar her maid "
17:23 And Abraham t' Ishmael his son, "
18: 8 he t' butter, and milk, and the calf "
20: 2 king of Gerar sent, and t' Sarah. "
14 And Abimelech t' sheep, and oxen, "
21:14 and t' bread, and a bottle of water, "
21 mother t' him a wife out of the land "
27 And Abraham t' sheep and oxen, "
22: 3 t' two of his young men with him, "
6 Abraham t' the wood of the burnt "
6 he t' the fire in his hand, and a "
10 and t' the knife to slay his son. "
13 and Abraham went and t' the ram, "
24: 7 which t' me from my father's house, "
10 the servant t' ten camels of the "
22 that the man t' a golden earring of "
61 the servant t' Rebekah, and went "
65 therefore she t' a vail, and covered "
67 and t' Rebekah, and she became "
25: 1 Then again Abraham t' a wife, and "
20 old when he t' Rebekah to wife, "
26 his hand t' hold on Esau's heel; *
26:34 old when he t' to wife Judith the 3947
27:15 Rebekah t' goodly raiment of her "
36 he t' away my birthright; and, "
28: 9 and t' unto the wives which he had "
11 and he t' of the stones of that place, "
18 t' the stone that he had put for his "
29:23 that he t' Leah his daughter, and "
30: 9 she t' Zilpah her maid, and gave "
37 Jacob t' him rods of green poplar, "
31:23 And he t' his brethren with him, "
45 And Jacob t' a stone, and set it up "
46 they t' stones, and made an heap: "
32:13 t' of that which came to his hand "
22 that night, and t' his two wives, "
23 And he t' them, and sent them over "
33:11 And he urged him, and he t' it. "
34: 2 he t' her, and lay with her, and "
25 t' each man his sword, and came "
26 t' Dinah out of Shechem's house, "
28 They t' their sheep, and their oxen, "
29 and their wives t' they captive, "
36: 2 Esau t' his wives of the daughters 3947
6 And Esau t' his wives, and his sons, "
37:24 they t' him, and cast him into a pit: "
31 they t' Joseph's coat, and killed a "
38: 2 and he t' her, and went in unto her. "
6 Judah t' a wife for Er his firstborn, "
28 the midwife t' and bound upon his "
39:20 And Joseph's master t' him, and "
Ge 40:11 I t' the grapes, and pressed them 3947
41:42 Pharaoh t' off his ring from his 5493
42:24 and t' from them Simeon, and 3947
30 and t' us for spies of the country. 5414
43:15 And the men t' that present, and 3947
15 they t' double money in their hand, "
34 he t' and sent messes unto them 5375
44:11 t' down every man his sack to the 3381
46: 1 Israel t' his journey with all that
6 And they t' their cattle, and their 3947
47: 2 And he t' some of his brethren, "
48: 1 and he t' with him his two sons, "
13 And Joseph t' them both, Ephraim "
22 I t' out of the hand of the Amorite "
50:25 Joseph t' an oath of the children
Ex 2: 1 and t' to wife a daughter of Levi. 3947
3 she t' for him an ark of bulrushes, "
9 the woman t' the child, and nursed "
4: 6 when he t' it out, behold, his hand3318
20 Moses t' his wife and his sons, 3947
20 Moses t' the rod of God in his hand. "
25 Then Zipporah t' a sharp stone, "
6:20 Amram t' him Jochebed his father's "
23 Aaron t' him Elisheba, daughter of "
25 Eleazar...t' him one of the daughters "
9:10 And they t' ashes of the furnace, "
10:19 wind, which t' away the locusts, 5375
12:34 the people t' their dough before it "
13:19 Moses t' the bones of Joseph with 3947
20 they t' their journey from Succoth,
22 t' not away the pillar of the cloud*4185
14: 6 and t' his people with him: 3947
7 he t' six hundred chosen chariots "
25 And t' off their chariot wheels, 5493
15:20 Miriam...t' a timbrel in her hand: 3947
16: 1 And they t' their journey from Elim,
17:12 they t' a stone, and put it under 3947
18: 2 Moses' father in law, t' Zipporah, "
12 t' a burnt offering and sacrifices for "
24: 6 Moses t' half of the blood, and put "
7 And he t' the book of the covenant, "
8 Moses t' the blood, and sprinkled it "
32:20 he t' the calf which they had made, "
33: 7 And Moses t' the tabernacle, and * "
34: 4 and t' in his hand the two tables of "
34 t' the vail off, until he came out. 5493
40:20 he t' and put the testimony into 3947
Le 6: 4 that which he t' violently away, "
8:10 And Moses t' the anointing oil, 3947
15 Moses t' the blood, and put it upon "
16 And he t' all the fat that was upon "
23 Moses t' of the blood of it, and put "
25 he t' the fat, and the rump, and all "
26 he t' one unleavened cake, and a "
28 Moses t' them from off their hands, "
29 Moses t' the breast, and waved it "
30 And Moses t' of the anointing oil, "
9:15 and t' the goat, which was the sin "
17 offering, and t' an handful thereof,*
10: 1 t' either of them his censer, and 3947
Nu 1:17 And Moses and Aaron t' these men "
3:49 Moses t' the redemption money of "
50 Of the firstborn...t' he the money; "
7: 6 Moses t' the wagons and the oxen, "
10:12 children of Israel t' their journeys*
13 they first t' their journey according
11:25 t' of the spirit that was upon him, 680
16: 1 of Peleth, sons of Reuben, t' men: 3947
18 And they t' every man his censer, "
39 Eleazar...t' the brasen censers, "
47 And Aaron t' as Moses commanded, "
17: 9 looked, and t' every man his rod. "
20: 9 Moses t' the rod from before the "
21: 1 and t' some of them prisoners. "
25 And Israel t' all these cities: and 3947
32 and they t' the villages thereof, 3920
22:41 morning, that Balak t' Balaam, 3947
23: 7 And he t' up his parable, and said,5375
11 I t' thee to curse mine enemies, 3947
18 And he t' up his parable, and said, 5375
24: 3, 15, 20 he t' up his parable, and said, "
21 and t' up his parable, and said, "
23 And he t' up his parable, and said, "
25: 7 and t' a javelin in his hand; 3947
27:22 and he t' Joshua, and set him "
31: 9 t' all the women of Midian captives, "
9 and t' the spoil of all their cattle, "
11 t' all the spoil, and all the prey, 3947
27 them that t' the war upon them, *8610
47 Moses t' one portion of fifty, both 3947
51, 54 Moses and Eleazar...t' the gold "
32:39 Manasseh went to Gilead, and t' it,3920
41 and t' the small towns thereof, "
42 And Nobah went and t' Kenath, "
33:12 they t' their journey out of the *5265
De 1:15 So I t' the chief of your tribes, 3947
23 and I t' twelve men of you, one of "
25 And they t' of the fruit of the land "
2: 1 t' our journey into the wilderness 5265
34 we t' all his cities at that time, 3920
35 cattle we t' for a prey unto ourselves,
35 the spoil of the cities which we t'.*3920
3: 4 we t' all his cities at that time, "
4 was not a city which we t' not 3947
7 cities, we t' for a prey to ourselves.
8 we t' at that time out of the hand 3947
14 son of Manasseh t' all the country "
9:17 I t' the two tables, and cast them 8610
21 I t' your sin, the calf which ye had3947
10: 6 children of Israel t' their journey*
22:14 I t' this woman, and when I came 3947
24: 3 die, which t' her to be his wife; "
29: 8 we t' their land, and gave it for an "
Jos 2: 4 woman t' the two men, and hid "
3: 6 they t' up the ark of the covenant,*5375
4: 8 t' up twelve stones out of the midst "
Jos 4:20 stones, which they t' out of Jordan,3947
6:12 priests t' up the ark of the Lord. 5375
20 before him, and they t' the city. 3920
7: 1 of Judah, t' of the accursed thing: 3947
17 he t' the family of the Zarhites: 3920
21 then I coveted them, and t' them; 3947
23 t' them out of the midst of the tent, "
24 Joshua, and all Israel...t' Achan "
8:12 he t' about five thousand men, "
19 entered into the city, and t' it, 3920
23 And the king of Ai they t' alive, 8610
27 Israel t' for a prey unto themselves,
9: 4 t' old sacks upon their asses, and 3947
12 bread we t' hot for our provision
14 men t' of their victuals, and asked 3947
10:27 they t' them down off the trees, 3381
28 Joshua t' Makkedah, and smote it 3920
32 t' it on the second day, and smote it "
35 they t' it on that day, and smote it "
37 they t' it, and smote it with the "
39 And he t' it, and the king thereof, "
11:10 time turned back, and t' Hazor,
14 Israel t' for a prey unto themselves;
16 So Joshua t' all that land, the 3947
17 all their kings he t', and smote 3920
19 Gibeon: all other they t' in battle. 3947
23 So Joshua t' the whole land, "
15:17 Kenaz, the brother of Caleb, t' it: 3920
16: 4 and Ephraim, t' their inheritance.
19:47 to fight against Leshem, and t' it, 3920
24: 3 I t' your father Abraham from 3947
26 t' a great stone, and set it up there "
J'g 1:13 Caleb's younger brother, t' it: 3920
18 Judah t' Gaza with the coast
3: 6 t' their daughters to be their wives,3947
21 t' the dagger from his right thigh, "
25 therefore they t' a key, and opened "
28 t' the fords of Jordan toward Moab,3920
4:21 Jael Heber's wife t' a nail of the 3947
21 t' an hammer in her hand, and 7760
5:19 Megiddo; they t' no gain of money.3947
6:27 Gideon t' ten men of his servants, "
7: 8 people t' victuals in their hand, "
24 t' the waters unto Beth-barah 3920
25 t' two princes of the Midianites, "
8:12 t' the two kings of Midian, Zebah "
16 And he t' the elders of the city, 3947
21 t' away the ornaments that were "
9:43 he t' the people, and divided them "
45 he t' the city, and slew the people 3920
48 Abimelech t' an axe in his hand, 3947
48 a bough from the trees, and t' it, 5375
50 encamped against Thebez, and t' it.3920
11:13 Israel t' away my land, when they 3947
15 Israel t' not away the land of Moab, "
12: 5 the Gileadites t' the passages of 3920
6 Then they t' him, and slew him at* 270
9 t' in thirty daughters from abroad*935
13:19 So Manoah t' a kid with a meat 3947
14: 9 And he t' thereof in his hands, and7287
19 men of them, and t' their spoil, 3947
15: 4 t' firebrands, and turned tail to "
15 and put forth his hand, and t' it, "
16: 3 t' the doors of the gate of the city,* 270
12 Delilah therefore t' new ropes, 3947
21 the Philistines t' him, and put out* 270
29 Samson t' hold of the two middle
31 and t' him, and brought him up, 5375
17: 2 behold, the silver is with me; I t' it.3947
4 his mother t' two hundred shekels "
18:17 in thither, and t' the graven image, "
20 he t' the ephod, and the teraphim, "
27 t' the things which Micah had made, "
19: 1 who t' to him a concubine out of "
15 no man that t' them into his house 622
25 the man t' his concubine, and 2388
28 the man t' her up upon an ass, 3947
29 he t' a knife, and laid hold on his "
20: 6 And I t' my concubine, and cut her 270
21:23 t' them wives, according to their 5375
Ru 1: 4 t' them wives of the women of Moab; "
2:18 she t' it up, and went into the city: "
4: 2 he t' ten men of the elders of the 3947
13 So Boaz t' Ruth, and she was his "
16 Naomi t' the child, and laid it in "
1Sa 1:24 him, she t' him up with her, 5927
2:14 brought up...priest t' for himself. 3947
5: 1 the Philistines t' the ark of God, * "
2 Philistines t' the ark of God, they "
3 they t' Dagon, and set him in his "
6:10 t' two milch kine, and tied them "
12 the kine t' the straight way to the
15 the Levites t' down the ark of the 3381
7: 9 And Samuel t' a sucking lamb, 3947
12 Then Samuel t' a stone, and set it "
8: 3 aside after lucre, and t' bribes, "
9:22 Samuel t' Saul and his servant, "
24 And the cook t' up the shoulder, 7311
10: 1 Then Samuel t' a vial of oil, and 3947
11: 7 And he t' a yoke of oxen, and hewed "
14:32 t' sheep, and oxen, and calves, and "
47 Saul t' the kingdom over Israel, *3920
52 valiant man, he t' him unto him. 622
15: 8 t' Agag the king of the Amalekites8610
21 But the people t' of the spoil, 3947
16:13 Then Samuel t' the horn of oil, "
20 Jesse t' an ass laden with bread, "
23 that David t' an harp, and played "
17:20 and t', and went, as Jesse had 5375
34 bear, and t' a lamb out of the flock: "
40 And he t' his staff in his hand, 3947
49 and t' thence a stone, and slang it, "
51 t' his sword, and drew it out of the "
54 David t' the head of the Philistine, "
57 Abner t' him, and brought him "
18: 2 Saul t' him that day, and would "

1Sa 19:13 Michal t' an image, and laid it in 3947
24: 2 Saul t' three thousand chosen men "
25:18 haste, and t' two hundred loaves, "
43 David also t' Ahinoam of Jezreel; "
26:12 David t' the spear and the cruse of "
27: 9 t' away the sheep, and the oxen, "
28:24 and t' flour, and kneaded it, and did "
30:20 David t' all the flocks and the herds, "
31: 4 Therefore Saul t' a sword, and fell "
12 t' the body of Saul and the bodies "
13 they t' their bones, and buried them "
2Sa 1:10 I t' the crown that was upon his "
11 Then David t' hold on his clothes, "
2: 8 t' Ish-bosheth the son of Saul, *3947
32 they t' up Asahel, and buried him 5375
3:15 and t' her from her husband, even 3947
27 Joab t' him aside in the gate to speak "
36 And all the people t' notice of it, 5384
4: 4 and his nurse t' him up, and fled: 5375
7 beheaded him, and t' his head, 3947
10 I t' hold of him, and slew him in "
12 they t' the head of Ish-bosheth, 3947
5: 7 David t' the strong hold of Zion: 3920
13 David t' him more concubines and 3947
6: 6 to the ark of God, and t' hold of it; "
7: 8 I t' thee from the sheepcote, from 3947
15 as I t' it from Saul, whom I put 5493
8: 1 David t' Metheg-ammah out of 3947
4 And David t' from him a thousand 3920
7 And David t' the shields of gold that 3947
8 king David t' exceeding much brass. "
10: 4 Hanun t' David's servants, "
11: 4 David sent messengers, and t' her; "
12: 4 but t' the poor man's lamb, and "
26 of Ammon, and t' the royal city. 3920
29 and fought against it, and t' it. "
30 he t' their king's crown from off 3947
13: 8 And she t' flour, and kneaded it, "
9 she t' a pan, and poured out before "
10 Tamar t' the cakes which she had "
11 he t' hold of her, and said unto "
15: 5 forth his hand, and t' him, and 2388
17:19 woman t' and spread a covering 3947
18:14 And he t' three darts in his hand, "
17 And they t' Absalom, and cast him "
20: 3 the king t' the ten women his "
9 Joab t' Amasa by the beard with 270
10 Amasa t' no heed to the sword that "
21: 8 the king t' the two sons of Rizpah 3947
10 the daughter of Aiah t' sackcloth, "
12 David went and t' the bones of Saul "
22:17 He sent from above, he t' me; he "
23:16 and t' it, and brought it to David: 5375
1Ki 1:39 the priest t' an horn of oil out of 3947
3: 1 and t' Pharaoh's daughter, and "
20 and t' my son from beside me, "
4:15 he also t' Basmath the daughter of "
8: 3 and the priests t' up the ark. 5375
11:18 and they t' men with them out of 3947
12:28 Whereupon the king t' counsel, "
13:29 the prophet t' up the carcase of 5375
14:26 he t' away the treasures of the 3947
26 king's house; he even t' away all: "
26 he t' away all the shields of gold "
15:12 he t' away the sodomites out of *5674
18 Then Asa t' all the silver and the 3947
22 they t' away the stones of Ramah, *5375
16:31 he t' to wife Jezebel the daughter 3947
17:19 And he t' him out of her bosom, "
23 Elijah t' the child, and brought him "
18: 4 Obadiah t' an hundred prophets, "
10 he t' an oath of the kingdom and "
26 they t' the bullock which was 3947
31 Elijah t' twelve stones, according "
40 they t' them: and Elijah brought 8610
19:21 t' a yoke of oxen, and slew them, 3947
20:34 which my father t' from thy father, "
41 t' the ashes away from his face; "
22:46 father Asa, he t' out of the land. *1197
2Ki 2: 8 Elijah t' his mantle, and wrapped 3947
12 and he t' hold of his own clothes, and "
13 He t' up also the mantle of Elijah 7311
14 he t' the mantle of Elijah that fell 3947
3:26 he t' with him seven hundred men "
27 t' his eldest son that should have "
4:37 and t' up her son, and went out. 5375
5: 5 t' with him ten talents of silver, 3947
24 he t' them from their hand, and "
6: 7 And he put out his hand, and t' it. "
8 t' counsel with his servants, "
7:14 t' therefore two chariot horses; 3947
8: 9 him, and t' a present with him, "
15 that he t' a thick cloth, and dipped "
9:13 t' every man his garment, and put "
10: 7 they t' the king's sons, and slew "
14 And they t' them alive, and slew 8610
16 he t' him up to him into the chariot. 5927
31 But Jehu t' no heed to walk in the law
11: 2 t' Joash the son of Ahaziah, and 3947
4 t' an oath of them in the house of
9 t' every man his men that were to 3947
19 And he t' the rulers over hundreds, "
12: 9 But Jehoiada the priest t' a chest, "
17 fought against Gath, and t' it: 3920
18 Jehoash...t' all the hallowed 3947
13:15 he t' unto him bow and arrows. "
18 Take the arrows. And he t' them. "
25 Jehoash...t' again out of the hand "
14: 7 t' Selah by war, and called the 8610
13 king of Israel t' Amaziah king of "
14 And he t' all the gold and silver, 3947
21 all the people of Judah t' Azariah, "
15:29 king of Assyria, and t' Ijon, "
16: 8 Ahaz t' the silver and gold that was "
9 up against Damascus, and t' it, 8610
17 t' down the sea from off the brasen 3381

2Ki 17: 6 the king of Assyria t' Samaria, 3920
18:10 at the end of three years they t' it: "
13 cities of Judah, and t' them. 8610
20: 7 And they t' and laid it on the boil, 3947
23:11 t' away the horses that the kings 7673
16 t' the bones out of the sepulchres, 3947
19 Josiah t' away, and did to them 5493
30 the people of the land t' Jehoahaz 3947
34 Jehoiakim, and t' Jehoahaz away: "
24:12 the king of Babylon t' him in the "
25: 6 So they t' the king, and brought 8610
14 they ministered, t' they away. 3947
15 the captain of the guard t' away. "
18 the captain of the guard t' Seraiah "
19 And out of the city he t' an officer "
20 captain of the guard t' these, "
1Ch 2:19 Caleb t' unto him Ephrath, which "
23 And he t' Geshur, and Aram, with "
4:18 of Pharaoh, which Mered t'. "
5:21 they t' away their cattle; of their
7:15 And Machir t' to wife the sister of 3947
10: 4 So Saul t' a sword, and fell upon it. "
9 they t' his head, and his armour, 5375
12 and t' away the body of Saul, and "
11: 5 David t' the castle of Zion, which 3920
18 and t' it, and brought it to David: 5375
14: 3 David t' more wives at Jerusalem: 3947
17: 7 I t' thee from the sheepcote, even "
13 him, as I t' it from him that was 5493
18: 1 t' Gath and her towns out the 3947
4 And David t' from him a thousand 3920
7 And David t' the shields of gold 3947
19: 4 Hanun t' David's servants, and "
20: 2 David t' the crown of their king "
23:22 brethren the sons of Kish t' them. 5375
27:23 David t' not the number of them "
2Ch 5: 4 and the Levites t' up the ark. "
8:18 t' thence four hundred and fifty *3947
10: 6 Rehoboam t' counsel with the old "
8 t' counsel with the young men that
11:18 Rehoboam t' him Mahalath the 3947
20 t' Maachah...daughter of Absalom; "
21 (for he t' eighteen wives, and 5375
12: 4 And he t' the fenced cities which 3920
9 t' away the treasures of the house 3947
9 of the king's house; he t' all: "
13:19 Jeroboam, and t' cities from him, 3920
14: 3 t' away the altars of the strange 5493
5 he t' away out of all the cities of "
15: 8 he t' courage, and put away the "
16: 6 Then Asa the king t' all Judah; 3947
17: 6 t' away the high places and groves
22:11 king, t' Joash the son of Ahaziah, 3947
23: 1 t' the captains of hundreds, Azariah "
8 t' every man his men that were to "
20 he t' the captains of hundreds, and "
24: 3 Jehoiada t' for him two wives; 5375
11 and emptied the chest, and t' it, "
25:13 of them, and t' much spoil.
17 Amaziah king of Judah t' advice,
23 the king of Israel t' Amaziah king 8610
24 he t' all the gold and the silver, and
26: 1 all the people of Judah t' Uzziah, 3947
28: 8 t' also away much spoil from them,
15 t' the captives, and with the spoil 2388
21 Ahaz t' away a portion out of the
29:16 And the Levites t' it, to carry it out 6901
30:14 and t' away the altars that were in
14 the altars for incense t' they away,
23 whole assembly t' counsel to keep
32: 3 He t' counsel with his princes and
33:11 t' Manasseh among the thorns, 3920
15 And he t' away the strange gods,
34:33 Josiah t' away all the abominations
35:24 His servants therefore t' him out 5674
36: 1 the people of the land t' Jehoahaz 3947
4 And Necho t' Jehoahaz his brother, "
Ezr 2:61 which t' a wife of the daughters 3947
5:14 Nebuchadnezzar t' out of the 5312
6: 5 Nebuchadnezzar t' forth out of the "
8:30 So t' the priests and the Levites *6901
Ne 2: 1 and I t' up the wine, and gave it 5375
4: 1 and t' great indignation, and mocked
5:12 the priests, and t' an oath of them,
7:63 t' one of the daughters of Barzillai 3947
9:25 And they t' strong cities, and a fat 3920
Es 2: 7 dead, t' for his own daughter. 3947
3:10 the king t' his ring from his hand, 5493
6:11 Then t' Haman the apparel and 3947
8: 2 And the king t' off his ring, which 5493
9:27 Jews ordained, and t' upon them, 6901
Job 1:15 fell upon them, and t' them away: 3947
2: 8 And he t' him a potsherd to scrape "
Ps 18:16 He sent from above, he t' me, he "
22: 9 art he that t' me out of the womb: 1518
31:13 while they t' counsel together
48: 6 Fear t' hold upon them there, and
55:14 We t' sweet counsel together, and
56: title the Philistines t' him in Gath. 270
69: 4 restored that which I t' not away. 1497
71: 6 t' me out of my mother's bowels: 1491
78:70 and t' him from the sheepfolds: 3947
Pr 12:27 not that which he t' in hunting:
Ec 2:20 to despair of all the labour which I t' *
Ca 5: 7 walls t' away my veil from me. 5375
Isa 8: 2 I t' unto me faithful witnesses to *
20: 1 fought against Ashdod, and t' it; 3920
36: 1 cities of Judah, and t' them. 8610
40:14 With whom t' he counsel, and who
Jer 13: 7 t' the girdle from the place where 3947
25:17 I t' the cup at the Lord's hand, and "
26: 8 prophets and all the people t' him. *8610
27:20 Which Nebuchadnezzar...t' not, 3947
28: 3 king of Babylon t' away from this "
10 Hananiah the prophet t' the yoke "
31:32 I t' them by the hand to bring 2388

Jer 32:10 and sealed it, and t' witnesses, *
11 I t' the evidence of the purchase, 3947
35: 3 Then I t' Jaazaniah the son of "
36:14 Baruch...t' the roll in his hand, "
21 he t' it out of Elishama the scribe's "
32 Then t' Jeremiah another roll, and "
37:13 and he t' Jeremiah the prophet, *8610
14 so Irijah t' Jeremiah, and brought* "
17 the king sent, and t' him out: *3947
38: 6 Then t' they Jeremiah, and cast "
11 Ebed-melech t' the men with him, "
11 t' thence old cast clouts and old "
13 and t' him up out of the dungeon: 5927
14 t' Jeremiah the prophet unto him 3947
39:14 and t' Jeremiah out of the court "
40: 2 captain of the guard t' Jeremiah, "
41:12 Then they t' all the men, and went "
16 Then t' Johanan the son of Kareah, "
43: 5 t' all the remnant of Judah, that "
50:33 all that t' them captives held them
43 anguish t' hold of him, and pangs
52: 9 Then they t' the king, and carried 8610
18 they ministered, t' they away. 3947
19 t' the captain of the guard away. "
24 the captain of the guard t' Seraiah "
25 He t' also out of the city an eunuch, "
26 the captain of the guard t' them, "
La 5:13 They t' the young men to grind, *5375
Eze 3:12 Then the spirit t' me up, and I * "
14 spirit lifted me up, and t' me away, 3947
8: 3 and t' me by a lock of mine head; "
10: 7 and t' thereof, and put it into the 5375
7 linen: who t' it, and went out. 3947
11:24 Afterwards the spirit t' me up, *5375
16:50 I t' them away as I saw good. 5493
17: 3 t' the highest branch of the cedar: 3947
5 He t' also of the seed of the land, "
19: 5 then she t' another of her whelps, "
23:10 they t' her sons and her daughters, "
13 was defiled, that they t' both one way.
29: 7 they t' hold of thee by thy hand, 8610
33: 5 of the trumpet, and t' not warning;
43: 5 So the spirit t' me up, and brought 5375
Da 1:16 Melzar t' away the portion of their "
3:22 those men that t' up Shadrach, 5267
5:20 and they t' his glory from him: 5709
31 And Darius...t' the kingdom, *6902
Ho 1: 3 t' Gomer the daughter of Diblaim 3947
12: 3 t' his brother by the heel in the womb,
13:11 and t' him away in my wrath. *3947
Am 7:15 And the Lord t' me as I followed the "
Jon 1:15 So they t' up Jonah, and cast him 5375
Zec 11: 7 I t' unto me two staves; the one I 3947
10 I t' my staff, even Beauty, and cut "
13 And I t' the thirty pieces of silver, "
M't 1:24 him, and t' unto him his wife: 3880
2:14 he t' the young child and his "
21 and t' the young child and his "
8:17 saying, Himself t' our infirmities, 2983
9:25 he went in, and t' her by the hand, 2902
13:31 mustard seed, which a man t', 2983
33 like unto leaven, which a woman t'. "
14:12 disciples came, and t' up the body, 142
19 and t' the five loaves, and the two 2983
20 they t' up of the fragments that 142
15:36 he t' the seven loaves and the 2983
37 they t' up of the broken meat that 142
39 t' ship,...came into the coasts *1684, 1519
16: 9, 10 and how many baskets ye t' up? 2983
22 Then Peter t' him, and began to 4355
18:28 and t' him by the throat, saying, 2902
20:17 t' the twelve disciples apart in the 3880
21:35 the husbandmen t' his servants, 2983
46 because they t' him for a prophet. 2192
22: 6 And the remnant t' his servants, *2902
15 t' counsel how they might entangle 2983
24:39 flood came, and t' them all away; 142
25: 1 ten virgins, which t' their lamps, 2983
3 foolish t' their lamps, and t' no oil "
4 the wise t' oil in their vessels with "
15 and straightway t' his journey. * 589
35 I was a stranger, and ye t' me in: 4863
38 we thee a stranger, and t' thee in? "
43 a stranger, and ye t' me not in: "
26:26 Jesus t' bread, and blessed it, and 2983
27 And he t' the cup, and gave thanks, "
37 And he t' with him Peter and the 3880
50 laid hands on Jesus, and t' him. 2902
27: 1 and elders of the people t' counsel 2983
6 chief priests t' the silver pieces, "
7 they t' counsel, and bought with "
9 they t' the thirty pieces of silver, "
24 he t' water, and washed his hands "
27 t' Jesus into the common hall, 3880
30 t' the reed, and smote him on the 2983
31 they t' the robe off from him, and 1562
48 and t' a spunge, and filled it with 2983
28:15 So they t' the money, and did as "
M'r 1:31 he came and t' her by the hand, 2902
2:12 he arose, t' up the bed, and went 142
3: 6 t' counsel with the Herodians 4160
4:36 t' him even as he was in the ship. *3880
5:41 And he t' the damsel by the hand, *2902
6:29 they came and t' up his corpse, and 142
43 they t' up twelve baskets full of the "
7:33 he t' him aside from the multitude, 618
8: 6 he t' the seven loaves, and gave 2983
8 they t' up of the broken meat that 142
19, 20 baskets full of fragments t' ye "
23 he t' the blind man by the hand, 1949
32 Peter t' him, and began to rebuke 4355
9:27 But Jesus t' him by the hand, and 2902
36 he t' a child, and set him in the 2983
10:16 he t' them up in his arms, put his 1723
32 he t' again the twelve, and began 3880
12: 8 they t' him, and killed him, and 2983

M'r 12:20 the first t' a wife, and dying left no 2983
21 And the second t' her, and died, "
14:22 Jesus t' bread, and blessed, and "
23 he t' the cup, and when he had "
46 their hands on him, and t' him. 2902
49 temple teaching, and ye t' me not: "
15:20 they t' off the purple from him, 1562
46 t' him down, and wrapped him in *2507
Lu 2:28 Then t' he him up in his arms, *1209
5:25 and t' up that whereon he lay, and 142
8:54 t' her by the hand, and called, *2902
9:10 And he t' them, and went aside 3880
16 Then he t' the five loaves and the 2983
28 he t' Peter and John and James, 3880
47 t' a child, and set him by him, 1949
10:34 him to an inn, and t' care of him. 1959
35 he t' out two pence, and gave them 1544
13:19 of mustard seed, which a man t', 2983
21 is like leaven, which a woman t' "
14:4 he t' him, and healed him, and let 1949
15:13 t' his journey into a far country, 589
18:31 Then he t' unto him the twelve, 3880
20:29 the first t' a wife, and died without 2983
30 And the second t' her to wife, and* "
31 And the third t' her, and in like "
22:17 he t' the cup, and gave thanks, *1209
19 And he t' bread, and gave thanks, 2983
54 Then t' they him, and led him, *4815
23:53 And he t' it down, and wrapped it 2507
24:30 he t' bread, and blessed it, and 2983
43 he t' it, and did eat before them. "
Joh 5:9 was made whole, and t' up his bed, 142
6:11 And Jesus t' the loaves; and when 2983
24 they also t' shipping, and *1684,1519
8:59 t' they up stones to cast at him: 142
10:31 the Jews t' up stones again to stone 941
11:41 t' away the stone from the place 142
53 they t' counsel together for to put 4823
12:3 Then t' Mary a pound of ointment 2983
13 T' branches of palm trees, and "
13:4 and t' a towel, and girded himself. "
18:12 and officers of the Jews t' Jesus, *4815
19:1 Pilate therefore t' Jesus, and 2983
16 they t' Jesus, and led him away. 3880
23 t' his garments, and made four 2983
27 disciple t' her unto his own home. "
38 therefore, and t' the body of Jesus. 142
40 Then t' they the body of Jesus, 2983
Ac 1:16 was guide to them that t' Jesus. 4815
3:7 And he t' him by the right hand, 4084
4:13 they t' knowledge of them, that 1921
5:33 heart, and t' counsel to slay them.*1011
7:21 Pharaoh's daughter t' him up, and 337
43 ye t' up the tabernacle of Moloch, 353
9:23 the Jews t' counsel to kill him: 4823
25 Then the disciples t' him by night, 2983
27 But Barnabas t' him, and brought 1949
10:26 Peter t' him up, saying, Stand up;*1453
23 and t' with them John, whose *4838
13:29 they t' him down from the tree, 2507
15:39 Barnabas t' Mark, and sailed unto 3880
16:3 t' and circumcised him because of 2983
33 he t' them the same hour of the 3880
17:5 t' unto them certain lewd fellows 4355
19 they t' him, and brought him unto 1949
18:17 Then all the Greeks t' Sosthenes, * "
18 and then t' his leave of the brethren, 657
26 t' him unto them, and expounded 4355
19:13 t' upon them to call over them 2021
20:14 we t' him in, and came to Mitylene. 353
21:6 we t' ship; and they returned*1910,1519
11 t' Paul's girdle, and bound his own*142
15 those days we t' up our carriages,* 643
26 Then Paul t' the men, and the 3880
30 they t' Paul, and drew him out of 1949
32 Who immediately t' soldiers and 3880
33 captain came near, and t' him, *1949
23:18 So he t' him, and brought him to 3880
19 chief captain t' him by the hand, 1949
31 as it was commanded them, t' Paul, 353
24:6 whom we t', and would have *2902
7 t' him away out of our hands, * 520
27:35 t' bread, and gave thanks to God *2983
36 cheer, and they also t' some meat. 4355
28:15 he thanked God, and t' courage. 2983
1Co 11:23 in which he was betrayed t' bread: "
25 the same manner also he t' the cup,* "
Ga 2:1 and t' Titus with me also. *4838
Ph'p 2:7 t' upon him the form of a servant,*2983
Col 2:14 and t' it out of the way, nailing * 142
Heb 2:14 himself likewise t' part of the *3348
16 he t' not on him the nature of †‡1949
16 he t' on him the seed of Abraham.†‡"
8:9 when I t' them by the hand to lead * "
9:19 he t' the blood of calves and of 2983
10:34 t' joyfully the spoiling of your 4327
Re 5:7 t' the book out of the right hand *2983
8:5 the angel t' the censer, and filled it*"
10:10 I t' the little book out of the "
18:21 a mighty angel t' up a stone like a 142

tookest
Ps 99:8 though thou t' vengeance of their
Eze 16:18 And t' thy broidered garments, 3947

tool
Ex 20:25 if thou lift up thy t' upon it, thou 2719
32:4 and fashioned it with a graving t', "
De 27:5 shalt not lift up any iron t' upon them.
1Ki 6:7 any t' of iron heard in the house, 3627

tooth See also TEETH; TOOTH'S.
Ex 21:24 Eye for eye, t' for t', hand for 8127
27 if he smite out his manservant's t', "
27 or his maidservant's t'; he shall let "
Le 24:20 for breach, eye for eye, t' for t': "
De 19:21 t' for t', hand for hand, foot for foot."
Pr 25:19 time of trouble is like a broken t', 8127
M't 5:38 An eye for an eye, and a t' for a t': 3599

tooth's
Ex 21:27 shall let him go free for his t' sake. 8127

top See also HOUSETOP; TOPS.
Ge 11:4 whose t' may reach unto heaven; 7218
28:12 and the t' of it reached to heaven: "
18 and poured oil upon the t' of it. "
Ex 17:9 I will stand on the t' of the hill "
10 Hur went up to the t' of the hill. "
19:20 mount Sinai, on the t' of the mount: "
20 Lord called Moses up to the t' of "
24:17 like...fire on the t' of the mount "
28:32 there shall be an hole in the t' of it,*"
30:3 gold, the t' thereof, and the sides 1406
34:2 there to me in the t' of the mount. 7218
37:26 both the t' of it, and the sides 1406
Nu 14:40 up into the t' of the mountain, 7218
44 presumed to go up unto the hill t': "
20:28 died there in the t' of the mount: "
21:20 to the t' of Pisgah, which looketh "
23:9 from the t' of the rocks I see him, "
14 field of Zophim, to the t' of Pisgah, "
28 brought Balaam unto the t' of Peor, "
De 3:27 Get thee up into the t' of Pisgah, "
28:35 of thy foot unto the t' of thy head.*6936
33:16 and upon the t' of the head of him* "
34:1 to the t' of Pisgah, that is over 7218
Jos 15:8 went up to the t' of the mountain "
9 was drawn from the t' of the hill "
J'g 6:26 an altar...upon the t' of this rock, "
9:7 stood in the t' of mount Gerizim, "
25 for him in the t' of the mountains,* "
36 down from the t' of the mountains.*"
51 gat them up to the t' of the tower.*1406
15:8 dwelt in the t' of the rock Etam. *5585
11 went to the t' of the rock Etam, * "
16:3 carried them up to the t' of an hill 7218
1Sa 9:25 with Saul upon the t' of the house.*1406
26 called Saul to the t' of the house,* "
26:13 stood on the t' of an hill afar off: 7218
2Sa 2:25 troop, and stood on the t' of an hill. "
15:32 was come to the t' of the mount, "
16:1 was a little past the t' of the hill, "
22 a tent upon the t' of the house; 1406
1Ki 7:17 were upon the t' of the pillars; 7218
18 the chapiters that were upon the t', "
19 that were upon the t' of the pillars "
22 the t' of the pillars was lily work: "
35 in the t' of the base was there a "
35 and on the t' of the base the ledges "
41 were on the t' of the two pillars; "
41 were upon the t' of the pillars; "
10:19 and the t' of the throne was round "
18:42 Elijah went up to the t' of Carmel; "
2Ki 1:9 behold, he sat on the t' of an hill. "
9:13 under him on the t' of the stairs, 1634
23:12 t' of the upper chamber of Ahaz, *1406
2Ch 3:15 that was on the t' of each of them 7218
4:12 were on the t' of the two pillars, "
12 which were on the t' of the pillars; "
25:12 brought them unto the t' of the rock, "
12 cast...down from the t' of the rock, "
Es 5:2 and touched the t' of the sceptre. "
Ps 72:16 upon the t' of the mountains; "
102:7 sparrow alone upon the house t'. *1406
Pr 8:2 standeth in the t' of high places, 7218
23:34 he that lieth upon the t' of a mast. "
Ca 4:8 Lebanon: look from the t' of Amana, "
8 from the t' of Shenir and Hermon, "
Isa 2:2 established in the t' of...mountains, 7218
17:6 in the t' of the uppermost bough, "
30:17 a beacon upon the t' of a mountain, "
42:11 shout from the t' of the mountains. "
La 2:19 for hunger in the t' of every street.*"
4:1 poured out in the t' of every street.*"
Eze 17:4 cropped off the t' of his young twigs,*"
22 off from the t' of his young twigs* "
24:7 she set it upon the t' of a rock; *6706
8 set her blood upon the t' of a rock,* "
26:4 and make her like the t' of a rock.* "
14 will make thee like the t' of a rock:*"
31:3 his t' was among the thick boughs.6788
10 up his t' among the thick boughs, "
14 up their t' among the thick boughs, "
43:12 Upon the t' of the mountain the 7218
Am 1:2 and the t' of Carmel shall wither. "
9:3 hide themselves in the t' of Carmel, "
Mic 4:1 in the t' of the mountains, "
Na 3:10 in pieces at the t' of all the streets: "
Zec 4:2 with a bowl upon the t' of it, and "
2 which are upon the t' thereof: "
M't 27:51 in twain from the t' to the bottom; 509
M'r 15:38 in twain from the t' to the bottom. "
Joh 19:23 seam, woven from the t' throughout."
Heb 11:21 leaning upon the t' of his staff. 206

topaz
Ex 28:17 first row shall be a sardius, a t', 6357
39:10 first row was a sardius, a t', and "
Job 28:19 t' of Ethiopia shall not equal it, "
Eze 28:13 sardius, t', and the diamond, "
Re 21:20 the eighth, beryl; the ninth, a t'; 5116

Tophel (to'-fel)
De 1:1 between Paran, and T', and 8603

Tophet (to'-fet) See also TOPHETH.
Isa 30:33 T' is ordained of old; yea, for the*8613
Jer 7:31 have built the high places of T', *8612
32 that it shall no more be called T',* "
32 for they shall bury in T', till there* "
19:6 place shall no more be called T', * "
11 and they shall bury them in T', * "
12 and even make this city as T': * "
13 shall be defiled as the place of T',* "
14 Then came Jeremiah from T', * "

Topheth (to'-feth) See also TOPHET.
2Ki 23:10 And he defiled T', which is in the 8612

tops See also HOUSETOPS.
Ge 8:5 were the t' of the mountains seen. 7218
2Sa 5:24 going in the t' of the mulberry trees, "
1Ki 7:16 to set upon the t' of the pillars: "
2Ki 19:26 herb, as the grass on the house t',*1406
1Ch 14:15 in the t' of the mulberry trees, 7218
Job 24:24 cut off as the t' of the ears of corn. "
Isa 2:21 into the t' of the ragged rocks, *5585
15:3 on the t' of their houses, and in *1406
Eze 6:13 in all the t' of the mountains, and 7218
Ho 4:13 upon the t' of the mountains, "
Joe 2:5 chariots on the t' of mountains shall "

torch See also TORCHES.
Zec 12:6 and like a t' of fire in a sheaf; 3940

torches
Na 2:3 chariots shall be with flaming t' *6393
4 they shall seem like t', they shall 3940
Joh 18:3 with lanterns and t' and weapons. 2985

tore See TARE.

torment See also TORMENTED; TORMENTS.
M't 8:29 art thou come hither to t' us before 928
M'r 5:7 thee by God, that thou t' me not. "
Lu 8:28 high? I beseech thee, t' me not. "
16:28 they also come into this place of t'. 931
1Jo 4:18 out fear, because fear hath t'. *2851
Re 9:5 their t' was as the t' of a scorpion, 929
14:11 the smoke of their t' ascendeth up "
18:7 so much t' and sorrow give her: "
10 Standing afar off for...fear of her t', "
15 stand afar off for the fear of her t', "

tormented
M't 8:6 home sick of the palsy, grievously t'.928
Lu 16:24 tongue; for I am t' in this flame. *3600
25 he is comforted, and thou art t'. * "
Heb 11:37 being destitute, afflicted, t'; *2558
Re 9:5 that they should be t' five months: 928
11:10 these two prophets t' them that "
14:10 he shall be t' with fire and brimstone"
20:10 shall be t' day and night for ever "

tormentors
M't 18:34 wroth, and delivered him to the t', 930

torments
M't 4:24 taken with divers diseases and t', 931
Lu 16:23 hell he lift up his eyes, being in t', "

torn
Ge 31:39 That which was t' of beasts I 2966
44:28 Surely he is t' in pieces; and I 2963
Ex 22:13 If it be t' in pieces, then let him "
13 not make good that which was t'. 2966
31 ye eat any flesh that is t' of beasts "
Le 7:24 fat of that which is t' with beasts, "
17:15 or that which was t' with beasts, "
22:8 dieth of itself, or is t' with beasts, "
1Ki 13:26 unto the lion, which hath t' him, 7665
28 eaten the carcase, nor t' the ass. "
Isa 5:25 carcases were t' in the midst of *5478
Jer 5:6 out thence shall be t' in pieces: 2963
Eze 4:14 dieth of itself, or is t' in pieces; 2966
44:31 any thing that is dead of itself, or t'."
Ho 6:1 for he hath t', and he will heal us; 2963
Mal 1:13 and ye brought that which was t',*1497
M'r 1:26 the unclean spirit had t' him, *4682

tortoise
Le 11:29 mouse, and the t' after his kind, *6632

tortured
Heb 11:35 and others were t', not accepting 5178

toss See also TOSSED; TOSSINGS.
Isa 22:18 violently turn and t' thee like a 6802
Jer 5:22 the waves thereof t' themselves, 1607

tossed
Ps 109:23 I am t' up and down as the locust. 5287
Pr 21:6 a vanity t' to and fro of them that *5086
Isa 54:11 O thou afflicted, t' with tempest, and
M't 14:24 the midst of the sea, t' with waves:*928
Ac 27:18 exceedingly t' with a tempest, *5492
Eph 4:14 t' to and fro, and carried about 2831
Jas 1:6 sea driven with the wind and t'. 4494

tossings
Job 7:4 I am full of t' to and fro unto the 5076

tottering
Ps 62:3 wall shall ye be, and as a t' fence. 1760

Tou (to'-u) See also TOI.
1Ch 18:9 T' king of Hamath heard how 8583
10 (for Hadarezer had war with T';) "

touch See also TOUCHED; TOUCHETH; TOUCHING.
Ge 3:3 it, neither shall ye t' it, lest ye die. 5060
20:6 suffered I thee not to t' her. "
Ex 19:12 the mount, or t' the border of it: "
13 There shall not an hand t' it, but he"
Le 5:2 Or if a soul t' any unclean thing, "
3 Or if he t' the uncleanness of man, "
6:27 t' the flesh thereof shall be holy: "
7:21 soul that shall t' any unclean thing, "
11:8 and their carcase ye shall not t'; "
31 whosoever doth t' them, when they "
12:4 she shall t' no hallowed thing, nor "
Nu 4:15 but they shall not t' any holy thing, "
16:26 t' nothing of theirs, lest ye be "
De 14:8 flesh, nor t' their dead carcase. "
Jos 9:19 now therefore we may not t' them. "
Ru 2:9 men that they shall not t' thee? "
2Sa 14:10 and he shall not t' thee any more. "
18:12 that none t' the young man Absalom. "
23:7 man that shall t' them must be *5060
1Ch 16:22 T' not mine anointed, and do my "
Job 1:11 and t' all that he hath, and he will "

Job 2: 5 and t' his bone and his flesh, and he 5060
5:19 in seven there shall no evil t' thee. "
6: 7 things that my soul refused to t' are "
Ps 105:15 T' not mine anointed, and do my "
144: 5 t' the mountains, and they shall "
Isa 52:11 from thence, t' no unclean thing; "
Jer 12:14 that t' the inheritance which I have "
La 4:14 men could not t' their garments. "
15 it is unclean; depart, depart, t' not: "
Hag 2:12 and with his skirt do t' bread, or "
13 by a dead body t' any of these, "
M't 9:21 If I may but t' his garment, I shall 680
14:36 might only t' the hem of his garment: "
M'r 3:10 they pressed upon him for to t' him. "
5:28 If I may t' but his clothes, I shall be "
6:56 t' if it were but the border of his "
8:22 him, and besought him to t' him. "
10:13 to him, that he should t' them: "
Lu 6:19 whole multitude sought to t' him: "
11:46 t' not the burdens with one of your 4379
18:15 also infants, that he would t' them: 680
Joh 20:17 Jesus saith unto her, T' me not; "
1Co 7: 1 is good for a man not to t' a woman. "
2Co 6:17 t' not the unclean thing; and I will "
Col 2:21 (T' not; taste not; handle not; "
Heb 11:28 destroyed the firstborn should t' 2345
12:20 And if so much as a beast t' the "

touched
Ge 26:29 us no hurt, as we have not t' thee. 5060
32:25 him, he t' the hollow of his thigh; "
32 he t' the hollow of Jacob's thigh "
Le 22: 6 The soul which hath t' any such "
Nu 19:18 and upon him that t' a bone, or one "
31:19 and whosoever hath t' any slain, "
J'g 6:21 t' the flesh and...unleavened cakes; "
1Sa 10:26 of men, whose hearts God had t'. "
1Ki 6:27 the wing of the one t' the one wall, "
27 the other cherub t' the other wall; "
27 their wings t' one another in the "
19: 5 then an angel t' him, and said unto "
7 and t' him, and said, Arise and eat; "
2Ki 13:21 let down, and t' the bones of Elisha, "
Es 5: 2 near, and t' the top of the sceptre. "
Job 19:21 for the hand of God hath t' me. "
Isa 6: 7 and said, Lo, this hath t' thy lips; "
Jer 1: 9 forth his hand, and t' my mouth. "
Eze 3:13 creatures that t' one another, 5401
Da 8: 5 earth, and t' not the ground: 5060
18 but he t' me, and set me upright. "
9:21 t' me about the time of the evening "
10:10 an hand t' me, which set me upon "
16 of the sons of men t' my lips: "
18 t' me one like the appearance of a "
M't 8: 3 put forth his hand, and t' him, 680
15 he t' her hand, and the fever left her: "
9:20 and t' the hem of his garment: "
29 Then t' he their eyes, saying, "
14:36 many as t' were made perfectly "
17: 7 Jesus came and t' them, and said, "
20:34 on them, and t' their eyes: "
M'r 1:41 put forth his hand, and t' him, and "
5:27 the press behind, and t' his garment. "
30 press, and said, Who t' my clothes? "
31 thee, and sayest thou, Who t' me? "
6:56 as many as t' him were made whole. "
7:33 ears, and he spit, and t' his tongue; "
Lu 5:13 he put forth his hand, and t' him, "
7:14 And he came and t' the bier: and "
8:44 and t' the border of his garment: "
45 And Jesus said, Who t' me? When "
45 thee, and sayest thou, Who t' me? * "
46 Jesus said, Somebody hath t' me: * "
47 people for what cause she had t' him, "
22:51 And he t' his ear, and healed him. "
Ac 27: 3 And the next day we t' at Sidon. 2609
Heb 4:15 t' with...feeling of our infirmities; 4834
12:18 unto the mount that might be t', 5584

toucheth
Ge 26:11 He that t' this man or his wife 5060
Ex 19:12 whosoever t' the mount shall be "
29:37 whatsoever t' the altar shall be holy. "
30:29 whatsoever t' them shall be holy. "
Le 6:18 every one that t' them shall be holy. "
7:19 the flesh that t' any unclean thing "
11:24 whosoever t' the carcase of them "
26 one that t' them shall be unclean. "
27 whoso t' their carcase shall be "
36 which t' their carcase shall be "
39 he that t' the carcase thereof shall* "
15: 5 whosoever t' his bed shall wash his "
7 And he that t' the flesh of him that "
10 whosoever t' any thing that was "
11 whomsoever he t' that hath the "
12 that he t' which hath the issue, "
19 whosoever t' her shall be unclean "
21 whosoever t' her bed shall wash his "
22 whosoever t' any thing that she "
23 when he t' it, he shall be unclean "
27 whosoever t' these things shall be "
22: 4 whoso t' any thing that is unclean "
5 Or whosoever t' any creeping thing, "
Nu 19:11 He that t' the dead body of any man "
13 Whosoever t' the dead body of any "
16 And whosoever t' one that is slain "
21 he that t' the water of separation * "
22 unclean person t' shall be unclean; "
22 the soul that t' it shall be unclean "
J'g 16: 9 of tow is broken when it t' the fire. 7306
Job 4: 5 it t' thee, and thou art troubled. 5060
Ps 104:32 he t' the hills, and they smoke. "
Pr 6:29 t' her shall not be innocent. "
Eze 17:10 wither, when the east wind t' it? "
Ho 4: 2 they break out, and blood t' blood. "
Am 9: 5 God of hosts is he that t' the land, "
Zec 2: 8 he that t' you t' the apple of his eye. "

Lu 7:39 manner of woman this is...t' him: 680
1Jo 5:18 and that wicked one t' him not. "

touching
Ge 27:42 Behold, thy brother Esau, as t' thee,
Nu 8:26 do unto the Levites t' their charge.
1Sa 20:23 And as t' the matter which thou and I
2Ki 22:18 As t' the words which thou hast heard;
Ezr 7:24 that t' any of the priests and Levites,
Job 37:23 T' the Almighty, we cannot find him
Ps 45: 1 things which I have made t' the king:
Isa 5: 1 a song of my beloved t' his vineyard.
Jer 1:16 them t' all their wickedness, 5921
21:11 And t' the house of the king of Judah,
22:11 For thus saith the Lord t' Shallum 413
Eze 7:13 the vision is t' the whole multitude "
M't 18:19 shall agree on earth as t' any thing 4012
22:31 as t' the resurrection of the dead, "
M'r 12:26 And as t' the dead, that they rise: "
Lu 23:14 no fault in this man t' those things
Ac 5:35 ye intend to do as t' these men. 1909
21:25 As t' the Gentiles which believe, 4012
24:21 T' the resurrection of the dead I "
26: 2 t'...the things whereof I am accused "
Ro 11:28 but as t' the election, they are 2596
1Co 8: 1 as t' things offered unto idols, *4012
16:12 As t' our brother Apollos, I greatly "
2Co 9: 1 as t' the ministering to the saints, "
Ph'p 3: 5 Hebrews; as t' the law, a Pharisee; 2596
6 t' the righteousness which is in the "
Col 4:10 Barnabas, (t' whom ye received 4012
1Th 4: 9 t' brotherly love ye need not that * "
2Th 3: 4 have confidence in the Lord t' you, 1909

tow
J'g 16: 9 as a thread of t' is broken when it 5296
Isa 1:31 the strong shall be as t', and the "
43:17 extinct, they are quenched as t'. 6594

toward See also UNTOWARD.
Ge 13:12 and pitched his tent t' Sodom. *5704
18:16 thence, and looked t' Sodom: 5921,6440
19: 1 himself with his face t' the ground;* "
28 And he looked t' Sodom and 5921,6440
28 and t' all the land of the plain, " "
25:18 Egypt, as thou goest t' Assyria: "
28:10 from Beer-sheba, and went t' Haran.
30:40 of the flocks t' the ringstraked, 413
31: 2 behold, it was not t' him as before.
5 that it is not t' me as before;
21 and set his face t' the mount Gilead.
48:13 in his right hand t' Israel's left hand,
13 in his left hand t' Israel's right hand,
Ex 16:10 that they looked t' the wilderness, 413
25:20 t' the mercy seat shall the faces of
28:27 t' the forepart thereof, over *4136
34: 8 and bowed his head t' the earth,
36:25 which is t' the north corner, *
39:20 underneath, t' the forepart of it, *4136
Le 9:22 lifted up his hand t' the people, 413
13:41 the part of his head t' his face, *
Nu 2: 3 on the east side t' the rising of the
3:38 before the tabernacle t' the east, *
16:42 they looked t' the tabernacle of the 413
21:11 which is before Moab, t' the sunrising.
20 which looketh t' Jeshimon. *5921,6440
23:28 that looketh t' Jeshimon. " "
24: 1 he set his face t' the wilderness. 413
32:14 fierce anger of the Lord t' Israel.
34:15 Jericho eastward, t' the sunrising.
De 4:41, 47 this side Jordan t' the sunrising;
28:54 his eye shall be evil t' his brother,
54 and t' the wife of his bosom,
54 t' the remnant of his children which
56 be evil t' the husband of her bosom,
56 and t' her son, and t' her daughter,
57 t' her young one that cometh out
57 t' her children which she shall bear:
Jos 1: 4 sea t' the going down of the sun,
15 on this side Jordan t' the sunrising.
3:16 came down t' the sea of the plain, 5921
8:18 the spear that is in thy hand t' Ai; 413
18 that he had in his hand t' the city. "
12: 1 side Jordan t' the rising of the sun,
13: 5 and all Lebanon, t' the sunrising.
15: 4 From thence it passed t' Azmon, and*
7 the border went up t' Debir from the*
7 so northward, looking t' Gilgal, 413
7 passed t' the waters of En-shemesh,* "
21 t' the coast of Edom southward
16: 6 went out t' the sea to Michmethah*
18:13 border went over from thence t' Luz,*
17 and went forth t' Geliloth, * 413
18 passed along t' the side over "
19:11 And their border went up t' the sea,*
12 from Sarid eastward t' the sunrising
18 And their border was t' Jezreel. *
27 t' the sunrising to Beth-dagon,
27 t' the north side of Beth-emek,
34 Judah upon Jordan t' the sunrising.
J'g 3:28 and took the fords of Jordan t' Moab,
4: 6 saying, Go and draw t' mount Tabor,*
5: 9 My heart is t' the governors of Israel,
11 acts t' the inhabitants of his villages*
8: 3 Then their anger was abated t' him,
13:20 went up t' heaven from off the altar,
19: 9 now the day draweth t' evening,
18 t' the side of mount Ephraim; 5704
20:43 over against Gibeah t' the sunrising.
45 turned and fled t' the wilderness
1Sa 13:18 the valley of Zeboim t' the wilderness.
17:30 he turned from him t' another, 413,4136
48 David hasted, and ran t' the army
20:12 if there be good t' David, and I 413
41 arose out of a place t' the south, 681
2Sa 14: 1 the king's heart was t' Absalom. 5921
15:23 t' the way of the wilderness. 5921,6440
24:20 his servants coming on t' him: 5921
1Ki 7: 9 on the outside t' the great court. *5704
25 oxen, three looking t' the north,
25 north, and three looking t' the west,
25 west, and three looking t' the south,
25 south, and three looking t' the east:
8:22 and spread forth his hands t' heaven:
29 eyes may be opened t' this house 413
29 t' the place of which thou hast said. "
29 thy servant shall make t' this place. "
30 when they shall pray t' this place: "
35 if they pray t' this place, and confess "
38 spread forth his hands t' this house: "
42 shall come and pray t' this house; "
44 Lord t' the city which thou hast 1870
44 and t' the house that I have built
48 and pray unto thee t' their land, 1870
14:13 some good thing t' the Lord God 413
18:43 Go up now, look t' the sea. 1870
2Ki 3:14 I would not look t' thee, nor see 413
25: 4 king went the way t' the plain. *1870
1Ch 9:24 t' the east, west, north, and south.
12:15 both t' the east, and t' the west.
26:17 a day, and t' Asuppim two and two.*
2Ch 4: 4 oxen, three looking t' the north,
4 north, and three looking t' the west,
4 west, and three looking t' the south,
4 south, and three looking t' the east:
6:13 and spread forth his hands t' heaven,
20 thy servant prayeth t' this place. 413
21 which they shall make t' this place: "
26 if they pray t' this place, and confess "
34 they pray unto thee t' this city 1870
38 and pray t' their land, which thou "
38 t' the city which thou hast chosen,*
38 and t' the house which I have built
16: 9 them whose heart is perfect t' him. 413
20:24 Judah came t' the watch tower *5921
24:16 done good in Israel, both t' God, 5973
16 and t' his house. *
31:14 the Levite, the porter t' the east, *
Ezr 3:11 mercy endureth for ever t' Israel. 5921
Ne 3:26 against the water gate t' the east,
12:31 hand upon the wall t' the dung gate:
Es 1:13 manner t' all that knew law and 6440
8: 4 held out the golden sceptre t' Esther.*
Job 2:12 dust upon their heads t' heaven.
11:13 stretch out thine hands t' him; 413
39:26 and stretch her wings t' the south?
Ps 5: 7 will I worship t' thy holy temple. 413
25:15 Mine eyes are ever t' the Lord; for "
28: 2 lift up my hands t' thy holy oracle. "
66: 5 his doing t' the children of men. 5921
85: 4 cause thine anger t' us to cease. 5973
86:13 For great is thy mercy t' me: and 5921
103:11 is his mercy t' them that fear him. "
116:12 the Lord for all his benefits t' me? "
117: 2 merciful kindness is great t' us: "
138: 2 I will worship t' thy holy temple, 413
Pr 14:35 The king's favour is t' a wise servant:
23: 5 they fly away as an eagle t' heaven.
Ec 1: 6 The wind goeth t' the south, and 413
11: 3 and if the tree fall t' the south, or
3 t' the north, in the place where the
Ca 7: 4 Lebanon which looketh t' Damascus.
10 beloved's, and his desire is t' me. 5921
Isa 7: 1 went up t' Jerusalem to war against*
11:14 of the Philistines t' the west: *
29:13 fear t' me is taught by the precept* 854
38: 2 turned his face t' the wall, * 413
49:23 to thee with their face t' the earth,*
63: 7 great goodness t' the house of Israel,
15 bowels and of thy mercies t' me? 413
66:14 shall be known t' his servants, 854
14 and his indignation t' his enemies.*
Jer 1:13 the face thereof is t' the north. *6440
3:12 proclaim these words t' the north,
4: 6 Set up the standard t' Zion: retire,
11 t' the daughter of my people,
12: 3 me, and tried mine heart t' thee: 854
15: 1 mind could not be t' this people: 413
29:10 perform my good word t' you, 5921
11 the thoughts that I think t' you, "
31:21 set thine heart t' the highway, even
40 corner of the horse gate t' the east,
46: 6 t' the north by the river Euphrates.*
49:36 will scatter them t' all those winds;
La 2:19 lift up thy hands t' him for the 5921
Eze 1:23 straight, the one t' the other: 413
4: 7 thy face t' the siege of Jerusalem, "
6: 2 thy face t' the mountains of Israel, "
14 than the wilderness t' Diblath,
8: 3 inner gate that looketh t' the north;
5 thine eyes now the way t' the north.
5 up mine eyes the way t' the north,
14 house which was t' the north; 5921
16 backs t' the temple of the Lord, 413
16 Lord, and their faces t' the east;
16 they worshipped the sun t' the east.
9: 2 higher gate, which lieth t' the north,
12:14 scatter t' every wind all that are
16:42 So will I make my fury t' thee to rest,*
17: 6 whose branches turned t' him, 413
7 vine did bend her roots t' him, 5921
7 and shot forth her branches t' him, "
21 shall be scattered t' all winds:
20:46 of man, set thy face t' the south, 1870
46 and drop thy word t' the south, 413
21: 2 man, set thy face t' Jerusalem, "
2 drop thy word t' the holy places, "
24:23 iniquities, and mourn one t' another. "
33:25 and lift up your eyes t' your idols, "
40: 6 the gate which looketh t' the east, 1870
20 court that looked t' the north, "
22 of the gate that looketh t' the east; "
23 the gate t' the north, and t' the east.*

Eze 40: 24 that he brought me t' the south, 1870
24 behold a gate t' the south: and he "
27 gate in the inner court t' the south: "
27 from gate to gate t' the south "
31 arches...were t' the utter court; 413
32 into the inner court t' the east: 1870
34 arches...were t' the outward court:
37 posts thereof were t' the utter court;
44 their prospect was t' the south: 1870
44 having the prospect t' the north. "
45 whose prospect is t' the south, "
46 whose prospect is t' the north is "
41: 11 were t' the place that was left,
11 one door t' the north, "
11 and another door t' the south: "
12 at the end t' the west was seventy "
14 and of the separate place t' the east,
19 face of a man was t' the palm tree 413
19 face of a young lion t' the palm tree "
42: 1 utter court, the way t' the north: 1870
1 before the building t' the north. 413
4 cubit; and their doors t' the north. "
7 t' the utter court on the forepart 1870
10 the wall of the court t' the east, "
11 chambers which were t' the north, "
12 chambers that were t' the south "
12 directly before the wall t' the east, "
15 he brought me forth t' the gate * "
15 whose prospect is t' the east, and "
43: 1 the gate that looketh t' the east: "
4 gate whose prospect is t' the east. "
17 and his stairs shall look t' the east.
44: 1 sanctuary which looketh t' the east;
46: 1 inner court that looketh t' the east
12 him the gate that looketh t' the east,
19 priests, which looked t' the north:
47: 1 of the house stood t' the east,
8 waters issue out t' the east country,
15 border of the land t' the north side.*
48: 10 t' the north five and twenty thousand
10 t' the west ten thousand in breadth,
10 t' the east ten thousand in breadth,
10 t' the south five and twenty thousand
17 t' the north two hundred and fifty,
17 t' the south two hundred and fifty,
17 t' the east two hundred and fifty,
17 t' the west two hundred and fifty.
21 the oblation t' the east border, 5704
21 and twenty thousand t' the west 5921
28 and to the river t' the great sea. * "
Da 4: 2 the high God hath wrought t' me. 5974
6: 10 open in his chamber t' Jerusalem, 5049
8: 8 ones t' the four winds of heaven.
9 exceeding great, t' the south, 413
9 t' the east, and t' the pleasant land. "
18 deep sleep on my face t' the ground: "
10: 9 my face, and my face t' the ground. "
15 unto me, I set my face t' the ground, "
11: 4 be divided t' the four winds of heaven; "
19 his face t' the fort of his own land: "
29 shall return, and come t' the south;* "
Ho 3: 1 the Lord t' the children of Israel, * 854
5: 1 for judgment is t' you, because ye* "
Joe 2: 20 with his face t' the east sea, and * 413
20 his hinder part t' the utmost sea, * "
Jon 2: 4 will look again t' thy holy temple. "
Zec 6: 6 grisled go forth t' the south country. "
8 these that go t' the north country "
9: 1 tribes of Israel, shall be t' the Lord. "
14: 4 thereof t' the east and t' the west, "
4 mountain shall remove t' the north, "
4 the north, and half of it t' the south. "
8 half of them t' the former sea, 413
8 and half of them t' the hinder sea: "
M't 12: 49 forth his hand t' his disciples, *1909
14: 14 moved with compassion t' them, * "
28: 1 to dawn t' the first day of the week, 1519
M'r 6: 34 moved with compassion t' them, *1909
Lu 2: 14 on earth peace, good will t' men. *1722
12: 21 himself, and is not rich t' God. 1519
13: 22 and journeying t' Jerusalem. * "
24: 29 for it is t' evening, and the day is 4314
Joh 6: 17 went over the sea t' Capernaum. *1519
Ac 1: 10 looked stedfastly t' heaven as he * "
8: 26 go t' the south unto the way that 2596
20: 21 to the Greeks, repentance t' God, 1519
21 and faith t' our Lord Jesus Christ. "
22: 3 and was zealous t' God, as ye all are* "
24: 15 And have hope t' God, which they 1519
16 conscience void of offence t' God, 4314
16 and t' men. "
27: 12 t' the south west and north west. *2596
40 to the wind, and made t' shore. *1519
28: 14 days: and so we went t' Rome. "
Ro 1: 27 burned in their lust one t' another; "
5: 8 God commendeth his love t' us,
11: 22 t' thee, goodness, if thou continue 1909
12: 16 of the same mind one t' another. 1519
15: 5 be likeminded one t' another *1722
1Co 7: 36 himself uncomely t' his virgin, 1909
2Co 1: 16 be brought on my way t' Judæa. *1519
18 word t' you was not yea and nay. 4314
2: 8 would confirm your love t' him. 1519
7: 4 is my boldness of speech t' you, 4314
7 your fervent mind t' me; *5228
15 affection is more abundant t' you, 1519
9: 8 to make all grace abound t' you; * "
10: 1 but being absent am bold t' you: "
13: 4 him by the power of God t' you. "
Gal 2: 8 was mighty in me t' the Gentiles:)* "
Eph 1: 8 hath abounded t' us in all wisdom "
2: 7 in his kindness t' us through 1909
Ph'p 2: 30 supply your lack of service t' me. 4314
3: 14 I press t' the mark for the prize 2596
Col 4: 5 Walk in wisdom t' them that are 4314
1Th 3: 12 abound in love one t' another, 1519

1Th 3: 12 t' all men, even as we do t' you: 1519
4: 10 indeed ye do it t' all the brethren "
12 ye may walk honestly t' them that 4314
5: 14 the weak, be patient t' all men.
2Th 1: 3 of you all t' each other aboundeth; 1519
Tit 3: 4 God our Saviour t' man appeared, 4314
Ph'm 5 thou hast t' the Lord Jesus, 4314
5 and t' all saints; 1519
Heb 6: 1 dead works, and of faith t' God, 1909
10 which ye have shewed t' his name, 1519
1Pe 2: 19 for conscience t' God endure grief,
3: 21 of a good conscience t' God,) 1519
1Jo 3: 21 then have we confidence t' God. 4314
4: 9 manifested the love of God t' us, *1722

towel
Joh 13: 4 and took a t', and girded himself. 3012
5 wipe them with the t' wherewith "

tower See also TOWERS; WATCHTOWER.
Ge 11: 4 to, let us build us a city and a t', 4026
5 down to see the city and the t', "
35: 21 his tent beyond the t' of Edar. "
J'g 8: 9 peace, I will break down this t'. "
17 he beat down the t' of Penuel, "
9: 46 men of the t' of Shechem heard "
47 men of the t' of Shechem were "
49 men of the t' of Shechem died also, "
51 there was a strong t' within the city, "
51 gat them up to the top of the t'. "
52 And Abimelech came unto the t', "
52 went hard unto the door of the t' to "
2Sa 22: 3 my high t', and my refuge, my 4869
51 He is the t' of salvation for his *1431
2Ki 5: 24 when he came to the t', he took *6076
9: 17 there stood a watchman on the t' 4026
17: 9 from the t' of the watchmen to the "
18: 8 from the t' of the watchmen to the "
2Ch 20: 24 Judah came toward the watch t' in* "
Ne 3: 1 even unto the t' of Meah they 4026
1 sanctified it, unto the t' of Hananeel. "
11 piece, and the t' of the furnaces. "
25 t' which lieth out from the king's "
26 the east, and the t' that lieth out. "
27 against the great t' that lieth out, "
12: 38 from beyond the t' of the furnaces "
39 fish gate, and the t' of Hananeel, "
39 and the t' of Meah, even unto the "
Ps 18: 2 of my salvation, and my high t'. 4869
61: 3 and a strong t' from the enemy. 4026
144: 2 my high t', and my deliverer; 4869
Pr 18: 10 name of the Lord is a strong t': 4026
Ca 4: 4 Thy neck is like the t' of David "
7: 4 Thy neck is as a t' of ivory; thine "
4 thy nose is as the t' of Lebanon "
Isa 2: 15 And upon every high t', and upon "
5: 2 and built a t' in the midst of it, "
Jer 6: 27 I have set thee for a t' and a ‡ 969
31: 38 from the t' of Hananeel unto the 4026
Eze 29: 10 from the t' of Syene even unto the 4024
30: 6 from the t' of Syene shall they fall "
Mic 4: 8 And thou, O t' of the flock, the 4026
Hab 2: 1 my watch, and set me upon the t', 4692
Zec 14: 10 and from the t' of Hananeel unto 4026
M't 21: 33 a winepress in it, and built a t', 4444
M'r 12: 1 place for the winefat, and built a t', "
Lu 13: 4 upon whom the t' in Siloam fell, "
14: 28 which of you, intending to build a t', "

towers
2Ch 14: 7 make about them walls, and t', 4026
26: 9 Uzziah built t' in Jerusalem at the "
10 Also he built t' in the desert, and "
15 be on the t' and upon the bulwarks, "
27: 4 the forests he built castles and t'. "
32: 5 broken, and raised it up to the t', "
Ps 48: 12 about her: tell the t' thereof. "
Ca 8: 10 I am a wall, and my breasts like t': "
Isa 23: 13 they set up the t' thereof, they 971
30: 25 great slaughter, when the t' fall. 4026
32: 14 the forts and t' shall be for dens * 975
33: 18 where is he that counted the t'? 4026
Eze 26: 4 of Tyrus, and break down her t': "
9 his axes he shall break down thy t'. "
27: 11 the Gammadims were in thy t': "
Zep 1: 16 cities, and against the high t'. *6438
3: 6 the nations: their t' are desolate;* "

to-wit See WIT.

town See also TOWNCLERK; TOWNS.
Jos 2: 15 for her house was upon the t' wall 7023
1Sa 16: 4 the elders of the t' trembled at his* "
23: 7 entering into a t' that hath gates 5892
27: 5 a place in some t' in the country, * "
Hab 2: 12 him that buildeth a t' with blood, "
M't 10: 11 city or t' ye shall enter, *2968
M'r 8: 23 the hand, and led him out of the t'; * "
26 saying, Neither go into the t', nor * "
26 nor tell it to any in the t'. * "
Lu 5: 17 were come out of every t' of Galilee, * "
Joh 7: 42 out of the t' of Bethlehem, where * "
11: 1 the t' of Mary and her sister Martha. * "
30 Jesus was not yet come into the t', * "

townclerk
Ac 19: 35 And when the t' had appeased the 1122

towns
Ge 25: 16 these are their names, by their t', *2691
Nu 32: 41 Jair...went and took the small t' 2333
De 3: 5 beside unwalled t' a great many. 5892
Jos 13: 30 t' of Jair, which are in Bashan, 2333
15: 45 Ekron, with her t' and her villages: 1323
47 Ashdod with her t' and her villages, "
47 Gaza with her t' and her villages, "
17: 11 in Asher Beth-shean and her t', "
11 and Ibleam and her t', "
11 the inhabitants of Dor and her t', "
11 inhabitants of En-dor and her t', "
11 inhabitants of Taanach and her t', "

Jos 17: 11 inhabitants of Megiddo and her t', 1323
16 who are of Beth-shean and her t', "
J'g 1: 27 of Beth-shean and her t', "
27 nor Taanach and her t', "
27 the inhabitants of Dor and her t', "
27 inhabitants of Ibleam and her t', "
27 inhabitants of Megiddo and her t': "
11: 26 Israel dwelt in Heshbon and her t', "
26 and in Aroer and her t', and in all "
1Ki 4: 13 to him pertained the t' of Jair the 2333
1Ch 2: 23 and Aram, with the t' of Jair, "
23 with Kenath, and the t' thereof, *1323
5: 16 in her t', and in all the suburbs of "
7: 28 were, Beth-el and the t' thereof, "
28 westward Gezer, with the t' thereof; "
28 Shechem also and the t' thereof, "
28 unto Gaza and the t' thereof: "
29 Manasseh, Beth-shean and her t', "
29 Taanach and her t', "
29 Megiddo and her t', "
29 Dor and her t'. "
8: 12 Ono, and Lod, with the t' thereof: 1323
18: 1 Gath and her t' out of the hand of "
2Ch 13: 19 him, Beth-el with the t' thereof, "
19 and Jeshanah with the t' thereof, "
19 and Ephrain with the t' thereof. "
Es 9: 19 that dwelt in the unwalled t', 5892
Jer 19: 15 upon this city and upon all her t' "
Zec 2: 4 inhabited as t' without walls for *6519
M'r 1: 38 Let us go into the next t', that I 2969
8: 27 into the t' of Cæsarea Philippi: *2968
Lu 9: 6 went through the t', preaching the* "
12 they may go into the t' and country* "

Trachonitis (*trak-o-ni'-tis*)
Lu 3: 1 of Ituræa and of the region of T', 5139

trade See also TRADED; TRADING.
Ge 34: 10 dwell and t' ye therein, and get 5503
21 dwell in the land, and t' therein; "
46: 32 for their t' hath been to feed cattle; 582
34 Thy servants' t' hath been about * "
Re 18: 17 sailors, and as many as t' by sea, *2038

traded
Eze 27: 12 tin, and lead, they t' in thy fairs. 5414
13 they t' the persons of men and "
14 house of Togarmah t' in thy fairs "
17 t' in thy market wheat of Minnith, "
M't 25: 16 talents went and t' with the same. 2038

trading
Lu 19: 15 much every man had gained by t'. 1281

tradition See also TRADITIONS.
M't 15: 2 transgress the t' of the elders? 3862
3 commandment of God by your t'? "
6 of God of none effect by your t'. "
M'r 7: 3 eat not, holding the t' of the elders. "
5 according to the t' of the elders, "
8 ye hold the t' of men, as the "
9 that ye may keep your own t'. "
13 God of none effect through your t', "
Col 2: 8 vain deceit, after the t' of men, "
2Th 3: 6 not after the t' which he received "
1Pe 1: 18 received by t' from your fathers; *

traditions
Ga 1: 14 zealous of the t' of my fathers. 3862
2Th 2: 15 hold the t'...ye have been taught, "

traffick
Ge 42: 34 brother, and ye shall t' in the land. 5503
1Ki 10: 15 of the t' of the spice merchants, 4536
Eze 17: 4 and carried it into a land of t'; 3667
28: 5 by thy t' hast thou increased thy 7404
18 iniquities, by the iniquity of thy t'; "

traffickers
Isa 23: 8 t' are the honourable of the earth? 3669

train See also TRAINED.
1Ki 10: 2 to Jerusalem with a very great t', 2428
Pr 22: 6 T' up a child in the way he should 2596
Isa 6: 1 up, and his t' filled the temple. 7757

trained
Ge 14: 14 captive, he armed his t' servants, 2593

traitor See also TRAITORS.
Lu 6: 16 Iscariot, which was also the t'. 4273

traitors
2Ti 3: 4 T', heady, highminded, lovers of 4273

trample
Ps 91: 13 dragon shalt thou t' under feet. 7429
Isa 63: 3 anger, and t' them in my fury; "
M't 7: 6 lest they t' them under their feet, 2662

trance
Nu 24: 4, 16 into a t', but having his eyes open:*
Ac 10: 10 they made ready, he fell into a t', 1611
11: 5 and in a t' I saw a vision, A certain "
22: 17 prayed in the temple, I was in a t'; "

tranquillity
Da 4: 27 it may be a lengthening of thy t'. 7963

transferred
1Co 4: 6 I have in a figure t' to myself and 3345

transfigured
M't 17: 2 And was t' before them: and his 3339
M'r 9: 2 and he was t' before them. "

transformed
Ro 12: 2 ye t' by the renewing of your mind, 3339
2Co 11: 14 Satan himself is t' into an angel *3345
15 t' as...ministers of righteousness; * "

transforming
2Co 11: 13 t' themselves into the apostles of *3345

transgress See also TRANSGRESSED; TRANGRESSEST; TRANGRESSETH; TRANSGRESSING.
Nu 14: 41 do ye t' the commandment of the 5674
1Sa 2: 24 ye make the Lord's people to t'. "

2Ch 24:20 Why t' ye the commandments of 5674
Ne 1: 8 If ye t', I will scatter you abroad *4603
13:27 to t' against our God in marrying * "
Ps 17: 3 that my mouth shall not t'. 5674
25: 3 ashamed which t' without cause. * 898
Pr 28:21 a piece of bread that man will t'. 6586
Jer 2:20 and thou saidst, I will not t'; *5647
Eze 20:38 and them that t' against me: 6586
Am 4: 4 Come to Beth-el, and t'; at Gilgal "
M't 15: 2 thy disciples t' the tradition of the 3845
3 do ye also t' the commandment "
Ro 2:27 and circumcision dost t' the law? 3848

transgressed
De 26:13 I have not t' thy commandments, 5674
Jos 7:11 and they have also t' my covenant "
15 because he hath t' the covenant of "
23:16 When ye have t' the covenant of the* "
J'g 2:20 this people hath t' my covenant "
1Sa 14:33 he said, Ye have t': roll a great * 898
15:24 for I have t' the commandment of 5674
1Ki 8:50 wherein they have t' against thee, 6586
2Ki 18:12 their God, but t' his covenant, 5674
1Ch 2: 7 Israel, who t' in...thing accursed. *4603
5:25 t' against the God of their fathers, "
2Ch 12: 2 they had t' against the Lord, * "
26:16 for he t' against the Lord his God, * "
28:19 naked, and t' sore against the Lord.* "
36:14 people, t' very much after all the * "
Ezr 10:10 Ye have t', and have taken strange* "
13 many that have t' in this thing. 6586
Isa 24: 5 because they have t' the laws, 5674
43:27 thy teachers have t' against me. 6586
66:24 the men that have t' against me: "
Jer 2: 8 the pastors also t' against me, and "
29 ye all have t' against me, saith the "
3:13 hast t' against the Lord thy God, "
33: 8 whereby they have t' against me. "
34:18 the men that have t' my covenant, 5674
La 3:42 We have t' and have rebelled: 6586
Eze 2: 3 their fathers have t' against me, "
18:31 transgressions, whereby ye have t'; "
Da 9:11 Yea, all Israel have t' thy law, 5674
Ho 6: 7 they like men have t' the covenant: "
7:13 because they have t' against me: *6586
8: 1 because they have t' my covenant, 5674
Zep 3:11 wherein thou hast t' against me: 6586
Lu 15:29 neither t' I at any time thy 3928

transgressest
Es 3: 3 Mordecai, Why t' thou the king's 5674

trangresseth
Pr 16:10 his mouth t' not in judgment. *4603
Hab 2: 5 Yea also, because he t' by wine, * 898
1Jo 3: 4 Whosoever committeth sin t' *458,4160
2Jo 9 Whosoever t', and abideth not in *3845

transgressing
De 17: 2 Lord thy God, in t' his covenant, 5674
Isa 59:13 In t' and lying against the Lord, 6586

transgression See also TRANSGRESSIONS.
Ex 34: 7 forgiving iniquity and t' and sin, 6588
Nu 14:18 forgiving iniquity and t', and by no "
Jos 22:22 or if in t' against the Lord, (save *4604
1Sa 24:11 is neither evil nor t' in mine hand, 6588
1Ch 9: 1 carried away to Babylon for their t'. 4604
10:13 So Saul died for his t' which he * "
2Ch 29:19 in his reign did cast away in his t', * "
Ezr 9: 4 the t' of those that had been * "
10: 6 he mourned because of the t' of * "
Job 7:21 why dost thou not pardon my t', 6588
8: 4 he have cast them away for their t'; "
13:23 make me to know my t' and my sin. "
14:17 My t' is sealed up in a bag, and "
33: 9 I am clean without t', I am "
34: 6 my wound is incurable without t'. "
Ps 19:13 shall be innocent from the great t'. "
32: 1 Blessed is he whose t' is forgiven, "
36: 1 The t' of the wicked saith within "
59: 3 not for my t' nor for my sin, O Lord. "
89:32 will I visit their t' with the rod, "
107:17 Fools because of their t', and "
Pr 12:13 The wicked is snared by the t' of "
17: 9 He that covereth a t' seeketh love; "
19 He loveth t' that loveth strife: and "
19:11 and it is his glory to pass over a t'. "
28: 2 For the t' of a land many are the "
24 his mother, and saith, It is no t'; "
29: 6 t' of an evil man there is a snare: "
16 are multiplied, t' increaseth: "
22 and a furious man aboundeth in t'. "
Isa 24:20 t' thereof shall be heavy upon it; "
53: 8 for the t' of my people was he "
57: 4 are ye not children of t', a seed of "
58: 1 and shew my people their t', and "
59:20 them that turn from t' in Jacob, "
Eze 33:12 not deliver him in the day of his t': "
Da 8:12 the daily sacrifice by reason of t', "
13 sacrifice, and the t' of desolation, "
9:24 to finish the t', and to make an end "
Am 4: 4 at Gilgal multiply t'; and bring 6586
Mic 1: 5 For the t' of Jacob is all this, and 6588
5 What is the t' of Jacob? is it not "
3: 8 to declare unto Jacob his t', and to "
6: 7 shall I give my firstborn for my t', "
7:18 passeth by the t' of the remnant of "
Ac 1:25 from which Judas by t' fell, that *3845
Ro 4:15 for where no law is, there is no t'. 3847
5:14 after the similitude of Adam's t', "
1Ti 2:14 woman being deceived was in the t'. "
Heb 2: 2 every t' and disobedience received "
1Jo 3: 4 the law: for sin is the t' of the law.* 458

transgressions
Ex 23:21 not; for he will not pardon your t': 6588
Le 16:16 because of their t' in all their sins: "
21 and all their t' in all their sins, "
Jos 24:19 not forgive your t' nor your sins. 6588
1Ki 8:50 all their t' wherein they have "
Job 31:33 If I covered my t' as Adam, by "
35: 6 if thy t' be multiplied, what doest "
36: 9 their t' that they have exceeded. "
Ps 5:10 out in the multitude of their t'; "
25: 7 not the sins of my youth, nor my t': "
32: 5 I will confess my t' unto the Lord; "
39: 8 Deliver me from all my t': make "
51: 1 thy tender mercies blot out my t'. "
3 For I acknowledge my t': and my "
65: 3 as for our t', thou shalt purge them "
103:12 hath he removed our t' from us. "
Isa 43:25 blotteth out thy t' for mine own "
44:22 blotted out, as a thick cloud, thy t', "
50: 1 your t' is your mother put away. "
53: 5 But he was wounded for our t', he "
59:12 our t' are multiplied before thee, "
12 for our t' are with us; and as for "
Jer 5: 6 because their t' are many, and their "
La 1: 5 her for the multitude of her t': "
14 yoke of my t' is bound by his hand: "
22 hast done unto me for all my t': "
Eze 14:11 polluted any more with all their t'; "
18:22 All his t' that he hath committed, "
28 away from all his t' that he hath "
30 turn yourselves from all your t'; "
31 Cast away from you all your t', "
21:24 in that your t' are discovered, so "
33:10 If our t' and our sins be upon us, "
37:23 things, nor with any of their t': "
39:24 according to their t' have I done "
Am 1: 3 For three t' of Damascus, and for "
6 For three t' of Gaza, and for four, "
9 For three t' of Tyrus, and for four, "
11 For three t' of Edom, and for four, "
13 For three t' of the children of "
2: 1 For three t' of Moab, and for four, "
4 For three t' of Judah, and for four, "
6 For three t' of Israel, and for four, "
3:14 shall visit the t' of Israel upon him "
5:12 your manifold t' and your mighty "
Mic 1:13 the t' of Israel were found in thee. "
Ga 3:19 It was added because of t', till the 3847
Heb 9:15 the t' that were under the first "

transgressor See also TRANSGRESSORS.
Pr 21:18 and the t' for the upright. * 898
22:12 overthroweth the words of the t'. * "
Isa 48: 8 wast called a t' from the womb. 6586
Ga 2:18 I destroyed, I make myself a t'. 3848
Jas 2:11 kill, thou art become a t' of the law. "

transgressors
Ps 37:38 But the t' shall be destroyed 6586
51:13 Then will I teach t' thy ways; and "
59: 5 be not merciful to any wicked t'. 898
119:158 I beheld the t', and was grieved;* "
Pr 2:22 and the t' shall be rooted out of it.* "
11: 3 the perverseness of t' shall destroy* "
6 t' shall be taken in their own * "
13: 2 the soul of the t' shall eat violence.* "
15 favour: but the way of t' is hard.* "
23:28 and increaseth the t' among men.* "
26:10 the fool, and rewardeth t'. *5674
Isa 1:28 the destruction of the t' and of the 6586
46: 8 men: bring it again to mind, O ye t'. "
53:12 and he was numbered with the t'; "
12 and made intercession for the t'. "
Da 8:23 when the t' are come to the full, "
Ho 14: 9 them: but the t' shall fall therein. "
M'r 15:28 And he was numbered with the t'.* 459
Lu 22:37 And he was reckoned among the t': "
Jas 2: 9 and are convinced of the law as t'. 3848

translate See also TRANSLATED.
2Sa 3:10 To t' the kingdom from the house 5674

translated
Col 1:13 hath t' us into the kingdom of his 3179
Heb 11: 5 By faith Enoch was t' that he 3346
5 not found, because God had t' him: "

translation
Heb 11: 5 for before his t' he had this 3331

transparent
Re 21:21 was pure gold, as it were t' glass. 1307

trap See also TRAPS.
Job 18:10 and a t' for him in the way. 4434
Ps 69:22 for their welfare, let it become a t'. 4170
Jer 5:26 they set a t', they catch men. 4889
Ro 11: 9 table he made a snare, and a t', 2339

traps
Jos 23:13 shall be snares and t' unto you. *4170

travail See also TRAVAILED; TRAVAILEST; TRAVAILETH; TRAVAILING; TRAVEL.
Ge 38:27 came to pass in the time of her t', 3205
Ex 18: 8 all the t' that had come upon them 8513
Ps 48: 6 and pain, as of a woman in t'. 3205
Ec 1:13 this sore t' hath God given to the 6045
2:23 days are sorrows, and his t' grief; "
26 to the sinner he giveth t', to gather "
3:10 I have seen the t', which God hath "
4: 4 I considered all t', and every right* 5999
6 hands full with t' and vexation of* "
8 is also vanity, yea, it is a sore t'. 6045
5:14 But those riches perish by evil t':* "
Isa 23: 4 I t' not, nor bring forth children, *2342
53:11 He shall see of the t' of his soul, 5999
54: 1 thou that didst not t' with child: 2342
Jer 4:31 heard a voice as of a woman in t', 2470
6:24 us, and pain, as of a woman in t'. 3205
13:21 sorrows take thee, as a woman in t'? 3205
22:23 thee, the pain as of a woman in t'! "
30: 6 whether a man doth t' with child? "
6 on his loins, as a woman in t', "
49:24 have taken her, as a woman in t'. "
50:43 him, and pangs as of a woman in t'. "
Mic 4: 9 have taken thee as a woman in t'. 3205
10 of Zion, like a woman in t': "
Joh 16:21 A woman...in t' hath sorrow, 5088
Ga 4:19 I t' in birth again until Christ be 5605
1Th 2: 9 brethren, our labour and t': 3449
5: 3 as t' upon a woman with child; 5604
2Th 3: 8 wrought with labour and t' night 3449

travailed
Ge 35:16 Rachel t', and she had hard labour, 3205
38:28 it came to pass, when she t', that "
1Sa 4:19 dead, she bowed herself and t'; * "
Isa 66: 7 Before she t', she brought forth; 2342
8 for as soon as Zion t', she brought "

travailest
Ga 4:27 forth and cry, thou that t' not: 5605

travaileth
Job 15:20 wicked man t' with pain all his 2342
Ps 7:14 he t' with iniquity, and hath 2254
Isa 13: 8 be in pain as a woman that t': *3205
21: 3 as the pangs of a woman that t': * "
Jer 31: 8 and her that t' with child together: "
Mic 5: 3 she which t' hath brought forth: "
Ro 8:22 and t' in pain together until now. 4944

travailing
Isa 42:14 now will I cry like a t' woman; I 3205
Ho 13:13 The sorrows of a t' woman shall "
Re 12: 2 being with child cried, t' in birth, 5605

travel See also TRAVAIL; TRAVELLED; TRAVELLETH; TRAVELLING.
Nu 20:14 all the t' that hath befallen us: *8513
La 3: 5 compassed me with gall and t'. * "
Ac 19:29 Macedonia, Paul's companions in t'. 4898
2Co 8:19 chosen of the churches to t' with us "

travelled
Ac 11:19 Stephen t' as far as Phenice, and 1330

traveller See also TRAVELLERS.
2Sa 12: 4 there came a t' unto the rich man, 1982
Job 31:32 but I opened my doors to the t'. 734

travellers
J'g 5: 6 the t' walked through byways. 1980,5410

travelleth
Pr 6:11 thy poverty come as one that t', *1980
24:34 thy poverty come as one that t'; * "

travelling
Isa 21:13 O ye t' companies of Dedanim. ‡ 736
63: 1 t' in the greatness of his strength? *6808
M't 25:14 is as a man t' into a far country, * 589

traversing
Jer 2:23 art a swift dromedary t' her ways; 8308

treacherous
Isa 21: 2 t' dealer dealeth treacherously, 898
24:16 t' dealers have dealt treacherously; "
16 the t' dealers have dealt very "
Jer 3: 7 And her t' sister Judah saw it. 901
8 yet her t' sister Judah feared not, 898
10 her t' sister Judah hath not 901
11 herself more than t' Judah. 898
9: 2 adulterers, an assembly of t' men. "
Zep 3: 4 prophets are light and t' persons: 900

treacherously
J'g 9:23 Shechem dealt t' with Abimelech: 898
Isa 21: 2 the treacherous dealer dealeth t'. "
24:16 treacherous dealers have dealt t'; "
16 dealers have dealt very t'. "
33: 1 wast not spoiled; and dealest t', "
1 and they dealt not t' with thee! "
1 thou shalt make an end to deal t', "
1 they shall deal t' with thee. "
48: 8 that thou wouldest deal very t', "
Jer 3:20 as a wife t' departeth from her "
20 so have ye dealt t' with me, "
5:11 have dealt very t' against me, "
12: 1 are all they happy that deal very t'? "
6 even they have dealt t' with thee; "
La 1: 2 her friends have dealt t' with her, "
Ho 5: 7 have dealt t' against the Lord: "
6: 7 there have they dealt t' against me. "
Hab 1:13 lookest thou upon them that deal t', "
Mal 2:10 we deal t' every man against his "
11 Judah hath dealt t', and an "
14 against whom thou hast dealt t': "
15 deal t' against the wife of his youth. "
16 to your spirit, that ye deal not t'. "

treachery
2Ki 9:23 Ahaziah, There is t', O Ahaziah. 4820

tread See also TREADER; TREADETH; TREADING; TRODDEN; TRODE.
De 11:24 the soles of your feet shall t' shall 1869
25 upon all the land...ye shall t' upon, "
33:29 thou shalt t' upon their high places. "
Jos 1: 3 the sole of your feet shall t' upon, "
1Sa 5: 5 t' on the threshold of Dagon in "
Job 24:11 t' their winepresses, and suffer "
40:12 t' down the wicked in their place. 1915
Ps 7: 5 let him t' down my life upon the 7429
44: 5 will we t' them under that rise up 947
60:12 it is that shall t' down our enemies. "
91:13 shalt t' upon the lion and adder: 1869
108:13 it is that shall t' down our enemies. 947
Isa 1:12 this at your hand, to t' my courts? *7429
10: 6 t' them down like the mire of 7760,4823
14:25 my mountains t' him under foot: 947
16:10 treaders shall t' out no wine in 1869
26: 6 The foot shall t' it down, even the 7429
63: 3 for I will t' them in mine anger, *1869
6 I will t' down the people in mine * 947
Jer 25:30 shout, as they that t' the grapes, 1869
48:33 none shall t' with shouting; their "
Eze 26:11 shall he t' down all thy streets: 7429
34:18 ye must t' down with your feet the "
Da 7:23 shall t' it down, and break it in 1759

Ho 10: 11 and loveth to t' out the corn; 1758
Mic 1: 3 t' upon the high places of the 1869
5: 5 and when he shall t' in our palaces, "
6: 15 thou shalt t' the olives, but thou "
Na 3: 14 go into clay, and t' the morter, 7429
Zec 10: 5 which t' down their enemies in the*947
Mal 4: 3 And ye shall t' down the wicked; 6072
Lu 10: 19 you power to t' on serpents and *3961*
Re 11: 2 holy city shall they t' under foot "

treader See also TREADERS.
Am 9: 13 the t' of grapes him that soweth 1869

treaders
Isa 16: 10 the t' shall tread out no wine in *1869

treadeth
De 25: 4 the ox when he t' out the corn. 1758
Job 9: 8 and t' upon the waves of the sea. 1869
Isa 41: 25 morter, and as the potter t' clay. 7429
63: 2 like him that t' in the winefat? 1869
Am 4: 13 t' upon the high places of the earth, "
Mic 5: 6 and when he t' within our borders. "
8 t' down, and teareth in pieces, 7429
1Co 9: 9 of the ox that t' out the corn. *248*
1Ti 5: 18 muzzle the ox that t' out the corn. "
Re 19: 15 and he t' the winepress of the *3961*

treading
Ne 13: 15 t' wine presses on the sabbath, 1869
Isa 7: 25 and for the t' of lesser cattle. 4823
22: 5 is a day of trouble, and of t' down,4001
Am 5: 11 as your t' is upon the poor, *1318

treason
1Ki 16: 20 and his t' that he wrought, 7195
2Ki 11: 14 rent her clothes, and cried, T', T'. "
2Ch 23: 13 rent their clothes, and said, T', T'. "

treasure See also TREASURED; TREASURES; TREASUREST.
Ge 43: 23 hath given you t' in your sacks: 4301
Ex 1: 11 they built for Pharaoh t' cities, *4543
19: 5 then ye shall be a peculiar t' unto me‡
De 28: 12 shall open unto thee his good t', 214
1Ch 29: 8 to the t' of the house of the Lord, "
Ezr 2: 69 their ability unto the t' of the work "
5: 17 be search made in the king's t' 1596
7: 20 it out of the king's t' house. "
Ne 7: 70 gave to the t' a thousand drams of*214
71 gave to the t' of the work twenty * "
10: 38 to the chambers, into the t' house. "
Ps 17: 14 whose belly thou fillest with thy hid t':
135: 4 himself, and Israel for his peculiar t'.‡
Pr 15: 6 house of the righteous is much t': 2633
16 Lord than great t' and trouble 214
21: 20 There is t' to be desired and oil in "
Ec 2: 8 the peculiar t' of kings and of the "
Isa 33: 6 the fear of the Lord is his t'. 214
Eze 22: 25 they have taken the t' and 2633
Da 1: 2 vessels into the t' house of his god. 214
Ho 13: 15 spoil the t' of all pleasant vessels. "
M't 6: 21 where your t' is, there will your *2344*
12: 35 good t' of the heart bringeth forth "
35 evil t' bringeth forth evil things. "
13: 44 heaven is like unto t' hid in a field; "
52 out of his t' things new and old. "
19: 21 and thou shalt have t' in heaven: "
M'r 10: 21 and thou shalt have t' in heaven: "
Lu 6: 45 good t' of his heart bringeth forth "
45 evil t' of his heart bringeth forth "
12: 21 he that layeth up t' for himself, *2343*
33 t' in the heavens that faileth not, *2344*
34 where your t' is, there will your "
18: 22 and thou shalt have t' in heaven: "
Ac 8: 27 who had the charge of all her t', *1047*
2Co 4: 7 we have this t' in earthen vessels, *2344*
Jas 5: 3 heaped t' together for the last *2343*

treasure-cities See TREASURE and CITIES.

treasured
Isa 23: 18 it shall not be t' nor laid up; for 686

treasure-house See TREASURE and HOUSE.

treasurer See also TREASURERS.
Ezr 1: 8 by the hand of Mithredath the t', 1489
Isa 22: 15 get thee unto this t', even unto 5532

treasurers
Ezr 7: 21 the t' which are beyond the river, 1490
Ne 13: 13 And I made t' over the treasuries, 686
Da 3: 2, 3 judges, the t', the counsellers, 1411

treasures
De 32: 34 me, and sealed up among my t'? 214
33: 19 the seas, and of t' hid in the sand. 8226
1Ki 7: 51 he put among the t' of the house of*214
14: 26 he took away the t' of the house of "
26 Lord, and the t' of the king's house;"
15: 18 in the t' of the house of the Lord, "
18 and the t' of the king's house, and "
2Ki 12: 18 in the t' of the house of the Lord, "
14: 14 and in the t' in the king's house, "
16: 8 and in the t' in the king's house, "
18: 15 and in the t' of the king's house. "
20: 13 and all that was found in his t': "
15 among my t' that I have not shewed "
24: 13 all the t' of the house of the Lord, "
13 and the t' of the king's house, and "
1Ch 26: 20 Ahijah was over the t' of the house* "
20 over the t' of the dedicated things. * "
22 were over the t' of the house of the* "
24 the son of Moses, was ruler of the t'.*"
26 were over all the t' of the dedicated* "
27: 25 over the king's t' was Azmaveth the*"
2Ch 5: 1 among the t' of the house of God.* "
8: 15 any matter, or concerning the t'. "
12: 9 took away the t' of the house of the "
9 and the t' of the king's house; he "
16: 2 gold out of the t' of the house of the "
25: 24 and the t' of the king's house, the "
36: 18 and the t' of the house of the Lord, "

2Ch 36: 18 and the t' of the king, and of his 214
Ezr 6: 1 the t' were laid up in Babylon. 1596
Ne 12: 44 over the chambers for the t', 214
Job 3: 21 and dig for it more than for hid t':4301
38: 22 entered into the t' of the snow? * 214
22 or hast thou seen the t' of the hail,* "
Pr 2: 4 and searchest for her as for hid t';4301
8: 21 substance; and I will fill their t'. * 214
10: 2 T' of wickedness profit nothing: but"
21: 6 The getting of t' by a lying tongue "
Isa 2: 7 neither is there any end of their t'; "
10: 13 people, and have robbed their t', 6259
30: 6 their t' upon the bunches of camels,214
39: 2 and all that was found in his t': "
4 there is nothing among my t' that I "
45: 3 I will give thee the t' of darkness, "
Jer 10: 13 bringeth forth the wind out of his t'.*"
15: 13 Thy substance and thy t' will I give "
17: 3 substance and all thy t' to the spoil, "
20: 5 and all the t' of the kings of Judah "
41: 8 we have t' in the field, of wheat, *4301
48: 7 trusted in thy works and in thy t', 214
49: 4 that trusted in her t', saying, Who "
50: 37 a sword is upon her t'; and they "
51: 13 abundant in t', thine end is come, "
16 bringeth forth the wind out of his t'.*"
Eze 28: 4 gotten gold and silver into thy t': "
Da 11: 43 have power over the t' of gold and 4362
Mic 6: 10 Are there yet the t' of wickedness 214
M't 2: 11 and when they had opened their t',*2344*
6: 19 not up for yourselves t' upon earth, "
20 lay up for yourselves t' in heaven, "
Col 2: 3 whom are hid all the t' of wisdom "
Heb 11: 26 greater riches than the t' in Egypt: "

treasurest
Ro 2: 5 t' up unto thyself wrath against *2343*

treasuries
1Ch 9: 26 and t' of the house of God. 214
28: 11 thereof, and of the t' thereof, 1597
12 about, of the t' of the house of God, 214
12 of the t' of the dedicated things: "
2Ch 32: 27 and he made himself t' for silver, "
Ne 13: 12 the new wine and the oil unto the t'. "
13 And I made treasurers over the t', "
Es 3: 9 to bring it into the king's t'. 1595
4: 7 had promised to pay to the king's t' "
Ps 135: 7 he bringeth the wind out of his t'. 214

treasury See also TREASURIES.
Jos 6: 19 shall come into the t' of the Lord. 214
24 into the t' of the house of the Lord. "
Jer 38: 11 the house of the king under the t', "
M't 27: 6 lawful for to put them into the t', *2878*
M'r 12: 41 And Jesus sat over against the t', *1049*
41 the people cast money into the t': "
43 all they which have cast into the t': "
Lu 21: 1 men casting their gifts into the t'. "
Joh 8: 20 These words spake Jesus in the t', "

treat See ENTREAT; INTREAT.

treatise
Ac 1: 1 The former t' have I made, O *3056*

tree See also TREES.
Ge 1: 11 the fruit t' yielding fruit after his 6086
12 t' yielding fruit, whose seed was in "
29 face of all the earth, and every t', "
29 is the fruit of a t' yielding seed; "
2: 9 grow every t' that is pleasant to the"
9 the t' of life also in the midst of the "
9 t' of knowledge of good and evil. "
16 every t' of the garden thou mayest "
17 of the t' of the knowledge of good "
3: 1 Ye shall not eat of every t' of the "
3 of the fruit of the t' which is in the "
6 woman saw that the t' was good "
6 a t' to be desired to make one wise, "
11 Hast thou eaten of the t', whereof I "
12 she gave me of the t', and I did eat. "
17 and hast eaten of the t', of which I "
22 take also of the t' of life, and eat, "
24 way, to keep the way of the t' of life."
18: 4 and rest yourselves under the t': "
8 and he stood by them under the t', "
30: 37 and of the hazel and chesnut t'; "
40: 19 thee, and shall hang thee on a t'; 6086
Ex 9: 25 field, and brake every t' of the field."
10: 5 shall eat every t' which groweth for "
15: 25 the Lord shewed him a t', which "
Le 27: 30 or of the fruit of the t', is the Lord's:"
Nu 6: 4 eat nothing...made of the vine t', *
De 12: 2 the hills, and under every green t':6086
19: 5 with the axe to cut down the t', "
20: 19 (for the t' of the field is man's life) "
21: 22 death, and thou hang him on a t': "
23 not remain all night upon the t', "
22: 6 be before thee in the way in any t', "
24: 20 When thou beatest thine olive t', thou
Jos 8: 29 the king of Ai he hanged on a t' 6086
29 take his carcase down from the t', "
J'g 4: 5 And she dwelt under the palm t' of
9: 8 they said unto the olive t', Reign thou
9 But the olive t' said unto them, Should
10 And the trees said to the fig t', 6086
11 But the fig t' said unto them, "
1Sa 14: 2 Gibeah under a pomegranate t' "
22: 6 Saul abode in Gibeah under a t' in 815
31: 13 buried them under a t' at Jabesh, "
1Ki 4: 25 under his vine and under his fig t', "
33 the cedar t' that is in Lebanon *6086
6: 23 he made two cherubims of olive t'.*"
31 the oracle he made doors of olive t':*"
32 The two doors also were of olive t':*"
33 door of the temple posts of olive t':*"
34 And the two doors were of fir t': * "
14: 23 high hill, and under every green t'.*"
19: 4 and sat down under a juniper t':

1Ki 19: 5 he lay and slept under a juniper t',
2Ki 3: 19 and shall fell every good t', and 6086
16: 4 hills, and under every green t'. "
17: 10 hills, and under every green t'. "
18: 31 vine, and every one of his fig t', "
2Ch 3: 5 greater house he cieled with fir t', 6086
28: 4 hills, and under every green t', "
Es 2: 23 they were both hanged on a t': "
Job 14: 7 For there is hope of a t', if it be cut "
19: 10 hope hath he removed like a t'. "
24: 20 wickedness shall be broken as a t'. "
Ps 1: 3 be like a t' planted by the rivers "
37: 35 himself like a green bay t'.
52: 8 like a green olive t' in the house of God:
92: 12 shall flourish like the palm t':
Pr 3: 18 She is a t' of life to them that lay 6086
11: 30 fruit of the righteous is a t' of life; "
13: 12 the desire cometh, it is a t' of life. "
15: 4 A wholesome tongue is a t' of life: "
27: 18 Whoso keepeth the fig t' shall eat
Ec 11: 3 and if the t' fall toward the south, 6086
3 the place where the t' falleth, there "
12: 5 and the almond t' shall flourish,
Ca 2: 3 As the apple t' among the trees of 6086
13 The fig t' putteth forth her green
7: 7 thy stature is like to a palm t',
8 I will go up to the palm t', I will
8: 5 raised thee up under the apple t':
Isa 6: 13 as a teil t', and as an oak, whose *
17: 6 as the shaking of an olive t', two or
24: 13 be as the shaking of an olive t', and
34: 4 as a falling fig from the fig t'.
36: 16 his vine, and every one of his fig t',
40: 20 chooseth a t' that will not rot; 6086
41: 19 wilderness the cedar, the shittah t', "
19 and the myrtle, and the oil t';
19 I will set in the desert the fir t',
19 the pine, and the box t' together:
44: 19 I fall down to the stock of a t'? 6086
23 O forest, and every t' therein:
55: 13 the thorn shall come up the fir t',
13 brier shall come up the myrtle t':
56: 3 eunuch say, Behold, I am a dry t'. 6086
57: 5 with idols under every green t',
60: 13 shall come unto thee, the fir t',
13 the pine t', and the box together. *
65: 22 as the days of a t' are the days of 6086
66: 17 gardens behind one t' in the midst,*
Jer 1: 11 said, I see a rod of an almond t'.
2: 20 and under every green t' thou 6086
3: 6 mountain and under every green t'. "
13 the strangers under every green t', "
8: 13 nor figs on the fig t', and the leaf
10: 3 one cutteth a t' out of the forest, 6086
5 They are upright as the palm t',
11: 16 A green olive t', fair, and of goodly
19 Let us destroy the t' with the fruit6086
17: 8 be as a t' planted by the waters,
Eze 6: 13 under every green t', and under
15: 2 What is the vine t' more than any t',"
6 As the vine t' among the trees of
17: 5 waters, and set it as a willow t'.
24 Lord have brought down the high t',6086
24 have exalted the low t', have
24 have dried up the green t', and have"
24 and have made the dry t' to flourish:"
20: 47 green t' in thee, and every dry t': "
21: 10 the rod of my son, as every t'. "
31: 8 nor any t' in the garden of God was "
34: 27 t' of the field shall yield her fruit, "
36: 30 I will multiply the fruit of the t', "
41: 18 a palm t' was between a cherub
19 toward the palm t' on the one side,
19 toward the palm t' on the other side:
Da 4: 10 a t' in the midst of the earth, 363
11 The t' grew, and was strong, and "
14 Hew down the t', and cut off his "
20 The t' that thou sawest, which grew, "
23 Hew the t' down, and destroy it; yet "
26 leave the stump of the t' roots; "
Ho 9: 10 as the firstripe in the fig t' at her
14: 6 and his beauty shall be as the olive t',
8 I am like a green fir t'. From me
Joe 1: 7 vine waste, and barked my fig t':
12 dried up, and the fig t' languisheth;
12 the pomegranate t', the palm t'
12 the apple t', even all the trees of
2: 22 spring, for the t' beareth her fruit,6086
22 the fig t' and the vine do yield
Mic 4: 4 under his vine and under his fig t';
Hab 3: 17 the fig t' shall not blossom,
Hag 2: 19 and the fig t', and the pomegranate,
19 the olive t', hath not brought forth:6086
Zec 3: 10 under the vine and under the fig t'.
11: 2 Howl, fir t'; for the cedar is fallen;
M't 3: 10 every t' which bringeth not forth *1186*
7: 17 good t' bringeth forth good fruit; "
17 corrupt t' bringeth forth evil fruit. "
18 good t' cannot bring forth evil fruit,"
18 a corrupt t' bring forth good fruit. "
19 every t' that bringeth not forth "
12: 33 Either make the t' good, and his "
33 or else make the t' corrupt, and his "
33 for the t' is known by his fruit. "
13: 32 among herbs, and becometh a t', "
21: 19 when he saw a fig t' in the way, he*4808*
19 presently the fig t' withered away. "
20 How soon is the fig t' withered "
21 do this which is done to the fig t', "
24: 32 Now learn a parable of the fig t'; "
M'r 11: 13 seeing a fig t' afar off having leaves,"
20 the fig t' dried up from the roots. "
21 fig t'...thou cursedst is withered "
13: 28 Now learn a parable of the fig t'; "
Lu 3: 9 every t' therefore which bringeth *1186*
6: 43 good t' bringeth not forth corrupt "

Lu 6:43 corrupt t' bring forth good fruit. *1186*
44 every t' is known by his own fruit. "
13: 6 certain man had a fig t' planted *4808*
7 come seeking fruit on this fig t'. "
19 it grew, and waxed a great t'; *1186*
17: 6 ye might say unto this sycamine t'. "
19: 4 climbed up into a sycomore t' to *4809*
21:29 Behold the fig t', and all the trees; *4808*
23:31 they do these things in a green t'. *3586*
Joh 1:48 when thou wast under the fig t', I *4808*
50 thee, I saw thee under the fig t'. "
Ac 5:30 whom ye slew and hanged on a t'. *3586*
10:39 whom they slew and hanged on a t':"
13:29 they took him down from the t'. "
Ro 11:17 and thou, being a wild olive t', * *65*
17 of the root and fatness of the olive t';
24 cut out of the olive t' which is wild *65*
24 to nature into a good olive t': *2565*
24 be graffed into their own olive t'?
Ga 3:13 is every one that hangeth on a t': *3586*
Jas 3:12 Can the fig t', my brethren, bear *4808*
1Pe 2:24 our sins in his own body on the t', *3586*
Re 2: 7 will I give to eat of the t' of life, "
6:13 a fig t' casteth her untimely figs, *4808*
7: 1 nor on the sea, nor on any t'. *1186*
9: 4 any green thing, neither any t'; "
22: 2 the river, was there the t' of life, *3586*
2 leaves of the t' were for the healing "
14 may have right to the t' of life, and "

trees See also AXLETREES.
Ge 3: 2 We may eat of the fruit of the t' 6086
8 God amongst the t' of the garden. "
23:17 all the t' that were in the field, that "
Ex 10:15 all the fruit of the t' which the hail "
15 not any green thing in the t', * "
15:27 and threescore and ten palm t': "
Le 19:23 planted all manner of t' for food, 6086
23:40 first day the boughs of goodly t', "
40 branches of palm t',
40 and the boughs of thick t', and 6086
26: 4 t' of the field shall yield their fruit. "
20 neither shall the t' of the land yield "
Nu 24: 6 t' of lign aloes which the Lord hath*
6 as cedar t' beside the waters. "
33: 9 and threescore and ten palm t'; "
De 6:11 vineyards and olive t', which thou "
8: 8 and barley, and vines, and fig t', "
16:21 plant thee a grove of any t' near *6086
20:19 thou shalt not destroy the t' "
20 the t' which thou knowest that they "
20 they be not t' for meat, thou shalt "
28:40 shalt have olive t' throughout all thy
42 All thy t' and fruit of thy land 6086
34: 3 of Jericho, the city of palm t', unto
Jos 10:26 them, and hanged them on five t': 6086
26 hanging upon the t' until...evening."
27 and they took them down off the t', "
J'g 1:16 went up out of the city of palm t'
3:13 and possessed the city of palm t'.
9: 8 t' went forth on a time to anoint 6086
9 and go to be promoted over the t'? "
10 And the t' said to the fig tree, Come"
11 and go to be promoted over the t'? "
12 Then said the t' unto the vine, "
13 and go to be promoted over the t'? "
14 said all the t' unto the bramble, "
15 And the bramble said unto the t', "
48 and cut down a bough from the t', "
2Sa 5:11 and cedar t', and carpenters, and "
23 over against the mulberry t'.
24 in the tops of the mulberry t',
1Ki 4:33 he spake of t', from the cedar 6086
5: 6 hew me cedar t' out of Lebanon; "
10 Hiram gave Solomon cedar t' *6086
10 fir t' according to all his desire. "
6:29 figures of cherubims and palm t'
32 carvings of cherubims and palm t'
32 cherubims, and upon the palm t',
35 thereon cherubims and palm t'
7:36 cherubims, lions, and palm t',
9:11 furnished Solomon with cedar t' 6086
11 and fir t', and with gold, according "
10:11 Ophir great plenty of almug t', "
12 king made of the almug t' pillars "
12 there came no such almug t', nor "
27 sycomore t' that are in the vale, "
2Ki 3:25 water, and felled all the good t': "
19:23 cut down the tall cedar t' thereof,*
23 and the choice fir t' thereof: and
1Ch 14:14 them over against the mulberry t'.
15 in the tops of the mulberry t',
16:33 Then shall the t' of the wood sing 6086
22: 4 Also cedar t' in abundance: for "
27:28 the olive t' and the sycomore t'
2Ch 1:15 as stones, and cedar t' made he as*
15 the sycomore t' that are in the vale
2: 8 also cedar t', [6086] fir t', and almug t',
3: 5 set thereon palm t' and chains.
9:10 algum t' and precious stones. 6086
11 king made of the algum t' terraces "
27 cedar t' made he as the sycomore*
27 made he as the sycomore t' that
28:15 to Jericho, the city of palm t',
Ezr 3: 7 to bring cedar t' from Lebanon to 6086
Ne 8:15 and branches of thick t', to make "
9:25 and fruit t' in abundance: "
10:35 the firstfruits of all fruit of all t', "
37 and the fruit of all manner of t', of "
Job 40:21 He lieth under the shady t', in the
22 The shady t' cover him with their
Ps 74: 5 lifted up axes upon the thick t'. 6086
78:47 and their sycomore t' with frost.
96:12 shall all the t' of the wood rejoice 6086
104:16 The t' of the Lord are full of sap; "
17 the stork, the fir t' are her house.
105:33 their vines also and their fig t';

Ps 105:33 and brake the t' of their coasts. 6086
148: 9 hills; fruitful t', and all cedars: "
Ec 2: 5 I planted t' in them of all kind of "
6 the wood that bringeth forth t': "
Ca 2: 3 tree among the t' of the wood, "
4:14 with all t' of frankincense; "
Isa 7: 2 as the t' of the wood are moved "
10:19 the rest of the t' of his forest shall "
14: 8 Yea, the fir t' rejoice at thee, and
37:24 and the choice fir t' thereof:
44:14 among the t' of the forest: 6086
55:12 all the t' of the field shall clap their "
61: 3 might be called t' of righteousness;352
Jer 5:17 eat up thy vines and thy fig t':
6: 6 Hew ye down t', and cast a mount 6097
7:20 upon the t' of the field, and upon 6086
17: 2 their groves by the green t' upon "
Eze 15: 2 a branch which is among the t' of "
6 vine tree among the t' of the forest, "
17:24 t' of the field shall know that I the 6086
20:28 every high hill, and all the thick t',*"
27: 5 thy ship boards of fir t' of Senir:
31: 4 rivers unto all the t' of the field. 6086
5 above all the t' of the field, "
8 the fir t' were not like his boughs,
8 and the chesnut t' were not like his
9 so that all the t' of Eden, that 6086
14 that none of all the t' by the waters "
14 neither their t' stand up in their * 352
15 all the t' of the field fainted for 6086
16 all the t' of Eden, the choice and "
18 in greatness among the t' of Eden? "
18 brought down with the t' of Eden "
40:16 and upon each post were palm t'.
22 their arches, and their palm t',
26 it had palm t', one on this side, and
31, 34, 37 palm t' were upon the posts
41:18 made with cherubims and palm t',
20 were cherubims and palm t' made,
25 the temple, cherubims and palm t',
26 windows and palm t' on the one
47: 7 were very many t' on the one side 6086
12 shall grow all t' for meat, whose "
Ho 2:12 I will destroy her vines and her fig t',
Joe 1:12 even all the t' of the field, are 6086
19 hath burned all the t' of the field. "
Am 4: 9 your vineyards and your fig t'
Na 2: 3 the fir t' shall be terribly shaken.*
3:12 strong holds shall be like fig t'
Zec 1: 8 he stood among the myrtle t' that
10 that stood among the myrtle t'
11 that stood among the myrtle t',
4: 3 two olive t' by it, one upon the right
11 What are these two olive t' upon the
M't 3:10 ax is laid unto the root of the t': *1186*
21: 8 cut down branches from the t', and "
M'r 8:24 and said, I see men as t', walking. "
11: 8 cut down branches off the t', and * "
Lu 3: 9 axe is laid unto the root of the t': "
21:29 Behold the fig tree, and all the t'; "
Joh 12:13 Took branches of palm t', and
Jude 12 t' whose fruit withereth, without *1186*
Re 7: 3 earth, neither the sea, nor the t', "
8: 7 the third part of t' was burnt up, "
11: 4 These are the two olive t', and the two

tremble See also TREMBLED; TREMBLETH; TREMBLING.
De 2:25 and shall t', and be in anguish 7264
20: 3 faint, fear not, and do not t', 2648
Ezr 10: 3 those that t' at the commandment2730
Job 9: 6 place, and the pillars thereof t'. 6426
26:11 The pillars of heaven t' and are 7322
Ps 60: 2 Thou hast made the earth to t'; 7493
99: 1 Lord reigneth; let the people t': 7264
114: 7 T', thou earth, at the presence of 2342
Ec 12: 3 the keepers of the house shall t', 2111
Isa 5:25 the hills did t', and their carcases 7264
14:16 the man that made the earth to t', "
32:11 T', ye women that are at ease; be 2729
64: 2 nations may t' at thy presence! 7264
66: 5 of the Lord, ye that t' at his word; 2730
Jer 5:22 will ye not t' at my presence, 2342
10:10 at his wrath the earth shall t', *7493
33: 9 they shall fear and t' for all the 7264
51:29 the land shall t' and sorrow: for *7493
Eze 26:16 shall t' at every moment, and be 2729
18 Now shall the isles t' in the day of "
32:10 they shall t' at every moment, "
Da 6:26 men t' and fear before the God of 2112
Ho 11:10 children shall t' from the west. *2729
11 shall t' as a bird out of Egypt, and* "
Joe 2: 1 all the inhabitants of the land t': 7264
10 before them; the heavens shall t':7493
Am 8: 8 Shall not the land t' for this, and 7264
Hab 3: 7 curtains of the land of Midian did t'."
Jas 2:19 the devils also believe, and t'. *5425*

trembled
Ge 27:33 And Isaac t' very exceedingly, 2729
Ex 19:16 the people that was in the camp t'. "
J'g 5: 4 earth t', and the heavens dropped,7493
1Sa 4:13 his heart t' for the ark of God. 2730
14:15 and the spoilers, they also t', 2729
16: 4 elders of the town t' at his coming,*"
28: 5 was afraid, and his heart greatly t'."
2Sa 22: 8 Then the earth shook and t'; the 7493
Ezr 9: 4 every one that t' at the words of 2730
Ps 18: 7 Then the earth shook and t'; the 7493
77:18 the world: the earth t' and shook.7264
97: 4 the world: the earth saw, and t'. 2342
Jer 4:24 the mountains, and, lo, they t', 7493
8:16 the whole land t' at the sound of * "
Da 5:19 t' and feared before him: 2112
Hab 3:10 mountains saw thee, and they t':*2342
16 When I heard, my belly t'; my 7264
16 I t' in myself, that I might rest in "

M'r 16: 8 for they t' and were amazed:*2192,5156
Ac 7:32 Then Moses t', and durst not 1790,1096
24:25 Felix t', and answered, Go thy*1719

trembleth
Job 37: 1 At this also my heart t', and is 2729
Ps 104:32 He looketh on the earth, and it t': 7460
119:120 My flesh t' for fear of thee; and 5568
Isa 66: 2 contrite spirit, and t' at my word. 2730

trembling
Ex 15:15 t' shall take hold upon them; 7460
De 28:65 shall give thee there a t' heart. 7268
1Sa 13: 7 and all the people followed him t'.2729
14:15 And there was t' in the host, in 2731
15 quaked: so it was a very great t'. "
Ezr 10: 9 t' because of this matter, and for 7460
Job 4:14 Fear came upon me, and t', which "
21: 6 and t' taketh hold on my flesh. *6427
Ps 2:11 Lord with fear, and rejoice with t'.7460
55: 5 Fearfulness and t' are come upon "
Isa 51:17 drunken the dregs of the cup of t',*8653
22 out of thine hand the cup of t', * "
Jer 30: 5 We have heard a voice of t', of 2731
Eze 12:18 drink thy water with t' and with 7269
26:16 shall clothe themselves with t'; 2731
Da 10:11 this word unto me, I stood t'. 7460
Ho 13: 1 When Ephraim spake t', he 7578
Zec 12: 2 I will make Jerusalem a cup of t' *7478
M'r 5:33 But the woman fearing and t', *5141*
Lu 8:47 she came t', and falling down "
Ac 9: 6 he t' and astonished said, Lord, * "
16:29 and sprang in, and came t', *1096,1790*
1Co 2: 3 and in fear, and in much t'. *5156*
2Co 7:15 with fear and t' ye received him. "
Eph 6: 5 with fear and t', in singleness of "
Ph'p 2:12 your own salvation with fear and t'."

trench
1Sa 17:20 he came to the t', as the host was*4570
26: 5 Saul lay in the t', and the people * "
7 Saul lay sleeping within the t', and*"
2Sa 20:15 the city, and it stood in the t': *2426
1Ki 18:32 and he made a t' about the altar, 8585
35 and he filled the t' also with water. "
38 up the water that was in the t'. "
Lu 19:43 enemies shall cast a t' about thee,*5482*

trespass See also TRESPASSED; TRESPASSES; TRESPASSING.
Ge 31:36 What is my t'? what is my sin, that6588
50:17 the t' of thy brethren, and their * "
17 forgive the t' of thy servants of the*"
Ex 22: 9 For all manner of t', whether it be "
Le 5: 6 he shall bring his t' offering unto † 817
7 then he shall bring for his t', which*"
15 If a soul commit a t', and sin 4604
15 shall bring for his t' unto the Lord†817
15 of the sanctuary, for a t' offering:† "
16 him with the ram of the t' offering,† "
18 for a t' offering, unto the priest: † "
19 It is a t' offering: he hath certainly† "
6: 2 and commit a t' against the Lord, 4604
5 in the day of his t' offering. * 819
6 bring his t' offering unto the Lord,†817
6 for a t' offering, unto the priest: † "
17 sin offering, and as the t' offering,† "
7: 1 this is the law of the t' offering: † "
2 shall they kill the t' offering: † "
5 unto the Lord: it is a t' offering. † "
7 sin offering is, so is the t' offering:† "
37 and of the t' offering, and of the † "
14:12 lamb, and offer him for a t' offering,† "
13 is the priest's, so is the t' offering:† "
14 some of the blood of the t' offering,† "
17 upon the blood of the t' offering: † "
21 take one lamb for a t' offering to be† "
24 take the lamb of the t' offering, † "
25 shall kill the lamb of the t' offering,†"
25 some of the blood of the t' offering,† "
28 place of the blood of the t' offering:† "
19:21 bring his t' offering unto the Lord,† "
21 even a ram for a t' offering. † "
22 the ram of the t' offering before the† "
22:16 them to bear the iniquity of t', *819
26:40 with their t' which they trespassed4604
Nu 5: 6 commit, to do a t' against the Lord," "
7 shall recompense his t' with the * 817
8 kinsman to recompense the t' unto,*"
8 t' be recompensed unto the Lord,* "
12 and commit a t' against him, 4604
27 have done t' against her husband, "
6:12 of the first year for a t' offering: † 817
18: 9 every t' offering of theirs, which † "
31:16 to commit t' against the Lord in 4604
Jos 7: 1 children of Israel committed a t' in "
22:16 What t' is this...ye have committed "
20 Achan the son of Zerah commit a t' "
31 have not committed this t' against "
1Sa 6: 3 any wise return him a t' offering:† 817
4 What shall be the t' offering which† "
8 ye return him for a t' offering. † "
17 for a t' offering unto the Lord; † "
25:28 forgive the t' of thine handmaid: 6588
1Ki 8:31 any man t' against his neighbour,*2398
2Ki 12:16 t' money and sin money was not * 817
1Ch 21: 3 will he be a cause of t' to Israel? * 819
2Ch 19:10 warn them that they t' not against*816
10 this do, and ye shall not t'. "
24:18 and Jerusalem for this their t'. * 819
28:13 add more to our sins and to our t': "
13 our t' is great, and there is fierce "
22 he t' yet more against the Lord: 4603
33:19 all his sins, and his t', and the 4604
Ezr 9: 2 rulers hath been chief in this t'. "
6 t' is grown up unto the heavens. * 819
7 we been in a great t' unto this day;* "
13 our evil deeds, and for our great t',* "

Ezr 10: 10 wives, to increase the t' of Israel. * 819
19 a ram of the flock for their t'. * "
Eze 15: 8 because they have committed a t', 4604
17: 20 will plead with him there for his t' "
18: 24 in his t' that he hath trespassed, "
20: 27 have committed a t' against me. "
40: 39 the sin offering and the t' offering. †817
42: 13 the sin offering, and the t' offering;* "
44: 29 the sin offering, and the t' offering;* "
46: 20 the priests shall boil the t' offering* "
Da 9: 7 their t' that they have trespassed 4604
M't 18: 15 if thy brother shall t' against thee,*264
Lu 17: 3 If thy brother t' against thee, rebuke*"
4 if he t' against thee seven times in* "

trespassed
Le 5: 19 certainly t' against the Lord. * 816
26: 40 trespass which they t' against me, 4604
Nu 5: 7 unto him against whom he hath t'.*816
De 32: 51 Because ye t' against me among 4603
2Ch 26: 18 the sanctuary; for thou hast t'; "
29: 6 For our fathers have t', and done "
30: 7 t' against the Lord God of their "
33: 23 but Amon t' more and more. 819
Ezr 10: 2 We have t' against our God, and 4603
Eze 17: 20 that he hath t' against me. 4604
18: 24 in his trespass that he hath t', "
39: 23 because they t' against me, 4603
26 whereby they have t' against me, "
Da 9: 7 that they have t' against thee. "
Ho 8: 1 my covenant, and t' against my law. "

trespasses
Ezr 9: 15 we are before thee in our t': for * 819
Ps 68: 21 as one as goeth on still in his t'. * 817
Eze 39: 26 and all their t' whereby they have 4604
M't 6: 14 For if ye forgive men their t', your 3900
15 But if ye forgive not men their t', "
15 will your Father forgive your t'. "
18: 35 not every one his brother their t'. * "
M'r 11: 25 heaven may forgive you your t'. "
26 which is in heaven forgive your t'.* "
2Co 5: 19 not imputing their t' unto them; "
Eph 2: 1 who were dead in t' and sin; "
Col 2: 13 him, having forgiven you all t'; "

trespassing
Le 6: 7 all that he hath done in t' therein.* 819
Eze 14: 13 land sinneth against me by t' *4603

trespass-money See TRESPASS and MONEY.

trespass-offering See TRESPASS and OFFERING.

trial
Job 9: 23 laugh at the t' of the innocent. 4531
Eze 21: 13 Because it is a t', and what if the 974
2Co 8: 2 How that in a great t' of affliction 1382
Heb 11: 36 others had t' of cruel mockings 3984
1Pe 1: 7 That the t' of your faith, being *1383
4: 12 the fiery t' which is to try you,

tribe See also TRIBES.
Ex 31: 2 the son of Hur, of the t' of Judah: 4294
6 son of Ahisamach, of the t' of Dan: "
35: 30 the son of Hur, of the t' of Judah; "
34 son of Ahisamach, of the t' of Dan. "
38: 22 the son of Hur, of the t' of Judah, "
23 son of Ahisamach, of the t' of Dan, "
Le 24: 11 daughter of Dibri, of the t' of Dan:) "
Nu 1: 4 there shall be a man of every t'; "
5 of the t' of Reuben; Elizur the son of*
21 of them, even of the t' of Reuben, 4294
23 of them, even of the t' of Simeon, "
25 of them, even of the t' of Gad, "
27 of them, even of the t' of Judah, "
29 of them, even of the t' of Issachar, "
31 of them, even of the t' of Zebulun, "
33 of them, even of the t' of Ephraim, "
35 of them, even of the t' of Manasseh, "
37 of them, even of the t' of Benjamin, "
39 of them, even of the t' of Dan, "
41 of them, even of the t' of Asher, "
43 of them, even of the t' of Naphtali, "
47 Levites after the t' of their fathers "
49 shalt not number the t' of Levi, "
2: 5 unto him shall be the t' of Issachar: "
7 Then the t' of Zebulun: and Eliab "
12 by him shall be the t' of Simeon: "
14 Then the t' of Gad: and the captain "
20 by him shall be the t' of Manasseh: "
22 Then the t' of Benjamin: and the "
27 by him shall be the t' of Asher: "
29 Then the t' of Naphtali: and the "
3: 6 Bring the t' of Levi near, and "
4: 18 Cut ye not off the t' of the families 7626
7: 12 of Amminadab, of the t' of Judah: 4294
10: 15 of the t' of the children of Issachar "
16 of the t' of the children of Zebulun "
19 of the t' of the children of Simeon "
20 host of the t' of the children of Gad "
23 the t' of the children of Manasseh "
24 the t' of the children of Benjamin "
26 of the t' of the children of Asher "
27 of the t' of the children of Naphtali "
13: 2 of every t' of their fathers shall ye "
4 of the t' of Reuben, Shammua the "
5 Of the t' of Simeon, Shaphat the "
6 Of the t' of Judah, Caleb the son of "
7 Of the t' of Issachar, Igal the son "
8 Of the t' of Ephraim, Oshea the son "
9 Of the t' of Benjamin, Palti the son "
10 Of the t' of Zebulun, Gaddiel the "
11 Of the t' of Joseph, namely, of the "
11 of the t' of Manasseh, Gaddi the "
12 Of the t' of Dan, Ammiel the son of "
13 Of the t' of Asher, Sethur the son of "
14 Of the t' of Naphtali, Nahbi the son "
15 Of the t' of Gad, Geuel the son of "
18: 2 thy brethren also of the t' of Levi, "
2 t' of thy father, bring thou with 7626
Nu 31: 4 Of every t' a thousand, 4294
5 a thousand of every t', twelve "
6 to the war, a thousand of every t', "
32: 33 and unto half the t' of Manasseh 7626
34: 13 the nine tribes, and to the half t': 4294
14 the t' of the children of Reuben "
14 and the t' of the children of Gad "
14 and half the t' of Manasseh have "
15 and the half t' have received their "
18 shall take one prince of every t', "
19 Of the t' of Judah, Caleb the son of "
20 of the t' of the children of Simeon, "
21 Of the t' of Benjamin, Elidad the "
22 of the t' of the children of Dan, "
23 the t' of the children of Manasseh, "
24 the t' of the children of Ephraim, "
25 the t' of the children of Zebulun, "
26 the t' of the children of Issachar, "
27 of the t' of the children of Asher, "
28 the t' of the children of Naphtali, "
36: 3 be put to the inheritance of the t' "
4 be put unto the inheritance of the t' "
4 inheritance of the t' of our fathers. "
5 t' of the sons of Joseph hath said "
6 t' of their father shall they marry. "
7 of Israel remove from t' to t': "
7 inheritance of the t' of his fathers. "
8 in any t' of the children of Israel, "
8 of the family of the t' of her father, "
9 remove from one t' to another t'; "
12 the t' of the family of their father. "
De 1: 23 twelve men of you, one of a t': 7626
3: 13 gave I unto the half t' of Manasseh; "
10: 8 the Lord separated the t' of Levi, "
18: 1 all the t' of Levi, shall have no part "
29: 8 and to the half t' of Manasseh. "
18 man, or woman, or family, or t', "
Jos 1: 12 to half the t' of Manasseh, spake "
3: 12 of Israel, out of every t' a man. "
4: 2 of the people, out of every t' a man, "
4 of Israel, out of every t' a man: "
12 half the t' of Manasseh, passed over "
7: 1 for Achan,...of the t' of Judah, 4294
14 that the t' which the Lord taketh 7626
16 and the t' of Judah was taken: "
18 and Achan,...of the t' of Judah, 4294
12: 6 and the half t' of Manasseh. 7626
13: 7 tribes, and the half t' of Manasseh, "
14 unto the t' of Levi he gave none "
15 the t' of the children of Reuben 4294
24 gave inheritance unto the t' of Gad, "
29 unto the half t' of Manasseh: 7626
29 half t' of the children of Manasseh 4294
33 unto the t' of Levi Moses gave not 7626
14: 2 the nine tribes, and for the half t'. 4294
3 an half t' on the other side Jordan: "
15: 1, 20, 21 the t' of the children of Judah "
16: 8 of the t' of the children of Ephraim "
17: 1 also a lot for the t' of Manasseh; "
18: 4 among you three men for each t': 7626
7 and half the t' of Manasseh, have "
11, 21 t' of the children of Benjamin 4294
19: 1 for the t' of the children of Simeon "
8 of the t' of the children of Simeon "
23 of the t' of the children of Issachar "
24 for the t' of the children of Asher "
31 of the t' of the children of Asher "
39 of the t' of the children of Naphtali "
40 out for the t' of the children of Dan "
48 of the t' of the children of Dan "
20: 8 the plain out of the t' of Reuben, "
8 in Gilead out of the t' of Gad, "
8 Bashan out of the t' of Manasseh. "
21: 4 had by lot out of the t' of Judah, "
4 and out of the t' of Simeon, "
4 and out of the t' of Benjamin, "
5 of the families of the t' of Ephraim, "
5 and out of the t' of Dan, "
5 out of the half t' of Manasseh, ten "
6 of the families of the t' of Issachar, "
6 and out of the t' of Asher, "
6 and out of the t' of Naphtali, "
6 the half t' of Manasseh in Bashan, "
7 families had out of the t' of Reuben, "
7 and out of the t' of Gad, "
7 and out of the t' of Zebulun, twelve "
9 of the t' of the children of Judah, "
9 of the t' of the children of Simeon, "
17 out of the t' of Benjamin, Gibeon "
20 their lot out of the t' of Ephraim. "
23 And out of the t' of Dan, Eltekeh "
25 of the half t' of Manasseh, Tanach "
27 the other half t' of Manasseh, they "
28 out of the t' of Issachar, Kishon "
30 And out of the t' of Asher, Mishal "
32 out of the t' of Naphtali, Kedesh "
34 out of the t' of Zebulun, Jokneam "
36 out of the t' of Reuben, Bezer with "
38 And out of the t' of Gad, Ramoth 4294
22: 1 and the half t' of Manasseh, "
7 the one half of the t' of Manasseh 7626
9 the half t' of Manasseh returned, "
10 the half t' of Manasseh built there "
11 the half t' of Manasseh have built "
13, 15 and to the half t' of Manasseh, "
21 the half t' of Manasseh answered, "
J'g 18: 1 the t' of the Danites sought them "
19 be a priest unto a t' and a family in "
30 sons were priests to the t' of Dan "
20: 12 men through all the t' of Benjamin, "
21: 3 be to day one t' lacking in Israel? "
6 There is one t' cut off from Israel "
17 a t' be not destroyed out of Israel. "
24 every man to his t' and to his family, "
1Sa 9: 21 the families of the t' of Benjamin? "
10: 20 near, the t' of Benjamin was taken. "
1Sa 10: 21 caused the t' of Benjamin to come 7626
1Ki 7: 14 widow's son of the t' of Naphtali, 4294
11: 13 but will give one t' to thy son 7626
32 have one t' for my servant David's "
36 And unto his son will I give one t', "
12: 20 of David, but the t' of Judah only. "
21 of Judah, with the t' of Benjamin, "
2Ki 17: 18 none left but the t' of Judah only. "
1Ch 5: 18 Gadites, and half the t' of Manasseh, "
23 children of the half t' of Manasseh "
26 Gadites, and the half t' of Manasseh, "
6: 60 And out of the t' of Benjamin; 4294
61 were left of the family of that t', "
61 were cities given out of the half t', "
61 out of the half t' of Manasseh, by lot,*
62 families out of the t' of Issachar, 4294
62 and out of the t' of Asher, "
62 and out of the t' of Naphtali, "
62 out of the t' of Manasseh in Bashan, "
63 families, out of the t' of Reuben, "
63 and out of the t' of Gad, "
63 and out of the t' of Zebulun, twelve "
65 of the t' of the children of Judah, "
65 of the t' of the children of Simeon, "
65 the t' of the children of Benjamin, "
66 coasts out of the t' of Ephraim. "
70 of the half t' of Manasseh; Aner "
71 family of the half t' of Manasseh, "
72 And out of the t' of Issachar; "
74 And out of the t' of Asher; Mashal "
76 And out of the t' of Naphtali; "
77 were given out of the t' of Zebulun, "
78 given them out of the t' of Reuben, "
80 And out of the t' of Gad; Ramoth "
12: 31 of the half t' of Manasseh eighteen "
37 and of the half t' of Manasseh, 7626
23: 14 sons were named of the t' of Levi. "
26: 32 Gadites, and the half t' of Manasseh, "
27: 20 of the half t' of Manasseh, Joel the "
21 Of the half t' of Manasseh in Gilead, "
Ps 78: 67 and chose not the t' of Ephraim: 7626
68 But chose the t' of Judah, the "
Eze 47: 23 in what t' the stranger sojourneth, "
Lu 2: 36 of Phanuel, of the t' of Aser: 5443
Ac 13: 21 Saul...a man of the t' of Benjamin, "
Ro 11: 1 of Abraham, of the t' of Benjamin. "
Ph'p 3: 5 of Israel, of the t' of Benjamin, "
Heb 7: 13 spoken pertaineth to another t', "
14 of which t' Moses spake nothing "
Re 5: 5 the Lion of the t' of Juda, the Root "
7: 5 Of the t' of Juda were sealed twelve "
5 Of the t' of Reuben were sealed "
5 Of the t' of Gad were sealed twelve "
6 Of the t' of Aser were sealed twelve "
6 Of the t' of Nepthalim were sealed "
6 Of the t' of Manasses were sealed "
7 Of the t' of Simeon were sealed "
7 Of the t' of Levi were sealed twelve "
7 Of the t' of Issachar were sealed "
8 Of the t' of Zabulon were sealed "
8 Of the t' of Joseph were sealed "
8 Of the t' of Benjamin were sealed "

tribes
Ge 49: 16 people, as one of the t' of Israel. 7626
28 All these are the twelve t' of Israel: "
Ex 24: 4 according to the twelve t' of Israel. "
28: 21 they be according to the twelve t'. "
39: 14 name, according to the twelve t'. "
Nu 1: 16 princes of the t' of their fathers, 4294
7: 2 who were the princes of the t', "
24: 2 in his tents according to their t'; 7626
26: 55 names of the t' of their fathers 4294
30: 1 spake unto the heads of the t' "
31: 4 throughout all the t' of Israel, "
32: 28 and the chief fathers of the t' of "
33: 54 according to the t' of your fathers "
34: 13 commanded to give unto the nine t', "
15 two t' and the half tribe...received "
36: 3 to any of the sons of the other t' 7626
9 every one of the t' of the children 4294
De 1: 13 and known among your t', 7626
15 So I took the chief of your t', wise "
15 tens, and officers among your t', "
5: 23 even all the heads of your t', and "
12: 5 God shall choose out of all your t' "
14 Lord shall choose in one of thy t', "
16: 18 God giveth thee, throughout thy t': "
18: 5 hath chosen him out of all thy t', "
29: 10 captains of your t', your elders, "
21 unto evil out of all the t' of Israel, "
31: 28 unto me all the elders of your t', "
33: 5 t' of Israel were gathered together. "
Jos 3: 12 twelve men out of the t' of Israel, "
4: 5 according unto the number of the t' "
8 according unto the number of the t' "
7: 14 be brought according to your t': "
16 and brought Israel by their t'; "
11: 23 to their divisions by their t'. "
12: 7 Joshua gave unto the t' of Israel "
13: 7 for an inheritance unto the nine t', "
14: 1 heads of the fathers of the t' of 4294
2 for the nine t', and for the half "
3 had given the inheritance of two t' "
4 the children of Joseph were two t', "
18: 2 And there remained...seven t', 7626
19: 51 heads of the fathers of the t' of 4294
21: 1 heads of the fathers of the t' of "
16 nine cities out of those two t'. 7626
22: 14 throughout all the t' of Israel; 4294
23: 4 to be an inheritance for your t', 7626
24: 1 Joshua gathered all the t' of Israel "
J'g 18: 1 not fallen unto them among the t' "
20: 2 people, even of all the t' of Israel, "
10 throughout all the t' of Israel, "
12 t' of Israel sent men through all "
21: 5 is there among all the t' of Israel "

J'g 21: 8 What one is there of the t· of Israel 7626
15 made a breach in the t· of Israel. "
1Sa 2: 28 choose him out of all the t· of Israel "
9: 21 of the smallest of the t· of Israel? "
10: 19 before the Lord by your t·, "
20 all the t· of Israel to come near, "
15: 17 made the head of the t· of Israel, "
2Sa 5: 1 came all the t· of Israel to David "
7: 7 I a word with any of the t· of Israel, "
15: 2 servant is of one of the t· of Israel. "
10 spies throughout all the t· of Israel, "
19: 9 strife throughout all the t· of Israel, "
20: 14 he went through all the t· of Israel "
24: 2 Go now through all the t· of Israel, "
1Ki 8: 1 Israel, and all the heads of the t·, 4294
16 no city out of all the t· of Israel 7626
11: 31 and will give ten t· to thee: "
32 chosen out of all the t· of Israel:) "
35 will give it unto thee, even ten t·. "
14: 21 did choose out of all the t· of Israel, "
18: 31 of the t· of the sons of Jacob, "
2Ki 21: 7 I have chosen out of all t· of Israel, "
1Ch 27: 16 Furthermore over the t· of Israel: "
22 were the princes of the t· of Israel. "
28: 1 princes of Israel,...princes of the t·, "
29: 6 and princes of the t· of Israel, "
2Ch 5: 2 Israel, and all the heads of the t·, 4294
6: 5 no city among all the t· of Israel 7626
11: 16 out of all the t· of Israel such as set "
12: 13 chosen out of all the t· of Israel, "
33: 7 chosen before all the t· of Israel, "
Ezr 6: 17 to the number of the t· of Israel. 7625
Ps 78: 55 t· of Israel to dwell in their tents. 7626
105: 37 one feeble person among their t·. "
122: 4 the t· go up, the t· of the Lord, "
Isa 19: 13 that are the stay of the t· thereof. "
49: 6 servant to raise up the t· of Jacob, "
63: 17 sake, the t· of thine inheritance. "
Eze 37: 19 and the t· of Israel his fellows, "
45: 8 house of Israel according to their t·. "
47: 13 according to the twelve t· of Israel: "
21 you according to the t· of Israel. "
22 with you among the t· of Israel. "
48: 1 Now these are the names of the t·. "
19 serve it out of all the t· of Israel. "
23 As for the rest of the t·, from the "
29 divide by lot unto the t· of Israel "
31 after the names of the t· of Israel: "
Ho 5: 9 among the t· of Israel have I made "
Hab 3: 9 according to the oaths of the t·, 4294
Zec 9: 1 of man, as of all the t· of Israel, 7626
M't 19: 28 judging the twelve t· of Israel. *5443*
24: 30 shall all the t· of the earth mourn, "
Lu 22: 30 judging the twelve t· of Israel. "
Ac 26: 7 Unto which promise our twelve t·, *1429*
Jas 1: 1 the twelve t· which are scattered *5443*
Re 7: 4 all the t· of the children of Israel. * "
21: 12 are the names of the twelve t· of "

tribulation See also TRIBULATIONS.
De 4: 30 When thou art in t·, and all these 6862
J'g 10: 14 deliver you in the time of your t·. *6869
1Sa 26: 24 and let him deliver me out of all t·. "
M't 13: 21 for when t· or persecution ariseth *2347*
24: 21 For then shall be great t·, such as "
29 after the t· of those days shall the "
M'r 13: 24 after that t·, the sun...be darkened, "
Joh 16: 33 In the world ye shall have t·: but "
Ac 14: 22 through much t· enter into the * "
Ro 2: 9 T· and anguish upon every soul of "
5: 3 knowing that t· worketh patience; "
8: 35 shall t·, or distress, or persecution, "
12: 12 Rejoicing in hope; patient in t·; "
2Co 1: 4 Who comforteth us in all our t·, "
7: 4 I am exceeding joyful in all our t·.* "
1Th 3: 4 before that we should suffer t·; **2346*
2Th 1: 6 t· to them that trouble you; **2347*
Re 1: 9 your brother, and companion in t·, "
2: 9 thy works, and t·, and poverty, "
10 and ye shall have t· ten days: "
22 adultery with her into great t·, "
7: 14 they which came out of great t·, "

tribulations
1Sa 10: 19 of all your adversities and your t·: *6869
Ro 5: 3 only so, but we glory in t· also; *2347*
Eph 3: 13 that ye faint not at my t· for you, "
2Th 1: 4 persecutions and t· that ye endure: * "

tributaries
De 20: 11 found therein shall be t· unto thee. *4522
J'g 1: 30 dwelt among them, and became t·. * "
33 Beth-anath became t· unto them. * "
35 prevailed, so that they became t·. * "

tributary See also TRIBUTARIES.
La 1: 1 provinces, how is she become t·! 4522

tribute See also DISTRIBUTE.
Ge 49: 15 and became a servant unto t·. *4522
Nu 31: 28 levy a t· unto the Lord of the men 4371
37 the Lord's t· of the sheep was six "
38 the Lord's t· was threescore and "
39 which the Lord's t· was threescore "
40 the Lord's t· was thirty and two "
41 Moses gave the t·, which was the "
De 16: 10 a t· of a freewill offering of thine 4530
Jos 16: 10 unto this day, and serve under t·. *4522
17: 13 that they put the Canaanites to t·; * "
J'g 1: 28 that they put the Canaanites to t·, * "
2Sa 20: 24 And Adoram was over the t·: and "
1Ki 4: 6 the son of Abda was over the t·. "
9: 21 Solomon levy a t· of bondservice "
12: 18 sent Adoram, who was over the t·; "
2Ki 23: 33 put the land to a t· of an hundred 6066
2Ch 8: 8 make to pay t· until this day. *4522
10: 18 sent Hadoram that was over the t·; * "
17: 11 brought...presents, and t· silver; 4853
Ezr 4: 13 then will they not pay toll, t·, and 1093
Ezr 4: 20 t·, and custom, was paid unto them. 1093
6: 8 even of the t· beyond the river, 4061
7: 24 lawful to impose toll, t·, or custom, 1093
Ne 5: 4 borrowed money for the king's t·, 4060
Es 10: 1 Ahasuerus laid a t· upon the land, 4522
Pr 12: 24 but the slothful shall be under t·. * "
M't 17: 24 they that receive t· money came *1323*
24 said, Doth not your master pay t·? * "
25 of the earth take custom or t·? *2778*
22: 17 Is it lawful to give t· unto Cæsar, "
19 Shew me the t· money. And they "
M'r 12: 14 Is it lawful to give t· to Cæsar, or "
Lu 20: 22 lawful for us to give t· unto Cæsar, *5411*
23: 2 and forbidding to give t· to Cæsar, "
Ro 13: 6 For for this cause pay ye t· also: "
7 t· to whom t· is due; custom to "

trickleth
La 3: 49 Mine eye t· down, and ceaseth *5064

tried
De 21: 5 controversy and every stroke be t·: * "
2Sa 22: 31 perfect; the word of the Lord is t·: 6884
Job 23: 10 when he hath t· me, I shall come 974
34: 36 is that Job may be t· unto the end, "
Ps 12: 6 as silver t· in a furnace of earth, 6884
17: 3 thou hast t· me, and shalt find "
18: 30 perfect: the word of the Lord is t·: "
66: 10 thou hast t· us, as silver is t·. "
105: 19 came: the word of the Lord t· him. "
Isa 28: 16 a stone, a t· stone, a precious 976
Jer 12: 3 me, and t· mine heart toward thee: *974
Da 12: 10 purified, and made white, and t·; *6884
Zec 13: 9 and will try them as gold is t·: 974
Heb 11: 17 when he was t·, offered up Isaac: *3985*
Jas 1: 12 for when he is t·, he shall receive *1384*
1Pe 1: 7 though it be t· with fire, might be *1381*
Re 2: 2 thou hast t· them which say they **3985*
10 you into prison, that ye may be t·; "
3: 18 to buy of me gold t· in the fire, **4448*

triest
1Ch 29: 17 my God, that thou t· the heart, and 974
Jer 11: 20 that t· the reins and the heart, "
20: 12 that t· the righteous, and seest the "

trieth
Job 34: 3 For the ear t· words, as the mouth 974
Ps 7: 9 for the righteous God t· the hearts "
11: 5 The Lord t· the righteous: but the "
Pr 17: 3 for gold: but the Lord t· the hearts. "
1Th 2: 4 but God, which t· our hearts. **1381*

trimmed
2Sa 19: 24 dressed his feet, nor t· his beard, 6213
M't 25: 7 virgins arose, and t· their lamps. *2885*

trimmest
Jer 2: 33 Why t· thou thy way to seek love? 3190

triumph See also TRIUMPHED; TRIUMPHING.
2Sa 1: 20 daughters of the uncircumcised t·. 5937
Ps 25: 2 let not mine enemies t· over me. 5970
41: 11 mine enemy doth not t· over me. 7321
47: 1 unto God with the voice of t·. 7440
60: 8 Philistia, t· thou because of me. *7321
92: 4 I will t· in the works of thy hands. 7442
94: 3 how long shall the wicked t·? 5937
106: 47 holy name, and to t· in thy praise. 7623
108: 9 my shoes; over Philistia will I t·. *7321
2Co 2: 14 always causeth us to t· in Christ, *2358*

triumphed
Ex 15: 1 the Lord, for he hath t· gloriously: 1342
21 the Lord, for he hath t· gloriously; "

triumphing
Job 20: 5 That the t· of the wicked is short, 7445
Col 2: 15 of them openly, t· over them in it. *2358*

Troas (*tro'-as*)
Ac 16: 8 passing by Mysia came down to T·. *5174*
11 Therefore loosing from T·, we "
20: 5 going before tarried for us at T·. "
6 came unto them to T· in five days; "
2Co 2: 12 I came to T· to preach Christ's "
2Ti 4: 13 cloke that I left at T· with Carpus, "

trod See TRODDEN; TRODE.

trodden
De 1: 36 give the land that he hath t· upon, 1869
Jos 14: 9 land whereon thy feet have t· shall "
J'g 5: 21 soul, thou hast t· down strength. * "
Job 22: 15 old way which wicked men have t'? "
28: 8 The lion's whelps have not t· it, nor "
Ps 119: 118 hast t· down all them that err *5541
Isa 5: 5 thereof, and it shall be t· down: 4823
14: 19 the pit; as a carcase t· under feet. 947
18: 2 a nation meted out and t· down, *4001
7 nation meted out and t· under foot, * "
25: 10 Moab shall be t· down under him, 1758
10 straw is t· down for the dunghill. "
28: 3 of Ephraim, shall be t· under feet; 7429
18 then ye shall be t· down by it. 4823
63: 3 I have t· the winepress alone; and 1869
18 our adversaries have t· down thy 947
Jer 12: 10 they have t· my portion under foot. "
La 1: 15 hath t· under foot all my mighty *5541
15 the Lord hath t· the virgin, the 1869
Eze 34: 19 which ye have t· with your feet; 7429
Da 8: 13 and the host to be t· under foot? 4823
Mic 7: 10 shall she be t· down as the mire of "
M't 5: 13 out, and to be t· under foot of men. *2662*
Lu 8: 5 it was t· down, and the fowls of the "
21: 24 Jerusalem shall be t· down of the *3961*
Heb 10: 29 who hath t· under foot the Son of *2662*
Re 14: 20 winepress was t· without the city, *3961*

trode
J'g 9: 27 their vineyards, and t· the grapes, 1869
20: 43 and t· them down with ease over "
2Ki 7: 17, 20 people t· upon him in the gate, 7429
9: 33 horses: and he t· her under foot. "
14: 9 in Lebanon, and t· down the thistle. "
2Ch 25: 18 in Lebanon, and t· down the thistle. 7429
Lu 12: 1 that they t· one upon another, *2662*

Trogyllium (*tro-jil'-le-um*)
Ac 20: 15 at Samos, and tarried at T·; **5175*

troop See also TROOPS.
Ge 30: 11 And Leah said, A t· cometh: and *1409
49: 19 Gad, a t· shall overcome him: but 1416
1Sa 30: 8 Shall I pursue after this t·? shall I "
2Sa 2: 25 after Abner, and became one t·, * 92
3: 22 and Joab came from pursuing a t·, *1416
22: 30 by thee I have run through a t·: by "
23: 11 were gathered together into a t·, 2416
13 the t· of the Philistines pitched in "
Ps 18: 29 by thee I have run through a t·; 1416
Isa 65: 11 that prepare a table for that t·, *1409
Jer 18: 22 bring a t· suddenly upon them: 1416
Hos 7: 1 the t· of robbers spoileth without. "
Am 9: 6 and hath founded his t· in the earth; *92

troops
Job 6: 19 The t· of Tema looked, the * 734
19: 12 His t· come together, and raise up 1416
Jer 5: 7 assembled themselves by t· in the "
Hos 6: 9 as t· of robbers wait for a man, 1416
Mic 5: 1 Now gather thyself in t·, 1413
1 O daughter of t·: he hath laid 1416
Hab 3: 16 he will invade them with his t·. "

Trophimus (*trof'-im-us*)
Ac 20: 4 and of Asia, Tychicus and T·. *5161*
21: 29 before with him in the city T· an "
2Ti 4: 20 but T· have I left at Miletum sick. "

troth See BETROTH.

trouble See also TROUBLED; TROUBLES; TROUBLEST; TROUBLETH; TROUBLING.
Jos 6: 18 camp of Israel a curse, and t· it. 5916
7: 25 us? the Lord shall t· thee this day. "
J'g 11: 35 thou art one of them that t· me: "
2Ki 19: 3 This day is a day of t·, and of 6869
1Ch 22: 14 in my t· I have prepared for the *6040
2Ch 15: 4 they in their t· did turn unto the *6862
29: 8 and he hath delivered them to t·, *2189
32: 18 to affright them, and to t· them; 926
Ne 9: 27 and in the time of their t·, when 6869
32 let not all the t· seem little before *8513
Job 3: 26 neither was I quiet; yet t· came. 7267
5: 6 doth t· spring out of the ground; 5999
7 Yet man is born unto t·, as the "
14: 1 is of few days, and full of t·. 7267
15: 24 T· and anguish shall make him *6862
27: 9 his cry when t· cometh upon him? 6869
30: 25 weep for him that was in t·? 7186, 3117
34: 29 quietness, who then can make t·? *7561
38: 23 reserved against the time of t·, 6862
Ps 3: 1 how are they increased that t· me! * "
9: 9 oppressed, a refuge in times of t·. 6869
13 consider my t· which I suffer of *6040
10: 1 hidest thou thyself in times of t·? 6869
13: 4 those that t· me rejoice when I am *6862
20: 1 Lord hear thee in the day of t·; 6869
22: 11 Be not far from me; for t· is near; "
27: 5 in the time of t· he shall hide me 7451
31: 7 for thou hast considered my t·; *6040
9 upon me, O Lord, for I am in t·: *6887
32: 7 thou shalt preserve me from t·; 6862
37: 39 is their strength in the time of t·. 6869
41: 1 Lord will deliver him in time of t·. *7451
46: 1 strength, a very present help in t·. 6869
50: 15 And call upon me in the day of t·: "
54: 7 he hath delivered me out of all t·: "
59: 16 and refuge in the day of my t·. *6862
60: 11 Give us help from t·: for vain is * "
66: 14 hath spoken, when I was in t·. * "
69: 17 from thy servant; for I am in t·: *6887
73: 5 They are not in t· as other men; 5999
77: 2 day of my t· I sought the Lord: 6869
78: 33 in vanity, and their years in t·. * 928
49 wrath, and indignation, and t·, 6869
81: 7 Thou calledst in t·, and I delivered "
86: 7 day of my t· I will call upon thee: "
91: 15 I will be with him in t·; I will deliver "
102: 2 me in the day when I am in t·; *6862
107: 6, 13 cried unto the Lord in their t·, "
19 they cry unto the Lord in their t·, "
26 their soul is melted because of t·. 7451
28 they cry unto the Lord in their t·, 6862
108: 12 Give us help from t·: for vain is the * "
116: 3 upon me: I found t· and sorrow. 6869
119: 143 T· and anguish have taken hold 6862
138: 7 Though I walk in the midst of t·, 6869
142: 2 him; I shewed before him my t·. "
143: 11 sake bring my soul out of t·. "
Pr 11: 8 The righteous is delivered out of t·, "
12: 13 but the just shall come out of t·. "
15: 6 in the revenues of the wicked is t·. 5916
16 great treasure and t· therewith. 4103
25: 19 in an unfaithful man in time of t· 6869
Isa 1: 14 they are a t· unto me; I am weary 2960
8: 22 behold t· and darkness, dimness *6869
17: 14 And behold at eveningtide t·; *1091
22: 5 For it is a day of t·, and of *4103
26: 16 Lord, in t· have they visited thee, 6862
30: 6 Into the land of t· and anguish, 6869
33: 2 our salvation also in the time of t·. "
37: 3 This day is a day of t·, and of "
46: 7 answer, nor save him out of his t·. "
65: 23 in vain, nor bring forth for t·; * 928
Jer 2: 27 in the time of their t· they will say, 7451
28 can save thee in the time of thy t·: "
8: 15 a time of health, and behold t·! *1205
11: 12 them at all in the time of their t·. 7451
14 that they cry unto me for their t·. "
14: 8 the saviour thereof in time of t·, 6869
19 the time of healing, and behold t·! *1205
30: 7 it is even the time of Jacob's t·; 6869
51: 2 for in the day of t· they shall be 7451

La 1:21 mine enemies have heard of my t':7451
Eze 7: 7 is come, the day of t' is near, *4103
32:13 neither shall the foot of man t' them"
13 nor the hoofs of beasts t' them. 1804
Da 4:19 the interpretation thereof, t' thee. 927
5:10 let not thy thoughts t' thee, nor let "
11:44 and out of the north shall t' him: 926
12: 1 and there shall be a time of t', 6869
Na 1: 7 good, a strong hold in the day of t'; "
Hab 3:16 that I might rest in the day of t': "
Zep 1:15 of wrath, a day of t' and distress, "
M't 26:10 them, Why t' ye the woman? 2873,3930
M'r 14: 6 said, Let her alone; why t' ye her? "
Lu 7: 6 unto him, Lord, t' not thyself: 4660
8:49 is dead; t' not the Master. "
11: 7 shall answer and say, T' me not: 2873
Ac 15:19 sentence is, that we t' not them, 3926
16:20 Jews, do exceedingly t' our city, 1613
20:10 T' not yourselves; for his life is *2350
1Co 7:28 such shall have t' in the flesh: *2347
2Co 1: 4 comfort them which are in any t',* "
8 our t' which came to us in Asia, * "
Ga 1: 7 but there be some that t' you, and 5015
5:12 were even cut off which t' you. * 387
6:17 henceforth let no man t' me: 2873,3930
2Th 1: 6 tribulation to them that t' you; *2346
2Ti 2: 9 Wherein I suffer t', as an evil doer,*2553
Heb12:15 of bitterness springing up t' you, 1776

troubled See also TROUBLEDST.
Ge 34:30 Ye have t' me to make me to stink 5916
41: 8 the morning that his spirit was t'; 6470
45: 3 for they were t' at his presence. 926
Ex 14:24 and t' the host of the Egyptians, *2000
Jos 7:25 Joshua said, Why hast thou t' us? 5916
1Sa 14:29 My father hath t' the land: see, "
16:14 evil spirit from the Lord t' him. *1204
28:21 Saul, and saw that he was sore t', 926
2Sa 4: 1 feeble, and all the Israelites were t'. "
1Ki 18:18 he answered, I have not t' Israel; 5916
2Ki 6:11 king of Syria was sore t' for this 5590
Ezr 4: 4 Judah, and t' them in building, 1089
Job 4: 5 it toucheth thee, and thou art t'. 926
21: 4 why should not my spirit be t'? *7114
23:15 Therefore am I t' at his presence: 926
34:20 the people shall be t' at midnight,*1607
Ps 30: 7 didst hide thy face, and I was t'. 926
38: 6 I am t'; I am bowed down greatly;*5753
46: 3 the waters thereof roar and be t', 2560
48: 5 they were t', and hasted away. * 926
77: 3 I remembered God, and was t': *1993
4 I am so t' that I cannot speak. 6470
16 afraid: the depths also were t'. *7264
83:17 Let them be confounded and t' for*926
90: 7 anger, and by thy wrath are we t'. "
104:29 Thou hidest thy face, they are t': "
Pr 25:26 the wicked is as a t' fountain, 7515
Isa 32:10 Many days and years shall ye be t',7264
11 are at ease; be t', ye careless ones: "
57:20 But the wicked are like the t' sea, 1644
Jer 31:20 my bowels are t' for him; I will ‡1993
La 1:20 my bowels are t'; mine heart is 2560
2:11 my bowels are t', my liver is poured"
Eze 7:27 of the people of the land shall be t':926
26:18 isles that are in the sea shall be t'* "
27:35 afraid, they shall be t' in their 7481
Da 2: 1 wherewith his spirit was t', and 6470
3 my spirit was t' to know the dream."
4: 5 and the visions of my head t' me. 927
19 one hour, and his thoughts t' him. "
5: 6 his thoughts t' him, so that the "
9 Then was king Belshazzar greatly t', "
7:15 and the visions of my head t' me. "
28 Daniel, my cogitations much t' me, "
Zec 10: 2 they were t', because there was no*6031
M't 2: 3 had heard these things, he was t', 5015
14:26 they were t', saying, It is a spirit; "
24: 6 see that ye be not t': for all these 2360
M'r 6:50 For they all saw him, and were t'. 5015
13: 7 and rumours of wars, be ye not t': 2360
Lu 1:12 when Zacharias saw him, he was t',5015
29 she was t' at his saying, and cast 1298
10:41 careful and t' about many things: 5182
24:38 Why are ye t'? and why do 5015
Joh 5: 4 into the pool, and t' the water: * "
7 have no man, when the water is t', "
11:33 groaned in the spirit,...was t', 5015,1438
12:27 Now is my soul t'; and what shall 5015
13:21 he was t' in spirit, and testified, "
14: 1 Let not your heart be t': ye believe "
27 Let not your heart be t', neither let "
Ac 15:24 out from us have t' you with words, "
17: 8 they t' the people and the rulers of "
2Co 4: 8 We are t' on every side, yet not *2346
7: 5 rest, but we were t' on every side;* "
2Th 1: 7 And to you who are t' rest with us,* "
2: 2 or be t', neither by spirit, nor by 2360
1Pe 3:14 afraid of their terror, neither be t';5015

troubledst
Eze 32: 2 and t' the waters with thy feet, 1804

troubler
1Ch 2: 7 Achar, the t' of Israel, who 5916

troubles
De 31:17 evils and t' shall befall them; 6869
21 evils and t' are befallen them, "
Job 5:19 He shall deliver thee in six t': yea, "
Ps 25:17 The t' of my heart are enlarged: O "
22 Israel, O God, out of all his t'. "
34: 6 him, and saved him out of all his t'. "
17 delivereth them out of all their t'. "
71:20 hast shewed me great and sore t', "
88: 3 For my soul is full of t': and my 7451
Pr 21:23 tongue keepeth his soul from t'. 6869
Isa 65:16 because the former t' are forgotten, "
M'r 13: 8 and there shall be famines and t':*5016

troublest
M'r 5:35 dead: why t' thou the Master any 4660

troubleth
1Sa 16:15 an evil spirit from God t' thee. 1204
1Ki 18:17 him, Art thou he that t' Israel? *5916
Job 22:10 about thee, and sudden fear t' thee;926
23:16 heart soft, and the Almighty t' me:* "
Pr 11:17 he that is cruel t' his own flesh. 5916
29 that t' his own house shall inherit "
15:27 is greedy of gain t' his own house; "
Da 4: 9 is in thee, and no secret t' thee. 598
Lu 18: 5 yet because this widow t' me, 3930,2873
Ga 5:10 but he that t' you shall bear his 5015

troubling
Job 3:17 There the wicked cease from t'; 7267
Joh 5: 4 the t' of the water stepped in was*5015

troublous
Da 9:25 and the wall, even in t' times. 5916

trough See also TROUGHS.
Ge 24:20 emptied her pitcher into the t', 8268

troughs See also KNEADINGTROUGHS.
Ge 30:38 watering t' when the flocks came 8268
Ex 2:16 filled the t' to water their father's 7298

trow
Lu 17: 9 were commanded him? I t' not. *1380

trucebreakers
2Ti 3: 3 Without natural affection, t', false* 786

true
Ge 42:11 we are t' men, thy servants are no 3651
19 If ye be t' men, let one of your "
31 We are t' men; we are no spies: "
33 shall I know that ye are t' men; "
34 are no spies, but that ye are t' men:"
De 17: 4 it be t', and the thing certain, 571
22:20 But if this thing be t', and the tokens"
Jos 2:12 house, and give me a t' token: "
Ru 3:12 it is t' that I am thy near kinsman: 551
2Sa 7:28 art that God, and thy words be t', 571
1Ki 10: 6 It was a t' report that I heard in "
22:16 tell me nothing but that which is t'* "
2Ch 9: 5 It was a t' report which I heard in "
15: 3 Israel hath been without the t' God, "
Ne 9:13 them right judgments, and t' laws, "
Ps 19: 9 the judgments of the Lord are t' "
119:160 Thy word is t' from the beginning:*"
Pr 14:25 A t' witness delivereth souls: but a "
Jer 10:10 But the Lord is the t' God, he is the "
42: 5 Lord be a t' and faithful witness "
Eze 18: 8 hath executed t' judgment between "
Da 3:14 Is it t', O Shadrach, Meshach, and*6656
24 said unto the king, T', O king. 3330
6:12 The thing is t', according to the "
8:26 the morning which was told is t': 571
10: 1 and the thing was t', but the time "
Zec 7: 9 Execute t' judgment, and shew "
M't 22:16 Master, we know that thou art t', 227
M'r 12:14 Master, we know that thou art t', "
Lu 16:11 commit to your trust the t' riches? 228
Joh 1: 9 That was the t' Light, which lighteth"
3:33 hath set to his seal that God is t'. 227
4:23 when the t' worshippers shall 228
37 herein is that saying t', One soweth, "
5:31 of myself, my witness is not t'. 227
32 which he witnesseth of me is t'. "
6:32 my Father giveth you the t' bread 228
7:18 glory that sent him, the same is t', 227
28 but he that sent me is t', whom ye 228
8:13 of thyself; thy record is not t'. 227
14 record of myself, yet my record is t':"
16 yet if I judge, my judgment is t': "
17 that the testimony of two men is t'. "
26 he that sent me is t'; and I speak to "
10:41 that John spake of this man were t'. "
15: 1 I am the t' vine, and my Father is 228
17: 3 might know thee the only t' God, "
19:35 it bear record, and his record is t': "
35 he knoweth that he saith t', that ye 227
21:24 and we know that his testimony is t'. "
Ac 12: 9 that it was t' which was done by the "
Ro 3: 4 let God be t', but every man a liar; "
2Co 1:18 But as God is t', our word toward *4103
6: 8 report: as deceivers, and yet t'; 227
Eph 4:24 righteousness and t' holiness. *3588,225
Ph'p 4: 3 I intreat thee also, t' yokefellow, 1103
8 brethren, whatsoever things are t', 227
1Th 1: 9 idols to serve the living and t' God; 228
1Ti 3: 1 This is a t' saying, If a man desire*4103
Tit 1:13 This witness is t'. Wherefore 227
Heb 8: 2 sanctuary, and of the t' tabernacle, 228
9:24 which are the figures of the t'; "
10:22 Let us draw near with a t' heart in "
1Pe 5:12 that this is the t' grace of God 227
2Pe 2:22 them according to the t' proverb, "
1Jo 2: 8 which thing is t' in him and in you: "
8 past, and the t' light now shineth. 228
5:20 that we may know him that is t', "
20 and we are in him that is t', even in "
20 This is the t' God, and eternal life. "
3Jo 12 and ye know that our record is t'. 227
Re 3: 7 saith he that is holy, he that is t', 228
14 the faithful and t' witness, the "
6:10 How long, O Lord, holy and t', "
15: 3 just and t' are thy ways, thou King "
16: 7 t' and righteous are thy judgments. "
19: 2 t' and righteous are his judgments: "
9 me, These are the t' sayings of God. "
11 him was called Faithful and T', "
21: 5 for these words are t' and faithful. "
22: 6 These sayings are faithful and t': "

truly
Ge 24:49 deal kindly and t' with my master, 571
47:29 and deal kindly and t' with me; "
48:19 but t' his younger brother shall be*199
Nu 14:21 But as t' as I live, all the earth * 199
28 As t' as I live, saith the Lord, as ye*
De 14:22 Thou shalt t' tithe all the increase*
Jos 2:14 will deal kindly and t' with thee. 571
24 T' the Lord hath delivered into 3588
J'g 9:16 if ye have done t' and sincerely, in 571
19 ye then have dealt t' and sincerely "
1Sa 20: 3 but t' as the Lord liveth, and as thy199
Job 36: 4 For t' my words shall not be false: 551
Ps 62: 1 T' my soul waiteth upon God: * 389
73: 1 T' God is good to Israel, even to * "
116:16 O Lord, t' I am thy servant; I am 577
Pr 12:22 they that deal t' are his delight. 530
Ec 11: 7 T' the light is sweet, and a pleasant
Jer 3:23 T' in vain is salvation hoped for 403
23 t' in the Lord...is the salvation of "
10:19 but I said, T' this is a grief, and I 389
28: 9 that the Lord hath t' sent him. 571
Eze 18: 9 hath kept my judgments, to deal t'; "
Mic 3: 8 t' I am full of power by the spirit 199
M't 9:37 The harvest t' is plenteous, but 3303
17:11 Elias t' shall first come, and * "
27:54 saying, T' this was the Son of God. 230
M'r 14:38 The spirit t' is ready, but the flesh*3303
15:39 T' this man was the Son of God. 230
Lu 10: 2 The harvest t' is great, but the *3303
11:48 T' ye bear witness that ye allow * 686
20:21 teachest the way of God t': *1909,225
22:22 t' the Son of man goeth, as it was *3303
Joh 4:18 thy husband: in that saidst thou t'.227
20:30 many other signs t' did Jesus *3303
Ac 1: 5 For John t' baptized with water; * "
3:22 For Moses t' said unto the fathers,* "
5:23 The prison t' found we shut with * "
2Co 12:12 T' the signs of an apostle were "
Heb 7:23 they t' were many priests, because*"
11:15 And t', if they had been mindful of* "
1Jo 1: 3 t' our fellowship is with...Father, *1161

trump See also TRUMPET.
1Co 15:52 twinkling of an eye, at the last t': 4536
1Th 4:16 archangel, and with the t' of God: "

trumpet See also TRUMP; TRUMPETS.
Ex 19:13 when the t' soundeth long, they 3104
16 the voice of the t' exceeding loud;7782
19 the voice of the t' sounded long, "
20:18 lightnings, and the noise of the t', "
Le 25: 9 cause the t' of the jubile to sound "
9 make the t' sound throughout all "
Nu 10: 4 And if they blow but with one t', then*
Jos 6: 5 when ye hear the sound of the t', 7782
20 people heard the sound of the t', "
J'g 3:27 that he blew a t' in the mountain "
6:34 upon Gideon, and he blew a t'; "
7:16 he put a t' in every man's hand, * "
18 When I blow with a t', I and all "
1Sa 13: 3 Saul blew the t' throughout all the "
2Sa 2:28 So Joab blew a t', and all the people"
6:15 and with the sound of the t'. "
15:10 soon as ye hear the sound of the t', "
18:16 Joab blew the t', and the people "
20: 1 blew a t', and said, We have no part"
22 he blew a t', and they retired from "
1Ki 1:34 blow ye with the t', and say, God "
39 they blew the t'; and all the people "
41 when Joab heard the sound of the t',"
Ne 4:18 he that sounded the t' was by me. "
20 place...ye hear the sound of the t', "
Job 39:24 he that it is the sound of the t'. "
Ps 47: 5 the Lord with the sound of a t'. "
81: 3 Blow up the t' in the new moon, in "
150: 3 Praise him with the sound of the t':"
Isa 18: 3 and when he bloweth a t', hear ye. "
27:13 that the great t' shall be blown, "
58: 1 spare not, lift up thy voice like a t', "
Jer 4: 5 and say, Blow ye the t' in the land: "
19 heard, O my soul, the sound of the t',"
21 and hear the sound of the t'? "
6: 1 and blow the t' in Tekoa, and set up"
17 Hearken to the sound of the t'. "
42:14 war, nor hear the sound of the t', "
51:27 blow the t' among the nations, "
Eze 7:14 They have blown the t', even to 8628
33: 3 blow the t', and warn the people; 7782
4 heareth the sound of the t', "
5 He heard the sound of the t', and "
6 if the watchman...blow not the t', "
Ho 5: 8 in Gibeah, and the t' in Ramah; 2689
8: 1 Set the t' to thy mouth. He shall 7782
Joe 2: 1 Blow ye the t' in Zion, and sound "
15 Blow the t' in Zion, sanctify a fast, "
Am 2: 2 and with the sound of the t': "
3: 6 Shall a t' be blown in the city, and "
Zep 1:16 A day of t' and alarm against the "
Zec 9:14 and the Lord God shall blow the t', "
M't 6: 2 alms, do not sound a t' before thee,4537
24:31 angels with a great sound of a t', 4536
1Co 14: 8 if the t' give an uncertain sound, "
15:52 for the t' shall sound, and the dead
Heb12:19 And the sound of a t', and the voice4536
Re 1:10 behind me a great voice, as of a t', "
4: 1 as it were of a t' talking with me; "
8:13 voices of the t' of the three angels, "
9:14 to the sixth angel which had the t', "

trumpeters
2Ki 11:14 the princes and the t' by the king,*2689
2Ch 5:13 as the t' and singers were as one, "
29:28 singers sang, and the t' sounded: 2690
Re 18:22 musicians, and of pipers, and t', 4538

trumpets
Le 23:24 a sabbath a memorial of blowing of t',
Nu 10: 2 Make thee two t' of silver; of a 2689
8 the priests, shall blow with the t'; "
9 ye shall blow an alarm with the t'; "
10 blow with the t' over your burnt "
29: 1 it is a day of blowing the t' unto you,

Nu 31: 6 and the t' to blow in his hand. 2689
Jos 6: 4 shall bear before the ark seven t' 7782
4 the priests shall blow with the t'. "
6 priests bear seven t' of rams' horns "
8 seven priests bearing the seven t' "
8 the Lord, and blew with the t': "
9 the priests that blew with the t'. "
9 going on, and blowing with the t'. "
13 And seven priests bearing seven t' "
13 continually, and blew with the t': "
13 going on, and blowing with the t'. "
16 when the priests blew with the t'. "
20 when the priests blew with the t': "
J'g 7: 8 victuals in their hand, and their t': "
18 blow ye the t' also on every side of "
19 and they blew the t', and brake the "
20 the three companies blew the t', "
20 the t' in their right hands to blow "
22 And the three hundred blew the t', "
2Ki 9: 13 blew with t', saying, Jehu is king.* "
11: 14 of the land rejoiced, and blew with t': "
12: 13 snuffers, basons, t', any vessels of 2689
1Ch 13: 8 and with cymbals, and with t'. "
15: 24 did blow with the t' before the ark "
28 sound of the cornet, and with t', "
16: 6 priests with t' continually before "
42 with t' and cymbals for those that "
2Ch 5: 12 twenty priests sounding with t':) "
13 they lifted up their voice with the t' "
7: 6 the priests sounded t' before them, "
13: 12 his priests with sounding t' to cry 2689
14 and the priests sounded with the t'." "
15: 14 with shouting, and with t', and with "
20: 28 harps and t' unto the house of the "
23: 13 the princes and the t' by the king: "
13 land rejoiced, and sounded with t', "
29: 26 of David, and the priests with the t'." "
27 the song...began also with the t', "
Ezr 3: 10 the priests in their apparel with t', "
Ne 12: 35 certain of the priests' sons with t'; "
41 Zechariah, and Hananiah, with t'; "
Job 39: 25 He saith among the t', Ha, ha; and*7782
Ps 98: 6 With t' and sound of cornet make 2689
Re 8: 2 and to them were given seven t'. 4536
6 the seven t' prepared themselves to" "

trust See also TRUSTED; TRUSTEST; TRUSTETH; TRUSTING.
J'g 9: 15 and put your t' in my shadow: ‡2620
Ru 2: 12 whose wings thou art come to t'. * "
2Sa 22: 3 God of my rock; in him will I t': ‡ "
31 a buckler to all them that t' in him.‡" "
2Ki 18: 20 Now on whom dost thou t', that 982
21 of Egypt unto all that t' on him. "
22 me, We t' in the Lord our God: "
24 put thy t' on Egypt for chariots and "
30 Hezekiah make you t' in the Lord, "
1Ch 5: 20 because they put their t' in him. "
Job 4: 18 he put no t' in his servants; and his539
8: 14 whose t' shall be a spider's web. 4009
13: 15 he slay me, yet will I t' in him: †‡3176
15: 15 he putteth no t' in his saints; yea, 539
31 not him that is deceived t' in vanity:" "
35: 14 him; therefore t' thou in him. *2342
39: 11 Wilt thou t' him, because his 982
Ps 2: 12 all they that put their t' in him. ‡2620
4: 5 and put your t' in the Lord. 982
5: 11 that put their t' in thee rejoice: ‡2620
7: 1 my God, in thee do I put my t': ‡ "
9: 10 thy name will put their t' in thee: 982
11: 1 In the Lord put I my t': how say ‡2620
16: 1 O God: for in thee do I put my t'. ‡ "
17: 7 them which put their t' in thee ‡ "
18: 2 God, my strength, in whom I will t';‡" "
30 buckler to all those that t' in him.‡ "
20: 7 Some t' in chariots, and some in "
25: 2 O my God, I t' in thee: let me * 982
25: 20 ashamed; for I put my t' in thee.‡2620
31: 1 In thee, O Lord, do I put my t'; let " "
6 lying vanities: but I t' in the Lord. 982
19 wrought for them that t' in thee ‡2620
34: 22 none of them that t' in him shall ‡ "
36: 7 children of men put their t' under* "
37: 3 T' in the Lord, and do good; so 982
5 t' also in him; and he shall bring it "
40 save them, because they t' in him.*2620
40: 3 it, and fear, and shall t' in the Lord.982
4 man that maketh the Lord his t', 4009
44: 6 For I will not t' in my bow, neither 982
49: 6 They that t' in their wealth, and "
52: 8 I t' in the mercy of God for ever and "
55: 23 half their days; but I will t' in thee. "
56: 3 time I am afraid, I will t' in thee. "
4 his word, in God I have put my t'; "
11 In God have I put my t': I will not "
61: 4 I will t' in the covert of thy wings.*2620
62: 8 T' in him at all times; ye people, 982
10 T' not in oppression, and become "
64: 10 in the Lord, and shall t' in him; ‡2620
71: 1 In thee, O Lord, do I put my t': let‡ "
5 thou art my t' from my youth. 4009
73: 28 I have put my t' in the Lord God, *4268
91: 2 fortress: my God; in him will I t'. 982
4 and under his wings shalt thou t':*2620
115: 9 O Israel, t' thou in the Lord: he is 982
10 O house of Aaron, t' in the Lord: "
11 Ye that fear the Lord, t' in the Lord:" "
118: 8, 9 It is better to t' in the Lord than2620
119: 42 reproacheth me: for I t' in thy word.982
125: 1 They that t' in the Lord shall be as "
141: 8 in thee is my t'; leave not my soul‡2620
143: 8 in thee do I t': cause me to know 982
144: 2 my shield, and he in whom I t'; ‡2620
146: 3 Put not your t' in princes, nor in 982
Pr 3: 5 T' in the Lord with all thine heart; "
22: 19 That thy t' may be in the Lord, I 4009
28: 25 he that putteth his t' in the Lord 982
29: 25 whoso putteth his t' in the Lord shall982
30: 5 unto them that put their t' in him.‡2620
31: 11 her husband doth safely t' in her. * 982
Isa 12: 2 I will t', and not be afraid: for "
14: 32 the poor of his people shall t' in it.*2620
26: 4 T' ye in the Lord for ever: for in 982
30: 2 and to t' in the shadow of Egypt! 2620
3 the t' in the shadow of Egypt your 2622
12 t' in oppression and perverseness, 982
31: 1 and t' in chariots, because they are "
36: 5 now on whom dost thou t', that thou" "
6 king of Egypt to all that t' in him. "
7 to me, We t' in the Lord our God: "
9 put thy t' on Egypt for chariots and "
15 Hezekiah make you t' in the Lord, "
42: 17 ashamed, that t' in graven images, "
50: 10 let him t' in the name of the Lord, "
51: 5 me, and on mine arm shall they t'.3176
57: 13 he that putteth his t' in me shall ‡2620
59: 4 they t' in vanity, and speak lies; 982
Jer 7: 4 T' ye not in lying words,...The temple" "
8 ye t' in lying words, that cannot "
14 wherein ye t', and unto the place "
9: 4 and t' ye not in any brother: "
28: 15 thou makest this people to t' in a lie." "
29: 31 and he caused you to t' in a lie: "
39: 18 thou hast put thy t' in me, saith the "
46: 25 Pharaoh, and all them that t' in him:" "
49: 11 alive; and let thy widows t' in me. "
Eze 16: 15 thou didst t' in thine own beauty, "
33: 13 if he t' to his own righteousness, "
Ho 10: 13 because thou didst t' in thy way, "
Am 6: 1 and t' in the mountain of Samaria,* "
Mic 7: 5 T' ye not in a friend, put ye not 539
Na 1: 7 he knoweth them that t' in him. ‡2620
Zep 3: 12 shall t' in the name of the Lord. ‡ "
M't 12: 21 in his name shall the Gentiles t'. *1679
M'r 10: 24 for them that t' in riches to enter 3982
Lu 16: 11 commit to your t' the true riches? 4100
Joh 5: 45 you, even Moses, in whom ye t'. *1679
Ro 15: 12 in him shall the Gentiles t'. * "
24 for I t' to see you in my journey, * "
1Co 16: 7 but I t' to tarry a while with you, * "
2Co 1: 9 that we should not t' in ourselves, 3982
10 in whom we t' that he will yet *1679
13 I t' ye shall acknowledge even to * "
3: 4 such t' have we through Christ to*4006
5: 11 I t' also are made manifest in *1679
10: 7 If any man t' to himself that he *3982
13: 6 I t' that ye shall know that we are*1679
Ph'p 2: 19 But I t' in the Lord Jesus to send* "
24 I t' in the Lord that I also myself 3982
3: 4 whereof he might t' in the flesh, * "
1Th 2: 4 to be put in t' with the gospel, *4100
1Ti 1: 11 which was committed to my t'. "
4: 10 because we t' in the living God, *1679
6: 17 nor t' in uncertain riches, but in "
20 that which is committed to thy t',* "
Ph'm 22 for I t' that through your prayers*1679
Heb 2: 13 again, I will put my t' in him. 3982
13: 18 we t' we have a good conscience, * "
2Jo 12 but I t' to come unto you, and *1679
3Jo 14 But I t' I shall shortly see thee, * "

trusted See also TRUSTEDST.
De 32: 37 gods, their rock in whom they t', ‡2620
J'g 11: 20 Sihon t' not Israel to pass through 539
20: 36 they t' unto the liers in wait which 982
2Ki 18: 5 He t' in the Lord God of Israel; so "
Ps 13: 5 But I have t' in thy mercy; my "
22: 4 Our fathers t' in thee: they t', and "
5 they t' in thee, and were not "
8 He t' on the Lord that he would *1556
26: 1 I have t' also in the Lord; therefore982
28: 7 my heart t' in him, and I am helped:" "
31: 14 But I t' in thee, O Lord: I said, "
33: 21 because we have t' in his holy name." "
41: 9 own familiar friend, in whom I t', "
52: 7 but t' in the abundance of his riches," "
78: 22 in God, and t' not in his salvation: "
Isa 47: 10 For thou hast t' in thy wickedness: "
Jer 13: 25 forgotten me, and t' in falsehood. "
48: 7 because thou hast t' in thy works "
49: 4 that t' in her treasures, saying, "
Da 3: 28 his servants that t' in him, and 7365
Zep 3: 2 she t' not in the Lord; she drew 982
M't 27: 43 He t' in God; let him deliver him 3982
Lu 11: 22 him all his armour wherein he t', "
18: 9 unto certain which t' in themselves" "
24: 21 we t' that it had been he which *1679
Eph 1: 12 of his glory, who first t' in Christ. *4276
13 In whom ye also t', after that ye * "
1Pe 3: 5 holy women also, who t' in God, *1679

trustedst
De 28: 52 walls come down, wherein thou t', 982
Jer 5: 17 thy fenced cities, wherein thou t',* "
12: 5 the land of peace, wherein thou t',* "

trustest
2Ki 18: 19 confidence is this wherein thou t'? 982
21 thou t' upon the staff of this bruised" "
19: 10 God in whom thou t' deceive thee, "
Isa 36: 4 confidence is this wherein thou t'? "
6 thou t' in the staff of this broken "
37: 10 Let not thy God, in whom thou t', "

trusteth
Job 40: 23 he t' that he can draw up Jordan * 982
Ps 21: 7 For the king t' in the Lord, and "
32: 10 but he that t' in the Lord, mercy "
34: 8 blessed is the man that t' in him. ‡2620
57: 1 for my soul t' in thee: yea, in the * "
84: 12 blessed is the man that t' in thee. 982
86: 2 save thy servant that t' in thee. "
115: 8 so is every one that t' in them. "
135: 18 so is every one that t' in them. "
Pr 11: 28 He that t' in his riches shall fall: "
16: 20 whoso t' in the Lord, happy is he. "
28: 26 He that t' in his own heart is a fool:982
Isa 26: 3 on thee: because he t' in thee. "
Jer 17: 5 Cursed be the man that t' in man, "
7 Blessed is the man that t' in...Lord, "
Hab 2: 18 the maker of his work t' therein, "
1Ti 5: 5 indeed, and desolate, t' in God, *1679

trusting
Ps 112: 7 his heart is fixed, t' in the Lord. 982

trusty
Job 12: 20 removeth away the speech of the t'.539

truth See also TRUTH'S.
Ge 24: 27 my master of his mercy and his t': 571
32: 10 of all the t', which thou hast shewed" "
42: 16 whether there be any t' in you: "
Ex 18: 21 such as fear God, men of t', hating "
34: 6 and abundant in goodness and t', "
De 13: 14 and, behold, if it be t', and the thing "
32: 4 a God of t' and without iniquity, * 530
Jos 24: 14 serve him in sincerity and in t': 571
J'g 9: 15 If in t' ye anoint me king over you, "
1Sa 12: 24 serve him in t' with all your heart: "
21: 5 Of a t' women have been kept 3588,518
2Sa 2: 6 shew kindness and t' unto you: 571
15: 20 mercy and t' be with thee. "
1Ki 2: 4 walk before me in t' with all their "
3: 6 as he walked before thee in t', "
17: 24 word of the Lord in thy mouth is t'. "
2Ki 19: 17 Of a t', Lord, the kings of Assyria 551
20: 3 how I have walked before thee in t'571
19 good, if peace and t' be in my days? "
2Ch 18: 15 that thou say nothing but the t' "
31: 20 and right and t' before the Lord * "
Es 9: 30 with words of peace and t', "
Job 9: 2 I know it is so of a t': but how 551
Ps 15: 2 and speaketh the t' in his heart. 571
25: 5 Lead me in thy t', and teach me: "
10 paths of the Lord are mercy and t' "
26: 3 eyes: and I have walked in thy t'. "
30: 9 praise thee? shall it declare thy t'? "
31: 5 hast redeemed me, O Lord God of t'. "
33: 4 and all his works are done in t'. * 530
40: 10 thy t' from the great congregation. 571
11 and thy t' continually preserve me. "
43: 3 O send out thy light and thy t': let "
45: 4 because of t' and meekness and "
51: 6 thou desirest t' in the inward parts: "
54: 5 mine enemies: cut them off in thy t'. "
57: 3 send forth his mercy and his t'. "
10 heavens, and thy t' unto the clouds. "
60: 4 be displayed because of the t'. 7189
61: 7 O prepare mercy and t', which may 571
69: 13 hear me, in the t' of thy salvation. "
71: 22 thee with the psaltery, even thy t', "
85: 10 Mercy and t' are met together; "
11 T' shall spring out of the earth; "
86: 11 way, O Lord; I will walk in thy t': "
15 and plenteous in mercy and t'. "
89: 14 mercy and t' shall go before thy face." "
49 thou swarest unto David in thy t'?* 530
91: 4 his t'...be thy shield and buckler. 571
96: 13 and the people with his t'. 530
98: 3 remembered his mercy and his t' * "
100: 5 his t' endureth to all generations.* "
108: 4 and thy t' reacheth unto the clouds.571
111: 8 and are done in t' and uprightness. "
117: 2 the t' of the Lord endureth for ever. "
119: 30 I have chosen the way of t': thy * 530
43 take not the word of t' utterly out 571
142 righteousness, and thy law is the t'. "
151 and all thy commandments are t'. "
132: 11 Lord hath sworn in t' unto David; "
138: 2 thy lovingkindness and for thy t': "
145: 18 him, to all that call upon him in t'. "
146: 6 therein is: which keepeth t' for ever:" "
Pr 3: 3 Let not mercy and t' forsake thee: "
8: 7 For my mouth shall speak t'; and "
12: 17 He that speaketh t' sheweth forth 530
19 The lip of t' shall be established 571
14: 22 t' shall be to them that devise good. "
16: 6 By mercy and t' iniquity is purged: "
20: 28 Mercy and t' preserve the king: and "
22: 21 the certainty of the words of t'; "
21 mightest answer the words of t' "
23: 23 Buy the t', and sell it not; also "
Ec 12: 10 was upright, even words of t'. "
Isa 5: 9 Of a t' many houses shall be 518,3808
10: 20 Lord, the Holy One of Israel, in t'. 571
16: 5 sit upon it in t' in the tabernacle "
25: 1 of old are faithfulness and t'. 544
26: 2 which keepeth the t' may enter in.‡ 529
37: 18 Of a t', Lord, the kings of Assyria 551
38: 3 walked before thee in t' and with a 571
18 into the pit cannot hope for thy t'. "
19 children shall make known thy t'. "
39: 8 shall be peace and t' in my days. "
42: 3 shall bring forth judgment unto t'. "
43: 9 or let them hear, and say, It is t'. "
48: 1 but not in t', nor in righteousness "
59: 4 for justice, nor any pleadeth for t': 530
14 for t' is fallen in the street, and 571
15 t' faileth; and he that departeth "
61: 8 I will direct their work in t', and I "
65: 16 shall bless himself in the God of t':543
16 earth shall swear by the God of t'; "
Jer 4: 2 The Lord liveth, in t', in judgment, 571
5: 1 judgment, that seeketh the t'; 530
3 Lord, are not thine eyes upon the t'? "
7: 28 t' is perished, and is cut off from "
9: 3 not valiant for the t' upon the earth; "
5 and will not speak the t': 571
26: 15 for of a t' the Lord hath sent me "
33: 6 them the abundance of peace and t'. "
Da 2: 47 Of a t' it is, that your God is a God7187
4: 37 whose works are t', and his ways "
7: 16 and asked him the t' of all this. 3330

Da 7:19 know the t' of the fourth beast, 3321
8:12 it cast down the t' to the ground; 571
9:13 iniquities, and understand thy t'. "
10:21 which is noted in the scripture of t': "
11: 2 And now will I shew thee the t'. "
Ho 4: 1 because there is no t', nor mercy, "
Mic 7:20 Thou wilt perform the t' to Jacob, "
Zec 8: 3 Jerusalem shall be called a city of t':"
8 God, in t' and in righteousness. "
16 Speak ye every man the t' to his "
16 execute the judgment of t' and "
19 therefore love the t' and peace. "
Mal 2: 6 The law of t' was in his mouth, and "
M't 14:33 Of a t' thou art the Son of God. 230
15:27 she said, T', Lord: yet the dogs *3483
22:16 and teachest the way of God in t', 225
M'r 5:33 before him, and told him all the t'. "
12:14 but teachest the way of God in t': "
32 Well, Master, thou hast said the t': "
Lu 4:25 I tell you of a t', many widows were "
9:27 But I tell you of a t', there be some 230
12:44 Of a t' I say unto you, that he will "
21: 3 Of a t' I say unto you, that this poor "
22:59 Of a t' this fellow also was with 225
Joh 1:14 of the Father,) full of grace and t'. "
17 grace and t' came by Jesus Christ. "
3:21 he that doeth t' cometh to the light, "
4:23 the Father in spirit and in t': "
24 must worship him in spirit and in t'. "
5:33 and he bare witness unto the t'. "
6:14 This is of a t' that prophet that 230
7:40 said, Of a t' this is the Prophet. "
8:32 And ye shall know the t', and the 225
32 and the t' shall make you free. "
40 a man that hath told you the t', "
44 beginning, and abode not in the t', "
44 because there is no t' in him. "
45 because I tell you the t', ye believe "
46 And if I say the t', why do ye not "
14: 6 I am the way, the t', and the life: "
17 Even the Spirit of t'; whom the "
15:26 the Father, even the Spirit of t', "
16: 7 Nevertheless I tell you the t'; It is "
13 when he, the Spirit of t', is come, he "
13 he will guide you into all t': for he "
17:17 Sanctify them through thy t': "
17 thy word is t'. "
19 might be sanctified through the t'. "
18:37 I should bear witness unto the t'. "
37 Every one that is of the t' heareth "
38 Pilate saith unto him, What is t'? "
Ac 4:27 of a t' against thy holy child Jesus, "
10:34 Of a t' I perceive that God is no "
26:25 forth the words of t' and soberness. "
Ro 1:18 who hold the t' in unrighteousness; "
25 Who changed the t' of God into a lie, "
2: 2 judgment of God is according to t' "
8 contentious, and do not obey the t', "
20 knowledge and of the t' in the law. "
3: 7 if the t' of God hath more abounded "
9: 1 I say the t' in Christ, I lie not, my "
15: 8 the circumcision for the t' of God, "
1Co 5: 8 unleavened bread of sincerity and t'."
13: 6 in iniquity, but rejoiceth in the t'; "
14:25 report that God is in you of a t'. *3689
2Co 4: 2 but by manifestation of the t' 225
6: 7 By the word of t', by the power of "
7:14 as we spake all things to you in t', "
14 I made before Titus, is found a t'. "
11:10 As the t' of Christ is in me, no man "
12: 6 not be a fool; for I will say the t': "
13: 8 nothing against the t', but for the t'. "
Ga 2: 5 the t' of the gospel might continue "
14 according to the t' of the gospel, "
3: 1 you, that ye should not obey the t',* "
4:16 enemy, because I tell you the t'? "
5: 7 you that ye should not obey the t'? 225
Eph 1:13 after that ye heard the word of t', "
4:15 speaking the t' in love, may grow 226
21 taught by him, as the t' is in Jesus: 225
25 speak every man t' with his 226
5: 9 goodness and righteousness and t';) "
6:14 having your loins girt about with t', "
Ph'p 1:18 whether in pretence, or in t', Christ "
Col 1: 5 in the word of the t' of the gospel; "
6 and knew the grace of God in t': "
1Th 2:13 but as it is in t', the word of God, 230
2Th 2:10 they received not the love of the t', 225
12 be damned who believed not the t', "
13 of the Spirit and belief of the t': "
1Ti 2: 4 come unto the knowledge of the t'. "
7 (I speak the t' in Christ, and lie not;)"
3:15 God, the pillar and ground of the t'. "
4: 3 them which believe and know the t'. "
6: 5 corrupt minds,...destitute of the t'. "
2Ti 2:15 rightly dividing the word of t'. "
18 Who concerning the t' have erred, "
25 to the acknowledging of the t'; "
3: 7 to come to the knowledge of the t'. "
8 Moses, so do these also resist the t': "
4: 4 turn away their ears from the t', "
Tit 1: 1 of the t' which is after godliness; "
14 of men, that turn from the t'. "
Heb10:26 received the knowledge of the t', "
Jas 1:18 will begat he us with the word of t', "
3:14 glory not, and lie not against the t'. "
5:19 if any of you do err from the t', and "
1Pe 1:22 purified your souls in obeying the t' "
2Pe 1:12 and be established in the present t'. "
2: 2 the way of t' shall be evil spoken of. "
1Jo 1: 6 darkness, we lie, and do not the t': "
8 ourselves, and the t' is not in us. "
2: 4 is a liar, and the t' is not in him. "
21 unto you because ye know not the t'," "
21 know it, and that no lie is of the t'. "
27 of all things, and is t', and is no lie,*227
1Jo 3:18 in tongue; but in deed and in t'. 225
19 we know that we are of the t', and "
4: 6 Hereby know we the spirit of t', and "
5: 6 witness, because the Spirit is t'. "
2Jo 1 her children, whom I love in the t'; "
1 also all they that have known the t'; "
3 Son of the Father, in t' and love. "
4 I found of thy children walking in t'," "
3Jo 1 Gaius, whom I love in the t'. "
3 and testified of the t' that is in thee, "
3 even as thou walkest in the t'. "
4 to hear that my children walk in t'. "
8 we might be fellowhelpers to the t'. "
12 report of all men, and of the t' itself:"

truth's
Ps 115: 1 for thy mercy, and for thy t' sake. 571
2Jo 2 For the t' sake, that dwelleth in us, 225

try See also TRIED; TRIEST; TRIETH; TRYING.
J'g 7: 4 and I will t' them for thee there: 6884
2Ch 32:31 God left him, to t' him, that he 5254
Job 7:18 morning, and t' him every moment? 974
12:11 Doth not the ear t' words? and the "
Ps 11: 4 his eyelids t' the children of men. "
26: 2 me; t' my reins and my heart. 6884
139:23 t' me, and know my thoughts: 974
Jer 6:27 thou mayest know and t' their way. "
9: 7 I will melt them, and t' them; "
17:10 Lord search the heart, I t' the reins. "
La 3:40 Let us search and t' our ways, 2713
Da 11:35 fall, to t' them, and to purge, and*6884
Zec 13: 9 and will t' them as gold is tried: * 974
1Co 3:13 the fire shall t' every man's work *1381
1Pe 4:12 fiery trial which is to t' you, 4314,3986
1Jo 4: 1 t' the spirits whether they are of *1381
Re 3:10 t' them that dwell upon the earth. 3985

trying
Jas 1: 3 t' of your faith worketh patience.†‡1383

Tryphena (*tri-fe'-nah*)
Ro 16:12 Salute T' and Tryphosa, who *5170

Tryphosa (*tri-fo'-sah*)
Ro 16:12 Salute Tryphena and T', who 5173

Tubal (*tu'-bal*) See also TUBAL-CAIN.
Ge 10: 2 and T', and Meshech, and Tiras. 8422
1Ch 1: 5 and T', and Meshech, and Tiras. "
Isa 66:19 to T', and Javan, to isles afar off, "
Eze 27:13 T', and Meshech, they were thy "
32:26 There is Meshech, T', and all her "
38: 2 chief prince of Meshech and T', "
3 chief prince of Meshech and T': "
39: 1 chief prince of Meshech and T': "

Tubal-cain (*tu'-bal-cain*)
Ge 4:22 And Zillah, she also bare T', an 8423
22 and the sister of T' was Naamah. "

tumbled
J'g 7:13 bread t' into the host of Midian, 2015

tumult See also TUMULTS.
1Sa 4:14 What meaneth the noise of this t'?1995
2Sa 18:29 I saw a great t', but I knew not "
2Ki 19:28 against me and thy t' is come up *7600
Ps 65: 7 waves, and the t' of the people. 1995
74:23 the t' of those that rise up against7588
83: 2 For, lo, thine enemies make a t': 1993
Isa 33: 3 the noise of the t' the people fled; 1995
37:29 thy t', is come up into mine ears, *7600
Jer 11:16 with the noise of a great t' he hath1999
Ho 10:14 shall a t' arise among thy people, 7588
Am 2: 2 and Moab shall die with t', with "
Zec 14:13 a great t' from the Lord shall be 4103
M't 27:24 but that rather a t' was made, he 2351
M'r 5:38 and seeth the t', and them that "
Ac 21:34 not know the certainty for the t', * "
24:18 neither with multitude, nor with t'. "

tumults
Am 3: 9 the great t' in the midst thereof, 4103
2Co 6: 5 in imprisonments, in t', in labours, 181
12:20 strifes,...whisperings, swellings, t': "

tumultuous
Isa 13: 4 a t' noise of the kingdoms of *7588
22: 2 that art full of stirs, a t' city, a 1993
Jer 48:45 of the head of the t' ones. 1121,7588

turn See also OVERTURN; RETURN; TURNED; TURNEST; TURNETH; TURNING.
Ge 19: 2 my lords, t' in, I pray you, into 5493
24:49 that I may t' to the right hand, or 6437
27:44 until thy brother's fury t' away: 7725
45 Until thy brother's anger t' away "
Ex 3: 3 I will now t' aside, and see this 5493
14: 2 that they t' and encamp before 7725
23:27 thine enemies t' their backs unto thee. "
32:12 T' from thy fierce wrath, and 7725
Le 13:16 Or if the raw flesh t' again, and be "
19: 4 T' ye not unto idols, nor make to 6437
Nu 14:25 To morrow t' you, and get you "
20:17 will not t' to the right hand nor 5186
21:22 we will not t' into the fields, or into"
22:23 Balaam smote the ass, to t' her "
26 was no way to t' either to the right "
32:15 if ye t' away from after him, he 7725
34: 4 your border shall t' from the south5437
De 1: 7 T' you, and take your journey, 6437
40 t' you, and take your journey into "
2: 3 long enough: t' you northward. "
27 I will neither t' unto the right nor5493
4:30 if thou t' to the Lord thy God, *7725
5:32 ye shall not t' aside to the right 5493
7: 4 will t' away thy son from following "
11:16 ye t' aside, and serve other gods, "
28 t' aside out of the way which I "
13: 5 spoken to t' you away from the *5627
17 Lord may t' from the fierceness of7725
14:25 Then shalt thou t' it into money, 5414
16: 7 and thou shalt t' in the morning. 6437
De 17:17 himself, that his heart t' not away:5493
20 and that he t' not aside from the "
23:13 shalt t' back and cover that which7725
14 in thee, and t' away from thee. "
30: 3 Lord thy God will t' thy captivity, "
10 t' unto the Lord thy God with all "
17 But if thine heart t' away, as that 6437
31:20 then will they t' unto other gods, "
29 t' aside from the way I have 5493
Jos 1: 7 t' not from it to the right hand or to"
22:16, 18 t' away this day from following 7725
23 altar to t' from following the Lord, "
29 t' this day from following the Lord," "
23: 6 that ye t' not aside therefrom to 5493
24:20 then he will t' and do you hurt, 7725
J'g 4:18 T' in, my lord, t' in to me; fear 5493
11: 8 Therefore we t' again to thee now,*7725
19:11 t' into this city of the Jebusites, 5493
12 will not t' aside hither into the city "
20: 8 will we any of us t' into his house. "
Ru 1:11 And Naomi said, T' again, my 7725
12 T' again, my daughter, go your "
4: 1 such a one! t' aside, sit down here.5493
1Sa 12:20 t' not aside from following the Lord,"
21 t' ye not aside: for then should ye "
14: 7 t' thee; behold, I am with thee 5186
15:25 pardon my sin,...t' again with me, 7725
30 and t' again with me, that I may "
22:17 T', and slay the priests of the 5437
18 T' thou, and fall upon the priests. "
2Sa 2:21 T' thee aside to thy right hand or5186
21 not t' aside from following of him.5493
22 T' thee aside from following me: "
23 Howbeit he refused to t' aside: "
14:19 none can t' to the right hand or to the
24 Let him t' to his own house, and 5437
15:31 t' the...of Ahithophel into foolishness.
18:30 unto him, T' aside, and stand 5437
19:37 servant, I pray thee, t' back again,7725
1Ki 8:33 shall t' again to thee, and confess "
35 thy name, and t' from their sin, "
9: 6 shall at all t' from following me, "
11: 2 they will t' away your heart after 5186
12:27 heart of this people t' again unto 7725
13: 9 nor t' again by the same way that* "
17 nor t' again to go by the way that "
17: 3 thee hence, and t' thee eastward, 6437
22:34 T' thine hand, and carry me out 2015
2Ki 1: 6 Go, t' again unto the king that 7725
4:10 to us, that he shall t' in thither. 5493
9:18, 19 with peace? t' thee behind me. 5437
17:13 T' ye from your evil ways, and 7725
18:24 then wilt thou t' away the face of "
19:28 I will t' thee back by the way by "
20: 5 T' again, and tell Hezekiah the "
1Ch 12:23 t' the kingdom of Saul to him, 5437
14:14 up after them; t' away from them, "
2Ch 6:26 thy name, and t' from their sin, 7725
37 t' and pray unto thee in the land of "
42 t' not away...face of thine anointed:"
7:14 face, and t' from thy wicked ways; "
19 But if ye t' away, and forsake my "
15: 4 they in their trouble did t' unto the*"
18:33 T' thine hand, that thou mayest 2015
25:27 that Amaziah did t' away from 5493
29:10 that his fierce wrath may t' away 7725
30: 6 t' again unto the Lord God of "
8 fierceness of his wrath may t' away "
9 if ye t' again unto the Lord, your "
9 not t' away his face from you, 5493
35:22 Josiah would not t' his face from 5437
Ne 1: 9 But if ye t' unto me, and keep my*7725
4: 4 t' their reproach upon their own "
9:26 against them to t' them to thee, "
Es 2:12 when every maid's t' was come to 8447
15 Now when the t' of Esther, the "
Job 5: 1 to which of the saints wilt thou t'? 6437
14: 6 T' from him, that he may rest, till *8159
23:13 in one mind, and who can t' him? 7725
24: 4 They t' the needy out of the way: 5186
34:15 and man shall t' again unto dust. 7725
Ps 4: 2 long will ye t' my glory into shame?* "
7:12 If he t' not, he will whet his 7725
18:37 I t' again till they were consumed. "
21:12 shalt thou make them t' their back, "
22:27 remember and t' unto the Lord: 7725
25:16 T' thee unto me, and have mercy 6437
40: 4 proud, nor such as t' aside to lies. 7750
44:10 us to t' back from the enemy: 7725
56: 9 thee, then shall mine eyes t' back: "
60: 1 displeased; O t' thyself to us again.*"
69:16 t' unto me according to the 6437
80: 3 T' us again, O God, and cause thy7725
7 T' us again, O God of hosts, and "
19 T' us again, O Lord God of hosts, "
85: 4 T' us, O God of our salvation, and "
8 but let them not t' again to folly. "
86:16 O t' unto me, and have mercy 6437
101: 3 hate...work of them that t' aside; 7750
104: 9 that they t' not again to cover the 7725
106:23 to t' away his wrath, lest he should "
119:37 T' away mine eyes from 5674
39 T' away my reproach which I fear: "
79 those that fear thee t' unto me, 7725
125: 5 As for such as t' aside unto their 5186
126: 4 T' again our captivity, O Lord, as 7725
132:10 t' not away the face of thine "
11 he will not t' from it; Of the fruit "
Pr 1:23 T' you at my reproof: behold, I "
4:15 by it, t' from it, and pass away. 7847
27 T' not to the right hand nor to 5186
9: 4, 16 is simple, let him t' in hither: 5493
24:18 he t' away his wrath from him. 7725
25:10 and thine infamy t' not away. "
29: 8 but wise men t' away wrath. "
Ec 3:20 the dust, and all t' to dust again. 7725

Ca 2:17 t', my beloved, and be thou like a 5437
6: 5 T' away thine eyes from me, for "
Isa 1:25 And I will t' my hand upon thee, 7725
10: 2 t' aside the needy from judgment, 5186
13:14 every man t' to his own people, 6437
14:27 out, and who shall t' it back? 7725
19: 6 they shall t' the rivers far away; *2186
22:18 surely violently t' and toss thee 6801
23:17 Tyre, and she shall t' to her hire, *7725
28: 6 them that t' the battle to the gate. "
29:21 and t' aside the just for a thing of 5186
30:11 of the way, t' aside out of the path, "
21 ye in it, when ye t' to the right hand,
21 and when ye t' to the left.
31: 6 T' ye unto him from whom the 7725
36: 9 wilt thou t' away the face of one "
37:29 t' thee back by the way by which "
58:13 t' away thy foot from the sabbath, "
59:20 t' from transgression in Jacob, "
Jer 2:24 in her occasion who can t' her way? "
35 surely his anger shall t' from me.* "
3: 7 these things, T' thou unto me. * "
14 T', O backsliding children, saith * "
19 and shalt not t' away from me. "
4:28 repent, neither will I t' back from it. "
6: 9 t' back thine hand as a "
8: 4 shall he t' away, and not return? "
13:16 he t' it into the shadow of death, 7760
18: 8 t' from their evil, I will repent of 7725
20 to t' away thy wrath from them. "
21: 4 I will t' back the weapons of war 5437
25: 5 T' ye again now every one from *7725
26: 3 and t' every man from his evil way, "
29:14 and I will t' away your captivity, "
31:13 I will t' their mourning into joy, 2015
18 t' thou me, and I shall be turned; 7725
21 t' again, O virgin of Israel, t' "
32:40 that I will not t' away from them, "
44: 5 ear to t' from their wickedness, "
49: 8 Flee ye, t' back, dwell deep, O 6437
50:16 shall t' every one to his people, "
La 2:14 iniquity, to t' away thy captivity; *7725
3:35 To t' aside the right of a man 5186
40 ways, and t' again to the Lord. 7725
5:21 T' thou us unto thee, O Lord, and "
Eze 3:19 he t' not from his wickedness, nor "
20 righteous man doth t' from his "
4: 8 shalt not t' thee from one side to 2015
7:22 My face will I t' also from them, 5437
8: 6 t' thee yet again, and thou shalt *7725
13 T' thee yet again, and thou shalt * "
15 t' thee yet again, and thou shalt * "
14: 6 and t' yourselves from your idols; "
6 and t' away your face from all your "
18:21 the wicked will t' from all his sins "
30 and t' yourselves from all your "
32 wherefore t' yourselves, and live "
33: 9 the wicked of his way to t' from it; "
9 if he do not t' from his way, he "
11 but that the wicked t' from his way "
11 t' ye, t' ye from your evil ways; for "
14 if he t' from his sin, and do that "
19 the wicked t' from his wickedness,* "
36: 9 am for you, and I will t' unto you, 6437
38: 4 I will t' thee back, and put hooks 7725
12 to t' thine hand upon the desolate "
39: 2 I will t' thee back, and leave but "
Da 9:13 we might t' from our iniquities, "
11:18 shall he t' his face unto the isles, "
18 he shall cause it to t' upon him. "
19 shall t' his face toward the fort of "
12: 3 they that t' many to righteousness, as
Ho 5: 4 their doings to t' unto their God: 7725
12: 6 Therefore t' thou to thy God: keep "
14: 2 you words, and t' to the Lord: * "
Joe 2:12 t' ye even to me with all your heart, "
13 and t' unto the Lord your God: "
Am 1: 3, 6 will not t' away the punishment "
8 I will t' mine hand against Ekron: "
9, 11, 13 not t' away the punishment "
2: 1, 4, 6 not t' away the punishment "
7 and t' aside the way of the meek: 5186
5: 7 Ye who t' judgment to wormwood, 2015
12 they t' aside the poor in the gate 5186
8:10 will t' your feasts into mourning, 2015
Jon 3: 8 let them t' every one from his evil 7725
9 can tell if God will t' and repent, "
9 and t' away from his fierce anger, "
Mic 7:19 He will t' again, he will have "
Zep 2: 7 them, and t' away their captivity.* "
3: 9 t' to the people a pure language, 2015
20 when I t' back your captivity *7725
Zec 1: 3 T' ye unto me, saith the Lord of * "
3 I will t' unto you, saith the Lord of* "
4 T' ye now from your evil ways, * "
9:12 T' you to the strong hold, ye "
10: 9 with their children, and t' again. * "
13: 7 t' mine hand upon the little ones. "
Mal 2: 6 did t' many away from iniquity. "
3: 5 that t' aside the stranger from his 5186
4: 6 t' the heart of the fathers to the 7725
M't 5:39 cheek, t' to him the other also. *4762*
42 borrow of thee t' not thou away. *654*
7: 6 feet, and t' again and rend you. *4762*
M'r 13:16 is in the field not t' back again **1994*
Lu 1:16 Israel shall he t' to the Lord their "
17 to t' the hearts of the fathers to the "
10: 6 it: if not, it shall t' to you again. *344*
17: 4 and seven times in a day t' again *1994*
21:13 it shall t' to you for a testimony. *576*
Ac 13: 8 t' away the deputy from the faith. *1294*
46 life, lo, we t' to the Gentiles. *4762*
14:15 ye should t' from these vanities **1994*
26:18 to t' them from darkness to light, "
20 they should repent and t' to God, "
Ro 11:26 t' away ungodliness from Jacob: *654*

2Co 3:16 when it shall t' to the Lord, *1994*
Ga 4: 9 how t' ye again to the weak and "
Ph'p 1:19 that this shall t' to my salvation *576*
2Ti 3: 5 power thereof: from such t' away. *665*
4: 4 they shall t' away their ears from *654*
Tit 1:14 of men, that t' from the truth. "
Heb 12:25 we t' away from him that speaketh "
Jas 3: 3 and we t' about their whole body. *3329*
2Pe 2:21 to t' from the holy commandment *1994*
Re 11: 6 over waters to t' them to blood, *4762*

turned See also OVERTURNED; RETURNED.
Ge 3:24 flaming sword which t' every way, 2015
18:22 men t' their faces from thence, 6437
19: 3 they t' in unto him, and entered 5493
38: 1 and t' in to a certain Adullamite, 5186
16 And he t' unto her by the way, "
42:24 he t' himself about from them, 5437
Ex 3: 4 Lord saw that he t' aside to see, 5493
4: 7 it was t' again as his other flesh. 7725
7:15 the rod which was t' to a serpent 2015
17 river, and they shall be t' to blood. "
20 were in the river were t' to blood. "
23 And Pharaoh t' and went into his 6437
10: 6 he t' himself, and went out from "
19 Lord t' a mighty strong west wind, 2015
14: 5 servants was t' against the people,* "
32: 8 They have t' aside quickly out of 5493
15 Moses t', and went down from the 6437
33:11 And he t' again into the camp: 7725
Le 13: 3 the hair in the plague is t' white, 2015
4 the hair thereof be not t' white; "
10 skin, and it have t' the hair white, "
13 hath the plague: it is all t' white: "
17 if the plague be t' into white; "
20 and the hair thereof be t' white; "
25 hair in the bright spot be t' white, "
Nu 14:43 ye are t' away from the Lord, 7725
20:21 wherefore Israel t' away from him. 5186
21:33 they t' and went up by the way of 6437
22:23 the ass t' aside out of the way, 5186
33 and the ass saw me, and t' from me "
33 unless she had t' from me, surely "
25: 4 anger of the Lord may be t' away *7725
11 hath t' my wrath away from the "
33: 7 and t' again unto Pi-hahiroth, "
De 1:24 t' and went up into the mountain, 6437
2: 1 Then we t', and took our journey "
8 we t' and passed by the way of the "
3: 1 Then we t', and went up the way "
9:12 are quickly t' aside out of the way 5493
15 t' and came down from the mount, 6437
16 t' aside quickly out of the way 5493
10: 5 t' myself and came down from the 6437
23: 5 the Lord thy God t' the curse into 2015
31:18 that they are t' unto other gods. 6437
Jos 7:12 t' their backs before their enemies,* "
26 the Lord t' from the fierceness of 7725
8:20 fled to the wilderness t' back 2015
21 they t' again, and slew the men of 7725
11:10 And Joshua at that time t' back, "
19:12 And t' from Sarid eastward toward "
J'g 2:17 they t' quickly out of the way 5493
3:19 himself t' again from the quarries 7725
4:18 And when he had t' in unto her 5493
8:33 that the children of Israel t' again, 7725
14: 8 he t' aside to see the carcase of 5493
15: 4 t' tail to tail, and put a firebrand 6437
18: 3 they t' in thither, and said unto 5493
15 they t' thitherward, and came to "
21 So they t' and departed, and put 6437
23 they t' their faces, and said unto 5437
26 t' and went back unto his house. 6437
19:15 they t' aside thither, to go in and 5493
20:41 when the men of Israel t' again, 2015
42 they t' their backs before the men 6437
45 t' and fled toward the wilderness "
47 six hundred men t' and fled to the "
48 the men of Israel t' again upon 7725
Ru 3: 8 man was afraid, and t' himself: 3943
4: 1 And he t' aside, and sat down. 5493
1Sa 6:12 t' not aside to the right hand or to "
8: 3 but t' aside after lucre, and took 5186
10: 6 and shalt be t' into another man. 2015
9 that when he had t' his back to go 6437
13:17 one company t' unto the way that "
18 And another company t' the way to "
18 another company t' to the way of "
14:21 they also t' to be with the Israelites
47 whithersoever he t' himself, he 6437
15:11 he is t' back from following me, 7725
27 as Samuel t' about to go away, he 5437
31 So Samuel t' again after Saul; and 7725
17:30 he t' from him toward another, 5437
22:18 Doeg the Edomite t', and he fell "
25:12 David's young men t' their way, 2015
2Sa 1:22 the bow of Jonathan t' not back, 7734
2:19 going he t' not to the right hand 5186
18:30 And he t' aside, and stood still. 5437
19: 2 victory that day was t' into mourning
22:38 and t' not again until I had *7725
1Ki 2:15 howbeit the kingdom is t' about, 5437
28 for Joab had t' after Adonijah, 5186
28 though he t' not after Absalom. "
8:14 And the king t' his face about, and 5437
10:13 t' and went to her own country, 6437
11: 3 and his wives t' away his heart. 5186
4 wives t' away his heart after other "
9 heart was t' from the Lord God of "
15: 5 t' not aside from any thing that he 5493
18:37 thou hast t' their heart back again. 5437
20:39 a man t' aside, and brought a man 5493
21: 4 upon his bed, and t' away his face, 5437
22:32 they t' aside to fight against him: 5493
33 they t' back from pursuing him. 7725
43 he t' not aside from it, doing that 5493
2Ki 1: 5 the messengers t' back unto him, *7725

2Ki 1: 5 them, Why are ye now t' back? *7725
2:24 he t' back, and looked on them, *6437
4: 8 by, he t' in thither to eat bread. 5493
11 he t' into the chamber, and lay "
5:12 So he t' and went away in a rage. 6437
26 man t' again from his chariot 2015
9:23 And Joram t' his hands, and fled, "
15:20 So the king of Assyria t' back, and 7725
16:18 t' he from the house of the Lord 5437
20: 2 Then he t' his face to the wall, and "
22: 2 t' not aside to the right hand or to 5493
23:16 as Josiah t' himself, he spied the 6437
25 that t' to the Lord with all his 7725
26 Lord t' not from the fierceness of "
34 t' his name to Jehoiakim, and took *5437
24: 1 he t' and rebelled against him. 7725
1Ch 10:14 t' the kingdom unto David the son 5437
21:20 Ornan t' back, and saw the angel; 7725
2Ch 6: 3 the king t' his face, and blessed 5437
9:12 she t', and went away to her own 2015
12:12 the wrath of the Lord t' from him, 7725
18:32 they t' back...from pursuing him. "
20:10 they t' from them, and destroyed 5493
29: 6 have t' away their faces from the 5437
6 of the Lord, and t' their backs. 5414
36: 4 and t' his name to Jehoiakim. *5437
Ezr 6:22 t' the heart of the king of Assyria "
10:14 God for this matter be t' from us. 7725
Ne 2:15 and viewed the wall, and t' back, "
9:35 t' they from their wicked works. "
13: 2 God t' the curse into a blessing. 2015
Es 9: 1 (though it was t' to the contrary, "
22 month which was t' unto them from "
Job 6:18 paths of their way are t' aside; *3943
16:11 t' me over into the hands of the *3399
19:19 whom I loved are t' against me. 2015
20:14 Yet his meat in his bowels is t', it is "
28: 5 and under it is t' up as it were fire. "
30:15 Terrors are t' upon me: they pursue "
31 My harp also is t' to mourning, and
31: 7 If my step hath t' out of the way, 5186
34:27 Because they t' back from him, 5493
37:12 is t' round about by his counsels: 2015
38:14 It is t' as clay to the seal; and they* "
41:22 sorrow is t' into joy before him. *1750
28 are t' with him into stubble. 2015
42:10 the Lord t' the captivity of Job, 7725
Ps 9: 3 When mine enemies are t' back, * "
17 The wicked shall be t' into hell, † "
30:11 hast t' for me my mourning into 2015
32: 4 my moisture is t' into the drought* "
35: 4 let them be t' back and brought 5472
44:18 Our heart is not t' back, neither "
66: 6 He t' the sea into dry land: they 2015
20 which hath not t' away my prayer, 5493
70: 2 let them be t' backward, and put 5472
3 Let them be t' back for a reward 7725
78: 9 bows, t' back in the day of battle. 2015
38 many a time t' he his anger away, 7725
41 Yea, they t' back and tempted God, "
44 And had t' their rivers into blood; 2015
57 But t' back, and dealt unfaithfully 5472
57 were t' aside like a deceitful bow. 2015
81:14 and t' my hand against their *7725
85: 3 hast t' thyself from the fierceness "
89:43 hast also t' the edge of his sword,* "
105:25 He t' their heart to hate his people, 2015
29 He t' their waters into blood, and "
114: 8 t' the rock into a standing water, "
119:59 t' my feet unto thy testimonies. 7725
126: 1 the Lord t' again the captivity of ‡ "
129: 5 and t' back that hate Zion. 5472
Ec 2:12 t' myself to behold wisdom, and 6437
Ca 6: 1 whither is thy beloved t' aside? "
Isa 5:25 all this his anger is not t' away, 7725
9:12, 17, 21 his anger is not t' away, but "
10: 4 For all this his anger is not t' away. "
12: 1 with me, thine anger is t' away, "
21: 4 my pleasure hath he t' into fear 7760
28:27 neither is a cart wheel t' about 5437
29:17 Lebanon...t' into a fruitful field, 7725
34: 9 streams...shall be t' into pitch, 2015
38: 2 Hezekiah t' his face toward the 5437
42:17 They shall be t' back, they shall 5472
44:20 a deceived heart hath t' him aside, 5186
50: 5 rebellious, neither t' away back. 5472
53: 6 have t' every one to his own way; 6437
59:14 judgment is t' away backward, 5253
63:10 he was t' to be their enemy, 2015
Jer 2:21 art thou t' into the degenerate plant "
27 they have t' their back unto me, 6437
3:10 sister Judah hath not t' unto me *7725
4: 8 anger of the Lord is not t' back "
5:25 Your iniquities have t' away these 5186
6:12 houses shall be t' unto others, 5437
8: 6 every one t' to his course, as the *7725
11:10 They are t' back to the iniquities of "
23:22 have t' them from their evil way, "
30: 6 and all faces are t' into paleness? 2015
31:18 turn thou me, and I shall be t'; 7725
19 after that I was t', I repented; "
32:33 they have t' unto me the back, and 6437
34:11 But afterward they t', and caused 7725
15 ye were now t', and had done right "
16 But ye t' and polluted my name, "
38:22 mire, and they are t' away back. 5472
46: 5 them dismayed and t' away back? "
21 they also are t' back, and are fled 6437
48:39 hath Moab t' the back with shame! "
50: 6 t' them away on the mountains: 7725
La 1:13 net for my feet, he hath t' me back: "
20 mine heart is t' within me; for I 2015
3: 3 Surely against me is he t'; *7725
11 He hath t' aside my ways, and 5493
5: 2 Our inheritance is t' to strangers, 2015
15 our dance is t' into mourning.

La 5:21 thee, O Lord, and we shall be t': 7725
Eze 1: 9 they t' not when they went; 5437
12, 17 and they t' not when they went. "
10:11 they t' not as they went, but to the "
11 followed it; they t' not as they went."
16 same wheels also t' not from beside"
17: 6 whose branches t' toward him, 6437
26: 2 she is t' unto me: I shall be 5437
42:19 He t' about to the west side, and "
Da 9:16 anger and thy fury be t' away 7725
10: 8 my comeliness was t' in me into 2015
16 vision my sorrows are t' upon me, "
Ho 7: 8 people; Ephraim is a cake not t'. "
11: 8 mine heart is t' within me, my "
14: 4 mine anger is t' away from him. 7725
Joe 2:31 The sun shall be t' into darkness, 2015
Am 6:12 for ye have t' judgment into gall, "
Jon 3:10 that they t' from their evil way; 7725
Na 2: 2 t' away the excellency of Jacob, * "
Hab 2:16 Lord's right hand shall be t' unto 5437
Zep 1: 6 that are t' back from the Lord; 5472
Hag 2:17 yet ye t' not to me, saith the Lord.
Zec 5: 1 Then I t', and lifted up mine eyes,*7725
6: 1 And I t', and lifted up mine eyes, * "
14:10 All the land shall be t' as a plain 5437
M't 2:22 t' aside into the parts of Galilee: * 402
9:22 But Jesus t' him about, and when*1994
16:23 But he t', and said unto Peter, Get 4772
M'r 5:30 t' him about in the press, and said,1994
8:33 when he had t' about and looked on*"
Lu 2:45 they t' back again to Jerusalem, *5290
7: 9 t' him about, and said unto the 4762
44 he t' to the woman, and said unto * "
9:55 But he t', and rebuked them, and "
10:23 And he t' him unto his disciples, * "
14:25 him: and he t', and said unto them, "
17:15 t' back, and with a loud voice 5290
22:61 Lord t', and looked upon Peter. 4762
Joh 1:38 Then Jesus t', and saw them "
16:20 your sorrow shall be t' into joy. 1096
20:14 she t' herself back, and saw Jesus 4762
16 She t' herself, and saith unto him,* "
Ac 2:20 The sun shall be t' into darkness, "
7:39 hearts t' back again into Egypt, "
42 Then God t', and gave them up to "
9:35 Saron saw him, and t' to the Lord. 1994
11:21 believed, and t' unto the Lord. "
15:19 among the Gentiles are t' to God: * "
16:18 grieved, t' and said to the spirit, "
17: 6 that have t' the world upside down 387
19:26 and t' away much people, 3179
1Th 1: 9 and how ye t' to God from idols to 1994
1Ti 1: 6 have t' aside unto vain jangling; 1824
5:15 are already t' aside after Satan. "
2Ti 1:15 are in Asia be t' away from me; 654
4: 4 truth, and shall be t' unto fables. * "
Heb11:34 t' to flight the armies of the aliens.2827
12:13 which is lame be t' out of the way;1624
Jas 3: 4 t' about with a very small helm, 3329
4: 9 let...laughter be t' to mourning, 3344
2Pe 2:22 dog is t' to his own vomit again; *1994
Re 1:12 I t' to see the voice that spake with "
12 And being t', I saw seven golden "

turnest
1Ki 2: 3 and whithersoever thou t' thyself:6437
Job 15:13 thou t' thy spirit against God, 7725
Ps 90: 3 Thou t' man to destruction; and "

turneth See also OVERTURNETH; RETURNETH.
Le 20: 6 the soul that t' after such as have 6437
De 29:18 whose heart t' away this day from "
Jos 7: 8 Israel t' their backs before their *2015
19:27 And t' toward the sunrising to *7725
29 And then the coast t' to Ramah, * "
29 Tyre; and the coast t' to Hosah; * "
34 And then the coast t' westward to* "
Job 39:22 neither t' he back from the sword. "
Ps 107:33 He t' rivers into a wilderness, and 7760
35 He t' the wilderness into a standing"
146: 9 the way of the wicked he t' upside 5791
Pr 15: 1 A soft answer t' away wrath: but 7725
17: 8 whithersoever it t', it prospereth. 6437
21: 1 he t' it whithersoever he will. 5186
26:14 As the door t' upon his hinges, so 5437
28: 9 that t' away his ear from hearing 5493
30:30 beasts, and t' not away for any; 7725
Ec 1: 6 south, and t' about unto the north;5437
Ca 1: 7 should I be as one that t' aside *5844
Isa 9:13 the people t' not unto him that *7725
24: 1 it waste, and t' it upside down, 5753
44:25 that t' wise men backward, and 7725
Jer 14: 8 as a wayfaring man that t' aside 5186
49:24 feeble, and t' herself to flee, and 6437
La 1: 8 yea, she sigheth, and t' backward. 7725
3: 3 t' his hand against me all the day. "
Eze18:24, 26 t' away from his righteousness, "
27 man t' away from his wickedness "
28 t' away from all his transgressions "
33:12 day that he t' from his wickedness; "
18 righteous t' from his righteousness, "
Am 5: 8 and t' the shadow of death into 2015

turning See also RETURNING.
2Ki 21:13 wiping it, and t' it upside down. 2015
2Ch 26: 9 gate, and at the t' of the wall, 4740
36:13 heart from t' unto the Lord God 7257
Ne 3:19 the armoury at the t' of the wall. 4740
20 from the t' of the wall unto the door"
24 of Azariah unto the t' of the wall, "
25 over against the t' of the wall, "
Pr 1:32 the t' away of the simple shall slay*4878
Isa 29:16 your t' of things upside down *2017
Eze 41:24 two leaves apiece, two t' leaves; 4142
Mic 2: 4 t' away he hath divided our fields.*7725
Lu 23:28 But Jesus t' unto them said, 4762
Joh 21:20 Peter, t' about, seeth the disciple 1994
Ac 3:26 in t' away every one of you from 654
Ac 9:40 t' him to the body said, Tabitha, 1994
Jas 1:17 variableness, neither shadow of t'. 5157
2Pe 2: 6 t' the cities of Sodom...into ashes 5077
Jude 4 t' the grace of our God into 3346

turtle See also TURTLEDOVE; TURTLES.
Ca 2:12 the voice of the t' is heard in our ‡8449
Jer 8: 7 and the t' and the crane and the ‡ "

turtledove See also TURTLEDOVES.
Ge 15: 9 old, and a t', and a young pigeon. 8449
Le 12: 6 pigeon, or a t', for a sin offering, "
Ps 74:19 O deliver not the soul of thy t' unto "

turtledoves
Le 1:14 he shall bring his offering of t', 8449
5: 7 two t', or two young pigeons, unto "
11 But if he be not able to bring two t'," "
14:22 And two t', or two young pigeons, "
30 And he shall offer the one of the t', "
15:14 day he shall take to him two t', "
Lu 2:24 A pair of t', or two young pigeons. 5167

turtles
Le 12: 8 lamb, then she shall bring two t', *8449
15:29 day she shall take unto her two t',* "
Nu 6:10 eighth day he shall bring two t', * "

tutors
Ga 4: 2 But is under t' and governors *2012

twain See also TWO.
1Sa 18:21 my son in law in the one of the t'.*8147
2Ki 4:33 and shut the door upon them t', "
Isa 6: 2 wings; with t' he covered his face, "
2 and with t' he covered his feet, "
2 and with t' he did fly. "
Jer 34:18 when they cut the calf in t', and "
Eze 21:19 both t' shall come forth out of one "
M't 5:41 thee to go a mile, go with him t'. 1417
19: 5 wife: and they t' shall be one flesh? "
6 Wherefore they are no more t', but "
21:31 Whether of them t' did the will of "
27:21 Whether of the t' will ye that I "
51 the veil of the temple was rent in t' "
M'r 10: 8 And they t' shall be one flesh: so "
8 so then they are no more t', but one"
15:38 the veil of the temple was rent in t' "
Eph 2:15 make in himself of t' one new man, "

twelfth
Nu 7:78 On the t' day Ahira the son of8147,6240
1Ki 19:19 before him, and he with the t': " "
2Ki 8:25 In the t' year of Joram the son " "
17: 1 In the t' year of Ahaz king of " "
25:27 in the t' month, on the seven " "
1Ch 24:12 to Eliashib, the t' to Jakim, " "
25:19 The t' to Hashabiah, he, his " "
27:15 The t' captain for the t' month " "
2Ch 34: 3 and in the t' year he began to " "
Ezr 8:31 the t' day of the first month, " "
Es 3: 7 the t' year of king Ahasuerus, " "
7 to the t' month, that is, the " "
13 thirteenth day of the t' month, " "
8:12 thirteenth day of the t' month, " "
9: 1 Now in the t' month, that is, " "
Jer 52:31 in the t' month, in the five and " "
Eze 29: 1 in the t' day of the month, the " "
32: 1 it came to pass in the t' year, " "
1 t' month, in the first day of the " "
17 came to pass also in the t' year, " "
33:21 it came to pass in the t' year of " "
Re 21:20 a jacinth; the t', an amethyst. 1428

twelve
Ge 5: 8 nine hundred and t' years: 8147,6240
14: 4 T' years they served " "
17:20 t' princes shall he beget, and I " "
25:16 t' princes according to their " "
35:22 Now the sons of Jacob were t': " "
42:13 Thy servants are t' brethren, " "
32 We be t' brethren, sons of our " "
49:28 these are the t' tribes of Israel: " "
Ex 15:27 where were t' wells of water, " "
24: 4 under the hill, and t' pillars, " "
4 according to the t' tribes of " "
28:21 of the children of Israel, t', " "
21 be according to the t' tribes. " "
39:14 of the children of Israel, t', " "
14 according to the t' tribes. " "
Le 24: 5 and bake t' cakes thereof: " "
Nu 1:44 princes of Israel, being t' men: " "
7: 3 covered wagons, and t' oxen; " "
84 of Israel: t' chargers of silver, " "
84 t' silver bowls, t' spoons of gold: " "
86 The golden spoons were t', full " "
87 were t' bullocks, the rams t', " "
87 the lambs of the first year t', " "
87 of the goats for sin offering t'. " "
17: 2 house of their fathers t' rods: " "
6 fathers' houses, even t' rods: " "
29:17 ye shall offer t' young bullocks, " "
31: 5 t' thousand armed for war. " "
33 And threescore and t' thousand 8147
38 Lord's tribute was threescore and t'. "
33: 9 were t' fountains of water, 8147,6240
De 1:23 and I took t' men of you, one of " "
Jos 3:12 take you t' men out of the " "
4: 2 Take you t' men out of the " "
3 t' stones, and ye shall carry " "
4 Then Joshua called the t' men, " "
8 t' stones out of the midst of " "
9 Joshua set up t' stones in the " "
20 And those t' stones, which they " "
8:25 and women, were t' thousand, " "
18:24 t' cities with their villages: " "
19:15 t' cities with their villages. " "
21: 7 the tribe of Zebulun, t' cities. " "
40 were by their lot t' cities. " "
J'g 19:29 with her bones, into t' pieces, " "
21:10 sent thither t' thousand men of " "
2Sa 2:15 by number t' of Benjamin, 8147,6240
15 and t' of the servants of David. " "
10: 6 of Ish-tob t' thousand men. " "
17: 1 me now choose out t' thousand " "
1Ki 4: 7 had t' officers over all Israel, " "
26 and t' thousand horsemen. " "
7:15 a line of t' cubits did compass " "
25 It stood upon t' oxen, three " "
44 sea, and t' oxen under the sea; " "
10:20 t' lions stood there on the one " "
26 t' thousand horsemen, whom " "
11:30 on him, and rent it in t' pieces: " "
16:23 to reign over Israel, t' years: " "
18:31 And Elijah took t' stones, " "
19:19 plowing with t' yoke of oxen " "
2Ki 3: 1 of Judah, and reigned t' years. " "
21: 1 Manasseh was t' years old when" "
1Ch 6:63 the tribe of Zebulun, t' cities. " "
9:22 gates were two hundred and t'." "
15:10 brethren an hundred and t'. " "
25: 9 his brethren and sons were t': " "
10, 11, 12, 13, 14, 15, 16, 17, 18, 19, 20,
21, 22, 23, 24, 25, 26, 27, 28, 29, 30
sons, and his brethren, were t':8147,6240
31 sons, and his brethren, were t'. " "
2Ch 1:14 and t' thousand horsemen, " "
4: 4 It stood upon t' oxen, three " "
15 One sea, and t' oxen under it. " "
9:19 t' lions stood there on the one " "
25 and t' thousand horsemen; " "
12: 3 With t' hundred chariots, and 505
33: 1 Manasseh was t' years old 8147,6240
Ezr 2: 6 thousand eight hundred and t'." "
18 of Jorah, an hundred and t'. " "
6:17 t' he goats, according to the 8648,6236
8:24 I separated t' of the chief 8147,6240
35 t' bullocks for all Israel, ninety" "
35 t' he goats for a sin offering: " "
Ne 5:14 t' years, I and my brethren " "
7:24 of Hariph, an hundred and t'. " "
Es 2:12 that she had been t' months, " "
Ps 60: *title* the valley of salt t' thousand." "
Jer 52:20 and t' brasen bulls that were " "
21 a fillet of t' cubits did compass " "
Eze 43:16 altar shall be t' cubits long, " "
16 t' broad, square in the four " "
47:13 to the t' tribes of Israel: " "
Da 4:29 end of t' months he walked in8648,6236
M't 9:20 with an issue of blood t' years, 1427
10: 1 called unto him his t' disciples, "
2 the names of the t' apostles are "
5 These t' Jesus sent forth, and "
11: 1 of commanding his t' disciples, "
14:20 that remained t' baskets full. "
19:28 ye also shall sit upon t' thrones, "
28 judging the t' tribes of Israel. "
20:17 took the t' disciples apart in the "
26:14 Then one of the t', called Judas "
20 was come, he sat down with the t'. "
47 lo, Judas, one of the t', came, and "
53 me more than t' legions of angels? "
M'r 3:14 he ordained t', that they should be "
4:10 that were about him with the t' "
5:25 had an issue of blood t' years, "
42 for she was of the age of t' years. "
6: 7 And he called unto him the t', and "
43 they took up t' baskets full of the "
8:19 ye up? They say unto him, T'. "
9:35 And he sat down, and called the t', "
10:32 he took again the t', and began to "
11:11 went out unto Bethany with the t'. "
14:10 Judas Iscariot, one of the t', went "
17 evening he cometh with the t'. "
20 It is one of the t', that dippeth "
43 spake, cometh Judas, one of the t', "
Lu 2:42 when he was t' years old, they "
6:13 of them he chose t', whom also he "
8: 1 of God: and the t' were with him, "
42 daughter, about t' years of age, "
43 having an issue of blood t' years, "
9: 1 he called his t' disciples together, "
12 then came the t', and said unto "
17 that remained to them t' baskets. "
18:31 Then he took unto him the t', and "
22: 3 being of the number of the t'. "
14 and the t' apostles with him. * "
30 judging the t' tribes of Israel. "
47 one of the t', went before them, "
Joh 6:13 filled t' baskets with the fragments "
67 Then said Jesus unto the t', Will ye "
70 Have not I chosen you t', and one "
71 betray him, being one of the t'. "
11: 9 Are there not t' hours in the day? "
20:24 But Thomas, one of the t', called "
Ac 6: 2 Then the t' called the multitude of "
7: 8 and Jacob begat the t' patriarchs. "
19: 7 And all the men were about t'. 1177
24:11 yet but t' days since I went up to "
26: 7 Unto which promise our t' tribes, 1429
1Co 15: 5 seen of Cephas, then of the t': 1427
Jas 1: 1 to the t' tribes which are scattered "
Re 7: 5 of Juda were sealed t' thousand. "
5 of Reuben were sealed t' thousand. "
5 of Gad were sealed t' thousand. "
6 of Aser were sealed t' thousand. "
6 Nepthalim were sealed t' thousand. "
6 Manasses were sealed t' thousand. "
7 of Simeon were sealed t' thousand. "
7 of Levi were sealed t' thousand. "
7 Issachar were sealed t' thousand. "
8 of Zabulon were sealed t' thousand. "
8 of Joseph were sealed t' thousand. "
8 Benjamin were sealed t' thousand. "
12: 1 upon her head a crown of t' stars: "
21:12 great and high, and had t' gates, "
12 at the gates t' angels, and names "

Re 21:12 of the t' tribes of the children of 1427
14 wall of the city had t' foundations, "
14 the names of the t' apostles of the "
16 with the reed, t' thousand furlongs. "
21 the t' gates were t' pearls; every "
22: 2 life, which bare t' manner of fruits, "

twelve-hundred See TWELVE and HUNDRED.

twelve-thousand See TWELVE and THOUSAND.

twentieth
Ge 8:14 the seven and t' day of the month, 6242
Ex 12:18 the one and t' day of the month at "
Nu 10:11 on the t' day of the second month, "
1Ki 15: 9 t' year of Jeroboam king of Israel "
2Ki 12: 6 three and t' year of king Jehoash "
13: 1 In the three and t' year of Joash the "
15:30 t' year of Jotham the son of Uzziah. "
25:27 the seven and t' day of the month, "
1Ch 24:16 to Pethahiah, the t' to Jehezekel, "
17 The one and t' to Jachin, the two "
17 to Jachin, the two and t' to Gamul, "
18 The three and t' to Delaiah, the "
18 the four and t' to Maaziah. "
25:27 The t' to Eliathah, he, his sons, "
28 The one and t' to Hothir, he, his "
29 The two and t' to Giddalti, he, his "
30 The three and t' to Mahazioth, he, "
31 The four and t' to Romamti-ezer, "
2Ch 7:10 and t' day of the seventh month "
Ezr 10: 9 on the t' day of the month; "
Ne 1: 1 the month Chisleu, in the t' year, "
2: 1 in the t' year of Artaxerxes the "
5:14 from the t' year even unto the two "
Es 8: 9 on the three and t' day thereof; "
Jer 25: 3 day, that is the three and t' year, * "
52:30 and t' year of Nebuchadrezzar "
31 in the five and t' day of the month, "
Eze 29:17 to pass in the seven and t' year, "
40: 1 five and t' year of our captivity, "
Da 10: 4 four and t' day of the first month, "
Hag 1:15 and t' day of the sixth month, "
2: 1 in the one and t' day of the month, "
10, 18 and t' day of the ninth month, "
20 four and t' day of the ninth month, "
Zec 1: 7 and t' day of the eleventh month, "

twenty See also TWENTY'S.
Ge 6: 3 shall be an hundred and t' years. 6242
11:24 And Nahor lived nine and t' years, "
18:31 there shall be t' found there. "
23: 1 hundred and seven and t' years old: "
31:38 t' years have I been with thee; thy "
41 have I been t' years in thy house; I "
32:14 hundred she goats, and t' he goats, "
14 two hundred ewes, and t' rams, "
15 bulls, t' she asses, and ten foals. "
37:28 Ishmeelites for t' pieces of silver: "
Ex 26: 2 curtain shall be eight and t' cubits, "
18 t' boards on the south side "
19 of silver under the t' boards; "
20 north side there shall be t' boards: "
27:10 And the t' pillars thereof and their "
10 their t' sockets shall be of brass; "
11 his t' pillars and their t' sockets of "
16 shall be an hanging of t' cubits, "
30:13 (a shekel is t' gerahs:) an half "
14 from t' years old and above, shall "
36: 9 one curtain was t' and eight cubits, "
23 t' boards for the south side "
24 he made under the t' boards; two "
25 north corner, he made t' boards, "
38:10 Their pillars were t', "
10 and their brasen sockets t'; "
11 their pillars were t', "
11 and their sockets of brass t'; "
18 t' cubits was the length, and the "
24 the offering, was t' and nine talents, "
26 from t' years old and upward, "
Le 27: 3 male from t' years old even unto "
5 years old even unto t' years old, "
5 shall be of the male t' shekels, "
25 t' gerahs shall be the shekel. "
Nu 1: 3 From t' years old and upward, all "
18, 20, 22, 24, 26, 28, 30, 32, 34, 36, 38, 40,
42, 45 from t' years old and upward, 6242
3:39 upward, were t' and two thousand. "
43 t' and two thousand two hundred "
47 them: (the shekel is t' gerahs:) "
7:86 was an hundred and t' shekels. "
88 were t' and four bullocks, the "
8:24 t' and five years old and upward "
11:19 days, neither ten days, nor t' days; "
14:29 from t' years old and upward, "
18:16 the sanctuary, which is t' gerahs. "
25: 9 plague were t' and four thousand. "
26: 2 from t' years old and upward, "
4 from t' years old and upward; "
14 t' and two thousand and two "
62 of them were t' and three thousand, "
32:11 from t' years old and upward, "
33:39 an hundred and t' and three years "
De 31: 2 I am an hundred and t' years old "
34: 7 hundred and t' years old when he "
Jos 15:32 all the cities are t' and nine, with "
19:30 t' and two cities with their villages. "
J'g 4: 3 t' years he mightily oppressed the "
7: 3 of the people t' and two thousand; "
8:10 hundred and t' thousand men that "
10: 2 he judged Israel t' and three years, "
3 and judged Israel t' and two years. "
11:33 come to Minneth, even t' cities, "
15:20 the days of the Philistines t' years. "
16:31 And he judged Israel t' years. "
20:15 t' and six thousand men that drew "
21 that day t' and two thousand men. "
35 t' and five thousand and an hundred "

J'g 20:46 t' and five thousand men that drew 6242
1Sa 7: 2 time was long; for it was t' years: "
14:14 was about t' men, within as it were "
2Sa 3:20 to David to Hebron, and t' men "
8: 4 and t' thousand footmen: "
5 Syrians two and t' thousand men. "
9:10 had fifteen sons and t' servants. "
10: 6 of Zoba, t' thousand footmen, "
18: 7 slaughter that day of t' thousand "
19:17 sons and his t' servants with him; "
21:20 six toes, four and t' in number; "
24: 8 end of nine months and t' days. "
1Ki 4:23 and t' oxen out of the pastures, "
5:11 gave Hiram t' thousand measures "
11 and t' measures of pure oil: "
6: 2 and the breadth thereof t' cubits, "
3 t' cubits was the length thereof, "
16 he built t' cubits on the sides of "
20 forepart was t' cubits in length, "
20 and t' cubits in breadth, "
20 t' cubits in the height thereof: and "
8:63 Lord, two and t' thousand oxen, "
63 an hundred and t' thousand sheep. "
9:10 came to pass at the end of t' years, "
11 king Solomon gave Hiram t' cities "
28 gold, four hundred and t' talents, "
10:10 an hundred and t' talents of gold, "
14:20 reigned were two and t' years: "
15:33 Israel in Tirzah, t' and four years. "
16: 8 the t' and sixth year of Asa king of "
10, 15 t' and seventh year of Asa king "
29 Israel in Samaria t' and two years. "
20:30 there a wall fell upon t' and seven "
22:42 and he reigned t' and five years in "
2Ki 4:42 of the firstfruits, t' loaves of barley, "
8:26 Two and t' years old was Ahaziah "
10:36 in Samaria was t' and eight years. "
14: 2 He was t' and five years old when "
2 t' and nine years in Jerusalem. "
15: 1 t' and seventh year of Jeroboam "
27 in Samaria, and reigned t' years. "
33 Five and t' years old was he when "
16: 2 T' years old was Ahaz when he "
18: 2 T' and five years old was he when "
2 he reigned t' and nine years in "
21:19 Amon was t' and two years old "
23:31 Jehoahaz was t' and three years "
36 Jehoiakim was t' and five years "
24:18 Zedekiah was t' and one years old "
1Ch 2:22 and t' cities in the land of Gilead. "
7: 2 and t' thousand and six hundred. "
7 t' and two thousand and thirty and "
9 was t' thousand and two hundred. "
40 was t' and six thousand men. "
12:28 father's house t' and two captains. "
30 of Ephraim t' thousand and eight "
35 war t' and eight thousand and six "
37 battle, an hundred and t' thousand. "
15: 5 his brethren an hundred and t': "
6 his brethren two hundred and t': "
18: 4 and t' thousand footmen: "
5 Syrians two and t' thousand men. "
20: 6 fingers and toes were four and t', "
23: 4 t' and four thousand were to set "
24 from the age of t' years and upward. "
27 were numbered from t' years old "
27: 1, 2 course were t' and four thousand. "
4 course...were t' and four thousand. "
5, 7, 8, 9, 10, 11, 12, 13, 14, 15 course
were t' and four thousand. 6242
23 them from t' years old and under: "
2Ch 2:10 t' thousand measures of...wheat, "
10 t' thousand measures of barley, "
10 and t' thousand baths of wine, "
10 and t' thousand baths of oil. "
3: 3 cubits, and the breadth t' cubits. "
4 the breadth of the house, t' cubits, "
4 the height was an hundred and t': "
8 the breadth of the house, t' cubits, "
8 and the breadth thereof t' cubits: "
11 the cherubims were t' cubits long: "
13 spread themselves forth t' cubits: "
4: 1 brass, t' cubits the length thereof, "
1 t' cubits the breadth thereof, and "
5:12 an hundred and t' priests sounding "
7: 5 of t' and two thousand oxen, and "
5 an hundred and t' thousand sheep: "
8: 1 came to pass at the end of t' years, "
9: 9 an hundred and t' talents of gold, "
11:21 and begat t' and eight sons, and "
13:21 and begat t' and two sons, and "
20:31 and he reigned t' and five years in "
25: 1 Amaziah was t' and five years old "
1 he reigned t' and nine years in "
5 them from t' years old and above, "
27: 1 Jotham was t' and five years old "
8 He was five and t' years old when "
28: 1 Ahaz was t' years old when he "
6 an hundred and t' thousand in one "
29: 1 when he was five and t' years old, "
1 nine and t' years in Jerusalem. "
31:17 Levites...t' years old and upward, "
33:21 Amon was two and t' years old "
36: 2 Jehoahaz was t' and three years "
5 Jehoiakim was t' and five years "
11 Zedekiah was one and t' years old "
Ezr 1: 9 of silver, nine and t' knives, "
2:11 of Bebai, six hundred t' and three. "
12 thousand two hundred t' and two. "
17 Bezai, three hundred t' and three. "
19 Hashum, two hundred t' and three. "
21 Beth-lehem, an hundred t' and three. "
23 Anathoth, an hundred t' and eight. "
26 and Gaba, six hundred t' and one. "
27 Michmas, an hundred t' and two. "
28 and Ai, two hundred t' and three. "

Ezr 2:32 of Harim, three hundred and t'. 6242
33 and Ono, seven hundred t' and five. "
41 of Asaph, an hundred t' and eight. "
67 six thousand seven hundred and t'. "
3: 8 Levites,...t' years old and upward, "
8:11 and with him t' and eight males. "
19 his brethren and their sons, t'; "
20 two hundred and t' Nethinims: "
27 t' basons of gold, of a thousand "
Ne 6:15 was finished in the t' and fifth day "
7:16 of Bebai, six hundred t' and eight. "
17 two thousand three hundred t' and "
22 Hashum, three hundred t' and eight. "
23 Bezai, three hundred t' and four. "
27 Anathoth, an hundred t' and eight. "
30 and Gaba, six hundred t' and one. "
31 an hundred and t' and two. "
32 and Ai, an hundred t' and three. "
35 of Harim, three hundred and t'. "
37 and Ono, seven hundred t' and one. "
69 seven hundred and t' asses. "
71 work t' thousand drams of gold, 7239
72 was t' thousand drams of gold, "
9: 1 t' and fourth day of this month 6242
11: 8 Sallai, nine hundred t' and eight. "
12 were eight hundred t' and two: "
14 valour, an hundred t' and eight: "
Es 1: 1 and seven and t' provinces:) "
8: 9 an hundred t' and seven provinces, "
9:30 hundred t' and seven provinces of "
Ps 68:17 chariots of God are t' thousand, 7239
Jer 52: 1 Zedekiah was one and t' years old 6242
28 thousand Jews and three and t': "
Eze 4:10 shall be by weight, t' shekels a day: "
8:16 were about five and t' men, with "
11: 1 door of the gate five and t' men; "
40:13 the breadth was five and t' cubits, "
21, 25 the breadth five and t' cubits. "
29 long, and five and t' cubits broad. "
30 about were five and t' cubits long, "
33 long, and five and t' cubits broad. "
36 and the breadth five and t' cubits. "
49 length of the porch was t' cubits, "
41: 2 cubits, and the breadth, t' cubits. "
4 the length thereof, t' cubits; "
4 the breadth, t' cubits, before the "
10 of t' cubits round about the house "
42: 3 the t' cubits which were for the "
45: 1 length of five and t' thousand reeds, "
3 the length of five and t' thousand, "
5 the five and t' thousand of length, "
5 for a possession for t' chambers. "
6 and five and t' thousand long, over "
12 And the shekel shall be t' gerahs: "
12 t' shekels, five and t' shekels, "
48: 8 of five and t' thousand reeds in "
9 of five and t' thousand in length, "
10 the north five and t' thousand "
10 the south five and t' thousand "
13 have five and t' thousand in length, "
13 length shall be five and t' thousand, "
15 against the five and t' thousand, "
20 shall be five and t' thousand "
20 by five and t' thousand: "
21, 21 against the five and t' thousand "
Da 6: 1 an hundred and t' princes, 6243
10:13 withstood me one and t' days: 6242
Hag 2:16 one came to an heap of t' measures, "
16 out of the press, there were but t'. "
Zec 5: 2 the length thereof is t' cubits, and "
Lu 14:31 against him with t' thousand? 1501
Joh 6:19 about five and t' or thirty furlongs, "
Ac 1:15 were about an hundred and t',) "
27:28 sounded, and found it t' fathoms: "
1Co 10: 8 in one day three and t' thousand. "
Re 4: 4 the throne were four and t' seats: "
4 I saw four and t' elders sitting, "
10 The four and t' elders fall down "
5: 8 the four and t' elders fell down "
14 the four and t' elders fell down * "
11:16 four and t' elders, which sat before "
19: 4 the four and t' elders and the four "

twenty's
Ge 18:31 I will not destroy it for t' sake. 6242

twenty-thousand See TWENTY and THOUSAND.

twice
Ge 41:32 was doubled unto Pharaoh t'; 6471
Ex 16: 5 t' as much as they gather daily. 4932
22 they gathered t' as much bread, "
Nu 20:11 with his rod he smote the rock t': 6471
1Sa 18:11 avoided out of his presence t'. "
1Ki 11: 9 which had appeared unto him t', "
2Ki 6:10 saved himself...not once nor t'. 8147
Ne 13:20 without Jerusalem once or t'. "
Job 33:14 For God speaketh once, yea t', yet "
40: 5 Once have I spoken;...yea, t'; but I "
42:10 gave Job t' as much as he had 4932
Ps 62:11 t' have I heard this; that power 8147
Ec 6: 6 he live a thousand years t' told, 6471
M'r 14:30 before the cock crow t', thou shalt 1364
72 Before the cock crow t', thou shalt "
Lu 18:12 I fast t' in the week, I give tithes of "
Jude 12 without fruit, t' dead, plucked up "

twigs
Eze 17: 4 cropped off the top of his young t', 3242
22 off from the top of his young t' a 3127

twilight
1Sa 30:17 David smote them from the t' 5399
2Ki 7: 5 they rose up in the t', to go unto "
7 they arose and fled in the t', and "
Job 3: 9 the stars of the t' thereof be dark; "
24:15 of the adulterer waiteth for the t', "
Pr 7: 9 In the t', in the evening, in the "
Eze 12: 6 and carry it forth in the t': *5939

Eze 12: 7 I brought it forth in the t', and I *5939
12 bear upon his shoulder in the t', * "

twined

Ex 26: 1 with ten curtains of fine t' linen, 7806
31 and fine t' linen of cunning work: "
36 and scarlet, and fine t' linen, "
27: 9 shall be hangings...of fine t' linen "
16 and scarlet, and fine t' linen, "
18 height five cubits of fine t' linen, "
28: 6 of scarlet, and fine t' linen, with "
8 and scarlet, and fine t' linen. "
15 of scarlet, of fine t' linen, shalt thou"
36: 8 made ten curtains of fine t' linen, "
35 and scarlet, and fine t' linen: "
37 and scarlet, and fine t' linen, of "
38: 9 of the court were of fine t' linen, "
16 round about were of fine t' linen. "
18 and scarlet, and fine t' linen: "
39: 2 and scarlet, and fine t' linen. "
5 and scarlet, and fine t' linen; "
8 and scarlet, and fine t' linen. "
24 purple, and scarlet, and t' linen. "
28 and linen breeches of fine t' linen, "
29 And a girdle of fine t' linen, and blue, "

twinkling

1Co 15: 52 In a moment, in the t' of an eye, 4493

twins

Ge 25: 24 behold, there were t' in her womb. 8380
38: 27 that, behold, t' were in her womb. "
Ca 4: 2 whereof every one bear t', and 8382
5 like two young roes that are t', 8380
6: 6 whereof every one beareth t', and 8382
7: 3 like two young roes that are t'. 8380

two See also TWAIN; TWOEDGED; TWOFOLD.

Ge 1: 16 And God made t' great lights; 8147
4: 19 Lamech took unto him t' wives: "
5: 18 lived an hundred sixty and t' years, "
20 nine hundred sixty and t' years: "
26 seven hundred eighty and t' years, "
28 an hundred eighty and t' years, "
6: 19 t' of every sort shalt thou bring "
20 t' of every sort shall come unto "
7: 2 of beasts that are not clean by t', "
9 There went in t' and t' unto Noah "
15 into the ark, t' and t' of all flesh, "
9: 22 and told his t' brethren without. "
10: 25 And unto Eber were born t' sons: "
11: 20 And Reu lived t' and thirty years, "
19: 1 And there came t' angels to Sodom "
8 I have t' daughters which have not "
15 take thy wife, and thy t' daughters, "
16 upon the hand of his t' daughters; "
30 and his t' daughters with him; "
30 in a cave, he and his t' daughters. "
22: 3 took t' of his young men with him, "
24: 22 and t' bracelets for her hands of ten "
25: 23 her, T' nations are in thy womb, "
23 and t' manner of people shall be "
27: 9 fetch me from thence t' good kids "
36 hath supplanted me these t' times: 6471
29: 16 Laban had t' daughters: the name 8147
31: 33 into the t' maidservants' tents; "
41 fourteen years for thy t' daughters, "
32: 7 herds, and the camels, into t' bands; "
10 and now I am become t' bands. "
14 T' hundred she goats, and twenty he "
14 t' hundred ewes, and twenty rams, "
22 that night, and took his t' wives, 8147
22 and his t' womenservants, and "
33: 1 Rachel, and unto the t' handmaids. "
34: 25 that t' of the sons of Jacob, Simeon "
40: 2 was wroth against t' of his officers, "
41: 1 to pass at the end of t' full years, that "
50 And unto Joseph were born t' sons 8147
42: 37 Slay my t' sons, if I bring him not "
44: 27 know that my wife bare me t' sons: "
45: 6 these t' years hath the famine been in "
46: 27 born him in Egypt, were t' souls: 8147
48: 1 and he took with him his t' sons, "
5 thy t' sons, Ephraim and Manasseh, "
49: 14 couching down between t' burdens: *
Ex 2: 13 t' men of the Hebrews strove 8147
4: 9 will not believe also these t' signs, "
12: 7 and strike it on the t' side posts "
22 and the t' side posts with the blood "
23 the lintel, and on the t' side posts, "
16: 22 much bread, t' omers for one man: "
29 on the sixth day the bread of t' days; "
18: 3 her t' sons; of which the name of 8147
6 thy wife, and her t' sons with her. "
21: 21 if he continue a day or t', he shall not
25: 10 t' cubits and a half shall be the length
12 t' rings shall be in the one side of 8147
12 and t' rings in the other side of it. "
17 t' cubits and a half shall be the length
18 shalt make t' cherubims of gold, 8147
18 in the t' ends of the mercy seat. "
19 cherubims on the t' ends thereof. "
22 from between the t' cherubims "
23 t' cubits shall be the length thereof,
35, 35, 35 a knop under t' branches of 8147
26: 17 T' tenons shall there be in one "
19 boards; t' sockets under one board "
19 under one board for his t' tenons, "
19 and t' sockets under another board "
19 another board for his t' tenons. "
21 silver; t' sockets under one board, "
21 and t' sockets under another board. "
23 t' boards shalt thou make for the "
23 of the tabernacle in the t' sides. *
24 they shall be for the t' corners. 8147
25 t' sockets under one board, "
25 and t' sockets under another board. "
27 tabernacle, for the t' sides westward. *

Ex 27: 7 be upon the t' sides of the altar, 8147
28: 7 It shall have the t' shoulderpieces "
7 joined at the t' edges thereof; "
9 And thou shalt take t' onyx stones, "
11 engrave the t' stones with the "
12 the t' stones upon the shoulders of "
12 upon his t' shoulders for a "
14 t' chains of pure gold at the ends; "
23 the breastplate t' rings of gold, "
23 put the t' rings on the t' ends of the "
24 put the t' wreathen chains of gold "
24 the t' rings which are on the ends "
25 t' ends of the t' wreathen chains "
25 thou shalt fasten in the t' ouches, "
26 thou shalt make t' rings of gold, "
26 put them upon the t' ends of the "
27 t' other rings of gold thou shalt "
27 them on the t' sides of the ephod "
29: 1 and t' rams without blemish, "
3 with the bullock and the t' rams. "
13, 22 the t' kidneys, and the fat that "
38 t' lambs of the first year day by day "
30: 2 t' cubits shall be the height thereof:
4 t' golden rings shalt thou make to 8147
4 of it, by the t' corners thereof, "
4 upon the t' sides of it shalt thou "
23 even t' hundred and fifty shekels,
23 calamus t' hundred and fifty shekels,
31: 18 t' tables of testimony, tables of 8147
32: 15 the t' tables of the testimony were "
34: 1 Hew thee t' tables of stone like "
4 he hewed t' tables of stone like "
4 in his hand the t' tables of stone. "
29 with the t' tables of testimony in "
36: 22 One board had t' tenons, equally "
24 boards; t' sockets under one board "
24 under one board for his t' tenons, "
24 t' sockets under another board for "
24 another board for his t' tenons. "
26 silver; t' sockets under one board, "
26 and t' sockets under another board. "
28 t' boards made he for the corners of "
28 of the tabernacle in the t' sides. *
30 under every board t' sockets. 8147
37: 1 t' cubits and a half was the length of
3 even t' rings upon the one side of 8147
3 t' rings upon the other side of it. "
6 t' cubits and a half was the length
7 And he made t' cherubims of gold, 8147
7 on the t' ends of the mercy seat; "
8 the cherubims on the t' ends "
10 t' cubits was the length thereof,
21, 21, 21 a knop under t' branches of 8147
25 and t' cubits was the height of it;
27 And he made t' rings of gold for it 8147
27 crown thereof, by the t' corners of "
27 upon the t' sides thereof, to be "
38: 29 t' thousand and four hundred shekels.
39: 4 by the t' edges was it coupled 8147
16 t' ouches of gold, and t' gold rings; "
16 put the t' rings in the t' ends of the "
17 they put the t' wreathen chains of "
17 in the t' rings on the ends of the "
18 t' ends of the t' wreathen chains "
18 they fastened in the t' ouches, "
19 And they made t' rings of gold, "
19 on the t' ends of the breastplate, "
20 they made t' other golden rings, "
20 them on the t' sides of the ephod "
Le 3: 4, 10, 15 the t' kidneys, and the fat "
4: 9 the t' kidneys, and the fat that is "
5: 7, 11 t' turtledoves, or t' young pigeons, "
7: 4 the t' kidneys, and the fat that is "
8: 2 t' rams, and a basket of unleavened "
16 and the t' kidneys, and their fat, "
25 and the t' kidneys, and their fat, "
12: 5 she shall be unclean t' weeks, as in
8 t' turtles, or t' young pigeons; 8147
14: 4 cleansed t' birds alive and clean, "
10 he shall take t' he lambs without "
22 t' turtledoves, or t' young pigeons, "
49 take to cleanse the house t' birds, "
15: 14 t' turtledoves, or t' young pigeons, "
29 her t' turtles, or t' young pigeons, "
16: 1 after the death of the t' sons of "
5 t' kids of the goats for a sin "
7 And he shall take the t' goats, and "
8 shall cast lots upon the t' goats; "
23: 13 t' tenth deals of fine floor mingled "
17 t' wave loaves of t' tenth deals: "
18 one young bullock, and t' rams: "
19 t' lambs of the first year for a "
20 before the Lord, with the t' lambs: "
24: 5 t' tenth deals shall be in one cake. "
6 And thou shalt set them in t' rows, "
Nu 1: 35 were thirty and t' thousand "
35 thousand and t' hundred.
39 t' thousand and seven hundred. 8147
2: 21 were thirty and t' thousand "
21 thousand and t' hundred.
26 t' thousand and seven hundred. 8147
3: 34 were six thousand and t' hundred.
39 were twenty and t' thousand. 8147
43 were twenty and t' thousand "
43 t' hundred and threescore and
46 be redeemed of the t' hundred and
4: 36 were t' thousand seven hundred and
40 were t' thousand and six hundred and
44 were three thousand and t' hundred.
6: 10 t' turtles, or t' young pigeons, 8147
7: 3 a wagon for t' of the princes, and "
7 T' wagons and four oxen he gave "
17, 23, 29, 35, 41, 47, 53, 59, 65, 71, 77,
83 offerings, t' oxen, five rams, 8147
85 silver vessels weighed t' thousand and
89 from between the t' cherubims: 8147

Nu 9: 22 Or whether it were t' days, or a
10: 2 Make thee t' trumpets of silver; of 8147
11: 19 shall not eat one day, nor t' days,
26 there remained t' of the men in 8147
31 it were t' cubits high upon the face of
13: 23 bare it between t' upon a staff; 8147
15: 6 offering t' tenth deals of flour "
16: 2 t' hundred and fifty princes of the
17 t' hundred and fifty censers;
35 the t' hundred and fifty men that
22: 22 and his t' servants were with him. 8147
26: 10 devoured t' hundred and fifty men:
14 twenty and t' thousand and 8147
14 thousand and t' hundred.
34 t' thousand and seven hundred. 8147
37 and t' thousand and five hundred. "
28: 3, 9 t' lambs of the first year without "
9 t' tenth deals of flour for a meat "
11 t' young bullocks, and one ram, "
12 t' tenth deals of flour for a meat "
19 t' young bullocks, and one ram, and "
20 and t' tenth deals for a ram; "
27 t' young bullocks, one ram, seven "
28 t' tenth deals unto one ram, "
29: 3 and t' tenth deals for a ram, "
9 and t' tenth deals to one ram, "
13 t' rams, and fourteen lambs of the "
14 t' tenth deals to each ram of the "
14 deals to each ram of the t' rams, "
17 twelve young bullocks, t' rams, "
20 third day eleven bullocks, t' rams, "
23 fourth day ten bullocks, t' rams, "
26 the fifth day nine bullocks, t' rams, "
29 sixth day eight bullocks, t' rams, "
32 day seven bullocks, t' rams, "
31: 35 and t' thousand persons in all, "
40 tribute was thirty and t' persons. "
34: 15 The t' tribes and the half tribe have "
35: 5 on the east side t' thousand cubits, "
5 the south side t' thousand cubits, "
5 on the west side t' thousand cubits, "
5 the north side t' thousand cubits; "
6 ye shall add forty and t' cities. 8147
De 3: 8 out of the hand of the t' kings "
21 God hath done unto these t' kings: "
4: 13 wrote them upon t' tables of stone. "
47 Bashan, t' kings of the Amorites, "
5: 22 he wrote them in t' tables of stone, "
9: 10 delivered unto me t' tables of stone "
11 Lord gave me the t' tables of stone, "
15 and the t' tables of the covenant "
15 were in my t' hands. "
17 I took the t' tables, and cast them "
17 cast them out of my t' hands, and "
10: 1 Hew thee t' tables of stone like unto "
3 hewed t' tables of stone like unto "
3 having the t' tables in mine hand. "
14: 6 and cleaveth the cleft into t' claws, "
17: 6 At the mouth of t' witnesses, or "
19: 15 at the mouth of t' witnesses, or at "
21: 15 If a man have t' wives, one beloved, "
32: 30 and t' put ten thousand to flight, "
Jos 2: 1 sent out of Shittim t' men to spy "
4 And the woman took the t' men, "
10 unto the t' kings of the Amorites, "
23 So the t' men returned, and "
3: 4 t' thousand cubits by measure: "
6: 22 the t' men that had spied out the 8147
7: 3 let about t' or three thousand men go
9: 10 to the t' kings of the Amorites, 8147
14: 3 given the inheritance of t' tribes "
4 children of Joseph were t' tribes, "
15: 60 t' cities with their villages. "
19: 30 twenty and t' cities with their "
21: 16 nine cities out of those t' tribes. "
25, 27 with her suburbs; t' cities. "
24: 12 even the t' kings of the Amorites; "
J'g 3: 16 him a dagger which had t' edges, "
5: 30 prey; to every man a damsel or t'; "
7: 3 the people twenty and t' thousand; 8147
25 took t' princes of the Midianites, "
8: 12 and took the t' kings of Midian, "
9: 44 t' other companies ran upon all the "
10: 3 judged Israel twenty and t' years. "
11: 37 let me alone t' months, that I may "
38 and he sent her away for t' months: "
39 came to pass at the end of t' months, "
12: 6 Ephraimites forty and t' thousand. "
15: 4 put a firebrand...between t' tails. "
13 they bound him with t' new cords, "
16: 3 the gate of the city, and the t' posts, "
28 of the Philistines for my t' eyes, "
29 Samson took hold of the t' middle "
17: 4 took t' hundred shekels of silver,
19: 10 were with him t' asses saddled, *6771
20: 21 day twenty and t' thousand men. 8147
45 and slew t' thousand men of them.
Ru 1: 1 he, and his wife, and his t' sons. 8147
2 the name of his t' sons Mahlon and "
3 and she was left, and her t' sons. "
5 the woman was left of her t' sons "
7 her t' daughters in law with her; "
8 said unto her t' daughters in law, "
19 So they t' went until they came to "
4: 11 t' did build the house of Israel: "
1Sa 1: 2 he had t' wives; the name of the "
3 And the t' sons of Eli, Hophni and "
2: 21 bare three sons and t' daughters. "
34 that shall come upon thy t' sons, "
4: 4, 11 the t' sons of Eli, Hophni and "
17 and thy t' sons also, Hophni and "
6: 7 take t' milch kine, on which there "
10 took t' milch kine, and tied them "
10: 2 thou shalt find t' men by Rachel's "
4 and give thee t' loaves of bread; "
11: 11 t' of them were not left together. "

1Sa 13: 1 when he had reigned t' years over 8147
2 t' thousand were with Saul in
14: 49 names of his t' daughters were 8147
15: 4 t' hundred thousand footmen, and
18: 27 slew of the Philistines t' hundred men;
23: 18 they t' made a covenant before 8147
25: 13 and t' hundred abode by the stuff.
18 haste, and took t' hundred loaves,
18 t' bottles of wine, and five sheep 8147
18 t' hundred cakes of figs, and laid them
27: 3 David with his t' wives, Ahinoam 8147
28: 8 and he went, and t' men with him, "
30: 5 And David's t' wives were taken "
10 t' hundred abode behind, which were
12 of figs, and t' clusters of raisins: 8147
18 and David rescued his t' wives. "
21 David came to the t' hundred men,
2Sa 1: 1 David...abode t' days in Ziklag; 8147
2: 2 up thither, and his t' wives also, "
10 over Israel, and reigned t' years. "
4: 2 Saul's son had t' men that were "
8: 2 even with t' lines measured he to "
5 the Syrians t' and twenty thousand "
12: 1 There were t' men in one city; the "
13: 23 it came to pass after t' full years,
14: 6 And thy handmaid had t' sons, 8147
6 and they t' strove together in the "
28 dwelt t' full years in Jerusalem,
15: 11 with Absalom went t' hundred men
27 peace, and your t' sons with you, 8147
36 have there with them their t' sons, "
16: 1 upon them t' hundred loaves of bread,
18: 24 David sat between the t' gates: 8147
21: 8 the king took the t' sons of Rizpah "
23: 20 he slew t' lionlike men of Moab: "
1Ki 2: 5 what he did to the t' captains of "
32 fell upon t' men more righteous "
39 t' of the servants of Shimei ran "
3: 16 Then came there t' women, that "
18 the house, save we t' in the house. "
25 said, Divide the living child in t', "
5: 12 and they t' made a league together. "
14 Lebanon, and t' months at home: "
6: 23 the oracle he made t' cherubims "
32 The t' doors also were of olive tree; "
34 And the t' doors were of fir tree: "
34 the t' leaves of the one door were "
34 the t' leaves of the other door were "
7: 15 For he cast t' pillars of brass, of "
16 made t' chapiters of molten brass, "
18 t' rows round about upon the one "
20 the chapiters upon the t' pillars "
20 the pomegranates were t' hundred in
24 the knops were cast in t' rows, 8147
26 it contained t' thousand baths.
41 The t' pillars, and the 8147
41 the t' bowls of the chapiters that "
41 were on top of the t' pillars; *8147
41 t' networks, to cover the t' bowls "
42 pomegranates for the t' networks, "
42 t' rows of pomegranates for one "
42 cover the t' bowls of the chapiters "
8: 7 spread forth their t' wings over *
9 the ark save the t' tables of stone, 8147
63 t' and twenty thousand oxen, and "
9: 10 Solomon had built the t' houses, "
10: 16 king Solomon made t' hundred targets
19 and t' lions stood beside the stays. 8147
11: 29 and they t' were alone in the field: "
12: 28 counsel, and made t' calves of gold, "
20 reigned were t' and twenty years: "
15: 25 and reigned over Israel t' years. "
16: 8 to reign over Israel in Tirzah, t' years,
21 of Israel divided into t' parts: 2677
24 of Shemer for t' talents of silver,
29 in Samaria twenty and t' years. 8147
17: 12 I am gathering t' sticks, that I "
18: 21 long halt ye between t' opinions? "
23 them therefore give us t' bullocks; "
32 would contain t' measures of seed.
20: 1 were thirty and t' kings with him, 8147
15 and they were t' hundred
15 hundred and thirty t': 8147
16 the thirty and t' kings that helped "
27 them the t' little flocks of kids; "
21: 10 set t' men, sons of Belial, before "
13 there came in t' men, children of "
22: 31 his thirty and t' captains that had "
51 and reigned t' years over Israel.
2Ki 1: 14 burnt up the t' captains of the 8147
2: 6 leave thee. And they t' went on. "
7 off: and they t' stood by Jordan. "
8 they t' went over on dry ground. "
12 clothes, and rent them in t' pieces. "
24 forth t' she bears out of the wood, "
24 tare forty and t' children of them. "
4: 1 come to take unto him my t' sons "
5: 17 servant t' mules' burden of earth? "
22 mount Ephraim t' young men of 8147
22 silver, and t' changes of garments. "
23 said, Be content, take t' talents.
23 bound t' talents of silver in t' bags, 8147
23 with t' changes of garments, and "
23 laid them upon t' of his servants; "
7: 1 t' measures of barley for a shekel, in
14 took therefore t' chariot horses; 8147
16 and t' measures of barley for a shekel,
18 T' measures of barley for a shekel,
8: 17 Thirty and t' years old was he 8147
26 T' and twenty years old was "
9: 32 out to him t' or three eunuchs. "
10: 4 t' kings stood not before him: "
8 Lay ye them in t' heaps at the "
14 t' and forty men; neither left he "
11: 7 t' parts of all you that go forth on "
15: 2 t' and fifty years in Jerusalem. "

2Ki 15: 27 In the t' and fiftieth year of Azariah 8147
17: 16 them molten images, even t' calves, "
18: 23 deliver thee t' thousand horses,
21: 5 t' courts of the house of the Lord. 8147
19 Amon was twenty and t' years old "
19 he reigned t' years in Jerusalem. "
23: 12 made in the t' courts of the house "
25: 16 The t' pillars, one sea, and the "
1Ch 1: 19 And unto Eber were born t' sons: "
4: 5 the father of Tekoa had t' wives, "
5: 21 of sheep t' hundred and fifty thousand,
21 of asses t' thousand, and of men an
7: 2 t' and twenty thousand and six 8147
7 twenty and t' thousand and thirty "
9 was twenty thousand and t' hundred.
11 thousand and t' hundred soldiers,
9: 22 the gates were t' hundred and twelve.
11: 21 was more honourable than the t'; 8147
22 he slew t' lionlike men of Moab: "
12: 28 house twenty and t' captains. "
32 the heads of them were t' hundred;
15: 6 his brethren t' hundred and twenty:
8 the chief, and his brethren t' hundred:
18: 5 Syrians t' and twenty thousand 8147
19: 7 thirty and t' thousand chariots, "
24: 17 the t' and twentieth to Gamul, "
25: 7 was t' hundred fourscore and eight.
29 The t' and twentieth to Giddalti, 8147
26: 8 were threescore...t' of Obed-edom. "
17 day, and toward Asuppim t' and t'. "
18 the causeway, and t' at Parbar. "
32 t' thousand and seven hundred chief
2Ch 3: 10 made t' cherubims of image work, 8147
15 he made before the house t' pillars "
4: 3 T' rows of oxen were cast, when it "
12 the t' pillars, and the pommels, and "
12 which were on the top of the t' pillars,
12 t' wreaths to cover the t' pommels 8147
13 pomegranates on the t' wreaths; "
13 t' rows of pomegranates on each "
13 to cover the t' pommels of the "
5: 10 nothing in the ark save the t' tables "
7: 5 of twenty and t' thousand oxen, "
8: 10 even t' hundred and fifty, that bare
9: 15 king Solomon made t' hundred targets
18 and t' lions standing by the stays: 8147
13: 21 and begat twenty and t' sons, and "
14: 8 drew bows, t' hundred and fourscore
17: 15 with him t' hundred and fourscore
16 t' hundred thousand mighty men of
17 bow and shield t' hundred thousand.
21: 5 Jehoram was thirty and t' years 8147
19 after the end of t' years, his bowels "
20 Thirty and t' years old was he when "
22: 2 Forty and t' years old was Ahaziah "
24: 3 And Jehoiada took for him t' wives; "
26: 3 and he reigned fifty and t' years in "
12 men of valour were t' thousand and six
28: 8 brethren t' hundred thousand,
29: 32 rams, and t' hundred lambs:
33: 5 t' courts of the house of the Lord, 8147
21 Amon was t' and twenty years old
21 and reigned t' years in Jerusalem.
35: 8 t' thousand and six hundred small
Ezr 2: 3 of Parosh, t' thousand an hundred
3 thousand an hundred seventy...t'. 8147
6 t' thousand eight hundred and twelve
7 a thousand t' hundred fifty and four
10 of Bani, six hundred forty and t'. 8147
12 a thousand t' hundred twenty
12 hundred twenty and t'. 8147
14 Bigvai, t' thousand fifty and six.
19 Hashum, t' hundred twenty and three.
24 children of Azmaveth, forty and t'. 8147
27 Michmas, an hundred twenty and t'. "
28 and Ai, t' hundred twenty and three.
29 The children of Nebo, fifty and t'. 8147
31 a thousand t' hundred fifty and four.
37 of Immer, a thousand fifty and t'. 8147
38 thousand t' hundred forty and seven.
58 were three hundred ninety and t'. 8147
60 of Nekoda, six hundred fifty and t'. "
64 and t' thousand three hundred and
65 among them t' hundred singing men
66 their mules, t' hundred forty and five;
6: 17 t' hundred rams, four hundred lambs;
8: 4 and with him t' hundred males.
9 him t' hundred and eighteen males.
20 t' hundred and twenty Nethinims:
27 and t' vessels of fine copper, 8147
10: 13 is this a work of one day or t': "
Ne 5: 14 t' and thirtieth year of Artaxerxes "
6: 15 the month Elul, in fifty and t' days. "
7: 8 t' thousand an hundred seventy...t'. "
9 three hundred seventy and t'. "
10 of Arah, six hundred fifty and t'. "
11 t' thousand and eight hundred and
12 a thousand t' hundred fifty and four.
17 of Azgad, t' thousand three 8147
17 three hundred twenty and t'. "
19 t' thousand threescore and seven.
28 of Beth-azmaveth, forty and t'. 8147
31 an hundred and twenty and t'. "
33 men of the other Nebo, fifty and t'. "
34 a thousand t' hundred fifty and four.
40 of Immer, a thousand fifty and t'. 8147
41 a thousand t' hundred forty and seven.
60 were three hundred ninety and t'. 8147
62 of Nekoda, six hundred forty and t'. "
66 together was forty and t' thousand
67 t' hundred forty and five singing men
68 their mules, t' hundred forty and five:
71 drams of gold, and t' thousand
71 and t' hundred pound of silver.
72 gold, and t' thousand pound of silver,
11: 12 were eight hundred twenty and t': 8147

Ne 11: 13 the fathers, t' hundred forty and
13 the fathers,...hundred forty and t': 8147
18 were t' hundred fourscore and four.
19 were an hundred seventy and t'. 8147
12: 31 t' great companies of them that "
40 stood the t' companies of them that "
13: 6 t' and thirtieth year of Artaxerxes "
Es 2: 21 t' of the king's chamberlains, "
6: 2 t' of the king's chamberlains, the "
9: 27 keep these t' days according to "
Job 13: 20 Only do not t' things unto me: then "
42: 7 thee and against thy t' friends: "
Pr 30: 7 T' things have I required of thee; "
15 The horseleach hath t' daughters, "
Ec 4: 9 T' are better than one; because "
11 Again, if t' lie together, then they "
12 against him, t' shall withstand him; "
Ca 4: 5 Thy t' breasts are like t' young roes "
6: 13 As it were the company of t' armies.*
7: 3 Thy t' breasts are like t' young 8147
8: 12 that keep the fruit thereof t' hundred.
Isa 7: 4 for the t' tails of these smoking 8147
21 nourish a young cow, and t' sheep; "
17: 6 t' or three berries in the top of the "
22: 11 also a ditch between the t' walls for "
36: 8 I will give thee t' thousand horses, if "
45: 1 to open before him the t' leaved gates;
47: 9 these t' things shall come to thee 8147
51: 19 These t' things are come unto thee; "
Jer 2: 13 my people have committed t' evils; "
3: 14 you one of a city, and t' of a family, "
24: 1 t' baskets of figs were set before the "
28: 3 Within t' full years will I bring again
11 within the space of t' full years.
33: 24 t' families...the Lord hath chosen, 8147
52: 20 The t' pillars, one sea, and twelve "
29 eight hundred thirty and t' persons: "
Eze 1: 11 t' wings of every one were joined "
11 and t' covered their bodies. "
23, 23 every one had t', which covered "
21: 19 son of man, appoint thee t' ways, "
21 the way, at the head of the t' ways, "
23: 2 there were t' women, the daughters "
35: 10 hast said, These t' nations and "
10 these t' countries shall be mine, "
37: 22 they shall be no more t' nations, "
22 they be divided into t' kingdoms "
40: 9 and the posts thereof, t' cubits; "
39 porch of the gate were t' tables on "
39 this side, and t' tables on that side,
40 of the north gate, were t' tables; 8147
40 porch of the gate, were t' tables. "
41: 3 the post of the door, t' cubits; "
18 and every cherub had t' faces; "
22 and the length thereof t' cubits; "
23 and the sanctuary had t' doors. "
24 And the doors had t' leaves apiece, "
24 leaves apiece, t' turning leaves; "
24 t' leaves for the one door, "
24 and t' leaves for the other door. "
43: 14 to the lower settle shall be t' cubits, "
45: 15 out of the flock, out of t' hundred,
46: 19 was a place on the t' sides westward.
47: 13 Israel: Joseph shall have t' portions.
48: 17 toward the north t' hundred and fifty,
17 toward the south t' hundred and fifty,
17 toward the east t' hundred and fifty,
17 toward the west t' hundred and fifty.
Da 5: 31 about threescore and t' years old. 8648
8: 3 the river a ram which had t' horns:
3 the t' horns were high; but one was
6 came to the ram that had t' horns,
7 the ram, and brake his t' horns: 8147
14 t' thousand and three hundred days;
20 ram...thou sawest having t' horns
9: 25 and threescore and t' weeks: 8147
26 after threescore and t' weeks shall "
12: 5 there stood other t', the one on this "
11 thousand t' hundred and ninety days.
Ho 6: 2 After t' days will he revive us: in the
10: 10 themselves in their t' furrows. 8147
Am 1: 1 Israel, t' years before the earthquake.
3: 3 Can t' walk together, except they 8147
12 out of the mouth of the lion t' legs, "
4: 8 So t' or three cities wandered unto "
Zec 4: 3 t' olive trees by it, one upon the "
11 What are these t' olive trees upon "
12 What be these t' olive branches "
12 through the t' golden pipes empty "
14 These are the t' anointed ones, "
5: 9 behold, there came out t' women, "
6: 1 out from between t' mountains; "
11: 7 And I took unto me t' staves; the "
13: 8 t' parts therein shall be cut off and "
M't 2: 16 from t' years old and under, 1332
4: 18 saw t' brethren, Simon called 1417
21 thence, he saw other t' brethren, "
6: 24 No man can serve t' masters: for "
8: 28 met him t' possessed with devils, "
9: 27 t' blind men followed him, crying, "
10: 10 neither t' coats, neither shoes, nor "
29 t' sparrows sold for a farthing? "
11: 2 Christ, he sent t' of his disciples, * "
14: 17 here but five loaves, and t' fishes. "
19 the five loaves, and the t' fishes. "
18: 8 having t' hands or t' feet to be cast "
9 having t' eyes to be cast into hell "
16 then take with thee one or t' more, "
16 the mouth of t' or three witnesses "
19 if t' of you shall agree on earth as "
20 For where t' or three are gathered "
20: 21 Grant that...my t' sons may sit, "
24 indignation against the t' brethren. "
30 t' blind men sitting by the way side, "
21: 1 Olives, then sent Jesus t' disciples, "
28 A certain man had t' sons: and he "

M't 22:40 On these *t*' commandments hang 1417
24:40 Then shall *t*' be in the field; the "
41 *T*' women shall be grinding at the "
25:15 he gave five talents, to another *t*', "
17 likewise, he that had received *t*', "
17 he also gained the other *t*'. "
22 that had received *t*' talents came "
22 thou deliveredst unto me *t*' talents: "
22 I have gained *t*' other talents "
26: 2 that after *t*' days is the feast of the "
37 Peter and the *t*' sons of Zebedee, "
60 At the last came *t*' false witnesses, "
27:38 the *t*' thieves crucified with him, "
M'r 5:13 (they were about *t*' thousand;) 1367
6: 7 to send them forth by *t*' and *t*'; 1417
9 sandals; and not put on *t*' coats. "
37 *t*' hundred pennyworth of bread, 1250
38 knew, they say, Five, and *t*' fishes. 1417
41 the five loaves and the *t*' fishes, "
41 *t*' fishes divided he among them all. "
9:43 than having *t*' hands to go into hell, "
45 having *t*' feet to be cast into hell, "
47 having *t*' eyes to be cast into hell "
11: 1 he sendeth forth *t*' of his disciples, "
4 in a place where *t*' ways met; * 296
12:42 widow, and she threw in *t*' mites, 1417
14: 1 After *t*' days was the feast of the "
13 he sendeth forth *t*' of his disciples, "
15:27 with him they crucify *t*' thieves; "
16:12 in another form unto *t*' of them, "
Lu 2:24 turtledoves, or *t*' young pigeons. "
3:11 He that hath *t*' coats, let him impart "
5: 2 saw *t*' ships standing by the lake: "
7:19 calling unto him *t*' of his disciples "
41 creditor which had *t*' debtors: "
9: 3 neither have *t*' coats apiece. "
13 more but five loaves and *t*' fishes; "
16 took the five loaves and the *t*' fishes, "
30 there talked with him *t*' men, "
32 the *t*' men that stood with him. "
10: 1 seventy others, and sent them *t*' "
1 and sent them...*t*' before his face 1417
35 he departed, he took out *t*' pence, "
12: 6 five sparrows sold for *t*' farthings, "
52 three against *t*', and *t*' against "
15:11 he said, A certain man had *t*' sons: "
16:13 No servant can serve *t*' masters: "
17:34 there shall be *t*' men in one bed; "
35 *T*' women shall be grinding "
36 *T*' men shall be in the field; the * "
18:10 *T*' men went up into the temple to "
19:29 Olives, he sent *t*' of his disciples, "
21: 2 widow casting in thither *t*' mites. "
22:38 Lord, behold, here are *t*' swords. "
23:32 there were also *t*' other, malefactors, "
24: 4 *t*' men stood by them in shining "
13 *t*' of them went that same day to a "
Joh 1:35 John stood, and *t*' of his disciples; "
37 the *t*' disciples heard him speak, "
40 One of the *t*' which heard John "
2: 6 containing *t*' or three firkins apiece. "
4:40 them: and he abode there *t*' days. "
43 after *t*' days he departed thence, "
6: 7 *T*' hundred pennyworth of bread 1250
9 barley loaves, and *t*' small fishes: 1417
8:17 that the testimony of *t*' men is true. "
Joh 11: 6 he abode *t*' days still in the same 1417
19:18 crucified him, and *t*' other with him, "
20:12 And seeth *t*' angels in white sitting, "
21: 2 and *t*' other of his disciples. "
8 but as it were *t*' hundred cubits,) 1250
Ac 1:10 *t*' men stood by them in white 1417
23 they appointed *t*', Joseph called "
24 of these *t*' thou hast chosen, "
7:29 of Madian, where he begat *t*' sons. "
9:38 they sent unto him *t*' men, desiring "
10: 7 called *t*' of his household servants, "
12: 6 was sleeping between *t*' soldiers, "
6 bound with *t*' chains: and the "
19:10 continued by the space of *t*' years; "
22 he sent into Macedonia *t*' of them "
34 the space of *t*' hours cried out, "
21:33 him to be bound with *t*' chains; "
23:23 he called unto him *t*' centurions, "
23 Make ready *t*' hundred soldiers to 1250
23 spearmen *t*' hundred, at the third "
24:27 after *t*' years Porcius Festus came 1333
27:37 *t*' hundred threescore and sixteen 1250
41 into a place where *t*' seas met, 1337
28:30 Paul dwelt *t*' whole years in his 1333
1Co 6:16 for *t*', saith he, shall be one flesh. *1417
14:27 let it be by *t*', or at the most by "
29 Let the prophets speak *t*' or three, "
2Co 13: 1 the mouth of *t*' or three witnesses "
Ga 4:22 Abraham had *t*' sons, the one by a "
24 for these are the *t*' covenants; the "
Eph 5:31 wife, and they *t*' shall be one flesh. * "
Ph'p 1:23 For I am in a strait betwixt *t*', "
1Ti 5:19 but before *t*' or three witnesses. "
Heb 6:18 That by *t*' immutable things, in "
10:28 mercy under *t*' or three witnesses: "
Re 2:12 the sharp sword with *t*' edges; *1366
9:12 there come *t*' woes more hereafter. 1417
16 *t*' hundred thousand thousand: * "
11: 2 under foot forty and *t*' months. "
3 give power unto my *t*' witnesses, "
3 *t*' hundred and threescore days, 1250
4 These are the *t*' olive trees, and 1417
4 the *t*' candlesticks standing before "
10 these *t*' prophets tormented them "
12: 6 thousand *t*' hundred and threescore "
14 given *t*' wings of a great eagle, "
13: 5 to continue forty and *t*' months. "
11 and he had *t*' horns like a lamb, "

twoedged
Ps 149: 6 and a *t*' sword in their hand; 6374
Pr 5: 4 wormwood, sharp as a *t*' sword. 6310
Heb 4:12 and sharper than any *t*' sword, 1366
Re 1:16 of his mouth went a sharp *t*' sword: "

twofold
M't 23:15 make him *t*' more the child of hell 1366

two-hundred See TWO and HUNDRED.

two-leaved See TWO and LEAVED.

two-thousand See TWO and THOUSAND.

Tychicus (*tik'-ik-us*)
Ac 20: 4 and of Asia, *T*' and Trophimus. 5190
Eph 6:21 *T*', a beloved brother and faithful "
subscr. Rome unto the Ephesians by *T*'. * "
Co 4: 7 All my state shall *T*' declare unto "
subscr. from Rome to the Colossians by *T*' * "
2Ti 4:12 And *T*' have I sent to Ephesus. 5190
Tit 3:12 send Artemas unto thee, or *T*', "

Tyrannus (*ti-ran'-nus*)
Ac 19: 9 daily in the school of one *T*'. 5181

Tyre (*tire*) See also TYRUS.
Jos 19:29 Ramah, and to the strong city *T*'; 6865
2Sa 5:11 Hiram king of *T*' sent messengers "
24: 7 And came to the strong hold of *T*', "
1Ki 5: 1 Hiram king of *T*' sent his servants "
7:13 sent and fetched Hiram out of *T*'. "
14 and his father was a man of *T*', 6876
9:11 king of *T*' had furnished Solomon 6865
12 Hiram came out from *T*' to see the "
1Ch 14: 1 Hiram king of *T*' sent messengers "
22: 4 they of *T*' brought much cedar 6876
2Ch 2: 3 sent to Huram the king of *T*', 6865
11 the king of *T*' answered in writing, "
14 his father was a man of *T*', skilful 6876
Ezr 3: 7 to them of *T*', to bring cedar trees "
Ne 13:16 There dwelt men of *T*' also therein, "
Ps 45:12 daughter of *T*' shall be there with 6865
83: 7 with the inhabitants of *T*'; "
87: 4 Philistia, and *T*', with Ethiopia; "
Isa 23: 1 The burden of *T*'. Howl, ye ships "
5 be sorely pained at the report of *T*'. "
8 hath taken this counsel against *T*', "
15 *T*' shall be forgotten seventy years, "
15 years shall *T*' sing as an harlot. "
17 years, that the Lord will visit *T*', "
Joe 3: 4 ye to do with me, O *T*', and Zidon, "
M't 11:21 had been done in *T*' and Sidon, 5184
22 be more tolerable for *T*' and Sidon "
15:21 into the coasts of *T*' and Sidon. "
M'r 3: 8 they about *T*' and Sidon, a great "
7:24 into the borders of *T*' and Sidon, "
31 departing from the coasts of *T*' and "
Lu 6:17 from the sea coast of *T*' and Sidon, "
10:13 works had been done in *T*' and "
14 be more tolerable for *T*' and Sidon "
Ac 12:20 highly displeased with them of *T*' 5185
21: 3 sailed into Syria, and landed at *T*': 5184
7 we had finished our course from *T*', "

Tyrus (*ti'-rus*) See also TYRE.
Jer 25:22 And all the kings of *T*', and all the * 6865
27: 3 to the king of *T*', and to the king * "
47: 4 and to cut off from *T*' and Zidon * "
Eze 26: 2 *T*' hath said against Jerusalem, * "
3 I am against thee, O, *T*', and will * "
4 they shall destroy the walls of *T*', * "
7 will bring upon *T*' Nebuchadrezzar * "
15 Thus saith the Lord God to *T*'; * "
27: 2 man, take up a lamentation for *T*'; * "
3 say unto *T*', O thou that art situate * "
3 O *T*', thou hast said, I am of perfect * "
8 thy wise men, O *T*', that were in * "
32 saying, What city is like *T*', like * "
28: 2 of man, say unto the prince of *T*', * "
12 a lamentation upon the king of *T*', * "
29:18 to serve a great service against *T*': * "
18 he no wages, nor his army, for *T*', * "
Ho 9:13 Ephraim, as I saw *T*', is planted in * "
Am 1: 9 For three transgressions of *T*', and * "
10 I will send a fire on the wall of *T*', * "
Zec 9: 2 *T*', and Zidon, though it be very * "
3 *T*' did build herself a strong hold, * "

U.

Ucal (*u'-cal*)
Pr 30: 1 Ithiel, even unto Ithiel and *U*'. 401

Uel (*u'-el*)
Ezr 10:34 of Bani; Maadai, Amram, and *U*', 177

Ulai (*u'-lahee*)
Da 8: 2 vision, and I was by the river of *U*'. 195
16 man's voice between the banks of *U*', "

Ulam (*u'-lam*)
1Ch 7:16 and his sons were *U*' and Rakem. 198
17 And the sons of *U*'; Bedan. These "
8:39 his brother were, *U*' his firstborn, "
40 the sons of *U*' were mighty men of "

Ulla (*ul'-lah*)
1Ch 7:39 And the sons of *U*'; Arah, and 5925

Ummah (*um'-mah*)
Jos 19:30 *U*' also, and Aphek, and Rehob: 5981

unaccustomed
Jer 31:18 as a bullock *u*' to the yoke: 3808,3925

unadvisedly
Ps 106:33 so that he spake *u*' with his lips. 981

unawares
Ge 31:20 Jacob stole away *u*' to Laban 3820,3824
26 thou hast stolen away *u*' to me, " "
Nu 35:11 which killeth any person at *u*'. *7684
15 that killeth any person *u*' may flee * "
De 4:42 should kill his neighbour *u*', 1097,1847
Jos 20: 3 slayer that killeth any person *u*' *7684
9 killeth any person at *u*' might flee * "
Ps 35: 8 destruction come upon him at *u*'; 3045
Lu 21:34 and so that day come upon you *u*'. * 160
Ga 2: 4 of false brethren *u*' brought in, 3920
Heb 13: 2 some have entertained angels *u*'. 2990
Jude 4 there are certain men crept in *u*', *3921

unbelief
M't 13:58 works there because of their *u*'. 570
17:20 said unto them, Because of your *u*': * "
M'r 6: 6 he marvelled because of their *u*'. "
9:24 Lord, I believe; help thou mine *u*'. "
16:14 upbraided them with their *u*' and "
Ro 3: 3 shall their *u*' make the faith of God * "
Ro 4:20 at the promise of God through *u*'; 570
11:20 because of *u*' they were broken off, "
23 also, if they abide not still in *u*', "
30 obtained mercy through their *u*': * 543
32 God hath concluded them all in *u*', * "
1Ti 1:13 because I did it ignorantly in *u*'. 570
Heb 3:12 be in any of you an evil heart of *u*', "
19 they could not enter in because of *u*'. "
4: 6 entered not in because of *u*': * 543
11 fall after the same example of *u*'. * "

unbelievers
Lu 12:46 him his portion with the *u*'. * 571
1Co 6: 6 with brother, and that before the *u*'. "
14:23 in those that are unlearned, or *u*', * "
2Co 6:14 unequally yoked together with *u*': "

unbelieving
Ac 14: 2 the *u*' Jews stirred up the Gentiles, *544
1Co 7:14 the *u*' husband is sanctified by the 571
14 *u*' wife is sanctified by the husband: "
15 But if the *u*' depart, let him depart. "
Tit 1:15 are defiled and *u*' is nothing pure; "
Re 21: 8 But the fearful, and *u*', and the "

unblameable
Col 1:22 to present you holy and *u*' and * 299
1Th 3:13 stablish your hearts *u*' in holiness "

unblameably
1Th 2:10 justly and *u*' we behaved ourselves 274

uncertain
1Co 14: 8 For if the trumpet gave an *u*' sound, 82
1Ti 6:17 nor trust in *u*' riches, but in the * 83

uncertainly
1Co 9:26 I therefore so run, not as *u*'; so fight 82

unchangeable
Heb 7:24 ever, hath an *u*' priesthood. 531

uncircumcised
Ge 17:14 And the *u*' man child whose flesh 6189
34:14 give our sister to one that is *u*'; 6190
Ex 6:12 hear me, who am of *u*' lips? 6189
30 I am of *u*' lips, and how shall "
12:48 for no *u*' person shall eat thereof. "
Le 19:23 shall count the fruit thereof as *u*': *6189
23 three years shall it be as *u*' unto "
26:41 if then their *u*' hearts be humbled, "
Jos 5: 7 for they were *u*', because "
J'g 14: 3 to take a wife of the *u*' Philistines? "
15:18 and fall into the hand of the *u*'? "
1Sa 14: 6 over unto the garrison of these *u*': "
17:26 who is this *u*' Philistine, that he "
36 this *u*' Philistine shall be as one of "
31: 4 lest these *u*' come and thrust me "
2Sa 1:20 the daughters of the *u*' triumph. "
1Ch 10: 4 lest these *u*' come and abuse me. "
Isa 52: 1 into thee the *u*' and the unclean. "
Jer 6:10 ear is *u*', and they cannot hearken: "
9:25 which are circumcised with the *u*'; *6190
26 for all these nations are *u*', and 6189
26 house of Israel are *u*' in the heart. "
Eze 28:10 Thou shalt die the deaths of the *u*' "
31:18 thou shalt lie in the midst of the *u*' "
32:19 down, and be thou laid with the *u*'. "
21 they lie *u*', slain by the sword. "
24 are gone down *u*' into the nether "
25 All of them *u*', slain by the sword: "
26 all of them *u*', slain by the sword, "
27 the mighty that are fallen of the *u*', "
28 be broken in the midst of the *u*', "
29 they shall lie with the *u*', and with "
30 and they lie *u*' with them that be "
32 shall be laid in the midst of the *u*' "
44: 7 *u*' in heart, and *u*' in flesh, to be "
9 stranger, *u*' in heart, nor *u*' in flesh, "
Ac 7:51 Ye stiffnecked and *u*' in heart and 564
11: 3 Thou wentest in to men *u*', 203,2192
Ro 4:11 which he had yet being *u*': *1722,3588,203
12 which he had being yet *u*'. * "
1Co 7:18 let him not become *u*'. 1986

uncircumcision
Ro 2:25 law, thy circumcision is made *u*'. 203
26 if the *u*' keep the righteousness "
26 shall not his *u*' be counted for "
27 And shall not *u*' which is by nature, "
3:30 by faith, and *u*' through faith. "
4: 9 or upon the *u*' also? for we say that "
10 he was in circumcision, or in *u*'? "

Ro 4:10 Not in circumcision, but in u'. 203
1Co 7:18 Is any called in u'? let him not be "
19 is nothing, and u' is nothing, "
Ga 2: 7 gospel of the u' was committed unto "
5: 6 availeth any thing, nor u'; but faith "
6:15 availeth any thing, nor u', but a "
Eph 2:11 who are called U' by that which "
Col 2:13 your sins and the u' of your flesh, "
3:11 Greek nor Jew, circumcision nor u'. "

uncle See also UNCLE'S.
Le 10: 4 the sons of Uzziel the u' of Aaron, 1730
25:49 Either his u', or his uncle's son, "
1Sa 10:14 Saul's u' said unto him and to his "
15 Saul's u' said, Tell me, I pray thee, "
16 Saul said unto his u', He told us "
14:50 Abner, the son of Ner, Saul's u'. "
1Ch 27:32 David's u' was a counseller, "
Es 2:15 of Abihail the u' of Mordecai, "
Jer 32: 7 Hanameel...thine u' shall come "
Am 6:10 And a man's u' shall take him up, "

unclean
Le 5: 2 Or if a soul touch any u' thing, 2931
2 whether it be a carcase of an u' beast, "
2 a carcase of u' cattle, or the carcase "
2 or the carcase of u' creeping things, "
2 he also shall be u', and guilty. "
7:19 flesh that toucheth any u' thing "
21 soul that shall touch any u' thing, 2932
21 of man, or any u' beast, 2931
21 or any abominable u' thing, and "
10:10 unholy, and between u' and clean; "
11: 4, 5, 6 not the hoof; he is u' unto you. "
7 not the cud; he is u' to you. "
8 ye not touch; they are u' to you. "
24 And for these ye shall be u': 2930
24 of them shall be u' until the even. "
25 his clothes, and be u' until the even. "
26 cheweth the cud, are u' unto you: 2931
26 that toucheth them shall be u'. 2930
27 on all four, those are u' unto you: 2931
27 carcase shall be u' until the even. 2930
28 clothes, and be u' until the even: "
28 the even: they are u' unto you: 2931
29 shall be u' unto you among the "
31 are u' to you among all that creep: "
31 be dead, shall be u' until the even. 2930
32 are dead, doth fall, it shall be u'; "
32 and it shall be u' until the even; "
33 whatsoever is in it shall be u'; "
34 such water cometh shall be u': "
34 in every such vessel shall be u'. "
35 their carcase falleth shall be u'; "
35 are u', and shall be u' unto you. 2931
36 toucheth their carcase shall be u'. 2930
38 thereon, it shall be u' unto you. 2931
39 thereof shall be u' until the even. 2930
40 clothes, and be u' until the even: "
40 clothes, and be u' until the even. "
43 ye make yourselves u' with them, "
47 a difference between the u' and 2931
12: 2 then she shall be u' seven days; 2930
2 for her infirmity shall she be u'. "
5 then she shall be u' two weeks, "
13: 3 on him, and pronounce him u'. "
8 the priest shall pronounce him u': "
11 the priest shall pronounce him u', "
11 shall not shut him up: for he is u'. 2931
14 appeareth in him, he shall be u'. 2930
15 flesh, and pronounce him to be u': "
15 for the raw flesh is u': it is a 2931
20, 22, 25, 27, 30 pronounce him u'. 2930
36 not seek for yellow hair; he is u'. 2931
44 He is a leprous man, he is u': "
44 shall pronounce him utterly u'; 2930
45 upper lip, and shall cry, U', u'. 2931
46 him he shall be defiled; he is u': "
51 plague is a fretting leprosy; it is u'. "
55 the plague be not spread; it is u': "
59 it clean, or to pronounce it u'. 2930
14:36 that is in the house be not made u': "
40 shall cast them into an u' place 2931
41 without the city into an u' place: "
44 leprosy in the house: it is u'. "
45 out of the city into an u' place. "
46 shut up shall be u' until the even. 2930
57 To teach when it is u', and when 2931
15: 2 flesh, because of his issue he is u'. "
4 he lieth that hath the issue, is u': 2930
4 whereon he sitteth, shall be u'. "
5, 6, 7, 8 and be u' until the even. "
9 that hath the issue shall be u'. "
10 him shall be u' until the even: "
10, 11, 16, 17, 18 be u' until the even. "
19 toucheth her shall be u' until the "
20 upon in her separation shall be u': "
20 also that she sitteth upon shall be u'. "
21, 22 and be u' until the even. "
23 it, he shall be u' until the even. "
24 him, he shall be u' seven days; 2930
24 bed whereon he lieth shall be u'. "
25 of her separation: she shall be u'. 2931
26 she sitteth upon shall be u', "
27 toucheth those things shall be u', 2930
27 in water, and be u' until the even. "
33 him that lieth with her that is u'. 2931
17:15 in water, and be u' until the even: 2930
20:21 brother's wife, it is an u' thing: *5079
25 between clean beasts and u', 2931
25 and between u' fowls and clean: "
25 I have separated from you as u'. 2930
22: 4 toucheth any thing that is u' by 2931
5 whereby he may be made u', or a 2930
6 hath touched any such shall be u' "
27:11 if it be any u' beast, of which they 2931
27 if it be of an u' beast, then he shall "

Nu 6: 7 not make himself u' for his father, 2930
9:10 be u' by reason of a dead body, 2931
18:15 the firstling of u' beasts shalt "
19: 7 priest shall be u' until the even. 2930
8 and shall be u' until the even. "
10 clothes, and be u' until the even: "
11 any man shall be u' seven days. "
13 upon him, he shall be u'; 2931
14 in the tent, shall be u' seven days. 2930
15 no covering bound upon it, is u'. 2931
16 or a grave, shall be u' seven days. 2930
17 for an u' person they shall take of 2931
19 shall sprinkle upon the u' on the "
20 But the man that shall be u', and 2930
20 sprinkled upon him; he is u'. 2931
21 separation shall be u' until even. 2930
22 whatsoever the u' person toucheth 2931
22 person toucheth shall be u'; 2930
22 toucheth it shall be u' until even. "
De 12:15 u' and the clean may eat thereof, 2931
22 the u' and the clean shall eat of "
14: 7 therefore they are u' unto you. "
8 not the cud, it is u' unto you: "
10 ye may not eat; it is u' unto you. "
19 creeping thing that flieth is u' unto "
15:22 u' and the clean person shall eat "
23:14 that he see no u' thing in thee, 6172
26:14 away ought thereof for any u' use, 2931
Jos 22:19 if the land of your possession be u', "
J'g 13: 4 drink, and eat not any u' thing: "
7 drink, neither eat any u' thing: 2932
14 strong drink, nor eat any u' thing: "
2Ch 23:19 none which was u' in any thing 2931
Ezr 9:11 an u' land with the filthiness of 5079
Job 14: 4 bring a clean thing out of an u'? 2931
36:14 and their life is among the u'. 6945
Ec 9: 2 and to the clean, and to the u'; 2931
Isa 6: 5 because I am a man of u' lips, and "
5 in the midst of a people of u' lips: "
35: 8 the u' shall not pass over it; but it "
52: 1 thee the uncircumcised and the u'. "
11 out from thence, touch no u' thing; "
64: 6 But we are all as an u' thing, and "
La 4:15 unto them, Depart ye; it is u'; "
Eze 22:26 between the u' and the clean, "
44:23 between the u' and the clean. "
Hos 9: 3 they shall eat u' things in Assyria. "
Hag 2:13 If one that is u' by a dead body "
13 touch any of these, shall it be u'? 2930
13 answered and said, It shall be u'. "
14 that which they offer there is u'. 2931
Zec 13: 2 u' spirit to pass out of the land. 2932
M't 10: 1 gave them power against u' spirits, 169
12:43 the u' spirit is gone out of a man, "
M'r 1:23 synagogue a man with an u' spirit; "
26 And when the u' spirit had torn him, "
27 commandeth he even the u' spirits, "
3:11 u' spirits, when they saw him, fell "
30 they said, He hath an u' spirit. "
5: 2 of the tombs a man with an u' spirit, "
8 Come out of the man, thou u' spirit. "
13 the u' spirits went out, and entered "
6: 7 gave them power over u' spirits; "
7:25 young daughter had an u' spirit, "
Lu 4:33 which had a spirit of an u' devil, "
36 power he commandeth the u' spirits, "
6:18 that were vexed with u' spirits: "
8:29 commanded the u' spirit to come "
9:42 Jesus rebuked the u' spirit, and "
11:24 the u' spirit is gone out of a man, "
Ac 5:16 which were vexed with u' spirits: "
8: 7 For u' spirits, crying with loud voice, "
10:14 any thing that is common or u'. "
28 not call any man common or u'. "
11: 8 nothing common or u' hath at any "
Ro 14:14 that there is nothing u' of itself: 2839
14 any thing to be u', to him it is u'. "
1Co 7:14 else were your children u'; but 169
2Co 6:17 Lord, and touch not the u' thing; "
Eph 5: 5 nor u' person, nor covetous man, "
Heb 9:13 of an heifer sprinkling the u', *2840
Re 16:13 I saw three u' spirits like frogs 169
18: 2 a cage of every u' and hateful bird. "

uncleanness See also UNCLEANNESSES.
Le 5: 3 Or if he touch the u' of man, 2932
3 whatsoever u' it be that a man "
7:20 the Lord, having his u' upon him, "
21 as the u' of man, or any unclean "
14:19 that is to be cleansed from his u'; "
15: 3 And this shall be his u' in his issue: "
3 stopped from his issue, it is his u'. "
25 all the days of the issue of her u' "
26 unclean, as the u' of her separation. "
30 the Lord for the issue of her u'. "
31 the children of Israel from their u'; "
31 they die not in their u', when they "
16:16 of the u' of the children of Israel, "
16 among them in the midst of their u'. "
19 from the u' of the children of Israel. "
18:19 as she is put apart for her u'. "
22: 3 having his u' upon him, that soul "
5 or a man of whom he may take u', 2930
5 whatsoever u' he hath; 2932
Nu 5:19 if thou hast not gone aside to u' "
19:13 be unclean; his u' is yet upon him. "
De 23:10 reason of u' that chanceth him by 7137
24: 1 he hath found some u' in her: *6172
2Sa 11: 4 for she was purified from her u': 2932
2Ch 29:16 out all the u' that they found "
Ezr 9:11 from end to another with their u'. "
Eze 36:17 me as the u' of a removed woman. "
39:24 According to their u' and according "
Zec 13: 1 of Jerusalem for sin and for u'. 5079
M't 23:27 of dead men's bones, and of all u'. 167
Ro 1:24 God also gave them up to u' through "
6:19 yielded your members servants to u' "

2Co 12:21 and have not repented of the u' and 167
Ga 5:19 are these; Adultery, fornication, u', "
Eph 4:19 to work all u' with greediness. "
5: 3 But fornication, and all u', or "
Col 3: 5 upon the earth; fornication, u', "
1Th 2: 3 not of deceit, nor of u', nor in guile: "
4: 7 For God hath not called us unto u', "
2Pe 2:10 after the flesh in the lust of u', *3394

uncleannesses
Eze 36:29 will also save you from all your u': 2932

uncle's
Le 20:20 if a man shall lie with his u' wife, 1733
20 hath uncovered his u' nakedness: 1730
25:49 Either his uncle, or his u' son, may 1733
Es 2: 7 that is, Esther his u' daughter: "
Jer 32: 8 Hanameel mine u' son came to me "
9 the field of Hanameel my u' son, "
12 the sight of Hanameel mine u' son, "

unclothed
2Co 5: 4 not for that we would be u', but 1562

uncomely
1Co 7:36 behaveth himself u' toward a virgin, 807
12:23 our u' parts have more abundant 809

uncondemned
Ac 16:37 They have beaten us openly u', 178
22:25 a man that is a Roman, and u'? "

uncorruptible See also INCORRUPTIBLE.
Ro 1:23 changed the glory of the u' God 862

uncorruptness
Tit 2: 7 in doctrine shewing u', gravity, 90

uncover See also UNCOVERED; UNCOVERETH.
Le 10: 6 U' not your heads, neither rend *6544
18: 6 kin to him, to u' their nakedness: 1540
7 of thy mother, shalt thou not u': "
7 thou shalt not u' her nakedness. "
8 thy father's wife shalt thou not u': "
9, 10 nakedness thou shalt not u'. "
11 thou shalt not u' her nakedness. "
12 not u' the nakedness of thy father's "
13 u' the nakedness of thy mother's "
14 not u' the nakedness of thy father's "
15 u' the nakedness of thy daughter "
15 thou shalt not u' her nakedness. "
16 u' the nakedness of thy brother's "
17 not u' the nakedness of a woman "
17 daughter, to u' her nakedness; "
18 to vex her, to u' her nakedness, "
19 unto a woman to u' her nakedness, "
20:18 her sickness, and shall u' her "
19 u' the nakedness of thy mother's "
21:10 shall not u' his head, nor rend his *6544
Nu 5:18 Lord, and u' the woman's head, * "
Ru 3: 4 and u' his feet, and lay thee down; 1540
Isa 47: 2 and grind meal: u' thy locks, "
2 make bare the leg, u' the thigh, "
Zep 2:14 for he shall u' the cedar work. *6168

uncovered
Ge 9:21 and he was u' within his tent. 1540
Le 20:11 wife hath u' his father's nakedness: "
17 he hath u' his sister's nakedness; "
18 and she hath u' the fountain of her "
20 he hath u' his uncle's nakedness: "
21 he hath u' his brother's nakedness; "
Ru 3: 7 and u' his feet, and laid her down. "
2Sa 6:20 who u' himself to day in the eyes of "
Isa 20: 4 foot, even with their buttocks u', 2834
22: 6 horsemen, and Kir u' the shield. 6168
47: 3 Thy nakedness shall be u', yea, 1540
Jer 49:10 bare, I have u' his secret places, "
Eze 4: 7 thine arm shall be u', and thou 2834
Hab 2:16 also, and let thy foreskin be u': *
M'r 2: 4 they u' the roof where he was: 648
1Co 11: 5 or prophesieth with her head u' * 177
13 that a woman pray unto God u'? * "

uncovereth
Le 20:19 sister; for he u' his near kin: *6168
De 27:20 because he u' his father's skirt: 1540
2Sa 6:20 fellows shamelessly u' himself! "

unction
1Jo 2:20 ye have an u' from the Holy One, *5545

undefiled
Ps 119: 1 Blessed are the u' in the way, 8549
Ca 5: 2 sister, my love, my dove, my u': 8535
6: 9 My dove, my u' is but one; she is "
Heb 7:26 who is holy, harmless, u', separate 283
13: 4 is honourable in all, and the bed u': "
Jas 1:27 Pure religion and u' before God "
1Pe 1: 4 an inheritance incorruptible, and u', "

under See also UNDERGIRDING; UNDERNEATH; UNDERSETTERS; UNDERSTAND; UNDERTAKE.
Ge 1: 7 which were u' the firmament 8478
9 waters u' the heaven be gathered "
6:17 the breath of life, from u' heaven; "
7:19 hills, that were u' the whole heaven, "
16: 9 and submit thyself u' her hands. "
18: 4 and rest yourselves u' the tree: "
8 and he stood by them u' the tree, "
19: 8 came they u' the shadow of my roof. "
21:15 cast the child u' one of the shrubs. 8478
35: 4 Jacob hid them u' the oak which "
8 buried beneath Beth-el u' an oak: "
39:23 to any thing that was u' his hand; "
41:35 lay up corn u' the hand of Pharaoh, 8478
47:29 I pray thee, thy hand u' my thigh, "
49:25 blessings of the deep that lieth u',* "
Ex 6: 6, 7 out from u' the burdens of the "
17:12 they took a stone, and put it u' him, "
14 of Amalek from u' heaven. "
18:10 from u' the hand of the Egyptians. "

Ex 20: 4 or that is in the water *u* the earth: 8478
21: 20 with a rod, and he die *u* his hand; "
23: 5 hateth thee lying *u* his burden, "
24: 4 and builded an altar *u* the hill, "
10 and there was *u* his feet as it were "
25: 35, 35, 35 *u* two branches of the same, "
26: 19 of silver *u* the twenty boards; "
19 two sockets *u* one board for his "
19 two sockets *u* another board for "
21 of silver; two sockets *u* one board, "
21 and two sockets *u* another board. "
25 two sockets *u* one board, and two "
25 and two sockets *u* another board. "
33 hang up the vail *u* the taches, "
30: 4 thou make to it *u* the crown of it, "
36: 24 he made *u* the twenty boards; "
24 two sockets *u* one board for his "
24 two sockets *u* another board for "
26 two sockets *u* one board, and two "
26 and two sockets *u* another board. "
30 silver, *u* every board two sockets. "
37: 21, 21, 21 *u* two branches of the same, "
27 of gold for it *u* the crown thereof, "
38: 4 grate of network *u* the compass "
Le 15: 10 any thing that was *u* him shall be "
22: 27 it shall be seven days *u* the dam; "
27: 32 of whatsoever passeth *u* the rod, "
Nu 3: 36 *u* the custody and charge of the sons*
4: 28, 33 *u* the hand of Ithamar the son of
6: 18 in the fire which is *u* the sacrifice 8478
7: 8 *u* the hand of Ithamar the son of
16: 31 clave asunder that was *u* them: 8478
22: 27 the Lord, she fell down *u* Balaam: "
31: 49 men of war which are *u* our charge,
33: 1 *u* the hand of Moses and Aaron.
De 2: 25 that are *u* the whole heaven, 8478
3: 17 sea, *u* Ashdoth-pisgah eastward. "
4: 11 near and stood *u* the mountain; "
19 all nations *u* the whole heaven. "
49 the plain, *u* the springs of Pisgah. "
7: 24 destroy their name from *u* heaven: "
9: 14 out their name from *u* heaven: "
12: 2 the hills, and *u* every green tree: "
25: 19 of Amalek from *u* heaven; "
28: 23 earth that is *u* thee shall be iron. "
29: 20 blot out his name from *u* heaven. "
Jos 7: 21 of my tent, and the silver *u* it. "
22 hid in his tent, and the silver *u* it. "
11: 3 to the Hivite *u* Hermon in the land "
17 of Lebanon *u* mount Hermon: "
12: 3 from the south, *u* Ashdoth-pisgah: "
13: 5 from Baal-gad *u* mount Hermon "
16: 10 unto this day, and serve *u* tribute.*
24: 26 and set it up there *u* an oak, 8478
J'g 1: 7 gathered their meat *u* my table: "
3: 16 he did gird it *u* his raiment upon "
30 that day *u* the hand of Israel. "
4: 5 dwelt *u* the palm tree of Deborah "
6: 11 sat *u* an oak which was in Ophrah, "
19 brought it out unto him *u* the oak, "
9: 29 to God this people were *u* my hand! "
Ru 2: 12 *u* whose wings thou art come to 8478
1Sa 7: 11 them, until they came *u* Beth-car. "
14: 2 *u* a pomegranate tree which is in "
21: 3 therefore what is *u* thine hand? "
4 is no common bread *u* mine hand, "
8 here *u* thine hand spear or sword? "
22: 6 abode in Gibeah *u* a tree in Ramah, "
31: 13 buried them *u* a tree at Jabesh, "
2Sa 2: 23 spear smote him *u* the fifth rib, * 413
3: 27 and smote him there *u* the fifth rib,*
4: 6 they smote him *u* the fifth rib: * 413
12: 31 were therein, and put them *u* saws,
31 *u* harrows of iron, and *u* axes of iron,
18: 2 part of the people *u* the hand of Joab,
2 third part *u* the hand of Abishai the
2 third part *u* the hand of Ittai the
9 the mule went *u* the thick boughs 8478
9 the mule that was *u* him went away. "
22: 10 and darkness was *u* his feet. "
37 Thou hast enlarged my steps *u* me; "
39 yea, they are fallen *u* my feet. "
40 me hast thou subdued *u* me. "
48 bringeth down the people *u* me, "
1Ki 4: 25 man *u* his vine and *u* his fig tree, "
5: 3 put them *u* the soles of his feet. "
7: 24 *u* the brim of it round about there "
30 *u* the laver were undersetters * "
32 *u* the borders were four wheels; * "
44 sea, and twelve oxen *u* the sea; "
8: 6 *u* the wings of the cherubims. 413, "
13: 14 and found him sitting *u* an oak: "
14: 23 high hill, and *u* every green tree. "
18: 23, 23 lay it on wood, and put no fire *u*: "
25 of your gods, but put no fire *u*. "
19: 4 and sat down *u* a juniper tree: 8478
5 he lay and slept *u* a juniper tree, "
2Ki 8: 20, 22 Edom revolted from *u* the hand "
9: 13 it *u* him on the top of the stairs, "
33 the horses: and he trode her *u* foot.
13: 5 they went out from *u* the hand of 8478
14: 27 the name of Israel from *u* heaven: "
16: 4 the hills, and *u* every green tree. "
17 off the brasen oxen that were *u* it, "
17: 7 from *u* the hand of Pharaoh king "
10 high hill, and *u* every green tree: "
1Ch 10: 12 their bones *u* the oak in Jabesh, "
17: 1 the ark...remaineth *u* curtains. "
24: 19 their manner, *u* Aaron their father,*
25: 2 the sons of Asaph *u* the hands of 5921
3 six, *u* the hands of their father "
6 were *u* the hands of their father "
26: 28 it was *u* the hand of Shelomith, "
27: 23 from twenty years old and *u*: 4295
2Ch 4: 3 *u* it was the similitude of oxen, 8478
15 One sea, and twelve oxen *u* it. "

2Ch 5: 7 even *u* the wings of the cherubims: 8478
13: 18 Israel were brought *u* at that time,
21: 8 revolted from *u* the dominion of 8478
10 revolted from *u* the hand of Judah "
10 did Libnah revolt from *u* his hand; "
26: 11 *u* the hand of Hananiah, one of 5921
13 And *u* their hand was an army, "
28: 4 the hills, and *u* every green tree. 8478
10 to keep *u* the children of Judah
31: 13 overseers *u* the hand of Cononiah
Ne 2: 14 the beast that was *u* me to pass. 8478
8: 17 made booths, and sat *u* the booths: *
Job 9: 13 proud helpers do stoop *u* him. 8478
20: 12 though he hide it *u* his tongue; "
26: 5 are formed from *u* the waters, * "
8 and the cloud is not rent *u* them. 5921
28: 5 *u* it is turned up as it were fire. *8478
24 and seeth *u* the whole heaven; "
30: 7 *u* the nettles they were gathered "
37: 3 He directeth it *u* the whole heaven, "
40: 21 He lieth *u* the shady trees, in the "
41: 11 whatsoever is *u* the whole heaven is "
30 Sharp stones are *u* him: he * "
Ps 8: 6 thou hast put all things *u* his feet: "
10: 7 *u* his tongue is mischief and "
17: 8 hide me *u* the shadow of thy wings,
18: 9 and darkness was *u* his feet. 8478
36 Thou hast enlarged my steps *u* me, "
38 to rise: they are fallen *u* my feet. "
39 subdued *u* me those that rose up "
36: 7 their trust *u* the shadow of thy wings.
44: 5 we tread them *u* that rise up against
45: 5 whereby the people fall *u* thee. 8478
47: 3 He shall subdue the people *u* us, "
3 and the nations *u* our feet. "
91: 1 shall abide *u* the shadow of the
4 and *u* his wings shalt thou trust: 8478
13 dragon shalt thou trample *u* feet.
106: 42 into subjection *u* their hand. 8478
140: 3 adders' poison is *u* their lips. "
144: 2 who subdueth my people *u* me. "
Pr 12: 24 but the slothful shall be *u* tribute.
22: 27 take away thy bed from *u* thee? 8478
Ec 1: 3 labour which he taketh *u* the sun? "
9 there is no new thing *u* the sun. "
13 all things that are done *u* heaven: "
14 the works that are done *u* the sun; "
2: 3 they should do *u* the heaven all the "
11 and there was no profit *u* the sun. "
17 work that is wrought *u* the sun is "
18 which I had taken *u* the sun: "
19 shewed myself wise *u* the sun. "
20 the labour which I took *u* the sun. "
22 he hath laboured *u* the sun? "
3: 16 *u* the sun the place of judgment, "
4: 1 that are done *u* the sun: "
3 evil work that is done *u* the sun. "
7 and I saw vanity *u* the sun. "
15 the living which walk *u* the sun, "
5: 13 evil which I have seen *u* the sun, "
18 labour that he taketh *u* the sun "
6: 1 evil which I have seen *u* the sun, "
12 what shall be after him *u* the sun? "
7: 6 the crackling of thorns *u* the pot, "
8: 9 every work that is done *u* the sun: "
15 hath no better thing *u* the sun, "
15 which God giveth him *u* the sun. "
17 the work that is done *u* the sun: "
9: 3 all things that are done *u* the sun, "
6 any thing that is done *u* the sun. "
9 he hath given thee *u* the sun, all "
9 labour...thou takest *u* the sun. "
11 and saw *u* the sun, that the race is "
13 wisdom have I seen also *u* the sun, "
10: 5 evil which I have seen *u* the sun, "
Ca 2: 3 I sat down *u* his shadow with great
6 His left hand is *u* my head, and 8478
4: 11 honey and milk are *u* thy tongue; "
8: 3 His left hand should be *u* my head, "
5 I raised thee up *u* the apple tree: "
Isa 3: 6 and let this ruin be *u* thy hand: "
10: 4 shall bow down *u* the prisoners, "
4 they shall fall *u* the slain. For all "
16 and *u* his glory he shall kindle a "
14: 11 the worm is spread *u* thee, and "
19 pit; as a carcase trodden *u* feet.
25 my mountains tread him *u* foot;
18: 7 meted out and trodden *u* foot, *
24: 5 also is defiled *u* the inhabitants 8478
25: 10 Moab shall be trodden down *u* him, "
28: 3 of Ephraim, shall be trodden *u* feet:
15 *u* falsehood have we hid ourselves:
34: 15 and hatch, and gather *u* her shadow:
57: 5 with idols *u* every green tree, 8478
5 valleys *u* the clifts of the rocks? "
58: 5 spread sackcloth and ashes *u* him?
Jer 2: 20 high hill and *u* every green tree 8478
3: 6 and *u* every green tree, and 413, "
13 the strangers *u* every green tree, "
10: 11 earth, and from *u* these heavens. 8460
12: 10 have trodden my portion *u* foot,
27: 8 will not put their neck *u* the yoke
11 that bring their neck *u* the yoke
12 your necks *u* the yoke of the king
33: 13 pass again *u* the hands of him 5921
38: 11 of the king *u* the treasury, 413, 8478
12 rags *u* thine armholes *u* the cords. "
48: 45 fled stood *u* the shadow of Heshbon
52: 20 bulls that were *u* the bases, 8478
La 1: 15 trodden *u* foot all my mighty men*
3: 34 crush *u* his feet all the prisoners 8478
66 them in anger from *u* the heavens "
4: 20 *U* his shadow we shall live among
5: 5 Our necks are *u* persecution: we *5921
13 and the children fell *u* the wood.
Eze 1: 8 the hands of a man *u* their wings 8478

Eze 1: 23 *u* the firmament were their wings 8478
6: 13 mountains, and *u* every green tree, "
13 *u* every thick oak, the place where "
10: 2 even *u* the cherub, and fill 413, "
8 of a man's hand *u* their wings. "
20 creature that I saw *u* the God of "
21 hands of a man was *u* their wings. "
17: 6 and the roots thereof were *u* him: "
23 *u* it shall dwell all fowl of every "
20: 37 I will cause you to pass *u* the rod, "
24: 5 and burn also the bones *u* it, and "
31: 6 *u* his branches did all the beasts "
6 and *u* his shadow dwelt all great
17 that dwelt *u* his shadow in the midst
32: 27 laid their swords *u* their heads, 8478
42: 9 *u* these chambers was the entry "
46: 23 with boiling places *u* the rows "
47: 1 issued out from *u* the threshold "
1 the waters came down from *u* "
Da 4: 12 beasts of...field had shadow *u* it, 8460
14 let the beasts get away from *u* it, 8478
21 *u* which the beasts of the field 8460
7: 27 the kingdom *u* the whole heaven, "
8: 13 and the host to be trodden *u* foot?
9: 12 for *u* the whole heaven hath not 8478
Ho 4: 12 gone a whoring from *u* their God. "
13 *u* oaks and poplars and elms, "
14: 7 They that dwell *u* his shadow shall
Joe 1: 17 The seed is rotten *u* their clods, 8478
Am 2: 13 I am pressed *u* you, as a cart is * "
Ob 7 bread have laid a wound *u* thee: "
Jon 4: 5 booth, and sat *u* it in the shadow, "
Mic 1: 4 mountains shall be molten *u* him, "
4: 4 man *u* his vine and *u* his fig tree; "
Zec 3: 10 *u* the vine and *u* the fig tree. "
Mal 4: 3 be ashes *u* the soles of your feet "
M't 2: 16 from two years old and *u*, 2736
5: 13 and to be trodden *u* foot of men. 2662
15 a candle, and put it *u* a bushel, 5259
7: 6 they trample them *u* their feet, 1722
8: 8 thou shouldest come *u* my roof: 5259
9 For I am a man *u* authority, "
9 having soldiers *u* me: and I say "
23: 37 her chickens *u* her wings, and "
M'r 4: 21 to be put *u* a bushel, or *u* a bed? "
32 air may lodge *u* the shadow of it. "
6: 11 shake off the dust *u* your feet for 5270
7: 28 yet the dogs *u* the table eat of the "
Lu 7: 6 thou shouldest enter *u* my roof: 5259
8 I also am a man set *u* authority, "
8 having *u* me soldiers, and I say "
8: 16 a vessel, or putteth it *u* a bed; 5270
11: 33 neither *u* a bushel, but on a 5259
13: 34 gather her brood *u* her wings, "
17: 24 out of the one part *u* heaven, "
24 unto the other part *u* heaven; "
Joh 1: 48 when thou wast *u* the fig tree, I "
50 thee, I saw thee *u* the fig tree, *5270
Ac 2: 5 out of every nation *u* heaven. 5259
4: 12 none other name *u* heaven given "
8: 27 of a great authority *u* Candace queen
23: 12 and bound themselves *u* a curse, 332
14 bound ourselves *u* a great curse, "
27: 4 we sailed *u* Cyprus, because the 5284
7 we sailed *u* Crete, over against "
16 running *u* a certain island which 5295
30 *u* colour as though they would have
Ro 3: 9 Gentiles, that they are all *u* sin; 5259
13 the poison of asps is *u* their lips: "
19 saith to them who are *u* the law: 1722
6: 14 ye are not *u* the law, but *u* grace. 5259
15 we are not *u* the law, but *u* grace? "
7: 14 but I am carnal, sold *u* sin. "
16: 20 bruise Satan *u* your feet shortly. "
1Co 6: 12 not be brought *u* the power of any. "
7: 15 sister is not *u* bondage in such cases:
9: 20 that are *u* the law, as *u* the law, 5259
20 gain them that are *u* the law; "
21 to God, but *u* the law to Christ,) 1772
27 I keep *u* my body, and bring it *5299
10: 1 all our fathers were *u* the cloud, 5259
14: 34 commanded to be *u* obedience, *5293
15: 25, 27 hath put all enemies *u* his feet. 5259
27 he saith all things are put *u* him, * "
27 which did put all things *u* him. *5293
28 unto him that put all things *u* him,* "
2Co 11: 32 the governor *u* Aretas the king
Ga 3: 10 works of the law are *u* the curse: 5259
22 hath concluded all *u* sin, that "
23 faith came, we were kept *u* the law, "
25 we are no longer *u* a schoolmaster. "
4: 2 is *u* tutors and governors until the "
3 *u* the elements of the world: "
4 made of a woman, made *u* the law, "
5 redeem them that were *u* the law, "
21 ye that desire to be *u* the law, do ye "
5: 18 of the Spirit, ye are not *u* the law. "
Eph 1: 22 And hath put all things *u* his feet, "
Ph'p 2: 10 in earth, and things *u* the earth, 2709
Col 1: 23 every creature which is *u* heaven; 5259
1Ti 5: 9 number *u* threescore years old, 1640
6: 1 servants as are *u* the yoke count 5259
Heb 2: 8 all things in subjection *u* his feet. 5270
8 he put all in subjection *u* him, *
8 left nothing that is not put *u* him.* 506
8 see not yet all things put *u* him. 5293
7: 11 *u* it the people received the law,) 1909
9: 15 the transgressions that were *u* the "
10: 28 mercy *u* two or three witnesses: * "
29 trodden *u* foot the Son of God, 2662
Jas 2: 3 there, or sit here *u* my footstool: 5259
1Pe 5: 6 *u* the mighty hand of God, "
Jude 6 in everlasting chains *u* darkness "
Re 5: 3 nor in earth, neither *u* the earth, 5270
13 and on the earth, and *u* the earth, "
6: 9 I saw *u* the altar the souls of them* "

Re 11: 2 shall they tread u' foot forty and two
12: 1 the sun, and the moon u' her feet, 5270

undergirding
Ac 27:17 up, they used helps, u' the ship; 5269

underneath
Ex 28:27 on the two sides of the ephod u'. 4295
39:20 on the two sides of the ephod u', "
De 33:27 u' are the everlasting arms: 8478

undersetters
1Ki 7:30 the four corners thereof had u': 3802
30 under the laver were u' molten, "
34 were four u' to the four corners "
34 the u' were of the very base itself. "

understand See also UNDERSTANDEST; UNDERSTANDETH; UNDERSTANDING; UNDERSTOOD.
Ge 11: 7 may not u' one another's speech. 8085
41:15 canst u' a dream to interpret it: * "
Nu 16:30 u' that these men have provoked 3045
De 9: 3 U' therefore this day, that the Lord* "
6 U' therefore, that the Lord thy * "
28:49 whose tongue thou shalt not u'; 8085
2Ki 18:26 the Syrian language; for we u' it: "
1Ch 28:19 Lord made me u' in writing by his 7919
Ne 8: 3 women, and those that could u'; 995
7 caused the people to u' the law: "
8 and caused them to u' the reading. "
13 even to u' the words of the law. *7919
Job 6:24 me to u' wherein I have erred. 995
23: 5 and u' what he would say unto me. "
26:14 thunder of his power who can u'? "
32: 9 neither do the aged u' judgment. "
36:29 any u' the spreadings of the clouds, "
Ps 14: 2 see if there were any that did u', 7919
19:12 Who can u' his errors? cleanse * 995
53: 2 see if there were any that did u', 7919
82: 5 They knew not, neither will they u';995
92: 6 not; neither doth a fool u' this. "
94: 8 U', ye brutish among the people: * "
107:43 u' the lovingkindness of the Lord. * "
119:27 to u' the way of thy precepts: * "
100 I u' more than the ancients, because "
Pr 1: 6 To u' a proverb, and the "
2: 5 shalt thou u' the fear of the Lord, "
9 Then shalt thou u' righteousness, "
8: 5 O ye simple, u' wisdom: and, ye "
14: 8 of the prudent is to u' his way: "
19:25 and he will u' knowledge. "
20:24 how can a man then u' his own way? "
28: 5 Evil men u' not judgment: but they "
5 they that seek the Lord u' all things. "
29:19 for though he u' he will not answer. "
Isa 6: 9 people, Hear ye indeed, but u' not; "
10 and u' with the heart, and convert, "
28: 9 whom shall he make to u' doctrine? "
19 be a vexation only to u' the report. "
32: 4 also of the rash shall u' knowledge, "
33:19 tongue, that thou canst not u'. 998
36:11 the Syrian language; for we u' it: 8085
41:20 and consider, and u' together, 7919
43:10 believe me, and u' that I am he: 995
44:18 their hearts, that they cannot u'. 7919
56:11 they are shepherds that cannot u': 995
Jer 9:12 is the wise man, that may u' this? "
Eze 3: 6 whose words thou canst not u'. 8085
Da 8:16 make this man to u' the vision. 995
17 he said unto me, U', O son of man: "
9:13 our iniquities, and u' thy truth. *7919
23 therefore u' the matter, and 995
25 Know therefore and u', that from *7919
10:11 u' the words that I speak unto thee,995
12 that thou didst set thine heart to u', "
14 make thee u' what shall befall thy "
11:33 they that u' among the people *7919
12:10 and none of the wicked shall u'; 995
10 but the wise shall u'. "
Ho 4:14 people that doth not u' shall fall. "
14: 9 is wise, and he shall u' these things? "
Mic 4:12 Lord, neither u' they his counsel: "
M't 13:13 they hear not, neither do they u'. 4920
14 ye shall hear, and shall not u'; "
15 and should u' with their heart, and "
15:10 and said unto them, Hear, and u': "
17 Do not ye yet u', that whatsoever *3539
16: 9 Do ye not yet u', neither remember* "
11 How is it that ye do not u' that I * "
24:15 place, (whoso readeth, let him u':) "
M'r 4:12 hearing they may hear, and not u';4920
7:14 unto me every one of you, and u': "
8:17 perceive ye not yet, neither u'? have "
21 them, How is it that ye do not u'? "
13:14 (let him that readeth u',) then let *3539
14:68 not, neither u' I what thou sayest. 1987
Lu 8:10 see, and hearing they might not u'.4920
24:45 that they might u' the scriptures, "
Joh 8:43 Why do ye not u' my speech? even 1097
12:40 nor u' with their heart, and be *3539
Ac 24:11 Because that thou mayest u', that*1097
28:26 ye shall hear, and shall not u'; 4920
27 u' with their heart, and should be "
Ro 15:21 they that have not heard shall u'. "
1Co 12: 3 Wherefore I give you to u', that no 1107
13: 2 of prophecy, and u' all mysteries. *1492
Eph 3: 4 u' my knowledge in mystery of *3539
Ph'p 1:12 I would ye should u', brethren, *1097
Heb 11: 3 Through faith we u' that the 3539
2Pe 2:12 speak evil of things that they u' not;*50

understandest
Job 15: 9 what u' thou, which is not in us? 995
Ps 139: 2 thou u' my thought afar off. "
Jer 5:15 not, neither u' what they say. 8085
Ac 8:30 said, U' thou what thou readest? 1097

understandeth
1Ch 28: 9 and u' all the imaginations of the 995
Job 28:23 God u' the way thereof, and he "

Ps 49:20 Man that is in honour, and u' not, 995
Pr 8: 9 They are all plain to him that u', "
14: 6 knowledge is easy unto him that u'. "
Jer 9:24 that he u' and knoweth me, that I 7919
M't 13:19 word of the kingdom, and u' it not,4920
23 he that heareth the word, and u' it; "
Ro 3:11 There is none that u', there is none "
1Co 14: 2 for no man u' him; howbeit in the 191
16 seeing he u' not what thou sayest?*1492

understanding
Ex 31: 3 of God, in wisdom, and in u', 8394
35:31 spirit of God, in wisdom, in u', "
36: 1 whom the Lord put wisdom and u' "
De 1:13 Take you wise men, and u', and 995
4: 6 your u' in the sight of the nations, 998
6 nation is a wise and u' people. 995
32:28 neither is there any u' in them. 8394
1Sa 25: 3 and she was a woman of good u', 7922
1Ki 3: 9 Give...thy servant an u' heart 8085
11 asked for thyself u' to discern 995
12 given thee a wise and an u' heart; "
4:29 God gave Solomon wisdom and u' 8394
7:14 he was filled with wisdom, and u', "
1Ch 12:32 were men that had u' of the times, 998
22:12 the Lord give thee wisdom and u', "
2Ch 2:12 son, endued with prudence and u', "
13 a cunning man, endued with u', "
26: 5 who had u' in the visions of God: 995
Ezr 8:16 and for Elnathan, men of u'. * "
18 us they brought us a man of u', *7922
Ne 8: 2 and all that could hear with u', 995
10:28 having knowledge, and having u'; "
Job 12: 3 But I have u' as well as you; I am 3824
12 wisdom; and in length of days u'.8394
13 strength, he hath counsel and u'. "
20 taketh away the u' of the aged. 2940
17: 4 thou hast hid their heart from u': 7922
20: 3 of my u' causeth me to answer. 998
26:12 by his u' he smiteth through the 8394
28:12, 20 and where is the place of u'? 998
28 and to depart from evil is u'. "
32: 8 of the Almighty giveth them u'. 995
34:10 hearken unto me, ye men of u': 3824
16 If now thou hast u', hear this: 998
34 Let men of u' tell me, and let a 3824
38: 4 the earth? declare, if thou hast u'. 998
36 or who hath given u' to the heart? "
39:17 neither hath he imparted to her u'. "
Ps 32: 9 or as the mule, which have no u': 995
47: 7 the earth: sing ye praises with u'.7919
49: 3 of my heart shall be of u'. 8394
111:10 a good u' have all they that do his 7922
119:34 Give me u', and I shall keep thy 995
73 give me u', that I may learn thy "
99 more u' than all my teachers: 7919
104 Through thy precepts I get u': 995
125 give me u', that I may know thy "
130 light; it giveth u' unto the simple. "
144 give me u', and I shall live. "
169 give me u' according to thy word. "
147: 5 of great power: his u' is infinite. 8394
Pr 1: 2 to perceive the words of u'; 998
5 a man of u' shall attain unto wise 995
2: 2 and apply thine heart to u'; 8394
3 and liftest up thy voice for u'; "
6 mouth cometh knowledge and u'. "
11 preserve thee, u' shall keep thee: "
3: 4 good u' in the sight of God and 7922
5 and lean not unto thine own u'. 998
13 and the man that getteth u'. 8394
19 earth; by u' hath he established the "
4: 1 of a father, and attend to know u'. 998
5 Get wisdom, get u': forget it not; "
7 and with all thy getting get u'. "
5: 1 and bow thine ear to my u': 8394
6:32 adultery with a woman lacketh u':3820
7: 4 sister; and call u' thy kinswoman: 998
7 youths, a young man void of u', 3820
8: 1 cry? and u' put forth her voice? 8394
5 and, ye fools, be ye of an u' heart. 995
14 wisdom: I am u'; I have strength. 998
9: 4 as for him that wanteth u', she 3820
6 live; and go in the way of u'. 998
10 and the knowledge of the holy is u'. "
16 as for him that wanteth u', she 3820
10:13 In the lips of him that hath u' * 995
13 the back of him that is void of u'. 3820
23 but a man of u' hath wisdom. 8394
11:12 but a man of u' holdeth his peace. "
12:11 vain persons is void of u'. 3820
13:15 Good u' giveth favour: but the 7922
14:29 is slow to wrath is of great u': 8394
33 in the heart of him that hath u': 995
15:14 that hath u' seeketh knowledge: "
21 a man of u' walketh uprightly. 8394
32 he that heareth reproof getteth u'.3820
16:16 u' rather to be chosen than silver! 998
22 U' is a wellspring of life unto 7922
17:18 A man void of u' striketh hands, 3820
24 is before him that hath u'; but the 995
27 and a man of u' is of an excellent 8394
28 his lips is esteemed a man of u'. * 995
18: 2 A fool hath no delight in u', but 8394
19: 8 he that keepeth u' shall find good. "
25 and reprove one that hath u', and 995
20: 5 but a man of u' will draw it out. 8394
21:16 wandereth out of the way of u' 7919
30 no wisdom nor u' nor counsel 8394
23:23 wisdom, and instruction, and u'. 998
24: 3 and by u' it is established: 8394
30 vineyard of the man void of u'; 3820
28: 2 by a man of u' and knowledge the 995
11 the poor that hath u' searcheth him "
16 The prince that wanteth u' is also 8394
30: 2 man, and have not the u' of a man. 998

Ec 9:11 nor yet riches to men of u', nor yet 995
Isa 11: 2 spirit of wisdom and u', the spirit 998
3 shall make him of quick u' in the*7306
27:11 on fire: for it is a people of no u': 998
29:14 u' of their prudent men shall be hid. "
16 him that framed it, He had no u'? 995
24 erred in spirit shall come to u', 998
40:14 and shewed to him the way of u'? 8394
28 there is no searching of his u'. "
44:19 is there knowledge nor u' to say, I "
Jer 3:15 feed you with knowledge and u'. 7919
4:22 children, and they have none u': 995
5:21 O foolish people, and without u'; 3820
51:15 stretched out the heaven by his u'.8394
Eze 28: 4 with thine u' thou hast gotten thee "
Da 1: 4 in knowledge, and u' science, 995
17 Daniel had u' in all visions and "
20 in all matters of wisdom and u', 998
2:21 knowledge to them that know u': 999
4:34 mine u' returned unto me, and I 4486
5:11 father light and u' and wisdom, 7924
12 and u', interpreting of dreams, "
14 u' and excellent wisdom is found in "
8:23 u' dark sentences, shall stand up. 995
9:22 come forth to give thee skill and u'.998
10: 1 the thing, and had u' of the vision. "
11:35 And some of them of u' shall fall, *7919
Ho 13: 2 idols according to their own u', 8394
Ob 7 under thee: there is none u' in him. "
8 and u' out of the mount of Esau? "
M't 15:16 said, Are ye also yet without u'? 801
M'r 7:18 them, Are ye so without u' also? "
12:33 all the heart, and with all the u', 4907
Lu 1: 3 having had perfect u' of all things*3877
2:47 him were astonished at his u' 4907
24:45 Then opened he their u', that they*3563
Ro 1:31 Without u', covenantbreakers, 801
1Co 1:19 to nothing the u' of the prudent. *4907
14:14 prayeth, but my u' is unfruitful. 3563
15 and I will pray with the u' also: "
15 and I will sing with the u' also. "
19 rather speak five words with my u', "
20 Brethren, be not children in u': *5424
20 be ye children, but in u' be men. * "
Eph 1:18 eyes of your u' being enlightened;*1271
4:18 Having the u' darkened, being "
5:17 u' what the will of the Lord is. *4920
Ph'p 4: 7 peace of God, which passeth all u',3563
Col 1: 9 in all wisdom and spiritual u'; 4907
2: 2 riches of the full assurance of u', "
1Ti 1: 7 u' neither what they say, nor *4920
2Ti 2: 7 Lord give thee u' in all things. 4907
1Jo 5:20 is come, and hath given us an u', 1271
Re 13:18 him that hath u' count the number3563

understood
Ge 42:23 knew not that Joseph u' them; 8085
De 32:29 they were wise, that they u' this, 7919
1Sa 4: 6 they u' that the ark of the Lord 3045
26: 4 u' that Saul was come in very deed. "
2Sa 3:37 all the people and all Israel u' that "
Ne 8:12 u' the words that were declared 995
13: 7 u' of the evil that Eliashib did for "
Job 13: 1 this, mine ear hath heard and u' it. "
42: 3 have I uttered that I u' not; "
Ps 73:17 of God; then u' I their end. * "
81: 5 I heard a language that I u' not. *3045
106: 7 Our fathers u' not thy wonders in 7919
Isa 40:21 ye not u' from the foundations of 995
44:18 They have not known nor u': for he* "
Da 8:27 at the vision, but none u' it. "
9: 2 I Daniel u' by books the number of "
10: 1 and he u' the thing, and had "
12: 8 And I heard, but I u' not: then said "
M't 13:51 them, Have ye u' all these things? 4920
16:12 Then u' they how that he bade "
17:13 the disciples u' that he spake unto "
26:10 When Jesus u' it, he said unto *1097
M'r 9:32 But they u' not that saying, and 50
Lu 2:50 u' not the saying which he spake 4920
9:45 they u' not this saying, and it was 50
18:34 And they u' none of these things: 4920
Joh 8:27 u' not that he spake to them of *1097
10: 6 u' not what things they were which "
12:16 These things u' not his disciples at "
Ac 7:25 his brethren would have u' how 4920
25 deliver them: but they u' not. "
23:27 having u' that he was a Roman. *3129
34 when he u' that he was of Cilicia; 4441
Ro 1:20 u' by the things that are made, *3539
1Co 13:11 I u' as a child, I thought as a child:*5426
14: 9 by the tongue words easy to be u', 2154
2Pe 3:16 are some things hard to be u', 1425

undertake See also UNDERTOOK.
Isa 38:14 Lord, I am oppressed; u' for me. *6148

undertook
Es 9:23 Jews u' to do as they had begun, 6901

undo See also UNDONE.
Isa 58: 6 to u' the heavy burdens, and to let 5425
Zep 3:19 that time I will u' all that afflict *6213

undone
Nu 21:29 thou art u', O people of Chemosh: 6
Jos 11:15 he left nothing u' of all that the 5493
Isa 6: 5 Woe is me! for I am u'; because 1820
M't 23:23 done, and not to leave the other u'.
Lu 11:42 done, and not to leave the other u'.

undressed
Le 25: 5 gather the grapes of thy vine u': 5139
11 the grapes in it of thy vine u'. "

unequal
Eze 18:25, 29 are not your ways u'? 3808,8505

unequally
2Co 6:14 not u' yoked together with 2086

unfaithful
Pr 25:19 Confidence in an u' man in time of 898
unfaithfully
Ps 78:57 and dealt u' like their fathers: *898
unfeigned
2Co 6: 6 by the Holy Ghost, by love u', 505
1Ti 1: 5 of a good conscience, and of faith u': "
2Ti 1: 5 the u' faith that is in thee, which "
1Pe 1:22 Spirit unto u' love of the brethren, "
unfruitful
M't 13:22 the word, and he becometh u'. 175
M'r 4:19 choke the word, and it becometh u' "
1Co 14:14 but my understanding is u'. "
Eph 5:11 with the u' works of darkness, "
Tit 3:14 necessary uses, that they be not u'. "
2Pe 1: 8 nor u' in the knowledge of our Lord "
ungirded
Ge 24:32 he u' his camels, and gave straw 6605
ungodliness
Ro 1:18 revealed from heaven against all u' 763
11:26 and shall turn away u' from Jacob: "
2Ti 2:16 for they will increase unto more u' "
Tit 2:12 denying u' and worldly lusts, we "
ungodly
2Sa 22: 5 floods of u' men made me afraid: *1100
2Ch 19: 2 Shouldest thou help the u', and *7563
Job 16:11 God hath delivered me to the u', 5760
34:18 wicked? and to princes, Ye are u'? *7563
Ps 1: 1 walketh not in the counsel of the u',*"
4 The u' are not so: but are like the*"
5 u' shall not stand in the judgment,*"
6 but the way of the u' shall perish.* "
3: 7 hast broken the teeth of the u'. * "
18: 4 floods of u' men made me afraid. *1100
43: 1 cause against an u' nation: 3808,2623
73:12 these are the u', who prosper in *7563
Pr 16:27 An u' man diggeth up evil: and in*1100
19:28 An u' witness scorneth judgment:* "
Ro 4: 5 on him that justifieth the u', his 765
5: 6 in due time Christ died for the u'. "
1Ti 1: 9 for the u' and for sinners, for "
1Pe 4:18 where shall the u' and the sinner "
2Pe 2: 5 in the flood upon the world of the u'; "
6 unto those that after should live u';764
3: 7 judgment and perdition of u' men. 765
Jude 4 u' men, turning the grace of our God "
15 to convince all that are u' among 763
15 all their u' deeds which they have* "
15 which they have u' committed, 764
15 speeches which u' sinners have 765
18 walk after their own u' lusts. 763
unholy
Le 10:10 difference between holy and u', *2455
1Ti 1: 9 for u' and profane, for murderers of 462
2Ti 3: 2 to parents, unthankful, u', "
Heb 10:29 he was sanctified, an u' thing, 2839
unicorn See also UNICORNS.
Nu 23:22 as it were the strength of an u'. *7214
24: 8 as it were the strength of an u': * "
Job 39: 9 Will the u' be willing to serve thee,*"
10 Canst thou bind the u' with his * "
Ps 29: 6 Lebanon and Sirion like a young u'.*"
92:10 thou exalt like the horn of an u': * "
unicorns
De 33:17 his horns are like the horns of u':*7214
Ps 22:21 heard me from the horns of the u'.*"
Isa 34: 7 the u' shall come down with them,* "
unite See also UNITED.
Ps 86:11 u' my heart to fear thy name. 3161
united
Ge 49: 6 mine honour, be not thou u': 3161
unity
Ps 133: 1 brethren to dwell together in u'! 3162
Eph 4: 3 to keep the u' of the Spirit in the 1775
13 we all come in the u' of the faith, "
unjust
Ps 43: 1 me from the deceitful and u' man. 5766
Pr 11: 7 and the hope of u' men perisheth.* 205
28: 8 u' gain increaseth his substance, *8636
29:27 An u' man is an abomination to 5766
Zep 3: 5 not; but the u' knoweth no shame. 5767
M't 5:45 rain on the just and on the u'. 94
Lu 16: 8 the lord commended the u' steward,*93
10 is u' in the least is u' also in much.* 94
18: 6 said, Hear what the u' judge saith.* 93
11 as other men are, extortioners, u', 94
Ac 24:15 of the dead, both of the just and u'. "
1Co 6: 1 go to law before the u', and not * "
1Pe 3:18 suffered for sins, the just for the u',* "
2Pe 2: 9 to reserve the u' unto the day of * "
Re 22:11 He that is u', let him be u' still: * 91
unjustly
Ps 82: 2 How long will ye judge u', and 5766
Isa 26:10 of uprightness will he deal u', *5765
unknown
Ac 17:23 this inscription, To The U' God. 57
1Co 14: 2 he that speaketh in an u' tongue *
4 in an u' tongue edifieth himself; *
14 if I pray in an u' tongue, my spirit*
19 ten thousand words in an u' tongue.*
27 If any man speak in an u' tongue, let*
2Co 6: 9 As u', and yet well known; as dying, 50
Gal 1:22 was u' by face unto the churches of "
unlade
Ac 21: 3 the ship was to u' her burden. 670
unlawful
Ac 10:28 an u' thing for a man that is a Jew 111
2Pe 2: 8 day to day with their u' deeds;) * 459

unlearned
Ac 4:13 that they were u' and ignorant men, 62
1Co 14:16 the u' say Amen at thy giving of 2399
23 there come in those that are u', "
24 one that believeth not, or one u', "
2Ti 2:23 foolish and u' questions avoid, * 521
2Pe 3:16 that are u' and unstable wrest, * 261
unleavened
Ge 19: 3 did bake u' bread, and they did 4682
Ex 12: 8 night, roast with fire, and u' bread; "
15 Seven days shall ye eat u' bread; "
17 shall observe the feast of u' bread; "
18 ye shall eat u' bread, until the one "
20 habitations shall ye eat u' bread. "
39 they baked u' cakes of the dough "
13: 6 Seven days thou shalt eat u' bread, "
7 U' bread shall be eaten seven "
23:15 shalt keep the feast of u' bread: "
15 (thou shalt eat u' bread seven days, "
29: 2 u' bread, and cakes u' tempered "
2 and wafers u' anointed with oil: "
23 out of the basket of the u' bread "
34:18 feast of u' bread shalt thou keep. "
18 Seven days thou shalt eat u' bread, "
Le 2: 4 u' cakes of fine flour mingled with "
4 oil, or u' wafers anointed with oil. "
5 a pan, it shall be of fine flour u', "
6:16 with u' bread shall it be eaten in * "
7:12 u' cakes mingled with oil, "
12 and u' wafers anointed with oil, "
8: 2 rams, and a basket of u' bread; "
26 And out of the basket of u' bread, "
26 he took one u' cake, and a cake of "
23: 6 the feast of u' bread unto the Lord: "
6 seven days ye must eat u' bread. "
Nu 6:15 and a basket of u' bread, cakes of "
15 wafers of u' bread anointed with "
17 Lord, with the basket of u' bread: "
19 and one u' cake out of the basket, "
19 one u' wafer, and shall put them "
9:11 eat it with u' bread and bitter "
28:17 seven days shall u' bread be eaten. "
De 16: 3 seven days shalt thou eat u' bread "
8 Six days thou shalt eat u' bread: "
16 in the feast of u' bread, and in the "
Jos 5:11 u' cakes, and parched corn in the "
J'g 6:19 and u' cakes of an ephah of flour: "
20 Take the flesh and the u' cakes, "
21 touched the flesh and the u' cakes; "
21 the flesh and the u' cakes. "
1Sa 28:24 kneaded it, and did bake u' bread "
2Ki 23: 9 did eat of the u' bread among their "
1Ch 23:29 for the u' cakes, and for that which "
2Ch 8:13 year, even in the feast of u' bread, "
30:13 people to keep the feast of u' bread "
21 the feast of u' bread seven days "
35:17 the feast of u' bread seven days. "
Ezr 6:22 the feast of u' bread seven days "
Eze 45:21 seven days; u' bread shall be eaten. "
M't 26:17 first day of the feast of u' bread 106
M'r 14: 1 of the passover, and of u' bread: "
12 the first day of u' bread, when they "
Lu 22: 1 Now the feast of u' bread drew nigh, "
7 Then came the day of u' bread, "
Ac 12: 3 (Then were the days of u' bread.) "
20: 6 Philippi after the days of u' bread, "
1Co 5: 7 ye may be a new lump, as ye are u'. "
8 the u' bread of sincerity and truth. "
unless
Le 22: 6 u' he wash his flesh with 3588,518
Nu 22:33 u' she had turned from me, surely 194
2Sa 2:27 u' thou hadst spoken, surely*3588,3884
Ps 27:13 u' I had believed to see the
94:17 U' the Lord had been my help, my "
119:92 U' thy law had been my delights, I "
Pr 4:16 u' they cause some to fall. 518,3808
1Co 15: 2 u' ye have believed in vain. *1622,1508
unloose See also LOOSE.
M'r 1: 7 not worthy to stoop down and u'. 3089
Lu 3:16 whose shoes I am not worthy to u': "
Joh 1:27 shoe's latchet I am not worthy to u'. "
unmarried
1Co 7: 8 say therefore to the u' and widows, 22
11 and if she depart, let her remain u', "
32 He that is u' careth for the things "
34 The u' woman careth for the things "
unmerciful
Ro 1:31 natural affection, implacable, u': 415
unmindful
De 32:18 Rock that begat thee thou art u', 7876
unmoveable
Ac 27:41 stuck fast, and remained u', 761
1Co 15:58 brethren, be ye stedfast, u', 277
Unni (*un'-ni*)
1Co 15:18 and Jehiel, and U', Eliab, and 6042
20 and Jehiel, and U', and Eliab, and "
Ne 12: 9 Also Bakbukiah and U', their "
unoccupied
J'g 5: 6 the highways were u', and the 2308
unperfect
Ps 139:16 did see my substance, yet being u':‡
unprepared
2Co 9: 4 come with me, and find you u', 532
unprofitable
Job 15: 3 Should he reason with u' talk? or 5532
M't 25:30 cast ye the u' servant into outer 888
Lu 17:10 you, say, We are u' servants: "
Ro 3:12 way, they are together become u'; 889
Tit 3: 9 the law; for they are u' and vain. 512
Ph'm 11 Which in time past was to thee u', 890
Heb 13:17 with grief: for that is u' for you. 255
unprofitableness
Heb 7:18 for the weakness and u' thereof. 512

unpunished
Pr 11:21 hand, the wicked shall not be u': 5352
16: 5 join in hand, he shall not be u'. "
17: 5 is glad at calamities shall not be u'. "
19: 5, 9 A false witness shall not be u', "
Jer 25:29 name, and should ye be utterly u'? "
29 Ye shall not be u': for I will call for "
30:11 will not leave thee altogether u'. "
46:28 yet will I not leave thee wholly u'. "
49:12 thou he that shall altogether go u'? "
12 thou shalt not go u', but thou shalt "
unquenchable
M't 3:12 will burn up the chaff with u' fire. 762
Lu 3:17 the chaff he will burn with fire u'. "
unreasonable
Ac 25:27 seemeth to me u' to send a prisoner, 249
2Th 3: 2 delivered from u' and wicked men: 824
unrebukeable
1Ti 6:14 commandment without spot, u', *423
unreproveable
Col 1:22 unblameable and u' in his sight: 410
unrighteous
Ex 23: 1 the wicked to be an u' witness. 2555
Job 27: 7 riseth up against me as the u'. 5767
Ps 71: 4 the hand of the u' and cruel man. 5765
Isa 10: 1 unto them that decree u' decrees, 205
55: 7 way, and the u' man his thoughts: "
Lu 16:11 not been faithful in the u' mammon, 94
Ro 3: 5 Is God u' who taketh vengeance? "
1Co 6: 9 u' shall not inherit the kingdom of "
Heb 6:10 God is not u' to forget your work "
unrighteousness
Le 19:15 Ye shall do no u' in judgment: 5766
35 Ye shall do no u' in judgment, in "
Ps 92:15 my rock, and there is no u' in him. "
Jer 22:13 that buildeth his house by u', 3808,6664
Lu 16: 9 friends of the mammon of u'; 93
Joh 7:18 the same is true, and no u' is in him. "
Ro 1:18 all ungodliness and u' of men, "
18 of men, who hold the truth in u'; "
29 Being filled with all u', fornication, "
2: 8 but obey u', indignation and wrath, "
3: 5 if our u' commend the righteousness "
6:13 as instruments of u' unto sin: "
9:14 we say then? Is there u' with God? "
2Co 6:14 hath righteousness with u'? * 458
2Th 2:10 deceivableness of u' in them that 93
12 not the truth, but had pleasure in u'. "
Heb 8:12 For I will be merciful to their u', * "
2Pe 2:13 And shall receive the reward of u',* "
15 Bosor, who loved the wages of u'; * "
1Jo 1: 9 sins, and to cleanse us from all u'. "
5:17 All u' is sin: and there is a sin not "
unrighteously
De 25:16 all that do u', are an abomination 5766
unripe
Job 15:33 shake off his u' grape as the vine, 1154
unruly
1Th 5:14 brethren, warn them that are u', *813
Tit 1: 6 children not accused of riot or u'. 506
10 there are many u' and vain talkers "
Jas 3: 8 it is an u' evil, full of deadly poison.*183
unsatiable
Eze 16:28 because thou wast u'; yea, 1115,7654
unsavoury
2Sa 22:27 froward thou wilt shew thyself u'.*6617
Job 6: 6 Can that which is u' be eaten 8602
unsearchable
Job 5: 9 doeth great things and u': 369,2714
Ps 145: 3 praised; and his greatness is u'. "
Pr 25: 3 and the heart of kings is u'. "
Ro 11:33 how u' are his judgments, and his 419
Eph 3: 8 Gentiles the u' riches of Christ; 421
unseemly
Ro 1:27 with men working that which is u'.*808
1Co 13: 5 Doth not behave itself u', seeketh not
unshod
Jer 2:25 Withhold thy foot from being u', 3182
unskilful
Heb 5:13 every one that useth milk is u' in * 552
unspeakable
2Co 9:15 Thanks be unto God for his u' gift. 411
12: 4 into paradise, and heard u' words, 731
1Pe 1: 8 with joy u' and full of glory: 412
unspotted
Jas 1:27 to keep himself u' from the world. 784
unstable
Ge 49: 4 U' as water, thou shalt not excel;‡6349
Jas 1: 8 A double minded man is u' in all 182
2Pe 2:14 cease from sin; beguiling u' souls:*793
3:16 that are unlearned and u' wrest, * "
unstopped
Isa 35: 5 and the ears of the deaf shall be u'. 6605
untaken
2Co 3:14 remaineth the same vail u' *3361,348
untempered
Eze 13:10 others daubed it with u' morter: 8602
11 them which daub it with u' morter, "
14 that ye have daubed with u' morter, "
15 that have daubed it with u' morter, "
22:28 have daubed them with u' morter, "
unthankful
Lu 6:35 is kind unto the u' and to the evil. 884
2Ti 3: 2 disobedient to parents, u', unholy, "

until See also TILL.
Ge 8: 5 continually *u'* the tenth month: 5704
7 *u'* the waters were dried up from "
26: 13 and grew *u'* he became very great: "
27: 44 *u'* thy brother's fury turn 5704,834
45 *U'* thy brother's anger turn 5704
28: 15 *u'* I have done that which I 5704,834
29: 8 *u'* all the flocks be gathered 5704
32: 4 Laban, and stayed there *u'* now: "
24 with him *u'* the breaking of the day. "
33: 3 *u'* he came near to his brother. "
14 *u'* I come unto my lord unto Seir. "
34: 5 held his peace *u'* they were come. "
39: 16 by her, *u'* his lord came home. "
41: 49 very much, *u'* he left numbering; "
46: 34 cattle from our youth even *u'* now, "
49: 10 his feet, *u'* Shiloh come; 5704,3588
Ex 9: 18 foundation thereof even *u'* now. 5704
10: 26 serve the Lord, *u'* we come thither. "
12: 6 keep it up *u'* the fourteenth day of "
10 nothing of it remain *u'*...morning; "
10 which remaineth of it *u'*...morning "
15 the first day *u'* the seventh day, "
18 *u'* the one and twentieth day of the "
22 door of his house *u'* the morning. "
16: 20 of them left of it *u'* the morning, "
23 for you to be kept *u'* the morning. "
35 *u'* they came to a land inhabited; "
35 *u'* they came unto the borders of "
17: 12 *u'* the going down of the sun. "
23: 18 sacrifice remain *u'* the morning. "
30 *u'* thou be increased, and inherit "
24: 14 for us, *u'* we come again unto you: "
33: 8 *u'* he was gone into the tabernacle. "
34: 34 he took the vail off, *u'* he came out. "
35 *u'* he went in to speak with him. "
Le 7: 15 not leave any of it *u'* the morning. "
8: 33 *u'* the days of your consecration be "
11: 24 them shall be unclean *u'* the even. "
25 clothes, and be unclean *u'* the even. "
27 shall be unclean *u'* the even. "
28 clothes, and be unclean *u'* the even: "
31 dead, shall be unclean *u'* the even. "
32 and it shall be unclean *u'* the even; "
39 shall be unclean *u'* the even. "
40 clothes, and be unclean *u'* the even: "
40 clothes, and be unclean *u'* the even. "
12: 4 *u'* the days of her purifying be "
14: 46 up shall be unclean *u'* the even. "
15: 5, 6, 7 and be unclean *u'* the even. "
10 him shall be unclean *u'* the even: "
10, 16, 17, 18, 19, 21, 22, 23, 27 be
unclean *u'* the even. 5704
16: 17 *u'* he come out, and have made an "
17: 15 water, and be unclean *u'* the even: "
19: 6 if ought remain *u'* the third day, it "
13 with thee all night *u'* the morning. "
22: 4 of the holy things, *u'* he be clean. "
6 any such shall be unclean *u'* even. "
30 leave none of it *u'* the morrow: "
23: 14 *u'* the selfsame day that ye have "
25: 22 eat...of old fruit *u'* the ninth year; "
22 *u'* her fruits come in ye shall "
28 bought it *u'* the year of jubile: "
Nu 4: 3 and upward even *u'* fifty years old, "
23 and upward *u'* fifty years old shalt "
6: 5 *u'* the days be fulfilled, in the "
9: 15 appearance of fire, *u'* the morning. "
11: 20 *u'* it come out at your nostrils, and "
14: 19 people, from Egypt even *u'* now. "
33 *u'* your carcases be wasted in the "
19: 7 priest shall be unclean *u'* the even. "
8 and shall be unclean *u'* the even. "
10 clothes, and be unclean *u'* the even: "
21 separation shall be unclean *u'* even. "
22 toucheth it shall be unclean *u'* even. "
20: 17 *u'* we have passed thy borders. "
21: 22 way, *u'* we be past thy borders. "
35 *u'* there was none left him alive: "
23: 24 not lie down *u'* he eat of the prey, "
24: 22 *u'* Asshur shall carry thee away "
32: 13 *u'* all the generation, that had "
17 *u'* we have brought them unto "
18 *u'* the children of Israel have "
21 *u'* he hath driven out his enemies "
35: 12 *u'* he stand before the congregation "
28 *u'* the death of the high priest: "
32 land, *u'* the death of the priest. "
De 1: 31 went, *u'* ye came into this place. "
2: 14 *u'* we were come over the brook "
14 *u'* all the generation of the men of "
15 the host, *u'* they were consumed. "
29 *u'* I shall pass over Jordan into the "
3: 3 we smote him *u'* none was left "
20 *U'* the Lord have given rest unto "
7: 20 *u'* they that are left, and hide "
23 destruction, *u'* they be destroyed. "
24 thee, *u'* thou have destroyed them. "
9: 7 *u'* ye came unto this place, ye have "
21 even *u'* it was as small as dust: "
11: 5 *u'* ye came into this place; "
16: 4 remain all night *u'* the morning. "
22: 2 thee *u'* thy brother seek after it, 5704
28: 20 for to do, *u'* thou be destroyed, "
20 and *u'* thou perish quickly; "
21 *u'* he have consumed thee from off "
22 shall pursue thee *u'* thou perish. "
24 upon thee, *u'* thou be destroyed. "
48 neck, *u'* he have destroyed thee. "
51 of thy land, *u'* thou be destroyed: "
51 sheep, *u'* he have destroyed thee. "
52 *u'* thy high and fenced walls come "
61 upon thee, *u'* thou be destroyed. "
31: 24 in a book, *u'* they were finished, "
30 of this song, *u'* they were ended. "
Jos 1: 15 *U'* the Lord have given your "
Jos 2: 16 days, *u'* the pursuers be returned: 5704
22 *u'* the pursuers were returned: "
3: 17 *u'* all the people were passed clean "
4: 10 *u'* every thing was finished that "
23 *u'* ye were passed over, as the Lord "
23 before us, *u'* we were gone over: "
5: 1 of Israel, *u'* we were passed over, "
6: 10 mouth, *u'* the day I bid you shout; "
7: 6 the ark of the Lord *u'* the eventide, "
13 *u'* ye take away the accursed thing "
8: 24 the sword, *u'* they were consumed, "
26 *u'* he had utterly destroyed all the "
29 he hanged on a tree *u'* eventide: "
10: 13 *u'* the people had avenged "
26 upon the trees *u'* the evening. "
27 which remain *u'* this very day. * "
33 *u'* he had left him none remaining. "
11: 8 *u'* they left them none remaining. "
14 *u'* they had destroyed them. "
13: 13 among the Israelites *u'* this day. * "
20: 6 *u'* he stand before the congregation "
6 *u'* the death of the high priest that "
9 *u'* he stood before the congregation. "
22: 17 we are not cleansed *u'* this day, * "
23: 13 *u'* ye perish from off this good land "
15 *u'* he have destroyed you from off "
J'g 4: 24 *u'* they had destroyed Jabin king "
5: 7 in Israel, *u'* that I Deborah arose, "
6: 18 *u'* I come unto thee, and bring "
13: 15 *u'* we shall have made ready a kid* "
18: 30 *u'* the day of the captivity of the "
19: 8 they tarried *u'* afternoon, and they "
25 her all the night *u'* the morning: "
20: 23 and wept before the Lord *u'* even, "
Ru 1: 19 went *u'* they came to Beth-lehem. "
2: 7 even from the morning *u'* now, "
17 she gleaned in the field *u'* even, "
21 *u'* they have ended all my 5704,518
3: 3 *u'* he shall have done eating and 5704
13 liveth: lie down *u'* the morning. "
14 she lay at his feet *u'* the morning: "
18 *u'* thou know how the matter 5704,834
18 *u'* he have finished the thing 3588,518
1Sa 1: 22 not go up *u'* the child be weaned, 5704
23 tarry *u'* thou have weaned him; "
23 her son suck *u'* she weaned him. "
3: 15 And Samuel lay *u'* the morning, "
7: 11 *u'* they came under Beth-car. "
9: 13 the people will not eat *u'* he come, "
11: 11 Ammonites *u'* the heat of the day: "
14: 9 Tarry *u'* we come to you; then we "
24 that eateth any food *u'* evening, "
36 spoil them *u'* the morning light, "
15: 7 Havilah *u'* thou comest to Shur, * "
18 against them *u'* they be consumed. 5704
35 to see Saul *u'* the day of his death: "
17: 52 *u'* thou come to the valley, "
19: 2 heed to thyself *u'* the morning, * "
23 *u'* he came to Naioth in Ramah. "
20: 41 with another, *u'* David exceeded. "
25: 36 less or more, *u'* the morning light. "
30: 4 *u'* they had no more power to 5704,834
2Sa 1: 12 and fasted *u'* even, for Saul, and 5704
4: 3 were sojourners there *u'* this day.) "
5: 25 from Geba *u'* thou come to Gazer. "
10: 5 Jericho *u'* your beards be grown, "
15: 24 *u'* all the people had done passing "
28 *u'* there come word from you to "
17: 13 *u'* there be not one small stone 5704,834
19: 7 befell thee from thy youth *u'* now. 5704
24 king departed *u'* the day he came "
21: 10 *u'* water dropped upon them out of "
22: 38 not again *u'* I had consumed them.* "
23: 10 *u'* his hand was weary, 5704,3588
1Ki 3: 1 *u'* he had made an end of building 5704
2 name of the Lord, *u'* those days. "
5: 3 *u'* the Lord put them under the "
6: 22 *u'* he had finished all the house: "
10: 7 *u'* I came, and mine eyes had seen "
11: 16 *u'* he had cut off every male in "
40 in Egypt *u'* the death of Solomon. "
15: 29 breathed, *u'* he had destroyed him, "
17: 14 *u'* the day that the Lord sendeth "
18: 26 Baal from morning even *u'* noon, "
29 *u'* the time of the offering of the "
22: 11 *u'* thou have consumed them. "
27 of affliction, *u'* I come in peace. "
2Ki 6: 25 *u'* an ass's head was sold for "
7: 3 another, Why sit we here *u'* we die? "
8: 6 that she left the land, even *u'* now. "
11 stedfastly, *u'* he was ashamed: "
10: 8 in of the gate *u'* the morning. "
11 *u'* he left him none remaining. "
17: 20 *u'* he had cast them out of his "
23 *U'* the Lord removed Israel out of "
18: 32 *U'* I come and take you away to a "
24: 20 *u'* he had cast them out from his "
1Ch 5: 22 in their steads *u'* the captivity. "
6: 32 *u'* Solomon had built the house of "
12: 22 *u'* it was a great host, like the host "
19: 5 at Jericho *u'* your beards be grown, "
28: 20 *u'* thou hast finished all the work "
2Ch 8: 8 make to pay tribute *u'* this day. * "
16 of the Lord, and *u'* it was finished. "
9: 6 *u'* I came, and mine eyes had seen "
16: 12 *u'* his disease was exceeding great:* "
18: 10 push Syria *u'* they be consumed. "
26 of affliction, *u'* I return in peace. "
34 against the Syrians *u'* the even: "
21: 15 *u'* thy bowels fall out by reason of "
24: 10 the chest, *u'* they had made an end. "
29: 28 *u'* the burnt offering was finished. "
34 *u'* the other priests had sanctified "
35: 14 burnt offerings and the fat *u'* night; "
36: 16 *u'* the wrath of the Lord arose "
20 *u'* the reign of the kingdom of "
2Ch 36: 21 *u'* the land had enjoyed her 5704
Ezr 4: 5 even *u'* the reign of Darius king of "
21 *u'* another commandment shall be "
5: 16 *u'* now hath it been in building, "
8: 29 *u'* ye weigh them before the chief "
9: 4 astonied *u'* the evening sacrifice. "
10: 14 *u'* the fierce wrath of our God for "
Ne 7: 3 be opened *u'* the sun be hot; "
8: 3 gate from the morning *u'* midday, "
12: 23 *u'* the days of Johanan the son of "
Job 14: 13 me secret, *u'* thy wrath be past, "
26: 10 *u'* the day and night come to an * "
Ps 36: 2 *u'* his iniquity be found to be hateful.*
57: 1 *u'* these calamities be overpast. 5704
71: 18 *u'* I have shewed thy strength unto "
94: 13 *u'* the pit be digged for the wicked. "
104: 23 and to his labour *u'* the evening. "
105: 19 *U'* the time that his word came: "
110: 1 *u'* I make thine enemies thy "
112: 8 *u'* he see his desire upon his "
123: 2 *u'* that he have mercy upon us. "
132: 5 *U'* I find out a place for the Lord, "
Pr 7: 18 take our fill of love *u'* the morning: "
Ca 2: 17 *U'* the day break, and the shadows "
3: 11 *u'* I had brought him into my "
4: 6 *U'* the day break, and the shadows "
8: 4 nor awake my love, *u'* he please. "
Isa 5: 11 that continue *u'* night, till wine * "
6: 11 *U'* the cities be wasted without 5704
26: 20 *u'* the indignation be overpast. "
32: 15 *U'* the spirit be poured upon us "
36: 17 *U'* I come and take you away to a "
39: 6 have laid up in store *u'* this day, "
62: 1 *u'* the righteousness...go forth as "
Jer 23: 20 not return, *u'* he have executed, "
27: 7 *u'* the very time of his land come: "
8 *u'* I have consumed them by his "
22 they be *u'* the day that I visit them, "
30: 24 shall not return, *u'* he have done it, "
24 *u'* he hath performed the intents of* "
32: 5 and there shall he be *u'* I visit him, "
36: 23 *u'* all the roll was consumed in the "
37: 21 *u'* all the bread in the city were "
38: 28 *u'* the day that Jerusalem was "
44: 27 famine, *u'* there be an end of them. "
52: 34 a portion *u'* the day of his death, "
Eze 21: 27 more, *u'* he come whose right it is; "
33: 22 *u'* he came to me in the morning; "
46: 2 shall not be shut *u'* the evening. "
Da 4: 32 *u'* thou know that the most High "
7: 22 *U'* the Ancient of days came, and "
25 *u'* a time...times and the dividing "
9: 27 desolate,...*u'* the consummation, * "
Ho 7: 4 the dough, *u'* it be leavened. "
Mic 5: 3 *u'* the time...she which travaileth "
7: 9 *u'* he plead my cause, and execute "
Zep 3: 8 *u'* the day that I rise up to the prey: "
M't 1: 17 *u'* the carrying away into Babylon *2193*
2: 13 be thou there *u'* I bring thee word: "
15 was there *u'* the death of Herod: "
11: 12 days of John the Baptist *u'* now "
13 and the law prophesied *u'* John. "
23 would have remained *u'* this day. *3360*
13: 30 both grow together *u'* the harvest: "
17: 9 *u'* the Son of man be risen again *2193*
18: 22 say not unto thee, *U'* seven times: "
22 times: but, *U'* seventy times seven. "
24: 38 *u'* the day that Noe entered into *891*
39 And knew not *u'* the flood came, *2193*
26: 29 *u'* that day when I drink it new "
27: 64 be made sure *u'* the third day, "
28: 15 among the Jews *u'* this day. *3360*
M'r 14: 25 *u'* that day that I drink it new *2193*
15: 33 the whole land *u'* the ninth hour. "
Lu 1: 20 *u'* the day that these things shall be *891*
13: 35 *u'* the time...when ye shall say, *2193*
15: 4 after that which is lost, *u'* he find it? "
16: 16 and the prophets were *u'* John: "
17: 27 *u'* the day that Noe entered into *891*
21: 24 *u'* the times of the Gentiles be "
22: 16 *u'* it be fulfilled in the kingdom of *2193*
18 *u'* the kingdom of God shall come. "
23: 44 over all the earth *u'* the ninth hour. "
24: 49 *u'* ye be endued with power from "
Joh 2: 10 hast kept the good wine *u'* now. "
9: 18 *u'* they called the parents of him "
Ac 1: 2 *U'* the day in which he was taken *891*
2: 35 *U'* I make thy foes thy footstool. **2193*
3: 21 *u'* the times of restitution of all *891*
10: 30 ago I was fasting *u'* this hour; *3360*
13: 20 fifty years, *u'* Samuel the prophet. *2193*
20: 7 continued his speech *u'* midnight. *3360*
21: 26 *u'*...an offering should be offered *2193*
23: 1 conscience before God *u'* this day. *891*
14 eat nothing *u'* we have slain Paul. *2193*
Ro 5: 13 (For *u'* the law sin was in the world: *891*
8: 22 travaileth in pain together *u'* now. "
11: 25 *u'* the fulness of the Gentiles "
1Co 4: 5 *u'* the Lord come, who both will *2193*
16: 8 will tarry at Ephesus *u'* Pentecost. "
2Co 3: 14 *u'* this day remaineth the same vail *891*
Ga 4: 2 *u'* the time appointed of the father. "
19 again *u'* Christ be formed in you, "
Eph 1: 14 *u'*...redemption of the purchased **1519*
Ph'p 1: 5 gospel from the first day *u'* now; *891*
6 it *u'* the day of Jesus Christ: "
2Th 2: 7 let, *u'* he be taken out of the way. *2193*
1Ti 6: 14 *u'* the appearing of our Lord *3360*
Heb 1: 13 *u'* I make thine enemies thy **2193*
9: 10 them *u'* the time of reformation. *3360*
Jas 5: 7 *u'* he receive the early and latter *2193*
2Pe 1: 19 *u'* the day dawn, and the day star "
1Jo 2: 9 brother, is in darkness even *u'* now. "
Re 6: 11 *u'* their fellowservants also and "
17: 17 *u'* the words of God...be fulfilled. *891*
20: 5 *u'*...thousand years were finished. *2193*

untimely
Job 3:16 a hidden u' birth I had not been; 5309
Ps 58: 8 like the u' birth of a woman, that "
Ec 6: 3 that an u' birth is better than he. "
Re 6:13 as a fig tree casteth her u' figs, *3653
unto See in the APPENDIX; also HEREUNTO; THEREUNTO; WHEREUNTO.
untoward
Ac 2:40 from this u' generation. *4646
unwalled
De 3: 5 beside u' towns a great many. 6521
Es 9:19 villages, that dwelt in the u' towns,6519
Eze 38:11 will go up to the land of u' villages;
unwashen
M't 15:20 to eat with u' hands defileth not a 449
M'r 7: 2 defiled, that is...with u', hands, "
5 elders, but eat bread with u' hands?*"
unweighed
1Ki 7:47 And Solomon left all the vessels u',*
unwise
De 32: 6 O foolish people and u'? 3808,2450
Ho 13:13 he is an u' son; for he should "
Ro 1:14 both to the wise, and to the u'. * 453
Eph 5:17 Wherefore be ye not u', but * 878
unwittingly
Le 22:14 if a man eat of the holy thing u', 7684
Jos 20: 3 any person unawares and u'*1097,1847
5 he smote his neighbour u', * "
unworthily
1Co 11:27 and drink this cup of the Lord, u',† 371
29 For he that eateth and drinketh u',* "
unworthy
Ac 13:46 u' of everlasting life, 3756,514
1Co 6: 2 u' to judge the smallest matters? 370
up See in the APPENDIX; also UPBRAID; UPHOLD; UPON; UPPER; UPRIGHT; UPRISING; UPROAR; UPSIDE; UPWARD.
upbraid See also UPBRAIDED; UPBRAIDETH.
J'g 8:15 with whom ye did u' me, saying, *2778
M't 11:20 Then began he to u' the cities 3679
upbraided
M'r 16:14 and u' them with their unbelief 3679
upbraideth
Jas 1: 5 to all men liberally, and u' not; 3679
Upharsin (u-far'-sin) See also PERES.
Da 5:25 written, Mene, Mene, Tekel, U'. 6537
Uphaz (u'-faz)
Jer 10: 9 Tarshish, and gold from U', the 210
Da 10: 5 were girded with fine gold of U':
upheld
Isa 63: 5 unto me; and my fury, it u' me. 5564
uphold See also UPHELD; UPHOLDEN; UPHOLDEST; UPHOLDETH; UPHOLDING.
Ps 51:12 and u' me with thy free spirit. 5564
54: 4 Lord is with them that u' my soul. "
119:116 U' me according unto thy word, "
Pr 29:23 but honour shall u' the humble in*8551
Isa 41:10 I will u' thee with the right hand of"
42: 1 Behold my servant, whom I u'; "
63: 5 I wondered...there was none to u':5564
Eze 30: 6 They also that u' Egypt shall fall; "
upholden
Job 4: 4 Thy words have u' him that was 6965
Pr 20:28 and his throne is u' by mercy. 5582
upholdest
Ps 41:12 me, thou u' me in mine integrity, 8551
upholdeth
Ps 37:17 but the Lord u' the righteous. 5564
24 for the Lord u' him with his hand. "
63: 8 after thee: thy right hand u' me. 8551
145:14 Lord u' all that fall, and raiseth 5564
upholding
Heb 1: 3 u' all things by the word of his 5342
upon See in the APPENDIX; also THEREUPON; WHEREUPON.
upper See also UPPERMOST.
Ex 12: 7 on the u' door post of the houses, *4947
Le 13:45 shall put a covering upon his u' lip,8222
De 24: 6 the nether or the u' millstone to 7393
Jos 15:19 And he gave her the u' springs, 5942
16: 5 unto Beth-horon the u'; 5945
J'g 1:15 Caleb gave her the u' springs and 5942
2Ki 1: 2 a lattice in his u' chamber that 5944
18:17 stood by the conduit of the u' pool,5945
23:12 the top of the u' chamber of Ahaz, 5944
1Ch 7:24 Beth-horon the nether, and the u',5945
28:11 and of the u' chambers thereof, 5944
2Ch 3: 9 he overlaid the u' chambers with "
8: 5 Also he built Beth-horon the u', 5945
32:30 also stopped the u' watercourse of "
Isa 7: 3 end of the conduit of the u' pool "
36: 2 stood by the conduit of the u' pool "
Eze 42: 5 Now the u' chambers were shorter: "
Zep 2:14 shall lodge in the u' lintels of it; *3730
M'r 14:15 shew you a large u' room furnished 508
Lu 22:12 shew you a large u' room furnished:"
Ac 1:13 they went up into an u' room, 5253
9:37 they laid her in an u' chamber. "
39 brought him into the u' chamber: "
19: 1 having passed through the u' coasts 510
20: 8 many lights in the u' chamber, 5250
uppermost
Ge 40:17 u' basket there was of all manner 5945
Isa 17: 6 berries in the top of the u' bough,
Isa 17: 9 a forsaken bough, and an u' branch,*
M't 23: 6 love the u' rooms at feasts, and *4411
M'r 12:39 and the u' rooms at feasts: * "
Lu 11:43 love the u' seats in...synagogues, *4410
upright
Ge 37: 7 lo, my sheaf arose, and also stood u';
Ex 15: 8 the floods stood u' as an heap,
Le 26:13 of your yoke, and made you go u'. 6968
1Sa 29: 6 thou hast been u', and thy going 3477
2Sa 22:24 was also u' before him, and have *8549
26 merciful, and with the u' man * "
26 thou wilt shew thyself u'. *8552
2Ch 29:34 the Levites were more u' in heart 3477
Job 1: 1 and that man was perfect and u', "
8 a perfect and an u' man, one that "
2: 3 a perfect and an u' man, one that "
8: 6 If thou wert pure and u'; surely "
12: 4 just u' man is laughed to scorn. *8549
17: 8 U' men shall be astonied at this, 3477
Ps 7:10 God, which saveth the u' in heart. "
11: 2 may privily shoot at the u' in heart."
7 his countenance doth behold the u'."
18:23 I was also u' before him, and I *8549
25 thyself merciful; with an u' man * "
25 thou wilt shew thyself u'; *8549,8552
19:13 then shall I be u', and I shall be * "
20: 8 fallen: but we are risen, and stand u'.
25: 8 Good and u' is the Lord: therefore3477
32:11 for joy, all ye that are u' in heart. "
33: 1 for praise is comely for the u'. "
36:10 thy righteousness to the u' in heart."
37:14 slay such as be of u' conversation. "
18 Lord knoweth the days of the u': *8549
37 perfect man, and behold the u': 3477
49:14 u' shall have dominion over them "
64:10 and all the u' in heart shall glory. "
92:15 To shew that the Lord is u': he is "
94:15 all the u' in heart shall follow it. "
97:11 and gladness for the u' in heart. "
111: 1 heart, in the assembly of the u', "
112: 2 generation of the u' shall be blessed."
4 Unto the u' there ariseth light in "
119:137 O Lord, and u' are thy judgments. "
125: 4 to them that are u' in their hearts. "
140:13 the u' shall dwell in thy presence. "
Pr 2:21 For the u' shall dwell in the land, "
10:29 of the Lord is strength to the u': 8537
11: 3 The integrity of the u' shall guide 3477
6 righteousness of the u' shall deliver"
11 By the blessing of the u' the city is "
20 are u' in their way are his delight.*8549
12: 6 mouth of the u' shall deliver them.3477
13: 6 keepeth him that is u' in the way: 8537
14:11 tabernacle of the u' shall flourish. 3477
15: 8 the prayer of the u' is his delight. "
16:17 The highway of the u' is to depart "
21:18 and the transgressor for the u'. "
29 as for the u', he directeth his way. "
28:10 the u' shall have good things in *8549
29:10 The bloodthirsty hate the u': but *8535
27 is u' in the way is abomination to 3477
Ec 7:29 found, that God had made man u'; "
12:10 that which was written was u', *3476
Ca 1: 4 more than wine: the u' love thee. *4339
Isa 26: 7 thou, most u', dost weigh the path3477
Jer 10: 5 They are u' as the palm tree, but *4749
Da 8:18 but he touched me, and set me u'. 5977
10:11 I speak unto thee, and stand u': "
11:17 kingdom, and u' ones with him; 3477
Mic 7: 2 and there is none u' among men: "
4 u' is sharper than a thorn hedge: "
Hab 2: 4 which is lifted up is not u' in him: 3474
Ac 14:10 a loud voice, Stand u' on thy feet. 3717
uprightly
Ps 15: 2 He that walketh u', and worketh 8549
58: 1 do ye judge u', O ye sons of men? 4339
75: 2 the congregation I will judge u'. "
84:11 withhold from them that walk u'. 8549
Pr 2: 7 is a buckler to them that walk u'.*8537
10: 9 He that walketh u' walketh surely: "
15:21 man of understanding walketh u'.*3474
28:18 Whoso walketh u' shall be saved: 8549
Isa 33:15 righteously, and speaketh u'; 4339
Am 5:10 they abhor him that speaketh u'. 8549
Mic 2: 7 do good to him that walketh u'? 3477
Ga 2:14 they walked not u' according to 3716
uprightness
De 9: 5 or for the u' of thine heart, dost 3476
1Ki 3: 6 and in u' of heart with thee; 3483
9: 4 in integrity of heart, and in u', 3476
1Ch 29:17 the heart, and hast pleasure in u'. "
17 u' of mine heart I have willingly 4339
Job 4: 6 thy hope, and the u' of thy ways? *8537
33: 3 shall be of the u' of my heart: 3476
23 thousand, to shew unto man his u':*"
Ps 9: 8 judgment to the people in u'. 4339
25:21 Let integrity and u' preserve me; 3476
111: 8 ever, and are done in truth and u'.3477
119: 7 I will praise thee with u' of heart, 3476
143:10 good; lead me into the land of u'. 4334
Pr 2:13 Who leave the paths of u', to walk 3476
14: 2 He that walketh in his u' feareth "
28: 6 is the poor that walketh in his u',*8537
Isa 26: 7 The way of the just is u': thou, 4339
10 land of u' will he deal unjustly, 5229
57: 2 beds, each one walking in his u'. 5228
uprising
Ps 139: 2 my downsitting and mine u', 6965
uproar
1Ki 1:41 noise of the city being in an u'? 1993
M't 26: 5 there be an u' among the people. *2351
M'r 14: 2 lest there be an u' of the people. * "
Ac 17: 5 and set all the city on an u'. 2350
Ac 19:40 called in question for this day's u',*4714
20: 1 And after the u' was ceased, Paul 2351
21:31 that all Jerusalem was in an u'. *4797
38 before these days madest an u', * 387
upside
2Ki 21:13 wiping it, and turning it u' 5921,6440
Ps 146: 9 way of the wicked he turneth u' down.
Isa 24: 1 waste, and turneth it u' down, 5921,6440
29:16 your turning of things u' down shall
Ac 17: 6 that have turned the world u' down 389
upward
Ge 7:20 Fifteen cubits u' did the waters 4605
Ex 38:26 from twenty years old and u', "
Nu 1: 3 From twenty years old and u', all "
18, 20, 22, 24, 26, 28, 30, 32, 34, 36, 38, 40, 42, 45 from twenty years old and u'. 4605
3:15 every male from a month old and u'"
22, 28, 34, 39, 40, 43 a month old and u'."
4: 3, 23, 30, 35, 39, 43, 47 years old and u' "
8:24 twenty and five years old and u' "
14:29 from twenty years old and u', "
26: 2 from twenty years old and u', "
4 from twenty years old and u'; "
62 all males from a month old and u': "
32:11 from twenty years old and u', "
J'g 1:36 to Akrabbim, from the rock, and u'."
1Sa 9: 2 from his shoulders and u' he was "
10:23 people from his shoulders and u'. "
2Ki 3:21 were able to put an armour, and u',"
19:30 root downward, and bear fruit u'. "
1Ch 23: 3 the age of thirty years and u': "
24 the age of twenty years and u'. "
2Ch 31:16 males, from three years old and u', "
17 from twenty years old and u', "
Ezr 3: 8 from twenty years old and u', "
Job 5: 7 unto trouble, as the sparks fly u'. 1361
Ec 3:21 the spirit of man that goeth u', 4605
Isa 8:21 king and their God, and look u'. "
37:31 root downward, and bear fruit u': "
38:14 mine eyes fail with looking u': 4791
Eze 1:11 their wings were stretched u'; *4605
27 the appearance of his loins even u',"
8: 2 from his loins even u', as the "
41: 7 a winding about still u' to the side* "
7 went still u' round about the * "
7 breadth of the house was still u', "
43:15 altar and u' shall be four horns. "
Hag 2:15 you, consider from this day and u', "
18 Consider now from this day and u'."
Ur (ur)
Ge 11:28 his nativity, in U' of the Chaldees. 218
31 with them from U' of the Chaldees, "
15: 7 thee out of U' of the Chaldees, "
1Ch 11:35 the Hararite, Eliphal the son of U', "
Ne 9: 7 him forth out of U' of the Chaldees, "
Urbane (ur'-bane)
Ro 16: 9 Salute U', our helper in Christ, 3779
urge See also URGED.
Lu 11:53 the Pharisees began to u' him *1758
urged
Ge 33:11 and he u' him, and he took it. 6484
J'g 16:16 daily with her words, and u' him, 509
19: 7 depart, his father in law u' him: 6484
2Ki 2:17 they u' him till he was ashamed, "
5:16 And he u' him to take it; but he "
23 he u' him, and bound two talents 6555
urgent
Ex 12:33 the Egyptians were u' upon the 2388
Da 3:22 the king's commandment was u', 2685
Uri (u'-ri)
Ex 31: 2 by name Bezaleel the son of U', 221
35:30 by name Bezaleel the son of U', "
38:22 And Bezaleel the son of U', the son "
1Ki 4:19 Geber the son of U' was in the "
1Ch 2:20 And Hur begat U', and U' begat "
2Ch 1: 5 that Bezaleel the son of U', the son "
Ezr 10:24 Shallum, and Telem, and U'. "
Uriah (u-ri'-ah) See also URIAH'S; URIAS; URIJAH.
2Sa 11: 3 Eliam, the wife of U' the Hittite? 223
6 saying, Send me U' the Hittite. "
6 And Joab sent U' to David. "
7 And when U' was come unto him, "
8 And David said to U', Go down to "
8 And U' departed out of the king's "
9 U' slept at the door of the king's "
10 U' went not down unto his house, "
10 David said unto U', Camest thou "
11 U' said unto David, The ark, and "
12 David said to U', Tarry here to day "
12 So U' abode in Jerusalem that day, "
14 Joab, and sent it by the hand of U'. "
15 Set ye U' in the forefront of the "
16 he assigned U' unto a place where "
17 David; and U' the Hittite died also. "
21 Thy servant U' the Hittite is dead "
24 thy servant U' the Hittite is dead "
26 the wife of U' heard that U' her "
12: 9 killed U' the Hittite with the sword, "
10 taken the wife of U' the Hittite to "
23:39 U' the Hittite: thirty and seven in "
1Ki 15: 5 in the matter of U' the Hittite. "
1Ch 11:41 U' the Hittite, Zabad the son of "
Ezr 8:33 the hand of Meremoth the son of U'"
Isa 8: 2 witnesses to record, U' the priest, "
Uriah's (u-ri'-ahz)
2Sa 12:15 Lord struck the child that U' wife 223
Urias (u-ri'-as) See also URIAH.
M't 1: 6 her that had been the wife of U':*3774
Uriel (u'-re-el)
1Ch 6:24 Tahath his son, U' his son, Uzziah 222
15: 5 the sons of Kohath; U' the chief. "

1Ch 15: 11 and for the Levites, for *U*', Asaiah, 222
2Ch 13: 2 the daughter of *U*' of Gibeah. "

Urijah (*u-ri'-jah*) See also URIAH.
2Ki 16: 10 Ahaz sent to *U*' the priest the 223
11 And *U*' the priest built an altar "
11 *U*' the priest made it against king "
15 Ahaz commanded *U*' the priest, "
16 Thus did *U*' the priest, according to "
Ne 3: 4 repaired Meremoth the son of *U*',* "
21 repaired Meremoth the son of *U*'* "
8: 4 and Anaiah, and *U*', and Hilkiah,* "
Jer 26: 20 *U*' the son of Shemaiah of "
21 when *U*' heard it, he was afraid, * "
23 they fetched forth *U*' out of Egypt,* "

Urim (*u'-rim*)
Ex 28: 30 the breastplate of judgment the *U*' 224
Le 8: 8 he put in the breastplate the *U*' "
Nu 27: 21 judgment of *U*' before the Lord: "
De 33: 8 thy Thummim and thy *U*' be with "
1Sa 28: 6 neither by dreams, nor by *U*', nor "
Ezr 2: 63 till there stood up a priest with *U*' "
Ne 7: 65 till there stood up a priest with *U*' "

us See in the APPENDIX; also US-WARD.

use See also ABUSE; USED; USES; USEST; USETH; USING.
Le 7: 24 may be used in any other *u*': *4399
19: 26 neither shall ye *u*' enchantment, 5172
Nu 10: 2 mayest *u*' them for the calling of the
15: 39 after which ye *u*' to go a whoring:
De 26: 14 ought thereof for any unclean *u*',*
2Sa 1: 18 children of Judah the *u*' of the bow:*
1Ch 12: 2 *u*' both the right hand and the 3231
28: 15 to the *u*' of every candlestick. 5656
Jer 23: 31 that *u*' their tongues, and say, He 3947
31: 23 shall *u*' this speech in the land of 559
46: 11 in vain shalt thou *u*' many medicines;
Eze 12: 23 more *u*' it as a proverb in Israel. 4912
16: 44 shall *u*' this proverb against thee, 4911
18: 2 *u*' this proverb concerning the "
3 more to *u*' this proverb in Israel. "
21: 21 of the two ways, to *u*' divination: 7080
M't 5: 44 them which despitefully *u*' you, **1908*
6: 7 when ye pray, *u*' not vain repetitions,
Lu 6: 28 them which despitefully *u*' you, *1908*
Ac 14: 5 to *u*' them despitefully, and to **5195*
Ro 1: 26 did change the natural *u*' into that *5540*
27 leaving...natural *u*' of the woman, "
1Co 7: 21 mayest be made free, *u*' it rather. *5530*
31 they that *u*' this world, as not "
2Co 1: 17 thus minded, did I *u*' lightness? * "
3: 12 we *u*' great plainness of speech: "
13: 10 being present I...*u*' sharpness, * "
Ga 5: 13 *u*' not liberty for an occasion to the
Eph 4: 29 is good to the *u*' of edifying, **5532*
1Ti 1: 8 is good, if a man *u*' it lawfully; *5530*
3: 10 then let them *u*' the office of a deacon,*
5: 23 *u*' a little wine for thy stomach's *5530*
2Ti 2: 21 and meet for the master's *u*',
Heb 5: 14 those who by reason of *u*' have *1838*
1Pe 4: 9 *U*' hospitality one to another **5382*

used See also ABUSED; MISUSED.
Ex 21: 36 the ox hath *u*' to push in time past,*
Le 7: 24 may be *u*' in any other use: 6213
J'g 14: 10 a beast, for so *u*' the young men to do.
20 whom he had *u*' as his friend.
2Ki 17: 17 *u*' divination and enchantments,
21: 6 times, and *u*' enchantments,
2Ch 33: 6 times, and *u*' enchantments,
6 and *u*' witchcraft, and dealt with a*
Jer 2: 24 A wild ass *u*' to the wilderness, 3928
Eze 22: 29 people of the land have *u*' oppression,
35: 11 envy which thou hast *u*' out of thy*6213
Ho 12: 10 multiplied visions, and *u*' similitudes,
M'r 2: 18 and of the Pharisees *u*' to fast: **1510*
Ac 8: 9 in the same city *u*' sorcery, *3096*
19: 19 of them also which *u*' curious arts**4238*
27: 17 they *u*' helps, undergirding the ship; *5530*
Ro 3: 13 their tongues they have *u*' deceit; *1387*
1Co 9: 12 we have not *u*' this power; **5530*
15 But I have *u*' none of these things: "
1Th 2: 5 time *u*' we flattering words, **1096,1722*
1Ti 3: 13 that have *u*' the office of a deacon**1247*
Heb 10: 33 companions of them that were so *u*'. *390*

uses
Tit 3: 14 good works for necessary *u*', *5532*

usest
Ps 119: 132 as thou *u*' to do unto those that 4941

useth
De 18: 10 or that *u*' divination, or an observer
Es 6: 8 be brought which the king *u*' to wear,
Pr 15: 2 of the wise *u*' knowledge aright: *
18: 23 The poor *u*' intreaties; but the 1696
Jer 22: 13 that *u*' his neighbour's service
Eze 16: 44 every one that *u*' proverbs shall
Heb 5: 13 For one that *u*' milk is unskilful *3348*

using See also ABUSING.
Col 2: 22 Which all are to perish with the *u*';)*671*
1Pe 2: 16 not *u*' your liberty for a cloke of *2192*

usurer
Ex 22: 25 thou shalt not be to him as an *u*', *5383

usurp
1Ti 2: 12 nor to *u*' authority over the man. *831*

usury
Ex 22: 25 shalt thou lay upon him *u*'. 5392
Le 25: 36 Take thou no *u*' of him, or increase: "
37 not give him thy money upon *u*', "
De 23: 19 not lend upon *u*' to thy brother; 5391
19 *u*' of money, *u*' of victuals, 5392
19 *u*' of any thing that is lent upon "
19 any thing that is lent upon *u*': 5391
20 a stranger thou mayest lend upon *u*';"
De 23: 20 thou shalt not lend upon *u*': 5391
Ne 5: 7 Ye exact *u*', every one of his 5383
10 I pray you, let us leave off this *u*'. 5383
Ps 15: 5 putteth not out his money to *u*', 5392
Pr 28: 8 He that by *u*' and unjust gain "
Isa 24: 2 as with the taker of *u*', so with 5383
2 so with the giver of *u*' to him. 5378
Jer 15: 10 I have neither lent on *u*', nor men 5383
10 nor men have lent to me on *u*'; "
Eze 18: 8 thou hath not given forth upon *u*',5392
13 Hath given forth upon *u*', and hath "
17 hath not received *u*' nor increase, "
22: 12 thou hast taken *u*' and increase, "
M't 25: 27 have received mine own with *u*'. **5110*
Lu 19: 23 have required mine own with *u*'? * "

us-ward
Ps 40: 5 and thy thoughts which are to *u*': 413
Eph 1: 19 his power to *u*' who believed, *1519,2248*
2Pe 3: 9 but is longsuffering to *u*', not " "

Uthai (*u'-thahee*)
1Ch 9: 4 *U*' the son of Ammihud, the son 5793
Ezr 8: 14 *U*', and Zabbud, and with them "

utmost See also OUTMOST; UTTERMOST.
Ge 49: 26 the *u*' bound of the everlasting hills:
Nu 22: 36 Arnon, which is in the *u*' coast. 7097
41 might see the *u*' part of the people. "
23: 13 shalt see but the *u*' part of them, "
De 34: 2 the land of Judah, unto the *u*' sea,* 314
Jer 9: 26 and all that are in the *u*' corners, *7112
25: 23 and all that are in the *u*' corners, * "
49: 32 them that are in the *u*' corners; * "
50: 26 against her from the *u*' border, 7093
Joe 2: 20 his hinder part toward the *u*' sea,* 314
Lu 11: 31 from the *u*' parts of the earth to **4009*

utter See also OUTER; UTTERED; UTTERETH; UTTERING; UTTERMOST.
Le 5: 1 if he do not *u*' it, then he shall 5046
Jos 2: 14 yours, if ye *u*' not this our business." "
20 And if thou *u*' this our business, "
J'g 5: 12 Deborah: awake, awake, *u*' a song:1696
1Ki 20: 42 I appointed to *u*' destruction, *
Job 8: 10 and *u*' words out of their heart? 3318
15: 2 a wise man *u*' vain knowledge, *6030
27: 4 nor my tongue *u*' deceit. 1897
33: 3 lips shall *u*' knowledge clearly. *4448
Ps 78: 2 I will *u*' dark sayings of old: 5042
94: 4 long shall they *u*' and speak hard* "
106: 2 Who can *u*' the mighty acts of the 4448
119: 171 My lips shall *u*' praise, when 5042
145: 7 shall abundantly *u*' the memory "
Pr 14: 5 but a false witness will *u*' lies. *6315
23: 33 heart shall *u*' perverse things. 1696
Ec 1: 8 are full of labour; man cannot *u*' it:"
5: 2 hasty to *u*' any thing before God: 3318
Isa 32: 6 and to *u*' error against the Lord, 1696
48: 20 *u*' it even to the end of the earth; 3318
Jer 1: 16 I will *u*' my judgments against 1696
25: 30 *u*' his voice from his holy 5414
Eze 24: 3 *u*' a parable unto the rebellious 4911
40: 31, 37 were toward the *u*' court; *2435
42: 1 brought me forth into the *u*' court,*"
3 pavement...was for the *u*' court, * "
7 toward the *u*' court on the forepart*"
8 chambers that were in the *u*' court*"
9 goeth into them from the *u*' court.* "
14 of the holy place into the *u*' court,* "
44: 19 they go forth into the *u*' court, * "
19 even into the *u*' court of the people,*"
46: 20 bear them not out into the *u*' court,*"
21 brought me forth into the *u*' court,*"
47: 2 *u*' gate by the way that looketh *2531
Joe 2: 11 Lord shall *u*' his voice before his *5414
3: 16 and *u*' his voice from Jerusalem; "
Am 1: 2 and *u*' his voice from Jerusalem; "
Na 1: 8 he will make an *u*' end of the place3617
9 he will make an *u*' end: affliction* "
Zec 14: 11 shall be no more *u*' destruction; *
M't 13: 35 *u*' things which have been kept *2044*
1Co 14: 9 except ye *u*' by the tongue words *1325*
2Co 12: 4 it is not lawful for a man to *u*'. *2980*

utterance
Ac 2: 4 tongues, as the Spirit gave them *u*'.*669*
1Co 1: 5 ye are enriched by him, in all *u*', *3056*
2Co 8: 7 in faith, and *u*', and knowledge, "
Eph 6: 19 that *u*' may be given unto me, that "
Col 4: 3 would open unto us a door of *u*', * "

uttered
Nu 30: 6 vowed, or *u*' ought out of her lips,*4008
8 that which she *u*' with her lips, * "
J'g 11: 11 Jephthah *u*' all his words before *1696
2Sa 22: 14 and the most High *u*' his voice. 5414
Ne 6: 19 me, and *u*' my words to him. *3318
Job 26: 4 To whom hast thou *u*' words? and5046
42: 3 have I *u*' that I understood not;
Ps 46: 6 he *u*' his voice, the earth melted. 5414
66: 14 Which my lips have *u*', and my 4475
Jer 48: 34 Jahaz, have they *u*' their voice, 5414
51: 55 waters, a noise of their voice is *u*': "
Hab 3: 10 the deep *u*' his voice, and lifted up "
Ro 8: 26 with groanings which cannot be *u*'. *215*
Heb 5: 11 things to say, and hard to be *u*', **3004*
Re 10: 3 seven thunders *u*' their voices. *2980*
4 seven thunders had *u*' their voices, "
4 which the seven thunders *u*', "

uttereth
Job 15: 5 For thy mouth *u*' thine iniquity, * 502
Ps 19: 2 Day unto day *u*' speech, and night5042
Pr 1: 20 she *u*' her voice in the streets: 5414
21 the city she *u*' her words, saying, 559
10: 18 and he that *u*' a slander, is a fool. 3318
29: 11 A fool *u*' all his mind: but a wise "
Jer 10: 13 When he *u*' his voice, there is a 5414
51: 16 When he *u*' his voice, there is a "
Mic 7: 3 he *u*' his mischievous desire: 1696

uttering
Isa 59: 13 conceiving and *u*' from the heart 1897

utterly
Ex 17: 14 I will *u*' put out the remembrance of
22: 17 father *u*' refuse to give her unto him,
20 only, he shall be *u*' destroyed.
23: 24 but thou shalt *u*' overthrow them,
Le 13: 44 priest...pronounce him *u*' unclean;*
26: 44 I abhor them, to destroy them *u*', 3615
Nu 15: 31 that soul shall be *u*' cut off;
21: 2 then I will *u*' destroy their cities.
3 they *u*' destroyed them and their
30: 12 husband hath *u*' made them void *
De 2: 34 and *u*' destroyed the men, and the
3: 6 And we *u*' destroyed them, as we
6 *u*' destroying the men, women,
4: 26 ye shall soon *u*' perish from off the
26 upon it, but shall *u*' be destroyed.
7: 2 smite them, and *u*' destroy them;
26 but thou shalt *u*' detest it, and thou
26 and thou shalt *u*' abhor it; for it is a
12: 2 Ye shall *u*' destroy all the places, *
13: 15 destroying it *u*', and all that is
20: 17 But thou shalt *u*' destroy them;
31: 29 death ye will *u*' corrupt yourselves,
Jos 2: 10 and Og, whom ye *u*' destroyed.
6: 21 they *u*' destroyed all that was in
8: 26 until he had *u*' destroyed all the
10: 1 taken Ai, and had *u*' destroyed it;
28 the king thereof he *u*' destroyed,
35 therein he *u*' destroyed that day,
37 destroyed it *u*', and all the souls
39 and *u*' destroyed all the souls that
40 but *u*' destroyed all that breathed,
11: 11 of the sword, *u*' destroying them:
12 he *u*' destroyed them, as Moses
20 that he might destroy them *u*',
21 destroyed them *u*' with their cities.
17: 13 tribute; but did not *u*' drive them out.
J'g 1: 17 Zephath, and *u*' destroyed it.
28 and did not *u*' drive them out.
15: 2 thought that thou hadst *u*' hated her;
21: 11 Ye shall *u*' destroy every male,
1Sa 15: 3 and *u*' destroy all that they have,
8 *u*' destroyed all the people with the
9 good, and would not *u*' destroy them:
9 and refuse, that they destroyed *u*'.
15 and the rest we have *u*' destroyed.
18 Go and *u*' destroy the sinners the
20 have *u*' destroyed the Amalekites.
21 which should have been *u*' destroyed,*
27: 12 his people Israel *u*' to abhor him;
2Sa 17: 10 is as the heart of a lion, shall *u*' melt:
23: 7 they shall be *u*' burned with fire in the
1Ki 9: 21 also were not able *u*' to destroy,
2Ki 19: 11 to all lands, by destroying them *u*':
1Ch 4: 41 destroyed them *u*' unto this day,
2Ch 20: 23 Seir, *u*' to slay and destroy them:
31: 1 until they had *u*' destroyed them *
32: 14 nations that my fathers *u*' destroyed,
Ne 9: 31 thou didst not *u*' consume them, *
Ps 37: 24 fall, he shall not be *u*' cast down:
73: 19 they are *u*' consumed with terrors.
89: 33 my lovingkindness will I not *u*' take
119: 8 thy statutes: O forsake me not *u*'. 3966
43 word of truth *u*' out of my mouth; "
Ca 8: 7 for love, it would *u*' be contemned.
Isa 2: 18 And the idols he shall *u*' abolish. 3632
6: 11 man, and the land be *u*' desolate,
11: 15 shall *u*' destroy the tongue of the
24: 3 shall be *u*' emptied, and *u*' spoiled:
19 The earth is *u*' broken down, the
34: 2 he hath *u*' destroyed them, he
37: 11 all lands by destroying them *u*';
40: 30 and the young men shall *u*' fall:
56: 3 *u*' separated me from his people:*
60: 12 yea, those nations shall be *u*' wasted.
Jer 9: 4 for every brother will *u*' supplant,
12: 17 I will *u*' pluck up and destroy that*
14: 19 Hast thou *u*' rejected Judah? hath
23: 39 behold, I, even I, will *u*' forget you,
25: 9 about, and will *u*' destroy them,
29 and should ye be *u*' unpunished?
50: 21 waste and *u*' destroy after them,
26 up as heaps, and destroy her *u*':
51: 3 men; destroy ye *u*' all her host.
58 walls of Babylon shall be *u*' broken.
La 5: 22 But thou hast *u*' rejected us; thou
Eze 9: 6 Slay *u*' old and young, both maids,
17: 10 shall it not *u*' wither, when the east
27: 31 make themselves *u*' bald for thee,*
29: 10 of Egypt *u*' waste and desolate,
Da 11: 44 destroy, and *u*' to make away many.
Ho 1: 6 Israel; but I will *u*' take them away.*
10: 15 shall the king of Israel *u*' be cut off.
Am 9: 8 I will not *u*' destroy the house of
Na 1: 15 through thee; he is *u*' cut off. 3605
Zep 1: 2 I will *u*' consume all things from off
Zec 11: 17 his right eye shall be *u*' darkened.
1Co 6: 7 there is *u*' a fault among you, **3654*
2Pe 2: 12 and shall *u*' perish in their own **2704*
Re 18: 8 she shall be *u*' burned with fire: *2618*

uttermost See also UTMOST.
Ex 26: 4 in the *u*' edge of another curtain, *7020
36: 11 in the *u*' side of another curtain, * "
17 upon the *u*' edge of the curtain * "
Nu 11: 1 were in the *u*' parts of the camp. 7097
20: 16 a city in the *u*' of thy border: "
De 11: 24 unto the *u*' sea shall your coast be.*314
Jos 15: 1 was the *u*' part of the south coast. 7097
5 of the sea at the *u*' part of Jordan:* "
21 the *u*' cities of the tribe of the "
1Sa 14: 2 tarried in the *u*' part of Gibeah "
1Ki 6: 24 from the *u*' part of the one wing 7098
24 wing unto the *u*' part of the other "

2Ki 7: 5 the *u'* part of the camp of Syria, *7097
8 came to the *u'* part of the camp, * "
Ne 1: 9 out unto the *u'* part of the heaven, "
Ps 2: 8 and the *u'* parts of the earth for thy657
65: 8 that dwell in the *u'* parts are afraid7098
139: 9 dwell in the *u'* parts of the sea; 319
Isa 7: 18 the *u'* part of the rivers of Egypt, 7097
24: 16 From the *u'* part of the earth have3671
M't 5: 26 till thou hast paid the *u'* farthing. *2078
12: 42 from the *u'* parts of the earth *4009
M'r 13: 27 from the *u'* part of the earth 206
27 to the *u'* part of heaven. "
Ac 1: 8 unto the *u'* part of the earth. 2078
24: 22 I will know the *u'* of your matter. *1231
1Th 2: 16 wrath is come upon them to the *u'*.5056
Heb 7: 25 able also to save them to the *u'* 3838

Uz (*uz*)
Ge 10: 23 children of Aram; *U'*, and Hul, 5780
36: 28 children of Dishan are these; *U'*. "
1Ch 1: 17 Aram, and *U'*, and Hul, and Gether," "
42 The sons of Dishan; *U'*, and Aran. "
Job 1: 1 There was a man in the land of *U'*, "
Jer 25: 20 and all the kings of the land of *U'*, "
La 4: 21 that dwellest in the land of *U'*; "

Uzai (*u'-zahee*)
Ne 3: 25 Palal the son of *U'*, over against 186

Uzal (*u'-zal*)
Ge 10: 27 Hadoram, and *U'*, and Diklah, 187
1Ch 1: 21 Hadoram also, and *U'*, and Diklah, "

Uzza (*uz'-zah*) See also UZZAH.
2Ki 21: 18 own house, in the garden of *U'*: 5798
26 his sepulchre in the garden of *U'*: "
1Ch 6: 29 son, Shimei his son, *U'* his son, * "
8: 7 he removed them, and begat *U'*, "
13: 7 and *U'* and Ahio drave the cart. "
9 *U'* put forth his hand to hold the "

1Ch 13: 10 the Lord was kindled against *U'*, 5798
11 Lord had made a breach upon *U'*: "
Ezr 2: 49 The children of *U'*, the children of "
Ne 7: 51 the children of *U'*, the children of "

Uzzah (*uz'-zah*) See also PEREZ-UZZAH; UZZA.
2Sa 6: 3 *U'* and Ahio, the sons of Abinadab,5798
6 *U'* put forth his hand to the ark of "
7 the Lord was kindled against *U'*; "
8 Lord had made a breach upon *U'*: "

Uzzen-sherah (*uz''-zen-she'-rah*)
1Ch 7: 24 built Beth-horon...and *U'*.) * 242

Uzzi (*uz'-zi*)
1Ch 6: 5 Bukki, and Bukki begat *U'*, 5813
6 *U'* begat Zerahiah, and Zerahiah "
51 Bukki his son, *U'* his son, Zerahiah"
7: 2 sons of Tola; *U'*, and Rephaiah, "
3 And the sons of *U'*; Izrahiah: "
7 sons of Bela; Ezbon, and *U'*, and "
9: 8 and Elah the son of *U'*, the son of "
Ezr 7: 4 Zerahiah, the son of *U'*, the son of "
Ne 11: 22 was *U'* the son of Bani, the son "
12: 19 Joiarib, Mattenai; of Jedaiah, *U'*; "
42 Eleazar, and *U'*, and Jehohanan, "

Uzzia (*uz-zi'-ah*)
1Ch 11: 44 *U'* the Ashterathite, Shama and 5814

Uzziah (*uz-zi'-ah*) See also OZIAS.
2Ki 15: 13 the nine and thirtieth year of *U'* 5818
30 year of Jotham the son of *U'*. "
32 Jotham the son of *U'*...to reign. "
34 to all that his father *U'* had done. "
1Ch 6: 24 Uriel his son, *U'* his son, and "
27: 25 was Jehonathan the son of *U'*: "
2Ch 26: 1 all the people of Judah took *U'*, "
3 Sixteen years old was *U'* when he "
8 the Ammonites gave gifts to *U'*: "
9 *U'* built towers in Jerusalem at "

2Ch 26: 11 *U'* had an host of fighting men, 5818
14 *U'* prepared for them...shields, "
18 And they withstood *U'* the king, "
18 It appertaineth not unto thee, *U'*, "
19 *U'* was wroth, and had a censer in "
21 *U'* the king was a leper unto the "
22 Now the rest of the acts of *U'*, first "
23 So *U'* slept with his fathers, and "
27: 2 according to all his father *U'* did: "
Ezr 10: 21 and Shemaiah, and Jehiel, and *U'*. "
Ne 11: 4 of Judah; Athaiah the son of *U'*, "
Isa 1: 1 in the days of *U'*, Jotham, Ahaz, "
6: 1 In the year that king *U'* died I saw"
7: 1 the son of Jotham, the son of *U'*, "
Ho 1: 1 in the days of *U'*, Jotham, Ahaz, "
Am 1: 1 in the days of *U'* king of Judah, "
Zec 14: 5 the earthquake in the days of *U'* "

Uzziel (*uz-zi'-el*) See also UZZIELITES.
Ex 6: 18 and Izhar, and Hebron, and *U'*: 5816
22 And the sons of *U'*; Mishael, and "
Le 10: 4 the sons of *U'* the uncle of Aaron, "
Nu 3: 19 and Izehar, Hebron, and *U'*. "
30 shall be Elizaphan the son of *U'*. "
1Ch 4: 42 Rephaiah, and *U'*, the sons of Ishi. "
6: 2 Amram, Izhar, and Hebron, and *U'*. "
18 and Izhar, and Hebron, and *U'*. "
7: 7 Ezbon, and Uzzi, and *U'*, and "
15: 10 Of the sons of *U'*; Amminadab "
23: 12 Amram, Izhar, Hebron, and *U'*, "
20 Of the sons of *U'*; Micah the first, "
24: 24 Of the sons of *U'*; Michah: "
25: 4 Bukkiah, Mattaniah, *U'*, Shebuel, "
2Ch 29: 14 of Jeduthun; Shemaiah, and *U'*. "
Ne 3: 8 Next unto him repaired *U'* the son "

Uzzielites (*uz-zi'-el-ites*)
Nu 3: 27 and the family of the *U'*: 5817
1Ch 26: 23 the Hebronites, and the *U'*: "

V.

vagabond See also VAGABONDS.
Ge 4: 12 a *v'* shalt thou be in the earth. *5110
14 a fugitive and a *v'* in the earth; * "
Ac 19: 13 Then certain of the *v'* Jews, *4022

vagabonds
Ps 109: 10 Let his children be continually *v'*, 5128

vail See also VAILS; VEIL.
Ge 24: 65 therefore she took a *v'*, and *6809
38: 14 and covered her with a *v'*, and * "
19 laid by her *v'* from her, and put on* "
Ex 26: 31 And thou shalt make a *v'* of blue,*6532
33 thou shalt hang up the *v'* under * "
33 bring in thither within the *v'* the * "
33 *v'* shall divide unto you between * "
35 shalt set the table without the *v'*,* "
27: 21 of the congregation without the *v'*,* "
30: 6 the *v'* that is by the ark of the * "
34: 33 them, he put a *v'* on his face. *4533
34 took the *v'* off, until he came out. * "
35 Moses put the *v'* upon his face * "
35: 12 seat, and the *v'* of the covering, *6532
36: 35 he made a *v'* of blue, and purple, * "
38: 27 sanctuary,...the sockets of the *v'*; * "
39: 34 skins, and the *v'* of the covering, * "
40: 3 and cover the ark with the *v'*. * "
21 and set up the *v'* of the covering, * "
22 northward, without the *v'*. * "
26 of the congregation before the *v'*: * "
Le 4: 6 before the *v'* of the sanctuary. * "
17 before the Lord, even before the *v'*.* "
16: 2 holy place within the *v'* before the* "
12 small, and bring it within the *v'*: * "
15 and bring his blood within the *v'*, * "
21: 23 Only he shall not go in unto the *v'*,* "
24: 3 Without the *v'* of the testimony, in* "
Nu 4: 5 shall take down the covering *v'*, * "
18: 7 of the altar, and within the *v'*, * "
Ru 3: 15 Bring the *v'* that thou hast upon *4304
2Ch 3: 14 And he made the *v'* of blue, and *6532
Isa 25: 7 *v'* that is spread over all nations. *4541
2Co 3: 13 which put a *v'* over his face, that *2571
14 the same *v'* untaken away in the * "
14 which *v'* is done away in Christ. * "
15 read, the *v'* is upon their heart. *2571
16 Lord, the *v'* shall be taken away. * "

vails
Isa 3: 23 linen, and the hoods, and the *v'*. *7289

vain See also VAINGLORY.
Ex 5: 9 let them not regard *v'* words. *8267
20: 7 name of the Lord thy God in *v'*; 7723
7 guiltless that taketh his name in *v'*." "
Le 26: 16 ye shall sow your seed in *v'*, for 7385
20 your strength shall be spent in *v'*: "
De 5: 11 name of the Lord thy God in *v'*: 7723
11 guiltless that taketh his name in *v'*. "
32: 47 For it is not a *v'* thing for you; 7386
J'g 9: 4 Abimelech hired *v'* and light "
11: 3 were gathered *v'* men to Jephthah, "
1Sa 12: 21 then should ye go after *v'* things, 8414
21 profit nor deliver; for they are *v'*. "
25: 21 in *v'* have I kept all that this 8267
2Sa 6: 20 one of the *v'* fellows shamelessly 7386
2Ki 17: 15 became *v'*, and went after the 1891
18: 20 sayest, (but they are but *v'* words,)8193
2Ch 13: 7 are gathered unto him *v'* men, ‡7386
Job 9: 29 wicked, why then labour I in *v'*? 1892
11: 11 For he knoweth *v'* men: he seeth 7723
12 For *v'* man would be wise, though 5014
15: 2 a wise man utter *v'* knowledge, and7307
16: 3 Shall *v'* words have an end? or "
21: 34 How then comfort ye me in *v'*, 1892

Job 27: 12 then are ye thus altogether *v'*? 1891
35: 16 doth Job open his mouth in *v'*; *1892
39: 16 her labour is in *v'* without fear; 7385
41: 9 the hope of him is in *v'*: shall not 3576
Ps 2: 1 and the people imagine a *v'* thing? 7385
26: 4 I have not sat with *v'* persons, ‡7723
33: 17 An horse is a *v'* thing for safety: 8267
39: 6 every man walketh in a *v'* shew: "
6 surely they are disquieted in *v'*: 1892
60: 11 trouble: for *v'* is the help of man. 7723
62: 10 and become not *v'* in robbery: 1891
73: 13 I have cleansed my heart in *v'*, 7385
89: 47 hast thou made all men in *v'*? *7723
108: 12 trouble: for *v'* is the help of man. "
119: 113 I hate *v'* thoughts: but thy law do I* "
127: 1 they labour in *v'* that build it: 7723
1 the watchman waketh but in *v'*. "
2 It is *v'* for you to rise up early, to "
139: 20 thine enemies take thy name in *v'*. "
Pr 1: 17 Surely in *v'* the net is spread in 2600
12: 11 he that followeth *v'* persons is 7386
28: 19 he that followeth after *v'* persons "
30: 9 and take the name of my God in *v'*.* "
31: 30 is deceitful, and beauty is *v'*: but 1892
Ec 6: 12 all the days of his *v'* life which he "
Isa 1: 13 Bring no more *v'* oblations; 7723
30: 7 For the Egyptians shall help in *v'*,1892
36: 5 thou, (but they are but *v'* words) 8193
45: 18 he created it not in *v'*, he formed *8414
19 Seek ye me in *v'*: I the Lord speak "
49: 4 Then I said, I have laboured in *v'*, 7385
4 strength for nought, and in *v'*: *1892
65: 23 They shall not labour in *v'*, nor 7385
Jer 2: 5 after vanity, and are become *v'*? 1891
30 *v'* have I smitten your children; 7723
3: 23 Truly in *v'* is salvation hoped for 8267
4: 14 thy *v'* thoughts lodge within thee? 205
30 in *v'* shalt thou make thyself fair; 7723
6: 29 the fire; the founder melteth in *v'*: "
8: 8 us? Lo, certainly in *v'* made he it;*8267
8 it; the pen of the scribes is in *v'*. * "
10: 3 customs of the people are in *v'*: *1892
23: 16 unto you: they make you *v'*: *1891
46: 11 in *v'* shalt thou use many 7723
50: 9 man; none shall return in *v'*. 7387
51: 58 and the people shall labour in *v'*, *7385
La 2: 14 have seen *v'* and foolish things *7723
4: 17 eyes as yet failed for our *v'* help: 1892
Eze 6: 10 said in *v'* that I would do this evil 2600
12: 24 shall be no more any *v'* vision 7723
13: 7 Have ye not seen a *v'* vision, and "
Zec 10: 2 false dreams; they comfort in *v'*: 1892
Mal 3: 14 have said, It is *v'* to serve God: 7723
M't 6: 7 when ye pray, use not *v'* repetitions, "
15: 9 But in *v'* they do worship me, 3155
M'r 7: 7 Howbeit in *v'* do they worship me, "
Ac 4: 25 and the people imagine *v'* things? 2756
Ro 1: 21 became *v'* in their imaginations, 3154
13: 4 for he beareth not the sword in *v'*: 1500
1Co 3: 20 of the wise, that they are *v'*. 3152
15: 2 you, unless ye have believed in *v'*. 1500
10 bestowed upon me was not in *v'*; 2756
14 risen, then is our preaching *v'*, "
14 and your faith is also *v'*. "
17 be not raised, your faith is *v'*; 3152
58 your labour is not in *v'* in the Lord.2756
2Co 6: 1 receive not the grace of God in *v'*. "
9: 3 boasting of you should be in *v'* *2761
Ga 2: 2 I should run, or had run, in *v'*. 2756
21 the law, then Christ is dead in *v'*. *1432
3: 4 many things in *v'*? if it be yet in *v'*.1500
4: 11 bestowed upon you labour in *v'*. "

Ga 5: 26 Let us not be desirous of *v'* glory,*2755
Eph 5: 6 man deceive you with *v'* words: *2756
Ph'p 2: 16 not run in *v'*, neither laboured in *v'*." "
Col 2: 8 through philosophy and *v'* deceit. "
1Th 2: 1 in unto you, that it was not in *v'*: "
3: 5 you, and our labour be in *v'*. "
1Ti 1: 6 have turned aside unto *v'* jangling;3150
6: 20 avoiding profane and *v'* babblings,*2757
2Ti 2: 16 shun profane and *v'* babblings: for* "
Tit 1: 10 unruly and *v'* talkers and deceivers,3151
3: 9 for they are unprofitable and *v'*. 3152
Jas 1: 26 own heart, this man's religion is *v'*." "
2: 20 O *v'* man, that faith without works2756
4: 5 think that the scripture saith in *v'*,2761
1Pe 1: 18 your *v'* conversation received by 3152

vainglory See also VAIN and GLORY.
Ph'p 2: 3 be done through strife or *v'*; 2754

vainly
Col 2: 18 *v'* puffed up by his fleshly mind, 1500

Vajezatha (*va-jez'-a-thah*)
Es 9: 9 and Arisai, and Aridai, and *V'*. *2055

vale See also VALLEY.
Ge 14: 3 together in the *v'* of Siddim, 6010
8 with them in the *v'* of Siddim; "
10 *v'* of Siddim was full of slimepits; "
37: 14 sent him out of the *v'* of Hebron, "
De 1: 7 in the hills, and in the *v'*, and in *8219
Jos 10: 40 of the south, and of the *v'*, and of * "
1Ki 10: 27 sycomore trees that are in the *v'*, * "
2Ch 1: 15 sycomore trees that are in the *v'* * "
Jer 33: 13 in the cities of the *v'*, and in the * "

valiant See also VALIANTEST.
1Sa 14: 52 any strong man, or any *v'* man, 2428
16: 18 a mighty *v'* man, and a man of war,* "
18: 17 only be thou *v'* for me, and 1121,2428
26: 15 said to Abner, Art not thou a *v'* man? "
31: 12 All the *v'* men arose, and went all 2428
2Sa 2: 7 strengthened, and be ye *v'*: 1121, "
11: 16 where he knew that *v'* men were. "
13: 28 be courageous, and be *v'*. 1121, "
17: 10 he also that is *v'*, whose heart "
10 and they be with him are *v'* men. "
23: 20 of Jehoiada, the son of a *v'* man, "
24: 9 eight hundred thousand *v'* men "
1Ki 1: 42 Come in; for thou art a *v'* man, * "
1Ch 5: 18 tribe of Manasseh, of *v'* men, "
7: 2 were *v'* men of might in their *1368
5 of Issachar were *v'* men of might,* "
10: 12 They arose, all the *v'* men, and 2428
11: 22 the son of a *v'* man of Kabzeel, "
26 Also the *v'* of the armies were, *1368
28: 1 all the *v'* men, unto Jerusalem. *2428
2Ch 13: 3 with an army of *v'* men of war, 1368
26: 17 of the Lord, that were *v'* men: 2428
28: 6 day, which were all *v'* men; "
Ne 11: 6 threescore and eight *v'* men. "
Ca 3: 7 threescore *v'* men are about it, of 1368
7 are about it, of the *v'* of Israel. * "
Isa 10: 13 the inhabitants like a *v'* man: 3524
33: 7 their *v'* ones shall cry without: 691
Jer 9: 3 they are not *v'* for the truth upon *1396
46: 15 Why are thy *v'* men swept away? * 47
Na 2: 3 red, the *v'* men are in scarlet: 2428
Heb 11: 34 waxed *v'* in fight, turned to flight*2478

valiantest
J'g 21: 10 thousand men of the *v'*, 1121,2428

valiantly
Nu 24: 18 enemies; and Israel shall do *v'*. 2428
1Ch 19: 13 and let us behave ourselves *v'* *2388

Ps 60:12 Through God we shall do v': for 2428
108:13 Through God we shall do v': for he "
118:15, 16 right hand of the Lord doeth v'. "

valley See also VALE; VALLEYS.
Ge 14:17 at the v' of Shaveh, which is the *6010
26:17 pitched his tent in the v' of Gerar, 5158
19 Isaac's servants digged in the v', "
Nu 14:25 the Canaanites dwelt in the v'.) 6010
21:12 and pitched in the v' of Zared. 5158
20 from Bamoth in the v', that is in 1516
32: 9 they went up unto the v' of Eshcol, 5158
De 1:24 and came unto the v' of Eshcol, "
3:16 unto the river Arnon half the v', "
29 So we abode in the v' over against 1516
4:46 in the v' over against Beth-peor, in "
21: 4 down the heifer unto a rough v', 5158
4 off the heifer's neck there in the v': "
6 heifer that is beheaded in the v': "
34: 3 and the plain of the v' of Jericho, 1237
6 he buried him in a v' in the land of 1516
Jos 7:24 brought them unto the v' of Achor. 6010
26 place was called, The v' of Achor, "
8:11 was a v' between them and Ai. 1516
13 that night into the midst of the v'. *6010
10:12 and thou, Moon, in the v' of Ajalon. "
11: 2 the v', and in the borders of Dor *8219
8 unto the v' of Mizpeh eastward; 1237
16 all the land of Goshen, and the v', *8219
16 of Israel, and the v' of the same; * "
17 Baal-gad in the v' of Lebanon 1237
12: 7 from Baal-gad in the v' of Lebanon "
13:19 in the mount of the v', 6010
27 And in the v', Beth-aram, and "
15: 7 toward Debir from the v' of Achor, "
8 up by the v' of the son of Hinnom 1516
8 before the v' of Hinnom westward, "
8 of the v' of the giants northward: *6010
33 in the v', Eshtaol, and Zoreah, *8219
17:16 the land of the v' have chariots of 6010
16 they who are of the v' of Jezreel. "
18:16 before the v' of the son of Hinnom, 1516
16 the v' of the giants on the north, *6010
16 descended to the v' of Hinnom, to 1516
21 Beth-hoglah, and the v' of Keziz, *6010
19:14 are in the v' of Jiphthah-el: 1516
27 to the v' of Jiphthah-el toward the "
J'g 1: 9 and in the south, and in the v'. *8219
19 drive out the inhabitants of the v'. 6010
34 suffer them to come down to the v': "
5:15 he was sent on foot into the v'. "
6:33 and pitched in the v' of Jezreel. "
7: 1 them, by the hill of Moreh, in the v'. "
8 Midian was beneath him in the v'. "
12 of the east lay along in the v' like "
16: 4 loved a woman in the v' of Sorek, 5158
18:28 in the v' that lieth by Beth-rehob. 6010
1Sa 6:13 their wheat harvest in the v': "
13:18 that looketh to the v' of Zeboim 1516
15: 5 of Amalek, and laid wait in the v'. 5158
17: 2 and pitched by the v' of Elah, *6010
3 and there was a v' between them. 1516
19 of Israel, were in the v' of Elah, *6010
52 until thou come to the v', and to *1516
21: 9 thou slewest in the v' of Elah, *6010
31: 7 were on the other side of the v', "
2Sa 5:18, 22 themselves in the v' of Rephaim. "
8:13 of the Syrians in the v' of salt, 1516
23:13 pitched in the v' of Rephaim. 6010
2Ki 2:16 some mountain, or into some v'. 1516
3:16 Lord, Make this v' full of ditches. 5158
17 yet that v' shall be filled with water, "
14: 7 He slew of Edom in the v' of salt 1516
23:10 in the v' of the children of Hinnom, "
1Ch 4:14 the father of the v' of Charashim; * "
39 even unto the east side of the v', "
10: 7 men of Israel that were in the v' 6010
11:15 encamped in the v' of Rephaim. "
14: 9 themselves in the v' of Rephaim. "
13 spread themselves abroad in the v'. "
18:12 of the Edomites in the v' of salt 1516
2Ch 14:10 in array in the v' of Zephathah "
20:26 themselves in the v' of Berachah; 6010
26 was called, The v' of Berachah, "
25:11 went to the v' of salt, and smote of 1516
26: 9 at the v' gate, and at the turning of "
28: 3 in the v' of the son of Hinnom, "
33: 6 fire in the v' of the son of Hinnom: "
14 west side of Gihon, in the v', even 5158
35:22 came to fight in the v' of Megiddo. 1237
Ne 2:13 out by night by the gate of the v', 1516
15 and entered by the gate of the v', "
3:13 The v' gate repaired Hanun, and "
11:30 Beer-sheba unto the v' of Hinnom. "
35 Lod, and Ono, the v' of craftsmen. "
Job 21:33 The clods of the v' shall be sweet 5158
39:21 He paweth in the v', and rejoiceth 6010
Ps 23: 4 through the v' of the shadow of 1516
60: *title* smote of Edom in the v' of salt "
6 and mete out the v' of Succoth. 6010
84: 6 Who passing through the v' of Baca "
108: 7 and mete out the v' of Succoth. "
Pr 30:17 ravens of the v' shall pick it out, 5158
Ca 6:11 of nuts to see the fruits of the v', "
Isa 17: 5 ears in the v' of Rephaim. 6010
22: 1 The burden of the v' of vision. 1516
5 God of hosts in the v' of vision, "
28: 4 which is on the head of the fat v', "
21 be wroth as in the v' of Gibeon, 6010
40: 4 Every v' shall be exalted, and 1516
63:14 As a beast goeth down into the v', 1237
65:10 v' of Achor a place for the herds to 6010
Jer 2:23 see thy way in the v', know what 1516
7:31 is in the v' of the son of Hinnom, "
32 nor the v' of the son of Hinnom, "
32 but the v' of slaughter: for they "
Jer 19: 2 unto the v' of the son of Hinnom, 1516
6 nor The v' of the son of Hinnom, "
6 but The v' of slaughter. "
21:13 O inhabitant of the v', and rock of 6010
31:40 the whole v' of the dead bodies, and "
32:35 are in the v' of the son of Hinnom, 1516
44 in the cities of the v', and in the *8219
47: 5 off with the remnant of their v': 6010
48: 8 v' also shall perish, and the plain "
49: 4 thy flowing v', O backsliding "
Eze 37: 1 midst of the v' which was full of 1237
2 were very many in the open v'; "
39:11 v' of the passengers on the east of 1516
11 shall call it The v' of Hamon-gog. "
15 buried it in the v' of Hamon-gog. "
Ho 1: 5 bow of Israel in the v' of Jezreel. 6010
2:15 the v' of Achor for a door of hope: "
Joe 3: 2 down into the v' of Jehoshaphat, "
12 come up to the v' of Jehoshaphat: "
14 multitudes in the v' of decision: "
14 Lord is near in the v' of decision. "
18 and shall water the v' of Shittim. 5158
Mic 1: 6 the stones thereof into the v', 1516
Zec 12:11 in the v' of Megiddon. 1237
14: 4 and there shall be a very great v'; 1516
5 shall flee to the v' of the mountains; "
5 the v' of the mountains shall reach "
Lu 3: 5 Every v' shall be filled, and every *5327*

valleys
Nu 24: 6 As the v' are they spread forth, as 5158
De 8: 7 and depths that spring out of v' 1237
11:11 possess it, is a land of hills and v', "
Jos 9: 1 Jordan, in the hills, and in the v', *8219
12: 8 In the mountains, and in the v', "
1Ki 20:28 hills, but he is not God of the v', 6010
1Ch 12:15 they put to flight all them of the v', "
27:29 over the herds that were in the v' "
Job 30: 6 To dwell in the cliffs of the v', in 5158
39:10 or will he harrow the v' after thee? 6010
Ps 65:13 v' also are covered over with corn; "
104: 8 they go down by the v' unto the 1237
10 He sendeth the springs into the v', 5158
Ca 2: 1 of Sharon, and the lily of the v'. 6010
Isa 7:19 rest all of them in the desolate v', 5158
22: 7 choicest v' shall be full of chariots, 6010
28: 1 head of the fat v' of them that are *1516
41:18 fountains in the midst of the v': 1237
57: 5 slaying the children in the v' 5158
Jer 49: 4 Wherefore gloriest thou in the v' 6010
Eze 6: 3 hills, to the rivers, and to the v'; 1516
7:16 the mountains like doves of the v', "
31:12 in all the v' his branches are fallen, "
32: 5 and fill the v' with thy height. "
35: 8 in thy hills, and in thy v', and in all "
36: 4, 6 hills, to the rivers, and to the v', "
Mic 1: 4 the v' shall be cleft, as wax before 6010

valour
Jos 1:14 all the mighty men of v', and 2428
6: 2 thereof, and the mighty men of v'. "
8: 3 thirty thousand mighty men of v', "
10: 7 him, and all the mighty men of v'. "
J'g 3:29 men, all lusty, and all men of v'; "
6:12 with thee, thou mighty man of v'. "
11: 1 Jephthah...was a mighty man of v', "
18: 2 men from their coasts, men of v', "
20:44 men; all these were men of v'. "
46 the sword; all these were men of v'. "
1Ki 11:28 Jeroboam was a mighty man of v': "
2Ki 5: 1 he was also a mighty man in v', but "
24:14 and all the mighty men of v', "
1Ch 5:24 mighty men of v', famous men, and "
7: 7 of their fathers, mighty men of v'; "
9, 11 their fathers, mighty men of v', "
40 choice and mighty men of v', chief "
8:40 of Ulam were mighty men of v', "
12:21 for they were all mighty men of v', "
25 mighty men of v' for the war, "
28 Zadok, a young man mighty of v', "
30 eight hundred, mighty men of v', "
26: 6 for they were mighty men of v'. "
30 and his brethren, men of v', "
31 among them mighty men of v' at "
32 his brethren, men of v', were two "
2Ch 13: 3 men, being mighty men of v'. "
8 all these were mighty men of v'. "
17:13 the men of war, mighty men of v', "
14 with him mighty men of v' three "
16 thousand mighty men of v'. "
17 Eliada a mighty man of v', and "
25: 6 mighty men of v' out of Israel "
26:12 fathers of the mighty men of v' "
32:21 cut off all the mighty men of v', "
Ne 11:14 their brethren, mighty men of v', "

value See also VALUED; VALUEST.
Le 27: 8 priest, and the priest shall v' him; 6186
8 that vowed shall the priest v' him. "
12 And the priest shall v' it, whether "
Job 13: 4 lies, ye are all physicians of no v'. 457
M't 10:31 of more v' than many sparrows. *1308*
27: 9 of the children of Israel did v'; *5091*
Lu 12: 7 of more v' than many sparrows. *1308*

valued
Le 27:16 barley seed shall be v' at fifty shekels
Job 28:16 be v' with the gold of Ophir, 5541
19 neither shall it be v' with pure gold. "
M't 27: 9 the price of him that was v', *5091*

valuest
Le 27:12 as thou v' it, who art the priest, so 6187

Vaniah (*va-ni'-ah*)
Ezr 10:36 V', Meremoth, Eliashib, 2057

vanish See also VANISHED; VANISHETH.
Job 6:17 time they wax warm, they v': 6789
Isa 51: 6 heavens shall v' away like smoke, 4414
1Co 13: 8 be knowledge, it shall v' away. *2673*
Heb 8:13 waxeth old is ready to v' away. *854*

vanished
Jer 49: 7 the prudent? is their wisdom v'? 5628
Lu 24:31 and he v' out of their sight. *1096, 855*

vanisheth
Job 7: 9 As the cloud is consumed and v' 3212
Jas 4:14 for a little time, and then v' away. *853*

vanities
De 32:21 me to anger with their v': 1892
1Ki 16:13, 26 of Israel to anger with their v'. "
Ps 31: 6 hated them that regard lying v': "
Ec 1: 2 Vanity of v', saith the Preacher, "
2 Preacher, vanity of v'; all is vanity. "
5: 7 words there are also divers v': "
12: 8 Vanity of v', saith the preacher; all "
Jer 8:19 images, and with strange v'? "
10: 8 the stock is a doctrine of v'. * "
14:22 any among the v' of the Gentiles "
Jon 2: 8 that observe lying v' forsake their "
Ac 14:15 from these v' unto the living God, *3152*

vanity See also VANITIES.
2Ki 17:15 they followed v', and became vain, 1892
Job 7: 3 I made to possess months of v', 7723
16 let me alone; for my days are v'. 1892
15:31 him that is deceived trust in v': 7723
31 for v' shall be his recompence. "
35 mischief, and bring forth v', * 205
31: 5 If I have walked with v', or if my 7723
35:13 Surely God will not hear v', neither "
Ps 4: 2 how long will ye love v', and seek 7385
10: 7 under his tongue is mischief and v'. *205
12: 2 They speak v' every one with his ‡7723
24: 4 hath not lifted up his soul unto v', "
39: 5 at his best state is altogether v'. 1892
11 a moth: surely every man is v'. "
41: 6 come to see me, he speaketh v': ‡7723
62: 9 Surely men of low degree are v', 1892
9 they are altogether lighter than v'. "
78:33 their days did he consume in v', "
94:11 thoughts of man, that they are v'. "
119:37 mine eyes from beholding v'; 7723
144: 4 Man is like to v': his days are as 1892
8 Whose mouth speaketh v', and ‡7723
11 children, whose mouth speaketh v', ‡ "
Pr 13:11 Wealth gotten by v' shall be 1892
21: 6 treasures by a lying tongue is a v' * "
22: 8 that soweth iniquity shall reap v': *205
30: 8 Remove far from me v' and lies: 7723
Ec 1: 2 V' of vanities, saith the Preacher, 1892
2 saith the Preacher, v' of vanities; "
2 saith the Preacher,...all is v'. "
14 all is v' and vexation of spirit. "
2: 1 and, behold, this also is v'. "
11 all was v' and vexation of spirit, "
15 in my heart, that this also is v'. "
17 for all is v' and vexation of spirit. "
19 under the sun. This is also v'. "
21 This also is v' and a great evil. "
23 rest in the night. This is also v'. "
26 also is v' and vexation of spirit. "
3:19 above a beast: for all is v'. "
4: 4 is also v' and vexation of spirit. "
7 and I saw v' under the sun. "
8 This is also v', yea, it is a sore "
16 also is v' and vexation of spirit. "
5:10 with increase: this is also v'. "
6: 2 this is v', and it is an evil disease. "
4 For he cometh in with v', and "
9 is also v' and vexation of spirit. "
11 be many things that increase v', "
7: 6 laughter of the fool: this is also v'. "
15 have I seen in the days of my v': "
8:10 they had so done: this is also v'. "
14 There is a v' which is done upon "
14 I said that this also is v'. "
9: 9 all the days of the life of thy v', "
9 the sun, all the days of thy v': "
11: 8 be many. All that cometh is v'. "
10 for childhood and youth are v'. "
12: 8 V' of vanities, saith the preacher; "
8 saith the preacher; all is v'. "
Isa 5:18 draw iniquity with cords of v', 7723
30:28 sift the nations with the sieve of v': "
40:17 to him less than nothing, and v'. 8414
23 the judges of the earth as v'. "
41:29 they are all v'; their works are 205
44: 9 a graven image are all of them v', 8414
57:13 all away; v' shall take them: *1892
58: 9 of the finger, and speaking v'; * 205
59: 4 they trust in v', and speak lies; 8414
Jer 2: 5 me, and have walked after v', 1892
10:15 They are v', and the work of errors: "
16:19 our fathers have inherited lies, v', "
18:15 they have burned incense to v', 7723
51:18 They are v', the work of errors: 1892
Eze 13: 6 They have seen v' and lying 7723
8 Because ye have spoken v', and "
9 be upon the prophets that see v', "
23 ye shall see no more v', nor divine "
21:29 Whiles they see v' unto thee, "
22:28 seeing v', and divining lies unto "
Ho 12:11 in Gilead? surely they are v': "
Hab 2:13 weary themselves for very v'? 7385
Zec 10: 2 For the idols have spoken v', and 205
Ro 8:20 creature was made subject to v', *3152*
Eph 4:17 walk, in the v' of their mind, "
2Pe 2:18 speak great swelling words of v'. "

vantage See ADVANTAGE.

vapour See also VAPOURS.
Job 36:27 rain according to the v' thereof: 108
33 the cattle also concerning the v'. *5927

Ac 2:19 blood, and fire, and v' of smoke: 822
Jas 4:14 a v', that appeareth for a little time, "
vapours
Ps 135: 7 He causeth the v' to ascend from 5387
148: 8 Fire, and hail; snow, and v'; *7008
Jer 10:13 he causeth the v' to ascend from 5387
51:16 he causeth the v' to ascend from "
variableness
Jas 1:17 with whom is no v', neither *3883
variance
M't 10:35 a man at v' against his father, 1369
Ga 5:20 v', emulations, wrath, strife, *2054
Vashni (vash'-ni)
1Ch 6:28 sons of Samuel: the firstborn V'. *2059
Vashti (vash'-ti)
Es 1: 9 V' the queen made a feast for the 2060
11 bring V' the queen before the king "
12 the queen V' refused to come at the "
15 unto the queen V' according to law, "
16 V' the queen hath not done wrong "
17 commanded V' the queen to be "
19 That V' come no more before king "
2: 1 he remembered V', and what she "
4 the king be queen instead of V'. "
17 and made her queen instead of V'. "
vaunt See also VAUNTETH.
J'g 7: 2 lest Israel v' themselves against 6286
vaunteth
1Co 13: 4 charity v' not itself, is not puffed 4068
vehement
Ca 8: 6 of fire, which hath a most v' flame.*3050
Jon 4: 8 that God prepared a v' east wind;*2759
2Co 7:11 yea, what fear, yea, what v' desire,*1972
vehemently
M'r 14:31 But he spake the more v', If I 1722,4053
Lu 6:48 stream beat v' upon that house, *4366
49 which the stream did beat v', * "
11:53 Pharisees began to urge him v', 1171
23:10 scribes stood and v' accused him. 2159
veil See also VAIL.
Ca 5: 7 the keepers...took away my v' *7289
M't 27:51 v' of the temple was rent in twain 2665
M'r 15:38 v' of the temple was rent in twain "
Lu 23:45 v' of the temple was rent in twain "
Heb 6:19 entereth into that within the v'; "
9: 3 after the second v', the tabernacle "
10:20 consecrated for us, through the v', "
vein
Job 28: 1 Surely there is a v' for the silver, *4161
venge See AVENGE; REVENGE.
vengeance
Ge 4:15 v' shall be taken on him sevenfold.5358
De 32:35 To me belongeth v', and 5359
41 I will render v' to mine enemies, "
43 will render v' to his adversaries, "
J'g 11:36 the Lord hath taken v' for thee of 5360
Ps 58:10 shall rejoice when he seeth the v': 5359
94: 1 Lord God, to whom v' belongeth; 5360
1 O God, to whom v' belongeth, shew "
99: 8 thou tookest v' of their inventions.5358
149: 7 To execute v' upon the heathen, 5360
Pr 6:34 he will not spare in the day of v'. 5359
Isa 34: 8 For it is the day of the Lord's v'; "
35: 4 your God will come with v', even "
47: 3 I will take v', and I will not meet "
59:17 he put on the garments of v' for "
61: 2 Lord, and the day of v' of our God; "
63: 4 For the day of v' is in mine heart, "
Jer 11:20 heart, let me see thy v' on them: 5360
20:12 heart, let me see thy v' on them: "
46:10 a day of v', that he may avenge him "
50:15 for it is the v' of the Lord: "
15 take v' upon her; as she hath 5358
28 declare in Zion the v' of the Lord 5360
28 Lord our God, the v' of his temple. "
51: 6 for this is the time of the Lord's v'; "
11 v' of the Lord, the v' of his temple. "
36 thy cause, and take v' for thee; "
La 3:60 Thou hast seen all their v' and all "
Eze 24: 8 cause fury to come up to take v'; 5359
25:12 the house of Judah by taking v'; "
14 I will lay my v' upon Edom by the 5360
14 they shall know my v', saith the "
15 taken v' with a despiteful heart, 5359
17 great v' upon them with furious 5360
17 when I shall lay my v' upon them. "
Mic 5:15 execute v' in anger and fury upon 5359
Na 1: 2 will take v' on his adversaries, 5358
Lu 21:22 For these be the days of v', that 1557
Ac 28: 4 the sea, yet v' suffereth not to live.*1349
Ro 3: 5 Is God unrighteous who taketh v'?*3709
12:19 V' is mine; I will repay, saith the 1557
2Th 1: 8 In flaming fire taking v' on them "
Heb 10:30 V' belongeth unto me, I will "
Jude 7 suffering the v' of eternal fire. *1349
venison
Ge 25:28 Esau, because he did eat of his v': 6718
27: 3 to the field, and take me some v'; 6720
5 went to the field to hunt for v', 6718
7 Bring me v', and make me savoury "
19 sit and eat of my v', that thy soul "
25 to me, and I will eat of my son's v', "
31 father arise, and eat of his son's v', "
33 where is he that hath taken v', and "
venom
De 32:33 dragons, and the cruel v' of asps. 7219
venomous
Ac 28: 4 saw the v' beast hang on his hand,*
vent See also INVENT; PREVENT.
Job 32:19 belly is as wine which hath no v'; 6605

venture See also ADVENTURE.
1Ki 22:34 a certain man drew a bow at a v', 8537
2Ch 18:33 a certain man drew a bow at a v', "
verified
Ge 42:20 so shall your words be v', and ye 539
1Ki 8:26 let thy word, I pray thee, be v', "
2Ch 6:17 God of Israel, let thy word be v', "
verily
Ge 42:21 We are v' guilty concerning our 61
Ex 31:13 V' my sabbaths ye shall keep: for 389
J'g 15: 2 I v' thought that thou hadst utterly559
1Ki 1:43 V' our lord king David hath made 61
2Ki 4:14 V' she hath no child, and her "
1Ch 21:24 I will v' buy it for the full price: 7069
Job 19:13 acquaintance are v' estranged * 389
Ps 37: 3 the land, and v' thou shalt be fed. †‡530
39: 5 v' every man at his best state is * 389
58:11 V' there is a reward for the "
11 v' he is a God that judgeth in the "
66:19 But v' God hath heard me; he hath403
Isa 45:15 V' thou art a God that hidest "
Jer 15:11 V' it shall be well with thy 518,3808
11 v' I will cause the enemy to entreat518
M't 5:18 For v' I say unto you, Till heaven 281
26 V' I say unto thee, Thou shalt by "
6: 2, 5, 16 V' I say unto you, They have "
8:10 V' I say unto you, I have not found "
10:15 V' I say unto you, It shall be more "
23 for v' I say unto you, Ye shall not "
42 v' I say unto you, he shall in no wise "
11:11 V' I say unto you, Among them that "
13:17 For v' I say unto you, That many "
16:28 V' I say unto you, There be some "
17:20 for v' I say unto you, If ye have faith "
18: 3 V' I say unto you, Except ye be "
13 v' I say unto you, he rejoiceth more "
18 V' I say unto you, Whatsoever ye "
19:23 V' I say unto you, That a rich man "
28 V' I say unto you, That ye which "
21:21 V' I say unto you, If ye have faith, "
31 V' I say unto you, That the "
23:36 V' I say unto you, All these things "
24: 2 v' I say unto you, There shall not be "
34 V' I say unto you, This generation "
47 V' I say unto you, That he shall "
25:12 V' I say unto you, I know you not. "
40, 45 V' I say unto you, Inasmuch as "
26:13 V' I say unto you, Wheresoever this "
21 V' I say unto you, that one of you "
34 V' I say unto thee, That this night, "
M'r 3:28 V' I say unto you, All sins shall be "
6:11 V' I say unto you, It shall be more* "
8:12 v' I say unto you, There shall no "
9: 1 V' I say unto you, That there be "
12 Elias v' cometh first, and restoreth*3303
41 v' I say unto you, he shall not lose 281
10:15 V' I say unto you, Whosoever shall "
29 V' I say unto you, There is no man "
11:23 v' I say unto you, That whosoever "
12:43 V' I say unto you, That this poor "
13:30 V' I say unto you, that this "
14: 9 V' I say unto you, Wheresoever this "
18 V' I say unto you, One of you which "
25 V' I say unto you, I will drink no "
30 V' I say unto thee, That this day, "
Lu 4:24 V' I say unto you, No prophet is "
11:51 v' I say unto you, It shall be *3483
12:37 v' I say unto you, that he shall gird 281
13:35 and v' I say unto you, Ye shall not * "
18:17 V' I say unto you, Whosoever shall "
29 V' I say unto you, There is no man "
21:32 V' I say unto you, This generation "
23:43 V' I say unto thee, To day shalt "
Joh 1:51 V', v', I say unto you, Hereafter ye "
3: 3, 5 V', v', I say unto thee, Except a "
11 V', v', I say unto thee, We speak "
5:19 V', v', I say unto you, The Son can "
24 V', v', I say unto you, He that "
25 V', v', I say unto you, The hour is "
6:26 V', v', I say unto you, Ye seek me, "
32 V', v', I say unto you, Moses gave "
47 V', v', I say unto you, He that "
53 V', v', I say unto you, Except ye eat "
8:34 V', v', I say unto you, Whosoever "
51 V', v', I say unto you, If a man keep "
58 V', v', I say unto you, Before "
10: 1 V', v', I say unto you, He that "
7 V', v', I say unto you, I am the door "
12:24 V', v', I say unto you, Except a corn "
13:16 V', v', I say unto you, The servant is "
20 V', v', I say unto you, He that "
21 V', v', I say unto you, that one of "
38 V', v', I say unto thee, The cock shall "
14:12 V', v', I say unto you, He that "
16:20 V', v', I say unto you, That ye shall "
23 V', v', I say unto you, Whatsoever "
21:18 V', v', I say unto thee, When thou "
Ac 16:37 nay v'; but let them come 1063
19: 4 John v' baptized with the baptism*3303
22: 3 I am v' a man which am a Jew, born* "
26: 9 I v' thought with myself, that 3303,3767
Ro 2:25 For circumcision v' profiteth, if *3303
10:18 Yes v', their sound went into all 3304
15:27 It hath pleased them v'; and their*1063
1Co 5: 3 For I v', as absent in body, but 3303
9:18 V', that, when I preach the gospel, I*
14:17 For thou v' givest thanks well, 3303
Ga 3:21 v' righteousness should have been 3689
1Th 3: 4 For v', when we were with you, we 2532
Heb 2:16 v' he took not on him the nature of1222
3: 5 Moses v' was faithful in all his *3303
6:16 For men v' swear by the greater: * "
7: 5 v' they that are of the sons of Levi,* "
18 For there is v' a disannulling of the* "
9: 1 Then v' the first covenant had also* "

Heb 12:10 For they v' for a few days chastened3303
1Pe 1:20 Who v' was foreordained before the* "
1Jo 2: 5 him v' is the love of God perfected: 230
verity
Ps 111: 7 The works of his hands are v' and* 571
1Ti 2: 7 of the Gentiles in faith and v'. *225
vermilion
Jer 22:14 with cedar, and painted with v'. 8350
Eze 23:14 of the Chaldeans pourtrayed with v'. "
very
Ge 1:31 made, and, behold, it was v' good. 3966
4: 5 And Cain was v' wroth, and his "
12:14 the woman that she was v' fair. "
13: 2 And Abram was v' rich in cattle, in "
18:20 because their sin is v' grievous; "
21:11 thing was v' grievous in Abraham's "
24:16 the damsel was v' fair to look upon, "
26:13 and grew until he became v' great: "
27:21 whether thou be my v' son Esau or2088
24 he said, Art thou my v' son Esau? "
33 Isaac trembled v' exceedingly, 1419
34: 7 they were v' wroth, because he 3966
41:19 and v' ill favoured and leanfleshed, "
31 following; for it shall be v' grievous. "
49 v' much, until he left numbering; "
47:13 for the famine was v' sore, so that "
50: 9 and it was a v' great company. "
10 a great and v' sore lamentation: "
Ex 1:20 multiplied, and waxed v' mighty. "
8:28 only ye shall not go v' far away: "
9: 3 shall be a v' grievous murrain. 3966
16 And in v' deed for this cause have I 199
18 cause it to rain a v' grievous hail, 3966
24 and fire...with the hail, v' grievous, "
10:14 v' grievous were they; before them "
11: 3 Moses was v' great in the land of "
12:38 and herds, even v' much cattle. "
30:36 thou shalt beat some of it v' small,1854
Nu 6: 9 any man die v' suddenly by him, 6621
11:33 the people with a v' great plague. 3966
12: 3 the man Moses was v' meek, above "
13:28 the cities are walled, and v' great: "
16:15 Moses was v' wroth, and said unto "
22:17 promote thee unto v' great honour, "
32: 1 had a v' great multitude of cattle: "
De 9:20 the Lord was v' angry with Aaron "
21 stamped it, and ground it v' small,3190
20:15 the cities which are v' far off from 3966
27: 8 all the words of this law v' plainly.3190
28:43 shall get up above thee v' high; *4605
43 and thou shalt come down v' low.*4295
54 tender among you, and v' delicate,3966
30:14 But the word is v' nigh unto thee, "
32:20 they are a v' froward generation,
Jos 1: 7 be thou strong and v' courageous,3966
3:16 an heap v' far from the city Adam,* "
8: 4 go not v' far from the city, but be ye "
9: 9 From a v' far country thy servants "
13 by reason of the v' long journey. "
22 We are v' far from you; when ye "
10:20 them with a v' great slaughter, "
27 which remain until this v' day. 6106
11: 4 with horses and chariots v' many. 3966
13: 1 there remaineth yet v' much land "
22: 8 your tents, and with v' much cattle, "
8 iron, and with v' much raiment: "
23: 6 Be ye therefore v' courageous to "
J'g 3:17 Moab: and Eglon was a v' fat man. "
11:33 vineyards, with a v' great slaughter. "
35 thou hast brought me v' low, and "
13: 6 of an angel of God, v' terrible: 3966
18: 9 the land, and, behold, it is v' good: "
Ru 1:20 hath dealt v' bitterly with me. "
1Sa 2:17 sin of the young men was v' great "
22 Now Eli was v' old, and heard all "
4:10 and there was a v' great slaughter; "
5: 9 the city with a v' great destruction: "
11 hand of God was v' heavy there. "
14:15 so it was a v' great trembling. * 430
20 there was a v' great discomfiture. 3966
31 and the people were v' faint. "
18: 8 And Saul was v' wroth, and the "
15 that he behaved himself v' wisely, "
19: 4 have been to thee-ward v' good: "
20: 7 but if he be v' wroth, then be sure* "
23:22 is told me that he dealeth v' subtilly. "
25: 2 and the man was v' great, and he 3966
15 But the men were v' good unto us, "
34 For in v' deed, as the Lord God of 199
36 him, for he was v' drunken: 5704,3966
26: 4 that Saul was come in v' deed. *3559
2Sa 1:26 v' pleasant hast thou been unto 3966
2:17 there was a v' sore battle that day; "
3: 8 Then was Abner v' wroth for the "
11: 2 the woman was v' beautiful to look "
12:15 bare unto David, and it was v' sick. "
13: 3 and Jonadab was a v' subtil man. 3966
21 of all these things, he was v' wroth. "
36 and all his servants wept v' sore. "
18:17 a v' great heap of stones upon him: "
19:32 Now Barzillai was a v' aged man, "
32 for he was a v' great man. "
24:10 for I have done v' foolishly. "
1Ki 1: 4 And the damsel was v' fair, and "
6 and he also was a v' goodly man; "
15 and the king was v' old; and "
7:34 undersetters were of the v' base *
10: 2 to Jerusalem with a v' great train,3966
2 and v' much gold, and precious "
10 and of spices v' great store, and "
19:10, 14 I have been v' jealous for the Lord "
21:26 he did v' abominably in following 3966
2Ki 14:26 of Israel, that it was v' bitter: "
17:18 the Lord was v' angry with Israel. "

2Ki 21:16 shed innocent blood v' much, 3966
1Ch 9:13 v' able men for the work of the
18: 8 brought David v' much brass, 3966
21: 8 servant; for I have done v' foolishly."
13 Lord; for v' great are his mercies: "
23:17 sons of Rehabiah were v' many. 4605
2Ch 6:18 God in v' deed dwell with men on 552
7: 8 with him, a v' great congregation, 3966
9: 1 with a v' great company, and "
14:13 they carried away v' much spoil. "
16: 8 host, with v' many chariots and * "
14 they made a v' great burning 5704,
20:35 king of Israel, who did v' wickedly: "
24:24 Lord delivered a v' great host 3966
30:13 month, a v' great congregation. "
32:29 had given him substance v' much. "
33:14 and raised it up a v' great height, "
36:14 transgressed v' much after all the
Ezr 10: 1 a v' great congregation of men 3966
1 children: for the people wept v' sore.
Ne 1: 7 We have dealt v' corruptly against "
2: 2 heart. Then I was v' sore afraid, 3966
4: 7 stopped, then they were v' wroth, "
5: 6 I was v' angry when I heard their "
8:17 And there was v' great gladness. "
Es 1:12 therefore was the king v' wroth, "
Job 1: 3 asses, and a v' great household; "
2:13 saw that his grief was v' great. "
15:10 the grayheaded and v' aged men, 3453
32: 6 said, I am young, and ye are v' old; "
Ps 5: 9 their inward part is v' wickedness;1942
35: 8 into that v' destruction let him fall.*
46: 1 a v' present help in trouble. 3966
50: 3 v' tempestuous round about him. "
71:19 righteousness...O God, is v' high, 5704
79: 8 us: for we are brought v' low. 3966
89: 2 shalt thou establish in the v' heavens.
92: 5 and thy thoughts are v' deep. 3966
93: 5 Thy testimonies are v' sure: "
104: 1 O Lord my God, thou art v' great; "
105:12 but a few men in number; yea, v' few,
119:107 I am afflicted v' much: 5704,3966
138 are righteous and v' faithful. "
140 Thy word is v' pure: therefore "
142: 6 my cry; for I am brought v' low: "
147:15 earth: his word runneth v' swiftly.5704
Pr 17: 9 a matter separateth v' friends. *
27:15 continual dropping in a v' rainy 5464
Isa 1: 9 left unto us a v' small remnant, 4592
5: 1 hath a vineyard in a v' fruitful hill: "
10:25 For yet a v' little while, and the 4213
16: 6 the pride of Moab; he is v' proud: 3966
14 the remnant shall be v' small and 4213
24:16 dealers have dealt v' treacherously.899
29:17 Is it not yet a v' little while, and 4213
31: 1 because they are v' strong; 3966
33:17 behold the land that is v' far off. *4801
40:15 up the isles as a v' little thing. 1851
47: 6 hast thou v' heavily laid thy yoke. 3966
48: 8 thou wouldest deal v' treacherously,898
52:13 and extolled, and be v' high. 3966
64: 9 Be not wroth v' sore, O Lord, "
12 thy peace, and afflict us v' sore? "
Jer 2:12 be ye v' desolate, saith the Lord. "
4:19 I am pained at my v' heart; my 7023
5:11 dealt v' treacherously against me,
12: 1 happy that deal v' treacherously? 899
14:17 breach, with a v' grievous blow. 3966
18:13 Israel hath done a v' horrible thing."
20:15 born unto thee; making him v' glad.
24: 2 One basket had v' good figs, even 3966
2 other basket had v' naughty figs, "
3 I said, Figs; the good figs, v' good; "
3 and the evil, v' evil, that cannot be "
27: 7 until the v' time of his land come: *
40:12 wine and summer fruits v' much. 3966
46:20 Egypt is like a v' fair heifer, but 3304
La 5:22 thou art v' wroth against us. 5704,3966
Eze 2: 3 against me, even unto this v' day. 6106
16:47 as if that were a v' little thing, 6985
27:25 made v' glorious in the midst of 3966
33:32 art unto them as a v' lovely song 5690
37: 2 were v' many in the open valley; 3966
2 valley; and, lo, they were v' dry. "
40: 2 set me upon a v' high mountain, "
47: 7 were v' many trees on the one side "
9 shall be a v' great multitude of fish."
Da 2:12 the king was angry and v' furious,7690
7:20 mouth that spake v' great things,*7260
8: 8 the he goat waxed v' great: *5704,3966
11:25 a v' great and mighty army; * " "
Joe 2:11 army: for his camp is v' great: "
11 of the Lord is great and v' terrible; "
Am 5:20 v' dark, and no brightness in it? 651
Jon 4: 1 exceedingly, and he was v' angry.*
Hab 2:13 people shall labour in the v' fire, 1767
13 weary themselves for v' vanity? * "
Zec 1:15 I am v' sore displeased with the
8: 4 his staff in his hand for v' age. 7230
9: 2 and Zidon, though it be v' wise. 3966
5 shall see it, and be v' sorrowful, * "
14: 4 and there shall be a v' great valley;"
M't 10:30 But the v' hairs of your head are 2532
15:28 made whole from that v' hour. *1565
17:18 child was cured from that v' hour.* "
18:31 was done, they were v' sorry, *4970
21: 8 a v' great multitude spread their *4118
24:24 they shall deceive the v' elect. *2532
26: 7 box of v' precious ointment, * 927
37 began to be sorrowful and v' heavy.*85
M'r 8: 1 the multitude being v' great, and *3827
14: 3 ointment of spikenard v' precious 4185
33 be sore amazed, and to be v' heavy;* 85
16: 2 v' early in the morning the first 3029
4 rolled away: for it was v' great. *4970
Lu 1: 3 of all things from the v' first, *
Lu 9: 5 shake off the v' dust from your *2532
10:11 Even the v' dust of your city, which*
12: 7 But even the v' hairs of your head 2532
59 till thou hast paid the v' last mite.
18:23 heard this, he was v' sorrowful: *4970
23 sorrowful: for he was v' rich. * "
24 saw that he was v' sorrowful, *4036
19:17 thou hast been faithful in a v' little,1646
48 were v' attentive to hear him. *1582
24: 1 v' early in the morning, they came*
Joh 7:26 indeed that this is the v' Christ? * 230
8: 4 was taken in adultery, in the v' act.*1888
12: 3 ointment of spikenard, v' costly, 4186
14:11 else believe me for the v' works' sake.
Ac 9:22 proving that this is v' Christ. * 846
24: 2 that v' worthy deeds are done unto*2735
25:10 no wrong, as thou v' well knowest.2566
Ro 10:20 Esaias is v' bold, and saith, I was 662
13: 6 continually upon this v' thing. 846
1Co 4: 3 it is a v' small thing that I should 1646
2Co 9: 2 your zeal hath provoked v' many. 4119
11: 5 behind the v' chiefest apostles. 5228
12:11 I behind the v' chiefest apostles. 3029
15 I will v' gladly spend and be spent*2236
Ph'p 1: 6 Being confident of this v' thing, that846
1Th 5:13 to esteem them v' highly in love *5228
23 the v' God of peace sanctify you * 846
2Ti 1:17 he sought me out v' diligently, *4708
18 at Ephesus, thou knowest v' well. 957
Heb10: 1 and not the v' image of the things, 846
Jas 3: 4 turned about with a v' small helm,1646
5:11 that the Lord is v' pitiful, and of *4184

vessel See also VESSELS.
Le 6:28 earthen v' wherein it is sodden 3627
11:32 whether it be any v' of wood, or "
32 whatsoever v' it be, wherein any "
33 every earthen v', whereinto any of "
34 in every such v' shall be unclean. "
14: 5 the birds be killed in an earthen v' "
50 an earthen v' over running water: "
15:12 And the v' of earth, that he toucheth"
12 every v' of wood shall be rinsed in "
Nu 5:17 take holy water in an earthen v'; "
19:15 And every open v', which hath no "
17 water shall be put thereto in a v': "
De 23:24 but thou shalt not put any in thy v'."
1Sa 21: 5 were sanctified this day in the v'. * "
1Ki 17:10 I pray thee, a little water in a v', "
2Ki 4: 6 unto her son, Bring me yet a v'. "
6 unto her, There is not a v' more. "
Ps 2: 9 them in pieces like a potter's v'. "
31:12 out of mind: I am like a broken v'. "
Pr 25: 4 shall come forth a v' for the finer. "
Isa 30:14 it as the breaking of the potters' v'5035
66:20 bring an offering in a clean v' into 3627
Jer 18: 4 And the v' that he made of clay was"
4 so he made it again another v', as "
19:11 as one breaketh a potter's v', that "
22:28 is he a v' wherein is no pleasure? "
25:34 and ye shall fall like a pleasant v'. "
32:14 and put them in an earthen v', that "
48:11 hath not been emptied from v' to v', "
38 have broken Moab like a v' wherein"
51:34 he hath made me an empty v', he "
Eze 4: 9 and fitches, and put them in one v', "
15: 3 a pin of it to hang any v' thereon? "
Hos 8: 8 as a v' wherein is no pleasure. "
M'r 11:16 carry any v' through the temple. 4632
Lu 8:16 a candle, covereth it with a v', "
Joh 19:29 there was set a v' full of vinegar: "
Ac 9:15 he is a chosen v' unto me, to bear "
10:11 a certain v' descending unto him, "
16 the v' was received up again into "
11: 5 saw a vision, A certain v' descend, "
Ro 9:21 lump to make one v' unto honour, "
1Th 4: 4 to possess his v' in sanctification "
2Ti 2:21 he shall be a v' unto honour, "
1Pe 3: 7 unto the wife, as unto the weaker v', "

vessels
Ge 43:11 best fruits in the land in your v', 3627
Ex 7:19 both in v' of wood, and in v' of stone.
25:39 shall he make it, with all these v'. 3627
27: 3 v' thereof thou shalt make of brass."
19 All the v' of the tabernacle in all * "
30:27 And the table and all his v', "
27 and the candlestick and his v', "
28 And the altar...with all his v', "
35:13 and his staves, and all his v', and "
16 grate, his staves, and all his v', "
37:16 he made the v' which were upon "
24 pure gold made he it, and all the v'"
38: 3 And he made all the v' of the altar, "
3 all the v' thereof made he of brass. "
30 for it, and all the v' of the altar, "
39:36 The table, and all the v' thereof, "
37 all the v' thereof, and the oil for "
39 brass, his staves, and all his v', "
40 and all the v' of the service of the* "
40: 9 hallow it, and all the v' thereof: * "
10 all his v', and sanctify the altar: "
Le 8:11 anointed the altar and all his v', "
Nu 1:50 over all the v' thereof, and over all*"
50 tabernacle, and all the v' thereof;* "
3:31 the v' of the sanctuary wherewith "
36 all the v' thereof, and all that * "
4: 9 all the oil v' thereof, wherewith "
10 put it and all the v' thereof within "
14 shall put upon it all the v' thereof, "
14 the basons, all the v' of the altar; "
15 and all the v' of the sanctuary, * "
16 sanctuary, and in the v' thereof. * "
7: 1 the altar and all the v' thereof, "
85 the silver v' weighed two thousand "
18: 3 come nigh the v' of the sanctuary "
19:18 and upon all the v', and upon the "
Jos 6:19 and gold, and v' of brass and iron, 3627
24 and the v' of brass and of iron, "
Ru 2: 9 go unto the v', and drink of that "
1Sa 9: 7 for the bread is spent in our v', "
21: 5 the v' of the young men are holy, "
2Sa 8:10 brought with him v' of silver, "
10 and v' of gold, and v' of brass: "
17:28 beds, and basons, and earthen v', "
1Ki 7:45 all these v', which Hiram made "
47 Solomon left all the v' unweighed, "
48 Solomon made all the v' that "
51 silver, and the gold, and the v', "
8: 4 holy v' that were in the tabernacle, "
10:21 Solomon's drinking v' were of gold, "
21 all the v' of the house of the forest "
25 present, v' of silver, and v' of gold, "
15:15 the Lord, silver, and gold, and v'. "
2Ki 4: 3 Go, borrow thee v' abroad of all "
3 even empty v'; borrow not a few. "
4 and shalt pour out into all those v'."
5 who brought the v' to her; and she
6 to pass, when the v' were full, 3627
7:15 way was full of garments and v', "
12:13 any v' of gold, or v' of silver, of the "
14:14 all the v' that were found in the "
23: 4 all the v' that were made for Baal, "
24:13 cut in pieces all the v' of gold "
25:14 all the v' of brass wherewith they "
16 all these v' was without weight. "
1Ch 9:28 the charge of the ministering v', "
29 were appointed to oversee the v', * "
18: 8 and the pillars, and the v' of brass. "
10 all manner of v' of gold and silver "
22:19 the holy v' of God, into the house "
23:26 any v' of it for the service thereof. "
28:13 for all the v' of service in the house "
2Ch 4:18 Solomon made all these v' in great "
19 Solomon made all the v' that were "
5: 5 holy v' that were in the tabernacle, "
9:20 the drinking v' of king Solomon "
20 all the v' of the house of the forest "
24 v' of silver, and v' of gold, and "
15:18 dedicated, silver, and gold, and v'. "
24:14 made v' for the house of the Lord, "
14 even v' to minister, and to offer "
14 spoons, and v' of gold and silver. "
25:24 all the v' that were found in the "
28:24 together the v' of the house of God, "
24 cut in pieces the v' of the house of "
29:18 offering, with all the v' thereof, "
18 table, with all the v' thereof. "
19 Moreover all the v', which king "
36: 7 Nebuchadnezzar also carried...v' of "
10 goodly v' of the house of the Lord, "
18 all the v' of the house of God, "
19 destroyed all the goodly v' thereof. "
Ezr 1: 6 their hands with v' of silver, with "
7 Cyrus...brought forth the v' of "
10 and ten, and other v' a thousand. "
11 All the v' of gold and of silver were "
5:14 the v' also of gold and silver of the3984
15 Take these v', go, carry them into "
6: 5 golden and silver v' of the house "
7:19 The v' also that are given thee for "
8:25 silver, and the gold, and the v', 3627
26 and silver v' an hundred talents, "
27 two v' of fine copper, precious as "
28 v' are holy also; and the silver "
30 the silver, and the gold, and the v', "
33 and the v' weighed in the house "
Ne 10:39 where are the v' of the sanctuary, "
13: 5 the frankincense, and the v', and "
9 I again the v' of the house of God, "
Es 1: 7 they gave them drink in v' of gold, "
7 v' being diverse one from another,)"
Isa 18: 2 v' of bulrushes upon the waters, "
22:24 the issue, all v' of small quantity,* "
24 the v' of cups, even to all the v' of "
52:11 clean, that bear the v' of the Lord. "
65: 4 abominable things is in their v'; "
Jer 14: 3 they returned with their v' empty; "
27:16 v' of the Lord's house shall now "
18 v' which are left in the house of "
19 concerning the residue of the v' "
21 concerning the v' that remain in "
28: 3 bring again into this place all the v'"
6 to bring again the v' of the Lord's "
40:10 and put them in your v', and dwell "
48:12 and shall empty his v', and break "
49:29 and all their v', and their camels; "
52:18 all the v' of brass wherewith they "
20 the brass of all these v' was without"
Eze 27:13 the persons of men and v' of brass "
Da 1: 2 part of the v' of the house of God: "
2 he brought the v' into the treasure "
5: 2 to bring the golden and silver v' 3984
3 Then they brought the golden v' "
23 have brought the v' of his house "
11: 8 precious v' of silver and of gold; 3627
Ho 13:15 spoil the treasure of all pleasant v'. "
Hag 2:16 to draw out fifty v' out of the press, "
M't 13:48 gathered the good into v', but cast 30
25: 4 wise took oil in their v' with their "
M'r 7: 4 cups, and pots, and brazen v', and "
Ro 9:22 v' of wrath fitted to destruction: 4632
23 of his glory on the v' of mercy, "
2Co 4: 7 have this treasure in earthen v', "
2Ti 2:20 are not only v' of gold and of silver,"
Heb 9:21 and all the v' of the ministry. "
Re 2:27 as the v' of a potter shall they be "
18:12 wood, and all manner v' of ivory, * "
12 manner v' of most precious wood,* "

vestments
2Ki 10:22 forth v' for all the worshippers 3830
22 And he brought them forth v'. 4403

vestry
2Ki 10:22 unto him that was over the *v*. 4458
vesture See also VESTURES.
De 22:12 upon the four quarters of thy *v*. 3682
Ps 22:18 them, and cast lots upon my *v*. 3830
102:26 as a *v*. shalt thou change them,
M't 27:35 and upon my *v*. did they cast lots.*2441
Joh 19:24 and for my *v*. they did cast lots. "
Heb 1:12 as a *v*. shalt thou fold them up, *4018
Re 19:13 clothed with a *v*. dipped in blood:*2440
16 on his *v*. and on his thigh a name* "
vestures
Ge 41:42 arrayed him in *v*. of fine linen, 899
vex See also VEXED.
Ex 22:21 Thou shalt neither *v*. a stranger, *3238
Le 18:18 take a wife to her sister, to *v*. her,*6887
19:33 in your land, ye shall not *v*. him. *3238
Nu 25:17 *V*. the Midianites, and smite 6887
18 For they *v*. you with their wiles,
33:55 shall *v*. you in the land wherein
2Sa 12:18 how will he then *v*. himself, 6213,7451
2Ch 15:6 God did *v*. them with all adversity.2000
Job 19:2 How long will ye *v*. my soul, and 3013
Ps 2:5 and *v*. them in his sore displeasure.926
Isa 7:6 us go up against Judah, and *v*. it, 6973
11:13 and Judah shall not *v*. Ephraim. 6887
Eze 32:9 I will also *v*. the hearts of many 3707
Hab 2:7 and awake that shall *v*. thee, 2111
Ac 12:1 hands to *v*. certain of the church. 2559
vexation See also VEXATIONS.
De 28:20 shall send upon thee cursing, *v*., *4103
Ec 1:14 all is vanity and *v*. of spirit. *7469
17 that this also is *v*. of spirit. *7475
2:11 all was vanity and *v*. of spirit, *7469
17 for all is vanity and *v*. of spirit. * "
22 labour, and of the *v*. of his heart, *7475
26 also is vanity and *v*. of spirit. *7469
4:4 This is also vanity and *v*. of spirit.* "
6 full with travail and *v*. of spirit. * "
16 this also is vanity and *v*. of spirit.*7475
6:9 this is also vanity and *v*. of spirit.*7469
Isa 9:1 shall not be such as was in her *v*.,*4164
28:19 shall be a *v*. only to understand *2113
65:14 and shall howl for *v*. of spirit. 7667
vexations
2Ch 15:5 but great *v*. were upon all the 4103
vexed
Nu 20:15 Egyptians *v*. us, and our fathers:‡†7489
J'g 2:18 that oppressed them and *v*. them. 1766
10:8 they *v*. and oppressed the children7492
16:16 so that his soul was *v*. unto death:7114
1Sa 14:47 he turned himself, he *v*. them. ‡7561
2Sa 13:2 Amnon was so *v*., that he fell sick 3334
2Ki 4:27 for her soul is *v*. within her: 4843
Ne 9:27 of their enemies, who *v*. them: *6887
Job 27:2 Almighty, who hath *v*. my soul; 4843
Ps 6:2 heal me; for my bones are *v*. 926
3 My soul is also sore *v*.: but thou "
10 enemies be ashamed and sore *v*.: "
Isa 63:10 rebelled, and *v*. his holy Spirit: *6087
Eze 22:5 which art infamous and much *v*.*4103
7 in thee have they *v*. the fatherless*3238
29 and have *v*. the poor and needy: "
M't 15:22 is grievously *v*. with a devil. 1139
17:15 for he is lunatick, and sore *v*.: *3958
Lu 6:18 that were *v*. with unclean spirits:*3791
Ac 5:16 which were *v*. with unclean spirits: "
2Pe 2:7 *v*. with the filthy conversation of *2669
8 *v*. his righteous soul from day to * 928
vial See also VIALS.
1Sa 10:1 Then Samuel took a *v*. of oil, and 6378
Re 16:2 poured out his *v*. upon the earth;*5357
3 poured out his *v*. upon the sea; * "
4 poured out his *v*. upon the rivers * "
8 poured out his *v*. upon the sun; * "
10 poured out his *v*. upon the seat * "
12 out his *v*. upon the great river * "
17 poured out his *v*. into the air; * "
vials
Re 5:8 and golden *v*. full of odours, which*5357
15:7 seven golden *v*. full of the wrath of*"
16:1 pour out the *v*. of the wrath of God*"
17:1 angels which had the seven *v*., * "
21:9 the seven *v*. full of the seven last * "
victory
2Sa 19:2 the *v*. that day was turned into 8668
23:10 the Lord wrought a great *v*. that "
12 and the Lord wrought a great *v*. "
1Ch 29:11 and the glory, and the *v*., and the 5331
Ps 98:1 holy arm, hath gotten him the *v*.,*3467
Isa 25:8 He will swallow up death in *v*.; *5331
M't 12:20 he send forth judgment unto *v*. 3534
1Co 15:54 Death is swallowed up in *v*.
55 thy sting? O grave, where is thy *v*.? "
57 *v*. through our Lord Jesus Christ. "
1Jo 5:4 the *v*. that overcometh the world, 3529
Re 15:2 had gotten the *v*. over the beast, *3528
victual See also VICTUALS.
Ex 12:39 prepared for themselves any *v*. 6720
J'g 20:10 to fetch *v*. for the people, that they "
1Ki 4:27 those officers provided *v*. for king 3557
2Ch 11:11 captains in them, and store of *v*. 3978
23 he gave them *v*. in abundance. 4202
victuals
Ge 14:11 and Gomorrah, and all their *v*., 400
Le 25:37 nor lend him thy *v*. for increase.
De 23:19 usury of money, usury of *v*., usury "
Jos 1:11 people, saying, Prepare you *v*.; 6720
9:11 Take *v*. with you for the journey, * "
14 And the men took up their *v*., and*6718
J'g 7:8 the people took *v*. in their hand. 6720
J'g 17:10 and a suit of apparel, and thy *v*. 4241
1Sa 22:10 and gave him *v*., and gave him 6720
1Ki 4:7 provided *v*. for the king and his 3557
11:18 appointed him *v*., and gave him 3899
Ne 10:31 ware or any *v*. on the sabbath day 7668
13:15 in the day wherein they sold *v*. 6718
Jer 40:5 captain of the guard gave him *v*. 737
44:17 for then had we plenty of *v*., and 3899
M't 14:15 villages, and buy themselves *v*. *1033
Lu 9:12 about, and lodge, and get *v*.: ‡1979
view See also VIEWED.
Jos 2:1 Go *v*. the land, even Jericho. 7200
7:2 saying, Go up and *v*. the country.*7270
2Ki 2:7 went, and stood to *v*. afar off: *5048
15 prophets...were to *v*. at Jericho * "
viewed
Jos 7:2 And the men went up and *v*. Ai. *7270
Ezr 8:15 and I *v*. the people, and the priests,995
Ne 2:13 and *v*. the walls of Jerusalem, 7663
15 night by the brook, and *v*. the wall, "
vigilant
1Ti 3:2 husband of one wife, *v*., sober, of *3524
1Pe 5:8 Be sober, be *v*.; because your *1127
vile See also REVILE; VILER; VILEST.
De 25:3 thy brother should seem *v*. unto 7034
J'g 19:24 this man do not so *v*. a thing. *5039
1Sa 3:13 his sons made themselves *v*., and*7043
15:9 but every thing that was *v*. and 5240
2Sa 6:22 I will yet be more *v*. than thus, 7043
Job 18:3 and reputed *v*. in your sight? *2933
40:4 I am *v*.; what shall I answer thee?*7043
Ps 15:4 eyes a *v*. person is contemned; * 959
Isa 32:5 The *v*. person shall be no more ‡5036
6 the *v*. person will speak villany, ‡ "
Jer 15:19 forth the precious from the *v*., 2151
29:17 will make them like *v*. figs, that 8182
La 1:11 and consider; for I am become *v*. 2151
Da 11:21 estate shall stand up a *v*. person,* 959
Na 1:14 make thy grave; for thou art *v*. 7043
3:6 filth upon thee, and make thee *v*., 5034
Ro 1:26 gave them up unto *v*. affections: 819
Ph'p 3:21 Who shall change our *v*. body, *5014
Jas 2:2 in also a poor man in *v*. raiment: 4508
vilely
2Sa 1:21 of the mighty is *v*. cast away, 1602
viler
Job 30:8 men: they were *v*. than the earth.*5217
vilest
Ps 12:8 when the *v*. men are exalted. *2149
village See also VILLAGES.
M't 21:2 Go into the *v*. over against you, 2968
M'r 11:2 Go your way into the *v*. over against"
Lu 8:1 went throughout every city and *v*.,*"
9:52 entered into a *v*. of the Samaritans,"
56 them. And they went to another *v*."
10:38 that he entered into a certain *v*.: "
17:12 And as he entered into a certain *v*., "
19:30 Go ye into the *v*. over against you; "
24:13 same day to a *v*. called Emmaus, "
28 And they drew nigh unto the *v*., "
villages
Ex 8:13 out of the *v*., and out of the fields.*2691
Le 25:31 houses of the *v*. which have no wall "
Nu 21:25 Heshbon, and in all the *v*. thereof.*1323
32 they took the *v*. thereof, and drove*"
32:42 took Kenath, and the *v*. thereof, "
Jos 13:23 the cities and the *v*. thereof. 2691
28 families, the cities, and their *v*. "
15:32 are twenty and nine, with their *v*. "
36 fourteen cities with their *v*. "
41 sixteen cities with their *v*. "
44 Mareshah; nine cities with their *v*.: "
45 Ekron, with her towns and her *v*.: "
46 that lay near Ashdod, with their *v*.: "
47 Ashdod with her towns and her *v*., "
47 Gaza with her towns and her *v*., "
51 Giloh; eleven cities with their *v*. "
54 and Zior; nine cities with their *v*. "
57 Timnah; ten cities with their *v*. "
59 Eltekon: six cities with their *v*. "
60 Rabbah; two cities with their *v*. "
62 En-gedi; six cities with their *v*. "
16:9 all the cities with their *v*. "
18:24 Gaba; twelve cities with their *v*.: "
28 fourteen cities with their *v*. "
19:6 thirteen cities and their *v*.: "
7 Ashan; four cities and their *v*.: "
8 all the *v*. that were round about "
15 twelve cities with their *v*. "
16 families, these cities with their *v*. "
22 Jordan: sixteen cities with their *v*. "
23 families, the cities and their *v*. "
30 twenty and two cities with their *v*. "
31 families, these cities with their *v*. "
38 nineteen cities with their *v*. "
39 families, the cities and their *v*. "
48 families, these cities with their *v*. "
21:12 fields of the city, and the *v*. thereof, "
J'g 5:7 The inhabitants of the *v*. ceased, *6520
11 the inhabitants of his *v*. in Israel:* "
1Sa 6:18 of fenced cities, and of country *v*. 3724
1Ch 4:32 And their *v*. were, Etam, and Ain, 2691
33 all their *v*. that were round about "
6:56 fields of the city, and the *v*. thereof,"
9:16 dwelt in the *v*. of the Netophathites."
22 by their genealogy in their *v*., "
25 brethren, which were in their *v*., "
27:25 and the cities, and in the *v*., and 3723
2Ch 28:18 and Shocho with the *v*. thereof, *1323
18 and Timnah with the *v*. thereof, * "
18 Gimzo also and the *v*. thereof: and*"
Ne 6:2 together in some one of the *v*. 3715
Ne 11:25 And for the *v*., with their fields, 2691
25 Kirjath-arba, and in the *v*. thereof.* "
25 at Dibon, and in the *v*. thereof, *1323
25 at Jekabzeel, and in the *v*. thereof,*"
27 Beer-sheba, and in the *v*. thereof,* "
28 at Mekonah, and in the *v*. thereof,* "
30 and in their *v*., at Lachish, 2691
30 at Azekah, and in the *v*. thereof. *1323
31 Aija, and Beth-el, and in their *v*. * "
12:28 and from the *v*. of Netophathi; 2691
29 for the singers had builded them *v*. "
Es 9:19 Therefore the Jews of the *v*., that 6521
Ps 10:8 in the lurking places of the *v*.: 2691
Ca 7:11 the field; let us lodge in the *v*. 3723
Isa 42:11 the *v*. that Kedar doth inhabit: 2691
Eze 38:11 go up to the land of unwalled *v*.; 6519
Hab 3:14 with his staves the head of his *v*.:*6518
M't 9:35 went about all the cities and *v*., 2968
14:15 that they may go into the *v*., and "
M'r 6:6 And he went round about the *v*., "
36 and into the *v*., and buy themselves"
56 he entered, into the *v*., or cities, or "
Lu 13:22 he went through the cities and *v*., "
Ac 8:25 preached the gospel in many *v*. "
villany
Isa 32:6 For the vile person will speak *v*., ‡5039
Jer 29:23 they have committed *v*. in Israel, * "
vine See also VINEDRESSERS; VINES; VINEYARD.
Ge 40:9 dream, behold, a *v*. was before me;1612
10 And in the *v*. were three branches: "
49:11 Binding his foal unto the *v*., and
11 his ass's colt unto the choice *v*.; 8321
Le 25:5 the grapes of thy *v*. undressed: 5139
11 the grapes in it of thy *v*. undressed.*"
Nu 6:4 eat nothing...made of the *v*. tree, 3196
De 32:32 For their *v*. is of the *v*. of Sodom, 1612
J'g 9:12 Then said the trees unto the *v*., "
13 the *v*. said unto them, Should I "
13:14 of any thing that cometh of the *v*., "
1Ki 4:25 every man under his *v*. and under "
2Ki 4:39 to gather herbs, and found a wild *v*.,"
18:31 eat ye every man of his own *v*., and "
2Ch 26:10 and *v*. dressers in the mountains,*3755
Job 15:33 off his unripe grape as the *v*., and 1612
Ps 80:8 hast brought a *v*. out of Egypt: "
14 and behold, and visit this *v*.; "
128:3 Thy wife shall be as a fruitful *v*. by "
Ca 6:11 to see whether the *v*. flourished, "
7:8 breasts shall be as clusters of the *v*.,"
12 let us see if the *v*. flourish, whether"
Isa 5:2 and planted it with the choicest *v*.,8321
16:8 languish, and the *v*. of Sibmah: 1612
9 weeping of Jazer the *v*. of Sibmah: "
24:7 wine mourneth, the *v*. languisheth, "
32:12 pleasant fields, for the fruitful *v*. "
34:4 as the leaf falleth off from the *v*., "
36:16 and eat ye every one of his *v*., and "
Jer 2:21 Yet I had planted thee a noble *v*., 8321
21 degenerate plant of a strange *v*. 1612
6:9 glean the remnant of Israel as a *v*.: "
8:13 there shall be no grapes on the *v*., "
48:32 O *v*. of Sibmah, I will weep for thee "
Eze 15:2 What is the *v*. tree more than any "
6 As the *v*. tree among the trees of "
17:6 a spreading *v*. of low stature, "
6 so it became a *v*., and brought forth"
7 this *v*. did bend her roots toward "
8 fruit, that it might be a goodly *v*. "
19:10 Thy mother is like a *v*. in thy blood,"
Ho 10:1 Israel is an empty *v*., he bringeth "
14:7 as the corn, and grow as the *v*.: "
Joe 1:7 He hath laid my *v*. waste, and "
12 The *v*. is dried up, and the fig tree "
2:22 and the *v*. do yield their strength. "
Mic 4:4 sit every man under his *v*. and "
Na 2:2 out, and marred their *v*. branches.2156
Hag 2:19 as yet the *v*., and the fig tree, and 1612
Zec 3:10 man his neighbour under the *v*. "
8:12 the *v*. shall give her fruit, and the "
Mal 3:11 neither shall your *v*. cast her fruit "
M't 26:29 henceforth of this fruit of the *v*., 288
M'r 14:25 drink no more of the fruit of the *v*., "
Lu 22:18 I will not drink of the fruit of the *v*.,"
Joh 15:1 I am the true *v*., and my Father is "
4 of itself, except it abide in the *v*.; "
5 I am the *v*., ye are the branches: He"
Jas 3:12 bear olive berries? either a *v*., figs? "
Re 14:18 gather the clusters of the *v*. of "
19 and gathered the *v*. of the earth, * "
vinedressers See also VINE and DRESSERS.
2Ki 25:12 the land to be *v*. and husbandmen.3755
Isa 61:5 shall be your plowmen and your *v*. "
Jer 52:16 the land for *v*. and for husbandmen."
Joe 1:11 howl, O ye *v*., for the wheat and for "
vinegar
Nu 6:3 no *v*. of wine, or *v*. of strong drink,2558
Ru 2:14 bread, and dip thy morsel in the *v*. "
Ps 69:21 my thirst they gave me *v*. to drink. "
Pr 10:26 As *v*. to the teeth, and as smoke to "
25:20 and as *v*. upon nitre, so is he that "
M't 27:34 *v*. to drink mingled with gall: *3690
48 took a spunge, and filled it with *v*., "
M'r 15:36 ran and filled a spunge full of *v*., "
Lu 23:36 coming to him, and offering him *v*.,"
Joh 19:29 there was set a vessel full of *v*.: "
29 and they filled a spunge with *v*., "
30 When Jesus...had received the *v*., "
vines
Nu 20:5 place of seed, or of figs, or of *v*., 1612
De 8:8 A land of wheat, and barley, and *v*.,"
Ps 78:47 He destroyed their *v*. with hail, "
105:33 He smote their *v*. also and their fig "
Ca 2:13 the *v*. with the tender grape give a "
15 the little foxes, that spoil the *v*.: *3754

Ca 2:15 for our *v* have tender grapes. *3754
Isa 7:23 were a thousand *v* at a thousand 1612
Jer 5:17 they shall eat up thy *v* and thy fig "
31: 5 yet plant *v* upon the mountains *3754
Ho 2:12 destroy her *v* and her fig trees, 1612
Hab 3:17 neither shall fruit be in the *v*; "

vineyard See also VINEYARDS.
Ge 9:20 husbandman, and he planted a *v*: 3754
Ex 22: 5 shall cause a field or *v* to be eaten, "
5 of the best of his own *v*, shall he "
23:11 manner thou shalt deal with thy *v*, "
Le 19:10 And thou shalt not glean thy *v*, "
10 thou gather every grape of thy *v*; "
25: 3 six years thou shalt prune thy *v*, "
4 sow thy field, nor prune thy *v*. "
De 20: 6 man is he that hath planted a *v*, "
22: 9 Thou shalt not sow thy *v* with "
9 and the fruit of thy *v*, be defiled. "
23:24 thou comest into thy neighbour's *v*, "
24:21 thou gatherest the grapes of thy *v*, "
28:30 thou shalt plant a *v*, and shalt not "
1Ki 21: 1 that Naboth the Jezreelite had a *v*, "
2 Give me thy *v*, that I may have it "
2 give thee for it a better *v* than it; "
2 Give me thy *v* for money; or else, "
6 I will give thee another *v* for it: "
6 I will not give thee my *v*. "
7 I will give thee the *v* of Naboth "
15 take possession of the *v* of Naboth "
16 up to go down to the *v* of Naboth "
18 behold, he is in the *v* of Naboth, "
Ps 80:15 the *v* which thy right hand hath *3657
Pr 24:30 and by the *v* of the man void of 3754
31:16 fruit of her hands she planteth a *v*. "
Ca 1: 6 but mine own *v* have I not kept. "
8:11 Solomon had a *v* at Baal-hamon; "
11 he let out the *v* unto keepers; "
12 My *v*, which is mine, is before me: "
Isa 1: 8 of Zion is left as a cottage in a *v*, "
3:14 ye have eaten up the *v*; the spoil "
5: 1 song of my beloved touching his *v*. "
1 hath a *v* in a very fruitful hill: "
3 I pray you, betwixt me and my *v*. "
4 have been done more to my *v*, "
5 tell you what I will do to my *v*: "
7 *v* of the Lord of hosts is the house "
10 ten acres of *v* shall yield one bath, "
27: 2 sing ye unto her, A *v* of red wine. "
Jer 12:10 Many pastors have destroyed my *v*, "
35: 7 house, nor sow seed, nor plant *v*, "
9 neither have we *v*, nor field, nor "
Mic 1: 6 the field, and as plantings of a *v*: "
M't 20: 1 to hire labourers into his *v*. *290*
2 a day, he sent them into his *v*. "
4 unto them; Go ye also into the *v*, "
7 unto them, Go ye also into the *v*; "
8 the lord of the *v* saith unto his "
21:28 said, Son, go work to day in my *v*. "
33 householder, which planted a *v*, "
39 cast him out of the *v*, and slew him. "
40 the lord therefore of the *v* cometh, "
41 and will let out his *v* unto other "
M'r 12: 1 A certain man planted a *v*, and set "
2 husbandmen of the fruit of the *v*. "
8 him, and cast him out of the *v*. "
9 shall therefore the lord of the *v* do? "
9 and will give the *v* unto others. "
Lu 13: 6 man had a fig tree planted in his *v*; "
7 said he unto the dresser of his *v*, * *289*
20: 9 A certain man planted a *v*, and let *290*
10 give him of the fruit of the *v*: "
13 Then said the lord of the *v*, What "
15 So they cast him out of the *v*, and "
15 shall the lord of the *v* do unto "
16 and shall give the *v* to others. "
1Co 9: 7 who planteth a *v*, and eateth not of "

vineyards
Nu 16:14 us inheritance of fields and *v*: 3754
20:17 the fields, or through the *v*, * "
21:22 turn into the fields, or into the *v*;* "
22:24 the Lord stood in a path of the *v*, "
De 6:11 *v* and olive trees, which thou "
28:39 Thou shalt plant *v*, and dress "
Jos 24:13 *v* and oliveyards which ye planted "
J'g 9:27 and gathered their *v*, and trode the "
11:33 cities, and unto the plain of the *v*,* "
14: 5 and came to the *v* of Timnath: "
15: 5 corn, with the *v* and olives. * "
21:20 saying, Go and lie in wait in the *v*; "
21 then come ye out of the *v*, and "
1Sa 8:14 will take your fields, and your *v*, "
15 tenth of your seed, and of your *v*, "
22: 7 give every one of you fields and *v*, "
2Ki 5:26 garments, and oliveyards, and *v*, "
18:32 and wine, a land of bread and *v*, "
19:29 year sow ye, and reap, and plant *v*, "
1Ch 27:27 the *v* was Shimei the Ramathite: "
27 over the increase of the *v* for the "
Ne 5: 3 We have mortgaged our lands, *v*, "
4 and that upon our lands and *v*. "
5 other men have our lands and *v*. "
11 even this day, their lands, their *v*, "
9:25 wells digged, *v*, and oliveyards, "
Job 24:18 he beholdeth not the way of the *v*. "
Ps 107:37 And sow the fields, and plant *v*, "
Ec 2: 4 me houses; I planted me *v*: "
Ca 1: 6 they made me the keeper of the *v*; "
14 of camphire in the *v* of En-gedi. "
7:12 Let us get up early to the *v*; let us "
Isa 16:10 in the *v* there shall be no singing, "
36:17 and wine, a land of bread and *v*. "
37:30 plant *v*, and eat the fruit thereof. "
65:21 they shall plant *v*, and eat the fruit "
Jer 32:15 and *v* shall be possessed again in "
39:10 gave them *v* and fields at the same "
Eze 28:26 shall build houses, and plant *v*: 3754
Ho 2:15 I will give her her *v* from thence, "
Am 4: 9 when your gardens and your *v* and "
5:11 ye have planted pleasant *v*, but ye "
17 And in all *v* shall be wailing: for I "
9:14 and they shall plant *v*, and drink "
Zep 1:13 they shall plant *v*, but not drink "

vintage
Le 26: 5 threshing shall reach unto the *v*, 1210
5 the *v* shall reach unto the sowing "
J'g 8: 2 better than the *v* of Abi-ezer? "
Job 24: 6 they gather the *v* of the wicked. 3754
Isa 16:10 I have made their *v* shouting to cease. "
24:13 grapes when the *v* is done. 1210
32:10 for the *v* shall fail, the gathering "
Jer 48:32 summer fruits and upon thy *v*: "
Mic 7: 1 as the grapegleanings of the *v*: "
Zec 11: 2 the forest of the *v* is come down. *1208

viol See also VIOLS.
Isa 5:12 And the harp, and the *v*, the *5035
Am 6: 5 That chant to the sound of the *v*, "

violated
Eze 22:26 Her priests have *v* my law, and *2554

violence
Ge 6:11 and the earth was filled with *v*. 2555
13 the earth is filled with *v* through "
Le 6: 2 or in a thing taken away by *v*, or*1498
2Sa 22: 3 saviour; thou savest me from *v*. 2555
Ps 11: 5 him that loveth *v* his soul hateth. "
55: 9 I have seen *v* and strife in the city. "
58: 2 ye weigh the *v* of your hands in "
72:14 their soul from deceit and *v*: "
73: 6 *v* covereth them as a garment. "
Pr 4:17 and drink the wine of *v*. "
10: 6, 11 but *v* covereth the mouth of the "
13: 2 of the transgressors shall eat *v*. "
28:17 A man that doeth *v* to the blood *6231
Isa 53: 9 because he had done no *v*, 2555
59: 6 and the act of *v* is in their hands. "
60:18 *V* shall no more be heard in thy "
Jer 6: 7 *v* and spoil is heard in her; before "
20: 8 I cried out, I cried *v* and spoil; "
22: 3 no wrong, do no *v* to the stranger, 2554
17 for oppression, and for *v*, to do it. 4835
51:35 The *v* done to me and to my flesh 2555
46 come a rumour, and *v* in the land, "
Eze 7:11 *V* is risen up into a rod of "
23 crimes, and the city is full of *v*. "
8:17 they have filled the land with *v*, "
12:19 of the *v* of all them that dwell "
18: 7 hath spoiled none by *v*, hath 1500
12 hath spoiled by *v*, hath not "
16 neither hath spoiled by *v*, but "
18 spoiled his brother by *v*, and did 1499
28:16 filled the midst of thee with *v*, 2555
45: 9 remove *v* and spoil, and execute "
Joe 3:19 *v* against the children of Judah, "
Am 3:10 who store up *v* and robbery in "
6: 3 cause the seat of *v* to come near; "
Ob 10 thy *v* against thy brother Jacob "
Jon 3: 8 from the *v* that is in their hands. "
Mic 2: 2 covet fields, and take them by *v*; *1497
6:12 rich men thereof are full of *v*, 2555
Hab 1: 2 even cry out unto thee of *v*, and "
3 for spoiling and *v* are before me: "
9 They shall come all for *v*: their "
2: 8 for the *v* of the land, of the city, "
17 the *v* of Lebanon shall cover thee, "
17 for the *v* of the land, of the city, "
Zep 1: 9 fill their masters' houses with *v* "
3: 4 they have done *v* to the law. 2554
Mal 2:16 one covereth *v* with his garment, 2555
M't 11:12 kingdom of heaven suffereth *v*, *971*
Lu 3:14 Do *v* to no man, neither accuse *1286*
Ac 5:26 and brought them without *v*: *970*
21:35 the soldiers for the *v* of the people. "
24: 7 with great *v* took him away out of* "
27:41 broken with the *v* of the waves. "
Heb 11:34 Quenched the *v* of fire, escaped **1411*
Re 18:21 *v* shall that great city Babylon be**3731*

violent
2Sa 22:49 delivered me from the *v* man. 2555
Ps 7:16 *v* dealing shall come down upon * "
18:48 hast delivered me from the *v* man. "
86:14 the assemblies of *v* men have 6184
140: 1, 4 preserve me from the *v* man; 2555
11 evil shall hunt the *v* man to "
Pr 16:29 A *v* man enticeth his neighbor, and* "
Ec 5: 8 *v* perverting of judgment and 1499
M't 11:12 and the *v* take it by force. * *973*

violently
Ge 21:25 servants had *v* taken away. 1497
Le 6: 4 restore that which he took *v* *1500
De 28:31 thine ass shall be *v* taken away 1497
Job 20:19 he hath *v* taken away an house "
24: 2 they *v* take away flocks, and feed "
Isa 22:18 *v* turn and toss thee like a ball *
La 2: 6 *v* taken away his tabernacle, 2554
M't 8:32 of swine ran *v* down a steep place*
M'r 5:13 the herd ran *v* down a steep place*
Lu 8:33 the herd ran *v* down a steep place*

viols
Isa 14:11 the grave, and the noise of thy *v*: 5035
Am 5:23 will not hear the melody of thy *v*. "

viper See also VIPER'S; VIPERS.
Isa 30: 6 the *v* and fiery flying serpent, 660
59: 5 is crushed breaketh out into a *v*. "
Ac 28: 3 there came a *v* out of the heat, *2191*

viper's
Job 20:16 asps: the *v* tongue shall slay him. 660

vipers
M't 3: 7 O generation of *v*, who hath *2191*
12:34 O generation of *v*, how can ye, "
23:33 ye generation of *v*, how can ye "
Lu 3: 7 O generation of *v*, who hath "

virgin See also VIRGIN'S; VIRGINS.
Ge 24:16 was very fair to look upon, a *v*, 1330
43 *v* cometh forth to draw water, *5959
Le 21: 3 for his sister a *v*, that is nigh 1330
14 he shall take a *v* of his own people "
De 22:19 an evil name upon a *v* of Israel: "
23 damsel that is a *v* be betrothed "
28 If a man find a damsel that is a *v*, "
32:25 both the young man and the *v*, the "
2Sa 13: 2 for she was a *v*; and Amnon "
1Ki 1: 2 for my lord the king a young *v*: "
2Ki 19:21 The *v* the daughter of Zion hath "
Isa 7:14 Behold, a *v* shall conceive, and 5959
23:12 O thou oppressed *v*, daughter of 1330
37:22 The *v*, the daughter of Zion, hath "
47: 1 O *v* daughter of Babylon, sit on "
62: 5 For as a young man marrieth a *v*, "
Jer 14:17 *v* daughter of my people is broken "
18:13 the *v* of Israel hath done a very "
31: 4 thou shalt be built, O *v* of Israel: "
13 shall the *v* rejoice in the dance, "
21 O *v* of Israel, turn again to these "
46:11 balm, O *v*, the daughter of Egypt: "
La 1:15 the Lord hath trodden the *v*, the "
2:13 thee, O *v* daughter of Zion? "
Joe 1: 8 Lament like a *v* girded with "
Am 5: 2 The *v* of Israel is fallen; she shall "
M't 1:23 Behold, a *v* shall be with child, *3933*
Lu 1:27 To a *v* espoused to a man whose "
1Co 7:28 if a *v* marry, she hath not sinned. "
34 also between a wife and a *v*. "
36 himself uncomely toward his *v*, "
37 his heart that he will keep his *v*, "
2Co 11: 2 you as a chaste *v* to Christ. "

virginity
Le 21:13 he shall take a wife in her *v*. 1331
De 22:15 forth the tokens of the damsel's *v* "
17 are the tokens of my daughter's *v*. "
20 tokens of *v* be not found for the "
J'g 11:37 bewail my *v*, I and my fellows. "
38 and bewailed her *v* upon the "
Eze 23: 3 they bruised the teats of their *v*. "
8 they bruised the breasts of her *v*, "
Lu 2:36 husband seven years from her *v*; *3932*

virgin's
Lu 1:27 and the *v* name was Mary. *3933*

virgins
Ex 22:17 according to the dowry of *v*. 1330
J'g 21:12 four hundred young *v*, that had "
2Sa 13:18 the king's daughters that were *v* "
Es 2: 2 Let there be fair young *v* sought "
3 together all the fair young *v* unto "
17 in his sight more than all the *v*; "
19 the *v* were gathered together "
Ps 45:14 the *v* her companions that follow "
Ca 1: 3 therefore do the *v* love thee. 5959
6: 8 and *v* without number. "
Isa 23: 4 up young men, nor bring up *v*. 1330
La 1: 4 priests sigh, her *v* are afflicted, "
18 my *v* and my young men are "
2:10 the *v* of Jerusalem hang down "
21 my *v* and my young men are "
Am 8:13 the fair *v* and young men faint for "
M't 25: 1 of heaven be likened unto ten *v*, *3933*
7 all those *v* arose, and trimmed "
11 Afterward came also the other *v*, "
Ac 21: 9 same man had four daughters, *v*, "
1Co 7:25 Now concerning *v* I have no "
Re 14: 4 with women; for they are *v*. "

virtue
M'r 5:30 that *v* had gone out of him, **1411*
Lu 6:19 for there went *v* out of him, and * "
8:46 perceive that *v* has gone out of me.* "
Ph'p 4: 8 there be any *v*, and if there be any *703*
2Pe 1: 3 that hath called us to glory and *v*: "
5 diligence, add to your faith *v*; "
5 and to *v* knowledge: "

virtuous
Ru 3:11 know that thou art a *v* woman. ‡2428
Pr 12: 4 A *v* woman is a crown to her ‡ "
31:10 Who can find a *v* woman? for her‡ "

virtuously
Pr 31:29 Many daughters have done *v*, but‡2428

visage
Isa 52:14 his *v* was so marred more than 4758
La 4: 8 Their *v* is blacker than a coal; 8389
Da 3:19 the form of his *v* was changed 600

visible See also INVISIBLE.
Col 1:16 that are in earth, *v* and invisible, *3707*

vision See also DIVISION; VISIONS.
Ge 15: 1 Lord came unto Abram in a *v*, 4236
Nu 12: 6 myself known unto him in a *v*, 4758
24: 4, 16 saw the *v* of the Almighty, 4236
1Sa 3: 1 those days; there was no open *v*. 2377
15 Samuel feared to shew Eli the *v*. 4758
2Sa 7:17 according to all this *v*, so did 2384
1Ch 17:15 according to all this *v*, so did 2377
2Ch 32:32 they are written in the *v* of Isaiah "
Job 20: 8 chased away as a *v* of the night. 2384
33:15 in a *v* of the night, when deep "
Ps 89:19 thou spakest in *v* to thy holy one, 2377
Pr 29:18 Where there is no *v*, the people "
Isa 1: 1 The *v* of Isaiah the son of Amoz, "
21: 2 grievous *v* is declared unto me; 2380
22: 1 The burden of the valley of *v*. 2384
5 God of hosts in the valley of *v*. "

Isa 28: 7 they err in v', they stumble in 7203
29: 7 shall be as a dream of a night v'. 2377
11 the v' of all is become unto you as 2380
Jer 14: 14 they prophesy unto you a false v' 2377
23: 16 they speak a v' of their own heart, "
La 2: 9 also find no v' from the Lord. "
Eze 7: 13 v' is touching the whole multitude "
26 shall they seek a v' of the prophet; "
8: 4 to the v' that I saw in the plain. *4758
11: 24 brought me in a v' by the Spirit of "
24 the v' that I had seen went up from "
12: 22 prolonged, and every v' faileth? 2377
23 at hand, and the effect of every v'. "
24 be no more any vain v' nor flattering "
27 The v' that he seeth is for many "
13: 7 Have ye not seen a vain v', and 4236
43: 3 appearance of the v' which I saw, 4758
3 according to the v' that I saw when "
3 were like the v' that I saw by the "
Da 2: 19 revealed unto Daniel in a night v'. 2376
7: 2 and said, I saw in my v' by night, "
8: 1 Belshazzar a v' appeared unto me, 2377
2 I saw in a v'; and it came to pass, "
2 I saw in a v', and I was by the river "
13 shall be the v' concerning the "
15 even I Daniel, had seen the v', and "
16 this man to understand the v'. 4758
17 the time of the end shall be the v'. "
26 v' of the evening and the morning "
26 wherefore shut thou up the v'; for 2377
27 I was astonished at the v', but 4758
9: 21 whom I had seen in the v' at the 2377
23 the matter, and consider the v'. "
24 and to seal up the v' and prophecy. "
10: 1 and had understanding of the v'. 4758
7 And I Daniel alone saw the v': for 4759
7 that were with me saw not the v'; "
8 left alone, and saw this great v', "
14 for yet the v' is for many days. 2377
16 by the v' my sorrows are turned 4758
11: 14 themselves to establish the v'; 2377
Ob 1 The v' of Obadiah. Thus saith the "
Mic 3: 6 you, that ye shall not have a v'; "
Na 1: 1 The book of the v' of Nahum the "
Hab 2: 2 Write the v', and make it plain "
3 the v' is yet for an appointed time, "
Zec 13: 4 be ashamed every one of his v', 2384
M't 17: 9 Tell the v' to no man, until the 3705
Lu 1: 22 he had seen a v' in the temple: 3701
24: 23 they had also seen a v' of angels, "
Ac 9: 10 and to him said the Lord in a v', 3705
12 seen in a v' a man named Ananias* "
10: 3 He saw in a v' evidently about the "
17 what this v' which he had seen "
19 While Peter thought on the v', the "
11: 5 and in a trance I saw a v', a certain "
12: 9 angel; but thought he saw a v'. "
16: 9 a v' appeared to Paul in the night; "
10 And after he had seen the v', "
18: 9 Lord to Paul in the night by a v', "
26: 19 disobedient unto the heavenly v': "
Re 9: 17 I saw the horses in the v', and 3706

visions See also DIVISIONS.
Ge 46: 2 unto Israel in the v' of the night, 4759
2Ch 9: 29 v' of Iddo the seer against 2378
26: 5 understanding in the v' of God: *7200
Job 4: 13 thoughts from the v' of the night, 2384
7: 14 and terrifiest me through v': "
Eze 1: 1 were opened, and I saw v' of God. 4759
8: 3 brought me in the v' of God to "
13: 16 which see v' of peace for her, and 2377
40: 2 In the v' of God brought he me 4759
43: 3 and the v' were like the vision "
Da 1: 17 understanding in all v' and 2377
2: 28 v' of thy head upon thy bed, are 2376
4: 5 and the v' of my head trouble me. "
9 tell me the v' of my dream that I "
10 Thus were the v' of mine head in "
13 I saw in the v' of my head upon my "
7: 1 and v' of his head upon his bed: "
7 After this I saw in the night v', "
13 I saw in the night v', and, behold, "
15 and the v' of my head troubled me. "
Ho 12: 10 I have multiplied v', and used 2377
Joe 2: 28 your young men shall see v': 2384
Ac 2: 17 and your young men shall see v', 3706
2Co 12: 1 I will come to v' and revelations 3701

visit See also VISITED; VISITEST; VISITETH; VISITING.
Ge 50: 24 God will surely v' you, and bring 6485
25 God will surely v' you, and ye shall "
Ex 13: 19 God will surely v' you; and ye shall "
32: 34 the day when I v' I will v' their sin "
Le 18: 25 I do v' the iniquity thereof upon it, "
Job 5: 24 and thou shalt v' thy habitation, "
7: 18 thou shouldest v' him every "
Ps 59: 5 Israel, awake to v' all the heathen: "
80: 14 heaven, and behold, and v' this "
89: 32 Then will I v' their transgression "
106: 4 people: O v' me with thy salvation; "
Isa 23: 17 that the Lord will v' Tyre, and she "
Jer 3: 16 it; neither shall they v' it; "
5: 9, 29 Shall I not v' for these things? "
6: 15 time that I v' them they shall be "
9: 9 Shall I not v' them for these things? "
14: 10 their iniquity, and v' their sins. "
15: 15 and v' me, and revenge me of my "
23: 2 v' upon you the evil of your doings, "
27: 22 they be until the day that I v' them, "
29: 10 at Babylon I will v' you, "
32: 5 and there shall he be until I v' him, "
49: 8 him, the time that I will v' him. "
50: 31 is come, the time that I will v' thee. "
La 4: 22 he will v' thine iniquity, O daughter "
Ho 2: 13 will v' upon her the days of Baalim, "
8: 13 their iniquity, and v' their sins: 6485
9: 9 their iniquity, he will v' their sins. "
Am 3: 14 shall v' the transgressions of Israel "
14 I will also v' the altars of Beth-el: "
Zep 2: 7 the Lord their God shall v' them, "
Zec 11: 16 shall not v' those that be cut off, "
Ac 7: 23 to v' his brethren the children of 1980
15: 14 God at the first did v' the Gentiles, "
36 Let us go again and v' our brethren "
Jas 1: 27 To v' the fatherless and widows in "

visitation
Nu 16: 29 visited after the v' of all men; 6486
Job 10: 12 thy v' hath preserved my spirit. "
Isa 10: 3 And what will ye do in the day of v', "
Jer 8: 12 the time of their v' they shall be "
10: 15 time of their v' they shall perish. "
11: 23 Anathoth, even the year of their v'. "
23: 12 them, even the year of their v', "
46: 21 upon them, and the time of their v'. "
48: 44 upon Moab, the year of their v', "
50: 27 day is come, the time of their v'. "
51: 18 time of their v' they shall perish. "
Ho 9: 7 The days of v' are come, the days "
Mic 7: 4 of thy watchmen and thy v' cometh; "
Lu 19: 44 knewest not the time of thy v'. 1984
1Pe 2: 12 behold, glorify God in the day of v'. "

visited
Ge 21: 1 the Lord v' Sarah as he had said, 6485
Ex 3: 16 I have surely v' you, and seen that "
4: 31 Lord had v' the children of Israel, "
Nu 16: 29 if they be v' after the visitation of "
J'g 15: 1 that Samson v' his wife with a kid; "
Ru 1: 6 the Lord had v' his people in giving "
1Sa 2: 21 And the Lord v' Hannah, so that she "
Job 35: 15 it is not so, he hath v' in his anger; "
Ps 17: 3 thou hast v' me in the night; thou "
Pr 19: 23 he shall not be v' with evil. "
Isa 24: 22 after many days shall they be v'. "
26: 14 hast thou v' and destroyed them, "
16 Lord, in trouble have they v' thee, "
29: 6 Thou shalt be v' of the Lord of "
Jer 6: 6 Jerusalem: this is the city to be v'; "
23: 2 them away, and have not v' them: "
Eze 38: 8 After many days thou shalt be v': "
Zec 10: 3 the Lord of hosts hath v' his flock "
M't 25: 36 I was sick, and ye v' me: I was in 1980
43 and in prison, and ye v' me not. "
Lu 1: 68 hath v' and redeemed his people, "
78 dayspring from on high hath v' us.* "
7: 16 and, That God hath v' his people. "

visitest
Ps 8: 4 the son of man, that thou v' him? 6485
65: 9 Thou v' the earth, and waterest it: "
Heb 2: 6 the son of man, that thou v' him? 1980

visiteth
Job 31: 14 when he v', what shall I answer 6485

visiting
Ex 20: 5 v' the iniquity of the fathers upon 6485
34: 7 v' the iniquity of the fathers upon "
Nu 14: 18 v' the iniquity of the fathers upon "
De 5: 9 v' the iniquity of the fathers upon "

vocation See also CONVOCATION.
Eph 4: 1 walk worthy of the v' wherewith *2821

voice See also VOICES.
Ge 3: 8 they heard the v' of the Lord God 6963
10 I heard thy v' in the garden, and "
17 hearkened unto the v' of thy wife, "
4: 10 v' of thy brother's blood crieth unto "
23 wives, Adah and Zillah, hear my v'; "
16: 2 hearkened to the v' of Sarai. "
21: 12 unto thee, hearken unto her v'; "
16 over against him, and lift up her v', "
17 And God heard the v' of the lad; "
17 God hath heard the v' of the lad "
22: 18 because thou hast obeyed my v'. "
26: 5 that Abraham obeyed my v', and "
27: 8 obey my v' according to that which "
13 only obey my v', and go fetch me "
22 The v' is Jacob's v', but the hands "
38 And Esau lifted up his v', and wept. "
43 Now therefore, my son, obey my v'; "
29: 11 and lifted up his v', and wept. "
30: 6 me, and hath also heard my v', "
39: 14 with me, and I cried with a loud v': "
15 he heard that I lifted up my v' and "
18 as I lifted up my v' and cried, that "
Ex 3: 18 they shall hearken to thy v': and "
4: 1 me, nor hearken unto my v': "
8 hearken to the v' of the first sign, "
8 will believe the v' of the latter sign. "
9 signs, neither hearken unto thy v', "
5: 2 should obey his v' to let Israel go? "
15: 26 hearken to the v' of the Lord thy "
18: 19 Hearken now unto my v', I will "
24 to the v' of his father in law, "
19: 5 if ye will obey my v' indeed, and "
16 v' of the trumpet exceeding loud; "
19 the v' of the trumpet sounded long, "
19 and God answered him by a v'. "
23: 21 Beware of him, and obey his v', "
22 if thou shalt indeed obey his v', "
24: 3 all the people answered with one v', "
32: 18 v' of them that shout for mastery, "
18 the v' of them that cry for being "
Le 5: 1 hear the v' of swearing, and is a "
Nu 7: 89 he heard the v' of one speaking "
14: 1 the congregation lifted up their v', "
22 and have not hearkened to my v'; "
20: 16 he heard our v', and sent an angel, "
21: 3 Lord hearkened to the v' of Israel, "
De 1: 34 Lord heard the v' of your words, "
45 Lord would not hearken to your v', "
4: 12 ye heard the v' of the words, but "
12 no similitude; only ye heard a v'. "
De 4: 30 and shalt be obedient unto his v'; 6963
33 v' of God speaking out of the midst "
36 he made thee to hear his v', that "
5: 22 the thick darkness, with a great v': "
23 ye heard the v' out of the midst of "
24 we have heard his v' out of the "
25 if we hear the v' of the Lord our "
26 hath heard the v' of the living God "
28 Lord heard the v' of your words, "
28 I have heard the v' of the words of "
8: 20 obedient unto the v' of the Lord "
9: 23 him not, nor hearkened to his v'. "
13: 4 commandments, and obey his v', "
18 shalt hearken to the v' of the Lord "
15: 5 hearken to the v' of the Lord thy "
18: 16 not hear again the v' of the Lord "
21: 18 will not obey the v' of his father, "
18 or the v' of his mother, and that, "
20 rebellious, he will not obey our v'; "
26: 7 Lord heard our v', and looked on "
14 hearkened to the v' of the Lord my "
17 and to hearken unto his v': "
27: 10 obey the v' of the Lord thy God, "
14 all the men of Israel with a loud v', "
28: 1 hearken...unto the v' of the Lord "
2 hearken unto the v' of the Lord thy "
15 not hearken unto the v' of the Lord "
45 not unto the v' of the Lord thy "
62 not obey the v' of the Lord thy God. "
30: 2 obey his v' according to all that I "
8 return and obey the v' of the Lord, "
10 hearken unto the v' of the Lord thy "
20 that thou mayest obey his v', and "
33: 7 said, Hear, Lord, the v' of Judah, "
Jos 5: 6 they obeyed not the v' of the Lord: "
6: 10 nor make any noise with your v', "
10: 14 hearkened unto the v' of a man: "
22: 2 have obeyed my v' in all that I "
24: 24 we serve, and his v' will we obey. "
J'g 2: 2 but ye have not obeyed my v': why "
4 that the people lifted up their v', "
20 have not hearkened unto my v'; "
6: 10 but ye have not obeyed my v'. "
9: 7 lifted up his v', and cried, and said "
13: 9 God hearkened to the v' of Manoah; "
18: 3 knew the v' of the young man the "
25 Let not thy v' be heard among us, "
20: 13 hearken to the v' of their brethren "
Ru 1: 9 they lifted up their v', and wept. "
14 they lifted up their v', and wept "
1Sa 1: 13 moved, but her v' was not heard: "
2: 25 not unto the v' of their father, "
8: 7 Hearken unto the v' of the people in "
9 therefore hearken unto their v': "
19 refused to obey the v' of Samuel; "
22 Hearken unto their v', and make "
12: 1 have hearkened unto your v' in all "
14 serve him, and obey his v', and not "
15 ye will not obey the v' of the Lord, "
15: 1 the v' of the words of the Lord. "
19 thou not obey the v' of the Lord, "
20 I have obeyed the v' of the Lord, "
22 as in obeying the v' of the Lord? "
24 the people, and obeyed their v'. "
19: 6 hearkened unto the v' of Jonathan: "
24: 16 said, Is this thy v', my son David? "
16 And Saul lifted up his v', and wept. "
25: 35 I have hearkened to thy v', and "
26: 17 And Saul knew David's v', and said, "
17 Is this thy v', my son David? And "
17 David said, It is my v', my lord, "
28: 12 Samuel, she cried with a loud v': "
18 obeyedst not the v' of the Lord, "
21 thine handmaid hath obeyed thy v', "
22 unto the v' of thine handmaid, "
23 and he hearkened unto their v'. "
30: 4 him lifted up their v' and wept, "
2Sa 3: 32 the king lifted up his v', and wept "
12: 18 he would not hearken unto our v': "
13: 14 he would not hearken unto her v': "
36 and lifted up their v' and wept: "
15: 23 all the country wept with a loud v', "
19: 4 the king cried with a loud v', O my "
35 any more the v' of singing men "
22: 7 he did hear my v' out of his temple, "
14 and the most High uttered his v'. "
1Ki 8: 55 congregation of Israel with a loud v', "
17: 22 the Lord heard the v' of Elijah; and "
18: 26 But there was no v', nor any that "
29 that there was neither v', nor any "
19: 12 and after the fire a still small v'. "
13 there came a v' unto him, and said, "
20: 25 he hearkened unto their v', and did "
36 hast not obeyed the v' of the Lord, "
2Ki 4: 31 there was neither v', nor hearing. "
7: 10 no man there, neither v' of man, "
10: 6 and if ye will hearken unto my v', "
18: 12 they obeyed not the v' of the Lord "
28 a loud v' in the Jews' language, "
19: 22 whom hast thou exalted thy v', "
1Ch 15: 16 by lifting up the v' with joy. "
2Ch 5: 13 lifted up their v' with the trumpets "
15: 14 sware unto the Lord with a loud v', "
20: 19 of Israel with a loud v' on high. "
30: 27 and their v' was heard, and their "
32: 18 with a loud v' in the Jews' speech "
Ezr 3: 12 their eyes, wept with a loud v'; "
10: 12 answered and said with a loud v', "
Ne 9: 4 cried with a loud v' unto the Lord "
Job 2: 12 they lifted up their v', and wept; "
3: 7 solitary, let no joyful v' come therein. "
18 hear not the v' of the oppressor. 6963
4: 10 the lion, and the v' of the fierce lion, "
16 there was silence, and I heard a v', "
9: 16 that he had hearkened unto my v'. "
30: 31 organ into the v' of them that weep. "

Job 33: 8 I have heard the v' of thy words, 6963
34:16 hearken to the v' of my words. "
37: 2 Hear attentively the noise of his v', "
4 After it a v' roareth: he thundereth "
4 with the v' of his excellency; "
4 not stay them when his v' is heard. "
5 marvellously with his v'; great "
38:34 thou lift up thy v' to the clouds, "
40: 9 thou thunder with a v' like him? "
Ps 3: 4 I cried unto the Lord with my v', "
5: 2 Hearken unto the v' of my cry, my "
3 My v' shalt thou hear in the "
6: 8 hath heard the v' of my weeping. "
18: 6 he heard my v' out of his temple, "
13 and the Highest gave his v'; "
19: 3 where their v' is not heard. "
26: 7 with the v' of thanksgiving, "
27: 7 O Lord, when I cry with my v': "
28: 2 Hear the v' of my supplications, "
6 heard the v' of my supplications. "
29: 3 v' of the Lord is upon the waters: "
4 The v' of the Lord is powerful; the "
4 the v' of the Lord is full of majesty. "
5 v' of the Lord breaketh the cedars; "
7 v' of the Lord divideth the flames "
8 The v' of the Lord shaketh the "
9 v' of the Lord maketh the hinds to "
31:22 heardest the v' of my supplications "
42: 4 with the v' of joy and praise, with a "
44:16 For the v' of him that reproacheth "
46: 6 he uttered his v', the earth melted. "
47: 1 unto God with the v' of triumph. "
55: 3 Because of the v' of the enemy, "
17 cry aloud: and he shall hear my v'. "
58: 5 not hearken to the v' of charmers, "
64: 1 Hear my v', O God, in my prayer: "
66: 8 the v' of his praise to be heard: "
19 attended to the v' of my prayer. "
68:33 lo, he doth send out his v', "
33 and that a mighty v'. "
74:23 Forget not the v' of thine enemies: "
77: 1 I cried unto God with my v', even "
1 unto God with my v'; and he gave "
18 The v' of thy thunder was in the "
81:11 people would not hearken to my v'; "
86: 6 attend to the v' of my supplications. "
93: 3 the floods have lifted up their v'; "
95: 7 hand. To day if ye will hear his v', "
98: 5 the harp, and the v' of a psalm. "
102: 5 By reason of the v' of my groaning "
103:20 hearkening unto the v' of his word. "
104: 7 at the v' of thy thunder they hasted "
106:25 not unto the v' of the Lord. "
116: 1 Lord, because he hath heard my v' "
118:15 The v' of rejoicing and salvation is "
119:149 Hear my v' according unto thy "
130: 2 Lord, hear my v': let thine ears "
2 thine ears be attentive to the v' of "
141: 1 give ear unto my v', when I cry "
142: 1 I cried unto the Lord with my v'; "
1 with my v' unto the Lord did I "
Pr 1:20 she uttereth her v' in the streets: "
2: 3 liftest up thy v' for understanding; "
5:13 not obeyed the v' of my teachers, "
8: 1 understanding put forth her v'? "
4 and my v' is to the sons of man. "
27:14 blesseth his friend with a loud v', "
Ec 5: 3 a fool's v' is known by multitude of "
6 should God be angry at thy v', "
10:20 a bird of the air shall carry the v', "
12: 4 he shall rise up at the v' of the bird, "
Ca 2: 8 The v' of my beloved! behold, he "
12 the v' of the turtle is heard in our "
14 me hear thy v'; for sweet is thy v', "
5: 2 v' of my beloved that knocketh, "
8:13 the companions hearken to thy v': "
Isa 6: 4 moved at the v' of him that cried, "
8 Also I heard the v' of the Lord, "
10:30 Lift up thy v', O daughter of "
13: 2 exalt the v' unto them, shake the "
15: 4 their v' shall be heard even unto "
24:14 They shall lift up their v', they shall "
28:23 Give ye ear, and hear my v'; "
29: 4 thy v' shall be, as of one that hath a "
30:19 unto thee at the v' of thy cry; "
30 cause his glorious v' to be heard, "
31 through the v' of the Lord shall the "
31: 4 he will not be afraid of their v', nor "
32: 9 hear my v', ye careless daughters; "
36:13 cried with a loud v' in the Jews' "
37:23 whom hast thou exalted thy v', "
40: 3 The v' of him that crieth in the "
6 The v' said, Cry. And he said, "
9 tidings, lift up thy v' with strength; "
42: 2 nor cause his v' to be heard in the "
11 and the cities thereof lift up their v', "
48:20 with a v' of singing declare ye, tell 6963
50:10 that obeyeth the v' of his servant, "
51: 3 thanksgiving, and the v' of melody. "
52: 8 Thy watchmen shall lift up the v'; "
8 with the v' together shall they sing: "
58: 1 not, lift up thy v' like a trumpet, "
4 make your v' to be heard on high. "
65:19 the v' of weeping shall be no more "
19 heard in her, nor the v' of crying. "
66: 6 A v' of noise from the city, "
6 a v' from the temple, "
6 a v' of the Lord that rendereth "
Jer 3:13 and ye have not obeyed my v', saith "
21 A v' was heard upon the high "
25 have not obeyed the v' of the Lord "
4:15 For a v' declareth from Dan, and "
16 give out their v' against the cities "
31 heard a v' as of a woman in travail, "
31 the v' of the daughter of Zion, that "
6:23 their v' roareth like the sea; and "

Jer 7:23 Obey my v', and I will be your God, 6963
28 that obeyeth not the v' of the Lord "
34 the v' of mirth,...the v' of gladness, "
34 the v' of the bridegroom, and "
34 the v' of the bride: for the land "
8:19 the v' of the cry of the daughter of "
9:10 can men hear the v' of the cattle; "
13 and have not obeyed my v', neither "
19 a v' of wailing is heard out of Zion, "
10:13 When he uttereth his v', there is a "
11: 4 iron furnace, saying, Obey my v', "
7 and protesting, saying, Obey my v'. "
16: 9 the v' of mirth,...the v' of gladness, "
9 the v' of the bridegroom, and "
9 and the v' of the bride. "
18:10 that it obey not my v', then I will "
19 hearken to the v' of them that "
22:20 and lift up thy v' in Bashan, and cry "
21 that thou obeyedst not my v'. "
25:10 the v' of mirth,...the v' of gladness, "
10 the v' of the bridegroom, and "
10 and the v' of the bride, the sound "
30 high, and utter his v' from his holy "
36 A v' of the cry of the shepherds, and "
26:13 obey the v' of the Lord your God; "
30: 5 We have heard a v' of trembling, of "
19 the v' of them that make merry: "
31:15 A v' was heard in Ramah, "
16 Refrain thy v' from weeping, and "
32:23 but they obeyed not thy v', neither "
33:11 The v' of joy, and the v' of gladness, "
11 the v' of the bridegroom, and "
11 and the v' of the bride, the "
11 v' of them that shall say, Praise the "
35: 8 we obeyed the v' of Jonadab the "
38:20 I beseech thee, the v' of the Lord, "
40: 3 Lord, and have not obeyed his v', "
42: 6 we will obey the v' of the Lord our "
6 when we obey the v' of the Lord our "
13 neither obey the v' of the Lord your "
21 have not obeyed the v' of the Lord "
43: 4 obeyed not the v' of the Lord, to "
7 they obeyed not the v' of the Lord: "
44:23 have not obeyed the v' of the Lord, "
46:22 v' thereof shall go like a serpent; * "
48: 3 A v' of crying shall be from * "
34 Jahaz, have they uttered their v', "
50:28 v' of them that flee and escape out "
42 their v' shall roar like the sea, and "
51:16 When he uttereth his v', there is a "
55 destroyed out of her the great v'; "
55 a noise of their v' is uttered: "
La 3:56 Thou hast heard my v': hide not "
Eze 1:24 waters, as the v' of the Almighty, "
24 the v' of speech, as the noise of * "
25 a v' from the firmament that was "
28 and I heard a v' of one that spake. "
3:12 behind me a v' of a great rushing, "
8:18 they cry in mine ears with a loud v', "
9: 1 also in mine ears with a loud v', "
10: 5 as the v' of the Almighty God when "
11:13 cried with a loud v', and said, Ah "
19: 9 that his v' should no more be heard "
21:22 to lift up the v' with shouting, to "
23:42 a v' of a multitude being at ease "
27:30 cause their v' to be heard against "
33:32 song of one that hath a pleasant v', "
43: 2 and his v' was like a noise of many "
Da 4:31 there fell a v' from heaven, saying, 7032
6:20 he cried with a lamentable v' unto "
7:11 the v' of the great words which the "
8:16 I heard a man's v' between the 6963
9:10 have we obeyed the v' of the Lord "
11 that they might not obey thy v'; "
14 he doeth: for we obeyed not his v'. "
10: 6 and the v' of his words like the "
6 like the v' of a multitude. "
9 Yet heard I the v' of his words: "
9 when I heard the v' of his words, "
Joe 2:11 shall utter his v' before his army: "
3:16 and utter his v' from Jerusalem; "
Am 1: 2 and utter his v' from Jerusalem; "
Jon 2: 2 cried I, and thou heardest my v'. "
9 thee with the v' of thanksgiving; "
Mic 6: 1 and let the hills hear thy v'. "
9 The Lord's v' crieth unto the city, "
Na 2: 7 lead her as with the v' of doves, "
13 v' of thy messengers shall no more "
Hab 3:10 the deep uttered his v', and lifted "
16 my lips quivered at the v': "
Zep 1:14 even the v' of the day of the Lord: "
2:14 their v' shall sing in the windows; "
3: 2 She obeyed not the v'; she received "
Hag 1:12 obeyed the v' of the Lord their God, "
Zec 6:15 diligently obey the v' of the Lord "
11: 3 v' of the howling of the shepherds; "
3 a v' of the roaring of young lions; "
M't 2:18 In Rama was there a v' heard, 5456
3: 3 v' of one crying in the wilderness, "
17 And lo a v' from heaven, saying, "
12:19 any man hear his v' in the streets. "
17: 5 and behold a v' out of the cloud, "
27:46 Jesus cried with a loud v', saying, "
50 he had cried again with a loud v', "
M'r 1: 3 v' of one crying in the wilderness, "
11 And there came a v' from heaven, "
26 cried with a loud v', he came out of "
5: 7 cried with a loud v', and said, What "
9: 7 a v' came out of the cloud, saying, "
15:34 hour Jesus cried with a loud v', "
37 Jesus cried with a loud v', and gave "
Lu 1:42 And she spake out with a loud v', "
44 v' of thy salutation sounded in mine "
3: 4 v' of one crying in the wilderness, "
22 a v' came from heaven, which said, "
4:33 devil, and cried out with a loud v', "

Lu 8:28 with a loud v' said, What have I to 5456
9:35 there came a v' out of the cloud, "
36 when the v' was past, Jesus was "
11:27 certain woman...lifted up her v', "
17:15 and with a loud v' glorified God, "
19:37 praise God with a loud v' for all the "
23:46 when Jesus had cried with a loud v', "
Joh 1:23 v' of one crying in the wilderness, "
3:29 because of the bridegroom's v': "
5:25 shall hear the v' of the Son of God: "
28 are in the graves shall hear his v', "
37 Ye have neither heard his v' at any "
10: 3 openeth; and the sheep hear his v': "
4 follow him: for they know his v'. "
5 they know not the v' of strangers. "
16 and they shall hear my v'; and "
27 My sheep hear my v', and I know "
11:43 he cried with a loud v', Lazarus, "
12:28 Then came there a v' from heaven, "
30 This v' came not because of me, "
18:37 that is of the truth heareth my v'. "
Ac 2:14 lifted up his v', and said unto them, "
4:24 they lifted up their v' to God with "
7:31 the v' of the Lord came unto him, "
57 Then they cried out with a loud v', "
60 cried with a loud v', Lord, lay not "
8: 7 spirits, crying with loud v', came "
9: 4 and heard a v' saying unto him, "
7 hearing a v', but seeing no man. "
10:13 there came a v' to him, Rise, Peter; "
15 the v' spake unto him again the "
11: 7 And I heard a v' saying unto me, "
9 But the v' answered me again from "
12:14 And when she knew Peter's v', she "
22 is the v' of a god, and not of a man. "
14:10 Said with a loud v', Stand upright "
16:28 Paul cried with a loud v', saying, "
19:34 one v' about the space of two hours "
22: 7 heard a v' saying unto me, Saul, "
9 heard not the v' of him that spake "
14 shouldest hear the v' of his mouth. "
24:21 Except it be for this one v', that I "
26:10 death, I gave my v' against them.*5586
14 I heard a v' speaking unto me, and 5456
24 Festus said with a loud v', Paul, "
1Co 14:11 if I know not the meaning of the v', "
19 that by my v' I might teach others*
Ga 4:20 you now, and to change my v'; 5456
1Th 4:16 with the v' of the archangel, and "
Heb 3: 7 saith, To day if ye will hear his v', "
15 said, To day if ye will hear his v', "
4: 7 said, To day if ye will hear his v', "
12:19 of a trumpet, and the v' of words; "
19 which v' they that heard intreated "
26 Whose v' then shook the earth: 5456
2Pe 1:17 came such a v' to him from the "
18 this v' which came from heaven we "
2:16 dumb ass speaking with man's v' "
Re 1:10 and heard behind me a great v', as "
12 I turned to see the v' that spake "
15 his v' as the sound of many waters. "
3:20 if any man hear my v', and open "
4: 1 the first v' which I heard was as it "
5: 2 angel proclaiming with a loud v', "
11 I heard the v' of many angels round "
12 Saying with a loud v', Worthy is the "
6: 6 I heard a v' in the midst of the four "
7 I heard the v' of the fourth beast "
10 And they cried with a loud v', "
7: 2 he cried with a loud v' to the four "
10 And cried with a loud v', saying, "
8:13 saying with a loud v', Woe, woe, "
9:13 I heard a v' from the four horns of "
10: 3 cried with a loud v', as when a lion "
4 I heard a v' from heaven saying "
7 days of the v' of the seventh angel, "
8 v' which I heard from heaven spake "
11:12 they heard a great v' from heaven "
12:10 I heard a loud v' saying in heaven, "
14: 2 And I heard a v' from heaven, as "
2 as the v' of many waters, and "
2 and as the v' of a great thunder: "
2 heard the v' of harpers harping "
7 Saying with a loud v', Fear God, "
9 them, saying with a loud v', "
13 I heard a v' from heaven saying "
15 loud v' to him that sat on the cloud, "
16: 1 a great v' out of the temple saying "
17 a great v' out of the temple of "
18: 2 he cried mightily with a strong v', "
4 I heard another v' from heaven, "
22 the v' of harpers, and musicians, "
23 the v' of the bridegroom and of the "
19: 1 I heard a great v' of much people "
5 And a v' came out of the throne, "
6 it were the v' of a great multitude, "
6 and as the v' of many waters, "
6 as the v' of mighty thunderings, "
17 and he cried with a loud v', saying "
21: 3 a great v' out of heaven saying, "

voices

J'g 21: 2 lifted up their v', and wept sore; 6963
1Sa 11: 4 people lifted up their v', and wept. "
Lu 17:13 And they lifted up their v', and 5456
23:23 And they were instant with loud v', "
23 v' of them and of the chief priests "
Ac 13:27 nor yet the v' of the prophets which "
14:11 they lifted up their v', saying in the "
22:22 and then lifted up their v', and said,*
1Co 14:10 so many kinds of v' in the world, "
Re 4: 5 lightnings and thunderings and v': "
8: 5 and there were v', and thunderings, "
13 of the other v' of the trumpet of "
10: 3 seven thunders uttered their v'. "
4 seven thunders had uttered their v', "
11:15 and there were great v' in heaven, "

Re 11:19 lightnings, and v', and thunderings, *5456*
16:18 there were v', and thunders, and "

void See also AVOID.
Ge 1: 2 the earth was without form, and v';922
Nu 30:12 made them v' on the day he heard 6565
12 her husband hath made them v'; "
13 or her husband may make it v'. "
15 make them v' after that he hath "
De 32:28 For they are a nation v' of counsel, 6
1Ki 22:10 in a v' place in the entrance of the*1637
2Ch 18: 9 sat in a v' place at the entering in* "
Ps 89:39 made v'...covenant of thy servant.*5010
119:126 for they have made v' thy law. 6565
Pr 7: 7 a young man v' of understanding, 2638
10:13 of him that is v' of understanding. "
11:12 He that is v' of wisdom despiseth "
12:11 vain persons is v' of understanding. "
17:18 A man v' of understanding striketh "
24:30 of the man v' of understanding; "
Isa 55:11 it shall not return unto me v', but 7387
Jer 4:23 and, lo, it was without form, and v';922
19: 7 make v' the counsel of Judah and 1238
Na 2:10 She is empty, and v', and waste: 4003
Ac 24:16 conscience v' of offence toward God, *677*
Ro 3:31 make v' the law through faith? **2673*
4:14 faith is made v', and the promise *2758*
1Co 9:15 man should make my glorying v'. "

volume
Ps 40: 7 in the v' of the book it is written *4039
Heb 10: 7 (in the v' of the book it is written **2777*

voluntarily
Eze 46:12 peace offerings v' unto the Lord, *5071

voluntary
Le 1: 3 offer it of his own v' will at the *7522
7:16 offering be a vow, or a v' offering, *5071
Eze 46:12 shalt prepare a v' burnt offering * "
Col 2:18 you of your reward in a v' humility*2309*

vomit See also VOMITED; VOMITETH.
Job 20:15 and he shall v' them up again: 6958
Pr 23: 8 thou hast eaten shalt thou v' up, "
25:16 thou be filled therewith, and v' it. "
26:11 a dog returneth to his v', so a fool 6892
Isa 19:14 drunken man staggereth in his v'. "
28: 8 For all tables are full of v' and "
Jer 48:26 Moab also shall wallow in his v', and "
2Pe 2:22 dog is turned to his own v' again; *1829*

vomited
Jon 2:10 it v' out Jonah upon the dry land. 6958

vomiteth
Le 18:25 land itself v' out her inhabitants. 6958

Vophsi (*vof'-si*)
Nu 13:14 of Naphtali, Nahbi the son of V'. 2058

vouch See AVOUCH.

vow See also VOWED; VOWEST; VOWETH; VOWS.
Ge 28:20 Jacob vowed a v', saying, If God 5088
31:13 where thou vowedst a v' unto me: "
Le 7:16 the sacrifice of his offering be a v', "
22:21 unto the Lord to accomplish his v', "
23 for a v' it shall not be accepted. "
27: 2 a man shall make a singular v', the "
Nu 6: 2 shall separate themselves to v' a 5087
2 v' of a Nazarite, to separate 5088
5 the days of the v' of his separation "
21 according to the v' which he vowed, "
15: 3, 8 a sacrifice in performing a v', or "
21: 2 Israel vowed a v' unto the Lord, "
30: 2 If a man v'...unto the Lord, *5087
2 v' unto the Lord, or swear 5088
3 a woman also v'...unto the Lord, *5087
3 v' unto the Lord, and bind 5088
4 her father hear her v', and her bond "
8 shall make her v' which she vowed, *"
9 But every v' of a widow, and of her "
13 Every v', and every binding oath to "
De 12:11 vows which ye v' unto the Lord: 5087
23:18 of the Lord thy God for any v': 5088
21 thou shalt v'... unto the Lord 5087
21 v' unto the Lord thy God, 5088
22 But if thou shalt forbear to v', it 5087
J'g 11:30 Jephthah vowed a v' unto the Lord, "
39 according to his v' which he had "
1Sa 1:11 And she vowed a v', and said, "
21 Lord the yearly sacrifice, and his v', "
2Sa 15: 7 pray thee, let me go and pay my v', "
8 servant vowed a v' while I abode "
Ps 65: 1 unto thee shall the v' be performed. "
76:11 V', and pay unto the Lord your 5087
Ec 5: 4 When thou vowest a v' unto God, 5088
5 is it that thou shouldest not v', 5087
5 that thou shouldest v' and not pay. "
Isa 19:21 yea, they shall v'...unto the Lord, "
21 a v' unto the Lord, and perform it. 5088
Ac 18:18 head in Cenchrea: for he had a v'. *2171*
21:23 four men which have a v' on them; "

vowed See also VOWEDST.
Ge 28:20 And Jacob v' a vow, saying, If God 5087
Le 27: 8 according to his ability that v' shall "
Nu 6:21 law of the Nazarite who hath v', and* "
21 according to the vow which he v',* "
21: 2 And Israel v' a vow unto the Lord, "
30: 6 at all an husband, when she v', *5088
8 shall make her vow which she v', * "
10 if she v' in her husband's house, 5087
De 23:23 as thou hast v' unto the Lord thy "
J'g 11:30 Jephthah v' a vow unto the Lord, "
39 to his vow which he had v': "
1Sa 1:11 And she v' a vow, and said, O Lord, "
2Sa 15: 7 I have v' unto the Lord, in Hebron. 5087
8 thy servant v' a vow while I abode "
Ps 132: 2 v' unto the mighty God of Jacob; "
Ec 5: 4 pay that which thou hast v'. * "
Jer 44:25 perform our vows that we have v', "
Jon 2: 9 I will pay that that I have v'. "

vowedst
Ge 31:13 and where thou v' a vow unto me: 5087

vowest
De 12:17 nor any of thy vows which thou v', 5087
Ec 5: 4 When thou v' a vow unto God, defer "

voweth
Mal 1:14 and v', and sacrificeth unto the 5087

vows
Le 22:18 offer his oblation for all his v', 5088
23:38 beside all your v', and beside all "
Nu 29:39 beside your v', and your freewill "
30: 4 then all her v' shall stand, and "
5 not any of her v', or of her bonds "
7 then her v' shall stand, and her "
11 then all her v' shall stand, and "
12 out of her lips concerning her v', "
14 then he establisheth all her v', or "
De 12: 6 your v', and your freewill offerings, "
11 all your choice v' which ye vow "
17 nor any of thy v' which thou "
26 and thy v', thou shalt take, and go "
Job 22:27 thee, and thou shalt pay thy v'. "
Ps 22:25 I will pay my v' before them that "
50:14 and pay thy v' unto the most High: "
56:12 Thy v' are upon me, O God: I will "
61: 5 For thou, O God, hast heard my v': "
8 that I may daily perform my v'. "
66:13 offerings: I will pay thee my v', "
116:14, 18 I will pay my v' unto the Lord "
Pr 7:14 me; this day have I payed my v'. "
20:25 holy, and after v' to make enquiry. "
31: 2 womb? and what, the son of my v'? "
Jer 44:25 will surely perform our v' that we "
25 ye will surely accomplish your v', "
25 and surely perform your v'. "
Jon 1:16 sacrifice unto the Lord, and made v'. "
Na 1:15 thy solemn feasts, perform thy v': "

voyage
Ac 27:10 I perceive that this v' will be with 4144

vulture See also VULTURE'S; VULTURES.
Le 11:14 the v', and the kite after his kind;*1676
De 14:13 the kite, and the v' after his kind.*1772

vulture's
Job 28: 7 which the v' eye hath not seen: * 344

vultures
Isa 34:15 the v' also be gathered, every *1772

W.

wafer See also WAFERS.
Ex 29:23 and one w' out of the basket of 7550
Le 8:26 a cake of oiled bread, and one w', "
Nu 6:19 the basket, and one unleavened w', "

wafers
Ex 16:31 of it was like w' made with honey. 6838
29: 2 w' unleavened anointed with oil: 7550
Le 2: 4 unleavened w' anointed with oil. "
7:12 unleavened w' anointed with oil, "
Nu 6:15 w' of unleavened bread anointed "

wag See also WAGGING.
Jer 18:16 be astonished, and w' his head. *5110
La 2:15 w' their head at the daughter of 5128
Zep 2:15 her shall hiss, and w' his hand. "

wages
Ge 29:15 tell me, what shall thy w' be? 4909
30:28 Appoint me thy w', and I will give 7939
31: 7 and changed my w' ten times; 4909
8 The speckled shall be thy w': 7939
41 hast changed my w' ten times. 4909
Ex 2: 9 me, and I will give thee thy w'. 7939
Le 19:13 w' of him that is hired shall not 6468
Jer 22:13 neighbour's service without w', 2600
Eze 29:18 yet had he no w', nor his army, for 7939
19 and it shall be the w' for his army. "
Hag 1: 6 and he that earneth w' earneth 7936
6 earneth w' to put it into a bag "
Mal 3: 5 that oppress the hireling in his w', 7939
Lu 3:14 and be content with your w'. *3800*
Joh 4:36 And he that reapeth receiveth w', *3408*
Ro 6:23 For the w' of sin is death; but the *3800*
2Co 11: 8 other churches, taking w' of them, "
2Pe 2:15 loved the w' of unrighteousness; **3408*

wagging
M't 27:39 by reviled him, w' their heads, *2795*
M'r 15:29 by railed on him, w' their heads, "

wagon See also WAGONS.
Nu 7: 3 a w' for two of the princes, and for 5699

wagons
Ge 45:19 take you w' out of the land of 5699
21 Joseph gave them w', according to "
27 when he saw the w' which Joseph "
46: 5 in the w' which Pharaoh had sent "
Nu 7: 3 before the Lord, six covered w', "
6 Moses took the w' and the oxen, "
7 Two w' and four oxen he gave unto "
8 four w' and eight oxen he gave "
Eze 23:24 against thee with chariots, w', *7393

wail See also BEWAILED; WAILED; WAILING.
Eze 32:18 w' for the multitude of Egypt, 5091
Mic 1: 8 Therefore I will w' and howl, I 5594
Re 1: 7 kindreds of the earth shall w' **2875*

wailed
M'r 5:38 and them that wept and w' greatly. **214*

wailing
Es 4: 3 and fasting, and weeping, and w';4553
Jer 9:10 will I take up a weeping and w', 5092
18 haste, and take up a w' for us, "
19 a voice of w' is heard out of Zion, "
20 and teach your daughters w', "
Eze 7:11 neither shall there be w' for them. *5089
27:31 bitterness of heart and bitter w'. *4553
32 in their w' they shall take up a 5204
Am 5:16 W' shall be in all streets; and 4553
16 as are skilful of lamentation to w'. "
17 And in all vineyards shall be w': "
Mic 1: 8 I will make a w' like the dragons, "
M't 13:42, 50 be w' and gnashing of teeth. **2805*
Re 18:15 of her torment, weeping and w', **3996*
19 cried, weeping and w', saying, * "

wait See also AWAIT; WAITED; WAITETH; WAITING.
Ex 21:13 if a man lie not in w', but God 6658
Nu 3:10 shall w' on their priest's office: *8104
8:24 in to w' upon the service of the 6633
35:20 or hurl at him by laying of w', 6660
22 him any thing without laying of w', "
De 19:11 and lie in w' for him, and rise up 693
Jos 8: 4 ye shall lie in w' against the city, * "
13 liers in w' on the west of the city, 6119
J'g 9:25 set liers in w' for him in the top of 693
32 with thee, and lie in w' in the field: "
34 and they laid w' against Shechem "
35 were with him, from lying in w'. *3993
43 laid w' in the field, and looked, 693
16: 2 laid w' for him all night in the gate "
9 Now there were men lying in w', "
12 there were liers in w' abiding in "
20:29 Israel set liers in w' round about "
33 liers in w' of Israel came forth "
36 they trusted unto the liers in w' "
37 liers in w' hasted, and rushed upon "
37 liers in w' drew themselves along, "
38 men of Israel and the liers in w', "
21:20 Go and lie in w' in the vineyards; "
1Sa 15: 2 how he laid w' for him in the way,* "
5 Amalek, and laid w' in the valley. 693
22: 8 my servant against me, to lie in w', "
13 should rise against me, to lie in w', "
2Ki 6:33 I w' for the Lord any longer? 3176
1Ch 23:28 was to w' on the sons of Aaron 3027
2Ch 5:11 and did not then w' by course: *8104
13:10 the Levites w' upon their business:* "
Ezr 8:31 and of such as lay in w' by the way. 693
Job 14:14 of my appointed time will I w'. 3176
Job 17:13 If I w', the grave is mine house: *6960
31: 9 if I have laid w' at my neighbour's 693
38:40 and abide in the covert to lie in w'? 695
Ps 10: 9 He lieth in w' secretly as a lion in* 693
9 he lieth in w' to catch the poor: he "
25: 3 none that w' on thee be ashamed: 6960
5 on thee do I w' all the day. "
21 preserve me; for I w' on thee. "
27:14 W' on the Lord: be of good "
14 thine heart: w', I say, on the Lord. "
37: 7 Lord, and w' patiently for him: 2342
9 but those that w' upon the Lord, 6960
34 W' on the Lord, and keep his way, "
39: 7 And now, Lord, what w' I for? "
52: 9 and I will w' on thy name; for it is* "
56: 6 steps, when they w' for my soul. * "
59: 3 For, lo, they lie in w' for my soul: 693
9 his strength will I w' upon thee: 8104
62: 5 My soul, w' thou only upon God; 1826
69: 3 eyes fail while I w' for my God. 3176
6 Let not them that w' on thee, 6960
71:10 and they that lay w' for my soul *8104
104:27 These w' all upon thee; that thou 7663
123: 2 so our eyes w' upon the Lord our * "
130: 5 I w' for the Lord, my soul doth w', 6960
145:15 The eyes of all w' upon thee; and 7663
Pr 1:11 let us lay w' for blood, let us lurk 693
18 And they lay w' for their own blood; "
7:12 and lieth in w' at every corner.) "
12: 6 the wicked are to lie in w' for blood: "
20:22 w' on the Lord, and he shall save 6960
23:28 She also lieth in w' as for a prey, 693
24:15 Lay not w', O wicked man, against "
Isa 8:17 And I will w' upon the Lord, that 2442
30:18 therefore will the Lord w', that he "
18 blessed are all they that w' for him. "
40:31 they that w' upon the Lord shall 6960
42: 4 and the isles shall w' for his law. 3176
49:23 not be ashamed that w' for me. 6960
51: 5 the isles shall w' upon me, and on "
59: 9 w' for light, but behold obscurity;* "
60: 9 Surely the isles shall w' for me, "
Jer 5:26 they lay w', as he that setteth *7789
9: 8 but in heart he layeth his w'. 696
14:22 therefore we will w' upon thee: for 6960
La 3:10 was unto me as a bear lying in w', 693
25 Lord is good unto them that w' 6960
26 quietly w' for the salvation of the 1748
4:19 laid w' for us in the wilderness. 693
Ho 6: 9 as troops of robbers w' for a man, 2442
7: 6 like an oven, whiles they lie in w': 693
12: 6 and w' on thy God continually. 6960
Mic 7: 2 they all lie in w' for blood; they 693
7 w' for the God of my salvation: 3176

Hab 2: 3 though it tarry, w' for it: because 2442
Zep 3: 8 Therefore w' ye upon me, saith the "
M'r 3: 9 a small ship should w' on him 4342
Lu 11:54 Laying w' for him, and seeking to 1748
12:36 like...men that w' for their lord, *4327
Ac 1: 4 w' for the promise of the Father, 4037
20: 3 the Jews laid w' for him, *1096,1917
19 by the lying in w' of the Jews: *1917
23:16 son heard of their lying in w', 1747
21 for there lie in w' for him of them 1748
30 the Jews laid w' for the man, *1917
25: 3 laying w' in the way to kill ‡4160,1747
Ro 8:25 then do we with patience w' for it. 553
12: 7 let us w' on our ministering: *
1Co 9:13 they which w' at the altar are 4332
Gal 5: 5 w' for the hope of righteousness by 553
Eph 4:14 whereby they lie in w' to deceive; *3180
1Th 1:10 And to w' for his Son from heaven, 362

waited
Ge 49:18 I have w' for thy salvation, O Lord. 6960
1Ki 20:38 and w' for the king by the way, 5975
2Ki 5: 2 and she w' on Naaman's wife. 1961,6440
1Ch 6:32 and then they w' on their office 5975
33 they that w' with their children. "
9:18 w' in the king's gate eastward: "
2Ch 7: 6 the priests w' on their offices: the*5975
17:19 These w' on the king, beside those 8334
35:15 and the porters w' at every gate; *
Ne 12:44 priests and for the Levites that w'. 5975
Job 6:19 the companies of Sheba w' for them. 6960
15:22 and he is w' for of the sword. 6822
29:21 Unto me men gave ear, and w', 3176
23 And they w' for me as for the rain; "
30:26 when I w' for light, there came "
32: 4 Elihu had w' till Job had spoken, 2442
11 Behold, I w' for your words; I 3176
16 When I had w', (for they spake not,*"
Ps 40: 1 I w' patiently for the Lord; and he 6960
106:13 they w' not for his counsel: 2442
119:95 wicked have w' for me to destroy 6960
Isa 25: 9 we have w' for him, and he will "
9 we have w' for him, we will be glad "
26: 8 O Lord, have we w' for thee; "
33: 2 we have w' for thee: be thou their "
Eze 19: 5 when she saw that she had w', 3176
Mic 1:12 of Maroth w' carefully for good: 2342
Zec 11:11 poor of the flock that w' upon me *8104
M'r 15:43 also w' for the kingdom of God, *4327
Lu 1:21 And the people w' for Zacharias, *4328
23:51 himself w' for the kingdom of God. *4327
Ac 10: 7 them that w' on him continually; 4342
24 And Cornelius w' for them, and *4328
17:16 while Paul w' for them at Athens, 1551
1Pe 3:20 of God w' in the days of Noah, "

waiteth
Job 24:15 the adulterer w' for the twilight, 8104
Ps 33:20 Our soul w' for the Lord: he is *2442
62: 1 Truly my soul w' upon God: from 1747
65: 1 Praise w' for thee, O God, in Sion: "
130: 6 My soul w' for the Lord more than† "
Pr 27:18 he that w' on his master shall be 8104
Isa 64: 4 prepared for him that w' for him. 2442
Da 12:12 Blessed is he that w', and cometh to "
Mic 5: 7 man, nor w' for the sons of men. 3176
Ro 8:19 w' for the manifestation of the 553
Jas 5: 7 husbandman w' for the precious 1551

waiting
Nu 8:25 cease w' upon the service thereof, 6635
Pr 8:34 gates, w' at the posts of my doors. 8104
Lu 2:25 w' for the consolation of Israel: *4327
8:40 him: for they were all w' for him. 4328
Joh 5: 3 w' for the moving of the water. *1551
Ro 8:23 w' for the adoption, to wit, the 553
1Co 1: 7 w' for the coming of our Lord Jesus "
2Th 3: 5 and into the patient w' for Christ.*

wake See also AWAKE; WAKED; WAKENED; WAKENETH; WAKETH; WAKING.
Jer 51:39, 57 a perpetual sleep, and not w', 6974
Joe 3: 9 w' up the mighty men, let all the *5782
1Th 5:10 whether we w' or sleep, we should 1127

waked
Zec 4: 1 with me came again, and w' me, 5782

wakened
Joe 3:12 Let the heathen be w', and come *5782
Zec 4: 1 a man that is w' out of his sleep, "

wakeneth
Isa 50: 4 he w' morning by morning, 5782
4 w' mine ear to hear as the learned. "

waketh
Ps 127: 1 the watchman w' but in vain. 8245
Ca 5: 2 I sleep, but my heart w': it is the *5782

waking
Ps 77: 4 Thou holdest mine eyes w': I am *8109

walk See also WALKED; WALKEST; WALKETH; WALKING.
Ge 13:17 Arise, w' through the land in the 1980
17: 1 w' before me, and be thou perfect. "
24:40 The Lord, before whom I w', will "
48:15 fathers Abraham and Isaac did w', "
Ex 16: 4 whether they will w' in my law, or 3212
18:20 the way wherein they must w', "
21:19 and w' abroad upon his staff, 1980
Le 18: 3 shall ye w' in their ordinances. 3212
4 mine ordinances, to w' therein: "
20:23 ye shall not w' in the manners of "
26: 3 If ye w' in my statutes, and keep "
12 I will w' among you, and will be 1980
21 ye w' contrary unto me, and will 3212
23 but will w' contrary unto me; 1980
24 will I also w' contrary unto you, "
27 unto me, but w' contrary unto me; "
28 Then I will w' contrary unto you "
De 5:33 Ye shall w' in all the ways which 3212
8: 6 to w' in his ways, and to fear him. "
19 w' after other gods, and serve 1980
10:12 to w' in all his ways, and to love 3212
11:22 to w' in all his ways, and to cleave "
13: 4 Ye shall w' after the Lord your God, "
5 thy God commanded thee to w' in. "
19: 9 thy God, and to w' ever in his ways; "
26:17 be thy God, and to w' in his ways, "
28: 9 Lord thy God, and w' in his ways. 1980
29:19 I w' in the imagination of mine 3212
30:16 Lord thy God, to w' in his ways, "
Jos 18: 8 Go and w' through the land, and 1980
22: 5 God, and to w' in all his ways, 3212
J'g 2:22 the way of the Lord to w' therein, "
5:10 in judgment, and w' by the way. 1980
1Sa 2:30 should w' before me for ever: "
35 he shall w' before mine anointed "
8: 5 and thy sons w' not in thy ways: "
1Ki 2: 3 to w' in his ways, to keep his 3212
4 to w' before me in truth with all "
3:14 if thou wilt w' in my ways, to keep "
14 as thy father David did w', 1980
6:12 if thou wilt w' in my statutes, 3212
12 my commandments to w' in them; "
8:23 thy servants that w' before thee 1980
25 w' before me as thou hast walked 3212
36 good way wherein they should w', "
58 unto him, to w' in all his ways, "
61 Lord our God, to w' in his statutes, "
9: 4 if thou wilt w' before me, as David "
11:38 wilt w' in my ways, and do that 1980
16:31 a light thing for him to w' in the 3212
2Ki 10:31 no heed to w' in the law of the Lord "
23: 3 the Lord, to w' after the Lord, "
2Ch 6:14 that w' before thee with all their 1980
16 heed to their way to w' in my law, 3212
27 good way, wherein they should w'; "
31 to w' in thy ways, so long as they "
7:17 for thee, if thou wilt w' before me, "
34:31 the Lord, and to w' after the Lord, "
Ne 5: 9 ye not to w' in the fear of our God "
10:29 into an oath, to w' in God's law, "
Ps 12: 8 The wicked w' on every side, 1980
23: 4 though I w' through the valley 3212
26:11 for me, I will w' in mine integrity: "
48:12 W' about Zion, and go round 5437
56:13 I may w' before God in the light 1980
78:10 God, and refused to w' in his law; 3212
82: 5 they w' on in darkness: 1980
84:11 from them that w' uprightly. "
86:11 O Lord; I will w' in thy truth: "
89:15 they shall w', O Lord, in the light "
30 and w' not in my judgments; 3212
101: 2 I will w' within my house with a 1980
115: 7 feet have they, but they w' not: "
116: 9 I will w' before the Lord in the "
119: 1 who w' in the law of the Lord. "
3 no iniquity: they w' in his ways. "
45 I will w' at liberty: for I seek thy "
138: 7 I w' in the midst of trouble, thou 3212
143: 8 know the way wherein I should w'; "
Pr 1:15 w' not thou in the way with them; "
2: 7 buckler to them that w' uprightly. 1980
13 to w' in the ways of darkness; 3212
20 thou mayest w' in the way of good "
3:23 shalt thou w' in thy way safely, "
Ec 4:15 the living which w' under the sun, 1980
6: 8 knoweth to w' before the living? "
11: 9 and w' in the ways of thine heart, "
Isa 2: 3 ways, and we will w' in his paths: 3212
5 let us w' in the light of the Lord. "
3:16 w' with stretched forth necks and "
8:11 not w' in the way of this people, "
30: 2 That w' to go down into Egypt, ‡1980
21 This is the way, w' ye in it, when 3212
35: 9 but the redeemed shall w' there: 1980
40:31 and they shall w', and not faint. 3212
42: 5 and spirit to them that w' therein: 1980
24 for they would not w' in his ways, "
50:11 w' in the light of your fire, and in 3212
59: 9 brightness, but we w' in darkness. 1980
Jer 3:17 neither shall they w' any more 3212
18 shall w' with the house of Israel, "
6:16 is the good way, and w' therein, "
16 they said, We will not w' therein. "
25 into the field, nor w' by the way; "
7: 6 w' after other gods to your hurt: "
9 w' after other gods whom ye know 1980
23 w' ye in all the ways that I have "
9: 4 neighbour will w' with slanders. * "
13:10 which w' in the imagination of "
10 and w' after other gods, to serve "
16:12 w' every one after the imagination "
18:12 we will w' after our own devices, "
15 to w' in paths, in a way not cast "
23:14 commit adultery, and w' in lies: "
26: 4 hearken to me, to w' in my law, "
31: 9 cause them to w' by the rivers of "
42: 3 us the way wherein we may w', "
La 5:18 is desolate, the foxes w' upon it. "
Eze 11:20 That they may w' in my statutes, 3212
20:18 W' ye not in the statutes of your "
19 w' in my statutes, and keep my "
33:15 w' in the statutes of life, without 1980
36:12 I will cause men to w' upon you, 3212
27 cause you to w' in my statutes, "
37:24 they shall also w' in my judgments, "
42: 4 chambers was a w' of ten cubits 4109
Da 4:37 those that w' in pride he is able to 1981
9:10 to w' in his laws, which he set 3212
Ho 11:10 They shall w' after the Lord: he "
14: 9 right, and the just shall w' in them: "
Joe 2: 8 they shall w' every one in his path:* "
Am 3: 3 Can two w' together, except they "
Mic 4: 2 ways, and we will w' in his paths: "
4: 5 will w' every one in the name of his 3212
5 will w' in the name of the Lord our "
6: 8 and to w' humbly with thy God? "
16 Ahab, and ye w' in their counsels; "
Na 2: 5 they shall stumble in their w'; *1979
Hab 3:15 didst w' through the sea with *1869
19 me to w' upon mine high places. "
Zep 1:17 that they shall w' like blind men, 1980
Zec 1:10 to w' to and fro through the earth. "
3: 7 If thou wilt w' in my ways, and if 3212
7 to w' among these that stand by. *4108
6: 7 w' to and fro through the earth: 1980
7 w' to and fro through the earth. "
10:12 shall w' up and down in his name, "
M't 9: 5 thee; or to say, Arise, and w'? 4043
11: 5 and the lame w', the lepers are "
15:31 the lame to w', and the blind to see:* "
M'r 2: 9 Arise, and take up thy bed, and w'? "
7: 5 Why w' not thy disciples according "
Lu 5:23 thee; or to say, Rise up and w'? "
7:22 how that the blind see, the lame w', "
11:44 the men that w' over them are not "
13:33 I must w' to day, and to morrow, *4198
20:46 which desire to w' in long robes, 4043
24:17 ye have one to another, as ye w', "
Joh 5: 8 him, Rise, take up thy bed, and w'. "
11 unto me, Take up thy bed, and w'. "
12 thee, Take up thy bed, and w'? "
7: 1 for he would not w' in Jewry, "
8:12 me shall not w' in darkness, "
11: 9 If any man w' in the day, he "
10 But if a man w' in the night, he "
12:35 W' while ye have the light, lest "
Ac 3: 6 Christ of Nazareth rise up and w'. "
12 we had made this man to w'? "
14:16 all nations to w' in their own ways. 4198
21:21 neither to w' after the customs. 4043
Ro 4:12 also w' in the steps of that faith 4748
6: 4 should w' in newness of life. 4043
8: 1 who w' not after the flesh, but * "
4 who w' not after the flesh, but "
13:13 Let us w' honestly, as in the day; "
1Co 3: 3 are ye not carnal, and w' as men? "
7:17 called every one, so let him w'. "
2Co 5: 7 (For we w' by faith, not by sight:) "
6:16 dwell in them, and w' in them; 1704
10: 3 For though we w' in the flesh, we 4043
Ga 5:16 W' in the Spirit, and ye shall not "
25 Spirit, let us also w' in the Spirit. 4748
6:16 many as w' according to this rule, "
Eph 2:10 that we should w' in them. 4043
4: 1 that ye w' worthy of the vocation "
17 w' not as other Gentiles w', "
5: 2 w' in love, as Christ also hath loved "
8 in the Lord: w' as children of light: "
15 See then that ye w' circumspectly, "
Ph'p 3:16 let us w' by the same rule, let us 4748
17 mark them which w' so as ye have 4043
18 (For many w', of whom I have told "
Col 1:10 That ye might w' worthy of the "
2: 6 Jesus the Lord, so w' ye in him: "
4: 5 W' in wisdom toward them that "
1Th 2:12 That ye would w' worthy of God, "
4: 1 ye ought to w' and to please God, "
12 w' honestly toward them that are "
2Th 3:11 which w' among you disorderly, "
2Pe 2:10 them that w' after the flesh in the 4198
1Jo 1: 6 with him, and w' in darkness, 4043
7 But if we w' in the light, as he is in "
2: 6 in him ought himself also so to w', "
2Jo 6 we w' after his commandments. "
6 the beginning, ye should w' in it. "
3Jo 4 hear that my children w' in truth. "
Jude 18 w' after their own ungodly lusts. *4198
Re 3: 4 they shall w' with me in white: 4043
9:20 neither can see, nor hear, nor w': "
16:15 lest he w' naked, and they see his "
21:24 are saved shall w' in the light of it: "

walked See also WALKEDST.
Ge 5:22 Enoch w' with God after he begat 1980
24 Enoch w' with God: and he was "
6: 9 generations, and Noah w' with God. "
Ex 2: 5 her maidens w' along by the river's "
14:29 children of Israel w' upon dry land "
Le 26:40 they have w' contrary unto me; "
41 I also have w' contrary unto them, 3212
Jos 5: 6 w' forty years in the wilderness, 1980
J'g 2:17 the way which their fathers w' in, "
5: 6 the travellers w' through byways. 3212
11:16 w' through the wilderness unto the "
1Sa 8: 3 And his sons w' not in his ways, 1980
12: 2 I have w' before you from my "
2Sa 2:29 and his men w' all that night * "
7: 6 w' in a tent and in a tabernacle. "
7 I have w' with all the children of "
11: 2 and w' upon the roof of the king's "
1Ki 3: 6 as he w' before thee in truth, and "
8:25 me as thou hast w' before me. "
9: 4 as David thy father w', in integrity "
11:33 have not w' in my ways, to do that "
15: 3 And he w' in all the sins of his 3212
26 and w' in the way of his father, and "
34 and w' in the way of Jeroboam, and "
16: 2 hast w' in the way of Jeroboam, "
26 he w' in all the way of Jeroboam "
22:43 And he w' in all the ways of Asa his "
52 and w' in the way of his father, and "
2Ki 4:35 and w' in the house to and fro; "
8:18 he w' in the way of the kings of "
27 he w' in the way of the house of "
13: 6 made Israel sin, but w' therein. 1980
11 made Israel sin: but he w' therein. "
16: 3 But he w' in the way of the kings 3212
17: 8 w' in the statutes of the heathen, "
19 w' in the statutes of Israel which "
22 children of Israel w' in all the sins "

2Ki 20: 3 w· before thee in truth and with a 1980
21: 21 And he w· in all the way that his 3212
21 in all the way that his father w· in,1980
22 and w· not in the way of the Lord. "
22: 2 and w· in all the way of David his 3212
1Ch 17: 6 I have w· with all Israel, 1980
8 thee whithersoever thou hast w·, *
2Ch 6: 16 law, as thou hast w· before me. "
7: 17 before me, as David thy father w·, 1980
11: 17 they w· in the way of David and "
17: 3 he w· in the first ways of his father "
4 w· in his commandments, and not "
20: 32 And he w· in the way of Asa his 3212
21: 6 And he w· in the way of the kings "
12 thou hast not w· in the ways of 1980
13 hast w· in the way of the kings of 3212
22: 3 also w· in the ways of the house of1980
5 He w· also after their counsel, and "
28: 2 he w· in the ways of the kings of 3212
34: 2 w· in the ways of David his father, "
Es 2: 11 Mordecai w· every day before the 1980
Job 29: 3 his light I w· through darkness; 3212
31: 5 If I have w· with vanity, or if my 1980
7 and mine heart w· after mine eyes, "
38: 16 thou w· in the search of the depth? "
Ps 26: 1 for I have w· in mine integrity: "
3 eyes: and I have w· in thy truth. "
55: 14 and w· unto the house of God in "
81: 12 they w· in their own counsels. *3212
13 and Israel had w· in my ways! *1980
142: 3 In the way wherein I w· have they* "
Isa 9: 2 people that w· in darkness have "
20: 3 my servant Isaiah hath w· naked "
38: 3 how I have w· before thee in truth "
Jer 2: 5 and have w· after vanity, and are 3212
8 w· after things that do not profit. 1980
7: 24 but w· in the counsels and in the 3212
8: 2 and after whom they have w·, and1980
9: 13 obeyed my voice, neither w· therein; "
14 w· after the imagination of their 3212
11: 8 w· every one in the imagination of "
16: 11 have w· after other gods, and have "
32: 23 thy voice, neither w· in thy law; 1980
44: 10 have they feared, nor w· in my law, "
23 of the Lord, nor w· in his law, nor "
Eze 5: 6 statutes, they have not w· in them. "
7 and have not w· in my statutes, "
11: 12 for ye have not w· in my statutes, "
16: 47 hast thou not w· after their ways, "
18: 9 Hath w· in my statutes, and hath "
17 judgments, hath w· in my statutes; "
20: 13 they w· not in my statutes, and "
16 and w· not in my statutes, but "
21 they w· not in my statutes, neither "
23: 31 hast w· in the way of thy sister; "
28: 14 hast w· up and down in the midst "
Da 4: 29 w· in the palace of the kingdom *1981
Ho 5: 11 he...w· after the commandment. *1980
Am 2: 4 the which their fathers have w·: * "
Na 2: 11 even the old lion, w·, and the lion's "
Zec 1: 11 We have w· to and fro through the "
6: 7 w· to and fro through the earth. "
Mal 2: 6 he w· with me in peace and equity "
3: 14 w· mournfully before the Lord "
M't 14: 29 he w· on the water, to go to Jesus. *4043*
M'r 1: 16 Now as he w· by the sea of Galilee,* "
5: 42 the damsel arose, and w·, for she "
16: 12 form unto two of them, as they w·, "
Joh 1: 36 looking upon Jesus as he w·, he "
5: 9 whole, and took up his bed, and w·: "
6: 66 back, and w· no more with him. "
7: 1 these things Jesus w· in Galilee: "
10: 23 Jesus w· in the temple in Solomon's* "
11: 54 w· no more openly among the "
Ac 3: 8 he leaping up stood, and w·, and * "
14: 8 mother's womb, who never had w·: "
10 on thy feet. And he leaped and w·. "
2Co 10: 2 as if we w· according to the flesh. "
12: 18 you? w· we not in the same spirit? "
18 spirit? w· we not in the same steps? "
Ga 2: 14 they w· not uprightly according to*3716*
Eph 2: 2 in time past ye w· according to the*4043*
Col 3: 7 In the which ye also w· some time, "
1Pe 4: 3 we w· in lasciviousness, lusts, *4198*
1Jo 2: 6 also so to walk, even as he w·. *4043*

walkedst
Joh 21: 18 and w· whither thou wouldest: *4043*

walkest
De 6: 7 and when thou w· by the way, 3212
11: 19 and when thou w· by the way, "
1Ki 2: 42 out, and w· abroad any whither, 1980
Isa 43: 2 when thou w· through the fire, 3212
Ac 21: 24 w· orderly, and keepest the law. *4748*
Ro 14: 15 meat, now w· thou not charitably. *4043*
3Jo 3 thee, even as thou w· in the truth. "

walketh
Ge 24: 65 man is this that w· in the field to 1980
De 23: 14 Lord thy God w· in the midst of "
1Sa 12: 2 behold, the king w· before you: "
Job 18: 8 own feet, and he w· upon a snare. "
22: 14 and he w· in the circuit of heaven. "
34: 8 iniquity, and w· with wicked men. 3212
Ps 1: 1 that w· not in the counsel of the 1980
15: 2 He that w· uprightly, and worketh "
39: 6 Surely every man w· in a vain shew: "
73: 9 and their tongue w· through the "
91: 6 the pestilence that w· in darkness; "
101: 6 he that w· in a perfect way, he shall "
104: 3 who w· upon the wings of the wind: "
128: 1 the Lord; that w· in his ways. "
Pr 6: 12 man, w· with a froward mouth. "
10: 9 that w· [1980] uprightly w· surely: 3212
13: 20 He that w· with wise men shall be *1980
14: 2 He that w· in his uprightness "
15: 21 of understanding w· uprightly. * "
Pr 19: 1 the poor that w· in his integrity, *1980
20: 7 The just man w· in his integrity: "
28: 6 poor that w· in his uprightness, "
18 Whoso w· uprightly shall be saved: "
26 but whoso w· wisely, he shall be "
Ec 2: 14 but the fool w· in darkness: and I "
10: 3 when he that is a fool w· by the way, "
Isa 33: 15 He that w· righteously, and "
50: 10 that w· in darkness, and hath no "
65: 2 w· in a way that was not good, "
Jer 10: 23 in man that w· to direct his steps. "
23: 17 one that w· after the imagination "
Eze 11: 21 whose heart w· after the heart of "
Mic 2: 7 do good to him that w· uprightly? "
M't 12: 43 he w· through dry places, seeking*1330*
Lu 11: 24 he w· through dry places, seeking* "
Joh 12: 35 he that w· in darkness knoweth *4043*
2Th 3: 6 every brother that w· disorderly, "
1Pe 5: 8 w· about, seeking whom he may "
1Jo 2: 11 w· in darkness, and knoweth not "
Re 2: 1 who w· in the midst of the seven "

walking
Ge 3: 8 of the Lord God w· in the garden 1980
De 2: 7 he knoweth thy w· through this 3212
1Ki 3: 3 w· in the statutes of David his "
16: 19 in w· in the way of Jeroboam, and "
Job 1: 7 and from w· up and down in it. 1980
2: 2 and from w· up and down in it. "
31: 26 or the moon w· in brightness; "
Ec 10: 7 and princes w· as servants upon the "
Isa 3: 16 w· and mincing as they go, and "
20: 2 he did so, w· naked and barefoot. "
57: 2 each one w· in his uprightness. * "
Jer 6: 28 revolters, w· with slanders: * "
Da 3: 25 loose, w· in the midst of the fire. 1981
Mic 2: 11 man w· in the spirit and falsehood1980
M't 4: 18 Jesus, w· by the sea of Galilee, *4043*
14: 25 went unto them, w· on the sea. "
26 the disciples saw him w· on the sea, "
M'r 6: 48 cometh unto them, w· upon the sea, "
49 when they saw him w· upon the sea, "
8: 24 up, and said, I see men as trees, w·. "
11: 27 and as he was w· in the temple, "
Lu 1: 6 w· in all the commandments and *4198*
Joh 6: 19 they see Jesus w· on the sea, and *4043*
Ac 3: 8 into the temple, w·, and leaping, "
9 saw him w· and praising God: "
9: 31 w· in the fear of the Lord, and in *4198*
2Co 4: 2 not w· in craftiness, nor handling *4043*
2Pe 3: 3 scoffers, w· after their own lusts, *4198*
2Jo 4 found of thy children w· in truth, *4043*
Jude 16 w· after their own lusts; *4198*

wall See also WALLED; WALLS.
Ge 49: 6 selfwill they digged down a w·. *7794
22 whose branches run over the w·: 7791
Ex 14: 22, 29 waters were a w· unto them 2346
Le 14: 37 in sight are lower than the w·; 7023
25: 31 which have no w· round about 2346
Nu 22: 24 vineyards, a w· being on this side,*1447
24 this side, and a w· on that side. * "
25 she thrust herself unto the w·, 7023
25 Balaam's foot against the w·: "
35: 4 shall reach from the w· of the city "
Jos 2: 15 her house was upon the town w·, 2346
15 and she dwelt upon the w·. "
6: 5 w· of the city shall fall down flat, "
20 shout, that the w· fell down flat, "
1Sa 18: 11 I will smite David even to the w· 7023
19: 10 to smite David even to the w· with "
10 he smote the javelin into the w·: "
20: 25 times, even upon a seat by the w·: "
25: 16 w· unto us both by night and day, 2346
22, 34 that pisseth against the w·. *7023
31: 10 his body to the w· of Beth-shan. 2346
12 his sons from the w· of Beth-shan, "
2Sa 11: 20 that they would shoot from the w·? "
21 a millstone upon him from the w·, "
21 Thebez? why went ye nigh the w·? "
24 shooters shot from off the w· upon "
18: 24 the roof over the gate unto the w·, "
20: 15 were with Joab battered the w·, "
21 shall be thrown to thee over the w·. "
22: 30 by my God have I leaped over a w·.7791
1Ki 3: 1 the w· of Jerusalem round about. 2346
4: 33 that springeth out of the w·: 7023
6: 5 And against the w· of the house he "
6 in the w· of the house he made "
27 of the one touched the one w·, 7023
27 other cherub touched the other w·; "
31 side posts were a fifth part of the w·. "
33 of olive tree, a fourth part of the w·. "
9: 15 Millo, and the w· of Jerusalem, 2346
14: 10 him that pisseth against the w·, *7023
16: 11 not one that pisseth against a w·,* "
20: 30 w· fell upon twenty and seven 2346
21: 21 him that pisseth against the w·, *7023
23 eat Jezebel by the w· of Jezreel. *2426
2Ki 3: 27 for a burnt offering upon the w·. 2346
4: 10 chamber, I pray thee, on the w·; 7023
6: 26 Israel was passing by upon the w·,2346
30 he passed by upon the w·, and the "
9: 8 him that pisseth against the w·, *7023
33 her blood was sprinkled on the w·, "
14: 13 brake down the w· of Jerusalem 2346
18: 26 of the people that are on the w·. "
27 me to the men which sit on the w·, "
20: 2 Then he turned his face to the w·, 7023
2Ch 3: 11, 12 reaching to the w· of the house: "
25: 23 brake down the w· of Jerusalem 2346
26: 6 and brake down the w· of Gath, "
6 w· of Jabneh, and the w· of Ashdod, "
9 turning of the w·, and fortified them. "
27: 3 on the w· of Ophel he built much. 2346
32: 5 built up all the w· that was broken, "
5 the towers, and another w· without, "
2Ch 32: 18 of Jerusalem that were on the w·, 2346
33: 14 built a w· without the city of David, "
36: 19 brake down the w· of Jerusalem, "
Ezr 5: 3 this house, and to make up this w·?846
9: 9 a w· in Judah and in Jerusalem. 1447
Ne 1: 3 w· of Jerusalem also is broken 2346
2: 8 and for the w· of the city, and for "
15 by the brook, and viewed the w·, "
17 let us build up the w· of Jerusalem, "
3: 8 Jerusalem unto the broad w·. "
13 a thousand cubits on the w· unto "
15 w· of the pool of Siloah by the king's "
19 the armoury at the turning of the w·. "
20 turning of the w· unto the door of the "
24 of Azariah unto the turning of the w·, "
25 over against the turning of the w·, "
27 out, even unto the w· of Ophel. 2346
4: 1 heard that we builded the w·, "
3 even break down their stone w·. "
6 So built we the w·; and all the "
6 all the w· was joined together unto "
10 that we are not able to build the w·. "
13 I in the lower places behind the w·, "
15 we returned all of us to the w·, "
17 They which builded on the w·, and "
19 we are separated upon the w·, one "
5: 16 I continued in the work of this w·, "
6: 1 heard that I had builded the w·, "
6 which cause thou buildest the w·, "
15 w· was finished in the twenty and "
7: 1 when the w· was built, and I had "
12: 27 dedication of the w· of Jerusalem "
30 people, and the gates, and the w·. "
31 the princes of Judah upon the w·, "
31 right hand upon the w· toward the "
37 at the going up of the w·, above the "
38 the half of the people upon the w·, "
38 furnaces even unto the broad w·; "
13: 21 them, Why lodge ye about the w·? "
Ps 18: 29 by my God have I leaped over a w·.7791
62: 3 as a bowing w· shall ye be, and as 7023
Pr 18: 11 as an high w· in his own conceit. 2346
24: 31 the stone w· thereof was broken 1444
Ca 2: 9 he standeth behind our w·, he 3796
8: 9 If she be a w·, we will build upon 2346
10 I am a w·, and my breasts like "
Isa 2: 15 high tower, upon every fenced w·, "
5: 5 break down the w· thereof, and it*1447
22: 10 ye broken down to fortify the w·. 2346
25: 4 ones is as a storm against the w·. 7023
30: 13 swelling out in a high w·, whose 2346
36: 11 of the people that are on the w·. "
12 me to the men that sit upon the w·, "
38: 2 turned his face toward the w·, 7023
59: 10 We grope for the w· like the blind, "
Jer 15: 20 this people a fenced brasen w·: 2346
49: 27 kindle a fire in the w· of Damascus, "
51: 44 yea, the w· of Babylon shall fall. "
La 2: 8 to destroy the w· of the daughter "
8 the rampart and the w· to lament; "
18 O w· of the daughter of Zion, let "
Eze 4: 3 set it for a w· of iron between thee7023
8: 7 I looked, behold a hole in the w·. "
8 me, Son of man, dig now in the w·: "
8 when I had digged in the w·, "
10 pourtrayed upon the w· round "
12: 5 Dig thou through the w· in their "
7 I digged through the w· with mine "
12 shall dig through the w· to carry "
13: 10 one built up a w·, and, lo, others 2434
12 when the w· was fallen, shall it not7023
14 will I break down the w· that ye "
15 accomplish my wrath upon the w·, "
15 The w· is no more, neither they "
23: 14 saw men pourtrayed upon the w·, "
38: 20 every w· shall fall to the ground. 2346
40: 5 a w· on the outside of the house "
41: 5 he measured the w· of the house, 7023
6 they entered into the w· which "
6 not hold in the w· of the house. "
9 The thickness of the w·, which was "
12 w· of the building was five cubits "
17 all the w· round about within and "
20 made, and on the w· of the temple. "
42: 7 And the w· that was without over 1447
10 thickness of the w· of the court 1444
12 the way directly before the w· 1448
20 it had a w· round about, five 2346
43: 8 and the w· between me and them, 7023
Da 5: 5 upon the plaister of the w· of the 3797
9: 25 shall be built again, and the w·, *2742
Ho 2: 6 and make a w·, that she shall not*1447
Joe 2: 7 climb the w· like men of war; 2346
9 they shall run upon the w·, they "
Am 1: 7 will send a fire on the w· of Gaza, "
10 will send a fire on the w· of Tyrus, "
14 kindle a fire in the w· of Rabbah, "
5: 19 and leaned his hand on the w·, 7023
7: 7 upon a w· made by a plumbline, 2346
Na 2: 5 make haste to the w· thereof, and "
3: 8 sea, and her w· was from the sea? "
Hab 2: 11 the stone shall cry out of the w·, 7023
Zec 2: 5 will be unto her a w· of fire round 2346
Ac 9: 25 let down by the w· in a basket. *5038*
23: 3 shall smite thee, thou whited w·: *5109*
2Co 11: 33 a basket was I let down by the w·, *5038*
Eph 2: 14 broken down the middle w· of
Re 21: 12 And had a w· great and high, and *5038*
14 the w· of the city had twelve "
15 gates thereof, and the w· thereof. "
17 And he measured the w· thereof, "
18 building of the w·...was of jasper: "
19 foundations of the w· of the city "

walled See also UNWALLED.
Le 25: 29 sell a dwelling house in a w· city, 2346
30 w· city shall be established for ever "

Nu 13:28 and the cities are w', and very *1219
De 1:28 are great and w' up to heaven; * "

wallow See also WALLOWED; WALLOWING.
Jer 6:26 sackcloth, and w' thyself in ashes:6428
25:34 w' yourselves in the ashes, ye "
48:26 Moab also shall w' in his vomit, 5606
Eze 27:30 shall w' themselves in the ashes: 6428

wallowed
2Sa 20:12 Amasa w' in blood in the midst of*1556
M'r 9:20 on the ground and w' foaming. 2947

wallowing
2Pe 2:22 was washed to her w' in the mire. 2946

walls
Le 14:37 plague be in the w' of the house 7023
39 plague be spread in the w' of the "
De 3:5 cities were fenced with high w', 2346
28:52 thy high and fenced w' come down, "
1Ki 4:13 great cities with w' and brasen "
6:5 against the w' of the house round 7023
6 be fastened in the w' of the house. "
15 he built the w' of the house within "
15 the house, and the w' of the ceiling: "
16 and the w' with boards of cedar: "
29 he carved all the w' of the house "
2Ki 25:4 way of the gate between two w', 2346
10 brake down the w' of Jerusalem "
1Ch 29:4 to overlay the w' of the houses 7023
2Ch 3:7 the w' thereof, and the doors "
7 and graved cherubims on the w'. "
8:5 fenced cities, with w', gates, and 2346
14:7 make about them w', and towers, "
Ezr 4:12 and have set up the w' thereof, 7791
13 be builded, and the w' set up again, "
16 again, and the w' thereof set up, "
5:8 and timber is laid in the w', and 3797
9 house, and to make up these w'? * 846
Ne 2:13 and viewed the w' of Jerusalem, 2346
4:7 the w' of Jerusalem were made up, "
Job 24:11 Which make oil within their w', 7791
Ps 51:18 build thou the w' of Jerusalem. 2346
55:10 go about it upon the w' thereof: "
122:7 Peace be within thy w', and 2426
Pr 25:28 is broken down, and without w'. *2346
Ca 5:7 keepers of the w' took away my veil "
Isa 22:5 breaking down the w', and of 7023
11 also a ditch between the two w' 2346
25:12 fortress of the high fort of thy w' "
26:1 salvation will God appoint for w' "
49:16 thy w' are continually before me. "
56:5 within my w' a place and a name "
60:10 of strangers shall build up thy w', "
18 thou shalt call thy w' Salvation, "
62:6 I have set watchmen upon thy w', "
Jer 1:15 all the w' thereof round about, "
18 brasen w' against the whole land, "
5:10 Go ye up upon her w', and destroy;8284
21:4 which besiege you without the w', 2346
39:4 by the gate betwixt the two w': "
8 brake down the w' of Jerusalem. "
50:15 are fallen, her w' are thrown down: "
51:12 standard upon the w' of Babylon, "
58 broad w' of Babylon shall be utterly "
52:7 way of the gate between the two w', "
14 brake down all the w' of Jerusalem "
La 2:7 of the enemy the w' of her palaces; "
Eze 26:4 they shall destroy the w' of Tyrus, "
9 set engines of war against thy w', "
10 thy w' shall shake at the noise of "
12 they shall break down thy w', and "
27:11 thine army were upon thy w' round "
11 hanged their shields upon thy w' "
33:30 are talking against thee by the w' 7023
38:11 all of them dwelling without w', 2346
41:13 the building, with the w' thereof, 7023
22 and the w' thereof, were of wood: "
25 like as were made upon the w'; "
Mic 7:11 the day that thy w' are to be built,1447
Zec 2:4 inhabited as towns without w' "
Heb 11:30 By faith the w' of Jericho fell 5038

wander See also WANDERED; WANDEREST; WANDERETH; WANDERING.
Ge 20:13 me to w' from my father's house, 8582
Nu 14:33 children shall w' in the wilderness*7462
32:13 he made them w' in the wilderness5128
De 27:18 he that maketh the blind to w' out7686
Job 12:24 causeth them to w' in a wilderness8582
38:41 unto God, they w' for lack of meat. "
Ps 55:7 then would I w' far off, and remain5074
59:15 them w' up and down for meat, 5128
107:40 them to w' in the wilderness, 8582
119:10 not w' from thy commandments. 7686
Isa 47:15 shall w' every one to his quarter; 8582
Jer 14:10 Thus have they loved to w', they 5128
48:12 that shall cause him to w', and *6808
Am 8:12 And they shall w' from sea to sea, 5128

wandered
Ge 21:14 and w' in the wilderness of 8582
Jos 14:10 of Israel w' in the wilderness: 1980
Ps 107:4 They w' in the wilderness in a 8582
Isa 16:8 they w' through the wilderness: "
La 4:14 They have w' as blind men in the*5128
15 when they fled away and w', they "
Eze 34:6 My sheep w' through all the 7686
Am 4:8 or three cities w' unto one city, 5128
Heb 11:37 they w' about in sheepskins and *4022
38 they w' in deserts, and in *4105

wanderers
Jer 48:12 that I will send unto him w', that*6808
Ho 9:17 shall be w' among the nations. 5074

wanderest
Jer 2:20 under every green tree thou w', *6808

wandereth
Job 15:23 He w' abroad for bread, saying, 5074
Pr 21:16 The man that w' out of the way of 8582
27:8 As a bird that w' from her nest, so 5074
8 so is a man that w' from his place. "
Isa 16:3 outcasts; bewray not him that w'.* "
Jer 49:5 none shall gather up him that w'.‡ "

wandering See also WANDERINGS.
Ge 37:15 behold, he was w' in the field: 8582
Pr 26:2 As the bird by w', as the swallow 5110
Ec 6:9 the eyes than the w' of the desire: 1981
Isa 16:2 as a w' bird cast out of the nest, 5074
1Ti 5:13 w' about from house to house; *4022
Jude 13 w' stars, to whom is reserved the 4107

wanderings
Ps 56:8 Thou tellest my w': put thou my 5112

want See also WANTED; WANTETH; WANTING; WANTS.
De 28:48 nakedness, and in w' of all things:2640
57 shall eat them for w' of all things "
J'g 18:10 a place where there is no w' of 4270
19:19 there is no w' of any thing. "
Job 24:8 embrace...rock for w' of a shelter. 1097
30:3 For w' and famine they were 2639
31:19 seen any perish for w' of clothing, 1097
Ps 23:1 is my shepherd; I shall not w'. 2637
34:9 is no w' to them that fear him. 4270
10 Lord shall not w' any good thing. 2637
Pr 6:11 and thy w' as an armed man. 4270
10:21 but fools die for w' of wisdom. *2638
13:23 is destroyed for w' of judgment. *3808
25 the belly of the wicked shall w'. 2637
14:28 but in the w' of people is the 657
21:5 every one that is hasty only to w'. 4270
22:16 to the rich, shall surely come to w'. "
24:34 and thy w' as an armed man. "
Isa 34:16 shall fail, none shall w' her mate: 6485
Jer 33:17 never w' a man to sit upon the 3772
18 Levites w' a man before me to offer "
35:19 not w' a man to stand before me for "
La 4:9 for w' of the fruits of the field.
Eze 4:17 they may w' bread and water, and2637
Am 4:6 and w' of bread in all your places:2640
M'r 12:44 she of her w' did cast in all that 5304
Lu 15:14 land; and he began to be in w'. 5302
2Co 8:14 may be a supply for their w', 5303
14 also may be a supply for your w': "
9:12 only supplieth the w' of the saints, "
Ph'p 4:11 Not that I speak in respect of w': 5304

wanted
Jer 44:18 we have w' all things, and have 2637
Joh 2:3 when they w' wine, the mother of *5302
2Co 11:9 I was present with you, and w', I * "

wanteth
De 15:8 for his need, in that which he w'. 2637
Pr 9:4 for him that w' understanding, *2638
16 as for him that w' understanding,* "
10:19 of words there w' not sin: but 2308
28:16 The prince that w' understanding*2638
Ec 6:2 so that he w' nothing for his soul* "
Ca 7:2 round goblet, which w' not liquor:*2637

wanting
2Ki 10:19 and all his priests; let none be w':6485
19 whosoever shall be w', he shall not "
Pr 19:7 with words, yet they are w' to him.*3808
Ec 1:15 which is w' cannot be numbered. 2642
Da 5:27 in the balances, and art found w'. 2627
Tit 1:5 set in order the things that are w',3007
3:13 that nothing be w' unto them. "
Jas 1:4 be perfect and entire, w' nothing.* "

wanton
Isa 3:16 stretched forth necks and w' eyes, 8265
1Ti 5:11 begun to wax w' against Christ, 2691
Jas 5:5 pleasure on the earth, and been w':*4684

wantonness
Ro 13:13 not in chambering and w', not in 766
2Pe 2:18 through much w', those that were* "

wants
J'g 19:20 let all thy w' lie upon me; only 4270
Ph'p 2:25 and he that ministered to my w'. *5532

war See also WARFARE; WARRED; WARRETH; WARRING; WARS.
Ge 14:2 these made w' with Bera king of 4421
Ex 1:10 when there falleth out any w', "
13:17 the people repent when they see w', "
15:3 The Lord is a man of w': the Lord "
17:16 the Lord will have w' with Amalek "
32:17 There is a noise of w' in the camp. "
Nu 1:3 able to go forth to w' in Israel: 6635
20, 22, 24, 26, 28, 30, 32, 34, 36, 38, 40, 42
all that were able to go forth to w';6635
45 were able to go forth to w' in Israel; "
10:9 if ye go to w' in your land against 4421
26:2 that are able to go to w' in Israel. 6635
31:3 some of yourselves unto the w', "
4 of Israel, shall ye send to the w'. "
5 twelve thousand armed for w'. "
6 And Moses sent them to the w', a "
6 of Eleazer the priest, to the w', "
21 men of w' which went to the battle, "
27 them that took the w' upon them, 4421
28 the men of w' which went out to "
32 which the men of w' had caught, 6635
36 of them that went out to w', "
49 men of w' which are under our 4421
53 the men of w' had taken spoil, 6635
32:6 Shall your brethren go to w', and 4421
20 go armed before the Lord to w', "
27 over, every man armed for w', 6635
De 1:41 on every man his weapons of w', 4421
2:14 generation of the men of w' were "
De 2:16 all the men of w' were consumed 4421
3:18 all that are meet for the w'. *2428
4:34 signs, and by wonders, and by w', 4421
20:12 but will make w' against thee, then "
19 in making w' against it to take it, 3898
20 the city that maketh w' with thee, 4421
21:10 When thou goest forth to w' * "
24:5 new wife, he shall not go out to w',6635
Jos 4:13 forty thousand prepared for w' "
5:4 even all the men of w', died in the 4421
6 all the people that were men of w', "
6:3 compass the city, all ye men of w', "
8:1 take all the people of w' with thee, "
3 arose, and all the people of w', to "
11 even the people of w' that were "
10:5 Gibeon, and made w' against it. 3898
7 and all the people of w' with him, 4421
24 captains of the men of w' which "
11:7 and all the people of w' with him, "
18 Joshua made w' a long time with "
23 And the land rested from w'. "
14:11 even so is my strength now, for w', "
15 And the land had rest from w'. "
17:1 he was a man of w', therefore he "
22:12 to go up to w' against them. 6635
J'g 3:2 might know, to teach them w', 4421
10 judged Israel, and went out to w': "
5:8 gods; then was w' in the gates: 3901
11:4, 5 the children of Ammon made w'3898
27 doest me wrong to w' against me: "
18:11 appointed with weapons of w'. 4421
16 appointed with their weapons of w', "
17 were appointed with weapons of w'. "
20:17 sword: all these were men of w'. "
21:22 not to each man his wife in the w':* "
1Sa 8:12 and to make his instruments of w', "
14:52 was sore w' against the Philistines "
16:18 and a man of w', and prudent in "
17:33 and he a man of w' from his youth. "
18:5 Saul set him over the men of w', "
19:8 there was w' again: and David "
23:8 called all the people together to w', "
28:15 Philistines make w' against me, 3898
2Sa 1:27 and the weapons of w' perished! 4421
3:1 long w' between the house of Saul "
6 was w' between the house of Saul "
11:7 did, and how the w' prospered. "
18 all the things concerning the w'; "
19 end of telling the matters of the w' "
17:8 thy father is a man of w', and will "
21:15 Philistines had yet w' again with "
22:35 He teacheth my hands to w'; so "
1Ki 2:5 and shed the blood of w' in peace, "
5 put the blood of w' upon his girdle "
9:22 but they were men of w', and his "
14:30 there was w' between Rehoboam "
15:6 there was w' between Rehoboam "
7 there was w' between Abijam and "
16, 32 there was w' between Asa and "
20:18 or whether they be come out for w', "
22:1 continued three years without w' "
2Ki 8:28 to the w' against Hazael king of "
13:25 hand of Jehoahaz his father by w'. "
14:7 took Selah by w', and called the "
16:5 Israel came up to Jerusalem to w': "
18:20 counsel and strength for the w'. "
24:16 that were strong and apt for w', "
25:4 men of w' fled by night by the way "
19 that was set over the men of w', "
1Ch 5:10 in the days of Saul they made w' "
18 to shoot with bow, and skilful in w', "
18 threescore, that went out to the w'.6635
19 they made w' with the Hagarites, 4421
22 slain, because the w' was of God. "
7:4 were bands of soldiers for w', six "
11 fit to go out for w' and battle. 6635
40 of them that were apt to the w' and "
12:1 the mighty men, helpers of the w'.4421
8 and men of w' fit for the battle, 6635
23 that were ready armed to the w', "
24 hundred, ready armed to the w'. "
25 mighty men of valour for the w', "
33 forth to battle, expert in w', *4421
33 with all instruments of w', fifty "
35 of the Danites expert in w' twenty* "
36 battle, expert in w', forty thousand.* "
37 all manner of instruments of w' 6635
38 All these men of w', that could 4421
18:10 (for Hadarezer had w' with Tou;)* "
20:4 there arose w' at Gezer with the "
5 And there was w' again with the "
6 yet again there was w' at Gath, "
28:3 thou hast been a man of w', and "
2Ch 6:34 If thy people go out to w' against * "
8:9 they were men of w', and chief of "
13:2 w' between Abijah and Jeroboam. "
3 with an army of valiant men of w', "
14:6 and he had no w' in those years; "
15:19 And there was no more w' unto the "
17:10 made no w' against Jehoshaphat. 3898
13 and the men of w', mighty men of 4421
18 ready prepared for the w'. 6635
18:3 and we will be with thee in the w'.4421
22:5 son of Ahab king of Israel to w' "
25:5 choice men, able to go forth to w', 6635
26:11 men, that went out to w' by bands, "
13 that made w' with mighty power, 4421
28:12 them that came from the w', 6635
32:6 And he set captains of w' over the 4421
33:14 and put captains of w' in all the *2428
35:21 the house wherewith I have w': 4421
Job 5:20 in w' from the power of the sword. "
10:17 changes and w' are against me. *6635
38:23 against the day of battle and w'? 4421
Ps 18:34 He teacheth my hands to w', so "
27:3 though w' should rise against me, "

Ps 55:21 butter, but w' was in his heart: 7128
68:30 thou the people that delight in w'.
120: 7 but when I speak, they are for w'. 4421
140: 2 are they gathered together for w'. "
144: 1 teacheth my hands to w', 4421,7128
Pr 20:18 and with good advice make w'. 4421
24: 6 counsel thou shalt make thy w': "
Ec 3: 8 a time of w', and a time of peace. "
8: 8 there is no discharge in that w'; "
9:18 is better than weapons of w': but 7128
Ca 3: 8 hold swords, being expert in w': 4421
Isa 2: 4 neither shall they learn w' any "
3: 2 mighty man, and the man of w', "
25 sword, and thy mighty in the w'. "
7: 1 toward Jerusalem to w' against it, "
21:15 and from the grievousness of w'. "
36: 5 I have counsel and strength for w': "
37: 9 come forth to make w' with thee. *3898
41:12 they that w' against thee shall be 4421
42:13 stir up jealousy like a man of w': "
Jer 4:19 of the trumpet, the alarm of w'. "
6: 4 Prepare ye w' against her; arise, "
23 set in array as men for w' against* "
21: 2 king of Babylon maketh w' 3898
4 I will turn back the weapons of w'4421
28: 8 of w', and of evil, and of pestilence. "
38: 4 the hands of the men of w' that "
39: 4 saw them, and all the men of w', "
41: 3 found there, and the men of w'. "
16 even mighty men of w', and the "
42:14 Egypt, where we shall see no w', "
48:14 mighty and strong men for the w'? "
49: 2 cause an alarm of w' to be heard in "
26 all the men of w' shall be cut off in "
50:30 all her men of w' shall be cut off in "
51:20 my battle axe and weapons of w': "
32 and the men of w' are affrighted. "
52: 7 all the men of w' fled, and went "
25 had the charge of the men of w'; "
Eze 17:17 company make for him in the w', "
26: 9 engines of w' against thy walls, *6904
27:10 in thine army, thy men of w': 4421
27 all thy men of w', that are in thee, "
32:27 to hell with their weapons of w': "
39:20 mighty men, and with all men of w', "
Da 7:21 horn made w' with the saints, 7129
9:26 unto the end of the w' desolations 4421
Joe 2: 7 shall climb the wall like men of w'; "
3: 9 Prepare w', wake up the mighty "
9 let all the men of w' draw near; "
Mic 2: 8 by securely as men averse from w'. "
3: 5 they even prepare w' against him. "
4: 3 neither shall they learn w' any "
Lu 14:31 to make w' against another king, 4171
23:11 Herod with his men of w' set him *4753
2Co 10: 3 flesh, we do not w' after the flesh: 4754
1Ti 1:18 them mightest w' a good warfare; "
Jas 4: 1 lusts that w' in your members? "
2 ye fight and w', yet ye have not, 4170
1Pe 2:11 lusts, which w' against the soul; 4754
Re 11: 7 pit shall make w' against them, 4171
12: 7 there was w' in heaven: Michael "
17 went to make w' with the remnant "
13: 4 who is able to make w' with him? 4170
7 him to make w' with the saints, 4171
17:14 These...make w' with the Lamb, 4170
19:11 he doth judge and make w'. "
19 to make w' against him that sat 4171

ward See also BACKWARD; DOWNWARD; EASTWARD; FORWARD; FROWARD; GOD-WARD; INWARD; NORTHWARD; ONWARD; OUTWARD; REREWARD; REWARD; SEATWARD; SOUTHWARD; THEEWARD; THITHERWARD; TOWARD; UPWARD; USWARD; WARDROBE; WARDS; WESTWARD; YOUWARD.
Ge 40: 3 he put them in w' in the house of 4929
4 and they continued a season in w'. "
7 with him in the w' of his lord's "
41:10 put me in w' in the captain of the "
42:17 he put them altogether into w' "
Le 24:12 they put him in w', that the mind "
Nu 15:34 they put him in w', because it was "
2Sa 20: 3 put them in w', and fed them, 4931
1Ch 12:29 kept the w' of the house of Saul. * "
25: 8 And they cast lots, w' against * "
8 against w', as well the small as the* "
26:16 of the going up, w' against w'. 4929
Ne 12:24 the man of God, w' over against w'. "
25 porters keeping the w' at the "
45 porters kept the w' of their God, 4931
45 and the w' of the purification, "
Isa 21: 8 I am set in my w' whole nights: "
Jer 37:13 a captain of the w' was there, 6488
Eze 19: 9 they put him in w' in chains, *5474
Ac 12:10 past the first and the second w', 5438

wardrobe
2Ki 22:14 son of Harhas, keeper of the w'; 899
2Ch 34:22 son of Hasrah, keeper of the w'; "

wards See also INWARDS; REWARDS.
1Ch 9:23 house of the tabernacle, by w'. 4931
26:12 having w' one against another, * "
Ne 13:30 appointed the w' of the priests and "

ware See also AWARE; BEWARE; WARES.
Ne 10:31 the people of the land bring w' or 4728
13:16 brought fish, and all manner of w',4377
20 sellers of all kind of w' lodged 4465
Lu 8:27 devils long time, and w' no clothes,*1737
Ac 14: 6 They were w' of it, and fled unto *4894
2Ti 4:15 Of whom be thou w' also; for he 5442

wares See also UNAWARES.
Jer 10:17 Gather up thy w' out of the land, 3666
Eze 27:16, 18 of the w' of thy making: *4639
33 thy w' went forth out of the seas, 5801
Jon 1: 5 forth the w' that were in the ship 3627

warfare
1Sa 28: 1 their armies together for w', 6635
Isa 40: 2 her, that her w' is accomplished, "
1Co 9: 7 Who goeth a w' any time at his *4754
2Co 10: 4 weapons of our w' are not carnal, 4752
1Ti 1:18 by them mightest war a good w'; "

warm See also LUKEWARM; WARMED; WARMETH; WARMING.
2Ki 4:34 the flesh of the child waxed w'. 2552
Job 6:17 What time they wax w', they 2215
37:17 How thy garments are w', when 2525
Ec 4:11 but how can one be w' alone? 3179
Isa 44:15 will take thereof, and w' himself;*2552
16 Aha, I am w', I have seen the fire: "
47:14 there shall not be a coal to w' at, "
Hag 1: 6 clothe you, but there is none w'; 2527

warmed
Job 31:20 he were not w' with the fleece of 2552
M'r 14:54 and w' himself at the fire. *2328
Joh 18:18 was cold: and they w' themselves:* "
18 stood with them, and w' himself. * "
25 Simon Peter stood and w' himself.* "
Jas 2:16 in peace, be ye w' and filled; "

warmeth
Job 39:14 the earth, and w' them in dust, 2552
Isa 44:16 yea, he w' himself, and saith, Aha, "

warming
M'r 14:67 when she saw Peter w' himself, 2328

warn See also WARNED; WARNING.
2Ch 19:10 w' them that they trespass not 2094
Eze 3:18 nor speakest to w' the wicked "
19 Yet if thou w' the wicked, and he "
21 if thou w' the righteous man, that "
33: 3 the trumpet, and w' the people; "
7 my mouth, and w' them from me.* "
8 dost not speak to w' the wicked "
9 if thou w' the wicked of his way to "
Ac 20:31 I ceased not to w' every one night*3560
1Co 4:14 but as my beloved sons I w' you. * "
1Th 5:14 w' them that are unruly, comfort* "

warned
2Ki 6:10 of God told him and w' him of, 2094
Ps 19:11 by them is thy servant w': and in "
Eze 3:21 shall surely live, because he is w';* "
33: 6 trumpet, and the people be not w'; "
M't 2:12 being w' of God in a dream that 5537
22 being w' of God in a dream, he "
3: 7 w' you to flee from the wrath to 5263
Lu 3: 7 w' you to flee from the wrath to "
Ac 10:22 w' from God by an holy angel to 5537
Heb 11: 7 being w' of God of things not seen "

warning
Jer 6:10 whom shall I speak, and give w', *5749
Eze 3:17 mouth, and give them w' from me.2094
18 givest him not w', nor speakest "
20 because thou hast not given him w'. "
33: 4 of the trumpet, and taketh not w'; "
5 of the trumpet, and took not w'; "
5 taketh w' shall deliver his soul "
Col 1:28 w' every man, and teaching every *3560

warp
Le 13:48 Whether it be in the w', or woof; 8359
49, 51 either in the w', or in the woof, "
52 whether the w' or woof, in woolen "
53 either in the w', or in the woof, or "
56 or out of the w', or out of the woof: "
57 either in the w', or in the woof, or "
58 the garment, either w', or woof, or "
59 either in the w', or woof, or any "

warred
Nu 31: 7 they w' against the Midianites, 6633
42 Moses divided from the men that w'. "
Jos 24: 9 Moab, arose and w' against Israel,*3898
1Ki 14:19 the acts of Jeroboam, how he w', "
20: 1 Samaria, and w' against it. * "
22:45 that he shewed, and how he w', "
2Ki 6: 8 the king of Syria w' against Israel, "
14:28 how he w', and how he recovered "
2Ch 26: 6 and w' against the Philistines, "

warreth
2Ti 2: 4 No man that w' entangleth himself*4754

warring
2Ki 19: 8 king of Assyria w' against Libnah:3898
Isa 37: 8 king of Assyria w' against Libnah: "
Ro 7:23 w' against the law of my mind, 497

warrior See also WARRIORS.
Isa 9: 5 battle of the w' is with confused *5431

warriors
1Ki 12:21 chosen men, which were w', 6213,4421
2Ch 11: 1 chosen men, which were w', "

wars
Nu 21:14 in the book of the w' of the Lord, 4421
J'g 3: 1 had not known all the w' of Canaan; "
2Sa 8:10 for Hadadezer had w' with Toi. "
1Ki 5: 3 the w' which were about him on "
1Ch 22: 8 abundantly, and hast made great w': "
2Ch 12:15 there were w' between Rehoboam "
16: 9 henceforth thou shalt have w'. "
27: 7 the acts of Jotham, and all his w', "
Ps 46: 9 maketh w' to cease unto the end of "
M't 24: 6 shall hear of w' and rumours of w':4171
M'r 13: 7 shall hear of w' and rumours of w', "
Lu 21: 9 ye shall hear of w' and commotions, "
Jas 4: 1 whence come w' and fightings "

was See in the APPENDIX; also WAST; WERE.

wash See also UNWASHEN; WASHED; WASHEST; WASHING; WASHPOT.
Ge 18: 4 w' your feet, and rest yourselves 7364
19: 2 tarry all night, and w' your feet, "
24:32 water to w' his feet, and the men's 7364
Ex 2: 5 daughter of Pharaoh came...to w' "
19:10 and let them w' their clothes, 3526
29: 4 and shalt w' them with water. 7364
17 and w' the inwards of him, and his "
30:18 his foot also of brass, to w' withal: "
19 and his sons shall w' their hands "
20 they shall w' with water, that they "
21 they shall w' their hands and their "
40:12 and w' them with water. "
30 and put water there, to w' withal. "
Le 1: 9 and his legs shall he w' in water: "
13 But he shall w' the inwards and the "
6:27 thou shalt w' that whereon it was 3526
9:14 he did w' the inwards and the *7364
11:25, 28 of them shall w' his clothes, 3526
40, 40 carcase of it shall w' his clothes, "
13: 6, 34 and he shall w' his clothes, and "
54 w' the thing wherein the plague is, "
58 of skin it be, which thou shalt w', "
14: 8 to be cleansed shall w' his clothes, "
8 and w' himself in water, that he *7364
9 and he shall w' his clothes, also 3526
9 also he shall w' his flesh in water,*7364
47 in the house shall w' his clothes; 3526
47 in the house shall w' his clothes. "
15: 5 toucheth...bed shall w' his clothes, "
6, 7 hath the issue shall w' his clothes, "
8 he shall w' his clothes, and bathe "
10 of those things shall w' his clothes, "
11 he shall w' his clothes, and bathe "
13 w' his clothes, and bathe his flesh "
16 he shall w' all his flesh in water, *7364
21 her bed shall w' his clothes, 3526
22 she sat upon shall w' his clothes, "
27 and shall w' his clothes, and bathe "
16: 4 shall he w' his flesh in water, and*7364
24 w' his flesh with water in the holy* "
26 the scapegoat shall w' his clothes,*3526
28 burneth them shall w' his clothes, "
17:15 he shall both w' his clothes, and "
16 if he w' them not, nor bathe his "
22: 6 unless he w' his flesh with water.*7364
Nu 8: 7 and let them w' their clothes, *3526
19: 7 Then the priest shall w' his clothes, "
8 that burneth her shall w' his clothes "
10 of the heifer shall w' his clothes, "
19 purify himself, and w' his clothes, "
21 of separation shall w' his clothes; "
31:24 w' your clothes on the seventh day, "
De 21: 6 w' their hands over the heifer 7364
23:11 on, he shall w' himself with water:* "
Ru 3: 3 W' thyself therefore, and anoint "
1Sa 25:41 to w' the feet of the servants of my "
2Sa 11: 8 down to thy house, and w' thy feet. "
2Ki 5:10 Go and w' in Jordan seven times, "
12 may I not w' in them, and be clean? "
13 he saith to thee, W', and be clean? "
2Ch 4: 6 and five on the left, to w' in them: "
6 the sea was for the priests to w' in. "
Job 9:30 If I w' myself with snow water, and "
Ps 26: 6 I will w' mine hands in innocency: "
51: 2 W' me throughly from mine 3526
7 w' me, and I shall be whiter than "
58:10 w' his feet in the blood of the 7364
Isa 1:16 W' you, make you clean; put away "
Jer 2:22 though thou w' thee with nitre, 3526
4:14 w' thine heart from wickedness, "
Eze 23:40 for whom thou didst w' thyself, 7364
M't 6:17 anoint thine head, and w' thy face;3538
15: 2 w' not their hands when they eat "
M'r 7: 3 except they w' their hands oft, eat "
4 except they w', they eat not. ‡ 907
Lu 7:38 began to w' his feet with tears, *1026
Joh 9: 7 him, Go, w' in the pool of Siloam, 3538
11 Go to the pool of Siloam, and w': "
13: 5 and began to w' the disciples' feet, "
6 him, Lord, dost thou w' my feet? "
8 him, Thou shalt never w' my feet. "
8 If I w' thee not, thou hast no part "
10 needeth not save to w' his feet, "
14 also ought to w' one another's feet. "
Ac 22:16 be baptized, and w' away thy sins, 628

washed See also UNWASHEN.
Ge 43:24 water, and they w' their feet; 7364
31 And he w' his face, and went out, "
49:11 he w' his garments in wine, and 3526
Ex 19:14 people; and they w' their clothes. "
40:31 Aaron and his sons w' their hands7364
32 came near unto the altar, they w'; "
Le 8: 6 his sons, and w' them with water. "
21 he w' the inwards and the legs in "
13:55 the plague, after that it is w': 3526
58 it shall be w' the second time, and "
15:17 shall be w' with water, and be "
Nu 8:21 purified, and they w' their clothes; "
J'g 19:21 they w' their feet, and did eat and 7364
2Sa 12:20 David arose from the earth, and w', "
19:24 his beard, nor w' his clothes, 3526
1Ki 22:38 one w' the chariot in the pool of 7857
38 his blood; and they w' his armour;7364
2Ch 4: 6 burnt offering they w' in them; 1740
Job 29: 6 When I w' my steps with butter, 7364
Ps 73:13 and w' my hands in innocency. "
Pr 30:12 yet is not w' from their filthiness. "
Ca 5: 3 I have w' my feet; how shall I "
12 rivers of waters, w' with milk, and "
Isa 4: 4 Lord shall have w' away the filth "
Eze 16: 4 thou w' in water to supple thee; "
9 Then w' I thee with water; yea, "
9 I throughly w' away thy blood 7857
40:38 where they w' the burnt offering. 1740
M't 27:24 w' his hands before the multitude, 633
Lu 7:44 she hath w' my feet with tears, *1026
11:38 he had not first w' before dinner. ‡ 907
Joh 9: 7 and w', and came seeing. 3538

Joh 9:11 I went and *w'*, and I received sight.3538
15 mine eyes, and I *w'*, and do see. "
13:10 He that is *w'* needeth not save to *3068
12 So after he had *w'* their feet, and 3538
14 and Master, have *w'* your feet; "
Ac 9:37 whom when they had *w'*, they laid3068
16:33 of the night, and *w'* their stripes; "
1Co 6:11 but ye are *w'*, but ye are sanctified, 628
1Ti 5:10 if she have *w'* the saints' feet, if 3538
Heb10:22 and our bodies *w'* with pure water.3068
2Pe 2:22 sow that was *w'* to her wallowing "
Re 1:5 *w'* us from our sins in his own * "
7:14 and have *w'* their robes, and made4150

washest
Job 14:19 thou *w'* away the things which *7857

washing See also WASHINGS.
Le 13:56 somewhat dark after the *w'* of it; 3526
2Sa 11:2 roof he saw a woman *w'* herself; *7364
Ne 4:23 that every one put them off for *w'*.*4325
Ca 4:2 which came up from the *w'*; 7367
6:6 of sheep which go up from the *w'*, "
M'r 7:4 received to hold, as the *w'* of cups, *909
8 of men, as the *w'* of pots and cups:* "
Lu 5:2 of them, and were *w'* their nets. 637
Eph 5:26 cleanse it with the *w'* of water by 3067
Tit 3:5 by the *w'* of regeneration, and "

washings
Heb 9:10 in meats and drinks, and divers *w'*.909

washpot
Ps 60:8 Moab is my *w'*; over Edom 5518,7366
108:9 Moab is my *w'*; over Edom " "

wast See also WERT.
Ge 3:11 Who told thee that thou *w'* naked?
19 ground; for out of it *w'* thou taken:
33:10 of God, and thou *w'* pleased with me.
40:13 manner when thou *w'* his butler. 1961
De 5:15 *w'* a servant in the land of Egypt, "
15:15 that thou *w'* a bondman in the land "
16:12 that thou *w'* a bondman in Egypt: "
23:7 thou *w'* a stranger in his land. "
24:18 remember that thou *w'* a bondman "
22 thou *w'* a bondman in the land of "
25:18 thee, when thou *w'* faint and weary; "
28:60 of Egypt, which thou *w'* afraid of; "
1Sa 15:17 When thou *w'* little in thine own sight, "
17 *w'* thou not made the head of the "
2Sa 1:14 How *w'* thou not afraid to stretch "
25 thou *w'* slain in thine high places.* "
5:2 thou *w'* he that leddest out and *1961
1Ch11:2 thou *w'* he that leddest out and * "
Job15:7 or *w'* thou made before the hills? "
38:4 Where *w'* thou when I laid the 1961
21 thou it, because thou *w'* then born? "
Ps 99:8 thou *w'* a God that forgavest them.1961
114:5 Jordan, that thou *w'* driven back?* "
Isa 12:1 though thou *w'* angry with me, thine "
14:3 wherein thou *w'* made to serve, "
33:1 spoilest, and thou *w'* not spoiled; "
43:4 Since thou *w'* precious in my sight,* "
48:8 and *w'* called a transgressor from the "
54:6 of youth, when thou *w'* refused, * "
57:10 hand; therefore thou *w'* not grieved. "
Jer 2:36 as thou *w'* ashamed of Assyria. "
50:24 O Babylon, and thou *w'* not aware: "
Eze16:4 day thou *w'* born thy navel was not "
4 neither *w'* thou washed in water to "
5 thou *w'* cast out in the open field, "
5 person, in the day that thou *w'* born. "
6, 6 thee when thou *w'* in thy blood,* "
7 whereas thou *w'* naked and bare. "
13 Thus *w'* thou decked with gold and "
13 thou *w'* exceeding beautiful, and thou "
22 when thou *w'* naked and bare, 1961
22 and *w'* polluted in thy blood. "
28 Assyrians, because thou *w'* unsatiable; "
29 yet thou *w'* not satisfied herewith. "
47 thou *w'* corrupted more than they "
21:30 in the place where thou *w'* created, "
24:13 thou *w'* not purged, thou shalt not "
26:17 that *w'* inhabited of seafaring men, "
17 which *w'* strong in the sea, she and "
27:25 thou *w'* replenished, and made very "
28:3 thee in the day that thou *w'* created. "
14 thou *w'* upon the holy mountain 1961
15 Thou *w'* perfect in thy ways from the "
15 from the day that thou *w'* created, "
Ob 1:11 even thou *w'* as one of them. "
M't 26:69 Thou also *w'* with Jesus of Galilee.2258
M'r 14:67 thou also *w'* with Jesus of Nazareth. "
Joh 1:48 when thou *w'* under the fig tree, 5607
9:34 Thou *w'* altogether born in sins, and "
21:18 When thou *w'* young, thou girdedst2258
Re 5:9 for thou *w'* slain, and hast redeemed "
11:17 God Almighty, which art, and *w'*, 2258
16:5 Lord, which art, and *w'*, and shalt "

waste See also WASTED; WASTES; WASTETH; WASTING.
Le 26:31 And I will make your cities *w'*, 2723
33 be desolate, and your cities *w'*. "
Nu 21:30 we have laid them *w'* even unto 8074
De 32:10 and in the *w'* howling wilderness;8414
1Ki 17:14 The barrel of meal shall not *w'*, 3615
2Ki 19:25 to lay *w'* fenced cities into ruinous7582
1Ch17:9 of wickedness *w'* them any more, 1086
Ne 2:3 of my fathers' sepulchres, lieth *w'*,2720
17 how Jerusalem lieth *w'*, and the "
Job 30:3 in former time desolate and *w'*. *4875
38:27 satisfy the desolate and *w'* ground;"
Ps 79:7 and laid *w'* his dwelling place. 8074
80:13 boar out of the wood doth *w'* it, *3765
Isa 5:6 I will lay it *w'*: it shall not be 1326
17 *w'* places of the fat ones shall 2723
15:1 in the night Ar of Moab is laid *w'*. 7703
Isa 15:1 the night Kir of Moab is laid *w'*, 7703
23:1 for it is laid *w'*, so that there is no "
14 for your strength is laid *w'*. "
24:1 and maketh it *w'*, and turneth it 1110
33:8 The highways lie *w'*, the 8074
34:10 to generation it shall lie *w'*; 2717
37:18 Assyria have laid *w'* all the nations,"
26 be to lay *w'* defenced cities into 7582
42:15 I will make *w'* mountains and 2717
49:17 they that made thee *w'* shall go "
19 thy *w'* and thy desolate places, 2723
51:3 he will comfort all her *w'* places; "
52:9 ye *w'* places of Jerusalem: "
58:12 thee shall build the old *w'* places: "
61:4 they shall repair the *w'* cities, the 2721
64:11 our pleasant things are laid *w'*. 2723
Jer 2:15 yelled, and they made his land *w'*:8047
4:7 and thy cities shall be laid *w'*, 5327
27:17 should this city be laid *w'*? *2723
46:19 Noph shall be *w'* and desolate *8047
49:13 a reproach, a *w'*, and a curse; 2721
50:21 *w'* and utterly destroy after them,*2717
Eze 5:14 Moreover I will make thee *w'*, *2723
6:6 dwellingplaces...shall be laid *w'*, 2717
6 your altars may be laid *w'* and "
12:20 are inhabited shall be laid *w'*, "
19:7 palaces, and he laid *w'* their cities; "
26:2 be replenished, now she is laid *w'*: "
29:9 of Egypt shall be desolate and *w'*;2723
10 of Egypt utterly *w'* and desolate, "
12 among the cities that are laid *w'* 2717
30:12 I will make the land *w'*, and all *8074
35:4 I will lay thy cities *w'*, and thou 2723
36:35 the *w'* and desolate and ruined 2720
38 so shall the *w'* cities be filled with "
38:8 which have been always *w'*: 2723
Joe 1:7 He hath laid my vine *w'*, and 8047
Am 7:9 of Israel shall be laid *w'*; 2717
9:14 and they shall build the *w'* cities, 8074
Mic 5:6 shall *w'* the land of Assyria with 7489
Na 2:10 She is empty, and void, and *w'*: 1110
3:7 thee, and say, Nineveh is laid *w'*: 7703
Zep 3:6 I made their streets *w'*, that none 2717
Hag 1:4 houses, and this house lie *w'*? 2720
9 Because of mine house that is *w'*. "
Mal 1:3 mountains and his inheritance *w'**8077
M't 26:8 To what purpose is this *w'*? 684
M'r 14:4 Why was this *w'* of the ointment "

wasted
Nu 14:33 carcases be *w'* in the wilderness. *8552
24:22 the Kenite shall be *w'*, until 1197
De 2:14 the men of war were *w'* out from *8552
1Ki 17:16 And the barrel of meal *w'* not, 3615
1Ch 20:1 *w'* the country of the children of 7843
Ps 137:3 they that *w'* us required of us 8437
Isa 6:11 cities be *w'* without inhabitant, 7582
19:5 the river shall be *w'* and dried up. 2717
60:12 those nations shall be utterly *w'*. "
Jer 44:6 and they are *w'* and desolate, as 2723
Eze 30:7 the midst of the cities that are *w'*. 2717
Joe 1:10 The field is *w'*, the land mourneth;7703
10 land mourneth; for the corn is *w'*: "
Lu 15:13 there *w'* his substance with riotous1287
16:1 unto him that he had *w'* his goods.* "
Ga 1:13 the church of God, and *w'* it: *4199

wasteness
Zep 1:15 a day of *w'* and desolation, a day 7722

waster
Pr 18:9 brother to him that is a great *w'*. *7843
Isa 54:16 I have created the *w'* to destroy. * "

wastes
Isa 61:4 And they shall build the old *w'*, 2723
Jer 49:13 cities thereof shall be perpetual *w'*. * "
Eze 33:24 those *w'* of the land of Israel * "
27 they that are in the *w'* shall fall by* "
36:4 to the desolate *w'*, and to the cities * "
10 and the *w'* shall be builded: * "
33 cities, and the *w'* shall be builded.* "

wasteth
Job 14:10 But man dieth, and *w'* away: ‡2522
Ps 91:6 destruction that *w'* at noonday. 7736
Pr 19:26 He that *w'* his father, and †‡7703

wasting
Isa 59:7 *w'* and destruction are in their *7701
60:18 *w'* nor destruction within thy * "

watch See also WATCHED; WATCHES; WATCHETH; WATCHFUL; WATCHING; WATCHMAN; WATCHTOWER.
Ge 31:49 the Lord *w'* between me and thee, 6822
Ex 14:24 in the morning *w'* the Lord looked 821
J'g 7:19 in the beginning of the middle *w'*; "
19 they had but newly set the *w'*: 8104
1Sa 11:11 midst of the host in the morning *w'* 821
19:11 unto David's house, to *w'* him, 8104
2Sa 13:34 the young man that kept the *w'* 6822
2Ki 11:5 keepers of the *w'* of the king's 4931
6 shall ye keep the *w'* of the house, "
7 they shall keep the *w'* of the house "
2Ch 20:24 Judah came toward the *w'* tower 4707
23:6 shall keep the *w'* of the Lord. 4931
Ezr 8:29 *W'* ye, and keep them, until ye 8245
Ne 4:9 set a *w'* against them day and 4929
7:3 of Jerusalem, every one in his *w'*, "
Job 7:12 that thou settest a *w'* over me? "
14:16 dost thou not *w'* over my sin? 8104
Ps 90:4 it is past, and as a *w'* in the night. 821
102:7 I *w'*, and am as a sparrow alone 8245
130:6 than they that *w'* for the morning:*8104
6 than they that *w'* for the morning.* "
141:3 Set a *w'*, O Lord, before my mouth:8108
Isa 21:5 the table, *w'* in the watchtower, 6822
29:20 all that *w'* for iniquity are cut off: 8245
Jer 5:6 a leopard shall *w'* over their cities: "
Jer 31:28 so will I *w'* over them, to build, and 8245
44:27 I will *w'* over them for evil, and not "
51:12 make the *w'* strong, set up the 4929
Na 2:1 *w'* the way, make thy loins strong,6822
Hab 2:1 I will stand upon my *w'*, and set 4931
1 will *w'* to see what he will say *6822
M't 14:25 fourth *w'* of the night Jesus went 5438
24:42 *W'* therefore: for ye know not 1127
43 in what *w'* the thief would come, 5438
25:13 *W'* therefore, for ye know neither 1127
26:38 tarry ye here, and *w'* with me. "
40 could ye not *w'* with me one hour? "
41 *W'* and pray, that ye enter not into "
27:65 Ye have a *w'*: go your way, make *2892
66 sealing the stone, and setting a *w'*.* "
28:11 some of the *w'* came into the city,* "
M'r 6:48 about the fourth *w'* of the night 5438
13:33 Take ye heed, *w'* and pray: for ye 69
34 and commanded the porter to *w'*. 1127
35 *W'* ye therefore: for ye know not "
37 I say unto you I say unto all, *W'*. "
14:34 unto death: tarry ye here, and *w'*. "
37 couldest not thou *w'* one hour? "
38 *W'* ye and pray, lest ye enter into "
Lu 2:8 keeping *w'* over their flock by 5438
12:38 if he shall come in the second *w'*, "
38 or come in the third *w'*, and find * "
21:36 *W'* ye therefore, and pray always, 69
Ac 20:31 Therefore *w'*, and remember, that 1127
1Co 16:13 *W'* ye, stand fast in the faith, quit "
Col 4:2 *w'* in the same with thanksgiving;* "
1Th 5:6 others; but let us *w'* and be sober. "
2Ti 4:5 But *w'* thou in all things, endure *3525
Heb13:17 they *w'* for your souls, as they that 69
1Pe 4:7 sober, and *w'* unto prayer. *3525
Re 3:3 If therefore thou shalt not *w'*, I 1127

watched
Ps 59: *title* and they *w'* the house to kill him.8104
Jer 20:10 All my familiars *w'* for my halting,* "
31:28 that like as I have *w'* over them, 8245
La 4:17 *w'* for a nation that could not save6822
Da 9:14 hath the Lord *w'* upon the evil, 8245
M't 24:43 he would have *w'*, and would not 1127
27:36 sitting down they *w'* him there; 5083
M'r 3:2 they *w'* him, whether he would 3906
Lu 6:7 the scribes and Pharisees *w'* him, "
12:39 he would have *w'*, and not have 1127
14:1 the sabbath day, that they *w'* him.*3906
20:20 they *w'* him, and sent forth spies, "
Ac 9:24 they *w'* the gates day and night to "

watcher See also WATCHERS.
Da 4:13 a *w'* and an holy one came down 5894
23 the king saw a *w'* and an holy one "

watchers
Jer 4:16 that *w'* come from a far country, 5341
Da 4:17 matter is by the decree of the *w'*, 5894

watches
Ne 7:3 *w'* of the inhabitants of Jerusalem,4931
12:9 were over against them in the *w'*.* "
Ps 63:6 meditate on thee in the night *w'*. 821
119:148 Mine eyes prevent the night *w'*, "
La 2:19 beginning of the *w'* pour out thine "

watcheth
Ps 37:32 The wicked *w'* the righteous, and 6822
Eze 7:6 the end is come: it *w'* for thee; *6974
Re 16:15 Blessed is he that *w'*, and keepeth 1127

watchful
Re 3:2 Be *w'*, and strengthen the things 1127

watching See also WATCHINGS.
1Sa 4:13 sat upon a seat by the wayside *w'*:6822
Pr 8:34 heareth me, *w'* daily at my gates, 8245
La 4:17 in our *w'* we have watched for a 6822
M't 27:54 they that were with him, *w'* Jesus,5083
Lu 12:37 lord when he cometh shall find *w'*:1127
Eph 6:18 and *w'* thereunto with all 69

watchings
2Co 6:5 in tumults, in labours, in *w'*, in 70
11:27 painfulness, in *w'* often, in hunger "

watchman See also WATCHMAN'S; WATCHMEN.
2Sa 18:24 the *w'* went up to the roof over the6822
25 And the *w'* cried, and told the king."
26 the *w'* saw another man running: "
26 and the *w'* called unto the porter, "
27 And the *w'* said, Me thinketh the "
2Ki 9:17 there stood a *w'* on the tower in "
18 the *w'* told, saying, The messenger "
20 And the *w'* told, saying, He came "
Ps 127:1 city, the *w'* waketh but in vain. 8104
Isa 21:6 set a *w'*, let him declare what he 6822
11, 11 *W'*, what of the night? 8104
12 The *w'* said, The morning cometh, "
Eze 3:17 thee a *w'* unto the house of Israel: 6822
33:2 coasts, and set him for their *w'*: "
6 But if the *w'* see the sword come, "
7 thee a *w'* unto the house of Israel; "
Ho 9:8 *w'* of Ephraim was with my God: "

watchman's
Eze 33:6 blood will I require at the *w'* hand.6822

watchmen
1Sa 14:16 *w'* of Saul in Gibeah of Benjamin 6822
2Ki 17:9 from the tower of the *w'* to the 5341
18:8 from the tower of the *w'* to the "
Ca 3:3 The *w'* that go about the city 8104
5:7 The *w'* that went about the city "
Isa 52:8 Thy *w'* shall lift up the voice; 6822
56:10 His *w'* are blind: they are all "
62:6 I have set *w'* upon thy walls, O 8104
Jer 6:17 I set *w'* over you, saying, Hearken6822
31:6 the *w'* upon the mount Ephraim 5341
51:12 the watch strong, set up the *w'*, 8104
Mic 7:4 the day of thy *w'* and thy visitation6822

watchtower See also WATCH and TOWER.
Isa 21: 5 the table, watch in the w·, eat, *6844
8 I stand continually upon the w· in4707
water See also WATERCOURSE; WATERED; WATEREST; WATERETH; WATERFLOOD; WATERING; WATERPOT; WATERS; WATERSPOUTS; WATERSPRINGS.
Ge 2:10 went out of Eden to w· the garden;8248
16: 7 found her by a fountain of w· in 4325
18: 4 Let a little w·, I pray you, be "
21:14 and took bread, and a bottle of w·, "
15 And the w· was spent in the bottle, "
19 her eyes, and she saw a well of w·, "
19 went, and filled the bottle with w·, "
25 Abimelech because of a well of w·, "
24:11 by a well of w· at the time of the "
11 time that women go out to draw w·. "
13 I stand here by the well of w·; 4325
13 of the city come out to draw w·: "
17 thee, drink a little w· of thy pitcher." "
32 and w· to wash his feet, and the "
43 I stand by the well of w·; and it "
43 virgin cometh forth to draw w·, * "
43 a little w· of thy pitcher to drink; 4325
26:18 Isaac digged again the wells of w·, "
19 found there a well of springing w·. "
20 herdmen, saying, The w· is ours: "
32 said unto him, We have found w·. "
29: 7 w· ye the sheep, and go and feed 8248
8 mouth; then we w· the sheep. "
37:24 was empty, there was no w· in it. 4325
43:24 and gave them w·, and they washed "
49: 4 Unstable as w·, thou shalt not excel;"
Ex 2:10 Because I drew him out of the w·. "
16 and they came and drew w·, and filled
16 troughs to w· their father's flock. 8248
19 and also drew w· enough for us, "
4: 9 shalt take of the w· of the river, 4325
9 the w· which thou takest out of the "
7:15 lo, he goeth out unto the w·; and "
18 lothe to drink of the w· of the river. "
19 upon all their pools of w·, that they "
21 not drink of the w· of the river; "
24 digged round about the river for w·" "
24 for they could not drink of the w· of" "
8:20 lo, he cometh forth to the w·; and "
12: 9 nor sodden at all with w·, but roast "
15:22 in the wilderness, and found no w·. "
27 where were twelve wells of w·, "
17: 1 was no w· for the people to drink. "
2 said, Give us w· that we may drink." "
3 the people thirsted there for w·; "
6 there shall come w· out of it, that "
20: 4 that is in the w· under the earth: "
23:25 shall bless thy bread, and thy w·; "
29: 4 and shalt wash them with w·. "
30:18 and thou shalt put w· therein. "
20 they shall wash with w·, that they "
32:20 powder, and strawed it upon the w·, "
34:28 did neither eat bread, nor drink w·. "
40: 7 the altar, and shalt put w· therein. "
12 and wash them with w·. "
30 and put w· there, to wash withal. "
Le 1: 9 and his legs shall he wash in w·: "
13 the inwards and the legs with w·: "
6:28 be both scoured, and rinsed in w·. "
8: 6 his sons, and wash them with w·. "
21 the inwards and the legs in w·; "
11:32 is done, it must be put into w·, and "
34 on which such w· cometh shall be "
36 wherein there is plenty of w·, shall "
38 But if any w· be put upon the seed, "
14: 5 an earthen vessel over running w·: "
6 was killed over the running w·: "
8 and wash himself in w·, that he "
9 he shall wash his flesh in w·, and "
50 an earthen vessel over running w·: "
51 in the running w·, and sprinkle the "
52 with the running w·, and with the "
15: 5, 6, 7, 8, 10 and bathe himself in w·, "
11 hath not rinsed his hands in w·, "
11 his clothes, and bathe himself in w·," "
12 vessel of wood shall be rinsed in w·. "
13 and bathe his flesh in running w·, "
16 he shall wash all his flesh in w·, "
17 shall be washed with w·, and be "
18 shall both bathe themselves in w·, "
21, 22, 27 and bathe himself in w·, "
16: 4 shall he wash his flesh in w·, and so "
24 shall wash his flesh with w· in the "
26, 28 and bathe his flesh in w·, "
17:15 and bathe himself in w·, and be "
22: 6 unless he wash his flesh with w·. "
Nu 5:17 And the priest shall take holy w· in "
17 shall take, and put it into the w·: "
18 bitter w· that causeth the curse: "
19 be thou free from this bitter w· "
22 And this w· that causeth the curse "
23 blot them out with the bitter w·: "
24 the woman to drink the bitter w· "
24 the w· that causeth the curse shall "
26 cause the woman to drink the w·. "
27 he hath made her to drink the w·, "
27 the w· that causeth the curse shall "
8: 7 Sprinkle w· of purifying upon "
19: 7 and he shall bathe his flesh in w·, "
8 her shall wash his clothes in w·, "
8 bathe his flesh in w·, and shall be "
9 of Israel for a w· of separation: "
13 the w· of separation was not "
17 running w· shall be put thereto in "
18 take hyssop, and dip it in the w·, "
19 clothes, and bathe himself in w·, "
20 the w· of separation hath not been "
21 that sprinkleth the w· of separation" "
21 that toucheth the w· of separation "

Nu 20: 2 was no w· for the congregation: 4325
5 neither is there any w· to drink. "
8 it shall give forth his w·, and thou "
8 forth to them w· out of the rock: "
10 we fetch you w· out of this rock? "
11 and the w· came out abundantly, "
13 This is the w· of Meribah; because* "
17 will we drink of the w· of the wells: "
19 if I and my cattle drink of thy w·, "
24 my word at the w· of Meribah. * "
21: 5 is no bread, neither is there any w·; "
16 together, and I will give them w·. "
24: 7 pour the w· out of his buckets, and "
27:14 sanctify me at the w· before their "
14 is the w· of Meribah in Kadesh in* "
31:23 purified with the w· of separation: "
23 ye shall make go through the w·. "
33: 9 Elim were twelve fountains of w·, "
14 was no w· for the people to drink. "
De 2: 6 also buy w· of them for money, "
28 and give me w· for money, that I "
8: 7 good land, a land of brooks and w·, "
15 drought, where there was no w·; "
15 forth w· out of the rock of flint; "
9: 9 neither did eat bread nor drink w·: "
18 did neither eat bread, nor drink w·, "
11: 4 he made the w· of the Red sea to "
11 drinketh w· of the rain of heaven: "
12:16, 24 pour it upon the earth as w·. "
15:23 shalt pour it upon the ground as w·." "
23: 4 met you not with bread and with w· "
11 on, he shall wash himself with w·: "
29:11 wood unto the drawer of thy w·: "
Jos 2:10 dried up the w· of the Red sea for "
3: 8 to the brink of the w· of Jordan, * "
15 were dipped in the brim of the w·, "
7: 5 people melted, and became as w·. "
9:21 and drawers of w· unto all the "
23 and drawers of w· for the house of "
27 drawers of w· for the congregation," "
15: 9 the fountain of the w· of Nephtoah,* "
19 land; give me also springs of w·. "
16: 1 unto the w· of Jericho on the east,* "
J'g 1:15 land; give me also springs of w·. "
4:19 Give me,...a little w· to drink; "
5: 4 the clouds also dropped w·. "
11 of archers in the places of drawing w·, "
25 He asked w·, and she gave him 4325
6:38 out of the fleece, a bowl full of w·. "
7: 4 bring them down unto the w·, and "
5 down the people unto the w·: "
5 Every one that lappeth of the w· "
6 down upon their knees to drink w·. "
15:19 jaw, and there came w· thereout; "
1Sa 7: 6 drew w·, and poured it out before "
9:11 maidens going out to draw w·, "
25:11 I then take my bread, and my w·, "
26:11 and the cruse of w·, and let us go. "
12 the cruse of w· from Saul's bolster; "
16 cruse of w· that was at his bolster. "
30:11 eat; and they made him drink w·; "
12 eaten no bread, nor drunk any w·, "
2Sa 14:14 and are as w· spilt on the ground, "
17:20 They be gone over the brook of w·. "
21 Arise, and pass quickly over the w·: "
21:10 until w· dropped upon them out of "
23:15 of the w· of the well of Beth-lehem," "
16 and drew w· out of the well of "
1Ki 13: 8 bread nor drink w· in this place: "
9 Eat no bread, nor drink w·, nor "
16 will I eat bread nor drink w· with "
17 eat no bread nor drink w· there, "
18 he may eat bread and drink w·. "
19 bread in his house, and drank w·. "
22 hast eaten bread and drunk w· in "
22 Eat no bread, and drink no w·; "
14:15 Israel, as a reed is shaken in the w·," "
17:10 I pray thee, a little w· in a vessel, "
18: 4 and fed them with bread and w·.) "
5 unto all fountains of w·, and unto "
13 and fed them with bread and w·? "
33 Fill four barrels with w·, and pour "
35 the w· ran round about the altar; "
35 he filled the trench also with w·. "
38 up the w· that was in the trench. "
19: 6 coals, and a cruse of w· at his head. "
22:27 affliction and with w· of affliction. "
2Ki 2:19 the w· is naught, and the ground "
3: 9 there was no w· for the host, and "
11 poured w· on the hands of Elijah. "
17 that valley shall be filled with w·, "
19 good tree, and stop all wells of w·, "
20 there came w· by the way of Edom," "
20 and the country was filled with w·. "
22 and the sun shone upon the w·, "
22 the Moabites saw the w· on the "
25 they stopped all the wells of w·, "
6: 5 beam the axe head fell into the w·: "
22 set bread and w· before them, that "
8:15 a thick cloth, and dipped it in w·, "
20:20 and brought w· into the city, are "
1Ch 11:17 of the w· of the well of Beth-lehem, "
18 drew w· out of...well of Beth-lehem, "
2Ch 18:26 affliction and with w· of affliction, "
32: 4 Assyria come, and find much w·? "
Ezr 10: 6 he did eat no bread, nor drink w·: "
Ne 3:26 against the w· gate toward the east," "
8: 1 street that was before the w· gate; "
3 street that was before the w· gate "
16 and in the street of the w· gate, "
9:15 forth w· for them out of the rock "
20 and gavest them w· for their thirst. "
12:37 even unto the w· gate eastward. "
13: 2 of Israel with bread and with w·, "
Job 8:11 can the flag grow without w·? "
9:30 I wash myself with snow w·, 1119

Job 14: 9 through the scent of w· it will bud,4325
15:16 which drinketh iniquity like w·? "
22: 7 not given w· to the weary to drink, "
34: 7 who drinketh up scorning like w·? "
36:27 he maketh small the drops of w·: "
Ps 1: 3 a tree planted by the rivers of w·, "
6: 6 I w· my couch with my tears. 4529
22:14 I am poured out like w·, and all 4325
42: 1 hart panteth after the w· brooks. "
63: 1 and thirsty land, where no w· is; "
65: 9 the river of God, which is full of w·: "
66:12 went through fire and through w·: "
72: 6 as showers that w· the earth. 2222
77:17 The clouds poured out w·: the 4325
79: 3 Their blood have they shed like w· "
88:17 came round about me daily like w·;" "
107:35 the wilderness into a standing w·, "
109:18 let it come into his bowels like w·, "
114: 8 turned the rock into a standing w·, "
Pr 8:24 no fountains abounding with w·. "
17:14 is as when one letteth out w·: "
20: 5 the heart of man is like deep w·; "
21: 1 of the Lord, as the rivers of w·: * "
25:21 he be thirsty, give him w· to drink: "
27:19 As in w· face answereth to face, so "
30:16 the earth that is not filled with w·; "
Ec 2: 6 I made me pools of w·, "
6 to w· therewith the wood that 8248
Isa 1:22 dross, thy wine mixed with w·: 4325
30 and as a garden that hath no w·. "
3: 1 bread, and the whole stay of w·, "
12: 3 draw w· out of the wells of salvation." "
14:23 for the bittern, and pools of w·: "
16: 9 I will w· thee with my tears, O 7301
21:14 brought w· to him that was thirsty,4325
22:11 two walls for the w· of the old pool: "
27: 3 I will w· it every moment: lest 8248
30:14 or to take w· withal out of the pit. 4325
20 adversity, and the w· of affliction, "
32: 2 as rivers of w· in a dry place, as "
35: 7 and the thirsty land springs of w·: "
37:25 I have digged, and drunk w·; and "
41:17 When the poor and needy seek w·, "
18 make the wilderness a pool of w·, "
18 and the dry land springs of w·. "
44: 3 pour w· upon him that is thirsty, "
4 as willows by the w· courses. * "
12 he drinketh no w·, and is faint. "
49:10 by the springs of w· shall he guide "
50: 2 stinketh, because there is no w·, "
58:11 like a spring of w·, whose waters "
63:12 dividing the w· before them, to "
Jer 2:13 broken cisterns, that can hold no w·." "
8:14 and given us w· of gall to drink, "
9:15 and give them w· of gall to drink. "
13: 1 thy loins, and put it not in w·. "
14: 3 came to the pits, and found no w·; "
23:15 and make them drink the w· of gall:" "
38: 6 in the dungeon there was no w·: "
La 1:16 mine eye runneth down with w·, "
2:19 pour out thine heart like w· before "
3:48 eye runneth down with rivers of w·" "
5: 4 We have drunken our w· for money;" "
Eze 4:11 shalt drink also w· by measure, "
16 and they shall drink w· by measure," "
17 That they may want bread and w·, "
7:17 and all knees shall be weak as w·. "
12:18 drink thy w· with trembling and "
19 drink their w· with astonishment, "
16: 4 neither wast thou washed in w· to "
9 Then washed I thee with w·; yea, "
17: 7 he might w· it by the furrows of 8248
21: 7 and all knees shall be weak as w·: 4325
24: 3 set it on, and also pour w· into it: "
26:12 and thy dust in the midst of the w·.*" "
31:14 in their height, all that drink w·: "
16 of Lebanon, all that drink w·, "
32: 6 also w· with thy blood the land 8248
36:25 will I sprinkle clean w· upon you, 4325
Da 1:12 us pulse to eat, and w· to drink. "
Ho 2: 5 that give me my bread and my w·, "
5:10 my wrath upon them that like w·. "
10: 7 is cut off as the foam upon the w·. "
Joe 3:18 and shall w· the valley of Shittim. 8248
Am 4: 8 unto one city, to drink w·; 4325
8:11 famine of bread, not a thirst for w·, "
Jon 3: 7 let them not feed, nor drink w·: "
Na 2: 8 Nineveh is of old like a pool of w·: "
Hab 3:10 overflowing of the w· passed by: * "
Zec 9:11 out of the pit wherein is no w·. "
M't 3:11 I indeed baptize you with w· unto 5204
16 went up straightway out of the w·: "
10:42 these little ones a cup of cold w· "
14:28 bid me come unto thee on the w·. *5204
29 he walked on the w·, to go to Jesus.*" "
17:15 into the fire, and oft into the w·. "
27:24 he took w·, and washed his hands "
M'r 1: 8 I indeed have baptized you with w·: "
10 coming up out of the w·, he saw "
9:41 you a cup of w· to drink in my name," "
14:13 you a man bearing a pitcher of w·: "
Lu 3:16 all, I indeed baptize you with w·; "
7:44 thou gavest me no w· for my feet: "
8:23 they were filled with w·, and were in "
24 wind and the raging of the w·: 5204
25 commandeth even the winds and w·, "
16:24 may dip the tip of his finger in w·, "
22:10 meet you, bearing a pitcher of w·; "
Joh 1:26 them, saying, I baptize with w·: "
31 am I come baptizing with w·. "
33 he that sent me to baptize with w·, "
2: 7 them, Fill the waterpots with w·. "
9 tasted the w· that was made wine, "
9 servants which drew the w· knew;) "
3: 5 Except a man be born of w· and of "
23 because there was much w· there: "

Joh 4: 7 a woman of Samaria to draw w·: 5204
10 he would have given thee living w·. "
11 then hast thou that living w·?
13 Whosoever drinketh of this w· shall "
14 whosoever drinketh of the w· that I "
14 w· that I shall give him shall be in "
14 him a well of w· springing up into "
15 Sir, give me this w·, that I thirst "
46 Galilee, where he made the w· wine. "
5: 3 waiting for the moving of the w·. * "
4 into the pool, and troubled the w·:* "
4 first after the troubling of the w· * "
7 when the w· is troubled, to put me "
7: 38 belly shall flow rivers of living w·. "
13: 5 that he poureth w· into a bason, "
19: 34 came there out blood and w·. "
Ac 1: 5 For John truly baptized with w·; "
8: 36 way, they came unto a certain w·: "
36 See, here is w·; what doth hinder "
38 they went down both into the w·, "
39 they were come up out of the w·, "
10: 47 Can any man forbid w·, that these "
11: 16 said, John indeed baptized with w·; "
Eph 5: 26 the washing of w· by the word, "
1Ti 5: 23 Drink no longer w·, but use a little 5202
Heb 9: 19 of calves and of goats, with w·, and 5204
10: 22 our bodies washed with pure w·. "
Jas 3: 11 at the same place sweet w· and bitter? "
12 both yield salt w· and fresh. 5204
1Pe 3: 20 is, eight souls were saved by w·. "
2Pe 2: 17 These are wells without w·, clouds 504
3: 5 standing out of the w· and in the w·: 5204
6 being overflowed with w·, perished: "
1Jo 5: 6 is he that came by w· and blood, "
6 not by w· only, but by w· and blood. "
8 earth, the spirit, and the w·, and "
Jude 12 clouds they are without w·, carried 504
Re 12: 15 out of his mouth w· as a flood 5204
16: 12 and the w· thereof was dried up, "
21: 6 the fountain of the w· of life freely. "
22: 1 shewed me a pure river of w· of life, "
17 will, let him take the w· of life freely. "

water-brooks See WATER and BROOKS.

watercourse See also WATER and COURSES.
2Ch 32: 30 the upper w· of Gihon, *4161,4325
Job 38: 25 w· for the overflowing of waters, *8585

watered See also WATEREDST.
Ge 2: 6 w· the whole face of the ground. 8248
13: 10 that it was well w· every where, 4945
29: 2 out of that well they w· the flocks: 8248
3 the well's mouth, and w· the sheep, "
10 w· the flock of Laban his mother's "
Ex 2: 17 helped them, and w· their flock. "
19 enough for us, and w· the flock. "
Pr 11: 25 watereth shall be w· also himself. 3384
Isa 58: 11 and thou shalt be like a w· garden, 7302
Jer 31: 12 their soul shall be as a w· garden; "
1Co 3: 6 I have planted, Apollos w·; but 4222

wateredst
De 11: 10 w· it with thy foot, as a garden of 8248

waterest
Ps 65: 9 Thou visitest the earth, and w· it: 7783
10 Thou w· the ridges thereof 7301

watereth
Ps 104: 13 He w· the hills from his chambers: 8248
Pr 11: 25 he that w· shall be watered also 7301
Isa 55: 10 w· the earth, and maketh it bring "
1Co 3: 7 any thing, neither he that w·; 4222
8 planteth and he that w· are one: "

waterflood
Ps 69: 15 Let not the w· overflow me, 7641,4325

watering
Ge 30: 38 in the gutters in the w· troughs 4325
Job 37: 11 by w· he wearieth the thick cloud: *7377
Lu 13: 15 stall, and lead him away to w·? 4222

waterpot See also WATERPOTS.
Joh 4: 28 The woman then left her w·, and 5201

waterpots
Joh 2: 6 were set there six w· of stone, 5201
7 unto them, Fill the w· with water. "

waters
Ge 1: 2 moved upon the face of the w·. 4325
6 firmament in the midst of the w·. "
6 and let it divide the w· from the w·. "
7 divided the w· which were under "
7 from the w· which were above the "
9 Let the w· under the heaven be "
10 together of the w· called he Seas: "
20 Let the w· bring forth abundantly "
21 the w· brought forth abundantly, "
22 multiply, and fill the w· in the seas, "
6: 17 bring a flood of w· upon the earth, "
7: 6 the flood of w· was upon the earth. "
7 ark, because of the w· of the flood. "
10 that the w· of the flood were upon "
17 the w· increased, and bare up the "
18 w· prevailed, and were increased "
18 ark went upon the face of the w·. "
19 w· prevailed exceedingly upon the "
20 cubits upward did the w· prevail; "
24 the w· prevailed upon the earth "
8: 1 the earth, and the w· asswaged; "
3 the w· returned from off the earth "
3 and fifty days the w· were abated. "
5 the w· decreased continually until "
7 until the w· were dried up from off "
8 to see if the w· were abated from "
9 the w· were on the face of the whole "
11 Noah knew that the w· were abated "
13 w· were dried up from off the earth "
9: 11 off any more by the w· of a flood; "
Ge 9: 15 the w· shall no more become a flood 4325
Ex 7: 17 upon the w· which are in the river, "
19 thine hand upon the w· of Egypt, "
20 smote the w· that were in the river, "
20 all the w·...in the river were turned "
8: 6 out his hand over the w· of Egypt; "
14: 21 dry land, and the w· were divided. "
22 the w· were a wall unto them on "
26 w· may come...upon the Egyptians, "
28 the w· returned, and covered the "
29 the w· were a wall unto them on "
15: 8 the w· were gathered together, "
10 they sank as lead in the mighty w·. "
19 brought again the w· of the sea "
23 could not drink of the w· of Marah, "
25 which when he had cast into the w·, "
25 the w· were made sweet: "
27 and they encamped there by the w·. "
Le 11: 9 shall ye eat of all that are in the w·: "
9 hath fins and scales in the w·, in "
10 of all that move in the w·, and of "
10 any living thing which is in the w·, "
12 hath no fins nor scales in the w·, "
46 living creature...moveth in the w·, "
Nu 21: 22 will not drink of the w· of the well: "
24: 6 and as cedar trees beside the w·. "
7 and his seed shall be in many w·, "
De 4: 18 that is in the w· beneath the earth:* "
5: 8 that is in the w· beneath the earth:* "
10: 7 to Jotbath, a land of rivers of w·. * "
14: 9 shall ye eat of all that are in the w·: "
32: 51 Israel at the w· of Meribah-Kadesh, "
33: 8 didst strive at the w· of Meribah; "
Jos 3: 13 shall rest in the w· of the Jordan, "
13 w· of the Jordan shall be cut off "
13 from the w· that come down from "
16 the w· which came down from above "
4: 7 the w· of Jordan were cut off before "
7 the w· of Jordan were cut off: "
18 the w· of Jordan returned unto "
23 God dried up the w· of Jordan from "
5: 1 Lord had dried up the w· of Jordan "
11: 5 pitched together at the w· of Merom, "
7 against them by the w· of Merom "
15: 7 toward the w· of En-shemesh, "
18: 15 out to the well of w· of Nephtoah: "
J'g 5: 19 in Taanach by the w· of Megiddo; "
7: 24 them the w· unto Beth-barah "
24 took the w· unto Beth-barah and "
2Sa 5: 20 before me, as the breach of w·. "
12: 27 and have taken the city of w·. "
22: 12 dark w·, and thick clouds of the "
17 he drew me out of many w·; "
2Ki 2: 8 smote the w·, and they were divided "
14 and smote the w·, and said, Where "
14 when he also had smitten the w·, "
21 forth unto the spring of the w·, "
21 the Lord, I have healed these w·; "
22 the w· were healed unto this day, "
5: 12 better than all the w· of Israel? "
18: 31 ye every one the w· of his cistern: "
19: 24 have digged and drunk strange w·, "
1Ch 14: 11 hand like the breaking forth of w·: "
2Ch 32: 3 men to stop the w· of the fountains "
Ne 9: 11 as a stone into the mighty w·. "
Job 3: 24 are poured out like the w·. * "
5: 10 and sendeth w· upon the fields: "
11: 16 remember it as w· that pass away: "
12: 15 Behold, he withholdeth the w·, "
14: 11 As the w· fail from the sea, and the "
19 The w· wear the stones: thou "
22: 11 and abundance of w· cover thee. "
24: 18 He is swift as the w·; their portion "
19 and heat consume the snow w·: so "
26: 5 are formed from under the w·, "
8 He bindeth up the w· in his thick "
10 compassed the w· with bounds, "
27: 20 Terrors take hold on him as w·, "
28: 4 even the w· forgotten of the foot:* "
25 he weigheth the w· by measure. 4325
29: 19 My root was spread out by the w·, "
30: 14 upon me as a wide breaking in of w·: *
37: 10 breadth of the w· is straitened. 4325
38: 25 for the overflowing of w·, "
30 The w· are hid as with a stone, 4325
34 abundance of w· may cover thee? "
Ps 18: 11 round about him were dark w· and "
15 Then the channels of w· were seen, "
16 me, he drew me out of many w·. "
23: 2 he leadeth me beside the still w·. "
29: 3 voice of the Lord is upon the w·: "
3 the Lord is upon many w·. "
32: 6 surely in the floods of great w· they "
33: 7 He gathereth the w· of the sea "
46: 3 Though the w· thereof roar and be "
58: 7 Let them melt away as w· which * "
69: 1 the w· are come in unto my soul. "
2 I am come into deep w·, where "
14 hate me, and out of the deep w·. "
73: 10 and w· of a full cup are wrung out "
74: 13 the heads of the dragons in the w·. "
77: 16 w· saw thee, O God, the w· saw thee; "
19 sea, and thy path in the great w·, "
78: 13 he made the w· to stand as an heap. "
16 caused w· to run down like rivers. "
20 the rock, that the w· gushed out, "
81: 7 I proved thee at the w· of Meribah. "
93: 4 mightier than the noise of many w·, "
104: 3 beams of his chambers in the w·: "
6 the w· stood above the mountains. "
105: 29 He turned their w· into blood, and "
41 the rock, and the w· gushed out; "
106: 11 And the w· covered their enemies: "
32 angered him also at the w· of strife, "
107: 23 ships, that do business in great w·; "
114: 8 the flint into a fountain of w·. "
Ps 119: 136 Rivers of w· run down mine eyes, *4325
124: 4 Then the w· had overwhelmed us, "
5 proud w· had gone over our soul. "
136: 6 stretched...the earth above the w·: "
144: 7 and deliver me out of great w·, "
147: 18 his wind to blow, and the w· flow. "
148: 4 ye w· that be above the heavens. "
Pr 5: 15 Drink w· out of thine own cistern, "
15 running w· out of thine own well. "
16 and rivers of w· in the streets. *4325
8: 29 that the w· should not pass his "
9: 17 Stolen w· are sweet, and bread "
18: 4 of a man's mouth are as deep w·, "
25: 25 As cold w· to a thirsty soul, so is "
30: 4 hath bound the w· in a garment? "
Ec 11: 1 Cast thy bread upon the w·: for "
Ca 4: 15 a well of living w·, and streams "
5: 12 eyes of doves by the rivers of w·, * "
8: 7 Many w· cannot quench love, "
Isa 8: 6 the w· of Shiloah that go softly, "
7 up upon them the w· of the river, "
11: 9 the Lord, as the w· cover the sea. "
15: 6 the w· of Nimrim shall be desolate: "
9 w· of Dimon shall be full of blood: "
17: 12 like the rushing of mighty w·! "
13 rush like the rushing of many w·: "
18: 2 in vessels of bulrushes upon the w·, "
19: 5 And the w· shall fail from the sea, "
8 they that spread nets upon the w· "
22: 9 gathered...the w· of the lower pool. "
23: 3 And by great w· the seed of Sihor, "
28: 2 a flood of mighty w· overflowing, "
17 w· shall overflow the hiding place. "
30: 25 high hill, rivers and streams of w· "
32: 20 Blessed...ye that sow beside all w·, "
33: 16 be given him; his w· shall be sure. "
35: 6 the wilderness shall w· break out, "
36: 16 every one the w· of his own cistern; "
40: 12 measured the w· in the hollow of "
43: 2 When thou passest through the w·, "
16 sea, and a path in the mighty w·; "
20 because I give w· in the wilderness, "
48: 1 come forth out of the w· of Judah, "
21 caused the w· to flow out of the rock "
21 rock also, and the w· gushed out. "
51: 10 the sea, the w· of the great deep; "
54: 9 this is as the w· of Noah unto me: "
9 the w· of Noah should no more go "
55: 1 that thirsteth, come ye to the w·, "
57: 20 whose w· cast up mire and dirt. "
58: 11 spring of water, whose w· fail not. "
64: 2 the fire causeth the w· to boil. "
Jer 2: 13 forsaken...the fountain of living w·, "
18 of Egypt, to drink the w· of Sihor? "
18 to drink the w· of the river? "
6: 7 As a fountain casteth out her w·, "
9: 1 Oh that my head were w·, and mine "
18 and our eyelids gush out with w·. "
10: 13 is a multitude of w· in the heavens, "
14: 3 have sent their little ones to the w·: "
15: 18 me as a liar, and as w· that fail? "
17: 8 shall be as a tree planted by the w·, "
13 the Lord, the fountain of living w·. "
18: 14 the cold flowing w· that come from "
31: 9 them to walk by the rivers of w· "
41: 12 by the great w· that are in Gibeon. "
46: 7 whose w· are moved as the rivers? "
8 his w· are moved like the rivers; "
47: 2 w· rise up out of the north, and "
48: 34 for the w· also of Nimrim shall be "
50: 38 A drought is upon her w·; and they "
51: 13 O thou that dwellest upon many w·, "
16 is a multitude of w· in the heavens; "
55 her waves do roar like great w·, "
La 3: 54 W· flowed over mine head; then I "
Eze 1: 24 wings, like the noise of great w·, "
17: 5 he placed it by great w·, and set it "
8 planted in a good soil by great w·, "
19: 10 in thy blood, planted by the w·: "
10 of branches by reason of many w·. "
26: 19 thee, and great w· shall cover thee; "
27: 26 have brought thee into great w·: "
34 by the seas in the depths of the w·, "
31: 4 The w· made him great, the deep "
5 because of the multitude of w·, "
7 for his root was by great w·. "
14 none of all the trees by the w· exalt "
15 and the great w· were stayed: "
32: 2 troubledst the w· with thy feet and "
13 thereof from beside the great w·; "
14 Then will I make their w· deep, and "
34: 18 and to have drunk of the deep w·, "
43: 2 voice was like a noise of many w·: "
47: 1 w· issued out from under the "
1 the w· came down from under from "
2 there ran out w· on the right side. "
3 and he brought me through the w·; "
3 the w· were to the ancles. "
4 and brought me through the w·; "
4 the w· were to the knees. "
4 through; the w· were to the loins. "
5 for the w· were risen, w· to swim in, "
8 These w· issue out toward the east "
8 the sea, the w· shall be healed. "
9 these w· shall come thither: "
12 their w· they issued out of the "
19 even to the w· of strife in Kadesh, "
48: 28 unto the w· of strife in Kadesh, "
Da 12: 6, 7 was upon the w· of the river, "
Joe 1: 20 for the rivers of w· are dried up, * "
3: 18 rivers of Judah shall flow with w·, "
Am 5: 8 that calleth for the w· of the sea, "
24 But let judgment run down as w·, "
9: 6 he that calleth for the w· of the sea, "
Jon 2: 5 The w· compassed me about, even "
Mic 1: 4 as the w· that are poured down a "

Na 3: 3 that had the *w'* round about it, *4325
14 Draw thee *w'* for the siege, fortify "
Hab 2:14 of the Lord, as the *w'* cover the sea." "
3:15 through the heap of great *w'*. "
Zec 14: 8 *w'* shall go out from Jerusalem; "
M't 8:32 the sea, and perished in the *w'*. *5204*
M'r 9:22 him into the fire, and into the *w'*, "
2Co 11:26 in perils of *w'*, in perils of robbers,*4215*
Re 1:15 his voice as the sound of many *w'*. *5204*
7:17 them unto living fountains of *w'*: "
8:10 and upon the fountains of *w'*; "
11 and the third part of the *w'* became "
11 and many men died of the *w'*, "
11: 6 have power over *w'* to turn them to "
14: 2 heaven, as the voice of many *w'*, "
7 the sea, and the fountains of *w'*. "
16: 4 upon...rivers and fountains of *w'*; "
5 I heard the angel of the *w'* say, "
17: 1 whore that sitteth upon many *w'*: "
15 The *w'* which thou sawest, where "
19: 6 and as the voice of many *w'*, "

waterspouts
Ps 42: 7 unto deep at the noise of thy *w'*: 6794

watersprings
Ps 107:33 and the *w'* into dry ground; 4161,4325
35 and dry ground into *w'*. "

wave See also WAVED; WAVES.
Ex 29:24 shalt *w'* them...before the Lord. 5130
24 for a *w'* offering before the Lord. 8573
26 and *w'* it...before the Lord: 5130
26 for a *w'* offering before the Lord: 8573
27 the breast of the *w'* offering, "
Le 7:30 for a *w'* offering before the Lord. "
34 *w'* breast and the heave shoulder "
8:27 for a *w'* offering before the Lord. "
29 it for a *w'* offering before the Lord: "
9:21 for a *w'* offering before the Lord; "
10:14 *w'* breast and heave shoulder shall "
15 *w'* breast shall they bring with the "
15 the fat, to *w'* it...before the Lord; 5130
15 for a *w'* offering before the Lord; 8573
14:12 and *w'* them...before the Lord: 5130
12 for a *w'* offering before the Lord: 8573
24 shall *w'* them...before the Lord: 5130
24 for a *w'* offering before the Lord: 8573
23:11 *w'* the sheaf before the Lord, 5130
11 after...sabbath the priest shall *w'* it." "
12 when ye *w'* the sheaf an he lamb "
15 the sheaf of the *w'* offering; 8573
17 two *w'* loaves of two tenth deals: "
20 priest shall *w'* them with the bread 5130
20 for a *w'* offering before the Lord, 8573
Nu 5:25 *w'* the offering before the Lord, 5130
6:20 And the priest shall *w'* them for a "
20 for a *w'* offering before the Lord: 8573
20 the *w'* breast and heave shoulder: "
18:11 the *w'* offerings of the children of "
18 *w'* breast and as the right shoulder "
Jas 1: 6 is like a *w'* of the sea driven with *2830*

waved
Ex 29:27 of the heave offering, which is *w'*, 5130
Le 7:30 the breast may be *w'* for a wave "
8:27 *w'* them for a wave offering before "
29 *w'* it for a wave offering before the "
9:21 Aaron *w'* for a wave offering before "
14:21 for a trespass offering to be *w'*, 8573

wave-loaf See WAVE and LOAF.

wave-offering See WAVE and OFFERING.

wavereth
Jas 1: 6 he that *w'* is like a wave of the sea*1252*

wavering
Heb 10:23 profession of our faith without *w'*;**186*
Jas 1: 6 let him ask in faith, nothing *w'*. **1252*

waves
2Sa 22: 5 the *w'* of death compassed me, 4867
Job 9: 8 treadeth upon the *w'* of the sea. 1116
38:11 here shall thy proud *w'* be stayed?1530
Ps 42: 7 all thy *w'* and thy billows are gone 4867
65: 7 of the seas, the noise of their *w'*, 1530
88: 7 hast afflicted me with all thy *w'*. 4867
89: 9 when the *w'* thereof arise, thou 1530
93: 3 voice; the floods lift up their *w'*. 1796
4 yea, than the mighty *w'* of the sea.*4867
107:25 which lifteth up the *w'* thereof. 1530
29 so that the *w'* thereof are still. "
Isa 48:18 righteousness as the *w'* of the sea: "
51:15 divided the sea, whose *w'* roared: "
Jer 5:22 the *w'* thereof toss themselves, yet "
31:35 the sea when the *w'* thereof roar; "
51:42 with the multitude of the *w'* "
55 her *w'* do roar like great waters, "
Eze 26: 3 the sea causeth his *w'* to come up. "
Jon 2: 3 billows and thy *w'* passed over me. "
Zec 10:11 and shall smite the *w'* in the sea, "
M't 8:24 the ship was covered with the *w'*: *2949*
14:24 midst of the sea, tossed with *w'*: "
M'r 4:37 the *w'* beat into the ship, so that it "
Lu 21:25 the sea and the *w'* roaring; **4535*
Ac 27:41 broken with the violence of the *w'*.*2949*
Jude 13 Raging *w'* of the sea, foaming out "

wax See also WAXED; WAXEN; WAXETH; WAXING.
Ex 22:24 And my wrath shall *w'* hot, and I
32:10 that my wrath may *w'* hot against
11 why doth thy wrath *w'* hot against
22 not the anger of my lord *w'* hot:
Le 25:47 if a sojourner or stranger *w'* rich *
47 that dwelleth by him *w'* poor,
1Sa 3: 2 his eyes began to *w'* dim, that he
Job 6:17 What time they *w'* warm, they
14: 8 Though the root thereof *w'* old in

Ps 22:14 my heart is like *w'*; it is melted in 1749
68: 2 as *w'* melteth before the fire, so let "
97: 5 The hills melted like *w'* at the "
102:26 all of them shall *w'* old like a garment;
Isa 17: 4 the fatness of his flesh shall *w'* lean.
29:22 neither shall his face now *w'* pale.
50: 9 they all shall *w'* old as a garment;
51: 6 earth shall *w'* old like a garment,
Jer 6:24 our hands *w'* feeble: anguish hath
Mic 1: 4 shall be cleft, as *w'* before the fire,1749
M't 24:12 the love of many shall *w'* cold. *5594*
Lu 12:33 yourselves bags which *w'* not old, *3822*
1Ti 5:11 to *w'* wanton against Christ,* *2691*
2Ti 3:13 and seducers shall *w'* worse and *4298*
Heb 1:11 all shall *w'* old as doth a garment;*3822*

waxed See also WAXEN.
Ge 18:12 After I am *w'* old shall I have
26:13 And the man *w'* great, and went
41:56 the famine *w'* sore in the land of *
Ex 1: 7 multiplied and *w'* exceeding mighty;
20 people multiplied, and *w'* very mighty.
16:21 when the sun *w'* hot, it melted.
19:19 long, and *w'* louder and louder,
32:19 Moses' anger *w'* hot, and he cast
Nu 11:23 Is the Lord's hand *w'* short? thou
De 8: 4 Thy raiment *w'* not old upon thee,
32:15 But Jeshurun *w'* fat, and kicked:
Jos 23: 1 Joshua *w'* old and stricken in age.*
1Sa 2: 5 hath many children is *w'* feeble. *
2Sa 3: 1 David *w'* stronger and stronger, 1980
1 the house of Saul *w'* weaker and "
21:15 Philistines: and David *w'* faint.
2Ki 4:34 and the flesh of the child *w'* warm.
1Ch 11: 9 So David *w'* greater and greater: 1980
2Ch 13:21 Abijah *w'* mighty, and married
17:12 And Jehoshaphat *w'* great 1980
24:15 Jehoiada *w'* old, and was full of
Ne 9:21 their clothes *w'* not old, and their
Es 9: 4 Mordecai *w'* greater and greater. 1980
Ps 32: 3 bones *w'* old through my roaring
Jer 49:24 Damascus is *w'* feeble, and
50:43 of them, and his hands *w'* feeble:*
Da 8: 8 Therefore the he goat *w'* very great:*
9 horn, which *w'* exceeding great,
10 And it *w'* great, even to the host of
M't 13:15 For this people's heart is *w'* gross,*3975*
Lu 1:80 child grew, and *w'* strong in spirit,*2901*
2:40 child grew, and *w'* strong in spirit, "
13:19 and it grew, and *w'* a great tree; **1096*
Ac 13:46 Then Paul and Barnabas *w'* bold,**3955*
28:27 the heart of this people is *w'* gross,*3975*
Heb 11:34 made strong, *w'* valiant in fight, *1096*
Re 18: 3 merchants of the earth are *w'* rich *4147*

waxen See also WAXED.
Ge 19:13 the cry of them is *w'* great before
Le 25:25 If thy brother be *w'* poor, and
35 And if thy brother be *w'* poor, and
39 that dwelleth by thee be *w'* poor,
De 29: 5 clothes are not *w'* old upon you,
5 thy shoe is not *w'* old upon thy foot.
31:20 and filled themselves, and *w'* fat;
32:15 thou art *w'* fat, thou art grown
Jos 17:13 children of Israel were *w'* strong,
Jer 5:27 are become great, and *w'* rich.
28 They are *w'* fat, they shine: yea,
Eze 16: 7 thou hast increased and *w'* great,*

waxeth
Ps 6: 7 it *w'* old because of all mine
Heb 8:13 and *w'* old is ready to vanish *1095*

waxing
Ph'p 1:14 *w'* confident by my bonds, are **3982*

way See also ALWAY; AWAY; CAUSEWAY; HIGHWAY; PATHWAY; STRAIGHTWAY; WAYFARING; WAYMARKS; WAYS; WAYSIDE.
Ge 3:24 sword which turned every *w'*,
24 to keep the *w'* of the tree of life.
6:12 for all flesh had corrupted his *w'*
12:19 thy wife, take her, and go thy *w'*.
14:11 their victuals, and went their *w'*. 3212
16: 7 by the fountain in the *w'* to Shur. 1870
18:16 them to bring them on the *w'*. 7971
19 they shall keep the *w'* of the Lord,1870
33 And the Lord went his *w'*, as soon 3212
21:16 over against him a good *w'* off,
24:27 I being in the *w'*, the Lord led me 1870
40 with thee, and prosper thy *w'*; "
42 thou do prosper my *w'* which I go: "
48 had led me in the right *w'* to take "
56 the Lord hath prospered my *w'*; "
61 took Rebekah, and went his *w'*. 3212
62 Isaac came from the *w'* of the well 935
25:34 and rose up, and went his *w'*: 3212
28:20 will keep me in this *w'* that I go, 1870
32: 1 And Jacob went on his *w'*, and the "
33:16 that day on his *w'* unto Seir. "
35: 3 with me in the *w'* which I went. "
16 but a little *w'* to come to Ephrath.‡ 776
19 was buried in the *w'* to Ephrath, 1870
38:14 which is by the *w'* to Timnath; "
16 And he turned unto her by the *w'*, "
21 that was openly by the *w'* side? "
42:25 to give them provision for the *w'*: "
38 if mischief befall him by the *w'* in "
45:21 gave them provision for the *w'*. "
23 and meat for his father by the *w'*. "
24 See that ye fall not out by the *w'*. "
48: 7 in the land of Canaan in the *w'*, "
7 a little *w'* to come unto Ephrath: ‡ 776
7 buried her...in the *w'* of Ephrath; 1870
49:17 Dan shall be a serpent by the *w'*, an "
Ex 2:12 he looked this *w'* and that *w'*, 3541
4:24 came to pass by the *w'* in the inn, 1870
5:20 and Aaron, who stood in the *w'*, 7125
13:17 *w'* of the land of the Philistines, 1870

Ex 13:18 *w'* of the wilderness of the Red sea:1870
21 of a cloud, to lead them the *w'*; "
18: 8 had come upon them by the *w'*, "
20 the *w'* wherein they must walk, "
27 he went his *w'* unto his own land.
23:20 to keep thee in the *w'*, and to 1870
32: 8 out of the *w'* which I commanded "
33: 3 lest I consume thee in the *w'*. "
13 shew me now thy *w'*, that I may * "
Nu 13:17 Get you up this *w'* southward, and
14:25 wilderness by...*w'* of the Red sea. 1870
20:17 we will go by the king's high *w'*, "
19 unto him, We will go by the high *w'*: "
21: 1 Israel came by the *w'* of the spies;1870
4 Hor by the *w'* of the Red sea, "
4 much discouraged because of the *w'*. "
22 will go along by the king's high *w'*, "
33 and went up by the *w'* of Bashan: "
22:22 stood in the *w'* for an adversary "
23 angel of the Lord standing in the *w'*, "
23 the ass turned aside out of the *w'*, "
23 the ass, to turn her into the *w'*. "
26 no *w'* to turn either to the right "
31 angel of the Lord standing in the *w'*, "
32 because thy *w'* is perverse before, "
34 not that thou stoodest in the *w'* "
24:25 place: and Balak also went his *w'*. "
De 1: 2 Horeb by the *w'* of mount Seir "
19 *w'* of the mountain of the Amorites, "
22 again by the *w'* we must go up, "
31 in all the *w'* that ye went, until ye "
33 Who went in the *w'* before you, to "
33 shew you by what *w'* ye should go, "
40 wilderness by the *w'* of the Red sea. "
2: 1 wilderness by the *w'* of the Red sea, "
8 the *w'* of the plain from Elath, "
8 by the *w'* of the wilderness of Moab. "
27 I will go along by the high *w'*, I "
3: 1 and went up the *w'* to Bashan: "
6: 7 when thou walkest by the *w'*, and "
8: 2 *w'* which the Lord thy God led thee "
9:12 quickly turned aside out of the *w'* "
16 turned aside quickly out of the *w'* "
11:19 when thou walkest by the *w'*, when "
28 but turn aside out of the *w'* which I "
30 the *w'* where the sun goeth down, "
13: 5 to thrust thee out of the *w'* which "
14:24 And if the *w'* be long for thee, so "
17:16 henceforth return no more that *w'*. "
19: 3 Thou shalt prepare thee a *w'*, and "
6 because the *w'* is long, and slay "
22: 4 ass or his ox fall down by the *w'*, "
6 chance to be before thee in the *w'* "
23: 4 bread and with water in the *w'*, "
24: 9 God did unto Miriam by the *w'*, "
25:17 Amalek did unto thee by the *w'*, "
18 How he met thee by the *w'*, and "
27:18 the blind to wander out of the *w'*. "
28: 7 shall come out against thee one *w'*, "
25 shalt go out one *w'* against them, "
68 the *w'* whereof I spake unto thee, "
31:29 and turn aside from the *w'* which I "
Jos 1: 8 thou shalt make thy *w'* prosperous, "
2: 7 the *w'* to Jordan unto the fords; "
16 and afterward may ye go your *w'*. "
22 sought them throughout all the *w'*, "
3: 4 know the *w'* by which ye must go: "
4 have not passed this *w'* heretofore. "
5: 4 died in the wilderness by the *w'*, "
5 in the wilderness by the *w'* as they "
7 not circumcised them by the *w'*. "
8:15 fled by the *w'* of the wilderness. "
20 no power to flee this *w'* or that *w'*:2008
10:10 *w'* that goeth up to Beth-horon, 1870
12: 3 the east, the *w'* to Beth-jeshimoth; "
23:14 I am going the *w'* of all the earth: "
24:17 us in all the *w'* wherein we went, "
J'g 2:17 *w'* which their fathers walked in, "
19 doings, nor from their stubborn *w'*. "
22 they will keep the *w'* of the Lord "
5:10 in judgment, and walk by the *w'*. "
8:11 *w'* of them that dwelt in tents "
9:25 that came along that *w'* by them: "
18: 5 *w'* which we go shall be prosperous. "
6 the Lord is your *w'* wherein ye go. "
22 a good *w'* from the house of Micah, "
26 the children of Dan went their *w'*:1870
19: 5 of bread, and afterward go your *w'*. "
9 morrow get you early on your *w'*, 1870
14 they passed on and went their *w'*; 3212
27 house, and went out to go his *w'*: 1870
20:42 unto the *w'* of the wilderness; "
Ru 1: 7 on the *w'* to return unto...Judah. "
1Sa 1:18 woman went her *w'*, and did eat, "
6: 9 goeth up by the *w'* of his own coast "
12 the kine took the straight *w'* "
12 to the *w'* of Beth-shemesh, "
9: 6 shew us our *w'* that we should go.* "
8 to the man of God, to tell us our *w'*. "
12:23 teach you the good and the right *w'*: "
13:17 unto the *w'* that leadeth to Ophrah, "
18 turned the *w'* to Beth-horon: "
18 turned to the *w'* of the border that "
15: 2 how he laid wait for him in the *w'*, "
20 gone the *w'* which the Lord sent "
17:52 fell down by the *w'* to Shaaraim, "
20:22 arrows are beyond thee; go thy *w'*:3212
24: 3 came to the sheepcotes by the *w'*, 1870
7 out of the cave, and went on his *w'*. "
25:12 David's young men turned their *w'*, "
26: 3 which is before Jeshimon, by the *w'*. "
25 So David went on his *w'*, and Saul "
28:22 strength, when thou goest on thy *w'*. "
30: 2 them away, and went on their *w'*. "
2Sa 2:24 the *w'* of the wilderness of Gibeon. "
13:30 to pass, while they were in the *w'*, "

2Sa 13:34 much people by the w' of the hill 1870
15: 2 and stood beside the w' of the gate: "
23 toward the w' of the wilderness. "
16:13 David and his men went by the w', "
18:23 Ahimaaz ran by the w' of the plain, "
19:36 servant will go a little w' over Jordan*
22:31 As for God, his w' is perfect; 1870
33 and he maketh my w' perfect. "
1Ki 1:49 rose up, and went every man his w'."
2: 2 I go the w' of all the earth: be thou "
4 If thy children take heed to their w'."
8:25 thy children take heed to their w', "
32 to bring his w' upon his head; "
36 good w' wherein they should walk. "
11:29 the Shilonite found him in the w'; "
13: 9 by the same w' that thou camest. "
10 went another w', and returned not "
10 by the w' that he came to Beth-el. "
12 said unto them, What w' went he? "
12 seen what w' the man of God went, "
17 to go by the w' that thou camest. "
24 a lion met him by the w', and slew "
24 and his carcase was cast in the w', "
25 and saw the carcase cast in the w', "
26 that brought him back from the w' "
28 and found his carcase cast in the w', "
33 returned not from his evil w' "
15:26 and walked in the w' of his father, "
34 and walked in the w' of Jeroboam, "
16: 2 hast walked in the w' of Jeroboam, "
19 in walking in the w' of Jeroboam, "
26 he walked in all the w' of Jeroboam "
18: 6 Ahab went one w' by himself, "
6 and Obadiah went another w' by "
7 And as Obadiah was in the w', "
19:15 return on thy w' to the wilderness "
20:38 and waited for the king by the w', "
22:24 Which w' went the Spirit of 2088
52 and walked in the w' of his father, 1870
52 and in the w' of his mother, "
52 and in the w' of Jeroboam the son "
2Ki 2:23 and as he was going up by the w', "
3: 8 he said, Which w' shall we go up? "
8 The w' through the wilderness of "
20 there came water by the w' of Edom, "
5:19 So he departed from him a little w'. 776
6:19 This is not the w', neither is this 1870
7:15 all the w' was full of garments "
8:18 in the w' of the kings of Israel, "
27 in the w' of the house of Ahab, "
9:27 fled by the w' of the garden house. "
10:12 at the shearing house in the w', "
11:16 w' by the which the horses came "
19 by the w' of the gate of the guard "
16: 3 in the w' of the kings of Israel, "
19:28 by the w' by which thou camest. "
33 By the w' that he came, by the same "
21:21 walked in all the w' that his father "
22 walked not in the w' of the Lord. "
22: 2 and walked in all the w' of David "
25: 4 w' of the gate between two walls, "
4 king went the w' toward the plain. "
2Ch 6:16 thy children take heed to their w' "
23 recompensing his w' upon his own "
27 thou hast taught them the good w', "
34 by the w' that thou shalt send them, "
11:17 they walked in the w' of David and "
18:23 Which w' went the Spirit of the "
20:32 he walked in the w' of Asa his "
21: 6, 13 in the w' of the kings of Israel, "
Ezr 8:21 to seek of him a right w' for us, "
22 us against the enemy in the w': "
31 and of such as lay in wait by the w'. "
Ne 9:12 to give them light in the w' wherein "
19 them by day, to lead them in the w'; "
19 and the w' wherein they should go. "
Es 4:17 So Mordecai went his w', and did "
Job 3:23 given to a man whose w' is hid, 1870
6:18 The paths of their w' are turned * "
8:19 Behold, this is the joy of his w', "
12:24 a wilderness where there is no w'. "
16:22 go the w' whence I shall not return. 734
17: 9 righteous...shall hold on his w', 1870
18:10 and a trap for him in the w'. 5410
19: 8 He hath fenced up my w' that I 734
12 and raise up their w' against me, 1870
21:29 not asked them that go by the w'? "
31 Who shall declare his w' to his face? "
22:15 Hast thou marked the old w' which 734
23:10 he knoweth the w' that I take: 1870
11 his w' have I kept, and not "
24: 4 They turn the needy out of the w': "
18 not the w' of the vineyards. "
24 are taken out of the w' as all other, "
28:23 God understandeth the w' thereof, "
26 w' for the lightning of the thunder: "
29:25 I chose out their w', and sat chief, "
31: 7 my step hath turned out of the w', "
36:23 Who hath enjoined him his w'? "
38:19 is the w' where light dwelleth? "
24 By what w' is the light parted, "
25 a w' for the lightning of thunder; "
Ps 1: 1 nor standeth in the w' of sinners, "
6 knoweth the w' of the righteous: "
6 the w' of the ungodly shall perish. "
2:12 angry, and ye perish from the w', "
5: 8 make thy w' straight before my face. "
18:30 As for God, his w' is perfect: "
32 strength, and maketh my w' perfect. "
25: 8 will he teach sinners in the w'. "
9 and the meek will he teach his w'. "
12 teach in the w' that he shall choose. "
27:11 Teach me thy w', O Lord, and lead "
32: 8 thee in the w' which thou shalt go: "
35: 3 and stop the w' against them that "
6 Let their w' be dark and slippery: 1870

Ps 36: 4 himself in a w' that is not good; 1870
37: 5 Commit thy w' unto the Lord; "
7 of him who prospereth in his w', "
23 Lord: and he delighteth in his w'. "
34 Wait on the Lord, and keep his w', "
44:18 our steps declined from thy w'; 734
49:13 This their w' is their folly: yet 1870
67: 2 thy w' may be known upon earth, "
77:13 Thy w', O God, is in the sanctuary: "
19 Thy w' is in the sea, and thy path "
78:50 He made a w' to his anger; *5410
80:12 they which pass by the w' do pluck 1870
85:13 shall set us in the w' of his steps. "
86:11 Teach me thy w', O Lord; I will "
89:41 All that pass by the w' spoil him: "
101: 2 behave myself wisely in a perfect w'. "
6 he that walketh in a perfect w', he "
102:23 He weakened my strength in the w'; "
107: 4 in the wilderness in a solitary w'; "
7 he led them forth by the right w', "
40 the wilderness, where there is no w'. "
110: 7 shall drink of the brook in the w': "
119: 1 Blessed are the undefiled in the w', "
9 shall a young man cleanse his w'? 734
14 rejoiced in...w' of thy testimonies. 1870
27 to understand the w' of thy precepts: "
29 Remove from me the w' of lying: "
30 I have chosen the w' of truth: thy "
32 run the w' of thy commandments, "
33 Teach me,...the w' of thy statutes; "
37 and quicken thou me in thy w'. * "
101 my feet from every evil w', 734
104 therefore I hate every false w'. "
128 be right; and I hate every false w'. "
139:24 if there be any wicked w' in me, 1870
24 and lead me in the w' everlasting. "
142: 3 In the w' wherein I walked have 734
143: 8 cause me to know the w' wherein 1870
146: 9 w' of the wicked he turneth upside "
Pr 1:15 walk not thou in the w' with them; "
31 eat of the fruit of their own w', "
2: 8 and preserveth the w' of his saints. "
12 deliver thee from the w' of the evil "
20 mayest walk in the w' of good men, "
3:23 shalt thou walk in thy w' safely, "
4:11 taught thee in the w' of wisdom; "
14 go not in the w' of evil men. "
19 w' of the wicked is as darkness: "
5: 8 Remove thy w' far from her, and "
6:23 of instruction are the w' of life: "
7: 8 and he went the w' to her house, "
27 Her house is the w' to hell, going "
8: 2 by the w' in the places of the paths. "
13 the evil w', and the froward mouth, "
20 I lead in the w' of righteousness, in 734
22 me in the beginning of his w', 1870
9: 6 and go in the w' of understanding. "
10:17 He is in the w' of life that keepeth 734
29 The w' of the Lord is strength to 1870
11: 5 of the perfect shall direct his w': "
20 upright in their w' are his delight. "
12:15 The w' of a fool is right in his own "
26 the w' of the wicked seduceth them. "
28 In the w' of righteousness is life; 734
13: 6 him that is upright in the w': 1870
15 but the w' of transgressors is hard. "
14: 8 the prudent is to understand his w': "
12 a w' which seemeth right unto a "
15: 9 w' of the wicked is an abomination "
10 unto him that forsaketh the w': 734
19 The w' of the slothful man is 1870
19 the w' of the righteous is made 734
24 The w' of life is above to the wise, "
16: 9 A man's heart deviseth his w': but 1870
17 keepeth his w' preserveth his soul. "
25 w' that seemeth right unto a man, "
29 him into the w' that is not good. "
31 be found in the w' of righteousness. "
19: 3 foolishness of man perverteth his w': "
20:14 but when he is gone his w', then he "
24 man then understand his own w'? 1870
21: 2 Every w' of a man is right in his "
8 w' of man is froward and strange: "
16 man that wandereth out of the w' of "
29 for the upright, he directeth his w'.* "
22: 5 snares are in the w' of the froward: "
6 Train up a child in the w' he should "
23:19 and guide thine heart in the w'. "
26:13 man saith, There is a lion in the w'; "
28:10 righteous to go astray in an evil w', "
29:27 and he that is upright in the w' is "
30:19 The w' of an eagle in the air; the "
19 w' of a serpent upon a rock; the "
19 w' of a ship in the midst of the sea; "
19 and the w' of a man with a maid. "
20 Such is the w' of an adulterous "
Ec 9: 7 Go thy w', eat thy bread with joy, "
10: 3 he that is a fool walketh by the w', 1870
11: 5 not what is the w' of the spirit, "
12: 5 high, and fears shall be in the w', "
Isa 3:12 err, and destroy the w' of thy paths. "
8:11 not walk in the w' of this people, "
9: 1 afflict her by the w' of the sea, "
15: 5 w' of Horonaim they shall raise up "
26: 7 The w' of the just is uprightness: 734
8 in the w' of thy judgments, O Lord, "
28: 7 strong drink are out of the w'; †‡8582
7 of the w' through strong drink; †‡ "
30:11 Get you out of the w', turn 1870
21 This is the w', walk ye in it, "
35: 8 an highway shall be there, and a w', "
8 shall be called The w' of holiness; "
37:29 the w' by which thou camest. "
34 By the w' that he came, by the "
40: 3 Prepare ye the w' of the Lord, "
14 to him the w' of understanding? "

Isa 40:27 My w' is hid from the Lord, and my 1870
41: 3 w' that be had not gone with his 734
42:16 blind by a w' that they knew not; 1870
43:16 which maketh a w' in the sea, and "
19 even make a w' in the wilderness, "
48:15 he shall make his w' prosperous. "
17 by the w' that thou shouldest go. "
49:11 I will make all my mountains a w', "
51:10 a w' for the ransomed to pass over? "
53: 6 turned every one to his own w'; "
55: 7 Let the wicked forsake his w', and "
56:11 they all look to their own w', every "
57:10 wearied in the greatness of thy w'; "
14 ye up, cast ye up, prepare the w', "
14 block out of the w' of my people. "
17 on frowardly in the w' of his heart. "
59: 8 The w' of peace they knew not; and "
62:10 prepare ye the w' of the people; "
65: 2 walketh in a w' that was not good, "
Jer 2:17 God, when he led thee by the w'? "
18 hast thou to do in the w' of Egypt, "
18 hast thou to do in the w' of Assyria, "
23 see thy w' in the valley, know what "
33 trimmest thou thy w' to seek love? "
36 about so much to change thy w'? "
3:21 for they have perverted their w', "
4: 7 of the Gentiles is on his w'; 5265
18 Thy w' and thy doings have 1870
5: 4 they know not the w' of the Lord, "
5 they have known the w' of the Lord, "
6:16 the old paths, where is the good w', "
25 into the field, nor walk by the w'; "
27 thou mayest know and try their w'. "
10: 2 Learn not the w' of the heathen, "
23 that the w' of man is not in himself: "
12: 1 doth the w' of the wicked prosper? "
18:11 ye now every one from his evil w', "
15 walk in paths, in a w' not cast up; "
21: 8 the w' of life, and the w' of death. "
23:12 their w' shall be unto them as "
22 have turned them from their evil w', "
25: 5 now every one from his evil w', "
35 shepherds shall have no w' to flee, 4498
26: 3 turn every man from his evil w', 1870
28:11 the prophet Jeremiah went his w'. "
31: 9 the rivers of waters in a straight w', "
21 even the w' which thou wentest: "
32:39 give them one heart, and one w', "
35:15 ye now every man from his evil w', "
36: 3 return every man from his evil w'; "
7 return every one from his evil w': "
39: 4 by the w' of the king's garden, by "
4 and he went out the w' of the plain. "
42: 3 God may shew us the w' wherein "
48:19 of Aroer, stand by the w', and espy; "
50: 5 They shall ask the w' to Zion with* "
52: 7 w' of the gate between the...walls, "
7 they went by the w' of the plain. "
Eze 3:18 the wicked from his wicked w', "
19 nor from his wicked w', he shall die "
7:27 I will do unto them after their w', "
8: 5 eyes now the w' toward the north. "
5 mine eyes the w' toward the north, "
9: 2 from the w' of the higher gate, "
10 I will recompense their w' upon "
11:21 I will recompense their w' upon "
13:22 not return from his wicked w', "
14:22 shall see their w' and their doings: "
16:25 high place at every head of the w', "
27 which are ashamed of thy lewd w'. "
31 place in the head of every w', "
43 I also will recompense thy w' upon "
18:25 say, The w' of the Lord is not equal. "
25 Is not my w' equal? are not your "
29 The w' of the Lord is not equal. "
21:16 Go thee one w' or other, either on* "
19 it at the head of the w' to the city. 1870
20 Appoint a w', that the sword may "
21 stood at the parting of the w', "
22:31 their own w' have I recompensed "
23:13 defiled, that they took both one w', "
31 hast walked in the w' of thy sister; "
33: 8 to warn the wicked from his w', "
9 warn the wicked of his w' to turn "
9 if he do not turn from his w', he "
11 that the wicked turn from his w' "
17 The w' of the Lord is not equal: "
17 as for them, their w' is not equal. "
20 The w' of the Lord is not equal. "
36:17 defiled it by their own w' and by "
17 their w' was before me as the "
19 according to their w' and according "
42: 1 court, the w' toward the north: "
4 breadth inward, a w' of one cubit; "
11 And the w' before them was like the "
12 was a door in the head of the w', "
12 even the w' directly before the wall "
43: 2 Israel came from the w' of the east: "
4 into the house by the w' of the gate "
44: 1 brought me back the w' of the gate "
3 enter by the w' of the porch of that "
3 shall go out by the w' of the same. "
4 he me the w' of the north gate "
46: 2 shall enter by the w' of the porch "
8 by the w' of the porch of that gate, "
8 he shall go forth by the w' thereof. "
9 in by the w' of the north gate "
9 out by the w' of the south gate; "
9 entereth by the w' of the south gate "
9 forth by the w' of the north gate. "
9 not return by the w' of the gate "
47: 2 out of the w' of the gate northward, "
2 and led me about the w' without "
2 by the w' that looketh eastward; "
15 the w' of Hethlon, as men go to "
48: 1 to the coast of the w' of Hethlon, "

Da 12: 9 And he said, Go thy w', Daniel: for
Ho 2: 6 I will hedge up thy w' with thorns,1870
6: 9 of priests murder in the w' by "
10: 13 because thou didst trust in thy w', "
13: 7 as a leopard by the w' will I observe"
Am 2: 7 and turn aside the w' of the meek: "
Jon 3: 8 turn every one from his evil w', "
10 that they turned from their evil w';"
Na 1: 3 Lord hath his w' in the whirlwind "
2: 1 watch the w', make thy loins strong,"
Zec 10: 2 they went their w' as a flock, they
Mal 2: 8 But ye are departed out of the w';1870
3: 1 he shall prepare the w' before me: "
M't 2: 12 into their own country another w' 3598
3: 3 Prepare ye the w' of the Lord, "
4: 15 by the w' of the sea, beyond Jordan,*"
5: 24 gift before the altar, and go thy w'; "
25 whiles thou art in the w' with him;3598
7: 13 and broad is the w', that leadeth to "
14 and narrow is the w', which leadeth"
8: 4 but go thy w', shew thyself to the ‡
13 said unto the centurion, Go thy w'; "
28 no man might pass by that w'. 3598
30 a good w' off from them an herd *3112
10: 5 Go not into the w' of the Gentiles, 3598
11: 10 shall prepare thy w' before thee. "
13: 4 some seeds fell by the w' side, "
19 which received seed by the w' side. "
25 sowed tares...and went his w'. *
15: 32 fasting, lest they faint in the w'. 3598
20: 4 will give you. And they went their w'.
14 Take that thine is, and go thy w': "
17 twelve disciples apart in the w', 3598
30 blind men sitting by the w' side, "
21: 8 spread their garments in the w'; "
8 trees, and strawed them in the w'. "
19 when he saw a fig tree in the w', "
32 came...in the w' of righteousness, "
22: 16 and teachest the w' of God in truth,"
22 and left him, and went their w'. "
27: 65 go your w', make it as sure as ye can.‡
M'r 1: 2 shall prepare thy w' before thee. 3598
3 Prepare ye the w' of the Lord, "
44 but go thy w', shew thyself to the ‡
2: 11 bed, and go thy w' into thine house.*
4: 4 he sowed, some fell by the w' side,3598
15 And these are they by the w' side, "
7: 29 unto her, For this saying go thy w'; "
8: 3 houses, they will faint by the w': 3598
27 by the w' he asked his disciples, "
9: 33 it that ye disputed...by the w'? "
34 by the w' they had disputed among "
10: 17 when he was gone forth into the w'," "
21 go thy w', sell whatsoever thou hast, "
32 in the w' going up to Jerusalem; *3598
52 Go thy w'; thy faith hath made thee "
52 and followed Jesus in the w'. 3598
11: 2 Go your w' into the village over "
4 they went their w', and found the colt*
8 spread their garments in the w': 3598
8 trees, and strawed them in the w'.* "
12: 12 and they left him, and went their w'.*
14 teachest the w' of God in truth: 3598
16: 7 But go your w', tell his disciples and*
Lu 1: 79 guide our feet into the w' of peace.3598
3: 4 Prepare ye the w' of the Lord, "
4: 30 through the midst of them went his w', "
5: 19 find by what w' they might bring him "
7: 22 Go your w', and tell John what things "
27 shall prepare thy w' before thee. 3598
8: 5 he sowed, some fell by the w' side; "
12 by the w' side are they that hear; "
39 And he went his w', and published "
9: 57 as they went in the w', a certain 3598
10: 4 and salute no man by the w'. "
31 came down a certain priest that w':" "
12: 58 as thou art in the w', give diligence"
14: 32 the other is yet a great w' off, 4206
15: 20 when he was yet a great w' off, *3112
17: 19 Arise, go thy w': thy faith hath made "
18: 35 blind man sat by the w' side 3598
19: 4 to see him: for he was to pass that w'. "
32 And they that were sent went their w',*
36 they spread their clothes in the w'.3598
20: 21 but teachest the w' of God truly: "
22: 4 he went his w', and communed with*
24: 32 while he talked with us by the w', 3598
35 what things were done in the w', "
Joh 1: 23 Make straight the w' of the Lord, "
4: 28 and went her w' into the city, *
50 unto him, Go thy w'; thy son liveth. "
50 spoken unto him, and he went his w'. "
8: 21 I go my w', and ye shall seek me,*
9: 7 He went his w' therefore, and washed,*
10: 1 but climbeth up some other w', "
11: 28 when she had so said, she went her w',*
14: 4 I go ye know, and the w' ye know. 3598
5 and how can we know the w'? "
6 I am the w', the truth, and the life: "
16: 5 now I go my w' to him that sent me;*
18: 8 ye seek me, let these go their w': "
Ac 8: 26 w' that goeth...from Jerusalem 3598
36 as they went on their w', they came"
39 and he went on his w' rejoicing. "
9: 2 that if he found any of this w', "
15 Go thy w': for he is a chosen "
17 Ananias went his w', and entered into "
17 that appeared unto thee in the w' 3598
27 how he had seen the Lord in the w'," "
15: 3 brought on their w' by the church,4311
16: 17 shew unto us the w' of salvation. 3598
18: 25 instructed in the w' of the Lord; "
26 him the w' of God more perfectly. "
19: 9 but spake evil of that w' before the "
23 arose no small stir about that w'. "
21: 5 we departed and went our w'; *4311

Ac 21: 5 and they all brought us on our w', 4311
22: 4 persecuted this w' unto the death, 3598
24: 14 after the w' which they call heresy, "
22 more perfect knowledge of that w', "
25 answered, Go thy w' for this time; "
25: 3 laying wait in the w' to kill him. 3598
26: 13 I saw in the w' a light from heaven," "
Ro 3: 2 Much every w': chiefly, because 5158
12 They are all gone out of the w', they*
17 w' of peace have they not known: 3598
14: 13 an occasion to fall in his brother's w'. "
15: 24 be brought on my w' thitherward 4311
1Co 10: 13 temptation...make a w' to escape, 1545
12: 31 I unto you a more excellent w'. 3598
16: 7 I will not see you now by the w'; 3938
2Co 1: 16 brought on my w' toward Judæa. *4311
Ph'p 1: 18 every w', whether in pretence, or 5158
Col 2: 14 took it out of the w', nailing it to 3319
1Th 3: 11 Christ, direct our w' unto you. 3598
2Th 2: 7 until he be taken out of the w'. 3319
Heb 5: 2 on them that are out of the w'; *4105
9: 8 the w' into the holiest of all was 3598
10: 20 By a new and living w', which he "
12: 13 is lame be turned out of the w'; 1624
Jas 1: 24 beholdeth himself, and goeth his w',*
2: 25 had sent them out another w'? 3598
5: 20 the sinner from the error of his w' "
2Pe 2: 2 w' of truth shall be evil spoken of. "
15 Which have forsaken the right w', "
15 following the w' of Balaam the son "
21 known the w' of righteousness, "
3: 1 minds by w' of remembrance: *1722
Jude 11 they have gone in the w' of Cain, 3598
Re 16: 12 the w' of the kings of the east "

wayfaring
J'g 19: 17 he saw a w' man in the street of 732
2Sa 12: 4 the w' man that was come unto him;"
Isa 33: 8 lie waste, the w' man ceaseth: 5674,734
35: 8 the w' men, though fools, 1980,1870
Jer 9: 2 a lodging place of w' men; 732
14: 8 as a w' men that turneth aside to "

waymarks
Jer 31: 21 Set thee up w', make thee high 6725

ways See also ALWAYS; HIGHWAYS.
Ge 19: 2 rise up early, and go on your w'. *1870
Le 20: 4 people...do any w' hide their eyes
26: 22 your high w' shall be desolate. 1870
Nu 30: 15 if he shall any w' make them void*
De 5: 33 walk in all the w' which the Lord*1870
8: 6 to walk in his w', and to fear him. "
10: 12 to walk in all his w', and to love "
11: 22 to walk in all his w', and to cleave "
19: 9 thy God, and to walk ever in his w';"
26: 17 to walk in his w', and to keep his "
28: 7 way, and flee before thee seven w'. "
9 Lord thy God, and walk in his w'. "
25 and flee seven w' before them: "
29 thou shalt not prosper in thy w': "
30: 16 to walk in his w', and to keep his "
32: 4 for all his w' are judgment: "
Jos 22: 5 to walk in all his w', and to keep "
1Sa 8: 3 And his sons walked not in his w', "
5 and thy sons walk not in thy w': "
18: 14 behaved...wisely in all his w'; "
2Sa 22: 22 For I have kept the w' of the Lord, "
1Ki 2: 3 God, to walk in his w', to keep his "
3: 14 And if thou wilt walk in my w', to "
8: 39 to every man according to his w', "
58 to walk in all his w', and to keep "
11: 33 and have not walked in my w', to do"
38 and wilt walk in my w', and do that "
22: 43 he walked in all the w' of Asa his * "
2Ki 17: 13 Turn ye from your evil w', and "
2Ch 6: 30 every man according unto all his w'," "
31 to walk in thy w', so long as they "
7: 14 and turn from their wicked w'; "
13: 22 acts of Abijah, and his w', and his "
17: 3 in the first w' of his father David, "
6 was lifted up in the w' of the Lord: "
21: 12 walked in the w' of Jehoshaphat "
12 nor in the w' of Asa king of Judah, "
22: 3 in the w' of the house of Ahab: "
27: 6 prepared his w' before the Lord "
7 acts of Jotham,...and his w', "
28: 2 in the w' of the kings of Israel, "
26 the rest of his acts and of all his w'," "
32: 13 any w' able to deliver their lands "
34: 2 and walked in the w' of David his 1870
Job 4: 6 and the uprightness of thy w'? "
13: 15 maintain mine own w' before him. "
21: 14 desire not the knowledge of thy w'. "
22: 3 that thou makest thy w' perfect? "
28 the light shall shine upon thy w'. "
24: 13 they know not the w' thereof, nor "
23 yet his eyes are upon their w'. "
26: 14 these are parts of his w': but how "
30: 12 me the w' of their destruction. 734
31: 4 Doth not he see my w', and count 1870
34: 11 man to find according to his w'. 734
21 his eyes are upon the w' of man, 1870
27 would not consider any of his w': "
40: 19 He is the chief of the w' of God: "
Ps 10: 5 His w' are always grievous; "
18: 21 For I have kept the w' of the Lord, "
25: 4 Shew me thy w', O Lord; teach me "
39: 1 I said, I will take heed to my w', "
51: 13 will I teach transgressors thy w'; "
81: 13 and Israel had walked in my w'! "
84: 5 in whose heart are the w' of them.4546
91: 11 thee, to keep thee in all thy w'. 1870
95: 10 and they have not known my w': "
103: 7 He made known his w' unto Moses," "
119: 3 do no iniquity: they walk in his w'. "
5 O that my w' were directed to keep "

Ps 119: 15 and have respect unto thy w'. 734
26 I have declared my w', and thou 1870
59 I thought on my w', and turned my "
168 for all my w' are before thee. "
125: 5 as turn aside unto their crooked w', "
128: 1 the Lord; that walketh in his w'. 1870
138: 5 shall sing in the w' of the Lord: "
139: 3 and art acquainted with all my w'. "
145: 17 The Lord is righteous in all his w', "
Pr 1: 19 the w' of every one that is greedy of734
2: 13 to walk in the w' of darkness; 1870
15 Whose w' are crooked, and they 734
3: 6 In all thy w' acknowledge him, 1870
17 Her w' are w' of pleasantness, and "
31 and choose none of his w'. "
4: 26 and let all thy w' be established. "
5: 6 path of life, her w' are moveable, 4570
21 the w' of man are before the eyes 1870
6: 6 consider her w', and be wise: "
7: 25 not thine heart decline to her w', "
8: 32 blessed are they that keep my w'. "
9: 15 passengers...go right on their w': 734
10: 9 he that perverteth his w' shall be 1870
14: 2 but he that is perverse in his w' "
12 the end thereof are the w' of death. "
14 shall be filled with his own w': "
16: 2 All the w' of a man are clean in his "
7 When a man's w' please the Lord, "
25 the end thereof are the w' of death. "
17: 23 to pervert the w' of judgment. 734
19: 16 he that despiseth his w' shall die. 1870
22: 25 Lest thou learn his w', and get a 734
23: 26 and let thine eyes observe my w'. 1870
28: 6 than he that is perverse in his w', "
18 that is perverse in his w' shall fall "
31: 3 nor thy w' to that which destroyeth "
27 well to the w' of her household, 1979
Ec 11: 9 and walk in the w' of thine heart, 1870
Ca 3: 2 in the broad w' I will seek him 7339
Isa 2: 3 and he will teach us of his w', and 1870
42: 24 for they would not walk in his w', "
45: 13 and I will direct all his w': "
49: 9 They shall feed in the w', and their "
55: 8 neither are your w' my w', saith "
9 so are my w' higher than your w', "
57: 18 I have seen his w', and will heal "
58: 2 daily, and delight to know my w', "
13 not doing thine own w', nor finding "
63: 17 thou made us to err from thy w', "
64: 5 that remember thee in thy w': "
66: 3 they have chosen their own w', and "
Jer 2: 23 swift dromedary traversing her w'; "
33 also taught the wicked ones thy w'. "
3: 2 In the w' hast thou sat for them, as "
13 scattered thy w' to the strangers "
6: 16 Stand ye in the w', and see, and ask "
7: 3 Amend your w' and your doings, "
5 amend your w' and your doings; "
23 walk ye in all the w' that I have * "
12: 16 diligently learn the w' of my people," "
15: 7 since they return not from their w'. "
16: 17 For mine eyes are upon all their w':" "
17: 10 give every man according to his w'," "
18: 11 and make your w' and your doings "
15 caused them to stumble in their w' "
23: 12 as slippery w' in the darkness: *
26: 13 amend your w' and your doings, 1870
32: 19 upon all the w' of the sons of men: "
19 give every one according to his w', "
La 1: 4 The w' of Zion do mourn, because "
3: 9 inclosed my w' with hewn stone, "
11 He hath turned aside my w', and "
40 Let us search and try our w', and "
Eze 7: 3 will judge thee according to thy w'," "
4 will recompense thy w' upon thee, "
8 will judge thee according to thy w'," "
9 recompense thee according to thy w'" "
14: 23 ye see their w' and their doings: "
16: 47 hast thou not walked after their w'," "
47 more than they in all thy w'. "
61 Then thou shalt remember thy w', "
18: 23 that he should return from his w'.* "
25 equal? are not your w' unequal? "
29 of Israel, are not my w' equal? "
29 are not your w' unequal? "
30 every one according to his w', "
20: 43 there shall ye remember your w', "
44 not according to your wicked w', "
21: 19 son of man, appoint thee two w', "
21 at the head of the two w', to use "
24: 14 according to thy w', and according "
28: 15 Thou wast perfect in thy w' from "
33: 11 turn ye, turn ye from your evil w'; "
20 will judge you every one after his w'. "
36: 31 ye remember your own evil w', "
32 and confounded for your own w', "
Da 4: 37 are truth, and his w' judgment: 735
5: 23 whose are all thy w', hast thou not "
Ho 4: 9 I will punish them for their w', 1870
9: 8 is a snare of a fowler in all his w', "
12: 2 punish Jacob according to his w'; "
14: 9 for the w' of the Lord are right, and "
Joe 2: 7 shall march every one on his w', "
Mic 4: 2 he will teach us of his w', and we "
Na 2: 4 against another in the broad w': "
Hab 3: 6 did bow: his w' are everlasting. *1979
Hag 1: 7 Lord of hosts; Consider your w'.1870
Zec 1: 4 Turn ye now from your evil w', "
6 to do unto us, according to our w', "
3: 7 If thou wilt walk in my w', and if "
Mal 2: 9 as ye have not kept my w', but "
M't 8: 33 fled, and went their w' into the city,*
22: 5 made light of it, and went their w', "
M'r 11: 4 in a place where two w' met; *296
Lu 1: 76 face of the Lord to prepare his w'; 3598
3: 5 the rough w' shall be made smooth;"

Lu 10: 3 Go your *w*: behold, I send you forth
10 go your *w* out into the streets of *
Joh 11: 46 them went their *w* to the Pharisees,*
Ac 2: 28 made known to me the *w* of life; *3598*
13: 10 not cease to pervert the right *w* of "
14: 16 all nations to walk in their own *w*. "
Ro 3: 16 and misery are in their *w*: "
11: 33 and his *w* past finding out! "
1Co 4: 17 of my *w* which be in Christ, "
Heb 3: 10 and they have not known my *w*. "
Jas 1: 8 man is unstable in all his *w*. "
11 the rich man fade away in his *w*. **4197*
2Pe 2: 2 shall follow their pernicious *w*; * *684*
Re 15: 3 just and true are thy *w*, thou King*3598*
16: 1 Go your *w*, and pour out the vials of*

wayside See also WAY and SIDE.
1Sa 4: 13 Eli sat upon a seat by the *w* *3197,1870
Ps 140: 5 have spread a net by the *w*; *3027,4570

we See in the APPENDIX; also OUR; US.

weak See also WEAKER.
Nu 13: 18 whether they be strong or *w*, 7504
J'g 16: 7, 11 then shall I be *w*, and be as 2470
17 I shall become *w*, and be like any "
2Sa 3: 39 And I am this day *w*, though 7390
17: 2 while he is weary and *w* handed, 7504
2Ch 15: 7 and let not your hands be *w*: *7503
Job 4: 3 hast strengthened the *w* hands. 7504
Ps 6: 2 upon me, O Lord; for I am *w*: * 536
109: 24 My knees are *w* through fasting; 3782
Isa 14: 10 Art thou also become *w* as we? 2470
35: 3 Strengthen ye the *w* hands, and 7504
Eze 7: 17 all knees shall be *w* as water. 3212
16: 30 How *w* is thine heart, saith the 535
21: 7 all knees shall be *w* as water: 3212
Joe 3: 10 let the *w* say, I am strong. 2523
M't 26: 41 is willing, but the flesh is *w*. *772*
M'r 14: 38 truly is ready, but the flesh is *w*. "
Ac 20: 35 ye ought to support the *w*, *770*
Ro 4: 19 being not *w* in faith, he considered* "
8: 3 in that it was *w* through the flesh, "
14: 1 Him that is *w* in the faith receive "
2 another, who is *w*, eateth herbs. "
21 or is offended, or is made *w*. * "
15: 1 to bear the infirmities of the *w*, *102*
1Co 1: 27 chosen the *w* things of the world *772*
4: 10 we are *w*, but ye are strong; "
8: 7 their conscience being *w* is defiled. "
9 stumblingblock to them that are *w*. *770*
10 the conscience of him which is *w* *772*
11 shall the *w* brother perish, *770*
12 and wound their *w* conscience, "
9: 22 To the *w* became I as *w*, "
22 that I might gain the *w*: I am "
11: 30 many are *w* and sickly among you, "
2Co 10: 10 but his bodily presence is *w*, and "
11: 21 as though we had been *w*. "
29 Who is *w*, and I am not *w*? who is "
12: 10 for when I am *w*, then am I strong. "
13: 3 which to you-ward is not *w*, but is "
4 For we also are *w* in him, but we "
9 when we are *w*, and ye are strong: "
Ga 4: 9 to the *w* and beggarly elements, *772*
1Th 5: 14 support the *w*, be patient toward "

weaken See also WEAKENED; WEAKENETH.
Isa 14: 12 which didst *w* the nations! *2522

weakened
Ezr 4: 4 *w* the hands of...people of Judah, 7503
Ne 6: 9 hands shall be *w* from the work, "
Ps 102: 23 He *w* my strength in the way; he 6031

weakeneth
Job 12: 21 *w* the strength of the mighty. *7503
Jer 38: 4 he *w* the hands of the men of war "

weaker
2Sa 3: 1 house of Saul waxed *w* and *w*. 1800
1Pe 3: 7 the wife, as unto the *w* vessel, *772*

weak-handed See WEAK and HANDED.

weakness
1Co 1: 25 *w* of God is stronger than men. *772*
2: 3 I was with you in *w*, and in fear, *769*
15: 43 it is sown in *w*; it is raised in power:"
2Co 12: 9 my strength is made perfect in *w*. "
13: 4 though he was crucified through *w*,"
Heb 7: 18 for the *w* and unprofitableness *772*
11: 34 out of *w* were made strong, *769*

wealth See also COMMONWEALTH.
Ge 34: 29 their *w*, and all their little ones, 2428
De 8: 17 mine hand hath gotten me this *w*. "
18 he that giveth thee power to get *w*,"
Ru 2: 1 a mighty man of *w*, of the family "
1Sa 2: 32 the *w* which God shall give Israel: "
2Ki 15: 20 even of all the mighty men of *w*, 2428
2Ch 1: 11 not asked riches, *w*, or honour, 5233
12 I will give thee riches, and *w*, and "
Ezr 9: 12 nor seek their peace or their *w* *2896
Es 10: 3 seeking the *w* of his people, and * "
Job 21: 13 They spend their days in *w*, and in*"
31: 25 rejoiced because my *w* was great,2428
Ps 44: 12 not increase thy *w* by their price.
49: 6 They that trust in their *w*, and 2428
10 perish, and leave their *w* to others. "
112: 3 *W* and riches...be in his house: 1952
Pr 5: 10 strangers be filled with thy *w*; *3581
10: 15 rich man's *w* is his strong city: 1952
13: 11 *W* gotten by vanity shall be "
22 the *w* of the sinner is laid up for 2428
18: 11 rich man's *w* is his strong city, 1952
19: 4 *W* maketh many friends; but the "
Ec 5: 19 God hath given riches and *w*, 5233
6: 2 to whom God hath given riches, *w*,"
Zec 14: 14 *w* of all the heathen round about 2428
Ac 19: 25 that by this craft we have our *w*. *2142*
1Co 10: 24 his own, but every one another's *w*.*

wealthy
Ps 66: 12 broughtest us out into a *w* place. 7310
Jer 49: 31 get you up unto the *w* nation, *7961

weaned
Ge 21: 8 And the child grew, and was *w*: 1580
8 the same day that Isaac was *w*. "
1Sa 1: 22 will not go up until the child be *w*, "
23 tarry until thou have *w* him; "
23 gave her son suck until she *w* him."
24 And when she had *w* him, she "
1Ki 11: 20 Tahpenes *w* in Pharaoh's house: "
Ps 131: 2 as a child that is *w* of his mother: "
2 my soul is even as a *w* child. "
Isa 11: 8 *w* child shall put his hand on the "
28: 9 them that are *w* from the milk, "
Ho 1: 8 Now when she had *w* Lo-ruhamah,"

weapon See also WEAPONS.
Nu 35: 18 smite him with an hand *w* of 3627
De 23: 13 shalt have a paddle upon thy *w*; * 240
2Ch 23: 10 man having his *w* in his hand, 7973
Ne 4: 17 and with the other hand held a *w*. "
Job 20: 24 He shall flee from the iron *w*, and5402
Isa 54: 17 No *w* that is formed against thee 3627
Eze 9: 1 with his destroying *w* in his hand. "
2 man a slaughter *w* in his hand; "

weapons
Ge 27: 3 therefore take, I pray thee, thy *w*,3627
De 1: 41 girded on every man his *w* of war, "
J'g 18: 11 six hundred men appointed with *w*"
16 men appointed with their *w* of war."
17 that were appointed with *w* of war. "
1Sa 21: 8 my sword nor my *w* with me, "
2Sa 1: 27 fallen, and the *w* of war perished! "
2Ki 11: 8 every man with his *w* in his hand: "
11 every man with his *w* in his hand, "
2Ch 23: 7 every man with his *w* in his hand; "
Ec 9: 18 Wisdom is better than *w* of war: "
Isa 13: 5 and the *w* of his indignation, to "
Jer 21: 4 I will turn back the *w* of war that "
22: 7 against thee, every one with his *w*: "
50: 25 forth the *w* of his indignation: "
51: 20 art my battle axe and *w* of war: "
Eze 32: 27 down to hell with their *w* of war: "
39: 9 shall set on fire and burn the *w*, 5402
10 for they shall burn the *w* with fire:"
Joh 18: 3 with lanterns and torches and *w*. *3696*
2Co 10: 4 *w* of our warfare are not carnal, "

wear See also WARE; WEARETH; WEARING.
Ex 18: 18 Thou wilt surely *w* away, both 5034
De 22: 5 woman shall not *w* that which 1961
11 not *w* a garment of divers sorts, 3847
1Sa 2: 28 incense, to *w* an ephod before me?5375
22: 18 persons that did *w* a linen ephod. "
Es 6: 8 brought which the king useth to *w*,3847
Job 14: 19 The waters *w* the stones: thou 7833
Isa 4: 1 bread, and *w* our own apparel: 3847
Da 7: 25 *w* out the saints of the most High,1080
Zec 13: 4 *w* a rough garment to deceive: 3847
M't 11: 8 they that *w* soft clothing are in *5409*
Lu 9: 12 when the day began to *w* away, *2827*

weareth
Jas 2: 3 to him that *w* the gay clothing, *5409*

wearied
Ge 19: 11 *w* themselves to find the door. 3811
Isa 43: 23 offering, nor *w* thee with incense.3021
24 hast *w* me with thine iniquities. "
47: 13 Thou art *w* in the multitude of 3811
57: 10 *w* in the greatness of thy way: 3021
Jer 4: 31 soul is *w* because of murderers. *5888
12: 5 and they have *w* thee, then how 3811
5 thou trustedst, they *w* thee, "
Eze 24: 12 She hath *w* herself with lies, and 3811
Mic 6: 3 wherein have I *w* thee? testify "
Mal 2: 17 *w* the Lord with your words. 3021
17 ye say, Wherein have we *w* him? "
Joh 4: 6 being *w* with his journey, sat *2872*
Heb 12: 3 ye be *w* and faint in your minds. *2577*

wearieth
Job 37: 11 by watering he *w* the thick cloud:*2959
Ec 10: 15 the foolish *w* every one of them, 3021

weariness
Ec 12: 12 much study is a *w* of the flesh. 3024
Mal 1: 13 said also, Behold, what a *w* is it! 4972
2Co 11: 27 In *w* and painfulness, in *2873*

wearing
1Sa 14: 3 priest in Shiloh, *w* an ephod. 5375
Joh 19: 5 Jesus forth, *w* the crown of thorns,*5409*
1Pe 3: 3 plaiting the hair, and of *w* of gold,*4025*

wearisome
Job 7: 3 and *w* nights are appointed to me.5999

weary See also WEARIED; WEARIETH; WEARISOME.
Ge 27: 46 I am *w* of my life because of the 6973
De 25: 18 when thou wast faint and *w*; 3023
J'g 4: 21 for he was fast asleep and *w*. *5774
8: 15 bread unto thy men that are *w*? 3286
2Sa 16: 14 that were with him, came *w*, 5889
17: 2 upon him while he is *w* and weak 3023
29 The people is hungry, and *w*, 5889
23: 10 Philistines until his hand was *w*, 3021
Job 3: 17 and there the *w* be at rest. 3019
10: 1 My soul is *w* of my life; I will 5354
16: 7 But now he hath made me *w*: 3811
22: 7 not given water to the *w* to drink,5889
Ps 6: 6 I am *w* with my groaning; all the 3021
68: 9 thine inheritance, when it was *w*. 3811
69: 3 I am *w* of my crying: my throat 3021
Pr 3: 11 neither be *w* of his correction: 6973
25: 17 lest he be *w* of thee, and so hate 7646
Isa 1: 14 unto me; I am *w* to bear them. 3811
5: 27 None shall be *w* nor stumble 5889

Isa 7: 13 a small thing for you to *w* men, 3811
13 but will ye *w* my God also? "
16: 12 that Moab is *w* on the high place,* "
28: 12 ye may cause the *w* to rest; 5889
32: 2 shadow of a great rock in a *w* land."
40: 28 earth, fainteth not, neither is *w*? 3021
30 the youths shall faint and be *w*, "
31 they shall run, and not be *w*; and "
43: 22 thou hast been *w* of me, O Israel. "
46: 1 they are a burden to the *w* beast. 5889
50: 4 word in season to him that is *w*: 3287
Jer 2: 24 all they that seek her will not *w* 3286
6: 11 the Lord; I am *w* with holding in:3811
9: 5 *w* themselves to commit iniquity. "
15: 6 thee, I am *w* with repenting. "
20: 9 I was *w* with forbearing, and I "
31: 25 For I have satiated the *w* soul, 5889
51: 58 in the fire, and they shall be *w*. 3286
64 upon her: and they shall be *w*. "
Hab 2: 13 the people shall *w* themselves for "
Lu 18: 5 her continual coming she *w* me. **5299*
Ga 6: 9 And let us not be *w* in well doing: *1573*
2Th 3: 13 brethren, be not *w* in well doing. "

weasel
Le 11: 29 the *w*, and the mouse, and the 2467

weather
Job 37: 22 Fair *w* cometh out of the north: *2091
Pr 25: 20 taketh away a garment in cold *w*,3117
M't 16: 2 evening, ye say, It will be fair *w*: *2105*
3 morning, It will be foul *w* to day: *5494*

weave See also WEAVEST; WOVE; WOVEN.
Isa 19: 9 and they that *w* networks, shall be 707
59: 5 eggs, and *w* the spider's web: "

weaver See also WEAVER'S.
Ex 35: 35 and in fine linen, and of the *w*, 707
Isa 38: 12 I have cut off like a *w* my life: he "

weaver's
1Sa 17: 7 of his spear was like a *w* beam; 707
2Sa 21: 19 of whose spear was like a *w* beam. "
1Ch 11: 23 hand was a spear like a *w* beam; "
20: 5 spear staff was like a *w* beam. "
Job 7: 6 days are swifter than a *w* shuttle, "

weavest
J'g 16: 13 If thou *w* the seven locks of my 707

web See also WEBS.
J'g 16: 13 locks of my head with the *w*. 4545
14 pin of the beam, and with the *w*. "
Job 8: 14 whose trust shall be a spider's *w*.1004
Isa 59: 5 eggs, and weave the spider's *w*: 6980

webs
Isa 59: 6 *w* shall not become garments, 6980

wed See WEDDING; WEDLOCK.

wedding
M't 22: 3 them that were bidden to the *w*: **1062*
8 The *w* is ready, but they which "
10 the *w* was furnished with guests. "
11 which had not on a *w* garment: "
12 in hither not having a *w* garment? "
Lu 12: 36 when he will return from the *w*; * "
14: 8 thou art bidden of any man to a *w*,*"

wedge
Jos 7: 21 *w* of gold of fifty shekels weight, 3956
24 the *w* of gold, and his sons, and his"
Isa 13: 12 a man than the golden *w* of Ophir.*

wedlock
Eze 16: 38 as women that break *w* and shed 5003

weeds
Jon 2: 5 *w* were wrapped about my head. 5488

week See also WEEKS.
Ge 29: 27 Fulfil her *w*, and we will give thee7620
28 Jacob did so, and fulfilled her *w*: "
Da 9: 27 the covenant with many for one *w*:"
27 and in the midst of the *w* he shall "
M't 28: 1 toward the first day of the *w*, *4521*
M'r 16: 2 the morning the first day of the *w*, "
9 risen early the first day of the *w*, "
Lu 18: 12 I fast twice in the *w*, I give tithes "
24: 1 Now upon the first day of the *w*, "
Joh 20: 1 the first day of the *w* cometh Mary "
19 being the first day of the *w*, when "
Ac 20: 7 And upon the first day of the *w*, "
1Co 16: 2 Upon the first day of the *w* let every"

weeks
Ex 34: 22 thou shalt observe the feast of *w*, 7620
Le 12: 5 then she shall be unclean two *w*, "
Nu 28: 26 after your *w* be out, ye shall have "
De 16: 9 Seven *w* shalt thou number unto "
9 begin to number the seven *w* from "
10 keep the feast of *w* unto the Lord "
16 in the feast of *w*, and in the feast "
2Ch 8: 13 in the feast of *w*, and in the feast "
Jer 5: 24 us the appointed *w* of the harvest. "
Da 9: 24 Seventy *w* are determined upon "
25 the Prince shall be seven *w*, "
25 and threescore and two *w*: the "
26 threescore and two *w* shall Messiah"
10: 2 Daniel was mourning three full *w*. "
3 till three whole *w* were fulfilled. "

weep See also WEEPEST; WEEPETH; WEEPING; WEPT.
Ge 23: 2 mourn for Sarah, and to *w* for her.1058
43: 30 and he sought where to *w*; and he "
Nu 11: 10 people *w* throughout their families,*"
13 for they *w* unto me, saying, Give "
1Sa 11: 5 What aileth the people that they *w*?"
30: 4 until they had no more power to *w*. "
2Sa 1: 24 daughters of Israel, *w* over Saul, "
12: 21 thou didst fast and *w* for the child, "
2Ch 34: 27 rend thy clothes, and *w* before me;*"
Ne 8: 9 Lord your God; mourn not, nor *w*, "

Job 27:15 death. and his widows shall not w'.*1058
30:25 Did not I w' for him that was in "
31 organ into the voice of them that w'. "
Ec 3: 4 A time to w', and a time to laugh; "
Isa 15: 2 to Dibon, the high places, to w': 1065
22: 4 I will w' bitterly, labour not to "
30:19 thou shalt w' no more: he will be 1058
33: 7 the ambassadors of peace shall w' "
Jer 9: 1 that I might w' day and night for "
13:17 my soul shall w' in secret places for "
17 and mine eye shall w' sore, and 1830
22:10 W' ye not for the dead, neither 1058
10 w' sore for him that goeth away: "
48:32 will w' for thee with the weeping of "
La 1:16 For these things I w'; mine eye, "
Eze 24:16 neither shalt thou mourn nor w', "
23 ye shall not mourn nor w'; but ye "
27:31 shall w' for thee with bitterness "
Joe 1: 5 Awake, ye drunkards, and w'; and "
2:17 w' between the porch and the altar, "
Mic 1:10 ye it not at Gath, w' ye not at all: "
Zec 7: 3 Should I w' in the fifth month, "
M'r 5:39 Why make ye this ado, and w'? 2799
Lu 6:21 Blessed are ye that w' now: for ye "
25 now! for ye shall mourn and w'. "
7:13 on her, and said unto her, W' not. "
8:52 he said, W' not; she is not dead, "
23:28 Daughters of Jerusalem, w' not for "
28 but w' for yourselves, and for your "
Joh 11:31 She goeth unto the grave to w' "
16:20 you, That ye shall w' and lament, "
Ac 21:13 What mean ye to w' and to break * "
Ro 12:15 rejoice, and w' with them that w'. "
1Co 7:30 they that w', as though they wept "
Jas 4: 9 Be afflicted, and mourn, and w': "
5: 1 w' and howl for your miseries that "
Re 5: 5 W' not: behold, the Lion of the tribe "
18:11 merchants of the earth shall w' "

weepest
1Sa 1: 8 to her, Hannah, why w' thou? 1058
Joh 20:13, 15 unto her, Woman, why w' thou? 2799

weepeth
2Sa 19: 1 w' and mourneth for Absalom. 1058
2Ki 8:12 And Hazael said, Why w' my lord? "
Ps 126: 6 He that goeth forth and w', bearing* "
La 1: 2 She w' sore in the night, and her "

weeping
Nu 25: 6 were w' before the door of the 1058
De 34: 8 days of w' and mourning for Moses 1065
2Sa 3:16 husband went with her along w' 1058
15:30 they went up, w' as they went up. "
Ezr 3:13 the noise of the w' of the people: 1065
10: 1 w' and casting himself down 1058
Es 4: 3 and fasting, and w', and wailing; 1065
Job 16:16 My face is foul with w', and on my "
Ps 6: 8 Lord hath heard the voice of my w'. "
30: 5 w' may endure for a night, but joy "
102: 9 and mingled my drink with w', "
Isa 15: 3 one shall howl, w' abundantly. "
5 Luhith with w' shall they go it up; "
16: 9 I will bewail with the w' of Jazer "
22:12 did the Lord God of hosts call to w', "
65:19 voice of w' shall be no more heard "
Jer 3:21 w' and supplications of the "
9:10 will I take up a w' and wailing, "
31: 9 They shall come with w', and with "
15 Ramah, lamentation, and bitter w'; "
15 Rahel w' for her children refused 1058
16 Refrain thy voice from w', and 1065
41: 6 them, w' all along as he went: 1058
48: 5 Luhith continual w' shall go up; 1065
32 weep for thee with the w' of Jazer: "
50: 4 of Judah together, going and w': 1058
Eze 8:14 there sat women w' for Tammuz. "
Joe 2:12 fasting, and with w', and with 1065
Mal 2:13 with tears, with w', and with crying "
M't 2:18 lamentation, and w', and great 2805
18 Rachel w' for her children, and 2799
8:12 shall be w' and gnashing of teeth. 2805
22:13 shall be w' and gnashing of teeth. "
24:51 shall be w' and gnashing of teeth. "
25:30 shall be w' and gnashing of teeth. "
Lu 7:38 stood at his feet behind him w', 2799
13:28 shall be w' and gnashing of teeth, 2805
Joh 11:33 When Jesus therefore saw her w', 2799
33 Jews also w' which came with her, "
20:11 stood without at the sepulchre w': "
Ac 9:39 and all the widows stood by him w', "
Ph'p 3:18 often, and now tell you even w', "
Re 18:15 fear of her torment, w' and wailing, "
19 w' and wailing, saying, Alas, alas "

weigh See also WEIGHED; WEIGHETH; WEIGHING.
1Ch 20: 2 and found it to w' a talent of gold, 4948
Ezr 8:29 ye w' them before the chief of the 8254
Ps 58: 2 ye w' the violence of your hands 6424
Isa 26: 7 dost w' the path of the just. * "
46: 6 w' silver in the balance, and hire 8254
Eze 5: 1 then take thee balances to w', and 4948

weighed See also UNWEIGHED.
Ge 23:16 Abraham w' to Ephron the silver, 8254
Nu 7:85 all the silver vessels w' two thousand*
1Sa 2: 3 and by him actions are w'. 8505
17: 7 spear's head w' six hundred shekels of
2Sa 14:26 he w' the hair of his head at two 8254
21:16 spear w' three hundred shekels *
Ezr 8:25 And w' unto them the silver, and 8254
26 I even w' unto their hand six "
33 the vessels w' in the house of our "
Job 6: 2 that my grief were throughly w', "
28:15 silver be w' for the price thereof. "
31: 6 Let me be w' in an even balance, "
Isa 40:12 and w' the mountains in scales, "
Jer 32: 9 w' him the money, even seventeen "
Jer 32:10 w' him the money in the balances. 8254
Da 5:27 Thou art w' in the balances, and 8625
Zec 11:12 they w' for my price thirty pieces 8254

weigheth
Job 28:25 he w' the waters by measure. *8505
Pr 16: 2 eyes; but the Lord w' the spirits. "

weighing
Nu 7:85 charges of silver w' an hundred and
86 full of incense, w' ten shekels apiece,

weight See also WEIGHTS.
Ge 24:22 golden earring of half a shekel w', 4948
22 her hands of ten shekels w' of gold; "
43:21 of his sack, our money in full w': "
Ex 30:34 of each shall there be a like w': "
Le 19:35 in meteyard, in w', or in measure. 4948
26:26 deliver you your bread again by w': "
Nu 7:13, 19, 25 w' whereof was an hundred
31 charger of the w' of an hundred 4948
37 w' whereof was an hundred and "
43 charger of the w' of an hundred "
49 w' whereof was an hundred and "
55 charger of the w' of an hundred "
61, 67, 73, 79 w' whereof was an "
De 25:15 shalt have a perfect and just w', a 68
Jos 7:21 wedge of gold of fifty shekels w', 4948
J'g 8:26 w' of the golden earrings that he "
1Sa 17: 5 w' of the coat was five thousand "
2Sa 12:30 the w' thereof was a talent of gold "
14:26 hundred shekels after the king's w'. 68
21:16 the w' of whose spear weighed 4948
16 hundred shekels of brass in w', "
1Ki 7:47 neither was the w' of the brass "
10:14 Now the w' of gold that came to "
2Ki 25:16 of all these vessels was without w'. "
1Ch 21:25 six hundred shekels of gold by w'. "
22: 3 brass in abundance without w'; "
14 and of brass and iron without w'; "
28:14 of gold by w' for things of gold, for "
14 for all instruments of silver by w', "
15 Even the w' for the candlesticks of "
15 of gold, by w' for every candlestick, "
15 for the candlesticks of silver by w', "
16 by w' he gave gold for the tables of "
17 he gave gold by w' for every bason; "
17 silver by w' for every bason of "
18 altar of incense refined gold by w'; "
2Ch 3: 9 And the w' of the nails was fifty "
4:18 for the w' of the brass could not be "
9:13 Now the w' of gold that came to "
Ezr 8:30 and the Levites the w' of the silver, "
34 By number and by w' of every one: "
34 and all the w' was written at that "
Job 28:25 To make the w' for the winds; and "
Pr 11: 1 Lord: but a just w' is his delight. 68
16:11 A just w' and balance are the *6425
Jer 52:20 all these vessels was without w'. 4948
Eze 4:10 thou shalt eat shall be by w'. 4946
16 and they shall eat bread by w', 4948
Zec 5: 8 he cast the w' of lead upon the 68
Joh 19:39 aloes, about an hundred pound w'. "
2Co 4:17 exceeding and eternal w' of glory; 922
Heb 12: 1 let us lay aside every w', and the 3591
Re 16:21 every stone about the w' of a talent: 5006

weightier
M't 23:23 omitted the w' matters of the law, 926

weights
Le 19:36 Just balances, just w', a just 68
Pr 16:11 all the w' of the bag are his work. "
20:10 Divers w', and divers measures, "
23 Divers w' are an abomination unto "
Mic 6:11 and with the bag of deceitful w'? "

weighty See also WEIGHTIER.
Pr 27: 3 A stone is heavy, and the sand w'; 5192
2Co 10:10 his letters, say they, are w' and 926

welfare
Ge 43:27 he asked them of their w', and 7965
Ex 18: 7 they asked each other of their w'; "
1Ch 18:10 to king David, to enquire of his w',* "
Ne 2:10 the w' of the children of Israel. 2896
Job 30:15 my w' passeth away as a cloud. 3444
Ps 69:22 should have been for their w', *7965
Jer 38: 4 seeketh not the w' of this people, "

well See also FAREWELL; WELFARE; WELL-BELOVED; WELLFAVOURED; WELLPLEASING; WELL'S; WELLS; WELLSPRING.
Ge 4: 7 If thou doest w', shalt thou not be 3190
7 if thou doest not w', sin lieth at the "
12:13 it may be w' with me for thy sake; "
16 And he entreated Abram w' for her "
13:10 of Jordan, that it was w' watered
16:14 the w' was called Beer-lahai-roi; 875
18:11 were old and w' stricken in age;
21:19 her eyes, and she saw a w' of water; 875
25 Abimelech because of a w' of water, "
30 unto me, that I have digged this w'. "
24: 1 was old, and w' stricken in age:
11 by a w' of water at the time of the 875
13 I stand here by the w' of water; *5869
16 she went down to the w', and filled* "
20 and ran again unto the w' to draw 875
29 ran out unto the man, unto the w'.*5869
30 he stood by the camels at the w'. * "
42 And I came this day unto the w', * "
43 Behold, I stand by the w' of water;* "
45 she went down unto the w', and * "
25:11 Isaac dwelt by the w' Lahai-roi. * 883
26:19 and found there a w' of springing 875
20 he called the name of the w' Esek; "
21 they digged another w', and strove "
22 digged another w'; and for that they "
25 there Isaac's servants digged a w'. "
32 told him concerning the w' which "
Ge 29: 2 looked, and behold a w' in the field, 875
2 for out of that w' they watered the "
6 And he said unto them, Is he w'? 7965
6 And they said, He is w': and,
17 was beautiful and w' favoured. 3303
32: 9 and I will deal w' with thee: *3190
37:14 see whether it be w' with thy 7965
14 w' with the flocks; and bring me "
39: 6 a goodly person, and w' favoured. 3303
40:14 think on me when it shall be w' 3190
41: 2 the river seven w' favoured kine 3303
4 the seven w' favoured and fat kine. "
18 kine, fatfleshed and w' favoured; "
43:27 Is your father w', the old man of 7965
45:16 and it pleased Pharaoh w', and his
49:22 even a fruitful bough by a w'; *5869
Ex 1:20 God dealt w' with the midwives: 3190
2:15 Midian: and he sat down by a w'. 875
4:14 brother? I know that he can speak w'.
10:29 Thou hast spoken w', I will see thy 3651
Le 24:16 as w' the stranger, as he that is born
22 w' for the stranger, as for one of your
Nu 11:18 for it was w' with us in Egypt: 2895
13:30 it; for we are w' able to overcome it.
21:16 the w' whereof the Lord spake unto 875
17 Spring up, O w'; sing ye unto it: "
18 The princes digged the w', the "
22 not drink of the waters of the w': * "
36: 5 of the sons of Joseph hath said w'.*3651
De 1:17 shall hear the small as w' as the great;*
23 And the saying pleased me w':
3:20 unto your brethren, as w' as unto you,*
4:40 that it may go w' with thee, and 3190
5:14 maidservant may rest as w' as thou.
16 that it may go w' with thee, in the 3190
28 w' said all that they have spoken. "
29 that it might be w' with them, and "
33 and that it may be w' with you, 2895
6: 3, 18 that it may be w' with thee, and 3190
7:18 shalt w' remember what the Lord thy
12:25, 28 that it may go w' with thee, 3190
15:16 house, because he is w' with thee; 2895
18:17 They have w' spoken that which 3190
19:13 Israel, that it may go w' with thee. 2895
20: 8 his brethren's heart faint as w' as his*
22: 7 that it may be w' with thee, and 3190
Jos 8:33 of the Lord, as w' the stranger,
18:15 to the w' of waters of Nephtoah: *4599
J'g 7: 1 and pitched beside the w' of Harod: *5878
9:16 if ye have dealt w' with Jerubbaal 2895
14: 3 for me; for she pleaseth me w'.
7 and she pleased Samson w'.
Ru 3: 1 thee, that it may be w' with thee? 3190
13 thee the part of a kinsman, w'; 2896
1Sa 9:10 said Saul to his servant, W' said; "
16:16 with his hand, and thou shalt be w'. 2895
17 me now that a man can play w', 3190
23 so Saul was refreshed, and was w', 2895
18:26 it pleased David w' to be the
19:22 came to a great w' that is in Sechu: 953
20: 7 If he say thus, It is w'; thy servant 2896
24:18 that thou hast dealt w' with me: "
19 enemy, will he let him go w' away? "
20 I know w'...thou shalt surely be king,*
25:31 shall have dealt w' with my lord, 3190
2Sa 3:13 he said, W'; I will make a league 2896
26 him again from the w' of Sirah: 953
6:19 Israel, as w' to the women as men,
11:25 devoureth one as w' as another: 2090
17: 4 the saying pleased Absalom w',
18 which had a w' in his court; 875
21 that they came up out of the w', and "
18:28 and said unto the king, All is w'. 7965
19: 6 then it had pleased thee w'.
23:15 the water of the w' of Beth-lehem, 953
16 water out of the w' of Beth-lehem,
1Ki 2:18 W'; I will speak for thee unto the 2896
8:18 thou didst w' that it was in thine 3190
18:24 answered and said, It is w' spoken. 2896
2Ki 4:23 And she said, It shall be w'. 7965
26 and say unto her, Is it w' with thee? "
26 is it w' with thy husband? "
26 is it w' with the child? "
26 And she answered, It is w'. "
5:21 to meet him, and said, Is all w'? "
22 And he said, All is w'. My master "
7: 9 said one to another, We do not w': 3651
9: 11 and one said unto him, Is all w'? 7965
10:30 thou hast done w' in executing 2895
25:24 and it shall be w' with you. 3190
1Ch 11:17 the water of the w' of Beth-lehem, 953
18 water out of the w' of Beth-lehem,
25: 8 ward, as w' the small as the great,
26:13 cast lots, as w' the small as the great,
2Ch 6: 8 thou didst w' in that it was in 2895
12:12 and also in Judah things went w'.*2896
31:15 as w' to the great as to the small:
Ne 2:13 even before the dragon w', and to 5869
Job 12: 3 I have understanding as w' as you; 71
33:31 Mark w', O Job, hearken unto me: 7181
Ps 48:13 Mark ye w' her bulwarks,
49:18 when thou doest w' to thyself. 3190
73: 2 gone; my steps had w' nigh slipped. 369
78:29 So they did eat, and were w' filled: 3966
84: 6 the valley of Baca make it a w'; *4599
87: 7 As w' the singers as the players on
119:65 Thou hast dealt w' with thy 2896
128: 2 be, and it shall be w' with thee.
139:14 and that my soul knoweth right w'.*
Pr 5:15 running waters out of thine own w'. 875
10:11 of a righteous man is a w' of life: *4726
11:10 When it goeth w' with the 2898
13:10 but with the w' advised is wisdom.
14:15 the prudent man looketh w' to his 995
27:23 flocks, and look w' to thy herds.
30:29 There be three things which go w',*3190

Pr 31:27 She looketh w· to the ways of her 6822
Ec 8:12 be w· with them that fear God, 2896
13 it shall not be w· with the wicked, "
Ca 4:15 of gardens, a w· of living waters, 875
Isa 1:17 Learn to do w·; seek judgment, 3190
3:10 that it shall be w· with him: 2896
24 instead of w· set hair baldness; 4639
25: 6 of wines on the lees w· refined.
33:23 not w· strengthen their mast, *3651
42:21 w· pleased for his righteousness' *2654
Jer 1:12 Lord unto me, Thou hast w· seen: 3190
7:23 you, that it may be w· unto you. "
15:11 Verily it shall be w· with thy *2896
11 to entreat thee w· in the time of evil*
22:15 and then it was w· with him? 2896
16 needy; then it was w· with him: "
38:20 so it shall be w· unto thee, and thy 3190
39:12 Take him, and look w· to him,
40: 4 and I will look w· unto thee:
9 and it shall be w· with you. 3190
42: 6 that it may be w· with us, when we2896
44:17 we plenty of victuals, and were w·, "
Eze24: 5 under it, and make it boil w·, 7571
10 consume the flesh, and spice it w·,*
33:32 and can play w· on an instrument:
44: 5 Son of man, mark w·, and
5 mark w· the entering in of the
47:14 shall inherit it, one as w· as another:
Da 1: 4 was no blemish, but w· favoured, 2896
3:15 the image which I have made; w·:
Jon 4: 4 Lord, Doest thou w· to be angry? 3190
9 thou w· to be angry for the gourd? "
9 he said, I do w· to be angry, even "
Zec 8:15 I thought in these days to do w· * "
M't 3:17 Son, in whom I am w· pleased. 2106
12:12 is lawful to do w· on the sabbath *2573
18 in whom my soul is w· pleased: 2106
15: 7 w· did Esaias prophesy of you, 2573
17: 5 Son, in whom I am w· pleased; 2106
25:21 W· done, thou good and faithful 2095
23 him, W· done, good and faithful "
M'r 1:11 Son, in whom I am w· pleased. 2106
7: 6 W· hath Esaias prophesied of 2573
9 Full w· ye reject the commandment "
37 He hath done all things w·: "
12:28 that he had answered them w·, "
32 W·, Master, thou hast said the * "
Lu 1: 7 were now w· stricken in years. 4260
18 and my wife w· stricken in years. "
3:22 Son; in thee I am w· pleased. 2106
6:26 all men shall speak w· of you! 2573
19:17 unto him, W·, thou good servant: 2095
20:39 said, Master, thou hast w· said. 2573
Joh 2:10 and when men have w· drunk, *3184
4: 6 Now Jacob's w· was there. Jesus 4077
6 his journey, sat thus on the w·: "
11 to draw with, and the w· is deep: 5421
12 father Jacob, which gave us the w·, "
14 a w· of water springing up into 4077
17 Thou hast w· said, I have no 2573
8:48 Say we not w· that thou art a "
11:12 Lord, if he sleep, he shall do w·. *4982
13:13 Master and Lord: and ye say w·; 2573
18:23 but if w·, why smitest thou me? "
Ac 10:33 thou hast w· done that thou art "
47 the Holy Ghost as w· as we? 2532
15:29 ye shall do w·. Fare ye w·. 2095
16: 2 was w· reported of by the brethren3140
25:10 wrong, as thou very w· knowest. 2573
28:25 W· spake the Holy Ghost by "
Ro 2: 7 by patient continuance in w· doing* 18
11:20 W·; because of unbelief they 2573
1Co 7:37 he will keep his virgin, doeth w·. "
38 giveth her in marriage doeth w·; "
9: 5 a wife, as w· as other apostles, *2532
10: 5 of them God was not w· pleased: 2106
14:17 For thou verily givest thanks w·, 2573
2Co 6: 9 As unknown, and yet w· known; 1921
11: 4 ye might w· bear with him. 2573
Gal 4:17 zealously affect you, but not w·; * "
5: 7 Ye did run w·; who did hinder you "
6: 9 let us not be weary in w· doing: 2570
Eph 6: 3 That it may be w· with thee, and 2095
Ph'p 4:14 Notwithstanding ye have w· done,*2573
Col 3:20 this is w· pleasing unto the Lord. 2101
2Th 3:13 be not weary in w· doing. *2569
1Ti 3: 4 One that ruleth w· his own house, 2573
12 children and their own houses w·. "
13 used the office of a deacon w· "
5:10 W· reported of for good works; if 3140
17 the elders that rule w· be counted 2573
2Ti 1:18 me at Ephesus, thou knowest very w·.957
Tit 2: 9 please them w· in all things; 1510,2101
Heb 4: 2 preached, as w· as unto them: *2509
13:16 such sacrifices God is w· pleased. 2100
Jas 2: 8 thy neighbour as thyself, ye do w·:2573
19 there is one God; thou doest w·: "
1Pe 2:14 for the praise of them that do w·. 17
15 that with w· doing ye may put to * 15
20 when ye do w·, and suffer for it, ye "
3: 6 ye are, as long as ye do w·, and "
17 ye suffer for w· doing, than for evil* "
4:19 of their souls to him in w· doing, * 16
2Pe 1:17 Son, in whom I am w· pleased. 2106
19 ye do w· that ye take heed, as unto2573
3Jo 6 after a godly sort, thou shalt do w·:"

wellbeloved
Ca 1:13 A bundle of myrrh is my w· unto *1730
Isa 5: 1 Now will I sing to my w· a song of3039
1 My w· hath a vineyard in a very "
M'r 12: 6 yet therefore one son, his w·, he * 27
Ro 16: 5 Salute my w· Epænetus, who is the* "
3Jo 1 The elder unto the w· Gaius, whom* "

well-doing See WELL and DOING.

wellfavoured See also WELL and FAVOURED.
Na 3: 4 whoredoms of the w· harlot, *2896,2580

well-nigh See WELL and NIGH.

wellpleasing See also WELL and PLEASING.
Ph'p 4:18 a sacrifice acceptable, w· to God. 2101
Heb13:21 you that which is w· in his sight, "

well's
Ge 29: 2 great stone was upon the w· mouth.875
3 rolled the stone from the w· mouth, "
3 the stone again upon the w· mouth "
8 roll the stone from the w· mouth: "
10 rolled the stone from the w· mouth, "
2Sa 17:19 a covering over the w· mouth, "

wells
Ge 26:15 the w· which his father's servants 875
18 Isaac digged again the w· of water, "
Ex 15:27 where were twelve w· of water, 5869
Nu 20:17 we drink of the water of the w·: 875
De 6:11 w· digged, which thou diggest not,* 953
2Ki 3:19 and stop all w· of water, and mar *4599
25 they stopped all the w· of water, * "
2Ch 26:10 the desert, and digged many w·: * 953
Ne 9:25 w· digged, vineyards, and * "
Isa 12: 3 water out of the w· of salvation. 4599
2Pe 2:17 These are w· without water, *4077

wellspring
Pr 16:22 Understanding is a w· of life unto 4726
18: 4 and the w· of wisdom as a flowing "

wen
Le 22:22 maimed, or having a w·, or scurvy,2990

wench
2Sa 17:17 and a w· went and told them; *8198

went See also OUTWENT; WENTEST.
Ge 2: 6 there w· up a mist from the earth, 5927
10 a river w· out of Eden to water 3318
4:16 Cain w· out from the presence of "
7: 7 And Noah w· in, and his sons, and 935
9 There w· in two and two unto Noah "
15 they w· in unto Noah into the ark, "
16 they that w· in, w· in male and "
18 the ark w· upon the face of the 3212
8: 7 a raven, which w· forth to and fro, 3318
18 Noah w· forth, and his sons, and "
19 their kinds, w· forth out of the ark. "
9:18 of Noah, that w· forth of the ark, "
23 and w· backward, and covered the3212
10:11 Out of that land w· forth Asshur, 3318
11:31 they w· forth with him from Ur "
12: 4 unto him; and Lot w· with him; 3212
5 they w· forth to go into the land of3318
10 and Abram w· down into Egypt to 3381
13: 1 Abram w· up out of Egypt, he, and5927
3 he w· on his journeys from the 3212
5 which w· with Abram, had flocks, 1980
14: 8 there w· out the king of Sodom, 3318
11 their victuals, and w· their way. 3212
17 king of Sodom w· out to meet him 3318
24 of the men which w· with me, 1980
15:17 when the sun w· down, and it was 935
16: 4 And he w· in unto Hagar, and she "
17:22 and God w· up from Abraham. 5927
18:16 Abraham w· with them to bring 1980
22 thence, and w· toward Sodom: 3212
33 And the Lord w· his way, as soon as"
19: 6 Lot w· out at the door unto them, 3318
14 Lot w· out, and spake unto his sons"
28 the smoke of the country w· up as5927
30 Lot w· up out of Zoar, and dwelt "
33 and the firstborn w· in, and lay 935
21:16 And she w·, and sat her down over3212
19 and she w·, and filled the bottle "
22: 3 w· unto the place of which God had"
6 and they w· both of them together. "
8 so they w· both of them together. "
13 Abraham w· and took the ram, and"
19 and w· together to Beer-sheba. "
23:10 all that w· in at the gate of his city,935
18 all that w· in at the gate of his city. "
24:10 he arose, and w· to Mesopotamia, 3212
16 and she w· down to the well, and 3381
45 and she w· down unto the well, and"
61 took Rebekah, and w· his way. 3212
63 Isaac w·...to meditate in the field 3318
25:22 And she w· to enquire of the Lord.3212
34 drink, and rose up, and w· his way:"
26: 1 Isaac w· unto Abimelech king of "
13 man waxed great, and w· forward,* "
23 w· up from thence to Beer-sheba. 5927
26 Abimelech w· to him from Gerar, 1980
27: 5 Esau w· to the field to hunt for 3212
14 And he w·, and fetched, and brought"
22 Jacob w· near...Isaac his father; 5066
28: 5 he w· to Padan-aram unto Laban, 3212
9 Then w· Esau unto Ishmael, and "
10 Jacob w· out from Beer-sheba, 3318
10 and w· toward Haran. 3212
29: 1 Then Jacob w· on his journey,5375,7272
10 that Jacob w· near, and rolled the 5066
23 her to him; and he w· in unto her. 935
30 And he w· in also unto Rachel, and "
30: 4 to wife: and Jacob w· in unto her. "
14 Reuben w· in the days of wheat 3212
16 and Leah w· out to meet him, 3318
31:19 And Laban w· to shear his sheep: 1980
33 And Laban w· into Jacob's tent, 935
33 Then w· he out of Leah's tent, and3318
32: 1 And Jacob w· on his way, and the 1980
21 So w· the present over before him:*5674
34: 1 w· out to see the daughters of the 3318
6 w· out unto Jacob to commune "
24 that w· out of the gate of his city; "
24 that w· out of the gate of his city. "
Ge 34:26 out of Shechem's house, and w· out.3318
35: 3 with me in the way which I w·. 1980
13 God w· up from him in the place 5927
22 Reuben w· and lay with Bilhah 3212
36: 6 w· into the country from the face "
37:12 brethren w· to feed their father's "
17 And Joseph w· after his brethren, "
38: 1 Judah w· down from his brethren,3381
2 he took her, and w· in unto her. 935
9 he w· in unto his brother's wife, "
11 Tamar w· and dwelt in her father's3212
12 w· up unto his sheepshearers to 5927
19 she arose, and w· away, and laid 3212
39:11 Joseph w· into the house to do his 935
41:45 Joseph w· out over all the land of 3318
46 Joseph w· out from the presence of"
46 and w· throughout all the land of 5674
42: 3 ten brethren w· down to buy corn 3381
43:15 w· down to Egypt, and stood before "
31 he washed his face, and w· out, 3318
44:28 And the one w· out from me, and "
45:25 And they w· up out of Egypt, and 5927
46:29 w· up to meet Israel his father, to "
47:10 and w· out from before Pharaoh. 3318
49: 4 thou it: he w· up to my couch. 5927
50: 7 Joseph w· up to bury his father: "
7 w· up all the servants of Pharaoh, "
9 there w· up with him both chariots "
14 w· up with him to bury his father, "
18 his brethren also w· and fell down3212
Ex 2: 1 w· a man of the house of Levi, "
8 w· and called the child's mother. "
11 he w· out unto his brethren, and 3318
13 And when he w· out the second day,"
4:18 Moses w· and returned to Jethro 3212
27 he w·, and met him in the mount "
29 Moses and Aaron w· and gathered "
5: 1 Moses and Aaron w· in, and told *935
10 taskmasters of the people w· out, 3318
7:10 and Aaron w· in unto Pharaoh, 935
23 turned and w· into his house, "
8:12 and Aaron w· out from Pharaoh: 3318
30 And Moses w· out from Pharaoh, "
9:33 w· out of the city from Pharaoh, "
10: 6 himself, and w· out from Pharaoh. "
14 the locusts w· up over all the land 5927
18 And he w· out from Pharaoh, 3318
11: 8 he w· out from Pharaoh in a great "
12:28 And the children of Israel w· away,3212
38 multitude w· up also with them; 5927
41 w· out from the land of Egypt. 3318
13:18 w· up harnessed out of the land 5927
21 Lord w· before them by day in a 1980
14: 8 Israel w· out with an high hand. 3318
19 God, which w· before the camp of 1980
19 removed and w· behind them; 3212
19 cloud w· from before their face, *5265
22 children of Israel w· into the midst 935
23 w· in after them to the midst of "
15:19 Pharaoh w· in with his chariots "
19 Israel w· on dry land in the midst*1980
20 w· out after her with timbrels, 3318
22 w· out into the wilderness of Shur;"
22 w· three days in the wilderness, 3212
16:27 w· out some of the people on the 3318
17:10 Hur w· up to the top of the hill. 5927
18: 7 Moses w· out to meet his father in 3318
27 he w· his way into his own land. 3212
19: 3 Moses w· up unto God, and the 5927
14 Moses w· down from the mount 3381
20 top of the mount; and Moses w· up.5927
25 So Moses w· down unto the people,3381
24: 9 They w· up Moses, and Aaron, 5927
13 Moses w· up into the mount of God."
15 Moses w· up into the mount, and a "
18 w· into the midst of the cloud, *935
32:15 and w· down from the mount, 3381
33: 7 w· out unto the tabernacle 3318
8 Moses w· out unto the tabernacle, "
34: 4 and w· up unto mount Sinai, 5927
34 w· in before the Lord to speak 935
35 until he w· in to speak with him. "
38:26 every one that w· to be numbered,*5674
40:32 When they w· into the tent of the 935
36 the children of Israel w· onward 5265
Le 9: 8 Aaron therefore w· unto the altar,*7121
23 and Aaron w· into the tabernacle 935
10: 2 there w· out fire from the Lord, *3318
5 So they w· near, and carried them*7126
16:23 on when he w· into the holy place, 935
24:10 w· out among the children of 3318
Nu 8:22 after that w· the Levites in to do 935
10:14 place w· the standard of the camp 5265
33 the covenant of the Lord w· before "
34 day, when they w· out of the camp."
11: 8 the people w· about, and gathered 7751
24 Moses w· out, and told the people 3318
26 but w· not out unto the tabernacle:"
31 w· forth a wind from the Lord, 5265
13:21 So they w· up, and searched the 5927
26 And they w· and came to Moses, 3212
31 the men that w· up with him said, 5927
14:24 into the land whereinto he w·; 935
38 men that w· to search the land, 1980
16:25 Moses rose up and w· unto Dathan3212
33 w· down alive into the pit, and the3381
17: 8 w· into the tabernacle of witness; 935
20: 6 Moses and Aaron w· from the "
15 our fathers w· down into Egypt, 3381
27 they w· up into mount Hor in the 5927
21:16 And from thence they w· to Beer:*
18 the wilderness they w· to Mattanah:*
23 and w· out against Israel into the 3318
33 and w· up by the way of Bashan: 5927
33 the king of Bashan w· out against 3318
22:14 rose up, and they w· unto Balak, 935

Nu 22:21 and w' with the princes of Moab. 3212
22 anger was kindled because he w': 1980
23 of the way, and w' into the field: 3212
26 the angel of the Lord w' further, 5674
32 I w' out to withstand thee, 3318
35 w' with the princes of Balak. 3212
36 he w' out to meet him unto a city 3318
39 And Balaam w' with Balak, and 3212
23: 3 thee. And he w' to an high place. "
24: 1 he w' not, as at other times, to 1980
25 and w' and returned to his place: 3212
25 place: and Balak also w' his way. 1980
25: 8 he w' after the man of Israel into 935
26: 4 w' forth out of the land of Egypt. *3318
31: 13 w' forth to meet them without the "
21 men of war which w' to the battle, 935
27 upon them, who w' out to battle, 3318
28 men of war which w' out to battle: "
36 portion of them that w' out to war, "
32: 9 w' up unto the valley of Eshcol, 5927
39 the son of Manasseh w' to Gilead, 3212
41 Jair...w' and took the small towns 1980
42 Nobah w' and took Kenath, and the "
33: 1 w' forth out of the land of Egypt 3318
3 Israel w' out with an high hand "
8 w' three days' journey in the 3212
23 And they w' from Kehelathah, and *5265
29 And they w' from Mithcah, and * "
33 And they w' from Hor-hagidgad, * "
38 the priest w' up into mount Hor 5927
De 1:19 we w' through all that great and 3212
24 and w' up into the mountain, 5927
31 in all the way that ye w', until ye 1980
33 Who w' in the way before you, to "
43 w' presumptuously up into the 5927
2:13 And we w' over the brook Zered. 5674
3: 1 and w' up the way to Bashan: 5927
5: 5 fire, and w' not up into the mount;) "
10: 3 w' up into the mount, having the two "
22 Thy fathers w' down into Egypt 3381
26: 5 he w' down into Egypt, and "
29:26 For they w' and served other gods, 3212
31: 1 Moses w' and spake these words "
14 And Moses and Joshua w', and "
33: 2 from his right hand w' a fiery law*
34: 1 w' up from the plains of Moab 5927
Jos 2: 1 they w', and came into an harlot's 3212
5 it was dark, that the men w' out: 3318
5 whither the men w' I wot not: 1980
22 And they w', and came unto the 3212
3: 2 the officers w' through the host; 5974
6 ark...and w' before the people. 3212
5:13 and Joshua w' unto him, and said "
6: 1 none w' out, and none came in. 3318
9 armed men w' before the priests 1980
13 ark of the Lord w' on continually, "
13 and the armed men w' before them; "
20 that the people w' up into the city, 5927
23 young men that were spies w' in, 935
7: 2 And the men w' up and viewed Ai. 5927
4 So there w' up thither of the people "
8: 9 and they w' to lie in ambush, and 3212
10 numbered the people, and w' up, 5927
11 of war that were with him, w' up, "
13 Joshua w' that night into the 3212
14 of the city w' out against Israel 3318
17 Beth-el, and w' not out after Israel: "
9: 4 w' and made as if they had been 3212
6 they w' to Joshua unto the camp "
10: 5 and w' up, they and all their hosts, 5927
9 and w' up from Gilgal all night. "
24 men of war which w' with him, 1980
36 And Joshua w' up from Eglon, 5927
11: 4 they w' out, they and all their 3318
14: 8 my brethren that w' up with me 5927
15: 3 And it w' out to the south side to 3318
3 to Hezron, and w' up to Adar, 5927
4 w' out unto the river of Egypt; 3318
6 the border w' up to Beth-hogla, 5927
6 border w' up to the stone of Bohan "
7 the border w' up toward Debir "
8 border w' up by the valley of the "
8 w' up to the top of the mountain "
9 and w' out to the cities of mount 3318
10 and w' down to Beth-shemesh, 3381
11 w' out unto the side of Ekron 3318
11 Baalah, and w' out unto Jabneel; "
15 he w' up thence to the inhabitants 5927
16: 6 the border w' out toward the sea 3318
6 border w' about eastward unto *5437
7 w' down from Janohah to Ataroth, 3381
7 to Jericho, and w' out at Jordan. 3318
8 The border w' out from Tappuah 3212
17: 7 border w' along on the right hand 1980
18: 8 and the men arose, and w' away: 3212
8 Joshua charged them that w' 1980
9 w' and passed through the land, 3212
12 border w' up to the side of Jericho 5927
12 and w' up through the mountains "
13 w' over from thence toward Luz, *5674
15 and the border w' out on the west, 3318
15 and w' out to the well of waters of "
17 north, and w' forth to En-shemesh, "
17 w' forth toward Geliloth, which is "
18 and w' down unto Arabah: 3381
19:11 their border w' up toward the sea, 5927
47 coast of the children of Dan w' out 3318
47 children of Dan w' up to fight 5927
22: 6 away: and they w' unto their tents. 3212
24: 4 his children w' down into Egypt. 3381
11 ye w' over Jordan, and came unto 5674
17 us in all the way wherein we w', 1980
J'g 1: 3 thy lot. So Simeon w' with him. 3212
4 And Judah w' up; and the Lord 5927
9 children of Judah w' down to fight 3381
10 Judah w' against the Canaanites 3212
J'g 1:11 w' against...inhabitants of Debir: 3212
16 w' up out of the city of palm trees 5927
16 w' and dwelt among the people. 3212
17 Judah w' with Simeon his brother, "
22 they also w' up against Beth-el: 5927
26 w' into the land of the Hittites, 3212
2: 6 w' every man unto his inheritance "
15 Whithersoever they w' out, the 3318
17 they w' a whoring after other gods, ‡
3:10 judged Israel, and w' out to war: 3318
13 Amalek, and w' and smote Israel, 3212
19 that stood by him w' out from him. 3318
22 the haft also w' in after the blade; 935
23 Ehud w' forth through the porch, 3318
27 w' down with him from the mount, 3381
28 they w' down after him, and took "
4: 9 and w' with Barak to Kedesh. 3212
10 w' up with the ten thousand men 5927
10 and Deborah w' up with him. "
14 So Barak w' down from mount 3381
18 Jael w' out to meet Sisera, and said 3318
21 w' softly unto him, and smote the 935
6:19 Gideon w' in, and made ready a kid, "
33 gathered together, and w' over, *5674
7:11 Then w' he down with Phurah, 3381
8: 8 And he w' up thence to Penuel, 5927
11 And Gideon w' up by the way of "
27 Israel w' thither a whoring after it: ‡
29 w' and dwelt in his own house. 3212
33 and w' a whoring after Baalim, ‡
9: 1 son of Jerubbaal w' to Shechem 3212
5 he w' unto his father's house at 935
6 w', and made Abimelech king, 3212
7 he w' and stood in the top of mount "
8 The trees w' forth on a time to 1980
21 ran away, and fled, and w' to Beer, 3212
26 brethren, and w' over to Shechem: 5674
27 And they w' out into the fields, 3318
27 and w' into the house of their god, 935
35 And Gaal the son of Ebed w' out, 3318
39 And Gaal w' out before the men "
42 the people w' out into the field; "
50 Then w' Abimelech to Thebez, 3212
52 w' hard unto the door of the tower ‡5066
11: 3 Jephthah, and w' out with him. 3318
5 of Gilead w' to fetch Jephthah out 3212
11 Then Jephthah w' with the elders "
18 w' along through the wilderness, * "
38 she w' with her companions, and * "
40 the daughters of Israel w' yearly "
12: 1 together, and w' northward, *5674
13:11 And Manoah...w' after his wife, 3212
20 the flame w' up toward heaven 5927
14: 1 And Samson w' down to Timnath, 3381
5 Then w' Samson down, and his "
7 And he w' down, and talked with "
9 in his hands, and w' on eating, 3212
10 So his father w' down unto the 3381
18 day before the sun w' down, 935
19 and he w' down to Ashkelon, 3381
19 and he w' up to his father's house. 5927
15: 4 Samson w' and caught three 3212
8 he w' down and dwelt in the top of 3381
9 Then the Philistines w' up, and 5927
11 of Judah w' to the top of the rock 3381
16: 1 Then w' Samson to Gaza, and 3212
1 an harlot, and w' in unto her. 935
3 posts, and w' away with them, *5265
14 w' away with the pin of the beam,* "
19 him, and his strength w' from him. 5493
17:10 thy victuals. So the Levite w' in. 3212
18:11 w' from thence of the family of *5265
12 And they w' up, and pitched in 5927
14 men that w' to spy out the country 1980
17 And the five men that w' to spy "
17 to spy out the land w' up, 5927
18 And these w' into Micah's house, 935
20 and w' in the midst of the people. "
26 the children of Dan w' their way: 3212
26 and w' back unto his house. 7725
19: 2 w' away from him unto her 3212
3 husband arose, and w' after her, "
14 they passed on and w' their way; "
14 the sun w' down upon them when 935
15 when he w' in, he sat him down "
18 I w' to Beth-lehem-judah, but I 3212
23 master of the house, w' out unto 3318
27 house, and w' out to go his way: "
20: 1 all the children of Israel w' out, "
18 and w' up to the house of God, 5927
20 the men of Israel w' out to battle 3318
23 children of Israel w' up and wept 5927
25 Benjamin w' forth against them 3318
26 w' up, and came unto the house 5927
30 children of Israel w' up against "
31 the children of Benjamin w' out 3318
21:23 they w' and returned unto their 3212
24 w' out from thence every man to 3318
Ru 1: 1 w' to sojourn in the country of 3212
7 Wherefore she w' forth out of the 3318
7 w' on the way to return unto the 3212
19 So they two w' until they came to "
21 I w' out full, and the Lord hath 1980
2: 3 she w', and came, and gleaned in 3212
18 took it up, and w' into the city: 935
3: 6 And she w' down unto the floor, 3381
7 he w' to lie down at the end of the 935
15 it on her: and she w' into the city. "
4: 1 Then w' Boaz up to the gate, and 5927
13 and when he w' in unto her, the 935
1Sa 1: 3 And this man w' up out of his city 5927
7 w' up to the house of the Lord, "
18 So the woman w' her way, and did 3212
21 w' up to offer unto the Lord the 5927
22 But Hannah w' not up; for she "
2:11 Elkanah w' to Ramah to his house, 3212
1Sa 2:20 And they w' unto their own home. 1980
3: 3 ere the lamp of God w' out in the *3518
5 again. And he w' and lay down. 3212
6 And Samuel arose and w' to Eli, "
8 he arose and w' to Eli, and said "
9 So Samuel w' and lay down in his "
4: 1 Now Israel w' out against the 3318
5:12 cry of the city w' up to heaven. 5927
6:12 w' along the highway, lowing as 1980
12 the highway, lowing as they w', "
12 the Philistines w' after them unto "
7: 7 Philistines w' up against Israel. 5927
11 men of Israel w' out of Mizpeh, 3318
16 he w' from year to year in circuit 1980
9: 9 when a man w' to enquire of God, 3212
10 w' unto the city where the man of "
11 as they w' up the hill to the city, 5927
14 And they w' up into the city: and "
26 they w' out both of them, he and 3318
10:14 and to his servant, Whither w' ye? 1980
26 Saul also w' home to Gibeah; and "
26 there w' with him a band of men, 3212
11:15 And all the people w' to Gilgal; "
13: 7 And some of the Hebrews w' over *5674
10 Saul w' out to meet him, that he 3318
20 all the Israelites w' down to the 3381
23 Philistines w' out to the passage 3318
14:16 w' on beating down one another. 3212
19 the Philistines w' on and increased: "
21 w' up with them into the camp 5927
46 Then Saul w' up from following "
46 Philistines w' to their own place. 1980
15:34 Then Samuel w' to Ramah; and 3212
34 Saul w' up to his house to Gibeah 5927
16:13 Samuel rose up, and w' to Ramah. 3212
17: 4 w' out a champion out of the camp 3318
7 one bearing a shield w' before 1980
12 man w' among men for an old man *935
13 sons of Jesse w' and followed *3212
13 three sons that w' to the battle 1980
15 David w' and returned from Saul "
20 w', as Jesse had commanded him; 3212
35 I w' out after him, and smote him, 3318
41 that bare the shield w' before him. "
18: 5 David w' out whithersoever Saul 3318
13 he w' out and came in before the "
16 he w' out and came in before them. "
27 Wherefore David arose and w', he 3212
30 princes of the Philistines w' forth: 3318
30 came to pass, after they w' forth, "
19: 8 David w' out, and fought with the "
12 and he w', and fled, and escaped. 3212
18 he and Samuel w' and dwelt in "
22 Then w' he also to Ramah, and "
23 he w' thither to Naioth in Ramah: "
23 and he w' on, and prophesied, "
20:11 w' out both of them into the field. 3318
35 Jonathan w' out into the field at "
42 and Jonathan w' into the city. 935
21:10 and w' to Achish the king of Gath. "
22: 1 it, they w' down thither to him. 3381
3 And David w' thence to Mizpeh of 3212
23: 5 David and his men w' to Keilah, "
13 w' whithersoever they could go. 1980
16 and w' to David into the wood, 3212
18 and Jonathan w' to his house. 1980
24 arose, and w' to Ziph before Saul: 3212
25 Saul...and his men w' to seek him. "
26 Saul w' on this side of the mountain, "
28 and w' against the Philistines: "
29 And David w' up from thence, 5927
24: 2 w' to seek David and his men 3212
3 and Saul w' in to cover his feet: 935
7 of the cave, and w' on his way. 3212
8 afterward, and w' out of the cave, 3318
22 And Saul w' home; but David 3212
25: 1 w' down to the wilderness of 3381
12 turned their way, and w' again, 7725
13 there w' up after David about 5927
42 damsels of hers that w' after her; 1980
42 she w' after the messengers of 3212
26: 2 w' down to the wilderness of Ziph, 3381
13 David w' over to the other side, 5674
25 So David w' on his way, and Saul 3212
27: 8 And David and his men w' up, and 5927
28: 8 and he w', and two men with him, 3212
25 rose up, and w' away that night. "
29:11 the Philistines w' up to Jezreel. 5927
30: 2 them away, and w' on their way. 3212
9 David w', he and the six hundred "
21 and they w' forth to meet David, 3318
22 of those that w' with David, 1980
22 Because they w' not with us, we "
31: 3 And the battle w' sore against Saul, "
12 men arose, and w' all night, and 3212
2Sa 1: 4 said unto him, How w' the matter? 1961
2: 2 David w' up thither, and his two 5927
12 w' out from Mahanaim to Gibeon. 3318
13 servants of David, w' out, and met "
15 and w' over by number twelve of 5674
24 sun w' down when they were come 935
29 w' through all Bithron, and they 3212
32 And Joab and his men w' all night, "
3:16 her husband w' with her along "
19 Abner w' also to speak in the ears "
21 Abner away; and he w' in peace. "
4: 5 w', and came about the heat of the "
5: 6 king and his men w' to Jerusalem "
10 David w' on, and grew great, and* "
17 of it, and w' down to the hold. 3381
6: 2 arose, and w' with all the people 3212
4 God: and Ahio w' before the ark. 1980
12 David w' and brought up the ark 3212
7:18 Then w' king David in, and sat 935
23 God w' to redeem for a people to 1980
8: 3 as he w' to recover his border at 3212

2Sa 8: 6, 14 David whithersoever he *w'*. 1980
10: 16 the host of Hadarezer *w'* before them.*
11: 9 and *w'* not down to his house. 3381
10 Uriah he *w'* not down unto his house. "
13 even he *w'* out to lie on his bed 3318
13 but *w'* not down to his house. 3381
17 And the men of the city *w'* out, 3318
21 why *w'* ye nigh the wall? then say 5066
22 So the messenger *w'*, and came 3212
12: 16 David fasted, and *w'* in, and lay 935
17 of his house arose, and *w'* to him,*
24 *w'* in unto her, and lay with her: 935
29 *w'* to Rabbah, and fought against it, 3212
13: 8 So Tamar *w'* to her brother
9 they *w'* out every man from him. 3318
19 on her head, and *w'* on crying. 3212
37 Absalom fled, and *w'* to Talmai, "
38 So Absalom fled, and *w'* to Geshur, "
14: 23 So Joab arose and *w'* to Geshur, "
15: 9 So he arose, and *w'* to Hebron. "
11 with Absalom *w'* two hundred 1980
11 and they *w'* in their simplicity, and "
16, 17 And the king *w'* forth, and all 3318
24 and Abiather *w'* up, until all the 5927
30 David *w'* up by the ascent of mount "
30 wept as he *w'* up, and had his head "
30 head covered, and he *w'* barefoot: 1980
30 man his head, and they *w'* up, 5927
30 weeping as they *w'* up. "
16: 13 David and his men *w'* by the way, 3212
13 Shimei *w'* along on the hill's side 1980
13 and cursed as he *w'*, and threw "
22 Absalom *w'* in unto his father's 935
17: 17 and a wench *w'* and told them; * 980
17 and they *w'* and told king David. 3212
18 they *w'* both of them away quickly, "
18 his court; whither they *w'* down. 3381
21 well, and *w'* and told king David, 3212
25 that *w'* in to Abigail the daughter 935
18: 6 people *w'* out into the field against 3318
9 mule *w'* under the thick boughs 935
9 mule that was under him *w'* away. 5674
24 the watchman *w'* up to the roof 3212
33 *w'* up to the chamber over the 5927
33 as he *w'*, thus he said, O my son 3212
19: 17 *w'* over Jordan before the king. 6743
18 there *w'* over a ferry boat to carry 5674
19 the king *w'* out of Jerusalem, 3318
31 and *w'* over Jordan with the king, 5674
39 all the people *w'* over Jordan. "
40 Then the king *w'* on to Gilgal, "
40 and Chimham *w'* on with him: and "
20: 2 So every man of Israel *w'* up from 5927
3 them, but *w'* not in unto them. 935
5 So Amasa *w'* to assemble the men 3212
7 there *w'* out after him Joab's men, 3318
7 they *w'* out of Jerusalem, to pursue "
8 in Gibeon, Amasa *w'* before them.* 935
8 and as he *w'* forth it fell out. 3318
13 all the people *w'* on after Joab, to 5674
14 *w'* through all the tribes of Israel "
14 together, and *w'* also after him. 935
22 woman *w'* unto all the people in her "
21: 12 David *w'* and took the bones of 3212
15 David *w'* down, and his servants 3381
22: 9 There *w'* up a smoke out of his 5927
23: 13 three of the thirty chief *w'* down, 3381
17 that *w'* in jeopardy of their lives? 1980
20 he *w'* down also and slew a lion 3381
21 but he *w'* down to him with a staff, "
24: 4 captains of the host *w'* out from 3318
7 they *w'* out to the south of Judah, "
19 *w'* up as the Lord commanded. *5927
20 and Araunah *w'* out, and bowed 3318
1Ki 1: 15 Bath-sheba *w'* in unto the king 935
38 and the Pelethites, *w'* down, and 3381
49 up, and *w'* every man his way. 3212
50 *w'*, and caught hold of the horns of "
2: 8 the day when I *w'* to Mahanaim: "
19 Bath-sheba therefore *w'* unto king 935
34 the son of Jehoiada *w'* up, and 5927
40 *w'* to Gath to Achish to seek his 3212
40 and Shimei *w'*, and brought his "
46 which *w'* out, and fell upon him. 3318
3: 4 the king *w'* to Gibeon to sacrifice 3212
6: 8 they *w'* up with winding stairs 5927
8: 66 *w'* unto their tents joyful and glad 3212
10: 5 *w'* up unto the house of the Lord; 5927
13 turned and *w'* to her own country, 3212
16 shekels of gold *w'* to one target. 5927
17 three pound of gold *w'* to one "
29 And a chariot...*w'* out of Egypt. 3318
11: 5 Solomon *w'* after Ashtoreth the 3212
6 *w'* not fully after the Lord, as did
24 they *w'* to Damascus, and dwelt 3212
29 Jeroboam *w'* out of Jerusalem, 3318
12: 1 And Rehoboam *w'* to Shechem: 3212
25 and *w'* out from thence, and built 3318
30 people *w'* to worship before the 3212
13: 10 So he *w'* another way, and returned "
12 said unto them, What way *w'* he? 1980
12 seen what way the man of God *w'*, "
14 And *w'* after the man of God, 3212
19 he *w'* back with him, and did eat 7725
28 he *w'* and found his carcase cast 3212
14: 4 *w'* to Shiloh, and came to the "
28 king *w'* into the house of the Lord, 935
15: 17 king of Israel *w'* up against Judah, 5927
16: 10 Zimri *w'* in and smote him, and 935
17 And Omri *w'* up from Gibbethon, 5927
18 he *w'* into the palace of the king's 935
31 and *w'* and served Baal, and 3212
17: 5 So he *w'* and did according unto "
5 *w'* and dwelt by the brook Cherith, "
10 So he arose and *w'* to Zarephath. "
15 she *w'* and did according to the "

1Ki 18: 2 Elijah *w'* to shew himself unto 3212
6 Ahab *w'* one way by himself, and 1980
6 and Obadiah *w'* another way by "
16 So Obadiah *w'* to meet Ahab, and 3212
16 and Ahab *w'* to meet Elijah. "
42 Ahab *w'* up to eat and to drink. 5927
42 Elijah *w'* up to the top of Carmel; "
43 he *w'* up, and looked, and said, "
45 And Ahab rode, and *w'* to Jezreel. 3212
19: 3 that, he arose, and *w'* for his life, "
4 he himself *w'* a day's journey into 1980
8 *w'* in the strength of that meat 3212
13 his face in his mantle, and *w'* out, 3318
21 *w'* after Elijah, and ministered 3212
20: 1 he *w'* up and besieged Samaria, 5927
16 And they *w'* out at noon. But 3318
17 of the provinces *w'* out first; "
21 king of Israel *w'* out, and smote "
26 *w'* up to Aphek, to fight against 5927
27 all present, and *w'* against them: 3212
39 Thy servant *w'* out into the midst 3318
43 the king of Israel *w'* to his house 3212
21: 27 lay in sackcloth, and *w'* softly. 1980
22: 24 the son of Chenaanah *w'* near, *5674
24 Which way *w'* the Spirit of the "
29 of Judah *w'* up to Ramoth-gilead. 5927
30 himself, and *w'* into the battle. 935
36 And there *w'* a proclamation 5674
48 but they *w'* not; for the ships 1980
2Ki 1: 9 And he *w'* up to him: and, behold, 5927
13 the third captain of fifty *w'* up, "
15 *w'* down with him unto the king. 3381
2: 1 Elijah *w'* with Elisha from Gilgal. 3212
2 thee. So they *w'* down to Beth-el. 3381
6 leave thee. And they two *w'* on. 3212
7 of the sons of the prophets *w'*, 1980
8 they two *w'* over on dry ground. 5674
11 it came to pass, as they still *w'* on, 1980
11 Elijah *w'* up by a whirlwind into 5927
13 *w'* back, and stood by the bank of 7725
14 and thither: and Elisha *w'* over. 5674
21 he *w'* forth unto the spring of the 3318
23 he *w'* up from thence unto Beth-el: 5927
25 *w'* from thence to mount Carmel, 3212
3: 6 king Jehoram *w'* out of Samaria 3318
7 he *w'* and sent to Jehoshaphat 3212
9 So the king of Israel *w'*, and the "
12 the king of Edom *w'* down to him. 3381
24 *w'* forward smiting the Moabites, 5221
25 howbeit the slingers *w'* about it, 5437
4: 5 So she *w'* from him, and shut the 3212
18 that he *w'* out to his father to the 3318
21 And she *w'* up, and laid him on 5927
21 the door upon him, and *w'* out. 3318
25 *w'* and came unto the man of God 3212
31 he *w'* again to meet him, and told 7725
33 He *w'* in therefore, and shut the 935
34 And he *w'* up, and lay upon the 5927
35 *w'* up, and stretched himself upon "
37 Then she *w'* in, and fell at his feet, 935
37 and took up her son, and *w'* out 3318
39 *w'* out into the field to gather herbs, "
5: 4 And one *w'* in, and told his lord. 935
11 Naaman was wroth, and *w'* away, 3212
12 So he turned and *w'* away in a rage. "
14 Then *w'* he down, and dipped 3381
25 But he *w'* in, and stood before his 935
25 said, Thy servant *w'* no whither. 1980
26 *W'* not mine heart with thee, when "
27 *w'* out from his presence a leper 3318
6: 4 So he *w'* with them. And when 3212
23 away, and they *w'* to their master. "
24 and *w'* up, and besieged Samaria. 5927
7: 8 they *w'* into one tent, and did eat 935
8 and raiment, and *w'* and hid it; 3212
15 they *w'* after them unto Jordan: "
16 the people *w'* out, and spoiled the 3318
8: 2 and she *w'* with her household, 3212
3 she *w'* forth to cry unto the king 3318
9 So Hazael *w'* to meet him, and 3212
21 So Joram *w'* over to Zair, and all 5674
28 he *w'* with Joram the son of Ahab 3212
29 king Joram *w'* back to be healed *7725
29 of Judah *w'* down to see Joram 3381
9: 4 the prophet, *w'* to Ramoth-gilead. 3212
6 he arose, and *w'* into the house; 935
16 in a chariot, and *w'* to Jezreel; 3212
18 So there *w'* one on horseback to "
21 Ahaziah king of Judah *w'* out, 3318
21 they *w'* out against Jehu, and met "
24 and the arrow *w'* out at his heart, "
35 And they *w'* to bury her: but they 3212
10: 9 he *w'* out, and stood, and said to 3318
23 Jehu *w'*, and Jehonadab the son of 935
24 when they *w'* in to offer sacrifices "
25 *w'* to the city of the house of Baal. 3212
11: 16 she *w'* by the way by the which the 935
18 people of the land *w'* into the house "
12: 17 Then Hazael king of Syria *w'* up, 5927
18 and he *w'* away from Jerusalem. "
13: 5 they *w'* out from under the hand 3318
14: 11 Jehoash king of Israel *w'* up; and 5927
15: 14 the son of Gadi *w'* up from Tirzah, "
16: 9 Assyria *w'* up against Damascus, "
10 king Ahaz *w'* to Damascus to 3212
17: 5 *w'* up to Samaria, and besieged it 5927
15 *w'* after...heathen that were round 3212
18: 7 he prospered whithersoever he *w'* 3318
17 they *w'* up and came to Jerusalem. 5927
19: 1 and *w'* into the house of the Lord. 935
14 *w'* up into the house of the Lord, 5927
35 that the angel of the Lord *w'* out, 3318
36 and returned, and dwelt at 3212
22: 14 *w'* unto Huldah the prophetess, "
23: 2 king *w'* up into the house of the 5927
29 king of Egypt *w'* up against the "

2Ki 23: 29 and king Josiah *w'* against him; 3212
24: 12 *w'* out to the king of Babylon, 3318
25: 4 king *w'* the way toward the plain. 3212
1Ch 2: 21 Hezron *w'* in to the daughter of 935
4: 39 they *w'* to the entrance of Gedor, 3212
42 hundred men, *w'* to mount Seir, 1980
5: 18 threescore, that *w'* out to the war.* 3318
25 *w'* a whoring after the gods of the‡
6: 15 And Jehozadak *w'* into captivity, 1980
7: 23 And when he *w'* in to his wife, she 935
23 because it *w'* evil with his house. 1961
10: 3 And the battle *w'* sore against Saul,
11: 4 and all Israel *w'* to Jerusalem, 3212
6 Joab the son of Zeruiah *w'* first up, 5927
15 captains *w'* down to the rock to 3381
22 he *w'* down and slew a lion in a pit "
23 he *w'* down to him with a staff, and "
12: 15 These are they that *w'* over Jordan 5674
17 And David *w'* out to meet them, 3318
20 As he *w'* to Ziklag, there fell to 3212
33 Zebulun, such as *w'* forth to battle,* 3318
36 of Asher, such as *w'* forth to battle,* "
13: 6 And David *w'* up, and all Israel, to 5927
14: 8 the Philistines *w'* up to seek David. "
8 of it, and *w'* out against them. 3318
17 the fame of David *w'* out into all "
15: 25 *w'* to bring up the ark of the 1980
16: 20 when they *w'* from nation to nation, "
17: 21 whom God *w'* to redeem to be his "
18: 3 as he *w'* to stablish his dominion 3212
6, 13 David whithersoever he *w'*. 1980
19: 5 Then there *w'* certain, and told 3212
16 host of Hadarezer *w'* before them.*
21: 4 and *w'* throughout all Israel, and 1980
19 David *w'* up at the saying of Gad, 5927
21 and *w'* out of the threshingfloor, 3318
27: 1 in and *w'* out month by month "
29: 30 and the times that *w'* over him, 5674
2Ch 1: 3 *w'* to the high place that was at 3212
6 *w'* up thither to the brasen altar 5927
8: 3 Solomon *w'* to Hamath-zobah, 3212
17 Then *w'* Solomon to Ezion-geber, 1980
18 *w'* with the servants of Solomon 935
9: 4 *w'* up into the house of the Lord; 5927
12 and *w'* away to her own land, 3212
15 shekels of...gold *w'* to one target. 5927
16 shekels of gold *w'* to one shield. "
21 the king's ships *w'* to Tarshish 1980
10: 1 And Rehoboam *w'* to Shechem: 3212
16 So all Israel *w'* to their tents. * "
12: 12 and also in Judah things *w'* well, *1961
14: 10 Then Asa *w'* out against him, and 3318
15: 2 And he *w'* out to meet Asa, and "
5 was no peace to him that *w'* out, "
17: 9 *w'* about throughout all the cities 5437
18: 2 certain years he *w'* down to Ahab 3381
12 messenger that *w'* to call Micaiah 1980
23 Which way *w'* the Spirit of the 5674
28 of Judah *w'* up to Ramoth-gilead. 5927
29 himself; and they *w'* to the battle. 935
19: 2 the seer *w'* out to meet him, 3318
4 *w'* out again through the people "
20: 20 and *w'* forth into the wilderness of "
20 and as they *w'* forth, Jehoshaphat "
21 as they *w'* out before the army, and "
21: 9 Jehoram *w'* forth with his princes,* 5674
22: 5 *w'* with Jehoram the son of Ahab 3212
6 *w'* down to see Jehoram the son 3381
7 he *w'* out with Jehoram against 3318
23: 2 And they *w'* about in Judah, and 5437
17 the people *w'* to the house of Baal, 935
25: 11 people, and *w'* to the valley of salt, 3212
21 So Joash the king of Israel *w'* up; 5927
26: 6 he *w'* forth and warred against the 3318
11 men, that *w'* out to war by bands, "
16 *w'* into the temple of the Lord to 935
17 Azariah the priest *w'* in after him, "
28: 9 *w'* out before the host that came 3318
29: 16 the priests *w'* into the inner part of 935
18 they *w'* in to Hezekiah the king, "
20 *w'* up to the house of the Lord. 5927
30: 6 posts *w'* with the letters from the 3212
31: 1 *w'* out to the cities of Judah, 3318
34: 22 *w'* to Huldah the prophetess, the 3212
30 *w'* up into the house of the Lord, 5927
35: 20 and Josiah *w'* out against him. 3318
Ezr 2: 1 that *w'* up out of the captivity, 5927
59 they which *w'* up from Tel-melah, "
4: 23 *w'* up in haste to Jerusalem unto 236
5: 8 we *w'* into the provinces of Judea, "
7: 6 This Ezra *w'* up from Babylon; 5927
7 there *w'* up some of the children of "
8: 1 that *w'* up with me from Babylon, "
10: 6 *w'* into the chamber of Johanan 3212
Ne 2: 13 I *w'* out by night by the gate of 3318
14 I *w'* on to the gate of the fountain, 5674
15 *w'* I up in the night by the brook, 5927
16 the rulers knew not whither I *w'*, 1980
7: 6 that *w'* up out of the captivity, 5927
61 which *w'* up also from Tel-melah, "
8: 12 all the people *w'* their way to eat, 3212
16 the people *w'* forth, and brought 3318
9: 11 *w'* through the midst of the sea on 5674
24 So the children *w'* in and possessed 935
12: 1 Levites that *w'* up with Zerubbabel 5927
31 one *w'* on the right hand upon the 1980
32 after them *w'* Hoshaiah, and half 3212
37 they *w'* up by the stairs of the city 5927
38 gave thanks *w'* over against them, 1980
Es 2: 14 In the evening she *w'*, and on the 935
3: 15 The posts *w'* out, being hastened 3318
4: 1 *w'* out into the midst of the city,
6 Hatach *w'* forth to Mordecai unto "
17 So Mordecai *w'* his way, and did 5674
5: 9 Then *w'* Haman forth that day 3318
7: 7 his wrath *w'* into the palace gardens:

Es 7: 8 word w' out of the king's mouth, 3318
8:14 upon mules and camels w' out, "
15 Mordecai w' out from the presence "
9: 4 his fame w' out throughout all the 1980
Job 1: 4 sons w' and feasted in their houses, "
12 Satan w' forth from the presence 3318
2: 7 So w' Satan forth from the presence "
18:20 they that w' before were affrighted. 6923
29: 7 When I w' out to the gate through 3318
30:28 I w' mourning without the sun: I* 1980
31:34 and w' not out of the door? 3318
42: 9 Zophar the Naamathite w', 3212
Ps 18: 8 w' up a smoke out of his nostrils, 5927
42: 4 I w' with them to the house of 1718
66: 6 they w' through the flood on foot: 5674
12 we w' through fire and through 935
68:25 The singers w' before, the 6923
73:17 Until I w' into the sanctuary of 935
77:17 thine arrows also w' abroad. 1980
81: 5 when he w' out through the land 3318
105:13 w' from one nation to another, 1980
106:32 it w' ill with Moses for their sakes: ‡
39 w' a whoring with their own
114: 1 When Israel w' out of Egypt, the 3318
119:67 Before I was afflicted I w' astray: 7683
133: 2 that w' down to the skirts of his *3381
Pr 7: 8 and he w' the way to her house, 6805
24:30 I w' by the field of the slothful, 5674
Ec 2:20 I w' about to cause my heart to *5437
Ca 5: 7 watchmen that w' about the city * "
6:11 I w' down into the garden of nuts 3381
Isa 7: 1 w' up toward Jerusalem to war 5927
8: 3 I w' unto the prophetess; and she 7126
37: 1 and w' into the house of the Lord. 935
14 Hezekiah w' up unto the house of 5927
36 the angel of the Lord w' forth, 3318
37 departed, and w' and returned, 3212
48: 3 they w' forth out of my mouth, 3318
51:23 the street, to them that w' over. *5674
52: 4 My people w' down aforetime into 3381
57:17 he w' on frowardly in the way of 3212
60:15 so that no man w' through thee, *5674
Jer 3: 8 but w' also, and played the harlot also. 3212
7:24 and w' backward, and not forward. 1961
11:10 they w' after other gods to serve *1980
13: 5 So I w', and hid it by Euphrates, 3212
7 Then I w' to Euphrates, and "
18: 3 I w' down to the potter's house, 3381
22:11 which w' forth out of this place; 3318
26:21 afraid, and fled, and w' into Egypt; 935
28: 4 of Judah, that w' into Babylon, "
11 prophet Jeremiah w' his way. 3212
31: 2 when I w' to cause him to rest. 1980
36:12 he w' down into the king's house, 3381
20 they w' in to the king into the 935
37: 4 in and w' out among the people: 3318
12 Jeremiah w' forth out of Jerusalem "
38: 8 w' forth out of the king's house, "
11 w' into the house of the king under 935
39: 4 w' forth out of the city by night, 3318
4 and he w' out the way of the plain. "
40: 6 Then w' Jeremiah unto Gedaliah 935
41: 6 Ishmael...w' forth from Mizpah 3318
6 them, weeping all along as he w': 1980
12 w' to fight with Ishmael the son 3212
14 and w' unto Johanan the son of "
15 men, and w' to the Ammonites. "
44: 3 in that they w' to burn incense, "
51:59 when he w' with Zedekiah the "
52: 7 w' forth out of the city by night by 3318
7 and they w' by the way of the plain. 3212
Eze 1: 9 they turned not when they w'; "
9 they w' every one straight forward. "
12 they w' every one straight forward: "
12 the spirit was to go, they w'; "
12 and they turned not when they w'. "
13 it w' up and down among the 1980
13 out of the fire w' forth lightning. 3318
17 When they w', they w' upon their 3212
17 and they turned not when they w'. "
19 living creatures w', the wheels w' "
20 the spirit was to go, they w', "
21 When those w', these w'; and when "
24 when they w', I heard the noise "
3:14 I w' in bitterness, in the heat of my "
23 and w' forth into the plain: 3318
8:10 So I w' in and saw; and behold 935
11 a thick cloud of incense w' up. 5927
9: 2 they w' in, and stood beside the 935
7 they w' forth, and slew in the city. 3318
10: 2 the city. And he w' in in my sight. 935
3 of the house, when the man w' in; "
4 glory of the Lord w' up from the *7311
6 then he w' in, and stood beside the 935
7 linen: who took it, and w' out. 3318
11 When they w', they w' upon their 3212
11 they turned not as they w', but to "
11 it; they turned not as they w'. "
16 the cherubims w', the wheels w' by "
19 when they w' out, the wheels also 3318
22 w' every one straight forward. 3212
11:23 glory of the Lord w' up from the 5927
24 vision that I had seen w' up from "
16:14 thy renown w' forth among the 3318
19: 6 he w' up and down among the 1980
20:16 for their heart w' after their idols. "
23:44 Yet they w' in unto her, as they go 935
44 so w' they in unto Aholah and unto "
24:12 scum w' not forth out of her: *3318
25: 3 of Judah, when they w' into captivity; "
27:33 thy wares w' forth out of the seas, 3318
31:15 day when he w' down to the grave 3381
17 They also w' down into hell with "
36:20 whither they w', they profaned my 935
21 among the heathen, whither they w'. "
22 among the heathen, whither ye w'. "
Eze 39:23 w' into captivity for their iniquity: "
40: 6 and w' up the stairs thereof, and 5927
22 they w' up unto it by seven steps; "
49 the steps whereby they w' up to it: "
41: 3 Then w' he inward, and measured 935
7 winding...of the house w' still upward
44:10 far from me, when Israel w' astray, 8582
10 which w' astray away from me after "
15 children of Israel w' astray from me, "
47: 3 line in his hand w' forth eastward, 3318
48:11 my charge, which w' not astray 8582
11 the children of Israel w' astray, "
11 as the Levites w' astray. "
Da 2:13 decree w' forth that the wise men 5312
16 Then Daniel w' in, and desired of 5954
17 Then Daniel w' to his house, and 236
24 Daniel w' in unto Arioch, whom 5954
24 he w' and said thus unto him; 236
6:10 was signed, he w' into his house; 5954
18 Then the king w' to his palace, 236
18 him: and his sleep w' from him. *5075
19 w' in haste unto the den of lions. 236
Ho 1: 3 So he w' and took Gomer the 3212
2:13 she w' after her lovers, and forgat "
5:13 then w' Ephraim to the Assyrian, "
9:10 but they w' to Baal-peor, and * 935
11: 2 called them, so they w' from them: 1980
Am 5: 3 city that w' out by a thousand 3318
3 that which w' forth by an hundred "
19 or w' into the house, and leaned his 935
Jon 1: 3 the Lord, and w' down to Joppa; 3381
3 fare thereof, and w' down into it, "
2: 6 I w' down to the bottoms of the "
3: 3 arose, and w' unto Nineveh, 3212
4: 5 So Jonah w' out of the city, and 3318
Na 3:10 carried away, she w' into captivity: 1980
Hab 3: 5 Before him w' the pestilence, and 3212
5 burning coals w' forth at his feet. 3318
11 the light of thine arrows they w', 1980
Zec 2: 3 angel that talked with me w' forth, 3318
3 another angel w' out to meet him, "
5: 5 angel that talked with me w' forth, "
6: 7 And the bay w' forth, and sought to "
8:10 peace to him that w' out or came in "
10: 2 they w' their way as a flock, they *5265
M't 2: 9 saw in the east, w' before them, 4254
3: 5 Then w' out to him Jerusalem, 1607
16 w' up straightway out of the water: 305
4:23 And Jesus w' about all Galilee, 4013
24 his fame w' throughout all Syria: 565
5: 1 he w' up into a mountain: 305
8:32 out, they w' into the herd of swine: 565
33 fled, and w' their ways into the city, "
9:25 he w' in, and took her by the hand, *1525
26 fame...w' abroad into all that land. 1831
32 As they w' out, behold, they "
35 Jesus w' about all the cities and 4013
11: 7 What w' ye out into the wilderness 1831
8 what w' ye out for to see? A man "
9 But what w' ye out for to see? A "
12: 1 Jesus w' on the sabbath through 4198
9 thence, he w' into their synagogue: 2064
14 Then the Pharisees w' out, and 1831
13: 1 same day w' Jesus out of the house, "
2 so that he w' into a ship, and sat; *1684
3 Behold, a sower w' forth to sow; 1831
25 among the wheat, and w' his way. 565
36 away, and w' into the house: 2064
46 w' and sold all that he had, and * 565
14:12 buried it, and w' and told Jesus. 2064
14 Jesus w' forth, and saw a great *1831
23 he w' up into a mountain apart to 305
25 of the night Jesus w' unto them, * 565
15:21 Then Jesus w' thence, and 1831
29 and w' up into a mountain, and sat 305
18:13 and nine which w' not astray. *4105
28 But the same servant w' out, and 1831
30 but w' and cast him into prison, 565
19:22 that saying, he w' away sorrowful: "
20: 1 which w' out early in the morning 1821
3 And he w' out about the third hour, "
4 give you. And they w' their way. 565
5 Again he w' out about the sixth 1831
6 about the eleventh hour he w' out, "
21: 6 And the disciples w', and did as 4198
9 the multitudes that w' before, 4254
12 Jesus w' into the temple of God, *1525
17 and w' out of the city into Bethany; 1831
29 but afterward he repented, and w'. 565
30 and said, I go, sir: and w' not. "
33 and w' into a far country: 589
22: 5 made light of it, and w' their ways, 565
10 servants w' out into the highways, 1831
15 Then w' the Pharisees, and took 4198
22 and left him, and w' their way. 565
24: 1 Jesus w' out, and departed from 1831
25: 1 w' forth to meet the bridegroom. "
10 And while they w' to buy, the 565
10 were ready w' in with him to the 1525
16 five talents w' and traded with the 4198
18 one w' and digged in the earth, and 565
25 w' and hid thy talent in the earth: "
26:14 Iscariot, w' unto the chief priests, 4198
30 w' out into the mount of Olives. 1831
39 he w' a little farther, and fell on 4281
42 He w' away again the second time, 565
44 And he left them, and w' away again, "
58 the high priest's palace, and w' in, *1525
75 And he w' out, and wept bitterly. 1831
27: 5 and w' and hanged himself. 565
53 w' into the holy city, and appeared *1525
58 He w' to Pilate, and begged the 4334
66 So they w', and made the sepulchre 4198
28: 9 as they w' to tell his disciples, * "
16 disciples w' away into Galilee, "
M'r 1: 5 w' out unto him all the land of 1607
M'r 1:20 hired servants, and w' after him. 565
21 And they w' into Capernaum; and *1531
35 he w' out, and departed into a 1831
45 he w' out, and began to publish it "
2:12 bed, and w' forth before them all; "
13 he w' forth again by the sea side; "
23 he w' through the corn fields on *3899
23 as they w', to pluck the ears of 3598, 4160
26 How he w' into the house of God *1525
3: 6 And the Pharisees w' forth, and 1831
19 him: and they w' into an house. 2064
21 it, they w' out to lay hold on him: 1831
4: 3 Behold, there w' out a sower to sow: "
5:13 And the unclean spirits w' out, * "
14 they w' out to see what it was that "
24 Jesus w' with him; and much 565
6: 1 he w' out from thence, and came 1831
6 he w' round about the villages, 4013
12 they w' out, and preached that 1831
24 she w' forth, and said unto her "
27 he w' and beheaded him in the 565
51 he w' up unto them into the ship; 305
7:24 w' into the borders of Tyre and 565
8:27 Jesus w' out, and his disciples, 1831
10:22 that saying, and w' away grieved: 565
32 and Jesus w' before them: and 4254
46 w' out of Jericho with his disciples 1607
11: 4 they w' their way, and found the 565
9 they that w' before, and they that 4254
11 he w' out unto Bethany with the 1831
15 and Jesus w' into the temple, and *1525
19 was come, he w' out of the city. 1607
12: 1 and w' into a far country. 589
12 and they left him, and w' their way. 565
13: 1 And as he w' out of the temple, 1607
14:10 twelve, w' unto the chief priests, 565
16 his disciples w' forth, and came 1831
26 w' out into the mount of Olives. "
35 he w' forward a little, and fell on 4281
39 again he w' away, and prayed, and 565
68 And he w' out into the porch; and 1831
15:43 and w' in boldly unto Pilate, and 1525
16: 8 they w' out quickly, and fled from 1831
10 she w' and told them that had 4198
12 walked, and w' into the country. * "
13 w' and told it unto the residue: 565
20 And they w' forth, and preached 1831
Lu 1: 9 he w' into the temple of the Lord. 1525
39 w' into the hill country with haste, 4198
2: 1 there w' out a decree from Cæsar 1831
3 all w' to be taxed, every one into 4198
4 And Joseph also w' up from Galilee, 305
41 his parents w' to Jerusalem every 4198
42 they w' up to Jerusalem after the 305
44 the company, w' a day's journey; 2064
51 he w' down with them, and came 2597
4:14 there w' out a fame of him through 1831
16 he w' into the synagogue on the *1525
30 the midst of them w' his way, 4198
37 fame of him w' out into every place 1607
42 he departed and w' into a desert 4198
5:15 the more w' there a fame abroad 1330
19 they w' upon the housetop, and let 305
27 And after these things he w' forth, 1831
6: 1 that he w' through the corn fields; *1279
4 How he w' into the house of God, *1525
12 he w' out into a mountain to pray, 1831
19 for there w' virtue out of him, and* "
7: 6 Then Jesus w' with them. And 4198
11 that he w' into a city called Nain, "
11 many of his disciples w' with him, 4848
17 rumour of him w' forth throughout 1831
24 What w' ye out into the wilderness "
25, 26 But what w' ye out for to see? "
36 he w' into the Pharisee's house, *1525
8: 1 that he w' throughout every city 1353
2 out of whom w' seven devils, *1831
5 A sower w' out to sow his seed: and "
22 w' into a ship with his disciples: *1684
27 And when he w' forth to land, *1831
33 Then w' the devils out of the man, * "
34 w' and told it in the city and in the *565
35 they w' out to see what was done; 1831
37 and he w' up into the ship, and *1684
39 And he w' his way, and published 565
42 as he w' the people thronged him. 5217
9: 6 and w' through the towns, 1330
10 w' aside privately into a desert *5298
28 and w' up into a mountain to pray. 305
52 they w', and entered into a village 4198
56 And they w' to another village. "
57 as they w' in the way, a certain man "
10:30 man w' down from Jerusalem to *2597
34 And w' to him, and bound up his *4334
38 as they w', that he entered into a 4198
11:37 he w' in, and sat down to meat. 1525
13:22 w' through the cities and villages, 1279
14: 1 as he w' into the house of one of 2064
25 w' great multitudes with him: and 4848
15:15 w' and joined himself to a citizen 4198
16:30 if one w' unto them from the dead, * "
17:11 as he w' to Jerusalem, that he * "
14 as they w', they were cleansed. 5217
29 day that Lot w' out of Sodom it 1831
18:10 Two men w' up into the temple to 305
14 this man w' down to his house 2597
39 they which w' before rebuked him, 4254
19:12 nobleman w' into a far country to 4198
28 he w' before, ascending up to "
32 they that were sent w' their way, 565
36 as he w', they spread their clothes 4198
45 he w' into the temple, and began *1525
20: 9 w' into a far country for a long time. 589
21:37 at night he w' out, and abode in the 1831
22: 4 he w' his way, and communed with 565
13 they w', and found as he had said "

Lu 22:39 w'. as he was wont, to the mount 4198
47 one of the twelve, w' before them, 4281
62 Peter w' out, and wept bitterly. 1831
23:52 This man w' unto Pilate, and 4344
24:13 two of them w' that same day to a*4198
15 drew near, and w' with them. 4848
24 were with us w' to the sepulchre, 565
28 unto the village, whither they w':*4198
29 And he w' in to tarry with them. 1525
Joh 2:12 this he w' down to Capernaum, 2597
13 and Jesus w' up to Jerusalem, 305
4:28 w' her way into the city, and saith 565
30 Then they w' out of the city, and 1831
43 departed thence, and w' into Galilee.565
45 for they also w' unto the feast. 2064
47 he w' unto him, and besought him 565
50 unto him, and he w' his way. 4198
5: 1 and Jesus w' up to Jerusalem. 305
4 For an angel w' down at a certain*2597
6: 1 Jesus w' over the sea of Galilee, 565
3 And Jesus w' up into a mountain, 424
16 disciples w' down unto the sea, 2597
17 w' over...sea toward Capernaum. *2064
21 was at the land whither they w'. *5217
22 Jesus w' not with his disciples *4897
66 time many of his disciples w' back, 565
7:10 then w' he also up unto the feast, 305
14 feast Jesus w' up into the temple, "
53 every man w' unto his own house. 4198
8: 1 Jesus w' unto the mount of Olives. "
9 w' out one by one, beginning at 1831
59 himself, and w' out of the temple, "
9: 7 He w' his way therefore, and 565
11 I w' and washed, and I received "
10:40 w' away again beyond Jordan into "
11:20 was coming, w' and met him: 5221
28 she had so said, she w' her way, 565
31 she rose up hastily and w' out, 1831
46 some of them w' their ways to the 565
54 w' thence unto a country near to * "
55 many w' out of the country up to 305
12:11 of him many of the Jews w' away, 5217
13 trees, and w' forth to meet him, 1831
13: 3 come from God, and w' to God; *5217
30 having received the sop w'...out: 1831
18: 1 w' forth with his disciples over the "
4 w' forth, and said unto them, "
6 they w' backward, and fell to the 565
15 w' in with Jesus into the palace of*4897
16 Then w' out that other disciple, 1831
28 w' not into the judgment hall, *1525
29 Pilate then w' out unto them, and 1831
38 he w' out again unto the Jews, "
19: 4 Pilate therefore w' forth again, and "
9 w' again into the judgment hall, *1525
17 w' forth into a place called the 1831
20: 3 Peter therefore w' forth, and that "
5 clothes lying; yet w' he not in. *1525
6 w' into the sepulchre, and seeth * "
8 Then w' in also that other disciple,* "
10 disciples w' away again unto their 565
21: 3 They w' forth, and entered into a 1831
11 Simon Peter w' up, and drew the 305
23 Then w' this saying abroad among1831
Ac 1:10 toward heaven as he w' up, 4198
13 they w' up into an upper room, 305
21 Lord Jesus w' in and out 1525,1831
3: 1 Now Peter and John w' up together305
4:23 they w' to their own company, *2064
5:26 w' the captain with the officers, 565
7:15 So Jacob w' down into Egypt, and 2597
8: 4 w' every where preaching the 1330
5 Then Philip w' down to the city of 2718
27 And he arose and w': and, behold,4198
36 And as they w' on their way, they "
38 they w' down both into the water, 2597
39 and he w' on his way rejoicing. 4198
9: 1 the Lord, w' unto the high priest, 4334
17 Ananias w' his way, and entered * 565
29 but they w' about to slay him. 2021
39 Peter arose and w' with them. 4905
10: 9 as they w' on their journey, and *3596
9 Peter w' up upon the housetop to 305
21 Then Peter w' down to the men 2597
23 morrow Peter w' away with them, 1831
27 he w' in, and found many that 1525
38 who w' about doing good, and 1330
12: 9 And he w' out, and followed him; 1831
10 they w' out, and passed on through "
17 and w' into another place. 4198
19 And he w' down from Judæa to 2718
13:11 he w' about seeking some to lead 4013
14 and w' into the synagogue on the 1525
14: 1 w' both together into the synagogue*"
25 Perga, they w' down into Attalia: 2597
15:24 certain which w' out from us have 1831
38 and w' not with them to the work. 4905
41 he w' through Syria and Cilicia, 1330
16: 4 as they w' through the cities, they 1279
13 on the sabbath we w' out of the 1831
16 as we w' to prayer, a certain *4198
40 And they w' out of the prison, and 1831
17: 2 his manner was, w' in unto them, 1525
10 w' into the synagogue of the Jews. 549
18:22 church, he w' down to Antioch. 2597
23 w' over all the country of Galatia 1330
19: 8 And he w' into the synagogue, *1525
12 the evil spirits w' out of them. 1831
20:10 Paul w' down, and fell on him, and2597
13 we w' before to ship, and sailed *4281
21: 2 we w' aboard, and set forth. 1910
5 we departed and w' our way; and 4198
15 carriages, and w' up to Jerusalem. 305
16 There w' with us also certain of 4905
18 Paul w' in with us unto James; 1524
31 And as they w' about to kill him, 2212
Ac 22: 5 w' to Damascus, to bring them *4198
26 he w' and told the chief captain, 4334
23:16 he w' and entered into the castle,*3854
19 and w' with him aside privately, *402
24:11 days since I w' up to Jerusalem 305
25: 6 days, he w' down unto Cæsarea; 2597
26:12 as I w' to Damascus with authority*4198
21 temple, and w' about to kill me. *3987
28:14 days: and so we w' toward Rome.*2064
Ro 10:18 their sound w' into all the earth, 1831
2Co 2:13 I w' from thence into Macedonia. "
8:17 of his own accord he w' unto you. "
Ga 1:17 Neither w' I up to Jerusalem to 424
17 but I w' into Arabia, and returned 565
18 Then after three years I w' up to 424
2: 1 I w' up again to Jerusalem with 305
2 And I w' up by revelation, and "
1Ti 1: 3 when I w' into Macedonia, *4198
18 to the prophecies which w' before 4254
Heb 9: 6 the priests w' always into the *1524
7 into the second w' the high priest* "
11: 8 obeyed; and he w' out, 1831
8 not knowing whither he w'. 2064
1Pe 3:19 he w' and preached unto the 4198
1Jo 2:19 They w' out from us, but they were1831
19 they w' out, that they might be made "
3Jo 7 for his name's sake they w' forth, 1831
Re 1:16 his mouth w' a sharp twoedged *1607
6: 2 he w' forth conquering, and to *1831
4 there w' out another horse that * "
10: 9 I w' unto the angel, and said unto 565
12:17 w' to make war with the remnant of "
16: 2 the first w', and poured out his vial "
20: 9 they w' upon the breadth of the 305

wentest
Ge 49: 4 thou w' up to thy father's bed; 5927
J'g 5: 4 Lord, when thou w' out of Seir, 3318
8: 1 when thou w' to fight with the 1980
1Sa 10: 2 asses which thou w' to seek are "
2Sa 7: 9 with thee whithersoever thou w', "
16:17 why w' thou not with thy friend? "
19:25 Wherefore w' not thou with me, "
Ps 68: 7 thou w' forth before thy people, 3318
Isa 57: 7 even thither w' thou up to offer 5927
9 thou w' to the king with ointment,7788
Jer 2: 2 thou w' after me in the wilderness,3212
31:21 even the way which thou w': 1980
Hab 3:13 Thou w' forth for the salvation of 3318
Ac 11: 3 Thou w' in to men uncircumcised,1525

wept
Ge 21:16 and lift up her voice, and w'. 1058
27:38 Esau lifted up his voice, and w'. "
29:11 and lifted up his voice, and w'. "
33: 4 neck, and kissed him: and they w'. "
37:35 Thus his father w' for him. "
42:24 himself about from them, and w'; "
43:30 into his chamber, and w' there. "
45: 2 And he w' aloud: 5414,853,6963,1065
14 brother Benjamin's neck, and w'; 1058
14 and Benjamin w' upon his neck. "
15 his brethren, and w' upon them: "
46:29 and w' on his neck a good while. "
50: 1 and w' upon him, and kissed him. "
17 Joseph w' when they spake unto "
Ex 2: 6 child: and, behold, the babe w'. "
Nu 11: 4 children of Israel also w' again, "
18 ye have w' in the ears of the Lord, "
20 and have w' before him, saying, "
14: 1 cried; and the people w' that night."
De 1:45 returned and w' before the Lord; "
34: 8 the children of Israel w' for Moses "
J'g 2: 4 people lifted up their voice, and w'. "
14:16 And Samson's wife w' before him, "
17 she w' before him the seven days, "
20:23 and w' before the Lord until even, "
26 came unto the house of God, and w', "
21: 2 lifted up their voices, and w' sore; "
Ru 1: 9 they lifted up their voice, and w'. "
14 lifted up their voice, and w' again: "
1Sa 1: 7 therefore she w', and did not eat. "
10 prayed unto the Lord, and w' sore. "
11: 4 people lifted up their voices, and w'. "
20:41 w' one with another, until David "
24:16 Saul lifted up his voice, and w'. "
30: 4 him lifted up their voice and w' "
2Sa 1:12 they mourned, and w', and fasted "
3:32 and w' at the grave of Abner; "
32 of Abner; and all the people w'. "
34 all the people w' again over him. "
12:22 child was yet alive, I fasted and w': "
13:36 and lifted up their voice and w': "
36 and all his servants w' very sore. "
15:23 all the country w' with a loud voice, "
30 mount Olivet, and w' as he went up, "
18:33 the chamber over the gate, and w': "
2Ki 8:11 ashamed: and the man of God w'. "
13:14 and w' over his face, and said, O my "
20: 3 thy sight. And Hezekiah w' sore. "
22:19 rent thy clothes, and w' before me; "
Ezr 3:12 their eyes, w' with a loud voice; "
10: 1 for the people w' very sore. "
Ne 1: 4 words, that I sat down and w', "
8: 9 For all the people w', when they "
Job 2:12 they lifted up their voice, and w'; "
Ps 69:10 When I w', and chastened my soul "
137: 1 we w', when we remembered Zion. "
Isa 38: 3 thy sight. And Hezekiah w' sore. "
Ho 12: 4 he w', and made supplication unto "
M't 26:75 And he went out, and w' bitterly. 2799
M'r 5:38 them that w' and wailed greatly. "
14:72 when he thought thereon, he w'. * "
16:10 with him, as they mourned and w'. "
Lu 7:32 to you, and ye have not w'. "
8:52 all w', and bewailed her: but he * "
19:41 he beheld the city, and w' over it, "
Lu 22:62 Peter went out, and w' bitterly. 2799
Joh 11:35 Jesus w'. 1145
20:11 and as she w', she stooped down, 2799
Ac 20:37 And they all w' sore, and fell on1096,2805
1Co 7:30 that weep, as though they w' not; 2799
Re 5: 4 And I w' much, because no man "

were See in the APPENDIX; also WERT.

wert See also WAST.
Job 8: 6 If thou w' pure and upright; surely
Ca 8: 1 O that thou w' as my brother, that
Ro 11:17 olive tree, w' graffed in among them,*
24 For if thou w' cut out of the olive tree
24 and w' graffed contrary to nature into
Re 3:15 nor hot: I would thou w' cold or hot.1498

west See also WESTERN; WESTWARD.
Ge 12: 8 having Beth-el on the w', and Hai 3220
28:14 thou shalt spread abroad to the w'. "
Ex 10:19 turned a mighty strong w' wind, "
27:12 the w' side shall be hangings of fifty"
38:12 the w' side were hangings of fifty "
Nu 2:18 On the w' side shall be the standard"
34: 6 this shall be your w' border. "
35: 5 on the w' side two thousand cubits, "
De 33:23 possess thou the w' and the south. "
Jos 8: 9 Beth-el and Ai, on the w' side of Ai:"
12 and Ai, on the w' side of the city. "
13 liers in wait on the w' of the city, "
11: 2 in the borders of Dor on the w', "
3 on the east and on the w', "
12: 7 on this side Jordan on the w', * "
15:12 the w' border was to the great sea, "
18:14 of Judah: this was the w' quarter. "
15 and the border went out on the w',*"
19:34 reacheth to Asher on the w' side, "
1Ki 7:25 and three looking toward the w', "
1Ch 9:24 toward the east, w', north, and "
12:15 the east, and toward the w'. 4628
2Ch 4: 4 and three looking toward the w', 3220
32:30 to the w' side of the city of David. 4628
33:14 on the w' side of Gihon, in the "
Ps 75: 6 from the east, nor from the w', "
103:12 As far as the east is from the w', "
107: 3 from the east, and from the w', "
Isa 11:14 of the Philistines toward the w'; 3220
43: 5 east, and gather thee from the w';4628
45: 6 and from the w', that there is none "
49:12 and from the w'; and these from 3220
59:19 the name of the Lord from the w', 4628
Eze 41:12 end toward the w' was seventy 3220
42:19 He turned about to the w' side, "
45: 7 city, from the w' side westward, "
7 from the w' border unto the east "
47:20 w' side also shall be the great sea "
20 Hamath. This is the w' side. "
48: 1 for these are his sides east and w'; "
2 from the east side unto the w' side, "
3 the east side even unto the w' side, "
4, 5 the east side unto the w' side, "
6 the east side even unto the w' side, "
7, 8 the east side unto the w' side, "
8 from the east side unto the w' side: "
10 and toward the w' ten thousand in "
16 the w' side four thousand and five "
17 toward the w' two hundred and "
21 and twenty thousand toward the w'" "
23, 24, 25, 26, 27 east side unto the w' "
34 At the w' side four thousand and "
Da 8: 5 an he goat came from the w' on 4628
Ho 11:10 children shall tremble from the w'.3220
Zec 8: 7 and from the w' country; 3996,8121
14: 4 toward the east and toward the w'.3220
M't 8:11 shall come from the east and w', 1424
24:27 east, and shineth even unto the w'; "
Lu 12:54 ye see a cloud rise out of the w', "
13:29 from the east, and from the w', "
Ac 27:12 toward the south w' and north 3047
12 toward the south...and north w'. 5566
Re 21:13 gates; and on the w' three gates. 1424

western
Nu 34: 6 And as for the w' border, ye shall 3220

westward
Ge 13:14 southward, and eastward, and w':3220
Ex 26:22 for the sides of the tabernacle w' "
27 the tabernacle, for the two sides w'."
36:27 for the sides of the tabernacle w' "
32 of the tabernacle for the sides w'. "
Nu 3:23 pitch behind the tabernacle w'. "
De 3:27 of Pisgah, and lift up thine eyes w', "
Jos 5: 1 were on the side of Jordan w', and "
15: 8 before the valley of Hinnom w', "
10 from Baalah w' unto mount Seir, "
16: 3 down w' to the coast of Japhleti, "
8 Tappuah w' unto the river Kanah; "
18:12 went up through the mountains w'; "
19:26 and reacheth to Carmel w', and to "
34 coast turneth w' to Aznoth-tabor, "
22: 7 brethren on this side Jordan w'. "
23: 4 even unto the great sea w'. *3996,8121
1Ch 7:28 and w' Gezer, with the towns 4628
26:16 and Hosah the lot came forth w', "
18 At Parbar w', four at the causeway,"
30 of Israel on this side Jordan w'. "
Eze 45: 7 of the city, from the west side w'. 3220
46:19 was a place on the two sides w'. "
48:18 eastward, and ten thousand w': "
21 and w' over against the five and "
Da 8: 4 I saw the ram pushing w', and "

west-wind See WEST and WIND.

wet
Job 24: 8 They are w' with the showers of 7372
Da 4:15, 23 be w' with the dew of heaven, 6647
25 w' thee with the dew of heaven, "

Da 4:33 and his body was w· with the dew 6647
5:21 and his body was w· with the dew "

whale See also WHALE'S; WHALES.
Job 7:12 Am I a sea, or a w·, that thou *8577
Eze 32: 2 and thou art as a w· in the seas: *8565

whale's
M't 12:40 and three nights in the w· belly; *2785

whales
Ge 1:21 And God created great w·, and *8577

what See also SOMEWHAT; WHATSOEVER.
Ge 2:19 to see w· he would call them: 4100
3:13 W· is this that thou hast done? "
4:10 And he said, W· hast thou done? "
9:24 w· his younger son had done 853,834
12:18 W· is this that thou hast done 4100
15: 2 Lord God, w· wilt thou give me, "
20: 9 him, W· hast thou done unto us? "
9 and w· have I offended thee, that* "
10 W· sawest thou, that thou hast "
21:17 unto her, W· aileth thee, Hagar? "
24:65 W· man is this that walketh in 4310
25:32 w· profit shall this birthright do 4100
26:10 W· is this thou hast done unto us? "
27:37 and w· shall I do now unto thee, "
46 land, w· good shall my life do me? "
29:15 tell me, w· shall thy wages be? "
25 W· is this thou hast done unto me? "
30:31 And he said, W· shall I give thee? "
31:26 W· hast thou done, that thou hast "
36 W· is my trespass? w· is my sin, "
43 w· can I do this day unto these my "
32:27 he said unto him, W· is thy name? "
33: 8 W· meanest thou by all this drove4310
15 And he said, W· needeth it? let 4100
34:11 w· ye shall say unto me I will give. 834
37:10 W· is this dream that thou hast 4100
15 him, saying, W· seekest thou? "
20 see w· will become of his dreams. "
26 W· profit is it if we slay our brother, "
38:16 And she said, W· wilt thou give me, "
18 said, W· pledge shall I give thee? 834
39: 8 not w· is with me in the house, 4100
41:25 Pharaoh w· he is about to do. 853,834
28 W· God is about to do he sheweth "
55 unto Joseph; w· he saith to you, do. "
42:28 W· is this that God hath done 4100
44:15 W· deed is this that ye have done? "
16 W· shall we say unto my lord? "
16 w· shall we speak? or how shall we "
46:33 shall say, W· is your occupation? "
47: 3 brethren, W· is your occupation? "
Ex 3:13 shall say to me, W· is his name? "
13 w· shall I say unto them? "
4: 2 unto him, W· is that in thine hand? "
12 and teach thee w· thou shalt say. 834
15 will teach you w· ye shall do. 853, "
10: 2 w· things I have wrought in " "
26 with w· we must serve the Lord, 4100
12:26 you, W· mean ye by this service? "
13:14 in time to come, saying, W· is this? "
15:24 Moses, saying, W· shall we drink? "
16: 7 w· are we, that ye murmur against "
8 w· are we? your murmurings are "
15 manna: for they wist not w· it was. "
17: 4 W· shall I do unto this people? "
18:14 W· is this thing that thou doest to "
19: 4 seen w· I did unto the Egyptians, 834
23:11 w· they leave the beasts of the field
32: 1 we wot not w· is become of him. 4100
21 W· did this people unto thee, that "
23 we wot not w· is become of him. "
Le 15: 9 w· saddle soever he rideth upon 834
17: 3 W· man soever there be of...Israel, 376
22: 4 W· man soever of the seed of Aaron "
25:20 W· shall we eat the seventh year? 4100
Nu 9: 8 hear w· the Lord will command "
10:32 that w· goodness the Lord shall do 834
13:18 And see the land, w· it is; and the4100
19 w· the land is that they dwell in, "
19 w· cities they be that they dwell in, "
20 w· the land is, whether it be fat or "
15:34 declared w· should be done to him. "
16:11 and w· is Aaron, that ye murmur "
21:14 W· he did in the Red sea, and in *853
22: 9 W· men are these with thee? 4310
19 may know w· the Lord will say 4100
28 W· have I done unto thee, that "
23:11 W· hast thou done unto me? "
17 him, W· hath the Lord spoken? "
23 of Israel, W· hath God wrought! "
24:13 w· the Lord saith, that will I speak?834
14 w· this people shall do to thy people "
26:10 w· time the fire devoured two hundred
31:50 w· every man hath gotten, of 834
De 1:22 again by w· way must we go up, * "
22 and into w· cities we shall come. * 853
33 shew you by w· way ye should go, 834
3:24 for w· God is there in heaven or 4310
4: 3 eyes have seen w· the Lord did 853,834
7 For w· nation is there so great, 4310
8 And w· nation is there so great, "
6:20 W· mean the testimonies, and 4100
7:18 remember w· the Lord thy God853,834
8: 2 to know w· was in thine heart, " "
10:12 w· doth the Lord thy God require 4100
11: 4 w· he did unto the army of Egypt, 834
5 w· he did unto you in the wilderness, "
6 w· he did unto Dathan and Abiram, "
12:32 W· thing soever I command you, 853
20: 5 W· man is there that hath built a 4310
6 w· man is he that hath planted a "
7 w· man is there that hath betrothed "
8 W· man is there that is fearful "
24: 9 w· the Lord...did unto Miriam 853,834
De 25:17 w· Amalek did unto thee 853,834
29:24 w· meaneth the heat of this great 4100
32:20 I will see w· their end shall be: "
Jos 2:10 w· ye did unto the two kings of the 834
4: 6 W· mean ye by these stones? 4100
21 saying, W· mean these stones? "
5:14 W· saith my lord unto his servant? "
7: 8 O Lord, w· shall I say, when Israel "
9 w· wilt thou do unto thy great "
19 tell me now w· thou hast done; "
9: 3 Gibeon heard w· Joshua had 853,834
15:18 said unto her, w· wouldest thou? 4100
22:16 W· trespass is this that ye have "
24 W· have ye to do with the Lord "
24: 7 seen w· I have done in Egypt: 853,834
J'g 1:14 Caleb said unto her, W· wilt thou?4100
7:11 And thou shalt hear w· they say; "
8: 2 W· have I done now in comparison "
3 w· was I able to do in comparison "
18 W· manner of men were they 375
9:48 W· ye have seen me do, make 4100
10:18 W· man is he that will begin to 4310
11:12 W· hast thou to do with me, that 4100
13: 8 teach us w· we shall do unto the "
17 W· is thy name, that when thy 4310
14: 6 or his mother w· he had done. 853,834
18 down, W· is sweeter than honey? 4100
18 w· is stronger than a lion? And he "
15:11 w· is this that thou hast done unto "
16: 5 w· means we may prevail against "
18: 3 and w· makest thou in this place? "
3 and w· hast thou here? "
8 said unto them, W· say ye? "
14 therefore consider w· ye have to do. "
18 the priest unto them, W· do ye? "
23 W· aileth thee, that thou comest "
24 gone away: and w· have I more? "
24 w· is this that ye say unto me, * "
24 ye say unto me, W· aileth thee? "
19:24 them w· seemeth good unto you: "
20:12 W· wickedness is this that is done4100
21: 8 W· one is there of the tribes of 4310
Ru 2:18 in law saw w· she had gleaned:853,834
3: 4 he will tell thee w· thou shalt do. " "
4: 5 W· day thou buyest the field
1Sa 1:23 Do w· seemeth thee good; tarry
3:17 W· is the thing that the Lord 4100
18 let him do w· seemeth him good.
4: 6, 14 W· meaneth the noise of this 4100
16 he said, W· is there done, my son?* "
5: 8 W· shall we do with the ark of the "
6: 2 W· shall we do to the ark of the "
4 W· shall be the trespass offering "
9: 7 we go, w· shall we bring the man? "
7 to the man of God: w· have we? "
10: 2 saying, W· shall I do for my son? "
8 shew thee w· thou shalt do. 853,834
11 W· is this that is come unto the 4100
15 thee, w· Samuel said unto you. "
11: 5 W· aileth the people that they "
13:11 Samuel said, W· hast thou done? "
14:40 Saul, Do w· seemeth good unto thee.
43 Tell me w· thou hast done. 4100
15:14 W· meaneth then this bleating of "
16 tell thee w· the Lord hath said 853,834
16: 3 will shew thee w· thou shalt do: " "
17:26 W· shall be done to the man that 4100
29 David said, W· have I now done? "
18: 8 w· can he have more but the kingdom?
18 and w· is my life, or my father's 4310
19: 3 and w· I see, that I will tell thee. *4100
20: 1 Jonathan, W· have I done? "
1 w· is mine iniquity? "
1 w· is my sin before thy father, that "
10 or w· if thy father answer thee * "
32 shall he be slain? w· hath he done? "
21: 2 and w· I have commanded thee: 834
3 w· is under thine hand? give 4100
3 in mine hand, or w· there is present.*
22: 3 till I know w· God will do for me. 4100
25:17 and consider w· thou wilt do; "
26:18 his servant? w· have I done? for "
18 or w· evil is in mine hand? "
28: 2 know w· thy servant can do. 853,834
9 thou knowest w· Saul hath done, " "
13 Be not afraid: for w· sawest thou?4100
14 said unto her, W· form is he of? "
15 make known unto me w· I shall do. "
29: 3 W· do these Hebrews here? And "
8 unto Achish, But w· have I done? "
8 w· hast thou found in thy servant "
2Sa 3:24 king, and said, W· hast thou done? "
7:18 and w· is in my house, that thou 4310
20 w· can David say more unto thee? 4100
23 w· one nation in the earth is like 4310
9: 8 W· is thy servant, that thou 4100
12:21 W· thing is this that thou hast "
14: 5 said unto her, W· aileth thee? "
15: 2 and said, Of w· city art thou? 4310
21 surely in w· place my lord the king 834
35 w· thing soever thou shalt hear 3605
16: 2 Ziba, W· meanest thou by these? 4100
10 W· have I to do with you, ye sons "
17: 5 let us hear likewise w· he saith.
18: 4 W· seemeth you best I will do. 834
21 Go tell the king w· thou hast seen.
29 tumult, but I knew not w· it was. 4100
19:18 and to do w· he thought good.
22 W· have I to do with you, ye sons 4100
27 do therefore w· is good in thine eyes.
28 W· right therefore have I yet to 4100
35 can thy servant taste w· I eat 853,834
35 I eat or w· I drink? can I hear "
37 w· shall seem good unto thee.
21: 3 Gibeonites, W· shall I do for you? 4100
4 W· ye shall say, that will I do for "
2Sa 21:11 was told David w· Rizpah the 853,834
24:13 w· answer I shall return to him 4100
17 these sheep, w· have they done? "
22 offer up w· seemeth good unto him:
1Ki 1:16 the king said, W· wouldest thou? 4100
2: 5 w· Joab the son of Zeruiah did 853,834
5 w· he did to the two captains of the "
9 knowest w· thou oughtest to do853, "
3: 5 God said, Ask w· I shall give thee.4100
8:38 W· prayer and supplication 3605
9:13 W· cities are these which thou 4100
11:22 But w· hast thou lacked with me, "
12: 9 W· counsel give ye that we may "
16 W· portion have we in David? "
13:12 unto them, W· way went he? 335,2088
12 seen w· way the man of God went, 834
14: 3 thee w· shall become of the child. 4100
14 of Jeroboam that day: but w·? "
16: 5 acts of Baasha, and w· he did, 834
17:18 W· have I to do with thee, O thou 4100
18: 9 W· have I sinned, that thou * "
13 w· I did when Jezebel slew the 853,834
19: 9, 13 W· doest thou here, Elijah? 4100
20 again: for w· have I done to thee? "
20:22 mark, and see w· thou doest: 853,834
22:14 w· the Lord saith unto me,3588, " "
2Ki 1: 7 W· manner of man was he which 4100
2: 9 Elisha, Ask w· I shall do for thee, "
3:13 Israel, W· have I to do with thee? "
4: 2 unto her, W· shall I do for thee? "
2 tell me, w· hast thou in the house? "
13 this care; w· is to be done for thee? "
14 said, W· then is to be done for her? "
43 W·, should I set this before an "
6:28 said unto her, W· aileth thee? "
33 w· should I wait for the Lord any* "
7:12 shew you w· the Syrians have 853,834
8:13 But w·, is thy servant a dog, that 4100
14 to him, W· said Elisha to thee? "
9:18, 19 W· hast thou to do with peace? "
22 W· peace, so long as the "
18:19 W· confidence is this wherein thou "
19:11 heard w· the kings of Assyria 853,834
20: 8 W· shall be the sign that the Lord4100
14 W· said these men? and from "
15 W· have they seen in thine house? "
22:19 heardest w· I spake against this 834
1Ch 12:32 to know w· Israel ought to do; 4100
17:16 Lord God, and w· is mine house, 4310
18 W· can David speak more to thee 4100
21 w· one nation in the earth is like 4310
21:12 w· word I shall bring again to 4100
29:14 who am I, and w· is my people, 4310
2Ch 1: 7 him, Ask w· I shall give thee. 4100
6:29 Then w· prayer or...supplication 834
29 w· supplication soever shall be *
10: 6 W· counsel give ye me to return 349
9 W· advice give ye that we may 4100
16 W· portion have we in David? "
18:13 liveth, even w· my God saith, 853,834
19: 6 the judges, Take heed w· ye do: 4100
10 w· cause soever shall come to you*3602
20:12 us; neither know we w· to do: 4100
24:11 w· time the chest was brought unto
25: 9 w· shall we do for the hundred 4100
32:13 Know ye not w· I and my fathers "
35:21 W· have I to do with thee, thou "
Ezr 5: 4 W· are the names of the men that4479
6: 8 w· ye shall do to the elders 3964,1768
8:17 w· they should say unto Iddo, 1697
9:10 God, w· shall we say after this? 4100
Ne 2: 4 For w· dost thou make request? "
12 w· my God had put in my heart "
16 not whither I went, or w· I did; "
19 W· is this thing that ye do? will ye "
4: 2 W· do these feeble Jews? will they "
20 In w· place therefore ye hear the 834
13:17 W· evil thing is this that ye do, 4100
Es 1:15 W· shall we do unto the queen "
2: 1 Vashti, and w· she had done, 853,834
1 and w· was decreed against her. "
11 did, and w· should become of her. 4100
15 but w· Hegai...appointed. 853,834
4: 5 to Mordecai, to know w· it was, 4100
5: 3 her, W· wilt thou, queen Esther? "
3 and w· is thy request? it shall be "
6 W· is thy petition? and it shall be "
6 and w· is thy request? even to "
6: 3 W· honour and dignity hath been "
6 W· shall be done unto the man "
7: 2 W· is thy petition, queen Esther? "
2 w· is thy request? and it shall be "
8: 1 Esther had told w· he was unto her. "
9: 5 did w· they would unto those that "
12 w· have they done in the rest of "
12 now w· is thy petition? and it shall "
12 w· is thy request further? and it "
Job 2:10 W·? shall we receive good at the 1571
6:11 W· is my strength, that I should 4100
11 w· is mine end, that I should "
17 W· time they wax warm, they vanish:
25 w· doth your arguing reprove? 4100
7:17 W· is man, that thou shouldest "
20 w· shall I do unto thee, O thou "
9:12 will say unto him, W· doest thou? "
11: 8 high as heaven; w· canst thou do? "
8 than hell; w· canst thou know? "
13: 2 W· ye know, the same do I know also:
13 speak, and let come on me w· will.4100
15: 9 W· knowest thou, that we know "
9 w· understandest thou, which is not "
12 and w· do thy eyes wink at, *4100
14 W· is man, that he should be "
16: 3 or w· emboldeneth thee that thou "
6 though I forbear, w· am I eased? "
21:15 W· is the Almighty, that we "

Job 21:15 *w'* profit should we have, if we pray*4100
21 *w'* pleasure hath he in his house "
31 shall repay him *w'* he hath done? "
22:17 *w'* can the Almighty do for them? 4100
23: 5 understand *w'* he would say unto "
13 and *w'* his soul desireth, even that he
27: 8 *w'* is the hope of the hypocrite, 4100
31: 2 *w'* portion of God is there from "
2 *w'* inheritance of the Almighty from
14 *W'* then shall I do when God 4100
14 visiteth, *w'* shall I answer him? "
32:11 whilst ye searched out *w'* to say,
34: 4 know among ourselves *w'* is good. 4100
7 *W'* man is like Job, who drinketh 4310
33 therefore speak *w'* thou knowest. 4100
35: 3 *W'* advantage will it be unto thee? "
3 and, *W'* profit shall I have, if I be "
6 *w'* doest thou against him? or if "
6 multiplied, *w'* doest thou unto him?"
7 be righteous, *w'* givest thou him? "
7 or *w'* receiveth he of thine hand? "
37:19 Teach us *w'* we shall say unto him;"
38:24 By *w'* way is the light parted, 335,2088
39:18 *W'* time she lifted up herself on high,
40: 4 I am vile; *w'* shall I answer thee? 4100
Ps 8: 4 *W'* is man, that thou art mindful "
11: 3 destroyed, *w'* can the righteous do?"
25:12 *W'* man is he that feareth the 4310
30: 9 *W'* profit is there in my blood, 4100
34:12 *W'* man is he that desireth life, 4310
39: 4 the measure of my days, *w'* it is; "
7 Lord, *w'* wait I for? my hope is in 4100
44: 1 us, *w'* work thou didst in their days,
46: 8 *w'* desolations he hath made in the 834
50:16 *W'* hast thou to do to declare my 4100
56: 3 *W'* time I am afraid, I will trust in
4 I will not fear *w'* flesh can do 4100
11 not be afraid *w'* man can do unto "
66:16 and I will declare *w'* he hath done 834
85: 8 hear *w'* God the Lord will speak: 4100
89:48 *W'* man is he that liveth, and 4310
114: 5 *W'* ailed thee, O thou sea, that 4100
116:12 *W'* shall I render unto the Lord "
118: 6 not fear: *w'* can man do unto me? "
120: 3 *W'* shall be given unto thee? "
3 *w'* shall be done unto thee, thou "
144: 3 Lord, *w'* is man, that thou takest "
Pr 4:19 they know not at *w'* they stumble.
10:32 the righteous know *w'* is acceptable:
23: 1 diligently *w'* is before thee: *853,834
25: 8 thou know not *w'* to do in the end 4100
27: 1 knowest not *w'* a day may bring "
30: 4 *w'* is his name, and *w'* is his son's "
31: 2 *W'*, my son? and "
2 and *w'*, the son of my womb? "
2 and *w'*, the son of my vows? "
Ec 1: 3 *W'* profit hath a man of all his "
2: 2 mad: and of mirth, *W'* doeth it? "
3 I might see *w'* was that good for 335
12 *w'* can the man do that cometh 4100
22 For *w'* hath man of all his labour, "
3: 9 *W'* profit hath he that worketh in "
22 him to see *w'* shall be after him? "
5:11 and *w'* good is there to the owners "
16 and *w'* profit hath he that hath "
6: 8 *w'* hath the wise more than the "
8 *w'* hath the poor, that knoweth to "
11 vanity, *w'* is man the better? "
12 who knoweth *w'* is good for man in"
12 can tell a man *w'* shall be after him"
7:10 *W'* is the cause that the former "
8: 4 may say unto him, *W'* doest thou? "
10: 14 a man cannot tell *w'* shall be; "
14 *w'* shall be after him, who can tell* "
11: 2 not *w'* evil shall be upon the earth. "
5 not *w'* is the way of the spirit, "
Ca 5: 9 *W'* is thy beloved more than "
9 *w'* is thy beloved more than "
6:13 *W'* will ye see in the Shulamite? * "
8: 8 *w'* shall we do for our sister in the "
Isa 1:11 To *w'* purpose is the multitude of "
3:15 *W'* mean ye that ye beat my people"
5: 4 *W'* could have been done more to "
5 you *w'* I will do to my vineyard:853,834
10: 3 And *w'* will ye do in the day of 4100
19:12 *w'* the Lord of hosts hath purposed "
21: 6 let him declare *w'* he seeth. 834
11 Seir, Watchman, *w'* of the night? 4100
11 night? Watchman, *w'* of the night? "
22: 1 *W'* aileth thee now, that thou art "
16 *W'* hast thou here? and whom "
33:13 ye that are far off, *w'* I have done; 834
37:11 *w'* the kings of Assyria have done "
38:15 *W'* shall I say? he hath both 4100
22 *W'* is the sign that I shall go up "
39: 3 *W'* said these men? and from "
4 *W'* have they seen in thine house? "
40: 6 *W'* shall I cry? All flesh is grass, "
18 *w'* likeness will ye compare unto "
41:22 and shew us *w'* shall happen: 853,834
22 the former things, *w'* they be, 4100
45: 9 fashioneth it, *W'* makest thou? "
10 unto his father, *W'* begettest thou?"
10 *W'* hast thou brought forth? "
52: 5 *w'* have I here, saith the Lord, "
64: 4 *w'* he hath prepared for him that *
Jer 1:11 saying, Jeremiah, *w'* seest thou? 4100
13 second time, saying, *W'* seest thou?"
2: 5 *W'* iniquity have your fathers "
18, 18 *w'* hast thou to do in the way of "
23 valley, know *w'* thou hast done: "
4:30 thou art spoiled, *w'* wilt thou do? "
5:15 neither understandest *w'* they say. "
31 *w'* will ye do in the end thereof? "
6:18 O congregation, *w'* is among 853,834
20 To *w'* purpose cometh there to 4100

Jer 7:12 and see *w'* I did to it for the 853,834
17 thou not *w'* they do in the cities 4100
8: 6 saying, *W'* have I done? "
9 Lord; and *w'* wisdom is in them? "
9:12 for *w'* the land perisheth and is * "
11:15 *W'* hath my beloved to do in mine "
13:21 *W'* wilt thou say when he shall "
16:10 *w'* is our iniquity? or *w'* is our sin "
18: 7 At *w'* instant I shall speak concerning
9 And at *w'* instant I shall speak
23:25 heard *w'* the prophets said, 853,834
28 *W'* is the chaff to the wheat? saith4100
33 *W'* is the burden of the Lord? "
33 then say unto them, *W'* burden? "
35 *W'* hath the Lord answered? "
35 and, *W'* hath the Lord spoken? "
37 *W'* hath the Lord answered thee? "
37 and, *W'* hath the Lord spoken? "
24: 3 *W'* seest thou, Jeremiah? And I "
32:24 *w'* thou hast spoken is come to 834
33:24 not *w'* this people have spoken, 4100
37:18 *W'* have I offended against thee, * "
38:25 Declare unto us now *w'* thou hast "
25 also *w'* the king said unto thee: "
48:19 escapeth, and say, *W'* is done? "
La 2:13 *W'* thing shall I take to witness for"
13 *w'* thing shall I liken to thee, "
13 *w'* shall I equal to thee, that I may "
5: 1 O Lord, *w'* is come upon us: "
Eze 2: 8 man, hear *w'* I say unto thee; 853,834
8: 6 Son of man, seest thou *w'* they do?4100
12 *w'* the ancients of the house of 834
12: 9 said unto thee, *W'* doest thou? 4100
22 *w'* is that proverb that ye have "
15: 2 *W'* is the vine tree more than any "
17:12 know ye not *w'* these things mean? "
18: 2 *W'* mean ye, that ye use this "
19: 2 *W'* is thy mother? A lioness: she "
21:13 *w'* if the sword condemn even the "
24:19 tell us *w'* these things are to us, "
27:32 *W'* city is like Tyrus, like the * "
33:30 hear *w'* is the word that cometh "
37:18 shew *w'* thou meanest by these? "
47:23 in *w'* tribe the stranger sojourneth,834
Da 2:22 he knoweth *w'* is in the darkness, 4101
23 me now *w'* we desired of thee: 1768
28 *w'* shall be in the latter days. 4101
29 *w'* should come to pass hereafter: "
29 known to thee *w'* shall come to pass."
45 *w'* shall come to pass hereafter: "
3: 5, 15 *w'* time ye hear the sound of the1768
4:35 or say unto him, *W'* doest thou? 4101
8:19 know *w'* shall be in the last end853,834
10:14 *w'* shall befall thy people in the " "
12: 8 *w'* shall be the end of these 4100
Ho 6: 4 Ephraim, *w'* shall I do unto thee? "
4 O Judah, *w'* shall I do unto thee? "
9: 5 *W'* will ye do in the solemn day, "
14 them, O Lord: *w'* wilt thou give? "
10: 3 *w'* then should a king do to us? "
14: 8 *W'* have I to do any more with "
Joe 3: 4 *w'* have ye to do with me, O Tyre, "
Am 4:13 unto man *w'* is his thought, that "
5:18 of the Lord! to *w'* end is it for you?*"
7: 8 said unto me, Amos, *w'* seest thou? "
Jon 1: 6 him, *W'* meanest thou, O sleeper? "
8 *W'* is thine occupation? and "
8 comest thou? *w'* is thy country? "
8 and of *w'* people art thou? 335,2088
11 *W'* shall we do unto thee, that the4100
4: 5 see *w'* would become of the city. "
Mic 1: 5 *W'* is the transgression of Jacob? 4310
5 *w'* are the high places of Judah? "
6: 1 Hear ye now *w'* the Lord saith; 834
3 people, *w'* have I done unto thee? 4100
5 *w'* Balak king of Moab consulted, "
5 *w'* Balaam...son of Beor answered "
8 shewed thee, O man, *w'* is good; "
8 *w'* doth the Lord require of thee, "
Na 1: 9 *W'* do ye imagine against the "
Hab 2: 1 and will watch to see *w'* he will say "
1 and *w'* I shall answer when I am "
18 *W'* profiteth the graven image that"
Zec 1: 9 Then said I, O my lord, *w'* are these?"
9 me, I will shew thee *w'* these be. "
19 that talked with me, *W'* be these? "
21 Then said I, *W'* come these to do? "
2: 2 to see *w'* is the breadth thereof, "
2 and *w'* is the length thereof. "
4: 2 And said unto me, *W'* seest thou? "
4 me, saying, *W'* are these, my lord? "
5 me, Knowest thou not *w'* these be? "
11 *W'* are these two olive trees upon "
12 *W'* be these two olive branches "
13 Knowest thou not *w'* these be? And "
5: 2 *W'* seest thou? And I answered, "
5 and see *w'* is this that goeth forth. "
6 And I said, *W'* is it? And he said, "
6: 4 with me, *W'* are these, my lord? "
13: 6 him, *W'* are these wounds in thine "
Mal 1:13 also, Behold, *w'* a weariness is it! "
3:13 say, *W'* have we spoken so much*4100
14 *w'* profit is it that we have kept "
M't 2: 7 diligently *w'* time...star appeared. 5588
5:46 which love you, *w'* reward have ye?5101
47 only, *w'* do ye more than others? "
6: 3 know *w'* thy right hand doeth: "
8 Father knoweth *w'* things ye have5739
25 *w'* ye shall eat, or *w'* ye shall drink;5101
25 for your body, *w'* ye shall put on. "
31 saying, *W'* shall we eat? or, "
31 or, *W'* shall we drink? or, "
7: 2 with *w'* judgment ye judge, ye shall5739
9 *w'* man is there of you, whom if 5101
8:27 saying, *W'* manner of man is this, 4217
29 *W'* have we to do with thee, Jesus,5101

M't 8:33 *w'* was befallen to the possessed 3588
9:13 go ye and learn *w'* that meaneth, 5101
10:19 thought how or *w'* ye shall speak: "
19 that same hour *w'* ye shall speak. "
27 *W'* I tell you in darkness, that 3739
27 *w'* ye hear in the ear, that preach ye"
11: 7 *W'* went ye out in the wilderness 5101
8 But *w'* went ye out for to see? A "
9 But *w'* went ye out for to see? A * "
12: 3 Have ye not read *w'* David did, "
7 if ye had known *w'* this meaneth, "
11 *W'* man shall there be among you, "
16:26 For *w'* is a man profited, if he shall "
26 *w'* shall a man give in exchange for"
17:25 *W'* thinkest thou, Simon? of whom"
18:31 his fellowservants saw *w'* was 3588
19: 6 *W'* therefore God hath joined 3739
16 *w'* good thing shall I do, that I 5101
20 from my youth up: *w'* lack I yet? "
27 thee; *w'* shall we have therefore? "
20:15 me to do *w'* I will with mine own? 3739
21 he said unto her, *W'* wilt thou? 5101
22 and said, Ye know not *w'* ye ask. "
32 *W'* will ye that I shall do unto you?"
21:16 Hearest thou *w'* these say? and "
23 By *w'* authority doest thou these 4169
24, 27 by *w'* authority I do these things."
28 But *w'* think ye? A certain man 5101
40 cometh, *w'* will he do unto those "
22:17 us therefore, *W'* thinkest thou? "
42 *W'* think ye of Christ? whose son is"
24: 3 *w'* shall be the sign of thy coming, "
42 for ye know not *w'* hour your Lord4169
43 known in *w'* watch the thief would "
26: 8 To *w'* purpose is this waste? 5101
15 *W'* will ye give me, and I will "
40 *W'*, could ye not watch with me 3779
62 *w'* is it which these witness 5101
65 *w'* further need have we of "
66 *W'* think ye? They answered and "
70 saying, I know not *w'* thou sayest. "
27: 4 *W'* is that to us? see thou to that. "
22 *W'* shall I do then with Jesus "
23 said, Why, *w'* evil hath he done? "
M'r 1:24 *w'* have we to do with thee, thou "
27 amazed,...saying, *W'* thing is this? "
27 *w'* new doctrine is this? "
2:25 Have ye never read *w'* David did, "
3: 8 had heard *w'* great things he did, 3745
4:24 with *w'* measure ye mete, it shall 3739
30 *w'* comparison shall we compare 4169
41 *W'* manner of man is this, that*5101,686
5: 7 *W'* have I to do with thee, Jesus, 5101
9 he asked him, *W'* is thy name? "
14 out to see *w'* it was that was done. "
33 knowing *w'* was done in her, came3739
6: 2 *w'* wisdom is this which is given 5101
10 In *w'* place soever ye enter into *3699
24 unto her mother, *W'* shall I ask? 5101
30 *w'* they had done, and *w'* they had*3745
8:36 For *w'* shall it profit a man, if he 5101
37 Or *w'* shall a man give in exchange "
9: 6 For he wist not *w'* to say; for they "
9 tell no man *w'* things they had 3739
10 *w'* the rising from the dead should5101
16 scribes, *W'* question ye with them? "
33 *W'* was it that ye disputed among "
10: 3 *W'* did Moses command you? "
9 *W'* therefore God hath joined 3739
17 *w'* shall I do that I may inherit 5101
32 *w'* things should happen unto him,*3588
36 *W'* would ye that I should do for 5101
38 unto them, Ye know not *w'* ye ask: "
51 *W'* wilt thou that I should do unto "
11: 5 them, *W'* do ye, loosing the colt? "
24 *W'* things soever ye desire, when*3745
28 By *w'* authority doest thou these 4169
29, 33 *w'* authority I do these things. "
12: 9 *W'* shall therefore the lord of the 5101
13: 1 Master, see *w'* manner of stones 4217
1 stones and *w'* buildings are here! "
4 *w'* shall be the sign when all these5101
11 beforehand *w'* ye shall speak, "
37 And *w'* I say unto you I say unto 3739
14: 8 She hath done *w'* she could: she is "
36 not *w'* I will, but *w'* thou wilt. 5101
40 neither wist they *w'* to answer him, "
60 *w'* is it which these witness thee "
63 *W'* need we any further witnesses? "
64 heard the blasphemy: *w'* think ye? "
68 understand I *w'* thou sayest. "
15:12 *W'* will ye then that I shall do unto "
14 them, Why, *w'* evil hath he done? "
24 them, *w'* every man should take. "
Lu 1:29 mind *w'* manner of salutation this 4217
66 *W'* manner of child shall this 5101,686
3:10 him, saying, *W'* shall we do then? 5101
12 unto him, Master, *w'* shall we do? "
14 of him, saying, And *w'* shall we do? "
4:34 *w'* have we to do with thee, thou "
36 saying, *W'* a word is this! for with "
5:19 by *w'* way they might bring him 4169
22 *W'* reason ye in your hearts? 5101
6: 3 *W'* David did, when himself was an3739
11 another *w'* they might do to Jesus.5101
32 which love you, *w'* thank have ye? 4169
33 do good to you, *w'* thank have ye? "
34 hope to receive, *w'* thank have ye? "
7:22 tell John *w'* things ye have seen 3739
24 John, *W'* went ye out into the 5101
25, 26 But *w'* went ye out for to see? A "
31 generation?...to *w'* are they like? "
39 and *w'* manner of woman this is 4217
8: 9 saying, *W'* might this parable be? 5101
25 *W'* manner of man is this! *5101,686
28 *W'* have I to do with thee, Jesus. 5101

Lu 8:30 asked him, saying, W' is thy name? 5101
34 they that fed them saw w' was done, 3588
35 they went out to see w' was done; "
36 by w' means he that was possessed* 4459
47 for w' cause she had touched him, 3739
56 they should tell no man w' was done. 3588
9:25 For w' is a man advantaged, if he 5101
33 for Elias: not knowing w' he said. 3739
55 Ye know not w' manner of spirit *3634
10:25 w' shall I do to inherit eternal life? 5101
26 W' is written in the law? how "
12:11 how or w' thing ye shall answer, "
11 ye shall answer, or w' ye shall say: "
12 the same hour w' ye ought to say. 3739
17 W' shall I do, because I have no 5101
22 for your life, w' ye shall eat; "
22 for the body, w' ye shall put on. "
29 And seek not ye w' ye shall eat, or "
29 ye shall eat, or w' ye shall drink, "
39 w' hour the thief would come, 4169
49 w' will I, if it be already kindled? 5101
57 yourselves judge ye not w' is right? 3588
13:18 w' is the kingdom of God like? 5101
14:31 Or w' king, going to make war "
15: 4 W' man of you, having an hundred "
8 Either w' woman having ten pieces "
26 and asked w' these things meant. "
16: 3 W' shall I do? for my lord taketh "
4 I am resolved w' to do, that, when "
18: 6 Hear w' the unjust judge saith. "
18 w' shall I do to inherit eternal life? "
36 passed by, he asked w' it meant. "
41 W' wilt thou that I shall do unto "
19:48 could not find w' they might do: "
20: 2 by w' authority doest thou these 4169
8 by w' authority I do these things. "
13 W' shall I do? I will send my 5101
15 W' therefore shall the lord of the "
17 W' is this then that is written, "
21: 7 w' sign will there be when these "
14 meditate before w' ye shall answer: *
22:49 about him saw w' would follow, 3588
60 Man, I know not w' thou sayest. 3739
71 W' need we any further witness? 5101
23:22 Why, w' evil hath he done? I have "
31 tree, w' shall be done in the dry? "
34 them; for they know not w' they do. "
47 the centurion saw w' was done, 3588
24:17 W' manner of communications 5101
19 he said unto them, W' things? 4169
35 they told w' things were done in the* 3588
Joh 1:21 him, W' then? Art thou Elias? 5101
22 sent us. W' sayest thou of thyself? "
38 and saith unto them, W' seek ye? "
2: 4 Woman, w' have I to do with thee? "
18 W' sign shewest thou unto us, "
25 man: for he knew w' was in man. "
3:32 w' he hath seen and heard, that he 3739
4:22 Ye worship ye know not w': we * "
22 we know w' we worship: for * "
27 W' seekest thou? or, Why talkest 5101
5:12 W' man is that which said unto *3739
19 but w' he seeth the Father do: 5100
19 for w' things soever he doeth, these "
6: 6 he himself knew w' he would do. 5101
9 but w' are they among so many? "
28 W' shall we do, that we might work "
30 W' sign shewest thou then, that "
30 believe thee? w' dost thou work? "
62 W' and if ye shall see the Son of man "
7:36 W' manner of saying is this that 5101
51 it hear him, and know w' he doeth? "
8: 5 be stoned: but w' sayest thou? "
9:17 W' sayest thou of him, that he hath "
21 But by w' means he now seeth, we* 4459
26 to him again, W' did he to thee? 5101
10: 6 understood not w' things they were "
11:46 told them w' things Jesus had done. 3739
47 W' do we? for this man doeth 5101
56 W' think ye, that he will not come "
12: 6 the bag, and bare w' was...therein. 3588
27 w' shall I say? Father, save me 5101
33 signifying w' death he should die. 4169
49 w' I should say, and w' I should 5101
13: 7 W' I do thou knowest not now; 3739
12 Know ye w' I have done to you? 5101
28 knew for w' intent he spake this "
15: 7 ye shall ask w' ye will, and it shall* 3739
15 knoweth not w' his lord doeth: 5101
16:17 W' is this that he saith unto us, "
18 therefore, W' is this that he saith, "
18 we cannot tell w' he saith. "
18:21 me, w' I have said unto them: "
21 behold, they know w' I said. * "
29 W' accusation bring ye against "
32 signifying w' death he should die. 4169
35 thee unto me: w' hast thou done? 5101
38 Pilate saith unto him, W' is truth? "
19:22 W' I have written I have written. 3739
21:19 by w' death he should glorify God. 4169
21 Lord, and w' shall this man do? 5101
22, 23 till I come, w' is that to thee? "
Ac 2:12 one to another, W' meaneth this? "
37 Men and brethren, w' shall we do? "
4: 7 By w' power, or by w' name, 4169
9 by w' means he is made whole; 5101
16 W' shall we do to these men? for "
5: 7 his wife, not knowing w' was done. 3588
35 w' ye intend to do as touching 5101
7:40 we wot not w' is become of him. "
49 w' house will ye build me? saith 4169
49 or, w' is the place of my rest? 5101
8:30 Understandest...w' thou readest? 3739
36 w' doth hinder me to be baptized? 5101
9: 6 Lord, w' wilt thou have me to do?* "
6 it shall be told thee w' thou must do. "

Ac 10: 4 was afraid, and said, W' is it, Lord? 5101
6 tell thee w' thou oughtest to do. * "
15 W' God hath cleansed, that call not 3739
17 w' this vision which he had seen 5101
21 w' is the cause wherefore ye are "
29 for w' intent ye have sent for me?* "
11: 9 W' God hath cleansed, that call *3739
17 w' was I, that I could withstand 5101
12:18 soldiers, w'...become of Peter. 5101,686
13:12 deputy, when he saw w' was done, 3588
14:11 the people saw w' Paul had done, 3739
15:12 declaring w' miracles and wonders 3745
16:30 Sirs, w' must I do to be saved? 5101
17:18 some said, W' will this babbler say? "
19 we know not w' this new doctrine, "
20 therefore w' these things mean. "
19: 3 Unto w' then were ye baptized? "
35 w' man is there that knoweth not "
20:18 after w' manner I have been with 4459
21:13 W' mean ye to weep and to break 5101
19 w' things God had wrought among* 3739
22 W' is it therefore? the multitude 5101
33 who he was, and w' he had done. "
22:10 And I said, W' shall I do, Lord? "
15 men of w' thou hast seen and heard. 3739
26 saying, Take heed w' thou doest: 5101
23:19 W' is that thou hast to tell me? "
30 thee w' they had against him. *3588
34 he asked of w' province he was. 4169
28:22 to hear of thee w' thou thinkest: 3739
Ro 3: 1 W' advantage then hath the Jew? 5101
1 w' profit is there of circumcision? "
3 For w' if some did not believe? "
5 w' shall we say? Is God "
9 W' then? are we better than they? "
19 w' things soever the law saith, 3745
27 By w' law? of works? Nay: but 4169
4: 1 W' shall we say then that 5101
3 w' saith the scripture? Abraham "
21 w' he had promised, he was able 3739
6: 1 W' shall we say then? Shall we 5101
15 W' then? shall we sin, because we "
21 W' fruit had ye then in those "
7: 7 W' shall we say then? Is the law "
15 not; for w' I would, that do I not; 3739
15 do I not; but w' I hate, that do I. "
8: 3 w' the law could not do, in that it 3588
24 for w' a man seeth, why doth he yet* "
26 know not w' we should pray for *5101
27 knoweth w' is the mind of the Spirit, "
31 W' shall we then say to these "
9:14 W' shall we say then? Is there "
22 W' if God, willing to shew his wrath, "
30 W' shall we say then? That the 5101
10: 8 But w' saith it? The word is nigh "
11: 2 w' the scripture saith of Elias? "
4 But w' saith the answer of God "
7 W' then? Israel hath not obtained "
15 w' shall the receiving of them be, "
12: 2 that ye may prove w' is that good, "
1Co 2:11 w' man knoweth the things of a * "
3:13 every man's work of w' sort it is. 3697
4: 7 w' hast thou that thou didst not 5101
21 w' will ye? shall I come unto you "
5:12 For w' have I to do to judge them "
6:16 W'? know ye not that he which is* 2228
19 W'? know ye not that your body is* "
7:16 For w' knowest thou, O wife, *5101
36 him do w' he will, he sinneth not: *3739
9:18 W' is my reward then? Verily that 5101
10:15 as to wise men; judge ye w' I say. 3739
19 W' say I then? that the idol is any 5101
11:22 W'? have ye not houses to eat...in? 1063
22 W' shall I say to you? shall I 5101
14: 6 w' shall I profit you, except I shall "
7 it be known w' is piped or harped? 3588
9 how shall it be known w' is spoken? "
15 W' is it then? I will pray with the 5101
16 understandeth not w' thou sayest? "
36 W'? came the word of God out 2228
15: 2 keep in memory w' I preached ‡5101
10 by the grace of God I am w' I am: 3739
29 Else w' shall they do which are 5101
32 w' advantageth it me, if the dead "
35 and with w' body do they come? 4169
2Co 6:14 w' fellowship hath righteousness 5101
14 w' communion hath light with "
15 w' concord hath Christ with Belial? "
15 w' part hath he that believeth with "
16 w' agreement hath the temple of "
7:11 w' carefulness it wrought in you, 4214
11 in you, yea, w' clearing of yourselves,
11 of yourselves, yea, w' indignation,
11 yea, w' fear, yea, w' vehement desire,
11 desire, yea, w' zeal, yea, w' revenge!
12:13 w' is it wherein ye were inferior 5101
Ga 4:30 Nevertheless w' saith the scripture? "
Eph 1:18 know w' is the hope of his calling, "
18 w' the riches of the glory of his "
19 w' is the exceeding greatness of "
3: 9 w' is the fellowship of the mystery, "
18 with all saints w' is the breadth, "
4: 9 w' is it but that he also descended "
5:10 Proving w' is acceptable unto the "
17 w' the will of the Lord is. "
Ph'p 1:18 W' then? notwithstanding, every "
22 yet w' I shall choose I wot not. "
3: 7 But w' things were gain to me, 3748
Col 1:27 w' is the riches of the glory of 5101
2: 1 knew w' great conflict I have for *2245
1Th 1: 5 know w' manner of men we were 3634
9 w' manner of entering in we had 3697
2:19 For w' is our hope, or joy, or 5101
3: 9 For w' thanks can we render to "
4: 2 know w' commandments we gave "
2Th 2: 6 w' withholdeth that he might be *3588

1Ti 1: 7 understanding neither w' they say, 3739
2Ti 2: 7 Consider w' I say; and the Lord give "
3:11 Lystra; w' persecutions I endured: 3634
Heb 2: 6 W' is man, that thou art mindful 5101
7:11 w' further need was there that "
11:32 w' shall I more say? for the time "
12: 7 for w' son is he whom the father "
13: 6 not fear w' man shall do unto me. "
Jas 1:24 forgetteth w' manner of man he 3697
2:14 W' doth it profit, my brethren, 5101
16 to the body; w' doth it profit? "
4:14 not w' shall be on the morrow. 3588
14 For w' is your life? It is even a 4169
1Pe 1:11 Searching w', or...manner of 1519,5101
11 or w' manner of time the Spirit 4169
2:20 For w' glory is it, if, when ye be "
4:17 w' shall the end be of them that 5101
2Pe 3:11 w' manner of persons ought ye to 4217
1Jo 3: 1 w' manner of love the Father hath "
2 not yet appear w' we shall be: 5101
Jude 10 but w' they know naturally, as 3745
Re 1:11 W' thou seest, write in a book 3739
2: 7, 11, 17, 29 hear w' the Spirit saith 5101
3: 3 shalt not know w' hour I will come 4169
6, 13, 22 hear w' the Spirit saith 5101
7:13 W' are these which are arrayed in "
18:18 W' city is like unto this great city!* "

whatsoever

Ge 2:19 w' Adam called every living 3605,834
8:19 and w' creepeth upon the earth, 3605
19:12 and w' thou hast in the city, *3605,834
31:16 w' God hath said unto thee, do. " "
39:22 w' they did there, he was the " "
Ex 13: 2 firstborn, w' openeth the womb 3605
21:30 ransom...w' is laid upon him. 3605,834
29:37 w' toucheth the altar shall be holy. 3605
30:29 w' toucheth them shall be holy. "
Le 5: 3 w' uncleanness it be that a man "
4 w'...a man shall pronounce 3605,834
6:27 W' shall touch the flesh thereof 3605
7:27 W' soul it be that eateth any * "
11: 3 W' parteth the hoof, and is "
9 w' hath fins and scales in the "
12 W' hath no fins nor scales in the "
27 w' goeth upon his paws, among all "
32 upon w' any of them, when they "
32 w' vessel it be, wherein any work is "
33 w' is in it shall be unclean; "
42 W' goeth upon the belly, "
42 and w' goeth upon all fours, "
42 or w' hath more feet among all "
13:58 w' thing of skin it be, which thou "
15:26 w' she sitteth upon shall be *3605,3627
17: 8 W' man there be of the house of 376,834
10 w' man there be of the house of " "
13 w' man there be of the children " "
21:18 w' man he be that hath a blemish, 3605
22: 5 w' uncleanness he hath; "
18 W' he be of the house of Israel, 376,834
20 w' hath a blemish, that shall ye 3605
23:29 w' soul it be that shall not be "
30 w' soul it be that doeth any work in "
27:32 even of w' passeth under the rod, "
Nu 5:10 w' any man giveth the priest, it 834
18:13 and w' is first ripe in the land, *3605, "
19:22 w' the unclean person toucheth 3605
22:17 I will do w' thou sayest unto 3605,834
23: 3 w' he sheweth me I will tell 1697,4100
30:12 then w' proceeded out of her lips 3605
De 2:37 w' the Lord our God forbad us. * "
12: 8 man w' is right in his own eyes. "
15 w' thy soul lusteth after, according* "
20 eat flesh, w' thy soul lusteth after.* "
21 thy gates w' thy soul lusteth after.* "
14:10 w' hath not fins and scales ye 3605,834
26 money for w' thy soul lusteth " "
26 or for w' thy soul desireth: " "
J'g 10:15 us w' seemeth good unto thee; 3605
11:31 w' cometh forth of the doors of my 834
1Sa 14:36 Do w' seemeth good unto thee. 3605
20: 4 W' thy soul desireth, I will even 4100
25: 8 w' cometh to thine hand unto 853,834
2Sa 3:36 as w' the king did pleased all 3605, "
15:15 ready to do w' my lord the king " "
19:38 w' thou shalt require of me, "
1Ki 8:37 w' plague, w' sickness there be; 3605
10:13 Sheba all her desire, w' she asked, 834
20: 6 that w' is pleasant in thine eyes, 3605
2Ch 6:28 w' sore or w' sickness there be: "
9:12 Sheba all her desire, w' she asked, "
Ezr 7:18 w' shall seem good to thee, 1401,1768
20 And w' more shall be needful for the
21 w' Ezra the priest, the scribe 3605,3627
23 W' is commanded by the God " "
Es 2:13 w' she desired was given 853,3605,834
Job 37:12 do w' he commandeth them "
41:11 w' is under the whole heaven is mine.
Ps 1: 3 and w' he doeth shall prosper. 3605,834
8: 8 w' passeth through the paths of the
115: 3 hath done w' he hath pleased. 3605,834
135: 6 W' the Lord pleased, that did " "
Ec 2:10 w' my eyes desireth I kept not " "
3:14 w' God doeth, it shall be for " "
8: 3 for he doeth w' pleaseth him. " "
9:10 W' thy hand findeth to do, do it, " "
Jer 1: 7 w' I command thee thou shalt "
44:17 w' thing goeth forth out of our *853, "
M't 5:37 w' is more than these cometh of evil. 3588
7:12 w' ye would that men should 3745,302
10:11 into w' city or town ye...enter, 3739, "
14: 7 to give her w' she would ask. " 1437
15: 5 by w' thou mightest be profited* " "
17 w' entereth in at the mouth goeth 3956
16:19 w' thou shalt bind on earth 3739,1437
19 w' thou shalt loose on earth shall

M't 17:12 have done unto him w' they listed.3745
18:18 W' ye shall bind on earth *3745,1437
18 w' ye shall loose on earth shall*" "
20: 4 and w' is right I will give you. 3739, "
7 w' is right that shall ye receive.*" "
21:22 w' ye shall ask in prayer, 3745,302
23: 3 w' they bid you observe, "
28:20 things w' I have commanded you: 3745
M'r 6:22 Ask of me w' thou wilt, and I 3739,1437
23 W' thou shalt ask of me, I will " "
7:11 by w' thou mightest be profited by*" "
18 w' thing from without entereth 3956
9:13 have done unto him w' they listed,3745
10:21 sell w' thou hast, and give to the "
35 do for us w' we shall desire. 3739,1437
11:23 pass; he shall have w' he saith.*" 302
13:11 w' shall be given you in that " 1437
Lu 4:23 w' we have heard done in 3745
9: 4 w' house ye enter into, there 3739,302
10: 5 And into w' house ye enter, first" "
8, 10 into w' city ye enter, and they" "
35 w' thou spendest more, when I3748,302
12: 3 w' ye have spoken in darkness 3745
Joh 2: 5 W' he saith unto you, do it. 3748,302
5: 4 made whole of w' disease he had. *1221
11:22 w' thou wilt ask of God, God 3748,302
12:50 w' I speak therefore, even as the *3739
14:13 w' ye shall ask in my name, 3748,302
26 remembrance, w' I have said unto*3739
15:14 friends, if ye do w' I command *3745
16 w' ye shall ask of the Father 3748,302
16:13 w' he shall hear, that shall he 3745, "
23 W' ye shall ask the Father in *3748, "
17: 7 w' thou hast given me are of thee. 3745
Ac 3:22 in all things w' he shall say 3748,302
4:28 to do w' thy hand and thy counsel 3745
Ro 14:23 faith: for w' is not of faith is sin. 3956
15: 4 w' things were written aforetime 3745
16: 2 ye assist her in w' business she 3739,302
1Co 10:25 W' is sold in the shambles, that 3956
27 w' is set before you, eat, asking "
31 w' ye do, do all to the glory of God.5100
Ga 2: 6 (w' they were, it maketh no 3697,4219
6: 7 w' a man soweth, that shall he3739,1437
Eph 5:13 w' doth make manifest is light. *3956
6: 8 w' good thing any man 3739,1437,5100
Ph'p 4: 8 brethren, w' things are true, 3745
8 w' things are honest, "
8 w' things are just, "
8 w' things are pure, "
8 w' things are lovely, "
8 w' things are of good report; "
11 w' state I am, therewith to be 3588,3739
Col 3:17 w' ye do in word or deed, 3956,3754,5100
23 w' ye do, do it heartily, as " 1437
1Jo 3:22 w' we ask, we receive of him. 3739, "
5: 4 w' is born of God overcometh the 3956
15 w' we ask, we know that we 3739,302
3Jo 5 w' thou doest to the brethren, " 1437
Re 18:22 craftsman, of w' craft he be, shall 3956
21:27 w' worketh abomination, or maketh*

wheat See also WHEATEN.
Ge 30:14 went in the days of w' harvest, 2406
Ex 9:32 the w' and the rie were not smitten "
34:22 the firstfruits of w' harvest, and the"
Nu 18:12 best of the wine, and of the w', *1715
De 8: 8 A land of w', and barley, and 2406
32:14 with the fat of kidneys of w'; "
J'g 6:11 his son Gideon threshed w' by the "
15: 1 after, in the time of w' harvest, "
Ru 2:23 barley harvest and of w' harvest; "
1Sa 6:13 were reaping their w' harvest in "
12:17 Is it not w' harvest to day? I will "
2Sa 4: 6 they would have fetched w'; "
17:28 vessels, and w', and barley, and "
1Ki 5:11 twenty thousand measures of w' "
1Ch 21:20 Now Ornan was threshing w'. "
23 and the w' for the meat offering; "
2Ch 2:10 thousand measures of beaten w', "
15 the w', and the barley, the oil, and "
27: 5 and ten thousand measures of w', "
Ezr 6: 9 w', salt, wine, and oil, according 2591
7:22 and to an hundred measures of w', "
Job 31:40 Let thistles grow instead of w', 2406
Ps 81:16 them also with the finest of the w'. "
147:14 filleth thee with the finest of the w'."
Pr 27:22 bray a fool in a mortar among w' *7383
Ca 7: 2 an heap of w' set about with lilies.2406
Isa 28:25 cast in the principal w' and the "
Jer 12:13 They have sown w', but shall reap "
23:28 What is the chaff to the w'? saith 1250
31:12 for w', and for wine, and for oil, *1715
41: 8 in the field, of w', and of barley, 2406
Eze 4: 9 Take thou also unto thee w', and "
27:17 traded in thy market w' of Minnith, "
45:13 part of an ephah of an homer of w',*"
Joe 1:11 for the w' and for the barley;
2:24 the floors shall be full of w', and 1250
Am 5:11 ye take from him burdens of w': "
8: 5 sabbath, that we may set forth w', "
6 yea, and sell the refuse of the w'? "
M't 3:12 and gather his w' into the garner; 4621
13:25 and sowed tares among the w', "
29 ye root up also the w' with them. "
30 but gather the w' into my barn. "
Lu 3:17 will gather the w' into his garner; "
16: 7 said, An hundred measures of w'. "
22:31 you, that he may sift you as w': "
Joh 12:24 a corn of w' fall into the ground "
Ac 27:38 and cast out the w' into the sea. "
1Co 15:37 it may chance of w', or of some "
Re 6: 6 A measure of w' for a penny, and "
18:13 and oil, and fine flour, and w', "

wheaten
Ex 29: 2 of w' flour shalt thou make them. 2406

wheel See also WHEELS.
1Ki 7:32 height of a w' was a cubit and half 212
33 was like the work of a chariot w': "
Ps 83:13 God, make them like a w'; as the *1534
Pr 20:26 and bringeth the w' over them. 212
Ec 12: 6 or the w' broken at the cistern. 1534
Isa 28:27 neither is a cart w' turned about 212
28 break it with the w' of his cart, 1536
Eze 1:15 behold one w' upon the earth by 212
16 it were a w' in the middle of a w'. "
10: 9 cherubim, one w' by one cherub, "
9 another w' by another cherub: "
10 a w' had been in the midst of a w'. "
13 unto them in my hearing, O w'. *1534

wheels
Ex 14:25 took off their chariot w', that they 212
J'g 5:28 why tarry the w' of his chariots? 6471
1Ki 7:30 And every base had four brasen w',212
32 under the borders were four w'; "
32 axletrees of the w' were joined to "
33 work of the w' was like the work of "
Isa 5:28 and their w' like a whirlwind: 1534
Jer 18: 3 he wrought a work on the w'. 70
47: 3 and at the rumbling of his w', the 1534
Eze 1:16 appearance of the w' and their 212
19 creatures went, the w' went by them:"
19 the earth, the w' were lifted up. "
20 the w' were lifted up over against "
20 of the living creature was in the w'. "
21 w' were lifted up over against them: "
21 of the living creature was in the w'. "
3:13 noise of the w' over against them, "
10: 2 Go in between the w', even under 1534
6 Take fire from between the w', "
6 went in, and stood beside the w'. * 212
9 the four w' by the cherubims, "
9 appearance of the w' was as the "
12 the w' were full of eyes round about,"
12 even the w' that they four had. "
13 As for the w', it was cried unto "
16 cherubims went, the w' went by "
16 the same w' also turned not from "
19 out, the w' also were beside them, "
11:22 wings, and the w' beside them; and "
23:24 with chariots, wagons, and w', *1534
26:10 of the horsemen, and of the w', * "
Da 7: 9 flame, and his w' as burning fire. 1535
Na 3: 2 the noise of the rattling of the w', 212

whelm See OVERWHELM.

whelp See also WHELPS.
Ge 49: 9 Judah is a lion's w': from the 1482
De 33:22 Dan is a lion's w': he shall leap "
Na 2:11 the lion's w', and none made them "

whelps
2Sa 17: 8 as a bear robbed of her w' in the field:
Job 4:11 the stout lion's w' are scattered 1121
28: 8 The lion's w' have not trodden it. * "
Pr 17:12 Let a bear robbed of her w' meet a
Jer 51:38 lions: they shall yell as lions' w'. 1484
Eze 19: 2 she nourished her w' among 1482
3 she brought one of her w': it "
5 she took another of her w', and "
Ho 13: 8 as a bear that is bereaved of her w',
Na 2:12 tear in pieces enough for his w', 1484

when See also WHENSOEVER.
Ge 2: 4 of the earth w' they were created,
3: 6 w' the woman saw that the tree was
4: 8 w' they were in the field, that Cain
12 W' thou tillest the ground, it 3588
5: 2 Adam, in the day w' they were created.
6: 1 w' men began to multiply on the 3588
4 w' the sons of God came in unto 834
7: 6 w' the flood of waters was upon the
9:14 w' I bring a cloud over the earth, that
12: 4 years old w' he departed out of Haran.
11 w' he was come near to enter into 834
12 w' the Egyptians shall see thee, 3588
14 w' Abram was come into Egypt, the
14:14 w' Abram heard that his brother 3588
15:11 w' the fowls came down upon the *
12 And w' the sun was going down, 1961
17 w' the sun went down, and it was "
16: 4, 5 w' she saw that she had conceived,
6 w' Sarai dealt hardly with her, she*
16 w' Hagar bare Ishmael to Abram.
17: 1 w' Abram was ninety years old 1961
24, 25 w' he was circumcised in the flesh
18: 2 w' he saw them, he ran to meet
19:15 And w' the morning arose, then 3644
17 w' they had brought them forth *
23 the earth w' Lot entered into Zoar.
29 w' God destroyed the cities of the
29 w' he overthrew the cities in the
33, 35 w' she lay down, nor w' she arose.
20:13 w' God caused me to wander from 834
21: 5 w' his son Isaac was born unto him.
24:36 a son to my master w' she was old. 310
52 w' Abraham's servant heard their
64 w' she saw Isaac, she lighted off the
25:20 years old w' he took Rebekah to wife,
24 w' her days to be delivered were
26 threescore years old w' she bare them.
26: 8 w' he had been there a long time, 3588
27:34 w' Esau heard the words of his father,
40 w' thou shalt have the dominion, 834
28: 6 W' Esau saw that Isaac had blessed*
29:10 w' Jacob saw Rachel the daughter 834
13 w' Laban heard the tidings of Jacob
31 w' the Lord saw that Leah was hated,*
30: 1 w' Rachel saw that she bare Jacob no
9 W' Leah saw that she had left
25 w' Rachel had born Joseph, that 834
30 w' shall I provide for mine own 4970

Ge 30:33 w' it shall come for my hire before 3588
38 troughs w' the flocks came to drink,"
38 conceive w' they came to drink. *
42 w' the cattle were feeble, he put them
31:49 w' we are absent one from another.3588
32: 2 w' Jacob saw them, he said, This 834
17 W' Esau my brother meeteth 3588
19 speak unto Esau, w' ye find him.
25 And w' he saw that he prevailed not
33:18 Canaan, w' he came from Padan-aram;
34: 2 And w' Shechem the son of Hamor the
7 came out of the field w' they heard it:
25 w' they were sore, that two of the sons
35: 1 w' thou fleddest from the face of Esau
7 w' he fled from the face of his
9 w' he came out of Padan-aram, and
17 w' she was in hard labour, that the
22 w' Israel dwelt in that land, that
37: 4 w' his brethren saw that their father*
18 w' they saw him afar off, even before*
23 w' Joseph was come unto his 834
38: 5 he was at Chezib, w' she bare him.
9 w' he went in unto his brother's 518
15 W' Judah saw her, he thought her to
25 W' she was brought forth, she
28 w' she travailed, that the one put out*
39:13 w' she saw that he had left his
15 w' he heard that I had lifted up my
19 w' his master heard the words of his
40:13 manner w' thou wast his butler. 834
14 on me w' it shall be well with thee. "
16 W' the chief baker saw that the
41:21 And w' they had eaten them up,
46 years old w' he stood before Pharaoh
55 w' all the land of Egypt was famished,
42: 1 w' Jacob saw that there was corn in*
21 w' he besought us, and we would not
35 w' both they and their father saw the
43: 2 w' they had eaten up the corn 834
21 w' we came to the inn, that we 3588
26 w' Joseph came home, they brought
44: 4 And w' they were gone out of the city,
4 w' thou dost overtake them, say unto
24 w' we came up unto thy servant 3588
30 w' I come to thy servant my father,
31 w' he seeth that the lad is not with us,
45:27 w' he saw the wagons that Joseph had
46:33 w' Pharaoh shall call you, and 3588
47:15 w' money failed in the land of Egypt,
18 W' the year was ended, they came
48: 7 w' I came from Padan, Rachel died by
7 w' yet there was but a little way 5750
17 w' Joseph saw that his father laid his
49:33 w' Jacob had made an end of
50: 4 w' the days of his mourning were past,
11 And w' the inhabitants of the land,
15 w' Joseph's brethren saw that their
17 Joseph wept w' they spake unto him.
Ex 1:10 that, w' there falleth out any war, 3588
16 W' ye do the office of a midwife to the
2: 3 w' she saw the ark among the flags,*
6 w' she had opened it, she saw the*
11 w' Moses was grown, that he went out
12 and w' he saw that there was no man,
13 and w' he went out the second day,*
15 Now w' Pharaoh heard this thing,
18 And w' they came to Reuel their father,
3: 4 w' the Lord saw that he turned aside
12 W' thou hast brought forth the
13 w' I came unto the children of Israel,
4: 6 w' he took it out, behold, his hand was
14 w' he seeth thee, he will be glad in his
21 W' thou goest to return into Egypt,
31 w' they heard that the Lord had
5:13 daily tasks, as w' they were straw. 834
6:28 day w' the Lord spake unto Moses in
7: 5 w' I stretch forth mine hand upon
7 years old, w' they spake unto Pharaoh.
9 W' Pharaoh shall speak unto you,3588
8: 9 w' shall I intreat for thee, and for*4970
15 w' Pharaoh saw that there was respite,
9:34 w' Pharaoh saw that the rain and the
10:13 and w' it was morning, the east wind
11: 1 w' he shall let you go, he shall surely
12:13 w' I see the blood, I will pass over
13 you, w' I smite the land of Egypt.
23 w' he seeth the blood upon the lintel,
25 w' ye be come to the land which 3588
26 w' your children shall say unto you,"
27 w' he smote the Egyptians, and
44 w' thou hast circumcised him, then
13: 5 w' the Lord shall bring thee into 3588
8 unto me w' I came forth out of Egypt.
11 w' the Lord shall bring thee into 3588
14 w' thy son asketh thee in time to "
15 w' Pharaoh would hardly let us go, "
17 pass, w' Pharaoh had let the people go,
17 the people repent w' they see war,
14:10 w' Pharaoh drew nigh, the children of
18 w' I have gotten me honour upon
27 his strength w' the morning appeared;
15:23 w' they came to Marah, they could not
25 w' he had cast into the waters, the*
16: 3 of Egypt, w' we sat by the flesh pots,
3 and w' we did eat bread to the full;
8 w' the Lord shall give you in the flesh
14 w' the dew that lay was gone up,
15 And w' the children of Israel saw it,
18 And w' they did mete it with an omer,
21 and w' the sun waxed hot, it melted.
32 w' I brought you forth from the land
17:11 pass, w' Moses held up his hand, 834
11 and w' he let down his hand,
18:14 w' Moses' father in law saw all that he
16 W' they have a matter, they come3588
19: 1 w' the children of Israel were gone*

Ex 19: 9 people may hear w' I speak with thee,
13 w' the trumpet soundeth long, they
19 And w' the voice of the trumpet 1961
20: 18 w' the people saw it, they removed,
22: 27 w' he crieth unto me, that I will 3588
23: 16 w' thou hast gathered in thy labours
28: 29 w' he goeth in unto the holy place,
30 heart, w' he goeth in before the Lord:
35 w' he goeth in unto the holy place
35 and w' he cometh out, that he die not.
43 w' they come in unto the tabernacle
43 or w' they come near unto the altar to
29: 30 w' he cometh into the tabernacle of 834
36 w' thou hast made an atonement for
30: 7 w' he dresseth the lamps, he shall
8 w' Aaron lighteth the lamps at even,
12 W' thou takest the sum of the 3588
12 the Lord, w' thou numberest them;
12 them, w' thou numberest them.
15 w' they give an offering unto the Lord,
20 W' they go into the tabernacle of the
20 or w' they come near to the altar to
31: 18 w' he made an end of communing
32: 1 w' the people saw that Moses delayed
5 w' Aaron saw it, he built an altar
17 w' Joshua heard the noise of the
25 w' Moses saw that the people were
34 nevertheless in the day w' I visit I
33: 4 w' the people heard these evil tidings,
8 w' Moses went out unto the tabernacle,
34: 24 w' thou shalt go up to appear before
29 w' Moses came down from mount
29 w' he came down from the mount,
30 w' Aaron and all the children of Israel
34 w' Moses went in before the Lord to
40: 32 W' they went into the tent of the
32 w' they came near unto the altar, they
36 w' the cloud was taken up from over
Le 2: 1 w' any will offer a meat offering unto
8 and w' it is presented unto the priest,
4: 14 W' the sin, which they have sinned
22 W' a ruler hath sinned, and done 834
5: 3, 4 w' he knoweth of it, then he shall be
5 w' he shall be guilty in one of 3588
6: 20 the Lord in the day w' he is anointed;
21 w' it is baken, thou shalt bring it in:*
27 w' there is sprinkled of the blood 834
7: 35 w' he presented them to minister unto
9: 24 w' all the people saw, they shouted,
10: 9 w' ye go into the tabernacle of the
20 w' Moses heard that, he was content.
11: 31 doth touch them, w' they be dead,
12: 6 w' the days of her purifying are
13: 2 W' a man shall have in the skin of 3588
3 w' the hair in the plague is turned*
9 W' the plague of leprosy is in a 3588
14 w' raw flesh appeareth in him, he* 3117
20 And if, w' the priest seeth it, behold,*
14: 34 W' ye be come into the land of 3588
57 To teach w' it is unclean, and 3117
57 and w' it is clean: this is the law of "
15: 2 W' any man hath a running issue 3588
13 w' he that hath an issue is cleansed "
31 w' they defile my tabernacle that is
16: 1 w' they offered before the Lord, and
17 w' he goeth in to make an atonement
20 w' he hath made the end of reconciling
23 put on w' he went into the holy place,
18: 28 spue not you out also, w' ye defile it,
19: 9 w' ye reap the harvest of your land,
23 And w' ye shall come into the land, 3588
20: 4 w' he giveth of his seed unto Molech,
22: 7 w' the sun is down, he shall be clean,
16 trespass, w' they eat their holy things:
27 W' a bullock, or a sheep, or a goat, is
29 And w' ye will offer a sacrifice of 3588
23: 10 W' ye be come into the land which "
12 offer that day w' ye wave the sheaf
22 w' ye reap the harvest of your land,
39 w' ye have gathered in the fruit of the
43 w' I brought them out of the land of
24: 16 w' he blasphemeth the name of the
25: 2 W' ye come into the land which I 3588
26: 17 ye shall flee w' none pursueth you.
25 w' ye are gathered together within*
26 And w' I have broken the staff of your
35 in your sabbaths, w' ye dwelt upon it.
36 and they shall fall w' none pursueth.
37 before a sword, w' none pursueth:
44 w' they be in the land of their enemies,
27: 2 W' a man shall make a singular 3588
14 w' a man shall sanctify his house "
21 the field, w' it goeth out in the jubile,
Nu 3: 4 w' they offered strange fire before the
4: 5 w' the camp setteth forward, Aaron
15 w' Aaron and his sons have made an
19 w' they approach unto the most holy
20 to see w' the holy things are covered,*
5: 6 W' a man or a woman shall 3588
21 w' the Lord doth make thy thigh to
27 And w' he hath made her to drink the
29 w' a wife goeth aside to another 834
30 Or w' the spirit of jealousy cometh "
6: 2 W' either man or woman shall 3588
7 brother, or for his sister, w' they die:
13 w' the days of his separation are
7: 84 altar, in the day w' it was anointed,
89 And w' Moses was gone into the
8: 2 W' thou lightest the lamps, the seven
19 w' the children of Israel come nigh
9: 17 w' the cloud was taken up from *6310
20 w' the cloud was a few days upon* 834
21 w' the cloud abode from even unto* "
22 but w' it was taken, they journeyed.
10: 3 But w' they shall blow with them,
5 W' ye blow an alarm, then the camps

Nu 10: 6 W' ye blow an alarm the second time
7 w' the congregation is to be gathered
28 to their armies, w' they set forward.*
34 by day, w' they went out of the camp.
35 came to pass, w' the ark set forward,
36 w' it rested, he said, Return, O Lord,
11: 1 And w' the people complained, it *
2 and w' Moses prayed unto the Lord,*
9 And w' the dew fell upon the camp
25 that, w' the spirit rested upon them,
12: 12 w' he cometh out of his mother's 834
15: 2 W' ye be come into the land of 3588
8 w' thou preparest a bullock for a "
18 W' ye come into the land whither I
19 w' ye eat of the bread of the land, ye
28 w' he sinneth by ignorance before the
16: 4 And w' Moses heard it, he fell upon his
42 w' the congregation was gathered
18: 26 W' ye take of the children of 3588
30 W' ye have heaved the best thereof
32 w' ye have heaved from it the best of
19: 14 the law, w' a man dieth in a tent: 3588
20: 3 we had died w' our brethren died
16 w' we cried unto the Lord, he heard
29 And w' all the congregation saw that
21: 1 And w' king Arad the Canaanite, *
8 bitten, w' he looketh upon it, shall live.
9 w' he beheld the serpent of brass, he
22: 25, 27 And w' the ass saw the angel of*
36 And w' Balak heard that Balaam was
23: 17 w' he came to him, behold, he stood*
24: 1 And w' Balaam saw that it pleased
20 w' he looked upon Amalek, he took*
23 Alas, who shall live w' God doeth this!
25: 7 And w' Phinehas, the son of Eleazar,
26: 9 w' they strove against the Lord:
10 with Korah, w' that company died,
61 w' they offered strange fire before the
64 w' they numbered the children of* 834
27: 13 w' thou hast seen it, thou also shalt
28: 26 w' ye bring a new meat offering unto
30: 6 had at all a husband, w' she vowed,*
32: 1 w' they saw the land of Jazer, and the
8 w' I sent them from Kadesh-barnea
9 For w' they went up unto the valley of
33: 39 years old w' he died in mount Hor.
51 W' ye are passed over Jordan 3588
34: 2 them, W' ye come into the land of "
35: 10 W' ye be come over Jordan unto "
19 w' he meeteth him, he shall slay him.
21 slay the murderer, w' he meeteth him.
36: 4 And w' the jubile of the children of 518
De 1: 19 w' we departed from Horeb, we went*
41 w' ye had girded on every man his*
2: 8 w' we passed by from our brethren*
12 w' they had destroyed them from*
16 w' all the men of war were 834
19 w' thou comest nigh over against the
22 w' he destroyed the Horims from 834
4: 10 w' the Lord said unto me, Gather me
19 w' thou seest the sun, and the moon,
25 W' thou shalt beget children, and 3588
30 W' thou art in tribulation, and all
5: 23 w' ye heard the voice out of the midst
28 of your words, w' ye spake unto me;
6: 7 of them w' thou sittest in thine house,
7 and w' thou walkest by the way,
7 and w' thou liest down,
7 and w' thou risest up.
10 w' the Lord thy God shall have 3588
11 w' thou shalt have eaten and be full;*
20 w' thy son asketh thee in time to 3588
7: 1 W' the Lord thy God shall bring "
2 w' the Lord thy God shall deliver
8: 10 W' thou hast eaten and art full, then*
12 Lest w' thou hast eaten and art full,
13 w' thy herds and thy flocks multiply,
9: 9 W' I was gone up into the mount to
23 Likewise w' the Lord sent you from
11: 19 of them w' thou sittest in thine house,
19 and w' thou walkest by the way,
19 w' thou liest down, and w' thou risest
29 w' the Lord thy God hath brought 3588
12: 10 But w' ye go over Jordan, and dwell
10 w' he giveth you rest from all your*
20 W' the Lord thy God shall enlarge 3588
25 w' thou shalt do that which is right "
28 w' thou doest that which is good "
29 W' the Lord thy God shall cut off "
13: 18 W' thou shalt hearken to the voice "
14: 24 w' the Lord thy God hath blessed "
15: 4 w' there shall be no poor among * "
10 shall not be grieved w' thou givest
13 And w' thou sendest him out free 3588
18 w' thou sendest him away free from
16: 3 w' thou camest forth out of the land
17: 14 W' thou art come unto the land 3588
18 w' he sitteth upon the throne of his
18: 9 W' thou art come into the land 3588
22 W' the prophet speaketh in the 834
19: 1 W' the Lord thy God hath cut off 3588
5 As w' a man goeth into the wood 834
20: 1 W' thou goest out to battle 3588
2 w' ye are come nigh unto the battle,
9 w' the officers have made an end of
10 W' thou comest nigh unto a city 3588
13 w' the Lord thy God hath delivered it
19 W' thou shalt besiege a city a 3588
21: 9 w' thou shalt do that which is right "
10 W' thou goest forth to war against "
16 w' he maketh his sons to inherit *3117
18 w' they have chastened him, will not*
22: 8 W' thou buildest a new house, 3588
14 w' I came to her, I found her not a
26 for as w' a man riseth against his
23: 4 way, w' ye came forth out of Egypt;

De 23: 9 W' the host goeth forth against 3588
11 w' evening cometh on, he shall wash
11 w' the sun is down, he shall come into
13 w' thou wilt ease thyself abroad, thou
21 W' thou shalt vow a vow unto the 3588
24 W' thou comest into thy "
25 W' thou comest into the standing "
24: 1 W' a man hath taken a wife, and "
2 w' she is departed out of his house,
5 W' a man hath taken a new wife, 3588
10 W' thou dost lend thy brother any "
13 pledge again w' the sun goeth down,
19 W' thou cuttest down thine 3588
20 W' thou beatest thine olive tree, "
21 W' thou gatherest the grapes of "
25: 4 the ox w' he treadeth out the corn.
11 W' men strive together one with 3588
17 w' ye were come forth out of Egypt;*
18 thee, w' thou wast faint and weary;
19 w' the Lord thy God hath given thee
26: 1 w' thou art come in unto the land 3588
7 w' we cried unto the Lord God of our*
12 W' thou hast made an end of 3588
27: 2 w' ye shall pass over Jordan unto 834
3 this law, w' thou art passed over,
4 it shall be w' ye be gone over Jordan,
12 people, w' ye are come over Jordan;
28: 6 Blessed shalt thou be w' thou comest
6 blessed shalt thou be w' thou goest
19 Cursed shalt thou be w' thou comest
19 cursed shalt thou be w' thou goest out.
29: 7 w' ye came unto this place, Sihon the
19 w' he heareth the words of this curse,
22 w' they see the plagues of that land,
25 w' he brought them forth out of the
30: 1 w' all these things are come upon 3588
31: 11 W' all Israel is come to appear before
20 w' I shall have brought them into 3588
21 w' many evils and troubles are "
24 w' Moses had made an end of writing
32: 8 W' the most High divided to the
8 w' he separated the sons of Adam, he
19 And w' the Lord saw it, he abhorred*
36 w' he seeth that their power is 3588
33: 5 w' the heads of the people and the
34: 7 and twenty years old w' he died:
Jos 2: 5 w' it was dark, that the men went out:
10 sea for you, w' ye came out of Egypt;
14 w' the Lord hath given us the land,
18 w' we come into the land, thou shalt
3: 3 W' ye see the ark of the covenant of
8 W' ye are come to the brink of the
14 w' the people removed from their
4: 1 w' all the people were clean passed 834
6 w' your children ask their fathers 3588
7 w' it passed over Jordan, the waters of
11 w' all the people were clean passed 834
18 w' the priests that bare the ark of the
21 W' your children shall ask their 834
5: 1 w' all the kings of the Amorites,
8 w' they had done circumcising all 834
13 to pass, w' Joshua was by Jericho,
6: 5 w' they make a long blast with the
5 w' ye hear the sound of the trumpet,
8 w' Joshua had spoken unto the people,
16 w' the priests blew with the trumpets,
18 w' ye take of the accursed thing, and
20 shouted w' the priests blew with the*
20 w' the people heard the sound of the
7: 8 w' Israel turneth their backs 6310
21 W' I saw among the spoils a goodly
8: 5 w' they come out against us, as at 3588
8 shall be, w' ye have taken the city,
13 w' they had set the people, even all*
14 w' the king of Ai saw it, that they
20 w' the men of Ai looked behind them,
21 w' Joshua and all Israel saw that the
24 w' Israel had made an end of slaying
24 w' they were all fallen on the edge of*
9: 1 w' all the kings which were on this
3 w' the inhabitants of Gibeon heard
22 far from you; w' ye dwell among us?
10: 12 in the day w' the Lord delivered up
20 w' Joshua and the children of Israel
24 w' they brought out those kings unto
11: 1 w' Jabin king of Hazor had heard
5 w' all these kings were met together,*
14: 7 w' Moses the servant of the Lord sent
17: 13 w' the children of Israel were 3588
19: 49 W' they had made an end of dividing*
20: 4 w' he that doth flee unto one of those*
22: 7 w' Joshua sent them away also 3588
10 w' they came unto the borders of
12 w' the children of Israel heard of it,
28 w' they should so say to us or to 3588
30 w' Phinehas the priest, and the princes
23: 16 W' ye have transgressed the covenant
24: 7 And w' they cried unto the Lord,
J'g 1: 14 it came to pass, w' she came to him,
25 w' he shewed them the entrance into*
28 w' Israel was strong, that they put the
2: 4 w' the angel of the Lord spake these
6 And w' Joshua had let the people go,
18 w' the Lord raised them up judges, 3588
19 w' the judge was dead, that they
21 nations which Joshua left w' he died:
3: 9, 15 w' the children of Israel cried unto
18 w' he had made an end to offer the 834
24 W' he was gone out, his servants came;
24 w' they saw that, behold, the doors of*
27 pass, w' he was come, that he blew a
4: 1 sight of the Lord, w' Ehud was dead.
18 w' he had turned in unto her into the*
20 w' any man doth come and enquire 518
22 And w' he came into her tent, behold,*
5: 2 w' the people willingly offered *

J'g 5: 4 Lord, *w*· thou wentest out of Seir,
4 *w*· thou marchedst out of the field of
26 *w*· she had pierced and stricken *
31 the sun *w*· he goeth forth in his might.
6: 3 And so it was, *w*· Israel had sown, 518
7 *w*· the children of Israel cried unto3588
22 *w*· Gideon perceived that he was an*
28 *w*· the men of the city arose early in
29 *w*· they enquired and asked, they said,
7: 13 And *w*· Gideon was come, behold,
15 *w*· Gideon heard the telling of the
17 *w*· I come to the outside of the camp,
18 *W*· I blow with a trumpet, I and all
8: 1 *w*· thou wentest to fight with the 3588
3 toward him, *w*· he had said that.
7 *w*· the Lord hath delivered Zeba and
9 *W*· I come again in peace, I will break
12 And *w*· Zeba and Zalmunna fled.*
9: 7 And *w*· they told it to Jotham, he went
22 *W*· Abimelech had reigned three years*
30 *w*· Zebul the ruler of the city heard
33 *W*· he and the people that is with him
36 And *w*· Gaal saw the people, he said to
46 And *w*· all the men of the tower of
55 And *w*· the men of Israel saw that
11: 5 *w*· the children of Ammon made * 834
7 unto me now *w*· ye are in distress? "
13 *w*· they came up out of Egypt, from
16 But *w*· Israel came up from Egypt, and
31 *w*· I return in peace from the children
35 to pass, *w*· he saw her, that he rent his
12: 2 *w*· I called you, ye delivered me not
3 And *w*· I saw that ye delivered me not,
5 *w*· those Ephraimites which were
13: 17 *w*· thy sayings come to pass we 3588
20 *w*· the flame went up toward heaven
14: 11 *w*· they saw him, that they brought
15: 5 And *w*· he had set the brands on fire,
14 *w*· he came unto Lehi, the Philistines
17 *w*· he had made an end of speaking,
19 *w*· he had drunk, his spirit came again,
16: 2 *w*· it is day, we shall kill him. 5704
9 of tow is broken *w*· it toucheth the fire.
15 thee, *w*· thine heart is not with me?
16 *w*· she pressed him daily with her 3588
18 *w*· Delilah saw that he had told her all
24 *w*· the people saw him, they praised
25 pass, *w*· their hearts were merry, 3588
17: 3 *w*· he had restored the eleven hundred*
18: 2 who *w*· they came to mount Ephraim,*
3 *W*· they were by the house of Micah,
10 *W*· ye go, ye shall come unto a people
22 *w*· they were a good way from the
26 *w*· Micah saw that they were too strong
19: 1 days, *w*· there was no king in Israel,
3 *w*· the father of the damsel saw him,
5 *w*· they arose early in the morning,*
7 And *w*· the man rose up to depart, his*
9 And *w*· the man rose up to depart,
11 *w*· they were by Jebus, the day was far
14 upon them *w*· they were by Gibeah,*
15 *w*· he went in, he sat him down in a*
17 *w*· he had lifted up his eyes, he saw a*
25 *w*· the day began to spring, they let
29 *w*· he was come into his house, he
20: 10 *w*· they come to Gibeah of Benjamin,
39 *w*· the men of Israel retired in the*
40 *w*· the flame began to arise up out of
41 *w*· the men of Israel turned again,*
21: 22 *w*· their fathers or their brethren 3588
Ru 1: 1 pass in the days *w*· the judges ruled,
18 *W*· she saw that she was stedfastly
19 *w*· they were come to Beth-lehem, that
2: 9 *w*· thou art athirst, go unto the
15 *w*· she was risen up to glean, Boaz
3: 4 be, *w*· he lieth down, that thou shalt
7 And *w*· Boaz had eaten and drunk,
15 And *w*· she held it, he measured six*
16 And *w*· she came to her mother in law,
4: 13 *w*· he went in unto her, the Lord gave
1Sa 1: 4 *w*· the time was that Elkanah offered,
7 *w*· she went up to the house of 1767
20 *w*· the time was come about after
24 *w*· she had weaned him, she took 834
2: 13 that, *w*· any man offered sacrifice,
19 *w*· she came up with her husband to
27 *w*· they were in Egypt in Pharaoh's
3: 2 *w*· Eli was laid down in his place,
12 *w*· I begin, I will also make an end.*
4: 2 *w*· they joined battle, Israel was
3 *w*· the people were come into the
3 *w*· it cometh among us, it may save us*
5 *w*· the ark of the covenant of the
6 *w*· the Philistines heard the noise of
13 *w*· he came, lo, Eli sat upon a seat by
13 *w*· the man came into the city, and
14 *w*· Eli heard the noise of the crying, he
18 *w*· he made mention of the ark of God,
19 *w*· she heard the tidings that the ark
5: 2 *W*· the Philistines took the ark of*
3 *w*· they of Ashdod arose early on the
4 *w*· they arose early on the morrow
7 *w*· the men of Ashdod saw that it was
6: 6 *w*· he had wrought wonderfully 834
16 *w*· the five lords of the Philistines had
7: 7 And *w*· the Philistines heard that the
7 *w*· the children of Israel heard it, they
8: 1 *w*· Samuel was old, that he made 834
6 *w*· they said, Give us a king to "
9: 5 *w*· they were come to the land of Zuph,
9 *w*· a man went to enquire of God,
14 and *w*· they were come into the city,*
17 *w*· Samuel saw Saul, the Lord said
25 *w*· they were come down from the
10: 2 *W*· thou art departed from me to day,
5 *w*· thou art come thither to the city,

1Sa 10: 7 *w*· these signs are come unto thee,3588
9 *w*· he had turned his back to go from
10 And *w*· they came thither to the hill,
11 *w*· all that knew him beforetime saw
13 And *w*· he had made an end of
14 *w*· we saw that they were no where,
20 *w*· Samuel had caused all the tribes*
21 *W*· he had caused the tribe of *
21 *w*· they sought him, he could not be
23 *w*· he stood among the people, he was
11: 6 upon Saul *w*· he heard those tidings,
8 *w*· he numbered them in Bezek, the*
12: 8 *W*· Jacob was come into Egypt, 834
9 *w*· they forgat the Lord their God, he*
12 *w*· ye saw that Nahash the king of the
12 *w*· the Lord your God was your king.
13: 1 and *w*· he had reigned two years over
6 *W*· the men of Israel saw that they
14: 17 And *w*· they had numbered, behold,
22 *w*· they heard that the Philistines fled,
26 And *w*· the people were come into the
27 not *w*· his father charged the people
52 *w*· Saul saw any strong man, or any
15: 2 in the way, *w*· he came up from Egypt.
6 Israel, *w*· they came up out of Egypt.
12 *w*· Samuel rose early to meet Saul*
17 *W*· thou wast little in thine own * 518
16: 6 *w*· they were come, that he looked on
16 *w*· the evil spirit from God is upon
23 *w*· the evil spirit from God was upon
17: 11 *w*· Saul and all Israel heard those
24 *w*· they saw the man, fled from him,
28 heard *w*· he spake unto the men;
31 *w*· the words were heard which David
35 *w*· he arose against me, I caught him
42 *w*· the Philistine looked about, and
48 *w*· the Philistine arose, and came 3588
51 *w*· the Philistines saw their champion
55 *w*· Saul saw David go forth against
18: 1 *w*· he had made an end of speaking
6 *w*· David was returned from the
15 Wherefore *w*· Saul saw that he behaved
19 *w*· Merab Saul's daughter should have
26 *w*· his servants told David these words,
19: 14 *w*· Saul sent messengers to take David,
16 And *w*· the messengers were come in,
20 and *w*· they saw the company of the
21 *w*· it was told Saul, he sent other
20: 12 *w*· I have sounded my father about3588
15 *w*· the Lord hath cut off the enemies
19 And *w*· thou hast stayed three days,
19 hide thyself *w*· the business was in
24 *w*· the new moon was come, the king
37 *w*· the lad was come to the place of the
21: 6 in the day *w*· it was taken away.
22: 1 *w*· his brethren and all his father's
6 *W*· Saul heard that David was *
17 because they knew *w*· he fled, *3588
22 *w*· Doeg the Edomite was there, "
23: 6 *w*· Abiathar the son of Ahimelech fled
25 *w*· Saul heard that, he pursued after
24: 1 *w*· Saul was returned from following834
8 *w*· Saul looked behind him, David
16 *w*· David had made an end of speaking
18 as *w*· the Lord had delivered me
25: 9 And *w*· David's young men came, they
15 with them, *w*· we were in the fields:
23 *w*· Abigail saw David, she hasted,
30 *w*· the Lord shall have done to my3588
31 *w*· the Lord shall have dealt well with
37 *w*· the wine was gone out of Nabal,
39 *w*· David heard that Nabal was dead,
40 *w*· the servants of David were come
26: 20 as *w*· one doth hunt a partridge in 834
28: 5 *w*· Saul saw the host of the Philistines,
6 And *w*· Saul enquired of the Lord,
12 *w*· the woman saw Samuel, she cried
22 strength, *w*· thou goest on thy way.3588
30: 1 *w*· David and his men were come to
12 *w*· he had eaten, his spirit came again
16 *w*· he had brought him down, behold,
21 *w*· David came near to the people, he
26 *w*· David came to Ziklag, he sent of
31: 5 *w*· his armourbearer saw that Saul
7 *w*· the men of Israel that were on the
8 *w*· the Philistines came to strip the
11 *w*· the inhabitants of Jabesh-gilead
2Sa 1: 1 *w*· David was returned from the
2 *w*· he came to David, that he fell to the
7 *w*· he looked behind him, he saw me,
2: 10 old *w*· he began to reign over Israel,
24 down *w*· they were come to the hill of
30 *w*· he had gathered all the people
3: 13 *w*· thou comest to see my face.
23 *W*· Joab and all the host that was
26 *w*· Joab was come out from David, he
27 *w*· Abner was returned to Hebron,
28 afterward *w*· David heard it, he said,
35 *w*· all the people came to cause David*
4: 1 *w*· Saul's son heard...Abner was dead
4 *w*· the tidings came of Saul and
7 For *w*· they came into the house, he
10 *W*· one told me, saying, Behold, Saul
11 *w*· wicked men have slain a 3588
5: 2 *w*· Saul was king over us, thou wast
17 *w*· the Philistines heard that they had
23 *w*· David enquired of the Lord, he
24 *w*· thou hearest the sound of a going
6: 6 And *w*· they came to Nachon's
13 *w*· they that bare the ark of the 3588
7: 1 *w*· the king sat in his house, and "
12 *w*· thy days be fulfilled, and thou "
8: 5 *w*· the Syrians of Damascus came to
9 *W*· Toi king of Hamath heard that
13 *w*· he returned from smiting of the
9: 2 *w*· they had called him unto David,*

2Sa 9: 6 Now *w*· Mephibosheth, the son of*
10: 5 *W*· they told it unto David, he sent to
6 *w*· the children of Ammon saw that
7 *w*· David heard of it, he sent Joab, and
9 *W*· Joab saw that the front of the
14 *w*· the children of Ammon saw that
15 *w*· the Syrians saw that they were
17 *w*· it was told David, he gathered all*
19 *w*· all the kings that were servants to
11: 1 time *w*· the kings go forth to battle,
7 *w*· Uriah was come unto him, David
10 *w*· they had told David, saying, Uriah
16 *w*· Joab observed the city, that he
19 *W*· thou hast made an end of telling
20 so nigh unto the city *w*· ye did fight?*
26 *w*· the wife of Uriah heard that Uriah
27 *w*· the mourning was past, David sent
12: 19 *w*· David saw that his servants
20 *w*· he required, they set bread before
21 *w*· the child was dead, thou didst 834
13: 5 *w*· thy father cometh to see thee, say
6 and *w*· the king was come to see him,
11 *w*· she had brought them unto him to
21 But *w*· king David heard of all these
28 ye now *w*· Ammon's heart is merry
28 and *w*· I say unto you, Smite Ammon;
14: 4 *w*· the woman of Tekoah spake to the
26 *w*· he polled his head, (for it was at
29 *w*· he sent again the second time, he*
33 *w*· he had called for Absalom, he came
15: 2 *w*· any man that had a controversy
5 *w*· any man came nigh to him to do
32 *w*· David was come to the top of the
16: 1 *w*· David was a little past the top of
5 And *w*· king David came to Bahurim,
7 thus said Shimei *w*· he cursed, Come
16 *w*· Hushai the Archite, David's 834
17: 6 And *w*· Hushai was come to Absalom,
9 *w*· some of them be overthrown at the
20 *w*· Absalom's servants came to the*
20 *w*· they had sought and could not find
23 *w*· Ahithophel saw that his counsel
27 *w*· David was come to Mahanaim,
18: 5 *w*· the king gave all the captains
29 *W*· Joab sent the king's servant, and
19: 3 steal away *w*· they flee in battle.
25 *w*· he was come to Jerusalem to 3588
39 *w*· the king was come over, the king*
20: 8 *W*· they were at the great stone
12 *w*· the man saw that all the people
13 *W*· he was removed out of the
17 *w*· he was come near unto her, the*
21: 12 *w*· the Philistines had slain Saul *3117
21 *w*· he defied Israel, Jonathan the son
22: 5 *W*· the waves of death compassed*3588
23: 4 of the morning, *w*· the sun riseth,
9 *w*· they defied the Philistines that
24: 8 So *w*· they had gone through all the
11 *w*· David was up in the morning, the
16 *w*· the angel stretched out his hand
17 *w*· he saw the angel that smote the
1Ki 1: 21 *w*· my lord the king shall sleep with
23 *w*· he was come in before the king, he
41 And *w*· Joab heard the sound of the
2: 7 to me *w*· I fled because of Absalom
8 in the day *w*· I went to Mahanaim:
3: 21 *w*· I rose in the morning to give my
21 but *w*· I had considered it in the
5: 7 *w*· Hiram heard...words of Solomon,
6: 7 *w*· it was in building, was built of
7: 24 were cast in two rows, *w*· it was cast.
8: 9 *w*· the Lord made a covenant with 834
9 *w*· they came out of the land of Egypt.
10 *w*· the priests were come out of the
21 *w*· he brought them out of the land of
30 *w*· they shall pray toward this 834
30 and *w*· thou hearest, forgive.
33 *W*· thy people Israel be smitten down
35 *W*· heaven is shut up, and there is no
35 there sin, *w*· thou afflictest them: 3588
42 *w*· he shall come and pray toward this
53 *w*· thou broughtest our fathers out of
54 *w*· Solomon had made an end of
9: 1 *w*· Solomon had finished the building
10 *w*· Solomon had built the two houses,*
10: 1 *w*· the queen of Sheba heard of the
2 and *w*· she was come to Solomon, she
4 *w*· the queen of Sheba had seen all
11: 4 *w*· Solomon was old, that his 6256
15 *w*· David was in Edom, and Joab the
21 *w*· Hadad heard in Egypt that David
24 a band, *w*· David slew them of Zobah:
29 *w*· Jeroboam went out of Jerusalem,
12: 2 *w*· Jeroboam the son of Nebat, who
16 So *w*· all Israel saw that the king
20 *w*· all Israel heard that Jeroboam was
21 *w*· Rehoboam was come to Jerusalem,
13: 4 *w*· king Jeroboam heard the saying of
24 *w*· he was gone, a lion met him by the
26 *w*· the prophet that brought him back
31 *W*· I am dead, then bury me in the
14: 5 it shall be, *w*· she cometh in, that she
6 *w*· Ahijah heard the sound of her feet,
12 and *w*· thy feet enter into the city, the
17 *w*· she came to the threshold of the*
21 one years old *w*· he began to reign,
28 *w*· the king went into the house *1767
15: 21 it came to pass, *w*· Baasha heard
29 *w*· he reigned, that he smote all the*
16: 11 *w*· he began to reign, as soon as he sat
18 *w*· Zimri saw that the city was taken,
17: 10 *w*· he came to the gate of the city,
18: 4 *w*· Jezebel cut off the prophets of
10 and *w*· they said, He is not there;
12 and so *w*· I come and tell Ahab,
13 *w*· Jezebel slew the prophets of the

1Ki 18: 17 w· Ahab saw Elijah, that Ahab said
29 w· midday was past, and they
39 w· all the people saw it, they fell on
19: 3 w· he saw that, he arose, and went for
13 w· Elijah heard it, that he wrapped
15 w· thou comest, anoint Hazael to be
20: 12 w· Ben-hadad heard this message,
21: 15 w· Jezebel heard that Naboth was
27 to pass, w· Ahab heard those words,
22: 25 w· thou shalt go into an inner 834
32, 33 w· the captains of the chariots
42 five years old w· he began to reign;
2Ki 1: 5 w· the messengers turned back unto*
2: 1 w· the Lord would take up Elijah into
9 came to pass, w· they were gone over,
10 thou see me w· I am taken from thee,
14 w· he also had smitten the waters,
15 w· the sons of the prophets which
17 w· they urged him till he was ashamed,
18 w· they came again to him, (for he*
3: 5 it came to pass, w· Ahab was dead,
15 came to pass, w· the minstrel played,
20 w· the meat offering was offered, *
21 w· all the Moabites heard that the
24 w· they came to the camp of Israel,
26 w· the king of Moab saw that the
4: 4 w· thou art come in, thou shalt shut*
6 came to pass, w· the vessels were full,
10 and it shall be, w· he cometh to us,
12 w· he had called her, she stood before
15 w· he had called her, she stood in the
18 w· the child was grown, it fell on a
20 w· he had taken him, and brought
25 w· the man of God saw her afar off,
27 w· she came to the man of God to the
32 w· Elisha was come into the house,
36 w· she was come in unto him, he said,
5: 6 Now w· this letter is come unto thee,
7 w· the king of Israel had read the
8 w· Elisha the man of God had heard
13 w· he saith to thee, Wash, and be 3588
18 w· my master goeth into the house
18 w· I bow down myself in the house of
21 w· Naaman saw him running after
24 w· he came to the tower, he took them
26 w· the man turned again from his 3588
6: 4 w· they came to Jordan, they cut down
15 w· the servant of the man of God was
18 w· they came down to him, Elisha
20 w· they were come into Samaria,
21 w· he saw them, My father, shall I
23 w· they had eaten and drunk, he sent
30 w· the king heard the words of the
32 w· the messenger cometh, shut the
7: 5 w· they were come to the uttermost
12 W· they come out of the city, we 3588
17 who spake w· the king came down to
8: 6 w· the king asked the woman, she
17 old was he w· he began to reign;
26 old was Ahaziah w· he began to reign;
29 w· he fought against Hazael king of
9: 2 w· thou comest thither, look out there
5 w· he came, behold, the captains of
15 w· he fought with Hazael king of
22 w· Joram saw Jehu, that he said, Is it
25 w· I and thou rode together after
27 w· Ahaziah the king of Judah saw
30 And w· Jehu was come to Jezreel,
34 w· he was come in, he did eat and
10: 7 pass, w· the letter came to them, that
15 w· he was departed thence, he lighted
17 w· he came to Samaria, he slew all that
11: 1 w· Athaliah the mother of Ahaziah
13 w· Athaliah heard the noise of the
14 w· she looked, behold, the king stood*
21 was Jehoash w· he began to reign.
12: 10 w· they saw that there was much
13: 21 and w· the man was let down, and
14: 2 five years old w· he began to reign,
15: 2, 33 old was he w· he began to reign,
16: 2 old was Ahaz w· he began to reign,
12 And w· the king was come from
18: 2 old was he w· he began to reign;
17 w· they were come up, they came and
18 w· they had called to the king, there
32 w· he persuadeth you, saying, The 3588
19: 1 to pass, w· king Hezekiah heard it,
9 w· he heard say of Tirhakah king of
35 w· they arose early in the morning,
21: 1 years old w· he began to reign,
19 two years old w· he began to reign,
22: 1 eight years old w· he began to reign,
11 w· the king had heard the words of
19 w· thou heardest what I spake against
23: 29 him at Megiddo, w· he had seen him.
31 three years old w· he began to reign;
36 five years old w· he began to reign;
24: 8 years old w· he began to reign, and
18 one years old w· he began to reign,
25: 23 w· all the captains of the armies, they
1Ch 1: 44 w· Bela was dead, Jobab the son of*
45 And w· Jobab was dead, Husham of*
46 w· Husham was dead, Hadad the son*
47 w· Hadad was dead, Samlah of *
48 w· Samlah was dead, Shaul of *
49 w· Shaul was dead, Baal-hanan the*
50 w· Baal-hanan was dead, Hadad *
2: 19 w· Azubah was dead, Caleb took unto*
21 w· he was threescore years old;
5: 7 w· the genealogy of their generations
6: 15 w· the Lord carried away Judah and
10: 5 w· his armourbearer saw that Saul
7 w· all the men of Israel that were in
8 w· the Philistines came to strip the
9 w· they had stripped him, they took*
11 w· all Jabesh-gilead heard all that the

1Ch 11: 2 time past, even w· Saul was king,
12: 15 w· it had overflown all his banks;
19 w· he came with the Philistines
13: 9 w· they came unto the threshingfloor
14: 8 w· the Philistines heard that David
12 And w· they had left their gods there,*
15 w· thou shalt hear a sound of going
15: 26 w· God helped the Levites that bare
16: 2 w· David had made an end of offering
19 W· ye were but few, even a few, and
20 w· they went from nation to nation,*
17: 11 w· thy days be expired that thou 3588
18: 5 w· the Syrians of Damascus came
9 w· Tou king of Hamath heard how
19: 6 w· the children of Ammon saw that
8 w· David heard of it, he sent Joab,
10 Now w· Joab saw that the battle was
15 w· the children of Ammon saw that
16 w· the Syrians saw that they were
17 w· David had put the battle in array
19 w· the servants of Hadarezer saw that
20: 7 w· he defied Israel, Jonathan the son
21: 28 that time w· David saw that the Lord
23: 1 w· David was old and full of days, he*
2Ch 4: 3 of oxen were cast, w· it was cast.
5: 10 w· the Lord made a covenant with 834
10 of Israel, w· they came out of Egypt.
11 w· the priests were come out of the
13 w· they lifted up their voice with the
6: 21 heaven; and w· thou hearest, forgive.
26 W· the heaven is shut up, and there
26 sin, w· thou dost afflict them, 3588
27 w· thou hast taught them the good "
29 w· every one shall know his own * 834
7: 1 w· Solomon had made an end of
3 w· all the children of Israel saw how
6 w· David praised by their ministry;
9: 1 w· the queen of Sheba heard of the
1 w· she was come to Solomon, she
3 w· the queen of Sheba had seen the
10: 2 w· Jeroboam the son of Nebat, who
16 w· all Israel saw that the king would
11: 1 w· Rehoboam was come to Jerusalem,
12: 1 w· Rehoboam had established the
7 w· the Lord saw that they humbled
11 w· the king entered into the house*1767
12 w· he humbled himself, the wrath of
13 forty years old w· he began to reign,
13: 7 w· Rehoboam was young and
14 w· Judah looked back, behold, the
15: 4 w· they in their trouble did turn
8 w· Asa heard these words, and the
9 w· they saw that the Lord his God was
16: 5 w· Baasha heard it, that he left off
18: 14 w· he was come to the king, the king
24 w· thou shalt go into an inner 834
31, 32 w· the captains of the chariots
19: 8 w· they returned to Jerusalem. *
20: 9 w· evil cometh upon us, as the sword,*
10 w· they came out of the land of Egypt,
21 w· he had consulted with the people,
22 w· they began to sing and to 6256
23 w· they had made an end of the
24 w· Judah came toward the watch
25 w· Jehoshaphat and his people came
29 w· they had heard that the Lord
31 and five years w· he began to reign,
21: 4 w· Jehoram was risen up to the
5 two years old w· he began to reign,
20 old was he w· he began to reign,
22: 2 was Ahaziah w· he began to reign,
6 w· he fought with Hazael king of
7 w· he was come, he went out with
8 w· Jehu was executing judgment
9 w· they had slain him, they buried*
10 w· Athaliah the mother of Ahaziah
23: 7 w· he cometh in, and w· he goeth out.
12 w· Athaliah heard the noise of the
15 w· she was come to the entering of the
24: 1 seven years old w· he began to reign,
14 w· they had finished it, they brought
15 and was full of days w· he died; *
15 thirty years old was he w· he died.
22 w· he died, he said, The Lord look
25 w· they were departed from him, (for
25: 1 five years old w· he began to reign,
3 w· the kingdom was established to 834
26: 3 old was Uzziah w· he began to reign,
16 w· he was strong, his heart was lifted
27: 1 five years old w· he began to reign,
8 twenty years old w· he began to reign,
28: 1 twenty years old w· he began to reign,
29: 1 to reign w· he was five and twenty
22 w· they had killed the rams, they*
27 w· the burnt offering began, the 6256
29 w· they had made an end of offering,
31: 1 w· all this was finished, all Israel that
8 w· Hezekiah and the princes came
32: 2 w· Hezekiah saw that Sennacherib
21 w· he was come into the house of his
33: 1 twelve years old w· he began to reign,
12 w· he was in affliction, he besought
21 twenty years old w· he began to reign,
34: 1 eight years old w· he began to reign,
7 w· he had broken down the altars and*
8 w· he had purged the land, and the
9 w· they came to Hilkiah the high*
14 w· they brought out the money that
19 w· the king had heard the word of the
27 w· thou heardest his words against
35: 20 w· Josiah had prepared the temple, 834
36: 2 three years old w· he began to reign,
5 five years old w· he began to reign,
9 eight years old w· he began to reign,
10 w· the year was expired, king *
11 twenty years old w· he began to reign,

Ezr 2: 68 w· they came to the house of the Lord
3: 1 w· the seventh month was come, and
10 w· the builders laid the foundation of
11 w· they praised the Lord, because the
4: 1 w· the adversaries of Judah and
23 Now w· the copy of king 4481,1768
10: 1 w· Ezra had prayed, and w· he had *
6 w· he came thither, he did eat no
Ne 1: 4 w· I heard these words, that I sat
2: 3 w· the city, the place of my fathers' 834
6 be? and w· wilt thou return? 4970
10 W· Sanballat the Horonite, and
19 w· Sanballat the Horonite, and Tobiah
4: 1 w· Sanballat heard that we builded 834
7 w· Sanballat, and Tobiah, and the "
12 w· the Jews which dwelt by them "
15 w· our enemies heard that it was "
5: 6 w· I heard their cry and these "
6: 1 w· Sanballat, and Tobiah, and "
16 w· all our enemies heard thereof "
7: 1 w· the wall was built, and I had set "
73 w· the seventh month came, the
8: 5 w· he opened it, all the people stood
9 w· they heard the words of the law.
9: 18 w· they had made them a molten 3588
27 w· they cried unto thee, thou heardest
28 w· they returned, and cried unto thee,
10: 38 the Levites, w· the Levites take tithes:
13: 3 w· they had heard the law, that they
19 w· the gates of Jerusalem began to 834
Es 1: 2 w· the king Ahasuerus sat on the
4 W· he shewed the riches of his
5 w· these days were expired, the king
10 w· the heart of the king was merry
17 in their eyes, w· it shall be reported,
20 w· the king's decree, which he shall
2: 1 w· the wrath of king Ahasuerus was
7 w· her father and mother were dead,
8 w· the king's commandment and his
8 and w· many maidens were gathered
12 w· every maid's turn was come to
15 w· the turn of Esther, the daughter of
19 w· the virgins were gathered together
20 as w· she was brought up with him. 834
23 w· inquisition was made of the matter,
3: 4 w· they spake daily unto him, and he
5 w· Haman saw that Mordecai bowed
4: 1 W· Mordecai perceived all that was
5: 2 w· the king saw Esther the queen
9 w· Haman saw Mordecai in the king's
10 w· he came home, he sent and called*
9: 1 w· the king's commandment and 834
25 w· Esther came before the king, he
Job 1: 5 w· the days of their feasting were 3588
6 was a day w· the sons of God came
13 w· his sons and his daughters were
2: 1 was a day w· the sons of God came
11 Now w· Job's three friends heard of
12 w· they lifted up their eyes afar off,
3: 11 the ghost w· I came out of the belly?
22 glad, w· they can find the grave? 3588
4: 13 night, w· deep sleep falleth upon men,
5: 21 afraid of destruction w· it cometh. 3588
6: 5 the wild ass bray w· he hath grass?
17 w· it is hot, they are consumed out of
7: 4 W· I lie down, I say, 4970
4 W· shall I arise, and the night "
13 W· I say, My bed shall comfort 3588
11: 3 w· thou mockest, shall no man make
16: 22 W· a few years are come, then I 3588
17: 16 w· our rest together is in the dust. 518
20: 23 W· he is about to fill his belly, God
21: 6 Even w· I remember I am afraid, 518
21 w· the number of his months is cut off
22: 29 W· men are cast down, then thou 3588
23: 10 w· he hath tried me, I shall come forth
15 w· I consider, I am afraid of him.
27: 8 w· God taketh away his soul? 3588
9 cry w· trouble cometh upon him? "
28: 26 W· he made a decree for the rain, and
29: 2 as in the days w· God preserved me;
3 W· his candle shined upon my head,
3 w· by his light I walked through *
4 w· the secret of God was upon my
5 W· the Almighty was yet with 5750
5 w· my children were about me; *
6 W· I washed my steps with butter,
7 W· I went out to the gate through the
7 w· I prepared my seat in the street!
11 W· the ear heard me, then it 3588
11 w· the eye saw me, it gave witness to
30: 26 W· I looked for good, then evil 3588
26 w· I waited for light, there came
31: 13 w· they contended with me;
14 shall I do w· God riseth up? and 3588
14 w· he visiteth, what shall I answer "
21 w· I saw my help in the gate: "
26 If I beheld the sun w· it shined, or "
29 lifted up myself w· evil found him: "
32: 5 W· Elihu saw there was no answer in
16 W· I had waited, (for they spake not,*
33: 15 night, w· deep sleep falleth upon men,
34: 29 W· he giveth quietness, who then can
29 w· he hideth his face, who then can
36: 13 they cry not w· he bindeth them. 3588
20 w· people are cut off in their place.
37: 4 stay them w· his voice is heard. 3588
15 Dost thou know w· God disposed *
38: 4 wast thou w· I laid the foundations
7 W· the morning stars sang together,
8 the sea with doors, w· it brake forth,
9 W· I made the cloud the garment
38 W· the dust groweth into hardness,
40 W· they couch in their dens, and 3588
41 w· his young ones cry unto God, "
39: 1 w· the wild goats of the rock bring

Job 39: 1 thou mark w· the hinds do calve?
2 thou the time w· they bring forth?
41: 25 W· he riseth up himself, the mighty
42: 10 of Job, w· he prayed for his friends:
Ps 2: 12 w· his wrath is kindled but a little.*3588
3: title w· he fled from Absalom his son.
4: 1 Hear me w· I call, O God of my
1 hast enlarged me w· I was in distress;
3 the Lord will hear w· I call unto him.
8: 3 W· I consider thy heavens, the 3588
9: 3 W· mine enemies are turned back
12 W· he maketh inquisition for *3588
10: 9 poor, w· he draweth him into his net.
12: 8 side, w· the vilest men are exalted.
13: 4 trouble me rejoice w· I am moved.3588
14: 7 w· the Lord bringeth back the
17: 15 satisfied, w· I awake, with thy likeness.
20: 9 Lord: let the king hear us w· we call.
21: 12 w· thou shalt make ready thine arrows*
22: 9 w· I was upon my mother's breasts.
24 but w· he cried unto me, he heard.
27: 2 W· the wicked, even mine enemies
7 w· I cry with my voice: have mercy
8 W· thou saidst, Seek ye my face; my
10 W· my father and my mother *3588
28: 2 my supplications, w· I cry unto thee,
2 w· I lift up my hands toward thy holy
30: 9 in my blood, w· I go down to the pit?
31: 22 my supplications w· I cried unto thee.
32: 3 W· I kept silence, my bones 3588
6 in a time w· thou mayest be found:
34: title w· he changed his behaviour before
35: 13 w· they were sick, my clothing was
37: 33 nor condemn him w· he is judged.
34 w· the wicked are cut off, thou shalt
38: 16 w· my foot slippeth, they magnify
39: 11 W· thou with rebukes dost correct
41: 5 me, W· shall he die, and his name4970
6 w· he goeth abroad, he telleth it.
42: 2 w· shall I come and appear before 4970
4 W· I remember these things, I pour
49: 5 w· the iniquity of my heels shall
16 Be not thou afraid w· one is made 3588
16 rich, w· the glory of his house is "
17 w· he dieth he shall carry nothing "
18 thee, w· thou doest well to thyself. "
50: 18 W· thou sawest a thief, then thou 518
51: title w· Nathan the prophet came unto
4 mightest be justified w· thou speakest,
4 speakest, and be clear w· thou judgest.
52: title w· Doeg the Edomite came and told
53: 6 W· God bringeth back the captivity of
54: title w· the Ziphims came and said to
56: title w· the Philistines took him in Gath.
6 my steps, w· they wait for my soul.*834
9 W· I cry unto thee, then shall mine
57: title w· he fled from Saul in the cave.
58: 7 w· he bendeth his bow to shoot his
10 rejoice w· he seeth the vengeance:3588
59: title w· Saul sent, and they watched the
60: title w· he strove with Aram-naharaim
title w· Joab returned, and smote of Edom*
61: 2 thee, w· my heart is overwhelmed:
63: 6 W· I remember thee upon my bed, 518
65: 9 corn, w· thou hast so provided for it.
66: 14 hath spoken, w· I was in trouble.
68: 7 God, w· thou wentest forth before thy
7 w· thou didst march through the
9 thine inheritance, w· it was weary.
14 W· the Almighty scattered kings in
69: 10 W· I wept, and chastened my soul
71: 9 forsake me not w· my strength faileth.
18 also w· I am old and grayheaded, 5704
23 greatly rejoice w· I sing unto thee:3588
72: 12 shall deliver the needy w· he crieth;
73: 3 w· I saw the prosperity of the wicked.
16 w· I thought to know this, it was too
20 a dream w· one awaketh; so, O Lord,
20 w· thou awakest, thou shalt despise
75: 2 W· I shall receive the congregation3588
76: 7 in thy sight w· once thou art angry?
9 W· God arose to judgment, to save all
78: 34 W· he slew them, then they sought518
42 w· he delivered them from the 834
59 W· God heard this, he was wroth, and
81: 5 w· he went out through the land of
87: 6 count, w· he writeth up the people,
89: 9 w· the waves thereof arise, thou stillest
90: 4 are but as yesterday w· it is past, 3588
92: 7 W· the wicked spring as the grass,
7 and w· all the workers of iniquity do
94: 8 and ye fools, w· will ye be wise? 4970
18 W· I said, My foot slippeth; thy 518
95: 9 W· your fathers tempted me, 834
101: 2 O w· wilt thou come unto me? I 4970
102: title w· he is overwhelmed, and 3588
2 me in the day w· I am in trouble;*
2 the day w· I call answer me speedily.
16 W· the Lord shall build up Zion, *3588
22 W· the people are gathered together,
105: 12 W· they were but a few men in
13 W· they went from one nation to*
38 Egypt was glad w· they departed: for
106: 44 their affliction, w· he heard their cry:
109: 7 W· he shall be judged, let him be
23 gone like the shadow w· it declineth:
25 w· they looked upon me they shaked
28 w· they arise, let them be ashamed;
114: 1 W· Israel went out of Egypt, the
119: 6 w· I have respect unto all thy
7 w· I shall have learned thy righteous
32 w· thou shalt enlarge my heart. 3588
74 fear thee will be glad w· they see me;*
82 saying, W· wilt thou comfort me?4970
84 w· wilt thou execute judgment on "
171 w· thou hast taught me thy *3588

Ps 120: 7 but w· I speak, they are for war. *3588
122: 1 I was glad w· they said unto me, Let
124: 2 our side, w· men rose up against us:
3 w· their wrath was kindled against
126: 1 W· the Lord turned again the
137: 1 yea, we wept, w· we remembered Zion.
138: 3 the day w· I cried thou answeredst me,*
4 w· they hear the words of thy *3588
139: 15 w· I was made in secret, and 834
16 w· as yet there was none of them.
18 w· I awake, I am still with thee.
141: 1 ear unto my voice, w· I cry unto thee.
6 W· their judges are overthrown in*
7 as w· one cutteth and cleaveth wood
142: title A Prayer w· he was in the cave.
3 W· my spirit was overwhelmed
Pr 1: 26 I will mock w· your fear cometh;
27 W· your fear cometh as desolation,
27 w· distress and anguish cometh upon
2: 10 W· wisdom entereth into thine *3588
3: 24 W· thou liest down, thou shalt not 518
25 of the wicked, w· it cometh. 3588
27 w· it is in the power of thine hand to
28 will give; w· thou hast it by thee.
4: 8 honour, w· thou dost embrace her.3588
12 W· thou goest, thy steps shall not be
12 w· thou runnest, thou shalt not * 518
5: 11 w· thy flesh and thy body are
6: 3 w· thou art come into the hand of*3588
9 w· wilt thou arise out of thy sleep?4970
22 W· thou goest, it shall lead thee;
22 w· thou sleepest, it shall keep thee;
22 w· thou awakest, it shall talk with
30 satisfy his soul w· he is hungry; 3588
8: 24 W· there were no depths, I was
24 w· there were no fountains abounding
27 W· he prepared the heavens, I was
27 w· he set a compass upon the face of
28 W· he established the clouds above:
28 w· he strengthened the fountains of
29 W· he gave to the sea his decree that
29 w· he appointed the fountains of the
11: 2 W· pride cometh, then cometh shame:
7 W· a wicked man dieth, his
10 W· it goeth well with the righteous,
10 w· the wicked perish, there is shouting.
13: 12 w· the desire cometh, it is a tree of
14: 7 w· thou perceivest not in him the lips*
16: 7 W· a man's ways please the Lord, he
17: 14 strife is as w· one letteth out water:
28 w· he holdeth his peace, is counted
18: 3 W· the wicked cometh, then cometh
20: 14 but w· he is gone his way, then he
21: 11 W· the scorner is punished, the
11 w· the wise is instructed, he receiveth
27 w· he bringeth it with a wicked 3588
22: 6 and w· he is old, he will not depart "
23: 1 W· thou sittest to eat with a ruler, "
16 rejoice, w· thy lips speak right things.
22 not thy mother w· she is old. 3588
31 not thou upon the wine w· it is red, "
31 w· it giveth his colour in the cup, "
31 in the cup, w· it moveth itself aright.
35 w· shall I awake? I will seek it 4970
24: 14 w· thou hast found it, then there * 518
17 Rejoice not w· thine enemy falleth,
17 thine heart be glad w· he stumbleth:
25: 8 w· thy neighbour hath put thee to
26: 25 W· he speaketh fair, believe him 3588
28: 1 The wicked flee w· no man pursueth:
12 W· righteous men do rejoice, there is
28 W· the wicked rise, men hide
28 w· they perish, the righteous increase.
29: 2 W· the righteous are in authority, the
2 w· the wicked beareth rule, the people*
16 W· the wicked are multiplied,
30: 22 For a servant w· he reigneth; and3588
22 and a fool w· he is filled with meat; "
23 odious woman w· she is married; "
31: 23 w· he sitteth among the elders of the
Ec 4: 10 woe to him that is alone w· he falleth:
5: 1 Keep thy foot w· thou goest to the 834
4 W· thou vowest a vow unto God, "
11 W· goods increase, they are increased
8: 7 can tell him w· it shall be? 3588,834
16 W· I applied mine heart to know "
9: 12 time, w· it falleth suddenly upon them.
10: 3 w· he that is a fool walketh by the
16 to thee, O land, w· thy king is a child,
17 land, w· thy king is the son of nobles,
12: 1 w· thou shalt say, I have no 834
3 day w· the keepers of the house shall
4 w· the sound of the grinding is low,
5 w· they shall be afraid of that which is
Ca 5: 6 my soul failed w· he spake: I sought
8: 1 w· I should find thee without, I would
8 in the day w· she shall be spoken for?
Isa 1: 12 W· ye come to appear before me, 3588
15 w· ye spread forth your hands, I will
15 w· ye make many prayers, I will 3588
2: 19, 21 w· he ariseth to shake terribly the
3: 6 W· a man shall take hold of his 3588
4: 4 W· the Lord shall have washed 518
5: 4 w· I looked that it should bring forth
6: 13 in them, w· they cast their leaves: 834
8: 19 w· they shall say unto you, Seek 3588
21 w· they shall be hungry, they shall "
9: 1 w· at the first he lightly afflicted *6256
3 men rejoice w· they divide the spoil.
10: 12 w· the Lord hath performed his 3588
18 be as w· a standardbearer fainteth.
13: 19 be as w· God overthrew Sodom and
16: 12 w· it is seen that Moab is weary on3588
17: 5 be as w· the harvestman gathereth the
18: 3 w· he lifteth up an ensign on the
3 and w· he bloweth a trumpet, hear ye.

Isa 20: 1 (w· Sargon the king of Assyria sent
24: 13 W· thus it shall be in the midst of*3588
13 grapes w· the vintage is done. 518
23 the Lord of hosts shall reign in*3588
25: 4 w· the blast of the terrible ones is "
26: 9 w· thy judgments are in the earth, 834
11 w· thy hand is lifted up, they will not*
16 w· thy chastening was upon them.
27: 8 In measure, w· it shooteth forth, thou
9 w· he maketh all the stones of the
11 W· the boughs thereof are withered,
28: 4 which w· he that looketh upon it seeth,
15, 18 w· the overflowing scourge 3588
25 W· he hath made plain the face 518
29: 8 w· an hungry man dreameth, and, 834
8 as w· a thirsty man dreameth, and, "
23 w· he seeth his children, the work 3588
30: 19 w· he shall hear it, he will answer
21 in it, w· ye turn to the right hand, 3588
21 hand, and w· ye turn to the left. "
25 the great slaughter, w· the towers fall.
29 the night w· a holy solemnity is kept;
29 w· one goeth with a pipe to come into
31: 3 W· the Lord shall stretch out his
4 w· a multitude of shepherds is * 834
32: 7 even w· the needy speaketh right.
19 W· it shall hail, coming down on the*
33: 1 w· thou shalt cease to spoil, thou shalt
1 w· thou shalt make an end to deal
37: 1 w· king Hezekiah heard it, that he
9 And w· he heard it, he sent messengers
36 w· they arose early in the morning,
38: 9 w· he had been sick, and was
41: 17 W· the poor and needy seek water,*
28 no counseller, that, w· I ask of them,
43: 2 W· thou passest through the 3588
12 w· there was no strange god among
48: 7 the day w· thou heardest them not;*
13 w· I call unto them, they stand up
21 thirsted not w· he led them through
50: 2 w· I came, was there no man?
2 w· I called, was there none to answer?
52: 8 w· the Lord shall bring again Zion.
53: 2 and w· we shall see him, there is no
10 w· thou shalt make his soul an 518
54: 6 youth, w· thou wast refused, saith 3588
57: 13 W· thou criest, let thy companies
20 troubled sea, w· it cannot rest, *3588
58: 7 w· thou seest the naked, that thou "
59: 19 W· the enemy shall come in like a*"
64: 2 w· the melting fire burneth, the fire
3 W· thou didst terrible things which
65: 12 because w· I called, ye did not answer;
12 w· I spake, ye did not hear; but did
66: 4 because w· I called, none did answer;
4 w· I spake, they did not hear: but
14 w· ye see this, your heart shall rejoice,*
Jer 2: 2 w· thou wentest after me in the *
7 w· ye entered, ye defiled my land, and
17 God, w· he led thee by the way? 6256
20 w· upon every high hill and under 3588
26 thief is ashamed w· he is found, "
3: 8 w· for all the causes whereby "
16 w· ye be multiplied and increased "
4: 30 w· thou art spoiled, what wilt thou do?
5: 7 w· I had fed them to the full, they then
19 w· ye shall say, Wherefore doeth 3588
6: 14 Peace, peace; w· there is no peace.
15 ashamed w· they had committed 3588
8: 11 Peace, peace; w· there is no peace.
12 ashamed w· they had committed 3588
18 W· I would comfort myself against*
10: 13 W· he uttereth his voice, there is a
11: 15 w· thou doest evil, then thou 3588
12: 1 thou, O Lord, w· I plead with thee: "
13: 21 thou say w· he shall punish thee? "
27 be made clean? w· shall it once be?*
14: 12 W· they fast, I will not hear their 3588
12 w· they offer burnt offering and an "
16: 10 w· thou shalt show this people all "
17: 6 and shall not see w· good cometh; "
8 and shall not see w· heat cometh, "
18: 22 w· thou shalt bring a troop "
21: 1 w· king Zedekiah sent unto him
22: 23 thou be w· pangs come upon thee,
23: 33 w· this people, or the prophet, or a 3588
25: 12 w· seventy years are accomplished,
26: 8 w· Jeremiah had made an end of
10 W· the princes of Judah heard these
21 w· Jehoiakim the king, with all his
21 w· Urijah heard it, he was afraid, and
27: 20 w· he carried away captive Jeconiah
28: 9 w· the word of the prophet shall come
29: 13 w· ye shall search for me with all 3588
31: 2 Israel, w· I went to cause him to rest.
23 w· I shall bring again their captivity;
35 the sea w· the waves thereof roar;*
32: 16 w· I had delivered the evidence of the
34: 1 w· Nebuchadnezzar king of Babylon,
7 W· the king of Babylon's army fought
10 w· all the princes, and all the people,*
14 w· he hath served thee six years, thou*
18 w· they cut the calf in twain, and
35: 11 w· Nebuchadrezzar king of Babylon
36: 11 W· Michaiah the son of Gemariah, the
13 w· Baruch read the book in the ears of
16 w· they had heard all the words, they
23 w· Jehudi had read three or four
37: 5 w· the Chaldeans that besieged
11 w· the army of the Chaldeans was
13 w· he was in the gate of Benjamin, a
16 W· Jeremiah was entered into 3588
38: 7 w· Ebed-melech the Ethiopian, one of
28 was there w· Jerusalem was taken.*834
39: 4 w· Zedekiah the king of Judah saw "
5 w· they had taken him, they brought

Jer 40: 1 w' he had taken him being bound in
7 Now w' all the captains of the forces
11 w' all the Jews that were in Moab,
41: 7 w' they came into the midst of the
11 But w' Johanan the son of Kareah,
13 that w' all the people which were with
42: 6 w' we obey the voice of the Lord 3588
18 you, w' ye shall enter into Egypt:
20 w' ye sent me unto the Lord your*3588
43: 1 w' Jeremiah had made an end of
11 w' he cometh, he shall smite the land
44: 19 w' we burned incense to the 3588
45: 1 w' he had written these words in a
51: 16 W' he uttereth his voice, there is a
55 w' her waves do roar like great waters,*
59 w' he went with Zedekiah the king of
61 W' thou comest to Babylon, and shalt
63 w' thou hast made an end of reading
52: 1 twenty years old w' he began to reign,
La 1: 7 w' her people fell into the hand of the
2: 12 w' they swooned as the wounded in
12 w' their soul was poured out into their
3: 8 w' I cry and shout, he shutteth 3588
37 pass, w' the Lord commanded it not?
4: 15 w' they fled away and wandered, 3588
Eze 1: 9 another; they turned not w' they went;
12 and they turned not w' they went.
17 W' they went, they went upon their
17 and they turned not w' they went.
19 w' the living creatures went, the
19 w' the living creatures were lifted up
21 W' those went, these went; and
21 w' those stood, these stood; and
21 w' those were lifted up from the earth,
24 w' they went, I heard the noise of
24 w' they stood, they let down their
25 w' they stood, and had let down their
28 w' I saw it, I fell upon my face, and
2: 2 into me w' he spake unto me, 834
9 w' I looked, behold, an hand was sent
3: 18 W' I say unto the wicked, Thou shalt
20 W' a righteous man doth turn from
27 w' I speak with thee, I will open thy
4: 6 And w' thou hast accomplished them,
5: 2 w' the days of the siege are fulfilled:
13 w' I have accomplished my fury in
15 w' I shall execute judgments in thee in
16 W' I shall send upon them the evil
6: 8 w' ye shall be scattered through the
13 w' their slain men shall be among
8: 7 w' I looked, behold a hole in the wall.
8 w' I had digged in the wall, behold a
10: 3 of the house, w' the man went in;
5 the Almighty God w' he speaketh.
6 that w' he had commanded the man
9 w' I looked, behold the four wheels*
11 W' they went, they went upon their
16 w' the cherubims went, the wheels
16 w' the cherubims lifted up their wings
17 W' they stood, these stood; and
17 w' they were lifted up, these lifted up
19 w' they went out, the wheels also were
11: 13 w' I prophesied, that Pelatiah the son
12: 15 w' I shall scatter them among the
13: 12 Lo, w' the wall is fallen, shall it not
14: 9 w' he hath spoken a thing, *3588
13 w' the land sinneth against me by "
21 w' I send my four sore judgments "
23 w' ye see their ways and their doings:
15: 5 w' it was whole, it was meet for no
5 w' the fire hath devoured it, and 3588
7 w' I set my face against them.
16: 6 w' I passed by thee, and saw thee
6 thee w' thou wast in thy blood, Live;*
6 thee w' thou wast in thy blood, Live.*
8 w' I passed by thee, and looked upon
22 w' thou wast naked and bare, and
53 W' I shall bring again their captivity,*
55 W' thy sisters, Sodom and her *
61 w' thou shalt receive thy sisters, thine*
63 w' I am pacified toward thee for all
17: 10 wither, w' the east wind toucheth it?
18 w', lo, he had given his hand, and*
18: 19 W' the son hath done that which is
24 w' the righteous turneth away from
26 W' a righteous man turneth away
27 w' the wicked man turneth away
19: 5 w' she saw that she had waited, and
20: 5 In the day w' I chose Israel, and
5 w' I lifted up mine hand unto them,
28 w' I had brought them into the land,
31 For w' ye offer your gifts,
31 w' ye make your sons to pass through
41 w' I bring you out from the people,
42 w' I shall bring you into the land of
21: 7 w' they say unto thee, Wherefore 3588
25 w' iniquity shall have an end, *6256
29 w' their iniquity shall have an end.*"
22: 28 God, w' the Lord hath not spoken.
23: 5 played the harlot w' she was mine;
14 w' she saw men pourtrayed upon the*
39 w' they had slain their children to
24: 24 w' this cometh ye shall know that I
25 w' I take from them their strength,
25: 3 w' it was profaned; and against 3588
3 land of Israel, w' it was desolate; "
3 Judah, w' they went into captivity; "
17 w' I shall lay my vengeance upon
26: 10 w' he shall enter into thy gates, as
15 w' the wounded cry, w' the slaughter
19 W' I shall make thee a desolate city,
19 w' I shall bring up the deep upon
20 W' I shall bring thee down with *
27: 33 W' thy wares went forth out of the
34 time w' thou shalt be broken by the*
28: 22 w' I shall have executed judgments in
Eze 28: 25 W' I shall have gathered the house of
26 w' I have executed judgments upon
29: 7 W' they took hold of thee by thy hand,
7 and w' they leaned upon thee, thou
30: 4 w' the slain shall fall in Egypt, and
8 Lord, w' I have set a fire in Egypt,
8 w' all her helpers shall be destroyed.*
18 w' I shall break there the yokes of
25 w' I shall put my sword into the hand
31: 5 multitude of waters, w' he shot forth.
15 the day w' he went down to the grave
16 w' I cast him down to hell with them
32: 7 w' I shall put thee out, I will cover
9 w' I shall bring thy destruction
10 w' I shall brandish my sword before
15 W' I shall make the land of Egypt
15 W' I shall smite all them that dwell
33: 2 W' I bring the sword upon a 3588
3 w' he seeth the sword come upon the
8 W' I say unto the wicked, O wicked
13 W' I shall say to the righteous, that
14 w' I say unto the wicked, Thou shalt
18 W' the righteous turneth from his
29 w' I have laid the land most desolate,
33 w' this cometh to pass, (lo, it will
34: 5 of the field, w' they were scattered.*
27 w' I have broken the bands of their
35: 11 among them, w' I have judged thee.834
14 W' the whole earth rejoiceth, I will
36: 17 w' the house of Israel dwelt in their
20 And w' they entered unto the heathen,
20 w' they said to them, These are the*
23 w' I shall be sanctified in you before
37: 8 w' I beheld, lo, the sinews and the*
13 w' I have opened your graves, O my
18 w' the children of thy people shall3588
28 w' my sanctuary shall be in the midst
38: 14 day w' my people of Israel dwelleth
16 w' I shall be sanctified in thee, O Gog,
18 w' Gog shall come against the 3117
39: 15 w' any seeth a man's bone, then shall
26 w' they dwelt safely in their land, and
27 W' I have brought them again from
42: 14 W' the priests enter therein, then
15 w' he had made an end of measuring
43: 3 I saw w' I came to destroy the city:
18 in the day w' they shall make it,
23 W' thou hast made an end of
27 w' these days are expired, it shall be,
44: 7 w' ye offer my bread, the fat and the
10 far from me, w' Israel went astray,
15 w' the children of Israel went astray
17 w' they enter in at the gates of the
19 w' they go forth into the utter court,
21 w' they enter into the inner court.
45: 1 w' ye shall divide by lot the land for
46: 8 w' the prince shall enter, he shall go
9 w' the people of the land shall come
10 in the midst of them, w' they go in,
10 and w' they go forth, shall go forth.
47: 3 w' the man that had the line in his
7 w' I had returned, behold, at the bank
48: 11 w' the children of Israel went astray,
Da 3: 7 w' all the people heard the sound 1768
5: 20 w' his heart was lifted up, and his "
6: 10 w' Daniel knew that the writing was"
14 king, w' he heard these words, "
20 w' he came to the den, he cried with
8: 2 pass, w' I saw, that I was at Shushan
8 w' he was strong, the great horn was
15 w' I, even I Daniel, had seen the
17 w' he came, I was afraid, and fell
23 w' the transgressors are come to the
10: 9 And w' I heard the voice of his words,
11 w' he had spoken this word unto me,
15 w' he had spoken such words unto
19 w' he had spoken unto me, I was
20 w' I am gone forth, lo, the prince of
11: 4 w' he shall stand up, his kingdom
12 w' he hath taken away the multitude,*
34 w' they shall fall, they shall be holpen
12: 7 w' he held up his right hand and his
7 and w' he shall have accomplished to
Ho 1: 8 w' she had weaned Lo-ruhamah, she
2: 15 day w' she came up out of the land of
4: 14 your daughters w' they commit 3588
14 spouses w' they commit adultery: "
5: 13 W' Ephraim saw his sickness, and
6: 11 w' I returned the captivity of my
7: 1 W' I would have healed Israel, then
12 W' they shall go, I will spread my 834
14 w' they howled upon their beds: *3588
9: 12 also to them w' I depart from them!
10: 10 w' they shall bind themselves in their
11: 1 W' Israel was a child, then I 3588
10 w' he shall roar, then the children* "
13: 1 W' Ephraim spake trembling, he
1 but w' he offended in Baal, he died.
Joe 2: 8 w' they fall upon the sword, they *
3: 1 w' I shall bring again the captivity 834
Am 3: 4 roar in the forest, w' he hath no prey?
4: 7 w' there were yet three months to the
9 w' your gardens and your vineyards*
7: 2 w' they had made an end of eating 518
8: 5 W' will the new moon be gone, 4970
Jon 2: 7 W' my soul fainted within me I
4: 2 w' I was yet in my country? 5704
7 w' the morning rose the next day,
8 it came to pass, w' the sun did arise,
Mic 2: 1 w' the morning is light, they practise
5: 5 w' the Assyrian shall come into 3588
5 w' he shall tread in our palaces, "
6 w' he cometh into our land, "
6 w' he treadeth within our borders. "
7: 1 w' they have gathered the summer
8 enemy: w' I fall, I shall arise; 3588
Mic 7: 8 w' I sit in darkness, the Lord shall be
Na 3: 17 w' the sun ariseth they flee away, and
Hab 1: 13 w' the wicked devoureth the man that
2: 1 I shall answer w' I am reproved. *5921
3: 16 W' I heard, my belly trembled; my*
16 w' he cometh up unto the people, he
Zep 3: 20 w' I turn back your captivity before
Hag 1: 9 w' ye brought it home, I did blow upon
2: 5 with you w' ye came out of Egypt,
16 w' one came to an heap of twenty
16 w' one came to the pressfat for to
Zec 7: 2 W' they had sent unto the house of*
5 W' ye fasted and mourned in the 3588
6 w' ye did eat, and w' ye did drink, "
7 w' Jerusalem was inhabited and in
7 w' men inhabited the south and the*
8: 14 w' your fathers provoked me to wrath,
9: 1 w' the eyes of man, as of all the *3588
13 W' I have bent Judah for me, filled*"
12: 2 w' they shall be in the siege both *
13: 3 that w' any shall yet prophesy, 3588
3 thrust him through w' he prophesieth.
4 of his vision, w' he hath prophesied;
14: 3 w' he fought in the day of battle. 3117
Mal 2: 17 w' ye say, Every one that doeth evil is*
3: 2 and who shall stand w' he appeareth?
17 that day w' I make up my jewels;* 834
M't 1: 18 W' as his mother Mary was espoused
2: 1 W' Jesus was born in Bethlehem of
3 W' Herod the king had heard these
4 And w' he had gathered all the chief*
7 w' he had privily called the wise men,*
8 w' ye have found him, bring me 1875
9 W' they had heard the king, they*
10 W' they saw the star, they rejoiced
11 w' they were come into the house, they*
11 w' they had opened their treasures,*
13 w' they were departed, behold, the
14 W' he arose, he took the young child*
16 Herod, w' he saw that he was mocked
19 w' Herod was dead, behold, an angel
22 w' he heard that Archelaus did reign
3: 7 w' he saw many of the Pharisees and
16 Jesus, w' he was baptized, went up
4: 2 w' he had fasted forty days and forty
3 w' the tempter came to him, he said,*
12 w' Jesus had heard that John was
5: 1 w' he was set, his disciples came unto
11 w' men shall revile you, and 3752
6: 2 w' thou doest thine alms, do not "
3 But w' thou doest alms, let not thy left
5 w' thou prayest, thou shalt not 3752
6 thou, w' thou prayest, enter into "
6 w' thou hast shut thy door, pray to*
7 w' ye pray, use not vain repetitions,*
16 w' ye fast, be not, as the hypocrites,3752
17 w' thou fastest, anoint thine head,
7: 28 w' Jesus had ended these sayings,3753
8: 1 W' he was come down from the
5 w' Jesus was entered into Capernaum,
10 W' Jesus heard it, he marvelled, and
14 w' Jesus was come into Peter's house,
16 W' the even was come, they brought
18 Now w' Jesus saw great multitudes
23 w' he was entered into a ship, his
28 w' he was come to the other side into
32 w' they were come out, they went into*
34 w' they saw him, they besought him
9: 8 But w' the multitudes saw it, they
11 w' the Pharisees saw it, they said
12 w' Jesus heard that, he said unto
15 w' the bridegroom shall be taken 3752
22 w' he saw her, he said, Daughter, be*
23 w' Jesus came into the ruler's house,
25 w' the people were put forth, 3753
27 w' Jesus departed thence, two blind*
28 w' he was come into the house, the
31 But they, w' they were departed, *
33 w' the devil was cast out, the dumb
36 w' he saw the multitudes, he was
10: 1 w' he had called unto him his twelve*
12 w' ye come into an house, salute it.*
14 w' ye depart out of that house or city,*
19 w' they deliver you up, take no 3752
23 w' they persecute you in this city, "
11: 1 w' Jesus had made an end of 3753
2 w' John had heard in the prison the
12: 2 w' the Pharisees saw it, they said
3 David did, w' he was an hungred, 3753
9 w' he was departed thence, he went*
15 But w' Jesus knew it, he withdrew*
24 w' the Pharisees heard it, they said,
43 W' the unclean spirit is gone out 3752
44 w' he is come, he findeth it empty,
13: 4 w' he sowed, some seeds fell *1722,3588
6 And w' the sun was up, they were
19 W' any one heareth the word of the
21 w' tribulation or persecution ariseth
26 But w' the blade was sprung up, 3753
32 w' it is grown, it is the greatest 3752
44 the which w' a man hath found, he*
46 w' he hath found one pearl of great*
48 w' it was full, they drew to shore, 3753
53 that w' Jesus had finished these "
54 w' he was come into his own country,
14: 5 w' he would have put him to death, he
6 w' Herod's birthday was kept, they
13 W' Jesus heard of it, he departed
13 w' the people had heard thereof, they
15 w' it was evening, his disciples came
23 w' he had sent the multitudes away,
23 w' the evening was come, he was
26 w' the disciples saw him walking on
29 w' Peter was come down out of the*
30 w' he saw the wind boisterous, he was
32 w' they were come into the ship, the

M't 14:34 w· they were gone over, they came
35 w· the men of that place had
15: 2 their hands w· they eat bread. 3752
31 w· they saw the dumb to speak,
16: 2 W· it is evening, ye say, it will be fair
5 w· his disciples were come to the *
8 Which w· Jesus perceived, he said*
13 W· Jesus came into the coasts of
17: 6 w· the disciples heard it, they fell on
8 w· they had lifted up their eyes, they*
14 w· they were come to the multitude,
24 w· they were come to Capernaum,
25 w· he was come into the house, 3753
27 w· thou hast opened his mouth, thou
18:24 w· he had begun to reckon, one was
31 w· his fellowservants saw what was
19: 1 that w· Jesus had finished these 3753
22 w· the young man heard that saying,
25 W· his disciples heard it, they were
28 w· the Son of man shall sit in the 3752
20: 2 w· he had agreed with the labourers
8 So w· even was come, the lord of the
9 w· they came that were hired about
10 But w· the first came, they supposed
11 And w· they had received it, they
24 w· the ten heard it, they were moved
30 w· they heard that Jesus passed by,
21: 1 And w· they drew nigh unto 3753
10 w· he was come into Jerusalem, all
15 w· the chief priests and scribes saw
19 w· he saw a fig tree in the way, he*
20 And w· the disciples saw it, they
23 And w· he was come into the temple,
32 and ye, w· ye had seen it, repented not
34 w· the time of the fruit drew near, 3753
38 But w· the husbandmen saw the son,
40 W· the lord therefore of the 3752
45 w· the chief priests and Pharisees had
46 w· they sought to lay hands on him,
22: 7 But w· the king heard thereof, he was*
11 w· the king came in to see the guests,
22 W· they had heard these words, they
25 the first, w· he had married a wife,*
33 And w· the multitude heard this, they
34 w· the Pharisees had heard that he
23:15 w· he is made, ye make him 3752
24: 3 Tell us, w· shall these things be? 4218
15 W· ye therefore shall see the 3752
32 W· his branch is yet tender, and "
33 w· ye shall see all these things, "
46 w· he cometh shall find so doing.
50 come in a day w· he looketh not for
25:31 W· the Son of man shall come in 3752
37 w· saw we thee an hungred, and 4218
38 W· saw we thee a stranger, and "
39 Or w· saw we thee sick, or in "
44 w· saw we thee an hungred, or "
26: 1 w· Jesus had finished all these 3753
6 w· Jesus was in Bethany, in the house
8 But w· his disciples saw it, they had
10 W· Jesus understood it, he said unto*
20 Now w· the even was come, he sat
29 until that day w· I drink it new 3752
30 And w· they had sung an hymn, they
71 w· he was gone out into the porch,
27: 1 W· the morning was come, all the
2 w· they had bound him, they led him*
3 w· he saw that he was condemned,
12 w· he was accused of the chief 1722,3588
17 w· they were gathered together,
19 W· he was set down on the judgment*
24 W· Pilate saw that he could prevail
26 and w· he had scourged Jesus, he *
29 w· they had platted a crown of thorns,*
33 w· they were come unto a place called*
34 w· he had tasted thereof, he would not
47 w· they heard that, said, This man
50 w· he had cried again with a loud *
54 w· the centurion, and they that were
57 W· the even was come, there came a
59 w· Joseph had taken the body, he *
28:12 And w· they were assembled with the
17 w· they saw him, they worshipped
M'r 1:19 And w· he had gone a little farther*
26 w· the unclean spirit had torn him,*
29 w· they were come out of the
32 w· the sun did set, they brought 3753
37 w· they had found him, they said unto*
2: 4 w· they could not come nigh unto him
4 w· they had broken it up, they let
5 W· Jesus saw their faith, he said *
8 immediately w· Jesus perceived in his*
16 w· the scribes and Pharisees saw him
17 W· Jesus heard it, he saith unto
20 w· the bridegroom shall be taken *3752
25 w· he had need, and was an 3753
3: 5 w· he had looked round about on
8 w· they had heard what great things*
11 unclean spirits, w· they saw him, *3752
21 w· his friends heard of it, they went
4: 6 w· the sun was up, it was scorched;
10 w· he was alone, they that were 3753
15 but w· they have heard, Satan 3752
16 w· they have heard the word, "
17 w· affliction or persecution ariseth for
29 w· the fruit is brought forth, 3752
31 w· it is sown in the earth, is less "
32 But w· it is sown, it groweth up,
34 w· they were alone, he expounded all*
35 the same day, w· the even was come,
36 w· they had sent away the multitude,*
5: 2 w· he was come out of the ship,
6 w· he saw Jesus afar off, he ran and
18 w· he was come unto the ship, he that*
21 w· Jesus was passed over again by
22 and w· he saw him, he fell at his feet,*

M'r 5:27 W· she heard of Jesus, came in the*
39 w· he was come in, he saith unto *
40 w· he had put them all out, he taketh*
6: 2 And w· the sabbath day was come, he
11 w· ye depart thence, shake off the*
16 w· Herod heard thereof, he said, It is
20 w· he heard him, he did many things,
21 w· a convenient day was come, that
22 w· the daughter of the said Herodias
29 w· his disciples heard of it, they came
34 And Jesus, w· he came out, saw much*
35 And w· the day was now far spent, his
38 w· they knew, they say, Five, and two
41 w· he had taken the five loaves and*
46 And w· he had sent them away, he*
47 w· even was come, the ship was in the
49 w· they saw him walking upon the
53 w· they had passed over, they came
54 w· they were come out of the ship,
7: 2 w· they saw some of his disciples eat*
4 w· they come from the market, except
14 w· he had called all the people unto*
17 w· he was entered into the house 3753
30 w· she was come to her house, she*
8:17 w· Jesus knew it, he saith unto
19 W· I brake the five loaves among 3753
20 w· the seven among four thousand, "
23 w· he had spit on his eyes, and put his
33 w· he had turned about and looked*
34 w· he had called the people unto him*
38 w· he cometh in the glory of his 3752
9: 8 w· they had looked round about, they *
14 w· he came to his disciples, he saw a
15 all the people, w· they beheld him,
20 w· he saw him, straightway the spirit
25 W· Jesus saw the people came
28 w· he was come into the house, his
36 w· he had taken him in his arms, he*
10:14 But w· Jesus saw it, he was much
17 w· he was gone forth into the way,*
41 w· the ten heard it, they began to be
47 w· he heard that it was Jesus of
11: 1 w· they came nigh to Jerusalem, 3753
11 w· he had looked round about upon all
12 w· they were come from Bethany,
13 w· he came to it, he found nothing but
19 w· even was come he went out of *3753
24 things soever ye desire, w· ye pray,*
25 w· ye stand praying, forgive, if ye*3752
12:14 w· they were come, they say unto him,
23 therefore, w· they shall rise, *3752
25 For w· they shall rise from the dead,"
34 And w· Jesus saw that he answered
13: 4 Tell us, w· shall these things be? 4218
4 sign w· all these things shall be 3752
7 And w· ye shall hear of wars and "
11 w· they shall lead you, and deliver "
14 w· ye shall see the abomination of "
28 W· her branch is yet tender, and "
29 w· ye shall see these things come to"
33 for ye know not w· the time is. 4218
35 w· the master of the house cometh, "
14:11 And w· they heard it, they were glad,
12 w· they killed the passover, his 3753
23 w· he had given thanks, he gave it to
26 And w· they had sung an hymn, they
40 w· he returned, he found them asleep*
67 w· she saw Peter warming himself,*
72 And w· he thought thereon, he wept.
15:15 Jesus, w· he had scourged him, to be
20 w· they had mocked him, they 3753
24 And w· he had crucified him, they*
33 w· the sixth hour was come, there was
35 w· they heard it, said, Behold, he
39 w· the centurion, which stood over
41 w· he was in Galilee, followed him,3753
42 now w· the even was come, because it
45 w· he knew it of the centurion, he gave
16: 1 w· the sabbath was past, Mary
4 And w· they looked, they saw that the*
9 w· Jesus was risen early in the first
11 w· they had heard that he was alive,
Lu 1: 9 w· he went into the temple of the Lord.*
12 w· Zacharias saw him, he was
22 w· he came out, he could not speak
29 w· she saw him, she was troubled at*
41 w· Elisabeth heard the salutation 5613
2: 2 w· Cyrenius was governor of Syria.*
17 w· they had seen it, they made known
21 w· eight days were accomplished 3753
22 w· the days of her purification "
27 w· the parents brought in the 1722,3588
39 w· they had performed all things 5613
42 w· he was twelve years old, they 3753
43 w· they had fulfilled the days, as they
45 w· they found him not, they turned
48 w· they saw him, they were amazed:
3:21 w· all the people were 1722,3588
4:17 w· he had opened the book, he found
25 w· the heaven was shut up three 3753
25 w· great famine was throughout 5613
28 synagogue, w· they heard these *
35 w· the devil had thrown him in the
40 Now w· the sun was setting, all they
42 And w· it was day, he departed and
5: 4 w· he had left speaking, he said 5613
6 w· they had this done, they inclosed a
8 W· Simon Peter saw it, he fell down
11 w· they had brought their ships to
12 w· he was in a certain city, *1722,3588
19 w· they could not find by what way*
20 w· he saw their faith, he said unto*
22 w· Jesus perceived their thoughts,*
35 w· the bridegroom shall be taken 3752
6: 3 did, w· himself was an hungred, 3698
13 w· it was day, he called unto him 3753

Lu 6:22 are ye w· men shall hate you, and 3752
22 w· they shall separate you from "
26 w· all men shall speak well of you: "
42 w· thou thyself beholdest not the
48 w· the flood arose, the stream beat
7: 1 w· he had ended all his sayings in*1893
3 w· he heard of Jesus, he sent unto him
4 w· they came to Jesus, they besought
6 w· he was now not far from the house,
9 W· Jesus heard these things, he
12 w· he came nigh to the gate of the 5613
13 And w· the Lord saw her, he had
20 W· the men were come unto him, they
24 And w· the messengers of John were
37 w· she knew that Jesus sat at meat in
39 w· the Pharisee which had bidden
42 w· they had nothing to pay, he frankly
8: 4 And w· much people were gathered
8 w· he had said these things, he cried,*
13 w· they hear, receive the word 3752
14 w· they have heard, go forth, and are*
16 No man, w· he hath lighted a candle,
27 w· he went forth to land, there met
28 W· he saw Jesus, he cried out, and
34 W· they that fed them saw what was
40 that, w· Jesus was returned, *1722,3588
45 W· all denied, Peter and they that
47 w· the woman saw that she was not
50 w· Jesus heard it, he answered him*
51 w· he came into the house, he suffered
9: 5 w· ye go out of that city, shake off the
10 apostles, w· they were returned, told
11 the people, w· they knew it, followed*
12 w· the day began to wear away, then*
26 w· he shall come in his own glory, 3752
32 and w· they were awake, they saw his
36 w· the voice was past, Jesus 1722,3588
37 w· they were come down from the hill,
51 w· the time was come that he 1722,3588
54 w· his disciples James and John saw
10:31 w· he saw him, he passed by on the
32 a Levite, w· he was at the place, came
33 w· he saw him, he had compassion on
35 on the morrow w· he departed, he*
35 w· I come again, I will repay 1722,3588
11: 1 w· he ceased, one of his disciples 5613
2 W· ye pray, say, Our Father which3752
14 w· the devil was gone out, the dumb
21 W· a strong man armed keepeth 3752
22 w· a stronger than he shall come 1875
24 W· the unclean spirit is gone out 3752
25 w· he cometh, he findeth it swept and
29 w· the people were gathered thick
33 No man, w· he hath lighted a candle,
34 w· thine eye is single, thy whole 1875
34 w· thine eye is evil, thy body also 3752
36 w· the bright shining of a candle "
38 w· the Pharisee saw it, he marvelled
12: 1 w· they were gathered together an
11 w· they bring you...the synagogues,3752
36 w· he will return from the 4218
36 that w· he cometh and knocketh,
37 lord w· he cometh shall find watching:
40 cometh at an hour w· ye think not.*
43 whom his lord w· he cometh shall find
46 come in a day w· he looketh not for
46 at an hour w· he is not aware, and will
54 W· ye see a cloud rise out of the 3752
55 w· ye see the south wind blow, ye 3753
58 W· thou goest with thine *5613
13:12 w· Jesus saw her, he called her to him,
17 w· he had said these things, all his*
25 W· once the master of the house is
28 w· ye shall see Abraham, and 3752
35 until the time come w· ye shall *3753
14: 7 w· he marked how they chose out the
8 W· thou art bidden of any man to 3752
10 w· thou art bidden, go and sit down"
10 w· he that bade thee cometh, he "
12 W· thou makest a dinner or a "
13 But w· thou makest a feast, call the"
15 w· one of them that sat at meat with
15: 5 w· he hath found it, he layeth it on his
6 And w· he cometh home, he calleth
9 w· she hath found it, she calleth her
14 w· he had spent all, there arose a
17 w· he came to himself, he said, How
20 w· he was yet a great way off, his
16: 4 w· I am put out of the stewardship,3752
9 w· ye fail, they may receive you "
17: 7 w· he is come from the field, Go and
10 w· ye shall have done all those 3752
14 w· he saw them, he said unto them, Go
15 w· he saw that he was healed, turned
20 w· he was demanded of the Pharisees,*
20 w· the kingdom of God should 4218
22 w· ye shall desire to see one of the3753
30 the day w· the Son of man is revealed.*
18: 8 w· the Son of man cometh, shall he
15 w· his disciples saw it, they rebuked
22 w· Jesus heard these things, he
23 w· he heard this, he was very
24 w· Jesus saw that he was very *
40 w· he was come near, he asked him,
43 w· they saw it, gave praise unto God.
19: 5 And w· Jesus came to the place, he5613
7 w· they saw it, they all murmured,
15 w· he was returned, having 1722,3588
28 w· he had thus spoken, he went before,
29 w· he was come nigh to Bethphage5613
37 w· he was come nigh, even now at the*
41 w· he was come near, he beheld 5613
20:13 will reverence him w· they see him.*
14 w· the husbandmen saw him, they
16 And w· they heard it, they said, God
37 w· he calleth the Lord the God of 5613

Lu 21: 7 _w_· shall these things be? and what 4218
7 _w_· these things shall come to pass 3752
9 But _w_· ye shall hear of wars and "
20 _w_· ye...see Jerusalem compassed "
28 _w_· these things begin to come to pass,
30 _W_· they now shoot forth, ye see 3752
31 _w_· ye see these things come to pass, "
22: 7 _w_·...passover must be killed. *1722,3739
10 _w_· ye are entered into the city, there
14 _w_· the hour was come, he sat 3753,3588
32 _w_· thou art converted, strengthen 4218
35 _W_· I sent you without purse, and 3753
40 _w_· he was at the place, he said unto
45 _w_· he rose up from prayer, and was
49 _W_· they which were about him saw
53 _W_· I was daily with you in the temple,
55 _w_· they had kindled a fire in the midst
64 And _w_· they had blindfolded him,*
23: 6 _W_· Pilate heard of Galilee, he asked
8 _w_· Herod saw Jesus, he was...glad:
13 _w_· he had called together the chief*
33 _w_· they were come to the place, 3753
42 _w_· thou comest into thy kingdom. 3752
46 _w_· Jesus had cried with a loud voice,
47 _w_· the centurion saw what was done,
24: 6 unto you _w_· he was yet in Galilee,
23 _w_· they found not his body, they came,
40 _w_· he had thus spoken, he shewed
Joh 1:19 _w_· the Jews sent priests and 3753
42 _w_· Jesus beheld him, he said, Thou art
48 _w_· thou was under the fig tree, I saw
2: 3 _w_· they wanted wine, the mother of
9 _W_· the ruler of the feast had 5613
10 _w_· men have well drunk, then that3752
15 _w_· he had made a scourge of small*
22 _W_· therefore he was risen from 3753
23 _w_· he was in Jerusalem at the 5613
23 _w_· they saw the miracles which he did.*
3: 4 How can a man be born _w_· he is old?
4: 1 _W_· therefore the Lord knew how 5613
21 _w_· ye shall neither in this 3753
23 _w_· the true worshippers shall "
25 _w_· he is come, he will tell us all 3752
40 _w_· the Samaritans were come unto5613
45 Then _w_· he was come into Galilee,3753
47 _W_· he heard that Jesus was come out
52 hour _w_· he began to amend. 1722,3739
54 _w_· he was come out of Judæa into *
5: 6 _W_· Jesus saw him lie, and knew that
7 no man, _w_· the water is troubled, 3752
25 _w_· the dead shall hear the voice of 3753
6: 5 _W_· Jesus then lifted up his eyes, and*
11 _w_· he had given thanks, he distributed*
12 _W_· they were filled, he said unto 5613
14 _w_· they had seen the miracle that
15 _W_· Jesus therefore perceived that they*
16 _w_· even was now come, his 5613
19 So _w_· they had rowed about five and
22 _w_· the people which stood on the other*
24 _W_· the people therefore saw that 3753
25 _w_· they had found him on the 4218
25 him, Rabbi, _w_· camest thou hither?
60 disciples, _w_· they had heard this, said,
61 _W_· Jesus knew in himself that his*
7: 9 _W_· he had said these words unto *
10 _w_· his brethren were gone up, then5613
27 _w_· Christ cometh, no man knoweth 3752
31 _W_· Christ cometh, will he do more "
8: 3 _w_· they had set her in the midst, *
7 _w_· they continued asking him, he 5613
10 _W_· Jesus had lifted up himself, and*
28 _W_· ye have lifted up the Son of 3752
44 _W_· he speaketh a lie, he speaketh "
9: 4 night cometh, _w_· no man can work.3753
6 _W_· he had thus spoken, he spat on
14 sabbath day _w_· Jesus made the 3753
35 _w_· he had found him, he said unto him,*
10: 4 _w_· he putteth forth his own sheep, 3752
11: 4 _W_· Jesus heard that, he said, This
6 _W_· he had heard therefore that he5613
17 _w_· Jesus came, he found that he had
28 _w_· she had so said, she went her way,
31 _w_· they saw Mary, that she rose up
32 _w_· Mary was come where Jesus 5613
33 _W_· Jesus therefore saw her "
43 And _w_· he thus had spoken, he cried
12:12 _w_· they heard that Jesus was coming
14 Jesus, _w_· he had found a young ass,*
16 but _w_· Jesus was glorified, then 3753
17 _w_· he called Lazarus out of his "
41 _w_· he saw his glory, and spake of * "
13: 1 _w_· Jesus knew that his hour was come*
19 _w_· it is come to pass, ye may 3752
21 _W_· Jesus had thus said, he was
26 I shall give a sop, _w_· I have dipped it.*
26 _w_· he had dipped the sop, he gave 3753
31 _w_· he was gone out, Jesus said, "
14:29 _w_· it is come to pass, ye might 3752
15:26 _w_· the Comforter is come, whom I "
16: 4 _w_· the time shall come, ye may "
8 _w_· he is come, he will reprove the world
13 _w_· he, the Spirit of truth, is come, 3752
21 _w_· she is in travail hath sorrow, "
25 _w_· I shall no more speak unto you3753
18: 1 _W_· Jesus had spoken these words, he
22 _w_· he had thus spoken, one of the
38 _w_· he had said this, he went out again
19: 6 _W_· the chief priests therefore and3753
8, 13 _W_· Pilate therefore heard that "
23 _w_· they had crucified Jesus, took "
26 _W_· Jesus therefore saw his mother,
30 _W_· Jesus therefore had received 3753
33 But _w_· they came to Jesus, and 5613
20: 1 Magdalene early, _w_· it was yet dark,*
14 _w_· she had thus said, she turned
19 _w_· the doors were shut where the

Joh 20:20 And _w_· he had so said, he shewed
20 disciples glad, _w_· they saw the Lord.
22 _w_· he had said this, he breathed on
24 was not with them _w_· Jesus came. 3753
21: 4 _w_· the morning was now come, Jesus
7 _w_· Simon Peter heard that it was the
15 _w_· they had dined, Jesus saith to 3753
18 _W_· thou wast young, thou girdedst "
18 _w_· thou shalt be old, thou shalt 3752
19 _w_· he had spoken this, he saith unto
Ac 1: 6 _W_· they therefore were come together,
9 _w_· he had spoken these things, while
13 And _w_· they were come in, they 3753
2: 1 _w_· the day of Pentecost was 1722,3588
6 Now _w_· this was noised abroad, the
37 _w_· they heard this, they were pricked
3:12 _w_· Peter saw it, he answered unto the
13 _w_· he was determined to let him go.
19 _w_· the times of refreshing shall *3704
4: 7 _w_· they had set them in the midst, they
13 Now _w_· they saw the boldness of Peter
15 But _w_· they had commanded to go
21 _w_· they had further threatened them,
24 _w_· they heard that, they lifted up their
31 _w_· they had prayed, the place was
5: 7 _w_· his wife, not knowing what was
21 _w_· they heard that, they entered into
22 But _w_· the officers came, and found*
23 _w_· we had opened, we found no man
24 _w_· the high priest and the captain 5613
27 _w_· they had brought them, they set
33 _W_· they heard that, they were cut to
40 _w_· they had called the apostles, and
6: 1 _w_· the number of the disciples was
6 _w_· they had prayed, they laid their
7: 2 Abraham, _w_· he was in Mesopotamia,
4 _w_· his father was dead, he removed3326
5 after him, _w_· as yet he had no child.
12 _w_· Jacob heard that there was corn in
17 _w_· the time of the promise drew *2531
21 _w_· he was cast out, Pharaoh's daughter
23 _w_· he was full forty years old, it 5613
30 _w_· forty years were expired, there
31 _W_· Moses saw it, he wondered at the
54 _W_· they heard these things, they were
60 And _w_· he had said this, he fell asleep.
8:12 _w_· they believed Philip preaching 3753
13 _w_· he was baptized, he continued with*
14 _w_· the apostles which were at
15 Who, _w_· they were come down, prayed
18 _w_· Simon saw that through laying on
25 _w_· they had testified and preached the
39 _w_· they were come up out of...water,3753
9: 8 _w_· his eyes were opened, he saw no
19 _w_· he had received meat, he was *
26 _w_· Saul was come to Jerusalem, he
30 _w_· the brethren knew, they brought
37 whom _w_· they had washed, they laid
39 _W_· he was come, they brought him
40 eyes: and _w_· she saw Peter, she sat up.
41 _w_· he had called the saints and widows,*
10: 4 _w_· he looked on him, he was afraid, *
7 _w_· the angel which spake unto 5613
8 _w_· he had declared all these things*
32 who, _w_· he cometh, shall speak unto*
11: 2 _w_· Peter was come up to Jerusalem,3753
6 which _w_· I had fastened mine eyes,
18 _W_· they heard these things, they held
20 _w_· they were come to Antioch, spake
23 _w_· he came, and had seen the grace
26 _w_· he had found him, he brought him
12: 4 _w_· he had apprehended him, and put
6 _w_· Herod would have brought him3753
10 _W_· they were past the first and the
11 _w_· Peter was come to himself, he said,
12 _w_· he had considered the thing, he
14 _w_· she knew Peter's voice, she opened
16 _w_· they had opened the door, and saw
19 _w_· Herod had sought for him, and
25 _w_· they had fulfilled their ministry,
13: 3 _w_· they had fasted and prayed, and
5 _w_· they were at Salamis, they
6 _w_· they had gone through the isle
12 _w_· he saw what was done, believed,
13 _w_· Paul and his company loosed from*
14 _w_· they departed from Perga, they*
17 _w_· they dwelt as strangers in 1722,3588
19 _w_· he had destroyed seven nations in
22 _w_· he had removed him, he raised up
24 _W_· John had first preached before his
29 _w_· they had fulfilled all that was 5613
42 _w_· the Jews were gone out of the
43 _w_· the congregation was broken up,
45 _w_· the Jews saw the multitudes, they
48 _w_· the Gentiles heard this, they were*
14: 5 _w_· there was an assault made both5613
11 _w_· the people saw what Paul had done,
21 And _w_· they had preached the gospel
23 _w_· they had ordained them elders in
25 _w_· they had preached the word in
27 _w_· they had come, and had gathered
15: 2 _W_· therefore Paul and Barnabas had
4 _w_· they were come to Jerusalem, they
7 _w_· there had been much disputing,
30 So _w_· they were dismissed, they came
31 _w_· they had gathered the multitude*
31 Which _w_· they had read, they rejoiced
16: 6 _w_· they had gone throughout Phrygia
15 _w_· she was baptized, and her 5613
19 _w_· her masters saw that the hope of
23 _w_· they had laid many stripes upon
34 _w_· he had brought them into his *
35 _w_· it was day, the magistrates sent the
38 _w_· they heard that they were Romans.
40 _w_· they had seen the brethren, they
17: 1 _w_· they had passed through

Ac 17: 6 _w_· they found them not, they drew
8 the city, _w_· they heard these things.
9 _w_· they had taken security of Jason,
13 But _w_· the Jews of Thessalonica 5613
16 _w_· he saw the city wholly given to*
32 _w_· they heard of the resurrection of
18: 5 _w_· Silas and Timotheus were come5613
6 _w_· they opposed themselves, and
12 _w_· Gallio was the deputy of Achaia,
14 _w_· Paul was now about to open his
20 _W_· they desired him to tarry longer
22 _w_· he had landed at Cæsarea, and
26 _w_· Aquila and Priscilla had heard,
27 _w_· he was disposed to pass into
27 _w_· he was come, helped them much
19: 5 _W_· they heard this, they were baptized
6 _w_· Paul had laid his hands upon them,
9 But _w_· divers were hardened, and 5613
21 _w_· he had passed through Macedonia
28 And _w_· they heard these sayings, they
30 _w_· Paul would have entered in unto
34 But _w_· they knew that he was a Jew,
35 _w_· the townclerk had appeased the
41 _w_· he had thus spoken, he dismissed
20: 2 _w_· he had gone over those parts, and
3 _w_· the Jews laid wait for him, as he
7 _w_· the disciples came together to
11 _W_· he therefore was come again, and
14 And _w_· he met with us at Assos, 5613
18 _w_· they were come to him, he said "
36 _w_· he had thus spoken, he kneeled,
21: 3 Now _w_· we had discovered Cyprus, we
5 _w_· we had accomplished those 3753
6 _w_· we had taken our leave one of*
7 _w_· we had finished our course from
11 _w_· he was come unto us, he took Paul's
12 _w_· we heard these things, both we,5613
14 _w_· he would not be persuaded, we
17 _w_· we were come to Jerusalem, the
19 _w_· he had saluted them, he declared
20 _w_· they heard it, they glorified the
27 And _w_· the seven days were almost5613
27 _w_· they saw him in the temple, stirred
32 _w_· they saw the chief captain and the
34 _w_· he could not know the certainty for
35 _w_· he came upon the stairs, so it 3753
40 _w_· he had given him licence, Paul
40 _w_· there was made a great silence, he
22: 2 _w_· they heard that he spake in the
11 _w_· I could not see for the glory of 5613
17 _w_· I was come again to Jerusalem,
20 And _w_· the blood of thy martyr 3753
26 _W_· the centurion heard that, he went
23: 6 _w_· Paul perceived that the one part
7 _w_· he had so said, there arose a
10 _w_· there arose a great dissension, the
12 _w_· it was day, certain of the Jews
16 _w_· Paul's sister's son heard of their*
28 _w_· I would have known the cause
30 _w_· it was told me how that the Jews
33 Who, _w_· they came to Cæsarea, and
34 _w_· the governor had read the letter,
35 _w_· thine accusers are also come. 3752
24: 2 _w_· he was called forth, Tertullus
22 _w_· Felix heard these things, having*
22 _W_· Lysias the chief captain shall 3752
24 _w_· Felix came with his wife Drusilla,*
25 _w_· I have a convenient season, I will
25: 1 _w_· Festus was come into the province,*
6 _w_· he had tarried among them more
7 _w_· he was come, the Jews which came
12 _w_· he had conferred with the council,
14 _w_· they had been there many *5613
15 About whom, _w_· I was at Jerusalem,
17 _w_· they were come hither, without
18 Against whom _w_· the accusers stood
21 _w_· Paul had appealed to be reserved
23 _w_· Agrippa was come, and Bernice,
25 _w_· I found that he had committed*
26:10 _w_· they were put to death, I gave my
14 _w_· we were all fallen to the earth, I
30 _w_· he had thus spoken, the king rose*
31 _w_· they were gone aside, they talked
27: 1 _w_· it was determined that we 5613
4 _w_· we had launched from thence, we*
5 _w_· we had sailed over the sea of
7 _w_· we had sailed slowly many days,
9 Now _w_· much time was spent, and
9 _w_· sailing was now dangerous, *
13 _w_· the south wind blew softly,
15 _w_· the ship was caught, and could not
17 _w_· they had taken up, they used helps,
20 _w_· neither sun nor stars in many days
27 _w_· the fourteenth night was come, 5613
28 _w_· they had gone a little further, they*
35 And _w_· he had thus spoken, he took
35 _w_· he had broken it, he began to eat.*
38 _w_· they had eaten enough, they
39 _w_· it was day, they knew not the 3753
40 _w_· they had taken up the anchors, they*
28: 1 _w_· they were escaped, then they knew
3 _w_· Paul had gathered a bundle of
4 And _w_· the barbarians saw the 5613
6 they looked _w_· he should have swollen,*
9 So _w_· this was done, others also,
10 _w_· we departed, they laded us with
15 _w_· the brethren heard of us, they came
15 _w_· Paul saw, he thanked God, and
16 And _w_· we came to Rome, the 3753
17 _w_· they were come together, he said
18 Who, _w_· they had examined me,
19 _w_· the Jews spake against it, I was
23 _w_· they had appointed him a day,
29 _w_· he had said these words, the Jews*
Ro 1:21 _w_· they knew God, they glorified him*
2:14 For _w_· the Gentiles, which have 3752

Ro 2:16 In the day w· God shall judge the 3753
3: 4 overcome w· thou art judged. 1722,3588
4:10 w· he was in circumcision, or in
19 w· he was about an hundred years*
5: 6 w· we were yet without strength, in*
10 if, w· we were enemies, we were "
13 sin is not imputed w· there is no law.
6:20 For w· ye were the servants of sin,3753
7: 5 For w· we were in the flesh, the "
9 but w· the commandment came, sin
21 w· I would do good, evil is present*
9:10 w· Rebecca also had conceived by one,*
11:27 w· I shall take away their sins. 3752
13:11 nearer than w· we believed. 3753
15:28 W· therefore I have performed this,
29 w· I come unto you, I shall come in the
1Co 2: 1 And I, brethren, w· I came to you,
5: 4 w· ye are gathered together, and my*
8:12 w· ye so sin against the brethren, and*
9:18 w· I preach the gospel, I may make
27 w· I have preached to others, I myself*
11:18 w· ye come together in the church, I
20 W· ye come together therefore into
24 w· he had given thanks, he brake it,
25 he took the cup, w· he had supped,*3326
32 But w· we are judged, we are
33 w· ye come together to eat, tarry one
34 rest will I set in order w· I come. *5613
13:10 w· that which is perfect is come, 3752
11 W· I was child, I spake as a child,3753
11 w· I became a man, I put away * "
14:16 w· thou shalt bless with the spirit,*1437
26 w· ye come together, every one of 3752
15:24 w· he shall have delivered up the "
24 w· he shall have put down all rule, "
27 w· he saith all things are put under "
28 w· all things shall be subdued unto "
54 So w· this corruptible shall have "
16: 2 there be no gatherings w· I come. "
3 w· I come, whomsoever ye shall "
5 w· I shall pass through Macedonia: "
12 w· he shall have convenient time. "
2Co 1:17 W· I therefore was thus minded, I did
2: 3 lest, w· I came, I should have sorrow
12 w· I came to Troas to preach Christ's
3:15 w· Moses is read, the vail is upon *2259
16 w· it shall turn to the Lord, * "
7: 5 w· we were come into Macedonia, our
7 w· he told us your earnest desire,*
10: 2 I may not be bold w· I am present
6 w· your obedience is fulfilled. 3752
11 in word by letters w· we are absent,
11 we be also in deed w· we are present.
15 w· your faith is increased, that we*
11: 9 And w· I was present with you, and
12:10 w· I am weak, then am I strong. 3752
20 w· I come, I shall not find you such as
21 w· I come again, my God will humble
13: 9 For we are glad, w· we are weak, 3752
Ga 1:15 But w· it pleased God, who 3753
2: 7 w· they saw that the gospel of the
9 And w· James, Cephas, and John, who
11 w· Peter was come to Antioch, I 3753
12 w· they were come, he withdrew "
14 But w· I saw that they walked not "
4: 3 so we, w· we were children, were in "
4 But w· the fulness of the time was "
8 w· ye knew not God, ye did service*
18 and not only w· I am present 1722,3588
6: 3 to be something, w· he is nothing,
Eph 1:20 w· he raised him from the dead, and
2: 5 Even w· we were dead in sins, hath
3: 4 w· ye read, ye may understand my
Ph'p 2:19 good comfort, w· I know your state.
28 w· ye see him again, ye may rejoice,
4:15 w· I departed from Macedonia, no 3753
Col 3: 4 W· Christ, who is our life, shall 3752
7 some time, w· ye lived in them. 3753
4:16 w· this epistle is read among you, 3752
1Th 2: 6 w· we might have been burdensome,
13 w· ye received the word of God which
3: 1 w· we could no longer forbear, we
4 w· we were with you, we told you 3753
5 w· I could no longer forbear, I sent
6 w· Timotheus came from you unto us,
5: 3 For w· they shall say, Peace and 3752
2Th 1: 7 w· the Lord Jesus shall be *1722,3739
10 W· he shall come to be glorified 3752
2: 5 w· I was yet with you, I told ye these
3:10 even w· we were with you, this we 3753
1Ti 1: 3 w· I went into Macedonia, that thou
5:11 for w· they have begun to wax 3752
2Ti 1: 5 W· I call to remembrance the *
17 But w· he was in Rome, he sought me
4: 3 w· they will not endure sound 3753
13 w· thou comest, bring with thee, and
Tit 3:12 W· I shall send Artemas unto 3752
Heb 1: 3 w· he had by himself purged our sins,
6 w· he bringeth in the firstbegotten3752
3: 9 W· your fathers tempted me, *3756
16 some, w· they had heard, did provoke:
5: 7 w· he had offered up prayers and*
12 For w· for the time ye ought to be
6:13 w· God made promise to Abraham,
7:10 father, w· Melchisedec met him. 3753
27 he did once, w· he offered up himself.
8: 5 of God w· he was about to make the
8 w· I will make a new covenant with*
9 w· I took them by the hand to lead*
9: 6 w· these things were thus ordained,*
19 w· Moses had spoken every precept to
10: 5 w· he cometh into the world, he saith,
8 w· he said, Sacrifice and offering and*
11: 8 w· he was called to go out into a place
11 of a child w· she was passed age,
17 Abraham, w· he was tried, offered*

Heb11:21 w· he was a dying, blessed both the
22 By faith Joseph, w· he died, made
23 Moses, w· he was born, was hid three
24 Moses, w· he was come to years,
31 w· she had received the spies with*
12: 5 nor faint w· thou art rebuked of him:
17 w· he would have inherited the
Jas 1: 2 w· ye fall into divers temptations; 3752
12 w· he is tried, he shall receive the
13 Let no man say w· he is tempted,
14 w· he is drawn away of his own lust,
15 w· lust hath conceived, it bringeth
15 sin, w· it is finished, bringeth forth
2:21 w· he had offered Isaac his son upon*
25 w· she had received the messengers,
1Pe 1:11 w· it testified beforehand the
2:20 w· ye be buffeted for your faults, ye
20 w· ye do well, and suffer for it, ye take
23 w· he was reviled, reviled not again;
23 w· he suffered, he threatened not; but
3:20 w· once the longsuffering of God 3753
4: 3 w· we walked in lasciviousness, lusts,*
13 w· his glory shall be revealed,*1722,3588
5: 4 w· the chief Shepherd shall appear,
2Pe 1:16 w· we made known unto you the power
17 w· there came such a voice to him
18 w· we were with him in the holy
2:18 w· they speak great swelling words of*
1Jo 2:28 w· he shall appear, we may have *3752
3: 2 w· he shall appear, we shall be like*1437
5: 2 w· we love God, and keep his 3752
3Jo 3 w· the brethren came and testified of
Jude 3 w· I gave all diligence to write unto
9 w· contending with the devil he 3753
12 w· they feast with you, feeding
Re 1:17 w· I saw him, I fell at his feet as 3753
4: 9 w· those beasts give glory and 3752
5: 8 And w· he had taken the book, the3753
6: 1 I saw w· the Lamb opened one of
3 w· he had opened the second seal, I "
5 w· he had opened the third seal, I "
7 w· he had opened the fourth seal, I "
9 w· he had opened the fifth seal, I "
12 w· he had opened the sixth seal,
13 w· she is shaken of a mighty wind.
14 as a scroll w· it is rolled together;
8: 1 w· he had opened the seventh seal,3753
9: 5 scorpion, w· he striketh a man. 3752
10: 3 a loud voice, as w· a lion roareth:*
3 w· he had cried, seven thunders 3753
4 And w· the seven thunders had
7 w· he shall begin to sound, the 3752
11: 7 w· they shall have finished their "
12:13 w· the dragon saw that he was 3753
17: 6 w· I saw her, I wondered with great*
8 w· they behold the beast that was, and
10 w· he cometh, he must continue a 3752
18: 9 w· they shall see the smoke of their "
18 w· they saw the smoke of her burning,*
20: 7 w· the thousand years are expired,3752
22: 8 And w· I had heard and seen, I fell 3753

whence

Ge 16: 8 Sarai's maid, w· comest thou? 335,2088
29: 4 unto them, My brethren, w· be ye? 370
42: 7 he said unto them, W· come ye? "
Nu 11:13 W· should I have flesh to give unto "
23:13 w· thou mayest see them: 834,8033
De 9:28 land w· thou broughtest us out " "
11:10 Egypt, from w· ye came out, " "
Jos 2: 4 me, but I wist not w· they were: 370
9: 8 Who are ye? and from w· come ye? "
20: 6 unto the city from w· he fled. 834,8033
J'g 13: 6 but I asked him not w· he was,335,2088
19: 9 said unto him, W· comest thou? 370
19:17 goest thou? and w· comest thou? "
1Sa 25:11 whom I know not w· they be? 834,2088
30:13 belongest thou?...w· art thou? 335, "
2Sa 1: 3 unto him, From w· comest thou?" "
13 man that told him, W· art thou?" "
2Ki 5:25 him, W· comest thou, Gehazi? 370
6:27 not help thee, w· shall I help thee? "
20:14 and from w· came they unto thee? "
Job 1: 7 said unto Satan, W· comest thou? "
2: 2 unto Satan, From w· comest 335,2088
10:21 Before I go w· I shall not return,
16:22 go the way w· I shall not return.
28:20 W· then cometh wisdom? and 370
Ps 121: 1 the hills, from w· cometh my help.
Ec 1: 7 the place from w· the rivers come,*
Isa 30: 6 w· come the young and the old lion,1992
39: 3 and from w· came they unto thee? 370
51: 1 look unto the rock w· ye are hewn,
1 the hole of the pit w· ye are digged.
Jer 29:14 w· I caused you to be carried 834,8033
Jon 1: 8 and w· comest thou? what is thy 370
Na 3: 7 w· shall I seek comforters for thee? "
M't 12:44 my house from w· I came out; 3606
13:27 thy field? from w· hath it tares? 4159
54 W· hath this man this wisdom, "
56 W· then hath this man all these "
15:33 W· should we have so much bread "
21:25 The baptism of John, w· was it? "
M'r 6: 2 w· hath this man these things? "
8: 4 w· can a man satisfy these men "
12:37 Lord; and w· is he then his son? "
Lu 1:43 And w· is this to me, that the
11:24 unto my house w· I came out. 3606
13:25 you, I know you not w· ye are: 4159
27 tell you, I know you not w· ye are; "
20: 7 that they could not tell w· it was. "
Joh 1:48 unto him, W· knowest thou me? "
2: 9 wine, and knew not w· it was: "
3: 8 but canst not tell w· it cometh, "
4:11 w· then hast thou that living water?"
6: 5 W· shall we buy bread, that these "
7:27 Howbeit we know this man w· he is:"

Joh 7:27 cometh, no man knoweth w· he is. 4159
28 know me, and ye know w· I am: "
8:14 for I know w· I came, and whither "
14 ye cannot tell w· I come, and "
9:29 fellow, we know not from w· he is. "
30 that ye know not from w· he is, "
19: 9 saith unto Jesus, W· art thou? "
Ac 14:26 to Antioch, from w· they had been 3606
Ph'p 3:20 w· also we look for the Saviour, 3739
Heb11:15 country from w· they came out, * "
19 from w· also he received him in a 3606
Jas 4: 1 w· come wars and fightings 4159
Re 2: 5 therefore from w· thou art fallen, "
7:13 in white robes? and w· came they? "

whensoever

Ge 30:41 w· the stronger cattle did conceive,3605
M'r 14: 7 w· ye will ye may do them good: 3752
Ro 15:24 W· I take my journey into 5613,1437

where See also WHEREABOUT; WHEREAS; WHEREBY; WHEREFORE; WHEREIN; WHEREINSOEVER; WHEREINTO; WHEREOF; WHEREON; WHERESOEVER; WHERETO; WHEREUNTO; WHEREUPON; WHEREWITH; WHEREWITHAL.

Ge 2:11 of Havilah, w· there is gold; 834,8033
3: 9 and said unto him, W· art thou? 335
4: 9 unto Cain, W· is Abel thy brother? "
13: 3 place w· his tent had been at the 834
10 that it was well watered every w·,
18: 9 unto him, W· is Sarah thy wife? 346
19: 5 W· are the men which came in to
27 place w· he stood before the Lord: 834
20:15 before thee: dwell w· it pleaseth thee.
21:17 the voice of the lad w· he is. 834
27:33 w· is he that hath taken venison, * 645
31:13 Bethel, w·...anointedst the pillar, 834
13 w· thou vowedst a vow unto me: "
33:19 field, w· he had spread his tent, "
35:13 in the place w· he talked with him. "
15 the place w· God spake with him, "
27 w· Abraham and Isaac sojourned. "
37:16 I pray thee, w· they feed their flocks.375
38:21 W· is the harlot, that was openly 346
39:20 w· the king's prisoners were bound:834
40: 3 the place w· Joseph was bound. "
43:30 and he sought w· to weep; and he
Ex 2:20 w· is he? why is it that ye have 346
5:11 ye, get you straw w· ye can find it: 834
12:13 a token upon the houses w· ye are: "
30 a house w· there was not one dead. "
15:27 w· were twelve wells of water, 8033
18: 5 w· he encamped at the mount 834, "
20:21 the thick darkness w· God was." "
24 w· I record my name I will come 834
29:42 w· I will meet you, to speak 834,8033
30: 6 w· I will meet with thee. " "
36 w· I will meet with thee: it " "
Le 4:12 place, w· the ashes are poured out; 413
12 w· the ashes are poured out shall 5921
24 in the place w· they kill the burnt 834
33 w· they kill the burnt offering "
6:25 place w· the burnt offering is killed. "
7: 2 place w· they kill the burnt offering "
14:13 place w· he shall kill the sin offering "
Nu 13:22 w· Ahiman, Sheshai, and Talmai, *8033
17: 4 w· I will meet with you. 834, "
22:26 w· was no way to turn either to the 834
33:14 w· was no water for the people to 8033
54 place w· his lot falleth; *413,834,
De 1:31 w· thou hast seen how that the 834
8:15 drought, w· there was no water; "
11:10 w· thou sowedst thy seed, and "
30 by the way w· the sun goeth down, in*
18: 6 of all Israel, w· he sojourned, 834,8033
23:16 one of thy gates, w· it liketh him best:
32:37 W· are their gods, their rocks in 335
Jos 4: 3 place w· the priests' feet stood firm,
3 place, w· ye shall lodge this night. 834
8 unto the place w· they lodged, 413
9 in the place w· the feet of the priests
J'g 5:27 w· he bowed, there he fell down 834
6:13 w· be all his miracles which our 346
9:38 W· is now thy mouth, wherewith "
17: 8 to sojourn w· he could find a place: 834
9 to sojourn w· I could find a place. "
18:10 w· there is no want of any thing. "
19:26 man's house w· her lord was, 834,8033
20:22 w· they put themselves in array" "
Ru 1: 7 out of the place w· she was, "
16 and w· thou lodgest, I will lodge: 834
17 W· thou diest, will I die, and there "
2:19 her, W· hast thou gleaned to day? 645
19 w· wroughtest thou? blessed be he 375
3: 4 mark the place w· he shall lie, 834,8033
1Sa 3: 3 w· the ark of God was, and "
6:14 there, w· there was a great stone: "
9:10 city w· the man of God was. 834,
18 thee, w· the seer's house is. 335,2088
10: 5 God, w· is the garrison of the 834,8033
14 when we saw that they were no w·*370
14:11 out of the holes w· they hid 834,8033
19: 3 my father in the field w· thou art, 834
22 said, W· are Samuel and David? 375
20:19 to the place w· thou didst hide 834,8033
23:22 and see his place w· his haunt is, 834
23 lurking places w· he hideth 834,8033
24: 3 by the way, w· was a cave, and Saul"
26: 5 the place w· Saul had pitched:834, "
5 David beheld the place w· Saul" "
16 And now see w· the king's spear is, 335
30: 9 Besor, w· those that were left behind
31 places w· David himself and 834,8033
2Sa 2:23 to the place w· Asahel fell down" "
9: 4 the king said unto him, W· is he? 375
11:16 w· he knew that valiant men were 834
15:32 the mount, w· he worshipped 834,8033

2Sa 16: 3 said, And w· is thy master's son? 346
17: 12 place w· he shall be found, 834,8033
20 said, W· is Ahimaaz and Jonathan?346
18: 7 W· the people of Israel were slain*8033
21: 12 w· the Philistines had hanged, 8033
19 w· Elhanan the son of Jaare-oregim,*
20 w· was a man of great stature, that
23: 11 w· was a piece of ground full of 8033
1Ki 4: 28 the place w· the officers were, 834, "
7: 7 the throne w· he might judge, " "
8 his house w· he dwelt had " "
13: 25 in the city w· the old prophet dwelt.834
17: 19 him up into a loft w· he abode,834,8033
21: 19 w· dogs licked the blood of Naboth 834
2Ki 2: 14 said, W· is the Lord God of Elijah? 346
4: 8 Shunem, w· was a great woman; 8033
6: 1 w· we dwelt with thee is too 834, "
2 a place there, w· we may dwell. "
6 the man of God said, W· fell it? 575
13 Go and spy w· he is, that I may 351
18: 34 W· are the gods of Hamath, and 346
34 w· are the gods of Sepharvaim, "
19: 13 W· is the king of Hamath, and the "
23: 7 w· the women wove hangings 834,8033
8 w· the priests had burned " "
1Ch 11: 4 is Jebus; w· the Jebusites were, "
13: 2 abroad unto our brethren every w·, "
20: 6 Gath, w· was a man of great stature, "
2Ch 3: 1 w· the Lord appeared unto David 834
25: 4 of Moses, w· the Lord commanded,* "
36: 20 w· they were servants to him and his*
Ezr 1: 4 in any place w· he sojourneth,834,8033
6: 1 w· the treasures were laid up in 8536
3 the place w· they offered sacrifices,1768
Ne 10: 39 w· are the vessels of the sanctuary,8033
13: 5 w· aforetime they laid the meat "
Es 1: 6 W· were white, green, and blue *
7: 5 Who is he, and w· is he, that durst 335
Job 4: 7 or w· were the righteous cut off? 375
9: 24 thereof; if not, w·, and who is he?* 645
10: 22 order, and w· the light is as darkness.
12: 24 in a wilderness w· there is no way.
15: 23 abroad for bread, saying, W· is it? 346
17: 15 w· is now my hope? as for my 346,645
20: 7 have seen him shall say, W· is he? 335
21: 28 say, W· is the house of the prince? 346
28 w· are the dwelling places of the "
23: 3 Oh that I knew w· I might find him!
9 w· he doth work, but I cannot behold*
28: 1 and a place for gold w· they fine it.*
12 But w· shall wisdom be found? 370
12 and w· is...understanding? 335,2088
20 w· is the place of understanding? 335
34: 22 w· the workers of iniquity may 8033
35: 10 W· is God my maker, who giveth 335
36: 16 broad place, w· there is no straitness;
38: 4 W· wast thou when I laid the 375
19 W· is the way w· light dwelleth? 335
19 darkness, w· is the place thereof, "
26 it to rain on the earth, w· no man is;
39: 30 and w· the slain are, there is she. 834
40: 20 w· all the beasts of the field play. 8033
Ps 19: 3 language, w· their voice is not heard.*
26: 8 the place w· thine honour dwelleth.
42: 3 say unto me, W· is thy God? 346
10 say daily unto me, W· is thy God? "
53: 5 there in great fear, w· no fear was:
63: 1 a dry and thirsty land, w· no water is;
69: 2 in deep mire, w· there is no standing:
2 deep waters, w· the floods overflow me.
79: 10 W· is their God? let him be known 346
81: 5 w· I heard a language that I
84: 3 herself, w· she may lay her young, 834
89: 49 w· are thy former lovingkindnesses,346
104: 17 W· the birds make their nests:834,8033
107: 40 the wilderness, w· there is no way.
115: 2 heathen say, W· is now their God? 346
Pr 11: 14 W· no counsel is, the people fall: but
14: 4 W· no oxen are, the crib is clean: but
15: 17 is a dinner of herbs w· love is, 8033
26: 20 W· no wood is, the fire goeth out: 657
20 w· there is no talebearer, the strife
29: 18 W· there is no vision the people
Ec 1: 5 hasteth to his place w· he arose. 8033
8: 4 W· the word of a king is, there is 834
10 in the city w· they had so done: * "
11: 3 place w· the tree falleth, there it shall
Ca 1: 7 w· thou feedest, w· thou makest 349
Isa 7: 23 w· there were a thousand vines at 834
10: 3 and w· will ye leave your glory? 575
19: 12 W· are they?...thy wise men? * 335
12 w· are thy wise men? and let them 645
29: 1 to Ariel, the city w· David dwelt!
30: 32 w· the grounded staff shall pass; *
33: 18 W· is the scribe? w· is the receiver?346
18 w· is he that counted the towers? "
35: 7 the habitation of dragons, w· each lay,
36: 19 W· are the gods of Hamath and 346
19 w· are the gods of Sepharvaim? "
37: 13 W· is the king of Hamath, and the "
49: 21 left alone; these, w· had they been?375
50: 1 W· is the bill of your mother's 335
51: 13 and w· is the fury of the oppressor?346
57: 8 lovedst their bed w· thou sawest it.3027
63: 11 W· is he that brought them up out 346
11 w· is he that put his holy Spirit "
15 w· is thy zeal and thy strength, the "
64: 11 house w· our fathers praised thee, 834
66: 1 w· is the house that ye build unto* 335
1 and w· is the place of my rest? * "
Jer 2: 6 W· is the Lord that brought us up 346
6 through, and w· no man dwelt? 8033
8 priests said not, W· is the Lord? 346
28 w· are thy gods that thou hast made "
3: 2 see w· thou hast not been lien with.375
6: 16 paths, w· is the good way, and walk335

Jer 7: 12 w· I set my name at the first, 834,8033
13: 7 from the place w· I hid it: " "
20 w· is the flock that was given thee, 346
16: 13 w· I will not shew you favour. * 834
17: 15 W· is the word of the Lord? let it 346
22: 26 country, w· ye were not born; 834,8033
35: 7 in the land w· ye be strangers.* " "
36: 19 and let no man know w· ye be. 375
37: 19 W· are now your prophets which 346
38: 9 die for hunger in the place w· he 8478
39: 5 w· he gave judgment upon him. *
42: 14 of Egypt, w· we shall see no war, 834
52: 9 w· he gave judgment upon him. *
La 2: 12 mothers, W· is corn and wine? 346
Eze 3: 15 of Chebar, and I sat w· they sat, 8033
6: 13 place w· they did offer sweet 834,8033
8: 3 w· was the seat of the image of " "
11: 16 countries w· they shall come. " "
17 w· ye have been scattered, and I 834
13: 12 W· is the daubing wherewith ye 346
17: 10 wither in the furrows w· it grew. 5921
16 in the place w· the king dwelleth that
20: 38 out of the country w· they sojourn,
21: 30 in the place w· thou wast created, 834
34: 12 w· they have been scattered, *834,8033
40: 38 w· they washed the burnt offering.* "
42: 13 w· the priests that approach 834, "
43: 7 w· I will dwell in the midst of " "
46: 20 place w· the priests shall boil "
20 w· they shall bake the meat 834
24 w· the ministers of the house 834,833
Da 8: 17 So he came near w· I stood: and when
Ho 1: 10 the place w· it was said unto them, 834
13: 10 w· is any other that may save thee 645
Joe 2: 17 among the people, W· is their God?346
Am 3: 5 upon the earth, w· no gin is for him?
Mic 7: 10 unto me, W· is the Lord thy God? 346
Na 2: 11 W· is the dwelling of the lions, and "
11 w· the lion, even the old lion, 834,8033
3: 17 place is not known w· they are. 335
Zep 3: 19 land w· they have been put to shame.*
Zec 1: 5 Your fathers, w· are they? and 346
Mal 1: 6 I be a father, w· is mine honour? "
6 and if I be a master, w· is my fear? "
2: 17 or, W· is the God of judgment? "
M't 2: 2 W· is he that is born King of the 4226
4 of them w· Christ should be born. "
9 stood over w· the young child was.3757
6: 19 w· moth and rust doth corrupt, 3699
19 w· thieves break through and steal: "
20 w· neither moth nor rust doth "
20 w· thieves do not break through "
21 w· your treasure is, there will your "
8: 20 man hath not w· to lay his head. 4226
13: 5 w· they had not much earth: 3699
18: 20 For w· two or three are gathered 3757
25: 24 reaping w· thou hast not sown, 3699
24 and gathering w· thou hast not 3606
26 knewest that I reap w· I sowed 3699
26 and gather w· I have not strawed: 3606
26: 17 W· wilt thou that we prepare for 4226
57 w· the scribes and the elders were 3699
28: 6 Come, see the place w· the Lord lay."
16 w· Jesus had appointed them. 3757
M'r 2: 4 uncovered the roof w· he was: 3699
4: 5 ground, w· it had not much earth; "
15 the way side, w· the word is sown; "
5: 40 and entereth in w· the damsel was "
6: 55 were sick, w· they heard he was. "
9: 44, 46 W· their worm dieth not, and * "
48 W· their worm dieth not, and "
11: 4 without in a place w· two ways met;*296
13: 14 standing w· it ought not, (let him 3699
14: 12 W· wilt thou that we go and 4226
14 saith, W· is the guestchamber, "
14 w· I shall eat the passover with my3699
15: 47 of Joses beheld w· he was laid. 4226
16: 6 behold the place w· they laid him. 3699
20 went forth, and preached every w·,*3837
Lu 4: 16 w· he had been brought up: 3757
17 found the place w· it was written, "
8: 25 said unto them, W· is your faith? 4226
9: 6 the gospel, and healing every w·. *3837
58 of man hath not w· to lay his head.4226
10: 33 as he journeyed, came w· he was; 2596
12: 17 no room w· to bestow my fruits? 4226
33 w· no thief approacheth, neither 3699
34 w· your treasure is, there will your "
17: 17 ten cleansed? but w· are the nine? 4226
37 and said unto him, W·, Lord? "
22: 9 him, W· wilt thou that we prepare?"
10 into the house w· he entereth in. *3757
11 thee, W· is the guestchamber, 4226
11 w· I shall eat the passover with 3699
Joh 1: 28 Jordan, w· John was baptizing, "
38 Master,) w· dwellest thou? 4226
39 They came and saw w· he dwelt, "
3: 8 The wind bloweth w· it listeth, and3699
4: 20 the place w· men ought to worship. "
46 Galilee, w· he made the water wine. "
6: 23 the place w· they did eat bread, "
62 man ascend up w· he was before? "
7: 11 at the feast, and said, W· is he? 4226
34 w· I am, thither ye cannot come. 3699
36 w· I am, thither ye cannot come? "
42 town of Bethlehem w· David was? "
8: 10 her, Woman, w· are those thine 4226
19 said unto him, W· is thy Father? "
9: 12 him, W· is he? He said, I know not."
10: 40 the place w· John at first baptized;3699
11: 6 days still in the same place w· he was. "
30 in that place w· Martha met him. 3699
32 when Mary was come w· Jesus was,"
34 And said, W· have ye laid him? 4226
41 the place w· the dead was laid. *3757
57 if any man knew w· he were, he 4226

Joh 12: 1 w· Lazarus was which had been 3699
26 and w· I am, there shall also my "
14: 3 that w· I am, there ye may be also. "
17: 24 hast given me, be with me w· I am: "
18: 1 w· was a garden, into the which he "
19: 18 W· they crucified him, and two "
20 place w· Jesus was crucified was "
41 the place w· he was crucified there "
20: 2 we know not w· they have laid 4226
12 feet, w· the body of Jesus had lain.3699
13 I know not w· they have laid him. 4226
15 tell me w· thou hast laid him, and I "
19 w· the disciples were assembled 3699
Ac 1: 13 w· abode both Peter, and James, 3757
2: 2 all the house w· they were sitting. "
4: 31 w· they were assembled *1722,3739
7: 29 of Madian, w· he begat two sons. 3757
33 w· thou standest is holy *1722,3739
8: 4 went every w· preaching the word.*1330
11: 11 come unto the house w· I was,*1722,3739
12: 12 w· many were together praying. 3757
15: 36 city w· we have preached *1722,3739
16: 13 w· prayer was wont to be made; *3757
17: 1 w· was a synagogue of the Jews: 3699
30 all men every w· to repent: *3837
20: 6 days; w· we abode seven days. 3757
8 w· they were gathered together. "
21: 28 men every w· against the people, *3837
25: 10 seat, w· I ought to be judged: 3757
27: 41 falling into a place w· two seas met,1337
28: 14 W· we found brethren, and were 3757
22 that every w· it is spoken against.*3837
Ro 3: 27 W· is boasting then? It is 4226
4: 15 for w· no law is, there is no 3757
5: 20 But w· sin abounded, grace did "
9: 26 place w· it was said unto them, "
15: 20 not w· Christ was named, lest I 3699
1Co 1: 20 W· is the wise? w· is the scribe? 4226
20 w· is the disputer of this world? "
4: 17 I teach every w· in every church. *3837
12: 17 were an eye, w· were the hearing? 4226
17 hearing, w· were the smelling? "
19 one member, w· were the body? "
15: 55 O death, w· is thy sting? O grave, "
55 sting? O grave, w· is thy victory? "
2Co 3: 17 and w· the Spirit of the Lord is, 3757
Ga 4: 15 W· is then the blessedness ye 5101
Ph'p 4: 12 every w· and in all things I *1722,3956
Col 3: 1 w· Christ sitteth on the right 3757
11 W· there is neither Greek nor 3699
1Ti 2: 8 that men pray every w·, *1722,5117
Heb 9: 16 w· a testament is, there must also 3699
10: 18 w· remission of these is, there is "
Jas 3: 16 w· envying and strife is, there is "
1Pe 4: 18 w· shall the ungodly and the 4226
2Pe 3: 4 W· is the promise of his coming? "
Re 2: 13 thy works, and w· thou dwellest, "
13 dwellest, even w· Satan's seat is: 3699
13 slain among you, w· Satan dwelleth."
11: 8 w· also our Lord was crucified. "
12: 6 w· she hath a place prepared of "
14 w· she is nourished for a time, and "
17: 15 w· the whore sitteth, are peoples, 3757
20: 10 w· the beast and the false prophet 3699

whereabout
1Sa 21: 2 thing of the business w· I send thee,834

whereas
Ge 31: 37 W· thou hast searched all my 3588
De 19: 6 w· he was not worthy of death,
28: 62 w· ye were as the stars of heaven 834
1Sa 24: 17 good, w· I have rewarded thee evil.
2Sa 7: 6 W· I have not dwelt in any house*3588
15: 20 W· thou camest but yesterday, should
1Ki 8: 18 W· it was in thine heart to 3282,834
12: 11 w· my father did lade you with a
2Ki 13: 19 w· now thou shalt smite Syria but 6258
2Ch 10: 11 w· my father put a heavy yoke
28: 13 w· we have offended against the *3588
Job 22: 20 W· our substance is not cut down,*518
Ec 4: 14 w· also he that is born in his *3588
Isa 37: 21 W· thou hast prayed to me 834
60: 15 W· thou hast been forsaken and 8478
Jer 4: 10 w· the sword reacheth unto the soul.
Eze 13: 7 W· ye say, The Lord saith it;
16: 7 W· thou wast naked and bare. *
34 w· none followeth thee to commit*
35: 10 possess it; w· the Lord was there:
36: 34 w· it lay desolate in the sight 8478,834
Da 2: 41 w· thou sawest the feet and toes, 1768
43 w· thou sawest iron mixed with "
4: 23 w· the king saw a watcher and an "
26 w· they commanded to leave the "
8: 22 w· four stood up for it, four *
Mal 1: 4 W· Edom saith, We are 3588
Joh 9: 25 that, w· I was blind, now I see.
1Co 3: 3 w· there is among you envying, 3699
Jas 4: 14 W· ye know not what shall be on 3748
1Pe 2: 12 w· they speak against you as *1722,3759
3: 16 w· they speak evil of you, as of* "
2Pe 2: 11 W· angels, which are greater in 3699

whereby
Ge 15: 8 w· shall I know that I shall inherit4100
44: 5 drinketh, and w· indeed he divineth?
Le 22: 5 w· he may be made unclean, 834
Nu 5: 8 w· an atonement shall be made for "
17: 5 w· they murmur against you. * "
De 7: 19 w· the Lord thy God brought thee "
28: 20 doings, w· thou hast forsaken me. "
1Sa 20: 33 w· Jonathan knew that it was
Ps 45: 5 w· the people fall under thee.
8 w· they have made thee glad. *4482
68: 9 w· thou didst confirm thine *
Jer 3: 8 w· backsliding Israel committed * 834
17: 19 w· the kings of Judah come in, "
23: 6 is his name w· he shall be called, "

Jer 33: 8 *w·* they have sinned against me; 834
8 iniquities, *w·* they have sinned, "
8 *w·* they have transgressed against "
Eze 18: 31 *w·* ye have transgressed; and * "
20: 25 judgments *w·* they should not live;* "
39: 26 *w·* they have trespassed against 834
40: 49 by the steps *w·* they went up to it: "
46: 9 the way of the gate *w·* he came in, "
47: 13 border, *w·* ye shall inherit the land "
Zep 2: 8 *w·* they have reproached my people,* "
Lu 1: 18 *W·* shall I know this? for I *2596,5101*
78 *w·* the dayspring from on high *1722,3739*
Ac 4: 12 men, *w·* we must be saved. * "
11: 14 *w·* thou and all thy house shall " "
19: 40 *w·* we may give an account of**4012,3757*
Ro 8: 15 *w·* we cry, Abba, Father. *1722,3739*
14: 21 thing *w·* thy brother stumbleth," "
Eph 3: 4 *W·*, when ye read, ye may *4314,* "
4: 30 *w·* ye are sealed unto the day**1722,* "
Ph'p 3: 21 *w·* he is able even to subdue all *3588*
Heb 12: 28 grace, *w·* we may serve God *1223,3739*
2Pe 1: 4 *W·* are given unto us...great " "
3: 6 *W·* the world that then was, * "
1Jo 2: 18 *w·* we know that it is the last time.*3606*
wherefore See also THEREFORE.
Ge 10: 9 *w·* it is said, Even as Nimrod 5921,3651
16: 14 *W·* the well was called "
18: 13 *W·* did Sarah laugh, saying, Shall 4100
21: 10 *W·* she said unto Abraham, Cast out
26: 27 unto them, *W·* come ye to me, 4069
29: 25 *w·* then hast thou beguiled 4100,2063
31: 27 *W·* didst thou flee away secretly, 4100
30 yet, *w·* hast thou stolen my gods? "
32: 29 *W·* is it that thou dost ask after my "
38: 10 the Lord: *w·* he slew him also. *
40: 7 saying, *W·* look ye so sadly to day?4069
43: 6 *W·* dealt ye so ill with me, as to 4100
44: 4 *W·* have ye rewarded evil for good?"
7 him, *W·* saith my lord these words?"
47: 19 *W·* shall we die before thine eyes, "
22 *w·* they sold not their lands. 5921,3651
50: 11 *w·* the name of it was called "
Ex 2: 13 wrong, *W·* smitest thou thy fellow?4100
5: 4 *W·* do ye, Moses and Aaron, let the "
14 *W·* have ye not fulfilled your task 4069
15 *W·* dealest thou thus with thy 4100
22 *w·* hast thou so evil entreated this "
6: 6 *W·* say unto the children of Israel,3651
14: 11 *w·* hast thou dealt with us, 4100,2063
15 *W·* criest thou unto me? speak 4100
17: 2 *W·* the people did chide with Moses,
2 with me? *w·* do ye tempt the Lord?4100
3 *W·* is this that thou hast brought "
20: 11 day: *w·* the Lord blessed the 5921,3651
31: 16 *W·* the children of Israel shall keep
32: 12 *W·* should the Egyptians speak, 4100
Le 10: 17 *W·* have ye not eaten the sin 4069
13: 25 *w·* the priest shall pronounce him*
25: 18 *W·* ye shall do my statutes, and keep
Nu 9: 7 *w·* are we kept back, that we may 4100
11: 11 *W·* hast thou afflicted thy servant?"
12: 8 *w·* then were ye not afraid to speak4069
14: 3 *w·* hath the Lord brought us into 4100
41 *W·* now do ye transgress the "
16: 3 *w·* then lift ye up yourselves 4069
20: 5 *w·* have ye made us to come up out4100
21 *w·* Israel turned away from him.
21: 5 *W·* have ye brought us up out of 4100
14 *W·* it is said in the book of 5921,3651
27 *W·* they that speak in proverbs" "
22: 32 *W·* hast thou smitten thine ass 4100
37 *w·* camest thou not unto me? am I "
25: 12 *W·* say, Behold, I give unto him 3651
32: 5 *W·*, said they, if we have found grace*
De 7: 12 *W·* it shall come to pass, if ye "
10: 9 *W·* Levi hath no part nor 5921,3651
19: 7 *W·* I command thee, saying, " "
29: 24 *W·* hath the Lord done thus 4100
Jos 5: 9 *W·* the name of the place is called
7: 5 *w·* the hearts of the people melted,*
7 *w·* hast thou at all brought this 4100
10 *w·* liest thou thus upon thy face? "
26 *W·* the name of that place 5921,3651
9: 11 *W·* our elders and all the inhabitants*
22 *W·* have ye beguiled us, saying, 4100
10: 3 *W·* Adoni-zedec king of Jerusalem
J'g 2: 3 *W·* I also said, I will not drive them
10: 13 gods: *w·* I will deliver you no more.3651
11: 27 *W·* I have not sinned against thee,*
12: 1 *W·* passedst thou over to fight 4069
3 *w·* then are ye come up unto me 4100
18: 12 *w·* they called that place 5921,3651
Ru 1: 7 *W·* she went forth out of the place*
1Sa 1: 20 *W·* it came to pass, when the time*
2: 17 *W·* the sin of the young men was *
29 *W·* kick ye at my sacrifice and at 4100
30 *W·* the Lord God of Israel saith, *3651
4: 3 *W·* hath the Lord smitten us to 4100
6: 5 *W·* ye shall make images of your
6 *W·* then do ye harden your hearts,4100
9: 21 *w·* then speakest thou so to me? "
14: 27 *W·* he put forth the end of the rod
15: 19 *W·* then didst thou not obey the 4100
16: 19 *W·* Saul sent messengers unto Jesse,
18: 15 *W·* when Saul saw that he behaved*
21 *W·* Saul said to David, Thou shalt this
27 *W·* David arose and went, he and his*
19: 5 *w·* then wilt thou sin against 4100
24 *W·* they say, Is Saul also 5921,3651
20: 27 *W·* cometh not the son of Jesse to4069
31 *W·* now send and fetch him unto me,
32 *W·* shall he be slain? what hath 4100
21: 14 *w·* then have ye brought him to me?"
23: 25 *w·* he came down into a rock, and
28 *W·* Saul returned from pursuing after*
24: 9 *W·* hearest thou men's words, 4100

1Sa 24: 19 *w·* the Lord reward thee good for that
25: 8 *W·* let the young men find favour in
36 *w·* she told him nothing, less or more,
26: 15 *w·* then hast thou not kept thy 4100
18 *W·* doth my lord thus pursue after "
27: 6 *w·* Ziklag pertaineth unto the 3651
28: 9 *w·* then layest thou a snare for my4100
16 *W·* then dost thou ask of me, "
29: 7 *W·* now return, and go in peace,
10 *W·* now rise up early in the
2Sa 2: 16 together: *w·* that place was called
22 *w·* should I smite thee to the 4100
23 *w·* Abner with the hinder end of the
3: 7 *W·* hast thou gone in unto my 4069
7: 22 *W·* thou art great, O Lord 5921,3651
10: 4 *W·* Hanun took David's servants,*
11: 20 *W·* approached ye so nigh unto 4069
12: 9 *W·* hast thou despised the "
23 now he is dead, *w·* should I fast? 4100
14: 13 *W·* then hast thou thought such a "
31 *W·* have thy servants set my field "
32 say, *W·* am I come from Geshur? "
15: 19 *W·* goest thou also with us? return "
16: 10 then say, *W·* hast thou done so? 4069
18: 22 *W·* wilt thou run, my son, 4100,2088
19: 12 *w·* then are ye the last to bring 4100
25 *W·* wentest not thou with me, "
35 *w·* then should thy servant be yet "
42 *W·* then be ye angry for this "
21: 3 *W·* David said unto the Gibeonites,*
24: 21 *W·* is my lord the king come to 4069
1Ki 1: 2 *W·* his servants said unto him, Let
11 *W·* Nathan spake unto Bath-sheba*
41 *W·* is this noise of the city being 4069
16: 16 *w·* all Israel made Omri, the captain
20: 9 *W·* he said unto the messengers of
22: 34 *w·* he said unto the driver of his
2Ki 4: 23 *W·* wilt thou go to him to day? 4069
31 *W·* he went again to meet him, and
5: 7 *w·* consider, I pray you, and *3588,389
8 *W·* hast thou rent thy clothes? 4100
7: 7 *W·* they arose and fled in the twilight,
9: 11 *w·* came this mad fellow to thee? 4069
36 *W·* they came again, and told him.
17: 26 *W·* they spake to the king of Assyria,
19: 4 *w·* lift up thy prayers for the remnant
1Ch 19: 4 *W·* Hanun took David's servants, and
21: 4 *W·* Joab departed, and went
29: 10 *W·* David blessed the Lord before all
2Ch 5: 3 *W·* all the men of Israel assembled*
19: 7 *W·* now let the fear of the Lord be*
22: 4 *W·* he did evil in the sight of the Lord*
25: 10 *W·* their anger was greatly kindled
15 *W·* the anger of the Lord was kindled
28: 5 *W·* the Lord his God delivered him
29: 8 *W·* the wrath of the Lord was upon
34 *w·* their brethren the Levites did help
33: 11 *W·* the Lord brought upon them the
Ne 2: 2 *W·* the king said unto me, Why is*
Es 3: 6 *W·* Haman sought to destroy all the
9: 26 *W·* they called these days 5921,3651
Job 3: 20 *W·* is light given to him that is in 4100
10: 2 *w·* thou contendest with me. 5921, "
18 *W·* then hast thou brought me "
13: 14 *W·* do I take my flesh in my 5921, "
24 *W·* hidest thou thy face, and "
18: 3 *W·* we are counted as beasts, and 4069
21: 7 *W·* do the wicked live, become old, "
32: 6 *w·* I was afraid, and durst not5921,3651
33: 1 *W·*, Job, I pray thee, hear my * 199
42: 6 *W·* I abhor myself, and 5921,3651
Ps 10: 13 *W·* doth the wicked contemn " 4100
44: 24 *W·* hidest thou thy face, and "
49: 5 *W·* should I fear in the days of evil," "
79: 10 *W·* should the heathen say, Where "
89: 47 *W·* hast thou made all men *5921, "
115: 2 *W·* should the heathen say, Where "
Pr 17: 16 *W·* is there a price in the 4100,2088
Ec 4: 2 *W·* I praised the dead which are
5: 6 *w·* should God be angry at thy 4100
Isa 5: 4 *w·*, when I looked that it should 4069
10: 12 *W·* it shall come to pass, that when
16: 11 *W·* my bowels shall sound 5921,3651
24: 15 *W·* glorify ye the Lord in the " "
28: 14 *W·* hear the word of the Lord, ye " "
29: 13 *W·* the Lord said, Forasmuch as *
30: 12 *W·* thus saith the Holy One of 3651
37: 4 *w·* lift up thy prayer for the remnant
50: 2 *W·*, when I came, was there no 4069
55: 2 *W·* do ye spend money for that 4100
58: 3 *W·* have we fasted, say they, and "
3 *w·* have we afflicted our soul, and thou
63: 2 *W·* art thou red in thine apparel, 4069
Jer 2: 9 *W·* I will yet plead with you, 3651
29 *W·* will ye plead with me? ye all 4100
31 *w·* say my people, We are lords; 4069
5: 6 *W·* a lion out of the forest 5921,3651
14 *W·* thus saith the Lord God of "
19 *W·* doeth the Lord our God 8478,4100
12: 1 *W·* doth the way of the wicked 4069
1 *w·* are all they happy that deal very
13: 22 *W·* come these things upon me? 4069
16: 10 *W·* hath the Lord pronounced5921,4100
22: 8 *W·* hath the Lord done thus "
28 *w·* are they cast out, he and his 4069
23: 12 *W·* their way shall be unto them 3651
27: 17 *w·* should this city be laid waste, 4100
30: 6 *w·* do I see every man with his 4069
32: 3 *W·* dost thou prophesy, and say, "
37: 15 *W·* the princes were wroth with *
40: 15 *w·* should he slay thee, that all the4100
44: 6 *W·* my fury and mine anger was
7 *W·* commit ye this great evil 4100
46: 5 *W·* have I seen them dismayed 4069
49: 4 *W·* gloriest thou in the valleys, 4100
51: 52 *W·*, behold, the days come, saith 3651

La 3: 39 *W·* doth a living man complain, a 4100
5: 20 *W·* dost thou forget us forever, "
Eze 5: 11 *W·*, as I live, saith the Lord God; 3651
7: 24 *W·* I will bring the worst of the
13: 20 *W·* thus saith the Lord God; 3651
16: 35 *W·*, O harlot, hear the word of the "
18: 32 *w·* turn yourselves, and live ye.
20: 10 *W·* I caused them to go forth out of *
25 *W·* I gave them also statutes that*
30 *W·* say unto the house of Israel, 3651
21: 7 *W·* sighest thou? that thou 5981,4100
23: 9 *W·* I have delivered her unto the 3651
24: 6 *W·* thus saith the Lord God; Woe "
33: 25 *W·* say unto them, Thus saith the "
36: 18 *W·* I poured my fury upon them
43: 8 *w·* I have consumed them in mine
Da 3: 8 *W·* at that time certain 3605,6903,1836
4: 27 *W·*, O king, let my counsel be 3861
6: 9 *W·* king Darius signed 3605,6903,1836
8: 26 *w·* shut thou up the vision; for it*
10: 20 Knowest thou *w·* I come unto thee?4100
Joe 2: 17 *w·* should they say among the "
Jon 1: 14 *W·* they cried unto the Lord, and
Hab 1: 13 *w·* lookest thou upon them that 4100
Mal 2: 14 Yet ye say, *W·*? Because the 5921, "
15 *w·* one? That he might seek a
M't 6: 30 *W·*, if God so clothe the grass of **1161*
7: 20 *W·* by their fruits ye shall **686,1065*
9: 4 *W·* think ye evil in your *2443,5101*
12: 12 *W·* it is lawful to do well on the *5620*
31 *W·* I say unto you, All **1223,5124*
14: 31 faith, *w·* didst thou doubt? *1519,5101*
18: 8 *W·* if thy hand or thy foot offend **1161*
19: 6 *W·* they are no more twain, but **5620*
23: 31 *W·* ye be witnesses unto yourselves," "
34 *W·*, behold, I send unto you **1223,5124*
24: 26 *W·* if they shall say unto you, **3767*
26: 50 Friend, *w·* art thou come? **1909,3739*
27: 8 *W·* that field was called, The field *1352*
Lu 7: 7 *W·* neither thought I myself "
47 *W·* I say unto thee, Her sins, *3739,5484*
19: 23 *W·* then gavest not thou my *1302*
Joh 9: 27 hear: *w·* would ye hear it again? *5101*
Ac 1: 21 *W·* of these men which have **3767*
6: 3 *W·*, brethren, look ye out among* "
10: 21 is the cause *w·* ye are come? *1223,3739*
13: 35 *W·* he saith also in another psalm,**1352*
15: 19 *W·* my sentence is, that we trouble" "
19: 32 *w·* they were come together. *5101,1752*
38 *W·* if Demetrius, and the **3303,3767*
20: 26 *W·* I take you to record this day, *1352*
22: 24 *w·* they cried so against him.**1223,3739*
30 *w·* he was accused of the Jews, *5101*
23: 28 the cause *w·* they accused him,*1223,3739*
24: 26 *w·* he sent for him the oftener, *1352*
25: 26 *W·* I have brought him forth before" "
26: 3 *w·* I beseech thee to hear me "
27: 25 *W·*, sirs, be of good cheer: for I "
34 *W·* I pray you to take some meat: "
Ro 1: 24 *W·* God also gave them up to "
5: 12 *W·*, as by...man sin entered **1223,5124*
7: 4 *W·*, my brethren, ye also are *5620*
12 *W·* the law is holy, and the * "
9: 32 *W·*? Because they sought it not *1302*
13: 5 *W·* ye must needs be subject, not *1352*
15: 7 *W·* receive ye one another, as "
1Co 4: 16 *W·* I beseech you, be ye followers**3767*
8: 13 *W·*, if meat make my brother to *1355*
10: 12 *W·* let him that thinketh he *5620*
14 *W·*, my dearly beloved, flee from *1355*
11: 27 *W·* whosoever shall eat this bread,*5620*
33 *W·*, my brethren, when ye come "
12: 3 *W·* I give you to understand, that *1352*
14: 13 *W·* let him that speaketh in an *1355*
22 *W·* tongues are for a sign, not to *5620*
39 *W·*, brethren, covet to prophesy, "
2Co 2: 8 *W·* I beseech you that ye would *1352*
5: 9 *W·* we labour, that, whether "
16 *W·* henceforth know we no man *5620*
6: 17 *W·* come out from among them, *1352*
7: 12 *W·*, though I wrote unto you, I did *686*
8: 24 *W·* shew ye to them, and before the*3767*
11: 11 *W·*? because I love you not? God *1302*
Ga 3: 19 *W·* then serveth the law? It was *5101*
24 *W·* the law was our schoolmaster**5620*
4: 7 *W·* thou art no more a servant, * "
Eph 1: 15 *W·* I also, after I heard of **1223,5124*
2: 11 *W·* remember, that ye being in *1352*
3: 13 *W·* I desire that ye faint not at my "
4: 8 *W·* he saith, When he ascended "
25 *W·* putting away lying, speak "
5: 14 *W·* he saith, Awake thou that "
17 *W·* be ye not unwise, but *1223,5124*
6: 13 *W·* take unto you the whole " "
Ph'p 2: 9 *W·* God also hath highly exalted *1352*
12 *W·*, my beloved, as ye have always**5620*
Col 2: 20 *W·* if ye be dead with Christ from**3767*
1Th 2: 18 *W·* we would have come unto you,**1352*
3: 1 *W·* when we could no longer "
4: 18 *W·* comfort one another with *5620*
5: 11 *W·* comfort yourselves together, *1352*
2Th 1: 11 *W·* also we pray always for **1519,3739*
2Ti 1: 6 *W·* I put thee in remembrance**1223,*
Tit 1: 13 *W·* rebuke them sharply, that* "
Ph'm 8 *W·*, though I might be much bold *1352*
Heb 2: 17 *W·* in all things it behoved him to *3606*
3: 1 *W·*, holy brethren, partakers of "
7 *W·* (as the Holy Ghost saith, To *1352*
10 *W·* I was grieved with that "
7: 25 *W·* he is able also to save them *3606*
8: 3 *w·* it is of necessity that this man "
10: 5 *W·* when he cometh into the *1352*
11: 16 *w·* God is not ashamed to be called "
12: 1 *W·* seeing we also are compassed**5105*
12 *W·* lift up the hands which hang *1352*
28 *W·* we receiving a kingdom which "

Heb13:12 W' Jesus also, that he might 1352
Jas 1:19 W', my beloved brethren, let *5620
21 W' lay apart all filthiness and 1352
4: 6 W' he saith, God resisteth the "
1Pe 1:13 W' gird up the loins of your mind, "
2: 1 W' laying aside all malice, and *3767
6 W' also it is contained in the *1352
4:19 W' let them that suffer according 5620
2Pe 1:10 W' the rather, brethren, give 1352
12 W' I will not be negligent to put "
3:14 W', beloved, seeing that ye look "
1Jo 3:12 w' slew he him? Because his 5484,5101
3Jo 10 W', if I come, I will *1223,3739
Re 17: 7 W' didst thou marvel? I will tell 1302

wherein See also WHEREINSOEVER; WHEREINTO.
Ge 1:30 w' there is life, I have given every 834
6:17 w' is the breath of life, from under "
7:15 of all flesh, w' is the breath of life. "
17: 8 the land w' thou art a stranger, all*
21:23 the land w' thou hast sojourned. 834
28: 4 the land w' thou art a stranger, *
36: 7 the land w' they were strangers, *
37: 1 in the land w' his father was a *
Ex 1:14 w' they made them serve, was with834
6: 4 pilgrimage, w' they were strangers. "
12: 7 of the houses, w' they shall eat it. "
18:11 in the thing w' they dealt proudly "
20 shew them the way w' they must walk,
22:27 w' shall he sleep? and it shall 4100
33:16 w' shall it be known here that I "
Le 4:23 w' he hath sinned, come to his 834
5:18 w' he erred and wist it not, and it "
6:28 vessel w' it is sodden shall be "
11:32 w' any work is done, it must be put* "
36 w' there is plenty of water, shall be "
13:46 days w' the plague shall be in him 834
52 any thing of skin, w' the plague is: "
54 wash the thing w' the plague is, "
57 burn that w' the plague is with fire. "
18: 3 land of Egypt, w' ye dwelt, shall ye "
Nu 12:11 upon us, w' we have done foolishly,* "
11 foolishly, and w' we have sinned.* "
19: 2 w' is no blemish, and upon which "
31:10 burnt all their cities w' they dwelt, "
35:55 vex you in the land w' ye dwell. 834
35:33 shall not pollute the land w' ye are: "
34 shall inhabit, w' I dwell: 834,8432
De 8: 9 A land w' thou shalt eat bread 834
15 wilderness, w' were fiery serpents, "
12: 2 w' the nations which ye shall 834,8033
7 w' the Lord thy God hath blessed 834
17: 1 or sheep, w' is blemish, or any "
28:52 w' thou trustedst, throughout834,2004
Jos 8:24 wilderness w' they chased them, 834
10:27 cave w' they had been hid, 834,8033
22:19 w' the Lord's tabernacle "
33 land w' the children of Reuben 834
24:17 us in all the way w' we went, and "
J'g 16: 5 see w' his great strength lieth, 4100
6 w' thy great strength lieth, and "
15 told me w' thy great strength lieth. "
18: 6 the Lord is your way w' ye go. 834
1Sa 6:15 w' the jewels of gold were, and put "
14:38 see w' this sin hath been this day.4100
2Sa 7: 7 all the places w' I have walked 834
1Ki 8:21 ark, w' is the covenant of the 834,8033
36 the good way w' they should walk, 834
50 w' they have transgressed against "
13:31 sepulchre w' the man of God is "
2Ki 12: 2 w' Jehoiada the priest instructed "
14: 6 w' the Lord commanded, saying, "
17:29 in their cities w' they dwelt. 834,8033
18:19 confidence is this w' thou trustest? 834
23:23 w' this passover was holden to the*
2Ch 3: 3 w' Solomon was instructed for the*
6:11 w' is the covenant of the Lord.834,8033
27 good way, w' they should walk; 834
8: 1 w' Solomon had built the house of "
33:19 the places w' he built high places, "
Ezr 5: 7 unto him, w' was written thus; 1459
Ne 6: 6 W' was written, It is reported
13:15 them in the day w' they sold victuals.
Es 5:11 w' the king had promoted him, 834
8:11 W' the king granted the Jews "
9:22 days w' the Jews rested from their "
Job 3: 3 Let the day perish w' I was born, and
6:16 of the ice, and w' the snow is hid:
24 me to understand w' I have erred.4100
38:26 on the wilderness, w' there is no man;
Ps 74: 2 this mount Zion, w' thou hast dwelt.
90:15 to the days w' thou hast afflicted us,
15 and the years w' we have seen evil.
104:20 w' all the beasts of the forest do
25 wide sea, w' are things creeping 8033
142: 3 In the way w' I walked have they 2098
143: 8 to know the way w' I should walk; "
Ec 2:19 all my labour w' I have laboured,
19 w' I have shewed myself wise under
22 w' he hath laboured under the sun?
8: 9 worketh in that w' he laboureth? 834
8: 9 is a time w' one man ruleth over "
Isa 2:22 for w' is he to be accounted of? 4100
14: 3 bondage w' thou wast made to 834
33:21 w' shall go no galley with oars,
36: 4 confidence is this w' thou trustest? 834
47:12 w' thou hast laboured from thy
65:12 did choose that w' I delighted not.
Jer 5:17 fenced cities, w' thou trustedst,834,2004
7:14 called by my name, w' ye trust, and 834
12: 5 the land of peace, w' thou trustedst,*
16:19 vanity, and things w' there is no profit.
20:14 Cursed be the day w' I was born: 834
14 not the day w' my mother bare me "
22:28 idol? is he a vessel w' is no pleasure?
31: 9 way, w' they shall not stumble:
36:14 roll w' thou hast read in the ears of834
Jer 41: 9 pit w' Ishmael had cast all the dead834
42: 3 shew us the way w' we may walk,
48:38 Moab like a vessel w' is no pleasure,
51:43 a land w' no man dwelleth, 834
Eze 20:34 the countries w' ye are scattered, "
41 countries w' ye have been scattered;
43 doings, w' ye have been defiled; 834
23:19 w' she had played the harlot in the "
26:10 enter into a city w' is made a breach.
32: 6 thy blood the land w' thou swimmest,
37:23 w' they have sinned, and will 834
42:14 their garments w' they minister; "
Ho 2:13 w' she burned incense to them, and*"
8: 8 Gentiles as a vessel w' is no pleasure.
Jon 4:11 w' are more than sixscore thousand
Mic 6: 3 thee? and w' have I wearied thee? 4100
Zep 3:11 w' thou hast transgressed against 834
Zec 9:11 prisoners out of the pit w' is no water.
Mal 1: 2 Yet ye say, W' hast thou loved us?4100
6 W' have we despised thy name? "
7 W' have we polluted thee? In that "
2:17 ye say, W' have we wearied him? "
3: 7 But ye said, W' shall we return? "
8 ye say, W' have we robbed thee? "
M't 11:20 w' most of his mighty works 1722,3739
25:13 w' the Son of man cometh. * "
M'r 2: 4 w' the sick of the palsy lay. *1909, "
Lu 1: 4 w' thou hast been instructed. 4012, "
25 in the days w' he looked on me, "
11:22 all his armour w' he trusted, 1909, "
23:53 w' never man before was laid. *3757
Joh 19:41 w' was never man yet laid. 1722, "
Ac 2: 8 own tongue, w' we were born? "
7: 4 into this land, w' ye now dwell.1519, "
10:12 W'...all manner of fourfooted 1722, "
Ro 2: 1 for w' thou judgest another, "
5: 2 into this grace w' we stand, "
7: 6 being dead w' we were held; "
1Co 7:20 same calling w' he was called. "
24 w' he is called, therein abide "
15: 1 have received, and w' ye stand; "
2Co 11:12 that w' they glory, they may be "
12:13 For what is it w' ye were inferior to "
Eph 1: 6 w' he hath made us accepted *1722, "
8 W' he hath abounded toward us * "
2: 2 W' in time past ye walked 1722, "
5:18 drunk with wine, w' is excess; "
Ph'p 4:10 w' ye were also careful, but 1909, "
Col 2:12 w' also ye are risen with him 1722, "
2Ti 2: 9 W' I suffer trouble, as an evil "
Heb 6:17 W' God, willing more "
9: 2 first, w' was the candlestick, "
4 w' was the golden pot that had "
1Pe 1: 6 W' ye greatly rejoice, though 1519, "
3:20 w' few, that is, eight souls 1519, "
4: 4 W' they think it strange that 1722, "
5:12 true grace of God w' ye stand.*1519, "
2Pe 3:12 w' the heavens being on fire *1223, "
13 w' dwelleth righteousness. 1722, "
Re 2:13 w' Antipas was my...martyr, * "
18:19 w' were made rich all that had "

whereinsoever
2Co 11:21 w' any is bold, (I speak 1722,3739,302

whereinto
Le 11:33 w' any of them falleth, 834,413,8432
Nu 14:24 into the land w' he went; 824, "
Joh 6:22 one w' his disciples...entered,*1519,3739

whereof
Ge 3:11 w' I commanded thee that thou 834
Le 6:30 w' any of the blood is brought into "
13:24 skin w' there is a hot burning, and*
27: 9 w' men bring an offering unto the 834
Nu 5: 3 their camps, in the midst w' I dwell."
7:19, 37, 49, 61, 67, 73, 79 weight w' was
an hundred and thirty shekels, *
21:16 well w' the Lord spake unto Moses,834
De 13: 2 to pass, w' he spake unto thee, "
28:27 itch w' thou canst not be healed.
68 by the way w' I spake unto thee, "
Jos 20: 2 w' I spake unto you by the hand of "
22: 9 w' they were possessed, according "
1Sa 10:16 of the kingdom, w' Samuel spake, "
13: 2 w' two thousand were with Saul in
2Sa 12:30 weight w' was a talent of gold with
2Ki 13:14 sick of this sickness w' he died. 834
17:12 w' the Lord had said unto them, "
2Ch 3: 8 w' was according to the breadth *
6:20 place w' thou hast said that thou 834
24:14 w' were made vessels for the house of
33: 4 w' the Lord had said, In Jerusalem834
Ne 12:31 w' one went on the right hand upon
Job 6: 4 poison w' drinketh up my spirit: 834
Ps 46: 4 w' shall make glad the city of God,
57: 6 midst w' they are fallen themselves.*
126: 3 great things for us; w' we are glad.
Ec 1:10 Is there any thing w' it may be said,
Ca 4: 2 w' every one bear twins, and none is
6: 6 w' every one beareth twins, and there
Jer 32:36 concerning this city, w' ye say, It 834
43 this land, w' ye say, It is desolate "
42:16 and the famine, w' ye were afraid "
Eze 32:15 be destitute of that w' it was full,
39: 8 this is the day w' I have spoken. 834
Da 9: 2 w' the word of the Lord came to "
Ho 2:12 w' she hath said, These are my "
Lu 23:14 those things w' ye accuse him:
Ac 2:32 raised up, w' we all are witnesses. 3739
3:15 raised from the dead; w' we are "
17:19 new doctrine, w' thou speakest, is?*
31 w' he hath given assurance unto all
21:24 w' they were informed concerning
24: 8 all these things, w' we accuse him.3739
13 things w' they now accuse 4012, "
25:11 of these things w' these accuse me, "
26: 2 things w' I am accused of the Jews: "
Ro 4: 2 he hath w' to glory; but not before
6:21 w' ye are now ashamed? 1909,3739
15:17 w' I may glory through Jesus Christ*
1Co 7: 1 things w' ye wrote unto me: 4012,3739
2Co 9: 5 your bounty, w' ye had notice before,*
Eph 3: 7 W' I was made a minister, 3739
Ph'p 3: 4 he hath w' he might trust in the flesh,*
Col 1: 5 w' ye heard before in the word of 3739
23 w' I Paul am made a minister; "
25 W' I am made a minister, "
1Ti 1: 7 they say, nor w' they affirm. 4012,5101
6: 4 words, w' cometh envy, strife,1537,3739
Heb 2: 5 world to come, w' we speak. 4012, "
10:15 W' the Holy Ghost also is a witness*
12: 8 chastisement, w' all are partakers,3739
13:10 w' they have no right to eat 1537, "
1Jo 4: 3 w' ye have heard that it should "

whereon
Ge 28:13 land w' thou liest, to thee will 834,5921
Ex 3: 5 place w' thou standest is holy " "
8:21 also the ground w' they are. " "
Le 6:27 wash that w' it was sprinkled " "
15: 6 sitteth on any thing w' he sat " "
17 w' is the seed of copulation, " "
23 or on any thing w' she sitteth, " "
24 all the bed w' he lieth shall be " "
26 bed w' she lieth all the days of " "
De 11:24 w' the soles of your feet shall tread834
Jos 5:15 place w' thou standest is holy. 834,5921
14: 9 land w' thy feet have trodden shall 834
1Sa 6:18 Abel, w' they set down the ark834,5921
2Ch 4:19 tables w' the shewbread was set; "
32:10 W' do ye trust, that ye abide 5921,4100
Job 24:23 him to be in safety, w' he resteth;*
Ca 4: 4 w' there hang a thousand bucklers,5921
Isa 36: 6 w' if a man lean, it will go 834, "
Eze 37:20 sticks w' thou writest shall be " "
M'r 11: 2 a colt tied, w' never man sat; 1909,3739
Lu 4:29 the hill w' their city was built, " "
5:25 and took up that w' he lay, and " "
19:30 a colt tied, w' never man sat; " "
Joh 4:38 to reap w' ye bestowed no labour: "

wheresoever
Le 13:12 to his foot, w' the priest looketh; *3605
2Ki 8: 1 and sojourn w' thou canst sojourn: 834
12: 5 w' any breach shall be found. 834,8033
1Ch 17: 6 W' I...walked with all Israel, *3605,834
Jer 40: 5 go w' it seemeth convenient 413,3605
Da 2:38 w' the children of men dwell, 3606,1768
M't 24:28 w' the carcase is, there will 3699,1437
26:13 W' this gospel shall be " "
M'r 9:18 w' he taketh him, he teareth " 302
14: 9 W' this gospel shall be " "
14 w' he shall go in, say ye to the " 1437
Lu 17:37 W' the body is, thither will the 3699

whereto See also WHEREUNTO.
Job 30: 2 w' might the strength of their 4100
Isa 55:11 prosper in the thing w' I sent it. 834
Ph'p 3:16 w' we have already attained, *1519,3739

whereunto
Nu 36: 4 of the tribe w' they are received: 834
De 4:26 perish from off the land w' ye go "
2Ch 8:11 w' the ark of the Lord hath come. "
Es 10: 2 w' the king advanced him, "
Ps 71: 3 w' I may continually resort:
Jer 22:27 the land w' they desire to return, 834
Eze 5: 9 w' I will not do any more the like, "
20:29 is the high place w' ye go? 834,8033
M't 11:16 w' shall I liken this generation? 5101
M'r 4:30 W' shall we liken the kingdom of* "
Lu 7:31 W' then shall I liken the men of "
13:18 like? and w' shall I resemble it? "
20 W' shall I liken the kingdom of "
Ac 5:24 of them w' this would grow. "
13: 2 for the work w' I have called them.3739
27: 8 nigh w' was the city of Lasea. "
Ga 4: 9 w' ye desire again to be in "
Col 1:29 W' I also labour, striving 1519, "
2Th 2:14 W' he called you by our gospel," "
1Ti 2: 7 W' I am ordained a preacher, " "
4: 6 doctrine, w' thou hast attained. "
6:12 w' thou art also called, and 1519, "
2Ti 1:11 W' I am appointed a preacher, " "
1Pe 2: 8 w' also they were appointed. " "
3:21 like figure w' even baptism doth * "
2Pe 1:19 w' ye do well that ye take heed, as "

whereupon
Le 11:35 w' any part of their carcase 834,5921
J'g 16:26 pillars w' the house standeth, " "
1Ki 7:48 of gold, w' the shewbread was, " "
12:28 W' the king took counsel, and made
2Ch 12: 6 W' the princes of Israel and the king*
Job 38: 6 W' are the foundations 5921,4100
Eze 9: 3 from the cherub, w' he was, 834,5921
23:41 w' thou hast set thine incense and "
24:25 that w' they set their minds, their sons
40:41 tables, w' they slew their sacrifices.413
42 w' also they laid the instruments "
Am 4: 7 and the piece w' it rained not 834,5921
M't 14: 7 W' he promised with an oath to 3606
Ac 24:18 W' certain Jews from Asia *1722,3739
26:12 W' as I went to Damascus with "
19 W', O king Agrippa, I was not 3606
Heb 9:18 W' neither the first testament was*"

wherewith See also WHEREWITHAL.
Ge 27:41 blessing w' his father blessed him: 834
Ex 4:17 thine hand, w' thou shalt do signs. "
16:32 may see the bread w' I have fed you "
17: 5 thy rod, w' thou smotest the river, "
29:33 things w' the atonement was made, "
Nu 3:31 of the sanctuary w' they minister, "
48 w' the odd number of them is to be "
4: 9 thereof, w' they minister unto it: 834

Nu 4:12 w· they minister in the sanctuary, 834
14 w· they minister about it, even the "
16:39 w· they that were burnt had offered;*"
25:18 w· they have beguiled you in the "
30: 4 her bond w· she hath bound her soul"
4 bond w· she hath bound her soul "
5 bonds w· she hath bound her soul, "
6 of her lips, w· she bound her soul; "
7 w· she bound her soul shall stand. "
8 lips, w· she bound her soul, of none "
9 w· they have bound their souls, "
11 w· she bound her soul shall stand. "
35:17 throwing a stone, w· he may die, * "
18 weapon of wood, w· he may die, * "
23 with any stone, w· a man may die,* "
De 9:19 w· the Lord was wroth against you "
15:14 w· the Lord thy God hath blessed * "
22:12 of thy vesture, w· thou coverest "
28:53 w· thine enemies shall distress thee:"
55 w· thine enemies shall distress thee "
57 w· thine enemy shall distress thee "
67 of thine heart w· thou shalt fear, * "
33: 1 w· Moses the man of God blessed "
Jos 8:26 w· he stretched out the spear, until "
J'g 6:15 my Lord, w· shall I save Israel? 4100
9: 4 w· Abimelech hired vain and light
9 w· by me they honour God and man,834
38 is now thy mouth, w· thou saidst,* "
16: 6 w· thou mightest be bound to 4100
10 thee, w· thou mightest be bound. "
1Sa 6: 2 tell us w· we shall send it to his "
8: 8 w· they have forsaken me, and served*
29: 4 for w· should he reconcile himself 4100
2Sa 13:15 hatred w· he hated her was greater834
15 than the love w· he had loved her. "
21: 3 w· shall I make the atonement, 4100
1Ki 8:59 w· I have made supplication before834
15:22 thereof, w· Baasha had builded; "
26 in his sin w· he made Israel to sin. "
30 w· he provoked the Lord God of "
34 in his sin w· he made Israel to sin. "
16:26 in his sin w· he made Israel to sin, "
21:22 w· thou hast provoked me to anger, "
22:22 And the Lord said unto him, W·? 4100
2Ki 13:12 w· he fought against Amaziah 834
21:16 his sin w· he made Judah to sin, "
23:26 w· his anger was kindled against "
25:14 vessels of brass w· they ministered, "
1Ch 18: 8 w· Solomon made the brasen sea, "
2Ch 2:17 w· David his father had numbered 834
16: 6 thereof, w· Baasha was building; "
18:20 And the Lord said unto him, W·? 4100
35:21 but against the house w· I have war: "
Ne 9:34 w· thou didst testify against them. 834
Job 15: 3 with speeches w· he can do no good? "
Ps 79:12 w· they have reproached thee, O 834
89:51 W· thine enemies have reproached, "
51 w· they have reproached the "
93: 1 strength, w· he hath girded himself:?*
109:19 a girdle w· he is girded continually. "
119:42 w· to answer him that reproacheth*1697
129: 7 W· the mower filleth not his hand; "
Ca 3:11 crown w· his mother crowned him "
Isa 28:12 w· ye may cause the weary to rest;* "
37: 6 w· the servants of the king of 834
Jer 18:10 w· I said I would benefit them. "
19: 9 w· their enemies, and they that seek "
21: 4 w· ye fight against the king of "
33:16 is the name w· she shall be called,* "
52:18 vessels of brass w· they ministered, "
La 1:12 w· the Lord hath afflicted me in the "
Eze 13:20 w· ye there hunt the souls to make "
16:19 and oil, and honey, w· I fed thee, "
29:20 labour w· he served against it, 834
32:16 lamentation w· they shall lament her: "
36:18 their idols w· they had polluted it: "
Da 2: 1 dreams, w· his spirit was troubled,* "
Mic 6: 6 W· shall I come before the Lord, 4100
Zec 14:12 plague w· the Lord shall smite all 834
18 w· the Lord will smite the heathen "
Mal 2: 5 to him for the fear w· he feared me,* "
M't 5:13 savour, w· shall it be salted? 1722,5101
M'r 3:28 w· soever they shall blaspheme: 3745
9:50 saltness, w· will ye season it? 1722,5101
Lu 14:34 savour, w· shall it be seasoned?" "
17: 8 Make ready w· I may sup, and "
Joh 13: 5 with the towel w· he was girded. 3739
17:26 the love w· thou hast loved me may "
Ro 14:19 things w· one may edify another. * "
2Co 1: 4 w· we ourselves are comforted of 3739
7: 7 w· he was comforted in you, "
10: 2 w· I think to be bold against some, "
Ga 5: 1 liberty w· Christ hath made us free.*"
Eph 2: 4 for his great love w· he loved us, "
4: 1 of the vocation w· ye are called, "
6:16 w· ye shall be able to quench 1722, "
1Th 3: 9 joy w· we joy for your sakes before "
Heb 10:29 w· he was sanctified, an unholy 1722,"

wherewithal
M't 6:31 drink? or, W· shall we be clothed? 5101

whet
De 32:41 If I w· my glittering sword, and 8150
Ps 7:12 he turn not, he will w· his sword; 3913
64: 3 Who w· their tongue like a sword, 8150
Ec 10:10 blunt, and he do not w· the edge, 7043

whether
Ge 18:21 see w· they have done altogether
27:21 w· thou be my very son Esau or not.
31:39 w· stolen by day, or stolen by night.
37:14 w· it be well with thy brethren, and
32 now w· it be thy son's coat or no.
42:16 proved, w· there be any truth in you:
43: 6 the man w· ye had yet a brother? 5750
Ex 4:18 Egypt, and see w· they be yet alive.
12:19 w· he be a stranger, or born in the

Ex 16: 4 w· they will walk in my law, or no.
19:13 w· it be beast or man, it shall not 518
21:31 W· he have gored a son, or have 176
22: 4 hand alive, w· it be ox, or ass, 5704
8 to see w· he have put his hand 518,3808
9 w· it be for ox, for ass, for sheep,
34:19 cattle, w· ox or sheep, that is male.*
Le 3: 1 w· it be a male or female, he shall 518
5: 1 w· he hath seen or known of it; 176
2 w· it be a carcase of an unclean "
7:26 blood, w· it be of fowl or of beast,
11:32 w· it be any vessel of wood, or
35 w· it be oven, or ranges for pots, they
13:47 w· it be a woolen garment, or a linen
48 W· it be in the warp, or woof, of 176
48 w· in a skin, or any thing made of "
52 w· warp or woof, in woollen or in "
55 w· it be bare within or without.
15: 3 w· his flesh run with his issue, or his
16:29 w· it be one of your own country, or *
17:15 w· it be one of your own country, or *
18: 9 w· she be born at home, or born
27:12 shall value it, w· it be good or bad: 996
14 estimate it, w· it be good or bad: "
26 w· it be ox, or sheep: it is the 518
30 w· of the seed of the land, or of the
33 not search w· it be good or bad, 996
Nu 9:21 w· it was by day or by night that 176
22 Or w· it were two days, or a month, "
11:23 w· my word shall come to pass unto
13:18 w· they be strong or weak, few or
19 they dwell in, w· it be good or bad;
19 w· in tents, or in strong holds;
20 what the land is, w· it be fat or lean,
20 lean, w· there be wood therein, or not.
15:30 w· he be born in the land, or a 4480
18:15 w· it be of men or beasts, shall be
De 4:32 w· there hath been any such thing as
8: 2 w· thou wouldest keep his
13: 3 to know w· ye love the Lord with
18: 3 a sacrifice, w· it be ox or sheep; 518
22: 6 w· they be young ones, or eggs, *
24:14 w· he be of thy brethren, or of thy
Jos 24:15 w· the gods which your fathers 518
J'g 2:22 w· they will keep the way of the Lord
3: 4 know w· they would hearken unto the
9: 2 W· is better for you, either that 4100
18: 5 may know w· our way which we go
Ru 3:10 not young men, w· poor or rich. 518
2Sa 12:22 Who can tell w· God will be gracious
15:21 w· in death or life, even there also 518
1Ki 20:18 W· they be come out for peace, "
18 or w· they be come out for war, "
33 observe w· any thing would come
2Ki 1: 2 w· I shall recover of this disease. 518
2Ch 14:11 w· with many, or with them that * 996
15:13 be put to death, w· small or great,4480
13 small or great, w· man or woman.
Ezr 2:59 their seed, w· they were of Israel: 518
5:17 w· it be so, that a decree was made2006
7:26 judgment...w· it be unto death, or "
Ne 7:61 their seed, w· they were of Israel. 518
Es 3: 4 w· Mordecai's matters would stand:
4:11 w· man or woman, shall come unto
14 w· thou art come to the kingdom 518
Job 34:29 w· it be done against a nation, or
33 w· thou refuse, or w· thou choose;*3588
37:13 w· for correction, or for his land, 518
Pr 20:11 w· his work be pure, and w· it be "
Ec 2:19 w· he shall be a wise man or a fool?
5:12 is sweet, w· he eat little or much: 518
11: 6 knowest not w· shall prosper, * 335
6 or w· they both shall be alike good. 518
12:14 things, w· it be good, or w· it be evil. "
Ca 6:11 and to see w· the vine flourished,
7:12 flourish, w· the tender grape appear,
Jer 30: 6 and see w· a man doth travail with 518
42: 6 W· it be good, or w· it be evil, we "
Eze 2: 5 w· they...hear, or w· they will forbear."
7 w· they...hear, or w· they will forbear:"
3:11 w· they...hear, or w· they will forbear."
44:31 or torn, w· it be fowl or beast. 4480
M't 9: 5 w· is easier, to say, Thy sins be 5101
21:31 W· of them twain did the will of "
23:17 for w· is greater, the gold, or the "
19 w· is greater, the gift, or the altar "
26:63 thou tell us w· thou be the Christ, 1487
27:21 W· of the twain will ye that I 5101
49 w· Elias will come to save him. 1487
M'r 2: 9 W· it is easier to say to the sick of 5101
3: 2 w· he would heal him on the 1487
15:36 w· Elias will come to take him down."
44 him w· he had been any while dead."
Lu 3:15 w· he were the Christ, or not; 3379
5:23 W· is easier, to say, Thy sins be 5101
6: 7 w· he would heal on the sabbath 1487
14:28 w· he have sufficient to finish it? "
31 w· he be able with ten thousand to "
22:27 w· is greater, he that sitteth at 5101
23: 6 asked w· the man were a Galilæan.1487
Joh 7:17 of the doctrine, w· it be of God, 4220
17 or w· I speak of myself.
9:25 W· he be a sinner or no, I know 1487
Ac 1:24 w· of these two thou hast 3739,1520
4:19 W· it be right in the sight of God 1487
5: 8 w· ye sold the land for so much? "
9: 2 w· they were men or women 5037
10:18 and asked w· Simon, which was 1487
17:11 daily, w· those things were so. "
19: 2 heard w· there be any Holy Ghost. "
25:20 him w· he would go to Jerusalem, "
Ro 6:16 ye obey; w· of sin unto death, 2273
12: 6 w· prophecy, let us prophesy 1535
14: 8 w· we live, we live unto the 1437,5037
8 w· we die, we die unto the "
8 w· we live therefore, or die, we "

1Co 1:16 I know not w· I baptized any other.1487
3:22 W· Paul, or Apollos, or Cephas, or1535
7:16 w· thou shalt save thy husband? 1487
16 man, w· thou shalt save thy wife? "
8: 5 gods, w· in heaven or in earth, 1535
10:31 W· therefore ye eat, or drink, or "
12:13 body, w· we be Jews or Gentiles, "
13 w· we be bond or free; and have "
26 And w· one member suffer, all the "
13: 8 w· there be prophecies, they shall "
8 w· there be tongues, they shall "
8 w· there be knowledge, it shall "
14: 7 w· pipe or harp, except they give a "
15:11 Therefore w· it were I or they, so "
2Co 1: 6 And w· we be afflicted, it is for your"
6 w· we be comforted, it is for your "
2: 9 w· ye be obedient in all things. 1487
5: 9 w· present or absent, we may be 1535
10 he hath done, w· it be good or bad. "
13 w· we be beside ourselves, it is to "
13 w· we be sober, it is for your cause. "
8:23 W· any do enquire of Titus, he is "
12: 2 (w· in the body, I cannot tell; "
2 or w· out of the body, I cannot tell: "
3 (w· in the body, or out of the body, "
13: 5 yourselves, w· ye be in the faith; 1487
Eph 6: 8 the Lord, w· he be bond or free. 1535
Ph'p 1:18 w· in pretence, or in truth, Christ "
20 body, w· it be by life, or by death. "
27 w· I come and see you, or else be "
Col 1:16 w· they be thrones, or dominions, "
20 w· they be things in earth, or things"
1Th 5:10 w· we wake or sleep, we should live"
2Th 2:15 taught, w· by word, or our epistle. "
1Pe 2:13 w· it be to the king, as supreme; "
1Jo 4: 1 try the spirits w· they are of God: 1487

which See also WHO.
Ge 1: 7 the waters w· were under the 834
7 waters w· were above the firmament:"
21 w· the waters brought forth "
29 w· is upon the face of all the earth, "
29 in the w· is the fruit of a tree "
2: 2 ended his work w· he had made; "
2 from all his work w· he had made. "
3 from all his work w· God created "
11 is it w· compasseth the whole land of "
14 that is it w· goeth toward the east of "
22 rib, w· the Lord God had taken 834
3: 1 beast...w· the Lord God had made. "
3 tree w· is in the midst of the garden,"
17 the tree, of w· I commanded thee, "
24 flaming sword w· turned every way, "
4:11 earth, w· hath opened her mouth 834
5:29 ground w· the Lord hath cursed. "
6: 2 them wives of all w· they chose. * "
4 became mighty men w· were of old,‡"
15 fashion w· thou shalt make it of:* "
7:23 w· was upon the face of the ground. "
8: 6 window of the ark w· he had made: "
7 forth a raven, w· went forth to and fro.
12 w· returned not again unto him any*
9: 4 life thereof, w· is the blood thereof, "
12 covenant w· I make between me 834
15 covenant, w· is between me and you "
17 the covenant, w· I have established "
11: 5 w· the children of men builded. "
6 w· they have imagined to do. 3605, "
13: 4 altar, w· he had made there at the "
5 And Lot also, w· went with Abram,‡
15 For all the land w· thou seest, to 834
14: 2 and the king of Bela, w· is Zoar. *1931
3 vale of Siddim, w· is the salt sea. * "
6 El-paran, w· is by the wilderness. 834
15 w· is on the left hand of Damascus. "
17 of Shaveh, w· is the king's dale. *1931
20 w· hath delivered thine enemies 834
24 that w· the young men have eaten,‡ "
24 of the men w· went with me, "
16:15 son's name, w· Hagar bare, Ishmael.‡"
17:10 is my covenant, w· ye shall keep, "
12 any stranger, w· is not of thy seed.‡ "
21 w· Sarah shall bare unto thee at a ‡ "
18: 8 milk, and the calf w· he had dressed,"
10 the tent door, w· was behind him. 1931
13 a surety bear a child, w· am old? ‡ 589
17 from Abraham that thing w· I do; 834
19 that w· he hath spoken of him. "
21 to the cry of it, w· is come unto me; "
27 Lord, w· am but dust and ashes: ‡ 595
19: 5 w· came in to thee this night? ‡ 834
8 daughters w· have not known man; "
14 sons in law, w· married his daughters,‡
15 and thy two daughters, w· are here;‡
19 w· thou hast shewed unto me in 834
21 city for the w· thou hast spoken. "
25 and that w· grew upon the ground. "
29 the cities in the w· Lot dwelt. 834,2004
20: 3 for the woman w· thou hast taken;‡834
13 is thy kindness w· thou shalt shew "
21: 2 set time of w· God had spoken to "
9 w· she had born unto Abraham, "
25 well...w· Abimelech's servants had "
24:48 w· had led me in the right way to ‡ "
60 possess the gate of those w· hate them.‡
25: 7 years of Abraham's life w· he lived,834
9 the Hittite, w· is before Mamre; "
26: 2 in the land w· I shall tell thee of; "
3 oath w· I sware unto Abraham thy "
15 the wells w· his father's servants "
18 w· they had digged in the days of "
18 by w· his father had called them. "
32 concerning the well w· they had "
27:17 and the bread, w· she had prepared,"
27 of a field w· the Lord hath blessed: "
45 forget that w· thou hast done to him:"
46 w· are of the daughters of the land,*"

Ge 28: 4 land...*w'* God gave unto Abraham. 834
9 and took unto the wives *w'* he had
15 done that *w'* I have spoken to thee 834
22 this stone, *w'* I have set for a pillar, "
29: 27 service *w'* thou shalt serve with me "
30: 26 knowest my service *w'* I have done* "
30 little *w'* thou hadst before I came, "
37 white appear *w'* was in the rods. "
38 set the rods *w'* he had pilled before "
31: 1 of that *w'* was our father's hath he "
10 the rams *w'* leaped upon the cattle
12 the rams *w'* leap upon the cattle are
16 riches *w'* God hath taken from our 834
18 and all his goods *w'* he had gotten, "
18 *w'* he had gotten in Padan-aram, "
39 *w'* was torn of beasts I brought not "
43 their children *w'* they have born? ‡ 834
51 *w'* I have cast betwixt me and thee; "
32: 8 other company *w'* is left shall escape.
9 the Lord *w'* saidst unto me, Return‡
10 *w'* thou hast shewed unto thy 834
12 the sand...*w'* cannot be numbered "
13 took of that *w'* came to his hand a
32 Israel eat not of the sinew *w'* shrank,*
32 *w'* is upon the hollow of the thigh. 834
33: 5 the children *w'* God hath graciously‡"
8 thou by all this drove *w'* I met? "
18 Shechem, *w'* is in the land of Canaan,"
34: 1 of Leah, *w'* she bare unto Jacob, ‡ "
7 *w'* things ought not to be done. 3651
28 asses, and that *w'* was in the city, 834
29 the city, and that *w'* was in the field."
35: 3 was with me in the way *w'* I went. "
4 strange gods *w'* were in their hand, "
4 their earrings *w'* were in their ears; "
4 under the oak *w'* was by Shechem. "
6 Luz, *w'* is in the land of Canaan, "
12 And the land *w'* I gave Abraham "
19 way to Ephrath, *w'* is Beth-lehem. 1958
26 of Jacob, *w'* were born to him in ‡ 834
27 *w'* is Hebron, where Abraham and* "
36: 5 *w'* were born unto him in the land! "
6 *w'* he had got in the land of Canaan;"
37: 6 you, this dream *w'* I have dreamed: "
38: 10 thing *w'* he did displeased the Lord:"
14 place, *w'* is by the way to Timnath; "
39: 1 *w'* had brought him down thither. ‡ "
6 he had, save the bread *w'* he did eat,"
17 *w'* thou hast brought unto us, ‡ "
19 his wife, *w'* she spake unto him, "
23 that *w'* he did, the Lord made it to "
40: 5 of Egypt, *w'* were bound in prison.‡ "
20 day, *w'* was Pharaoh's birthday, "
41: 28 *w'* I have spoken unto Pharaoh: 834
36 *w'* shall be in the land of Egypt; "
43 in the second chariot *w'* he had; "
48 *w'* were in the land of Egypt, and "
48 field, *w'* was round about every city, "
50 sons...*w'* Asenath...bare unto him.‡ "
42: 9 the dreams *w'* he dreamed of them, "
38 him by the way in the *w'* ye go, "
43: 2 corn *w'* they had brought out of "
26 the present *w'* was in their hand "
32 the Egyptians *w'* did eat with him,‡
44: 5 not this it in *w'* my lord drinketh, 834
8 *w'* we found in our sacks' mouths, "
45: 6 in...*w'* there shall neither be earing "
27 Joseph, *w'* he had said unto them:‡ "
27 wagons *w'* Joseph had sent to carry "
46: 5 wagons *w'* Pharaoh had sent to "
6 *w'* they had gotten in the land of "
8 children of Israel, *w'* came into Egypt,
15 of Leah, *w'* she bare unto Jacob ‡ 834
20 *w'* Asenath...bare unto him. ‡ "
22 of Rachel, *w'* were born to Jacob:‡ "
25 Bilhah, *w'* Laban gave unto Rachel‡"
26 into Egypt, *w'* came out of his loins,‡
27 Joseph, *w'* were born him in Egypt,‡834
27 *w'* came into Egypt, were threescore‡
31 *w'* were in the land of Canaan, are ‡834
47: 14 for the corn *w'* they brought: "
22 their portion *w'* Pharaoh gave them:"
26 priests only, *w'* became not Pharaoh's.*
48: 5 *w'* were born unto thee in the land of‡
6 issue, *w'* thou begettest after them,‡834
15 the God *w'* fed me all my life long ‡
16 The angel *w'* redeemed me from all‡
22 *w'* I took out of the hand of the 834
49: 1 that *w'* shall befall you in the last "
30 of Machpelah, *w'* is before Mamre, "
30 *w'* Abraham bought with the field of"
50: 3 the days of those *w'* are embalmed:*
5 my grave *w'* I have digged for me 834
10 threshingfloor of Atad, *w'* is beyond "
11 Abel-mizraim, *w'* is beyond Jordan. "
13 *w'* Abraham bought with the field "
15 us all the evil *w'* we did unto him. "
24 land *w'* he sware unto Abraham, "
Ex 1: 1 of Israel, *w'* came into Egypt; ‡
8 over Egypt, *w'* knew not Joseph. ‡ 834
15 of *w'* the name of one was Shiphrah,‡"
3: 7 of my people *w'* are in Egypt, and ‡ "
4: 9 water *w'* thou takest out of the river"
19 the men are dead *w'* sought thy life.‡
21 *w'* I have put in thine hand: 834
28 signs *w'* he had commanded him. * "
5: 8 bricks, *w'* they did make heretofore, "
14 *w'* Pharaoh's taskmasters had set "
6: 8 concerning the *w'* I did swear to "
27 are they *w'* spake to Pharaoh king of ‡
7: 17 the waters *w'* are in the river, 834
8: 3 *w'* shall go up and come into thine
22 of Goshen, in *w'* my people dwell, 834
9: 3 is upon the cattle *w'* is in the field, "
19 beast *w'* shall be found in the field, "
10: 2 signs *w'* I have done among them; "

Ex 10: 5 eat the residue of that *w'* is escaped,
5 *w'* remaineth unto you from the hail,
5 every tree *w'* groweth for you out of
6 *w'* neither thy fathers, nor thy * 834
15 fruit of the trees *w'* the hail left: "
19 west wind, *w'* took away the locusts,
21 Egypt, even darkness *w'* may be felt.
12: 16 save that *w'* every man must eat, 834
19 whosoever eateth that *w'* is leavened,
25 the land *w'* the Lord will give you, 834
39 dough *w'* they brought forth out of "
13: 3 day, in *w'* ye came out from Egypt, "
5 *w'* he sware unto thy fathers to give"
8 of that *w'* the Lord did unto me
12 cometh of a beast *w'* thou hast; 834
14: 13 Lord, *w'* he will shew to you to day: "
19 *w'* went before the camp of Israel,‡
31 work *w'* the Lord did put upon the 834
15: 7 wrath *w'* consumed them as stubble.*
13 the people *w'* thou hast redeemed:‡2098
16 pass over, *w'* thou hast purchased.‡"
17 *w'* thou hast made for thee to dwell
17 Lord, *w'* thy hands have established.
25 *w'* when he had cast into the waters,*
26 wilt do that *w'* is right in his sight,
26 diseases, *w'* I have brought upon the834
16: 1 of Sin, *w'* is between Elim and Sinai,"
5 shall prepare that *w'* they bring in; "
8 *w'* ye murmur against him: "
15 *w'* the Lord hath given you to eat. "
16 thing *w'* the Lord hath commanded,"
16 man for them *w'* are in his tents. ‡ "
23 This is that *w'* the Lord hath said, "
23 bake that *w'* ye will bake to day, "
23 that *w'* remaineth over lay up for you
26 on the seventh day, *w'* is the sabbath.*
32 the thing *w'* the Lord commanded,834
18: 3 *w'* the name of the one was Gershom;‡"
9 *w'* the Lord had done to Israel, "
19: 7 words *w'* the Lord commanded "
22 priests also, *w'* come near to the Lord,‡
20: 2 *w'* have brought thee out of the ‡ 834
12 the land *w'* the Lord thy God giveth "
21: 1 *w'* thou shalt set before them. "
22: 9 *w'* another challengeth to be his, "
13 shall not make good that *w'* was torn.
23: 16 *w'* thou hast sown in the field: 834
16 *w'* is in the end of the year, "
20 into the place *w'* I have prepared. 834
28 thee, *w'* shall drive out the Hivite, "
24: 3 the words *w'* the Lord hath said 834
5 of Israel, *w'* offered burnt offerings,‡
8 *w'* the Lord hath made with you 834
12 commandments *w'* I have written; "
25: 3 offering *w'* ye shall take of them; "
16 the testimony *w'* I shall give thee. "
22 *w'* are upon the ark of the testimony,"
22 of all things *w'* I will give thee in "
40 *w'* was shewed thee in the mount. "
26: 10 of the curtain *w'* coupleth the second.*
13 that *w'* remaineth in the length of the
30 *w'* was shewed thee in the mount. 834
27: 21 the vail, *w'* is before the testimony, "
28: 4 the garments *w'* they shall make; "
8 girdle of the ephod, *w'* is upon it, "
24 *w'* are on the ends of the breastplate.*
26 *w'* is in the side of the ephod inward.834
38 *w'* the children of Israel shall hallow"
29: 27 *w'* is waved, and *w'* is heaved up, of "
27 even of that *w'* is for Aaron, "
27 and of that *w'* is for his sons: "
35 things *w'* I have commanded thee: "
38 *w'* thou shalt offer upon the altar; "
30: 37 for the perfume *w'* thou shalt make, "
32: 1 make us gods, *w'* shall go before us;"
2 *w'* are in the ears of your wives, "
3 earrings *w'* were in their ears, "
4 *w'* brought thee up out of the land‡ "
7 *w'* thou broughtest out of the land‡ "
8 of the way *w'* I commanded them: "
8 *w'* have brought up out of the land‡ "
11 *w'* thou hast brought forth out of the‡"
14 of the evil *w'* he thought to do "
20 took the calf *w'* they had made, and "
23 Make us gods, *w'* shall go before us: "
32 out of thy book *w'* thou hast written."
34 place of *w'* I have spoken unto thee:"
35 they made the calf, *w'* Aaron made. "
33: 1 people *w'* thou hast brought up out‡"
1 the land *w'* I sware unto Abraham, "
7 every one *w'* sought the Lord went out‡
7 *w'* was without the camp. 834
34: 1 in the first tables, *w'* thou brakest. "
10 people among *w'* thou art shall see "
11 that *w'* I commanded thee this day: "
34 Israel that *w'* he was commanded. "
35: 1 words *w'* the Lord hath commanded,"
4 the thing *w'* the Lord commanded, "
25 and brought that *w'* they had spun, "
29 *w'* the Lord had commanded to be 834
36: 3 *w'* the children of Israel had brought"
4 man from his work *w'* they made; "
5 *w'* the Lord commanded to make. "
12 the curtain *w'* was in the coupling* "
17 of the curtain *w'* coupleth the second.
25 *w'* is toward the north corner, he made*
37: 16 the vessels *w'* were upon the table, 834
38: 8 *w'* assembled at the door of the ‡ "
39: 19 *w'* was on the side of the ephod "
Le 1: 8, 12 is on the fire *w'* is upon the altar:"
2: 10 And that *w'* is left of the meat offering
11 *w'* ye shall bring unto the Lord, 834
3: 4 *w'* is by the flanks, and the caul "
5 *w'* is upon the wood that is on the "
10, 15 *w'* is by the flanks, and the caul "
4: 2 things *w'* ought not to be done, "

Le 4: 3 for his sin, *w'* he hath sinned, 834
7 *w'* is in the tabernacle of the "
7 *w'* is at the door of the tabernacle "
9 *w'* is by the flanks, and the caul "
13 things *w'* should not be done, "
14 sin, *w'* they have sinned against it,* "
18 of the altar *w'* is before the Lord, "
18 *w'* is at the door of the tabernacle "
22 things *w'* should not be done, "
27 things *w'* ought not to be done, "
28 Or of his sin, *w'* he hath sinned, "
28 for his sin *w'* he hath sinned. "
5: 6 Lord for his sin *w'* he hath sinned, "
7 his trespass, *w'* he hath committed, "
8 offer that *w'* is for the sin offering "
10 him for his sin *w'* he hath sinned, "
17 things *w'* are forbidden to be done "
6: 2 that *w'* was delivered him to keep,*
3 Or have found that *w'* was lost, and
4 restore that *w'* he took violently 834
4 thing *w'* he hath deceitfully gotten, "
4 that *w'* was delivered him to keep, "
4 or the lost thing *w'* he found, "
5 that about *w'* he hath sworn falsely; "
10 the ashes *w'* the fire hath consumed*"
15 *w'* is upon the meat offering, and "
20 *w'* they shall offer unto the Lord in "
7: 4 *w'* is by the flanks, and the caul that"
8 burnt offering *w'* he hath offered. "
11 *w'* he shall offer unto the Lord, "
21 offerings, *w'* pertain unto the Lord, "
24 the fat of that *w'* is torn with beasts,
25 of *w'* men offer an offering made by834
36 *W'* the Lord commanded to be "
38 *W'* the Lord commanded Moses in "
8: 5 is the thing *w'* the Lord commanded"
30 of the blood *w'* was upon the altar, "
32 And that *w'* remaineth of the flesh and
36 *w'* the Lord commanded by the 834
9: 5 brought that *w'* Moses commanded "
8 the sin offering, *w'* was for himself. "
12 *w'* he sprinkled round about upon the*
15 *w'* was the sin offering for the 834
18 offerings, *w'* was for the people: "
18 *w'* he sprinkled upon the altar round *
19 and that *w'* covereth the inwards, "
24 *w'* when all the people saw, they *
10: 1 Lord, *w'* he commanded them not. 834
6 burning *w'* the Lord hath kindled. "
11 statutes *w'* the Lord hath spoken "
14 *w'* are given out of the sacrifices of*
16 sons of Aaron *w'* were left alive, *
11: 2 These are the beasts *w'* ye shall eat834
10 any living thing *w'* is in the waters,*"
13 they *w'* ye shall have in abomination*
21 *w'* have legs above their feet, to 834
23 creeping things, *w'* have four feet, "
26 of every beast *w'* divideth the hoof, "
34 Of all meat *w'* may be eaten, "
34 that on *w'* such water cometh shall "
36 that *w'* toucheth their carcase shall be
37 any sowing seed *w'* is to be sown, 834
39 if any beast, of *w'* ye may eat, die; "
13: 18 The flesh also, in *w'*, even in the skin*
58 of skin it be, *w'* thou shalt wash, 834
14: 32 get that *w'* pertaineth to his cleansing.
34 *w'* I give to you for a possession, 834
37 *w'* in sight are lower than the wall;*
40 the stones in *w'* the plague is, 834
15: 12 that he toucheth *w'* hath the issue, "
16: 2 the mercy seat, *w'* is upon the ark; "
6 of the sin offering, *w'* is for himself, "
9 the goat upon *w'* the Lord's lot fell, "
10 on *w'* the lot fell to be the scapegoat,"
11 of the sin offering, *w'* is for himself, "
11 of the sin offering *w'* is for himself: "
23 *w'* he put on when he went into the "
17: 2 thing *w'* the Lord hath commanded, "
5 *w'* they offer in the open field, "
8 the strangers *w'* sojourn among you*"
13 *w'* hunteth and catcheth any beast‡ "
15 soul that eateth that *w'* died of itself,
15 that *w'* was torn with beasts, whether
18: 5 *w'* if a man do, he shall live in them:834
27 the land done, *w'* were before you,‡ "
30 *w'* were committed before you, "
19: 22 Lord for his sin, *w'* he hath done: "
22 sin *w'* he hath done shall be forgiven
36 *w'* brought you out of the land of ‡ 834
20: 8 I am the Lord *w'* sanctify you. ‡
23 the nation, *w'* I cast out before you.834
24 *w'* have separated you from other‡ "
25 *w'* I have separated from you as "
21: 3 virgin,...*w'* hath had no husband; ‡ "
8 I the Lord, *w'* sanctify you, am holy.‡
22: 2 things *w'* they hallow unto me: 834
3 *w'* the children of Israel hallow unto"
8 *w'* dieth of itself, or is torn with beasts,
15 Israel, *w'* they offer unto the Lord; 834
18 *w'* they will offer unto the Lord for a"
24 offer unto the Lord that *w'* is bruised,
23: 2 *w'* ye shall proclaim to be holy 834
4 *w'* ye shall proclaim in their seasons."
10 unto the land *w'* I give unto you, "
37 *w'* ye shall proclaim to be holy "
38 offerings, *w'* ye give unto the Lord. "
25: 2 come into the land *w'* I give you, "
5 That *w'* groweth of its own accord
11 neither reap that *w'* groweth of itself
25 he redeem that *w'* his brother sold.
28 then that *w'* is sold shall remain in
31 *w'* have no wall round about them. 834
38 *w'* brought you forth out of the land‡"
42 *w'* I brought forth out of the land of‡"
44 thy bondmaids, *w'* thou shalt have,‡"
45 with you, *w'* they begat in your land:

Le 26:13 w' brought you forth out of the ‡ 834
22 w' shall rob you of your children, and
32 enemies w' dwell therein shall be‡
40 trespass w' they trespassed against834
46 and laws, w' the Lord made "
27:11 of w' they do not offer a sacrifice "
22 the Lord a field w' he hath bought,
22 w' is not of the fields of his 834
26 w' should be the Lord's firstling. "
29 devoted, w' shall be devoted of men, "
34 w' the Lord commanded Moses for "
Nu 1:17 these men w' are expressed by their‡"
44 w' Moses and Aaron numbered, and‡"
2:12 those w' pitch by him shall be the*
32 those w' were numbered of the *
3: 3 the priests w' were anointed, whom‡
26 the court, w' is by the tabernacle, 834
39 w' Moses and Aaron numbered at‡ "
46 Israel, w' are more than the Levites;‡
4:37 w' Moses and Aaron did number * 834
5: 7 confess their sin w' they have done: "
9 Israel, w' they bring unto the priest,"
18 hands, w' is the jealousy offering:1958
6: 5 in the w' he separateth himself 834
18 in the fire w' is under the sacrifice "
21 according to the vow w' he vowed, "
10: 4 w' are heads of the thousands of *
25 w' was the rereward of all the camps
29 unto the place of w' the Lord said, 834
11: 5 fish, w' we did eat in Egypt freely; "
12 the land w' thou swarest unto their "
17 take of the spirit w' is upon thee, "
20 despised the Lord w' is among you,‡"
12: 3 men w' were upon the face of the‡
13: 2 w' I give unto the children of Israel:"
16 w' Moses sent to spy out the land.* "
24 w' the children of Israel cut down "
32 of the land w' they had searched "
32 through w' we have gone to search "
33 of Anak, w' come of the giants: ‡
14: 6 w' were of them that searched the ‡
7 w' we passed through to search it, 834
8 us; a land w' floweth with milk and "
11 the signs w' I have shewed among "
15 nations w' have heard the fame of‡ "
16 the land w' he sware unto them, "
22 all those men w' have seen my glory,‡
22 w' I did in Egypt and in the 834
23 the land w' I sware unto their fathers,
27 congregation, w' murmur against‡ 834
27 Israel, w' they murmur against me. "
29 w' have murmured against me, ‡ "
30 w' I sware to make you dwell * "
31 ones, w' ye said should be a prey,‡
31 know the land w' ye have despised.834
34 the days in w' ye search the land, "
36 w' Moses sent to search the land,‡
38 w' were of the men that went to *
40 place w' the Lord hath promised: 834
45 the Canaanites w' dwell in that hill,‡
15: 2 habitations, w' I give unto you. 834
39 after w' ye use to go a whoring: "
41 w' brought you out of the land of ‡ "
16:11 For w' cause both thou and all thy*
12 Eliab: w' said, We will not come up:*
40 w' is not of the seed of Aaron, come‡834
18: 9 theirs, w' they shall render unto me,"
12 w' they shall offer unto the Lord, "
13 w' they shall bring unto the Lord, "
15 flesh, w' they bring unto the Lord, "
16 the sanctuary, w' is twelve gerahs.*1958
19 w' the children of Israel offer unto 834
21 for their service w' they serve, "
24 w' they offer as an heave offering "
26 the tithes w' I have given you from "
28 w' ye receive of the children of "
19: 2 law w' the Lord hath commanded, "
2 and upon w' never came yoke. "
15 w' hath no covering bound upon it, "
20:12 unto the land w' I have given them. "
24 unto the land w' I have given unto "
21: 1 the Canaanite, w' dwelt in the south,‡
11 the wilderness w' is before Moab, 834
13 w' is in the wilderness that cometh "
20 Pisgah, w' looketh toward Jeshimon.
30 Nophah, w' reacheth unto Medeba. 834
34 the Amorites, w' dwelt at Heshbon.‡"
22: 5 Pethor, w' is by the river of the land "
11 w' covereth the face of the earth:*
20 the word w' I shall say unto thee, 834
30 upon w' thou hast ridden ever since "
36 Moab, w' is in the border of Arnon, "
36 Arnon, w' is in the utmost coast. "
23:12 w' the Lord hath put in my mouth? "
24: 4 said, w' heard the words of God, ‡ "
4 w' saw the vision of the Almighty,‡
6 lign aloes w' the Lord hath planted,
12 messengers w' thou sentest unto ‡ 834
16 w' heard the words of God, and knew‡
16 w' saw the vision of the Almighty,‡
25:18 w' was slain in the day of the plague‡
26: 4 w' went forth out of the land of Egypt.‡
9 w' were famous in the congregation,‡
27:12 land w' I have given unto the 834
17 W' may go out before them, and ‡ "
17 and w' may go in before them, and‡ "
17 and w' may lead them out, and ‡ "
17 w' may bring them in; that the ‡ "
17 not as sheep w' have no shepherd. "
28: 3 fire w' ye shall offer unto the Lord; "
6 w' was ordained in mount Sinai for a
23 w' is for a continual burnt offering.834
30: 1 thing w' the Lord hath commanded."
8 shall make her vow w' she vowed, "
8 and that w' she uttered with her lips, *
14 or all her bonds, w' are upon her: 834

Nu 30:16 w' the Lord commanded Moses, 834
31:12 plains of Moab, w' are by Jordan "
14 hundreds, w' came from the battle.‡
21 the men of war w' went to the battle,‡
21 w' the Lord commanded Moses; 834
28 the men of war w' went out to battle:*
30 w' keep the charge of the tabernacle‡
32 prey w' the men of war had caught 834
36 w' was the portion of them that went
38, 39, 40 of w' the Lord's tribute was
41 w' was the Lord's heave offering,
42 w' Moses divided from the men ‡ 834
47 w' kept the charge of the tabernacle‡
48 officers w' were over thousands ‡ 834
49 men of war w' are under our charge,‡"
32: 4 country w' the Lord smote before "
7 land w' the Lord hath given them? "
9 land w' the Lord hath given them: "
11 the land w' I sware unto Abraham, "
24 w' hath proceeded out of your mouth.
38 unto the cities w' they builded. 834
39 the Amorite w' was in it. ‡ "
33: 1 w' went forth out of the land of ‡ "
4 firstborn, w' the Lord had smitten‡ "
6 w' is in the edge of the wilderness. "
7 w' is before Baal-zephon: "
36 wilderness of Zin, w' is Kadesh. *1958
55 those w' ye let remain of them shall‡834
34:17 w' shall divide the land unto you:‡ "
35: 4 w' ye shall give unto the Levites, "
6 w' ye shall give unto the Levites "
7 cities w' ye shall give to the Levites "
8 the cities w' ye shall give shall be "
8 to his inheritance w' he inheriteth. "
11 w' killeth any person at unawares.‡
13 And of these cities w' ye shall give, 834
14 of Canaan, w' shall be cities of refuge.*
25 w' was anointed with the holy oil.‡ 834
31 a murderer, w' is guilty of death:‡ "
34 the land w' ye shall inhabit, "
36: 6 thing w' the Lord doth command "
13 w' the Lord commanded by the "
De 1: 1 w' Moses spake unto all Israel "
4 the Amorites, w' dwelt in Heshbon,‡"
4 w' dwelt at Astaroth in Edrei: ‡ "
8 the land w' the Lord sware unto "
14 thing w' thou hast spoken is good "
18 time all the things w' ye shall do. "
19 wilderness, w' ye saw by the way "
20 w' the Lord our God doth give unto "
25 w' the Lord our God doth give us "
30 Lord your God w' goeth before you,*
35 land, w' I sware to give unto your 834
38 son of Nun, w' standeth before thee,‡
39 ones, w' ye said should be a prey,‡ 834
39 w' in that day had no knowledge ‡ "
44 Amorites, w' dwelt in that mountain,‡
2: 4 the children of Esau, w' dwelt in Seir;‡
8 children of Esau, w' dwelt in Seir,‡
11 W' also were accounted giants, *1992
12 w' the Lord gave unto them. 834
14 the space in w' we came from "
22 the children of Esau, w' dwelt in Seir,‡
23 And the Avims w' dwelt in Hazerim,‡
23 w' came forth out of Caphtor, *
29 the children of Esau w' dwell in Seir,‡
29 Moabites w' dwell in Ar, did unto me;)‡
29 into the land w' the Lord our God 834
35 the spoil of the cities w' we took. "
36 Aroer, w' is by the brink of the river "
3: 2 the Amorites, w' dwelt at Heshbon.‡"
4 not a city w' we took not from them,"
9 (W' Hermon the Sidonians call
12 land, w' we possessed at that time,*
12 w' is by the river Arnon, and half 834
13 w' was called the land of giants, *1931
16 w' is the border of the children of
19 your cities w' I have given you; 834
20 w' the Lord your God hath given "
20 possession, w' I have given you. "
28 inherit the land w' thou shalt see. "
4: 1 judgments, w' I teach you, for to do "
2 unto the word w' I command you, "
2 Lord your God w' I command you. "
6 w' shall hear all these statutes, and‡"
8 law, w' I set before you this day? "
9 the things w' thine eyes have seen, "
13 w' he commanded you to perform, "
19 w' the Lord thy God hath divided "
21 w' the Lord thy God giveth thee for "
23 covenant...w' he made with you, "
23 w' the Lord thy God hath forbidden "
28 w' neither see, nor hear, nor eat, "
31 fathers w' he sware unto them. "
32 that are past, w' were before thee, "
40 w' I command thee this day, "
40 w' the Lord thy God giveth thee, "
42 w' should kill his neighbour ‡ "
44 law w' Moses set before the children"
45 w' Moses spake unto the children of "
47 w' were on this side Jordan toward‡"
48 w' is by the bank of the river Arnon "
5: 1 w' I speak in your ears this day, "
6 God, w' brought thee out of the land‡"
16 land w' the Lord thy God giveth "
28 w' they have spoken unto thee: "
31 judgments, w' thou shalt teach them,"
31 them in the land w' I give them "
33 w' the Lord your God...commanded "
33 in the land w' ye shall possess. "
6: 1 w' the Lord your God commanded "
2 commandments, w' I command thee,"
6 words, w' I command thee this day, "
10 land w' he sware unto thy fathers, "
10 goodly cities, w' thou buildedst not, "
11 good things, w' thou filledst not, "

De 6:11 wells digged, w' thou diggedst not, 834
11 olive trees, w' thou plantedst not; "
12 w' brought thee forth out of the ‡ "
14 the people w' are round about you;‡ "
17 w' he hath commanded thee. "
18 shalt do that w' is right and good "
18 w' the Lord sware unto thy fathers, "
20 w' the Lord our God...commanded "
23 land w' he sware unto our fathers. "
7: 8 w' he had sworn unto your fathers, "
9 w' keepeth covenant and mercy ‡ "
11 w' I command thee this day, to do "
12 land w' he sware unto thy fathers: "
13 land w' he sware unto thy fathers "
15 diseases of Egypt, w' thou knowest, "
16 w' the Lord thy God shall deliver "
19 temptations w' thine eyes saw, "
8: 1 commandments w' I command thee "
1 land w' the Lord sware unto your "
2 way w' the Lord thy God led thee "
3 with manna, w' thou knewest not, "
10 good land w' he hath given thee. "
11 w' I command thee this day: "
14 w' brought thee forth out of the land‡
16 manna, w' thy fathers knew not, 834
18 w' he sware unto thy fathers, as it "
20 nations w' the Lord destroyeth ‡ "
9: 3 God, is he w' goeth over before thee;‡
5 w' the Lord sware unto thy fathers,834
9 covenant w' the Lord made with "
10 words w' the Lord spake with you "
12 w' thou hast brought forth out of ‡ "
16 way w' the Lord had commanded "
18 your sins w' ye sinned, in doing "
21 your sin, the calf w' ye had made, "
23 the land w' I have given you; "
26 w' thou hast redeemed through thy‡"
26 w' thou hast brought forth out of ‡ "
28 into the land w' he promised them, "
29 w' thou broughtest out by thy ‡ "
10: 2 in the first tables w' thou brakest, "
4 w' the Lord spake unto you in the "
5 the tables in the ark w' I had made;"
11 w' I sware unto their fathers to "
13 w' I command thee this day for "
17 w' regardeth not persons, nor ‡ "
21 terrible things, w' thine eyes have "
11: 2 your children w' have not known, ‡ "
3 acts, w' he did in the midst of Egypt"
7 great acts of the Lord w' he did. "
8 commandments w' I command you "
9 w' the Lord sware unto your fathers "
12 A land w' the Lord thy God careth "
13 commandments w' I command you "
21 w' the Lord sware unto your fathers"
22 commandments w' I command you, "
27 w' I command you this day: "
28 the way w' I command you this day, "
28 other gods, w' ye have not known. "
30 w' dwell in the champaign over ‡
31 w' the Lord your God giveth you, 834
32 judgments w' I set before you this "
12: 1 w' ye shall observe to do in the land,"
1 w' the Lord God of thy fathers hath "
2 the nations w' ye shall possess ‡ "
5 w' the Lord your God shall choose "
9 w' the Lord your God giveth you. "
10 w' the Lord your God giveth you "
11 w' the Lord your God shall choose "
11 vows w' ye vowed unto the Lord: "
14 the place w' the Lord shall choose "
15 Lord thy God w' he hath given thee:"
17 nor any of thy vows w' thou vowest, "
18 w' the Lord thy God shall choose, "
21 w' the Lord thy God hath chosen "
21 flock, w' the Lord hath given thee, "
25 do that w' is right in the sight of the
26 Only thy holy things w' thou hast, 834
26 the place w' the Lord shall choose: "
28 all these words w' I command thee, "
28 doest that w' is good and right in
31 abomination...w' he hateth, 834
13: 2 other gods, w' thou hast not known, "
5 w' brought you out of the land of ‡
6 friend, w' is as thine own soul, ‡ 834
6 other gods, w' thou hast not known, "
7 the people w' are round about you, "
10 w' brought thee out of the land of‡
12 w' the Lord thy God hath given 834
13 other gods, w' ye have not known, "
18 commandments w' I command thee "
18 do that w' is right in the eyes of the
14: 4 are the beasts w' ye shall eat: 834
12 these are they of w' ye shall not eat: "
23 in the place w' he shall choose to "
24 w' the Lord thy God shall choose "
25 w' the Lord thy God shall choose: "
29 the widow, w' are within thy gates,‡ "
29 work of thine hand w' thou doest. "
15: 3 that w' is thine with thy brother * "
4 land w' the Lord thy God giveth "
5 w' I command thee this day, "
7 land w' the Lord thy God giveth "
8 for his need, in that w' he wanteth. "
20 the place w' the Lord shall choose, "
16: 2 the place w' the Lord shall choose "
4 w' thou sacrificedst the first day at "
5 w' the Lord thy God giveth thee: "
6 w' the Lord thy God shall choose "
7 place w' the Lord thy God shall "
10 w' thou shalt give unto the Lord "
11 w' the Lord thy God hath chosen "
15 the place w' the Lord shall choose: "
16 God in the place w' he shall choose; "
17 Lord thy God w' he hath given thee. "
18 w' the Lord thy God giveth thee, "

De 16:20 That *w·* is altogether just shalt thou
20 land *w·* the Lord thy God giveth 834
21 thy God, *w·* thou shalt make thee. "
22 image; *w·* the Lord thy God hateth. "
17: 2 *w·* the Lord thy God giveth thee, "
3 heaven, *w·* I have not commanded; "
5 *w·* have committed that wicked ‡ "
8 *w·* the Lord thy God shall choose. "
10 sentence, *w·* they of that place "
10 place *w·* the Lord shall choose "
11 of the law *w·* they shall teach thee, "
11 judgment *w·* they shall tell thee, "
11 sentence *w·* they shall shew thee, "
14 land *w·* the Lord thy God giveth thee, "
15 over thee, *w·* is not thy brother. ‡ "
18 out of that *w·* is before the priests "
18: 6 the place *w·* the Lord shall choose; 834
7 do, *w·* stand there before the Lord. ‡
8 that *w·* cometh of the sale of his
9 land *w·* the Lord thy God giveth 834
14 these nations, *w·* thou shalt possess, "
17 spoken that *w·* they have spoken. "
19 my words *w·* he shall speak in my "
20 *w·* shall presume to speak a word in‡"
20 *w·* I have not commanded him to "
21 word *w·* the Lord hath not spoken? 834
22 thing *w·* the Lord hath not spoken, "
19: 2, 3 *w·* the Lord thy God giveth thee to "
4 the slayer, *w·* shall flee thither, ‡ "
8 land *w·* he promised to give unto "
9 them, *w·* I command thee this day, "
10 land, *w·* the Lord thy God giveth thee "
14 *w·* they of old time have set in thine "
14 *w·* thou shalt inherit in the land "
16 testify against him that *w·* is wrong;*
17 judges, *w·* shall be in those days; ‡ 834
20 And those *w·* remain shall hear, ‡
20: 1 *w·* brought thee up out of the land‡ 834
14 *w·* the Lord thy God hath given "
15 all the cities *w·* are very far off from
15 *w·* are not of the cities of these 834
16 *w·* the Lord thy God doth give thee "
18 *w·* they have done unto their gods; "
20 Only the trees *w·* thou knowest that "
21: 1 land *w·* the Lord thy God giveth "
2 cities *w·* are round about him that "
3 the city *w·* is next unto the slain man, "
3 *w·* had not been wrought with, 834
3 and *w·* hath not drawn in the yoke; "
4 valley, *w·* is neither eared nor sown, "
9 do that *w·* is right in the sight of the "
16 his sons to inherit that *w·* he hath, 834
16 the hated, *w·* is indeed the firstborn:‡
18 *w·* will not obey the voice of his father,‡
23 *w·* the Lord thy God giveth thee 834
22: 3 of thy brother's, *w·* he hath lost, "
5 wear that *w·* pertaineth unto a man, "
9 fruit of thy seed *w·* thou hast sown,834
28 is a virgin, *w·* is not betrothed, ‡ "
23: 15 the servant *w·* is escaped from his‡ "
16 in that place *w·* he shall choose "
23 That *w·* is gone out of thy lips thou "
23 *w·* thou hast promised with thy "
24: 3 die, *w·* took her to be his wife; ‡ 834
4 former husband, *w·* sent her away,‡ "
4 *w·* the Lord thy God giveth thee for "
25: 6 the firstborn *w·* she beareth shall ‡ "
6 in the name of his brother *w·* is dead, ‡
15, 19 land *w·* the Lord thy God giveth 834
26: 1 the land *w·* the Lord giveth thee for "
2 *w·* thou shalt bring of thy land "
2 place *w·* the Lord God shall choose "
3 *w·* the Lord sware unto our father "
10 *w·* thou, O Lord, hast given me. "
11 good thing *w·* the Lord hath given "
12 third year, *w·* is the year of tithing, "
13 *w·* thou hast commanded me: 834
15 and the land *w·* thou hast given us, "
19 above all nations *w·* he hath made,‡ "
27: 1 commandments *w·* I command you "
2, 3 *w·* the Lord thy God giveth thee, "
4 stones, *w·* I command you this day, "
10 statutes, *w·* I command thee this day. "
28: 1 commandments *w·* I command you "
8 land *w·* the Lord thy God giveth "
11 *w·* the Lord sware unto thy fathers "
13 thy God, *w·* I command thee this day, "
14 words *w·* I command thee this day, "
15 statutes *w·* I command thee this day; "
33 nation *w·* thou knowest not eat up;‡ "
34 sight of thine eyes *w·* thou shalt see. "
36 thy king *w·* thou shalt set over thee, "
36 nation *w·* neither thou nor thy fathers‡
45 his statutes *w·* he commanded thee. 834
48 *w·* the Lord shall send against thee, "
50 *w·* shall not regard the person of ‡ "
51 *w·* also shall not leave thee either‡ "
52, 53 *w·* the Lord thy God hath given "
54 of his children *w·* he shall leave: ‡ "
56 *w·* would not adventure to set the‡ "
57 her children *w·* she shall bear: ‡ "
60 of Egypt, *w·* thou wast afraid of; "
61 *w·* is not written in the book of this "
64 *w·* neither thou nor thy fathers "
67 sight of thine eyes *w·* thou shalt see. "
29: 1 *w·* the Lord commanded Moses to "
3 *w·* thine eyes have seen, the signs, "
12 *w·* the Lord thy God maketh with "
16 through...nations *w·* ye passed by;‡ "
17 and gold, *w·* were among them:) "
22 *w·* the Lord hath laid upon it; * "
23 *w·* the Lord overthrew in his anger, "
25 *w·* he made with them when he "
29 those things *w·* are revealed belong *
30: 1 the curse, *w·* I have set before thee,834
5 the land *w·* thy fathers possessed, "

De 30: 7 that hate thee, *w·* persecuted thee. 834
8 commandments *w·* I commanded "
10 statutes *w·* are written in this book "
11 commandment *w·* I command thee 834
20 *w·* the Lord sware unto thy fathers, "
31: 5 *w·* I have commanded you. "
7 land *w·* the Lord hath sworn unto "
9 *w·* bare the ark of the covenant of "
11 God in the place *w·* he shall choose,834
13 children *w·* have not known any ‡ "
18 evils *w·* they shall have wrought, "
20 land *w·* I sware unto their fathers, "
21 their imagination *w·* they go about, "
21 them into the land *w·* I sware. "
23 into the land *w·* I sware unto them: "
25 *w·* bare the ark of the covenant of ‡ "
29 from the way *w·* I have commanded "
32: 15 then he forsook God *w·* made him, "
21 jealously with that *w·* is not God; "
21 with those *w·* are not a people; ‡ "
38 *W·* did eat the fat of their 834
46 all the words *w·* I testify among you "
46 *w·* ye shall command your children "
49 Nebo, *w·* is in the land of Moab, "
49 Canaan, *w·* I give unto the children "
52 land *w·* I give the children of Israel. "
34: 4 the land *w·* I sware unto Abraham, "
11 the wonders, *w·* the Lord sent him "
12 the great terror *w·* Moses shewed "
Jos 1: 2 unto the land *w·* I do give to them, "
6 *w·* I sware unto their fathers to give "
7 *w·* Moses my servant commanded "
11 *w·* the Lord your God giveth you to "
13 word *w·* Moses the servant of the "
14 in the land *w·* Moses gave you on this "
15 *w·* the Lord your God giveth them: "
15 *w·* Moses the Lord's servant gave "
2: 3 *w·* are entered into thine house: "
6 *w·* she had laid in order upon the "
7 they *w·* pursued after them were ‡ 834
17 oath *w·* thou hast made us swear. "
18 window *w·* thou didst let us down by: "
20 oath *w·* thou hast made us to swear. "
3: 4 know the way by *w·* ye must go: "
16 the waters *w·* came down from above "
4: 9 priests *w·* bare the ark of the covenant‡
10 priests *w·* bare the ark stood in the‡
20 stones *w·* they took out of Jordan, 834
23 sea, *w·* he dried up from before us, "
5: 1 *w·* were on the side of Jordan ‡ "
1 the Canaanites, *w·* were by the sea,‡ "
6 men of war, *w·* came out of Egypt,‡
6 land, *w·* the Lord sware unto their 834
6: 25 *w·* Joshua sent to spy out Jericho.‡
7: 2 Jericho to Ai, *w·* is beside Beth-aven, "
11 my covenant *w·* I commanded them: "
14 tribe *w·* the Lord taketh shall come‡ "
14 the family *w·* the Lord shall take ‡ "
8: 27 Lord...*w·* he commanded Joshua. "
31 over *w·* no man hath lifted up any "
32 *w·* he wrote in the presence of the "
33 *w·* bare the ark of the covenant of the
35 *w·* Joshua read not before all the 834
9: 1 kings *w·* were on this side Jordan,‡ "
10 king of Bashan, *w·* was at Ashtaroth.‡ "
13 And these bottles of wine *w·* we filled, "
20 of the oath *w·* we sware unto them. "
27 in the place *w·* he should choose. "
10: 11 more *w·* died with hailstones than‡ "
20 the rest *w·* remained of them entered‡
24 of the men of war *w·* went with him,‡
27 mouth, *w·* remain until this very day.*
32 of Israel, *w·* took it on the second day,*
12: 1 *w·* the children of Israel smote, * 834
2 *w·* is upon the bank of the river "
2 *w·* is the border of the children of* "
4 *w·* was of the remnant of the giants,*
7 *w·* Joshua and the children of * 834
7 *w·* Joshua gave unto the tribes of* "
9 the king of Ai, *w·* is beside Beth-el,834
13: 3 From Sihor, *w·* is before Egypt, "
3 *w·* is counted to the Canaanite: "
8 inheritance, *w·* Moses gave them, 834
10 Amorites, *w·* reigned in Heshbon, ‡ "
12 *w·* reigned in Ashtaroth and in ‡ "
21 Amorites, *w·* reigned in Heshbon, ‡ "
21 and Reba, *w·* were dukes of Sihon,‡
30 towns of Jair, *w·* are in Bashan, 834
32 countries *w·* Moses did distribute "
14: 1 *w·* the children of Israel inherited "
1 *w·* Eleazar the priest, and Joshua "
15 *w·* Arba was a great man among the
15: 7 *w·* is on the south side of the river: 834
8 *w·* is at the end of the valley of the "
9 to Baalah, *w·* is Kirjath-jearim: *1958
10 of mount Jearim, *w·* is Chesalon, * 834
13 father of Anak, *w·* city is Hebron.*1958
25 Kerioth, and Hezron, *w·* is Hazor,* "
49 and Kirjath-sannah, *w·* is Debir, * "
54 and Kirjath-arba, *w·* is Hebron, * "
60 Kirjath-baal, *w·* is Kirjath-jearim,* "
17: 5 *w·* were on the other side Jordan; 834
18: 2 tribes, *w·* had not yet received their‡ "
3 *w·* the Lord God of your fathers "
7 *w·* Moses the servant of the Lord "
13 to the side of Luz, *w·* is Beth-el, *1958
14 Kirjath-baal, *w·* is Kirjath-jearim,* "
16 and *w·* is in the valley of the giants 834
17 *w·* is over against the going up of "
28 and Jebusi, *w·* is Jerusalem, *1958
19: 50 they gave him the city *w·* he asked,834
51 *w·* Eleazar the priest, and Joshua "
20: 7 and Kirjath-arba, *w·* is Hebron, *1958
21: 4 the priest, *w·* were of the Levites,‡
9 these cities *w·* are mentioned by 834
10 *W·* the children of Aaron, being of*

Jos 21: 11 father of Anak, *w·* city is Hebron,*1958
20 Levites *w·* remained of the children*
40 *w·* were remaining of the families of*
43 land *w·* he sware to give unto their 834
45 good thing *w·* the Lord had spoken "
22: 4, 5 *w·* Moses the servant of the Lord "
9 Shiloh, *w·* is in the land of Canaan, "
17 from *w·* we are not cleansed until "
28 of the Lord, *w·* our fathers made, "
30 of Israel *w·* were with him, heard ‡ "
23: 13 *w·* the Lord your God hath given "
14 things *w·* the Lord your God spake "
15 *w·* the Lord your God promised you; "
15 *w·* the Lord your God hath given "
16 your God, *w·* he commanded you, "
16 good land *w·* he hath given unto you "
24: 5 according to that *w·* I did among "
8 *w·* dwelt on the other side Jordan;‡
12 *w·* drave them out from before you, "
13 you a land for *w·* ye did not labour,*834
13 cities *w·* ye built not, and ye dwell in "
13 olive yards *w·* ye planted not do ye "
14, 15 the gods *w·* your fathers served‡ "
17 *w·* did those great signs in our sight,* "
18 the Amorites *w·* dwelt in the land:‡ "
23 strange gods *w·* are among you, ‡ 834
27 words of the Lord *w·* he spake unto "
30 *w·* is in mount Ephraim, on the north "
31 *w·* had known all the works of the* "
32 *w·* the children of Israel brought up "
32 parcel of ground *w·* Jacob bought "
33 his son, *w·* was given him in mount "
J'g 1: 16 Judah, *w·* lieth in the south of Arad; "
26 *w·* is the name thereof unto this 1931
2: 1 land *w·* I sware unto your fathers; 834
10 after them, *w·* knew not the Lord, "
12 *w·* brought them out of the land of‡ "
16 *w·* delivered them out of the hand of‡
17 the way *w·* their fathers walked in,*834
20 my covenant *w·* I commanded their "
21 nations *w·* Joshua left when he died:‡ "
3: 1 are the nations *w·* the Lord left, ‡ "
4 *w·* he commanded their fathers by "
16 made him a dagger *w·* had two edges, "
20 *w·* he had made for himself alone:*834
31 *w·* slew of the Philistines six hundred‡
4: 2 was Sisera, *w·* dwelt in Harosheth "
11 *w·* was of the children of Hobab the* "
11 plain of Zaanaim, *w·* is by Kedesh. 834
14 in *w·* the Lord hath delivered Sisera "
6: 2 the dens *w·* are in the mountains, "
8 children of Israel, *w·* said unto them,*
11 sat under an oak *w·* was in Ophrah,834
13 miracles *w·* our fathers told us of, "
26 the grove *w·* thou shalt cut down. "
8: 27 *w·* thing became a snare unto Gideon,*
35 goodness *w·* he had shewed unto 835
9: 2 *w·* are threescore and ten persons,‡
4 and light persons, *w·* followed him.‡
13 my wine, *w·* cheereth God and man, "
24 their brother, *w·* slew them; ‡ 834
24 *w·* aided him in the killing of his ‡ "
56 Abimelech *w·* he did unto his father, "
10: 4 *w·* are called Havoth-jair unto this "
4 day, *w·* are in the land of Gilead. 834
8 land of the Amorites, *w·* is in Gilead. "
14 unto the gods *w·* ye have chosen; ‡ "
11: 24 possess that *w·* Chemosh thy god "
28 words of Jephthah *w·* he sent him. "
36 *w·* hath proceeded out of thy mouth; "
39 to his vow *w·* he had vowed: "
12: 5 those Ephraimites *w·* were escaped*
13: 8 the man of God *w·* thou didst send*834
14: 19 unto them *w·* expounded the riddle.*
15: 19 *w·* is in Lehi unto this day. 834
16: 8 green withs *w·* had not been dried, "
24 of our country, *w·* slew many of us.‡ "
29 pillars upon *w·* the house stood, "
29 and on *w·* it was borne up, of the one*
30 So the dead *w·* he slew at his death‡834
30 than they *w·* he slew in his life. ‡ "
17: 2 from thee; about *w·* thou cursedst, "
6 man did that *w·* was right in his own "
18: 5 way *w·* we go shall be prosperous. 834
16 *w·* were of the children of Dan, stood‡ "
24 have taken away my gods *w·* I made, "
27 took the things *w·* Micah had made, "
27 and the priest *w·* he had, and came‡ "
31 Micah's graven image, *w·* he made, "
19: 10 against Jebus, *w·* is Jerusalem; *1958
14 Gibeah, *w·* belongeth to Benjamin. 834
16 even, *w·* was also of mount Ephraim;*
19 young man *w·* is with thy servants:‡ "
20: 9 the thing *w·* we will do to Gibeah; 834
13 children of Belial, *w·* are in Gibeah,‡ "
15 *w·* were numbered seven hundred‡
18 *W·* of us shall go up first to the *4310
31 of *w·* one goeth up to the house of 834
36 wait *w·* they had set beside Gibeah.‡ "
42 them *w·* came out of the cities they‡ "
46 all *w·* fell that day of Benjamin were‡
21: 12 Shiloh, *w·* is in the land of Canaan. 834
14 them wives *w·* they had saved alive‡ "
19 *w·* is on the north side of Beth-el "
25 did that *w·* was right in his own eyes. "
Ru 1: 22 her, *w·* returned out of the country of‡
2: 9 that *w·* the young men have drawn.834
11 *w·* thou knewest not heretofore. "
4: 3 *w·* was our brother Elimelech's: "
11 *w·* two did build the house of Israel:‡ "
12 the seed *w·* the Lord shall give thee "
14 Lord, *w·* hath not left thee this day‡ "
15 daughter in law *w·* loveth thee, "
15 *w·* is better to thee than seven‡834,1931
1Sa 1: 27 me my petition *w·* I asked of him: 834
2: 20 for the loan *w·* is lent to the Lord. "

1Sa 2:29 offering, w· I have commanded in 834
32 wealth w· God shall give Israel: "
35 to that w· is in mine heart and in my"
3:11 at w· both the ears of every one that "
12 Eli all things w· I have spoken "
13 for the iniquity w· he knoweth; "
4: 4 w· dwelleth between the cherubims: "
6: 4 offering w· we shall return to him? 834
7 kine, on w· there hath come no yoke, "
8 w· ye return him for a trespass "
17 golden emerods w· the Philistines "
18 w· stone remaineth unto this day in
7:14 cities w· the Philistines had taken 834
8: 8 to all the works w· they have done "
18 king w· ye shall have chosen you; "
9:22 bidden, w· were about thirty persons.
23 Bring the portion w· I gave thee, 834
23 of w· I said unto thee, Set it by thee. "
24 shoulder, and that w· was upon it,
24 Behold that w· is left! set it before
10: 2 asses w· thou wentest to seek are 834
4 w· thou shalt receive of their hands.
11:11 that they w· remained were scattered,‡
12: 7 w· he did to you and to your fathers.834
8 w· brought forth your fathers out of*
16 w· the Lord will do before your 834
17 w· ye have done in the sight of the "
21 things, w· cannot profit nor deliver: "
13: 5 as the sand w· is on the sea shore in "
13 thy God, w· he commanded thee: "
14 that w· the Lord commanded thee. "
14: 2 pomegranate tree w· is in Migron: "
4 w· Jonathan sought to go over unto "
14 w· Jonathan and his armourbearer "
14 land, w· a yoke of oxen might plow.*
21 w· went up with them into the ‡ 834
22 men of Israel w· had hid themselves
30 of their enemies w· they found? ‡ 834
39 as the Lord liveth, w· saveth Israel,‡
15: 2 I remember that w· Amalek did to 834
14 the lowing of the oxen w· I hear? "
20 gone the way w· the Lord sent me,
21 w· should have been utterly destroyed,
16: 4 Samuel did that w· the Lord spake,834
16 thy servants, w· are before thee, ‡
19 thy son, w· is with the sheep. 834
17: 1 at Shochoh, w· belongeth to Judah, "
31 words were heard w· David spake, "
40 them in a shepherd's bag w· he had, "
20:23 matter w· thou and I have spoken "
27 w· was the second day of the month,
36 out now the arrows w· I shoot. 834
37 of the arrow w· Jonathan had shot, "
22: 9 w· was set over the servants of ‡1931
14 as David, w· is the king's son in law,‡
23:13 his men, w· were about six hundred,‡
19 w· is on the south of Jeshimon? 834
24: 4 the day of w· the Lord said unto thee,"
25: 7 now thy shepherds w· were with us,*"
27 this blessing w· thine handmaid "
32 w· sent thee this day to meet me: ‡ "
33 be thou, w· hast kept me this day ‡ "
34 w· hath kept me back from hurting‡"
35 hand that w· she had brought him, "
44 the son of Laish, w· was of Gallim.‡ "
26: 1 Hachilah, w· is before Jeshimon? "
3 Hachilah, w· is before Jeshimon, "
28:21 words w· thou spakest unto me. "
29: 1 by a fountain w· is in Jezreel. "
3 w· hath been with me these days, ‡ "
4 to his place w· thou hast appointed*"
30:10 w· were so faint that they could not‡"
14 the coast w· belongeth to Judah, "
17 men, w· rode upon camels, and fled.‡"
20 w· they drave before those other
21 w· were so faint that they could ‡ 834
23 that w· the Lord hath given us, "
27 To them w· were in Beth-el, and to‡ "
27 to them w· were in south Ramoth,‡ "
27 and to them w· were in Jattir, ‡ "
28 And to them w· were in Aroer, ‡ "
28 and to them w· were in Siphmoth,‡ "
28 and to them w· were in Eshtemoa,‡ "
29 to them w· were in Rachal, and to‡ "
29, 29 them w· were in the cities of the‡ "
30 to them w· were in Hormah, and to‡ "
30 and to them w· were in Chor-ashan,‡ "
30 and to them w· were in Athach, ‡ "
31 to them w· were in Hebron, and to‡ "
31:11 w· the Philistines had done to Saul;
2Sa 2:15 w· pertained to Ish-bosheth the son*
16 Helkath-hazzurim, w· is in Gibeon.834
32 of his father, w· is in Beth-lehem. "
3: 8 w· against Judah do shew kindness*"
14 wife Michal, w· I espoused to me ‡ "
26 w· brought him again from the well‡
4: 8 thine enemy, w· sought thy life; ‡ 834
5: 6 w· spake unto David, saying, Except‡
6: 4 of Abinadab w· was at Gibeah, "
21 Lord, w· chose me before thy father,‡"
22 maidservants w· thou hast spoken‡ "
7:12 w· shall proceed out of thy bowels,‡ "
23 w· thou redeemest to thee from ‡ "
8:11 W· also king David did dedicate unto
11 of all nations w· he subdued; ‡ 834
9: 3 hath yet a son, w· is lame on his feet.‡
10: 12 Lord do that w· seemeth him good.
12: 3 w· he had bought and nourished 834
13:10 took the cakes w· she had made, "
23 Baal-hazor, w· is beside Ephraim: "
14: 7 they shall quench my coal w· is left, "
13 speak this thing as one w· is faulty,‡
14 w· cannot be gathered up again; 834
15: 4 every man w· hath any suit or cause‡"
7 w· I have vowed unto the Lord, in "
16 left ten women, w· were concubines,‡

2Sa 15:18 six hundred men w· came after ‡ 834
16:11 my son w· came forth of my bowels,‡ "
21 w· he had left to keep the house; ‡ "
23 w· he counselled in those days, "
17:10 they w· be with him are valiant ‡ "
18 Bahurim, w· had a well in his court;*
25 w· Amasa was a man's son, whose*
18:18 a pillar, w· is in the king's dale: 834
28 w· hath delivered up the men that‡ "
19: 5 w· this day have saved thy life, ‡
16 a Benjamite, w· was of Bahurim, ‡ 834
19 remember that w· thy servant did "
38 that w· shall seem good unto thee: "
20: 5 set time w· he had appointed him. 834
8 the great stone w· is in Gibeon, "
21:12 w· had stolen them from the street‡ "
16 w· was of the sons of the giant, ‡ "
18 w· was of the sons of the giant. ‡ "
22:44 a people w· I knew not shall serve me.‡
23:15 of Beth-lehem, w· is by the gate! 834
24: 2 of the host, w· was with him, ‡ "
1Ki 1: 8 mighty men w· belonged to David,‡ "
9 of Zoheleth, w· is by En-rogel, "
48 w· hath given one to sit on my ‡ "
2: 4 word w· he spake concerning me, "
8 w· cursed me with a grievous *1931
24 liveth, w· hath established me, * 834
27 w· he spake concerning the house of"
31 the innocent blood, w· Joab shed, "
44 wickedness w· thine heart is privy to,"
46 w· went out, and fell upon him, that*
3: 8 thy people w· thou hast chosen, ‡ 834
13 thee that w· thou hast not asked, "
21 it was not my son, w· I did bear. ‡ "
28 judgment w· the king had judged; "
4: 2 These were the princes w· he had;‡ "
7 w· provided victuals for the king and‡
11 w· had Taphath the daughter of * "
12 w· is by Zartanah beneath Jezreel,
13 son of Manasseh, w· are in Gilead; 834
13 region of Argob, w· is in Bashan, "
19 the only officer w· was in the land.‡ "
20 sand w· is by the sea in multitude, "
34 earth, w· had heard of his wisdom.‡ "
5: 3 for the wars w· were about him "
7 w· hath given unto David a wise son‡"
8 things w· thou sentest to me for: "
16 Solomon's officers w· were over the*"
16 w· ruled over the people that wrought‡
6: 1 month Zif, w· is the second month,1931
2 house w· king Solomon built for 834
12 this house w· thou art building, "
12 w· I spake unto David thy father: "
20 covered the altar w· was of cedar.
38 Bul, w· is the eighth month, 1931
7: 8 the porch, w· was of the like work.
17 chapiters w· were upon the top of 834
20 the belly w· was by the network: "
41 chapiters w· were upon the tops of* "
45 w· Hiram made to king Solomon "
51 the things w· David his father had
8: 1 out of the city of David, w· is Zion.1958
2 w· is the seventh month. 1931
9 w· Moses put there at Horeb, 834
15 w· spake with his mouth unto "
21 Lord, w· he made with our fathers, "
26 w· thou spakest unto thy servant "
28 w· thy servant prayeth before thee "
29 the place of w· thou hast said, * "
29 prayer w· thy servant shall make "
34 w· thou gavest unto their fathers. "
36 w· thou hast given unto thy people "
38 w· shall know every man the plague‡"
40 land w· thou gavest unto our fathers."
43 house w· I have builded, is called by"
44 toward the city w· thou hast chosen,"
48 enemies, w· led them away captive,‡"
48 w· thou gavest unto their fathers, "
48 the city w· thou hast chosen, and "
48 house w· I have built for thy name: "
51 w· thou broughtest forth out of "
56 w· he promised by the hand of Moses"
58 w· he commanded our fathers. "
63 w· he offered unto the Lord, two and"
9: 1 desire w· he was pleased to do, "
3 this house w· thou hast built, "
6 statutes w· I have set before you, "
7 of the land w· I have given them; "
7 w· I have hallowed for my name, "
8 And at this house, w· is high, *
12 cities w· Solomon had given him; 834
13 are these w· thou hast given me, "
15 the levy w· king Solomon raised; "
19 w· Solomon desired to build in "
20 w· were not of the children of Israel,‡"
23 w· bare rule over the people that ‡
24 unto her house w· Solomon had 834
25 the altar w· he built unto the Lord, "
26 Ezion-geber, w· is beside Eloth, "
10: 3 from the king, w· he told her not. "
5 by w· he went up into the house of "
7 exceedeth the fame w· I heard. "
8 w· stand continually before thee, ‡
9 w· delighted in thee, to set thee on‡834
10 w· the queen of Sheba gave to king "
13 w· Solomon gave her of his royal "
24 wisdom, w· God had put in his heart."
11: 2 nations concerning w· the Lord said‡"
8 w· burnt incense and sacrificed unto‡
9 w· had appeared unto him twice,‡
10 not that w· the Lord commanded. 834
11 w· I have commanded thee, "
13 Jerusalem's sake w· I have chosen. "
20 w· gave him an house, and appointed‡
23 w· fled from his lord Hadadezer ‡ 834
32 the city w· I have chosen out of all "

1Ki 11:33 to do that w· is right in mine eyes,
37 city w· I have chosen me to put my 834
12: 4 his heavy yoke w· he put upon us, "
8 the old men, w· they had given him,"
8 with him, and w· stood before him:‡"
9 yoke w· thy father did put upon us* "
15 w· the Lord spake by Ahijah the "
17 Israel w· dwelt in the cities of Judah,‡
21 chosen men, w· were warriors, ‡
28 w· brought thee up out of the land‡834
31 w· were not of the sons of Levi. ‡ "
32 the high places w· he had made. "
33 upon the altar w· he had made in "
33 month w· he had devised of his own "
13: 3 the sign w· the Lord hath spoken; "
4 w· had cried against the altar in ‡ "
4 hand, w· he put forth against him, "
5 sign w· the man of God had given "
11 the words w· he had spoken unto "
12 God went, w· came from Judah. ‡ "
21 w· the Lord thy God commanded "
22 w· the Lord did say to thee, Eat no "
26 the lion, w· hath torn him, and slain
26 of the Lord, w· he spake unto him.834
32 For the saying w· he cried by the "
32 high places w· are in the cities of "
14: 2 w· told me that I should be king ‡1931
8 that only w· was right in mine eyes;
15 land, w· he gave to their fathers, 834
18 w· he spake by the hand of his "
20 the days w· Jeroboam reigned were "
21 the city w· the Lord did choose out "
22 their sins w· they had committed, "
24 nations w· the Lord cast out before‡"
26 shields of gold w· Solomon had made."
27 w· kept the door of the king's house.‡
15: 3 father, w· he had done before him:834
5 w· was right in the eyes of the Lord,
11 Asa did that w· was right in the eyes
15 the things w· his father had dedicated,*
15 the things w· himself had dedicated,*
20 hosts w· he had against the cities*‡834
23 did, and the cities w· he had built, "
27 w· belonged to the Philistines; "
29 w· he spake by his servant Ahijah "
30 sins of Jeroboam w· he sinned, "
30 and w· he made Israel sin, * "
16:12 w· he spake against Baasha by "
13 of Elah his son, by w· they sinned, "
13 and by w· they made Israel to sin,* "
15 w· belonged to the Philistines. "
19 his sins w· he sinned in doing evil "
19 his sin, w· he did, to make Israel "
24 the name of the city w· he built, "
27 rest of the acts of Omri w· he did, "
32 Baal, w· he had built in Samaria. "
34 w· he spake by Joshua the son of "
17: 9 to Zarephath, w· belongeth to Zidon,"
16 of the Lord, w· he spake by Elijah. "
18: 3 w· was the governor of his house. ‡ "
19 four hundred, w· eat at Jezebel's table.‡
26 took the bullock w· was given them,
26 leaped upon the altar w· was made.834
19: 3 Beer-sheba, w· belongeth to Judah, "
18 knees w· have not bowed unto Baal."
18 every mouth w· hath not kissed "
20:19 and the army w· followed them. ‡ "
34 w· my father took from thy father, "
21: 1 had a vineyard, w· was in Jezreel, "
4 w· Naboth the Jezreelite had spoken"
11 letters w· she had sent unto them. "
15 w· he refused to give thee for "
18 king of Israel, w· is in Samaria: ‡ "
25 Ahab, w· did sell himself to work "
22:13 of them, and speak that w· is good.*
16 but that w· is true in the name of the*
24 W· way went the Spirit of the335,2088
38 the word of the Lord w· he spake. 834
39 and the ivory house w· he made, "
43 w· was right in the eyes of the Lord "
46 w· remained in the days of his father "
2Ki 1: 4, 6 that bed on w· thou art gone up,*834
7 was he w· came up to meet you, ‡ "
16 off that bed on w· thou art gone up,*"
17 of the Lord w· Elijah had spoken. "
18 of the acts of Ahaziah w· he did, "
2:15 of the prophets w· were to view at‡ "
22 the saying of Elijah w· he spake. "
3: 3 son of Nebat, w· made Israel to sin;*"
8 he said, W· way shall we go 335,2088
11 w· poured water on the hands of ‡ 834
4: 4 and thou shalt set aside that w· is full.
9 of God w· passeth by us continually.‡
5:20 at his hands that w· he brought: 834
6:10 place w· the man of God told him "
11 w· of us is for the king of Israel? ‡4310
7:13 that remain, w· are left in the city, 834
15 w· the Syrians had cast away in "
8:21 Edomites w· compassed him about, ‡
29 w· the Syrians had given him. 834
9: 5 And Jehu said, Unto w· of all us? 4310
15 w· the Syrians had given him, 834
19 second on horseback, w· came to them,‡
27 going up to Gur, w· is by Ibleam. 834
36 w· he spake by his servant Elijah "
10: 5 do thou that w· is good in thine eyes.
6 men of the city, w· brought them up.‡
10 w· the Lord spake concerning the 834
10 that w· he spake by his servant "
30 executing that w· is right in mine eyes,
31 of Jeroboam, w· made Israel to sin.*834
33 Aroer, w· is by the river Arnon, "
11: 2 among the king's sons w· were slain;*
16 by the way by the w· the horses came*
12: 2 w· was right in the sight of the Lord
20 house of Millo, w· goeth down to Silla.*

2Ki 13: 2 w' was evil in the sight of the Lord,
2 son of Nebat, w' made Israel to sin;*
11 w' was evil in the sight of the Lord;
25 w' he had taken out of the hand of 834
14: 3 w' is right in the sight of the Lord,
6 unto that w' is written in the book
11 Beth-shemesh, w' belongeth to 834
15 of the acts of Jehoash w' he did, "
21 Azariah, w' was sixteen years old,*1931
24 w' was evil in the sight of the Lord:
25 w' he spake by the hand of his 834
25 prophet, w' was of Gath-hepher. ‡ "
28 and Hamath, w' belonged to Judah,
15: 3 w' was right in the sight of the Lord,
9 w' was evil in the sight of the Lord:
12 the Lord w' he spake unto Jehu, 834
15 and his conspiracy w' he made, "
18, 24, 28 that w' was evil in the sight of
34 w' was right in the sight of the Lord:
16: 2 w' was right in the sight of the Lord
7 king of Israel, w' rise up against me.‡
14 altar, w' was before the Lord, 834
19 rest of the acts of Ahaz w' he did, "
17: 2 w' was evil in the sight of the Lord,
7 w' had brought them up out of the‡
8 kings of Israel, w' they had made.‡ 834
13 law w' I commanded your fathers, "
13 and w' I sent to you by my servants "
15 w' he testified against them; and "
19 statutes of Israel w' they made. "
22 all the sins of Jeroboam w' he did; "
25 among them, w' slew some of them. "
26 The nations w' thou hast removed,‡834
29 high places w' the Samaritans had "
32 w' sacrificed for them in the ‡1961
34 w' the Lord commanded the 834
37 commandment, w' he wrote for you, "
18: 3 w' was right in the sight of the Lord,
6 w' the Lord commanded Moses. 834
9 w' was the seventh year of Hoshea1958
14 w' thou puttest on me will I bear. 834
16 w' Hezekiah king of Judah had "
17 w' is in the highway of the fuller's "
18 Hilkiah, w' was over the household,‡"
21 Egypt, on w' if a man lean, it will go*"
27 sent me to the men w' sit on the wall, ‡
37 Hilkiah, w' was over...household, ‡ 834
19: 2 Eliakim, w' was over the household,‡"
4 words w' the Lord thy God hath "
6 of the words w' thou hast heard, * "
6 with w' the servants of the king of* "
12 them w' my fathers have destroyed;‡"
12 of Eden w' were in Thelasar? ‡ "
15 w' dwellest between the cherubims,‡
16 w' hath sent him to reproach the * 834
20 That w' thou hast prayed to me * "
28 by the way by w' thou camest. "
29 year that w' springeth of the same;
20: 3 done that w' is good in thy sight.
17 that w' thy fathers have laid up in 834
18 w' thou shalt beget, shall they take‡ "
19 of the Lord w' thou hast spoken. "
21: 2 w' was evil in the sight of the Lord,
3 high places w' Hezekiah his father "
4 of the Lord, of w' the Lord said, * "
7 house, of w' the Lord said to David, "
7 w' I have chosen out of all tribes "
8 of the land w' I gave their fathers; "
11 Amorites did, w' were before him,‡ "
15 done that w' was evil in my sight, "
16 w' was evil in the sight of the Lord,
20 w' was evil in the sight of the Lord,
25 of the acts of Amon w' he did, 834
22: 2 w' was right in the sight of the Lord,
4 sum the silver w' is brought into the
4 w' the keepers of the door have 834
5 work w' is in the house of the Lord, "
13 all that w' is written concerning us.
16 book w' the king of Judah hath 834
18 w' sent you to enquire of the Lord,*
18 the words w' thou hast heard; 834
20 evil w' I will bring upon this place. "
23: 2 covenant w' was found in the house of
8 w' were on a man's left hand at the834
10 w' is in the valley of the children of "
11 w' was in the suburbs, and burned "
12 w' the kings of Judah had made, "
12 the altars w' Manasseh had made "
13 w' were on the right hand of the "
13 w' Solomon the king of Israel had "
15 high place w' Jeroboam the son of "
16 Lord w' the man of God proclaimed, "
17 man of God, w' came from Judah, ‡ "
19 w' the kings of Israel had made to "
24 w' were written in the book that "
27 city Jerusalem w' I have chosen, 834
27 the house of w' I said, My name shall"
32, 37 did that w' was evil in the sight of
24: 2 w' he spake by his servants the 834
4 blood; w' the Lord would not pardon.*
9 w' was evil in the sight of the Lord,
13 w' Solomon king of Israel had made834
19 w' was evil in the sight of the Lord,
25: 4 walls, w' is by the king's garden: 834
8 w' is the nineteenth year of king 1958
16 w' Solomon had made for the house834
19 w' were found in the city, and the‡
19 w' mustered the people of the land,‡
1Ch 1: 46 w' smote Midian in the field of Moab,‡
2: 3 w' three were born unto him of the‡
19 unto him Ephrath, w' bare him Hur.‡
42 w' was the father of Ziph; ‡1931
55 of the scribes w' dwelt at Jabez; ‡
3: 1 w' were born unto him in Hebron :‡834
4: 10 granted him that w' he requested. "
11 w' was the father of Eshton. ‡1931
1Ch 4: 18 daughter of Pharaoh, w' Mered ‡ 834
6: 61 w' were left of the family of that tribe,*
65 w' are called by their names. 834
9: 22 these w' were chosen to be porters in‡
25 brethren, w' were in the villages,*
10: 13 w' he committed against the Lord, 834
13 word of the Lord, w' he kept not, "
11: 4 went to Jerusalem, w' is Jebus; *1958
5 of Zion, w' is the city of David. * "
12: 31 w' were expressed by name, * 834
33 fifty thousand, w' could keep rank:*
13: 2 and Levites w' are in their cities *
6 Kirjath-jearim, w' belonged to 834
14: 4 of his children w' had in Jerusalem;‡"
15: 3 place, w' he had prepared for it. "
16: 15 the word w' he commanded to a "
16 of the covenant w' he made with "
40 Lord, w' he commanded Israel; "
17: 11 after thee, w' shall be of thy sons;‡ "
19: 13 Lord do that w' is good in his sight.
18 seven thousand men w' fought in‡
20: 4 at w' time Sibbechai the * 227
21: 19 w' he spake in the name of the 834
23 king do that w' is good in his eyes:
24 take that w' is thine for the Lord, 834
29 w' Moses made in the wilderness, "
22: 13 w' the Lord charged Moses with "
23: 4 Of w' twenty and four thousand * 428
5 with the instruments w' I made, 834
29 and for that w' is baked in the pan,
25: 2 w' prophesied according to the order*
26: 22 w' were over the treasures of the ‡
26 W' Shelomith and his brethren *1931
26 w' David the king, and the chief 834
27: 1 w' came in and went out month by‡
31 substance w' was king David's. 834
29: 3 w' I have given to the house of my
17 joy thy people, w' are present here,to‡
19 for the w' I have made provision. 834
2Ch 1: 3 w' Moses the servant of the Lord "
4 to the place w' David had prepared*
6 w' was at the tabernacle of the
14 w' he placed in the chariot cities, ‡
2: 5 And the house w' I build is great: 834
9 house w' I am about to build shall "
11 in writing, w' he sent to Solomon,
14 device w' shall be put to him, * 834
15 wine, w' my lord hath spoken of, "
3: 5 w' he overlaid with fine gold, and
4: 3 of oxen, w' did compass it round
12 chapiters w' were on the top of the two
12 w' were on the top of the pillars; * 834
13 chapiters w' were upon the pillars.* "
5: 2 of the city of David, w' is Zion. 1958
3 feast w' was in the seventh month.1931
6 and oxen, w' could not be told nor 834
10 two tables w' Moses put therein "
12 Also the Levites w' were the singers,‡
6: 4 his hands fulfilled that w' he spake834
9 thy son w' shall come forth out of thy*
14 w' keepest covenant, and shewest*
15 Thou w' hast kept with thy servant*
15, 16 father that w' thou hast promised834
17 w' thou hast spoken unto thy "
18 less this house w' I have built! "
19 w' thy servant prayeth before thee: "
20 the prayer w' thy servant prayeth "
21 w' they shall make toward this * "
25 w' thou gavest to them and to their "
27 w' thou hast given unto thy people "
31 w' thou gavest unto our fathers. "
32 w' is not of thy people Israel, * "
33 house w' I have built is called by thy"
34 this city w' thou hast chosen, "
34 house w' I have built for thy name; "
36 (for there is no man w' sinneth not,)*"
38 w' thou gavest unto their fathers, "
38 toward the city w' thou hast chosen,"
38 house w' I have built for thy name: "
39 thy people w' have sinned against ‡ "
7: 6 w' David the king had made to "
7 brasen altar w' Solomon had made "
14 people, w' are called by my name, ‡ "
19 w' I have set before you, and shall go"
20 of my land w' I have given them; "
20 w' I have sanctified for my name, "
21 And this house, w' is high, shall be "
22 w' brought them forth out of the ‡ "
8: 2 w' Huram had restored to Solomon,‡"
4 store cities, w' he built in Hamath. "
7 the Jebusites, w' were not of Israel,‡"
12 w' he had built before the porch, "
9: 2 from Solomon w' he told her not. "
4 his ascent by w' he went up into the "
5 a true report w' I heard in mine * "
7 w' stand continually before thee, ‡
8 w' delighted in thee to set thee on ‡ 834
10 w' brought gold from Ophir, ‡ "
12 that w' she had brought unto the
14 w' chapmen and merchants brought.
18 gold, w' were fastened to the throne,
10: 8 counsel w' the old men gave him, 834
9 w' have spoken to me, saying, Ease*"
15 w' he spake by the hand of Ahijah
11: 1 men, w' were warriors, to fight ‡
10 w' are in Judah and in Benjamin, 834
15 and for the calves w' he had made. "
19 W' bare him children; Jeush, and*
20 w' bare him Abijah, and Attai, and*
12: 4 cities w' pertained to Judah, 834
9 the shields of gold w' Solomon had "
10 Instead of w' king Rehoboam made
13 the city w' the Lord had chosen out834
13: 4 w' is in mount Ephraim, and said,
8 w' Jeroboam made you for gods.
10 the priests, w' minister unto the Lord,‡
2Ch 14: 2 w' was good and right in the eyes of
15: 8 cities w' he had taken from mount 834
11 time, of the spoil w' they had brought,
16: 14 w' he had made for himself in the 834
14 in the bed w' was filled with sweet "
17: 2 w' Asa his father had taken.
18: 23 W' way went the Spirit of the 335,2088
20: 2 in Hazazon-tamar; w' is En-gedi.*1958
11 w' thou hast given us to inherit. 834
22 Seir, w' were come against Judah;‡
25 w' they stripped off for themselves,
32 w' was right in the sight of the Lord.
21: 6 w' was evil in the eyes of the Lord.
9 the Edomites w' compassed him in,‡
13 house, w' were better than thyself: ‡
22: 6 of the wounds w' were given him 834
23: 9 w' were in the house of God. "
19 that none w' was unclean in any thing‡
24: 2 w' was right in the sight of the Lord
20 the priest, w' stood above the people,*
22 kindness w' Jehoiada his father 834
25: 2 w' was right in the sight of the Lord,
9 talents w' I have given to the army834
13 of the army w' Amaziah sent back,‡ "
15 w' said unto me, Why hast thou ‡
15 w' could not deliver their own ‡ 834
21 Beth-shemesh, w' belongeth...Judah."
26: 4 w' was right in the sight of the Lord,
23 burial w' belonged to the kings; 834
27: 2 w' was right in the sight of the Lord,
28: 1 w' was right in the sight of the Lord,
6 in one day, w' were all valiant men;*
11 w' ye have taken captive of your ‡ 834
15 the men w' were expressed by name‡"
23 the gods of Damascus, w' smote him:‡
29: 2 w' was right in the sight of the Lord,
6 w' was evil in the eyes of the Lord
19 w' king Ahaz in his reign did cast 834
32 w' the congregation brought,
30: 7 w' trespassed against the Lord God‡"
8 w' he hath sanctified for ever: "
16 w' they received of the hands of the
31: 6 holy things w' were consecrated unto
10 and that w' is left is this great store.
12 over w' Cononiah the Levite was ruler,*
19 w' were in the fields of the suburbs of‡
20 that w' was good and right and truth
32: 3 fountains w' were without the city:834
19 w' were the work of the hands of man.‡
21 w' cut off all the mighty men of valour,‡
33: 2 w' was evil in the sight of the Lord,
3 w' Hezekiah his father had broken 834
7 idol w' he had made, in the house of "
7 of w' God had said to David and to "
7 w' I have chosen before all the tribes"
8 land w' I have appointed for your "
11 w' took Manasseh among the thorns,‡
22 w' was evil in the sight of the Lord,
22 w' Manasseh his father had made, 834
34: 2 w' was right in the sight of the Lord,
9 w' the Levites that kept the door 834
11 houses w' the kings of Judah had "
24 w' they have read before the king of "
26 the words w' thou hast heard; "
31 covenant w' are written in this book.
35: 3 all Israel, w' were holy unto the Lord,‡
3 the house w' Solomon the son of 834
26 w' was written in the law of the Lord,
36: 5 w' was evil in the sight of the Lord
8 and his abominations w' he did, 834
8 w' was found in him, behold, they are
9 w' was evil in the sight of the Lord.
12 w' was evil in the sight of the Lord
14 w' he had hallowed in Jerusalem. 834
23 house in Jerusalem, w' is in Judah. "
Ezr 1: 2 house at Jerusalem, w' is in Judah. "
3 go up to Jerusalem, w' is in Judah, "
3 (he is the God,) w' is in Jerusalem. "
5 of the Lord w' is in Jerusalem. "
7 w' Nebuchadnezzar had brought "
2: 1 of those w' had been carried away,‡
2 W' came with Zerubbabel: ‡ 834
59 were they w' went up from Tel-melah,‡
61 w' took a wife of the daughters of‡ 834
68 of the Lord w' is at Jerusalem, "
4: 2 of Assur, w' brought us up hither.‡
12 that the Jews w' came up from ‡1768
15 time: for w' cause was this city 1836
18 The letter w' ye sent unto us hath1768
20 w' have ruled over all countries ‡
24 house of God w' is at Jerusalem. 1768
5: 2 the house of God w' is at Jerusalem"
6 w' were on this side the river, ‡ "
8 w' is builded with great stones, 1931
11 w' a great king of Israel builded and
14 w' Nebuchadnezzar took out of 1768
16 house of God w' is at Jerusalem: "
17 house, w' is there at Babylon, ‡ "
6: 5 w' Nebuchadnezzar took forth out "
5 unto the temple w' is at Jerusalem,"
6 w' are beyond the river, be ye far‡
9 And that w' they have need of both
9 the priests w' are at Jerusalem, ‡1768
12 house of God w' is at Jerusalem. "
13 that w' Darius the king had sent, * "
15 w' was in the sixth year of the "
18 service of God, w' is at Jerusalem; "
21 w' were come again out of captivity,‡
7: 6 w' the Lord God of Israel had ‡ 834
8 w' was in the seventh year of the 1958
13 w' are minded of their...freewill ‡1768
14 law of thy God w' is in thine hand; "
15 w' the king and his counsellers "
16 of their God w' is in Jerusalem: "
17 of your God w' is in Jerusalem. "
20 w' thou shalt have occasion to "

Ezr 7:21 treasurers w· are beyond the river,‡1768
25 w· may judge all the people that ‡ "
27 w· hath put such a thing as this in‡834
27 of the Lord w· is in Jerusalem: "
8:25 w· the king, and his counsellers, and
35 w· were come out of captivity, offered‡
9:11 W· thou hast commanded by thy 834
11 land unto w· ye go to possess it, is "
11 w· have filled it from one end to ‡ "
10:14 all them w· have taken strange wives‡
Ne 1: 2 w· were left of the captivity, ‡ 834
6 w· I pray before thee now, day and "
6 w· we have sinned against thee: "
7 w· thou commandedst thy servant "
2: 8 place w· appertained to the house, "
13 Jerusalem, w· were broken down, "
18 of my God w· was good upon me; "
3:25 tower w· lieth out from the king's
4: 2 of the rubbish w· are burned? *1992
3 Even that w· they build, if a fox 834
12 when the Jews w· dwelt by them came,‡
14 the Lord, w· is great and terrible,‡
17 They w· builded on the wall, and they*
23 men of the guard w· followed me,‡ 834
5: 8 Jews, w· were sold unto the heathen; ‡
18 Now that w· was prepared for me 834
6: 6 w· cause thou buildest the wall, 3651
7: 5 of them w· came up at the first, ‡
61 they w· went up also from Tel-melah,‡
63 w· took one of the daughters of ‡ 834
72 w· the rest of the people gave was "
8: 1 w· the Lord had commanded to "
4 w· they had made for the purpose; "
9 Nehemiah, w· is the Tirshatha, ‡1931
14 law w· the Lord had commanded* 834
9: 5 w· is exalted above all blessing and‡
15 w· thou hadst sworn to give them. 834
23 w· thou hadst promised to their "
26 slew thy prophets w· testified ‡ "
29 (w· if a man do, he shall live in "
35 fat land w· thou gavest before them,"
10:29 w· was given by Moses the servant "
12: 8 w· was over the thanksgiving, he ‡
37 gate, w· was over against them, *
13: 5 w· was commanded to be given to the
15 w· they brought into Jerusalem on the
16 of Tyre also therein, w· brought fish,‡
Es 1: 1 (this is Ahasuerus w· reigned, from ‡
2 w· was in Shushan the palace, 834
9 house w· belonged to king Ahasuerus.
13 to the wise men, w· knew the times,‡
14 and Media, w· saw the king's face,‡
14 and w· sat the first in the kingdom,)‡
18 w· have heard of the deed of the ‡ 834
20 the king's decree w· he shall make, "
2: 4 the maiden w· pleaseth the king be ‡ "
6 w· had been carried away with ‡ "
9 maidens w· were meet to be given her,‡
14 chamberlain, w· kept the concubines:‡
16 tenth month, w· is the month Tebeth,
21 of those w· kept the door, were wroth,‡
3: 3 servants, w· were in the king's * 834
13 month, w· is the month Adar, 1931
4: 6 city, w· was before the king's gate. 834
16 king, w· is not according to the law:"
6: 8 brought w· the king useth to wear, "
8 crown royal w· is set upon his head:"
7: 9 w· Haman had made for Mordecai, "
8: 2 ring, w· he had taken from Haman, "
5 w· he wrote to destroy the Jews "
5 w· are in all the king's provinces: "
8 writing w· is written in the king's "
9 w· are from India unto Ethiopia, "
11 the Jews w· were in every city ‡ "
12 month, w· is the month Adar. 1931
9:13 to the Jews w· are in Shushan ‡ 834
22 w· was turned unto them from "
25 w· he devised against the Jews, "
26 w· they had seen concerning this 4100
26 matter, and w· had come unto them,"
Job 3: 3 night in w· it was said, There is a man
14 w· built desolate places...themselves;‡
16 been; as infants w· never saw light.‡
21 W· long for death, but it cometh not;‡
22 W· rejoice exceedingly, and are glad,‡
25 thing w· I greatly feared is come upon
25 that w· I was afraid is come unto 834
4:14 w· made all my bones to shake.
19 dust, w· are crushed before the moth?‡
21 their excellency w· is in them go away?
5: 1 to w· of the saints wilt thou turn?‡4310
9 W· doeth great things and ‡
11 those w· mourn may be exalted to‡
6: 6 Can that w· is unsavoury be eaten
16 W· are blackish by reason of the ice,
26 one that is desperate, w· are as wind?
9: 5 W· removeth the mountains, and‡
5 w· overturneth them in his anger.*834
6 W· shaketh the earth out of her place,‡
7 W· commandeth the sun, and it riseth‡
8 W· alone spreadeth out the heavens,‡
9 W· maketh Arcturus, Orion, and‡
10 W· doeth greater things past finding ‡
11: 6 and they are double to that w· is!*
14:19 things w· grow out of the dust of the*
15: 9 understandest thou, w· is not in 1931
14 and he w· is born of a woman, that he*
16 man, w· drinketh iniquity like water?*
17 and that w· I have seen I will declare:
18 W· wise men have told from their 834
28 and in houses w· no man inhabiteth,
28 w· are ready to become heaps. 834
16: 8 wrinkles, w· is a witness against me:
20: 7 they w· have seen him shall say, ‡
9 eye also w· saw him shall see him no
11 w· shall be down with him in the dust.*

Job 20:18 That w· he laboured for shall he
19 away an house w· he builded not;*
20 he shall not save of that w· he desired.*
21:27 devices w· ye wrongfully imagine
22:15 way w· wicked men have trodden? 834
16 W· were cut down out of time, * "
17 W· said unto God, Depart from us:*
23: 5 the words w· he would answer me,
24:11 W· make oil within their walls, and*
16 w· they had marked for themselves in*
19 doth the grave those w· have sinned.‡
25: 6 and the son of man, w· is a worm?‡
27:11 w· is with the Almighty will I not 834
13 w· they shall receive of the Almighty,
28: 7 There is a path w· no fowl knoweth,*
7 w· the vulture's eye hath not seen:*
29:16 cause w· I knew not I searched out.*
32:19 my belly is as wine w· hath no vent;
33:27 that w· was right, and it profited me
34: 8 W· goeth in company with...workers‡
32 That w· I see not teach thou me:
36:16 and that w· should be set on thy table
24 magnify his work, w· men behold.* 834
28 W· the clouds do drop and distil "
37: 5 doeth he, w· we cannot comprehend.
16 of him w· is perfect in knowledge?‡
18 w· is strong, and as a molten looking
21 the bright light w· is in the clouds:1931
38:23 W· I have reserved against the 834
24 W· scattereth the east wind upon the*
39:14 W· leaveth her eggs in the earth, 3588
40:15 behemoth, w· I made with thee; 834
41: 1 with a cord w· thou lettest down?*
42: 3 too wonderful for me, w· I knew not.
8 spoken of me the thing w· is right,*
Ps 1: 4 the chaff w· the wind driveth away. 834
3: 2 Many there be w· say of my soul, ‡
7: title David, w· he sang unto the Lord, 834
10 w· saveth the upright in heart. ‡
15 fallen into the ditch w· he made.
8: 3 the stars, w· thou hast ordained; 834
9:11 to the Lord, w· dwelleth in Zion: ‡
13 trouble w· I suffer of them that hate
15 net w· they hid is their own foot 2098
16 by the judgment w· he executeth:*
17: 7 them w· put their trust in thee from‡
13 soul from the wicked, w· is thy sword:*
14 From men w· are thy hand, O Lord,‡
14 w· have their portion in this life, ‡
18:17 enemy, and from them w· hated me:*
19: 5 W· is as a bridegroom coming out of
21:11 device, w· they are not able to perform.
25: 3 ashamed w· transgress without *
28: 3 w· speak peace to their neighbours,‡
31:18 w· speak grievous things proudly‡
19 w· thou hast laid up for them that 834
19 w· thou hast wrought for them that
32: 8 thee in the way w· thou shalt go: 2098
9 the mule, w· have no understanding:
35: 7 w· without cause they have digged*
10 w· deliverest the poor from him that ‡
27 w· hath pleasure in the prosperity of‡
40: 5 wonderful works w· thou hast done,
5 and thy thoughts w· are to us-ward:
41: 9 I trusted, w· did eat of my bread, ‡
44:10 they w· hate us spoil for themselves.‡
45: 1 w· I have made touching the king:
51: 8 that the bones w· thou hast broken
58: 5 W· will not hearken to the voice of 834
7 away as waters w· run continually:*
8 As a snail w· melteth, let every one of
59:12 for cursing and lying w· they speak.
60:10 not thou, O God, w· hadst cast us off?*
10 w· didst not go out with our armies?*
61: 7 and truth, w· may preserve him. *
65: 6 W· by his strength setteth fast the‡
7 W· stilleth the noise of the seas, the‡
9 the river of God, w· is full of water:*
66: 9 W· holdeth our soul in life, and ‡
14 W· my lips have uttered, and my 834
20 God, w· hath not turned away my‡ "
68: 6 he bringeth out those w· are bound*
16 the hill w· God desireth to dwell in;
28 w· thou hast wrought for us. 2098
33 heavens of heavens, w· were of old;
69: 4 restored that w· I took not away, 834
22 w· should have been for their welfare,*
71:20 w· hast shewed me great and sore‡ 834
23 my soul, w· thou hast redeemed. "
74: 2 w· thou hast purchased of old; ‡
2 inheritance, w· thou hast redeemed;
78: 3 W· we have heard and known, 834
5 w· he commanded our fathers, "
6 even the children w· should be born;‡
45 flies among them, w· devoured them;
45 and frogs, w· destroyed them.
54 w· his right hand had purchased.
60 the tent w· he placed among men;
68 Judah, the mount Zion w· he loved.834
69 like the earth w· he hath established
79:10 the blood of thy servants w· is shed.
80:12 they w· pass by the way do pluck her?‡
15 vineyard w· thy right hand hath 834
81:10 God, w· brought thee out of the land‡
83:10 W· perished at En-dor: they became‡
85:12 Lord shall give that w· is good; and
86:17 that they w· hate me may see it, ‡
89:49 w· thou swarest unto David in thy‡
90: 5 they are like the grass w· groweth up.
91: 9 hast made the Lord, w· is my refuge,*
94:20 thee, w· frameth mischief by a law?
102:18 the people w· shall be created shall‡
104: 8 place w· thou hast founded for 2088
10 the valleys, w· run among the hills.*
12 fowls...w· sing among the branches.*
15 and bread w· strengtheneth man's*

Ps 104:16 of Lebanon, w· he hath planted; 834
105: 8 the word w· he commanded to a
9 W· covenant he made with 834
106:21 w· had done great things in Egypt;‡
36 idols: w· were a snare unto them.
107:25 wind, w· lifteth up the waves thereof.
37 w· may yield fruits of increase. *
109:19 him as the garment w· covereth him,*
114: 8 W· turned the rock into a standing‡
115:15 the Lord w· made heaven and earth.‡
118:20 into w· the righteous shall enter.*
22 The stone w· the builders refused is
24 is the day w· the Lord hath made;
27 is the Lord, w· hath shewed us light:*
119:21 w· do err from thy commandments.‡
39 Turn away my reproach w· I fear:*834
47 commandments, w· I have loved. "
48 commandments, w· I have loved; "
49 w· thou hast caused me to hope. * "
85 for me, w· are not after thy law. * "
165 peace have they w· love thy law: ‡
121: 2 the Lord, w· made heaven and earth.‡
125: 1 as mount Zion, w· cannot be moved,
129: 6 w· withereth afore it groweth up:
8 Neither do they w· go by say, The‡
134: 1 w· by night stand in the house of the‡
135:21 of Zion, w· dwelleth at Jerusalem.*
136:13 To him w· divided the Red sea into‡
16 To him w· led his people through the‡
17 To him w· smote great kings: for his‡
138: 8 will perfect that w· concerneth me:
139:16 w· in continuance were fashioned,
140: 2 W· imagine mischiefs in their ‡ 834
141: 5 oil, w· shall not break my head: *
9 the snares w· they have laid for me,
144: 1 w· teacheth my hands to war, ‡
146: 6 W· made heaven, and earth, the sea,‡
6 therein is: w· keepeth truth for ever:‡
7 W· executeth judgment for the ‡
7 w· giveth food to the hungry. ‡
147: 9 and to the young ravens w· cry. 834
148: 6 hath made a decree w· shall not pass.‡
Pr 1:19 w· taketh away the life of the owners*
2:16 stranger w· flattereth with her words;‡
17 W· forsaketh the guide of her youth,‡
6: 7 W· having no guide, overseer, or 834
7: 5 stranger w· flattereth with her words.‡
9: 5 drink of the wine w· I have mingled.
11:22 fair woman w· is without discretion.‡
12:27 not that w· he took in hunting:
14:12 is a way w· seemeth right unto a man,
33 that w· is in the midst of fools is made
19:17 that w· he hath given will he pay him*
20:25 man who devoureth that w· is holy,*
22:28 landmark, w· thy fathers have set. 834
23: 5 set thine eyes upon that w· is not?
8 morsel w· thou hast eaten shalt thou
24:13 honeycomb, w· is sweet to thy taste:
25: 1 w· the men of Hezekiah king of 834
27:16 of his right hand, w· bewrayeth itself.*
28: 3 a sweeping rain w· leaveth no food.
30:18 be three things w· are too wonderful
21 and for four w· it cannot bear:
24 things w· are little upon the earth,
29 There be three things w· go well, yea,
30 A lion w· is strongest among beasts,
31: 3 thy ways to that w· destroyeth kings.
Ec 1: 3 his labour w· he taketh under the sun?*
9 that hath been, it is that w· shall be;
9 w· is done is that w· shall be done:
10 of old time, w· was before us. 834
15 That w· is crooked cannot be made
15 and that w· is wanting cannot be
2: 3 w· they should do under the heaven*834
12 that w· hath been already done.
16 seeing that w· now is in the days to*
18 hated all my labour w· I had taken*
20 despair of all the labour w· I took*
3: 2 a time to pluck up that w· is planted;
10 w· God hath given to the sons of 834
15 That w· hath been is now; and that
15 that w· is to be hath already been; 834
15 and God requireth that w· is past.
19 For that w· befalleth the sons of men
4: 2 praised the dead w· are already dead‡
2 than the living w· are yet alive. ‡ 834
3 w· hath not yet been, who hath not‡ "
15 all the living w· walk under the sun,‡
5: 4 pay that w· thou hast vowed. ‡ 834
13 evil w· I have seen under the sun,
15 w· he may carry away in his hand.‡
18 Behold that w· I have seen: it is ‡ 834
18 days of his life, w· God giveth him: "
6:12 vain life w· he spendeth as a shadow?
7:13 w· he hath made crooked? 834
19 ten mighty men w· are in the city.‡ "
24 That w· is far off, and exceeding 4100
28 W· yet my soul seeketh, but I find 834
8: 7 he knoweth not that w· shall be: 4100
12 that fear God, w· fear before him.‡ 834
13 prolong his days, w· are as a shadow;
14 vanity w· is done upon the earth; 834
15 w· God giveth him under the sun. "
9: 9 w· he hath given thee under the sun,"
9 in thy labour w· thou takest under*
10: 5 an evil w· I have seen under the sun,
5 error w· proceedeth from the ruler:
20 and that w· hath wings shall tell
12: 5 shall be afraid of that w· is high,
10 and that w· was written was upright,
11 w· are given from one shepherd.
Ca 1: 1 song of songs, w· is Solomon's. 834
3: 7 Behold his bed, w· is Solomon's; *
4: 2 w· came up from the washing;
5 are twins, w· feed among the lilies.*
6: 6 of sheep w· go up from the washing,

Ca 7: 2 goblet, w· wanteth not liquor: *
4 Lebanon w· looketh toward Damascus.
13 and old, w· I have laid up for thee,
8: 6 w· hath a most vehement flame.
12 My vineyard, w· is mine, is before
Isa 1: 1 w· he saw concerning Judah and 834
29 of the oaks w· ye have desired, "
2: 8 w· their own fingers have made: "
20 w· they made each for himself to "
3: 12 they w· lead thee cause thee to err,‡
5: 23 W· justify the wicked for reward,‡
6: 6 w· he had taken with the tongs
8: 18 of hosts, w· dwelleth in mount Zion.‡
10: 1 grievousness w· they have prescribed;*
3 the desolation w· shall come from far?
11: 10 w· shall stand for an ensign of the 834
11, 16 of his people, w· shall be left, ‡ "
13: 1 w· Isaiah the son of Amoz did see. "
17 them, w· shall not regard silver; ‡ "
14: 12 ground, w· didst weaken the nations!
15: 7 and that w· they have laid up,
17: 2 shall be for flocks, w· shall lie down,
8 that w· his fingers have made, 834
9 w· they left because of the children "
12 w· make a noise like the noise of the‡
18: 1 w· is beyond the rivers of Ethiopia:834
19: 15 w· the head or tail, branch or rush,
16 of hosts, w· he shaketh over it. 834
17 w· he hath determined against it. "
21: 10 that w· I have heard of the Lord of "
22: 3 together, w· have fled from far. *
15 unto Shebna, w· is over the house, ‡834
26: 2 w· keepeth the truth may enter in.‡
27: 13 shall come w· were ready to perish‡
28: 1 w· are on the head of the fat 834
2 w· as a tempest of hail and a *
4 w· is on the head of the fat valley, 834
4 w· when he that looketh upon it "
14 this people w· is in Jerusalem. ‡ "
29 hosts, w· is wonderful in counsel,‡
29: 11 w· men deliver to one that is 834
30: 10 W· say to the seers, See not; and‡ "
24 w· hath been winnowed with the "
31 be beaten down, w· smote with a rod.‡
32 w· the Lord shall lay upon him, 834
31: 7 w· your own hands have made unto "
36: 3 son, w· was over the house, and ‡ "
37: 4 w· the Lord thy God hath heard: "
12 delivered them w· my fathers have‡ "
12 of Eden w· were in Telassar? ‡ "
17 w· hath sent to reproach the living‡ "
22 word w· the Lord hath spoken "
29 back by the way w· thou camest. "
30 year that w· springeth of the same:
38: 3 have done that w· is good in thy sight.
8 w· is gone down in the sun dial of 834
8 by w· degrees it was gone down. *
39: 6 that w· thy fathers have laid up in 834
7 w· thou shalt beget, shall they take‡"
8 of the Lord w· thou hast spoken.
42: 5 earth, and that w· cometh out of it;
43: 16 the Lord, w· maketh a way in the sea,‡
17 W· bringeth forth the chariot and‡
44: 2 thee from the womb, w· will help thee;*
14 w· he strengtheneth for himself *
45: 3 the Lord, w· call thee by thy name,‡
46: 3 w· are borne by me from the belly,‡
3 belly, w· are carried from the womb:‡
47: 11 thee suddenly, w· thou shalt not know.
48: 1 w· are called by the name of Israel,‡
1 w· swear by the name of the Lord,
14 w· among them hath declared ‡4310
17 thy God w· teacheth thee to profit,‡
17 w· leadeth thee by the way that thou‡
49: 20 The children w· thou shalt have, after*
50: 1 w· of my creditors is it to whom ‡4310
51: 10 Art thou not it w· hath dried the sea,‡
12 son of man w· shall be made as grass;‡
17 w· hast drunk at the hand of the ‡ 834
23 w· have said to my soul, Bow down,‡"
52: 15 w· had not been told them shall ‡ "
15 that w· they had not heard shall they"
55: 11 it shall accomplish that w· I please, "
56: 8 Lord God w· gathereth the outcasts‡
11 dogs w· can never have enough, *
57: 16 me, and the souls w· I have made.‡
59: 5 that w· is crushed breaketh out into a
61: 9 the seed w· the Lord hath blessed.‡
62: 2 w· the mouth of the Lord shall 834
6 w· shall never hold their peace day*
8 for the w· thou hast laboured: 834
63: 7 w· he hath bestowed on them "
64: 3 terrible things w· we looked not for,
65: 2 w· walketh in a way that was not ‡
4 W· remain among the graves, and‡
4 w· eat swine's flesh, and broth of ‡
7 w· have burned incense upon the 834
18 for ever in that w· I create: "
66: 4 and chose that in w· I delighted not.*"
22 the new earth, w· I will make, shall "
Jer 2: 11 their gods, w· are yet no gods? ‡1992
11 glory for that w· did not profit. "
3: 15 w· shall feed you with knowledge and‡
5: 17 w· thy sons and thy daughters should
21 w· have eyes, and see not; ‡
21 w· have ears, and hear not: ‡
22 w· have placed the sand for the ‡ 834
7: 10 w· is called by my name, and say, "
11 w· is called by my name, become "
12 unto my place w· was in Shiloh, "
14 house, w· is called by my name, "
14 the place w· I gave to you and to "
30 the house w· I called by my name, "
31 w· is in the valley of the son of "
31 w· I commanded them not, neither "
8: 3 w· remain in all the places whither I‡

Jer 8: 17 among you, w· will not be charmed,834
9: 13 my law w· I set before them, "
14 w· their fathers taught them: "
24 the Lord w· exercise lovingkindness,‡
25 punish all them w· are circumcised‡
10: 1 word w· the Lord speaketh unto 834
11: 4 W· I commanded your fathers in "
4 to all w· I commanded you: "
5 oath w· I have sworn unto your "
8 w· I commanded them to do; "
10 w· refused to hear my words; and‡ "
10 w· I made with their fathers. "
11 w· they shall not be able to escape; "
17 w· they have done against "
12: 14 w· I have caused my people Israel to"
13: 4 thou hast got, w· is upon thy loins, "
6 w· I commanded thee to hide there. "
10 people, w· refuse to hear my words,‡
10 w· walk in the imagination of their ‡
10 this girdle, w· is good for nothing. 834
15: 4 for that w· he did in Jerusalem. "
14 into a land w· thou knowest not:
14 mine anger, w· shall burn upon you.
18 incurable, w· refuseth to be healed?
17: 4 in the land w· thou knowest not: 834
4 in mine anger, w· shall burn for ever.
16 that w· came out of my lips was right
19 by the w· they go out, and in all 834
18: 1 The word w· came to Jeremiah "
14 snow of Lebanon w· cometh from the*
19: 2 w· is by the entry of the east gate, 834
3 the w· whosoever heareth, his ears "
5 w· I commanded not, nor spake it, "
20: 2 w· was by the house of the Lord. "
5 w· shall spoil them, and take them,‡
16 the cities w· the Lord overthrew, 834
21: 1 word w· came unto Jeremiah from "
4 w· besiege you without the walls,‡
13 w· say, Who shall come down against‡
22: 6 and cities w· are not inhabited.
11 w· reigned instead of Josiah his ‡
11 w· went forth out of this place; He‡834
28 cast into a land w· they know not? "
23: 4 over them w· shall feed them: ‡
7 w· brought up the children of ‡ 834
8 w· brought up and w· led the seed of‡"
27 W· think to cause my people to forget‡
27 w· they tell every man to his 834
40 shame, w· shall not be forgotten. "
24: 2 naughty figs, w· could not be eaten, "
8 as the evil figs, w· cannot be eaten, "
25: 2 The w· Jeremiah the prophet spake "
13 words w· I have pronounced against"
13 w· Jeremiah hath prophesied "
22 of the isles w· are beyond the sea, "
26 w· are upon the face of the earth: "
27 sword w· I will send among you. "
29 on the city w· is called by my name, "
26: 2 w· come to worship in the Lord's ‡
3 evil w· I purpose to do unto them 834
4 in my law w· I have set before you, "
19 of the evil w· he had pronounced "
27: 3 the messengers w· come to Jerusalem‡
8 kingdom w· will not serve the ‡ 834
9 your sorcerers, w· speak unto you,‡ "
18 w· are left in the house of the Lord,
20 W· Nebuchadnezzar king of 834
28: 1 Azur the prophet, w· was of Gibeon,‡"
6 thy words w· thou hast prophesied, "
9 prophet w· prophesieth of peace, ‡ "
29: 1 elders w· were carried away captives,*
8 dreams w· ye caused to be dreamed.834
19 w· I sent unto them by my servants*"
21 w· prophesy a lie unto you in my ‡
22 of Judah w· are in Babylon, ‡ 834
23 w· I have not commanded them; "
27 w· maketh himself a prophet to you?‡
31: 2 The people w· were left of the sword‡
21 even the way w· thou wentest:
32 w· my covenant they brake, 834
35 w· giveth the sun for a light by day,*
35 w· divideth the sea when the waves‡
32: 1 w· was the eighteenth year of 1958
2 w· was in the king of Judah's 834
8 w· is in the country of Benjamin: "
11 both that w· was sealed according to
11 and custom, and that w· was open:
14 of the purchase, both w· is sealed,
14 and this evidence w· is open; and put
20 W· hast set signs and wonders in‡ 834
22 w· thou didst swear to their fathers "
32 w· they have done to provoke me to "
34 w· is called by my name, to defile it. "
35 w· are in the valley of the son of "
35 w· I commanded them not, neither "
33: 3 mighty things, w· thou knowest not.
4 w· are thrown down by the mounts,
9 w· shall hear all the good that I do ‡834
10 w· ye say shall be desolate without* "
12 w· is desolate without man and
14 good thing w· I have promised 834
24 families w· the Lord hath chosen, "
34: 1 The word w· came unto Jeremiah "
5 former kings w· were before thee,‡ "
8 all the people w· were at Jerusalem,‡"
10 w· had entered into the covenant, ‡ "
14 w· hath been sold unto thee; ‡ "
15 the house w· is called by my name: "
18 w· have not performed the words of‡"
18 covenant w· they had made before "
19 w· passed between the parts of the‡
21 army, w· are gone up from you. ‡
35: 1 The word w· came unto Jeremiah 834
4 w· was by the chamber of the "
4 w· was above the chamber of "
15 in the land w· I have given to you

Jer 35: 16 father, w· he commanded them: 834
36: 3 evil w· I purpose to do unto them; "
4 w· he had spoken unto him, upon a "
6 w· thou hast written from my "
21 the princes w· stood beside the king.‡
27 w· Baruch wrote at the mouth of 834
28 w· Jehoiakim the king of Judah hath"
32 w· Jehoiakim king of Judah had "
37: 2 Lord, w· he spake by the prophet "
7 army, w· is come forth to help you,‡
19 prophets w· prophesied unto you,‡ 834
38: 3 of Babylon's army, w· shall take it.‡
7 w· was in the king's house, heard‡1931
20 of the Lord, w· I speak unto thee: 834
39: 10 of the people, w· had nothing, ‡ "
40: 1 The word w· came to Jeremiah from "
1 w· were carried away captive unto‡
4 chains w· were upon thine hand. 834
7 of the forces w· were in the field, "
10 Chaldeans w· will come unto us: ‡ "
15 all the Jews w· are gathered unto thee‡
41: 13 the people w· were with Ishmael ‡ 834
17 of Chimham, w· is by Beth-lehem, "
42: 5 for the w· the Lord thy God shall * "
8 of the forces w· were with him, "
16 sword, w· ye feared, shall overtake "
21 for the w· he hath sent me unto you. "
43: 1 for w· the Lord their God had sent* "
9 w· is at the entry of Pharaoh's "
44: 1 Jews w· dwell in the land of Egypt,‡
1 w· dwell at Migdol, and at Tahpanhes,‡
3 w· they have committed to provoke834
9 w· they have committed in the land "
14 w· are gone into the land of Egypt to‡
14 to the w· they...desire to return 834
15 men w· knew that their wives had‡
20 people w· had given him that answer,‡
22 of the abominations w· ye have 834
45: 4 that w· I have built will I break "
4 that w· I have planted I will pluck "
46: 1 The word...w· came to Jeremiah "
2 w· was by the river Euphrates in "
2 w· Nebuchadrezzar king of Babylon "
49: 28 w· Nebuchadrezzar king of Babylon "
31 nations,...w· have neither gates nor‡
31 neither gates nor bars w· dwell alone.‡
50: 3 w· shall make her land desolate, ‡1931
51: 12 and done that w· he spake against 834
25 the Lord, w· destroyest all the earth:
44 mouth that w· he hath swallowed up:
59 The word w· Jeremiah the prophet 834
52: 2 that w· was evil in the eyes of the
7 walls, w· was by the king's garden:834
12 w· was the nineteenth year of 1958
12 guard, w· served the king of Babylon,‡
19 that w· was of gold in gold, and 834
19 and that w· was of silver in silver, "
20 w· king Solomon had made in the "
25 w· had...charge of the men of war;‡ "
25 person, w· were found in the city;‡ "
La 1: 12 my sorrow, w· is done unto me,
2: 3 fire, w· devoureth round about.
17 hath done that w· he had devised; 834
5: 18 the mountain of Zion, w· is desolate,
Eze 1: 2 w· was the fifth year of king 1958
23 one had two, w· covered on this side,
23 one had two, w· covered on that side,
3: 20 his righteousness w· he hath done 834
23 glory w· I saw by the river of Chebar:"
4: 10 And the meat w· thou shalt eat shall"
14 I not eaten of that w· dieth of itself,
5: 9 do in thee that w· I have not done, 834
16 w· shall be for their destruction, "
16 and w· I will send to destroy you: "
6: 9 heart, w· hath departed from me, "
9 eyes, w· go a whoring after their idols:‡
9 evils w· they have committed in all 834
7: 13 shall not return to that w· is sold,
13 multitude thereof, w· shall not return;‡
8: 3 of jealousy, w· provoketh to jealousy.
14 house w· was toward the north; 834
17 abominations w· they commit here? "
9: 2 gate, w· lieth toward the north, "
3 w· had the writer's inkhorn by his‡ "
6 men w· were before the house. ‡ "
11 w· had the inkhorn by his side, ‡
10: 22 w· I saw by the river of Chebar,
11: 1 Lord's house, w· looketh eastward:
3 W· say, It is not near; let us build‡
23 w· is on the east side of the city. 834
12: 2 w· have eyes to see, and see not; ‡ "
28 word w· I have spoken shall be done,"
13: 11 w· daub it with untempered morter,*
16 w· prophesy concerning Jerusalem,‡
16 and w· see visions of peace for her,‡
17 w· prophesy out of their own heart;‡
14: 7 w· separateth himself from me, ‡
15: 2 w· is among the trees of the forest?834
6 w· I have given to the fire for fuel, "
16: 14 comeliness, w· I had put upon thee, "
17 of my silver, w· I had given thee, "
19 My meat also w· I gave thee, fine "
27 w· are ashamed of thy lewd way; ‡
32 w· taketh strangers instead of her*
36 w· thou didst give unto them; 834
45 w· lothed their husbands and their‡ "
51 abominations w· thou hast done. "
52 also, w· hast judged thy sisters, * "
57 Philistines w· despise thee round‡
59 w· hast despised the oath in ‡ 834
17: 3 of feathers, w· had divers colours, "
18: 5 and do that w· is lawful and right, "
14 his father's sins w· he hath done, 834
18 w· is not good among his people, "
19 the son hath done that w· is lawful
21 and do that w· is lawful and right, he

Eze 18:27 doeth that w' is lawful and right, he
19:14 w' hath devoured her fruit, so that she*
20: 6 honey, w' is the glory of all lands: 1958
11, 13 w' if a man do, he shall even live 834
15 into the land w' I have given them, "
15 honey, w' is the glory of all lands; 1958
21 w' if a man do, he shall even live in 834
28 w' I lifted up mine hand to give it to "
32 that w' cometh into your mind shall
42 for the w' I lifted up mine hand 834
21:14 w' entereth into their privy chambers.‡
22: 4 in thine idols w' thou hast made; 834
5 w' art infamous and much vexed. ‡
13 dishonest gain w' thou hast made, 834
13 thy blood w' hath been in the midst "
23: 6 W' were clothed with blue, captains‡
24 w' shall set against thee buckler and*
42 w' put bracelets upon their hands,*
24:21 eyes, and that w' your soul pitieth;
27 mouth be opened to him w' is escaped,‡
25: 9 from his cities w' are on his frontiers,
26: 6 her daughters w' are in the field ‡ 834
17 w' wast strong in the sea, she and‡ "
17 w' cause their terror to be on all ‡ "
27: 3 w' art a merchant for the people on‡
7 that w' thou spreadest forth to be thy*
7 of Elishah was that w' covered thee.*
27 company w' is in the midst of thee,‡834
29: 3 w' hath said, My river is mine own,‡
16 Israel w' bringeth their iniquity to*
30:22 the strong, and that w' was broken;
32: 9 countries w' thou hast not known. 834
23 w' caused terror in the land of the‡ "
24 w' are gone down uncircumcised ‡ "
24 w' caused their terror in the land of‡"
27 w' are gone down to hell with their‡ "
29 w' with their might are laid by them‡"
30 w' are gone down with the slain; ‡ "
33:14 and do that w' is lawful and right;
16 he hath done that w' is lawful and
29 all their abominations w' they have 834
34: 4 have ye healed that w' was sick,
4 have ye bound up that w' was broken,
4 ye brought again that w' was driven
4 have ye sought that w' was lost;
16 I will seek that w' was lost, and bring
16 bring again that w' was driven away,
16 and will bind up that w' was broken,
16 and will strengthen that w' was sick:
19 eat that w' ye have trodden with your
19 they drink that w' ye have fouled with
35:11 w' thou hast used out of thy hatred 834
12 blasphemies w' thou hast spoken "
36: 4 w' became a prey and derision to ‡ "
5 w' have appointed my land into "
21 w' the house of Israel had profaned "
22 w' ye have profaned among the "
23 w' was profaned among the heathen,
23 w' ye have profaned in the midst of 834
37: 1 of the valley w' was full of bones, *1958
19 w' is in the hand of Ephraim, 834
38: 8 Israel, w' have been always waste: "
12 w' have gotten cattle and goods, ‡
17 w' prophesied in those days many‡
39:19 of my sacrifice w' I have sacrificed 834
28 w' caused them to be led into *
40: 2 w' was as the frame of a city on the*
6 gate, w' looketh toward the east, 834
6 of the gate, w' was one reed broad;*
6 of the gate, w' was one reed broad.*
40 w' was at the porch of the gate, 834
44 w' was at the side of the north gate; "
46 w' come near to the Lord to minister‡
41: 1 w' was the breadth of the tabernacle.
6 into the wall w' was of the house 834
9 w' was for the side chamber without"
9 that w' was left was the place of the
15 separate place w' was behind it, 834
42: 1 w' was before the building toward "
3 cubits w' were for the inner court, "
3 the pavement w' was for the utter "
11 chambers w' were toward the north,"
13 w' are before the separate place, "
14 to those things w' are for the people."
43: 3 appearance of the vision w' I saw, "
19 seed of Zadok, w' approach unto me,‡
44: 1 sanctuary w' looketh toward the east;
10 w' went astray away from me after‡834
13 their abominations w' they have "
45: 4 w' shall come near to minister unto‡
14 cor, w' is an homer of ten baths; 4480
46:19 w' was at the side of the gate, 834
19 priests, w' looked toward the north:
47: 8 w' being brought forth into the sea,
9 every thing that liveth, w' moveth, 834
14 concerning the w' I lifted up mine "
16 w' is between the border of "
16 w' is by the coast of Hauran. "
22 w' shall beget children among you:‡ "
48: 8 be the offering w' ye shall offer "
11 of Zadok; w' have kept my charge,‡ "
11 w' went not astray when the ‡ "
22 the midst of that w' is the prince's, "
29 This is the land w' ye shall divide "
Da 1: 2 w' he carried into the land of Shinar*
5 meat, and of the wine w' he drank:
8 meat, nor with the wine w' he drank:
10 the children w' are of your sort? ‡ 834
15 w' did eat the portion of the king's‡
2:14 w' was gone forth to slay the wise 1768
26 unto me the dream w' I have seen, "
27 secret w' the king hath demanded "
34 w' smote the image upon his feet that
39 w' shall bear rule over all the 1768
44 w' shall never be destroyed: "
3: 2 image w' Nebuchadnezzar the king"

Da 3:12 golden image w' thou hast set up. 1768
14 the golden image w' I have set up? "
15 worship the image w' I have made; "
18 golden image w' thou hast set up. "
29 w' speak any thing amiss against‡ "
4: 5 I saw a dream w' made me afraid,
20 tree that thou sawest, w' grew, 1768
21 under w' the beasts of the field dwelt,
24 w' is come upon my lord the king: 1768
5: 2 w' his father Nebuchadnezzar had "
2 of the temple w' was in Jerusalem; "
3 house of God w' was at Jerusalem; "
13 Daniel, w' art of the children of the‡"
23 w' see not, nor hear, nor know: ‡ "
6: 1 w' should be over the whole kingdom;‡
8, 12 Medes and Persians, w' altereth 1768
13 Daniel, w' is of the children of the ‡"
15 statute w' the king established "
24 those men w' had accused Daniel,‡ "
26 that w' shall not be destroyed, "
7: 6 w' had upon the back of it four "
11 the great words w' the horn spake: "
14 dominion, w' shall not pass away, "
14 that w' shall not be destroyed. "
17 These great beasts, w' are four, are"
17 w' shall arise out of the earth. ‡
19 w' was diverse from all the others, 1768
19 w' devoured, brake in pieces, and
20 and of the other w' came up, and 1768
23 earth, w' shall be diverse from all "
8: 1 that w' appeared unto me at the first.
2 w' is in the province of Elam; and 834
3 the river a ram w' had two horns:
6 w' I had seen standing before the 834
9 horn, w' waxed exceeding great,
13 said unto that certain saint w' spake,‡
16 w' called, and said, Gabriel, make this‡
20 The ram w' thou sawest having 834
26 the vision...w' was told is true: "
9: 1 w' was made king over the realm of‡"
6 w' spake in thy name to our kings,‡ "
10 w' he set before us by his servants "
12 his words, w' he spake against us, "
14 in all his works w' he doeth: for we "
18 the city w' is called by thy name: "
10: 4 of the great river, w' is Hiddekel; 1931
10 touched me, w' set me upon my knees,‡
21 that w' is noted in the scripture of
11: 4 to his dominion w' he ruled: * 834
7 estate, w' shall come with an army,‡
16 w' by his hand shall be consumed.*
24 that w' his fathers have not done, 834
12: 1 prince w' standeth for the children‡
6, 7 w' was upon the waters of the ‡ 834
Ho 1: 3 w' conceived, and bare him a son.‡
10 the sand...w' cannot be measured 834
2: 8 and gold, w' they prepared for Baal.
23 will say to them w' are not my people,‡
5: 9 made known that w' shall surely be.
Joe 1: 4 That w' the palmerworm hath left
4 and that w' the locust hath left hath
4 and that w' the cankerworm hath left
2:25 great army w' I sent among you. ‡ 834
Am 1: 1 w' he saw concerning Israel in the "
4 w' shall devour the palaces of *
7 w' shall devour the palaces thereof:*
10 w' shall devour the palaces thereof.*
12 w' shall devour the palaces of *
2: 4 the w' their fathers have walked: 834
3: 1 w' I brought up from the land of ‡ "
4: 1 of Bashan,...w' oppress the poor, ‡
1 the poor, w' crush the needy, ‡
1 w' say to their masters, Bring, and let‡
3 every cow at that w' is before her;
5: 1 word w' I take up against you, 834
3 and that w' went forth by an hundred
26 god, w' ye made for yourselves. 834
6: 1 w' are named chief of the nations,*
13 Ye w' rejoice in a thing of nought,‡
13 w' say, Have we not taken to us horns‡
9:10 w' say, The evil shall not overtake nor‡
12 heathen, w' are called by my name,‡834
15 of their land w' I have given them, "
Ob 20 of Jerusalem, w' is in Sepharad, "
Jon 1: 9 w' hath made the sea and the dry ‡ "
4:10 for the w' thou hast not laboured, "
10 w' came up in a night, and perished in
Mic 1: 1 w' he saw concerning Samaria and 834
2: 3 evil, from w' ye shall not remove "
5: 3 time that she w' travaileth hath ‡
6:14 and that w' thou deliverest will I 834
7:10 shame shall cover her w' said unto‡
14 w' dwell solitarily in the wood, ‡
20 w' thou hast sworn unto our 834
Na 3:17 w' camp in the hedges in the cold day,
Hab 1: 1 The burden w' Habakkuk the 834
5 w' ye will not believe, though it
6 w' shall march through the breadth‡
2: 4 his soul w' is lifted up is not upright
6 him that increaseth that w' is not his!
17 spoil of beasts, w' made them afraid,
Zep 1: 1 the Lord w' came unto Zephaniah 834
9 w' fill their masters' houses with ‡
2: 3 w' have wrought his judgment; ‡834
Hag 1:11 that w' the ground bringeth forth, "
2:14 that w' they offer there is unclean. "
Zec 1: 6 w' I commanded my servants the "
7 month, w' is the month Sebat, 1931
12 Judah, against w' thou hast had 834
19, 21 horns w' have scattered Judah, "
21 w' lifted up their horn over the land of
2: 8 me unto the nations w' spoiled you:‡
4: 2 lamps, w' are upon the top thereof:
10 w' run to and fro through the whole*
12 w' through the two golden pipes 834
6: 5 w' go forth from standing before the‡

Zec 6: 6 The black horses w' are therein go* 834
10 w' are come from Babylon, and * "
7: 3 the priests w' were in the house * "
7 the words w' the Lord hath cried "
12 and the words w' the Lord of hosts "
8: 9 w' were in the day that the ‡ "
10: 5 w' tread down their enemies in the*
11:10 w' I had made with all the people. 834
16 w' shall not visit those that be cut off,‡
12: 1 Lord, w' stretcheth forth the heavens,‡
13: 6 Those with w' I was wounded in 834
14: 4 w' is before Jerusalem on the east, "
7 day w' shall be known to the Lord, 1931
16 of all the nations w' came against‡
Mal 1:13 and ye brought that w' was torn, and
14 w' hath in his flock a male, ‡3426
2:11 holiness of the Lord w' he loved, 834
4: 4 w' I commanded unto him in "
M't 1:20 w' is conceived in her is of the Holy
22 fulfilled w' was spoken of the Lord 3588
23 Emmanuel, w' being interpreted 3739
2: 9 lo, the star w' they saw in the east, "
15 fulfilled w' was spoken of the 3588
16 the time w' he had diligently 3739
17 that w' was spoken by Jeremy 3588
20 w' sought the young child's life. * "
23 w' was spoken by the prophets, * "
3:10 tree w' bringeth not forth good fruit*
4:13 in Capernaum, w' is upon the sea 3588
14 fulfilled w' was spoken by Esaias "
16 people w' sat in darkness saw * "
16 w' sat in the region and shadow * "
24 those w' were possessed with devils,*
24 and those w' were lunatick, and those*
5: 6 Blessed are they w' do hunger *3588
10 w' are persecuted for righteousness'*
12 the prophets w' were before you. ‡3588
16 glorify your Father w' is in heaven.‡"
44 pray for them w' despitefully use * "
45 the children of your Father w' is in* "
46 For if ye love them w' love you, "
48 Father w' is in heaven is perfect. * "
6: 1 of your Father w' is in heaven. * "
4 Father w' seeth in secret himself ‡ "
6 pray to thy Father w' is in secret;‡ "
6 Father w' seeth in secret shall ‡ "
9 Our Father w' art in heaven, ‡ "
18 unto thy Father w' is in secret: ‡ "
18 and thy Father, w' seeth in secret,‡ "
27 W' of you by taking thought can ‡5101
30 w' to day is, and to morrow is cast
7: 6 not that w' is holy unto the dogs, 3588
11 w' is in heaven give good things ‡ "
13 and many there be w' go in thereat:* "
14 narrow is the way, w' leadeth unto* "
15 w' come to you in sheep's ‡3748
21 will of my Father w' is in heaven.‡3588
24 w' built his house upon a rock: ‡3748
26 w' built his house upon the sand:‡ "
8:17 w' was spoken by Esaias the 3588
9: 8 w' had given such power unto men.‡"
16 that w' is put in to fill it up taketh
20 w' was diseased with an issue of ‡
10:20 your Father w' speaketh in you. ‡3588
28 And fear not them w' kill the body,‡"
28 fear him w' is able to destroy ‡ "
32, 33 before my Father w' is in heaven.‡"
11: 4 those things w' ye do hear and 3739
10 w' shall prepare thy way before * "
14 this is Elias, w' was for to come. ‡3588
21 works, w' were done in you, had "
23 w' art exalted unto heaven, * "
23 works, w' have been done in thee, "
12: 2 do that w' is not lawful to do upon 3739
4 w' was not lawful for him to eat, "
4 neither for them w' were with him,*
10 was a man w' had his hand withered.*
17 w' was spoken by Esaias the 3588
50 will of my Father w' is in heaven, ‡ "
13:14 w' saith, By hearing ye shall hear, "
17 to see those things w' ye see, 3739
17 to hear those things w' ye hear, "
19 that w' was sown in his heart. 3588
19 is he w' received by the way side. * "
23 w' also beareth fruit, and bringeth* 3739
24 unto a man w' sowed good seed in his*
31 w' a man took, and sowed in his 3739
32 W' indeed is the least of all seeds; "
33 w' a woman took, and hid in three "
35 w' was spoken by the prophet, 3588
35 I will utter things w' have been kept*
41 that offend, and them w' do iniquity;*
44 w' when a man hath found, he 3739
48 W', when it was full, they drew to "
52 w' is instructed unto the kingdom of*
52 w' bringeth forth out of his ‡3748
14: 9 and them w' sat with him at meat,‡
15: 1 Pharisees, w' were of Jerusalem, *3588
11 Not that w' goeth into the mouth
11 but that w' cometh out of the mouth,
13 w' my heavenly Father hath not 3739
18 w' proceed out of the mouth 3588
20 are the things w' defile a man: "
27 crumbs w' fall from their masters' "
16: 8 W' when Jesus perceived, he said*
17 but my Father w' is in heaven. ‡3588
28 w' shall not taste of death, till ‡3748
17: 5 a voice out of the cloud, w' said, *
18: 6 these little ones w' believe in me, *3588
10 face of my Father w' is in heaven.‡ "
11 is come to save that w' was lost. "
12 seeketh that w' is gone astray? "
13 ninety and nine w' went not astray "
14 will of your Father w' is in heaven,‡"
19 them of my Father w' is in heaven.‡"
23 w' would take account of his ‡3739

M't 18:24 w' owed him ten thousand talents.‡
28 w' owed him an hundred pence: ‡3739
19: 4 w' made them at the beginning ‡3588
9 marrieth her w' is put away doth ‡ "
12 w' were so born from their ‡3748
12 w' were made eunuchs of men: ‡ "
12 w' have made themselves eunuchs‡"
18 He saith unto him, W'? Jesus 4169
28 That ye w' have followed me, in ‡3588
20: 1 w' went out early in the morning ‡3748
12 w' have borne the burden and ‡3588
21: 4 w' was spoken by the prophet, "
21 do this w' is done to the fig tree, *
24 w' if ye tell me, I in like wise will 3739
33 householder, w' planted a ‡3748
41 w' shall render him the fruits in ‡ "
42 The stone w' the builders rejected,3739
22: 2 w' made a marriage for his son, ‡3748
4 Tell them w' are bidden, Behold, I*
8 they w' were bidden were not worthy.‡
11 w' had not on a wedding garment:‡
21 unto Cæsar the things w' are Cæsar's;
23 w' say that there is no resurrection,‡3588
31 w' was spoken unto you by God, "
35 Then one of them, w' was a lawyer,*
36 w' is the great commandment in 4169
23: 9 is your Father, w' is in heaven. ‡3588
16 unto you, ye blind guides, w' say,‡ "
24 blind guides, w' strain at a gnat, ‡ "
26 first that w' is within the cup and* "
27 w' indeed appear beautiful 3748
31 of them w' killed the prophets. *
37 stonest them w' are sent unto thee,*
24:17 Let him w' is on the housetop not*
18 Neither let him w' is in the field *
25: 1 ten virgins, w' took their lamps, ‡3748
24 Then he w' had received the one *
28 give it unto him w' hath ten talents.*
29 be taken away even that w' he hath.
26:25 Then Judas, w' betrayed him, ‡3588
28 w' is shed for many for the "
51 one of them w' were with Jesus ‡
62 is it w' these witness against thee?
75 word of Jesus, w' said unto him, ‡3588
27: 3 Then Judas, w' had betrayed him,‡ "
9 that w' was spoken by Jeremy "
17 or Jesus w' is called Christ? ‡ "
22 then with Jesus w' is called Christ?‡"
35 w' was spoken by the prophet, "
44 also, w' were crucified with him, ‡ "
52 bodies of the saints w' slept arose,* "
55 w' followed Jesus from Galilee, ‡3748
56 Among w' was Mary Magdalene, *3739
28: 5 ye seek Jesus, w' was crucified. ‡3588
M'r 1: 2 w' shall prepare thy way before *3739
44 those things w' Moses commanded, "
2: 3 sick of the palsy, w' was borne of*
24 sabbath day that w' is not lawful? 3739
26 w' is not lawful to eat but for the "
26 gave also to them w' were with him?‡
3: 1 a man there w' had a withered hand.‡
3 unto the man w' had the withered*
17 Boanerges, w' is, The sons of ‡3739
19 Judas Iscariot, w' also betrayed ‡2076
22 the scribes w' came down from ‡3588
34 about on them w' sat about him, ‡ "
4:16 likewise w' are sown on stony ground;*
18 are they w' are sown among thorns;*
20 are they w' are sown on good ground;
22 hid, w' shall not be manifested; *3739
31 w', when it is sown in the earth, "
5:25 w' had an issue of blood twelve years,‡
35 w' said, Thy daughter is dead: *
41 w' is, being interpreted, Damsel, 3739
6: 2 wisdom is this w' is given unto him,*
26 for their sakes w' sat with him, *3588
7: 1 the scribes w' came from Jerusalem.‡
4 be, w' they have received to hold, 3739
13 tradition, w' ye have delivered: "
15 but the things w' come out of him, "
20 That w' cometh out of the man, that
9: 1 here, w' shall not taste of death, ‡3748
17 thee my son, w' hath a dumb spirit;‡
39 man w' shall do a miracle in my ‡3739
10:42 that they w' are accounted to rule‡
11:21 the fig tree w' thou cursedst is 3739
23 w' he saith shall come to pass; * "
25 your Father also w' is in heaven ‡3588
26 Father w' is in heaven forgive your*"
12:10 The stone w' the builders rejected 3739
18 w' say there is no resurrection; ‡3748
25 as the angels w' are in heaven. ‡3588
28 W' is the first commandment of *4169
38 w' love to go in long clothing, ‡3588
40 W' devour widows' houses, and ‡3739
42 in two mites, w' make a farthing. 2076
43 they w' have cast into the treasury:‡
13:19 the creation w' God created unto 3739
32 not the angels w' are in heaven, *3588
14:18 One of you w' eateth with me ‡ "
24 testament, w' is shed for many. "
60 what is it w' these witness against
15: 7 w' lay bound with them that had *
22 w' is, being interpreted, The place 3739
28 scripture was fulfilled, w' saith, *3588
34 w' is, being interpreted, My God, 3739
39 centurion, w' stood over against ‡3588
41 women w' came up with him unto‡ "
43 w'...waited for the kingdom ‡3739,846
46 sepulchre w' was hewn out of a 3739
16: 6 Jesus...Nazareth, w' was crucified:‡3588
14 w' had seen him after he was risen.*
Lu 1: 1 things w' are most surely believed
2 w' from the beginning were ‡3588
20 w' shall be fulfilled in their 3748
35 holy thing w' shall be born of thee

Lu 1:45 things w' were told her from the Lord.
70 w' have been since the world 3588
73 oath w' he sware to our father 3739
2: 4 of David, w' is called Bethlehem; 3748
10 great joy, w' shall be to all people. "
11 a Saviour, w' is Christ the Lord. ‡3739
15 see this thing w' is come to pass, *3588
15 w' the Lord hath made known unto "
17 w' was told them concerning the "
18 things w' were told them by the "
21 w' was so named of the angel "
24 that w' is said in the law of the Lord,
31 W' thou hast prepared before the 3739
33 those things w' were spoken of him.
34 and for a sign w' shall be spoken
37 w' departed not from the temple, ‡3739
50 the saying w' he spake unto them. "
3: 9 w' bringeth not forth good fruit is*
13 more than that w' is appointed you.
19 all the evils w' Herod had done, 3739
22 a voice came from heaven, w' said,*
23 son of Joseph, w' was the son of Heli,*
24 W' was the son of Matthat, *
24 of Matthat, w' was the son of Levi,*
24 son of Levi, w' was the son of Melchi,*
24 of Melchi, w' was the son of Janna,*
24 of Janna, w' was the son of Joseph,*
25 W' was the son of Mattathias, *
25 Mattathias, w' was the son of Amos,*
25 son of Amos, w' was the son of Naum,*
25 son of Naum, w' was the son of Esli,*
25 son of Esli, w' was the son of Nagge,*
26 W' was the son of Maath, *
26 Maath, w' was the son of Mattathias,*
26 Mattathias, w' was the son of Semei,*
26 of Semei, w' was the son of Joseph,*
26 son of Joseph, w' was the son of Juda,*
27 W' was the son of Joanna, *
27 of Joanna, w' was the son of Rhesa,*
27 of Rhesa, w' was the son of Zorobabel,*
27 Zorobabel, w' was the son of Salathiel,*
27 of Salathiel, w' was the son of Neri,*
28 W' was the son of Melchi, *
28 son of Melchi, w' was the son of Addi,*
28 son of Addi, w' was the son of Cosam,*
28 Cosam, w' was the son of Elmodam,*
28 son of Elmodam, w' was the son of Er,*
29 W' was the son of Jose, *
29 son of Jose, w' was the son of Eliezer,*
29 of Eliezer, w' was the son of Jorim,*
29 of Jorim, w' was the son of Matthat,*
29 of Matthat, w' was the son of Levi,*
30 W' was the son of Simeon, *
30 son of Simeon, w' was the son of Juda,*
30 son of Juda, w' was the son of Joseph,*
30 of Joseph, w' was the son of Jonan,*
30 of Jonan, w' was the son of Eliakim,*
31 W' was the son of Melea, *
31 son of Melea, w' was the son of Menan,*
31 Menan, w' was the son of Mattatha,*
31 Mattatha, w' was the son of Nathan,*
31 of Nathan, w' was the son of David,*
32 W' was the son of Jesse, *
32 son of Jesse, w' was the son of Obed,*
32 son of Obed, w' was the son of Booz,*
32 of Booz, w' was the son of Salmon,*
32 of Salmon, w' was the son of Naasson,*
33 W' was the son of Aminadab, *
33 w' was the son of Aram, *
33 w' was the son of Esrom, *
33 w' was the son of Phares, *
33 of Phares, w' was the son of Juda,*
34 W' was the son of Jacob, *
34 w' was the son of Isaac, *
34 w' was the son of Abraham, *
34 w' was the son of Thara, *
34 of Thara, w' was the son of Nachor,*
35 W' was the son of Saruch, *
35 w' was the son of Ragau, *
35 w' was the son of Phalec, *
35 w' was the son of Heber, *
35 of Heber, w' was the son of Sala, *
36 W' was the son of Cainan, *
36 w' was the son of Arphaxad, *
36 w' was the son of Sem, *
36 w' was the son of Noe, *
36 of Noe, w' was the son of Lamech,*
37 W' was the son of Mathusala, *
37 w' was the son of Enoch, *
37 w' was the son of Jared, *
37 w' was the son of Maleleel, *
37 of Maleleel, w' was the son of Cainan,*
38 W' was the son of Enos, *
38 w' was the son of Seth, *
38 w' was the son of Adam, *
38 w' was the son of God. *
4:22 w' proceeded out of his mouth. 3588
33 man, w' had a spirit of an unclean‡
5: 3 one of the ships, w' was Simon's, 3739
7 w' were in the other ship, ‡3588
9 of fishes w' they had taken: 3739
10 Zebedee, w' were partners with ‡ "
17 w' were come out of every town of‡ "
18 a man w' was taken with a palsy:‡ "
21 is this w' speaketh blasphemies? * "
6: 2 do ye that w' is not lawful to do on "
3 hungred, and they w' were with "
4 w' it is not lawful to eat but for the
8 man w' had the withered hand, *3739
16 Judas Iscariot, w' also was the ‡ "
17 w' came to hear him, and to be ‡ "
27 I say unto you w' hear, Love your‡
27 do good to them w' hate you, *3588
28 for them w' despitefully use you. *
32 if ye love them w' love you, what *
33 ye do good to them w' do good to you.*

Lu 6:45 heart bringeth forth that w' is good;
45 heart bringeth forth that w' is evil:
46 and do not the things w' I say? 3739
48 is like a man w' built a house, and*"
49 against w' the stream did beat "
7:25 they w' are gorgeously apparelled,‡
27 w' shall prepare thy way before *3739
37 woman in the city, w' was a *3748
39 w' had bidden him saw it, he ‡3588
41 a certain creditor w' had two debtors:*
42 w' of them will love him most? 5101
47 Her sins, w' are many, are 3588
8: 2 w' had been healed of evil spirits ‡3739
3 w' ministered unto him of their ‡3748
13 w', when they hear, receive the ‡3739
13 no root, w' for a while, believe, ‡ "
14 that w' fell among thorns are they,
14 w', when they have heard, go forth,*
15 w' in an honest and good heart, *3748
16 they w' enter in may see the light.‡
18 even that w' he seemeth to have. 3739
20 was told him by certain w' said, Thy*
21 these w' hear the word of God, ‡3588
26 w' is over against Galilee. 3748
27 man w' had devils long time, and *3739
36 They also w' saw it told them by what*
43 w' had spent all her living upon ‡3748
9:27 w' shall not taste of death, till ‡3739
30 men, w' were Moses and Elias: ‡3748
31 w' he should accomplish at 3739
36 of those things w' they had seen. "
43 every one at all things w' Jesus did,*"
46 w' of them should be greatest. ‡5101
61 farewell, w' are at home at my house,‡
10:11 dust of your city, w' cleaveth on 3588
13 Sidon, w' have been done in you, 3739
15 w' art exalted to heaven, shalt *3588
23 eyes w' see the things that ye see: "
24 desired to see those things w' ye 3739
24 to hear those things w' ye hear, "
30 w' stripped him of his raiment, ‡ "
36 W' now of these three, thinkest ‡5101
39 w' also sat at Jesus' feet, and heard‡
42 w' shall not be taken away from 3748
11: 2 Our Father w' art in heaven, *3588
5 W' of you shall have a friend, and‡5101
27 and the paps w' thou hast sucked.*3739
33 w' come in may see the light. *3588
35 light w' is in thee be not darkness.*"
40 he, that made that w' is without * "
40 make that w' is within also? *
44 ye are as graves w' appear not, 3588
50 prophets, w' was shed from the "
51 w' perished between the altar and‡ "
12: 1 the Pharisees, w' is hypocrisy. 3748
3 w' ye have spoken in the ear, in 3739
5 w' after he hath killed hath power‡
15 abundance of the things w' he
20 things be, w' thou hast provided? 3739
24 w' neither have storehouse nor "
25 And w' of you with taking thought‡5101
26 be not able to do that thing w' is least,
28 the grass, w' is to day in the field,
33 yourselves bags w' wax not old,
47 servant, w' knew his lord's will, ‡3588
13:11 a woman w' had a spirit of infirmity‡
14 six days in w' men ought to work: 3739
19 of mustard seed, w' a man took, "
21 leaven, w' a woman took and hid "
30 there are last w' shall be first; ‡ "
30 and there are first w' shall be last. ‡"
34 Jerusalem, w' killest the prophets,3588
14: 2 man before him w' had the dropsy.‡
5 W' of you shall have an ass or an‡5101
7 a parable to those w' were bidden,‡
24 men w' were bidden shall taste ‡3588
28 w' of you, intending to build a ‡5101
15: 4 go after that w' is lost, until he find it?
6 have found my sheep w' was lost. 3588
7 persons w' need no repentance. ‡3748
9 have found the piece w' I had lost.3739
30 w' hath devoured thy living with ‡3588
16: 1 rich man, w' had a steward; ‡3739
10 is faithful in that w' is least is faithful*
12 faithful in that w' is another man's,
12 shall give you that w' is your own?
19 man w' was clothed in purple and*2532
20 Lazarus, w' was laid at his gate, *3739
21 crumbs w' fell from the rich *3588
26 they w' would pass from hence to you‡
17: 7 w' of you, having a servant *5101
10 those things w' are commanded you,
10 done that w' was our duty to do. 3739
12 that were lepers, w' stood afar off:‡ "
31 he w' shall be upon the housetop,‡ "
18: 2 a judge, w' feared not God, neither‡
7 own elect, w' cry day and night ‡3588
9 certain w' trusted in themselves ‡ "
27 things w' are impossible with men are
34 knew they the things w' were spoken.*
39 they w' went before rebuked him,*
19: 2 w' was the chief among the *2532,846
10 to seek and to save that w' was lost.
20 w' I have kept laid up in a napkin:3739
26 every one w' hath shall be given; *3588
27 w' would not that I should reign ‡ "
30 in the w' at your entering ye shall 3739
42 the things w' belong unto thy peace!
20:17 The stone w' the builders rejected,3739
20 w' should feign themselves just men,‡
25 unto Cæsar the things w' be Cæsar's,*
25 and unto God the things w' be God's.*
27 w' deny that there is any ‡3588
35 they w' shall be accounted worthy to‡
46 w' desire to walk in long robes, ‡3588
47 W' devour widows' houses, and ‡3739

Lu 21: 6 As for these things w' ye behold, 3739
6 in the w' there shall not be left one ‡
15 w' all your adversaries shall not be* "
21 them w' are in Judæa flee to the *
21 let them w' are in the midst of it‡
22 that all things w' are written 3588
26 those things w' are coming on the
22: 1 drew nigh, w' is called the Passover.
19 is my body w' is given for you: 3588
20 in my blood, w' is shed for you.
23 w' of them it was that should do ‡5101
23 w' of them should be accounted ‡ "
28 w' have continued with me in my ‡
49 w' were about him saw what would*
52 the elders, w' were come to him, ‡
23: 27 w' also bewailed and lamented *3739
29 in the w' they shall say, Blessed
29 and the paps w' never gave suck, * "
33 to the place w' is called Calvary, 3588
39 malefactors w' were hanged railed on‡
48 beholding the things w' were done,*
55 w' came with him from Galilee, ‡3748
24: 1 the spices w' they had prepared, 3739
10 w' told these things unto the * "
12 himself at that w' was come to pass.
13 w' was from Jerusalem about
14 of all these things w' had happened.
18 known the things w' are come to pass
19 w' was a prophet mighty in deed ‡3739
21 he w' should have redeemed Israel:‡
22 w' were early at the sepulchre; *
23 angels, w' said that he was alive. ‡3739
24 w' were with us went to the sepulchre,*
44 the words w' I spake unto you, 3739
44 w' were written in the law of
Joh 1: 9 w' lighteth every man that cometh3739
13 W' were born, not of blood, nor of‡ "
18 w' is in the bosom of the Father, ‡3588
24 w' were sent were of the Pharisees.* "
29 w' taketh away the sin of the
30 a man w' is preferred before me; ‡3739
33 he w' baptizeth with the Holy Ghost.‡
38 (w' is to say, being interpreted, 3739
40 One of the two w' heard John *3588
41 w' is, being interpreted, the Christ.3739
42 w' is by interpretation, A stone, "
2: 9 servants w' drew the water knew;‡3588
10 well drunk then that w' is worse:
22 and the word w' Jesus had said. 3739
23 they saw the miracles w' he did. "
3: 6 That w' is born of the flesh is flesh;
6 that w' is born of the Spirit is spirit.
13 the Son of man w' is in heaven. ‡3588
29 w' standeth and heareth him, ‡ "
4: 5 city of Samaria, w' is called Sychar,*
9 of me, w' am a woman of Samaria?‡
12 Jacob, w' gave us the well, ‡3739
25 Messias cometh, w' is called ‡3588
29 w' told me all things that ever I *3739
39 w' testified, He told me all that ever I‡
53 in the w' Jesus said unto him, 3739
5: 2 w' is called in the Hebrew tongue 3588
5 w' had an infirmity thirty and eight‡
12 w' said unto thee, Take up thy *3588
15 Jesus, w' had made him whole. ‡ "
23 not the Father w' hath sent him. ‡
28 in the w' all that are in the graves‡3739
30 will of the Father w' hath sent me.‡"
32 witness w' he witnesseth of me is "
36 works w' the Father hath given me "
37 Father himself, w' hath sent me, hath‡
39 and they are they w' testify of me.
44 w' receive honour one of another, and‡
6: 1 of Galilee, w' is the sea of Tiberias.
2 miracles w' he did on them that 3739
9 lad here, w' hath five barley loaves,‡"
13 w' remained over and above unto "
22 people w' stood on the other side ‡3588
27 not for the meat w' perisheth, but "
27 meat w' endureth unto everlasting "
27 w' the Son of man shall give unto 3739
33 is he w' cometh down from heaven,‡3588
39 the Father's will w' hath sent me,* "
39 all w' he hath given me I should lose
40 that every one w' seeth the Son, ‡3588
41 bread w' came down from heaven. "
44 except the Father w' hath sent me‡"
46 save he w' is of God, he hath seen‡"
50 bread w' cometh down from heaven, "
51 bread w' came down from heaven: "
51 w' I will give for the life of the *3739
58 bread w' came down from heaven: 3588
7: 31 than these w' this man hath done?3739
39 w' they that believe on him should "
8: 9 And they w' heard it, being convicted*
26 those things w' I have heard of him.3739
31 to those Jews w' believed on him, ‡3588
38 I speak that w' I have seen with "
38 ye do that w' ye have seen with "
40 the truth, w' I have heard of God: "
46 W' of you convinceth me of sin? ‡5101
53 our father Abraham, w' is dead? ‡3748
9: 1 a man w' was blind from his birth.‡
7 (w' is by interpretation, Sent.) 3739
8 w' before had seen him that he was‡
39 world, that they w' see not might see;‡
39 that they w' see might be made blind.‡
40 Pharisees w' were with him heard‡3588
10: 6 things they were w' he spake 3739
16 sheep I have, w' are not of this fold:"
29 My Father, w' gave them me, is ‡ "
32 w' of those works do ye stone me? 4169
11: 2 Mary w' anointed the Lord with ‡3588
16 said Thomas, w' is called Didymus,‡"
27 God, w' should come into the world.‡"
31 Jews then w' were with her in the‡ "
Joh 11: 33 Jews also weeping w' came with her,‡
37 w' opened the eyes of the blind, ‡3588
42 because of the people w' stand by I‡"
45 many of the Jews w' came to Mary,‡"
45 the things w' Jesus did, believed 3739
12: 1 where Lazarus was w' had been ‡3588
4 Simon's son, w' should betray him,‡"
21 Philip, w' was of Bethsaida of Galilee,‡
38 w' he spake, Lord, who hath 3739
49 but the Father w' sent me, he ‡3588
13: 1 loved his own w' were in the world,‡"
14: 24 the word w' ye hear is not mine, 3739
24 mine, but the Father's w' sent me.‡3588
26 the Comforter, w' is the Holy Ghost,‡
15: 3 the word w' I have spoken unto 3739
24 the works w' none other man did, "
26 w' proceedeth from the Father, ‡ "
17: 4 the work w' thou gavest me to do. "
5 w' I had with thee before the world "
6 men w' thou gavest me out of the‡ "
8 them the words w' thou gavest me; "
9 for them w' thou hast given me; ‡ "
20 w' shall believe on me through their*
22 glory w' thou gavest me I have 3739
24 my glory, w' thou hast given me: "
18: 1 a garden, into the w' he entered,
2 Judas also, w' betrayed him, knew‡3588
5 w' betrayed him, stood with them.‡ "
9 might be fulfilled, w' he spake, 3739
9 Of them w' thou gavest me have I* "
11 cup w' my Father hath given me, "
14 he, w' gave counsel to the Jews, ‡3588
16 w' was known unto the high priest,‡3739
21 ask them w' heard me, what I have‡
22 the officers w' stood by struck Jesus‡
32 w' he spake signifying what death3739
19: 17 w' is called in the Hebrew Golgotha:"
24 w' saith, They parted my raiment 3588
32 the other w' was crucified with him.‡"
39 w' at the first came to Jesus by ‡ "
20: 8 w' came first to the sepulchre, ‡ "
16 him, Rabboni; w' is to say, Master.3739
30 w' are not written in this book: "
21: 10 of the fish w' ye have now caught. "
20 w' also leaned on his breast at ‡ "
20 Lord, w' is he that betrayeth thee?*5101
24 w' testifieth of these things, ‡3588
25 many other things w' Jesus did, 3745
25 w', if they should be written every 3748
Ac 1: 2 the day in w' he was taken up, 3739
4 w', saith he, ye have heard of me. "
7 w' the Father hath put in his own "
11 W' also said, Ye men of Galilee, ‡ "
11 w' is taken up from you, into ‡3588
12 w' is from Jerusalem a sabbath 3739
16 w' the Holy Ghost by the mouth of "
16 w' was guide to them that took *3588
21 these men w' have companied with us‡
24 Lord, w' knowest the hearts of all men,‡
25 w' Judas by transgression fell, and 3739
2: 7 not all these w' speak Galilæans? ‡3588
16 w' was spoken by the prophet Joel;
22 w' God did by him in the midst of 3739
33 forth this, w' ye now see and hear. "
3: 2 the temple w' is called Beautiful, 3588
10 he w' sat for alms at the Beautiful‡ "
10 at that w' had happened unto him.
11 as the lame man w' was healed held‡
16 the faith w' is by him hath given him
18 w' God before had shewed by the 3739
20 w' before was preached unto you:*
21 w' God hath spoken by the mouth*3739
23 soul, w' will not hear that ‡3748, 302
25 covenant w' God made with our 3739
4: 4 many of them w' heard the word *
11 stone w' was set at nought of you 3588
11 w' is become the head of the corner."
14 man w' was healed standing with‡
20 the things w' we have seen and 3739
21 glorified God for that w' was done.
24 w' hast made heaven, and earth, *3588
32 things w' he possessed was his own;
36 (w' is, being interpreted, The son 3739
5: 9 feet of them w' have buried thy ‡
16 them w' were vexed with unclean*
17 (w' is the sect of the Sadducees,) 3588
6: 9 w' is called the synagogue of the * "
10 and the spirit by w' he spake. 3739
11 they suborned men, w' said, We have‡
13 set up false witnesses, w' said, This‡
14 the customs w' Moses delivered us.3739
7: 3 into the land w' I shall shew thee. "
17 w' God had sworn to Abraham, "
18 king arose, w' knew not Joseph. ‡ "
20 In w' time Moses was born, and "
34 of my people w' is in Egypt, 3588
35 of the angel w' appeared to him in‡3588
37 w' said unto the children of Israel,‡"
38 angel w' spake to him in the mount‡"
40 w' brought us out of the land of ‡3739
43 figures w' ye made to worship "
45 W' also our fathers that came after"
52 W' of the prophets have not your‡5101
52 slain them w' shewed before of the*3588
8: 1 the church w' was at Jerusalem;
6 unto those things w' Philip spake,*
6 and seeing the miracles w' he did.
9 w' beforetime in the same city used‡
13 the miracles and signs w' were done.*
14 apostles w' were at Jerusalem ‡3588
24 of these things w' ye have spoken 3739
26 Jerusalem unto Gaza, w' is desert.*3778
32 of the scripture w' he read was this,
9: 7 men w' journeyed with him stood*3588
11 into the street w' is called Straight,"
19 the disciples w' were at Damascus.‡
Ac 9: 21 them w' called on this name in ‡3588
22 the Jews w' dwelt at Damascus, ‡ "
30 W' when the brethren knew, they*
32 to the saints w' dwelt at Lydda. ‡3588
33 w' had kept his bed eight years, ‡
36 w' by interpretation is called 3739
36 works and almsdeeds w' she did. "
39 and garments w' Dorcas made, 3745
10: 2 w' gave much alms to the people, and*
7 the angel w' spake unto Cornelius*3588
17 vision w' he had seen should mean,3739
17 men w' were sent from Cornelius *3588
18 Simon, w' was surnamed Peter, ‡ "
21 to the men w' were sent unto him‡ "
36 word w' God sent unto the children3739
37 w' was published throughout all
37 after the baptism w' John 3739
39 things w' he did both in the land "
42 w' was ordained of God to be the 3588
44 fell on all them w' heard the word.‡
45 w' believed were astonished, ‡
47 w' have received the Holy Ghost ‡3748
11: 6 the w' when I had fastened mine 3739
13 w' stood and said unto him, Send men*
19 they w' were scattered abroad upon*
20 w', when they were come to ‡3748
22 the church w' was in Jerusalem: 3588
28 w' came to pass in the days of 3748
29 unto the brethren w' dwelt in Judæa:*
30 W' also they did, and sent it to 3739
12: 9 true w' was done by the angel; 3588
10 w' opened to them of his own 3748
13: 1 w' had been brought up with Herod*
7 W' was with the deputy of the ‡3739
27 the prophets w' are read every ‡3588
31 of them w' came up with him from‡
32 the promise w' was made unto the*
39 from w' ye could not be justified 3739
40 you, w' is spoken of in the prophets;
41 work w' ye shall in no wise believe,
45 those things w' were spoken by Paul,
14: 3 w' gave testimony unto the word ‡3588
13 of Jupiter, w' was before their city,*"
14 W' when the apostles, Barnabas and*
15 the living God, w' made heaven, *3739
26 God for the work w' they fulfilled. "
15: 1 certain men w' came down from *
5 the sect of the Pharisees w' believed,*
8 And God, w' knoweth the hearts, ‡
10 w' neither our fathers nor we 3739
16 of David, w' is fallen down; 3588
19 w' from among the Gentiles are ‡ "
23 brethren w' are of the Gentiles in‡ "
24 certain w' went out from us have‡
29 from w' if ye keep yourselves, ye 3739
31 W' when they had read, they rejoiced*
16: 1 of a certain woman, w' was a Jewess,‡
2 W' was well reported of by the *3739
3 Jews w' were in those quarters: ‡3588
4 and elders w' were at Jerusalem. * "
12 w' is the chief city of that part of 3748
13 unto the women w' resorted thither.‡
14 Thyatira, w' worshipped God, heard*
14 the things w' were spoken of Paul.
16 w' brought her masters much gain‡3748
17 God, w' shew unto us the way of ‡ "
17: 5 But the Jews w' believed not, moved‡
12 of honourable women w' were *3588
21 strangers w' were there, spent "
31 in the w' he will judge the world 3739
34 among the w' was Dionysius the * "
18: 27 much w' had believed through grace:‡
19: 4 on him w' should come after him, ‡
10 they w' dwelt in Asia heard the word‡
13 to call over them w' had evil spirits‡
14 and chief of the priests, w' did so.‡
19 of them also w' used curious arts*
24 w' made silver shrines for Diana,‡
26 no gods, w' are made with hands: 3588
31 chief of Asia, w' were his friends, sent‡
35 the image w' fell down from Jupiter?
37 w' are neither robbers of churches,‡
38 and the craftsmen w' are with him,*
20: 19 w' befell me by the lying in wait 3588
24 w' I have received of the Lord 3739
28 w' the Holy Ghost hath made you "
28 w' he hath purchased with his own "
32 grace, w' is able to build you up, 3588
32 among all them w' are sanctified.*
38 most of all for the words w' he 3739
21: 8 evangelist, w' was one of the seven;‡
9 daughters, virgins, w' did prophesy.*
20 of Jews there are w' believe; and ‡3588
21 the Jews w' are among the Gentiles‡
23 four men w' have a vow on them;*
25 As touching the Gentiles w' believe,‡
27 the Jews w' were of Asia, when they‡
38 w' before these days madest an ‡
39 I am a man w' am a Jew of Tarsus, a*
22: 1 my defence w' I make now unto you.
3 a man w' am a Jew, born in Tarsus,*
5 bring them w' were there bound unto*
10 things w' are appointed for thee 3739
12 report of all the Jews w' dwelt there,*
29 w' should have examined him: ‡3588
23: 13 forty w' had made this conspiracy.‡"
21 w' have bound themselves with ‡3748
24: 14 after the way w' they call heresy, 3739
14 all things w' are written in the 3588
15 w' they themselves also allow, 3739
24 his wife Drusilla, w' was a Jewess,‡
25: 5 w' among you are able, go down *
7 Jews w' came down from Jerusalem‡
7 Paul, w' they could not prove. 3588
16 w' is accused have the accusers face*
19 and of one Jesus, w' was dead, whom*

Ac 25:24 all men w' are here present with ‡3588
26: 3 and questions w' are among the Jews:
4 w' was at first among mine own 3588
5 W' knew me from the beginning, if*
7 w' promise our twelve tribes, 3739
7 w' hope's sake, king Agrippa, I am"
10 W' thing I also did in Jerusalem:* "
13 me and them w' journeyed with me.*
16 of these things w' thou hast seen,*3739
16 in the w' I will appear unto thee;* "
18 among them w' are sanctified by‡
27: 8 a place w' is called The fair havens;*
11 those things w' were spoken of by
12 w' is an haven of Crete, and lieth
16 a certain island w' is called Clauda,*
17 W' when they had taken up, they*3739
39 into the w' they were minded, * "
43 w' could swim should cast themselves‡
28: 9 w' had diseases in the island, ‡3588
11 w' had wintered in the isle,
24 some believed the things w' were
31 those things w' concern the Lord*
Ro 1: 2 (W' he had promised afore by his 3739
3 w' was made of the seed of David *3588
19 w' may be known of God is manifest
26 into that w' is against nature:
27 men working that w' is unseemly,
27 recompence of their error w' was 3739
28 those things w' are not convenient;
32 w' commit such things are worthy of‡
2: 2 against them w' commit such things.*
3 that judgest them w' do such things,*
14 the Gentiles, w' have not the law, ‡3588
15 W' shew the work of the law *3748
19 a light of them w' are in darkness,*
20 w' hast the form of knowledge and of‡
21 Thou therefore w' teachest *3588
27 not uncircumcision w' is by nature,
28 he is not a Jew, w' is one outwardly;‡
28 w' is outward in the flesh:
29 But he is a Jew, w' is one inwardly;‡
3: 22 w' is by faith of Jesus Christ unto all*
26 justifier of him w' believeth in Jesus.*
30 w' shall justify the circumcision *3739
4: 11 of the faith w' he had yet being 3588
12 that faith...w' he had being yet
14 For if they w' are of the law be heirs,‡
16 seed; not to that only w' is of the law,
16 also w' is of the faith of Abraham;
17 things w' be not as though they were.*
18 according to that w' was spoken,
5: 5 Holy Ghost w' is given unto us. 3588
15 w' is by one man, Jesus Christ, * "
17 much more they w' receive abundance*
6: 17 form of doctrine w' was delivered*3739
7: 2 For the woman w' hath an husband is*
5 sins, w' were by the law, did work3588
10 w' was ordained to life, I found
13 that w' is good made death unto me?
13 death in me by that w' is good;
15 For that w' I do I allow not: for 3739
16 If then I do that w' I would not, I* "
18 but how to perform that w' is good I
19 not: but the evil w' I would not, 3739
23 law of sin w' is in my members. 3588
8: 1 to them w' are in Christ Jesus, *
18 the glory w' shall be revealed in
23 w' have the firstfruits of the Spirit,‡
26 with groanings w' cannot be uttered.
9: 6 are not all Israel, w' are of Israel: ‡3588
8 They w' are the children of the flesh,*
23 w' he had afore prepared unto 3739
25 my people, w' were not my people;‡
25 and her beloved, w' was not beloved.‡
30 w' followed not...righteousness, ‡3588
30 the righteousness w' is of faith. "
31 Israel, w' followed after the law of*
10: 5 the righteousness w' is of the law, 3588
5 man w' doeth those things shall live‡
6 w' is of faith speaketh on this wise,
11: 2 away his people w' he foreknew. ‡3739
7 not obtained that w' he seeketh "
14 to emulation them w' are my flesh,*
22 on them w' fell, severity; but toward‡
24 cut out of the olive tree w' is wild
24 w' be the natural branches, be graffed
12: 1 God, w' is your reasonable service.
9 dissimulation. Abhor that w' is evil;
9 cleave to that w' is good.
14 Bless them w' persecute you: bless,*
13: 3 do that w' is good, and thou shalt
4 But if thou do that w' is evil, be
14: 3 and let not him w' eateth not judge*
19 after the things w' make for peace,
22 in that thing w' he alloweth. 3739
15: 17 in those things w' pertain to God.*
18 those things w' Christ hath not 3739
22 w' cause also I have been much *1352
26 poor saints w' are at Jerusalem. *3588
31 service w' I have for Jerusalem
16: 1 you Phebe our sister, w' is a servant*
1 of the church w' is at Cenchrea: *3588
10 Salute them w' are of Aristobulus'*
11 of Narcissus, w' are in the Lord. ‡3588
12 Persis, w' laboured much in the ‡3748
14 and the brethren w' are with them.*
15 and all the saints w' are with them.*
17 them w' cause divisions and offences‡
17 the doctrine w' ye have learned; 3739
19 have you wise unto that w' is good,
25 w' was kept secret since the world
1Co 1: 2 the church of God w' is at Corinth,3588
4 the grace of God w' is given you by *
11 by them w' are of the house of Chloe,‡
18 unto us w' are saved it is the power‡
24 them w' are called, both Jews and*3588

1Co 1: 27 confound the things w' are mighty;*
28 things w' are despised, hath God *
28 things w' are not, to bring to *3588
2: 7 w' God ordained before the world 3739
8 W' none of the princes of this "
9 things w' God hath prepared for "
11 the spirit of man w' is in him? 3588
12 world, but the spirit w' is of God; "
13 W' things also we spake, not in 3739
13 the words w' man's wisdom teacheth,
13 but w' the Holy Ghost teacheth;
3: 10 to the grace of God w' is given 3588
11 that is laid, w' is Jesus Christ. 3739
14 man's work abide w' he hath built "
17 of God is holy, w' temple ye are. 3748
4: 6 of men above that w' is written, 3739
17 of my ways w' be in Christ, 3588
19 the speech of them w' are puffed up,‡
6: 16 that he w' is joined to a harlot is one‡
19 of the Holy Ghost w' is in you, ‡
19 w' ye have of God, and ye are not 3739
20 and in your spirit, w' are God's, *3748
7: 13 woman w' hath an husband that ‡ "
35 upon you, but for that w' is comely,
8: 10 man see thee w' hast knowledge ‡3588
10 conscience of him w' is weak be *
10 those things w' are offered to idols;*
9: 13 they w' minister about holy things‡
13 and they w' wait at the altar are ‡
14 that they w' preach the gospel should‡
24 that they w' run in a race run all,‡
10: 16 The cup of blessing w' we bless, is3739
16 bread w' we break, is it not "
18 not they w' eat of the sacrifices ‡
19 or that w' is offered in sacrifice to
20 that the things w' the Gentiles 3739
30 of for that for w' I give thanks?
11: 19 they w' are approved may be made‡
23 of the Lord that w' also I delivered3739
23 same night in w' he was betrayed, "
24 this is my body, w' is broken for 3588
12: 6 the same God w' worketh all in all.‡ "
22 of the body, w' seem to be more feeble,
23 w' we think to be less honourable, 3739
24 honour to that part w' lacked:
13: 10 But when that w' is perfect is come,
10 that w' is in part shall be done away.
14: 22 believe not, but for them w' believe.*
15: 1 the gospel w' I preached unto you, 3739
1 w' also ye have received, and "
2 w' also ye are saved, if ye keep in "
3 first of all that w' I also received, "
10 his grace w' was bestowed upon me
10 but the grace of God w' was with 3588
18 also w' are fallen asleep in Christ are‡
27 w' did put all things under him. *
29 they do w' are baptized for the dead,‡
31 w' I have in Christ Jesus our Lord,3739
36 fool, that w' thou sowest is not "
37 And that w' thou sowest, thou "
46 that was not first w' is spiritual,
46 but that w' is natural; and afterward
46 and afterward that w' is spiritual.
57 w' giveth us the victory through ‡3588
16: 17 that w' was lacking on your part they
2Co 1: 1 church of God w' is at Corinth, 3588
1 all the saints w' are in all Achaia:‡ "
4 comfort them w' are in any trouble,*
6 w' is effectual in the enduring of 3588
6 same sufferings w' ye also suffer: "
8 our trouble w' came to us in Asia, "
9 but in God w' raiseth the dead: ‡ "
21 Now he w' stablisheth us with you in‡
2: 2 the same w' is made sorry by me?*
4 ye might know the love w' I have 3739
6 this punishment, w' was inflicted 3588
14 w' always causeth us to triumph in‡
17 not as many, w' corrupt the word of*
3: 7 w' glory was to be done away: 3588
10 w' was made glorious had no glory in
11 that w' is done away was glorious,
11 more that w' remaineth is glorious.
13 as Moses, w' put a vail over his face,‡
13 to the end of that w' is abolished:
14 w' vail is done away in Christ. 3748
4: 4 the minds of them w' believe not,‡
11 we w' live are alway delivered ‡3588
14 he w' raised up the Lord Jesus shall‡
16 For w' cause we faint not; but *1352
17 affliction, w' is but for a moment, 3588
18 we look not at the things w' are seen,
18 but at the things w' are not seen:
18 the things w' are seen are temporal;
18 things w' are not seen are eternal.
5: 2 with our house w' is from heaven: 3588
12 them w' glory in appearance, ‡
15 they w' live should not henceforth‡
15 unto him w' died for them, and rose*
7: 14 w' I made before Titus, is found a 3588
8: 11 performance also...of that w' ye have.
16 w' put the same earnest care into ‡3588
19 w' is administered by us to the "
20 abundance w' is administered by us:"
22 great confidence w' I have in you.
9: 2 for w' I boast of you to them of 3739
6 He w' soweth sparingly shall reap*
11 w' causeth...us thanksgiving 3748
14 w' long after you for the exceeding*
10: 2 w' think of us as if we walked ‡3588
8 w' the Lord hath given us for 3739
13 rule w' God hath distributed to us, "
11: 4 spirit, w' ye have not received,
4 gospel, w' ye have not accepted,
9 for that w' was lacking to me, the*
9 brethren w' came from Macedonia*
12 from them w' desire occasion; ‡

2Co 11: 17 That w' I speak, I speak it not 3739
28 that w' cometh upon me daily, the3588
30 glory of the things w' concern mine*
31 Christ, w' is blessed for evermore,*3588
12: 4 w' it is not lawful for a man to 3739
6 above that w' he seeth me to be, "
21 bewail many w' have sinned *3588
21 and lasciviousness w' they have 3739
13: 2 to them w' heretofore have sinned,*
3 w' to you-ward is not weak, but *3739
7 that ye should do that w' is honest,
10 the power w' the Lord hath given 3739
Ga 1: 2 And all the brethren w' are with me,‡
7 W' is not another; but there be 3739
8 you than that w' we have preached "
11 the gospel w' was preached of me 3588
17 to them w' are apostles before me;‡
20 Now the things w' I write unto 3739
22 of Judæa w' were in Christ: 3588
23 he w' persecuted us in times past now*
23 the faith w' once he destroyed. 3739
2: 2 that gospel w' I preach among the "
2 but privately to them w' were of *
4 liberty w' we have in Christ Jesus,3739
10 same w' I also was forward to do. "
12 them w' were of the circumcision.*
18 again the things w' I destroyed, 3739
20 the life w' I now live in the flesh I "
3: 7 ye therefore that they w' are of faith,‡
9 So then they w' be of faith are ‡
10 w' are written in the book of the *3588
16 And to thy seed, w' is Christ. 3739
17 w' was four hundred and thirty years
21 been a law given w' could have 3588
4: 8 unto them w' by nature are no gods.‡
14 my temptation w' was in my flesh ye
24 W' things are an allegory: for 3748
24 Sinai w' gendereth to bondage, *
24 to bondage, w' is Agar. ‡3748
25 answereth to Jerusalem, w' now *3588
26 But Jerusalem w' is above is free,*
26 is free, w' is the mother of us all. 3748
27 more children than she w' hath an‡
5: 6 but faith w' worketh by love. *
12 were even cut off w' trouble you. *
19 manifest, w' are these; Adultery, 3748
21 of the w' I tell you before, as I 3739
21 w' do such things shall not inherit‡
6: 1 w' are spiritual, restore such an ‡3588
Eph 1: 1 to the saints w' are at Ephesus, ‡ "
9 good pleasure w' he hath 3739
10 w' are in heaven, and w' are on 3588
14 W' is the earnest of our 3739
20 W' he wrought in Christ, when he "
21 world, but also in that w' is to come:
23 W' is his body, the fulness of him 3748
2: 10 w' God hath before ordained that 3739
11 w' is called the Circumcision in 3588
17 peace to you w' were afar off, * "
3: 2 of God w' is given me to you-ward:"
5 W' in other ages was not made 3739
9 w' from the beginning of the 3588
11 w' he purposed in Christ Jesus our3739
13 my tribulations for you, w' is your3748
19 love of Christ, w' passeth knowledge,
4: 15 him in all things w' is the head, ‡3739
16 by that w' every joint supplieth,
22 w' is corrupt according to the ‡3588
24 man, w' after God is created in ‡ "
28 with his hands the thing w' is good,*
29 w' is good to the use of edifying, *1536
5: 4 nor jesting, w' are not convenient:3588
12 things w' are done of them in secret.
6: 2 w' is the first commandment with 3748
17 of the Spirit, w' is the word of God:3739
20 w' I am an ambassador in bonds:
Ph'p 1: 1 in Christ Jesus w' are at Philippi,‡3588
6 w' hath begun a good work in you‡
11 w' are by Jesus Christ, unto the 3588
12 things w' happened unto me have
23 to be with Christ; w' is far better:*
28 w' is to them an evident token of 3748
30 the same conflict w' ye saw in me, 3634
2: 5 you, w' was also in Christ Jesus: 3739
9 a name w' is above every name: 3588
13 it is God w' worketh in you both ‡ "
21 not the things w' are Jesus Christ's.*
3: 3 w' worship God in the spirit, and *3588
6 the righteousness w' is in the law, "
9 own righteousness w' is of the law, "
9 but that w' is the faith of Christ. "
9 righteousness w' is of God by faith:"
12 that for w' also I am apprehended 3739
13 forgetting those things w' are behind,
13 unto those things w' are before,
17 and mark them w' walk so as ye have‡
4: 3 women w' laboured with me in *3748
7 God, w' passeth all understanding,3588
9 things w' ye have both learned 3739
13 through Christ w' strengtheneth ‡3588
18 the things w' were sent from you,*
21 The brethren w' are with me greet*
Col 1: 2 brethren in Christ w' are at Colosse:*
4 love w' ye have to all the saints, 3588
5 For the hope w' is laid up for you "
6 W' is come unto you, as it is in all "
12 w' hath made us meet to be "
23 hope of the gospel, w' ye have heard,
23 w' was preached to every creature3588
23 to every creature w' is under heaven;*
24 that w' is behind of the afflictions of
24 his body's sake, w' is the church: 3739
25 of God w' is given to me for you, 3588
26 Even the mystery w' hath been "
27 w' is Christ in you, the hope of 3739
29 w' worketh in me mightily. 3588

Col 2:10 w' is the head of all principality *3739
14 against us, w' was contrary to us, "
17 W' are a shadow of things to "
18 those things w' he hath not seen, "
19 w' all the body by joints and bands*"
22 W' all are to perish with the using;)"
23 W' things have indeed a shew of 3748
3: 1 seek those things w' are above, *
5 members w' are upon the earth; 3588
5 and covetousness, w' is idolatry: 3748
6 w' things' sake the wrath of God 3739
7 the w' ye also walked some time, "
10 w' is renewed in knowledge after 3588
14 w' is the bond of perfectness. ‡3748
15 w' also ye are called in one body; 3739
25 for the wrong w' he hath done: "
4: 1 unto your servants that w' is just and
3 Christ, for w' I am also in bonds: 3739
9 you all things w' are done here. *3588
11 Jesus, w' is called Justus, who are‡ "
11 w' have been a comfort unto me. ‡3748
15 the brethren w' are in Laodicea, *
15 and the church w' is in his house.*
17 ministry w' thou hast received in 3739
1Th 1: 1 w' is in God the Father, and in *
10 w' delivered us from the wrath ‡3588
2: 4 but God w' trieth our hearts. ‡
13 the word of God w' ye heard of us, ye
13 w' effectually worketh also in you‡3739
14 God w' in Judæa are in Christ: 3588
3:10 that w' is lacking in your faith?
4: 5 the Gentiles w' knew not God: ‡3588
10 brethren w' are in all Macedonia: ‡ "
13 concerning them w' are asleep, ‡
13 even as others w' have no hope. ‡3588
14 them also w' sleep in Jesus will God*
15 w' are alive and remain unto the *3588
15 not prevent them w' are asleep. * "
17 w' are alive and remain shall be * "
5:12 know them w' labour among you,* "
15 but ever follow that w' is good, "
21 things; hold fast that w' is good. "
2Th 1: 5 W' is a manifest token of the "
5 of God, for w' ye also suffer: 3739
2:15 traditions w' ye have been taught, "
16 our Father, w' hath loved us, ‡3588
3: 4 do the things w' we command you.3739
6 the tradition w' he received of us. "
11 there are some w' walk among you*
17 w' is the token in every epistle: "
1Ti 1: 1 Lord Jesus Christ, w' is our hope:‡3588
4 endless genealogies, w' minister 3748
4 than godly edifying w' is in faith: 3588
6 From w' some having swerved 3739
11 w' was committed to my trust. "
14 faith and love w' is in Christ 3588
16 to them w' should hereafter believe‡
18 prophecies w' went before on thee, "
19 w' some having put away 3739
2:10 (w' becometh women professing "
3: 7 good report of them w' are without*
13 in the faith w' is in Christ Jesus. 3588
15 w' is the church of the living 3748
4: 3 w' God hath created to be received3739
3 w' believe and know the truth. *
8 now is, and of that w' is to come, "
14 w' was given thee by prophecy, 3739
5:13 speaking things w' they ought not.3588
6: 3 to the doctrine w' is according to "
9 w' drown men in destruction and *3748
10 w' while some coveted after, they 3739
15 W' in his times he shall shew, "
16 light w' no man can approach unto;"
20 that w' is committed to thy trust, "
subscr. w' is the chiefest city of 3748
2Ti 1: 1 of life w' is in Christ Jesus, 3588
5 w' dwelt first in thy grandmother, 3748
6 w' is in thee by the putting on of 3739
9 w' was given us in Christ Jesus 3588
12 w' cause I also suffer these things:3739
12 w' I have committed unto him "
13 words w' thou hast heard of me, 3739
13 and love w' is in Christ Jesus. 3588
14 thing w' was committed unto thee "
14 the Holy Ghost w' dwelleth in us. ‡3588
15 w' are in Asia be turned away *
2:10 the salvation w' is in Christ Jesus 3588
3: 6 sort are they w' creep into houses,‡
11 w' came unto me at Antioch, *3634
14 thou in the things w' thou hast 3739
15 w' are able to make thee wise 3588
15 through faith w' is in Christ Jesus. "
4: 8 w' the Lord, the righteous judge, 3739
Tit 1: 1 the truth w' is after godliness; 3588
2 w' God, that cannot lie, promised 3739
3 w' is committed unto me ‡ "
11 teaching things w' they ought not "
2: 1 things w' become sound doctrine: "
3: 5 righteousness w' we have done, "
6 W' he shed on us abundantly "
8 they w' have believed in God might be‡
Ph'm 5 w' thou hast toward the Lord 3739
6 good thing w' is in you in Christ 3588
8 enjoin thee that w' is convenient, "
11 W' in time past was to thee 3588
Heb 1: 5 w' of the angels said he at any 5101
13 to w' of the angels said he at any "
2: 1 to the things w' we have heard, *
3 w' at the first began to be spoken 3748
11 for w' cause he is not ashamed 3739
13 children w' God hath given me. ‡ "
3: 5 things w' were to be spoken after; "
4: 3 we w' have believed do enter into ‡3588
15 not an high priest w' cannot be *
5: 8 by the things w' he suffered; 3739
12 w' be the first principles of the *5101

Heb 6: 7 earth w' drinketh in the rain that 3588
8 that w' beareth thorns and briers "
10 w' ye have shewed toward his 3739
18 in w' it was impossible for God "
19 W' hope we have as an anchor of "
19 w' entereth into that within the veil; "
7: 2 of Salem, w' is, King of peace; ‡3739
13 of w' no man gave attendance at "
14 of w' tribe Moses spake nothing "
19 by the w' we draw nigh unto God. "
28 men high priests w' have infirmity;*
28 of the oath, w' was since the law, 3588
8: 1 things w' we have spoken this is
2 the true tabernacle, w' the Lord 3739
6 w' was established upon better 3748
13 Now that w' decayeth and waxeth old
9: 2 the shewbread; w' is called the 3748
3 the tabernacle w' is called the 3588
4 W' had the golden censer, and the*
5 seat; of w' we cannot now speak 3739
9 W' was a figure for the time then 3748
9 in w' were offered both gifts and 3739
10 W' stood only in meats and "
15 they w' are called might receive the*
20 testament w' God hath enjoined 3739
24 w' are the figures of the true; *
10: 1 w' they offered year by year 3739
8 w' are offered by the law; 3748
10 By the w' will we are sanctified 3739
11 sacrifices, w' can never take away 3748
20 w' he hath consecrated for us, 3739
27 w' shall devour the adversaries. "
32 in w', after ye were illuminated, 3739
35 w' hath great recompense of 3748
11: 3 things w' are seen were not made*3588
3 were not made of things w' do appear.
4 by w' he obtained witness that he 3739
7 by the w' he condemned the world, "
7 of the righteousness w' is by faith. "
8 place w' he should after receive 3739
10 looked for a city w' hath foundations,
12 as the sand w' is by the sea shore 3588
29 w' the Egyptians assaying to do 3739
12: 1 the sin w' doth so easily beset us, and
5 w' speaketh unto you as unto 3748
9 fathers of our flesh w' corrected us,*
11 unto them w' are exercised thereby.*
12 lift up the hands w' hang down, and*
13 lest that w' is lame be turned out of
14 w' no man shall see the Lord: 3739
19 words, w' voice they that had heard"
20 not endure that w' was commanded,
23 firstborn, w' are written in heaven,*
27 those things w' cannot be shaken may
28 a kingdom w' cannot be moved, *
13: 3 and them w' suffer adversity, as being*
7 Remember them w' have the rule over*
9 w' have not profited them that *3739
10 right to eat w' serve the tabernacle.‡
21 that w' is wellpleasing in his sight,
Jas 1: 1 twelve tribes w' are scattered ‡3739
12 w' the Lord hath promised to them"
21 word, w' is able to save your souls.3588
2: 5 w' he hath promised to them that 3739
7 name by the w' ye are called? 3588
16 things w' are needful to the body;*
23 was fulfilled w' saith, Abraham 3588
3: 4 the ships, w' though they be so great,*
9 w' are made after the similitude ‡3588
5: 4 w' is of you kept back by fraud, "
4 the cries of them w' have reaped are*
11 we count them happy w' endure. ‡
20 that he w' converteth the sinner from‡
1Pe 1: 3 w' according to his abundant *3588
10 Of w' salvation the prophets have 3739
11 Spirit of Christ w' was in them did3588
12 w' are now reported unto you by 3739
12 w' things the angels desire to look "
15 But as he w' hath called you is holy,‡
23 of God, w' liveth and abideth for ever.
25 word w' by the gospel is preached 3588
2: 7 therefore w' believe he is precious:‡"
7 but unto them w' be disobedient,*
7 the stone w' the builders disallowed,
8 to them w' stumble at the word, *3739
10 W' in time past were not a people,‡3588
10 w' had not obtained mercy, but ‡ "
11 lusts, w' war against the soul; 3748
12 your good works, w' they shall behold,
3: 4 heart, in that w' is not corruptible,*
4 w' is in the sight of God of great 3739
13 if ye be followers of that w' is good?
19 By w' also he went and preached 3739
20 W' sometime were disobedient, when‡
4:11 as of the ability w' God giveth: 3739
12 the fiery trial w' is to try you,
5: 1 The elders w' are among you I exhort,*
2 the flock of God w' is among you,
2Pe 1:18 this voice w' came from heaven we*
2:11 w' are greater in power and might,*
15 W' have forsaken the right way, and*
3: 1 in both w' I stir up your pure *3739
2 of the words w' were spoken before
7 heavens and the earth, w' are now,*
10 w' the heavens shall pass away 3739
16 in w' are some things hard to be * "
16 w' they that are unlearned and "
1Jo 1: 1 That w' was from the beginning, "
1 w' we have heard, w' we have seen "
1 w' we have looked upon, and our "
2 life, w' was with the Father, and 3748
3 That w' we have seen and heard 3739
5 message w' we have heard of him "
2: 7 w' ye had from the beginning. "
7 the word w' ye have heard "
8 w' thing is true in him and in you: "

1Jo 2:24 in you, w' ye have heard from the 3739
24 If that w' ye have heard from the "
27 w' ye have received of him abideth "
3:24 by the Spirit w' he hath given us. "
5: 9 God, w' he hath testified of his Son.*"
16 sin a sin w' is not unto death, *
2Jo 2 the truth's sake, w' dwelleth in us,3588
5 w' we had from the beginning, 3739
8 those things w' we have wrought, "
3Jo 6 W' have borne witness of thy * "
10 remember his deeds w' he doeth, "
11 Beloved, follow not that w' is evil,*
11 but that w' is good. He that doeth
Jude 3 faith w' was once delivered unto the
6 angels w' kept not their first estate,‡
10 evil of those things w' they know 3745
15 w' they have ungodly committed, 3739
15 w' ungodly sinners have spoken "
17 the words w' were spoken before 3588
Re 1: 1 w' God gave unto him, to shew 3739
1 things w' must shortly come to "
3 those things w' are written therein: "
4 the seven churches w' are in Asia:3588
4 w' is, and w' was, and w' is to come;‡ "
4 the seven Spirits w' are before ‡3739
7 and they also w' pierced him: ‡3748
8 w' is, and w' was, and w' is to come,‡3588
11 the seven churches w' are in Asia;*"
19 Write the things w' thou hast seen,3739
19 hast seen, and the things w' are, "
19 the things w' shall be hereafter; "
20 w' thou sawest in my right hand, "
20 w' thou sawest are the seven * "
2: 2 thou canst not bear them w' are evil:*
2 tried them w' say they are apostles,*
6 the Nicolaitanes, w' I also hate. ‡3739
7 w' is in the midst of the paradise "
8 first and the last, w' was dead, and,‡"
9 of them w' say they are Jews, *3588
10 those things w' thou shalt suffer: 3739
12 saith he w' hath the sharp sword*
15 the Nicolaitanes, w' thing I hate. *3739
17 w' no man knoweth saving he that "
20 Jezebel, w' calleth herself a ‡3588
23 he w' searcheth the reins and ‡3739
24 w' have not known the depths of ‡3748
25 that w' ye have already hold fast till I
3: 2 and strengthen the things w' remain,*
4 Sardis w' have not defiled their ‡3739
9 w' say they are Jews, and are not,‡3588
10 w' shall come upon all the world, "
11 hold that fast w' thou hast, that 3739
12 of my God, w' is new Jerusalem, 3588
12 w' cometh down out of heaven from"
4: 1 first voice w' I heard was as it 3739
1 w' said, Come up hither, and I will
1 thee things w' must be hereafter. 3739
5 w' are the seven Spirits of God. "
8 w' was, and is, and is to come. ‡3588
5: 6 w' are the seven Spirits of God 3739
8 odours, w' are the prayers of saints."
13 And every creature w' is in heaven,‡
6: 9 and for the testimony w' they held:"
7: 4 the number of them w' were sealed:‡"
9 w' no man could number, of all 3739
10 God w' sitteth upon the throne, *3588
13 w' are arrayed in white robes? "
14 These are they w' came out of great‡
17 For the Lamb w' is in the midst of ‡3588
8: 2 the seven angels w' stood before ‡3739
3 golden altar w' was before the 3588
4 w' came with the prayers of the *
6 seven angels w' had the seven ‡3588
9 of the creatures w' are in the sea, "
13 three angels w' are yet to sound! * "
9: 4 men w' have not the seal of God *3748
11 w' is the angel of the bottomless pit,*
13 the golden altar w' is before God. 3588
14 sixth angel w' had the trumpet, ‡3739
14 w' are bound in the great river ‡3588
15 w' are prepared for an hour, and a ‡ "
18 w' issued out of their mouths. "
20 rest of the men w' were not killed ‡3739
20 w' neither can see, nor hear, nor "
10: 4 things w' the seven thunders "
5 the angel w' I saw stand upon the‡ "
6 sea, and the things w' are therein,*
8 the voice w' I heard from heaven 3739
8 book w' is open in the hand of the 3588
8 angel w' standeth upon the sea * "
11: 2 the court w' is without the temple,
8 w' spiritually is called Sodom and 3748
11 fear fell upon them w' saw them. *
16 w' sat before God on their seats, ‡3588
17 w' art, and wast, and art to come:‡ "
18 destroy them w' destroy the earth.‡
12: 4 w' was ready to be delivered, *3588
9 w' deceiveth the whole world: "
10 w' accused them before our God ‡ "
13 w' brought forth the man child. ‡3748
16 the flood w' the dragon cast out 3739
17 w' keep the commandments of ‡3588
13: 2 beast w' I saw was like unto a 3739
4 dragon w' gave power unto the *
12 and them w' dwell therein to worship*
14 miracles w' he had power to do 3739
14 w' had the wound by a sword, * "
14: 3 w' were redeemed from the earth.*3588
4 These are they w' are not defiled ‡3739
4 are they w' follow the Lamb ‡3588
10 w' is poured out without mixture "
13 the dead w' die in the Lord from ‡ "
17 out of the temple w' is in heaven, "
18 from the altar w' had power over fire;*
16: 2 w' had the mark of the beast, ‡3588
2 upon them w' worshipped his image,‡

Re 16: 5 O Lord, w' art, and wast, and ‡3588
9 w' hath power over these plagues:‡ "
14 w' go forth unto the kings of the
17: 1 seven angels w' had the seven *3588
7 w' hath the seven heads and ten "
9 here is the mind w' hath wisdom. "
9 on w' the woman sitteth. 3699,846
12 ten horns w' thou sawest are *3739
12 w' have received no kingdom as ‡3748
15 The waters w' thou sawest, where 3739
16 ten horns w' thou sawest upon "
18 woman w' thou sawest is that * "
18 w' reigneth over the kings of the 3588
18: 6 in the cup w' she hath filled fill 3739
14 things w' were dainty and goodly *3588
15 w' were made rich by her, shall * "
19: 2 w' did corrupt the earth with her ‡3748
9 they w' are called unto the marriage‡
14 And the armies w' were in heaven ‡3588
20 with w' he deceived them that *3739
21 w' sword proceeded out of his 3588
20: 2 that old serpent, w' is the Devil, ‡3739
4 w' had not worshipped the beast,*3748
8 nations w' are in the four quarters‡3588
12 opened, w' is the book of life: 3739
12 those things w' were written in the
13 gave up the dead w' were in it; ‡3588
13 up the dead w' were in them: ‡ "
21: 8 in the lake w' burneth with fire *3739
8 brimstone: w' is the second death. "
9 seven angels w' had the seven *3588
12 w' are the names of the twelve 3739
24 them w' are saved shall walk in the*
27 w' are written in the Lamb's book of ‡
22: 2 life, w' bare twelve manner of fruits,*
8 angel w' shewed me these things.‡3588
9 w' keep the sayings of this book: ‡
11 and he w' is filthy, let him be filthy*
19 the things w' are written in this book
20 He w' testifieth these things saith,*

while See also WHILES; WHILST.
Ge 8: 22 W' the earth remaineth, seedtime 5750
19: 16 w' he lingered, the men laid hold upon
25: 6 from Isaac his son, w' he yet lived,
29: 9 w' he yet spake with them, Rachel
45: 1 w' Joseph made himself known unto
46: 29 and wept on his neck a good w'. 5750
Ex 33: 22 w' my glory passeth by, that I will 5704
22 thee with my hand w' I pass by: "
34: 29 his face shone w' he talked with him.*
Le 4: 27 ignorance, w' he doeth somewhat*
14: 46 the house all the w' that it is shut up
Nu 11: 33 w' the flesh was yet between their
15: 32 w' the children of Israel were in the
23: 15 offering, w' I meet the Lord yonder.
De 19: 6 pursue the slayer, w' his heart is 3588
31: 27 w' I am yet alive with you this day,
Jos 14: 10 w' the children of Israel wandered 834
J'g 3: 26 And Ehud escaped w' they tarried, 5704
11: 26 W' Israel dwelt in Heshbon and her
15: 1 a w' after, in the time of the wheat
16: 27 that beheld w' Samson made sport.
1Sa 2: 13 came w' the flesh was in seething,
7: 2 to pass, w' the ark abode in 3117
9: 27 but stand thou still a w', that I * "
14: 19 w' Saul talked unto the priest, 5704
20: 14 w' yet I live shew me the kindness 518
22: 4 the w' that David was in the hold. 3117
25: 7 all the w' they were in Carmel. "
16 w' we were with them keeping the "
27: 11 the w' he dwelleth in the country "
2Sa 3: 6 w' there was war between the house
35 David to eat meat w' it was yet day,
7: 19 house for a great w' to come. 7350
12: 18 w' the child was yet alive, we spake
21 weep for the child, w' it was alive;
22 W' the child was yet alive, I fasted
13: 30 w' they were in the way, that tidings
15: 8 vow w' I abode at Geshur in Syria,
12 from Giloh, w' he offered sacrifices.
17: 2 upon him w' he is weary and weak
18: 14 w' he was yet alive in the midst of 5750
19: 32 sustenance w' he lay at Mahanaim;
24: 13 thine enemies, w' they pursue thee?
1Ki 1: 14 w' thou yet talkest there with the
22 lo, w' she yet talked with the king,
42 w' he yet spake, behold, Jonathan
3: 20 beside me, w' thine handmaid slept,
6: 7 in the house, w' it was in building.
12: 6 Solomon his father w' he yet lived,
17: 7 after a w', that the brook dried 3117
18: 45 the mean w', that the heaven was 3541
2Ki 6: 33 And w' he yet talked with them,
1Ch 12: 1 Ziklag, w' he yet kept himself close
17: 17 servant's house for a great w' to come.
2Ch 10: 6 Solomon his father w' he yet lived,
14: 7 bars, w' the land is yet before us;*
15: 2 Lord is with you, w' ye be with him;
26: 19 w' he was wroth with the priests, the
34: 3 w' he was yet young, he began to
Ne 7: 3 w' they stand by, let them shut 5704
Es 2: 21 w' Mordecai sat in the king's gate, two
6: 14 w' they were yet talking with him,
Job 1: 16, 17, 18 W' he was yet speaking,
20: 23 shall rain it upon him w' he is eating.
24: 24 They are exalted for a little w', but
27: 3 All the w' my breath is in me, *5750
Ps 7: 2 in pieces, w' there is none to deliver.
31: 13 w' they took counsel together against
37: 10 yet a little w', and the wicked shall
39: 1 bridle, w' the wicked is before me. 5750
3 me, w' I was musing the fire burned:
42: 3 w' they continually say unto me,
10 w' they say daily unto me, Where is
49: 18 Though w' he lived he blest his soul:
63: 4 Thus will I bless thee w' I live: I will

Ps 69: 3 mine eyes fail w' I wait for my God.
78: 30 w' their meat was yet in their *
88: 15 w' I suffer thy terrors I am distracted.
104: 33 to my God w' I have my being. 5750
146: 2 W' I live will I praise the Lord: I
2 unto my God w' I have any being. 5750
Pr 8: 26 W' as yet he had not made the
19: 18 Chasten thy son w' there is hope, 3588
31: 15 She riseth also w' it is yet night,
Ec 9: 3 madness is in their heart w' they live,
12: 1 w' the evil days come not, nor the †5704
2 W' the sun or the light or the † "
Ca 1: 12 W' the king sitteth at his table, "
Isa 10: 25 For yet a very little w', and the
28: 4 w' it is yet in his hand he eateth it
29: 17 Is it not yet a very little w', and
55: 6 Seek ye the Lord w' he may be found,
6 call ye upon him w' he is near:
63: 18 have possessed it but a little w': 4705
65: 24 w' they are yet speaking, I will
Jer 13: 16 w' ye look for light, he turn it into the
15: 9 is gone down w' it was yet day:
33: 1 w' he was yet shut up in the court
39: 15 w' he was shut up in the court of the
40: 5 now w' he was not yet gone back,
51: 33 yet a little w', and the time of her
La 1: 19 w' they sought their meat to 3588
Eze 9: 8 to pass, w' they were slaying them,
Da 4: 31 W' the word was in the king's 5751
Ho 1: 4 for yet a little w', and I will avenge
Na 1: 10 For w' they be folden together as †5704
10 w' they are drunken as drunkards,*
Hag 2: 6 it is a little w', and I will shake the
Zec 14: 12 away w' they stand upon their feet,
M't 1: 20 But w' he thought on these things,*
9: 18 W' he spake these things unto them,
12: 46 W' he yet talked to the people,
13: 21 in himself, but dureth for a w': 4340
25 w' men slept his enemy came 1722,3588
29 Nay; lest w' ye gather up the tares,
14: 22 w' he sent the multitudes away. *2193
17: 5 W' he yet spake, behold, a bright
22 And w' they abode in Galilee, Jesus
22: 41 W' the Pharisees were gathered
25: 5 W' the bridegroom tarried they all
10 w' they went to buy, the bridegroom
26: 36 ye here, w' I go and pray yonder. 2193
47 w' he yet spake, lo, Judas, one of the
73 after a w' came unto him they that 3397
27: 63 deceiver said, w' he was yet alive,
28: 13 and stole him away w' we slept.
M'r 1: 35 rising up a great w' before day, he
2: 19 w' the bridegroom is with 1722,3739
5: 35 W' he yet spake, there came from the
6: 31 into a desert place, and rest a w': 3641
45 w' he sent away the people. 2193
12: 35 and said, w' he taught in the temple,*
14: 32 Sit ye here, w' I shall pray. 2193
43 w' he yet spake cometh Judas, one of
15: 44 whether he had been any w' dead. 3819
Lu 1: 8 w' he executed...priest's office 1722,3588
2: 6 w' they were there, the days were
5: 34 w' the bridegroom is with 1722,3739
8: 13 for a w' believe, and in time of 2540
49 W' he yet spake, there cometh one
9: 34 W' he thus spake, there came a cloud,
43 w' they wondered every one at all
10: 13 they had a great w' ago repented,*
14: 32 w' the other is yet a great way off, he
18: 4 And he would not for a w': but 5550
22: 47 w' he yet spake, behold a multitude,
58 And after a little w' another saw him,
60 w' he yet spake, the cock crew.
24: 15 w' they communed together 1722,3588
32 w' he talked with us by the way, 5613
32 w' he opened to us the scriptures? "
41 w' they yet believed not for joy, and*
44 w' I was yet with you, that all things
51 w' he blessed them, he was 1722,3588
Joh 4: 31 mean w' his disciples prayed him,
5: 7 but w' I am coming, another 1722,3739
7: 33 Yet a little w' am I with you, and 5550
9: 4 of him that sent me, w' it is day: 2193
12: 35 Yet a little w' is the light with you. 5550
35 w' ye have the light, lest darkness 2193
36 W' ye have light, believe in the "
13: 33 children, yet a little w' I am with you.
14: 19 Yet a little w', and the world seeth me
16: 16 A little w', and ye shall not see me:
16 again, a little w', and ye shall see me,
17 A little w', and ye shall not see me:
17 again, a little w', and ye shall see me:
18 What is this that he saith, A little w'?
19 A little w', and ye shall not see me:
19 again, a little w', and ye shall see me?
17: 12 W' I was with them in the world, 3753
Ac 1: 9 w' they beheld, he was taken up;*
10 w' they looked stedfastly toward 5613
9: 39 Dorcas made, w' she was with them.
10: 10 but w' they made ready, he fell into a
17 w' Peter doubted in himself what 5613
19 W' Peter thought on the vision, the
44 W' Peter yet spake these words, the
15: 7 that a good w' ago God made 2250
17: 16 w' Paul waited for them at Athens,
18: 18 this tarried there yet a good w', *2250
19: 1 w' Apollos was at Corinth, 1722,3588
20: 11 talked a long w', even till break of
22: 17 w' I prayed in the temple, I was in a
24: 20 in me, w' I stood before the council,*
25: 8 W' he answered for himself, neither
27: 33 w' the day was coming on, 891,3739
28: 6 but after they had looked a great w',*
Ro 2: 15 their thoughts the mean w' accusing*
5: 8 w' we were yet sinners, Christ died for
7: 3 So then if, w' her husband liveth, she

1Co 3: 4 For w' one saith, I am of Paul; *3752
8: 13 eat no flesh w' the world standeth,*
16: 7 I trust to tarry a w' with you, 5550,5099
2Co 4: 18 W' we look not at the things which
Ga 2: 17 w' we seek to be justified by Christ,
1Ti 5: 6 in pleasure is dead w' she liveth.
6: 10 which w' some coveted after, they*
Heb 3: 13 daily, w' it is called To day; *891,3739
15 W' it is said, To day if ye will 1722,3588
9: 8 w' as the first tabernacle was yet
17 at all w' the testator liveth. 3753
10: 37 For yet a little w', and he that 3397
1Pe 3: 2 W' they behold your chaste
20 w' the ark was preparing, wherein
5: 10 after that ye have suffered a w', 3641
2Pe 2: 13 deceivings w' they feast with you;
19 W' they promise them liberty, they

whiles See also WHILE; WHILST.
Eze 21: 29 W' they see vanity unto thee,
29 w' they divine a lie unto thee,
44: 17 w' they minister in the gates of the
Da 5: 2 Belshazzar, w' he tasted the wine,
9: 20 w' I was speaking and praying, 5750
21 Yea, w' I was speaking in prayer, "
Ho 7: 6 like an oven, w' they lie in wait:
M't 5: 25 w' thou art in the way with 2193,3755
Ac 5: 4 W' it remained, was it not thine own?
2Co 9: 13 W' by the experiment of this *

whilst See also WHILE.
J'g 6: 31 put to death w' it is yet morning: 5704
Ne 6: 3 the work cease, w' I leave it, 834
Job 32: 11 w' ye searched out what to say. 5704
Ps 141: 10 own nets, w' that I withal escape. "
Jer 17: 2 W' their children remember their
2Co 5: 6 w' we are at home in the body, we are
7: 15 w' he remembereth the obedience
Heb 10: 33 w' ye were made a gazingstock both*
33 w' ye became companions of them*

whip See also WHIPS.
Pr 26: 3 A w' for the horse, a bridle for the 7752
Na 3: 2 The noise of a w', and the noise of "

whips
1Ki 12: 11 father hath chastised you with w', 7752
14 father also chastised you with w', "
2Ch 10: 11, 14 my father chastised you with w'."

whirleth
Ec 1: 6 it w' about continually, and *1980

whirlwind See also WHIRLWINDS.
2Ki 2: 1 up Elijah into heaven by a w'. 5591
11 Elijah went up by a w' into heaven."
Job 37: 9 Out of the south cometh the w': *5492
38: 1 Lord answered Job out of the w', 5591
40: 6 the Lord unto Job out of the w', "
Ps 58: 9 shall take them away as with a w', 8175
Pr 1: 27 your destruction cometh as a w'; 5492
10: 25 As the w' passeth, so is the wicked "
Isa 5: 28 flint, and their wheels like a w': "
17: 13 like a rolling thing before the w'. * "
40: 24 the w' shall take them away as 5591
41: 16 and the w' shall scatter them:
66: 15 and with his chariots like a w', 5492
Jer 4: 13 and his chariots shall be as a w': "
23: 19 a w' of the Lord is gone forth in *5591
19 forth in fury, even a grievous w': * "
25: 32 great w' shall be raised up from * "
30: 23 w' of the Lord goeth forth with fury,*"
23 forth with fury, a continuing w': * "
Eze 1: 4 a w' came out of the north, a*7307,5591
Da 11: 40 shall come against him like a w', 8175
Ho 8: 7 wind, and they shall reap the w': 5492
13: 3 chaff that is driven with the w' 5590
Am 1: 14 a tempest in the day of the w': 5492
Na 1: 3 the Lord hath his way in the w' "
Hab 3: 14 came out as a w' to scatter me: 5590
Zec 7: 14 But I scattered them with a w' "

whirlwinds
Isa 21: 1 As w' in the south pass through; 5492
Zec 9: 14 and shall go with w' of the south. 5591

whisper See also WHISPERED; WHISPERINGS.
Ps 41: 7 All that hate me w' together 3907
Isa 29: 4 and thy speech shall w' out of the 6850

whispered
2Sa 12: 19 David saw that his servants w', 3907

whisperer See also WHISPERERS.
Pr 16: 28 and a w' separateth chief friends. 5372

whisperers
Ro 1: 29 debate, deceit, malignity; w', 5588

whisperings
2Co 12: 20 w', swellings, tumults: 5587

whit
De 13: 16 and all the spoil thereof every w', 3632
1Sa 3: 18 And Samuel told him every w', 1697
Joh 7: 23 I have made a man every w' whole 3650
13: 10 wash his feet, but is clean every w':"
2Co 11: 5 not a w' behind the very chiefest 3367

white See also WHITED; WHITER.
Ge 30: 35 every one that had some w' in it, 3836
37 and pilled w' strakes in them, and "
37 w' appear which was in the rods. "
40: 16 had three w' baskets on my head: 2751
49: 12 wine, and his teeth w' with milk. 3836
Ex 16: 31 and it was like coriander seed, w'; "
Le 13: 3 the hair in the plague is turned w', "
4 If the bright spot be w' in the skin "
4 the hair thereof be not turned w'; "
10 if the rising be w' in the skin,
10 and it have turned the hair w', and "
13 hath the plague: it is all turned w':"
16 again, and be changed unto w', "

Le 13:17 if the plague be turned into w': 3836
19 place of a boil there be a w' rising, "
19 or a bright spot, w', and somewhat "
20 and the hair thereof be turned w'; "
21 there be no w' hairs therein, and "
24 that burneth have a w' bright spot,*"
24 spot, somewhat reddish, or w'; "
25 in the bright spot be turned w', "
26 there be no w' hair in the bright "
38 bright spots, even w' bright spots; "
39 skin of their flesh be darkish w'; "
42 or bald forehead, a w' reddish sore;*"
43 rising of the sore be w' reddish in* "
Nu 12:10 Miriam became leprous, w' as snow: "
J'g 5:10 Speak, ye that ride on w' asses, 6715
2Ki 5:27 his presence a leper as w' as snow. "
2Ch 5:12 brethren, being arrayed in w' linen,* "
Es 1: 6 Where were w', green, and blue, *2353
6 and blue, and w', and black, marble.1858
8:15 king in royal apparel of blue and w',2353
Job 6: 6 any taste in the w' of an egg? 7388
Ps 68:14 in it, it was w' as snow in Salmon.* "
Ec 9: 8 Let thy garments be always w'; 3836
Ca 5:10 My beloved is w' and ruddy, the 6703
Isa 1:18 they shall be as w' as snow; 3835
Eze 27:18 the wine of Helbon, and w' wool. 6713
Da 7: 9 whose garment was w' as snow, and "
11:35 to purge, and to make them w', 3835
12:10 shall be purified, and made w', and "
Joe 1: 7 the branches thereof are made w'. "
Zec 1: 8 there red horses, speckled, and w'.3836
6: 3 And in the third chariot w' horses; "
6 and the w' go forth after them; "
M't 5:36 not make one hair w' or black. 3022
17: 2 his raiment was w' as the light. "
28: 3 and his raiment w' as snow: "
M'r 9: 3 shining, exceeding w' as snow; "
3 as no fuller on earth can w' them.*3021
16: 5 side, clothed in a long w' garment;3022
Lu 9:29 his raiment was w' and glistering. "
Joh 4:35 for they are w' already to harvest. "
20:12 And seeth two angels in w' sitting, "
Ac 1:10 two men stood by them in w' "
Re 1:14 His head and his hairs were w' like "
14 as w' as snow; and his eyes were as "
2:17 will give him a w' stone, and in the "
3: 4 and they shall walk with me in w': "
5 shall be clothed in w' raiment; "
18 w' raiment, that thou mayest be "
4: 4 sitting, clothed in w' raiment; and "
6: 2 And I saw, and behold a w' horse: "
11 w' robes were given unto every one "
7: 9 clothed with w' robes, and palms "
13 which are arrayed in w' robes? "
14 made them w' in the blood of the 3021
14:14 I looked, and behold a w' cloud, 3022
15: 6 clothed in pure and w' linen, *2986
19: 8 arrayed in fine linen, clean and w':*"
11 opened and behold a w' horse; 3022
14 followed him upon w' horses, "
14 clothed in fine linen, w' and clean. "
20:11 I saw a great w' throne, and him "

whited
M't 23:27 for ye are like unto w' sepulchres, 2867
Ac 23: 3 God shall smite thee, thou w' wall: "

whiter
Ps 51: 7 me, and I shall be w' than snow. 3835
La 4: 7 snow, they were w' than milk, 6705

whither See also WHITHERSOEVER.
Ge 16: 8 camest thou? and w' wilt thou go? 575
20:13 every place w' we shall come, 834,8033
28:15 thee in all places w' thou goest, * 834
32:17 Whoso art thou? and w' goest thou?575
37:30 child is not; and I, w' shall I go? "
Ex 21:13 a place w' he shall flee. 834,8033
34:12 inhabitants of the land w' thou" 5921
Le 18: 3 w' I bring you, shall ye not do: 8033
20:22 w' I bring you to dwell therein. "
Nu 13:27 unto the land w' thou sentest us, 834
15:18 into the land w' I bring you, 834,8033
35:25 of his refuge, w' he was fled: "
26 of his refuge, w' he was fled; "
De 1:28 W' shall we go up? our brethren 575
3:21 unto all the kingdoms w' thou834,8033
4: 5 unto the land w' ye go to possess it. "
14 w' ye go over to possess it. "
27 w' the Lord shall lead you. "
6: 1 the land w' ye go to possess it: "
7: 1 land w' thou goest to possess "
11: 8 the land, w' ye go to possess it; "
10 w' thou goest in to possess it, "
11 the land, w' ye go to possess it, "
29 land w' thou goest to possess "
12:29 w' thou goest to possess them, "
21:14 then thou shalt let her go w' she will;
23:12 w' thou shalt go forth abroad: 8033
20 land w' thou goest to possess 834,
28:21 w' thou goest to possess it. "
37 nations w' the Lord shall lead "
63 land w' thou goest to possess "
30: 1, 3 w' the Lord thy God hath "
16 land w' thou goest to possess "
18 w' thou passest over Jordan to "
31:13 w' ye go over Jordan to possess "
16 w' they go to be among them, "
32:47 w' ye go over Jordan to possess "
50 in the mount w' thou goest up, "
Jos 2: 5 out: w' the men went I wot not: 575
J'g 19:17 W' goest thou? and whence comest "
Ru 1:16 for w' thou goest, I will go: 413,834
1Sa 10:14 and to his servant, W' went ye? 575
27:10 W' have ye made a road to day? 413
2Sa 2: 1 And David said, W' shall I go up? 575
13:13 w' shall I cause my shame to go? "
15:20 seeing I go w' I may, return 5921,834
2Sa 17:18 in his court; w' they went down. *8033
1Ki 2:36 and go not forth thence any w', 575
42 out, and walkest abroad any w', "
8:47 the land w' they were carried 834,8033
18:10 w' my lord hath not sent to "
12 shall carry thee w' I know 5921,834
21:18 w' he is gone down to possess 834,8033
2Ki 5:25 he said, Thy servant went no w'. 575
2Ch 6:37 the land w' they are carried 834,8033
38 w' they have carried them captives,834
10: 2 w' he had fled from the presence of "
Ne 2:16 And the rulers knew not w' I went, 575
Ps 122: 4 W' the tribes go up, the tribes of 8033
139: 7 W' shall I go from thy spirit? 575
7 or w' shall I flee from thy presence? "
Ec 9:10 in the grave, w' thou goest. 834,8033
Ca 6: 1 W' is thy beloved gone, O thou 575
1 w' is thy beloved turned aside? that "
Isa 20: 6 w' we flee for help to be 834,8033
Jer 8: 3 places w' I have driven them, " "
15: 2 unto thee, W' shall we go forth? 575
16:15 lands w' he had driven them: 834,8033
19:14 Tophet, w' the Lord had sent him 834
22:12 the place w' they have led him 834,8033
23: 3 countries w' I have driven them," "
8 countries w' I had driven them; " "
24: 9 all places w' I shall drive them." "
29: 7 city w' I have caused you to be " "
14 the places w' I have driven you," "
18 nations w' I have driven them:" "
30:11 nations w' I have driven them:" "
32:37 w' I have driven them in mine " "
40: 4 w' it seemeth good and convenient 413
45: 5 in all places w' thou goest. 834,8033
46:28 nations w' I have driven thee: " "
49:36 nation w' the outcasts of Elam " "
Eze 1:12 w' the spirit was to go, they " "
4:13 Gentiles, w' I will drive them. " "
6: 9 nations w' they shall be carried" "
10:11 to the place w' the head looked 834
12:16 among the heathen w' they 834,8033
29:13 people w' they were scattered:" "
36:20 unto the heathen, w' they went," "
21, 22 the heathen, w' they went. " "
37:21 the heathen, w' they be gone, " "
47: 9 live w' the river cometh. *413,
Da 9: 7 w' thou hast driven them, " "
Joe 3: 7 the place w' ye have sold them, " "
Zec 2: 2 Then said I, W' goest thou? And 575
5:10 me, W' do these bear the ephah? "
Lu 10: 1 place, w' he himself would come. 3757
24:28 nigh unto the village, w' they went: "
Joh 3: 8 whence it cometh, and w' it goeth:4226
6:21 was at the land w' they went. 1519,3739
7:35 W' will he go, that we shall not 4226
8:14 I know whence I came, and w' I go;"
14 tell whence I come, and w' I go; "
21 sins: w' I go, ye cannot come. 3699
22 he saith, W' I go, ye cannot come. "
12:35 darkness knoweth not w' he goeth.4226
13:33 Jews, W' I go, ye cannot come; 3699
36 said unto him, Lord, w' goest thou?4226
36 W' I go, thou canst not follow me3699
14: 4 w' I go ye know, and the way ye "
5 we know not w' thou goest; and 4226
16: 5 of you asketh me, W' goest thou? "
18:20 temple, w' the Jews always resort;3699
21:18 and walkedst w' thou wouldest: "
18 carry thee w' thou wouldest not. "
Heb 6:20 W' the forerunner is...entered, "
11: 8 went out, not knowing w' he went.4226
1Jo 2:11 and knoweth not w' he goeth. "

whithersoever
Jos 1: 7 mayest prosper w' thou goest. 3605,834
9 God is with thee w' thou goest. " "
16 w' thou sendest us, we will 413, " "
J'g 2:15 W' they went out, the hand of " "
1Sa 14:47 w' he turned himself, he vexed " "
18: 5 David went out w' Saul sent him," "
23:13 Keilah, and went w' they could go. "
2Sa 7: 9 was with thee w' thou wentest,3605, "
8: 6, 14 preserved David w' he went. " "
1Ki 2: 3 w' thou turnest thyself: 3605,834,8033
8:44 w' thou shalt send them, 1870,834
2Ki 18: 7 he prospered w' he went forth:3605, "
1Ch 17: 8 with thee w' thou hast walked, " "
18: 6, 13 preserved David w' he went. " "
Es 4: 3 w' the king's commandment 4725, "
8:17 w' the king's commandment and his" "
Pr 17: 8 w' it turneth, it prospereth.413,3605, "
21: 1 he turneth it w' he will. 5921, "
Eze 1:20 W' the spirit was to go, they" 834,8033
21:16 or on the left, w' thy face is set. "
47: 9 w' the rivers...come,* 413,3605,834,8033
M't 8:19 will follow thee w' thou goest.3699,1437
M'r 6:56 And w' he entered, into * 302
Lu 9:57 I will follow thee w' thou goest. " "
1Co 16: 6 me on my journey w' I go. 3757,1437
Jas 3: 4 helm, w' the governor listeth, *3699,302
Re 14: 4 follow the Lamb w' he goeth. " "

who See also WHICH; WHOM; WHOSE; WHOSOEVER.
Ge 3:11 W' told thee that thou wast 4310
14:12 brother's son, w' dwelt in Sodom, 1931
21: 7 W' would have said unto 4310
26 I wot not w' hath done this thing: "
24:15 w' was born to Bethuel, son of 834
27:32 said unto him, W' art thou? 4310
33 Isaac trembled...and said, W'? "
30: 2 w' hath withheld from thee the 834
33: 5 and said, W' are those with thee? 4310
35: 3 w' answered me in the day of my "
36: 1 generations of Esau, w' is Edom. *1931
19 are the sons of Esau, w' is Edom,*
20 Seir, the Horite, w' inhabited the land;*
Ge 36:35 w' smote Midian in the field of Moab,
42:30 The man, w' is the lord of the land,*
43:22 tell w' put our money in our sacks.4310
48: 8 sons, and said, W' are these? "
14 Ephraim's head, w' was...younger,1931
49: 9 old lion; w' shall rouse him up? 4310
25 God of thy father, w' shall help thee
25 w' shall bless thee with blessings of
Ex 2:14 W' made thee a prince and a judge4310
3:11 And Moses said unto God, W' am I,"
4:11 him, W' hath made man's mouth? "
11 or w' maketh the dumb, or deaf, or "
28 words of the Lord w' had sent him,834
5: 2 And Pharaoh said, W' is the Lord,4310
6:12 me, w' am of uncircumcised lips? 589
10: 8 God: but w' are they that shall go?4310
12:40 of Israel w' dwelt in Egypt, was 834
15:11 W' is like unto thee, O Lord, 4310
11 w' is like thee, glorious in holiness, "
18:10 w' hath delivered you out of the 834
10 w' hath delivered the people from "
21: 8 w' hath betrothed her to himself,
32:26 said, W' is on the Lord's side? *4310
Le 5: 8 w' shall offer that which is for the sin
12: 7 W' shall offer it before the Lord, and*
27:12 as thou valuest it, w' art the priest,*
Nu 6:21 law of the Nazarite w' hath vowed, 834
7: 2 w' were the princes of the tribes, 1992
9: 6 w' were defiled by the dead body of 834
11: 4 said, W' shall give us flesh to eat?4310
18 saying, W' shall give us flesh to eat?"
12: 7 so, w' is faithful in all mine house.1931
14:36 w' returned, and made all the
21:26 w' had fought against the former 1931
23:10 W' can count the dust of Jacob, 4310
24: 9 as a great lion: w' shall stir him up?"
23 w' shall live when God doeth this! "
25: 6 w' were weeping before the door *1992
26: 9 w' strove against Moses and against834
47 w' were fifty and three thousand and
63 w' numbered the children of Israel 834
27:21 w' shall ask council for him after the
31:27 war upon them, w' went out to battle,
De 1:33 W' went in the way before you, to
2:25 w' shall hear report of thee, and 834
4: 7 w' hath God so nigh unto them,
46 the Amorites, w' dwelt at Heshbon, "
5: 3 w' are all of us here alive this day. 428
26 w' is there of all flesh, that hath 4310
8:15 W' led thee through that great and
15 w' brought thee forth water out of the
16 W' fed thee in the wilderness with
9: 2 W' can stand before the children 4310
21: 1 it be not known w' had slain him: "
30:12 W' shall go up for us to heaven, "
13 W' shall go over the sea for us, "
33: 9 W' said unto his father and to his
26 w' rideth upon the heaven in thy help,
29 w' is like unto thee, O people 4310
29 w' is the sword of thy excellency!* 834
Jos 9: 8 W' are ye? and from whence 4310
11: 8 the hand of Israel, w' smote them,*
12: 2 of the Amorites, w' dwelt in Heshbon,
13:12 w' remained of the remnant of the*1931
15:19 W' answered, Give me a blessing;
17:16 they w' are of Beth-shean and her 834
16 they w' are of the valley of Jezreel. "
21:10 w' were of the children of Levi, had:
J'g 1: 1 W' shall go up for us against the 4310
2: 7 w' had seen all the great works of 834
3: 9 up a deliverer...w' delivered them,
19 thee, O King: w' said, Keep silence.*
6:29 another, W' hath done this thing?4310
35 w' also was gathered after him:
8:34 w' had delivered them out of the hands
9:28 Gaal...said, W' is Abimelech, and 4310
28 w' is Shechem, that we shall "
38 W' is Abimelech, that we should "
11:39 w' did with her according to his vow
15: 6 said, W' hath done this? 4310
17: 4 w' made thereof a graven image and a
5 one of his sons, w' became his priest.
7 a young man...w' was a Levite, 1931
18: 2 w' when they came to mount *
3 him, W' brought thee hither? 4310
29 father, w' was born unto Israel: 834
19: 1 w' took to him a concubine out of
21: 5 W' is there among all the tribes 4310
Ru 2: 3 w' was of the kindred of Elimelech.834
20 w' hath not left off his kindness to "
3: 9 And he said, W' art thou? And 4310
16 said, W' art thou, my daughter? "
1Sa 2:25 the Lord, w' shall intreat for him? "
4: 8 w' shall deliver us out of the hand "
6:20 W' is able to stand before this holy"
10:19 w' himself saved you out of all 834
11:12 W' is he that said, Shall Saul 4310
14:17 now and see w' is gone from us. "
45 w' hath wrought this great 834
16:16 man, w' is a cunning player on an harp;
17:25 be, that the man w' killeth him, 834
26 for w' is this uncircumcised 4310
18:18 David said unto Saul, W' am I? "
20:10 to Jonathan, W' shall tell me? "
22:14 w' is so faithful among all thy "
23:22 is, and w' hath seen him there: "
25:10 W' is David? and w' is the son of "
26: 6 W' will go down with me to Saul to"
9 for w' can stretch forth his hand "
14 W' art thou that criest to the king?"
15 and w' is like to thee in Israel? "
30:23 w' hath preserved us, and delivered
24 w' will hearken unto you in this 4310
2Sa 1: 8 And he said unto me, W' art thou? "
4: 9 w' hath redeemed my soul out of 834
10 w' thought that I would have given

2Sa 6:20 w· uncovered himself to day in the 834
7:18 W· am I, O Lord God? and what is 4310
10:18 the captain of their host, w· died there.*
12:22 W· can tell whether God will be 4310
16:10 W· shall then say, Wherefore hast "
22: 4 the Lord, w· is worthy to be praised:*
32 For w· is God, save the Lord? 4310
32 and w· is a rock, save our God? "
23: 1 and the man w· was raised up on high,
20 Benaiah...w· had done many acts,
1Ki 1:20, 27 w· shall sit on the throne of 4310
2:24 and w· hath made me an house, 834
3: 9 for w· is able to judge this thy so 4310
8:23 w· keepest covenant and mercy with
24 W· hast kept with thy servant 834
50 before them w· carried them captive,
9: 9 w· brought forth their fathers out* 834
12: 2 Jeroboam...w· was yet in Egypt, 1931
9 w· have spoken to me, saying, 834
18 Adoram, w· was over the tribute; "
13:26 w· was disobedient unto the word of "
14: 8 David, w· kept my commandments, "
8 w· followed me with all his heart, to "
14 w· shall cut off the house of "
16 w· did sin, and w· made Israel to * "
17: 1 w· was of the inhabitants of Gilead,
19:19 w· was plowing with twelve yoke 1931
20:14 he said, W· shall order the battle? 4310
21:11 the nobles w· were the inhabitants 834
22:20 W· shall persuade Ahab, that he 4310
52 of Nebat, w· made Israel to sin: * 834
2Ki 4: 5 w· brought the vessels to her; 1992
7:17 w· spake when the king came 834
9:31 Had Zimri peace, w· slew his master?*
32 and said, W· is on my side? w·? 4310
10: 9 slew him: but w· slew all these? "
13 king of Judah, and said, W· are ye?"
29 of Nebat, w· made Israel sin, * 834
13: 6 Jeroboam, w· made Israel sin, "
11 son of Nebat, w· made Israel to sin:*"
14:24 son of Nebat, w· made Israel to sin.* "
15: 9, 18, 24, 28 w· made Israel to sin. * "
17:36 w· brought you up out of the land of"
18:35 W· are they among all the gods 4310
23:15 son of Nebat, w· made Israel to sin, 834
16 w· proclaimed these words. "
1Ch 2: 7 w· transgressed in the thing "
22 w· had three and twenty cities in the
5: 8 w· dwelt in Aroer, even unto Nebo 1931
10 the Hagarites, w· fell by their hand:
6:39 Asaph, w· stood on his right hand,
7:24 w· built Beth-horon the nether,
31 w· is the father of Birzavith. 1931
8:13 w· were heads of the fathers of 1992
13 w· drove away the inhabitants of "
9: 1 w· were carried away to Babylon for*
18 W· hitherto waited in the king's gate
31 w· was the firstborn of Shallum 1931
33 w· remaining in the chambers were
11:10 w· strengthened themselves with him
12 w· was one of the three mighties. 1931
22 Benaiah...w· had done many acts;
12:18 Amasai, w· was chief of the captains,
16:41 chosen, w· were expressed by name, 834
17:16 W· am I, O Lord God, and what is 4310
19: 7 w· came and pitched before Medeba.
21:16 Israel, w· were clothed in sackcloth,* "
22: 9 to thee, w· shall be a man of rest; 1931
24:28 Mahli came Eleazar, w· had no sons.
25: 1 w· should prophesy with harps,
3 Jeduthun, w· prophesied with a harp,
9 w· with his brethren and sons 1931
27: 6 w· was mighty among the thirty,
29: 5 w· then is willing to consecrate 4310
14 w· am I, and what is my people, "
2Ch 1:10 for w· can judge this thy people, "
2: 6 w· is able to build him an house, "
6 w· am I then, that I should build "
12 w· hath given to David the king a 834
6: 4 w· hath with his hands fulfilled that
8: 8 w· were left after them in the land,* 834
10: 2 the son of Nebat, w· was in Egypt, 1931
17:16 w· willingly offered himself unto the
18:19 W· shall entice Ahab king of 4310
19: 6 Lord, w· is with you in the judgment.
20: 7 w· didst drive out the inhabitants of
34 w· is mentioned in the book of * 834
35 of Israel, w· did very wickedly: *1931
22: 9 w· sought the Lord with all his 834
26: 1 Uzziah, w· was sixteen years old, 1931
5 w· had understanding in the visions
28: 5 w· smote him with a great slaughter
30: 7 w· therefore gave them up to *
32: 4 together, w· stopped all the fountains,
14 W· was there among all the gods 4310
31 w· sent unto him to enquire of the
34:26 w· sent you to enquire of the Lord,
35:21 w· is with me, that he destroy thee 834
36:13 w· had made him swear by God:
17 w· slew their young men with the
23 W· is there among you of all his *4310
Ezr 1: 3 W· is there among you of all his * "
3:12 of the fathers, w· were ancient men,
5: 3 W· hath commanded you to 4479
9 W· commanded you to build this "
12 Chaldean, w· destroyed this house,
Ne 1:11 servants, w· desire to fear thy name:
3: 3 w· also laid the beams thereof, *1992
6:10 of Mehetabeel, w· was shut up; 1931
11 w· is there, that, being as I am, 4310
7: 7 W· came with Zerubbabel, Jeshua,
9: 7 the God, w· didst choose Abram, 834
27 hand of their enemies, w· vexed them:
27 w· saved them out of the hand of their
32 God, w· keepest covenant and mercy,
13:26 like him, w· was beloved of his God,

Es 2: 6 W· had been carried away from 834
15 w· had taken her for his daughter, "
22 w· told it unto Esther the queen:
4:11 the inner court, w· is not called, 834
14 w· knoweth whether thou art 4310
6: 2 w· sought to lay hand on the king 834
4 the king said, W· is in the court? 4310
7: 5 W· is he, and where is he, that "
9 w· had spoken good for the king, 834
Job 3: 8 day, w· are ready to raise up their
15 gold, w· filled their houses with silver:
4: 2 but w· can withhold himself from 4310
7 w· ever perished, being innocent? "
5:10 W· giveth rain upon the earth, and
9: 4 w· hath hardened himself against 4310
12 taketh away, w· can hinder him? "
12 w· will say unto him, What doest "
19 w· shall set me a time to plead? "
24 thereof; if not, where, and w· is he?"
11:10 together, then w· can hinder him? "
12: 3 w· knoweth not such things as "
4 w· calleth upon God, and he
9 W· knoweth not in all these that 4310
13:19 W· is he that will plead with me? "
14: 4 W· can bring a clean thing out of "
16: 9 me in his wrath, w· hateth me:
17: 3 w· is he that will strike hands 4310
15 as for my hope, w· shall see it? "
21:31 W· shall declare his way to his "
31 w· shall repay him what he hath "
23:13 one mind, and w· can turn him? "
24:25 so now, w· will make me a liar, "
26:14 of his power w· can understand? "
27: 2 w· hath taken away my judgment;
2 the Almighty, w· hath vexed my soul;
30: 4 W· cut up mallows by the bushes,
34: 7 w· drinketh up scorning like water?
13 W· hath given him a charge over 4310
13 w· hath disposed the whole world? "
29 w· then can make trouble? "
29 his face, w· then can behold him? "
35:10 maker, w· giveth songs in the night;
11 W· teacheth us more than the beasts
36:22 his power: w· teacheth like him? 4310
23 W· hath enjoined him his way? "
23 or w· can say, Thou hast wrought "
38: 2 W· is this that darkeneth counsel "
5 W· hath laid the measures thereof, "
5 w· hath stretched the line upon it? "
6 or w· laid the corner stone thereof, "
8 Or w· shut up the sea with doors, "
25 W· hath divided a watercourse 4310
28 w· hath begotten the drops of dew?"
29 of heaven, w· hath gendered it? "
36 W· hath put wisdom in the inward "
36 or w· hath given understanding to "
37 W· can number the clouds in "
37 w· can stay the bottles of heaven, "
41 W· provideth for the raven his "
39: 5 W· hath sent out the wild ass free? "
5 w· hath loosed the bands of the "
41:10 w· then is able to stand before me? "
11 W· hath prevented me, that I "
13 W· can discover the face of his "
13 w· can come to him with his double"
14 W· can open the doors of his face? "
33 not his like, w· is made without fear.*
42: 3 W· is he that hideth counsel 4310
Ps 4: 6 say, W· will shew us any good? "
6: 5 grave w· shall give thee thanks? "
8: 1 w· hast set thy glory above the 834
12: 4 W· have said, With our tongue will "
4 are our own: w· is lord over us? 4310
14: 4 w· eat up my people as they eat
15: 1 w· shall abide in thy tabernacle? 4310
1 w· shall dwell in thy holy hill? "
16: 7 Lord, w· hath given me counsel: 834
17: 9 enemies, w· compass me about. *
18: title w· spake unto the Lord the 834
3 the Lord, w· is worthy to be praised:
31 For w· is God save the Lord? 4310
31 or w· is a rock save our God? "
19:12 W· can understand his errors? "
24: 3 W· shall ascend into the hill of the "
3 w· shall stand in his holy place? "
4 w· hath not lifted up his soul unto 834
8, 10 W· is this King of glory? The 4310
34: title w· drove him away, and he departed.
35:10 say, Lord, w· is like unto thee, 4310
37: 7 of him w· prospereth in his way,
7 the man w· bringeth wicked devices
42:11 w· is the health of my countenance,
43: 5 w· is the health of my countenance,
53: 4 w· eat up my people as they eat
59: 7 lips: for w·, say they, doth hear? 4310
60: 9 W· will bring me into the strong "
9 city? w· will lead me into Edom? "
64: 3 W· whet their tongue like a sword, 834
5 they say, W· shall see them? 4310
65: 5 w· art the confidence of all the ends of*
68:19 w· daily loadeth us with benefits,
71:19 high, w· hast done great things: 834
19 O God, w· is like unto thee! 4310
72:18 w· only doeth wondrous things,
76: 7 w· may stand in thy sight when 4310
77:13 w· is so great a God as our God? "
78: 6 w· should arise and declare them to
83:12 W· said, Let us take to ourselves 834
84: 6 W· passing through the valley of
89: 6 w· in the heaven can be compared 4310
6 w· among the sons of the mighty can
8 w· is a strong Lord like unto thee? 4310
90:11 W· knoweth the power of thine "
94:16 W· will rise up for me against the "
16 w· will stand up for me against the "
103: 3 W· forgiveth all thine iniquities;

Ps 103: 3 iniquities; w· healeth all thy diseases;
4 W· redeemeth thy life from
4 w· crowneth thee with lovingkindness
5 W· satisfieth thy mouth with good
104: 2 W· coverest thyself with light as with
2 w· stretchest out the heavens like a
3 W· layeth the beams of his chambers
3 w· maketh the clouds his chariot:
3 w· walketh upon the wings of the
4 W· maketh his angels spirits; his
5 W· laid the foundations of the earth,
105:17 Joseph, w· was sold for a servant:
106: 2 W· can utter the mighty acts of 4310
2 w· can shew forth all his praise? *
108:10 W· will bring me into the strong 4310
10 city? w· will lead me into Edom? "
11 not thou, O God, w· hast cast us off? "
113: 5 W· is like unto the Lord our God, 4310
5 Lord our God, w· dwelleth on high,
6 W· humbleth himself to behold the*
119: 1 way, w· walk in the law of the Lord.
38 servant, w· is devoted to thy fear.* 834
124: 1, 2 been the Lord w· was on our side,
6 w· hath not given us as a prey to their
8 the Lord, w· made heaven and earth.
130: 3 iniquities, O Lord, w· shall stand? 4310
135: 8 W· smote the firstborn of Egypt, both
9 W· sent tokens and wonders into the*
10 W· smote great nations, and slew
136: 4 To him w· alone doeth great wonders:
23 W· remembered us in our low estate:
25 W· giveth food to all flesh: for his*
137: 7 w· said, Rase it, rase it, even to the
8 of Babylon, w· art to be destroyed;*
140: 4 w· have purposed to overthrow my 834
144: 2 w· subdueth my people under me.
10 w· delivereth David his servant from
147: 8 W· covereth the heaven with clouds,
8 w· prepareth rain for the earth,
8 w· maketh grass to grow upon the
17 w· can stand before his cold? 4310
Pr 2:13 W· leave the paths of uprightness, to
14 W· rejoice to do evil, and delight in
9:15 passengers w· go right on their ways:
18:14 a wounded spirit w· can bear? 4310
20: 6 but a faithful man w· can find? "
9 W· can say, I have made my heart "
25 man w· devoureth that which is holy,*
21:24 his name w· dealeth in proud wrath.*
23:29 W· hath woe? w· hath sorrow? 4310
29 w· hath contentions? w· hath "
29 w· hath wounds without cause? "
29 w· hath redness of eyes? "
24:22 w· knoweth the ruin of them both? "
26:18 As a mad man w· casteth firebands,
27: 4 w· is able to stand before envy? 4310
30: 4 W· hath ascended up into heaven, "
4 w· hath gathered the wind in his "
4 w· hath bound the waters in a "
4 w· hath established all the ends of "
9 thee, and say, W· is the Lord? "
31:10 W· can find a virtuous woman? "
Ec 2:25 w· can eat, or w· else can hasten "
3:21 W· knoweth the spirit of man that "
22 w· shall bring him to see what shall"
4: 3 w· hath not seen the evil work 834
13 w· will no more be admonished. "
6:12 w· knoweth what is good for man 4310
7:13 for w· can make that straight, "
24 exceeding deep, w· can find it out? "
8: 1 W· is as the wise man? and "
1 w· knoweth the interpretation of a "
7 w· can tell him when it shall be? "
10 w· had come and gone from the place*
10:14 be after him, w· can tell him? 4310
11: 5 the works of God w· maketh all. 834
12: 7 shall return unto God w· gave it. "
Ca 3: 6 W· is this that cometh out of the 4310
6:10 W· is she that looketh forth as the "
8: 2 mother's house, w· would instruct me:
5 W· is this that cometh up from 4310
Isa 1:12 w· hath required this at your "
6: 8 shall I send, and w· will go for us? "
14: 6 He w· smote the people in wrath *
27 purposed, and w· shall disannul it? 4310
27 out, and w· shall turn it back? "
23: 8 W· hath taken this counsel against"
24:18 w· fleeth from the noise of the fear
27: 4 w· would set the briers and thorns 4310
29:15 W· seeth us? and w· knoweth us? "
22 the Lord, w· redeemed Abraham, 834
33:14 W· among us shall dwell with the 4310
14 w· among us shall dwell with "
36:20 W· are they among all the gods of "
37: 2 w· was over the household, 834
40:12 W· hath measured the waters in 4310
13 W· hath directed the Spirit of the "
14 w· instructed him, and taught him in
26 and behold w· hath created these 4310
41: 2 W· raised up the righteous man "
4 W· hath wrought and done it, "
26 W· hath declared from the "
42:19 W· is blind, but my servant? or "
19 w· is blind as he that is perfect, "
23 W· among you will give ear to "
23 w· will hearken and hear for the time*
24 W· gave Jacob for a spoil, and 4310
43: 9 w· among them can declare this, "
13 I will work, and w· shall let it? "
44: 7 And w·, as I, shall call, and shall "
10 W· hath formed a god, or molten "
45:21 w· hath declared this from ancient "
21 w· hath told it from that time? "
49:21 W· hath begotten me these, 4310
50: 8 w· will contend with me? let us "
8 w· is mine adversary? let him come"

Isa 50: 9 w· is he that shall condemn me? 4310
10 W· is among you that feareth the "
51:12 w· art thou, that thou shouldest be "
19 thee; w· shall be sorry for thee? "
53: 1 W· hath believed our report? and "
8 w· shall declare his generation? "
60: 8 W· are these that fly as a cloud, "
63: 1 W· is this that cometh from Edom, "
65:16 That he w· blesseth himself in the 834
66: 8 W· hath heard such a thing? 4310
8 w· hath seen such things? Shall 834
Jer 1:16 w· have forsaken me, and have *
2:24 occasion w· can turn her away? 4310
9:12 W· is the wise man, that may "
12 w· is he to whom the mouth of the "
10: 7 W· should not fear thee, O king 4310
15: 5 For w· shall have pity upon thee, "
5 or w· shall bemoan thee? "
5 or w· shall go aside to ask how thou "
17: 9 desperately wicked: w· can know 4310
18:13 w· hath heard such things: "
20: 1 w· was also chief governor in the 1931
15 w· brought tidings to my father, 834
21:13 W· shall come down against us? 4310
13 w· shall enter into our habitations? "
23:18 w· hath stood in the counsel of the "
18 w· hath marked his word, and "
26:20 w· prophesied against this city and
23 w· slew him with the sword, and cast
30:21 w· is this that engaged his heart 4310
36:32 w· wrote therein from the mouth of
46: 7 W· is this that cometh up as a 4310
49: 4 saying, W· shall come unto me? "
19 and w· is a chosen man, that I may*"
19 w· is like me? and w· will appoint "
19 w· is that shepherd that will stand "
50:44 and w· is a chosen man, that I may*"
44 w· is like me? and w· will appoint "
44 w· is that shepherd that will stand "
52:25 w· mustered the people of the land;
La 2:13 like the sea: w· can heal thee? 4310
3:37 W· is he that saith, and it cometh "
Eze 10: 7 with linen: w· took it, and went out.
Da 1:10 w· hath appointed your meat and 834
2:23 w· hast given me wisdom and 1768
3:15 w· is that God that shall deliver 4479
28 w· hath sent his angel, and 1768
6:27 w· hath delivered Daniel from the "
Ho 3: 1 w· look to other gods, and love *1992
7: 4 w· ceaseth from raising after he hath
14: 9 W· is wise, and he shall 4310
Joe 2:11 very terrible; and w· can abide it? "
14 W· knoweth if he will return and "
Am 1: 1 w· was among the herdmen of 834
3: 8 lion hath roared, w· will not fear? 4310
8 hath spoken, w· can but prophesy? "
10 store up violence and robbery in
5: 7 Ye w· turn judgment to wormwood,
Ob 3 W· shall bring me down to the 4310
Jon 3: 9 W· can tell if God will turn and "
Mic 5: 8 w·, if he go through, both treadeth 834
6: 9 the rod, and w· hath appointed it. 4310
7:18 W· is a God like unto thee, that "
Na 1: 6 W· can stand before his "
6 w· can abide in the fierceness of his"
3: 7 is laid waste: w· will bemoan her? "
Hab 2: 5 w· enlargeth his desire as hell, 834
Zep 3:18 the solemn assembly, w· are of thee,
Hag 2: 3 W· is left among you that saw 4310
Zec 4: 7 W· art thou, O great mountain? "
10 w· hath despised the day of small "
Mal 1:10 W· is there even among you that * "
3: 2 But w· may abide the day of his "
2 w· shall stand when he appeareth? "
M't 1:16 born Jesus, w· is called Christ. *3588
3: 7 w· hath warned you to flee from 5101
10: 2 first, Simon, w· is called Peter, 3588
4 Judas Iscariot, w· also betrayed "
11 enter, enquire w· in it is worthy; 5101
12:48 said unto him... W· is my mother? "
48 and w· are my brethren? "
13: 9, 43 W· hath ears to hear, let him *3588
46 W·, when he had found one pearl*3739
18: 1 W· is the greatest in the kingdom 5101
19:25 saying, W· then can be saved? "
21:10 city was moved, saying, W· is this? "
23 and w· gave thee this authority? "
24:45 W· then is a faithful and wise "
25:14 w· called his own servants, and *
26: 3 priest, w· was called Caiaphas, 3588
68 Christ, W· is he that smote thee? 5101
27:57 w·...himself was Jesus' disciple: 3739
M'r 1:19 w· also were in the ship mending 841
24 I know thee w· thou art, the Holy 5101
2: 7 w· can forgive sins but God only? "
3:33 W· is my mother, or my brethren? "
4:16 w·, when they have heard the 3739
5: 3 W· had his dwelling among the "
30 and said, W· touched my clothes? 5101
31 and sayest thou, W· touched me? "
9:34 w· should be the greatest. "
10:26 themselves, W· then can be saved? "
11:28 w· gave thee this authority to do "
13:34 w· left his house, and gave authority*
15: 7 w· had committed murder in the 3748
21 one Simon a Cyrenian, w· passed by,*
41 W· also, when he was in Galilee, 3739
16: 3 W· shall roll us away the stone 5101
Lu 1:36 with her, w· was called barren. *3588
3: 7 w· hath warned you to flee from 5101
4:34 I know thee w· thou art; the Holy "
5:12 w· seeing Jesus fell on his face, *2532
21 saying, W· is this which speaketh 5101
21 W· can forgive sins, but God alone? "
7: 2 servant, w· was dear unto him, 3739
39 w· and what manner of woman 5101
Lu 7:49 W· is this that forgiveth sins also?5101
8:45 And Jesus said, W· touched me? "
45 and sayest thou, W· touched me?* "
9: 9 but w· is this, of whom I hear such "
31 W· appeared in glory, and spake 3739
10:22 no man knoweth w· the Son is, 5101
22 and w· the Father is, but the Son, "
29 Jesus, And w· is my neighbour? "
12:14 w· made me a judge or a divider "
42 W· then is that faithful and wise "
16:11 w· will commit to your trust the "
12 w· shall give you that which is your"
14 the Pharisees also, w· were covetous,
18:26 it said, W· then can be saved? 5101
30 W· shall not receive manifold 3739
19: 3 he sought to see Jesus w· he was; 5101
20: 2 or w· is he that gave thee this "
22:64 Prophesy, w· is it that smote thee? "
23: 7 w· himself also was at Jerusalem
19 (W· for a certain sedition made in 3748
51 w· also himself waited for the 3739
Joh 1:19 to ask him, W· art thou? 5101
22 said they unto them, W· art thou? "
27 w· coming after me is preferred *3588
4:10 and w· it is that saith to thee, 5101
5:13 that was healed wist not w· it was: "
6:60 is an hard saying; w· can hear it? "
64 w· they were that believed not, "
64 and w· should betray him. "
7:20 a devil: w· goeth about to kill thee?"
49 people w· knoweth not the law *3588
8:25 said they unto him, W· art thou? 5101
9: 2 w· did sin, this man, or his parents,"
19 son, w· ye say was born blind? 3739
21 w· hath opened his eyes, we know 5101
36 W· is he, Lord, that I might "
12:34 be lifted up? w· is this Son of man? "
38 Lord, w· hath believed our report? "
13:11 he knew w· should betray him; *3588
24 w· it should be of whom he spake. 5101
25 saith unto him, Lord, w· is it? "
18:18 w· had made a fire of coals; for it was
21:12 durst ask him, W· art thou? 5101
Ac 1:23 w· was surnamed Justus, and 3739
3: 3 W· seeing Peter and John about "
4:25 W· by the mouth of thy servant 3588
36 w· by the apostles was surnamed "
5:36 rose up Theudas,...w· was slain; 3739
7:27 W· made thee a ruler and a judge5101
35 W· made thee a ruler and a judge? "
38 w· received the lively oracles to 3739
46 W· found favour before God, and "
53 W· have received the law by the 3748
8:15 W·, when they were come down, "
27 w· had the charge of all her 3739
33 w· shall declare his generation? 5101
9: 5 And he said, W· art thou, Lord? "
10:32 w·, when he cometh, shall speak *3739
38 w· went about doing good, and "
41 w· did eat and drink with him 3748
11:14 W· shall tell thee words, whereby 3739
17 w· believed on the Lord Jesus *
23 W·, when he came, and had seen 3739
13: 7 w· called for Barnabas and Saul, *3778
9 Then Saul, (w· is also called Paul,)3739
31 W· are his witnesses unto the 3748
43 w·, speaking to them, persuaded "
14: 8 a cripple...w· never had walked: 3739
9 w· stedfastly beholding him, and "
16 W· in times past suffered all nations"
19 w· persuaded the people, and, 2532
15:17 Lord, w· doeth all these things. 3588
27 w· shall also tell you the same 846
38 w· departed from them from 3588
16:24 W·, having received such a 3739
17:10 w· coming thither went into the 3748
18:27 w·, when he was come, helped *3739
19:15 and Paul I know; but w· are ye? 5101
21: 4 w· said to Paul through the *3748
32 W· immediately took soldiers and*3739
33 demanded w· he was, and what 5101
37 W· said, Canst thou speak Greek?*3588
22: 8 I answered, W· art thou, Lord? 5101
23:18 w· hath something to say unto thee.
33 W·, when they came to Cæsarea, 3748
24: 1 w· informed the governor against* "
6 W· also hath gone about to 3739
19 W· ought to have been here before "
26:15 And I said, W· art thou, Lord? 5101
28: 7 w· received us, and lodged us 3739
10 W· also honoured us with many "
18 W·, when they had examined me, 3748
Ro 1:18 w· hold...truth in unrighteousness;3588
25 W· changed the truth of God into;3748
25 the Creator, w· is blessed for ever. 3739
32 W· knowing the judgment of God,3748
2: 6 W· will render to every man 3739
7 To them w· by patient continuance
27 w· by the letter and circumcision 3588
3: 5 unrighteous w· taketh vengeance? "
19 it saith to them w· are under the law:
4:12 w· are not of the circumcision 3588
12 w· also walk in the steps of that "
16 of Abraham; w· is father of us all,3739
17 God, w· quickeneth the dead, 3588
18 W· against hope believed in hope,3739
25 W· was delivered for our offences, "
5:14 w· is the figure of him that is to "
7: 4 to him w· is raised from the dead,
24 w· shall deliver me from the body 5101
8: 1 w· walk not after the flesh, but after*
4 w· walk not after the flesh, but after
20 w· hath subjected the same in hope;
28 w· are the called according to his*
31 be for us, w· can be against us? 5101
33 W· shall lay any thing to the "
Ro 8:34 W· is he that condemeth? It is 5101
34 w· is even at the right hand of 3739
34 w· also maketh intercession for us. "
35 W· shall separate us from the 5101
9: 4 W· are Israelites; to whom 3748
5 w· is over all, God blessed for ever.3588
19 For w· hath resisted his will? 5101
20 w· art thou that repliest against "
10: 6 W· shall ascend into heaven? "
7 Or, W· shall descend into the deep?"
16 Lord, w· hath believed our report? "
11: 4 w· have not bowed the knee to the 3748
34 w· hath known the mind of the 5101
34 or w· hath been his counsellor? "
35 Or w· hath first given to him, and it"
14: 2 another, w· is weak, eateth herbs.*3588
4 W· art thou that judgest another 5101
20 that man w· eateth with offence. 3588
16: 4 W· have for my life laid down 3748
5 w· is the firstfruits of Achaia unto3739
6 w bestowed much labour on us. 3748
7 w· are of note among the apostles, "
7 w· also were in Christ before me. 3739
12 Tryphosa, w· labour in the Lord. 3588
22 I Tertius, w· wrote this epistle, "
1Co 1: 8 W· shall also confirm you unto 3739
30 w· of God is made unto us wisdom, "
2:16 w· hath known the mind of the 5101
3: 5 W· then is Paul, and w· is Apollos,* "
4: 5 w· both will bring to light the 3739
7 w· maketh thee to differ from 5101
17 w· is my beloved son, and faithful 3739
17 the Lord, w· shall bring you into "
6: 4 to judge w· are least esteemed in the
9: 7 W· goeth a warfare any time at *5100
7 w· planteth a vineyard, and eateth "
7 w· feedeth a flock, and eateth not "
10:13 w· will not suffer you to be 3739
14: 8 w·, shall prepare himself to the 5101
2Co 1: 4 W· comforteth us in all our 3588
10 W· delivered us from so great a
19 w· was preached among you by 3588
22 W· hath also sealed us, and given "
2: 2 w· is he then that maketh me 5101
16 w· is sufficient for these things? "
3: 6 W· also hath made us able 3739
4: 4 w· is the image of God, should
6 w· commanded the light to shine *3588
5: 5 w· also hath given unto us the
18 w· hath reconciled us to himself by "
21 him to be sin for us, w· knew no sin;
8:10 for you, w· have begun before, 3748
19 w· was also chosen of the churches
10: 1 w· in presence am base among 3739
11:29 W· is weak, and I am not weak? 5101
29 w· is offended, and I burn not? "
Ga 1: 1 w· raised him from the dead;) 3588
4 W· gave himself for our sins, that "
15 w· separated me from my mother's "
2: 3 neither Titus, w· was with me,
4 w· came in privily to spy out our 3748
6 of these w· seemed to be somewhat,
6 for they w· seemed to be somewhat
9 and John, w· seemed to be pillars, 3588
15 We w· are Jews by nature, and not*
20 w· loved me, and gave himself for 3588
3: 1 Galatians, w· hath bewitched you, 5101
4:23 he w· was of the bondwoman was born*
5: 7 w· did hinder you that ye should 5101
6:10 them w· are of the household of faith,*
13 they themselves w· are circumcised
Eph 1: 3 Jesus Christ, w· hath blessed us 3588
11 purpose of him w· worketh all things
12 glory, w· first trusted in Christ. 3588
19 of his power to us-ward w· believe, "
2: 1 w· were dead in trespasses and sins,
4 But God, w· is rich in mercy, for his*
11 w· are called Uncircumcision by 3588
13 ye w· sometimes were far off are *3739
14 our peace, w· hath made both "
3: 8 w· am less than the least of all
9 w· created all things by Jesus 3588
4: 6 and Father of all, w· is above all,
19 W· being past feeling have given 3748
5: 5 covetous man, w· is an idolater, 3739
Ph'p 2: 6 W·, being in the form of God, *
20 w· will naturally care for your 3748
3:19 shame, w· mind earthly things.) 3588
Col 1: 8 W· also declared unto us your love "
13 W· hath delivered us from the 3739
15 W· is the image of the invisible "
18 w· is the beginning, the firstborn "
24 W· now rejoice in my sufferings *
2:12 w· hath raised him from the dead.3588
3: 4 When Christ, w· is our life, shall
4: 7 w· is a beloved brother, and a
9 beloved brother, w· is one of you. 3739
11 w· are of the circumcision. 3588
12 Epaphras, w· is one of you, a "
1Th 2:15 W· both killed the Lord Jesus,
5: 8 But let us, w· are of the day, be sober,
10 W· died for us, that, whether we 3588
24 that calleth you, w· also will do it. "
2Th 1: 7 to you w· are troubled rest with us,*
9 W· shall be punished with 3748
2: 4 W· opposeth and exalteth himself*3588
7 only he w· now letteth will let, until he*
12 all might be damned w· believed 3588
3: 3 W· shall stablish you, and keep 3739
1Ti 1:12 our Lord, w· hath enabled me, 3588
13 W· was before a blasphemer, and* "
2: 4 W· will have all men to be saved, 3739
6 W· gave himself a ransom for all, 3588
4:10 God, w· is the Saviour of all men, 3739
5:17 w· labour in the word and doctrine.
6:13 of God, w· quickeneth all things, 3588

1Ti 6:13 w' before Pontius Pilate witnessed 3588
15 w' is the...only Potentate, "
16 W' only hath immortality, "
17 w' giveth us richly all things to "
2Ti 1: 9 W' hath saved us, and called us "
10 Christ, w' hath abolished death,
2: 2 w' shall be able to teach others 3748
4 w' hath chosen him to be a soldier.
18 W' concerning the truth have 3748
26 w' are taken captive by him at his*
4: 1 w' shall judge the quick and the 3588
Tit 1:11 w' subvert whole houses, teaching 3748
2:14 W' gave himself for us, that he 3739
Heb 1: 1 W' at sundry times and in divers*
3 W' being the brightness of his
7 W' maketh his angels spirits, 3739
14 them w' shall be heirs of salvation?*
2: 9 w' was made a little lower than 3588
11 sanctifieth and they w' are sanctified
15 them w' through fear of death 3745
3: 2 W' was faithful to him that appointed
3 as he w' hath builded the house *
5: 2 W' can have compassion on the
7 W' in the days of his flesh, when 3739
14 w' by reason of use have their senses
6: 4 for those w' were once enlightened,
12 w' through faith and patience inherit
18 w' have fled for refuge to lay hold 3588
7: 1 w' met Abraham returning from "
5 Levi, w' receive the office of the * "
9 Levi also, w' receiveth tithes,
16 W' is made, not after the law of a 3739
26 w' is holy, harmless, undefiled, *
27 W' needeth not daily, as those 3739
28 Son, w' is consecrated for evermore.*
8: 1 w' is set on the right hand of the 3739
5 W' serve unto the example and 3748
9:14 w' through the eternal Spirit 3739
10:29 w' hath trodden under foot the 3588
39 of them w' draw back unto perdition;*
11:11 judge him faithful w' had promised.
27 endured, as seeing him w' is invisible.
33 W' through faith subdued 3739
12: 2 w' for the joy that was set before "
16 w' for one morsel of meat sold his "
25 w' refused him that spake on earth,*
13: 7 w' have spoken unto you the word 3748
Jas 3:13 W' is a wise man and endued 5101
4:12 w' is able to save and to destroy: 3588
12 destroy: w' art thou that judgest 5101
5: 4 w' have reaped down your fields, 3588
10 w' have spoken in the name of the 3739
1Pe 1: 5 W' are kept by the power of God 3588
10 w' prophesied of the grace that "
17 w' without respect of persons "
20 W' verily was foreordained before the
21 W' by him do believe in God, that 3588
2: 9 w' hath called you out of darkness
22 W' did no sin, neither was guile 3739
23 W', when he was reviled, reviled "
24 W' his own self bare our sins in
3: 5 women also, w' trusted in God, 3588
13 w' is he that will harm you, if ye 5101
22 W' is gone into heaven, and is on 3739
4: 5 W' shall give account to him that "
5: 1 w' am also an elder, and a witness 3588
10 w' hath called us unto his eternal "
2Pe 2: 1 w' privily shall bring in damnable 3748
15 w' loved the wages of 3739
18 escaped from them w' live in error.*
1Jo 2:22 W' is a liar but he that denieth 5101
3:12 as Cain, w' was of that wicked one,*
4:21 he w' loveth God love his brother
5: 5 W' is he that overcometh the 5101
2Jo 7 w' confess not that Jesus Christ *3588
3Jo 9 w' loveth to have the preeminence "
Jude 4 w' were before of old ordained to "
18 w' should walk after their own *
19 These be they w' separate themselves,
Re 1: 2 W' bare record of the word of 3739
5 Christ, w' is the faithful witness,
9 John, w' am also your brother, *3588
2: 1 w' walketh in the midst of the * "
13 martyr, w' was slain among you, 3739
14 w' taught Balac to cast a
18 w' hath his eyes like unto a flame 3588
4: 9 throne, w' liveth for ever and ever,*"
5: 2 W' is worthy to open the book, 5101
6:17 and w' shall be able to stand? "
12: 5 w' was to rule all nations with 3739
13: 4 W' is like unto the beast? 5101
4 w' is able to make war with him? "
14:11 w' worship the beast and his 3588
15: 4 W' shall not fear thee, O Lord, 5101
7 God w' liveth for ever and ever. 3588
18: 8 is the Lord God w' judgeth her. * "
9 w' have committed fornication "

whole See also WHOLESOME.
Ge 2: 6 and watered the w' face of the 854,3605
11 the w' land of Havilah, " "
13 the w' land of Ethiopia. " "
7:19 that were under the w' heaven, "
8: 9 were on the face of the w' earth: "
9:19 them was the w' earth overspread. "
11: 1 the w' earth was of one language. "
4 upon the face of the w' earth. "
13: 9 Is not the w' land before thee? "
47:28 the w' age of Jacob was an hundred*
Ex 12: 6 w' assembly of the congregation 3605
16: 2 the w' congregation of the children "
3 to kill this w' assembly 854, "
10 the w' congregation of the children "
19:18 and the w' mount quaked greatly. "
29:18 thou shalt burn the w' ram 854, "
Le 3: 9 the fat thereof, and the w' rump, *8549
4:12 Even the w' bullock shall he 854,3605
13 the w' congregation of Israel sin 3605
7:14 shall offer one out of the w' oblation "
8:21 and Moses burnt the w' ram 854, "
10: 6 the w' house of Israel, bewail the "
25:29 may redeem it within a w' year 8552
Nu 3: 7 charge of the w' congregation 3605
8: 9 shalt gather the w' assembly 854, "
10: 2 of a w' piece shalt thou make *4749
11:20 But even a w' month, until it 3117
21 that they may eat a w' month, "
14: 2 the w' congregation said unto 3605
29 according to your w' number, from "
20: 1 w' congregation, into the desert of "
22 the w' congregation, journeyed "
De 2:25 that are under the w' heaven, "
4:19 all nations under the w' heaven. "
27: 6 of the Lord thy God of w' stones: *8003
29:23 the w' land thereof is brimstone, 3605
33:10 w' burnt sacrifice upon thine 3632
Jos 5: 8 in the camp, till they were w'. 8421
8:31 an altar of w' stones, over which *8003
10:13 not to go down about a w' day. 8549
11:23 So Joshua took the w' land, 854,3605
18: 1 w' congregation of the children of "
22:12 w' congregation of the children of "
16 the w' congregation of the Lord, "
18 with the w' congregation of Israel "
J'g 19: 2 and was there four w' months. *3117
21:13 w' congregation sent some to 3605
2Sa 1: 9 because my life is yet w' in me. "
3:19 good to the w' house of Benjamin. "
6:19 among the w' multitude of Israel, "
14: 7 w' family is risen against thine "
1Ki 6:22 w' house be overlaid with gold, "
22 the w' altar that was by the oracle "
11:34 w' kingdom out of his hand. 854, "
2Ki 9: 8 the w' house of Ahab shall perish: "
2Ch 6: 3 blessed the w' congregation of *854, "
15:15 sought him with their w' desire; "
26:12 w' number of the chief of the fathers "
30:23 w' assembly took counsel to keep "
33: 8 according to the w' law and the * "
Ezr 2:64 w' congregation together was forty "
Ne 7:66 w' congregation together was forty "
Es 3: 6 the w' kingdom of Ahasuerus, "
Job 5:18 woundeth, and his hands make w'. 7495
28:24 and seeth under the w' heaven; 3605
34:13 who hath disposed the w' world? "
37: 3 directeth it under the w' heaven, "
41:11 is under the w' heaven is mine. "
Ps 9: 1 thee, O Lord, with my w' heart; "
48: 2 joy of the w' earth, is mount Zion, "
51:19 offering and w' burnt offering: 3632
72:19 w' earth be filled with his glory; 854,3605
97: 5 presence of the Lord of the w' earth. "
105:16 he brake the w' staff of bread. "
111: 1 praise the Lord with my w' heart, "
119: 2 that seek him with the w' heart. "
10 my w' heart have I sought thee: "
34 shall observe it with my w' heart. "
58 thy favour with my w' heart: "
69 thy precepts with my w' heart. "
145 I cried with my w' heart; hear me, O "
Pr 1:12 w', as those that go down into 8549
16:33 the w' disposing thereof is of the 3605
26:26 be shewed before the w' congregation.*
Ec 12:13 the conclusion of the w' matter: 3605
13 for this is the w' duty of man. "
Isa 1: 5 w' head is sick, and the w' heart "
3: 1 the staff, the w' stay of bread, "
1 and the w' stay of water, "
6: 3 the w' earth is full of his glory. "
10:12 his w' work upon mount Zion 854, "
13: 5 indignation, to destroy the w' land. "
14: 7 The w' earth is at rest, and is quiet: "
26 is purposed upon the w' earth: "
29 Rejoice not thou, w' Palestina, * "
31 thou, w' Palestina, art dissolved: * "
21: 8 I am set in my ward w' nights: "
28:22 even determined upon the w' earth. "
54: 5 God of the w' earth shall he be "
Jer 1:18 brasen walls against the w' land, "
4:20 cried; for the w' land is spoiled: "
27 The w' land shall be desolate; "
29 The w' city shall flee for the noise‡ "
7:15 even the w' seed of Ephraim. "
8:16 the w' land trembled at the sound "
12:11 the w' land is made desolate, "
13:11 unto me the w' house of Israel "
11 Israel and the w' house of Judah, "
15:10 man of contention to the w' earth! "
19:11 that cannot be made w' again: 7495
24: 7 unto me with their w' heart. 3605
25:11 this w' land shall be a desolation, "
31:40 the w' valley of the dead bodies, "
32:41 my w' heart and with my w' soul. "
35: 3 the w' house of the Rechabites; "
37:10 had smitten the w' army of the "
45: 4 I will pluck up, even the w' land. "
50:23 hammer of the w' earth cut asunder "
51:41 praise of the w' earth surprised! "
47 her w' land shall be confounded, "
La 2:15 of beauty, The joy of the w' earth? "
Eze 5:10 the w' remnant of thee will I "
7:13 touching the w' multitude thereof, "
10:12 their w' body, and their backs, and "
15: 5 when it was w', it was meet for no 8549
32: 4 beasts of the w' earth with thee. 3605
35:14 When the w' earth rejoiceth, I will "
37:11 bones are the w' house of Israel: "
39:25 mercy upon the w' house of Israel, "
43:11 may keep the w' form thereof, "
12 the w' limit thereof round about "
45: 6 shall be for the w' house of Israel. "
Da 2:35 mountain, and filled the w' earth. 3606
48 him ruler over the w' province "
6: 1 should be over the w' kingdom; 3606
3 to set him over the w' realm. "
7:23 and shall devour the w' earth, "
27 the kingdom under the w' heaven, "
8: 5 west on the face of the w' earth. 3605
9:12 for under the w' heaven hath not "
10: 3 three w' weeks were fulfilled. 3117
11:17 the strength of his w' kingdom, 3605
Am 1: 6 away captive the w' captivity, 8003
9 they delivered up the w' captivity "
3: 1 against the w' family which I 3605
Mic 4:13 unto the Lord of the w' earth. "
Zep 1:18 w' land shall be devoured by the "
Zec 4:10 to and fro through the w' earth. "
14 stand by the Lord of the w' earth. "
5: 3 forth over the face of the w' earth: "
Mal 3: 9 robbed me, even the w' nation. "
M't 5:29, 30 thy w' body should be cast into 3650
6:22 thy w' body shall be full of light. "
23 w' body shall be full of darkness. "
8:32 the w' herd of swine ran violently 3956
34 the w' city came out to meet Jesus:*"
9:12 that be w' need not a physician, 2480
21 touch his garment, I shall be w'. 4982
22 thy faith hath made thee w'. "
22 woman was made w' from that "
12:13 it was restored w', like as the 5199
13: 2 w' multitude stood on the shore. *3956
33 of meal, till the w' was leavened. *3650
14:36 as touched were made perfectly w'. 1295
15:28 was made w' from that very hour. *2390
31 the maimed to be w', the lame to 5199
16:26 if he shall gain the w' world, and 3650
26:13 shall be preached in the w' world, "
27:27 unto him the w' band of soldiers. "
M'r 2:17 They that are w' have no need of 2480
3: 5 hand was restored w' as the other. *5199
4: 1 the w' multitude was by the sea *3956
5:28 but his clothes, I shall be w'. 4982
34 thy faith hath made thee w'; "
34 peace, and be w' of thy plague. 5199
6:55 ran through that w' region round 3650
56 as touched him were made w'. 4982
8:36 if he shall gain the w' world, and 3650
10:52 way; thy faith hath made thee w'. 4982
12:33 is more than all w' burnt offerings 3646
14: 9 preached throughout the w' 3650
15: 1 scribes and the w' council, and "
16 and they call together the w' band. "
33 was darkness over the w' land until "
Lu 1:10 the w' multitude of the people 3956
5:31 that are w' need not a physician; 5198
6:10 hand was restored w' as the other. *5199
19 w' multitude sought to touch him: *3956
7:10 servant w' that had been sick. 5198
8:37 the w' multitude of the country 587
39 published throughout the w' city 3650
48 thy faith hath made thee w'; go in 4982
50 only, and she shall be made w'. "
9:25 if he gain the w' world, and lose 3650
11:34 thy w' body also is full of light; "
36 w' body therefore be full of light, "
36 dark, the w' shall be full of light, * "
13:21 of meal, till the w' was leavened. * "
17:19 thy faith hath made thee w'. 4982
19:37 w' multitude of the disciples began 587
21:35 dwell on the face of the w' earth. *3956
23: 1 the w' multitude of them arose, 587
Joh 4:53 believed, and his w' house. 3650
5: 4 w' of whatsoever disease he had. *5199
6 unto him, Wilt thou be made w'? "
9 immediately the man was made w'. "
11 He that made me w', the same said "
14 him, Behold, thou art made w': "
15 was Jesus, which had made him w'. "
7:23 every whit w' on the sabbath day? "
11:50 and that the w' nation perish not. 3650
Ac 4: 9 by what means he is made w'; 4982
10 this man stand here before you w'. 5199
6: 5 saying pleased the w' multitude: 3956
9:34 Jesus Christ maketh thee w': *2390
11:26 that a w' year they assembled 3650
13:44 came almost the w' city together 3956
15:22 and elders, with the w' church, 3650
19:29 w' city was filled with confusion: * "
28:30 two w' years in his own hired "
Ro 1: 8 spoken of throughout the w' world. "
8:22 that the w' creation groaneth 3956
16:23 of the w' church, saluteth you. 3650
1Co 5: 6 little leaven leaveneth the w' lump? "
12:17 If the w' body were an eye, "
17 If the w' were hearing, "
14:23 w' church become together into one "
Ga 5: 3 he is a debtor to do the w' law. "
9 little leaven leaveneth the w' lump. "
Eph 3:15 w' family in heaven and earth is 3956
4:16 the w' body fitly joined together * "
6:11 Put on the w' armour of God, that ye
13 take unto you the w' armour of God,
1Th 5:23 your w' spirit and soul and body *3648
Tit 1:11 who subvert w' houses, teaching 3650
Jas 2:10 whosoever shall keep the w' law, "
3: 2 able also to bridle the w' body. "
3 and we turn about their w' body. "
6 that it defileth the w' body, and "
1Jo 2: 2 also for the sins of the w' world. "
5:19 the w' world lieth in wickedness. "
Re 12: 9 which deceiveth the w' world: "
16:14 of the earth and of the w' world, "

wholesome
Pr 15: 4 A w' tongue is a tree of life: but 4832
1Ti 6: 3 and consent not to w' words, even *5198

wholly
Le 6:22 the Lord; it shall be w' burnt. 3632
23 offering...shall be w' burnt:

Le 19: 9 not w· reap the corners of thy field,3615
Nu 3: 9 they are w· given unto him out of
4: 6 spread over it a cloth w· of blue. *3632
8:16 For they are w· given unto me from
32:11 they have not w· followed me: 4390
12 they have w· followed the Lord. "
De 1:36 he hath w· followed the Lord. "
Jos 14: 8 I w· followed the Lord my God. "
9 hast w· followed the Lord my God. "
14 that he w· followed the Lord God "
J'g 17: 3 w· dedicated the silver unto the *6942
1Sa 7: 9 a burnt offering w· unto the Lord:*3632
1Ch 28:21 people...w· at thy commandment. 3605
Job 21:23 full strength, being w· at ease and "
Isa 22: 1 art w· gone up to the housetops? "
Jer 2:21 thee a noble vine, w· a right seed: "
6: 6 is w· oppression in the midst of her."
13:19 it shall be w· carried away captive.7965
42:15 ye w· set your faces to enter into 7760
46:28 I not leave thee w· unpunished. *5352
50:13 but it shall be w· desolate: 3605
Eze 11:15 and all the house of Israel w·, * "
Am 8: 8 and it shall rise up w· as a flood; "
9: 5 and it shall rise up w· like a flood; "
Ac 17:16 he saw the city w· given to idolatry.*
1Th 5:23 very God of peace sanctify you w· ;3651
1Ti 4:15 give thyself w· to them; that 1510,1722

whom See also WHOMSOEVER.
Ge 2: 8 he put the man w· he had formed. 834
3:12 The woman w· thou gavest to be "
4:25 seed instead of Abel, w· Cain slew.*3588
6: 7 will destroy man w· I have created 834
10:14 (out of w· came Philistim,) and * "
15:14 w· they shall serve, will I judge: "
21: 3 him, w· Sarah bare to him, Isaac. "
24:40 before w· I walk, will send his angel "
25:12 w· Hagar the Egyptian, Sarah's "
30:26 children, for w· I have served thee, "
41:38 is, a man in w· the Spirit of God is? "
43:27 well, the old man of w· ye spake? "
29 younger brother, of w· ye spake? "
44:10 w· it is found shall be my servant; "
16 he also with w· the cup is found. "
45: 4 your brother, w· ye sold into Egypt. "
46:18 w· Laban gave to Leah his daughter,*"
48: 9 w· God hath given me in this place. "
15 w· my fathers Abraham and Isaac "
49: 8 art he w· thy brethren shall praise:*
Ex 4:13 by the hand of him w· thou wilt send.
6: 5 w· the Egyptians keep in bondage;*834
26 and Moses, to w· the Lord said, "
14:13 Egyptians w· ye have seen to day, "
18: 9 w· he had delivered out of the land* "
22: 9 w· the judges shall condemn, he "
23:27 the people to w· thou shalt come, "
28: 3 w· I have filled with the spirit of "
32:13 w· thou swarest by thine own self, "
33:12 know w· thou wilt send with me.853, "
19 gracious to w· I will be gracious," "
19 mercy on w· I will shew mercy. " "
35:21 every one w· his spirit made willing, "
23 every man, with w· was found blue, "
24 with w· was found shittim wood "
36: 1 in w· the Lord put wisdom 834,1992
Le 6: 5 it unto him to w· it appertaineth, 834
13:45 And the leper in w· the plague is, "
14:32 him in w· is the plague of leprosy, "
15:18 woman also with w· man shall lie "
16:32 And the priest, w· he shall anoint,* "
32 w· he shall consecrate to minister * "
17: 7 after w· they have gone a 834,1992
22: 5 of w· he may take uncleanness, 834
25:27 unto the man to w· he sold it; "
55 my servants w· I brought forth 834,853
26:45 w· I brought forth out of the " "
27:24 unto him of w· it was bought, " "
24 w·...possession of the land...belong.834
Nu 3: 3 w· he consecrated to minister in "
4:41 w· Moses and Aaron did number "
45 w· Moses and Aaron numbered "
46 w· Moses and Aaron and the chief of"
5: 7 him against w· he hath trespassed, "
11:16 w· thou knowest to be the elders of "
21 The people, among w· I am, are six "
12: 1 woman w· he had married: "
12 of w· the flesh is half consumed when
16: 5 even him w· he hath chosen will 834
7 the man w· the Lord doth choose, "
17: 5 w· I shall choose, shall blossom: "
22: 6 that he w· thou blessest is blessed, "
6 and he w· thou cursest is cursed. "
23: 8 shall I curse, w· God hath not cursed?
8 I defy, w· the Lord hath not defied?
26: 5 of w· cometh the family of the *
64 w· Moses and Aaron the priest *
27:18 of Nun, a man in w· is the spirit, 834
34:29 are they w· the Lord commanded to "
36: 6 Let them marry to w· they think best;
De 4:46 w· Moses and the children of Israel834
7:19 people of w· thou art afraid. 834,6440
9: 2 of the Anakims, w· thou knowest, 834
2 and of w· thou hast heard say, "
17:15 w· the Lord thy God shall choose: "
19: 4 w· he hated not in time past; *
17 between w· the controversy is,834,1992
21: 8 Israel, w· thou hast redeemed, 834
24:11 man to w· thou dost lend shall bring"
28:55 flesh of his children w· he shall eat: "
29:26 them, gods w· they knew not, "
26 and w· he had not given unto them: "
31: 4 land of them, w· he destroyed. 834,853
32:17 to gods w· they knew not, to new gods
17 newly up, w· your fathers feared not.
20 generation, children in w· is no faith.
37 gods, their rock in w· they trusted,*

De 33: 8 one, w· thou didst prove at Massah,834
8 with w· thou didst strive at the waters
34:10 w· the Lord knew face to face, 834
Jos 2:10 and Og, w· ye utterly destroyed.834,853
4: 4 w· he had prepared of the children 834
5: 6 w· the Lord sware that he 834,1992
7 w· he raised up in their stead, "
10:11 w· the children of Israel slew with 834
25 enemies against w· ye fight. 834,853
13: 8 With w· the Reubenites and the *5973
21 w· Moses smote with the princes 834
24:15 you this day w· ye will serve; 4310
17 the people through w· we passed: 834
J'g 4:22 shew thee the man w· thou seekest. "
7: 4 shall be, that of w· I say unto thee, "
8:15 with w· ye did upbraid me, saying, "
18 men were they w· ye slew at Tabor? "
12: 9 thirty daughters, w· he sent abroad,*
14:20 w· he had used as his friend. 834
21:23 them that danced, w· they caught: "
Ru 2:19 with w· she had wrought, and 834,5973
19 w· I wrought to day is Boaz. " "
4: 1 kinsman of w· Boaz spake came by;834
1 unto w· he said, Ho, such a one!
12 w· Tamar bare unto Judah, of the 834
1Sa 2:33 w· I shall not cut off from mine altar,
6:20 and to w· shall he go up from us? 4310
9:17 Behold the man w· I spake to thee 834
20 on w· is all the desire of Israel? 4310
10:24 See ye him w· the Lord hath 834
12: 3 I taken? or w· have I defrauded? 4310
3 w· have I oppressed? or of whose
13 the king w· ye have chosen, 4310
13 chosen, and w· ye have desired!
16: 3 unto me him w· I name unto thee. 834
17:28 w· hast thou left those few sheep 4310
45 of Israel, w· thou hast defied. * 834
21: 9 w· thou slewest in the valley of "
24:14 After w· is the king of Israel come4310
14 after w· dost thou pursue? after a "
25:11 w· I know not whence they be? 834
25 men of my lord, w· thou didst send. "
28: 8 up, w· I shall name unto thee. 853, "
11 W· shall I bring up unto thee? " 4310
29: 5 of w· they sang one to another 834
30:13 unto him, To w· belongest thou? 4310
21 w· they had made also to abide at the
2Sa 7: 7 w· I commanded to feed my people 834
15 Saul, w· I put away before thee. "
23 w· God went to redeem for a people "
14: 7 the life of his brother w· he slew; "
15:33 Unto w· David said, If thou passest*
16:18 but w· the Lord, and this people, 834
19 And again, w· should I serve? 4310
17: 3 man w· thou seekest is as if all 834
19:10 Absalom, w· we anointed over us, "
20: 3 w· he had left to keep the house, and"
21: 6 of Saul, w· the Lord did choose. *
8 w· she bare unto Saul, Armoni and 834
8 w· she brought up for Adriel the son
23: 8 of the mighty men w· David had: 834
8 hundred, w· he slew at one time.
1Ki 2: 5 Amasa the son of Jether, w· he slew,
5: 5 son, w· I will set upon thy throne 834
7: 8 daughter, w· he had taken to wife, "
9:21 w· the children of Israel also were not
10:26 w· he bestowed in the cities for *
11:20 w· Tahpenes weaned in Pharaoh's
34 w· I chose, because he kept my 834
13:23 prophet w· he had brought back. "
17: 1 of Israel liveth, before w· I stand, "
20 upon the widow with w· I sojourn, "
18:15 of hosts liveth, before w· I stand, "
31 unto w· the word of the Lord came, "
20:14 And Ahab said, By w·? And he 4310
42 w· I appointed to utter destruction,
21:25 w· Jezebel his wife stirred up. 834
26 the Amorites, w· the Lord cast out
22: 8 by w· we may enquire of the Lord:
2Ki 3:14 of hosts liveth, before w· I stand, 834
5:16 As the Lord liveth, before w· I stand, "
6:19 bring you to the man w· ye seek. "
22 those w· thou hast taken captive "
8: 5 her son, w· Elisha restored to life. "
10:24 of the men w· I have brought into "
16: 3 w· the Lord cast out from before "
17: 8 w· the Lord cast out from before "
11 heathen w· the Lord carried away "
15 w· the Lord had charged them, "
27 priests w· ye brought from thence; "
28 priests w· they had carried away "
33 the nations w· they carried away "
34 of Jacob, w· he named Israel; "
35 w· the Lord had made a covenant, "
18:20 Now on w· dost thou trust, that 4310
19: 4 w· the king of Assyria his master 834
10 thy God in w· thou trustest deceive "
22 W· hast thou reproached and 853,4310
22 against w· hast thou exalted thy "
21: 2 w· the Lord cast out before the 834
9 the nations w· the Lord destroyed "
23: 5 priests, w· the kings of Judah had "
25:22 w· Nebuchadnezzar king of "
1Ch 1:12 (of w· came the Philistines,) * "
2:21 w· he married when he was "
5: 6 w· Tilgath-pilneser...carried 834
25 w· God destroyed before them. "
6:31 they w· David set over the service "
7:14 of Manasseh; Ashriel, w· she bare: "
9:22 w· David and Samuel the seer 834,1922
11:10 of the mighty men w· David had, 834
11 of the mighty men w· David had; "
17: 6 w· I commanded to feed my people, "
21 w· God went to redeem to be his "
21 w· thou hast redeemed out of * "
26:32 w· king David made rulers over the

1Ch 29: 1 my son, w· alone God hath chosen,
8 w· precious stones were found 834
2Ch 1:11 w· I have made thee king: 834,5921
2: 7 w· David my father did provide. 834
8: 8 w· the children of Israel consumed "
9:25 w· he bestowed in the chariot cities,*
17:19 w· the king put in fenced cities 834
18: 7 by w· we may enquire of the Lord:
20:10 w· thou wouldest not let Israel 834
22: 7 w· the Lord had anointed to cut off "
23:18 w· David had distributed in the "
28: 3 w· the Lord had cast out before the "
33: 2 w· the Lord had cast out before the "
9 heathen, w· the Lord had destroyed "
Ezr 2: 1 w· Nebuchadnezzar the king of "
65 of w· there were seven thousand 428
4:10 w· the great and noble Asnapper 1768
5:14 w· he had made governor; "
8:20 w· David and the princes had
10:44 had wives by w· they had children.
Ne 1:10 w· thou hast redeemed by thy 834
7: 6 w· Nebuchadnezzar the king of
67 of w· there were seven thousand 428
8:10 them for w· nothing is prepared:
9:37 kings w· thou hast set over us 834
Es 2: 6 w· Nebuchadnezzar the king of
7 w· Mordecai, when her father and
4: 5 w· he had appointed to attend 834
11 to w· the king shall hold out the
6: 6 man w· the king delighteth to honour?
6 To w· would the king delight to do
7 w· the king delighteth to honour 4310
9 w· the king delighteth to honour, 834
9, 11 w· the king delighteth to honour. "
13 before w· thou hast begun to fall,
Job 3:23 is hid, and w· God hath hedged in?
5:17 happy is the man w· God correcteth:
9:15 W·, though I were righteous, yet 834
15:19 w· alone the earth was given, 1992
19:19 w· I loved are turned against me.
27 w· I shall see for myself, and mine 834
25: 3 upon w· doth not his light arise? 4310
26: 4 To w· hast thou uttered words? "
30: 2 me, in w· old age was perished? 5921
Ps 10: 3 the covetous, w· the Lord abhorreth.*
16: 3 the excellent, in w· is all my delight.
18: 2 God, my strength, in w· I will trust;*
43 w· I have not known shall serve me.
27: 1 my salvation; w· shall I fear? 4310
1 of my life; of w· shall I be afraid? "
32: 2 w· the Lord imputeth not iniquity,
33:12 people w· he hath chosen for his own
41: 9 familiar friend, in w· I trusted, 834
45:16 w· thou mayest make princes in all
47: 4 excellency of Jacob w· he loved. 834
65: 4 Blessed is the man w· thou choosest
69:26 him w· thou hast smitten; 834
26 grief of those w· thou hast wounded.
73:25 W· have I in heaven but thee? 4310
80:17 w· thou madest strong for thyself.
86: 9 All nations w· thou hast made 834
88: 5 w· thou rememberest no more: "
89:21 With w· my hand...be established: "
94: 1 God, to w· vengeance belongeth;
1 O God, to w· vengeance belongeth,
12 is the man w· thou chastenest, O 834
95:11 Unto w· I sware in my wrath that* "
104:26 w· thou hast made to play therein.
105:26 and Aaron w· he had chosen. 834
106:34 w· the Lord commanded them: * "
38 w· they sacrificed unto the idols of "
107: 2 w· he hath redeemed from the hand "
144: 2 my shield, and he in w· I trust;
146: 3 the son of man, in w· there is no help.
Pr 3:12 For w· the Lord loveth he 853,834
12 a father the son in w· he delighteth.
27 not good from them to w· it is due,
25: 7 prince w· thine eyes have seen. 834
30:31 against w· there is no rising up. 5973
Ec 4: 8 For w· do I labour, and bereave 4310
5:19 man also to w· God hath given 834
6: 2 A man to w· God hath given riches, "
8:14 just men, unto w· it happeneth 834,413
14 to w· it happeneth according to the "
9: 9 with the wife w· thou lovest all the 834
Ca 1: 7 Tell me, O thou w· my soul loveth,
3: 1 I sought him w· my soul loveth:
2 I will seek him w· my soul loveth:
3 the city found me: to w· I said,
3 Saw ye him w· my soul loveth? 853
Isa 6: 8 W· shall I send, and who will 853,4310
8:12 them to w· this people shall say, 834
18 children w· the Lord hath give me "
10: 3 to w· will ye flee for help? and 4310
19:25 W· the Lord of hosts shall bless, * 834
22:16 w· hast thou here, that thou hast 4310
23: 2 thou w· the merchants of Zidon, that
28: 9 W· shall he teach knowledge?853,4310
9 and w· shall he make to 834,413
12 To w· he said, This is the rest
31: 6 unto him from w· the children 834
36: 5 now on w· dost thou trust, that 4310
37: 4 w· the king of Assyria his master 834
10 not thy God, in w· thou trustest, "
23 W· hast thou reproached and 853,4310
23 against w· hast thou exalted thy "
40:14 With w· took he counsel, and who "
18 To w· then will ye liken God? or "
25 To w· then will ye liken me, or "
41: 8 servant, Jacob w· I have chosen, 834
9 Thou w· I have taken from the "
42: 1 Behold my servant, w· I uphold;
1 mine elect, in w· my soul delighteth;
24 he against w· we have sinned? 2098
43:10 and my servant w· I have chosen: 834
44: 1 and Israel, w· I have chosen:

Isa 44: 2 and thou, Jesurun, w' I have chosen.
46: 5 To w' will ye liken me, and make 4310
47: 15 thee with w' thou hast laboured, 834
49: 3 O Israel, in w' I will be glorified.
7 Holy One, to him w' man despiseth,
7 to him w' the nation abhorreth,
50: 1 divorcement, w' I have put away? 834
1 creditors is it to w' I have sold you? "
51: 18 the sons w' she hath brought forth;
19 by w' shall I comfort thee? 4310
53: 1 and to w' is the arm of the Lord "
57: 4 Against w' do ye sport yourselves? "
4 against w' make ye a wide mouth, "
11 And of w' hast thou been afraid or "
66: 13 As one w' his mother comforteth, 834
Jer 1: 12 w' the word of the Lord came in the "
6: 10 To w' shall I speak, and give 4310
7: 9 after other gods w' ye know not; 834
8: 2 w' they have loved, and w' they "
2 and after w' they have walked,
2 and w' they have sought, and
2 w' they have worshipped: they 834
9: 12 who is he to w' the mouth of the "
16 w' neither they nor their fathers "
11: 12 unto w' they offer incense: 834,1992
14: 16 people to w' they prophesy " "
18: 8 against w' I have pronounced, * 834
19: 4 w' neither they nor their fathers "
20: 6 to w' thou hast prophesied 834,1992
23: 9 like a man w' wine hath overcome,
24: 5 w' I have sent out of this place 834
25: 15 to w' I send thee, to drink it. 834,413
17 unto w' the Lord hath sent me: "
26: 5 the prophets, w' I sent unto you, 834
27: 5 unto w' it seemed meet unto me. "
29: 1 w' Nebuchadnezzar had carried "
3 (w' Zedekiah king of Judah sent "
4 w' I have caused to be carried away "
20 w' I have sent from Jerusalem to "
22 w' the king of Babylon roasted in "
30: 9 king, w' I will raise up unto them. "
17 is Zion, w' no man seeketh after. "
33: 5 w' I have slain in mine anger and 834
34: 11 handmaids, w' they had let go free, "
16 w' he had set at liberty at their "
37: 1 w' Nebuchadrezzar king of Babylon "
38: 9 w' they have cast into the 853,
39: 17 men of w' thou art afraid. 834,6440
40: 5 w' the king of Babylon hath made 834
41: 2 w' the king of Babylon had made "
9 w' he had slain because of "
10 w' Nebuzar-adan the captain of the "
16 w' he had recovered from Ishmael "
16 w' he had brought again from "
18 w' the king of Babylon made "
42: 6 Lord our God, to w' we send thee; "
9 w' ye sent me to present your 834,413
11 Babylon, of w' ye are afraid; " 6440
44: 3 other gods, w' they knew not, 834
52: 28 people w' Nebuchadrezzar carried "
La 1: 10 w' thou didst command that they "
14 from w' I am not able to rise up.
2: 20 consider to w' thou hast done 4310
4: 20 w' we said, Under his shadow we 834
Eze 9: 6 any man upon w' is the mark;
11: 1 among w' I saw Jaazaniah the son of *
7 Your slain w' ye have laid in the 834
15 w' the inhabitants of Jerusalem "
13: 22 sad, w' I have not made sad; "
16: 20 w' thou hast borne unto me, 834
37 with w' thou hast taken pleasure, "
20: 9 the heathen, among w' they were, "
23: 7 and with all on w' she doted: "
9 the Assyrians, upon w' she doted. "
22 from w' thy mind is alienated, 834,1992
28 the hand of them w' thou hatest, 834
28 from w' thy mind is alienated: "
37 their sons, w' they bare unto me, "
40 unto w' a messenger was sent; 834,413
40 for w' thou didst wash thyself, 834
24: 21 daughters w' ye have left shall fall "
28: 25 people among w' they are scattered, "
31: 2 W' art thou like in thy 413,4310
18 To w' art thou thus like in glory "
32: 19 W' doest thou pass in beauty? go "
38: 17 Art thou he of w' I have spoken in 834
Da 1: 4 Children in w' was no blemish, 834,1992
4 w' they might teach the learning *
7 Unto w' the prince of the eunuchs*1992
11 w' the prince of the eunuchs had 834
2: 24 w' the king had ordained to 1768
3: 12 Jews w' thou hast set over the 3487
17 God w' we serve is able to deliver 1768
4: 8 in w' is the spirit of the holy gods: "
5: 11 in w' is the spirit of the holy gods: "
11 w' the king Nebuchadnezzar thy *
12 w' the king named Belteshazzar: 1768
13 w' the king my father brought "
19 before him: w' he would he slew; "
19 and w' he would he kept alive; "
19 alive; and w' he would he set up; "
19 up; and w' he would he put down. "
6: 2 of w' Daniel was first: 1768,2006
16 God w' thou servest continually, 1768
20 God, w' thou servest continually, "
7: 8 before w' there were three of the*
20 came up, and before w' three fell;*4479
9: 21 w' I had seen in the vision at the 834
11: 21 w' they shall not give the honour 5921
38 a god w' his fathers knew not 834
39 w' he shall acknowledge and * "
Ho 13: 10 and thy judges of w' thou saidst, "
Joe 2: 32 the remnant w' the Lord shall call. "
3: 2 w' they have scattered among the "
Am 6: 1 to w' the house of Israel came! 1992
7: 2, 5 by w' shall Jacob arise? for he *4310

Na 3: 19 w' hath not thy wickedness passed*4310
Zep 3: 18 to w' the reproach...was a burden 5921
Zec 1: 4 w' the former prophets have 834,413
10 These are they w' the Lord hath 834
7: 14 all the nations w' they knew not. "
12: 10 look upon me w' they...pierced, 854. "
Mal 1: 4 people against w' the Lord hath "
2: 14 w' thou hast dealt treacherously: "
3: 1 w' ye seek, shall suddenly come "
1 of the covenant, w' ye delight in: "
M't 1: 16 of Mary, of w' was born Jesus, 3739
3: 17 Son, in w' I am well pleased. "
7: 9 w' if his son ask bread, will he give* "
11: 10 he, of w' it is written, Behold, I "
12: 18 my servant, w' I have chosen; "
18 in w' my soul is well pleased: "
27 w' do your children cast them out? 5101
16: 13 W' do men say that I the Son of * "
15 them, But w' say ye that I am? * "
17: 5 Son, in w' I am well pleased; 3739
25 w' do the kings of the earth take 5101
18: 7 that man by w' the offence cometh! 3739
19: 11 saying, save they to w' it is given. "
20: 23 for w' it is prepared of my Father. "
23: 35 w' ye slew between the temple and "
24: 45 w' his lord hath made ruler over "
46 w' his lord when he cometh shall "
26: 24 by w' the Son of man is betrayed! "
27: 9 w'...the children of Israel did value; "
15 people a prisoner, w' they would. "
17 W' will ye that I release unto you? 5101
M'r 1: 11 Son, in w' I am well pleased. *3739
3: 13 and calleth unto him w' he would: "
6: 16 he said, It is John, w' I beheaded: "
8: 27 them, W' do men say that I am? *5101
29 them, But w' say ye that I am? * "
10: 40 to them for w' it is prepared. 3739
13: 20 the elect's sake, w' he hath chosen, "
14: 21 by w' the Son of man is betrayed! "
71 I know not this man of w' ye speak. "
15: 12 him w' ye call the King of the Jews? "
40 among w' was Mary Magdalene, "
16: 9 out of w' he had cast seven devils. "
Lu 6: 13 twelve, w' also he named apostles; "
14 Simon, (w' he also named Peter,) "
34 to them of w' ye hope to receive, "
47 I will shew you to w' he is like: 5101
7: 27 This is he, of w' it is written, 3739
43 that he, to w' he forgave most. "
47 to w' little is given, the same loveth "
8: 2 out of w' went seven devils, "
35 out of w' the devils were departed, "
38 out of w' the devils were departed "
9: 9 is this, of w' I hear such things? "
18 W' say the people that I am? *5101
20 them, But w' say ye that I am? "
10: 22 he to w' the Son will reveal him. *3739
11: 19 by w' do your sons cast them out? 5101
12: 5 will forewarn you w' ye shall fear: "
37 w' the lord when he cometh shall 3739
42 w' his lord shall make ruler over "
43 w' his lord when he cometh shall "
48 to w' men have committed much, "
13: 4 upon w' the tower in Siloam fell, "
16 w' Satan hath bound, lo, these "
17: 1 unto him, through w' they come! "
19: 15 to w' he had given the money, that "
22: 22 that man by w' he is betrayed! "
23: 25 into prison, w' they had desired; "
Joh 1: 15 This was he of w' I spake, He that "
26 one among you, w' ye know not; "
30 This is he of w' I said, After me "
33 Upon w' thou shalt see the Spirit* "
45 of w' Moses in the law, and the "
47 Israelite indeed, in w' is no guile! "
3: 26 to w' thou barest witness, behold, "
34 For he w' God hath sent speaketh "
4: 18 he w' thou now hast is not thy "
5: 21 so the Son quickeneth w' he will. "
38 w' he...sent, him ye believed not. "
45 you, even Moses, in w' ye trust. "
6: 29 ye believe on him w' he hath sent. "
68 him, Lord, to w' shall we go? 5101
7: 25 Is not this he, w' they seek to kill? 3739
28 sent me is true, w' ye know not. "
8: 53 dead: w' makest thou thyself? 5101
54 of w' ye say, that he is your God: 3739
10: 35 unto w' the word of God came, "
36 him, w' the Father hath sanctified, "
11: 3 behold, he w' thou lovest is sick. "
12: 1 dead, w' he raised from the dead. "
9 w' he had raised from the dead. "
38 to w' hath the arm of the Lord 5101
13: 18 I know w' I have chosen: but that 3739
22 another, doubting of w' he spake. 5101
23 one of his disciples, w' Jesus loved. 3739
24 who it should be of w' he spake. "
26 He it is, to w' I shall give a sop, "
14: 17 w' the world cannot receive, "
26 w'...Father will send in my name, "
15: 26 w' I will send unto you from the "
17: 3 Jesus Christ, w' thou hast sent. "
11 name those w' thou hast given me, "
24 w' thou hast given me, be with me* "
18: 4 and said unto them, W' seek ye? 5101
7 asked he them again, W' seek ye? "
19: 26 disciple standing by, w' he loved, 3739
37 shall look on him w' they pierced. "
20: 2 the other disciple, w' Jesus loved, "
15 weepest thou? w' seekest thou? 5101
21: 7 disciple w' Jesus loved saith unto 3739
20 seeth the disciple w' Jesus loved "
Ac 1: 2 unto the apostles w' he had chosen: "
3 To w' also he shewed himself alive "
2: 24 W' God hath raised up, having "
36 same Jesus, w' ye have crucified. "

Ac 3: 2 w' they laid daily at the gate of the 3739
13 w' ye delivered up, and denied him "
15 w' God hath raised from the dead; "
4: 10 Christ of Nazareth, w' ye crucified, "
10 w' God raised from the dead, "
22 on w' this miracle of healing was "
5: 25 the men w' ye put in prison are "
30 w' ye slew and hanged on a tree. "
32 w' God hath given to them that "
36 to w' a number of men, about four "
6: 6 W' they set before the apostles: "
7: 7 to w' they shall be in bondage "
35 This Moses w' they refused, saying, "
39 To w' our fathers would not obey, "
45 w' God drave out before the face of "
52 of w' ye have been...the betrayers "
8: 10 To w' they all gave heed, from the "
34 of w' speaketh the prophet this? 5101
9: 5 I am Jesus w' thou persecutest: 3739
37 w' when they had washed, they *
10: 21 said, Behold, I am he w' ye seek: 3739
39 w' they slew and hanged on a tree: "
13: 22 to w' also he gave testimony, "
25 w' think ye that I am? I am not *5101
37 But he, w' God raised again, saw 3739
14: 23 to the Lord, on w' they believed. "
15: 17 upon w' my name is called, "
24 to w' we gave no...commandment: "
17: 7 W' Jason hath received: and these "
23 W'...ye ignorantly worship, * "
31 by that man w' he hath ordained; "
18: 26 w' when Aquila and Priscilla had* 846
19: 13 you by Jesus w' Paul preacheth. 3739
16 the man in w' the evil spirit was "
27 w' all Asia and...world worshippeth. "
20: 25 among w' I have gone preaching "
21: 16 disciple, with w' we should lodge. "
29 w' they supposed that Paul had "
22: 5 from w' also I received letters unto "
8 of Nazareth, w' thou persecutest. "
23: 29 W' I perceived to be accused of "
24: 6 w' we took, and would have judged "
8 w' thyself mayest take knowledge "
25: 15 About w', when I was at "
16 w' I answered, It is not the manner "
18 w' when the accusers stood up, "
19 dead, w' Paul affirmed to be alive. "
24 w' all the multitude of the Jews "
26 w' I have no certain thing to write "
26: 15 I am Jesus w' thou persecutest. "
17 Gentiles, unto w' now I send thee, "
26 before w' also I speak freely: "
27: 23 God, whose I am, and w' I serve, "
28: 4 w', though he hath escaped the sea, "
8 to w' Paul entered in, and prayed, "
15 w' when Paul saw, he thanked God, "
23 to w' he expounded and testified "
Ro 1: 5 By w' we have received grace and "
6 Among w' are ye also the called of "
9 w' I serve with my spirit in the "
3: 25 W' God had set forth to be a "
4: 6 unto w' God imputed righteousness "
8 to w' the Lord will not impute sin. "
17 before him w' he believed, even "
24 us also, to w' it shall be imputed, "
5: 2 By w' also we have access by faith "
11 by w' we have now received the "
6: 16 to w' ye yield yourselves servants "
16 his servants ye are to w' ye obey; "
8: 30 Moreover w' he did predestinate, "
30 w' he called, them he also "
30 w' he justified, them he also "
9: 4 to w' pertaineth the adoption, and* "
5 of w' as concerning the flesh * "
15 have mercy on w' I will have mercy, "
15 on w' I will have compassion "
18 he mercy on w' he will have mercy, "
18 mercy, and w' he will he hardeneth. "
24 Even us, w' he hath called, not of "
10: 14 him in w' they have not believed? "
14 in him of w' they have not heard? "
11: 36 things: to w' be glory for ever. * 846
13: 7 dues: tribute to w' tribute is due; 3588
7 custom to w' custom; "
9 fear to w' fear; "
9 honour to w' honour. "
14: 15 with thy meat, for w' Christ died. 3739
15: 21 To w' he was not spoken of, they "
16: 4 unto w' not only I give thanks, but "
1Co 1: 9 by w' ye were called unto the "
3: 5 but ministers by w' ye believed, "
7: 39 to be married to w' she will; "
8: 6 of w' are all things, and we in him; "
6 by w' are all things, and we by "
11 brother perish, for w' Christ died?* "
10: 11 upon w' the ends of the world are "
15: 6 of w' the greater part remain unto "
15 w' he raised not up, if so be that "
2Co 1: 10 in w' we trust that he will yet "
2: 3 from them of w' I ought to rejoice; "
10 To w' ye forgive any thing, I forgive "
10 forgave any thing, to w' I forgave it,* "
4: 4 In w' the god of this world hath "
8: 22 w' we have oftentimes proved "
10: 18 but w' the Lord commendeth. "
11: 4 another Jesus, w' we have not "
12: 17 any of them w' I sent unto you? "
Ga 1: 5 To w' be glory for ever and ever. "
2: 5 To w' we gave place by subjection, "
3: 19 come to w' the promise was made; "
4: 19 of w' I travail in birth again "
6: 14 by w' the world is crucified unto * "
Eph 1: 7 In w' we have redemption through "
11 In w' also we have obtained an "
13 In w' ye also trusted, after that ye "
2: 3 Among w' also we all had our "

Eph 2:21 In w' all the building fitly framed 3739
22 In w' ye also are builded together "
3:12 In w' we have boldness and access "
15 Of w' the whole family in heaven "
4:16 w' the whole body fitly joined "
6:22 W' I have sent unto you for the "
Ph'p 2:15 among w' ye shine as lights in the "
3: 8 for w' I have suffered the loss of "
18 walk, of w' I have told you often, "
Col 1:14 In w' we have redemption through "
27 To w' God would make known what "
28 W' we preach, warning every man, "
2: 3 In w' are hid all the treasures of "
11 In w' also ye are circumcised with "
4: 8 W' I have sent unto you for the "
10 w' ye received commandments: "
1Th 1:10 w' he raised from the dead, even "
2Th 2: 8 w' the Lord shall consume with the "
1Ti 1:15 save sinners; of w' I am chief. "
20 w' is Hymenæus and Alexander; "
20 w' I have delivered unto Satan, "
6:16 w' no man hath seen, nor can see: "
16 to w' be honour and power "
2Ti 1: 3 w' I serve from my forefathers "
12 I know w' I have believed, and am "
15 w' are Phygellus and Hermogenes. "
2:17 of w' is Hymenæus and Philetus; "
3:14 of w' thou hast learned them; 5101
4:15 Of w' be thou ware also; for he 3739
18 to w' be glory for ever and ever. "
Ph'm 10 w' I have begotten in my bonds: "
12 W' I have sent again: thou "
13 W' I would have retained with me. "
Heb 1: 2 w' he hath appointed heir of all "
2 by w' also he made the worlds; "
2:10 became him, for w' are all things, "
10 and by w' are all things, in "
3:17 with w' was he grieved forty years? 5101
18 to w' sware he that they should not "
4: 6 they to w' it was first preached "
13 eyes of him with w' we have to do. 3739
5:11 Of w' we have many things to say, "
6: 7 meet for them by w' it is dressed,* "
7: 2 To w' also Abraham gave a tenth "
4 w' even the patriarch Abraham "
8 of w' it is witnessed that he liveth. "
13 he of w' these things are spoken 3739
11:18 Of w' it was said, That in Isaac "
38 (Of w' the world was not worthy:) "
12: 6 w' the Lord loveth he chasteneth, "
6 and scourgeth every son w' he "
7 what son is he w' the father "
13:21 to w' be glory for ever and ever. "
23 with w', if he come shortly, I will "
Jas 1:17 lights, with w' is no variableness, "
1Pe 1: 8 W' having not seen, ye love; "
8 w', though now ye see him not, yet "
12 Unto w' it was revealed, that not 3739
2: 4 To w' coming, as unto a living "
4:11 w' be praise and dominion for ever.* "
5: 8 about, seeking w' he may devour: 5101
9 W' resist stedfast in the faith, 3739
2Pe 1:17 Son, in w' I am well pleased. "
2: 2 by reason of w' the way of truth "
17 w' the mist of darkness is reserved "
19 for of w' a man is overcome, of the "
1Jo 4:20 not his brother w' he hath seen, "
20 he love God w' he hath not seen? "
2Jo 1 her children, w' I love in the truth; "
3Jo 6 w' if thou bring forward on their "
Jude 13 to w' is reserved the blackness of "
Re 7: 2 to w' it was given to hurt the earth "
17: 2 With w' the kings of the earth have "
20: 8 the number of w' is as the sand of "

whomsoever
Ge 31:32 With w' thou findest thy gods, 834
44: 9 With w' of thy servants it be found, "
Le 15:11 w' he toucheth that hath the 3605,
J'g 7: 4 w' I say unto thee, This shall not go "
11:24 w' the Lord our God shall drive 3605,
Da 4:17 giveth it to w' he will, and setteth 4479
25, 32 men, and giveth it to w' he will. "
5:21 appointeth over it w' he will. 4479,1768
M't 11:27 to w' the Son will reveal him. 3739,1437
21:44 but on w' it shall fall, it will " 302
26:48 W' I shall kiss, that same is he: " "
M'r 14:44 W' I shall kiss, that same is he; " "
15: 6 one prisoner, w' they desired. *3746
Lu 4: 6 me; and to w' I will I give it. 3739,1437
12:48 For unto w' much is given, of 3956,3739
20:18 w' it shall fall, it shall grind 3739,302
Joh 13:20 receiveth w' I send receiveth 1437,5100
Ac 8:19 that on w' I lay hands, he may 3739,302
1Co 16: 3 w' ye shall approve by your 1437

whore See also WHOREMONGER; WHORE'S; WHORES; WHORING; WHORISH.
Le 19:29 daughter, to cause her to be a w'; *2181
21: 7 shall not take a wife that is a w', * "
9 profane herself by playing the w', * "
De 22:21 to play the w' in her father's house: * "
23:17 no w' of the daughters of Israel, *6948
18 shalt not bring the hire of a w', ‡2181
J'g 19: 2 And his concubine played the w' * "
Pr 23:27 For a w' is a deep ditch; and a ‡ "
Isa 57: 3 seed of the adulterer and the w'. ‡ "
Eze 16:28 hast played the w' also with the ‡ "
Re 17: 1 judgment of the great w' that *4204
15 where the w' sitteth, are peoples, * "
16 these shall hate the w', and shall * "
19: 2 for he hath judged the great w', * "

whoredom See also WHOREDOMS.
Ge 38:24 behold, she is with child by w'. 2183
Le 19:29 lest the land fall to w', and the 2181
20: 5 to commit w' with Molech, from ‡ "
Nu 25: 1 people began to commit w' with ‡ "
Jer 3: 9 through the lightness of her w', 2184
13:27 the lewdness of thy w', and thine "
Eze 16:17 and didst commit w' with them, *2181
33 unto thee on every side for thy w'. *8457
20:30 commit ye w' after their ‡2181
23: 8 and poured their w' upon her. 8457
17 and they defiled her with their w', "
27 thy w' brought from the land of 2184
43: 7 they, nor their kings, by their w', "
9 Now let them put away their w', "
Ho 1: 2 land hath committed great w', ‡2181
4:10 they shall commit w', and shall not ‡ "
11 W' and wine and new wine take 2184
13 your daughters shall commit w', ‡2181
14 daughters when they commit w', ‡ "
18 have committed w' continually: ‡ "
5: 3 O Ephraim, thou committest w', ‡ "
6:10 there is the w' of Ephraim, Israel 2184

whoredoms
Nu 14:33 and bear your w', until your 2184
2Ki 9:22 as the w' of thy mother Jezebel 2183
2Ch 21:13 to the w' of the house of Ahab, *2181
Jer 3: 2 hast polluted the land with thy w' 2184
Eze 16:20 Is this of thy w' a small matter, 8457
22 thy w' thou hast not remembered "
25 that past by, and multiplied thy w'. * "
26 hast increased thy w', to provoke * "
34 thee from other women in thy w', "
34 none followeth thee to commit w': ‡‡2181
36 discovered through thy w' with 8457
23: 3 And they committed w' in Egypt; ‡
3 they committed w' in their youth: ‡
7 she committed her w' with them, 8457
8 left she her w' brought from Egypt: "
11 and in her w' more than her sister "
11 more than her sister in her w'. 2183
14 And that she increased her w': 8457
18 So she discovered her w', and "
19 Yet she multiplied her w', in "
29 of thy w' shall be discovered, 2183
29 both thy lewdness and thy w'. 8457
35 thou also thy lewdness and thy w'. "
43 Will they now commit w' with her, ‡ "
Ho 1: 2 a wife of w' and children of w': 2183
2: 2 put away her w' out of her sight, "
4 for they be the children of w'. * "
4:12 of w' hath caused them to err, "
5: 4 spirit of w' is in the midst of them, * "
Na 3: 4 the w' of the wellfavoured harlot, "
4 that selleth nations through her w', "

whoremonger See also WHOREMONGERS.
Eph 5: 5 we know, that no w', nor unclean *4205

whoremongers
1Ti 1:10 For w', for them that defile *4205
Heb 13: 4 w' and adulterers God will judge.* "
Re 21: 8 and w', and sorcerers, and * "
22:15 are dogs, and sorcerers, and w', * "

whore's
Jer 3: 3 thou hadst a w' forehead, thou ‡2181

whores
Eze 16:33 They give gifts to all w': but thou *2181
Ho 4:14 themselves are separated with w', ‡ "

whoring
Ex 34:15 and they go a w' after their gods, ‡2181
16 daughters go a w' after their gods, ‡ "
16 thy sons go a w' after their gods. ‡ "
Le 17: 7 after whom they have gone a w'. ‡ "
20: 5 off, and all that go a w' after him, ‡ "
6 wizards, to go a w' after them, I ‡ "
Nu 15:39 after which ye used to go a w': ‡ "
De 31:16 and go a w' after the gods of the ‡ "
J'g 2:17 but they went a w' after other gods, ‡ "
8:27 all Israel went thither a w' after it: ‡ "
33 again, and went a w' after Baalim, ‡ "
1Ch 5:25 and went a w' after the gods of the ‡ "
2Ch 21:13 inhabitants of Jerusalem...go a w', ‡ "
Ps 73:27 all them that go a w' from thee. ‡ "
106:39 went a w' with their own inventions. ‡ "
Eze 6: 9 which go a w' after their idols: ‡ "
23:30 hast gone a w' after the heathen, ‡ "
Ho 4:12 gone a w' from under their God. ‡ "
9: 1 thou hast gone a w' from thy God, ‡ "

whorish
Pr 6:26 by means of a w' woman a man is ‡2181
Eze 6: 9 I am broken with their w' heart. ‡ "
16:30 work of an imperious w' woman; ‡ "

whose See also WHOSOEVER.
Ge 1:11 w' seed is in itself, upon the earth: *834
12 w' seed was in itself, after his kind: * "
7:22 in w' nostrils was the breath of life, "
11: 4 tower, w' top may reach unto heaven; "
16: 1 an Egyptian, w' name was Hagar. "
17:14 w' flesh of his foreskin is not * 834
24:23 W' daughter art thou? tell me, I 4310
32:17 W' art thou? and whither goest "
17 thou? and w' are these before thee? "
38: 1 Adullamite, w' name was Hirah. "
2 Canaanite, w' name was Shuah; "
6 Er his firstborn, w' name was Tamar.* "
25 man, w' these are, am I with child: 834
25 Discern, I pray thee, w' are these, "
44:17 man in w' hand the cup is found. "
49:22 well; w' branches run over the wall: * "
Ex 34:14 the Lord, w' name is Jealous, is a "
35:21 every one w' heart stirred him up, 834
26 the women w' heart stirred them up "
29 w' heart made them willing to bring "
36: 2 in w' heart the Lord had put wisdom, "
2 one w' heart stirred him up to come "
Le 13:40 man w' hair is fallen off his head, 3588
14:32 w' hand is not able to get that * 834
15:32 and of him w' seed goeth from him, "
16:27 w' blood was brought in to make "
Le 21:10 w' head the anointing oil was poured, 834
22: 4 or a man w' seed goeth from him; "
24:10 woman, w' father was an Egyptian, "
Nu 24: 3, 15 and the man w' eyes are open hath
De 8: 9 a land w' stones are iron, and out 834
9 out of w' hills thou mayest dig brass.
19: 1 w' land the Lord thy God giveth 834
28:49 a nation w' tongue thou shalt not "
29:18 w' heart turneth away this day from "
Jos 24:15 of the Amorites, in w' land ye dwell: "
J'g 4: 2 the captain of w' host was Sisera,
6:10 the Amorites, in w' land ye dwell: 834
8:31 son, w' name he called Abimelech.* 853
13: 2 of the Danites, w' name was Manoah;
16: 4 valley of Sorek, w' name was Delilah.
17: 1 mount Ephraim, w' name was Micah.
Ru 2: 2 him in w' sight I shall find grace. 834
5 the reapers, W' damsel is this? 4310
12 under w' wings thou art come to 834
3: 2 kindred, with w' maidens thou wast? "
1Sa 9: 1 w' name was Kish, the son of Abiel,
2 And he had a son, w' name was Saul,
10:26 of men, w' hearts God had touched. 834
12: 3 his anointed: w' ox have I taken? 4310
3 or w' ass have I taken? "
3 of w' hand have I received any "
17: 4 w' height was six cubits and a span.
12 w' name was Jesse; and he had
55 host, Abner, w' son is this youth? 4310
56 Enquire...w' son the stripling is. "
58 W' son art thou, thou young man? "
25: 2 Maon, w' possessions were in Carmel;
2Sa 3: 7 a concubine, w' name was Rizpah,
12 his behalf, saying, W' is the land? 4310
6: 2 w' name is called by the name of * 834
9: 2 of Saul a servant w' name was Ziba.
12 had a young son, w' name was Micha.
13: 1 had a fair sister, w' name was Tamar;
3 had a friend, w' name was Jonadab,
14:27 one daughter, w' name was Tamar:
16: 5 w' name was Shimei, the son of Gera:
8 Saul, in w' stead thou hast reigned; 834
17:10 w' heart is as the heart of a lion, "
25 son, w' name was Ithra an Israelite,
20: 1 w' name was Sheba, the son of Bichri,
21:16 weight of w' spear weighed three
19 of w' spear was like a weaver's beam.
1Ki 3:26 woman w' the living child was unto 834
8:39 to his ways, w' heart thou knowest; "
11:26 servant, w' mother's name was Zeruah,
2Ki 7: 2 a lord on w' hand the king leaned 834
17 the lord on w' hand he leaned to "
8: 1, 5 w' son he had restored to life, "
12:15 w' hand they delivered the money to "
18:22 is it not he, w' high places and 834,853
22 and w' altars Hezekiah hath taken "
1Ch 2:16 W' sisters were Zeruiah, and Abigail.*
26 another wife, w' name was Atarah;
34 an Egyptian, w' name was Jarha.
7: 2 w' number was in the days of David*
15 w' sister's name was Maachah;)
8:29 Gibeon; w' wife's name was Maachah:
38 Azel had six sons, w' names are these,
9:35 Jehiel, w' wife's name was Maachah:
44 Azel had six sons, w' names are these,
12: 8 w' faces were like the faces of lions,
20: 5 w' spear staff was like a weaver's beam.
6 w' fingers and toes were four and
26: 7 w' brethren were strong men, Elihu,
2Ch 6:30 ways, w' heart thou knowest; 834,853
16: 9 them w' heart is perfect toward him.
28: 9 Lord was there, w' name was Obed:
Ezr 1: 5 all them w' spirit God had raised, 853
5:14 unto one, w' name was Sheshbazzar,
7:15 w' habitation is in Jerusalem, 1768
Es 2: 5 a certain Jew, w' name was Mordecai,
Job 1: 1 the land of Uz, w' name was Job;
3:23 light given to a man w' way is hid, 834
4:19 of clay, w' foundation is in the dust, "
5: 5 W' harvest the hungry eateth up, "
8:14 W' hope shall be cut off, and "
14 and w' trust shall be a spider's web.
12: 6 w' hand God bringeth abundantly. 834
10 In w' hand is the soul of every living "
22:16 w' foundation was overflown with a "
26: 4 and w' spirit came from thee? 4310
30: 1 w' fathers I would have disdained 834
38:29 Out of w' womb came the ice? and 4310
39: 6 W' house I have made the 834
Ps 15: 4 In w' eyes a vile person is contemned;
17:14 w' belly thou fillest with thy hid
26:10 In w' hands is mischief, and their 834
32: 1 Blessed is he w' transgression is
1 is forgiven, w' sin is covered.
2 and in w' spirit there is no guile.
9 w' mouth must be held in with bit and
33:12 is the nation w' God is the Lord; 834
38:14 not, and in w' mouths are no reproofs.
57: 4 w' teeth are spears and arrows, and
78: 8 w' spirit was not stedfast with God.
83:18 that thou, w' name alone is Jehovah,
84: 5 is the man w' strength is in thee;
5 in w' heart are the ways of them.
105:18 W' feet they hurt with fetters: he was*
144: 8 W' mouth speaketh vanity, and 834
11 w' mouth speaketh vanity, and their "
15 is that people, w' God is the Lord.
146: 5 help, w' hope is in the Lord his God:
Pr 2:15 W' ways are crooked, and they * 834
26:26 W' hatred is covered by deceit, his*
30:14 a generation, w' teeth are as swords,
Ec 7:26 w' heart is snares and nets, 834,1931
Isa 1:30 shall be as an oak w' leaf fadeth,
2:22 man, w' breath is in his nostrils: 834
5:28 W' arrows are sharp, and all their "
6:13 as an oak, w' substance is in them, "

Isa 10:10 w' graven images did excel them of
14: 2 them captives, w' captives they were;
18: 2 w' land the rivers have spoiled! 834
7 w' land the rivers have spoiled, the "
23: 7 city, w' antiquity is of ancient days?
8 city, w' merchants are princes, 834
8 w' traffickers are the honourable of
26: 3 peace, w' mind is stayed on thee:
28: 1 w' glorious beauty is a fading flower,*
30:13 w' breaking cometh suddenly at an834
31: 9 w' fire is in Zion, and his furnace in "
36: 7 is it not he, w' high places and 834,853
7 and w' altars Hezekiah hath taken "
43:14 the Chaldeans, w' cry is in the ships.*
45: 1 w' right hand I have holden, 834
51: 7 the people in w' heart is my law;
15 that divided the sea, w' waves roared:
57:15 w' name is Holy; I dwell in the
20 rest, w' waters cast up mire and dirt.*
58:11 spring of water, w' waters fail not. 834
Jer 5:15 nation w' language thou knowest not,
17: 5 and w' heart departed from the Lord.
7 the Lord, and w' hope the Lord is.
19:13 upon w' roofs they have burned 834
22:25 the hand of them w' face thou fearest,*
32:29 w' roofs they have offered incense 834
33: 5 w' wickedness I have hid my face "
37:13 w' name was Irijah, the son of
44:28 know w' words shall stand, mine, 4310
46: 7 w' waters are moved as the rivers?
18 king, w' name is the Lord of hosts,
48:15 king, w' name is the Lord of hosts.
49:12 they w' judgment was not to drink*834
51:57 king, w' name is the Lord of hosts.
Eze 3: 6 w' words...canst not understand. 834
11:21 w' heart walketh after the heart of
17: 6 w' branches turned toward him,
16 him king, w' oath he despised, 834,853
16 w' covenant he brake, even with "
20: 9 w' sight I made myself known unto "
14 in w' sight I brought them out. 834
22 in w' sight I brought them forth. "
21:25 w' day is come, when iniquity shall "
27 more, until he come w' right it is; "
29 w' day is come, when their iniquity "
23:20 w' flesh is as the flesh of asses,
20 w' issue is like the issue of horses.
24: 6 city, to the pot w' scum is therein, 834
6 and w' scum is not gone out of it! "
32:23 W' graves are set in the sides of 834
40: 3 w' appearance was like the appearance
45 w' prospect is toward the south, 834
46 w' prospect is toward the north "
42:15 w' prospect is toward the east, "
43: 4 gate w' prospect is toward the east. "
47:12 trees for meat, w' leaf shall not fade,
Da 2:11 gods, w' dwelling is not with flesh.1768
26 Daniel, w' name was Belteshazzar, "
31 image, w' brightness was excellent,
3: 1 w' height was threescore cubits, 1768
27 w' bodies the fire had no power, * "
4: 8 w' name was Belteshazzar, "
19 Daniel, w' name was Belteshazzar, "
20 w' height reached unto the heaven,
21 W' leaves were fair, and the fruit
21 upon w' branches the fowls of the
34 w' dominion is an everlasting *1768
5:23 the God in w' hand thy breath is,
23 and w' are all thy ways, hast thou not
7: 9 sit, w' garment was white as snow,*
19 dreadful, w' teeth were of iron, 1768
20 w' look was more stout than his
27 w' kingdom is an everlasting kingdom,*
10: 1 w' name was called Belteshazzar; 834
5 w' loins were girded with fine gold of
Joe 1: 6 w' teeth are the teeth of a lion, and *
Am 2: 9 w' height was like the height of 834
5:27 Lord, w' name is The God of hosts.
Ob 3 of the rock, w' habitation is high;
Jon 1: 7 for w' cause this evil is upon us. 4310
8 w' cause this evil is upon us; 834, "
Mic 5: 2 w' goings forth have been from of old,
Na 3: 8 w' rampart was the sea, and her 834
Zec 6:12 the man w' name is The Branch;
11: 5 W' possessors slay them, and hold 834
M't 3:11 w' shoes I am not worthy to bear; 3739
12 W' fan is in his hand, and he will "
10: 3 w' surname was Thaddæus; *3588
22:20 W' is this image and 5101
28 W' wife shall she be of the seven? "
42 think ye of Christ? w' son is he? "
M'r 1: 7 latchet of w' shoes I am not worthy 3739
7:25 w' young daughter had an unclean "
12:16 them, W' is this image and 5101
23 w' wife shall she be of them? for
Lu 1:27 to a man w' name was Joseph, 3739
2:25 Jerusalem, w' name was Simeon; "
3:16 w' shoes I am not worthy to "
17 W' fan is in his hand, and he will "
6: 6 w' right hand was withered. *2532,846
12:20 w' shall those things be, which 5101
13: 1 w' blood Pilate had mingled with 3739
20:24 W' image and superscription 5100
33 w' wife of them is she?
24:18 w' name was Cleopas, answering *3739
Joh 1: 6 sent from God, w' name was John. 846
27 w' shoe's latchet I am not worthy 3739
4:46 w' son was sick at Capernaum. "
6:42 w' father and mother we know? "
10:12 w' own the sheep are not, seeth the "
11: 2 hair, w' brother Lazarus was sick. "
18:26 his kinsman w' ear Peter cut off, "
19:24 but cast lots for it, w' it shall be: 5101
20:23 W' soever sins ye remit, they are 5100
23 w' soever sins ye retain, they are "
Ac 7:58 young man's feet, w' name was Saul.*
Ac 10: 5 Simon, w' surname was Peter: *3739
6 tanner, w' house is by the sea side: "
32 Simon, w' surname is Peter; * "
11:13 Simon, w' surname is Peter; 3588
12:12 of John, w' surname was Mark; "
25 them John, w' surname was Mark. "
13:25 w' shoes of his feet I am not 3739
15:37 them John, w' surname was Mark.*3588
16:14 w' heart the Lord opened, that she3739
18: 7 w' house joined hard to the "
27:23 God, w' I am, and whom I serve, "
28: 7 of the island, w' name was Publius;*
11 isle, w' sign was Castor and Pollux.*
Ro 2:29 w' praise is not of men, but of God.3739
3: 8 may come? w' damnation is just. "
14 W' mouth is full of cursing and "
4: 7 are they w' iniquities are forgiven, "
7 forgiven, and w' sins are covered. "
9: 5 W' are the fathers, and of whom "
2Co 8:18 w' praise is in the gospel "
11:15 w' end shall be according to their "
Ga 3: 1 before w' eyes Jesus Christ hath "
Ph'p 3:19 W' end is destruction, w' God is "
19 w' glory is in their shame, who 3588
4: 3 w' names are in the book of life. 3739
2Th 2: 9 w' coming is after the working of "
Tit 1:11 W' mouths must be stopped, who "
Heb 3: 6 w' house are we, if we hold fast the "
17 w' carcases fell in the wilderness? "
6: 8 cursing; w' end is to be burned. "
7: 6 he w' descent is not counted from
11:10 w' builder and maker is God. 3739
12:26 W' voice then shook the earth: but "
13: 7 w' faith follow, considering the end*"
11 w' blood is brought into the holy "
1Pe 2:24 by w' stripes ye were healed. "
3: 3 W' adorning, let it not be that "
6 w' daughters ye are, as long as ye "
2Pe 2: 3 w' judgment now of a long time "
Jude 12 trees w' fruit withereth, without *
Re 13: 8 w' names are not written in the 3739
12 beast, w' deadly wound was healed."
17: 8 w' names were not written in the "
20:11 from w' face the earth and the "

whoso See also WHOSOEVER.
Ge 9: 6 W' sheddeth man's blood, by man
Le 11:27 w' toucheth their carcase shall be 3605
22: 4 w' toucheth any thing that is unclean
Nu 35:30 W' killeth any person, the 3605
De 19: 4 W' killeth...neighbour ignorantly, 834
2Ch 23:14 w' followeth her, let him be slain with
Ps 50:23 W' offereth praise glorifieth me: and
101: 5 W' privily slandereth his neighbour,
107:43 W' is wise, and will observe these4310
Pr 6:32 But w' committeth adultery with a*
8:35 For w' findeth me findeth life, and
9: 4, 16 W' is simple, let him turn in 4310
12: 1 W' loveth instruction loveth
13:13 W' despiseth the word shall be
16:20 w' trusteth in the Lord, happy is he.
17: 5 W' mocketh the poor reproacheth his
13 W' rewardeth evil for good, evil shall
20: 2 W' provoketh him to anger sinneth*
20 W' curseth his father or his mother,
21:13 W' stoppeth his ears at the cry of the
23 W' keepeth his mouth and his
25:14 W' boasteth himself of a false *376,834
26:27 W' diggeth a pit shall fall therein:
27:18 W' keepeth the fig tree shall eat the
28: 7 W' keepeth the law is a wise son:
10 W' causeth the righteous to go
13 w' confesseth and forsaketh them
18 W' walketh uprightly shall be saved:
24 W' robbeth his father or his mother,
26 but w' walketh wisely, he shall be
29: 3 W' loveth wisdom rejoiceth his
24 W' is partner with a thief hateth his
25 but w' putteth his trust in the Lord
Ec 7:26 w' pleaseth God shall escape from
8: 5 W' keepeth the commandment shall
10: 8 w' breaketh an hedge, a serpent shall
9 W' removeth stones shall be hurt
Da 3: 6 w' falleth not...worshippeth 4479,1768
11 w' falleth not...worshippeth, "
Zec 14:17 that w' will not come up of all the 834
M't 18: 5 w' shall receive one such 3739,302
6 w' shall offend one of these "
19: 9 w' marrieth her which is put *3588
23:20 W' therefore shall swear by the * "
21 And w' shall swear by the temple,* "
24:15 (w' readeth, let him understand:)
M'r 7:10 W' curseth father or mother, let * "
Joh 6:54 W' eateth my flesh, and drinketh * "
Jas 1:25 w' looketh into the perfect law of * "
1Jo 2: 5 w' keepeth his word, in him 3739,302

whosoever See also WHOSO.
Ge 4:15 W' slayeth Cain, vengeance shall 3605
Ex 19:12 w' toucheth the mount shall be "
22:19 w' lieth with a beast shall surely "
30:33 W' compoundeth any like it, 376
33 or w' putteth any of it upon a 834
38 W' shall make like unto that, to376, "
31:14 for w' doeth any work therein, that
15 w' doeth any work in the sabbath 3605
32:24 W' hath any gold, let them break 4310
33 W' hath sinned against me, 4310,834
35: 2 w' doeth work therein shall be 3605
5 w' is of a willing heart, let him "
Le 7:25 For w' eateth the fat of the beast, "
11:24 w' toucheth the carcase of them "
25 w' beareth ought of the carcase of "
31 w' doth touch them, when they be "
15: 5 w' toucheth his bed shall wash 376,834
10 w' toucheth any thing that was 3605
19 w' toucheth her shall be unclean "
Le 15:21 w' toucheth her bed shall wash 3605
22 w' toucheth any thing that she sat "
27 w' toucheth those things shall be "
17:14 w' eateth it shall be cut off. "
18:29 w' shall commit any of these 3605,834
19:20 w' lieth carnally with a woman, 376, "
20: 2 W' he be of the children of Israel, 376
21:17 W' he be of thy seed in their 376,834
22: 3 W' he be of all your seed " "
5 w' toucheth any creeping thing, " "
21 w' offereth a sacrifice of peace " "
24:15 W' curseth his God shall bear " "
Nu 5: 2 and w' is defiled by the dead: 3605
15:14 or w' be among you in your 834
17:13 W' cometh any thing near unto *3605
19:13 W' toucheth the dead body of any "
16 w' toucheth one that is slain 3605,834
31:19 w' hath killed any person, and 3605
19 w' hath touched any slain, purify "
De 18:19 w' will not hearken unto my 376,834
Jos 1:18 W' he be that doth rebel "
2:19 w' shall go out of the doors 3605, "
19 w' shall be with thee in the "
20: 9 w' killeth any person at unawares3605
J'g 7: 3 W' is fearful and afraid, let him 4310
1Sa 11: 7 W' cometh not forth after Saul 834
2Sa 5: 8 W' getteth up to the gutter, and
14:10 W' saith ought unto thee, bring him
17: 9 w' heareth it will say, There is a
1Ki 13:33 w' would, he consecrated him,
2Ki 10:19 w' shall be wanting, he shall 3605,834
1Ch 11: 6 w' smiteth the Jebusites first shall3605
26:28 and w' had dedicated any thing, "
2Ch 13: 9 w' cometh to consecrate himself "
15:13 w' would not seek the Lord God "
23: 7 and w' else cometh into the house, he
Ezr 1: 4 w' remaineth in any place where 3605
6:11 that w' shall alter this word, "
7:26 w' will not do the law of thy God, "
10: 8 w' would not come within three "
Es 4:11 that w', whether man or woman, 834
Pr 6:29 w' toucheth her shall not be 3605
20: 1 w' is deceived thereby is not wise. "
27:16 W' hideth her hideth the wind, and*
Isa 54:15 w' shall gather together against 4310
59: 8 w' goeth therein shall not know 3605
Jer 19: 3 which w' heareth, his ears shall "
Eze 33: 4 Then w' heareth the sound of the "
Da 5: 7 W' shall read this writing, and 3605
6: 7 w' shall ask a petition of any God "
Joe 2:32 w' shall call on the name of the 834
M't 5:19 W' therefore shall break one 3739,1437
19 w' shall do and teach them, " 302
21 w' shall kill shall be in danger " "
22 w' is angry with his brother *3956,3588
22 w' shall say to his brother, 3739,302
22 but w' shall say, Thou fool, " "
28 w' looketh on a woman to *3956,3588
31 W' shall put away his wife, 3739,302
32 w' shall put away his wife, * "
32 w' shall marry her that is " 1437
39 w' shall smite thee on thy right 3748
41 w' shall compel thee to go a mile, "
7:24 w' heareth these sayings of *3956, "
10:14 And w' shall not receive you, 3739,1437
32 W' therefore shall confess *3956,3748
33 w' shall deny me before men, 3748,302
42 w' shall give to drink unto 3739,1437
11: 6 w' shall not be offended in me. "
12:32 w' speaketh a word against " 302
32 w' speaketh against the Holy " "
50 w' shall do the will of my 3748, "
13:12 For w' hath, to him shall be given, 3748
12 w' hath not, from him shall be "
15: 5 W' shall say to his father or 3739,302
16:25 w' will save his life shall lose " "
25 w' will lose his life for my " "
18: 4 W' therefore shall humble 3748
19: 9 W' shall put away his wife, 3739,302
20:26 w' will be great among you, " 1437
27 w' will be chief among you, " "
21:44 w' shall fall on this stone shall *3588
23:12 w' shall exalt himself shall be 3748
16 W' shall swear by the temple 3739,302
16 w' shall swear by the gold of " "
18 W' shall swear by the altar, it " 1437
18 w' sweareth by the gift that is " 302
M'r 3:35 w' shall do the will of God, the " "
6:11 w' shall not receive you, nor 3745, "
8:34 W' will come after me, let him *3748
35 w' will save his life shall lose 3736,302
35 w' shall lose his life for my sake " "
38 W' therefore shall be ashamed " "
9:37 W' shall receive one of such 3739,1437
37 w' shall receive me, receiveth " "
41 w' shall give you a cup of water " 302
42 w' shall offend one of these " "
10:11 W' shall put away his wife, and " 1437
15 W' shall not receive the " "
43 w' will be great among you, " "
44 w' of you will be the chiefest, " 302
11:23 That w' shall say unto this " "
Lu 6:47 W' cometh to me, and *3956,3588
7:23 w' shall not be offended in me.*3739,1437
8:18 w' hath, to him shall be given; " 302
18 w' hath not, from him shall be " "
9: 5 And w' will not receive you, *3745, "
24 For w' will save his life shall 3739, "
24 w' will lose his life for my sake, " "
26 w' shall be ashamed of me and " "
48 W' shall receive this child in " 1437
48 w' shall receive me receiveth " "
12: 8 W' shall confess me *3956,3739,302
10 w' shall speak a word against 3956,3739
14:11 w' exalted himself shall be * " 3588
27 w' doth not bear his cross, and 3748

Lu 14:33 w' he be of you that forsaketh not 3956
16:18 W' putteth away his wife, *3956,3588
18 w' marrieth her that is put " "
17:33 W' shall seek to save his life 3739,1437
33 w' shall lose his life shall " "
18:17 W' shall not receive the " "
20:18 W' shall fall upon that stone*3956,3588
Joh 3:15,16 w' believeth in him should " "
4:13 W' drinketh of this water shall" "
14 But w' drinketh of the water 3739,302
5:4 w' then first after the troubling of*3588
8:34 W' committeth sin is the *3956, "
11:26 w' liveth and believeth in me " "
12:46 w' believeth on me should not " "
16:2 w' killeth you will think that " "
19:12 w' maketh himself a king " "
Ac 2:21 w' shall call on the name of the" 3739
10:43 w' believeth in him shall * " 3588
13:26 w' among you feareth God, to you* "
Ro 2:1 man, w' thou art that judgest:3956, "
9:33 w' believeth on him shall not* " "
10:11 W' believeth on him shall not " "
13 w' shall call upon the 3956,3739,302
13:2 W' therefore resisteth the power,*3588
1Co 11:27 w' shall eat this bread, and 3739,302
Ga 5:4 w' of you are justified by the law;*3748
10 bear his judgment, w' he be. 3748,302
Jas 2:10 w' shall keep the whole law, and 3748
4:4 w' therefore will be a friend 3739,302
1Jo 2:23 W' denieth the Son, the same3956,3588
3:4 W' committeth sin * "
6 W' abideth in him sinneth not: " "
6 w' sinneth hath not seen him, " "
9 W' is born of God doth not " "
10 w' doeth not righteousness is " "
15 W' hateth his brother is a " "
4:15 W' shall confess that Jesus is 3739,302
5:1 W' believeth that Jesus is 3956,3588
18 w' is born of God sinneth not; " "
2Jo 9 W' transgresseth, and abideth " "
Re 14:11 w' receiveth the mark of his name.*1536
20:15 w' was not found written in the * "
22:15 w' loveth and maketh a lie. *3956,3588
17 w' will, let him take the water of* "

why
Ge 4:6 unto Cain, W' art thou wroth? 4100
6 and w' is thy countenance fallen? "
12:18 w' didst thou not tell me that she "
19 W' saidst thou, She is my sister? "
25:22 she said, If it be so, w' am I thus? "
27:45 w' should I be deprived also of you "
42:1 W' do you look one upon another? "
47:15 w' should we die in thy presence? "
Ex 1:18 W' have ye done this thing, and 4069
2:20 w' is it that ye have left the man? 4100
3:3 this great sight, w' the bush is 4069
5:22 people? w' is it thou hast sent me?4100
14:5 W' have we done this, that we * "
17:2 unto them, W' chide ye with me? "
18:14 w' sittest thou thyself alone, and 4069
32:11 w' doth thy wrath wax hot against4100
Nu 11:20 W' came we forth out of Egypt? "
20:4 And w' have ye brought up the "
27:4 W' should the name of our father "
De 5:25 Now therefore w' should we die? "
Jos 7:25 W' hast thou troubled us? the "
17:14 W' hast thou given me but one 4069
J'g 2:2 my voice: w' have ye done this? 4100
5:16 W' abodest thou among the "
17 and w' did Dan remain in ships? "
28 W' is his chariot so long in 4069
28 w' tarry the wheels of his chariot? "
6:13 w' then is all this befallen us? 4100
8:1 W' hast thou served us thus, that "
9:28 Shechem:...w' should we serve him?"
11:7 w' are ye come unto me now when4069
26 w' therefore did ye not recover * "
13:18 W' askest thou thus after my *4100
15:10 W' are ye come up against us? "
21:3 w' is this come to pass in Israel, "
Ru 1:11 w' will ye go with me? are there "
21 w' then call ye me Naomi, seeing "
2:10 W' have I found grace in thine 4069
1Sa 1:8 w' weepest thou? and w' eatest 4100
8 w' is thy heart grieved? am I not "
2:23 unto them, W' do ye such things? "
6:3 you w' his hand is not removed "
17:8 W' are ye come out to set your "
28 said, W' camest thou down hither?"
19:17 W' hast thou deceived me so, and "
17 Let me go; w' should I kill thee? "
20:2 w' should my father hide this 4060
8 for w' shouldest thou bring me to 4100
21:1 W' art thou alone, and no man 4069
22:13 W' have ye conspired against me,4100
27:5 for w' should thy servant dwell in "
28:12 W' hast thou deceived me? for "
15 W' hast thou disquieted me, to "
2Sa 3:24 w' is it that thou hast sent him "
7:7 W' build ye not me an house of "
11:10 w' then didst thou not go down *4069
21 w' went ye nigh the wall? then say4100
13:4 W' art thou, being the king's son,4069
26 him, W' should he go with thee? 4100
16:9 W' should this dead dog curse my "
17 w' wentest thou not with thy "
18:11 w' didst thou not smite him there 4069
19:10 w' speak ye not a word of bringing4100
11 W' are ye the last to bring the king "
29 W' speakest thou any more of thy "
36 w' should the king recompense it "
41 W' have our brethren the men of 4069
43 w' then did ye despise us, that our "
20:19 w' wilt thou swallow up the 4100
24:3 w' doth my lord the king delight "
1Ki 1:6 in saying, W' hast thou done so? 4069

1Ki 1:13 w' then doth Adonijah reign? 4069
2:22 And w' dost thou ask Abishag the 4100
43 W' then hast thou not kept the "
9:8 W' hath the Lord done thus 5921, "
14:6 w' feignest thou thyself to be "
21:5 W' is thy spirit so sad, that thou "
2Ki 1:5 them, W' are ye now turned back? "
7:3 W' sit we here until we die? "
8:12 Hazael said, W' weepeth my lord?4069
12:7 W' repair ye not the breaches of "
1Ch 17:6 W' have ye not built me an house 4100
21:3 w' then doth my lord require this "
3 w' will he be a cause of trespass to "
2Ch 7:21 W' hath the Lord done thus unto4100
24:6 W' hast thou not required of the 4069
20 W' transgress ye the 4100
25:15 W' hast thou sought after the gods "
16 w' shouldest thou be smitten? "
19 w' shouldest thou meddle to thine "
32:4 W' should the king of Assyria come, "
Ezr 4:22 w' should damage grow to the 4101
7:23 w' should there be wrath against "
Ne 2:2 W' is thy countenance sad, 4069
3 w' should not my countenance be "
6:3 w' should the work cease, whilst 4100
13:11 W' is the house of God forsaken? 4069
21 them, W' lodge ye about the wall? "
Es 3:3 W' transgressest thou the king's "
4:5 know what it was, and w' it was. 4100
Job 3:11 W' died I not from the womb? "
11 w' did I not give up the ghost when I "
12 W' did the knees prevent me? 4069
12 or w' the breasts that I should suck?"
20 W' is light given to a man whose way "
23 W' is light given to a man whose way "
7:20 w' hast thou set me as a mark 4100
21 And w' dost thou not pardon my "
9:29 be wicked, w' then labour I in vain?"
15:12 W' doth thine heart carry thee "
19:22 W' do ye persecute me as God, "
28 W' persecute we him, seeing the "
21:4 so, w' should not my spirit be 4069
24:1 W', seeing times are not hidden "
27:12 w' then are ye thus altogether 4100
31:1 w' then should I think upon a * "
33:13 W' dost thou strive against him? 4069
Ps 2:1 W' do the heathen rage, and the 4100
10:1 W' standest thou afar off, O Lord? "
1 w' hidest thou thyself in times of "
22:1 My God, my God, w' hast thou 4100
1 w' art thou so far from helping me, "
42:5 w' art thou disquieted in me? "
9 rock, W' hast thou forgotten me? 4100
9 w' go I mourning because of the "
11 W' art thou cast down, O my soul? "
11 w' art thou disquieted within me? "
43:2 strength: w' dost thou cast me off? "
2 w' go I mourning because of the "
5 W' art thou cast down, O my soul? "
5 w' art thou disquieted within me? "
44:23 Awake, w' sleepest thou, O Lord? "
52:1 W' boastest thou thyself in "
68:16 W' leap ye, ye high hills? this is "
74:1 w' hast thou cast us off for ever? "
1 w' doth thine anger smote against the "
11 W' withdrawest thou thy hand, 4100
80:12 W' hast thou then broken down "
88:14 Lord, w' castest thou off my soul? "
14 w' hidest thou thy face from me? "
Pr 22:27 w' should he take away thy bed 4100
Ec 2:15 me; and w' was I then more wise? "
7:16 w' shouldest thou destroy thyself? "
17 w' shouldest thou die before thy "
Ca 1:7 w' should I be as one that turneth "
Isa 1:5 W' should ye be stricken any 5921, "
40:27 W' sayest thou, O Jacob, and "
63:17 w' hast thou made us to err from "
Jer 2:14 homeborn slave? w' is he spoiled? 4069
33 W' trimmest thou thy way to *4100
36 W' gaddest thou about so much "
8:5 W' then is this people of 4069
14 W' do we sit still? assemble 5921,4100
19 W' have they provoked me to 4069
22 w' then is not the health of the "
14:8 w' shouldest thou be as a stranger4100
9 W' shouldest thou be as a man "
19 w' hast thou smitten us, and 4069
15:18 W' is my pain perpetual, and my 4100
26:9 W' hast thou prophesied in the 4069
27:13 W' will ye die, thou and thy 4100
29:27 w' hast thou not reproved Jeremiah "
30:15 W' criest thou for thine affliction? "
36:29 W' hast thou written therein, 4069
46:15 W' are thy valiant men swept "
49:1 w' then doth their king inherit "
Eze 18:19 W'? doth not the son bear the * "
31 w' will ye die, O house of Israel? 4100
33:11 w' will ye die, O house of Israel? "
Da 1:10 for w' should he see your faces "
2:15 W' is the decree so hasty *5922,4101
Jon 1:10 him, W' hast thou done this? *4100
Mic 4:9 Now w' dost thou cry out aloud? "
Hab 1:3 W' dost thou shew me iniquity, "
Hag 1:9 W'? saith the Lord of hosts. 3282, "
Mal 2:10 w' do we deal treacherously 4069
M't 6:28 w' take ye thought for raiment? 5101
7:3 w' beholdest thou the mote that is "
8:26 W' are ye fearful, O ye of little faith?"
9:11 W' eateth your Master with 1302
14 W' do we and the Pharisees fast "
13:10 W' speakest thou unto them in "
15:2 W' do thy disciples transgress the "
3 W' do ye also transgress the "
16:8 w' reason ye among yourselves, 5101
17:10 W' then say the scribes that Elias "
19 W' could not we cast him out? 1302
19:7 W' did Moses then command to 5101

M't 19:17 W' callest thou me good? there is 5101
20:6 W' stand ye here all the day idle? "
21:25 us, W' did ye not then believe him?1302
22:18 W' tempt ye me, ye hypocrites? 5101
26:10 W' trouble ye the woman? for she "
27:23 said, W', what evil hath he done? 1063
46 my God, w' hast thou forsaken me?2444
M'r 2:7 W' doth this man thus speak 5101
8 W' reason ye these things in your "
18 W' do the disciples of John and 1302
24 w' do they on the sabbath day 5101
4:40 W' are ye so fearful? how is it that "
5:35 w' troublest thou the Master any "
39 W' make ye this ado, and weep? "
7:5 W' walk not thy disciples 1302
8:12 W' doth this generation seek 5101
17 W' reason ye, because ye have no "
9:11 W' say the scribes that Elias *3754
28 W' could not we cast him out? * "
10:18 W' callest thou me good? there is 5101
11:3 man say unto you, W' do ye this? "
31 W' then did ye not believe him? 1302
12:15 said unto them, W' tempt ye me? 5101
14:4 W' was this waste of the *1519, "
6 Let her alone; w' trouble ye her? "
15:14 them, W', what evil hath he done? 1063
34 my God, w' hast thou forsaken1519,5101
Lu 2:48 w' hast thou thus dealt with us? "
5:30 W' do ye eat and drink with 1302
33 W' do the disciples of John fast * "
6:2 W' do ye that which is not lawful 5101
41 w' beholdest thou the mote that is "
46 w' call ye me, Lord, Lord, and do "
12:26 w' take ye thought for the rest? "
57 w' even of yourselves judge ye not "
13:7 down; w' cumbereth it the ground?2444
18:19 him, W' callest thou me good? 5101
19:31 man ask you, W' do ye loose him?1302
33 unto them, W' loose ye the colt? 5101
20:5 say, W' then believed ye him not? 1302
23 said unto them, W' tempt ye me?*5101
22:46 them, W' sleep ye? rise and pray, "
23:22 time, W', what evil hath he done? 1063
24:5 W' seek ye the living among the 5101
38 said unto them, W' are ye troubled?"
38 w' do thoughts arise in...hearts? *1302
Joh 1:25 W' baptizest thou then, if thou be5101
4:27 thou? or, W' talkest thou with her?"
7:19 the law? W' go ye about to kill me?"
45 them, W' have ye not brought him?1302
8:43 W' do ye not understand my "
46 truth, w' do ye not believe me? "
9:30 W' herein is a marvellous thing, 1063
10:20 devil, and is mad; w' hear ye him?5101
12:5 W' was not this ointment sold 1302
13:37 Lord, w' cannot I follow thee now? "
18:21 W' askest thou me? ask them 5101
23 but if well, w' smitest thou me? "
20:13,15 her, Woman, w' weepest thou? "
Ac 1:11 w' stand ye gazing up into heaven? "
3:12 w' marvel ye at this? or w' look ye "
4:25 W' did the heathen rage, and the 2444
5:3 w' hath Satan filled thine heart to 1302
4 w' hast thou conceived this thing *5101
7:26 w' do ye wrong one to another? 2444
9:4 Saul, w' persecutest thou me? 5101
14:15 Sirs, w' do ye these things? "
15:10 Now therefore w' tempt ye God, to "
22:7 Saul, Saul, w' persecutest thou me?"
16 And now w' tarriest thou? arise, "
26:8 W' should it be thought a thing "
14 Saul, Saul, w' persecutest thou me?"
Ro 3:7 w' yet am I also judged as a sinner?"
8:24 man seeth, w' doth he yet hope for?"
9:19 unto me, W' doth he yet find fault?"
20 it, W' hast thou made me thus? "
14:10 But w' dost thou judge thy brother?"
10 w' dost thou set at nought thy "
1Co 4:7 w' dost thou glory, as if thou hadst"
6:7 W' do ye not rather take wrong? 1302
7 w' do ye not rather suffer "
10:29 w' is my liberty judged of 2444,5101
30 w' am I evil spoken of for that "
15:29 w' are they then baptized for the "
30 w' stand ye in jeopardy every hour?"
Ga 2:14 w' compellest thou the Gentiles to* "
5:11 w' do I yet suffer persecution? "
Col 2:20 w', as though living in the world, "

wicked
Ge 13:13 the men of Sodom were w' and 7451
18:23 destroy the righteous with the w'?7563
25 slay the righteous with the w': "
25 the righteous should be as the w', "
38:7 was w' in the sight of the Lord; 7451
Ex 9:27 and I and my people are w'. 7563
23:1 put not thine hand with the w' to "
7 not: for I will not justify the w'. "
Le 20:17 it is a w' thing; and they shall *2617
Nu 16:26 from the tents of these w' men, 7563
De 15:9 be not a thought in thy w' heart, *1100
17:5 have committed that w' thing, *7451
23:9 keep thee from every w' thing. * "
25:1 righteous, and condemn the w'. 7563
2 w' man be worthy to be beaten, "
1Sa 2:9 the w' shall be silent in darkness; "
24:13 proceedeth from the w': "
30:22 answered all the w' men and 7451
2Sa 3:34 as a man falleth before w' men, *5766
4:11 w' men have slain a righteous 7563
1Ki 8:32 thy servants, condemning the w', "
2Ki 17:11 wrought w' things to provoke 7451
2Ch 6:23 thy servants, by requiting the w', 7563
7:14 face, and turn from their w' ways;7451
24:7 sons of Athaliah, that w' woman, 4849
Ne 9:35 turned they from their w' works. 7451

Es 7: 6 and enemy is this *w*· Haman. 7451
9: 25 by letters that his *w*· device. "
Job 3: 17 the *w*· cease from troubling; 7563
8: 22 of the *w*· shall come to nought. "
9: 22 destroyeth the perfect and the *w*·. "
24 is given into the hand of the *w*·: "
29 If I be *w*·, why then labour I in *7561
10: 3 shine upon the counsel of the *w*·? 7563
7 Thou knowest that I am not *w*·; 7561
15 If I be *w*·, woe unto me; and if I be"
11: 20 But the eyes of the *w*· shall fail, 7563
15: 20 The *w*· man travaileth with pain "
16: 11 me over into the hands of the *w*·. "
18: 5 the light of the *w*· shall be put out, "
21 such are the dwellings of the *w*·, 5767
20: 5 the triumphing of the *w*· is short, 7563
22 hand of the *w*· shall come upon *6001
29 This is the portion of the *w*· man 7563
21: 7 Wherefore do the *w*· live, become "
16 counsel of the *w*· is far from me. "
17 oft is the candle of the *w*· put out! "
28 are the dwelling places of the *w*·? "
30 the *w*· is reserved to the day of *7451
22: 15 way which *w*· men have trodden? 205
18 counsel of the *w*· is far from me. 7563
24: 6 they gather the vintage of the *w*·. "
27: 7 Let mine enemy be as the *w*·, and "
13 the portion of a *w*· man with God, "
29: 17 And I brake the jaws of the *w*·. *5767
31: 3 Is not destruction to the *w*·? and * "
34: 8 and walketh with *w*· men. *7562
18 fit to say to a king, Thou art *w*·? *1100
26 He striketh them as *w*· men in the 7563
36 because of his answers for *w*· men. 205
36: 6 preserveth not the life of the *w*·: 7563
17 fulfilled the judgment of the *w*·: "
38: 13 the *w*· might be shaken out of it? "
15 from the *w*· their light is withholden, "
40: 12 tread down the *w*· in their place. "
Ps 7: 9 wickedness of the *w*· come to an "
11 God is angry with the *w*· every day.* "
9: 5 thou hast destroyed the *w*·, thou 7563
16 the *w*· is snared in the work of his "
17 *w*· shall be turned into hell, and "
10: 2 *w*· in his pride doth persecute the "
3 *w*· boasteth of his heart's desire, "
4 The *w*·, through the pride of his "
13 doth the *w*· contemn God? "
15 Break thou the arm of the *w*· and "
11: 2 For, lo, the *w*· bend their bow, they "
5 the *w*· and him that loveth violence "
6 Upon the *w*· he shall rain snares, "
12: 8 The *w*· walk on every side, when "
17: 9 the *w*· that oppress me, from my "
13 deliver my soul from the *w*·, which "
22: 16 assembly of the *w*· have inclosed *7489
26: 5 doers; and will not sit with the *w*·. 7563
27: 2 When the *w*·, even mine enemies *7489
28: 3 Draw me not away with the *w*·, 7563
31: 17 let the *w*· be ashamed, and let "
32: 10 Many sorrows shall be to the *w*·: "
34: 21 Evil shall slay the *w*·: and they "
36: 1 transgression of the *w*· saith "
11 not the hand of the *w*· remove me. "
37: 7 who bringeth *w*· devices to pass. 4209
10 while, and the *w*· shall not be: 7563
12 The *w*· plotteth against the just, "
14 The *w*· have drawn out the sword, "
16 better than the riches of many *w*·. "
17 the arms of the *w*· shall be broken: "
20 But the *w*· shall perish, and the "
21 The *w*· borroweth, and payeth not "
28 the seed of the *w*· shall be cut off. "
32 The *w*· watcheth the righteous, "
34 when the *w*· are cut off, thou shalt "
35 I have seen the *w*· in great power, "
38 the end of the *w*· shall be cut off. "
40 shall deliver them from the *w*·, and "
39: 1 bridle, while the *w*· is before me. "
50: 16 But unto the *w*· God saith, What "
55: 3 of the oppression of the *w*·: "
58: 3 *w*· are estranged from the womb: "
10 wash his feet in the blood of the *w*·. "
59: 5 merciful to any *w*· transgressors. 205
64: 2 from the secret counsel of the *w*·; 7489
68: 2 *w*· perish at the presence of God. 7563
71: 4 my God, out of the hand of the *w*·. "
73: 3 I saw the prosperity of the *w*·. "
74: 19 unto the multitude of the *w*·: *
75: 4 and to the *w*·, Lift not up the horn: 7563
8 all the *w*· of the earth shall wring "
10 horns of the *w*· also will I cut off; "
82: 2 and accept the persons of the *w*·? "
4 rid them out of the hand of the *w*·. "
91: 8 and see the reward of the *w*·. "
92: 7 When the *w*· spring as the grass, "
11 my desire of the *w*· that rise up *7489
94: 3 Lord, how long shall the *w*·, how 7563
3 how long shall the *w*· triumph? "
13 until the pit be digged for the *w*·. "
97: 10 them out of the hand of the *w*·. "
101: 3 set no *w*· thing before mine eyes: *1100
4 me: I will not know a *w*· person. *7451
8 destroy all the *w*· of the land; 7563
8 that I may cut off all the *w*· doers 205
104: 35 earth, and let the *w*· be no more. 7563
106: 18 the flame burned up the *w*·. "
109: 2 the mouth of the *w*· and the mouth "
6 Set thou a *w*· man over him: and "
112: 10 The *w*· shall see it, and be grieved; "
10 the desire of the *w*· shall perish. "
119: 53 of the *w*· that forsake thy law. "
61 bands of the *w*· have robbed me: "
95 *w*· have waited for me to destroy "
110 The *w*· have laid a snare for me: "
119 puttest away all the *w*· of the earth "
Ps 119: 155 Salvation is far from the *w*·: for 7563
125: 3 the rod of the *w*· shall not rest *7562
129: 4 cut asunder the cords of the *w*·. 7563
139: 19 Surely thou wilt slay the *w*·, O God: "
24 see if there be any *w*· way in me, 6090
140: 4 O Lord, from the hands of the *w*·; 7563
8 not, O Lord, the desires of the *w*·: "
8 further not his *w*· device; lest *2162
141: 4 to practise *w*· works with men *7562
10 Let the *w*· fall into their own nets, 7563
145: 20 him: but all the *w*· will he destroy. "
146: 9 the way of the *w*· he turneth upside "
147: 6 casteth the *w*· down to the ground. "
Pr 2: 14 in the frowardness of the *w*·; *7451
22 *w*· shall be cut off from the earth, 7563
3: 25 neither of the desolation of the *w*·, "
33 the Lord is in the house of the *w*·: "
4: 14 Enter not into the path of the *w*·, "
19 The way of the *w*· is as darkness: "
5: 22 iniquity shall take the *w*· himself, "
6: 12 *w*· man, walketh with a froward * 205
18 heart that deviseth *w*· imaginations, "
9: 7 he that rebuketh a *w*· man getteth 7563
10: 3 away the substance of the *w*·. "
6 covereth the mouth of the *w*·. "
7 but the name of the *w*· shall rot. "
11 violence covereth...mouth of the *w*·. "
16 to life: the fruit of the *w*· to sin. "
20 the heart of the *w*· is little worth. "
24 The fear of the *w*·, it shall come "
25 passeth, so is the *w*· no more: "
27 years of the *w*· shall be shortened. "
28 expectation of the *w*· shall perish. "
30 the *w*· shall not inhabit the earth. "
32 of the *w*· speaketh frowardness. "
11: 5 *w*· shall fall by his own wickedness. "
7 When a *w*· man dieth, his "
8 and the *w*· cometh in his stead. "
10 the *w*· perish, there is shouting. "
11 overthrown by the mouth of the *w*·. "
18 The *w*· worketh a deceitful work: "
21 the *w*· shall not be unpunished: *7451
23 the expectation of the *w*· is wrath. 7563
31 much more the *w*· and the sinner. "
12: 2 man of *w*· devices will...condemn. 4209
5 the counsels of the *w*· are deceit. 7563
6 words of the *w*· are to lie in wait "
7 *w*· are overthrown, and are not: "
10 tender mercies of the *w*· are cruel. "
12 The *w*· desireth the net of evil men: "
13 *w*· is snared by the transgression 7451
21 *w*· shall be filled with mischief. 7563
26 the way of the *w*· seduceth them. "
13: 5 a *w*· man is loathsome, and cometh "
9 the lamp of the *w*· shall be put out. "
17 *w*· messenger falleth into mischief: "
25 but the belly of the *w*· shall want. "
14: 11 The house of the *w*· shall be "
17 and a man of *w*· devices is hated. 4209
19 *w*· at the gates of the righteous. 7563
32 The *w*· is driven away in his "
15: 6 in the revenues of the *w*· is trouble. "
8 sacrifice of the *w*· is an abomination "
9 way of the *w*· is an abomination "
26 The thoughts of the *w*· are an *7451
28 mouth of the *w*· poureth out evil 7563
29 The Lord is far from the *w*·: but he "
16: 4 yea, even the *w*· for the day of evil. "
17: 4 A *w*· doer giveth heed to false lips; *7489
15 He that justifieth the *w*·, and he 7563
23 A *w*· man taketh a gift out of the "
18: 3 When the *w*· cometh, then cometh "
5 good to accept the person of the *w*·, "
19: 28 mouth of the *w*· devoureth iniquity. "
20: 26 A wise king scattereth the *w*·, and "
21: 4 and the plowing of the *w*·, is sin. "
7 The robbery of the *w*· shall destroy "
10 The soul of the *w*· desireth evil: "
12 considereth the house of the *w*·: "
12 God overthroweth the *w*· for their "
18 The *w*· shall be a ransom for the "
27 sacrifice of the *w*· is abomination: "
27 he bringeth it with a *w*· mind? 2154
29 A *w*· man hardeneth his face: but 7563
24: 15 Lay not wait, O *w*· man, against the "
16 but the *w*· shall fall into mischief. "
19 neither be thou envious at the *w*·: "
20 candle of the *w*· shall be put out. "
24 He that saith unto the *w*·, Thou art "
25: 5 Take...the *w*· from before the king, "
26 man falling down before the *w*· "
26: 23 Burning lips and a *w*· heart are 7451
28: 1 *w*· flee when no man pursueth: 7563
4 that forsake the law praise the *w*·: "
12 when the *w*· rise, a man is hidden. "
15 is a *w*· ruler over the poor people. "
28 the *w*· rise, men hide themselves: "
29: 2 but when the *w*· beareth rule, the "
7 the *w*· regardeth not to know it. "
12 to lies, all his servants are *w*·. "
16 When the *w*· are multiplied, "
27 the way is abomination to the *w*·. "
Ec 3: 17 judge the righteous and the *w*·: "
7: 15 a *w*· man that prolongeth his life "
17 Be not over much *w*·, neither be 7561
8: 10 And so I saw the *w*· buried, who 7563
13 it shall not be well with the *w*·, "
14 according to the work of the *w*·; "
14 again, there be *w*· men, to whom it "
9: 2 to the righteous, and to the *w*·; "
Isa 3: 11 Woe unto the *w*·! it shall be ill "
5: 23 Which justify the *w*· for reward, "
11: 4 of his lips shall he slay the *w*·. "
13: 11 evil, and the *w*· for their iniquity; "
14: 5 Lord...broken the staff of the *w*·, "
26: 10 Let favour be shewed to the *w*·, yet "
Isa 32: 7 he deviseth *w*· devices to destroy 2154
48: 22 peace, saith the Lord, unto the *w*·. 7563
53: 9 And he made his grave with the *w*·, "
55: 7 Let the *w*· forsake his way, and the "
57: 20 the *w*· are like the troubled sea, "
21 no peace, saith my God, to the *w*·. "
Jer 2: 33 also taught the *w*· ones thy ways. 7451
5: 26 among my people are...*w*· men: 7563
28 they overpass the deeds of the *w*·: *7451
6: 29 for the *w*· are not plucked away. "
12: 1 doth the way of the *w*· prosper? 7563
15: 21 thee out of the hand of the *w*·. 7451
17: 9 all things, and desperately *w*·: * 605
23: 19 upon the head of the *w*·. 7563
25: 31 give them that are *w*· to the sword, "
30: 23 with pain upon the head of the *w*·. "
Eze 3: 18 When I say unto the *w*·, Thou shalt "
18 to warn the *w*· from his *w*· way, "
18 *w*· man shall die in his iniquity; "
19 if thou warn the *w*·, and he turn "
19 wickedness, nor from his *w*· way, "
7: 21 to the *w*· of the earth for a spoil; "
8: 9 the *w*· abominations that they do 7451
11: 2 and give *w*· counsel in this city: "
13: 22 the hands of the *w*·, that he should "
22 should not return from his *w*· way, 7563
18: 20 wickedness of the *w*· shall be upon "
21 if the *w*· will turn from all his sins "
23 pleasure...that the *w*· should die? "
24 abominations...the *w*· man doeth, "
27 *w*· man turneth away from his "
20: 44 not according to your *w*· ways, *7451
21: 3 from thee the righteous and the *w*·. 7563
4 from thee the righteous and the *w*·. "
25 thou, profane *w*· prince of Israel, "
29 of the *w*·, whose day is come, when "
30: 12 the land into the hand of the *w*·: *7451
33: 8 When I say unto the *w*·, O *w*· man, 7563
8 speak to warn the *w*· from his way, "
8 *w*· man shall die in his iniquity; "
9 warn the *w*· of his way to turn from "
11 no pleasure in the death of the *w*·; "
11 the *w*· turn from his way and live: "
12 as for the wickedness of the *w*·, he "
14 when I say unto the *w*·, Thou shalt "
15 If the *w*· restore the pledge, give "
19 if the *w*· turn from his wickedness, "
Da 12: 10 tried; but the *w*· shall do wickedly: "
10 none of the *w*· shall understand; "
Mic 6: 10 wickedness in the house of the *w*·, "
11 them pure with the *w*· balances, 7562
Na 1: 3 and will not at all acquit the *w*·: *
11 against the Lord, a *w*· counsellor. *1100
15 *w*· shall no more pass through thee; "
Hab 1: 4 *w*· doth compass about the 7563
13 when the *w*· devoureth the man "
3: 13 the head out of the house of the *w*·. "
Zep 1: 3 the stumblingblocks with the *w*·; "
Mal 3: 18 between the righteous and the *w*·. "
4: 3 And ye shall tread down the *w*·; "
M't 12: 45 other spirits more *w*· than himself, *4191
45 be also unto this *w*· generation. *4190
13: 19 then cometh the *w*· one, and * "
38 are the children of the *w*· one; * "
49 sever the *w*· from among the just, "
16: 4 A *w*· and adulterous generation * "
18: 32 O thou *w*· servant, I forgave thee "
21: 41 miserably destroy those *w*· men, *2556
25: 26 Thou *w*· and slothful servant, 4190
Lu 11: 26 other spirits more *w*· than himself; *4191
19: 22 will I judge thee, thou *w*· servant. 4190
Ac 2: 23 *w*· hands have crucified and slain: * 459
18: 14 a matter of wrong or *w*· lewdness, 4190
1Co 5: 13 among yourselves that *w*· person. "
Eph 6: 16 quench all the fiery darts of the *w*·. * "
Col 1: 21 enemies in your mind by *w*· works, * "
2Th 2: 8 then shall that *W*· be revealed, * 459
3: 2 from unreasonable and *w*· men: *4190
2Pe 2: 7 the filthy conversation of the *w*·: 113
3: 17 led away with the error of the *w*·, "
1Jo 2: 13 ye have overcome the *w*· one. 4190
14 and ye have overcome the *w*· one.* "
3: 12 as Cain, who was of that *w*· one, * "
5: 18 and that *w*· one toucheth him not.* "

wickedly

Ge 19: 7 I pray you, brethren, do not so *w*·. 7489
De 9: 18 doing *w*· in the sight of the Lord, *7451
J'g 19: 23 nay, I pray you, do not so *w*·; 7489
1Sa 12: 25 if ye shall still do *w*·, ye shall be "
2Sa 22: 22 have not *w*· departed from my God. 7561
24: 17 have sinned, and I have done *w*·: *5753
2Ki 21: 11 done *w*· above all...the Amorites 7489
2Ch 6: 37 done amiss, and have dealt *w*·: 7561
20: 35 king of Israel, who did very *w*·: "
22: 3 mother was his counsellor to do *w*·. "
Ne 9: 33 done right, but we have done *w*·: "
Job 13: 7 Will ye speak *w*· for God? and *5766
34: 12 Yea, surely God will not do *w*·, 7561
Ps 18: 21 have not *w*· departed from my God. "
73: 8 speak *w*· concerning oppression: *7451
74: 3 hath done *w*· in the sanctuary. *7489
106: 6 iniquity, we have done *w*·. 7561
139: 20 For they speak against thee *w*·, 4209
Da 9: 5 have done *w*·, and have rebelled, 7561
15 we have sinned, we have done *w*·. "
11: 32 such as do *w*· against the covenant "
12: 10 tried; but the wicked shall do *w*·: "
Mal 4: 1 all that do *w*·, shall be stubble: *7564

wickedness

Ge 6: 5 saw that the *w*· of man was great 7451
39: 9 then can I do this great *w*·, and sin "
Le 18: 17 are her near kinswomen: it is *w*·. 2154
19: 29 and the land became full of *w*·. "
20: 14 a wife and her mother, it is *w*·: "
14 that there be no *w*· among you. "

De 9: 4, 5 but for the *w*· of these nations 7564
27 nor to their *w*·, nor to their sin: 7562
13:11 do no more any such *w*· as this is 7451
17: 2 wrought *w*· in the sight of the Lord* "
28:20 because of the *w*· of thy doings, *7455
J'g 9:56 God rendered the *w*· of Abimelech,7451
20: 3 Israel, Tell us, how was this *w*·? "
12 What *w*· is this that is done among "
1Sa 12:17 and see that your *w*· is great, "
20 Fear not: ye have done all this *w*·:* "
24:13 *W*· proceedeth from the wicked: 7562
25:39 hath returned the *w*· of Nabel *7451
2Sa 3:39 the doer of evil according to his *w*·. "
7:10 children of *w*· afflict them any 5766
1Ki 1:52 but if *w*· shall be found in him, 7451
2:44 *w*· which thine heart is privy to, "
44 return thy *w*· upon thine own head: "
8:47 perversely, we...committed *w*·; *7561
21:25 which did sell himself to work *w*·*7451
2Ki 21: 6 wrought much *w*· in the sight of * "
1Ch 17: 9 the children of *w*· waste them 5766
Job 4: 8 that plow iniquity, and sow *w*·, *5999
11:11 he seeth *w*· also; will he not then* 205
14 not *w*· dwell in thy tabernacles. *5766
20:12 Though *w*· be sweet in his mouth, 7451
22: 5 Is not thy *w*· great? and thine "
24:20 and *w*· shall be broken as a tree. *5766
27: 4 My lips shall not speak *w*·, nor my* "
34:10 from God, that he should do *w*·; 7562
35: 8 Thy *w*· may hurt a man as thou art; "
Ps 5: 4 not a God that hath pleasure in *w*·: "
9 their inward part is very *w*·; their1942
7: 9 Oh let the *w*· of the wicked come 7451
10:15 seek out his *w*· till thou find none.7562
28: 4 according to the *w*· of their 7455
45: 7 righteousness, and hatest *w*·: 7562
52: 7 strengthened himself in his *w*·. 1942
55:11 *W*· is in the midst thereof: deceit "
15 for *w*· is in their dwellings, and 7451
58: 2 Yea, in heart ye work *w*·; ye 5766
84:10 than to dwell in the tents of *w*·. 7562
89:22 him; nor the son of *w*· afflict him. 5766
94:23 shall cut them off in their own *w*·;*7451
107:34 the *w*· of them that dwell therein. "
Pr 4:17 For they eat the bread of *w*·, and 7562
8: 7 *w*· is an abomination to my lips. "
10: 2 Treasurers of *w*· profit nothing: "
11: 5 wicked shall fall by his own *w*·. 7564
12: 3 shall not be established by *w*·: 7562
13: 6 but *w*· overthroweth the sinner. 7564
14:32 wicked is driven away in his *w*·: *7451
16:12 abomination...kings to commit *w*·:7562
21:12 the wicked for their *w*·. *7451
26:26 his *w*· shall be shewed before the "
30:20 and saith, I have done no *w*·. 205
Ec 3:16 of judgment, that *w*· was there; 7562
7:15 that prolongeth his life in his *w*·. *7451
25 and to know the *w*· of folly, even 7562
8: 8 neither shall *w*· deliver those that "
Isa 9:18 For *w*· burneth as the fire: it shall7564
47:10 For thou hast trusted in thy *w*·: 7451
58: 4 and to smite with the fist of *w*·: 7562
6 to loose the bands of *w*·, to undo "
Jer 1:16 against them touching all their *w*·,7451
2:19 Thine own *w*· shall correct thee, "
3: 2 thy whoredoms and with thy *w*·. "
4:14 wash thine heart from *w*·, that "
18 this is thy *w*·, because it is bitter, "
6: 7 waters, so she casteth out her *w*·; "
7:12 to it for the *w*· of my people Israel. "
8: 6 no man repented him of his *w*·, "
12: 4 the *w*· of them that dwell therein? "
14:16 I will pour their *w*· upon them. "
20 We acknowledge, O Lord, our *w*·, 7562
22:22 and confounded for all thy *w*·. 7451
23:11 in my house have I found their *w*·, "
14 that none doth return from his *w*·: "
33: 5 for all whose *w*· I have hid my face "
44: 3 of their *w*·...they have committed "
5 their ear to turn from their *w*·, "
9 ye forgotten the *w*· of your fathers, "
9 and the *w*· of the kings of Judah, "
9 and the *w*· of their wives, "
9 of their wives, and your own *w*·, "
9 and the *w*· of your wives, which "
La 1:22 Let all their *w*· come before thee; "
Eze 3:19 and he turn not from his *w*·, nor 7562
5: 6 changed my judgments into *w*· 7564
7:11 is risen up into a rod of *w*·: 7562
16:23 it came to pass after all thy *w*·, 7451
57 Before thy *w*· was discovered, as at "
18:20 the *w*· of the wicked shall be upon7564
27 wicked...turneth away from his *w*· "
31:11 I have driven him out for his *w*·. 7562
33:12 as for the *w*· of the wicked, he 7564
12 day that he turneth from his *w*·; 7562
19 But if the wicked turn from his *w*·,7564
Ho 7: 1 discovered, and the *w*· of Samaria:7451
2 hearts that I remember all their *w*·: "
3 make the king glad with their *w*·, "
9:15 All their *w*· is in Gilgal: for there I "
15 for the *w*· of their doings I will 7455
10:13 Ye have plowed *w*·, ye have reaped7562
15 unto you because of your great *w*·:7451
Joe 3:13 fats overflow; for their *w*· is great. "
Jon 1: 2 for their *w*· is come up before me. "
Mic 6:10 treasures of *w*· in the house of the 7562
Na 3:19 not thy *w*· passed continually? 7451
Zec 5: 8 And he said, This is *w*·. And he 7564
Mal 1: 4 shall call them, The border of *w*·, "
3:15 yea, they that work *w*· are set up; "
M't 22:18 But Jesus perceived their *w*·, and 4189
M'r 7:22 Thefts, covetousness, *w*·, deceit, "
Lu 11:39 part is full of ravening and *w*·. "
Ac 8:22 Repent therefore of this thy *w*·, 2549
25: 5 man, if there be any *w*· in him.*5129,824

Ro 1:29 *w*·, covetousness, maliciousness; 4189
1Co 5: 8 with the leaven of malice and *w*·: "
Eph 6:12 against spiritual *w*· in high places, "
1Jo 5:19 and the whole world lieth in *w*·. *4190

wide
De 15: 8 open thine hand *w*· unto him, *6605
11 thine hand *w*· unto thy brother, * "
1Ch 4:40 the land was *w*·, and quiet, 7342,3027
Job 29:23 opened their mouth *w*· as for the latter
30:14 as a *w*· breaking in of waters: 7342
Ps 35:21 opened their mouth *w*· against 7337
81:10 open thy mouth *w*·, and I will fill "
104:25 So is this great and *w*· sea, 7342,3027
Pr 13: 3 he that openeth *w*· his lips shall have
21: 9 a brawling woman in a *w*· house. 2267
25:24 brawling woman and in a *w*· house. "
Isa 57: 4 against whom make ye a *w*· mouth,7337
Jer 22:14 I will build me a *w*· house and 4060
Na 3:13 the gates...shall be set *w*· open 6605
M't 7:13 for *w*· is the gate, and broad is the 4116

wideness
Eze 41:10 the *w*· of twenty cubits round 7341

widow See also WIDOW'S; WIDOWS.
Ge 38:11 Remain a *w*· at thy father's house, 490
Ex 22:22 Ye shall not afflict any *w*·, or "
Le 21:14 A *w*·, or a divorced woman, or "
22:13 But if the priest's daughter be a *w*·, "
Nu 30: 9 But every vow of a *w*·, and of her "
De 10:18 judgment of the fatherless and *w*·, "
14:29 and the fatherless, and the *w*·, "
16:11, 14 and the fatherless, and the *w*·, "
24:19 for the fatherless, and for the *w*·: "
20, 21 for the fatherless, and for the *w*·. "
26:12 stranger, the fatherless, and the *w*·, "
13 to the fatherless, and to the *w*·, "
27:19 of the stranger, fatherless, and *w*·. "
2Sa 14: 5 answered, I am indeed a *w*· woman, "
1Ki 11:26 name was Zeruah, a *w*· woman, "
17: 9 commanded a *w*· woman there to "
10 the *w*· woman was there gathering "
20 evil upon the *w*· with whom I "
Job 24:21 not: and doeth not good to the *w*·. "
31:16 caused the eyes of the *w*· to fail; "
Ps 94: 6 They slay the *w*· and the stranger, "
109: 9 be fatherless, and his wife a *w*·. "
146: 9 he relieveth the fatherless and *w*·: "
Pr 15:25 will establish the border of the *w*·. "
Isa 1:17 the fatherless, plead for the *w*·. "
23 the cause of the *w*· come unto them. "
47: 8 I shall not sit as a *w*·, neither shall I "
Jer 7: 6 stranger, the fatherless, and the *w*·, "
22: 3 stranger, the fatherless, nor the *w*·, "
La 1: 1 how is she become as a *w*·! she that "
Eze 22: 7 they vexed the fatherless and the *w*·. "
44:22 shall they take for their wives a *w*·, "
22 or a *w*· that had a priest before. "
Zec 7:10 And oppress not the *w*·, nor the "
Mal 3: 5 the hireling in his wages, the *w*·, "
M'r 12:42 And there came a certain poor *w*·, 5503
43 That this poor *w*· hath cast more in, "
Lu 2:37 a *w*· of about fourscore and four "
4:26 Sidon, unto a woman that was a *w*·. "
7:12 of his mother, and she was a *w*·: "
18: 3 And there was a *w*· in that city; "
5 Yet because this *w*· troubleth me, I "
21: 2 *w*· casting in thither two mites. "
3 *w*· hath cast in more than they all: "
1Ti 5: 4 if any *w*· have children or nephews, "
5 that is a *w*· indeed, and desolate, "
9 not a *w*· be taken into the number "
Re 18: 7 I sit a queen, and am no *w*·, and "

widowhood
Ge 38:19 and put on the garments of her *w*·. 491
2Sa 20: 3 the day of their death, living in *w*·. "
Isa 47: 9 day, the loss of children, and *w*·: 489
54: 4 remember the reproach of thy *w*· 491

widow's
Ge 38:14 And she put her *w*· garments off * 491
De 24:17 nor take the *w*· raiment to pledge: 490
1Ki 7:14 was a *w*· son of the tribe of Naphtali,* "
Job 24: 3 they take the *w*· ox for a pledge. "
29:13 I caused the *w*· heart to sing for joy. "

widows See also WIDOWS'.
Ex 22:24 and your wives shall be *w*·, and 490
Job 22: 9 Thou hast sent *w*· away empty, and "
27:15 in death: and his *w*· shall not weep. "
Ps 68: 5 the fatherless, and a judge of the *w*·, "
78:64 and their *w*· made no lamentation. "
Isa 9:17 mercy on their fatherless and *w*·: "
10: 2 people, that *w*· may be their prey, "
Jer 15: 8 Their *w*· are increased to me above "
18:21 bereaved of their children, and be *w*·; "
49:11 alive; and let thy *w*· trust in me. "
La 5: 3 fatherless, our mothers are as *w*·. "
Eze 22:25 made her many *w*· in the midst "
Lu 4:25 many *w*· were in Israel in the days5503
Ac 6: 1 their *w*· were neglected in the daily "
9:39 all the *w*· stood by him weeping, "
41 he had called the saints and *w*·, "
1Co 7: 8 therefore to the unmarried and *w*·, "
1Ti 5: 3 Honour *w*· that are *w*· indeed. "
11 But the younger *w*· refuse: for "
16 or woman that believeth have *w*·, "
16 relieve them that are *w*· indeed. "
Jas 1:27 fatherless and *w*· in their affliction, "

widows'
M't 23:14 for ye devour *w*· houses, and for a*5503
M'r 12:40 Which devour *w*· houses, and for a "
Lu 20:47 Which devour *w*· houses, and for a "

width See WIDENESS.

wife See also MIDWIFE; WIFE'S; WIVES.
Ge 2:24 and shall cleave unto his *w*·: 802
25 both naked, the man and his *w*·, "

Ge 3: 8 Adam and his *w*· hid themselves 802
17 hearkened unto the voice of thy *w*·, "
21 Unto Adam also and to his *w*· did "
4: 1 Adam knew Eve his *w*·; and she "
17 Cain knew his *w*·; and she conceived, "
25 Adam knew his *w*· again; and she "
6:18 ark, thou, and thy sons, and thy *w*·, "
7: 7 Noah went in,...his sons, and his *w*·, "
13 the sons of Noah, and Noah's *w*·, and "
8:16 Go forth of the ark, thou, and thy *w*·, "
18 went forth, and his sons, and his *w*·, "
11:29 the name of Abram's *w*· was Sarai; "
29 the name of Nahor's *w*·, Milcah, the "
31 daughter in law, his son Abram's *w*·; "
12: 5 Abram took Sarai his *w*·, and Lot "
11 he said unto Sarai his *w*·, Behold "
12 that they shall say, This is his *w*·: "
17 plagues because of Sarai Abram's *w*·. "
18 thou not tell me that she was thy *w*·? "
19 I might have taken her to me to *w*·: "
19 behold thy *w*·, take her, and go thy "
20 and they sent him away, and his *w*·, "
13: 1 went up out of Egypt, he, and his *w*·, "
16: 1 Abram's *w*· bare him no children: "
3 Abram's *w*· took Hagar her maid "
3 to her husband Abram to be his *w*·. "
17:15 As for Sarai thy *w*·, thou shalt not "
19 Sarah thy *w*· shall bare thee a son "
18: 9 unto him, Where is Sarah thy *w*·? "
10 lo, Sarah thy *w*· shall have a son. "
19:15 take thy *w*·, and thy two daughters, "
16 hand, and upon the hand of his *w*·, "
26 his *w*· looked back from behind him, "
20: 2 Abraham said of Sarah his *w*·, She "
3 hast taken; for she is a man's *w*·.1166
7 therefore restore the man his *w*·; 802
12 my mother; and she became my *w*·. "
14 and restored him Sarah his *w*·. "
17 God healed Abimelech, and his *w*·, "
18 because of Sarah Abraham's *w*·. "
21:21 him a *w*· out of the land of Egypt. "
23:19 Abraham buried Sarah his *w*· in "
24: 3 thou shalt not take a *w*· unto my son "
4 and take a *w*· unto my son Isaac. "
7 thou shalt take a *w*· unto my son "
15 the *w*· of Nahor, Abraham's brother, "
36 Sarah my master's *w*· bare a son to "
37 Thou shalt not take a *w*· to my son "
38 kindred, and take a *w*· unto my son. "
40 take a *w*· for my son of my kindred, "
51 and let her be thy master's son's *w*·, "
67 Rebekah, and she became his *w*·; "
25: 1 Then again Abraham took a *w*·, "
10 Abraham buried, and Sarah his *w*·. "
20 old when he took Rebekah to *w*·, "
21 Isaac intreated the Lord for his *w*·, "
21 him, and Rebekah his *w*· conceived. "
26: 7 men of the place asked him of his *w*·; "
7 for he feared to say, She is my *w*·; "
8 was sporting with Rebekah his *w*·. "
9 Behold, of a surety she is thy *w*·: "
10 might lightly have lien with thy *w*·, "
11 He that toucheth this man or his *w*· "
34 he took to *w*· Judith the daughter of "
27:46 if Jacob take a *w*· of the daughters "
28: 1 shalt not take a *w*· of the daughters "
2 take thee a *w*· from thence of the "
6 to take him a *w*· from thence; and "
6 shalt not take a *w*· of the daughters "
9 the sister of Nebajoth, to be his *w*·. "
29:21 Give me my *w*·, for my days are "
28 gave him Rachel his daughter to *w*· "
30: 4 gave him Bilhah her handmaid to *w*·: "
9 her maid, and gave her Jacob to *w*·. "
34: 4 saying, Get me this damsel to *w*·. "
8 I pray you give her him to *w*·. "
12 me: but give me the damsel to *w*·. "
36:10 the son of Adah the *w*· of Esau, "
10 son of Bashemath the *w*· of Esau. "
12 were the sons of Adah Esau's *w*·. "
13 the sons of Bashemath Esau's *w*·. "
14 the daughter of Zibeon, Esau's *w*·: "
17 the sons of Bashemath Esau's *w*·. "
18 the sons of Aholibamah Esau's *w*·: "
18 the daughter of Anah, Esau's *w*·. "
38: 6 Judah took a *w*· for Er his firstborn, "
8 Go in unto thy brother's *w*·, and "
9 he went in unto his brother's *w*·, "
12 daughter of Shuah Judah's *w*· died; "
14 she was not given unto him to *w*·. "
39: 7 his master's *w*· cast her eyes upon "
8 and said unto his master's *w*·, "
9 but thee, because thou art his *w*·: "
19 his master heard the words of his *w*·, "
41:45 gave him to *w*· Asenath the daughter "
44:27 know that my *w*· bare me two sons: "
46:19 The sons of Rachel Jacob's *w*·; "
49:31 buried Abraham and Sarah his *w*·; "
31 buried Isaac and Rebekah his *w*·; "
Ex 4:20 And Moses took his *w*· and his sons, "
6:20 Jochebed his father's sister to *w*·; "
23 Amminadab, sister of Naashon, to *w*·; "
25 one of the daughters of Putiel to *w*·; "
18: 2 in law took Zipporah, Moses' *w*·, "
5 with his sons and his *w*· unto Moses "
6 and thy *w*·, and her two sons with "
20:17 shalt not covet thy neighbour's *w*·, "
21: 3 then his *w*· shall go out with him. "
4 If his master have given him a *w*·, "
4 the *w*· and her children shall be her "
5 I love my master, my *w*·, and my "
10 If he take him another *w*·; her food, "
22:16 shall surely endow her to be his *w*·.802
Le 18: 8 father's *w*· shalt thou not uncover: "
14 thou shalt not approach to his *w*·; "
15 she is thy son's *w*·; thou shalt not "

Le 18:16 the nakedness of thy brother's *w*·: 802
18 shalt thou take a *w*· to her sister, †
20 lie carnally with thy neighbour's *w*·, "
20:10 adultery with another man's *w*·, "
10 adultery with his neighbour's *w*·, "
11 man that lieth with his father's *w*· "
14 if a man take a *w*· and her mother, "
20 a man shall lie with his uncle's *w*·, 1753
21 if a man shall take his brother's *w*·, 802
21: 7 shall not take a *w*· that is a whore,* "
13 he shall take a *w*· in her virginity. "
14 take a virgin of his own people to *w*·. "
Nu 5:12 If any man's *w*· go aside, and commit "
14, 14 and he be jealous of his *w*·, "
15 the man bring his *w*· unto the priest, "
29 when a *w*· goeth aside to another "
30 him, and he be jealous over his *w*·, "
26:59 name of Amram's *w*· was Jochebed, "
30:16 between a man and his *w*·, between "
36: 8 shall be *w*· unto one of the family of "
De 5:21 shalt thou desire thy neighbour's *w*·, "
13: 6 or the *w*· of thy bosom, or thy friend, "
20: 7 is there that hath betrothed a *w*·, "
21:11 thou wouldest have her to thy *w*·; "
13 her husband, and she shall be thy *w*·. "
22:13 If a man take a *w*·, and go in unto "
16 my daughter unto this man to *w*·, "
19 and she shall be his *w*·; he may not "
24 he hath humbled his neighbour's *w*·: "
29 of silver, and she shall be his *w*·; "
30 A man shall not take his father's *w*·, "
24: 1 When a man hath taken a *w*·, and "
2 she may go and be another man's *w*·. "
3 die, which took her to be his *w*·; 802
4 may not take her again to be his *w*·, "
5 When a man hath taken a new *w*·, "
5 shall cheer up his *w*· which he hath "
25: 5 the *w*· of the dead shall not marry "
5 take her to him to *w*·, and perform "
7 like not to take his brother's *w*·. 2994
7 his brother's *w*· go up to the gate "
9 his brother's *w*· come unto him "
11 and the *w*· of the one draweth near 802
27:20 he that lieth with his father's *w*·; "
28:30 Thou shalt betroth a *w*·, and another "
54 and toward the *w*· of his bosom, "
Jos 15:16 I give Achsah my daughter to *w*·. "
17 gave him Achsah his daughter to *w*·. "
J'g 1:12 I give Achsah my daughter to *w*·. "
13 gave him Achsah his daughter to *w*·. "
4: 4 a prophetess, the *w*· of Lapidoth, "
17 to the tent of Jael the *w*· of Heber "
21 Then Jael Heber's *w*· took a nail of "
5:24 Jael the *w*· of Heber the Kenite be, "
11: 2 Gilead's *w*· bare him sons; and his "
13: 2 and his *w*· was barren, and bare not. "
11 Manoah arose, and went after his *w*·, "
19 and Manoah and his *w*· looked on. "
20 And Manoah and his *w*· looked on it, "
21 appear to Manoah and to his *w*·. "
22 Manoah said unto his *w*·, We shall "
23 But his *w*· said unto him, If the Lord "
14: 2 now therefore get her for me to *w*·. "
3 to take a *w*· of the uncircumcised "
15 that they said unto Samson's *w*·, "
16 And Samson's *w*· wept before him, "
20 But Samson's *w*· was given to his "
15: 1 Samson visited his *w*· with a kid; "
1 will go in to my *w*· into the chamber. "
6 because he had taken his *w*·, and "
21: 1 his daughter unto Benjamin to *w*·. "
18 be he that giveth a *w*· to Benjamin. "
21 catch you every man his *w*· of the "
22 we reserved not to each man his *w*· "
Ru 1: 1 the country of Moab, he, and his *w*·, "
2 and the name of his *w*· Naomi, "
4: 5 the Moabitess, the *w*· of the dead, "
10 Ruth the Moabitess,...*w*· of Mahlon, "
10 have I purchased to be my *w*·, to "
13 Boaz took Ruth, and she was his *w*·: "
1Sa 1: 4 offered, he gave to Peninnah his *w*·, "
19 and Elkanah knew Hannah his *w*·; "
2:20 And Eli blessed Elkanah and his *w*·, "
4:19 his daughter in law, Phinehas' *w*·, "
14:50 the name of Saul's *w*· was Ahinoam, "
18:17 Merab, her will I give thee to *w*·: "
19 unto Adriel the Meholathite to *w*·. "
27 gave him Michal his daughter to *w*·. "
19:11 and Michal David's *w*· told him, "
25: 3 and the name of his *w*· Abigail: "
14 young men told Abigail, Nabal's *w*·, "
37 his *w*· had told him these things, "
39 with Abigail, to take her to him to *w*·. "
40 unto thee, to take thee to him to *w*·. "
42 of David, and became his *w*·. "
44 Michal his daughter, David's *w*·, to "
27: 3 Abigail the Carmelitess, Nabal's *w*·. "
30: 5 Abigail...*w*· of Nabal the Carmelite. "
22 save to every man his *w*· and his "
2Sa 2: 2 Abigail Nabal's *w*· the Carmelite. "
3: 3 Abigail...*w*· of Nabal the Carmelite; "
5 Ithream, by Eglah David's *w*·. "
14 Deliver me my *w*· Michal, which I "
11: 3 Eliam, the *w*· of Uriah the Hittite? "
11 and to drink, and to lie with my *w*·? "
26 when the *w*· of Uriah heard that "
27 she became his *w*·, and bare him a "
12: 9 and hast taken his *w*· to be thy *w*·, "
10 me, and hast taken the *w*· of Uriah "
10 of Uriah the Hittite to be thy *w*·. "
15 which Uriah's *w*· bare unto David, "
24 David comforted Bath-sheba his *w*·, "
1Ki 2:17 me Abishag the Shunammite to *w*·. "
21 given to Adonijah thy brother to *w*·. "
4:11, 15 the daughter of Solomon to *w*·: "
7: 8 daughter, whom he had taken to *w*·, "

1Ki 9:16 unto his daughter, Solomon's *w*·. 802
11:19 him to *w*· the sister of his own *w*·, "
14: 2 And Jeroboam said to his *w*·, Arise, "
2 not known to be the *w*· of Jeroboam; "
4 Jeroboam's *w*· did so, and arose, "
5 the *w*· of Jeroboam cometh to ask a "
6 said, Come in, thou *w*· of Jeroboam; "
17 Jeroboam's *w*· arose, and departed, "
16:31 he took to *w*· Jezebel the daughter "
21: 5 But Jezebel his *w*· came to him, and "
7 Jezebel his *w*· said unto him, Dost "
25 whom Jezebel his *w*· stirred up. "
2Ki 5: 2 and she waited on Naaman's *w*·. "
8:18 for the daughter of Ahab was his *w*·: "
14: 9 Give thy daughter to my son to *w*·: "
22:14 the prophetess, the *w*· of Shallum "
1Ch 2:18 begat children of Azubah his *w*·, "
24 Abiah Hezron's *w*· bare him Ashur "
26 Jerahmeel had also another *w*·, "
29 of the *w*· of Abishur was Abihail, "
35 daughter to Jarha his servant to *w*·; "
3: 3 the sixth, Ithream by Eglah his *w*·. "
4:18 And his *w*· Jehudijah bare Jered the "
19 the sons of his *w*· Hodiah the sister "
7:15 And Machir took to *w*· the sister of "
16 Maachah the *w*· of Machir bare a "
23 And when he went in to his *w*·, she "
8: 9 he begat of Hodesh his *w*·, Jobab, "
2Ch 8:11 My *w*· shall not dwell in the house "
11:18 of Jerimoth the son of David to *w*·, "
21: 6 he had the daughter of Ahab to *w*·: "
22:11 the *w*· of Jehoiada the priest, "
25:18 Give thy daughter to my son to *w*·: "
34:22 the prophetess, the *w*· of Shallum "
Ezr 2:61 a *w*· of the daughters of Barzillai "
Ne 7:63 of Barzillai the Gileadite to *w*·, "
Es 5:10 for his friends, and Zeresh his *w*·. "
14 Then said Zeresh his *w*· and all his "
6:13 Haman told Zeresh his *w*· and all his "
13 his wise men and Zeresh his *w*· "
Job 2: 9 Then said his *w*· unto him, Dost "
19:17 My breath is strange to my *w*·, "
31:10 Then let my *w*· grind unto another, "
Ps 109: 9 be fatherless, and his *w*· a widow. "
128: 3 Thy *w*· shall be as a fruitful vine by "
Pr 5:18 and rejoice with the *w*· of thy youth. "
6:29 that goeth in to his neighbour's *w*·; "
18:22 Whoso findeth a *w*· findeth a good "
19:13 contentions of a *w*· are a continual "
14 and a prudent *w*· is from the Lord. "
Ec 9: 9 Live joyfully with the *w*· whom thou "
Isa 54: 1 the children of the married *w*·, "
6 and a *w*· of youth, when thou wast 802
Jer 3: 1 If a man put away his *w*·, and she "
20 as a *w*· treacherously departeth "
5: 8 one neighed after his neighbour's *w*·. "
6:11 husband with the *w*· shall be taken, "
16: 2 Thou shalt not take thee a *w*·, "
Eze 16:32 as a *w*· that committeth adultery, "
18: 6 hath defiled his neighbour's *w*·, "
11 and defiled his neighbour's *w*·, "
15 hath not defiled his neighbour's *w*·, "
22:11 abomination with his neighbour's *w*·; "
24:18 at even my *w*· died; and I did in the "
33:26 defile every one his neighbour's *w*·: "
Ho 1: 2 take unto thee a *w*· of whoredoms "
2: 2 she is not my *w*·, neither am I her "
12:12 of Syria, and Israel served for a *w*·, "
12 and for a *w*· he kept sheep. "
Am 7:17 Thy *w*· shall be an harlot in the city, "
Mal 2:14 between thee and...*w*· of thy youth, "
14 and the *w*· of thy covenant. "
15 deal treacherously against the *w*· of "
M't 1: 6 of her that had been the *w*· of Urias; "
20 not to take unto thee Mary thy *w*·: *1135*
24 him, and took unto him his *w*·: "
5:31 Whosoever shall put away his *w*·, "
32 whosoever shall put away his *w*·, "
14: 3 sake, his brother Philip's *w*·. "
18:25 to be sold, and his *w*·, and children, "
19: 3 lawful for a man to put away his *w*· "
5 mother, and shall cleave to his *w*·: "
9 Whosoever shall put away his *w*·, "
10 case of the man be so with his *w*·, "
29 or father, or mother, or *w*·, or "
22:24 his brother shall marry his *w*·, and "
25 first, when he had married a *w*·, *
25 issue, left his *w*· unto his brother: *1135*
28 whose *w*· shall she be of the seven? "
27:19 seat, his *w*· sent unto him, saying, "
M'r 6:17 sake, his brother Philip's *w*·: "
18 for thee to have thy brother's *w*·. "
10: 2 for a man to put away his *w*·? "
7 and mother, and cleave to his *w*·; "
11 Whosoever shall put away his *w*·, "
29 or father, or mother, or *w*·, or "
12:19 die, and leave his *w*· behind him, "
19 that his brother should take his *w*·, "
20 the first took a *w*·, and dying left "
23 rise, whose *w*· shall she be of them? "
23 for the seven had her to *w*·. "
Lu 1: 5 his *w*· was of the daughters of "
13 *w*· Elisabeth shall bear thee a son, "
18 and my *w*· well stricken in years. "
24 days his *w*· Elisabeth conceived, "
2: 5 taxed with Mary his espoused *w*·, *
3:19 Herodias his brother Philip's *w*·, "
8: 3 the *w*· of Chuza Herod's steward, "
14:20 I have married a *w*·, and therefore "
26 his father, and mother, and *w*·, "
16:18 Whosoever putteth away his *w*·, "
17:32 Remember Lot's *w*·. "
18:29 or parents, or brethren, or *w*·, "
20:28 any man's brother die, having a *w*·, "
28 that his brother should take his *w*·, "
29 the first took a *w*·, and died without "

Lu 20:30 the second took her to *w*·, and he **1135*
33 whose *w*· of them is she? "
33 for seven had her to *w*·. "
Joh 19:25 sister, Mary the *w*· of Cleophas,
Ac 5: 1 Ananias, with Sapphira his *w*·, *1135*
2 price, his *w*· also being privy to it, "
7 his *w*·, not knowing what was done, "
18: 2 from Italy, with his *w*· Priscilla; "
24:24 Felix came with his *w*· Drusilla, "
1Co 5: 1 one should have his father's *w*·. "
7: 2 let every man have his own *w*·, and "
3 husband render unto the *w*· due "
3 also the *w*· unto the husband. "
4 *w*· hath not power of her own body, "
4 power of his own body, but the *w*·. "
10 Let not the *w*· depart from her "
11 not the husband put away his *w*·. "
12 brother hath a *w*· that believeth "
14 husband is sanctified by the *w*·, "
14 *w*· is sanctified by the husband: "
16 For what knowest thou, O *w*·, "
16 whether thou shalt save thy *w*·? "
27 Art thou bound unto a *w*·? seek not "
27 loosed from a *w*·? seek not a *w*·. "
33 world, how he may please his *w*·. "
34 is difference also between a *w*· and "
39 The *w*· is bound by the law as long "
9: 5 power to lead about a sister, a *w*·, "
Eph 5:23 the husband is the head of the *w*·, "
28 that loveth his *w*· loveth himself. "
31 and shall be joined unto his *w*·, "
33 so love his *w*· even as himself; and "
33 the *w*· see that she reverence her "
1Ti 3: 2 the husband of one *w*·, vigilant, "
12 deacons be the husbands of one *w*·, "
5: 9 having been the *w*· of one man, "
Tit 1: 6 the husband of one *w*·, having "
1Pe 3: 7 giving honour unto the *w*·, as unto**1134*
Re 19: 7 his *w*· hath made herself ready. *1135*
21: 9 shew thee the bride, the Lamb's *w*·. "

wife's
Ge 3:20 And Adam called his *w*· name Eve; 802
20:11 they will slay me for my *w*· sake. "
36:39 and his *w*· name was Mehetabel, "
Le 18:11 The nakedness of thy father's *w*· "
J'g 11: 2 and his *w*· sons grew up, and they "
1Ch 1:50 and his *w*· name was Mehetabel, "
8:29 whose *w*· name was Maachah: "
9:35 whose *w*· name was Maachah: "
M't 8:14 house, he saw his *w*· mother laid, *3994*
M'r 1:30 Simon's *w*· mother lay sick of a "
Lu 4:38 And Simon's *w*· mother was taken "

wild
Ge 16:12 And he will be a *w*· man; his hand*6501
Le 26:22 also send *w*· beasts among you, *7704
De 14: 5 the fallow deer, and the *w*· goat, 689
5 the pygarg, and the *w*· ox, and the*8377
1Sa 17:46 and to the *w*· beasts of the earth; 2416
24: 2 upon the rocks of the *w*· goats. 3277
2Sa 2:18 was as light of foot as a *w*· roe. 7704
2Ki 4:39 gather herbs, and found a *w*· vine, "
39 gathered thereof *w*· gourds his lap "
14: 9 a *w*· beast that was in Lebanon, 7704
2Ch 25:18 a *w*· beast that was in Lebanon, "
Job 6: 5 *w*· ass bray when he hath grass? 6501
11:12 may be born like a *w*· ass's colt. "
24: 5 as *w*· asses in the desert, go they "
39: 1 *w*· goats of the rock bring forth? 3277
5 Who hath sent out the *w*· ass free? 6501
5 loosed the bands of the *w*· ass? 6171
15 that the *w*· beast may break them. 7704
Ps 50:11 the *w*· beasts of the field are mine. 2123
80:13 *w*· beasts of the field doth devour it. "
104:11 the *w*· asses quench their thirst. 6501
18 hills are a refuge for the *w*· goats; 3277
Isa 5: 2 and it brought forth *w*· grapes. 891
4 grapes, brought it forth *w*· grapes? "
13:21 *w*· beasts of the desert shall lie 6728
22 *w*· beasts of the islands shall cry * 338
32:14 a joy of *w*· asses, a pasture of 6501
34:14 *w*· beasts of the desert shall also 6728
14 also meet with the *w*· beasts of the*338
51:20 the streets, as a *w*· bull in a net: *8377
Jer 2:24 A *w*· ass used to the wilderness, 6501
14: 6 *w*· asses did stand in the high "
50:39 the *w*· beasts of the desert with 6728
39 *w*· beasts of the islands shall dwell*338
Da 5:21 dwelling was with the *w*· asses: 6167
Hos 8: 9 Assyria, a *w*· ass alone by himself: 6501
13: 8 the *w*· beast shall tear them. 7704
M't 3: 4 his meat was locusts and *w*· honey *66*
M'r 1: 6 he did eat locusts and *w*· honey; "
13 and was with the *w*· beasts; *2342*
Ac 10:12 *w*· beasts, and creeping things, * "
11: 6 *w*· beasts, and creeping things, and "
Ro 11:17 being a *w*· olive tree, wert graffed *65*
24 the olive tree which is *w*· by nature, "

wild-ass See WILD and ASS.

wilderness
Ge 14: 6 El-paran, which is by the *w*·. 4057
16: 7 by a fountain of water in the *w*·, "
21:14 wandered in the *w*· of Beer-sheba. "
20 and he grew, and dwelt in the *w*·, "
21 And he dwelt in the *w*· of Paran: "
36:24 that found the mules in the *w*·, "
37:22 him into this pit that is in the *w*·, "
Ex 3:18 three days' journey into the *w*·, that "
4:27 Go into the *w*· to meet Moses. "
5: 1 may hold a feast unto me in the *w*·. "
7:16 that they may serve me in the *w*·: "
8:27 go three days' journey into the *w*·, "
28 to the Lord your God in the *w*·; "
13:18 the way of the *w*· of the Red sea: "
20 in Etham, in the edge of the *w*·. "

Ex 14: 3 the land, the w' hath shut them in.4057
11 taken us away to die in the w'? "
12 than that we should die in the w'. "
15: 22 they went out into the w' of Shur; "
22 and they went three days in the w', "
16: 1 of Israel came unto the w' of Sin, "
2 against Moses and Aaron in the w': "
3 have brought us forth into this w', "
10 that they looked toward the w', "
14 upon the face of the w' there lay a "
32 wherewith I have fed you in the w', "
17: 1 Israel journeyed from the w' of Sin, "
18: 5 his wife unto Moses into the w', "
19: 1 came they into the w' of Sinai. "
2 Sinai, and had pitched in the w'; "
Le 7: 38 unto the Lord, in the w' of Sinai. "
16: 10 him go for a scapegoat into the w'. "
21 the hand of a fit man into the w': "
22 he shall let go the goat in the w'. "
Nu 1: 1 spake unto Moses in the w' of Sinai, "
19 numbered them in the w' of Sinai. "
3: 4 before the Lord, in the w' of Sinai, "
14 unto Moses in the w' of Sinai, "
9: 1 unto Moses in the w' of Sinai, "
5 month at even in the w' of Sinai: "
10: 12 journeys out of the w' of Sinai; "
12 cloud rested in the w' of Paran. "
31 how we are to encamp in the w', "
12: 16 and pitched in the w' of Paran. "
13: 3 sent them from the w' of Paran: "
21 from the w' of Zin unto Rehob, "
26 unto the w' of Paran, to Kadesh; "
14: 2 would God we had died in this w'! "
16 he hath slain them in the w'. "
22 which I did in Egypt and in the w', "
25 into the w' by the way of the Red "
29 Your carcases shall fall in this w'; "
32 carcases, they shall fall in this w'. "
33 shall wander in the w' forty years, "
33 your carcases be wasted in the w'. "
35 in this w' they shall be consumed, "
15: 32 children of Israel were in the w', "
16: 13 to kill us in the w', except thou "
20: 4 of the Lord into this w', "
21: 5 us up out of Egypt to die in the w'? "
11 in the w' which is before Moab, "
13 which is in the w' that cometh out "
18 the w' they went to Mattanah: "
23 went out against Israel into the w': "
24: 1 but he set his face toward the w'. "
26: 64 of Israel in the w' of Sinai. "
65 They shall surely die in the w'. "
27: 3 Our father died in the w', and he "
14 Meribah in Kadesh in the w' of Zin. "
32: 13 them wander in the w' forty years, "
15 he will yet leave them in the w'; "
33: 6 which is in the edge of the w'. "
8 the midst of the sea into the w', "
8 went three days' journey in the w' "
11 and encamped in the w' of Sin. "
12 their journey out of the w' of Sin, "
15 and pitched in the w' of Sinai. "
36 pitched in the w' of Zin, which is "
34: 3 w' of Zin along by the coast of Edom, "
De 1: 1 Israel on this side Jordan in the w', "
19 all that great and terrible w', "
31 And in the w', where thou hast "
40 take your journey into the w' by "
2: 1 took our journey into the w' by the "
7 thy walking through this great w': "
8 by the way of the w' of Moab. "
26 I sent messengers out of the w' of "
4: 43 Bezer in the w', in the plain "
8: 2 thee these forty years in the w', "
15 through that great and terrible w', "
16 Who fed thee in the w' with manna, "
9: 7 Lord thy God to wrath in the w': "
28 them out to slay them in the w'. "
11: 5 what he did unto you in the w', "
24 from the w' and Lebanon, from the "
29: 5 have led you forty years in the w': "
32: 10 and in the waste howling w'; 3452
51 Meribah-Kadesh, in the w' of Zin; 4057
Jos 1: 4 From the w' and this Lebanon even "
5: 4 of war, died in the w' by the way, "
5 that were born in the w' by the way "
6 Israel walked forty years in the w', "
8: 15 and fled by the way of the w'. "
20 people that fled to the w' turned "
24 in the w' wherein they chased them, "
12: 8 in the w', and in the south country; "
14: 10 of Israel wandered in the w': "
15: 1 of Edom the w' of Zin southward "
61 In the w', Beth-arabah, Middin, "
16: 1 the w' that goeth up from Jericho "
18: 12 were at the w' of Beth-aven. "
20: 8 assigned Bezer in the w' upon the "
24: 7 ye dwelt in the w' a long season. "
J'g 1: 16 of Judah into the w' of Judah, "
8: 7 your flesh with the thorns of the w' "
16 and thorns of the w' and briers, "
11: 16 walked through the w' unto the "
18 they went along through the w', "
22 and from the w' even unto Jordan. "
20: 42 of Israel unto the way of the w'; "
45 fled toward the w' unto the rock of "
47 fled to the w' unto the rock "
1Sa 4: 8 with all the plagues in the w'. "
13: 18 valley of Zeboim toward the w'. "
17: 28 thou left those few sheep in the w'? "
23: 14 David abode in the w' in strong "
14 in a mountain in the w' of Ziph. "
15 David was in the w' of Ziph in a "
24 his men were in the w' of Maon, "
25 rock, and abode in the w' of Maon. "
25 after David in the w' of Maon. "
1Sa 24: 1 David is in the w' of En-gedi. 4057
25: 1 and went down to the w' of Paran. "
4 David heard in the w' that Nabal "
14 sent messengers out of the w' to "
21 all that this fellow hath in the w', "
26: 2 and went down to the w' of Ziph, "
2 to seek David in the w' of Ziph. "
3 But David abode in the w', and he "
3 Saul came after him into the w'. "
2Sa 2: 24 by the way of the w' of Gibeon. "
15: 23 over, toward the way of the w'. "
28 I will tarry in the plain of the w', "
16: 2 as be faint in the w' may drink. "
17: 16 this night in the plains of the w', "
29 and weary, and thirsty, in the w'. "
1Ki 2: 34 buried in his own house in the w'. "
9: 18 Baalath, and Tadmor in the w', "
19: 4 went a day's journey into the w', "
15 on thy way to the w' of Damascus: "
2Ki 3: 8 The way through the w' of Edom. "
1Ch 5: 9 unto the entering in of the w' "
6: 78 Bezer in the w' with her suburbs, "
12: 8 unto David into the hold to the w' "
21: 29 Lord, which Moses made in the w', "
2Ch 1: 3 of the Lord had made in the w'. "
8: 4 And he built Tadmor in the w', "
20: 16 the brook, before the w' of Jeruel. "
20 went forth into the w' of Tekoa: "
24 toward the watch tower in the w', "
24: 9 of God laid upon Israel in the w'. "
Ne 9: 19 forsookest them not in the w': "
21 didst thou sustain them in the w', "
Job 1: 19 came a great wind from the w', "
12: 24 causeth them to wander in a w' 8414
24: 5 the w' yieldeth food for them and 6160
30: 3 fleeing into the w' in former time*6723
38: 26 the w', wherein there is no man; 4057
39: 6 Whose house I have made the w', 6160
Ps 29: 8 voice of the Lord shaketh the w'; 4057
8 Lord shaketh the w' of Kadesh. "
55: 7 far off, and remain in the w'. "
63: *title* when he was in the w' of Judah. "
65: 12 drop upon the pastures of the w': "
68: 7 thou didst march through the w'; 3452
72: 9 They that dwell in the w' shall 6728
74: 14 to the people inhabiting the w'. "
78: 15 He clave the rocks in the w', and 4057
17 provoking...most High in the w'. *6723
19 Can God furnish a table in the w'?4057
40 oft did they provoke him in the w', "
52 guided them in the w' like a flock. "
95: 8 in the day of temptation in the w': "
102: 6 I am like a pelican of the w': I am "
106: 9 the depths, as through the w'. "
14 But lusted exceedingly in the w', "
26 them, to overthrow them in the w': "
107: 4 wandered in...w' in a solitary way; "
33 He turneth rivers into a w', and the "
35 turneth the w' into a standing "
40 causeth them to wander in the w', *8414
136: 16 led his people through the w': 4057
Pr 21: 19 It is better to dwell in the w', than* "
Ca 3: 6 is this that cometh out of the w' "
8: 5 is this that cometh up from the w', "
Isa 14: 17 That made the world a w', and "
16: 1 of the land from Sela to the w', "
8 they wandered through the w': "
23: 13 it for them that dwell in the w': 6728
27: 10 forsaken, and left like a w': 4057
32: 15 high, and the w' be a fruitful field, "
16 judgment shall dwell in the w', "
33: 9 Sharon is like a w'; and Bashan *6160
35: 1 w' and the solitary place...be glad 4057
6 in the w' shall waters break out, "
40: 3 voice of him that crieth in the w', "
41: 18 I will make the w' a pool of water, "
19 I will plant in the w' the cedar, "
42: 11 Let the w' and the cities thereof "
43: 19 I will even make a way in the w', "
20 because I give waters in the w', "
50: 2 the sea, I make the rivers a w': "
51: 3 and he will make her w' like Eden, "
63: 13 the deep, as an horse in the w', "
64: 10 Thy holy cities are a w', Zion is a "
10 Zion is a w', Jerusalem a "
Jer 2: 2 thou wentest after me in the w', "
6 Egypt, that led us through the w', "
24 A wild ass used to the w', that "
31 Have I been a w' unto Israel? "
3: 2 for them, as the Arabian in the w'; "
4: 11 wind of the high places in the w' "
26 and, lo, the fruitful place was a w', "
9: 2 that I had in the w' a lodging place "
10 and for the habitations of the w' "
12 and is burned up like a w', "
26 corners, that dwell in the w': "
12: 10 my pleasant portion a desolate w'. "
12 all high places through the w': "
13: 24 passeth away by the wind of the w'. "
17: 6 the parched places in the w', "
22: 6 yet surely I will make thee a w', "
23: 10 places of the w' are dried up, "
31: 2 of the sword found grace in the w'; "
48: 6 and be like the heath in the w'. "
50: 12 of the nations shall be a w', "
51: 43 a desolation, a dry land, and a w',*6160
La 4: 3 cruel, like the ostriches in the w'. 4057
19 they laid wait for us in the w'. "
5: 9 because of the sword of the w'. "
Eze 6: 14 than the w' toward Diblath, "
19: 13 And now she is planted in the w', "
20: 10 and brought them into the w'. "
13 rebelled against me in the w': "
13 out my fury upon them in the w', "
15 up my hand unto them in the w', "
17 I make an end of them in the w'. "
Eze 20: 18 said unto their children in the w'. 4057
21 my anger against them in the w'. "
23 mine hand unto them also in the w', "
35 bring you into the w' of the people, "
36 pleaded with your fathers in the w' "
23: 42 were brought Sabeans from the w', "
29: 5 will leave thee thrown into the w', "
34: 25 they shall dwell safely in the w', "
Hos 2: 3 and make her as a w', and set her "
14 her, and bring her into the w', "
9: 10 found Israel like grapes in the w'; "
13: 5 I did know thee in the w', in the land "
15 Lord shall come up from the w', "
Joe 1: 19 devoured the pastures of the w', "
20 devoured the pastures of the w'. "
2: 3 and behind them a desolate w'; "
22 for the pastures of the w' do spring, "
3: 19 and Edom shall be a desolate w', "
Am 2: 10 led you forty years through the w', "
5: 25 and offerings in the w' forty years, "
6: 14 Hemath unto the river of the w'. *6166
Zep 2: 13 a desolation, and dry like a w'. 4057
Mal 1: 3 waste for the dragons of the w'. "
M't 3: 1 preaching in the w' of Judæa, 2048
3 The voice of one crying in the w', "
4: 1 Jesus led up of the spirit in the w' "
11: 7 What went ye out into the w' to see? "
15: 33 we have so much bread in the w', *2047
M'r 1: 3 The voice of one crying in the w', 2048
4 John did baptize in the w', and "
12 the spirit driveth him into the w'. "
13 he was there in the w' forty days, "
8: 4 men with bread here in the w'? *2047
Lu 3: 2 the son of Zacharias in the w'. 2048
4 The voice of one crying in the w', "
4: 1 was led by the Spirit into the w', "
5: 16 he withdrew himself into the w', * "
7: 24 went ye out into the w' for to see? "
8: 29 was driven of the devil into the w'.)* "
15: 4 leave the ninety and nine in the w', "
Joh 1: 23 the voice of one crying in the w', "
3: 14 lifted up the serpent in the w', "
6: 49 fathers did eat manna in the w', "
11: 54 unto a country near to the w', "
Ac 7: 30 in the w' of mount Sina an angel "
36 Red sea, and in the w' forty years. "
38 he, that was in the church in the w' "
42 the space of forty years in the w'? "
44 the tabernacle of witness in the w', "
13: 18 suffered he their manners in the w'. "
21: 38 leddest out into the w' four "
1Co 10: 5 for they were overthrown in the w'. "
2Co 11: 26 in the city, in perils in the w', 2047
Heb 3: 8 in the day of temptation in the w': 2048
17 whose carcases fell in the w'? "
Re 12: 6 And the woman fled into the w', "
14 that she might fly into the w', "
17: 3 me away in the spirit into the w': "

wild-goat See WILD and GOAT.

wild-ox See WILD and OX.

wiles
Nu 25: 18 For they vex you with their w', 5231
Eph 6: 11 stand against the w' of the devil. 3180

wilfully
Heb10: 26 For if we sin w' after that we have 1596

wilily
Jos 9: 4 They did work w', and went and 6195

will See also FREEWILL; SELFWILL; WILFULLY; WILLETH; WILLING; WILT; WOULD.
Ge 2: 18 I w' make him an help meet for him.
3: 15 I w' put enmity between thee and the
16 I w' greatly multiply thy sorrow and
6: 7 I w' destroy man whom I have
13 I w' destroy them with the earth.
18 with thee w' I establish my covenant;
7: 4 I w' cause it to rain upon the earth
4 that I have made w' I destroy from
8: 21 I w' not again curse the ground any
21 neither w' I again smite any more
9: 5 your blood of your lives w' I require;
5 hand of every beast w' I require it,
5 every man's brother w' I require the
11 I w' establish my covenant with you;
15 I w' remember my covenant, which is
16 I w' look upon it, that I may remember
11: 6 nothing w' be restrained from them,
12: 1 house, unto a land that I w' show thee:
2 I w' make of thee a great nation,
2 I w' bless thee, and make thy name
3 And I w' bless them that bless thee,
7 Unto thy seed w' I give this land:
12 w' kill me, but they w' save thee alive.
13: 9 left hand, then I w' go to the right;
9 right hand, then I w' go to the left.
15 to thee w' I give it, and to thy seed for
16 I w' make thy seed as the dust of the
17 breadth of it; for I w' give it unto thee.
14: 23 I w' not take from a thread even to a
23 I w' not take any thing that is thine,*
15: 14 whom they shall serve, w' I judge:
16: 10 I w' multiply thy seed exceedingly,
12 And he w' be a wild man; his hand*
12 his hand w' be against every man, and*
17: 2 I w' make my covenant between me
2 and w' multiply thee exceedingly.
6 I w' make thee exceeding fruitful,
6 and I w' make nations of thee, and
7 I w' establish my covenant between
8 I w' give unto thee, and unto thy
8 possession; and I w' be their God.
16 I w' bless her, and give thee a son
16 I w' bless her, and she shall be a
19 I w' establish my covenant with him
20 blessed him, and w' make him fruitful.

Ge 17:20 and *w'* multiply him exceedingly;
20 and I *w'* make him a great nation.
21 But my covenant *w'* I establish with
18: 5 I *w'* fetch a morsel of bread, and
10 said, I *w'* certainly return unto thee
14 At the time appointed I *w'* return
19 he *w'* command his children and his*
21 I *w'* go down now, and see whether
21 come unto me; and if not, I *w'* know.
26 I *w'* spare all the place for their sakes.
28 forty and five, I *w'* not destroy it.
29 he said, I *w'* not do it for forty's sake.
30 not the Lord be angry, and I *w'* speak:
30 he said, I *w'* not do it, if I find thirty
31 I *w'* not destroy it for twenty's sake.
32 and I *w'* speak yet but this once:
32 said, I *w'* not destroy it for ten's sake.
19: 2 and we *w'* abide in the street all night.
9 sojourn, and he *w'* needs be a judge:
9 *w'* we deal worse with thee, than with
13 For we *w'* destroy this place, because
14 for the Lord *w'* destroy this city.
21 that I *w'* not overthrow this city, for
32 and we *w'* lie with him, that we may
20:11 and they *w'* slay me for my wife's sake.
21: 6 that all that hear *w'* laugh with me.
13 of the bondwoman *w'* I make a nation,
18 for I *w'* make him a great nation.
24 And Abraham said, I *w'* swear.
22: 2 mountains which I *w'* tell thee of.
5 and I and the lad *w'* go yonder and
8 son, God *w'* provide himself a lamb
17 That in blessing I *w'* bless thee,
17 multiplying I *w'* multiply thy seed as
23:13 I *w'* give thee money for the field;
24: 3 I *w'* make thee swear by the Lord,
5 woman *w'* not be willing to follow
7 Unto thy seed *w'* I give this land;
8 woman *w'* not be willing to follow*
14 and I *w'* give thy camels drink also:
19 *w'* draw water for thy camels also,
33 I *w'* not eat, until I have told mine
39 the woman *w'* not follow me.
40 *w'* send his angel with thee, and
44 and I *w'* also draw for thy camels:
46 and I *w'* give thy camels drink also:
49 if ye *w'* deal kindly and truly with my
57 We *w'* call the damsel, and enquire at
58 with this man? And she said, I *w'* go.
26: 3 I *w'* be with thee, and *w'* bless thee;
3 thy seed, I *w'* give all these countries,
3 I *w'* perform the oath which I sware
4 I *w'* make thy seed to multiply as the
4 and *w'* give unto thy seed all these
24 for I am with thee, and *w'* bless thee,
27: 9 I *w'* make them savoury meat for thy
12 My father peradventure *w'* feel me,
25 me, and I *w'* eat of my son's venison,
41 then *w'* I slay my brother Jacob.
45 then I *w'* send, and fetch thee from
28:13 thou liest, to thee *w'* I give it,
15 *w'* keep thee in all places whither thou
15 and *w'* bring thee again into this land;
15 for I *w'* not leave thee, until I have
20 a vow, saying, If God *w'* be with me,
20 and *w'* keep me in this way that I go,
20 *w'* give me bread to eat, and raiment
22 I *w'* surely give the tenth unto thee.
29:18 I *w'* serve thee seven years for Rachel
27 and we *w'* give thee this also for the
32 now therefore my husband *w'* love me.
34 this time *w'* my husband be joined
35 she said, Now *w'* I praise the Lord:
30:13 for the daughters *w'* call me blessed:
20 now *w'* my husband dwell with me,
28 me thy wages, and I *w'* give it.
31 I *w'* again feed and keep thy flock.
32 I *w'* pass through all thy flock to day,
31: 3 to thy kindred; and I *w'* be with thee.
52 I *w'* not pass over this heap to thee,
32: 9 and I *w'* deal well with thee:
11 him, lest he *w'* come and smite me,
12 thou saidst, I *w'* surely do thee good,
20 I *w'* appease him with the present
20 me, and afterward I *w'* see his face;
20 peradventure he *w'* accept of me.
26 said, I *w'* not let thee go, except thou
33:12 and let us go, and I *w'* go before thee.
13 them one day, all the flock *w'* die.
14 his servant; and I *w'* lead on softly,
34:11 what ye shall say unto me I *w'* give.
12 I *w'* give according as ye shall say
15 But in this *w'* we consent unto you:
15 If ye *w'* be as we be, that every male
16 Then *w'* we give our daughters unto
16 and we *w'* take your daughters to us,
16 and we *w'* dwell with you,
16 and we *w'* become one people.
17 But if ye *w'* not hearken unto us, to
17 then *w'* we take our daughter,
17 and we *w'* be gone.
22 herein *w'* the men consent unto us
23 unto them, and they *w'* dwell with us.
35: 3 I *w'* make there an altar unto God,
12 to thee I *w'* give it, and to thy seed
12 seed after thee *w'* I give the land.
37:13 come, and I *w'* send thee unto them.
20 and we *w'* say, Some evil beast hath
20 see what *w'* become of his dreams.
35 I *w'* go down into the grave unto my
38:17 I *w'* send thee a kid from the flock.
41:32 and God *w'* shortly bring it to pass.
40 the throne *w'* I be greater than thou.
42:34 *w'* I deliver you your brother, and ye
36 and ye *w'* take Benjamin away:
37 and I *w'* bring him to thee again.

Ge 43: 4 us, we *w'* go down and buy thee food:
5 wilt not send him, we *w'* not go down:
8 lad with me, and we *w'* arise and go;
9 I *w'* be surety for him; of my hand
44: 9 and we also *w'* be my lord's bondmen.
26 be with us, then *w'* we go down:
31 the lad is not with us, that he *w'* die:
45:11 And there *w'* I nourish thee; for yet
18 I *w'* give you the good of the land of
28 I *w'* go and see him before I die.
46: 3 for I *w'* there make of thee a great
4 I *w'* go down with thee into Egypt;
4 I *w'* also surely bring thee up again:
31 I *w'* go up, and shew Pharaoh, and say
47:16 I *w'* give you for your cattle, if money
18 We *w'* not hide it from my lord, how
19 and we and our land *w'* be servants
25 and we *w'* be Pharaoh's servants.
30 But I *w'* lie with my fathers, and thou*
30 And he said, I *w'* do as thou hast said.
48: 4 I *w'* make thee fruitful, and multiply
4 and I *w'* make of thee a multitude of
4 *w'* give this land to thy seed after thee
9 thee, unto me, and I *w'* bless them.
49: 7 I *w'* divide them in Jacob, and scatter
50: 5 bury my father, and I *w'* come again.
15 said, Joseph *w'* peradventure hate us,
15 *w'* certainly requite all the evil which
21 I *w'* nourish you, and your little ones.
24 and God *w'* surely visit you, and bring
25 God *w'* surely visit you, and ye shall
Ex 2: 9 it for me, and I *w'* give thee thy wages.
3: 3 Moses said, I *w'* now turn aside, and
10 and I *w'* send thee unto Pharaoh, that
12 he said, Certainly I *w'* be with thee;
17 I *w'* bring you up out of the affliction
19 the king of Egypt *w'* not let you go,
20 And I *w'* stretch out my hand, and
20 which I *w'* do in the midst thereof:
20 and after that he *w'* let you go.
21 I *w'* give this people favour in the
4: 1 they *w'* not believe me, nor hearken
1 for they *w'* say, The Lord hath not
8 if they *w'* not believe thee, neither
8 *w'* believe the voice of the latter sign.
9 *w'* not believe also these two signs,
12 and I *w'* be with thy mouth, and
14 thee, he *w'* be glad in his heart.
15 and I *w'* be with thy mouth, and with
15 and *w'* teach you what ye shall do.
21 but I *w'* harden his heart, that he
23 behold, I *w'* slay thy son, even thy
5: 2 the Lord, neither *w'* I let Israel go.
10 Pharaoh, I *w'* not give you straw.
6: 1 thou see what I *w'* do to Pharaoh:
6 I *w'* bring you out from under the
6 and I *w'* rid you out of their bondage,
6 I *w'* redeem you with a stretched out
7 I *w'* take you to me for a people, and I
7 I *w'* be to you a God: and ye shall
8 And I *w'* bring you unto the land,
8 and I *w'* give it you for an heritage:
7: 3 I *w'* harden Pharaoh's heart, and
17 I *w'* smite with the rod that is in mine
8: 2 I *w'* smite all thy borders with frogs:
8 I *w'* let the people go, that they may
21 I *w'* send swarms of flies upon thee,
22 And I *w'* sever in that day the land of
23 I *w'* put a division between my people
26 their eyes, and *w'* they not stone us?
27 We *w'* go three day's journey into the
28 Pharaoh said, I *w'* let you go, that ye
29 I *w'* entreat the Lord that the swarms
9:14 I *w'* send at this time all my plagues
15 I *w'* stretch out my hand, that I may*
18 I *w'* cause it to rain a very grievous
29 I *w'* spread abroad my hands unto the
30 I know that ye *w'* not yet fear the Lord
10: 4 *w'* I bring the locusts into thy coast:
9 We *w'* go with our young and with our
9 flocks and with our herds *w'* we go;
10 I *w'* let you go, and your little ones:
29 well, I *w'* see thy face again no more.
11: 1 Yet *w'* I bring one plague more upon
1 afterwards he *w'* let you go hence:
4 About midnight *w'* I go out into the
8 thee: and after that I *w'* go out.
12:12 I *w'* pass through the land of Egypt
12 *w'* smite all the firstborn in the land
12 gods of Egypt I *w'* execute judgment:
13 I *w'* pass over you, and the plague
23 the Lord *w'* pass through to smite the
23 posts, the Lord *w'* pass over the door,
23 *w'* not suffer the destroyer to come in
25 the land which the Lord *w'* give you,
48 and *w'* keep the passover to the Lord,
13:19 saying, God *w'* surely visit you;
14: 3 Pharaoh *w'* say of the children of
4 And I *w'* harden Pharaoh's heart, that
4 and I *w'* be honoured upon Pharaoh,
13 Lord, which he *w'* shew to you to day:
17 I *w'* harden the hearts of the
17 I *w'* get me honour upon Pharaoh,
15: 1 I *w'* sing unto the Lord, for he hath
2 and I *w'* prepare him an habitation;
2 my father's God, and I *w'* exalt him.
9 said, I *w'* pursue, I *w'* overtake,
9 I *w'* divide the spoil; my lust shall be
9 I *w'* draw my sword, my hand shall
26 I *w'* put none of these diseases upon
16: 4 I *w'* rain bread from heaven for you;
4 they *w'* walk in my law, or no.
23 bake that which ye *w'* bake to day,
23 to day, and seethe that ye *w'* seethe;
17: 6 I *w'* stand before thee there upon the
9 I *w'* stand on the top of the hill

Ex 17:14 I *w'* utterly put out the remembrance
16 the Lord *w'* have war with Amalek
18:19 I *w'* give thee counsel, and God shall
19: 5 if ye *w'* obey my voice indeed,
8 that the Lord hath spoken we *w'* do.
11 Lord *w'* come down in the sight of all
20: 7 for the Lord *w'* not hold him guiltless
19 Speak thou with us, and we *w'* hear:
24 record my name I *w'* come unto thee,
24 come unto thee, and I *w'* bless thee.
21: 5 my children; I *w'* not go out free:
13 I *w'* appoint thee a place whither he
22 woman's husband *w'* lay upon him;*
22:23 all unto me, I *w'* surely hear their cry;
24 and I *w'* kill you with the sword;
27 he crieth unto me, that I *w'* hear;
23: 7 not: for I *w'* not justify the wicked.
21 he *w'* not pardon your transgressions:
22 I *w'* be an enemy unto thy enemies,
23 the Jebusites: and I *w'* cut them off.
25 I *w'* take sickness away from the
26 the number of thy days I *w'* fulfil.
27 I *w'* send my fear before thee, and
27 and *w'* destroy all the people to whom
27 and I *w'* make all thine enemies turn
28 And I *w'* send hornets before thee,
29 I *w'* not drive them out from before
30 I *w'* drive them out from before thee,
31 I *w'* set thy bounds from the Red sea
31 I *w'* deliver the inhabitants of the land
33 it *w'* surely be a snare unto thee.
24: 3 which the Lord hath said *w'* we do.
7 that the Lord hath said *w'* we do,
12 and I *w'* give thee tables of stone,
25:22 And there I *w'* meet with thee, and
22 I *w'* commune with thee from above
22 I *w'* give thee in commandment
29:42 I *w'* meet you, to speak there unto
43 I *w'* meet with the children of Israel,
44 And I *w'* sanctify the tabernacle
44 I *w'* sanctify also both Aaron and his
45 And I *w'* dwell among the children
45 of Israel, and *w'* be their God.
30: 6 testimony, where I *w'* meet with thee.
36 where I *w'* meet with thee:
32:10 and I *w'* make of thee a great nation.
13 I *w'* multiply your seed as the stars
13 spoken of *w'* I give unto your seed,
30 and now I *w'* go up unto the Lord;
33 me, him *w'* I blot out of my book.
34 I visit I *w'* visit their sin upon them.
33: 1 saying, Unto thy seed *w'* I give it:
2 And I *w'* send an angel before thee;
2 and I *w'* drive out the Canaanite
3 I *w'* not go up in the midst of thee;
5 I *w'* come up into the midst of thee*
14 with thee, and I *w'* give thee rest.
17 I *w'* do this thing also that thou hast
19 I *w'* make all my goodness pass
19 I *w'* proclaim the name of the Lord
19 and *w'* be gracious unto whom I *w'* be
19 *w'* shew mercy to whom I *w'* shew
22 that I *w'* put thee in a clift of a rock,
22 *w'* cover thee with my hand while I
23 I *w'* take away mine hand, and thou
34: 1 I *w'* write upon these tables the words
7 that *w'* by no means clear the guilty;
10 before all thy people I *w'* do marvels,
10 for it is a terrible thing that I *w'* do*
24 I *w'* cast out the nations before thee,
Le 1: 3 offer it of his own voluntary *w'* *7522
2: 1 when any *w'* offer a meat offering*
9: 4 for to day the Lord *w'* appear unto*
10: 3 I *w'* be sanctified in them that come
3 before all the people I *w'* be glorified.
16: 2 for I *w'* appear in a cloud upon the
17:10 I *w'* even set my face against that
10 and *w'* cut him off from among his
19: 5 ye shall offer it at your own *w'*. *7522
20: 5 I *w'* set my face against that man,
6 I *w'* even set my face against that
6 and *w'* cut him off from among his
24 I *w'* give it unto you to possess it,
22:18 *w'* offer his oblation for all his vows,*
18 which they *w'* offer unto the Lord*
19 at your own *w'* a male without *7522
29 And when ye *w'* offer a sacrifice *
29 the Lord, offer it at your own *w'*. *7522
32 I *w'* be hallowed among the children
23:30 *w'* I destroy from among his people.
25:21 I *w'* command my blessing upon you
26: 4 I *w'* give you rain in due season,
6 I *w'* give peace in the land, and ye
6 I *w'* rid evil beasts out of the land,
9 I *w'* have respect unto you, and make
11 I *w'* set my tabernacle among you:
12 I *w'* walk among you,
12 and *w'* be your God, and ye shall
14 But if ye *w'* not hearken unto me,
14 *w'* not do all these commandments;
15 Ye *w'* not do all my commandments,
16 I also *w'* do this unto you;
16 I *w'* even appoint over you terror,
17 I *w'* set my face against you, and ye
18 if ye *w'* not yet for all this hearken
18 I *w'* punish you seven times more for
19 I *w'* break the pride of your power;
19 and I *w'* make your heaven as iron,
21 me, and *w'* not hearken unto me; 14
21 I *w'* bring seven times more plagues
22 I *w'* also send wild beasts among
23 And if ye *w'* not be reformed by me
23 but *w'* walk contrary unto me;
24 Then *w'* I also walk contrary unto
24 *w'* punish you yet seven times for
25 And I *w'* bring a sword upon you,

Le 26:25 I w· send the pestilence among you;
27 if ye w· not for all this hearken unto
28 Then I w· walk contrary unto you
28 I, w· chastise you seven times for
30 I w· destroy your high places, and cut
31 I w· make your cities waste, and bring
31 I w· not smell the savour of your
32 I w· bring the land into desolation:
33 I w· scatter you among the heathen,
33 and w· draw out a sword after you:
36 I w· send a faintness into their hearts
42 Then w· I remember my covenant
42 with Abraham w· I remember;
42 and I w· remember the land.
44 I w· not cast them away, neither
44 neither w· I abhor them, to destroy
45 I w· for their sakes remember the
27:15 that sanctified it w· redeem his house,
19 the field w· in any wise redeem it,
20 And if he w· not redeem the field,
31 if a man w· at all redeem ought of
Nu 6:27 of Israel; and I w· bless them.
9: 8 and I w· hear what the Lord *
8 Lord w· command concerning you.
14 w· keep the passover unto the Lord;
10:29 which the Lord said, I w· give it you:
29 thou with us, and we w· do thee good:
30 And he said unto him, I w· not go;
30 I w· depart to mine own land, and to
32 unto us, the same w· we do unto thee.
11:17 I w· come down and talk with thee
17 I w· take of the spirit which is upon
17 w· put it upon them; and they shall
18 therefore the Lord w· give you flesh,
21 I w· give them flesh, that they may eat
12: 6 I the Lord w· make myself known unto
6 and w· speak unto you in a dream.
8 With him w· I speak mouth to mouth,
14: 8 he w· bring us into this land, and give
11 How long w· this people provoke me?
11 how long w· it be ere they believe me,
12 I w· smite them with the pestilence,
12 and w· make of thee a greater nation
14 they w· tell it to the inhabitants of this
15 the fame of thee w· speak, saying,
24 him w· I bring into the land whereunto
28 spoken in mine ears, so w· I do to you:
31 them w· I bring in, and they shall
35 I w· surely do it unto all this evil
40 and w· go up unto the place which the
43 therefore the Lord w· not be with you.
15: 3 w· make an offering by fire unto the
14 and w· offer an offering made by fire,
16: 5 morrow the Lord w· show who are his,
5 w· cause him to come near unto him:
5 chosen w· he cause to come near unto
12 Eliab: which said, We w· not come up:
17: 4 testimony, where I w· meet with you.*
5 I w· make to cease from me the
20:17 we w· not pass through the fields,
17 w· we drink of the water of the wells:
17 we w· go by the king's high way,
17 we w· not turn to the right hand nor to
19 unto him, We w· go by the high way:
19 of thy water, then w· I pay for it:
19 I w· only, without doing any thing else,*
21: 2 then I w· utterly destroy their cities.
16 together, and I w· give them water.
22 we w· not turn into the fields, or into
22 w· not drink of the waters of the well:
22 we w· go along by the king's high way,
22: 8 I w· bring you word again, as the Lord
17 For I w· promote thee unto very great
17 I w· do whatsoever thou sayest unto
19 what the Lord w· say unto me more.
34 displease thee, I w· get me back again.
23: 3 Stand by thy burnt offering, and I w· go:
3 the Lord w· come to meet me:
3 whatever he sheweth me I w· tell thee.
27 I w· bring thee unto another place;
27 it w· please God that thou mayest
24:13 what the Lord saith, that w· I speak?
14 I w· advertise thee what this people
32:15 he w· yet again leave them in the
16 We w· build sheepfolds here for our
17 But we ourselves w· go ready armed
18 We w· not return unto our houses,
19 For we w· not inherit with them on
20 said unto them, If ye w· do this thing,
20 ye w· go armed before the Lord to war,
21 w· go all of you armed over Jordan
23 But if ye w· not do so, behold, ye have
23 and be sure your sin w· find you out.
25 w· do as my lord commandeth.
27 thy servants w· pass over, every man
29 Reuben w· pass with you over Jordan,
30 But if they w· not pass over with you
31 said unto thy servants, so w· we do.
32 w· pass over armed before the Lord
33:55 if ye w· not drive out the inhabitants
De 1:13 and I w· make them rulers over you.
17 you, bring it unto me, and I w· hear it.
22 We w· send men before us, and they*
36 to him w· I give the land that he hath
39 and unto them w· I give it, and they
41 we w· go up and fight, according to all
2: 5 for I w· not give you of their land, no,
9 for I w· not give thee of their land
19 for I w· not give thee of the land of the
25 This day w· I begin to put the dread
27 land: I w· go along by the high way,
27 I w· neither turn unto the right hand
28 only I w· pass through on my feet;
3: 2 for I w· deliver him, and all his people,
4:10 I w· make them hear my words, that
31 he w· not forsake thee, neither destroy

De 5:11 Lord w· not hold them guiltless that
25 for this great fire w· consume us: if we
27 unto thee; and we w· hear it, and do it.
31 and I w· speak unto thee all the
7: 4 For they w· turn away thy son from
4 so w· the anger of the Lord be kindled
10 he w· not be slack to him that hateth
10 him, he w· repay him to his face.
13 And he w· love thee, and bless thee,
13 he w· also bless the fruit of thy womb,
15 the Lord w· take away from thee all
15 and w· put none of the evil diseases
15 w· lay them upon all them that hate
16 for that w· be a snare unto thee.
20 God w· send the hornet among them,
22 thy God w· put out those nations
9:14 I w· make of thee a nation mightier
10: 2 I w· write on the tables the words
11:14 I w· give you the rain of your land
15 I w· send grass in thy fields for thy
23 w· the Lord drive out all these
28 if ye w· not obey the commandments
12:20 I w· eat flesh, because thy soul
30 their gods? even so w· I do likewise.
15:16 I w· not go away from thee; because
17:12 man that w· do presumptuously, and*
12 w· not hearken unto the priest that*
14 I w· set a king over me, like as all the
18:15 God w· raise up unto thee a Prophet
18 I w· raise them up a Prophet from
18 and w· put my words in his mouth;
19 w· not hearken unto my words
19 in my name, I w· require it of him.
20:12 if it w· make no peace with thee,
12 w· make war against thee, then thou
21:14 shalt let her go whither she w·; 5315
18 w· not obey the voice of his father,
18 him, w· not hearken unto them.
20 rebellious, he w· not obey our voice;
23:21 thy God w· surely require it of thee;
25: 7 w· not perform the duty of my 14
9 w· not build up his brother's house.*
28: 1 thy God w· set thee on high above all
27 w· smite thee with the botch of Egypt,
55 that he w· not give to any of them
59 Lord w· make thy plagues wonderful,
60 he w· bring upon thee all the diseases
61 them w· the Lord bring upon thee,
63 so the Lord w· rejoice over you
29:20 The Lord w· not spare him, but then
30: 3 Lord thy God w· turn thy captivity,
3 w· return and gather thee from all
4 from thence w· the Lord thy God
4 and from thence w· he fetch thee:
5 thy God w· bring thee into the land
5 he w· do thee good, and multiply thee
6 the Lord...w· circumcise thine heart,
7 God w· put all these curses upon thine
9 Lord thy God w· make thee plenteous
9 for the Lord w· again rejoice over thee
31: 3 thy God, he w· go over before thee,
3 and he w· destroy these nations from
6 he w· not fail thee, nor forsake thee.
8 he w· be with thee, he w· not fail thee.
16 and this people w· rise up, and go
16 and w· forsake me, and break my
17 I w· forsake them, and I w· hide my
17 so that they w· say in that day, Are
18 I w· surely hide my face in that day
20 then w· they turn unto other gods,
23 unto them: and I w· be with thee.
29 after my death ye w· utterly corrupt
29 evil w· befall you in the latter days;
29 because ye w· do evil in the sight of
32: 1 ear, O ye heavens, and I w· speak;
3 I w· publish the name of the Lord:
7 ask thy father, and he w· shew thee;
7 thy elders, and they w· tell thee.
20 he said, I w· hide my face from them,
20 I w· see what their end shall be:
21 I w· move them to jealousy with those
21 I w· provoke them to anger with a
23 I w· heap mischiefs upon them;
23 I w· spend mine arrows upon them.
24 I w· also send the teeth of beasts upon
41 I w· render vengeance to mine
41 and w· reward them that hate me.
42 I w· make mine arrows drunk with
43 for he w· avenge the blood of his
43 and w· render vengeance to his
43 w· be merciful unto his land, and to
33:16 for the good w· of him that dwell in 7522
34: 4 saying, I w· give it unto thy seed: I
Jos 1: 5 was with Moses, so I w· be with thee:
5 I w· not fail thee, nor forsake thee.
16 that thou commandest us we w· do,
16 thou sendest us, we w· go.
17 things, so w· we hearken unto thee:
18 and w· not hearken unto thy words*
2:12 that ye w· also shew kindness unto
13 that ye w· save alive my father, and
14 we w· deal kindly and truly with thee.
17 We w· be blameless of this thine oath
19 upon his head, and we w· be guiltless:
20 then we w· be quit of thine oath
3: 5 the Lord w· do wonders among you.
7 This day w· I begin to magnify thee in
7 I was with Moses, so I w· be with thee.
10 and that he w· without fail drive out
7:12 neither w· I be with you any more,
8: 5 with me, w· approach unto the city:
5 the first, that we w· flee before them,
6 (For they w· come out after us) till we
6 for they w· say, They flee before us, as
6 first: therefore we w· flee before them.
7 the Lord your God w· deliver it into

Jos 8:18 Ai; for I w· give it into thy hand.
9:20 This we w· do to them;
20 we w· even let them live, lest *
11: 6 about this time w· I deliver them up
13: 6 w· I drive out from before the children
14:12 if so be the Lord w· be with me, then I
15:16 w· I give Achsah my daughter to wife.
18: 4 I w· send them, and they shall rise,
22:18 it w· be, seeing ye rebel to day against
18 to morrow he w· be wroth with the
23:13 Lord your God w· no more drive out
24:15 choose you this day whom ye w· serve;
15 and my house, we w· serve the Lord.
18 therefore w· we serve the Lord;
19 he w· not forgive your transgressions
20 then he w· turn and do you hurt, and
21 Nay; but we w· serve the Lord.
24 God w· we serve, and his voice w· we
J'g 1: 3 I likewise w· go with thee unto thy lot
12 to him w· I give Achsah my daughter
24 the city, and we w· shew thee mercy.
2: 1 I w· never break my covenant with
3 I w· not drive them out from before
21 w· not henceforth drive out any from
22 they w· keep the way of the Lord
4: 7 And I w· draw unto thee to the river
7 and I w· deliver him into thine hand.
8 If thou wilt go with me, then I w· go:
8 wilt not go with me, then I w· not go.
9 And she said, I w· surely go with thee:
22 I w· shew thee the man whom thou
5: 3 I, even I, w· sing unto the Lord;
3 I w· sing praise to the Lord God of
6:16 Surely I w· be with thee, and thou
18 said, I w· tarry until thou come again.
31 W· ye plead for Baal? w· ye save him?
31 he that w· plead for him, let him be put
37 I w· put a fleece of wool in the floor;
39 me, and I w· speak but this once:
7: 4 and I w· try them for thee there:
7 men that lapped w· I save you,
8: 7 I w· tear your flesh with the thorns of
9 in peace, I w· break down this tower.
23 unto them, I w· not rule over you,
25 answered, We w· willingly give
10:13 wherefore I w· deliver you no more.
18 What man is he that w· begin to fight
11:24 from before us, them w· we possess.
31 I w· offer it up for a burnt offering.
12: 1 w· burn thine house upon thee with
13:16 detain me, I w· not eat of thy bread:
14:12 I w· now put forth a riddle unto you:*
12 I w· give you thirty sheets and thirty
15: 1 I w· go in to my wife into the chamber.
7 done this, yet w· I be avenged of you,
7 avenged of you, and after...I w· cease.
12 ye w· not fall upon me yourselves.
13 but we w· bind thee fast, and deliver
13 hand: but surely we w· not kill thee.
16: 5 we w· give thee every one of us eleven
17 then my strength w· go from me,
20 I w· go out as at other times before,
17: 3 therefore I w· restore it unto thee.
10 I w· give thee ten shekels of silver by
19:12 We w· not turn aside hither into the
12 of Israel; we w· pass over to Gibeah.
24 them I w· bring out now, and humble
20: 8 We w· not any of us go to his tent,
8 neither w· we any of us turn into his
9 the thing which we w· do to Gibeah;
9 Gibeah; we w· go up by lot against it;
10 And we w· take ten men of an hundred
21: 7 we w· not give them of our daughters
22 complain, that we w· say unto them,
Ru 1:10 we w· return with thee unto thy people.
11 my daughters: why w· ye go with me?
16 for whither thou goest, I w· go: and
16 and where thou lodgest, I w· lodge:
17 w· I die, and there w· I be buried:
3: 4 and he w· tell thee what thou shalt do.
5 All that thou sayest unto me I w· do.
11 I w· do to thee all that thou requirest:
13 if he w· perform unto thee the
13 but if he w· not do the part of a 2654
13 then w· I do the part of a kinsman to
18 thou know how the matter w· fall:
18 for the man w· not be in rest, until he
4: 4 thee. And he said, I w· redeem it.
1Sa 1:11 then I w· give him unto the Lord all
22 I w· not go up until the child be
22 and then I w· bring him, that he may
2: 9 He w· keep the feet of his saints, and
15 he w· not have sodden flesh of thee,
16 now; and if not, I w· take it by force.
30 for them that honour me I w· honour,
31 days come, that I w· cut off thine arm,
35 And I w· raise me up a faithful priest,
35 I w· build him a sure house; and he
3:11 Behold, I w· do a thing in Israel,
12 I w· perform against Eli all things
12 when I begin, I w· also make an end.
13 him that I w· judge his house for ever
6: 5 peradventure he w· lighten his hand
7: 3 he w· deliver you out of the hand of the
5 and I w· pray for you unto the Lord.
8 he w· save us out of the hand of the
8:11 This w· be the manner of the king that
11 w· take your sons, and appoint them
12 he w· appoint him captains over
12 w· set them to ear his ground, and to
13 he w· take your daughters to be
14 And he w· take your fields, and your
15 And he w· take the tenth of your seed,
16 And he w· take your menservants,
17 He w· take the tenth of your sheep:
18 the Lord w· not hear you in that day.

1Sa 8:19 Nay; but we *w*' have a king over us;
9: 8 *w*' I give to the man of God, to tell us
13 the people *w*' not eat until he come,
16 I *w*' send thee a man out of the land of
19 to day, and to morrow I *w*' let thee go,
19 *w*' tell thee all that is in thine heart.
10: 2 and they *w*' say unto thee, The asses
4 they *w*' salute thee, and give thee two
6 Spirit of the Lord *w*' come upon thee,
8 I *w*' come down unto thee, to offer
11: 1 with us, and we *w*' serve thee.
2 condition *w*' I make a covenant with
3 to save us, we *w*' come out to thee.
10 To morrow we *w*' come out unto you,
12: 3 there with? and I *w*' restore it you.
10 of our enemies, and we *w*' serve thee.
14 If ye *w*' fear the Lord, and serve him,
15 ye *w*' not obey the voice of the Lord,
16 the Lord *w*' do before your eyes.
17 I *w*' call unto the Lord, and he shall
22 the Lord *w*' not forsake his people
23 I *w*' teach you the good and the right
13:12 The Philistines *w*' come down now
14: 6 may be that the Lord *w*' work for us:
8 we *w*' pass over unto these men,
8 we *w*' discover ourselves unto them.
9 then we *w*' stand still in our place,
9 and *w*' not go up unto them.
10 Come up unto us; then we *w*' go up:
12 up to us, and we *w*' shew you a thing.
40 my son *w*' be on the other side.
15:16 I *w*' tell thee what the Lord hath said
26 unto Saul, I *w*' not return with thee:
29 also the Strength of Israel *w*' not lie
16: 1 go, I *w*' send thee to Jesse the
2 can I go? If Saul hear it, he *w*' kill me.
3 I *w*' shew thee what thou shalt do:
11 for we *w*' not sit down till he come
17: 9 kill me, then *w*' we be your servants:
25 the king *w*' enrich him with great
25 and *w*' give him his daughters,
32 thy servant *w*' go and fight with this
37 he *w*' deliver me out of the hand of
44 and I *w*' give thy flesh unto the fowls
46 This day *w*' the Lord deliver thee into
46 I *w*' smite thee, and take thine head
46 and I *w*' give the carcases of the host
47 and he *w*' give you into our hands.
18:11 I *w*' smite David...to the wall with it.
17 Merab, her *w*' I give thee to wife:
21 I *w*' give him her, that she may be a
19: 3 I *w*' go out and stand beside my father
3 I *w*' commune with my father of thee;
3 and what I see, that *w*' I tell thee.
20: 2 my father *w*' do nothing either great*
2 but that he *w*' shew it me: and why*
4 desireth, I *w*' even do it for thee.
13 I *w*' shew it thee, and send thee away.*
18 missed, because thy seat *w*' be empty.
20 I *w*' shoot three arrows on the side
21 I *w*' send a lad, saying, Go, find out
22: 3 till I know what God *w*' do for me.
7 *w*' the son of Jesse give every one
23: 4 I *w*' deliver the Philistines into thine
11 *W*' the men of Keilah deliver me up
11 *w*' Saul come down, as thy servant
11 And the Lord said, He *w*' come down.
12 *W*' the men of Keilah deliver me and
12 the Lord said, They *w*' deliver thee up.
23 the certainty, and I *w*' go with you:
23 I *w*' search him out throughout all the
24: 4 I *w*' deliver thine enemy into thine
10 I *w*' not put forth mine hand against
19 enemy, *w*' he let him go well away?
25: 8 young men, and they *w*' shew thee.
28 *w*' certainly make my lord a sure
26: 6 Who *w*' go down with me to Saul
6 Abishai said, I *w*' go down with thee.
8 I *w*' not smite him the second time.
21 for I *w*' no more do thee harm,
27:11 and so *w*' be his manner all the while*
28: 2 *w*' I make thee keeper of mine head
19 the Lord *w*' also deliver Israel with
23 he refused, and said, I *w*' not eat.
30:15 I *w*' bring thee down to this company.
22 we *w*' not give them ought of the spoil
24 who *w*' hearken unto you in this
2Sa 2: 6 I also *w*' requite you this kindness,
26 it *w*' be bitterness in the latter end?
3:13 Well; I *w*' make a league with thee:
18 I *w*' save my people Israel out of the
21 I *w*' arise and go, and *w*' gather all
5:19 I *w*' doubtless deliver the Philistines
6:21 therefore *w*' I play before the Lord.
22 I *w*' yet be more vile than thus, and
22 *w*' be base in mine own sight:
7:10 I *w*' appoint a place for my people
10 *w*' plant them, that they may dwell
11 that he *w*' make thee an house.
12 I *w*' set up thy seed after thee,
12 and I *w*' establish his kingdom.
13 and I *w*' stablish the throne of his
14 I *w*' be his father, and he shall be my
14 I *w*' chasten him with the rod of men,
27 saying, I *w*' build thee an house:
9: 7 for I *w*' surely shew thee kindness
7 *w*' restore thee all the land of Saul
10: 2 I *w*' shew kindness unto Hanun
11 thee, then *w*' I come and help thee.
11:11 soul liveth, I *w*' not do this thing.
12 and to morrow I *w*' let thee depart.
12:11 I *w*' raise up evil against thee out of
11 I *w*' take thy wives before thine eyes,
12 I *w*' do this thing before all Israel,
18 how *w*' he then vex himself, if we tell
22 whether God *w*' be gracious to me,

2Sa 13:13 for he *w*' not withhold me from thee.
14: 7 and we *w*' destroy the heir also: *
8 and I *w*' give charge concerning thee.
15 said, I will now speak unto the king;
15 that the king *w*' perform the request
16 For the king *w*' hear, to deliver his
17 the Lord thy God *w*' be with thee.*
15: 8 Jerusalem, then *w*' I serve the Lord.
21 even there also *w*' thy servant be.
25 he *w*' bring me again, and shew me
28 I *w*' tarry in the plain of the
34 Absalom, I *w*' be thy servant, O king;
34 so *w*' I now also be thy servant:
16:12 that the Lord *w*' look on my affliction,
12 that the Lord *w*' requite me good
18 his *w*' I be, and with him *w*' I abide.
19 presence, so *w*' I be in thy presence.
17: 1 and I *w*' arise and pursue after David
2 *w*' come upon him while he is weary
2 handed, and *w*' make him afraid:
2 flee; and I *w*' smite the king only:
3 And I *w*' bring back all the people
8 and *w*' not lodge with the people.
9 and it *w*' come to pass, when some of
9 that whosoever heareth it *w*' say,
12 and we *w*' light upon him as the dew
13 and we *w*' draw it into the river,
18: 2 I *w*' surely go forth with you myself
3 we flee away, they *w*' not care for us;
3 if half of us die, *w*' they care for us:
4 them, What seemeth you best I *w*' do.
19: 7 *w*' not tarry one with thee this night:
7 *w*' be worse unto thee than all the evil
26 I *w*' saddle me an ass, that I may ride
33 I *w*' feed thee with me in Jerusalem.
36 servant *w*' go a little way over Jordan*
38 I *w*' do to him that which shall seem
38 require of me, that *w*' I do for thee.
20:21 only, and I *w*' depart from the city.
21: 4 We *w*' have no silver nor gold of Saul,*
4 ye shall say, that *w*' I do for you.
6 we *w*' hang them up unto the Lord
6 And the king said, I *w*' give them.
22: 3 God of my rock; in him *w*' I trust:
4 I *w*' call on the Lord, who is worthy
29 and the Lord *w*' lighten my darkness.
50 Therefore I *w*' give thanks unto thee,
50 and I *w*' sing praises unto thy name.
24:24 I *w*' surely buy it of thee at a price:
24 neither *w*' I offer burnt offerings
1Ki 1: 5 himself, saying, I *w*' be a king:
14 I also *w*' come in after thee,
30 even so *w*' I certainly do this day.
51 that he *w*' not slay his servant with
52 If he *w*' shew himself a worthy man,*
2: 8 I *w*' not put thee to death with the
17 king, (for he *w*' not say thee nay,)
18 I *w*' speak for thee unto the king.
20 mother: for I *w*' not say thee nay.
26 I *w*' not at this time put thee to death,
30 And he said, Nay; but I *w*' die here.
38 king hath said, so *w*' thy servant do.
3:14 did walk, then I *w*' lengthen thy days.
5: 5 whom I *w*' set upon thy throne in thy
6 thee *w*' I give hire for thy servants
8 I *w*' do all thy desire concerning
9 I *w*' convey them by sea in floats unto
9 *w*' cause them to be discharged there,
6:12 *w*' I perform my word with thee,
13 *w*' dwell among the children of Israel,
13 and *w*' not forsake my people Israel.
8:27 *w*' God indeed dwell on the earth?
9: 5 I *w*' establish the throne of thy
6 *w*' not keep my commandments and*
7 *w*' I cut off Israel out of the land
7 my name, *w*' I cast out of my sight;
11: 2 *w*' turn away your heart after their
11 I *w*' surely rend the kingdom from
11 thee, and *w*' give it to thy servant.
12 I *w*' not do it for David thy father's
12 I *w*' rend it out of the hand of thy son.
13 I *w*' not rend away all the kingdom;
13 *w*' give one tribe to thy son for David
31 I *w*' rend the kingdom out of the hand
31 and *w*' give ten tribes to thee.
34 I *w*' not take the whole kingdom out
34 I *w*' make him prince all the days of
35 I *w*' take the kingdom out of his son's
35 *w*' give it unto thee, even ten tribes.
36 And unto his son *w*' I give one tribe,
37 I *w*' take thee, and thou shalt reign
38 I *w*' be with thee, and build thee a
38 David, and *w*' give Israel unto thee.
39 I *w*' for this afflict the seed of David,
12: 4 us, lighter, and we *w*' serve thee.
7 they *w*' be thy servants for ever.
11 heavy yoke, I *w*' add to your yoke:
11 but I *w*' chastise you with scorpions.
14 heavy, and I *w*' add to your yoke:
14 but I *w*' chastise you with scorpions.
13: 7 thyself, and I *w*' give thee a reward.
8 thine house, I *w*' not go with thee,
8, 16 neither *w*' I eat bread nor drink
14:10 I *w*' bring evil upon the house of
10 *w*' cut off from Jeroboam him that
10 *w*' take away the remnant of the
16: 3 *w*' take away the posterity of Baasha,
3 *w*' make thy house like the house
18: 1 and I *w*' send rain upon the earth.
15 I *w*' surely shew myself unto him to
23 I *w*' dress the other bullock, and lay
24 I *w*' call on the name of the Lord:
19:20 mother, and then I *w*' follow thee.
20: 6 I *w*' send my servants unto thee to
9 for to thy servants at first I *w*' do:
13 I *w*' deliver it into thine hand this day;

1Ki 20:22 king of Syria *w*' come up against thee.
25 we *w*' fight against them in the plain,
28 *w*' I deliver all this great multitude
31 peradventure he *w*' save thy life.
34 took from thy father, I *w*' restore;
34 *w*' send thee away with this covenant.
21: 2 I *w*' give thee for it a better vineyard
2 *w*' give thee the worth of it in money.
4 I *w*' not give thee the inheritance of
6 I *w*' give thee another vineyard for it:
6 I *w*' not give thee my vineyard.
7 I *w*' give thee the vineyard of Naboth
21 Behold, I *w*' bring evil upon thee,
21 and *w*' take thy posterity, and
21 and *w*' cut off from Ahab him that
22 *w*' make thine house like the house
29 I *w*' not bring the evil in his days:
29 in his son's day *w*' I bring the evil
22:14 the Lord saith to me, that *w*' I speak.
21 Lord, and said, I *w*' persuade him.
22 I *w*' go forth, and I *w*' be a lying spirit
30 I *w*' disguise myself, and enter into
2Ki 2: 2 thy soul liveth, I *w*' not leave thee.
3 Lord *w*' take away thy master from
4 as thy soul liveth, I *w*' not leave thee.
5 Lord *w*' take away thy master from
6 as thy soul liveth, I *w*' not leave thee.
3: 7 he said, I *w*' go up: I am as thou art,
18 *w*' deliver the Moabites also into your
4:30 as thy soul liveth, I *w*' not leave thee.
5: 5 I *w*' send a letter unto the king of
11 He *w*' surely come out to me, and
16 whom I stand, I *w*' receive none.
17 servant *w*' henceforth offer neither
20 I *w*' run after him, and take somewhat
6: 3 And he answered, I will go.
11 *W*' ye not shew me which of us is for
19 I *w*' bring you to the man whom ye
28 and we *w*' eat my son to morrow.
7: 4 We *w*' enter into the city, then the
9 light, some mischief *w*' come upon us:*
12 I *w*' now shew you what the Syrians
9: 8 I *w*' cut off from Ahab him that
9 I *w*' make the house of Ahab like the
26 I *w*' requite thee in this plat, saith
10: 5 and *w*' do all that thou shalt bid us;
5 we *w*' not make any king: do thou
6 if ye *w*' hearken unto my voice, take
18:14 which thou puttest on me *w*' I bear.
21 *w*' go into his hand, and pierce it:
23 I *w*' deliver thee two thousand horses,
30 The Lord *w*' surely deliver us, and
32 you saying, The Lord *w*' deliver us.
19: 4 thy God *w*' hear all the words of
4 *w*' reprove the words which the Lord
7 I *w*' send a blast upon him, and he
7 I *w*' cause him to fall by the sword in
23 and *w*' cut down the tall cedar trees
23 I *w*' enter into the lodgings of his
28 I *w*' put my hook in thy nose,
28 I *w*' turn thee back by the way by
34 For I *w*' defend this city, to save it,
20: 5 thy tears: behold, I *w*' heal thee:
6 I *w*' add unto thy days fifteen years;
6 I *w*' deliver thee and this city out of
6 I *w*' defend this city for mine own
8 be the sign that the Lord *w*' heal me,
9 Lord *w*' do the thing he hath spoken:
21: 4 In Jerusalem *w*' I put my name.
7 of Israel, *w*' I put my name for ever:
8 Neither *w*' I make the feet of Israel
8 if they *w*' observe to do according to
13 I *w*' stretch over Jerusalem the line of
13 I *w*' wipe Jerusalem as a man wipeth
14 I *w*' forsake the remnant of mine
22:16 I *w*' bring evil upon this place, and
20 I *w*' gather thee unto thy fathers,
20 evil which I *w*' bring upon this place.
23:27 I *w*' remove Judah also out of my
27 *w*' cast off this city Jerusalem which
1Ch 12:19 He *w*' fall to his master Saul to the
14:10 I *w*' deliver them into thine hand.
16:18 Unto thee *w*' I give the land of Canaan,
17: 9 I *w*' ordain a place for my people
9 and *w*' plant them, and they shall
10 I *w*' subdue all thine enemies.
10 that the Lord *w*' build thee an house.
11 that I *w*' raise up thy seed after thee,
11 and I *w*' establish his kingdom.
12 and I *w*' stablish his throne for ever.
13 I *w*' be his father, and he shall be my
13 I *w*' not take my mercy away from
14 I *w*' settle him in mine house and in
19: 2 I *w*' shew kindness unto Hanun the
12 strong for thee, then I *w*' help thee.
21: 3 *w*' he be a cause of trespass to Israel?
24 I *w*' verily buy it for the full price:
24 I *w*' not take that which is thine for
22: 5 I *w*' therefore now make preparation
9 I *w*' give him rest from all his enemies
9 I *w*' give peace and quietness unto
10 be my son, and I *w*' be his father;
10 and I *w*' establish the throne of his
28: 6 to be my son, and I *w*' be his father.
7 I *w*' establish his kingdom for ever,
9 seek him, he *w*' be found of thee;
9 forsake him, he *w*' cast thee off for
20 God, even my God *w*' be with thee;*
20 he *w*' not fail thee, nor forsake thee,
21 *w*' be wholly at thy commandment.
2Ch 1:12 I *w*' give thee riches, and wealth, and
2:10 I *w*' give to thy servants, the hewers
16 *w*' cut wood out of Lebanon, as much
16 *w*' bring it to thee in floats by sea
6:18 *w*' God in every deed dwell with men
7:14 ways, then *w*' I hear from heaven.

2Ch 7:14 and w· forgive their sin,
14 and w· heal their land.
18 w· I stablish the throne of thy
20 w· I pluck them up by the roots out of
20 my name, w· I cast out of my sight,
20 and w· make it to be a proverb and a
10: 4 he put upon us, and we w· serve thee.
11 upon you, I w· put more to your yoke:
11 but I w· chastise you with scorpions.
14 your yoke heavy, but I w· add thereto:
14 but I w· chastise you with scorpions.
12: 7 therefore I w· not destroy them,
7 I w· grant them some deliverance;
15: 2 if ye seek him, he w· be found of you;
2 if ye forsake him, he w· forsake you.
18: 3 and we w· be with thee in the war.
5 for God w· deliver it into the king's*
13 what my God saith, that w· I speak.
20 the Lord, and said, I w· entice him.
21 I w· go out, and be a lying spirit
29 Jehoshaphat, I w· disguise myself,
29 and w· go to the battle; but put thou*
20:17 them: for the Lord w· be with you.*
21:14 a great plague w· the Lord smite thy
28:23 them, therefore w· I sacrifice to them,
30: 6 he w· return to the remnant of you,*
9 w· not turn away his face from you,
33: 7 of Israel, w· I put my name for ever:
8 Neither w· I any more remove the foot
8 so that they w· take heed to do all that
34:24 I w· bring evil upon this place,
28 I w· gather thee to thy fathers,
28 evil that I w· bring upon this place,
Ezr 4: 3 together w· build unto the Lord God
13 then w· they not pay toll, tribute,
7:18 that do after the w· of your God. 7470
26 And whosoever w· not do the law of
10: 4 we also w· be with thee: be of good*
Ne 1: 8 I w· scatter you abroad among the
9 yet w· I gather them from thence,
9 w· bring them unto the place that
2:19 ye do? w· ye rebel against the king?
20 The God of heaven, he w· prosper us;
20 we his servants w· arise and build:
4: 2 Jews? w· they fortify themselves?
2 w· they sacrifice? w· they make an
2 w· they revive the stones out of the
12 return unto us they w· be upon you.*
5: 8 w· ye even sell your brethren? or shall*
12 We w· restore them, and w· require
12 of them; so w· we do as thou sayest.
6:10 temple: for they w· come to slay thee;
10 in the night w· they come to slay thee.
10:39 w· not forsake the house of our God.
13:21 ye do so again, I w· lay hands on you.
Es 3: 9 I w· pay ten thousand talents of silver
4:16 and my maidens w· fast likewise;
16 so w· I go in unto the king, which is not
5: 8 w· do to morrow as the king hath said.
7: 8 W· he force the queen also before me
Job 1:11 hath, and he w· curse thee to thy face.
2: 4 that a man hath w· he give for his life.
5 flesh, and he w· curse thee to thy face.
5: 1 if there be any that w· answer thee;
6:24 Teach me, and I w· hold my tongue:
7:11 Therefore I w· not refrain my mouth;
11 I w· speak in the anguish of my spirit;
11 I w· complain in the bitterness of my
8:20 God w· not cast away a perfect man,
20 neither w· he help the evil doers:
9: 3 If he w· contend with him, he cannot*
12 who w· say unto him, What doest
13 If God w· not withdraw his anger,
18 w· not suffer me to take my breath,
23 w· laugh at the trial of the innocent.
27 If I say, I w· forget my complaint,
27 I w· leave off my heaviness,
10: 1 I w· leave my complaint upon myself;
1 I w· speak in the bitterness of my soul.
2 I w· say unto God, Do not condemn
15 righteous, yet w· I not lift up my head.
11:11 also; w· he not then consider it? *
13: 7 W· ye speak wickedly for God?
8 W· ye accept his person? w· ye
10 He w· surely reprove you, if ye do
13 speak, and let come on me what w·.
15 Though he slay me, yet w· I trust him:‡
15 but I w· maintain mine own ways
19 Who is he that w· plead with me?
20 then w· I not hide myself from thee.
22 Then call thou, and I w· answer:
14: 7 be cut down, that it w· sprout again,
7 tender branch thereof w· not cease.
9 through the scent of water it w· bud,
14 days of my appointed time w· I wait,*
15 Thou shalt call, and I w· answer thee:*
15:17 I w· shew thee, hear me; and that
17 that which I have seen I w· declare;
17: 3 is he that w· strike hands with me?
18: 2 How long w· it be ere ye make an end
2 mark, and afterwards we w· speak.
19: 2 How long w· ye vex my soul,
5 If indeed ye w· magnify yourselves
22: 4 W· he reprove thee for fear of thee?
4 w· he enter with thee into judgment?*
23: 6 W· he plead against me with his great*
24:25 who w· make me a liar, and make my
27: 5 w· not remove mine integrity from me.
6 I hold fast, and w· not let it go:
9 W· God hear his cry when trouble
10 W· he delight himself in the Almighty?
10 w· he always call upon God? *
11 I w· teach you by the hand of God:
11 with the Almighty w· I not conceal.
30:24 he w· not stretch out his hand to the
32:10 to me; I also w· shew mine opinion.

Job 32:14 neither w· I answer him with your
17 I said, I w· answer my part, I also
17 part, I also w· shew mine opinion.
20 I w· speak, that I may be refreshed:
20 I w· open my lips and answer.
33:12 I w· answer thee, that God is greater
26 and he w· be favourable unto him:*
26 w· render...man his righteousness.*
28 He w· deliver his soul from going *
31 hold thy peace, and I w· speak.
34:12 Yea, surely God w· not do wickedly,
12 w· the Almighty pervert judgment.
23 For he w· not lay upon man more than*
31 I w· not offend any more:
32 I have done iniquity, I w· do no more.
33 he w· recompense it, whether thou*
35: 3 What advantage w· it be unto thee?
4 I w· answer thee, and thy companions
13 Surely God w· not hear vanity,
13 neither w· the Almighty regard it.
36: 2 and I w· shew thee that I have yet to
3 I w· fetch my knowledge from afar,
3 w· ascribe righteousness to my Maker.
19 W· he esteem thy riches? no, not gold,
37: 4 he w· not stay them when his voice is*
23 in plenty of justice: he w· not afflict.
38: 3 for I w· demand of thee, and answer
39: 9 W· the unicorn be willing to serve
10 or w· he harrow the valleys after thee?
12 that he w· bring home thy seed,
40: 4 I w· lay mine hand upon my mouth.*
5 have I spoken; but I w· not answer:
5 twice; but I w· proceed no further.
7 I w· demand of thee, and declare thou
14 Then w· I also confess unto thee that
41: 3 W· he make many supplications unto
3 w· he speak soft words unto thee?
4 W· he make a covenant with thee?
12 I w· not conceal his parts, nor his
42: 4 Hear, I beseech thee, and I w· speak:
4 I w· demand of thee, and declare thou
8 for him w· I accept: lest I deal with
Ps 2: 7 I w· declare the decree: the Lord hath
3: 6 I w· not be afraid of ten thousands of
4: 2 w· ye turn my glory into shame?*
2 how long w· ye love vanity, and seek
3 the Lord w· hear when I call unto him.
6 that say, Who w· shew us any good?
8 I w· both lay me down in peace,
5: 2 and my God: for unto thee w· I pray.*
3 in the morning w· direct my prayer
3 my prayer unto thee, and w· look up.
6 the Lord w· abhor the bloody and*
7 I w· come unto thy house in the
7 and in thy fear w· I worship toward
6: 9 the Lord w· receive my prayer.
7:12 If he turn not, he w· whet his sword;
17 I w· praise the Lord according to his
17 w· sing praise to the name of the Lord
9: 1 I w· praise thee, O Lord, with my
1 I w· shew forth all thy marvellous
2 I w· be glad and rejoice in thee:
2 I w· sing praise to thy name, O thou
9 The Lord also w· be a refuge for the
10 thy name w· put their trust in thee:
14 Zion: I w· rejoice in thy salvation.
10: 4 countenance, w· not seek after God:
11 hideth his face; he w· never see it.
12: 4 said, With our tongue w· we prevail;
5 needy, now w· I arise, saith the Lord;
5 I w· set him in safety from him that
13: 6 I w· sing unto the Lord, because he
16: 4 offerings of blood w· I not offer,
7 I w· bless the Lord, who hath given
17:15 I w· behold thy face in righteousness:*
18: 1 I w· love thee, O Lord, my strength.*
2 my strength, in whom I w· trust;
3 I w· call upon the Lord, who is worthy
28 my God w· enlighten my darkness.
49 Therefore w· I give thanks unto thee,
20: 5 We w· rejoice in thy salvation, and in
5 name of our God we w· set up our
6 w· hear him from his holy heaven
7 w· remember the name of the Lord
21:13 so w· we sing and praise thy power.
22:22 I w· declare thy name unto my
22 of the congregation w· I praise thee.
25 I w· pay my vows before them that
23: 4 shadow of death, I w· fear no evil:
6 I w· dwell in the house of the Lord for
25: 8 w· he teach sinners in the way.
9 The meek w· he guide in judgment:
9 and the meek w· he teach his way.
14 and he w· shew them his covenant.
26: 4 neither w· I go in with dissemblers.
5 doers; and w· not sit with the wicked.
6 I w· wash mine hands in innocency:
6 so w· I compass thine altar, O Lord:
11 for me, I w· walk in mine integrity:
12 the congregations w· I bless the Lord.
27: 3 against me, in this w· I be confident.
4 of the Lord, that w· I seek after;
6 therefore w· I offer in his tabernacle
6 I w· sing, yea, I w· sing praises unto
8 unto thee, Thy face, Lord, w· I seek.
10 me, then the Lord w· take me up.
12 over unto the w· of mine enemies: 5315
28: 1 Unto thee w· I cry, O Lord my rock;
7 and with my song w· I praise him.
29:11 The Lord w· give strength unto his
11 Lord w· bless his people with peace.
30: 1 I w· extol thee, O Lord; for thou hast
12 I w· give thanks unto thee for ever.
31: 7 I w· be glad and rejoice in thy mercy:
32: 5 I w· confess my transgressions unto
8 I w· instruct thee and teach thee in

Ps 32: 8 go: I w· guide thee with mine eye.
34: 1 I w· bless the Lord at all times: his
11 I w· teach you the fear of the Lord.
35:18 I w· give thee thanks in the great
18 I w· praise thee among much people.
37:33 Lord w· not leave him in his hand,
38:18 For I w· declare mine iniquity;
18 iniquity; I w· be sorry for my sin.
39: 1 I said, I w· take heed to my ways, that
1 I w· keep my mouth with a bridle,
40: 8 I delight to do thy w·, O my God: 7522
41: 1 the Lord w· deliver him in time of
2 The Lord w· preserve him, and
2 him unto the w· of his enemies. 5315
3 Lord w· strengthen him upon the bed
42: 6 w· I remember thee from the land of*
8 Lord w· command his lovingkindness
9 I w· say unto God my rock, Why hast
43: 4 Then w· I go unto the altar of God,
4 upon the harp w· I praise thee, O God
44: 5 Through thee w· we push down our
5 through thy name w· we tread them
6 For I w· not trust in my bow, neither
45:17 w· make thy name to be remembered
46: 2 Therefore w· not we fear, though the
10 I w· be exalted among the heathen,
10 heathen, I w· be exalted in the earth.
48: 8 God w· establish it for ever. Selah.
14 w· be our guide even unto death.
49: 4 I w· incline mine ear to a parable:
4 I w· open my dark saying upon the
15 But God w· redeem my soul from
18 and men w· praise thee, when thou*
50: 7 Hear, O my people, and I w· speak;
7 Israel, and I w· testify against thee:
8 I w· not reprove thee for thy sacrifices
9 I w· take no bullock out of thy house,
13 W· I eat the flesh of bulls, or drink
15 w· deliver thee, and thou shalt glorify
21 but I w· reprove thee, and set them in
23 aright w· I shew the salvation of God.
51:13 w· I teach transgressors thy ways;
52: 9 I w· praise thee for ever, because thou
9 and I w· wait on thy name; for it is
54: 6 w· freely sacrifice unto thee:
6 I w· praise thy name, O Lord;
55:16 As for me, I w· call upon God; and the
17 at noon, w· I pray, and cry aloud:
23 their days; but I w· trust in thee.
56: 3 time I am afraid, I w· trust in thee.
4 In God I w· praise his word, in God I
4 I w· not fear what flesh can do unto
10 In God w· I praise his word:
10 in the Lord w· I praise his word.
11 I w· not be afraid what man can do
12 God: I w· render praises unto thee.
57: 1 of thy wings w· I make my refuge,
2 I w· cry unto God most high; unto
7 is fixed: I w· sing and give praise.
8 and harp: I myself w· awake early.
9 I w· praise thee, O Lord, among the
9 I w· sing unto thee among the nations.
58: 5 w· not hearken to the voice of *
59: 9 of his strength w· I wait upon thee:
16 but I w· sing of thy power; yea,
16 I w· sing aloud of thy mercy in the
17 Unto thee, O my strength, w· I sing:
60: 6 I w· rejoice, I w· divide Shechem, and
8 over Edom w· I cast out my shoe:
9 Who w· bring me into the strong city?
9 city? who w· lead me unto Edom?*
61: 2 end of the earth w· I cry unto thee,
4 I w· abide in thy tabernacle for ever:
4 I w· trust in the covert of thy wings.
8 So w· I sing praise unto thy name for
62: 3 How long w· ye imagine mischief
63: 1 art my God; early w· I seek thee:
4 Thus w· I bless thee while I live:
4 I w· lift up my hands in thy name.
7 the shadow of thy wings w· I rejoice.
66:13 I w· go into thy house with burnt
13 offerings: I w· pay thee my vows,
15 I w· offer unto thee burnt sacrifices of
15 rams: I w· offer bullocks with goats.
16 and I w· declare what he hath done
18 my heart, the Lord w· not hear me.
68:16 yea, the Lord w· dwell in it for ever.
22 said, I w· bring again from Bashan,
22 I w· bring my people again from the
69:30 I w· praise the name of God with a
30 w· magnify him with thanksgiving.
35 For God w· save Zion, and w· build
71:14 But I w· hope continually, and
14 and w· yet praise thee more and more.
16 I w· go in the strength of the Lord
16 I w·...mention of thy righteousness,
22 I w· also praise thee with the psaltery,
22 unto thee w· I sing with the harp,
73:15 If I say, I w· speak thus; behold, I
75: 2 the congregation I w· judge uprightly.
9 I w· declare for ever; I w· sing praises
10 horns of the wicked also w· I cut off;
77: 7 W· the Lord cast off for ever? and
7 w· he be favourable no more?
10 I w· remember the years of the right
11 I w· remember the works of the Lord:
11 I w· remember thy wonders of old.
12 I w· meditate also of all thy work,
78: 2 I w· open my mouth in a parable:
2 I w· utter dark sayings of old:
4 We w· not hide them from their
79:13 pasture w· give thee thanks for ever:
13 we w· shew forth thy praise to all
80:18 So w· not we go back from thee:
18 us, and we w· call upon thy name.
81: 8 people, and I w· testify unto thee:

Ps 81:10 open thy mouth wide, and I w' fill it.
82: 2 How long w' ye judge unjustly,
5 know not, neither w' they understand;*
84: 4 house: they w' be still praising thee.
11 the Lord w' give grace and glory:
11 no good thing w' he withhold from
85: 8 I w' hear what God the Lord w' speak:
8 for he w' speak peace unto his people,
86: 7 day of my trouble I w' call upon thee:
11 way, O Lord; I w' walk in thy truth:
12 I w' praise thee, O Lord my God,
12 I w' glorify thy name for evermore.
87: 4 I w' make mention of Rahab and
89: 1 I w' sing of the mercies of the Lord
1 w' I make known thy faithfulness
4 Thy seed w' I establish for ever,
23 And I w' beat down his foes before his
25 I w' set his hand also in the sea,
27 Also I w' make him my firstborn,
28 My mercy w' I keep for him for
32 Then w' I visit their transgression
33 my lovingkindness w' I not utterly
34 My covenant w' I not break,
35 holiness that I w' not lie unto David.
91: 2 I w' say of the Lord, He is my refuge
2 my God; in him w' I trust. *
14 upon me, therefore w' I deliver him:
14 I w' set him on high, because he hath
15 call upon me, and I w' answer him:
15 I w' be with him in trouble;
15 I w' deliver him, and honour him.
16 With long life w' I satisfy him,
92: 4 w' triumph in the works of thy hands.
94: 8 and ye fools, when w' ye be wise?
14 For the Lord w' not cast off his people,
14 neither w' he forsake his inheritance.
16 Who w' rise up for me against the
16 or who w' stand up for me against
95: 7 To day if ye w' hear his voice, *
101: 1 I w' sing of mercy and judgment:
1 unto thee, O Lord, w' I sing.
2 I w' behave myself wisely in a perfect
2 I w' walk within my house with a
3 I w' set no wicked thing before mine
4 I w' not know a wicked person.
5 his neighbour, him w' I cut off:
5 and a proud heart w' not I suffer.
8 I w' early destroy all the wicked
102: 17 He w' regard the prayer of the *
103: 9 He w' not always chide: neither
9 neither w' he keep his anger for ever.
104: 33 w' sing unto the Lord as long as I live:
33 I w' sing praise to my God while I have
34 be sweet: I w' be glad in the Lord.
105: 11 Unto thee w' I give the land of Canaan,
107: 43 is wise, and w' observe these things,*
108: 1 I w' sing and give praise, even with
2 and harp: I myself w' awake early.
3 I w' praise thee, O Lord, among the
3 and I w' sing praises unto thee
7 I w' rejoice, I w' divide Shechem,
9 over Edom w' I cast out my shoe;
9 my shoe; over Philistia w' I triumph.
10 Who w' bring me into the strong city?
10 who w' lead me into Edom? *
109: 30 I w' greatly praise the Lord with my
30 I w' praise him among the multitude.
110: 4 Lord hath sworn, and w' not repent,
111: 1 I w' praise the Lord with my whole
5 w' ever be mindful of his covenant.
112: 5 he w' guide his affairs with discretion.*
115: 12 he w' bless us; he w' bless the house
12 he w' bless the house of Aaron.
13 He w' bless them that fear the Lord,
18 But we w' bless the Lord from this
116: 2 therefore w' I call upon him as long
9 I w' walk before the Lord in the land
13 I w' take the cup of salvation, and call
14 I w' pay my vows unto the Lord now
17 I w' offer to thee the sacrifice of
17 and w' call upon the name of the Lord.
18 I w' pay my vows unto the Lord now
118: 6 The Lord is on my side; I w' not fear:
10 name of the Lord w' I destroy them.
11, 12 name of the Lord I w' destroy them.
19 I w' go into them, and I w' praise the
21 I w' praise thee: for thou hast heard
24 made; we w' rejoice and be glad in it.
28 Thou art my God, and I w' praise thee:
28 thou art my God, I w' exalt thee.
119: 7 I w' praise thee with uprightness
8 I w' keep thy statutes: O forsake me
15 I w' meditate in thy precepts,
16 I w' delight myself in thy statutes:
16 statutes: I w' not forget thy word.
32 I w' run the way of...commandments,
45 And I w' walk at liberty; for I seek
46 I w' speak of thy testimonies also
46 kings, and w' not be ashamed.
47 And I w' delight myself in thy
48 My hands also w' I lift up unto thy
48 and I w' meditate in thy statutes.
62 At midnight I w' rise to give thanks
69 but I w' keep thy precepts with my
74 They that fear thee w' be glad when*
78 but I w' meditate in thy precepts.
93 I w' never forget thy precepts:
95 but I w' consider thy testimonies.
106 I have sworn, and I w' perform it,*
106 w' keep thy righteous judgments.
115 for I w' keep the commandments of*
117 I w' have respect unto thy statutes*
134 of man: so w' I keep thy precepts.
145 me, O Lord: I w' keep thy statutes.
121: 1 I w' lift up mine eyes unto the hills,
3 He w' not suffer thy foot to be moved:

Ps 121: 3 he that keepeth thee w' not slumber.
122: 8 I w' now say, Peace be within thee.
9 the Lord our God I w' seek thy good.
132: 3 I w' not come into the tabernacle
4 I w' not give sleep to mine eyes,
7 We w' go into his tabernacles:
7 we w' worship at his footstool.
11 unto David; he w' not turn from it;
11 of thy body w' I set upon thy throne.
12 If thy children w' keep my covenant
14 here w' I dwell; for I have desired it.
15 I w' abundantly bless her provision:
15 I w' satisfy her poor with bread.
16 I w' also clothe her priest with
17 There w' I make the home of David
18 His enemies w' I clothe with shame:
135: 14 For the Lord w' judge his people,*
14 w' repent himself concerning his*
138: 1 I w' praise thee with my whole heart:
1 before the gods w' I sing praise unto
2 I w' worship toward thy holy temple,
8 Lord w' perfect that which concerneth
139: 14 I w' praise thee; for I am fearfully
140: 12 that the Lord w' maintain the cause
143: 10 Teach me to do thy w'; for thou 7522
144: 9 I w' sing a new song unto thee, O God
9 ten strings w' I sing praises unto thee.
145: 1 I w' extol thee, my God, O king;
1 and I w' bless thy name for ever and
2 Every day w' I bless thee; and I
2 and I w' praise thy name for ever and
5 I w' speak of the glorious honour
6 acts: and I w' declare thy greatness.
19 He w' fulfil the desire of them that
19 w' hear their cry, and w' save them.
20 but all the wicked w' he destroy.
146: 2 While I live w' I praise the Lord:
2 I w' sing praises unto my God while I
149: 4 w' beautify the meek with salvation.
Pr 1: 5 A wise man w' hear, *
5 and w' increase learning; *
22 ye simple ones, w' ye love simplicity?
23 I w' pour out my spirit unto you,
23 I w' make known my words unto you.
26 I also w' laugh at your calamity;
26 I w' mock when your fear cometh;
28 call upon me, but I w' not answer;
3: 28 come again, and to morrow I w' give;
6: 26 adulteress w' hunt for...precious life.*
34 w' not spare in the day of vengeance.
35 He w' not regard any ransom;
35 neither w' he rest content,
7: 20 w' come home at the day appointed.
8: 6 for I w' speak of excellent things;
21 and I w' fill their treasures.*
9: 8 a wise man, and he w' love thee.
9 to a wise man, and he w' be yet wiser:
9 man, and he w' increase in learning.
10: 3 The Lord w' not suffer the soul of the
8 in heart w' receive commandments:
12: 2 man of wicked devices w' he condemn.
14: 5 A faithful witness w' not lie:
5 but a false witness w' utter lies. *
15: 12 neither w' he go unto the wise.
25 The Lord w' destroy the house of the
25 w' establish the border of the widow.
16: 14 of death: but a wise man w' pacify it.
18: 14 a man w' sustain his infirmity;
19: 6 w' intreat the favour of the prince:
17 he hath given w' he pay him again.
24 and w' not so much as bring it to his
25 a scorner, and the simple w' beware:
25 and he w' understand knowledge.
20: 3 strife: but every fool w' be meddling.
4 The sluggard w' not plow by reason of
5 man of understanding w' draw it out.
6 Most men w' proclaim every one his
22 Say not thou, I w' recompense evil;
21: 1 he turneth it whithersoever he w'. 2654
22: 6 he is old, he w' not depart from it.
23 For the Lord w' plead their cause,
23: 9 he w' despise the wisdom of thy words,
35 shall I awake? I w' seek it yet again.
24: 29 w' do so to him as he hath done to me:
29 I w' render to the man according to
26: 27 rolleth a stone, it w' return upon him.*
27: 22 yet w' not his foolishness depart
28: 8 gather it for him that w' pity the poor.*
21 piece of bread that man w' transgress.*
29: 19 servant w' not be corrected by words:
19 he understand he w' not answer.
31: 12 She w' do him good and not evil all*
Ec 2: 1 Go to now, I w' prove thee with mirth,
4: 10 fall, the one w' lift up his fellow:
13 who w' no more be admonished. *3045
5: 12 abundance of the rich w' not suffer
7: 2 and the living w' lay it to his heart.
23 I w' be wise; but it was far from me.
10: 11 Surely the serpent w' bite without*
12 lips of a fool w' swallow up himself.
11: 9 God w' bring thee into judgment.
Ca 1: 4 Draw me, we w' run after thee: the
4 we w' be glad and rejoice in thee,
4 w' remember thy love more than wine:
11 We w' make thee borders of gold with
3: 2 I w' rise now, and go about the city in
2 I w' seek him whom my soul loveth:
4: 6 I w' get me to the mountain of myrrh,
6: 13 What w' ye see in the Shulamite?
7: 8 I said, I w' go up to the palm tree,
8 I w' take hold of the boughs thereof:
12 forth: there w' I give thee my loves.
8: 9 wall, we w' build upon her a palace of
9 w' inclose her with boards of cedar.
Isa 1: 5 ye w' revolt more and more: the
15 hands, I w' hide mine eyes from you;

Isa 1: 15 ye make many prayers, I w' not hear:
24 Ah, I w' ease me of mine adversaries,
25 I w' turn my hand upon thee, and
26 And I w' restore thy judges as at the
2: 3 and he w' teach us of his ways,
3 and we w' walk in his paths: for out
3: 4 I w' give children to be their princes,
7 swear, saying, I w' not be an healer;
14 Lord w' enter into judgment with the
17 the Lord w' smite with a scab the
17 and the Lord w' discover their secret
18 Lord w' take away the bravery of their
4: 1 We w' eat our own bread, and wear
5 And the Lord w' create upon every
5: 1 Now w' I sing my wellbeloved a song
5 I w' tell you what I w' do to my
5 I w' take away the hedge thereof, and
6 And I w' lay it waste: it shall not be
6 I w' also command the clouds that
26 And he w' lift up an ensign to the
26 and w' hiss unto them from the end of
6: 8 shall I send, and who w' go for us?
7: 9 If ye w' not believe, surely ye shall
12 I w' not ask, neither w' I tempt,
13 men, but w' ye weary my God also?
8: 17 I w' wait upon the Lord, that hideth
17 house of Jacob, and I w' look for him.
9: 7 of the Lord of hosts w' perform this.*
10 but we w' build with hewn stones:
10 but we w' change them into cedars.
14 the Lord w' cut off from Israel head
10: 3 And what w' ye do in the day of
3 from far? to whom w' ye flee for help?
3 and where w' ye leave your glory?
6 I w' send him against an hypocritical
6 of my wrath w' I give him a charge,
12 I w' punish the fruit of the stout heart
12: 1 shalt say, O Lord, I w' praise thee:
2 I w' trust, and not be afraid:
13: 11 And I w' punish the world for their
11 I w' cause the arrogancy of the proud
11 and w' lay low the haughtiness of the
12 I w' make a man more precious than
13 Therefore I w' shake the heavens, and
17 I w' stir up the Medes against them,
14: 1 For the Lord w' have mercy on Jacob,
1 and w' yet choose Israel, and set
13 thine heart, I w' ascend into heaven,
13 I w' exalt my throne above the stars of
13 I w' sit also upon the mount of the
14 I w' ascend above the heights of the
14 I w' be like the most High.
22 For I w' rise up against them, saith
23 I w' also make it a possession for the
23 I w' sweep it with the besom of
25 That I w' break the Assyrian in my
30 I w' kill thy root with famine, and he
15: 9 for I w' bring more upon Dimon, lions
16: 9 I w' bewail with the weeping of Jazer
9 I w' water thee with my tears, O
18: 4 Lord said unto me, I w' take my rest,
4 and I w' consider in my dwelling place
19: 2 I w' set the Egyptians against the
3 and I w' destroy the counsel thereof:
4 And the Egyptians w' I give over into
21: 12 if ye w' enquire, enquire ye: return,
22: 4 I w' weep bitterly, labour not to
17 Lord w' carry thee away with a
17 and w' surely cover thee.
18 He w' surely violently turn and toss
19 And I w' drive thee from thy station,
20 I w' call my servant Eliakim the son
21 I w' clothe him with thy robe, and
21 I w' commit thy government into his
22 the key...w' I lay upon his shoulder;
23 And I w' fasten him as a nail in a sure
23: 17 that the Lord w' visit Tyre, and she
25: 1 I w' exalt thee, I w' praise thy name;
7 he w' destroy in this mountain the
8 He w' swallow up death in victory;*
8 Lord God w' wipe away tears from off
9 waited for him, and he w' save us:
9 him, we w' be glad and rejoice in his
26: 1 salvation w' God appoint for walls and
9 spirit within me w' I seek thee early:
9 of the world w' learn righteousness.*
10 yet w' he not learn righteousness:
10 of uprightness w' he deal unjustly,
10 w' not behold the majesty of the Lord.
11 thy hand is lifted up, they w' not see:*
13 by thee only w' we make mention of
27: 3 keep it; I w' water it every moment:
3 hurt it, I w' keep it night and day.
11 them w' not have mercy on them,
11 formed them w' shew them no favour.
28: 11 another tongue w' he speak to this
17 Judgment also w' I lay to the line, and
28 he w' not ever be threshing it, nor
29: 2 Yet I w' distress Ariel, and there shall
3 I w' camp against thee round about,
3 and w' lay siege against thee with a
3 and I w' raise forts against thee.
14 I w' proceed to do a marvellous work
30: 6 they w' carry their riches upon the*
9 children that w' not hear the law of 14
16 said, No; for we w' flee upon horses;
16 We w' ride upon the swift; therefore;
18 And therefore w' the Lord wait, that
18 you, and therefore w' he be exalted,
19 he w' be very gracious unto thee at
19 he shall hear it, he w' answer thee.
32 and in battles of shaking w' he fight
31: 2 Yet he also is wise, and w' bring evil,
2 evil, and w' not call back his words:
2 but w' arise against the house of the
4 he w' not be afraid of their voice, nor

Isa 31: 5 so w· the Lord of hosts defend
5 defending also he w· deliver it; and
5 and passing over he w· preserve it.*
32: 6 For the vile person w· speak villany,
6 and his heart w· work iniquity, to
6 he w· cause the drink of the thirsty to*
33: 10 Now w· I arise, saith the Lord; now
10 w· I be exalted; now w· I lift up
21 Lord w· be unto us a place of broad
22 the Lord is our king; he w· save us.
35: 4 your God w· come with vengeance,
4 recompence; he w· come and save you.
36: 6 it w· go into his hand, and pierce it:
8 I w· give thee two thousand horses,
15 saying, The Lord w· surely deliver us;
18 you, saying, The Lord w· deliver us.
37: 4 Lord thy God w· hear the words of
4 and w· reprove the words which the
24 I w· cut down the tall cedars thereof,
24 I w· enter into the height of his border,
29 w· I put my hook in thy nose,
29 I w· turn thee back by the way by
38: 5 I w· add unto thy days fifteen years.
6 And I w· deliver thee and this city
6 Assyria: and I w· defend this city.
7 Lord w· do this thing that he hath
8 I w· bring again the shadow of the
12 he w· cut me off with pining sickness:
13 as a lion, so w· he break all my bones:*
20 we w· sing my songs to the stringed
40: 10 the Lord God w· come with strong
18 To whom then w· ye liken God? or
18 or what likeness w· ye compare unto
20 chooseth a tree that w· not rot;
25 To whom then w· ye liken me, or shall
41: 10 I w· strengthen thee;
10 yea, I w· help thee;
10 I w· uphold thee with the right hand of
13 Lord thy God w· hold thy right hand,
13 unto thee, Fear not; I w· help thee.
14 I w· help thee, saith the Lord, and thy
15 I w· make thee a new sharp threshing
17 I the Lord w· hear them, I the God of
17 God of Israel w· not forsake them.
18 I w· open rivers in high places, and
18 I w· make the wilderness a pool of
19 I w· plant in the wilderness the cedar,
19 I w· set in the desert the fir tree, and
27 I w· give to Jerusalem one that
42: 6 w· hold thine hand, and w· keep thee,
8 my glory w· I not give to another,
14 now w· I cry like a travailing woman;
14 I w· destroy and devour at once.
15 I w· make waste mountains and hills,
15 and I w· make the rivers islands, and
15 islands, and I w· dry up the pools.
16 I w· bring the blind by a way that
16 I w· lead them in paths that they have
16 I w· make darkness light before them,
16 These things w· I do unto them, and
21 he w· magnify the law, and make it*
23 Who among you w· give ear to this?
23 who w· hearken and hear for the time
43: 2 the waters, I w· be with thee;
4 therefore w· I give men for thee, and
5 I w· bring thy seed from the east,
6 I w· say to the north, Give up; and to
13 hand: I w· work, and who shall let it?
19 Behold, I w· do a new thing; now it
19 I w·...make a way in the wilderness,
25 sake, and w· not remember thy sins.
44: 2 from the womb, which w· help thee;
3 For I w· pour water upon him that
3 I w· pour my spirit upon thy seed,
15 for he w· take thereof, and warm *
26 and I w· raise up the decayed places
27 Be dry, and I w· dry up thy rivers:
45: 1 and I w· loose the loins of kings,
2 I w· go before thee, and make the
2 I w· break in pieces the gates of brass,
3 w· give thee the treasures of darkness,
13 and I w· direct all his ways:
46: 4 and even to hoar hairs w· I carry you:
4 carry you: I have made, and I w· bear;
4 even I w· carry, and w· deliver you.
5 To whom w· ye liken me, and make
10 stand, and I w· do all my pleasure:
11 spoken it, I w· also bring it to pass;
11 I have purposed it, I w· also do it.
13 w· place salvation in Zion for Israel
47: 3 shall be seen: I w· take vengeance,
3 and I w· not meet thee as a man.
48: 6 see all this; and w· not ye declare it?
9 name's sake w· I defer mine anger,
9 for my praise w· I refrain for thee,
11 even for mine own sake, w· I do it:
11 I w· not give my glory unto another.
14 he w· do his pleasure on Babylon,*
49: 3 O Israel, in whom I w· be glorified.
6 I w· also give thee for a light to the
8 and I w· preserve thee, and give thee
11 I w· make all my mountains a way,
13 w· have mercy upon his afflicted.
15 may forget, yet w· I not forget thee.
22 I w· lift up mine hand to the Gentiles,
25 w· contend with him that contendeth
25 with thee, and I w· save thy children.
26 And I w· feed them that oppress thee
50: 7 For the Lord God w· help me;
8 me; who w· contend with thee?
9 Behold, the Lord God w· help me;
51: 3 he w· comfort all her desolate places;*
3 w· make her wilderness like Eden,*
4 and I w· make my judgment to rest
23 But I w· put it into the hand of them
52: 12 for the Lord God w· go before you;
Isa 52: 12 God of Israel w· be your rereward.
53: 12 Therefore w· I divide him a portion
54: 7 with great mercies w· I gather thee.
8 everlasting kindness w· I have mercy
11 I w· lay thy stones with fair colours,
12 And I w· make thy windows of agates,
55: 3 and I w· make an everlasting covenant
7 Lord, and he w· have mercy upon him;
7 our God, for he w· abundantly pardon.
56: 5 unto them w· I give in mine house
5 I w· give them an everlasting name,
7 w· I bring to my holy mountain,
8 Yet w· I gather others to him, besides
12 Come ye, say they, I w· fetch wine,
12 we w· fill ourselves with strong drink;
57: 12 I w· declare thy righteousness,
16 For I w· not contend for ever, neither
16 neither w· I be always wroth: for the
18 have seen his ways, and w· heal him:
18 I w· lead him also, and restore
19 saith the Lord; and I w· heal him.
58: 14 and I w· cause thee to ride upon the
59: 2 his face from you, that he w· not hear.
18 he w· repay, fury to his adversaries,
18 to the islands he w· repay recompence.
60: 7 and I w· glorify the house of my glory.
12 and kingdom that w· not serve thee
13 w· make the place of my feet glorious.
15 I w· make thee an eternal excellency,
17 For brass I w· bring gold, and for iron
17 and for iron I w· bring silver, and for
17 I w· also make thy officers peace,
22 I the Lord w· hasten it in his time.
61: 8 and I w· direct their work in truth,
8 I w· make an everlasting covenant
10 I w· greatly rejoice in the Lord,
11 the Lord God w· cause righteousness
62: 1 For Zion's sake I w· not hold my peace,
1 and for Jerusalem's sake I w· not rest,
8 Surely I w· no more give thy corn to
63: 3 for I w· tread them in mine anger,*
3 and I w· stain all my raiment. *
6 I w· tread down the people in mine*
6 I w· bring down their strength to the*
7 I w· mention the lovingkindnesses
8 my people, children that w· not lie:
65: 6 I w· not...silence, but w· recompense
7 therefore w· I measure their former
8 so w· I do for my servants' sakes, that
9 I w· bring forth a seed out of Jacob,
12 w· I number you to the sword,
19 And I w· rejoice in Jerusalem,
24 that before they call, I w· answer;
24 they are yet speaking, I w· hear.
66: 2 but to this man w· I look, even to him
4 I also w· choose their delusions,
4 and w· bring their fears upon them;
12 I w· extend peace to her like a river,
13 comforteth, so w· I comfort you;
15 the Lord w· come with fire, and with
16 and by his sword w· the Lord plead
18 I w· gather all nations and tongues;
19 And I w· set a sign among them,
19 I w· send those that escape of them
21 And I w· also take of them for priests
22 and the new earth, which I w· make,
Jer 1: 12 for I w· hasten my word to perform it.*
15 I w· call all the families of the
16 And I w· utter my judgments against
2: 9 Wherefore I w· yet plead with you,
9 your children's children w· I plead.
20 and thou saidst, I w· not transgress;
24 all they that seek her w· not weary
25 strangers, and after them w· I go.
27 of their trouble they w· say, Arise,
29 Wherefore w· ye plead with me? ye all
31 lords; we w· come no more unto thee?
35 Behold, I w· plead with thee, because
3: 5 W· he reserve his anger for ever?
5 w· he keep it to the end? Behold, thou
12 I w· not cause mine anger to fall upon
12 Lord, and I w· not keep anger for ever.
14 I w· take you one of a city, and two of
14 a family, and I w· bring you to Zion.
15 I w· give you pastors according to
22 and I w· heal your backslidings.
4: 6 for I w· bring evil from the north,
12 also w· I give sentence against them.
27 desolate; yet w· I not make a full end.
28 have purposed it, and w· not repent,*
28 neither w· I turn back from it.
30 fair; thy lovers w· despise thee, *
30 despise thee, they w· seek thy life.*
5: 1 seeketh the truth; and I w· pardon it.
5 I w· get me unto the great men,
5 and w· speak unto them; for they
14 I w· make my words in thy mouth
15 w· bring a nation upon you from far,
18 I w· not make a full end with you.
22 w· ye not tremble at my presence,
31 and what w· ye do in the end thereof?
6: 11 I w· pour it out upon the children *
12 for I w· stretch out my hand upon the
16 But they said, We w· not walk therein.
17 But they said, We w· not hearken.
19 I w· bring evil upon this people,
21 I w· lay stumblingblocks before this
7: 3 I w· cause you to dwell in this place.
7 w· I cause you to dwell in this place,
9 W· ye steal, murder, and commit
14 Therefore w· I do unto this house,
15 And I w· cast you out of my sight,
16 to me: for I w· not hear thee.
23 Obey my voice, and I w· be your God,
27 but they w· not hearken to thee:
27 them; but they w· not answer thee.
Jer 7: 34 w· I cause to cease from the cities
8: 10 w· I give their wives unto others,
13 I w· surely consume them, saith the
17 I w· send serpents, cockatrices,
17 which w· not be charmed, and they
9: 4 for every brother w· utterly supplant,
4 neighbour w· walk with slanders.
5 w· deceive every one his neighbour,
5 w· not speak the truth: they have
7 I w· melt them, and try them; for
10 For the mountains w· I take up a
11 I w· make Jerusalem heaps, and a
11 I w· make the cities of Judah desolate,
15 I w· feed them, even this people,
16 I w· scatter them also among the
16 I w· send a sword after them, till I
25 that I w· punish all them that are
10: 18 I w· sling out the inhabitants of the
18 w· distress them, that they may find it
11: 4 be my people, and I w· be your God:
8 I w· bring upon them all the words*
11 I w· bring evil upon them, which they
11 unto me, I w· not hearken unto them.
14 for I w· not hear them in the time
22 of hosts, Behold, I w· punish them:
23 for I w· bring evil upon the men of
12: 14 I w· pluck them out of their land,
15 I have plucked them out I w· return,
15 w· bring them again, every man to his
16 if they w·diligently learn the ways of
17 But if they w· not obey,
17 I w· utterly pluck up and destroy
13: 9 After this manner w· I mar the pride
13 I w· fill all the inhabitants of this
14 I w· dash them one against another,
14 I w· not pity, nor spare, nor have
17 But if ye w· not hear it, my soul shall
24 w· I scatter them as the stubble
26 w· I discover thy skirts upon thy face,
14: 10 he w· now remember their iniquity,
12 they fast, I w· not hear their cry;
12 and an oblation, I w· not accept them:
12 I w· consume them by the sword, and
13 but I w· give you assured peace in
16 I w· pour their wickedness upon them.
22 God? therefore we w· wait upon thee:
15: 3 I w· appoint over them four kinds,
4 I w· cause them to be removed into
6 therefore w· I stretch out my hand*
7 I w· fan them with a fan in the gates*
7 I w· bereave them of children, *
7 I w· destroy my people, since they*
9 residue of them w· I deliver to the
11 verily I w· cause the enemy to entreat
13 treasures w· I give to the spoil
14 I w· make thee to pass with thine
19 return, then w· I bring thee again,
20 I w· make thee unto this people as
21 I w· deliver thee out of the hand of
21 I w· redeem thee out of the hand of
16: 9 I w· cause to cease out of this place
13 w· I cast you out of this land into
13 where I w· not shew you favour.
15 I w· bring them again into their land
16 I w· send for many fishers, saith the
16 after w· I send for many hunters, and
18 first I w· recompense their iniquity
21 I w· this once cause them to know,
21 I w· cause them to know mine hand
17: 3 I w· give thy substance and all thy
4 I w· cause thee to serve thine enemies
27 But if ye w· not hearken unto me
27 then w· I kindle a fire in the gates
18: 2 and there w· I cause thee to hear my
8 I w· repent of the evil that I thought
10 then w· I repent of the good,
12 but we w· walk after our own devices,
12 we w· every one do the imagination of
14 W· a man leave the snow of Lebanon*
17 I w· scatter them as with an east wind
17 I w· shew them the back, and not the
19: 3 I w· bring evil upon this place, the
7 I w· make void the counsel of Judah
7 I w· cause them to fall by the sword
7 their carcases w· I give to be meat for
8 I w· make this city desolate, and a
9 I w· cause them to eat the flesh of
11 Even so w· I break this people and
12 Thus w· I do unto this place, saith the
15 I w· bring upon this city and upon all
20: 4 I w· make thee a terror to thyself,
4 I w· give all Judah into the hand of
5 I w· deliver all the strength of this
5 w· I give into the hand of their enemies,
9 I w· not make mention of him, nor
10 Report, say they, and we w· report it.
10 Peradventure he w· be enticed, and
21: 2 if so be that the Lord w· deal with us
4 I w· turn back the weapons of war
4 I w· assemble them into the midst of
5 And I myself w· fight against you
6 I w· smite the inhabitants of this city,
7 I w· deliver Zedekiah king of Judah,
14 I w· punish you according to the fruit
14 and I w· kindle a fire in the forest
22: 5 But if ye w· not hear these words, I
6 surely I w· make thee a wilderness,
7 I w· prepare destroyers against thee,
14 I w· build me a wide house and large
21 but thou saidst, I w· not hear.
25 And I w· give thee in the hand of them
26 I w· cast thee out, and thy mother
23: 2 I w· visit upon you the evil of your
3 I w· gather the remnant of my flock
3 w· bring them again to their folds;
5 that I w· raise unto David a righteous

Jer 23:12 for I w' bring evil upon them, even the
15 I w' feed them with wormwood, and
33 I w' even forsake you, saith the Lord.
39 I, even I, w' utterly forget you,
39 and I w' forsake you, and the city that
40 I w' bring an everlasting reproach
24: 5 so w' I acknowledge them that are
6 I w' set mine eyes upon them for
6 I w' bring them again to this land:
6 I w' build them, and not pull them
6 I w' plant them, and not pluck them
7 I w' give them an heart to know me,
7 be my people, and I w' be their God:
8 So w' I give Zedekiah the king of
9 I w' deliver them to be removed into
10 And I w' send the sword, the famine,
25: 6 your hands; and I w' do you no hurt.
9 I w' send and take all the families
9 and w' bring them against this land,
9 and w' utterly destroy them, and
10 I w' take from them the voice of mirth,
12 that I w' punish the king of Babylon,
12 and w' make it perpetual desolations.
13 I w' bring upon that land all my words
14 I w' recompense them according to
16 sword that I w' send among them.
27 the sword which I w' send among you.
29 I w' call for a sword upon all the
31 nations: he w' plead with all flesh;
31 w' give them that are wicked to the
26: 3 so be they w' hearken, and turn every
4 If ye w' not hearken to me, to walk
6 w' I make this house like Shiloh,
6 w' make this city a curse to all the
13 and the Lord w' repent him of the evil
27: 8 w' not serve the same Nebuchadnezzar
8 w' not put their neck under the yoke
8 that nation w' I punish, saith the Lord,
11 those w' I let remain still in their own
13 Why w' ye die, thou and thy people,
13 that w' not serve the king of Babylon?
22 then w' I bring them up, and restore
28: 3 w' I bring again into this place all
4 w' bring again to this place Jeconiah
4 for I w' break the yoke of the king of
11 Even so w' I break the yoke of
16 I w' cast thee from off the face of the
29: 10 be accomplished at Babylon I w' visit
12 unto me, and I w' hearken unto you.
14 And I w' be found of you, saith the
14 and I w' turn away your captivity,
14 I w' gather you from all the nations,
14 I w' bring you again into the place
17 I w' send upon them the sword, the
17 and w' make them like vile figs, that
18 I w' persecute them with the sword,
18 w' deliver them to be removed to all
21 I w' deliver them into the hand of
32 w' punish Shemaiah the Nehelamite,
32 the good that I w' do for my people,
30: 3 I w' bring again the captivity of my
3 I w' cause them to return to the land
8 I w' break his yoke from off thy neck,
8 w' burst thy bonds, and strangers
9 king, whom I w' raise up unto them.
10 I w' save thee from afar, and thy
11 yet w' I not make a full end of thee:
11 I w' correct thee in measure, and
11 and w' not leave thee altogether
16 prey upon thee w' I give for a prey.
17 For I w' restore health unto thee,
17 I w' heal thee of thy wounds, saith
18 w' bring again the captivity of Jacob's
19 I w' multiply them, and they shall
19 I w' also glorify them, and they shall
20 I w' punish all that oppress them.
21 and I w' cause him to draw near,
22 be my people, and I w' be your God.
31: 1 w' I be the God of all the families of
4 I w' build thee, and thou shalt be
8 I w' bring them from the north
9 and with supplications w' I lead them:
9 I w' cause them to walk by the rivers
10 that scattered Israel w' gather him,
13 for I w' turn their mourning into joy,
13 and w' comfort them, and make them
14 I w' satiate the soul of the priests
20 I w' surely have mercy upon him,
27 I w' sow the house of Israel and the
28 so w' I watch over them, to build, and
31 I w' make a new covenant with the
33 that I w' make with the house of
33 I w' put my law in their inward parts,
33 and w' be their God, and they shall be
34 for I w' forgive them their iniquity,
34 I w' remember their sin no more.
37 I w' also cast off all the seed of Israel
32: 3, 28 I w' give this city into the hand of
37 I w' gather them out of all countries,
37 I w' bring them again unto this place,
37 and I w' cause them to dwell safely:
38 be my people, and I w' be their God:
39 And I w' give them one heart, and
40 I w' make an everlasting covenant
40 that I w' not turn away from them,
40 but I w' put my fear in their hearts,
41 I w' rejoice over them to do them
41 I w' plant them in this land assuredly
42 so w' I bring upon them all the good
33: 3 I w' answer thee, and shew thee great
6 I w' bring it health and cure, and
6 I w' cure them, and w' reveal unto
7 And I w' cause the captivity of Judah
7 and w' build them, as at the first.
8 I w' cleanse them from all their
8 and I w' pardon all their iniquities,

Jer 33:11 I w' cause to return the captivity of
14 I w' perform that good thing which I
15 w' I cause the Branch of righteousness
22 so w' I multiply the seed of David my
26 Then w' I cast away the seed of Jacob,
26 so that I w' not take any of his seed
26 for I w' cause their captivity to return,
34: 2 I w' give this city into the hand of
5 and they w' lament thee, saying, Ah*
17 I w' make you to be removed into all
18 And I w' give the men that have
20 I w' even give them into the hand of
21 his princes w' I give into the hand of
22 I w' command, saith the Lord,
22 and I w' make the cities of Judah a
35: 6 But they said, We w' drink no wine:
13 W' ye not receive instruction to
17 I w' bring upon Judah and upon all
36: 3 house of Judah w' hear all the evil
7 they w' present their supplication
7 w' return every one from his evil way:
16 We w' surely tell the king all these
31 I w' punish him and his seed and his
31 and I w' bring upon them, and upon
38: 14 unto Jeremiah, I w' ask thee a thing;
16 this soul, I w' not put thee to death,
16 neither w' I give thee into the hand
25 and we w' not put thee to death;
39: 16 I w' bring my words upon this city
17 But I w' deliver thee in that day,
18 For I w' surely deliver thee, and thou
40: 4 and I w' look well unto thee: but if it
10 I w' dwell at Mizpah, to serve the
10 which w' come unto us: but ye, *
15 w' slay Ishmael the son of Nethaniah,
42: 4 I w' pray unto the Lord your God
4 answer you, I w' declare it unto you;
4 I w' keep nothing back from you.
6 we w' obey the voice of the Lord our
10 If ye w' still abide in this land, then
10 then w' I build you, and not pull you
10 I w' plant you, and not pluck you up:
12 And I w' shew mercies unto you,
13 say, We w' not dwell in this land,
14 but we w' go into the land of Egypt,
14 of bread; and there w' we dwell:
17 the evil that I w' bring upon them.
20 so declare unto us, and we w' do it.
43: 12 I w' kindle a fire in the houses of the
44: 11 I w' set my face against you for evil,
12 And I w' take the remnant of Judah,
13 For I w' punish them that dwell in the
16 Lord, we w' not hearken unto thee.
17 But we w' certainly do whatsoever
25 We w' surely perform our vows that
25 ye w' surely accomplish your vows,*
27 Behold, I w' watch over them for evil,
29 that I w' punish you in this place,
30 I w' give Pharaoh-hophra king of
45: 4 which I have built, w' I break down,
4 which I have planted I w' pluck up,
5 I w' bring evil upon all flesh, saith
5 thy life w' I give unto thee for a prey
46: 8 I w' go up, and w' cover the earth;
8 I w' destroy the city and the
25 I w' punish the multitude of No, and
26 And I w' deliver them into the hand
27 behold, I w' save thee from afar off,
28 for I w' make a full end of all the
28 but I w' not make a full end of thee,
28 yet w' I not leave thee wholly
47: 4 for the Lord w' spoil the Philistines,
6 how long w' it be ere thou be quiet?
48: 12 that I w' send unto him wanderers,
31 Therefore w' I howl for Moab, and
31 and I w' cry out for all Moab; mine
32 I w' weep for thee with the weeping
35 I w' cause to cease in Moab, saith
44 I w' bring upon it, even upon Moab,
47 w' I bring again the captivity of Moab
49: 2 that I w' cause an alarm of war to be
5 I w' bring fear upon thee, saith the
6 I w' bring again the captivity
8 I w' bring the calamity of Esau upon
8 him, the time that I w' visit him. *
9 they w' destroy till they have enough.*
11 I w' preserve them alive; and let thy
15 I w' make thee small among the *
16 I w' bring thee down from thence,
19 I w' suddenly make him run away
19 and who w' appoint me the time?
19 who is that shepherd that w' stand
27 And I w' kindle a fire in the wall of
32 I w' scatter into all winds them that
32 I w' bring their calamity from all
35 I w' break the bow of Elam, the chief
36 upon Elam w' I bring the four winds
36 w' scatter them towards all those
37 For I w' cause Elam to be dismayed
37 I w' bring evil upon them, even my
37 and I w' send the sword after them,
38 And I w' set my throne in Elam, and
38 w' destroy from thence the king and
39 I w' bring again the captivity of Elam,
50: 9 I w' raise and cause to come up
18 I w' punish the king of Babylon and
19 And I w' bring Israel again to his
20 I w' pardon them whom I reserve.
31 is come, the time that I w' visit thee.
32 I w' kindle a fire in his cities, and it
42 are cruel, and w' not shew mercy:*
44 I w' make them suddenly run away
44 and who w' appoint me the time?
44 shepherd that w' stand before me?
51: 1 I w' raise up against Babylon, and
2 And w' send unto Babylon fanners,

Jer 51: 6 he w' render unto her a recompense.
14 Surely I w' fill thee with men,
20 w' I break in pieces the nations,
20 and with thee w' I destroy kingdoms;
21 thee w' I break in pieces the horse
21 thee w' I break in pieces the chariot
23 I w' also break in pieces with thee
23 w' I break in pieces the husbandman
23 w' I break in pieces captains and
24 I w' render unto Babylon and to all
25 I w' stretch out mine hand upon thee,
25 and w' make thee a burnt mountain.
36 I w' plead thy cause, and take
36 I w' dry up her sea, and make her
39 In their heat I w' make their feasts,
39 I w' make them drunken, that they
40 I w' bring them down like lambs
44 And I w' punish Bel in Babylon,
44 I w' bring forth out of his mouth that
47 I w' do judgment upon the graven
52 I w' do judgment upon her graven
57 I w' make drunk her princes, and her
64 the evil that I w' bring upon her:
La 3: 24 my soul; therefore w' I hope in him.
31 For the Lord w' not cast off for ever:
32 yet w' he have compassion
4: 16 them; he w' no more regard them:
22 he w' no more carry thee away into
22 he w' visit thine iniquity, O daughter
22 of Edom; he w' discover thy sins.
Eze 2: 1 thy feet, and I w' speak unto thee.
5 whether they w' hear, or whether they
5 or whether they w' forbear, (for they
7 unto them, whether they w' hear,
7 or whether they w' forbear: for they
3: 7 house of Israel w' not hearken unto 14
7 for they w' not hearken unto me: "
11 saith the Lord; whether they w' hear,
11 or whether they w' forbear.
18, 20 blood w' I require at thine hand.
22 plain, and I w' there talk with thee.
26 I w' make thy tongue cleave to the
27 with thee, I w' open thy mouth,
4: 8 I w' lay bands upon thee, and thou*
13 the Gentiles, whither I w' drive them.
16 I w' break the staff of bread in
5: 2 and I w' draw out a sword after them.
8 w' execute judgments in the midst of
9 I w' do in thee that which I have not
9 I w' not do any more the like,
10 and I w' execute judgments in thee,
10 thee w' I scatter unto all the winds.
11 therefore w' I also diminish thee;
11 eye spare, neither w' I have any pity.
12 I w' scatter a third part into all
12 and I w' draw out a sword after them.
13 I w' cause my fury to rest upon them,
13 and I w' be comforted: and they shall
14 I w' make thee waste, and a reproach
16 which I w' send to destroy you:
16 I w' increase the famine upon you,
16 and w' break your staff of bread:
17 w' I send upon you famine and evil
17 and I w' bring the sword upon thee.
6: 3 I, even I, w' bring a sword upon you,
3 and I w' destroy your high places.
4 I w' cast down your slain men before
5 And I w' lay the dead carcases of the
5 I w' scatter your bones round about
8 Yet w' I leave a remnant, that ye may
12 w' I accomplish my fury upon them.
14 So w' I stretch out my hand upon
7: 3 and I w' send mine anger upon thee,
3 w' judge thee according to thy ways,
3 w' recompense upon thee all thine
4 not spare thee, neither w' I have pity:
4 w' recompense thy ways upon thee,
8 Now w' I shortly pour out my fury
8 w' judge thee according to thy ways,
8 w' recompense thee for all thine
9 not spare, neither w' I have pity:
9 I w' recompense thee according to thy
21 I w' give it into the hands of the
22 My face w' I turn also from them,
24 I w' bring the worst of the heathen,
24 I w' also make the pomp of the strong
27 I w' do unto them after their way,
27 to their deserts w' I judge them;
8: 18 Therefore w' I also deal in fury: mine
18 not spare, neither w' I have pity:
18 a loud voice, yet w' I not hear them.
9: 10 not spare, neither w' I have pity,
10 but I w' recompense their way upon
11: 7 But I w' bring you forth out of the*
8 I w' bring a sword upon you, saith the
9 And I w' bring you out of the midst
9 and w' execute judgment among you.
10 I w' judge you in the border of Israel;
11 I w' judge you in the border of Israel:
16 yet w' I be to them as a little
17 I w' even gather you from the people,
17 and I w' give you the land of Israel.
19 And I w' give them one heart,
19 and I w' put a new spirit within you;
19 I w' take the stony heart out of their
19 and w' give them a heart of flesh:
20 be my people, and I w' be their God.
21 I w' recompense their way upon their
12: 3 it may be they w' consider, though
13 My net also w' I spread upon him,
13 I w' bring him to Babylon to the land
14 I w' scatter toward every wind all that
14 I w' draw out the sword after them.
16 I w' leave a few men of them from the
23 I w' make this proverb to cease,
25 I w' speak, and the word that I shall

Eze 12: 25 O rebellious house, *w'* I say the word,
25 and *w'* perform it, saith the Lord God.
13: 13 I *w'* even rend it with a stormy wind
14 *w'* I break down the wall that ye have
15 *w'* I accomplish my wrath upon the
15 *w'* say unto you, The wall is no more,
18 *W'* ye hunt the souls of my people,
18 *w'* ye save the souls alive that come*
19 *w'* ye pollute me among my people for*
20 and I *w'* tear them from your arms,
20 *w'* let the souls go, even the souls that
21 Your kerchiefs also *w'* I tear, and
23 *w'* deliver my people out of your hand:
14: 4 I the Lord *w'* answer him that cometh
7 I the Lord *w'* answer him by myself:
8 I *w'* set my face against that man,
8 *w'* make him a sign and a proverb,
8 I *w'* cut him off from the midst of my
9 I *w'* stretch out my hand upon him,
9 *w'* destroy him from the midst of my
13 *w'* I stretch out mine hand upon it,*
13 and *w'* break the staff of the bread*
13 and *w'* send famine upon it, and *
13 and *w'* cut off man and beast from it:*
15: 3 or *w'* men take a pin of it to hang any
6 fuel, so *w'* I give the inhabitants of
7 And I *w'* set my face against them;
8 And I *w'* make the land desolate,
16: 27 delivered thee unto the *w'* of them5314
37 therefore I *w'* gather all thy lovers,
37 I *w'* even gather them round about
37 *w'* discover thy nakedness unto them,
38 And I *w'* judge thee, as women that
38 and I *w'* give thee blood in fury and
39 I *w'* also give thee into their hand,
41 I *w'* cause thee to cease from playing
42 So *w'* I make my fury toward thee
42 and I *w'* be quiet, and *w'* be no more
43 I also *w'* recompense thy way upon
53 then *w'* I bring again the captivity
59 I *w'* even deal with thee as thou hast
60 I *w'* remember my covenant with thee
60 I *w'* establish unto thee an everlasting
61 *w'* give them unto thee for daughters,
62 I *w'* establish my covenant with thee;
17: 19 even it *w'* I recompense upon his own
20 And I *w'* spread my net upon him,
20 snare, and I *w'* bring him to Babylon,
20 and *w'* plead with him there for his
22 I *w'* also take of the highest branch
22 branch of the high cedar, and *w'* set it;
22 I *w'* crop off from the top of his young
22 and *w'* plant it upon an high mountain
23 of the height of Israel *w'* I plant it:
18: 21 if the wicked *w'* turn from all his sins*
30 Therefore I *w'* judge you, O house of
31 for why *w'* ye die, O house of Israel?
20: 3 God, I *w'* not be enquired of by you.
8 I *w'* pour out my fury upon them,*
31 God, I *w'* not be enquired of by you.
32 *w'* be as the heathen, as the families
33 fury poured out, *w'* I rule over you:
34 I *w'* bring you out from the people,
34 *w'* gather you out of countries wherein
35 I *w'* bring you into the wilderness
35 there *w'* I plead with you face to face.
36 so *w'* I plead with you, saith the Lord
37 I *w'* cause you to pass under the rod,
37 I *w'* bring you into the bond of the
38 I *w'* purge out from among you the
38 I *w'* bring them forth out of the
39 also, if ye *w'* not hearken unto me:
40 serve me: there *w'* I accept them,
40 there *w'* I require your offerings,
41 I *w'* accept you with your sweet
41 I *w'* be sanctified in you before the
47 I *w'* kindle a fire in thee, and it shall
21: 3 *w'* draw forth my sword out of the
3, 4 *w'* cut off from thee the righteous
17 I *w'* also smite mine hands together,
17 I *w'* cause my fury to rest: I the Lord
23 but he *w'* call to remembrance the*
27 I *w'* overturn, overturn, overturn, it:
27 right it is; and I *w'* give it him.
30 I *w'* judge thee in the place where
31 I *w'* pour out mine indignation upon
31 I *w'* blow against thee in the fire of my
22: 14 the Lord have spoken it, and *w'* do it.
15 I *w'* scatter thee among the heathen,
15 *w'* consume thy filthiness out of thee.
19 I *w'* gather you into the midst of
20 so *w'* I gather you in mine anger and
20 I *w'* leave you there, and melt you.
21 I *w'* gather you, and blow upon you
23: 22 I *w'* raise up thy lovers against thee,
22 I *w'* bring them against thee on every
24 and I *w'* set judgment before them,
25 And I *w'* set my jealousy against thee,
27 Thus *w'* I make thy lewdness to cease
28 I *w'* deliver thee into the hand of them
30 I *w'* do these things unto thee, *
31 *w'* I give her cup into thine hand.
43 *W'* they now commit whoredoms with
46 I *w'* bring up a company upon them,
46 and *w'* give them to be removed and
48 Thus *w'* I cause lewdness to cease
24: 9 I *w'* even make the pile for fire great.
14 and I *w'* do it; I *w'* not go back,
14 neither *w'* I spare, neither *w'* I repent;
21 Behold, I *w'* profane my sanctuary,
25: 4 I *w'* deliver thee to the men of the east
5 *w'* make Rabbah a stable for camels,
7 I *w'* stretch out mine hand upon thee,*
7 and *w'* deliver thee for a spoil to the
7 and I *w'* cut thee off from the people,
7 and I *w'* cause thee to perish out of

Eze 25: 7 I *w'* destroy thee; and thou shalt
9 I *w'* open the side of Moab from the
10 and *w'* give them in possession, that
11 I *w'* execute judgments upon Moab;
13 I *w'* also stretch out mine hand upon
13 and *w'* cut off man and beast from it;
13 I *w'* make it desolate from Teman;
14 I *w'* lay my vengeance upon Edom by
16 I *w'* stretch out mine hand upon the
16 and I *w'* cut off the Cherethims, and
17 I *w'* execute great vengeance upon
26: 3 *w'* cause many nations to come up
4 I *w'* also scrape her dust from her,
7 Behold, I *w'* bring upon Tyrus
13 I *w'* cause the noise of thy songs to
14 I *w'* make thee like the top of a rock:
21 I *w'* make thee a terror, and thou shalt
28: 7 I *w'* bring strangers upon thee,
16 I *w'* cast thee as profane out of the*
16 I *w'* destroy thee, O covering cherub,*
17 I *w'* cast thee to the ground, *
17 I *w'* lay thee before kings, that they*
18 *w'* I bring forth a fire from the
18 and I *w'* bring thee to ashes upon the
22 I *w'* be glorified in the midst of thee:
23 For I *w'* send into her pestilence, and
29: 4 But I *w'* put hooks in thy jaws, and
4 I *w'* cause the fish of the rivers to
4 I *w'* bring thee up out of the midst of
5 And I *w'* leave thee thrown into the
8 I *w'* bring a sword upon thee, and
10 I *w'* make the land of Egypt utterly
12 I *w'* make the land of Egypt desolate
12 I *w'* scatter the Egyptians among the
12 and *w'* disperse them through the
13 forty years *w'* I gather the Egyptians
14 I *w'* bring the captivity of Egypt,
14 *w'* cause them to return into the land
15 for I *w'* diminish them, that they shall
19 I *w'* give the land of Egypt unto
21 day *w'* I cause the horn of the house
21 I *w'* give thee the opening of the
30: 10 I *w'* also make the multitude of Egypt
12 And I *w'* make the rivers dry, and sell
12 I *w'* make the land waste, and all that
13 I *w'* also destroy the idols, and I
13 I *w'* cause their images to cease out
13 I *w'* put a fear in the land of Egypt.
14 And I *w'* make Pathros desolate, and
14 desolate, and *w'* set fire in Zoan,
14 Zoan, and *w'* execute judgments in No.
15 And I *w'* pour my fury upon Sin,
15 and I *w'* cut off the multitude of No.
16 And I *w'* set fire in Egypt: Sin shall
19 *w'* I execute judgments in Egypt:
22 king of Egypt, and *w'* break his arms,
22 I *w'* cause the sword to fall out of his
23 I *w'* scatter the Egyptians among the
23 and *w'* disperse them through the
24 I *w'* strengthen the arms of the king
24 I *w'* break Pharaoh's arms, and he
25 I *w'* strengthen the arms of the king
26 I *w'* scatter the Egyptians among the
32: 3 I *w'* therefore spread out my net over
4 Then *w'* I leave thee upon the land,
4 I *w'* cast thee forth upon the open
4 *w'* cause all the fowls of the heaven to
4 I *w'* fill the beasts of the whole earth
5 I *w'* lay thy flesh upon the mountains,
6 I *w'* also water with thy blood the
7 I *w'* cover the heaven, and make the
7 I *w'* cover the sun with a cloud, and
8 lights of heaven *w'* I make dark over
9 I *w'* also vex the hearts of many
10 I *w'* make many people amazed at thee,
12 *w'* I cause thy multitude to fall,
13 I *w'* destroy also all the beasts thereof
14 Then *w'* I make their waters deep, and
33: 6 but his blood *w'* I require at the
8 his blood *w'* I require at thine hand.
11 for why *w'* ye die, O house of Israel?
20 I *w'* judge you every one after his
27 in the open field *w'* I give to the beasts
28 For I *w'* lay the land most desolate,
31 thy words, but they *w'* not do them:*
33 this cometh to pass, (lo, it *w'* come,)
34: 10 I *w'* require my flock at their hand,
10 for I *w'* deliver my flock from their
11 I, *w'* both search my sheep, and seek
12 *w'* I seek out my sheep, and *w'* deliver
13 I *w'* bring them out from the people,
13 *w'* bring them to their own land, and
14 I *w'* feed them in a good pasture, and
15 I *w'* feed my flock, and
15 I *w'* cause them to lie down,
16 I *w'* seek that which was lost, and
16 *w'* bind up that which was broken,
16 *w'* strengthen that which was sick:
16 I *w'* destroy the fat and the strong;
16 I *w'* feed them with judgment.
20 even I, *w'* judge between the fat cattle
22 *w'* I save my flock, and they shall
22 I *w'* judge between cattle and cattle.
23 I *w'* set up one shepherd over them,
24 I the Lord *w'* be their God, and my
25 I *w'* make with them a covenant of
25 *w'* cause the evil beast to cease out of
26 I *w'* make them and the places round
26 I *w'* cause the shower to come down in
29 I *w'* raise up for them a plant of
35: 3 I *w'* stretch out mine hand against
3 and I *w'* make thee most desolate,
4 I *w'* lay thy cities waste, and thou
6 I *w'* prepare thee unto blood, and
7 *w'* I make mount Seir most desolate,
8 I *w'* fill his mountains with his slain

Eze 35: 9 I *w'* make thee perpetual desolations,
10 shall be mine, and we *w'* possess it;
11 I *w'* even do according to thine anger,
11 I *w'* make myself known among them,
14 rejoiceth, I *w'* make thee desolate.
15 it was desolate, so *w'* I do unto thee:
36: 9 and I *w'* turn unto you, and ye shall
10 I *w'* multiply men upon you, all the
11 And I *w'* multiply upon you man and
11 I *w'* settle you after your old estates,
11 *w'* do better unto you than at your
12 I *w'* cause men to walk upon you,
15 *w'* I cause men to hear in thee the
23 I *w'* sanctify my great name, which
24 For I *w'* take you from among the
24 and *w'* bring you into your own land.
25 *w'* I sprinkle clean water upon you,
25 from all your idols, *w'* I cleanse you.
26 A new heart also *w'* I give you,
26 and a new spirit *w'* I put within you:
26 I *w'* take away the stony heart out of
26 and I *w'* give you an heart of flesh.
27 I *w'* put my spirit within you, and
28 be my people, and I *w'* be your God.
29 I *w'* also save you from all your
29 I *w'* call for the corn, and *w'* increase
30 I *w'* multiply the fruit of the tree, and
33 I *w'* also cause you to dwell in the
36 Lord have spoken it, and I *w'* do it.
37 I *w'* yet for this be enquired of by the
37 I *w'* increase them with men like a
37: 5 I *w'* cause breath to enter into you,
6 And I *w'* lay sinews upon you, and
6 *w'* bring up flesh from you, and cover
12 I *w'* open your graves, and cause
19 I *w'* take the stick of Joseph, which is
19 *w'* put them with him, even with the
21 I *w'* take the children of Israel from
21 *w'* gather them on every side, and
22 I *w'* make them one nation in the
23 but I *w'* save them out of all their
23 have sinned, and *w'* cleanse them:
23 be my people, and I *w'* be their God.
26 I *w'* make a covenant of peace with
26 I *w'* place them, and multiply them,
26 *w'* set my sanctuary in the midst of
27 I *w'* be their God, and they shall be
38: 4 I *w'* turn thee back, and put hooks
4 I *w'* bring thee forth, and all thine
11 I *w'* go up to the land of unwalled
11 I *w'* go to them that are at rest, that
16 I *w'* bring thee against my land, that
21 And I *w'* call for a sword against him
22 I *w'* plead against him with pestilence
22 and I *w'* rain upon him, and upon his
23 *w'* I magnify myself, and sanctify
23 and I *w'* be known in the eyes of many
39: 2 I *w'* turn thee back, and leave but the
2 *w'* cause thee to come up from the
2 *w'* bring thee upon the mountain of
3 and I *w'* smite thy bow out of thy left
3 and *w'* cause thine arrows to fall out
4 I *w'* give thee unto the ravenous birds
6 I *w'* send a fire on Magog, and among
7 So *w'* I make my holy name known in
7 and I *w'* not let them pollute my holy
11 I *w'* give unto Gog a place there of
21 I *w'* set my glory among the heathen,
25 Now *w'* I bring again the captivity of
25 and *w'* be jealous for my holy name;
29 *w'* I hide my face any more from
43: 7 I *w'* dwell in the midst of the children
9 I *w'* dwell in the midst of them for
27 I *w'* accept you, saith the Lord God.
44: 14 But I *w'* make them keepers of the
Da 2: 4 and we *w'* shew the interpretation.
5 if ye *w'* not make known unto me the*
7 we *w'* shew the interpretation of it.
9 if ye *w'* not make known unto me the*
24 I *w'* shew unto the king the
25 *w'* make known unto the king the
36 we *w'* tell the interpretation thereof.
3: 17 he *w'* deliver us out of thine hand, O
18 king, that we *w'* not serve thy gods,
4: 17 and giveth it to whomsoever he *w'*.6634
25, 32 giveth it to whomsoever he *w'*. "
35 to his *w'* in the army of heaven, "
5: 12 and he *w'* shew the interpretation.
17 I *w'* read the writing unto the king,
21 over it whomsoever he *w'*. 6634
6: 16 servest continually, he *w'* deliver thee.
8: 4 but he did according to his *w'*, and7522
19 I *w'* make thee known what shall be in
10: 20 *w'* I return to fight with the prince
21 I *w'* shew thee that which is noted in
11: 2 And now *w'* I shew thee the truth.
3 and do according to his *w'*. 7522
16 shall do according to his own *w'*, "
36 king shall do according to his *w'*; "
Ho 1: 4 I *w'* avenge the blood of Jezreel upon
4 *w'* cause to cease the kingdom of the
5 I *w'* break the bow of Israel in the
6 I *w'* no more have mercy upon the
6 but I *w'* utterly take them away. *
7 I *w'* have mercy upon the house
7 *w'* save them by the Lord their God,
7 *w'* not save them by bow, nor by
9 my people, and I *w'* not be your God.
2: 4 *w'* not have mercy upon her children;
5 I *w'* go after my lovers, that give me
6 I *w'* hedge up thy way with thorns,
7 *w'* go and return to my first husband;
9 *w'* I return, and take away my corn
9 *w'* recover my wool and my flax given
10 And now *w'* I discover her lewdness in
11 I *w'* also cause all her mirth to cease,

Ho 2:12 I w' destroy her vines and her fig
12 and I w' make them a forest, and
13 And I w' visit upon her the days of
14 I w' allure her, and bring her into
15 I w' give her her vineyards from
17 I w' take away the names of Baalim
18 day w' I make a covenant for them
18 I w' break the bow and the sword
18 and w' make them to lie down safely.
19 I w' betroth thee unto me for ever;
19 yea, I w' betroth thee unto me in
20 I w' even betroth thee unto me in
21 in that day, I w' hear, saith the Lord,
21 I w' hear the heavens, and they
23 I w' sow her unto me in the earth;
23 I w' have mercy upon her that had
23 I w' say to them which were not my
3: 3 another man: so w' I also be for thee.
4: 5 night, and I w' destroy thy mother.
6 I w' also reject thee, that thou shalt
6 God, I w' also forget thy children.
7 w' I change their glory into shame.
9 I w' punish them for their ways,
14 I w' not punish your daughters when
16 now the Lord w' feed them as a lamb
5: 4 w' not frame their doings to turn
10 I w' pour out my wrath upon them
12 w' I be unto Ephraim as a moth, *
14 For I w' be unto Ephraim as a lion,
14 w' tear and go away; I w' take away,
15 I w' go and return to my place, till
15 their affliction they w' seek me early.
6: 1 he hath torn us, and he w' heal us;
1 hath smitten, and he w' bind us up.
2 After two days w' he revive us;
2 in the third day he w' raise us up,
7: 12 go, I w' spread my net upon them;
12 I w' bring them down as the fowls of
12 I w' chastise them, as their
8: 5 how long w' it be ere they attain to
10 now w' I gather them, and they shall
13 now w' he remember their iniquity,
14 but I w' send a fire upon his cities,
9: 5 What w' ye do in the solemn day,
9 he w' remember their iniquity,
9 he w' visit their sins.
12 yet w' I bereave them, that there shall
15 I w' drive them out of mine house,
15 mine house, I w' love them no more:
16 yet w' I slay even the beloved fruit
17 My God w' cast them away, because
10: 11 I w' make Ephraim to ride; Judah
11: 9 I w' not execute the fierceness of
9 I w' not return to destroy Ephraim:
9 and I w' not enter into the city.
11 I w' place them in their houses,
12: 2 and w' punish Jacob according to his
2 to his doings w' he recompense him.
9 of Egypt w' yet make thee to dwell
13: 7 Therefore I w' be unto them as a lion:*
7 leopard by the way w' I observe them:
8 I w' meet them as a bear that is
8 and w' rend the caul of their heart,
8 there w' I devour them like a lion:
10 I w' be thy king: where is any * 165
14 I w' ransom them from the power
14 I w' redeem them from death:
14 O death, I w' be thy plagues; * 165
14 O grave, I w' be thy destruction: * "
14: 2 so w' we render the calves of our lips.
3 save us; we w' not ride upon horses:
3 neither w' we say any more to the
4 I w' heal their backsliding,
4 I w' love them freely: for mine anger
5 I w' be as the dew unto Israel:
Joe 1: 19 O Lord, to thee w' I cry: for the fire*
2: 14 Who knoweth if he w' return and
18 w' the Lord be jealous for his land,*
19 Lord w' answer and say unto his
19 I w' send you corn, and wine, and oil,
19 I w' no more make you a reproach
20 But I w' remove far off from you the
20 and w' drive him into a land barren
21 for the Lord w' do great things. *
23 he w' cause to come down for you the*
25 And I w' restore to you the years that
28 I w' pour out my Spirit upon all flesh;
29 in those days w' I pour out my spirit.
30 I w' shew wonders in the heavens
3: 2 I w' also gather all nations, and
2 w' bring them down into the valley
2 and w' plead with them there for my
4 w' ye render me a recompence?
4 speedily w' I return your recompence
7 I w' raise them out of the place
7 w' return your recompence upon your
8 I w' sell your sons and your daughters
12 there w' I sit to judge all the heathen
16 the Lord w' be the hope of his people,
21 I w' cleanse their blood that I have
Am 1: 2 The Lord w' roar from Zion, and utter*
3 I w' not turn away the punishment
4 I w' send a fire into the house of
5 I w' break also the bar of Damascus,
6 I w' not turn away the punishment
7 I w' send a fire on the wall of Gaza,
8 And I w' cut off the inhabitant from
8 I w' turn mine hand against Ekron:
9 I w' not turn away the punishment
10 I w' send a fire on the wall of Tyrus,
11 I w' not turn away the punishment
12 But I w' send a fire upon Teman,
13 I w' not turn away the punishment
14 But I w' kindle a fire in the wall of
2: 1 I w' not turn away the punishment
2 But I w' send a fire upon Moab,

Am 2: 3 I w' cut off the judge from the midst
3 w' slay all the princes thereof with
4 I w' not turn away the punishment
5 But I w' send a fire upon Judah,
6 I w' not turn away the punishment
7 father w' go in unto the same maid,
3: 2 I w' punish you for all your iniquities.
4 W' a lion roar in the forest, when he
4 w' a young lion cry out of his den,
7 Surely the Lord God w' do nothing,
8 lion hath roared, who w' not fear?
14 I w' also visit the altars of Beth-el:
15 I w' smite the winter house with the
4: 2 that he w' take you away with hooks,*
12 thus w' I do unto thee, O Israel:
12 because I w' do this unto thee,
5: 15 w' be gracious unto the remnant of
17 w' pass through thee, saith the Lord.
21 and I w' not smell in your solemn
22 meat offerings, I w' not accept them:
22 neither w' I regard the peace offerings
23 I w' not hear the melody of thy viols.
27 w' I cause you to go into captivity
6: 8 w' I deliver up the city with all that
11 he w' smite the great house with *
12 rock? w' one plow there with oxen?
14 I w' raise up against you a nation,
7: 8 I w' set a plumbline in the midst
8 I w' not again pass by them any more:
9 w' rise against the house of Jeroboam
8: 2 I w' not again pass by them any more.
5 When w' the new moon be gone,
7 I w' never forget any of their works.
9 I w' cause the sun to go down at noon,
9 I w' darken the earth in the clear day:
10 I w' turn your feasts into mourning,
10 I w' bring up sackcloth upon all loins,
10 I w' make it as the mourning of an
11 that I w' send a famine in the land.
9: 1 I w' slay the last of them with the
2 thence w' I bring them down:
3 I w' search and take them out thence;
3 thence w' I command the serpent,
4 thence w' I command the sword,
4 w' set mine eyes upon them for evil,
8 I w' destroy it from off the face of the
8 I w' not utterly destroy the house of
9 I w' command, and I w' sift the house
11 that day w' I raise up the tabernacle
11 and I w' raise up his ruins,
11 I w' build it as in the days of old:
14 I w' bring again the captivity of my
15 And I w' plant them upon their land,
Ob 4 thence w' I bring thee down, saith the
Jon 1: 6 if so be that God w' think upon us,
2: 4 yet I w' look again toward thy holy
9 I w' sacrifice unto thee with the voice
9 I w' pay that that I have vowed.
3: 9 can tell if God w' turn and repent,
Mic 1: 3 w' come down, and tread upon the
6 I w' make Samaria as an heap of the
6 and I w' pour down the stones thereof
6 I w' discover the foundations thereof.
7 all the idols thereof w' I lay desolate:
8 Therefore I w' wail and howl,
8 and howl, I w' go stripped and naked:
8 I w' make a wailing like the dragons,
15 Yet w' I bring an heir unto thee,
2: 11 I w' prophesy unto thee of wine
12 I w' surely assemble, O Jacob, all of
12 I w' surely gather the remnant of
12 I w' put them together as the sheep
3: 4 the Lord, but he w' not hear them:
4 he w' even hide his face from them
11 w' they lean upon the Lord, and say,
4: 2 and he w' teach us of his ways,
2 ways, and we w' walk in his paths:
5 w' walk every one in the name of his
5 we w' walk in the name of the Lord
6 w' I assemble her that halteth,
6 and I w' gather her that is driven out,
7 I w' make her that halted a remnant,
13 for I w' make thine horn iron, and I
13 iron, and I w' make thy hoofs brass:
13 I w' consecrate their gain unto the*
5: 3 Therefore w' he give them up, until
10 I w' cut off thy horses out of the midst
10 of thee, and I w' destroy thy chariots:
11 And I w' cut off the cities of thy land,
12 I w' cut off witchcrafts out of thine
13 Thy graven images also w' I cut off,
14 I w' pluck up thy groves out of the
14 of thee: so w' I destroy thy cities.
15 I w' execute vengeance in anger
6: 2 people, and he w' plead with Israel.
7 W' the Lord be pleased with
13 w' I make thee sick in smiting thee,*
14 which thou deliverest w' I give up
7: 7 Therefore I w' look unto the Lord;
7 I w' wait for the God of my salvation:
7 of my salvation: My God w' hear me.
9 I w' bear the indignation of the Lord,
9 he w' bring me forth to the light,
15 w' I shew unto him marvellous things.
19 He w' turn again, he
19 he w' have compassion upon us;*
19 he w' subdue our iniquities; and thou
Na 1: 2 Lord w' take vengeance on his *
3 and w' not at all acquit the wicked:
8 he w' make an utter end of the place
9 w' make an utter end: affliction shall
12 thee, I w' afflict thee no more.
13 now w' I break his yoke from off thee,
13 and w' burst thy bonds in sunder.
14 gods w' I cut off the graven image
14 I w' make thy grave; for thou art vile.

Na 2: 13 I w' burn her chariots in the smoke,
13 I w' cut off thy prey from the earth,
3: 5 w' discover thy skirts upon thy face,
5 I w' shew the nations thy nakedness,
6 w' cast abominable filth upon thee,
6 and w' set thee as a gazingstock.
7 is laid waste: who w' bemoan her?
Hab 1: 5 for I w' work a work in your days,*
5 which ye w' not believe, though it be
2: 1 I w' stand upon my watch, and set
1 and w' watch to see what he w' say
3 it w' surely come, it w' not tarry.
3: 16 he w' invade them with his troops.*
18 Yet I w' rejoice in the Lord,
18 I w' joy in the God of my salvation.
19 and he w' make my feet like hind's*
19 he w' make me to walk upon mine
Zep 1: 2 I w' utterly consume all things from
3 I w' consume man and beast;
3 I w' consume the fowls of the heaven.
3 I w' cut off man from off the land,
4 I w' also stretch out mine hand upon
4 and I w' cut off the remnant of Baal
8 that I w' punish the princes, and the
9 same day also w' I punish all those
12 I w' search Jerusalem with candles,
12 The Lord w' not do good,
12 neither w' he do evil.
17 And I w' bring distress upon men,
2: 5 Philistines, I w' even destroy thee,
11 The Lord w' be terrible unto them:
11 he w' famish all the gods of the earth;
13 he w' stretch out his hand against the
13 and w' make Nineveh a desolation,
3: 5 midst thereof; he w' not do iniquity:
9 then w' I turn to the people a pure
11 w' take away out of the midst of thee
12 I w' also leave in the midst of thee
17 he w' save, he w' rejoice over thee
17 he w' rest in his love, he w' joy over
18 I w' gather them that are sorrowful
19 time I w' undo all that afflict thee:
19 I w' save her that halteth, and gather
19 I w' get them praise and fame in
20 At that time w' I bring you again,
20 I w' make you a name and a praise
Hag 1: 8 house; and I w' take pleasure in it,
8 and I w' be glorified, saith the Lord.
2: 6 I w' shake the heavens, and the earth,
7 I w' shake all nations, and the desire
7 I w' fill this house with glory, saith
9 in this place w' I give peace, saith the
19 from this day w' I bless you.
21 I w' shake the heavens and the earth;
22 I w' overthrow the throne of
22 I w' destroy the strength of the
22 and I w' overthrow the chariots,
23 w' I take thee, O Zerubbabel, my
23 Lord, and w' make thee as a signet:
Zec 1: 3 I w' turn unto you, saith the Lord
9 me, I w' shew thee what these be.
2: 5 w' be unto her a wall of fire round
5 and w' be glory in the midst of her.
9 I w' shake mine hand upon them,
10, 11 and I w' dwell in the midst of thee,
3: 4 I w' clothe thee with change of
7 I w' give thee places to walk among
8 I w' bring forth my servant the
9 I w' engrave the graving thereof,
9 I w' remove the iniquity of that land
5: 4 I w' bring it forth, saith the Lord of
6: 15 if ye w' diligently obey the voice of the
8: 3 w' dwell in the midst of Jerusalem:
7 I w' save my people from the east
8 And I w' bring them, and they shall
8 be my people, and I w' be their God,
11 I w' not be unto the residue of this
12 I w' cause the remnant of this people
13 so w' I save you, and ye shall be a
21 seek the Lord of hosts: I w' go also.
23 is a Jew, saying, We w' go with you:
9: 4 Behold, the Lord w' cast her out,
4 and he w' smite her power in the sea;
6 and I w' cut off the pride of the
7 And I w' take away his blood out of
8 And I w' encamp about mine house
10 I w' cut off the chariot from Ephraim,
12 that I w' render double unto thee;
10: 6 I w' strengthen the house of Judah,
6 and I w' save the house of Joseph,
6 I w' bring them again to place them;
6 the Lord their God, and w' hear them.
8 I w' hiss for them, and gather them;
9 I w' sow them among the people:
10 I w' bring them again also out of the
10 w' bring them into the land of Gilead
12 I w' strengthen them in the Lord;
11: 6 For I w' no more pity the inhabitants
6 I w' deliver the men every one into his
6 of their hand I w' not deliver them.
7 And I w' feed the flock of slaughter,*
9 Then said I, I w' not feed you: that
16 I w' raise up a shepherd in the land,
12: 2 I w' make Jerusalem a cup of
3 w' I make Jerusalem a burdensome
4 I w' smite every horse with
4 I w' open mine eyes upon the house
4 and w' smite every horse of the
6 In that day w' I make the governors
9 I w' seek to destroy all the nations
10 I w' pour upon the house of David,
13: 2 I w' cut off the names of the idols
2 and also I w' cause the prophets and
7 I w' turn mine hand upon the ones.
9 And I w' bring the third part through
9 and w' refine them as silver is refined,

Zec 13: 9 and w' try them as gold is tried:
9 on my name, and I w' hear them:
9 I w' say, It is my people: and they
14: 2 For I w' gather all nations against
12 the Lord w' smite all the people
17 that whoso w' not come up of all the*
18 the Lord w' smite the heathen
Mal 1: 4 we w' return and build the desolate
4 shall build, but I w' throw down;
5 The Lord w' be magnified from the*
8 w' he be pleased with thee, or accept
9 God that he w' be gracious unto us:
9 w' he regard your persons? saith the
10 neither w' I accept an offering at your
2: 2 w' not hear, and...w' not lay it to heart,
2 I w' even send a curse upon you,
2 you, and I w' curse your blessings:
3 Behold, I w' corrupt your seed, and
12 The Lord w' cut off the man that
13 or receiveth it with good w' at 7522
3: 1 Behold, I w' send my messenger, *
5 I w' come near to you to judgment;
5 I w' be a swift witness against the
7 unto me, and I w' return unto you,
8 W' a man rob God? Yet ye have
10 if I w' not open you the windows of
11 I w' rebuke the devourer for your
17 I w' spare them, as a man spareth
4: 5 I w' send you Elijah the prophet
M't 2: 13 Herod w' seek the young child to 3195
3: 12 and he w' throughly purge his floor,
12 but he w' burn up the chaff with
4: 9 All these things w' I give thee, if thou
19 me, and I w' make you fishers of men,
5: 40 if any man w' sue thee at the law, *2309
6: 10 Thy w' be done in earth, as it is in 2307
14 heavenly Father w' also forgive you:
15 neither w' your Father forgive your
21 is, there w' your heart be also.
24 for either he w' hate the one, and love
24 or else he w' hold to the one, and
7: 9 ask bread, w' he give him a stone?
10 ask a fish, w' he give him a serpent?
21 he that doeth the w' of my Father 2307
22 Many w' say to me in that day, Lord,
23 And then w' I profess unto them, I
24 I w' liken him unto a wise man, *
8: 3 him, saying, I w'; be thou clean. 2309
7 unto him, I w' come and heal him.
19 I w' follow thee whithersoever thou
9: 13 I w' have mercy, and not sacrifice:*2309
15 but the days w' come, when the
38 he w' send forth labourers into his*
10: 17 they w' deliver you up to the councils,
17 and they w' scourge you in their
32 him w' I confess also before my Father
33 him w' I also deny before my Father
11: 14 And if ye w' receive it, this is *2309
27 whomsoever the Son w' reveal him.*1014
28 heavy laden, and I w' give you rest.
12: 7 I w' have mercy, and not sacrifice,*2309
11 w' he not lay hold on it, and lift it
18 I w' put my spirit upon him, and he
29 man? and then he w' spoil his house.
44 I w' return into my house from
50 do the w' of my Father which is in 2307
13: 30 of harvest I w' say to the reapers,
35 I w' open my mouth in parables;
35 I w' utter things which have been
15: 32 I w' not send them away fasting, *2309
16: 2 It w' be fair weather: for the sky is
3 It w' be foul weather to day: for the
18 upon this rock I w' build my church;
19 And I w' give unto thee the keys of
24 If any man w' come after me, let *2309
25 w' save his life shall lose it: * "
25 w' lose his life for my sake shall find*
18: 14 so it is not the w' of your Father 2307
16 But if he w' not hear thee, then take*
26, 29 with me, and I w' pay thee all.
20: 4 and whatsoever is right I w' give you.
14 I w' give unto this last, even as 2309
15 me to do what I w' with mine own? "
26 whosoever w' be great among you,* "
27 whosoever w' be chief among you,* "
32 What w' ye that I shall do unto you? "
21: 3 and straightway he w' send them.
24 I also w' ask you one thing, which if
24 I in like wise w' tell you by what
25 he w' say unto us, Why did ye not then
29 He answered and said, I w' not: 2309
31 twain did the w' of his father? 2307
37 saying, They w' reverence my son.
40 what w' he do unto those husbandmen?
41 He w' miserably destroy those wicked
41 and w' let out his vineyard unto other
44 shall fall, it w' grind him to powder.
23: 4 themselves w' not move them 2309
24: 28 there w' the eagles be gathered
25: 21, 23 I w' make thee ruler over many
26: 15 unto them, What w' ye give me, *2309
15 and I w' deliver him unto you?
18 I w' keep the passover at thy house*
29 I w' not drink henceforth of this fruit‡
31 it is written, I w' smite the shepherd,
32 again, I w' go before you into Galilee.
33 of thee, yet w' I never be offended.
35 die with thee, yet w' I not deny thee.
39 nevertheless not as I w', but as 2309
42 except I drink it, thy w' be done. 2307
27: 17 Whom w' ye that I release unto 2309
21 of the twain w' ye that I release "
42 from the cross, and we w' believe him.
43 deliver him...if he w' have him: *2309
49 whether Elias w' come to save him.*
63 alive, After three days I w' rise again.*
M't 28: 14 we w' persuade him, and secure you.
M'r 1: 41 saith unto him, I w'; be thou clean.2309
2: 20 But the days w' come, when the
22 spilled, and the bottles w' be marred:*
3: 27 except he w' first bind the strong *
27 and then he w' spoil his house.
35 whosoever shall do the w' of God, 2307
4: 13 then w' ye know all the parables?*
6: 22 thou wilt, and I w' give it thee.
23 I w' give it thee, unto the half of my
25 I w' that thou give me by and by 2309
8: 3 houses, they w' faint by the way:
34 Whosoever w' come after me, let *2309
35 whosoever w' save his life shall * "
9: 50 saltness, wherewith w' ye season it?
10: 43 whosoever w' be great among you,2309
44 whosoever of you w' be...chiefest, * "
11: 3 straightway, he w' send him hither.
26 neither w' your Father which is in*
29 I w' also ask of you one question,
29 I w' tell you by what authority I do
31 he w' say, Why then did ye not believe
12: 6 saying, They w' reverence my son.
9 w' come and destroy the husbandmen,
9 w' give the vineyard unto others.
14: 7 whensoever ye w' ye may do them 2309
15 he w' shew you a large upper room
25 I w' drink no more of the fruit of the‡
27 is written, I w' smite the shepherd,
28 risen, I w' go before you into Galilee.
29 all shall be offended, yet w' not I.
31 thee, I w' not deny thee in any wise.
36 nevertheless not what I w', but 2309
58 I w' destroy this temple that is made
58 and within three days I w' build
15: 9 W' ye that I release unto you the 2309
12 What w' ye then that I shall do * "
36 whether Elias w' come to take him*
Lu 2: 14 peace, good w' toward men. *2107
3: 17 and he w' throughly purge his floor,*
17 w' gather the wheat into his garner;*
17 but the chaff he w' burn with fire
4: 6 power w' I give thee, and the glory
6 and to whomsoever I w' I give it. 2309
23 w' surely say unto me this proverb,
5: 5 at thy word I w' let down the net.
13 him, saying, I w': be thou clean. 2309
35 days w' come, when the bridegroom
37 else the new wine w' burst the bottles,
6: 9 unto them, I w' ask you one thing;*
47 I w' shew you to whom he is like:
7: 42 which of them w' love him most?
9: 5 And whosoever w' not receive you,*
23 If any man w' come after me, let *2309
24 whosoever w' save his life shall * "
24 whosoever w' lose his life for my sake,*
57 I w' follow thee whithersoever thou
61 also said, Lord, I w' follow thee;
10: 22 he to whom the Son w' reveal him.*1014
35 when I come again, I w' repay thee.
11: 2 Thy w' be done, as in heaven, so *2307
8 Though he w' not rise and give him,
8 because of his importunity he w' rise
11 that is a father, w' he give him a stone?*
11 w' he for a fish give him a serpent?*
12 an egg, w' he offer him a scorpion?
24 I w' return unto my house whence I
49 I w' send them prophets and apostles,
12: 5 I w' forewarn you whom ye shall fear:
18 And he said, This w' I do:
18 I w' pull down my barns, and build
18 there w' I bestow all my fruits and
19 I w' say to my soul, Soul, thou hast
28 how much more w' he clothe you,*
34 there w' your heart be also.
36 when he w' return from the wedding;*
37 and w' come forth and serve them.*
44 he w' make him ruler over all that he
46 lord of that servant w' come in a day*
46 not aware, and w' cut him in sunder,*
46 w' appoint him his portion with the*
47 knew his lord's w', and prepared 2307
47 neither did according to his w', "
48 much, of him they w' ask the more.
49 what w' I, if it be already kindled?‡2309
55 wind blow, ye say, There w' be heat;
13: 24 I say unto you, w' seek to enter in,*
31 hence: for Herod w' kill thee. *2309
14: 5 w' not straightway pull him out on the
15: 18 I w' arise and go to my father,
18 w' say unto him, Father, I have sinned
16: 11 who w' commit to your trust the true
13 for either he w' hate the one, and love
13 or else he w' hold to the one, and
30 them from the dead, they w' repent.
31 neither w' they be persuaded, though
17: 1 impossible but that offences w' come:*
7 w' say unto him by and by, when he is
8 And w' not rather say unto him,
22 The days w' come, when ye shall
37 thither w' the eagles be gathered
18: 5 I w' avenge her, lest by her continual
8 that he w' avenge them speedily.
19: 14 We w' not have this man to reign 2309
22 of thine own mouth w' I judge thee,
20: 3 I w' ask you one thing; and answer
5 he w' say, Why then believed ye him
6 Of men; all the people w' stone us:
13 I w' send my beloved son: it may be
13 may be they w' reverence him when
18 shall fall, it w' grind him to powder.
21: 6 the days w' come, in the which there
7 what sign w' there be when these*
15 For I w' give you a mouth and
22: 16 you, I w' not any more eat thereof,‡
18 I w' not drink of the fruit of the vine.‡
Lu 22: 42 nevertheless not my w', but thine, 2307
67 If I tell you, ye w' not believe:
68 ye w' not answer me, nor let me go.
23: 16 I w' therefore chastise him, and
22 I w' therefore chastise him, and let
25 but he delivered Jesus to their w'. 2307
Joh 1: 13 w' of the flesh, nor of the w' of man, "
2: 19 and in three days I w' raise it up.
4: 25 he is come, he w' tell us all things.
34 is to do the w' of him that sent me,2307
48 signs and wonders, ye w' not believe.
5: 20 and he w' shew him greater works
21 the Son quickeneth whom he w'. 2309
30 because I seek not mine own w', 2307
30 w' of the Father which...sent me, "
40 And ye w' not come to me, that ye 2309
43 in his own name, him ye w' receive.
45 Do not think that I w' accuse you
6: 37 cometh to me I w' in no wise cast out.
38 heaven, not to do mine own w', 2307
38 but the w' of him that sent me. "
39 the Father's w' which hath sent me, "
40 this is the w' of him that sent me, "
40, 44 I w' raise him up at the last day.
51 the bread that I w' give is my flesh,
51 I w' give for the life of the world.*
54 and I w' raise him up at the last day.
67 the twelve, W' ye also go away? *2309
7: 17 If any man w'...he shall know * "
17 If any man...do his w', he shall 2307
31 w' he do more miracles than these
35 Whither w' he go, that we shall not3195
35 w' he go unto the dispersed among "
8: 22 said the Jews, W' he kill himself?
44 the lusts of your father ye w' do. 2309
9: 27 w' ye also be his disciples? * "
31 and doeth his w', him he heareth. 2307
10: 5 And a stranger w' they not follow,
5 w' flee from him: for they know not
11: 22 wilt ask of God, God w' give it thee.
48 thus alone, all men w' believe on him:
56 that he w' not come to the feast?
12: 26 serve me, him w' my Father honour.
28 glorified it, and w' glorify it again.
32 the earth, w' draw all men unto me.
13: 37 I w' lay down my life for thy sake.
14: 3 I w' come again, and receive you unto*
13 that w' I do, that the Father may be
14 ask any thing in my name, I w' do it.
16 I w' pray the Father, and he shall give
18 I w' not leave you comfortless:
18 you comfortless: I w' come to you.*
21 I w' love him, and w' manifest myself
23 a man love me, he w' keep my words:
23 w' love him, and we w' come unto him,
26 whom the Father w' send in my name,
30 Hereafter I w' not talk much with you:
15: 7 ye shall ask what ye w', and it 2309
20 me, they w' also persecute you;
20 my sayings, they w' keep yours also.
21 all these things w' they do unto you
26 I w' send unto you from the Father,
16: 2 w' think that he doeth God service.*
3 And these things w' they do unto you,
7 the Comforter w' not come unto you;
7 if I depart, I w' send him unto you.
8 he w' reprove the world of sin, and of
13 come, he w' guide you into all truth:*
13 and he w' shew you things to come.*
22 but I w' see you again, and your
23 Father in my name, he w' give it you.
26 that I w' pray the Father for you:
17: 24 Father, I w' that they also, whom ‡2309
26 unto them thy name, and w' declare it:
18: 39 w' ye therefore that I release unto 1014
20: 15 hast laid him, and I w' take him away.
25 hand into his side, I w' not believe.
21: 22, 23 If I w' that he tarry till I come, 2309
Ac 2: 17 God, I w' pour out my Spirit upon all
18 I w' pour out in those days of my
19 I w' shew wonders in heaven above,
3: 23 soul, which w' not hear that prophet,*
5: 38 be of men, it w' come to nought:
6: 4 we w' give ourselves continually to
7: 7 they shall be in bondage w' I judge,
34 now come, I w' send thee into Egypt.
43 w' carry you away beyond Babylon.
49 what house w' ye build me? saith the
9: 16 I w' shew him how great things he
13: 22 heart, which shall fulfil all my w'. 2307
34 I w' give you the sure mercies of
36 own generation by the w' of God, *1012
15: 16 After this I w' return, and w' build
17: 18 said, What w' this babbler say? *2309
31 which he w' judge the world in 3195
32 w' hear thee again of this matter.
18: 6 henceforth I w' go unto the Gentiles.
15 I w' be no judge of such matters. *1014
21 but I w' return again unto you, *
21 again unto you, if God w'. 2309
21: 14 The w' of the Lord be done. 2307
22 for they w' hear that thou art come.
22: 14 that thou shouldest know his w', 2307
18 for they w' not receive thy testimony
21 I w' send thee far hence unto the
23: 14 we w' eat nothing until we have slain*
21 they w' neither eat nor drink till they*
35 I w' hear thee, said he, when thine
24: 22 I w' know the uttermost of your
25 convenient season, I w' call for thee.
26: 16 in the which I w' appear unto thee;
27: 10 that this voyage w' be with hurt 3195
28: 28 the Gentiles, and that they w' hear it.
Ro 1: 10 by the w' of God to come unto you.2307
2: 6 Who w' render to every man according
18 knowest his w', and approvest the 2307

Ro 4: 8 to whom the Lord w· not impute sin.
5: 7 for a righteous man w· one die:
7: 18 for to w· is present with me; but 2309
8: 27 the saints according to the w· of God.
9: 9 At this time w· I come, and Sarah
15 I w· have mercy on whom I...have
15 mercy on whom I w· have mercy, *
15 I w· have compassion on whom I
15 on whom I w· have compassion. *
18 mercy on whom he w· have mercy, 2309
18 and whom he w· he hardeneth. "
19 For who hath resisted his w·? 1013
25 I w· call them my people, which were
28 For he w· finish the work, and cut it
28 a short work w· the Lord make upon*
10: 19 I w· provoke you to jealousy by them
19 by a foolish nation I w· anger you.
12: 2 acceptable, and perfect, w· of God. 2307
19 Vengeance is mine; I w· repay, saith
15: 9 For this cause I w· confess to thee
18 I w· not dare to speak of any of those
24 journey into Spain, I w· come to you:*
28 fruit, I w· come by you into Spain.
32 you with joy by the w· of God, 2307
1Co 1: 1 Jesus Christ through the w· of God, "
19 I w· destroy the wisdom of the wise,
19 w· bring to nothing the understanding
4: 5 who both w· bring to light the hidden
5 and w· make manifest the counsels*
19 But I w· come to you shortly,
19 if the Lord w·, 2309
19 w· know, not the speech of them
21 What w· ye? shall I come unto you 2309
6: 12 I w· not be brought under the power
14 w· also raise up us by his own power.
7: 36 let him do what he w·, he sinneth 2309
37 but hath power over his own w·, 2307
37 heart that he w· keep his virgin, *
39 to be married to whom she w·; 2309
8: 13 I w· eat no flesh while the world
9: 17 but if against my w·, a dispensation 210
10: 13 who w· not suffer you to be tempted
13 w· with the temptation also make a
11: 34 rest w· I set in order when I come.
12: 11 to every man severally as he w·. 1014
14: 15 is it then? I w· pray with the spirit,
15 and I w· pray with the understanding
15 I w· sing with the spirit,
15 and I w· sing with the understanding
21 other lips w· I speak unto this people;
21 yet for all that w· they not hear me,
23 w· they not say that ye are mad?
25 down on his face he w· worship God,
35 And if they w· learn any thing, *2309
15: 35 some man w· say, How are the dead
16: 3 them w· I send to bring your liberality
5 Now I w· come unto you, when I shall
6 And it may be that I w· abide, yea,*
7 I w· not see you now by the way; *2309
8 I w· tarry at Ephesus until Pentecost.
12 his w· was not at all to come at 2307
12 but he w· come when he shall have
2Co 1: 1 of Jesus Christ by the w· of God, 2307
10 we trust that he w· yet deliver us;
6: 16 I w· dwell in them, and walk in them,
16 and I w· be their God, and they shall
17 unclean thing; and I w· receive you,
18 And w· be a Father unto you, and ye
8: 5 and unto us by the w· of God. 2307
11 as there was a readiness to w·, 2309
10: 11 such w· we be also in deed when we*
13 we w· not boast of things without our
11: 12 But what I do, that I w· do, that I may
18 glory after the flesh, I w· glory also.
30 I w· glory of the things which concern
12: 1 I w· come to visions and revelations of
5 Of such an one w· I glory: yet of
5 of myself I w· not glory, but in mine
6 not be a fool; for I w· say the truth:*
9 w· I rather glory in mine infirmities,
14 and I w· not be burdensome to you:
15 I w· very gladly spend and be spent
21 my God w· humble me among you,*
13: 2 that, if I come again, I w· not spare:
Ga 1: 4 according to the w· of God and our 2307
5: 10 that ye w· be none otherwise minded:
Eph 1: 1 of Jesus Christ by the w· of God, 2307
5 to the good pleasure of his w·, "
9 unto us the mystery of his w·, "
11 after the counsel of his own w·: "
5: 17 but...what the w· of the Lord is. "
6: 6 doing the w· of God from the heart;"
7 With good w· doing service, as 2133
Ph'p 1: 6 w· perform it until the day of Jesus
15 strife; and some also of good w·: 2107
18 therein do rejoice, yea, and w· rejoice.
2: 13 both to w· and to do of his good 2309
20 who w· naturally care for your state.
23 as I shall see how it w· go with me.
Col 1: 1 of Jesus Christ by the w· of God, 2307
9 filled with the knowledge of his w· "
2: 23 a shew of wisdom in w· worship, 1479
4: 12 and complete in all the w· of God. 2307
1Th 4: 3 w· of God, even your sanctification, "
14 which sleep in Jesus w· God bring
5: 18 for this is the w· of God in Christ 2307
24 that calleth you, who also w· do it.
2Th 2: 7 only he who now letteth w· let, until*
3: 4 w· do the things which we command
1Ti 2: 4 Who w· have all men to be saved,†2309
8 I w· therefore that men pray *1014
5: 11 against Christ, they w· marry; *2309
14 I w· therefore that the younger *1014
6: 9 that w· be rich fall into temptation†‡ "
2Ti 1: 1 of Jesus Christ by the w· of God, 2307
2: 12 if we deny him, he also w· deny us:

2Ti 2: 16 w· increase unto more ungodliness.
17 their word w· eat as doth a canker:
25 if God...w· give them repentance *
26 are taken captive by him at his w·. 2307
3: 12 and all that w· live godly in Christ *2309
4: 3 time w· come when they w· not endure
18 and w· preserve me unto his heavenly
Tit 3: 8 these things I w· that thou affirm 1014
Ph'm 19 with mine own hand, I w· repay it:
Heb 1: 5 I w· be to him a Father, and he shall
2: 4 Ghost, according to his own w·? 2308
12 I w· declare thy name unto my
12 the church w· I sing praise unto thee.
13 And again, I w· put my trust in him.
3: 7 saith, To day if ye w· hear his voice,
15 To day if ye w· hear his voice, *
4: 7 To day if ye w· hear his voice, harden*
6: 3 And this w· we do, if God permit.
14 Saying, Surely blessing I w· bless thee,
14 and multiplying I w· multiply thee.
7: 21 The Lord sware and w· not repent,
8: 8 when I w· make a new covenant
10 I w· make with the house of Israel
10 I w· put my laws into their mind,
10 and I w· be to them a God, and they
12 For I w· be merciful to their
12 iniquities w· I remember no more.
10: 7 written of me,) to do thy w·, O God. 2307
9 he, Lo, I come to do thy w·, O God. "
10 By the which w· we are sanctified "
16 covenant that I w· make with them
16 I w· put my laws into their hearts,
16 and in their minds w· I write them;
17 and iniquities w· I remember no more.
30 me, I w· recompense, saith the Lord.
36 after ye have done the w· of God, 2307
37 shall come w· come, and w· not tarry.*
13: 4 and adulterers God w· judge.
5 I w· never leave thee, nor forsake
6 I w· not fear what man shall do unto
21 in every good work to do his w·, 2307
23 if he come shortly, I w· see you.
Jas 1: 18 Of his own w· begat he us with the 1014
2: 18 I w· shew thee my faith by my works.
4: 4 therefore w· be a friend of the *1014
7 Resist the devil, and he w· flee from
8 to God, and he w· draw nigh to you.
13 to morrow we w· go into such a city,
15 If the Lord w·, we shall live, and 2309
1Pe 2: 15 For so is the w· of God, that with 2307
3: 10 For he that w· love life, and see *2309
13 And who is he that w· harm you, if ye
17 it is better, if the w· of God be so, 2307
4: 2 lusts of men, but to the w· of God. "
3 wrought the w· of the Gentiles, * "
19 suffer according to the w· of God "
2Pe 1: 12 I w· not be negligent to put you *
15 I w· endeavour that ye may be able
21 not in old time by the w· of man: 2307
3: 10 day of the Lord w· come as a thief
1Jo 2: 17 he that doeth the w· of God abideth 2307
5: 14 according to his w·, he heareth us: "
3Jo 10 I w· remember his deeds which he
13 I w· not with ink and pen write *2309
Jude 5 I w·...put you in remembrance, *1014
Re 2: 5 or else I w· come unto thee quickly,*
5 w· remove thy candlestick out of his
7 To him that overcometh w· I give to
10 and I w· give thee a crown of life.
16 or else I w· come unto thee quickly,*
16 w· fight against them with the sword
17 To him that overcometh w· I give to
17 and w· give him a white stone, and in
22 Behold, I w· cast her into a bed, and*
23 I w· kill her children with death;
23 and I w· give unto every one of you
24 I w· put upon you none other burden.*
26 to whom w· I give power over the
28 And I w· give him the morning star.
3: 3 I w· come on thee as a thief, and
3 know what hour I w· come upon thee.
5 I w· not blot out his name out of the
5 but I w· confess his name before my
9 I w· make them of the synagogue of*
9 I w· make them to come and worship
10 I also w· keep thee from the hour of
12 Him that overcometh w· I make a
12 I w· write upon him the name of my
12 I w· write upon him my new name.*
16 I w· spue thee out of my mouth. 3195
20 I w· come in to him, and w· sup with
21 To him that overcometh w· I grant to
4: 1 I w· shew thee things which must be
11: 3 w· give power unto my two witnesses,
5 And if any man w· hurt them, *2309
5 and if any man w· hurt them, he * "
6 all plagues, as often as they w·. * "
17: 1 I w· shew unto thee the judgment of
7 I w· tell thee the mystery of the
17 put in their hearts to fulfil his w·,*1106
21: 3 and he w· dwell with them, and they*
6 I w· give unto him that is athirst of
7 and I w· be his God, and he shall be
9 hither, I w· shew thee the bride, the
22: 17 whosoever w·, let him take the 2309

willeth
Ro 9: 16 So then it is not of him that w·, 2309

willing
Ge 24: 5 the woman will not be w· to follow 14
8 woman will not be w· to follow thee, "
Ex 35: 5 whosoever is of a w· heart, let him 5081
21 one whom his spirit made w·, 5068
22 as many as were w· hearted, 5081
29 of Israel brought a w· offering *5071
29 whose heart made them w· to 5068

1Ch 28: 9 perfect heart and with a w· mind: 2655
21 workmanship every w· skilful 5081
29: 5 who then is w· to consecrate his 5068
Job 39: 9 Will the unicorn be w· to serve thee,*14
Ps 110: 3 Thy people shall be w· in the day 5071
Isa 1: 19 If ye be w· and obedient, ye shall eat 14
M't 1: 19 w· to make her a publick example, 2309
26: 41 the spirit indeed is w·, but the 4289
M'r 15: 15 Pilate, w· to content the people, *1014
Lu 10: 29 But he, w· to justify himself, said *2309
22: 42 Father, if thou be w·, remove this 1014
23: 20 Pilate...w· to release Jesus, spake *2309
Joh 5: 35 ye were w· for a season to rejoice * "
Ac 24: 27 w· to shew the Jews a pleasure, * "
25: 9 w· to do the Jews a pleasure, * "
27: 43 But the centurion, w· to save Paul,*1014
Ro 9: 22 if God, w· to show his wrath, and 2309
2Co 5: 8 w· rather to be absent from the 2106
8: 3 power they were w· of themselves; *830
12 For if there be first a w· mind, *4288
1Th 2: 8 were w· to have imparted unto you,*2106
1Ti 6: 18 to distribute, w· to communicate; 2843
Heb 6: 17 w· more abundantly to shew unto*1014
13: 18 in all things w· to live honestly. *2309
2Pe 3: 9 not w· that any should perish, 1014

willingly
Ex 25: 2 every man that giveth it w· with 5068
J'g 5: 2 the people w· offered themselves. "
9 that offered themselves w· among "
8: 25 answered, We will w· give them. 5414
1Ch 29: 6 of the king's work, offered w·, 5068
9 rejoiced, for that they offered w·. "
9 with perfect heart they offered w· "
14 should be able to offer so w· after "
17 I have w· offered all these things: "
17 present here, to offer w· unto thee. "
2Ch 17: 16 w· offered himself unto the Lord; "
35: 8 princes gave w· unto the people, *5071
Ezr 1: 6 beside all that was w· offered. 5068
3: 5 that w· offered a freewill offering "
7: 16 offering w· for the house of their God"
Ne 11: 2 that w· offered themselves to dwell at
Pr 31: 13 and worketh w· with her hands. 2656
La 3: 33 For he doth not afflict w·, nor 3820
Ho 5: 11 because he w· walked after the *2974
Joh 6: 21 they w· received him into the ship:*2309
Ro 8: 20 subject to vanity, not w·, but *1635
1Co 9: 17 For if I do this thing w·, I * "
Ph'm 14 it were of necessity, but w·. *2596,1595
1Pe 5: 2 thereof, not by constraint, but w·; 1596
2Pe 3: 5 For this they w· are ignorant of, *2309

willow See also WILLOWS.
Eze 17: 5 waters, and set it as a w· tree. 6851

willows
Le 23: 40 thick trees, and w· of the brook; 6155
Job 40: 22 the w· of the brook compass him "
Ps 137: 2 We hanged our harps upon the w· "
Isa 15: 7 carry away to the brook of the w·. "
44: 4 grass, as w· by the water courses. "

will-worship See WILL and WORSHIP.

wilt
Ge 13: 9 if thou w· take the left hand, then I
15: 2 what w· thou give me, seeing I go
16: 8 thou? and whither w· thou go? *
18: 23 W· thou also destroy the righteous
24 w· thou also destroy and not spare
28 w· thou destroy all the city for lack of
20: 4 w· thou slay also a righteous nation?
21: 23 that thou w· not deal falsely with me,
23: 13 But if thou w· give it, I pray thee,
24: 58 unto her, W· thou go with this man?
30: 31 if thou w· do this thing for me, I will
38: 16 What w· thou give me, that thou
17 W· thou give me a pledge, till thou
43: 4 If thou w· send our brother with us,
5 But if thou w· not send him, we will
Ex 4: 13 the hand of him whom thou w· send.
8: 21 if thou w· not let my people go,
9: 2 let them go, and w· hold them still,
17 people, that thou w· not let them go?
10: 3 long w· thou refuse to humble thyself
13: 13 and if thou w· redeem it, then thou
15: 26 w· diligently hearken to the voice
26 and w· do that which is right in his
26 w· give ear to his commandments,
18: 18 Thou w· surely wear away, both thou
20: 25 And if thou w· make an altar of stone,*
32: 32 now, if thou w· forgive their sin—;
33: 12 know whom thou w· send with me.
Nu 16: 14 w· thou put out the eyes of these men?
22 and w· thou be wroth with all the
21: 2 If thou w· indeed deliver this people
De 30: 17 so that thou w· not hear, but shall be
Jos 7: 9 what w· thou do unto thy great name?
J'g 1: 14 Caleb said unto her, What w· thou?*
4: 8 If thou w· go with me, then I will go:
8 but if thou w· not go with me, then I
6: 36 If thou w· save Israel by mine hand,
37 thou w· save Israel by mine hand,
11: 24 W· not thou possess that which
13: 16 and if thou w· offer a burnt offering,
Ru 4: 4 If thou w· redeem it, redeem it:
4 but if thou w· not redeem it, then tell
1Sa 1: 11 thou w· indeed look on the affliction
11 but w· give unto thine handmaid a
14 How long w· thou be drunken?
14: 37 w· thou deliver them into the hand
16: 1 How long w· thou mourn for Saul,
19: 5 then w· thou sin against innocent
21: 9 if thou w· take that, take it: for there
24: 21 thou w· not cut off my seed after me,
21 that thou w· not destroy my name
25: 17 know and consider what thou w· do;
30: 15 by God; that thou w· neither kill me,

2Sa 13: 4 w· thou not tell me? And Amnon said
18: 22 Wherefore w· thou run, my son,
20: 19 why w· thou swallow up the
22: 26 thou w· shew thyself merciful,
26 man thou w· shew thyself upright.
27 the pure thou w· shew thyself pure;
27 thou w· shew thyself unsavoury.
28 And the afflicted people thou w· save:
24: 13 or w· thou flee three months before
1Ki 3: 14 And if thou w· walk in my ways,
6: 12 if thou w· walk in my statutes,
9: 4 And if thou w· walk before me,
4 and w· keep my statutes and my
11: 38 w· hearken unto all that I command
38 and w· walk in my ways, and do that
12: 7 If thou w· be a servant unto this
7 and w· serve them, and answer them,
13: 8 If thou w· give me half thine house,
22: 4 W· thou go with me to battle to
2Ki 3: 7 w· thou go with me against Moab to
4: 23 Wherefore w· thou go to him to day?
8: 12 the evil that thou w· do unto the
12 their strong holds w· thou set on fire,
12 men w· thou slay with the sword,
12 and w· dash their children, and rip up
18: 24 How then w· thou turn away the face*
1Ch 14: 10 w· thou deliver them into mine hand?
17: 25 that thou w· build him an house:
2Ch 7: 17 if thou w· walk before me, as David
18: 3 king of Judah, W· thou go with me
20: 9 affliction, then thou w· hear and help.
12 O our God, w· thou not judge them?
25: 8 But if thou w· go, do it, be strong for
Ne 2: 6 and when thou w· return?
Es 5: 3 unto her, What w· thou, queen Esther?
Job 4: 2 with thee, w· thou be grieved?
5: 1 to which of the saints w· thou turn?
7: 19 How long w· thou not depart from me,
8: 2 How long w· thou not speak these
9: 28 that thou w· not hold me innocent.
10: 9 and w· thou bring me into dust again?
14 and thou w· not acquit me from mine
13: 25 W· thou break a leaf driven to and
25 and w· thou pursue the dry stubble?
14: 15 w· have a desire to the work of thine*
30: 23 I know that thou w· bring me to death,
34: 17 w· thou condemn him that is most
38: 39 W· thou hunt the prey for the lion?
39: 11 W· thou trust him, because his
11 or w· thou leave thy labour to him?
12 W· thou believe him, that he will
40: 8 W· thou also disannul my
8 w· thou condemn me, that thou
41: 4 w· thou take him for a servant for*
5 W· thou play with him as with a bird,
5 or w· thou bind him for thy maidens?
Ps 5: 12 Lord, w· thou bless the righteous;
12 with favour w· thou compass him as
10: 13 in his heart, Thou w· not require it.
17 w· prepare their heart, thou w· cause
13: 1 How long w· thou forget me, O Lord?
1 long w· thou hide thy face from me?
16: 10 For thou w· not leave my soul in hell;
10 w· thou suffer thine Holy One to see
11 Thou w· shew me the path of life:
17: 6 thee, for thou w· hear me, O God:
18: 25 thou w· shew thyself merciful;
25 man thou w· shew thyself upright;
26 the pure thou w· shew thyself pure;
26 thou w· shew thyself froward.
27 For thou w· save the afflicted people;
27 but w· bring down high looks.
28 thou w· light my candle: the Lord my
35: 17 Lord, how long w· thou look on?
38: 15 thou w· hear, O Lord my God.
41: 2 thou w· not deliver him unto the will*
3 w· make all his bed in his sickness.*
51: 17 heart, O God, thou w· not despise.
56: 13 w· not thou deliver my feet from *
60: 10 W· not thou, O God, which hadst*
61: 6 Thou w· prolong the king's life: and
65: 5 in righteousness w· thou answer us,
79: 5 Lord? w· thou be angry for ever?
80: 4 how long w· thou be angry against
81: 8 O Israel, if thou w· hearken unto me;*
85: 5 W· thou be angry with us for ever?
5 w· thou draw out thine anger to all
6 W· thou not revive us again: that thy
86: 7 upon thee: for thou w· answer me.
88: 10 W· thou shew wonders to the dead?
89: 46 Lord? w· thou hide thyself for ever?
101: 2 O when w· thou come unto me? I will
108: 11 W· not thou, O God, who hast cast*
11 w· not thou, O God, go forth with our*
119: 82 saying, When w· thou comfort me?
84 w· thou execute judgment on them
138: 7 midst of trouble, thou w· revive me:
139: 19 Surely thou w· slay the wicked, O God:
Pr 2: 1 My son, if thou w· receive my words,
5: 20 why w· thou, my son, be ravished*
6: 9 How long w· thou sleep, O sluggard?
9 when w· thou arise out of thy sleep?
23: 5 W· thou set thine eyes upon that
Isa 26: 3 Thou w· keep him in perfect peace,
12 Lord, thou w· ordain peace for us:
27: 8 shooteth forth, thou w· debate with it:*
36: 9 How then w· thou turn away the face*
38: 12, 13 w· thou make an end of me.
16 so w· thou recover me, and make*
58: 5 w· thou call this a fast, and an
64: 12 W· thou refrain thyself for these
12 w· thou hold thy peace, and afflict us
Jer 3: 4 W· thou not from this time cry unto
4: 1 If thou w· return, O Israel, saith the
1 and if thou w· put away thine
30 thou art spoiled, what w· thou do?
Jer 12: 5 w· thou do in the swelling of Jordan?
13: 21 What w· thou say when he shall
27 w· thou not be made clean?
15: 18 w· thou be...unto me as a liar,
31: 22 How long w· thou go about, O thou
38: 15 w· thou not surely put me to death?
15 w· thou not hearken unto me?
17 If thou w· assuredly go forth unto the
18 But if thou w· not go forth to the
47: 5 valley: how long w· thou cut thyself?
La 1: 21 thou w· bring the day that thou hast
Eze 9: 8 w· thou destroy all the residue of
11: 13 w· thou make a full end of the
20: 4 W· thou judge them, son of man,
4 w· thou judge them? cause them to
22: 2 thou son of man, w· thou judge,
2 w· thou judge the bloody city?
23: 36 w· thou judge Aholah and Aholibah?
24: 19 W· thou not tell us these things are
28: 9 W· thou yet say before him that
37: 18 W· thou not shew us what thou
Hos 9: 14 O Lord: what w· thou give? give them
Mic 7: 19 w· cast all their sins into the depths of
20 Thou w· perform the truth to Jacob,
Hab 1: 2 shall I cry, and thou w· not hear!
2 out of violence, and thou w· not save!
Zep 3: 7 I said, Surely thou w· fear me,
7 thou w· receive instruction; so their
Zec 1: 12 how long w· thou not have mercy on
3: 7 If thou w· walk in my ways, and if
7 and if thou w· keep my charge,
M't 4: 9 if thou w· fall down and worship me.
8: 2 Lord, if thou w·, thou canst make 2309
13: 28 W· thou then that we go and "
15: 28 be it unto thee even as thou w·. "
17: 4 if thou w·, let us make here three "
19: 17 but if thou w· enter into life, keep* "
21 If thou w· be perfect, go and sell * "
20: 21 he said unto her, What w· thou? "
26: 17 Where w· thou that we prepare for "
39 not as I will, but as thou w·. "
M'r 1: 40 If thou w·, thou canst make me 2309
6: 22 Ask of me whatsoever thou w·, and "
10: 51 What w· thou that I should do unto "
14: 12 Where w· thou that we go and "
36 not what I will, but what thou w·. "
Lu 4: 7 If thou therefore w· worship me, all
5: 12 Lord, if thou w·, thou canst make 2309
9: 54 w· thou that we command fire to "
22: 9 Where w· thou that we prepare? "
Joh 2: 20 and w· thou rear it up in three days?
5: 6 him, W· thou be made whole? *2309
11: 22 whatsoever thou w· ask of God, *
13: 38 W· thou lay down thy life for my
14: 22 that thou w· manifest thyself unto us,
Ac 1: 6 w· thou at this time restore again the*
2: 27 thou w· not leave my soul in hell,
27 neither w· thou suffer thine Holy One
7: 28 W· thou kill me as thou diddest *2309
9: 6 Lord, what w· thou have me to do?* "
13: 10 w· thou not cease to perverse the
25: 9 W· thou go up to Jerusalem, and
Ro 9: 19 Thou w· say then unto me, Why doth
11: 19 Thou w· say then, The branches were
13: 3 W· thou then not be afraid of the *2309
Ph'm 21 thou w· also do more than I say.
Jas 2: 20 But w· thou know, O vain man, 2309

wimples
Isa 3: 22 and the w·, and the crisping pins,*4304

win See also WINNETH; WON.
2Ch 32: 1 thought to w· them for himself. 1234
Ph'p 3: 8 but dung, that I may w· Christ. 2770

wind See also WHIRLWIND; WINDING; WINDS; WOUND.
Ge 8: 1 God made a w· to pass over the 7307
41: 6 blasted with the east w· sprung up
23 blasted with the east w·, sprung up
27 empty ears blasted with the east w·
Ex 10: 13 Lord brought an east w· upon the 7307
13 the east w· brought the locusts. "
19 turned a mighty strong west w·, "
14: 21 sea to go back by a strong east w· "
15: 10 Thou didst blow with thy w·, the "
Nu 11: 31 went forth a w· from the Lord, and "
2Sa 22: 11 was seen upon the wings of the w·. "
1Ki 18: 45 was black with clouds and w·, "
19: 11 and strong w· rent the mountains, "
11 but the Lord was not in the w·: "
11 and after the w· an earthquake; "
2Ki 3: 17 Ye shall not see w·, neither shall "
Job 1: 19 a great w· from the wilderness, "
6: 26 is desperate, which are as w·? "
7: 7 O remember that my life is w·: ‡ "
8: 2 of thy mouth be like a strong w·? "
15: 2 and fill his belly with the east w·? "
21: 18 They are as stubble before the w·, "
27: 21 The east w· carrieth him away, and "
30: 15 they pursue my soul as the w·: 7307
22 Thou liftest me up to the w·; thou "
37: 17 quieteth the earth by the south w·? "
21 but the w· passeth, and cleanseth 7307
38: 24 scattereth the east w· upon the earth? "
Ps 1: 4 chaff which the w· driveth away. 7307
18: 10 he did fly upon the wings of the w·. "
42 small as the dust before the w·: "
35: 5 Let them be as chaff before the w·: "
48: 7 ships of Tarshish with an east w·.* "
78: 26 He caused an east w· to blow in the "
26 power he brought in the south w·. "
39 a w· that passeth away, and 7307
83: 13 wheel; as the stubble before the w·. "
103: 16 For the w· passeth over it, and it is "
104: 3 walketh upon the wings of the w·: "
107: 25 and raiseth the stormy w·, "
135: 7 bringeth the w· out of his treasuries. "
Ps 147: 18 he caused his w· to blow, and the 7307
148: 8 stormy w· fulfilling his word: "
Pr 11: 29 his own house shall inherit the w·: "
25: 14 like clouds and w· without rain. "
23 The north w· driveth away rain: "
27: 16 hideth her hideth the w·, and "
30: 4 hath gathered the w· in his fists? "
Ec 1: 6 w· goeth toward the south, and "
6 w· returneth again according to the "
5: 16 he that hath laboured for the w·? "
11: 4 observeth the w· shall not sow; "
Ca 4: 16 Awake, O north w·; and come, thou
Isa 7: 2 the wood are moved with the w·. 7307
11: 15 with his mighty w· shall he shake "
17: 13 of the mountains before the w·, "
26: 18 have as it were brought forth w·; "
27: 8 he stayeth his rough w· * "
8 in the day of the east w·. "
32: 2 be as an hiding place from the w·, 7307
41: 16 and the w· shall carry them away, "
29 molten images are w· and confusion. "
57: 13 the w· shall carry them all away; "
64: 6 iniquities, like the w·, have taken "
Jer 2: 24 snuffeth up the w· at her pleasure; "
4: 11 A dry w· of the high places in the "
12 w· from those places shall come "
5: 13 And the prophets shall become w·, "
10: 13 forth the w· out of his treasures. "
13: 24 away by the w· of the wilderness. "
14: 6 snuffed up the w· like dragons; * "
18: 17 will scatter them as with an east w· "
22: 22 The w· shall eat up all thy pastors, "
51: 1 up against me, a destroying w·; "
16 forth the w· out of his treasures. "
Eze 5: 2 part thou shalt scatter in the w·; "
12: 14 scatter toward every w· all that are "
13: 11 fall; and a stormy w· shall rend it. "
13 rend it with a stormy w· in my fury; "
17: 10 when the east w· toucheth it? "
19: 12 and the east w· dried up her fruit: "
27: 26 the east w· hath broken thee in "
37: 9 he unto me, Prophesy unto the w·, "
9 son of man, and say to the w·, "
Da 2: 35 and the w· carried them away, that 7308
Ho 4: 19 The w· hath bound her up in her 7307
8: 7 they have sown the w·, and they "
12: 1 Ephraim feedeth on w·, "
1 and followeth after the east w·: "
13: 15 brethren, an east w· shall come, "
15 the w· of the Lord shall come up *7307
Am 4: 13 mountains, and createth the w·, "
Jon 1: 4 sent out a great w· into the sea "
4: 8 God prepared a vehement east w·; "
Hab 1: 9 their faces shall sup up as the east w·. "
Zec 5: 9 and the w· was in their wings; 7307
M't 11: 7 to see. A reed shaken with the w·? 417
14: 24 with waves: for the w· was contrary. "
30 But when he saw the w· boisterous, "
32 come into the ship, the w· ceased. "
M'r 4: 37 And there arose a great storm of w·, "
39 And he arose, and rebuked the w·, "
39 the w· ceased, and there was a great "
41 even the w· and the sea obey him? "
6: 48 for the w· was contrary unto them: "
51 into the ship; and the w· ceased: "
Lu 7: 24 to see? A reed shaken with the w·? "
8: 23 down a storm of w· on the lake; "
24 rebuked the w· and the raging of "
12: 55 And when ye see the south w· blow, "
Joh 3: 8 The w· bloweth where it listeth, 4151
6: 18 by reason of the great w· that blew. 417
Ac 2: 2 heaven as of a rushing mighty w·, 4157
27: 7 the w· not suffering us, we sailed 417
13 And when the south w· blew softly, "
14 arose against it a tempestuous w·, 417
15 and could not bear up into the w·, "
40 hoised up the mainsail to the w·, 4154
28: 13 and after one day the south w· blew, "
Eph 4: 14 about with every w· of doctrine, 417
Jas 1: 6 wave of the sea driven with the w· 416
Re 6: 13 when she is shaken of a mighty w·. 417
7: 1 the w· should not blow on the earth, "

winding
1Ki 6: 8 and they went up with w· stairs 3583
Eze 41: 7 a w· about still upward to the side *5437
7 w· about of the house went still *4141

window See also WINDOWS.
Ge 6: 16 A w· shalt thou make to the ark, *6672
8: 6 Noah opened the w· of the ark 2474
26: 8 the Philistines looked out at a w·, "
Jos 2: 15 down by a cord through the w·: "
18 bind this line of...thread in the "
21 she bound the scarlet line in the w·. "
J'g 5: 28 of Sisera looked out at a w·, "
1Sa 19: 12 let David down through a w·: "
2Sa 6: 16 daughter looked through a w·, "
2Ki 9: 30 her head, and looked out at a w·. "
32 And he lifted up his face to the w·, "
13: 17 And he said, Open the w· eastward. "
1Ch 15: 29 looking out at a w· saw king David "
Pr 7: 6 at the w· of my house I looked "
Ac 20: 9 sat in a w· a certain young man 2376
2Co 11: 33 through a w· in a basket was I let "

windows
Ge 7: 11 and the w· of heaven were opened. 699
8: 2 and the w· of heaven were stopped, "
1Ki 6: 4 he made w· of narrow lights. 2474
7: 4 And there were w· in three rows, *8261
5 posts were square, with the w·: *8260
2Ki 7: 2 Lord would make w· in heaven, 699
19 Lord should make w· in heaven, "
Ec 12: 3 that look out of the w· be darkened, "
Ca 2: 9 he looketh forth at the w·, 2474
Isa 24: 18 for the w· from on high are opened, 699
54: 12 I will make thy w· of agates, and *8121

Isa 60: 8 and as the doves to their *w*? 699
Jer 9: 21 For death is come up into our *w*. 2474
22: 14 chambers, and cutteth him out *w*; "
Eze 40: 16 narrow *w* to the little chambers, "
16 and *w* were round about inward: "
22 And their *w*, and their arches, and "
25 were *w* in it and in the arches "
25 thereof round about, like those *w*: "
29 were *w* in it and in the arches "
33 were *w* therein and in the arches "
36 and the *w* to it round about: "
41: 16 The door posts, and the narrow *w*, "
16 and from the ground up to the *w*, "
16 and the *w* were covered; "
26 were narrow *w* and palm trees "
Da 6: 10 his *w* being open in his chamber 3551
Joe 2: 9 shall enter in at the *w* like a thief. 2474
Zep 2: 14 their voice shall sing in the *w*; "
Mal 3: 10 will not open you the *w* of heaven, 699

winds See also WHIRLWINDS.
Job 28: 25 To make the weight for the *w*; *7307
Jer 49: 32 I will scatter into all *w* them that "
36 upon Elam will I bring the four *w* "
36 scatter them toward all those *w*; "
Eze 5: 10 of thee will I scatter into all the *w*. "
12 scatter a third part into all the *w*, "
17: 21 shall be scattered toward all *w*: * "
37: 9 Come from the four *w*, O breath, "
Da 7: 2 the four *w* of the heaven strove 7308
8: 8 ones toward the four *w* of heaven. 7307
11: 4 toward the four *w* of heaven; "
Zec 2: 6 as the four *w* of the heaven, "
M't 7: 25, 27 the floods came, and the *w* blew, 417
8: 26 and rebuked the *w* and the sea; "
27 even the *w* and the sea obey him! "
24: 31 together his elect from the four *w*, "
M'r 13: 27 together his elect from the four *w*, "
Lu 8: 25 commandeth even the *w* and water, "
Ac 27: 4 because the *w* were contrary. "
Jas 3: 4 are driven of fierce *w*, yet are they "
Jude 12 without water, carried about of *w*; "
Re 7: 1 holding the four *w* of the earth, "

windy
Ps 55: 8 my escape from the *w* storm 7307

wine See also WINEBIBBER; WINEFAT; WINEPRESS; WINES.
Ge 9: 21 And he drank of the *w*, and was 3196
24 Noah awoke from his *w*, and knew "
14: 18 Salem brought forth bread and *w*: "
19: 32 let us make our father drink *w*, "
33 they made their father drink *w* "
34 make him drink *w* this night also; "
35 they made their father drink *w* "
27: 25 he brought him *w*, and he drank. "
28 earth, and plenty of corn and *w*: 8492
37 corn and *w* have I sustained him: "
49: 11 he washed his garments in *w*, 3196
12 His eyes shall be red with *w*, "
Ex 29: 40 the fourth part of an hin of *w* "
Le 10: 9 Do not drink *w* nor strong drink, "
23: 13 drink offering thereof shall be of *w*, "
Nu 6: 3 He shall separate himself from *w* "
3 and shall drink no vinegar of *w*, "
20 that the Nazarite may drink *w*. "
15: 5 the fourth part of an hin of *w* "
7 offer the third part of an hin of *w*, "
10 a drink offering half an hin of *w*, "
18: 12 all the best of the *w*, and of the *8492
28: 7 cause the strong *w* to be poured 7941
14 offerings shall be half an hin of *w* 3196
De 7: 13 of thy land, thy corn, and thy *w*, 8492
11: 14 gather in thy corn, and thy *w*, "
12: 17 the tithe of thy corn, or of thy *w*, "
14: 23 the tithe of thy corn, of thy *w*, "
26 for sheep, or for *w*, or for strong 3196
16: 13 gathered in thy corn and thy *w*: *3342
18: 4 also of the corn, of thy *w*, and of 8492
28: 39 but shalt neither drink of the *w*, 3196
51 leave thee either corn, *w*, or oil, 8492
29: 6 neither have ye drunk *w* or strong 3196
32: 33 Their *w* is the poison of dragons, "
38 and drank the *w* of their drink "
33: 28 be upon a land of corn and *w*; 8492
Jos 9: 4 and *w* bottles, old, and rent, and *3196
13 these bottles of *w*, which we filled.* "
J'g 9: 13 Should I leave my *w*, which 8492
13: 4 and drink not *w* nor strong drink, 3196
7 now drink no *w* nor strong drink, "
14 let her drink *w* or strong drink, "
19: 19 there is bread and *w* also for me, "
1Sa 1: 14 put away thy *w* from thee. "
15 drunk neither *w* nor strong drink, "
24 ephah of flour, and a bottle of *w*, "
10: 3 another carrying a bottle of *w*: "
16: 20 with bread, and a bottle of *w*, "
25: 18 hundred loaves, two bottles of *w*, "
37 when the *w* was gone out of Nabal, "
2Sa 6: 19 piece of flesh, and a flagon of *w*. *
13: 28 Amnon's heart is merry with *w*, 3196
16: 1 summer fruits, and a bottle of *w*. "
2 and the *w*, that such as be faint "
2Ki 18: 32 own land, a land of corn and *w*, 8492
1Ch 9: 29 fine flour, and the *w*, and the oil, 3196
12: 40 bunches of raisins, and *w*, and oil, "
16: 3 good piece of flesh, and a flagon of *w*.*
27: 27 of the vineyards for the *w* cellars 3196
2Ch 2: 10 and twenty thousand baths of *w*, "
15 and the *w*, which my lord hath "
11: 11 store of victual, and of oil and *w*. "
31: 5 the firstfruits of corn, *w*, and oil, 8492
32: 28 increase of corn, and *w*, and oil; "
Ezr 6: 9 God of heaven, wheat, salt, *w*, 2562
7: 22 and to an hundred baths of *w*, "
Ne 2: 1 the king, that *w* was before him: 3196
1 and I took up the *w*, and gave it "
Ne 5: 11 the *w*, and the oil, that ye exact 8492
15 had taken of them bread and *w*, 3196
18 ten days store of all sorts of *w*: "
10: 37 of *w* and of oil, unto the priests, 8492
39 offering of the corn, of the new *w*, "
13: 5 tithes of the corn, the new *w*, "
12 the new *w* and the oil unto the "
15 some treading *w* presses on the *1660
15 as also *w*, grapes, and figs, and 3196
Es 1: 7 and royal *w* in abundance, "
10 of the king was merry with *w*, "
5: 6 unto Esther at the banquet of *w*, "
7: 2 second day at the banquet of *w*, "
7 arising from the banquet of *w* in "
8 into the place of the banquet of *w*; "
Job 1: 13, 18 and drinking *w* in their eldest "
32: 19 belly is as *w* which hath no vent; "
Ps 4: 7 their corn and their *w* increased. 8492
60: 3 to drink the *w* of astonishment. 3196
75: 8 there is a cup, and the *w* is red; "
78: 65 man that shouteth by reason of *w*. "
104: 15 *w* that maketh glad the heart of "
Pr 3: 10 shall burst out with new *w*. 8492
4: 17 and drink the *w* of violence. 3196
9: 2 beasts; she hath mingled her *w*; "
5 and drink of the *w* which I have "
20: 1 *W* is a mocker, strong drink is "
21: 17 he that loveth *w* and oil shall not "
23: 30 They that tarry long at the *w*; "
30 they that go to seek mixed *w*. 4469
31 Look not thou upon the *w* when 3196
31: 4 it is not for kings to drink *w*; "
6 and *w* unto those that be of heavy "
Ec 2: 3 mine heart to give myself unto *w*, "
9: 7 drink thy *w* with a merry heart; "
10: 19 for laughter, and *w* maketh merry: "
Ca 1: 2 for thy love is better than *w*. "
4 remember thy love more than *w*: "
4: 10 much better is thy love than *w*! "
5: 1 I have drunk my *w* with my milk: "
7: 9 like the best *w* for my beloved, "
8: 2 cause thee to drink of spiced *w* "
Isa 1: 22 dross, thy *w* mixed with water: 5435
5: 11 until night, till *w* inflame them! 3196
12 pipe, and *w*, are in their feasts: "
22 them that are mighty to drink *w*, "
16: 10 tread out no *w* in their presses; "
22: 13 eating flesh, and drinking *w*: "
24: 7 The new *w* mourneth, the vine 8492
9 shall not drink *w* with a song; 3196
11 is a crying for *w* in the streets; "
27: 2 ye unto her, A vineyard of red *w*. 2561
28: 1 them that are overcome with *w*! 3196
7 they also have erred through *w*, "
7 drink, they are swallowed up of *w*, "
29: 9 they are drunken, but not with *w*; "
36: 17 own land, a land of corn and *w*, 8492
49: 26 their own blood, as with sweet *w*: 6071
51: 21 and drunken, but not with *w*: 3196
55: 1 buy *w* and milk without money "
56: 12 Come ye, say they, I will fetch *w*, "
62: 8 the stranger shall not drink thy *w*, 8492
65: 8 new *w* is found in the cluster, "
Jer 13: 12 bottle shall be filled with *w*: 3196
12 every bottle shall be filled with *w*? "
23: 9 like a man whom *w* hath overcome, "
25: 15 Take the *w* cup of this fury at my "
31: 12 for wheat, and for *w*, and for oil, 8492
35: 2 chambers, and give them *w* to drink. 3196
5 of the Rechabites pots full of *w*, "
5 and I said unto them, Drink ye *w*. "
6 they said, We will drink no *w*: "
6 Ye shall drink no *w*, neither ye, "
8 us, to drink no *w* all our days, "
14 his sons not to drink *w*, "
40: 10 gather ye *w*, and summer fruits, "
12 gathered *w* and summer fruits very "
48: 33 *w* to fail from the winepresses: "
51: 7 the nations have drunken of her *w*; "
La 2: 12 mothers, Where is corn and *w*? "
Eze 27: 18 in the *w* of Helbon, and white wool. "
44: 21 Neither shall any priest drink *w*, "
Da 1: 5 meat, and of the *w* which he drank: "
8 nor with the *w* which he drank: "
16 and the *w* that they should drink; "
5: 1 and drank *w* before the thousand. 2562
2 Belshazzar, whiles he tasted the *w*, "
4 They drank *w*, and praised the "
23 concubines, have drunk *w* in them; "
10: 3 came flesh nor *w* in my mouth, 3196
Ho 2: 8 know that I gave her corn, and *w*, 8492
9 and my *w* in the season thereof, "
22 shall hear the corn, and the *w*, "
3: 1 other gods, and love flagons of *w*. *6025
4: 11 Whoredom and *w* and new 3196
11 and new *w* take away the heart. 8492
7: 5 made him sick with bottles of *w*; 3196
14 themselves for corn and *w*, 8492
9: 2 and the new *w* shall fail in her. "
4 They shall not offer *w* offerings "
14: 7 shall be as the *w* of Lebanon. "
Joe 1: 5 and howl, all ye drinkers of *w*, 3196
5 because of the new *w*; for it is cut 6071
10 the new *w* is dried up, the oil 8492
2: 19 I will send you corn, and *w*, and "
24 fats shall overflow with *w* and oil. "
3: 3 sold a girl for *w*, that they might 3196
18 shall drop down new *w*, 6071
Am 2: 8 drink the *w* of the condemned in 3196
12 ye gave the Nazarites *w* to drink; "
5: 11 but ye shall not drink *w* of them. "
6: 6 That drink *w* in bowls, and anoint "
9: 13 the mountains shall drop sweet *w*, 6071
14 plant vineyards, and drink the *w* 3196
Mic 2: 11 I will prophesy unto thee of *w* "
6: 15 anoint thee with oil; and sweet *w*, *8492
Mic 6: 15 but shalt not drink *w*. 3196
Hab 2: 5 because he transgresseth by *w*, "
Zep 1: 13 but not drink the *w* thereof. "
Hag 1: 11 upon the new *w*, and upon the oil, 8492
2: 12 do touch bread, or pottage, or *w*, 3196
Zec 9: 15 and make a noise as through *w*; "
17 cheerful, and new *w* the maids. 8492
10: 7 heart shall rejoice as through *w*: 3196
M't 9: 17 men put new *w* into old bottles: 3631
17 and the *w* runneth out, and the "
17 they put new *w* into new bottles, "
M'r 2: 22 putteth new *w* into old bottles; "
22 the new *w* doth burst the bottles, "
22 and the *w* is spilled, and the "
22 but new *w* must be put into new "
15: 23 to drink *w* mingled with myrrh: "
Lu 1: 15 drink neither *w* nor strong drink; "
5: 37 putteth new *w* into old bottles; "
37 the new *w* will burst the bottles, "
38 But new *w* must be put into new "
39 also having drunk old *w* straightway "
7: 33 eating bread nor drinking *w*; 3631
10: 34 his wounds, pouring in oil and *w*, "
Joh 2: 3 when they wanted *w*, the mother "
3 saith unto him, They have no *w*. "
9 tasted the water that was made *w*, "
10 beginning doth set forth good *w*; "
10 hast kept the good *w* until now. "
4: 46 where he made the water *w*. "
Ac 2: 13 said, These men are full of new *w*. 1098
Ro 14: 21 to eat flesh, nor to drink *w*, 3631
Eph 5: 18 And be not drunk with *w*, wherein "
1Ti 3: 3 Not given to *w*, no striker, not *3943
3: 8 not given to much *w*, not greedy 3631
5: 23 use a little *w* for thy stomach's "
Tit 1: 7 not given to *w*, no striker, not *3943
2: 3 not given to much *w*, teachers of 3631
1Pe 4: 3 lusts, excess of *w*, revellings, *3632
Re 6: 6 thou hurt not the oil and the *w*. 3631
14: 8 drink of the *w* of the wrath of her "
10 drink of the *w* of the wrath of God, "
16: 19 the cup of the *w* of the fierceness "
17: 2 drunk with the *w* of her fornication. "
18: 3 have drunk of the *w* of the wrath "
13 and *w*, and oil, and fine flour, and "

winebibber See also WINEBIBBERS.
M't 11: 19 and a *w*, a friend of publicans and 3630
Lu 7: 34 and a *w*, a friend of publicans and "

winebibbers
Pr 23: 20 Be not among *w*; among 5433, 3196

wine-cellars See WINE and CELLARS.

wine-cup See WINE and CUP.

winefat
Isa 63: 2 like him that treadeth in the *w*? ‡1660
M'r 12: 1 and digged a place for the *w*, and *5276

wine-offerings See WINE and OFFERINGS.

winepress See also WINEPRESSES.
Nu 18: 27 and as the fulness of the *w*. 3342
30 and as the increase of the *w*. "
De 15: 14 out of thy floor, and out of thy *w*: "
J'g 6: 11 Gibeon threshed wheat by the *w*, 1660
7: 25 Zeeb they slew at the *w* of Zeeb, 3342
2Ki 6: 27 of the barnfloor, or out of the *w*? "
Isa 5: 2 of it, and also made a *w* therein: "
63: 3 I have trodden the *w* alone; and 6333
La 1: 15 the daughter of Judah, as in a *w*. 1660
Ho 9: 2 The floor and the *w* shall not feed 3342
M't 21: 33 and digged a *w* in it, and built a 3025
Re 14: 19 great *w* of the wrath of God. "
20 *w* was trodden without the city, "
20 and blood came out of the *w*, even "
19: 15 treadeth the *w* of the fierceness 3025, 3631

winepresses See also WINE and PRESSES.
Job 24: 11 tread their *w*, and suffer thirst. 3342
Jer 48: 33 caused wine to fail from the *w*: "
Zec 14: 10 of Hananeel unto the king's *w*. "

wines
Isa 25: 6 a feast of *w* on the lees, of fat 8105
6 of *w* on the lees well refined. "

wing See also LAPWING; WINGED; WINGS.
1Ki 6: 24 was the one *w* of the cherub, 3671
24 cubits the other *w* of the cherub: "
24 uttermost part of the one *w* unto "
27 *w* of the one touched the one wall, "
27 *w* of the other cherub touched the "
2Ch 3: 11 one *w* of the one cherub was five "
11 other *w* was likewise five cubits, "
11 reaching to the *w* of the other "
12 one *w* of the other cherub was five "
12 and the other *w* was five cubits "
12 joining to...*w* of the other cherub. "
Isa 10: 14 there was none that moved the *w*, "
Eze 17: 23 it shall dwell all fowl of every *w*; "

winged See also LONGWINGED.
Ge 1: 21 and every *w* fowl after his kind: 3671
De 4: 17 likeness of any *w* fowl that flieth in "

wings
Ex 19: 4 and how I bare you on eagles' *w*, 3671
25: 20 cherubims...stretch forth their *w* "
20 the mercy seat with their *w*, "
37: 9 the cherubims spread out their *w* "
9 and covered with their *w* over the "
Le 1: 17 shall cleave it with the *w* thereof, "
De 32: 11 her young, spreadeth abroad her *w*, "
11 them, beareth them on her *w*: * 84
Ru 2: 12 under whose *w* thou art come to 3671
2Sa 22: 11 was seen upon the *w* of the wind. "
1Ki 6: 27 they stretched forth the *w* of "
27 their *w* touched one another in the "
8: 6 even under the *w* of the cherubims. "

1Ki 8: 7 spread forth their two *w*· over the 3671
1Ch 28: 18 cherubims, that spread out their *w*·, "
2Ch 3: 11 *w*· of the cherubims were twenty 3671
13 The *w*· of these cherubims spread "
5: 7 even under the *w*· of the cherubims: "
8 cherubims spread forth their *w*· "
Job 39: 13 the goodly *w*· unto the peacocks?* "
13 or *w*· and feathers unto the ostrich?*84
26 stretch her *w*· toward the south? 3671
Ps 17: 8 hide me under the shadow of thy *w*·, "
18: 10 he did fly upon the *w*· of the wind. "
36: 7 trust under the shadow of thy *w*·. "
55: 6 said, Oh that I had *w*· like a dove! 83
57: 1 in the shadow of thy *w*· will I 3671
61: 4 I will trust in the covert of thy *w*·. "
63: 7 the shadow of thy *w*· will I rejoice. "
68: 13 *w*· of a dove covered with silver, "
91: 4 and under his *w*· shalt thou trust: "
104: 3 walketh upon the *w*· of the wind: "
139: 9 If I take the *w*· of the morning, and "
Pr 23: 5 for riches...make themselves *w*·; "
Ec 10: 20 which hath *w*· shall tell the matter. "
Isa 6: 2 the seraphims: each one had six *w*·; "
8: 8 the stretching out of his *w*· shall "
18: 1 Woe to the land shadowing with *w*·, "
40: 31 shall mount up with *w*· as eagles; 83
Jer 48: 9 Give *w*· unto Moab, that it may 6731
40 and shall spread his *w*· over Moab. 3671
49: 22 and spread his *w*· over Bozrah: and "
Eze 1: 6 faces, and every one had four *w*·. "
8 the hands of a man under their *w*·. "
8 four had their faces and their *w*·. "
9 Their *w*· were joined one to "
11 their *w*· were stretched upward; "
11 two *w*· of every one were joined one to "
23 firmament were their *w*· straight, 3671
24 I heard the noise of their *w*·, like "
24 they stood, they let down their *w*·. "
25 stood, and had let down their *w*·. "
3: 13 of the *w*· of the living creatures "
10: 5 the sound of the cherubims *w*· was "
8 of a man's hand under their *w*·. "
12 and their hands, and their *w*·, and "
16 the cherubims lifted up their *w*· to "
19 the cherubims lifted up their *w*·, "
21 apiece, and every one four *w*·; and "
21 hands of a man was under their *w*·. "
11: 22 did the cherubims lift up their *w*·, "
17: 3 A great eagle with great *w*·, "
7 another great eagle with great *w*· "
Da 7: 4 was like a lion, and had eagle's *w*·: 1611
4 till the *w*· thereof were plucked, "
6 the back of it four *w*· of a fowl; "
Ho 4: 19 wind hath bound her up in her *w*·. 3671
Zec 5: 9 and the wind was in their *w*·; for "
9 they had *w*· like the *w*· of a stork: "
Mal 4: 2 arise with healing in his *w*·; "
M't 23: 37 her chickens under her *w*·, 4420
Lu 13: 34 gather her brood under her *w*·, "
Re 4: 8 four beasts had each of them six *w*· "
9: 9 sound of their *w*· was as the sound "
12: 14 given two *w*· of a great eagle, "

wink See also WINKED; WINKETH.
Job 15: 12 away? and what do thy eyes *w*· at, ‡7335
Ps 35: 19 them *w*· with the eye that hate me 7169

winked
Ac 17: 30 times of this ignorance God *w*· at; *5237

winketh
Pr 6: 13 He *w*· with his eyes, he speaketh 7169
10: 10 He that *w*· with the eye causeth "

winneth
Pr 11: 30 life; and he that *w*· souls is wise. 3947

winnowed
Isa 30: 24 hath been *w*· with the shovel and 2219

winnoweth
Ru 3: 2 he *w*· barley to night in the 2219

winter See also WINTERED; WINTERHOUSE.
Ge 8: 22 cold and heat, and summer and *w*·, 2779
Ps 74: 17 thou hast made summer and *w*·. "
Ca 2: 11 the *w*· is past, the rain is over and 5638
Isa 18: 6 the beasts...shall *w*· upon them. 2778
Am 3: 15 I will smite the *w*· house with the 2779
Zec 14: 8 in summer and in *w*· shall it be. 2778
M't 24: 20 that your flight may not be in *w*·, 5494
M'r 13: 18 that your flight may not be in *w*·. "
Joh 10: 22 of the dedication, and it was in *w*·. "
Ac 27: 12 haven was not commodious to *w*· in, 3915
12 attain to Phenice, and there to *w*·; 3914
1Co 16: 6 I will abide, yea, and *w*· with you, "
2Ti 4: 21 thy diligence to come before *w*·. 5494
Tit 3: 12 for I have determined there to *w*·. 3914

wintered
Ac 28: 11 which had *w*· in the isle, whose 3916

winterhouse See also WINTER and HOUSE.
Jer 36: 22 the king sat in the *w*· in the ninth 2779

wipe See also WIPED; WIPETH; WIPING.
2Ki 21: 13 and I will *w*· Jerusalem as a man 4229
Ne 13: 14 *w*· not out my good deeds that I "
Isa 25: 8 Lord God will *w*· away tears from "
Lu 7: 38 did *w*· them with the hairs of her *1591
10: 11 on us, we do *w*· off against you: 631
Joh 13: 5 and to *w*· them with the towel 1591
Re 7: 17 God shall *w*· away all tears from 1813
21: 4 God shall *w*· away all tears from "

wiped
Pr 6: 33 his reproach shall not be *w*· away. 4229
Lu 7: 44 *w*· them with the hairs of her head. 1591
Joh 11: 2 and *w*· his feet with her hair, "
12: 3 and *w*· his feet with her hair: "

wipeth
2Ki 21: 13 Jerusalem as a man *w*· a dish, 4229
Pr 30: 20 she eateth, and *w*· her mouth, and "

wiping
2Ki 21: 13 *w*· it, and turning it upside down. 4229

wires
Ex 39: 3 into thin plates, and cut it into *w*·, 6616

wisdom
Ex 28: 3 I have filled with the spirit of *w*·, 2451
31: 3 with the spirit of God, in *w*·, "
6 are wise hearted I have put *w*·, "
35: 26 whose heart stirred them up in *w*· "
31 with the spirit of God, in *w*·, "
35 hath he filled with *w*· of heart, "
36: 1 in whom the Lord put *w*· and "
2 in whose heart the Lord had put *w*·, "
De 4: 6 is your *w*· and your understanding "
34: 9 of Nun was full of the spirit of *w*·; "
2Sa 14: 20 according to the *w*· of an angel of "
20: 22 went unto all the people in her *w*·. "
1Ki 2: 6 Do therefore according to thy *w*·, "
3: 28 saw that the *w*· of God was in him, "
4: 29 And God gave Solomon *w*· and "
30 Solomon's *w*· excelled the *w*· of all "
30 country, and all the *w*· of Egypt. "
34 people to hear the *w*· of Solomon, "
34 earth, which had heard of his *w*·. "
5: 12 And the Lord gave Solomon *w*·, "
7: 14 filled with *w*·, and understanding, "
10: 4 Sheba had seen all Solomon's *w*·, "
6 own land of thy acts and of thy *w*·. "
7 thy *w*· and prosperity exceedeth "
8 before thee, and that hear thy *w*·. "
23 of the earth for riches and for *w*·. "
24 sought to Solomon, to hear his *w*·, "
11: 41 and his *w*·, are they not written "
1Ch 22: 12 Only the Lord give thee *w*· and *7922
2Ch 1: 10 Give me now *w*· and knowledge, 2451
11 but hast asked *w*· and knowledge "
12 *W*· and knowledge is granted unto "
9: 3 Sheba had seen the *w*· of Solomon, "
5 land of thine acts, and of thy *w*·: "
6 greatness of thy *w*· was not told "
7 before thee, and hear thy *w*·. "
22 kings of the earth in riches and *w*·. "
23 of Solomon, to hear his *w*·, "
Ezr 7: 25 thou, Ezra, after the *w*· of thy God, 2452
Job 4: 21 go away? they die, even without *w*·. 2451
6: 13 and is *w*· driven quite from me? †8454
11: 6 would shew thee the secrets of *w*·, 2451
12: 2 people, and *w*· shall die with you. "
12 With the ancient is *w*·; and in "
13 With him is *w*· and strength, he "
16 With him is strength and *w*·: the †8454
13: 5 peace! and it should be your *w*·. 2451
15: 8 dost thou restrain *w*· to thyself? "
26: 3 counselled him that hath no *w*·? "
28: 12 But where shall *w*· be found? "
18 for the price of *w*· is above rubies. "
20 Whence then cometh *w*·? and "
28 the fear of the Lord, that is *w*·; "
32: 7 multitude of years shall teach *w*·. "
13 should say, We have found out *w*·: "
33: 33 peace, and I shall teach thee *w*·. "
34: 35 and his words were without *w*·. 7919
36: 5 he is mighty in strength and *w*·. *3820
38: 36 hath put *w*· in the inward parts? 2451
37 Who can number the clouds in *w*·? "
39: 17 God hath deprived her of *w*·, "
26 Doth the hawk fly by thy *w*·, and 998
Ps 37: 30 of the righteous speaketh *w*·, 2451
49: 3 My mouth shall speak of *w*·; and 2454
51: 6 thou shalt make me to know *w*·. 2451
90: 12 we may apply our hearts unto *w*·. "
104: 24 in *w*· hast thou made them all: "
105: 22 and teach his senators *w*·. 2449
111: 10 the Lord is the beginning of *w*·: 2451
136: 5 him that by *w*· made the heavens: *8394
Pr 1: 2 To know *w*· and instruction; 2451
3 To receive the instruction of *w*·, *7919
7 fools despise *w*· and instruction. 2451
20 *W*· crieth without; she uttereth 2454
2: 2 thou incline thine ear unto *w*·, 2451
6 For the Lord giveth *w*·: out of his "
7 He layeth up sound *w*· for the 8454
10 *w*· entereth into thine heart, and 2451
3: 13 Happy is the man that findeth *w*·, "
19 Lord by *w*· hath founded the earth; "
21 keep sound *w*· and discretion: 8454
4: 5 Get *w*·, get understanding: forget 2451
7 *W*· is the principal thing; "
7 principal thing; therefore get *w*·: "
11 have taught thee in the way of *w*·; "
5: 1 My son, attend unto my *w*·, and "
7: 4 Say unto *w*·, Thou art my sister; "
8: 1 Doth not *w*· cry? and understanding "
5 O ye simple, understand *w*·: and, 6195
11 For *w*· is better than rubies; and 2451
12 I *w*· dwell with prudence, and find "
14 Counsel is mine, and sound *w*·: *8454
9: 1 *W*· hath builded her house, she 2454
10 of the Lord is the beginning of *w*·: 2451
10: 13 hath understanding *w*· is found: "
21 but fools die for want of *w*·. *3820
23 man of understanding hath *w*·. 2451
31 mouth of the just bringeth forth *w*·: "
11: 2 shame: but with the lowly is *w*·. "
12 He that is void of *w*· despiseth his 3820
12: 8 commended according to his *w*·: 7922
13: 10 but with the well advised is *w*·. 2451
14: 6 A scorner seeketh *w*·, and findeth "
8 *w*· of the prudent is to understand "
33 *W*· resteth in the heart of him that "
15: 21 joy to him that is destitute of *w*·: 3820
33 the Lord is the instruction of *w*·; 2451
16: 16 better is it to get *w*· than gold! "
17: 16 price in the hand of a fool to get *w*·, "
24 *W*· is before him that hath "
Pr 18: 1 and intermeddleth with all *w*·. 8454
4 wellspring of *w*· as a flowing 2451
19: 8 getteth *w*· loveth his own soul: 3820
21: 30 There is no *w*· nor understanding 2451
23: 4 be rich: cease from thine own *w*·. 998
9 will despise the *w*· of thy words. 7922
23 also *w*·, and instruction, and 2451
24: 3 Through *w*· is an house builded; "
7 *W*· is too high for a fool: he 2454
14 knowledge of *w*· be unto thy soul: 2451
29: 3 Whoso loveth *w*· rejoiceth his "
15 The rod and reproof give *w*·: but "
30: 3 I neither learned *w*·, nor have the "
31: 26 She openeth her mouth with *w*·; "
Ec 1: 13 search out by *w*· concerning all "
16 have gotten more *w*· than all they "
16 my heart had great experience of *w*· "
17 And I gave my heart to know *w*·, "
18 For in much *w*· is much grief: "
2: 3 acquainting mine heart with *w*·; "
9 also my *w*· remained with me. "
12 And I turned myself to behold *w*·, "
13 Then I saw that *w*· excelleth folly, "
21 is a man whose labour is in *w*·, "
26 a man that is good in his sight *w*·, "
7: 11 *W*· is good with an inheritance: "
12 For *w*· is a defence, and money is a "
12 *w*· giveth life to them that have it. "
19 *W*· strengtheneth the wise more "
23 All this have I proved by *w*·: "
25 to seek out *w*·, and the reason of "
8: 1 a man's *w*· maketh his face to "
16 I applied mine heart to know *w*·, "
9: 10 nor device, nor knowledge, nor *w*·, "
13 This *w*· have I seen also under the "
15 he by his *w*· delivered the city; "
16 said I, *W*· is better than strength: "
16 the poor man's *w*· is despised, "
18 *W*· is better than weapons of war: "
10: 1 in reputation for *w*· and honour. "
3 his *w*· faileth him, and he saith *3820
10 but *w*· is profitable to direct. 2451
Isa 10: 13 hand I have done it, and by my *w*·; "
11: 2 the spirit of *w*· and understanding, "
29: 14 *w*· of their wise men shall perish, "
33: 6 *w*· and knowledge shall be the "
47: 10 Thy *w*· and thy knowledge, it hath "
Jer 8: 9 the Lord; and what *w*· is in them? "
9: 23 not the wise man glory in his *w*·, "
10: 12 hath established the world by his *w*·, "
49: 7 Is *w*· no more in Teman? is counsel "
7 the prudent? is their *w*· vanished? "
51: 15 hath established the world by his *w*·, "
Eze 28: 4 With thy *w*· and with thine "
5 By thy great *w*· and by thy traffick "
7 swords against the beauty of thy *w*·, "
12 Thou sealest up the sum, full of *w*·, "
17 thou hast corrupted thy *w*· by "
Da 1: 4 and skilful in all *w*·, and cunning "
17 and skill in all learning and *w*·: "
20 matters of *w*· and understanding, "
2: 14 answered with counsel and *w*· to *2942
20 ever: for *w*· and might are his: 2452
21 he giveth *w*· unto the wise, and "
23 who hast given me *w*· and might, "
30 is not revealed to me for any *w*· "
5: 11 light and understanding and *w*·, "
11 like the *w*· of the gods, was found "
14 and excellent *w*· is found in thee. "
Mic 6: 9 the man of *w*· shall see thy name: 8454
M't 11: 19 But *w*· is justified of her children. 4678
12: 42 earth to hear the *w*· of Solomon; "
13: 54 Whence hath this man this *w*·, and "
M'r 6: 2 *w*· is this which is given unto him, "
Lu 1: 17 disobedient to the *w*· of the just; 5428
2: 40 strong in spirit, filled with *w*·: 4678
52 Jesus increased in *w*· and stature, "
7: 35 *w*· is justified of all her children. "
11: 31 earth to hear the *w*· of Solomon; "
49 Therefore also said the *w*· of God, "
21: 15 For I will give you a mouth and *w*·, "
Ac 6: 3 full of the Holy Ghost and *w*·, "
10 they were not able to resist the *w*· "
7: 10 gave him favour and *w*· in the sight "
22 in all the *w*· of the Egyptians, "
Ro 11: 33 depth of the riches both of the *w*· "
1Co 1: 17 not with *w*· of words, lest the cross "
19 I will destroy the *w*· of the wise, "
20 made foolish the *w*· of this world? "
21 For after that in the *w*· of God "
21 the world by *w*· knew not God, "
22 sign, and the Greeks seek after *w*·: "
24 the power of God, and the *w*· of God. "
30 who of God is made unto us *w*·, "
2: 1 with excellency of speech or of *w*·, "
4 with enticing words of man's *w*·, "
5 should not stand in the *w*· of men, "
6 we speak *w*· among them that are "
6 yet not the *w*· of this world, nor of "
7 we speak the *w*· of God in a "
7 even the hidden *w*·, which God "
13 words which man's *w*· teacheth, 4678
3: 19 *w*· of this world is foolishness with "
12: 8 given by the Spirit the word of *w*·; "
2Co 1: 12 not with fleshly *w*·, but by the grace "
Eph 1: 8 hath abounded toward us in all *w*· "
17 you the spirit of *w*· and revelation "
3: 10 the church the manifold *w*· of God, "
Col 1: 9 the knowledge of his will in all *w*· "
28 and teaching every man in all *w*·; "
2: 3 whom are hid all the treasures of *w*· "
23 indeed a shew of *w*· in will worship, "
3: 16 Christ dwell in you richly in all *w*·; "
4: 5 Walk in *w*· toward them that are "
Jas 1: 5 If any of you lack *w*·, let him ask "
3: 13 his works with meekness of *w*·. "

Jas 3:15 This w· descendeth not from above,4678
17 But the w· that is from above is "
2Pe 3:15 according to the w· given unto him "
Re 5:12 and w·, and strength, and honour, "
7:12 Blessing, and glory, and w·, and "
13:18 Here is w·. Let him that hath "
17: 9 here is the mind which hath w·. "

wise See also CONTRARIWISE; LIKEWISE; OTHERWISE; UNWISE; WISER.
Ge 3: 6 tree to be desired to make one w·, 7919
41: 8 and all the w· men thereof: 2450
33 look out a man discreet and w·, "
39 so discreet and w· as thou art: "
Ex 7:11 Pharaoh also called the w· men "
22:23 If thou afflict them in any w·, and 6031
23: 8 the gift blindeth the w·, and *6493
28: 3 speak unto all that are w· hearted,2450
31: 6 the hearts of all that are w· hearted"
35:10 every w· hearted among you shall "
25 the women that were w· hearted "
36: 1 every w· hearted man, in whom "
2 every w· hearted man, in whose "
4 And all the w· men, that wrought "
8 every w· hearted man among them "
Le 7:24 use: but ye shall in no w· eat of it.
19:17 thou shalt in any w· rebuke thy *3198
27:19 the field will in any w· redeem it.*
Nu 6:23 On this w· ye shall bless the children
De 1:13 Take you w· men, and 2450
15 the chief of your tribes, w· men, "
4: 6 is a w· and understanding people. "
16:19 a gift doth blind the eyes of the w·, "
17:15 shalt in any w· set him king over ‡
21:23 shalt in any w· bury him that day;*
22: 7 thou shalt in any w· let the dam go,‡
32:29 O that they were w·, that they 2449
Jos 6:18 in any w· keep yourselves from the
23:12 if ye do in any w· go back, and cleave
J'g 5:29 Her w· ladies answered her, yea, 2450
1Sa 6: 3 any w· return him a trespass offering:
2Sa 14: 2 and fetched thence a w· woman, 2450
20 and my lord is w·, according to the "
20:16 Then cried a w· woman out of the "
1Ki 2: 9 for thou art a w· man, and knowest"
3:12 a w· and an understanding heart; "
26 the living child, and in no w· slay it.
27 the living child, and in no w· slay it:
5: 7 hath given unto David a w· son 2450
11:22 Nothing: howbeit let me go in any w·.
1Ch 26:14 Zechariah his son, a w· counseller,*7922
27:32 counseller, a w· man, and a scribe:*995
2Ch 2:12 given to David the king a w· son, 2450
Es 1:13 Then the king said to the w· men, "
6:13 Then said his w· men and Zeresh "
Job 5:13 He taketh the w· in their own "
9: 4 He is w· in heart, and mighty in "
11:12 vain man would be w·, though *3823
15: 2 a w· man utter vain knowledge, 2450
18 w· men have told from their fathers,"
17:10 cannot find one w· man among you."
22: 2 he that is w· may be profitable 7919
32: 9 Great men are not always w·: 2449
34: 2 Hear my words, O ye w· men; 2450
34 and let a w· man hearken unto me. "
37:24 not any that are w· of heart. "
Ps 2:10 Be w· now therefore, O ye kings: 7919
19: 7 is sure, making w· the simple. 2449
36: 3 he hath left off to be w·, and to do 7919
37: 8 fret not thyself in any w· to do evil.*
49:10 For he seeth that w· men die, 2450
94: 8 and ye fools, when will ye be w·? 7919
107:43 Whoso is w·, and will observe 2450
Pr 1: 5 w· man will hear, and will increase "
5 man...shall attain unto w· counsels:
6 the words of the w·, and their dark2450
3: 7 Be not w· in thine own eyes: fear
35 The w· shall inherit glory: but "
6: 6 consider her ways, and be w·: 2449
8:33 Hear instruction, and be w·, and "
9: 8 rebuke a w· man, and he will love 2450
9 Give instruction to a w· man, and "
12 If thou be w·, thou shalt be w· for 2449
10: 1 A w· son maketh a glad father: 2450
5 gathereth in summer is a w· son: 7919
8 The w· in heart will receive 2450
14 W· men lay up knowledge: but "
19 he that refraineth his lips is w·. *7919
11:29 be servant to the w· of heart. 2450
30 and he that winneth souls is w·. "
12:15 hearkeneth unto counsel is w·. "
18 but the tongue of the w· is health. "
13: 1 A w· son heareth his father's "
14 law of the w· is a fountain of life, "
20 He that walketh with w· men shall "
20 shall be w·: but a companion of 2449
14: 1 Every w· woman buildeth her 2454
3 the lips of the w· shall preserve 2450
16 A w· man feareth, and departeth "
24 The crown of the w· is their riches:"
35 favour is toward a w· servant: 7919
15: 2 the w· useth knowledge aright: 2450
7 lips of the w· disperse knowledge: "
12 neither will he go unto the w·. "
20 A w· son maketh a glad father: but"
24 The way of life is above to the w·, 7919
31 of life abideth among the w·. 2450
16:14 death: but a w· man will pacify it. "
21 w· in heart shall be called prudent:"
23 heart of the w· teacheth his mouth, "
17: 2 A w· servant shall have rule over *7919
10 A reproof entereth more into a w·* 995
28 holdeth his peace, is counted w·: 2450
18:15 the ear of the w· seeketh knowledge."
19:20 that thou mayest be w· in thy 2449
20: 1 is deceived thereby is not w·. "
26 A w· king scattereth the wicked, 2450
Pr 21:11 punished, the simple is made w·: 2449
11 and when the w· is instructed, he 2450
20 and oil in the dwelling of the w·; "
22 A w· man scaleth the city of the "
22:17 and hear the words of the w·, and "
23:15 My son, if thine heart be w·, my 2449
19 Hear thou, my son, and be w·, and "
24 he that begetteth a w· child shall 2450
24: 5 A w· man is strong; yea, a man of "
6 by w· counsel thou shalt make thy
23 These things also belong to the w·.2450
25:12 a w· reprover upon an obedient ear."
26: 5 lest he be w· in his own conceit. "
12 thou a man w· in his own conceit? "
27:11 be w·, and make my heart glad, 2449
28: 7 Whoso keepeth the law is a w· son: 995
11 rich man is w· in his own conceit;2450
29: 8 snare: but w· men turn away wrath."
9 a w· man contendeth with a foolish "
11 but a w· man keepeth it in till "
30:24 earth, but they are exceeding w·: "
Ec 2:14 The w· man's eyes are in his head; "
15 me; and why was I then more w·?2449
16 no remembrance of the w· more 2450
16 how dieth the w· man? as the fool. "
19 he shall be a w· man or a fool? "
19 wherein I have shewed myself w·*2449
4:13 Better is a poor and a w· child, 2450
6: 8 hath the w· more than the fool? "
7: 4 heart of the w· is in the house of "
5 better to hear the rebuke of the w·, "
7 oppression maketh a w· man mad; "
16 neither make thyself over w·: 2449
19 Wisdom strengtheneth the w· 2450
23 I said, I will be w·; but it was far 2449
8: 1 Who is as the w· man? and who 2450
5 a w· man's heart discerneth both "
17 though a w· man think to know it, "
9: 1 that the righteous, and the w·, and "
11 neither yet bread to the w·, nor "
15 there was found in it a poor w· man,"
17 The words of w· men are heard in "
10: 2 A w· man's heart is at his right "
12 of a w· man's mouth are gracious; "
12: 9 because the preacher was w·, he "
11 The words of the w· are as goads, "
Isa 5:21 unto them that are w· in their own "
19:11 the w· counsellers of Pharaoh is * "
11 I am the son of the w·, the son of "
12 are they? where are thy w· men? "
29:14 the wisdom of their w· men shall "
31: 2 Yet he also is w·, and will bring "
44:25 that turneth w· men backward, "
Jer 4:22 they are w· to do evil, but to do "
8: 8 We are w·, and the law of the Lord "
9 w· men are ashamed, they are "
9:12 Who is the w· man, that may "
23 the w· man glory in his wisdom, "
10: 7 among all the w· men of the nations,"
18:18 nor counsel from the w·, nor the "
50:35 her princes, and upon her w· men. "
51:57 drunk her princes, and her w· men, "
Eze 27: 8 thy w· men, O Tyrus, that were in "
9 Gebal and the w· men thereof were "
Da 2:12 destroy all the w· men of Babylon.2445
13 that the w· men should be slain; "
14 to slay the w· men of Babylon: "
18 the rest of the w· men of Babylon. "
21 he giveth wisdom unto the w·, and "
24 to destroy the w· men of Babylon: "
24 Destroy not the w· men of Babylon:"
27 hath demanded cannot the w· men, "
48 over all the w· men of Babylon. "
4: 6 bring in all the w· men of Babylon "
18 w· men of my kingdom are not able"
5: 7 and said to the w· men of Babylon, "
8 Then came in all the king's w· men:"
15 now the w· men, the astrologers, "
12: 3 And they that be w· shall shine 7919
10 but the w· shall understand. "
Ho 14: 9 Who is w·, and he shall understand2450
Ob 8 destroy the w· men out of Edom, "
Zec 9: 2 and Zidon, though it be very w·. 2449
M't 1:18 of Jesus Christ was on this w·: 3779
2: 1 there came w· men from the east 3097
7 he had privily called the w· men, "
16 that he was mocked of the w· men, "
16 diligently enquired of the w· men. "
5:18 one tittle shall in no w· pass from the
7:24 I will liken him unto a w· man, 5429
10:16 be ye therefore w· as serpents, and "
42 you, he shall in no w· lose his reward.
11:25 hast hid these things from the w· 4680
21:24 I in like w· will tell you by what
23:34 unto you prophets, and w· men, 4680
24:45 then is a faithful and w· servant, 5429
25: 2 And five of them were w·, and five "
4 But the w· took oil in their vessels "
8 And the foolish said unto the w·, "
9 the w· answered, saying, Not so; "
M'r 14:31 thee, I will not deny thee in any w·.*
Lu 10:21 hast hid these things from the w· 4680
12:42 is that faithful and w· steward, 5429
13:11 could in no w· lift up herself. 3588,3838
18:17 child shall in no w· enter therein.
Joh 6:37 cometh to me I will in no w· cast out.
21: 1 and on this w· shewed he himself. 3779
Ac 7: 6 And God spake on this w·, that his "
13:34 he said on this w·, I will give you "
41 work which ye shall in no w· believe.
Ro 1:14 both to the w·, and to the unwise. 4680
22 Professing themselves to be w·, "
3: 9 No, in no w·: for we have before 3843
10: 6 is of faith speaketh on this w·, *3779
11:25 should be w· in your own conceits;5429
12:16 Be not w· in your own conceits.
Ro 16:19 you w· unto that which is good, 4680
27 To God only w·, be glory through "
1Co 1:19 I will destroy the wisdom of the w·,"
20 Where is the w·? where is the scribe"
26 not many w· men after the flesh, "
27 of the world to confound the w·; "
3:10 as a w· masterbuilder, I have laid "
18 you seemeth to be w· in this world, "
18 become a fool, that he may be w·. "
19 He taketh the w· in their own "
20 knoweth the thoughts of the w·, "
4:10 sake, but ye are w· in Christ; 5429
6: 5 there is not a w· man among you? 4680
10:15 I speak as to w· men; judge ye 5429
2Co 10:12 among themselves, are not w·. *4920
11:19 seeing ye yourselves are w·. 5429
Eph 5:15 not as fools, but as w·, 4680
1Ti 1:17 the only w· God, be honour and * "
2Ti 3:15 to make thee w· unto salvation 4679
Heb 4: 4 of the seventh day on this w·, 3779
Jas 3:13 Who is a w· man and endued with 4680
Jude 25 To the only w· God our Saviour, * "
Re 21:27 there shall in no w· enter into it any

wise-hearted See WISE and HEARTED

wisely
Ex 1:10 Come on, let us deal w· with them;2449
1Sa 18: 5 sent him, and behaved himself w·:7919
14 And David behaved himself w· "
15 that he behaved himself very w·, "
30 David behaved himself more w· "
2Ch 11:23 And he dealt w·, and dispersed of 995
Ps 58: 5 charmers, charming never so w·. 2449
64: 9 they shall w· consider of his doing.7919
101: 2 behave myself w· in a perfect way. "
Pr 16:20 He that handeth a matter w· shall* "
21:12 The righteous man w· considereth "
28:26 but whoso walketh w·, he shall be 2451
Ec 7:10 for thou dost not enquire w· "
Lu 16: 8 steward, because he had done w·: 5430

wise-men See WISE and MEN.

wiser
1Ki 4:31 For he was w· than all men; than 2449
Job 35:11 and maketh us w· than the fowls "
Ps 119:98 commandments hast made me w· "
Pr 9: 9 a wise man, and he will be yet w·: "
26:16 sluggard is w· in his own conceit 2450
Eze 28: 3 Behold, thou art w· than Daniel; "
Lu 16: 8 w· than the children of light. 5429
1Co 1:25 foolishness of God is w· than men;4680

wise-woman See WISE and WOMAN.

wish See also WISHED; WISHING.
Job 33: 6 I am according to thy w· in God's*6310
Ps 40:14 and put to shame that w· me evil.*2655
73: 7 have more than heart could w·. 4906
Ro 9: 3 could w· that myself were accursed2172
2Co 13: 9 and this also we w·, even your * "
3Jo 2 I w· above all things that thou * "

wished
Jon 4: 8 and w· in himself to die, and said, 7592
Ac 27:29 of the stern, and w· for the day. 2172

wishing
Job 31:30 to sin by w· a curse to his soul. 7592

wist See also WIT; WOT.
Ex 16:15 for they w· not what it was. ‡3045
34:29 Moses w· not that the skin of his ‡ "
Le 5:17 though he w· it not, yet is he guilty,*"
18 wherein he erred and w· it not, * "
Jos 2: 4 me, but I w· not whence they were:‡"
8:14 he w· not that there were liers in ‡ "
J'g 16:20 w· not that the Lord was departed‡ "
M'r 9: 6 For he w· not what to say; for they1492
14:40 neither w· they what to answer "
Lu 2:49 w· ye not that I must be about my "
Joh 5:13 that was healed w· not who it was: "
Ac 12: 9 w· not that it was true which was "
23: 5 Then said Paul, I w· not, brethren, "

wit See also WIST; WIT'S; WITTINGLY; WOT.
Ge 24:21 to w· whether the Lord had made*3045
Ex 2: 4 to w· what would be done to him.* "
Jos 17: 1 to w·, for Machir the firstborn of *
1Ki 2:32 to w·, Abner the son of Ner, captain of
7:50 doors of the house, to w·, of the temple.
13:23 to w·, for the prophet whom he had
2Ki 10:29 to w·, the golden calves that were in
1Ch 7: 2 of their father's house, to w·, of Tola:
27: 1 to w·, the chief fathers and
2Ch 4:12 To w·, the two pillars, and the *
25: 7 Israel, to w·, with all the children of
10 to w·, the army that was come
31: 3 to w·, for the morning and evening
Es 2:12 to w·, six months with oil of myrrh,
Jer 25:18 To w·, Jerusalem, and the cities of
34: 9 of them, to w·, of a Jew his brother.
Eze 13:16 To w·, the prophets of Israel which
Ro 8:23 to w·, the redemption of our body.
2Co 5:19 To w·, that God was in Christ, 5613
8: 1 do you to w· of the grace of God *1107

witch See also BEWITCH; WITCHCRAFT.
Ex 22:18 Thou shalt not suffer a w· to live.*3784
De 18:10 of times, or an enchanter, or a w·,* "

witchcraft See also WITCHCRAFTS.
1Sa 15:23 For rebellion is as the sin of w·, 7081
2Ch 33: 6 used enchantments, and used w·,*3784
Ga 5:20 Idolatry, w·, hatred, variance, *5331

witchcrafts
2Ki 9:22 Jezebel and her w· are so many? 3785
Mic 5:12 will cut off w· out of thine hand; "
Na 3: 4 the mistress of w·, that selleth "
4 and families through her w·. "

with See in the APPENDIX; also HEREWITH; THEREWITH; WHEREWITH; WITHAL; WITHDRAW; WITHHOLD; WITHIN; WITHOUT; WITHS; WITHSTAND.

withal See also WHEREWITHAL.
Ex 25:29 and bowls thereof, to cover *w'*. ‡2004
30: 4 places for the staves to bear it *w'*.‡1992
18 and his foot also of brass, to wash *w'*:
36: 3 of the sanctuary, to make it *w'*.
37:16 covers to cover *w'*, of pure gold. ‡2004
27 places for the staves to bear it *w'*.
38: 7 the sides of the altar, to bear it *w'*;
40:30 and put water there, to wash *w'*.
Le 5: 3 it be that a man shall be defiled *w'*.*
6:30 to reconcile *w'* in the holy place,*
11:21 feet, to leap *w'* upon the earth; ‡2004
19:24 shall be holy to praise the Lord *w'*.*
Nu 4: 7 the bowls, and covers to cover *w'*:
J'g 7:20 in their right hands to blow *w'*:
1Sa 16:12 *w'* of a beautiful countenance, 5973
1Ki 19: 1 *w'* how he had slain all the 834,3605
1Ch 29: 4 to overlay the walls of the houses *w'*:
2Ch 24:14 vessels to minister, and to offer *w'*,
26:15 to shoot arrows and great stones *w'*.
Es 6: 9 array the man *w'* whom the king
Job 2: 8 him a potsherd to scrape himself *w'*;
Ps 141:10 own nets, whilst that I *w'* escape. 3162
Pr 22:18 they shall *w'* be fitted in thy lips. "
Isa 30:14 or to take water *w'* out of the pit. ‡
23 that thou shalt sow the ground *w'*;‡
M'r 10:39 I am baptized *w'* shall ye be baptized:
Lu 6:38 that ye mete *w'* it shall be measured*
Ac 25:27 not *w'* to signify the crimes laid
1Co 12: 7 is given to every man to profit *w'*.
Col 4: 3 *W'* praying also for us, that God 260
1Ti 5:13 *w'* they learn to be idle, wandering "
Ph'm 22 But *w'* prepare me also a lodging: "

withdraw See also WITHDRAWEST; WITHDRAWETH; WITHDRAWN; WITHDREW.
1Sa 14:19 unto the priest, *W'* thine hand. 622
Job 9:13 If God will not *w'* his anger, the 7725
13:21 *W'* thine hand far from me: and 7368
33:17 he may *w'* man from his purpose, 5493
Pr 25:17 *W'* thy foot from thy neighbour's*3365
Ec 7:18 also from this *w'* not thine hand: 3240
Isa 60:20 neither shall thy moon *w'* itself: 622
Joe 2:10 and the stars shall *w'* their shining: "
3:15 and the stars shall *w'* their shining. "
2Th 3: 6 *w'* yourselves from every brother 4724
1Ti 6: 5 godliness: from such *w'* thyself. * 868

withdrawest
Ps 74:11 Why *w'* thou thy hand, even thy *7725

withdraweth
Job 36: 7 He *w'* not his eyes from the 1639

withdrawn
De 13:13 *w'* the inhabitants of their city, *5080
Ca 5: 6 but my beloved had *w'* himself, 2559
La 2: 8 not *w'* his hand from destroying: 7725
Eze 18: 8 hath *w'* his hand from iniquity, "
Ho 5: 6 he hath *w'* himself from them. 2502
Lu 22:41 And he was *w'* from them about a* 645

withdrew
Ne 9:29 and *w'* the shoulder, and 5414,5437
Eze 20:22 Nevertheless I *w'* mine hand, 7725
M't 12:15 it, he *w'* himself from thence: 402
M'r 3: 7 Jesus *w'* himself with his disciples "
Lu 5:16 he *w'* himself into the wilderness, 5298
Ga 2:12 he *w'* and separated himself, *5288

wither See also WITHERED; WITHERETH.
Ps 1: 3 his leaf also shall not *w'*; and 5034
37: 2 grass, and *w'* as the green herb. "
Isa 19: 6 up: the reeds and flags shall *w'*. 7060
7 sown by the brooks, shall *w'*, *3001
40:24 blow upon them, and they shall *w'*, "
Jer 12: 4 and the herbs of every field *w'*, "
Eze 17: 9 cut off the fruit thereof, that it *w'*? "
9 *w'* in all the leaves of her spring, "
10 shall it not utterly *w'*, when the "
10 *w'* in the furrows where it grew. "
Am 1: 2 and the top of Carmel shall *w'*. "

withered
Ge 41:23 seven ears, *w'*, thin, and blasted 6798
Ps 102: 4 heart is smitten, and *w'* like grass;3001
Isa 15: 6 for the hay is *w'* away, the grass "
27:11 When the boughs thereof are *w'*, "
La 4: 8 it is *w'*, it is become like a stick. "
Eze 19:12 strong rods were broken and *w'*; "
Joe 1:12 all the trees of the field, are *w'*: "
12 joy is *w'* away from the sons of men. "
17 broken down; for the corn is *w'*. "
Am 4: 7 piece whereupon it rained not *w'*. "
Jon 4: 7 and it smote the gourd that it *w'*. "
M't 12:10 a man which had his hand *w'*. 3584
13: 6 they had no root, they *w'* away. 3583
21:19 And presently the fig tree *w'* away. "
20 How soon is the fig tree *w'* away!* "
M'r 3: 1 man there which had a *w'* hand. "
3 the man which had the *w'* hand, "
4: 6 because it had no root, it *w'* away. "
11:21 which thou cursedst is *w'* away. "
Lu 6: 6 a man whose right hand was *w'*. 3584
8 man which had the *w'* hand, Rise "
8: 6 it *w'*...because it lacked moisture. 3583
Joh 5: 3 halt, *w'*, waiting for the moving of 3584
15: 6 cast forth as a branch, and is *w'*; 3583

withereth
Job 8:12 down, it *w'* before any other herb.3001
Ps 90: 6 the evening it is cut down, and *w'*. "
129: 6 which *w'* afore it groweth up: "
Isa 40: 7, 8 The grass *w'*, the flowers fadeth: "
Jas 1:11 burning heat, but it *w'* the grass, 3583
1Pe 1:24 The grass *w'*, and the flower "
Jude 12 trees whose fruit *w'*, without fruit,*5352

withheld See also WITHHELDEST; WITHHOLDEN.
Ge 20: 6 I also *w'* thee from sinning 2820
22:12 seeing thou hast not *w'* thy son, "
16 hast not *w'* thy son, thine only son:"
30: 2 who hath *w'* from thee the fruit of 4513
Job 31:16 If I have *w'* the poor from their "
Ec 2:10 I *w'* not my heart from any joy; "

withheldest
Ne 9:20 *w'* not thy manna from their 4513

withhold See also WITHHELD; WITHHOLDEN; WITHHOLDETH.
Ge 23: 6 shall *w'* from thee his sepulchre, 3607
2Sa 13:13 for he will not *w'* me from thee. 4513
Job 4: 2 can *w'* himself from speaking? 6113
Ps 40:11 *W'* not thou thy tender mercies 3607
84:11 good thing will he *w'* from them 4513
Pr 3:27 *W'* no good from them to whom it "
23:13 *W'* not correction from a child: "
Ec 11: 6 in the evening *w'* not thine hand: 3240
Jer 2:25 *W'* thy foot from being unshod, 4513

withholden See also WITHHELD.
1Sa 25:26 *w'* thee from coming to shed 4513
Job 22: 7 hast *w'* bread from the hungry. "
38:15 from the wicked their light is *w'*, "
42: 2 no thought can be *w'* from thee. *1219
Ps 21: 2 hast not *w'* the request of his lips.4513
Jer 3: 3 the showers have been *w'*, "
5:25 your sins have *w'* good things from "
Eze 18:16 hath not *w'* the pledge, neither *2254
Joe 1:13 drink offering is *w'* from the 4513
Am 4: 7 also I have *w'* the rain from you, "

withholdeth
Job 12:15 he *w'* the waters, and they dry up:6113
Pr 11:24 is that *w'* more than is meet, 2820
26 He that *w'* corn, the people shall 4513
2Th 2: 6 what *w'* that he might be revealed*2722

within
Ge 6:14 pitch it *w'* and without with pitch. 1004
9:21 and he was uncovered *w'* his tent. 8432
18:12 Sarah laughed *w'* herself, saying, 7130
24 be fifty righteous *w'* the city: 8432
26 Sodom fifty righteous *w'* the city, "
25:22 children struggled together *w'* 7130
39:11 of the men of the house there *w'*. 1004
40:13, 19 Yet *w'* three days shall Pharaoh
Ex 20:10 nor thy stranger that is *w'* thy gates:
25:11 *w'* and without shalt thou overlay 1004
26:33 in thither *w'* the vail of the ark of "
37: 2 it with pure gold *w'* and without, "
Le 10:18 not brought in *w'* the holy place: 6441
13:55 whether it be bare *w'* or without. 7146
14:41 caused the house to be scraped *w'* 1004
16: 2 holy place *w'* the vail before the "
12 small, and bring it within the vail: "
15 and bring his blood *w'* the vail, "
25:29 it *w'* a whole year after it is sold; 5704
29 *w'* a full year may he redeem it. *8537
30 redeemed *w'* the space of a...year, 5704
26:25 gathered together *w'* your cities, 413
Nu 4:10 *w'* a covering of badgers' skins, "
18: 7 of the altar, and *w'* the vail; 1004
De 5:14 thy stranger that is *w'* thy gates;
12:17 Thou mayest not eat *w'* thy gates the
18 and the Levite that is *w'* thy gates:
14:27 And the Levite that is *w'* thy gates;
28 and shalt lay it up *w'* thy gates:
29 the widow, which are *w'* thy gates,
15: 7 of thy brethren *w'* any of thy gates
22 Thou shalt eat it *w'* thy gates: the
16: 5 the passover *w'* any of thy gates,
11 and the Levite that is *w'* thy gates
14 the widow, that are *w'* thy gates.
17: 2 *w'* any of thy gates which the Lord
8 matters of controversy *w'* thy gates:
23:10 he shall not come *w'* the camp: 8432
24:14 that are in thy land *w'* thy gates:
26:12 that they may eat *w'* thy gates, and
28:43 stranger that is *w'* thee shall get *7130
31:12 thy stranger that is *w'* thy gates.
32:25 The sword without, and terror *w'*,*2315
Jos 1:11 *w'* three days ye shall pass over 5750
19: 1 *w'* the inheritance of the children*8432
9 inheritance *w'* the inheritance of * "
21:41 *w'* the possession of the children * "
J'g 7:16 and lamps *w'* the pitchers. "
9:51 was a strong tower *w'* the city, "
11:18 came not *w'* the border of Moab:
26 not recover them *w'* that time?
14:12 declare it me *w'* the seven days
15: 1 But it came to pass *w'* a while after,*
1Sa 13:11 camest not *w'* the days appointed,
14:14 *w'* as it were an half acre of land,
25:36 Nabal's heart was merry *w'* him, 5921
37 that his heart died *w'* him, and 7130
26: 7 Saul lay sleeping *w'* the trench,
2Sa 7: 2 ark of God dwelleth *w'* curtains. 8432
20: 4 me the men of Judah *w'* three days,
1Ki 6:15 house *w'* with boards of cedar, 1004
16 he even built them for it *w'*, even "
18 cedar of the house *w'* was carved 6441
19 oracle he prepared in the house *w'*,"
21 the house *w'* with pure gold: "
23 *w'* the oracle he made two cherubims
27 cherubims *w'* the inner house: 8432
29 and open flowers, *w'* and without. 6441
30 overlaid with gold, *w'* and without. "
7: 8 had another court *w'* the porch, 1004
9 sawed with saws, *w'* and without, "
31 mouth of it *w'* the chapiter and "
2Ki 4:27 alone; for her soul is vexed *w'* her:
6:30 had sackcloth *w'* upon his flesh. 1004
7:11 they told it to the king's house *w'*.6441
11: 8 and he that cometh *w'* the ranges,
2Ch 3: 4 he overlaid it *w'* with pure gold. 6441
Ezr 4:15 sedition *w'* the same of old time: 4481
10: 9 unto Jerusalem *w'* three days.
Ne 4:22 his servant lodge *w'* Jerusalem, 8432
6:10 the house of God, *w'* the temple,
Job 6: 4 arrows of the Almighty are *w'* me,5978
14:22 and his soul *w'* him shall mourn. 5921
19:27 my reins be consumed *w'* me. 2436
20:13 but keep it still *w'* his mouth; 8432
14 it is the gall of asps *w'* him. 7130
24:11 Which make oil *w'* their walls, and 996
32:18 the spirit *w'* me constraineth me. 990
Ps 36: 1 of the wicked saith *w'* my heart, 7130
39: 3 My heart was hot *w'* me, while I "
40: 8 God: yea, thy law is *w'* my heart. 8432
10 hid thy righteousness *w'* my heart;"
42: 6 God, my soul is cast down *w'* me: 5921
11 why art thou disquieted *w'* me? "
43: 5 why art thou disquieted *w'* me? "
45:13 king's daughter is all glorious *w'*: 6441
51:10 and renew a right spirit *w'* me. 7130
55: 4 My heart is sore pained *w'* me: "
94:19 multitude of my thoughts *w'* me "
101: 2 walk *w'* my house with a perfect "
7 deceit shall not dwell *w'* my house:"
103: 1 all that is *w'* me, bless his holy "
109:22 and my heart is wounded *w'* me. "
122: 2 Our feet shall stand *w'* thy gates,
7 Peace be *w'* thy walls, and prosperity
7 walls, and prosperity *w'* thy palaces.
8 I will now say, Peace be *w'* thee.
142: 3 my spirit was overwhelmed *w'* me,5921
143: 4 is my spirit overwhelmed *w'* me; "
4 my heart *w'* me is desolate. 8432
147:13 hath blessed thy children *w'* thee. 7130
Pr 22:18 thing if thou keep them *w'* thee; 990
26:24 lips, and layeth up deceit *w'* him; 7130
Ec 9:14 was a little city, and a few men *w'* it;
Ca 4: 1 thou hast doves' eyes *w'* thy locks:*1157
3 of a pomegranate *w'* thy locks. * "
6: 7 are thy temples *w'* thy locks. * "
Isa 7: 8 *w'* threescore and five years shall
16:14 *W'* three years, as the years of an
21:16 *W'* a year, according to the years 5750
26: 9 my spirit *w'* me will I seek thee 7130
56: 5 mine house and *w'* my walls a place
60:18 nor destruction *w'* thy borders;
63:11 he that put his holy Spirit *w'* him?*7130
Jer 4:14 thy vain thoughts lodge *w'* thee? "
23: 9 Mine heart *w'* me is broken because"
28: 3 *W'* two full years will I bring 5750
11 *w'* the space of two full years.
La 1:20 mine heart is turned *w'* me; for I 7130
Eze 1:27 of fire round about *w'* it, 1004
2:10 it was written *w'* and without: 6440
3:24 Go, shut thyself *w'* thine house. 8432
7:15 the pestilence and the famine *w'*: 1004
11:19 and I will put a new spirit *w'* you; 7130
12:24 divination *w'* the house of Israel. 8432
36:26 and a new spirit will I put *w'* you: 7130
27 And I will put my spirit *w'* you,
40: 7 porch of the gate *w'* was one reed.*1004
8 also the porch of the gate *w'*. * "
16 posts *w'* the gate round about, 6441
43 *w'* were hooks, an hand broad, 1004
41: 9 of the side chambers that were *w'*. "
17 wall round about *w'* and without, 6442
44:17 gates of the inner court, and *w'*. 1004
Da 6:12 of any God or man *w'* thirty days, 5705
11:20 but *w'* few days he shall be destroyed.
Ho 11: 8 mine heart is turned *w'* me, my
Jon 2: 7 When my soul fainteth *w'* me I 5921
Mic 3: 3 pot, and as flesh *w'* the caldron. 8432
5: 6 and when he treadeth *w'* our borders.
Zep 3: 3 princes *w'* her are roaring lions; 7130
Zec 12: 1 formeth the spirit of man *w'* him. "
M't 3: 9 think not to say *w'* yourselves, 1722
9: 3 of the scribes said *w'* themselves, "
21 For she said *w'* herself, If I may "
23:25 *w'* they are full of extortion and 2081
26 first that which is *w'* the cup and *1787
27 are *w'* full of dead men's bones, *2081
28 but *w'* ye are full of hypocrisy and* "
M'r 2: 8 they so reasoned *w'* themselves, 1722
7:21 from *w'*, out of the heart of men, 2081
23 All these evil things come from *w'*, "
14: 4 had indignation *w'* themselves, *4314
58 *w'* three days I will build another*1223
Lu 3: 8 begin not to say *w'* yourselves, We1722
7:39 he spake *w'* himself, saying, This "
49 him began to say *w'* themselves, "
11: 7 he from *w'* shall answer and say, 2081
40 make that which is *w'* also? * "
12:17 And he thought *w'* himself, saying,1722
16: 3 Then the steward said *w'* himself, "
17:21 the kingdom of God is *w'* you. 1787
18: 4 but afterward he said *w'* himself, 1722
19:44 ground, and thy children *w'* thee; "
24:32 Did not our heart burn *w'* us, while "
Joh 20:26 days again his disciples were *w'*, 2080
Ac 5:23 had opened, we found no man *w'*. "
Ro 8:23 we ourselves groan *w'* ourselves, 1722
1Co 5:12 do not ye judge them that are *w'*? 2080
2Co 7: 5 were fightings, *w'* were fears. 2081
Heb 6:19 entereth into that *w'* the vail; 2082
Re 4: 8 and they were full of eyes *w'*: 2081
5: 1 on the throne a book written *w'* "

without
Ge 1: 2 earth was *w'* form, and void; *8414
6:14 pitch it within and *w'* with pitch. 2351
9:22 and told his two brethren *w'*. "
19:16 him forth, and set him *w'* the city. "
24:11 camels to kneel down *w'* the city by "
31 wherefore standeth thou *w'*? for I "
37:33 Joseph is *w'* doubt rent in pieces. 2963
41:44 *w'* thee shall no man lift up his 1107
49 numbering; for it was *w'* number. 369

Ex 12: 5 Your lamb shall be w' blemish, 8549
25: 11 and w' shalt thou overlay it, 2351
26: 35 thou shalt set the table w' the vail, "
27: 21 of the congregation w' the vail, "
29: 1 bullock and two rams w' blemish, 8549
14 thou burn with fire w' the camp: 2351
33: 7 and pitched it w' the camp, "
7 which was w' the camp. "
37: 2 it with pure gold within and w', "
40: 22 tabernacle northward, w' the vail. "
Le 1: 3 let him offer a male w' blemish: 8549
10 he shall bring it a male w' blemish. "
3: 1 he shall offer it w' blemish before "
6 female, he shall offer it w' blemish. "
4: 3 a young bullock w' blemish unto "
12 shall he carry forth w' the camp 2351
21 forth the bullock w' the camp, "
23 of the goats, a male w' blemish: 8549
28 of the goats, a female w' blemish, "
32 shall bring it a female w' blemish. "
5: 15 a ram w' blemish out of the flocks, "
18 a ram w' blemish out of the flock, "
6: 6 a ram w' blemish out of the flock, "
11 carry forth the ashes w' the camp 2351
8: 17 he burnt with fire w' the camp; "
9: 2 for a burnt offering, w' blemish, 8549
3 both of the first year, w' blemish, "
11 he burnt with fire w' the camp. 2351
10: 12 eat it w' leaven beside the altar: 4682
13: 46 w' the camp shall his habitation 2351
55 whether it be bare within or w'. 1372
14: 10 take two he lambs w' blemish, 8549
10 lamb of the first year w' blemish, "
40 into an unclean place w' the city: 2351
41 w' the city into an unclean place: "
16: 27 shall one carry forth w' the camp; "
22: 19 your own will a male w' blemish, 8549
23: 12 an he lamb w' blemish of the first "
18 seven lambs w' blemish of the first "
24: 3 W' the vail of the testimony, in 2351
14 him that hath cursed w' the camp; "
26: 43 while she lieth desolate w' them: "
Nu 5: 3 w' the camp shall ye put them; 2351
4 so, and put them out w' the camp: "
6: 14, 14 lamb of the first year w' blemish 8549
14 and one ram w' blemish for peace "
15: 24 w' the knowledge of the congregation, "
35 him with stones w' the camp. 2351
36 brought him w' the camp, "
19: 2 bring thee a red heifer w' spot, 8549
3 may bring her forth w' the camp, 2351
9 up w' the camp in a clean place, "
20: 19 w' doing any thing else, go through 369
28: 3 two lambs of the first year w' spot 8549
9 two lambs of the first year w' spot, "
11 lambs of the first year w' spot; "
19 they shall be unto you w' blemish: "
31 they shall be unto you w' blemish) "
29: 2 lambs of the first year w' blemish: "
8 they shall be unto you w' blemish: "
13 first year; they shall be w' blemish: "
17 lambs of the first year w' spot: "
20 lambs of the first year w' blemish; "
23 lambs of the first year w' blemish: "
26 lambs of the first year w' spot: "
29, 32, 36 of the first year w' blemish: "
31: 13 forth to meet them w' the camp. 2351
19 ye abide w' the camp seven days: "
35: 5 shall measure from w' the city on "
22 thrust him suddenly w' enmity, 3808
22 him any thing w' laying of wait, "
26 time come w' the border of the city* "
27 find him w' the borders of the city 2351
De 8: 9 thou shalt eat bread w' scarceness, 3808
23: 12 have a place also w' the camp, 2351
25: 5 shall not marry w' unto a stranger: "
32: 4 a God of truth and w' iniquity, 369
25 The sword w', and terror within 2351
Jos 3: 10 he will w' fail drive out from before
6: 23 left them w' the camp of Israel. 2351
J'g 2: 23 w' driving them out hastily; 1115
6: 5 and their camels were w' number: 369
7: 12 and their camels were w' number, "
11: 30 thou shalt w' fail deliver the children
Ru 4: 14 left thee this day w' a kinsman,
1Sa 19: 5 blood, to stay David w' a cause? 2600
30: 8 overtake them, and w' fail recover all.
2Sa 23: 4 riseth, even a morning w' clouds; 3808
1Ki 6: 6 for w' in the wall of the house he *2351
29 and open flowers, within and w'. 2435
30 overlaid with gold, within and w'. "
7: 9 sawed with saws, within and w', 2351
8: 8 oracle, and they were not seen w': "
2Ki 10: 24 Jehu appointed fourscore men w', "
11: 15 Have her forth w' the ranges: *413,1004
16: 18 the king's entry w', turned he 2435
18: 25 come up w' the Lord against 1107
23: 4 he burned them w' Jerusalem in 2351
6 w' Jerusalem, unto the brook "
25: 16 all these vessels was w' weight. 3808
1Ch 2: 30 but Seled died w' children. "
32 and Jether died w' children. "
21: 24 nor offer burnt offerings w' cost. 2600
22: 14 and of brass and iron w' weight; 369
2Ch 5: 9 oracle; but they were not seen w'. 2351
12: 3 people were w' number that came 369
15: 3 Israel hath been w' the true God, 3808
3 w' a teaching priest, and w' law. "
21: 20 and departed w' being desired. "
24: 8 set it w' at the gate of the house 2351
32: 3 fountains which were w' the city: "
5 the towers, and another wall w', "
33: 14 built a wall w' the city of David, *2435
Ezr 6: 9 it be given them day by day w' fail:
7: 22 salt w' prescribing how much. 3809
10: 13 and we are not able to stand w', 2351

Ne 13: 20 ware lodged w' Jerusalem once or 2351
Job 2: 3 him, to destroy him w' cause. 2600
4: 20 perish forever w' any regarding it.
21 away? they die, even w' wisdom. 3808
5: 9 marvellous things w' number: 5704,369
6: 6 is unsavoury be eaten w' salt? 1097
7: 6 shuttle, and are spent w' hope. 657
8: 11 Can the rush grow up w' mire? 3808
11 can the flag grow w' water? 1097
9: 10 yea, and wonders w' number. 5704,369
17 multiplieth my wounds w' cause. 2600
10: 22 shadow of death, w' any order, 3808
11: 15 shalt thou lift up thy faces w' spot;
12: 25 They grope in the dark w' light, 3808
24: 7 the naked to lodge w' clothing, 1097
10 him to go naked w' clothing, "
26: 2 thou helped him that is w' power? 3808
30: 28 I went mourning w' the sun:
31: 19 clothing, or any poor w' covering;* 369
39 eaten the fruits thereof w' money, 1097
33: 9 I am clean w' transgression, I am
34: 6 is incurable w' transgression.
20 shall be taken away w' hand. 3808
24 in pieces mighty men w' number,* "
35 Job hath spoken w' knowledge, "
35 and his words were w' wisdom. "
35: 16 multiplieth words w' knowledge. 1097
36: 12 and they shall die w' knowledge. "
38: 2 counsel by words w' knowledge? "
39: 16 her labour is in vain w' fear; "
41: 33 not his like, who is made w' fear. "
42: 3 that hideth counsel w' knowledge? "
Ps 7: 4 him that w' cause is mine enemy:)7387
25: 3 which transgress w' cause.
31: 11 that did see me w' fled from me. 2351
35: 7 w' cause have they hid for me 2600
7 w' cause they have digged for my "
19 the eye that hate me w' a cause. "
69: 4 They that hate me w' a cause are "
105: 34 caterpillers, and that w' number. 369
109: 3 and fought against me w' a cause. 2600
119: 78 perversely with me w' a cause: *8267
161 have persecuted me w' a cause: 2600
Pr 1: 11 privily for the innocent w' cause: "
20 Wisdom crieth w'; she uttereth *2351
3: 30 Strive not with a man w' cause, 2600
5: 23 He shall die w' instruction; and * 369
6: 15 shall he be broken w' remedy. "
7: 12 Now is she w', now in the streets, *2351
11: 22 fair woman which is w' discretion. 5493
15: 22 W' counsel purposes are * 369
16: 8 than great revenues w' right. *3808
19: 2 that the soul be w' knowledge,
22: 13 There is a lion w', I shall be slain 2351
23: 29 who hath wounds w' cause? 2600
24: 27 Prepare thy work w', and make it 2351
28 against thy neighbour w' cause; 2600
25: 14 gift is like clouds and wind w' rain. 369
28 that is broken down, and w' walls.* "
29: 1 be destroyed, and that w' remedy. "
Ec 10: 11 serpent will bite w' enchantment; *3808
Ca 6: 8 concubines, and virgins w' number. 369
8: 1 when I should find thee w', I 2351
Isa 5: 9 even great and fair, w' inhabitant. 369
14 opened her mouth w' measure: 1097
6: 11 the cities be wasted w' inhabitant, 369
11 and the houses w' man, and the "
10: 4 W' me they shall bow down under 1115
33: 7 their valiant ones shall cry w': 2351
36: 10 now come up w' the Lord against 1107
45: 17 confounded world w' end. 5769,5703
52: 3 ye shall be redeemed w' money. 3808
4 oppressed them w' cause. 657
55: 1 and milk w' money and w' price. 3808
Jer 2: 15 cities are burned w' inhabitant. 1097
32 have forgotten me days w' number. 369
4: 23 the earth, and, lo, it was w' form, *8414
5: 21 people, and w' understanding; 369
9: 11 Judah desolate, w' an inhabitant. 1097
21 to cut off the children from w', 2351
21: 4 which besiege you w' the walls, "
22: 13 his neighbour's service w' wages, 2600
26: 9 shall be desolate w' an inhabitant? 369
32: 43 say, It is desolate w' man or beast: "
33: 10 be desolate w' man and w' beast, "
10 that are desolate, w' man, "
10 and w' inhabitant, and w' beast. "
12 desolate w' man and w' beast, 369,5704
34: 22 Judah a desolation w'...inhabitant. 369
44: 19 offerings unto her, w' our men? 1107
22 and a curse, w' an inhabitant, 369
46: 19 and desolate w' an inhabitant. "
48: 9 desolate, w' any to dwell therein. "
49: 31 nation, that dwelleth w' care,
51: 29 a desolation w' an inhabitant. 369
37 and an hissing, w' an inhabitant. "
52: 20 of all these vessels was w' weight. 3808
La 1: 6 w' strength before the pursuer.
3: 49 ceaseth not, w' any intermission, 369
52 me sore, like a bird, w' cause. 2600
Eze 2: 10 and it was written within and w': 268
7: 15 sword is w', and the pestilence 2351
14: 23 w' cause all that I have done in it, 2600
17: 9 w' great power or many people to‡3808
33: 15 of life, w' committing iniquity; *1115
38: 11 all of them dwelling w' walls, 369
40: 19 the forefront of the inner court w', 2351
40 at the side w', as one goeth up to "
44 w' the inner gate were the "
41: 9 which was for the side chamber w',*"
17 even unto the inner house, and w', "
17 wall round about within and w', 2435
25 upon the face of the porch w'. 2351
42: 7 wall that was w' over against the "
43: 21 of the house, w' the sanctuary. "
22 offer a kid of the goats w' blemish 8549

Eze 43: 23 offer a young bullock w' blemish, 8549
23 a ram out of the flock w' blemish. "
25 a ram out of the flock, w' blemish. "
45: 18 take a young bullock w' blemish, "
23 and seven rams w' blemish daily "
46: 2 way of the porch of that gate w', 2351
4 shall be six lambs w' blemish, 8549
4 and a ram w' blemish. "
6 be a young bullock w' blemish, "
6 a ram: they shall be w' blemish. "
13 a lamb of the first year w' blemish: "
47: 2 led me about the way w' unto 2351
Da 2: 34 a stone was cut out w' hands, 1768,3809
45 out of the mountain w' hands, "
8: 25 but he shall be broken w' hand. 657
11: 18 w' his own reproach he shall *1115
Ho 3: 4 days w' a king, and w' a prince, 369
4 w' a sacrifice, and w' an image, "
4 w' [369] an ephod, and w' teraphim:
7: 1 the troop of robbers spoileth w'. 2351
11 also is like a silly dove w' heart: 369
Joe 1: 6 my land, strong, and w' number, "
Zec 2: 4 shall be inhabited as towns w' walls
M't 5: 22 angry with his brother w' a cause *1500
10: 29 fall on the ground w' your Father. 427
12: 46 mother and his brethren stood w', 1854
47 mother and thy brethren stand w', "
13: 34 w' a parable spake he not unto 5565
57 A prophet is not w' honour, save 820
15: 16 Are ye also yet w' understanding? 801
26: 69 Peter sat w' in the palace: and a 1854
M'r 1: 45 city, but was w' in desert places: "
3: 31 and, standing w', sent unto him, "
32 and thy brethren w' seek for thee. "
4: 11 unto them that are w', all these "
34 w' a parable spake he not unto 5565
6: 4 A prophet is not w' honour, but in 820
7: 15 There is nothing from w' a man, 1855
18 Are ye so w' understanding also? 801
18 from w' entereth into the man, 1855
11: 4 the colt tied by the door w' in a 1854
14: 58 will build another made w' hands. 886
Lu 1: 10 praying w' at the time of incense. 1854
74 enemies might serve him w' fear, 870
6: 49 a man that w' a foundation built 5565
8: 20 mother and thy brethren stand w', 1854
11: 40 he that made that which is w' 1855
13: 25 ye begin to stand w', and to knock 1854
20: 28 a wife, and he die w' children, * 815
29 took a wife, and died w' children. * "
22: 35 When I sent you w' purse, and 817
Joh 1: 3 w' him was not any thing made 5565
8: 7 He that is w' sin among you, let 361
15: 5 for w' me ye can do nothing. *5565
25 law, They hated me w' a cause. 1432
18: 16 But Peter stood at the door w'. 1854
19: 23 now the coat was w' seam, woven 729
20: 11 Mary stood w' at the sepulchre 1854
Ac 5: 23 the keepers standing w' before the* "
26 and brought them w' violence: 3756,3326
9: 9 And he was three days w' sight, 3361
10: 29 came I unto you w' gainsaying, 369
12: 5 prayer was made w' ceasing of *1618
14: 17 he left not himself w' witness, 267
25: 17 w' any delay on the morrow I 3367,4160
Ro 1: 9 w' ceasing I make mention of you* 89
20 so that they are w' excuse: 379
31 W' understanding, 801
31 w' natural affection, implacable, 794
2: 12 For as many as have sinned w' law 460
12 shall also perish w' law; and as "
3: 3 make the faith of God w' effect? *2673
21 righteousness of God w' the law *5565
28 by faith w' the deeds of the law. * "
4: 6 imputeth righteousness w' works,* "
5: 6 For when we were yet w' strength, *772
7: 8 For w' the law sin was dead. *5565
9 I was alive w' the law once: but * "
10: 14 how shall they hear w' a preacher? "
11: 29 calling of God are w' repentance. 278
12: 9 Let love be w' dissimulation. 505
1Co 4: 8 ye have reigned as kings w' us: 5565
5: 12 do to judge them also that are w'? 1854
13 But them that are w' God judgeth. "
6: 18 that a man doeth is w' the body; 1622
7: 32 I would have you w' carefulness. * 275
35 attend upon the Lord w' distraction. 563
9: 18 the gospel of Christ w' charge, 77
21 To them that are w' law, as w' law, 459
21 not w' law to God, but under the law" "
21 I might gain them that are w' law. "
11: 11 neither is the man w' the woman, 5565
11 neither the woman w' the man, in "
14: 7 even things w' life giving sound, 895
10 none of them is w' signification. 880
16: 10 that he may be with you w' fear: 870
2Co 7: 5 w' were fightings, within were 1855
10: 13 boast of things w' our measure, * 280
15 boasting of things w' our measure,* "
11: 28 Beside those things that are w', 3924
Eph 1: 4 and w' blame before him in love: 299
2: 12 at that time ye were w' Christ, 5565
12 no hope, and w' God in the world: 112
3: 21 throughout all ages, world w' end.*
5: 27 it should be holy and w' blemish. 299
Ph'p 1: 10 w' offence till the day of Christ, *677
14 bold to speak the word w' fear. 870
2: 14 Do all things w' murmurings 5565
15 the sons of God, w' rebuke, in the 298
Col 2: 11 the circumcision made w' hands, * 886
4: 5 wisdom toward them that are w', 1854
1Th 1: 3 Remembering w' ceasing your work 89
2: 13 also thank we God w' ceasing, "
4: 12 honestly toward them that are w', 1854
5: 17 Pray w' ceasing. 89
1Ti 2: 8 hands, w' wrath and doubting. 5565

1Ti 3: 7 good report of them which are w.: 1855
16 w' controversy great is the mystery 3672
5: 21 w' preferring one before another, 5565
6: 14 keep this commandment w' spot, 784
2Ti 1: 3 w' ceasing I have remembrance of* 88
3: 3 W'...affection, trucebreakers, 794
Ph'm 14 w' thy mind would I do nothing; 5565
Heb 4: 15 tempted like as we are, yet w' sin. "
7: 3 W' father, [540] w' mother 282
3 w' descent, having neither 35
7 w' all contradiction the less is 5565
20 not w' an oath he was made priest: "
21 priests were made w' an oath; "
9: 7 not w' blood, which he offered for "
14 offered himself w' spot to God, 299
18 testament was dedicated w' blood. 5565
22 and w' shedding of blood is no * "
28 second time w' sin unto salvation.* "
10: 23 profession of our faith w' wavering;* 186
28 despised Moses' law died w' mercy 5565
11: 6 w' faith it is impossible to please "
40 w' us should not be made perfect.* "
12: 8 But if ye be w' chastisement, "
14 w' which no man shall see the "
13: 5 conversation be w' covetousness;* 866
11 for sin, are burned w' the camp. 1854
12 own blood, suffered w' the gate. "
13 therefore unto him w' the camp, "
Jas 2: 13 he shall have judgment w' mercy, 448
18 shew me thy faith w' thy works, *5565
20 man, that faith w' works is dead?* "
26 as the body w' the spirit is dead, * "
26 so faith w' works is dead also. * "
3: 17 w' partiality, [87] and w' hypocrisy. 505
1Pe 1: 17 who w' respect of persons judgeth 678
19 lamb w' blemish [299] and w' spot: 784
3: 1 they also may w' the word be won 427
4: 9 one to another w' grudging. "
2Pe 2: 17 These are wells w' water, clouds 504
3: 14 in peace, w' spot, and blameless. 784
Jude 12 you, feeding themselves w' fear: 870
12 clouds they are w' water, carried 504
12 w' fruit, twice dead, plucked up 175
Re 11: 2 court which is w' the temple leave 1855
14: 5 w' fault before the throne of God. 299
10 poured out w' mixture into the cup* 194
20 winepress was trodden w' the city, 1854
22: 15 For w' are dogs, and sorcerers, "

withs
J'g 16: 7 they bind me with seven green w' 3499
8 brought up to her seven green w' "
9 he brake the w', as a thread of tow "

withstand See also NOTWITHSTANDING; WITHSTOOD.
Nu 22: 32 I went out to w' thee, because thy* 7854
2Ch 13: 7 and could not w' them. 2388
8 to w' the kingdom of the Lord "
20: 6 so that none is able to w' thee? 3320
Es 9: 2 and no man could w' them; for 5975
Ec 4: 12 against him, two shall w' him; "
Da 11: 15 the arms of the south shall not w'. "
15 shall there be any strength to w'. "
Ac 11: 17 what was I, that I could w' God? 2967
Eph 6: 13 ye may be able to w' in the evil day, 436

withstood
2Ch 26: 18 And they w' Uzziah the king, and 5975
Da 10: 13 of the kingdom of Persia w' me "
Ac 13: 8 w' them, seeking to turn away the 436
Ga 2: 11 I w' him to the face, because he was* "
2Ti 3: 8 as Jannes and Jambres w' Moses, "
4: 15 for he hath greatly w' our words. "

witness See also EYEWITNESS; WITNESSED; WITNESSES; WITNESSETH; WITNESSING.
Ge 21: 30 that they may be a w' unto me, 5713
31: 44 be for a w' between me and thee. 5707
48 heap is a w' between me and thee "
50 see, God is w' betwixt me and thee. "
52 This heap be w', and this pillar "
52 and this pillar be w', that I will 5711
Ex 20: 16 shalt not bear false w' against thy 5707
22: 13 then let him bring it for w', and he "
23: 1 the wicked to be an unrighteous w'. "
Le 5: 1 the voice of swearing, and is a w'. "
Nu 5: 13 and there be no w' against her, "
17: 7 the Lord in the tabernacle of w'. *5715
8 went into the tabernacle of w'; * "
18: 2 before the tabernacle of w'. * "
35: 30 but one w' shall not testify against 5707
De 4: 26 I call heaven and earth to w' 5749
5: 20 shalt thou bear false w' against 5707
17: 6 at the mouth of one w' he shall not "
19: 15 One w' shall not rise up against a "
16 a false w' rise up against any man "
18 if the w' be a false w', and hath "
31: 19 that this song may be a w' for me "
21 shall testify against them as a w'; "
26 may be there for a w' against thee. "
Jos 22: 27 But that it may be a w' between us, "
28 but it is a w' between us and you. "
34 be a w' between us that the Lord is "
24: 27 this stone shall be a w' unto us; 5713
27 it shall be therefore a w' unto you, "
J'g 11: 10 The Lord be w' between us, if we 8085
1Sa 12: 3 w' against me before the Lord, 6030
5 The Lord is w' against you, and 5707
5 and his anointed is w' this day, "
5 And they answered, He is w'. "
1Ki 21: 10 to bare w' against him, saying, 5749
2Ch 24: 6 Israel, for the tabernacle of w'? *5715
Job 16: 8 which is a w' against me: 5707
8 up in me beareth w' to my face *6030
19 my w' is in heaven, and my record 5707
29: 11 the eye saw me, it gave w' to me: 5749
Ps 89: 37 and as a faithful w' in heaven. 5707
Pr 6: 19 A false w' that speaketh lies, and 5707
12: 17 righteousness: but a false w' deceit. "
14: 5 A faithful w' will not lie: but a false "
5 lie: but a false w' will utter lies. "
25 A true w' delivereth souls: but a "
25 but a deceitful w' speaketh lies. *
19: 5, 9 A false w' shall not be 5707
28 An ungodly w' scorneth judgment: "
21: 28 A false w' shall perish: but the "
24: 28 Be not a w' against thy neighbour "
25: 18 that beareth false w' against his "
Isa 3: 9 countenance doth w' against them; "
19: 20 it shall be for a sign and for a w' "
55: 4 given him for a w' to the people, "
Jer 29: 23 I know, and am a w', saith the Lord. "
42: 5 The Lord be a true and faithful w' "
La 2: 13 thing shall I take to w' for thee? *5749
Mic 1: 2 the Lord God be w' against you, 5707
Mal 2: 14 the Lord hath been w' between 5749
3: 5 a swift w' against the sorcerers, 5707
M't 15: 19 thefts, false w', blasphemies: 5577
19: 18 steal, Thou shalt not bare false w', 5576
24: 14 preached in all the world for a w' *3142
26: 59 sought false w' against Jesus, 5577
62 is it which these w' against thee? 2649
27: 13 many things they w' against thee? "
M'r 10: 19 Do not bare false w', Defraud not, 5576
14: 55 sought for w' against Jesus 3141
56 many bare false w' against him, 5576
56 but their w' agreed not together. 3141
57 and bare false w' against him, 5576
59 neither so did their w' agree 3141
60 is it which these w' against thee? 2649
15: 4 many things they w' against thee.* "
Lu 4: 22 all bare him w', and wondered at 3140
11: 48 Truly ye bare w' that ye allow the "
18: 20 Do not bare false w', Honour thy 5576
22: 71 What need we any further w'? 3141
Joh 1: 7 The same came for a w', to bear "
7 to bear w' of the Light, that all 3140
8 was sent to bear w' of that Light. "
15 John bare w' of him, and cried, "
3: 11 seen; and ye receive not our w'. 3141
26 Jordan, to whom thou barest w', 3140
28 Ye yourselves bear me w', that I "
5: 31 If I bear w' of myself, "
31 my w' is not true. 3141
32 is another that beareth w' of me; 3140
32 I know that the w' which he 3141
33 and he bare w' unto the truth. 3140
36 have greater w' than that of John: 3141
36 works that I do, bear w' of me, 3140
37 hath sent me, hath borne w' of me. "
8: 18 I am one that bear w' of myself, "
18 that sent me beareth w' of me. "
10: 25 Father's name, they bear w' of me. "
15: 27 ye also shall bear w', because ye "
18: 23 spoken evil, bear w' of the evil: "
37 I should bear w' unto the truth. "
Ac 1: 22 be a w' with us of his resurrection. 3144
4: 33 the apostles w' of the resurrection 3142
7: 44 tabernacle of w' in the wilderness, * "
10: 43 To him give all the prophets w', 3140
14: 17 he left not himself without w', 267
15: 8 knoweth the hearts, bare them w', 3140
22: 5 the high priest doth bear me w', "
15 thou shalt be his w' unto all men 3144
23: 11 must thou bear w' also at Rome. 3140
26: 16 and a w' both of these things 3144
Ro 1: 9 For God is my w', whom I serve "
2: 15 their conscience also bearing w', 4828
8: 16 itself beareth w' with our spirit, "
9: 1 not, my conscience bearing me w' "
13: 9 Thou shalt not bear false w', *5576
1Th 2: 5 a cloke of covetousness; God is w': 3144
Tit 1: 13 This w' is true. Wherefore rebuke* 3141
Heb 2: 4 God also bearing them w', both 4901
10: 15 the Holy Ghost also is a w' to us: 3140
11: 4 obtained w' that he was righteous, "
Jas 5: 3 the rust of them shall be a w' *3142
1Pe 5: 1 a w' of the sufferings of Christ, 3144
1Jo 1: 2 we have seen it, and bear w', 3140
5: 6 And it is the Spirit that beareth w', "
8 are three that bear w' in earth, "
9 If we receive the w' of men, 3141
9 the w' of God is greater: "
9 this is the w' of God which he hath "
10 Son of God hath the w' in himself: "
3Jo 6 have borne w' of thy charity 3140
Re 1: 5 Christ, who is the faithful w', 3144
3: 14 the faithful and the true w', the "
20: 4 beheaded for the w' of Jesus, *3141

witnessed
1Ki 21: 13 the men of Belial w' against him, 5749
Ro 3: 21 being w' by the law and the 3140
1Ti 6: 13 Pontius Pilate w' a good confession; "
Heb 7: 8 them, of whom it w' that he liveth. "

witnesses See also EYEWITNESSES.
Nu 35: 30 be put to death by the mouth of w': 5707
De 17: 6 At the mouth of two w', "
6 or three w', shall he that is worthy "
7 The hands of the w' shall be first "
19: 15 sinneth: at the mouth of two w', "
15 or at the mouth of three w', shall "
Jos 24: 22 Ye are w' against yourselves that "
22 him. And they said, We are w'. "
Ru 4: 9 Ye are w' this day, that I have "
10 of his place: ye are w' this day. "
11 and the elders, said, We are w'. "
Job 10: 17 Thou renewest thy w' against me, "
Ps 27: 12 false w' are risen up against me, "
35: 11 False w' did rise up; they laid to "
Isa 8: 2 took unto me faithful w' to record, "
43: 9 let them bring forth their w', that "
10 Ye are my w', saith the Lord, and "
Isa 43: 12 ye are my w', saith the Lord, that I 5707
44: 8 declared it? ye are even my w'. "
9 and they are their own w'; they "
Jer 32: 10 evidence, and sealed it, and took w' "
12 presence of the w' that subscribed "
25 the field for money, and take w'; "
44 take w' in the land of Benjamin, "
M't 18: 16 in the mouth of two or three w' 3144
23: 31 ye be w' unto yourselves, that 3140
26: 60 though many false w' came, yet 5575
60 At the last came two false w', "
65 what further need have we of w'? 3144
M'r 14: 63 What need we any further w'? "
Lu 24: 48 And ye are w' of these things. "
Ac 1: 8 and ye shall be w' unto me both in "
2: 32 raised up, whereof we all are w'. "
3: 15 from the dead; whereof we are w'. "
5: 32 And we are his w' of these things; "
6: 13 And set up false w', which said, "
7: 58 and the w' laid down their clothes "
10: 39 we are w' of all things which he did "
41 but unto w' chosen before of God, "
13: 31 who are his w' unto the people. "
1Co 15: 15 and we are found false w' of God; 5575
2Co 13: 1 In the mouth of two or three w' 3144
1Th 2: 10 Ye are w', and God also, how holily "
1Ti 5: 19 but before two or three w'. "
6: 12 a good profession before many w'. "
2Ti 2: 2 hast heard of me among many w', "
Heb 10: 28 mercy under two or three w': "
12: 1 about with so great a cloud of w', "
Re 11: 3 I will give power unto my two w', "

witnesseth
Joh 5: 32 witness which he w' of me is true. 3140
Ac 20: 23 the Holy Ghost w' in every city, *1263

witnessing
Ac 26: 22 w' both to small and great, saying* 3140

wit's
Ps 107: 27 man, and are at their w' end. *2451

wittingly
Ge 48: 14 head, guiding his hands w'; 7919

witty
Pr 8: 12 find out knowledge of w' inventions.*

wives See also MIDWIVES; WIVES'.
Ge 4: 19 Lamech took unto him two w': the 802
23 And Lamech said unto his w', Adah "
23 ye w' of Lamech, hearken unto my "
6: 2 them w' of all which they chose. "
18 wife, and thy sons' w' with thee. "
7: 7 his sons' w' with him, into the ark, "
13 the three w' of his sons with them, "
8: 16 thy sons, and thy sons' w' with thee. "
18 his wife, and his sons' w' with him: "
11: 29 Abram and Nahor took them w': "
28: 9 and took unto the w' which he had "
30: 26 Give me my w' and my children, "
31: 17 set his sons and his w' upon camels; "
50 take other w' beside my daughters, "
32: 22 up that night, and took his two w', "
34: 21 us take their daughters to us for w', "
29 ones, and their w' took they captive, "
36: 2 Esau took his w' of the daughters of "
6 And Esau took his w', and his sons, "
37: 2 the sons of Zilpah, his father's w': "
45: 19 for your little ones, and for your w', "
46: 5 and their little ones, and their w', "
26 besides Jacob's sons' w', all the souls "
Ex 19: 15 the third day: come not at your w'.* "
22: 24 your w' shall be widows, and your "
32: 2 which are in the ears of your w', "
Nu 14: 3 that our w' and our children should "
16: 27 and their w', and their sons, and "
32: 26 Our little ones, our w', our flocks, "
De 3: 19 But your w', and your little ones, "
17: 17 Neither shall he multiply w' to "
21: 15 If a man have two w', one beloved, "
29: 11 Your little ones, your w', and thy "
Jos 1: 14 Your w', your little ones, and your "
J'g 3: 6 took their daughters to be their w', "
8: 30 body begotten: for he had many w'. "
21: 7 How shall we do for w' for them that "
7 give them of our daughters to w'? "
14 gave them w' which they had saved* "
16 How shall we do for w' for them that "
18 not give them w' of our daughters: "
23 and took them w', according to "
Ru 1: 4 them w' of the women of Moab; "
1Sa 1: 2 And he had two w'; the name of the "
25: 43 they were also both of them his w'. "
27: 3 even David with his two w', "
30: 3 and their w', and their sons, and "
5 David's two w' were taken captives, "
18 away: and David rescued his two w'. "
2Sa 2: 2 up thither, and his two w' also, "
5: 13 took him more concubines and w' "
12: 8 and thy master's w' into thy bosom, "
11 I will take thy w' before thine eyes, "
11 he shall lie with thy w' in the sight "
19: 5 daughters, and the lives of thy w', "
1Ki 11: 3 And he had seven hundred w', "
3 and his w' turned away his heart. "
4 his w' turned away his heart after "
8 did he for all his strange w', which "
20: 3 thy w' also and thy children, even "
5 gold, and thy w', and thy children; "
7 for he sent unto me for my w', "
2Ki 4: 1 certain woman of the w' of the sons "
24: 15 and the king's w', and his officers, "
1Ch 4: 5 the father of Tekoa had two w', "
7: 4 for they had many w' and sons. "
8: 8 Hushim and Baara were his w'. "
14: 3 And David took more w' at

2Ch 11:21 of Absalom above all his w' and 802
21 (for he took eighteen w', and "
23 And he desired many w'. "
13:21 mighty, and married fourteen w', "
20:13 ones, their w', and their children, "
21:14 and thy children, and thy w', and "
17 and his sons also, and his w'; "
24: 3 And Jehoiada took for him two w'; "
29: 9 and our w' are in captivity for this. "
31:18 their w', and their sons, and their "
Ezr 10: 2 have taken strange w' of the people* "
3 with our God to put away all the w', "
10 and have taken strange w', to * "
11 the land, and from the strange w'. * "
14 have taken strange w' in our cities* "
17 the men that had taken strange w'* "
18 found that had taken strange w': * "
19 that they would put away their w'; "
44 All these had taken strange w': and "
44 some of them had w' by whom they "
Ne 4:14 daughters, your w', and your houses. "
5: 1 of their w' against their brethren "
10:28 their w', and their sons, and their "
12:43 w' also and the children rejoiced: * "
13:23 Jews that had married w' of Ashdod,* "
27 our God in marrying strange w'? * "
Es 1:20 w' shall give to their husbands * "
Isa 13:16 be spoiled, and their w' ravished. "
Jer 6:12 with their fields and w' together: "
8:10 will I give their w' unto others, "
14:16 none to bury them, their w', "
18:21 let their w' be bereaved of their "
29: 6 Take ye w', and begat sons and "
6 take w' for your sons, and give your "
23 adultery with their neighbours' w', "
35: 8 our w', our sons, nor our daughters; "
38:23 So they shall bring out all thy w' "
44: 9 and the wickedness of their w', "
9 and the wickedness of your w', "
15 that their w' had burned incense "
25 Ye and your w' have both spoken "
Eze 44:22 shall they take for their w' a widow, "
Da 5: 2 his w', and his concubines, might 7695
3 his w', and his concubines, drank "
23 thy w', and thy concubines, have "
6:24 them, their children, and their w':5389
Zec 12:12 of David apart, and their w' apart; 802
12 of Nathan apart, and their w' apart; "
13 of Levi apart, and their w' apart; "
13 of Shimei apart, and their w' "
14 family apart, and their w' apart. "
M't 19: 8 suffered you to put away your w': *1135*
Lu 17:27 they drank, they married w', they* "
Ac 21: 5 on our way, with w' and children. *1135*
1Co 7:29 have w' be as though they had none; "
Eph 5:22 W', submit yourselves unto your "
24 let the w' be to their own husbands "
25 Husbands, love your w', even as "
28 to love their w' as their own bodies. "
Col 3:18 W', submit yourselves unto your "
19 Husbands, love your w', and be not "
1Ti 3:11 Even so must their w' be grave, * "
1Pe 3: 1 ye w', be in subjection to your own "
1 won by the conversation of the w'; "

wives'
1Ti 4: 7 refuse profane and old w' fables. *1126*

wizard See also WIZARDS.
Le 20:27 or that is a w', shall surely be put 3049
De 18:11 spirits, or a w', or a necromancer. "

wizards
Le 19:31 neither seek after w', to be defiled 3049
20: 6 and after w', to go a whoring after "
1Sa 28: 3 spirits, and the w', out of the land. "
9 spirits, and the w', out of the land: "
2Ki 21: 6 dealt with familiar spirits and w': "
23:24 with familiar spirits, and the w', "
2Ch 33: 6 with a familiar spirit, and with w': "
Isa 8:19 unto w' that peep, and that mutter: "
19: 3 have familiar spirits, and to the w'. "

woe See also WOEFUL; WOES.
Nu 21:29 W' to thee, Moab! thou art undone. 188
1Sa 4: 7 W' unto us! for there hath not "
8 W' unto us! who shall deliver us "
Job 10:15 If I be wicked, w' unto me; and if I 480
Ps 120: 5 W' is me, that I sojourn in Mesech, 190
Pr 23:29 Who hath w'? who hath sorrow? 188
Ec 4:10 but w' to him that is alone when 337
10:16 W' to thee, O land, when thy king "
Isa 3: 9 W' unto their soul! for they have 188
11 W' unto the wicked! it shall be ill "
5: 8 W' unto them that join house to 1945
11 W' unto them that rise up early in "
18 W' unto them that draw iniquity "
20 W' unto them that call evil good, "
21 W' unto them that are wise in "
22 W' unto them that are mighty to "
6: 5 said I, W' is me! for I am undone: 188
10: 1 W' unto them that decree 1945
17:12 W' to the multitude of many * "
18: 1 W' to the land shadowing with * "
24:16 leanness, my leanness, w' unto me! 188
28: 1 W' to the crown of pride, to the 1945
29: 1 W' to Ariel, to Ariel, the city * "
15 W' unto them that seek deep to "
30: 1 W' to the rebellious children, saith "
31: 1 W' to them that go down to Egypt "
33: 1 W' to thee that spoilest, and thou "
45: 9 W' unto him that striveth with his "
10 W' unto him that saith unto his "
Jer 4:13 W' unto us! for we are spoiled. 188
31 W' is me now! for my soul is "
6: 4 W' unto us! for the day goeth away. "
10:19 W' is me for my hurt! my wound "
13:27 W' unto thee, O Jerusalem! wilt "
15:10 W' is me, my mother, that thou "
Jer 22:13 W' unto him that buildeth his 1945
23: 1 W' be unto the pastors that "
45: 3 Thou didst say, W' is me now! 188
48: 1 W' unto Nebo! for it is spoiled: 1945
46 W' be unto thee, O Moab! the 188
50:27 w' unto them! for their day is 1945
La 5:16 w' unto us, that we have sinned! 188
Eze 2:10 and mourning, and w'. 1958
13: 3 W' unto the foolish prophets, 1945
18 W' to the women that sew pillows "
16:23 (w', w' unto thee! saith the Lord 188
24: 6 W' to the bloody city, to the pot "
9 W' to the bloody city! I will even "
30: 2 God; Howl ye, W' worth the day! 1929
34: 2 W' be to the shepherds of Israel 1945
Ho 7:13 W' unto them! for they have fled 188
9:12 w' also to them when I depart "
Am 5:18 W' unto you that desire the day 1945
6: 1 W' to them that are at ease in "
Mic 2: 1 W' to them that devise iniquity, "
7: 1 W' is me! for I am as when they 480
Na 3: 1 W' to the bloody city! it is all full 1945
Hab 2: 6 W' to him that increaseth that "
9 W' to him that coveteth an evil "
12 W' to him that buildeth a town "
15 W' unto him that giveth his "
19 W' unto him that saith to the wood, "
Zep 2: 5 W' unto the inhabitants of the sea "
3: 1 W' to her that is filthy and "
Zec 11:17 W' to the idol shepherd that "
M't 11:21 W' unto thee, Chorazin! *3759*
21 w' unto thee, Bethsaida! for if the "
18: 7 W' unto the world because of "
7 but w' to that man by whom the "
23:13 w' unto you, scribes and Pharisees, "
14 W' unto you, scribes and Pharisees.* "
15 W' unto you, scribes and Pharisees, "
16 W' unto you, ye blind guides, "
23, 25, 27, 29 W' unto you, scribes and "
24:19 w' unto them that are with child, "
26:24 w' unto that man by whom the Son "
M'r 13:17 w' to them that are with child, and "
14:21 w' to that man by whom the Son of "
Lu 6:24 But w' unto you that are rich! "
25 W' unto you that are full! for ye "
25 W' unto you that laugh now! for "
26 W' unto you, when all men shall "
10:13 W' unto thee, Chorazin! "
13 w' unto thee, Bethsaida! for if the "
11:42 But w' unto you, Pharisees! for ye "
43 W' unto you, Pharisees! for ye "
44 W' unto you, scribes and Pharisees, "
46 W' unto you also, ye lawyers! "
47 W' unto you! for ye build the "
52 W' unto you, lawyers! for ye have "
17: 1 w' unto him, through whom they "
21:23 w' unto them that are with child, "
22:22 w' unto that man by whom he is "
1Co 9:16 w' is unto me, if I preach not the "
Jude 11 W' unto them! for they have gone "
Re 8:13 W', w', w', to the inhabiters of the "
9:12 One w' is past; and, behold, there "
11:14 The second w' is past; and, "
14 behold, the third w' cometh quickly. "
12:12 W' to the inhabiters of the earth "

woeful
Jer 17:16 neither have I desired the w' day; 605

woes
Re 9:12 there come two w' more hereafter. *3759*

wolf See also WOLVES.
Ge 49:27 Benjamin shall ravin as a w': 2061
Isa 11: 6 w' also shall dwell with the lamb, "
65:25 The w' and the lamb shall feed "
Jer 5: 6 and a w' of the evenings shall spoil "
Joh 10:12 seeth the w' coming, and leaveth *3074*
12 and the w' catcheth them, and "

wolves
Eze 22:27 are like w' ravening the prey, 2061
Hab 1: 8 more fierce than the evening w': "
Zep 3: 3 her judges are evening w'; they "
M't 7:15 but inwardly they are ravening w'. *3074*
10:16 forth as sheep in the midst of w': "
Lu 10: 3 send you forth as lambs among w'. "
Ac 20:29 grievous w' enter in among you, "

woman See also BONDWOMAN; FREEWOMAN; KINSWOMAN; WOMANKIND; WOMAN'S; WOMEN.
Ge 2:22 made he a w', and brought her 802
23 she shall be called W', because she "
3: 1 he said unto the w', Yea, hath God "
2 w' said unto the serpent, We may "
4 serpent said unto the w', Ye shall "
6 the w' saw that the tree was good "
12 The w' whom thou gavest to be "
13 Lord God said unto the w', what is "
13 w' said, The serpent beguiled me, "
15 put enmity between thee and the w', "
16 Unto the w' he said, I will greatly "
12:11 that thou art a fair w' to look upon: "
14 the Egyptians beheld the w' that she "
15 w' was taken into Pharaoh's house. "
20: 3 for the w' which thou hast taken; "
24: 5 w' will not be willing to follow me "
8 if the w' will not be willing to follow "
39 Peradventure the w' will not follow "
44 same be the w' whom the Lord "
46:10 and Shaul the son of a Canaanitish w'. "
Ex 2: 2 the w' conceived and bare a son: 802
9 w' took the child, and nursed it. "
3:22 But every w' shall borrow of her "
6:15 and Shaul the son of a Canaanitish w': "
11: 2 every w' of her neighbour, jewels 802
21:22 men strive, and hurt a w' with child, "
28 If an ox gore a man or a w', that "
29 that he hath killed a man or a w'; "
Ex 35:29 every man and w', whose heart 802
36: 6 neither man nor w' make any more "
Le 12: 2 If a w' have conceived seed, and "
13:29 If a man or w' have a plague upon "
38 a man also or a w' have in the skin "
15:18 The w' also with whom man shall "
19 And if a w' have an issue, and her "
25 if a w' have an issue of her blood "
33 issue, of the man, and of the w', 5347
18:17 not uncover the nakedness of a w' 802
19 not approach unto a w' to uncover "
23 neither shall any w' stand before a "
19:20 whosoever lieth carnally with a w', "
20:13 as he lieth with a w', both of them* "
16 And if a w' approach unto any beast, "
16 thou shalt kill the w', and the beast: "
18 lie with a w' having her sickness, "
27 or w' that hath a familiar spirit, "
21: 7 neither shall they take a w' put away "
24:10 And the son of an Israelitish w', "
10 and this son of the Israelitish w' "
Nu 5: 6 man or w' shall commit any sin 802
18 shall set the w' before the Lord, "
19 say unto the w', If no man have lain "
21 shall charge the w' with an oath of "
21 and the priest shall say unto the w', "
22 And the w' shall say, Amen, amen. "
24 cause the w' to drink the bitter "
26 cause the w' to drink the water. "
27 the w' shall be a curse among her "
28 And if the w' be not defiled, but be "
30 and shall set the w' before the Lord, "
31 and this w' shall bear her iniquity. "
6: 2 either man or w' shall separate "
12: 1 Ethiopian w' whom he had married: "
1 for he had married an Ethiopian w'. "
25: 6 a Midianitish w' in the sight of Moses, "
8 and the w' through her belly. 802
15 Midianitish w' that was slain was "
30: 3 a w' also vow a vow unto the Lord, "
31:17 kill every w' that hath known man "
De 15:12 or an Hebrew w', be sold unto thee, "
17: 2 man or w', that hath wrought 802
5 bring forth that man or that w', "
5 gates, even that man or that w', "
21:11 among the captives a beautiful w', "
22: 5 The w' shall not wear that which "
14 I took this w', and when I came to "
22 found lying with a w' married to an "
22 both the man that lay with the w', "
22 and the w': so shalt thou put away "
28:56 The tender and delicate w' among you, "
29:18 should be among you man, or w', 802
Jos 2: 4 w' took the two men, and hid them, "
6:21 both man and w', young and old, "
22 house, and bring out thence the w', "
J'g 4: 9 shall sell Sisera into the hand of a w'. "
9:53 And a certain w' cast a piece of a "
54 men say not of me, A w' slew him. "
11: 2 for thou art the son of a strange w'. "
13: 3 of the Lord appeared unto the w', "
6 the w' came and told her husband, "
9 angel of God came again unto the w' "
10 w' made haste, and ran, and told "
11 the man that spakest unto the w'? "
13 I said unto the w' let her beware. "
24 And the w' bare a son, and called "
14: 1 and saw a w' in Timnath of the "
2 I have seen a w' in Timnath of the "
3 never a w' among the daughters "
7 went down, and talked with the w'; "
10 So his father went down unto the w': "
16: 4 loved a w' in the valley of Sorek, "
19:26 came the w' in the dawning of the "
27 the w' his concubine was fallen "
20: 4 husband of the w' that was slain, "
21:11 and every w' that hath lain by man. "
Ru 1: 5 and the w' was left of her two sons "
3: 8 and, behold, a w' lay at his feet. "
11 know that thou art a virtuous w'. "
14 not be known that a w' came into "
4:11 The Lord make the w' that is come "
12 Lord shall give thee of this young w'. 5291
1Sa 1:15 lord, I am a w' of a sorrowful spirit: 802
18 So the w' went her way, and did eat, "
23 So the w' abode, and gave her son "
26 I am the w' that stood by thee here, "
2:20 The Lord give thee seed of this w' "
15: 3 but slay both man and w', infant and "
20:30 Thou son of the perverse rebellious w',* "
25: 3 she was a w' of good understanding, 802
27: 9 and left neither man nor w' alive, "
11 And David saved neither man nor w' "
28: 7 a w' that hath a familiar spirit, "
7 is a w' that hath a familiar spirit "
8 and they came to the w' by night: "
9 the w' said unto him, Behold, thou "
11 said the w', Whom shall I bring "
11 when the w' saw Samuel, she cried "
12 and the w' spake to Saul, saying, "
13 the w' said unto Saul, I saw gods "
21 the w' came unto Saul, and saw that "
23 together with the w', compelled him; "
24 the w' had a fat calf in the house; "
2Sa 3: 8 day with a fault concerning this w'? "
11: 2 roof he saw a w' washing herself; "
2 w' was very beautiful to look upon. "
3 David sent and enquired after the w'. "
5 the w' conceived, and sent and told "
21 did not a w' cast a piece of a "
13:17 put now this w' out from me, and bolt "
14: 2 and fetched thence a wise w', 802
2 be as a w' that had a long time "
4 when the w' of Tekoah spake to "
5 answered, I am indeed a widow w',‡ "
8 king said unto the w', Go to thine "

2Sa 14: 9 w· of Tekoah said unto the king, 802
12 the w· said, Let thine handmaid, "
13 the w· said, Wherefore then hast "
18 king answered and said unto the w·, "
18 the w· said, Let my lord the king "
19 the w· answered and said, As thy "
27 she was a w· of a fair countenance. "
17: 19 the w· took and spread a covering "
20 Absalom's servants came to the w· "
20 And the w· said unto them, They be "
20: 16 Then cried a wise w· out of the city, "
17 unto her, the w· said, Art thou Joab? "
21 And the w· said unto Joab, Behold, "
22 the w· went unto all the people "
1Ki 3: 17 And the one w· said, O my lord, I "
17 I and this w· dwell in one house; "
18 that this w· was delivered also: "
22 the other w· said, Nay; but the "
26 Then spake the w· whose the living "
11: 26 name was Zeruah, a widow w·, "
14: 5 shall feign herself to be another w·. "
17: 9 a widow w· there to sustain thee. ‡ 802
10 widow w· was...gathering of sticks: ‡ "
17 that the son of the w·, the mistress "
24 the w· said to Elijah, Now by this "
2Ki 4: 1 Now there cried a certain w· of the "
8 to Shunem, where was a great w·; "
17 the w· conceived, and bare a son "
6: 26 there cried a w· unto him, saying, "
28 This w· said unto me, Give thy son, "
30 the king heard the words of the w·, "
8: 1 Then spake Elisha unto the w·, "
2 And the w· arose, and did after the "
3 the w· returned out of the land of "
5 the w·, whose son he had restored "
5 O king, this is the w·, and this is "
6 when the king asked the w·, she "
9: 34 see now this cursed w·, and bury her: "
1Ch 16: 3 both man and w·, to every one a 802
2Ch 2: 14 son of a w· of the daughters of Dan, "
15: 13 small or great, whether man or w·. "
24: 7 sons of Athaliah, that wicked w·, "
Es 4: 11 whether man or w·, shall come 802
Job 14: 1 Man that is born of a w· is of few "
15: 14 he which is born of a w·, that he "
25: 4 can he be clean that is born of a w·? "
31: 9 heart have been deceived by a w·, "
Ps 48: 6 and pain, as of a w· in travail. "
58: 8 like the untimely birth of a w·, 802
113: 9 maketh the barren w· to keep house, "
Pr 2: 16 deliver thee from the strange w·, 802
6: 24 To keep thee from the evil w·, "
24 of the tongue of a strange w·. "
26 by means of a whorish w· a man is‡802
32 committeth adultery with a w· "
7: 5 may keep thee from the strange w·, "
10 met him a w· with the attire of a "
9: 13 A foolish w· is clamorous: she is "
11: 16 A gracious w· retaineth honour: "
22 fair w· which is without discretion. "
12: 4 A virtuous w· is a crown to her "
14: 1 Every wise w· buildeth her house: "
20: 16 a pledge of him for a strange w·. * "
21: 9 with a brawling w· in a wide house. 802
19 a contentious and an angry w·. "
23: 27 and a strange w· is a narrow pit. "
25: 24 a brawling w· in a wide house. 802
27: 13 a pledge of him for a strange w·. "
15 and a contentious w· are alike. 802
30: 20 Such is the way of an adulterous w·;"
23 an odious w· when she is married; "
31: 10 Who can find a virtuous w·? for 802
30 a w· that feareth the Lord, she "
Ec 7: 26 find more bitter than death the w·, "
28 a w· among all those have I not "
Isa 13: 8 be in pain as a w· that travaileth: "
21: 3 as the pangs of a w· that travaileth: "
26: 17 Like as a w· with child, that draweth "
42: 14 now will I cry like a travailing w·; "
45: 10 or to the w·, What hast thou 802
49: 15 Can a w· forget her sucking child, "
54: 6 as a w· forsaken and grieved in * "
Jer 4: 31 heard a voice as of a w· in travail, "
6: 2 of Zion to a comely and delicate w·.* "
24 of us, and pain, as of a w· in travail. "
13: 21 take thee, as a w· in travail? 802
22: 23 thee, the pain as of a w· in travail! "
30: 6 hands on his loins, as a w· in travail, "
31: 8 lame, the w· with child and her that "
22 earth, A w· shall compass a man. 5347
44: 7 to cut off from you man and w·, 802
48: 41 be as the heart of a w· in her pangs. "
49: 22 be as the heart of a w· in her pangs. "
24 have taken her, as a w· in travail. "
50: 43 him, and pangs as of a w· in travail. "
51: 22 will I break in pieces man and w·; 802
La 1: 17 Jerusalem is as a menstruous w· "
Eze 16: 30 work of an imperious whorish w·;* 802
18: 6 hath come near to a menstruous w·, "
23: 44 unto a w· that playeth the harlot: * "
44 unto Aholibah, the lewd w·. "
36: 17 as the uncleanness of a removed w·. "
Ho 3: 1 love a w· beloved of her friend, 802
13: 13 sorrows of a travailing w· shall come "
Mic 4: 9 have taken thee as a w· in travail. "
10 daughter of Zion, like a w· in travail; "
Zec 5: 7 this is a w· that sitteth in the midst802
M't 5: 28 whosoever looketh on a w· to lust 1135
9: 20 a w·, which was diseased with an "
22 the w· was made whole from that "
13: 33 like unto leaven, which a w· took, "
15: 22 a w· of Canaan came out of the "
28 unto her, O w·, great is thy faith: "
22: 27 And last of all the w· died also. "
26: 7 him a w· having an alabaster box of "
10 unto them, Why trouble ye the w·? "
M't 26: 13 that this w· hath done, be told for
M'r 5: 25 certain w·, which had an issue of 1135
33 But the w· fearing and trembling, "
7: 25 a certain w·, whose young daughter "
26 The w· was a Greek, a "
10: 12 if a w· shall put away her husband,* "
12: 22 seed: last of all the w· died also. "
14: 3 came a w· having an alabaster box "
Lu 4: 26 unto a w· that was a widow. "
7: 37 behold, a w· in the city, which was "
39 what manner of w· this is that "
44 he turned to the w·, and said unto "
44 said unto Simon, Seest thou this w·? "
45 this w· since the time I came in * "
46 this w· hath anointed my feet with* "
50 he said to the w·, Thy faith hath 1135
8: 43 a w· having an issue of blood "
47 the w· saw that she was not hid, "
10: 38 a certain w· named Martha "
11: 27 certain w· of the company lifted up "
13: 11 there was a w· which had a spirit "
12 W·, thou art loosed from thine "
16 And ought not this w·, being a "
21 which a w· took and hid in three 1135
15: 8 what w· having ten pieces of silver, "
20: 32 Last of all the w· died also. "
22: 57 him, saying, W·, I know him not. "
Joh 2: 4 W·, what have I to do with thee? "
4: 7 a w· of Samaria to draw water: "
9 saith the w· of Samaria unto him, "
9 of me, which am a w· of Samaria? "
11 w· saith unto him, Sir, Thou hast "
15 The w· saith unto him, Sir, give "
17 The w· answered and said, I have "
19 The w· saith unto him, Sir, I "
21 W·, believe me, the hour cometh, "
25 The w· saith unto him, I know that "
27 that he talked with the w·: "
28 The w· then left her waterpot, and "
39 on him for the saying of the w·, "
42 said unto the w·, Now we believe, "
8: 3 brought unto him a w· taken in "
4 this w· was taken in adultery, "
9 and the w· standing in the midst. "
10 saw none but the w·, he said unto* "
10 W·, where are...thine accusers? "
16: 21 A w· when she is in travail hath "
19: 26 his mother, W·, behold thy son! "
20: 13, 15 unto her, W·, why weepest thou? "
Ac 9: 36 this w· was full of good works "
16: 1 Timotheus, the son of a certain w·,*1135
14 a certain w· named Lydia, a seller "
17: 34 a w· named Damaris, and others "
Ro 1: 27 leaving the natural use of the w·, 2338
7: 2 w· which hath an husband is bound1135
1Co 7: 1 good for a man not to touch a w·. "
2 every w· have her own husband. "
13 the w· which hath an husband 1135
34 w· careth for the things of the Lord,* "
11: 3 the head of the w· is the man; "
5 w· that prayeth or prophesieth "
6 if the w· be not covered, let her "
6 it be a shame for a w· to be shorn "
7 but the w· is the glory of the man. "
8 For the man is not of the w·; "
8 but the w· of the man. "
9 was the man created for the w·; "
9 but the w· for the man. "
10 cause ought the w· to have power "
11 neither is the man without the w·, "
11 neither the w· without the man, "
12 For as the w· is of the man, even so "
12 even so is the man also by the w·; "
13 a w· pray unto God uncovered? "
15 if a w· have long hair, it is a glory "
Ga 4: 4 sent forth his Son, made of a w·, "
1Th 5: 3 as travail upon a w· with child; "
1Ti 2: 11 Let the w· learn in silence with 1135
12 I suffer not a w· to teach, nor to "
14 but the w· being deceived was in "
5: 16 If any man or w· that believeth have "
Re 2: 20 thou sufferest that w· Jezebel, 1135
12: 1 a w· clothed with the sun, and the "
4 w· which was ready to be delivered, "
6 w· fled into the wilderness, where "
13 w· which brought forth the man "
14 to the w· were given two wings "
15 mouth water as a flood after the w·, "
16 the earth helped the w·, and the "
17 the dragon was wroth with the w·, "
17: 3 a w· sit upon a scarlet coloured "
4 w· was arrayed in purple and "
6 I saw the w· drunken with the "
7 tell thee the mystery of the w·, "
9 mountains, on which the w· sitteth. "
18 w· which thou sawest is that great "

womankind
Le 18: 22 not lie with mankind, as with w·: 802

woman's
Ge 38: 20 his pledge from the w· hand: 802
Ex 21: 22 according as the w· husband will "
Le 24: 11 Israelitish w· son blasphemed the * "
Nu 5: 18 uncover the w· head, and put the "
25 jealousy offering out of the w· hand, "
De 22: 5 shall a man put on a w· garment; "
1Ki 3: 19 And this w· child died in the night; "

womb See also WOMBS.
Ge 25: 23 Two nations are in thy w·, and two 990
24 behold, there were twins in her w·. "
29: 31 Leah was hated, he opened her w·: 7358
30: 2 from thee the fruit of the w·? 990
22 to her, and opened her w·. 7358
38: 27 that, behold, twins were in her w·. 990
49: 25 of the beasts, and of the w·: 7356
Ex 13: 2 whatsoever openeth the w· among7358
Nu 8: 16 instead of such as open every w·. 7358
12: 12 he cometh out of his mother's w·. "
De 7: 13 will also bless the fruit of thy w·,* 990
J'g 13: 5 be a Nazarite unto God from the w·: "
7 be a Nazarite to God from the w· "
16: 17 unto God from my mother's w·: "
Ru 1: 11 there yet any more sons in my w·, 4578
1Sa 1: 5 but the Lord had shut up her w·. 7358
6 the Lord had shut up her w·. "
Job 1: 21 came I out of my mother's w·, and 990
3: 10 not up the doors of my mother's w·, "
11 Why died I not from the w·? why 7358
10: 18 brought me forth out of the w·? "
19 carried from the w· to the grave. 990
24: 20 The w· shall forget him; the worm7358
31: 15 that made me in the w· make him? 990
15 did not one fashion us in the w·? 7358
18 guided her from my mother's w·;) 990
38: 8 as if it had issued out of the w·? 7358
29 Out of whose w· came the ice? 990
Ps 22: 9 art he that took me out of the w·: "
10 I was cast upon thee from the w·: 7358
58: 3 wicked are estranged from the w·: "
71: 6 have I been holden up from the w·: 990
110: 3 from the w· of the morning: 7358
127: 3 the fruit of the w· is his reward. 990
139: 13 hast covered me in my mother's w·. "
Pr 30: 16 The grave; and the barren w·; 7356
31: 2 son? and what, the son of my w·? 990
Ec 5: 15 As he came forth of his mother's w·, "
11: 5 the bones do grow in the w· of her "
Isa 13: 18 have no pity on the fruit of the w·; "
44: 2 thee, and formed thee from the w·, "
24 he that formed thee from the w·, "
46: 3 which are carried from the w·: 7356
48: 8 called a transgressor from the w·. 990
49: 1 Lord hath called me from the w·; "
5 formed me from the w· to be his "
15 compassion on the son of her w·? "
66: 9 cause to bring forth, and shut the w·? "
Jer 1: 5 thou camest forth out of the w· I 7358
20: 17 he slew me not from the w·; "
17 her w· to be always great with me. "
18 I forth out of the w· to see labour "
Eze 20: 26 the fire all that openeth the w·, 7356
Ho 9: 11 from the birth, and from the w·, * 990
14 give them a miscarrying w· and 7358
16 even the beloved fruit of their w·. 990
12: 3 his brother by the heel in the w·, "
M't 19: 12 so born from their mother's w·: 2836
Lu 1: 15 Ghost, even from his mother's w·. "
31 thou shalt conceive in thy w·, and 1064
41 the babe leaped in her w·; and 2836
42 and blessed is the fruit of thy w·. "
44 the babe leaped in my w· for joy. "
2: 21 before he was conceived in the w·. "
23 Every male that openeth the w· 3388
11: 27 Blessed is the w· that bare thee, 2836
Joh 3: 4 second time into his mother's w·, "
Ac 3: 2 man lame from his mother's w· was "
14: 8 a cripple from his mother's w·, "
Ro 4: 19 yet the deadness of Sarah's w·: 3388
Ga 1: 15 me from my mother's w·, and 2836

wombs
Ge 20: 18 Lord had fast closed up all the w· 7358
Lu 23: 29 and the w· that never bare, and

women See also BONDWOMEN; KINSWOMEN; WOMEN'S; WOMENSERVANTS.
Ge 14: 16 and the w· also, and the people. 802
18: 11 with Sarah after the manner of w·. "
31: 35 for the custom of w· is upon me. "
33: 5 and saw the w· and the children; "
Ex 1: 16 office of a midwife to the Hebrew w·, "
19 w· are not as the Egyptian w·; 802
2: 7 call to thee a nurse of the Hebrew w·, "
15: 20 all the w· went out after her with 802
35: 22 And they came, both men and w·, "
25 all the w· that were wise hearted "
26 all the w· whose heart stirred them "
38: 8 lookingglasses of the w· assembling, "
Le 26: 26 ten w· shall bake your bread in one802
Nu 31: 9 took all the w· of Midian captives, "
15 Have ye saved all the w· alive? 5347
18 all the w· children, that have not 802
35 of w· that had not known man by "
De 2: 34 destroyed the men, and the w·, and "
3: 6 utterly destroying the men, w·, and "
20: 14 But the w·, and the little ones, and "
31: 12 the people together, men, and w·, "
Jos 8: 25 fell that day, both of men and w·, "
35 congregation of Israel, with the w·, "
J'g 5: 24 Blessed above w· shall Jael the wife "
24 blessed shall she be above w· in the "
9: 49 also, about a thousand men and w·. "
51 and thither fled all the men and w·, "
16: 27 the house was full of men and w·; "
27 about three thousand men and w·, "
21: 10 sword, with the w· and the children. "
14 alive of the w· of Jabesh-gilead: "
16 w· are destroyed out of Benjamin? "
Ru 1: 4 took them wives of the w· of Moab; "
4: 14 w· said unto Naomi, Blessed be "
17 the w· her neighbours gave it a name,
1Sa 2: 22 how they lay with the w· that 802
4: 20 time of her death the w· that stood by "
15: 33 thy sword hath made w· childless, 802
33 thy mother be childless among w·. "
18: 6 w· came out of all cities of Israel, "
7 w· answered one another as they "
21: 4 kept themselves at least from w·. "
5 Of a truth w· have been kept from us "
22: 19 edge of the sword, both men and w·, "
30: 2 had taken the w· captives, that were "
2Sa 1: 26 wonderful, passing the love of w·. "
6: 19 as well to the w· as men, to every "

2Sa 15:16 the king left ten w', which were 802
19:35 voice of singing men and singing w'? "
20: 3 and the king took the ten w' his 802
1Ki 3:16 Then came there two w', that were "
11: 1 Solomon loved many strange w', "
1 w' of the Moabites, Ammonites, "
2Ki 8:12 and rip up their w' with child. "
15:16 w' therein that were with child he "
23: 7 the w' wove hangings for the grove.802
2Ch 28: 8 thousand, w', sons, and daughters, "
35:25 singing w' spake of Josiah in their "
Ezr 2:65 hundred singing men and singing w'. "
10: 1 great congregation of men and w' 802
Ne 7:67 and five singing men and singing w'. "
8: 2 congregation both of men and w', 802
3 before the men and the w', and "
13:26 him did outlandish w' cause to sin. "
Es 1: 9 the queen made a feast for the w' "
17 queen shall come abroad unto all w'. "
2: 3 the palace, to the house of the w', "
3 chamberlain, keeper of the w'; "
8 custody of Hegai, keeper of the w'. "
9 best place of the house of the w'. "
12 according to the manner of the w', "
12 things for the purifying of the w';) "
13 house of the w' unto the king's house. "
14 into the second house of the w', "
15 chamberlain, the keeper of the w', "
17 king loved Esther above all the w', "
3:13 young and old, little children and w', "
8:11 both little ones and w', and to take "
Job 42:15 all the land were no w' found so fair "
Ps 45: 9 were among thy honourable w': "
Pr 22:14 mouth of strange w' is a deep pit: "
31: 3 Give not thy strength unto w', nor 802
Ec 2: 8 I gat me men singers and w' singers, "
Ca 1: 8 know not, O thou fairest among w', 802
5: 9 beloved, O thou fairest among w'? "
6: 1 gone, O thou fairest among w'? "
Isa 3:12 oppressors, and w' rule over them. "
4: 1 seven w' shall take hold of one man, "
19:16 day shall Egypt be like unto w': "
27:11 the w' come, and set them on fire: "
32: 9 Rise up, ye w' that are at ease; hear "
11 Tremble, ye w' that are at ease; be "
Jer 7:18 the w' knead their dough, to make 802
9:17 ye, and call for the mourning w', "
17 send for cunning w', that they may "
20 hear the word of the Lord, O ye w', 802
38:22 all the w' that are left in the king "
22 and those w' shall say, Thy friends "
40: 7 committed unto him men, and w', 802
41:16 and the w', and the children, and "
43: 6 Even men, and w', and children, "
44:15 and all the w' that stood by, a great "
20 to the men, and to the w', and to all "
24 and to all the w', Hear the word "
50:37 her; and they shall become as w': "
51:30 hath failed; they became as w': "
La 2:20 Shall the w' eat their fruit, and "
4:10 pitiful w' have sodden their own "
5:11 They ravished the w' in Zion, and "
Eze 8:14 there sat w' weeping for Tammuz. "
9: 6 maids, and little children, and w': "
13:18 Woe to the w' that sew pillows to all "
16:34 from other w' in thy whoredoms, 802
38 judge thee, as w' that break wedlock "
41 upon thee in the sight of many w': 802
23: 2 there were two w', the daughters "
10 and she became famous among w'; "
44 and unto Aholibah, the lewd w'. "
48 that all w' may be taught not to do "
Da 11:17 shall give him the daughter of w', "
37 nor the desire of w', nor regard any "
Ho 13:16 their w' with child shall be ripped up. "
Am 1:13 they have ripped up the w' with child "
Mic 2: 9 w' of my people have ye cast out 802
Na 3:13 people in the midst of thee are w': "
Zec 5: 9 behold, there came out two w', "
8: 4 men and old w' dwell in the streets "
14: 2 houses rifled, and the w' ravished; 802
M't 11:11 Among them that are born of w' 1135
14:21 five thousand men, beside w' and "
15:38 four thousand men, beside w' and "
24:41 Two w' shall be grinding at the mill; "
27:55 many w' were there beholding 1135
28: 5 answered and said unto the w', "
M'r 15:40 were also w' looking on afar off: "
41 other w' which came up with him "
Lu 1:28 blessed art thou among w'. *1135
42 said, Blessed art thou among w', "
7:28 Among those that are born of w' "
8: 2 certain w', which had been healed "
17:35 Two w' shall be grinding together; "
23:27 company of people, and of w', 1135
49 w' that followed him from Galilee, "
55 the w' also, which came with him "
24:10 and other w' that were with them, "
22 and certain w' also of our company 1135
24 it even so as the w' had said: "
Ac 1:14 and supplication, with the w', "
5:14 multitudes both of men and w'.) "
8: 3 haling men and w' committed them "
12 were baptized, both men and w'. "
9: 2 whether they were men or w', he "
13:50 the devout and honourable w', "
16:13 spake unto the w' which resorted "
17: 4 and of the chief w' not a few. "
12 honourable w' which were Greeks, "
22: 4 into prisons both men and w'. "
Ro 1:26 their w' did change the natural use 2338
1Co 14:34 w' keep silence in the churches: 1135
35 for w' to speak in the church. "
Ph'p 4: 3 help those w' which laboured with me "
1Ti 2: 9 w' adorn themselves in modest 1135
10 (which becometh w' professing "

1Ti 5: 2 The elder w' as mothers; the younger "
14 therefore that the younger w' marry,*
2Ti 3: 6 captive silly w' laden with sins, 1133
Tit 2: 3 The aged w' likewise, that they be 4247
4 may teach the young w' to be sober, "
Heb 11:35 W' received their dead raised to 1135
1Pe 3: 5 in the old time the holy w' also, "
Re 9: 8 they had hair as the hair of w' "
14: 4 which were not defiled with w'; "

women's
Es 2:11 before the court of the w' house, 802

womenservants
Ge 20:14 and w', and gave them unto 8198
32: 5 flocks, and menservants, and w': "
22 his two w', and his eleven sons, * "

won
1Ch 26:27 Out of the spoils w' in battles did they
Pr 18:19 brother offended is harder to be w'
1Pe 3: 1 may without the word be w' *2770

wonder See also WONDERED; WONDERFUL; WONDERING; WONDERS.
De 13: 1 and giveth thee a sign or a w', 4159
2 the sign or the w' come to pass, "
28:46 upon thee for a sign and for a w', "
2Ch 32:31 enquire of the w' that was done "
Ps 71: 7 I am as a w' unto many; but thou "
Isa 20: 3 for a sign and w' upon Egypt "
29: 9 Stay yourselves, and w'; cry ye 8539
14 even a marvellous work and a w': 6382
Jer 4: 9 and the prophets shall w'. 8539
Hab 1: 5 and regard, and w' marvellously: "
Ac 3:10 and they were filled with w' and 2285
13:41 Behold, ye despisers, and w', 2296
Re 12: 1 appeared a great w' in heaven; *4592
3 appeared another w' in heaven; * "
17: 8 that dwell on the earth shall w', 2296

wondered
Isa 59:16 w' that there was no intercessor: 8074
63: 5 w' that there was none to uphold: "
Zec 3: 8 thee: for they are men w' at: *4159
M't 15:31 Insomuch that the multitude w', 2296
M'r 6:51 beyond measure, and w'. * "
Lu 2:18 that heard it w' at those things "
4:22 and w' at the gracious words which "
8:25 they being afraid w', saying one to*"
9:43 they w' every one at all things * "
11:14 dumb spake; and the people w'. * "
24:41 they yet believed not for joy, and w',"
Ac 7:31 Moses saw it, he w' at the sight: "
8:13 and w', beholding the miracles *1839
Re 13: 3 and all the world w' after the beast2296
17: 6 her, I w' with great admiration. "

wonderful
De 28:59 the Lord will make thy plagues w',6381
2Sa 1:26 thy love to me was w', passing the "
2Ch 2: 9 am about to build shall be w' great. "
Job 42: 3 things too w' for me, which I knew "
Ps 40: 5 thy w' works which thou hast done, "
78: 4 and his w' works that he hath done.*"
107: 8, 15, 21, 31 w' works to the children of"
111: 4 his w' works to be remembered: "
119:129 Thy testimonies are w': 6382
139: 6 Such knowledge is too w' for me; 6383
Pr 30:18 be three things which are too w' 6381
Isa 9: 6 and his name shall be called W', 6382
25: 1 for thou hast done w' things; thy "
28:29 which is w' in counsel, and 6381
Jer 5:30 w' and horrible thing is committed8047
M't 7:22 name done many w' works? *1411
21:15 saw the w' things that he did, 2297
Ac 2:11 our tongues the w' works of God. *3167

wonderfully
1Sa 6: 6 he had wrought w' among them, 5953
Ps 139:14 for I am fearfully and w' made: 6395
La 1: 9 therefore she came down w': she 6382
Da 8:24 and he shall destroy w', and shall 6381

wondering
Ge 24:21 the man w' at her held his peace, *7583
Lu 24:12 w' in himself at that which was 2296
Ac 3:11 is called Solomon's, greatly w'. 1569

wonderously See also WONDROUSLY.
J'g 13:19 and the angel did w'; and Manoah*6381

wonders
Ex 3:20 smite Egypt with all my w' which 6381
4:21 do all those w' before Pharaoh, 4159
7: 3 and my w' in the land of Egypt. "
11: 9 that my w' may be multiplied in "
10 did all these w' before Pharaoh: "
15:11 fearful in praises, doing w'? 6382
De 4:34 by signs, and by w', and by war, 4159
6:22 And the Lord shewed signs and w', "
7:19 and the w', and the mighty hand, "
26: 8 and with signs and with w': "
34:11 the w', which the Lord sent him to "
Jos 3: 5 the Lord will do w' among you. 6381
1Ch 16:12 his w', and the judgments of his 4159
Ne 9:10 signs and w' upon Pharaoh, "
17 neither were mindful of thy w' 6381
Job 9:10 out; yea, and w' without number.* "
Ps 77:11 I will remember thy w' of old. 6382
14 Thou art the God that doest w': "
78:11 his w' that he had shewed them. *6381
43 and his w' in the field of Zoan: 4159
88:10 Wilt thou shew w' to the dead? 6382
12 Shall thy w' be known in the dark? "
89: 5 And the heavens shall praise thy w'," "
96: 3 heathen, his w' among all people.*6381
105: 5 his w', and the judgments of his 4159
27 them, and w' in the land of Ham. "
106: 7 Our fathers understood not thy w' 6381
107:24 the Lord, and his w' in the deep. "
135: 9 Who sent tokens and w' into the 4159

Ps 136: 4 To him who alone doeth great w': 6381
Isa 8:18 for w' in Israel from the Lord 4159
Jer 32:20 signs and w' in the land of Egypt, "
21 with signs, and with w', and with a "
Da 4: 2 w' that the high God hath wrought8540
3 and how mighty are his w'! "
6:27 he worketh signs and w' in heaven "
12: 6 shall it be to the end of these w'? 6382
Joe 2:30 And I will shew w' in the heavens 4159
M't 24:24 and shall shew great signs and w';5059
M'r 13:22 rise, and shall shew signs and w', "
Joh 4:48 Except ye see signs and w', ye will "
Ac 2:19 And I will shew w' in heaven above, "
22 you by miracles and w' and signs, "
43 and many w' and signs were done "
4:30 and that signs and w' may be done "
5:12 were many signs and w' wrought "
6: 8 did great w' and miracles among "
7:36 that he had shewed w' and signs "
14: 3 granted signs and w' to be done "
15:12 declaring what miracles and w' God"
Ro 15:19 Through mighty signs and w', by "
2Co 12:12 signs, and w', and mighty deeds. "
2Th 2: 9 all power and signs and lying w', "
Heb 2: 4 witness, both with signs and w', "
Re 13:13 And he doeth great w', so that he *4592

wondrous
1Ch 16: 9 him, talk ye of all his w' works. *6381
Job 37:14 and consider the w' works of God. "
16 w' work of him which is perfect 4652
Ps 26: 7 and tell of all thy w' works. 6381
71:17 have I declared thy w' works. "
72:18 of Israel, who only doeth w' things. "
75: 1 name is near thy w' works declare. "
78:32 and believed not for his w' works. "
86:10 thou art great, and doest w' things: "
105: 2 him: talk ye of all his w' works. * "
106:22 W' works in the land of Ham, and "
119:18 behold w' things out of thy law. "
27 so shall I talk of thy w' works. "
145: 5 of thy majesty, and of thy w' works. "
Jer 21: 2 us according to all his w' works, "

wondrously See also WONDEROUSLY.
Joe 2:26 God, that hath dealt w' with you: 6381

wont
Ex 21:29 ox were w' to push with his horn 5056
Nu 22:30 was I ever w' to do so unto thee? 5532
1Sa 30:31 and his men were w' to haunt. 1980
2Sa 20:18 They were w' to speak in old time, 1696
Da 3:19 seven times more than it was w' 2370
M't 27:15 governor was w' to release unto 1486
M'r 10: 1 and, as he was w', he taught them "
Lu 22:39 and went, as he was w', to *2596,1486
Ac 16:13 where prayer was w' to be made; *3543

wood See also WOODS; WORMWOOD.
Ge 6:14 Make thee an ark of gopher w'; 6086
22: 3 clave the w' for the burnt offering, "
6 took the w' of the burnt offering, "
7 he said, Behold the fire and the w': "
9 and laid the w' in order, and bound "
9 laid him on the altar upon the w'. "
Ex 7:19 both in vessels of w', and in vessels "
25: 5 and badgers' skins, and shittim w', "
10 shall make an ark of shittim w': "
13 shalt make staves of shittim w', "
23 also make a table of shittim w': "
28 shalt make the staves of shittim w', "
26:15 for the tabernacle of shittim w' "
26 thou shalt make bars of shittim w'; "
32 four pillars of shittim w' overlaid *
27: 1 shalt make an altar of shittim w', 6086
6 staves of shittim w', and overlay "
30: 1 of shittim w' shalt thou make it. "
5 shalt make the staves of shittim w', "
35: 7 and badgers' skins, and shittim w', "
24 with whom was found shittim w' "
33 and in carving of w', to make any "
36:20 for the tabernacle of shittim w', "
31 and he made bars of shittim w'; five "
36 thereunto four pillars of shittim w',*
37: 1 made the ark of shittim w': 6086
4 And he made staves of shittim w', "
10 he made the table of shittim w': "
15 he made the staves of shittim w', "
25 made the incense altar of shittim w': "
28 he made the staves of shittim w', "
38: 1 altar of burnt offering of shittim w': "
6 he made the staves of shittim w', "
Le 1: 7 lay the w' in order upon the fire: "
8 order upon the w' that is on the fire "
12 order on the w' that is on the fire "
17 upon the w' that is upon the fire: "
3: 5 is upon the w' that is on the fire: "
4:12 and burn him on the w' with fire: "
6:12 the priest shall burn w' on it every "
11:32 whether it be any vessel of w', or "
14: 4 and cedar w', and scarlet, and "
6 and the cedar w', and the scarlet, "
49 and cedar w', and scarlet, and "
51 the cedar w', and the hyssop, "
52 with the cedar w', and with the "
15:12 every vessel of w' shall be rinsed "
Nu 13:20 whether there be w' therein, "
19: 6 shall take cedar w', and hyssop, "
31:20 hair, and all things made of w'. "
35:18 him with an hand weapon of w', "
De 4:28 work of men's hands, w' and stone, "
10: 1 mount, and make thee an ark of w'. "
3 And I made an ark of shittim w', "
19: 5 As when a man goeth into the w' *3293
5 with his neighbour to hew w', 6086
28:36 thou serve other gods, w' and stone. "
64 have known, even w' and stone. "
29:11 hewer of thy w' unto the drawer "

De 29:17 and their idols, *w*. and stone, silver 6086
Jos 9:21 but let them be hewers of *w*. and "
23, 27 hewers of *w*...drawers of water "
17:15 then get thee up to the *w*. country,*3293
18 for it is a *w*. and thou shalt cut it* "
J'g 6:26 sacrifice with the *w*. of the grove 6086
1Sa 6:14 and they clave the *w*. of the cart, "
14:25 all they of the land came to a *w*.; *3293
26 the people were come into the *w*.,* "
23:15 in the wilderness of Ziph in a *w*. 2793
16 and went to David into the *w*., and "
18 and David abode in the *w*., and "
19 with us in strong holds in the *w*., "
2Sa 6: 5 of instruments made of fir *w*., 6086
18: 6 battle was in the *w*. of Ephraim; *3293
8 the *w*. devoured more people that* "
17 cast him into a great pit in the *w*.,* "
24:22 instruments of the oxen for *w*. 6086
1Ki 6:15 covered them on the inside with *w*., "
18:23, 23 and lay it on *w*., and put no fire "
33 And he put the *w*. in order, and cut "
33 in pieces, and laid him on the *w*., "
33 the burnt sacrifice, and on the *w*. "
38 the burnt sacrifice, and the *w*., "
2Ki 2:24 forth two she bears out of the *w*. 3293
6: 4 came to Jordan, they cut down *w*. 6086
19:18 work of men's hands, *w*. and stone: "
1Ch 16:33 shall the trees of the *w*. sing out 3293
21:23 the threshing instruments for *w*., 6086
22: 4 of Tyre brought much cedar *w*. to* "
29: 2 of iron, and *w*. for things of *w*.; "
2Ch 2:16 And we will cut *w*. out of Lebanon, "
Ne 8: 4 the scribe stood upon a pulpit of *w*., "
10:34 and the people, for the *w*. offering, "
13:31 And for the *w*. offering, at times "
Job 41:27 as straw, and brass as rotten *w*. "
Ps 80:13 boar out of the *w*. doth waste it, 3293
83:14 As the fire burneth a *w*., and as * "
96:12 shall all the trees of the *w*. rejoice. "
132: 6 we found it in the fields of the *w*. "
Pr 26:20 Where no *w*. is, there the fire 6086
21 to burning coals, and *w*. to fire; "
Ec 2: 6 the *w*. that bringeth forth trees: *3293
10: 9 and he that cleaveth *w*. shall be 6086
Ca 2: 3 tree among the trees of the *w*., 3293
3: 9 a chariot of the *w*. of Lebanon. 6086
Isa 7: 2 as the trees of the *w*. are moved *3293
10:15 lift up itself, as if it were no *w*. 6086
30:33 pile thereof is fire and much *w*.; "
37:19 work of men's hands, *w*. and stone: "
45:20 set up the *w*. of their graven image. "
60:17 for *w*. brass, and for stones iron: "
Jer 5:14 thy mouth fire, and this people *w*., "
7:18 The children gather *w*., and the "
28:13 Thou hast broken the yokes of *w*.; "
46:22 her with axes, as hewers of *w*. "
La 5: 4 for money; our *w*. is sold unto us. "
13 and the children fell under the *w*. "
Eze 15: 3 *w*. be taken thereof to do any work? "
20:32 countries, to serve *w*. and stone. "
24:10 Heap on *w*., kindle the fire, "
39:10 shall take no *w*. out of the field, "
41:16 door, cieled with *w*. round about, "
22 altar of *w*. was three cubits high, "
22 and the walls thereof, were of *w*.: "
Da 5: 4 brass, of iron, of *w*., and of stone. 636
23 gold, of brass, iron, *w*., and stone, "
Mic 7:14 which dwell solitarily in the *w*., *3293
Hab 2:19 him that saith to the *w*., Awake; 6086
Hag 1: 8 up to the mountain, and bring *w*., "
Zec 12: 6 an hearth of fire among the *w*., "
1Co 3:12 precious stones, *w*., hay, stubble; *3586*
2Ti 2:20 silver, but also of *w*. and of earth; *3585*
Re 9:20 and brass, and stone, and of *w*.: "
18:12 and scarlet, and all thyine *w*., *3586*
12 manner vessels of most precious *w*., "

wood-offering See WOOD and OFFERING.

woods
Eze 34:25 wilderness, and sleep in the *w*. 3264

woof
Le 13:48 Whether it be in the warp, or *w*.; 6154
49, 51 either in the warp, or in the *w*., "
52 whether warp or *w*., in woollen or "
53 either in the warp, or in the *w*., or "
56 or out of the warp, or out of the *w*.: "
57 either in the warp, or in the *w*., "
58 the garment, either warp, or *w*., "
59 either in the warp, or *w*., or any "

wool
J'g 6:37 will put a fleece of *w*. in the floor; 6785
2Ki 3: 4 thousand rams, with the *w*. "
Ps 147:16 He giveth snow like *w*.: he "
Pr 31:13 She seeketh *w*., and flax, and "
Isa 1:18 like crimson, they shall be as *w*. "
51: 8 the worm shall eat them like *w*.: "
Eze 27:18 the wine of Helbon, and white *w*. "
34: 3 fat, and ye clothe you with the *w*., "
44:17 and no *w*. shall come upon them, "
Da 7: 9 hair of his head like the pure *w*.: 6015
Ho 2: 5 my *w*. and my flax, mine oil and 6785
9 will recover my *w*. and my flax "
Heb 9:19 and scarlet *w*. and hyssop, and *2053*
Re 1:14 and his hairs were white like *w*., "

woollen
Le 13:47 whether it be a *w*. garment, or a 6785
48 warp, or woof; of linen, or of *w*.; "
52 warp or woof, in *w*. or in linen, "
59 leprosy in a garment of *w*. or linen, "
19:19 garment mingled of linen and *w*. *8162
De 22:11 sorts, as of *w*. and linen together.*6785

word See also WORD'S; WORDS.
Ge 15: 1 *w*. of the Lord came unto Abram 1697
4 the *w*. of the Lord came unto him, "
30:34 it might be according to thy *w*. "
37:14 the flocks; and bring me *w*. again. 1697
41:40 according unto thy *w*. shall all my 6310
44: 2 to the *w*. that Joseph had spoken. 1697
18 thee, speak a *w*. in my lord's ears, "
Ex 8:10 he said, Be it according to thy *w*.: "
13 did according to the *w*. of Moses; "
31 Lord according to the *w*. of Moses; "
9:20 He that feared the *w*. of the Lord "
21 regarded not the *w*. of the Lord "
12:35 did according to the *w*. of Moses; "
14:12 the *w*. that we did tell thee in Egypt, "
32:28 did according to the *w*. of Moses: "
Le 10: 7 did according to the *w*. of Moses. "
Nu 3:16, 51 according to the *w*. of the Lord, 6310
4:45 according to the *w*. of the Lord * "
11:23 whether my *w*. shall come to pass 1697
13:26 and brought back *w*. unto them, "
14:20 have pardoned according to thy *w*.: "
15:31 hath despised the *w*. of the Lord, "
20:24 rebelled against my *w*. at the 6310
22: 8 I will bring you *w*. again, as the 1697
18 go beyond the *w*. of the Lord 6310
20 the *w*. which I shall say unto thee, 1697
35 the *w*. that I shall speak unto thee, "
38 *w*. that God putteth in my mouth, "
23: 5 Lord put a *w*. in Balaam's mouth, "
16 Balaam, and put a *w*. in his mouth, "
27:21 Lord: at his *w*. shall they go out, 6310
21 and at his *w*. they shall come in, "
30: 2 he shall not break his *w*., he shall 1697
36: 5 according to the *w*. of the Lord, 6310
De 1:22 bring us *w*. again by what way we 1697
25 and brought us *w*. again, and said, "
4: 2 add unto the *w*. which I command "
5: 5 to shew you the *w*. of the Lord: "
8: 3 but by every *w*. that proceedeth out* "
9: 5 the *w*. which the Lord sware unto 1697
18:20 presume to speak a *w*. in my name, "
21 know the *w*. which the Lord hath "
21: 5 by their *w*. shall every controversy 6310
30:14 But the *w*. is very nigh unto thee, 1697
33: 9 for they have observed thy *w*., and 565
34: 5 according to the *w*. of the Lord. 6310
Jos 1:13 Remember the *w*. which Moses 1697
6:10 neither shall any *w*. proceed out "
8:27 according unto the *w*. of the Lord "
35 was not a *w*. of all that Moses "
14: 7 I brought him *w*. again as it was "
10 the Lord spake this *w*. unto Moses, "
19:50 According to the *w*. of the Lord *6310
22: 9 according to the *w*. of the Lord by* "
32 and brought them *w*. again. 1697
1Sa 1:23 him; only the Lord establish his *w*. "
3: 1 the *w*. of the Lord was precious "
7 neither was the *w*. of the Lord yet "
21 in Shiloh by the *w*. of the Lord. "
4: 1 *w*. of Samuel came to all Israel. "
9:27 that I may shew thee the *w*. of God. "
15:10 the *w*. of the Lord unto Samuel, "
23, 26 hast rejected the *w*. of the Lord, "
2Sa 3:11 could not answer Abner a *w*. again, "
7: 4 *w*. of the Lord came unto Nathan, "
7 spake I a *w*. with any of the tribes "
25 the *w*. that thou hast spoken "
14:12 speak one *w*. unto my lord the king. "
17 The *w*. of my lord the king shall "
15:28 until there come *w*. from you to "
19:10 speak ye not a *w*. of bringing the king "
14 that they sent this *w*. unto the king, "
22:31 perfect; the *w*. of the Lord is tried: 565
23: 2 me, and his *w*. was in my tongue. 4405
24: 4 king's *w*. prevailed against Joab, 1697
11 the *w*. of the Lord came unto the "
1Ki 2: 4 Lord may continue his *w*. which he "
23 spoken this *w*. against his own life. "
27 he might fulfil the *w*. of the Lord, "
30 Benaiah brought the king *w*. again, "
42 The *w*. that I have heard is good.* "
6:11 *w*. of the Lord came to Solomon, "
12 will I perform my *w*. with thee, "
8:20 Lord hath performed his *w*. that he "
26 let thy *w*., I pray thee, be verified, "
56 hath not failed one *w*. of all his "
12:22 the *w*. of God came unto Shemaiah "
24 therefore to the *w*. of the Lord, "
24 according to the *w*. of the Lord. "
13: 1 by the *w*. of the Lord unto Beth-el: "
2 the altar in the *w*. of the Lord, "
5 had given by the *w*. of the Lord. "
9 charged me by the *w*. of the Lord, "
17 said to me by the *w*. of the Lord, "
18 unto me by the *w*. of the Lord, "
20 the *w*. of the Lord came unto the "
21 disobedient unto the *w*. of the *6310
26 according to the *w*. of the Lord, 1697
32 he cried by the *w*. of the Lord "
14:18 according to the *w*. of the Lord, "
16: 1 the *w*. of the Lord came to Jehu "
7 *w*. of the Lord against Baasha, "
12, 34 according to the *w*. of the Lord, "
17: 1 years, but according to my *w*. "
2 the *w*. of the Lord came unto him, "
5 according unto the *w*. of the Lord: "
8 the *w*. of the Lord came unto him, "
16 according to the *w*. of the Lord, "
24 the *w*. of the Lord in thy mouth "
18: 1 *w*. of the Lord came to Elijah "
21 the people answered him not a *w*. "
31 unto whom the *w*. of the Lord came, "
36 have done all these things at thy *w*. "
19: 9 the *w*. of the Lord came to him, "
20: 9 departed, and brought him *w*. again. "
35 neighbour in the *w*. of the Lord, "
21: 4 *w*. which Naboth the Jazreelite had "
17, 28 *w*. of the Lord came to Elijah "
22: 5 thee, at the *w*. of the Lord to day. "
1Ki 22:13 one mouth: let thy *w*., I pray thee, 1697
13 be like the *w*. of one of them, and "
19 thou therefore the *w*. of the Lord: "
38 according unto the *w*. of the Lord "
2Ki 1:16 God in Israel to enquire of his *w*.? "
17 according to the *w*. of the Lord "
3:12 The *w*. of the Lord is with him. "
4:44 according to the *w*. of the Lord. "
6:18 according to the *w*. of Elisha. "
7: 1 said, Hear ye the *w*. of the Lord; "
16 according to the *w*. of the Lord. "
9:26 according to the *w*. of the Lord. "
36 This is the *w*. of the Lord, which he "
10:10 earth nothing of the *w*. of the Lord, "
14:25 according to the *w*. of the Lord God "
15:12 This was the *w*. of the Lord which "
18:28 Hear the *w*. of the great king, the "
36 peace, and answered him not a *w*.: "
19:21 the *w*. that the Lord hath spoken "
20: 4 the *w*. of the Lord came to him, "
16 Hezekiah, hear the *w*. of the Lord. "
19 Good is the *w*. of the Lord which "
22: 9 and brought the king *w*. again, "
20 they brought the king *w*. again. "
23:16 according to the *w*. of the Lord "
24: 2 according to the *w*. of the Lord, "
1Ch 10:13 even against the *w*. of the Lord, "
11: 3, 10 according to the *w*. of the Lord "
12:23 according to the *w*. of the Lord. 6310
15:15 according to the *w*. of the Lord. 1697
16:15 the *w*. which he commanded to a "
17: 3 the *w*. of God came to Nathan, "
6 spake I a *w*. to any of the judges of "
21: 4 king's *w*. prevailed against Joab. "
6 king's *w*. was abominable to Joab. "
12 what *w*. I shall bring again to him* "
22: 8 but the *w*. of the Lord came to me, "
2Ch 6:10 hath performed his *w*. that he hath "
17 God of Israel, let thy *w*. be verified, "
10:15 the Lord might perform his *w*., "
11: 2 *w*. of the Lord came to Shemaiah "
12: 7 *w*. of the Lord came to Shemaiah, "
18: 4 thee, at the *w*. of the Lord to day. "
12 let thy *w*. therefore, I pray thee, be "
18 Therefore hear the *w*. of the Lord; "
30:12 the princes, by the *w*. of the Lord. "
34:16 brought the king *w*. back again, "
21 have not kept the *w*. of the Lord, "
28 So they brought the king *w*. again. "
35: 6 do according to the *w*. of the Lord "
36:21 To fulfil the *w*. of the Lord by the "
22 that the *w*. of the Lord spoken by "
Ezr 1: 1 *w*. of the Lord by the mouth of "
6:11 that whosoever shall alter this *w*., 6600
10: 5 should do according to this *w*. 1697
Ne 1: 8 *w*. that thou commandest thy "
Es 1:21 according to the *w*. of Memucan: "
7: 8 *w*. went out of the king's mouth, "
Job 2:13 and none spake a *w*. unto him: "
Ps 17: 4 *w*. of thy lips I have kept me from "
18:30 the *w*. of the Lord is tried: he is a 565
33: 4 For the *w*. of the Lord is right; 1697
6 By the *w*. of the Lord were the "
56: 4 In God I will praise his *w*., in God I "
10 In God will I praise his *w*.: "
10 in the Lord will I praise his *w*. "
68:11 The Lord gave the *w*.: great was 562
103:20 unto the voice of his *w*. 1697
105: 8 the *w*. which he commanded to a "
19 Until the time that his *w*. came: "
19 the *w*. of the Lord tried him. 565
28 they rebelled not against his *w*. *1697
106:24 land, they believed not his *w*.: "
107:20 He sent his *w*., and healed them, "
119: 9 heed thereto according to thy *w*. "
11 Thy *w*. have I hid in mine heart, 565
16 statutes: I will not forget thy *w*. 1697
17 that I may live, and keep thy *w*. "
25 quicken...me according to thy *w*. "
28 thou me according unto thy *w*. "
38 Stablish thy *w*. unto thy servant, 565
41 thy salvation, according to thy *w*. "
42 me: for I trust in thy *w*. 1697
43 take not the *w*. of truth utterly out "
49 Remember the *w*. unto thy servant, "
50 for thy *w*. hath quickened me. 565
58 unto me according to thy *w*. "
65 O Lord, according unto thy *w*. 1697
67 astray: but now have I kept thy *w*. 565
74 because I have hoped in thy *w*. 1697
76 to thy *w*. unto thy servant. 565
81 salvation: but I hope in thy *w*. 1697
82 Mine eyes fail for thy *w*., saying, 565
89 Lord, thy *w*. is settled in heaven. 1697
101 evil way, that I might keep thy *w*. "
105 Thy *w*. is a lamp unto my feet, and "
107 O Lord, according unto thy *w*. "
114 and my shield: I hope in thy *w*. "
116 Uphold me according unto thy *w*. 565
123 and for the *w*. of thy righteousness. "
133 Order my steps in thy *w*.: and let not "
140 Thy *w*. is very pure: therefore thy "
147 and cried: I hoped in thy *w*. *1697
148 that I might meditate in thy *w*. 565
154 quicken me according to thy *w*. "
158 because they kept not thy *w*. "
160 Thy *w*. is true from the beginning: 1697
161 heart standeth in awe of thy *w*. * "
162 I rejoice at thy *w*., as one that 565
169 according to thy *w*. 1697
170 deliver me according to thy *w*. 565
172 My tongue shall speak of thy *w*.: "
130: 5 doth wait, and in his *w*. do I hope. 1697
138: 2 hast magnified thy *w*. above all 565
139: 4 there is not a *w*. in my tongue, 4405
147:15 earth: his *w*. runneth very swiftly. 1697

Ps 147:18 He sendeth out his w', and melteth 1697
19 He sheweth his w' unto Jacob, "
148: 8 stormy wind fulfilling his w': "
Pr 12:25 but a good w' maketh it glad. "
13:13 despiseth the w' shall be destroyed: "
14:15 The simple believeth every w': "
15:23 and a w' spoken in due season, "
25:11 A w' fitly spoken is like apples of "
30: 5 Every w' of God is pure: he is a 565
Ec 8: 4 Where the w' of a king is, there is 1697
Isa 1:10 Hear the w' of the Lord, ye rulers "
2: 1 The w' that Isaiah the son of Amoz "
3 the w' of the Lord from Jerusalem. "
5:24 despised the w' of the Holy One of 565
8:10 speak the w', and it shall not 1697
20 speak not according to this w', "
9: 8 The Lord sent a w' into Jacob, and "
16:13 is the w' that the Lord hath spoken "
24: 3 for the Lord hath spoken this w'. "
28:13 the w' of the Lord was unto them "
14 Wherefore hear the w' of the Lord, "
29:21 make a man an offender for a w',* "
30:12 Because ye despise this w', and "
21 ears shall hear a w' behind thee, "
36:21 peace, and answered him not a w': "
37:22 the w' which the Lord hath spoken "
38: 4 came the w' of the Lord to Isaiah, "
39: 5 Hear the w' of the Lord of hosts: "
8 Good is the w' of the Lord which "
40: 8 w' of our God shall stand for ever. "
41:28 I asked of them, could answer a w'. "
44:26 confirmeth the w' of his servant, "
45:23 the w' is gone out of my mouth in "
50: 4 speak a w' in season to him that is* "
55:11 So shall my w' be that goeth forth "
66: 2 spirit, and trembleth at my w'. "
5 Hear the w' of the Lord, ye that "
5 ye that tremble at his w'; Your "
Jer 1: 2 To whom the w' of the Lord came "
4, 11 the w' of the Lord came unto me, "
12 I will hasten my w' to perform it. "
13 the w' of the Lord came unto me "
2: 1 the w' of the Lord came to me, "
4 Hear ye the w' of the Lord, O "
31 see ye the w' of the Lord. "
5:13 wind, and the w' is not in them: 1699'
14 Because ye speak this w', behold, 1697
6:10 the w' of the Lord is unto them a "
7: 1 w' that came to Jeremiah from the "
2 house, and proclaim there this w', "
2 Hear ye the w' of the Lord, all ye "
8: 9 have rejected the w' of the Lord; "
9:20 Yet hear the w' of the Lord, O ye "
20 ear receive the w' of his mouth, "
10: 1 Hear ye the w' which the Lord "
11: 1 The w' that came to Jeremiah "
13: 2 according to the w' of the Lord, "
3 the w' of the Lord came unto me "
8 the w' of the Lord came unto me, "
12 thou shalt speak unto them this w'; "
14: 1 The w' of the Lord that came to "
17 thou shalt say this w' unto them; "
15:16 and thy w' was unto me the joy *
16: 1 w' of the Lord came also unto me, "
17:15 Where is the w' of the Lord? let it "
20 Hear ye the w' of the Lord, ye "
18: 1 w' which came to Jeremiah from "
5 the w' of the Lord came to me, "
18 wise, nor the w' from the prophet. "
19: 3 Hear ye the w' of the Lord, O kings "
20: 8 the w' of the Lord was made a "
9 w' was in mine heart as a burning* "
21: 1 w' which came unto Jeremiah 1697
11 say, Hear ye the w' of the Lord; "
22: 1 of Judah, and speak there this w', "
2 Hear the w' of the Lord, O king of "
29 earth, hear the w' of the Lord. "
23:18 hath perceived and heard his w'? "
18 who hath marked his w', and heard "
28 and he that hath my w', "
28 let him speak my w' faithfully. "
29 Is not my w' like as a fire? saith the "
36 every man's w' shall be his burden; "
38 Because ye say this w', the burden "
24: 4 the w' of the Lord came unto me, "
25: 1 The w' that came to Jeremiah "
3 w' of the Lord hath come unto me, "
26: 1 Judah came this w' from the Lord, "
2 unto them; diminish not a w': "
27: 1 w' unto Jeremiah from the Lord, "
18 if the w' of the Lord be with them, "
28: 7 hear thou now this w' that I speak "
9 the w' of the prophet shall come to "
12 the w' of the Lord came unto "
29:10 perform my good w' toward you, "
20 Hear ye...the w' of the Lord, "
30 w' of the Lord unto Jeremiah, "
30: 1 w' that came to Jeremiah from the "
31:10 Hear the w' of the Lord, O ye "
32: 1 The w' that came to Jeremiah "
6 The w' of the Lord came unto me, "
8 according to the w' of the Lord, "
8 that this was the w' of the Lord. "
26 the w' of the Lord unto Jeremiah, "
33: 1, 19 the w' of the Lord came unto "
23 the w' of the Lord came to "
34: 1 The w' which came unto Jeremiah "
4 Yet hear the w' of the Lord, O "
5 for I have pronounced the w', "
8 w' that came unto Jeremiah from "
12 the w' of the Lord came to "
35: 1 w' which came unto Jeremiah from "
12 the w' of the Lord unto Jeremiah, "
36: 1 that this w' came unto Jeremiah "
27 the w' of the Lord came to "
37: 6 w' of the Lord unto the prophet "
Jer 37:17 Is there any w' from the Lord? 1697
38:21 w' that the Lord hath shewed me: "
39:15 the w' of the Lord came unto "
40: 1 The w' that came to Jeremiah from "
42: 7 that the w' of the Lord came unto "
15 therefore hear the w' of the Lord, "
43: 8 the w' of the Lord unto Jeremiah "
44: 1 The w' that came to Jeremiah "
16 w' that thou hast spoken unto us "
24 Hear the w' of the Lord, all Judah "
26 hear ye the w' of the Lord, all "
45: 1 The w' that Jeremiah the prophet "
46: 1 The w' of the Lord which came to "
13 The w' that the Lord spake to "
47: 1 The w' of the Lord that came to "
49:34 The w' of the Lord that came to "
50: 1 w' that the Lord spake against "
51:59 w' which Jeremiah the prophet "
La 2:17 he hath fulfilled his w' that he had 565
Eze 1: 3 w' of the Lord came expressly 1697
3:16 the w' of the Lord came unto me, "
17 hear the w' at my mouth, and give "
6: 1 the w' of the Lord came unto me, "
3 hear the w' of the Lord God; "
7: 1 the w' of the Lord came unto me, "
11:14 the w' of the Lord came unto me, "
12: 1 w' of the Lord also came unto me, "
8 came the w' of the Lord unto me, "
17 the w' of the Lord came to me, "
21 the w' of the Lord came unto me, "
25 w' that I shall speak shall come to "
25 will I say the w', and will perform "
26 the w' of the Lord came to me, "
28 w' which I have spoken shall be "
13: 1 the w' of the Lord came unto me, "
2 hearts, Hear ye the w' of the Lord; "
6 that they would confirm the w'. "
14: 2 the w' of the Lord came unto me, "
12 The w' of the Lord came unto me, "
15: 1 the w' of the Lord came unto me, "
16: 1 the w' of the Lord came unto me, "
35 O harlot, hear the w' of the Lord: "
17: 1, 11 the w' of the Lord came unto me, "
18: 1 The w' of the Lord came unto me "
20: 2 came the w' of the Lord unto me, "
45 the w' of the Lord came unto me, "
46 and drop thy w' toward the south, "
47 south, Hear the w' of the Lord; 1697
21: 1 the w' of the Lord came unto me, "
2 drop thy w' toward the holy places, "
8 the w' of the Lord came unto me, 1697
18 The w' of the Lord came unto me "
22: 1, 17, 23 the w' of the Lord came "
23: 1 w' of the Lord came again unto me, "
24: 1, 15 the w' of the Lord came unto me, "
20 The w' of the Lord came unto me, "
25: 1 w' of the Lord came again unto me, "
3 Hear the w' of the Lord God; "
26: 1 the w' of the Lord came unto me, "
27: 1 w' of the Lord came again unto me, "
28: 1 w' of the Lord came again unto me, "
11, 20 w' of the Lord came unto me, "
29: 1, 17 w' of the Lord came unto me, "
30: 1 w' of the Lord came again unto me, "
20 the w' of the Lord came unto me, "
31: 1 the w' of the Lord came unto me, "
32: 1, 17 w' of the Lord came unto me, "
33: 1 the w' of the Lord came unto me, "
7 shalt hear the w' at my mouth, "
23 the w' of the Lord came unto me, "
30 what is the w' that cometh forth "
34: 1 the w' of the Lord came unto me, "
7, 9 hear the w' of the Lord; "
35: 1 the w' of the Lord came unto me, "
36: 1 Israel, hear the w' of the Lord: "
4 Israel, hear the w' of the Lord God; "
16 the w' of the Lord came unto me, "
37: 4 dry bones, hear the w' of the Lord. "
15 w' of the Lord came again unto me, "
38: 1 the w' of the Lord came unto me, "
Da 3:28 and have changed the king's w', 4406
4:17 demand by the w' of the holy ones: 3983
31 the w' was in the king's mouth, 4406
9: 2 w' of the Lord came to Jeremiah 1697
10:11 he had spoken this w' unto me, "
Ho 1: 1 The w' of the Lord that came unto "
2 of the w' of the Lord by Hosea. *1699'
4: 1 Hear the w' of the Lord, ye 1697
Joe 1: 1 w' of the Lord that came to Joel "
2:11 he is strong that executeth his w': "
Am 3: 1 Hear this w' that the Lord hath "
4: 1 Hear this w', ye kine of Bashan, "
5: 1 Hear ye this w' which I take up "
7:16 hear thou the w' of the Lord: "
16 not thy w' against the house of Isaac. "
8:12 and fro to seek the w' of the Lord, 1697
Jon 1: 1 the w' of the Lord came unto Jonah "
3: 1 the w' of the Lord came unto Jonah "
3 according to the w' of the Lord. "
6 w' came unto the king of Nineveh,* "
Mic 1: 1 w' of the Lord that came to Micah "
4: 2 the w' of the Lord from Jerusalem. "
Hab 3: 9 the oaths of the tribes, even thy w'. 562
Zep 1: 1 w' of the Lord which came unto 1697
2: 5 the w' of the Lord is against you; "
Hag 1: 1, 3 came the w' of the Lord by Haggai "
2: 1 the w' of the Lord by the prophet "
5 the w' that I covenanted with you "
10 came the w' of the Lord by Haggai "
20 w' of the Lord came unto Haggai "
Zec 1: 1, 7 w' of the Lord unto Zechariah, "
4: 6 w' of the Lord unto Zerubbabel, "
8 the w' of the Lord came unto me, "
6: 9 the w' of the Lord came unto me, "
7: 1 that the w' of the Lord came unto "
4 came the w' of the Lord of hosts "
Zec 7: 8 And the w' of the Lord came unto 1697
8: 1, 18 w' of the Lord of hosts came to me, "
9: 1 The burden of the w' of the Lord "
11:11 knew that it was the w' of the Lord. "
12: 1 The burden of the w' of the Lord "
Mal 1: 1 The burden of the w' of the Lord "
M't 2: 8 bring me w' again, that I may 518
13 thou there until I bring thee w': *2036
4: 4 by every w' that proceedeth out of 4487
8: 8 but speak the w' only, and my 3056
16 he cast out the spirits with his w', "
12:32 speaketh a w' against the Son of "
36 every idle w' that men shall speak, 4487
13:19 one heareth the w' of the kingdom, 3056
20 the same is he that heareth the w', "
21 ariseth because of the w', "
22 thorns is he that heareth the w'; "
22 choke the w', and he becometh "
23 ground is he that heareth the w', "
15:23 But he answered her not a w'. "
18:16 every w' may be established. 4487
22:46 man was able to answer him a w', 3056
26:75 remembered the w' of Jesus, 4487
27:14 he answered him to never a w'; "
28: 8 did run to bring his disciples w'. 518
M'r 2: 2 he preached the w' unto them. 3056
4:14 The sower soweth the w'. "
15 the way side, where the w' is sown; "
15 taketh away the w' that was sown "
16 when they have heard the w', "
18 thorns: such as hear the w', "
19 choke the w', and it becometh "
20 such as hear the w', and receive it, "
33 parables spake he the w' unto them, "
5:36 Jesus heard the w' that was spoken, "
7:13 Making the w' of God of none "
14:72 the w' that Jesus said unto him, 4487
16:20 and confirming the w' with signs 3056
Lu 1: 2 and ministers of the w'; "
38 be it unto me according to thy w'. 4487
2:29 in peace, according to thy w': "
3: 2 the w' of God came unto John the "
4: 4 alone, but by every w' of God. *
32 for his w' was with power. 3056
36 saying, What a w' is this! for with "
5: 1 upon him to hear the w' of God, "
5 at thy w' I will let down the net. 4487
7: 7 but say in a w', and my servant 3056
8:11 is this: The seed is the w' of God. "
12 away the w' out of their hearts, "
13 they hear, receive the w' with joy; "
15 heart, having heard the w', keep it, "
21 these which hear the w' of God, "
10:39 sat at Jesus' feet, and heard his w'. "
11:28 that hear the w' of God, and keep it. "
12:10 speak a w' against the Son of man, "
22:61 remembered the w' of the Lord, "
24:19 mighty in deed and w' before God "
Joh 1: 1 In the beginning was the W', "
1 and the W' was with God, "
1 and the W' was God. "
14 the W' was made flesh, and dwelt "
2:22 and the w' which Jesus had said. "
4:41 believed because of his own w'; "
50 man believed the w' that Jesus had "
5:24 He that heareth my w', and "
38 ye have not his w' abiding in you: "
8:31 If ye continue in my w', then are "
37 because my w' hath no place in you, "
43 even because ye cannot hear my w'. "
10:35 unto whom the w' of God came, "
12:48 the w' that I have spoken, the same "
14:24 the w' which ye hear is not mine, "
15: 3 w' which I have spoken unto you. "
20 Remember the w' that I said unto "
25 that the w' might be fulfilled that "
17: 6 me; and they have kept thy w'. "
14 I have given them thy w'; and the "
17 through thy truth: thy w' is truth. "
20 believe on me through their w'; "
Ac 2:41 received his w' were baptized: "
4: 4 them which heard the w' believed; "
29 boldness they may speak thy w', "
31 spake the w' of God with boldness. "
6: 2 that we should leave the w' of God, "
4 and to the ministry of the w'. "
7 And the w' of God increased; and "
8: 4 went every where preaching the w'. "
14 had received the w' of God, they "
25 and preached the w' of the Lord, "
10:36 The w' which God sent unto the "
37 That w', I say, ye know, which *4487
44 on all them which heard the w'. 3056
11: 1 had also received the w' of God. "
16 remembered I the w' of the Lord. 4487
19 preaching the w' to none but unto 3056
12:24 the w' of God grew and multiplied. "
13: 5 they preached the w' of God in the "
7 and desired to hear the w' of God. "
15 if ye have any w' of exhortation for "
26 to you is the w' of this salvation "
44 together to hear the w' of God. "
46 It was necessary that the w' of God "
48 and glorified the w' of the Lord: "
49 the w' of the Lord was published "
14: 3 which gave testimony unto the w' "
25 they had preached the w' in Perga, "
15: 7 should hear the w' of the gospel, "
35 and preaching the w' of the Lord, "
36 have preached the w' of the Lord, "
16: 6 of the Holy Ghost to preach the w' "
32 spake unto him the w' of the Lord, "
17:11 received the w' with all readiness "
13 w' of God was preached of Paul "
18:11 teaching the w' of God among them. "
19:10 in Asia heard the w' of the Lord

Ac 19:20 So mightily grew the w' of God and 3056
20:32 to God, and to the w' of his grace, "
22:22 gave him audience unto this w', "
28:25 after that Paul had spoken one w', 4487
Ro 9: 6 Not as though the w' of God hath 3056
9 For this is the w' of promise, At "
10: 8 w' is nigh thee, even in thy mouth, 4487
8 the w' of faith, which we preach; "
17 and hearing by the w' of God. "
15:18 obedient, by w' and deed, 3056
1Co 4:20 the kingdom of God is not in w', "
12: 8 given by the Spirit the w' of wisdom; "
8 to another the w' of knowledge by "
14:36 came the w' of God out from you? "
2Co 1:18 our w' toward you was not yea and "
2:17 many, which corrupt the w' of God: "
4: 2 the w' of God deceitfully; "
5:19 unto us the w' of reconciliation. "
6: 7 By the w' of truth, by the power of "
10:11 such as we are in w' by letters when "
13: 1 shall every w' be established. 4487
Ga 5:14 all the law is fulfilled in one w', "
6: 6 Let him that is taught in the w' "
Eph 1:13 after that ye heard the w' of truth, "
5:26 the washing of water by the w', "
6:17 the Spirit, which is the w' of God: "
Ph'p 1:14 bold to speak the w' without fear. 3056
2:16 Holding forth the w' of life; that I "
Col 1: 5 heard before in the w' of the truth "
25 me for you, to fulfil the w' of God; "
3:16 Let the w' of Christ dwell in you "
17 whatsoever ye do in w' or deed, do "
1Th 1: 5 came not unto you in w' only, "
6 received the w' in much affliction, "
8 you sounded out the w' of the Lord "
2:13 w' of God which ye heard of us, "
13 ye received it not as the w' of men, "
13 but as it is in truth, the w' of God, "
4:15 say unto you by the w' of the Lord, "
2Th 2: 2 neither by spirit, nor by w', "
15 whether by w', or our epistle. "
17 and stablish you in every good w' "
3: 1 the w' of the Lord may have free "
14 obey not our w' by this epistle, "
1Ti 4: 5 is sanctified by the w' of God and "
12 an example of the believers, in w', "
5:17 they who labour in the w' and "
2Ti 2: 9 but the w' of God is not bound. "
15 rightly dividing the w' of truth. "
17 their w' will eat as doth a canker: "
4: 2 Preach the w'; be instant in "
Tit 1: 3 in due times manifested his w' "
9 Holding fast the faithful w' as he "
2: 5 the w' of God be not blasphemed. "
Heb 1: 3 all things by the w' of his power, 4487
2: 2 For if the w' spoken by angels was 3056
4: 2 w' preached did not profit them, "
12 For the w' of God is quick, and "
5:13 unskilful in the w' of righteousness: "
6: 5 have tasted the good w' of God, 4487
7:28 but the w' of the oath, which was 3056
11: 3 were framed by the w' of God, 4487
12:19 that the w' should not be spoken 3056
27 this w', Yet once more, signifieth "
13: 7 spoken unto you the w' of God: 3056
22 suffer the w' of exhortation: "
Jas 1:18 begat he us with the w' of truth, "
21 with meekness the engrafted w', "
22 But be ye doers of the w', and not "
23 For if any be a hearer of the w', "
3: 2 If any man offend not in w', the "
1Pe 1:23 by the w' of God, which liveth and "
25 w' of the Lord endureth for ever. 4487
25 w' which by the gospel is preached "
2: 2 desire the sincere milk of the w', *3050
8 to them which stumble at the w', 3056
3: 1 that, if any obey not the w', they "
1 also may without the w' be won "
2Pe 1:19 also a more sure w' of prophecy; "
3: 5 by the w' of God the heavens were "
7 by the same w' are kept in store, "
1Jo 1: 1 have handled, of the W' of life; "
10 him a liar, and his w' is not in us. "
2: 5 But whoso keepeth his w', in him "
7 the w' which ye have heard from "
14 and the w' of God abideth in you, "
3:18 children, let us not love in w', "
5: 7 the Father, the W', and the Holy* "
Re 1: 2 Who bare record of the w' of God, "
9 for the w' of God, and for the "
3: 8 and hast kept my w', and hast not "
10 hast kept the w' of my patience, "
6: 9 that were slain for the w' of God, "
12:11 and by the w' of their testimony; "
19:13 his name is called The W' of God, "
20: 4 and for the w' of God, and which "

word's
2Sa 7:21 For thy w' sake, and according to 1697
M'r 4:17 persecution ariseth for...w' sake, *3056

words
Ge 24:30 when he heard the w' of Rebekah 1697
52 Abraham's servant heard their w', "
27:34 Esau heard the w' of his father, "
42 w' of Esau her elder son were told "
31: 1 he heard the w' of Laban's sons, "
34:18 And their w' pleased Hamor, and "
37: 8 more for his dreams, and for his w'. "
39:17 unto him according to these w', "
19 master heard the w' of his wife, "
42:16 prison, that your w' may be proved, "
20 so shall your w' be verified, and ye "
43: 7 according to the tenor of these w': "
44: 6 he spake unto them these same w'. "
7 Wherefore saith my lord these w'? "
10 let it be according unto your w' "
Ge 44:24 we told him the w' of my lord. 1697
45:27 they told him all the w' of Joseph, "
49:21 hind let loose: he giveth goodly w'. 561
Ex 4:15 him, and put w' in his mouth: 1697
28 told Aaron all the w' of the Lord "
30 spake all the w' which the Lord "
5: 9 and let them not regard vain w'. "
19: 6 are the w' which thou shalt speak "
7 w' which the Lord commanded him. "
8 Moses returned the w' of the people "
9 Moses told the w' of the people "
20: 1 God spake all these w', saying, "
23: 8 perverteth the w' of the righteous. "
24: 3 the people all the w' of the Lord, "
3 w' which the Lord hath said will "
4 Moses wrote all the w' of the Lord, "
8 with you concerning all these w'. "
34: 1 the w' that were in the first tables, "
27 unto Moses, Write thou these w': "
27 after the tenor of these w' I have "
28 the tables the w' of the covenant, "
35: 1 are the w' which the Lord hath "
Nu 11:24 told the people the w' of the Lord, "
12: 6 And he said, Hear now my w': If "
16:31 an end of speaking all these w', "
22: 7 and spake unto him the w' of Balak. "
24: 4, 16 which heard the w' of God, 561
De 1: 1 the w' which Moses spake unto all 1697
34 the Lord heard the voice of your w', "
2:26 king of Heshbon with w' of peace, "
4:10 and I will make them hear my w', "
12 ye heard the voice of the w', but "
36 heardest his w' out of the midst "
5:22 w' the Lord spake unto all your "
28 Lord heard the voice of your w', "
28 the voice of the w' of this people, "
6: 6 these w', which I command thee "
9:10 written according to all the w', "
10: 2 the w' that were in the first tables "
11:18 lay up these my w' in your heart "
12:28 hear all these w' which I command "
13: 3 hearken unto the w' of that prophet, "
16:19 and pervert the w' of the righteous. "
17:19 to keep all the w' of this law and "
18:18 and will put my w' in his mouth; "
19 w' which he shall speak in my name, "
27: 3 upon them all the w' of this law, "
8 upon the stones all the w' of this law "
26 not all the w' of this law to do them. "
28:14 w' which I command thee this day, "
58 w' of this law that are written in "
29: 1 These are the w' of the covenant, "
9 therefore the w' of this covenant, "
19 he heareth the w' of this curse, "
29 we may do all the w' of this law. "
31: 1 and spake these w' unto all Israel. "
12 observe to do all the w' of this law: "
24 an end of writing the w' of this law "
28 I may speak these w' in their ears, "
30 of Israel the w' of this song, "
32: 1 hear, O earth, the w' of my mouth. 561
44 and spake all the w' of this song 1697
45 end of speaking all these w' to all "
46 hearts unto all the w' which I testify "
46 observe to do, all the w' of this law. "
33: 3 every one shall receive of thy w'. 1703
Jos 1:18 and will not hearken unto thy w' 1697
2:21 According unto your w', so be it. "
3: 9 hear the w' of the Lord your God. "
8:34 he read all the w' of the law, "
22:30 the w' that the children of Reuben "
24:26 Joshua wrote these w' in the book "
27 it hath heard all the w' of the Lord 561
J'g 2: 4 angel of the Lord spake these w' 1697
9: 3 all the men of Shechem all these w': "
30 of the city heard the w' of Gaal "
11:10 we do not so according to thy w'. * "
11 Jephthah uttered all his w' before "
28 not unto the w' of Jephthah "
13:12 said, Now let thy w' come to pass. "
16:16 she pressed him daily with her w', "
1Sa 3:19 none of his w' fall to the ground. "
8:10 Samuel told all the w' of the Lord "
21 heard all the w' of the people, "
15: 1 unto the voice of the w' of the Lord. "
24 of the Lord, and thy w': "
17:11 heard those w' of the Philistine, "
23 spake according to the same w': "
31 w' were heard which David spake, "
18:23 Saul's servants spake those w' in "
26 his servants told David these w', "
21:12 And David laid up these w' in his "
24: 7 stayed his servants with these w', "
9 Wherefore hearest thou men's w', "
16 made an end of speaking these w' "
25: 9 according to all those w' in the "
24 and hear the w' of thine handmaid. "
26:19 the king hear the w' of his servant. "
28:20 afraid, because of the w' of Samuel: "
21 hearkened unto the w' which thou "
2Sa 3: 8 wroth for the w' of Ish-bosheth, "
7:17 According to all these w', and "
28 and thy w' be true, and thou hast "
14: 3 So Joab put the w' in her mouth. "
19 w' in the mouth of thine handmaid: "
19:43 w' of the men of Judah were fiercer "
43 than the w' of the men of Israel. "
20:17 Hear the w' of thine handmaid. "
22: 1 unto the Lord the w' of this song "
23: 1 Now these be the last w' of David. "
1Ki 1:14 in after thee, and confirm thy w'. "
3:12 I have done according to thy w': * "
5: 7 Hiram heard the w' of Solomon, "
8:59 And let these my w', wherewith "
10: 7 Howbeit I believed not the w', "
12: 7 speak good w' to them, that they "
1Ki 13:11 w' which he had spoken unto the 1697
21:27 when Ahab heard those w', that he "
22:13 w' of the prophets declare good "
2Ki 1: 7 to meet you, and told you these w'? "
6:12 the w' that thou speakest in thy "
30 king heard the w' of the woman, "
18:20 (but they are but vain w',) I have "
27 and to thee, to speak these w'? "
37 told him the w' of Rab-shakeh. "
19: 4 will hear all the w' of Rab-shakeh, "
4 reprove the w' which the Lord thy "
6 of the w' which thou hast heard, "
16 hear the w' of Sennacherib, which "
22:11 king had heard the w' of the book "
13 w' of this book that is found: "
13 hearkened unto the w' of this book, "
16 the w' of the book which the king "
18 the w' which thou hast heard; "
23: 2 the w' of the book of the covenant "
3 to perform the w' of this covenant "
16 who proclaimed these w'. * "
24 might perform the w' of the law "
1Ch 17:15 According to these w', and "
23:27 by the last w' of David the Levites "
25: 5 the king's seer in the w' of God, "
2Ch 9: 6 I believed not their w', until I came, "
10: 7 speak good w' to them, they will "
11: 4 they obeyed the w' of the Lord, "
15: 8 And when Asa heard these w', and "
18:12 the w' of the prophets declare good "
29:15 of the king, by the w' of the Lord, "
30 unto the Lord with the w' of David, "
32: 8 the w' of Hezekiah king of Judah. "
33:18 w' of the seers that spake to him "
34:19 king had heard the w' of the law, "
21 the w' of the book that is found: "
26 the w' which thou hast heard; "
27 heardest his w' against this place, "
30 the w' of the book of the covenant "
31 to perform the w' of the covenant "
35:22 hearkened not unto the w' of Necho "
36:16 despised his w', and misused his "
Ezr 7:11 of the w' of the commandments "
9: 4 trembled at the w' of the God of "
Ne 1: 1 The w' of Nehemiah the son of "
4 when I heard these w', that I sat "
2:18 king's w' that he had spoken unto "
5: 6 when I heard their cry and these w'. "
6: 6 be their king, according to these w'. "
7 to the king, according to these w'. "
19 me, and uttered my w' to him. "
8: 9 when they heard the w' of the law. "
12 the w' that were declared unto "
13 to understand the w' of the law. "
9: 8 seed, and hast performed thy w'; "
Es 4: 9 and told Esther the w' of Mordecai. "
12 they told to Mordecai Esther's w'. "
9:26 for all the w' of this letter, "
30 with w' of peace and truth, "
Job 4: 4 Thy w' have upholden him that 4405
6: 3 therefore my w' are swallowed up. 1697
10 concealed the w' of the Holy One. 561
25 How forcible are right w'! but what "
26 Do ye imagine to reprove w', and 4405
8: 2 w' of thy mouth be like a strong 561
10 and utter w' out of their heart? 4405
9:14 out my w' to reason with him? 1697
11: 2 the multitude of w' be answered? "
12:11 Doth not the ear try w'? and the 4405
15:13 lettest such w' go out of thy mouth? "
16: 3 Shall vain w' have an end? 1697
4 I could heap up w' against you, 4405
18: 2 will it be ere ye make an end of w'? "
19: 2 and break me in pieces with w'? "
23 Oh that my w' were now written! "
22:22 and lay up his w' in thine heart. 561
23: 5 w' which he would answer me, 4405
12 have esteemed the w' of his mouth 561
26: 4 To whom hast thou uttered w'? 4405
29:22 After my w' they spake not again; 1697
31:40 The w' of Job are ended. "
32:11 I waited for your w'; I gave ear "
12 Job, or that answered his w': 561
14 not directed his w' against me: 4405
33: 1 and hearken to all my w'. 1697
3 My w' shall be of the uprightness 561
5 me, set thy w' in order before me, "
8 I have heard the voice of thy w', 4405
34: 2 Hear my w', O ye wise men; and "
3 For the ear trieth w', as the mouth "
16 hearken to the voice of my w'. "
35 and his w' were without wisdom. 1697
37 and multiplieth his w' against God. 561
35:16 he multiplieth w' without knowledge. 4405
36: 4 For truly my w' shall not be false: "
38: 2 counsel by w' without knowledge? "
41: 3 will he speak soft w' unto thee? "
42: 7 had spoken these w' unto Job, 1697
Ps 5: 1 Give ear to my w', O Lord, consider 561
7: *title* concerning the w' of Cush 1697
12: 6 The w' of the Lord are pure w': 565
18: *title* unto the Lord the w' of this song 1697
19: 4 their w' to the end of the world. 4405
14 Let the w' of my mouth, and the 561
22: 1 and from the w' of my roaring? 1697
36: 3 The w' of his mouth are iniquity "
50:17 and castest my w' behind thee. "
52: 4 Thou lovest all devouring w', "
54: 2 give ear to the w' of my mouth. 561
55:21 w' of his mouth were smoother * "
21 his w' were softer than oil, yet were 1697
56: 5 Every day they wrest my w': all "
59:12 the w' of their lips let them even "
64: 3 shoot their arrows, even bitter w': "
78: 1 your ears to the w' of my mouth. 561
106:12 Then believed they his w'; they 1697

Ps 107: 11 rebelled against the w' of God, 561
109: 3 me about also with w' of hatred; 1697
119: 57 have said that I would keep thy w'. "
103 sweet are thy w' unto my taste! 565
130 entrance of thy w' giveth light; 1697
139 mine enemies have forgotten thy w'. "
138: 4 they hear the w' of thy mouth. 561
141: 6 they shall hear my w'; for they are "
Pr 1: 2 to perceive the w' of understanding; "
6 the w' of the wise, and their dark 1697
21 in the city she uttereth her w', 561
23 will make known my w' unto you. 1697
2: 1 My son, if thou wilt receive my w', 561
16 which flattereth with her w'; "
4: 4 Let thine heart retain my w': 1697
5 decline from the w' of my mouth. 561
20 My son, attend to my w'; incline 1697
5: 7 not from the w' of my mouth. 561
6: 2 snared with the w' of thy mouth, "
2 are taken with the w' of thy mouth. "
7: 1 My son, keep my w', and lay up my "
5 which flattereth with her w'. "
24 and attend to the w' of my mouth. "
8: 8 All the w' of my mouth are in "
10: 19 multitude of w' there wanteth not 1697
12: 6 w' of the wicked are to lie in wait "
15: 1 but grievous w' stir up anger. "
26 the w' of the pure are pleasant w'.*
16: 24 Pleasant w' are as an honeycomb, 561
17: 27 that hath knowledge spareth his w': "
18: 4 The w' of the man's mouth are as 1697
8 w' of a talebearer are as wounds, "
19: 7 he pursueth them with w', yet they 561
27 to err from the w' of knowledge. "
22: 12 the w' of the transgressor. 1697
17 hear the w' of the wise, and apply "
21 the certainty of the w' of truth; 561
21 mightest answer the w' of truth "
23: 8 vomit up, and lose thy sweet w'. 1697
9 will despise the wisdom of thy w'. 4405
12 thine ears to the w' of knowledge. 561
26: 22 w' of a talebearer are as wounds, 1697
29: 19 servant will not be corrected by w': "
20 thou a man that is hasty in his w'? "
30: 1 The w' of Agur the son of Jakeh, "
6 Add thou not unto his w', lest he "
31: 1 The w' of king Lemuel, the "
Ec 1: 1 The w' of the Preacher, the son of "
5: 2 earth: therefore let thy w' be few. "
3 voice is known by multitude of w'. "
7 and many w' there are also divers "
7: 21 heed unto all w' that are spoken; "
9: 16 despised, and his w' are not heard. "
17 w' of wise men are heard in quiet "
10: 12 The w' of a wise man's mouth are "
13 beginning of the w' of his mouth "
14 A fool also is full of w': a man "
12: 10 sought to find out acceptable w': "
10 was upright, even w' of truth. "
11 The w' of the wise are as goads, "
Isa 29: 11 as the w' of a book that is sealed, "
18 the deaf hear the w' of the book, "
31: 2 evil, and will not call back his w': "
32: 7 to destroy the poor with lying w', 561
36: 5 thou, (but they are but vain w') I 1697
12 and to thee to speak these w'? "
13 Hear ye the w' of the great king, "
22 and told him the w' of Rabshakeh. "
37: 4 God will hear the w' of Rabshakeh, "
4 will reprove the w' which the Lord "
6 of the w' that thou hast heard, "
17 and hear all the w' of Sennacherib, "
41: 26 there is none that heareth your w'. 561
51: 16 I have put my w' in thy mouth, 1697
58: 13 nor speaking thine own w': "
59: 13 from the heart w' of falsehood. "
21 w' which I have put in thy mouth, "
Jer 1: 1 w' of Jeremiah the son of Hilkiah, "
9 I have put my w' in thy mouth. "
3: 12 Go and proclaim these w' toward "
5: 14 I will make my w' in thy mouth fire, "
6: 19 have not hearkened unto my w', "
7: 4 Trust ye not in lying w', saying, "
8 Behold, ye trust in lying w', that "
27 shalt speak all these w' unto them; "
11: 2 Hear ye the w' of this covenant, "
3 obeyeth not the w' of this covenant, "
6 Proclaim all these w' in the cities "
6 Hear ye the w' of this covenant, "
8 them all the w' of this covenant, "
10 which refused to hear my w'; "
12: 6 though they speak fair w' unto thee. "
13: 10 which refuse to hear my w', which 1697
15: 16 Thy w' were found, and I did eat "
16: 10 shalt shew this people all these w', "
18: 2 I will cause thee to hear my w'. "
18 us not give heed to any of his w'. "
19: 2 there the w' that I shall tell thee, "
15 that they might not hear my w'. "
22: 5 But if ye will not hear these w', I "
23: 9 because of the w' of his holiness. "
16 not unto the w' of the prophets "
22 caused my people to hear my w', "
30 steal my w' every one from his "
36 perverted the w' of the living God, "
25: 8 Because ye have not heard my w', "
13 my w' which I have pronounced "
30 thou against them all these w', "
26: 2 w' that I command thee to speak "
5 hearken to the w' of my servants "
7 Jeremiah speaking these w' in the "
12 city all the w' that ye have heard. "
15 to speak all these w' in your ears. "
20 according to all the w' of Jeremiah: "
21 and all the princes, heard his w', "
27: 12 of Judah according to all these w', "

Jer 27: 14 not unto the w' of the prophets 1697
16 not to the w' of your prophets "
28: 6 perform thy w' which thou hast "
29: 1 w' of the letter that Jeremiah "
19 they have not hearkened to my w', "
23 have spoken lying w' in my name, "
30: 2 all the w' that I have spoken unto "
4 are the w' that the Lord spake "
34: 6 spake all these w' unto Zedekiah "
18 w' of the covenant which they had "
35: 13 instruction to hearken to my w'? "
14 w' of Jonadab the son of Rechab, "
36: 2 write...all the w' that I have spoken "
4 of Jeremiah all the w' of the Lord, "
6 the w' of the Lord in the ears of the "
8 in the book the w' of the Lord "
10 in the book the w' of Jeremiah "
11 of the book all the w' of the Lord, "
13 them all the w' that he had heard, "
16 when they had heard all the w', "
16 surely tell the king of all these w'. "
17 write all these w' at his mouth? "
18 pronounced all these w' unto me "
20 all the w' in the ears of the king. "
24 servants that heard all these w'. "
27 w' which Baruch wrote at the "
28 the former w' that were in the first "
32 w' of the book which Jehoiakim "
32 besides unto them many like w'. "
37: 2 hearken unto the w' of the Lord, "
38: 1 the w' that Jeremiah had spoken "
4 in speaking such w' unto them: "
24 Let no man know of these w', and "
27 w' that the king had commanded. "
39: 16 bring my w' upon this city for evil, "
42: 4 your God according to your w'; "
43: 1 the people all the w' of the Lord "
1 him to them, even all these w'. "
44: 28 shall know whose w' shall stand, * "
29 know that my w' shall surely stand "
45: 1 he had written these w' in a book "
51: 60 all these w' that are written against "
61 see, and shalt read all these w'; "
64 Thus far are the w' of Jeremiah. "
Eze 2: 6 them, neither be afraid of their w', "
6 be not afraid of their w', nor be "
7 thou shalt speak my w' unto them, "
3: 4 and speak with my w' unto them. "
6 w' thou canst not understand. "
10 my w' that I shall speak unto thee "
12: 28 shall none of my w' be prolonged "
33: 31 they hear thy w', but they will not "
32 for they hear thy w', but they do "
35: 13 have multiplied your w' against me: "
Da 2: 9 corrupt w' to speak before me, 4406
5: 10 by reason of the w' of the king and "
6: 14 the king, when he heard these w', "
7: 11 great w' which the horn spake: "
25 great w' against the most High, "
9: 12 And he hath confirmed his w', 1697
10: 6 his w' like the voice of a multitude. "
9 Yet heard I the voice of his w': "
9 when I heard the voice of his w', "
11 understand the w' that I speak "
12 before thy God, thy w' were heard, "
12 heard, and I am come for thy w'. * "
15 he had spoken such w' unto me, "
12: 4 O Daniel, shut up the w', and seal "
9 for the w' are closed up and sealed "
Ho 6: 5 slain them by the w' of my mouth: 561
10: 4 They have spoken w', swearing 1697
14: 2 Take with you w', and turn to the "
Am 1: 1 The w' of Amos, who was among "
7: 10 land is not able to bear all his w'. "
8: 11 but of hearing the w' of the Lord: "
Mic 2: 7 do not my w' do good to him that "
Hag 1: 12 and the w' of Haggai the prophet, "
Zec 1: 6 But my w' and my statutes, which "
13 with good w' and comfortable w'. "
7: 7 the w' which the Lord hath cried "
12 w' which the Lord of hosts hath "
8: 9 w' by the mouth of the prophets, "
Mal 2: 17 wearied the Lord with your w'. "
3: 13 Your w' have been stout against "
M't 10: 14 nor hear your w', when ye depart 3056
12: 37 by thy w' thou shalt be justified, "
37 by thy w' thou shalt be condemned. "
22: 22 When they had heard these w', *
24: 35 but my w' shall not pass away. 3056
26: 44 third time, saying the same w'. "
M'r 8: 38 be ashamed of me and of my w' "
10: 24 disciples were astonished at his w'. "
12: 13 Herodians, to catch him in his w'. * "
13: 31 but my w' shall not pass away. "
14: 39 prayed, and spake the same w'. "
Lu 1: 20 because thou believest not my w', "
3: 4 in the book of the w' of Esaias "
4: 22 wondered at the gracious w' which "
9: 26 be ashamed of me and of my w', * "
20: 20 they might take hold of his w', "
26 they could not take hold of his w' 4487
21: 33 but my w' shall not pass away. 3056
23: 9 questioned with him in many w'; "
24: 8 And they remembered his w', 4487
11 their w' seemed to them as idle "
44 These are the w' which I spake 3056
Joh 3: 34 hath sent speaketh the w' of God: 4487
5: 47 how shall ye believe my w'? "
6: 63 the w' that I speak unto you, they "
68 go? thou hast the w' of eternal life. "
7: 9 he had said these w' unto them, *
8: 20 w' spake Jesus in the treasury, 4487
30 As he spake these w', many believed*
47 that is of God heareth God's w': 4487
9: 22 These w' spake his parents, because*
40 which were with him heard these w'.*

Joh 10: 21 the w' of him that hath a devil. *4487
12: 47 And if any man hear my w', and * "
48 and receiveth not my w', hath one* "
14: 10 w' that I speak unto you I speak "
23 man love me, he will keep my w':*3056
15: 7 my w' abide in you, ye shall ask 4487
17: 8 them the w' which thou gavest me; "
18: 1 When Jesus had spoken these w', he
Ac 2: 14 unto you, and hearken to my w': 4487
22 Ye men of Israel, hear these w'; 3056
40 with many other w' did he testify "
5: 5 Ananias hearing these w' fell down, "
20 to the people all the w' of this life. 4487
6: 11 blasphemous w' against Moses, "
13 blasphemous w' against this holy "
7: 22 was mighty in w' and in deeds. 3056
10: 22 his house, and to hear w' of thee. 4487
44 While Peter yet spake these w', "
11: 14 Who shall tell thee w', whereby "
13: 42 that these w' might be preached "
15: 15 this agree the w' of the prophets; 3056
24 from us have troubled you with w', "
32 exhorted...brethren with many w'. "
16: 38 told these w' unto the magistrates: 4487
18: 15 it be a question of w' and names, 3056
20: 35 remember the w' of the Lord Jesus, "
38 of all for the w' which he spake, * "
24: 4 hear us of thy clemency a few w'.
26: 25 but speak forth the w' of truth 4487
28: 29 And when he had said these w', *
Ro 10: 18 w' unto the ends of the world. 4487
16: 18 good w' and fair speeches deceive*5542
1Co 1: 17 not with wisdom of w', lest the 3056
2: 4 with enticing w' of man's wisdom, "
13 w' which man's wisdom teacheth, "
14: 9 tongue w' easy to be understood, * "
19 five w' with my understanding, "
19 thousand w' in an unknown tongue. "
2Co 12: 4 and heard unspeakable w', which 4487
Eph 3: 3 mystery; (as I wrote afore in few w', "
5: 6 no man deceive you with vain w': 3056
Col 2: 4 beguile you with enticing w'. *4086
1Th 2: 5 any time used we flattering w', 3056
4: 18 comfort one another with these w'. "
1Ti 4: 6 nourished up in the w' of faith and "
6: 3 and consent not to wholesome w', "
3 the w' of our Lord Jesus Christ, "
4 about questions and strifes of w', 3055
2Ti 1: 13 Hold fast the form of sound w', 3056
2: 14 strive not about w' to no profit, 3054
4: 15 he hath greatly withstood our w'. 3056
Heb 12: 19 a trumpet, and the voice of w'; 4487
13: 22 a letter unto you in a few w'. "
2Pe 2: 3 with feigned w' make merchandise 3056
18 speak great swelling w' of vanity, "
3: 2 of the w' which were spoken 4487
3Jo 10 against us with malicious w': 3056
Jude 16 mouth speaketh great swelling w', "
17 the w' which were spoken before 4487
Re 1: 3 that hear the w' of this prophecy, 3056
17: 17 the w' of God shall be fulfilled. 4487
21: 5 for these w' are true and faithful. 3056
22: 18 w' of the prophecy of this book, "
19 w' of the book of this prophecy, "

wore See WARE.

work See also HANDYWORK; NETWORK; WORKETH; WORKFELLOW; WORKING; WORKMAN; WORK'S; WORKS; WROUGHT.
Ge 2: 2 the seventh day God ended his w' 4399
2 on the seventh day from all his w' "
3 in it he had rested from all his w' "
5: 29 comfort us concerning our w' 4639
Ex 5: 9 more w' be laid upon the men, 5656
11 of your w' shall be diminished. "
18 Go therefore now, and w'; for 5647
12: 16 no manner of w' shall be done in 4399
14: 31 saw that great w' which the Lord 3027
18: 20 and the w' that they must do. 4640
20: 9 thou labour, and do all thy w': 4399
10 in it thou shalt not do any w', thou "
23: 12 Six days thou shalt do thy w', and 4639
24: 10 a paved w' of a sapphire stone, "
25: 18 beaten w' shalt thou make them, 4749
31 of beaten w' shall the candlestick "
36 shall be one beaten w' of pure gold. "
26: 1 cherubims of cunning w' shalt 4639
31 fine twined linen of cunning w': "
28: 6 fine twined linen, with cunning w'. "
8 same, according to the w' thereof; "
11 the w' of an engraver in stone, like "
14 wreathen w' shalt thou make them, "
15 of judgment with cunning w'; "
15 after the w' of the ephod thou shalt "
22 ends of wreathen w' of pure gold. "
32 a binding of woven w' round about "
31: 4 to w' in gold, and in silver, and in 6213
5 w' in all manner of workmanship. "
14 whosoever doeth any w' therein, 4399
15 Six days may w' be done; but in "
15 doeth any w' in the sabbath day, "
32: 16 the tables were the w' of God, and 4639
34: 10 art shall see the w' of the Lord: "
21 Six days thou shalt w', but on 5627
35: 2 Six days shall w' be done, but on 4399
2 whosoever doeth w' therein shall be "
21 offering to the w' of the tabernacle "
24 wood for any w' of the service, "
29 to bring for all manner of w', "
32 to w' in gold, and in silver, and in 6213
33 make any manner of cunning w'. 4399
35 wisdom of heart, to w' all manner 6213
35 manner of w', of the engraver, *4399
35 even of them that do any w', * "
35 of those that devise cunning w'. * "
36: 1 understanding to know how to w' 6213

Ex 36: 1 all manner of w' for the service 4399
2 up to come unto the w' to do it: "
3 brought for the w' of the service "
4 wrought all the w' of the sanctuary, "
4 came every man from his w' which "
5 enough for the service of the w', "
6 man nor woman make any more w' "
7 had was sufficient for all the w' "
8 wrought the w' of the tabernacle "
8 cherubims of cunning w' made he 4639
35 made he it of cunning w'. "
37: 17 beaten w' made he the candlestick; 4749
22 it was one beaten w' of pure gold. "
29 to the w' of the apothecary. *4639
38: 24 gold that was occupied for the w' 4399
24 all the w' of the holy place, even "
39: 3 w' it in the blue, and in the purple, 6213
3 in the fine linen, with cunning w'. 4639
5 same, according to the w' thereof; "
8 the breastplate of cunning w', "
8 like the w' of the ephod; of gold, "
15 ends, of wreathen w' of pure gold. "
22 the robe of the ephod of woven w', "
27 of fine linen of woven w' for Aaron, "
32 was all the w' of the tabernacle 5656
42 children of Israel made all the w'. "
43 Moses did look upon all the w', 4399
40: 33 gate. So Moses finished the w'. "
Le 11: 32 wherein any w' is done, it must be "
13: 51 or in any w' that is made of skin;* "
16: 29 and do no w' at all, whether it be "
23: 3 Six days shall w' be done: but the "
3 ye shall do no w' therein: it is the "
7, 8 ye shall do no servile w' therein. "
21 ye shall do no servile w' therein: "
25 Ye shall do no servile w' therein: "
28 ye shall do no w' in that same day: "
30 that doeth any w' in that same day, "
31 Ye shall do no manner of w': it "
35, 36 ye shall do no servile w' therein. "
Nu 4: 3 to do the w' in the tabernacle of "
23 to do the w' in the tabernacle of 5656
30 to do the w' of the tabernacle of "
35, 39, 43 for the w' in the tabernacle of "
8: 4 this w' of the candlestick was of 4639
4 flowers thereof, was beaten w': "
28: 18 shall do no manner of servile w' 4399
25 ye shall do no servile w'. "
26 ye shall do no servile w': "
29: 1 ye shall do no servile w': "
7 ye shall not do any w' therein: "
12 ye shall do no servile w', and ye "
35 ye shall do no servile w' therein: "
31: 20 of skins, and all w' of goats' hair, 4639
De 4: 28 serve gods, the w' of men's hands, "
5: 13 shalt labour, and do all thy w': 4399
14 in it thou shalt not do any w', thou, "
14: 29 thee in all the w' of thine hand 4639
15: 19 shalt do no w' with the firstling 5647
16: 8 God: thou shalt do no w' therein. 4399
24: 19 thee in all the w' of thine hands. 4639
27: 15 w' of the hands of the craftsman, "
28: 12 to bless all the w' of thine hand: "
30: 9 plenteous in every w' of thine hand, "
31: 29 through the w' of your hands. "
32: 4 He is the Rock, his w' is perfect: 6467
33: 11 and accept the w' of his hands: "
Jos 9: 4 They did w' wilily, and went and 6213
J'g 19: 16 came an old man from his w' out 4639
Ru 2: 12 The Lord recompense thy w', and 6467
1Sa 8: 16 asses, and put them to his w'. 4399
14: 6 be that the Lord will w' for us: 6213
1Ki 5: 16 officers which were over the w', 4399
16 the people that wrought in the w'. "
6: 35 with gold fitted upon the carved w'. "
7: 8 porch, which was of the like w'. 4649
14 cunning to w' all works in brass. 6213
14 Solomon, and wrought all his w'. 4399
17 And nets of checker w', 4639
17 and wreaths of chain w', "
19 pillars were of lily w' in the porch, "
22 the top of the pillars was lily w': "
22 was the w' of the pillars finished. 4399
28 the w' of the bases was on this 4639
29 certain additions made of thin w'. "
31 was round after the w' of the base, "
33 And the w' of the wheels was like "
33 was like the w' of a chariot wheel: "
40 made an end of doing all the w' 4399
51 ended all the w' that king Solomon "
9: 23 that were over Solomon's w', "
23 the people that wrought in the w'. "
16: 7 to anger with the w' of his hands, 4639
21: 20 w' evil in the sight of the Lord. 6213
25 did sell himself to w' wickedness "
2Ki 12: 11 the hands of them that did the w', 4399
19: 18 but the w' of men's hands, wood 4639
22: 5 the hand of the doers of the w', *4399
5 them give it to the doers of the w',* "
9 the hand of them that do the w', * "
25: 17 and the wreathen w', and *7639
17 second pillar with wreathen w'. * "
1Ch 4: 23 dwelt with the king for his w', 4399
6: 49 all the w' of the place most holy, "
9: 13 able men for the w' of the service "
19 were over the w' of the service, "
33 employed in that w' day and night. "
16: 37 as every day's w' required: 1697
22: 15 men for every manner of w'. 4399
23: 4 the w' of the house of the Lord; "
24 the w' for the service of the house "
28 the w' of the service of the house 4639
27: 26 did the w' of the field for tillage 4399
28: 13 the w' of the service of the house "
20 the w' for the service of the house "
29: 1 and tender, and the w' is great: "

1Ch 29: 5 of w' to be made by the hands 4399
6 with the rulers of the king's w', "
2Ch 2: 7 a man cunning to w' in gold, 6213
14 man of Tyre, skilful to w' in gold, "
18 overseers to set the people a w'. 5647
3: 10 made two cherubims of image w', 4639
4: 5 it like the w' of the brim of a cup,* "
11 Huram finished the w' that he 4399
5: 1 all the w' that Solomon made for "
8: 9 make no servants for his w': "
16 all the w' of Solomon was prepared "
15: 7 for your w' shall be rewarded. 6468
16: 5 of Ramah, and let his w' cease. 4399
24: 12 such as did the w' of the service "
13 and the w' was perfected by them, "
29: 34 till the w' was ended, and until the "
31: 21 in every w' that he began in the 4639
32: 19 were the w' of the hands of man. "
34: 12 the men did the w' faithfully: 4399
13 of all that wrought the w' in any "
Ezr 2: 69 ability unto the treasure of the w' "
3: 8 to set forward the w' of the house "
4: 24 ceased the w' of the house of God 5673
5: 8 and this w' goeth fast on, and "
6: 7 Let the w' of this house of God "
22 in the w' of the house of God, 4399
10: 13 is this a w' of one day or two: "
Ne 2: 16 nor to the rest that did the w'. "
18 their hands for this good w'. "
3: 5 necks to the w' of their Lord. 5656
4: 6 for the people had a mind to w'. 6213
11 them, and cause the w' to cease. 4399
15 to the wall, every one unto his w'. "
16 of my servants wrought in the w', "
17 one of his hands wrought in the w', "
19 The w' is great and large, and we "
21 So we laboured in the w': and half "
5: 16 continued in the w' of this wall, "
16 were gathered thither unto the w'. "
6: 3 I am doing a great w', so that I "
3 why should the w' cease, whilst I "
9 shall be weakened from the w', "
16 this w' was wrought of our God. "
7: 70 of the fathers gave unto the w'. "
71 gave to the treasure of the w' "
10: 33 all the w' of the house of our God. "
11: 12 that did the w' of the house "
13: 10 and the singers, that did the w', "
Job 1: 10 hast blessed the w' of his hands, 4639
7: 2 looketh for the reward of his w': *6467
10: 3 despise the w' of thine hands, 3018
14: 15 a desire to the w' of thine hands, 4639
23: 9 the left hand, where he doth w', 6213
24: 5 desert, go they forth to their w'; 6467
34: 11 the w' of a man shall he render "
19 they all are the w' of his hands. 4639
36: 9 Then he sheweth them their w', 6467
24 that thou magnify his w', "
37: 7 that all men may know his w'. *4639
Ps 8: 3 thy heavens, the w' of thy fingers, "
9: 16 snared in the w' of his own hands. 6467
28: 4 them after the w' of their hands, *4639
44: 1 what w' thou didst in their days, 6467
58: 2 Yea, in heart ye w' wickedness; 6466
62: 12 to every man according to his w'. 4639
64: 9 and shall declare the w' of God; 6467
74: 6 they break down the carved w' 6603
77: 12 I will meditate also of all thy w', 6467
90: 16 thy w' appear unto thy servants, "
17 establish thou the w' of our hands 4639
17 w' of our hands establish thou it. "
92: 4 made me glad through thy w': 6467
95: 9 me, proved me, and saw my w'. "
101: 3 I hate the w' of them that turn 6213
102: 25 heavens are the w' of thy hands. 4639
104: 23 Man goeth forth unto his w' and 6467
111: 3 His w' is honourable and glorious: "
115: 4 and gold, the w' of men's hands. 4639
119: 126 It is time for thee, Lord, to w': 6213
135: 15 and gold, the w' of men's hands. 4639
141: 4 works with men that w' iniquity: 5950
143: 5 I muse on the w' of thy hands. 4639
Pr 11: 18 wicked worketh a deceitful w': *6468
16: 11 the weights of the bag are his w'. 4639
18: 9 He also that is slothful in his w' 4399
20: 11 doings, whether his w' be pure, 6467
21: 8 as for the pure, his w' is right. "
24: 27 Prepare thy w' without, and make 4399
29 to the man according to his w'. 6467
Ec 2: 17 w' that is wrought under the sun 4639
3: 11 find out the w' that God maketh "
17 every purpose and for every w'. "
4: 3 not seen the evil w' that is done "
4 all travail, and every right w', "
5: 6 and destroy the w' of thine hands? "
7: 13 Consider the w' of God: for who "
8: 9 applied my heart unto every w' "
11 sentence against an evil w' is not "
14 according to the w' of the wicked; "
14 to the w' of the righteous: "
17 Then I beheld all the w' of God, "
17 cannot find out the w' that is done "
9: 10 for there is no w', nor device, nor "
12: 14 bring every w' into judgment, "
Ca 7: 1 w' of the hands of a cunning "
Isa 2: 8 worship the w' of their own hands, "
5: 12 regard not the w' of the Lord, 6467
19 make speed, and hasten his w', 4639
10: 12 Lord hath performed his whole w' "
17: 8 to the altars, the w' of his hands, "
19: 9 Moreover they that w' in fine flax, 5647
14 Egypt to err in every w' thereof, 4639
15 shall there be any w' for Egypt, "
25 and Assyria the w' of my hands, "
28: 21 he may do his w', his strange w'; "
29: 14 marvellous w' among this people, 6381

Isa 29: 14 a marvellous w' and a wonder: 6381
16 the w' say of him that made it, *4639
23 his children, the w' of mine hands, "
31: 2 the help of them that w' iniquity. 6213
32: 6 and his heart will w' iniquity, to "
17 the w' of righteousness shall be 4639
37: 19 the w' of men's hands, wood and "
40: 10 with him, and his w' before him. *6468
41: 24 nothing, and your w' of nought: 6467
43: 13 I will w', and who shall let it? 6466
45: 9 What makest thou? or thy w', 6467
11 concerning the w' of my hands "
49: 4 Lord, and my w' with my God. *6468
54: 16 forth an instrument for his w'; 4639
60: 21 my planting, the w' of my hands, "
61: 8 and I will direct their w' in truth,*6468
62: 11 with him, and his w' before him.* "
64: 8 and we all are the w' of thine hand. 4639
65: 7 will I measure their former w' 6468
22 long enjoy the w' of their hands. 4639
Jer 10: 3 w' of the hands of the workman, "
9 the w' of the workman, and of "
9 are all the w' of cunning men. "
15 are vanity, and the w' of errors: "
17: 22 neither do ye any w', but hallow 4399
24 sabbath day, to do no w' therein; "
18: 3 he wrought a w' on the wheels. "
22: 13 and giveth him not for his w'; *6467
31: 16 for thy w' shall be rewarded, saith 6468
32: 19 in counsel, and mighty in w': 5950
30 anger with the w' of their hands, 4639
48: 10 the w' of the Lord deceitfully, 4399
50: 25 this is the w' of the Lord God of "
29 her according to her w'; 6467
51: 10 declare in Zion the w' of the Lord 4639
18 They are vanity, the w' of errors: "
La 3: 64 according to the w' of their hands. "
4: 2 the w' of the hands of the potter! "
Eze 1: 16 their w' was like unto the colour "
16 and their w' was as it were a wheel "
15: 3 be taken thereof to do any w'? 4399
4 is burned. It is meet for any w'? "
5 was whole, it was meet for no w': "
5 less shall it be meet for any w', "
16: 10 thee also with broidered w', 7553
13 linen, and silk, and broidered w'; "
30 the w' of an imperious whorish 4639
27: 7 Fine linen with broidered w' 7553
16 and broidered w', and fine linen, "
24 in blue clothes, and broidered w', "
33: 26 ye w' abomination, and ye defile 6213
Da 11: 23 with him he shall w' deceitfully: "
Ho 6: 8 a city of them that w' iniquity, 6466
13: 2 all of it the w' of the craftsman: 4639
14: 3 any more to the w' of our hands, "
Mic 2: 1 and w' evil upon their beds! 6466
5: 13 worship the w' of thine hands. 4639
Hab 1: 5 marvellously: for I will w' 6466
5 a w' in your days, which ye will 6467
2: 18 maker of his w' trusteth therein, 3336
3: 2 revive thy w' in the midst of the 6467
Zep 2: 14 for he shall uncover the cedar w'. 731
Hag 1: 14 did w' in the house of the Lord 4399
2: 4 the land, saith the Lord, and w': 6213
14 and so is every w' of their hands; 4639
Mal 3: 15 that w' wickedness are set up; 6213
M't 7: 23 from me, ye that w' iniquity. 2038
21: 28 Son, go w' to day in my vineyard. "
26: 10 hath wrought a good w' upon me. 2041
M'r 6: 5 he could there do no mighty w', 1411
13: 34 servants, and to every man his w', 2041
14: 6 she hath wrought a good w' on me. "
Lu 13: 14 days in which men ought to w': 2038
Joh 4: 34 that sent me, and to finish his w'. 2041
5: 17 worketh hitherto, and I w'. 2038
6: 28 that we might w' the works of God?" "
29 This is the w' of God, that ye 2041
30 believe thee? what dost thou w'? *2038
7: 21 I have done one w', and ye all 2041
9: 4 I must w' the works of him that 2038
4 night cometh, when no man can w'. "
10: 33 For a good w' we stone thee not; 2041
17: 4 finished the w' which thou gavest "
Ac 5: 38 or this w' be of men, it will come "
13: 2 for the w' whereunto I have called "
41 for I w' [2038] a w' in your days, 2040
41 a w' which ye shall in no wise 2041
14: 26 for the w' which they fulfilled. "
15: 38 and went not with them to the w'. "
27: 16 we had much w' to come by *3433, 2480
Ro 2: 15 shew the w' of the law written in 2041
7: 5 did w' in our members to bring *1754
8: 28 all things w' together for good to 4903
9: 28 For he will finish the w', and cut *3056
28 short w' will the Lord make upon* "
11: 6 otherwise w' is no more w'. *2041
14: 20 meat destroy not the w' of God. "
1Co 3: 13 man's w' shall be made manifest: "
13 fire shall try every man's w' "
14 If any man's w' abide which he "
15 If any man's w' shall be burned, he "
9: 1 are not ye my w' in the Lord? "
15: 58 abounding in the w' of the Lord, "
16: 10 for he worketh the w' of the Lord, "
2Co 9: 8 may abound to every good w': "
Ga 6: 4 But let every man prove his own w', "
Eph 4: 12 for the w' of the ministry, for the "
19 to w' all uncleanness with 2039
Ph'p 1: 6 which hath begun a good w' in you 2041
2: 12 w' out your own salvation with 2716
30 for the w' of Christ he was nigh 2041
Col 1: 10 being fruitful in every good w', and "
1Th 1: 3 without ceasing your w' of faith, "
4: 11 and to w' with your own hands, 2038
2Th 1: 11 and the w' of faith with power: 2041
2: 7 of iniquity doth already w': 1754

2Th 2:17 you in every good word and w'. 2041
3:10 that if any would not w', neither 2038
12 that with quietness they w', and "
1Ti 3: 1 of a bishop, he desireth a good w'. 2041
5:10 diligently followed every good w'. "
2Ti 2:21 and prepared unto every good w'. "
4: 5 do the w' of an evangelist, make "
18 shall deliver me from every evil w', "
Tit 1:16 and unto every good w' reprobate. "
3: 1 to be ready to every good w', "
Heb 6:10 forget your w' and labour of love, "
13:21 Make you perfect in every good w' "
Jas 1: 4 let patience have her perfect w', "
25 but a doer of the w', this man shall* "
3:16 is confusion and every evil w'. *4229
1Pe 1:17 according to every man's w', 2041
Re 22:12 man according as his w' shall be. "

worked See WROUGHT.

worker See also WORKERS.
1Ki 7:14 was a man of Tyre, a w' in brass: 2790

workers See also FELLOWWORKERS.
2Ki 23:24 Moreover the w' with familiar spirits,*
1Ch 22:15 and w' of stone and timber, and 2796
Job 31: 3 punishment to the w' of iniquity? 6466
34: 8 in company with the w' of iniquity, "
22 where the w' of iniquity may hide "
Ps 5: 5 thou hatest all w' of iniquity. "
6: 8 from me, all ye w' of iniquity; "
14: 4 the w' of iniquity no knowledge? "
28: 3 with the w' of iniquity, which speak "
36:12 There are the w' of iniquity fallen: "
37: 1 against the w' of iniquity. *6213
53: 4 the w' of iniquity no knowledge? 6466
59: 2 Deliver me from the w' of iniquity, "
64: 2 insurrection of the w' of iniquity: "
92: 7 all the w' of iniquity do flourish; "
9 w' of iniquity shall be scattered. "
94: 4 w' of iniquity boast themselves? "
16 for me against the w' of iniquity? "
125: 5 them forth with the w' of iniquity: "
141: 9 and the gins of the w' of iniquity. "
Pr 10:29 shall be to the w' of iniquity. "
21:15 shall be to the w' of iniquity. "
Lu 13:27 from me, all ye w' of iniquity. 2040
1Co 12:29 teachers? are all w' of miracles? 1411
2Co 6: 1 We then, as w' together with him,*4903
11:13 are false apostles, deceitful w', 2040
Ph'p 3: 2 Beware of dogs, beware of evil w', "

worketh
Job 33:29 these things w' God oftentimes *6466
Ps 15: 2 and w' righteousness, and speaketh "
101: 7 He that w' deceit shall not dwell 6213
Pr 11:18 The wicked w' a deceitful work: * "
26:28 and a flattering mouth w' ruin. "
31:13 and w' willingly with her hands. "
Ec 3: 9 What profit hath he that w' in that "
Isa 44:12 with the tongs both w' in the coals,6466
12 w' it with the strength of his arms: "
64: 5 rejoiceth and w' righteousness, 6213
Da 6:27 w' signs and wonders in heaven 5648
Joh 5:17 My Father w' hitherto, and I work.2038
Ac 10:35 w' righteousness, is accepted with "
Ro 2:10 peace, to every man that w' good, "
4: 4 to him that w' is the reward not "
5 But to him that w' not, but "
15 Because the law w' wrath: for 2716
5: 3 knowing...tribulation w' patience; "
13:10 Love w' no ill to his neighbour: 2038
1Co 12: 6 the same God which w' all in all. 1754
11 w' that one and the selfsame Spirit, "
16:10 he w' the work of the Lord, as I 2038
2Co 4:12 So then death w' in us, but life in 1754
17 w' for us a far more exceeding 2716
7:10 godly sorrow w' repentance unto "
10 the sorrow of the world w' death. "
Ga 3: 5 Spirit, and w' miracles among you, 1754
5: 6 but faith which w' by love. "
Eph 1:11 purpose of him who w' all things "
2: 2 spirit that now w' in the children "
3:20 to the power that w' in us, "
Ph'p 2:13 is God which w' in you both to will "
Col 1:29 working, which w' in me mightily. "
1Th 2:13 which effectually w' also in you "
Jas 1: 3 trying of your faith w' patience. 2716
20 w' not the righteousness of God. * "
Re 21:27 whatsoever w' abomination, or *4160

workfellow See also FELLOWWORKERS.
Ro 16:21 Timotheus my w', and Lucius, *4904

working
Ps 52: 2 like a sharp rasor, w' deceitfully. 6213
74:12 w' salvation in the midst of the 6466
Isa 28:29 in counsel, and excellent in w'. *8454
Eze 46: 1 east shall be shut the six w' days;4639
M'r 16:20 the Lord w' with them, and 4903
Ro 1:27 men w' that which is unseemly, 2716
7:13 w' death in me by that which is "
1Co 4:12 labour, w' with our own hands: 2038
9: 6 have not we power to forbear w'? "
12:10 To another the w' of miracles; *1755
Eph 1:19 to the w' of his mighty power, 1753
3: 7 me by the effectual w' of his power. "
4:16 to the effectual w' in the measure "
28 w' with his hands the thing which 2038
Ph'p 3:21 according to the w' whereby he is 1753
Col 1:29 striving according to his w', which "
2Th 2: 9 coming is after the w' of Satan "
3:11 w' not at all, but are busybodies. *2038
Heb 13:21 his will, w' in you that which is 4160
Re 16:14 the spirits of devils, w' miracles, "

workman See also WORKMANSHIP; WORKMEN.
Ex 35:35 engraver, and of the cunning w', 2803
38:23 an engraver, and a cunning w', "
Ca 7: 1 work of the hands of a cunning w'. 542
Isa 40:19 The w' melteth a graven image, 2796
20 seeketh unto him a cunning w' to "
Jer 10: 3 the work of the hands of the w', "
9 from Uphaz, the work of the w', * "
Ho 8: 6 the w' made it; therefore it is not "
M't 10:10 for the w' is worthy of his meat. *2040
2Ti 2:15 a w' that needeth not to be "

workmanship
Ex 31: 3 and in all manner of w', 4399
5 to work in all manner of w'. "
35:31 and in all manner of w'; "
2Ki 16:10 according to all the w' thereof. 4639
1Ch 28:21 be with thee for all manner of w' *4399
Eze 28:13 w' of thy tabrets and of thy pipes "
Eph 2:10 For we are his w', created in 4161

workmen See also WORKMEN'S.
2Ki 12:14 But they gave that to the w', *6213,4399
15 money to be bestowed on w': * "
1Ch 22:15 are w' with thee in abundance, " "
25: 1 number of the w' according * 582, "
2Ch 24:13 So the w' wrought, and the 6213, "
34:10 w' that had the oversight " "
10 w' that wrought in the house " "
17 and to the hand of the w', " "
Ezr 3: 9 the w' in the house of God: " "
Isa 44:11 and the w', they are of men: 2796
Ac 19:25 with the w' of like occupation, 2040

workmen's
J'g 5:26 her right hand to the w' hammer; 6001

work's
1Th 5:13 highly in love for their w' sake. 2041

works See also NETWORKS.
Ex 5: 4 let the people from their w'? 4639
13 Fulfil your w', your daily tasks, "
23:24 serve them, nor do after their w': "
31: 4 To devise cunning w', to work in
35:32 And to devise curious w', to work *
Nu 16:28 hath sent me to do all these w'; 4639
De 2: 7 thee in all the w' of thy hand: * "
3:24 that can do according to thy w', * "
15:10 God shall bless thee in all thy w', * "
16:15 and in all the w' of thine hands, * "
Jos 24:31 had known all the w' of the Lord, * "
J'g 2: 7 seen all the great w' of the Lord, * "
10 w' which he had done for Israel. * "
1Sa 8: 8 to all the w' which they have done "
19: 4 his w' have been to thee-ward "
1Ki 7:14 cunning to work all w' in brass. 4399
13:11 w' that the man of God had done 4639
2Ki 22:17 with all the w' of their hands; * "
1Ch 16: 9 talk ye of all his wondrous w'.
12 Remember his marvellous w' that he
24 his marvellous w' among all nations
28:19 even all the w' of this pattern. 4399
2Ch 20:37 the Lord hath broken thy w'. 4639
32:30 Hezekiah prospered in all his w'. "
34:25 with all the w' of their hands; "
Ne 6:14 according to these their w', "
9:35 turned they from their wicked w'. 4611
Job 34:25 Therefore he knoweth their w', 4566
37:14 consider the wondrous w' of God.
16 wondrous w' of him which is perfect
Ps 8: 6 dominion over the w' of thy hands 4639
9: 1 shew forth all thy marvellous w'.
14: 1 they have done abominable w', 5949
17: 4 Concerning the w' of men, by the 6468
26: 7 and tell of all thy wondrous w'.
28: 5 regard not the w' of the Lord, 6468
33: 4 and all his w' are done in truth. *4640
15 alike; he considereth all their w'. "
40: 5 wonderful w' which thou hast done,
46: 8 Come, behold the w' of the Lord, 4659
66: 3 How terrible art thou in thy w'! 4639
5 Come and see the w' of God: he is 4659
71:17 have I declared thy wondrous w'.
73:28 God, that I may declare all thy w'. 4399
75: 1 is near thy wondrous w' declare.
77:11 remember the w' of the Lord: *4611
78: 4 wonderful w' that he hath done.
7 God, and not forget the w' of God, 4611
11 forgat his w', and his wonders *5949
32 believed not for his wondrous w'.
86: 8 neither are there any w' like unto
8 are there any...like unto thy w'. 4639
92: 4 triumph in the w' of thy hands. "
5 O Lord, how great are thy w'! "
103:22 his w' in all places of his dominion: "
104:13 is satisfied with the fruit of thy w'. "
24 O Lord, how manifold are thy w'! "
31 the Lord shall rejoice in his w'. "
105: 2 talk ye of all his wondrous w'.
5 Remember his marvellous w' that
106:13 They soon forgat his w'; they 4639
22 Wondrous w' in the land of Ham,
35 the heathen, and learned their w'. 4639
39 they defiled with their own w', "
107: 8, 15, 21 for his wonderful w' to the
22 and declare his w' with rejoicing, 4639
24 These see the w' of the Lord, and "
31 his wonderful w' to the children
111: 2 The w' of the Lord are great, 4639
4 wonderful w' to be remembered:
6 his people the power of his w', 4639
7 The w' of his hands are verity "
118:17 and declare the w' of the Lord. "
119:27 so shall I talk of thy wondrous w'.
138: 8 not the w' of thine own hands. 4639
139:14 marvellous are thy w'; and that "
141: 4 practise wicked w' with men that*5949
143: 5 I meditate on all thy w'; I muse *6467
145: 4 shall praise thy w' to another, 4639
5 and of thy wondrous w'. 1697
9 tender mercies are over all his w'. 4639
10 All thy w' shall praise thee, O "
Ps 145:17 all his ways, and holy in all his w'.4639
Pr 7:16 with carved w', with fine linen *
8:22 of his way, before his w' of old. 4659
16: 3 Commit thy w' unto the Lord, 4639
24:12 every man according to his w'? *6467
31:31 her own w' praise her in the gates.4639
Ec 1:14 have seen all the w' that are done "
2: 4 I made me great w'; I builded me "
11 w' that my hands had wrought, "
3:22 man should rejoice in his own w'; "
9: 1 and their w', are in the hand of 5652
7 for God now accepteth thy w'. 4639
11: 5 thou knowest not the w' of God * "
Isa 26:12 hast wrought all our w' in us. "
29:15 their w' are in the dark, and they "
41:29 all vanity; their w' are nothing: "
57:12 thy righteousness, and thy w'; "
59: 6 cover themselves with their w': "
6 their w' are w' of iniquity, and the "
66:18 know their w' and their thoughts: "
Jer 1:16 the w' of their own hands. "
7:13 because ye have done all these w', "
21: 2 according to all his wondrous w', "
25: 6 anger with the w' of your hands; *4639
7 to anger with the w' of your hands "
14 to the w' of their own hands. * "
44: 8 wrath with the w' of your hands, "
48: 7 thou hast trusted in thy w' and in "
Eze 6: 6 and your w' may be abolished. "
Da 4:37 heaven, all whose w' are truth, 4567
9:14 our God is righteous in all his w' 4639
Am 8: 7 I will never forget any of their w'. "
Jon 3:10 And God saw their w', that they "
Mic 6:16 and all the w' of the house of Ahab, "
M't 5:16 that they may see your good w', 2041
7:22 name done many wonderful w'?
11: 2 in the prison the w' of Christ, 2041
20 most of his mighty w' were done,
21 if the mighty w', which were done
23 if the mighty w', which have been
13:54 this wisdom, and these mighty w'?
58 he did not many mighty w' there
14: 2 therefore mighty w' do shew forth*
16:27 every man according to his w'. *4234
23: 3 but do not ye after their w': 2041
5 w' they do for to be seen of men: "
M'r 6: 2 even such mighty w' are wrought
14 mighty w' do shew forth...in him.
Lu 10:13 mighty w. had been done in Tyre
19:37 the mighty w' that they had seen;
Joh 5:20 shew him greater w' than these, 2041
36 w' which the Father hath given me "
36 same w' that I do, bear witness "
6:28 that we might work the w' of God? "
7: 3 may see the w' that thou doest. "
7 of it, that the w' thereof are evil. "
8:39 ye would do the w' of Abraham. "
9: 3 w' of God should be made manifest "
4 work the w' of him that sent me, "
10:25 w' that I do in my Father's name, "
32 Many good w' have I shewed you "
32 which of those w' do ye stone me? "
37 If I do not the w' of my Father, "
38 ye believe not me, believe the w': "
14:10 dwelleth in me, he doeth the w'. "
12 the w' that I do shall he do also; "
12 greater w' than these shall he do; "
15:24 the w' which none other man did, "
Ac 2:11 tongues the wonderful w' of God.
7:41 in the w' of their own hands. 2041
9:36 this woman was full of good w' and "
15:18 Known unto God are all his w' * "
26:20 and do w' meet for repentance. "
Ro 3:27 By what law? of w'? Nay: but by "
4: 2 if Abraham were justified by w', "
6 imputeth righteousness without w', "
9:11 not of w', but of him that calleth;) "
32 but as it were by the w' of the law. "
11: 6 by grace, then is it no more of w': "
6 But if it be of w', then is it no more* "
13: 3 rulers are not a terror to good w', * "
12 cast off the w' of darkness, and "
2Co 11:15 end shall be according to their w'. "
Ga 2:16 not justified by the w' of the law, "
16 and not by the w' of the law: "
16 by the w' of the law shall no flesh "
3: 2 Received ye the Spirit by the w' of "
5 doeth he it by the w' of the law, "
10 many as are of the w' of the law "
5:19 the w' of the flesh are manifest, "
Eph 2: 9 Not of w', lest any man should "
10 in Christ Jesus unto good w', "
5:11 with the unfruitful w' of darkness, "
Col 1:21 enemies in your mind by wicked w',"
1Ti 2:10 godliness) with good w'. "
5:10 Well reported of for good w'; if she "
25 the good w' of some are manifest "
6:18 that they be rich in good w', ready "
2Ti 1: 9 calling, not according to our w', "
3:17 furnished unto all good w'. "
4:14 reward him according to his w': "
Tit 1:16 but in w' they deny him, being "
2: 7 thyself a pattern of good w': "
14 peculiar people, zealous of good w'. "
3: 5 Not by w' of righteousness which "
8 be careful to maintain good w'. "
14 to maintain good w' for necessary "
Heb 1:10 heavens are the w' of thine hands: "
2: 7 set him over the w' of thy hands: "
3: 9 me, and saw my w' forty years. "
4: 3 the w' were finished from the "
4 the seventh day from all his w'. "
10 also hath ceased from his own w', "
6: 1 of repentance from dead w', and of "
9:14 purge your conscience from dead w' "
10:24 provoke unto love and to good w': "

Jas 2:14 say he hath faith, and have not *w*? 2041
17 so faith, if it hath not *w*, is dead, "
18 say, Thou hast faith, and I have *w*: "
18 shew me thy faith without thy *w*, "
18 I will shew thee my faith by my *w*. "
20 man, that faith without *w* is dead? "
21 Abraham our father justified by *w* "
22 how faith wrought with his *w*, "
22 and by *w* was faith made perfect? "
24 how that by *w* a man is justified, "
25 Rahab the harlot justified by *w*, "
26 so faith without *w* is dead also. "
3:13 out of a good conversation his *w* "
1Pe 2:12 they may by your good *w*, which "
2Pe 3:10 *w* that are therein shall be burned "
1Jo 3: 8 might destroy the *w* of the devil. "
12 Because his own *w* were evil, and "
Re 2: 2 I know thy *w*, and thy labour, and "
5 and repent, and do the first *w*; "
9 I know thy *w*, and tribulation, and* "
13 I know thy *w*, and where thou * "
19 I know thy *w*, and charity, and "
19 faith, and thy patience, and thy *w*; "
23 one of you according to your *w*. "
26 and keepeth my *w* unto the end, "
3: 1 I know thy *w*, that thou hast a name "
2 for I have not found thy *w* perfect "
8 I know thy *w*: behold, I have set "
15 I know thy *w*, that thou art neither "
9:20 yet repented not of the *w* of their "
14:13 and their *w* do follow them. "
15: 3 Great and marvellous are thy *w*, "
18: 6 her double according to her *w*: "
20:12 in the books, according to their *w*. "
13 every man according to their *w*. "

works'
Joh 14:11 believe me for the very *w* sake. 2041

world See also WORLD'S; WORLDS.
1Sa 2: 8 and he hath set the *w* upon them. 8398
2Sa 22:16 the foundations of the *w* were "
1Ch 16:30 the *w* also shall be stable, that it "
Job 18:18 darkness, and chased out of the *w*. "
34:13 or who hath disposed the whole *w*? "
37:12 upon the face of the *w* in the earth. "
Ps 9: 8 shall judge the *w* in righteousness, "
17:14 from men of the *w*, which have 2465
18:15 the foundations of the *w* were 8398
19: 4 their words to the end of the *w*. "
22:27 ends of the *w* shall remember * 776
24: 1 the *w*, and they that dwell therein. 8398
33: 8 inhabitants of the *w* stand in awe "
49: 1 ear, all ye inhabitants of the *w*: 2465
50:12 for the *w* is mine, and the fulness 8398
73:12 ungodly, who prosper in the *w*; *5769
77:18 the lightnings lightened the *w*: 8398
89:11 for the *w* and the fulness thereof, "
90: 2 hadst formed the earth and the *w*, "
93: 1 the *w* also is stablished, that it "
96:10 the *w* also shall be established that "
13 judge the *w* with righteousness, "
97: 4 His lightnings enlightened the *w*: "
98: 7 the *w*, and they that dwell therein. "
9 righteousness shall he judge the *w*, "
Pr 8:26 highest part of the dust of the *w*. "
Ec 3:11 he hath set the *w* in their heart, ‡5769
Isa 13:11 I will punish the *w* for their evil, 8398
14:17 That made the *w* as a wilderness, "
21 fill the face of the *w* with cities. "
18: 3 All ye inhabitants of the *w*, and "
23:17 with all the kingdoms of the *w* 776
24: 4 *w* languisheth and fadeth away, 8398
26: 9 of the *w* will learn righteousness. "
18 the inhabitants of the *w* fallen. "
27: 6 and fill the face of the *w* with fruit. "
34: 1 the *w*, and all things that come "
38:11 with the inhabitants of the *w*. 2309
45:17 nor confounded *w* without end. 5769
62:11 proclaimed unto the end of the *w*, *776
64: 4 since the beginning of the *w* men *5769
Jer 10:12 established the *w* by his wisdom, 8398
25:26 and all the kingdoms of the *w*, 776
51:15 established the *w* by his wisdom, 8398
La 4:12 and all the inhabitants of the *w*, "
Na 1: 5 the *w*, and all that dwell therein. "
M't 4: 8 him all the kingdoms of the *w*, 2889
5:14 Ye are the light of the *w*. A city "
12:32 forgiven him, neither in this *w*, 165
32 neither in the *w* to come. *
13:22 the word; and the care of this *w*, 165
35 from the foundation of the *w*. 2889
38 The field is the *w*; the good seed "
39 the harvest is the end of the *w*; 165
40 so shall it be in the end of this *w*. "
49 So shall it be at the end of the *w*: "
16:26 if he shall gain the whole *w*, and 2889
18: 7 Woe unto the *w* because of "
24: 3 coming, and of the end of the *w*? 165
14 shall be preached in all the *w* for 3625
21 not since the beginning of the *w* 2889
25:34 you from the foundation of the *w*: "
26:13 shall be preached in the whole *w*, "
28:20 alway, even unto the end of the *w*. 165
M'r 4:19 And the cares of this *w*, and the "
8:36 if he shall gain the whole *w*, and 2889
10:30 and in the *w* to come eternal life. 165
14: 9 preached throughout the whole *w*, 2889
16:15 Go ye into all the *w*, and preach "
Lu 1:70 have been since the *w* began: ‡ 165
2: 1 that all the *w* should be taxed. 3625
4: 5 unto him all the kingdoms of the *w* "
9:25 if he gain the whole *w*, and lose 2889
11:50 shed from the foundation of the *w*, "
12:30 do the nations of the *w* seek "
16: 8 the children of this *w* are in their 165
18:30 in the *w* to come life everlasting. "

Lu 20:34 The children of this *w* marry, and 165
35 accounted worthy to obtain that *w*, "
Joh 1: 9 every man that cometh into the *w*. 2889
10 He was in the *w*, "
10 and the *w* was made by him, "
10 and the *w* knew him not. "
29 which taketh away the sin of the *w*. "
3:16 For God so loved the *w*, that he "
17 Son into the *w* to condemn the *w*; "
17 the *w* through him might be saved. "
19 that light is come into the *w*, and "
4:42 the Christ, the Saviour of the *w*. "
6:14 that should come into the *w*. "
33 and giveth light unto the *w*. "
51 I will give for the life of the *w*. "
7: 4 these things, shew thyself to the *w*. "
7 The *w* cannot hate you; but me it "
8:12 saying, I am the light of the *w*: "
23 am from above: ye are of this *w*; "
23 I am not of this *w*. "
26 I speak to the *w* those things which "
9: 5 As long as I am in the *w*, "
5 I am the light of the *w*. "
32 Since the *w* began was it not heard 165
39 judgment I am come into this *w*, 2889
10:36 sanctified, and sent into the *w*, "
11: 9 he seeth the light of this *w*. "
27 God, which should come into the *w*. "
12:19 behold, the *w* is gone after him. "
25 that hateth his life in this *w* shall "
31 Now is the judgment of this *w*: "
31 the prince of this *w* be cast out. "
46 I am come a light into the *w*, that "
47 to judge the *w*, but to save the *w*. "
13: 1 he should depart out of this *w* unto "
1 loved his own which were in the *w*, "
14:17 whom the *w* cannot receive, "
19 while, and the *w* seeth me no more; "
22 unto us, and not unto the *w*? "
27 not as the *w* giveth, give I unto you. "
30 for the prince of this *w* cometh, "
31 *w* may know that I love the Father; "
15:18 If the *w* hate you, ye know that it "
19 of the *w*, the *w* would love his own: "
19 but because ye are not of the *w*, "
19 I have chosen you out of the *w*, "
19 therefore the *w* hateth you. "
16: 8 he will reprove the *w* of sin, and of "
11 the prince of this *w* is judged. "
20 lament, but the *w* shall rejoice: "
21 joy that a man is born into the *w*. "
28 Father, and am come into the *w*: "
28 I leave the *w*, and go to the Father. "
33 In the *w* ye shall have tribulation: "
33 cheer; I have overcome the *w*. "
17: 5 I had with thee before the *w* was. "
6 thou gavest me out of the *w*: "
9 I pray not for the *w*, but for them "
11 And now I am no more in the *w*, "
11 but these are in the *w*, and I come "
12 While I was with them in the *w*, "
13 and these things I speak in the *w*, "
14 word; and the *w* hath hated them, "
14 because they are not of the *w*, "
14 even as I am not of the *w*. "
15 shouldest take them out of the *w*, "
16 They are not of the *w*, "
16 even as I am not of the *w*. "
18 As thou hast sent me into the *w*, "
18 so have I also sent them into the *w*. "
21 *w* may believe...thou hast sent me. "
23 *w* may know...thou hast sent me, "
24 me before the foundation of the *w*. "
25 the *w* hath not known thee: but I "
18:20 I spake openly to the *w*; I ever "
36 My kingdom is not of this *w*: "
36 if my kingdom were of this *w*, then "
37 for this cause came I into the *w*, "
21:25 even the *w* itself could not contain "
Ac 3:21 holy prophets since the *w* began. ‡ 165
11:28 dearth throughout all the *w*: 3625
15:18 from the beginning of the *w*. ‡ 165
17: 6 have turned the *w* upside down 3625
24 God that made the *w* and all 2889
31 will judge the *w* in righteousness 3625
19:27 all Asia and the *w* worshippeth. "
24: 5 all the Jews throughout the *w*, "
Ro 1: 8 spoken of throughout the whole *w*. 2889
20 from the creation of the *w* are "
3: 6 then how shall God judge the *w*? "
19 all the *w* may become guilty before "
4:13 that he should be the heir of the *w*, "
5:12 by one man sin entered into the *w*, "
13 (For until the law sin was in the *w*: "
10:18 words unto the ends of the *w*. 3625
11:12 of them be the riches of the *w*, 2889
15 them be the reconciling of the *w*, "
12: 2 And be not conformed to this *w*: 165
16:25 kept secret since the *w* began, * 166
1Co 1:20 where is the disputer of this *w*? 165
20 foolish the wisdom of this *w*? 2889
21 the *w* by wisdom knew not God, "
27 chosen the foolish things of the *w* "
27 chosen the weak things of the *w* "
28 And base things of the *w*, and "
2: 6 yet not the wisdom of this *w*, 165
6 nor of the princes of this *w*, that "
7 God ordained before the *w* unto * "
8 of the princes of this *w* knew: "
12 received, not the spirit of the *w*, 2889
3:18 you seemeth to be wise in this *w*, 165
19 wisdom of this *w* is foolishness 2889
22 or the *w*, or life, or death, or "
4: 9 are made a spectacle unto the *w*, "
13 we are made as the filth of the *w*, "
5:10 with the fornicators of this *w*, "

1Co 5:10 must ye needs go out of the *w*. 2889
6: 2 that the saints shall judge the *w*? "
2 if the *w* shall be judged by you, "
7:31 And they that use this *w*, as not "
31 fashion of this *w* passeth away. "
33 for the things that are of the *w*, "
34 careth for the things of the *w*, "
8: 4 that an idol is nothing in the *w*, "
13 no flesh while the *w* standeth, * 165
10:11 whom the ends of the *w* are come.* "
11:32 not be condemned with the *w*. 2889
14:10 so many kinds of voices in the *w*, "
2Co 1:12 had our conversation in the *w*, "
4: 4 the god of this *w* hath blinded the 165
5:19 reconciling the *w* unto himself, 2889
7:10 sorrow of the *w* worketh death. "
Ga 1: 4 deliver us from the present evil *w*, 165
4: 3 under the elements of the *w*: 2889
6:14 whom the *w* is crucified unto me, "
14 and I unto the *w*. "
Eph 1: 4 before the foundation of the *w*, "
21 that is named, not only in this *w*, 165
2: 2 according to the course of this *w*, 2889
12 hope, and without God in the *w*: "
3: 9 the beginning of the *w* hath been* 165
21 throughout all ages, *w* without end.* "
6:12 rulers of the darkness of this *w*, * "
Ph'p 2:15 whom ye shine as lights in the *w*; 2889
Col 1: 6 come unto you, as it is in all the *w*; "
2: 8 after the rudiments of the *w*, and "
20 from the rudiments of the *w*, why, "
20 as though living in the *w*, are ye "
1Ti 1:15 came into the *w* to save sinners; "
3:16 believed on in the *w*, received up "
6: 7 we brought nothing into this *w*, "
17 them that are rich in this *w*, 165
2Ti 1: 9 Christ Jesus before the *w* began,* 166
4:10 me, having loved this present *w*, 165
Tit 1: 2 promised before the *w* began; * 166
2:12 and godly, in this present *w*; 165
Heb 1: 6 in the firstbegotten into the *w*, 3625
2: 5 put in subjection the *w* to come, "
4: 3 from the foundation of the *w*. 2889
6: 5 and the powers of the *w* to come,* 165
9:26 since the foundation of the *w*: 2889
26 but now once in the end of the *w* * 165
10: 5 when he cometh into the *w*, he 2889
11: 7 by the which he condemned the *w*, "
38 (Of whom the *w* was not worthy:) "
Jas 1:27 himself unspotted from the *w*. "
2: 5 the poor of this *w* rich in faith, "
3: 6 tongue is a fire, a *w* of iniquity: "
4: 4 the friendship of the *w* is enmity "
4 be a friend of the *w* is the enemy "
1Pe 1:20 before the foundation of the *w*, "
5: 9 your brethren that are in the *w*. "
2Pe 1: 4 the corruption that is in the *w* "
2: 5 And spared not the old *w*, but "
5 flood upon the *w* of the ungodly; "
20 escaped the pollutions of the *w* "
3: 6 Whereby the *w* that then was, "
1Jo 2: 2 also for the sins of the whole *w*. "
15 Love not the *w*, neither "
15 the things that are in the *w*. "
15 If any man love the *w*, the love of "
16 For all that is in the *w*, the lust of "
16 not of the Father, but is of the *w*. "
17 And the *w* passeth away, and the "
3: 1 therefore the *w* knoweth us not, "
13 my brethren, if the *w* hate you. "
4: 1 prophets are gone out into the *w*. "
3 even now already is it in the *w*. "
4 is in you, than he that is in the *w*. "
5 They are of the *w*: therefore "
5 therefore speak they of the *w*, "
5 and the *w* heareth them. "
9 his only begotten Son into the *w*, "
14 Son to be the Saviour of the *w*. "
17 as he is, so are we in this *w*. "
5: 4 born of God overcometh the *w*: "
4 the victory that overcometh the *w*, "
5 Who is he that overcometh the *w*, "
19 the whole *w* lieth in wickedness. "
2Jo 7 deceivers are entered into the *w*, "
Re 3:10 which shall come upon all the *w*, 3625
11:15 kingdoms of this *w* are become 2889
12: 9 which deceiveth the whole *w*: 3625
13: 3 the *w* wondered after the beast. *1092
8 from the foundation of the *w*. 2889
16:14 of the earth and of the whole *w*, 3625
17: 8 from the foundation of the *w*, 2889

worldly
Tit 2:12 denying ungodliness and *w* lusts, 2886
Heb 9: 1 service, and a *w* sanctuary. * "

world's
1Jo 3:17 But whoso hath this *w* good, 2889

worlds
Heb 1: 2 by whom also he made the *w*; 165
11: 3 the *w* were framed by the word of "

worm See also CANKERWORM; PALMERWORM; WORMS; WORMWOOD.
Ex 16:24 neither was there any *w* therein. 7415
Job 17:14 to the *w*, Thou art my mother, "
24:20 the *w* shall feed sweetly on him; "
25: 6 How much less man, that is a *w*? "
6 the son of man, which is a *w*? 8438
Ps 22: 6 But I am a *w*, and no man; "
Isa 14:11 the *w* is spread under thee, and 7415
41:14 Fear not, thou *w* Jacob, and ye 8438
51: 8 the *w* shall eat them like wool: 5580
66:24 for their *w* shall not die, neither 8438
Jon 4: 7 But God prepared a *w* when the "
M'r 9:44, 46 Where their *w* dieth not, *4668
48 Where their *w* dieth not, "

worms
Ex 16:20 and it bred *w'*, and stank: 8438
De 28:39 grapes; for the *w'* shall eat them.* "
Job 7: 5 My flesh is clothed with *w'* and 7415
19:26 after my skin *w'* shall destroy this* "
21:26 dust, and the *w'* shall cover them.*7415
Isa 14:11 under thee, and the *w'* cover thee.*8438
Mic 7:17 of their holes like *w'* of the earth: 2119
Ac 12:23 he was eaten of *w'*, and gave up *4662*

wormwood
De 29:18 a root that beareth gall and *w'*; 3939
Pr 5: 4 But her end is bitter as *w'*, sharp "
Jer 9:15 them, even this people, with *w'*, "
23:15 I will feed them with *w'*, and make "
La 3:15 hath made me drunken with *w'*. "
19 my misery, the *w'* and the gall. "
Am 5: 7 Ye who turn judgment to *w'*, and "
Re 8:11 the name of the star is called *W'*: *894*
11 part of the waters became *w'*; "

worse
Ge 19: 9 now will we deal *w'* with thee, 7489
2Sa 19: 7 that will be *w'* unto thee than all "
1Ki 16:25 did *w'* than all that were before * "
2Ki 14:12 Judah was put to the *w'* before 5062
1Ch 19:16, 19 were put to the *w'* before Israel, "
2Ch 6:24 thy people Israel be put to the *w'** "
25:22 Judah was put to the *w'* before "
33: 9 to do *w'* than the heathen, whom *7451
Jer 7:26 they did *w'* than their fathers. 7489
16:12 have done *w'* than your fathers; * "
Da 1:10 faces *w'* liking than the children 2196
M't 9:16 garment, and the rent is made *w'*. *5501*
12:45 of that man is *w'* than the first. "
27:64 last error shall be *w'* than the first. "
M'r 2:21 the old, and the rent is made *w'*. "
5:26 bettered, but rather grew *w'*, "
Lu 11:26 of that man is *w'* than the first. "
Joh 2:10 well drunk, then that which is *w'*: *1640*
5:14 lest a *w'* thing come unto thee. *5501*
1Co 8: 8 if we eat not, are we the *w'*. *5302*
11:17 not for the better, but for the *w'*. *2276*
1Ti 5: 8 faith, and is *w'* than an infidel. *5501*
2Ti 3:13 and seducers shall wax *w'* and *w'*, "
2Pe 2:20 the latter end is *w'* with them than "

worship See also WORSHIPPED; WORSHIPPETH; WORSHIPPING.
Ge 22: 5 and the lad will go yonder and *w'*, 7812
Ex 24: 1 of Israel; and *w'* ye afar off. "
34:14 For thou shalt *w'* no other god: "
De 4:19 shouldest be driven to *w'* them, "
8:19 and serve them, and *w'* them, "
11:16 and serve other gods, and *w'* them; "
26:10 and *w'* before the Lord thy God: "
30:17 *w'* other gods, and serve them; "
Jos 5:14 on his face to the earth, and did *w'*, "
1Sa 1: 3 went up out of his city yearly to *w'* "
15:25 with me, that I may *w'* the Lord, "
30 that I may *w'* the Lord thy God. "
1Ki 9: 6 and serve other gods, and *w'* them: "
12:30 the people went to *w'* before the one, "
2Ki 5:18 the house of Rimmon to *w'* there, 7812
17:36 shall ye fear, and him shall ye *w'*,* "
18:22 *w'* before the altar in Jerusalem? "
1Ch 16:29 *w'* the Lord in the beauty of "
2Ch 7:19 and serve other gods, and *w'* them; "
32:12 Ye shall *w'* before one altar, and "
Ps 5: 7 will I *w'* toward thy holy temple. "
22:27 the nations shall *w'* before thee. "
29 fat upon earth shall eat and *w'*: "
29: 2 *w'* the Lord in the beauty of "
45:11 he is thy Lord; and *w'* thou him. "
66: 4 All the earth shall *w'* thee, and "
81: 9 shalt thou *w'* any strange god. "
86: 9 shall come and *w'* before thee; "
95: 6 O come, let us *w'* and bow down: "
96: 9 O *w'* the Lord in the beauty of "
97: 7 of idols: *w'* him, all ye gods. "
99: 5 our God, and *w'* at his footstool; "
9 our God, and *w'* at his holy hill; "
132: 7 we will *w'* at his footstool. "
138: 2 I will *w'* toward thy holy temple, "
Isa 2: 8 *w'* the work of their own hands, "
20 made each one for himself to *w'*, "
27:13 shall *w'* the Lord in the holy mount "
36: 7 Ye shall *w'* before this altar? "
46: 6 a god: they fall down, yea, they *w'*. "
49: 7 see and arise, princes also shall *w'*, "
66:23 all flesh come to *w'* before me, "
Jer 7: 2 in at these gates to *w'* the Lord. "
13:10 gods, to serve them, and to *w'* them, "
25: 6 gods to serve them, and to *w'* them, "
26: 2 come to *w'* in the Lord's house, "
44:19 did we make her cakes to *w'* her, 6087
Eze 46: 2 *w'* at the threshold of the gate: 7812
3 shall *w'* at the door of this gate "
9 by the way of the north gate to *w'* "
Da 3: 5 fall down and *w'* the golden image 5457
10 fall down and *w'* the golden image: "
12 nor *w'* the golden image which thou "
14 nor *w'* the golden image which I "
15 ye fall down and *w'* the image "
15 but if ye *w'* not, ye shall be cast "
18 nor *w'* the golden image which thou "
28 might not serve nor *w'* any god, "
Mic 5:13 more *w'* the work of thine hands. 7812
Zep 1: 5 them that *w'* the host of heaven "
5 *w'* and that swear by the Lord, "
2:11 and men shall *w'* him, every one "
Zec 14:16 from year to year to *w'* the King, "
17 unto Jerusalem to *w'* the King, "
M't 2: 2 the east, and are come to *w'* him. *4352*
8 that I may come and *w'* him also. "
4: 9 if thou wilt fall down and *w'* me. "
10 Thou shalt *w'* the Lord thy God, "
M't 15: 9 But in vain do they *w'* me, teaching *4576*
M'r 7: 7 Howbeit in vain do they *w'* me, "
Lu 4: 7 If thou therefore wilt *w'* me, *4352, 1799*
8 Thou shalt *w'* the Lord thy God, *4352*
14:10 have *w'* in the presence of them *1391
Joh 4:20 the place where men ought to *w'*. *4352*
21 yet at Jerusalem, *w'* the Father. "
22 Ye *w'* ye know not what: "
22 we know what we *w'*: for salvation "
23 shall *w'* the Father in spirit and in "
23 the Father seeketh such to *w'* him.* "
24 is a Spirit: and they that *w'* him "
24 must *w'* him in spirit and in truth. "
12:20 that came up to *w'* at the feast: "
Ac 7:42 them up to *w'* the host of heaven; *3000*
43 which ye made to *w'* them: *4352*
8:27 had come to Jerusalem for to *w'*, "
17:23 Whom therefore ye ignorantly *w'*, *2151*
18:13 fellow persuadeth men to *w'* God *4576*
24:11 I went up to Jerusalem for to *w'*. *4352*
14 so *w'* I the God of my fathers, *3000
1Co 14:25 down on his face he will *w'* God, *4352*
Ph'p 3: 3 which *w'* God in the spirit, and *3000*
Col 2:23 indeed a shew of wisdom in will *w'*, *1479*
Heb 1: 6 let all the angels of God *w'* him. *4352*
Re 3: 9 to come and *w'* before thy feet, "
4:10 and *w'* him that liveth for ever and "
9:20 that they should not *w'* devils, and "
11: 1 altar, and them that *w'* therein. "
13: 8 dwell upon the earth shall *w'* him, "
12 dwell therein to *w'* the first beast, "
15 not *w'* the image of the beast "
14: 7 and *w'* him that made heaven, and "
9 If any man *w'* the beast and his * "
11 who *w'* the beast and his image, "
15: 4 shall come and *w'* before thee; "
19:10 And I fell at his feet to *w'* him. "
10 *w'* God: for the testimony of Jesus "
22: 8 I fell down to *w'* before the feet of "
9 the sayings of this book: *w'* God. "

worshipped
Ge 24:26 down his head, and *w'* the Lord. 7812
48 down my head, and *w'* the Lord, "
52 heard their words, he *w'* the Lord, "
Ex 4:31 they bowed their heads and *w'*. "
12:27 the people bowed the head and *w'*. "
32: 8 them a molten calf, and have *w'* it. "
33:10 and all the people rose up and *w'*, "
34: 8 his head toward the earth, and *w'*. "
De 17: 3 and served other gods, and *w'* them, "
29:26 and served other gods, and *w'* them, "
J'g 7:15 interpretation thereof, that he *w'*, "
1Sa 1:19 *w'* before the Lord, and returned, "
28 Lord. And he *w'* the Lord there. "
15:31 after Saul; and Saul *w'* the Lord. "
2Sa 12:20 into the house of the Lord, and *w'*: "
15:32 top of the mount, where he *w'* God, "
1Ki 9: 9 upon other gods, and have *w'* them, "
11:33 have *w'* Ashtoreth the goddess of "
16:31 went and served Baal, and *w'* him. "
22:53 For he served Baal, and *w'* him, "
2Ki 17:16 and *w'* all the host of heaven, and "
21: 3 and *w'* all the host of heaven, and "
21 that his father served, and *w'* them: "
1Ch 29:20 down their heads, and *w'* the Lord, "
2Ch 7: 3 and *w'*, and praised the Lord, "
22 hold on other gods, and *w'* them, "
29:28 And all the congregation *w'*, and "
29 him bowed themselves, and *w'*. "
30 and they bowed their heads and *w'*. "
33: 3 and *w'* all the host of heaven, "
Ne 8: 6 and *w'* the Lord with their faces to "
9: 3 and *w'* the Lord their God. "
Job 1:20 fell down upon the ground, and *w'*, "
Ps 106:19 in Horeb, and *w'* the molten image. "
Jer 1:16 *w'* the works of their own hands. "
8: 2 sought, and whom they have *w'*: "
16:11 served them, and have *w'* them, "
22: 9 *w'* other gods, and served them. "
Eze 8:16 they *w'* the sun toward the east. "
Da 2:46 and *w'* Daniel, and commanded 5457
3: 7 fell down and *w'* the golden image "
M't 2:11 mother, and fell down and *w'* him: *4352*
8: 2 there came a leper and *w'* him, "
9:18 came a certain ruler, and *w'* him, "
14:33 were in the ship came and *w'* him, "
15:25 Then came she and *w'* him, saying, "
18:26 fell down, and *w'* him, saying, Lord, "
28: 9 held him by the feet, and *w'* him. "
17 they *w'* him: but some doubted. "
M'r 5: 6 Jesus afar off, he ran and *w'* him, "
15:19 and bowing their knees *w'* him. "
Lu 24:52 And they *w'* him, and returned to "
Joh 4:20 Our fathers *w'* in this mountain; "
9:38 Lord, I believe. And he *w'* him. "
Ac 10:25 fell down at his feet, and *w'* him. "
16:14 Thyatira, which *w'* God, heard us; *4576*
17:25 Neither is *w'* with men's hands, *2323
18: 7 named Justus, one that *w'* God, *4576*
Ro 1:25 and *w'* and served the creature *4573*
2Th 2: 4 all that is called God, or that is *w'*; *4574*
Heb 11:21 and *w'*, leaning upon the top of *4352*
Re 5:14 and *w'* him that liveth for ever and "
7:11 throne on their faces, and *w'* God, "
11:16 fell upon their faces, and *w'* God, "
13: 4 *w'* the dragon which gave power "
4 and they *w'* the beast, saying, Who "
16: 2 and upon them which *w'* his image. "
19: 4 four beasts fell down and *w'* God "
20 beast, and them that *w'* his image. "
20: 4 which had not *w'* the beast, neither "

worshipper See also WORSHIPPERS.
Joh 9:31 but if any man be a *w'* of God, and *2318*
Ac 19:35 a *w'* of the great goddess Diana, *3511

worshippers
2Ki 10:19 he might destroy the *w'* of Baal. 5647
21 all the *w'* of Baal came, so that "
22 vestments for all the *w'* of Baal. "
23 said unto the *w'* of Baal, Search, "
23 the Lord, but the *w'* of Baal only. "
Joh 4:23 true *w'* shall worship the Father *4353*
Heb 10: 2 the *w'* once purged should have *3000*

worshippeth
Ne 9: 6 and the host of heaven *w'* thee. 7812
Isa 44:15 yea, he maketh a god, and *w'* it; "
17 he falleth down unto it, and *w'* it, "
Da 3: 6 whoso falleth not down and *w'* 5457
11 And whoso falleth not down and *w'*, "
Ac 19:27 whom all Asia and the world *w'*. *4576*

worshipping
2Ki 19:37 *w'* in the house of Nisroch his god, 7812
2Ch 20:18 fell before the Lord, *w'* the Lord. "
Isa 37:38 *w'* in the house of Nisroch his god, "
M't 20:20 *w'* him, and desiring a certain *4352*
Col 2:18 humility and *w'* of angels, *2356*

worst
Eze 7:24 I will bring the *w'* of the heathen, 7451

worth See also PENNYWORTH.
Ge 23: 9 money as it is *w'* he shall give it *4392
Le 27:23 unto him the *w'* of thy estimation, 4373
De 15:18 been *w'* a double hired servant *7939
2Sa 18: 3 thou art *w'* ten thousand of us: 3644
1Ki 21: 2 give thee the *w'* of it in money. 4242
Job 24:25 and make my speech nothing *w'*?
Pr 10:20 the heart of the wicked is little *w'*.
Eze 30: 2 God; Howl ye, Woe *w'* the day!

worthies
Na 2: 5 He shall recount his *w'*: they shall 117

worthily See also UNWORTHILY.
Ru 4:11 do thou *w'* in Ephratah, and be 2428

worthy See also THANKWORTHY; UNWORTHY; WORTHIES.
Ge 32:10 I am not *w'* of the least of all the 6994
De 17: 6 is *w'* of death to be put to death; *
19: 6 whereas he was not *w'* of death,
21:22 have committed a sin *w'* of death,
22:26 is in the damsel no sin *w'* of death:
25: 2 wicked man be *w'* to be beaten, 1121
1Sa 1: 5 unto Hannah he gave a *w'* portion: *639
26:16 ye are *w'* to die, because ye have 1121
2Sa 22: 4 the Lord, who is *w'* to be praised:
1Ki 1:52 will shew himself a *w'* man, 2428
2:26 fields; for thou art *w'* of death: 376
Ps 18: 3 the Lord, who is *w'* to be praised:
Jer 26:11 saying, This man is *w'* to die;
16 This man is not *w'* to die: for he
M't 3:11 whose shoes I am not *w'* to bear: *2425*
8: 8 I am not *w'* that thou shouldest "
10:10 for the workman is *w'* of his meat. *514*
11 shall enter, enquire who in it is *w'*; "
13 if the house be *w'*, let your peace "
13 if it be not *w'*, let your peace return "
37 more than me is not *w'* of me: "
37 more than me is not *w'* of me. "
38 followeth after me, is not *w'* of me. "
22: 8 which were bidden were not *w'*. "
M'r 1: 7 shoes I am not *w'* to stoop down *2425*
Lu 3: 8 therefore fruits *w'* of repentance, *514*
16 shoes I am not *w'* to unloose: *2425*
7: 4 he was *w'* for whom he should do *514*
6 I am not *w'* that thou shouldest *2425*
7 thought I myself *w'* to come *515*
10: 7 for the labourer is *w'* of his hire. *514*
12:48 did commit things *w'* of stripes, "
15:19 am no more *w'* to be called thy son: "
21 am no more *w'* to be called thy son. "
20:35 accounted *w'* to obtain that world, *2661*
21:36 accounted *w'* to escape all these "
23:15 nothing *w'* of death is done unto *514*
Joh 1:27 latchet I am not *w'* to unloose. "
Ac 5:41 were counted *w'* to suffer shame *2661*
13:25 of his feet I am not *w'* to loose. *514*
23:29 laid to his charge *w'* of death "
24: 2 very *w'* deeds are done unto this *2735
25:11 committed any thing *w'* of death, *514*
25 had committed nothing *w'* of death, "
26:31 nothing *w'* of death or of bonds. "
Ro 1:32 such things are *w'* of death, "
8:18 time are not *w'* to be compared "
Eph 4: 1 that ye walk *w'* of the vocation * *516*
Col 1:10 might walk *w'* of the Lord unto * "
1Th 2:12 That ye would walk *w'* of God, who* "
2Th 1: 5 may be counted *w'* of the kingdom *2661*
11 count you *w'* of this calling, *515*
1Ti 1:15 saying, and *w'* of all acceptation, *514*
4: 9 saying and *w'* of all acceptation. "
5:17 be counted *w'* of double honour, *515*
18 The labourer is *w'* of his reward. *514*
6: 1 their own masters *w'* of all honour, "
Heb 3: 3 man was counted *w'* of more glory *515*
10:29 shall he be thought *w'*, who hath "
11:38 (Of whom the world was not *w'*:) *514*
Jas 2: 7 they blaspheme that *w'* name *2570
Re 3: 4 with me in white: for they are *w'*. *514*
4:11 Thou art *w'*, O Lord, to receive "
5: 2 Who is *w'* to open the book, and to "
4 no man was found *w'* to open and "
9 Thou art *w'* to take the book, and "
12 *W'* is the lamb that was slain to "
16: 6 blood to drink; for they are *w'*. "

wot See also WIST; WIT; WOTTETH.
Ge 21:26 I *w'* not who hath done this thing: *3045
44:15 *w'* ye not that such a man as I can* "
Ex 32: 1, 23 *w'* not what is become of him.* "
Nu 22: 6 I *w'* that he whom thou blessest is* "
Jos 2: 5 whither the men went I *w'* not: "

Ac 3:17 I w' that through ignorance ye did1492
7:40 we w' not what is become of him. "
Ro 11: 2 W' ye not what the scripture saith "
Ph'p 1:22 yet what I shall choose I w' not. 1107

wotteth
Ge 39: 8 my master w' not what is with me*3045

would See also WOULDEST.
Ge 2:19 Adam to see what he w' call them:
21: 7 Who w' have said unto Abraham, that
30:34 I w' that it might be according 3863
42:21 he besought us, and we w' not hear;
22 and ye w' not hear? therefore, behold,
43: 7 certainly know that he w' say, Bring
44:22 leave his father, his father w' die.
Ex 2: 4 afar off, to wit what w' be done to him.
8:32 neither w' he let the people go. *
9:35 neither w' he let the children of *
10:20 he w' not let the children of Israel*
27 heart, and he w' not let them go. 14
11:10 he w' not let the children of Israel*
13:15 when Pharaoh w' hardly let us go,
16: 3 W' to God we had died by 4310,5414
Nu 11:29 w' God that all the Lord's "
29 Lord w' put his spirit upon them!
14: 2 W' God that we had died in the 3863
2 w' God we...died in the wilderness! "
20: 3 W' God that we had died when "
21:23 And Sihon w' not suffer Israel to pass
22:18 If Balak w' give me his house full of
29 I w' there were a sword in mine 3863
29 in mine hand, for now I w' kill thee.*
24:13 If Balak w' give me his house full of
De 1:26 Notwithstanding ye w' not go up, 14
43 and ye w' not hear, but rebelled *
45 Lord w' not hearken to your voice,*
2:30 king of Heshbon w' not let us pass 14
3:26 for your sakes, and w' not hear me:
5:29 a heart in them, that they w' fear me,
7: 8 because he w' keep the oath which he
8:20 ye w' not be obedient unto the voice
9:25 the Lord had said he w' destroy you.
10:10 and the Lord w' not destroy thee. 14
23: 5 God w' not hearken unto Balaam; "
21 it of thee; and it w' be sin in thee.
28:56 w' not adventure to set the sole of
67 say, W' God it were even! 4310,5414
67 say, W' God it were morning! " "
32:26 I said, I w' scatter them into corners,
26 I w' make the remembrance of them
29 they w' consider their latter end!
Jos 5: 6 that he w' not shew them the land,
6 unto their fathers that he w' give us,
7: 7 w' to God we had been content, 3863
17:12 Canaanites w' dwell in that land. 2974
24:10 But I w' not hearken unto Balaam; 14
J'g 1:27 Canaanites w' dwell in that land. 2974
34 for they w' not suffer them to come
35 Amorites w' dwell in mount Heres2974
2:17 w' not hearken unto their judges,*
3: 4 to know whether they w' hearken
8:19 saved them alive, I w' not slay you.
24 them, I w' desire a request from you,
24 w' give me every man the earrings
9:29 w' to God this people were 4310,5414
29 then w' I remove Abimelech. And he
11:17 the king of Edom w' not hearken*
17 king of Moab: but he w' not consent:14
13:23 he w' not have received a burnt
23 neither w' he have shewed us all
23 nor w' as at this time have told us
14: 6 he rent him as he w' have rent a kid,
15: 1 her father w' not suffer him to go in.
19:10 But the man w' not tarry that night, 14
25 the men w' not hearken to him: "
20:13 of Benjamin w' not hearken to the "
Ru 1:13 W' ye tarry for them till they were
13 w' ye stay for them from having
1Sa 2:16 then he w' answer him, Nay; but
25 because the Lord w' slay them. 2654
13:13 for now w' the Lord have established
15: 9 and w' not utterly destroy them: 14
18: 2 and w' let him go no more home to his
20: 9 come upon thee, then w' not I tell it
22:17 servants of the king w' not put forth14
22 was there, that he w' surely tell Saul:
26:23 but I w' not stretch forth mine hand 14
31: 4 But his armourbearer w' not; for he "
2Sa 2:21 But Asahel w' not turn aside from "
4: 6 though they w' have fetched wheat;
10 that I w' have given him a reward*
6:10 So David w' not remove the ark of 14
11:20 knew ye not that they w' shoot from
12: 8 I w' moreover have given unto thee
17 but he w' not, neither did he eat 14
18 he w' not hearken unto our voice:*
13:14 he w' not hearken unto her voice: 14
16 me. But he w' not hearken unto her."
25 howbeit he w' not go, but blessed "
14:16 man that w' destroy me and my son
29 king; but he w' not come to him: 14
29 second time, he w' not come. "
15: 4 unto me, and I w' do him justice!
18:11 I w' have given thee ten shekels of
12 yet w' I not put forth mine hand
33 w' God I had died for thee, O 4310,5414
23:15 that one w' give me drink of the water
16 nevertheless he w' not drink 14
17 therefore he w' not drink it. These "
1Ki 8:12 he w' dwell in the thick darkness.
13:33 whosoever w', he consecrated him,2655
18:32 as great as w' contain two measures of
20:33 whether any thing w' come from him,*
21: 4 away his face, and w' eat no bread.
22:18 w' prophesy no good concerning me,
49 the ships. But Jehoshaphat w' not. 14
2Ki 2: 1 when the Lord w' take up Elijah into
3:14 I w' not look toward thee, nor see
5: 3 W' God my lord were with the 305
3 for he w' recover him of his leprosy.
7: 2 the Lord w' make windows in heaven,*
8:19 Yet the Lord w' not destroy Judah 14
13:23 and w' not destroy them, neither "
14:11 But Amaziah w' not hear. Therefore
27 that he w' blot out the name of Israel
17:14 Notwithstanding they w' not hear,
18:12 and w' not hear them, nor do them.
24: 4 which the Lord w' not pardon. 14
1Ch 10: 4 But his armourbearer w' not; for he "
11:17 that one w' give me drink of the water
18 but David w' not drink of it, but 14
19 Therefore he w' not drink it. "
13: 4 congregation said that they w' do so:
19:19 neither w' the Syrians help the 14
27:23 he w' increase Israel like to the stars
2Ch 6: 1 that he w' dwell in the thick darkness.
10:16 saw that the king w' not hearken *
12:12 that he w' not destroy him altogether:
15:13 whosoever w' not seek the Lord God of
18:17 that he w' not prophesy good unto me,
21: 7 w' not destroy the house of David, 14
24:19 them: but they w' not give ear.
25:20 But Amaziah w' not hear; for it came
33:10 his people: but they w' not hearken.*
35:22 Josiah w' not turn his face from him,
Ezr 10: 8 w' not come within three days,
19 that they w' put away their wives;
Ne 6:11 w' go into the temple to save his life?
14 prophets, that w' have put me in fear.
9:24 they might do with them as they w'.
29 hardened their neck, and w' not hear.
30 yet w' they not give ear: therefore
10:30 we w' not give our daughters unto the
31 w' not buy it of them on the sabbath,
31 that we w' leave the seventh year,
Es 3: 4 whether Mordecai's matters w' stand:
6: 6 To whom w' the king delight to do
8:11 and province that w' assault them,
9: 5 what they w' unto those that hated
27 that they w' keep these two days
Job 5: 8 I w' seek unto God,
8 and unto God w' I commit my cause:
6: 3 it w' be heavier than the sand of the
8 that God w' grant me the thing that
9 that it w' please God to destroy me;
9 that he w' let loose his hand, and cut
10 I w' harden myself in sorrow: let‡
7:16 I loathe it, I w' not live alway: let me
8: 6 surely now he w' awake for thee, and
9:15 I were righteous, yet w' I not answer,
15 I w' make supplication to my judge.
16 w' I not believe that he had hearkened
21 perfect, yet w' I not know my soul:*
21 I w' despise my life. "
35 Then w' I speak, and not fear him; *
11: 5 But oh that God w' speak, and open
6 he w' shew thee the secrets of wisdom,
12 For vain man w' be wise, though man*
13: 3 Surely I w' speak to the Almighty, and
5 ye w' altogether hold your peace!
16: 5 I w' strengthen you with my mouth,
23: 4 I w' order my cause before him, and
5 I w' know the words which
5 he w' answer me, and understand
5 understand what he w' say unto me.
6 No; but he w' put strength in me.
27:22 spare: he w' fain flee out of his hand.
30: 1 whose fathers I w' have disdained to*
31:12 and w' root out all mine increase.
35 Oh that one w' hear me! behold, my*
35 that the Almighty w' answer me, and*
36 Surely I w' take it upon my shoulder,
37 I w' declare unto him the number of
37 as a prince w' I go near unto him.
32:22 in so doing my maker w' soon take me
34:27 and w' not consider any of his ways:
36:16 Even so w' he have removed thee out
41:32 one w' think the deep to be hoary.
Ps 22: 8 on the Lord that he w' deliver him:*
35:25 their hearts, Ah, so w' we have it: 5315
40: 5 if I w' declare and speak of them,
50:12 If I were hungry, I w' not tell thee:
51:16 not sacrifice; else w' I give it: thou
55: 6 for then w' I fly away, and be at rest.
7 Lo, then w' I wander far off, and
8 I w' hasten my escape from the
12 then I w' have hid myself from him:
56: 1 O God: for man w' swallow me up;
2 Mine enemies w' daily swallow me up:
57: 3 reproach of him that w' swallow me
69: 4 w' destroy me, being mine enemies
81:11 people w' not hearken to my voice;
11 and Israel w' none of me. 14
106:23 he said that he w' destroy them,
107: 8, 15, 21, 31 men w' praise the Lord for
119:57 I have said that I w' keep thy words.
142: 4 there was no man that w' know me:
Pr 1:25 counsel, and w' none of my reproof:14
30 They w' none of my counsel: they
Ca 3: 4 I held him, and w' not let him go,
8: 1 find thee without, I w' kiss thee;
2 I w' lead thee, and bring thee into
2 mother's house, who w' instruct me:
2 w' cause thee to drink of spiced wine
7 if a man w' give all the substance of
7 for love, it w' utterly be contemned.
Isa 27: 4 who w' set the briers and thorns
4 I w' go through them,
4 I w' burn them together.
28:12 refreshing: yet they w' not hear. 14
30:15 be your strength: and ye w' not. "
42:24 for they w' not walk in his ways, "
Isa 54: 9 that I w' not be wroth with thee,
Jer 8:18 I w' comfort myself against sorrow,*
10: 7 Who w' not fear thee, O King of
13:11 for a glory: but they w' not hear.
18:10 wherewith I said I w' benefit them.
22:24 hand, yet w' I pluck thee hence;
29:19 but ye w' not hear, saith the Lord.
36:25 the king that he w' not burn the roll:
25 but he w' not hear them.
38:26 that he w' not cause me to return to
49: 9 w' they not leave some gleaning
51: 9 We w' have healed Babylon, but she
La 4:12 w' not have believed that the *
Eze 3: 6 they w' have hearkened unto thee.
6:10 that I w' do this evil unto them.
13: 6 hope that they w' confirm the word.*
20: 8 me, and w' not hearken unto me: 14
13 I w' pour out my fury upon them
15 I w' not bring into the land which I
21 I w' pour out my fury upon them,
23 I w' scatter them among the heathen,
38:17 that I w' bring thee against them?
Da 1: 8 heart that he w' not defile himself
2: 8 of certainty that ye w' gain the time,
16 of the king that he w' give him time,
16 w' shew the king the interpretation.
18 they w' desire mercies of the God of
5:19 before him: whom he w' he slew; 6634
19 and whom he w' he kept alive; "
19 and whom he w' he set up; "
19 and whom he w' he put down. "
7:19 I w' know the truth of the fourth * "
9: 2 that he w' accomplish seventy years*
Ho 7: 1 When I w' have healed Israel, then
11: 7 most High, none at all w' exalt him.*
Ob 5 w' they not have stolen till they had
Jon 3:10 he had said that he w' do unto them;
4: 5 see what w' become of the city.
Zec 7:13 as he cried, and they w' not hear;
13 so they cried, and I w' not hear, *
Mal 1:10 that w' shut the doors for nought?
M't 2:18 children, and w' not be comforted, 2309
5:42 him that w' borrow of thee turn not "
7:12 ye w' that men should do to you, "
8:34 he w' depart out of their coasts.
11:21 they w' have repented long ago in
23 it w' have remained until this day.
12: 7 ye w' not have condemned the
38 we w' see a sign from thee. 2309
14: 5 when he w' have put him to death,
7 to give her whatsoever she w' ask.
16: 1 he w' shew them a sign from heaven.*
18:23 w' take account of his servants. 2309
30 he w' not: but went and cast him "
22: 3 wedding: and they w' not come. "
23:30 we w' not have been partakers with*
37 w' I have gathered thy children 2309
37 under her wings, and ye w' not!
24:43 in what watch the thief w' come, *
43 come, he w' have watched, and
43 w' not have suffered his house to be
27:15 people a prisoner, whom they w'. 2309
34 tasted thereof, he w' not drink. "
M'r 3: 2 whether he w' heal on the sabbath
13 and calleth unto him whom he w': 2309
5:10 that he w' not send them away out
6:19 and w' have killed him; but she *2309
26 sat with him, he w' not reject her. "
48 sea, and w' have passed by them. "
7:24 and w' have no man know it: "
26 that he w' cast forth the devil out of
9:30 he w' not that any man should 2309
10:35 Master, we w' that thou shouldest "
36 What w' ye that I should do for you?"
11:16 And w' not suffer that any man should
Lu 1:62 father, how he w' have him called.2309
74 That he w' grant unto us, that we *
5: 3 w' thrust out a little from the land.*
6: 7 whether he w' heal on the sabbath
31 ye w' that men should do to you, 2309
7: 3 that he w' come and heal his servant.
36 desired him that he w' eat with him.
39 w' have known who and what manner
8:31 he w' not command them to go out
32 that he w' suffer them to enter into
41 him that he w' come into his house:*
9:53 as though he w' go to Jerusalem.*
10: 1 whither he himself w' come. *3195
2 that he w' send forth labourers *
12:39 known what hour the thief w' come,*
39 he w' have watched, and not have
13:34 w' I have gathered thy children 2309
34 under her wings, and ye w' not!
15:16 he w' fain have filled his belly with
28 he was angry, and w' not go in: 2309
16:26 which w' pass from hence to you
26 to us, that w' come from thence. *
18: 4 And he w' not for a while: but 2309
13 w' not lift up so much as his eyes
15 infants, that he w' touch them: *
19:27 which w' not that I should reign 2309
40 the stones w' immediately cry out.*
22:49 were about him saw what w' follow,
24:28 as though he w' have gone further.
Joh 1:43 Jesus w' go forth into Galilee, *2309
4:10 he w' have given thee living water.
40 him that he w' tarry with them; *
47 besought him that he w' come down,
5:46 Moses, ye w' have believed me:
6: 6 he himself knew what he w' do. 3195
11 of the fishes as much as they w'. 2309
15 w' come and take him by force, 3195
7: 1 for he w' not walk in Jewry, 2309
44 some of them w' have taken him;
8:39 ye w' do the works of Abraham.
42 God were your Father, ye w' love me:

Ps 90: 7 and by thy w' are we troubled. 2534
9 days are passed away in thy w': 5678
11 according to thy fear, so is thy w'. "
95: 11 Unto whom I sware in my w' that 639
102: 10 of thine indignation and thy w': 7110
106: 23 to turn away his w', lest he should 2534
40 the w' of the Lord kindleth against 639
110: 5 through kings in the day of his w'. "
124: 3 their w' was kindled against us: "
138: 7 against the w' of mine enemies, "
Pr 11: 4 Riches profit not in the day of w': 5678
23 expectation of the wicked is w'. "
12: 16 A fool's w' is presently known: *3708
14: 29 He that is slow to w' is of great * 639
35 his w' is against him that causeth 5678
15: 1 A soft answer turneth away w': 2534
16: 14 The w' of a king is as messengers "
19: 12 The king's w' is as the roaring of 2197
19 A man of great w' shall suffer 2534
21: 14 a reward in the bosom strong w'. "
24 name, who dealeth in proud w'. *5678
24: 18 and he turn away his w' from him. 639
27: 3 a fool's w' is heavier than them *3708
4 W' is cruel, and anger is 2534
29: 8 snare: but wise men turn away w'. 639
30: 33 forcing of w' bringeth forth strife. "
Ec 5: 17 he hath much sorrow and w' with 7110
Isa 9: 19 Through the w' of the Lord of 5678
10: 6 against the people of my w' will I "
13: 9 cruel both with w' and fierce anger, "
13 in the w' of the Lord of hosts, and "
14: 6 He who smote the people in w' "
16: 6 and his pride, and his w': "
54: 8 In a little w' I hid my face from 7110
60: 10 in my w' I smote thee, but in my "
Jer 7: 29 forsaken the generation of his w'. 5678
10: 10 at his w' the earth shall tremble, 7110
18: 20 to turn away thy w' from them. †2534
21: 5 and in fury, and in great w'. ‡7110
32: 37 and in my fury, and in great w'; ‡ "
44: 8 me unto w' with the works *3707
48: 30 I know his w', saith the Lord; 5678
50: 13 Because of the w' of the Lord it 7110
La 2: 2 down in his w' the strong holds 5678
3: 1 seen affliction by the rod of his w'. "
Eze 7: 12, 14 w' is upon all the multitude 2740
19 in the day of the w' of the Lord: 5678
13: 15 accomplish my w' upon the wall, ‡2534
21: 31 against thee in the fire of my w', 5678
22: 21 blow upon you in the fire of my w', ‡ "
31 them with the fire of my w': "
38: 19 in the fire of my w' have I spoken, "
Ho 5: 10 I will pour out my w' upon them "
13: 11 and took him away in my w'. "
Am 1: 11 and he kept his w' for ever: "
Na 1: 2 and he reserveth w' for his enemies. "
Hab 3: 2 known; in w' remember mercy. 7267
8 was thy w' against the sea, that 5678
Zep 1: 15 That day is a day of w', a day of "
18 them in the day of the Lord's w'; "
Zec 7: 12 came a great w' from the Lord of 7110
8: 14 your fathers provoked me to w', 7107
M't 3: 7 you to flee from the w' to come? 3709
Lu 3: 7 you to flee from the w' to come? "
4: 28 these things, were filled with w'. 2372
21: 23 the land, and w' upon his people. 3709
Joh 3: 36 but the w' of God abideth on him. "
Ac 19: 28 these sayings, they were full of w', 2372
Ro 1: 18 For the w' of God is revealed from 3709
2: 5 heart treasurest up unto thyself w' "
5 against the day of w' and "
8 unrighteousness, indignation...w'. "
4: 15 Because the law worketh w': for "
5: 9 be saved from w' through him. "
9: 22 What if God, willing to shew his w', "
22 vessels of w' fitted to destruction: "
12: 19 but rather give place unto w': "
13: 4 to execute w' upon him that doeth "
5 needs be subject, not only for w', "
Ga 5: 20 hatred, variance, emulations, w', *2372
Eph 2: 3 were by nature the children of w', 3709
4: 26 the sun go down upon your w': 3950
31 and w', and anger, and clamour, 2372
5: 6 things cometh the w' of God 3709
6: 4 provoke not your children to w': 3949
Col 3: 6 things' sake the w' of God cometh 3709
8 anger, w', malice, blasphemy, 2372
1Th 1: 10 delivered us from the w' to come. 3709
2: 16 for the w' is come upon them to "
5: 9 God hath not appointed us to w', "
1Ti 2: 8 hands, without w' and doubting. "
Heb 3: 11 So I sware in my w', They shall "
4: 3 As I have sworn in my w', If they "
11: 27 not fearing the w' of the king: 2372
Jas 1: 19 hear, slow to speak, slow to w': 3709
20 For the w' of man worketh not the "
Re 6: 16 and from the w' of the Lamb: "
17 the great day of his w' has come; "
11: 18 were angry, and thy w' is come, "
12: 12 having great w', because he 2372
14: 8 wine of the w' of her fornication. "
10 drink of the wine of the w' of God, "
19 great winepress of the w' of God. "
15: 1 in them is filled up the w' of God. "
7 golden vials full of the w' of God, "
16: 1 pour out the vials of the w' of God "
19 wine of the fierceness of his w'. 3709
18: 3 wine of the w' of her fornication, 2372
19: 15 fierceness and w' of Almighty God. 3709

wrathful See also WROTH.
Ps 69: 24 thy w' anger take hold of them. *2740
Pr 15: 18 A w' man stirreth up strife: but 2534

wraths
2Co 12: 20 debates, envyings, w', strifes, 2372

wreath See also WREATHED; WREATHS.
2Ch 4: 13 rows of pomegranates on each w', *7639

wreathed See also WREATHEN.
La 1: 14 they are w', and come up upon *8276

wreathen See also WREATHED.
Ex 28: 14 of w' work shalt thou make them, 5688
14 fasten the w' chains to the ouches. "
22 the ends of w' work of pure gold. "
24 shalt put the two w' chains of gold "
25 of the two w' chains thou shalt "
39: 15 the ends, of w' work of pure gold. "
17 they put the two w' chains of gold "
18 of the two w' chains they fastened "
2Ki 25: 17 the w' work, and pomegranates *7639
17 had the second pillar with w' work.* "

wreaths
1Ki 7: 17 w' of chain work, for the chapiters 1434
2Ch 4: 12 two w' to cover the two pommels *7639
13 hundred pomegranates on...two w'; * "

wreck See SHIPWRECK.

wrest
Ex 23: 2 after many to w' judgment: 5186
6 shalt not w' the judgment of thy "
De 16: 19 Thou shalt not w' judgment; thou "
Ps 56: 5 Every day they w' my words: 6087
2Pe 3: 16 are unlearned and unstable w', 4761

wrestle See also WRESTLED; WRESTLINGS.
Eph 6: 12 For we w' not against flesh *2076, 3823

wrestled
Ge 30: 8 have I w' with my sister, and I 6617
32: 24 there w' a man with him until the 79
25 was out of joint, as he w' with him. "

wrestlings
Ge 30: 8 With great w' have I wrestled 5319

wretched
Ro 7: 24 O w' man that I am! who shall 5005
Re 3: 17 and knowest not that thou art w', "

wretchedness
Nu 11: 15 sight; and let me not see my w'. 7451

wring See also WRINGED; WRINGING; WRUNG.
Le 1: 15 w' off his head, and burn it on the 4454
5: 8 and w' off his head from his neck, "
Ps 75: 8 of the earth shall w' them out, ‡4680

wringed See also WRUNG.
J'g 6: 38 and w' the dew out of the fleece, 4680

wringing
Pr 30: 33 the w' of the nose bringeth forth 4330

wrinkle See also WRINKLES.
Eph 5: 27 spot, or w', or any such thing; 4512

wrinkles
Job 16: 8 And thou hast filled me with w', 7059

write See also WRITEST; WRITETH; WRITING; WRITTEN; WROTE.
Ex 17: 14 W' this for a memorial in a book, 3789
34: 1 will w' upon these tables the words "
27 unto Moses, W' thou these words: "
Nu 5: 23 priest shall w' these curses in a "
17: 2 w' thou every man's name upon "
3 w' Aaron's name upon the rod of "
De 6: 9 thou shalt w' them upon the posts "
10: 2 I will w' on the tables the words "
11: 20 shalt w' them upon the door posts "
17: 18 he shall w' him a copy of this law "
24: 1, 3 w' her a bill of divorcement, "
27: 3 shalt w' upon them all the words "
8 w' upon the stones all the words "
31: 19 therefore w' ye this song for you, "
2Ch 26: 22 the prophet, the son of Amoz, w'. "
Ezr 5: 10 we might w' the names of the men 3790
Ne 9: 38 make a sure covenant, and w' it; 3789
Es 8: 8 W' ye also for the Jews, as it "
Pr 3: 3 w' them upon the table of thine "
7: 3 w' them upon the table of thine "
Isa 8: 1 and w' in it with a man's pen "
10: 1 that w' grievousness which they "
19 be few, that a child may w' them. "
30: 8 go, w' it before them in a table, "
Jer 22: 30 W' ye this man childless, a man "
30: 2 W' thee all the words that I have "
31: 33 parts, and w' it in their hearts; "
36: 2 w' therein all the words that I have "
17 How didst thou w' all these words "
28 w' in it all the former words that "
Eze 24: 2 man, w' thee the name of the day, "
37: 16 take thee one stick, and w' upon it, "
16 take another stick, and w' upon it, "
43: 11 w' it in their sight, that they may "
Hab 2: 2 W' the vision, and make it plain "
M'r 10: 4 to w' a bill of divorcement, 1125
Lu 1: 3 very first, to w' unto thee in order, "
16: 6 and sit down quickly, and w' fifty. "
7 Take thy bill, and w' fourscore. "
Joh 1: 45 in the law, and the prophets, did w', "
19: 21 W' not, The King of the Jews; "
Ac 15: 20 But that we w' unto them, that 1989
25: 26 I have no certain thing to w' unto 1125
26 had, I might have somewhat to w'. "
1Co 4: 14 I w' not these things to shame you, "
14: 37 that the things that I w' unto you "
2Co 1: 13 we w' none other things unto you, "
2: 9 For to this end also did I w', that I "
9: 1 is superfluous for me to w' to you: "
13: 2 I w' to them which heretofore have* "
10 I w' these things being absent, lest "
Ga 1: 20 the things which I w' unto you, "
Ph'p 3: 1 To w' the same things to you, "
1Th 4: 9 ye need not that I w' unto you: "
5: 1 have no need that I w' unto you. * "
2Th 3: 17 token in every epistle: so I w'. 1125
1Ti 3: 14 These things w' I unto thee, "
Heb 8: 10 mind, and w' them in their hearts: 1924
10: 16 and in their minds will I w' them; "
2Pe 3: 1 beloved, I now w' unto you; 1125
1Jo 1: 4 And these things w' we unto you, "
2: 1 these things w' I unto you, that ye "
7 I w' no new commandment unto "
8 new commandment I w' unto you, "
12 I w' unto you, little children, "
13 I w' unto you, fathers, because ye "
13 I w' unto you, young men, because "
13 I w' unto you, little children, "
2Jo 12 Having many things to w' unto you, "
12 I would not w' with paper and ink: "
3Jo 13 I had many things to w', but I will 1125
13 not with ink and pen w' unto thee: "
Jude 3 to w' unto you of the common "
3 needful for me to w' unto you, "
Re 1: 11 What thou seest, w' in a book, "
19 W' the things which thou hast "
2: 1 angel of the church of Ephesus w'; "
8 angel of the church in Smyrna w'; "
12 of the church in Pergamos w'; "
18 angel of the church in Thyatira w'; "
3: 1 angel of the church in Sardis w'; "
7 of the church in Philadelphia w'; "
12 I will w' upon him the name of my "
12 I will w' upon him my new name.* "
14 the church of the Laodiceans w'; 1125
10: 4 their voices, I was about to w': "
4 thunders uttered, and w' them not. "
14: 13 W', Blessed are the dead which die "
19: 9 W', Blessed are they which are "
21: 5 W': for these words are true "

writer See also WRITER'S.
J'g 5: 14 they that handle the pen of the w'. *5608
Ps 45: 1 my tongue is the pen of a ready w'. "

writer's
Eze 9: 2 with a w' inkhorn by his side: 5608
3 had the w' inkhorn by his side; "

writest
Job 13: 26 thou w' bitter things against me, 3789
Eze 37: 20 sticks whereon thou w' shall be in "

writeth
Ps 87: 6 count, when he w' up the people, 3789

writing See also HANDWRITING; WRITINGS.
Ex 32: 16 the w' was the w' of God, graven 4385
39: 30 pure gold, and wrote upon it a w', "
De 10: 4 according to the first w', the ten "
31: 24 an end of w' the words of this law 3789
1Ch 28: 19 Lord made me understand in w' 3791
2Ch 2: 11 the king of Tyre answered in w', "
21: 12 came a w' to him from Elijah the 4385
35: 4 to the w' of David king of Israel, 3791
4 to the w' of Solomon his son. 4385
36: 22 his kingdom, and put it also in w', "
Ezr 1: 1 his kingdom, and put it also in w', "
4: 7 w' of the letter was written in the 3791
Es 1: 22 every province according to the w' "
3: 12 every province according to the w' "
14 copy of the w' for a commandment "
4: 8 the copy of the w' of the decree "
8: 8 w' which is written in the king's "
9 every province according to the w' "
9 to the Jews according to their w', "
13 copy of the w' for a commandment "
9: 27 two days according to their w', "
Isa 38: 9 w' of Hezekiah king of Judah, 4385
Eze 13: 9 in the w' of the house of Israel, 3791
Da 5: 7 Whosoever shall read this w', 3792
8 but they could not read the w', "
15 that they should read this w', "
16 now if thou canst read the w', "
17 I will read the w' unto the king, "
24 from him; and this w' was written. "
25 And this is the w' that was written, "
6: 8 the decree, and sign the w', "
9 king Darius signed the w' and the "
10 Daniel knew that the w' was signed, "
M't 5: 31 let him give her a w' of divorcement:
19: 7 to give a w' of divorcement, and to 975
Lu 1: 63 And he asked for a w' table, and 4093
Joh 19: 19 And the w' was, Jesus Of Nazareth 1125

writings
Joh 5: 47 if ye believe not his w', how shall 1121

writing-table See WRITING and TABLE.

written
Ex 24: 12 commandments which I have w'; 3789
31: 18 stone, w' with the finger of God. "
32: 15 tables were w' on both their sides; "
15 and on the other were they w'. "
32 out of thy book which thou hast w'. "
Nu 11: 26 they were of them that were w', "
De 9: 10 stone w' with the finger of God; "
10 was w' according to all the words, "
28: 58 this law that are w' in this book, 3789
61 is not w' in the book of this law, "
29: 20 the curses that are w' in this book "
21 covenant that are w' in this book "
27 the curses that are w' in this book: "
30: 10 statutes which are w' in this book "
Jos 1: 8 according to all that is w' therein: "
8: 31 as it is w' in the book of the law of "
34 all that is w' in the book of the law. "
10: 13 not this w' in the book of Jasher? "
23: 6 all that is w' in the book of the law "
2Sa 1: 18 it is w' in the book of Jasher.) "
1Ki 2: 3 as it is w' in the law of Moses, "
11: 41 not w' in the book of the acts of "
14: 19, 29 w' in the book of the chronicles "
15: 7, 23, 31 not w' in the book of the "
16: 5, 14, 20, 27 not w' in the book of the "

1Ki 21:11 as it was w· in the letters which 3789
22:39, 45 w· in the book of the chronicles "
2Ki 1:18 not w· in the book of the chronicles "
8:23 not w· in the book of the chronicles "
10:34 not w· in the book of the chronicles "
12:19 not w· in the book of the chronicles "
13:8, 12 w· in the book of the chronicles "
14:6 which is w· in the book of the law "
15, 18, 28 not w· in the book of the "
15:6, 11, 15, 21, 26, 31, 36 not w· in the book "
16:19 not w· in the book of the chronicles "
20:20 not w· in the book of the chronicles "
21:17, 25 w· in the book of the chronicles "
22:13 all that which is w· concerning us. "
23:3 covenant that were w· in this book. "
21 w· in the book of this covenant. "
24 which were w· in the book of Hilkiah "
28 not w· in the book of the chronicles "
24:5 not w· in the book of the chronicles "
1Ch 4:41 these w· by name came in the days "
9:1 were w· in the book of the kings of "
16:40 that is w· in the law of the Lord. "
29:29 w· in the book of Samuel the seer. "
2Ch 9:29 not w· in the book of Nathan the "
12:15 not w· in the book of Shemaiah the "
13:22 w· in the story of the prophet Iddo. "
16:11 w· in the book of the kings of Judah "
20:34 they are w· in the book of Jehu "
23:18 as it is w· in the law of Moses. "
24:27 are w· in the story of the book "
25:4 w· in the law in the book of Moses. "
26 w· in the book of the kings of Judah "
27:7 w· in the book of the kings of Israel "
28:26 w· in the book of the kings of Judah "
30:5 long time in such sort as it was w·. "
18 passover otherwise than it was w·. "
31:3 as it is w· in the law of the Lord. "
32:32 they are w· in the vision of Isaiah "
33:18 w· in the book of the kings of Israel. "
19 w· among the sayings of the seers. 3789
34:21 do after all that is w· in this book. "
24 the curses that are w· in the book "
31 covenant which are w· in this book. "
35:12 as it is w· in the book of Moses. "
25 they are w· in the lamentations. "
26 was w· in the law of the Lord. "
27 w· in the book of the kings of Israel "
36:8 w· in the book of the kings of Israel "
Ezr 3:2 as it is w· in the law of Moses "
4 feast of tabernacles, as it is w·. "
4:7 letter was w· in the Syrian tongue. "
5:7 was w· thus; Unto Darius the 3790
6:2 a roll, and therein was a record w·: "
18 as it is w· in the book of Moses. 3792
8:34 the weight was w· at that time. 3789
Ne 6:6 Wherein was w·, It is reported "
7:5 at the first, and found w· therein. "
8:14 found w· in the law which the Lord "
15 trees, to make booths, as it is w·. "
10:34 Lord our God, as it is w· in the law: "
36 of our cattle, as it is w· in the law. "
12:23 w· in the book of the chronicles, "
13:1 and therein was found w·, that the "
Es 1:19 w· among the laws of the Persians "
2:23 w· in the book of the chronicles "
3:9 it be w· that they may be destroyed: "
12 w· according to all that Haman had "
12 name of king Ahasuerus was it w·. "
6:2 it was found w·, that Mordecai had "
8:5 let it be w· to reverse the letters "
8 which is w· in the king's name, "
9 w· according to all that Mordecai "
9:23 as Mordecai had w· unto them; "
32 Purim; and it was w· in the book. "
10:2 not w· in the book of the chronicles "
Job 19:23 Oh that my words were now w·! "
31:35 that mine adversary had w· a book. "
Ps 40:7 volume of the book it is w· of me. "
69:28 and not be w· with the righteous. "
102:18 be w· for the generation to come: "
139:16 thy book all my members were w·. "
149:9 upon them the judgment w·: "
Pr 22:20 not I w· to thee excellent things "
Ec 12:10 that which was w· was upright, "
Isa 4:3 one that is w· among the living "
65:6 it is w· before me: I will not keep "
Jer 17:1 sin of Judah is w· with a pen of "
13 from me shall be w· in the earth, "
25:13 even all that is w· in this book, "
36:6 thou hast w· from my mouth, "
29 saying, Why hast thou w· therein, "
45:1 when he had w· these words in a * "
51:60 words that are w· against Babylon. "
Eze 2:10 and it was w· within and without: "
10 there was w· therein lamentations,* "
13:9 neither shall they be w· in the "
Da 5:24 him; and this writing was w·. *7560
25 And this is the writing that was w·.* "
9:11 oath that is w· in the law of Moses 3789
13 As it is w· in the law of Moses, all "
12:1 that shall be found w· in the book. "
Ho 8:12 I have w· to him the great things†‡ "
Mal 3:16 and a book of remembrance was w· "
M't 2:5 for thus it is w· by the prophet, 1125
4:4 It is w·, Man shall not live by "
6 for it is w·, He shall give his angels "
7 It is w· again, Thou shalt not tempt "
10 for it is w·, Thou shalt worship the "
11:10 For this is he, of whom it is w·, "
21:13 It is w·, My house shall be called "
26:24 Son of man goeth as it is w· of him: "
31 it is w·, I will smite the shepherd, "
27:37 up over his head his accusation w·, "
M'r 1:2 As it is w· in the prophets, Behold, "
7:6 it is w·, This people honoureth me "
9:12 how it is w· of the Son of man, that "
M'r 9:13 they listed, as it is w· of him. 1125
11:17 it not w·, My house shall be called "
14:21 indeed goeth, as it is w· of him: "
27 it is w·, I will smite the shepherd, "
15:26 of his accusation was w· over, 1924
Lu 2:23 (As it is w· in the law of the Lord, 1125
3:4 As it is w· in the book of the words "
4:4 It is w·, That man shall not live by "
8 it is w·, Thou shalt worship the "
10 it is w·, He shall give his angels "
17 he found the place where it was w·, "
7:27 This is he, of whom it is w·, Behold, "
10:20 your names are w· in heaven. "
26 What is w· in the law? how readest "
18:31 things that are w· by the prophets "
19:46 It is w·, My house is the house of "
20:17 said, What is this then that is w·, "
21:22 that all things...w· may be fulfilled. "
22:37 that is w· must yet be accomplished "
23:38 a superscription...was w· over him "
24:44 which were w· in the law of Moses, "
46 is w·, and thus it behoved Christ "
Joh 2:17 remembered that it was w·, "
6:31 as it is w·, He gave them bread "
45 It is w· in the prophets, And they "
8:17 It is also w· in your law, that the "
10:34 Is it not w· in your law, I said, Ye "
12:14 young ass, sat thereon; as it is w·, "
16 that these things were w· of him, "
15:25 be fulfilled that is w· in their law, "
19:20 it was w· in Hebrew, and Greek, "
22 What I have w· I have w·. "
20:30 which are not w· in this book: "
31 these are w·, that ye might believe "
21:25 if they should be w· every one, I "
25 the books that should be w·. "
Ac 1:20 it is w· in the book of Psalms, "
7:42 it is w· in the book of the prophets, "
13:29 had fulfilled all that was w· of him, "
33 it is also w· in the second psalm, "
15:15 words of the prophets; as it is w·, "
21:25 we have w· and concluded that *1989
23:5 for it is w·, Thou shalt not speak 1125
24:14 all things which are w· in the law* "
Ro 1:17 as it is w·, The just shall live by "
2:15 work of the law w· in their hearts, 1123
24 Gentiles through you, as it is w·. 1125
3:4 but every man a liar; as it is w·, "
10 it is w·, There is none righteous, "
4:17 As it is w·, I have made thee a "
23 it was not w· for his sake alone, "
8:36 As it is w·, For thy sake we are "
9:13 As it is w·, Jacob have I loved, but "
33 As it is w·, Behold, I lay in Sion a "
10:15 it is w·, How beautiful are the feet "
11:8 (According as it is w·, God hath "
26 as it is w·, There shall come out of "
12:19 for it is w·, Vengeance is mine; "
14:11 For it is w·, As I live, saith the "
15:3 as it is w·, The reproaches of them "
4 For whatsoever things were w· 4270
4 were w· for our learning, that we "
9 as it is w·, For this cause I will 1125
15 I have w· the more boldly unto you* "
21 But as it is w·, To whom he was not "
subscr. W· to the Romans from Corinthus.* "
1Co 1:19 it is w·, I will destroy the wisdom "
31 as it is w·, He that glorieth, "
2:9 But as it is w·, Eye hath not seen, "
3:19 For it is w·, He taketh the wise in "
4:6 of men above that which is w·, "
5:11 w· unto you not to keep company,†‡ "
9:9 For it is w· in the law of Moses, "
10 For our sakes, no doubt, this is w·: "
15 neither have I w· these things, * "
10:7 as it is w·, The people sat down to "
11 they are w· for our admonition, "
14:21 In the law it is w·, With men of "
15:45 so it is w·, The first man Adam was "
54 to pass the saying that is w·, "
subscr. to the Corinthians was w· * "
2Co 3:2 Ye are our epistle w· in our hearts, 1449
3 ministered by us, w· not with ink, "
7 w· and engraven in stones, 1722, 1121
4:13 according as it is w·, I believed, 1125
8:15 As it is w·, He that had gathered "
9:9 (As it is w·, He hath dispersed "
subscr. epistle to the Corinthians was w·* "
Ga 3:10 for it is w·, Cursed is every one "
10 which are w· in the book of the law "
13 for it is w·, Cursed is every one "
4:22 is w·, that Abraham had two sons, "
27 For it is w·, Rejoice, thou barren "
6:11 large a letter I have w· unto you "
subscr. Unto the Galatians w· from Rome.* "
Eph *subscr.* W· from Rome unto...Ephesians* "
Ph'p *subscr.* It was w· to the Philippians * "
Col *subscr.* W· from Rome to the Colossians * "
1Th *subscr.* unto the Thessalonians was w· * "
2Th *subscr.* to the Thessalonians was w· * "
1Ti *subscr.* The first to Timothy was w· from * "
2Ti *subscr.* Ephesians, was w· from Rome, * "
Tit *subscr.* It was w· to Titus, ordained the "
Ph'm 19 I Paul have w· it with mine own "
subscr. W· from Rome to Philemon, by * "
Heb 10:7 volume of the book it is w· of me,) "
12:23 firstborn, which are w· in heaven, * 583
13:22 w· a letter unto you in few words. 1989
subscr. W· to the Hebrews from Italy *1125
1Pe 1:16 Because it is w·, Be ye holy; "
5:12 I have w· briefly, exhorting, and "
2Pe 3:15 given unto him hath w· unto you;* "
1Jo 2:14 I have w· unto you, fathers, "
14 I have w· unto you, young men, "
21 I have not w· unto you because ye "
26 These things have I w· unto you "
1Jo 5:13 These things have I w· unto you 1125
Re 1:3 those things which are w· therein: "
2:17 and in the stone a new name w·, "
5:1 book w· within and on the backside. "
13:8 names are not w· in the book of life "
14:1 Father's name w· in their foreheads. "
17:5 upon her forehead was a name w·, "
8 names...not w· in the book of life "
19:12 had a name w·, that no man knew, "
16 and on his thigh a name w·, "
20:12 things which were w· in the books, "
15 was not found w· in the book of life "
21:12 and names w· thereon, which are 1924
27 are w· in the Lamb's book of life. 1125
22:18 plagues that are w· in this book: "
19 things which are w· in this book. "

wrong See also WRONGED; WRONGETH; WRONGFULLY.
Ge 16:5 unto Abram, My w· be upon thee: 2555
Ex 2:13 he said to him that did the w·, 7563
De 19:16 against him that which is w·; 5627
J'g 11:27 doest me w· to war against me: 7451
1Ch 12:17 there is no w· in mine hands, 2555
16:21 suffered no man to do them w·: 6231
Es 1:16 the queen hath not done w· to the 5753
Job 19:7 Behold, I cry out of w·, but I am 2555
Ps 105:14 suffered no man to do them w·: 6231
Jer 22:3 and do no w·, do no violence 3238
13 and his chambers by w·; *3808, 4941
La 3:59 O Lord, thou hast seen my w·: 5792
Hab 1:4 w· judgment proceedeth. *6127
M't 20:13 Friend, I do thee no w·: didst not 91
Ac 7:24 And seeing one of them suffer w·, "
26 why do ye w· one to another? "
27 he that did his neighbour w· thrust "
18:14 matter of w· or wicked lewdness, 92
25:10 to the Jews have I done no w·, 91
1Co 6:7 Why do ye not rather take w·? why "
8 Nay, ye do w·, and defraud, and that "
2Co 7:12 for his cause that had done the w·, "
12 for his cause that suffered w·, but "
12:13 to you? forgive me this w·. 93
Col 3:25 But he that doeth w· shall receive 91
25 for the w· which he hath done: "

wronged
2Co 7:2 we have w· no man, we have 91
Ph'm 18 If he hath w· thee, or oweth thee "

wrongeth
Pr 8:36 against me w· his own soul: 2554

wrongfully
Job 21:27 which ye w· imagine against me. 2554
Ps 35:19 mine enemies w· rejoice over me: 8267
38:19 that hate me w· are multiplied. "
69:4 being mine enemies w·, are "
119:86 they persecute me w·; help thou "
Eze 22:29 oppressed the stranger w·. 3808, 4941
1Pe 2:19 God endure grief, suffering w·. 95

wrote
Ex 24:4 Moses w· all the words of the 3789
34:28 he w· upon the tables the words of "
39:30 pure gold, and w· upon it a writing, "
Nu 33:2 And Moses w· their goings out "
De 4:13 w· them upon two tables of stone. "
5:22 he w· them in two tables of stone. "
10:4 he w· on the tables, according to "
31:9 Moses w· this law, and delivered it "
22 Moses therefore w· this song the "
Jos 8:32 he w· there upon the stones a copy "
32 which he w· in the presence of the "
24:26 Joshua w· these words in the book "
1Sa 10:25 and w· it in a book, and laid it up "
2Sa 11:14 that David w· a letter to Joab, and "
15 he w· in the letter, saying, Set ye "
1Ki 21:8 So she w· letters in Ahab's name, "
9 And she w· in the letters, saying, "
2Ki 10:1 And Jehu w· letters, and sent to "
6 Then he w· a letter the second time "
17:37 commandment, which he w· for you, "
1Ch 24:6 Levites, w· them before the king, "
2Ch 30:1 w· letters also to Ephraim and "
32:17 w· also letters to rail on the Lord "
Ezr 4:6 w· they unto him an accusation "
7 days of Artaxerxes w· Bishlam, "
8 Shimshai the scribe w· a letter 3790
9 Then w· Rehum the chancellor, and "
Es 8:5 which he w· to destroy the Jews 3789
10 w· in the king Ahasuerus' name, "
9:20 And Mordecai w· these things, and "
29 Mordecai...w· with all authority, "
Jer 36:4 w· from the mouth of Jeremiah "
18 I w· them with ink in the book. "
27 w· at the mouth of Jeremiah, "
32 w·...from the mouth of Jeremiah "
51:60 Jeremiah w· in a book all the evil "
Da 5:5 w· over against the candlestick 3790
5 saw the part of the hand that w·. "
6:25 king Darius w· unto all people, "
7:1 he w· the dream, and told the sum "
M'r 10:5 your heart he w· you this precept. 1125
12:19 Master, Moses w· unto us, If a "
Lu 1:63 and w·, saying, His name is John. "
20:28 Master, Moses w· unto us, If any "
Joh 5:46 have believed me: for he w· of me. "
8:6 with his finger w· on the ground. "
8 down, and w· on the ground. "
19:19 And Pilate w· a title, and put it on "
21:24 these things, and w· these things: "
Ac 15:23 they w· letters by them after this "
18:27 the brethren w·, exhorting the "
23:25 he w· a letter after this manner: "
Ro 16:22 I Tertius, who w· this epistle, * "
1Co 5:9 I w· unto you in an epistle not to "
7:1 the things whereof ye w· unto me: "
2Co 2:3 And I w· this same unto you, lest, "

2Co 2: 4 I *w'* unto you with many tears; 1125
7:12 though I *w'* unto you, I did it not "
Eph 3: 3 (as I *w'* afore in few words, 1270
Ph'm 21 in thy obedience I *w'* unto thee, *1125
2Jo 5 though I *w'* a new commandment "
3Jo 9 I *w'* unto the church: but "

wroth See also WRATHFUL.
Ge 4: 5 And Cain was very *w'*, and his 2734
6 said unto Cain, Why art thou *w'*? "
31: 36 Jacob was *w'*, and chode with "
34: 7 and they were very *w'*, because he "
40: 2 Pharaoh was *w'* against two of his 7107
41: 10 Pharaoh was *w'* with his servants, "
Ex 16: 20 and Moses was *w'* with them. "
Nu 16: 15 And Moses was very *w'*, and said 2734
22 be *w'* with all the congregation? 7107
31: 14 Moses was *w'* with the officers of "
De 1: 34 words, and was *w'*, and sware, "
3: 26 the Lord was *w'* with me for your 5674
9: 19 the Lord was *w'* against you to 7107
Jos 22: 18 he will be *w'* with the whole "
1Sa 18: 8 Saul was very *w'*, and the saying 2734
20: 7 but if he be very *w'*, then be sure "
29: 4 the Philistines were *w'* with him; 7107
2Sa 3: 8 was Abner very *w'* for the words 2734
13: 21 all these things, he was very *w'*. "
22: 8 and shook, because he was *w'*. "
2Ki 5: 11 Naaman was *w'*, and went away, 7107
13: 19 the man of God was *w'* with him, "
2Ch 16: 10 Then Asa was *w'* with the seer, 3707
26: 19 Then Uzziah was *w'*, and had a 2196
19 while he was *w'* with the priests, "
28: 9 of your fathers was *w'* with Judah, 2534
Ne 4: 1 we builded the wall, he was *w'*, 2734
7 be stopped, then they were very *w'*, "
Es 1: 12 therefore was the king very *w'*, 7107
2: 21 were *w'*, and sought to lay hand on "
Ps 18: 7 were shaken, because he was *w'*. 2734
78: 21 the Lord heard this, and was *w'*: 5674
59 When God heard this, he was *w'*, "
62 and was *w'* with his inheritance. "
89: 38 hast been *w'* with thine anointed. "
Isa 28: 21 he shall be *w'* as in the valley of 7264
47: 6 I was *w'* with my people, I have 7107
54: 9 that I would not be *w'* with thee, "
57: 16 ever, neither will I be always *w'*: "
17 of his covetousness was I *w'*, "
17 I hid me, and was *w'*, and he went "
64: 5 thou art *w'*; for we have sinned: "
9 Be not *w'* very sore, O Lord, "
Jer 37: 15 the princes were *w'* with Jeremiah, "
La 5: 22 thou art very *w'* against us. "
M't 2: 16 was exceeding *w'*, and sent forth, 2373
18: 34 his lord was *w'*, and delivered 3710

M't 22: 7 the king heard thereof, he was *w'*: 3710
Re 12: 17 dragon was *w'* with the woman, "

wrought See also WROUGHTEST.
Ge 34: 7 because he had *w'* folly in Israel 6213
Ex 10: 2 what things I have *w'* in Egypt, 5953
27: 16 twined linen, *w'* with needlework:* "
36: 1 Then *w'* Bezaleel and Aholiab, *6213
4 *w'* all the work of the sanctuary, "
8 *w'* the work of the tabernacle "
39: 6 *w'* onyx stones inclosed in ouches "
Le 20: 12 they have *w'* confusion; their blood" "
Nu 23: 23 and of Israel, What hath God *w'*! 6466
31: 51 gold of them, even all *w'* jewels. 4639
De 13: 14 abomination is *w'* among you; 6213
17: 2 hath *w'* wickedness in the sight * "
4 such abomination is *w'* in Israel: "
21: 3 which hath not been *w'* with, 5647
22: 21 she hath *w'* folly in Israel, to play 6213
31: 18 the evils which they shall have *w'*, "
Jos 7: 15 because he hath *w'* folly in Israel. "
J'g 20: 10 folly that they have *w'* in Israel. "
Ru 2: 19 in law with whom she had *w'*, and "
19 with whom I *w'* to day is Boaz. "
1Sa 6: 6 *w'* wonderfully among them, 5953
11: 13 Lord hath *w'* salvation in Israel. 6213
14: 45 *w'* this great salvation in Israel? "
45 for he hath *w'* with God this day. "
19: 5 the Lord *w'* a great salvation for all" "
2Sa 18: 13 I should have *w'* falsehood against* "
23: 10 Lord *w'* a great victory that day; "
12 and the Lord *w'* a great victory. "
1Ki 5: 16 over the people that *w'* in the work." "
7: 14 king Solomon, and *w'* all his work. "
26 was *w'* like the brim of a cup, 4639
9: 23 the people that *w'* in the work. 6213
16: 20 his treason that he *w'*, are they 7194
25 But Omri *w'* evil in the eyes of the*6213
2Ki 3: 2 he *w'* evil in the sight of the Lord;* "
12: 11 that *w'* upon the house of the Lord, "
17: 11 *w'* wicked things to provoke the "
21: 6 he *w'* much wickedness in the "
1Ch 4: 21 house of them that *w'* fine linen, 5656
22: 2 set masons to hew *w'* stones to 1496
2Ch 3: 14 linen, and *w'* cherubims thereon. 5927
21: 6 and he *w'* that which was evil in *6213
24: 12 such as *w'* iron and brass to mend 2790
13 So the workmen *w'*, and the work 6213
31: 20 *w'* that which was good and right "
33: 6 he *w'* much evil in the sight of the "
34: 10 workmen that *w'* in the house of "
13 all that *w'* the work in any manner*" "
Ne 4: 16 half of my servants *w'* in the work, "
17 one of his hands *w'* in the work, "
6: 16 that this work was *w'* of our God. "

Ne 9: 18 and had *w'* great provocations; 6213
26 and they *w'* great provocations. "
Job 12: 9 the hand of the Lord hath *w'* this? "
36: 23 can say, Thou hast *w'* iniquity? 6466
Ps 31: 19 thou hast *w'* for them that trust in "
45: 13 within: her clothing is of *w'* gold.*4865
68: 28 that which thou hast *w'* for us. 6466
78: 43 How he had *w'* his signs in Egypt,*7760
139: 15 curiously *w'* in the lowest parts of 7551
Ec 2: 11 the works that my hands had *w'*, 6213
17 the work that is *w'* under the sun is" "
Isa 26: 12 also hast *w'* all our works in us. 6466
18 we have not *w'* any deliverance in 6213
41: 4 Who hath *w'* and done it, calling 6466
Jer 11: 15 she hath *w'* lewdness with many, 6213
18: 3 he *w'* a work on the wheels. "
Eze 20: 9, 14, 22 *w'* for my name's sake, "
44 *w'* with you for my name's sake, "
29: 20 because they *w'* for me, saith the "
Da 4: 2 the high God hath *w'* toward me. 5648
Jon 1: 11 unto us, for the sea *w'*, and was 1980
13 sea *w'*, and was tempestuous. * "
Zep 2: 3 which have *w'* his judgment; 6466
M't 20: 12 These last have *w'* but one hour, *4160
26: 10 she hath *w'* a good work upon me. 2038
M'r 6: 2 mighty works are *w'* by his hands?1096
14: 6 she hath *w'* a good work on me. 2038
Joh 3: 21 manifest, that they are *w'* in God. "
Ac 5: 12 and wonders *w'* among the people;1096
15: 12 God had *w'* among the Gentiles 4160
18: 3 he abode with them, and *w'*: 2038
19: 11 God *w'* special miracles by the 4160
21: 19 God had *w'* among the Gentiles by "
Ro 7: 8 *w'* in me all manner of 2716
15: 18 which Christ hath not *w'* by me, "
2Co 5: 5 that hath *w'* us for the selfsame "
7: 11 what carefulness it *w'* in you, yea, "
12: 12 signs of an apostle were *w'* among "
Ga 2: 8 (For he that *w'* effectually in 1754
Eph 1: 20 Which he *w'* in Christ, when he "
2Th 3: 8 *w'* with labour and travail night *2038
Heb 11: 33 *w'* righteousness, obtained "
Jas 2: 22 thou how faith *w'* with his works, 4903
1Pe 4: 3 have *w'* the will of the Gentiles, 2716
2Jo 8 not those things which we have *w'*, 2038
Re 19: 20 the false prophet that *w'* miracles 4160

wroughtest
Ru 2: 19 to day? and where *w'* thou? 6213

wrung See also WRINGED.
Le 1: 15 the blood thereof shall be *w'* out *4680
5: 9 rest of the blood shall be *w'* out * "
Ps 73: 10 of a full cup are *w'* out to them. ‡ "
Isa 51: 17 cup of trembling, and *w'* them out.*"

Y.

yard See METEYARD; OLIVEYARD; VINEYARD.

yarn
1Ki 10: 28 out of Egypt, and linen *y'*: *4723
28 received the linen *y'* at a price. * "
2Ch 1: 16 out of Egypt, and linen *y'*: * "
16 received the linen *y'* at a price. * "

ye See in the APPENDIX; also YOU.

yea See also YES.
Ge 3: 1 *Y'*, hath God said, Ye shall 637, 3588
17: 16 *y'*, I will bless her, and she shall be a "
20: 6 *Y'*, I know that thou didst this in 1571
27: 33 him? *y'*, and he shall be blessed. "
Le 25: 35 *y'*, though he be a stranger, or a *
Nu 10: 32 *y'*, it shall be, that what goodness the "
De 33: 3 *Y'*, he loved the people; all his 637
J'g 5: 29 *y'*, she returned answer to herself, "
1Sa 15: 20 *Y'*, I have obeyed the voice of the 834
21: 5 *y'*, though it were sanctified this * 637
24: 11 *y'*, see the skirts of thy robe in my "
2Sa 19: 30 unto the king, *Y'*, let him take all, "
22: 39 *y'*, they are fallen under my feet. "
2Ki 2: 3, 5 *Y'*, I know it; hold...your peace. 1571
16: 3 *y'*, and made his son to pass "
1Ch 16: 21 *y'*, he reproved kings for their sakes. "
Ezr 9: 2 *y'*, the hand of the princes and rulers "
Ne 5: 15 *y'*, even their servants bare rule 1571
16 *Y'*, also I continued in the work "
6: 10 *y'*, in the night will they come to slay "
9: 18 *Y'*, when they had made them a 637
21 *Y'*, forty years didst thou sustain "
Es 5: 12 *Y'*, Esther the queen did let no man "
Job 1: 17 *y'*, and slain the servants with the "
2: 4 *y'*, all that a man hath will he give "
5: 19 *y'*, in seven there shall no evil touch "
6: 10 *y'*, I would harden myself in sorrow: "
27 *Y'*, ye overwhelm the fatherless, 637
29 *y'*, return again, my righteousness is "
9: 10 out; *y'*, and wonders without number. "
11: 15 *y'*, thou shalt be stedfast, and shalt "
18 *y'*, thou shalt dig about thee, and thou "
19 *y'*, many shall make suit unto thee. "
12: 3 *y'*, who knoweth not such things as "
14: 10 *y'*, man giveth up the ghost, and where "
15: 4 *Y'*, thou castest off fear, and 637
6 *y'*, thine own lips testify against thee. "
15 *y'*, the heavens are not clean in his "
18: 5 *Y'*, the light of the wicked shall 1571
19: 18 *Y'*, young children despised me; * "
20: 8 *y'*, he shall be chased away as a "
25 *y'*, the glittering sword cometh out "
21: 7 old, *y'*, are mighty in power? 1571
22: 25 *Y'*, the Almighty shall be thy "
25: 5 *y'*, the stars are not pure in his sight.* "
28: 27 he prepared it, *y'*, and searched it 1571
30: 2 *Y'*, whereto might the strength "

Job 30: 8 of fools, *y'*, children of base men: 1571
9 I their song, *y'*, I am their byword. "
31: 8 *y'*, let my offspring be rooted out. "
11 *y'*, it is an iniquity to be punished "
32: 12 *Y'*, I attended unto you, and, behold, "
33: 14 For God speaketh once, *y'* twice, yet "
22 *Y'*, his soul draweth near unto the "
34: 12 *Y'*, surely God will not do 637
36: 7 *y'*, he doth establish them for ever.* "
40: 5 not answer: *y'*, twice; but I will "
41: 24 *y'*, as hard as a piece of the nether "
Ps 7: 4 (*y'*, I have delivered him that without "
5 *y'*, let him tread down my life upon "
8: 7 *y'*, and the beasts of the field; 1571
16: 6 *y'*, I have a goodly heritage. 637
18: 10 *y'*, he did fly upon the wings of the "
14 *Y'*, he sent out his arrows, and "
48 *y'*, thou liftest me up above those 637
19: 10 than gold, *y'*, than much fine gold: "
25: 3 *Y'*, let none that wait on thee be 1571
27: 6 *y'*, I will sing praises unto the Lord. "
29: 5 *y'*, the Lord breaketh the cedars of "
10 *y'*, the Lord sitteth King for ever. "
31: 9 with grief, *y'*, my soul and my belly. "
35: 10 *y'*, the poor and the needy from him "
15 *y'*, the abjects gathered themselves* "
21 *Y'*, they opened their mouth wide "
37: 10 *y'*, thou shalt diligently consider his "
36 *y'*, I sought him, but he could not "
40: 8 God: *y'*, thy law is within my heart. "
41: 9 *Y'*, mine own familiar friend, 1571
44: 22 *Y'*, for thy sake are we killed all 3588
57: 1 *y'*, in the shadow of thy wings will I "
58: 2 *Y'*, in heart ye work wickedness; ‡ 637
59: 16 *y'*, I will sing aloud of thy mercy "
68: 3 God: *y'*, let them exceedingly rejoice. "
16 *y'*, the Lord will dwell in it for ever. 637
18 for men: *y'*, for the rebellious also, "
72: 11 *Y'*, all kings shall fall down before "
78: 19 *Y'*, they spake against God; they "
38 *y'*, many a time turned he his anger "
41 *Y'*, they turned back and tempted* "
83: 11 Zeeb: *y'*, all their princes as Zebah, "
17 *y'*, let them be put to shame, and "
84: 2 My soul longeth, *y'*, even fainteth 1571
3 *Y'*, the sparrow hath found an "
85: 12 *Y'*, the Lord shall give that which "
90: 17 *y'*, the work of our hands establish "
93: 4 *y'*, than the mighty waves of the sea.* "
94: 23 *y'*, the Lord our God shall cut them* "
102: 13 her, *y'*, the set time, is come. 3588
26 *y'*, all of them shall wax old like a "
105: 12 *y'*, very few, and strangers in it. "
14 *y'*, he reproved kings for their sakes; "
106: 24 *Y'*, they despised the pleasant land, "
37 *Y'*, they sacrificed their sons and "
109: 30 *y'*, I will praise him among the "

Ps 116: 5 righteous; *y'*, our God is merciful. "
118: 11 *y'*, they compassed me about: 1571
119: 34 *y'*, I shall observe it with my...heart. "
103 *y'*, sweeter than honey to my mouth. "
127 above gold; *y'*, above fine gold. "
128: 6 *Y'*, thou shalt see thy children's "
137: 1 *y'*, we wept, when we remembered 1571
138: 5 *Y'*, they shall sing in the ways of the "
139: 12 *Y'*, the darkness hideth not from *1571
144: 15 *y'*, happy is that people, whose God "
Pr 2: 3 *Y'*, if thou criest after knowledge, 3588
9 and equity; *y'*, every good path. "
3: 24 *y'*, thou shalt lie down, and thy sleep "
6: 16 *y'*, seven are an abomination unto "
7: 26 *y'*, many strong men have been slain "
8: 18 *y'*, durable riches and righteousness. "
19 better than gold, *y'*, than fine gold; "
16: 4 *y'*, even the wicked for the day of 1571
22: 10 *y'*, strife and reproach shall cease. "
23: 16 *Y'*, my reins shall rejoice, when thy "
34 *Y'*, thou shalt be as he that lieth "
24: 5 *y'*, a man of knowledge increaseth "
29: 17 *y'*, he shall give delight unto thy soul. "
30: 15 *y'*, four things say not, It is enough: "
18 for me, *y'*, four which I know not: "
29 go well, *y'*, four are comely in going. "
31: 20 *y'*, she reacheth forth her hands to the "
Ec 1: 16 *y'*, my heart had great experience of "
2: 18 *Y'*, I hated all my labour which I had* "
23 *y'*, his heart taketh not rest in the 1571
3: 19 *y'*, they have all one breath; so that "
4: 3 *Y'*, better is he than both they, which "
8 *y'*, he hath neither child nor 1571
8 is also vanity, *y'*, it is a sore travail. "
6: 6 *Y'*, though he live a thousand years 432
7: 18 *y'*, also from this withdraw not 1571
8: 17 *y'* farther; though a wise man "
9: 3 *y'*, also the heart of the sons of men" "
10: 3 *Y'* also, when he that is a fool "
12: 9 *y'*, he gave good heed, and sought out "
Ca 1: 16 art fair, my beloved, *y'*, pleasant: 637
5: 1 *y'*, drink abundantly, O beloved. "
16 most sweet: *y'*, he is altogether lovely "
6: 9 *y'*, the queens and the concubines, "
8: 1 *y'*, I should not be despised. 1571
Isa 1: 15 *y'*, when ye make many prayers, "
5: 10 *Y'*, ten acres of vineyard shall *3588
29 *y'*, they shall roar, and lay hold of the "
14: 8 *Y'*, the fir trees rejoice at thee, 1571
19: 21 *y'*, they shall vow a vow unto the "
24: 16 *y'*, the treacherous dealers have dealt "
26: 8 *Y'*, in the way of thy judgments, 637
9 *y'*, with my spirit within me will I "
11 *y'*, the fire of thine enemies shall "
29: 5 *y'*, it shall be at an instant suddenly. "
30: 33 *y'*, for the king it is prepared; 1571
32: 13 *y'*, upon all the houses of joy in 3588

Isa 40:24 Y', they shall not be planted; 637
24 y', they shall not be sown: "
24 y', their stock shall not take root in "
41:10 y', I will help thee; y', I will uphold "
23 y', do good, or do evil, that we may "
26 y', there is none that sheweth, "
26 y', there is none that declareth, "
26 y', there is none that heareth your "
42:13 he shall cry, y', roar; he shall "
43: 7 formed him; y', I have made him. "
44: 8 y', there is no God; I know not any.
12 y', he is hungry, and his strength 1571
15 y', he kindleth it, and baketh 637
15 y', he maketh a god, and "
16 y', he warmeth himself, and saith, "
19 y', also I have baked bread upon "
45:21 y', let them take counsel together: "
46: 6 they fall down, y', they worship. "
7 y', one shall cry unto him, yet can "
11 y', I have spoken it, I will also bring "
47: 3 y', thy shame shall be seen: I will 1571
48: 8 Y', thou heardest not; y', thou "
8 y', from that time that thine ear "
15 have spoken; y', I have called him: 637
49:15 y', they may forget, yet will I not 1571
55: 1 y', come, buy wine and milk without
56: 9 devour, y', all ye beasts in the forest.
11 y', they are greedy dogs which can
59:15 Y', truth faileth; and he that
60:12 y', these nations shall be utterly
66: 3 Y', they have chosen their own 1571
Jer 2:37 y', thou shalt go forth from him, "
5:28 y', they overpass the deeds of the "
8: 7 Y', the stork in the heaven "
12: 2 them, y', they have taken root: "
2 grow, y', they bring forth fruit: "
6 y', they have called a multitude * "
14: 5 Y', the hind also calved in 3588, "
18 y', both the prophet and the * "
23:11 y', in my house have I found their "
26 y', they are prophets of the deceit of*
27:21 Y', thus saith the Lord of hosts, 3588
31: 3 Y', I have loved thee with an
19 was ashamed, y', even confounded, 1571
32:41 Y', I will rejoice over them to do
46:16 many to fall, y', one fell upon another:
51:44 y', the wall of Babylon shall fall. 1571
La 1: 8 y', she sigheth, and turneth
Eze 6:14 desolate, y', more desolate than the*
16: 6 y', I said unto thee when thou wast in
8 y', I sware unto thee, and entered
9 y', I throughly washed away thy
28 y', thou hast played the harlot with
52 y', be thou confounded also, and 1571
17:10 Y', behold, being planted, shall it
22: 2 y', thou shalt shew her all her *
21 Y', I will gather you, and blow upon
29 y', they have oppressed the stranger
23:36 Aholibah? y', declare unto them *
26:18 y', the isles that are in the sea shall be
28:26 y', they shall dwell with confidence,
32:10 Y', I will make many people amazed
28 Y', thou shalt be broken in the midst*
34: 6 y', my flock was scattered upon all
36:12 Y', I will cause men to walk upon
37:27 y', I will be their God, and they *
39:13 Y', all the people of the land shall
Da 8:11 Y', he magnified himself even to the
9:11 Y', all Israel have transgressed thy
21 Y', whiles I was speaking in prayer,
10:19 be unto thee; be strong, y', be strong.
11:22 y', also the prince of the covenant. 1571
24 y', and he shall forecast his devices
26 Y', they that feed of the portion of
Ho 2:19 y', I will betroth thee unto me in
4: 3 y', the fishes of the sea also shall 1571
7: 9 y', gray hairs are here and there "
8:10 Y', though they have hired among "
9:12 y', woe also to them when I 3588
12: 4 Y', he had power over the angel, and
11 y', their altars are as heaps in the 1571
Joe 1:16 y', joy and gladness from the house of
18 y', the flocks of sheep are made 1571
2: 3 y', and nothing shall escape them. "
19 Y', the Lord will answer and say*
3: 4 Y', and what have ye to do with 1571
Am 8: 6 y', and sell the refuse of the wheat!*
Ob 13 y', thou shouldest not have looked 1571
16 y', they shall drink, and they shall
Jon 3: 8 y', let them turn every one from his
Mic 3: 7 y', they shall all cover their lips;
Na 1: 5 y', the world, and all that dwell
Hab 2: 5 Y' also, because he transgresseth 637
Zep 2: 1 y', gather together, O nation not
Hag 2:19 y', as yet the vine, and the fig tree,
Zec 7:12 Y', they made their hearts as an
8:22 Y', many people and strong nations
10: 7 y', their children shall see it, and be
14: 5 y', ye shall flee, like as ye fled from
21 Y', every pot in Jerusalem and in
Mal 2: 2 y', I have cursed them already, 1571
3:15 y', they that work wickedness are "
15 y', they that tempt God are even "
4: 1 proud, y', and all that do wickedly,
M't 5:37 let your communication be, Y', y'; 3483
9:28 They said unto him, Y', Lord.
11: 9 A prophet? y', I say unto you, and
13:51 They say unto him, Y', Lord.
21:16 Y'; have ye never read, Out of the "
26:60 y', though many false witnesses *2532
Lu 2:35 (Y', a sword shall pierce through 1161
7:26 A prophet? Y', I say unto you, 3483
11:28 Y' rather, blessed are they that 3304
12: 5 hell; y', I say unto you, Fear him. 3483
57 Y', and why even of yourselves judge*
24:22 Y', and certain women also of our *235

Joh 11:27 Y', Lord: I believe that thou art 3483
16: 2 y', the time cometh, that whosoever 235
32 the hour cometh, y', is now come, 2532
21:15, 16 Y', Lord; thou knowest that I 3483
Ac 3:16 y', the faith which is by him hath 2532
24 Y', and all the prophets from 1161
5: 8 And she said, Y', for so much. 3483
7:43 Y', ye took up the tabernacle of *2532
20:34 Y', ye yourselves know, that these 1161
22:27 art thou a Roman? He said, Y'. 3483
Ro 3: 4 y', let God be true, but every man a 1161
31 forbid: y', we establish the law. * 235
14: 4 Y', he shall be holden up: for God "
15:20 Y', so have I strived to preach the "
1Co 1:28 chosen, y', and things which are not,
2:10 things, y', the deep things of God. 2532
4: 3 y', I judge not mine own self. 235
9:16 y', woe is unto me, if I preach not*1161
15:15 Y', and we are found false witnesses"
16: 6 will abide, y', and winter with you, 2228
2Co 1:17 that with me there should be y' y'. 3483
18 toward you was not y' and nay.
19 not y' and nay, but in him was y'. "
20 the promises of God in him are y', "
5:16 y', though we have known Christ*1161
7:11 y', what clearing of yourselves, 235
11 y', what indignation, y', what fear, "
11 y', what vehement desire, "
11 y', what zeal, y', what revenge! "
13 y', and exceedingly the more joyed we*
8: 3 y', and beyond their power they were
Ga 4:17 y', they would exclude you, that ye*235
Ph'p 1:18 do rejoice, y', and will rejoice.
2:17 Y', and if I be offered upon the "
3: 8 Y' doubtless, and I count all "
2Ti 3:12 Y', and all that will live godly in 1161
Ph'm 20 Y', brother, let me have joy of 3483
Heb11:36 y', moreover of bonds and 1161
Jas 2:18 Y', a man may say, Thou hast 235
5:12 your y' be y'; and your nay, nay; 3483
1Pe 5: 5 Y', all of you be subject one to 1161
2Pe 1:13 Y', I think it meet, as long as I am "
3Jo 12 y', and we also bear record; and ye "
Re 14:13 Y', saith the Spirit, that they may 3483

year See also YEAR'S; YEARS.
Ge 7:11 six hundredth y' of Noah's life, 8141
8:13 in the six hundredth and first y', "
14: 4 in the thirteenth y' they rebelled. "
5 fourteenth y' came Chedorlaomer, "
17:21 thee at this set time in the next y'. "
26:12 in the same y' an hundredfold: "
47:17 bread for all their cattle for that y'. "
18 When that y' was ended, they came "
18 they came unto him the second y', "
Ex 12: 2 be the first month of the y' to you. "
5 blemish, a male of the first y': "
13:10 in his season from y' to y'. 3117
23:11 the seventh y' thou shalt let it rest
14 keep a feast unto me in the y'. 8141
16 which is in the end of the y', when "
17 Three times in the y' all thy males "
29 out from before thee in one y'; "
29:38 two lambs of the first y' day by day "
30:10 upon the horns of it once in a y' "
10 once in the y' shall he make "
34:23 Thrice in the y' shall all your "
24 the Lord thy God thrice in the y'. "
40:17 in the first month in the second y', "
Le 9: 3 calf and a lamb, both of the first y', "
12: 6 shall bring a lamb of the first y' "
14:10 one ewe lamb of the first y' without "
16:34 of Israel for all their sins once a y'. "
19:24 in the fourth y' all the fruit thereof "
25 the fifth y' shall ye eat of the fruit "
23:12 lamb without blemish of the first y' "
18 without blemish of the first y', "
19 two lambs of the first y' for a "
41 unto the Lord seven days in the y'. "
25: 4 the seventh y' shall be a sabbath "
5 it is a y' of rest unto the land. "
10 And ye shall hallow the fiftieth y', "
11 A jubile shall that fiftieth y' be "
13 In the y' of this jubile ye shall "
20 What shall we eat the seventh y'? "
21 blessing upon you in the sixth y', "
22 ye shall sow the eight y', and eat "
22 yet of old fruit until the ninth y'; "
28 bought it until the y' of jubile: "
29 within a whole y' after it is sold; "
29 within a full y' may he redeem it. 3117
30 within the space of a full y', 8141
33 shall go out in the y' of jubile: *
40 serve thee unto the y' of jubile: 8141
50 him that bought him from the y' "
50 sold to him unto the y' of jubile "
52 but few years unto the y' of jubile, "
54 he shall go out in the y' of jubile, "
27:17 his field from the y' of jubile, "
18 even unto the y' of the jubile, "
23 even unto the y' of the jubile: "
24 In the y' of the jubile the field shall "
Nu 1: 1 in the second y' after they were "
6:12 bring a lamb of the first y' for a "
14 one he lamb of the first y' without "
14 one ewe lamb of the first y' without "
7:15 one ram, one lamb of the first y', "
17 he goats, five lambs of the first y': "
21 one ram, one lamb of the first y', "
23 he goats, five lambs of the first y': "
27 one ram, one lamb of the first y', "
29 he goats, five lambs of the first y': "
33 one ram, one lamb of the first y', "
35 he goats, five lambs of the first y': "
39 one ram, one lamb of the first y', "
41 he goats, five lambs of the first y': "
45 one ram, one lamb of the first y', "

Nu 7:47 he goats, five lambs of the first y': 8141
51 one ram, one lamb of the first y', "
53 he goats, five lambs of the first y': "
57 one ram, one lamb of the first y', "
59 he goats, five lambs of the first y': "
63 one ram, one lamb of the first y', "
65 he goats, five lambs of the first y': "
69 one ram, one lamb of the first y', "
71 he goats, five lambs of the first y': "
75 one ram, one lamb of the first y', "
77 he goats, five lambs of the first y': "
81 one ram, one lamb of the first y', "
83 he goats, five lambs of the first y': "
87 the lambs of the first y' twelve, "
88 the lambs of the first y' sixty. "
9: 1 of the second y' after they were "
22 month, or a y', that the cloud 3117
10:11 in the second y', that the cloud 8141
14:34 each day for a y', shall ye bear your "
15:27 shall bring a she goat of the first y' "
28: 3 lambs of the first y' without spot "
9 lambs of the first y' without spot, "
11 lambs of the first y' without spot; "
14 throughout the months of the y'. "
19 and seven lambs of the first y': "
27 ram, seven lambs of the first y'; "
29: 2 seven lambs of the first y' without "
8 and seven lambs of the first y'; "
13 and fourteen lambs of the first y'; "
17, 20, 23, 26, 29, 32 fourteen lambs of
the first y' without 8141
36 seven lambs of the first y' without "
33:38 the fortieth y' after the children "
De 1: 3 it came to pass in the fortieth y', "
11:12 from the beginning of the y' "
12 even unto the end of the y'. "
14:22 the field bringeth forth y' by y'. "
28 tithe of thine increase the same y', "
15: 9 The seventh y', the y' of release, "
12 the seventh y' thou shalt let him go "
20 before the Lord thy God y' by y' "
16:16 Three times in a y' shall all thy "
24: 5 but he shall be free at home one y', "
26:12 tithes of thine increase the third y', "
12 which is the y' of tithing, and hast "
31:10 in the solemnity of the y' of release, "
Jos 5:12 fruit of the land of Canaan that y'. "
J'g 10: 8 that y' they vexed and oppressed "
11:40 the Gileadite four days in a y'. "
17:10 ten shekels of silver by the y', 3117
1Sa 1: 7 And as he did so y' by y', when she 8141
2:19 brought it to him from y' to y'. 3117
7:16 he went from y' to y' in circuit to 8141
13: 1 Saul reigned one y'; and when he* "
27: 7 of the Philistines was a full y' "
2Sa 11: 1 after the y' was expired, at the 8141
21: 1 of David three years, y' after y'; "
1Ki 4: 7 each man his month in a y' made "
5:11 gave Solomon to Hiram y' by y'. "
6: 1 and eightieth y' after the children "
1 in the fourth y' of Solomon's reign "
37 In the fourth y' was the foundation "
38 in the eleventh y', in the month "
9:25 three times in a y' did Solomon "
10:14 that came to Solomon in one y' "
25 horses, and mules, a rate y' by y'. "
14:25 in the fifth y' of king Rehoboam, "
15: 1 the eighteenth y' of king Jeroboam "
9 in the twentieth y' of Jeroboam "
25 the second y' of Asa king of Judah, "
28, 33 the third y' of Asa king of Judah "
16: 8 twenty and sixth y' of Asa king "
10, 15 twenty and seventh y' of Asa king "
23 thirty and first y' of Asa king of "
29 thirty and eighth y' of Asa king of "
18: 1 Lord came to Elijah in the third y', "
20:22 at the return of the y' the king "
26 to pass at the return of the y', "
22: 2 And it came to pass in the third y', "
41 the fourth y' of Ahab king of Israel. "
51 the seventeenth y' of Jehoshaphat "
2Ki 1:17 in the second y' of Jehoram the son "
3: 1 the eighteenth y' of Jehoshaphat "
8:16 fifth y' of Joram the son of Ahab "
25 twelfth y' of Joram the son of Ahab "
26 he reigned one y' in Jerusalem. "
9:29 the eleventh y' of Joram the son of "
11: 4 the seventh y' Jehoiada sent and "
12: 1 In the seventh y' of Jehu Jehoash "
6 three and twentieth y' of...Jehoash "
13: 1 three and twentieth y' of Joash "
10 thirty and seventh y' of Joash king "
20 the land at the coming in of the y'. "
14: 1 second y' of Joash son of Jehoahaz "
23 fifteenth y' of Amaziah the son of "
15: 1 twenty and seventh y' of Jeroboam "
8 thirty and eighth y' of Azariah king "
13 nine and thirtieth y' of Uzziah "
17 nine and thirtieth y' of Azariah "
23 fiftieth y' of Azariah king of Judah "
27 two and fiftieth y' of Azariah king "
30 twentieth y' of Jotham the son of "
32 the second y' of Pekah the son of "
16: 1 seventeenth y' of Pekah the son of "
17: 1 twelfth y' of Ahaz king of Judah "
4 of Assyria, as he had done y' by y': "
6 the ninth y' of Hoshea the king of "
18: 1 to pass in the third y' of Hoshea "
9 the fourth y' of king Hezekiah, "
9 which was the seventh y' of Hoshea "
10 even in the sixth y' of Hezekiah, "
10 that is the ninth y' of Hoshea king "
13 the fourteenth y' of king Hezekiah "
19:29 eat this y' such things as grow "
29 the second y' that which springeth "
29 in the third y' sow ye, and reap,

2Ki 22: 3 in the eighteenth y' of king Josiah, 8141
23:23 in the eighteenth y' of king Josiah, "
24:12 him in the eighth y' of his reign. "
25: 1 to pass in the ninth y' of his reign, "
2 the eleventh y' of king Hezekiah. "
8 which is the nineteenth y' of king "
27 and thirtieth y' of the captivity "
27 in the y' that he began to reign "
1Ch 20: 1 pass, that after the y' was expired, "
26:31 fortieth y' of the reign of David "
27: 1 throughout all the months of the y'. "
2Ch 3: 2 month, in the fourth y' of his reign. "
8:13 solemn feasts, three times in the y', "
9:13 that came to Solomon in one y' "
24 horses, and mules, a rate y' by y'. "
12: 2 in the fifth y' of king Rehoboam "
13: 1 the eighteenth y' of king Jeroboam "
15:10 the fifteenth y' of the reign of Asa. "
19 thirtieth y' of the reign of Asa. "
16: 1 and thirtieth y' of the reign of Asa "
12 Asa in the thirty and ninth y' of his "
13 the one and fortieth y' of his reign. "
17: 7 third y' of his reign he sent to his "
22: 2 he reigned one y' in Jerusalem. "
23: 1 And in the seventh y' Jehoiada "
24: 5 the house of your God from y' to y', "
23 it came to pass at the end of the y', "
27: 5 the same y' an hundred talents of "
5 pay unto him, both the second y', "
29: 3 He in the first y' of his reign, "
34: 3 For in the eighth y' of his reign, "
3 in the twelfth y' he began to purge "
8 in the eighteenth y' of his reign, "
35:19 In the eighteenth y' of the reign of "
36:10 when the y' was expired, king "
22 the first y' of Cyrus king of Persia, "
Ezr 1: 1 the first y' of Cyrus king of Persia, "
3: 8 in the second y' of their coming "
4:24 unto the second y' of the reign 8140
5:13 in the first y' of Cyrus the king of "
6: 3 In the first y' of Cyrus the king "
15 the sixth y' of the reign of Darius "
7: 7 in the seventh y' of Artaxerxes 8141
8 was in the seventh y' of the king. "
Ne 1: 1 month Chisleu, in the twentieth y', "
2: 1 the twentieth y' of Artaxerxes the "
5:14 the twentieth y' even unto the two "
14 two and thirtieth y' of Artaxerxes "
10:31 we would leave the seventh y', "
34 at times appointed y' by y', to burn "
35 of all fruit of all trees, y' by y', "
13: 6 two and thirtieth y' of Artaxerxes "
Es 1: 3 In the third y' of his reign, he made "
2:16 in the seventh y' of his reign. "
3: 7 in the twelfth y' of king Ahasuerus, "
9:27 to their appointed time every y'; "
Job 3: 6 be joined unto the days of the y', "
Ps 65:11 crownest the y' with thy goodness; "
Isa 6: 1 In the y' that king Uzziah died I "
14:28 In the y' that king Ahaz died was "
20: 1 y' that Tartan came unto Ashdod, "
21:16 Within a y', according to the years "
29: 1 add ye y' to y'; let them kill "
34: 8 and the y' of recompences for the "
36: 1 the fourteenth y' of king Hezekiah, "
37:30 Ye shall eat this y' such as groweth "
30 the second y' that which springeth "
30 in the third y' sow ye, and reap, "
61: 2 the acceptable y' of the Lord, "
63: 4 and the y' of my redeemed is come. "
Jer 1: 2 in the thirteenth y' of his reign. "
3 end of the eleventh y' of Zedekiah "
11:23 even the y' of their visitation. "
17: 8 not be careful in the y' of drought, "
23:12 even the y' of their visitation, said "
25: 1 fourth y' of Jehoiakim the son of "
1 was the first y' of Nebuchadrezzar "
3 thirteenth y' of Josiah the son of "
3 that is the three and twentieth y', "
28: 1 And it came to pass the same y', "
1 in the fourth y', and in the fifth "
16 this y' thou shalt die, because thou "
17 the prophet died the same y' "
32: 1 in the tenth y' of Zedekiah king of "
1 eighteenth y' of Nebuchadrezzar "
36: 1 pass in the fourth y' of Jehoiakim "
9 to pass in the fifth y' of Jehoiakim "
39: 1 In the ninth y' of Zedekiah king of "
2 And in the eleventh y' of Zedekiah, "
45: 1 in the fourth y' of Jehoiakim the "
46: 2 smote in the fourth y' of Jehoiakim "
48:44 Moab, the y' of their visitation, "
51:46 a rumour shall both come one y', "
46 in another y' shall come a rumour, "
59 in the fourth y' of his reign. "
52: 4 to pass in the ninth y' of his reign, "
5 the eleventh y' of king Zedekiah. "
12 the nineteenth y' of Nebuchadrezzar "
28 the seventh y' three thousand Jews "
29 eighteenth y' of Nebuchadrezzar "
30 and twentieth y' of Nebuchadrezzar "
31 and thirtieth y' of the captivity "
31 in the first y' of his reign lifted up "
Eze 1: 1 it came to pass in the thirtieth y', "
2 the fifth y' of king Jehoiachin's "
4: 6 appointed thee each day for a y'. "
8: 1 it came to pass in the sixth y', "
20: 1 it came to pass in the seventh y', "
24: 1 in the ninth y', in the tenth month, "
26: 1 came to pass in the eleventh y', "
29: 1 In the tenth y', in the tenth month, "
17 pass in the seven and twentieth y', "
30:20 it came to pass in the eleventh y', "
31: 1 it came to pass in the eleventh y', "
32: 1 it came to pass in the twelfth y', "
17 came to pass also in the twelfth y', "

Eze 33:21 in the twelfth y' of our captivity, 8141
40: 1 and twentieth y' of our captivity, "
1 in the beginning of the y', in the "
1 fourteenth y' after that the city "
46:13 of a lamb of the first y' without "
17 it shall be his to the y' of liberty; "
Da 1: 1 third y' of the reign of Jehoiakim "
21 even unto the first y' of king Cyrus. "
2: 1 in the second y' of the reign of "
7: 1 In the first y' of Belshazzar king 8140
8: 1 In the third y' of the reign of king 8141
9: 1 In the first y' of Darius the son of "
2 In the first y' of his reign I Daniel "
10: 1 the third y' of Cyrus king of Persia "
11: 1 I in the first y' of Darius the Mede, "
Mic 6: 6 offerings, with calves of a y' old? "
Hag 1: 1 the second y' of Darius the king, "
15 the second y' of Darius the king. "
2:10 in the second y' of Darius, came "
Zec 1: 1, 7 in the second y' of Darius, came "
7: 1 pass in the fourth y' of king Darius, "
14:16 even go up from y' to y' to worship "
Lu 2:41 parents went to Jerusalem every y' 2094
3: 1 fifteenth y' of the reign of Tiberius "
4:19 the acceptable y' of the Lord. 1763
13: 8 Lord, let it alone this y' also, till I 2094
Joh 11:49 being the high priest that same y', 1763
51 but being high priest that y', he "
18:13 was the high priest that same y'. "
Ac 11:26 that a whole y' they assembled "
18:11 he continued there a y' and six "
2Co 8:10 but also to be forward a y' ago. 4070
9: 2 Achaia was ready a y' ago; "
Heb 9: 7 the high priest alone once every y', 1763
25 into the holy place every y' with * "
10: 1 they offered y' by y' continually, "
3 again made of sins every y'. * "
Jas 4:13 and continue there a y', and buy "
Re 9:15 and a day, and a month, and a y', "

yearly
Le 25:53 as a y' hired servant shall he be *8141
J'g 11:40 of Israel went y' to lament 3117
21:19 is a feast of the Lord in Shiloh y' * "
1Sa 1: 3 up out of his city y' to worship "
21 offer unto the Lord the y' sacrifice, "
2:19 husband to offer the y' sacrifice. "
20: 6 there is a y' sacrifice there for all "
Ne 10:32 charge ourselves y' with the third 8141
Es 9:21 the fifteenth day of the same, y', "

yearn See also YEARNED.
Ge 43:30 bowels did y' upon his brother: 3648

yearned
1Ki 3:26 for her bowels y' upon her son, 3648

year's
Ex 34:22 feast of ingathering at the y' end. 8141
2Sa 14:26 at every y' end that he polled it: 3117

years
Ge 1:14 for seasons, and for days, and y': 8141
5: 3 lived an hundred and thirty y', "
4 Seth were eight hundred y', "
5 were nine hundred and thirty y': "
6 Seth lived an hundred and five y', "
7 Enos eight hundred and seven y', "
8 were nine hundred and twelve y': "
9 Enos lived ninety y', and begat "
10 eight hundred and fifteen y', "
11 were nine hundred and five y': "
12 Cainan lived seventy y', and begat "
13 eight hundred and forty y', and "
14 were nine hundred and ten y': "
15 Mahalaleel lived sixty and five y', "
16 Jared eight hundred and thirty y', "
17 eight hundred ninety and five y': "
18 lived an hundred sixty and two y', "
19 he begat Enoch eight hundred y', "
20 nine hundred sixty and two y': "
21 Enoch lived sixty and five y', and "
22 Methuselah three hundred y', "
23 three hundred sixty and five y': "
25 an hundred eighty and seven y', "
26 seven hundred eighty and two y', "
27 nine hundred sixty and nine y': "
28 an hundred eighty and two y', "
30 five hundred ninety and five y', "
31 hundred seventy and seven y': "
32 Noah was five hundred y' old: "
6: 3 shall be an hundred and twenty y'. "
7: 6 Noah was six hundred y' old when "
9:28 flood three hundred and fifty y'. "
29 were nine hundred and fifty y': "
11:10 Shem was an hundred y' old, "
10 Arphaxad two y' after the flood: "
11 begat Arphaxad five hundred y', "
12 Arphaxad lived five and thirty y', "
13 Salah four hundred and three y', "
14 Salah lived thirty y', and begat "
15 Eber four hundred and three y', "
16 And Eber lived four and thirty y', "
17 Peleg four hundred and thirty y', "
18 Peleg lived thirty y', and begat "
19 begat Reu two hundred and nine y', "
20 And Reu lived two and thirty y', "
21 Serug two hundred and seven y', "
22 Serug lived thirty y', and begat "
23 he begat Nahor two hundred y', "
24 Nahor lived nine and twenty y', "
25 Terah an hundred and nineteen y', "
26 Terah lived seventy y', and begat "
32 were two hundred and five y': "
12: 4 Abram was seventy and five y' old "
14: 4 Twelve y' they served "
15: 9 Take me an heifer of three y' old, 8027
9 and a she goat of three y' old,

Ge 15: 9 and a ram of three y' old, and a 8027
13 shall afflict them four hundred y'; 8141
16: 3 Abram had dwelt ten y' in the land "
16 Abram was fourscore and six y' old, "
17: 1 Abram was ninety y' old and nine, "
17 unto him that is an hundred y' old? "
17 Sarah, that is ninety y' old, bear? "
24 Abraham was ninety y' old and "
25 his son was thirteen y' old, "
21: 5 Abraham was an hundred y' old, "
23: 1 and seven and twenty y' old: "
1 were the y' of the life of Sarah. "
25: 7 days of the y' of Abraham's life "
7 hundred threescore and fifteen y'. "
8 old age, an old man, and full of y'; "
17 are the y' of the life of Ishmael, 8141
17 hundred and thirty and seven y': "
20 Isaac was forty y' old when he took "
26 Isaac was threescore y' old when "
26:34 Esau was forty y' old when he took "
29:18 will serve thee seven y' for Rachel "
20 Jacob served seven y' for Rachel; "
27 serve with me yet seven other y'. "
30 served with him yet seven other y'. "
31:38 twenty y' have I been with thee; "
41 have I been twenty y' in thy house; "
41 I served thee fourteen y' for thy "
41 six y' for thy cattle: and thou hast "
35:28 were an hundred and fourscore y'. "
37: 2 Joseph, being seventeen y' old, was "
41: 1 to pass at the end of two full y', "
26 The seven good kine are seven y'; "
26 the seven good ears are seven y': "
27 came up after them are seven y'; "
27 wind shall be seven y' of famine. "
29 there come seven y' of great plenty "
30 after them seven y' of famine; "
34 of Egypt in the seven plenteous y'. "
35 food of those good y' that come, "
36 against the seven y' of famine, "
46 Joseph was thirty y' old when he "
47 in the seven plenteous y' the earth "
48 up all the food of the seven y', "
50 sons before the y' of famine came,* "
53 And the seven y' of plenteousness, "
54 seven y' of dearth began to come, "
45: 6 these two y' hath the famine been "
6 and yet there are five y', in which "
11 for yet there are five y' of famine; "
47: 9 days of the y' of my pilgrimage are "
9 are an hundred and thirty y': "
9 the days of the y' of my life been, "
9 of the y' of the life of my fathers "
28 in the land of Egypt seventeen y': "
28 was an hundred forty and seven y'. "
50:22 lived an hundred and ten y'. "
26 being an hundred and ten y' old: "
Ex 6:16 the y' of the life of Levi were an "
16 an hundred thirty and seven y'. "
18 the y' of the life of Kohath were an "
18 an hundred thirty and three y'. "
20 the y' of the life of Amram were an "
20 hundred and thirty and seven y'. "
7: 7 Moses was fourscore y' old, "
7 Aaron fourscore and three y' old, "
12:40 was four hundred and thirty y'. "
41 of the four hundred and thirty y', "
16:35 of Israel did eat manna forty y', "
21: 2 servant, six y' he shall serve: "
23:10 And six y' thou shalt sow thy land, "
30:14 from twenty y' old and above, shall "
38:26 from twenty y' old and upward, "
Le 19:23 three y' shall it be as "
25: 3 Six y' thou shalt sow thy field, "
3 y' thou shalt prune thy vineyard, "
8 number seven sabbaths of y' unto "
8 unto thee, seven times seven y'; "
8 space of the seven sabbaths of y' "
8 be unto thee forty and nine y'. "
15 the number of y' after the jubile "
15 the number of y' of the fruits "
16 According to the multitude of y' "
16 according to the fewness of y' thou "
16 according to the number of the y'* "
21 shall bring forth fruit for three y'. "
27 let him count the y' of the sale "
50 according unto the number of y', "
51 If there be yet many y' behind, "
52 but few y' unto the year of jubile, "
52 according unto his y' shall he give "
54 if he be not redeemed in these y',* "
27: 3 twenty y' old even unto sixty y' old, "
5 five y' old even unto twenty y' old, "
6 a month old even unto five y' old, "
7 if it be from sixty y' old and above; "
18 according to the y' that remain, "
Nu 1: 3 From twenty y' old and upward, "
18, 20, 22, 24, 26, 28, 30, 32, 34, 36, 38,
40, 42, 45 from twenty y' old and 8141
4: 3 thirty y' old...until fifty y' old, "
23 thirty y' old...until fifty y' old, "
30 thirty y' old...unto fifty y' old "
35, 39, 43, 47 thirty y' old...unto fifty y' "
8:24 twenty and five y' old and upward "
25 the age of fifty y' they shall cease "
13:22 Hebron was built seven y' before "
14:29 from twenty y' old and upward, "
33 wander in the wilderness forty y', "
34 even forty y', and ye shall know "
26: 2 from twenty y' old and upward, "
4 from twenty y' old and upward; "
32:11 from twenty y' old and upward, "
13 wander in the wilderness forty y'. "
33:39 and twenty and three y' old "
De 2: 7 these forty y' the Lord thy God "
14 Zered, was thirty and eight y'; "

De 8: 2 thy God led thee these forty y'. 8141
4 did thy foot swell, these forty y'. "
14:28 end of three y' thou shalt bring "
15: 1 end of every seven y' thou shalt "
12 unto thee, and serve thee six y'; "
18 to thee, in serving thee six y': "
29: 5 And I have led you forty y' in the "
31: 2 hundred and twenty y' old this day; "
10 At the end of every seven y', "
32: 7 the y' of many generations: "
34: 7 was an hundred and twenty y' old "
Jos 5: 6 children of Israel walked forty y' "
13: 1 Joshua was old and stricken in y'; "
1 Thou art old and stricken in y', "
14: 7 Forty y' old was I when Moses the "
10 these forty and five y', even since "
10 this day fourscore and five y' old. "
24:29 being an hundred and ten y' old. "
J'g 2: 8 being an hundred and ten y' old. "
3: 8 Chushan-rishathaim eight y'. "
11 And the land had rest forty y'. "
14 the king of Moab eighteen y'. "
30 And the land had rest fourscore y'. "
4: 3 twenty y' he mightily oppressed "
5:31 And the land had rest forty y'. "
6: 1 into the hand of Midian seven y'. "
25 the second bullock of seven y' old, "
8:28 country was in quietness forty y' "
9:22 Abimelech had reigned three y' "
10: 2 judged Israel twenty and three y', "
3 judged Israel twenty and two y'. "
8 eighteen y', all the children of "
11:26 coasts of Arnon, three hundred y'? "
12: 7 And Jephthah judged Israel six y'. "
9 And he judged Israel seven y'. "
11 Israel; and he judged Israel ten y'. "
14 and he judged Israel eight y'. "
13: 1 the hand of the Philistines forty y'. "
15:20 days of the Philistines twenty y'. "
16:31 And he judged Israel twenty y'. "
Ru 1: 4 they dwelled there about ten y'. "
1Sa 4:15 Eli was ninety and eight y' old; "
18 And he had judged Israel forty y'. "
7: 2 time was long; for it was twenty y': "
13: 1 he had reigned two y' over Israel, "
29: 3 with me these days, or these y', "
2Sa 2:10 Saul's son was forty y' old when "
10 over Israel, and reigned two y'. "
11 Judah was seven y' and six "
4: 4 He was five y' old when the tidings "
5: 4 David was thirty y' old when he "
4 to reign, and he reigned forty y'. "
5 he reigned over Judah seven y' and "
5 thirty and three y' over all Israel "
13:23 it came to pass after two full y', "
38 to Geshur, and was there three y'. "
14:28 So Absalom dwelt two full y' in "
15: 7 And it came to pass after forty y', "
19:32 aged man, even fourscore y' old: "
35 I am this day fourscore y' old: "
21: 1 famine in the days of David three y', "
24:13 Shall seven y' of famine come unto "
1Ki 1: 1 David was old and stricken in y': 3117
2:11 reigned over Israel were forty y': 8141
11 seven y' reigned he in Hebron, "
11 thirty and three y' reigned he in "
39 came to pass at the end of three y', "
6:38 So was he seven y' in building it. "
7: 1 building his own house thirteen y', "
9:10 to pass at the end of twenty y', "
10:22 once in three y' came the navy of "
11:42 over all Israel was forty y'. "
14:20 reigned were two and twenty y': "
21 Rehoboam was forty and one y' old "
21 reigned seventeen y' in Jerusalem, "
15: 2 Three y' reigned he in Jerusalem. "
10 And forty and one y' reigned he in "
25 and reigned over Israel two y'. "
33 Israel in Tirzah, twenty and four y'. "
16: 8 reign over Israel in Tirzah, two y'. "
23 to reign over Israel, twelve y': "
23 six y' reigned he in Tirzah. "
29 in Samaria twenty and two y'. "
17: 1 shall not be dew nor rain these y', "
22: 1 they continued three y' without war "
42 thirty and five y' old when he "
42 he reigned twenty and five y' in "
51 and reigned two y' over Israel. "
2Ki 3: 1 of Judah, and reigned twelve y'. "
8: 1 also come upon the land seven y'. "
2 land of the Philistines seven y'. "
17 Thirty and two y' old was he when "
17 he reigned eight y' in Jerusalem. "
26 Two and twenty y' old was Ahaziah "
10:36 Samaria was twenty and eight y'. "
11: 3 hid in the house of the Lord six y'. "
21 Seven y' old was Jehoash when he "
12: 1 forty y' reigned he in Jerusalem. "
13: 1 Samaria, and reigned seventeen y'. "
10 Samaria, and reigned sixteen y'. "
14: 2 twenty and five y' old when he "
2 twenty and nine y' in Jerusalem. "
17 Jehoahaz king of Israel fifteen y'. "
21 which was sixteen y' old, and made "
23 and reigned forty and one y'. "
15: 2 Sixteen y' old was he when he "
2 two and fifty y' in Jerusalem. "
17 and reigned ten y' in Samaria. "
23 in Samaria, and reigned two y'. "
27 in Samaria, and reigned twenty y'. "
33 Five and twenty y' old was he when "
33 he reigned sixteen y' in Jerusalem. "
16: 2 Twenty y' old was Ahaz when he "
2 reigned sixteen y' in Jerusalem, "
17: 1 in Samaria over Israel nine y'. "
5 Samaria, and besieged it three y'. "

2Ki 18: 2 Twenty and five y' old was he when 8141
2 twenty and nine y' in Jerusalem. "
10 at the end of three y' they took it: "
20: 6 will add unto thy days fifteen y'; "
21: 1 Manasseh was twelve y' old when "
1 fifty and five y' in Jerusalem. "
19 Amon was twenty and two y' old "
19 he reigned two y' in Jerusalem. "
22: 1 Josiah was eight y' old when he "
1 thirty and one y' in Jerusalem. "
23:31 Jehoahaz was twenty and three y' "
36 Jehoiakim was twenty and five y' "
36 reigned eleven y' in Jerusalem. "
24: 1 became his servant three y': "
8 Jehoiachin was eighteen y' old "
18 Zedekiah was twenty and one y' old "
18 he reigned eleven y' in Jerusalem. "
1Ch 2:21 when he was threescore y' old; "
3: 4 reigned seven y' and six months: "
4 he reigned thirty and three y'. "
23: 3 the age of thirty y' and upward: "
24 the age of twenty y' and upward. "
27 from twenty y' old and above: "
27:23 from twenty y' old and under: "
29:27 he reigned over Israel was forty y'; "
27 seven y' reigned he in Hebron, "
27 and thirty and three y' reigned he "
2Ch 8: 1 to pass at the end of twenty y', "
9:21 every three y' once came the ships "
30 Jerusalem over all Israel forty y'. "
11:17 son of Solomon strong, three y': "
17 three y' they walked in the way of "
12:13 Rehoboam was one and forty y' old "
13 reigned seventeen y' in Jerusalem, "
13: 2 He reigned three y' in Jerusalem. "
14: 1 his days the land was quiet ten y'. "
6 rest, and he had no war in those y'; "
18: 2 after certain y' he went down to "
20:31 he was thirty and five y' old when "
31 he reigned twenty and five y' in "
21: 5 Jehoram was thirty and two y' old "
5 he reigned eight y' in Jerusalem. "
19 of time, after the end of two y', 3117
20 Thirty and two y' old was he "
20 he reigned in Jerusalem eight y', 8141
22: 2 Forty and two y' old was Ahaziah "
12 them hid in the house of God six y': "
24: 1 Joash was seven y' old when he "
1 he reigned forty y' in Jerusalem. "
15 an hundred and thirty y' old was he "
25: 1 Amaziah was twenty and five y' old "
1 he reigned twenty and nine y' in "
5 from twenty y' old and above, "
25 Jehoahaz king of Israel fifteen y'. "
26: 1 Uzziah, who was sixteen y' old, "
3 Sixteen y' old was Uzziah when he "
3 and he reigned fifty and two y' in "
27: 1 Jotham was twenty and five y' old "
1 he reigned sixteen y' in Jerusalem. "
8 He was five and twenty y' old "
8 reigned sixteen y' in Jerusalem. "
28: 1 Ahaz was twenty y' old when he "
1 he reigned sixteen y' in Jerusalem: "
29: 1 when he was five and twenty y' old, "
1 he reigned nine and twenty y' in "
31:16 from three y' old and upward, even "
17 from twenty y' old and upward, "
33: 1 Manasseh was twelve y' old when "
1 and he reigned fifty and five y' in "
21 Amon was two and twenty y' old "
21 and reigned two y' in Jerusalem. "
34: 1 Josiah was eight y' old when he "
1 in Jerusalem one and thirty y'. "
36: 2 Jehoahaz was twenty and three y' "
5 Jehoiakim was twenty and five y' "
5 he reigned eleven y' in Jerusalem: "
9 Jehoiachin was eight y' old when "
11 Zedekiah was one and twenty y' old "
11 reigned eleven y' in Jerusalem. "
21 to fulfill threescore and ten y'. "
Ezr 3: 8 from twenty y' old and upward, "
5:11 was builded these many y' ago, 8140
Ne 5:14 twelve y', I and my brethren have 8141
9:21 forty y' didst thou sustain them in "
30 Yet many y' didst thou forbear "
Job 10: 5 of man? are thy y' as man's days, "
15:20 the number of y' is hidden to the "
16:22 When a few y' are come, then I "
32: 7 and multitude of y' should teach "
36:11 and their y' in pleasures. "
26 number of his y' be searched out. "
42:16 lived Job an hundred and forty y', "
Ps 31:10 with grief, and my y' with sighing: "
61: 6 and his y' as many generations. "
77: 5 days of old, the y' of ancient times. "
10 remember the y' of the right hand "
78:33 in vanity, and their y' in trouble. "
90: 4 For a thousand y' in thy sight are "
9 we spend our y' as a tale that is "
10 The days of our y' are threescore y' "
10 of strength they be fourscore y', "
15 the y' wherein we have seen evil. "
95:10 Forty y' long was I grieved with "
102:24 y' are throughout all generations. "
27 same, and thy y' shall have no end. "
Pr 4:10 and the y' of thy life shall be many. "
5: 9 others, and thy y' unto the cruel: "
9:11 the y' of thy life shall be increased. "
10:27 y' of the wicked shall be shortened "
Ec 6: 3 hundred children, and live many y', "
3 so that the days of his y' be many, "
6 though he live a thousand y' twice "
11: 8 But if a man live many y', and "
12: 1 nor the y' draw nigh, when thou "
Isa 7: 8 within threescore and five y' shall "
15: 5 unto Zoar, an heifer of three y' old: *

Isa 16:14 Within three y', as the y' of an 8141
20: 3 walked naked and barefoot three y' "
21:16 according to the y' of an hireling, "
23:15 Tyre shall be forgotten seventy y', "
15 end of seventy y' shall Tyre sing "
17 to pass after the end of seventy y', "
32:10 days and y' shall ye be troubled, * "
38: 5 I will add unto thy days fifteen y'. "
10 deprived of the residue of my y'. "
15 I shall go softly all my y' in the "
65:20 child shall die an hundred y' old; "
20 the sinner being an hundred y' old "
Jer 25:11 the king of Babylon seventy y'. "
12 when seventy y' are accomplished, "
28: 3 Within two full y' will I bring "
11 within the space of two full y'. "
29:10 after seventy y' be accomplished "
34:14 At the end of seven y' let ye go "
14 when he hath served thee six y', "
48:34 as an heifer of three y' old: *
52: 1 Zedekiah was one and twenty y' 8141
1 he reigned eleven y' in Jerusalem. "
Eze 4: 5 upon thee the y' of their iniquity, "
22: 4 and art come even unto thy y': "
29:11 shall it be inhabited forty y'. "
12 waste shall be desolate forty y': "
13 At the end of forty y' will I gather "
38: 8 in the latter y' thou shalt come "
17 in those days many y' that I would "
39: 9 shall burn them with fire seven y': "
Da 1: 5 so nourishing them three y', that at "
5:31 about threescore and two y' old. 8140
9: 2 by books the number of the y', 8141
2 he would accomplish seventy y' in "
11: 6 and in the end of y' they shall join "
8 continue more y' than the king "
13 come after certain y' with a great "
Joe 2: 2 after it, even to the y' of many "
25 restore to you the y' that the locust "
Am 1: 1 two y' before the earthquake. "
2:10 led you forty y' through the "
4: 4 and your tithes after three y': *3117
5:25 in the wilderness forty y', 8141
Hab 3: 2 thy work in the midst of the y', "
2 in the midst of the y' make known; "
Zec 1:12 these threescore and ten y'? "
7: 3 as I have done these so many y'? "
5 even those seventy y', did ye all "
Mal 3: 4 the days of old, and as in former y'. "
M't 2:16 from two y' old and under, 1332
9:20 with an issue of blood twelve y', 2094
M'r 5:25 had an issue of blood twelve y', "
42 for she was of the age of twelve y'. "
Lu 1: 7 both were now well stricken in y'. 2250
18 and my wife well stricken in y'. "
2:36 had lived with an husband seven y' 2094
37 of about fourscore and four y', "
42 when he was twelve y' old, they "
3:23 began to be about thirty y' of age, "
4:25 shut up three y' and six months, "
8:42 daughter, about twelve y' of age, "
43 having an issue of blood twelve y', "
12:19 much goods laid up for many y'; "
13: 7 these three y' I come seeking fruit "
11 had a spirit of infirmity eighteen y', "
16 hath bound, lo, these eighteen y', "
15:29 Lo, these many y' do I serve thee, "
Joh 2:20 Forty and six y' was this temple in "
5: 5 had an infirmity thirty and eight y'. "
8:57 Thou art not yet fifty y' old, and "
Ac 4:22 the man was above forty y' old, "
7: 6 entreat them evil four hundred y'. "
23 And when he was full forty y' old, 5063
30 And when forty y' were expired, 2094
36 and in the wilderness forty y'. "
42 space of forty y' in the wilderness? "
9:33 which had kept his bed eight y', "
13:18 And about the time of forty y' 5063
20 space of four hundred and fifty y', 2094
21 Benjamin, by the space of forty y'. "
19:10 continued by the space of two y'; "
20:31 the space of three y' I ceased not 5148
24:10 thou hast been of many y' a judge 2094
17 after many y' I came to bring alms "
27 after two y' Porcius Festus came 1333
28:30 Paul dwelt two whole y' in his own "
Ro 4:19 he was about an hundred y' old, 1541
15:23 a great desire these many y' to 2094
2Co 12: 2 in Christ above fourteen y' ago, "
Ga 1:18 Then after three y' I went up to "
2: 1 fourteen y' after I went up again "
3:17 four hundred and thirty y' after, "
4:10 and months, and times, and y'. 1763
1Ti 5: 9 number under threescore y' old, 2094
Heb 1:12 the same, and thy y' shall not fail. "
3: 9 me, and saw my works forty y'. "
17 whom was he grieved forty y'? "
11:24 when he was come to y', *1096,3173
Jas 5:17 earth by the space of three y' and 1763
2Pe 3: 8 is with the Lord as a thousand y', 2094
8 and a thousand y' as one day. "
Re 20: 2 and bound him a thousand y', "
3 the thousand y' should be fulfilled: "
4 reigned with Christ a thousand y'. "
5 until the thousand y' were finished. "
6 shall reign with him a thousand y'. "
7 when the thousand y' are expired, "

years'
2Ki 8: 3 came to pass at the seven y' end. 8141
1Ch 21:12 Either three y' famine; or three "

yell See also YELLED.
Jer 51:38 they shall y' as lions' whelps. *5286

yelled
Jer 2:15 lions roared upon him, and y',5414,6963

yellow
Le 13:30 and there be in it a y' thin hair; 6669
32 and there be in it no y' hair, "
36 the priest shall not seek for y' hair;"
Ps 68:13 and her feathers with y' gold. 3422

yes See also YEA.
M't 17:25 He saith, Y'. And when he was *3483
M'r 7:28 and said unto him, Y', Lord: * "
Ro 3:29 Gentiles? Y', of the Gentiles also:* "
10:18 Y', verily, their sound went into *3304

yesterday
Ex 5:14 task in making brick both y' 8543
1Sa 20:27 to meat, neither y', nor to day? "
2Sa 15:20 Whereas thou camest but y', "
2Ki 9:26 I have seen y' the blood of Naboth, 570
Job 8: 9 (For we are but of y', and know 8543
Ps 90: 4 years in thy sight are but as y' 865
Joh 4:52 Y' at the seventh hour the fever 5504
Ac 7:28 as thou diddest the Egyptian y'? "
Heb 13: 8 Jesus Christ the same y', and to day,"

yesternight
Ge 19:34 Behold, I lay y' with my father: 570
31:29 God of your father spake unto me y'."
42 of my hands, and rebuked thee y'. "

yet
Ge 6: 3 y' his days shall be an hundred and
7: 4 y' seven days, and I will cause it 5750
8:10, 12 And he stayed y' other seven days;
15:16 of the Amorites is not y' full. 5704,2008
18:22 but Abraham stood y' before the 5750
29 And he spake unto him y' again, "
32 and I will speak y' but this once: 389
20:12 And y' indeed she is my sister; *1571
21:26 neither y' heard I of it, but to day. "
25: 6 Isaac his son, while he y' lived,
27:30 Jacob was y' scarce gone out from 389
29: 7 And he said, Lo, it is y' high day, 5750
9 And while he y' spake with them, "
27 serve with me y' seven other years. "
30 with him y' other seven years. "
31:14 Is there y' any portion or "
30 y' wherefore hast...stolen my gods?*
37: 5 and they hated him y' the more. 5750
8 And they hated him y' the more "
9 And he dreamed y' another dream, "
38: 5 And she y' again conceived, and "
40:13, 19 Y' within three days shall "
23 Y' did not the chief butler remember
43: 6 man whether ye had y' a brother? 5750
7 saying, Is your father y' alive? "
27 of whom ye spake? Is he y' alive? 5750
28 is in good health, he is y' alive. "
44: 4 gone out of the city, and not y' far off,
14 house; for he was y' there: 5750
45: 3 am Joseph; doth my father y' live? "
6 y' there are five years, in the which "
11 for y' there are five years of famine;"
26 told him, saying, Joseph is y' alive, "
28 Joseph my son is y' alive: I will go "
46:30 thy face, because thou art y' alive. "
48: 7 when y' there was but a little way* "
Ex 4:18 and see whether they be y' alive. "
5:11 y' not ought of your work shall *3588
18 y' shall ye deliver the tale of bricks.
9:17 y' exaltest thou thyself against 5750
30 ye will not y' fear the Lord God. 2962
34 he sinned y' more, and hardened
10: 7 knowest thou not y' that Egypt is 2962
11: 1 Y' will I bring one plague more 5750
21:22 from her, and y' no mischief follow:
33:12 Y' thou hast said, I know thee by
36: 3 brought y' unto him free offerings5750
Le 5:17 though he wist it not, y' is he guilty,
11: 7 y' he cheweth not the cud; *
21 Y' these may ye eat of every flying 389
13:40 his head, he is bald; y' is he clean.
41 he is forehead bald; y' is he clean.
25:22 eat y' of old fruit until the ninth year;*
51 If there be y' many years behind, 5750
26:18 ye will not y' for all this hearken 5704
24 you y' seven times for your sins. *
44 y' for all that, when they be in the 637
Nu 9:10 y' he shall keep the passover unto
11:33 flesh was y' between their teeth, 5750
22:15 And Balak sent y' again princes, "
20 y' the word which I shall say unto*389
30:16 y' in her youth in her father's house.*
32:14 to augment y' the fierce anger of 5750
15 he will y' again leave them in the "
De 1:32 Y' in this thing ye did not believe the
9:29 Y' they are thy people and thine
12: 9 not as y' come to the rest 5704,6258
14: 8 the hoof, y' cheweth not the cud, *
20: 6 vineyard, and hath not y' eaten of it?*
22:17 and y' these are the tokens of my
29: 4 Y' the Lord hath not given you *
31:27 while I am y' alive with you this 5750
32:52 Y' thou shalt see the land before *3588
Jos 3: 4 Y' there shall be a place between 389
13: 1 there remaineth y' very much land
2 This is the land that y' remaineth:
14:11 As y' I am as strong this day as I 5750
17:12 Y' the children of Manasseh could
13 Y' it came to pass, when the children*
18: 2 had not y' received their inheritance.
J'g 1:35 y' the hand of the house of Joseph
2:10 nor y' the works which he had 1571
17 y' they would not hearken unto
6:24 is y' in Ophrah of the Abi-ezrites. 5750
31 to death whilst it is y' morning:
7: 4 The people are y' too many; 5750
8: 4 with him, faint, y' pursuing them.
20 feared, because he was y' a youth.5750
9: 5 y' Jotham the youngest son of *

J'g 10:13 Y' ye have forsaken me, and served
15: 7 y' will I be avenged of you, *3588,518
17: 4 Y' he restored the money unto his*
19:19 Y' there is both straw and 1571
20:28 Shall I y' again go out to battle 5750
21:14 and y' so they sufficed them not.
Ru 1:11 are there y' any more sons in my 5750
1Sa 3: 6 the Lord called y' again, Samuel. "
7 Samuel did not y' know the Lord, 2962
7 word of the Lord y' revealed unto "
8: 9 y' protest solemnly unto them, *3588
10:22 if the man shall y' come thither. 5750
12:20 y' turn not aside from following 389
13: 7 As for Saul, he was y' in Gilgal, 5750
21 Y' they had a file for the mattocks,
15:30 I have sinned: y' honour me now,
16:11 There remaineth y' the youngest, 5750
18:29 Saul was y' the more afraid of "
20:14 not only while y' I live shew me 5750
23: 4 enquired of the Lord y' again. "
22 Go, I pray you, prepare y', and know "
24:11 y' thou huntest my soul to take it.*
25:29 Y' a man is risen to pursue thee,*
2Sa 1: 9 because my life is y' whole in me. 5750
3:35 to eat meat while it was y' day, "
5:13 were y' sons and daughters born "
22 the Philistines came up y' again, "
6:22 I will y' be more vile than thus, "
7:19 was y' a small thing in thy sight, "
9: 1 there y' any that is left of the house "
3 not y' any of the house of Saul, "
3 Jonathan hath y' a son, which is "
12:18 while the child was y' alive, we
14:14 y' doth he devise means, that his *
18:12 y' would I not put forth mine hand
14 was y' alive in the midst of the oak.
22 the son of Zadok y' again 5750
19:28 y' didst thou set thy servant among
28 What right therefore have I y' to cry
35 servant be y' a burden unto my 5750
21:15 the Philistines had y' war again * "
20 there was y' a battle in Gath, * "
23: 5 y' he hath made with me an 3588
1Ki 1:14 y' talkest there with the king, 5750
22 while she y' talked with the king, "
42 And while he y' spake, behold, "
8:28 Y' have thou respect unto the prayer
47 Y' if they shall bethink themselves
11:17 Egypt; Hadad being y' a little child.
12: 2 Nebat, who was y' in Egypt, heard5750
5 Depart y' for three days, then "
6 Solomon his father while he y' lived,
14: 8 y' thou hast not been as my servant
19:18 Y' I have left me seven thousand in
20: 6 Y' I will send my servants unto *3588
32 And he said, Is he y' alive? he is "
22: 8 There is y' one man, Micaiah the "
43 burn incense y' in the high places.*"
2Ki 3:17 y' that valley shall be filled with water,
4: 6 unto her son, bring me y' a vessel.
6:33 And while he y' talked with them, 5750
8:19 Y' the Lord would not destroy Judah*
22 Y' Edom revolted from under the*
13:23 them from his presence as y'.5704,6258
14: 3 y' not like David his father: 7535
4 as y' the people did sacrifice *5750
17:13 Y' the Lord testified against Israel,
19:30 Judah shall y' again take root *
1Ch 12: 1 while he y' kept himself close 5750
14:13 the Philistines y' again spread "
17:17 y' this was a small thing in thine*
20: 6 y' again there was war at Gath, *5750
26:10 y' his father made him the chief;)
29: 1 hath chosen, is y' young and tender,
2Ch 1:11 neither y' hast asked long life; 1571
6:16 y' so that thy children take heed *7535
26 y' if they pray toward this place, and*
37 Y' if they bethink themselves in the
10: 6 Solomon his father while he y' lived,
13: 6 Y' Jeroboam the son of Nebat,
14: 7 while the land is y' before us; 5750
16: 8 y', because thou didst rely on the
12 y' in his disease he sought not to 1571
18: 7 There is y' one man, by whom we 5750
20:33 as y' the people had not prepared "
24:19 Y' he sent prophets to them, to bring
28:22 trespass y' more against the Lord:
30:18 y' did they eat the passover 3588
32:15 this manner, neither y' believe him:*
16 And his servants spake y' more 5750
33:17 y' unto the Lord their God only. *
34: 3 while he was y' young, he began 5750
Ezr 3: 6 the temple of the Lord was not y' laid.
5:16 in building, and y' it is not finished.
9: 9 y' our God hath not forsaken us in
15 for we remain y' escaped, as it is this*
10: 2 y' now there is hope in Israel
Ne 1: 9 y' will I gather them from thence,
2:16 neither had I as y' told it to 5704,3651
5: 5 Y' now our flesh is as the flesh of our
18 y' for all this required not I the bread
6: 4 Y' they sent unto me four times *
9:19 Y' thou in thy manifold mercies
28 y' when they returned, and cried unto
29 y' they dealt proudly, and hearkened
30 Y' many years didst thou forbear
30 prophets: y' would they not give ear:
13:18 y' ye bring more wrath upon Israel by
26 y' among many nations was there no
Es 2:20 Esther had not y' shewed her
5:13 Y' all this availeth me nothing,
6:14 they were y' talking with him, 5750
8: 3 Esther spake y' again before the
Job 1:16, 17, 18 While he was y' speaking,
3:26 neither was I quiet; y' trouble came.*
5: 7 Y' man is born to trouble, as the *3588

Job 6:10 Then should I y' have comfort; ‡5750
8: 7 y' thy latter end should greatly
12 Whilst it is y' in his greenness, 5750
9:15 righteous, y' would I not answer,
16 y' would I not believe that he had
21 y' would I not know my soul: *
31 Y' shalt thou plunge me in the 227
10: 8 about; y' thou dost destroy me.
15 y' will I not lift up my head.
13:15 he slay me, y' will I trust in him:‡
14: 9 Y' through the scent of water it will
19:26 body, y' in my flesh shall I see God:‡
20: 7 Y' he shall perish for ever like his
14 Y' his meat in his bowels is turned,
21:32 Y' shall he be brought to the grave,
22:18 Y' he filled their houses with good
24:12 y' God layeth not folly to them.
23 y' his eyes are upon their ways. *
29: 5 the Almighty was y' with me, 5750
32: 3 answer, and y' had condemned Job.
33:14 yea twice, y' man perceiveth it not.*
35:14 y' judgment is before him; *
15 anger; y' he knoweth it not in great*
36: 2 have y' to speak on God's behalf. 5750
Ps 2: 6 Y' have I set my king upon my holy
37:10 For y' a little while, and the 5750
25 y' have I not seen the righteous
36 Y' he passed away, and, lo, he was*
40:17 needy; y' the Lord thinketh upon me:
42: 5 I shall y' praise him for the help 5750
8 Y' the Lord will command his
11 for I shall y' praise him, who is 5750
43: 5 for I shall y' praise him, who is "
44:17 y' have we not forgotten thee, neither
49:13 y' their posterity approve their
55:21 than oil, y' were they drawn swords.
68:13 y' shall ye be as the wings of a dove*
71:14 will y' praise thee more and more.
78:17 sinned y' more against him 5750
30 their meat was y' in their mouths, "
56 Y' they tempted and provoked the
90:10 years, y' is their strength labour and
94: 7 Y' they say, The Lord shall not see.*
107:41 Y' setteth he the poor on high from
119:51 y' have I not declined from thy law.
83 smoke; y' do I not forget thy statutes.
109 my hand: y' do I not forget thy law.
110 me: y' I erred not from thy precepts.
141 y' do not I forget thy precepts.
143 me: y' thy commandments are my
157 y' do I not decline from thy
129: 2 y' they have not prevailed 1571
138: 6 y' hath he respect unto the lowly:
139:16 my substance, y' being unperfect;*
16 when as y' there was none of them.
141: 5 for y' my prayer also shall be in *5750
Pr 6:10 Y' a little sleep, a little slumber,
8:26 While as y' he had not made the 5704
9: 9 man, and he will be y' wiser: 5750
11:24 that scattereth, and y' increaseth; "
13: 7 maketh himself rich, y' hath nothing:
7 himself poor, y' hath great riches.
19: 7 words, y' they are wanting to him.*
19 him, y' thou must do it again. 5750
23:35 awake? I will seek it y' again. "
24:33 Y' a little sleep, a little slumber,
27:22 y' will not his foolishness depart from
30:12 y' is not washed from their filthiness.
25 y' they prepare...meat in the summer;
26 y' make they...houses in the rocks;
27 y' go they forth all of them by bands;
31:15 riseth also while it is y' night, 5750
Ec 1: 7 run into the sea; y' the sea is not full;
2: 3 y' acquainting mine heart with
19 y' shall he have rule over all my
21 y' to a man that hath not laboured
4: 2 than the living which are y' alive. 5728
3 both they, which have not y' been, "
8 y' is there no end of all his labour; "
6: 2 y' God giveth him not power to eat
6 twice told, y' hath he seen no good:
7 and y' the appetite is not filled. 1571
7:28 Which y' my soul seeketh, but I *5750
8:12 y' surely I know that it shall be 3588
17 to seek it out, y' he shall not find it;
17 y' shall he not be able to find it.
9:11 neither y' bread to the wise, 1571
11 y' riches to men of understanding, "
11 nor y' favour to men of skill; "
15 y' no man remembered that same
11: 8 y' let him remember the days of *
Isa 6:13 But y' it shall be a tenth, and it 5750
10:22 y' a remnant of them shall return:*
25 For y' a very little while, and the 5750
32 y' shall he remain at Nob that day:*"
14: 1 and will y' choose Israel, and set "
15 Y' thou shalt be brought down to 389
17: 6 Y' gleaning grapes shall be left in it,
26:10 y' will he not learn righteousness:
27:10 Y' the defenced city shall be desolate,*
28: 4 is y' in his hand he eateth it up. 5750
12 refreshing: y' they would not hear.
29: 2 Y' I will distress Ariel, and there*
17 Is it not y' a very little while, and 5750
30:20 y' shall not thy teachers be removed
31: 2 Y' he also is wise, and will bring evil,
42:25 fire round about, y' he knew not;
25 burned him, y' he laid it not to heart.
44: 1 Y' now hear, O Jacob my servant;
11 y' they shall fear, and they shall be
46: 7 y' can he not answer, nor save him
10 the things that are not y' done,
49: 4 y' surely my judgment is with the
5 y' shall I be glorious in the eyes of*
15 may forget, y' will I not forget thee.
53: 4 y' we did esteem him stricken,

Isa 53: 7 afflicted, y' he opened not his mouth:†‡
10 Y' it pleased the Lord to bruise him;
56: 8 Y' will I gather others to him, 5750
57: 10 y' saidst thou not, There is no hope:
58: 2 Y' they seek me daily, and delight to
65: 24 while they are y' speaking, I will 5750
Jer 2: 9 Wherefore I will y' plead with you, "
11 their gods, which are y' no gods?
21 Y' I had planted thee a noble vine,
22 y' thine iniquity is marked before me,
32 y' my people have forgotten me days
35 Y' thou sayest, Because I am
3: 1 y' return again to me, saith the Lord.
8 y' her treacherous sister Judah
10 And y' for all this her treacherous
4: 27 desolate; y' will I not make a full end.
5: 22 themselves, y' can they not prevail;
22 roar, y' can they not pass over it?
28 of the fatherless, y' they prosper;*
7: 26 Y' they hearkened not unto me, nor
9: 20 Y' hear the word of the Lord, 3588
11: 8 Y' they obeyed not, nor inclined their
12: 1 y' let me talk with thee of thy 389
14: 9 y' thou, O Lord, art in the midst of
15 not, y' they say, Sword and famine
15: 1 y' my mind could not be toward this
9 sun is gone down while it is y' day: 5750
10 y' every one of them doth curse me.
18: 23 Y', Lord, thou knowest all their
22: 6 y' surely I will make thee a
24 hand, y' would I pluck thee hence; 3588
23: 21 not sent these prophets, y' they ran:
21 spoken to them, y' they prophesied.
32 y' I sent them not, nor commanded
25: 7 Y' ye have not hearkened unto me,
27: 15 y' they prophesy a lie in my name;*
30: 11 y' will I not make a full end of * 389
31: 5 Thou shalt y' plant vines upon 5750
23 As y' they shall use this speech in "
39 the measuring line shall y' go forth"
32: 33 y' they have not hearkened to receive
33: 1 he was y' shut up in the court 5750
34: 4 Y' hear the word of the Lord, 389
36: 24 Y' they were not afraid, nor rent*
37: 10 y' should they rise up every man in
40: 5 while he was not y' gone back, 5750
44: 28 Y' a small number that escape the*
46: 28 y' will I not leave thee wholly *
48: 47 Y' will I bring again the captivity of
51: 33 y' a little while, and the time of 5750
53 y' from me shall spoilers come
La 3: 32 y' will he have compassion according
4: 17 eyes as y' failed for our vain help: 5750
Eze 2: 5 y' shall know that there hath been a
3: 19 Y' if thou warn the wicked, and he
6: 8 Y' will I leave a remnant, that ye may
7: 13 sold, although they were y' alive: 5750
8: 6 turn thee y' again, and thou shalt "
13 Turn thee y' again, and thou shalt "
15 turn thee y' again, and thou shalt "
18 a loud voice, y' will I not hear them.
11: 16 y' will I be to them as a little
12: 13 y' shall he not see it, though he shall
14: 22 Y', behold, therein shall be left a
15: 5 less shall it be meet y' for any work.
16: 28 and y' couldest not be satisfied.
29 and y' thou wast not satisfied 1571
47 Y' hast thou not walked after their
18: 19 Y' say ye, Why? doth not the son
25 Y' ye say, The way of the Lord is not
29 Y' saith the house of Israel, The way
20: 15 Y' also I lifted up my hand unto *
27 Y' in this your fathers have *5750
23: 19 Y' she multiplied her whoredoms,
44 Y' they went in unto her, as they*
24: 16 y' neither shalt thou mourn nor weep,
26: 21 y' shalt thou never be found again,
28: 2 y' thou art a man, and not God,
9 Wilt thou y' say before him that 559
29: 13 Y' thus saith the Lord God; At *3588
18 y' had he no wages, nor his army,
31: 18 y' shalt thou be brought down with
32: 24, 25 y' have they borne their shame*
33: 17 Y' the children of thy people say,
20 Y' ye say, The way of the Lord is not
36: 37 I will y' for this be enquired of by*5750
44: 11 Y' they shall be ministers in my
Da 4: 23 y' leave the stump of the roots *1297
5: 17 y' I will read the writing unto the* "
7: 12 y' their lives were prolonged for a
9: 13 y' made we not our prayer before the
10: 9 Y' heard I the voice of his words: and
14 for y' the vision is for many days: 5750
11: 2 stand up y' three kings in Persia; "
27 for y' the end shall be at the time "
33 y' they shall fall by the sword, and by
35 it is y' for a time appointed. 5750
45 y' he shall come to his end, and none
Ho 1: 4 for y' a little while, and I will 5750
10 Y' the number of the children of
3: 1 Go y', love a woman beloved of 5750
1 of her friend, y' an adulteress, *
4: 4 Y' let no man strive, nor reprove 389
15 the harlot, y' let not Judah offend;
5: 13 y' could he not heal you, nor cure you*
7: 9 there upon him, y' he knoweth not:*
13 y' they have spoken lies against me.
15 y' do they imagine mischief against
9: 12 their children, y' will I bereave them,
16 y' will I slay even the beloved fruit of
11: 12 but Judah y' ruleth with God, and 5750
12: 8 Y' I am become rich, I have found*389
9 Egypt will y' make thee to dwell 5750
13: 4 Y' I am the Lord thy God from the
Am 2: 9 Y' destroyed I the Amorite before
9 y' I destroyed his fruit from above.

Am 4: 6 y' have ye not returned unto me, saith
7 when there was y' three months 5750
8, 9, 10, 11 y' have ye not returned unto
6: 10 the house, Is there y' any with thee?
9: 9 y' shall not the least grain fall upon
Jon 2: 4 y' I will look again toward thy holy 389
6 y' hast thou brought up my life from
3: 4 Y' forty days, and Nineveh shall 5750
4: 2 when I was y' in my country? 5704
Mic 1: 15 Y' will I bring an heir unto thee, 5750
3: 11 y' will they lean upon the Lord, and
5: 2 y' out of thee shall he come forth unto*
6: 10 Are there y' the treasures of 5750
Na 1: 12 many, y' thus shall they be cut down,*
2: 8 of water: y' they shall flee away.
3: 10 Y' was she carried away, she 1571
Hab 2: 3 vision is y' for an appointed time, 5750
3: 18 Y' I will rejoice in the Lord, I will
Hag 2: 4 Y' now be strong, O Zerubbabel, saith
6 Y' once, it is a little while, and I 5750
17 y' ye turned not to me, saith the Lord.
19 Is the seed y' in the barn? yea, 5750
19 as y' the vine, and the fig tree, *5704
Zec 1: 17 Cry y', saying, Thus saith the 5750
17 through prosperity shall y' be "
17 the Lord shall y' comfort Zion, "
17 and shall y' choose Jerusalem. "
8: 4 shall y' old men and old women "
20 It shall y' come to pass, that there "
11: 15 Take unto thee y' the instruments "
13: 3 that when any shall y' prophesy, "
Mal 1: 2 Y' ye say, Wherein hast thou loved
2 saith the Lord: y' I loved Jacob,
2: 14 Y' ye say, Wherefore? Because the
14 y' is she thy companion, and the wife*
15 Y' had he the residue of the spirit.*
17 Y' ye say, Wherein have we wearied
3: 8 rob God? Y' have ye robbed me.
13 Y' ye say, What have we spoken so
M't 6: 25 y' for your body, what ye shall put
26 y' your heavenly Father feedeth them.*
29 y' I say unto you, That even Solomon
10: 10 coats, neither shoes, nor y' staves:*
12: 46 While he y' talked to the people, 2089
13: 21 Y' hath he not root in himself, but 1161
15: 16 ye also y' without understanding? 188
17 Do ye not y' understand, that *3768
27 y' the dogs eat of the crumbs *1063
16: 9 Do ye not y' understand, neither 3768
17: 5 While he y' spake, behold, a bright 2089
19: 20 from my youth up: what lack I y'? "
24: 6 come to pass, but the end is not y'. 3768
32 When his branch is y' tender, and*2236
26: 33 of thee, y' will I never be offended.*
35 die with thee, y' will I not deny 3364
47 And while he y' spake, lo, Judas, 2089
60 witnesses came, y' found they none.*
27: 63 said, while he was y' alive, 2089
M'r 5: 35 While he y' spake, there came "
6: 26 y' for his oath's sake, and for their*
7: 28 y' the dogs under the table eat *1063
8: 17 perceive ye not y', neither 3768
17 have ye your heart y' hardened? *2089
11: 13 for the time of figs was not y'. *
12: 6 Having y' therefore one son, his 2089
13: 7 be; but the end shall not be y'. 3768
28 When her branch is y' tender, and*2236
14: 29 all shall be offended, y' will not I. 235
43 while he y' spake, cometh Judas, 2089
15: 5 But Jesus y' answered nothing; *3765
Lu 3: 20 Added y' this above all, that he ‡2596
8: 49 While he y' spake, there cometh 2089
9: 42 And as he was y' a coming, the "
11: 8 y' because of his importunity he 1065
12: 27 y' I say unto you, that Solomon in all
14: 22 commanded, and y' there is room. 2089
32 while the other is y' a great way off,"
35 the land, nor y' for the dunghill; *
15: 20 when he was y' a great way off, 2089
29 y' thou never gavest me a kid, that I
18: 5 Y' because this widow troubleth 1065
22 him, Y' lackest thou one thing: 2089
19: 30 colt tied, whereon y' never man sat:
22: 37 written must y' be accomplished *2089
47 And while he y' spake, behold a "
60 while he y' spake, the cock crew. "
23: 15 No, nor y' Herod: for I sent you to
24: 6 you when he was y' in Galilee, 2089
41 while they y' believed not for joy,* "
44 unto you, while I was y' with you, "
Joh 2: 4 thee? mine hour is not y' come. 3768
3: 24 John was not y' cast into prison. "
4: 21 mountain, nor y' at Jerusalem, *
27 y' no man said, What seekest 3305
35 There are y' four months, and 2089
7: 6 unto them, My time is not y' come: 3768
8 I go not up y' unto this feast; ‡ "
8 for my time is not y' full come. "
19 and y' none of you keepeth the law?
30 because his hour was not y' come. 3768
33 Y' a little while am I with you, 2089
39 the Holy Ghost was not y' given; 3768
39 that Jesus was not y' glorified.) 3764
8: 14 record of myself, y' my record is true:*
16 y' if I judge, my judgment is true:*
20 him; for his hour was not y' come. 3768
55 Y' ye have not known him; but I*
57 Thou art not y' fifty years old, and 2532
9: 30 and y' he hath opened mine eyes.
11: 25 though he were dead, y' shall he live:
30 Jesus was not y' come into the 3768
12: 35 Y' a little while is the light with 2089
37 them, y' they believed not on him:
13: 33 y' a little while I am with you. 2089
14: 9 y' hast thou not known me, Philip?*
19 Y' a little while, and the world 2089

Joh 14: 25 unto you, being y' present with you.
16: 12 I have y' many things to say unto 2089
32 y' I am not alone, because the Father
19: 41 wherein was never man y' laid. 3764
20: 1 when it was y' dark, unto the 2089
5 clothes lying; y' went they not in. 3305
9 as y' they knew not the scripture, 3764
17 I am not y' ascended to my Father: 3768
29 have not seen, and y' have believed.
21: 11 so many, y' was not the net broken.*
23 y' Jesus said not unto him, He shall 2532
Ac 7: 5 y' he promised that he would give* "
5 him, when as y' he had no child.
8: 16 as y' he was fallen upon none of 3768
9: 1 y' breathing out threatenings and 2089
10: 44 While Peter y' spake these words, "
13: 27 nor y' the voices of the prophets *
28 y' desired they Pilate that he should
18: 18 this tarried there y' a good while, 2089
19: 37 nor y' blasphemers of your *
22: 3 y' brought up in this city at the feet*
24: 11 there are y' but twelve days since*
25: 8 the temple, nor y' against Cæsar,*
28: 4 y' vengeance suffereth not to live.
17 y' was I delivered prisoner from
Ro 3: 7 why y' am I also judged as a *2089
4: 11 which he had y' being uncircumcised:*
12 which he had being y' uncircumcised.*
19 y' the deadness of Sarah's womb:*
5: 6 we were y' without strength, 2089
7 y' peradventure for a good man *1063
8 while we were y' sinners, Christ 2089
8: 24 man seeth, why doth he y' hope for?*
9: 11 (For the children being not y' born, 3380
19 me, Why doth he y' find fault? *2089
11: 30 y' have now obtained mercy through*
16: 19 y' I would have you wise unto that*1161
1Co 2: 6 y' not the wisdom of this world, nor"
15 y' he himself is judged of no man.* "
3: 2 bear it, neither y' now are ye able.*2089
3 For ye are y' carnal: for whereas
15 shall be saved; y' so as by fire. 1161
4: 4 y' am I not hereby justified: but he 235
15 Christ, y' have ye not many fathers: "
5: 10 Y' not altogether with the *2532
7: 10 y' not I, but the Lord, Let not the wife*
25 y' I give my judgment, as one that*1161
8: 2 knoweth nothing y' as he ought 3764
9: 2 others, y' doubtless I am to you: 235
19 y' have I made myself servant unto*
12: 20 many members, y' but one body. *1161
31 and y' shew I unto you a more †‡2089
14: 19 Y' in the church I had rather * 235
21 y' for all that will they not hear me,*
15: 10 y' not I, but the grace of God which 1161
17 is vain; ye are y' in your sins. 2089
2Co 1: 10 we trust that he will y' deliver us;* "
23 you I came not as y' unto Corinth. 3765
4: 8 on every side, y' not distressed; 235
16 y' the inward man is renewed day "
5: 16 y' now henceforth know we him "
6: 8 good report: as deceivers, and y' true;
9 As unknown, and y' well known;
10 As sorrowful, y' alway rejoicing; 1161
10 as poor, y' making many rich; "
10 nothing, and y' possessing all things.
8: 9 y' for your sakes he became poor,
9: 3 Y' have I sent the brethren, lest 1161
11: 6 in speech, y' not in knowledge; 235
16 y' as a fool receive me, that I may 2579
12: 5 y' of myself I will not glory, but in*1161
13: 4 y' he liveth by the power of God. 235
Ga 1: 10 for if I y' pleased men, I should *2089
2: 20 y' not I, but Christ liveth in me: †‡3765
3: 4 things in vain? if it be y' in vain. *2596
15 y' if it be confirmed, no man
5: 11 if I y' preach circumcision, *2089
11 why do I y' suffer persecution? * "
Eph 5: 29 no man ever y' hated his own flesh;*
Ph'p 1: 9 love may abound y' more and 2089
22 y' what I shall choose I wot not. 2532
Col 1: 21 works, y' now hath he reconciled 1161
2: 5 y' am I with you in the spirit, 235
1Th 2: 6 nor y' of others, when we might have*
2Th 2: 5 when I was y' with you, I told you 2089
3: 15 Y' count him not as an enemy, but 2532
2Ti 2: 5 for masteries, y' is he not crowned,*
13 we believe not, y' he abideth faithful:*
Ph'm 9 Y' for love's sake I rather beseech
Heb 2: 8 not y' all things put under him. 3768
4: 15 tempted like as we are, y' without sin.
5: 8 y' learned he obedience by the things
7: 10 he was y' in the loins of his father, 2089
15 And it is y' far more evident: "
9: 8 of all was not y' made manifest, "
8 first tabernacle was y' standing: 2089
25 Nor y' that he should offer himself
10: 37 For y' a little while, and he that 2089
11: 4 by it he being dead y' speaketh. "
7 of God of things not seen as y', 3369
12: 4 Ye have not y' resisted unto blood, 3768
26 Y' once more I shake not the 2089
27 word, Y' once more, signifieth the "
Jas 2: 10 y' offend in one point, he is guilty of
11 commit no adultery, y' if thou kill, *1161
3: 4 y' are they turned about with a very
4: 2 y' ye have not, because ye ask not.*1161
1Pe 1: 8 now ye see him not, y' believing,
4: 16 Y' if any man suffer as a Christian,*"
1Jo 3: 2 not y' appear what we shall be: 3768
Jude 9 Y' Michael the archangel, when *1161
Re 6: 11 should rest y' for a little season, 2089
8: 13 angels, which are y' to sound. 3195
9: 20 by these plagues y' repented not *
17: 10 one is, and the other is not y' come: 3768
12 have received no kingdom as y'; "

yield See also YIELDED; YIELDETH; YIELDING.
Ge 4:12 not henceforth y' unto thee fruits. 5414
49:20 fat, and he shall y' royal dainties. "
Le 19:25 it may y' unto you the increase 3254
25:19 And the land shall y' her fruit, 5414
26: 4 and the land shall y' her increase, "
4 trees of the field shall y' their fruit. "
20 your land shall not y' her increase, "
20 the trees of the land y' their fruits. "
De 11:17 and that the land y' not her fruit; "
2Ch 30: 8 y' yourselves unto the Lord, 5414,3027
Ps 67: 6 shall the earth y' her increase; *5414
85:12 and our land shall y' her increase. "
107:37 which may y' fruits of increase. *6213
Pr 7:21 fair speech she caused him to y'. 5186
Isa 5:10 of vineyard shall y' one bath, 6213
10 seed of an homer shall y' an ephah. "
Eze 34:27 tree of the field shall y' her fruit, 5414
27 and the earth shall y' her increase, "
36: 8 and y' your fruit to my people of 5375
Ho 8: 7 stalk: the bud shall y' no meal: 6213
7 if so be it y', the strangers shall "
Joe 2:22 and the vine do y' their strength. 5414
Hab 3:17 fail, and the field shall y' no meat; 6213
M'r 4: 8 and did y' fruit that sprang up *1325
Ac 23:21 But do not thou y' unto them: 3982
Ro 6:13 Neither y' ye your members as *3936
13 but y' yourselves unto God, as * "
16 ye y' yourselves servants to obey,* "
19 so now y' your members servants* "
Jas 3:12 no fountain both y' salt water and 4160

yielded
Ge 49:33 y' up the ghost, and was gathered 1478
Nu 17: 8 blossoms, and y' almonds. 1580
Da 3:28 king's word, and y' their bodies, 3052
M't 27:50 with a loud voice, y' up the ghost. 863
M'r 4: 7 and choked it, and it y' no fruit. 1325
Ac 5:10 at his feet, and y' up the ghost: *1634
Ro 6:19 have y' your members servants *3936
Re 22: 2 and y' her fruit every month: * 591

yieldeth
Ne 9:37 it y' much increase unto the kings 7235
Job 24: 5 the wilderness y' food for them and
Pr 12:12 the root of the righteous y' fruit. 5414
Heb 12:11 afterward it y' the peaceable fruit 591

yielding
Ge 1:11 forth grass, the herb y' seed, 2232
11 fruit tree y' fruit after his kind, *6213
12 and herb y' seed after his kind, 2232
12 and the tree y' fruit, whose seed *6213
29 is the fruit of a tree y' seed; 2232
Ec 10: 4 for y' pacifieth great offences. 4832
Jer 17: 8 neither shall cease from y' fruit. 6213

yoke See also YOKED; YOKEFELLOW; YOKES.
Ge 27:40 break his y' from off thy neck. 5923
Le 26:13 I have broken the bands of your y', "
Nu 19: 2 and upon which never came y': "
De 21: 3 which hath not drawn in the y'; "
28:48 shall put a y' of iron upon thy neck, "
1Sa 6: 7 on which there hath come no y', "
11: 7 And he took a y' of oxen, and 6776
14:14 which a y' of oxen might plow * "
1Ki 12: 4 Thy father made our y' grievous: 5923
4 his heavy y' which he put upon us, "
9 y' which thy father did put upon us? "
10 Thy father made our y' heavy, but "
11 father did lade you with a heavy y', "
11 I will add to your y': my father "
14 My father made your y' heavy, and "
14 and I will add to your y': my "
19:19 plowing with twelve y' of oxen 6776
21 took a y' of oxen, and slew them, "
2Ch 10: 4 Thy father made our y' grievous: 5923
4 his heavy y' that he put upon us, "
9 y' that thy father did put upon us? "
10 Thy father made our y' heavy, "
11 my father put a heavy y' upon you, "
11 will put more to your y': my father "
14 My father made your y' heavy, "
Job 1: 3 and five hundred y' of oxen, 6776
42:12 and a thousand y' of oxen, and a "
Isa 9: 4 hast broken the y' of his burden, 5923
10:27 and his y' from off thy neck, "
27 and the y' shall be destroyed "
14:25 shall his y' depart from off them, "
47: 6 hast thou very heavily laid thy y'. "
58: 6 free, and that ye brake every y'? 4133
9 away from the midst of thee the y', "
Jer 2:20 of old time I have broken thy y', 5923
5: 5 have altogether broken the y', "
27: 8, 11, 12 the y' of the king of Babylon, "
28: 2 the y' of the king of Babylon. "
4 brake the y' of the king of Babylon. "
10 took the y' from off the prophet *4133
11 I break the y' of Nebuchadnezzar 5923
12 the prophet had broken the y' *4133
14 a y' of iron upon the neck of all 5923
30: 8 break his y' from off thy neck, "
31:18 as a bullock unaccustomed to the y': "
51:23 husbandman and his y' of oxen; 6776
La 1:14 The y' of my transgressions is 5923
3:27 that he bear the y' in his youth. "
Eze 34:27 have broken the bands of their y', "
Ho 11: 4 that take off the y' on their jaws, "
Na 1:13 will I break his y' from off thee, 4132
M't 11:29 Take my y' upon you, and learn of 2218
30 For my y' is easy, and my burden "
Lu 14:19 I have bought five y' of oxen, 2201
Ac 15:10 y' upon the neck of the disciples, 2218
Ga 5: 1 again with the y' of bondage. "
1Ti 6: 1 many servants as are under the y' "

yoked
2Co 6:14 y' together with unbelievers: 2086

yokefellow
Ph'p 4: 3 true y', help those women which 4805

yokes
Jer 27: 2 Make thee bonds and y', and put *4133
28:13 Thou hast broken the y' of wood;* "
13 shalt make for them y' of iron. * "
Eze 30:18 shall break there the y' of Egypt: "

yonder
Ge 22: 5 lad will go y' and worship. 5704,3541
Nu 16:37 and scatter thou the fire y'; 1973
23:15 offering, while I meet the Lord y'. 3541
32:19 inherit with them on y' side Jordan, 5676
2Ki 4:25 Behold, y' is that Shunammite:
M't 17:20 Remove hence to y' place; 1563
26:36 Sit ye here, while I go and pray y'. "

you See in the APPENDIX; also YOUR; YOUWARD.

young See also YOUNGER; YOUNGEST.
Ge 4:23 and a y' man to my hurt. 3206
14:24 which the y' men have eaten, 5288
15: 9 and a turtledove, and a y' pigeon. 1469
18: 7 good, and gave it unto a y' man; *5288
19: 4 the house round, both old and y', "
22: 3 took two of his y' men with him, "
5 Abraham said unto his y' men, "
19 Abraham returned unto his y' men, "
31:38 thy she goats have not cast their y', "
33:13 and herds with y' are with me: *5763
34:19 y' man deferred not to do the 5288
41:12 there was there with us a y' man, "
Ex 10: 9 go with our y' and with our old, "
23:26 There shall nothing cast their y', nor
24: 5 y' men of the children of Israel, 5288
29: 1 Take one y' bullock, and 1121,1241
33:11 Joshua, the son of Nun, a y' man, 5288
Le 1:14 of turtledoves, or of y' pigeons. 1121
4: 3 a y' bullock without blemish 1121,1241
14 offer a y' bullock for the sin, "
5: 7 or two y' pigeons, unto the Lord; 1121
11 two y' pigeons, then he that sinned "
9: 2 a y' calf for a sin offering, ††1121,1241
12: 6 a y' pigeon, or a turtledove, 1121
8 two turtles, or two y' pigeons; "
14:22 two y' pigeons, such as he is able "
30 y' pigeons, such as he can get; "
15:14 or two y' pigeons, and come before "
29 or two y' pigeons, and bring them "
16: 3 a y' bullock for a sin offering, 1121,1241
22:28 kill it and her y' both in one day. 1121
23:18 one y' bullock, and two rams: 1121,1241
Nu 6:10 or two y' pigeons, to the priest, 1121
7:15, 21, 27, 33, 39, 45, 51, 57, 63, 69, 75,
81 One y' bullock, one ram, one 1121,1241
8: 8 Then let them take a y' bullock " "
8 y' bullock shalt thou take " "
11:27 ran a y' man, and told Moses, 5288
28 one of his y' men, answered * 979
15:24 offer one y' bullock for a burnt 1121,1241
23:24 and lift up himself as a y' lion: *
28:11, 19, 27 y' bullocks,...one ram, 1121,1241
29: 2, 8 one y' bullock, one ram, and "
13 thirteen y' bullocks, two rams, "
17 shall offer twelve y' bullocks, "
De 22: 6 whether they be y' ones, or eggs, 667
6 and the dam sitting upon the y', "
6 not take the dam with the y': 1121
7 dam go, and take the y' to thee; "
28:50 old, nor shew favour to the y': 5288
57 toward her y' one that cometh out 7988
32:11 fluttereth over her y', spreadeth 1469
25 shall destroy both the y' man and 970
Jos 6:21 both man and woman, y' and old, 5288
23 y' men that were spies went in, "
J'g 6:25 Take thy father's y' bullock, even *6499
8:14 a y' man of the men of Succoth, 5288
9:54 unto the y' man his armourbearer, "
54 his y' man thrust him through, and "
14: 5 a y' lion roared against him. 3715
10 feast; for so used the y' men to do. 970
17: 7 a y' man out of Beth-lehem-judah 5288
11 y' man was unto him as one of his "
12 and the y' man became his priest, "
18: 3 the voice of the y' man the Levite: "
15 the house of the y' man the Levite, "
19:19 y' man which is with thy servants: "
21:12 four hundred y' virgins, that had 5291
Ru 2: 9 have I not charged the y' men 5288
9 that which the y' men have drawn. "
15 Boaz commanded his y' men, "
21 shalt keep fast by my y' men, "
3:10 as thou followedst not y' men, 970
4:12 shall give thee of this y' woman. 5291
1Sa 1:24 in Shiloh: and the child was y'. 5288
2:17 the sin of the y' men was very great "
8:16 your goodliest y' men, and your 970
9: 2 Saul, a choice y' man, and a goodly: "
11 y' maidens going out to draw 5291
14: 1 son of Saul said unto the y' man 5288
6 Jonathan said to the y' man that "
17:58 Whose son art thou, thou y' man? "
20:22 But if I say thus unto the y' man, *5958
21: 4 if the y' men have kept themselves 5288
5 vessels of the y' men are holy, "
25: 5 And David sent out ten y' men, "
5 David said unto the y' men, Get "
8 Ask thy y' men, and they will shew "
8 let the y' men find favour in thine "
9 And when David's y' men came, "
12 So David's y' men turned their way, "
14 But one of the y' men told Abigail, "
25 thine handmaid saw not the y' men "
27 the y' men that follow my lord. "
26:22 let one of the y' men come over and "
30:13 he said, I am a y' man of Egypt, "
1Sa 30:17 save four hundred y' men, which 5288
2Sa 1: 5 David said unto the y' man that "
6 And the y' man that told him said, "
13 And David said unto the y' man "
15 David called one of the y' men, and "
2:14 Let the y' men now arise, and "
21 lay thee hold on one of the y' men, "
4:12 And David commanded his y' men, "
9:12 Mephibosheth had a y' son, whose 6996
13:32 all the y' men the king's sons; 5288
34 the y' man that kept the watch "
14:21 bring the y' man Absalom again. "
16: 2 summer fruit for the y' men to eat; "
18: 5 gently for my sake with the y' man, "
12 none touch the y' man Absalom. "
15 y' men that bare Joab's armour "
29 said, Is the y' man Absalom safe? "
32 Is the y' man Absalom safe? And "
32 do thee hurt, be as that y' man is. "
1Ki 1: 2 for my lord the king a y' virgin: 5291
11:28 Solomon seeing the y' man that 5288
12: 8 consulted with the y' men that 3206
10 y' men that were grown up with "
14 after the counsel of the y' men, "
20:14, 15, 17, 19 y' men of the princes of 5288
2Ki 4:22 me, I pray thee, one of the y' men,* "
5:22 two y' men of the sons of the "
6:17 Lord opened the eyes of the y' man; "
8:12 their y' men wilt thou slay with 970
9: 4 So the y' man, even the 5288
4 even the y' man the prophet, "
1Ch 12:28 Zadok, a y' man mighty of valour, "
22: 5 Solomon my son is y' and tender, "
29: 1 hath chosen, is yet y' and tender, "
2Ch 10: 8 took counsel with the y' men that 3206
10 y' men that were brought up with "
14 after the advice of the y' men, "
13: 7 when Rehoboam was y' and 5288
9 himself with a y' bullock 1121,1241
34: 3 while he was yet y', he began to 5288
36:17 who slew their y' men with the 970
17 had no compassion upon y' man or "
Ezr 6: 9 both y' bullocks, and rams, 1123
Es 2: 2 there be fair y' virgins sought 5291
3 together all the fair y' virgins "
3:13 perish, all Jews, both y' and old, 5288
8:10 camels, and y' dromedaries: *1121
Job 1:19 it fell upon the y' men, and they 5288
4:10 and the teeth of the y' lions, are 3715
19:18 Yea, y' children despised me; "
29: 8 The y' men saw me, and hid 5288
32: 6 I am y', and ye are very old; 6810,3117
38:39 or fill the appetite of the y' lions, 3715
41 when his y' ones cry unto God, 3206
39: 3 they bring forth their y' ones, "
4 Their y' ones are in good liking, 1121
16 is hardened against her y' ones, "
30 Her y' ones also suck up blood: 667
Ps 17:12 a y' lion lurking in secret places. 3715
29: 6 and Sirion like a y' unicorn. 1121
34:10 The y' lions do lack, and suffer 3715
37:25 I have been y', and now am old; 5288
58: 6 out the great teeth of the y' lions, 3715
78:63 The fire consumed their y' men; 970
71 following the ewes great with y' †5763
84: 3 where she may lay her y', even 667
91:13 y' lion and the dragon shalt thou 3715
104:21 The y' lions roar after their prey, "
119: 9 shall a y' man cleanse his way? 5288
147: 9 and to the y' ravens which cry. 1121
148:12 Both y' men, and maidens; old 970
Pr 1: 4 y' man knowledge and discretion. 5288
7: 7 a y' man void of understanding, "
20:29 glory of y' men is their strength: 970
30:17 out, and the y' eagles shall eat it. 1121
Ec 11: 9 Rejoice, O y' man, in thy youth; 970
Ca 2: 9 beloved is like a roe or a y' hart: 6082
17 roe or a y' hart upon the mountains "
4: 5 are like two y' roes that are twins,* "
7: 3 are like two y' roes that are twins.* "
8:14 be thou like to a roe or to a y' hart "
Isa 5:29 lion, they shall roar like y' lions: 3715
7:21 that a man shall nourish a y' cow, 1241
9:17 shall have no joy in their y' men, 970
11: 6 and the y' lion and the fatling 3715
7 y' ones shall lie down together: 3206
13:18 shall dash the y' men to pieces; 5288
20: 4 Ethiopians captives, y' and old, "
23: 4 neither do I nourish up y' men, 970
30: 6 whence come the y' and old lion, *3833
6 riches upon the shoulders of y' asses, "
24 y' asses that ear the ground shall eat
31: 4 the y' lion roaring on his prey, 3715
8 his y' men shall be discomfited. 970
40:11 gently lead those that are with y'. †5763
30 the y' men shall utterly fall: 5288,970
62: 5 For as a y' man marrieth a virgin, "
Jer 2:15 The y' lions roared upon him, and 3715
6:11 the assembly of y' men together: 970
9:21 and the y' men from the streets. "
11:22 the y' men shall die by the sword; "
15: 8 against the mother of the y' men "
18:21 their y' men be slain by the sword "
31:12 the y' of the flock and of the herd: 1121
13 both y' men and old together: 970
48:15 his chosen y' men are gone down to "
49:26 her y' men shall fall in her streets, "
50:30 shall her y' men fall in the streets, "
51: 3 spare ye not her y' men; destroy ye "
22 will I break in pieces old and y'; 5288
22 in pieces the y' man and the maid; 970
La 1:15 against me to crush my y' men: "
18 my y' men are gone into captivity. "
2:19 him for the life of thy y' children, "
21 y' and the old lie on the ground in 5288
21 virgins and my y' men are fallen 970

La 4: 3 they give suck to their y' ones: 1482
4 the y' children ask bread, and no man
5: 13 They took the y' men to grind, and 970
14 gate, the y' men from their musick. "
Eze 9: 6 Slay utterly old and y', both maids, "
17: 4 off the top of his y' twigs, and 3242
22 off from the top of his y' twigs 3127
19: 2 her whelps among y' lions. 3715
3 it became a y' lion, and it learned "
5 whelps, and made him a y' lion. "
6 he became a y' lion, and learned "
23: 6 all of them desirable y' men, 970
12 all of them desirable y' men. "
23 them: all of them desirable y' men, "
30: 17 y' men of Aven and of Pi-beseth "
31: 6 of the field bring forth their y', "
32: 2 art like a y' lion of the nations, 3715
38: 13 of Tarshish, with all the y' lions "
41: 19 face of a y' lion toward the palm "
43: 19 y' bullock for a sin offering. 1121,1241
23 a y' bullock without blemish, " "
25 shall also prepare a y' bullock, " "
45: 18 a y' bullock without blemish, " "
46: 6 a y' bullock without blemish. " "
Ho 5: 14 as a y' lion to the house of Judah: 3715
Joe 2: 28 your y' men shall see visions: 970
Am 2: 11 and of your y' men for Nazarites. "
3: 4 will a y' lion cry out of his den, 3715
4: 10 your y' men have I slain with the 970
8: 13 virgins and y' men faint for thirst. "
Mic 5: 8 as a y' lion among the flocks of 3715
Na 2: 11 the feedingplace of the y' lions, "
13 sword shall devour thy y' lions: "
3: 10 her y' children also were dashed in
Zec 2: 4 Run, speak to this y' man, saying, 5288
9: 17 shall make the y' men cheerful, 970
11: 3 a voice of the roaring of y' lions; 3715
16 neither shall seek the y' one, *5288
M't 2: 8 search diligently for the y' child; 3813
9 stood over where the y' child was. "
11 the y' child with Mary his mother, "
13 take the y' child and his mother, "
13 seek the y' child to destroy him. "
14 he took the y' child and his mother "
20 take the y' child and his mother, "
20 which sought the y' child's life. "
21 took the y' child and his mother, "
19: 20 The y' man saith unto him, All 3495
22 the y' man heard that saying, he "
M'r 7: 25 y' daughter had an unclean spirit, *2365
10: 13 they brought y' children to him, *3813
14: 51 followed him a certain y' man, 3495
51 and the y' men laid hold on him: * "
16: 5 saw a y' man sitting on the right "
Lu 2: 24 of turtledoves, or two y' pigeons. 3502
7: 14 Y' man, I say unto thee, Arise. 3495
Joh 12: 14 when he had found a y' ass, sat 3678
21: 18 When thou wast y', thou girdedst 3501
Ac 2: 17 and your y' men shall see visions, 3495
5: 6 the y' men arose, wound him up, 3501
10 y' men came in, and found her 3495
7: 19 they cast out their y' children, *1025
58 their clothes at a y' man's feet, 3494
20: 9 a certain y' man named Eutychus, "
12 they brought the y' man alive, *3816
23: 17 this y' man unto the chief captain: 3494
18 prayed me to bring this y' man "
22 then let the y' man depart, "
Tit 2: 4 teach the y' women to be sober, 3501
6 Y' men likewise exhort to be * "
1Jo 2: 13 I write unto you, y' men, because 3495
14 written unto you, y' men, because "

younger
Ge 9: 24 knew what his y' son had done *6996
19: 31, 34 the firstborn said unto the y', 6810
35 and the y' arose, and lay with him; "
38 And the y', she also bare a son, "
25: 23 and the elder shall serve the y'. "
27: 15 put them upon Jacob her y' son: 6996
42 sent and called Jacob her y' son, "
29: 16 and the name of the y' was Rachel. "
18 years for Rachel the y' daughter. "
26 to give the y' before the firstborn. 6810
43: 29 Is this your y' brother, of whom *6996
48: 14 Ephraim's head, who was the y', 6810
19 his y' brother shall be greater 6996
J'g 1: 13 Kenaz, Caleb's y' brother, took it: "
3: 9 son of Kenaz, Caleb's y' brother. "
15: 2 is not her y' sister fairer than she? "
1Sa 14: 49 and the name of the y' Michal: "
1Ch 24: 31 over against their y' brethren. "
Job 30: 1 y' than I have me in derision, 6810,3117
Eze 16: 46 thy y' sister, that dwelleth at thy 6996
61 thy sisters, thine elder and thy y': "
Lu 15: 12 the y' of them said to his father, 3501
13 the y' son gathered all together, "
22: 26 among you, let him be as the y'; "
Ro 9: 12 her, The elder shall serve the y'. 1640
1Ti 5: 1 and the y' men as brethren; 3501
2 the y' as sisters, with all purity. "
11 But the y' widows refuse: for when "
14 therefore that the y' women marry, "
1Pe 5: 5 ye y', submit yourselves unto the "

youngest
Ge 42: 13 the y' is this day with our father, 6996
15 your y' brother come hither. "
20 bring your y' brother unto me; "
32 the y' is this day with our father "
34 bring your y' brother unto me: "
43: 33 and the y' according to his youth: 6810
44: 2 cup, in the sack's mouth of the y', 6996
12 at the eldest, and left at the y': "
23 Except your y' brother come down "
26 if our y' brother be with us, then "
26 except our y' brother be with us. "

Jos 6: 26 and in his y' son shall he set up 6810
J'g 9: 5 the y' son of Jerubbaal was left; 3996
1Sa 16: 11 said, There remaineth yet the y', "
17: 14 And David was the y': and the "
1Ki 16: 34 gates thereof in his y' son Segub, 6810
2Ch 21: 17 save Jehoahaz, the y' of his sons. 6996
22: 1 made Ahaziah his y' son king in "

your See also YOURS; YOURSELVES.
Ge 3: 5 thereof, then y' eyes shall be opened,
9: 2 sea; into y' hand are they delivered.
5 y' blood of y' lives will I require;
9 with you, and with y' seed after you;
17: 11 circumcise the flesh of y' foreskin;
12 every man child in y' generations, he
13 my covenant shall be in y' flesh for
18: 4 you, be fetched, and wash y' feet,
5 of bread, and comfort ye y' hearts;
5 therefore are ye come to y' servant.
19: 2 I pray you, into y' servant's house,
2 and tarry all night, and wash y' feet,
2 rise up early, and go on y' ways.
8 do ye to them as is good in y' eyes:
23: 8 y' mind that I should bury my dead
31: 5 I see y' father's countenance, that it
6 my power I have served y' father.
7 And y' father hath deceived me,
9 taken away the cattle of y' father,
29 the God of y' father spake unto me
34: 8 Shechem longeth for y' daughter:
9 give y' daughters unto us, and take
11 Let me find grace in y' eyes, and what
16 we will take y' daughters, and we
35: 2 be clean, and change y' garments:
37: 7 y' sheaves stood round about,
42: 15 except y' youngest brother come
16 of you, and let him fetch y' brother,
16 that y' words may be proved, whether
19 true men, let one of y' brethren
19 bound in the house of y' prison:
19 corn for the famine of y' houses:
20 bring y' youngest brother unto me;
20 so shall y' words be verified, and ye
33 one of y' brethren here with me,
33 food for the famine of y' households,
34 bring y' youngest brother unto me:
34 so will I deliver you y' brother, and
43: 3, 5 except y' brother be with you.
7 saying, Is y' father yet alive?
7 would say, Bring y' brother down?
11 best fruits in the land in y' vessels,
12 And take double money in y' hand;
12 again in the mouth of y' sacks,
12 carry it again in y' hand;
13 Take also y' brother, and arise, go
14 he may send away y' other brother,
23 y' God, and the God of y' father,
23 hath given you treasure in y' sacks:
23 I had y' money. And he brought
27 Is y' father well, the old man of whom
29 Is this y' younger brother, of whom
44: 10 let it be according unto y' words:
17 get you up in peace unto y' father.
23 Except y' youngest brother come
45: 4 I am Joseph y' brother, whom ye sold
7 and to save y' lives by a great *
12 y' eyes see, and the eyes of my brother
17 lade y' beasts, and go, get you unto
18 take y' father, and y' households,
19 the land of Egypt for y' little ones,
19 and for y' wives, and bring y' father,
20 Also regard not y' stuff; for the good
46: 33 shall say, What is y' occupation?
47: 3 his brethren, What is y' occupation?
16 And Joseph said, Give y' cattle;
16 I will give you for y' cattle, if money
23 I have bought you this day and y' land
24 and four parts shall be y' own, for seed
24 y' food, and for them of y' households,
24 and for food for y' little ones.
48: 21 you again unto the land of y' fathers.
49: 2 and hearken unto Israel y' father.
50: 4 now I have found grace in y' eyes,
21 I will nourish you, and y' little ones.
Ex 3: 13 God of y' fathers hath sent me unto
15, 16 The Lord God of y' fathers,
22 upon y' sons, and upon y' daughters;
5: 4 works? get you unto y' burdens.
11 ought of y' work shall be diminished.
13 hasted them, saying, Fulfil y' works,
13 y' daily tasks, as when there was
14 have ye not fulfilled y' task
19 ought from y' bricks of y' daily task.
6: 7 shall know that I am the Lord y' God,
8: 25 Go ye, sacrifice to y' God in the land.
28 ye may sacrifice to the Lord y' God
10: 8 unto them, Go, serve the Lord y' God:
10 I will let you go, and y' little ones:
16 have sinned against the Lord y' God,
17 and intreat the Lord y' God, that he
24 let y' flocks and y' herds be stayed:
24 let y' little ones also go with you.
12: 4 to his eating shall make y' count
5 Y' lamb shall be without blemish,
11 y' loins girded, y' shoes on y' feet,
11 and y' staff in y' hand;
14 the Lord throughout y' generations;
15 put away leaven out of y' houses:
17 y' armies out of the land of Egypt:
17 ye observe this day in y' generations
19 there be no leaven found in y' houses:
20 in all y' habitations shall ye eat
21 you a lamb according to y' families,
23 destroyer to come in unto y' houses to
26 when y' children shall say unto you,
32 Also take y' flocks and y' herds,
14: 14 for you, and ye shall hold y' peace.

Ex 16: 7 he heareth y' murmurings against
8 y' murmurings which ye murmur
8 y' murmurings are not against us,
9 for he hath heard y' murmurings.
12 shall know that I am the Lord y' God.
16 to the number of y' persons;
32 of it to be kept for y' generations;
33 Lord, to be kept for y' generations.
19: 15 the third day: come not at y' wives.*
20: 20 that his fear may be before y' faces,*
22: 24 and y' wives shall be widows,
24 and y' children fatherless.
23: 21 he will not pardon y' transgressions:
25 And ye shall serve the Lord y' God,
31 inhabitants of the land into y' hand;
29: 42 offerings throughout y' generations
30: 8 the Lord throughout y' generations.
10 upon it throughout y' generations:
15, 16 to make an atonement for y' souls.
31 unto me throughout y' generations.
31: 13 and you throughout y' generations;
32: 2 which are in the ears of y' wives,
2 of y' sons, and of y' daughters,
13 I will multiply y' seed as the stars of
13 spoken of will I give unto y' seed,
30 I shall make an atonement for y' sin.
34: 23 all y' menchildren appear before the
35: 3 no fire throughout y' habitations
Le 1: 2 ye shall bring y' offering of the cattle,
3: 17 a perpetual statute for y' generations
17 throughout all y' dwellings, that ye
6: 18 a statute for ever in y' generations
7: 26 or of beast, in any of y' dwellings.
32 of the sacrifices of y' peace offerings.
8: 33 until the days of y' consecration be
10: 4 carry y' brethren from before the
6 his sons, Uncover not y' heads,
6 neither rend y' clothes; lest ye die,
6 but let y' brethren, the whole house
9 for ever throughout y' generations:
11: 43 not make y' selves abominable? 5315
44 For I am the Lord y' God: ye shall
45 of the land of Egypt, to be y' God:
14: 34 a house of the land of y' possession;
16: 29 ye shall afflict y' souls, and do no
29 whether it be one of y' own country,*
30 ye may be clean from all y' sins
31 and ye shall afflict y' souls, by a
17: 11 to make an atonement for y' souls:
15 whether it be one of y' own country,*
18: 2 say unto them, I am the Lord y' God.
4 walk therein: I am the Lord y' God.
26 neither any of y' own nation, nor any*
19: 2 holy: for I the Lord y' God am holy.
3 my sabbaths: I am the Lord y' God.
4 molten gods: I am the Lord y' God.
5 Lord, ye shall offer it at y' own will.*
9 when ye reap the harvest of y' land,
10 and stranger: I am the Lord y' God.
25 thereof: I am the Lord y' God.
27 not round the corners of y' heads,
28 not make any cuttings in y' flesh
31 defiled by them: I am the Lord y' God.
33 stranger sojourn with thee in y' land,
34 land of Egypt: I am the Lord y' God.
36 I am the Lord y' God, which brought
20: 7 be ye holy: for I am the Lord y' God.
24 I am the Lord y' God, which have
25 shall not make y' souls abominable
22: 3 of all y' seed among y' generations,
19 Ye shall offer at y' own will a male*
24 make any offering thereof in y' land.
25 offer the bread of y' God of any of
29 unto the Lord, offer it at y' own will.*
33 of the land of Egypt, to be y' God:
23: 3 of the Lord in all y' dwellings.
10 sheaf of the firstfruits of y' harvest
14 brought an offering unto y' God:
14 y' generations in all y' dwellings.
17 Ye shall bring out of y' habitations
21 statute for ever in all y' dwellings
21 throughout y' generations.
22 when ye reap the harvest of y' land,
22 the stranger: I am the Lord y' God.
27 and ye shall afflict y' souls, and offer
28 for you before the Lord y' God.
31 y' generations in all y' dwellings.
32 of rest, and ye shall afflict y' souls:
32 even, shall ye celebrate y' sabbath.
38 beside y' gifts, and beside all y' vows,
38 and beside all y' freewill offerings,
40 shall rejoice before the Lord y' God
41 a statute for ever in y' generations:
43 That y' generations may know that I
43 land of Egypt: I am the Lord y' God.
24: 3 a statute for ever in y' generations.
22 as for one of y' own country: *
22 for I am the Lord y' God.
25: 9 sound throughout all y' land.
17 thy God: for I am the Lord y' God.
19 and ye shall eat y' fill, and dwell
24 And in all the land of y' possession
38 I am the Lord y' God, which brought
38 the land of Canaan, and to be y' God.
45 you, which they begat in y' land:
45 and they shall be y' possession.
46 inheritance for y' children after you,
46 they shall be y' bondmen for ever:
46 over y' brethren the children of Israel,
55 land of Egypt: I am the Lord y' God.
26: 1 set up any image of stone in y' land,
1 unto it: for I am the Lord y' God.
5 y' threshing shall reach unto the
5 and ye shall eat y' bread to the full,
5 to the full, and dwell in y' land safely.
6 shall the sword go through y' land.

Le 26: 7 And ye shall chase y' enemies, and
8 and y' enemies shall fall before you
12 walk among you, and will be y' God,
13 I am the Lord y' God, which brought
13 I have broken the bands of y' yoke,
15 or if y' soul abhor my judgments, so
16 and ye shall sow y' seed in vain,
16 for y' enemies shall eat it.
17 ye shall be slain before y' enemies:
18 you seven times more for y' sins.
19 I will break the pride of y' power;
19 y' heaven...iron, and y' earth as brass:
20 And y' strength shall be spent in vain:
20 y' land shall not yield her increase,
21 plagues upon you according to y' sins.
22 of y' children, and destroy y' cattle,
22 and y' high ways shall be desolate.
24 you yet seven times for y' sins.
25 are gathered together within y' cities,
26 I have broken the staff of y' bread,
26 ten women shall bake y' bread in one
26 deliver you y' bread again by weight:
29 And ye shall eat the flesh of y' sons,
29 the flesh of y' daughters shall ye eat.
30 I will destroy y' high places,
30 and cut down y' im s,
30 cast y' carcases upon the carcases
30 upon the carcases of y' idols,
31 And I will make y' ities waste,
31 bring y' sanctu ries unto desolation,
31 smell the savour f y' swe t odours.
32 and y' enemies whic dwell therein
33 y' land shall be de olate, and y' cities
34 and ye be in y' ene ies' land;
35 because it did not rest in y' sabbaths,
37 no power t stand bef re y' enemies.
38 land of y' enemie shall eat ou up.
39 in their iniquity in y' enemies' lands;
Nu 9: 10 If any man of yo or of y' p sterity
10: 8 for ever throughout y' generations.
9 And if ye g to war in y' land against
9 remembered before the Lord y' God,
9 ye shall be saved fron y' en mies.
10 of y' gladness, and in y' solemn days,
10 and in the b ginnings of y' months,
10 the trumpets over y' burnt offerings,
10 the sacrifices of y' peace offerings;
10 you for a memorial before y' God:
10 I am the Lord y' God.
11: 20 until it come out at y' nostrils, and it
14: 29 Y' carcases shall fall in this
29 you, according to y' whole number,
31 But y' little ones, whi h ye said
32 as for you, y' carcases, they shall
33 y' children shall wander in the
33 years and bear y' whoredoms,
33 until y' carcases be wasted
34 shall ye bear y' iniquities, even forty
42 ye be not smitten before y' enemies.
15: 2 come into the land of y' habitations,
3 offering, or in y' solemn feasts,
14 be among you in y' generations,
15 ordinance for ever in y' generations:
20 of y' dough for an heave offering:
21 Of the first of y' dough ye shall give
21 an heave offering in y' generations.
23 henceforward among y' generations;
39 after y' own heart and y' own eyes,
40 and be holy unto y' God.
41 I am the Lord y' God, which brought
41 to be y' God: I am the Lord y' God.
18: 1 bear the iniquity of y' priesthood.
6 I have taken y' brethren the Levites
7 with thee shall keep y' priest's office
7 I have given y' priest's office unto*
23 for ever throughout y' generations,
26 you from them for y' inheritance,
27 y' heave offering shall be reckoned
28 offering unto the Lord of all y' tithes,
29 Out of all y' gifts ye shall offer
31 every place, ye and y' households:
31 for it is y' reward for y' service in
22: 13 Get you into y' land: for the Lord
28: 11 And in the beginning of y' months ye
26 unto the Lord, after y' weeks be out,
29: 7 and ye shall afflict y' souls: ye shall
39 Lord in y' set feasts, beside y' vows,
39 y' freewill offerings, for y' burnt
39 y' meat offerings, and for y' drink
39 offerings, and for y' peace offerings.
31: 19 both yourselves and y' captives
20 And purify all y' raiment, and all*
24 wash y' clothes on the seventh day,
32: 6 Shall y' brethren go to war, and shall
8 Thus did y' fathers, when I sent
14 ye are risen up in y' fathers' stead,
22 and this land shall be y' possession *
23 and be sure y' sin will find you out.
24 Build you cities for y' little ones,
24 and folds for y' sheep;
24 hath proceeded out of y' mouth.
33: 54 for an inheritance among y' families:
54 to the tribes of y' fathers ye
55 in y' eyes, and thorns in y' sides,
34: 3 Then y' south quarter shall be from
3 y' south border shall be the outmost
4 y' border shall turn from the south
5 border: this shall be y' west border.
7 And this shall be y' north border:
8 Hor ye shall point out y' border *
9 this shall be y' north border.
10 ye shall point out y' east border from
12 this shall be y' land with the coasts
35: 29 y' generations in all y' dwellings.
De 1: 7 Turn you, and take y' journey, and go
8 the Lord sware unto y' fathers,

De 1: 10 The Lord y' God hath multiplied you,
11 (The Lord God of y' fathers make you
12 I myself alone bear y' cumbrance,
12 and y' burden, and y' strife?
13 and known among y' tribes, and I
15 So I took the chief of y' tribes,
15 over tens, and officers among y' tribes.
16 And I charged y' judges at that time,
16 Hear the causes between y' brethren,
26 commandment of the Lord y' God:
27 And ye murmured in y' tents, and
30 Lord y' God which goeth before you,
30 did for you in Egypt before y' eyes;
32 ye did not believe the Lord y' God,
33 you out a place to pitch y' tents in,
34 the Lord heard the voice of y' words,
35 which I sware to give unto y' fathers,
37 was angry with me for y' sakes,
39 Moreover y' little ones, which ye said
39 y' children, which in that day had no
40 take y' journey into the wilderness
42 lest ye be smitten before y' enemies.
45 Lord would not hearken to y' voice,
2: 4 pass through the coast of y' brethren
3: 18 The Lord y' God hath given you this
18 pass over armed before y' brethren
19 But y' wives, and y' little ones,
19 and y' cattle, (for I know that ye have
19 shall abide in y' cities which I have
20 Lord have given rest unto y' brethren,
20 the Lord y' God hath given them
21 all that the Lord y' God hath done
22 Lord y' God he shall fight for you.
26 Lord was wroth with me for y' sakes,
4: 1 Lord God of y' fathers giveth you.
2 commandments of the Lord y' God
3 Y' eyes have seen what the Lord did
4 that did cleave unto the Lord y' God
6 is y' wisdom and y' understanding
21 Lord was angry with me for y' sakes,
26 ye shall not prolong y' days upon it,
34 to all that the Lord y' God did
34 for you in Egypt before y' eyes?
5: 22 the Lord spake unto all y' assembly
28 the Lord heard the voice of y' words,
30 to them, Get you into y' tents again.
32 Lord y' God hath commanded you:
33 Lord y' God hath commanded you,
33 ye may prolong y' days in the land
6: 1 the Lord y' God commanded to teach
16 Ye shall not tempt the Lord y' God,
17 commandments of the Lord y' God,
7: 8 which he had sworn unto y' fathers,
14 barren among you, or among y' cattle.
8: 1 which the Lord sware unto y' fathers.
20 the Lord destroyeth before y' face,*
20 unto the voice of the Lord y' God.
9: 16 had sinned against the Lord y' God,
17 hands, and brake them before y' eyes.
18 of all y' sins which ye sinned,
21 And I took y' sin, the calf which ye
23 the commandment of the Lord y' God,
10: 16 therefore the foreskin of y' heart,
17 For the Lord y' God is God of gods,
11: 2 I speak not with y' children which
2 chastisement of the Lord y' God,
7 y' eyes have seen all the great acts
9 ye may prolong y' days in the land,
9 Lord sware unto y' fathers to give
13 this day, to love the Lord y' God,
13 with all y' heart and with all y' soul,
14 I will give you the rain of y' land
16 that y' heart be not deceived, and ye
18 my words in y' heart and in y' soul,
18 bind them for a sign upon y' hand,
18 may be as frontlets between y' eyes.
19 And ye shall teach them y' children,
21 That y' days may be multiplied,
21 and the days of y' children, in the
21 Lord sware unto y' fathers to give
22 to love the Lord y' God, to walk in all
24 the soles of y' feet shall tread shall be
24 the uttermost sea shall y' coast be.
25 the Lord y' God shall lay the fear of
27, 28 commandments of the Lord y' God,
31 which the Lord y' God giveth you,
12: 4 shall not do so unto the Lord y' God.
5 y' God shall choose out of all y' tribes
6 y' burnt offerings, and y' sacrifices,
6 y' tithes, and heave offerings of y'
6 and y' vows, and y' freewill offerings,
6 firstlings of y' herds and of y' flocks,
7 ye shall eat before the Lord y' God,
7 rejoice in all that ye put y' hand unto,
7 ye and y' household, wherein the
9 which the Lord y' God giveth you.*
10 which the Lord y' God giveth you
10 rest from all y' enemies round about,
11 which the Lord y' God shall choose
11 I command you; y' burnt offerings,
11 and y' sacrifices, y' tithes,
11 and the heave offering of y' hand,
11 and all y' choice vows which ye vow
12 shall rejoice before the Lord y' God,
12 ye, and y' sons, and y' daughters,
12 y' menservants, and y' maidservants,
12 the Levite that is within y' gates;
13: 3 for the Lord y' God proveth you, to
3 whether ye love the Lord y' God,
3 with all y' heart and with all y' soul.
4 Ye shall walk after the Lord y' God,
5 turn you away from the Lord y' God,
14: 1 are the children of the Lord y' God:
1 make any baldness between y' eyes
20: 3 day unto battle against y' enemies:
3 let not y' hearts faint, fear not, and

De 20: 4 y' God is he that goeth with you,
4 to fight for you against y' enemies,
18 should ye sin against the Lord y' God.
28: 68 ye shall be sold unto y' enemies
29: 2 did before y' eyes in the land of Egypt
5 y' clothes are not waxen old upon you,
6 know that I am the Lord y' God.
10 day all of you before the Lord y' God;
10 y' captains of y' tribes, y' elders,
10 y' officers, with all the men of Israel,
11 Y' little ones, y' wives, and thy
22 y' children that shall rise up after you,
30: 18 not prolong y' days upon the land,
31: 5 shall give them up before y' face,*
12 may learn, and fear the Lord y' God,
13 and learn to fear the Lord y' God,
26 of the covenant of the Lord y' God,
28 elders of y' tribes, and y' officers,
29 anger through the work of y' hands.
32: 17 up, whom y' fathers feared not.
38 and help you, and be y' protection.
46 Set y' hearts unto all the words
46 command y' children to observe
47 thing for you, because it is y' life:
47 shall prolong y' days in the land,
Jos 1: 3 the sole of y' foot shall tread upon,
4 down of the sun, shall be y' coast.
11 Lord y' God giveth you to possess
13 The Lord y' God hath given you rest,
14 Y' wives, y' little ones, and y' cattle,
14 shall pass before y' brethren armed,
15 the Lord hath given y' brethren rest,
15 which the Lord y' God giveth them:
15 unto the land of y' possession,
2: 9 and that y' terror is fallen upon us,‡
11 the Lord y' God, he is God in heaven
16 and afterward may ye go y' way.
21 According unto y' words, so be it.
3: 3 of the covenant of the Lord y' God,
3 then ye shall remove from y' place,
9 hear the words of the Lord y' God.
4: 5 over before the ark of the Lord y' God
6 when y' children ask their fathers
21 y' children shall ask their fathers
22 Then ye shall let y' children know,
23 the Lord y' God dried up the waters
23 as the Lord y' God did to the Red sea,
24 that ye might fear the Lord y' God for
6: 10 nor make any noise with y' voice,
10 any word proceed out of y' mouth,
7: 14 be brought according to y' tribes:
8: 7 y' God will deliver it into y' hand.
9: 11 say unto them, We are y' servants:
10: 19 ye not, but pursue after y' enemies,
19 y' God...delivered them into y' hand.
24 y' feet upon the necks of these kings.
25 shall the Lord do to all y' enemies
15: 4 the sea: this shall be y' south coast.
18: 3 Lord God of y' fathers hath given you?
20: 3 shall be y' refuge from the avenger*
22: 3 Ye have not left y' brethren these
3 commandment of the Lord y' God.
4 the Lord y' God hath given rest
4 hath given rest unto y' brethren,
4 return ye, and get you unto y' tents,
4 and unto the land of y' possession,
5 to love the Lord y' God, and to walk
5 with all y' heart and with all y' soul.
8 with much riches unto y' tents,
8 spoil of y' enemies with y' brethren.
19 the land of y' possession be unclean,
24 time to come y' children might speak
25 y' children make our children cease
27 y' children may not say to our
23: 3 all that the Lord y' God hath done
3 the Lord y' God is he that hath fought
4 to be an inheritance for y' tribes,
5 the Lord y' God, he shall expel them
5 and drive them from out of y' sight;
5 Lord y' God hath promised unto you.
8 But cleave unto the Lord y' God,
10 Lord y' God, he it is that fighteth for
11 heed therefore unto y' selves,
11 that ye love the Lord y' God.
13 Lord y' God will no more drive out
13 unto you, and scourges in y' sides,
13 and thorns in y' eyes, until ye perish
13 the Lord y' God hath given you.
14 in all y' hearts and in all y' souls,
14 things which the Lord y' God spake
15 the Lord y' God promised you;
15 the Lord y' God hath given you.
16 the covenant of the Lord y' God,
24: 2 Y' fathers dwelt on the other side of
3 I took y' father Abraham from the
6 I brought y' fathers out of Egypt:
6 Egyptians pursued after y' fathers
7 y' eyes have seen what I have done in
8 and I gave them into y' hand,
11 and I delivered them into y' hand.
14, 15 the gods which y' fathers served
19 forgive y' transgressions nor y' sins.
23 incline y' heart unto the Lord God
27 unto you, lest ye deny y' God.
J'g 2: 1 land which I sware unto y' fathers;
3 they shall be as thorns in y' sides,
3: 28 y' enemies the Moabites into y' hand.
6: 10 said unto you, I am the Lord y' God;
7: 15 delivered into y' hand the host of
8: 3 delivered into y' hand the princes
7 I will tear y' flesh with the thorns
9: 2 also that I am y' bone and y' flesh.
15 come and put y' trust in my shadow:‡
18 Shechem, because he is y' brother;)
10: 14 you in the time of y' tribulation.
11: 9 them before me, shall I be y' head?

J'g 18: 6 the Lord is y' way wherein ye go.
10 for God hath given it into y' hands;
19: 5 of bread, and afterward go y' way.
9 to morrow get you early on y' way,
30 take advice, and speak y' minds. *
20: 7 give here y' advice and counsel.
Ru 1:11 womb, that they may be y' husbands?
12 again, my daughters, go y' way;
13 for it grieveth me much for y' sakes
1Sa 2: 3 not arrogancy come out of y' mouth:
23 for I hear of y' evil dealings by all
6: 4 was on you all, and on y' lords.
5 ye shall make images of y' emerods,
5 images of y' mice that mar the land;
5 from off y' gods, and from off y' land.
6 then do ye harden y' hearts,
7: 3 unto the Lord with all y' hearts,
3 and prepare y' hearts unto the Lord,
8:11 He will take y' sons, and appoint
13 y' daughters to be confectionaries,
14 he will take y' fields, and y' vineyards,
14 y' oliveyards, even the best of them,
15 tenth of y' seed, and of y' vineyards,
16 y' menservants, and y' maidservants,
16 y' goodliest young men, and y' asses,
17 He will take the tenth of y' sheep:
18 cry out in that day because of y' king
10:19 And ye have this day rejected y' God,
19 all y' adversities and y' tribulations;
19 by y' tribes, and by y' thousands.
11: 2 that I may thrust out all y' right eyes,
12: 1 I have hearkened unto y' voice
6 brought y' fathers up out of the land
7 which he did to you and to y' fathers.
8 and y' fathers cried unto the Lord,
8 brought forth y' fathers out of Egypt,
11 you out of the hand of y' enemies
12 when the Lord y' God was y' king.
14 continue following the Lord y' God:
15 you, as it was against y' fathers.
16 which the Lord will do before y' eyes.
17 and see that y' wickedness is great,
20 but serve the Lord with all y' heart;
24 serve him in truth with all y' heart:
25 be consumed, both ye and y' king.
17: 8 ye come out to set y' battle in array?
9 kill me, then will we be y' servants:
26:16 because ye have not kept y' master,
2Sa 1:24 on ornaments of gold upon y' apparel.
2: 5 shewed this kindness unto y' lord,
7 now let y' hands be strengthened,
7 for y' master Saul is dead, and also
3:31 Rend y' clothes, and gird you with
4:11 require his blood of y' hand, and take
10: 5 at Jericho until y' beards be grown,
15:27 in peace, and y' two sons with you,
1Ki 1:33 take with you the servants of y' lord,
8:61 Let y' heart therefore be perfect with
9: 6 from following me, ye or y' children,
11: 2 turn away y' heart after their gods:
12:11 a heavy yoke, I will add to y' yoke:
14 My father made y' yoke heavy, and I
14 and I will add to y' yoke: my father
16 to y' tents, O Israel: now see to thine
24 nor fight against y' brethren the
18:24 And call ye on the name of y' gods,
25 call on the name of y' gods, but put
2Ki 2: 3, 5 Yea, I know it; hold ye y' peace.
3:17 both ye, and y' cattle, and y' beasts.
18 deliver the Moabites...into y' hand.
9:15 If it be y' minds, then let none go
10: 2 seeing y' master's sons are with you,
3 best and meetest of y' master's sons,
3 throne, and fight for y' master's house.
6 heads of the men y' master's sons,
24 I have brought into y' hands escape,
12: 7 no more money of y' acquaintance,
17:13 Turn ye from y' evil ways, and keep
13 law which I commanded y' fathers,
39 But the Lord y' God ye shall fear;
39 you out of the hand of all y' enemies.
18:32 you away to a land like y' own land,
19: 6 Thus shall ye say to y' master, Thus
23:21 the passover unto the Lord y' God,
1Ch 15:12 yourselves, both ye and y' brethren,
16:18 of Canaan, the lot of y' inheritance;
19: 5 at Jericho until y' beards be grown,
22:18 Is not the Lord y' God with you? and
19 Now set y' heart and y' soul to
19 seek the Lord y' God; arise
28: 8 commandments of the Lord y' God:
8 inheritance for y' children after you
29:20 Now bless the Lord y' God. And all
2Ch 10:11 upon you, I will put more to y' yoke:
14 My father made y' yoke heavy, but I
16 every man to y' tents, O Israel: and
11: 4 go up, nor fight against y' brethren:
13:12 against the Lord God of y' fathers;
15: 7 and let not y' hands be weak:
7 for y' work shall be rewarded.
18:14 they shall be delivered into y' hand.
19:10 y' brethren that dwell in their cities,
10 come upon you, and upon y' brethren:
20:20 Believe in the Lord y' God, so shall
24: 5 repair the house of y' God from year
28: 9 the Lord God of y' fathers was wroth
9 he hath delivered them into y' hand,
10 you, sins against the Lord y' God?
11 ye have taken captive of y' brethren:
29: 5 house of the Lord God of y' fathers,
8 and to hissing, as ye see with y' eyes.
30: 7 like y' fathers, and like y' brethren,
8 not stiffnecked, as y' fathers were,
8 and serve the Lord y' God, that the
9 y' brethren and y' children shall find
9 the Lord y' God is gracious and

2Ch 32:14 y' God should be able to deliver you
15 much less shall y' God deliver you
33: 8 which I have appointed for y' fathers;
35: 3 not be a burden upon y' shoulders:
3 serve now the Lord y' God, and his
4 by the houses of y' fathers,
4 after y' courses, according to the
5 families of the fathers of y' brethren
6 and prepare y' brethren, that they
Ezr 4: 2 for we seek y' God, as ye do; and we
6: 6 y' companions the Apharsachites,
7:17 altar of the house of y' God which is
18 gold, that do after the will of y' God.
8:28 unto the Lord God of y' fathers.
9:12 not y' daughters unto their sons,
12 take their daughters unto y' sons,
12 an inheritance to y' children for ever.
10:11 unto the Lord God of y' fathers,
Ne 4:14 and fight for y' brethren, y' sons, and
14 y' daughters, y' wives, and y' houses.
5: 8 and will ye even sell y' brethren?
8: 9 day is holy unto the Lord y' God;
10 Go y' way, eat the fat, and drink the
10 for the joy of the Lord is y' strength.
11 Hold y' peace, for the day is holy;
9: 5 bless the Lord y' God for ever and
13:18 Did not y' fathers thus, and did not
25 give y' daughters unto their sons,
25 take their daughters unto y' sons,
Job 6:22 a reward for me of y' substance?
25 but what doth y' arguing reprove?
27 and ye dig a pit for y' friend.
13: 5 ye would altogether hold y' peace!
5 and it should be y' wisdom.
12 Y' remembrances are like unto
12 ashes, y' bodies to bodies of clay.
13 Hold y' peace, let me alone, that I
17 and my declaration with y' ears.
16: 4 if y' souls were in my soul's stead,
5 of my lips should asswage y' grief.
18: 3 beasts, and reputed vile in y' sight?
21: 2 and let this be y' consolations.
5 and lay y' hand upon y' mouth.
27 I know y' thoughts, and the devices
34 seeing in y' answers there remaineth
32:11 Behold, I waited for y' words;
11 I gave ear to y' reasons, whilst ye
14 will I answer him with y' speeches.
42: 8 lest I deal with you after y' folly,
Ps 4: 4 with y' own heart upon y' bed,
5 and put y' trust in the Lord.
11: 1 Flee as a bird to y' mountain?
22:26 seek him: y' heart shall live for ever.
24: 7 Lift up y' heads, O ye gates; and be
9 Lift up y' heads, O ye gates; even lift
31:24 he shall strengthen y' heart, all ye
47: 1 O clap y' hands, all ye people;
58: 2 the violence of y' hands in the earth.
9 Before y' pots can feel the thorns,
62: 8 people, pour out y' heart before him:
10 increase, set not y' heart upon them.
69:32 y' heart shall live that seek God.
75: 5 Lift not up y' horn on high: speak
76:11 Vow, and pay unto the Lord y' God:
78: 1 incline y' ears to the words of my
95: 8 Harden not y' heart, as in the
9 When y' fathers tempted me, proved
105:11 of Canaan, the lot of y' inheritance:
115:14 more and more, you and y' children.
134: 2 Lift up y' hands in the sanctuary,
146: 3 Put not y' trust in princes, nor in
Pr 1:26 I also will laugh at y' calamity;
26 I will mock when y' fear cometh;
27 When y' fear cometh as desolation,
27 y' destruction cometh as a whirlwind;
Isa 1: 7 Y' country is desolate, y' cities are
7 y' land, strangers devour it in y'
11 is the multitude of y' sacrifices
12 who hath required this at y' hand,
14 Y' new moons and y' appointed feasts
15 And when ye spread forth y' hands,
15 not hear: y' hands are full of blood.
16 put away the evil of y' doings from
18 though y' sins be as scarlet, they
3:14 the spoil of the poor is in y' houses.
8:13 be y' fear, and let him be y' dread.
10: 3 and where will ye leave y' glory?
23: 7 Is this y' joyous city, whose antiquity
14 for y' strength is laid waste.
28:18 y' covenant with death shall be
18 y' agreement with hell shall not stand;
22 lest y' bands be made strong:
29:10 deep sleep, and hath closed y' eyes:
10 the prophets and y' rulers, the seers
16 Surely y' turning of things upside
30: 3 the strength of Pharaoh be y' shame,
3 in the shadow of Egypt y' confusion.
15 in confidence shall be y' strength:
31: 7 which y' own hands have made unto
32:11 and gird sackcloth upon y' loins.
33: 4 y' spoil shall be gathered like the
11 y' breath, as fire, shall devour you.
35: 4 y' God will come with vengeance,
36:17 you away to a land like y' own land,
37: 6 Thus shall ye say unto y' master,
40: 1 comfort ye my people, saith y' God.
9 the cities of Judah, Behold y' God!
26 Lift up y' eyes on high, and behold
41:21 Produce y' cause, saith the Lord;
21 bring forth y' strong reasons, saith
24 of nothing, and y' work of nought:
26 there is none that heareth y' words.
43:14 Thus saith the Lord, y' redeemer,
14 For y' sake I have sent to Babylon,
15 I am the Lord, y' Holy One,
15 the creator of Israel, y' King.

Isa 46: 1 y' carriages were heavy laden; they*
4 And even to y' old age I am he; *
50: 1 the bill of y' mother's divorcement,
1 y' iniquities have ye sold yourselves,
1 for y' transgressions is y' mother put
11 walk in the light of y' fire, and in
51: 2 Look unto Abraham y' father, and
6 Lift up y' eyes to the heavens, and
52:12 the God of Israel will be y' rereward.
55: 2 y' labour for that which satisfieth not?
2 let y' soul delight itself in fatness.
3 Incline y' ear, and come unto me:
3 hear, and y' soul shall live; and I
8 For my thoughts are not y' thoughts,
8 neither are y' ways my ways, saith
9 so are my ways higher than y' ways,
9 and my thoughts than y' thoughts.
58: 3 in the day of y' fast ye find pleasure,
3 and exact all y' labours.
4 to make y' voice to be heard on high.
59: 2 But y' iniquities have separated
2 y' God and y' sins have hid his face
3 For y' hands are defiled with blood,
3 and y' fingers with iniquity;
3 y' lips have spoken lies,
3 y' tongue hath muttered perverseness.
61: 5 shall stand and feed y' flocks,
5 be y' plowmen and y' vinedressers.
7 For y' shame ye shall have double;
65: 7 Y' iniquities, and the iniquities of
7 iniquities of y' fathers together,
15 ye shall leave y' name for a curse
66: 5 Y' brethren that hated you, that cast
5 but he shall appear to y' joy, and
14 ye see this, y' heart shall rejoice,
14 y' bones shall flourish like an herb:
20 And they shall bring all y' brethren
22 so shall y' seed and y' name remain.
Jer 2: 5 What iniquity...y' fathers found in me,
9 with y' children's children will I
30 In vain have I smitten y' children;
30 y' own sword...devoured y' prophets,
3:18 for an inheritance unto y' fathers.
22 and I will heal y' backslidings.
4: 3 Break up y' fallow ground, and sow
4 take away the foreskins of y' heart,
4 it, because of the evil of y' doings.
5:19 and served strange gods in y' land,
25 Y' iniquities have turned away these
25 y' sins have withholden good things
6:16 and ye shall find rest for y' souls.
20 y' burnt offerings are not acceptable,
20 nor y' sacrifices sweet unto me,
7: 3 Amend y' ways and y' doings, and I
5 amend y' ways and y' doings; if ye
6 walk after other gods to y' hurt:
7 in the land that I gave to y' fathers,
11 become a den of robbers in y' eyes?
14 which I gave to you and to y' fathers,
15 as I have cast out all y' brethren,
21 y' burnt offerings unto y' sacrifices,
22 For I spake not unto y' fathers,
23 Obey my voice, and I will be y' God,
25 Since the day that y' fathers came
9:20 let y' ear receive the word at his
20 and teach y' daughters wailing, and
11: 4 I commanded y' fathers in the day
4 be my people, and I will be y' God:
5 which I have sworn unto y' fathers,
7 I earnestly protested unto y' fathers
12:13 they shall be ashamed of y' revenues
13:16 Give glory to the Lord y' God, before
16 before y' feet stumble upon the dark
17 weep in secret places for y' pride;
18 for y' principalities shall come down,
18 even the crown of y' glory.
20 Lift up y' eyes, and behold them that
16: 9 this place in y' eyes, and in y' days,
11 Because y' fathers have forsaken me,
12 have done worse than y' fathers;
13 know not, neither ye nor y' fathers;
17: 1 and upon the horns of y' altars;
22 carry forth a burden out of y' houses
22 day, as I commanded y' fathers.
18:11 and make y' ways and y' doings good.
21: 4 weapons of war that are in y' hands,
12 it, because of the evil of y' doings.
14 according to the fruit of y' doings,
23: 2 visit upon you the evil of y' doings,
39 city that I gave you and y' fathers,
25: 4 hearkened, nor inclined y' ear to hear.
5 evil way, and the evil of y' doings,
5 unto you and to y' fathers for ever
6 to anger with the works of y' hands;
7 the works of y' hands to y' own hurt.
34 for the days of y' slaughter and
34 of y' dispersions are accomplished;*
26:11 city, as ye have heard with y' ears.
13 now amend y' ways and y' doings,
13 obey the voice of the Lord y' God;
14 As for me, behold, I am in y' hand:
15 to speak all these things in y' ears.
27: 4 Thus shall ye say unto y' masters;
9 hearken not ye to y' prophets,
9 to y' diviners, nor to y' dreamers,
9 to y' enchanters, nor to y' sorcerers,
10 to remove you far from y' land;
12 Bring y' necks under the yoke of the
16 not to the words of y' prophets that
29: 6 and take wives for y' sons,
6 and give y' daughters to husbands,
8 Let not y' prophets and y' diviners
8 hearken to y' dreams which ye
13 shall search for me with all y' heart.
14 and I will turn away y' captivity, and
16 y' brethren that are not gone forth

Jer 29:21 and he shall slay them before y' eyes.
30:22 be my people, and I will be y' God.
34:13 I made a covenant with y' fathers in
14 y' fathers hearkened not unto me.
35: 6 wine, neither ye, nor y' sons for ever:
7 but all y' days ye shall dwell in tents;
15 amend y' doings, and go not after
15 I have given to you and to y' fathers:
15 but ye have not inclined y' ear, nor
18 commandment of Jonadab y' father,
37:19 now y' prophets which prophesied
38: 5 king said, Behold, he is in y' hand:
40:10 and oil, and put them in y' vessels,
10 and dwell in y' cities that ye have
42: 4 I will pray unto the Lord y' God
4 according to y' words; and it shall
9 present y' supplication before him;
12 cause you to return to y' own land.
13 obey the voice of the Lord y' God,
15 If ye wholly set y' faces to enter into
20 ye dissembled in y' hearts, when ye
20 ye sent me unto the Lord y' God,
21 obeyed the voice of the Lord y' God,
44: 3 not, neither they, ye, nor y' fathers.
7 ye this great evil against y' souls,
8 wrath with the works of y' hands,
9 forgotten the wickedness of y' fathers,
9 of their wives, and y' own wickedness,
9 and the wickedness of y' wives,
10 I set before you and before y' fathers.
21 y' fathers, y' kings, and y' princes,
22 because of the evil of y' doings, and
22 therefore is y' land a desolation, and
25 Ye and y' wives have both spoken
25 y' mouths, and fulfilled with y' hand,
25 ye will surely accomplish y' vows,
25 and surely perform y' vows.
46: 4 and stand forth with y' helmets;
48: 6 Flee, save y' lives, and be like the
50:12 Y' mother shall be sore confounded;
51:24 they have done in Zion in y' sight,
46 And lest y' heart faint, and ye fear
50 and let Jerusalem come into y' mind.
Eze 5:16 you, and will break y' staff of bread:
6: 3 you, and I will destroy y' high places.
4 And y' altars shall be desolate,
4 and y' images shall be broken: and I
4 down y' slain men before y' idols.
5 y' bones round about y' altars.
6 In all y' dwellingplaces the cities
6 that y' altars may be laid waste and
6 y' idols may be broken and cease,
6 and y' images may be cut down,
6 and y' works may be abolished.
9: 5 let not y' eye spare, neither have ye
11: 5 the things that come into y' mind,
6 have multiplied y' slain in this city,
7 Y' slain whom ye have laid in the
11 This city shall not be y' caldron,
12:11 Say, I am y' sign: like as I have done,
25 for in y' days, O rebellious house, will
13:19 by y' lying to my people that hear
19 to my people that hear y' lies? *
20 Behold, I am against y' pillows,
20 and I will tear them from y' arms,
21 Y' kerchiefs also will I tear, and
21 and deliver my people out of y' hand,
21 be no more in y' hand to be hunted;
23 will deliver my people out of y' hand:
14: 6 and turn yourselves from y' idols;
6 y' faces from all y' abominations.
16:45 y' mother was an Hittite,
45 and y' father an Amorite.
55 shall return to y' former estate.
18:25 way equal? are not y' ways unequal?
29 ways equal? are not y' ways unequal?
30 yourselves from all y' transgressions;
30 so iniquity shall not be y' ruin.
31 away from you all y' transgressions,
20: 5 them, saying, I am the Lord y' God;
7 idols of Egypt: I am the Lord y' God.
18 ye not in the statutes of y' fathers,
19 I am the Lord y' God; walk in my
20 may know that I am the Lord y' God.
27 in this y' fathers have blasphemed
30 after the manner of y' fathers?
31 For when ye offer y' gifts, when ye
31 make y' sons to pass through the fire,
31 pollute yourselves with all y' idols,
32 And that which cometh into y' mind
36 Like as I pleaded with y' fathers
39 more with y' gifts, and with y' idols.
40 and there will I require y' offerings,
40 y' oblations, with all y' holy things.
41 will accept you with y' sweet savour,*
42 up mine hand to give it to y' fathers.
43 And there shall ye remember y' ways,
43 and all y' doings, wherein ye have
43 shall lothe yourselves in y' own sight
43 all y' evils that ye have committed.
44 not according to y' wicked ways,
44 nor according to y' corrupt doings,
21:24 made y' iniquity to be remembered,
24 that y' transgressions are discovered,
24 that in all y' doings y' sins do appear;
23:48 be taught not to do after y' lewdness.
49 they shall recompense y' lewdness
49 and ye shall bear the sins of y' idols:
24:21 of y' strength, the desire of y' eyes,
21 and that which y' soul pitieth;
21 and y' sons and y' daughters whom
22 ye shall not cover y' lips, nor eat the
23 And y' tires shall be upon y' heads,
23 and y' shoes upon y' feet: ye shall
23 ye shall pine away for y' iniquities,
33:11 turn ye from y' evil ways; for why will

Eze 33:25 and lift up y' eyes toward y' idols, and
26 Ye stand upon y' sword, ye work
34:18 with y' feet the residue of y' pastures?
18 ye must foul the residue with y' feet?
19 which ye have trodden with y' feet;
19 which ye have fouled with y' feet.
21 pushed all the diseased with y' horns,
31 men, and I am y' God, saith the Lord
35:13 Thus with y' mouth ye have boasted
13 have multiplied y' words against me:
36: 8 ye shall shoot forth y' branches,
8 yield y' fruit to my people of Israel;
11 I will settle you after y' old estates,
11 unto you than at y' beginnings:
22 I do not this for y' sakes, O house of
24 and will bring you into y' own land.
25 all y' filthiness, and from all y' idols,
26 away the stony heart out of y' flesh,
28 in the land that I gave to y' fathers;
28 be my people, and I will be y' God.
29 save you from all y' uncleannesses:
31 shall ye remember y' own evil ways,
31 and y' doings that were not good,
31 lothe yourselves in y' own sight for
31 y' iniquities and for y' abominations.
32 Not for y' sakes do I this, saith the
32 and confounded for y' own ways,
33 cleansed you from all y' iniquities
37:12 O my people, I will open y' graves,
12 cause you to come up out of y' graves,
13 when I have opened y' graves, O my
13 and brought you up out of y' graves,
14 and I shall place you in y' own land:
25 wherein y' fathers have dwelt;
43:27 y' burnt offerings upon the altar,
27 and y' peace offerings; and I will
44: 6 it suffice you of all y' abominations,
7 because of all y' abominations.
30 every sort of y' oblations, shall be
30 unto the priest the first of y' dough,
45: 9 away y' exactions from my people,
12 fifteen shekels, shall be y' maneh.
47:14 mine hand to give it unto y' fathers:
Da 1:10 hath appointed y' meat and y' drink:
10 for why should he see y' faces worse
10 the children which are of y' sort?
2: 5 y' houses shall be made a dunghill.
47 it is, that y' God is a God of gods,
10:21 in these things, but Michael y' prince.
Ho 1: 9 my people, and I will not be y' God.
2: 1 Say ye unto y' brethren, Ammi;
1 and to y' sisters, Ruhamah.
2 Plead with y' mother, plead: for she
4:13 y' daughters shall commit
13 y' spouses shall commit adultery.
14 I will not punish y' daughters when
14 nor y' spouses when they commit
5:13 heal you, nor cure you of y' wound.
6: 4 y' goodness is as a morning cloud,
9:10 I saw y' fathers as the firstripe in the
10:12 in mercy, break up y' fallow ground:
15 you because of y' great wickedness:
Joe 1: 2 the land. Hath this been in y' days,
2 or even in the days of y' fathers?
3 Tell ye y' children of it, and let
3 let y' children tell their children,
5 wine; for it is cut off from y' mouth.
13 withholden from the house of y' God.
14 into the house of the Lord y' God,
2:12 turn ye even to me with all y' heart,
13 rend y' heart, and not y' garments,
13 and turn unto the Lord y' God: for he
14 drink offering unto the Lord y' God?
23 Zion, and rejoice in the Lord y' God:
26 praise the name of the Lord y' God,
27 and that I am the Lord y' God,
28 and y' sons and y' daughters shall
28 y' old men shall dream dreams,
28 y' young men shall see visions:
3: 4 y' recompence upon y' own head;
5 and have carried into y' temple my
7 y' recompence upon y' own head:
8 I will sell y' sons and y' daughters
10 Beat y' plowshares into swords,
10 and y' pruninghooks into spears:
17 ye know that I am the Lord y' God
Am 2:11 I raised up of y' sons for prophets,
11 and of y' young men for Nazarites.
3: 2 I will punish you for all y' iniquities.
4: 2 hooks, and y' posterity with fishhooks.
4 and bring y' sacrifices every morning,
4 and y' tithes after three years:
6 you cleanness of teeth in all y' cities,
6 and want of bread in all y' places:
9 when y' gardens and y' vineyards
9 and y' fig trees and y' olive trees
10 y' young men have I slain with the
10 and have taken away y' horses;
10 I have made the stink of y' camps
10 to come up unto y' nostrils: yet have
5:11 as y' treading is upon the poor, *
12 I know y' manifold transgressions
12 y' mighty sins: they afflict the just,
21 I hate, I despise y' feast days,
21 will not smell in y' solemn assemblies.
22 burnt offerings and y' meat offerings,
22 the peace offerings of y' fat beasts.
26 borne the tabernacle of y' Moloch
26 Chiun y' images, the star of y' god,
6: 2 or their border greater than y' border?
8:10 I will turn y' feasts into mourning,
10 and all y' songs into lamentation;
Mic 2: 3 which ye shall not remove y' necks;
10 and depart; for this is not y' rest:
3:12 shall Zion for y' sake be plowed as
Hab 1: 5 for I will work a work in y' days,

Zep 3:20 turn back y' captivity before y' eyes,
Hag 1: 4 O ye, to dwell in y' cieled houses,
5 the Lord of hosts; Consider y' ways.
2: 3 is it not in y' eyes in comparison of it
17 hail in all the labours of y' hands;
Zec 1: 2 been sore displeased with y' fathers.
4 Be ye not as y' fathers, unto whom
4 turn ye now from y' evil ways,
4 and from y' evil doings: but they did
5 Y' fathers, where are they? and the
6 did they not take hold of y' fathers?
6:15 obey the voice of the Lord y' God.
7:10 evil against his brother in y' heart.
8: 9 Let y' hands be strong, ye that hear
13 fear not, but let y' hands be strong.
14 when y' fathers provoked me to wrath,
16 of truth and peace in y' gates:
17 none of you imagine evil in y' hearts
Mal 1: 5 And y' eyes shall see, and ye shall say,
9 unto us: this hath been by y' means:
9 will he regard y' persons? saith
10 will I accept an offering at y' hand.
13 should I accept this of y' hand? saith
2: 2 I will curse y' blessings: yea, I have
3 Behold I will corrupt y' seed,
3 and spread dung upon y' faces,
3 even the dung of y' solemn feasts;
13 it with good will at y' hand.
15 Therefore take heed to y' spirit, and
16 therefore take heed to y' spirit, that
17 have wearied the Lord with y' words.
3: 7 Even from the days of y' fathers
11 will rebuke the devourer for y' sakes,
11 not destroy the fruits of y' ground;
11 shall y' vine cast her fruit before the
13 Y' words have been stout against me,
4: 3 be ashes under the soles of y' feet
M't 5:12 for great is y' reward in heaven: 5216
16 Let y' light so shine before men, "
16 that they may see y' good works, "
16 and glorify y' Father which is in "
20 except y' righteousness exceed "
37 But let y' communication be, Yea, "
44 Love y' enemies, bless them that "
45 ye may be the children of y' Father "
47 And if ye salute y' brethren only, "
48 as y' Father which is in heaven is "
6: 1 that ye do not y' alms before men, "
1 ye have no reward of y' Father "
8 for y' Father knoweth what things "
14 y' heavenly Father will also forgive "
15 will y' Father forgive y' trespasses. "
21 For where y' treasure is, "
21 there will y' heart be also. * "
25 Take no thought for y' life, what ye "
25 nor yet for y' body, what ye shall "
26 y' heavenly Father feedeth them. "
32 for y' heavenly Father knoweth "
7: 6 cast ye y' pearls before swine, "
11 give good gifts unto y' children, "
11 how much more shall y' Father "
9: 4 Wherefore think ye evil in y' hearts? "
11 eateth y' Master with publicans "
29 According to y' faith be it unto you. "
10: 9 nor silver, nor brass in y' purses, "
10 Nor scrip for y' journey, neither "
13 worthy, let y' peace come upon it: 5216
13 worthy, let y' peace return to you. "
14 not receive you, nor hear y' words, "
14 city, shake off the dust of y' feet. "
20 Spirit of y' Father which speaketh "
29 on the ground without y' Father. "
30 hairs of y' head are all numbered. "
11:29 ye shall find rest unto y' souls. "
12:27 by whom do y' children cast them "
27 therefore they shall be y' judges. "
13:16 blessed are y' eyes, for they see: "
16 and y' ears, for they hear. "
15: 3 of God by y' tradition? "
6 God of none effect by y' tradition. "
17:20 Because of y' unbelief: for verily I "
24 Doth not y' master pay tribute? "
18:14 will of y' Father which is in heaven. "
35 ye from y' hearts forgive not every "
19: 8 because of the hardness of y' hearts "
8 suffered you to put away y' wives: "
20:26 among you, let him be y' minister; "
27 among you, let him be y' servant: "
23: 8 for one is y' Master, even Christ; "
9 no man y' father upon the earth: "
9 for one is y' Father, which is in "
10 for one is y' Master, even Christ. "
11 among you shall be y' servant. "
32 up then the measure of y' fathers. "
34 shall ye scourge in y' synagogues, "
38 y' house is left unto you desolate. "
24:20 that y' flight be not in the winter, "
42 not what hour y' Lord doth come. "
25: 8 Give us of y' oil; for our lamps are "
26:45 Sleep on now, and take y' rest: "
27:65 go y' way, make it as sure as you ‡
M'r 2: 8 reason ye these things in y' hearts? 5216
6:11 shake off the dust under y' feet "
7: 9 that ye may keep y' own tradition. "
13 of none effect through y' tradition, "
8:17 have ye y' heart yet hardened? "
10: 5 For the hardness of y' heart he "
43 among you, shall be y' minister: "
11: 2 Go y' way into the village over "
25 y' Father also which is in heaven 5216
25 may forgive you y' trespasses. "
26 neither will y' Father which is in "
26 is in heaven forgive y' trespasses. "
13:18 that y' flight be not in the winter. * "
14:41 Sleep on now, and take y' rest: it is
16: 7 But go y' way, tell his disciples and*

Lu 3:14 and be content with y' wages. 5216
4:21 is this scripture fulfilled in y' ears. "
5: 4 and let down y' nets for a draught. "
22 What reason ye in y' hearts? "
6:22 and cast out y' name as evil, for "
23 y' reward is great in heaven: "
24 ye have received y' consolation. "
27 Love y' enemies, do good to them "
35 But love ye y' enemies, and do good, "
35 and y' reward shall be great, and "
36 as y' Father also is merciful. "
38 shall men give into y' bosom. "
7:22 Go y' way, and tell John what things
8:25 unto them, Where is y' faith? 5216
9: 3 Take nothing for y' journey, 3588
5 shake off the very dust from y' feet 5216
44 sayings sink down into y' ears: "
10: 3 Go y' ways: behold, I send you
6 there, y' peace shall rest upon it: 5216
10 go y' ways out into the streets of *
11 Even the very dust of y' city, 5216
20 y' names are written in heaven. "
11:13 to give good gifts unto y' children: "
13 more shall y' heavenly Father 3588
19 by whom do y' sons cast them out? 5216
19 therefore shall they be y' judges. "
39 y' inward part is full of ravening "
46 the burdens with one of y' fingers. "
47 prophets,...y' fathers killed them. "
48 ye allow the deeds of y' fathers: "
12: 7 hairs of y' head are all numbered. "
22 Take no thought for y' life, what ye "
30 y' Father knoweth that ye have "
32 for it is y' Father's good pleasure "
34 For where y' treasure is, "
34 there will y' heart be also. "
35 Let y' loins be girded about, and "
35 and y' lights burning; 3588
13:35 y' house is left unto you desolate: 5216
16:11 commit to y' trust the true riches? 5213
12 give you that which is y' own? 5212
15 but God knoweth y' hearts: for 5216
19:30 at y' entering ye shall find a colt *
21:14 Settle it therefore in y' hearts, not 5216
15 y' adversaries shall not be able 5213
18 shall not an hair of y' head perish. 5216
19 In y' patience possess ye y' souls. "
28 then look up, and lift up y' heads; "
28 for y' redemption draweth nigh. "
30 ye see and know of y' own selves 1438
34 any time y' hearts be overcharged 5216
22:53 but this is y' hour, and the power of "
23:28 for yourselves, and for y' children. "
24:38 why do thoughts arise in y' hearts? "
Joh 4:35 Lift up y' eyes, and look on the "
6:49 Y' fathers did eat manna in the "
58 not as y' fathers did eat manna, * "
7: 6 but y' time is alway ready. 5212
8:17 It is also written in y' law, that the "
21 seek me, and shall die in y' sins: 5216
24 you, that ye shall die in y' sins: "
24 that I am he, ye shall die in y' sins. "
38 which ye have seen with y' father. "
41 Ye do the deeds of y' father. Then "
42 If God were y' Father, ye would "
44 Ye are of y' father the devil, "
44 the lusts of y' father ye will do. 5216
54 of whom ye say, that he is y' God: "
56 Y' father Abraham rejoiced to see "
9:19 Is this y' son, who ye say was born "
41 We see; therefore y' sin remaineth. "
10:34 Is it not written in y' law, I said, "
11:15 glad for y' sakes that I was not 5209
12:30 not because of me, but for y' sakes. "
13:14 If I then, y' Lord and Master, *3588
14 have washed y' feet; ye also ought 5216
14: 1 Let not y' heart be troubled; "
26 all things to y' remembrance, 5209
27 Let not y' heart be troubled, 5216
15:11 and that y' joy might be full. "
16 and that y' fruit should remain: "
16: 6 you, sorrow hath filled y' heart. "
20 y' sorrow shall be turned into joy. "
22 again, and y' heart shall rejoice, "
22 and y' joy no man taketh from you. "
24 receive, that y' joy may be full. "
18:31 and judge him according to y' law. "
19:14 unto the Jews, Behold y' King! "
15 unto them, Shall I crucify y' King? "
20:17 unto my Father, and y' Father; "
17 and to my God, and y' God. "
Ac 2:17 y' sons and y' daughters shall "
17 and y' young men shall see visions "
17 y' old men shall dream dreams: "
39 is unto you, and to y' children, "
3:17 ye did it, as did also y' rulers. "
19 that y' sins may be blotted out, "
22 A prophet shall the Lord y' God * "
22 raise up unto you of y' brethren, "
5:28 filled Jerusalem with y' doctrine, "
7:37 A prophet shall the Lord y' God * "
37 raise up unto you of y' brethren, "
43 and the star of y' god Remphan, * "
51 Ghost: as y' fathers did, so do ye. "
52 have not y' fathers persecuted? "
13:41 for I work a work in y' days, "
15:24 subverting y' souls, saying, Ye "
17:23 passed by, and beheld y' devotions, "
28 also of y' own poets have said, 2596,5209
18: 6 Y' blood be upon y' own heads; 546
15 and names, and of y' law, 2596,5209
19:37 yet blasphemers of y' goddess. 5216
20:30 of y' own selves shall men arise, "
24:22 know...uttermost of y' matter. 2596,5209
27:34 meat: for this is for y' health: 5212
Ro 1: 8 y' faith is spoken of throughout 5216

Ro 6:12 therefore reign in y' mortal body, 5216
13 yield ye y' members as instruments "
13 and y' members as instruments of "
19 because of the infirmity of y' flesh: "
19 have yielded y' members servants "
19 so now yield y' members servants "
22 ye have y' fruit unto holiness, and "
8:11 quicken y' mortal bodies by his "
11:25 be wise in y' own conceits; 3844,1438
28 they are enemies for y' sakes: 5209
31 through y' mercy they also may *5212
12: 1 y' bodies a living sacrifice, 5216
1 which is y' reasonable service. "
2 by the renewing of y' mind, "
16 Be not wise in y' own conceits. "
14:16 then y' good be evil spoken of: "
15:24 somewhat filled with y' company. "
30 together with me in y' prayers 3588
16:19 For y' obedience is come abroad 5216
19 I am glad therefore on y' behalf: *5213
20 bruise Satan under y' feet shortly. 5216
1Co 1: 4 thank my God always on y' behalf, * "
26 For ye see y' calling, brethren, "
2: 5 That y' faith should not stand in "
4: 6 myself and to Apollos for y' sakes; 5209
5: 6 Y' glorifying is not good. Know 5216
6: 5 I speak to y' shame. Is it so, that *5213
8 and defraud, and that y' brethren. "
15 that y' bodies are the members of 5216
19 ye not that y' body is the temple 1438
19 of God, and ye are not y' own? 5216
20 therefore glorify God in y' body, "
20 and in y' spirit, which are God's. * "
7: 5 tempt you not for y' incontinency. "
14 else were y' children unclean; "
35 And this I speak for y' own profit; "
9:11 if we shall reap y' carnal things? "
14:34 Let y' women keep silence in the * "
15:14 vain, and y' faith is also vain. "
17 be not raised, y' faith is vain; "
17 ye are yet in y' sins. "
31 I protest by y' rejoicing which I *5212
34 of God: I speak this to y' shame. *5213
58 ye know that y' labour is not 5216
16: 3 ye shall approve by y' letters, *
3 will I send to bring y' liberality 5216
14 y' things be done with charity. * "
17 that which was lacking on y' part "
2Co 1: 6, 6 it is for y' consolation and "
14 that we are y' rejoicing, even as ye "
24 we have dominion over y' faith, "
24 are helpers of y' joy: for by faith "
2: 8 would confirm y' love toward him.
10 for y' sakes forgave I it in the 5209
4: 5 ourselves y' servants for Jesus' 5216
15 For all things are for y' sakes, 5209
5:11 made manifest in y' consciences. 5216
13 we be sober, it is for y' cause. *5213
6:12 ye are straitened in y' own bowels. 5216
7: 7 when he told us y' earnest desire, "
7 y' mourning, y' fervent mind "
13 we were comforted in y' comfort: *5213
8: 7 and in y' love to us, see that ye 5209
8 to prove the sincerity of y' love. 5212
9 yet for y' sakes he became poor, 5216
14 y' abundance may be a supply for "
14 also may be a supply for y' want: "
19 and declaration of y' ready mind: * "
24 the churches, the proof of y' love, "
24 and of our boasting on y' behalf. "
9: 2 know the forwardness of y' mind, "
2 y' zeal hath provoked very many. "
5 and make up beforehand y' bounty, "
10 both minister bread for y' food, *
10 and multiply y' seed sown, 5216
10 the fruits of y' righteousness;) "
13 y' professed subjection unto the "
13 y' liberal distribution unto them, 3588
10: 6 when y' obedience is fulfilled. 5216
8 and not for y' destruction, I should * "
15 when y' faith is increased, that we "
11: 3 so y' minds should be corrupted "
12:19 dearly beloved, for y' edifying. "
13: 5 in the faith; prove y' own selves. 1438
5 Know ye not y' own selves, how "
9 we wish, even y' perfection. 5216
Ga 4: 6 the Spirit of his Son into y' hearts, "
15 have plucked out y' own eyes, "
16 Am I therefore become y' enemy, "
6:13 that they may glory in y' flesh. 5212
18 Lord Jesus Christ be with y' spirit. "
Eph 1:13 truth, the gospel of y' salvation: 5216
15 of y' faith in the Lord Jesus, *5209
18 eyes of y' understanding being 5216
3:13 tribulations for you, which is y' glory. "
17 that Christ may dwell in y' hearts 5216
4: 4 are called in one hope of y' calling; "
23 renewed in the spirit of y' mind; "
26 the sun go down upon y' wrath: "
29 proceed out of y' mouth, "
5:19 melody in y' heart to the Lord; "
22 yourselves unto y' own husbands; 3588
25 Husbands, love y' wives, even as 1438
6: 1 obey y' parents in the Lord: 5216
4 provoke not y' children to wrath: "
5 to them that are y' masters "
5 in singleness of y' heart, as unto 5216
9 that y' Master also is in heaven; * "
14 y' loins girt about with truth, "
15 y' feet shod with the preparation 3588
22 that he might comfort y' hearts. 5216
Ph'p 1: 5 For y' fellowship in the gospel "
9 that y' love may abound yet more "
19 my salvation through y' prayer, "
25 with you all for y' furtherance and "
26 y' rejoicing may be more abundant "

Ph'p 1:27 y' conversation be as it becometh
27 I may hear of y' affairs, that ye 5216
28 nothing terrified by y' adversaries: 3588
2:12 work out y' own salvation with fear 1438
17 sacrifice and service of y' faith, 5216
19 comfort, when I know y' state. "
20 who will naturally care for y' state. "
25 but y' messenger, and he that "
30 to supply y' lack of service toward "
4: 5 y' moderation be known unto all "
6 let y' requests be made known unto "
7 keep y' hearts and minds through "
10 last y' care of me hath flourished 3588
17 may abound unto y' account. 5216
19 my God shall supply all y' need * "
Col 1: 4 Since we heard of y' faith in Christ "
8 unto us y' love in the Spirit. "
21 enemies in y' mind by wicked 3588
2: 5 joying and beholding y' order, 5216
5 stedfastness of y' faith in Christ. "
13 And you, being dead in y' sins and "
13 and the uncircumcision of y' flesh, "
18 no man beguile you of y' reward
3: 2 Set y' affection on things above, not
3 y' life is hid with Christ in God. 5216
5 Mortify therefore y' members "
8 communication out of y' mouth. "
15 the peace of God rule in y' hearts, "
16 singing with grace in y' hearts to "
18 yourselves unto y' own husbands, 2398
19 Husbands, love y' wives, and be not 3588
20 Children, obey y' parents in all "
21 provoke not y' children to anger, 5216
22 obey in all things y' masters 3588
4: 1 unto y' servants that which is just "
6 y' speech be alway with grace, 5216
8 that he might know y' estate, * "
8 and comfort y' hearts; "
1Th 1: 3 ceasing y' work of faith, 5209
4 beloved, y' election of God. 5216
5 we were among you for y' sake. 5209
8 every place y' faith to God-ward 5216
2:14 like things of y' own countrymen, 2398
17 to see y' face with great desire. 5216
3: 2 to comfort you concerning y' faith: "
5 I sent to know y' faith, lest by "
6 brought us good tidings of y' faith "
7 affliction and distress by y' faith: "
9 we joy for y' sakes before our God; 5209
10 that we might see y' face, and 5216
10 that which is lacking in y' faith? "
13 the end he may stablish y' hearts "
4: 3 will of God, even y' sanctification, "
11 quiet, and to do y' own business, 2398
11 and to work with y' own hands, "
5:23 I pray God y' whole spirit and soul 3588
2Th 1: 3 that y' faith groweth exceedingly, 5216
4 of God for y' patience and faith "
4 y' persecutions and tribulations "
2:17 Comfort y' hearts, and stablish you "
3: 5 Lord direct y' hearts into the love "
Ph'm 22 for I trust that through y' prayers "
25 Lord Jesus Christ be with y' spirit. "
Heb 3: 8 Harden not y' hearts, as in the "
9 When y' fathers tempted me, "
15 hear his voice, harden not y' hearts, "
4: 7 hear his voice, harden not y' hearts. "
6:10 forget y' work and labour of love, "
9:14 purge y' conscience from dead "
10:34 joyfully the spoiling of y' goods, "
35 not away therefore y' confidence, "
12: 3 ye be wearied and faint in y' minds. "
13 make straight paths for y' feet, "
13: 5 Let y' conversation be without *3588
17 for they watch for y' souls, 5216
Jas 1: 3 trying of y' faith worketh patience. "
21 which is able to save y' souls. "
22 only, deceiving y' own selves. 1438
2: 2 come unto y' assembly a man 5216
3:14 envying and strife in y' hearts, "
4: 1 y' lusts that war in y' members? "
3 ye may consume it upon y' lusts. "
8 Cleanse y' hands, ye sinners; "
8 and purify y' hearts, ye double minded. "
9 y' laughter be turned to mourning, 5216
9 and y' joy to heaviness. 3588
14 For what is y' life? It is even a 5216
16 now ye rejoice in y' boastings: "
5: 1 weep and howl for y' miseries that "
2 Y' riches are corrupted, and "
2 and y' garments are motheaten. "
3 Y' gold and silver is cankered; "
3 shall eat y' flesh as it were fire. "
4 who have reaped down y' fields, "
5 ye have nourished y' hearts, as in a "
8 ye also patient; stablish y' hearts: "
12 oath: but let y' yea be yea; "
12 and y' nay, nay; lest ye fall 3588
16 Confess y' faults one to another, "
1Pe 1: 7 That the trial of y' faith, being 5216
9 Receiving the end of y' faith, "
9 even the salvation of y' souls. "
13 gird up the loins of y' mind, 5216
14 to the former lusts in y' ignorance: "
17 time of y' sojourning here in fear: "
18 from y' vain conversation received "
18 by tradition from y' fathers; "
21 y' faith and hope might be in God. "
22 Seeing ye have purified y' souls in "
2:12 Having y' conversation honest "
12 they may by y' good works, which 3588
16 and not using y' liberty for a cloke "
18 subject to y' masters with all fear; "
20 when ye be buffeted for y' faults, *
25 Shepherd and Bishop of y' souls. 5216
3: 1 in subjection to y' own husbands; 3588

1Pe 3: 2 behold y' chaste conversation 5216
7 that y' prayers be not hindered. "
15 the Lord God in y' hearts: "
16 accuse y' good conversation "
4:14 of, but on y' part he is glorified. *5209
5: 7 Casting all y' care upon him; for 5216
8 because y' adversary the devil, "
9 are accomplished in y' brethren "
2Pe 1: 5 add to y' faith virtue; and to "
10 give diligence to make y' calling "
19 the day star arise in y' hearts: "
3: 1 both which I stir up y' pure minds "
17 fall from y' own stedfastness. 3588
1Jo 1: 4 unto you, that y' joy may be full. *5216
2:12 because y' sins are forgiven you for 3588
2Jo 10 receive him not into y' house, neither
Jude 12 are spots in y' feasts of charity, 5216
20 yourselves on y' most holy faith, "
Re 1: 9 I John, who also am y' brother, "
2:23 one of you according to y' works. "
16: 1 Go y' ways, and pour out the vials of*

yours See also YOURSELVES.
Ge 45:20 the good of all the land of Egypt is y'.
De 11:24 of your feet shall tread shall be y':
Jos 2:14 Our life for y', if ye utter not this our
2Ch 20:15 for the battle is not y', but God's.
Jer 5:19 strangers in a land that is not y'.
Lu 6:20 poor: for y' is the kingdom of God. 5212
Joh 15:20 my saying, they will keep y' also.
1Co 3:21 in men; for all things are y'. 5216
22 or things to come; all are y'; "
8: 9 means this liberty of y' become a "
16:18 have refreshed my spirit and y': "
2Co 12:14 for I seek not y', but you: for the "

yourselves See also YOUR and SELVES.
Ge 18: 4 your feet, and rest y' under the tree:
45: 5 be not grieved, nor angry with y', 5869
49: 1 Gather y' together, that I may tell
2 Gather y' together, and hear, ye
Ex 19:12 Take heed to y', that ye go not up
30:37 ye shall not make to y' according to
32:29 Consecrate y' to day to the Lord, 3027
Le 11:43 neither shall ye make y' unclean 5315
44 ye shall therefore sanctify y', and "
44 neither shall ye defile y' with any "
18:24 Defile not ye y' in any of these
30 and that ye defile not y' therein:
19: 4 idols, nor make to y' molten gods:
20: 7 Sanctify y' therefore, and be ye
Nu 11:18 Sanctify y' against to morrow, and ye
16: 3 lift ye up y' above the congregation
21 Separate y' from among this
31: 3 Arm some of y' unto the war, and* 853
18 lying with him, keep alive for y'.
19 purify both y' and your captives on
De 2: 4 take ye good heed unto y' therefore:
4:15 ye therefore good heed unto y'; 5315
16 Lest ye corrupt y', and make you
23 Take heed unto y', lest ye forget
25 corrupt y', and make a graven image,
11:16 Take heed to y', that your heart
23 greater nations and mightier than y'.
14: 1 ye shall not cut y', nor make any
31:14 and present y' in the tabernacle of the
29 my death ye will utterly corrupt y',
Jos 2:16 and hide y' there three days, until the
3: 5 Sanctify y': for to morrow the Lord
6:18 keep y' from the accursed thing,
18 lest ye make y' accursed, when ye*
7:13 say, Sanctify y' against to morrow:
8: 2 shall ye take for a prey unto y':
23: 7 serve them, nor bow y' unto them:
16 other gods, and bowed y' to them;
24:22 Ye are witnesses against y' that ye
J'g 15:12 that ye will not fall upon me y'. 859
1Sa 2:29 to make y' fat with the chiefest of
4: 9 Be strong, and quit y' like men,
9 to you: quit y' like men, and fight.
10:19 therefore present y' before the Lord
14:34 said, Disperse y' among the people,
16: 5 sanctify y', and come with me to
1Ki 18:25 Choose you one bullock for y',
20:12 unto his servants, Set y' in array.
2Ki 17:35 nor bow y' to them, nor serve them,
1Ch 15:12 sanctify y', both ye and your brethren,
2Ch 20:17 set y', stand ye still, and see the
29: 5 ye Levites, sanctify now y', and
31 have consecrated y' unto the Lord, 3027
30: 8 but yield y' unto the Lord, and
32:11 to give over y' to die by famine *
35: 4 And prepare y' by the houses of
6 So kill the passover, and sanctify y',
Ezr 10:11 separate y' from the people of the
Ne 13:25 daughters unto your sons, or for y'.
Job 19: 3 that ye make y' strange to me. *
5 ye will magnify y' against me.
27:12 Behold, all ye y' have seen it;
42: 8 and offer up for y' a burnt offering;
Isa 8: 9 Associate y', O ye people, and ye
9, 9 gird y', and ye shall be broken in
Isa 29: 9 Stay y', and wonder; cry ye out,
45:20 Assemble y' and come; draw near
46: 8 Remember this, and shew y' men:
48:14 All ye, assemble y', and hear;
49: 9 them that are in darkness, Shew y'.
50: 1 for your iniquities have ye sold y'.*
11 that compass y' about with sparks:
52: 3 Ye have sold y' for nought; *
57: 4 Against whom do ye sport y'?
5 Enflaming y' with idols under every
61: 6 and in their glory shall ye boast y'.
Jer 4: 4 Circumcise y' to the Lord, and take
5 Assemble y', and let us go into the
6: 1 gather y' to flee out of the midst of*
8:14 assemble y', and let us enter into
13:18 to the queen, Humble y', sit down:
17:21 Take heed to y', and bear no 5315
25:34 and wallow y' in the ashes, ye
26:15 surely bring innocent blood upon y',
37: 9 Deceive not y', saying, The 5315
44: 8 that ye might cut y' off, and that *
50:14 Put y' in array against Babylon
Eze 14: 6 and turn y' from your idols;
18:30 y' from all your transgressions;
32 wherefore turn y', and live ye.
20: 7 defile not y' with the idols of Egypt:
18 nor defile y' with their idols:
31 ye pollute y' with all your idols,
43 ye shall lothe y' in your own sight
36:31 and shall lothe y' in your own sight
39:17 of the field, Assemble y', and come;
17 gather y' on every side to my
44: 8 my charge in my sanctuary for y'.
Ho 10:12 Sow to y' in righteousness, reap
Joe 1:13 Gird y', and lament, ye priests:
3:11 Assemble y', and come, all ye *
11 and gather y' together round about:
Am 3: 9 Assemble y' upon the mountains of
5:26 of your God, which ye made to y'.
Zep 2: 1 Gather y' together, yea, gather
Zec 7: 6 not ye eat for y', and drink for y'?
M't 3: 9 And think not to say within y', 1438
6:19 up for y' treasures upon earth, 5213
20 lay up for y' treasures in heaven,
16: 8 why reason ye among y', because 1438
23:13 for ye neither go in y', neither suffer
15 more the child of hell than y'. 5216
31 Wherefore ye be witnesses unto y', 1438
25: 9 to them that sell, and buy for y'.
M'r 6:31 Come ye y' apart into a desert 5210,846
9:33 ye disputed among y' by the way?*1438
50 Have salt in y', and have peace one "
13: 9 But take heed to y': for they shall "
Lu 3: 8 to say within y', We have Abraham "
11:46 and ye y' touch not the burdens 846
52 ye entered not in y', and them that "
12:33 provide y' bags which wax not old, 1438
36 And ye y' like unto men that wait
57 why even of y' judge ye not what 1438
13:28 of God, and you y' thrust out.
16: 9 to y' friends of the mammon of 1438
15 they which justify y' before men; "
17: 3 Take heed to y': If thy brother "
14 them, Go shew y' unto the priests. "
21:34 And take heed to y', lest at any "
22:17 Take this, and divide it among y': "
23:28 weep not for me, but weep for y', "
Joh 3:28 Ye y' bear me witness, that I 5210,846
6:43 unto them, Murmur not among y'. 240
16:19 enquire among y' of that I said, "
Ac 2:22 midst of you, as ye y' also know: 846
40 y' from this untoward generation.
5:35 take heed to y' what ye intend to 1438
13:46 y' unworthy of everlasting life, "
15:29 from which if ye keep y', ye shall "
20:10 Trouble not y'; for his life is in him.*
28 Take heed therefore unto y', and 1438
34 Yea, ye y' know, that these hands 846
Ro 6:11 also y' to be dead indeed unto sin, 1438
13 but yield y' unto God, as those "
16 whom ye yield y' servants to obey, "
12:19 Dearly beloved, avenge not y', "
1Co 5:13 from among y' that wicked 5216,846
6: 7 not rather suffer y' to be defrauded?*
7: 5 may give y' to fasting and prayer;
11:13 Judge in y': is it comely that a 5213,846
16:16 That ye submit y' unto such, and *
2Co 7:11 in you, yea, what clearing of y',
11 have approved y' to be clear in this 1438
11:19 fools gladly, seeing ye y' are wise.
13: 5 Examine y', whether ye be in *1438
Eph 2: 8 and that not of y': it is the gift of 5216
5:19 Speaking to y' in psalms and *1438
21 Submitting y' one to another
22 submit y' unto your own husbands,*
Col 3:18 submit y' unto your own husbands,*
1Th 2: 1 For y', brethren, know our entrance 846
3: 3 for y' know that we are appointed "
4: 9 for ye y' are taught of God to love "
5: 2 For y' know perfectly that the day "
11 Wherefore comfort y' together, * 240
1Th 5:13 And be at peace among y'. 1438
15 that which is good, both among y',* "
2Th 3: 6 ye withdraw y' from every brother
7 For y' know how ye ought to follow 846
Heb 10:34 knowing in y' that ye have in 1438
13: 3 as being y' also in the body. 846
17 the rule over you, and submit y': *5216
Jas 2: 4 Are ye not then partial in y', *1438
4: 7 Submit y' therefore to God.
10 Humble y' in the sight of the Lord,
1Pe 1:14 not fashioning y' according to the
2:13 Submit y' to every ordinance *
4: 1 arm y' likewise with the same mind:
8 have fervent charity among y': 1438
5: 5 ye younger, submit y' unto the elder.*
6 Humble y' therefore under the
1Jo 5:21 Little children, keep y' from idols. 1438
2Jo 8 Look to y', that we lose not those "
Jude 20 building up y' on your most holy "
21 Keep y' in the love of God, looking "
Re 19:17 gather y' together unto the supper*

youth See also YOUTHFUL; YOUTHS.
Ge 8:21 of man's heart is evil from his y'; 5271
43:33 the youngest according to his y': 6812
46:34 cattle from our y' even until now, 5271
Le 22:13 her father's house, as in her y', "
Nu 30: 3 in her father's house in her y'; "
16 yet in her y' in her father's house.
J'g 8:20 But the y' drew not his sword: 5288
20 feared, because he was yet a y'.
1Sa 17:33 with him: for thou art but a y', 5288
33 and he a man of war from his y'. 5271
42 for he was but a y', and ruddy, 5288
55 host, Abner, whose son is this y'?
2Sa 19: 7 evil that befell thee from thy y' 5271
1Ki 18:12 servant fear the Lord from my y'. "
Job 13:26 to possess the iniquities of my y'. "
20:11 bones are full of the sin of his y', 5934
29: 4 As I was in the days of my y', *2779
30:12 Upon my right hand rise the y'; *6526
31:18 from my y' he was brought up 5271
33:25 shall return to the days of his y': 5934
36:14 They die in y', and their life is 5290
Ps 25: 7 Remember not the sins of my y', 5271
71: 5 thou art my trust from my y'. "
17 thou hast taught me from my y': "
88:15 and ready to die from my y' up: 5290
89:45 The days of his y' hast thou 5934
103: 5 thy y' is renewed like the eagle's. 5271
110: 3 thou hast the dew of thy y'. 3208
127: 4 man; so are children of the y'. 5271
129: 1 have they afflicted me from my y', "
2 have they afflicted me from my y': "
144:12 be as plants grown up in their y'; "
Pr 2:17 forsaketh the guide of her y', "
5:18 rejoice with the wife of thy y'. "
Ec 11: 9 Rejoice, O young man, in thy y'; 3208
9 cheer thee in the days of thy y', 979
10 for childhood and y' are vanity. 7839
12: 1 thy Creator in the days of thy y', 979
Isa 47:12 thou hast laboured from thy y'; 5271
15 even thy merchants, from thy y': "
54: 4 shalt forget the shame of thy y', 5934
6 and a wife of y', when thou wast 5271
Jer 2: 2 the kindness of thy y', the love "
3: 4 father, thou art the guide of my y'? "
24 labour of our fathers from our y'; "
25 from our y' even unto this day, "
22:21 been thy manner from thy y', "
31:19 I did bear the reproach of my y'. "
32:30 done evil before me from their y': "
48:11 hath been at ease from his y', "
La 3:27 that he bear the yoke in his y'. "
Eze 4:14 from my y' up even till now have I "
16:22, 43 remembered the days of thy y', "
60 with thee in the days of thy y', "
23: 3 committed whoredoms in their y': "
8 for in her y' they lay with her, "
19 to remembrance the days of her y', "
21 the lewdness of thy y', "
21 Egyptians for the paps of thy y'. "
Ho 2:15 sing there, as in the days of her y', "
Joe 1: 8 for the husband of her y'. "
Zec 13: 5 me to keep cattle from my y'. "
Mal 2:14 thee and the wife of thy y', "
15 against the wife of his y'. "
M't 19:20 have I kept from my y' up: *3503
M'r 10:20 these have I observed from my y'. "
Lu 18:21 these have I kept from my y' up. "
Ac 26: 4 My manner of life from my y', "
1Ti 4:12 Let no man despise thy y'; but be "

youthful
2Ti 2:22 Flee also y' lusts: but follow 3512

youths
Pr 7: 7 I discerned among the y', a young 1121
Isa 40:30 the y' shall faint and be weary, 5288

you-ward
2Co 1:12 and more abundantly to y'. 4314,5209
13: 3 which to y' is not weak, but is 1519, "
Eph 3: 2 grace...which is given me to y': "

Z.

Zaanaim (*za-an-a'-im*) See also ZAANANNIM.
J'g 4:11 his tent unto the plain of Z', *6815

Zaanan (*za'-an-an*) See also ZENAN.
Mic 1:11 inhabitant of Z' came not forth 6630

Zaanannim (*za-an-an'-nim*) See also ZAANAIM.
Jos 19:33 from Heleph, from Allon to Z', 6815

Zaavan (*za'-av-an*) See also ZAVAN.
Ge 36:27 of Ezer are these; Bilhan, and Z'. 2190

Zabad (*za'-bad*) See also JOSABAD; JOZACHAR.
1Ch 2:36 Nathan, and Nathan begat Z', 2066
37 And Z' begat Ephlal, and Ephlal "
7:21 And Z' his son, and Shuthelah "
11:41 the Hittite, Z' the son of Ahlai, "
2Ch 24:26 Z' the son of Shimeath an "
Ezr 10:27 Mattaniah, and Jeremoth, and Z', "
33 Mattathah, Z', Eliphelet, Jeremai, "
43 Mattithiah, Z', Zebina, Jadau, "

Zabbai (*zab'-bahee*) See also ZACCAI.
Ezr 10:28 Hananiah, Z', and Athlai. 2079
Ne 3:20 Baruch the son of Z' earnestly "

Zabbud (*zab'-bud*) See also ZACCUR.
Ezr 8:14 Uthai, and Z', and with them 2072

Zabdi (*zab'-di*) See also ZACCHUR; ZICHRI.
Jos 7: 1 the son of Carmi, the son of Z', 2067
17 man by man; and Z' was taken.

Jos 7:18 the son of Carmi, the son of Z·, 2067
1Ch 8:19 And Jakim, and Zichri, and Z·, "
27:27 wine cellars was Z· the Shiphmite: "
Ne 11:17 the son of Z·, the son of Asaph, "

Zabdiel (*zab'-de-el*)
1Ch 27: 2 was Jashobeam the son of Z·: 2068
Ne 11:14 and their overseer was Z·, the son "

Zabud (*za'-bud*)
1Ki 4: 5 Z· the son of Nathan was principal 2071

Zabulon (*zab'-u-lon*) See also ZEBULUN.
M't 4:13 borders of Z· and Nephthalim: *2194
15 The land of Z·, and the land of * "
Re 7: 8 Of the tribe of Z· were sealed * "

Zaccai (*zac'-cahee*) See also ZABBAI.
Ezr 2: 9 The children of Z·, seven hundred 2140
Ne 7:14 The children of Z·, seven hundred "

Zacchæus (*zak-ke'-us*)
Lu 19: 2 there was a man named Z·, 2195
5 and unto him, Z·, make haste, "
8 Z· stood, and said unto the Lord; "

Zacchur (*zac'-cur*) See also ZACCUR.
1Ch 4:26 Hamuel his son, Z· his son, 2139

Zaccur (*zac'-cur*) See also ZABBUD; ZABDI; ZACCHUR; ZICHRI.
Nu 13: 4 Reuben, Shammua the son of Z·. 2139
1Ch 24:27 and Shoham, and Z·, and Ibri. "
25: 2 Z·, and Joseph, and Nethaniah, "
10 The third to Z·, he, his sons, and "
Ne 3: 2 them builded Z· the son of Imri. "
10:12 Z·, Sherebiah, Shebaniah, "
12:35 the son of Michaiah, the son of Z·, "
13:13 to them was Hanan the son of Z·, "

Zachariah (*zak-a-ri'-ah*) See also ZECHARIAH.
2Ki 14:29 Z·, his son reigned in his stead. *2148
15: 8 did Z· the son of Jeroboam reign * "
11 And the rest of the acts of Z·, * "
18: 2 also was Abi, the daughter of Z·. * "

Zacharias (*zak'-a-ri'-as*) See also ZECHARIAH.
M't 23:35 blood of Z· son of Barachias, *2197
Lu 1: 5 a certain priest named Z·, of the "
12 And when Z· saw him, he was "
13 angel said unto him, Fear not, Z·: "
18 And Z· said unto the angel, "
21 And the people waited for Z·, "
40 And entered into the house of Z·, "
59 they called him Z·, after the name "
67 And his father Z· was filled with "
3: 2 came unto John the son of Z· "
11:51 of Abel unto the blood of Z·, * "

Zacher (*za'-kur*) See also ZECHARIAH.
1Ch 8:31 And Gedor, and Ahio, and Z·. 2144

Zadok (*za'-dok*) See also ZADOK'S.
2Sa 8:17 And Z· the son of Ahitub, and 6659
15:24 And lo Z· also, and all the Levites "
25 the king said unto Z·, Carry back "
27 king said also unto Z· the priest, "
29 Z· therefore and Abiathar carried "
35 hast thou not there with thee Z· "
35 thou shalt tell it to Z· and Abiathar "
17:15 Then said Hushai unto Z· and to "
18:19 Then said Ahimaaz the son of Z·, "
22 Then said Ahimaaz the son of Z· "
27 running of Ahimaaz the son of Z·, "
19:11 David sent to Z· and to Abiathar "
20:25 Z· and Abiathar were the priests: "
1Ki 1: 8, 26 Z· the priest, and Benaiah...son "
32 Call me Z· the priest, and Nathan "
34 let Z· the priest, and Nathan the "
38 So Z· the priest, and Nathan the "
39 And Z· the priest took an horn of oil "
44 hath sent with him Z· the priest, "
45 And Z· the priest and Nathan the "
2:35 Z· the priest did the king put in "
4: 2 Azariah the son of Z· the priest, "
4 Z· and Abiathar were the priests: "
2Ki 15:33 was Jerusha, the daughter of Z·. "
1Ch 6: 8, 12 Ahitub begat Z·, and Z· begat "
53 Z· his son, Ahimaaz his son. "
9:11 son of Meshullam, the son of Z·, "
12:28 And Z·, a young man mighty of "
15:11 David called for Z· and Abiathar "
16:39 And Z· the priest, and his brethren "
18:16 And Z· the son of Ahitub, and "
24: 3 both Z· of the sons of Eleazar, "
6 and the princes, and Z· the priest, "
31 presence of David the king, and Z·, "
27:17 of Kemuel: of the Aaronites, Z·: "
29:22 chief governor, and Z· to be priest. "
2Ch 27: 1 was Jerushah, the daughter of Z·. "
31:10 chief priest of the house of Z· "
Ezr 7: 2 The son of Shallum, the son of Z·, "
Ne 3: 4 repaired Z· the son of Baana. "
29 repaired Z· the son of Immer "
10:21 Meshezabeel, Z·, Jaddua, "
11:11 son of Meshullam, the son of Z·, "
13:13 the priest, and Z· the scribe, "
Eze 40:46 these are the sons of Z· among the "
43:19 Levites that be of the seed of Z·, "
44:15 the sons of Z·, that kept the charge "
48:11 are sanctified of the sons of Z·; "

Zadok's (*za'-doks*)
2Sa 15:36 Ahimaaz Z· son, and Jonathan 6659

Zaham (*za'-ham*)
2Ch 11:19 Jeush, and Shamariah, and Z·. 2093

Zair (*za'-ur*)
2Ki 8:21 So Joram went over to Z·, and all 6811

Zalaph (*za'-laf*)
Ne 3:30 and Hanun the sixth son of Z·, 6764

Zalmon (*zal'-mon*) See also ILAI; SALMON.
J'g 9:48 got him up to mount Z·, 6756
2Sa 23:28 Z· the Ahohite, Maharai the "

Zalmonah (*zal-mo'-nah*)
Nu 33:41 mount Hor, and pitched in Z·. 6758
42 And they departed from Z·, and "

Zalmunna (*zal-mun'-nah*)
J'g 8: 5 am pursuing after Zebah and Z·, 6759
6 Are the hands of Zebah and Z· now "
7 Lord hath delivered Zebah and Z· "
10 Zebah and Z· were in Karkor, "
12 And when Zebah and Z· fled, he "
12 two kings of Midian, Zebah and Z·, "
15 Behold Zebah and Z·, with whom "
15 Are the hands of Zebah and Z· now "
18 Then said he unto Zebah and Z·, "
21 Zebah and Z· said, Rise thou, "
21 arose, and slew Zebah and Z·, "
Ps 83:11 their princes as Zebah, and as Z·: "

Zamzummims (*zam-zum'-mims*) See also ZUZIMS.
De 2:20 and the Ammonites call them Z·; *2157

Zanoah (*za-no'-ah*)
Jos 15:34 Z·, and En-gannim, Tappuah, 2182
56 And Jezreel, and Jokdeam, and Z·, "
1Ch 4:18 and Jekuthiel the father of Z·. "
Ne 3:13 Hanun, and the inhabitants of Z·; "
11:30 Z·, Adullam, and in their villages, "

Zaphnath-paaneah (*zaf''-nath-pa-a-ne'-ah*)
Ge 41:45 called Joseph's name Z·; *6847

Zaphon (*za'-fon*)
Jos 13:27 and Z·, the rest of the kingdom 6829

Zara (*za'-rah*) See also ZARAH; ZERAH.
M't 1: 3 Judas begat Phares and Z· of *2196

Zarah (*za'-rah*) See also ZARA; ZERAH.
Ge 38:30 and his name was called Z·. *2226
46:12 and Shelah, and Pharez, and Z·: * "

Zareah (*za'-re-ah*) See also ZAREATHITES; ZORAH.
Ne 11:29 And at En-rimmon, and at Z·, *6881

Zareathites (*za'-re-ath-ites*) See also ZORATHITES.
1Ch 2:53 of them came the Z·, and the *6882

Zared (*za'-red*) See also ZERED.
Nu 21:12 and pitched in the valley of Z·. *2218

Zarephath (*zar'-e-fath*) See also SAREPTA.
1Ki 17: 9 Arise, get thee to Z·, which 6886
10 So he arose and went to Z·. "
Ob 20 of the Canaanites, even unto Z·; "

Zaretan (*zar'-e-tan*) See also ZARTANAH; ZEREDATHAH.
Jos 3:16 the city Adam, that is beside Z·: *6891

Zareth-shahar (*za''-reth-sha'-har*)
Jos 13:19 and Z· in the mount of the valley, 6890

Zarhites (*zar'-hites*)
Nu 26:13 Of Zerah, the family of the Z·: *2227
20 of Zerah, the family of the Z·. * "
Jos 7:17 and he took the family of the Z·: * "
17 he brought the family of the Z· * "
1Ch 27:11 Sibbecai the Hushathite, of the Z·: * "
13 the Netophathite, of the Z·: * "

Zartanah (*zar'-ta-nah*) See also ZARETAN; ZARTHAN.
1Ki 4:12 which is by Z· beneath Jezreel, *6891

Zarthan (*zar'-than*) See also ZARETAN; ZARTANAH.
1Ki 7:46 ground between Succoth and Z·. *6891

Zatthu (*zath'-u*) See also ZATTU.
Ne 10:14 Parosh, Pahath-moab, Elam, Z·, *2240

Zattu (*zat'-tu*) See also ZATTHU.
Ezr 2: 8 The children of Z·, nine hundred 2240
10:27 sons of Z·; Elioenai, Eliashib, "
Ne 7:13 The children of Z·, eight hundred "

Zavan (*za'-van*) See also ZAAVAN.
1Ch 1:42 Ezer; Bilhan, and Z·, and Jakan. *2190

Zaza (*za'-zah*)
1Ch 2:33 sons of Jonathan; Peleth and Z·. 2117

zeal
2Sa 21: 2 slay them in his z· to the children 7065
2Ki 10:16 and see my z· for the Lord. 7068
19:31 z· of the Lord of hosts shall do this. "
Ps 69: 9 z· of thine house hath eaten me up; "
119:139 My z· hath consumed me, because "
Isa 9: 7 The z· of the Lord of hosts will "
37:32 z· of the Lord of hosts shall do this. "
59:17 and was clad with z· as a cloke. "
63:15 where is thy z· and thy strength, "
Eze 5:13 I the Lord have spoken it in my z·, "
Joh 2:17 z· of thine house hath eaten me 2205
Ro 10: 2 record that they have a z· of God, "
2Co 7:11 yea, what z·, yea, what revenge! "
9: 2 your z· hath provoked very many. "
Ph'p 3: 6 Concerning z·, persecuting the "
Col 4:13 that he hath a great z· for you, * "

zealous
Nu 25:11 while he was z· for my sake *7065
13 because he was z· for his God, and * "
Ac 21:20 and they are all z· of the law: 2207
22: 3 and was z· toward God, as ye all "
1Co 14:12 as ye are z· of spiritual gifts, "
Ga 1:14 z· of the traditions of my fathers. "
Tit 2:14 a peculiar people, z· of good works. "
Re 3:19 be z· therefore, and repent. 2206

zealously
Ga 4:17 They z· affect you, but not well; 2206
18 good to be z· affected always in a "

Zebadiah (*zeb-ad-i'-ah*)
1Ch 8:15 And Z·, and Arad, and Ader, 2069
17 And Z·, and Meshullam, and "
12: 7 and Z·, the sons of Jeroham "
26: 2 Jediael the second, Z· the third, "
27: 7 Joab, and Z· his son after him: "
2Ch 17: 8 and Nethaniah, and Z·, and Asahel, "
19:11 Z· the son of Ishmael, the ruler "
Ezr 8: 8 Z· the son of Michael, and with "
10:20 sons of Immer; Hanani, and Z·. "

Zebah (*ze'-bah*)
J'g 8: 5 and I am pursuing after Z· and 2076
6 Are the hands of Z· and Zalmunna "
7 when the Lord hath delivered Z· "
10 Now Z· and Zalmunna were in "
12 And when Z· and Zalmunna fled, "
12 kings of Midian, Z· and Zalmunna, "
15 Behold Z· and Zalmunna, with "
15 Are the hands of Z· and Zalmunna "
18 said he unto Z· and Zalmunna, "
21 Z· and Zalmunna said, Rise thou, "
21 slew Z· and Zalmunna, and took "
Ps 83:11 all their princes as Z·, and as "

Zebaim (*ze-ba'-im*)
Ezr 2:57 the children of Pochereth of Z·, *6380
Ne 7:59 the children of Pochereth of Z·. * "

Zebedee (*zeb'-e-dee*) See also ZEBEDEE'S.
M't 4:21 James the son of Z·, and John his 2199
21 in a ship with Z· their father, "
10: 2 James the son of Z·, and John his "
26:37 him Peter and the two sons of Z·, "
M'r 1:19 he saw James the son of Z·, and "
20 left their father Z· in the ship "
3:17 And James the son of Z·, and John "
10:35 James and John, the sons of Z·, "
Lu 5:10 James, and John, the sons of Z·, "
Joh 21: 2 and the sons of Z·, and two other "

Zebedee's (*zeb'-e-dees*)
M't 20:20 came...the mother of Z· children *2199
27:56 and the mother of Z· children. * "

Zebina (*ze-bi'-nah*)
Ezr 10:43 Zabad, Z·, Jadan, and Joel, 2081

Zeboiim (*ze-boy'-im*) See also ZEBOIM.
Ge 14: 2 Shemeber king of Z·, and the 6636
8 king of Z·, and the king of Bela "

Zeboim (*ze-bo'-im*) See also ZEBOIIM.
Ge 10:19 Gomorrah, and Admah, and Z·, *6636
De 29:23 and Gomorrah, Admah, and Z·, * "
1Sa 13:18 that looketh to the valley of Z· 6650
Ne 11:34 Hadid, Z·, Neballat, "
Ho 11: 8 how shall I set thee as Z·? 6636

Zebub See BAAL-ZEBUB.

Zebudah (*ze-bu'-dah*)
2Ki 23:36 And his mother's name was Z·. *2081

Zebul (*ze'-bul*)
J'g 9:28 And Z· his officer? serve the men 2083
30 when Z· the ruler of the city heard "
36 he said to Z·, Behold, there come "
36 And Z· said unto him, Thou seest "
38 Then said Z· unto him, Where is "
41 Z· thrust out Gaal and his brethren, "

Zebulonite (*zeb'-u-lon-ite*) See also ZEBULUNITES.
J'g 12:11 after him Elon, a Z·, judged *2075
12 And Elon the Z· died, and was * "

Zebulun (*zeb'-u-lun*) See also ZABULON; ZEBULONITE; ZEBULUNITES.
Ge 30:20 and she called his name Z·. 2074
35:23 and Judah, and Issachar, and Z·: "
46:14 sons of Z·; Sered, and Elon, "
49:13 Z· shall dwell at the haven "
Ex 1: 3 Issachar, Z·, and Benjamin, "
Nu 1: 9 Of Z·; Eliab the son of Helon. "
30 Of the children of Z·, by their "
31 even of the tribe of Z·, were fifty "
2: 7 Then the tribe of Z·: and Eliab "
7 be captain of the children of Z·. "
7:24 Helon, prince of the children of Z·, "
10:16 of the children of Z· was Eliab "
13:10 Of the tribe of Z·, Gaddiel the "
26:26 sons of Z· after their families: "
34:25 of the tribe of the children of Z·, "
De 27:13 Gad, and Asher, and Z·, Dan, "
33:18 of Z· he said, Rejoice, Z·, in thy "
Jos 19:10 came up for the children of Z· "
16 inheritance of the children of Z· "
27 reacheth to Z·, and to the valley "
34 reacheth to Z· on the south side, "
21: 7 out of the tribe of Z·, twelve cities. "
34 out of the tribe of Z·, Jokneam "
J'g 1:30 Z· drive out the inhabitants "
4: 6 Naphtali and of the children of Z·? "
10 Barak called Z· and Naphtali to "
5:14 out of Z· they that handle the pen "
18 Z· and Naphtali were a people that "
6:35 and unto Z·, and unto Naphtali; "
12:12 in Aijalon in the country of Z·. "
1Ch 2: 1 and Judah, Issachar, and Z·, "
6:63 out of the tribe of Z·, twelve cities. "
77 were given out of the tribe of Z·, "
12:33 Of Z·, such as went forth to battle, "
40 even unto Issachar and Z· and "
27:19 Of Z·, Ishmaiah the son of "
2Ch 30:10 and Manasseh even unto Z·: "
11 and Manasseh and of Z· humbled "
18 Issachar and Z·, had not cleansed "
Ps 68:27 princes of Z·, and the princes of "
Isa 9: 1 he lightly afflicted the land of Z· "
Ezr 48:26 unto the west side, Z· a portion. "
27 And by the border of Z·, from the "
33 gate of Issachar, one gate of Z·, "

Zebulunites (*zeb'-u-lun-ites*) See also ZEBULONITE.
Nu 26:27 These are the families of the Z· 2075

Zechariah (*zek-a-ri'-ah*) See also ZACCUR; ZACHARIAH; ZACHARIAS; ZACHER.
1Ch 5: 7 were the chief, Jeiel, and Z·. 2148
9:21 And Z· the son of Meshelemiah "
37 And Gedor, and Ahio, and Z·, "
15:18 Z·, Ben, and Jaaziel, and "
20 And Z·, and Aziel, and "
24 and Z·, and Benaiah, and Eliezer, "
16: 5 the chief, and next to him Z·, "
24:25 of the sons of Isshiah; Z·. "
26: 2 Z· the firstborn, Jediael the "
11 Tebaliah the third, Z· the fourth: "
14 for Z· his son, a wise counseller, "
27:21 in Gilead, Iddo the son of Z·: "
2Ch 17: 7 and to Obadiah, and to Z·, and "
20:14 Then upon Jahaziel the son of Z·, "
21: 2 and Jehiel, and Z·, and Azariah, "
24:20 Spirit of God came upon Z· the son "
26: 5 he sought God in the days of Z·, "
29: 1 was Abijah, the daughter of Z·. "
13 sons of Asaph; Z·, and Mattaniah: "
34:12 and Z· and Meshullam, of the sons "
35: 8 Hilkiah and Z· and Jehiel, "
Ezr 5: 1 prophet, and Z· the son of Iddo, "
6:14 prophet and Z· the son of Iddo. "
8: 3 of the sons of Pharosh; Z·: "
11 Z· the son of Bebai, and with him "
16 for Z·, and for Meshullam, chief "
10:26 Mattaniah, Z·, and Jehiel, and "
Ne 8: 4 Hashbadana, Z·, and Meshullam. "
11: 4 the son of Z·, the son of Amariah, "
5 the son of Joiarib, the son of Z·, "
12 the son of Z·, the son of Pashur, "
12:16 Of Iddo, Z·; of Ginnethon, "
35 namely, Z· the son of Jonathan, "
41 Z·, and Hananiah, with trumpets; "
Isa 8: 2 and Z· the son of Jeberechiah. "
Zec 1: 1, 7 came the word of the Lord unto Z·," "
7: 1 the word of the Lord came unto Z· "
8 the word of the Lord came unto Z·," "

Zedad (*ze'-dad*)
Nu 34: 8 forth of the border shall be to Z·: 6657
Eze 47:15 way of Hethlon, as men go to Z·; "

Zedekiah (*zed-e-ki'-ah*) See also MATTANIAH; ZEDEKIAH'S; ZIDKIJAH.
1Ki 22:11 Z· the son of Chenaanah made 6667
24 Z· the son of Chenaanah went near," "
2Ki 24:17 stead, and changed his name to Z·." "
18 Z· was twenty and one years old "
20 that Z· rebelled against the king "
25: 2 unto the eleventh year of king Z·. "
7 slew the sons of Z· before his eyes, "
7 put out the eyes of Z·, and bound "
1Ch 3:15 second Jehoiakim, the third Z·, "
16 Jeconiah his son, Z· his son. "
2Ch 18:10 Z· the son of Chenaanah had made "
23 Z· the son of Chenaanah came "
36:10 made Z· his brother king over "
11 Z· was one and twenty years old "
Jer 1: 3 eleventh year of Z· the son of "
21: 1 king Z· sent unto him Pashur the "
3 them, Thus shall ye say to Z·: "
7 I will deliver Z· king of Judah, "
24: 8 will I give Z· the king of Judah, "
27: 3 come to Jerusalem unto Z· king of "
12 I spake also to Z· king of Judah "
28: 1 in the beginning of the reign of Z· "
29: 3 (whom Z· king of Judah sent unto "
21 and of Z· the son of Maaseiah, "
22 The Lord make thee like Z· and "
32: 1 the Lord in the tenth year of Z· "
3 For Z· king of Judah had shut him "
4 Z· king of Judah shall not escape "
5 And he shall lead Z· to Babylon, "
34: 2 Go and speak to Z· king of Judah, "
4 of the Lord, O Z· king of Judah; "
6 spake all these words unto Z· king "
8 the king Z· had made a covenant "
21 Z· king of Judah and his princes "
36:12 and Z· the son of Hananiah, "
37: 1 king Z· the son of Josiah reigned "
3 Z· the king sent Jehucal the son "
17 Z· the king sent, and took him out: "
18 Jeremiah said unto king Z·, What "
21 Z· the king commanded that they "
38: 5 Z· the king said, Behold, he is in "
14 Then Z· the king sent, and took "
15 Jeremiah said unto Z·, If I declare "
16 So Z· the king sware secretly unto "
17 Then said Jeremiah unto Z·, Thus "
19 Z· the king said unto Jeremiah, I "
24 said Z· unto Jeremiah, Let no man "
39: 1 ninth year of Z· king of Judah, "
2 And in the eleventh year of Z·, "
4 when Z· the king of Judah saw "
5 and overtook Z· in the plains of "
6 king of Babylon slew the sons of Z· "
44:30 as I gave Z· king of Judah into "
49:34 in the beginning of the reign of Z· "
51:59 went with Z· the king of Judah "
52: 1 Z· was one and twenty years old "
3 that Z· rebelled against the king "
5 unto the eleventh year of king Z·. "
8 and overtook Z· in the plains of "
10 slew the sons of Z· before his eyes: "
11 Then he put out the eyes of Z·; "

Zedekiah's (*zed-e-ki'-ahs*)
Jer 39: 7 Moreover he put out Z· eyes 6667

Zeeb (*ze'-eb*)
J'g 7:25 of the Midianites, Oreb and Z·; 2062
25 Z· they slew at the winepress of Z·," "
7:25 heads of Oreb and Z· to Gideon 2062
8: 3 princes of Midian, Oreb and Z·: "
Ps 83:11 nobles like Oreb, and like Z·: "

Zelah (*ze'-lah*)
Jos 18:28 Z·, Eleph, and Jebusi, which is 6762
2Sa 21:14 in the country of Benjamin in Z·,* "

Zelek (*ze'-lek*)
2Sa 23:37 Z· the Ammonite, Nahari the 6768
1Ch 11:39 Z· the Ammonite, Naharai the "

Zelophehad (*ze-lo'-fe-had*)
Nu 26:33 Z· the son of Hepher had no sons,6765
33 the names of the daughters of Z· "
27: 1 Then came the daughters of Z·, "
7 The daughters of Z· speak right: "
36: 2 the inheritance of Z· our brother "
6 concerning the daughters of Z·, "
10 Moses, so did the daughters of Z·: "
11 the daughters of Z·, were married "
Jos 17: 3 Z·, the son of Hepher, the son of "
1Ch 7:15 was Z·: and Z· had daughters. "

Zelotes (*ze-lo'-teze*) See also CANAANITE; SIMON.
Lu 6:15 of Alphæus, and Simon called Z·,*2208
Ac 1:13 Simon Z·, and Judas the brother* "

Zelzah (*zel'-zah*)
1Sa 10: 2 in the border of Benjamin at Z·; 6766

Zemaraim (*zem-a-ra'-im*) See also ZEMARITE.
Jos 18:22 Beth-arabah, and Z·, and Beth-el,6787
2Ch 13: 4 Abijah stood up upon mount Z·, "

Zemarite (*zem'-a-rite*)
Ge 10:18 and the Z·, and the Hamathite: 6786
1Ch 1:16 and the Z·, and the Hamathite. "

Zemira (*ze-mi'-rah*)
1Ch 7: 8 sons of Becher; Z·, and Joash, *2160

Zenan (*ze'-nan*) See also ZAANAN.
Jos 15:37 Z·, and Hadashah, Migdal-gad, 6799

Zenas (*ze'-nas*)
Tit 3:13 Bring Z· the lawyer and Apollos *2211*

Zephaniah (*zef-a-ni'-ah*)
2Ki 25:18 priest, and Z· the second priest, 6846
1Ch 6:36 the son of Azariah, the son of Z·, "
Jer 21: 1 Z· the son of Maaseiah the priest, "
29:25 to Z· the son of Maaseiah the priest," "
29 And Z· the priest read this letter "
37: 3 Z· the son of Maaseiah the priest "
52:24 priest, and Z· the second priest, "
Zep 1: 1 came unto Z· the son of Cushi, "
Zec 6:10 the house of Josiah the son of Z·; "
14 Jedaiah, and to Hen the son of Z·, "

Zephath (*ze'-fath*) See also HORMAH.
J'g 1:17 the Canaanites that inhabited Z·, 6857

Zephathah (*zef'-a-thah*)
2Ch 14:10 in the valley of Z· at Mareshah. 6859

Zephi (*ze'-fi*) See also ZEPHO.
1Ch 1:36 Eliphaz; Teman, and Omar, Z·, 6825

Zepho (*ze'-fo*) See also ZEPHI.
Ge 36:11 Eliphaz were Teman, Omar, Z·, 6825
15 duke Omar, duke Z·, duke Kenaz, "

Zephon (*ze'-fon*) See also BAAL-ZEPHON; ZEPHONITES; ZIPHION.
Nu 26:15 families: of Z·, the family of the 6827

Zephonites (*zef'-on-ites*)
Nu 26:15 of Zephon, the family of the Z·: 6831

Zer (*zur*)
Jos 19:35 the fenced cities are Ziddim, Z·, 6863

Zerah (*ze'-rah*) See also EZRAHITE; ZARAH; ZARHITES; ZOHAR.
Ge 36:13 sons of Reuel; Nahath, and Z·, 2226
17 Nahath, duke Z·, duke Shammah, "
33 and Jobab the son of Z· of Bozrah "
Nu 26:13 Of Z·, the family of the Zarhites: "
20 of Z·, the family of the Zarhites. "
Jos 7: 1, 18 the son of Z·, of the tribe of "
24 took Achan the son of Z·, and the "
22:20 Did not Achan the son of Z· "
1Ch 1:37 of Reuel; Nahath, Z·, Shammah, "
44 Jobab the son of Z· of Bozrah "
2: 4 in law bare him Pharez and Z·. "
6 sons of Z·; Zimri, and Ethan, "
4:24 and Jamin, Jarib, Z·, and Shaul: "
6:21 Iddo his son, Z· his son, Jeaterai "
41 The son of Ethni, the son of Z·, "
9: 6 of the sons of Z·; Jeuel and their "
2Ch 14: 9 out against them Z· the Ethiopian "
Ne 11:24 children of Z· the son of Judah, "

Zerahiah (*zer-a-hi'-ah*)
1Ch 6: 6 Uzzi begat Z·, and Z· begat 2228
51 his son, Uzzi his son, Z· his son, "
Ezr 7: 4 The son of Z·, the son of Uzzi, "
8: 4 Elihoenai the son of Z·, and with "

Zered (*ze'-red*) See also ZARED.
De 2:13 and get you over the brook Z·. 2218
13 And we went over the brook Z·. "
14 we were come over the brook Z·, "

Zereda (*zer'-e-dah*)
1Ki 11:26 an Ephrathite of Z·, Solomon's *6868

Zeredathah (*ze-red'-a-thah*) See also ZARTHAN; ZERERATH.
2Ch 4:17 ground between Succoth and Z·. *6868

Zererath (*zer'-e-rath*) See also ZARTHAN; ZEREDATHAH.
J'g 7:22 host fled to Beth-shittah in Z·, *6888

Zeresh (*ze'-resh*)
Es 5:10 for his friends, and Z· his wife. 2238
14 said Z· his wife and...his friends "
Es 6:13 Haman told Z· his wife and all his 2238
13 said his wise men and Z· his wife "

Zereth (*ze'-reth*)
1Ch 4: 7 And the sons of Helah were, Z·, 6889

Zeri (*ze'-ri*) See also IZRI.
1Ch 25: 3 of Jeduthun; Gedaliah, and Z·, 6874

Zeror (*ze'-ror*)
1Sa 9: 1 the son of Abiel, the son of Z·, 6872

Zeruah (*ze-ru'-ah*)
1Ki 11:26 whose mother's name was Z·, 6871

Zerubbabel (*ze-rub'-ba-bel*) See also SHESHBAZZAR; ZOROBABEL.
1Ch 3:19 and the sons of Pedaiah were, Z·, 2216
19 and the sons of Z·; Meshullam, "
Ezr 2: 2 Which came with Z·: Jeshua, "
3: 2 priests, and Z· the son of Shealtiel," "
8 began Z· the son of Shealtiel, "
4: 2 Then they came to Z·, and to the "
3 But Z·, and Jeshua, and the rest "
5: 2 rose up Z· the son of Shealtiel, 2217
Ne 7: 7 Who came with Z·, Jeshua, 2216
12: 1 the Levites that went up with Z· "
47 And all Israel in the days of Z·, "
Hag 1: 1 by Haggai the prophet unto Z· the "
12 Then Z· the son of Shealtiel, "
14 Lord stirred up the spirit of Z· "
2: 2 Speak now to Z· the son of "
4 Yet now be strong, O Z·, saith "
21 Speak to Z·, governor of Judah, "
23 will I take thee, O Z·, my servant, "
Zec 4: 6 is the word of the Lord unto Z·, "
7 before Z· thou shalt become a "
9 The hands of Z· have laid the "
10 plummet in the hand of Z· with "

Zeruiah (*ze-ru-i'-ah*)
1Sa 26: 6 Abishai the son of Z·, brother to 6870
2Sa 2:13 And Joab the son of Z·, and the "
18 were three sons of Z· there, Joab, "
3:39 the sons of Z· be too hard for me: "
8:16 the son of Z· was over the host; "
14: 1 the son of Z· perceived that the "
16: 9 Then said Abishai the son of Z· "
10 I to do with you, ye sons of Z·? "
17:25 sister to Z· Joab's mother. "
18: 2 the hand of Abishai the son of Z·, "
19:21 Abishai the son of Z· answered "
22 ye sons of Z·, that ye should this "
21:17 the son of Z· succoured him, "
23:18 son of Z·, was chief among three. "
37 armourbearer to Joab the son of Z·." "
1Ki 1: 7 conferred with Joab the son of Z·, "
2: 5 also what Joab the son of Z· did "
22 priest, and for Joab the son of Z·. "
1Ch 2:16 Whose sisters were Z·, and Abigail." "
16 sons of Z·; Abishai, and Joab, and "
11: 6 Joab the son of Z· went first up, "
39 armourbearer to Joab the son of Z·," "
18:12 son of Z· slew of the Edomites "
15 the son of Z· was over the host; "
26:28 Joab the son of Z·, had dedicated; "
27:24 the son of Z· began to number, "

Zetham (*ze'-tham*)
1Ch 23: 8 the chief was Jehiel, and Z·, and 2241
26:22 Z·, and Joel his brother, which "

Zethan (*ze'-than*)
1Ch 7:10 and Chenaanah, and Z·, and 2133

Zethar (*ze'-thar*)
Es 1:10 Bigtha, and Abagtha, Z·, and 2242

Zia (*zi'-ah*)
1Ch 5:13 and Jorai, and Jachan, and Z·, 2127

Ziba (*zi'-bah*)
2Sa 9: 2 a servant whose name was Z·. 6717
2 king said unto him, Art thou Z·? "
3 Z· said unto the king, Jonathan "
4 Z· said unto the king, Behold, he "
9 Then the king called to Z·, Saul's "
10 Now Z· had fifteen sons and "
11 Then said Z· unto the king, "
12 all that dwelt in the house of Z· "
16: 1 Z· the servant of Mephibosheth "
2 king said unto Z·, What meanest "
2 Z· said, The asses be for the king's" "
3 Z· said unto the king, Behold, "
4 Then said the king to Z·, Behold, "
4 Z· said, I humbly beseech thee "
19:17 and Z· the servant of the house "
29 said, Thou and Z· divide the land. "

Zibeon (*zib'-e-un*)
Ge 36: 2 the daughter of Z· the Hivite; 6649
14 the daughter of Z·, Esau's wife: "
20 and Shobal, and Z·, and Anah, "
24 And these are the children of Z·; "
24 as he fed the asses of Z· his father. "
29 duke Shobal, duke Z·, duke Anah, "
1Ch 1:38 and Shobal, and Z·, and Anah, "
40 the sons of Z·; Aiah, and Anah. "

Zibia (*zib'-e-ah*)
1Ch 8: 9 Hodesh his wife, Jobab, and Z·, 6644

Zibiah (*zib'-e-ah*)
2Ki 12: 1 And his mother's name was Z· of 6645
2Ch 24: 1 His mother's name also was Z· of "

Zichri (*zik'-ri*) See also ZITHRI.
Ex 6:21 Korah, and Nepheg, and Z·. 2147
1Ch 8:19 And Jakim, and Z·, and Zabdi, "
23 And Abdon, and Z·, and Hanan, "
27 and Z·, the sons of Jeroham. "
9:15 the son of Micah, the son of Z·, "
26:25 and Joram his son, and Z· his son, "
27:16 was Eliezer the son of Z·: "
2Ch 17:16 him was Amasiah the son of Z·, "

2Ch 23: 1 and Elishaphat the son of Z'. 2147
28: 7 And Z', a mighty man of Ephraim, "
Ne 11: 9 the son of Z' was their overseer: "
12:17 Of Abijah, Z'; of Miniamin, of "

Ziddim (*zid'-dim*)
Jos 19:35 And the fenced cities are Z', Zer, 6661

Zidkijah (*zid-ki'-jah*) See also Zedekiah.
Ne 10: 1 the son of Hachaliah, and Z', *6667

Zidon (*zi'-don*) See also Sidon; Zidonians.
Ge 49:13 and his border shall be unto Z'. 6721
Jos 11: 8 and chased them unto great Z', "
19:28 and Kanah, even unto great Z'; "
J'g 1:31 Accho, nor the inhabitants of Z', "
10: 6 gods of Syria, and the gods of Z', "
18:28 because it was far from Z', "
2Sa 24: 6 came to Dan-jaan, and about to Z', "
1Ki 17: 9 Zarephath, which belongeth to Z', "
1Ch 1:13 And Canaan begat Z' his firstborn, "
Ezr 3: 7 drink, and oil, unto them of Z', 6722
Isa 23: 2 thou whom the merchants of Z', 6721
4 Be thou ashamed, O Z': for the "
12 oppressed virgin, daughter of Z': "
Jer 25:22 of Tyrus, and all the kings of Z', "
27: 3 and to the king of Z', by the hand "
47: 4 to cut off from Tyrus and Z' every "
Eze 27: 8 inhabitants of Z' and Arvad were "
28:21 Son of man, set thy face against Z', "
22 Behold, I am against thee, O Z'; "
Joe 3: 4 ye to do with me, O Tyre, and Z', "
Zec 9: 2 Tyrus, and Z', though it be very "

Zidonians (*zi-do'-ne-uns*) See also Sidonians.
J'g 10:12 The Z' also, and the Amalekites, 6722
18: 7 after the manner of the Z', quiet "
7 and they were far from the Z', and "
1Ki 11: 1 Ammonites, Edomites, Z', and "
5, 33 Ashtoreth the goddess of the Z', "
16:31 daughter of Ethbaal king of the Z', "
2Ki 23:13 the abomination of the Z', "
1Ch 22: 4 for the Z' and they of Tyre brought "
Eze 32:30 north, all of them, and all the Z', "

Zif (*zif*)
1Ki 6: 1 reign over Israel, in the month Z', *2099
37 of the Lord laid, in the month Z': * "

Ziha (*zi'-hah*)
Ezr 2:43 children of Z', the children of 6727
Ne 7:46 children of Z', the children of "
11:21 and Z' and Gispa were over the "

Ziklag (*zik'-lag*)
Jos 15:31 And Z', and Madmannah, and 6860
19: 5 And Z', and Beth-marcaboth, "
1Sa 27: 6 Then Achish gave him Z' that day: "
6 Z' pertaineth unto the kings of "
30: 1 and his men were come to Z', "
1 had invaded the south, and Z', "
1 smitten Z', and burnt it with fire; "
14 Caleb; and we burned Z' with fire. "
26 when David came to Z', he sent of "
2Sa 1: 1 David had abode two days in Z'; "
4:10 hold of him, and slew him in Z', "
1Ch 4:30 Bethuel, and at Hormah, and at Z', "
12: 1 are they that came to David to Z', "
20 As he went to Z', there fell to him "
Ne 11:28 And at Z', and at Mekonah, and "

Zillah (*zil'-lah*)
Ge 4:19 and the name of the other Z'. 6741
22 And Z', she also bare Tubal-cain, "
23 said unto his wives, Adah and Z', "

Zilpah (*zil'-pah*)
Ge 29:24 gave unto his daughter Leah Z' 2153
30: 9 she took Z' her maid, and gave "
10 Z' Leah's maid bare Jacob a son. "
12 And Z' Leah's maid bare Jacob a "
35:26 the sons of Z', Leah's handmaid; "
37: 2 with sons of Z', his father's wives: "
46:18 These are the sons of Z', whom "

Zilthai (*zil'-thahee*)
1Ch 8:20 And Elienai, and Z', and Eliel, *6769
12:20 and Z', captains of the thousands* "

Zimmah (*zim'-mah*)
1Ch 6:20 son, Jahath his son, Z' his son, 2155
42 the son of Z', the son of Shimei, "
2Ch 29:12 Joah the son of Z', and Eden "

Zimran (*zim'-ran*)
Ge 25: 2 she bare him Z', and Jokshan, 2175
1Ch 1:32 she bare Z', and Jokshan, and "

Zimri (*zim'-ri*)
Nu 25:14 the Midianitish woman, was Z', 2174
1Ki 16: 9 And his servant Z', captain of half "
10 And Z' went in and smote him, "
12 Thus did Z' destroy all the house "
15 of Judah did Z' reign seven days "
16 Z' hath conspired, and hath also "
18 Z' saw that the city was taken, "
20 the rest of the acts of Z', and his "
2Ki 9:31 said, Had Z' peace, who slew his "
1Ch 2: 6 sons of Zerah; Z', and Ethan, and "
8:36 and Z'; and Z' begat Moza; "
9:42 and Z'; and Z' begat Moza; "
Jer 25:25 And all the kings of Z', and all the "

Zin (*zin*)
Nu 13:21 the wilderness of Z' unto Rehob, 6790
20: 1 congregation, into the desert of Z' "
27:14 commandment in the desert of Z', "
14 in Kadesh in the wilderness of Z'. "
33:36 and pitched in the wilderness of Z', "
34: 3 shall be from the wilderness of Z' "
4 of Akrabbim, and pass on to Z', "
De 32:51 Kadesh, in the wilderness of Z'; "
Jos 15: 1 of Edom the wilderness of Z' "
3 passed along to Z', and ascended "

Zina (*zi'-nah*) See also Zizah.
1Ch 23:10 sons of Shimei were, Jahath, Z', 2126

Zion (*zi'-un*) See also Sion; Zion's.
2Sa 5: 7 David took the strong hold of Z': 6726
1Ki 8: 1 of the city of David, which is Z'. "
2Ki 19:21 daughter of Z' hath despised thee, "
31 they that escape out of mount Z': "
1Ch 11: 5 David took the castle of Z', "
2Ch 5: 2 of the city of David, which is Z', "
Ps 2: 6 my king upon my holy hill of Z'. "
9:11 to the Lord, which dwelleth in Z': "
14 in the gates of the daughter of Z': "
14: 7 of Israel were come out of Z'! "
20: 2 and strengthen thee out of Z'; "
48: 2 of the whole earth, is mount Z', "
11 Let mount Z' rejoice, let the "
12 Walk about Z', and go round "
50: 2 Out of Z' the perfection of beauty, "
51:18 good in thy good pleasure unto Z': "
53: 6 of Israel were come out of Z'! "
69:35 For God will save Z', and will "
74: 2 this mount Z', wherein thou hast "
76: 2 and his dwelling place in Z'. "
78:68 the mount Z' which he loved. "
84: 7 every one of them in Z' appeareth "
87: 2 The Lord loveth the gates of Z' "
5 And of Z' it shall be said, This and "
97: 8 Z' heard, and was glad; and the "
99: 2 The Lord is great in Z'; and he is "
102:13 arise, and have mercy upon Z': "
16 when the Lord shall build up Z', "
21 declare the name of the Lord in Z', "
110: 2 the rod of thy strength out of Z': "
125: 1 in the Lord shall be as mount Z', "
126: 1 turned again the captivity of Z', "
128: 5 The Lord shall bless thee out of Z': "
129: 5 and turned back that hate Z'. "
132:13 For the Lord hath chosen Z'; "
133: 3 upon the mountains of Z': "
134: 3 and earth bless thee out of Z'. "
135:21 Blessed be the Lord out of Z', "
137: 1 we wept, when we remembered Z'. "
3 Sing us one of the songs of Z'. "
146:10 reign for ever, even thy God, O Z', "
147:12 O Jerusalem; praise thy God, O Z'. "
149: 2 let the children of Z' be joyful in "
Ca 3:11 Go forth, O ye daughters of Z', and "
Isa 1: 8 daughter of Z' is left as a cottage "
27 Z' shall be redeemed with "
2: 3 for out of Z' shall go forth the law, "
3:16 the daughters of Z' are haughty, "
17 of the head of the daughters of Z', "
4: 3 to pass, that he that is left in Z', "
4 the filth of the daughters of Z', "
5 every dwelling place of mount Z', "
8:18 hosts, which dwelleth in mount Z'. "
10:12 his whole work upon mount Z' "
24 O my people that dwellest in Z', "
32 the mount of the daughter of Z', "
12: 6 and shout, thou inhabitant of Z': "
14:32 That the Lord hath founded Z', "
16: 1 the mount of the daughter of Z'. "
18: 7 of the Lord of hosts, the mount Z'. "
24:23 of hosts shall reign in mount Z', "
28:16 I lay in Z' for a foundation a stone, "
29: 8 be, that fight against mount Z'. "
30:19 shall dwell in Z' at Jerusalem: "
31: 4 come down to fight for mount Z', "
9 the Lord, whose fire is in Z', "
33: 5 he hath filled Z' with judgment "
14 The sinners in Z' are afraid; "
20 Look upon Z', the city of our "
34: 8 for the controversy of Z'. "
35:10 and come to Z' with songs and "
37:22 daughter of Z', hath despised thee, "
32 they that escape out of mount Z': "
40: 9 O Z', that bringest good tidings, "
41:27 The first shall say to Z', Behold, "
46:13 place salvation in Z' for Israel my "
49:14 Z' said, The Lord hath forsaken "
51: 3 For the Lord shall comfort Z': "
11 and come with singing unto Z'; "
16 say unto Z', Thou art my people. "
52: 1 awake; put on thy strength, O Z'; "
2 thy neck, O captive daughter of Z'. "
7 saith unto Z', Thy God reigneth! "
8 the Lord shall bring again Z'. "
59:20 the Redeemer shall come to Z', "
60:14 The Z' of the Holy One of Israel. "
61: 3 unto them that mourn in Z', "
62:11 Say ye to the daughter of Z', "
64:10 Z' is a wilderness, Jerusalem a "
66: 8 for as soon as Z' travailed, she "
Jer 3:14 family, and I will bring you to Z': "
4: 6 Set up the standard toward Z': "
31 the voice of the daughter of Z', "
6: 2 have likened the daughter of Z' to "
23 war against thee, O daughter of Z'. "
8:19 Is not the Lord in Z'? is not her "
9:19 voice of wailing is heard out of Z', "
14:19 Judah? hath thy soul lothed Z'? "
26:18 Z' shall be plowed like a field, and "
30:17 This is Z', whom no man seeketh "
31: 6 let us go up to Z' unto the Lord "
12 come and sing in the height of Z', "
50: 5 They shall ask the way to Z' with "
28 to declare in Z' the vengeance of the "
51:10 declare in Z' the work of the Lord "
24 evil that they have done in Z' "
35 shall the inhabitant of Z' say; "
La 1: 4 The ways of Z' do mourn, because "
6 from the daughter of Z' all her "
17 Z' spreadeth forth her hands, and "
2: 1 covered the daughter of Z' with a "
4 tabernacle of the daughter of Z': "
La 2: 6 and sabbaths to be forgotten in Z', 6726
8 the wall of the daughter of Z': "
10 The elders of the daughter of Z' sit "
13 thee, O virgin daughter of Z'? "
18 O wall of the daughter of Z', let "
4: 2 The precious sons of Z', "
11 and hath kindled a fire in Z', "
22 is accomplished, O daughter of Z'; "
5:11 They ravished the women in Z', "
18 Because of the mountain of Z', "
Joe 2: 1 Blow ye the trumpet in Z', and "
15 Blow the trumpet in Z', sanctify "
23 Be glad then, ye children of Z', "
32 for in mount Z' and in Jerusalem "
3:16 Lord also shall roar out of Z', "
17 the Lord your God dwelling in Z', "
21 for the Lord dwelleth in Z'. "
Am 1: 2 The Lord will roar from Z', and "
6: 1 Woe to them that are at ease in Z', "
Ob 17 upon mount Z' shall be deliverance, "
21 come up on mount Z' to judge "
Mic 1:13 of the sin to the daughter of Z': "
3:10 They build up Z' with blood, and "
12 shall Z' for your sake be plowed "
4: 2 for the law shall go forth of Z', "
7 shall reign over them in mount Z' "
8 strong hold of the daughter of Z', "
10 to bring forth, O daughter of Z', "
11 and let our eye look upon Z'. "
13 and thresh, O daughter of Z': "
Zep 3:14 Sing, O daughter of Z'; shout, "
16 and to Z', Let not thine hands be "
Zec 1:14 jealous for Jerusalem and for Z' "
17 and the Lord shall yet comfort Z', "
2: 7 Deliver thyself, O Z', that dwellest "
10 and rejoice, O daughter of Z': "
8: 2 jealous for Z' with great jealousy, "
3 I am returned unto Z', and will "
9: 9 Rejoice greatly, O daughter of Z'; "
13 and raised up thy sons, O Z', "

Zion's (*zi'-uns*)
Isa 62: 1 For Z' sake will I not hold my 6726

Zior (*zi'-or*)
Jos 15:54 which is Hebron, and Z'; nine 6730

Ziph (*zif*) See also Ziphites.
Jos 15:24 Z', and Telem, and Bealoth, 2128
55 Maon, Carmel, and Z', and Juttah, "
1Sa 23:14 mountain in the wilderness of Z', "
15 David was in the wilderness of Z' "
24 arose, and went to Z' before Saul: "
26: 2 went down to the wilderness of Z', "
2 seek David in the wilderness of Z'. "
1Ch 2:42 which was the father of Z'; "
4:16 Z', and Ziphah, Tiria, and Asareel. "
2Ch 11: 8 And Gath, and Mareshah, and Z', "

Ziphah (*zi'-fah*)
1Ch 4:16 Ziph, and Z', Tiria, and Asareel. 2129

Ziphims (*zif'-ims*) See also Ziphites.
Ps 54: *title* the Z' came and said to Saul, *2130

Ziphion (*zif'-e-on*) See also Zephon.
Ge 46:16 the sons of Gad; Z', and Haggi, 6837

Ziphites (*zif'-ites*) See also Ziphims.
1Sa 23:19 came up the Z' to Saul to Gibeah, 2130
26: 1 the Z' came unto Saul to Gibeah, "

Ziphron (*zif'-ron*)
Nu 34: 9 And the border shall go on to Z', 2202

Zippor (*zip'-por*)
Nu 22: 2 And Balak the son of Z' saw all 6834
4 Balak the son of Z' was king of "
10 Balak the son of Z', king of Moab, "
16 Thus saith Balak the son of Z', "
23:18 hearken unto me, thou son of Z': "
Jos 24: 9 Balak the son of Z', king of Moab, "
J'g 11:25 Balak the son of Z', king of Moab? "

Zipporah (*zip-po'-rah*)
Ex 2:21 he gave Moses Z' his daughter. 6855
4:25 Then Z' took a sharp stone, and "
18: 2 father in law, took Z', Moses' wife, "

Zithri (*zith'-ri*) See also Zichri.
Ex 6:22 Mishael, and Elzaphan, and Z'. 5644

Ziz (*ziz*)
2Ch 20:16 they come up by the cliff of Z'; 6732

Ziza (*zi'-zah*) See also Zizah.
1Ch 4:37 Z' the son of Shiphi, the son of 2124
2Ch 11:20 and Attai, and Z', and Shelomith. "

Zizah (*zi'-zah*) See also Zina; Ziza.
1Ch 23:11 was the chief, and Z' the second: 2125

Zoan (*zo'-an*)
Nu 13:22 seven years before Z' in Egypt. 6814
Ps 78:12 the land of Egypt, in the field of Z'. "
43 and his wonders in the field of Z': "
Isa 19:11 Surely the princes of Z' are fools, "
13 The princes of Z' are become fools, "
30: 4 For his princes were at Z', and his "
Eze 30:14 will set fire in Z', and will execute "

Zoar (*zo'-ar*)
Ge 13:10 of Egypt, as thou comest unto Z'. 6820
14: 2 and the king of Bela, which is Z'. "
8 the king of Bela, (the same is Z';) "
19:22 the name of the city was called Z'. "
23 earth when Lot entered into Z'. "
30 Lot went up out of Z', and dwelt "
30 for he feared to dwell in Z': and "
De 34: 3 the city of palm trees, unto Z'. "
Isa 15: 5 his fugitives shall flee unto Z', "
Jer 48:34 from Z' even unto Horonaim, "

Zoba (*zo'-bah*) See also Zobah.
2Sa 10: 6 and the Syrians of Z', twenty *6678
8 the Syrians of Z', and of Rehob, * "

Zobah (*zo'-bah*) See also ARAM-ZOBAH; HAMATH-ZOBAH; ZOBA.
1Sa 14: 47 and against the kings of Z', and 6678
2Sa 8: 3 the son of Rehob, king of Z', as he "
5 to succour Hadadezer king of Z', "
12 son of Rehob, king of Z'. "
23: 36 Igal the son of Nathan of Z', Bani "
1Ki 11: 23 his lord Hadadezer king of Z': "
24 band, when David slew them of Z': "
1Ch 18: 3 David smote Hadarezer king of Z' 6678
5 came to help Hadarezer king of Z', "
9 the host of Hadarezer king of Z'; "
19: 6 of Syria-maachah, and out of Z', "

Zobebah (*zo-be'-bah*)
1Ch 4: 8 And Coz begat Anub, and Z', and 6637

Zohar (*zo'-har*) See also ZERAH; ZEROR.
Ge 23: 8 for me to Ephron the son of Z', 6714
25: 9 the field of Ephron the son of Z' "
46: 10 and Ohad, Jachin, and Z', "
Ex 6: 15 and Ohad, and Jachin, and Z', "

Zoheleth (*zo'-he-leth*)
1Ki 1: 9 and fat cattle by the stone of Z', 2120

Zoheth (*zo'-heth*) See also BEN-ZOHETH.
1Ch 4: 20 and the sons of Ishi were, Z', and 2105

Zophah (*zo'-fah*)
1Ch 7: 35 Z', and Imna, and Shelesh, and 6690
36 sons of Z'; Suah, and Harnepher, "

Zophai (*zo'-fahee*) See also ZUPH.
1Ch 6: 26 sons of Elkanah; Z' his son, and 6689

Zophar (*zo'-far*)
Job 2: 11 Shuhite, and Z' the Naamathite: 6691
11: 1 answered Z' the Naamathite, and "
20: 1 answered Z' the Naamathite, and "
42: 9 Z' the Naamathite went, and did "

Zophim (*zo'-fim*) See also RAMATHAIM-ZOPHIM.
Nu 23: 14 brought him into the field of Z', 6839

Zorah (*zo'-rah*) See also ZAREAH; ZORATHITES; ZOREAH; ZORITES.
Jos 19: 41 coast of their inheritance was Z', 6881
J'g 13: 2 there was a certain man of Z', "
25 the camp of Dan between Z' and "
16: 31 and buried him between Z' and "
18: 2 men of valour, from Z', and from "
8 came unto their brethren to Z' "
11 family of the Danites, out of Z' "
2Ch 11: 10 And Z', and Aijalon, and Hebron, "

Zorathites (*zo'-rath-ites*) See also ZAREATHITES; ZORITES.
1Ch 4: 2 These are the families of the Z'. 6882

Zoreah (*zo'-re-ah*) See also ZORAH.
Jos 15: 33 in the valley, Eshtaol, and Z', *6881

Zorites (*zo'-rites*) See also ZAREATHITES; ZORATHITES.
1Ch 2: 54 half of the Manahethites, the Z'. 6882

Zorobabel (*zo-rob'-a-bel*) See also ZERUBBABEL.
M't 1: 12 and Salathiel begat Z'; Salathiel; **2216*
1: 13 And Z' begat Abiud; and Abiud **2216*
Lu 3: 27 which was the son of Z', which * "

Zuar (*zu'-ar*)
Nu 1: 8 Issachar; Nethaneel the son of Z'. 6686
2: 5 Nethaneel the son of Z' shall be "
7: 18 day Nethaneel the son of Z', "
23 of Nethaneel the son of Z'. "
10: 15 was Nethaneel the son of Z'. "

Zuph (*zuf*) See also RAMATHAIM-ZOPHIM.
1Sa 1: 1 the son of Z', an Ephrathite: 6689
9: 5 they were come to the land of Z', "
1Ch 6: 35 The son of Z', the son of Elkanah, "

Zur (*zur*) See also BETH-ZUR.
Nu 25: 15 was Cozbi, the daughter of Z'; 6698
31: 8 namely, Evi, and Rekem, and Z', "
Jos 13: 21 Midian, Evi, and Rekem, and Z', "
1Ch 8: 30 his firstborn son Abdon, and Z', "
9: 36 firstborn son Abdon, then Z', "

Zuriel (*zu'-re-el*)
Nu 3: 35 of the families of Merari was Z' 6700

Zurishaddai (*zu-re-shad'-da-i*)
Nu 1: 6 Simeon; Shelumiel the son of Z'. 6701
2: 12 shall be Shelumiel the son of Z'. "
7: 36 fifth day Shelumiel the son of Z', "
41 of Shelumiel the son of Z'. "
10: 19 was Shelumiel the son of Z'. "

Zuzims (*zu'-zims*) See also ZAMZUMMIMS.
Ge 14: 5 the Z' in Ham, and the Emins in *2104

ADDENDA.

A.

about
Ex 11: 4 A' midnight will I go out into...Egypt:
12: 37 a' six hundred thousand on foot that
Re 7: 11 and a' the elders and the four beasts,

above
2Ch 24: 20 priest, which stood a' the people, 5921
Es 5: 11 he had advanced him a' the princes "
2Co 11: 23 abundant, in stripes a' measure, *5234*

according
Ge 6: 22 a' to all that God commanded him,
7: 5 a' unto all that the Lord commanded
18: 14 a' to the time of life, and Sarah shall*
21 done altogether a' to the cry of it,
21: 23 a' to the kindness that I have done
27: 19 I have done a' as thou badest me: arise,
Ex 6: 26 land of Egypt a' to their armies. 5921
2Ch 35: 12 that they might give a' to the divisions
Ps 119: 170 before thee: deliver me a' to thy word,
M't *general title* Gospel A' To S. [St.] Matthew. *2596*
M'r *general title* The Gospel A' To S. [St.] Mark. "
Lu *general title* The Gospel A' To S. [St.] Luke. "
Joh *general title* The Gospel A' To S. [St.] John. "

acts
Ac *general title* The A' Of The Apostles. *4234*

afar
2Ki 4: 25 when the man of God saw her a' off, 5048

afflicted
Isa 54: 11 O thou a', tossed with tempest, and 6041

after
Ge 1: 26 man in our image, a' our likeness:
18: 11 be with Sarah a' the manner of women
25 to do a' this manner, 3651
19: 31 come in unto us a' the manner of all
Ex 25: 9 a' the pattern of the tabernacle, *
1Ki 18: 28 and cut themselves a' their manner
2Ch 17: 4 and not a' the doings of Israel.
Job 10: 6 iniquity, and searchest a' my sin?
42: 8 lest I deal with you a' your folly,
Ps 119: 85 The proud...which are not a' thy law.
M'r 9: 31 a' that he is killed, he shall rise *
2Pe 2: 20 For if a' they have escaped

again
Ge 24: 20 ran a' unto the well to draw water, 5750
Nu 12: 15 not till Miriam was brought in a'.
2Ch 28: 17 For a' the Edomites had come 5750
Eze 11: 14 A' the word of the Lord came unto me,*

against
Ex 9: 17 yet exaltest thou thyself a' my people,
Nu 12: 9 anger of the Lord was kindled a' them;
J'g 12: 1 over to fight a' the children of Ammon,
1 Sa 5: 9 the hand of the Lord was a' the city
Ne 3: 30 Meshullam...over a' his chamber. 5048
Ps 3: 1 many are they that rise up a' me. 5921
Pr 30: 31 a' whom there is no rising up. 5973
Eze 14: 8 And I will set my face a' that man, and
30: 11 shall draw their swords a' Egypt, 5921
42: 3 was gallery a' gallery in three 413, 6440
Jas 5: 3 rust of them shall be a witness a' you,

age
Lu 8: 42 about twelve years of a', and she lay

Ain (*ah'-yin*)
Ps 119: 121 *title* [ע] A'.

Aleph (*aw'-lef*)
Ps 119: 1 *title* [א] A'.

all
Ge 12: 5 a' their substance that they had 3605
13: 1 and his wife, and a' that he had, "
21: 22 with thee in a' that thou doest: "
22: 18 the nations of the earth be blessed; "
23: 10 of a' that went in at the gate "
18 before a' that went in at the gate "
24: 1 had blessed Abraham in a' things. "
2 that ruled over a' that he had, "
10 a' the goods of his master were in his "
20 and drew for a' his camels, "
36 hath he given a' that he hath. "
Ex 1: 5 and a' the souls that came out of "
3: 20 and smite Egypt with a' my wonders "
4: 19 a' the men are dead which sought "
8: 16 throughout a' the land of Egypt. "
17 throughout a' the land of Egypt. "
9: 24 none like it in a' the land of Egypt "
12: 33 they said, We be a' dead men. "
13: 7 seen with thee in a' thy quarters. "
Le 4: 34 shall pour out a' the blood thereof "
13: 13 it is a' turned white: he is clean. "
Nu 14: 29 and a' that were numbered of you, "
17: 12 we die, we perish, we a' perish. "
30: 2 according to a' that proceedeth out "
Jos 9: 19 But a' the princes said unto a' the "
1Sa 13: 3 the trumpet throughout a' the land, "
14: 34 And a' the people brought every man "
2Sa 7: 17 And according to a' this vision, so "
2Ki 10: 9 but who slew a' these? "
1Ch 23: 28 in the purifying of a' holy things, "
2Ch 10: 16 So a' Israel went to their tents. "
12: 1 and a' Israel with him. "
16: 4 and a' the store cities of Naphtali. "
20: 6 over a' the kingdoms of the heathen? "
Ps 85: 5 out thine anger to a' generations? "
91: 11 thee, to keep thee in a' thy ways. "
105: 7 his judgments are in a' the earth. "
119: 96 I have seen an end of a' perfection: "
138: 2 thy word above a' thy name. "
148: 7 the earth, ye dragons, and a' deeps: "
Pr 5: 19 her breasts satisfy thee at a' times: "
Ec 12: 4 and a' the daughters of musick shall "
Isa 21: 2 a' the sighing thereof have I made "
30: 5 They were a' ashamed of a people "
51: 18 by the hand of a' the sons that she "
65: 12 shall a' bow down to the slaughter: "
Jer 27: 7 And a' nations shall serve him, and "
39: 1 king of Babylon and a' his army "
La 3: 51 heart because of a' the daughters "
Eze 14: 5 they are a' estranged from me "
29: 7 and madest a' their loins to be at a "
35: 15 Seir, and a' Idumea, even a' of it: "
Zec 1: 11 and, behold, a' the earth sitteth still, "
2Pe 3: 11 ye to be in a' holy conversation "

alone
Ps 86: 10 wondrous things: thou art God a'. 905
148: 13 Lord: for his name a' is excellent; "

already
Ex 1: 5 souls: for Joseph was in Egypt a'.

also
Ge 20: 6 I a' withheld thee from sinning 1571
24: 14 I will give thy camels drink a': "
19 I will draw water for thy camels a', "
44 and I will a' draw for thy camels: "
46 and I will give thy camels drink a': "
46 and she made the camels drink a'. "
Ex 8: 21 and a' the ground whereon they are. "
18: 23 this people shall a' go to their place "
Le 26: 39 a' in the iniquities of their fathers 637
1Ch 16: 25 he a' is to be feared above all gods.
Ps 93: 1 the world a' is stablished, that it 389
Jer 35: 15 I have sent a' unto you all my servants
38: 25 death: a' what the king said unto thee:
Eze 20: 12 a' I gave them my sabbaths, to be 1571
M't 27: 41 a' the chief priests mocking him, *1161*
Lu 3: 21 Jesus a' being baptized, *2532*
Joh 4: 45 for they a' went unto the feast. "
18: 2 and Judas a', which betrayed him, "
Ac 14: 1 Jews and a' of the Greeks believed,* "
20: 21 to the Jews, and a' to the Greeks,* "
Ro 1: 6 are ye a' the called of Jesus Christ: "
15 preach...to you that are at Rome a'. "
5: 2 By whom a' we have access by faith "
8: 32 shall he not with him a' freely give "
11: 23 and they a', if they abide not still *1161*
31 mercy they a' may obtain mercy. *2532*
16: 7 who a' were in Christ before me. "
Ph'p 2: 24 that I a' myself shall come shortly. "
Col 4: 1 knowing that ye a' have a Master "
Tit 3: 3 we...a' were sometimes foolish, "
14 let ours a' learn to maintain good "
Ph'm 9 now a' a prisoner of Jesus Christ. "
Jas 2: 11 commit adultery, said a', Do not kill. "

altogether
Ca 5: 16 is most sweet: yea, he is a' lovely. 3605

am
Le 19: 18 neighbour as thyself: I a' the Lord.
28 any marks upon you: I a' the Lord.
Ps 139: 21 a' not I grieved with those that rise
Jer 50: 31 Behold, I a' against thee,
Eze 6: 9 I a' broken with their whorish heart.*
Jas 1: 13 he is tempted, I a' tempted of God: for

among
Ex 10: 2 my signs which I have done a' them:
Nu 3: 42 the firstborn a' the children of Israel.
1Sa 10: 11, 12 Is Saul also a' the prophets?
22 he hath hid himself a' the stuff. 413
24 there is none like him a' all the people?

Amos
Am *general title* A'. 5986

anger
Ps 103: 9 neither will he keep his a' for ever.

another
Ge 26: 31 and sware to one a': 251
1Sa 18: 7 answered one a' as they played,

answereth
M'r 10: 24 But Jesus a' again, and saith unto *611*

any
Ge 43: 34 five times as much as a' of theirs. 3605
Ex 1: 10 when there falleth out a' war, they join
10: 15 there remained not a' green thing 3605
12: 39 prepared for themselves a' victual.
22: 25 If thou lend money to a' of my people
Le 7: 24 may be used in a' other use: 3605
11: 32 vessel it be, wherein a' work is done,
Isa 44: 8 yea, there is no God; I know not a'.
Eze 15: 2 is the vine tree more than a' tree, 3605
36: 15 cause thy nations to fall a' more,
M't 10: 5 and into a' city of the Samaritans enter
Lu 4: 40 that had a' sick with divers diseases

apostle
Ro *general title* The Epistle of Paul The A' ‡ *652*
1Co *general title* First Epistle of Paul The A' ‡ "
2Co *general title* Second Epistle of Paul The A' ‡ "
Ga *general title* The Epistle of Paul [The A']* "

Eph *general title* The Epistle Of Paul The *A'* ‡ *652*
Ph'p *general title* The Epistle Of Paul The *A'* ‡ "
Col *general title* The Epistle Of Paul The *A'* ‡ "
1Th *general title* First Epistle Of Paul The *A'* ‡ "
2Th *general title* Second Epistle Of Paul The *A'* ‡ "
1Ti *general title* First Epistle Of Paul The *A'* ‡ "
2Ti *general title* Second Epistle Of Paul The *A'* ‡ "
Heb *general title* The Epistle Of Paul The *A'* ‡ "

apostles
Ac *general title* The Acts Of The *A'*. [*40*,] *652*

art
Heb12: 5 nor faint when thou *a'* rebuked of him:

asked
M'r 7:17 his disciples *a'* him concerning the *1905*

away
Le 16:21 shall send him *a'* by the hand of a fit
2Sa 3:22 for he had sent him *a'*, and he is gone

B.

bear
Isa 54: 1 O barren, thou that didst not *b'*; 3205

became
Ge 21:20 in the wilderness, and *b'* an archer. 1961
1Ch 18:13 the Edomites *b'* David's servants. "
Re 16: 3 it *b'* as the blood of a dead man: *1096*

because
Ge 21:31 *b'* there they sware both of them. 3588
De 9:18 *b'* of all your sins which ye sinned, 5921
25 *b'* the Lord had said he would 3588
28 say, *B'* the Lord was not able to bring
28 *b'* he hated them, he hath brought
23: 4 *b'* they hired against thee Balaam 834
31:17 *b'* our God is not among us? 5921, 3588
32:51 *b'* ye sanctified me not in the " 834
1Sa 15:24 thy words: *b'* I feared the people, 3588
Ne 6:18 *b'* him, *b'* he was the son in law of
Es 9:24 *B'* Haman the son of Hammedatha, "
Job 8: 9 *b'* our days upon earth are a shadow:)"
Ps 119:53 taken hold upon me *b'* of the wicked
Jer 39:18 *b'* thou hast put thy trust in me, 3588
Eze35: 5 *B'* thou hast had a perpetual 3282
Hab 2: 8 *b'* thou hast spoiled many nations, 3588
8 *b'* of men's blood, and for the violence

become
Pr 29:21 have him *b'* his son at the length. 1961

been
Ge 46:32 their trade hath *b'* to feed cattle; 1961
2Ki 20:12 he had heard that Hezekiah had *b'* sick.
Isa 42:14 I have *b'* still, and refrained
Jer 15: 9 she hath *b'* ashamed and confounded:
34:14 Hebrew, which hath *b'* sold unto thee;
48:11 hath not *b'* emptied from vessel to
Eze16:31 hast not *b'* as an harlot, in that 1961
Ph'p 2:26 ye had heard that he had *b'* sick.*

before
Ge 24:15 to pass, *b'* he had done speaking, 2962
2Sa 19:28 but dead men *b'* my lord the king:
1Ki 1:23 he bowed himself *b'* the king with his
Job 2: 1 to present himself *b'* the Lord. 5921
26: 6 Hell is naked *b'* him, and 5048
Ps 22:25 pay my vows *b'* them that fear "
69:19 mine adversaries are all *b'* thee. "
89:36 his throne as the sun *b'* me. "
101: 3 set no wicked thing *b'* mine eyes: "
Pr 15:11 and destruction are *b'* the Lord: "
Isa 40:17 all nations *b'* him are as nothing; "
Jer 47: 1 *b'* that Pharaoh smote Gaza. 2962
Eze42: 1 which was *b'* the building toward *5048
Da 10:16 and said unto him that stood *b'* me, "
Zep 2: 2 *B'* the decree bring forth, 2962
2 forth, *b'* the day pass as the chaff,
2 *b'* the fierce anger of the Lord 2962, 3808
2 *b'* the day of the Lord's anger "
2Ti *subscr.* Paul was brought *b'* Nero the **3936*

behold
Ge 22: 7 he said, *B'*, the fire and the wood: 2009
13 and *b'* behind him a ram caught in "
20 *B'*, Milcah, she hath also born "
24:13 *B'*, I stand here by the well "
15 that, *b'*, Rebekah came out, who was "
30 and, *b'*, he stood by the camels at "
43 *B'*, I stand by the well of water; and "
45 *b'*, Rebekah came forth with her "
37:29 and, *b'*, Joseph was not in the pit; "
47:23 *B'*, I have brought you this day 2005
Ex 1: 9 *B'*, the people of the children of 2009
2: 6 the child: and, *b'*, the babe wept. "
9: 3 *B'*, the hand of the Lord is upon thy "
39:43 and, *b'*, they had done it as the Lord "
Le 13:43 and, *b'*, if the rising of the sore be "
Nu 18: 8 *B'*, I...have given thee the charge "
22: 5 *B'*, there is a people come out from "
5 *b'*, they cover the face of the earth, "
24:10 *b'*, thou hast altogether blessed "
De 9:13 and, *b'*, it is a stiffnecked people: "
1Sa 12: 3 *B'*, here I am: witness against me* "
15:12 *b'*, he set him up a place, "
22 *B'*, to obey is better than sacrifice, "
19:19 *B'*, David is at Naioth in Ramah. "
2Sa 18:10 and said, *B'*, I saw Absalom hanged "
Jer 29:21 *B'*, I will deliver them into the hand "
49:19 *B'*, he shall come up like a lion "
50:41 *B'*, a people shall come from the "
Eze37: 7 and *b'* a shaking, and the bones "
Joe 3: 1 For, *b'*, in those days, and in that "
Am 6:11 For, *b'*, the Lord commandeth, and "

being
Es 1: 7 (the vessels *b'* diverse one from
Eze47: 8 which *b'* brought forth into the sea.*
Ac 16:18 But Paul, *b'* grieved, turned and said

Beth (*bayth*)
Ps 119: 9 *title* [ב] *B'*.

between
Ex 9: 4 the Lord shall sever *b'* the cattle of 996
J'g 16:31 and buried him *b'* Zorah and Eshtaol "

book
Ge *general title* The First *B'* Of Moses, Called
Ex *general title* The Second *B'* Of Moses, Called
Le *general title* The Third *B'* Of Moses, Called
Nu *general title* The Fourth *B'* Of Moses, Called
De *general title* The Fifth *B'* Of Moses, Called
Jos *general title* The *B'* Of Joshua.
J'g *general title* The *B'* Of Judges.
Ru *general title* The *B'* Of Ruth.
1Sa *general title* The First *B'* Of Samuel,
general title Called, The First *B'* Of The Kings.*
2Sa *general title* The Second *B'* Of Samuel,
general title The Second *B'* Of The Kings.*
1Ki *general title* The First *B'* Of The Kings,
general title The Third *B'* Of The Kings.*
2Ki *general title* The Second *B'* Of The Kings,
general title The Fourth *B'* Of The Kings.*
1Ch *general title* The First *B'* Of The Chronicles.
2Ch *general title* The Second *B'* Of The Chronicles.
Ne *general title* The *B'* Of Nehemiah.
Es *general title* The *B'* Of Esther.
Job *general title* The *B'* Of Job.
Ps *general title* The *B'* Of Psalms. *
Isa *general title* The *B'* Of The Prophet Isaiah.
Jer *general title* The *B'* Of The Prophet Jeremiah.
Eze *general title* The *B'* Of The Prophet Ezekiel.
Da *general title* The *B'* Of Daniel.

both
Ex 7:19 *b'* in vessels of wood, and in vessels
9:25 all...in the field, *b'* man and beast;
12:12 firstborn...of Egypt, *b'* man and beast;
1Sa 6:18 five lords, *b'* of fenced cities, and of
1Ch 24: 3 distributed them, *b'* Zadok of the sons*
Isa 31: 3 *b'* he that helpeth shall fall, and he
2Th 3: 4 you, that ye *b'* do and will do the *2532*

bound
J'g 16:12 new ropes, and *b'* him therewith. 631

bows
Eze 39: 9 bucklers, the *b'* and the arrows. 7198

brought
Isa 43:23 hast not *b'* me the small cattle 935

build
Ezr 5:11 and *b'* the house that was builded 1124
Ps 127: 1 house, they labor in vain that *b'* it: 1129

built
Jer 32:31 from the day that they *b'* it even 1129

burned
2Ki 23:15 brake down, and *b'* the high place, 8313

C.

call
Ps 116: 2 therefore will I *c'* upon him as long 7121
M't 10:25 shall they *c'* them of his household.

called
Ge *general title* First Book Of Moses, *C'* Genesis.
Ex *general title* Second Book Of Moses, *C'* Exodus.
Le *general title* Third Book Of Moses, *C'* Leviticus.
Nu *general title* Book Of Moses, *C'* Numbers.
De *general title* Book Of Moses, *C'* Deuteronomy.
1Sa *general title* Otherwise *C'*, The First Book*
2Sa *general title* Otherwise *C'*, The Second Book*
1Ki *general title* Commonly *C'*, The Third Book*
2Ki *general title* Commonly *C'*, The Fourth Book*

came
Ge 35:17 it *c'* to pass, when she was in hard 1961
18 it *c'* to pass, as her soul was in "
36:30 these are the dukes that *c'* of Hori,
Le 9: 1 it *c'* to pass on the eighth day, 1961
1Ki 19:13 And, behold, there *c'* a voice unto him,
1Ch 17: 3 that the word of God *c'* to Nathan, 1961

can
De 1:12 How *c'* I myself alone bear your
1Ki 5: 6 not among us any that *c'* skill to hew‡
Isa 38:18 death *c'* not celebrate thee: they that

cannot
Le 14:21 be poor, and *c'* get so much; 369, 3027
Job 19: 8 fenced up my way that I *c'* pass, 3808
Ps 88: 8 I am shut up, and I *c'* come forth. "
Isa 38:18 death [*c'*] celebrate thee: they that go
Jer 5:22 perpetual decree, that it *c'* pass it: 3808

canst
Jer 2:23 How *c'* thou say, I am not polluted, I

Caph (*kaf*)
Ps 119:81 *title* [כ] *C'*.

carcases
Le 11:26 The *c'* of every beast which divideth*

caused
2Ch 34:32 And he *c'* all...to stand to it.
Jer 29:31 him not, and he *c'* you to trust in a lie:

cave
1Ki 19:13 stood in the entering in of the *c'*. 4631

certainly
Ge 18:10 I will *c'* return unto thee 7725

chains
Ex 28:25 two ends of the two wreathen *c'* thou

Cheth (*khayth*)
Ps 119:57 *title* [ח] *C'*.

child
Ge 17:17 Shall a *c'* be born unto him that is an
18:13 Shall I of a surety bear a *c'*,

chronicles
1Ch *general title* The First Book Of The *C'*. 1697, 3117
2Ch *general title* The Second Book Of The *C'*. " "

Colossians
Col *general title* The Epistle Of Paul...To...*C'*. *2858*

come
Ge 9:14 And it shall *c'* to pass, when I bring 1961
24:14 And let it *c'* to pass, that the damsel "
Jer 12:15 it shall *c'* to pass, after that I have "
16 And it shall *c'* to pass, if they will "
Zec 14: 7 but it shall *c'* to pass, that at "

cometh
Jer 51:54 A sound of a cry *c'* from Babylon, and*

committed
Jer 29:23 and have *c'* adultery with their 6213

commonly
1Ki *general title* The Kings, *C'* Called, The Third*
2Ki *general title* The Kings, *C'* Called, The Fourth*

concerning
Ge 12:20 commanded his men *c'* him: 5921
1Ch 22:13 Lord charged Moses with *c'* Israel: "

Corinthians
1Co *general title* First Epistle Of Paul...To...*C'*. *2881*
2Co *general title* Second Epistle...Paul...To...*C'*. "

corn
2Ki 19:26 and as *c'* blasted before it be grown up.

D.

Daleth (*daw'-leth*)
Ps 119:25 *title* [ד] *D'*.

Daniel
Da *general title* The Book Of *D'*. 1840

David
1Ch 23: 5 I made, said *D'*, to praise therewith.

day
Ge 8: 5 on the first *d'* of the month,
2Ki 25: 1 month, in the tenth *d'* of the month,
Jer 39: 2 the ninth *d'* of the month, the city was

despised
Jer 22:28 Is this man Coniah a *d'* broken idol? 959

Deuteronomy (*doo''-tur-on'-o-mee*)
De *general title* Book Of Moses, Called *D'*. 428, 1697

did
J'g 6:13 *D'* not the Lord bring us up from
11:25 or *d'* he ever fight against them, *
1Sa 1: 7 her; therefore she wept, and *d'* not eat.
2Ki 23:12 of the Lord, *d'* the king beat down,
2Ch 35:18 neither *d'* all the kings of Israel keep
Jer 41: 1 and there they *d'* eat bread together in
Ac 26:10 the saints *d'* I shut up in prison, *

didst
Nu 21:34 do to him as thou *d'* unto Sihon 6213
J'g 12: 1 and *d'* not call us to go with thee? we
13: 8 man of God which thou *d'* send come
1Ki 8:53 For thou *d'* separate them from among
M't 13:27 Sir, *d'* not thou sow good seed in thy

displeased
Nu 11:10 greatly; Moses also was *d'*. 5869, 7541

divine
Re *general title* Revelation Of...John The *D'*. ‡*2312*

do
De 17:19 and these statutes, to *d'* them: 6213
Ps 31: 1 In thee, O Lord, *d'* I put my trust; let
34:10 young lions *d'* lack, and suffer hunger:
80:12 which pass by the way *d'* pluck her?
Jer 23:32 and *d'* tell them, and cause my people
Eze 23:30 I will *d'* these things unto thee, *6213
M't 8:29 What have we to *d'* with thee, Jesus,
15: 9 In vain they *d'* worship me, teaching
M'r 11:33 neither *d'* I tell you by what authority*
Ac 7:51 ye *d'* always resist the Holy Ghost:
Ph'm 19 albeit I *d'* not say to thee how thou*

doest
2Sa 3:25 in, and to know all that thou *d'*. 6213

doings
Eze 20:43 all your *d'*, wherein ye have been 5949

down
Nu 34:12 the border shall go *d'* to Jordan, 3381
M't 14:19 the multitude to sit *d'* on the grass, *347*
Heb10:12 sat *d'* on the right hand of God; *2523*
12: 2 sit *d'* at the right hand of the throne "

drew
Ge 24:20 water, and *d'* for all his camels. 7579

duties
Eze 18:11 And that doeth not any of those *d'*, but

dwelt
Isa 37:37 and returned, and *d'* at Nineveh. 3427

Jer 2: 6 through, and where no man *d*? 3427
Re 11:10 them that *d* on the earth. *2730

E.

each
Le 24: 7 put pure frankincense upon *e* row.

eat
De 15:22 and the clean person shall *e* it alike,

Ecclesiastes *(ek-kle"-ze-as'-teze)*
Ec *general title* *E*; Or, The Preacher. 6953

edge
Eze 43:13 by the *e* thereof round about shall 8193

Elpalet *(el-pa'-let)*
1Ch 14: 5 And Ibhar, and Elishua, and *E* *467

else
1Ki 20:39 or *e* thou shalt pay a talent of silver.
21: 6 or *e*, if it please thee, I will give thee

entering
1Sa 23: 7 by *e* into a town that hath gates 935
2Ki 14:25 *e* of Hamath unto the sea of the

Ephesians
Eph *general title* The Epistle...To The *E*. 2180

epistle
Ro *general title* The *E* Of Paul...Romans. 1992
1Co *general title* First *E*...Corinthians. "
2Co *general title* Second *E*...Corinthians. "
Ga *general title* *E* Of Paul...Galatians. "
Eph *general title* *E* Of Paul...Ephesians. "
Ph'p *general title* *E* Of Paul...Philippians. "
Col *general title* *E* Of Paul...Colossians. "
1Th *general title* First *E*...Thessalonians. "
2Th *general title* Second *E*...Thessalonians. "
1Ti *general title* First *E* Of Paul...Timothy. "
2Ti *general title* Second *E*...Timothy. "
Tit *general title* The *E* Of Paul To Titus. "
Ph'm *general title* The *E* Of Paul To Philemon. "
Heb *general title* The *E* Of Paul...Hebrews. "
Jas *general title* The General *E* Of James. "
1Pe *general title* First *E* General Of Peter. "
2Pe *general title* Second *E* General Of Peter. "
1Jo *general title* First *E* General Of John. "
2Jo *general title* The Second *E* Of John. "
3Jo *general title* The Third *E* Of John. "
Jude *general title* The General *E* Of Jude. "

Esther
Es *general title* The Book Of *E*. 635

even
Ge 23:10 *e* of all that went in at the gate of the
Le 20: 6 I will *e* set my face against that soul.
De 17:12 unto the judge, *e* that man shall die:
1Ki 14:26 he *e* took away all: and he took away
1Ch 11: 8 city round about, *e* from Millo 5704
Eze 8: 6 *e* the great abominations that the
Eph 1:10 and which are on earth; *e* in him:*

every
Ge 2:19 Adam called *e* living creature that was
9: 2 and upon *e* fowl of the air, upon 3605
10 of the ark, to *e* beast of the earth. "
19: 4 all the people from *e* quarter:
Ex 12:44 But *e* man's servant that is bought 3605
27:18 and the breadth fifty *e* where,
Le 11:15 *E* raven after his kind; 853, "
15: 4 *e* thing, whereon he sitteth, shall "
Nu 36: 8 *e* daughter, that possesseth an "
1Ch 28:17 silver by weight for *e* bason of silver:
2Ch 1: 2 and to *e* governor in all Israel, 3605
8:14 porters also by their courses at *e* gate:
Jer 5: 6 *e* one that goeth out thence shall 3605

Exodus *(ex'-o-dus)*
Ex *general title* Of Moses, Called *E*. 428,8031

Ezekiel
Eze *general title* Book Of The Prophet *E*. 3168

Ezra
Ezr *general title* *E*. 5830

F.

far
Ec 2:13 folly, as *f* as light excelleth darkness.

father's
Ne 7:61 they could not shew their *f* house,*

fathers
Nu 1:42 by the house of their *f*, according 1

fellow
Ge 19: 9 This one *f* came in to sojourn,

female
De 7:14 there shall not be male or *f* barren

fifth
De *general title* *F* Book Of Moses, Called

findeth
Pr 14: 6 scorner seeketh wisdom, and *f* it not:

fine
Ge 18: 6 quickly three measures of *f* meal, 5560

fire
Jer 32:35 their daughters to pass through the *f*

first
Ge *general title* The *F* Book Of Moses, Called
1Sa *general title* The *F* Book Of Samuel, [א]
1Sa *general title* The *F* Book Of The Kings. *
1Ki *general title* The *F* Book Of The Kings. [א]
1Ch *general title* The *F* Book Of The Chronicles. [א]
1Co *general title* The *F* Epistle Of Paul The 4413
1Th *general title* The *F* Epistle Of Paul The "
1Ti *general title* The *F* Epistle Of Paul The "
1Pe *general title* The *F* Epistle General Of "
1Jo *general title* The *F* Epistle General Of "

foolishly
1Sa 13:13 Thou hast done *f*: thou hast not 5528

foot
Eki 9:33 the horses: and he trode her under *f*.

forth
Nu 12: 5 and they both came *f*.
1Ki 8:16 I brought *f* my people Israel out 3318
Heb 1:14 sent *f* to minister for them who 649

forty
Ge 7:12 upon the earth *f* days and *f* nights, 705

fourth
Nu *general title* The *F* Book Of Moses, Called
2Ki *general title* The *F* Book Of The Kings. *

fowl
Ge 1:28 and over the *f* of the air, and over 5775

free
Am 4: 5 and publish the *f* offerings: *5071

full
Ge 14:10 the vale of Siddim was *f* of slimepits;

G.

Galatians
Ga *general title* Paul [The Apostle] To The *G*. 1052

gate
Re 21:21 every...*g* was of one pearl: *3588,4440

general
Jas *general title* The *G* Epistle Of James. ‡2526
1Pe *general title* The First Epistle *G* Of Peter.‡ "
2Pe *general title* Second Epistle *G* Of Peter. ‡ "
1Jo *general title* The First Epistle *G* Of John.‡ "
Jude *general title* The *G* Epistle of Jude. ‡ "

Genesis *(jen'-e-sis)*
Ge *general title* Book Of Moses, Called *G*. 7225

Gimel *(ghee'-mel)*
Ps 119:17 *title* [ג] *G*.

glad
Ps 40:16 seek thee rejoice and be *g* in thee: 8055

go
Ex 9:17 that thou wilt not let them *g*? 7971
J'g 20: 9 will *g* up by lot against it;
1Sa 12:21 for then should ye *g* after vain things,
1Ki 12:27 and *g* again to Rehoboam king *7725
Jer 46:19 furnish thyself to *g* into captivity:

God
1Ki 8:20 the name of the Lord *G* of Israel. 430
Ps 140: 7 O *G* the Lord, the strength of my ‡3069

goest
M't 8:19 follow thee whithersoever thou *g*. 565

good
Pr 28:10 the upright shall have *g* things *2896

gospel
M't *general title* *G* According To...Matthew. 2098
M'r *general title* The *G* According To...Mark. "
Lu *general title* The *G* According To...Luke. "
Joh *general title* The *G* According To...John. "

gray [*most editions* GREY *here*].
Pr 20:29 beauty of old men is the *g* head. *7872

grayheaded [*most editions* GREYHEADED *here*].
Ps 71:18 Now also when I am old and *g*, O 7872

great
2Ch 20: 2 There cometh a *g* multitude 7227

greatly
Isa 61:10 I will *g* rejoice in the Lord, my soul

grow
Job 8:11 can the flag *g* without water? 1342

guilty
Ex 34: 7 and that will by no means clear the *g*;

H.

Habakkuk
Hab *general title* *H*. 2265

had
Ex 2: 6 And when she *h* opened it, she saw*
Nu 30: 6 And if she *h* at all an husband, *1961
1Sa 15:35 repented that he *h* made Saul king
25:21 Now David *h* said, Surely in vain have
2Sa 8: 9 that David *h* smitten all the host of
12: 3 ewe lamb, which he *h* bought and
21:12 when the Philistines *h* slain Saul*
1Ki 5: 1 for he *h* heard that they *h* anointed
6:22 until he *h* finished all the house: *
7: 8 daughter, whom he *h* taken to wife,
Ne 10:28 all they that *h* separated themselves
Ps 51: *title* after he *h* gone in to Bath-sheba
Jer 41: 9 Asa the king *h* made for fear of
52:25 which *h* the charge of the men of *1961
Lu 12:39 if the goodman of the house *h* known
Ac 10:17 Cornelius *h* made enquiry for Simon's*

Haggai
Hag *general title* *H*. 2292

hand
2Sa 18:14 And he took three darts in his *h*, 3709
2Ki 11:11 man with his weapons in his *h*, 3027
23: 8 were on a man's left *h* at the gate
Job 1:12 upon himself put not forth thine *h*. 3027
Isa 30:21 when we turn to the right *h*, and

hast
Ru 2:13 and for that thou *h* spoken friendly
1Sa 19:17 Why *h* thou deceived me so, and sent
1Ki 1: 6 Why *h* thou done so? and he also was
Job 33: 8 Surely thou *h* spoken in mine hearing,
Ps 3: 7 thou *h* broken the teeth of the ungodly.
31: 8 And *h* not shut me up into the hands
8 thou *h* set my feet in a large room.
Eze 16:24 and *h* made thee a high place in every
Da 5:23 are all thy ways, *h* thou not glorified:*
Hab 1:12 thou *h* established them for correction.
2:10 people, and *h* sinned against thy soul.
Joh 4:18 and he whom thou now *h* is not thy 2192
Ac 23:22 thou *h* shewed these things to me.

hated
Ps 106:10 from the hand of him that *h* them, 8130
41 and they that *h* them ruled over

hath
1Sa 25:21 and he *h* requited me evil for good.
Ne 9:32 that *h* come upon us, on our kings, on
Job 16:11 God *h* delivered me to the ungodly,*
Ps 132:13 *h* chosen Zion: he *h* desired it for his
Pr 30: 4 who *h* gathered the wind in his fists?
4 who *h* bound the waters in a garment?
4 who *h* established all the ends of the
Ec 5: 4 to pay it; for he *h* no pleasure in fools:
Isa 14: 4 and say, How *h* the oppressor ceased!
Jer 48:11 and he *h* settled on his lees,
11 and *h* not been emptied from vessel to
11 neither *h* he gone into captivity:
La 1: 5 for the Lord *h* afflicted her for the
14 the Lord *h* delivered me into their
M't 15:13 my heavenly Father *h* not planted,*
Lu 11:33 No man, when he *h* lighted a candle,
Ac 24: 6 Who also *h* gone about to profane the*

have
Ge 4: 1 said, I *h* gotten a man from the Lord.
21: 7 for I *h* borne him a son in his old age.
26:10 thou shouldest *h* brought guiltiness
46:32 and their herds, and all that they *h*.
Nu 35: 3 the cities shall they *h* to dwell in; 1961
1Sa 11: 9 time the sun be hot, ye shall *h* help. "
19: 4 his works *h* been to thee-ward *
20: 3 certainly knoweth that I *h* found grace
1Ki 1:45 This is the noise that ye *h* heard.
11:36 my servant may *h* a light alway 1961
Ezr 4:14 therefore *h* we sent and certified the
Isa 14:24 and as I *h* purposed, so shall it stand:
43:10 and my servant whom I *h* chosen:
49:21 me these, seeing I *h* lost my children,
Jer 14:13 the sword, neither shall ye *h* famine;
25:35 the shepherds shall *h* no way to flee,
29: 7 the peace thereof shall ye *h* peace. 1961
30:11 end of all nations whither I *h* scattered
48: 4 little ones *h* caused a cry to be heard.
Eze 23:34 for I *h* spoken it, saith the Lord God.
28:26 when I *h* executed judgments upon all
39:29 for I *h* poured out my spirit upon the
Ob 7 that eat thy bread *h* laid a wound*
Hag 2:23 I *h* chosen thee, saith the Lord of hosts.
M't 13:17 which ye hear, and *h* not heard them.*
Ac 17:28 certain also of your own poets *h* said,

having
Ro 15:23 *h* a great desire these many years 2192
Heb 11:13 but *h* seen them afar off,

He *(hay)*
Ps 119:33 *title* [ה] *H*.

hearing
M'r 4:12 and *h* they may hear, and not 191

hearkened
1Ki 20:25 and he *h* unto their voice, and did 8085

Hebrews
Heb *general title* Paul The Apostle To The *H*. 1445

henceforth
Mic 4: 7 over them in mount Zion from *h*, 6258

here
2Ch 18: 6 there not *h* a prophet of the Lord 6311
Ac 8:36 See, *h* is water; what doth hinder

high
1Ch 11:23 man of great stature, five cubits *h*;

himself
Le 15:13 shall number to *h* seven days for his
2Sa 18:18 taken and reared up for *h* a pillar,*

hither
Pr 25: 7 it be said unto thee, Come up *h*; 2008

ho
Ru 4: 1 unto whom he said, *H*, such a one!

holds
2Co 10: 4 to the pulling down of strong *h*;) 3794

horns
Jos 6: 8 the seven trumpets of rams' *h* 3104

horses
2Sa 8: 4 David houghed all the chariot *h*, but

Hosea
Ho *general title* H·. 1954

host
1Ki 22:19 And all the h· of heaven standing 6635

houses
1Ch 28:11 and of the h· thereof, and of the 1004
Ne 7: 4 therein, and the h· were not builded. "
Pr 30:26 yet make they their h· in the rocks; "

how
Ex 6:12 h· then shall Pharaoh hear me, 349
10: 7 H· long shall this man be a snare 4970
11: 7 may know h· that the Lord doth put a
2Sa 6: 9 H· shall the ark of the Lord come 349
Isa 14:12 h· art thou cut down to the ground,
Jer 47: 5 h· long wilt thou cut thyself? 5704
La 4: 2 h· are they esteemed as earthen 349
Ac 19:35 knoweth not h· that the city of the

I.

if
Ex 1:16 i· it be a son, then ye shall kill 518
16 but i· it be a daughter, then she "
Le 5: 2 things, and i· it be hidden from him;* "
13:58 i· the plague be departed from them, "
Nu 19:12 i· he purify not himself the third 518
De 30:17 But i· thine heart turn away, so that "
2Sa 15:25 i· I shall find favour in the eyes of "
2Ch 6:26 yet i· they pray toward this place, and "
Job 21:15 we have, i· we pray unto him? 3588
Ps 62:10 i· riches increase, set not your "
Pr 6:30 do not despise a thief, i· he steal "
30: 4 is his son's name, i· thou canst tell? "
Ec 4:11 Again, i· two lie together, then 518
12 And i· one prevail against him, two "
11: 3 and i· the tree fall toward the south, "
8 But i· a man live many years, and "
Ca 7:12 let us see i· the vine flourish, * "
8: 9 and i· she be a door, we will inclose "
Isa 51:13 as i· he were ready to destroy? * 834
Jer 2:10 and see i· there be such a thing, 2005
28 i· they can save thee in the time of 518
3: 1 I· a man put away his wife, and 2005
4: 1 and i· thou wilt put away thine 518
42: 5 i· we do not even according to all "
Eze 18:21 But i· the wicked will turn from 3588
Da 3:18 But i· not, be it known unto thee, 2006
M't 16:26 i· he shall gain the whole world, *1437*
M'r 7:16 I· any man have ears to hear, **1437*
8:23 he asked him i· he saw ought. * "
Lu 14:26 I· any man come to me, and hate "

insomuch
Ps 106:40 i· that he abhorred his own *

into
Nu 4: 3 all that enter i· the host, to do the*
Job 34:23 that he should enter i· judgment with*
Jer 43: 3 to deliver us i· the hand of the
Eze 12:11 shall remove and go i· captivity.

Isaiah
Isa *general title* The Book Of The Prophet I·.3470

Israel
Jer 51:19 and I· is the rod of his inheritance:
Eze 18:15 eyes to the idols of the house of I·,3478

J.

Jair
De 3:14 J· the son of Manasseh took all 2971

James
Jas *general title* The General Epistle Of J·. *2385*

Jeremiah
Jer *general title* The Book Of The Prophet J·.3414
La *general title* The Lamentations Of J·.

Job
Job *general title* The Book of J·. 347

Jod (*yode*)
Ps 119:73 *title* [י] J·.

Joel
Joe *general title* J·. 3100

John
Joh *general title* Gospel According To S.[St.] J·.*2491*
1Jo *general title* The First Epistle General Of J·. "
2Jo *general title* The Second Epistle Of J·. "
3Jo *general title* The Third Epistle Of J·. "
Re *general title* The Revelation Of S. [St.] J· "

Jonah
Jon *general title* The Book Of J·. 3124

Joshua
Jos *general title* The Book Of J· 3091

Judah
1Ch 6:57 Aaron then gave the cities of J·,*[3063]

Jude
Jude *general title* The General Epistle Of J·. *2455*

judges
J'g *general title* The Book Of J·. 8199

judgments
De 30:16 And his statutes and his j·, that 4941

K.

Karnaim (*kar'-na-im*) See also ASHTEROTH.
Ge 14: 5 the Rephaims in Ashteroth K·, 6255

king
1Ki 14:25 in the fifth year of k· Rehoboam, 4428

kings
1Sa *general title* Called, The First Book Of The K·.*
2Sa *general title* The Second Book Of The K·.*
1Ki *general title* The First Book Of The K·. 4428
general title Called, The Third Book Of The K·.*
2Ki *general title* The Second Book Of The K·. 4428
general title The Fourth Book Of The K·.*

Koph (*kofe*)
Ps 119:145 *title* [ק] K·.

L.

laid
2Ch 24:27 greatness of the burdens l· upon him,

Lamed (*law'-med*)
Ps 119:89 *title* [ל] L·.

lamentations
La *general title* The L· Of Jeremiah. 349

land
Ge 41:36 that the l· perish not 776

less
Job 34:19 How much l· to him that accepteth
Eze 15: 5 how much l· shall it be meet yet for

lest
De 1:42 you; l· ye be smitten before your 3808
Ps 91:12 l· thou dash thy foot against a 6435
Pr 30: 9 or l· I be poor, and steal, and take "

let
Ge 1: 9 place, and l· the dry land appear:
Ex 22: 7 the thief be found, l· him pay double.*
1Sa 14:36 L· us draw near hither unto God.
Eze 45: 9 L· it suffice you, O prince of Israel:
M't 5:16 L· your light so shine before men, that
6: 3 l· not thy left hand know what thy

Leviticus (*le-vit'-i-cus*)
Le *general title* Third Book Of Moses, Called L·.7121

lie
Re 11: 8 dead bodies shall l· in the street of the

like
Ex 8:10 that there is none l· unto the Lord*
1Sa 8:20 That we also may be l· all the nations;
2Ki 5:14 again l· unto the flesh of a little child,
2Ch 4: 5 of it l· the work of the brim of a cup,
6:14 no God l· thee in the heavens, nor 3644
30:26 there was not the l· in Jerusalem. 2063
Job 38: 3 Gird up now thy loins l· a man;
Ps 31:12 out of mind: I am l· a broken vessel.
72:16 city shall flourish l· grass of the earth.
105:41 they ran in the dry places l· a river.
119:119 all the wicked of the earth l· dross.
Isa 18: 4 l· a clear heat upon herbs, and
33: 4 l· the gathering of the caterpiller:*
36:17 you away to a land l· your own land,
Jer 48:38 for I have broken Moab l· a vessel
La 4: 8 it is withered, it is become l· a stick.
Eze 31: 8 chesnut trees were not l· his branches;
Da 10:16 one l· the similitude of the sons of

lo
Ex 7:15 l·, he goeth out unto the water: 2009
2Sa 24:17 said, L·, I have sinned, and done "
2Ki 7: 6 L·, the king of Israel hath hired "
15 l·, all the way was full of garments "
1Ch 17: 1 L·, I dwell in an house of cedars, "
Eze 33:33 cometh to pass, (l·, it will come,)* "

loft
Ac 20: 9 and fell down from the third l·. **5152*

long
1Sa 1:14 How l· wilt thou be drunken? put 5704
Ne 2: 6 For how l· shall thy journey be? and "
Ps 79: 5 How l·, Lord? wilt thou be angry "

lord (Lord)
2Ch 17: 4 But sought to the L· God of his father.*
Ps 68:18 that the L· God might dwell among3050

lord's (Lord's)
Le 27:30 of the fruit of the tree, is the L·: 3068

Luke
Lu *general title* Gospel According To S. [St.] L·.*3065*

M.

made
1Ki 14: 9 hast gone and m· thee other gods, 6213
1Ch 28: 2 and had m· ready for the building:
Joh 1:31 he should be m· manifest to Israel, *5319*
Ac 8: 3 for Saul, he m· havock of the church,*

Mahli
1Ch 23:21 The sons of M·; Eleazar, and 4249

make
Job 41: 6 the companions m· a banquet of him?
28 The arrow cannot m· him flee:
Ps 132:17 will I m· the horn of David to bud:
Eze 35:11 I will m· myself known among them,
Eph 5:13 for whatsoever doth m· manifest **5319*

Malachi
Mal *general title* M·. 4401

man
Ge 20: 3 thou art but a dead m·,
Ps 12: 1 Help, Lord; for the godly m· ceaseth;
Pr 24:15 Lay not wait, O wicked m·, against
28:17 flee to the pit; let no m· stay him.
Ec 8: 1 Who is as the wise m·? and who
Isa 28:20 is shorter than that a m· can stretch
Joh 18:40 saying, Not this m·, but Barabbas.
19:12 If thou let this m· go, thou art not
Eph 5: 5 nor unclean person, nor covetous m·,

manner
2Ch 32:15 nor persuade you on this m·, neither

many
Isa 61: 4 the desolations of m· generations.

Mark
M'r *general title* According To S. [St.] M·. *3138*

Matthew
M't *general title* According To S. [St.] M·. *3156*

may
Ex 31: 6 that they m· make all that I have
Nu 27:20 of the children of Israel m· be obedient.
2Sa 18:14 Joab, I m· not tarry thus with thee.
Jer 46:10 he m· avenge him of his adversaries:
Eze 34:10 that they m· not be meat for them.

mean
Ge 21:29 What m· these seven ewe lambs which

meat
Ge 24:33 there was set m· before him

Mem (*mame*)
Ps 119:97 *title* [מ] M·.

men
Ge 4:26 then began m· to call upon the name
Nu 31:32 pray which the m· of war had 5971
2Sa 19:35 hear any more the voice of singing m·
1Ch 11:22 he slew two lionlike m· of Moab:*
12:32 were m· that had understanding of
2Ch 22: 1 for the band of m· that came with the
Ezr 2:65 two hundred singing m· and singing
7:28 together out of Israel chief m· to go
Ne 13:16 There dwelt m· of Tyre also therein,
Pr 7:26 many...m· have been slain by her.*
Ec 3:14 that m· should fear before him. *
Isa 35: 8 the wayfaring m·, though fools, shall
M't 21:41 miserably destroy those wicked m·,
1Th 3:12 toward one another, and toward all m·,
1Ti 5: 1 and the younger m· as brethren;
Heb 12:23 the spirits of just m· made perfect,
Jas 1: 5 that giveth to all m· liberally, and*

Micah
Mi *general title* M·. 4318

might
Ph'm 8 though I m· be much bold in Christ*

mine
Ge 49: 6 m· honour, be not thou united: for in*
Nu 8:17 firstborn of the children...are m·,
1Ki 2:15 knowest that the kingdom was m·,
Ne 7: 5 my God put into m· heart to gather*
Ps 138: 7 against the wrath of m· enemies,
Pr 8:14 counsel is m·, and sound wisdom: I

money
Ge 23:16 current m· with the merchant.

more
1Co 12:22 body, which seem to be m· feeble, are
23 have m· abundant comeliness. *4055*
Ph'p 2:28 I sent him...the m· carefully, *4708*

moreover
Ge 24:25 She said m· unto him, We have both
Ex 3: 6 M· he said, I am the God of thy father,
11: 3 M· the man Moses was very great 1571
1Ki 1:47 and m· the king's servants came "
Ne 12: 8 M· the Levites: Jeshua, Binnui,
Isa 8: 1 M· the Lord said unto me, Take thee*
Eze 35: 1 M· the word of the Lord came unto me,

Moses
Ge *general title* Book Of M·, Called Genesis.
Ex *general title* Book Of M·, Called Exodus.
Le *general title* Book Of M·, Called Leviticus.
Nu *general title* Book Of M·, Called Numbers.
De *general title* Book Of M·, Called Deuteronomy.

most
Ezr 2:63 should not eat of the m· holy things,
Ps 82: 6 you are children of the m· High. 5945

much
Ge 23: 9 for as m· money as it is worth he shall*
De 31:27 and how m· more after my death?
Ezr 7:22 and salt without prescribing how m·,
Eze 15: 5 how m· less shall it be meet 637,3588

must
Ge 17:13 m· needs be circumcised:
24: 5 m· I needs bring my son again unto
1Ch 17:11 that thou m· go to be with thy fathers,
Ezr 10:12 As thou hast said, so m· we do. 5921
Isa 28:10 For precept m· be upon precept, *

myself
Ne 5: 7 Then I consulted with m·, and I

N.

Nahum
Na *general title* N'. 5151
name
2Sa 6: 8 called the n' of the place Perez-uzzah*
namely
Nu 13:11 Of the tribe of Joseph, n', of the tribe
nay
Ge 19: 2 And they said, N'; but we will 3808
near
Nu 33:48 plains of Moab by Jordan n' Jericho.*
35: 1 plains of Moab by Jordan n' Jericho.*
needs
Ge 17:13 money, must n' be circumcised: 4135
19: 9 and he will n' be a judge: 8199
24: 5 must I n' bring thy son again unto 7725
Nehemiah
Ne *general title* The Book Of N'. 5166
neither
Ge 3: 3 not eat of it, n' shall ye touch it. 3808
8:21 n' will I again smite any more every "
Ex 34:25 n' shall the sacrifice of the feast of "
Nu 6: 3 n' shall he drink any liquor of "
1Ki 3:12 n' after thee shall any arise like "
Ps 6: 1 thine anger, n' chasten me in thy "
never
2Ch 21:17 so that there was n' a son left him, 3808
Jer 20:11 confusion shall n' be forgotten. "
nevertheless
Eze 3:21 N' if thou warn the righteous man,
night
Ps 63: 6 and meditate on thee in the n' watches.
no
Nu 20: 2 was n' water for the congregation:3808
Job 28: 7 is a path which n' fowl knoweth, "
Re 22: 5 they need n' candle, neither light *3756*
none
Ps 139:16 as yet there was n' of them. 3808,259
nor
Ge 19:35 when she lay down, n' when she arose.
De 10: 9 Levi hath no part n' inheritance with
Isa 44:18 have not known n' understood: *3808
nothing
2Ch 14:11 said, Lord, it is n' with thee to help,*369
Ezr 4: 3 Ye have n' to do with us to build 3808
Ps 17: 3 hast tried me, and shalt find n'; 1077
Isa 40:23 That bringeth the princes to n'; 369
now
Ge 22: 2 Take n' thy son, thine only son 4994
24:42 if n' thou do prosper my way "
27: 2 he said, Behold n', I am old, "
47:29 If n' I have found grace in thy sight, "
Ex 7:11 n' the magicians of Egypt, they *
10:11 go n' ye that are men, and serve 4994
1Sa 9: 6 to pass: n' let us go thither; 6258
2Sa 7:29 Therefore n' let it please thee to "
1Ki 8:26 And n', O God of Israel, let thy "
2Ki 13: 8 N' the rest of the acts of Jehoahaz, "
Isa 7:13 said, Hear ye n', O house of David; 4994
37:26 n' have I brought it to pass, that 6258
Jer 29:27 N' therefore why hast thou not "
Eze 4:14 even till n' have I not eaten of that "
Joe 2:12 Therefore also n', saith the Lord, "
Ac 16: 6 N'...they had gone throughout **1161*
Ro 6: 8 N' if we be dead with Christ, we * "
1Co 7:25 N' concerning virgins I have no "
Jas 2:11 N' if thou commit no adultery, yet "
numbers
Nu *general title* Book Of Moses, Called N'. 4057
Nun (*noon*)
Ps 119:105 *title* [נ] N'.

O.

Obadiah
Ob *general title* O'. 5662
off
De 11:17 ye perish...from o' the good land 5921
Da 4:14 shake o' his leaves, and scatter his "
Lu 9: 5 shake o' the very dust from your *660*
on
Le 14:23 bring them o' the eighth day for his
Nu 30: 8 husband disallowed her o' the day*
Job 38:26 To cause it to rain o' the earth, 5921
26 o' the wilderness, wherein there "
Eze 10: 3 cherubims stood o' the right side of "
48:21 o' the one side and o' the other of the "
Lu 4:40 and he laid his hands o' every one *2007*
21:35 as a snare shall it come o' all them**1909*
1Ti 4:14 with the laying o' of the hands of *1936*
one
Ge 24:41 if they give not thee o', thou shalt*
Le 11:26 every o' that toucheth them shall be
Nu 17: 2 take of every o' of them a rod
26:54 to every o' shall his inheritance be
De 21: 1 If o' be found slain in the land which
28:64 from o' end of the earth even unto
1Sa 26:20 as when o' doth hunt a partridge in
2Ki 19:22 even against the Holy O' of Israel.
Ne 13:28 and o' of the sons of Joiada, the son of
Isa 10:14 and as o' gathereth eggs that are left,
41:27 give to Jerusalem o' that bringeth
Jer 30:16 thine adversaries, every o' of them.
Eze 40:40 as o' goeth up to the entry of the north
Ro 14: 2 For o' believeth that he may eat all *3739*
2Co 2:16 To the o' we are the savour of *3303*
1Ti 3: 4 O' that ruleth well his own house,
one's
Ec 7: 1 day of death than the day of o' birth.
ones
2Ch 31:18 all their little o', their wives, and their
Ps 83: 3 and consulted against thy hidden o'.
Jer 46: 5 and their mighty o' are beaten down,
Lu 17: 2 he should offend one of these little o'.
only
Ge 14:24 Save o' that which the young men 7535
19: 8 eyes: o' unto these men do nothing; "
24: 8 o' bring not my son thither again. "
27:13 o' obey my voice, and go fetch 389
Ex 8: 9 they may remain in the river o'? 7535
28 o' ye shall not go very far away: "
10:17 forgive,...my sin o' this once, and 389
17 take away from me this death o' 7535
24 o' let your flocks and your herds "
12:16 that o' may be done of you. 905
2Sa 20:21 deliver him o', and I will depart "
2Ch 6:30 (for thou o' knowest the hearts of the "
Pr 5:17 Let them be o' thine own, and not* "
or
Ps 18:31 o' who is a rock save our God? *
Ec *general title* Ecclesiastes; O', The Preacher.
Jer 16: 2 sons o' [*some eds.* NOR] daughters in
order
Ge 22: 9 there, and laid the wood in o', 6186
other
Ge 20:16 that are with thee, and with all o':*
25:23 shall be stronger than the o' people;
Nu 24: 1 he went not, as at o' times, to seek for
32:38 and give o' names unto the cities
Es 2:12 and with o' things for the purifying*
Jer 12:12 the land even to the o' end of the land:
otherwise
1Sa *general title* Samuel, O' Called, The First
2Sa *general title* Samuel, O' Called, The Second
ought
Ge 20: 9 hast done deeds unto me that o' not to
over
Ex 30: 6 mercy seat that is o' the testimony, 5921
own
Ge 5: 3 begat a son in his o' likeness,
14:14 trained servants, born in his o' house,*
15: 4 come forth out of thine o' bowels
2Sa 17:11 go to battle in thine o' person.
1Ki 10:13 she turned and went to her o' country,
2Ki 2:12 he took hold of his o' clothes, and rent
2Ch 24:25 his o' servants conspired against him
Ps 17:10 They are inclosed in their o' fat: with
141:10 Let the wicked fall into their o' nets,
Pr 5:17 Let them be only thine o', and not*
27:10 Thine o' friend, and thy father's friend,
Isa 14:18 lie in glory, every one in his o' house.
53: 6 have turned every one to his o' way;
Jer 1:16 worshipped the works of their o' hands.

P.

part
Da 11:31 And arms that shall stand on his p',
Re 8: 7 and the third p' of trees was burnt up,
parts
Eze 37:11 we are cut off for our p'.
pass
Ge 4: 8 and it came to p', when they were in the
9:14 And it shall come to p', when I bring a
12:11 And it came to p', when he was come
12 Therefore it shall come to p', when the
14 And it came to p', that, when Abram
14: 1 it came to p' in the days of Amraphel
15:17 And it came to p', that, when the sun
19:17 it came to p', when they had brought
29 it came to p', when God had destroyed
34 And it came to p' on the morrow, that
21:22 And it came to p' at that time, that
22: 1, 20 And it come to p' after these things,
24:14 And let it come to p', that the damsel
15 And it came to p', before he had done
22 And it came to p', as the camels had
30 And it came to p', when he saw the
43 it shall come to p', that when the virgin
26:32 And it came to p' the same day,
35:17 And it came to p', when she was in
Nu 10:11 it came to p' on the twentieth day of
J'g 14:17 and it came to p' on the seventh day,
1Sa 10: 9 And all those signs came to p' that day.
2Sa 15: 7 And it came to p' after forty years, that
Jer 12:15 come to p', after that I have plucked
16 shall come to p', if they will diligently
Eze 20: 1 And it came to p' in the seventh year,
Zec 14: 7 but it shall come to p' that at evening
Paul
Ro *general title* P'...To The Romans. *3972*
1Co *general title* P'...To The Corinthians. "
2Co *general title* P'...To The Corinthians. "
Ga *general title* P' [...] To The Galatians. "
Eph *general title* P'...To The Ephesians. "
Ph'p *general title* P'...To The Philippians. "
Col *general title* P'...To The Colossians. "
1Th *general title* P'...To The Thessalonians. "
2Th *general title* P'...To The Thessalonians. *3972*
1Ti *general title* P'...The Apostle To Timothy. "
2Ti *general title* P'...The Apostle To Timothy. "
Tit *general title* The Epistle Of P' To Titus. "
Ph'm *general title* Epistle Of P' To Philemon. "
Heb *general title* P'...To The Hebrews. ‡ "
Pe (*pay*)
Ps 119:129 *title* [פ] P'.
peradventure
Ge 24: 5 P' the woman will not be willing to 194
39 P' the woman will not follow me "
27:12 my father p' will feel me, and I shall "
person
Nu 19:19 And the clean p' shall sprinkle upon
Eph 5: 5 nor unclean p', nor covetous man, who
Peter
1Pe *general title* First Epistle General Of P'. *4074*
2Pe *general title* Second Epistle General Of P'. "
Philemon
Ph'm *general title* The Epistle Of Paul To P'. *5371*
Philippians
Ph'p *general title* Epistle Of Paul...To The P'. *5374*
pit
Job 6:27 and ye dig a p' for your friend. *
place
Ex 28:29 when he goeth in unto the holy p',
pray
Ge 24: 2 Put, I p' thee, thy hand under my 4994
12 I p' thee, send me good speed this "
14 Let down thy pitcher, I p' thee, that "
17 Let me, I p' thee, drink a little water "
23 daughter art thou? tell me, I p' thee: "
43 Give me, I p' thee, a little water of "
45 unto her, Let me drink, I p' thee. * "
27: 3 take, I p' thee, thy weapons, thy "
38:25 Discern, I p' thee, whose are these, "
44:18 let thy servant, I p' thee, speak a "
48: 9 Bring them, I p' thee, unto me, and "
1Sa 25:28 I p' thee, forgive the trespass of "
2Sa 15:31 O Lord, I p' thee, turn the counsel "
1Ki 20:35 Smite me, I p' thee. And the man "
2Ki 2:16 let them go, we p' thee, and seek thy "
6: 3 Be content, I p' thee, and go with "
18:26 Speak, I p' thee, to thy servants in "
Job 4: 7 Remember, I p' thee, whoever "
Ps 119:76 Let, I p' thee, thy merciful kindness "
Isa 29:12 saying, Read this, I p' thee: "
preacher
Ec *general title* Ecclesiastes; Or, The P'.
presence
Ps 116:18 now in the p' of all his people, 5048
present
Lu 18:30 receive manifold more in this p' time, *
prophet
Isa *general title* The Book Of The P' Isaiah.
Jer *general title* The Book Of The P' Jeremiah.
Eze *general title* The Book Of The P' Ezekiel.
proverbs
Pr *general title* The P'. 4912
provocation
Jer 32:31 For this city hath been to me as a p'5921
psalms
Ps *general title* The Book Of P'. 8416
put
2Sa 20: 8 Joab's garment that he had p' on 3830
1Ch 11:19 men that have p' their lives in jeopardy?

R.

ran
J'g 9:21 And Jotham r' away, and fled, and 5127
rather
Jer 8: 3 And death shall be chosen r' than life
reach
Isa 30:28 overflowing stream, shall r' to the 2673
reason
1Ki 14: 4 for his eyes were set by r' of his age.*
Job 41:25 by r' of breakings...purify themselves.
remove
Eze 12:11 they shall r' and go into captivity.*1473
Resh (*raysh*)
Ps 119:153 *title* [ר] R'.
revelation
Re *general title* The R' Of S. [St.] John The *602*
right
Ps 139:14 and that my soul knoweth r' well. 3966
ripe
Nu 18:13 And whatsoever is first r' in the 1001
Romans
Ro *general title* Of Paul The Apostle To The R'. *4514*
room
1Ki 19:16 thou anoint to be prophet in thy r'.*8478
2Ch 6:10 for I am risen up in the r' of David "
ruin
2Ch 28:23 But they were the r' of him, and *3782

rule
Isa 44:13 carpenter stretcheth out his *r*˙; *6957

rulers
1Ki 9:22 captains, and *r*˙ of his chariots, 8269

S.

S. [for St. or Saint]
M't *general title* According To *S*˙ [St.] Matthew.‡*40*
M'r *general title* According To *S*˙ [St.] Mark. ‡ "
Lu *general title* According To *S*˙ [St.] Luke. ‡ "
Joh *general title* According To *S*˙ [St.] John. ‡ "
Re *general title* Revelation Of *S*˙ [St.] John. ‡ "

said
Ge 22: 5 And Abraham *s*˙ unto his young 559
2Ch 31:10 Azariah...answered him, and *s*˙, "

sake
1Ch 17:19 Lord, for thy servant's *s*˙, and 5668
2Ch 6:32 far country for thy great name's *s*˙, 4616
Ps 6: 4 oh save me for thy mercies' *s*˙. "
69: 7 for thy *s*˙ I have borne reproach: 5921
79: 9 away our sins, for thy name's *s*˙. 4616
Isa 45: 4 For Jacob my servant's *s*˙ and "
54:15 against thee shall fall for thy *s*˙. *5921
62: 1 and for Jerusalem's *s*˙ I will not 4616
66: 5 that cast you out for my name's *s*˙, "
Eze 20:44 wrought with you for my name's *s*˙, "

sakes
Ps 106:32 it went ill with Moses for their *s*˙: 5668

same
Ge 23: 2 the *s*˙ as Hebron in the land of 1931
19 Mamre: the *s*˙ is Hebron in the "
24:14 lot the *s*˙ be she that thou hast
Ex 19: 1 *s*˙ day came they into...wilderness 2088
27: 2 his horns shall be of the *s*˙: and thou*
Nu 4: 8 cover the *s*˙ with a covering of 853
2Ch 18: 7 always evil: the *s*˙ is Micaiah the 1931
20:26 therefore the name of the *s*˙ place* "
Isa 20: 2 At the *s*˙ time spake the Lord * "
Lu 23:12 And the *s*˙ day Pilate and Herod *846*
Eph 4:10 is the *s*˙ also that ascended up "
Ph'p 2: 2 ye be likeminded, having the *s*˙ love, "

Samech (*saw'-mek*)
Ps 119:113 *title* [ס] *S*˙.

Samuel
1Sa *general title* The First Book Of *S*˙, 8050
2Sa *general title* The Second Book Of *S*˙, "

save
2Ki 4: 2 in the house, *s*˙ a pot of oil. *3588,518
2Ch 21:17 left him, *s*˙ Jehoahaz, the "

say
Pr 23:35 They have stricken me, shalt thou *s*˙,
M'r 12:43 Verily I *s*˙ unto you, That this *3004*

Schin (*sheen*)
Ps 119:161 *title* [ש] *S*˙.

season
1Ch 21:29 offering, were at that *s*˙ in the *6256

second
Ex *general title* The *S*˙ Book Of Moses, Called
2Sa *general title* The *S*˙ Book Of Samuel, [ב]
general title Called, The *S*˙ Book Of...Kings.* "
2Ki *general title* The *S*˙ Book Of The Kings, [ב]
2Ch *general title* The *S*˙ Book Of The Chronicles.[ב]
2Co *general title* The *S*˙ Epistle Of Paul The *1208*
2Th *general title* The *S*˙ Epistle Of Paul The "
2Ti *general title* The *S*˙ Epistle Of Paul The "
2Pe *general title* The *S*˙ Epistle General Of "
2Jo *general title* The *S*˙ Epistle Of John. "

see
2Ki 5: 7 *s*˙ how he seekest a quarrel 7200
Eph 5:33 and the wife *s*˙ that she reverence her

seeing
Ge 22:12 *s*˙ thou hast not withheld thy son,
26:27 *s*˙ ye hate me, and have sent me away
Job 24: 1 *s*˙ times are not hidden from thee *
Pr 3:29 thy neighbour, *s*˙ he dwelleth securely

selves [*in most editions here* (YOUR)SELVES]
Le 11:43 Ye shall not make your *s*˙ *5315
Jos 23:11 good heed therefore unto your *s*˙,* "

separate
Jude 19 These be they who *s*˙ themselves, *592*

serve
Ex 10: 7 they may *s*˙ the Lord their God: 5647

served
1Ch 19: 5 how the men were *s*˙. And he sent 5921

set
1Sa 8:12 and will *s*˙ them to ear his ground,
1Ch 20: 2 in it; and it was *s*˙ upon David's head:
2Ch 4: 4 and the sea was *s*˙ above upon them,

shekels
Ge 24:22 bracelets...of ten *s*˙ weight of gold;

shew
Eze 22: 2 yea, thou shalt *s*˙ her all her *3645

should
Le 11:43 unclean with them, that he *s*˙ be defiled

shoulder
Ge 24:46 and let down her pitcher from her *s*˙,

side
2Ki 9:32 and said, Who is on my *s*˙?
2Ch 11:12 having Judah and Benjamin on his *s*˙.*

since
Ex 9:24 all the land of Egypt *s*˙ it became a 227

sing
Isa 38:20 therefore we will *s*˙ my songs to 5057

so
Ge 27: 1 old, and his eyes were dim, *s*˙ that he
Ex 8: 7 the magicians did *s*˙ with their *3651
17 And they did *s*˙: for Aaron stretched "
18 the magicians did *s*˙ with their "
18 *s*˙ there were lice upon man, and upon
26 Moses said, It is not meet *s*˙ to do; 3651
16:17 And the children of Israel did *s*˙, "
32:21 that thou hast brought *s*˙ great a sin*
Nu 8: 3 And Aaron did *s*˙; 3651
22:30 was I ever wont to do *s*˙ unto thee?*3541
35:29 *S*˙ these things shall be for a statute of
De 32:12 *S*˙ the Lord alone did lead him, and*
Jos 10:13 *S*˙ the sun stood still in the midst of*
1Ki 2:23 God do *s*˙ to me, and more also, if 3541
21: 5 Why is thy spirit *s*˙ sad, that thou 2088
22:12 prophesied *s*˙, saying, Go up to 3651
2Ki 4:36 *S*˙ he called her. And when she was
13: 5 a saviour, *s*˙ that they went out from
1Ch 17:15 all this vision, *s*˙ did Nathan speak 3651
Ezr 4:13 and *s*˙ thou shalt endamage the *
Job 21: 4 and if it were *s*˙, why should not my*
Ps 68: 2 As smoke is driven away, *s*˙ drive them
103:15 flower of the field, *s*˙ he flourisheth.3652
119:134 the oppression of man: *s*˙ will I keep
Ec 11: 5 even *s*˙ thou knowest not the 3602
Isa 5:24 *s*˙ their root shall be as rottenness,
14:24 as I have thought, *s*˙ shall it come 3652
29: 8 *s*˙ shall the multitude of all the "
31: 5 as birds flying, *s*˙ will the Lord of "
Jer 35:11 Syrians: *s*˙ we dwell at Jerusalem.
48:39 *s*˙ shall Moab be a derision and a
Eze 3:14 *S*˙ the spirit lifted me up, and took me
19:14 *s*˙ that she hath no strong rod to be a
21:24 *s*˙ that in all your doings your sins do
Da 7:16 *S*˙ he told me, and made me know the
Ho 13: 6 to their pasture, *s*˙ were they filled;
Jon 1: 6 if *s*˙ be that God will think upon us,
Zec 4: 4 *S*˙ I answered and spake to the angel*
8:13 *s*˙ will I save you, 3651
M't 27:66 *S*˙ they went, and made the *1161*
1Pe 5:13 you; and *s*˙ doth Marcus my son. *
Re 17: 3 *S*˙ he carried me away in the spirit**2532*

Solomon
Ca *general title* The Song of *S*˙. *7892

some
Ge 27: 3 to the field, and take me *s* venison:*
33:15 Let me...leave with thee *s*˙ of the folk
Le 14:25 the priest shall take *s*˙ of the blood of*
Re 2:10 devil shall cast *s*˙ of you into prison,

song
Ca *general title* The *S*˙ Of Solomon. 7892

sons
De 28:41 Thou shalt beget *s*˙ and daughters,1121
1Ch 9:14 Hashabiah, of the *s*˙ of Merari; "

sooner
Jas 1:11 sun is no *s*˙ risen with a burning heat,*

sort
Eze 23:42 men of the common *s*˙ were brought120

sounded
Ex 19:19 when the voice of the trumpet *s*˙ *1961

space
Ac 7:42 by the *s*˙ of forty years in the *

spake
Nu 21:16 whereof the Lord *s*˙ unto Moses, * 559

spread
M'r 6:14 (for his name was *s*˙ abroad:) and * *5318*

St. See S.; SAINT.

stead
1Ki 14:20 Nadab his son reigned in his *s*˙. 8478
16:28 and Ahab his son reigned in his *s*˙. "
1Ch 29:28 Solomon his son reigned in his *s*˙. "
2Ch 9:31 Rehoboam his son reigned in his *s*˙. "
26:23 Jotham his son reigned in his *s*˙. "
Ec 4:15 child that shall stand up in his *s*˙. "

still
Ex 9: 2 and wilt hold them *s*˙, 5750
Ru 3:18 Then said she, Sit *s*˙, my daughter,
2Sa 14:32 good for me to have been there *s*˙: 5750
Isa 9:12 but his hand is stretched out *s*˙. "

stories
Eze 41:16 galleries round about on their three *s*˙,

strange
Ps 144:11 me from the hand of *s*˙ children, †‡5236

such
Ge 27: 9 meat for thy father, *s*˙ as he loveth:*
14 savoury meat, *s*˙ as his father loved.
Ex 9:18 hail, *s*˙ as hath not been in Egypt 834
24 hail,...*s*˙ as there was none like it in "
11: 6 cry...*s*˙ as there was none like it, "

sunder
Isa 45: 2 and cut in *s*˙ the bars of iron:

surely
Ps 140:13 *S*˙ the righteous shall give thanks 389
Isa 45:24 *S*˙, shall one say, in the Lord have I* "
Am 8: 7 *S*˙ I will never forget any of their
Mic 2:12 I will *s*˙ gather the remnant of Israel:
Zep 3: 7 I said, *S*˙ thou wilt fear me, thou 389

sware
1Ki 2:23 Then King Solomon *s*˙ by the Lord,7650

T.

tabernacle
Le 8:33 not go out of the door of the *t*˙ * 168

take
Ge 13: 9 if thou wilt *t*˙ the left hand, then I will
Es 3:13 and to *t*˙ the spoil of them for a prey.

takest
Ps 144: 3 is man, that thou *t*˙ knowledge of him!

Tau (*tawv*)
Ps 119:169 *title* [ת] *T*˙.

Teth (*tayth*)
Ps 119:65 *title* [ט] *T*˙.

than
Ge 39: 9 none greater in this house *t*˙ I; 4480
Nu 14:12 a greater nation and mightier *t*˙ they.
2Sa 18: 8 more people that day *t*˙ the sword 834
1Ki 16:25 did worse *t*˙ all that were before him.*
33 to anger *t*˙ all the kings of Israel that
2Ki 6:16 us are more *t*˙ they that be with them.
2Ch 20:25 more *t*˙ they could carry away: and 369
30:18 passover otherwise *t*˙ it was written.
Ezr 9:13 punished us less *t*˙ our iniquities
Job 32: 2 he justified himself rather *t*˙ God. 4480
Ps 8: 5 made him a little lower *t*˙ the angels,
45: 2 Thou art fairer *t*˙ the children of men:
51: 7 wash me, and I shall be whiter *t*˙ snow.
61: 2 lead me to the rock that is higher *t*˙ I.
62: 9 they are altogether lighter *t*˙ vanity.
76: 4 excellent *t*˙ the mountains of prey.*
89:27 higher *t*˙ the kings of the earth. *
118: 8 trust...Lord *t*˙ to put confidence in man.
119:103 yea, sweeter *t*˙ honey to my mouth!
Pr 26:12 there is more hope of a fool *t*˙ of him.
16 is wiser in his own conceit *t*˙ seven men
Ec 4: 6 *t*˙ both the hands full with travail
9 Two are better *t*˙ one: because they
13 wise child *t*˙ an old and foolish king,
Ca 1: 2 mouth: for thy love is better *t*˙ wine.
4 will remember thy love more *t*˙ mine:
Isa 57: 8 hast discovered thyself to another *t*˙ me,
Jer 3:11 herself more *t*˙ treacherous Judah.
46:23 they are more *t*˙ the grasshoppers, and
La 4: 6 greater *t*˙ the punishment of the sin of
Lu 11:22 a stronger *t*˙ he shall come upon him,
Ac 17:11 These were more noble *t*˙ those in
1Ti 5: 8 the faith, and is worse *t*˙ an infidel.

themselves
Ge 21:28 set seven ewe lambs of the flock by *t*˙.
29 ewe lambs which thou hast set by *t*˙?
2Ki 17:32 and made unto *t*˙ of the lowest of *
Job 39: 3 They bow *t*˙, they bring forth their
Hab 2:13 people shall weary *t*˙ for very vanity?
2Pe 2:13 sporting *t*˙ with their own deceivings*

then
Ex 9: 1 *T*˙ the Lord said unto Moses, Go in
18: 2 *T*˙ Jethro, Moses' father in law, *
Nu 15:19 *T*˙ it shall be, that, when ye eat of the
30: 8 *t*˙ he shall make her vow which she
32:29 *t*˙ ye shall give them the land of Gilead
De 20:11 *t*˙ it shall be, that all the people that is
23:24 vineyard, *t*˙ thou mayest eat grapes
25 *t*˙ thou mayest pluck the ears with
2Sa 2:26 how long shall it be *t*˙, ere thou bid the
15:33 *t*˙ thou shalt be a burden unto me:
24: 6 *T*˙ they came to Gilead, and to the
1Ki 2:43 Why *t*˙ hast thou not kept the oath of
Jer 17:27 *t*˙ will I kindle a fire in the gates

thence
Ge 24: 7 take a wife unto my son from *t*˙. 8033
27: 9 fetch me from *t*˙ two good kids of "
Nu 21:16 And from *t*˙ they went to Beer: that "
De 5:15 thy God brought thee out *t*˙ through "
Jer 22:24 hand, yet would I pluck thee *t*˙; "

there
Ex 8:22 that no swarms of flies shall be *t*˙; 8033
Le 11:36 pit, wherein *t*˙ is plenty of water, *
Nu 13:28 we saw the children of Anak *t*˙. 8033
De 13:12 thy God hath given thee to dwell *t*˙, "
2Sa 18:25 he be alone, *t*˙ is tidings in his mouth.
24:13 or that *t*˙ be three days' pestilence in
Job 6: 6 is *t*˙ any taste in the white of an egg?
M't 9:18 *t*˙ came a certain ruler, and worshipped

thereby
Ge 24:14 *t*˙ shall I know that thou hast shewed

therefore
Ge 23:15 me and thee? bury *t*˙ thy dead.
Jer 44:23 *t*˙ this evil is happened unto 5921,3652

thereof
Ge 2:17 thou eatest *t*˙ thou shalt surely die.
45:16 the fame *t*˙ was heard in Pharaoh's
Le 13:20 skin, and the hair *t*˙ be turned white:

these
Ge 22: 1 after *t*˙ things, that God did tempt 428
20 pass after *t*˙ things, that it was told "
23 *t*˙ eight Milcah did bear to Nahor, "
23: 1 *t*˙ were the years of the life of Sarah.
24:28 told....her mother's house *t*˙ things. 428
31:43 I do this day unto *t*˙ my daughters. "
Ex 6:27 *t*˙ are that Moses and Aaron. 1931

Ex 19: 6 *T'* are the words which thou shalt 428
De 6: 6 And *t'* words, which I command thee "
1Sa 25:37 his wife had told him *t'* things, that "
Ne 13:26 king of Israel sin by *t'* things? "
Jer 45: 1 when he had written *t'* words in "
1Co 12: 2 carried away unto *t'* dumb idols, *3588*
Col 3: 8 put off all *t'*; anger, wrath, malice,
2Pe 3:17 seeing ye know *t'* things before,

Thessalonians
1Th *general title* Paul The Apostle To The *T'*. *2331*
2Th *general title* Paul The Apostle To The *T'*. "

thine
Le 18:14 approach to his wife: she is *t'* aunt.
De 5:14 nor *t'* ox, nor *t'* ass, nor any of thy
7:13 and thy wine, and *t'* oil, the increase
11:19 when thou sittest in *t'* house, and
13: 8 neither shall *t'* eye pity him, neither
18: 4 of thy wine, and of *t'* oil, and the first

thing
Ge 8:21 smite any more every *t'* living,
14:23 will not take any *t'* that is thine,*
18:17 hide from Abraham that *t'* which I do;*
19:22 cannot do any *t'* till thou be come 1697
22:12 neither do thou any *t'* unto him: for

things
Ge 24: 1 the Lord had blessed Abraham in all *t'*.

third
Le *general title* The *T'* Book Of Moses, Called
1Ki *general title* Called.... *T'* Book Of The Kings.*
3Jo *general title* The *T'* Epistle Of John. *5154*

this
Ge 22:14 as it is said to *t'* day,
16 because thou hast done *t'* thing, 2088
23:19 after *t'*, Abraham buried Sarah 3651
24: 5 willing to follow me unto *t'* land: 2063
7 unto thy seed will I give *t'* land; "
12 send me good speed *t'* day,
41 shalt thou be clear from *t'* my oath,*
42 And I came *t'* day unto the well,
38:29 *t'* breach be upon thee: *
41:28 *T'* is the thing which I have *1931
44:15 What deed is *t'* that ye have done? 2088
48:15 fed me all my life long unto *t'* day, "
Ex 3:12 and *t'* shall be a token unto thee, "
21 I will give *t'* people favour in the "
12:25 that ye shall keep *t'* service *2063
43 Aaron, *T'* is the ordinance of the "
16: 8 *T'* shall be, when the Lord shall give
Le 26:16 I also will do *t'* unto you; I will 2063
Nu 28: 3 *T'* is the offering made by fire 2088
De 1:31 until ye came into *t'* place. "
11: 5 until ye came into *t'* place; "
Ru 4:14 hath not left thee *t'* day without a
1Sa 12: 8 and made them dwell in *t'* place. *2088
24:10 *t'* day thine eyes have seen "
2Ki 8:22 under the hand of Judah unto *t'* day. "
19:32 He shall not come into *t'* city, 2063
1Ch 4:41 destroyed them utterly unto *t'* day, 2088
26:30 on *t'* side Jordan westward in all *
2Ch 6:15 hast fulfilled it...as it is *t'* day. 2088
Job 20: 2 answer, and for *t'* I make haste. *
Ps 119:50 *T'* is my comfort in my affliction: 2063
56 *T'* I had, because I kept...precepts. "
132:14 *T'* is my rest for ever:
Isa 9: 5 but *t'* shall be with burning
29:13 Forasmuch as *t'* people draw near 2068
Jer 5:29 avenged on such a nation as *t'*?
19:15 I will bring upon *t'* city 2063
32:37 I will bring them again into *t'* place, 2088
Eze 36:37 I will yet for *t'* be enquired of 2063
Zep 1: 4 the remnant of Baal from *t'* place, 2088
M't 11:14 *t'* is Elias, which was for to come. *846*
1Ti 3: 1 *T'* is a true saying, If a man desire *3588*
Heb 7:21 but *t'* with an oath by him that *
24 But *t'* man, because he continueth *3588*

thither
Ge 19:20 Oh, let me escape *t'*, (is it not a little 8033
22 Haste thee, escape *t'*; for I cannot "
22 do any thing till thou be come *t'*. "
24: 6 thou bring not my son *t'* again. "
1Sa 9: 6 now let us go *t'*; peradventure he "
Eze 47: 9 because these waters shall come *t'*: "
Joe 3:11 *t'* cause thy mighty ones to come

those
Nu 2:32 all *t'* that were numbered of the *
13: 3 all *t'* men were heads of the children*
De 29:29 but *t'* things which are revealed *
Jos 20: 6 high priest that shall be in *t'* days: 1992
Ezr 2:62 *t'* that were reckoned by genealogy
Eze 39:10 shall spoil *t'* that spoiled them, and
10 rob *t'* that robbed them, saith
Lu 21:26 looking after *t'* things which are *3588*
Ph'p 4: 3 help *t'* women which laboured with *846*

though
Nu 18:27 unto you, as *t'* it were the corn of the
Pr 29:19 words: for *t'* he understand he will not
Jer 46:23 the Lord, *t'* it cannot be searched; 3588

through
2Ch 31:18 their daughters, *t'* all the congregation:

throughout
Ex 11: 6 a great cry *t'* all the land of Egypt,

thus
Ge 31:32 *T'* they made a covenant at
Ex 7:17 *T'* saith the Lord, In this thou 3541
Jer 35:19 Therefore *t'* saith the Lord of hosts, "
Eze 14:21 For *t'* saith the Lord God; "
37: 9 *T'* saith the Lord God; Come from "
Hag 1: 2 *T'* speaketh the Lord of hosts,

Hag 1: 5 therefore *t'* saith the Lord of hosts: 3541
7 *T'* saith the Lord of hosts; Consider "
2: 6 For *t'* saith the Lord of hosts; Yet "
11 *T'* saith the Lord of hosts; Ask now "
Mal 1: 4 *t'* saith the Lord of hosts, They shall "
13 *t'* ye brought an offering: should I "

thyself
Ge 14:21 the persons, and take the goods to *t'*.

till
2Ki 13:17 Aphek, *t'* thou have consumed 5704
19 Syria *t'* thou hadst consumed it: "
Jer 49: 9 they will destroy *t'* they have enough.

time
Nu 14:14 them, by day *t'* in a pillar of a cloud,*
De 16: 9 such *t'* as thou beginnest to put the
Lu 12: 1 In the mean *t'*, when there were

Timothy
1Ti *general title* First Epistle Of Paul...To *T'*. *5095*
2Ti *general title* Second Epistle Of Paul...To *T'*. "

Titus
Ti *general title* The Epistle Of Paul To *T'*. *5103*

together
Nu 24:10 Balaam, and he smote his hands *t'*:
Ec 4: 5 fool foldeth his hands *t'*, and eateth his

too
J'g 7: 2 people that are with thee are *t'* many for
4 The people are yet *t'* many; bring them
Isa 49:19 shall even now be *t'* narrow by reason

touching
Le 5:13 an atonement for him as *t'* his sin 5921

toward
Ge 2:14 which goeth *t'* the east of Assyria.*
12: 9 journeyed, going on still *t'* the south.
15: 5 Look now *t'* heaven, and tell the stars,
18: 2 door, and bowed himself *t'* the ground,*
22 faces from thence, and went *t'* Sodom:
20: 1 journeyed from thence *t'* the south
Ex 9: 8 let Moses sprinkle it *t'* the heaven in
10 and Moses sprinkled it up *t'* heaven;
22 Stretch forth thine hand *t'* heaven 5921
23 Stretched forth his rod *t'* heaven: "
10:21 Stretch out thine hand *t'* heaven, "
22 stretched forth his hand *t'* heaven; "
26:35 the side of the tabernacle *t'* the south:
2Sa 24: 5 of the river of Gad, and *t'* Jazer: * 413
Ps 98: 3 and his truth *t'* the house of Israel:
Eze 16:63 when I am pacified *t'* thee for all that*

travail [*in some editions*]
Nu 20:14 all the *t'* that hath befallen us: 8513
La 3: 5 compassed me with gall and *t'*.

truly
Ge 4:24 *t'* Lamech seventy and sevenfold.

trust
2Ch 32:10 Whereon do ye *t'*, that ye abide in 982

two
Ge 11:10 begat Arphaxad *t'* years after the flood:
21 Reu lived...*t'* hundred and seven years,
23 Serug lived...*t'* hundred years,
32 were *t'* hundred and five years:
Nu 31:27 And divide the prey into *t'* parts; 2673
De 18: 3 the shoulder, and the *t'* cheeks, and
Jos 7:21 and *t'* hundred shekels of silver, and
2Sa 14:26 *t'* hundred shekels after the king's
2Ki 15:23 Israel in Samaria, and reigned *t'* years.
25: 4 the way of the gate between *t'* walls,
Ezr 2: 4 three hundred seventy and *t'*. 8147
Jer 39: 4 by the gate betwixt the *t'* walls:
52: 7 way of the gate between the *t'* walls,

Tzaddi (*tsaw-day'*)
Ps 119: 137 *title* [צ] *T'*.

U.

under
Ge 24: 2 I pray thee, thy hand *u'* my thigh: 8478
9 servant put his hand *u'* the thigh of "
Ex 27: 5 *u'* the compass of the altar beneath, "
Ps 18:47 and subdueth the people *u'* me, "
Ec 3: 1 time to every purpose *u'* the heaven: "

unknown
1Co 14:13 that speaketh in an *u'* tongue pray*

until
Ge 24:19 *u'* they have done drinking. 5704,515
33 *u'* I have told mine errand. " "
De 3:20 you, and *u'* they also possess the land*
20:20 war with thee, *u'* it be subdued. 5704
J'g 20:26 fasted that day *u'* even, and offered "
2Ch 31: 1 *u'* they had utterly destroyed them "
Ps 73:17 *U'* I went into the sanctuary of God; "

utterly
Mic 2: 4 and say, We be *u'* spoiled: 7703

V.

Vau (*vawv*)
Ps 119:41 *title* [ו] *V'*.

verily
Ps 73:13 *V'* I have cleansed my heart in * 389

very
Ps 146: 4 in that *v'* day his thoughts perish.
Isa 30:19 he will be *v'* gracious unto thee at the
Da 6:19 the king arose *v'* early in the morning,
Ac 10:10 he became *v'* hungry, and would *4361*

W.

wast
Ru 3: 2 with whose maidens thou *w'*? 1961

water
Ge 24:19 I will draw *w'* for thy camels also,*
20 ran again unto the well to draw *w'*,*
45 down unto the well, and drew *w'*:*

way
Ru 1:12 Turn again, my daughters, go your *w'*;
2Ki 4:29 take thy staff...and go thy *w'*:
Ne 8:10 Go your *w'*, eat the fat, and drink the
12 all the people went their *w'* to eat, and
Ca 1: 8 go thy *w'* forth by the footsteps
Da 12:13 go thou thy *w'* till the end be: for thou

weights
De 25:13 shalt not have in thy bag divers *w'*. 68

well
Ge 24:62 from the way of the *w'* Lahai-roi;* 875
J'g 20:48 sword, as *w'* the men of every city,*
Pr 24:32 I saw, and considered it *w'*: I looked
Lu 13: 9 And if it bear fruit, *w'*: and if not, then

went
2Ki 7: 8 carried thence...and *w'* and hid it. 935

what
Ge 21:29 *W'* mean these seven ewe lambs 4100
23:15 *w'* is that betwixt me and thee? "
31:32 discern thou *w'* is thine with me, "
37 *w'* hast thou found of all thy...stuff? "
Ex 2: 4 afar off, to wit *w'* would be done to him.
6: 1 see *w'* I will do to Pharaoh: 834
33: 5 that I may know *w'* to do unto thee. 4100
2Sa 16:20 counsel among you *w'* we shall do. "
2Ki 23:17 *W'* title is that that I see? "
Isa 14:32 *W'* shall one then answer the "
36: 4 *W'* confidence is this wherein thou "
Eze 20:29 *W'* is the high place whereunto ye "
Am 8: 2 he said, Amos, *w'* seest thou? "
M't 7: 2 with *w'* measure ye mete, it shall *3739*
2Co 1:13 that *w'* ye read or acknowledge; "
11:12 But *w'* I do, that I will do, that I may "

when
Ge 24:19 And *w'* she had done giving him drink,
30 *w'* he saw the earring and bracelets
43 that *w'* the virgin cometh forth to draw*
43:16 *w'* Joseph saw Benjamin with them,
Ex 2: 2 and *w'* she saw him that he was a
3 And *w'* she could not longer hide him,
3:21 that, *w'* ye go, ye shall not go empty:
12:48 And *w'* a stranger shall sojourn 3588
18: 1 *W'* Jethro, the priest of Midian, *
Le 11:32 any of them, *w'* they are dead, doth
15:23 *w'* he toucheth it, he shall be unclean
Nu 1:51 And *w'* the tabernacle setteth forward,
51 and *w'* the tabernacle is to be pitched,
9:19 And *w'* the cloud tarried long upon the
Jos 10: 1 *w'* Adoni-zedec king of Jerusalem
2Sa 5: 4 David was thirty years old *w'* he began
11:13 And *w'* David had called him, he did
1Ki 21:16 *w'* Ahab heard that Naboth was dead,
2Ki 7: 8 *w'* these lepers came to the uttermost
10:24 And *w'* they went in to offer sacrifices
1Ch 7:23 *w'* he went in to his wife, she conceived,*
2Ch 24:11 and *w'* they saw that there was much
Ezr 3:12 *w'* the foundation of this house was
9: 1 now *w'* these things were done, the
3 *w'* I heard this thing, I rent my
Job 37:17 warm, *w'* he quieteth the earth by the
Pr 28:12 *w'* the wicked rise, a man is hidden.
Isa 18: 5 afore the harvest, *w'* the bud is perfect,
43: 2 *w'* thou walkest through the fire, 3588
Eze 20:44 *w'* I have wrought with you for my
23:11 And *w'* her sister Aholibah saw this,*
29:16 *w'* they shall look after them:
Na 1:12 cut down, *w'* he shall pass through.*
M't 28:11 Now, *w'* they were going, behold, *
Lu 4: 2 and *w'* they were ended, he afterward
13 *w'* the devil had ended all the
Joh 7:40 the people...*w'* they heard this saying,
Ac 14:14 Which *w'* the apostles, Barnabas and
23:34 *w'* he understood that he was of
27:30 *w'* they had let down the boat into the*
28:25 And *w'* they agreed not among
Eph 4: 8 *W'* he ascended up on high, he led
2Ti *subscr.* *w'* Paul was brought before Nero *3753*

whence
Ge 3:23 ground from *w'* he was taken. 834,8033
24: 5 the land from *w'* thou camest? " "
Ne 4:12 From all places *w'* ye shall return * 834
Isa 47:11 shalt not know from *w'* it riseth: *

where
Ge 13:14 look from the place *w'* thou art 834,8033
22: 7 *w'* is the lamb for a burnt offering? 346
Ex 9:26 Goshen, *w'* the children...were, 834,8033
27:18 cubits, and the breadth fifty every *w'*,
Nu 9:17 in the place *w'* the cloud abode, 834
Job 14:10 giveth up the ghost, and *w'* is he? 346

whereby
Eph 4:14 *w'* they lie in wait to deceive; *3314*

wherefore
Ge 21:31 *W'* he called that place 5921,3651
24:31 *w'* standeth thou without? for I* 4100
Nu 11:11 and *w'* have I not found favour in "
32: 7 And *w'* discourage ye the heart of "
J'g 15:19 *w'* he called the name thereof 5921,3651
2Sa 5: 8 *W'* they said, The blind and 5921,3651
1Ki 11:11 *W'* the Lord said unto Solomon,
12:15 *W'* the king hearkened not unto the*

1Ch 13:11 *W*· that place is called Perez-uzza to*
Ec 3:22 *W*· I perceive that there is nothing
Jer 20:18 *W*· came I forth out of the womb 4100

wherein
1Ki 2:26 afflicted in all *w*· my father was 834
Ne 9:12 light in the way *w*· they should go. "
19 light, and the way *w*· they should go." "
Eze 37:25 servant, *w*· your fathers have dwelt; "
44:19 their garments *w*· they ministered, "

whereof
Jos 14:12 *w*· the Lord spake in that day; 834

whereon
Le 15: 4 every thing, *w*· he sitteth, *834,5921
Es 7: 8 upon the bed *w*· Esther was. " "

wherewith
Ex 3: 9 the oppression *w*· the Egyptians 834
J'g 16:13 tell me *w*· thou mightest be bound. 4100
Eze 13:12 Where is the daubing *w*· ye have 834
40:42 instruments *w*· they slew the burnt "

wherewithal
Ps 119: 9 *w*· shall a young man cleanse his 4100

whether
Ge 24:21 to wit *w*· the Lord had made his
Le 22:28 And *w*· it be cow or ewe, ye shall not
Pr 29: 9 man, *w*· he rage or laugh, there is no

which
Ge 21:29 seven ewe lambs *w*· thou hast set 834
22: 2 the mountains *w*· I will tell thee of. "
9 to the place *w*· God had told him of; "
17 as the sand *w*· is upon the sea shore; "
23: 9 *w*· he hath, *w*· is in the end of his "
16 the silver, *w*· he had named in the "
17 the field of Ephron, *w*· was in "
17 Machpelah, *w*· was before Mamre, "
17 field, and the cave *w*· was therein, "
24: 7 *w*· took me from my father's house,* "
7 my kindred, and *w*· spake unto me,* "
24 the son of Milcah, *w*· she bare unto "
26:35 *W*· were a grief of mind unto Isaac*
27: 8 according to that *w*· I command 834
Ex 3:16 and seen that *w*· is done to you in 853
20 my wonders *w*· I will do in the 834
4:18 unto my brethren *w*· are in Egypt,‡ "
30 the words *w*· the Lord had spoken "
6: 7 God, *w*· bringeth you out from under‡
7:15 the rod *w*· was turned to a serpent 834
8:12 the frogs *w*· he had brought against "
12:10 and that *w*· remaineth of it until the
19: 6 These are the words *w*· thou shalt 834
Le 9: 6 is the thing *w*· the Lord commanded "
22: 6 The soul *w*· hath touched any such "
32 I am the Lord *w*· hallow you, ‡
Nu 4:26 the court, *w*· is by the tabernacle 834
15:22 *w*· the Lord hath spoken unto "
33:40 Canaanite, *w*· dwelt in the south ‡1931
34:13 This is the land *w*· ye shall inherit 834
13 *w*· the Lord commanded to give "
De 4:48 unto mount Sion, *w*· is Hermon. *1931
11: 2 known, and *w*· have not seen the ‡ 834
17 good land *w*· the Lord giveth you. "
13: 5 of the way *w*· the Lord thy God "
23:13 and cover that *w*· cometh from thee:
24: 5 cheer up his wife *w*· he hath taken.‡834
Jos 7:14 household *w*· the Lord shall take "
J'g 2:10 nor yet the works *w*· he had done "
2Sa 24:24 God of that *w*· doth cost me nothing. "
2Ki 10:17 of the Lord, *w*· he spake to Elijah. 834
20:11 by *w*· it had gone down in the dial of "
1Ch 12:32 *w*· were men that had understanding*
23:29 in the pan, and for that *w*· is fried,
Job 35: 5 the clouds *w*· are higher than thou.
Ec 6: 1 There is an evil *w*· I have seen 834
10 That *w*· hath been is named already,*
Isa 55: 2 spend money for that *w*· is not bread?
2 your labour for that *w*· satisfieth not?
2 eat ye that *w*· is good, and let your
59:21 words *w*· I have put in thy mouth, 834
65: 5 *W*· say, Stand by thyself, come not‡
Jer 3: 6 seen that *w*· backsliding Israel 834
41: 9 was it *w*· Asa the king had made for "
Eze 33:19 do that *w*· is lawful and right, he shall
M't 24:16 Then let them *w*· be in Judæa flee *
27:60 *w*· he had hewn out in the rock: *3739*
M'r 4:25 shall be taken even that *w*· he hath. "
Lu 16:15 they *w*· justify yourselves before **3588*
15 for that *w*· is highly esteemed among
Joh 18:13 Caiaphas, *w*· was the high priest ‡*3739*
Ac 13:22 heart, *w*· shall fulfil all my will. * "
16:21 *w*· are not lawful for us to receive, "
26:22 *w*· the prophets and Moses did say* "
Ro 8:39 the love of God, *w*· is in Christ *3588*
10: 8 the word of faith, *w*· we preach; *3739*
2Co 9: 6 he *w*· soweth bountifully shall reap*
Ga 3:23 faith *w*· should afterward be revealed.
1Ti 6:21 *W*· some professing have erred *3739*
Heb 9: 7 blood, *w*· he offered for himself, "
Re 22: 6 the things *w*· must shortly be done. "

while
Le 26:43 *w*· she lieth desolate without them:
Nu 25:11 *w*· he was zealous for my sake among*
J'g 14:17 seven days, *w*· their feast lasted;
1Ch 21:12 *w*· that the sword of thine enemies

whilst
Job 8:12 *W*· it is yet in his greenness, and not

whither
Jer 40:12 all places *w*· they were driven, 834,8033
42:22 in the place *w*· ye desire to go " "
43: 5 nations, *w*· they had been driven, " "
44: 8 Egypt, *w*· ye be gone to dwell, " "

who
Ge 24:27 *w*· hath left destitute my master 834
27:18 Here am I; *w*· art thou, my son? 4310
Ex 5:20 Moses and Aaron, *w*· stood in the way,
12:27 *w*· passed over the houses of 834
Nu 16: 5 the Lord will shew *w*· are his, 853,834
5 and *w*· is holy; and will cause him 853
J'g 7: 1 Then Jerubbaal, *w*· is Gideon, and 1931
1Sa 10:12 and said, But *w*· is their father? 4310
2Sa 1:24 *w*· clothed you in scarlet, with other
24 *w*· put on ornaments of gold
4: 5 Ish-bosheth, *w*· lay on a bed at *1931
11:21 *W*· smote Abimelech the son of 4310
1Ki 2:32 *w*· fell upon two men more * 834
1Ch 4:22 *w*· had the dominion in Moab, and "
8:12 and Shamed, *w*· built Ono, and 1931
Ps 39: 6 knoweth not *w*· shall gather them. 4310
73:12 the ungodly, *w*· prosper in the world;*
Ec 2:19 And *w*· knoweth whether he shall 4310
6:12 for *w*· can tell a man what shall be "
8: 4 *w*· may say unto him, What doest? "
Mic 3: 2 *W*· hate the good, and love the evil;
2 *w*· pluck off their skin from off
3 *W*· also eat the flesh of my people, 834
Col 1: 7 *w*· is for you a faithful minister of *3739*
1Th 2:12 of God, *w*· hath called you unto his *3588*

whole
Ex 10:15 covered the face of the *w*· earth, 3605
2Ch 16: 9 run to and fro through the *w*· earth, "
Ps 138: 1 I will praise thee with my *w*· heart: "
Jer 3:10 turned unto me with her *w*· heart, "

whom
Ge 22: 2 only son Isaac, *w*· thou lovest, 834
24: 3 the Canaanites, among *w*· I dwell; "
14 the damsel to *w*· I shall say, Let "
44 woman *w*· the Lord hath appointed "
44 Nahor's son, *w*· Milcah bare unto "
Nu 26:59 *w*· her mother bare to Levi in *834,853
1Ch 7:21 *w*· the men of Gath that were born
Ca 3: 4 I found him *w*· my soul loveth: I held
Jer 50:20 I will pardon them *w*· I reserve. 834
Lu 7: 4 worthy for *w*· he should do this: **3739*
Ac 3:16 made this man strong, *w*· ye see "
21 *W*· the heaven must receive until "
4:27 child Jesus, *w*· thou hast anointed, "
6: 3 *w*· we may appoint over this "
17: 3 Jesus, *w*· I preach unto you, is "
19:25 *W*· he called together with the "
Ro 8:29 For *w*· he did foreknow, he also did "
Eph 1:13 in *w*· also after that ye believed, "
3Jo 1 Gaius, *w*· I love in the truth. "

whose
Ge 24:37 Canaanites, in *w*· land I dwell: 834
47 and said, *W*· daughter art thou? 4310
1Ch 13: 6 cherubims, *w*· name is called on it.*834
Ezr 8:13 sons of Adonikam, *w*· names are these,*
Ec 2:21 For there is a man *w*· labour is in
Da 4:37 all *w*· works are truth, and all his *1768
Ac 13: 6 a Jew, *w*· name was Bar-jesus: *3739*
Re 9:11 *w*· name in the Hebrew tongue is * *846*

whoso
Pr 1:33 But *w*· hearkeneth unto me shall dwell
18:22 *W*· findeth a wife findeth a good thing,
1Jo 3:17 But *w*· hath this world's good, *3739,302*

whosoever
Ex 12:15 for *w*· eateth leavened bread from 3605
2Ki 21:12 *w*· heareth of it, both his ears shall "

why
Jos 5: 4 cause *w*· Joshua did circumcise: 834
2Ki 14:10 for *w*· shouldest thou meddle to 4100
Ps 42: 5 *W*· art thou cast down, O my soul? "
Pr 5:20 *w*· wilt thou, my son, be ravished "

wife
Ex 2: 1 Levi, and took to *w*· a daughter of Levi

will
Le 27:13 if he *w*· at all redeem it, then he shall
2Ch 10: 7 them, they *w*· be thy servants for ever.
Isa 37: 7 I *w*· send a blast upon him, and he shall
7 I *w*· cause him to fall by the sword in
35 For I *w*· defend this city to save it for
Jer 23: 4 And I *w*· set up shepherds over them
34 *w*· even punish that man and his house.
Jer 32:44 I *w*· cause their captivity to return,
43:10 I *w*· send and take Nebuchadrezzar
10 and *w*· set his throne upon these stones
51:22 *w*· I break in pieces man and woman.
22 *w*· I break in pieces old and young;
22 *w*· I break in pieces the young man and
M'r 1:17 *w*· make you to become fishers of men.
Ac 15:16 *w*· build again the ruins thereof, and I
16 the ruins thereof, and I *w*· set it up:
2Co 11: 9 unto you, and so *w*· I keep myself.

wilt
2Sa 5:19 *w*· thou deliver them into mine hand?
M't 7: 4 *w*· thou say to thy brother, Let me pull
Lu 18:41 What *w*· thou that I shall do unto *2309*

wit
Ne 11: 3 cities, to *w*·, Israel, the priests, and the

withal
2Ki 23:26 that Manasseh had provoked him *w*·.

withered
Ps 102:11 and I am *w*· like grass. 3001

within
De 12:12 the Levite that is *w*· your gates;
Ezr 10: 8 would not come *w*· three days,

without
Ex 21:11 then shall she go out free *w*· money. 369
1Ki 22: 1 three years *w*· war between Syria and "
Ps 59: 4 prepare themselves *w*· my fault: 1097
Jer 4: 7 be laid waste, *w*· an inhabitant. 369
15:13 will I give to the spoil *w*· price. 3808

woman
Le 21:14 A widow, or a divorced *w*·, or profane,
Nu 25:14 was slain with the Midianitish *w*·,
Pr 5: 3 For the lips of a strange *w*· drop as an
20 my son, be ravished with a strange *w*·.

women
Ge 24:11 the time that *w*· go out to draw water.
Job 2:10 as one of the foolish *w*· speaketh.
Pr 23:33 Thine eyes shall behold strange *w*·.*
Isa 32:10 shall ye be troubled, ye careless *w*·:
Eze 23:45 after the manner of *w*· that shed blood:

wood
Ex 26:37 the hanging five pillars of shittim *w*·.*
Ps 141: 7 and cleaveth *w*· upon the earth. *

words
Joh 17: 1 These *w*· spake Jesus, and lifted up*

worth
Ge 23:15 is *w*· four hundred shekels of silver;

would
Ga 3: 8 foreseeing that God *w*· justify the
2Jo 12 I *w*· not write with paper and ink: *1014*
3Jo 10 forbiddeth them that *w*·, and casteth "

wrought
Ex 26:36 twined linen, *w*· with needlework.*4639

Y.

yea
2Ch 26:20 *y*·, himself hasted also to go out, because
Job 1:15 *y*·, they have slain the servants
Ps 23: 4 *y*·, though I walk through the valley 1571
35:27 *y*·, let them say continually, Let the
43: 4 *y*·, upon the harp will I praise thee, O
Isa 43:13 *y*·, before the day was I am he; and 1571
Ho 9:16 *y*·, though they bring forth, yet will "
Lu 14:26 *y*·, and his own life also, he cannot *2089*
Ro 8:34 died, *y*· rather, that is risen again, *1161*

yet
Nu 19:13 his uncleanness is *y*· upon him. 5750
2Sa 12:22 While the child was *y*· alive, I fasted "
2Ch 27: 2 And the people did *y*· corruptly. "
Ph'p 2:25 *Y*· I supposed it necessary to send* *1161*
Re 17: 8 that was, and is not, and *y*· is. * *2589*

your
Le 18:30 I am the Lord *y*· God.
26:28 chastise you seven times for *y*· sins.
De 5: 1 which I speak in *y*· ears this day,
23 the heads of *y*· tribes, and *y*· elders:

yourselves [*so most editions in these places*]
Le 11:43 not make [*your selves*] abominable 5315
Jos 23:11 heed therefore unto [*your selves*], "

Z.

Zain (*zah'-yin*)
Ps 119:49 *title* [ז] *Z*·.

Zechariah
Zec *general title Z*·. 2148

Zephaniah
Zep *general title Z*·. 6846

APPENDIX,

GIVING

THE OCCURRENCES OF THE FORTY-SEVEN WORDS CITED BY REFERENCE ONLY.

(See "Directions and Explanations" following the Preface of the MAIN CONCORDANCE.)

Main Concordance, p. 1220.

APPENDIX,

GIVING REFERENCES, BY CHAPTER AND VERSE, TO ALL THE PASSAGES IN WHICH A FEW UNIMPORTANT PARTICLES OF VERY FREQUENT OCCURRENCE ARE FOUND.

N. B.—1. The small superior figures (^{2}, ^{3}, ^{4}, etc.) denote the number of times the word occurs in the verses to which they are attached.

2. The Hebrew or Greek term, of which the words in this Appendix are respectively the proper or strict (but not uniform) translation (when such term exists), is indicated (by its appropriate number in the accompanying DICTIONARIES) once for all at the head of each; but (inasmuch as those terms are, as a rule, only expressed when more or less emphatic) the English words are usually the rendering merely of some inflection (such as by declension, conjugation, mood, tense, affix, etc.), construction, or implication of the principal word in the sentence (as an auxiliary, pronoun, preposition, etc.); and they are frequently supplied (not always in *italics*) in the A. V. merely for the sake of greater clearness or fullness of meaning. Many of them, moreover, often stand in the English text as renderings of various other words in the original, which are elsewhere represented by very different ones from those here indicated.

APPENDIX TO THE MAIN CONCORDANCE.

a See also AN.

GEN.
1:6 29 2:5 6 7 8 10 21 22 24 3:6 24 4:1 2[2] 12[2] 14[2] 15 17 23[2] 26 5:3 6:9 16[2] 17 8:1 7 8 21 9:11[2] 13[2] 14 15 23 25 10:8 9 12 30 11:2 4[3] 12:1 2[2] 8 10 11 13:7 16 14:23[2] 15:1 9[4] 12 13[3] 15 17[2] 18 16:7 11 12 15 17:4 5 7 8 11 16[2] 17 19 20 18:4 5 7[2] 10 13[2] 14 18 19:3 9 20[2] 26 28 30 31 37 38 20:3[3] 4 6 7 9 16[2] 21:2 7 8 13 14 16[2] 18 19 21 25 27 30 32 33

GEN.
22:2 6 7 8 13[3] 23:4[4] 6 9[2] 18 20[2] 24:3 4 7 11 16 17 22[2] 29 36 37 38 40 43 55 65 25:1 8 27[3] 26:1 8[2] 9 19 25 28 30 35 27:11[2] 12[3] 27 34 36 44 46 28:1 2 3 4 6[3] 11 12 18 20 22 29:2[2] 14 20 22 32 33 34 35 30:5 6 7 10 11 12 15 20 21 23 30 31:10 11 13 24 44[2] 45[2] 48 32:13 16 18 24 28 33:18 19[2] 34:14 35:11[2] 14[3] 16 20 37:1 3 5 9 15 24 25 31 38:1 2[2] 3 4 5

GEN.
38:6 11 14 17[2] 28 39:2 6 14 20 40:4 5 8 9 19 20 41:2 7 11 12 15[2] 18 33 38[2] 42 43:2 6 11[3] 44:15 18 19[2] 20[3] 25 33 45:7[2] 8[2] 46:3 10 29 47:11 22 48:4 7 16 19[2] 49:6[2] 9[2] 10 14 17 19 21 22[3] 27 30[2] 50:9 10[2] 11 13[2] 16 26

EXOD.
1:8 16[3] 2:1[2] 2[2] 7 14[2] 15 22[3] 3:2[2] 8[3] 12 17 19 4:2 3 4 10 16 25[2] 26 5:1 21 6:1[2] 6 7[2] 13 15 7:1 9[2] 10 15 8:23 24 9:3 5 9 10 18 24 10:7 9 19

EXOD.
10:22 11:6 7[2] 8 12:3[2] 5 13 14[3] 19 21 22 30[2] 38 42 45 46 48 13:5 6 9[3] 12 13 16 21[3] 14:20 21 22 29 15:3 5 16 20 25[2] 16:4 14 25 33 35 17:12 14[2] 18:3 12 16 19:5 6 9 16 18[2] 19 20:5 21:4 7[2] 8 12 13[2] 14 16 18 20[2] 21 22 26 28[2] 29[2] 30 31[2] 32[2] 33[4] 22:1[3] 2 5[2] 7 10[2] 14 16[2] 18 19 21 23:1 2[2] 3 7 9[2] 14 19 33 24:10[2] 12 15 25:8 10[5] 11 17[4] 23[4] 24 25[2] 31 33[4] 35[3] 39 26:7 13[2] 14[2] 16[3]

EXOD.
26:31 27:4 21 28:4[5] 11 12 16[2] 17[3] 18[2] 19 20[2] 21 28 29 32 34[4] 36[2] 37 43 29:9 10 14 18[2] 22 24 25[2] 26 28 33 36[2] 40[2] 41 42 30:2[2] 3 8 10 12 13[2] 15 16 18 21 33 34 35[2] 31:13 16 17 32:4[2] 5 8 9 10 11 17 21 29 30 31 33:3[2] 5[2] 11[2] 21[2] 22 34:9 10[2] 12[2] 14 15[2] 16[2] 20 26 27 33 35:2 5 29 36:19[2] 21[3] 35 37:1[5] 2 6[2] 10[3] 11 12[2] 19[4] 21[3] 24 25[2] 26 38:4 23 25 26[2] 27[2] 39:7 9[2] 10[3] 11[2] 12 13[2] 14

EXOD.
39:21 23 26[4] 28 29 30[2] 31 40:34

LEVIT.
1:3[2] 9[2] 10[2] 13[2] 17[2] 2:1 2 3 4 5[2] 6 7 9[2] 10 12 14 15 3:1[2] 5 6 7 12 16 17 4:2 3[2] 12 14 20 21 22 23[2] 24 28[2] 31 32[3] 33 5:1[2] 2[3] 3 4[2] 6[4] 7[3] 9 10 11[2] 12[2] 13 15[4] 17 18[2] 19 6:2[3] 3 6[2] 11 15 18 20 21[2] 22 28 7:5 12 16[2] 30 34 36 8:2[2] 21[2] 26 27 28 29 9:2[4] 3[5] 4[3] 18 21 24 10:9 14 15[2] 11:36 47 12:2[2] 5 6[7] 7[2] 8[2] 13:2[3] 3 5 6

LEVIT.
13:8 9 12 15 18 19[2] 20 22 23 24[2] 25 28 29[2] 30[3] 37 38[2] 39 42[2] 44 45 47[2] 48 49 51[2] 52 57 59 14:10 12[2] 21[3] 22[2] 24 31[2] 34[2] 35 44 55[2] 56[3] 15:2 15[2] 19 25 30[2] 16:3[4] 4 5[2] 9 10 12 21 22 29[2] 31[2] 34 17:6 7[2] 8 15 18:5 17 18 19 23 19:5 14 16 19[2] 20[3] 21[2] 29 33 36[2] 20:5 6 12 13[2] 14[2] 15[2] 16 17[2] 18[2] 20 21 24 27[3] 21:3 4 7[3] 13 14[3] 18[4] 19 20[2] 21[2] 23 22:4[3] 5 10 12 13 14 18 19 20

LEVIT.
22:21[2] 22 23[4] 25 27[3] 29 23:10 12 13 14 16 18 19[2] 20 21 24[2] 27 28 31 32 36 37[3] 39[3] 41[2] 24:3 6 7 9 10 18 19[2] 20[2] 21[2] 25:2 4[2] 5 10 24 29[5] 30 33 35[2] 39 40 46 47 53 26:1 25 33 36[3] 37 27:2[2] 4 6 7 9 10[4] 11 13 14 16[2] 21 22[2] 23 27 28 31

NUM.
1:4 3:15 22 28 34 39 40 43 50 4:6 7 8[2] 9 10[2] 11[2] 12[3] 13 14 5:6[2] 12 13 21 23 27 29 6:2 11[2] 12[2] 14[2] 15 17 20 7:3 13

NUM.
7:15 16 17 19 21 22 23 25 27 28 29 31 33 34 35 37 39 40 41 43 45 46 47 49 51 52 53 55 57 58 59 61 63 64 65 67 69 70 71 73 75 76 77 79 81 82 83 8:8[2] 12[2] 19 9:6 7 10[2] 13 14 20 22[2] 10:2 10 33 11:4 8 12 20 21 25 27 31[2] 33 12:6[3] 13:2[2] 23[2] 32[2] 14:3 4 8 12 14[3] 31 34 36 15:3[5] 4[2] 5 6[2] 7[2] 8[4] 9[2] 10[2] 11[2] 13 14[2] 20 24[3] 25 27[2] 30 32 38 39[2] 16:9 13[3] 14 21

NUM.
16:30 35 38[2] 39 40 45 46 17:2 6 10 18:4 6 7 11 16 17[4] 19[2] 23 26 19:2 9[4] 10 14[2] 16[5] 17 18[3] 21 20:15 16 20 21:2 8[2] 9[3] 28[2] 22:5 11 24[3] 26 27 29 36 23:2 4[2] 5 14[2] 16 19 21 24[2] 30[2] 24:4 9[2] 16 17[2] 18[2] 21 25:6 7 14[2] 15[2] 18 26:10 51 62 64 65 27:4 7 8 11 16 18 19 23 28:2 3 5[2] 6[3] 7 8[2] 9 11 12[2] 13[5] 14[4] 15 19[2] 20[2] 21 22 23 24 26 27 29 29:1 2[2] 3[2] 5 6[2] 8[2] 9 10 11

NUM.
29:12 13[3] 15 16 19 22 25 28 31 34 35 36[3] 38 30:2[3] 3[3] 9 10 16 31:4 5 6 16 18 28 54 32:1[2] 4 5 29 33:3 34:5 6 35:4 15 16 17[2] 18 21 23 29 31

DEU.
1:11 23 25 31 33[2] 39 2:5[2] 9[2] 10 19 20 21 35 3:4 5 7 11[2] 4:6 12 16 20 23 24[2] 25 31 34[3] 5:2 9 15[3] 22 6:8 15 21 7:6 8 9 16 21 23 26[2] 8:5 7[2] 8[2] 9[2] 9:2 3 6 12 13 14 16 26 10:7 15 17[3] 11:9 10 11 12 18 26[3]

DEU.
11:27 28 12:11 13:1[4] 14:2 21 15:1 3 7 9 15 18 16:8 10[2] 12 15 16 19[2] 21 17:8 14 15 18 18:3 6 10 11[4] 15 18 20 22 19:3 5[2] 15 16 18 20:1 5 6 7 10 19[2] 21:4 11[2] 13 15 17 18[2] 20[2] 22[3] 22:5[3] 6 8[2] 11 13 14 17 19 22[2] 23[4] 25[2] 26 28[3] 30 23:2 5 7 12 13 17 18[2] 20 21 23 25 24:1[3] 3 5[2] 6 7 17 18 19 22 25:1 2 5 7 13[2] 14[2] 15[2] 26:2 5[3] 8 9 15 27:3 15 28:22[2] 30[2] 33 35 36 37[2]

DEU.
28:46[2] 48 49[2] 50 65 29:13[2] 18 22 31:6 7 14 15[2] 16 19 21 23[2] 24 26 32:4 5 10 20 21[2] 22 28 30 47 49 33:2 4 20 21 28 34:6 10

JOSH.
1:6 9 18 2:12 15 3:4 12 4:2 4 5 6 7 5:6 13 6:5[2] 18 20 7:1 21[2] 26 8:2 11 14 17 27 28 29[2] 32 35 9:6[2] 7 9 11 15 16 10:2 8 10 13 14 16 17 20 11:14 18 19 12:6 7 14:15 15:3 13 18 19[2] 17:1 2 14 15 17 18 18:9 14 20:4 21:13 21 27 32 38

JOSH.
21:44 22:10 14 17 20 25 27 28 34 23:1 10 13 24:7 13 19 25[2] 26 27[2] 32 33

JUD.
1:14 15[2] 24 26 2:3 17 3:15[4] 16[2] 17 19 20[2] 25 27 28 29 4:4 9 16 18 19[2] 21 5:7 8 12 14 18 25 28 30[3] 6:8 17 19[3] 26 31 34 37 38 7:5 13[6] 14 16 18 8:14 18 20 24 25 26 27[2] 31 32 33 9:8[2] 48 49 51 53[3] 54 10:1 3 11:1 2 30 31 33 39 40 12:11 13 13:2 3 5[2] 6 7[2] 15 16 19[3] 23[2] 24 14:1 2 3[2]

JUD.
14:5 6 8[2] 10 12 16 18 15:1[2] 3 4 8 15[2] 16 16:4 9 12 17[2] 19 23 17:3[2] 4[2] 7[2] 8 9[2] 10[3] 13 18:10[3] 14[2] 19[6] 22 23 27 28 19:1[2] 3 5 12 15 17 24[2] 29 20:10[2] 38 21:5 15 17 18 19[2]

RUTH
1:1[2] 2:1[2] 3 7 10 11 12 3:8 9 11 12 13[3] 14 4:1 3 7[2] 13 14 15[2] 17[2]

1 SAM.
1:1 9[2] 11[2] 15[2] 16 24 25 2:3 13 18[2] 19 25 27 34 35[2] 36[3] 3:11 20 4:5 7 10 12 13 17 20 5:9 11 6:3 7 8[2] 14[3] 17

1 SAM.
6:19 7:9[2] 10 12 8:5 6 10 19 22 9:1[3] 2[4] 6 7 8 9[3] 12 15 16 21 27 10:1 3 5[6] 10 12 19 25 26 11:1 2[2] 7 13 12:1 12 13 17 19 13:2 4 6 9 12 14 21 14:1 2 4[2] 10 12 14 15 20 25 29 30 33 36 39 41 43 15:5 12 18 28 29 16:1 16[2] 17 18[4] 20[2] 17:3[3] 4[2] 5 6 7[2] 8[2] 10 20 29 33[2] 34[3] 38 40[2] 42[2] 43 45[3] 46 49 50[2] 18:3 10 13 21 23[3] 19:5[2] 8 12 13[2] 16 22 20:3 6 8 16

1 SAM.
20:20 21 25 29 33 35 41 21:2[2] 5[2] 7 9 22:2 6 8 13 18 23:5 7 14 15 18 25 27 24:3 14[2] 19 25:2[2] 3[2] 8 10 16 17[2] 28 29[2] 36[2] 37 41 26:12 13 15 20[2] 27:5 7 10 28:7[4] 9 12 14 22 24 29:1 30:12[2] 13 17 25 26 31:4 13

2 SAM.
1:2 13 2:17 18 28 3:7 8[2] 11 13 21 22[2] 29[2] 33 34 38[2] 4:2 4 5 10 11 5:2 3 23 24 6:3 8 14 16 19[3] 7:6[2] 7 9 10[2] 19[2] 23[2] 24 8:2 4 13 9:2 3 8 12 10:6

2 SAM.
11:2 8 14 16 21[2] 27 12:3 4 24 30 13:1 3[2] 6 9 18 14:2[4] 5 13 27[2] 15:2 8 13 17 19 23 27 33 16:1[3] 5 8 22 23 17:8[2] 9 10[2] 13 17 18[3] 19 25 18:2[3] 7 9[2] 10 11 12 17[2] 18 24 27 29 19:4 10 16 17 18 32[2] 35 36[2] 20:1[3] 8[6] 12 15 19[2] 21 22 26 21:1 16 18 19[3] 20[2] 22:9 11 20 30[2] 31 32 35 44 23:4 7 10 11[2] 12 20[3] 21[3] 29 24:14 15 23 24

1 KINGS
1:2 3[2] 6 42 52 2:2 4 8[2] 9 19

1 KINGS 2:42, 3:4, 5, 6, 7, 8, 9, 12, 15^2, 17, 14^2, 4:7, 32, 5:1, 7, 12, 13, 14^2, 6:21, 31, 33, 36, 7:3, 6, 7, 12, 14^3, 15, 23^2, 24, 26, 29, 31^2, 32^3, 33, 35, 8:9, 13, 21, 25, 41^2, 55, 63, 65^2, 9:5, 16, 21, 25, 26, 10:6, 18, 22, 25, 26, 28, 29, 11:17, 24, 26, 28, 29, 36, 38, 12:7, 11, 30, 32, 33, 13:1, 2, 3, 7, 18, 24, 14:3, 5, 10, 14, 15, 15:4, 13, 19^2, 22, 16:11, 31, 33, 17:7, 9, 10^2, 11, 12^4, 13, 19, 18:2, 4, 13, 21, 22, 27^2, 32, 41, 44^2, 45, 19:2, 4^2, 5, 6^2, 9, 11, 12^2, 13, 21, 20:13, 21, 28, 30, 34

1 KINGS 20:35, 36^2, 39^3, 42, 21:1, 2^3, 9, 12, 22:7, 10, 17, 21, 22, 23, 34^3, 36, 47

2 KINGS 1:2, 3, 6^2, 8, 9^2, 10, 12, 13, 2:1, 9, 10, 11^2, 20, 3:4, 9, 11, 15, 18, 27, 4:1, 2, 3, 6^2, 8^2, 10^5, 11, 16, 17, 18, 19, 28, 38, 39, 42, 5:1^3, 2, 5, 7^2, 8, 10, 12, 14, 15, 19, 22, 26, 27, 6:2^2, 5, 6, 8, 9, 14, 25^2, 26, 32^2, 7:1^3, 2, 6^3, 9, 16^3, 18^3, 19, 8:1, 5, 6, 8, 9, 13, 15, 19, 20, 9:16, 17^2, 19, 24, 28, 30, 34, 10:2, 6, 8, 18, 19, 20, 21, 27, 11:4, 5, 6^2, 14, 17, 12:9^2, 20, 13:5, 21^2, 14:9, 19

2 KINGS 15:5^2, 13, 19, 25, 30, 16:8, 17, 17:16, 21, 35, 36, 18:17, 21, 28, 31, 32^4, 36, 19:3, 7^2, 17, 29, 31, 32, 20:3, 7, 10, 12, 14, 20^2, 21:3, 7, 13^2, 14^2, 22:10, 12, 19^2, 23:3^2, 8, 22, 30, 33^2, 24:16, 25:8, 23, 30^2

1 CHRON. 2:34, 5:25, 6:33, 7:16, 23, 9:13, 10:4, 13, 11:3, 13, 14, 20, 22^4, 23^4, 42, 12:2, 4, 14, 22, 28, 34, 38, 13:7, 11, 14:12, 15, 15:1^2, 13, 27, 28, 29, 16:3^3, 5, 15, 17, 19, 42, 17:4, 6, 8, 9, 17^3, 21, 24, 18:4, 19:6, 20:2, 5, 6, 21:3, 5, 13, 16, 22:9^2, 14, 25:3, 26:14, 17^2, 30, 27:5, 32^3, 28:3, 9^2, 29:15, 19, 21^3, 28

2 CHRON. 1:4

2 CHRON. 1:6, 9, 14, 16, 17, 2:7, 12, 13, 14^2, 4:2^2, 3, 5^2, 5:10, 13, 6:2, 5, 13, 16, 22, 32, 36, 7:5, 8, 9, 18, 20^2, 8:13, 9:1, 17, 18, 24, 10:11, 13:5, 8, 9^2, 15, 17, 14:9, 15:3^2, 12, 14, 16, 16:3, 8, 10^2, 14, 17:17, 18:6, 9, 20, 21, 22, 33^3, 19:9, 20:2, 3, 8, 14, 19, 21:7, 8, 12, 13, 14, 17, 22:11, 23:3, 4, 5^2, 16, 24:8, 9, 24^2, 26, 25:2, 7, 15, 18, 27, 26:19, 21^3, 23, 28:5^2, 7, 9^2, 21, 29:10, 21, 31, 32, 30:5^2, 13, 18, 24^3, 32:18, 24, 33:6, 7, 14^2, 34:14, 18, 20, 31, 35:1, 3, 18, 36:3, 22

EZRA. 1:1, 9, 10^2, 2:7, 12, 31, 37

EZRA. 2:38, 39, 61, 63, 3:11, 12, 13, 4:8, 10, 11, 15, 17, 5:7, 11, 13, 17, 6:1, 2^2, 3, 4, 8, 11^2, 12, 17, 7:6, 11, 12^2, 13, 21, 27, 8:18, 21^2, 22, 27, 28, 35^2, 9:7^2, 8^4, 9^2, 10:1, 3, 12, 13^2, 19

NEH. 2:6, 8, 10, 17, 3:13, 4:2, 3, 4, 6, 9, 17, 22, 5:1, 7, 6:3, 7, 11, 7:2, 5, 12, 34, 40, 41, 42, 65, 70, 8:4, 18, 9:4, 8, 10, 11, 12^2, 17^2, 18, 25, 29, 31, 38, 10:29, 32, 11:23, 13:2, 5, 7

ESTHER 1:3, 5, 6, 9, 19, 2:5^2, 18^2, 23, 3:4, 8, 13, 14, 4:1^2, 5, 14, 5:9, 14, 8:11, 13, 15^2, 17^2, 9:17, 18, 19^2

ESTHER 9:22, 10:1

JOB 1:1, 3, 6, 8, 13, 14, 19, 2:1, 3, 4, 8, 13, 3:3, 5, 23, 4:12^2, 15, 16, 17, 5:26^2, 6:15, 22, 27, 7:2^2, 6, 12^3, 20^2, 8:2, 9, 14, 20, 9:2, 3, 17, 19, 25, 32, 10:16, 20, 22, 11:2, 12, 12:5, 14, 18, 25, 13:25, 27, 28^2, 14:1, 2^2, 4, 7, 9, 13, 14, 15, 17, 15:2, 14, 21, 24, 16:8, 14, 21^2, 22, 17:3, 6^2, 7, 18:8^2, 10, 19:10, 15, 23, 29, 20:5, 8^2, 26, 29, 21:11, 13, 22:2, 6, 14, 16, 28, 24:3, 5, 8, 9, 14, 20, 24, 25, 25:4, 6^2, 26:14, 27:13, 18^2, 20, 21, 28:1^2, 7, 26^2, 29:14^2, 16, 25, 30:5, 14, 15, 29^2, 31:1^2, 3

JOB 31:9, 12, 18, 23, 30, 34, 35, 36, 37, 32:8, 33:15^2, 23^2, 24, 25, 34:9, 11, 13, 18, 20, 29^2, 34, 35:8, 36:2, 16, 18, 37:4, 18, 20, 38:3, 9, 14, 25^2, 28, 30, 39:20, 40:7, 9, 17, 23, 41:1, 2, 4^2, 5, 6, 15, 18, 20, 21, 24^2, 29, 31^2, 32, 34, 42:8, 11, 12^2

PSALMS 1:3, 2:1, 9^2, 12, 3 *title*, 3, 4 *title*, 5 ", 5:4, 12, 6 *title*, 7:2, 15, 8 *title*, 5, 9 *title*, 6, 9^2, 10:9, 11 *title*, 1, 12 *title*, 2, 6, 13 *title*, 14 ", 15 ", 3, 4, 16:6, 17 *title*, 12^2, 18 *title*, 8, 10, 19, 29^2, 30, 31, 34, 43, 19 *title*, 4, 5^3, 20 *title*, 21 ", 3, 9, 11, 22 *title*, 6^2, 13^2, 15, 30^2, 31, 23 *title*, 5, 24 *title*, 4

PSALMS 25 *title*, 26 ", 27 ", 5, 11, 28 *title*, 29 ", 6^2, 30 *title*, 5^2, 31 *title*, 8, 11^2, 12^2, 20, 21, 32 *title*, 6, 33:3^2, 16, 17, 34 *title*, 18^2, 35 *title*, 7, 19, 36 *title*, 4, 6, 37 *title*, 10, 16^2, 23, 35, 38 *title*, 7, 13^2, 14, 39 *title*, 1, 6, 11, 12^2, 40 *title*, 2, 3, 15, 41 *title*, 42:4, 10, 44:3, 13^3, 14^2, 20, 45 *title*, 1^2, 6, 12, 46 *title*, 1, 4, 47 *title*, 2, 5^2, 48 *title*, 3, 6, 49 *title*, 4, 7, 50 *title*, 3, 5, 10, 18, 51 *title*, 10^2, 17^3, 52 *title*, 2, 8, 53 *title*, 54 ", 55 ", 2, 6, 13, 57:4, 6^2, 58:4, 8^2, 9, 11^3, 59:6^2, 14^2, 60:4, 61 *title*, 3^2, 62 *title*, 3^3, 8, 9, 63 *title*, 1, 10, 64 *title*, 3, 6, 65 *title*, 66 ", 1, 12, 67 *title*, 68 ", 5^2, 6, 9

PSALMS 68:13, 33, 69 *title*, 4, 8, 11, 22^2, 30, 70 *title*, 3, 71:7, 72 *title*, 73 ", 1, 6^2, 10, 19, 20, 22, 27, 74:5, 75 *title*, 5, 8, 76 *title*, 6, 77 *title*, 13, 17, 20, 78:2, 5^2, 8^2, 14^2, 19, 21, 38, 39, 50, 52, 57, 65, 66, 79 *title*, 4^2, 80 *title*, 1, 6, 8, 81 *title*, 1, 2, 4^2, 5^2, 82 *title*, 83 ", 2, 4, 13, 14, 84 *title*, 3, 6, 10^3, 11, 85 *title*, 86 ", 15, 17, 87 *title*, 88 ", 4, 89:3, 8, 13, 37, 41, 90 *title*, 4^2, 5^2, 9, 91:7, 12, 92 *title*, 1, 3, 6^2, 12, 94:2, 20, 95:1, 2, 3^2, 10, 96:1, 97:3, 98 *title*, 1, 4^2, 5, 6, 99:8, 100 *title*, 1, 101 *title*, 4^2, 5, 6, 102 *title*, 6, 7, 11, 26^2, 103 *title*, 13, 15, 104:2^2

PSALMS 104:4, 6, 9, 18, 105:8, 10, 12, 16, 17^2, 39^2, 41, 106:18, 19, 36, 39, 107:4, 7, 27, 29, 33, 34, 35, 36, 41, 108 *title*, 109 ", 2, 3, 6, 9, 19, 25, 29, 110 *title*, 4, 111:10, 112:5, 113:9, 114:1, 8^2, 118:5, 119:19, 63, 69, 78, 83, 105^2, 110, 161, 164, 176, 120 *title*, 2, 121 *title*, 122 ", 3, 123 *title*, 2, 124 *title*, 6, 7, 125 *title*, 126 ", 127 ", 4, 128 *title*, 3, 129 *title*, 1, 2, 130 *title*, 131 ", 2^2, 132 *title*, 5, 17, 133 *title*, 134 ", 135:12^2, 136:12^2, 137:3, 138 *title*, 139 ", 4, 140 *title*, 3, 5^2, 141 *title*, 3, 5, 142 *title*, 3, 143 *title*, 6, 144 *title*, 4, 8, 9^2, 11, 12, 15, 147:10, 148:6, 14, 149:1, 6

PROV. 1:5^2, 6, 27, 2:7, 3:12, 18, 30, 4:1, 9

PROV. 4:24, 5:3, 4, 10, 20^2, 6:1, 5^2, 10^3, 12^3, 17^2, 19, 23, 24, 26^3, 27, 30, 32, 33, 34, 7:7, 10, 19, 20, 22, 23^2, 8:27, 9:7^2, 8^2, 9^2, 13, 14, 10:1^3, 4, 5^2, 8, 10, 11^2, 13, 18^2, 23^2, 11:1^2, 7, 12, 13^2, 15, 16, 18^2, 20, 22^3, 28, 30, 12:2^2, 3, 4^2, 8^2, 9, 10, 14^2, 15, 16^2, 17, 18, 19^2, 23, 25, 27, 13:1^2, 2, 5^2, 8, 12, 14, 16, 17^2, 20, 22, 14:3, 5^2, 6, 7, 9, 10, 12^2, 14, 16, 17, 25^2, 26, 27, 30, 34^2, 35, 15:1, 4^3, 5, 12, 13^2, 15^2, 17^2, 18, 20^3, 21, 23^2, 30, 16:2, 7, 8, 9, 10, 11, 14^2, 15, 18, 20, 22, 25^2, 27

PROV. 16:28^2, 29, 31, 32, 17:1, 2^2, 4^3, 7^2, 8^2, 9^2, 10^3, 11, 12^3, 16^2, 17^2, 18, 20^2, 21^2, 22^3, 23^2, 24, 25^2, 27, 28^2, 18:1, 2, 4^2, 6, 7, 8, 9, 10, 13, 14^2, 16, 19^3, 20, 22^3, 24^3, 19:1, 5, 6, 9, 10^2, 11^2, 12, 13^3, 14, 15, 19, 21, 22^3, 24, 25, 26, 20:1, 2^2, 3, 5, 6, 8, 11, 15^2, 16^3, 17, 19, 23, 24, 25, 26, 30, 21:2, 4, 6^2, 9^3, 14^2, 17, 18, 19, 20, 22, 27, 28, 29, 22:1, 3, 6, 9, 13, 14, 15, 18, 24, 25, 29, 23:1, 2^2, 9, 21, 24, 27^4, 28, 32, 34, 24:5^2, 7, 8, 14, 16, 26, 28, 33^3, 25:2^3, 4, 9, 11, 12

PROV. 25:13, 14, 15^2, 18^4, 19^2, 20, 23, 24^2, 25^2, 26^3, 28, 26:1, 3^3, 4, 5, 6^2, 7, 8^3, 9^3, 11^2, 12^2, 13^2, 16, 17, 18, 21, 22, 23^2, 27^2, 28^2, 27:1, 2, 3^2, 6, 8^2, 9, 10^2, 12, 13^3, 14^2, 15^3, 17, 21, 22^3, 28:1, 2^2, 8^2, 7^2, 12, 15^3, 16, 17, 20, 21, 23, 24, 25, 26, 27, 29:5^2, 6, 8^2, 9^2, 11^2, 12, 15, 19, 20^2, 21, 22, 23, 24, 25, 30:2, 4, 5, 6, 10, 11, 12, 13, 14, 19^5, 22^2, 25, 26, 30, 31^2, 31:10, 15, 16^2, 30

ECCL. 1:3, 2:19^2, 21^3, 24, 26, 3:1^2, 2^4, 3^4, 4^4, 5^4, 6^4, 7^4, 8^4, 12, 17, 19^2, 22, 4:4, 8^2, 9, 12, 13^2, 5:3^2

ECCL. 5:4, 8, 12, 13, 14, 16, 6:2^2, 3, 6, 12^2, 7:1, 5, 6, 7^2, 8, 12^2, 15^2, 20, 28^2, 8:1^2, 4, 5, 9, 12, 13, 14, 15, 17^3, 9:4^2, 5, 6, 7, 14^2, 15, 10:1^2, 2^2, 3^2, 8^3, 11, 12^2, 14^2, 16, 19, 20, 11:2, 7, 8, 12:5, 12

CANT. 1:8, 13, 14, 2:9^2, 13, 17^2, 3:4, 9, 4:1, 2, 3^3, 4, 12^3, 15^2, 5:11, 13, 6:5, 6, 7^2, 7:1, 2, 4, 7, 13, 8:6^3, 7, 8, 9^3, 10, 11^2, 12, 14^2

ISAIAH 1:4^3, 8^5, 9, 14, 30, 31, 2:20, 3:6, 7, 16, 17, 24^4, 4:5^3, 6^4, 5:1^3, 2^2, 7, 9, 18, 28, 29, 6:1, 5^2, 6, 12, 13^2, 7:6^2, 8, 11, 13, 14^3, 20

ISAIAH 7:21^2, 23^2, 8:1^2, 3, 11, 12^2, 14^5, 19, 9:2, 6^2, 8, 10:6, 7, 13, 14, 16^2, 17^2, 18, 19, 22, 23, 24, 25, 26, 34, 11:1^2, 6, 10, 13:2, 4^3, 5, 6, 8, 12^2, 14, 14:6, 17, 19^2, 23, 29^2, 31, 15:5, 16:2, 4, 17:1^2, 7, 9, 11, 12^2, 13, 18:2^3, 3, 4^2, 7^3, 19:1, 4^2, 14^2, 17, 19, 20^4, 21, 23, 24, 20:3, 21:1, 2, 3, 6, 7^4, 8, 9^2, 16, 22:2^2, 5, 11, 16^3, 17, 18^2, 21, 23^3, 23:3, 10, 11, 24:9, 11, 20^2, 25:2^4, 4^5, 5^2, 6^2, 26:1, 16, 17, 20, 27:2, 10, 11, 28:1, 2^4, 4, 5^2, 6, 10^2, 13^2, 15, 16^5, 19, 20, 22, 27^4, 29:3, 4, 7^2, 8, 11, 14^3, 17^3

ISAIAH 29:21^4, 30:1, 5^3, 6, 8^2, 9, 13^2, 14, 17^2, 18, 20, 21, 22, 27, 28, 29^3, 30, 31, 33, 31:4, 7, 8^2, 32:1, 2^5, 14^2, 15^2, 18, 19, 33:9, 19^4, 20^2, 21, 23, 34:4^2, 6^2, 13, 14, 35:4^2, 7, 8, 36:2, 6, 13, 16, 17^3, 21, 37:3, 7^2, 18, 30, 32, 33, 36, 38:3, 7, 12^2, 13, 14^3, 21^2, 39:1, 3, 40:3, 11, 12^2, 15^3, 16, 19, 20^3, 22^2, 41:12, 15, 18, 28, 42:3, 6^2, 10, 13^2, 14, 16, 22^3, 24, 43:16^2, 19^2, 44:8, 9, 10^2, 13^3, 15^3, 17, 19, 20^2, 22^2, 45:15, 19, 20, 21^2, 46:1, 6^2, 11^2, 47:3, 7, 8, 9, 14, 48:8, 18, 20, 49:2^2, 6^2, 7, 8^2, 11, 15, 18, 21, 50:2, 4

ISAIAH 50:7, 9, 11, 51:4^2, 6, 8, 10, 12, 20^2, 53:2^3, 3, 7^2, 12, 54:6^2, 7, 8^2, 55:4^2, 5, 13, 56:3, 5^2, 57:4^2, 6^2, 7, 8, 15, 58:1, 2, 5^5, 11^2, 13, 59:5, 15, 17^2, 19^2, 60:8, 15, 22^4, 61:10^2, 62:1, 2, 3^2, 5^2, 7, 10, 12, 63:14^2, 18, 64:6, 10^3, 65:1, 2^2, 3, 5^2, 8, 9, 10^2, 11, 15, 17, 18^2, 22, 66:2, 3^3, 6^3, 7, 8^2, 12^2, 15, 19, 20

JER. 1:5, 6, 7, 11, 13, 18, 2:2, 6^3, 7, 10, 11, 14^2, 21^3, 23, 24, 27^2, 30, 31^2, 32^2, 3:1, 3, 8, 14^2, 19^2, 20, 21, 4:6, 11, 12, 13, 15, 16, 17, 19, 20, 26, 27, 29, 31^2, 5:1, 3, 6^3, 9, 10

JER. 5:15^3, 18, 19, 22, 23^2, 26, 27, 29, 30, 6:1, 2, 6, 7, 8, 9^2, 10, 20, 22^2, 24, 27^2, 7:5, 11, 28, 29, 8:5, 15, 19, 9:1, 2, 9, 10^2, 11, 12, 16, 18, 19, 10:3, 8, 13, 19, 22^2, 11:5, 9, 14, 16^2, 19, 12:6, 8, 9, 10, 13:1, 2, 4, 11^5, 21, 14:8^3, 9^2, 14^2, 17^2, 18, 15:7, 8, 10^2, 14^2, 18, 20, 16:2, 13, 20, 17:1^2, 4, 6, 8, 11, 12, 16, 17, 22, 27^2, 18:3, 7^2, 9^2, 11, 13, 14, 15, 16, 20, 22^3, 19:1, 11, 20:4, 8^2, 9, 11, 15, 21:5, 6, 9, 14, 22:5, 6, 14, 23, 28^3, 30, 23:5^2, 9^2, 16, 19^2, 23^2, 28^2, 29^2, 33, 40, 24:9^4, 25:11

JER.
25:18[2], 29, 30, 31[2], 32, 34, 36, 26:2, 6, 15, 18[2], 20, 27:10, 14, 15, 16, 28:14, 15, 29:18[2], 21, 22, 23, 26, 27, 31, 32, 30:2, 5, 6[2], 11[2], 14, 16[2], 23, 31:6, 8, 9[2], 10, 12, 15, 18, 20, 22[3], 29, 31, 35[2], 36, 32:20, 21[2], 22, 31, 33:9[2], 17, 18, 21, 24, 34:8, 9, 13, 15, 17, 22, 35:4, 19, 36:2[2], 4[2], 9, 22, 37:13, 21, 38:2, 14, 39:18, 40:5, 8, 11, 42:2, 5, 18[2], 43:12[2], 44:2, 8[2], 12[2], 14, 15, 22[2], 28, 29, 45:1, 5, 46:7, 8, 10[2], 17, 20, 22, 28[2], 47:7, 48:2, 3, 4, 5, 27, 38, 39[2], 41, 42, 45[2], 49:2, 5, 13[4], 14, 17, 18, 19[2], 22, 24, 27

JER.
49:30, 32[2], 33[2], 50:2, 3, 5, 9, 10, 12[3], 17, 22, 23, 24, 32, 35, 36[2], 37[2], 38, 41[2], 42, 43, 44[2], 51:1, 6, 7, 14, 16, 25, 26[3], 27[2], 29, 33[2], 34, 37, 39, 43[4], 46[2], 54[2], 55, 57, 59, 60, 63, 52:21, 22, 23, 34[2]

LAM.
1:1, 13, 15, 17, 2:1, 3, 6, 7[2], 8, 18, 20, 22, 3:10[2], 12, 14, 26, 27, 35, 36, 39[2], 44, 47, 52, 53, 64, 4:6, 8[2], 11, 17

EZEKIEL
1:4[4], 5, 7, 8, 10[2], 14, 16[3], 25, 26[3], 28, 2:3, 5[2], 6, 9[2], 3:5[2], 6, 9, 12[2], 13[2], 17, 20[2], 26[2], 27, 4:1, 2[2], 3[2], 6, 10, 5:1[2], 2[5], 3, 4, 14, 15[2], 6:3, 8, 9

EZEKIEL
7:11, 21[2], 23, 26, 8:2, 3, 7, 8, 11, 17, 18, 9:1, 2[2], 4, 10:1[2], 8, 9, 10[2], 14[3], 21, 11:8, 13[2], 16, 19, 24, 12:2[2], 3, 6, 16, 23, 13:7[2], 10, 11, 13, 14:7, 8[2], 9, 17, 19, 22, 15:2, 3, 8, 16:8, 11, 12[2], 13, 19, 20, 32, 34, 40, 47, 54, 17:2[2], 3, 4[2], 5[2], 6[2], 8[2], 13, 22, 23, 18:5, 6, 7, 10[3], 14, 16, 26, 31[2], 19:1, 2, 3, 5, 6, 10, 13, 14[4], 20:6, 11, 12, 20, 21, 27, 33[2], 34[2], 47, 21:9[2], 10, 13, 19, 20, 22[2], 23, 29, 22:4[2], 25[2], 30, 23:30, 40, 41[2], 42[2], 44, 46, 24:3[2], 7, 8, 16, 24, 27, 25:4, 5[2], 7, 15, 26:4, 5[2]

EZEKIEL
26:7, 8[2], 10[2], 12[2], 14[2], 17, 19, 21, 27:2, 3, 15, 32, 36, 28:2[2], 9, 12, 18, 19, 24, 29:6, 7, 8, 14, 18, 30:3, 8, 13[2], 18, 21, 24, 31:3[2], 15, 32:2[3], 3, 7, 25, 33:2[2], 7, 32[2], 33, 34:8, 12, 14[3], 18, 22, 24, 25, 26, 28, 29, 35:5, 36:3, 4, 5, 17, 26[2], 37, 37:7[2], 26, 38:4, 7, 9[2], 12[2], 13[3], 15[2], 16, 19, 21, 39:6, 11, 13, 15[2], 17, 40:2[2], 3[3], 5[2], 17, 24, 27, 42[2], 41:7, 8, 18[3], 19[2], 42:4[2], 12, 20[2], 43:2, 13[4], 17[2], 19[2], 22[2], 23[2], 24, 25[4], 44:13, 22[3], 45:4, 5, 7, 10[2], 14, 15[2], 18, 21, 22[2], 23[3], 24[3], 46:4, 5, 6[2], 7[3], 11[2], 12, 13[2], 14[3], 15

EZEKIEL
46:16, 17, 19, 21, 23, 47:3, 4[2], 5[3], 9, 10, 20, 48:1, 2, 3, 4, 5, 6, 7, 12, 15, 23, 24, 25, 26, 27

DANIEL
1:5, 2:3, 5, 10, 11, 19, 25, 28, 31, 34, 35, 37[2], 44, 47[4], 48, 3:6, 10, 11, 15, 29[2], 4:5, 6, 10, 15, 16, 23[2], 27, 31, 5:1[2], 5, 7, 11, 16, 18, 29[2], 6:7[3], 10, 12[2], 13, 17, 20, 26, 7:1, 4[3], 5[2], 6[2], 7, 8, 10, 12, 14, 20, 25, 8:1, 2[2], 3, 5, 9, 15, 16, 18, 9:12, 15, 16, 26, 10:1, 5, 6, 7, 9, 11, 18, 11:3, 7, 10, 11, 13[2], 15, 18, 20, 21, 22, 23, 25[2], 34, 35, 38, 39, 40, 12:1[2]

DANIEL
12:7, 11

HOSEA
1:2, 3, 4, 6, 8, 2:3[2], 6, 12, 15, 18, 3:1, 4[3], 4:1, 12, 16[3], 5:1[2], 2, 7, 12, 14[2], 6:4, 8, 9, 7:6, 8, 11, 16, 8:8, 9, 10, 12, 14, 9:1[2], 7, 8[2], 11, 12, 13, 14, 10:3, 4, 6, 14, 15, 11:1, 4, 10, 11[2], 12:1, 2, 7, 12[2], 13[2], 13:7[2], 8[2], 10, 11, 13, 14:8

JOEL
1:6[3], 8, 14[2], 15, 2:2[4], 3[3], 5[2], 9, 14[3], 15[2], 19, 20, 3:3[2], 4, 8, 18, 19[2]

AMOS
1:4, 7, 10, 12, 14[2], 2:2, 5, 6, 7, 13, 3:4[2], 5[3], 6[2], 12[3], 4:5, 11, 5:1, 3, 12, 19[4], 24, 6:10, 13, 14, 7:4, 7[3], 8[2], 14[2], 17, 8:1, 2, 6, 8

AMOS
8:10, 11[3], 9:5, 9

OBADIAH
1, 7, 12, 18[2]

JONAH
1:3, 4[2], 16, 17, 3:4, 5, 4:2, 5, 6[2], 7, 8, 10[2]

MICAH
1:4, 6, 8, 14, 2:2[2], 4[2], 5, 10, 11, 3:6, 12, 4:3, 7[2], 9, 10, 5:1, 7, 8[2], 6:6, 16, 7:2, 3, 4[2], 5[2], 6, 8, 17, 18

NAHUM
1:7, 11, 14, 2:8, 3:2, 3[2], 6

HABAK.
1:5, 10, 2:5, 6[2], 12[2], 18, 3:1, 14

ZEPH.
1:7, 10[2], 13[2], 15[5], 16, 18, 2:4, 9, 13[2], 15[2], 3:9, 13, 18, 20[2]

HAGGAI
1:6, 11, 2:6, 13, 15[2], 23

ZECH.
1:8[2], 14, 15, 16, 2:1[2], 5, 9, 3:2, 5[2], 4:1, 2[2], 7, 5:1, 2, 7[2], 9, 6:13

ZECH.
6:14, 7:12, 14, 8:3, 13[2], 23, 9:3, 6, 7[2], 9, 13, 15, 16, 10:2[2], 7, 11:3[2], 13, 15, 16, 12:2, 3, 6[2], 11, 13:1, 4, 14:4, 10, 13

MALACHI
1:6[4], 11, 13, 14[3], 2:2, 11, 15, 3:2, 3, 5, 8, 9, 10, 12, 16, 17, 4:6

MATT.
1:19[2], 20, 21, 23[2], 2:6, 12, 13, 18, 19, 22, 23[2], 3:4, 16, 17, 4:5, 6, 18, 21, 5:1, 14, 15[3], 22, 28, 31, 38[2], 41, 6:2, 16, 7:9, 10[2], 17, 18[2], 24[2], 25, 26, 8:2, 4, 5, 9, 14, 19, 23, 24, 26, 30, 32[2], 9:1, 2[2], 9, 12, 16, 18, 20, 23, 32[2], 10:18, 29, 34, 35, 36, 41[6], 42[2], 11:7, 8, 9[2], 11, 18, 19[3]

MATT.
12:10, 11, 12[2], 14, 20, 22, 29, 32, 35, 38, 39, 41, 42, 43, 13:2, 3, 21, 24, 31[2], 32, 33, 34, 42, 44[2], 45, 47, 52, 57, 14:5, 8, 11, 13, 14, 15, 22, 23, 26, 33, 15:5, 11[2], 20[2], 22[2], 23, 29, 33, 34, 16:1, 4[2], 26[2], 17:5[2], 14, 20, 27, 18:2, 6, 12, 17, 23, 19:3, 5, 7, 23, 24[3], 20:1, 2[2], 9, 10, 13, 20, 28, 29, 21:2, 5, 8, 13, 19, 26, 28, 33[5], 43, 46, 22:2[2], 11[2], 12, 19, 24, 25, 35[2], 46, 23:14, 16, 24[2], 37, 24:14, 31[2], 32, 45, 50, 25:6, 14[2], 19, 21, 23, 32, 35, 38, 43, 44, 26:7, 10, 13, 18, 36, 39, 47, 48, 51

MATT.
26:55, 69, 73, 27:14, 15, 16, 19, 24, 28, 29[2], 32, 33[3], 46, 48[2], 50, 57, 59, 60, 65, 66, 28:2, 16

MARK
1:6[2], 10, 11, 16, 19, 23, 26, 30, 35[2], 40, 44, 2:21, 3:1[2], 7, 8, 9, 13, 24, 25, 27, 4:1[2], 3, 17, 21[4], 26, 31, 34, 37, 38, 39, 5:2, 7, 11, 13, 25, 42, 6:4, 5, 8, 11, 15, 19, 20, 21[2], 25, 28, 29, 31[2], 32, 34, 35, 46, 49, 7:11, 15, 26[2], 36, 8:4, 7, 10, 11, 12, 22, 36, 37, 9:7[2], 14, 17, 21, 36, 39, 41, 42, 10:2, 4, 7, 12, 15, 25[3], 45, 46, 48, 11:2, 4, 13, 17, 32, 12:1[5], 2, 15, 19, 20, 40

MARK
12:42[2], 13:9, 28, 34[2], 14:3, 6, 9, 13[2], 15, 32, 35, 43, 44, 47[2], 48, 51[2], 69, 70[2], 15:1, 17, 19, 21, 22, 34, 36[2], 37, 46[3], 16:5[2]

LUKE
1:1, 5, 13, 17, 22, 26, 27[2], 31, 34, 36, 39, 42, 45, 57, 63, 2:7, 11, 12[2], 13, 16, 24[2], 25, 32, 34, 35, 36[2], 37, 44, 3:22[3], 4:5, 9, 11, 13, 14, 25, 26[3], 31, 33[3], 36, 38, 42, 5:3, 4, 6, 8, 12[2], 14, 15, 17, 18[3], 27, 29[2], 31, 36[4], 6:6, 12, 17, 39, 43[2], 44, 45, 48[3], 49[2], 7:2, 5, 7, 8, 11, 12[2], 16[2], 24, 25, 26[2], 28, 33, 34[3], 37[2], 39[2], 41, 8:4, 5, 6, 13, 16[4], 22[2], 23, 24

LUKE
8:27, 28, 33, 41[2], 42, 43, 9:5, 10, 12, 14, 25, 27, 28, 34, 35, 38, 39, 42, 47, 52, 57, 10:13, 25, 30, 31, 32, 33, 38[2], 39, 11:1, 5, 6, 11[6], 12, 14, 16, 17[2], 21, 22, 24, 27, 29, 30, 31, 32, 33[4], 36, 37, 12:10, 14[2], 15, 16[2], 33, 44, 46, 50, 54[2], 13:6[2], 11[2], 16, 19[3], 21, 33, 34, 14:2, 5, 7, 8[2], 12[3], 13, 16[2], 18, 20, 28, 32, 15:8, 11, 13, 14, 15, 20, 22, 29, 16:1[2], 19, 20, 26, 17:2, 4[2], 6, 7, 12, 15, 16, 18:1, 2[2], 3, 4, 10[2], 13, 17, 18, 25[3], 35, 19:2, 4, 7[2], 9, 11, 12[3], 14, 17, 20, 30, 37, 43, 46

LUKE
20:6, 9[4], 10, 12, 24, 28, 29, 38, 47, 21:2, 3, 13, 15, 27, 29, 35, 22:10[2], 12, 24, 29, 36, 41, 47, 48, 52, 55, 56, 58, 59[2], 23:2, 6, 8, 11, 19, 26, 27, 31, 38, 44, 46, 47, 50[4], 51, 53, 24:13, 18, 19, 23, 37, 39, 42[2]

JOHN
1:6, 7, 30, 32, 42, 2:1, 15, 3:1[2], 2, 3, 4, 5, 10, 25, 27, 4:5, 7, 9[2], 14, 19, 24, 29, 44, 46, 5:1, 2, 3, 4, 5, 6, 13, 14, 35[3], 6:2, 3, 4, 5, 7, 9, 14, 15[2], 17, 18, 50, 70, 7:12, 20, 22, 23[2], 33, 40, 43, 8:3, 7, 40, 44[3], 48[2], 49, 51, 52[2], 55, 9:1, 11, 16[3]

JOHN
9:17, 24, 25, 30, 31, 10:1[2], 5, 19, 20, 21[2], 33[2], 11:1, 10, 38[2], 43, 44, 47, 54[2], 57, 12:2, 3, 6, 14, 24, 28, 35, 46, 49, 13:4, 5, 26, 33, 34, 14:2, 3, 19, 23, 15:6[2], 13, 25, 16:16[2], 17[2], 18, 19[2], 21[2], 18:1, 3, 10, 18, 30, 35, 37[2], 39, 40, 19:2[2], 7, 12, 13, 17[2], 19, 23, 29[2], 34, 36, 38, 39, 20:7, 21:3[2], 8, 9

ACTS
1:9, 12, 18, 22, 2:2[2], 22, 30, 3:2, 14, 22, 4:16, 27, 36, 5:1[2], 2, 16, 30, 31[2], 34[3], 36, 6:1, 5[2], 7, 7:5, 6, 11, 16, 27[2], 29, 30[2], 35[4], 37, 41, 46, 57, 58, 60, 8:1, 9, 27, 32[2], 36, 9:3, 4, 7

ACTS
9:10[2], 12[2], 15, 25, 26, 33, 36, 43, 10:1[2], 2, 3, 4, 6, 7, 10, 11[2], 13, 22, 26, 28[2], 30, 32, 34, 39, 11:5[4], 7, 21, 24, 26, 12:7, 9, 11, 13, 21, 22[3], 13:6[3], 7, 11[3], 21[2], 22, 23, 29, 41[3], 47, 14:1, 8[2], 10, 15:7, 10, 14, 33, 16:1[3], 3, 9[2], 11, 12, 13, 14[2], 16[2], 24, 26, 28, 29, 17:1, 4[2], 5, 12, 18, 31, 34, 18:2, 7, 9, 11, 14, 15, 18[2], 24, 19:14, 22, 24[2], 34, 35, 38, 39, 20:9[3], 11, 12, 21:1, 2, 10, 23, 39[4], 40, 22:3[3], 6, 7, 12, 17, 22, 25[2], 26, 27, 28, 29, 23:6[2], 7, 9[2], 10, 12, 14, 17, 21, 25, 27, 24:1, 4

ACTS
24:5[3], 10, 15, 16, 23, 24, 25, 27, 25:9, 14, 27, 26:5, 8, 13, 14, 16[2], 24, 26, 28, 27:1[2], 5, 6, 8, 14, 16, 18, 26, 28, 39[2], 41, 28:2, 3[2], 4, 6[2], 8[2], 11, 13, 16, 23

ROMANS
1:1, 10, 25, 28, 2:14, 17, 19[2], 20, 21, 22, 25, 28, 29, 3:4, 5, 7, 25, 28, 4:11, 17, 5:7[2], 7:1, 21, 8:24, 9:9, 27, 28, 29, 33, 10:2, 14, 19, 21, 11:5, 9[4], 17, 24, 12:1, 13:3, 4, 14:13, 15:8, 12, 23, 26, 16:1, 2, 23

1 COR.
1:22, 23, 2:7, 11, 3:10, 14, 18, 4:1, 2, 3, 6, 9, 21, 5:6, 7, 11[4], 6:1, 5, 7, 18, 20, 7:1[2], 5, 12, 15[2], 21

1 COR.
7:22, 23, 26, 27[2], 28, 34[2], 35, 8:7, 9, 9:5[2], 7[3], 8, 11, 17[2], 20, 24, 25, 27, 10:13, 27, 30, 11:6[2], 7, 13, 14[2], 15[3], 28, 12:31, 13:1, 11[5], 12, 14:7, 11[2], 22, 25, 26[4], 35, 37, 15:38, 44[4], 45[2], 51, 52, 16:7, 9

2 COR.
1:10, 15, 23, 2:6, 7, 12, 15, 3:13, 18, 4:17[2], 5:1, 17, 6:2, 13, 18, 7:8[2], 9, 11, 14, 8:2, 10, 11[2], 12[2], 14[2], 9:2, 5, 7, 10:6, 13, 11:1, 2, 5, 16[3], 20[5], 23, 25[2], 32, 33[2], 12:2, 3, 4, 6, 7, 11, 17, 18[2], 13:3, *subscr.*

GAL.
2:3, 14, 16, 18, 3:13[2], 15, 19, 20[2], 21, 25, 4:1[2], 4, 7[3], 18, 22[2], 5:3, 9, 6:1[2], 3, 7

GAL.
6:11, 12, 15

EPHES.
3:7, 4:13, 5:2[2], 12, 27, 31, 32, 6:21

PHIL.
1:6, 23[2], 2:7, 8, 9, 15, 22, 3:5, 4:17, 18[2]

COLOS.
1:7, 23, 25, 2:15, 17, 18, 23, 3:13, 4:1, 3, 7[2], 9, 11, 12, 13

1 THESS.
2:5, 7, 11, 17, 4:16, 5:2, 3, 4

2 THESS.
1:5, 6, 2:3, 11, 3:15

1 TIM.
1:5[2], 8, 9, 13[2], 15, 16, 18, 19, 2:2, 6, 7[2], 12, 3:1[4], 2, 3, 5, 6, 7, 9, 10, 13[2], 4:2, 6, 9, 5:1, 5, 9, 23, 6:9, 12, 13, 19

2 TIM.
1:7, 11[2], 2:3, 4, 5, 11, 15, 17, 20, 21[2], 22, 3:5, 15, 4:7, 8

TITUS
1:1, 7, 8[2], 12, 2:7, 14

TITUS 3:8, 10 PHILE. 1, 9, 15, 16[3], 17, 22, *subscr.* HEB. 1:4, 5[2], 7, 8, 11

HEB. 1:12, 2:2, 6, 7, 9, 17, 3:5[2], 6, 4:1, 4, 7[2], 9, 12, 14, 5:6, 8, 13, 6:18

HEB. 7:2, 3, 7:5, 12, 16, 17, 18, 19, 21, 22[2], 8:2, 4, 6[2], 8, 10[2], 13, 9:1, 2

HEB. 9:9, 11, 16, 17, 10:1, 3, 5, 15, 20, 22, 27, 31, 32, 33, 34, 37, 11:2, 4

HEB. 11:6, 8, 9, 10, 11, 14, 16[2], 19, 21, 23, 25, 35, 39, 12:1, 10, 19, 20[2], 28

HEB. 12:29, 13:9, 18, 22 JAMES 1:1, 6, 8, 11, 18, 23[4], 25[2], 2:2[3], 3, 11, 14, 15

JAMES 2:18, 24, 3:2, 4, 5[3], 6[2], 11, 12, 13[2], 4:4, 11[2], 13[2], 14[2], 5:3, 5, 16, 17, 20[2]

1 PETER 1:3, 6, 19, 22, 2:4, 5, 6, 8[2], 9[3], 10, 16, 19, 3:4, 9, 15, 16, 20, 21

1 PETER 4:15[3], 16, 19, 5:1[2], 2, 4, 8, 10, 12, 14 2 PETER 1:1, 17, 19[3], 2:3, 5, 17

2 PETER 2:19, 3:8[2], 10[2], 13 1 JOHN 1:10, 2:4, 8, 22, 3:15, 4:20[2], 5:10, 16[2], 17 2 JOHN 1:4

2 JOHN 5, 7, 8 3 JOHN 6 JUDE 9, 22 REV. 1:10[2], 11, 13[2], 14, 15, 16

REV. 2:10, 14, 17[2], 18, 20[2], 22, 27[2], 3:1, 3, 4, 8, 12, 4:1[2], 2, 3[3], 6, 7[5], 5:1

REV. 5:2[2], 6, 9, 12, 6:2[3], 4, 5[2], 6[4], 8, 10, 11, 12, 13[2], 14, 7:2, 9, 10, 8:3

REV. 8:10[2], 12, 13, 9:1, 2[2], 5[2], 11, 13, 15[3], 10:1[2], 2, 3[2], 4, 11:1[2], 3, 12[2], 13, 12:1[3]

REV. 12:3, 5[2], 6[2], 10, 12, 14[3], 15, 13:1, 2[3], 5, 11[2], 14, 16, 18, 14:1, 2[2], 3, 7

REV. 14:9, 13, 14[3], 15, 17, 18, 20, 15:2, 16:1, 2, 3, 15, 16, 17, 18, 21[2], 17:3[2], 4

REV. 17:5, 10, 18:2[6], 7, 21[3], 22, 23, 19:1, 5, 6, 11, 12[2], 13, 15[2], 16, 17, 20, 20:1

REV. 20:2, 3[2], 4, 6[3], 11, 21:1[2], 2, 3, 10, 11[2], 12, 15, 17, 19, 20[2], 27, 22:1, 15

an See also A.

GEN. 2:18, 20, 4:3, 22, 5:3, 6, 18, 25, 28, 6:3, 14, 7:24, 8:11, 20, 9:20, 11:10, 25, 12:7, 8, 13:18, 15:9, 16:1[2], 17:7, 8, 13, 17, 19, 21:5, 20, 22:9, 23:1, 25:7, 8, 17, 25, 26:12, 25, 28, 27:30, 29:24, 31:46, 33:17, 19, 20, 34:31, 35:1, 3, 7, 8, 28, 37:33, 36, 38:14, 15, 39:1[2], 14, 41:12, 16, 42:23, 43:12, 32, 44:20, 46:34, 47:9, 28, 49:9, 13, 17, 33, 50:22, 25, 26 EXOD. 2:3, 11[2], 19, 4:20, 6:8, 16, 18, 20, 10:13, 26, 12:3, 14, 16[2], 17, 24, 45, 13:13, 14:8, 15:2

EXOD. 15:8, 25, 16:16, 18, 32, 33, 36[2], 17:15, 18:3, 19:6, 13, 20:24, 25, 21:2, 6, 28, 33[2], 22:1[2], 10[2], 11, 15, 25, 23:1, 20, 22[2], 24:4, 25:2, 10, 25, 26:36, 27:1, 9, 11, 16, 18, 28:4, 11, 18, 19[2], 20, 32[2], 29:18, 25, 28[2], 36, 37[2], 40[2], 41, 30:1, 10, 13, 14, 15[2], 16, 24, 25[3], 31, 31:18, 32:5, 30, 33:2, 34:20, 35:2, 5[2], 22, 24, 36:37, 37:12, 38:9, 11, 23[2], 25, 27, 39:11, 12[2], 13, 23[2], 40:10, 15 LEVIT. 1:2, 9, 13, 17, 2:2, 4, 9, 16, 3:3, 5, 9

LEVIT. 3:14, 4:20, 26, 31, 35, 5:2, 4, 6, 10, 11, 13, 16, 18, 6:7, 20, 7:5, 14, 18, 25, 32, 8:21, 28, 33, 34, 9:7[2], 17, 11:10, 11, 12, 13, 20, 23, 41, 42, 12:7, 8, 13:11, 28, 14:5, 18, 19, 20, 21, 29, 31, 40, 41, 45, 50, 53, 15:13, 15, 19, 25, 30, 32, 33, 16:6, 10, 11, 16, 17[2], 18, 20, 24, 30, 33[3], 34[2], 17:3, 4, 11[2], 19:20, 22, 20:13, 21, 21:14, 22:10, 12, 22, 27, 23:3, 7, 8[2], 13[2], 14, 18, 21, 24, 25, 27[2], 28, 35, 36[3]

LEVIT. 23:37, 24:7, 8, 10[2], 25:40, 46, 50, 26:8[2], 27:9, 16, 27 NUM. 2:9, 16, 24[2], 31, 4:15, 5:2, 8, 15[3], 17, 19, 21[2], 26, 6:11, 7:3, 13, 19, 25, 31, 37, 43, 49, 55, 61, 67, 73, 79, 85, 86, 8:11, 12, 13, 15, 19, 21[2], 9:7, 10:5, 6[2], 7, 8, 9, 12:1, 13:32, 14:7, 15:3, 4, 5, 6, 7, 9, 10[2], 13, 14, 15, 19, 20, 21, 25, 28[2], 16:31, 46, 47, 18:8, 17, 21, 24, 26, 28, 19:17, 20:16, 22:22, 23:3, 22, 24:8, 25:13[2], 26:53, 27:7, 28:5[2], 7, 14[3], 18

NUM. 28:22, 25, 26, 30, 29:5, 7, 12, 30:2, 6, 10, 31:29, 50[2], 32:14, 33:3, 39, 34:2, 35:16, 18, 36:2, 8 DEU. 4:21, 38, 5:29, 7:6, 25, 26, 10:1, 3, 13:16, 14:2, 21[2], 15:4, 12[2], 17, 17:1, 18:10[2], 12, 19:10, 20:9, 16, 19, 21:3, 23, 22:10[2], 14, 19[2], 22, 23, 23:3, 7[2], 24:4, 14, 25:5, 16, 19, 26:1, 8, 12, 19, 27:5[2], 15, 25, 28:9, 22[2], 30, 37, 29:4, 8, 31:2, 24, 32:11, 45, 33:7, 34:7 JOSH. 1:6, 2:1, 3:13, 16, 7:13, 8:2, 24, 28, 30, 31, 10:20, 11:23, 13:6, 7, 14:3

JOSH. 14:13, 17:4[2], 6, 19:49[2], 51[2], 22:10, 11, 14, 16, 19, 23, 26, 29, 23:4, 24:19, 25, 26, 29, 32 JUD. 2:1, 8, 3:18, 31, 4:21, 6:11[2], 19, 22[2], 24, 26, 8:10, 27, 9:23, 46, 48, 11:1, 12:5, 13:6, 16, 21, 14:4, 15:15, 16[2], 17, 19, 16:1, 3, 17:5[2], 18:1, 14, 19:9, 16, 28, 20:10[2], 16, 35, 38, 21:4, 17 RUTH 1:12[2], 2:17 1 SAM. 1:1, 2:28, 31, 32[2], 3:12, 4:18, 7:17, 9:6, 10:13, 13:10, 14:3, 14, 27, 28, 35, 48, 16:2, 14, 15, 16, 20, 23, 17:5, 12, 17, 38, 18:1

1 SAM. 18:25, 19:13, 16, 20:36, 21:7, 23:6, 24:16, 25:18, 42, 26:13, 19, 28:14, 29:4, 9, 30:11, 13, 14, 25 2 SAM. 1:8, 13, 2:25, 3:14, 29, 5:11, 6:18, 7:2, 5, 7, 11, 13, 27, 8:4, 11:2, 19, 13:36, 14:17, 20, 15:19, 16:1[2], 17:25, 18:10, 19:26, 27, 23:5, 14, 21, 38[2], 24:3, 18, 21, 25 1 KINGS 1:39, 41[2], 52, 2:24, 36, 3:1, 9, 12, 4:23, 5:3, 5[2], 7:2, 8, 26, 31, 40, 8:13, 16, 17, 18, 20, 31, 36, 54, 63, 10:10, 29[2], 11:7, 14, 18, 25, 26, 12:21, 31, 13:11, 14, 18, 14:21

1 KINGS 14:31, 15:13, 16:32, 17:12, 18:4, 10, 13, 32, 19:5, 11, 20:20, 25, 29, 30, 22:9, 25 2 KINGS 1:8, 9, 3:4[2], 4:9, 24, 43, 6:15, 25, 9:2, 5, 17, 10:25, 11:4, 16:10, 11, 18:31, 19:32, 23:33, 25:19 1 CHRON. 2:34, 5:21, 6:49, 8:40, 11:11, 23, 12:14, 37, 14:1, 15:5, 7, 10, 27, 16:2, 17, 29, 17:1, 4, 5, 6, 10, 12, 25, 18:4, 21:3, 5, 15, 18, 22, 26, 22:6, 7, 8, 10, 14, 27:4, 28:2, 3, 8, 10, 29:16 2 CHRON. 1:17[2], 2:1[2], 3, 4[2], 6[2], 12[2], 17, 3:4, 16, 4:1, 5

2 CHRON. 4:8, 5:12, 6:2, 5, 7, 8, 22, 27, 7:1, 5, 12, 21, 9:9, 11:1, 12:13, 13:3, 13, 14:8, 9, 15:16, 17:18, 18:24, 20:23, 21:18, 24:10, 15, 26, 25:6[2], 26:11, 13, 27:5, 28:6, 29:17, 24, 29, 32, 32:8, 21, 35:25, 36:3, 23 EZRA 1:2, 2:3, 18, 21, 23, 27, 30, 41, 42, 4:3, 6, 17, 6:17, 7:22[4], 8:3, 10, 12, 26[2], 9:11, 12, 10:17 NEH. 4:2, 5:12, 17, 6:5, 13, 7:8, 24, 26, 27, 31, 32, 44, 45, 10:29, 33, 11:14, 19 ESTHER 1:1, 4, 8:9 JOB 1:8, 10, 2:3

JOB 2:11, 3:16, 4:16, 6:6, 7:1[2], 2, 13:16, 14:3, 4, 6, 16:3, 18:2, 19:15, 24, 20:19, 26:10, 28:3, 31:6, 11[2], 28, 33:23, 40:9, 15, 41:1, 2, 42:11, 16 PSALMS 5:9, 7:9, 11:6, 18:25, 26:12, 27:3, 31:2, 33:2, 7, 16, 17, 38:4, 40:2, 41:8, 43:1, 48:7, 50:21, 55:12, 64:5, 7, 68:15, 21, 69:8, 31, 72:16, 78:13, 26, 55, 84:3, 88:8, 92:3, 10, 96:8, 101:5, 102:3, 6, 105:10, 106:20, 119:96, 111, 142, 127:3, 132:5, 135:12[2], 136:21, 22, 140:11, 141:5, 144:9, 145.13 PROV. 1:9, 4:9, 5:3, 6:11, 16, 18, 7:10, 13, 22, 8:5, 7, 10:25

PROV. 11:9, 13:22, 15:8, 9, 19, 26, 16:5, 12, 18, 19, 24, 27, 17:1, 10, 11, 27, 18:11, 19:15, 28, 20:3, 21, 23, 21:4, 19, 22:24, 23:5, 6, 18, 32, 24:3, 9, 34, 25:12[3], 19, 23, 27:6, 7, 28:10, 22, 29:6, 22, 27[2], 30:19, 20, 23[2], 31 ECCL. 4:6, 13, 5:6, 6:1, 2, 3[2], 7:11, 8:3, 11, 12, 9:2, 3, 12[2], 10:5[2] CANT. 4:4, 13, 6:4, 10, 7:2 ISAIAH 1:13, 21, 30, 3:7, 5:10[2], 26, 6:13, 9:17[2], 10:6, 11:10, 12, 16, 14:19, 15:5, 16:4, 11, 14, 17:6, 9, 18:3, 19:19, 21:16

ISAIAH 22:16, 23:15, 16, 24:13, 25:2, 29:5, 8, 21, 30:5, 13, 17[2], 28, 32:2, 33:1, 34:13, 35:6, 8, 36:16, 37:33, 38:12, 13, 41:24, 43:23, 44:14, 45:17, 48:4, 49:8, 18, 53:10, 54:16, 55:3, 13, 56:5, 58:5, 59:17, 60:15, 19, 61:8, 63:12, 13, 64:6, 65:9, 20[4], 66:3[3], 14, 20[2], 24 JER. 1:11, 14, 18, 2:7, 19, 3:18, 4:7, 5:15, 16, 6:26, 9:2, 8, 11, 10:10, 11:19, 14:12, 18:17, 19:8, 21:5, 22:19, 23:40, 24:7, 25:9[2], 11, 18[2], 36, 26:8, 9, 29:11, 18[2], 30:14, 17, 31:3, 32, 32:14, 40, 33:9, 12, 34:9[2], 14, 22, 42:18[2], 43:1, 44:12[2]

JER. 44:22[2], 27, 46:19, 22, 47:2, 48:34, 40, 49:2, 14, 50:9, 51:29, 34, 37[3], 41, 63, 52:23, 25 LAM. 1:15, 2:4[2], 5, 5:10 EZEKIEL 1:10[2], 24, 2:9, 3:5, 6, 9, 4:3, 11, 5:15[2], 7:2, 5[2], 6, 8:3, 10:14, 11:19, 13:11, 13, 16:3[2], 24[2], 30, 31, 45[2], 60, 17:13, 22, 20:17, 21:25, 29, 23:24, 31:3, 33:32, 35:5, 36:26, 37:10, 26, 38:10, 22, 40:5, 19, 23, 27, 42[2], 43, 47[2], 41:7, 13[2], 14, 15, 42:2, 8, 15, 43:13, 23, 44:28, 45:1[2], 4, 11[2], 13[4], 14[2], 24[4], 46:5[3], 7[4], 11[4], 14[2], 47:22

DANIEL 2:46, 3:1, 4, 27, 4:3, 13, 23, 34, 5:12, 6:1, 3, 7:14, 27, 8:5, 12, 9:24, 10:10, 11:6, 7, 12:7 HOSEA 3:1, 2[2], 4[2], 6:10, 11, 7:4, 6, 7, 8:1, 10:1, 11, 13:13, 15 JOEL 2:1, 3:3 AMOS 3:11, 12, 15, 5:3[2], 13, 7:2, 14, 17, 8:10 OBADIAH 1 JONAH 1:9, 3:3 MICAH 1:6, 7[2], 15, 2:3, 8, 6:16 NAHUM 1:8[2], 9 HABAK. 2:3, 9 ZEPH. 1:10, 3:12 HAGGAI 2:16 ZECH. 5:6, 11, 7:12, 9:9[2], 16, 12:6, 13:5

MALACHI 1:10, 13, 2:11, 12, 3:3, 4:1 MATT. 2:19, 4:8, 5:14, 38[2], 8:30, 9:16, 20, 10:12, 11:1, 12:1, 3, 35, 39, 13:8, 23, 28, 52, 14:7, 16:23, 17:1, 27, 18:12, 17, 28, 19:29, 20:1, 21:2, 5[2], 24:44, 50, 25:24, 35, 37, 42, 44, 26:5, 7, 30, 72 MARK 1:23, 2:21, 25, 3:19, 26, 30, 4:8, 20, 5:2, 25, 6:10, 20, 27, 7:22, 24, 25, 32, 9:2, 10:30, 12:1, 14:2, 3, 26, 15:43 LUKE 1:11, 18, 69, 2:36, 4:5, 33, 5:36, 6:3, 7, 45, 48, 49, 7:37, 8:8, 15, 32, 43

LUKE 9:28, 10:34, 11:12, 29, 12:1, 40, 46, 14:5[2], 32, 15:4, 16:2, 6, 7, 19:21, 22, 21:18, 22:37, 43, 44, 24:42 JOHN 1:22, 47, 2:16, 5:4, 5, 6:60, 10:12, 13, 12:15, 29, 13:15, 19:31, 39, 21:11 ACTS 1:13, 15, 2:30, 3:3, 6:15, 7:30, 47, 8:27, 9:37, 10:3, 22, 28, 11:13, 12:21, 13:17, 14:5, 17:5, 23, 18:24, 19:40, 20:32, 21:16, 26, 29, 31, 38, 23:9, 21, 27, 25:11, 27:12, 34 ROMANS 1:1, 23, 2:20, 3:13, 4:19, 7:2, 3, 11:1, 14:13, 16:16 1 COR. 1:1, 5:5, 9, 11[3], 6:15, 16

1 COR. 8:4, 7, 9:1, 2, 25, 12:17, 14:2, 4, 8, 13, 14, 19, 26, 27, 15:9, 52, 16:20 2 COR. 1:1, 2:11, 5:1, 6:15, 8:14, 10:11, 11:7, 14, 12:2, 5, 12, 13:13 GAL. 1:1, 8, 2:5, 4:7, 14, 24, 27, 5:13, 6:1 EPHES. 1:1, 11, 2:21, 22, 5:2, 5, 6:20 PHIL. 1:28, 3:5, 17, 4:18 COLOS. 1:1, 2:16 1 THESS. 5:8, 26 2 THESS. 3:9, 15 1 TIM. 1:1, 2:7, 4:12, 5:1, 8, 19[2] 2 TIM. 1:1, 9, 11, 2:9, 4:5 TITUS 1:1, 3:10

PHILE. 9 HEB. 3:12, 4:15, 5:5, 10, 6:6, 16[2], 17, 19, 20, 7:16, 20, 21[2], 24, 26, 8:1, 9:11, 13, 10:21, 22, 29, 34, 11:7, 8, 16, 12:22, 13:10 JAMES 3:8, 5:10 1 PETER 1:1, 4, 2:5, 9, 21, 3:15, 4:15, 5:1 2 PETER 1:1, 11, 2:6[2], 14 1 JOHN 2:1, 7, 20, 5:20 2 JOHN 1:7 JUDE 7 REV. 2:7, 11, 17, 29, 3:6, 8, 13, 22, 4:3, 7:4, 8:1, 5, 13, 9:15, 11:9, 11, 19, 13:9, 14, 14:1, 16:18, 19:17, 20:1, 21:17, 19, 20

and

2532

GEN. 1:1 2[4] 3[2] 4[2] 5[4] 6[2] 7[3] 8[3] 9[3] 10[3] 11[3] 12[4] 13[2] 14[5] 15[2] 16[2] 17 18[4] 19[2] 20[2] 21[4] 22[4] 23[2] 24[4] 25[4] 26[6] 27 28[3] 29[2] 30[4] 31[4] 2:1[2] 2[2] 3[3] 4[2] 5[3] 6 7[3] 8[2] 9[4] 10[3] 12[2] 13 14[2] 15[3] 16 17 18 19[4] 20[3] 21[4] 22[2] 23[2] 24[3] 25[2] 3:1 2 4 5[2] 6[6] 7[4] 8[3] 9[2] 10[3] 11 12[2] 13[3] 14[3] 15[5] 16[3] 17[2] 18[2] 19 20 21[2] 22[6] 24[2] 4:1[4] 2[2] 3 4[4] 5[3] 6[2] 7[3] 8[3] 9[2] 10 11 12 13 14[3] 15[2] 16[2] 17[5] 18[4] 19[2] 20[2] 21[2] 22[3] 23[3] 24 25[3] 26[2] 5:2[3] 3[4] 4[3] 5[3] 6[3] 7[4] 8[8] 9[2] 10[4] 11[3] 12[2] 13[4]

GEN. 5:14[3] 15[3] 16[4] 17[3] 18[3] 19[3] 20[3] 21[3] 22[3] 23[2] 24[2] 25[3] 26[4] 27[3] 28 29 30[4] 31[3] 32[3] 6:1[2] 2 3[2] 4[2] 5[2] 6[2] 7[4] 9[2] 10[2] 11 12[2] 13[2] 15 16[3] 17[2] 18[4] 19[2] 20 21[4] 7:1[2] 2[3] 3 4[3] 5 6 7[4] 8[3] 9[2] 10 11 12[2] 13[5] 14[4] 15[2] 16[3] 17[4] 18[3] 19[2] 20 21[5] 23[7] 24[2] 8:1[5] 2[2] 3[3] 4 5 6 7[2] 9[3] 10[2] 11[2] 12[2] 13[5] 14[2] 15 16[3] 17[4] 18[4] 19[2] 20[4] 21[2] 22[7] 9:1[5] 2[4] 5[2] 7[3] 8[2] 9[2] 10[2] 11 12[3] 13[2] 14 15[4] 16[3] 17[2] 18[4] 19 20[2] 21[3] 22[2] 23[7] 24[2] 25 26[2] 27[2] 28[2] 29[3] 10:1[2] 2[6] 3[3] 4[3] 6[4] 7[7] 8

GEN. 10:10[4] 11[3] 12[2] 13[4] 14[3] 15[2] 16[3] 17[1] 18[4] 19[4] 20 22[4] 23[4] 24[2] 25[2] 26[4] 27[3] 28[3] 29[3] 30 32 11:1[2] 2[2] 3[4] 4[3] 5[2] 6[4] 7 8 9 10 11[3] 12[3] 13[4] 14[2] 15[4] 16[3] 17[4] 18[2] 19[4] 20[3] 21[4] 22[2] 23[3] 24[3] 25[4] 26[3] 27[2] 28 29[4] 31[6] 32[3] 12:1[2] 2[4] 3[3] 4[3] 5[6] 6[2] 7[3] 8[5] 9 10[3] 11 12 13 14 15[2] 16[8] 17[2] 18[2] 19 20[4] 13:1[4] 2[2] 3[2] 4 5[3] 6 7[4] 8[4] 10[3] 11[2] 12[2] 13[2] 14[5] 15 16 17 18[4] 14:1[2] 2[3] 4 5[5] 6 7[4] 8[6] 9[3] 10[5] 11[4] 12[3] 13[4] 14[3] 15[4] 16[5] 17[2] 18[3] 19[3] 20[2] 21[2] 22[2] 23 24[2] 15:1 2[2] 3[2]

GEN. 15:4 5[4] 6[2] 7 8 9[5] 10[3] 11 12[2] 13[3] 14[2] 15 17[3] 19[2] 20[3] 21[4] 16:1 2[3] 3 4[3] 5[3] 6 7 8[3] 9[2] 10 11[2] 12[3] 13 14 15[2] 16[2] 17:1[4] 2[3] 3[2] 4 6[3] 7[4] 8[3] 9[2] 10[2] 11[3] 12 13[2] 14 15 16[3] 17[3] 18 19[4] 20[4] 22[2] 23[4] 24[2] 25 26 27[2] 18:1[2] 2[5] 3 4[2] 5[3] 6[3] 7[5] 8[6] 9[2] 10[3] 11[3] 13 14 15 16[3] 17 18[2] 19[3] 20[3] 21[2] 22[2] 23[2] 24 25 26 27[3] 28[2] 29[3] 30[3] 31[2] 32[3] 33[2] 19:1[4] 2[6] 3[6] 4 5[2] 6[2] 7 8 9[5] 10[2] 11[2] 12[4] 13 14[3] 15[2] 16[5] 17 18 19[3] 20[2] 21 24[2] 25[4] 26 27 28[5]

GEN. 19:29[2] 30[5] 31[2] 32 33[4] 34[3] 35[4] 37[4] 38[2] 20:1[4] 2[3] 3 4 5[2] 6 7[4] 8[3] 9[3] 10 11[2] 12[2] 13 14[6] 15 16[2] 17[4] 21:1[2] 2 3 4 5 6 7 8[3] 9 10 11 12[2] 13 14[8] 15[2] 16[5] 17[3] 18 19[5] 20[4] 21[2] 22[2] 23 24 25 26 27[4] 28 29 30 32[2] 33[2] 34 22:1[3] 2[3] 3[7] 4 5[5] 6[6] 7[8] 8 9[5] 10[2] 11[3] 12 13[6] 14 15 16 17[3] 18 19[3] 20 21[2] 22[5] 23 24[4] 23:1[3] 2[3] 3[2] 4 5 7[2] 8[2] 10[2] 11 12 13[2] 14 15 16[2] 17[3] 19 20[2] 24:1[3] 2 3[2] 4[2] 5 6 7[3] 8 9[2] 10[4] 11 12[2] 13 14[3] 15

GEN. 24:16[4] 17[2] 18[4] 19 20[4] 21 22[2] 23 24 25[2] 26[2] 27[2] 28[2] 29[3] 30[4] 31[2] 32[6] 33[2] 34 35[10] 36[2] 37 38[2] 39 40[4] 41 42[2] 43[2] 44[2] 45[4] 46[5] 47[5] 48[3] 49[3] 50[2] 51[2] 52 53[5] 54[6] 55[2] 56 57[2] 58[3] 59[4] 60[3] 61[6] 62 63[4] 64[2] 65[2] 66 67[5] 25:1 2[6] 3[5] 4[5] 5 6 7[2] 8[3] 9[2] 10 11[2] 13[4] 14[3] 15[2] 16[2] 17[6] 18[2] 19 20 21[3] 22[3] 23[4] 24 25[2] 26[4] 27[3] 28 29[3] 30 31 32[2] 33[3] 34[5] 26:1[2] 2[2] 3[4] 4[3] 5[2] 6 7[2] 8[3] 9[4] 10[2] 11 12[2] 13[3] 14[3] 15 16 17[3] 18[2] 19[2] 20[2] 21[3] 22[6] 23 24[4] 25[4] 26[2] 27[2] 28[4] 29[2] 30[3]

GEN. 26:31[4] 32[3] 33 34[2] 35 27:1[4] 2 3[3] 4[2] 5[3] 6 7[2] 9[2] 10[2] 11[2] 12[3] 13[2] 14[4] 15[2] 16[2] 17[2] 18[3] 19[2] 20[2] 21 22[3] 23 24[2] 25[6] 26[2] 27[5] 28[3] 29[3] 30[2] 31[4] 32[2] 33[6] 34[3] 35[2] 36[3] 37[6] 38[3] 39[3] 40[3] 41[2] 42[4] 43 44 45[2] 46 28:1[4] 2 3[3] 4[2] 5[3] 6[2] 7[3] 8 9 10[2] 11[5] 12[5] 13[4] 14[7] 15[3] 16[3] 17[3] 18[4] 19 20[4] 22[2] 29:1 2[4] 3[4] 4[2] 5[2] 6[3] 7[3] 8[2] 9 10[4] 11[3] 12[4] 13[5] 14[3] 15 16[2] 17 18[2] 19 20[2] 21 22[2] 23[3] 24 25[2] 26 27 28[3] 29 30[3] 31 32[3] 33[4] 34[3] 35[4] 30:1[2] 2[2] 3[2] 4[2] 5[2] 6[3] 7[2] 8[3] 9

GEN. 30:10 11[2] 12 13[2] 14[3] 15[3] 16[4] 17[3] 18[2] 19[2] 20[2] 21[2] 22[3] 23[3] 24[2] 25[2] 26[2] 27 28[2] 29[2] 30[3] 31[3] 32[5] 33[2] 34 35[7] 36[3] 37[5] 38 39[3] 40[5] 41 42 43[5] 31:1[2] 2[2] 3[3] 4[3] 5 6 7[2] 8 9 10[4] 11[2] 12[3] 13[2] 14[3] 15 16 17[2] 18[2] 19[2] 20 21[3] 22 23[3] 24[2] 25 26[2] 27[4] 28[2] 30 31[2] 32 33[4] 34[3] 35[2] 36[4] 37 38[2] 40[2] 41[2] 42[3] 43[6] 44[3] 45[2] 46[4] 47 48[2] 49[2] 50 51[3] 52[3] 53[2] 54[3] 55[6] 32:1[2] 2[2] 3 4[2] 5[5] 6[3] 7[5] 8[2] 9[4] 10[2] 11[2] 12[2] 13[2] 14[2] 15[2] 16[4] 17[4] 18 19[3] 20[2] 21 22[5] 23[3] 24[2] 25[2] 26[2] 27[2] 28[3]

GEN. 32:29[4] 30[2] 31[2] 33:1[7] 2[6] 3[2] 4[5] 5[5] 6[2] 7[5] 8[2] 9 10[2] 11[3] 12[3] 13[4] 14[2] 15[2] 17[3] 18[2] 19 20[2] 34:1 2[3] 3[3] 4 5[2] 6 7[3] 8 9[3] 10[4] 11[3] 12[3] 13[2] 14 16[3] 17 18[2] 19[2] 20[3] 21[2] 23[3] 24[3] 25[4] 26[4] 27 28[4] 29[4] 30[7] 31 35:1[3] 2[3] 3[4] 4[3] 5[3] 6 7[2] 8[2] 9[2] 10[2] 11[4] 12[3] 13 14[3] 15 16[4] 17 18 19[2] 20 21[2] 22[3] 23[5] 24 25[2] 26[2] 27[2] 28[2] 29[3] 36:2 3 4[2] 5[3] 6[8] 7 9 11[3] 12[2] 13[3] 14[4] 16 17 18 19 20[3] 21[3] 22[3] 23[4] 24[2] 25[2] 26[4] 27[2] 28 31 32[2] 33[2] 34[2] 35[3] 36[2] 37[2] 38[2] 39[4] 40 37:1

GEN. 37:2[3] 3 4[2] 5[3] 6 7[4] 8[3] 9[6] 10[6] 11 12 13[3] 14[4] 15[3] 16 17[3] 18 19 20[4] 21[3] 22[2] 23 24[3] 25[6] 26[2] 27[4] 28[4] 29[3] 30[3] 31[3] 32[3] 33[2] 34[3] 35[3] 36 38:1[2] 2[3] 3[3] 4[3] 5[4] 6 7[2] 8[3] 9[2] 10 11[2] 12[4] 13 14[5] 16[3] 17[2] 18[7] 19[4] 20 21 22[3] 23[3] 24[4] 25[3] 26[3] 27 28[3] 29[2] 30[2] 39:1[2] 2[3] 3[2] 4[4] 5[4] 6[4] 7[2] 8[2] 9 10 11[2] 12[4] 13[2] 14[2] 15[4] 16 17 18[3] 19 20[3] 21[2] 22[2] 23 40:1[2] 2[2] 3 4[3] 5[2] 6[3] 7 8[3] 9[2] 10[4] 11[4] 12 13[2] 14[3] 15 16 17[2] 18[2] 19[2] 20[3] 21[2] 41:1[2] 2[3] 3[3] 4[3] 5[4] 6[2] 7[4]

GEN. 41:8[5] 10[2] 11[2] 12[3] 13[2] 14[5] 15[3] 16 17 18[3] 19[3] 20[2] 21 22[3] 23[2] 24[2] 25 26 27[4] 30[3] 31 32[2] 33[2] 34[2] 35[3] 36 37[2] 38 39[2] 40 41 42[4] 43[3] 44[2] 45[3] 46[3] 47 48[2] 49 50 51[2] 52 53 54[2] 55[2] 56[4] 57 42:2[3] 3 5 6[4] 7[5] 8 9[2] 10 12 13[3] 14 16[2] 17 18[2] 20[2] 21[2] 22[2] 23 24[6] 25[3] 26[2] 27 28[4] 29[2] 30 31 32 33[3] 34[2] 35[3] 36[3] 37[2] 38[2] 43:1 2 3 4 6 7[3] 8[6] 9 11[5] 12[2] 13 14 15[6] 16[3] 17[2] 18[5] 19[2] 20 21[3] 22 23[3] 24[4] 25 26[2] 27[2] 28[3] 29[4] 30[4] 31[4] 32[3] 33[3] 34[4] 44:1[2] 2[3] 3

GEN. 44:4[3] 5 6[2] 7 9 10[2] 11 12[4] 13[2] 14[3] 15 16[2] 17[2] 18[2] 20[5] 21 22 23 24 25[2] 26 27 28[3] 29[2] 30 31 33 34 45:1[2] 2[3] 3[2] 4[3] 6 7[2] 8[3] 9[2] 10[7] 11[3] 12[2] 13[4] 14[3] 15[2] 16[3] 17[2] 18[5] 19[3] 21[3] 22 23[4] 24[2] 25[2] 26[3] 27[2] 28[2] 46:1[3] 2[3] 3 4[2] 5[4] 6[4] 7[3] 8[2] 9[4] 10[6] 11[2] 12[9] 13[4] 14[3] 15[2] 16[5] 17[7] 18 19 20[2] 21[7] 22 23 24[4] 25 26 27[2] 28[2] 29[5] 30 31[5] 32[4] 33[2] 34 47:1[7] 2[2] 3[3] 5[2] 6[2] 7[3] 8 9[4] 10[2] 11[3] 12[3] 13[2] 14[3] 15[3] 16[2] 17[6] 18[2] 19[5] 20 21[2] 23[2] 24[5] 25[2] 26 27[4] 28[2] 29[5]

GEN. 47:30[3] 31[3] 48:1[3] 2[4] 3[2] 4[4] 5[3] 6[2] 7[2] 8[2] 9 10[2] 11[2] 12[2] 13[3] 14[3] 15[3] 16[4] 17[2] 18 19[4] 20[3] 21[2] 22 49:1[2] 2[2] 3[2] 5 6 7[2] 9 10 11[2] 12 13[2] 15[4] 20 23[2] 24 25[2] 26 27 28[2] 29[2] 31[3] 32 33[3] 50:1[3] 2[2] 3[3] 4 5[2] 6[2] 7[3] 8[5] 9[3] 10[4] 11 12 13 14[3] 15[2] 16 17[3] 18[3] 19 21[3] 22[4] 23 24[4] 25[2] 26[3]

EXOD. 1:1 2 3 4 5 6[3] 7[5] 9[2] 10 11[2] 12[2] 13 14[3] 15[2] 16[2] 17 18[3] 19[2] 20[2] 21 22[2] 2:1[2] 2[3] 3[5] 4 5[3] 6[4] 7 8[3] 9[5] 10[5] 11[3] 12[4] 13[2] 14[4] 15[2] 16[3] 17[4] 18 19[3] 20[2]

EXOD. 2:21[2] 22[2] 23[4] 24[3] 25[2] 3:1[2] 2[4] 3[2] 4[3] 5 6[2] 7[2] 8[9] 9 10 11[2] 12[2] 13[3] 14[2] 15[3] 16[4] 17[7] 18[5] 19 20[3] 21[2] 22[6] 4:1[2] 2[2] 3[4] 4[5] 5 6[3] 7[4] 8 9[3] 10[2] 11 12[2] 13 14[4] 15[5] 16[3] 17 18[6] 19 20[5] 21 22 23[2] 24[2] 25[3] 27[4] 28[2] 29[3] 30[2] 31[4] 5:1[3] 2 3[2] 4[2] 5[2] 6[2] 7 8[2] 9 10[3] 11 13 14[3] 15 16[2] 17 18 19 20[2] 21[3] 22[2] 6:1 2[2] 3[2] 4 5[2] 6[4] 7[3] 8[3] 9[2] 10 12 13[4] 14[2] 15[6] 16[5] 17 18[6] 19[2] 20[6] 21[3] 22[3] 23[4] 24[3] 25[2] 26 27 28 30[2] 7:1[2] 2 3[3] 4[2] 5[2] 6[2] 7[3] 8[2] 9[2]

EXOD. 7:10[6] 11 12 13 14 15[2] 16[2] 17 18[3] 19[6] 20[6] 21[4] 22[2] 23[2] 24 25 8:1[2] 2 3[8] 4[3] 5[3] 6[3] 7[2] 8[4] 9[4] 10[2] 11[4] 12[3] 13[3] 14[2] 15 16[2] 17[4] 18[2] 19[2] 20[3] 21[5] 22 23[2] 24[4] 25[2] 26[2] 27 28 29[3] 30[2] 31[3] 32 9:1 2 3 4[3] 5 6[2] 7[4] 8[3] 9[3] 10[5] 11[2] 12[2] 13[3] 14[2] 15[2] 16[2] 19[5] 20 21[2] 22[3] 23[5] 24 25[4] 27[6] 28[3] 29[2] 30 31[3] 32 33[5] 34[5] 35 10:1[2] 2[3] 3[3] 5[3] 6[5] 7 8[3] 9[4] 10[2] 11[2] 12[2] 13[4] 14[2] 15[3] 16[3] 17 18[2] 19[2] 21 22[2] 24[3] 25[2] 26 27 28 29 11:1[2] 2[3] 3[2] 4 5[2] 6 7 8[5] 9

EXOD. 11:10[3] 12:1[2] 4[2] 6[2] 7[3] 8[3] 9 10[2] 11[3] 12[3] 13[3] 14[2] 16[2] 17 18 21[3] 22[5] 23[3] 24[2] 25 26 27[3] 28[3] 29[2] 30[4] 31[6] 32[3] 33 34 35[4] 36[2] 37 38[3] 39[2] 40 41[2] 43[2] 45 48[5] 49 50 51 13:1 2 3 5[6] 6 7 8 9[2] 11[3] 12 13[3] 14 15[2] 16[2] 17[2] 18 19[2] 20[2] 21[3] 14:1 2[2] 4[4] 5[4] 6[2] 7[3] 8[3] 9[4] 10[4] 11 13[2] 15 16[3] 17[5] 18[2] 19[4] 20[4] 21[4] 22[3] 23[3] 24[3] 25 26[2] 27[4] 28[4] 29[2] 30 31 15:1[3] 2[4] 4 7 8[2] 14 16 17 18 19[2] 20[3] 21[2] 22[3] 23 24 25[4] 26[4] 27[4] 16:1[3] 2[2] 3[2] 4[2] 5[2] 6[2] 7[2] 8[3]

EXOD. 16:9 10[2] 11 12[2] 13[3] 14 15[2] 17[2] 18[2] 19 20[3] 21[2] 22[3] 23[3] 24[2] 25 27[2] 28[2] 31[3] 32 33[3] 35 17:1[3] 2[2] 3[5] 4 5[4] 6[3] 7[3] 8 9[2] 10[3] 11[2] 12[7] 13[2] 14[2] 15[2] 18:1 2 3 4[2] 5[2] 6[3] 7[5] 8[4] 9 10[2] 12[4] 13[2] 14[2] 15 16[4] 17 18 19 20[4] 21[3] 22[3] 23[2] 24 25[3] 26 27[2] 19:2[3] 3[3] 4[2] 5 6[2] 7[3] 8[3] 9[3] 10[4] 11 12 14[3] 15 16[4] 17[2] 18[3] 19[4] 20[3] 21[2] 22 23[2] 24[4] 25 20:1 5 6[2] 9 11[4] 12 18[6] 19[2] 20 21[2] 22 24[4] 25 21:2 4[3] 5[2] 6[2] 7 9 10 11 13 15 16[2] 17 18[3] 19[2] 20[2] 22[3]

EXOD. 21:23 26 27 28 29[3] 32 33[3] 34[2] 35[3] 36[2] 22:1[2] 2 5[3] 6 7 9 10 11[3] 12 13 14[2] 16[2] 23 24[4] 27 29 30 31 23:5 7[2] 8[2] 10[2] 11[3] 12[4] 13[2] 15 16[2] 20 21 22[2] 23[6] 24 25[4] 27[2] 28[2] 29 30[2] 31[3] 24:1[5] 2 3[5] 4[4] 5[2] 6[3] 7[4] 8[3] 9[3] 10[3] 11[5] 12[5] 13[3] 14[8] 15[2] 16[3] 17 18[4] 25:1 3[3] 4[5] 5[3] 6 7[2] 8 9 10[6] 11[3] 12[4] 13[2] 14 16 17[4] 18 19[2] 20[2] 21[2] 22[2] 23[3] 24[2] 25[2] 26[2] 28[2] 29[3] 30 31 32[4] 33[3] 34[2] 35[3] 36 37[2] 38[2] 40 26:1[3] 2[3] 3 4[2] 5 6[3] 7 8[2] 9[3] 10[2] 11[3] 12 13[3]

EXOD. 26:14[2] 15 16[2] 18 19[2] 20 21[2] 22 23 24[2] 25[3] 26 27[2] 28 29[2] 31[4] 32 33[2] 34 35[3] 36[4] 37[4] 27:1[2] 2[2] 3[5] 4[2] 5 6[2] 7[2] 9 10[2] 11[4] 12[2] 13 14 15[2] 16[6] 17 18[3] 19[2] 20 21 28:1[4] 2[2] 3 4[7] 5[5] 6[3] 7 8[4] 9[2] 10 12[2] 13 14[2] 15[4] 16 17[4] 18[4] 19[4] 20[4] 21 22 23[2] 24 25[2] 26[2] 27[2] 28[2] 29 30[4] 31 32 33[4] 34[3] 35[4] 36[4] 37 38[2] 39[2] 40[2] 41[6] 42 43[4] 29:1[2] 2[2] 3[2] 4[2] 5[6] 6[2] 7[2] 8[2] 9[6] 10[3] 11 12[3] 13[5] 14[2] 15[2] 16[2] 17[5] 18 19[3] 20[6] 21[10] 22[6] 23[3] 24[3] 25[2] 26[3] 27[4] 28[3] 29[2] 30 31[2] 32[2] 33[2]

EXOD. 29:34 35[2] 36[3] 37[2] 39 40[2] 41[3] 43[2] 44[3] 45[2] 46 30:1 2[2] 3[4] 4[2] 5[2] 6 7 8 10 11 14 15 16[2] 17 18[4] 19[2] 21[3] 23[4] 24[2] 25 26[3] 27[5] 28[3] 29 30[3] 31 32 34[3] 35[2] 36[2] 37 31:1 3[4] 4[2] 5[2] 6[2] 7[3] 8[4] 9[3] 10[3] 11[2] 12 13 17[4] 18 32:1[2] 2[3] 3[2] 4[3] 5[3] 6[5] 7 8[3] 9[2] 10[2] 11[3] 12[3] 13[4] 14 15[4] 16[2] 17 18 19[5] 20[5] 21 22 24[2] 25 26[2] 27[6] 28[2] 29 30[2] 31[3] 32 33 35 33:1[4] 2[5] 3 4[2] 5 6 7[4] 8[3] 9[3] 10[3] 11[2] 12[3] 13 14[2] 15 16[2] 17[2] 18 19[4] 20[2] 21[2] 22[2] 23[2] 34:1[3] 2[3] 3 4[4] 5[3]

EXOD. 34:6[5] 7[5] 8[3] 9[4] 10[2] 11[5] 13 15[4] 16[3] 19 20[2] 21 22[2] 24 27[2] 28[3] 29 30[3] 31[4] 32[2] 33 34[2] 35[2] 35:1[2] 4 5[2] 6[5] 7[3] 8[3] 9[3] 10[2] 11[3] 12[2] 13[3] 14[2] 15[5] 16[2] 17[2] 18[2] 19 20 21[5] 22[7] 23[7] 24[2] 25[5] 26 27[3] 28[4] 29 30[2] 31[3] 32[3] 33[2] 34[2] 35[6] 36:1[3] 2[3] 3[2] 4 5 6[2] 7 8[4] 9[2] 10[2] 11 12 13[2] 14 15 16[2] 17[2] 18 19[2] 20 21[2] 23 24[2] 25 26[2] 27 28 29[2] 30[2] 31 32[2] 33 34[3] 35[4] 36[3] 37[4] 38[3] 37:1[6] 2[3] 3[2] 4[2] 5 6[4] 7 8 9[2] 10[4] 11[2] 12 13[2] 15[2] 16[4] 17[3] 18[2] 19[3] 20[2] 21[3] 22 23[3] 24 25[3]

EXOD. 37:26[3] 27 28[2] 29[2] 38:1[3] 2[2] 3[5] 4 5 6[2] 7 8[2] 9 10[2] 11[3] 12[3] 13 14 15[3] 17[4] 18[6] 19[4] 20[2] 22 23[6] 24[3] 25[4] 26[4] 27[2] 28[4] 29[2] 30[4] 31[4] 39:1[4] 2[4] 3[5] 5[4] 6 7 8[4] 9 10[2] 11[2] 12[2] 13[2] 14 15 16[3] 17 18[2] 19[2] 20[2] 21[2] 22 23 24[4] 25[2] 26[2] 27[2] 28[3] 29[4] 30[2] 31 32 33[4] 34[3] 35[2] 36[2] 37[2] 38[4] 39[3] 40[4] 41[2] 43[3] 40:1 3[2] 4[4] 5[2] 6 7[3] 8[2] 9[6] 10[4] 11[2] 12[3] 13[3] 14[2] 15 17 18[5] 19[2] 20[4] 21[3] 22 23 24 25 26 27 28 29[3] 30[3] 31[4] 32 33[3] 34 35[2] 36 38

LEVIT. 1:1[2] 2[3] 4[2] 5[3] 6[3]

LEVIT. 1:7[2] 8[2] 9[2] 10 11[2] 12[3] 13[3] 14 15[4] 16[2] 17[2] 2:1[3] 2[4] 3[2] 4 5 6 7 8[2] 9[2] 10[2] 13 14 15 16[2] 3:1 2[3] 3[2] 4[3] 5 6 8[3] 9[4] 10[3] 11 12 13[3] 14[2] 15[3] 16 4:1 2 4[3] 5[2] 6[2] 7[2] 8[2] 9[3] 10 11[5] 12 13[4] 14 15[2] 16 17[2] 18[2] 19[2] 20[3] 21[2] 22[2] 24[2] 25[3] 26[3] 27[2] 29[2] 30[3] 31[4] 32 33[2] 34[3] 35[4] 5:1[3] 2[2] 3 4 5 6[2] 7[2] 8[2] 9[2] 10[3] 12[2] 13[3] 14 15 16[5] 17[3] 18[4] 6:1 2[2] 3[2] 4 5[2] 6 7 8 9[2] 10[4] 11[3] 12[4] 14 15[4] 16[2] 17 19 20[2] 21[2] 22 24 25 27 28[2] 30 7:2 3 4[3]

LEVIT. 7:5 8 9[3] 10[2] 11 12[2] 14[2] 15 16 18[2] 19[2] 21 22 24[2] 28 31 32 33 34[3] 35 37[4] 8:1 2[6] 3 4[2] 5 6[3] 7[6] 8[2] 9 10[4] 11[4] 12[2] 13[4] 14[3] 15[6] 16[5] 17[2] 18[3] 19[2] 20[4] 21[4] 22[2] 23[4] 24[5] 25[7] 26[6] 27[3] 28[2] 29[2] 30[10] 31[4] 32[2] 33 35[2] 36 9:1[3] 2[3] 3[3] 4[2] 5[3] 6[2] 7[7] 8 9[4] 10[2] 11[2] 12[2] 13[3] 14[3] 15[4] 16[2] 17[3] 18[2] 19[5] 20[2] 21[2] 22[5] 23[5] 24[4] 10:1[5] 2[3] 3[2] 4[3] 5 6[4] 7[2] 8 10[4] 11 12[4] 13[2] 14[5] 15[3] 16[4] 17 19[4] 20 11:1[2] 3[2] 5 6 7[2] 8 9[2] 10[4] 13[3] 14[2] 16[4] 17[3] 18[3] 19[3] 22[3] 24 25[2] 26 27

LEVIT. 11:28[2] 29[2] 30[5] 32[2] 33[2] 34 35[2] 37 38 39 40[6] 41 42 44 46[3] 47[3] 12:1 2 3 4[2] 5[2] 6[2] 7[2] 8[4] 13:1[2] 2 3[5] 4[2] 5[3] 6[5] 8 10[4] 11[2] 12[2] 13 15[2] 16 17[2] 18 19[3] 20[2] 21[2] 22 23[2] 24 25[2] 26[2] 27[2] 28[3] 30[2] 31[3] 32[4] 33 34[4] 36 37[2] 39 40 41 42 43 45[4] 49[2] 50[2] 51 53[2] 54 55[3] 56[2] 57 58[2] 14:1 3[3] 4[4] 5 6[5] 7[3] 8[5] 9[4] 10[4] 11[2] 12[4] 13[2] 14[4] 15[2] 16[2] 17[3] 18[2] 19[3] 20[4] 21[4] 22[3] 23 24[3] 25[5] 26 27 28[3] 29 30 31[2] 33[2] 34 35[2] 36 37[2] 38 39[3] 40 41[2] 42[4] 43[4] 44[2] 45[4] 47[2] 48[3] 49[4]

LEVIT. 14:50 51[7] 52[6] 53[2] 54 55[2] 56[3] 57 15:1[2] 2 3 4 5[3] 6[3] 7[3] 8[3] 9 10[4] 11[4] 12[2] 13[4] 14[3] 15[3] 16[2] 17[3] 18 19[3] 20 21[3] 22[3] 23 24[3] 25 26 27[4] 28 29[2] 30[3] 32[2] 33[4] 16:1[2] 2 3 4[4] 5[2] 6[3] 7[2] 8[2] 9[2] 10 11[4] 12[3] 13 14[3] 15[4] 16[3] 17[4] 18[5] 19[3] 20[3] 21[4] 22[2] 23[3] 24[7] 25 26[3] 27[5] 28[3] 29[2] 31 32[3] 33[5] 34[2] 17:1 2[3] 4[2] 5 6[2] 7 8 9 10[2] 11 13[3] 15[3] 18:1 2 3 4 5 17 21 25[2] 26[2] 27 30 19:1 2 3[2] 5 6[2] 7 8 9 10[2] 12 16 17 19 20[2] 21 22[2] 23[2] 25 29 30 32[2]

LEVIT. 19:33 34 36 37[2] 20:1 3[3] 4[2] 5[3] 6[3] 7 8[2] 10[2] 11 12 14[3] 15[2] 16[3] 17[4] 18[4] 19 20 21 22[2] 23[2] 24[2] 25[4] 26[2] 21:1[2] 2[4] 3 6[2] 9 10[2] 13 16 22 24[3] 22:1 2[2] 4 6 7[2] 9 11 13[2] 14[2] 15 17 18[4] 21 25 26 27[2] 28[2] 29 31 23:1 2 6 9 10[2] 11 12 13[2] 14 15 16 18[4] 19 20 21 22[2] 23 26 27[2] 28 30 32 33 36[2] 37[2] 38[3] 39 40[4] 41 44 24:1 5[2] 6 7 9[3] 10[3] 11[4] 12 13 14[2] 15 16[2] 17 18 19 21[2] 23[3] 25:1 2 3[2] 6[5] 7[2] 8[3] 10[4] 14 15 16 18[3] 19[3] 20 21

LEVIT. 25:22[2] 23 24 25[2] 26[2] 27 28[2] 29 30 31 32 33[2] 35[2] 38 39[2] 40[2] 41[4] 44[2] 45[2] 46 47[3] 50[2] 52[2] 53[2] 54[2] 26:2 3[2] 4[2] 5[4] 6[4] 7[2] 8[3] 9[3] 10[2] 11[2] 12[3] 13[2] 14 15 16[3] 17[3] 18 19[3] 20 21[2] 22[3] 23 24 25[3] 26[4] 27 28 29[2] 30[4] 31[3] 32[2] 33[4] 34[2] 36[4] 37[2] 38[2] 39[2] 40[2] 41[3] 42[3] 43[3] 44[2] 46[3] 27:1 2 3 4 5[2] 6[2] 7[3] 8 9 10[2] 11 12 14 15[2] 16 18 19[2] 20 22 23 25 27[2] 28[2] 30 31 32 33[2]

NUM. 1:1 3[2] 4 5 17[2] 18[3] 20[2] 21[2] 22 23[2] 24 25[2] 26 27[2] 28 29[2] 30 31[2] 32 33

NUM. 1:34 35[2] 36 37[2] 38 39[2] 40 41[2] 42 43[2] 44[2] 45 46[3] 50[5] 51[3] 52[2] 53 54 2:1[2] 3[2] 4[4] 5[2] 6[4] 7 8[4] 9[3] 10 11[4] 12[2] 13[4] 14 15[5] 16[5] 18 19[3] 20[2] 21[4] 22 23[4] 24[3] 25 26[4] 27[2] 28[4] 29 30[4] 31[3] 32[3] 34[2] 3:1 2[3] 4[5] 5 6 7[2] 8[2] 9[2] 10[4] 11 12 13 14 15 16 17[3] 18[2] 19[3] 20[2] 21 22[2] 24 25[3] 26[4] 27[4] 28 30 31[7] 32[2] 33 34[3] 35 36[7] 37[4] 38[3] 39[3] 40[3] 41[2] 42 43[5] 44 45[2] 46[3] 48[2] 49[2] 50[2] 51[2] 4:1[2] 3 5[4] 6[3] 7[6] 8[3] 9[6] 10[2] 11[3] 12[4] 13[2] 14[5] 15[3] 16[7] 17[2] 19[4] 21 23 24 25[4] 26[6]

NUM. 4:27[3] 28 30 31[4] 32[6] 34[4] 35 36[2] 37 38[2] 39 40[2] 41 42 43 44 45 46[2] 47[2] 48[2] 49 5:1 2[2] 3 4[2] 5 6 7[3] 9 10 11 12[2] 13[5] 14[5] 15 16[2] 17[3] 18[4] 19[3] 20[2] 21[3] 22[3] 23[2] 24[3] 25[2] 26[3] 27[6] 28[2] 29 30[3] 31 6:1 2 3[2] 5 9[2] 10 11[4] 12[2] 13 14[3] 15[4] 16[3] 17[2] 18[3] 19[4] 20[3] 21 22 23 24 25 26 27[2] 7:1[7] 2 3[4] 4 5 6[3] 7 8[2] 10 11 12 13[2] 17 19 23 25 29 31 35 37 41 43 47 49 53 55 59 61 65 67 71 73 77 79 83 85[2] 86 87 88[2] 89[2] 8:1 2 3

NUM. 8:4 5 6 7[4] 8 9[2] 10[2] 11 12[3] 13[3] 14 15[3] 17 18 19[3] 20[3] 21[4] 22[2] 23 24[2] 25[2] 26 9:1 3 4 5 6[3] 7 8[2] 9 11[2] 13[2] 14[4] 15[2] 16 17[2] 18 19[2] 20[2] 21[2] 22 23 10:1 2 3 4 8[2] 9[3] 10[3] 11 12[2] 13 14 15 16 17[3] 18[2] 19 20 21[2] 22[2] 23 24 25[2] 26 27 29[2] 30[2] 31[2] 32 33[2] 34 35[3] 36 11:1[5] 2[2] 3 4[3] 5[4] 7[2] 8[6] 9 10 11[2] 15[2] 16[3] 17[5] 18[3] 20[2] 21[2] 22 23 24[4] 25[6] 26[4] 27[4] 28[2] 29[2] 30[2] 31[5] 32[5] 33[2] 34 35[2] 12:1[2] 2[2] 4[4] 5[5] 6[2] 8[2] 9[2] 10[4] 11[2] 13 14[2] 15[2] 16[2]

NUM. 13:1 3 4 16 17[3] 18[2] 20[3] 22[3] 23[3] 25 26[7] 27[5] 28[3] 29[5] 30[3] 32[2] 33[3] 14:1[3] 2[3] 3[2] 4[2] 5 6[2] 7 8[2] 9 10 11[2] 12[3] 13 14[4] 17 18[4] 19 20 22[4] 24[2] 25[2] 26[2] 29[2] 30 31 33[2] 34 35 36[2] 38 39[2] 40[3] 41 43[2] 44 45[3] 15:1 2 3 5 7 8 10 14[2] 15 16[2] 17 18 22[2] 23 24[2] 25[4] 26[2] 27 28[2] 29 30 31 32 33[3] 34 35 36[3] 37 38[2] 39[5] 40[2] 16:1[3] 2[2] 3[4] 4 5[4] 6 7[3] 8 9 10[3] 11[2] 12[2] 13 14[2] 15[2] 16[4] 17[5] 18[5] 19[2] 20[2] 22[3] 23 24 25[4] 26[2] 27[7] 28 30[3] 31 32[5] 33[3] 34 35[3]

NUM. 16:36 37 38 39[2] 40 41 42[4] 43[2] 44 45 46[5] 47[5] 48[3] 49 50[2] 17:1 2 3 4 5[2] 6[3] 7 8[5] 9[3] 10[2] 11 12 18:1[5] 2[3] 3[3] 4[3] 5[2] 6 7[4] 8[2] 9[3] 11[3] 12[2] 13 15 16 17 18[2] 19[3] 20[2] 21 22 23 25 26 27[2] 28 30 31[2] 32 19:1[2] 2 3[2] 4[2] 5[3] 6[4] 7[3] 8[3] 9[3] 10[4] 12 13 14 15 16 17[2] 18[6] 19[6] 20 21[2] 22[2] 20:1[3] 2[3] 3[2] 4[2] 5 6[4] 7 8[6] 9 10[3] 11[5] 12[2] 13 14 15[3] 16[4] 18 19[3] 20[3] 22[2] 23[2] 25[2] 26[4] 27[2] 28[5] 29 21:1[2] 2[2] 3[5] 4[2] 5[3] 6[3] 7[3] 8[3] 9[3] 10[2] 11[2] 12 13[2] 14 15[2]

NUM. 21:16[2] 18 19[2] 20 21 23[4] 24[2] 25[3] 26 27 28 29 30 32[3] 33[4] 34[4] 35[3] 22:1[2] 2 3[2] 4[2] 5 6[2] 7[4] 8[3] 9[2] 10 11 12 13[2] 14[3] 15[2] 16[2] 17 18[3] 20[3] 21[3] 22[3] 23[5] 24 25[3] 26[2] 27[3] 28[2] 29 30[2] 31[4] 32 33[3] 34 35 36 37 38 39 40[4] 41[2] 23:1[3] 2[4] 3[4] 4[4] 5[3] 6[3] 7[3] 9[2] 10[2] 11[2] 12[2] 13[3] 14[4] 15 16[4] 17[3] 18[3] 19[2] 20[2] 21 23 24[2] 25 26 27 28 29[3] 30[3] 24:1 2[3] 3[3] 5 6 7[3] 8[3] 9[2] 10[4] 12 13 14[2] 15[3] 16 17[3] 18[2] 19 20[2] 21[4] 23[2] 24[4] 25[4] 25:1[2] 2[3] 3[2] 4[2] 5 6[3] 7[2] 8[3] 9[2] 10

NUM. 25:13[3] 15[2] 16 17 18 26:1[2] 2 3[2] 4[2] 7[4] 8 9[5] 10[4] 14[2] 18 19[3] 20 21 22[2] 25[2] 27 28 29 31[2] 32[2] 33[4] 34[3] 36 37[2] 40[3] 41[3] 43[2] 46 47[2] 50[3] 51[2] 52 54 56 57 58 59[4] 60[3] 61[2] 62[3] 63 64 65[2] 27:1[4] 2[4] 3[2] 5 6 7 8[2] 9 10 11[3] 12[2] 13 15 17[3] 18[2] 19[3] 20 21[3] 22[4] 23[2] 28:1 2[2] 3 4 5 7 8[2] 9[3] 10 11[2] 12[2] 13 14[3] 15[2] 16 17 19[2] 20[2] 22 24 25 28 30 31[2] 29:1 2[2] 3[2] 4 5 6[4] 7[2] 8 9[2] 11[3] 12[2] 13[2] 14 15 16[2] 17 18[2] 19[3] 20 21[3] 22[3] 23[2] 24[2] 25[2] 26[3]

NUM. 29:27[3] 28[2] 29[2] 30[3] 31[2] 32[2] 33[3] 34[2] 37[2] 38[2] 39[4] 40 30:1 3 4[4] 5 6 7[2] 8[2] 9 10 11[4] 12 13 16[2] 31:1 3[2] 6[2] 7[2] 8[3] 9[3] 10[2] 11[2] 12[5] 13[2] 14[2] 15 16 17 19[4] 20[4] 21 22[2] 23[2] 24[2] 25 26[3] 27[2] 28[4] 29 30[2] 31[2] 32[2] 33[2] 34[2] 35[2] 36[4] 37[2] 38[2] 39[3] 40[2] 41 42 43[2] 44[2] 45[2] 46 47[2] 48[2] 49[2] 50[2] 51[2] 52[3] 54[4] 32:1[3] 2[4] 3[2] 4 5 6[3] 7 9 10[2] 11[2] 12 13[2] 14 15 16[2] 17 20 21 22[4] 23 24[2] 25[2] 26 28[2] 29[3] 31[2] 33[4] 34[3] 35[3] 36[3] 37[3] 38[4] 39[3] 40[2] 41[3] 42[4] 33:1 2[2] 3 5[2] 6[2] 7[3] 8[4]

NUM. 33:9^6 10^2 11^2 12^2 13^2 14^2 15^2 16^2 17^2 18^2 19^2 20^2 21^2 22^2 23^2 24^2 25^2 26^2 27^2 28^2 29^2 30^2 31^2 32^2 33^2 34^2 35^2 36^2 37^2 38^2 39^3 40 41^2 42^2 43^2 44^2 45^2 46^2 47^2 48^2 49 50 51 52^3 53^2 54^3 55^2 34:1 2 3 4^5 5^2 6 7 8 9^2 10 11^3 12^2 13^2 14^2 15 16 17 18 19 20 22 24 25 26 27 28 35:1 2 3^4 4^2 5^5 6^3 7 8 9 10 12 13 14 15^2 16 17^2 18 23^2 24 25^3 27^2 32 33 36:1^3 2^2 3^2 4 5 8 11^3 12^2 13

DEU. 1:1^4 3 4 7^7 8^3 9 10 11 12^2 13^3

DEU. 1:14^2 15^6 16^4 17^2 18 19^3 20 21 22^5 23^2 24^4 25^4 27^2 28^3 31 33 34^3 36^2 39^4 40 41^3 42 43^2 44^3 45^2 2:1^2 2 4^2 6 8^3 9 10^2 12 13^2 14^2 16 19 20 21^4 22^2 23^2 24^3 25^3 26 28 29 30 31^2 32 33^4 34^4 35 36 3:1^3 2^4 3^2 4 5 6^2 7 8 9 10^3 11 12^4 13^2 14^2 15 16^3 17^2 18 19^2 20^2 21 23 24^2 25^2 26^2 27^5 28^3 4:1^3 5 6^4 8^2 9^3 10^2 11^4 12 13^2 14^2 16 19^5 20 21^2 22 23 25^5 26 27^2 28^2 29 30^2 32 33 34^6 36^2 37^2 38 39^2 40^3 42^2 43^2 44 45^2 46 47^2 49

DEU. 5:1^5 5^2 9 10^2 13 14 15^3 16^2 22^4 23^2 24^4 26 27^3 28^2 29^2 31^3 33^2 6:1 2^4 3^3 5^3 6 7^5 8^2 9^2 10^3 11^4 13^2 15 17^2 18^4 20^3 21 22^4 23 24 25 7:1^8 2^2 4 5^3 8^2 9^2 10 11^2 12^3 13^7 15^2 16 18 19^4 20 21 22^2 23 24^2 26 8:1^3 2^2 3^3 6 7^2 8^5 9 10 11^2 12^3 13^5 14 15^3 16 17^2 19^4 9:1^2 2^2 3^2 5^2 7 9 10^2 11^2 12 13 14^3 15^3 16^3 17^3 18^2 19 20^2 21^5 22^3 23^2 25 26^2 27 28 29^2 10:1^2 2^2 3^3 4^2 5^4 6^3 7 8 10^4 11^2 12^4 13 14 15 16 17^2 18^3 20^2 21^2

DEU. 10:22^2 11:1^4 2^3 3^3 4^3 5 6^6 8^2 9^3 10 11^2 13^3 14^3 15^2 16^3 17^4 18^2 19^3 20^2 21 22 23^2 24 25 26 28 29^2 31^2 32^2 12:1 2 3^5 5 6^8 7^3 9 10^2 11^3 12^6 14 15^3 18^6 20 21^2 22^2 23 25 26^2 27^4 28^3 29^2 30 31 13:1 2^2 3 4^5 5^2 6 9 10 11^3 13^2 14^4 15^2 16^4 17^4 14:2 4 5^6 6^3 7^2 8 9 10^2 12^2 13^3 14 15^4 16^2 17^3 18^4 19 23^4 24 25^2 26^4 27 28 29^6 15:2 6^2 8 9^4 10^2 11 12^2 13 14^2 15^2 16^2 17^3 18 19 20 21 22^2 16:1 2 4 7^4 8 10 11^9 12^3 13 14^8

DEU. 16:15 16^3 18^2 19 20 17:3^3 4^5 5 7 8^5 9^4 10^2 11 12^3 13^3 14^3 17 18 19^3 20^2 18:1^2 3^4 4^2 5 6^2 12 14 17 18^2 19 21 19:1^3 3 4 5^4 6^2 8^2 9 10 11^4 12^2 17 18^3 20^3 21 20:1^3 2^2 3^2 5^4 6^4 7^4 8^4 9 11^3 12 13 14^4 17^3 19 20^2 21:1 2^2 3^2 4^2 5^4 6 7^2 8^2 10^2 11^2 12^2 13^7 14 15^4 18^2 19^3 20^3 21^3 22^3 22:1 2^3 3^3 4 6 7^2 9 10 11 13^2 14^4 15^2 16^2 17^3 18^2 19^3 20 21 22 23^2 24^2 25^2 26 27^2 28^3 29 23:4^2 11 13^4 14^2 21 23 24:1^4 2^2 3^4 4 5 7^2

DEU. 24:8 11 12 13^2 14 15^2 18 19^2 20 21 22 25:1^2 2^2 3^2 5^4 6 7^2 8^3 9^4 10 11^3 13 14 15^2 16 18^3 26:1^3 2^2 3^2 4^2 5^6 6^3 7^4 8^5 9^3 10^3 11^4 12^3 13^3 14 15^3 16^3 17^5 18^2 19^4 27:1 2^2 3^2 4 5 6 7^3 8 9^3 10^2 11 12^5 13^4 14^2 15^3 16 17 18 19^2 20 21 22 23 24 25 26 28:1^2 2^2 3 4^2 5 6 7 8^2 9 10^2 11^3 12^3 13^5 14 15^2 16 17 18^2 19 20^2 22^7 23^2 24 25^2 26^3 27^3 28^2 29^5 30^3 31^3 32^4 33^3 35 36^3 37^2 38 39 41 42 43 44^2 45^3 46^3 47 48^4 51^2

DEU. 28:52^3 53^3 54^3 55 56^4 57^3 58 59^4 60 61 62 63^4 64^3 65^3 66^4 67^2 68^3 29:2^4 3 4^2 5^2 7^3 8^4 9 10 11 12 13^3 14 15 16 17^4 18^2 19 20^3 21 22^2 23^6 26^3 27 28^4 29 30:1^3 2^4 3^3 4 5^4 6^3 7^2 8^3 9^3 10^3 12^2 13^2 14 15^3 16^5 17^2 18 19^4 20^4 31:1^2 2^3 3^3 4^3 5 6 7^4 8 9^3 10 12^6 13^2 14^5 15^2 16^5 17^5 18 19 20^7 21^2 22 23^4 24 26 27^2 28^3 29^2 30 32:1^2 2 4^2 5 6^2 7^2 10 12 13^2 14^4 15^2 18 19^2 20 21 22^3 24^2 25^2 27^2 30^2 32 33 34 35^2 36^2 37 38^3 39^3

DEU. 32:40 41^2 42^3 43^3 44^3 45 46 47 48 49 50^3 33:1 2^3 3 5^2 6^2 7^4 8^3 9^2 10^2 11^2 12^3 13^2 14^2 15^2 16^4 17^3 18^2 19 20^2 21^3 22 23^3 24^2 25^2 26 27^3 28 29^3 34:1^2 2^4 3^2 4^2 6 7^2 8^2 9^3 10 11^3 12^2

JOSH. 1:2 4^2 6 7 8 9 11 12^3 13 14^2 15^2 16^2 18^2 2:1^4 2 3 4^3 5 6 7^2 8^2 9^3 10^2 11^2 12 13^6 14^3 15 16^3 17 18^4 19^3 20 21^4 22^4 23^4 24 3:1^5 2 3^3 4 5 6^4 7 8 9^2 10^8 13^2 14^2 15^2 16^4 17^2 4:1 3^3 5^2 7 8^3 9^2 10^2 11^2 12^3 14 15 18^3 19^2

JOSH. 4:20 21 5:1^2 2 3^2 4 6 7 8 9 10^2 11^2 12 13^5 14^4 15^2 6:1 2^3 3^3 4^3 5^4 6^3 7^3 8^3 9^3 10 11^2 12^2 13^4 14^2 15^2 16 17^3 18^3 19^3 20^3 21^6 22^2 23^8 24^5 25^4 26^3 27 7:1 2^5 3^4 4 5^4 6^4 7^2 9^4 10 11^4 13 14^3 15^3 16^2 17^4 18^2 19^3 20^4 21^5 22^3 23^4 24^13 25^3 26 8:1^5 2^4 3^3 4 5^3 7 8 9^3 10^4 11^5 12^3 13^2 14^4 15^3 16^3 17^3 18^2 19^6 20^4 21^4 22^3 23^2 24^3 25^2 27 28^2 29^4 31^2 32 33^6 34^2 35^2 9:1^5 2 3^2 4^6 5^5 6^3 7^2 8^3 9^2 10^2 11^3 12 13^4 14^2 15^3 16^2 17^5 18^2

JOSH. 9:21^2 22^2 23^3 24^3 25^2 26^2 27^3 10:1^5 2^2 3^3 4^2 5^4 6^3 7^2 8 9 10^5 11^3 12^2 13^3 14 15^2 16 17 18^2 19^2 20^2 21 22 23^3 24^4 25^2 26^4 27^4 28^5 29^2 30^4 31^4 32^3 33^2 34^4 35^3 36^3 37^6 38^3 39^7 40^4 41^2 42^2 43^2 11:1^3 2^4 3^7 4^3 5^2 6^2 7^2 8^5 9^2 10^3 11^2 12^4 14^2 15 16^6 17^3 20 21^4 22 23^2 12:1^2 2^3 3^3 4^2 5^5 6^4 7^2 8^7 24 13:1^4 2 3^2 4 5^2 6 7 8 9^2 10 11 12^2 13 15 16^3 17^3 18^3 19^3 20^3 21^6 23^3 24 25^3 26^3 27^5 28 29^2 30^2 31^3 14:1^3 2 3 4^2 5 6^2 7 9^2 10^4

JOSH. 14:11 12^2 13^2 15^2 15:2 3^6 4^2 5^2 6^3 7^4 8^2 9^3 10^4 11^5 12^2 13 14^3 15^2 16^2 17^2 18^3 19^2 21^3 22^3 23^3 24^2 25^3 26^2 27^3 28^3 29^2 30^3 31^3 32^5 33^3 34^3 35^2 36^4 37^2 38^3 39^2 40^2 41^3 42^2 43^3 44^3 45 47^4 48^3 49^2 50^3 51^3 52^2 53^3 54^3 55^2 56^3 57 58 59^3 60 61 62^3 16:1 2^2 3^3 4 5 6^3 7^4 8 9 10^2 17:1 2^5 3^3 4^3 5^2 6 7^2 9^2 10^4 11^13 14^2 15^3 16^4 17^3 18^3 18:1^3 2 3 4^5 5^2 6 7^3 8^6 9^4 10^2 11^3 12^4 13^2 14^3 15^3 16^4 17^4 18^2 19^2 20 21^2 22^3 23^3 24^3 25^2 26^3 27^3 28^3 19:1^2

JOSH. 19:2^3 3^3 4^3 5^3 6^3 7^3 8 10^2 11^4 12^3 13^2 14^2 15^5 17 18^3 19^3 20^3 21^4 22^4 23 24 25^4 26^5 27^5 28^4 29^4 30^3 33^4 34^5 35^3 36^3 37^3 38^4 39 40 41^3 42^3 43^3 44^3 45^3 46^2 47^6 50^2 51^2 20:3^2 4^3 5^2 6^4 7^3 8^3 9^2 21:1^2 2 3^2 4^4 5^3 6^4 7^2 8 9^2 11 12 13 14^2 15^2 16^3 17 18 20 21 22^2 23 25^2 27^2 28 30 31 32^3 34^2 36^2 37 38^2 41 43^3 44^2 22:1^2 2^2 4^3 5^6 6^2 7 8^6 9^4 10^3 11^3 12 13^3 14^2 15^4 18 19 20^2 21^3 22 24 25^2 27^4 28 29 30^5 31^3 32^4 33^4 34^2 23:1^2 2^7 3

JOSH. 23:5^3 6 9 12^4 13^3 14^4 16^4 24:1^6 2^3 3^4 4^4 5^3 6^4 7^6 8^4 9^3 11^9 12 13^4 14^5 15^2 16^2 17^4 18 19 20^3 21 22^2 23 24^2 25^2 26^3 27 29^2 30 31^3 32^2 33^2

JUD. 1:2 3^2 4^4 5^4 6^4 7^5 8^3 9^3 10^4 11^2 12^2 13^2 14^3 15^3 16^3 17^4 18^2 19^2 20^2 21 22^2 23 24^3 25^2 26^3 27^5 28^2 30 33 34 35 36^2 2:1^4 2 3 4^2 5^2 6 7^2 8^2 9 10^2 11^2 12^4 13^3 14^3 15^2 17^2 18^3 19^3 20^3 3:3^3 4 5^5 6^3 7^4 8^2 9 10^5 11^2 12^2 13^5 15 16 17^2 18 19^2 20^4 21^3 22^3 23^2 24 25^4 26^3 27^3 28^4 29^3

JUD. 3:30 31^2 4:1 2 3^2 4 5^3 6^6 7^3 8 9^3 10^4 11 12 13^2 14^2 15^4 16^3 17 18^3 19^4 20^3 21^5 22^5 24^2 5:1 4 6 10 12 14 15^2 17^2 18 19 25 26^3 28 31 6:1^2 2^4 3^3 4^3 5^4 6^2 7 8 9^4 10 11^3 12^2 13^3 14^3 15^2 16^2 17 18^3 19^6 20^5 21^5 22 23 24 25^3 26^3 27^3 28^3 29^3 30 31 33^4 34^2 35^5 36 37^2 38^3 39^3 40^2 7:1^2 2 3^5 4^4 5 6 7^3 8^4 9 11^2 12^4 13^6 14^3 15^4 16^3 17^3 18^3 19^4 20^6 21^4 22^4 23^4 24^5 25^7 8:1^2 2 3^2 4^3 5^3 6^2 7^3 8^3 9 10^3 11^3 12^5 13 14^5 15^4

JUD. 8:16^4 17^2 18^2 19 20^2 21^5 22^2 23 24 25^3 26^5 27^4 28 29^2 30^2 31 32^2 33^3 34 9:1^3 2^2 3^2 4^3 5^3 6^4 7^5 8 9^2 10^2 11^2 12 13^3 14 15^4 16^4 17^2 18^4 19^3 20^5 21^4 23^2 24^3 25^3 26^3 27^8 28^3 29^3 30 31^3 32^2 33^4 34^3 35^4 36^2 37^3 38 39^2 40^4 41^3 42^2 43^7 44^5 45^5 46 47 48^8 49^5 50^2 51^5 52^3 53^2 54^4 55 57^2 10:1^2 2^4 3^3 4^2 5 6^10 7^3 8^2 9^2 10^2 11^3 12^4 13 14 15 16^3 17^3 18^2 11:1^2 2^4 3^3 4 5 6^2 7^3 8^3 9^2 10 11^3 12 13^2 14 15 16^2 17^2 18^4 19^2 20^2 21^3 22^2 23 25 26^4

JUD. 11:27 29^4 30^2 31 32 33^2 34^4 35^4 37^4 38^4 39^4 12:1^4 2^3 3^3 4^3 5^2 6^4 7^2 8 9^3 10 11^2 12^2 13 14^4 15^2 13:1^2 2^3 3^4 4^2 5^3 6^2 7^2 8^2 9^2 10^4 11^5 12^2 13 15 16^2 17 18 19^4 20^2 21 22 23 24^4 25^2 14:1^2 2^4 3^2 4 5^4 6^3 7^3 8^4 9^6 10 11 12^3 13^2 14^3 15^2 16^6 17^3 18^3 19^7 15:1 2 3 4^5 5^4 6^5 7^2 8^4 9^2 10^2 11^2 12^2 13 14^4 15^4 16 17^2 18^5 19^3 20 16:1^2 2^4 3^8 4 5^5 6^2 7^2 8 9^2 10^2 11^2 12^4 13^3 14^5 15^2 16^2 17^3 18^3 19^5 20^5 21^4 23 24^2 25^4 26 27^4 28^3 29^3

JUD. 16:30^4 31^6 17:1 2^3 3^2 4^4 5^4 7^2 8^2 9^3 10^6 11^2 12^3 18:1 2^4 3^4 4^4 5 6 7^6 8^3 9^4 10 11^2 12^2 13^2 14^4 15^3 16 17^7 18^4 19^5 20^5 21^4 22^2 23^3 24^5 25^2 26^3 27^6 28^5 29 30^3 31 19:1 2^3 3^6 4^4 5^3 6^5 7 8^4 9^4 10^3 11^4 12 13^2 14^3 15^3 16^2 17^3 18^3 19^5 20 21^4 22^2 23^2 24^3 25^4 26 27^5 28^4 29^4 30^2 20:1 2 4^2 5^4 6^4 7 8 10^3 12 13 15^2 16 17 18^5 19^2 20^2 21^3 22^2 23^4 24 25^2 26^7 27 28^2 29 30^2 31^5 32^2 33^3 34^2 35^4 37^4 38 39^2 40 41 42 43^2 44 45^5 46 47^2 48^3

JUD. 21:2^4 3 4^4 5 6^2 8^2 9 10^4 11^2 12^3 13^2 14^3 15 17 19 20 21^4 22 23^6 24^3

RUTH 1:1^3 2^6 3^3 4^2 5^4 7^2 8^2 9^2 10 11 12 14^3 15^2 16^2 17^3 19^2 20 21^2 22^2 2:1^2 2^3 3^4 4^3 6^2 7^3 9^3 10^2 11^6 12 13 14^6 15^2 16^3 17^2 18^5 19^6 20^3 21 22 23^3 3:2 3^4 4^5 5 6^2 7^6 8^3 9^2 10 11 12 13 14^3 15^4 16^2 17 4:1^4 2^3 3 4^4 6 7^3 9^4 10 11^5 12 13^3 14 15^2 16^3 17^2 19^2 20^2 21^2 22^2

1 SAM. 1:1 2^3 3^4 4^3 6 7^2 8^2 9 10^3 11^5 12 14 15^2 16 17^2 18^3 19^6 20

1 SAM. 1:21[3], 22[2], 23[2], 24[5], 25[2], 26, 27, 28, 2:1[2], 3, 4, 5[2], 6[2], 7[2], 8[3], 9, 10[2], 11[2], 13, 14, 15, 16[3], 19, 20[3], 21[4], 22[2], 23, 26[3], 27[2], 28[2], 29[2], 30[2], 31, 32[2], 33[3], 34[2], 35[4], 36[4], 3:1, 2[2], 3[2], 4, 5[5], 6[5], 8[5], 9[2], 10[3], 11, 13, 14, 15[3], 16[2], 17[2], 18[3], 19[3], 20, 21, 4:1[3], 2[3], 3, 4[2], 5, 6[2], 7[2], 9[2], 10[4], 11[3], 12[3], 13[3], 14[3], 15[2], 16[3], 17[6], 18[5], 19[5], 20, 21[3], 22, 5:1[2], 2, 3[3], 4[2], 6[3], 7[2], 8[4], 10[2], 11[4], 12[2], 6:1, 2[2], 3[2], 4[2], 5[4], 6[2], 7[3], 8[4], 9, 10[4], 11[3], 12[4], 13[4], 14[4], 15[5], 16, 17, 18[2], 19[4], 20[3], 21[2], 7:1[4], 2[2], 3[5], 4[2], 5[2], 6[6], 7[2], 8

1 SAM. 7:9[4], 10[3], 11[3], 12[3], 13[2], 14[4], 15, 16[4], 17[3], 8:1, 2, 3[3], 4, 5[2], 6, 7, 8, 9, 10, 11[4], 12[6], 13[3], 14[4], 15[4], 16[5], 17, 18[2], 19, 20[3], 21[2], 22[3], 9:2[4], 3[3], 4[4], 5[3], 6[2], 7, 8[2], 9, 11[2], 12[2], 13, 14[2], 16, 17, 18, 19[4], 20[3], 21[3], 22[4], 23, 24[5], 25, 26[5], 27[2], 10:1[3], 2[3], 3[4], 4[2], 5[5], 6[3], 7, 8[4], 9[2], 10[3], 11, 12[2], 13, 14[4], 15, 16, 17, 18[4], 19[4], 20, 21[2], 22, 23[4], 24[3], 25[2], 26[2], 27[2], 11:1[3], 2[2], 3[2], 4[3], 5[3], 6[2], 7[6], 8[2], 9[4], 10, 11[4], 12, 13, 14[2], 15[5], 12:1[2], 2[5], 3[2], 4, 5[3], 6[3], 7[3], 8[3], 9[4], 10[5], 11[6], 12, 13[2], 14[4], 16, 17[3], 18[4], 19, 20, 21

1 SAM. 12:23, 24, 25, 13:1, 2[3], 3[2], 4[3], 5[5], 6[4], 7[3], 8[2], 9[3], 10[2], 11[4], 12[2], 13, 14, 15[3], 16[3], 17, 18[2], 20[3], 21[4], 22[2], 23, 14:1, 2[2], 3[2], 4[4], 5, 6[2], 7, 8, 9, 10, 11[2], 12[5], 13[5], 14[2], 15[4], 16[3], 17[3], 18, 19[3], 20[5], 21, 23, 24, 25[2], 26, 27[3], 28[2], 31[2], 32[6], 33, 34[8], 35, 36[4], 37, 38[3], 40[3], 41[2], 42[3], 43[3], 44[2], 45, 46, 47[6], 48[3], 49[4], 50[2], 51[2], 52[2], 15:3[7], 4[3], 5[2], 6, 7, 8[2], 9[8], 11[3], 12[5], 13[2], 14[2], 15[3], 16[2], 17[2], 18[4], 19, 20[4], 21, 22[3], 23[2], 24[3], 25, 26[2], 27[2], 28[2], 29, 30[2], 31, 32[2], 33[2], 34, 35[2], 16:1[2], 2[3], 3[3], 4[4], 5[5], 6[2], 8[2], 9, 10, 11[5], 12[5], 13[3]

1 SAM. 16:14, 15, 16[2], 17[2], 18[6], 19, 20[4], 21[4], 22, 23[4], 17:1[3], 2[4], 3[3], 4[2], 5[3], 6[2], 7[3], 8[5], 9[3], 10, 11[2], 12[2], 13[5], 14[2], 15, 16[3], 17[3], 18[3], 19[2], 20[6], 21, 22[4], 23[3], 24[2], 25[4], 26[2], 27, 28[5], 29, 30[3], 31[2], 32[2], 33[2], 34[4], 35[6], 36[2], 37[3], 38[2], 39[4], 40[5], 41[3], 42[4], 43[2], 44[3], 45[2], 46[4], 47[3], 48[4], 49[5], 50[3], 51[6], 52[7], 53[2], 54[2], 55[2], 56, 57[2], 58[2], 18:1[2], 2[2], 3, 4[5], 5[5], 6[3], 7[3], 8[5], 9[2], 10[4], 11[2], 12[2], 13[3], 14[2], 16[2], 17[2], 18[2], 20[3], 21[2], 22[3], 23[3], 24, 25, 26[2], 27[6], 28[3], 29[2], 30, 19:1[2], 2[3], 3[4], 4[3], 5[3], 6[2], 7[4], 8[5], 9[2], 10[4], 11[2], 12[3], 13[4], 14, 15, 16, 17[3], 18[6], 19, 20[4], 21[4]

1 SAM. 19:22[5], 23[4], 24[4], 20:1[4], 2[2], 3[5], 5[2], 9, 11[3], 12[4], 13[3], 14, 17, 18, 19[3], 20, 21[2], 23[3], 24, 25[4], 27[2], 28, 29[4], 30[2], 31, 32[2], 33, 34, 35[2], 36[2], 37[2], 38[3], 39, 40[2], 41[5], 42[7], 21:1[3], 2[5], 4[2], 5[4], 7, 8[2], 9[2], 10[3], 11[2], 12[2], 13[4], 22:1[3], 2[5], 3[4], 4[2], 5[3], 6[2], 7[3], 8[2], 9, 10[3], 11[2], 12[2], 13[4], 14[4], 16[2], 17[4], 18[6], 19[6], 20[2], 21, 22, 23:1, 2[4], 3, 4[2], 5[4], 6, 7[3], 8[2], 9[2], 11, 12[2], 13[5], 14[3], 15[2], 16[3], 17[4], 18[3], 20, 21, 22[3], 23[4], 24[3], 25[4], 26[6], 27, 28, 29[2], 24:1, 2[2], 3[4], 4[2], 5, 6, 7[2], 8[4], 9, 10[2], 11[3], 12[2], 15[5], 16[3], 17, 18, 20[2], 21, 22[3], 25:1[6], 2[5], 3[5]

1 SAM. 25:4, 5[4], 6[3], 7, 8[2], 9[2], 10[3], 11[3], 12[3], 13[5], 14, 15, 16, 17[2], 18[7], 19, 20[4], 21, 22, 23[4], 24[4], 25, 26[3], 27, 28, 29[2], 30[2], 32, 33[3], 34, 35[2], 36[3], 37[2], 38, 39[4], 40, 41[3], 42[5], 43, 26:1, 2, 3[2], 4, 5[6], 6[3], 7[4], 8, 9[2], 10, 11[2], 12[3], 13, 14[3], 15[2], 16[2], 17[3], 18, 21, 22[4], 23, 24[2], 25[2], 27:1[2], 2[2], 3[3], 4[2], 5, 7[2], 8[5], 9[9], 10[4], 11[2], 12, 28:1[3], 2[2], 3[4], 4[5], 5[2], 6, 7[2], 8[7], 9[2], 10, 11, 12[2], 13[2], 14[6], 15[4], 16, 17[2], 19[2], 20[2], 21[5], 22[2], 23[3], 24[6], 25[4], 29:1, 2[3], 3[2], 4[3], 5, 6[3], 7, 8[2], 9[2], 10[2], 11[2], 30:1[5], 2[2], 3[5], 4[2], 5[2], 6[2], 7[2], 8[3], 9[2]

1 SAM. 30:10, 11[5], 12[4], 13[4], 14[3], 15[3], 16[4], 17[3], 18[2], 19, 20[3], 21[4], 22[4], 23, 25[2], 26, 27[2], 28[3], 29[3], 30[3], 31[3], 31:1[2], 2[5], 3[3], 4[4], 5[2], 6[3], 7[7], 8[2], 9[4], 10[2], 11, 12[5], 13[3]

2 SAM. 1:1, 2[3], 3[2], 4[6], 5[2], 6[3], 7[3], 8[2], 9, 10[4], 11[2], 12[6], 13[2], 14, 15[4], 16, 17[2], 19[2], 22, 23[3], 27, 2:1[4], 2[2], 3[2], 4[3], 5[3], 6[3], 7[2], 8, 9[6], 10, 11[2], 12[2], 13[5], 14[3], 15[2], 16[2], 17[3], 18[4], 19[2], 20[2], 21[3], 22, 23[4], 24[2], 25[3], 26, 27, 28[2], 29[5], 30[3], 31[2], 32[5], 3:1[4], 2[2], 3[2], 4, 5, 6[2], 7[2], 8[3], 9, 10[2], 11, 12[2], 13, 14, 15[2], 16[2], 17, 18, 19[3], 20[3], 21[6], 22[4], 23[3], 24[2], 25[3], 26, 27[2], 28[2]

2 SAM. 3:29[2], 30, 31[5], 32[4], 33[2], 34, 35[2], 36[2], 37, 38[2], 39[2], 4:1[2], 2[2], 3[2], 4[7], 5[3], 6[4], 7[5], 8[4], 9[3], 10, 11, 12[6], 5:1[2], 2[3], 3[2], 4, 5[4], 6[3], 8[6], 9[3], 10[3], 11[5], 12[2], 13[4], 14[4], 15[3], 16[3], 17[2], 18, 19[2], 20[3], 21[3], 22[2], 23[2], 24, 25, 6:2[2], 3[4], 4[2], 5[6], 6[2], 7[3], 8[2], 9[2], 11[3], 12[3], 13[2], 14[2], 15[2], 16[4], 17[4], 18[2], 19[3], 20[2], 21[2], 22[3], 7:1[2], 3, 4, 5, 6, 9[3], 10[2], 11[2], 12[3], 13, 14[2], 16[2], 17, 18[3], 19[2], 20, 21, 23[5], 24, 25, 26[2], 28[3], 29, 8:1[3], 2[5], 4[4], 5[2], 6[3], 7[2], 8[2], 9, 10[5], 11, 12[5], 13, 14[3], 15[3], 16[2], 17[3], 18[3], 9:1, 2[3], 3[2], 4[2], 5, 6[3], 7[3], 8[2], 9[2], 10[4]

2 SAM. 9:12[2], 13, 10:1[2], 2, 3[3], 4[3], 5[2], 6[5], 7[2], 8[6], 9[2], 10, 11[2], 12[3], 13[3], 14[3], 15, 16[4], 17[5], 18[4], 19[2], 11:1[5], 2[4], 3[3], 4[5], 5[4], 6[2], 7[3], 8[4], 9, 10, 11[8], 12[3], 13[4], 14[2], 15[3], 16, 17[4], 18, 19, 20, 22[2], 23[3], 24[3], 25[2], 26, 27[2], 12:1[2], 2, 3[3], 4[4], 5[2], 6[2], 7[2], 8[6], 9[2], 10, 11[3], 12, 13, 15, 16[3], 17[2], 18[3], 19, 20[7], 21[2], 22[2], 24[6], 25[2], 26[2], 27[3], 28[3], 29[4], 30[3], 31[7], 13:1[2], 2[2], 3, 4[2], 5[5], 6[3], 7, 8[5], 9[4], 10[4], 11[2], 12, 13[2], 14, 15, 16, 17[2], 18[2], 19[4], 20, 22, 23[2], 24[3], 25[2], 26, 37, 28[2], 29[3], 30[2], 31[3], 32[2], 34[3], 35, 36[5], 37[2], 38[2], 39, 14:2[5], 3[2], 4[3], 5[3]

2 SAM. 14:6[4], 7[5], 8[2], 9[4], 10[2], 11, 12, 13, 14, 15, 16, 17, 18[2], 19[4], 20, 21, 22[4], 23[2], 24[3], 26, 27[2], 28, 29, 30[3], 31[2], 32[2], 33[4], 15:1[3], 2[5], 3[2], 4, 5[3], 6, 7[2], 9[2], 11[3], 12[2], 13, 14[4], 15, 16[3], 17[3], 18[4], 19[2], 20[3], 21[3], 22[5], 23[3], 24[4], 25[3], 27[2], 29, 30[6], 31[2], 32[2], 34, 35[3], 36[2], 37, 16:1[5], 2[5], 3[3], 4, 5[2], 6[5], 7[2], 8[2], 9, 10, 11[3], 12, 13[5], 14[3], 15[3], 16, 17, 18[4], 19, 21[2], 22, 23[2], 17:1[2], 2[5], 3, 4[2], 5, 6, 7, 8[4], 9, 10[2], 11, 12[3], 13, 14[2], 15[5], 16[2], 17[5], 18[2], 19[4], 20[5], 21[5], 22[2], 23[7], 24[2], 25, 26, 27[3], 28[9], 29[7], 18:1[3], 2[4], 4[4], 5[4], 6, 7, 9[7]

2 SAM. 18:10[3], 11[5], 12[3], 13, 14[2], 15[3], 16[2], 17[4], 18[3], 19, 20, 21[2], 22, 23[2], 24[5], 25[5], 26[4], 27[3], 28[4], 29[3], 30[4], 31[2], 32[3], 33[4], 19:1[2], 2, 3, 4, 5[5], 6[2], 7[2], 8[3], 9[3], 10, 11[2], 12, 13[3], 14, 15, 16[2], 17[5], 18[3], 19, 21, 23, 24[2], 25, 26[2], 27, 29[2], 30, 31[2], 32, 33[2], 34, 35[3], 36, 37[3], 38[3], 39[4], 40[3], 41[5], 42, 43[4], 20:1[3], 2, 3[4], 4, 6[3], 7[5], 8[3], 9[2], 10[4], 11[3], 12[3], 14[5], 15[5], 17[3], 18, 19[2], 20[2], 21[2], 22[5], 23[2], 24[2], 25[3], 26, 21:1[3], 2[5], 3, 4[2], 5[2], 6[2], 7, 8[2], 9[4], 10[3], 11, 12[3], 13[3], 14[4], 15[4], 16, 17[2], 18, 19, 20[4], 21, 22[2], 22:1[2], 2[3], 3[2], 7[3], 8[2], 9, 10[2], 11[3]

2 SAM. 22:12[2], 14, 15[3], 16, 18, 22, 23, 24, 26, 27, 28, 29, 32, 33[2], 34, 36, 38[2], 39[2], 43, 46, 47[2], 48, 49, 50, 51[2], 23:1[2], 2, 4, 5[2], 7[2], 9[2], 10[4], 11[3], 12[3], 13[3], 14[2], 15[2], 16[4], 17, 18[4], 20[2], 21[4], 22, 23, 39, 24:1[3], 2, 3[2], 4[3], 5[3], 6[3], 7[4], 8, 9[3], 10[3], 12, 13[3], 14[2], 15, 16[3], 17[4], 18[2], 19, 20[5], 21[2], 22[4], 23, 24[2], 25[4]

1 KINGS 1:1[2], 2[3], 3[2], 4[3], 5[3], 6[3], 7[3], 8[5], 9[5], 10[3], 11[2], 12, 13[3], 14, 15[3], 16[3], 17[2], 18[2], 19[6], 20, 21, 22, 23, 24, 25[9], 26[3], 27, 28[3], 29[2], 30, 31[2], 32[4], 33[2], 34[4], 35[3], 36[2], 37, 38[6], 39[4], 40[3], 41[3], 42[3], 43[2], 44[6], 45[3], 46

1 KINGS 1:47[3], 48, 49[3], 50[4], 51, 52, 53[4], 2:1, 2, 3[5], 4, 5[5], 6, 7, 8[2], 9, 10, 11[3], 12, 13[3], 14, 15[3], 16[2], 17, 18, 19[5], 20, 21, 22[5], 23, 24[2], 25[2], 26[2], 28[2], 29[2], 30[5], 31[4], 32[4], 33[4], 34[3], 35[2], 36[5], 37, 38[2], 39, 40[5], 41[2], 42[6], 43, 45[2], 46[2], 3:1[5], 3[2], 4, 5, 6[4], 7[2], 8, 9, 10, 11[2], 12, 13[2], 14[2], 15[7], 16, 17[3], 18[2], 19, 20[4], 21, 22[4], 23[3], 24[2], 25[3], 26[2], 27[2], 28[2], 4:2, 3, 4[3], 5[3], 6[2], 7[2], 8, 9[3], 10, 12[2], 16, 19[2], 20[3], 21[3], 22[2], 23[5], 24, 25[3], 26[2], 27[2], 28, 29[3], 30[2], 31[4], 32[3], 33[4], 34, 5:1, 2, 5, 6, 7[2], 8[3], 9[4], 10, 11[2], 12[4], 13, 14[3]

1 KINGS 5:15[3], 16, 17[3], 18[4], 6:1[2], 2[3], 3[2], 4, 5[3], 6[2], 7, 8[2], 9[3], 10[2], 11, 12[2], 13[2], 14, 15[4], 16[2], 17, 18[2], 19, 20[5], 21[2], 22, 23, 24[2], 25[2], 26, 27[4], 28, 29[4], 30[2], 31[2], 32[6], 34[2], 35[4], 36[2], 38[2], 7:1, 2[2], 3, 4[2], 5[3], 6[5], 7, 8, 9[2], 10[2], 11[2], 12[3], 13[2], 14[6], 15, 16[2], 17[3], 18[3], 19, 20[2], 21[5], 22, 23[3], 24, 25[5], 26[2], 27[3], 28[2], 29[5], 30[3], 31[4], 32[4], 33[4], 34[2], 35[3], 36[3], 37, 38[2], 39[3], 40[3], 41[2], 42, 43[2], 44[2], 45[4], 46, 47, 48[2], 49[4], 50[7], 51[3], 8:1, 2, 3[2], 4[4], 5[3], 6, 7[2], 8[3], 9, 14[3], 15[2], 17, 18, 20[4], 21, 22[2], 23, 24, 26, 27, 28[2], 29, 30[4], 31[2], 32[3], 33[4]

1 KINGS 8:34[2], 35[3], 36[3], 38[2], 39[3], 42[3], 43[2], 44[2], 45[2], 46[2], 47[3], 48[4], 49[2], 50[3], 51, 52, 54, 55, 58[3], 59[3], 60, 61, 62[2], 63[5], 64[4], 65[3], 66[4], 9:1[3], 3[4], 4[4], 6[4], 7[3], 8[4], 9[4], 10[2], 11[2], 12[2], 13[2], 14, 15[7], 16[4], 17[2], 18[2], 19[6], 20[2], 22[5], 23, 25[3], 26, 27, 28[4], 10:1, 2[4], 3, 4[2], 5[6], 6[2], 7[3], 8, 9, 10[4], 11[2], 12[3], 13[3], 14, 15[3], 16, 17[2], 18, 19[3], 20[2], 21[2], 22[3], 23, 24, 25[6], 26[6], 27, 28[2], 29[6], 11:1, 3[3], 4, 5, 6[2], 7, 8[2], 9, 10, 11[3], 13, 14, 15, 17, 18[6], 19, 20[2], 21[2], 22, 23, 24[5], 25[3], 26, 27[2], 28[2], 29[3], 30[2], 31[2], 32, 33[5], 34, 35, 36, 37[3], 38[6], 39, 40[3]

1 KINGS 11:41[3], 42, 43[3], 12:1, 2[2], 3[4], 4[2], 5[2], 6[2], 7[4], 8[2], 9, 10, 11, 12, 13[2], 14[2], 18, 20[3], 21[2], 23[3], 24, 25[3], 26, 27[2], 28[2], 29[2], 30, 31[2], 32[3], 33[3], 13:1[2], 2[4], 3[2], 4[2], 5, 6[6], 7[3], 8, 10, 11[2], 12, 13[2], 14[4], 15, 16, 18[2], 19[2], 20, 21[2], 22[3], 23[2], 24[4], 25[5], 26[2], 27[2], 28[4], 29[5], 30[2], 31, 32, 33, 34[2], 14:2[3], 3[4], 4[4], 5[2], 6, 7, 8[4], 9[3], 10[4], 11, 12, 13[2], 15[2], 16[2], 17[4], 18[2], 19[2], 20[4], 21[4], 22[2], 23[3], 24[2], 25, 26[3], 27[2], 28[2], 29, 30[2], 31[4], 15:2, 3[2], 4, 5, 6[2], 7[3], 8[3], 9, 10[3], 11, 12[2], 13[3], 15[4], 16[2], 17[2], 18[4], 19[5], 20[5], 21[2], 22[4], 23[3], 24[3], 25[2], 26[3], 27[3]

1 KINGS 15:28, 29, 30, 31, 32[2], 33, 34[3], 16:2[3], 3[2], 4, 5, 6[2], 7[3], 8, 9, 10[5], 11, 13[2], 14, 15[2], 16[2], 17[3], 18[3], 19, 20, 21, 22, 23, 24[3], 25, 26, 27, 28[2], 29[4], 30, 31[4], 32, 33[2], 34, 17:1, 2, 3[2], 4[2], 5[2], 6[5], 7, 8, 9, 10[4], 11[2], 12[6], 13[5], 15[5], 16, 17[2], 18[2], 19[4], 20[2], 21[3], 22[3], 23[4], 24[2], 18:1[2], 2[2], 3, 4[3], 5[3], 6, 7[4], 8, 9, 10[2], 11, 12[4], 13[2], 14[2], 15, 16[2], 17, 18[3], 19[4], 20, 21[3], 22, 23[7], 24[5], 25[3], 26[4], 27[3], 28[3], 29[2], 30[3], 31, 32[2], 33[6], 34[4], 35[2], 36[5], 37, 38[5], 39[2], 40[4], 41[2], 42[4], 43[5], 44[3], 45[5], 46[3], 19:1[2], 2, 3[4], 4[4], 5[4], 6[6], 7[4], 8[5], 9[4]

1 KINGS 19:10[4], 11[7], 12[2], 13[5], 14[4], 15[2], 16[2], 17[2], 18, 19[2], 20[6], 21[8], 20:1[8], 2[2], 3[2], 4[3], 5[5], 6[4], 7[6], 8[2], 9[2], 10[3], 11[2], 12[3], 13[2], 14[3], 15[3], 16[3], 17[3], 18, 19, 20[4], 21[4], 22[4], 23[2], 24[2], 25[6], 26[2], 27[4], 28[4], 29[3], 30[4], 31[3], 32[4], 33[3], 34[3], 35[3], 36[3], 37[2], 38[3], 39[5], 40[3], 41[3], 42[2], 43[3], 21:1, 2[2], 3, 4[5], 5, 6[3], 7[3], 8[3], 9[2], 10[4], 11[3], 12, 13[5], 14, 15[2], 16, 17, 19[3], 20[2], 21[4], 22[3], 23, 24, 26, 27[6], 28, 22:1[2], 2, 3[3], 4[3], 5, 6[2], 7, 8[3], 9, 10[3], 11[2], 12[2], 13[2], 14, 15[3], 16, 17[2], 18, 19[3], 20[4], 21[3], 22[6], 23, 24[2], 25, 26[3], 27[3], 28[2], 29, 30[4], 31, 32[3], 33, 34[3], 35[4], 36

1 KINGS

22:37^2 38^3 39^3 40 41 42^4 43^2 44 45^2 46 50^3 51 52^4 53^2

2 KINGS

1:2^4 3 4 5 6^3 7^2 8^3 9^3 10^7 11^2 12^7 13^7 14 15^3 16 17 2:1 2^3 3^3 4^3 5^3 6^4 7^3 8^5 9^2 10 11^5 12^6 13^2 14^6 15^3 16^4 17^2 18 19^2 20^3 21^3 23^4 24^6 25^2 3:1 2^2 4^3 6^2 7^4 8^2 9^5 10 11^2 12^3 13^3 14 15 16 17^2 18 19^5 20^2 21^3 22^3 23^2 24^2 25^6 26 27^4 4:1^2 2^2 4^4 5^3 6^3 7^5 8^3 9 10^5 11^3 12^2 13^2 14^3 15^2 16^2 17^2 18 19^2 20^3 21^4 22^4 23^2 24^2 25^2 26^2 27^4 29^4 30^4 31^3 32^2 33 34 35^6 36^3 37^4 38^5

2 KINGS

4:39^5 40^3 41^3 42^4 43^2 44^2 5:1 2^3 3 4^3 5^6 6 7^4 8^2 9^2 10^4 11^6 12^3 13^3 14^3 15^5 16 17 18^2 19 20 21^2 22^2 23^5 24^4 25^3 26^8 27 6:1 2^3 3^3 4 5^2 6^5 7^2 8^2 9 10^3 11^2 12 13^4 14^4 15^4 16 17^6 18^3 19^2 20^4 21 22^5 23^4 24^3 25^3 26 27 28^3 29^3 30^4 31 32^3 33^2 7:1 2^2 3^2 4^4 5^2 6^3 7^5 8^{13} 9^2 10^5 11^2 12^3 13^4 14^2 15^5 16^3 17^3 18^2 19^3 20^2 8:1^4 2^4 3^3 4 5^4 6^2 7^3 8^3 9^4 10 11^2 12^5 13^2 14^2 15^4 16 17^2 18^2 19 20 21^5 23^2 24^3 26^3 27^2 28^2 29^2 9:1^4 2^4 3^4 5^4

2 KINGS

9:6^4 7^2 8^3 9^2 10^4 11^3 12^3 13^3 14 15 16^2 17^6 18^3 19^2 20^3 21^6 22^3 23^3 24^4 25^2 26^3 27^5 28^2 29 30^4 31 32^3 33^4 34^4 35^3 36^2 37 10:1^4 2^3 3^3 4 5^4 6^2 7^4 8^3 9^4 11^3 12^4 13^4 14^4 15^6 16^2 17 18^2 19 20^2 21^4 22^2 23^4 24^3 25^7 26^2 27^3 29 30^2 32 33^3 34^2 35^3 36^2 11:1^2 2^3 3^2 4^7 5 6^2 7 8^4 9^3 10^2 11^2 12^7 13^2 14^7 15^2 16^3 17^4 18^5 19^7 20^3 12:1^2 2 3 4^2 5 6 7^2 8 9^3 10^4 11^3 12^5 14 16 17^3 18^8 19 20^3 21^4 13:1^2 2^2 3^3 4^2 5^2 6 7^3 8^2 9^3 10^2 11 12^3 13^3

2 KINGS

13:14^4 15^4 16^3 17^5 18^5 19^2 20^3 21^5 23^5 24 25^2 14:2^4 3 4 5 7^2 9^3 10^3 11^2 12^2 13^3 14^6 15^2 16^3 17 18 19^2 20^2 21^2 22 23^2 24 27 28^4 29^2 15:1 2^3 3 4 5^3 6^2 7^2 8 9 10^4 11 12 13^2 14^4 15^2 16^3 17^2 18 19^2 20^2 21^2 22^2 23 24 25^5 26^2 27^2 28 29^8 30^4 31^2 33^3 34 35 36 37 38^3 16:2^2 3 4^4 5^2 6^3 7^3 8^4 9^4 10^4 11 12^2 13^4 14^3 15^9 17^4 18^2 20^3 17:2 3^2 4^3 5^2 6^4 7 8^2 9^2 10^3 11^2 13^5 15^6 16^5 17^5 18 20^3 21^3 24^8 25 26^2 27^3 28^2 29 30^3 31^4 32 33 34

2 KINGS

17:35 36^3 37^5 38 39 41^2 18:2^3 3 4^4 6 7^4 8 9^2 10 11^4 12^2 13 14^3 15^2 16^2 17^7 18^3 19 20 21 22^3 23 24 25 26^3 27^2 28^2 30 31^4 32^6 34^2 37^3 19:1^3 2^2 3^4 4 6 7^3 8 11 12^3 13^3 14^4 15^3 16^3 17 18^2 21 22^3 23^5 24^2 25 26^3 27^3 28^3 29^6 30^2 31 33 34 35^4 36^3 37^4 20:1^3 2 3^3 4 5 6^5 7^4 8^2 9 10 11^2 12 13^7 14^3 15^2 16 17 18^2 19^2 20^5 21^2 21:1^3 2 3^4 4 5 6^5 7^3 8 9 10 11^2 12 13^4 14^4 15 17^2 18^3 19^3 20 21^3 22^2 23^2 24^2 26^2 22:1^3 2^3 3 5^2

2 KINGS

22:6^4 8^3 9^4 10^2 11 12^5 13^2 14^5 15 16 17^2 19^5 20^3 23:1^3 2^8 3^7 4^7 5^5 6^4 7 8^3 10 11^2 12^4 13^3 14^3 15^5 16^5 17^2 18 19^2 20^3 21 24^5 25^3 27^3 28 29^2 30^6 31^3 32 33^3 34^5 35^3 36^3 37 24:1^2 2^5 4 5 6 7 8^2 9 10 11^2 12^6 13^3 14^5 15^5 16^4 17^2 18^3 19 20 25:1^4 2 3^2 4^3 5^3 6^2 7^4 8 9^4 10 11 12 13^4 14^5 15^4 16 17^5 18^3 19^4 20^2 21^2 22 23^6 24^5 25^4 26^4 27^3 28^2 29^2 30

1 CHRON.

1:4 5^6 6^3 7^3 8^2 9^7 10 11^4 12^3 13^2 14^2 15^3 16^3 17^8 18^2 19^2 20^4 21^2 22^3 23^3

1 CHRON.

1:28 29^2 30^2 31 32^7 33^5 34^2 35^3 36^4 37 38^7 39^3 40^5 41^4 42^3 43^2 44 45 46^2 47 48 49 50^3 51 2:1^2 2^2 3^4 4^2 5 6^5 7 8 9^2 10^2 11^2 12^2 13^3 16^4 17^2 18^4 19 20^2 21^2 22^2 23^3 24 25^5 27^3 28^4 29^3 30^2 31^3 32^3 33^2 34 35^2 36^2 37^2 38^2 39^2 40^2 41^2 42 43^4 44^2 45^2 46^4 47^6 48 49^2 52^2 53^5 54^2 55^2 3:4^4 5^4 6^2 7^3 8^3 9 10 15 16 17 18^3 19^5 20^4 21^2 22^6 23^3 24^7 4:1^3 2^3 3^4 4^2 5^2 6^4 7^3 8^3 9^2 10^5 11 12^3 13^3 14^2 15^3 16^3 17^7 18^4 19^2 20^5 21^2 22^6 23^2 24^2 26 27^2

1 CHRON.

4:28^3 29^3 30^3 31^4 32^4 33^2 34^3 35^2 36^7 37 38 39 40^5 41^5 42^4 43^2 5:1 2 3^2 7^2 8^2 9 10^2 11 12^3 13^7 16^3 17 18^7 19^3 20^4 21^5 22 23^3 24^8 25^2 26^9 6:1 2^3 3^5 5^2 6^2 7 8^2 9^2 10 11^2 12^2 13^2 14^2 15^2 16 17^2 18^4 19^2 23^2 24 25^2 26 28^2 31 32^2 33 39 44 49^4 50 55^2 56 57^4 58 59^2 60^3 61 62^4 63^2 64 65^3 66 67 68^2 69^2 70^2 71 72 73^2 74^2 75^2 76^3 78^2 79 80^2 81^2 7:1^2 2^8 3^4 4^3 5^2 6^2 7^9 8^9 9^2 10^7 11^2 12^2 13^3 15^4 16^5 17 18^3 19^4 20^5 21^4 22^2 23^3 24^3 25^3

1 CHRON.

7:28^7 29^5 30^4 31^2 32^4 33^3 34^3 35^4 36^4 37^5 38^3 39^3 40^4 8:1 2 3^3 4^3 5^3 6^2 7^5 8^2 9^4 10^3 11^2 12^3 13 14 15^3 16^3 17^4 18^2 19^3 20^3 21^3 22^3 23^3 24^3 25^2 26^3 27^3 29 30^5 31^3 32^2 33^6 34^2 35^4 36^5 37 38^5 39^2 40^4 9:1^2 2 3^4 5^2 6^3 7 8^3 9^3 10^3 11 12^2 13^3 14 15^3 16^2 17^5 19^3 20^2 21 22^2 23 24 25 26^2 27^2 28^2 29^5 30 31 32 33^2 35 36^5 37^4 38^2 39^6 40^2 41^4 42^5 43^2 44^5 10:1^2 2^5 3^3 4^3 5^2 6^2 7^6 8^2 9^4 10^2 11 12^5 13 14^2 11:1 2^4 3^2 4^2 5 6^3 7 8^2 9 10

1 CHRON.

11:11 12 13^2 14^4 15 16^2 17^2 18^4 19 20^2 22 23^5 24 25 42 43 44 45 46^3 47^2 12:1 2^3 3^4 4^6 5^4 6^4 7^2 8^4 14 15^2 16^2 17^4 18^4 19 20^6 21^2 23^2 24^2 25 26 27^3 28^3 29 30^2 31^2 32^2 34^4 35^3 36 37^4 38 39^2 40^{11} 13:1^3 2^5 3 4 6^2 7^3 8^8 9 10^3 11 12 14^3 14:1^2 2 3^3 4^2 5^3 6^3 7^3 8^3 9^2 10^3 11 12^2 13 14^2 15 16 17^2 15:1^3 2 3 4^2 5^2 6^2 7^2 8 9 10^2 11^6 12^2 14 15 16^3 17^2 18^{12} 19 20^8 21^6 22 23^2 24^9 25^2 26^2 27^4 28^4 29^3 16:1^3 2^2 3^4 4^4 5^9 6 7

1 CHRON.

16:11 12 16 17^2 19 20^2 22 25 27^2 28 29 31^2 32^2 35^4 36^3 37 38^3 39^2 40^2 41^3 42^5 43^2 17:3 4 5 8^3 9^3 10 11^2 13^2 14^2 15 16^4 17^2 19 21^2 22 23^2 24 26^2 27 18:1^3 2^3 3 4^3 5^2 6^2 7^2 8^3 10^5 11^5 13^2 14^2 15^2 16^3 17^3 19:1 2^2 3^2 4^3 5^4 6^5 7^6 8^2 9^3 10^2 11^2 12 13^3 14^2 15^2 16^3 17^5 18^3 19^2 20:1^6 2^5 3^6 4^2 5^2 6^5 8^2 21:1^2 2^3 3 4^2 5^5 6 7 8 9 10 11 12 13 14 15^5 16^4 17^3 18 19 20^3 21^4 23^4 24 26^5 27^2 29 22:1 2^2 3^3 4 5^4 6 7 8 9^3

1 CHRON.

22:10^3 11^2 12^2 13^2 14^5 15^3 16^4 18^2 19^3 23:1 2^2 3^3 4^3 5 6^2 7 8^2 9^2 10^3 11^3 12 13^4 15 17^2 19 20 21^2 22^3 23^2 24 26 27 28^3 29^6 30^3 31^2 32^3 24:1^2 2^3 3^2 4^3 5^2 6^7 17^2 18^2 20 23 26 27^3 30^2 31^4 25:1^5 2^3 3^4 4^3 5^2 6^2 7 8 9 10 11 12 13 14 15 16 17 18 19 20 21 22 23 24 25 26 27 28^2 29^2 30^2 31^2 26:2 4^2 7^3 8^3 9^2 11 13 14^2 15 16 17^2 18 19 20^2 22 23^2 24 25^5 26^4 28^6 29^2 30^4 31 32^4 27:1^5 2^2 4^3 5^2 6^2 7^3 8^2 9^2 10^2 11^2 12^2

1 CHRON.

27:13^2 14^2 15^2 23 25^4 26 27 28^3 29^2 30 31 32^2 33^2 34^3 28:1^9 2^4 3 4^2 5 6^3 7 8^3 9^4 10 11^5 12^3 13^3 15^4 16^2 17^4 18^3 20^3 21^4 29:1^2 2^7 3^2 4 5^3 6^3 7^5 8 9 10^2 11^6 12^6 13 14^2 15^2 16 17^2 18^2 19^4 20^5 21^4 22^5 23 24^3 25^2 27^3 28^3 29^3 30^4

2 CHRON.

1:1^3 2^3 3 5^2 6^2 7 8^2 10^2 11^3 12^4 13 14^6 15^3 16^2 17^6 2:1^2 2^5 3^2 4^6 5 6 7^8 8^2 10^4 12^3 13 14^7 15^2 16^3 17^5 18^5 3:2 3 4^4 5^3 6^2 7^3 8^3 9^2 10^2 11^2 12^2 13^2 14^5 15^2 16^4 17^4 4:1^2 2^2 3 4^5 5^4 6^2

2 CHRON.

4:7^3 8^3 9^3 10 11^4 12^3 13 14 15 16^3 17 19^2 21^4 22^6 5:1^4 2 4^2 5^4 6^2 7 8^2 9^2 11^2 12^5 13^6 6:2 3^3 4 6 10^2 11 12^2 13^6 14^2 15^2 18 19^2 20 21^2 22^2 23^3 24^5 25^3 26^3 27^3 29^2 30^2 32^3 33^3 34^2 35^2 36^3 37^3 38^4 39^3 40 41^2 7:1^3 2 3^4 4 5^5 6^3 7^3 8 9^2 10^5 11^3 12^3 14^5 15 16^3 17^4 19^5 20^3 21^2 22^4 8:1^2 2 3^2 4^2 5^2 6^7 7^4 9^3 10^2 11 13^4 14^3 15^2 16 17 18^6 9:1^5 2^2 3^2 4^6 5^2 6^2 7^2 8 9^4 10^3 11^5 12^2 13^2 14^4 15 16^2 17 18^3 19^2 20^2 21^3 22^2 23 24^5

2 CHRON.

9:25^4 26^2 27^2 28^2 29^3 30 31^3 10:1 2 3^4 4^2 5^2 6 7^3 8 9 10 12 13^2 14 16^3 18 19 11:1^3 3^2 4^2 5^2 6^2 7^3 8^3 9^3 10^4 11^5 12^4 13^2 14^4 15^3 16 17^2 18^2 19^2 20^4 21^6 22 23^5 12:1^3 2 3^3 4^2 5^3 6^2 7^2 8 9^2 10 11^3 12^2 13^4 14 15^4 16^3 13:2^2 3 4^3 5 6 7^4 8^3 9^3 10^3 11^4 12^2 13 14^4 15^3 16^2 17^2 18 19^4 20^2 21^4 22^3 14:1^2 2^2 3^2 4^3 5^2 6^2 7^5 8^5 9^3 10 11^3 12^2 13^5 14^2 15^3 15:1 2^5 3^2 4 5 6^2 7 8^6 9^5 11^2 12^2 14^4 15^4 16^4 18^4 19^2 16:1^2 2^3 3^3 4^6

2 CHRON.

16:5^2 6^4 7^2 8^2 9 10^2 11^3 12^2 13^3 14^4 17:1^2 2^3 3^2 4^2 5^3 6^2 7^4 8^{11} 9^4 10 11^5 12^3 13^2 14^2 15^3 16^2 17^3 18^3 18:1^2 2^5 3^4 4 5^2 7^2 8^2 9^4 10^2 11^2 12^2 13 14^4 15 16 17 18^2 19^4 20^3 21^5 22 23^2 24 25^2 26^3 27^2 28 29^3 31^3 33^2 34^2 19:1 2^3 3 4^3 5 6 7 8^3 9^2 10^7 11^3 20:1^2 2 3^3 4 5^2 6^4 7 8^2 9^3 10^4 13^2 15^3 16 17^2 18^3 19^2 20^5 21^3 22^4 23^3 24^3 25^4 26 27^2 28^3 29 31^5 32^2 34 35 36^2 37 21:1^2 2^6 3^3 4^2 5^2 6^2 7^2 8 9^4 11^2 12 13^3 14^3 15 16

2 CHRON.

21:17^5 18 19^2 20^3 22:1 2^2 5^2 6^2 7 8^3 9^4 10 11^3 12^2 23:1^6 2^4 3^2 4 5^3 6 7^3 8^2 9^2 10^2 11^6 12 13^8 14^2 15 16^3 17^4 18 19 20^6 21^2 24:1 2 3^3 4 5^5 6^4 7 8^2 9^2 10^4 11^6 12^6 13^3 14^7 15^2 16^2 17 18^5 19 20^2 21^2 22^2 23^5 24 25^4 26^2 27^3 25:1^4 2 5^7 8 9^2 10 11^4 12^8 13^2 14^3 15 16^3 17 18^3 19^2 21^2 22^2 23^3 24^5 25 26^2 27^2 28 26:1 2 3^2 4 5^2 6^7 7^3 8^2 9^3 10^{11} 11 12 13^3 14^6 15^4 16 17^2 18^2 19^2 20^4 21^3 22 23^2 27:1^2 2^2 3 4^2 5^5 7^3 8^2 9^3 28:1

2 CHRON.

28:2 3 4^3 5^4 6 7^3 8^4 9^3 10^3 11 12^3 13^3 14^2 15^{10} 17^2 18^8 19 20^2 21^3 22 23^2 24^4 25^2 26^3 27^2 29:1^4 2 3 4^3 5^3 6^4 7^2 8^3 9^3 11^2 12^5 13^4 14^4 15^3 16^3 17^2 18^3 19^2 20^2 21^7 22^3 23^3 24^3 25^4 26^2 27^3 28^4 29^3 30^5 31^6 32^3 33^2 34 35^2 36^2 30:1^4 2^2 4^2 6^5 7^2 8 9^3 10^2 11^3 12 13 14^4 15^4 16 18^2 20^2 21^3 22^3 23^2 24^4 25^5 27^5 31:1^6 2^6 3^4 4 5^5 6^5 7 8^4 9 10^4 11 12^4 13^1 14^9 15^5 16 17^2 18^3 19 20^4 21^4 32:1^4 2^2 3^2 4^2 5^6 6^3 7 8^2 9^2 11 12^4 13 15 16^3

2 CHRON. 32:17, 18, 19, 20[3], 21[4], 22[3], 23[2], 24[3], 25[2], 26, 27[8], 28[4], 29[2], 30[2], 32[3], 33[5], 33:1[2], 3[4], 5, 6[5], 7[3], 8[2], 9[2], 10[2], 11[2], 12[2], 13[4], 14[3], 15[5], 16[4], 18[2], 19[6], 20[2], 21[2], 22, 23[2], 24[2], 25, 34:1[2], 2[3], 3[5], 4[7], 5[3], 6[3], 7[4], 8[3], 9[6], 10[3], 11[3], 12[6], 13[4], 14, 15[3], 16[2], 17[3], 18, 19, 20[5], 21[2], 22[3], 23, 24, 25[2], 26, 27[5], 28[2], 29[2], 30[8], 31[6], 32[3], 33[3], 35:1, 2[2], 3[2], 4[2], 5[2], 6[2], 7[3], 8[6], 9[6], 10[2], 11[3], 12[2], 13[4], 14[4], 15[5], 16, 17[2], 18[6], 20, 22, 23[2], 24[6], 25[5], 26, 27[3], 36:1, 2[2], 3[3], 4[5], 5[3], 6, 7, 8[4], 9[3], 10[4], 11[2], 12[2], 13[2], 14[2], 15[3], 16[3], 17, 18[5], 19[4], 20[2], 21

2 CHRON. 36:22, 23[2]

EZRA 1:1, 2, 3[2], 4[4], 5[3], 6[3], 7, 8, 9[2], 10[2], 11[2], 2:1[2], 3, 4, 5, 6[2], 7, 8, 9, 10, 11, 12, 13, 14, 15, 16, 17, 18, 19, 20, 21, 22, 23, 24, 25[3], 26[2], 27, 28[2], 29, 30, 31, 32, 33[2], 34, 35[2], 36, 37, 38, 39, 40[2], 41, 42, 58[2], 59[3], 60, 61[2], 63[2], 64[2], 65[4], 66[2], 67[2], 68, 69[3], 70[6], 3:1[2], 2[4], 3[3], 4, 5[3], 7[5], 8[5], 9[3], 10[2], 11[3], 12[3], 13, 4:1, 2[3], 3[2], 4, 5, 6[2], 7[4], 8, 9[3], 10[5], 11, 12[3], 13[3], 14[2], 15[4], 16, 17[4], 19[5], 20[2], 21, 23[4], 5:1[2], 2[3], 3[4], 5, 6[2], 8[3], 9[2], 11[4], 12, 14[4], 15[2], 16[3], 17, 6:1, 2[2]

EZRA 6:3[2], 4[2], 5[5], 6, 7, 9[4], 10[2], 11[2], 12[3], 13, 14[8], 15, 16[3], 17[2], 18[2], 19, 20[4], 21[2], 22[2], 7:6[2], 7[6], 8, 9, 10[3], 11, 12, 13[2], 14[2], 15[3], 16[3], 17[2], 18[3], 20, 21, 22[4], 23, 24, 25[3], 26[2], 28[5], 8:1, 3[2], 4, 5, 6, 7[2], 8[2], 9[2], 10[3], 11[3], 12[3], 13[3], 14[2], 15[5], 16[7], 17[3], 18[3], 19[3], 20[2], 21[2], 22[2], 23[2], 24, 25[6], 26[3], 27, 28[3], 29[3], 30[3], 31[3], 32[2], 33[5], 34[2], 35[2], 36[4], 9:1[3], 2[2], 3[5], 4, 5[4], 6[3], 7[4], 8[3], 9[3], 10, 12[2], 13[3], 14, 10:1[4], 2[3], 3[3], 4, 5[3], 6[2], 7[2], 8[3], 9[3], 10[3], 11[3], 12, 13[2], 14[3], 15[3], 16[4], 17, 18[5], 19[2], 20[2], 21[5], 22[2], 23[3], 24[3], 25[6], 26[5], 27[4], 28, 29[4]

EZRA 10:30[4], 31, 32, 33, 34, 37, 38[2], 39[3], 41, 42, 43, 44

NEH. 1:1, 2[3], 3[3], 4[5], 5[4], 6[4], 7, 9[3], 10[2], 11[3], 2:1[3], 3[2], 5[2], 6[3], 8[4], 9[2], 10, 11, 12[2], 13[4], 14, 15[4], 16, 17[2], 18[2], 19[4], 20[2], 3:1[2], 2[2], 3[2], 4[3], 5, 6[4], 7[3], 8, 9, 10[2], 11[2], 12[2], 13[4], 14[2], 15[5], 16[2], 19, 22, 23, 25, 26, 30, 31[2], 32[2], 4:1[2], 2[3], 3, 4[2], 5[2], 6, 7[5], 8[3], 9[2], 10[2], 11[3], 12, 13[2], 14[9], 15[2], 16[5], 17[2], 18[2], 19[5], 21, 22, 5:1[2], 2[2], 3, 4[2], 5[4], 6[2], 7[4], 8[3], 10[3], 11[3], 12[2], 13[6], 14[2], 15[2], 16, 17[2], 18[2], 6:1[4], 2, 3[2], 4, 6[2], 7[3], 10[2], 11[2], 12[2], 13[3], 14[3], 15[2], 16[2], 17

NEH. 6:18, 19[2], 7:1[4], 2[2], 3[5], 4[2], 5[5], 6[2], 8, 9, 10, 11[3], 12, 13, 14, 15, 16, 17, 18, 19, 20, 21, 22, 23, 24, 25, 26[2], 27, 28, 29[2], 30[2], 31[2], 32[2], 33, 34, 35, 36, 37[2], 38, 39, 40, 41, 42, 43[2], 44, 45, 60[2], 61[2], 62, 63[2], 65[2], 66[2], 67[5], 68[2], 69[2], 70[2], 71[3], 72[4], 73[7], 8:1[2], 2[3], 3[4], 4[13], 5[2], 6[4], 7[4], 8[2], 9[3], 10[2], 12[4], 13[2], 14, 15[8], 16[6], 17[3], 18[2], 9:1[3], 2[4], 3[4], 4[3], 5[6], 6[4], 7[2], 8[6], 9[2], 10[4], 11[2], 12, 13[4], 14[3], 15[3], 16[3], 17[5], 18[2], 19, 20[2], 21, 22[4], 23, 24[4], 25[8], 26[4], 27[2], 28[2], 29[5], 30, 31, 32[6], 34, 35[3], 36[2], 37[3], 38[4], 10:1, 9, 10, 26

NEH. 10:28[4], 29[6], 30, 31[3], 33[5], 34[2], 35[2], 36[3], 37[5], 38[2], 39[6], 11:1[2], 2, 3[3], 4[2], 5, 6, 7, 8[2], 9[2], 12[3], 13[3], 14[3], 16[2], 17[3], 18, 19[2], 20[2], 21[2], 24, 25[6], 26[3], 27[3], 28[3], 29[3], 30[4], 31[3], 32, 35, 36[2], 12:1[2], 6, 7, 8[2], 9, 10[2], 11[2], 12, 19, 22[2], 24[3], 25, 26[2], 27[3], 28[2], 29[2], 30[5], 31, 32[2], 33[2], 34[3], 35, 36[4], 37, 38[3], 39[6], 40[2], 41[2], 42[9], 43[2], 44[4], 45[4], 46[3], 47[5], 13:1[2], 2, 4, 5[7], 6[2], 7[2], 8, 9[3], 10[2], 11[3], 12[2], 13[5], 14[2], 15[5], 16[3], 17[2], 18[2], 19[3], 20, 21, 22[4], 23, 24[2], 25[5], 26, 28, 29[2], 30[2], 31[3]

ESTHER 1:1[2], 3[3], 4[2], 5[2], 6[7], 7[2], 8, 10[2], 11, 12, 13, 14[4]

ESTHER 1:16[3], 18[2], 19[3], 20[2], 21[3], 22[2], 2:1[2], 3[2], 4[3], 7[4], 8[2], 9[6], 11[2], 12[2], 14[2], 15, 17[4], 18[3], 19, 21[2], 22[2], 23[2], 3:1[2], 2[2], 4, 5, 6, 7, 8[3], 9, 10[2], 11, 12[5], 13[5], 15[3], 4:1[4], 2, 3[7], 4[4], 5[2], 7[2], 8[3], 9[2], 10, 11, 12, 14[3], 16[5], 17, 5:1[2], 2[3], 3, 4[2], 5, 6[3], 7[2], 8[4], 9, 10, 11[5], 12, 14[4], 6:1[2], 2[2], 3[2], 4, 5[2], 6, 7, 8[2], 9[4], 10[3], 11[4], 12[2], 13[3], 14[2], 7:1, 2[4], 3[3], 4[3], 5[2], 6[3], 7[2], 8, 9, 8:1, 2[3], 3[4], 4, 5[4], 7[2], 8[2], 9[9], 10[5], 11[5], 13, 14[3], 15[7], 16[3], 17[6], 9:1, 2, 3[4], 4[2], 5[3], 6[2], 7[3], 8[3], 9[4], 12[5], 13, 14[3], 15, 16[4], 17[3], 18[4], 19[3]

ESTHER 9:20[3], 21, 22[5], 23[2], 24[2], 25[2], 26[2], 27[4], 28[4], 29, 30[3], 31[4], 32[2], 10:1[2], 2[4], 3[3]

JOB 1:1[4], 2[2], 3[4], 4[5], 5[5], 6, 7[5], 8[3], 9, 10[3], 11[2], 12, 13[3], 14[3], 15[3], 16[5], 17[5], 18[3], 19[5], 20[4], 21[3], 2:1, 2[6], 3[4], 4[2], 5[3], 6, 7, 8[2], 9, 10, 11[3], 12[5], 13[2], 3:1, 2[2], 3, 5, 13, 14, 17, 19[2], 20, 21, 22, 23, 24, 25, 4:1, 3, 4, 5[2], 6, 8, 9, 10[2], 11, 12, 14, 16, 18, 5:1, 2, 4, 5[2], 8[2], 9, 10, 13, 14, 15, 16, 18[2], 20, 22, 23, 24[3], 25, 27, 6:1, 2, 8, 9, 11, 13, 15, 16, 18, 20, 21, 24[2], 26, 27, 7:2, 3, 4[3], 5[2], 6, 8

JOB 7:9, 14, 15, 17, 18[2], 21[3], 8:1, 2, 4, 5, 6[2], 8, 9, 10, 12, 13, 14, 16, 17, 19, 21, 22, 9:1, 4[2], 5[2], 6, 7[2], 8, 9[2], 10, 11, 14, 16, 17, 19, 22, 24, 27, 30, 31, 32, 34, 35, 10:3, 6, 7, 8, 9, 10, 11[3], 12[2], 13, 14, 15, 16, 17[2], 18, 20, 21, 22[2], 11:1, 2, 3, 4, 5, 6, 9, 10, 13, 14, 15, 16, 17, 18[2], 19, 20[2], 12:1[2], 2, 4, 6, 7[3], 8[2], 10, 11, 12, 13[2], 14[2], 15[2], 16[2], 17, 18, 19, 20, 21, 22, 23[2], 24, 25, 13:1, 3, 5, 6, 7, 11, 13, 14, 17, 21, 22[2], 23[2], 24, 25[2], 26, 27, 28, 14:1, 2[2]

JOB 14:3[2], 7, 8, 9, 10[2], 11[2], 12, 13, 15, 17, 18[2], 19, 20[2], 21[2], 22, 15:1, 2, 4, 5, 6, 8, 10, 12, 13, 14, 16, 17, 18, 19, 20, 22, 24, 25, 27, 28[2], 30, 32, 33, 34, 35[2], 16:1, 4, 5, 6, 8[2], 11, 12[2], 13, 15, 16, 18, 19, 17:2, 6, 7, 8, 9[2], 10, 14, 15, 18:1, 2, 3, 4, 5, 6, 7, 8, 9, 10, 11, 12, 14, 16, 17, 18, 21, 19:1, 2, 4, 5, 6, 8, 9, 10[2], 11, 12[2], 13, 14, 15, 16, 18, 19, 20[2], 22, 24, 25, 26, 27[2], 20:1, 2, 3, 5, 6, 8, 10, 13, 15, 17, 18[2], 19, 23, 24, 25, 27, 28, 29

JOB 21:1, 2, 3, 4, 5[2], 6, 8, 10[2], 11, 12[2], 13, 15, 17, 18, 19, 20, 23, 24, 25[2], 26, 27, 28, 29, 31, 32, 33, 22:1, 5, 6, 7, 8, 9, 10, 11, 12, 13, 14, 17, 19[2], 21, 22, 24, 25, 26, 27[2], 28[2], 29, 30, 23:1, 4, 5, 8, 11, 13[2], 14, 16, 24:2, 5, 6, 8, 9, 10, 11[2], 12, 14[2], 15, 19, 20, 21, 22, 24[2], 25[2], 25:1, 2, 3, 5, 6, 26:1, 3, 4, 5, 6, 7, 8, 9, 10, 11, 12, 27:1, 2, 3, 6, 7, 13, 14, 15, 16, 17, 18, 19, 21[2], 22, 23, 28:1, 2, 3[2], 5, 6, 7, 10, 11, 12, 14, 17[2], 20, 21, 22

JOB 28:23, 24, 25, 26, 27[2], 28[2], 29:1, 3, 6, 8[3], 9, 10, 11, 12[2], 13, 14[2], 15, 16, 17[2], 18, 19, 20, 21[2], 22, 23[2], 24, 25[2], 30:3[2], 4, 6, 9, 10, 11, 12, 15, 16, 17, 19[2], 20[2], 22, 23, 26, 27, 28, 29, 30, 31, 31:2, 3, 4, 7[2], 8, 10, 12, 14, 15, 17, 18, 20, 22, 23, 25, 27, 34, 35, 36, 40, 32:3, 6[4], 7, 8, 12, 16, 20, 33:1, 3, 4, 8, 16, 17, 18, 19, 20, 21, 22, 24, 26[2], 27[3], 28, 31, 33, 34:1, 2, 5, 8, 10, 11, 14, 15, 17, 18, 20[3], 24, 25, 27, 28, 29, 33, 34, 35, 37, 35:1, 3, 4, 5[2], 8, 11

JOB 36:1, 2, 3, 5[2], 7, 8[2], 9, 10, 11[2], 12, 14, 15, 16, 17, 26, 28, 30, 32, 37:1, 2, 3, 4, 6, 8, 9, 10, 12, 14, 15, 18, 21[2], 23[2], 38:1, 3, 7, 9, 10[3], 11[2], 12, 14, 15[2], 19, 20, 23, 27[2], 29, 30, 35, 38, 40, 39:4, 6, 8, 12, 13, 14, 15, 18, 21, 22, 23, 24, 25[2], 26, 27, 28[2], 29, 30, 40:1, 3, 6, 7, 10[3], 11[2], 12[2], 13, 16, 21, 23, 41:18, 19, 21, 22, 27, 42:1, 2, 4[2], 6[2], 7[2], 8[4], 9[3], 10, 11[6], 12[3], 13, 14[3], 15[2], 16[3], 17

PSALMS 1:2[2], 3[2], 2:1, 2[2], 3, 5, 8[2], 11, 12, 3:3, 4, 5, 4:1, 2, 4[2], 5

PSALMS 4:7, 8, 5:2, 3, 6, 7, 6:10[2], 7:1, 5[2], 6, 8, 9, 11, 12, 14[2], 15[2], 16, 17, 8:2[2], 3, 4, 5[2], 7[2], 8[2], 9:2, 3, 4, 5, 6, 8, 10, 17, 10:3, 7[3], 10, 14, 15, 16, 18, 11:5, 6[2], 12:2, 3, 13:3, 4, 14:2, 4, 7, 15:2[2], 4, 16:3, 5, 9, 17:3, 6, 12, 14[2], 18 *tit.*[2], 2[4], 4, 6[2], 7[2], 8, 9[2], 10[2], 11, 12, 13[2], 14[3], 15, 17, 21, 22, 23, 26, 29, 32, 33, 35[2], 37, 43, 45, 46[2], 47, 49, 50[2], 19:1, 2, 4, 5, 6[2], 9, 10, 11, 13, 14[2], 20:2, 3, 4, 5, 7, 8[2], 21:1, 2, 4[2], 5, 7, 9, 10, 13, 22:1, 2[2], 4, 5[2], 6[2], 13, 14

PSALMS 22:15[2], 16, 17, 18, 23, 26, 27[2], 28, 29[2], 31, 23:4, 6[2], 24:1[2], 2, 4, 5, 7[2], 8, 9, 25:5, 6, 8, 9, 10[2], 13, 14, 16[2], 18[2], 19, 20, 21, 26:2[2], 3, 5, 7, 8, 10, 11, 27:1, 2[2], 4, 6, 7, 10, 11, 12, 14, 28:3, 4, 5, 7[3], 8, 9[2], 29:1, 6, 9[2], 30 *title*, 1, 2, 4, 6, 7, 8, 10, 11, 12, 31:3[2], 7, 8, 9, 10[2], 11, 15, 17, 18, 23, 24, 32:2, 4, 5[2], 8, 9, 11[2], 33:2, 4, 5, 6, 9[2], 12, 19, 20, 34 *title*, 2, 3, 4[2], 5[2], 6[2], 7, 8, 10, 12, 13, 14[2], 15, 17[2], 18, 21, 22, 35:2[2], 3, 4[2], 5, 6[2], 8, 9, 10, 13

PSALMS 35:15[3], 21, 23[2], 24, 26[2], 27, 28[2], 36:3[2], 5, 6, 8, 10, 11, 12, 37:2, 3[2], 4, 5, 6[2], 7, 8, 10[2], 11, 12, 14[3], 15, 18, 19, 20, 21[2], 22, 23, 25, 26[2], 27[2], 28, 29, 30, 32, 34[2], 35, 36, 37, 40[3], 38:2, 5, 7, 8, 9, 11[2], 12[2], 13, 14, 17, 19[2], 39:2, 4, 5, 6, 7, 12[2], 13, 40:1, 2[2], 3[3], 4, 5[2], 6[2], 10[2], 11, 14[2], 16, 17[2], 41:2[3], 5, 6, 8, 10, 12[2], 13[2], 42:2, 3, 4, 5, 6, 7, 8[2], 11[2], 43:1[2], 3[2], 5[2], 44:2[2], 3[2], 7, 8, 9[2], 10, 11, 12, 13, 15, 16[2], 19, 24[2], 26, 45:3, 4[4], 6, 7, 8[2], 10[3], 11, 12, 15, 17, 46:1, 2

PSALMS 46:3, 5, 9, 10, 47:3, 48 *title*, 1, 5[2], 6, 12, 14, 49:2[2], 3, 6, 8, 9, 10[2], 11, 14[2], 18, 20, 50:1, 3[2], 4, 6, 7[2], 10, 11, 12, 14, 15[2], 17, 18, 19, 20, 21[2], 22, 23, 51:2, 3, 4[2], 5, 6, 7[2], 8, 9, 10, 11, 12, 13, 14, 15, 17[2], 19, 52 *tit.*[2], 3, 5[2], 6[2], 7, 8, 9, 53:1, 6, 54 *title*, 1, 3, 7, 55:1, 2[2], 3, 4, 5[2], 6[2], 7, 8, 9[2], 10[2], 11, 13, 14, 15[2], 16, 17[4], 19, 22, 23, 57:3[2], 4[3], 7, 8, 10, 58:9, 59 *title*, 2, 4[2], 6, 11, 12[3], 13, 14[3], 15[2], 16, 17, 60 *tit.*[2], 5, 6, 7, 10, 61:3, 6, 7, 62:2, 3, 6, 7[2], 9, 10

PSALMS 63:1, 2, 5[2], 6, 64:3, 4, 6, 9[2], 10[2], 65 *title*, 1, 4, 5, 7, 8, 9, 11, 12, 66:4, 5, 8, 9, 12, 14, 16[2], 17, 67:1[2], 4[2], 6, 7, 68:4, 5, 12, 13, 20, 21, 23, 27[2], 33, 34, 35, 69:5, 8, 9, 10, 11, 12, 14[2], 15, 17, 18, 19[2], 20[3], 21, 22, 23, 24, 25, 26, 27, 28, 29, 30, 31, 32[2], 33, 34[2], 35[2], 36, 70:2[2], 4[2], 5[2], 71:2[2], 3, 4, 8, 10, 11, 13[2], 14[2], 15, 17, 18[2], 20[2], 21, 23, 72:1, 2, 3, 4, 5, 7, 8, 9, 10[2], 12, 13[2], 14[2], 15[3], 16, 17, 19[3], 73:8, 9, 10, 11[2], 13, 14, 21, 22, 24, 25, 26[2], 74:6, 14, 15, 16

ISAIAH	ISAIAH	ISAIAH	JER.	JER.	JER.	JER.	JER.	JER.	JER.	JER.	JER.	LAM.	EZEKIEL	EZEKIEL	EZEKIEL	EZEKIEL	EZEKIEL
49:1	58:2^{2}	66:12^{2}	5:30	11:22	18:17	25:15	31:1	36:1	42:10^{3}	48:46	51:61^{3}	5:21	7:19^{2}	13:22	18:24^{3}	23:18	28:18
2^{2}	3^{3}	13	31^{3}	23	18^{3}	16^{3}	4^{2}	2^{3}	11	49:1	63^{2}		20	23	26^{2}	20	19
3	4^{2}	14^{4}	6:1^{3}	12:2	19	17	5	3	12^{2}	2^{2}	64^{3}	EZEKIEL	21^{3}	14:1	27	22	21
4^{2}	5^{3}	15^{2}	2	3^{2}	20	18^{4}	6	4	14	3^{4}	52:1^{3}	1:1	22^{2}	2	28	23^{6}	22^{4}
5^{2}	6^{2}	16^{2}	4	4^{2}	21^{4}	19^{3}	7^{2}	5	15^{2}	5^{2}	2	3	23	3	30	24^{7}	23^{3}
6^{2}	7^{2}	17^{3}	5^{2}	5^{2}	22	20^{7}	8^{3}	6^{2}	16^{2}	6	3	4^{5}	24^{2}	4^{3}	31^{2}	25^{6}	24^{2}
7^{4}	8^{2}	18^{4}	6	6	19:1^{3}	21^{2}	9^{2}	7^{2}	17	10^{4}	4^{4}	5	25^{2}	6^{2}	32	26	25
8^{3}	9^{3}	19^{5}	7^{2}	9	2^{2}	22^{3}	10^{3}	8	18^{6}	11	6	6^{2}	26^{2}	7^{3}	19:2	27	26^{4}
9	10^{3}	20^{5}	10^{2}	11	3^{2}	23^{3}	11	9^{2}	20^{2}	12	7^{3}	7^{3}	27^{4}	8^{5}	3^{2}	29^{6}	29:2^{2}
11^{2}	11^{5}	21^{2}	11	13	4^{3}	24^{2}	12^{8}	12^{6}	21	13^{2}	8^{2}	8^{3}	8:1^{2}	9^{3}	4	30	3^{2}
12^{3}	12^{2}	22^{2}	12^{2}	14	7^{6}	25^{3}	13^{3}	14^{2}	22^{2}	14^{3}	9	10^{2}	2^{2}	10	5^{2}	32^{2}	4^{3}
13^{3}	13^{2}	23^{2}	13	15^{4}	8^{3}	26^{4}	14^{2}	15^{2}	43:1	15	10	11^{2}	3^{5}	11	6^{4}	33^{2}	5^{3}
14	14^{2}	24^{3}	16^{4}	16	9^{5}	27^{4}	15	16^{2}	2^{2}	16	11^{3}	12^{2}	4	13^{4}	7^{4}	34^{3}	6
17	59:2^{2}		18	17	11^{3}	28	16^{2}	17	3	17	13^{4}	13^{3}	5	14	8	35^{2}	7^{3}
18^{3}	3	JER.	20	13:1^{3}	12^{2}	29	17	18	4^{2}	18^{2}	14	14^{2}	6	15	9^{2}	36	8^{2}
19^{3}	4^{2}	1:5^{2}	21^{3}	2	13^{3}	30^{2}	18^{2}	19^{2}	5	19^{3}	15^{3}	16^{4}	7^{2}	17^{2}	10	37^{3}	9^{4}
21^{4}	5^{2}	7	22	3	14^{2}	32	19	20^{2}	6^{6}	20	16	17	8	19^{2}	11^{3}	38	10^{3}
22^{3}	6	9^{2}	23^{3}	4^{2}	15	33	23^{2}	21^{3}	9	22^{3}	17^{3}	18	9^{2}	20	12^{2}	39	12^{4}
23^{4}	7^{2}	10^{5}	24	5	20:2	34^{4}	24^{3}	23^{2}	10^{4}	23	18^{5}	19^{2}	10^{4}	21^{4}	13^{2}	40^{3}	14^{3}
25^{2}	8	11	25	6^{2}	3	35	25	25^{2}	11^{4}	24^{3}	19^{8}	21^{2}	11^{3}	22^{4}	14^{2}	41^{3}	16
26^{4}	10	13^{3}	26	7^{3}	4^{6}	36	26^{2}	26^{3}	12^{5}	26	20	22	13	23^{3}	20:1^{2}	42^{3}	17^{2}
50:1	11	15^{4}	27^{2}	9	5^{5}	37	27^{2}	27	13	27^{2}	21^{3}	23^{2}	14	15:1	3	43	18
2	12^{2}	16^{3}	28	10^{2}	6^{6}	38	28^{6}	28	44:1^{3}	28^{2}	22^{4}	24	15	4	5^{3}	44	19^{4}
3	13^{4}	17^{2}	7:2^{2}	11^{4}	7^{2}	26:2	29	29^{4}	2^{3}	29^{4}	23^{3}	25	16^{6}	5	6	45^{3}	21^{2}
5	14^{3}	18^{3}	5^{2}	12	8^{2}	3	31	30^{2}	3	30	24^{3}	26^{2}	17^{2}	7^{3}	7	46^{2}	30:2
6^{2}	15^{3}	19	6^{2}	13^{3}	9^{2}	4	33^{3}	31^{6}	4	32^{3}	25^{3}	27^{3}	18	8	8	47^{4}	4^{4}
10^{2}	16^{3}	2:2	7	14^{2}	10^{3}	5	34^{3}	32^{2}	6^{5}	33^{2}	26	28^{2}	9:2^{5}	16:3^{3}	10	49^{3}	5^{6}
11	17^{3}	3	9^{4}	15	11	6	35^{2}	37:1	7^{2}	36^{3}	27^{2}	2:1^{2}	3^{2}	4	11^{2}	24:3^{3}	6
51:1	19	4	10^{3}	16^{3}	12^{2}	7^{2}	37	3^{2}	8^{2}	37^{3}	28^{2}	2^{2}	4^{3}	6^{2}	12	4	7^{2}
2^{3}	20^{2}	5^{2}	12	17^{2}	16^{4}	8^{2}	39^{2}	4	9^{5}	38^{3}	29	3^{2}	5^{2}	7^{5}	13^{2}	5^{3}	8
3^{4}	21^{2}	6^{3}	13^{4}	18	17	9^{2}	40^{3}	5	10	50:1	30^{3}	4^{2}	6^{4}	8^{5}	15	6	9
4^{2}	60:1	7^{3}	14^{2}	19	18	10	32:2	8^{4}	11	2^{3}	31^{4}	5	7^{4}	9	16	10^{2}	11^{3}
5^{2}	2^{2}	8^{3}	15	20	21:1	11^{2}	3^{2}	10^{2}	12^{9}	3^{2}	32^{2}	6^{3}	8^{4}	10^{3}	19^{2}	11^{2}	12^{4}
6^{4}	3^{2}	9	17	21	4^{2}	12^{2}	4^{3}	11	13	4^{4}	33^{2}	7	9^{4}	11^{2}	20^{3}	12	13^{3}
8^{2}	4^{2}	10^{4}	18^{3}	22^{2}	5^{4}	13^{3}	5^{2}	13^{2}	15	5	34	8	10	12^{3}	22	13	14^{3}
9	5^{3}	12	20^{5}	25	6^{2}	14	6	14	17^{6}	7		9^{2}	11	13^{8}	23	14^{2}	15^{2}
11^{5}	6^{3}	13	21	27^{2}	7^{8}	15	8^{2}	15^{2}	18^{3}	8^{2}	LAM.	10^{6}	10:1	14	24^{2}	17^{3}	16^{3}
12	7	15^{2}	23^{3}	14:2^{2}	8^{2}	16^{2}	9^{2}	16^{2}	19^{3}	9^{2}	1:1	3:1	2^{5}	15^{2}	25	18^{2}	17^{2}
13^{4}	8	16	24^{3}	3^{4}	9^{4}	17	10^{4}	17^{4}	20^{2}	10	2	2	3	16^{3}	26	19	18^{2}
14	9^{3}	18	25	5	10^{2}	18^{3}	11^{2}	21	21^{5}	12	3	3^{3}	4^{3}	17^{3}	27	21^{3}	19
16^{4}	10^{2}	19^{4}	28	6	11	19^{3}	12^{2}	38:1^{3}	22^{3}	13	4	4^{2}	5	18^{4}	28^{4}	22	20
17	11	20^{8}	29^{3}	8	12^{2}	20^{2}	13	2^{2}	23^{2}	16^{2}	6^{2}	5	6^{2}	19^{3}	29	23^{3}	21
19^{3}	12	22	31^{2}	9	13	21^{4}	14^{2}	4	24	17	7^{3}	6	7^{4}	20^{2}	30	24	22^{3}
21	13^{2}	25^{2}	33^{3}	10	14^{2}	22^{2}	15^{2}	6^{3}	25^{4}	18	8	7	8	21	31	25^{2}	23^{2}
22	14^{2}	26^{2}	34^{3}	12^{4}	22:1	23^{3}	17^{3}	8	27^{3}	19^{5}	11	8	9^{3}	22^{4}	32^{2}	27^{4}	24^{3}
23^{2}	15	27^{3}	8:1^{4}	14^{3}	2^{3}	27:2^{2}	18	9	28	20^{4}	12	10	10	23	33^{2}	25:2	25^{3}
52:1	16^{3}	37^{2}	2^{7}	15^{3}	3^{3}	3^{5}	19^{2}	10	29	21^{3}	13^{3}	11^{3}	12^{5}	24	34^{4}	3^{3}	26^{3}
2	17^{4}	3:1^{2}	3	16^{3}	4^{2}	4	20^{4}	11^{4}	30^{2}	22	14	12	14^{4}	25^{3}	35^{2}	4^{3}	31:1
3	18	2^{3}	4^{2}	17^{2}	6^{2}	5^{3}	21^{5}	12^{3}	45:3	23	17	13^{2}	15	26	37^{2}	5^{3}	2
4	19	3^{2}	6	18^{2}	7^{3}	6^{2}	22^{2}	13^{2}	4	24^{3}	18^{2}	14^{2}	16^{2}	27	38^{4}	6^{2}	3^{2}
5	20	5	7^{3}	19^{4}	8^{2}	7^{5}	23^{2}	14^{2}	5	25	19	15^{2}	17	28	39^{2}	7^{4}	4
10	22	6^{2}	8	20	9^{2}	8^{5}	24^{5}	15	46:3^{2}	26	20	16	18	29	40^{2}	8	5^{2}
12	61:1	7^{2}	9^{2}	15:1^{2}	12	10^{2}	25^{2}	17^{3}	4^{3}	28	21	17	19^{4}	31^{2}	41^{2}	9	6^{2}
13^{2}	2	8^{3}	10	2^{4}	13^{2}	11^{3}	28^{2}	18^{2}	5^{4}	30	22^{2}	18	20	33	42	10	8
14	4^{2}	9^{3}	13^{2}	3^{5}	14^{2}	12^{3}	29^{4}	19^{2}	6	32^{5}	25	19	21^{2}	34^{3}	43^{3}	11^{2}	10^{2}
15	5^{4}	10	14^{3}	4	15^{4}	13^{2}	30	20	8^{4}	33^{2}	2:1^{2}	20^{3}	22^{2}	36^{3}	44	12^{2}	12^{6}
53:1	6	11	15^{2}	6	16	15^{2}	31	22^{4}	9^{5}	34	2^{2}	21	11:1^{4}	37^{2}	46^{2}	13^{4}	13
2^{2}	7	12^{4}	16^{3}	7	17^{4}	16	32^{4}	23^{3}	10^{3}	35^{3}	3	22^{3}	2	38^{4}	47^{4}	14^{4}	15^{4}
3^{4}	8^{2}	13^{2}	17	8	19	17	33^{3}	24	11	36^{2}	4	23^{3}	3	39^{6}	48	15	16^{2}
4^{2}	9^{2}	14^{3}	19	9^{2}	20^{3}	18^{3}	35^{2}	25^{3}	12^{2}	37^{4}	5^{2}	24^{3}	5^{2}	40^{2}	21:1	16^{2}	17
5	10	15^{2}	20	10	22^{2}	19^{3}	36^{3}	27^{2}	13	38^{2}	6^{4}	25^{2}	6	41^{4}	2^{2}	17^{2}	18^{2}
6	11^{2}	16^{2}	9:1^{2}	11	25^{3}	20^{2}	37^{4}	28	14^{4}	39^{2}	8	26^{2}	7	42^{3}	3^{4}	26:1	32:1
7^{2}	62:1^{2}	17	2	12	26^{3}	21^{2}	38^{2}	39:1^{2}	16^{3}	40^{2}	9^{2}	27^{2}	8	43	4	3	2^{5}
8^{2}	2^{3}	18	3^{2}	13^{2}	28^{2}	22^{2}	39^{3}	2	18	41^{2}	10	4:1^{2}	9^{3}	45^{4}	6	4^{3}	3
9^{2}	3	19^{3}	4^{2}	14	30	28:1^{3}	40	3^{2}	19	42^{3}	11	2^{4}	10	46^{4}	7^{6}	5	4^{2}
10	4^{2}	21^{2}	5^{3}	15^{2}	23:1	3	41^{2}	4^{4}	21^{2}	43^{2}	12	3^{5}	12	48	9^{2}	6^{2}	5^{2}
11	5	22	7	16^{3}	2^{2}	4	43	5^{2}	22	44^{2}	14^{3}	4	13^{3}	49^{3}	11^{2}	7^{4}	6
12^{4}	7^{2}	23	10^{3}	18^{2}	3^{4}	5	44^{8}	7	23	45	15	5	15	50^{2}	12	8^{3}	7^{3}
54:1	8^{2}	24^{2}	11^{3}	19^{2}	4^{2}	6	33:3^{3}	8^{3}	25^{4}	46	16	6^{2}	16	51	13	9^{2}	8
2^{2}	9^{2}	25^{3}	12^{2}	20^{3}	5^{4}	7	4^{2}	9	26^{4}	51:1	17^{2}	7	17^{2}	52	14^{2}	10^{2}	10^{2}
3^{3}	11	4:1	13^{2}	21^{2}	6^{2}	8^{4}	5^{2}	10^{2}	27^{5}	2^{2}	18	8^{2}	18^{3}	53^{3}	15	11	12^{2}
4	12^{2}	2^{4}	14	16:3^{3}	8^{3}	10	6^{4}	12^{2}	47:2^{5}	3^{2}	20^{3}	9^{8}	19^{4}	54	17	12^{7}	14
5	63:2	3^{2}	15	4^{4}	9^{2}	11^{2}	7^{3}	13^{3}	3	4	21^{3}	10	20^{4}	55^{5}	19	13^{2}	15
6^{2}	3^{4}	4^{3}	16	5	10^{2}	13	8^{3}	14^{2}	4^{2}	6	22	12^{2}	21	57	20	14	16
10	4	5^{4}	17^{2}	6	11	14^{2}	9^{5}	16^{3}	6	8	3:2	13	22^{2}	58	22	16^{3}	18^{2}
11^{2}	5^{4}	6	18^{3}	8	12	29:1^{3}	10^{4}	17	7	9^{2}	4	15	23^{2}	60	23	17^{3}	19
12^{2}	6^{3}	7^{2}	20^{3}	9^{3}	13	2^{5}	11^{3}	18	48:1^{2}	10	5	16^{4}	24	61^{3}	25	19	20
13^{2}	7^{3}	8	21^{2}	10^{2}	14^{2}	3	12^{2}	40:1	2	12	8	17^{3}	12:2^{2}	62^{2}	26^{2}	20^{2}	22
14	9^{4}	9^{4}	22	11^{5}	15	5^{3}	13^{4}	2^{2}	3	13	10	5:1^{4}	3^{2}	63^{2}	27^{2}	21	23
16^{2}	10^{2}	10	24^{2}	12	16	6^{6}	14	3^{2}	6	14	11	2^{4}	4	17:1	28^{3}	27:3	24
17^{2}	11	11	26^{6}	13^{2}	17	7^{2}	15^{3}	4^{3}	7^{3}	15	12	3	5	2	31^{3}	7	26
55:1^{4}	15^{4}	13	10:2	15^{2}	18^{3}	8	16^{2}	5^{3}	8^{3}	16^{2}	14	4^{2}	6	3^{2}	22:3	8	27^{2}
2^{3}	16	15	4^{2}	16^{5}	20	10	18^{2}	6	9	17	17	5	7^{3}	4	4^{4}	9	28
3^{3}	17	16	6	18^{3}	22^{2}	11	19	7^{5}	10	19	18^{2}	6^{3}	8	5^{2}	5^{2}	10^{6}	29^{2}
4	64:5^{2}	18	7	19^{4}	23	12^{3}	20^{3}	8^{6}	11^{3}	20^{2}	19^{2}	7^{2}	10	6^{6}	7^{2}	11	30^{3}
5^{2}	6^{3}	20	8	20	24	13^{2}	21	9^{4}	12^{2}	21^{4}	20	8	11	7^{3}	8	12	31^{2}
7^{4}	7^{2}	21	9^{3}	21^{2}	28	14^{5}	22	10^{4}	13	22^{5}	26	9^{2}	12^{2}	8	9	13^{2}	32^{2}
9	8^{2}	22	10^{2}	17:1^{2}	29	16^{2}	25^{3}	11^{4}	14	23^{5}	28	10^{3}	13^{2}	9	11^{3}	14^{2}	33:2^{2}
10^{5}	11^{2}	23^{4}	11^{2}	2	31	17^{2}	26^{3}	12^{3}	15^{2}	24^{2}	37	11	14^{3}	12^{3}	12^{3}	15	3
11	12	24^{2}	12	3^{2}	32^{3}	18^{6}	34:1^{4}	13	16	25^{3}	38	12^{4}	15^{2}	13^{3}	13	16^{4}	4^{2}
12^{3}	65:3	25^{2}	13^{2}	4^{2}	33	19	2^{3}	14	17^{2}	26	40^{2}	13^{3}	16^{2}	15^{2}	14	17^{5}	5
13^{2}	4^{2}	26^{3}	14	5^{2}	34^{4}	21^{2}	3^{5}	15^{3}	18^{2}	27	42	14	18^{2}	16	15^{3}	18	6^{3}
56:1^{2}	7^{2}	28^{2}	15	6^{2}	35^{2}	22^{2}	5^{2}	41:1^{2}	19^{3}	28	43	15^{4}	19^{3}	17^{2}	16^{2}	19^{3}	7
2^{2}	8	29^{3}	16	7	36	23^{3}	7^{2}	2^{3}	20	29^{2}	47^{2}	16^{3}	20^{3}	18	17	21^{3}	10^{2}
4^{2}	9^{4}	30	18	8^{3}	37	25^{3}	9	3^{2}	21^{3}	31	49	17^{5}	21	19	18^{3}	22^{3}	11
5^{3}	10^{2}	31	19	9	38	26^{2}	10^{3}	4^{2}	22^{3}	32^{3}	50	6:1	22	20^{4}	20^{7}	23^{3}	13
6^{2}	11	5:1^{5}	20^{3}	10	39^{4}	28^{3}	11^{4}	5^{4}	23^{3}	33	53	2	23^{2}	21^{3}	21^{2}	24^{3}	14^{2}
7^{2}	12^{2}	2	21^{2}	11^{3}	40^{2}	29	14	6^{2}	24^{3}	35^{2}	60	3^{4}	25^{2}	22^{3}	22	25^{2}	16
11	14	5^{3}	22^{2}	13	24:1^{4}	31^{2}	15^{3}	7^{3}	25	36^{3}	61	4^{3}	27	23^{4}	23	27^{5}	18
12^{3}	15^{2}	6^{2}	25^{4}	14^{2}	2	32	16^{5}	8^{4}	26	37^{2}	62	5^{2}	13:1	24^{3}	25	29^{2}	19^{2}
57:1^{2}	16^{2}	7^{3}	11:2^{2}	18	3^{2}	30:3^{3}	17^{3}	9	28^{2}	39^{3}	63	6^{6}	2	18:2	26^{5}	30^{3}	21
3	17^{2}	9	3	19^{3}	6^{5}	4^{2}	18^{2}	10^{3}	29^{3}	41	66	7^{2}	3	5^{2}	27	31^{4}	22^{3}
4	18^{2}	10	4^{2}	20^{3}	7^{3}	5	19^{3}	11	31	43	4:4	9^{3}	6^{3}	6	28^{2}	32^{2}	24
7	19^{3}	11	5^{2}	21	8^{4}	6^{2}	20^{3}	12^{2}	32	44^{3}	6	10^{2}	7	7^{2}	29^{3}	33	25^{3}
8^{3}	21^{4}	12	6^{2}	24	9^{3}	8^{2}	21^{4}	13	33^{4}	45	11^{2}	11^{3}	8	8	30^{2}	34	26^{2}
9^{4}	22^{3}	13^{2}	7	25^{5}	10^{3}	9	22^{5}	14^{2}	34	46^{4}	12^{2}	12^{8}	9^{3}	9	23:3^{2}	35	27^{3}
11^{3}	23	14^{2}	9^{2}	26^{10}	25:2	10^{5}	35:2^{3}	15	35	47^{2}	13	13^{2}	10^{3}	10	4^{6}	36	28^{2}
12	24^{2}	17^{5}	10^{2}	27^{3}	3^{3}	11	3^{3}	16^{4}	36	48^{2}	15	14^{2}	11^{2}	11^{2}	5^{2}	28:2^{2}	30^{3}
13	25^{3}	19^{2}	11	18:2^{2}	4^{2}	12	4	17^{2}	37^{2}	50	21	7:3^{3}	13^{2}	12^{2}	6	4^{3}	31^{3}
14	66:1^{2}	20	12^{2}	3	5^{4}	16^{3}	5^{3}	42:1^{3}	38	52	5:1	4^{3}	14^{4}	13	7	5^{2}	32^{2}
15^{4}	2^{3}	21^{3}	13	4	6^{4}	17	10^{2}	2^{2}	39	53	3	7	15^{2}	14^{2}	8^{2}	7^{2}	33
16	3	22	15	7^{3}	9^{6}	18^{3}	11^{2}	3	40	54	5	8^{3}	16^{2}	16	10^{3}	8	34:1
17^{3}	4^{2}	23^{2}	16^{2}	9^{3}	10^{3}	19^{5}	13^{2}	4	41^{2}	55	6	9^{3}	17	18	11^{2}	9	2
18^{3}	5	24	17	11^{4}	11^{3}	20^{2}	14	5	42	56	7^{2}	15^{4}	18^{3}	19^{3}	12	12^{2}	3
19^{2}	9^{2}	25	18^{2}	12^{2}	12^{4}	21^{4}	15^{5}	6	43^{2}	57^{6}	11	16	19^{4}	20	14	13^{5}	4
20	10	27	19^{2}	15	13	22^{2}	17^{2}	8^{2}	44	58^{4}	13	17	20^{2}	21^{3}	16^{2}	14^{2}	5^{2}
58:1^{3}	11^{2}	28	20	16^{2}	14^{3}	24	18^{3}	9	45^{3}	59	20	18^{3}	21^{3}	23^{2}	17^{4}	16^{2}	6^{2}

EZEKIEL 34:8^{2}, 10^{2}, 11, 12^{2}, 13^{5}, 14^{2}, 15, 16^{4}, 17^{3}, 18, 19^{2}, 20, 21^{2}, 22^{3}, 23^{3}, 24^{2}, 25^{4}, 26^{3}, 27^{5}, 28^{2}, 29^{2}, 30, 31, 35:2, 3^{3}, 4^{2}, 5, 6, 7^{2}, 8^{3}, 9^{2}, 10^{2}, 11^{2}, 12^{2}, 13, 15^{2}, 36:1, 3^{4}, 4^{4}, 5, 6^{4}, 8, 9^{3}, 10^{3}, 11^{7}, 12^{3}, 13, 17, 18, 19^{3}, 20^{2}, 23^{2}, 24^{2}, 25^{2}, 26^{3}, 27^{4}, 28^{3}, 29^{3}, 30^{2}, 31^{3}, 32, 33, 34, 35^{5}, 36^{2}, 38, 37:1^{2}, 2^{3}, 3^{2}, 4, 5, 6^{6}, 7^{3}, 8^{3}, 9^{2}, 10^{3}, 11, 12^{3}, 13^{2}, 14^{4}, 16^{4}, 17^{2}, 18, 19^{4}, 20, 21^{3}, 22^{3}, 23^{2}, 24^{4}, 25^{5}, 26^{3}, 27, 28, 38:1, 2^{2}, 3^{2}, 4^{6}, 5^{2}, 6^{3}, 7^{3}, 8^{2}, 9^{3}, 10, 11^{2}, 12^{3}, 13^{4}, 14, 15^{3}, 16^{2}, 19, 20^{7}, 21, 22^{7}, 23^{3}, 39:1^{2}, 2^{4}, 3^{2}

EZEKIEL 39:4^{3}, 6^{3}, 7^{2}, 8, 9^{8}, 10^{2}, 11^{5}, 12, 13, 14, 15, 16, 17^{4}, 18^{2}, 19^{2}, 20^{2}, 21^{3}, 22, 23^{2}, 24^{2}, 25^{2}, 26^{2}, 27^{2}, 28, 40:1^{2}, 2, 3^{4}, 4^{3}, 5^{4}, 6^{3}, 7^{4}, 9^{2}, 10^{4}, 11^{2}, 12^{3}, 13, 15, 16^{5}, 17^{2}, 18, 19, 20^{2}, 21^{6}, 22^{5}, 23^{3}, 24^{3}, 25^{4}, 26^{4}, 27^{2}, 28^{2}, 29^{7}, 30^{3}, 31^{3}, 32^{2}, 33^{6}, 34^{4}, 35^{2}, 36^{4}, 37^{4}, 38^{2}, 39^{4}, 40^{2}, 41, 42^{6}, 43^{2}, 44^{2}, 45, 46, 47^{2}, 48^{5}, 49^{4}, 41:1^{2}, 2^{5}, 3^{3}, 4^{2}, 5, 6^{3}, 7^{3}, 9, 10, 11^{3}, 12^{2}, 13^{2}, 14, 15^{4}, 16^{4}, 17^{3}, 18^{4}, 19, 20^{2}, 21, 22^{5}, 23^{2}, 24^{2}, 25^{3}, 26^{5}, 42:1^{2}, 2, 3, 4^{2}, 5, 6, 7, 8, 9, 10, 11^{4}, 12, 13^{4}, 14^{2}, 15, 19, 20^{2}, 43:2^{3}, 3^{3}, 4, 5^{2}

EZEKIEL 43:6^{2}, 7^{3}, 8^{3}, 9^{2}, 10, 11^{11}, 13^{5}, 14^{4}, 15^{2}, 16, 17^{5}, 18^{2}, 19, 20^{5}, 21, 22^{2}, 23, 24^{3}, 25, 26^{2}, 27^{4}, 44:1, 2, 3, 4^{3}, 5^{5}, 6, 7^{3}, 8, 10, 11^{3}, 12^{2}, 13^{2}, 14, 15^{2}, 16^{2}, 17^{3}, 18, 19^{4}, 23^{4}, 24^{5}, 25, 26, 27, 28^{2}, 29^{3}, 30^{7}, 45:1^{2}, 2, 3^{5}, 4^{2}, 5^{3}, 6^{3}, 7^{6}, 8^{2}, 9^{3}, 10^{2}, 11^{2}, 12^{2}, 13, 15^{3}, 17^{8}, 18, 19^{4}, 20^{2}, 22^{2}, 23^{3}, 24^{3}, 25^{2}, 46:1, 2^{5}, 3, 4^{2}, 5^{3}, 6^{3}, 7^{4}, 8^{2}, 9, 10^{2}, 11^{5}, 12^{3}, 14^{2}, 15^{2}, 19, 20, 21^{2}, 22, 23^{2}, 47:1^{2}, 2^{2}, 3^{2}, 4^{2}, 5, 6^{2}, 7, 8^{2}, 9^{3}, 10, 11, 12^{4}, 14^{2}, 15, 16, 17^{4}, 18^{5}, 19^{2}, 22^{3}, 23, 48:1, 2, 3, 4, 5, 6, 7, 8^{4}, 9^{2}

EZEKIEL 48:10^{7}, 12, 13^{5}, 14, 15^{4}, 16^{8}, 17^{8}, 18^{4}, 19, 20^{2}, 21^{8}, 22^{2}, 24, 25, 26, 27, 28^{2}, 29, 30^{2}, 31, 32^{4}, 33^{3}, 34, 35

DANIEL 1:1, 2^{2}, 3^{3}, 4^{6}, 5^{2}, 6, 7^{3}, 9, 10^{2}, 11, 12^{2}, 13^{2}, 14, 15^{2}, 16^{2}, 17^{4}, 19^{3}, 20^{3}, 21, 2:1^{2}, 2^{4}, 3^{2}, 4, 5^{2}, 6^{4}, 7^{2}, 8, 9^{2}, 10, 11^{2}, 12^{2}, 13^{3}, 14, 15, 16^{2}, 17^{2}, 18, 20^{3}, 21^{4}, 22^{2}, 23^{3}, 24^{2}, 25, 26^{2}, 27, 28^{2}, 29, 30, 31^{2}, 32^{2}, 33, 34^{2}, 35^{5}, 36, 37^{2}, 38^{3}, 39^{2}, 40^{4}, 41^{3}, 42^{3}, 43, 44^{4}, 45^{4}, 46^{3}, 47^{3}, 48^{3}, 49^{2}, 3:1, 2^{2}, 3^{3}, 4, 5^{2}, 6^{2}, 7^{3}, 8, 9, 10^{3}, 11^{2}, 12, 13^{2}, 14^{2}, 15^{4}, 16^{2}, 17, 19^{3}, 20^{3}, 21^{3}, 22^{2}, 23^{2}, 24^{4}, 25^{3}

DANIEL 3:26^{5}, 27^{3}, 28^{5}, 29^{3}, 30, 4:1, 2, 3^{2}, 4, 5^{2}, 7^{2}, 8^{2}, 9^{2}, 10^{2}, 11^{3}, 12^{4}, 13^{2}, 14^{4}, 15^{3}, 16^{2}, 17^{3}, 19^{4}, 20^{2}, 21^{3}, 22^{3}, 23^{7}, 24, 25^{5}, 26, 27^{2}, 30^{2}, 32^{4}, 33^{4}, 34^{6}, 35^{4}, 36^{6}, 37^{4}, 5:1, 2^{3}, 3^{3}, 4^{3}, 5^{2}, 6^{2}, 7^{6}, 9^{2}, 10^{3}, 11^{4}, 12^{5}, 13^{2}, 14^{3}, 15^{2}, 16^{5}, 17^{3}, 18^{3}, 19^{6}, 20^{2}, 21^{5}, 22, 23^{9}, 24, 25, 26, 27, 28^{2}, 29^{3}, 31^{2}, 6:1, 2^{2}, 3^{2}, 4, 6^{2}, 7^{3}, 8^{2}, 9, 10^{3}, 11^{2}, 12^{3}, 13, 14^{2}, 15^{2}, 16^{3}, 17^{4}, 18^{2}, 19, 20^{3}, 22^{2}, 23^{2}, 24^{6}, 25, 26^{4}, 27^{4}, 28, 7:1^{2}, 2^{2}, 3, 4^{4}, 5^{4}, 6^{2}, 7^{8}, 8^{3}, 9^{3}, 10^{3}, 11^{2}, 12, 13^{3}, 14^{5}, 15, 16^{2}, 18^{2}, 19^{2}, 20^{4}, 21^{2}, 22^{2}, 23^{3}, 24^{4}, 25^{7}, 26^{2}

DANIEL 7:27^{5}, 28, 8:2^{4}, 3^{4}, 4^{3}, 5^{3}, 6^{2}, 7^{7}, 8^{2}, 9^{3}, 10^{4}, 11^{2}, 12^{4}, 13^{3}, 14^{2}, 15^{2}, 16^{2}, 17^{2}, 18, 19, 20, 21^{2}, 23^{2}, 24^{6}, 25^{3}, 26^{2}, 27^{4}, 9:3^{4}, 4^{6}, 5^{4}, 6^{2}, 7^{3}, 8, 9, 11, 12^{2}, 13, 14, 15^{2}, 16^{3}, 17^{2}, 18^{3}, 19^{2}, 20^{5}, 22^{4}, 23^{2}, 24^{7}, 25^{5}, 26^{6}, 27^{5}, 10:1^{3}, 4^{2}, 5^{2}, 6^{5}, 7, 8^{3}, 9^{2}, 10^{2}, 11^{3}, 12^{2}, 13^{2}, 15^{2}, 16^{4}, 18^{2}, 19^{3}, 20^{2}, 21, 11:1, 2^{3}, 3^{2}, 4^{3}, 5^{4}, 6^{4}, 7^{3}, 8^{4}, 9, 10^{5}, 11^{4}, 12^{2}, 13^{3}, 14, 15^{3}, 16^{2}, 17^{2}, 18, 19^{2}, 21^{2}, 22^{2}, 23^{2}, 24^{4}, 25^{4}, 26^{2}, 27^{2}, 28^{3}, 29, 30^{3}, 31^{4}, 32^{3}, 33^{3}, 35^{3}, 36^{5}, 38^{4}, 39^{3}, 40^{7}, 41^{3}, 42, 43^{4}, 44^{2}, 45^{2}, 12:1^{3}, 2^{3}, 3^{3}, 4^{3}, 5^{2}, 6, 7^{5}, 8

DANIEL 12:9^{2}, 10^{3}, 11^{3}, 12^{3}, 13

HOSEA 1:1^{2}, 2^{2}, 3^{2}, 4^{3}, 5, 6^{3}, 7^{2}, 8, 9, 10, 11^{3}, 2:1, 2, 3^{4}, 4, 5^{3}, 6, 7^{3}, 8^{4}, 9^{4}, 10^{2}, 11^{2}, 12^{4}, 13^{5}, 14^{2}, 15^{4}, 16^{2}, 17, 18^{7}, 19^{4}, 20, 21^{2}, 22^{4}, 23^{4}, 3:1, 2^{2}, 3^{2}, 4^{5}, 5^{4}, 4:2^{5}, 3^{2}, 5, 8, 9^{3}, 10^{2}, 11^{2}, 12^{2}, 13^{4}, 14, 15, 19, 5:1^{3}, 2, 3^{2}, 4, 5^{2}, 6, 8, 11, 12, 13^{2}, 14^{3}, 15^{2}, 6:1^{3}, 2, 3^{2}, 4, 5, 6^{2}, 8, 9, 7:1^{3}, 2, 3, 7, 9^{2}, 10^{2}, 14^{3}, 15, 8:1, 4^{2}, 7, 10, 13^{2}, 14^{3}, 9:2^{2}, 3, 5, 7, 8, 10^{2}, 11^{2}, 14, 17, 10:5, 6, 8^{3}, 10, 11^{3}, 12, 14, 11:1, 2, 4^{2}, 6^{3}, 7, 9^{2}, 11^{2}, 12^{2}, 12:1^{4}

HOSEA 12:2, 3, 4^{3}, 6^{2}, 8, 9, 10^{2}, 12^{3}, 13^{2}, 14, 13:2^{4}, 3^{2}, 4, 6, 8^{2}, 10^{2}, 11, 15^{2}, 16, 14:2^{2}, 5, 6^{2}, 7, 8, 9^{3}

JOEL 1:2, 3^{2}, 4^{2}, 5^{2}, 6^{2}, 7^{2}, 9, 11, 12^{2}, 13^{2}, 14^{2}, 15, 16, 19, 20, 2:1, 2^{3}, 3^{3}, 4, 7^{2}, 8, 9, 10^{2}, 11^{3}, 12^{3}, 13^{6}, 14^{3}, 16^{2}, 17^{3}, 18, 19^{5}, 20^{5}, 21, 22, 23^{3}, 24^{3}, 25^{3}, 26^{4}, 27^{4}, 28^{3}, 29^{2}, 30^{4}, 31^{2}, 32^{3}, 3:1^{2}, 2^{4}, 3^{3}, 4^{5}, 5^{2}, 6, 7, 8^{3}, 10, 11^{2}, 12, 15^{2}, 16^{4}, 17, 18^{5}, 19, 20

AMOS 1:1, 2^{4}, 3, 5^{3}, 6, 8^{4}, 9^{2}, 11^{4}, 13, 14, 15^{2}, 2:1, 2^{3}, 3^{2}, 4^{3}, 5, 6^{2}, 7^{3}, 8^{2}, 9^{2}, 10, 11^{2}, 12, 14, 15, 16, 3:5

AMOS 3:6^{2}, 9^{4}, 10, 11^{2}, 12, 13, 14^{2}, 15^{3}, 4:1, 2, 3^{2}, 4^{3}, 5^{3}, 6^{2}, 7^{4}, 9^{4}, 10^{2}, 11^{2}, 12, 13^{3}, 5:3, 4, 5^{2}, 6^{3}, 7, 8^{4}, 10, 11, 12^{2}, 14^{2}, 15^{2}, 16^{3}, 17, 18, 19^{3}, 20^{2}, 21, 22, 24, 26, 6:1, 2^{2}, 3, 4^{3}, 5, 6, 7, 8, 9, 10^{4}, 11^{2}, 12, 14, 7:1^{2}, 2, 4^{3}, 7, 8^{2}, 9^{3}, 11, 12^{2}, 13, 14^{2}, 15^{2}, 16, 17^{5}, 8:1, 2^{2}, 3, 5^{3}, 6^{2}, 8^{4}, 9^{2}, 10^{6}, 12^{4}, 13, 14^{3}, 9:1^{4}, 3^{4}, 4^{4}, 5^{5}, 6^{2}, 7^{2}, 8, 9, 11^{3}, 12, 13^{3}, 14^{6}, 15^{2}

OBADIAH 1^{2}, 4, 7, 8, 9, 10, 11^{2}, 16^{2}, 17^{2}, 18^{6}, 19^{5}, 20^{2}, 21^{2}

JONAH 1:2, 3^{3}, 4, 5^{4}, 6, 7^{2}, 8^{2}, 9^{3}, 10, 11

JONAH 1:12^{2}, 13, 14^{2}, 15^{2}, 16^{2}, 17^{2}, 2:2^{3}, 3^{2}, 7, 10^{2}, 3:1, 2, 3, 4^{4}, 5^{2}, 6^{4}, 7^{3}, 8^{3}, 9^{2}, 10^{3}, 4:1, 2^{5}, 5^{3}, 6^{2}, 7, 8^{4}, 9^{2}, 10, 11^{3}

MICAH 1:1^{2}, 2^{2}, 3^{2}, 4^{3}, 5^{2}, 6^{3}, 7^{4}, 8^{3}, 16, 2:1, 2^{6}, 4^{2}, 10, 11^{2}, 13^{4}, 3:1^{2}, 2^{2}, 3^{4}, 5^{2}, 6^{3}, 7, 8^{3}, 9^{2}, 10, 11^{3}, 12^{2}, 4:1^{2}, 2^{7}, 3^{4}, 4^{2}, 5^{2}, 6^{2}, 7^{3}, 8, 10^{3}, 11, 13^{5}, 5:4^{3}, 5^{3}, 6^{3}, 7, 8^{3}, 9, 10^{2}, 11^{2}, 12^{2}, 13^{2}, 14, 15^{2}, 6:1, 2^{2}, 3, 4^{3}, 5, 6, 8^{2}, 9^{2}, 10, 11, 12^{2}, 14^{3}, 15, 16^{3}, 7:2, 3^{2}, 4, 9^{2}, 10, 12^{4}, 14, 16, 17, 18, 19, 20

NAHUM 1:2^{3}, 3^{4}, 4^{4}, 5^{3}, 6^{2}, 7, 8, 10, 12

NAHUM 1:13, 14^{2}, 2:2, 3, 5, 6, 7^{2}, 9, 10^{6}, 11^{3}, 12^{3}, 13^{4}, 3:1, 2^{3}, 3^{4}, 4, 5^{3}, 6^{3}, 7^{2}, 8, 9^{3}, 10^{2}, 14, 16, 17^{2}, 18

HABAK. 1:2^{2}, 3^{4}, 4, 5^{2}, 6, 7^{2}, 8^{3}, 9, 10^{3}, 11^{2}, 12, 13^{2}, 14, 15^{2}, 16^{2}, 17, 2:1^{3}, 2^{3}, 3, 5^{3}, 6^{3}, 7^{2}, 8^{2}, 10, 11, 12, 13, 15, 16^{2}, 17^{3}, 18, 19^{2}, 3:2, 3^{2}, 4^{2}, 5, 6^{3}, 7, 8, 10^{2}, 11^{2}, 16, 17^{2}, 19^{2}

ZEPH. 1:3^{4}, 4^{3}, 5^{4}, 6^{2}, 8^{3}, 9, 10^{3}, 12^{2}, 13^{2}, 14, 15^{4}, 16^{2}, 17^{3}, 2:4^{2}, 6^{3}, 7^{2}, 8^{2}, 9^{4}, 10, 11, 13^{4}, 14^{2}, 15^{2}, 3:1, 4, 7, 11, 12^{2}, 13^{2}, 14, 16, 19^{4}, 20

HAGGAI 1:1, 4, 6^{2}, 8^{4}, 9^{3}, 10, 11^{9}, 12^{3}

HAGGAI 1:14^{5}, 15, 2:1, 2^{2}, 3, 4^{3}, 6^{4}, 7^{2}, 8, 9, 10, 12^{3}, 13^{2}, 14^{4}, 15^{2}, 17^{2}, 18^{2}, 19^{3}, 20^{2}, 21, 22^{6}, 23

ZECH. 1:3, 4, 5, 6^{4}, 7, 8^{4}, 9, 10^{3}, 11^{5}, 12^{3}, 13^{2}, 14, 15^{2}, 16, 17^{2}, 18^{2}, 19^{3}, 20, 21, 2:1^{2}, 2^{2}, 3^{2}, 4^{2}, 5, 6, 9^{2}, 10^{2}, 11^{4}, 12^{2}, 3:1^{2}, 2, 3, 4^{4}, 5^{3}, 6, 7^{3}, 8, 9, 10, 4:1^{2}, 2^{5}, 3^{2}, 4, 5^{2}, 6, 7, 9, 10^{2}, 11^{2}, 12^{2}, 13^{3}, 5:1^{3}, 2^{3}, 3, 4^{5}, 5^{2}, 6^{2}, 7^{2}, 8^{3}, 9^{5}, 11^{3}, 6:1^{5}, 2, 3^{3}, 4, 5^{2}, 6^{2}, 7^{6}, 8, 9, 10^{3}, 11^{3}, 12^{3}, 13^{5}, 14^{4}, 15^{4}, 7:1, 2^{2}, 3^{2}, 5^{3}, 6^{3}, 7^{3}, 8, 9^{2}, 10^{2}, 11^{2}, 12, 13^{2}, 8:2, 3^{3}, 4^{2}, 5^{2}, 7

ZECH. 8:8^{5}, 12^{3}, 13^{3}, 14, 15, 16, 17^{2}, 18, 19^{6}, 20, 21^{2}, 22^{2}, 9:1, 2^{2}, 3^{3}, 4^{2}, 5^{5}, 6^{2}, 7^{4}, 8^{3}, 9^{3}, 10^{6}, 13^{2}, 14^{4}, 15^{6}, 16, 17^{2}, 10:1, 2^{2}, 3^{2}, 5^{3}, 6^{5}, 7^{3}, 8^{2}, 9^{4}, 10^{4}, 11^{5}, 12^{3}, 11:5^{3}, 6^{3}, 7^{4}, 8^{2}, 9^{2}, 10^{2}, 11^{2}, 12^{2}, 13^{3}, 14, 15, 16, 17^{2}, 12:1^{2}, 2, 3, 4^{3}, 5, 6^{4}, 7, 8^{2}, 9, 10^{6}, 12^{3}, 13^{2}, 14, 13:1^{2}, 2^{4}, 3^{4}, 4, 6, 7^{3}, 8^{2}, 9^{5}, 14:1, 2^{5}, 3, 4^{6}, 5^{3}, 6, 8^{3}, 9^{2}, 10^{3}, 11^{2}, 12^{3}, 13^{3}, 14^{4}, 15^{3}, 16^{2}, 17, 18^{2}, 19, 20, 21^{5}

MALACHI 1:3^{3}, 4^{3}, 5^{2}, 6^{3}, 7, 8^{3}, 9, 11^{2}, 12, 13^{4}, 14^{3}, 2:1, 2^{2}, 3^{2}, 4, 5^{3}, 6^{3}, 7, 9, 11^{3}, 12^{2}, 13^{2}, 14^{2}

MALACHI 2:15^{3}, 17, 3:1^{2}, 2^{2}, 3^{5}, 4^{2}, 5^{8}, 7^{2}, 8, 9, 10^{2}, 11^{2}, 12, 14^{2}, 15, 16^{4}, 17^{2}, 18^{3}, 4:1^{3}, 2^{2}, 3, 4, 5, 6^{3}

MATT. 1:2^{3}, 3^{4}, 4^{3}, 5^{3}, 6^{2}, 7^{3}, 8^{3}, 9^{3}, 10^{3}, 11^{2}, 12^{2}, 13^{3}, 14^{3}, 15^{3}, 16, 17^{2}, 19, 21^{2}, 23^{2}, 24, 25^{2}, 2:2, 3, 4^{2}, 5, 6, 8^{5}, 9^{2}, 11^{6}, 12, 13^{5}, 14^{2}, 15, 16^{4}, 18^{3}, 20^{3}, 21^{4}, 23^{2}, 3:2, 4^{4}, 5^{2}, 6, 7, 9, 10^{2}, 11, 12^{2}, 14, 15, 16^{4}, 17, 4:2^{2}, 3, 4, 5, 6^{2}, 8^{2}, 9^{2}, 10, 11^{2}, 13^{3}, 15, 16^{2}, 17, 18^{2}, 19^{2}, 20^{2}, 21^{3}, 22^{3}, 23^{4}, 24^{7}, 25^{5}, 5:1^{2}, 2^{2}, 6, 11^{2}, 12, 13, 15^{2}, 16, 18, 19^{2}, 20, 21, 22, 23, 24^{3}, 25^{2}, 29^{3}, 30^{3}, 32

MATT. 5:38, 40^{2}, 41, 42, 43, 44^{2}, 45^{3}, 47, 6:2, 4, 5, 6^{2}, 8, 12, 13^{3}, 17, 18, 19^{3}, 20, 24^{3}, 25, 28, 29, 30, 33^{2}, 7:2, 3, 4, 5, 6^{2}, 7^{3}, 8^{2}, 12, 13^{2}, 14^{2}, 19, 22^{2}, 23, 24, 25^{5}, 26^{2}, 27^{6}, 28, 29, 8:2^{2}, 3^{3}, 4^{2}, 5, 6, 7^{2}, 8^{2}, 9^{6}, 10, 11^{5}, 12, 13^{3}, 14^{2}, 15^{4}, 16^{2}, 17, 19^{2}, 20^{2}, 21^{2}, 22, 23, 24, 25^{2}, 26^{4}, 27, 28, 29, 30, 32^{4}, 33^{4}, 34^{2}, 9:1^{3}, 2^{2}, 3, 4, 5, 6, 7, 8, 9^{4}, 10^{4}, 11^{2}, 13^{2}, 14, 15^{2}, 16, 17^{3}, 18^{3}, 19^{3}, 20^{2}, 22^{2}, 23^{3}, 24, 25^{2}, 26, 27^{2}, 28^{2}, 30^{2}, 33^{2}, 35^{5}, 36, 10:1^{3}, 2^{2}, 3^{3}, 4, 5^{2}, 7, 11^{2}, 12, 13, 14, 15, 16

MATT. 10:17, 18^{3}, 21^{4}, 25, 26, 27, 28^{2}, 29, 35^{2}, 36, 37, 38^{2}, 39, 40, 41, 42, 11:1^{2}, 3, 4^{3}, 5^{3}, 6, 7, 9, 12^{2}, 13, 14, 16, 17^{3}, 18, 19^{4}, 21^{2}, 22, 23, 25^{4}, 27^{2}, 28^{2}, 29^{3}, 30, 12:1^{3}, 3, 4, 5, 7, 9, 10^{2}, 11^{3}, 13^{2}, 14, 15^{2}, 16, 18, 20, 21, 22^{4}, 23^{2}, 25^{3}, 26, 27, 29^{2}, 30, 31, 32, 33^{2}, 35, 37, 38, 39^{3}, 40^{2}, 41^{2}, 42^{2}, 43, 44^{2}, 45^{4}, 46, 47, 48^{2}, 49^{3}, 50^{2}, 13:1, 2^{3}, 3, 4^{3}, 5, 6^{2}, 7^{3}, 8, 10^{2}, 11, 12, 13, 14^{4}, 15^{6}, 16, 17^{4}, 19^{2}, 20, 21, 22^{3}, 23^{2}, 25^{2}, 26, 27, 28, 30^{2}, 31, 32^{2}, 33, 34, 36^{2}, 37, 39, 40, 41, 42^{2}, 44^{3}, 46^{2}, 47

MATT. 13:48^{2}, 49, 50^{2}, 52, 53, 54^{3}, 55^{4}, 56, 57^{2}, 58, 14:2^{2}, 3^{2}, 5, 6, 8, 9^{2}, 10^{2}, 11^{3}, 12^{5}, 13, 14^{4}, 15^{3}, 17^{2}, 19^{7}, 20^{3}, 21^{2}, 22^{2}, 23^{2}, 25, 26^{2}, 28^{2}, 29^{2}, 30, 31^{3}, 32, 33, 34, 35^{2}, 36^{2}, 15:1, 3, 4^{2}, 6, 8, 10^{3}, 12, 13, 14, 15, 16, 17, 18, 21^{2}, 22^{2}, 23^{2}, 24, 25, 26^{2}, 27, 28^{2}, 29^{4}, 30^{4}, 31^{2}, 32^{3}, 33, 34^{3}, 35, 36^{6}, 37^{3}, 38^{2}, 39^{3}, 16:1, 2, 3^{2}, 4^{4}, 5, 6^{2}, 7, 9, 10, 11, 12, 14^{2}, 16^{2}, 17^{3}, 18^{3}, 19^{3}, 21^{5}, 22, 23, 24^{2}, 25, 26, 27, 17:1^{3}, 2^{3}, 3^{2}, 4^{3}, 5, 6^{2}, 7^{4}, 8, 9, 10, 11^{3}, 12, 14^{2}, 15^{2}, 16^{2}, 17^{2}, 18^{3}, 19, 20^{3}, 21, 22, 23, 24^{2}

MATT. 17:25, 27^{5}, 18.2^{2}, 3^{2}, 5, 6, 8, 9^{2}, 12^{4}, 13^{2}, 15^{2}, 17^{2}, 18, 21^{2}, 24, 25^{4}, 26^{2}, 27^{2}, 28^{3}, 29^{3}, 30^{2}, 31^{2}, 34^{2}, 19:1^{2}, 2^{2}, 3, 4^{3}, 5^{4}, 7, 9^{3}, 12^{2}, 13^{2}, 14, 15^{2}, 16^{2}, 17, 19^{2}, 21^{5}, 24, 26, 27^{2}, 28, 29^{2}, 30, 20:2, 3^{2}, 4^{3}, 5^{2}, 6^{3}, 7, 8, 9, 10, 11, 12^{2}, 13, 14, 16, 17^{2}, 18^{3}, 19^{4}, 20, 21^{2}, 22^{2}, 23^{3}, 24, 25^{2}, 27, 28, 29, 30, 31, 32^{3}, 34^{3}, 21:1^{2}, 2^{3}, 3^{2}, 5^{2}, 6^{2}, 7^{4}, 8^{2}, 9^{2}, 10, 11, 12^{5}, 13, 14^{3}, 15^{4}, 16^{3}, 17^{3}, 19^{4}, 20, 21^{3}, 22, 23^{4}, 24^{2}, 25, 27^{3}, 28^{2}, 29^{2}, 30^{5}, 31, 32^{3}, 33^{3}, 34, 35^{4}, 36, 38, 39^{3}, 41, 42, 43, 44, 45^{3}, 22:1^{3}, 3^{2}, 4^{3}

MATT.
22:5
6[3]
7[8]
9
10[3]
11
12[2]
13[4]
15
16[2]
18
19
20[2]
21
22[2]
23
24
25[2]
26
27
29
32[2]
33
35
37[2]
38
39
40
46
23:1
2
3[2]
4[2]
5
6[2]
7[2]
8
9
12[2]
13
14[2]
15[3]
17
18
19
20
21[2]
22[2]
23[6]
24
25[3]
26
27[2]
28
29[2]
30
34[6]
35
37[2]
24:1[3]
2
3[3]
4[2]
5
6[2]
7[4]
9[2]
10[3]
11[2]
12
14[2]
19[2]
22
24[3]
27
29[3]
30[4]
31[2]
32
35
36
38[2]
39[2]
40
41
43
45
48
49[3]
50
51[3]
25:1
2[2]
3
5
6
7
8
9[2]
10[3]
12
14
15[3]
16[2]
17
18[2]
19
20[2]
21
22
23
24[2]
25[3]
26[3]
27
28
29

MATT.
25:30[2]
31
32[2]
33
35[2]
36[3]
37[2]
38[2]
39
40[2]
41
42[2]
43[4]
44
46
26:1
2
3[2]
4[2]
7
9
15[3]
16
18[2]
19[2]
21
22[2]
23[2]
25
26[5]
27[3]
30
31
33
36[2]
37[4]
38
39[3]
40[3]
41
42
43[2]
44[3]
45[3]
47[4]
49[2]
50[3]
51[4]
53
55[2]
56
57[2]
58[2]
59[2]
61[2]
62[2]
63[2]
64
66
67[2]
69
71[2]
72
73[2]
74[2]
75[3]
27:1
2[2]
3[2]
4
5[4]
6[2]
7[2]
9
10
11[3]
12[2]
14
16
20[2]
21
23
24
25[2]
26
27
28[2]
29[3]
30[3]
31[3]
32
33
34
35[3]
36
37
38
39
40[2]
41
42
46
48[5]
51[3]
52[2]
53[3]
54[2]
55
56[3]
58
59
60[3]
61[2]
62
64[2]
66[2]
28:1

MATT.
28:2[4]
3
4[2]
5[2]
7[3]
8[3]
9[4]
10
11
12[2]
13
14[2]
15[2]
17
18[3]
19[3]
20

MARK
1:4
5[3]
6[4]
7[2]
9[2]
10
11
12
13[3]
15[3]
16
17[2]
18[2]
19[2]
20[3]
21[3]
22[2]
23[2]
25[2]
26[2]
27[2]
28
29[3]
30
31[5]
32[2]
33
34[3]
35[3]
36[2]
37
38
39[2]
40[3]
41[3]
42[2]
43[2]
44[2]
45[3]
2:1[2]
2[2]
3
4[2]
6
8
9[2]
11[2]
12[3]
13[3]
14[4]
15[4]
16[5]
18[5]
19
20
21
22[3]
23[2]
24
25[3]
26[2]
27[2]
3:1[2]
2
3
4
5[3]
6[2]
7[2]
8[5]
9
11[2]
12
13[3]
14[2]
15[2]
16
17[3]
18[8]
19[2]
20
21
22[2]
23[2]
25
26[2]
27[2]
28
31[2]
32[3]
33
34[3]
35[2]
4:1[3]
2[2]
4[3]
5[2]
6

MARK
4:7[4]
8[6]
9
10
11
12[4]
13
15[2]
16
17[2]
18
19[4]
20[4]
21[2]
24[2]
25
26
27[5]
30
32[2]
33
34
35
36[2]
37[2]
38[3]
39[5]
40
41[3]
5:1
2
3
4[3]
5[4]
6
7[2]
9[2]
10
12
13[5]
14[4]
15[6]
16[2]
17
18
19[2]
20[3]
21[2]
22[2]
23[3]
24[2]
25
26[3]
27
29[2]
30[2]
31[2]
32
33[3]
34[2]
37[3]
38[4]
39[2]
40[4]
41[2]
42[3]
43[2]
6:1[3]
2[3]
3[5]
4[2]
5[2]
6[2]
7[4]
8
9
10
11[2]
12[2]
13[3]
14[3]
15
17[2]
19
20[4]
21[2]
22[5]
23
24[3]
25[3]
26[2]
27[4]
28[3]
29[3]
30[3]
31[4]
32
33[5]
34[3]
35[3]
36[2]
37[4]
38[3]
39
40[2]
41[6]
42[2]
43[2]
44
45[2]
46
47[2]
48[3]
49
50[3]
51[4]
53[2]

MARK
6:54
55[2]
56[3]
7:1
2
3
4[4]
5
6
8[2]
12
13
14[2]
17
18
19
20
23
24[5]
25[2]
26
27
28[2]
29
30[2]
31[2]
32[3]
33[4]
34[2]
35[3]
36
37[2]
8:1[2]
2
3
4
5[2]
6[6]
7[3]
8[2]
9[2]
10[2]
11[2]
12[2]
13[2]
15[2]
16
17
18
20[2]
21
22[3]
23[4]
24[2]
25[3]
26
27[3]
28[2]
29[3]
30
31[6]
32[3]
33
34[3]
35
36
38[2]
9:1
2[5]
3
4[2]
5[5]
7[2]
8
9
10
11
12[5]
13
14[2]
15[2]
16
17[2]
18[6]
19
20[4]
21[2]
22[3]
24[2]
25[2]
26[4]
27[2]
28
29[2]
30[3]
31[3]
32
33[2]
35[4]
36[3]
37
38[3]
42[2]
43
44
45
46
47
48
49
50
10:1[4]
2[2]
3[2]
4[2]
5[2]
6

MARK
10:7[2]
8
10
11[2]
12[2]
13[2]
14[2]
16[2]
17[3]
18
19
20[2]
21[5]
22[2]
23[2]
24[2]
26
27
28
29[3]
30[6]
31
32[6]
33[4]
34[5]
35[2]
36
37
38
39[3]
40
41[2]
42[2]
44
45
46[3]
47[2]
48
49[3]
50[2]
51[2]
52[3]
11:1[2]
2[3]
3[2]
4[3]
5
6[2]
7[3]
8[3]
9[2]
11[4]
12
13[2]
14[3]
15[6]
16
17
18[3]
19
20
21
22
23[2]
24
25
27[4]
28[2]
29[4]
31
33[3]
12:1[6]
2
3[2]
4[4]
5[4]
7
8[3]
9[2]
10
11
12[3]
13[2]
14[2]
16[4]
17[3]
18
19[3]
20[2]
21[3]
22[2]
24
26[3]
28[3]
29
30[4]
31
32[2]
33[6]
34[2]
35[2]
37[2]
38[2]
39[2]
40
41[3]
42[2]
43[2]
13:1[2]
2
3[4]
4
5
6
7[2]
8[4]
9[3]

MARK
13:10
11
12[3]
13
15
16
17
18
20
21
22[3]
24
25[2]
26[2]
27[2]
28
31
32
33
34[3]
37
14:1[4]
3[3]
4[2]
5[2]
6
7
10
11[3]
12[2]
13[3]
14
15[2]
16[4]
17
18[2]
19[3]
20[2]
22[5]
23[3]
24
26
27[2]
30
32[2]
33[5]
34[2]
35[3]
36
37[3]
38
39[3]
40
41[3]
43[5]
44[2]
45[3]
46[2]
47[3]
48[3]
49
50[2]
51[2]
52[2]
53[4]
54[3]
55[3]
57[2]
58
60[2]
61[2]
62[3]
63
64
65[5]
66
67[3]
68[2]
69[2]
70[3]
71
72[3]
15:1[6]
2[2]
3
4
7
8
12[2]
13
14
15[2]
16[2]
17[3]
18
19[3]
20[3]
21[2]
22
23
24
25[2]
26
27[2]
28[2]
29[3]
30
32[2]
33
34
35
36[4]
37[2]
38
39[2]
40[3]
41[2]

MARK
15:42
43[2]
44[2]
45
46[5]
47[2]
16:1[4]
2
3
4
5[2]
6
7
8[3]
10[3]
11[2]
12
13[2]
14[2]
15[2]
16
17
18[2]
19
20[3]

LUKE
1:2
5[2]
6[2]
7[2]
8
10
11
12[2]
13[2]
14[3]
15[2]
16
17[3]
18[2]
19[3]
20[2]
21[2]
22[3]
23
24[2]
26
27
28[2]
29[2]
30
31[3]
32[2]
33[2]
35[3]
36[2]
38[2]
39[2]
40[2]
41[2]
42[3]
43
45
46
47
49
50
52
53
55
56[2]
57
58[3]
59[2]
60[2]
61
62
63[3]
64[4]
65[2]
66[2]
67[2]
68
69
71
72
75
76
79
80[3]
2:1
2
3
4[2]
6
7[3]
8
9[3]
10
12
13[2]
14
15[2]
16[4]
17
18
19
20[3]
21
22
24
25[4]
26
27[2]
28[2]
32

LUKE
2:33[2]
34[4]
36[2]
37[4]
38[2]
39
40[3]
42
43[3]
44[2]
45
46[2]
47[2]
48[3]
49
50
51[3]
52[4]
3:1[4]
2
3
5[4]
6
8
9[2]
10
11[2]
12
13
14[4]
15[2]
16
17[2]
18
19
21
22[2]
23
4:1[2]
2[2]
3
4
5
6[3]
8[3]
9[3]
11
12
13
14[2]
15
16[3]
17[2]
18
20[4]
21
22[3]
23
24
25
27[2]
28
29[3]
31[2]
33[2]
35[4]
36[4]
37
38[4]
39[5]
40[2]
41[3]
42[5]
43
44
5:1
2[2]
3[4]
4
5[2]
6[2]
7[4]
9
10[3]
11[2]
12[2]
13[3]
14[3]
15
16[2]
17[5]
18[3]
19[2]
20
21[2]
23
24[2]
25[3]
26[3]
27[3]
28[2]
29[3]
30[3]
31
33[4]
34
35
36[2]
37[3]
38
6:1[3]
2
3[2]
4[3]
5
6[3]
7[2]

LUKE
6:8[4]
10[3]
11[2]
12[2]
13[2]
14[3]
15[2]
16[2]
17[8]
18[2]
19[2]
20[2]
22[3]
23
25
28
29[2]
30
31
33
34
35[5]
37[3]
38[3]
39
41
42
45
46[2]
47[2]
48[4]
49[3]
7:2[2]
3[2]
4
5
6
7
8[6]
9[2]
10
11[3]
12[2]
13[2]
14[4]
15[3]
16[3]
17[2]
18
19
21[4]
22[2]
23
24
25
26
29[2]
30
31[2]
32[4]
33
34[4]
36[3]
37
38[5]
39
40[2]
41
42
43
44[3]
48
49
50
8:1[4]
2[2]
3[3]
4[2]
5[3]
6[2]
7[3]
8[4]
9
10[2]
12
13[2]
14[5]
15[2]
17
18
19[2]
20[2]
21[4]
22[2]
23[3]
24[6]
25[4]
26
27[2]
28[2]
29[4]
30[2]
31
32[3]
33[3]
34[3]
35[4]
37[2]
39[3]
40
41[4]
42
43
44[2]
45[6]
46
47[3]

LUKE
8:48
50
51[5]
52[2]
53
54[3]
55[3]
56
9:1[3]
2[2]
3
4[2]
5
6[3]
7
8[2]
9[2]
10[3]
11[4]
12[5]
13[3]
14
15[2]
16[4]
17[3]
18[2]
19
21[2]
22[5]
23[3]
25
26[3]
28[4]
29[3]
30[2]
31
32[3]
33[4]
34[2]
35
36[3]
37
38
39[4]
40[2]
41[3]
42[5]
43
45[2]
46
47[2]
48[2]
49[3]
50
51
52[3]
53
54[3]
55[2]
56
57
58[2]
59[2]
60
61
62[2]
10:1[3]
4
5
6
7[2]
8[2]
9[2]
10[2]
13[2]
14
15
16[2]
17
18
19[3]
21[4]
22[3]
23[2]
24[4]
25[2]
27[5]
28[2]
29
30[4]
31[2]
32[3]
33
34[6]
35[4]
37[2]
38
39[2]
40[2]
41[3]
42
11:1
2
4[2]
5[3]
6
7[4]
8[2]
9[4]
10[2]
14[4]
16
17
19
22[2]
24
25[2]

LUKE
11:26[4]
27[3]
28
29[2]
31[2]
32[2]
37[3]
38
39[3]
41
42[5]
43
44[2]
45
46[2]
47
48
49[3]
51
52
53[3]
54
12:3
4[2]
6
10
11[3]
13
14
15[2]
16
17
18[4]
19[2]
21
22
23
24
25
27
28
29
30
31
33
35
36[2]
37[3]
38[2]
39[2]
42[2]
45[6]
46[3]
47[2]
48[2]
49
50
52
53[3]
54[2]
55[2]
56
57
58[2]
13:2
4
6[3]
7
8[2]
9[2]
10
11[3]
12[2]
13[3]
14[4]
15[2]
16
17[2]
18
19[4]
20
21
22[3]
23
24
25[5]
26[2]
28[5]
29[5]
30[2]
31
32[5]
33[2]
34[2]
35
14:1
2
3[2]
4[4]
5[2]
6
7
9[4]
10
11
12
14
15
16
17
18[3]
19[2]
20[2]
21[6]
22[2]
23[3]
25[3]

LUKE
14:26[7]
27[2]
28
29
30
31
32
15:1
2[3]
3
4[2]
5
6[2]
7
8[2]
9[2]
11
12[2]
13[3]
14[2]
15[3]
16[2]
17[3]
18[3]
19
20[6]
21[3]
22[3]
23[4]
24[3]
25[2]
26[2]
27[3]
28[3]
29[2]
31[2]
32[4]
16:1[2]
2[2]
5
6[4]
7[4]
8
9
10
12
13[3]
14[2]
15
16[2]
17[2]
18[2]
19[2]
20
21[2]
22[3]
23[3]
24[4]
25[2]
26[2]
29
30
31[2]
17:2
3
4[2]
5
6[3]
7[2]
8[6]
11[2]
12
13[2]
14[2]
15[2]
16[2]
17
19
20[2]
22[2]
23
25
26
27[2]
29[2]
31[2]
33
34
35
36
37[3]
18:1[2]
3[2]
4
6
7[2]
9[2]
10
11
13
14
15
16[2]
18
19
20
21
22[3]
23
24
26
27
28
29
30
31[2]
32[3]

LUKE
18:33[3]
34[2]
35
36
37
38
39
40[3]
41
42
43[3]
19:1[2]
2[2]
3[2]
4[2]
5[4]
6[3]
7
8[3]
9
10
11[3]
12
13[3]
14
15
17
18
19
20
21
22[2]
24[2]
25
26
27
28
29[2]
30
31
32[2]
33
34
35[3]
36
37[2]
38
39
40[2]
41[2]
43[2]
44[3]
45[3]
47[3]
48
20:1[3]
2
3[3]
5
6
7
8
9[2]
10[2]
11[4]
12[3]
15
16[3]
17[2]
19[3]
20[3]
21[2]
23
24[2]
25[2]
26[3]
27
28[2]
29[2]
30[2]
31[4]
34[2]
35
36
37[3]
40
41
42
46[3]
47
21:1[2]
2
3
5[2]
7[2]
8[2]
9[2]
10
11[5]
12[3]
13
15
16[5]
17
20
21[2]
23[2]
24[3]
25[5]
26
27[2]
28[2]
29[2]
30
33
34[4]
36[2]

LUKE
21:37[3]
38
22:1[2]
4[3]
5[2]
6[2]
8[3]
9
10
11
12
13[3]
14[2]
15
17[4]
19[4]
22
23
24
25[2]
26
29
30[2]
31
32
33[2]
34
35[4]
36[3]
37
38[2]
39[3]
40
41[3]
43
44[2]
45[2]
46[2]
47[3]
50[2]
51[4]
52[3]
53
54[3]
55[2]
56[2]
57
58[3]
59
60[2]
61[3]
62[2]
63[2]
64[2]
65
66[4]
67
68
70
71
23:1[2]
2[2]
3[3]
4
5
7
8[2]
10[3]
11[4]
12[2]
13[3]
14
15
16
18[2]
19
22[2]
23[3]
24
25[2]
26[2]
27[3]
28
29[2]
30
32
33[3]
34[2]
35[2]
36[2]
37
38[3]
39[2]
41
42
43
44[2]
45[2]
46[2]
48[2]
49[2]
50[3]
51
52
53[3]
54[2]
55[3]
56[4]
24:1
2
3[2]
4
5[2]
7[2]
8
9[3]
10[3]

LUKE
24:11[2]
12[3]
13
14
15[3]
17[2]
18[2]
19[4]
20[3]
21
22
23
24[2]
25
26
27[2]
28[2]
29[2]
30[4]
31[3]
32[2]
33[4]
34
35[2]
36[2]
37[2]
38[2]
39[3]
40[2]
41[2]
42[2]
43[2]
44[3]
46[3]
47[2]
48
49
50[3]
51[2]
52[2]
53[2]

JOHN
1:1[2]
3
4
5[2]
10[2]
11
14[4]
15
16[2]
17
19[2]
20[2]
21[3]
24
25[2]
29
31
32[2]
33[2]
34[2]
35
36
37[2]
38[2]
39[3]
40
41
42[2]
43[2]
44
45[2]
46[2]
47
48
49
50
51[3]
2:1[2]
2[2]
3
6
7
8[3]
9
10[2]
11[2]
12[4]
13[2]
14[4]
15[5]
16
17
18
19[2]
20[2]
22[2]
25
3:2
3
4
5
6
8[2]
9
10[2]
11[2]
12
13
14
19[2]
22[3]
23[3]
25
26[3]

JOHN
3:27
29
31
32[3]
35
36
4:1
3
4
6
10[3]
11
12[3]
13
16
17
18
20
23[2]
24[2]
27[2]
28[2]
30
34
35[2]
36[3]
37[2]
38
39
40
41
42[2]
43
46
47[2]
48
50[2]
51[2]
52
53[2]
5:1
4
5[2]
6
8
9[4]
11
12
13
14
15
16[2]
17
19
20[2]
21
24[2]
25[2]
27
29[2]
30
32
33
35[2]
37
38
39
40
43
44
6:2
3[2]
4
5
6
9
10
11[4]
13[2]
15
16
17[4]
18
19[3]
21
22
24
25
26[2]
29
30
33
35[2]
36
37
39
40[3]
42[2]
43
44
45[2]
49
50
51
53
54[2]
55
56[2]
57
58
62
63
64
65
66
69[2]
70

JOHN
7:3
4
11
12
14
15
16
18
19
20
21[2]
22
26
28[2]
29
31[2]
32[2]
33
34[2]
35
36[2]
37[2]
42
44
45[2]
51
52[2]
53
8:2[4]
3[3]
6
7
8[2]
9[3]
10
11[2]
14[3]
16[2]
18
20
21[2]
23
25
26[2]
28
29
32[2]
33
35
38
39
42
44[3]
45
46
48[2]
49
50[2]
52[2]
53
55[2]
56[2]
57
59[2]
9:1
2
6[2]
7[3]
8[2]
11[7]
14[2]
15[2]
16
18
19
20[2]
24
25
27
28
30[2]
31
34[3]
35
36
37[2]
38[2]
39[2]
40[2]
10:1
3[3]
4[2]
5
8
9[2]
10[3]
12[5]
13
14[2]
15
16[4]
18
20[2]
22[2]
23
24
25
27[2]
28[2]
29
30
33
35
36
38[2]
40[2]
41[2]

JOHN
10:42 11:1 2 5[2] 8 11 15 19[2] 20 25 26[2] 28[3] 29 31[2] 32 33[2] 34[2] 37 38 41[2] 42 43 44[4] 45 46 47[2] 48[3] 49 50 51 52 54 55[2] 56 57 12:1 3[3] 5 6[2] 9 11 13[2] 14 16 17 20 21 22[3] 23 24 25 26 27 28 29 30 32 34 36[2] 38 40[3] 41 44 45 47[2] 48 49 50 13:2 3[2] 4[3] 5[2] 6 7 9 10 12[2] 13[2] 14 20 21[2] 26 27 30 31 32 33 14:3[3] 4[2] 5 6 7[2] 8 9[2] 10 11 12 13 16[2] 17 19 20[2] 21[4] 22 23[4] 24 26 28 29 30 31 15:1 2 4 5 6[4] 7[2]

JOHN
15:10 11 16[3] 22 24[2] 27 16:3 4 5 8[3] 10 13 14 15 16[3] 17[4] 19[4] 20[2] 22[3] 23 24 26 27 28[2] 29 30 32[2] 17:1[2] 3[2] 5 6[2] 8[3] 10[3] 11[2] 12 13[2] 14 19 21 22 23[3] 25 26[3] 18:1 2 3[2] 4 5 6 7 10[2] 13[5] 13 15[3] 16[2] 18[5] 19 20[2] 22 25[3] 27 28[2] 29 30 31 33[2] 35 37 38[2] 19:1 2[3] 3[2] 4 5[2] 6[2] 7 9[2] 10 12 13 14[3] 16[2] 17 18[2] 19[3] 20[3] 23[2] 24 25[2] 26 27 29[3] 30[2] 31 32[2] 33 34[2] 35[3] 37 38[3] 39[3] 40 41 20:1 2[4] 3[2] 4[2] 5[2] 6[2] 7 8[2] 11[2] 12[2] 13[2] 14[3] 15 16

JOHN
20:17[4] 18[2] 19[2] 20[2] 22[2] 23 25[2] 26[4] 27[4] 28[3] 29 30 31 21:1 2[4] 3[2] 6[3] 7 8 9[2] 11[4] 12[2] 13[3] 17 18[3] 19 20 21 24[2] 25

ACTS
1:1 3 4 7 8[4] 9[2] 10 13[8] 14[3] 15[3] 16 17 18[2] 19 20[2] 21 23[2] 24[2] 25 26[3] 2:1 2[2] 3[2] 4[2] 5 6 7[2] 8 9[6] 10[4] 11 12[2] 14[3] 17[5] 18[3] 19[4] 20[2] 21 22[2] 23[3] 26 29[3] 30 33[2] 36 37[3] 38[2] 39[2] 40[2] 41 42[4] 43[3] 44[2] 45[3] 46[3] 47[2] 3:1 2 3 4 5 6[2] 7[4] 8[5] 9[2] 10[3] 11[2] 12 13[3] 14[2] 15 16[2] 17 19 20 23 24[2] 25[2] 4:1[3] 2 3[2] 4 5[3] 6[5] 7

ACTS
4:8 10 13[4] 14 16 18[2] 19[2] 20 23[3] 24[5] 25 26[2] 27[2] 28 29[2] 30[2] 31[3] 32[2] 33[2] 34 35[2] 36[2] 37[2] 5:2[3] 3 4 5[3] 6[3] 7 8[2] 9 10[4] 11[2] 12[3] 13 14[2] 15[2] 16[2] 17[2] 18[2] 19[2] 20 21[6] 22[2] 23 24[2] 25[2] 26 27[2] 28[2] 29[2] 30 31[2] 32[2] 33 34 35 36[2] 37[2] 38[2] 40[4] 41 42[3] 6:1 2[2] 3 4 5[9] 6 7[3] 8[3] 9[4] 10[2] 11 12[6] 13[2] 14 15 7:2[2] 3[3] 4[2] 5[2] 6[3] 7[3] 8[5] 9 10[5] 11[3] 13[2] 14[3] 15[2] 16[2] 17 19 20[2] 21[2] 22[3] 23 24[3] 26[2] 27 29 30 31 32[3] 34[3] 35[2] 36[3] 38 39 41[3] 42[2] 43[2] 46 49 51[2] 52[2]

ACTS
7:53 54 55[2] 56[2] 57[2] 58[3] 59[2] 60[3] 8:1[4] 2[2] 3[2] 5 6[2] 7[2] 8 9 11 12[2] 13[3] 14 17 18 22 23 24 25[3] 26[2] 27[4] 28 29 30[3] 31[3] 32 33 34[2] 35[2] 36[2] 37[3] 38[4] 39[2] 40 9:1 2 3[2] 4[2] 5[2] 6[5] 7 8[3] 9[2] 10[3] 11[3] 12[2] 14 15[2] 17[4] 18[4] 19 20 21[2] 22 23 24[2] 25 26[2] 27[4] 28[2] 29[2] 30 31[5] 32 33[2] 34[3] 35[3] 36 37[2] 38[2] 39[4] 40[5] 41[4] 42[2] 43 10:2[2] 3 4[4] 5[2] 7[2] 8 9 10[2] 11[3] 12[3] 13[2] 15 16 17 18[2] 20[2] 21 22[4] 23[3] 24[4] 25[3] 27[2] 28 30[3] 31[2] 32 33 34 35 37 38[2] 39[3] 40 41 42[3]

ACTS
10:45 46 48 11:1[2] 2 3 4 5[2] 6[4] 7[2] 10[2] 11 12[2] 13[3] 14 15 18 19[2] 20[2] 21[3] 22 23[2] 24[3] 26[4] 27 28[2] 30[2] 12:2 3 4[2] 6[2] 7[5] 8[5] 9[3] 10[4] 11[3] 12 13 14[2] 15 16[2] 17[4] 19[5] 20[3] 21[2] 22[2] 23[3] 24 25[3] 13:1[5] 2[2] 3[3] 4 5[2] 6 7[2] 10[2] 11[5] 13[2] 14[2] 15[3] 16[2] 17[2] 18 19 20[2] 21[2] 22[2] 25 26[2] 27 28 29[2] 31 32 34 36[2] 38 39 41[2] 42 43[2] 44 45[2] 46[3] 48[3] 49 50[5] 51 52[2] 14:1[3] 2 3[2] 4[2] 5[3] 6[3] 7 8 9 10[2] 11 12[2] 13[2] 14[2] 15[5] 17[3] 18 19[3] 20[2] 21[4] 22[2] 23[2] 24 25 26 27[3] 28

ACTS
15:1[2] 2[5] 3[3] 4[4] 5 6[2] 7[4] 8 9[2] 12[3] 13[2] 15 16[3] 17 20[3] 22[3] 23[5] 24 25 27 28 29[3] 30 32[3] 33 35[2] 36[3] 37 38 39[3] 40[2] 41[2] 16:1[3] 2 3[2] 4[2] 5[2] 6[2] 8 9[3] 10 11 12[3] 13[3] 14 15[4] 16 17[2] 18[3] 19[3] 20 21 22[3] 23 24 25[4] 26[3] 27[3] 29[3] 30[2] 31[3] 32[2] 33[4] 34[2] 35 36[2] 37[3] 38[2] 39[4] 40[4] 17:1 2[2] 3[3] 4[5] 5[4] 6[2] 7 8[2] 9[2] 10[2] 11 12 13 14[2] 15[3] 17[2] 18[3] 19[2] 21 22 23 24[2] 25[2] 26[3] 27 28[2] 29 30 32[2] 34[3] 18:1 2[2] 3[2] 4[3] 5[3] 6[3] 7[2] 8[3] 9 10 11[2] 12[2] 14 15[2] 16 17[2] 18[5]

ACTS
18:19[3] 21 22[3] 23[3] 24[2] 25[2] 26[3] 27 28 19:1[2] 3[2] 6[3] 7 8[3] 9[2] 10[2] 11 12[2] 14[2] 15[3] 16[4] 17[4] 18[3] 19[3] 20 21 22 23 25 26[2] 27[2] 28[2] 29[3] 30 31 32[2] 33[3] 35[2] 36 38[2] 41 20:1[3] 2[2] 3[2] 4[7] 6[2] 7[2] 8 9[4] 10[3] 11[3] 12[2] 13[2] 14[2] 15[5] 17[2] 18 19[2] 20[3] 21[2] 22 23 24 25 28 31[2] 32[3] 34 35 36[2] 37[3] 38 21:1[4] 2[2] 3[2] 4 5[6] 6[2] 7[3] 8[4] 9 10 11[5] 12[2] 13 14 15[2] 16 17 18[2] 19 20[3] 21 24[4] 25[4] 26 27[2] 28[4] 30[5] 31 32[4] 33[4] 34[2] 35 37 38 39 40[3] 22:1 2[2] 3[2] 4[3] 5[2] 6[2] 7[2] 8[2] 9[2]

ACTS
22:10[4] 11 12 13[3] 14[3] 15 16[3] 17 18[2] 19[2] 20[3] 21 22[3] 23[3] 24 25[2] 26 27 28[2] 29[2] 30[4] 23:1[2] 2 3 4 6[3] 7[3] 9[3] 10[3] 11[2] 12[2] 13 14[3] 15 16[3] 17 18[3] 19[2] 20 21 22 23[4] 24[2] 25 27[2] 28 30[2] 31 32 33 34[2] 35 24:1[2] 2[2] 3 5[2] 6 7 9 12 14 15[2] 16[2] 17 19 22[2] 23[3] 24[2] 25[3] 26 27 25:2[2] 3 4 5 6[2] 7[3] 9[2] 13[2] 14 15 16 17 19 20[2] 23[4] 24[3] 25 26 27 26:1 3 6[2] 7 10[2] 11[3] 12 13 14[2] 15[2] 16[3] 17 18[3] 20[5] 21 22[2] 23[3] 24 25 29[2] 30[4] 31 27:1[2] 2 3[3] 4 5[2]

ACTS
27:6[2] 7[2] 8 9 10[3] 11 12[2] 13 15[2] 16 17[2] 18 19 20[2] 21[4] 22 23 24 27 28[4] 29 30 31 32 33[2] 35[3] 36 37[2] 38[2] 39 40[4] 41[3] 42[2] 43[2] 44[3] 28:1 2[3] 3[3] 4 5[2] 6[2] 7 8[5] 9 10 11[2] 12 13[4] 14[2] 15[3] 16 17[3] 20 21 23[3] 24[2] 25 26[4] 27[6] 28 29[2] 30[2] 31

ROMANS
1:4 5 7[2] 12 14[2] 16 18 20 21 23[4] 25[2] 27[2] 28 2:3[2] 4[2] 5[2] 7[2] 8[2] 9[2] 10[2] 12 15 17[2] 18[2] 19 20[2] 27[2] 29[2] 3:4 8[2] 9 14 16 17 19 21 22 23 26 30 4:3 7 11 12 14 17 19 21 22 25 5:2 3

ROMANS
5:4[2] 5 11 12[2] 15 16 17 6:13 19 22[2] 7:6 9 10 11 12[3] 23 8:2 3 6 10 17[2] 22 23 27 28 30[2] 9:2 4[5] 5 9 10 15 17 18 21 22 23 25 26 28 29[2] 33[2] 10:1 3 8 9 10 12 14[2] 15[2] 17 18 19 20 21 11:3[3] 6 7 8 9[4] 10 12 14 16 17[4] 20 22 23 24 26[2] 29 33[2] 35 36[2] 12:2[3] 4 5 14 15 13:2 3 9 11 12 13[3] 14 14:3 6[3] 7 8 9[3] 11 14 17[3] 18 19 23 15:1 4 5 6 9[2] 10 11[2] 12[2] 13 14 18 19[2] 21 23 24 26 27 28 29 30

ROMANS
15:31 32 16:2[2] 3 7[2] 9 12 13[2] 14 15[4] 17[2] 18[2] 19 20 21[3] 23[2] 25 26 *subscr.*

1 COR.
1:1 2 3[2] 5 10[2] 12[3] 14 16 19 22 23 24[2] 25 27 28[3] 30[3] 2:1 2 3[3] 4[3] 3:1 2 3[3] 4 5 8[2] 10 13 16 20 23[2] 4:1 5[2] 6[2] 7 8 9[2] 11[4] 12 13 17 19 21 5:1 2[2] 4 8[2] 6:1 2 6 8[2] 11[2] 13[3] 14[2] 15 19 20 7:2 3 4 5[2] 6 7 8 10 11[2] 12 13[2] 14 17 19 28[2] 30[3] 31 34[2] 35[2] 36 37 40 8:2 4 5 6[3] 7 11 12 9:4 5[2] 6 7[2] 10 13 20 23 25 27

1 COR.
10:1 2[2] 3 4[2] 7[2] 8[2] 9 10 11 17 20[2] 21[2] 26 27 28 11:2 3[2] 7 18 21[2] 22[2] 24[2] 26 27[2] 28[2] 29[2] 30[2] 34[2] 12:3 5 6 11 12[2] 13 16 19 21 23[2] 26 27 28 31 13:1[2] 2[5] 3[3] 4 9 13 14:1 3[2] 7 10 11 15[2] 21[2] 23[2] 24 25[3] 27[2] 28[2] 29 31 32 35 39 40 15:1 4[2] 5 8 10 11 14[2] 15 17 20 24[2] 28 30 32 34 35 37 38 39 40[2] 41[2] 44 45 46 48 49 50 52[2] 53 54 56 16:3 4 6[2] 9[2] 15 16[2] 17[2] 18 19 *subscr.*[3]

2 COR.
1:1 2[2] 3 6[3] 7 10 12[2] 13

2 COR.
1:15 16[3] 17 18 19[3] 20 21 22 2:3 4 7 12 14 15 16[2] 3:2 4 7 13 17 4:5 7 13[2] 14 17 5:8[2] 11 12 15[2] 18[2] 19 6:2 7 8[3] 9[3] 10 14 15 16[4] 17[3] 18[3] 7:1 3 7 13 15[2] 8:2 3 4 5[2] 7[4] 8 10 12 13 15 18 19[2] 22 23[2] 24[2] 9:2 4 5[2] 6 8 10[2] 13[2] 14 10:1 5[2] 6 8 10[2] 12 16 11:1 9[4] 14 25 27[3] 29[2] 31 33 12:1 3 4 7 9 12[2] 14 15[2] 18 20 21[5] 13:2[3] 9[2] 10 11[2] 14 *subscr.*

GAL.
1:1 2 3[2] 4 5 7 13 14 15 16 17 18 21 22

GAL.
1:24 2:1 2 4 9[4] 12 13 14 15 16 20[2] 3:5 6 8 12 16[3] 17[2] 19 29[2] 4:2 6 7 9 10[3] 14 15 18 20 25[2] 27 30 5:1 11 15 16 17[2] 21 24[2] 6:2 4[2] 9 14 16[3]

EPHES.
1:1 2[2] 3 4 8 10 15 17 18 19 20 21[4] 22[2] 2:1[2] 3[2] 6[2] 8 12[2] 14 16 17[3] 19[2] 20[2] 3:5 6[2] 9 10 12 15 17 18[3] 19 4:2 4 6[3] 8 11[5] 13 14[3] 16 17 21 23 24[2] 26 30 31[4] 32 5:2[3] 3 5 9[2] 11 14[2] 18 19[3] 20 23 25 26 27 29 30 31[3] 32 33 6:2 3 4[2] 5 7 9

EPHES.
6:10 12 13 14 15 17[2] 18[3] 19 21[2] 22 23[2]

PHIL.
1:1[2] 2[2] 7[2] 9[3] 10 11 13 14 15[2] 18[2] 19 20 21 23 25[3] 27 28[2] 30 2:1 7[2] 8[2] 9 10[2] 11 12 13 14 15[2] 17[3] 18 25[3] 26 27 28 29 3:3[2] 8[2] 9 10 13 15 17 18 19 4:1[2] 2 3 4 6 7[2] 8 9[4] 12[4] 15 16 18 20

COLOS.
1:1 2[3] 3 4 6[2] 9[2] 10 11 13 16[3] 17[2] 18 20 21[2] 22[2] 23[3] 24 26 28 2:1[2] 2[2] 3 4 5[2] 7[2] 8[2] 10 13[2] 14 15[2] 18 19[3] 22 23[2] 3:3 5 10 11 12 13 14 15[2] 16[3] 17[2] 19

COLOS.
3:23[2] 25 4:1 2 7 8 9 10 11 12 13[2] 14 15[2] 16[2] 17 *subscr.*

1 THESS.
1:1[5] 3[3] 5[2] 6[2] 7 8 9[2] 2:2 9[2] 10[3] 11[2] 12 15[4] 18 20 3:2[4] 4 5 6[3] 7 10[2] 11[2] 12[3] 4:1[3] 4 6[2] 10[2] 11[3] 12 14 15 16[2] 17[2] 5:1 3[2] 5 6 7 8[2] 11 12[3] 13[2] 15 23[4]

2 THESS.
1:1[3] 2[2] 3 4[2] 7 8 9 10 11[2] 12[2] 2:1 3 4 6 8[2] 9[2] 10 11 13 15 16[3] 17[2] 3:1 2[2] 3 4[2] 5[2] 6 8[2] 12[2] 14[2]

1 TIM.
1:1 2 4 5 9[4] 10 12 13[2] 14[2] 15 17[2] 19 20 2:1 2 3 4 5[3] 7[3] 8

1 TIM.
2:9 14 15[2] 3:7 10 12 13 15 16 4:1 3[2] 4 5 6 7[2] 8 9 10 11 16[2] 5:1 4[2] 5[4] 7 8[2] 13[3] 16 17 18 21 23 24 25 6:1 2[5] 3[2] 4 5 7 8[2] 9[4] 10 11 12 13 15 16 20[2]

2 TIM.
1:2 3 5[2] 7[2] 9[2] 10[2] 11[2] 12 13 15 16 17 18 2:2 5 7 16 17[2] 18 20[4] 21[2] 23 24 26 3:6 7 8 12 13[3] 14 15 16 4:1[2] 2 4[2] 6 8 10 11 12 13 17[3] 18[3] 19[2] 21[4]

TITUS
1:1[2] 4[2] 5 9 10[2] 14 15[2] 16[2] 2:9 12[2] 13[2] 14 15[2] 3:1 3[3] 4 5 8[2] 9[4] 10

TITUS 3:11 13 14 PHILE. 1 2^{3} 3^{2} 5^{2} 7 9 11 16 HEB. 1:1 3^{2} 5^{2} 6^{2} 7^{2} 8 9 10^{2} 11 12^{3} 2:2^{2} 3 4^{3} 7^{2} 9 10 11 13^{3} 14 15 17 3:1 5 6 9 10^{2} 18 4:4 5 6 12^{7} 13 16

HEB. 5:1 2 3 4 7^{3} 9 11 12^{2} 14 6:1 2^{3} 3 4^{2} 5^{2} 6 7 8^{2} 9 10^{2} 11 12 14 15 16 19^{2} 7:1 2 5 6 7 8 9 11 15 18 20 21 23 26 27 8:2^{2} 3 5 8 9 10^{3} 11^{2} 12^{2}

HEB. 8:13 9:1 2^{2} 3 4^{3} 5 7 9 10^{3} 11 12 13^{2} 15 19^{5} 21 22^{3} 27 28 10:1 4 5 6 8^{3} 11^{2} 16 17^{2} 20 21 22 24^{2} 25 27 29^{2} 30 33^{2} 34^{2} 37^{2} 11:4 5 6 7 8 9 10 11 12^{2} 13^{4} 15

HEB. 11:17 20 21 22 23 28 32^{6} 35 36^{3} 37 38^{3} 39 12:1^{2} 2^{2} 3 5 6 8 9^{2} 12 13 14 15 18^{3} 19^{2} 20 21^{2} 22^{2} 23^{3} 24^{2} 27 28 13:3 4^{2} 5 6 8^{2} 9 16 17^{2} 21 22 24 JAMES 1:1 4

JAMES 1:5^{2} 6 11^{2} 14 15 17^{2} 21^{2} 22 23 24^{2} 25 26 27^{4} 2:2 3^{3} 4 5 6 9 10 12 13 14 15 16^{2} 18^{2} 19 22 23^{3} 24 25 3:2 3 4 5 6^{3} 7^{4} 9 10 11 12 13 14^{2} 16^{2} 17^{3} 18 4:1 2^{4}

JAMES 4:3 4 7 8^{2} 9^{3} 10 11^{2} 12 13^{4} 14 15 17 5:1 2 3^{3} 4 5 6^{2} 7^{2} 10 11^{2} 12 14 15^{3} 16 17^{3} 18^{3} 19 20 1 PETER 1:1 2^{2} 3 4^{2} 7^{2} 8 10 11 13 17 18 19 21^{2} 23 24^{2} 25

1 PETER 2:1^{4} 4 6 8^{2} 11 14 16 18 20 25 3:3 4 6 7 10^{2} 11^{2} 12 13 14^{2} 15^{2} 19 22^{3} 4:3 5 7 8 11^{2} 14 17 18^{2} 5:1^{2} 4 5^{2} 11^{2} 12 13 2 PETER 1:1^{2} 2^{2} 3^{2} 4 5^{2} 6^{3} 7^{2} 8 9^{2}

2 PETER 1:10 11 12 16 17 18 19 2:1 2 3^{2} 4 5 6^{2} 7 8 9 10 11 12^{2} 13^{2} 14 15 20^{2} 22 3:2^{3} 4 5^{2} 7^{2} 8 10^{2} 11 12^{2} 13 14 15 16 18^{3} 1 JOHN 1:1 2^{4} 3^{3} 4 5^{2} 6^{2} 7 8 9^{2}

1 JOHN 1:10 2:1 2^{3} 3 4 8^{2} 9 10 11^{2} 14^{2} 16^{2} 17^{2} 18 20 21 22 24 25 27^{4} 28^{2} 3:2 3 5^{2} 9 10 12^{3} 15 16 17^{2} 18 19^{2} 20 22^{2} 23^{2} 24^{3} 4:3^{3} 4 5 6 7^{2} 10 12 13 14^{2} 15 16^{4} 20 21

1 JOHN 5:1 2 3 4 6^{3} 7^{2} 8^{4} 11^{2} 12 13 14 15 16 17 18 19 20^{4} 2 JOHN 1^{2} 2 3^{3} 5 6 7 9^{2} 10 12^{2} 3 JOHN 2 3 5 10^{3} 12^{3} 13 14 JUDE 1^{3} 2^{2} 3 4^{2} 6 7^{3}

JUDE 8 11^{2} 14 15^{2} 16 22 23 24 25^{3} REV. 1:1^{2} 2^{2} 3^{2} 4^{4} 5^{4} 6^{5} 7^{2} 8^{4} 9^{4} 10 11^{10} 12^{2} 13^{2} 14^{2} 15^{2} 16^{3} 17^{3} 18^{4} 19^{2} 20^{2} 2:2^{6} 3^{4} 5^{3} 8^{3} 9^{4} 10^{2} 12 13^{3} 14 16 17^{2} 18^{2} 19^{6} 20^{2} 21^{2} 22 23^{4}

REV. 2:24^{2} 26^{2} 27 28 3:1^{3} 2 3^{4} 4 5^{2} 7^{4} 8^{3} 9^{3} 12^{4} 14^{2} 16 17^{7} 18^{3} 19^{2} 20^{4} 21 4:1^{3} 2^{3} 3^{3} 4^{5} 5^{4} 6^{4} 7^{4} 8^{6} 9^{4} 10^{4} 11^{4} 5:1^{2} 2^{2} 3 4^{2} 5^{2} 6^{5} 7^{2} 8^{4} 9^{6} 10^{3} 11^{6} 12^{6} 13^{10} 14^{5} 6:1^{3} 2^{6} 3^{2}

REV. 6:4^{4} 5^{5} 6^{4} 7^{2} 8^{8} 9^{2} 10^{3} 11^{3} 12^{4} 13 14^{3} 15^{8} 16^{4} 17 7:1 2^{3} 4^{4} 9^{6} 10^{2} 11^{5} 12^{7} 13^{2} 14^{4} 15^{3} 17^{2} 8:1 2^{2} 3^{3} 4 5^{7} 6 7^{5} 8^{3} 9^{3} 10^{4} 11^{3} 12^{6} 13^{2} 9:1^{3} 2^{4} 3^{2} 4 5^{2} 6^{4} 7^{3} 8 9^{2} 10^{3}

REV. 9:11 12 13^{2} 15^{4} 16^{2} 17^{8} 18^{2} 19^{3} 20^{6} 10:1^{4} 2^{3} 3^{2} 4^{3} 5^{2} 6^{7} 8^{4} 9^{5} 10^{4} 11^{4} 11:1^{5} 2^{3} 3^{3} 4 5^{3} 6^{2} 7^{3} 8^{2} 9^{6} 10^{3} 11^{4} 12^{3} 13^{5} 14 15^{5} 16^{3} 17^{3} 18^{8} 19^{7} 12:1^{3} 2^{2} 3^{4} 4^{3} 5^{3} 6^{2} 7^{4} 8 9^{3} 10^{5}

REV. 12:11^{3} 12^{2} 13 14^{3} 15 16^{3} 17^{3} 13:1^{5} 2^{6} 3^{3} 4^{2} 5^{4} 6^{3} 7^{5} 8 10 11^{3} 12^{3} 13 14^{2} 15^{2} 16^{4} 17 18^{2} 14:1^{4} 2^{3} 3^{6} 4 5 6^{5} 7^{5} 8 9^{3} 10^{3} 11^{5} 12 13^{2} 14^{4} 15^{2} 16^{3} 17 18^{3} 19^{3} 20^{3} 15:1^{2} 2^{5} 3^{4} 4^{2}

REV. 15:5^{2} 6^{3} 7^{2} 8^{3} 16:1^{2} 2^{5} 3^{3} 4^{3} 5^{3} 6^{2} 7^{2} 8^{2} 9^{3} 10^{3} 11^{3} 12^{2} 13^{3} 14 15^{2} 16 17^{2} 18^{5} 19^{3} 20^{2} 21^{2} 17:1^{2} 2 3^{2} 4^{6} 5^{2} 6^{3} 7^{3} 8^{6} 9 10^{4} 11^{4} 12 13^{2} 14^{5} 15^{4} 16^{5} 17^{2} 18 18:1^{2} 2^{5} 3^{2} 4^{2} 5

REV. 18:6 7^{4} 8^{3} 9^{3} 11^{2} 12^{13} 13^{14} 14^{3} 15 16^{6} 17^{4} 18 19^{3} 20^{2} 21^{3} 22^{5} 23^{3} 24^{3} 19:1^{4} 2^{2} 3^{3} 4^{4} 5^{3} 6^{3} 7^{3} 8^{2} 9^{2} 10^{3} 11^{6} 12^{2} 13^{2} 14^{2} 15^{4} 16^{3} 17^{3} 18^{7} 19^{4} 20^{3} 21^{2} 20:1^{2} 2^{3} 3^{4} 4^{8} 6^{3} 7 8^{2} 9^{5} 10^{6}

REV. 20:11^{4} 12^{5} 13^{4} 14^{2} 15 21:1^{4} 2 3^{5} 4^{2} 5^{3} 6^{3} 7^{2} 8^{8} 9^{2} 10^{3} 11 12^{5} 13 14^{2} 15^{2} 16^{5} 17^{3} 18^{2} 19 21^{2} 22^{2} 23^{2} 24^{3} 25 26 27 22:1 2^{2} 3^{3} 4^{2} 5^{4} 6^{3} 8^{4} 9^{2} 10 11^{3} 12^{2} 13^{3} 14 15^{6} 16^{3} 17^{5} 19^{3}

are

1526

GEN. 2:4 6:9 7:2 8 9:2 19 10:1 20 31 32 11:10 27 18:15 24 19:5 15 21 20:7 16 25:6 12 13 16 17 19 23 27:22 41 46 29:4 31:12 15 43^{3} 49 32:17 33:5 8 13^{2} 15 34:21 22 35:2 26 36:1 5 9 10 13 16 17^{3} 18 19^{2} 20 21 24 26 27 28 29 30 31 40 37:2 17

GEN. 38:25^{2} 40:12 18 41:26 27 42:9^{2} 10 11^{3} 12 13 14 16 21 31^{2} 33 34^{2} 36 43:18 44:16 45:6 11 16 46:8 18 22 25 31 32 47:1^{2} 3 4 5 9 48:5 8 9 49:5^{2} 28 50:3 EXOD. 1:1 9 19^{3} 2:18 3:7 4:18 19 5:5 16 17^{2} 6:15 16 19 24 25 26 27^{2} 7:17 8:21 9:27 10:8 11 12:13

EXOD. 14:3 15:4 16:7 8^{2} 16 19:6 21:1 24:14 25:22 26 28:3 4 24 29:33 30:13 14 31:6 32:2 22 33:5 16 35:1 39:6 40:4 LEVIT. 4:12^{2} 13 5:17 10:14 11:2^{2} 8 9 13^{2} 26 27 28 31 32 35 42 12:6 14:37 16:4 18:17 24 23:2 4 17 37 42 25:7 23 33 42 44 45 55^{2} 26:25 36 39 46 27:34

NUM. 1:3 5 17 44 2:32 3:1 2 3 9 13 18 20 21 27 33 46^{2} 4:15 20 41 6:13 8:16 17 9:7^{2} 10:4 29 31 11:21 13:16 28 30 31 32 14:9 35 43^{2} 15:13 15 16 16:3 5 11 37 18:6 17 18 20:16 22:4 6 9 12 24:3 5 6 15 26:2 7 14 18 22 25 27 30 34 35

NUM. 26:36 37^{2} 41 42^{2} 47 50 57 58 63 27:1 30:14 16 31:12 49 32:14 51 33:1 2 34:17 19 29 35:33 36:3 4 13 DEU. 1:2 10 11 20 28 2:4 25 3:18 4:4 20 30 32 45 5:3 6:1 14 7:6 17 20 8:9 9:12 29 11:12 30 12:1 9 13:7 13 14:1 2 4 7 9 12 29 16:11 14

DEU. 17:14 18:12 20:2 15^{2} 21:2 6 22:5 17 23:8 18 24:14 25:16 27:12 28:58 29:1 5 20 21 29 30:1 10 31:17 18 21 32:4 5 20 21 28 32^{2} 37 33:3 17^{3} 27 JOSH. 1:3 3:8 4:9 6:17^{2} 19 7:3 29 8:5 9:8^{2} 9 11 13 22 23 25 10:6 17 12:1 7 13:14 17 30 32 14:1 32 16:3 17:3 9

JOSH. 17:16^{2} 18:3 19:14 29 35 51 21:9 22:10 17 23:14 15 24:22^{2} 23 JUD. 3:1 5:11 6:2 7:2^{2} 3 18 8:6 15^{2} 9:2 18 10:4^{2} 11:7 12:3 4 15:10^{2} 11 12 18:9 24 19:18 20:7 13 32 39 21:16 RUTH 1:11 4:9 10 11 18 1 SAM. 2:3 4 8 4:8 17 6:17 9:20 10:2 7 12:2 22 16:11 16 17:8 19:22

1 SAM. 20:21 22 21:5 26:16 29:10 2 SAM. 1:4^{3} 19 25 27 3:28 5:1 8 7:9 11:11 13:33 14:14 20 15:3 13 15 16:4 21 17:2 10 12 16 19:11 12^{3} 19 22:28 39 24:14 1 KINGS 1:20 45 4:8 13 8:8 13 10:8^{2} 27 11:41 13:3 32 14:19 29 15:7 23 31 16:5 14 20 27 18:22 25 20:3 17 23 31 22:39 45

2 KINGS 1:5 18 3:23 5:12 6:9 16 7:12 13^{5} 8:23 9:22 10:2^{2} 5 13^{2} 34 12:19 13:8 12 14:15 18 28 15:6 11 15 21 26 31 36 16:19 18:20 26 34^{2} 35 19:3 4 20:14 15 20 21:17 25 23:28 24:5 1 CHRON. 1:29 31 33 54 2:1 18 55 4:2 4 12 18 22 5:14 6:19 31 33 50 54 65 7:8 33

1 CHRON. 8:6^{2} 38 40 9:33 44 11:1 10 12:1 15 18 23 13:2^{2} 14:4 15:12 16:14 26 27^{2} 17:8 19:3 21:3 13 22:15 24:1 26:19 29:15^{2} 17 29 2 CHRON. 1:15 2:7 3:3 6:37 7:14 8:11 9:7^{2} 27 29 11:10 12:15 13:7 8 9 10 22 16:11 17:14 19:3 20:12 34 23:6 24:26 27 25:26 26:18 27:7 28:10 26 29:9 19 30:6 32:32 33:18 19

2 CHRON. 34:21 24 31 35:25 27 36:8 EZRA 2:1 4:10 12 5:4 11 6:6 9 7:13 19 21 25 8:1 13 28^{3} 9:6 15 10:3 13^{2} NEH. 1:3^{3} 10 2:3 17^{2} 4:2 4 10 19 5:2 5 17 6:8 7:6 9:6 36^{2} 37 10:39 11:3 7 12:1 ESTHER 1:16 3:8 4:16 7:4 8:5 9 9:13 10:2 JOB 1:19 3:8 19 22

JOB 3:24 4:9 10 11 19 20 5:4^{2} 6:3 4 7 16 17 18 21^{2} 25 26 7:1 3 6^{2} 8 16 8:9^{2} 13 17 9:25 26 10:5^{2} 17 20 11:16 12:2 6 16 13:4^{2} 12 23 14:5^{2} 21 15:10 11 15 28 16:2 22 17:1^{2} 2 7 11^{2} 18:3 21 19:3 13 19 22 20:11 25 21:7 9 18 22 24^{2} 28 33 22:10

JOB 22:12 14 19 29 23:14 24:1 8 13 17 23 24^{3} 25:2 5 26:5 11 14 27:12 28:4^{2} 6 30:1 15 17 30 31:40 32:6 9 34:18 19 21 25 35:5 36:7^{2} 20 37:17 24 38:6 30 35 39:4 30 40:17 18^{2} 41:14 15 17 18 23^{2} 25 28 29 30 PSALMS 1:4^{2} 2:12 3:1^{2} 6:2 9:3 6 15 10:5^{2} 8 16 12:4

PSALMS 12:6 8 14:1 3^{2} 16:3 6 11 17:2 10 14^{2} 18:38 19:8 9 10 20:8^{2} 21:11 22:14 25:10 15 17 19 27:12 31:10 15 32:11 33:4 34:15^{2} 18 19 35:19 20 36:3 6 12^{2} 37:23 28 34 38:4^{2} 5 7 14 19^{3} 20 39:6 40:5^{3} 12 42:7 44:13 22^{2} 45:5 47:9 49:14 50:11 51:17 53:1 3 54:3 55:4 5 10 56:5 8 12 57:4^{2}

PSALMS 57:6 58:3 4 59:3 7 62:9^{3} 65:5 8 13^{2} 68:6 17 69:1 4^{2} 5 9 19 71:13 24^{2} 72:20 73:1 4 5^{2} 8 10 12 19^{2} 27 74:20 75:3 76:5 6 77:19 79:1 4^{2} 8 11 82:5 6^{2} 83:5 84:1 4 5 85:10 86:8 14 87:3 7 88:5 89:7 11 14 49 90:4 5^{2} 7^{2} 9 10 92:5^{2} 93:5 94:11 95:4 7 96:5 6^{3}

PSALMS 97:2^{2} 100:3 102:3^{2} 8^{2} 11 20 22 24 25 103:6 14 15 104:16 17 18 24 25 28 29 30 105:7 106:3 107:17 27 29 30 38 39 109:2 4 24 111:2 7^{2} 8 113:6 115:4 8 15 16 116:10 118:12 119:1 2 21 24 39 75^{2} 84 85 86 91 98 99 103 111 129 137 138 143 150 151 156 157 168

PSALMS 119:172 120:7 122:5 123:3 4 124:7 125:2 4 126:3 127:3 4^{2} 135:15 139:12 140:2 141:6 7 8 142:6 144:4 145:9 146:8 PROV. 1:19 2:15 3:15 17^{2} 20 4:22 23 5:6 11 21 6:16 23 8:8 9 11 18 32 9:17 18^{2} 10:6 11:20^{4} 12:5^{2} 6 7^{2} 10 22^{2} 13:8 14:4 12 18 15:3 11 15 22^{2} 26^{2} 16:2 11^{2} 13 24 25 17:6^{2}

PROV. 17:15 24 18:4 7 8 19 21 19:7 13 14 21 29 20:7 10 15 23 24 22:3 4 5 26 23:3 24:11^{2} 21 25:1 26:7 21 22 23 25 28 27:6^{2} 12 15 20^{2} 24 25 26^{2} 28:1 2 29:2 12 16 30:12 13^{2} 14 15^{2} 18 24^{2} 25 26 29 31:8 21 25 ECCL. 1:8 11 13 14 2:14 23 3:18

ECCL.
3:20
4:1
2[2]
9
5:7
11
7:19
21
8:8
13
9:1
3
12[3]
16
17
10:12
11:10
12:3
11[2]

CANT.
1:10
17
3:7
4:2[2]
3[2]
5[2]
11
13
5:11
12
13
14
15
6:6
7
8
7:1[2]
3[2]
9
13

ISAIAH
1:4[2]
7
14
15
23
2:6
13
14
3:8
12
16
4:2
5:12
13[2]
21
22
28
7:2
8:18
9:10[2]
16
10:8
14
20
29
14:19
16:4
7
8[3]
17:2
19:11
12[2]
13[2]
21:3
22:2
3[4]
9

ISAIAH
23:8
24:6
17
18
21
22
25:1
26:9
14[2]
27:7
9
11
28:1[2]
7[3]
8
9
15
27[2]
29:9
15
20
30:18
27
31:1[2]
3
32:7
9
11
33:13[2]
14
23
35:4
36:5
11
19[2]
20
37:3
39:3
40:11
15[2]
17[2]
22
41:23[2]
24
29[3]
42:9
17
22[3]
43:10
12
17[2]
44:7
8
9[2]
11
45:16
19
20
24
46:1
2
3[2]
10
12
48:1[2]
7
49:9
51:1[2]
19
20
52:7
53:5
54:1
55:8[2]
9[2]
56:8
10[3]
11[2]
57:1
4

ISAIAH
57:6
20
58:7
59:3
6
7[2]
10
12[2]
60:8
61:1[2]
9
11
63:8
19
64:6[2]
8[2]
9
10
11
65:5
11
16[2]
22
23
24

JER.
2:5
11
15
28[2]
31
4:13[2]
17
20
22[2]
5:3
4[2]
6[2]
7
10
16
23
26
27[2]
28
6:4
20
23
28[3]
29[2]
7:4
10
8:8
9[2]
16
20
9:3
10[3]
19[2]
25
26[3]
10:2
3
5
8
9
15
20
12:1
4
12
13:22
23
14:2
7
9
18
22
15:2[4]

JER.
15:8
16:3
17[2]
20
18:6
21:4
7
22:6
17
20
28[2]
23:10
11
14
26
24:2
3
5
8
25:12
22
23
26
31
34
37
27:5
18
29:1
4
16
17
22
25
30:4
6
31:20
29
32:19
24
35
33:4
34:21
35:14
37:19
38:19
22[3]
40:15
41:12
42:2
11
43:11[3]
44:2
6
10
14
24
27
28
46:5[2]
7
8
12
15
21[3]
23[2]
48:14
15
17
32
36
41
46
49:23
32
50:2[2]
11
15[2]
37
38

JER.
50:43
51:4
7
18
30
32[2]
43
51[2]
56
60
64

LAM.
1:2[2]
4[2]
5[2]
6[2]
14
16
18
20
21
22
2:9[2]
11
21
3:22
23
4:1
2
5
8
9
18
19
5:3[2]
5
7
12
17

EZEKIEL
2:4
5
7
3:7
26
27
5:2
5
6
7[2]
12[4]
14
15
7:9
11:2
7
12
15
12:2
10
14
20
22
23
27
13:4
14:5
16:7
27
38
52
57
18:2
4
25
29[2]
20:3
30

EZEKIEL
20:34
21:14
24[2]
29
22:9
18[2]
19
27
23:45
24:19
25:9
26:6
18
19
27:4
27
28:8
24
25
29:12[2]
30:7[2]
31:12[3]
14
32:20
21
22
23
24
25
26
27[2]
28
29
30[2]
32
33:24
27
30
34:3
12
30
31
35:8
35:12[2]
36:2
3[2]
4[2]
7
8
20[2]
35[2]
37:11[3]
38:7
11
12[2]
20
22
40:46
42:13
14[2]
43:13
18
27
44:10
45:14
46:24
48:1[2]
11
15
29
30

DANIEL
1:10
2:20
28
3:12
16
4:3[2]
18

DANIEL
4:35
37
5:23
7:17[2]
24
8:20
23
9:7[2]
16[2]
19
24
26
10:16
12:9

HOSEA
1:9
10[2]
2:12
4:4
6
14
5:2
6:5
7:2
4
7[2]
9
16
8:9
9:6
7[2]
15
11:7
8
12:7
11[2]
14:3
9

JOEL
1:6
7
12
17[2]
18[2]
20

AMOS
4:1
5:16
6:1[2]
6
9:7
8
12

OBADIAH
6[2]

JONAH
4:11

MICAH
1:4
5[2]
16
2:7
13
4:11
6:10
12
7:6
11

NAHUM
1:3
6
10
2:3

NAHUM
3:13
17[2]

HABAK.
1:3[2]
6
7
8[2]
15
3:6

ZEPH.
1:6
8
11[2]
12
3:3[2]
4
6[2]
18[2]

HAGGAI
1:6

ZECH.
1:5
9
10
15
19
21[2]
3:8
4:2
4
10
11
14
6:4
5
6
10
15
8:16
17
11:2
13:6

MALACHI
1:4
2:8
3:6
7
15[2]

MATT.
1:17[3]
2:2
18
20
5:3
4
5
6
7
8
9
10[2]
11
13
14
15[2]
26
7:15
8:26
9:12
17
37
10:2
28
29

MATT.
10:30
31
11:5[2]
8
11
27
28
12:5
48
13:15
16
38[2]
39
40
56
18:20
19:12[2]
26
30
20:22[2]
25
22:4[3]
14[2]
21[2]
30[2]
23:8
13
25
27[2]
28
31
37
24:8
19
25:8
26:55

MARK
2:17[2]
4:11[2]
15
16[2]
17
18[2]
20[2]
40
5:9
6:2
3
7:15
18
9:23
10:8
27
31
42
12:17[2]
25[3]
13:1
8
17
25
32
14:36
48

LUKE
1:1
4:18
5:20
31[2]
38
6:21[2]
22
24
25
7:22[2]
25[2]
28
31

LUKE
7:32
47[2]
48
8:12
13
14[2]
15
21
9:12
55
61
10:2
8
9
17
20[2]
22
23
11:7
21
28
41
44[2]
12:6
7[2]
24
37
38
13:14
23
25
27
30[2]
34
14:17
16:8
15
17:10[2]
17
18
18:11
27[2]
31
42
20:34
35
36[2]
21:21[3]
22
23
26
22:10
25
28
38
23:29[2]
24:17[2]
18
38
44
48

JOHN
3:21
4:35[2]
38
5:28
39
6:9
49
58
63[2]
64
69
7:7
23
47
49
8:10
22[2]

JOHN
8:31
37
44
47
53
9:28
40
10:8
12
16
21
26
30
34
11:9
13:10
11
17
35
14:2
15:3
5
6
14
19
16:15
30
17:7
9
10[2]
11[2]
14
16
22
20:23[2]
29
30
31
21:25

ACTS
2:7
13
15
32
39
3:15
25
5:9
25
32
7:1
26
10:4
21
31
33[2]
39
13:27
31
39
14:11
15[2]
15:18
19
23
16:17
21
28
17:6
22
28
29
19:15
26
37
38[2]
40
20:32

ACTS
21:20[2]
21[2]
24
22:3
10
23:15
21
35
24:2
11
14
25:5
24
26:3
18
26
28:27

ROMANS
1:6
15
20[3]
28
32
2:2
8
13
14
18
19
3:9[2]
12[2]
15
16
19
25
4:7[3]
12
14
6:2
4
13
14
15
16
21
7:4
6
8:1
5[2]
8
9
12
14[2]
16
18
24
28
36[2]
37
9:4
5
6[2]
7[2]
8[3]
26
10:15
19
11:14
16
28[2]
29
33
36
12:5
13:1
3
6
14:8

ROMANS
14:20
15:1
14
26
27
6:7
10
11
14
15
18

1 COR.
1:2
5
11[2]
18
24
26
27
28[2]
30
2:6
12
14[2]
3:2
3[2]
4
8
9[3]
16
17
20
21
22
23
4:8[2]
9
10[6]
11[2]
13[2]
18
19
5:2
4
7
12[2]
13
6:2
4
11[3]
12[3]
15
19
20[2]
7:14
23
33
8:4
5
6[2]
8[2]
9
10
9:1
2
12
13
20[2]
21[2]
10:11[2]
13
17[2]
18
22
23[3]
11:19
32[2]
12:4

1 COR.
12:5
6
12
13
20
22
27
29[4]
14:10
12
22
23[2]
32
34
37
15:2
6
15
17
18[2]
19
23
27
29[2]
35
40
48[4]
16:9
18

2 COR.
1:1
4[2]
7
14[2]
20
24
2:11
15[2]
16
17
3:2
3
5
18
4:3
8[2]
11
15
18[6]
5:4
6[3]
8
11[2]
17[2]
18
20
6:12
16
7:3
6
8:23
10:4
7
10
11[3]
12
14
11:13
19
22[3]
23
28
13:4
6
9[3]

GAL.
1:2
6

GAL.
2:15
17
3:3[2]
7[2]
9
10[2]
25
26
28
29
4:6
8
9
12
24[2]
28
31
5:4[2]
17
18
19[2]
24
6:1
10
13

EPHES.
1:1
10[2]
2:5
8
10
11
13
19
20
22
4:1
4
25
30
5:4
8
12
13
16
30
6:5

PHIL.
1:1
7
10
11
13
14
2:21
3:3
13[2]
18
4:3
8[6]
21
22

COLOS.
2:3
10
11
12
17
20
22
3:1
3
5
15
4:5
9

COLOS.
4:11[2]
13
15

1 THESS.
2:10
14
15
19
20
3:3
4:9
10
12
13
15[2]
17
5:4
5[2]
7
8
12
14

2 THESS.
1:3
7
2:13
3:11[2]
12
5:15

1 TIM.
2:2
3:7
5:3
16
24
25[2]
6:1
2
17

2 TIM.
1:15[2]
2:19
20
26
3:3
6
15

TITUS
1:5
10
12
15[2]
3:8
9
15

PHILE.
7

HEB.
1:10
14
2:10[2]
11[2]
14
18
3:6
14
4:13
15
5:2
11
12
14
6:9

HEB.
7:5
13
8:4
9:15
17
22
24
10:8
10
14
39
11:3
12:1
8[2]
11
18
22
23
27[2]
13:3
11

JAMES
1:1
2:4[2]
7
9
16
3:4[2]
9
5:2[2]
4
17

1 PETER
1:5
6
12
2:5
9
10
14
25
3:6[2]
9
12[2]
14
4:6
13
14
5:1
9[2]
14

2 PETER
1:4
2:10[2]
11
13
15
17[2]
19
20
3:5
7[2]
10
16[2]

1 JOHN
2:5
12
14
15
18
3:2
10
19
22
4:1[2]
4

1 JOHN
4:5
6
17
5:3
7[2]
8
19
20

2 JOHN
7

JUDE
1
4
7
12[2]
15
16

REV.
1:3
4[2]
11
19
20[2]
2:2[3]
9[3]
18
3:2
4
9[2]
4:5
11
5:6
8
13[2]
7:13[2]
14
15
8:13
9:14
10:6[3]
11:4
15
13:8
14:4[2]
5
12
13
18
15:3[2]
4
16:6
7
14
17:9
10[2]
12
14[2]
15
18:3
14[2]
19:2
9[3]
20:7
8
10
21:4
5
12
16
22
24
27
22:6
14
15
18
19

as

5612

GEN.
3:5
22
4:20
21
7:9
16
8:21
9:3
10:9
19[2]
11:2
12:4
13:10
16
16:6
17:4
15
20
23
18:5
25
33[2]
19:8
14
28
21:1[2]
4
16
22:14
17[2]
23:9[2]
24:22

GEN.
24:51
25:18
26:4
29[2]
27:4
9
12
14
19
23
27
30
42
46
28:6
14
31:2
5
26
32:12
25
28
31
33:10
14
34:12
15
22
31
35:18
36:24
38:11

GEN.
38:29
39:10
18
40:10
22
41:13
19
21
38
39[2]
49
54
42:27
35
43:6
17
34
44:1
3
15
17
18
47:11
21
30
48:5
7
49:4
9
16
27
50:6

GEN.
50:12
20[2]

EXOD.
1:17
19
2:14
4:6
7
5:7
13
14
20
7:6
10
13
20
22
8:15
19
27
9:12
17
18
24
29[2]
30
35
10:10
14
11:6
12:25

EXOD.
12:28
31
32
36
48
50
13:11
14:28
15:5
7
8
10
16[2]
16:5[2]
10
14[2]
22
24
34
17:10
18:21
19:18
21:7
22[2]
22:25
23:15
24:10[2]
27:8
28:32
30:37
32:1
13

EXOD.
32:17
19[2]
23
33:9
11
34:4
10
18
35:22[2]
38:21
39:1
5
6
7
21
23
26
29
31
43
40:15
19
21
23
25
27
29
32

LEVIT.
2:12
4:10

LEVIT.
4:20
21
25[2]
31
35
5:13[2]
6:17[2]
7:7
10[2]
19
21
8:4
9
13
17
21
29
31
34
9:7
10
15
21
10:5
15
18
11:4
12:5
13:43
14:6
13
22

LEVIT.
14:30
31
35
15:25
26[2]
16:15
34
18:19[2]
22
28
19:16
18
23[2]
34[2]
20:6
13
25
22:13
24:16[2]
19
20
22[2]
23
25:31
39
40[2]
42
46
53
26:19[2]
34[2]
35[2]

LEVIT.
26:36
37
27:12
14
21
23

NUM.
1:19
2:17
33
3:16
42
51
4:15
29
49
5:4
8:3
16
19
21
22
9:15
18[2]
10:31
11:7[2]
8
12
31[3]
12:10
12

NUM.
13:21
33
14:15
17
19
21[2]
28[3]
32
15:14
15
20
36
16:31
40[3]
45
47
49
17:11
18:6
7
18[2]
24
27[2]
30[2]
20:9
27
21:34
22:4
8
23:2
22
24[2]
30

NUM.
24:1
6[4]
8
9[2]
26:4
27:11
13
17
22
23
28:8[2]
31:7
31
41
47
32:25
27
31
33:56
34:6
36:10

DEU.
1:10
11[2]
17[2]
19
21
31
40
44
2:1

DEU.
2:5
10
11
12
14
21
22
29
30
3:2
6
20[2]
4:5
7
8
20
32
33
38
5:12
14[2]
16
26
31
32
6:3
8
16
19
24
25
8:5

DEU.
8:18
20
9:3[3]
18
21[2]
25
10:5
9
15
22
11:4
10[2]
18
21
25
12:9
12
15[2]
16
19[2]
20
21
22
24
13:6
11
17
14:7
15:6
21
22[2]
23

DEU.
16:9
10
17
17:14
16
18:2
7
14
19:5
19
20:6
8[2]
17
22:11
26
23:23
24:8
26:15
18
19
27:3
28:9
29
49[2]
62
63
29:13[2]
28
30:9
31:3
4
13[2]

DEU.
31:21
32:2[4]
10
11
31
50
33:20
25
34:9

JOSH.
1:3
5
15
17[2]
2:7[2]
11[2]
3:7
13[2]
15
4:8[2]
12
14
18
23
5:5
14
6:22
7:5
8:2
5
6

JOSH.
8:15
19[2]
29[2]
31[2]
33[3]
9:4
21
25
10:1
2
11
28
30
39[2]
40
11:4
9
12
13
15
20
13:6
8
14
33
14:2
5
7
10
11
12
15:18

JOSH.
15:63
17:14
21:8
22:4
23:5
8
9
10
15
24:15

JUD.
1:7
20
2:3
15[2]
22
3:1[2]
2
4:22
5:31
6:5
16
27
36
37
7:5
12
17
8:8
18
19

JUD.
8:21
33[2]
9:33[3]
36
48
11:36
13:9
23[2]
14:6
20
15:10
11
14
16:7
9
11
20
17:8
11
19:22
20:1
8
11
30
31
32
39
48[2]

RUTH
1:8
3:10
13

1 SAM.
1:7
12
26
28[2]
2:2
16[2]
3:10
4:9
5:10
6:6
12
7:10
9:11
13[2]
20
27
10:7
12:15
23
13:5
7
10[2]
14:14
39
45
15:22[2]
23[2]
27
33
16:7
17:20[2]
23
36
55
57
18:1
3
6
7
10
19:6
7
9
20
20:3[2]
13
17
20
21
23
25
31[2]
36
41[2]
42
22:8
13
14
23:11
24:4
13
18
25:15[2]
20
25
26[3]
29
34
37
26:10
16
20
24
27:8
28:10
17
29:6
8
9
10[2]
30:24

2 SAM.
1:6
21
2:18[2]
23
27
3:9
33
34
36
4:4
6
9
5:20
25
6:16
18
19
20
7:10
11
15
25
8:3
9:8
11
10:2
11:11
25
12:3
5
13:13[2]
29
35
36

2 SAM.
14:2
11
13
14
17
19
25
15:10
21
26
30
34
16:2
5
13[2]
19
23
17:3
8
10
11
12[2]
18:33
19:3
14
18
27
30
20:8
22:23
31
43[3]
45[2]
23:4[2]
6
24:19
23

1 KINGS
1:29
30
37
41
2:3
24[2]
31
38
3:6[2]
14
4:20
29
5:5
12
8:20
24
25
43
53
57
59
61
9:2
4
5
10
10:27[2]
11:4
6
11
33
38[2]
12:12
17
13:6
18
20
21
14:6
7
8
10
15
15:3
11
16:2
9
11[2]
31
17:1
11
12
13
18:7
10
12[2]
15
32[2]
19:2
5
20:11
12
34
36[4]
39
40
21:11[2]
26
22:4[3]
14
17

2 KINGS
1:16
2:2[2]
4[2]
6[2]
11

2 KINGS
2:19
23
3:7[3]
14
22[2]
4:8[2]
30[2]
40
5:16
20
27[2]
6:5
26
7:7
10
13[2]
17
18
8:5
18
19
27
9:17
22
31
37
10:2[2]
12
15
25[2]
11:8[2]
14
12:9
13:5
21
23
14:3
4
5[2]
15:9
17:2
4
11
23
41
19:13
26[4]
29
37
21:3
13
20
22:18
23:16
21
27
24:13
25:15
22

1 CHRON.
5:1
6:26
12:8[2]
20
33
36
14:16
15:15
29
16:37
17:1
9
13
23
18:3
21:3
15
17
21
22:7
11
23:24
24:19
25:8[3]
26:13[2]
21
28:2
7
29:11
15[2]
17
23
25

2 CHRON.
1:12
15[3]
2:3
16[2]
3:16
4:6
5:13[2]
6:8
10
15
16
31
33
7:17[2]
18
8:7
14
9:9
27[2]
10:12
17

2 CHRON.
11:16
13:10
15
16:3
18:3[2]
13
16
20:9
20
21
33
21:6
7
23:3
13
18[2]
24:12[2]
25:4
16
26:5[2]
29:8
31[2]
30:5
7
8
31:3
5[2]
15[2]
32:17
19
33:22
23
34:26
35:12
18
36:21[2]

EZRA
2:62
3:1
2
4[2]
5
4:2
3
6:18
21
7:14
25
27
28
8:27
31
9:7
13
15
10:3
12

NEH.
1:1
2:16
18
5:5[2]
12
6:8
11[2]
7:64
8:1
15
9:10
11
23
24
10:34
36
13:15

ESTHER
2:9
20[2]
3:11
4:14
5:5
8
13
6:10
7:8
8:8
9:2
22
23[2]
27[2]
31[2]

JOB
2:10
3:6
16[2]
4:8
5:7
14
25
26
6:7
15[2]
26
7:2[2]
9
20
9:26[2]
32
10:4
5[2]
9
10
16

JOB
10:19
22[2]
11:8[2]
16
17
20
12:3[3]
4
5
13:9
28[2]
14:2
6
11
15:24
33[2]
16:4
21
17:6
7
10
15
18:3
20
19:11
22
20:8[2]
21:4
18[2]
33
22:2
8
24[2]
23:10
24:5
14
17
18
20
24[2]
26:3
27:2
6
7[2]
16[2]
18[2]
20
21
28:5[2]
29:2[2]
4
14
18
23[2]
25[2]
30:5
14
15[2]
18
31:18
33
36
37
32:19
34:3
26
35:8
37:18
38:8
14[2]
19
30
39:16
20
40:15
18
41:5
15
20
24[4]
27[2]
29
42:7
9
10[2]
15

PSALMS
5:7
12
10:5
9
11:1
12:6
14:4
17:8
12[2]
15
18:30
42[2]
44[2]
19:5[2]
21:9
22:13
25:10
26:11
27:12
31:12
32:9[2]
33:7
22
34:18
35:5
13
14[2]
37:2
6[2]

PSALMS
37:14
20
22
38:4
10
13[2]
14
39:5[2]
12
40:4
16
41:12
42:1
10
44:22
48:6
8
50:21
53:4
55:16
20
58:3[2]
7[2]
8
9
61:6
62:3[2]
2
5
65:3
66:10
68:2[2]
13
14
15[2]
17
21
69:13
70:4
71:7
72:5[2]
6
7
17[2]
73:1
2
5
6[2]
19
20
22
74:5
77:13
78:8
13
15
27[2]
65
83:9[3]
10
11[2]
13
14[2]
87:7[2]
88:4
89:10
11
29
36
37[2]
90:4[2]
5[2]
9
92:7
95:8
102:3
7
26
103:11
12[2]
13
15[3]
18
104:2
6
17
33[2]
106:9
107:10
109:17[2]
18[2]
19
23
29
116:2[2]
118:12
119:14[2]
70[2]
111
132
162
122:3
123:2[2]
124:6
7
125:1
2
5[2]
126:4
127:4
128:3
129:6
131:2[2]
133:1
3[2]
137:8
139:12

PSALMS
139:16
140:9
141:2[2]
7
143:3
6
144:4
12[2]
147:20

PROV.
1:12[2]
27[2]
2:14[4]
3:12
4:18
19
5:3
4
19
6:5[2]
11[2]
7:2
22
23
8:26
30
9:4
16
10:20
23
25
26
11:19
20
22
28
12:4
15:19
16:14
15
24
27
17:8
14
18:4[2]
8
11
19:12[2]
24
20:2
19
21:1
8
29
23:5
7
28
34[2]
24:29
34[2]
25:12
13
16
20[2]
25
26
26:1[2]
2
8
9
11
14
18
21
22
27:8
19
21
28:1
4
15
30:14
31:8

ECCL.
2:8
13
15
16
3:19
4:1
5:15[2]
16
6:12
7:6
26
8:1
13
9:2[2]
12[2]
10:5
7
11:5
12:7
11[2]

CANT.
1:3
5
7
14
2:2
3
4:1
11
5:11[2]

CANT.
5:12
13
14[2]
15[3]
6:4[3]
5
6
7
10[4]
13
7:4[2]
8
8:1
6[4]
10

ISAIAH
1:7
8[3]
9
18[4]
26[2]
30[2]
31[2]
3:9
12
16
5:18
24[3]
6:13
7:2
8:6
9:1
3
4
18
19
10:9[3]
10
11
14[2]
15[3]
18
20
22
26
32
11:9
16
13:4
6
8[2]
14[2]
17
19
14:10
17
19[2]
24[2]
16:2
3
14
17:3
5[2]
6
9
13
19:14
20:3
21:1
3
22:16
23
23:5
10
15
24:2[6]
13[2]
22
25:4
5
10
11
26:17
18
19
20
27:7
9
28:2
4
21[2]
29:2[2]
4
5
7
8[2]
11
13
16
17
30:13
14
17[2]
22
26[2]
27
28
29[2]
31:4
5
32:2[3]
33:4
11
12[2]
34:4[3]
35:1

ISAIAH
35:6
37:12
27[4]
30
38
38:12
13
14
19
40:6
15[3]
17
22[3]
23
24
31
41:2[2]
11
12[2]
15
25[2]
42:13
19[3]
43:17
44:4[2]
7
22[2]
47:3
4'
8
14
48:18[2]
19
49:18[3]
26
50:4
9
51:9
12
13
20
23[2]
52:14
53:2[2]
3
7[2]
54:6
9[2]
55:9
10
56:12
58:2
4
5
8
10
59:10[3]
12
17[2]
21
60:8[2]
61:10[2]
11[2]
62:1[2]
5[2]
63:13
14
64:2
6[3]
65:8
22
66:3[4]
8[2]
13
20
22

JER.
2:26
36
3:2
5
20
4:13[2]
17
31[2]
5:8
9
16
19
26
27
29
6:7
9[2]
23
24
26
7:14
15
8:6
9:8
9
22[2]
10:5
6
7
11:5
12:8
9
16
13:5
10
11
21[2]
24
14:8[2]

JER.
14:9[2]
15:2[4]
18[2]
19
16:4
17:8
11
16
22
18:4
6[2]
17
19:11
12
13
20:9
11
21:7
22:23
24
23:12
14[2]
27
29
34
24:8
25:18
30
38
26:11
14[2]
18
27:13
30:6
20
31:5
10
12
18
23
28
32:20
31
42
33:7
11
22
38:16
39:12
40:3
10
41:6[2]
42:2
18
43:11[3]
12
44:6
13
14
16
17
22
23
30
46:7[2]
18[3]
22
26
48:8
13
34
40
41
49:16[2]
18
22[2]
24
50:8
9
11[2]
15
18
26
37
40
43
51:14
27
30
38
49

LAM.
1:1
15
17
20
22
2:4
5
6
7
12
22
3:6
10[2]
12
45
4:2
6
14
17[2]
5:3
21

EZEKIEL
1:1

EZEKIEL
1:4
10
13
14
15
16
18
22
24[2]
26[2]
27[3]
28
3:3
9
23
4:12
5:11
7:17
20
8:1
2[3]
9:10
11
10:1[2]
5
9
10[2]
11[2]
13
11:16
21
12:4[2]
7[2]
11
23
14:10
16
18
20
15:6
16:4
7
31
32
38
44
47
48[2]
50
57
59
17:5
16
19
18:3
4
18
20:3
31
32[2]
33
36
39
21:7
10
23
22:20
22
23:16[2]
18
20
44
24:18
22
26:3
10
28:2
6
16
30:9
18
32:2
33:11
12
17
27
31[2]
32
34:8
12
17
19
35:6
11
15
36:17
38[2]
37:7[2]
10
38:16
40:2
40
41:21
25
42:6
9
11[4]
12
43:22
46:5
7
11
12
47:10
14[2]
15
22

EZEKIEL
48:1
8
11
23

DANIEL
1:4
13
17
2:29
30
40[3]
41
42
43
45
4:18
25
32
33
35
5:12
6:4
10
22
7:4
9[2]
12
28
8:5
15
18
9:7
12
13
15
10:4
6[2]
17
11:29[2]
32
12:1
3[2]

HOSEA
1:10
2:3[2]
15[2]
4:4
7
16[2]
5:12[2]
14[2]
6:3[2]
4[2]
5
9
7:4
6
7
12[2]
8:1
8
12
9:1
4
9
10[2]
11
13
10:4
7[2]
11
14
11:2
4
8[2]
11[2]
12:9
11
13:3[4]
7[2]
8
14:5[3]
6[2]
7[3]

JOEL
1:15
2:2
3
4[2]
5
32

AMOS
2:9
13
3:12
4:11[2]
5:11
14
16
19
24[2]
7:15
8:8[2]
10[2]
9:5
7
9
11

OBADIAH
4
11
15
16[2]

JONAH
1:14

MICAH
1:4[2]
6[2]
8
16
2:8[2]
12[2]
3:3[2]
4
12[2]
4:9
12
5:7[2]
8[2]
15
7:1[2]
4
10
14

NAHUM
1:10[3]
2:2
7
3:6
15[2]
17[2]

HABAK.
1:8
9[2]
14[2]
2:5[2]
14
3:4
14[2]

ZEPH.
1:8
17[2]
2:2
9

HAGGAI
1:12
2:3
19
23

ZECH.
1:4
6
2:4
6
4:1
5:3[2]
7:3
12
13
8:11
13
14
9:1
3[2]
7[2]
11
13
14
15[2]
16[3]
10:2
3
5
6
7
8
12:8[3]
10[2]
11
13:9[2]
14:3
5
10
15

MALACHI
2:9
3:3[2]
4[2]
17
4:1
2

MATT.
1:18
24
5:48
6:2
5
7
10
12
16
7:29[2]
8:13
9:9
10
15[2]
32
36
10:7
16[3]
25[2]
11:7
12:13
40

MATT.
13:40
43
14:5
36[2]
15:28
33
17:2[2]
9
20
18:3
4
17
19
25
33
19:19
20:14
28
29
21:6
18
23
26
22:9[2]
10[2]
30
31
39
23:37
24:3
21
27
37
38
44
25:14
32
40
45
26:7
19
21
24
26
39[2]
55
27:10
32
65[2]
28:1
3
4
6
9
15

MARK
1:2
16
22[2]
42[2]
2:2
14
15
19[2]
23
3:5
10[2]
20
4:4
18
20
26
33
36
5:36
6:15
31
34
56[2]
7:4
6
8
8:24
9:3[2]
9
13
26
10:1
15
32
46
11:2[2]
6
20
27
12:25
26
31
12:33
13:1
3
19
34
14:3
16
18
21
22
45[2]
48
66
15:8
16:7
10
12
14

LUKE
1:1
2
23[2]
44[2]
55
70
2:15
20
23
43
3:4
15
23
4:16
5:1
14
17
6:3
10
22
31
34
36
40
8:5
6[2]
23
42
9:18
29
33
34
42
53
54
57
10:3
7
8
18
27
33
38
11:1[2]
2
8[2]
27
30
36
37
41
44
53
12:58
13:34
14:1
22
15:19
25
30[2]
17:6
11
12
14
24
26
28
18:11[2]
13
17
35
19:9
11
32
33
36
20:1
21:5
6
35
22:13
26[2]
27
29
31
39
44
52
56
66[2]
23:7[2]
14
24
26
24:4
5
11
17
24
28
36
39
50[2]

JOHN
1:12[2]
14
23
36
3:14
4:51
5:21
23
26
30
6:11[2]
31

JOHN
6:57
58
59
7:10
28
38
8:6
20
28
30
9:1
5[2]
29
10:15
26
11:20[2]
29[2]
56
12:14
50
13:15
33
34
14:27
31
15:4
6
9
10
12
16:21[2]
17:2[3]
11
14,16
18
21
22
23
18:6[2]
19:40
20:9
11
21
21:8
9[2]

ACTS
1:10
11
19
2:2
3
4
15
22
39[2]
45
47
3:6
11
12
17
24[2]
4:1
6[2]
34[2]
35
5:11[2]
35
36[2]
37[2]
6:15
7:5[2]
26
28
31
40
42
44
48
51
8:3
16
32
36
9:3
17
18
32
38
10:9
11
25
27
29[2]
45
47[2]
11:15[2]
17[2]
19[2]
22[2]
12:13
18[2]
13:1
2
17
25
33
34
48[2]
14:20
15:8
11
15
24
16:4
16

ACTS
17:2
14
23
25
28
29
19:2
20:3
9
21:10
25
31
37
22:3
5
6
23
25
23:11
15
20
31
24:10
25
25:10
18
26:12
24
29
27:25
27
30[2]
28:10
15[2]
22

ROMANS
1:13
15
17
21
28
2:12[4]
24
3:4
5
7
8[2]
10
4:1
6
17[2]
5:12
15
16
18
19
21
6:3
4
13[3]
19
7:1[2]
2
8:14[2]
26
36[2]
9:5
6
13
25
27
29[2]
32
33
10:15
11:8
13
26
28[2]
30
12:3
4
18[2]
13:9
13
14:11
15:3
7
9
15
21
16:2

1 COR.
1:6
31
2:9
3:1[3]
3
5
10
15
4:1
7
8
9
13
14
17
18
5:1[2]
3[2]
7
7:7
8
17[3]

1 COR.
7:25
29
30[3]
31
39[2]
8:1
2
4
5
7
9:5[3]
8
20[2]
21
22
26[2]
10:6
7[2]
8
9
10
13
15
10:33
11:1
2
5
7
12
25[2]
26[2]
12:2
11
12
18
13:1
11[3]
12
14:12
33
34
15:8
22
38
48[2]
49
58
16:1
2
10
12

2 COR.
1:5
7
14[2]
18
28
2:17[3]
3:1
3
5
13
18[2]
4:1
13
5:20
6:1
4
8
9[3]
10[3]
13
16
7:14
8:5
6
7
11
15
9:1
3
5[2]
7
9
10:2
7
9
11
14[3]
11:2
3
10
12
15
16
17
21[2]

2 COR.
11:23
12:20
13:2
7

GAL.
1:9
2:7
14[2]
3:6
10[2]
16[2]
27[2]
4:1[2]
12[2]
14[2]
28
29

GAL. 5:14, 21, 6:10, 12[2], 16[2], EPHES. 1:4, 2:3, 3:3, 5, 4:4, 17, 21, 32, 5:1, 2

EPHES. 5:3, 8, 15, 22, 23, 24, 25, 28, 29, 33, 6:5[2], 6, 7, 20, PHIL. 1:7

PHIL. 1:20, 27, 2:8, 12[2], 15, 22, 23, 3:5, 12, 15, 17, 4:15, COLOS. 1:6[2], 7, 2:1

COLOS. 2:6, 7, 20, 3:12, 13, 18, 22, 23, 4:4, 1 THESS. 1:5, 2:2, 4[2], 5, 6, 7

1 THESS. 2:11[2], 13, 14, 3:4, 6, 12, 4:1, 5, 6, 9, 11, 13, 5:2, 3, 4, 6, 11

2 THESS. 1:3, 2:2, 4, 3:1, 15[2], 1 TIM. 1:3, 5:1[2], 2, 6:1, 2 TIM. 2:3, 9, 17, 3:8, 9

TITUS 1:5, 7, 9, 2:3, PHILE. 9, 14, 16, 17, HEB. 1:4, 11, 12, 2:14, 3:2

HEB. 3:3, 5, 6, 7, 8, 15, 4:2[2], 3[2], 7, 10, 15, 5:3, 4, 6, 12, 6:19, 7:9

HEB. 7:20, 27, 8:5, 9:8, 9, 25, 27, 10:25[2], 11:7, 9, 12[4], 27, 29, 12:5, 7, 16, 20

HEB. 12:27, 13:3[2], 5, 17, JAMES 1:10, 2:8, 9, 12, 26, 5:3, 5, 17, 1 PETER 1:14

1 PETER 1:15, 18[2], 19, 24[2], 2:2, 4, 5, 11, 12, 13, 14, 16[2], 25, 3:6[3], 7[2], 8, 16

1 PETER 4:1, 10[2], 11[2], 12, 13, 15[4], 16, 19, 5:3, 8, 12, 2 PETER 1:3, 13, 14, 19

2 PETER 1:21, 2:1, 12, 13, 3:4, 8[2], 9, 10, 15, 16[2], 1 JOHN 1:7, 2:6, 18, 27[2]

1 JOHN 3:2, 3, 7, 12, 23, 4:17, 2 JOHN 4, 5, 6, 3 JOHN 2, 3

JUDE 7, 10, REV. 1:10, 14[3], 15[2], 16, 17, 2:24[3], 27[2], 3:3, 19[2], 21, 4:1, 7

REV. 5:6, 13, 6:1, 11, 12[2], 13, 14, 8:8, 10, 12, 9:2, 3, 5, 7[2], 8[2], 9[2], 17

REV. 10:1[2], 3, 7, 9, 10[3], 11:6[2], 12:4[4], 15, 13:2[2], 3, 11, 15[2], 14:2[2], 3, 15:2, 16:3

REV. 16:15, 18, 17:12[2], 18:6, 17[2], 19:6[3], 12, 20:8, 21:2, 11, 16[2], 21, 22:1, 12

be

1961, *1510*

GEN. 1:3, 6, 9[2], 14[2], 15, 22, 28, 29, 2:18, 23, 24, 3:5[2], 6, 12, 16, 4:7[2], 12, 14[2], 15, 24, 6:3, 15, 19, 21, 8:17, 9:1[2], 2, 3, 6, 7, 11[2], 13, 14, 15, 16, 20, 25[2], 26[2], 27, 10:8, 11:4, 6, 12:2, 3, 13, 13:8[2], 16, 14:19, 20, 15:4[2], 5[2], 13, 15, 16:2, 3, 5, 10, 12, 17:1, 4, 5[2], 7, 8, 10, 11, 12, 13[2], 14, 15, 16, 17, 18:4, 11, 18, 24, 25[2], 29, 30[2], 31, 32[2], 19:9, 15, 17, 22, 20:9, 21:10, 12[2], 30, 22:14, 17, 23:8, 24:5, 8[2], 14, 27

GEN. 24:41[2], 44, 51, 60, 25:22, 23[2], 26:3, 4, 11, 22, 28, 27:13, 21, 29[2], 33, 39, 45, 28:3, 9, 14[2], 20, 21, 22, 29:4, 7, 8, 15, 26, 29, 34, 30:32, 33, 34, 31:3, 8[2], 30, 44, 52[2], 32:12, 18, 28, 33:14, 34:7, 10, 15[3], 17[2], 22[2], 23, 30, 35:2, 10[2], 11[2], 36:43, 37:14, 27, 32, 35, 38:9, 11, 15, 23, 24, 29, 39:10, 40:14, 27, 36[2], 41:21, 30, 31[2], 40[3], 52, 42:15, 16[3], 19[2], 20, 32, 33, 43:3, 5, 9, 11, 14, 23, 29, 44:9[2], 10[3], 17, 26[2], 30, 34, 45:5, 6, 10, 46:15

GEN. 47:19[2], 24, 25, 48:5, 6[2], 16, 19[2], 21, 49:6, 7, 8, 10, 12, 13[2], 17, 20, 26, 29, 50:18, EXOD. 1:16[2], 2:4, 3:12[2], 4:12, 14, 15, 16[4], 18, 5:8, 9, 11, 18, 21, 6:7, 14[2], 7:1, 17, 19, 8:20, 21, 22, 23, 9:3, 9, 15, 16, 19[2], 22, 28, 29, 10:5, 7, 10, 14, 21[2], 24, 26, 11:6[2], 9, 12:2[2], 15, 16[2], 19, 25, 32, 42[2], 46, 48, 13:3, 7[3], 14:4, 15:9, 15, 16:12, 23, 32, 33, 34, 19:12, 13, 20:26, 21:8, 12, 15, 16[2], 17, 19, 20, 21, 22, 28[2], 29[2], 30, 31

EXOD. 21:32, 22:2[3], 3[3], 4[2], 5, 6, 7[2], 8[2], 9[2], 10, 11, 12, 13, 14, 15[2], 16, 19, 20, 24, 25, 30, 31, 23:1, 12[2], 13[2], 22, 26, 30, 33, 24:7, 12, 25:7, 10, 12, 14, 15[2], 17, 20, 23, 27, 28, 31[2], 34, 35, 36[2], 38, 26:2, 3[2], 6, 7, 8[2], 11, 16[2], 17, 20, 24[4], 25, 31, 32, 37, 27:1[2], 2, 5, 7[2], 9, 10[2], 11, 12, 13, 14, 15, 16[2], 17[2], 18, 19, 21, 28:7, 8, 11, 16[3], 17[2], 18, 20, 21[2], 28[2], 30, 32[2], 35[2], 37[2], 38[3], 43[2], 29:9, 10, 21, 26

EXOD. 29:28[2], 29[3], 34, 37[2], 42, 43, 45, 30:2[4], 4, 12, 13, 16, 21, 25, 29[2], 31, 32[2], 33, 34, 36, 37, 38, 31:14[2], 15[2], 32:5, 8, 33:16[2], 19[2], 23, 34:2, 3, 12, 25, 35:2[3], 9, 27, 29, 36:6, 18, 34, 37:3, 27, 38:5, 26, 39:7, 21[2], 37, 40:4, 9, 10, 15, LEVIT. 1:3, 4, 9, 10, 14, 15, 2:1, 2, 3, 4, 5[2], 7[2], 10, 11, 12, 13, 3:1[2], 6, 12, 17, 4:2, 12, 13[2], 15, 20, 22, 26, 27[2], 31, 35, 5:2[3], 3[4], 4[3], 5[2], 7, 9, 10, 11, 13[2], 16, 17, 18

LEVIT. 6:4, 7, 9, 12[2], 13, 16, 17, 18[2], 21, 22, 23[2], 25, 26, 27, 28[3], 30[2], 7:6, 9, 14, 15, 16[2], 17, 18[4], 19[3], 20, 21, 24, 25, 26, 27[2], 30, 31, 36, 8:5, 33, 10:3[2], 9, 14, 15, 11:7, 10, 11, 12, 13, 20, 23, 24[2], 25, 26, 27, 28, 29, 31[2], 32[6], 33, 34[4], 35[4], 36[2], 37[2], 38[2], 39, 40[2], 41[2], 43, 44, 45[2], 47[2], 12:2[2], 3, 4, 5, 7, 8[2], 13:2[2], 3, 4[3], 5, 6[2], 7, 9, 10[2], 14, 15, 16, 17, 19[2], 20[2], 21[3], 24, 25[2], 26[3], 27, 28, 30[2], 31

LEVIT. 13:32[2], 33, 34[3], 36, 37, 39, 42, 43, 45, 46[3], 47, 48, 49[2], 51, 52, 53, 55[2], 56, 58[4], 14:2[2], 3, 4, 5, 7, 8[2], 9[2], 11, 14, 17, 18, 19, 20, 21[2], 22, 25, 28, 29, 31, 34, 36, 37, 39, 41, 44, 46, 54, 15:3[2], 4, 5, 6, 7, 8, 9, 10[2], 11, 12[2], 13, 16, 17[2], 18, 19[3], 20[2], 21, 22, 23[2], 24[3], 25[2], 26[2], 27[2], 28[2], 16:4[2], 10[2], 17, 29[2], 30, 31, 34, 17:3, 4[2], 7, 8, 9, 10, 13[2], 14, 15[3], 18:9, 29, 19:3, 6[2], 7[2], 8, 20[2], 22, 23[2]

LEVIT. 19:24, 29, 31, 34, 20:2[2], 7, 9[2], 10, 11[2], 12[2], 13[2], 14[2], 15, 16[2], 17, 18, 21, 26[2], 27[2], 21:1, 8, 6[2], 8, 9, 17, 18, 20, 22:3[2], 4, 5, 6, 7, 12, 13, 18, 20, 21[3], 23, 25[2], 27[2], 28, 30, 32, 33, 23:2, 3, 10, 11, 13[2], 14, 15, 17[2], 18, 20, 21[2], 27[2], 29[3], 30, 31, 32, 34, 35, 36, 37, 39[2], 41, 24:3, 5, 7, 9, 12, 16[2], 17, 19, 20, 21, 25:4, 6, 7, 8, 10, 11, 12, 23, 25, 26, 28, 30[2], 31[2], 34, 35[2], 38, 39[2], 40, 42

LEVIT. 25:44, 45, 46, 48, 49, 50[2], 51, 53, 54, 26:12[2], 13, 17, 20, 22, 23, 25, 26, 32, 33, 34, 41, 43, 44, 45, 27:2, 3[2], 4[2], 5[2], 6[3], 7[3], 8, 9[2], 10, 11, 12[2], 14[2], 15, 16[2], 18, 19, 20, 21[2], 25[2], 26[2], 27[3], 28, 29[3], 32, 33[3], NUM. 1:4, 51[2], 53, 2:3, 5[2], 7, 10[2], 12[2], 14, 18[2], 20[2], 22, 25[2], 27[2], 29, 3:10, 12, 13, 24, 25, 30, 31, 32, 36, 38[2], 45, 46, 48, 4:4, 7, 27, 28, 45, 5:6, 8[2], 9, 10[2], 13[5], 14[4], 19, 20, 27[2], 28[3], 30

NUM. 5:31, 6:5[2], 12, 13, 25, 7:5, 8:14, 19, 9:10[2], 13, 10:7, 8, 9[2], 10, 31, 32[2], 35, 11:16, 20, 22[2], 12:6, 12, 14[3], 13:18, 19[2], 20[3], 28, 31, 14:3, 11, 17, 21, 31, 33, 35, 40, 42, 43, 15:2, 11, 14, 15[2], 16, 19, 24[2], 25, 26, 28, 30[2], 31[2], 34, 35, 39, 40, 41, 16:7[2], 16, 22, 26, 29, 38, 40[2], 17:3, 10, 13, 18:2, 4, 5, 7, 9[2], 10, 13, 14, 15[2], 16, 17, 18, 19:7, 8, 9, 10[2], 11, 12[2], 13[2], 14, 16, 17, 19, 20[2], 21[2], 22[2], 20:24

NUM. 20:26, 21:22, 22:11, 23:9, 10, 23, 24:7[3], 18[2], 20, 22, 25:4, 26:53, 54, 55, 56, 27:4, 11, 13, 17, 20, 28:7[2], 14, 15, 17, 18, 19, 20, 24, 26, 31, 29:3, 8, 9, 13, 14, 18, 21, 24, 29:27, 30, 33, 37, 31:2, 23[2], 24, 32:5, 22[3], 23, 26, 29, 32, 54, 55, 34:3[2], 4, 5, 6, 7, 8, 9[2], 12[2], 35:3, 5[2], 6, 7, 8, 10, 11, 12, 14, 15, 16, 17, 18, 21, 27, 29, 30, 31, 33, 36:3[4], 4[3], 8, DEU. 1:1, 17, 21, 29, 39, 42, 2:4, 25, 4:19

DEU. 4:20, 26, 27, 30, 5:16, 29, 33, 6:2, 3, 6, 8, 10, 11, 15, 18, 25, 7:4, 6, 10, 14[2], 16, 18, 20, 21, 23, 24, 25, 26, 8:14, 19, 20, 10:5, 16, 11:8, 15, 16, 17[2], 18, 21, 24[2], 25, 12:11, 21, 23, 27, 30[2], 13:5, 9, 14, 16[2], 14:2, 19, 24[2], 29, 15:4, 7, 9[3], 10, 12, 16, 17, 21[2], 16:4, 8, 17:2, 4[2], 6[2], 7, 9, 18, 19, 20, 18:3[2], 10, 13, 22, 19:2, 9, 10[2], 15, 17, 18, 20:1, 3, 11[3], 20[2], 21:1[2], 3, 6, 8[2], 13[2], 14, 15, 16, 22[2]

DEU. 21:23, 22:2[2], 6[2], 7, 9, 19, 20[2], 22, 23, 23:10, 11, 13, 14, 17, 21, 22, 24:2, 3, 4, 5[2], 7, 12, 13, 14, 15, 16[3], 19, 20, 21, 25:1, 2[4], 6[2], 9, 10, 15, 19, 26:1, 3, 12, 17, 18, 19, 27:2, 4[2], 15, 16, 17, 18, 19, 20, 21, 22, 23, 24, 25, 26, 28:3[2], 4, 5, 6[2], 7, 10, 13[2], 16, 17, 18, 19[2], 20, 23[2], 24, 25[2], 26, 27, 29, 31[4], 32[2], 33, 34, 35, 44[2], 45, 46, 51, 54, 56, 61, 62, 63, 68, 29:13, 18[2], 30:4, 17, 31:6[2], 7

DEU. 31:8[2], 16, 17[2], 19, 21, 23[2], 26, 32:20, 24, 38, 43, 50, 33:6, 7[2], 8, 13, 20, 24[2], 25[2], 28, 29, JOSH. 1:4, 5[2], 6, 7, 9[3], 17, 18[3], 2:3, 14, 16, 17, 19[6], 20, 21, 3:4, 7, 13, 4:6, 7, 6:17, 26, 7:12, 14[2], 15[2], 8:1, 4, 8, 9:6, 13, 20, 21, 23, 10:25, 11:6, 13:1, 14:9, 12[3], 15:4, 17:15[2], 18[3], 20:3, 6, 21:13, 21, 27, 32, 38, 22:18[2], 19, 22, 27, 28, 34, 23:4, 6, 13, 16, 24:27[2], JUD. 2:3[2], 6, 4:9, 20, 5:24[2], 31, 6:13[2], 16, 23, 31[2], 37[2], 39[3]

JUD. 7:4, 11, 17, 8:5, 9:9, 11, 13, 24, 31, 33, 10:18, 11:6, 8, 9, 10, 26, 27, 31[2], 37, 13:5, 7, 8, 14:11, 15:3, 7, 16:6, 7[2], 9, 10, 11[2], 12, 13, 14, 17[2], 20, 28, 17:2, 10, 18:5, 9, 19[3], 25, 19:6[2], 9, 20, 28, 20:9, 21:3, 5, 17[3], 18, 22[3], RUTH 1:11, 16, 17, 2:4, 9, 12, 13, 19, 20, 3:1, 4, 10, 13, 14, 18, 4:10[2], 11, 12, 14[2], 15, 1 SAM. 1:14, 22, 28, 2:9, 10, 28, 30[2], 31, 32, 33, 34, 3:9, 14, 20, 4:9[2], 19, 5:8, 6:3[2], 4

1 SAM. 8:11[2], 13[3], 17, 20, 9:13[2], 16, 10:1, 6, 7, 21, 11:3, 7, 9, 13, 12:15, 25, 13:14, 14:6, 10, 21, 24[2], 28, 39, 40[2], 15:1, 11, 13, 18, 33, 16:16, 17:9[3], 25, 26, 27, 36, 37, 18:17[3], 18, 21[3], 22, 23, 25, 26, 27, 19:6, 11, 22, 20:3, 7[2], 8, 9, 12, 13, 18[2], 23, 29, 31, 32, 42, 22:3, 15, 23, 23:3, 17[2], 20, 21, 23, 24:12, 13, 15, 20[2], 25:6[3], 10, 11, 24, 26, 27, 29, 31, 32, 33[2], 39, 41, 26:9, 19[2], 24, 25, 27:11, 12, 28:18, 19, 29:4[2], 10, 30:24

2 SAM. 1:5, 16, 2:5, 7[2], 26, 3:12, 35, 39, 5:2, 14, 24, 6:22[2], 7:8, 11, 12, 14[2], 16[2], 24, 26[2], 28, 29, 10:5, 11[2], 12, 11:15, 20, 24, 12:9, 10, 22, 28, 13:12, 13, 15, 25, 28, 14:2[2], 9, 14[2], 15, 17[2], 25, 32, 15:20, 21[2], 33, 34[2], 35, 16:2[2], 12, 18, 19, 21, 17:3, 8[2], 9, 10, 11, 12[2], 13[2], 16, 17, 20, 18:25, 28, 32, 19:7, 13, 21, 22[2], 35, 37, 42, 43, 20:1, 4, 20, 21, 21:5, 6, 22:4[2], 44, 45, 46, 47[2], 23:1, 3, 4, 5, 6[2], 7[2], 8, 17, 24:3, 13

2 SAM. 24:17, 21, 22, 1 KINGS 1:2, 5, 21, 35[2], 37, 48, 52, 2:2, 7, 19, 21, 24, 33, 37, 39, 45, 3:13, 26, 5:6, 7, 9, 6:6, 8:5, 15, 16, 26, 29[2], 31, 33, 37[3], 38, 46, 51, 52[2], 56, 57, 59, 61, 9:3, 7, 8, 10:9, 27[2], 11:37, 38[2], 12:7[2], 10, 13:2[2], 3[2], 6, 14:2[3], 5[2], 6, 10, 17:1, 4, 18:21, 24, 27, 31, 36, 19:15, 16[2], 20:6, 18[2], 23, 25, 39[2], 40, 21:7, 22:3, 13, 22, 2 KINGS 1:10, 12, 13, 14, 15, 2:9[2], 10[2], 16, 21, 3:17, 4:1, 10, 13[2], 14, 23

2 KINGS
5:10, 12, 13, 17, 22, 23, 6:3, 6^{2}, 8, 7:1, 2, 12, 18, 19, 8:13, 29, 9:10, 15^{2}, 37, 10:6, 9, 15, 19^{2}, 23, 24, 11:5, 6^{2}, 8^{2}, 15, 17, 12:5, 15, 14:6^{3}, 15:19, 16:15, 18:23, 29, 30, 19:4, 6, 10, 11, 25, 26, 29, 20:8, 17^{2}, 18, 19, 22:17^{2}, 20, 23:27, 25:12, 24^{2}

1 CHRON.
1:10, 4:10, 5:2, 6:17, 9:22, 11:2, 6, 12:17^{3}, 18^{2}, 13:2, 14:15, 15:16, 16:15, 25^{2}, 30^{2}, 31, 36, 38, 17:7, 9, 10, 11^{3}, 13^{2}, 14, 21, 23, 24^{3}, 27^{2}, 19:5, 12^{2}, 13, 21:3^{2}, 12, 17^{3}, 22, 22:5^{2}, 9^{3}, 10^{2}, 11, 13^{2}, 16^{2}, 19, 28:4^{2}, 6^{2}, 7, 9, 10, 20^{3}, 21^{3}, 29:2^{2}, 5, 10, 14, 22^{2}

2 CHRON.
1:9, 2:8, 9, 12, 14

2 CHRON.
2:18^{2}, 4:18, 5:6, 13, 6:4, 5^{2}, 6, 17, 20, 22, 24, 28^{4}, 29, 36, 40^{2}, 41, 7:13, 15, 16^{2}, 18, 20, 21, 22, 9:8^{2}, 10:3, 4^{2}, 7^{2}, 10, 11:22, 12:7, 8, 13:8, 9, 15:2^{2}, 7^{3}, 13, 18:3, 10, 12, 14, 21, 19:7, 11^{2}, 20:2, 15, 17^{2}, 20, 22:6, 23:4, 5^{2}, 7^{2}, 14, 15, 16, 25:8, 14, 16, 26:15, 18, 29:11, 24, 30:7, 8, 19, 31:4, 32:7^{3}, 14, 33:4, 34:25^{2}, 28, 35:3, 36:22, 23

EZRA
1:1, 3, 4:12, 13^{2}, 15, 16, 21^{2}, 5:8, 15, 17^{2}, 6:3^{2}, 4, 5, 6, 8^{2}, 9, 11^{3}, 12, 7:20, 21, 23^{2}, 24, 26^{2}, 27, 9:12, 14^{2}, 10:3, 4^{2}, 8, 14

NEH.
1:6, 11, 2:3, 6, 7, 17, 4:5, 7, 12, 14

NEH.
4:22, 5:5, 8, 13, 14, 6:6, 7, 9^{2}, 13, 7:3^{3}, 5, 8:10, 11, 9:5, 10:38, 11:23, 13:5, 19^{4}

ESTHER
1:17^{2}, 19^{2}, 20, 22, 2:2, 3, 4, 9, 3:9^{2}, 14^{2}, 4:14, 5:3, 6^{2}, 14^{3}, 6:6, 8, 9^{2}, 11, 13, 7:2^{2}, 3, 4^{2}, 8:5^{2}, 13^{2}, 9:1, 12^{2}, 13^{2}, 14, 25, 28

JOB
1:5, 21, 3:4, 6, 7, 9, 17, 4:2, 17^{2}, 5:1, 11^{2}, 21^{2}, 22, 23^{2}, 24, 25, 6:3, 6, 14, 28, 29, 7:4, 21, 8:2, 14^{2}, 22, 9:2, 29, 10:15^{2}, 11:2^{2}, 12^{2}, 14, 15, 17^{2}, 18, 20, 12:14^{2}, 13:5, 16, 18, 14:7, 15:14^{2}, 29, 31, 32^{2}, 34, 17:8, 9, 18:2, 4^{2}, 5, 6^{2}, 7, 12^{2}, 14, 15, 16^{2}, 18, 20, 19:4, 27, 29, 20:8^{2}, 12, 18

JOB
20:21, 22, 26, 21:2, 4, 5, 30, 32, 33, 22:2^{2}, 21, 23, 25, 28, 23:7, 24:20^{2}, 23^{2}, 25, 25:4^{2}, 27:7, 14^{2}, 15, 19, 28:12, 15^{2}, 16, 17, 18, 19, 31:6, 8, 11, 22, 28, 31, 32:20, 33:3, 7, 21, 23, 25, 26, 30, 34:10, 20^{2}, 29, 30, 31, 33, 36, 35:2, 3^{2}, 6, 7, 36:4, 8^{2}, 16^{2}, 26, 37:6, 20^{2}, 38:11, 13, 15, 39:9, 40:8, 41:9, 17, 23, 32, 42:2

PSALMS
1:3, 2:10^{2}, 12, 3:2, 6, 4:3, 4, 6, 5:11, 6:10^{2}, 7:3, 9:2, 9, 17, 18, 19, 20, 10:2, 6^{2}, 11:3, 6, 13:2, 14:7, 15:5, 16:4, 8, 17:15, 18:3^{2}, 45, 46^{2}, 19:10, 13^{2}, 14, 21:7, 13, 22:3, 11, 19, 25, 26, 29, 30, 31, 24:7, 25:2

PSALMS
25:3^{2}, 20, 26:11, 27:1, 2, 6, 14, 28:1^{2}, 6, 30:6, 10, 12, 31:1, 2, 7, 17^{3}, 18, 21, 24, 32:6, 9^{2}, 10, 11, 33:22, 34:1, 2, 18, 21, 22, 35:4^{2}, 5, 6, 9, 22, 26^{2}, 27^{2}, 36:2^{2}, 3, 8, 12, 37:1, 2, 3, 9, 10^{2}, 14, 15, 17, 18, 19^{2}, 20, 22^{3}, 24, 28, 36, 38^{2}, 38:18, 21, 39:13, 40:5^{2}, 13, 14^{2}, 15, 16^{2}, 41:2, 4, 10, 13, 42:8, 45:12, 14^{2}, 15, 16, 17, 46:2^{2}, 3, 5, 10^{3}, 48:1, 11, 14, 49:3, 16, 50:3, 22, 51:4^{2}, 7^{2}, 13, 19, 53:6, 55:6, 20, 22, 56:1, 2, 11, 57:1^{3}, 5^{2}, 11^{2}, 58:3, 7, 59:5, 12, 13, 15, 60:4, 5, 62:2, 3^{2}, 6, 9, 63:5, 10, 11^{2}, 64:7, 10, 65:1

PSALMS
65:4, 66:8, 9, 20, 67:1, 2, 4, 68:1, 3, 13, 19, 23, 35, 69:6^{2}, 14, 23, 25, 28^{2}, 32, 70:2^{2}, 3, 4^{2}, 71:1, 3, 6, 8, 12, 13^{2}, 72:14, 15^{3}, 16, 17^{2}, 18, 19^{2}, 74:14, 75:10, 76:7, 8, 11^{2}, 77:2, 7, 9, 78:6, 8, 79:2, 5, 10, 80:3, 4, 7, 17, 19, 81:9, 83:1, 4, 17^{2}, 84:4, 10, 85:6, 86:3, 17, 87:5, 7, 88:11, 12, 89:2, 6^{2}, 7^{2}, 16, 17, 21, 24^{2}, 37, 52, 90:10, 14, 17, 91:4, 5, 15, 92:7, 9, 10, 13, 14, 93:1, 94:8, 13, 96:4^{2}, 10^{2}, 11, 12, 97:1, 7, 98:8, 99:1, 100:4, 101:6, 102:18^{2}, 26, 28, 104:5, 12, 34^{2}, 35^{2}, 106:8, 46, 48, 107:30, 108:5, 6, 109:7^{2}, 8, 9, 10, 12^{2}, 13^{2}

PSALMS
109:14^{2}, 15, 17, 19, 20, 28, 29, 110:3, 111:4, 5, 112:2^{2}, 3, 6^{2}, 7, 8, 9, 10, 113:2, 3, 9, 118:26, 119:6, 46, 58, 74, 76, 78, 80^{2}, 116, 117, 122, 128, 132, 120:3^{2}, 121:3, 122:7, 8, 124:6, 125:1^{2}, 4, 5, 127:5, 128:1^{2}, 3, 4, 129:5, 6, 8, 130:2, 4, 132:9, 135:21, 137:8^{2}, 138:6, 139:11, 140:10, 11, 141:2, 5^{3}, 143:2, 7, 144:1, 12^{2}, 13, 14^{3}, 145:3, 14, 148:4, 149:2, 5, 6

PROV.
1:9, 31, 33, 2:22^{2}, 3:7, 8, 10, 11, 15, 22, 24^{2}, 25, 26, 35, 4:10, 12, 26, 5:10^{2}, 16, 17, 18, 19, 20, 22, 6:1, 6, 15, 18, 27, 28, 29, 31, 33, 8:5, 6, 11^{2}, 33, 9:9, 11^{2}, 12^{2}, 10:9, 24, 27, 28

PROV.
10:29, 30, 31, 11:6, 9, 18, 21^{2}, 25^{2}, 26, 29, 31, 12:3^{2}, 8^{2}, 11, 14^{2}, 19, 21, 24, 13:4, 9, 11, 13^{2}, 18^{2}, 20^{2}, 21, 14:11, 14^{2}, 22, 16:3, 5, 7, 16, 19, 21, 31, 17:5, 11, 14, 18:19, 20^{2}, 19:2, 5, 9, 20, 23, 20:3, 11^{2}, 13, 17, 20, 21^{2}, 21:13, 15, 17^{2}, 18, 20, 22:1, 5, 9, 11, 13, 18, 19, 26, 23:2, 3, 4, 15, 17, 18, 19, 20, 25, 34, 24:1, 4, 8, 11, 14^{3}, 17, 19, 20^{2}, 25, 28, 25:5, 7^{2}, 16, 17, 21^{2}, 26:4, 5, 26, 27:11, 14, 18, 23, 28:2, 6, 9, 18, 20, 22, 25, 26, 29:1, 14, 19, 25, 30:6, 9^{2}, 10, 18, 24, 29, 31:6, 30

ECCL.
1:9^{2}, 10, 11, 13, 15^{2}, 2:16, 18, 19, 3:2, 10^{2}, 14^{2}, 15, 22, 4:11, 13, 5:1, 2^{3}, 6, 8, 10, 6:8^{2}, 4, 11, 12, 7:9^{2}, 14, 16, 17^{2}, 23, 26, 8:1, 3, 7^{2}, 12^{2}, 13, 14, 15, 17, 9:8, 10:9^{2}, 10, 14^{2}, 11:2, 3^{2}, 6, 8, 12:2, 3, 4^{2}, 5^{3}, 6^{3}, 12, 14^{2}

CANT.
1:4, 7, 2:17, 7:8, 8:1, 3, 7, 8, 9^{2}, 14

ISAIAH
1:5, 18^{4}, 19, 20, 26, 27, 28^{2}, 29^{2}, 30, 31, 2:2^{2}, 6, 11^{3}, 12^{2}, 17^{3}, 22, 3:4, 5, 6, 7, 10, 11^{2}, 24, 4:1, 2^{2}, 3, 5, 6, 5:5^{2}, 6, 8^{2}, 9, 15^{3}, 16^{2}, 24, 27^{3}, 28, 29, 6:10, 11^{2}, 12, 13^{3}, • 7:4, 8^{2}, 9, 16, 23^{2}, 25^{2}, 8:4, 9^{3}

ISAIAH
8:12, 13^{2}, 14, 15^{3}, 20, 21, 22, 9:1, 5, 6^{2}, 7, 19, 20, 21, 10:2, 17, 18, 19, 22, 24, 27^{2}, 30, 33^{2}, 11:5, 9, 10^{2}, 11, 13, 16^{2}, 12:2, 13:6, 7, 8^{3}, 10, 14, 15, 16^{2}, 19, 20^{2}, 21, 22, 14:1, 14, 15, 20^{2}, 29, 30, 15:2, 4^{2}, 6, 9, 16:2^{2}, 4, 5, 6, 10^{2}, 14, 17:1, 2, 3, 4, 5^{2}, 6, 9^{2}, 11, 13, 18:6, 7, 19:1, 5, 6, 7^{2}, 9, 10, 15, 16^{2}, 17^{2}, 18, 19, 20, 21, 22, 23, 24, 25, 20:5, 6, 21:17, 22:14, 18, 21, 23, 25^{3}, 23:2, 4, 5, 15, 16, 18, 24:2, 3, 9, 13^{2}, 16, 18, 20^{3}, 22^{3}, 23, 25:2^{2}, 5, 9^{2}, 10, 26:6, 10, 20, 27:9, 10

ISAIAH
27:11, 12, 13, 28:3, 4, 5, 10, 13, 18^{2}, 19, 21, 22^{2}, 28, 29:2^{2}, 4^{3}, 5^{2}, 6, 7, 8^{2}, 14, 16, 17^{2}, 22, 30:3, 5, 8, 13, 14, 15^{2}, 16, 17, 18^{2}, 19, 20, 23, 25, 26^{2}, 28, 30, 31, 32, 31:4, 8, 9, 32:2, 3, 4, 5^{3}, 11, 14^{3}, 15^{3}, 17, 19, 33:1, 2^{2}, 4, 6, 10, 12^{2}, 16^{3}, 20^{3}, 21, 24, 34:3^{2}, 4^{2}, 5, 7, 9, 10, 12^{2}, 13, 15, 35:1, 2, 4, 5^{2}, 7, 8^{3}, 9^{2}, 36:8, 14, 15, 37:4, 6, 10, 11, 26, 27, 30, 38:7, 39:6^{2}, 7, 8, 40:4^{3}, 5, 9, 20, 24^{2}, 25, 30, 31, 41:6, 7, 10, 11^{2}, 12, 22, 23, 42:2, 4, 17^{2}, 43:2^{2}, 9^{3}, 10, 26, 44:8, 9

ISAIAH
44:11^{3}, 15, 21, 26^{2}, 27, 28^{2}, 45:1, 14, 16, 17^{2}, 18, 22, 24, 25, 46:5, 13, 47:1, 3^{2}, 5, 7, 11, 12^{2}, 14^{2}, 15, 48:11, 14, 49:3, 5^{4}, 6^{2}, 9, 11, 13, 19^{2}, 22, 23^{3}, 24, 25^{2}, 26, 50:7^{2}, 51:3, 6^{2}, 7, 8, 11, 12^{2}, 14, 19, 52:3, 11, 12, 13^{2}, 53:11, 54:3, 4^{3}, 5, 9, 10^{2}, 13^{2}, 14^{2}, 55:6^{2}, 12^{2}, 13, 56:1, 5, 7^{2}, 57:16, 58:4, 8, 10, 11, 12^{2}, 60:2, 4, 5^{2}, 7, 11^{3}, 12, 18, 19^{2}, 20^{2}, 21^{2}, 61:3^{2}, 5, 6, 7, 9, 10, 62:2, 3, 4^{4}, 8, 10, 12, 16, 63:3, 64:5, 9, 65:10, 13^{3}, 17, 18, 19, 20^{2}, 25, 66:5, 8^{2}, 10, 12^{2}, 13, 14, 16, 17, 24^{2}

JER.
1:8, 17

JER.
2:10, 12^{3}, 36, 3:1, 3, 16^{2}, 17, 4:7, 9, 11, 13, 14, 27, 28, 29, 5:1, 6, 9, 13, 29, 6:6, 8, 11, 12, 15, 22, 7:20^{2}, 23^{3}, 32^{2}, 33, 34, 8:2^{3}, 3, 12, 13, 14, 17, 9:2, 9, 10:2, 5^{2}, 10, 21, 11:3, 4, 5, 11, 19, 23, 12:13, 16, 13:10, 11, 12^{2}, 15, 19^{3}, 21, 27^{2}, 14:8, 9, 15^{2}, 16, 15:1, 4, 11, 18^{2}, 19, 16:4^{5}, 6, 14, 17:5, 6, 8^{3}, 11, 13^{2}, 14^{2}, 17, 18^{4}, 27, 18:14, 16, 20, 21^{4}, 22, 23, 19:6, 7, 8, 11^{2}, 13, 20:6, 10, 11^{2}, 14^{2}, 15, 16, 17, 18, 21:2, 9, 10, 22:19, 22, 23, 23:1, 3, 4^{2}, 6^{2}, 12^{2}, 26, 36, 40, 24:2, 3, 7^{2}, 8, 9^{2}

JER.
25:10, 11, 16^{2}, 27, 28, 29^{2}, 32, 33^{3}, 36, 26:3, 9^{2}, 18, 27:16, 17, 18^{2}, 22^{2}, 28:9, 29:4, 6, 7, 8^{2}, 10, 14^{2}, 17, 18^{2}, 22, 26, 30:7, 10^{3}, 13, 16^{2}, 18, 19^{2}, 20^{2}, 21, 22^{2}, 31:1, 4^{2}, 6, 12, 14, 15, 16, 18, 30, 33^{3}, 27, 38, 40^{2}, 32:4, 5, 15, 36, 38^{2}, 43, 33:9, 10^{2}, 12, 16^{2}, 20, 21, 22, 24, 25, 26, 34:3, 16, 17, 20, 35:7, 36:3, 7, 19, 30, 37:17, 20, 38:3, 4, 17, 18, 20, 22, 23^{2}, 39:16, 17, 18, 40:9, 15, 42:2, 5, 6^{3}, 11^{2}, 17, 18^{2}, 44:8^{2}, 12^{3}, 26, 27^{2}, 29, 46:10, 11, 19, 23, 24^{2}, 26, 27^{2}, 47:2, 6^{3}, 7, 48:2^{2}, 3, 4, 6, 7, 8, 9, 10^{2}

JER.
48:13, 26, 28, 30, 33, 34, 37^{2}, 38, 39, 41, 42, 43, 44, 46, 49:2^{4}, 5^{2}, 10, 13, 17^{2}, 22, 23, 26, 32, 33, 36, 37, 50:5, 8, 9^{2}, 10^{2}, 12^{3}, 13^{3}, 19, 20^{3}, 26, 30, 33, 36, 37, 38, 39^{2}, 41, 51:2, 6, 8^{2}, 26, 29, 35, 46, 47, 58^{3}, 62, 63, 64

LAM.
1:12, 17, 21, 2:6, 20, 3:6, 29^{2}, 4:9^{2}, 21^{2}, 5:6, 21

EZEKIEL
2:6^{6}, 8, 3:9^{2}, 12, 20, 23, 26^{2}, 4:3^{2}, 7, 10, 17, 5:12, 13^{2}, 15, 16, 6:4^{2}, 6^{6}, 8, 9, 13, 7:4, 11, 16, 17^{2}, 18, 19^{2}, 24, 25, 26, 27^{2}, 9:4, 11:3, 11^{2}, 16, 20^{2}, 12:3^{2}, 11, 13, 19, 20^{2}, 24, 25, 28^{2}, 13:9^{3}, 11, 12, 13, 14^{2}

EZEKIEL
13:20, 21^{2}, 14:3, 9, 10, 11^{3}, 15, 16^{2}, 18, 22^{3}, 15:3, 5, 16:16, 20, 25, 28, 42^{2}, 52, 54, 61, 63, 17:8, 14, 15, 20, 21, 23, 18:5, 13, 20^{2}, 22, 24, 30, 19:9, 14^{2}, 20:3, 9, 12, 14, 20, 22, 31, 32^{2}, 41, 47^{2}, 48, 21:7^{4}, 11^{2}, 12^{3}, 13, 14, 15, 23^{2}, 24^{2}, 26, 27, 32^{3}, 22:5^{2}, 14, 21, 22, 25, 29, 32, 33, 46, 48, 24:8, 10, 11^{3}, 12, 13, 23, 25, 27^{3}, 25:10, 26:1, 5, 6, 13, 14^{2}, 16, 17, 18, 20, 21^{3}, 27:7, 30, 34, 35^{2}, 36^{2}, 28:9, 19^{3}, 22^{2}, 23, 24, 25, 29:5, 7, 9, 11, 12, 14, 15, 16, 19, 30:3, 4^{2}, 7^{2}, 8, 11, 13, 16, 18, 21^{2}, 31:13, 16

EZEKIEL
31:17, 18^{2}, 32:6, 10, 12, 15, 19, 25, 27, 28, 30^{2}, 31, 32, 33:4, 5, 6, 10, 12, 13, 27^{2}, 28, 34:2, 10, 14, 16, 22, 23, 24, 26, 27, 28, 29, 35:4, 10, 15, 36:3, 9, 10^{2}, 12, 23, 25, 28^{2}, 32^{2}, 33, 34, 37, 38, 37:19, 20, 21, 22^{3}, 23^{2}, 24, 25, 26, 27^{3}, 28, 38:7^{2}, 8, 9, 16^{2}, 19, 20, 21, 23, 39:4, 12, 13^{2}, 16, 19^{2}, 20, 25, 28, 42:13, 43:10, 11, 12, 13^{3}, 14^{2}, 15^{2}, 16, 17^{3}, 19, 27, 44:2^{3}, 7, 11, 14, 17, 28, 29, 30, 31, 45:1^{3}, 2, 3, 4^{2}, 6, 7^{2}, 8, 11^{2}, 12^{2}, 17, 21, 46:1^{3}, 2, 4, 5^{2}, 6^{2}, 11, 16^{2}, 17^{2}, 18, 47:5, 8, 9^{2}, 10^{2}

EZEKIEL
47:11^{2}, 12^{2}, 13, 15, 17, 20, 22, 48:8^{2}, 9, 10^{2}, 11, 12, 13, 15^{2}, 16, 17, 18^{3}, 20, 21^{3}, 22, 28, 31, 35

DANIEL
1:13, 2:5^{2}, 9, 13^{2}, 20, 28, 40, 41^{2}, 42, 44^{2}, 3:6, 11, 15^{2}, 17, 18, 19, 28, 29^{2}, 4:1, 15^{2}, 16^{2}, 19, 23^{2}, 25, 26, 27^{2}, 32, 5:7^{2}, 10, 12, 16^{2}, 17, 29, 6:1, 7, 8, 12, 15, 17, 25, 26^{2}, 7:14, 23^{2}, 24, 25, 27, 8:13^{2}, 14, 17, 19^{2}, 24, 25, 26, 9:16, 25^{2}, 26^{2}, 27, 10:19^{2}, 11:2, 4^{3}, 5^{3}, 6, 10^{2}, 11^{2}, 12^{2}, 15, 16, 17, 19, 20, 22^{2}, 25, 27^{2}, 28, 29, 30, 32, 34, 36^{2}, 41, 43, 12:1^{3}, 3, 4, 6, 7^{2}, 8, 10, 11^{2}, 13

HOSEA 1:9, 10[3], 11[2], 2:4, 16, 17, 3:3[2], 4:3, 6, 9, 19, 5:9[2], 12, 14, 7:4[2], 16, 8:4, 5, 6, 7, 8, 11, 9:4[3], 6, 12, 17, 10:2, 6[2], 8, 10, 14, 15, 11:5, 13:3, 7, 10, 14[2], 15[2], 16[2], 14:5, 6, 7
JOEL 1:11, 2:2, 6, 8, 10, 18, 19, 21, 22, 23, 24, 26[2], 27, 31, 32[2], 3:12, 15, 16, 17, 19[2]
AMOS 3:4, 6[3], 11[2], 12, 14, 5:6, 14, 15[2], 16, 17, 20, 6:2, 7, 7:3, 6, 9[2], 11, 17[2], 8:3[2], 5, 7, 8, 9:1, 2, 5, 15
OBADIAH 1:9, 10, 15, 16

OBADIAH 1:17[2], 18[2], 21
JONAH 1:4, 6, 11, 12, 3:4, 7, 8, 4:4, 6, 9[2]
MICAH 1:2, 4[2], 7[2], 14, 2:4, 11, 3:6[3], 7, 12, 4:1[2], 10[2], 11, 5:2, 4, 5, 7, 8, 9[2], 6:7, 14[2], 7:4, 8, 10, 11[2], 13, 16[2], 17
NAHUM 1:10[2], 12[2], 14, 2:3[2], 5, 6[2], 7[2], 13, 3:11[2], 12[2], 13
HABAK. 1:5, 10, 2:5, 7, 9, 14, 16[3], 3:17[3]
ZEPH. 1:10, 17, 18[2], 2:3[2], 4[2], 5, 6, 7, 9, 11, 12, 14, 3:7, 8, 11[2], 13, 14, 16[2]
HAGGAI 1:2, 8, 2:4[3], 9, 12, 13[2]
ZECH. 1:4

ZECH. 1:9, 16[2], 17, 19, 2:4, 5[2], 9, 11[2], 13, 3:9, 4:5, 12, 13, 5:3[2], 11, 6:13[2], 14, 8:3, 5, 6[2], 8[2], 9[2], 11, 12, 13[2], 19, 9:1[2], 2, 4, 5[3], 7[2], 10[2], 14, 15, 16, 10:5[2], 6, 7[2], 10, 11, 11:5, 9[2], 16, 17[3], 12:2, 3[2], 5, 6, 8[2], 10, 11, 13:1, 2, 4, 7, 8[2], 14:1, 2[2], 4, 6, 7[3], 8[2], 9[2], 10[2], 11[2], 12, 13, 14, 15[2], 17[2], 18, 19, 20[2], 21[2]
MALACHI 1:5, 6[2], 8, 9, 11[3], 14, 2:4, 3:4, 5, 10[2], 12, 17, 4:1, 3
MATT. 1:22, 23, 2:4, 13, 15, 18

MATT. 2:23[2], 3:15, 4:1, 3[2], 6, 14, 5:4, 6, 9, 12, 13[3], 14, 18, 19[2], 21, 22[3], 24, 25, 29, 30, 37, 45, 48, 6:1, 4, 5[2], 7, 8, 9, 10, 16, 21, 22[2], 23[3], 31, 33, 7:1, 2[2], 7[2], 8, 13, 14, 26, 8:3, 8, 12[2], 13, 17, 9:2[2], 5, 12, 15, 21, 22, 29, 10:13[2], 14, 16, 18, 19, 21, 22[2], 23, 25, 26[2], 36, 11:6, 22, 23, 24, 12:11, 17, 27, 31[2], 32[2], 37[2], 39, 40, 45, 13:12[2], 15, 35, 40, 42, 49, 50, 14:9, 27[2], 28, 15:5, 6, 13, 14, 28, 31, 16:2, 3, 4

MATT. 16:19[2], 21[2], 22[2], 23[2], 28, 17:4, 7, 9, 17, 20, 22, 23, 18:3, 7, 8, 9, 12, 13, 16, 17, 18[2], 19, 25[2], 19:5, 9, 10, 12, 21, 25, 30[2], 20:16[2], 18, 22, 23[2], 26[3], 27[2], 28, 33, 21:4, 13, 21[3], 43, 44, 22:13, 28, 23:4, 5, 7, 8, 10, 11, 12[2], 26, 31, 24:2[2], 3[2], 6, 7, 9[2], 10, 13, 14, 16, 20, 21[2], 22[3], 27, 28, 29[2], 34, 37, 39, 40[2], 41[2], 43, 44, 51, 25:1, 9, 29[2], 30, 32, 26:2, 5, 13[2], 31[2], 33[2], 37, 39, 42, 46, 54[2], 56, 63[2], 27:22, 23, 25, 26

MATT. 27:35, 40, 42, 49, 58, 64[2], 28:10
MARK 1:41, 2:5, 9, 20, 22[2], 3:14, 24, 25, 26, 28, 4:12[2], 21[2], 22, 24[2], 25[2], 31, 39, 5:18, 23, 28, 34, 36, 43, 6:9, 11, 27, 50, 7:4, 11[2], 24, 27, 34, 8:12, 31[2], 33[2], 38[2], 9:1, 5, 12, 19, 34, 35[2], 43, 45[2], 47, 49, 10:8, 12, 26, 31, 33, 38, 39, 40, 41, 43[3], 44[2], 45, 49[2], 11:2, 10, 17, 22[2], 12:7, 23, 13:2[2], 4[3], 7[3], 8[2], 9[2], 10, 11, 12, 13[2], 14, 18, 19[2], 20, 24, 25, 30, 14:2, 9[2], 19, 27[2], 29, 33[2], 49, 64

MARK 15:15, 16:6, 16[2]
LUKE 1:15[2], 20[3], 29, 32[2], 33, 34, 35[2], 37, 38, 45, 57, 60, 66, 68, 71, 76, 2:1, 3, 5, 6, 10, 12, 23, 34, 35, 49, 3:5[4], 7, 12, 14, 23, 4:7, 9, 5:13, 15, 23, 35, 37, 38, 6:17, 20, 21, 35[2], 36, 37[3], 38[2], 40, 7:23, 8:9, 12, 17[2], 18[2], 38, 43, 48, 50, 9:22[3], 25, 26[2], 27, 33, 41, 44, 46, 48, 51, 10:5, 6, 11, 12, 14, 15, 42, 11:2[2], 9[2], 10, 18, 19, 29, 30, 35, 36[2], 46, 50, 51, 12:2[2], 3[2], 4, 9, 10[2], 19, 20[2], 26

LUKE 12:29, 31, 34, 35, 39, 40, 45, 47, 48[2], 49, 50[2], 52, 53, 55, 58, 13:14, 16, 23, 24, 28, 30[2], 32, 33, 14:8, 11[2], 12, 14[2], 23, 26, 27, 31, 33[2], 34, 15:7, 14, 19, 21, 23, 24, 32, 16:2, 21, 31, 17:6[2], 24, 25, 26, 30, 31, 34[3], 35[2], 36[2], 37, 18:13, 14[2], 26, 31, 32[2], 40, 19:7, 15, 19, 26[2], 38, 20:6, 13, 14, 18, 25[2], 35, 21:6[2], 7[2], 8, 9, 11[2], 15, 16[2], 17, 22[2], 23, 24[3], 25, 26, 32, 34, 36, 22:7, 16, 24, 26[2], 37, 42[2], 52, 23:23, 24, 31, 32, 35

LUKE 13:37, 39, 43, 24:7[2], 20, 36, 44, 47, 49
JOHN 1:25, 31, 42, 3:2, 3, 4[2], 5, 7, 9, 14, 17, 20, 21, 27, 4:14, 5:6, 34, 6:12, 20, 45, 7:4, 17, 23, 8:5, 33[2], 36, 41, 55, 9:3, 22, 25, 27, 31, 39, 10:9, 16, 24, 35, 11:4, 12:23, 26, 31, 32, 34, 36, 38, 40, 42, 13:18, 24, 22, 14:1, 3, 13, 17, 21, 27[2], 15:7, 8, 11, 25, 16:1, 20[2], 24, 32, 33, 17:11, 12, 19, 21[2], 22, 23, 24, 26, 18:9, 28, 32, 36, 19:16, 24[2], 28, 31[2], 36[2], 20:15, 19, 21, 26

JOHN 20:27, 21:18, 25[2]
ACTS 1:5, 8, 20, 22[2], 2:14, 20, 21, 24, 25, 38, 47, 3:14, 19[2], 23, 25, 4:9, 10, 12, 19, 28, 30, 5:31, 36, 38, 39[2], 7:7, 35, 8:20, 22, 36, 9:6, 17, 10:42, 47, 48, 11:14, 16, 28, 12:19, 13:11, 22, 28, 38, 39, 42, 47[2], 14:3, 9, 15:1[2], 11, 24, 16:13, 15, 30, 31, 17:18, 27, 18:6, 9, 15[2], 19:2, 26, 27[3], 36[2], 39, 40, 20:16, 21:13, 14[2], 24, 26, 33, 34, 37, 22:5, 10, 15, 16, 24[2], 23:3, 11, 29, 35, 24:4, 15, 21, 25:4, 5, 6, 9, 10, 11[2], 17

ACTS 25:19, 20, 21[2], 26:3, 8, 23, 28, 27:10, 20, 22[2], 24, 25[2], 26, 31, 28:27, 28
ROMANS 1:1, 4, 7[2], 11, 12, 19, 22, 2:12, 13, 25, 26, 3:4[2], 8, 19, 20, 25, 26, 4:11[3], 13, 14, 16[2], 17, 18, 24, 5:9, 10, 15, 19, 6:5, 6, 8, 11, 17, 7:2, 3[4], 4, 10, 8:4, 6[2], 7, 9, 10, 17[2], 18[2], 21, 26, 29[2], 31[2], 39, 9:7, 17, 26, 27[2], 33, 10:1, 9, 11, 13, 15, 11:6, 9, 10, 13, 15[2], 16[2], 17, 19, 20, 22, 23, 24[2], 25[3], 26, 35, 36, 12:2[2], 9, 10, 16[2], 18

ROMANS 12:21, 13:1[2], 3, 4, 5, 9, 14:4, 5, 9, 14, 15, 16, 15:5, 12, 16[2], 24[2], 31[2], 32, 33, 16:11, 20, 24, 27
1 COR. 1:1, 2, 8, 8, 10[2], 17, 3:13[2], 15[2], 18[2], 4:2, 3, 6, 16, 17, 5:2, 5, 7, 11, 6:2, 5, 7, 9, 12, 16, 7:5, 11, 12, 13, 18, 21, 23, 25, 26, 27, 29, 34, 39[2], 8:5[2], 10, 9:2, 10, 12, 15, 19, 23, 27, 10:1, 7, 13[2], 21, 27, 30, 33, 11:1, 5, 6, 16, 18, 19[2], 27, 31, 32, 12:13[2], 22, 23, 25, 26, 13:3, 8[3], 10, 14:7, 9[2], 10

1 COR. 14:11[2], 20[3], 23, 26, 27, 28, 30, 31, 34, 37, 38[2], 40, 15:9, 12, 13, 14, 15, 17, 22, 26, 28[3], 33, 37, 51, 52[2], 54, 57, 58, 16:2, 4, 6, 10, 13, 14, 22, 23, 24
2 COR. 1:2, 3, 4, 6[2], 7, 11, 16, 17, 2:4, 7, 9, 14, 3:3, 7, 8, 9, 16, 4:3, 7, 10, 11, 5:2, 3[2], 4[2], 8[2], 9, 10, 13[2], 17, 20, 21, 6:3, 13, 14, 16[2], 17, 18[2], 7:10, 11, 8:9, 10, 11, 12, 13, 14[2], 16, 23, 9:3[2], 4, 5, 15, 10:2[2], 8, 11, 15, 11:3, 6, 7

2 COR. 11:12, 15[2], 12:6, 7[2], 11, 13, 14, 15[2], 16[2], 20[2], 13:1, 5[2], 7, 11[4], 14
GAL. 1:3, 5, 7, 8, 9, 10, 2:3, 6[2], 9, 11, 16[2], 17, 3:4, 8, 9, 15[2], 18, 22, 23, 24, 29, 4:1, 9, 12, 18, 19, 20, 21, 30, 5:1, 2, 10[2], 15, 18, 26, 6:1[2], 3, 7, 9, 12, 16, 18
EPHES. 1:2, 3, 4, 12, 23, 3:6, 10, 16, 18, 19, 21, 4:14, 21, 23, 26, 31, 32, 5:1, 3, 7, 17, 18[2], 24, 27, 31[2], 6:3, 5, 8, 10, 11, 13, 16, 19, 23, 24

PHIL. 1:2, 10, 20[3], 23, 26, 27, 30, 2:1, 2, 3, 5, 6, 15, 17, 19, 28, 3:9, 15[3], 17, 21, 4:2, 5, 6[2], 8[2], 9, 11, 12[3], 20, 23
COLOS. 1:2, 9, 12, 16, 20, 23, 2:2, 5, 20, 3:1, 15, 19, 21, 4:6, 16, 18
1 THESS. 1:1, 2:4, 9, 16, 3:1, 3, 5, 4:11, 13, 17, 5:6, 7, 8, 13, 14, 23, 27, 28
2 THESS. 1:5, 7, 9, 10[2], 12, 2:2[2], 3, 6, 7, 8, 10, 12, 14, 15, 3:1, 2, 8, 13, 14, 16, 18
1 TIM. 1:7, 10, 17, 2:1, 4, 6

1 TIM. 2:12, 15, 3:2, 8, 10, 11, 12, 4:3, 4[2], 6, 12, 5:7, 9, 13, 16, 17, 22, 25, 6:1, 8, 9, 16, 17, 18, 21
2 TIM. 1:4, 8, 15, 2:1, 2, 4, 6, 11, 15, 21, 24, 3:2, 9, 17, 4:2, 4, 6, 15, 16, 17, 18, 22
TITUS 1:6, 7, 9, 11, 13, 2:2, 3, 4, 5[2], 6, 8[2], 9, 3:1, 2, 7, 8, 12, 13, 14, 15
PHILE. 1:8, 14, 22
HEB. 1:5[2], 12, 14, 25, 2:3, 17[2], 3:5, 12, 13, 4:15, 5:5, 11, 12[2], 6:8, 12, 7:11, 8:4, 10[2], 12, 9:6

HEB. 9:23, 10:2, 13, 29, 11:16, 18, 24, 40, 12:3, 8, 9, 10, 11, 13[2], 15, 16, 18, 19, 20, 27, 28, 13:2, 5, 9[2], 19, 21, 25
JAMES 1:4, 5, 13, 18, 19, 22, 23, 25, 26, 2:12, 15, 16, 3:1, 4, 10, 17, 4:4, 9[2], 14, 5:3, 7, 8, 9, 12, 15, 16
1 PETER 1:2, 3, 5, 6, 7[2], 13[2], 15, 16, 21, 2:3, 6, 7, 13, 18, 20, 3:1[2], 3, 4, 7, 8[2], 13, 14, 15, 16, 17, 4:6, 7, 11[2], 13[2], 14, 16, 17, 18, 5:1, 5, 8, 11, 14
2 PETER 1:2

2 PETER 1:4, 8[2], 11, 12[2], 15, 2:1, 2, 4, 9, 12, 3:2, 8, 11[2], 12, 14[2], 16, 18
1 JOHN 1:4, 2:19, 28, 3:1, 2[2], 4:10, 14
2 JOHN 1:2, 3, 12
3 JOHN 1:2, 8, 14
JUDE 1:2, 18, 19, 25
REV. 1:4, 6, 19, 2:10[2], 11, 19, 27, 3:2, 5, 18[2], 19, 4:1, 5:18, 6:11[2], 17, 7:12, 9:5, 10:6, 7, 9, 11:5, 9, 18, 12:2, 4, 15, 13:15, 14:10, 16:5, 12, 17:17, 18:4, 9, 21[2], 22[4], 23, 19:7, 8, 20:8[2], 6, 7, 10, 21:3[2], 4[2], 7[2], 25[2], 22:3[2], 4, 5, 6, 11[4], 12, 21

but

285

GEN. 2:6, 17, 20, 3:3, 4:2, 5, 6:8, 18, 8:9, 9:4, 11:30, 12:12, 13:13, 15:4

GEN. 15:10, 16, 16:6, 17:5, 15, 21, 18:15, 22, 27, 32, 19:2, 4, 10

GEN. 19:14, 26, 20:3[2], 4, 12, 21:23, 26, 22:7, 23:6, 13, 24:4, 33, 38, 25:6

GEN. 25:28, 26:29, 27:22, 38, 28:17, 19, 29:17, 20, 31, 30:42, 31:5, 7, 29, 36

GEN. 31:34, 35, 47, 32:28, 34:12, 15, 17, 35:8, 10, 16, 18, 37:11, 22, 35

GEN. 38:20, 39:8, 9, 21, 40:14, 22, 23, 41:8, 21, 24, 54, 42:4, 7, 8

GEN. 42:10, 12, 20, 34, 43:5, 34, 44:17, 45:8, 22, 46:12, 47:18, 30, 48:7, 19

GEN. 48:21, 49:19, 24, 50:20[2]
EXOD. 1:12, 16, 17[2], 2:15, 17, 3:22, 4:1, 10

EXOD. 4:21, 5:16, 17, 6:3, 9, 7:4, 12, 8:15, 18, 29, 9:6, 30, 32, 10:8

EXOD. 10:20, 23, 27, 11:7, 12:9, 44, 13:15, 18, 14:9, 16, 20, 29, 15:19, 16:8

EXOD. 16:20, 26, 17:12, 18:22, 19:13, 24, 20:10, 19, 21:13, 14, 18, 28, 29[2]

EXOD. 22:15, 23:11, 22, 24, 24:2, 29:14, 33, 31:15, 18, 33:11, 23, 34:13, 20, 21

EXOD. 34:34, 35:2, 36:38, 40:37
LEVIT. 1:9, 13, 17, 2:12, 5:8, 11, 6:28, 7:16

LEVIT. 7:17, 20, 24, 31, 8:17, 10:6, 11:4, 5, 6, 11, 23, 36, 38, 12:5

LEVIT. 13:6, 7, 14, 21[2], 26[2], 28, 33, 35, 37, 14:9, 53, 15:28, 16:10

LEVIT. 17:16, 19:14, 15, 18, 24, 34, 20:24, 21:2, 4, 14, 22:11, 13[2], 20, 23

LEVIT. 22:32, 23:3, 8, 25, 25:4, 17, 28, 31, 25:34, 36, 40, 43, 46, 52

LEVIT. 26:14, 15, 23, 27, 45, 27:8, 13, 18, 21, 29
NUM. 1:47, 50

NUM. 1:53 2:33 3:38 4:15 19 20 5:8 20 28 6:12 7:9 8:26 9:13 22 10:4 7[2] 30 11:6 20 26[2] 12:14 13:31 14:10 21 24 31 32 38 41 44 15:30 16:9 30 41 18:2 17 23 24 19:12 20 21:22 23 22:20 24 35 23:13 26 24:1 4 11 13 16 17[2] 20 26:33 64 27:3 28:19 27 29:8 36 30:5 8 9 12 14 15 31:18 32:17 23 27 30 33:55 35:8 20 22 26 28 30 31 33 36:9

DEU. 1:11 12 17 21 26 28 30 38 40 43 45 3:7 19 26 4:4 9 12 20 22[2] 26 29 5:3 14 31 7:5 8 15 18 23 26 8:3 18 9:4 9:5 19 10:12 11:7 11 28 12:5 10 14 18 13:9 14:7 12 20 15:3 6[2] 8 16:6 17:6 16 18:14 20 22 19:11 13 21 20:12 14 16 17 21:14 17 23 22:7 20 25 26 28 29 23:5 11 20 22 24 25 24:5 18 25:15 26:14 27:15 28:38 39 40 41 65 29:15 20 29 30:14 17[2] 32:15 52 34:4 6

JOSH. 1:8 14 2:4 6 22 5:5 12 14 6:13 19 22 7:1 3[2] 12 8:4 9 14 9:12 19 21 10:16 19 30 37 40 11:13 14 20 13:13 33 14:3 8 15:63 16:10 17:3[2] 8 12 13 14 18 18:7 21:12 22:3 5 7 18 19 27 28 23:8 9 23:13 24:4 10 12 15 21

JUD. 1:6 19 21 25 27 29 30 32 33 35 2:2 3 17[2] 3:15 16 19 4:8 16 5:31 6:10 13 34 39[2] 7:6 10 19 8:20 9:9 11 20 51 11:16 17[2] 18 20[2] 27 13:3 6 7 9 21 23 14:4 6 9 13 16 20 15:1[2] 13[2] 19 16:21 17:6 19:10[2] 16 18 24 25 28 20:9 13 14 32 34 40 42 47

RUTH 1:14 17 2:8 3:3 13 4:4

1 SAM. 1:2 5[2] 11 13 15 22 2:15 16 18 25 30 4:20 5:6 6:3 9 7:10 8:3 6 7 19 9:4[2] 7 27 10:12 16 19 27[2] 12:10 12 15[2] 20 23 12:25 13:8 14 16 20 22 14:1 10 26 27 37 39 41 43 15:3 9[2] 19 21 16:7[2] 14 17:9 15 33 42 45 50 54 18:8[2] 16 17 19 25[2] 19:2 10 20:2 3[2] 5 7 13 15 22 39 21:4 6 22:17 23 23:14 24 27 24:7 10 12 13 22 25:3 14 15 19 25 29 31 37 44 26:3 7 11 19 23 28:23[2] 29:2 8 30:2 6 10 24 31:4

2 SAM. 2:8 10 30 31 3:1 13 22 26 4:12 5:17 23 6:10 7:2 6 15 19 8:4 9:10 10:11 11:1 9 13 27 12:3 4 12 17 19 21 23 13:3 14 16 20 21 25 27 34 37 14:2 6 25 29 15:3 10 20 26 34 16:18 17:16 18 18:3[2] 20 22 23 29 19:4 21 27 28 37 20:2 3 5 10 21 21:2 7 8 17 22:19 28 42[2] 23:6 7 12 16 21 23 24:3 17 24

1 KINGS 1:1 4 8 10 19 26 52 2:7 8 9 26 30 33 3:7 11 21 22[2] 23 26[2] 5:4 7:1 31 8:16 19 27 41 9:6[2] 22 24 11:1 10 12 13 22 32 34 35 39 12:8 10 11 14 17 20 22 13:13 18 22 14:4 9 14 15:14 16:22 25 17:1 12 13 18:12 18 21 22 25 26 19:4 11[2] 12 20:9 16 23 27 28 30 21:5 15 25 29 22:8[2] 16 18 24 30 31 48 49

2 KINGS 1:3 4 6 16 2:10 17 19 3:2 5 11 15 18 24 26 4:27 31 41 5:1 11 15 16[2] 17 20[2] 25 6:5 12 19 32[2] 7:2 4 10 19 8:13 9:15 18 27 35 10:4 9 18 19 23 31 33 11.2 15 12:3 6 7 9 14 13:6 7 11 19 22 14:6[2] 11 19 27 15:25 16:3 5 17:2 14 18 19 36 39 40 18:6 12 20[2] 22 27 36 19:18 27 20:10 21:9 22:18 23:9 23 35 25:12 25

1 CHRON. 2:30 34 4:27 5:1 2 6:49 56 7:14 10:4 11:18[2] 25 12:17 19 13:13 15:2 16:5 16:19 26 17:1 5 14 18:4 19:3 12 18 20:1 7 21:3 6 8 13 17 24 30 22:8 23:11 17 22 24:2 27:23 24 28:3 9 29:1 14

2 CHRON. 1:4 11 2:6 4:6 5:9 6:2 6 8 9 18 32 7:19 8:8 9[2] 10:8 10 11 14[2] 17 18 11:2 12:7 13:10 11 13 21 15:2 4 5 17 16:12 17:4 18:6 7[2] 15 17 29 31 19:6 20:10 12 15 21:3 13 20 22:10 11 23:6[2] 7 24:15 19 22 25 25:2 4[3] 7 8 9 13 20 27 26:16 18 28:1 9 10 20 21 23 27 29:34 30:8 10 18 32:8 9 25 33:2 10 22 23 25 35:13 21[2] 22 36:13 36:16

EZRA 2:59 62 3:6 12 4:3[2] 5:5 12 13 8:22 9:9 10:13

NEH. 1:9 2:2 14 19 20 3:3 4 5 15 4:1 7 5:15[2] 6:2 8 12 7:4 61 64 9:16 17[2] 28 29 33 11:3 21 13:2 6 24

ESTHER 1:12 16 17 2:15 3:2 15 4:4 11 14 5:9 12 6:12 13 7:4 9:10 15 16[2] 18 25

JOB 1:11 2:5 6 10 3:9 21 4:2 5 16 5:3 15 6:1 14 25 7:21 8:9 15[2] 9:2 11 15 18 35 11:5 20 12:2 3 7 13:4 15 14:10 12[2] 13 21 22 16:5 7 12 20 17:10 19:7[2] 28 20:5 13 21:1 22:8 18 20 23:6 8[2] 9 23:10 13 24:24 26:1 27:14[2] 17 19 28:12 30:1 31:32 32:8 16 35:10 12 15 36:6 7 12 13 17 37:21 38:11 40:5[2] 42:5

PSALMS 1:2 4 6 2:12 3:3 5:7 11 6:3 7:9 9:7 20 11:5 13:5 15:4 16:3 18:18 27 41[2] 20:7 8 22:2 6 9 19 24 26:11 28:3 30:5 31:6 11 14 32:11 34:10 19 35:13 15 20 37:9 11 17 20 21 28 36 38 39 38:13 19 40:17 41:10 44:3 7 9 49:15 50:16 21 52:7 8 55:13 21 23[2] 59:8 16 62:4 63:9 11[2] 64:7 66:19 68:3 6 21 69:13 20[2] 29 70:5 71:7 14 73:2 4 25 26 28 74:6 75:7 8 9 10 77:10 78:7 30 38 78:50 52 53 57 68 81:7 11 15 85:8 86:15 88:13 89:24 38 90:4 91:7 92:8 10 94:15 22 96:5 102:12 26 27 103:17 105:12 106:7 14 15 25 35 43 109:4 16 21 28[2] 115:1 3 5[2] 6[2] 7[2] 16 18 118:10 11 13 17 18 119:23 61 67 69 70 78 81 87 95 96 113 161 163 120:7 125:1 5 127:1 5 130:4 132:18 135:16[2] 17 136:15 138:6 139:4 12 141:8 142:4 145:20 146:9

PROV. 1:7 25 28[2] 33 2:22 3:1 32 33 34 35 4:18 5:4 6:31 32 8:36 9:12 18 10:1 2 3 4 5 6 7 8 9 10 11 12 13 14 17 19 21 23 24 25 27

PROV. 10:28 29 30 31 32 11:1 2 3 4 5 6 9 11 12 13 14 17 18 20 21 23 24 26 27 28 12:1 2 3 4 5 6 7 8 10 11 12 13 15 16 17 18 19[2] 20 21 22 23 24 25 26 27 13:1 2 3 4 5 6 8 9 10 11 12 13 15 16 17 18 19 20 21 23 24 25 14:1 2 3 4 5 6 8 9 11 12 15 16 18 20 21 22 23 24 25 28 29 30 31 32 33 34 35 15:1 2 4 5 6 7 8 9 13 14 15 18 19 20 21 22 25 26

PROV. 15:27 28 29 32 16:2 9 14 22 25 33 17:3 9 22 24 18:2 14 17 23 19:4 12 16 20:3 5 6 14 15 17 21 22 21:2 5 8 12 13 15 20 26 28 29 31 22:3 15 23:7 17 24:16 25 25:2 27:3 4 6 7 12 28:1 2 4 5 7 10 11 12 13 14 16 18 19 20 25 26 27 28 29:2 3 4 6 7 8 10 11 15 16 18 23 25 26 30:24 26 31:29 30

ECCL. 1:4 2:14 26 3:12 4:1 10 11 5:7 12 14 6:2 7:4 12 14 23 26 28[2] 29 8:13 9:5 11 18 10:2 10 12 19 11:8 9

CANT. 1:5 6 3:1 2 4[2] 5:2 6:6[3] 9

ISAIAH 1:3 6 20 21 5:6 7[2] 12 16 25 6:9[2] 13 7:1 12 13 25 8:14 9:5 10[2] 12 17 21 10:4 7 20 11:4 14 13:21 14:19 16:6 12 14 17:11 13 22:11 24:16 26:11 13 28:7 13 27 29:8[2] 9[2] 13 23 30:1[2] 5[2] 16 20 31:1 2 8 32:8 33:21 34:11 12 35:8 9 36:5[2] 7 12 21 37:19 28 38:17 40:8 31 41:8 42:19 20[2] 22 43:1 22[2] 24 45:17 46:2 47:9 48:1 10 49:14 25 51:6 8 15 21 23 53:5 54:7 8 10 15 55:10 11 57:3 13[2] 20 59:2 9[2] 11[2] 60:2 10 18 19 61:6 62:4 9 63:10 18 64:6 8 65:6 11 12 13[3] 14 18 20 66:2 4 5

JER. 1:7 19 2:7 11 25 27 28 34 3:1 7 8 10 19 22 5:3[2] 5 10 23 6:16 17 19 7:12 13[2] 23 24[2] 26 27[2] 28 32 8:6 7 15 9:3 8 14 24 10:5 8 10 19 24 11:8[2] 12 19 20 12:3 13[2] 17 13:11 14 17 14:12 13 15:19 20 16:4 15 17:6 8 18[2] 22 23[2] 24 27 18:12 23 19:6 20:3 9 11 12 21:9 14 22:5 10 12 17[2] 21 27 23:8 22 38 25:3 4 26:5 15 21 37 38 42 46 27:11 18 28:13 15 29:19 30:7 9 11 31:30 33 32:4 23 32:34 40 33:5 34:3 5 11 14 16 35:6 7 10 11 14[2] 15 16 17[3] 36:20 25 26[2] 31 37[2] 37:14 38:2 4 18 20 21 23 25 39:5 10 12 17 18 40:4 10 14 16 41:8 11 15 42:13 14 21 43:1 3 5 44:5 14 17 18 45:5 46:20 27 28[2] 48:30 45 49:10 12 19 39 50:13 44 51:9 26 62 52:8 16

LAM. 1:19 2:14 3:2 32 5:22

EZEKIEL 2:8 3:5 7 14 18 19 20 25 27 7:4 14 16 20 26 8:6 9:6 10 10:11 11:7 11 12 21 12:16 23 28 14:11 14 16 18 20 16:5 15 32 33 43 47 51 61 17:14 15 18:5 7 11 16 21 24 19:12 20:8 9 13 14 16 18 24 39 21:23 22:30 24:23 28:9 29:4 16 30:24 25 32:27 33:5 6[2] 8 9 11 13 17 19 24 31[2] 32 34:3 4 8 16 18[2] 28 36:8 21 22 37:8 23 38:8 28 39:2 41:6 42:6 14 44:8 13 14 15 22 25 46:1 2 9[2] 17[2] 18 47:11

DANIEL 1:4 8 2:6 9[2] 28 30[2] 41 43 44 49 3:15 18 4:7 8 18 5:8 15 20 23 6:4 13 7:18 26 28 8:3 4 7 17 18 22 24 25 27 9:7 18 26 10:1 7 13[2] 21[2] 11:6[2] 7 10 11 12 14 16 17 18 19 20 11:21 25 27 29 32 34 38 41 43 44 12:4 8 10[2] 13

HOSEA 1:6 7 2:7[2] 5:6 6:7 7:16 8:4 6 12 13 14 9:3 8 10 13 10:11 11:3 5 12 13:1 4 9 14:9

JOEL 2:20 3:16 20

AMOS 1:4 7 10 12 14 2:2 5 12 3:7 8 4:8 5:5 11[2] 24 26 6:6 14 7:13 14 8:11

OBADIAH 12 17

JONAH 1:3 4 5 13 2:9 3:8 4:1 7

MICAH 1:12 3:4 8 4:1 4 12 5:2 6:8 14[2] 15[3]

NAHUM 1:7 2:8[2] 3:17

HABAK. 2:1 4 5 20

ZEPH. 1:13[2] 18 3:5 7

HAGGAI 1:6[3] 2:16

ZECH. 1:4 6 15 1:21 4:6 7:11 14 8:11 13 9:7 11:6 16 13:5 8 14:7[2] 11

MALACHI 1:4[2] 12 14 2:8 9 3:2 7 8 4:2

MATT. 1:20 2:19 22 3:7 11 12 14 4:4[2] 5:13[2] 15 17 19 22[2] 28 32 33 34 37 39[2] 44 6:3 6 7 13 15 17 18 20 23 33 7:3 15 17 21 8:4 8 12 20 22 24 27 9:6 8 12[2] 13[2] 14 15 17 18 21 22 24 25 31 34 36 37 10:6 13 17 19 20 22 28 28[2] 30 33 34 11:8 9 16 19 22 24 27 12:2 3 4 6 7 15 24[2] 28 31 32 36 39[2] 48 13:8 11

MATT. 13:12, 16, 20, 21, 23, 25, 26, 29, 30, 32, 38, 48, 57, 14:6, 16, 17, 24, 27, 30, 15:3, 5, 8, 9, 11, 13, 18, 20, 23, 24[2], 26, 16:3, 4, 12, 15, 17, 28[2], 17:12[2], 21, 18:6, 7, 16, 17, 22, 25, 28, 30, 19:6, 8, 11, 14, 17[2], 22, 26[2], 30, 20:10, 12, 13, 16, 20, 22, 23[2], 25, 26[2], 28, 31, 21:13, 19, 21, 26, 28, 29, 32, 37, 38, 44, 46, 22:5, 7, 8, 14, 18, 30, 31, 32, 34

MATT. 23:3, 4, 5, 8, 11, 13, 16, 18, 25, 27, 28, 24:6, 13, 20, 22, 35, 36[2], 37, 43, 48, 25:4, 9[2], 12, 18, 29, 33, 46, 26:5, 8, 11, 24, 29, 32, 39, 41, 54, 56, 58, 60, 63, 70, 27:20, 23, 24, 28:17

MARK 1:8, 30, 44, 45[2], 2:6, 7, 10, 17[2], 18, 20, 22, 26, 3:4, 7, 26, 29[2], 4:6, 11, 15, 17, 22, 29, 32, 34, 5:6, 19, 26, 28, 33, 39, 40, 6:4[2], 9, 16, 19, 49, 56, 7:5

MARK 7:6, 11, 15, 19, 24, 27, 36, 8:27, 29, 33[2], 35, 9:13, 22, 27, 29, 32, 34, 37, 39, 50, 10:6, 8, 14, 18, 24, 27, 30, 31, 38, 40[2], 42, 43[2], 45, 48, 11:13, 17, 23, 26, 32, 12:7, 12, 14, 15, 25, 27, 32, 44, 13:7, 9, 11[3], 13, 14, 17, 20, 23, 24, 31, 32[2], 14:2, 7, 21, 28, 29, 31, 36, 38, 49, 56, 59, 61, 68, 71, 15:3, 5, 9, 11, 23, 16:7, 16

LUKE 1:13, 60, 2:19, 37

LUKE 2:44, 51, 3:16, 17, 19, 4:4, 25, 26, 30, 5:2, 14, 15, 21, 22, 24, 30, 31, 32, 33, 35, 38, 6:4, 8, 24, 27, 35, 40, 41, 49, 7:7, 25, 26, 28, 30, 35, 44, 45, 46, 47, 8:10, 15, 16, 23, 27, 35, 38, 42, 50, 52, 56, 9:9, 13[2], 19, 20, 24, 27, 32, 43, 45, 55, 56, 58, 59, 60, 61, 10:2, 10, 12, 14, 20, 22[2], 29, 33, 40, 42, 11:4, 15, 17, 20, 22, 28, 29, 33, 34, 39

LUKE 11:41, 42, 12:5, 7, 9, 10, 20, 31, 45, 48, 50, 51, 56, 13:3, 5, 27, 14:10, 13, 34, 35, 15:20, 22, 30, 16:15, 25[2], 30, 17:1[2], 7, 17, 25, 29, 18:4, 13, 15, 16, 39, 19:14, 27, 42, 46, 47, 20:6, 10, 14, 18, 21, 23, 35, 38, 21:4, 7, 9[2], 12, 18, 23, 33, 22:21, 22, 26[2], 27, 32, 36, 42, 48, 53, 56, 23:9, 21, 25, 28[2], 40, 41, 24:6, 16, 21, 24, 29, 37, 49

JOHN 1:8, 12, 13, 17

JOHN 1:20, 26, 31, 33, 2:9, 10, 21, 24, 3:8, 13, 15, 16, 17, 18, 21, 28, 29, 30, 36, 4:2, 14[2], 23, 32, 5:7, 17, 18, 19, 22, 24, 30, 34[2], 36, 42, 47, 6:9, 20, 22, 26, 27, 32, 36, 38, 39, 64, 7:6, 7, 10[2], 12, 16, 18, 22, 24, 26, 27, 28, 29, 30, 39, 41, 44, 49, 8:5, 6, 10, 12, 14, 16, 26, 28, 35, 37, 40, 42, 49, 55[2], 59, 9:3, 9, 18, 21, 28, 31, 41, 10:1, 2

JOHN 10:5, 6, 8, 10, 12, 18, 26, 33, 38, 39, 41, 11:4, 10, 11, 13, 20, 22, 30, 42, 46, 51, 52, 54, 12:2, 6, 8, 9, 10, 16, 24, 27, 30, 37, 42, 44, 47, 49, 13:7, 9, 10[2], 18, 36, 14:6, 10, 17, 19, 24, 26, 31, 15:15, 16, 19[2], 21, 22, 24, 25, 26, 16:4, 5, 6, 7, 12, 13, 20[2], 21, 22, 25[2], 33, 17:9, 11, 12, 15, 20, 25, 18:16, 23, 28, 36, 39, 40, 19:9, 12, 13, 15[2], 21

JOHN 19:24, 33, 34, 38, 20:7, 11, 17, 24, 25, 27, 31, 21:4[2], 8, 18, 23

ACTS 1:4, 5, 8, 2:14, 15, 16, 34, 3:6, 14, 18, 4:15, 17, 19, 20, 32, 5:1, 3, 4, 13, 19, 21, 22, 23, 39, 6:4, 7:9, 12, 17, 25, 27, 39, 47, 55, 8:9, 12, 20, 40, 9:7, 8, 15, 21, 22, 24, 26, 27, 29, 40, 10:10, 14, 26, 28, 35, 41, 11:4, 8, 9, 16, 19, 12:5, 9, 14, 15, 16, 17, 20, 24, 13:8, 14

ACTS 13:25, 30, 37, 45, 46, 50, 51, 14:2, 4, 15:5, 11, 20, 38, 16:1, 7, 18, 28, 37[2], 17:5, 13, 14, 21, 30, 18:9, 15, 19, 21[2], 19:9[2], 15, 22, 26, 27, 34, 39, 20:20, 24, 21:13, 24, 39, 22:9, 28, 23:6, 8, 9, 21, 29, 24:7, 11, 14, 27, 25:4, 9, 11, 19, 21, 25, 26:16, 20, 25[2], 29, 27:10, 14, 21, 22, 27, 39, 41, 43, 28:6, 16, 19, 22

ROMANS 1:13, 21, 32, 2:2, 5, 8[2], 10, 13, 25, 29[2], 3:4

ROMANS 3:5, 21, 27, 4:2, 4, 5[2], 10, 12, 13, 16, 20, 24, 5:3, 8, 11, 13, 15, 16, 20, 6:10, 11, 13, 14, 15, 17[2], 22, 23, 7:2, 3, 6, 7, 8, 9, 13, 14, 15, 17, 18, 19, 20, 23, 25, 8:1, 4, 5, 6, 9[2], 10, 11, 13, 15, 20, 23, 24, 25, 26, 32, 9:7, 8, 10, 11, 13, 16, 20, 24, 31, 32, 10:2, 6, 8, 16, 18, 19, 20, 21, 11:4, 6, 7, 11, 15, 18[2], 20, 22, 28, 12:2

ROMANS 12:3, 16, 19, 21, 13:1, 3, 4, 5, 8, 14, 14:1, 10, 13, 14, 15, 17, 20, 15:3, 21, 23, 25, 16:4, 18, 19, 26

1 COR. 1:10, 17, 18, 23, 24, 27, 30, 2:4, 5, 7, 9, 10, 12, 13, 14, 15, 16, 3:1, 6, 7, 10, 15, 4:3, 4, 10[3], 14, 19[2], 20, 5:3, 8, 11, 13, 6:6, 11, 12[2], 13[2], 17, 18, 7:4[2], 6, 7, 9, 10, 11, 14, 15[2], 17, 19, 21, 28[2], 29, 32, 33, 34, 35, 36, 37, 38

1 COR. 7:39, 40, 8:1, 3, 4, 6[2], 8, 9, 12, 9:12, 15, 17, 21, 24, 25, 27, 10:5, 13[2], 20, 23[2], 24, 28, 29, 33, 11:3, 5, 6, 7, 8, 9, 12, 15, 16, 17, 28, 32, 12:3, 4, 5, 6, 7, 11, 14, 18, 20[2], 24, 25, 31, 13:6, 8, 10, 11, 12[2], 13, 14:1, 2, 3, 4, 5, 14, 17, 20, 22[3], 24, 28, 33, 34, 38, 15:6, 10[3], 13, 20, 23, 27, 35, 37, 38, 39, 40, 46, 51, 57, 16:7, 8, 11

1 COR. 16:12[2]

2 COR. 1:9[2], 12, 18, 19, 24, 2:1, 4, 5[2], 13, 17[2], 3:3[2], 5, 6[2], 7, 14, 15, 18, 4:2[2], 3, 5, 7, 8, 9[2], 12, 16, 17, 18[2], 5:4, 11, 12, 15, 6:4, 12, 7:5, 7, 8, 9, 10, 12, 14, 8:5, 8, 10, 14, 16, 17, 19, 21, 22, 9:6, 12, 10:1, 2, 4, 10, 12, 13[2], 15, 17, 18, 11:3, 6[2], 12, 17, 12:5, 6, 14[2], 16, 19, 13:3, 4, 6, 7, 8

GAL. 1:1, 7, 8, 11, 12

GAL. 1:15, 17, 19, 23, 2:2, 3, 6, 7, 11, 12, 14, 16, 17, 20, 3:11, 12, 15, 16, 18, 20, 22, 23, 25, 4:2, 4, 7, 9, 14, 17, 18, 23[2], 26, 29, 31, 5:6, 10, 13, 15, 18, 22, 6:4, 8, 13, 14, 15

EPHES. 1:21, 2:4, 13, 19, 4:7, 9, 15, 20, 28, 29, 5:3, 4, 8, 11, 13, 15, 17, 18, 27, 29, 32, 6:4, 6, 12, 21

PHIL. 1:12, 17, 20, 22, 28, 29, 2:3, 4, 7, 12, 19

PHIL. 2:22, 24, 25, 27[2], 3:1, 7, 8[2], 9, 12, 13, 4:6, 10[2], 15, 17, 18, 19

COLOS. 1:26, 2:17, 3:8, 11, 22, 25

1 THESS. 1:5, 8, 2:2, 4[2], 7, 8, 13, 17, 18, 3:6, 4:7, 8, 9, 10, 13, 5:1, 4, 6, 8, 9, 15

2 THESS. 2:12, 13, 3:3, 8, 9, 11, 13, 15

1 TIM. 1:8, 9, 13, 2:10, 12[2], 14, 3:3, 15, 4:7, 8, 12, 5:1, 4, 6, 8, 11, 13, 19, 23, 6:2, 4, 6, 9, 11, 17

2 TIM. 1:7, 8, 9, 10, 17, 2:9, 14, 16, 20[2], 22, 23, 24, 3:5, 9, 10, 11, 13, 14, 4:3, 5, 8, 13, 16, 20

TITUS 1:3, 8, 15[2], 16, 2:1, 10, 3:2, 4, 5, 9

PHILE. 1:11, 14[2], 16[2], 22

HEB. 1:8, 11, 12, 13, 2:6, 8, 9, 16, 3:4, 6, 13, 17, 18, 4:2, 13, 15, 5:4, 5, 14, 6:8, 9, 12, 7:3, 6, 8, 16, 19, 21, 24, 28, 8:6, 9:7, 11, 12, 23, 24, 26, 27

HEB. 10:3, 5, 25, 27, 32, 38, 39[2], 11:6, 13, 16, 12:8, 10, 11, 13, 22, 26[2], 13:4, 14, 15, 19

JAMES 1:4, 6, 10, 11, 14, 22, 25[2], 26, 2:6, 9, 20, 3:8, 14, 15, 17, 4:6[2], 11[2], 16, 5:12[2]

1 PETER 1:12, 15, 19, 20, 23, 25, 2:4, 7, 9, 10[2], 16, 18, 20, 23, 25, 3:4, 9, 12, 14, 15, 18, 21, 4:2, 6, 7, 13, 14, 15, 16, 5:2[2], 3, 10

2 PETER 1:9, 16, 21, 2:1

2 PETER 2:4, 5, 10, 12, 16, 22, 3:7, 8, 9[2], 10, 18

1 JOHN 1:7, 2:2, 5, 7, 11, 16, 17, 19[2], 20, 21, 22, 23, 27[2], 3:2, 17, 18, 4:1, 10, 18, 5:5, 6, 18

2 JOHN 1:1, 5, 8, 12

3 JOHN 1:11[2], 9, 13, 14

JUDE 1:6, 9, 10[2], 17, 20

REV. 2:6, 9[2], 14, 24, 25, 3:5, 9, 9:4, 5, 11, 10:7, 9, 11:2, 12:12, 14:3, 19:12, 20:5, 6, 21:8, 27, 22:3

by

GEN. 7:22, 8, 9:6, 11, 10:5, 32, 14:6, 15, 16:2, 7, 18:2, 8, 19:36, 20:3, 21:23, 28, 29, 22:13, 16, 23:20, 24:3, 11, 13, 30, 43, 25:11, 13

GEN. 25:16, 26:18, 27:40, 29:2, 30:3, 27, 40, 31:24, 31, 39, 40, 53, 32:16, 33:8, 35:4, 36:37, 40, 37:28, 38:14, 16, 18, 19, 20, 21, 24, 25, 39:10[2]

GEN. 39:12, 16, 41:1, 3, 31, 32, 47, 42:15, 16, 23, 38, 43:32[3], 45:1, 7, 23, 24, 47:13, 48:7, 49:17, 22, 24, 25[2]

EXOD. 2:3, 5, 15

EXOD. 2:23[2], 3:7, 19, 4:4, 13, 24, 6:3[2], 7:4, 15, 8:24, 9:35, 12:14, 26, 31, 51, 13:3, 14, 16, 21[3], 22, 14:2, 9, 20, 21, 15:16, 27, 16:3[2]

EXOD. 18:8, 13, 14, 19, 20:26, 21:3[2], 4, 22:25, 26, 23:30, 25:14, 26:9[2], 28:28, 29:11, 18, 25, 28, 32, 38, 41, 43, 30:4, 6, 20, 31:2, 32:13, 27

EXOD. 33:6, 12, 17, 21, 22[2], 34:6, 7, 35:29, 30, 36:16[2], 37:3, 5, 27, 38:21, 39:4, 21, 40:29, 38[2]

LEVIT. 1:5, 9, 13, 16, 17, 2:2

LEVIT. 2:3, 9, 10, 11, 14, 16, 3:3, 4, 5, 9[2], 10, 11, 14, 15, 16, 4:9, 35, 5:12, 15, 17, 6:2, 17, 18, 7:4, 5, 25, 30

LEVIT. 7:34, 35, 36, 8:21, 28, 36, 10:11, 12, 13, 15[2], 16:21, 31, 19:12, 31, 20:25[3], 21:6, 9, 21, 22:4, 22, 27, 23:8, 13, 18, 25, 27, 36[2]

LEVIT. 23:37, 24:7, 8, 9[2], 25:39, 47[2], 26:7, 8, 23[2], 26, 46, 27:2

NUM. 1:2[2], 3, 17, 18[2], 20[3], 22[3], 24[2], 26[2], 28[2], 30[2], 32[2], 34[2], 36[2]

NUM. 1:38[2], 40, 42, 45, 52[2], 2:2, 12, 17, 20, 25, 27, 32, 34, 3:15, 17, 18, 19, 20, 26[2], 43, 47, 49, 4:2, 22, 26[2], 29, 32

NUM. 4:36, 37, 38, 40, 42, 45, 49, 5:2, 19, 6:9, 11, 7:84, 9:6, 7, 10, 16[2], 21[2], 23, 10:13, 34, 11:31, 12:2, 13:3, 22, 29[2], 14:3, 14[2]

NUM. 14:18, 25, 36, 37, 43, 15:3, 10, 13, 14, 23, 24, 25, 28, 16:40, 18:8[2], 11, 19, 32, 20:17, 18, 19, 23, 21:1, 4, 18, 22, 27

NUM. 21:33, 22:1, 5, 23:3, 6, 15, 17, 24:6, 26:3, 55, 63[2], 27:2, 23, 28:2, 3[2], 6, 8, 13, 19, 24, 29:6, 13, 36, 30:3, 10, 31:12, 17

NUM. 31:18, 35, 33:2, 10, 48, 49, 50, 54, 34:3, 13, 18, 35:1, 20, 30, 33, 36:2[2], 13[2]

DEU. 1:2, 7, 19, 22, 33[3], 40, 2:1, 8[2]

DEU. 2:27, 30, 36[2], 3:12, 4:34[7], 48, 5:5, 15, 31, 6:7, 13, 7:22, 8:3[2], 9:29[2], 10:20, 11:19, 30, 12:30, 14:22, 15:20, 16:1, 18:1, 20:19, 21:5, 17, 22:4, 23:10[2]

DEU. 24:9, 25:2, 11, 17, 18, 27:16, 28:10, 68, 29:16, 33:12, 14[2], 29

JOSH. 2:12, 15, 18, 3:4[2], 4:6, 5:1, 4, 7, 13, 7:14[2], 16, 17, 18

JOSH. 8:3, 15, 9:13, 18, 19, 10:18, 11:7, 23, 13:6, 14, 16, 22, 29, 31, 32, 14:2[2], 15:1, 6, 8, 16:1, 6, 8, 17:2[2], 18:9, 20, 19:49, 51

JOSH. 20:2, 8, 9, 21:2, 4, 5, 6, 7, 8[2], 9, 40[2], 22:9, 10, 23:4, 7, 24:26

JUD. 2:18, 3:1, 4[2], 15, 19[2], 4:11, 5:10, 19, 22

JUD. 6:11 25 27[2] 28 30 36 37 7:1 5 7 12 8:11 9:6 9 25 32 34 37[2] 11:18 26 16:5 26 17:10 18:3 16 28 19:11 14 20:5 9 21:7 11 12
RUTH 2:8 21 23 4:1
1 SAM. 1:7 9 25 2:3 9 16 23 28 3:21 4:13 18 20 5:2 8 9 9:23 10:2 19[2] 21 11:7 9 14:4 6[2] 36 16:9 20 17:2 23 26 35 43 52 18:25 30 20:7 9 19 25[2] 23:7 24:3 21 25:13 16 20 22 34 26:3 7 24[2] 27:1 28:6[3] 8[2] 10 15[2] 17 29:1 2[2] 30:15 24
2 SAM. 1:6 12 2:13 15 16 24 3:5 18 6:2 7 10:2 8 11:14 12:14 25 13:31 32 34 15:30 36 16:2 13 17:11 17 22 18:4[3] 23 19:3 7 37 20:9 11 12 21 21:10[2] 22[2] 22:9 30[2] 35 23:2 4 15 16 24:16
1 KINGS 1:9[2] 17 27 30 2:8 23 25 42 3:5 4:12 20 5:9 11 14 21 22 7:20 8:38[2] 43 53 56 9:8 10:5 25 29 12:15 13:1[2] 2 5 9[2] 10 17[2] 18 24[3] 25[2] 28 32 14:4 18 15:13 29 30 16:7 12 13[2] 34 17:3 5 16 20 24 18:4 6[2] 13 24 19:2 11 19 20:14[2] 38 20:39[2] 21:1 23 22:8 19 28
2 KINGS 2:1 7 11 13 23 3:11 20 4:8 9 27 5:1 6:14 26 30 8:8 21 9:27[2] 36 10:6 10 33 11:11 14[2] 16[2] 19 13:7 25 14:7 9 25 27 16:15 17:4 6 13[3] 23 18:11 17 31 19:7 11 23 28[2] 33[2] 20:11 21:10 23:3 11 24:2 25:4[3]
1 CHRON. 1:48 3:3 4:38 41 5:7 10 17 6:15 61 63 65[2] 78 7:4 5 7 9 11 29 8:28 9:1 22 23 28 11:3 11 14 18 12:22 31 14:11 15:16 16:41 17:21 18:3 19:4 9 20:8[2] 21:15 25 26 23:3[2] 24[2] 27 31 24:5 27 26:16 25 27:1 28:1 12 14[2] 15[2] 16 17[2] 18 19 29:5 8
2 CHRON. 1:17 2:16 3:3 5:11 14 6:23[4] 33 34 7:6 12 14 20 21 8:14 18 9:4 18 24 10:15 12:7 13:5 16:14 18:7 27 19:5 20:15 16 21:9 15[3] 19 22:7 23:10[2] 13 18[2] 24:11[2] 13 25:18 26:11[2] 15 28:15 29:9 15 25 27 30:12 21 31:6 15 17[2] 19[2] 32:11[2] 33:8 34:14 35:4 6 20 36:13 15 21 22
EZRA 1:1 8 2:62 3:4 11 4:16 23 5:5 6:9 7:23 8:3 18 20 31 33 34[2] 9:11 10:16 17 44
NEH. 1:10[2] 2:6 13[2] 2:15[2] 3:15 23 25 4:3 12 18[2] 7:3 5 64 8:14 18 9:9 12[2] 14 19[2] 30 10:29 34 35 12:37 13:18 25 26
ESTHER 1:12 15 2:14 3:13 15 7:7 8:5 10 14[2] 9:25
JOB 4:9[2] 6:16 9:11 11:7 15:30 16:12 17:7 18:8 9 20:29 21:29 22:30 26:12 13 27:11 28:8 9 25 29:3 19 30:4 18 31:9 11 23 28 30 33 33:18 35:9[2] 36:12 22 31 32 37:10 11 12 17 19 38:2 24 39:9 26 41:18 25 42:5
PSALMS 1:3 5:10 9:16 10:10 17:4 7 18:8 29[2] 34 19:11 30:7 33:6[2] 16[2] 17 37:23 38:8 39:10 41:11 44:3 12 16 48:4 49:7 50:5 54:1[2] 56:7 59:11 63:10 65:5 6 66:7 12 68:4 71:6 72:3 73:23 74:7 13 77:20 78:17 18 26 49 55 64 65 72 79:10 80:12 88:9 89:35 39 41 90:7[2] 10 91:5[2] 94:20 102:5 104:8[2] 106:22 107:7 119:9 121:6[2] 128:3 129:8 134:1 136:5 137:1 140:5 147:4
PROV. 3:19[2] 20 28 29 4:15 6:26 7:26 8:2 15 16 30 9:11 11:5 11[2] 12:3 13 14 13:2 10 11[2] 14:4 15:13 23 16:6 12 20:4 11 18 28 21:6 22:4 24:3 4 6 30[2] 25:15 26:2 6 17[2] 26 28 27:9 28:2 8 29:19 30:27 31:18
ECCL. 1:13 5:3 9 14 7:3 11 23 26 27 9:1 15 10:3 18 12:11 12
CANT. 1:7 8 2:7 3:1 5 5:4 12 7:4
ISAIAH 1:7 3:5[2] 25 4:1 4[2] 5[2] 7:20[2] 9:1 10:13[2] 34 13:15 15:5 18:2 19:7[3] 20:2 22:3 5 14 23:3 26:13 27:7 9 12 29:13 32:8 34:17 36:2 16 37:7 11 24[2] 29[2] 34[2] 38:8 16 40:26[3] 41:3 42:16 43:1 7 44:4 5[2] 24 45:3 4 23 46:3 48:1[2] 17 49:10 19 50:4 51:18 19 52:12 53:11 54:15 60:19 62:2 8[2] 63:12 19 64:4 65:1 5 15 16 66:16[2]
JER. 2:8 17 34 4:26 5:7[2] 22 31 6:5 6:25 7:10 11 14 30 8:2 5 10:12[3] 14 11:21 22[2] 12:16[2] 13:5 24 14:9 12[3] 15 15:16 16:4[2] 17:2 8[2] 11 19 20 21 18:21[2] 19:2 7 20:2 4 21:9[3] 22:2 4 5 8 13[2] 23:27 32[2] 25:29 27:3 5[2] 8 13[3] 29:3 19 22 31:9 32 35[2] 32:17 34 36[3] 33:4[2] 34:4 15 37:2 38:2[3] 11 23 39:4[3] 18 41:12 17 42:17[3] 22[3] 44:12[4] 13[3] 15 18[2] 26 27[2] 46:2 6 10 18 48:19 49:3 9 13 17 50:1 13 51:14 15[3] 17[2] 52:7[5]
LAM. 1:12 2:15 21 3:1 5:12
EZEKIEL 1:1 3 15 19 3:15 4:10 11 16[2] 5:12 5:14 6:11[3] 12[2] 8:3 9:2 3 11 10:9[3] 15 16 20 22 11:10 24 12:3 4 7 13:19 22 14:3 7 13 14 20 16:6 8 15 25 36 56 61 17:5 7 8 9 14 17 18 21 18:7 12 16 18 19:7 10[2] 20:3 31[2] 21:12 22:7[2] 12 23:21 25[2] 24:6 21 25:12 13 14 15 26:6 10 11 27:12 16 34 28:5[2] 10 16 17 18[2] 23 29:7 30:5 6 10 12 17 31:7 9 12 14 18 32:12 20 21 22 23 24 25 26 29[2] 30 31 34:27 30 13 35:5 36:17[2] 34 37 37:2 18 38:17 39:15 23 40:2 5 7 18 22 28 38 41 49[2] 41:7 17[2] 42:20 43:3 4 6 7[2] 8[3] 13 44:2[2] 3[2] 45:1 46:2[2] 8[2] 9[5] 14 16 18 21 47:2 12 16 18 22 48:2 3 4 5 6 7 8 12 20 24 25 26 17 28 29
DANIEL 4:17[2] 27[2] 30 5:10 7:2 8 16 8:2 11 12 24 25 9:2 3 5 10 11 12 18 19 10:4 16 11:2 12 16 18 21 32 33[4] 12:7
HOSEA 1:2 7[6] 2:17 4:2 6:5[2] 9 7:16 8:4 9 11:3 12:3[2] 10 13[2] 13:7 16 14:1
AMOS 2:8 4:2 5:3[2] 6:8 10 13 7:2 4 5 7 8 11 17[2] 8:2 5 8 14 9:5 10 12
OBADIAH 5 9
JONAH 2:4 3:7
MICAH 2:2 5 8 12 13 3:8 7:18
NAHUM 1:6
HABAK. 1:16 2:4 5 10 12 3:10 13
ZEPH. 1:5[2] 18 2:12 15
HAGGAI 1:1 3 2:1 10 13 22 3:6
ZECH. 1:8 3:5 7 4:3 6[3] 14 5:4 7:7 12 8:9 9:8 11
MALACHI 1:1 9 2:10
MATT. 1:22 2:5 14 15 17 23 3:3 4:4[2] 14 15 18 5:21 26 27 33 34 35[2] 36 6:27 7:16 20 8:17 28 9:25 11:12 12:17 24 27[2] 28 33 37[2] 13:1 4 14 19 21[2] 35 14:13 15:3 5[2] 17:21 18:7 28 20:30 21:4 23 24 27 22:1 31 23:16[2] 18[2] 20[3] 21[3] 22[3] 24:15 26:4 24 73 27:9 32 35 39 64 28:9 13
MARK 1:16 31 2:13 14 3:22 4:1[2] 2 4 15 5:4 7 21 22 41 6:2 7 25 32 39 40[2] 48 7:11[2] 26 8:3 23 27 9:2 27 29[2] 33 34 10:1 46 11:4 20 28 29 33 12:1 36 13:14 14:1 19 21 47 69 70 15:21 29 35
LUKE 1:61 70 77 2:8 18 2:26 27 3:19 4:1 3[2] 4[2] 5:1 2 15 17 19 6:44 7:7 8:4 5 12 20 36 54 9:7 14 47 10:4 19 31[2] 32 11:3 19[2] 13:17 16:22 17:6 7 18:5 31 35 36 37 19:8 15 24 20:2 8 21:9 16 24 22:22 56 23:8 24:4 12 32
JOHN 1:3 10 17[2] 42 3:2 34 5:2 6:15 18 57[2] 7:50 8:9[2] 59 9:1 7 21 10:1 2 3 9 11:39 42 12:11 29 13:35 14:6 16:30 19:7 25 39 20:7 21:19
ACTS 1:3 10 16 25 2:16 22[2] 23[2] 33 43 3:7 12 16 18 21 4:7[2] 9 10[2] 4:16 25 30[2] 36 5:10 12 15 19 6:10 7:25 35 42 53 9:8 13 25[2] 36 39 10:6 22 32 36 11:4 5 28 30 12:9 20 13:4 8 11 19 21 36 39[2] 45 14:3 15:3 7 9 12 23 27 40 16:2 8 13 16 17:10 23 29 31 18:3 9 21 28 19:10 11 13 25 20:16 19 31 21:19 22:10 11 24 25 23:2 4 10 11 19 31 24:2[2] 8 14 21 26:18 27:2 11 12 13 16 23 28:16 25
ROMANS 1:2 4 5 10[2] 12 17 20 2:7 12 14 16 27[2] 3:20[2] 21 22 3:24 27[2] 28 30 4:2 16 5:1 2[2] 5 9 10[2] 11 12[2] 15[2] 16[2] 17[3] 18[2] 19[2] 21 6:4[2] 7:2 4 5 7 8 11 13[2] 8:11 14 20 24 9:10[2] 32[2] 10:5 17[2] 19[2] 11:6 14 20 24 12:1 2 14:14 15:16 18[2] 19 24 28 32 16:18 25 *subscr.*
1 COR. 1:4 5 9 10 11 21[2] 2:10 3:5 13 15 4:4 6:2 11 14 7:6 14[2] 39 8:6[2] 9 9:22 27 10:30 11:12 12:3[2] 8[2] 9[2] 13 14:6[4] 9 19 27[3] 30 31 15:2 10 21[2] 31 16:2 3 7 *subscr.*
2 COR. 1:1 4 5 11[3] 12 16 1:19[2] 20 24 2:2 14 3:3 10 18 4:2 14 16 5:7[2] 18 20 6:6[6] 7[3] 8[2] 7:6 7[2] 9 13 8:5 8[2] 14 19 20 9:12 13 14 10:1 9 11 12 15 11:3 26[2] 33 12:17 13:4[2] *subscr.*
GAL. 1:1[2] 15 22 2:2[2] 15 16[5] 17 20 21 3:2[2] 3 5[2] 11[2] 18 19 21 22 24 26 4:8 22 23 5:4 5 6 13 6:14
EPHES. 1:1 5 2:3 5 8 11[2] 13 16 18 3:3 5 6 7 9 10 12 16 17 21 4:14 16 21 5:13 26 *subscr.*
PHIL. 1:11 14 20 26 28 3:9 3:11 16 4:6 19 *subscr.*
COLOS. 1:1 16 17 20 21 2:11 18 19 3:17 4:18 *subscr.*
1 THESS. 3:3 5 7 4:1 2 15 5:9 27
2 THESS. 2:1[2] 2[3] 3 3:12 14 16
1 TIM. 1:1 18 4:5 14 5:21
2 TIM. 1:1 6 10 14 2:26 3:16 4:17
TITUS 1:9 3:5[2] 7
PHILE. 1:6 7 *subscr.*
HEB. 1:1 2[2] 3[2] 4 2:2 3[2] 9 10 3:4 16 5:3 8 14 6:7 13[2] 16 17 18 7:2 11 19 21 22 23 25 8:6 9 9:11 12[2] 15 22 26 10:1 8 10 14 19 10:20 33 38 11:2 3 4[3] 5 7[3] 8 9 12 17 20 21 22 23 24 27 29[2] 30 31 13:11 15 *subscr.*
JAMES 2:7 12 18 21 22 24[2] 25 5:4 12[3] 17
1 PETER 1:3 5 12 18 21 23 25 2:5 12 14 24 3:1 18 19 20 21 5:2 12
2 PETER 1:4 13 21[2] 2:2 3:1 2 5 7
1 JOHN 3:24 5:2 6[3]
3 JOHN 14
JUDE 1 12 23
REV. 1:1 5:9 8:13 9:2 18[4] 20 10:6 12:11[2] 13:14[2] 14:20 17:12 18:15 17 19 23 21:25

for

3588, *1063*

GEN. 1:14[3] 15 29 30 2:5 9 17 18 2:20 3:5 6 17 19 22 23 25 5:24 6:3 7 12 13 21 7:1 4 8:9[2] 21[2] 9:3 6 12 13 25 11:3 12:10 13 16 13:6 8 15[2] 17 14:13 15:6 16 16:10 13 17:4 5 7 8 17:13 15 19 20 18:5 14 15 19 18:24 26 28 29 31 32 19:8 13 19:14 17 21 22 30 20:3 6 7 20:11 18 21:2 7 10 12 16 17 21:18 30 22:2 3 7 12 13 16 23:2 8 9 13 18 20 24:10 19 24:20 22 23 31 32 40 44[2] 62 24:65 25:21 30 26:3 7[2] 9 14 15 26:16 18 21 22[2] 24[2] 27:5 9 36[2] 27:37 41 28:11 15 18 22 29:2 9 29:15 18 20[2] 21 24 25 27 32 30:13 15 16 26[2] 27[2] 30[2] 31 33[2]

GEN. 31:12 14 15 16 18 31 32 35 41 44 45 49 52 32:10 11 12 13 20 26 28 30 33:10 17 19 34:8 14 18 21[3] 22 36:7 37:7 8[2] 17 27 28 34 35[2] 38:6 11 14 16 39:5 40:15 17 41:8 19 31 32 36 49 51 52 55 57 42:2 4 5 18 19 23 25 27 30 33 38 43:5 9[2] 10 16 18 25 30 32[4] 44:4 14 17 18 22 26 32[3] 34 45:3 5 6 11 19[2] 20 21 23 26 46:3 32 34 47:4[3] 13 14 15[2] 16 17[6] 19 20[2] 21 22 23[2] 24[5] 48:4 7 10 14 18 49:6 7[2] 13 18 30 50:3[3] 5

GEN. 50:10 13[2] 17 19 20 EXOD. 1:5 11 18 19 2:3 7 9 19 22 3:5 6 7 15 4:1 19 5:7 8 18 23 6:1 7 8 9[2] 7:9 12 24[2] 8:8 9[3] 17 25[2] 26 28 9:2 11 14 15 16[2] 19 27 28 30 31 32 10:1 5 9 10 11 12 15 16 23 26 28 12:3 4[2] 12 13 14[2] 15 17[2] 19 21 23 24[2] 30 31 33 39[2] 42 44 48 13:3 9[3] 16[3] 17 19 14:3 12[2] 13[2] 14 25[2] 15:1 17 18 19 21 23 25 26 16:3 4 7 8 9 15 16[2] 22 23 25 27 29 32 33 17:1 3 14[2] 16 18:1[2] 3

EXOD. 18:4 8 9 11 12 18[2] 19 22 19:2 5 7 9 11 23 20:5 7 11 20 25 21:2 6 19 21 23 24[4] 25[3] 26 27 30 36 22:1[2] 2 3[3] 9[6] 13 15 21 27[3] 23:7 8 9 15 21[2] 23 31 33 24:14 25:6[3] 12 26 27 26:14 15 17 18 19[2] 20 22 23 24[2] 26 27[3] 29[2] 36 37[2] 27:4 6 9[3] 11 12 16 20 21 28:2[3] 4 12[2] 29 40[5] 43 29:9 22 24 25[2] 26 27[2] 28[2] 36[3] 37 40 41 30:4[2] 12 15 16[2] 19 21 37[2] 31:10 11 13 14[2] 16 17[2] 32:1[2] 7 12 13 18[2] 23[3] 25 29 30 33:3[2] 5 16 17 20

EXOD. 34:7 9[2] 10 12 14[2] 18 24 27 35:8[3] 9[2] 14[2] 15 17 19 21[2] 24 27[2] 28[3] 29 36:1 3 5 6 7[2] 14 19 20 22 23[2] 24[2] 25 27 28 31 32[3] 34 36 37 37:3 12 13 14 27[2] 38:4 5[2] 11 12 13 15 17 18 21 24 26[3] 27 28 30 39:1 4 7 27 37 38 40[2] 41 40:5 15 38 LEVIT. 1:4[2] 10 14 2:11 12[2] 14 3:6 7 16 17 4:3[2] 14 20[2] 21 26 28 31[2] 32 33 35 5:6[3] 7[3] 8 10[3] 11[3] 13 15[2] 16[2] 18[2] 6:6 7[2] 15 17 18 20 21 22 23[2] 26 7:5 7 12 13 14 15 19 25

LEVIT. 7:30 32 33 34[2] 36 8:2 14[2] 21 27 28 29[2] 33 34 35 9:2[2] 3[2] 4[2] 7[3] 8 15[2] 18[2] 21 10:7 9 12 13 14 15[2] 17 11:24 35[2] 42 44[2] 45[2] 12:2 6[4] 7[2] 8[3] 13:7 11 15 28 36 52 14:4 6 10 12[2] 13 18 19 20 21[3] 23 24 29 31[3] 34 53 54 55 56[3] 15:13 15[4] 30[4] 16:2 3[2] 5[2] 6[3] 8[2] 9 10 11[4] 15 16[2] 17[3] 18 24[2] 26 27[2] 29 30[2] 31 33[5] 34[2] 17:5 6 7 11[4] 14[3] 18:10 13 17 19 24 27 29 19:2 10 21 22[2] 23 28 34 20:7 9 19 23 26 21:1 2[6] 3[2] 6 7 8[2] 11[2] 12

LEVIT. 21:15 18 23 22:9 16 18[3] 20[2] 23[2] 25 27 23:11 12 13 14 18 19[2] 20[2] 21 28[2] 29 31 34 41 24:2 3 7 9 18 20[3] 22[2] 25:4 5 6[6] 7[2] 12 16 17 21 23[3] 24 30 33 34 37 46[3] 51 55 26:1 9 16 18[2] 20 24 27 28 44[2] 45 27:2 5 6 7 10[3] 34 NUM. 1:44 48 3:13 25 26[2] 38 41 46 4:16 24 25 26[2] 29 35 39 43 5:8 15[2] 6:7[4] 11[4] 12 14[3] 17 20[2] 21 7:3[2] 10 11 13 15 16 17 19[2] 21 22 23 25 27 28 29 31 33 34 35 37 39 40 41 43 45 46 47

NUM. 7:49 51 52 53 55 57 58 59 61 63 64 65 67 69 70 71 73 75 76 77 79 81 82 83 87[2] 88 8:8 11 12[3] 13 15 16 17[2] 18 19 21 9:14[2] 10:2[2] 6 8[2] 10 29 33 11:13 14 18[2] 22 29 31 12:1 13:30 31 14:3 9[2] 11 13 14 32 34 40 42 43 15:5[2] 6[2] 7[2] 8[2] 10[2] 11[3] 15[3] 16[2] 20 24[3] 25[3] 27 28[2] 29[3] 39 16:11 28 34 37 38[2] 39 46[2] 47 17:3[2] 6 8 10 18:4 6 7 8 9[2] 11 16 17[2] 19[2] 21[2] 23 26[2] 31[2] 19:9[3] 10[2] 17[2] 20:2 19 24 29 21:5 7[2] 13 24 26 28 34 22:6[3]

NUM. 22:12 13 17 22 29 34 23:9 24:1 18 20 24 25:11 13[2] 18[2] 26:53 62 65 27:14 21 28:2[2] 3 5 6 7[2] 9 12[4] 13[2] 15 19 20[2] 21 22[2] 23 27 30 29:2 3[2] 4 5[2] 6 8 10 11 16 18[3] 19 21[3] 22 24[3] 25 27[3] 28 30[3] 31 33[3] 34 37[3] 38 39[4] 31:18 29 50[2] 53[2] 54[2] 32:1 4 5 9 12 15 16[2] 19 24[2] 27 29 36 33:4 14 53 54 34:2 6[2] 7 14 23 35:2 3[3] 6[3] 11 12 13 15[3] 21 29 31 32 33 34 36:2 7 11 DEU. 1:10 14 17[2] 30[2] 37 38 40 42 2:5[2] 6[2] 7 9[3] 15 19[2]

DEU. 2:28[2] 30 35 36 3:2 7 11 18 19 22[2] 24 26 27 28 4:1 3 6 7[2] 15 21[2] 24 31 32 34 38 40 5:5 9 11 23 25 26 29 31 6:8 15 24 7:4 6 7 16 21 25 26 8:7 10 18 9:4[2] 5[3] 6[2] 12 19 20 10:13 17 19 21 22 11:2 10 12 15 18 22 25 31 12:9 23 28 31[2] 13:3 16[2] 14:1 2 7 21 24 26[6] 27 15:4[2] 6 8 10 11 17 18 16:1 3 19 17:1 8 18:5[2] 12 14[2] 19:5 9 10 11 15[2] 21[5] 20:1 4[2] 7 16 19[2] 20 21:5 14 17[2] 23[2] 22:5 8 20 26 27 23:3 6

DEU. 23:7 14 18[2] 21 24:4[2] 6 15 16[3] 19[3] 20[3] 21[3] 25:11 16 19 26:1 3 14[2] 28:20 32 34 38 39 40 41 46[3] 47 56 57[2] 62 67[2] 68 29:8 13 16 26 29 30:9[2] 11 12 13 20 31:6 7 18 19[2] 20 21[2] 23 26 27 29 32:4 9 20 22 28 31 32 35 36[2] 40[2] 43 47[2] 49 33:2 7 9 13[3] 14[2] 15[2] 16[2] 19 21 34:8[2] 9 JOSH. 1:6[2] 8 9 11 2:3 5 10[2] 11 14 15 24 3:4 5 15 4:7[2] 10 13 23 24 5:6 7 13[2] 15 6:16 7:1 3 5 9 11 13 8:2[2] 6[2] 7 18 26 27 28 9:9 11 12

JOSH. 9:22 23 27[2] 10:4 6 8 14[2] 18 19 24 25 42 11:6 10 13 14 20 23 12:6 7 13:6 7 12 32 14:1 2[2] 3 4[3] 9 11 12 13 15:19 63 16:9 17:1[3] 2[7] 15[2] 16 18[2] 18:4 6 7 8 10 19:1 9[2] 10 17 24 32 40 47 49 51 20:2 6 9[2] 21:2 4 10 12 13 21[2] 26 27 32 38 40 22:17 24 25 26[2] 28[2] 29[3] 34 23:2[5] 3[2] 4 9[2] 10[2] 13 24:1[4] 13 15 17 18 19 27 31 32 JUD. 1:1 15 32 34 2:7 10 15 18 28 4:3 5 9[2] 14 17 19 21 5:2 15 16 30 6:4 5[3] 22 31[3]

JUD. 6:38 40 7:2 4 9 12[2] 14 15 8:5 10 11 20 21 22 24 30 9:2 3 5 17[2] 21 25 28 10:16 11:2 18 35 36 37 38 12:6 9 13:5[2] 7 15 16 20 14:2 3[2] 4 10 15:18 16:2 17 18[2] 19 23[2] 24 25[2] 28 17:3 18:1 9 10 19 26 19:6 15 19[4] 20:6 10 27 28 36 39 41 21:5 6 7[2] 9 15 16[2] 17 18 22[2] RUTH 1:6 12 13[4] 16 20 2:13[2] 16 3:1 9 10 11 17 18 4:4 6[2] 7 8 15 1 SAM. 1:5 6 16[2] 22[2] 27 2:2 3 5 8 9 14 15[2] 17 20 23 24 25 30[2] 32 35

1 SAM. 2:36 3:5 6 8 9 10 13[2] 14 21 4:7[2] 10 13[2] 18 19 20 22 5:7 11 6:2 4 8 17[6] 7:2 5 8 9[2] 17 8:7 11[2] 9:5[2] 7 9 12[2] 13[2] 14 16 19 20[2] 24[2] 10:2[3] 7 11:2 13 12:19[2] 21[2] 22[2] 23[2] 24[2] 13:6 7 13[2] 19 21[4] 14:6[2] 10 12 18 24 26 31 39 44 45 15:2 6 11 15 23 24 26 29 35 16:1[2] 7[2] 11 12 22 17:8 12 17 20 21 26 28 31 33 39[2] 42 47 18:11 17[2] 19:5[2] 13 16 20:4 6[2] 8[2] 9 15 17 21 22 23 26 29 31[2] 34[2] 42 21:6 8 9 10 22:3 8 10 13 15[2]

1 SAM. 22:23 23:4 7 10 17 21 22 26[2] 27 24:10 11 17 19 25:8 11 17[2] 21 25 28 34 36 39 26:9 12 15 18 19 20 21 23 27:1 4 5 8 12 28:1 2 9 10 12 13 15 17 20 29:4 6 30:6[3] 8 10 12 24 25 26 31:4 2 SAM. 1:9 12[4] 16 21 26 2:7 26 3:6 8 14 17 18 22 27 28 37 39 4:2 7 10 5:12 19 24 6:6 7 17 7:3 5 10 13[2] 16[2] 19 20 21 22 23[3] 24[2] 25 26 27 29[3] 8:4 10 9:1 7[2] 10 11 13 10:2 11[2] 12[2] 11:4 22 25 26 12:4[2] 12 16 18 21 22

2 SAM. 13:2[3] 12 13[2] 18 22 32[2] 33 37 39 14:2 7 13 14 16 17 19 25 26 29 32 33 15:2 6 8 12[2] 14 19 34 16:2[2] 3 11 12 17:8 10 11 14 17 21 29[2] 18:3[3] 5 8 12 13 16 18[2] 31 19:1 2[2] 6[2] 7 8 9 20 21 22 26 28 32 38 42 20:11 21:1[2] 3 4 8 10 14 22:18[2] 22 23[3] 29 30 31 32 51[2] 23:5 24:2 10 14 22 24 25 1 KINGS 1:2 3 31 35 42 51 2:7 9 15 17 18 19[2] 20 22[6] 26 28 33[2] 36 37[2] 42[2] 45 3:4 8 9 11[2] 26 27 4:7 21 22 24 26

1 KINGS 4:27[2] 28 5:1[2] 3 6[2] 8 9 11 6:2 4 6 16[3] 31 33 7:7 8 12[2] 15 17[3] 18 36 40 42 45 50[2] 51 8:5 7 11 13 17 20 21 36 39 42 43 44 46 48 51 52 53 64 66[3] 9:3 5 7 15 16[2] 19[2] 22 24 10:9 12[3] 23[2] 26 27 29[4] 11:2 4 5 7 8 12 13[2] 15 16 31 32[2] 34 38 39[2] 12:1 2 5 7 15 17 24 28 30 13:6 9 12 17 23[2] 32 14:4 5[3] 6 9 11 13[2] 15 18 23 15:4 27 16:7 13 19 24 26 31 32 17:5 12 13[2] 14 18:4 23 25[2] 26 27 41 19:3

1 KINGS 19:4[2] 7 10[2] 14 20 20:7[5] 9 10[2] 18[2] 22 25[2] 34 38 39 42[2] 21:2[2] 4 6[2] 15[2] 22 22:6 8 12 15 34 43 48[2] 53 2 KINGS 2:2 4 6 9 18 3:2 9[2] 13 17 26[2] 4:2 10 13[2] 14 24 27 38 39 40 41 43 5:3 17 27 6:1 5 9 11[2] 16 23 25[2] 33 7:1[2] 6 7 16[2] 18[2] 20 8:1[2] 3[2] 5[2] 18 19 27 9:8 16 20 25 34 10:3 10 16 19 20 22 24 31 11:15 12:7[2] 12[2] 13 15 20 13:4 7[2] 14:6[3] 10 26[3] 28 15:14 16:8 9 15 18[2] 17:4 7 12 21 22 32 37[2] 18:4 6 20 24[2] 26 29

2 KINGS 18:31 36 19:3 4 8 18 31 34[3] 20:1 6[2] 10 12 21:3[2] 5 7 22:13[4] 23:4[3] 7 13[3] 24:3 4[2] 7 16 20 25:3 16 22 26 30 1 CHRON. 4:14 23 39 40 41 42 5:1 2 20 22 6:26 49[2] 54 70 7:4[2] 11 9:1 13 26 33 10:4 13[2] 11:9 19 20 21 12:8 18 19 21 22 25 29 37 39[2] 40 13:3 4 9 14:2 10 15 15:1[2] 2[2] 3 11[3] 12 13[2] 22 23 24 16:1 17[2] 21 25 26 34[3] 36 41 42 17:2 5 9 12 14[3] 17[3] 18[3] 19 22[3] 23 24 25 27[3] 18:10 19:3 5 12[2] 13[2] 21:6 8 13 17 22 23[3] 24[3] 25

1 CHRON. 21:29 30 22:1 3^3 4 5^2 6^2 7 9 10^2 14^2 15 18 23:13^2 24 25^2 26 27 28 29^7 24:5 6^2 25:6^2 9 26:5 6 8^2 10 13 14 29^2 31 32 27:2 3 5 7 8 9 10 11 12 13 14 15 24 26 27 28:2^4 3 4^2 5 6 7 8^4 9^2 10^2 13^3 14^4 15^7 16^3 17^4 18^2 20^2 21^3 29:1^3 2^6 3 5^3 7 9 10 11 14 15 16 17 18 19 21

2 CHRON. 1:3 4^3 9 10 11 15 17^4 2:1^2 4^3 5 8 9 12^2 3:3 6 4:6^2 9 11^2 16 18 19 22 5:1 6 8 11 13^3 14 6:2^3 7 8 9 10^2 13 27

2 CHRON. 6:30 32 33 34 36 38 7:3^3 6 7 9 10 12 16^2 17 20 8:7 9 11^2 14 9:6 8^2 11 21 25 10:1 7 10 11 15 17 11:4 5 14^2 15^3 17 21 22 12:13 13:5 8 10 11 12^2 14:3 6 11 13 14^2 15:3 6 7 9 15 16:9 10 14^2 17:18 18:2^2 5 7 8 11 32 33 19:6^3 7 8^2 11 20:7 8 9 12 15 17 21^2 23 25 26 27 30 33 21:6 7 19 22:1 3 4 7 9 11 23:6 8 14 24:3 6^2 7 14 18 24 25^2 25:4^3 6 7 8^2 9 20 26:8 10^2 14 15 16 18^2 21 23 28:2^2 6 10

2 CHRON. 28:11 13^2 17 19^2 21 23 29:6 9^2 11 21^4 23 24^3 25 32 34 35 36 30:2 3 5 8 9^2 14 17^2 18^2 24 26 31:2^2 3^5 10 16 18 32:1 7^3 15 20 25 26 27^6 28^3 29 33:3^2 4 5 7 8 22 34:3 11 21^3 26 35:7^2 8 9 14^4 15^2 21 23 24 25 36:17 21

EZRA 1:4 2:68 3:3 11^2 12 13 4:2 14 15 6:8 9 10 11 17^2 18 20^4 22 7:9 10 16 19 20 23^2 8:16^{11} 17 20 21^3 22^2 23 35^2 9:2^3 6 7 8 9 10 12^3 13^2 15^2 10:1 4 6 9 13 14 19

NEH. 1:5 6 11 2:3 4

NEH. 2:6 8^3 14 18 4:4^2 5 6 14 18 20 23 5:2^2 4 5 18^3 19^2 6:6 9 10 12 13 16 18 7:2 8:4 5 9 10^3 11 17 9:5 8 10 15^3 20 31^2 33 35 36 10:30 31^2 33^8 34 39 11:23^3 25 12:29 43 44^8 46 13:1 5 6 7 10 13 14^2 25 31^3

ESTHER 1:8 9 11 13 17 20 22 2:2 3 7^2 9 10 12^2 15 20 3:2 4 6 8 13 14 4:2 5 7 8 14^2 16 5:4 8 9 10 6:3^2 4 7 7:4^2 7^2 9^2 10 8:1 6 8^2 11^2 13 17 9:2 4^2 15 16 26 31^2 10:3

JOB 1:4 5 9

JOB 2:4^2 11 13 3:6 9 13 14 21^3 24 25 4:11 20 5:2 18 23 27 6:3 4 8 10 19 21 22 27 28 7:2 16 21 8:4 6 8 9 9:17 32 10:16 11:4 11 12 15 13:7^2 8 16 19 24 26 14:7 16 20 15:5 22 23 25 31 34 16:12 17 21^2 17:1 4 10^2 15 18:4 8 10^2 19:15 17 21 24 25 27 29 20:2 5 7 18 21 21:4 14 19 21 28 22:4 6^2 8 17 26 23:7 14^2 16 24:3 5^3 8 15 16 17 24 27:8 14 22 28:1^2 5 15^2 17 18 24 25 26^2 29:13 23^3 30:3 4 23^2 25^2 26^2 31:2 11 12

JOB 31:18 19 23 28 32:11 16 18 22 33:10 13 14 26 32 34:3 5 9 11 19 21 23 36 37 35:3 36:4 7 21 27 31 37:6 13^2 19 38:3 7 9 10 19 25^2 39 41^2 41:4^2 5 42:3 7 8^3 10 12

PSALMS 1:6 2:8^2 3:2 3 5 7 4:3 8 5:2 4 7 9 10 11 12 6:2^2 4 5 8 7:6 7 9 13 8:5 9:4 5 7^2 9 10 12 18^2 10:3 5 6 14 16 11:2 7 12:1^2 5^2 7 13:1 14:5 16:1 10 11 17:6 15 18:17^2 21 22 23 27 28 29 30 31 39 50 19:4 9 21:3 4 6^2 7 11 22:11^2 16 21

PSALMS 22:24 26 28 30 23:3 4 6 24:2 25:5 6 7 11^2 15 16 19 20 21 26:1 3 11 27:5 12 28:9 29:10 30:1 5^2 11 12 31:2 3^2 4^2 7 9 10 13 16 17 19^2 21 22 23 32:4 6 11 33:1^2 4 9 11 12 17 20 21 34:9 35:2 7^3 10 12 13 14 20 27 36:2 9 37:2 7 9 10 13 17 18 22 24 27 28^2 29 37 38:2 4^2 7 10 12 15 16 17 18^2 20 39:7 11 12 40:1 12 15 41:4 12^2 42:2^2 4 5^2 11 43:2 5 44 *title* 3 4 6 8 10 11 12 16 21 22^2 23 25 26^2 45 *title* 2 6

PSALMS 45:11 17 46 *title* 47 *title* 2 4 7 9 48 *title* 2 3 4 8 14^2 49 *title* 7 8^2 9 10 11 15 17 50:6 8 10 12 51:3 16 52:5 8 9^2 53:5 54:3 6 7 55:3 6 9 12 15 16 18 56:1 2 5 6 9^2 13 57:1 2 6 10 58:11 59:3^4 7 9 12^2 15 16 17 60:2 11 12 61:3^2 4 5 7 8 62 *title* 5 8 12 63:1^2 10 64:9 65:1 3 9 13 66:7 10 16 67:4^2 68:10 16 18^2 28 69:1 3 6^2 7 9 13 16 17 20^2 21 22 26 33 35 70:3 71:3 5 10^2 11 12 15 24^2 72:12 15 17 19 73:2 3 4 14

PSALMS 73:16 26 27 28 74:1 4 10 12 19 20 75:1 6 8 9 77:7 8^2 78:5 18 20 29 32^2 37 39 58 69 79:5 7 8 9^2 13 80:15 17 81:4^2 5 15 82:8 83:2 5 10 17 84 *title* 2^2 3 10 11 85 *title* 5 8 86:1 2 3 4 5 7 10 12 13 17 87 *title* 88 *title* 3 89:1 2^2 4 6 11 17 18 28^2 29 36 37 46 52 90:4 7 9 10 91:5^2 6^2 11 92 *title* 4 7 8 9^2 93:5 94:13 14 16^2 95:3 7 96:4 5 13^2 97:9 11^2 98:1 9 99:3 5 9 100:5 102:3 9 10 12 13 14 18 19 103:6 9 11 14 15 16

PSALMS 104:5 8 14^2 17 18^2 19 31 105:8 10^2 14 16 17 32 38 39 42 106:1^3 8 13 31^2 32 43 45 107:1^3 8^2 9 15^2 16 21^2 25 31^2 34 36 108:4 13 109:2 4 5^2 19 21^2 22 31 110:4 111:3 8 9 10 112:3 6 9 113:2 115:1^2 18 116:7 8 12 117:2^2 118:1^2 2 3 4 12 21 29^3 119:20 22 28 35 39 42 43 44 45 50 66 71 76 77 78 81 82 83 85 89 91 93 94 95 98 99 102 110 111^2 115 118 120 122^2 123^2 126^2 131^2 152 153 155 160 166 168 172 173 174 176 120:7^2 121:8 122:5 6 8 123:3 125:1

PSALMS 125:2 3 5 126:2 3 127:2^2 128:2 130:5 6^3 7 131:1 3 132:5^2 9 10 12 13^2 14^2 16 17 133:1 3^2 135:3^3 4^2 5 7 12 13 14 136:1^3 2^3 3^2 4^2 5^2 6^2 7^2 8^2 9^2 10^2 11^2 12^2 13^2 14^2 15^2 16^2 17^2 18^2 19^2 20^2 21^3 22^2 23^2 24^2 25^2 26^2 137:3 138:2^3 5 8 139:4 6 13 14 20 140:2 5^2 9 141:5 6 9 142:3 4 6^2 7 143:2 3 8^2 10 11^2 12 145:1 2 21 146:5 6 7 10 147:1^2 8 13 20 148:5 6 13 149:4 150:2

PROV. 1:9 11^2 16 18^2 29 32 2:3 4^2 6 7 18 21 3:2 12 14 26 32 4:2 3

PROV. 4:13 16 17 22 23 5:3 21 6:1 23 26^2 34 7:6 19 23 26 8:6 7 11 32 35 9:4 11 12 14 16 10:13 21 11:15^2 12:6 19^2 13:22 23 16:4^2 12 25 26 17:3^2 13 17 26 18:6 16 19:10^2 18 19 29^2 20:3 16^2 21:8 12 18^2 25 29 22:9 11 18 23 26 23:3 5 7 9 11 13 18 21 27 28 24:2 6 7 16 20 22 27 25:3^2 4 7 13 16 22 27 26:1 3^3 25 27:1 10 13^2 21^2 24^2 26 27^4 28:2 8 21^2 29:5 14 19 30:8 18 21^2 22 23 30 31:4^3 8 10 21^2

ECCL. 1:4 18 2:3 10 12 16^2 17

ECCL. 2:21^2 22 23 24 25 26 3:12 14 17^3 19^2 22^2 4:4 8 9 10^2 14 5:1 2 3 4 7 8 9 13 16 18^2 20 6:2 4 7 8 12^3 7:2 3 5 6 9 10 12 13 18 20 22 8:3 7^2 15 16 9:1 4^2 5^2 6 7 9 10 12 10:1 4 17^2 19 20 11:1 2 6 7 8 9 10 12:13 14

CANT. 1:2 7 2:5 11 14 15 3:10 4:4 5:2 4 6:5 7:6 9 13 8:6 7 8^2 11

ISAIAH 1:2 17 20 29^2 30 2:3 10^2 12 19^2 20 21 22 3:1 7 8 9 10 11 12 14 4:2 5 6^3 5:7 20^4 23

ISAIAH 5:25 6:5^2 8 7:4^2 6 8 13 16 18^2 22^2 23 25^2 8:2 10 11 14^5 17 18^2 19 9:4 5 6 7 12 13 16 17^2 18 21 10:3 4 8 13^2 17^2 22 23 25 26 11:4 9 10 12 16 12:2 5 6 13:3 6 10 11^2 17 14:1 2 9^2 13 21^2 22 23 27 29 31 15:5^3 6^2 8 9^2 16:2 4 7^2 8 9^3 11^2 17:2 18:4 5 19:10 15 20^3 20:3 6 21:6 15 16 17 22:5 11 13 16 23 25 23:1 4 13 14 18^3 24:3 11 14 18 25:1 2 4 8 9^2 10^2 26:1 4^2 5 8 9 11 12^2 19 20 21^2 27:11 28:5^2 6^2

ISAIAH 28:8 10 11 15 16 18 19^3 20 21 22 26 27 29:10 11 14 16 20^2 21^3 30:4 7 8^2 15 16 18 19 31 33^2 31:1 4^4 7^2 9 32:6 10 12^3 14^2 15 17 33:2 5 22 34:2 5 6 8^2 10^2 13 14 16 17^2 35:1 6 8 36:5 9^2 11 14 16 21 37:3 4 8 19 32 35^2 38:1 14 17^2 18^2 21^2 39:1 8 40:2^2 3 5 8 10 16 26 41:7 10^2 13 17 22 28 42:4 6^2 21 22^2 23 24^2 43:1 3^3 4^2 5 7^2 14 21 25 44:3 7 10 14 15^2 17 18 21 22 23^2 45:4 13 18 22 46:9 13 47:1 4 5

ISAIAH 47:7 9^2 10 48:2 8 9^3 11^3 21 49:4 6 8 10 13 19 20 23^2 25 50:1^2 2 7 51:2 3 4^2 6^2 8^2 10 19 52:1 3^2 4 5 8 9 12^2 15 53:2 5^2 8^2 10 11 12 54:1 3 4^3 5 6 7 8 9^2 10 14^2 15 16 55:2^2 4 5^2 7 8 9 10 12 13^2 56:1 4 7^2 11 57:8 12 15 16^3 17 58:4 5 14 59:3 4^2 9^2 10 11^2 12^3 14 17^2 21^2 60:1 2 9 10 12 17^4 19 20 21 61:3^3 7^2 8^2 10 11 62:1^2 4 5 8^2 10 63:3 4 8 17 64:3 4^3 5 7 9 12 65:1 5 8 10^2 11

ISAIAH 65:14^3 15^2 17 18^2 20 22 23^2 66:2 5 8 10^2 12 15 16 18 20 21^2 22 24

JER. 1:6 7 8 12 15 18 19 2:10 11 13 20 22 25 27 28 37 3:2 5 8 10 12^2 14 18 21 22 23 24 25 4:3 6 8^2 13 15 20 22 27 28 29 31^2 5:4 5 7 9 10 11 22 26 29 6:1 4^2 6 11 12 13 16^2 22 25 26^2 27 29 7:5 7 12 16^3 22 29 30 32 33^2 34 8:2 10 11 14 15^2 16 17 21 9:1 2 3^2 4 7^2 9 10^2 12 17^2 18 19 21 24 26 10:2 3^2 5

JER. 10:7 14 16 18 19 21 25 11:7 13 14^4 17^2 20 23 12:3^2 4 6 12 13:7 10 11^5 15 16 17 18 21 22 14:4 7^2 8 11^2 16 17 19^3 20 21 22 15:2^4 4 5 13 14 15 16 17 20 16:3 4^2 5^2 6^2 7^4 9 12 16^2 17 17:3 4^2 6 8 14 16 25 18:18 20^4 22^2 19:5 7^2 20:4 8 10^2 11 12 13 21:2^2 9 10 22:4 6 10^3 11 13 17^4 18^2 20 22 30 23:10^2 11 12 15 18 27 34 36^2 24:5 6^2 7 9 25:5 12 14 15 29^3 31 34 36 38 26:11 14 15^2 16 27:10 14 15 16 19 28:4 13

JER. 28:14, 29:6, 7[2], 8, 9, 10, 11, 13, 26, 28, 32, 30:3, 5, 7, 8, 10, 11, 12, 14[2], 15[2], 16, 17, 21, 31:6, 7[2], 9, 11, 12[4], 13, 15[2], 16, 18, 20[2], 22, 25, 30, 34[2], 35[2], 36, 37, 40, 32:2, 3, 7, 8[2], 15, 17, 19, 25[2], 27, 30[2], 31, 39[2], 42, 44[2], 33:4, 5, 9[2], 11[4], 17, 26, 34:5[2], 7, 11[2], 16[2], 17, 20, 35:6[2], 9, 11[2], 14, 19, 36:7, 31, 37:2, 3, 4, 9, 10, 11, 15, 17, 38:2[2], 4[2], 5, 9[2], 27, 39:16[2], 18[2], 40:4, 10, 16, 41:8, 9, 18, 42:2[3], 5, 10, 11, 18, 20[2], 21, 43:1, 3, 7, 11[3], 44:11, 13, 14, 16, 17, 27[2], 29, 45:3[4], 5[3], 46:5, 10[2]

JER. 46:11, 12, 14, 19, 21, 22, 27, 28[2], 47:3, 48:1, 5[2], 7, 9, 14, 18, 20, 26, 27[3], 31[3], 32, 34, 36[2], 37, 38, 40, 44, 46, 49:3[2], 8, 12, 13, 15, 19, 23, 30, 33, 37, 50:3, 9, 14, 15, 16, 20[2], 24, 25, 27, 29, 31, 38, 39, 44, 51:2, 5, 6, 8[2], 9, 11, 12, 17, 19, 20, 26[3], 29, 33, 36, 37, 46, 48[2], 51, 56, 62, 52:3, 6, 16[2], 34

LAM. 1:5[2], 9, 10, 11[2], 13, 16, 18, 19, 20[2], 22[2], 2:11, 13[2], 14[2], 16, 19[2], 3:12, 25, 26, 27, 31, 33, 39, 48, 4:4, 6, 9[2], 13, 17[3], 18, 19, 5:4, 17[2], 19, 20

EZEKIEL 1:10, 13, 18

EZEKIEL 1:20, 21, 2:1, 2, 7, 3:3, 5, 7[2], 26, 27, 4:3, 5, 6, 14, 15, 17, 5:4, 6, 16, 6:9, 11[2], 7:6, 8, 11, 12, 13[2], 14, 16, 20, 21[2], 22, 23, 8:12, 14, 17, 9:4, 9, 10, 10:10, 13, 17, 11:5, 12, 21, 12:2, 3, 4, 6[2], 7, 24, 25[2], 27, 13:5, 16, 19[2], 23, 14:7, 21, 15:4[2], 5[2], 6, 16:4, 14[2], 19, 21, 33, 52, 56, 59, 61, 63, 17:17, 20, 18:17, 18, 24, 26, 31, 32, 19:1, 11, 14, 20:6, 9, 14, 16, 22, 28[2], 31, 39, 40, 42, 43, 44, 21:7, 12, 15, 21, 22, 28, 32[2], 22:10, 30[2], 23:8, 10, 14, 20, 21, 28, 34, 37, 39, 40[2], 46, 24:7, 9, 17

EZEKIEL 24:23, 25:4, 5[2], 6, 7, 15, 26:5[5], 7, 17, 19, 21, 27:2, 3, 5, 15, 18, 20, 31[2], 32, 28:10, 23, 29:3, 5, 15, 18[2], 19, 20[2], 30:3, 9, 18, 31:7, 11, 14[2], 15[3], 32:2, 10[2], 11, 16[3], 18, 32, 33:2, 11, 12[2], 18[2], 17, 24, 28, 31, 32, 34:8, 10[2], 11, 17, 19, 29, 36:5, 8, 9[2], 18[2], 21, 22[2], 24, 29, 31[2], 32[2], 37[2], 37:10, 16[4], 25[2], 26, 28, 38:7, 19, 21, 39:5, 10, 17, 19, 23, 25, 29, 40:4, 17, 42, 45, 46, 41:6, 7, 9, 24[2], 42:3[2], 5, 6, 8, 13, 14[2], 43:7, 9, 19, 22, 24, 25, 44:3, 8, 11, 14[2], 22, 25[6], 28, 45:1, 2[2], 4[3], 5[3], 6, 7, 14, 15[4]

EZEKIEL 45:16, 17, 20[2], 22[3], 23, 24[3], 46:5[2], 7[3], 14, 15, 17, 47:1, 5, 9, 12[3], 14, 22, 48:1[2], 2, 3, 4, 5, 6, 7, 10[2], 11, 14, 15[3], 18, 21[2], 22, 23, 29

DANIEL 1:7, 10, 17, 2:2, 4, 9[2], 12, 20[2], 23, 29, 30[3], 35, 37, 44, 3:9, 4:12, 18, 19, 21, 22, 30[2], 34, 36, 5:10, 19, 6:6, 7, 21, 23, 26[2], 7:12, 18[2], 28, 8:8, 15, 17, 19, 22, 26[3], 9:12, 14[2], 16[2], 17, 18[3], 19[2], 20, 23, 24, 26, 27[2], 10:7, 8, 11, 12[2], 14[2], 17[3], 19, 11:4[2], 6, 13, 17, 18, 23, 24, 25, 27, 30, 35, 36, 37, 39, 12:1, 3, 7[2], 9, 13

HOSEA 1:2, 4, 6, 9

HOSEA 1:11, 2:2, 4, 5[2], 7, 8[2], 15, 17, 18, 19, 3:2[2], 3[3], 4, 4:1, 4, 6, 9, 10, 12, 14, 16, 5:1, 3, 4, 7, 14, 6:1, 4, 6, 9[2], 11, 7:1, 6, 10, 13, 14, 16, 8:6, 7, 9, 10, 12, 13, 9:1[2], 4[2], 6[2], 7, 11, 15[2], 10:3, 5[2], 6, 7, 12, 11:9, 12:12[2], 13:4, 13, 16, 14:1, 3, 4, 9

JOEL 1:5, 6, 8, 10, 11[2], 13, 15[2], 17, 19, 20, 2:1[2], 11[3], 13, 18, 21, 22[2], 23[2], 32, 3:1, 2[2], 3[3], 8, 12, 13[3], 14, 19, 20, 21[2]

AMOS 1:3[2], 6[2], 9[2], 11[3], 13[2], 2:1[2], 4[2], 6[4], 11[2], 3:2, 5, 10, 4:5, 13, 5:3, 4, 5, 8, 12, 13, 17

AMOS 5:18, 23, 6:6, 10, 11, 12, 7:2, 3, 5, 6, 11, 13, 8:6[2], 8, 11, 13, 9:4[2], 6, 9

OBADIAH 10[2], 15, 16, 18[2]

JONAH 1:2, 7, 8, 10, 11, 12[2], 13, 14[2], 2:3, 6, 3:6, 4:2, 3[2], 8, 9, 10

MICAH 1:3, 5[2], 7, 9[2], 12[2], 13, 16[2], 2:4, 9, 10, 3:1, 3, 7, 11[3], 12, 4:2, 4, 5[2], 7, 9, 10, 12, 13, 5:4, 7[2], 6:2, 4, 7[2], 12, 16, 7:1, 2, 3, 6, 7, 9, 13, 18

NAHUM 1:2, 10, 13, 14, 15, 2:2[2], 9, 12[2], 3:7, 10, 14, 19

HABAK. 1:3, 4, 5, 6, 9, 10, 12[2], 2:3[3], 7, 8, 11, 13, 14, 16, 17[2], 3:13[2]

ZEPH. 1:6, 7[2], 11, 18, 2:4, 6[2], 7[2], 10, 11, 14, 15, 3:8[2], 9, 11[2], 13, 18, 20

HAGGAI 1:4, 9, 11, 2:4, 6, 16, 23

ZECH. 1:5, 14[2], 15, 2:4, 5, 6, 8[2], 9, 10, 13, 3:8[2], 9, 4:10[2], 5:3, 9, 6:14, 7:6[2], 14, 8:2[2], 4, 10[4], 12, 14, 17, 23, 9:5, 7, 8, 11, 18, 16, 17, 10:2, 3, 6[2], 8[2], 10, 11:2[2], 3[2], 5, 6, 12, 16, 12:1, 3, 10[4], 13:1[2], 3, 5, 14:2, 5

MALACHI 1:3, 4, 8, 10[2], 11[2], 14, 2:1, 5, 7[2], 11, 16[2], 3:2, 6, 9, 11, 12, 16, 4:1, 3, 4

MATT. 1:20, 21, 2:2, 5, 6, 8, 13, 18, 20, 3:2, 3, 8, 9, 15

MATT. 4:6, 10, 17, 18, 5:3, 4, 5, 6, 7, 8, 9, 10[2], 11, 12[2], 13, 18, 20, 29[2], 30[2], 32, 34, 35[2], 37, 38[2], 41, 45, 46, 6:5, 7[2], 8, 13[2], 14, 16, 19, 20, 21, 24, 25[2], 26, 28, 32[2], 34[3], 7:2, 8, 12, 13, 29, 8:4, 9, 9:5, 13, 16, 21, 24, 10:10[2], 15[2], 17, 18[2], 19, 20, 22, 23, 25, 26, 29, 35, 39, 11:3, 8, 9, 10, 13, 14, 18, 21, 22[2], 23, 24[2], 26, 29, 30, 12:4[3], 8, 33, 34, 37, 40, 42, 50, 13:12, 15, 16[2], 17, 21[2], 44, 14:3[2], 4[2], 9, 24, 26, 15:2, 4, 9, 19, 23, 16:2, 3, 17, 23, 25[2], 26[2], 27, 17:4[4], 15[2], 20, 27, 18:6

MATT. 18:7, 8, 9, 10, 11, 19, 20, 19:3[2], 5, 9, 12[2], 14, 22, 24[2], 29, 20:1, 2, 13, 15, 16, 23, 28, 21:19, 26, 32, 46, 22:2, 14, 16[2], 28, 30, 23:3, 4, 5, 8, 9, 10, 13[2], 14[2], 15, 17, 19, 23, 25, 27, 39, 24:1, 5, 6, 7, 9, 14, 21, 22, 24, 27, 28, 38, 42, 44, 50, 25:8, 9[2], 13, 14, 29, 34, 35, 41, 42, 26:9[2], 10, 11, 12[2], 13, 15, 17, 24, 28[3], 31, 43, 52, 55, 73, 27:6, 10, 18[2], 19, 43, 47, 28:2, 4, 5, 6

MARK 1:4, 16, 22, 27, 37, 38, 44[2], 2:4, 15, 26, 27[2], 3:5, 10[2], 21, 32, 35, 4:17[2], 22, 25, 28, 5:8

MARK 5:9, 19, 20, 28, 42, 6:8, 11[3], 14, 17[3], 18[2], 20, 26[2], 31, 36, 48, 50, 52[2], 7:3, 7, 8, 10, 12, 21, 25, 27, 29, 8:3, 33, 35[2], 36, 37, 9:5[4], 6[2], 31, 34, 39, 40, 41, 42, 43, 45, 47, 49, 10:2, 5, 7, 14, 22, 24, 25[2], 27, 29, 35, 36, 40, 45[2], 11:13, 14, 18, 23, 32, 12:1, 12, 14[2], 23, 25, 32, 36, 40, 44, 13:6, 7, 8, 9[3], 11, 13, 16, 19, 20, 22, 33, 34, 35, 14:5[2], 7, 9, 15, 21, 24, 27, 40, 55, 56, 70, 15:10[2], 43, 16:4, 8[2]

LUKE 1:13, 15, 17, 18, 21, 22, 30, 33, 37, 44[2], 45, 48[2], 49, 55, 63, 68, 69

LUKE 1:76, 2:7, 10, 11, 20, 21, 25, 27, 30, 34[2], 38, 3:3, 8, 19[2], 4:6, 8, 10, 13, 16, 32, 36, 38, 41, 43, 5:4, 8, 9, 14[2], 39, 6:4, 19, 20, 21[2], 22, 23[3], 24, 25[2], 26, 28, 32[2], 33, 34, 35[2], 38, 43, 44[2], 45, 48, 7:4, 5, 6, 8, 19, 20, 24, 25, 26, 28, 33, 39, 44, 47, 8:13, 17, 18, 19, 25, 29[2], 37, 40[2], 42, 46, 47, 9:3, 5, 12, 13, 14, 24[2], 25, 26, 33[4], 38, 44, 48, 51[2], 52, 56, 62, 10:7, 12[2], 13, 14[2], 21, 24, 11:4, 6, 10, 11, 30, 31, 32, 42, 43, 44, 46, 47, 48, 52, 54, 12:2, 6, 12, 15, 19, 21, 22[2]

LUKE 12:24, 26, 30, 32, 34, 36, 40, 46, 48, 52, 13:17, 24, 31, 33, 14:11, 14[2], 17, 24, 28, 35[2], 15:1, 6, 9, 24, 30, 32, 16:2, 3, 8, 13, 15, 17, 24, 28, 17:2, 21, 24, 18:4, 14, 16, 23, 25[3], 29, 32, 19:3, 4, 5, 10, 12, 21, 26, 37, 43, 48, 20:6, 9, 19, 22, 33, 36, 38[2], 48, 21:4, 6, 8, 9, 12, 13, 15, 17, 22, 23, 26[3], 28, 35, 38, 22:2, 16, 18, 19, 20, 27, 32, 37[2], 45, 59, 71, 23:8, 12, 15, 17, 19[2], 25, 28[3], 29, 31, 34, 41, 51, 24:29, 39, 41

JOHN 1:7, 15, 16, 17, 30, 39, 2:25, 3:2, 16, 17, 20, 24, 34[2]

JOHN 4:8, 9, 18, 22, 23, 35, 39, 42, 44, 45, 47, 5:3, 4, 10, 13, 19, 20, 21, 22, 26, 28, 35, 36, 38, 39, 46[2], 6:6, 7, 24, 27[3], 83, 38, 51[2], 55, 58, 64, 71, 7:1, 4, 5, 8, 12, 13, 29, 39, 52, 8:14, 16, 20, 24, 29, 35, 42, 44, 9:21, 22, 29, 39, 10:4, 5, 10, 11, 13, 15, 19, 32, 33[2], 11:4, 15, 28, 39, 47, 50[2], 51, 52, 53, 56, 12:5, 6, 8, 9, 18[2], 27, 30, 34, 35, 43, 47, 49, 13:11, 13, 15, 28, 29, 37, 38, 14:2, 3, 11, 16, 17, 28, 30, 15:5, 13, 15[2], 21, 22, 16:7[2], 13, 14, 21, 26, 27, 17:8, 9[4], 19

JOHN 17:20[2], 24, 18:2, 13, 14, 18, 31, 37, 19:6, 20, 24[2], 31, 36, 38, 42, 20:9, 17, 19, 21:6, 7, 8, 11

ACTS 1:4, 5, 7, 17, 20, 2:15, 25[2], 34, 38, 39, 3:10, 22, 4:3, 12, 16, 20, 21[2], 22, 27, 28, 34, 5:8[2], 26, 31, 36, 38, 41, 6:14, 7:5, 16, 21, 25, 33, 40[2], 46, 8:3, 7, 15, 16, 21, 23, 24, 27, 33, 9:5, 11[2], 15, 16[2], 21, 10:4, 5, 14, 17, 20, 22, 24, 28, 29[2], 38, 46, 11:8, 13, 24, 25, 12:5, 14, 19, 13:2, 7, 8, 11, 15, 27, 36, 41, 47[2], 14:26, 15:6, 14, 21, 26, 28, 31, 16:3, 4, 10, 21, 28, 29, 17:15, 16, 20, 21

ACTS 17:23, 26, 28[2], 18:3, 10[2], 15, 17, 18, 28, 19:8, 22, 24[2], 32, 37, 40[2], 20:1, 3, 5, 10, 13, 16[3], 27, 29, 38, 21:3, 13[2], 22, 26, 29, 34, 35, 36, 22:5, 10, 11, 15, 18, 21, 22, 25, 26, 23:3, 5, 8, 11, 17, 21[3], 30, 24:5, 10, 11, 21, 24, 25[2], 26, 25:3, 8, 11, 16, 27, 26:1[2], 2, 6, 7, 14, 16[2], 20, 21, 24, 26[3], 27:22, 23, 25, 29, 34[3], 28:2, 20[3], 22, 27

ROMANS 1:5[2], 8, 9, 11, 16[2], 17, 18, 19, 20, 25, 26[2], 2:1[2], 7, 11, 12, 13, 14, 24, 25, 26, 28, 3:3, 6, 7, 9, 20, 22, 23, 25, 4:2, 3[2], 5, 9[2], 13, 14, 15

ROMANS 4:22, 23, 24, 25[2], 5:6[2], 7[3], 8, 10, 12, 13, 15, 16, 17, 19, 6:5, 7, 10, 14[2], 19, 20, 21, 23, 7:1, 2, 5, 7, 8, 9, 11, 14, 15[2], 18[2], 19, 22, 8:2[2], 3[2], 5, 6, 7, 13, 14, 15, 18, 19[2], 20, 22, 23, 24[3], 25[2], 26[3], 27, 28, 29, 31, 32, 34, 36[2], 38, 9:3[2], 5, 6, 8, 9, 11, 15, 17[2], 19, 28, 32, 10:1, 2, 3, 4[2], 5, 10, 11, 12[2], 13, 16, 11:1, 7, 11, 13, 15, 16, 21, 23, 24, 25, 27, 28[2], 29, 30, 32, 34, 36[2], 12:3, 4, 17, 19, 20, 13:1, 3, 4[4], 5[2], 6[3], 8, 9, 11, 14, 14:2, 3, 4, 6, 7, 8, 9

ROMANS 14:10, 11, 15, 17, 18, 19, 20[2], 23, 15:2, 3, 4[2], 8, 9[2], 18, 22, 24, 26[2], 27, 30[3], 31, 16:2, 4, 18, 19, 26, 27

1 COR. 1:4, 7, 11, 13, 17, 18, 19, 21, 22, 26, 2:2, 8, 9, 10, 11, 14, 16, 3:2, 3[2], 4, 9, 11, 13, 17, 19[2], 21, 4:4, 6[2], 7, 9[2], 10, 15, 17, 20, 5:3, 5, 7[2], 10, 12, 6:12, 13[5], 16, 20, 7:1, 5, 7, 8, 9, 14, 16, 21, 22, 26[2], 31, 32, 33, 34[2], 35[2], 8:5, 7, 8, 9, 10, 9:2, 9[2], 10[2], 15[2], 16[2], 17, 19, 23, 25, 10:4, 5, 11[2], 17[2], 23[2], 25, 26, 27, 28, 29, 30[3], 11:5, 6, 7, 8, 9[2], 10

FOR—*continued.*

1 COR.	1 COR.	2 COR.	2 COR.	GAL.	EPHES.	PHIL.	COLOS.	1 THESS.	1 TIM.	PHILE.	HEB.	HEB.	HEB.	1 PETER	2 PETER	JUDE	REV.
11:12	15:34	4:16	9:12	2:5	1:16	1:21	3:6	5:10	5:8^{2}	1:7	6:18^{2}	10:10	13:9	1:23	2:21^{2}	11^{2}	15:4^{3}
15^{2}	41	17^{3}	13^{2}	6	2:4	23	20	13	10	9	20^{2}	12^{2}	11^{2}	24	3:4	13	7
17^{2}	52	18	14^{2}	8	8	24	24	15	11	10	7:1^{2}	14^{2}	14	25	5	21	16:6^{2}
18	53	5:1	15	12	10	25	25	18	15	15^{3}	10	15	16	2:13	12	REV.	10
19	16:1	2	10:3	16	14	26	4:3^{2}	25	18	22	11	18	17^{4}	14^{2}	13	1:3	14
21	5	4^{2}	4	18	15	27	8		23		12	20	18^{2}	15	14	6	21
23	7	5	8^{3}	19	18	29^{2}	12	2 THESS.	6:7	HEB.	13	23	21	16	18	9^{2}	17:14
24	9	7	10	20	22	2:13	13^{2}	1:3	10	1:5	14	26^{2}	22	19^{2}	1 JOHN	18	17
26	10	10	12	21	3:1^{2}	18		4	19	8	15	27		20^{3}	1:2	2:3	18:3
29	11^{2}	12	14^{2}	3:6	13	20^{2}	1 THESS.	5		14	17^{2}	30	JAMES	21^{2}	2:2^{3}	3:2	5
30	17	13^{2}	18	10^{2}	14	21	1:2	11	2 TIM.	2:2	18^{2}	34	1:6	25	12	4	7
31	18	14^{2}	11:2^{2}	11	4:12^{3}	26	5^{2}	2:3	1:7	5	19	36	7	3:5	16	8	8
33		15^{2}	4	13^{2}	25	27	8	7	12^{2}	8	21^{2}	37	11	9^{2}	17	4:9	9
12:8	2 COR.	20	5	18	32	30	9	11	16	9^{2}	25	11:1	12	10	19	10	10^{2}
12	1:5	21^{2}	9	21	5:2^{2}	3:1	10	13	2:5	10^{2}	26	2	13	12	3:2	11^{2}	11
13	6^{2}	6:2	13	26	5	3	2:1	3:1	10	11	27^{3}	5	20	14	4	5:9	15
14	8	13	14	27	6	7	3	2	11	16	28^{2}	6	23	17^{3}	8^{2}	13	17
24	11^{2}	14	19	28	8	8^{2}	5	5	16	17	8:3	8	24	18^{3}	9	14	19
25	12	16	20	4:12	9	12	9^{2}	7^{2}	21	18	4	10^{2}	2:2	4:1^{2}	11	6:6^{2}	20
13:9	13	7:3	31	15	12	14	13	8	3:2	3:3	5	14	10	6^{2}	16^{2}	9^{2}	23^{2}
12	19	5	12:1	20	13	17	14^{2}	10	6	4	7^{2}	16^{2}	11	8	20	11	19:2^{2}
14:2^{2}	20	8^{3}	4	22	20	18	16	11	9	5	8	25	13	11	4:7	17	3
5	23	9	6^{2}	24	23	20^{2}	17		16^{4}	14	10	26	23	14^{2}	8	7:12	6
8	24^{2}	10	8	25	25	4:1	19	1 TIM.	4:3	16	11	27	26	17	10	17	7
9	2:2	11	9^{2}	27^{2}	29	6	20	1:9^{7}	6	4:2	12	32	3:2	5:2	20	8:12	8
14	4	12^{3}	10^{2}	30	30	11	3:3	10^{5}	8	3	9:2	40	7	5	5:3	9:15^{2}	10
17	9	13	11^{2}	5:3	31	16	4	12	10	4	7^{2}	12:2	16	7^{2}	4	19^{2}	20:4^{2}
21	10^{2}	14	13	5^{2}	6:1	20	5	16^{2}	11^{2}	8	9	3	4:14^{2}	11	7	10:6	10
22^{3}	11	8:3	14^{4}	6	12		8	17	15	10	12	6	15	2 PETER	9	11:2	11
31	15	9^{2}	15	13^{2}	18	COLOS.	9^{4}	2:1	18	12	13	7	5:1	1:8	16^{2}	15	21:1
33	16	10^{2}	19	14	19	1:3	4:2	2^{2}	TITUS	15	15^{2}	10^{3}	3	10	2 JOHN	12:4	2
34	17	12	20	17	20	5^{2}	3	3	1:5	5:1^{3}	16^{2}	11	7^{2}	11	2^{2}	10	4
35^{2}	3:6	13	13:4^{2}	6:3	22	7	7	5	7	2	17	13	8	16	7	12	5
15:3^{2}	7	14^{2}	8^{2}	5		9^{2}	9	6	10	3^{3}	19	16	10	17	11	14	22
9	9	16	9	7	PHIL.	16	14	13	11	6	24^{2}	17^{2}	14	21	3 JOHN	13:18	23
16	10	17		8		19	15	3:5	2:11	12^{2}	26	18	16	2:4	3	14:4	25
21	11	21	GAL.	9	1:4	24^{2}	16	13	13	13^{2}	28	20	1 PETER	8	7	5	22:2
22	14	9:1^{2}	1:4	12	5	25	5:2	4:4	14	6:4^{2}	10:1	25	1:4	16	JUDE	7	5^{2}
25	4:5^{2}	2^{2}	5	13	7	2:1^{4}	3	5	3:3	7^{2}	2	29	6	17	3^{2}	11	9
27	6	7	10^{2}	15	8	5	7	8	9	10	4	13:2	13	18	4	15^{3}	10
29^{2}	11^{2}	9	12	17	17	9	8	10	12	13	6	5	16	19	7	18	15
32	15^{2}	10	13		19	3:3	9	5:4	14	16^{2}	8	8	20	20		15:1	18

from

575

GEN.	GEN.	EXOD.	EXOD.	LEVIT.	NUM.	NUM.	NUM.	DEU.	DEU.	JOSH.	JUD.	1 SAM.	1 SAM.	2 SAM.	1 KINGS	2 KINGS	1 CHRON.
1:4	24:50	2:15	23:31^{2}	16:30	5:13	21:19^{2}	33:49	12:10	33:2^{4}	15:7	9:20^{3}	6:5	25:39^{2}	17:11	13:5	13:23	18:8^{2}
6	62	3:5	25:15	17:4	19	20	52	21	7	9	35	7	26:12^{2}	18:13	12	14:13	11^{6}
7	25:6	4:3	22^{2}	9	31	24	55	29	16	10	36	20	19	16	14	24	19:7
14	18	5:4	26:4	10	6:3	28	34:3	30	22	46	48	7:3	28:15	19:7	21	25	20:2
18	23	5	28	18:29	4	22:5	4^{2}	32	27	16:1^{2}	10:11^{4}	14^{2}	16	24	26	27	21:2
2:2	29	19	27:21	19:8	7:89	16	5	13:5^{2}	34:1	2	16	16	23	31	33	15:9	22
3	26:16	20	28:1	20:3	8:6	33^{2}	7	7^{2}		7	11:3	9:2	30:17	20:2^{2}	34	14	26
6	22	6:6	28	4	14	23:7	8	10^{2}	JOSH.	8	13	25	25	20	14:7	16	22:9
10	23	7	42	5	16	9^{2}	10	13	1:4	17:7	16	10:2	31:1	21	8	18	23:3
22	26	26	29:28^{2}	6	19	13^{2}	11	17	7	18:4	22^{2}	3	12	22	10	24	24
3:8	27	27	30:14	18	24	27	35:4	24	2:13	12	23	5		21:5	15:5	28	27
23	31	7:5	33	24	25	24:11	5	15:7	23	13	24	9	2 SAM.	10	13	16:3	27:23
4:1	27:9	8:8^{2}	38	25	9:13	24	8^{2}	12	3:1	14	29	23	1:1	12^{2}	19	6	
10	30^{2}	9	31:14	26	17	25:4	12	13	3	15	31	12:2	2	22:3	16:17	11^{2}	2 CHRON.
11^{2}	39	11^{4}	32:12^{2}	21:7	21	7	36:3^{2}	16	9	17	33	20	3	4	18:12^{2}	12	1:4
14	40	12	15	22:2	10:9	8	4	18	13^{2}	19:12	12:9	13:5	4	14	19:17	14^{2}	13^{2}
16	45^{2}	29^{4}	27	3	11	11	7	16:9	14	13	13:5	8	22^{2}	17	21	17^{2}	4:2
6:7	28:2	30	33:5	4	33	26:2	9	17:7	16^{2}	29	7	11	2:12	18^{2}	20:33	18	5:9
17	6	31^{3}	7	25	11:31^{2}	4		11	4:23^{2}	33^{2}	20	15	19	22	34	17:7	6:21^{2}
7:4	10	9:15	16	27	35	62	DEU.	12	5:1	34	15:13	14:17	21	23	36^{2}	8	23
23	29:3	33	34:18	23:15^{2}	12:10	27:4	1:2	15	9	20:3	14	21	22	24	41	9	25
8:2	8	10:5	29^{2}	29	14	30:14	19	20	15	6	16:12	31	26	44	21:21	13	26
3	10	6	35:5	30	15	31:14	2:8^{3}	18:3^{2}	6:18	22:9	17^{2}	46	27	49^{2}	22:24	21	27
7	30:2	11	20	32	16	42	12	6	7:2	16	19	15:2	30	23:11	33	22	30
8^{2}	32	17	36:4	24:3	13:3	32:7	14^{2}	12	5	17	20	6^{2}	3:10^{2}	17	43	24^{5}	32
11	31:13	18	6	8	21	8	15	15	9	18	17:2	7	15^{2}	24:2		27	33^{2}
13	16	23	11	25:41	23	11	16	18	12	23	3	11	22	4	2 KINGS	28	35
21	27	28	22	50	24	15	22	19:2	13	25	8	15	26^{2}	15	1:4	33	39^{2}
9:10	31	11:5	33	26:36	25	21	36^{2}	13	19	29	18:2^{3}	23	28	21	6	18:6	7:1
24	40	8	38:26	27:3	14:9	33:3	3:4	19	26	32^{2}	7	26	4:11	25	10^{2}	8	8
10:19	49	12:5^{2}	39:21	5	13	5	8	20:15	8:4	23:1	11	28	5:9		12^{2}	14	14^{2}
30	32:11^{2}	15^{2}	40:36	6	19	6	12	21:9	6	4	22	16:1	13	1 KINGS	14	16^{2}	8:15
11:2	33:18	19		7	29	7	16	13	7	5^{2}	28	13	25	1:45	2:1	17	9:2
6	35:1	29	LEVIT.	17	43	8	17	21	16	9	19:2	14^{2}	6:2^{2}	53	3	19:8	10
8	7	31	2:9	18	15:23	9	4:2	22:1	29	13^{2}	16	15	12	2:13	5	20:14^{3}	26
9	13	37	13		30	10	3	4	9:6	15	18^{2}	16	7:1	27	9	18	10:2
31	16	41	4:8	NUM.	16:9	11	9	8	8	16	30	22^{2}	8^{2}	31^{2}	10	21:16	11:4
12:1	36:6	42	10	1:3	15	13	26	21	9	24:3	20:1	17:15	11	33	13	23:6	14
8	37:25	13:3^{2}	13	18	21	14	29	22	22	8	13	24	15^{2}	40	14	8	12:12
13:3	38:14	10	19	20	24	15	32	24	23	12	31	26	23	41	21	12	13:19
9	17	14^{2}	31	22	26	16	34	23:9	24	17	32	30	8:4	3:20	23	17	15:8
11	19	20	35	24	27	17	38	13	10:6	18	21:6	33	13	4:12	25^{2}	22	16
14^{2}	20	22	5:2	26	33	18	48	14	7		8	46	9:5	21	3:26	26	16:3
17	39:5	14:5	3	28	35	19	5:6	15	9	JUD.	19	53	10:14	24	4:5	30	9
14:23	9	19	4	30	45	20	6:12	24:7	11^{2}	1:11	24	57	11:2^{2}	25	27	24:7	18:23
15:18	40:19^{2}	25	6	32	46^{2}	21	15	25:9	29	14		18:6	4	33	42	15	31
16:2	41:42	15:22	8	34	17:5	22	19	19^{2}	31	36^{2}	RUTH	9	8	34	5:19	20	32
6	46	16:1	7:20	36	9	23	23	26:15^{2}	34	2:1	1:6	10	10	5:9	21	25:5	19:2
8	42:2	4	21	38	10	24	7:4	28:14	36	3	13	12	15	6:24	22		4
17:14	7	6	25	40	18:6	25	8	21	41	19^{2}	16	13	20	7:7	24	1 CHRON.	20:2
22	24^{2}	32	27	42	9	26	15	24	11:17	21	2:4	19:8	21	9	26	2:23	10
18:2	43:34	17:1	34^{2}	45	16	27	20	31	21^{6}	3:3	7	9	24	23	27	4:10	32
3	44:28	14	8:28	3:12	26	28	24	35	23	19^{2}	8	20:1	12:10	8:35	6:32	5:9	21:8
16^{2}	29	16	9:22	15	30	29	8:14	49^{2}	12:1	20	4:10^{2}	2	17	51	8:14	23	10^{2}
22	45:1	18:4	24	22	32	30	9:4^{2}	57	2^{3}	21		9	20	53	20	9:25	12
25^{2}	46:5	10	10:2	28	19:13	31	5	63	3^{2}	27	1 SAM.	15^{2}	30	54^{2}	22	10:1	22:11^{2}
19:4	34	13	4	34	20	32	7	64	7	4:11	1:14	34	13:4	64	9:2	11:8	23:10
24	47:10	14	7	39	20:6	33	12	29:11	13:3	13	2:8	21:4	9^{2}	9:6	8	13	20
26	18	19:2	12:7	40	9	34	14	18	4	14	19	5	13	12	10:21	13:5^{2}	24:5
20:1	21	14	13:12	43	14	35	15	20	5	5:5^{2}	30	6	17	28	29^{2}	14:14	23
6	48:7	20:22	41	4:2	21	36	23	22	6^{2}	11	33	15	32	10:3	31	16	25
13	12	21:14	58	3	22	37	24	30:3	9	20	3:17^{2}	23:13	14:14	11^{2}	33^{2}	16:20^{2}	25:5
22:12	16	22	14:7	13	28	41	10:5	4^{2}	16	6:8	18	28	18	11:9	11:2^{2}	23	12
23:3	17	22:12	19	18	21:4	42	6	11	26^{2}	9	20	29	19	11	11	35	13
6	49:9	23:7	15:3	23	7	43	7^{2}	31:3	30	11	4:4	24:1	25	23	19	17:5^{2}	14
24:5	10^{2}	15	16	30	11	44	11:10	17	14:7	13	18	13	32	12:2	12:18	7^{2}	23
7^{2}	24	25	31	35	12	45	12	29	15	14	21	25:10	15:12^{2}	15	13:5	8	27
8	26	28	32	39	13	46	17	32:20	15:2^{2}	7:3	22	26^{2}	14	24	6	13^{2}	26:18
41^{2}	32	29	16:12	43	16	47	23	26	4	8:13	5:1	33^{2}	18	25	11	21	19
46	50:25	30	19	47	18	48	24^{2}	42	5	22	6:3	34	28	13:4	17	18:4	20

2 CHRON.
26:21, 28:8, 12, 29:6, 10, 30:5, 6, 8, 9, 10, 31:16, 17, 32:22[2], 23, 33:8, 34:3, 33, 35:11, 15, 18, 21, 22[2], 36:12, 13, 20

EZRA
1:11, 2:59, 62, 3:6, 7, 8, 13, 4:12, 14, 21, 6:6, 11, 21, 7:6, 9, 8:1, 31[2], 9:1, 5, 8, 11, 10:6, 8, 11[2], 14

NEH.
1:9, 3:15, 20, 21, 24, 25, 28, 4:5, 12, 16, 19, 21, 5:13[2], 14[2], 17, 6:9, 7:61, 64, 8:3, 18, 9:2, 13, 15, 19, 20, 27, 28, 35, 10:28, 11:30, 31, 12:28, 29, 38, 39, 13:3, 21, 28, 30

ESTHER
1:1, 7, 19, 2:6, 3:7[2], 8, 10, 4:4, 14, 7:7, 8:2, 9, 15, 9:16, 22[3], 28[2]

JOB
1:7[2], 12, 16, 19, 2:2[3], 7[2], 11, 3:4, 10, 11, 17, 19, 4:2, 13, 20, 5:4, 15[3], 20[2], 21, 6:13, 14, 23[2], 7:19, 8:18, 9:34, 10:14, 19, 13:20, 21, 14:6, 11, 15:18, 17:4, 18:17, 18, 19:9, 13[2], 20:24, 29, 21:9, 14, 16, 22:6, 7, 17, 18, 22, 23, 23:7, 12, 17, 24:1, 9, 10, 12, 26:4, 5, 27:5, 28:4[2], 11, 21[2], 28, 30:5, 10, 31:2[2], 16, 18[2], 22[2], 23, 33:17[2], 18[2], 24, 28, 30, 34:10[2], 27, 35:3, 36:3, 7, 10, 38:15, 39:22, 29, 42:2

PSALMS
2:3, 12, 3 *title*, 6:8, 7:1, 9:13, 12:1, 5, 7, 13:1, 14:2, 17:2, 4, 7, 9[2], 13, 14[2], 18 *title*, 3, 16, 17[2], 21, 22, 43, 18:48[2], 19:6[2], 12, 13[2], 20:2, 6, 21:10[2], 22:1[2], 10[2], 11, 19, 20[2], 21[2], 24, 24:5[2], 27:9, 30:3, 31:11, 15[2], 20[2], 22, 32:7, 33:13, 14, 19, 34:4, 13[2], 14, 16, 35:10[2], 17[2], 22, 37:8, 27, 40, 38:9, 10, 11, 21, 39:2, 8, 10, 40:10, 11, 41:13, 42:6[2], 43:1, 44:7, 10, 18, 49:14, 15, 50:1, 4, 51:2[2], 9, 11[2], 14, 53:2, 55:1, 8, 11, 12, 18, 56:13[2], 57:3[2], 58:3, 59 *title*, 1[2], 2[2], 60:11, 61:2, 3, 62:1, 4, 5, 64:1, 2[2], 66:20, 68:20, 22[2], 26, 69:5, 14, 17, 71:5, 6, 12, 17, 20, 72:8[2], 14, 73:27[2], 75:6[3], 76:8, 78:4, 23, 30, 42, 50, 70, 71, 80:14, 18, 81:6[2], 83:4, 84:7, 11, 85:3, 11, 86:13

PSALMS
88:5, 8, 14, 15, 18, 89:33, 48, 90:2, 91:3[2], 93:2, 94:13, 96:2, 101:4, 8, 102:2, 19[2], 103:4, 12[2], 17, 104:13, 21, 105:13[2], 106:10[2], 47, 48, 107:2, 3[4], 20, 41, 108:12, 109:15, 17, 20, 31, 110:3, 113:2, 3, 114:1, 115:18, 116:8[3], 119:10, 19, 21, 22, 29, 37, 51, 101, 102, 110, 115, 118, 134, 150, 155, 157, 160, 120:2[2], 121:1, 2, 7, 8, 125:2, 129:1, 2, 130:8, 131:3, 132:11, 135:7, 136:11, 24, 139:7[2], 12, 15, 19, 140:1[2], 4[2], 9, 142:6, 143:7, 9, 144:7[2], 10, 11, 148:1, 7

PROV.
1:15, 33, 2:12, 16[2], 22, 3:7, 21, 26, 27, 4:5, 15, 21, 24[2], 27, 5:7, 8, 6:5[2], 24[2], 7:5[2], 8:23[2], 10:2, 11:4, 13:14, 19, 14:7, 14, 16, 27, 15:24, 29, 16:1, 6, 17, 17:13, 19:4, 7, 14, 27, 20:3, 9, 21:23, 22:5, 6, 15, 27, 23:4, 13, 14, 24:18, 25:4, 5, 17, 25, 27:22, 28:9, 29:21, 26, 30:8, 12, 14[2], 31:14

ECCL.
1:7, 2:10[2], 24, 3:5, 11, 14, 7:18, 23, 26, 8:10, 10:5, 11:10[2], 12:11

CANT.
3:4, 4:1, 2, 8[6], 15, 5:7, 6:5[2], 6, 8:5

ISAIAH
1:6, 15, 16, 2:3, 6, 22, 3:1, 4:4, 6[3], 5:23, 26[2], 6:6, 7:17[2], 8:17[2], 18, 9:7, 14, 10:2[2], 3, 27[2], 11:11[8], 12, 16, 13:5[2], 6, 20, 14:3[3], 9[2], 12, 22, 25[2], 31, 15:1, 4, 16:1, 17:1, 3[2], 18:2, 7[2], 19:5, 20:2[2], 6, 21:1[2], 15[4], 22:3, 4, 14, 19[2], 24, 23:1, 24:14, 16, 18[2], 25:4[2], 8[2], 27:12, 28:9[2], 19, 22, 29, 29:13, 15, 30:6, 11, 14, 27, 31:6, 8, 32:2[2], 15, 33:15[3], 34:4[2], 10, 17, 36:2, 37:8, 14, 20, 38:7, 12[2], 13, 17, 39:3[2], 7, 40:21[2], 27[2], 41:2, 4, 9[2], 25[2], 26, 42:7, 10, 11, 43:5[2], 6[2], 44:2, 8, 24, 45:6[2], 8, 21[2], 46:3[2], 7, 10[2], 11[2], 12, 47:11, 12, 13, 14, 15, 48:3, 5, 6, 7, 8[2], 16[2], 19, 20, 49:1[3], 6, 12[4], 24, 50:6, 51:4, 8, 52:2[2], 11, 53:3, 8[2], 54:8, 10, 14[2], 55:10, 56:2[2], 3, 6, 11, 57:1, 58:7, 9, 13[2], 59:2, 9, 11, 13[2], 15, 19[2], 20, 21, 60:4, 6, 9, 63:1[2], 63:15[2], 16, 17[2], 64:7, 65:16, 66:6[2], 23[2]

JER.
2:5, 25[2], 35, 37, 3:1, 4, 19, 20, 23[2], 24, 25, 4:6, 7[2], 8, 12, 14, 15[2], 16, 28, 5:15, 25, 6:8, 13[2], 20[2], 22[2], 7:1, 28, 34[2], 8:10[2], 13, 16, 9:2, 3, 21[2], 10:9[2], 11[2], 13, 11:1, 4, 15, 19, 12:2, 12, 14, 13:6, 7, 20, 25, 15:7, 19, 16:5, 15[2], 16[2], 17[2], 19, 17:4, 5, 8, 12, 13, 16, 26[6], 18:1, 8, 11, 14[2], 15, 18[3], 20, 22, 23, 19:14, 20:2, 7[3], 13, 17, 21:1, 22:20, 21, 23:8, 14, 15, 22[2], 30, 24:1, 10, 25:3, 5[2], 10, 30[2], 32[2], 33, 26:1, 3, 10, 27:1, 10, 16, 20, 28:3, 6, 10, 28:11, 12, 16, 29:1[2], 2, 4, 14[2], 20, 30:1, 8, 10[2], 21, 31:8[2], 11, 13, 16[3], 34, 36[2], 38, 32:1, 30, 31[2], 40[2], 33:5, 8, 34:1, 8, 12, 14, 21, 35:1, 15, 36:1, 2[2], 3, 4, 6, 7, 9, 29, 32, 37:5, 9, 11, 17, 38:10, 14, 25, 40:1[2], 4, 41:5[3], 6, 14, 15, 16[3], 42:1, 4, 8, 11, 17, 43:5, 12, 44:7, 5, 12, 46:16, 27[2], 47:4, 48:2, 3, 10, 11[2], 18, 33[3], 34, 42, 44, 45, 49:5, 7, 14, 16, 19[2], 32, 36, 38, 50:6, 9[2], 16, 26, 39, 41[2], 44[2], 51:16, 25, 45, 48, 53, 54[2], 64, 52:3, 8, 29

LAM.
1:6, 13, 14, 16, 2:1, 2:3, 8, 9, 3:17, 18, 50, 66, 5:14[2], 16, 19

EZEKIEL
1:19, 21, 25, 27[2], 3:12, 17, 18, 19[2], 20, 4:8, 10, 11, 14, 6:9, 7:20, 22, 26[2], 8:2[2], 6, 9:2, 3, 10:2, 4, 6[2], 7, 16[2], 18, 19, 11:15, 17, 18, 23, 24, 12:3, 16[3], 19, 13:20, 22, 14:5, 6[2], 7, 8, 9, 11, 13, 17, 19, 21, 15:7, 16:9, 34, 41, 42, 17:22, 18:8, 17, 21, 23, 26, 27, 28, 30, 31, 19:8, 20:17, 34, 38, 41, 47, 21:3, 4[2], 22:5, 26, 23:8, 17, 18[2], 22, 27[2], 28, 40, 42, 24:13, 16, 25, 25:7, 9[2], 13[2], 26:4, 7, 16, 27:5, 7[2], 29, 28:3, 15, 16, 18, 25, 29:10, 13, 30:6, 9, 31:12, 32:13, 33:6, 7, 8, 9[2], 11[2], 12, 14, 18, 19, 30, 34:10[2], 13[2], 35:7, 36:24, 25[2], 29, 33, 37:9, 21, 38:8, 15, 39:2, 22, 23, 24, 27, 29, 40:13, 15, 19, 23, 27, 41:7, 16, 20, 42:6, 9[2], 43:2, 9, 14[2], 15, 44:10[2], 15, 45:7[3], 9, 46:18, 47:1[3], 10, 15, 17, 18[5], 19, 20, 48:1, 2, 3, 4, 5, 6, 7, 8[2], 22[2], 23, 24, 25, 26, 27, 28, 35

DANIEL
2:1, 5, 8, 15, 3:17, 4:3, 13, 14[2], 16, 23, 25, 31[2], 32, 33, 34, 5:20[2], 21, 24, 6:18, 20, 27, 7:3[2], 4, 7, 10, 19, 23, 24, 8:5, 9:5[2], 12, 16, 25, 10:12, 11:22, 12:11

HOSEA
1:2, 2:2, 15, 4:12, 5:3, 6, 7:4, 13, 8:6, 9:1, 11[3], 12, 10:5, 9, 11:2, 7, 10, 12:9, 13:4, 14[3], 15, 14:4, 8

JOEL
1:5, 9, 12, 13, 15, 16, 2:20, 3:6, 16, 20

AMOS
1:2[2], 5[2], 8[2], 2:3, 9[2], 10, 14, 3:1, 5, 11, 4:7, 5:11, 12, 19, 23, 6:2, 14, 8:12[2], 9:3, 7[2], 8

OBADIAH
1

JONAH
1:3[2], 10, 15, 2:6, 3:5, 6[2], 8[2], 9, 10, 4:3, 6

MICAH
1:2, 12, 16, 2:4, 8[2], 9[2], 3:2[2], 3, 4, 4:2, 7, 10, 5:2[2], 6, 7, 6:5, 7:5, 12[5], 20

NAHUM
1:13, 2:13, 3:7, 8

HABAK.
1:8, 12, 2:9, 3:3[2], 17

ZEPH.
1:2, 3, 4, 6, 10[3], 11, 3:10

HAGGAI
1:10[2], 2:15[2], 18[3], 19

ZECH.
1:4[2], 6, 3:4[2], 6:1, 5, 10, 12, 8:7[2], 9:5, 7, 10[4], 13:5, 14:2, 5, 8, 10[3], 13, 16

MALACHI
1:5, 11, 2:6, 3:5, 7[2]

MATT.
1:17[3], 21, 24, 2:1, 16, 3:7, 13, 17, 4:17, 21, 25[5], 5:18, 29, 30, 42, 6:13, 7:23, 8:1, 11, 30, 9:9, 15, 16, 22, 11:12, 25, 12:15, 38, 42, 44, 13:12, 27, 35, 49, 14:2, 15:8, 18, 27, 28, 29, 16:1, 21, 22, 17:9[2], 18, 18:8, 9, 35, 19:1, 8, 12, 20, 20:8, 29, 21:8, 25[2], 43, 22:46, 23:35, 24:1, 29, 31, 25:28, 29, 32[2], 34, 41, 26:16, 39, 42, 47, 27:31, 40, 42, 45, 51, 55, 64, 28:2[2], 7, 8

MARK
1:9, 11, 42, 45, 2:20, 21, 3:7[2], 8[3], 22, 4:25, 5:35, 6:1, 2, 10, 14, 16, 7:1, 4, 6, 15, 17, 18, 21, 23, 24, 31, 33, 8:3, 4, 11, 9:9[2], 10, 10:1, 6, 20, 11:12, 20, 30, 31, 12:2, 25, 34, 13:19, 27[2], 14:35, 36, 43, 52, 15:20, 30, 32, 38, 16:3, 8, 12

LUKE
1:2, 3, 15, 26, 38, 45, 48, 50, 52, 71[2], 78, 2:1, 4, 15, 36, 37, 3:7, 22, 4:1, 9, 13, 42, 5:3, 8, 10, 13, 35, 6:17, 22, 7:6, 18, 37, 8:49, 9:5, 7, 33, 37, 39, 45, 54, 10:7, 18, 21, 30, 42, 11:4, 7, 16, 22, 31, 50, 51, 12:36, 52, 58, 13:12, 15, 16, 27, 29[4], 16:3, 18, 21, 26[2], 30, 31, 17:7, 29, 18:21, 34, 19:8, 24, 26[2], 39, 42, 20:4, 5, 35, 21:11, 22:41, 42, 43, 45, 23:5, 49, 55, 24:2, 9, 13, 46, 49, 51

JOHN
1:6, 19, 31, 2:22, 3:2, 13, 27, 31[2], 4:11, 5:24, 34, 41, 44, 6:23, 31, 32[2], 33, 38, 41, 42, 50, 51, 58, 64, 66, 7:29, 8:23[2], 25, 42, 44, 9:29, 30, 10:5, 18, 32, 11:41, 53, 12:1, 9, 17, 27, 28, 32, 36, 13:3, 4, 14:7, 15:26[2], 15:27, 16:22, 27, 28, 30, 17:8, 15, 18:3, 28, 36, 19:11, 12, 23, 27, 20:1, 9, 21:8, 14

ACTS
1:4, 11, 12[2], 22[2], 25, 2:2, 40, 46, 3:2, 15, 19, 23, 24, 26, 4:2, 10, 5:38, 41, 7:3, 4, 33, 39, 8:10, 26, 33, 9:3, 8, 14, 18, 10:17, 21, 22, 23, 37, 41, 11:4, 5, 9, 11, 27, 12:7, 10, 11, 19, 25, 13:4, 8, 13[2], 14, 29, 30, 31, 34, 39[2], 46, 14:8, 15, 17, 19, 26, 15:1, 18, 19, 20[4], 24, 29[5], 33, 38[2], 39, 16:11, 12, 17:3, 27, 31, 33, 18:1, 2[2], 5, 6, 16, 21, 19:9, 12[2], 35, 20:6, 9, 17, 18, 20, 26, 21:1[2], 21:7, 10, 25[4], 22:5, 6, 22, 29, 30, 23:10, 21, 24:18, 25:1, 7, 26:4, 5, 10, 12, 13, 17[2], 18[2], 23, 26, 27:4, 21, 34, 43, 28:13, 15, 17, 23

ROMANS
1:4, 7, 17, 18, 20, 4:24, 5:9, 14, 6:4, 7, 9, 18, 17[2], 18, 20, 22, 7:2, 3, 4, 6, 24, 8:2, 11[2], 21, 35, 39, 9:3, 10:6, 7, 9, 11:15, 26, 15:19, 22, 31, *subscr.*

1 COR.
1:3[2], 4:7, 5:2, 13, 7:11, 27, 9:19, 10:14, 14:36, 15:12, 20, 41, 47, *subscr.*

2 COR.
1:2[2], 10, 2:3, 13, 3:1, 18, 5:2, 5, 6, 6:17, 7:1, 11:3, 9[2], 12, 12:8, *subscr.*

GAL.
1:1, 3[2], 4, 6, 8, 15, 2:12, 3:13, 4:1, 24, 5:4, 6:17, *subscr.*

EPHES.
1:2[2], 20, 2:12[2], 3:9, 4:16, 31, 18, 5:14, 6:23, 6, *subscr.*

PHIL.
1:2[2], 5, 3:20, 4:15, 18, *subscr.*

COLOS.
1:2, 13, 16, 18, 23, 26[2], 2:12, 19, 20, 4:16, *subscr.*

1 THESS.
1:1, 8, 9, 10[3], 2:17, 3:6, 4:3, 16, 5:22, *subscr.*

2 THESS.
1:2, 7, 9[2], 2:1, 13, 3:2, 3, 6, *subscr.*

1 TIM.
1:2, 6, 4:1, 3, 5:13, 6:5, 10, *subscr.*

2 TIM.
1:2, 3, 15, 2:8, 19, 21, 3:5, 15, 4:4, 18, *subscr.*

TITUS
1:4, 14, 2:14, *subscr.*

PHILE.
3, *subscr.*

HEB.
3:12, 4:3, 4, 10[2], 5:1, 7, 6:1, 7, 7:6, 26, 8:11, 9:14, 10:13, 22, 11:15, 19[2], 12:25[2], 13:20, *subscr.*

JAMES
1:17[2], 27, 3:15, 17, 4:1, 7, 5:19, 20[2]

1 PETER
1:3, 12, 18[2], 21, 2:11, 3:10, 4:1

2 PETER
1:9, 17[2], 18, 2:8, 14, 18, 21, 3:4, 17

1 JOHN
1:1, 7, 9, 2:7[2], 13, 14, 19, 20, 24[2], 3:8, 11, 14, 17, 4:21, 5:21

2 JOHN
3[2], 4, 5, 6

JUDE
14, 24

REV.
1:4[2], 5[2], 2:5, 3:10, 12, 6:4, 16[2], 7:2, 17, 8:10, 9:1, 6, 13, 10:1, 4, 8, 11:11, 12, 12:14, 13:8, 13, 14:2, 3, 4, 13[3], 18, 15:8[2], 16:17, 17:8, 18:1, 4, 14[2], 20:1, 9, 11, 21:2, 4, 10, 22:19[2]

he 1931, הוא

GEN. 1:5, 10, 16, 27[2], 31, 2:2[2], 3, 8[2], 19, 21[2], 22, 3:1, 6, 10, 11, 16, 17, 22, 23, 24, 4:4, 5, 9, 10, 17, 20, 21, 26, 5:1, 2, 4[2], 7, 8, 10, 11, 13, 14, 16, 17, 18, 19, 20, 22, 24, 26, 27, 29, 30, 31, 6:3, 6, 22, 8:6, 7, 8, 9, 10, 12, 9:6, 19, 21, 25, 26, 27, 29, 10:8, 9, 11:11, 13, 15, 17, 19, 23, 25, 12:4, 7, 8[2], 11[2], 16, 20, 26, 13:1[2], 3, 4, 14:13, 14, 15, 16, 18, 19, 20, 15:4, 5[2], 6, 7, 8, 9, 10[2], 13, 16:3, 8, 12[3], 17:12, 13, 14, 20, 22, 24, 25, 18:1, 2[2], 7, 8[2], 9

GEN. 18:10, 15, 19[2], 28, 29[2], 30[2], 31[2], 32[2], 33, 19:1, 2, 3[2], 9, 14, 16, 17, 21, 25, 27, 28, 29, 30[2], 33, 35, 20:4, 5[2], 7, 13, 16[2], 21:1, 13, 17, 20, 21, 30, 31, 22:1, 2, 6, 7[2], 11, 12, 23:8, 9[3], 13, 16, 24:2, 7, 10, 11, 12, 15, 27, 30[4], 31, 32, 33[2], 34, 35, 36, 40, 52, 53, 54[2], 56, 62, 63, 66, 67, 25:5, 6, 7, 17, 18, 20, 28, 29, 33, 34, 26:7[3], 8, 11, 13, 14, 18, 20, 21, 22[3], 23, 25, 30, 33, 34, 27:1[3], 2, 9, 10, 14, 18, 20, 22, 23[2], 24, 25[5], 27, 29, 31, 32, 33[2], 34, 35, 36[6], 45, 28:5

GEN. 28:6, 9, 11[2], 12, 16, 17, 18, 19, 29:1, 5, 6, 7, 9, 12, 13[2], 14, 20, 23[2], 25, 28, 30, 31, 33, 30:2, 15, 16, 28, 29, 31, 35[2], 36, 38, 40, 42, 31:1[2], 8[2], 12, 15, 18[3], 20, 21, 23, 33[2], 35, 49, 32:2[2], 4, 6, 7, 11, 13, 14, 16, 17, 18, 19, 20[2], 22, 23[2], 25[4], 26[2], 27[2], 28, 29[2], 31[2], 32, 33:1, 2, 3[2], 5[2], 8[2], 11[2], 12, 13, 15, 18, 19[2], 20, 34:2, 3, 5, 7, 13, 19[2], 31, 35:6, 7[2], 9, 10, 13, 14[3], 36:6, 24, 43, 37:3[2], 5, 6, 9, 10, 13, 14[3], 15, 16, 18, 21, 22, 27, 29, 30, 33, 35[2], 38:2, 3, 5

GEN. 38:9[3], 10[2], 11[2], 12, 15, 16[2], 17, 18[2], 20, 21, 22, 26, 29, 39:2[2], 3, 4[4], 5[3], 6[5], 8[3], 9, 10, 12, 13, 14[2], 15[2], 18, 20, 22, 23, 40:3, 4, 7, 16, 20[2], 21[2], 22, 41:1, 5, 8, 11, 12[2], 13[3], 14, 25, 28, 43[3], 45, 46, 48[2], 49, 51, 52, 55, 42:2, 4, 6, 7[2], 9, 12, 17, 21, 23, 24, 25, 27, 28, 38[2], 43:7, 14, 16, 18, 23[2], 24, 27[2], 28, 29[2], 30[2], 31, 34, 44:1, 2, 5, 6[2], 10[2], 12, 14, 16, 17[2], 20, 22, 28, 31[2], 45:1, 2, 4, 8, 14, 15, 22[2], 23, 24[2], 26[2], 27[2], 46:1, 2, 3, 7, 28, 29, 47:2, 17, 21, 22, 29

GEN. 47:30, 31[2], 48:1, 9, 10[3], 12, 15, 17, 19[3], 20[2], 49:4, 8, 9[2], 11, 13, 15, 19, 20, 21, 27[2], 28, 29, 33, 50:6, 10, 12, 14[2], 16, 21, 22, 24, 26

EXOD. 1:9, 16, 21, 2:2, 10, 11[2], 12[3], 13[2], 14, 15[2], 18, 20[3], 21, 22, 3:1, 2, 4[2], 5, 6[2], 12, 14, 20, 4:2, 3[2], 4, 6[2], 7[2], 13, 14[5], 16[3], 20, 21, 23, 26, 27, 28, 31, 5:3, 17, 23, 6:1, 11, 7:2, 13[2], 14, 15[2], 20, 22, 23, 8:8, 10[2], 12, 15, 19, 20, 27, 31, 32, 9:7, 12, 20, 21, 34[2], 35, 10:6, 8, 10, 16, 17, 18, 20, 27, 11:1[3], 8, 10, 12:19, 23, 25, 27, 30

EXOD. 12:31, 44, 48, 13:5, 11, 19, 22, 14:4, 6, 7, 8, 13, 15:1[2], 2[2], 4, 21[2], 25[4], 16:7, 9, 18[2], 23, 29, 17:7, 11, 12, 16, 18:2, 3, 4, 5, 6, 9, 11, 14, 24, 27, 19:13, 15, 24, 21:2[2], 3[3], 4, 6[2], 8[3], 9[2], 10[2], 11, 12[2], 13, 14, 15, 16[3], 17, 18, 19[3], 20[2], 21[3], 22[2], 26, 27[2], 29[2], 30, 31, 32, 35, 36, 22:1, 2, 3[3], 4, 5, 6, 8, 9, 11[2], 12, 13, 14, 15, 16, 17, 20[2], 27[2], 23:21, 25, 24:1, 5, 6, 7, 11, 14, 16, 25:39, 28:1, 3, 4, 29, 30, 35[3], 29:21, 30, 30:7[2], 8, 10, 31:15, 17, 18[2], 32:4[2], 5, 12, 14, 17, 18, 19[3]

EXOD. 32:20, 27, 29, 33:8, 11, 14, 15, 18, 19, 20, 34:4, 9, 10, 28[3], 29[2], 32, 33, 34[4], 35, 35:31, 34[3], 35, 36:8, 10[2], 11[2], 12[2], 13, 14[2], 16, 17[2], 18, 19, 20, 22, 23, 24, 25, 27, 28, 29, 31, 33, 34, 35[2], 36[2], 37, 38, 37:2, 3, 4, 5, 6, 7[2], 8, 10, 11, 12, 13, 15, 16, 17[2], 23, 24, 25, 26[2], 27, 28, 29, 38:1, 2[2], 3[2], 4, 5, 6, 7[2], 8, 9, 28, 30, 39:2, 7, 8, 22, 40:13, 16, 19, 20, 21, 22, 23, 24, 25, 26, 27, 28, 29, 30, 33

LEVIT. 1:3, 4, 5, 6, 9, 10, 11, 12, 13, 14, 16, 17, 2:1, 2[2]

LEVIT. 2:8, 3:1[2], 2, 3, 4, 6, 7[2], 8, 9[2], 10, 12, 13, 14, 15, 4:3, 4, 8, 9, 12[2], 18, 19, 20[3], 21[2], 23[2], 24, 26, 27, 28[3], 29, 31, 32[2], 33, 35[2], 5:1[3], 2, 3[3], 4[2], 5[3], 6, 7[3], 8, 9, 10[2], 11[4], 12, 13, 15, 16[2], 17[2], 18[2], 19, 6:4[5], 5[2], 6, 7, 10[2], 11, 12, 15, 20, 7:2, 3, 4, 8, 11, 12[2], 13, 14, 15, 16, 29, 30, 33, 35, 36, 38, 8:7[2], 8[2], 9[2], 11, 12, 14, 15, 16, 17, 18, 19, 20, 21, 22, 23, 24, 25, 26, 27, 33, 34, 9:2, 9, 10, 11, 12[2], 13, 14, 15, 16, 17, 18[2], 20, 10:1, 16, 20, 11:4[2], 5[2]

LEVIT. 11:6[2], 7[3], 28, 39, 40[2], 13:2, 6, 7[2], 9, 11, 13[2], 14, 16, 17, 33[2], 34, 36, 37, 39, 40[2], 41[3], 44[2], 45, 46[3], 51, 52, 54, 56, 14:2, 6, 7, 8[3], 9[5], 10[2], 12, 13[2], 18, 19, 20, 21[2], 22, 23, 25, 29, 30[2], 31, 35, 37, 41, 42, 43[2], 45[2], 46, 47[2], 49, 50, 51, 52, 53, 15:2, 4[2], 6[2], 7, 8[2], 9, 10, 11[2], 12, 13[2], 14, 16, 23, 24[2], 16:2[2], 4[4], 5, 7, 12, 13[2], 14[2], 15[2], 16[2], 17[2], 18, 19, 20[2], 22, 23[2], 24, 25, 26, 28[2], 32[2], 33[3], 34, 17:4, 13, 15[2], 16[2], 18:5, 19:8, 21, 22[2], 20:2[2], 3, 4, 9, 10, 13, 14, 15, 17[2], 18, 19

LEVIT. 20:20, 21, 21:3, 4, 7, 8[2], 10, 11, 13, 14[2], 15, 17, 18[3], 21[2], 22, 23[3], 22:3, 4[2], 5[3], 6, 7, 8, 11[2], 14, 18, 23:11, 12, 29, 24:4, 8, 9, 16[4], 17, 18, 19, 20, 21[4], 25:15, 16, 25, 27[2], 28[2], 29[2], 35[2], 40, 41[3], 48[2], 49[2], 50[2], 51[2], 52[2], 53, 54[3], 27:8[2], 10[2], 11, 13[2], 15[2], 17, 18, 19[2], 20[2], 22, 23, 27, 28, 31, 33[3]

NUM. 1:19, 3:3, 16, 50, 5:7[2], 14[2], 15[2], 23, 24, 27, 30, 6:3[2], 4, 5[2], 6[2], 7, 8, 9[3], 10, 11, 12, 13, 14[2], 17, 21[2], 7:7, 8, 9, 12, 17, 19, 23, 29, 35, 41, 47, 53, 59, 65, 71, 77, 83, 89[2], 8:3

NUM. 8:4, 9:10, 13, 14, 10:30, 31, 36, 11:3, 30, 32, 34, 12:1[2], 2, 6, 8, 9, 12, 14:8, 16[2], 24[2], 15:4, 9, 14, 27, 28, 30, 31, 36, 16:4, 5[3], 7, 10, 26, 31, 37, 40, 47, 48, 17:11, 19:3, 5, 7[2], 8, 10, 11, 12[4], 13, 19, 20[2], 21[2], 20:9, 10, 11, 13, 16, 20, 24, 21:1, 3, 7, 8, 9[2], 14, 23, 29, 33, 22:5, 6[2], 8, 22[2], 25, 27, 30, 31[2], 36, 41, 23:3[2], 4, 6[3], 7, 12, 14, 15, 17[2], 18, 19[6], 20, 21[2], 22, 24[2], 24:1[2], 2, 3, 4, 7, 8[2], 9[4], 10, 15, 16, 19, 20[3], 21, 23, 24, 25:7, 8, 11, 13[2], 15, 27:3, 4, 9, 10

NUM. 27:11, 21[2], 22, 23, 30:2[2], 5, 7, 8[2], 12, 14[4], 15[3], 32:10, 13, 15, 21, 40, 33:39, 35:6, 8, 12, 16[3], 17[4], 18[4], 19[2], 20[2], 21[4], 22, 23, 25[2], 26, 27, 28, 31, 32

DEU. 1:4, 11, 27, 30[2], 36[3], 38[2], 2:7, 22[2], 30, 32, 3:1, 22, 28[2], 4:13[3], 23, 31[2], 35, 36[3], 37[2], 39, 42, 5:22[2], 24, 6:10, 17, 23[3], 24, 25, 7:8[2], 9, 10[2], 12, 13[3], 24, 8:3[2], 10, 16[2], 18[3], 9:3[3], 5, 25, 28[3], 10:4, 6, 15, 18, 21[2], 11:3, 4[2], 5, 6, 7, 17, 25, 12:10, 12, 15, 20, 31, 13:2, 5, 10[2], 17, 14:21, 23, 27, 29, 15:2, 6, 8, 9, 16[3], 17, 18, 16:16, 17[2], 17:6[2], 16[2]

DEU. 17:17[2], 18[2], 19[2], 20[3], 18:2, 6, 7, 18, 19, 19:4[2], 5[2], 6[2], 8[2], 11, 12, 15, 19, 20:4, 5, 6[2], 7, 21:16[3], 17[3], 20[2], 21, 22, 23, 22:3, 16, 17, 19[2], 24, 27, 29[2], 23:1, 2, 6, 7, 10[2], 11[2], 14, 16[2], 24:1, 5[4], 13, 14, 15[2], 25:3[2], 4, 7, 8, 18[2], 26:5, 9, 18, 19[2], 27:16, 17, 18, 19, 20[2], 21, 22, 23, 24, 25, 26, 28:8, 9, 21, 44[2], 45, 48[2], 51[2], 52[2], 54, 55[3], 60, 29:1, 13[4], 19[2], 25[2], 26, 30:4, 5, 9, 20, 31:2, 3[3], 4[2], 6[2], 8[3], 11, 23, 32:4[2], 6[2], 7, 8[2], 10[4], 13[3], 15, 19, 20, 36, 37, 39, 43, 44, 46, 33:2[3], 3, 5, 7, 8

DEU. 33:9, 12[2], 13, 17, 18, 20[3], 21[4], 22[2], 23, 24, 27, 34:6, 7

JOSH. 1:15, 17, 18[2], 2:11, 3:1, 10, 4:4, 21, 23, 5:6[2], 7, 13, 14, 6:7, 26[2], 7:6, 15[5], 17[3], 18, 24, 8:4, 10, 12, 14[2], 18, 19, 26[2], 27, 29, 32[2], 33, 34, 9:9, 10, 22, 26, 27, 10:1[2], 7, 12, 28[4], 30[3], 32, 33, 35[2], 37[2], 39[5], 40, 11:1, 9, 11, 12, 15, 17, 20[2], 13:14[2], 33, 14:3, 10, 14, 15:13, 15, 16, 17, 19, 17:1[3], 4, 19:50[2], 20:4[2], 5, 6[3], 9, 21:43, 44, 22:4, 7, 8, 18, 22[2], 23:3, 5, 10[2], 15, 16[2], 24:7, 10, 17, 18, 19[3], 20[2], 23, 27, 31

JUD. 1:3, 5, 6[2], 7

JUD. 1:11, 12, 13, 19, 20, 25, 33, 2:7, 10, 14[2], 20, 21, 23, 3:4, 8, 10, 13, 16, 17, 18[2], 19, 20[3], 22, 24[2], 25, 27[3], 28, 31, 4:3[2], 10, 18, 19, 20, 21[2], 22, 5:13, 15, 25, 27[7], 31, 6:15, 17, 18, 19[2], 20, 22, 27[3], 30[3], 31[2], 32[2], 34, 35[2], 38, 7:5, 8, 11, 15, 16[2], 17, 8:2, 3, 4, 5, 8, 9, 12, 14, 15, 16[2], 17, 18, 19, 20[3], 26, 30, 31, 35, 9:3, 5, 7, 18, 28, 29, 31, 33, 36, 40, 43[2], 45, 48, 54[2], 56, 10:1, 2, 4, 7, 18[2], 11:1, 17, 25[2], 28, 29[2], 33, 34, 35[2], 38[2], 39, 12:5, 6[2], 9[3], 11, 14[2], 13:5, 6[2]

JUD. 13:7, 11, 16, 21, 23[3], 14:2, 4, 6[5], 7, 8[2], 9[4], 14, 15, 16, 17, 18, 19[2], 20, 15:1, 5[2], 6, 8[2], 10, 11, 14, 15, 17[2], 18, 19[3], 20, 16:4, 9, 11, 12, 13, 14, 17, 18[2], 20[2], 21, 22, 25[2], 30[3], 31, 17:2, 3, 4, 7, 8[3], 9, 18:4, 20, 24, 26, 27, 30, 31, 19:3, 4, 5, 7, 8, 9, 10, 13, 15[2], 16, 17[2], 18, 21, 28, 29[2], 21:5, 18

RUTH 1:1, 2:14, 19, 20, 21, 3:2, 3, 4[3], 7, 9, 10, 13[2], 14, 15[2], 17[2], 18, 4:1[2], 2, 3, 4, 8, 13, 15, 17

1 SAM. 1:2, 4, 5[2], 7, 22, 28[3], 2:6, 7, 8[2], 9

1 SAM. 2:10[2], 14, 15, 16, 23, 35, 3:2, 4, 5[3], 6, 8, 9, 13[2], 16, 17[2], 18, 4:13, 14, 15, 16[2], 18[5], 5:6, 9, 6:5, 6, 9, 19[2], 20, 7:3, 8, 16, 17[2], 8:1, 11[2], 12, 13, 14, 15, 16, 17, 21, 9:2[3], 4[2], 6[4], 9[2], 12[3], 13[3], 16, 26, 27, 10:9, 10, 11, 13[2], 14, 16[2], 21[2], 22, 23[2], 27, 11:6, 7, 8, 12, 12:5[2], 7, 9, 17, 24, 13:1, 2, 7, 8, 9, 10[2], 13, 14:1, 27, 33, 35, 37, 39, 40, 45[2], 47[2], 48, 52, 15:2[2], 8, 11[2], 12, 16, 23, 27, 29[2], 30, 35, 16:2, 5[2], 6, 8, 9, 11[3], 12[3], 16, 21[2], 22, 17:5[2], 6, 8, 9, 12, 20, 23

1 SAM. 17:25, 26, 28[2], 30, 31, 33, 35, 36, 37, 38[2], 39[2], 40[3], 42[2], 47, 49, 54, 55, 18:1, 3, 5, 8[2], 10, 11, 13, 15[2], 16, 27[2], 19:4, 5, 6, 7, 9, 10[2], 12, 14, 17[2], 18, 21, 22[2], 23[3], 24, 20:1, 2[2], 3[2], 6, 7[2], 13, 17[3], 26[3], 29[3], 30, 31, 32[2], 34, 36[2], 42, 21:13, 22:2, 3, 4, 10, 12, 13, 17, 18, 19, 22, 23, 23:6, 7, 9, 11, 13, 17, 22, 23[2], 25[2], 24:3, 5, 6[2], 10, 17, 19, 25:2[2], 3, 14, 17, 21, 25, 29, 30, 36[2], 37, 38, 39, 26:3, 10, 18, 27:2, 3, 4, 11, 12[2], 28:5, 8[2], 9, 11, 14[4], 17, 20, 21, 23[3], 29:3, 4[2]

1 SAM.
29:9
30:8
9
10
11
12[2]
13
15
16
21
25
26
31:3
4
5

2 SAM.
1:2[2]
3
4
7[2]
8
9
10[2]
13
15[2]
18
21
2:1
10
19
20
23[2]
30
3:11[2]
13
16
21
22[2]
23[2]
24
25
26
27
28
30
4:4[2]
7
5:2
4[2]
5[2]
8
12
18
20
23
6:7
8
13
18
19
7:11
13
14[2]
18
8:2[2]
3
6
10
11[2]
13
14[3]
9:2[2]
4[2]
6[2]
8
11
13
10:3
5
7
9
10[2]
11
17
11:2
4
13[3]
15[2]
16[2]
20
21
12:1
3
4
5
6[3]
11
17[2]
18[2]
19
20[3]
22
23[2]
24
25
30
31[2]
13:2
4
8
9
11
13
14
15[2]
16

2 SAM.
13:17
20
21
22
25[2]
26
27
32
36
39[2]
14:7
10
11
12
14
15
19[2]
26[4]
29[3]
30[2]
33[2]
15:2
5
9
12
14
25
26
30[2]
32
16:3[2]
5[2]
13
21
23
17:2
5
9
10
12
13
23
24
18:9
14[2]
18[2]
23[2]
25[2]
26
27
28
30
33[2]
19:9[2]
14
18[2]
21
24
25
26
27
32[3]
39
42
20:1
3
5[2]
6
8[2]
10[2]
11[2]
12[2]
13
14
17[4]
22
21:1
4
9
13
16
20
21
22:2
3
7
8
10
11[2]
12
15
17[3]
18
20[3]
21
31
33
34
35
42
51
23:3
4
5[2]
8[2]
10
12
16
17[2]
18
19[3]
20[2]
21[2]
23[2]
24:1
10
17

1 KINGS
1:1
5
6
7
10
13
17
19[2]
23[3]
24
25
26
30
35[2]
37
41
42
51[2]
52
53
2:1
4[2]
5[2]
8
11[2]
13
14
15
17[3]
22
24
25[2]
27[2]
28
29
30[2]
31
32
34
46
3:1
3
6
15
4:2
15
24[2]
31
32
33[2]
5:1
5
7
12
14
6:4
5[2]
6
9
10
15[2]
16[2]
19
20
21[2]
22[3]
23
27
28
29
30
31
32
33
35
36
38
7:1
2
6
7[2]
8[2]
14[3]
15
16
18[2]
21[3]
23
27
37
38
39[3]
40
51
8:12
15
19
20
21[2]
23
42
54
55
56[2]
57
58
59
63
64
66
9:1
2
13[2]
24
25[3]
10:3
4

1 KINGS
10:5
9
15
17
26[2]
27
11:2
8
10[2]
14
15
16
17
19
22
24
25[2]
26
27
28[2]
29
31
32
34
41
12:2
4
5
6
8
9
15
18
21
29[2]
31
32[5]
33[4]
13:2[2]
3
4[3]
10[2]
11
12
13[2]
14[2]
15
16
18[3]
19
21
23[4]
24
26[2]
27
28
30
31[2]
32
33[2]
14:3
5
6
13
15[2]
16
18
19[2]
20
21[2]
26[3]
29
15:2
3[2]
5
7
10
12
13
15
17
19
20
21
23[3]
26[2]
29[5]
30[3]
31
34[2]
16:5
7[2]
9
11[4]
12
14
18
19[2]
20
23
24[2]
26[2]
27[2]
31
32
34[2]
17:5[2]
6
10[3]
11
15
16
19[3]
20
21
22
18:7

1 KINGS
18:8
9
10[2]
12[2]
14
17
18
27[5]
30
32[2]
33
34[2]
35
39[2]
42
43[2]
44[2]
46
19:1
3[2]
4[3]
5
6[2]
8
9[2]
10
11
13
14
19[2]
20[2]
21[2]
20:1
2
7
9
11
12[3]
14[3]
15[2]
16
18
25
28
31
32[3]
33[2]
34
36[2]
37[2]
39[3]
40
41[2]
42
21:4[2]
6[2]
10
13
15
18[2]
20
26
27
29
22:4
8
11
15[2]
17
18
19
20
22[2]
28
34
38
39[3]
42[2]
43[2]
45[2]
46
52
53

2 KINGS
1:2
5
7[2]
8[2]
9[3]
11[2]
13
15
16
17[2]
18
2:3
4
5
6
10
12[3]
13
14[2]
16
17[2]
18[2]
20
21
22
23[2]
24
25[2]
3:2[2]
3[2]
7[2]
8[2]

2 KINGS
3:16
18
26
27
4:3
6
7
8[2]
10[2]
11[2]
12[2]
13
14
15[2]
16
18
19[2]
20[2]
23
25
29
30
31
33
34[2]
35
36[3]
38
41[3]
42
43
44
5:1[2]
3
5
6
7[2]
8[2]
11
12
13
14[2]
15[3]
16[3]
18
19[2]
20
21
22
23
24[3]
25[2]
26
27
6:2
3
4
5
6[2]
7[2]
11
13[3]
14
16
17[2]
18
19
21
22
23[2]
27
30[3]
31
32
33[2]
7:2
11
17[2]
19
20
8:1
5[3]
10
11[2]
12
13
14[3]
15[2]
17[3]
18[2]
19
21
23
26[2]
27[2]
28
29[2]
9:5[3]
6[2]
10
11
12[2]
14
15
17[2]
18
19
20[2]
22[2]
24
27[2]
32
33[2]
34[2]
36[2]
10:5[2]
6

2 KINGS
10:8
9
10
11
12[2]
14[2]
15[5]
16
17[4]
19[2]
22[2]
24
25
31
34
11:2
3
5
8[3]
12
19[2]
21
12:1
18
19
21
13:2[2]
3
4
7
8
11[3]
12[2]
14
15
16[2]
17[4]
18[4]
21
23
25
14:2[2]
3[2]
5
6
7
11
14
15[2]
19
20
22
24[2]
25[2]
27[2]
28[3]
15:2[3]
3
5
6
9[2]
12
13
15
16[2]
18[2]
21
24[2]
25
26
28[2]
31
33[3]
34[2]
35
36
16:2
3
4
13
14
18
19
17:2
4[2]
15[2]
20
21
22
23
26
34
37
39
18:2[3]
3
4[2]
5
6
7[3]
8
22
27
29
32
19:1
2
7
8[2]
9[3]
32
33[2]
37
20:7
9
11
12

2 KINGS
20:15
19
20
21:1
2
3[2]
4
5
6[2]
7[2]
16[2]
17[2]
19[2]
20
21
22
25
26
22:1[2]
2
4
8
11
23:2
4
5
6
7
8
10
11
14
15
16
17
18
19
20
24
28
29[2]
31[2]
32
33
34
35[2]
36[2]
37
24:1
2
3
4[2]
5
8[2]
9
12
13
14
15[2]
18[2]
19
20
25:1
9[2]
19
22
25
27
28
29

1 CHRON.
1:10
2:3
21[2]
23
3:4[2]
4:10
5:1[2]
6
9
20
26
6:10
7:23[2]
8:7
8
9
11
10:3
4
5
13[2]
14
11:2
8
11
13
19
20[2]
21[3]
22[2]
23[2]
25
12:1
18
19[2]
20
13:10[3]
14
14:4
15:3
22[2]
16:2
3
4
12

1 CHRON.
16:14
15
16
21[2]
25
33
34
37
40
17:12
13
18:2
3
6
10[2]
11
13[2]
19:3
5
8
10
11
12
17
20:2
3
6
7
21:3
6
7
15[2]
19
26
27
28
30
22:2
6
10[2]
11
18[2]
23:1
2
13[2]
25:10
11
12
13
14
15
16
17
18
19
20
21
22
23
24
25
26
27
28
29
30
31
26:10
27:23
24
28:4[2]
5
6[2]
7
9[2]
12
14
16
17
20
29:27[3]
28

2 CHRON.
1:4
5
14[2]
15
2:11[2]
18
3:2
4
5[2]
6
7
8[2]
9
10
14
15
16
17
4:1
2
6
7
8[2]
9
10
11
14[2]
21
5:1
13
6:1
4[2]
9

2 CHRON.
6:10
11
12
13
7:3
7
10
11
21
22
8:4[2]
5
11[2]
12
14
9:2
3
4
8
15
25
26
27
31
10:2
4
5
6
8
9
15
18
11:1[2]
6
11
12
15[2]
20
21
22
23[3]
12:1
4
9[2]
12[2]
13[2]
14[2]
13:2
20
14:3
5
6[2]
7[2]
15:2[3]
4
8[2]
9
15
16
18[2]
16:1
3
5
6
8
10
12
14
17:2
3
5
6
7
8
11
12
13
18:2[2]
3
7
14[2]
16
17
18
19
21
27
33
34
19:4
5
9
20:15
21[2]
31[3]
32
36
21:2
3[2]
4
5[2]
6[2]
7[2]
9
10
11
19
20[3]
22:2[2]
3
4
5
6[3]
7[2]
8
9[3]
12

2 CHRON.
23:3
7[3]
10
19
20
24:1[2]
3
5
15[3]
16
19
20
22[2]
25
25:1[2]
2
3
4
5
6
14
15
16
20
21
24
27
26:2
3[2]
4
5[2]
6
8
10[2]
15[3]
16[2]
19
20
21
23
27:1[2]
2[2]
3[2]
4[2]
5
6
8[2]
28:1[3]
2
3
4
5
9[2]
19
21
22
23[2]
24
25
29:1[2]
2
3
4
8
21[2]
23
25
30:6
8
19
31:3
4
21[2]
32:2
3
5
6
9
17
21[2]
23
24[2]
26
27
29
31
33:1[2]
3[2]
4
5
6[3]
7[2]
12[2]
13[2]
14
15[2]
16
19[2]
21
22
34:1[2]
2
3[3]
4[2]
5
6
7[2]
8[2]
19
30
32
35:2
21[2]
22
24[2]
36:2[2]
5[3]

2 CHRON.
36:8
9[3]
11
12
13[2]
14
15
17[2]
18
20
22
23

EZRA.
1:1
2
3
4
3:11
12
14
6:17
7:6
8
9[2]
8:23
31
35
10:1
6[3]

NEH.
1:2
2:8
18
20
3:12
14
15
4:1
2
3[2]
18
5:13
6:10
12
13
18
7:2
8:3
5[2]
10
18
9:29
12:8
13:2
5

ESTHER
1:3
4
10
20
22
2:1
4
7
9[2]
17
18
3:4[3]
6
4:4
5
8
11
5:5
9[2]
10[2]
11
14
6:1
4
7:5[2]
7
8
10
8:1
2
3
5
7
10
9:25[3]
30

JOB
1:10
11[2]
12
16
17
18
2:3
4
5
6
8[2]
10
4:18[2]
5:12
13
15
18[2]
19
20

JOB
6:5
9
14
7:9
10
8:4
6
15[2]
16
18
20
21
9:3[2]
4
11[2]
12
16[2]
17
18
19
22
23
24[2]
32
11:6
10
12:4
5
13
14[2]
15[2]
17
18
19
20
21
22
23[2]
24
25
13:9
10
15
16
19
28
14:2[2]
5
6[2]
10
14
20
21[2]
15:3[2]
14[3]
15
23[2]
25
26
27
28
29[2]
30[2]
33
16:7
9[2]
12[2]
13[2]
14[2]
17:3
5
6
9
18:4
8[2]
17
18
19
19:8[2]
9
10[2]
11[2]
13
16
25
20:7[2]
8[2]
12
13
15[2]
16
17
18[3]
19[3]
20[3]
22
23[2]
24
21:19[2]
20
21
22
31
32
22:2
4[2]
8
13
14[2]
28
27
29
30
23:5[2]
6[2]
8
9[2]

JOB
23:10[2]
13[3]
14
17
24:18[2]
20
21
22[2]
23
25:2
4
26:7
8
9
10
12[2]
13
27:7
9
10[2]
16
17
18
19[3]
21
22
28:3
9[2]
10
11[2]
23
24
25
26
27[2]
28
30:11
19
24
31:4
14
15
18
20
32:1
2
4
14
33:10[2]
11[2]
13
16
17
18
19
24
25
26[3]
27
28
34:9[2]
10[2]
11
14[2]
17
21
23[2]
24
25[2]
26
28
29[2]
33
37[2]
35:7
15[2]
16
36:4
5
6
7[2]
9
10
13
15
16
18
19
22
27
30
31[2]
32
37:3
4[2]
5
6
7
11[2]
12
13
17
20
23[2]
24
39:7[2]
8
10
12
17
21[2]
22[2]
24[2]
25[2]
40:2[2]
15
17

JOB
40:19[2]
21
23[3]
24
41:3[2]
4
25
26
29
30
31[2]
32
34[2]
42:3
10[2]
12
13
14

PSALMS
1:2
3[2]
2:4
5
12
3 *title*
3:4
7 *title*
2
12[3]
13[2]
14
15[2]
9:7
8[2]
12[3]
16
10:5
6
8[2]
9[4]
10
11[3]
13
11:6
13:6
15:2
3
4[2]
5[2]
16:8
18 *title*
6
7
10[2]
11
14[2]
16[3]
17
19[3]
20
30
33
34
41
48
50
19:4
20:6
21:1
4
7
22:8[3]
9
24[4]
28
31
23:2[2]
3[2]
24:2
4
5
10
25:8
9[2]
12[3]
14
15
27:5[3]
14
28:5
6
8
29:6
31:21
24
32:1
10
33:5
7[2]
9[2]
10
12
13
14
15[2]
17
20
34 *title*[2]
4
12[2]
20
35:8
14
36:2
3

PSALMS
36:4[3]
37:4
5
6
13
23
24[2]
26
33
34
36[3]
39
40
39:6
40:1
2
3
41:1
2
5
6[4]
8[2]
44:21
45:11
46:6
8
9[3]
47:2
3
4[2]
9
48:14
49:9
10
12
15
17
18[2]
19
50:4[2]
9
51 *title*
52:5
54:5
7
55:12
17
18
19
20[2]
22[2]
56:1
57 *title*
3
58:7
9
10[2]
11
60 *title*
12
61:7
62:2[2]
6[2]
63 *title*
65:4
66:5
6
7
16
17
19
68:6
20
33
35
71:6
72:2
4[2]
6
8
12[2]
13
14
74:5
75:7
8
76:3
12[2]
77:1
7
9
78:4
5[2]
11
12
13[2]
14
15
16
20[3]
23
25
26[2]
27
28
29
33
34
38[2]
39
42
43
45
46
47
48
49

PSALMS
78:50[3]
53
54
55
59
60[2]
62
66[2]
67
68
69[2]
70
71
72
81:5[2]
16
82:1
84:11
85:8
87:6
89:26
41
48[2]
91:1
2
3
4
11
14[2]
15
92:12
15
93:1[2]
94:9[4]
10[4]
14
23
95:5
7
96:4
10
13[3]
97:10[2]
98:1
2
3
9[2]
99:1
2
5
6
7[2]
100:3[2]
101:6[2]
7[2]
102 *title*
102:16
17
19
23[2]
103:7
9[2]
10
12
14[2]
15
104:10
13
14[2]
16
19
32[2]
105:5
7
8[2]
9
14[2]
16[2]
17
18
21
24
25
26[2]
28
29
31
32
33
34
36
37
39
40
41
42
43
106:1
3
8[2]
9[2]
10
15
23[3]
26
33
40
41
43
44[2]
45
46
107:1
2
6
7
9

PSALMS
107:12
13
14
16
19
20
25
28
29
30
33
35
36
38
40
41
108:12
109:7
11
15
16[2]
17[2]
18
19
31
110:6[3]
7[2]
111:4
5[2]
6[2]
9[2]
112:4
5
6
7
8[2]
9[2]
10
113:7
8
9
115:3[2]
9
10
11
12[3]
13
16
116:1
2
6
118:1
18
26
29
120:1
121:3[2]
4
7
123:2
126:6
127:2
129:4
7
130:8
132:2
11
13
135:6
7[3]
14
136:1
137:8
9
138:6[2]
142 *title*
143:3[2]
144:2
10
145:19[2]
20
146:4
5
9
147:2
3
4[2]
6
9
10[2]
13[2]
14
15
16[2]
17
18[3]
19
20
148:5
6[2]
14
149:4

PROV.
2:7[3]
8
3:6
12[2]
19
29
30
33
34[2]
4:4
5:21
22

PROV.
5:23^2
6:13^3
14^2
15
19
29
30^2
31^3
32
33
34
35^2
7:8
19
20
22
8:26
27^2
28^2
29^2
36
9:7^2
8^2
9^2
18
10:3
4
5^2
9
10
17^2
18^2
19
22
11:12
13
15^2
17
19
25
26
27^2
28
29
30
12:1
2
8
9^2
11^2
15
17
27
13:3^2
11
13
18
20
24^2
14:2^2
17
21^3
29^2
31^2
15:5
9
10
12
15
18
24
25
27^2
29
32^2
16:5
7
17
20^2
26
30^2
32^3
17:5
9^2
15^2
16
19^2
20^2
21
27
28^2
18:9
13^2
17
20
19:1
2
5
7
8^2
9
16^2
17^3
23^2
25
26
20:4
14^2
19
22
21:1^2
11
13
17^2
21
26
27

PROV.
21:29
22:5
6^3
8
9^2
11
12
14
16^2
22
27
29^2
23:7^3
9
11
13
24
34^2
24:7
8
12^4
17
18
24
29
25:10
13
17
20^2
21
28
26:5
6
8^2
17
24
25
27
27:14
18
28:6^2
7
8^2
9
10
13
14
16
18
19^2
20
22
23^2
25^2
26^2
27^2
29:1
3
4
9
17^2
18^2
19^2
21
24
27
30:5
6
10
22^2
31
31:11
23
28

ECCL.
1:3
5
18
2:19^2
21
22
24^2
26^2
3:9^3
11^2
4:3
8^2
10^2
14^2
5:4
8
10^2
12
14
15^4
16^3
17^2
18
20
6:2^2
3^2
4
5
6^2
10^2
12
7:13
18
8:3
7
8
13^2
17^2
9:2^2
9
15

ECCL.
10:3^3
8
9
10^2
15
11:4^2
12:4
9^2

CANT.
1:13
2:3
8
9^2
16
3:10
5:6^2
16
6:3
8:11

ISAIAH
1:1
11
2:3
4
12
18
19
21
22
3:7
4:3^2
5:2^2
7
14
25
26
6:2^3
6
7
9
11
7:13
15^2
22
8:7
8^3
14
9:1
15^2
20^2
10:7
8
13
16
24
26
28^3
32^2
34
11:3
4^3
12
15
16
12:2
5
13:9
14:6^2
30
15:8
16:5
6
12^2
17:5
8
14
18:3^2
5
19:16
17
20^2
22^2
20:2
21:4
6
7^2
8
9^2
11
22:8
16
19
21
22^2
23
23:11^2
12
13
24:18^2
25:7
8^2
9
11^3
12
26:3
5
10^2
27:1
5^2
6
7^3
8
9
10
11^2

ISAIAH
28:4^2
9^2
11
12
16
20
21^2
24
25^2
28
29:8^5
10
11
12
16^2
23
30:14^2
18^3
19^3
23
32
33
31:2
3^2
4
5^2
8
9
32:6
7
8
33:4
5^2
8^3
15^2
16
18
22
34:2^2
11
17
35:4
36:2
7
12
14
37:1
2
7
8^2
9^4
33
34^2
38
38:7
9
12
13
15
19
21
39:1^2
4
8
40:5
6
11^2
14
15
20^3
22
23
24
26^2
29^2
41:2
3^2
4
7^2
24
25^3
26
42:1
2
3^3
4^2
5^3
13^3
19
20
21
24
25^3
43:1
10
13
25
44:12^2
13^3
14^3
15^4
16^4
17^2
18
20^2
24
28
45:9
13^2
18^3
46:4
6
7^3
48:12
14
15
21^3

ISAIAH
49:1
2^3
6
7
10^2
50:4^2
8
9
51:3^2
12
13
14^2
52:6
9
13
15
53:2^2
3^2
4
5^2
7^4
8^3
9^2
10^3
11^2
12^4
54:5
55:1
5
6^2
7^2
57:2
13
17
58:9
59:2
5
15
16
17^2
18^2
60:9
61:1
3
10^2
62:7^2
63:7
8^2
9^3
10^2
11^3
64:4
65:16^2
66:3^8
5

JER.
2:14^2
17
26
3:1
5^2
4:7
13
5:12
24
26
8:4
8
9:8
12^2
24
10:10
12^2
13^3
16
11:16
12:4
13:16^2
21
14:10
22
15:4
16:15
17:6
8
11
18:3
4^2
19:4
20:4
10
18
17
21:2
7^2
9^3
10
22:4
10
11
12
16
19
28^2
23:6
17
20^2
28
31
25:30^2
31^2
38
26:11
13
16
19^2

JER.
26:21
27:20
29:21
28
31
32^3
30:7
21
24^2
31:10
11
20
32:3
5^2
28
33:1
15
21
24
34:2
3
14
16
35:8
14
16
18
36:4
12
13
18
21
23
25^2
30
37:2^2
13^2
14
17
38:2^3
4
5^2
9^2
10
26
27
28
39:4
5
7
12
14^2
15
40:1
3
5^2
11
15
41:4
6^3
7
9
16^3
42:8
12
21
43:10
11^2
12^3
13^2
45:1
46:8
10
16
17
18
47:7
48:10
11^2
18
26
27
29
36
40
42
44^2
49:1
10^2
12
19
20^3
22
50:8
19
34^2
44
45^3
51:6
12
15^2
16^3
19
34^5
40
44
59
52:1
2
3
4
9
10
11
13
25
29

JER.
52:33

LAM.
1:13^4
14
15
2:2^3
3^3
4^3
5^3
6^2
7^2
8^3
9
17^6
3:2
3^2
4^2
5
6
7^2
8
9^2
10
11^2
12
13
15^2
16^2
27
28
29
30
32^2
33
37
4:11
16
22^3

EZEKIEL
2:1
2
3
10
3:1
2
3
4
10
19^2
20^3
21^3
22
27^2
4:15
16
6:12^3
7:15^2
20
8:3
5
6
7
8
9
12
13
14
15
16
17
9:1
3^2
5
7
9
11:2
12:12^2
13^3
27^2
13:22
14:9
17:4^2
5^7
7
9
13
15^4
16^3
18^3
19^2
20^2
18:8
9^2
10
13^4
14^2
17^2
18^2
19
21^3
22^3
23
24^6
26^2
27^2
28^4
19:4
6^2
7^2
8
20:11
13
21
49

EZEKIEL
21:11
21^3
23
27
24:24
26
26:8^2
9^2
10
11^2
29:9
18^2
19
20
30:11
24
25
31:5
10
11
15
32:25
32
33:3^2
5^2
6
9^2
12^3
13^4
14
15^3
16^3
18
19
22^2
24
34:12
17
23^3
37:3
4
9
10
11
38:17
39:15
40:2
3^2
5
6
8
9
11
13
14
17
19
20
23
24^2
27
28^2
32^2
35
45
47
48
49
41:1
2
3
4^2
5
13
15
22
42:1^2
13
15^2
16
17
18
19
20
43:1
7
18
21
44:1
3^2
4
26
27^2
30
45:17
23
24
25
46:2^2
5
7
8^2
9^4
11
12^3
17
18
19
20
21
24
47:1
2
3^2
4^2
5
6^2

EZEKIEL
47:8

DANIEL
1:2^2
3
5
7
8^4
10
14
18
20
2:15
16^2
21^3
22^2
24
29
38
49
3:1
11
17
19
20
25
4:14
17
25
29
32
33
35
37
5:2
12
19^9
20
21^4
29
6:4
7
10^3
14^2
16
20^2
23
26
27^2
7:1
16
23
24^2
25
8:4
5
6
7^2
8^2
11
14
17^3
18^2
19
24
25^4
9:2
10
12^2
14
22
27^3
10:1
11^2
12
15
18
19
20
11:2
4^2
5
6^3
8
10
11
12^3
16^2
17^3
18^2
19^2
20
21
23^2
24^4
25^2
28^2
29
30^3
32
36
37^2
38^2
39^3
40
41
42
43
44
45^2
12:7^2
9
12

HOSEA
1:3
5:6

HOSEA
5:11
13
6:1^4
2^2
3
11
7:4
5
8
9^2
8:1
13
9:9^2
10:1^2
2^2
12
11:5
10^2
12:1
2
3^2
4^4
7^2
12
13
13:1^3
13^2
15^2
14:5
9^2

JOEL
1:6
7^2
2:11
13
14
20
23^2

AMOS
1:1
2
11^2
15
2:1
9
15^3
16
3:4^2
7
11
4:2
13
5:6
6:10^3
11
7:1
2
5
7
8:2
9:1^3
3
5
6^2

OBADIAH
12

JONAH
1:3^2
5
9
10^2
12
2:2
3:4
6^2
7
10^3
4:1
2
5
8
9

MICAH
1:1
9
11
15
2:4^3
11
3:4^2
5
4:2
3
12
5:1
2
3
4^2
5
6^3
8
6:2
8
7:3
9^2
12
18^2
19^3

NAHUM
1:2
4
7
8
9
12
15
2:1
5

HABAK.
1:11
13
2:1
2
5^2
9^2
3:4
6^2
16^2
19^2

ZEPH.
1:7
12
18
2:11
13
14
3:5^3
15
17^4

HAGGAI
6

ZECH.
1:6
8
19
21
2:2
8^2
13
3:1
4^2
4:6
7
9
13
14
5:2
3
6^2
8^3
11
6:7
8
12^2
13^3
7:13
9:4
7^3
9
10
10:11
11:16
12:8
13:3
4
5
6
14:3

MALACHI
1:8
9^2
2:5
6
7
11
13
15^3
16
17
3:1^2
2^2
3^2
11
4:6

MATT.
1:20
21
25
2:2
3
4^2
7
8
14^2
16^3
21
22^3
23^2
3:3
7^2
11^2
12^2
15
16^2
4:2^2
3
4
6
12
13

MATT.
4:19
21^2
24
5:1^2
2
19
45
6:24^2
30
7:8
9
10^2
21
29
8:1
9^3
10
14
15
16
18
23
24
26^2
28
32
34
9:1
6
7
9^3
12
18
22
24
25
28
29
34
36^2
37
38
10:1^2
22
25
37^2
38
39^2
40^2
41^2
42
11:1
2
3
6
10
11^2
15
18
20
27
12:3^2
4
9^2
11^2
13^2
15^2
18
19
20^3
22
26
29^2
30^2
39
43
44^3
45
46
48
49
13:2
3
4
11
12^2
19
20^2
21^2
22^3
23^2
24
28
29
31
33
34
37^2
44^2
46^2
52
53
54^2
58
14:2
5^2
7
9
10
13
14
18
19^2
22
23^3
29^2
30^3

MATT.
15:3
4
6
10
13
23
24
26
30
35
36
39
16:1
2
4
8
12
13
15
20^2
21
23
26
27
17:5
13
15^2
18
23
25^2
18:6
12
13^2
15
16
17^2
24
25^2
28
30^2
32
34
19:1
2
4^2
8
11
12
13
15
17
18
22^2
20:2^2
3
5
6
7
13
19
21
23
21:3
9
10
14
15
17^2
18^2
19^2
23^2
25
27
28
29^2
30^2
31
34
36
37
40
41
45
22:4
7^2
8
11
12
20
21
25
34
42
43
45
23:11
12
15
16
18
22
39
24:3
13
26^2
31
43
46
47
50^2
25:12
15
16
17^2
18
20
22

MATT.
25:24
29^2
31
32
33
41
45
26:1
7
10
16
18
20
21
23^2
24
25
27
37
38
39
40
42
43
44
45
46
47
48^2
49
53
65
66
68
70
71
72
74
75
27:3^2
5
12^2
14
18
19
23
24^2
26^3
34^2
42^3
43^3
50
58
59
60^2
63
64
28:6^3
7^2

MARK
1:6
8
10
13
16^2
19^2
20
21
22
23
26
27
31
34
35
38
39
42^2
43
45
2:1^2
2
4
5
8
10
12
13^2
14^3
16
17
23
25^3
26
27
3:1
2
3
4
5^3
8
9
10
12
13^2
14^2
16
17
21
22^2
23
26
27^2
29
30
33

MARK
3:34
4:1^2
2
4
9^2
10
11
13
21
24
25^3
26
27
29
30
33
34^2
35
36
38^2
39
40
5:2
4
5
6^2
8
9^2
10^2
18^3
21
22^2
32
34
35
36
37
38
39^2
40^2
41
43
6:1
2
5
6^2
7
10
14
16^2
17
20^2
23
26
27
31
34^2
37
38
39
41^3
45^2
46^2
47
48^2
50
51
55
56
7:6
9
11
14^2
17
18
20
24^2
26
29
31
33^2
34
35
36^2
37^2
8:5
6^2
7
9
10
12
13
15
17
21
22
23^4
24
25^2
26
27
29
30
31
32
33^2
34^2
36
38
9:1
2
6
9
12^2
14^2
16
18^3

MARK
9:19
20^2
21
25
26^2
27
28
29
30
31^3
33^2
35
36^3
38^2
40
41
42
10:1^3
3
5
11
13
14
15
16
17
20
22^2
30
32
34
36
46
47^2
48^2
49
50
52
11:1
3
7
9
11^2
12
13^4
17
19
21
23^3
27
31
32
12:1
2^2
4
5
6
9
12
15
16
21
27
28
32
34^2
35
37
38
43
13:1
3
13
20^2
21
27
36
14:3
11^2
13
14
15
16
17
20
21
23^3
24
31
32
33
35
36
37
39
40^2
41
42
43
44^2
45^2
52
54
61
68^2
70
71
72^2
15:2
3
6
8
10
11
14
15
23

MARK
15:28
31^2
35
39^2
41
44^3
45^2
46
47
16:6^3
7^2
9^2
11
12
14^2
15
16^2
19

LUKE
1:8
9
12
15^2
16
17
21
22^4
23
25
32
33
48
49
51^2
52
53^2
54
55
60
62
63
64
68
70
73
74
2:4
21
26^2
27
28
42
49
50
51
3:3
7
11^3
13
14
15
16
17^5
18
20
4:2^2
9
10
13
15
16^3
17^2
18^2
20^2
21
23
24
30
35
36
38
39
40
41^2
42^2
43
5:1
3^3
4^2
8
9
12
13
14
16
17
20^2
22
24
25^2
27^2
28
34
36
39
6:1
4
5
6
7
8^2
10^2
12
13^3
14
17

LUKE
6:20
35
39
47
48
49
7:1^2
3^3
4^2
5^2
6
8^3
9
11
12
13
14^2
15^2
19
20
21^2
23
24
27
28^2
33
36^2
39^2
40
42
43^3
44
48
50
8:1
4
5
8^3
10
16
18
21
22^2
23
24
25^2
27
28^2
29^3
30
31
32^2
36
37
38
39
41^2
42^2
44
48
49
50
51^2
52
54
55
56
9:1
2
3
7
9
10
11
13
14
16^2
18^2
20
21
23
25
26
28
29
31
33
34
38
39^2
42
48
48
49
50
51^2
53
55
59^2
10:1
2^2
16^3
18
22
23
26
27
28
29
31^2
32
33^4
35^2
37^2
38
11:1^2
2

LUKE 11:5 7 8^4 10 11^3 12^2 14 15 17 22^3 23^2 24^2 25^2 26 27 28 29 33 37^2 38^2 40 46 53 12:1 5 9 13 14 15^2 16 17 18 21 22 28 36^2 37^2 38 39 43 44^2 46^2 48 54 58 13:6^2 7 8 10 12 13 17 18 20 22 23 25 27 32 35 14:1 4 7^2 9 10^2 11 12 15^2 16 25 26 28 29 31 32 33^3 35 15:3 4^2 5^2 6^2 11

LUKE 15:12 14^2 15^2 16 17^2 20^3 24 25^2 26 27^2 28 29 31 16:1^2 2 5 6^2 7^3 8 10^2 13^2 15 23 24^2 25 27 28 30 31 17:1 2^2 3 4 7 9^2 11^2 12 14^2 15^2 16 19 20^2 22 25 31^2 37 18:1 4^2 7 8^2 9 14 15 21 22 23^3 24^2 27 29 31 32 33 35 36 38 39^2 40^2 41 43 19:1 3^3 4^2 5 6 7 9 11^2 12 13 15^4 17 19

LUKE 19:22 24 25 26 28^2 29^2 32 36 37 40 41^2 45 47 20:1 2 3 5 9 10 11 12 16 17 19 23 25 28 30 37 38 41 44 21:1 2 3 5 8 10 29 37^2 22:4^2 6 8 10^2 12 13 14 15 17 19 22 25 26^3 27^4 31 33 34 35 36^3 37 38 39^2 40^2 41 44 45^2 47^2 51 56 57 59 60 61 67 70 23:2 3 5 6 7^3 8^4 9^2

LUKE 23:13 17 22^2 23 25^2 26 35^2 42 46^2 47 50 51 53 24:6^3 12 17 19 21 23 25 27 28^2 29 30^2 31 32^2 35 38 40^2 41 43 44 45 50^2 51^2 JOHN 1:8 10 11 12 15^3 18 20 21^2 23 27 30^2 31 33^2 36^2 39^2 41 42^2 51 2:5 8 12 15^2 21 22^2 23^2 24 25 3:3 4^2 5 13 16 18^3 21 22 26 29 30 31^3 32^2 33 34 36^2 4:4 5

JOHN 4:10 18 25^2 26 27 32 36^3 39 40^2 43 45^2 46 47^4 50 51 52^2 54 5:4 6^2 11^2 13 16 18 19^2 20 21 23 24 26 27 32 33 35 38 46 6:2 3 5 6^3 11^2 12 15 20 29 31 33 35^2 39 41 42 46 47 51 56 57^2 58 59^2 61 62 65 71^2 7:1 4 9^2 10 11 12^2 17 18^2 25 26 27^2 28^2 29 31 35^2 36 38 39 50 51 8:2^2

JOHN 8:6 7^2 8 10 12 20 22^2 23 24 26 27 28 29 30 42 44^4 47 51 52 54 56 9:1 2 6^3 7 8^2 9^4 11 12^2 15^3 16 17^3 18 19 20 21^3 22^2 23 25^2 26^2 27 29 30^2 31 33 35^2 36^2 37 38^2 10:1 2 3 4^2 6 9 12 13 20 35 39 40 11:3 4 6^4 7 8 9^2 10 11^2 12^2 13 17^2 24 25^3 33 36 39^2 43^2 44 51^2 52 56

JOHN 11:57^2 12:1 6^3 9^2 14 17 18 25^2 33^2 35^2 37 38 40 41 44 45 48 49 13:1^2 3 4 5^2 6 10 11^2 12^2 16^2 18 19 20^2 21 22 24^2 25 26^3 28 29 30 31 14:9 10 12^3 16^2 17 21^3 23 24 26 15:2^2 5 6 23 26 16:2 8^2 13^6 14^2 15 17 18^2 23 17:2 18:1^2 5 6^2 7 8 9 13 14 17 22 25 30 32^2 38^2 19:7^2 8 11 13 14 16

JOHN 19:17 21 26^2 27 30^2 33 35^3 38^2 41 20:5^2 8 9 18 20^2 22^2 25 27 21:1 6 7^2 14 15^2 16^3 17^3 19^4 20 22 23^2 ACTS 1:2^3 3 4 7 9^2 10 17 18 22 25^2 26 2:24 25 29 30 31 33 34 40 3:5 7 8 10 12 13 18 20 22 4:9 32 35 5:37 6:10 7:2^3 4^2 5^4 8 10 12 15 21 23 24 25 26 27 29 31^2 36^2 38 44^3 55

ACTS 7:60^3 8:3 6 11 13^2 16 18 19 27 31^3 32^3 37 38^2 39 40^2 9:2^2 3^2 4 5 6 8 9 10 11 12 13 14 15 16 18 19^2 20^2 21^2 26^2 27^3 28 29 32 33 34 38 39 41^2 43 10:3 4^3 6^2 7 8^2 10^2 17^2 21 23 27^2 28 32^2 35 36 39 41 42^2 48 11:13^2 16 17 22 23 24 26^2 12:2 3^2 4^2 7 8^2 9^2 11 12^2 17^3 19^2 23^2 13:11 12

ACTS 13:17 18 19^2 20 22^3 25^2 28 31 33 34^2 35 36 37 14:9 10 12 17^2 19 20^2 27 15:8 41 16:1 10 18 27 29 33^2 34^2 17:16 17 18^2 24 25^2 27 31^4 18:3^2 4 6 7 11 16 18 19^2 20 21 22^2 23^2 25 26 27^2 28 19:2 3 8 9 21 22^2 25 31 34 35 41^2 20:2^2 3^2 9 11^2 13 14 16^2 17 18 28 35 36^2 38 21:4 11^2 14 19^2 33^2 34

ACTS 21:35^2 37 40^2 22:2^2 8 14 21 22 24^2 26 27 29^3 30^3 23:5 6 7 15^2 16 17 18 20 23 25 27 34^4 35^2 24:2 22 23^2 24 25 26^3 25:1 3 4 5 6^2 7 8 12 16 20 22 24 25^2 26:15 23 24 25 30 32 27:6 35^4 28:4 5 6^2 15 17 23 29 ROMANS 1:2 2:28 29 3:26 29^2 4:2 10 11^3 12 13 17 18 19^2 20 21^2 6:7 10^4 7:1 2 8:9

ROMANS 8:11 24 27^2 29^3 30^6 32^2 34 9:15 18^4 19 23^2 24 25 28 10:21 11:2^2 7 21 32 12:3 7 8^4 20 13:4^3 8 14:2 4^2 6^7 9 18 22^2 23^3 15:10 12 21 1 COR. 1:31 2:14 15^2 16 3:7^2 8^2 10 14^2 15^2 18 19 4:4 5:2 6:16^2 17 18 7:13 20 22^2 24 32^2 33^2 36^3 37^2 38^2 8:2^3 9:10^3 10:12^2 22 11:7 23 24^2 25^2 26 29 12:11 14:2^2 3 4^2 5^3 11 13 16^2 24^2 25

1 COR. 15:4^2 5 6 7 8 12 15^2 24^2 25^2 27^3 16:10^2 11 12^2 2 COR. 1:10 21 2:2 5 4:14 5:5 10 15 17 21 6:2 15 7:7^2 15 8:6^2 9^2 12 15^2 17^2 23 9:6^2 7 9^2 10 10:7^2 17 18 11:4 12:4 6^2 9 13:4^2 GAL. 1:4 23^2 2:8 11 12^2 3:5^2 16 4:1^2 23^2 29 5:3 10^2 6:3^2 4 7 8^2 EPHES. 1:4 6 8 9 10 20^2 2:1 4 7 14 16 3:3 11 16 4:8^3

EPHES. 4:9^2 10^2 11 28 5:14 23 26 27 28 6:8^2 22 PHIL. 1:6 2:8 22 25 26^2 27 30 3:4^2 21 COLOS. 1:17 18^2 21 2:13 15 18 3:25^2 4:8 10 13 1 THESS. 1:10 3:13 4:8 5:24 2 THESS 1:10 2:4^2 6 7^2 14 3:6 10 14 1 TIM. 1:12 3:1 5 6 7 5:8 6:4 15 2 TIM. 1:12 16 17^2 18^2 2:4 5 12 13^2 21 4:11 15 TITUS 1:9^2 2:8 14

TITUS 3:5 6 11 PHILE. 13 15 18 HEB. 1:2^2 3 4 5^2 6^2 7 8 13 2:5 8^2 9 11^2 14^2 16^2 17 18^2 3:3 4 17 18 4:3 4 7 8 10^2 5:1 2 3 4 5 6 7^2 8^3 9 13 6:13^2 15^2 7:6 8^2 10 13 17 20 24 25^2 27^2 8:4^2 5^2 6^2 8 13^2 9:7 12 15 19 21 25 26^2 28 10:5^2 8 9^3 12 14 15 20 23 28 29^2 37

HEB. 11:4^3 5^3 6^3 7 8^4 9 10 16 17^2 19 21 22 23^2 24 26 27^2 28^2 12:6^2 7 10 17^4 26 13:5 12 23 JAMES 1:6 7 9 10^2 12^2 13^2 14 18 23 24^2 25 2:5 10 11 13 14 21 23 4:6^2 7 8 10 11 5:6 7 15 17 18 20 1 PETER 1:15 2:6 7 23^3 3:10 13 18 19 4:1 2 14^2 5:6 7 8 2 PETER 1:9^2 17 2:19 1 JOHN 1:7 9

1 JOHN 2:2 4 6^3 9^2 10 11^2 17 22^2 23 25 28 29 3:2^2 3 5 7^2 8^2 9^2 10 12 14 16 23 24^4 4:4^2 6^2 8 10 13^2 15 16 17 18 19 20^5 21 5:5^2 6 9 10^3 12^2 14 15 16^3 18 2 JOHN 9^2 11 3 JOHN 10^2 11^2 JUDE 6 9 REV. 1:1 2 3 7 16 17 18 2:1 7 11^2 12 17^2 23 26 27 29 3:1 5 6 7^4

REV. 3:12 13 20 23 4:3 5:7 8 6:2^2 3 5^2 7 9 12 7:2 14 15 8:1 3 9:2 5 10:2^2 3 7^2 9 11 11:5 15 12:9 12^2 13^2 15 13:6 10^2 11^2 12 13^2 14 15 16 17 14:4 10 16 17 16:15^2 16 17:3 10^2 11 14 15 18:2 22 19:2 9^2 10 11^2 12^2 13 15^3 16 17 20 20:2 3^2 6 21:3 5^2 6 7^2 10 15 16 17 22:1 6 7 9 10 11^4 20

her

846

GEN. 2:22 3:6^2 15 4:11 12 8:9^2 11 15 12:16 19^2 16:2 3^3 4 5 6^3 7^2 9 10 11 13 17:15 16^2 19:33 20:4 6 7 13 21:10 12 14^2

GEN. 21:16^2 17 19 23:2 24:15 16^2 17 18 20 21 22 28 43 45^2 46 47^2 51 53 55 57 58 59 60 61 64 67^2 25:1 22 23^3 26:9

GEN. 27:6 15^3 17 42^2 29:9 12^2 19 20 21 23 27 28 29 31 30:1 3^2 4^2 9^2 15 16 21 22^2 31:19 35 33:2 7 34:2^4 8 11^2 35:17

GEN. 35:18 20 38:2^2 8 11 14^3 15^3 16 18^2 19^3 20 22 23^3 24^2 25 26^2 27^2 39:7 10^3 12 13 14 16 40:10 48:7 EXOD. 2:5^2 8 9

EXOD. 2:10 3:22^3 4:25 11:2 15:20^2 18:2 3 6^2 21:4^2 8^5 9^2 10^3 11 22^2 22:16^2 17^2 LEVIT. 11:19 12:2 4^2 5^2 6 7^3 8 15:19^3 20 21 23 24^2

LEVIT. 15:25^5 26^4 28 29 30^2 33^3 18:7 11 15 17^5 18^4 19^2 20 25 19:20 29 20:14 17 18^4 21:3 7 9 13 22:13^3 28 25:19 22 26:4 10 20

LEVIT. 26:34^2 43 NUM. 5:13^3 15^2 16^2 18 19 24 27^6 29 30 31 12:12 13 14^4 16:30 32 19:3^3 4^2 5^4 8 22:23 25 33 25:8 26:59 30:3 4^8

NUM. 30:5^8 6^2 7^5 8^6 9^2 10^2 11^5 12^6 13^2 14^6 15 16^2 36:8 DEU. 11:6 17 14:18 20:7^2 21:11^2 12^3 13^6 14^5 22:13^2 14^4 15 16 17 19 21^4

DEU. 22:23^2 25^3 27^2 28^2 29^3 24:1^5 3^5 4^3 25:5^4 8 11^2 12^2 28:30 56^5 57^3 32:11^4 22 JOSH. 2:14 15 17 6:17 22 23^4 25 8:2^2 10:1^2 39 13:17

JOSH. 15:18^3 19 45^2 47^4 17:11^6 16 21:13^2 14^2 15^2 16^3 17^2 18^2 21^2 22^2 23^2 24^2 25^2 27^2 28^2 29^2 30^2 31^2 32^3 34^2 35^2 36^2 37^2 38^2 39^2

JUD. 1:14^3 15 27^5 4:5 8 18 19 20 21 22 5:26^2 27^2 29^2 11:26^2 34 35 37 38^3 39^2 13:3 6 9^2 10 13 14^3 14:3^2 8 16 17^2 15:1

JUD. 15:2^6 6^3 16:1 5^2 7 8 9 11 13 16 17^2 18^2 19 19:2 3^5 25^4 26 27^2 28^2 29^3 20:6^2 RUTH 1:3 5^2 6 7^2 8^2 9 10

RUTH 1:14^2 15^2 18^2 22^2 2:1 2 3 10 11 14^2 15^2 16^2 18^2 19^3 20^2 22 23 3:1^2 5 6^2 7 15 16^3 4:13^2 16 17 1 SAM. 1:4^2 5

1 SAM. 1:6^4 7 8^2 12 13^3 14 18^2 19 22 23^3 24 2:19 4:19^4 20^3 21^2 18:17 21 25:19^2 20 23 35^2 39 40 41 42 28:7^2 10 13 14

2 SAM. 3:15^2 16^3 6:16 23 11:4^4 26^2 27 12:24^2 13:1 2 5 6 8 10 11^2 14^3 15^4 16 17 18^3 19^5 20^3 22 14:2 3 4 5 16:8 20:17 22

2 SAM. 21:10 1 KINGS 1:2^3 3 4 19^2 20 2:1 17 3:20 26^3 27 9:24^2 10:2 3^3 5 13^4 14:5^2 6 15:13^2 17:10 11 13 15 19^2 20 21:6

2 KINGS 4:2 5^3 6^2 9 12 13 14^2 15^2 17 20 22 24 25 26^2 27^4 30 36 37 5:3 6:28 29^2 8:2 3^2 5^3 6 10 9:22 30^2 33^4 34

2 KINGS 9:35^3 11:1 3 14 15^3 16 19:21 22:14 1 CHRON. 2:18 5:16 6:57^2 58^2 59^2 60^2 67^2 68^2 69^2 70^2 71^2 72^2 73^2 74^2 75^2 76^2 77^2 78^2 79^2 80^2

1 CHRON. 6:81^2, 7:29^4, 15:29, 18:1, 2 CHRON. 8:11, 9:1, 2^3, 4, 12^3, 10:20, 15:16^2, 22:10, 23:13, 14^3, 15^2, 34:22, 36:21, ESTHER 1:11, 19, 2:1, 7, 9^6, 10^3, 11, 13^2, 14, 15^2, 17^2, 20^3, 4:4^2, 5, 8^3, 5:1, 3, 12, 8:1

JOB 5:16, 9:6, 21:10, 31:10, 18, 39:14, 16^2, 17^2, 26, 27, 29, 30, PSALMS 34:2, 45:13, 14^2, 46:5^2, 48:3, 12, 18^2, 55:11, 58:4, 67:6, 68:13, 31, 69:15, 80:11^2, 12^2, 84:3, 85:12, 87:5^2, 102:13, 14, 104:17, 107:42, 123:2, 132:13^2, 16^2, 137:5

PROV. 1:20, 21, 2:4^2, 16, 17^2, 18^2, 19, 3:15, 16^2, 17^2, 18^2, 4:6^2, 8^2, 13^2, 5:3, 4, 5^2, 6, 8^2, 19^3, 6:6, 8^2, 25^3, 29, 7:5, 8^2, 11^2, 21^2, 22, 25^2, 26, 27, 8:1, 9:1^2, 2^3, 3, 14, 18, 12:4, 14:1^2, 17:12

PROV. 17:25, 27:8, 16, 30:20, 23, 28, 31:10, 11^2, 12, 13, 14, 15^2, 16, 17^2, 18^2, 19^2, 20^2, 21^2, 22, 23, 25, 26^2, 27, 28^4, 31^3, ECCL. 7:26^3, 11:5, CANT. 2:13, 3:4, 6:9^6, 8:5, 9^2, ISAIAH 1:27, 3:26, 4:5

ISAIAH 5:14, 7:16, 9:10, 10:11^2, 13:10, 13, 22^2, 16:8, 21:9, 23:3, 7^2, 17, 18^2, 24:2, 26:17^2, 21^2, 27:2, 29:7^3, 34:12, 13, 15^3, 16, 37:22, 40:2^4, 49:15^2, 51:2^2, 3^3, 18^2, 52:11, 53:7, 61:10, 11, 65:10, 19, 66:7, 8, 10^4, 11^2, 12^3

JER. 2:23, 24^5, 32^2, 3:1, 7, 8^3, 9, 10^2, 20, 4:17, 31^3, 5:10^2, 6:3^2, 4, 5, 7^3, 8:7, 19^2, 9:1, 20, 12:7, 9, 15:9, 17:8^2, 19:15, 20:17, 30:18, 31:8, 15^2, 44:17, 18, 19^4, 25, 46:21^2, 22, 23, 48:4, 15, 41, 49:2, 4

JER. 49:19^2, 22, 24, 26^2, 50:2^2, 3^2, 9, 10, 13, 14, 15^6, 26^5, 27, 29^3, 30^2, 35^2, 36, 37^2, 38, 44^2, 51:2^3, 3^2, 4, 6^2, 7, 8^2, 9^2, 27^3, 28, 30^2, 33^2, 36^2, 43, 45, 47^3, 48, 52^2, 53^2, 55^2, 56^2, 57^5

JER. 51:58, 64, LAM. 1:2^7, 3, 4^3, 5^5, 6, 7^7, 8^3, 9^3, 10^2, 11, 17^2, 2:5, 7, 9^4, 16, 4:6, 7, 13^3, EZEKIEL 5:5, 6, 12:19, 13:16, 16:2, 32, 44, 45^2, 46^2, 48, 49^2, 53^2, 55^2, 57, 17:7^3, 9, 19:2

EZEKIEL 19:3, 5^2, 11^3, 12^2, 14^2, 22:2^2, 3, 10, 24, 25^2, 26, 27, 28, 23:4, 5^2, 7, 8^5, 9^2, 10^5, 11^5, 12, 14, 16, 17^3, 18^4, 19^2, 31, 42, 43^2, 44, 24:7, 8, 12^3, 26:4^4, 6, 17, 28:22^2, 23^4, 29:12, 19^3, 30:4^2

EZEKIEL 30:6, 7, 8, 18^5, 31:4^2, 32:7, 16^4, 18, 20^2, 22, 23^2, 24^2, 25^3, 26^2, 29^2, 33:28, 34:27^2, 36:38, 44:22, DANIEL 11:6^3, 7, 17, HOSEA 1:6, 2:2^6, 3^5, 4, 6, 7, 8, 9, 10^3, 11^5, 12^2, 13^4, 14^3, 15^3, 17

HOSEA 2:23^2, 3:1, 2, 3, 4:18, 19^2, 9:2, 10, 10:7, 11, 14, 13:8, 16, JOEL 1:8, 2:16, 22, 3:17, AMOS 4:3, 5:2^2, OBADIAH 1, JONAH 1:15, 2:6, MICAH 1:9, 4:6^3, 7^2, 11, 7:5, 6^2, 10^2

NAHUM 2:7^2, 13, 3:4^2, 7, 8, 9, 10^3, ZEPH. 2:14, 15^2, 3:1, 2, 3^3, 4^2, 19^2, HAGGAI 1:10, 2:3, ZECH. 2:5^2, 5:11, 7:7, 8:2, 12^2, 9:4^2, 5, 12:6, 14:10, MALACHI 3:11, MATT. 1:6, 19^3, 20, 25^2, 2:18

MATT. 5:28^2, 31, 32, 8:15, 9:18, 22, 25, 10:35, 11:19, 14:4, 7, 8, 9, 11, 15:23^2, 28^2, 19:7, 9, 20:20, 21, 21:2, 22:28, 23:37^2, 24:29, 26:13, MARK 1:30, 31^3, 5:23, 29^2, 32, 33, 34, 41, 43, 6:17, 23, 24, 26, 28

MARK 7:26, 27, 29, 30^2, 10:4, 11, 12, 12:21, 22, 23, 44^2, 13:24, 28, 14:5, 6^2, 9, 16:11, LUKE 1:5, 28, 29, 30, 35, 36^2, 38, 41, 45, 56^2, 58^4, 61, 2:7, 19, 22, 36, 51, 4:38, 39^2, 7:12, 13^3, 35

LUKE 7:38, 44, 47, 48, 8:43, 48, 52, 54, 55^2, 56, 10:38, 40, 41, 42, 11:27, 12:53^2, 13:12^3, 13, 34^2, 15:9^2, 16:18, 18:5^2, 20:30, 31, 33, 21:4, JOHN 2:4, 4:7, 10, 13, 16, 17, 21, 26, 27, 28^2, 8:3, 7, 10

JOHN 8:11, 11:1, 2, 5, 23, 25, 28^2, 31^3, 33^2, 40, 12:3, 7, 16:21, 18:16, 19:27, 20:13, 15, 16, 17, 18, ACTS 5:8, 9, 10^4, 7:21, 8:27, 9:37, 40, 41^3, 12:15, 16:15, 16, 18, 19, 19:27, 21:3, 27:15, 32

ROMANS 7:2^2, 3^2, 9:12, 25, 16:2^2, 1 COR. 7:2, 4, 10, 11, 12, 13^2, 34, 36, 38^2, 39^2, 11:5^2, 6^2, 10, 15^2, 13:5, GAL. 4:25, 30, EPHES. 5:33, 1 THESS. 2:7, JAMES 1:4, 5:18, 2 PETER 2:22, 2 JOHN 1

REV. 2:21^2, 22^2, 23, 6:13, 12:1^2, 4, 5, 6, 14, 15, 16, 17, 14:8, 18, 16:19, 17:2, 4^2, 5, 6, 7, 16^2, 18:3^3, 4^3, 5^2, 6^4, 7^2, 8^2, 9^4, 10, 11, 15^2, 18, 19, 20^2, 24, 19:2^2, 3, 8, 21:2, 11, 22:2

him *846*

GEN. 1:27, 2:15, 18, 20, 3:9, 23, 4:7, 8, 15^3, 19, 26, 5:1, 24, 6:22, 7:5, 16^2, 23, 8:1, 8, 9^2, 11, 12, 18, 9:8, 24, 10:21, 12:3, 4, 7, 20^2, 13:1, 11, 14, 14:5, 17^2, 19, 20, 15:4, 5^2, 6, 7, 9, 10, 12, 16:1, 12, 13, 17:1, 3, 17, 19, 20^2, 22, 23, 27, 18:1, 9, 10, 18, 19^2, 29, 30, 19:5, 6, 16^2, 21, 26, 30, 32, 34^2, 35

GEN. 20:3, 6, 9, 14, 21:2, 3, 4, 5, 7, 16^2, 18, 21, 22:1, 2, 3^2, 9^2, 11, 12, 13^2, 23:5, 14, 24:5, 6, 9, 18, 19, 24, 25, 32, 33, 35, 36, 47, 54, 25:2, 9, 21, 33, 26:2, 7, 9, 12, 14, 20, 24, 26, 31, 32^2, 27:1, 13, 22, 23^2, 25^2, 26, 27^2, 32, 33, 37^3, 39, 41, 42, 44, 45, 28:1^2, 6^2, 29:5, 13^2, 14^2, 20, 23, 28

GEN. 29:30, 34, 30:4, 16, 20, 27, 29, 36, 31:2, 7, 14, 15, 20, 23^2, 24, 32, 32:1, 3, 6, 7, 11, 19, 20, 21, 24, 25^2, 27, 29^2, 31, 33:1, 4^3, 11, 13, 17, 34:6, 8, 35:2, 7, 9, 10, 11, 13^2, 14, 15, 18, 26, 29, 36:5, 37:3, 4^3, 5, 8^2, 10^2, 11, 13, 14^2, 15^2, 18^3, 20^3, 21^2, 22^4, 23, 24^2, 27^2, 33, 35^2, 36, 38:5, 7, 10, 14

GEN. 38:18, 39:1^2, 3, 4^2, 5, 12^2, 15, 17, 19, 20, 21^2, 23, 40:7, 8, 9, 12, 23, 41:12, 13, 14, 33, 34, 42, 43^3, 45, 50, 42:4, 6, 8, 10, 16, 24, 29, 31, 37^3, 38, 43:3, 5, 7, 9^4, 19, 26^2, 32^2, 33, 34^2, 44:7, 9, 14, 18, 20, 21^2, 24, 28, 29, 32, 45:1^2, 3, 9, 15, 26, 27^2, 28, 46:5, 6, 7^2, 20, 27, 28, 29, 31, 47:7

GEN. 47:18^2, 29, 31, 48:1, 10, 13, 17, 49:9, 10, 19, 23^3, 26, 50:1^2, 8^2, 7, 9, 12, 13^2, 14, 15, 17, 26, EXOD. 1:16, 2:2^2, 3^2, 4, 6, 10^2, 12, 13, 20, 22, 3:2, 4, 18, 4:2, 6, 11, 13, 15, 16, 18, 23, 24^2, 26, 27^2, 28^2, 6:2, 20^2, 23^2, 25^2, 7:16, 8:1, 20, 9:1, 13, 29, 10:1, 3, 7, 28, 12:4, 44, 48, 49, 13:14, 19, 14:6, 15:2^2

EXOD. 15:25, 16:8, 17:10, 12, 18:7, 17, 19:3, 7, 19, 24, 20:7, 21:3, 4^2, 6^3, 10, 13, 14^2, 16, 19^2, 22, 26, 27, 29, 30^2, 31, 36, 22:2, 3^2, 7, 12, 13, 17, 21, 25^2, 26, 23:4, 5^3, 21^3, 24:2, 14, 18, 28:1, 3, 41, 43^2, 29:5, 7, 17, 21, 29, 30:21, 31:3, 6, 18, 32:1^2, 23, 26^2, 33, 33:4, 15, 34:4, 5, 6, 20, 29, 30, 31, 32, 34, 35, 35:5

EXOD. 35:21, 31, 36:2, 3, 38:23, 40:13^2, 16, LEVIT. 1:1, 3, 4^2, 6, 4:3, 12, 14, 19, 21, 26^2, 31^2, 35, 5:2, 3, 4, 6, 10^2, 13^2, 16^2, 18^2, 6:2, 4, 5, 7^2, 18, 7:20, 8:2, 4, 7^6, 8, 12^2, 30^2, 9:9, 12, 13, 18, 13:3^2, 4, 5^2, 6^2, 8, 10, 11^2, 12, 13, 14, 15, 17^2, 20, 21, 22, 23, 25, 26, 27^2, 28, 30, 31, 33, 34, 36, 37

LEVIT. 13:44, 46, 14:4, 7^2, 11, 12, 14, 17, 18^2, 19, 20, 21, 25, 28, 29^2, 31, 32, 15:7, 8, 10, 14, 15, 16, 24, 32^3, 33^2, 16:9, 10^2, 21^2, 22, 17:10, 18:6, 19:13^2, 17, 22^2, 33, 34, 20:2, 3, 4, 5^2, 6, 9, 21:2, 8, 12, 15, 17, 22:3, 4, 11, 12, 14^3, 16, 19, 20, 23^2, 27, 28^2, 30, 35, 36, 37^2, 25:39, 41, 43, 47, 48, 49^3, 50^4, 52^2

LEVIT. 25:53^2, 54, 26:46, 27:8^2, 18, 19, 23, 24^2, NUM. 2:5, 20, 27, 3:6, 9, 42, 4:49, 5:7, 8, 12, 14^2, 30, 6:9, 11, 7:89^3, 8:2, 9:7, 14, 10:30, 11:20, 25^2, 29, 30, 12:6^2, 8, 13:27, 31, 14:24^2, 36, 15:28^2, 29^2, 31, 33^2, 34^2, 35, 36^2, 16:5^4, 10, 11, 25, 40, 17:6, 11, 19:13^2, 18, 20, 20:9, 18, 19, 20, 21, 21:24, 34^3, 35^2, 22:5, 7, 16, 20, 22^2, 36, 40

NUM. 22:41, 23:4, 6, 9^2, 13, 14, 17^3, 21, 24:2, 8, 9, 17^2, 19, 25:12, 13, 26:54, 27:11, 18, 19^2, 20, 21^2, 22^2, 23, 31:17, 18, 35, 32:15, 16, 21, 35:16, 17, 18, 19^2, 20^2, 21^3, 22^2, 23^2, 25, 27, 30, 32, 33, DEU. 1:3, 16, 36, 38, 2:24, 30^2, 33^2, 3:2^3, 3^2, 28^2, 4:7, 20, 25, 29^2, 34, 35, 42, 5:11, 6:13, 16, 7:9, 10^4, 8:6, 9:18, 20, 23, 10:8

DEU. 10:9, 12, 18, 20^2, 11:13, 22, 13:4^3, 8^4, 9^3, 10, 14:27, 15:8, 9, 10^2, 12, 13^2, 14^2, 18, 17:7^2, 15, 18, 19, 18:4, 5^2, 15, 18, 19, 20, 22, 19:6^3, 11^3, 12^2, 13, 16, 19, 20:5, 6, 7, 8, 21:1, 2, 5, 15, 17, 18, 19^2, 21, 22, 23, 22:2^2, 4, 18, 19, 26, 23:10, 16^2, 24:1, 7^2, 13, 15, 25:2, 3^2, 5, 8^2, 9, 10, 11^3, 26:3, 28:44, 55, 29:15^2

DEU. 29:20^2, 21, 30:20, 31:7, 14, 29, 32:10^4, 12^2, 13^2, 15, 16^2, 33:7^3, 9, 11^2, 12^2, 16^2, 24^2, 34:1, 4, 6, 9^2, 11, JOSH. 1:18, 2:19, 23, 4:14, 5:3, 13^3, 14, 6:5, 7, 20, 7:3, 19, 24, 25, 26, 8:11, 14, 23, 9:6, 9^2, 10:7, 15, 23, 24, 29, 31, 33^2, 34, 36, 38, 43, 11:7, 9, 13:1, 14:6, 7, 13, 15:16, 17, 18^2, 19:50, 20:4^2, 5^2, 22:5^2, 14, 27

JOSH. 22:30, 23:3^2, 14, 24:22, 30, 33^2, JUD. 1:7, 12, 13, 14^2, 15, 24, 25, 2:9, 3:10, 13, 15, 16, 19^2, 20, 23, 27, 28, 31, 4:6, 7, 13, 14, 18^2, 19^2, 21, 22^2, 25, 5:13, 25, 28^2, 31, 6:12^2, 13, 14, 15, 16, 17, 19, 20, 23, 25, 27, 31^5, 32^2, 34, 35, 7:1, 3, 5, 8, 9, 19, 8:1^2, 3, 4, 8^2, 14^2, 31, 9:3, 4^2, 5^2, 16, 19, 24

JUD. 9:25, 26, 28^2, 33, 34, 35, 36, 38^2, 40^2, 44, 48^3, 54^3, 10:3, 6, 11:2^2, 3, 11, 15, 19, 28, 34, 36, 12:5, 6^3, 8, 11, 13, 13:6, 10, 11, 12, 18, 23, 24, 25, 14:3, 5, 6^2, 11^2, 13, 16, 17^2, 18, 19, 15:1, 10, 12, 13^3, 14^2, 16:2^3, 5^4, 8, 9, 12^2, 14, 15, 16^2, 19^4, 20, 21^3, 24, 25, 26, 31^3, 17:9^2, 10, 11, 18:3, 5, 15, 16

JUD. 18:25, 26, 19:1, 2^2, 3^4, 4^2, 7, 9, 10^2, 12, 15, 18, 21, 22, 25, 28, 20:23, 21:5, RUTH 2:2, 4, 10, 3:13, 4:1, 15, 1 SAM. 1:11, 17, 20, 22, 23^2, 24^3, 27, 28, 2:3, 16^2, 19^2, 25^2, 27, 28, 35, 36, 3:7, 13, 18^4, 19, 5:3, 4, 6:3, 4, 8, 7:3, 9, 8:5, 10, 12, 9:5, 6, 13^2, 16, 17, 10:1, 9, 10^2, 11, 14, 16, 19, 21

1 SAM. 10:23, 24^2, 26, 27^2, 11:3, 5, 12:14, 24, 13:2, 7, 8, 10^2, 14^2, 15^2, 14:2, 7, 13^2, 17, 20, 34, 37, 39, 43, 52^2, 15:2, 12, 13, 16, 28, 32, 16:1, 3, 6, 7, 8, 11, 12^2, 13, 14, 15, 17, 18, 21^2, 23, 17:7, 8, 9^2, 13, 20, 24, 25^3, 26, 27^2, 30^2, 31, 32, 33, 35^5, 38, 39, 40, 41, 42, 50, 51, 57^2, 58, 18:1, 2^2, 3, 4

1 SAM. 18:5^2, 8, 12, 13^3, 14, 15, 17^2, 20, 21^3, 24, 27, 28, 19:4, 7, 8, 11^3, 15^2, 18^2, 23, 20:2, 7, 17^2, 24, 26, 30, 31, 32, 33^2, 34, 35, 36, 40, 21:1, 5, 6, 11^2, 14, 22:1, 2^2, 4, 6^2, 7, 10^3, 13^3, 15, 17, 23:3, 4, 7, 9, 14^2, 17, 20, 22, 23, 25, 24:1, 4^2, 5, 6, 8, 19, 25:1^2, 5, 6, 12, 17, 21, 22, 25, 35

1 SAM. 25:36^2, 37^2, 39, 40, 26:2, 3, 5, 7, 8^2, 9, 10, 19, 24, 27:2, 4, 6, 12, 28:3^2, 6, 7, 8^2, 9, 17, 20, 21, 23, 29:3, 4^4, 6, 30:4, 6, 8, 9, 11^3, 12^2, 13, 15, 16, 21, 31:3, 5, 2 SAM. 1:3^2, 4, 5, 6^2, 7, 8, 10^2, 11, 13, 14, 15^2, 16, 2:1, 3, 5, 8, 9, 20, 21^2, 23^2, 32, 3:9, 11, 16, 20^2, 22, 23^2, 24

2 SAM. 3:26, 27[3], 31, 34, 4:4, 6, 7[3], 10[3], 5:10, 12, 13, 14, 25, 6:2, 7, 10, 12, 16, 7:1, 14, 15, 23, 8:4, 10[3], 9:1, 2[2], 3, 4, 5, 7, 10, 10:1, 2, 9, 12, 13[2], 17, 11:1, 4, 7, 8, 13[3], 15, 21, 22, 25, 27, 12:1[2], 3, 4, 9, 17[2], 18[3], 20, 21, 23[2], 24, 13:2, 4[2], 5[2], 6, 7, 9[2], 11, 12, 16, 17, 25[2], 26, 27[2], 28, 29, 34, 14:3, 6, 7[2], 10, 14, 24[2], 25, 26, 29[2], 31, 32, 33, 15:1[2], 2, 3, 4, 5[4], 9, 14, 16, 17, 18[2], 22, 24, 26[2], 30, 32, 16:1, 10[2], 11[3], 13[2], 14, 15, 18, 17:2[3], 6, 10, 12, 16, 22, 23, 24, 29, 18:1

2 SAM. 18:9, 11[3], 15, 17[2], 19, 20, 23, 30, 19:17[2], 23, 25, 29, 30, 31, 37[2], 38, 39, 40, 41, 20:5, 6[2], 7, 8, 9, 10[2], 11[2], 12[2], 14, 15, 17, 21, 21:4, 15, 17[3], 21, 22:1, 3, 13, 24, 31, 23:9, 10, 11, 21[2], 23, 24:2, 10, 13[3], 16, 18, 20, 22

1 KINGS 1:1, 2[2], 4, 5[2], 6[2], 7, 13, 17, 20, 25, 27, 33, 34, 35[2], 38, 40, 41, 42, 44[2], 45, 52[2], 53[2], 2:8, 9[2], 16, 19, 22[2], 25, 29, 30, 31, 34[2], 36, 42, 46, 3:6[2], 11, 16, 28, 4:10, 12, 13[2], 24, 5:1, 3, 12, 8:5[2], 24, 25, 31[2], 32, 57, 58, 62, 65, 9:2, 3, 12, 10:1, 2, 11:9, 10, 17

1 KINGS 11:18[3], 19, 20, 22, 23, 24, 28, 29, 30, 34, 12:1, 3, 7, 8[2], 10[2], 13, 18[2], 20[2], 13:4[3], 6, 11, 13, 14[2], 18[3], 19, 20, 23, 24[2], 26[5], 29, 30, 31, 33, 14:3, 10[2], 11[2], 13[3], 14, 18[2], 22, 15:3, 4[2], 5, 8, 27[2], 28, 29, 16:4[2], 7[2], 9, 10[2], 11, 17, 18, 21, 25, 30, 31[2], 33, 17:2, 6, 8, 17, 19[3], 21, 22, 23[2], 18:7[2], 8, 15, 16, 17, 21[3], 24, 30, 33, 19:5[2], 6, 7, 9[2], 13, 15, 17[2], 18, 19[3], 20, 21[2], 20:1, 2, 7, 8[2], 9, 10, 11[2], 16, 17, 22, 23, 31, 33[4], 34[3], 35, 36[4], 37[2], 40, 41, 42, 21:4[2], 5[2], 6, 7, 10[4], 13[4], 19[2], 21[2], 24[2], 22:7

1 KINGS 22:8, 11, 13, 15[2], 16, 19, 21, 22[2], 26, 27, 32, 33, 53

2 KINGS 1:5, 6[2], 8, 9[3], 10, 11[2], 12, 13[2], 15[3], 16, 2:2, 3, 4, 5, 6, 12, 13, 14, 15[3], 16[3], 17[2], 18, 20, 23[2], 3:11, 12[2], 13, 15, 26[2], 27[2], 4:1, 5, 8, 10, 12, 13, 19, 20[2], 21[2], 23, 27, 29[2], 31[2], 35, 36, 38, 5:1, 3, 5, 6, 8, 10, 13, 15, 16, 19[2], 20[2], 21[3], 23[2], 25, 26, 6:6, 10[2], 13[2], 15, 18, 26, 28, 29[2], 31, 32[5], 33, 7:17[2], 20[2], 8:6, 7, 8, 9[3], 10[2], 14, 19[2], 21[2], 29, 9:1, 2[2], 6, 8[2], 11, 13, 15, 17, 18, 21, 25[2], 26, 27[2], 28[2], 32, 36, 10:3, 4, 7

2 KINGS 10:8, 9, 11, 15[6], 16, 17, 18, 22, 24[2], 35, 11:2[3], 4, 8, 12[4], 15, 12:2, 21[2], 13:4, 9, 14, 15[2], 19, 20, 25, 14:19[3], 20, 21, 15:7, 10[3], 14, 16, 19, 25[4], 30[2], 16:5, 9, 17:2, 3[2], 4[2], 17, 27, 36[3], 18:5[3], 6, 7[2], 15, 21, 36[2], 37, 19:3, 7[2], 16, 21, 37, 20:1[2], 2, 4, 14, 21:6, 11, 23, 22:18, 23:1, 2, 17, 18, 25[4], 26, 29[3], 30[5], 33, 24:1, 2, 12, 25:5[2], 6[2], 7[2], 25[2], 28[2], 29, 30

1 CHRON. 2:3[2], 4, 9, 19[2], 21, 24, 29, 35, 3:1, 4, 5, 4:6, 9, 10, 5:2, 20, 7:22, 9:20, 10:3, 9, 14, 11:9, 10[2], 11, 12, 28[2], 25, 42, 12:19, 20, 22, 23, 27, 13:10

1 CHRON. 14:1, 2, 10, 14, 16, 17, 15:1, 2, 13, 27, 29, 16:5, 9[2], 29, 30, 17:13[2], 14, 25, 18:4, 10[3], 19:2[2], 10, 14[2], 17, 20:7, 21:11, 12, 15, 20, 26, 28, 22:6, 9, 23:13, 24:19, 25:5, 26:10, 27:7, 28:6, 9[3], 29:22, 23, 25[2], 30

2 CHRON. 1:1[2], 3, 7, 2:3[2], 4[2], 6[4], 14, 15, 5:6, 6:15, 16, 22[2], 23, 7:8, 12, 8:18, 9:1, 10:1, 3, 7, 8[3], 10[2], 18[2], 11:13, 15, 18, 19, 20, 22, 12:1, 3, 12[2], 13:3, 5, 7, 10, 11, 19, 20, 14:1, 5, 6, 7, 10, 18, 15:2[4], 4, 5[2], 9[2], 15, 16:7, 9, 10[2], 14[3], 17:11, 14, 15[2], 16[2], 17, 18[2], 18:2[4], 3, 6, 7, 10, 12, 14, 15, 20[2], 21, 25

2 CHRON. 18:26, 30, 31[3], 32, 19:2, 20:30, 36, 21:7, 9[2], 12, 17, 18, 19, 20, 22:6, 9[4], 11[4], 23:1, 11[4], 14, 16, 24:3, 6, 16, 21[2], 22, 23, 25[6], 26, 27, 25:3, 7, 10, 13, 15[2], 16[2], 23, 27[3], 28, 26:1, 5, 7, 17[2], 18, 20[3], 23, 27:5[2], 9, 28:5[3], 16, 20[3], 21, 23[2], 24, 27[2], 29:6, 11[3], 29, 30:9, 31:10, 15, 32:3, 6, 7[2], 8, 9, 15, 17, 21, 24[2], 25[2], 29[2], 31[3], 33[2], 33:6, 11[2], 13[3], 18, 19, 20, 24[2], 34:26, 35:20, 21, 22[2], 24[3], 36:1, 3, 4, 6[3], 8, 10, 13, 17, 20, 23[3]

EZRA 1:2, 3[2], 4, 4:2, 6, 11, 5:7, 15, 6:11, 7:6[2], 9, 26, 8:3, 4, 5, 6, 7, 8, 9

EZRA 8:10, 11, 12, 19, 21, 22[2], 33, 10:1

NEH. 1:5, 11, 2:1, 6[2], 3:2, 8[2], 10, 12, 16, 17[2], 18, 19, 20, 21, 22, 23[2], 24, 25, 29, 30[2], 31, 4:3, 6:8, 12[2], 18, 19, 8:4, 9:7[2], 8, 11:8, 13:5, 7, 26[3], 28

ESTHER 1:3, 12, 14, 17, 19, 2:2, 9[2], 20, 3:1[2], 2[2], 4, 5, 6, 4:4, 5, 7[2], 8[3], 10, 11, 17, 5:4, 9, 11[2], 14, 6:3[2], 4, 5[2], 6, 9[2], 11[2], 13[4], 14, 7:7, 9, 8:3, 7, 10:2

JOB 1:2, 8, 10, 2:3[3], 8, 9, 11[3], 12, 13[2], 3:20, 4:4, 6:10, 14, 7:8, 10, 17[2], 18[2], 8:4, 18[2], 9:3[2], 4, 11[2], 12[2], 13, 14[2], 32, 34, 35, 11:10, 13, 12:4, 5

JOB 12:13, 16, 13:7, 9, 15[2], 16, 14:6, 20[2], 22[2], 15:21, 24[2], 26, 31, 18:6, 7, 9[2], 10[2], 11[2], 14, 20, 21, 19:11, 16, 28, 20:7, 9[3], 11, 14, 16, 22, 23[2], 24, 25, 26[2], 27, 29, 21:15[2], 19, 21, 31, 33[3], 22:3, 14, 27, 23:3, 4, 7, 8, 9[2], 13, 14, 15, 24:1, 10, 20[2], 23, 25:2, 26:2, 3, 6, 14, 27:9, 15, 20[2], 21[2], 22, 23[2], 29:12[2], 13, 30:25, 31:14, 15, 29[2], 37[2], 32:13, 14, 33:13, 23, 24[2], 26, 34:11, 13, 17, 19, 27, 28, 29, 35:6[2], 7, 14[3], 36:11, 22, 23, 26, 37:16, 18, 19, 20, 23, 24, 39:11[2], 12, 20, 23, 40:2[2], 9, 11, 12, 19[2], 20, 22[2], 41:4, 5[2], 6[2], 8, 9[2], 10

JOB 41:11, 13, 22, 26[2], 28[2], 30, 32, 42:8, 11[6]

PSALMS 2:12, 3:2, 4:3[2], 5:12, 7:4[2], 5, 13, 8:4[2], 5[2], 6, 10:9, 11:5, 12:5[3], 13:4, 17:13[2], 18 *title*, 6, 11, 12, 23, 30, 20:6, 21:2, 3, 4, 5, 6[2], 22:8[3], 23[3], 24[2], 25, 26, 29, 30, 24:6, 25:12, 14, 28:7[2], 32:6, 10, 33:2, 3, 8, 18, 21, 34 *title*, 5, 6[2], 7, 8, 9, 19, 22, 35:8[2], 10[4], 25, 37:5, 7[2], 12, 13, 22[2], 24, 32, 33[2], 36, 40, 41:1, 2[3], 3, 8, 42:5, 11, 43:5, 44:16, 45:11, 49:7, 17, 50:3[2], 18, 23, 51 *title*, 52 *title*, 6, 53:5, 55:12, 20, 56 *title*, 57:3, 59 *title*, 61:7, 62:1, 4, 5, 8[2], 63:11, 64:4, 10, 66:6, 17, 67:7, 68:1[2], 4[2], 33, 69:26, 30, 34

PSALMS 71:11[3], 72:9, 11[2], 12, 15[2], 17[2], 74:14, 76:11[2], 78:17, 34, 36[2], 37, 40[2], 58[2], 70, 71, 79:10, 81:15, 85:9, 13, 89:7, 20, 21, 22[2], 23, 24, 27, 28[2], 33, 41, 43, 45, 91:2, 14[2], 15[4], 16[2], 92:15, 94:12, 13, 95:2, 96:6, 9, 97:2, 3, 7, 98:1, 100:4, 101:5[2], 103:11, 13, 17, 104:34, 105:2[2], 19, 20[2], 21, 106:7, 10, 23, 29, 31, 32, 43, 107:32[2], 41, 109:6, 7, 12, 17[2], 19[2], 30, 31, 111:5, 113:8, 116:2, 117:1, 2, 119:2, 42, 120:6, 126:6, 130:7, 135:1, 136:4, 5, 6, 7, 10, 13, 16, 17, 140:11, 141:5, 142:2[2], 144:3[2], 145:18, 19, 20, 147:11, 148:1, 2[2], 3[2], 4, 14, 149:2[2], 3, 150:1, 2[2], 3[2], 4[2], 5[2]

PROV. 3:6, 6:16, 7:10, 13[3]

PROV. 7:20, 21[2], 8:9, 30[3], 9:4[3], 16[3], 10:13[2], 24, 26, 11:18, 26[2], 27, 12:14, 13:6, 18, 24[2], 14:2, 6, 7, 31, 33, 35, 15:9, 10, 12, 14, 21, 16:7, 13, 22, 26, 29, 17:8, 11, 24, 25, 18:9, 13, 16[2], 17, 19:6, 7[3], 17, 19, 20:2, 7, 16, 19, 21:25, 22:15, 23:6, 13, 14, 24, 24:18[2], 24[2], 25, 29, 25:13, 21[2], 26:4, 12, 15, 17, 24, 25, 27, 27:11, 13, 22, 28:8, 11, 17, 22, 29:20, 21, 23, 30:5, 31:1, 6, 7, 12

ECCL. 2:26, 3:14, 22[2], 4:10[2], 12[2], 16, 5:12, 18, 19, 20, 6:2, 10, 12, 7:14, 8:3, 4, 6, 7, 12, 15[2], 9:2[2], 4, 10:1, 3, 8, 14[2], 11:8

CANT. 1:2, 3:1[3], 2[3]

CANT. 3:3, 4[4], 11, 5:4, 6[3], 8, 6:1

ISAIAH 3:10, 11[2], 5:19, 23, 7:4, 8:13[2], 17, 9:11, 13, 10:6, 15[2], 22, 26, 11:2, 3, 14:25, 29, 15:4, 9, 16:3, 20:1, 21:6, 14[2], 22:11, 16, 21[2], 23, 24, 24:2, 25:9[2], 10, 26:3, 27:5, 7[3], 28:6, 26[2], 29:12, 16[2], 21, 23, 30:18, 32, 31:4, 6, 8, 33:16, 36:3, 6, 21[2], 22, 37:3, 7[2], 22, 38, 38:1[2], 39:3, 40:3, 10[3], 13, 14[4], 17[2], 18, 20, 41:2[3], 7, 42:1, 25[3], 43:7[3], 44:3, 14, 20, 45:1[2], 9[2], 10, 13, 24[2], 46:7[5], 48:14, 15[2], 49:5, 7[2], 25, 50:4, 8, 10, 51:2[3], 52:10, 15, 53:2[3], 3[2], 4, 5, 6, 10[2], 12, 55:4, 6, 7[2], 56:6, 8[2], 57:15, 17, 18[3], 19[3], 58:5, 7, 11, 59:15

ISAIAH 59:16[2], 19, 62:7, 11[2], 63:2, 11, 14, 64:4[2], 5, 66:2

JER. 2:3, 15, 37, 3:1, 4:2[2], 6:11, 8:6, 9:24, 10:25[2], 11:19, 15:8, 18:18, 19:4, 20:2, 3, 9, 10[2], 15, 16, 21:1, 9, 12, 22:10[2], 12, 13[2], 14, 15, 16, 18[2], 23:24, 28[2], 26:8[2], 13, 19[2], 21, 22, 23[2], 24[2], 27:6[2], 7[2], 11, 12, 28:9, 14[2], 29:26, 31, 30:8, 10, 11, 21, 31:2, 10[2], 11[2], 20[4], 32:3, 4, 5, 9, 10, 33:13, 34:2, 14, 36:4, 8, 15, 22, 31, 37:4, 14[2], 15[2], 17[2], 21, 38:6, 11, 13, 14, 27[2], 39:5[3], 7[2], 9, 12[4], 14[2], 40:1[2], 2, 5[3], 6, 7, 14, 41:1, 2[2], 3, 7, 11, 12, 13, 16, 42:8, 9, 11, 43:1, 44:20, 45:4, 46:10, 25, 27

JER. 48:11, 12[2], 17[2], 19, 26, 27, 35[2], 39, 49:5, 8[2], 19, 50:16, 32[2], 43, 51:3[2], 44, 52:8, 9[2], 11[3], 31, 32[2], 33, 34

LAM. 1:17, 2:19, 3:24, 25[2], 28, 30, 32

EZEKIEL 1:3, 2:2, 3:18, 20[2], 27[2], 7:15, 9:4, 5, 10:7, 12:13[2], 14[2], 13:22, 14:4, 7[2], 8[2], 9[2], 10[2], 17:6[2], 7[2], 12, 13[2], 15[2], 16[2], 17, 20[3], 18:13, 20[2], 22, 32, 19:4[2], 5, 8[2], 9[3], 21:26[2], 27, 24:27, 28:9[2], 12, 29:2, 20, 30:11, 24, 31:4[2], 8[2], 9[2], 11[3], 12[3], 15[3], 16, 17, 32:2, 21[2], 22, 25, 26, 33:2, 4, 5, 12, 16, 27, 35:7[2], 37:19, 38:2, 21, 22[3], 40:46, 43:6, 44:26, 45:20, 46:12, 47:23

DANIEL 2:1, 16, 22, 24, 25, 46, 48[2], 3:28, 4:8

DANIEL 4:16[2], 19, 23, 34, 35, 5:6, 9, 11, 17, 19[2], 20, 21, 24, 29, 6:3[2], 4, 5, 6, 14[2], 16, 18[2], 22, 23[2], 7:10[3], 13[2], 14[2], 16, 27, 8:4, 6, 7[5], 11, 12, 9:4, 9, 11, 10:16, 11:1, 5, 11, 16[2], 17[3], 18[2], 22, 23, 25, 26, 30, 40[2], 44, 45, 12:7

HOSEA 1:3, 4, 6, 4:17, 5:6, 14, 7:5, 9, 10, 8:3, 11, 12, 9:4, 17, 11:1, 7, 12:2, 4[2], 14[3], 13:11, 13, 14:2, 4, 8[2]

JOEL 2:13, 14, 20

AMOS 1:5, 8, 2:3, 3:5, 14, 5:8, 10[2], 11, 19[2], 6:10[3], 9:13

OBADIAH 1:7

JONAH 1:6[2], 8, 10, 11, 15, 3:6[2], 4:5, 6

MICAH 1:4, 2:7, 3:5, 5:5, 6:5, 6

MICAH 7:9, 15

NAHUM 1:5, 6, 7, 15, 2:4, 5[2], 6[4], 9, 12, 15[3], 2:19, 20, 3:5

ZEPH. 1:6, 2:11, 3:9

HAGGAI 1:12

ZECH. 1:8, 2:3, 4, 3:1, 4[3], 5, 4:11, 12, 5:4, 6:12, 8:10, 23, 9:8[2], 10:4[4], 12:1, 10[2], 13:3[4], 6

MALACHI 2:5[2], 12, 17, 3:16, 17, 18[3], 4:4

MATT. 1:20, 24[2], 2:2, 3, 5, 8[2], 11[2], 15, 3:5, 6, 13, 14, 15[2], 16[2], 4:5[2], 6, 7, 8[2], 9, 10[2], 11[2], 20, 22, 24, 25, 5:1, 25, 31, 39, 40, 41, 42[2], 6:8, 7:8, 9, 10, 11, 24, 8:1, 2, 3, 4, 5[2], 7[2], 16, 18, 19, 20, 21, 22, 23, 25[2], 27, 28, 31, 34, 9:2, 9[2], 10, 14, 18

MATT. 9:19, 20, 22, 24, 27, 28[2], 32, 10:1, 4, 28, 32, 33, 40, 11:3, 15, 27, 12:2, 3, 4[2], 10[2], 14[2], 15, 16, 18, 22[2], 32[2], 46, 47, 48[2], 13:2, 9, 10, 12[2], 27, 28, 36, 43, 51, 57, 14:2, 3[2], 4, 5[2], 9, 13, 15, 17, 22, 26, 28, 31[2], [illegible], 35[2], 36, 15:4, 12, 15, 22, 23, 25, 30, 32, 33, 16:1, 17, 22[2], 24, 17:3, 5, 10, 12[2], 14[2], 16[2], 17, 18, 19, 23, 25, 26[2], 18:2[2], 6, 15[2], 17, 21[2], 22, 24[2], 25, 26, 27[2], 28[3], 29, 30, 32[2], 34[2], 19:2, 3[3], 7, 10, 12, 13, 16, 17, 18, 20, 21, 27, 20:18, 19[2], 20[3], 21, 22, 25, 26, 27, 29, 33, 34

MATT. 21:7, 14, 16, 23, 25, 31, 32[3], 38, 39[3], 41[2], 44, 46[2], 22:12, 13[3], 15, 16, 19, 21, 22, 23[2], 35[2], 37, 42, 43, 45, 46[2], 23:15, 21, 22, 24:1[2], 3, 15, 17, 18, 47, 50, 51[2], 25:6, 10, 21, 23, 26, 28[2], 29, 31, 32, 37, 44, 26:4, 7, 15[2], 16, 17, 18, 22, 24, 25[2], 33, 34, 35, 37, 47, 48[2], 49, 50[2], 52, 56, 57, 58, 59, 62, 63, 64, 67[2], 69, 71, 73, 75, 27:1, 2[3], 3, 9, 11, 13, 14, 18, 19[2], 22[2], 23, 26, 27, 28[2], 29[2], 30[2], 31[5]

MATT. 27:32, 34, 35, 36, 38, 39, 41, 42[2], 43[3], 44, 48, 49, 54, 55, 64, 28:4, 7, 9[2], 13, 14, 17[2]

MARK 1:5[2], 10, 12, 13, 18, 20, 25[2], 26[2], 27, 30, 32, 34, 36[2], 37[2], 40[4], 41[2], 42, 43[2], 44, 45, 2:3, 4, 13, 14, 15, 16, 18, 24, 25, 26, 3:2[3], 6[2], 7, 8, 9[2], 10[2], 11[2], 12, 13[2], 14, 19, 21, 23, 31[2], 32[2], 34, 4:1, 9, 10[2], 23, 25, 36[2], 38[2], 41, 5:2, 3, 4[2], 6, 8, 9, 10, 12, 15, 16, 17, 18[2], 19[2], 20, 21, 22, 23, 24[3]

MARK 5:30[2], 31, 33[2], 37, 40[2], 6:1, 2[2], 3, 7, 14[2], 17, 19[2], 20[3], 22, 26, 27, 30, 33[2], 35, 37, 49, 50, 54, 56[2], 7:1, 5, 10, 12, 14, 15[3], 16, 17, 18, 25, 26, 28, 32[2], 33, 34, 8:1, 4, 11[3], 19, 22[3], 23[3], 25, 26, 29, 30, 32[2], 34[2], 38, 9:2, 7, 11, 13[2], 15[3], 18[3], 19[2], 20[4], 21[2], 22[2], 23[2], 25[3], 26[2], 27[2], 28[2], 31, 32, 36[2], 37, 38[2], 39, 42, 10:1, 2[2], 10, 13, 17[2], 18, 20, 21[3], 28, 32, 33[2], 34[4], 35, 37, 39, 42, 48, 49[2], 51[2], 52, 11:2[2]

MARK 11:3[2], 4, 7[2], 18[2], 27, 28, 31, 12:3[2], 4[3], 5, 6, 7, 8[3], 12[2], 13, 14, 16, 17, 18[2], 19, 26, 28, 29, 32, 34[2], 37[2], 43, 13:1, 2, 3, 14, 15, 16, 21, 14:1[2], 10, 11[2], 12, 13, 19, 21, 29, 30, 33, 35, 40, 43, 44[3], 45[2], 46[2], 50, 51[2], 53, 54, 55, 56, 57, 58, 61[2], 64, 65[4], 67, 69, 72, 15:1[2], 2[2], 3, 4, 7, 8, 10, 12, 13, 14, 15, 16, 17, 18, 19[3], 20[5], 22, 23, 24, 25, 27, 29, 32[2], 36[2], 39, 41[3], 44[2], 46[3], 16:1, 6, 7

MARK 16:10, 14

LUKE 1:11, 12[2], 13, 17, 19, 29, 32, 50, 59, 62, 66, 74, 75, 2:7[2], 22[2], 25, 26, 27, 28, 33, 38, 40, 44[2], 45[2], 46[2], 47, 48[2], 3:7, 10, 11[3], 12, 14, 19, 22, 4:3, 4, 5[2], 6, 8[2], 9[3], 12, 13, 14, 17, 20, 22, 29[3], 35[5], 37, 38, 40, 42[3], 5:3, 5, 9, 11, 12, 13[2], 14, 15[2], 18[3], 19[2], 20, 27, 28, 29, 33, 6:3, 4, 7[2], 13, 17, 19[2], 29[2], 30, 7:2, 3[2], 4, 6[2], 9[3], 11, 14, 15, 17, 18, 19, 20, 29, 30, 36[2], 38

LUKE 7:39[2], 40, 42, 43, 49, 8:1, 3, 4, 8, 9, 18[2], 19[2], 20, 24[2], 25, 27, 28, 29, 30[2], 31, 32, 37, 38[3], 39, 40[3], 41, 42, 44, 45, 47[3], 49, 50, 53, 9:7, 9, 10, 11, 12, 18, 23, 26, 30, 32[2], 33, 35, 37, 39[4], 40, 42[3], 45, 47[2], 48, 49, 50[2], 52, 53, 57, 58, 60, 62, 10:16, 22, 23, 25, 26, 28, 30[3], 31, 32, 33[2], 34[4], 35[2], 36, 37[3], 38, 40, 11:1, 5[2], 6, 8[2], 10, 11[2], 12, 13, 16[2], 22[3], 26, 27, 37[2], 39, 45, 53[2], 54[2], 12:5[2], 8

LUKE 12:10[2], 13, 14, 20, 36, 41, 44, 46[3], 48[2], 58, 13:1, 8, 12, 15[2], 17, 23, 31, 14:1, 2, 4[3], 5, 6, 8, 9, 12[2], 15[2], 16, 18, 25, 29, 31[2], 35, 15:1[2], 15, 16, 18, 20[2], 21, 22, 27[2], 28, 30, 31, 16:1, 2[2], 5, 6, 7, 14, 27, 29, 31, 17:1, 2, 3[2], 4, 7, 8, 9, 12, 16, 19, 31[2], 37, 18:3, 7, 15, 16, 18, 19, 22, 31, 33[2], 37, 39, 40[3], 42, 43, 19:4, 5[2], 6, 8, 9, 14[2], 15, 17, 19, 22, 24[2], 25, 26[2], 30[2], 31[3], 34, 35

LUKE 19:39, 47, 48, 20:1, 2, 5, 10[3], 11[3], 12[2], 13[2], 14[2], 15[2], 18, 19, 20[2], 21, 27[2], 38, 40, 44, 21:7, 38[2], 22:2, 4, 5, 6, 9, 10, 14, 21, 26, 33, 36[2], 39, 43[2], 47, 48, 49[2], 51, 52, 54[3], 56[3], 57[2], 58, 59, 61, 63[2], 64[3], 65, 66, 23:1, 2, 3[2], 7, 8[3], 9[2], 10, 11[4], 14[2], 15[2], 16[2], 21[2], 22[3], 25, 26[2], 27[2], 32, 33, 35[2], 36[3], 38, 39, 40, 43, 49, 55, 24:16, 18, 19, 20[2], 24, 29, 31, 42, 52

JOHN 1:3[2], 4, 7, 10[2], 11, 12, 15, 18

JOHN 1:19, 21, 22, 25[2], 29, 31, 32, 33[2], 37, 38, 39, 40, 41, 42[2], 43, 45[2], 46[2], 47[2], 48[2], 49, 50, 51, 2:3, 10, 11, 18, 3:2[2], 3, 4, 9, 10, 15, 16, 17, 18, 26[2], 27, 28, 29, 34, 36, 4:9, 11, 14[3], 15, 19, 23, 24[2], 25, 30, 31, 33, 34, 39, 40[2], 42, 45, 47[2], 48, 49, 50[2], 51[2], 52[2], 53, 5:6[2], 7, 8, 10, 12, 14[2], 15, 16, 18, 20[2], 23, 24, 27, 38, 43, 6:2, 5, 6, 7, 8, 15[2], 21, 25[2], 27, 28, 29, 30, 34, 37, 38, 40[3]

JOHN 6:41, 44[2], 54, 56, 64, 65, 66, 68, 71, 7:1, 3, 5, 11, 12, 13, 18[2], 26, 29[2], 30[2], 31, 32[2], 33, 35, 37, 39, 43, 44[2], 45, 48, 51, 52, 8:2, 3, 4, 6[2], 7[2], 13, 19, 20, 25, 26, 29, 30, 31, 33, 39, 41, 44, 48, 52, 55[4], 57, 59, 9:2, 3, 4, 7, 8, 9, 10, 12, 13, 15, 17, 18[2], 21, 23, 24, 26, 28, 31, 34[2], 35[3], 36, 37[2], 38, 40[2], 10:3, 4, 5, 20, 21, 24[2], 31, 33, 36, 38, 39, 41, 42, 11:3, 8, 10, 11, 15

JOHN 11:16, 20, 24, 27, 29, 30, 32[2], 34[2], 36, 39[2], 44[2], 45, 48[2], 53, 57, 12:2[2], 4, 11, 13, 16[2], 17[2], 18, 19, 21, 26[2], 29, 34, 37, 41, 42[2], 44, 45, 47, 48[2], 13:2, 6, 7, 8[2], 9, 10, 11, 16, 20, 24, 25, 27[2], 28, 29, 31, 32[3], 36[2], 37, 38, 14:5, 6, 7[2], 8, 9, 17[3], 21[2], 22, 23[4], 15:5, 21, 16:5, 7, 19, 29, 17:2[2], 18:2, 4, 5[2], 12, 13, 20, 23, 24, 25, 26, 30[2], 31[3], 33, 34, 37, 38, 19:1, 2, 3, 4[2], 6[6], 7, 9, 10, 12, 15[3]

JOHN 19:16[2], 18[2], 32, 36, 37, 38, 20:2, 6, 13, 15[5], 16, 25, 28, 29, 21:3, 5, 7, 12, 15[2], 16[3], 17[4], 19, 21, 22, 23

ACTS 1:6, 9, 11, 2:22, 23, 25, 30, 3:4, 7[2], 9, 10, 13[2], 16[2], 22, 26, 4:10, 5:6[3], 17, 21, 31, 32, 36, 37[2], 40, 6:11, 12[3], 14, 15, 7:3, 4, 5[3], 8[2], 9, 10[3], 14, 21[2], 24[2], 27, 30, 31, 33, 35, 37, 38, 39, 40, 47, 54, 55, 58[2], 8:2, 11, 30[2], 31, 35, 38, 39, 9:2, 3, 4, 6, 7, 8[2], 10, 11, 12, 15

ACTS 9:16, 17, 21, 23, 24, 25[2], 26, 27[3], 29, 30[2], 34, 35, 38[2], 39[2], 40, 10:3[2], 4[2], 7, 11, 13, 15, 19, 21, 23, 25[2], 26, 27, 35[2], 38, 40[2], 41, 43[2], 48, 11:2, 13, 26[2], 12:4[5], 5, 6, 7[2], 8[2], 9, 10, 16, 17, 19[2], 20, 23, 13:9, 11[2], 22, 27[2], 28, 29[3], 30, 31, 34, 39, 14:9, 19, 20, 15:21, 38, 16:3[3], 9, 32, 17:15[2], 16, 17, 18, 19[2], 23, 27[2], 28[2], 31, 34, 18:12, 17, 18, 20, 26[2], 27, 19:2, 4[2], 22, 30, 31[2], 33, 38, 20:1, 3, 4, 10[3], 14, 16

ACTS 20:18, 37, 38, 21:8, 11, 12, 20, 27[2], 29, 30, 31, 33[2], 34, 36, 40, 22:9, 13, 18, 20, 22, 24[2], 25, 27, 29[3], 30[2], 23:2[2], 3, 9, 10[2], 11, 15[3], 17[2], 18[3], 19[3], 20, 21[2], 22, 23, 24, 27, 28[2], 30, 31, 32, 33, 35, 24:2, 7, 8, 10, 23[2], 24, 26[4], 25:2[2], 3[3], 5, 15, 16, 19, 20, 21[2], 22, 25, 26, 27, 26:26, 27:3, 28:6, 8[2], 16, 21, 23[2], 30, 31

ROMANS 1:20, 21, 3:26, 4:3, 4, 5[2], 17, 22, 23, 24, 5:9, 14, 6:4, 6, 8, 9, 7:4, 8:11, 17

ROMANS 8:20, 32[2], 37, 9:11, 16[2], 20, 33, 10:9, 11, 12, 14[2], 11:4, 35[2], 36[3], 12:8, 20[2], 13:4, 14:1, 3[5], 4, 14[2], 15, 15:11, 12, 16:25

1 COR. 1:5, 30, 31, 2:2, 9, 11, 14, 16, 3:17, 18, 5:3, 7:12[2], 13, 15, 17, 18[2], 36, 8:3, 6[2], 10, 10:12, 11:14, 28, 34, 12:18, 14:2, 11, 13, 28[2], 37, 38, 15:27[2], 28[3], 38, 16:2[2], 11[3], 12, 22

2 COR. 1:19, 20[2], 2:7[2], 8, 5:9, 15, 16, 21[2], 6:1, 7:14, 15, 8:18, 9:7, 10:7, 19, 11:4, 12:18, 13:4[2]

GAL. 1:1, 6, 8, 9, 16, 18, 2:11, 13

GAL. 3:6, 4:29, 5:8, 6:6[7]

EPHES. 1:4[2], 10, 11, 17, 20[2], 22, 23, 2:18, 3:12, 20, 21, 4:15, 21[2], 28[3], 6:9

PHIL. 1:29, 2:7, 9[2], 22, 23, 27[2], 28[2], 29, 3:9, 10

COLOS. 1:16[3], 17, 19, 20[2], 2:6, 7, 9, 10, 12[3], 13, 3:4, 10[2], 17, 4:10, 13

1 THESS. 4:14, 5:10

2 THESS. 1:12, 2:1, 9, 3:14, 15[2]

1 TIM. 1:16, 5:1

2 TIM. 1:12, 18, 2:4[2], 11[2], 12[2], 26, 4:11, 14

TITUS 1:16

PHILE. 12, 15, 17

HEB. 1:5, 6, 2:3, 6[2], 7[2], 8[3], 10, 13, 14, 16[2], 17

HEB. 3:2[2], 4:13, 5:5, 7[2], 9, 6:6, 7:1, 6, 10, 21[2], 25, 9:9, 28, 10:30, 38, 11:5, 6[2], 9, 11, 12, 19[2], 27, 12:2, 3, 5, 25[3], 13:13, 15

JAMES 1:5[2], 6, 12, 2:3[2], 5, 14, 23, 3:13, 4:17[2], 5:13[2], 14[3], 15[2], 19, 20

1 PETER 1:8, 21[3], 2:6, 9, 14, 23, 3:6, 10, 11[2], 22, 4:5, 11[2], 16[2], 19, 5:7, 11

2 PETER 1:3, 17, 18, 3:14, 15, 18

1 JOHN 1:5[2], 6, 10, 2:3, 4[2], 5[2], 6, 8, 10, 13, 14, 15, 27[2], 28[2], 29, 3:1, 2[2], 3, 5, 6[3], 9, 12, 15, 17[2], 19

1 JOHN 3:22, 24[2], 4:9, 13, 15, 16, 19, 21, 5:1[3], 10, 14, 15, 16, 18, 20[2]

2 JOHN 10[2], 11

JUDE 9, 15, 24

REV. 1:1, 4, 5, 6, 7[3], 17, 2:7[2], 11, 17[6], 26, 28, 29, 3:6, 12[3], 13, 20[2], 21, 22, 4:8, 9, 10[2], 5:1, 7, 13, 14, 6:2[2], 4[2], 5, 8[2], 16, 7:14, 15, 8:3, 9:1, 10:6, 9, 12:9, 11, 13:2, 4, 5[2], 7[2], 8, 9, 12, 18, 14:1, 7[2], 15, 18, 16:8, 9, 17:14, 19:5, 7, 10, 11, 14, 19, 20[2], 21, 20:2, 3[2], 6, 11, 21:7, 22:3, 11[4], 17[3], 18

his

848

GEN. 1:11, 12[2], 21, 24[2], 25[2], 27, 2:2[2], 3, 7, 21, 24[2], 25, 3:8, 15, 20, 21, 22

GEN. 4:1, 2, 4[2], 5[2], 7, 8[2], 17[2], 20, 23, 25[2], 26, 5:3, 29, 6:3, 5, 6, 9

GEN. 6:12, 20, 7:2[2], 7, 13, 14[2], 8:9, 18, 21[2], 9:1, 6, 8, 21, 22, 24, 25, 26

GEN. 9:27, 10:5, 10, 15, 25, 11:28, 31[2], 12:5, 8, 11, 12, 17, 20[2], 13:1, 3[2], 10, 12

GEN. 13:18, 14:12, 14[2], 15, 16, 17, 16:3, 11, 12[2], 15, 17:3, 14, 17, 19[2], 23[2], 24, 25[2]

GEN. 17:26, 27, 18:2, 19, 33[2], 19:1, 3, 14[2], 16[2], 26, 30[2], 37, 38, 20:2, 7, 8, 14

GEN. 20:17, 21:2, 3, 4, 5, 7, 11, 21, 22, 32, 22:3[2], 4, 5, 6[2], 7, 9, 10

GEN. 22:13[3], 17, 19, 21, 24, 23:3, 6, 9, 10, 18, 19, 24:2, 7, 9, 10[2], 11, 20

GEN. 24:21, 26, 27, 29, 30[2], 32[2], 40, 48, 59, 61, 63, 67[3], 25:6, 8, 9, 10, 11

GEN. 25:17, 18, 21[2], 25, 26[2], 28, 30, 33, 34, 26:7, 8, 11[2], 15, 17, 18[2], 25, 26

GEN. 27:1[2], 5, 10, 11, 13, 14[2], 16, 18, 19, 20, 22, 23, 26, 27, 30, 31[2], 32

GEN. 27:34[2], 37, 38[2], 39, 40, 41[2], 28:7, 8, 9, 11, 16, 18, 29:1, 3, 6, 10[3], 11

GEN. 29:13[2], 23, 24, 28, 29, 32, 33, 34, 35, 30:6, 8, 11, 13, 14, 18, 20, 24

GEN 30:35, 40, 31:4, 17, 18[3], 19, 21, 23, 25[2], 46, 53, 54, 55[3], 32:1, 3, 13[2], 16[2]

GEN. 32:20, 22[3], 25, 31, 33:1, 3, 4, 5, 14, 16, 17, 18, 19, 34:3, 4, 5[4], 13

GEN. 34:19, 20, 24[3], 25, 26, 35:2, 7, 10, 18[2], 21, 22, 27, 29, 36:2, 6[8], 24, 32

GEN. 36:33, 34, 35[2], 36, 37, 38, 39[3], 37:1, 2[3], 3[2], 4[2], 5, 8[3], 9, 10[3], 11[3], 12

GEN. 37:17, 20, 22, 23[3], 26[2], 27, 29, 30, 34[3], 35[3], 38:1, 3, 4, 5, 6, 9[3], 11[2]

GEN.
38:12^2 13 16 20^2 28^2 29^3 30^3 39:2 3^2 4^3 5 7 8 9 11 12^2 13 15 16^2 18 19^3 23 40:1 2 5^2 7 9 13^2 20^2 21 41:8^2 10 11 12 14 37 38 42^3 44 42:1 4 7 8 21 22 25 27^4 28 35 37 38 43:8 16 21 29^3 30^3 31 33^2 44:1^2 2 4 11^2 13 14 19 20^4 22^3 30 33 45:1 3^3 4 8 14^2 15^2 16 23^2 24 46:1^2 4 6 7^5 8 15^3 18 25 26 28 29^4 31^2 47:2 3 7 11^2 12^3 20 29 48:1 9 12^2 13^2 14^3 17^3 18^2 19^3 49:1 10 11^4 12^2 13 15 16 17 20 24^2 26 28

GEN.
49:31^2 33^3 50:1 2^2 4 7^2 8^2 10 12 13 14^3 18^2 22 24

EXOD.
1:1 6 9 22 2:4 7 10 11^2 20 21 22 24 3:1 6 13 4:4^2 6^3 7^4 14 15^2 18 20^3 21 25 5:2 21 6:1 11 20 7:2 10^2 12 20 23^2 8:6 15 17^2 24 29^2 31^2 32 9:20^2 21^2 23 33 34^2 10:1^2 13 22 23 11:2 5 7 10 12:4^2 9^2 22 29 30 48 13:10 13 14:4 5 6^2 9^2 17^2 18^2 21 23^2 27^2 31 15:1 3 4^2 19^2 21 26^3 16:16^2 18 21 29^2 17:11^2 12^2 13 18:1 5^2 7 8 15 16 24 27^3 20:7 17^4 20 21:3 4 6^3 7

EXOD.
21:9 13 14 15^2 16 17^2 18^2 19^2 20^3 21 26^3 27^3 28 29^3 30 34 36^2 22:3 4 5^3 7 8^3 9^2 10 11^2 14 15 16 27^2 30 23:3 4 5 6 19 21 22 24:10^2 11 13 25:2 31^5 26:19^2 27:2 3^6 11 21 28:1 4 12 21 29 30 35 38 41 43^2 29:4 6 7 8 9^2 10 14^2 15 16 17^3 19 20^2 21^6 24 27 28 29 30 31 32 35 44 30:12 18 19 21 27^2 28^2 30 33 38 31:8^2 9^2 10 14 32:11 14 15 19 27^5 29^2 33:4 8 10 11^2 34:4 8 15 20 26 29 30 33 35 35:11^7 13^2 14^2 15 16^4 17

EXOD.
35:19 21^2 34 36:4 24^2 37:16^4 17^5 20^2 32^3 39:5 14 21 27 33^6 39^4 40^4 41 40:10 11 12 14 18^2 31

LEVIT.
1:3^2 4 9^2 10 11 12^3 14^2 15 16^2 2:1 2 3 10 3:1 2^2 6 7 8^2 12 13 14 4:3 4 6 11^5 17 19 22 23^3 24 25^2 26^2 28^4 29 30 33 34 35 5:1 4 6^3 7 8^2 10 11 12 13 15 17 18 6:2^2 5 6 9 10^3 11 15 16 20 22^2 25 7:18^2 15 16^2 18^2 20^2 21 25 27 29^3 30 31 33 34 35 8:2 6 9^2 11^2 14 15 17^3 18 22 23^2 27 30^6 31^2 36 9:1 9

LEVIT.
9:22 10:1 3 6 12 11:14 15 16 22^4 25 27 28 29 40^2 12:3 13:2^3 3 4 5 6 7 11 12^2 13 23 28 34 35 37 40 41^3 42^2 43^2 44^2 45^3 46 55 14:2 8^3 9^7 14^2 15 16^3 17^3 19 23 25^2 26 27^2 28^3 32 47^2 15:2^2 3^7 5^2 6 7 8 10 11^2 13^4 15 16 21 22 27 16:4^2 6^2 11 12 14^2 15 17 19 21 24^3 26^2 28^2 32 17:2 4 9 10 14 15 16^2 19:8^2 8^2 21 22 20:2 3^2 4 5 6 9^5 10 11 17^6 19 20^2 21^2 21:1 2^6 3^2 4 7 10^3 11^2 12^2 14 15^2 17 20^2 21 22

LEVIT.
21:24 22:2 3 6 7 11^3 18^3 21 23 23:29 30 37 24:9 11 14 15^2 19 25:10 13 25^3 27 28 30 33 41^3 48 49^3 50 51 52^2 54 27:8 14 15^2 16 17 18 22 28 31

NUM.
1:4 44 52^2 2:2 4 6 8 11 13 15 17 19 21 23 26 28 30 3:7 9 10 38 48 51 4:5 9^3 19^3 25 27 49 5:7 9 10^2 14^2 15 18 30 6:4 5^3 7^6 8 9^3 11 12^2 13 14 16^2 17^2 18^2 19 21^4 23 25 26 7:5 11 12 13 19 25 31 37 43 49 55 61 67 73 79 8:8 13 19 22 9:2 3

NUM.
9:7 13^3 10:14 18 22 25 11:1 10 28 29 12:12 14:24 15:4 24^2 30 31^2 16:4 5^2 6 17^3 18 40 17:2 9 19:3 4 5 7^2 8^2 10 13 19 21 20:8 11^2 21 24 25 26^3 28^2 21:23^2 24 26^2 29^2 33 34^2 35^3 22:5 18 21 22^2 23^2 31^4 23:6 7 10 16 17 18 21 24:1 2^2 3 4 7^4 8^2 10 13 15 16 18 20^2 21 23 25^2 25:5 6 7 13^2 26:54 27:1 3 4 8^2 9^2 10^2 11^4 21^2 23 28:10 15 24 31 29:6 16^2 22^2 25^2 28^2 31^2 34^2 38^2 30:2^3 4 7 11 14^2 16^2 31:6 32:18 21 42 33:54 35:8^2 21 23^2 25 26

NUM.
35:27 28^2 32 36:2 7 8 9

DEU.
1:16 31 36 41 2:12 24 30^2 31^2 32 33^2 34 3:1 2^2 3 4 11 14 4:13 20 30 36^3 37^2 40^2 42 47 5:11 21^5 24^3 6:2^2 13 17^2 7:3^2 7 9 10 22 8:2 5 6 11^3 18 9:23 10:6^2 8 9^2 12 13 20 11:1^4 2^3 3^3 14 22 12:5^2 8 11 21 13:4^2 17 18 14:13 14 15 21 23 24 15:2^2 8 17 16:2 6 11 17:2 17 18 19^2 20^5 18:1 5 6 7^2 8 10^2 18 19:4 5^3 6^3 9 11 12 18 19 20:5 6 7 8^3 21:16 17^2 18^2 19^4 20 21 23 22:1 3^2 4 19^2

DEU.
22:24 26 29^2 30^2 23:1 2 7 15^2 24:1^2 2 3^2 4 5 7 10^2 12 13 15^3 16 25:2^2 6^2 7^3 8 9^5 10^2 26:2 17^3 18^2 27:10^2 16^2 17 20^2 22^3 23 24 28:1 9 12^2 15^2 40 45^2 54^4 55 29:2 12 19 20^2 23^2 30:2 8 10^2 16^4 20 32:4^2 5 9^2 10 15 19^2 36^2 43^5 50 33:1 2 3 6 7^3 9^4 11^2 12 13 16 17^3 21 24^2 26 28 34:6 7^3 9 11^2

JOSH.
2:19^3 3:15 4:5 14 18 5:13^3 14^2 6:26^2 27 7:6^2 18 22 24^6 26 8:1^3 14 18 19 26 29 9:24 10:21 33 11:15 13:27 15:17 17:3 6 10 20:4 5^2 6^2 21:12 22:5^2

JOSH.
22:20 29 23:3 4 10 24:24 28 30 33

JUD.
1:2 3 6^2 13 17 2:6 9 3:10^2 16^2 20 21^3 22 24^3 4:7^2 10 11 13 15^4 17 21 22 5:11 17 26^2 31 6:11 13 21^2 27^2 31 32 7:5^2 7 8 11 13 14^2 21 22 8:20^2 21 24 25 27^2 29 30 31 32 9:1^2 3 5^2 7 16^2 17 18^2 19 21 24 26 28 30 31 41 48^2 49 53 54^2 55 56^2 10:16 11:2 3 11 20^2 21 23 32 34^2 35 39 12:9 13:2 5 6^2 7 11 19 20 21 22 23 24 14:2^2 3^3 4^2 5^2 6^3 9^2 10 19^2 20^2 15:1 6^2 14^3 15 17

JUD.
15:19 16:3 5 9 12 14 16 17 18^2 19^2 20 21 22 29^2 30^3 31^3 17:2^2 3^2 4^2 5^2 6 11 12 18:4 26 30 19:2 3 4 5 7 9^3 10 11 12 13 15^2 16 17 21 24 25 27^2 28 29^2 20:8^2 21:1 21 22 24^3 25

RUTH
1:1^2 2^2 6 2:1 5 15 20 22 3:4 7^2 8 14 4:5 7^2 8 10^3 13 14 17

1 SAM.
1:1 3 4 11^2 19 20 21^2 23 2:9 10^2 11 13 19 20 22 3:2^2 9 12 13^2 19 4:10 12^2 13 15 18 19 5:3^2 4^2 7 11 6:2 3 5 9^2 7:1 15 17^2 8:1 2^2 3^2 11^3 12^4 14

1 SAM.
8:15 16 17 22 9:2 3 5 7 10 15 22 10:1^2 9 14 16 23 25 27 11:6 7 12:3 5 14 22^3 13:2 14^2 16 20^4 22 14:1^2 6 7 12^2 13^4 14 17 20 26^2 27^5 34^3 45 47 49 50 15:1 27 34 35 16:1 4 5 7^2 10 13 16 17 20 21 23 17:5 6^2 7^2 13 15 17 22^2 25^2 28 33 34 35^2 38^2 39^2 40^4 48 49^5 51^2 54^2 57 18:1 2 3 4^4 7^2 10 11 13 14 22^2 26 27^2 30 19:1^2 4^3 5^2 7 9^4 13 16 24 20:6 17 25 27 32 33 34 36 38 40^2 41 21:7 11^2 12 13^3 14 22:1^2

1 SAM.
22:6^3 7 11 15 23:5 6 8 11 13 14 15 16 18 22^2 24 25 26^3 24:2 3^2 6 7^2 8 16 19 22 25:1 2 3^2 4 10 13^4 17 20 24 25^2 36 37^2 39^2 42 43 44 26:5 7^2 9 10 11 16 18 19 23^2 25^2 27:1^2 3^3 8 11 12 28:3 5 7^2 14 18 23 25 29:2 4^2 5^2 11 30:1 3 6^3 12 18 22^2 24^2 26 31 31:2 4^2 5^2 6^3 7 8 9^2 10 12

2 SAM.
1:2^2 4 5 6 10^2 11 12 17 2:2 3^2 16^3 21 27 29 32^2 3:2 3 8^2 12 27 29 30 32 38 39 4:1 4^3 6 7^3 8

2 SAM.
4:9 10 11^3 12 5:6 12^3 21 6:6 7 11 14 17 19 20^2 21 7:1^2 12 13 14 25 27 8:3 10 15 9:3 6 9 11 13 10:1^2 2^3 3 10 11:1 2 9^2 10 13^3 27^2 12:4^2 9^2 15 17 19^2 20^2 21 24^2 25 30 13:2 8 17 18 22 24 28 29 31^2 32 33 34 36 37 14:7^2 9 13 14 15 16 22^2 24^2 25^3 26^2 30 31 33 15:5 12 14 16 18 22 25 30^2 32^2 16:6^2 9 11 12 13 18 19 22 17:6 8 18 23^6 18:9 14 17 18^2 19 24 25 28 19:2 4 8 11^2 17^2 19 24^3 30 39 41 20:1 3^2

2 SAM.
20:8 10^2 21^2 22 21:1 2 4 6 12 13 14^2 15 22 22:1 7^2 9^2 10 14 23^2 25 31 51^3 23:2 8 10^2 18 21^2 23 24:14 16 20^2 21

1 KINGS
1:2 6^2 9 10 21 23 37 47 49 51 2:1 3^5 4 5^4 6 9 10 12^2 15 19^2 22 23 32 33^4 34 35 40^2 3:1 5 6 15 4:7 21 25^2 26 27 28 31 32 34 5:1^2 3^2 10 11 7:1^2 8 14^2 23 31 8:6 14 15^2 20 22 28 31 32^3 38^2 39 54^2 56^3 58^4 59^2 61^2 66^2 9:11 15 16 19^3 22^5 27 10:5^5 13 24^2 25 11:3^2 4^5 6 8 9 17 19 20

1 KINGS
11:21 23 26 27^2 33 34^2 35 36 41 43^4 12:4 6 15 18 24 26 33 13:4^2 11 12 13 19 24 27 28 30^2 31^2 33 14:2 4^2 8 18 20^3 21^2 31^5 15:2 3^4 4^2 5 6 8^3 10 11 12 13 14 15 18 23^3 24^5 26^2 28 29 30 34 16:3 4 5 6^3 7^2 9^3 10 11^3 13 19^2 20 26 27 28^3 34^3 17:17 19 23 18:3 7 42^2 43 46 19:3^2 6 13^2 19 20:1 11 12 20 24 31 35 38 39 41 42^2 43 21:4^3 5 7 8^2 11^2 25 27^2 29^3 22:3 10 17 19^3 22 31^2 34 35 36^2 38^2 40^3 42 43 45 46

1 KINGS
22:50^5 52^2 53

2 KINGS
1:2 8 9 10 11 12 13^2 16 17 2:8 12 3:2^3 25 27^2 4:12 18 19^2 20 25 32 34^6 35 37 38 39 43 5:1 3 4 6 7^2 8 9^2 11^2 13 14 15 20 23 25 26 27 6:7 8 11 12 15 17 24 30^2 32^2 7:12 13 8:11 14 15^2 18 19^2 20 24^4 26 9:2 3 6 11^2 13 21^2 23 24^4 25^2 26^2 28^3 31 32 36 10:3 10 11^3 15 16 19^2 24 31 34 35^3 11:2 8^2 9 11^2 18^2 12:1 2 5 17 18^2 20 21^4 13:8 9^3 12 13^2 14^2 16^2 21 23^2 24^2 25 14:2 3^2 5^3 6 15

2 KINGS
14:16^3 20 21 22 25 28 29^3 15:2 3 5 7^4 9 10 14 15 18 19^2 22^3 25^2 30 33 34 38^5 16:2^2 3 13^4 15 20^4 17:3 15^3 18 20 23^2 18:2 3 6 12 21 29 31^3 33 19:1 4 7^2 19 23^2 37^4 20:2 13^5 20 21^3 21:1 3 6 7 10 11 12 16 17 18^4 19 20 21^2 22 23 24^2 26^3 22:1 2 11 23:3^3 10^2 18^2 25^5 26^2 29 30^3 31 32 34^2 35 36 37 24:1^2 2 3 6^3 7 8 9 11 12^5 15 17^3 18 20 25:1^2 5 7 28 29^2 30^2

1 CHRON.
1:13 19^2 43 44 45 46^2 47 48 49 50^3 2:4 13

1 CHRON.
2:18
35[2]
42
3:3
10[2]
11[2]
12[2]
13[2]
14[2]
16[2]
17
4:9[2]
18
19
23
25[2]
26[2]
27
5:1[2]
2
4[2]
5[2]
6
7
6:20[2]
21[4]
22[2]
23[2]
24[4]
26[2]
27[2]
29[2]
30[2]
39[2]
49
50[2]
51[2]
52[2]
53[2]
7:14
16[2]
18
20[4]
21[2]
22
23[2]
24
25[2]
26[2]
27[2]
35
8:1
8
9
10
30
37[2]
39[2]
9:5
19[2]
36
43[2]
10:2
4[2]
5
6[2]
7
8
9[2]
10[2]
12
13
11:10
11
20
23
25
45
12:15
19
28
13:9
10
14
14:2[2]
4
15:3
5
6
7
8
9
10
17
16:7
8[2]
9
10
11[2]
12[2]
13[2]
14
15
16
23
24[2]
27[2]
29
34
37
39
41
43[2]
17:1
11
12
13

1 CHRON.
17:14
21
23
25
26
18:3
10[2]
14
19:1[2]
2[2]
3
7
11
13
15
19
20:2
8
21:3
13
16[2]
20
21
23
27
22:5
6
9[2]
10[2]
17
18
23:1
13[2]
14
25
25:9
10[2]
11[2]
12[2]
13[2]
14[2]
15[2]
16[2]
17[2]
18[2]
19[2]
20[2]
21[2]
22[2]
23[2]
24[2]
25[2]
26[2]
27[2]
28[2]
29[2]
30[2]
31[2]
26:6
10
14
15
22
25[5]
26
28
29
30
31
32
27:2
4[2]
5
6[2]
7[2]
8
9
10
11
12
13
14
15
28:1
2
6
7
11
19
20
29:5
23
28[2]
30[2]

2 CHRON.
1:1[2]
8
2:1
11
12
14
15
17
3:1
2
4:16
5:1
7
13
6:3
4[2]
10
12
13[2]
19
22
23[3]

2 CHRON.
6:29[3]
30
7:3
6
10
11
8:1
6
9[3]
14
18
9:4[5]
8
23[2]
24
31[4]
10:4
6
15
18
11:4
12
14
21[2]
22
23
12:8
13[2]
14
16[3]
13:2
5
6
12
17
22[2]
14:1[4]
2
11
13
15:9
17
18
16:4
5
12[4]
13[2]
14
17:1[2]
2
3
4[2]
5
6
7[2]
18:7
9
16
18[3]
21
33
34
19:1
20:18[2]
20
21
25
30
31
32
21:1[4]
4[2]
7
8
9[2]
10[2]
17[3]
18
19[4]
22:1[2]
2
3[2]
4[3]
9
11
23:7[2]
8
10[2]
11
13
17[2]
24:1
11
13
16
22[2]
25[2]
27[3]
25:1
3[2]
4
11
14
22
28
26:1
2
3
4
8
15
16[3]
19[2]
20
21[2]
23[4]
27:1

2 CHRON.
27:2
6[2]
7[2]
9[3]
28:1
3
5
22
25
26[2]
27[3]
29:1
2
8
10
19[2]
25
30:2
6
8[2]
9
19[2]
27
31:1
2
3
8
10
12
13
16
20
21[2]
32:3[2]
9[2]
12[2]
14
15
16[2]
17
21[3]
25
26
30
31
32
33[4]
33:3
6
7
10
12[2]
13[2]
18[2]
19[3]
20[4]
22[2]
23
24[2]
25[2]
34:2
3[2]
4
8[2]
19
27
31[6]
33
35:3
4
8
9
22
23
24[2]
26
27
36:1
4[3]
5
7
8[3]
10
12
13[2]
15[3]
16[3]
17
18
20
22
23[2]

EZRA
1:1
3[2]
4
7
2:1
68
3:2[2]
3
9[3]
11
4:6
5:6
15
17
6:5
7
10
11[2]
7:6[2]
9
10
11

EZRA.
7:13
14
15
23
28
8:17
18[2]
19
22[2]
25[2]
9:8
10:8
11
18

NEH.
1:5
2:1
20
3:1
10
12
17
23
28
29
30
4:2
15
17
18[2]
22
5:7
13[2]
6:5[2]
11
18
19
7:3[2]
6
8:4[2]
16
9:8[2]
10[2]
10:29[2]
11:3
13
17
20
12:8
36
45
47
13:10
26
30

ESTHER
1:2
3[2]
4[2]
8
12[2]
20
22
2:3
7[2]
8
15
16[2]
17
18[2]
3:1
10[2]
4:1
3
4
11
17
5:1
2[2]
10[2]
11[2]
14[2]
6:6
8
12[2]
13[3]
7:5
7[2]
8:2
3[2]
5[2]
7
17
9:1
4
25[3]
10:2[2]
3[3]

JOB
1:3
4[2]
10[3]
13[2]
20[2]
2:3
4
5[2]
6
7[2]
9
10
11
12
13

JOB
3:1[2]
19
4:9
17
18[2]
5:3
4
18
26
6:5
9
14
7:1
2
10[2]
8:12
15
16[2]
17
18
19
9:5
13
33
34[2]
11:5
11[3]
12:4
5
11
16
13:8
11[2]
14:5[3]
6
18
20
21
22[2]
15:2
15[2]
20
21
23
25
26[2]
27[3]
29
30[2]
31
32[2]
33[2]
16:9[3]
12
13
21
17:5[2]
9
18:4[2]
5
6[2]
7[2]
8
11
12[2]
13[2]
14[2]
15[3]
16[2]
17
19[2]
20
19:6
11[2]
12
20:6[2]
7
9
10[2]
11[2]
12[2]
13
14[2]
15
18
20
21[2]
22
23[2]
25
26
27
28[3]
21:17
19[2]
20[2]
21[2]
23
24[2]
25
31[2]
22:22[2]
23:3
6
11[2]
12[2]
13
15
24:1
6
15
22
23
25:2
3[2]
5
26:8

JOB
26:9[2]
11
12[2]
13[2]
14[2]
27:1
8
9
14[2]
15
18
19
21
22
23
28:9
10
29:1
3[2]
17
30:24[2]
31:20
23
30
31
32:1
2
3[2]
5
12
14
33:10
13
17
18[2]
19[2]
20[2]
21[2]
22[2]
23
25[2]
26[2]
28[2]
30
34:11
14[3]
19
21[2]
27
29
35
36
37[3]
35:15
16
36:7
15
18
23
24
26
29
30
37:1
2[2]
3
4[2]
5
6
7
11
12
13
15
38:12
32[2]
41[2]
39:6
8
10
11
18
19
20
21
40:16[4]
17[2]
18[2]
19
23
24[2]
41:1
2[2]
7[2]
12[3]
13[2]
14[2]
15[2]
18[2]
19[2]
20
21[2]
22
23
24
33
42:10
11[4]
12
16[2]

PSALMS
1:2[2]
3[3]
2:2
5[2]
12

PSALMS
3 *title*
4
7:12[2]
13
16[4]
17
8:6
9:7
11
16
10:2
3
4[2]
5[3]
6
7[2]
8
9[2]
10
11[2]
13
15
16
11:4[3]
5
7
12:2
14:1
6
7
15:2
3[3]
4
5
17:12
18 *title*
6[2]
8[2]
9[2]
11[2]
12
13
14
22[2]
24
30
50[3]
19:1
5
6[2]
12
20:6[3]
21:2[2]
3
5
9
22:24
29
31
23:3
24:3
4
5
25:9
10[2]
13[2]
14
22
27:4
5[2]
6
28:5
8
29:2
9[2]
11[2]
30:4[2]
5[2]
31:21
23
33:4
6
11
12
14
17
18
21
34:1
3
6
9
15
20
22
35:8
9
14
27
36:1
2[2]
3
4
37:7
10
12
13
18
23
24
25
26
28
30
31[3]
33
34
38:13

PSALMS
39:5
11
40:4
41:2
3[2]
5
6
9
42:5
8[2]
46:6
47:8
48:1
49:7
16
17
18
19
50:4
6
23
52:7[3]
53:1
54:7
55:20[2]
21[3]
56:4
10[2]
57:3[2]
58:7[2]
9
10
59:9
60:6
61:6
62:4
12
64:9
65:6
66:2[2]
5
7[2]
8
20
67:1
68:1
4[2]
5
21[2]
33
34[2]
35
69:33
36[2]
72:7
9
14
15[2]
17[2]
19[2]
73:10
76:1
2[2]
77:8[2]
9
78:4[2]
7
10
11[2]
20
22
26
32
37
38[2]
42
43[2]
49
50
52
54[2]
56
61[2]
62[2]
66
69
70
71[2]
72[2]
79:7
81:6[2]
85:8[2]
9
13
87:1
89:23[2]
24
25[2]
29[2]
30
36[2]
39
40[2]
41
42[2]
43
44[2]
45
48
91:4[2]
11
14
94:14[2]
95:2
4[2]
5[2]

PSALMS
95:7[3]
96:2[2]
3[2]
6
8[2]
13
97:2
3
4
6[2]
10
12
98:1[2]
2[2]
3[2]
99:5
6[2]
7
9
100:2
3[2]
4[2]
5[2]
101:5
102 *title*
16
19
21
103:1
2
7[2]
9
11
13
15
17
18[2]
19[2]
20[3]
21[3]
22[2]
104:3[2]
4[2]
8
13
15
19
23[2]
31
105:1[2]
2
3
4[2]
5[3]
6[3]
7
8
9
19
21[2]
22[3]
24
25[2]
26
27
28
42[3]
43[2]
45[2]
106:1
2
8[2]
12[2]
13[2]
23[2]
24
26
33[2]
40[2]
45[2]
107:1
8[2]
15[2]
20
21[2]
22
24
31[2]
108:7
109:6
7
8[2]
9[2]
10
11
12
13
14[2]
18[3]
31
110:5
111:3[2]
4
5
6[2]
7[2]
9[3]
10[2]
112:1
2
3[2]
5
7
8[3]
9[2]
10
113:4
8

PSALMS
114:2[2]
116:2
12
14
15
18
118:1
2
3
4
29
119:2
3
9
125:2
126:6
127:2
3
5
128:1
129:7[2]
130:5
8
131:2
132:1
7[2]
13
18[2]
133:2
135:3
4
7
9
12
14[2]
136:1
2
3
4
5
6
7
8
9
10
11
12
13
14
15[2]
16[2]
17
18
19
20
21
22[2]
23
24
25
26
140:8
144:4
10
145:3
9[2]
12[2]
17[2]
21
146:4[2]
5[2]
147:5
9
11
15[2]
17[2]
18[2]
19[3]
20
148:2[2]
8
13[2]
14[2]
149:1
3
4
9
150:1[2]
2[2]

PROV.
2:6
8
3:11
20
31
32
5:21
22[2]
23
6:13[3]
14
15
27[2]
28
29
30
31
32
33
7:23[2]
8:22[2]
29[2]
30
31
36
10:1

PROV.
10:9
15
19
11:1
5[2]
7
8
9[2]
12[2]
17[2]
19
20
28
29
12:4
8
10
11
13
14
15
25
26
13:1
2
3[2]
8
16
22
24[2]
25
14:2[2]
8
10[2]
14
15
20
21
26
31
32[2]
35
15:5
8
20
23
27
32
16:2
7
9[2]
10
11
15[2]
17[2]
23[2]
26
27
29
30
32
17:5
12
13
18
19
21
25
27
28[2]
18:2
6
7[3]
9
11[2]
14
17[2]
20[2]
19:1[2]
2
3[2]
4
7
8
11[2]
12
13
16[2]
18
22
24[3]
26[2]
20:2
6
7[2]
8
11[2]
14
16
17
19
20[3]
24
28
21:2
8
10[2]
13
18
23[3]
24
25
29[2]
22:5
8
9
11[2]
16

PROV.
22:25
29
23:3
6
7[2]
14
31
24:7
12
15
18
26
29
25:5
13
18
22
28
26:4
5[2]
11[2]
12
14[2]
15[3]
16
19
24
25
26
27:8
13
14
16
17
18
21
22
28:6[2]
7
8
9[2]
10
11
13
14
16
18
19
24[2]
25
26
27
29:1
3[2]
5[2]
10
11
12
14
15
20
21[2]
24
25
30:4[3]
6
10
17[2]
31:1
7[2]

ECCL.
1:3
5
6
2:14
21
22[2]
23[2]
24[2]
26
3:11
12
13
22[2]
4:4
5[2]
8[2]
10
14
15
5:14
15[3]
17[2]
18[3]
19[2]
20[2]
6:2
3[2]
4
7
12
7:2
15[3]
8:1[2]
3
9
12
13
15[2]
16
9:12
15
16
10:2[2]
3

ECCL.
10:18[2]
12:5
13

CANT.
1:2
4
12
2:3[2]
4
6[2]
16
3:8[2]
11[3]
4:16[2]
5:4
11[2]
12
13[2]
14[2]
15[2]
16
6:2
7:10
8:3[2]
7
10

ISAIAH
1:3[2]
2:3[2]
10
19
20[2]
21
22
3:5
6[2]
8
11
14
5:1
7
12
19
25[4]
6:1
2[2]
3
6
7:2[2]
14
8:3
7[5]
8
17
9:4[3]
6[2]
7[2]
11
12[2]
17[2]
19
20
21[2]
10:4[2]
7[2]
12[2]
16[2]
17[3]
18[2]
19
24
26
27[2]
28
32
11:1
3[2]
4[2]
5[2]
8
10
11[2]
15[2]
16
12:4[3]
13:6
10
13
14[2]
14:17
18
21
25[2]
27
29
31
32
15:4
5
16:6[4]
12
17:4
5
7[2]
8[2]
9
19:1
2[2]
14
22:21
22
23
24
23:11
24:2

ISAIAH
24:23
25:4
8
9
11[2]
26:21
27:1
8
9
28:4
5
21[4]
25
28[2]
29:8[2]
22
23
30:4[2]
26
27[3]
28
30[3]
31:2
3
4
7[2]
8
9[3]
32:6
33:6
15[3]
16[2]
17
34:2
14
16
17
36:6
16[3]
18
37:1
4
7[2]
20
24[2]
38[4]
38:2
9
39:2[5]
40:10[3]
11[3]
12
13
26
28
41:2[3]
3
6[2]
42:2
4
10
12
13
21
24[2]
25
44:5
6
11
12[2]
13
17
19
20
26[2]
45:1
9
10
11
18
46:3
47:4
15
48:2
14[2]
15
16
19
20
49:2[2]
5
7
13[2]
50:10[2]
51:14
15
17
22
52:9
10
14[2]
53:5
6
7[2]
8
9[3]
10[4]
11[2]
12
54:5
16
55:7[2]
56:2
3
6
10
11

ISAIAH
57:2
13
17[2]
18[2]
58:5[2]
59:1
2
16[2]
17
18[2]
19
60:2
21[4]
25
26
62:8[2]
11[2]
63:1[2]
7
9[3]
10
11[3]
12
65:15
20
66:5
6
13
14[3]
15[3]
16

JER.
1:2
9
15
2:3
15[2]
35
3:1
5
4:7[3]
13[2]
26
5:8
24
6:3
21
7:5
29
8:1
6[2]
16[2]
9:4
5
8[3]
20
23[3]
10:10[2]
12[3]
13[2]
14[2]
16[2]
23
25
11:19
12:15[2]
13:23[2]
16:12
17:5
10[2]
11[2]
18:11
12
16
18
19:3
9
20:9[2]
21:2
7
9
22:4[2]
6
7
8
10
11
13[4]
16[2]
18
28
30[2]
23:6
9
14
18[2]
20
27
30
34
35[2]
36
24:8
25:4
5
19[3]
30[3]
38[2]
26:3
21[2]
23
27:7[3]
8
12
28:11
29:32
30:6[3]
8

JER.
30:21
24
31:10
30[2]
34[2]
35
32:4[2]
18
19[2]
33:2
11
21
26
34:1[2]
3[2]
9[3]
10[2]
14
15
16[2]
17[2]
21
35:3[2]
14
15
18
36:3
7
14
17
18
24
30
31[2]
37:2
10
17
38:2
39:1
6
40:3
42:11
43:10[2]
12
44:21
23[3]
30[4]
46:8
10
26
47:3[3]
48:7
10
11[3]
12
15
16
17
25
26
29
30[2]
35
40
49:1[2]
2
3[2]
10[4]
20
22
50:16[2]
17
18
19[2]
25[2]
28
32
34
43
45
51:3[2]
5
6
9
11[2]
15[3]
16[2]
17[2]
19[2]
21[2]
23[2]
28
31
34
44
45
59
52:1
3
4[2]
8
10
11
27
31
32
33[2]
34[2]

LAM.
1:10
12
14
17
2:1[3]
2

LAM.
2:3[2]
4[2]
5
6[2]
7[2]
8
17
3:1
3
12
13
22
27
29
30
32
34
36
39
4:4
11
20

EZEKIEL
1:15
27[2]
3:12
18[4]
19[3]
20[4]
7:13
16
20
8:2[2]
11[2]
9:1[2]
2[2]
3
11
10:7
12:12[3]
14
13:22
14:4[5]
7[4]
16:15
17:4
14
15
17
18
19
20
21[2]
22
18:6
7[2]
8
11
12
13
14
15[2]
16
17[2]
18[4]
21
22
23
24[4]
26[2]
27[2]
28
30
19:7
9
20:7
39
21:3
4
5
21
23
30
22:11[4]
25:9[2]
26:3
9
10
11
29:3
18[2]
19
20
30:11
23
24
31:2
3
4
5[2]
6[2]
7[2]
8[2]
9
10[2]
11[2]
13[2]
16[2]
18
32:10
23[2]
31
32
33:4[2]
5[2]

EZEKIEL 33:6[2] 8[3] 9[3] 11 12[3] 13[3] 14 16 18 19 20 26 30 34:12[2] 26 35:8 36:20 37:7 16[2] 19 38:6 21 22 39:11 40:3 43:2[2] 17 44:27 45:8 46:2[2] 7 12[3] 16[2] 17[5] 18[3] 47:3 12 23 48:1

DANIEL 1:2[3] 3 8 20 2:1[2] 2 7 13 17[2] 18 20 32[4] 33[2] 34 46 3:13 19 20 24 28[2] 4:3[4] 14[4] 15[2] 16 19 23 33[3] 34 35[2] 37 5:1 2[4] 3[3] 6[3] 7 9[2] 10 20[4] 21[3] 22 23 29 6:5 10[5] 11 13

DANIEL 6:14 17[2] 18[2] 22 23 26[2] 7:1[2] 9[3] 11 14[2] 19[2] 20[2] 25 26 8:4[2] 5 6 7[2] 11 21 22 24[2] 25[3] 9:2 4 10[2] 12 14[2] 17 10:6[6] 9[2] 11:2[2] 3 4[4] 5[2] 6 7 9[2] 10[2] 11 12 15 16[2] 17[3] 18[3] 19[2] 20 21 24[3] 25[2] 26[2] 28[3] 31 36 37 39[2] 41 42 43 45[2] 12:7[2]

HOSEA 1:4 9 3:5 5:5 13[2] 6:2 3 7:5 9 10 8:14[2] 9:8[2] 13 10:1[2] 6 11 11:5 6[2] 12:2[2] 3[2] 5 7 14[3] 13:12

HOSEA 13:15[3] 14:5 6[3] 7

JOEL 2:7 8 11[4] 16 18[2] 19 20[4] 3:16[2]

AMOS 1:2 11[3] 15 2:4 7[2] 9[2] 14 3:4 7[2] 4:2 13[2] 5:8 19 6:8 7:7 10 17 9:6[3] 11

OBADIAH 3 6 11[2] 14[2]

JONAH 1:5 7 2:1 3:6[2] 7 8 9 4:6[2]

MICAH 1:2 3 11 2:2[2] 7 3:4 8[2] 4:2[2] 4[2] 5 12 5:3 4 6:2 7:2 8 6 9 18[2]

NAHUM 1:2[2] 3[2] 5 6[3] 8 14 2:3[2] 5 12[4]

HABAK. 1:11[3] 2:4[2] 5 6

HABAK. 2:9[2] 15 18 20 3:3[2] 4[3] 5 6 10[2] 14[2] 16

ZEPH. 1:7 18 2:3 11 13 15 3:5 17

HAGGAI 1:9 2:12[2] 22

ZECH. 1:21 2:1 8 12 13 3:1 5[2] 10 4:1 2 5:4 6:12 13[2] 7:9 10 12 8:4[2] 10 16 17 9:7[4] 10 14 16[2] 17[2] 10:3[2] 12 11:6[2] 17[4] 12:4 10[2] 13:3[4] 4 14:4 9 13[3]

MALACHI 1:3[2] 6[2] 12 14 2:6[2] 7 10 15 16 3:1 2 5[2] 14 16 17 4:2

MATT. 1:2 11 18

MATT. 1:21 23 24 25 2:2 11 13 14 20 22 3:3 4[3] 7 12[3] 4:6 18 21 24 5:1 2 13 22[2] 28 31 32 35 45 6:27 29 33 7:9 24 26 28 8:3[2] 13 14 16 20 21 23 25 9:1 7 10 11 19 20 21 31 37 38 10:1 2[2] 10 24[2] 25[3] 35 36 38 39[2] 42 11:1 2 20 12:1 10 19 21 26 29[2] 33[3] 46[2] 49[2] 13:19 24 25[2] 31 36 41[2] 52 54 55[2] 56 57[2] 14:2 3

MATT. 14:11 12 15 19 22 31 36 15:5[2] 6[2] 12 23 32 33 36 16:5 13 20 21 24[2] 25[2] 26[2] 27[3] 28 17:1 2[2] 10 27 18:6 15 23 25[2] 28 29[2] 31 32 34 35 19:3 5 9 10[2] 13 15 23 25 28 20:1 2 8 28 21:34 35 37 38 41 45 22:2 3 5[2] 6 7 8 15 24[3] 25[2] 33 45 23:1 24:1 17 18 31[2] 32 43 45[2] 46 47 48[2] 49 51 25:14[2] 15[2] 18 21 23 26 31[2]

MATT. 25:32 33 34 41 26:1 7 8 23 39 45 51[3] 52 63 65[2] 67 27:19 24 25 29[2] 31 32 35 37[2] 44 53 60 64 28:3[2] 7 8 9 13

MARK 1:3 6 16 19 22 28 41 2:8 15[2] 16 23 3:5 7 9 21 27[2] 31[2] 4:2 34 5:3 15 22 27 28 31 6:1[2] 2 3 4[3] 5 14 17 21[2] 26 27 28 29[2] 35 41 45 56 7:2 11 12[2] 17 19 25 32[2] 33[3] 35[2] 8:1 4 6

MARK 8:10 12 23[2] 25[2] 26 27[2] 33 34[2] 35[2] 36 37 38 9:3 14 18 21 28 31 36 41 42 50 10:2 7[2] 10 11 13 16[2] 23 24 45 46 48 50 52 11:1 18 23 12:6 13 19[4] 33 37 38 43 13:1 15 16 27[2] 34[3] 14:3 12 13 16 32 47 51 61 63 65 15:17 20 21 24 26 27[2] 16:7

LUKE 1:5 8 9 13 14 15 23 24 29 31 32 33 48 49 50 51 54[2] 55

LUKE 1:59 60 62 63 64[2] 67 68 69 70 72 76 77 80 2:3 5 21 28 33 34 41 43 47 48 51 3:1 4 17[3] 18 19 4:10 16 22 24 30 32[2] 40 5:12 13 19 25 29 30 6:1 10 13 14 17 20[2] 40[2] 44 45[3] 7:1 3 11 12 15 16 19 38[3] 8:5 9 19[2] 22 35 39 41 44 9:1 14 18 23 24[2] 26[2] 29[2] 31 32 42 43 51 52 53 54 58 62 10:1 2 7

LUKE 10:23 30 34[2] 39 11:1[2] 6 8[2] 18 21[2] 22[2] 54 12:1 22 25 27 39 42[2] 43 45[2] 46 47[2] 13:6 7 13 15[2] 17 19 14:17 21[2] 26[2] 27 34 15:5 6 12[2] 13[2] 15 16 20[3] 22[3] 25 28 29 16:1[2] 5 18 20 21 23[2] 24 17:2 16[2] 24 31 33[2] 18:7 13[2] 14 15 39 43 19:13 14 29 20:20 26[2] 28[3] 44 45 22:4 36[2] 39 44 45 50 51 71 23:11 34 49 55 24:8 23 26 40[2] 47 50

JOHN 1:11[2] 12 14 16 35 41 2:2 5 11[2] 12[3] 17 21 22 23 3:4 16 17 20 21 22 32 33[2] 35 4:2 3 5 6 8 12[2] 27 31 34 41 44 47 50 51 53 5:9 18 28 35 37[2] 38 43 47 6:2 3 5 8 12 16 22[3] 24 52 53 60 61 66 7:3 5 10 16 17 18[2] 30 38 53 8:6 20 44 55 9:1 2[2] 3 7 14 15 18[2] 20 21 22 23 27 28 31 10:3[2]

JOHN 10:4[2] 11 11:2 3 7 12 13 16 32 41 44 54 12:3 4 16 17 25[2] 41 50 13:1[2] 3 4 10 12 16 18 23 15:10 13[2] 15 19 20 16:17 29 32 17:1 18:1[2] 2 10 19[2] 22 25 26 19:2 17 23[2] 25[2] 26[2] 27 29 30 33 34 35 20:7 20[2] 25[2] 26 30 31 21:2 7 14 20 24

ACTS 1:3 7 14 18 20[2] 22 25 2:6 14 29 30[2] 31[2] 41 3:2 4 7 13 16[2] 18 21

ACTS 3:26[2] 4:26 32 5:1 2 7 10 31 32 41 6:15 7:4 5[2] 6 10[2] 13 14[2] 20 23[2] 25[2] 27 8:1 2 28 32[2] 33[4] 35 39 9:8 12[2] 17[2] 18 33 41 10:2 7 22 24 25 34 43 11:13 29 12:1 7[2] 10 11 15 21 13:8 9 13 16 23 24 25[2] 31 36[2] 14:3 8[2] 14 18 16:1 3 27[2] 32 33 34[2] 17:2 16 28 18:2 6 8 14 18[2] 19:6 12 31 33 20:7 10 28 32 38 21:11 19

ACTS 22:14[2] 15 20 30 23:29 30 24:8 23 24 27:3 28:3 4 8 23 30

ROMANS 1:2 3 5 9 20 2:4 6 18 26 3:7 20 24 25[2] 26 4:5 13 19 23 5:8 9 10[2] 6:3 5[2] 16 8:3 9 11 28 29 32 9:19 22[2] 23 11:1 2 22 33[2] 34 12:20 13:10 14:4 5 13 15:2[3] 9 10 16:13 15

1 COR. 1:9 29 2:10 3:8[2] 5:1 6:5 14 18 7:2 4 7 11 33 36 37[4] 9:7 10 10:24 28 11:4[2]

1 COR. 11:7 21 14:25[2] 30 15:10 23[2] 25 27 38 16:12

2 COR. 2:11 14 3:7 13 5:10 7:7 12[2] 13 15 8:9 17 9:7 9 15 10:10[3] 11:3 15 33

GAL. 1:15 16 3:16 4:4 6 5:10 6:4 5 8

EPHES. 1:5 6 7[2] 9[2] 11 12 14 18[2] 19[2] 20 22 23 2:4 7[2] 10 15 3:5 6 7 16[2] 4:25 28 5:28 29 30[3] 31[2] 33 6:10

PHIL. 1:29 2:4 13 30 3:10[3] 21 4:19

COLOS. 1:9 11 13 14 20

COLOS. 1:22[2] 24 26 29 2:14 18 3:9 4:15

1 THESS. 1:10 2:11 12 19 3:13 4:4 6 8

2 THESS. 1:7 9 10 11 2:6 8[2] 3:4[2] 5

1 TIM. 5:8[2] 18 6:1 15

2 TIM. 1:8 9 2:19 26 4:1[2] 8 14 18

TITUS 1:3 3:5 7

HEB. 1:2 3[3] 7[2] 2:4 8 3:2 5 6 7 15 18 4:1 4 7 10[3] 13 5:7 6:10 17 7:10 27 8:11[2] 9:12 10:13[2] 20 30 11:4 5 7 17 21 22 23 12:10 16 13:12

HEB. 13:13 15 21[2]

JAMES 1:8 11 14 18[2] 23 24 25 26[2] 2:21 22 3:13 4:11[2] 5:20

1 PETER 1:3 2:9 21 22 24[2] 3:10[2] 12 4:2 13 5:10

2 PETER 1:3 9 16 2:8 16 22 3:4 9 13 16

1 JOHN 1:3 7 10 2:3 4 5 9 10 11[2] 12 28 3:9 10 12[3] 14 15 16 17[2] 22[2] 23[2] 24 4:9 10 12 13 20[2] 21 5:2 3[2] 9 10 11 14 16 20

2 JOHN 6 11

3 JOHN 7 10

JUDE 14 24

REV. 1:1[3] 4 5 6 14[3] 15[2] 16[4] 17[2] 2:1 5 18[2] 3:5[3] 21 6:5 8 17 7:15 9:11 10:1[3] 2[3] 5 7 11:15 19[2] 12:3 4 5 7[2] 9 10 15 16 13:1[2] 2[4] 3[2] 6[2] 17 18 14:1 7 9[4] 10 11[2] 14[2] 16 19 15:2[3] 8 16:2[2] 3 4 8 10[2] 12 15[2] 17 19 17:17 18:1 19:2[2] 5 7 10 12[2] 13 15 16[2] 19 20 21 20:1 4[2] 7 21:3 7 22:3 4[2] 6[2] 12 14 19

I

589, *1473*

GEN. 1:25 30 2:18 3:10[2] 11 12 13 15 16 17 4:1 9 13 14 23 6:7[2] 13 17 18 7:1 4[2] 8:21[2] 9:3 5 9 11

GEN. 9:12 13 14 15 16 17 12:1 2 3 7 11 13 19 13:8 9[2] 15 16 17 22 23[3] 15:1 2 7 8 14 18

GEN. 16:2 5[2] 8 10 13 17:1 2 5 6 7 8[2] 16[2] 19 20[2] 21 18:3 4 5 10 12 13 14 15 17 19 21[2]

GEN. 18:26[2] 27 28 29 30[2] 31[2] 32 19:2 7 8[2] 19 21 22 34 20:5 6[3] 9 11 13 16 21:7 13 18 23 24 26[2]

GEN. 21:30 22:1 2 5 7 11 12 16 17 23:4[2] 8 11[2] 13[2] 24:2 3[2] 5 7 12 13 14[4] 17 19 23 24 27 31

GEN. 24:33 34 37 39 40 42[2] 43[2] 44 45[2] 46[2] 47[2] 48 49 56 58 25:22 30[2] 32 26:2 3[3] 4 9 24[2] 27:1 2 3

GEN. 27:4[2] 6 7 8 9 11 12 18 19[2] 21 24 25 32 33 37[3] 41 45[2] 46 28:13[2] 15[2] 16 20 21 22[2] 29:18 19[2]

GEN. 29:21 25 33 34 35 30:1 2 3 8 13 14 16 18 20 25 26[2] 27[2] 28 29 30[2] 31[2] 32 34 31:3 5 6

GEN. 31:10 11 12 13 31 35 38[2] 39[2] 40 41 43 44 51 52 32:4 5[3] 9 10[3] 11[2] 12 20[2] 26 29 30 33:8 9

GEN. 33:10[4] 11[2] 12 14[3] 34:8 11 12 30[3] 35:3[2] 11 12[3] 37:6[2] 9 10 13[2] 14 16[2] 17 30[2] 35 38:16 17 18 22 23 25[2]

GEN. 38:26[2] 39:9[2] 14 15 18 40:8 11[2] 14 15[2] 16[2] 41:9 11 15[2] 17 19 21 22 24 28 40 41 44 42:2 14 18 22

GEN 42:33 34[2] 37[2] 43:9[2] 14[2] 23 44:15 17 18 21 28[2] 30 32[2] 33 34[2] 45:3 4[2] 11 18 28[2] 46:2 3[2] 4[2] 30 31 47:16

GEN. 47:23 29[3] 30[2] 48:4[2] 5 7[2] 9 11 19[2] 21 22[2] 49:1 7 29 31 50:4[2] 5[4] 17 19 21 24

EXOD. 2:7 9 10

EXOD. 2:22 3:3 4 6 7[2] 8 9 10 11[3] 12[2] 13[2] 14[3] 16 17[2] 19 20[2] 21 4:10[2] 11 12 13 14 15 18 21[2] 23[2]

EXOD. 5:2[3] 10 23 6:1 2 3[2] 4 5[2] 6[4] 7[3] 8[4] 29[2] 30 7:1 2 3 4 5[2] 17[2] 8:2 8 9 21 22[2] 23 28

EXOD. 8:29[2] 9:14 15[2] 16 18 27 28 29[2] 30 10:1[2] 2[3] 4 10 16 17 29 11:1 4 8 12:8 12[3] 13[3] 15[2] 17 14:4[3] 17[3]

EXOD. 14:18[2] 15:1 2[2] 9[4] 26[3] 16:4[2] 12[2] 32[2] 17:4 6 9 14 18:3 6 11 16[2] 19 19:4[2] 9[2] 20:2 5 22 24[3] 21:5[2] 13 22:23

EXOD. 22:24 27[2] 23:7 13 15 20[2] 22[2] 23 25 26 27[2] 28 29 30 31[2] 24:12[2] 25:8 9 16 21 22[3] 28:3 29:35 42 43 44[2]

EXOD. 29:45, 46[3], 30:6, 36, 31:2, 8, 6[4], 11, 13, 32:8, 9, 10[2], 13[3], 18, 24[2], 30[2], 32, 33, 34[3], 33:1[2], 2[2], 3[2], 5[2], 12, 13[4], 14, 16[2], 17[2], 18, 19[4], 22[2], 23, 34:1, 9[2], 10[3], 11[2], 18, 24, 27, **LEVIT.** 6:17, 7:34, 8:31, 35, 10:3[2], 13, 18, 19, 11:44[2], 45[2], 14:34[2], 16:2, 17:10, 11, 12, 14, 18:2, 3, 4, 5, 6, 21, 24, 25, 30, 19:3, 4, 10, 12, 14, 16, 18, 25, 28, 30, 31, 32, 34, 36, 37, 20:2, 3, 5, 6, 7, 8, 22, 23[2], 24[3], 25, 26, 21:8, 12, 15, 23, 22:2, 3, 8, 9, 16, 30, 31, 32[2], 33, 23:10, 22, 30, 43[2], 25:2, 17, 21, 38, 42, 55[3], 26:1, 2

LEVIT. 26:4, 6[2], 9, 11, 12, 13[2], 16[2], 17, 18, 19[2], 21, 22, 24, 25[2], 26, 28[3], 30, 31[2], 32, 33, 36, 41, 27:42[3], 44[3], 45[4], **NUM.** 3:12, 13[3], 41, 45, 5:3, 6:27, 8:16, 17[2], 18, 19, 9:8, 10:10, 29, 30[2], 31, 11:11, 12[2], 13, 14, 15[2], 17[2], 21[2], 12:6, 8, 11, 13, 13:2, 14:11, 12, 17, 19, 20, 21, 22, 23, 24, 27[2], 28[2], 30, 31, 35[2], 15:2, 18, 41[2], 16:8, 15[2], 21, 26, 28, 45, 17:4, 5[2], 18:6[2], 7, 8[2], 11, 12, 19, 20, 21, 24[2], 26, 20:12, 17, 18, 19[3], 24, 21:2, 16, 34, 22:6[4], 8, 11, 16, 17[3], 18, 19[2], 20, 28, 29[2], 30[3], 32, 33, 34[3], 35, 37[2], 38[3], 23:3[2], 4[2], 8[2]

NUM. 23:9[2], 11, 12, 13, 15, 20[2], 26[2], 27[2], 24:10, 11, 12, 13[2], 14[2], 17[2], 25:11, 12, 27:12, 32:8, 11, 33:53, 56[2], 35:34[2], **DEU.** 1:8, 9[2], 12, 13, 15, 16, 17, 18, 20, 23, 29, 35, 36, 39, 42, 43, 2:5[2], 9[2], 13, 19[2], 24, 25, 26, 27[2], 28[3], 29, 31, 3:2, 12, 13, 15, 16, 18, 19[2], 20, 21, 23, 25, 4:1, 2[2], 5, 8, 10, 21[2], 22[2], 26, 40, 5:1, 5, 6, 9, 28, 31[2], 6:2, 6, 7:11, 17[2], 8:1, 11, 19, 9:9[3], 12, 13, 14[2], 15, 16, 17, 18[2], 19, 20, 21[2], 23, 24, 25[2], 26, 10:2, 3, 5[2], 10, 11, 13, 11:2, 8, 13, 14, 15, 22, 26, 27, 28, 32, 12:11, 14

DEU. 12:20, 21, 28, 30, 32, 13:18, 15:5, 11, 15, 16, 18:16, 18[2], 19, 20, 19:7, 9, 22:14[3], 16, 17, 24:8, 18, 22, 26:3[2], 8, 10, 13[3], 14[3], 27:1, 4, 10, 28:1, 13, 14, 15, 68, 29:5, 6, 14, 19[2], 30:1, 2, 8, 11, 15, 16, 18, 19[2], 31:2[2], 5, 14, 16, 17[2], 18, 20[2], 21[3], 23[2], 27[2], 28, 29[2], 32:1, 3, 20[2], 21[2], 23[2], 24, 26[3], 27, 39[6], 40[2], 41[2], 42, 46, 49, 52, 33:9, 34:4[3], **JOSH.** 1:2, 3[2], 5[3], 6, 9, 2:4, 5, 9, 12[2], 3:7[3], 5:9, 14, 6:2, 10, 7:8, 11, 12, 19, 20[2], 21[2], 8:1, 5, 8, 18, 10:8, 11:6, 13:6[2], 14:7[2], 8, 10, 11[2], 12, 15:16, 17:14, 18:4, 6, 8, 20:2, 22:2

JOSH. 23:2, 4[2], 14, 24:3, 4[2], 5[4], 6, 7, 8[3], 10[2], 11, 12, 13, **JUD.** 1:1, 2, 7, 12, 2:1[4], 3[2], 20, 21, 22, 3:19, 20, 4:7[2], 8[2], 9, 19[2], 22, 5:3[3], 7[2], 6:8, 9, 10[2], 14, 15[2], 16, 17, 18[3], 22, 37[2], 38[2], 7:4[3], 7, 9, 13, 17[2], 18[2], 8:2, 3, 5[2], 7, 9[2], 19, 23, 24, 9:2[2], 9, 11, 13, 29, 38, 48, 10:11, 12, 13, 11:9, 17, 27, 31[2], 35[2], 37[2], 12:2[2], 3[2], 13:4, 6, 11, 13, 14, 15, 16, 14:2, 12[2], 16[2], 15:1, 2[3], 3[2], 7[2], 11, 16, 18, 16:6, 7, 10, 11, 15, 17[3], 20, 26[2], 28[3], 17:2, 3[2], 9[3], 10, 13[2], 18:4, 24[2], 19:6, 8, 9, 11, 18[3], 23, 24, 20:4[3]

JUD. 20:6, 23, 28[3], **RUTH** 1:12[4], 16[2], 17[2], 21, 2:2, 7, 9, 10[2], 13, 19, 3:1, 5, 9, 11, 12[2], 13, 4:4[4], 6[3], 9, 10, **1 SAM.** 1:8, 11, 15[2], 16, 20, 22[2], 26, 27[2], 28, 2:1, 16, 23, 24, 27, 28[2], 29, 30[2], 31, 33, 35[2], 36[2], 3:4, 5[2], 6, 8, 11, 12[4], 13[2], 14, 16, 17, 4:16[2], 7:5, 7, 8, 9:8[2], 16[2], 17, 18, 19[2], 21, 23[2], 24[2], 26, 27, 10:2, 8[2], 15, 18, 11:2[2], 12:1, 2[2], 3[7], 7, 17, 23[2], 13:11, 12[3], 14:7, 24, 29[2], 37, 40, 43[2], 15:2, 6, 11, 13, 14, 16, 20, 24[3], 25[2], 26, 30[3], 16:1[3], 2[2], 3[2], 5, 7, 18, 22, 17:8, 9, 10, 28, 29, 35[2], 39[2], 43

1 SAM. 17:44, 45, 46[2], 55, 58, 18:11, 17, 18[2], 21, 23, 19:2, 3[4], 15, 17, 20:1, 3, 4, 5[2], 9[2], 12[2], 13, 14[2], 20[2], 21[2], 22, 23, 29[3], 30, 36, 21:2[3], 5, 8, 15, 22:3[2], 9, 12, 15, 22[2], 23:2, 4, 11, 17, 22, 23[2], 24:4, 6, 10[2], 11[2], 17[2], 20, 25:7, 8, 11[3], 19, 21, 22, 24, 25[2], 28, 35, 26:6, 8[2], 11[2], 18, 19, 21[3], 23, 27:1[3], 5[2], 28:2, 7, 8[2], 11, 13, 15[3], 21, 22, 23, 29:3, 6, 8[3], 9, 30:7, 8[2], 13[2], 15, **2 SAM.** 1:3, 4, 6, 7[2], 8[2], 9, 10[3], 13, 16, 26, 2:1[2], 6, 20, 22[2], 3:8, 9, 13[2], 14, 18, 21, 28, 35, 39, 4:10[2], 11, 5:19[2], 6:21, 22[2], 7:2

2 SAM. 7:6[2], 7[3], 8, 9, 10, 11, 12[2], 13, 14[2], 15, 18, 27, 9:1, 3, 7, 8, 9, 10:2, 11, 11:5, 11[2], 12:7, 8[2], 11[2], 12, 13, 22, 23[3], 27, 28, 13:4, 5[2], 6[2], 10, 12[3], 24, 26, 28[2], 14:2, 5, 8, 11, 12, 15[2], 18[2], 21, 22, 32[3], 15:4[2], 7[2], 8[2], 20[3], 25, 26, 28, 31, 34[3], 16:4[2], 9, 10, 18[2], 19[4], 17:1, 2[2], 3, 11, 15, 18:2, 4, 10, 11, 12[2], 13, 14, 18, 22, 29[2], 33, 19:6, 7, 20[2], 22[3], 26[2], 28, 29, 33, 34[2], 35[5], 37[2], 38[2], 20:16[2], 17[2], 19, 20, 21, 21:3[2], 4, 6, 22:3, 4[2], 7, 22, 23, 24, 30[2], 38[2], 39, 41, 43[2], 44, 50[2], 23:17, 24:2, 10[4], 12[2], 13, 14

2 SAM. 24:17, 24[2], **1 KINGS** 1:5, 12, 14, 21, 30, 35, 2:2, 7, 8[3], 14, 15, 16, 17, 18, 20[3], 26, 30, 42[2], 43, 3:5, 7[2], 9, 12, 13, 14, 17, 18, 21[3], 5:5[2], 6, 8, 9, 6:12[2], 13, 8:12, 16[3], 20, 21, 26, 27, 43, 44, 48, 59, 9:3[2], 4, 5, 6, 7[4], 10:6, 7[3], 11:11[2], 12[2], 13[2], 21, 31, 32, 34[3], 35, 36[2], 37, 38[3], 39, 12:6, 11[2], 14, 13:7, 8[2], 14, 16[2], 18, 31, 14:2[2], 6, 7, 10, 15:19, 16:2, 3, 17:1, 4, 9, 10[2], 12[3], 18, 20, 21, 24, 18:1, 8, 9, 12[4], 13[2], 15[2], 18, 22[2], 23, 24, 36[2], 19 2, 4, 10[3], 14[3], 18, 20[3], 20:4[2], 5, 6, 7[2], 9[2], 13[2], 28[2], 31

1 KINGS 20:32, 34[2], 35, 37, 42, 21:2[3], 3, 4, 6[3], 7, 20, 21, 29[2], 22:4, 5, 6[2], 8, 13, 14, 16, 17, 18, 19, 21, 22[2], 27, 30, 34, **2 KINGS** 1:2, 10, 12, 13, 2:2[2], 3, 4[2], 5, 6[2], 9[3], 10, 18, 19, 21, 3:7[2], 13, 14[3], 4:2, 9, 10, 13, 22[2], 24, 26, 28[2], 30, 43, 5:5, 6, 7[2], 11, 12, 15[2], 16[2], 17, 18[2], 20, 22, 6:3[2], 13, 17, 18, 19, 21[2], 27, 29, 33, 7:12, 13[2], 8:4, 8, 9, 12, 9:3, 5, 6, 7, 8, 9, 12, 17, 25, 26[2], 10:9, 19, 24, 16:7, 17:13[2], 38, 18:14[2], 20, 23[2], 25, 26, 32, 19:7[2], 19, 20, 23[2], 24[2], 25[3], 27, 28[2], 34, 20:3[2], 5[3], 6[3]

2 KINGS 20:8, 15, 21:4, 7[2], 8[3], 13[2], 14, 22:8, 16, 19[2], 20[2], 23:17, 27[4], **1 CHRON.** 4:9, 5:3, 11:19[2], 13:12, 14:10[2], 15:12, 16:18, 17:1, 5[2], 6[3], 7, 8, 9, 10[3], 11[2], 12, 13[3], 14, 16, 19:2, 12, 21:2, 8[4], 10[2], 12, 13, 17[3], 22, 23[2], 24[2], 22:5, 9[2], 10[2], 14[2], 23:5, 28:2, 6[2], 7, 29:2, 3[4], 14, 17[3], 19, **2 CHRON.** 1:7, 10, 11, 12, 2:4, 5, 6[2], 8, 9, 10, 13, 6:2, 5[3], 6, 10, 11, 18, 33, 34, 38, 40, 7:12, 13[3], 14, 16, 17, 18[2], 19, 20[4], 9:5, 6[3], 10:11, 14[2], 12:5, 7[2], 16:3, 18:3, 4, 5, 7, 12, 13, 14, 15, 16, 17, 18, 20, 21, 26, 29, 33, 20:11, 25:9, 16, 28:23, 32:13

2 CHRON. 33:7[2], 8[3], 34:15, 24, 27, 28[2], 35:21[3], 23, **EZRA** 4:19, 6:8, 11, 12, 7:13, 21[2], 28[2], 8:15[2], 16, 17[2], 21, 22, 24, 26, 28, 9:3[2], 4, 5[2], 6, **NEH.** 1:1, 2, 4[2], 5, 6[2], 8[2], 9[2], 11[3], 2:1[2], 2, 4, 5[2], 6, 7[2], 8, 9, 11, 12[4], 13, 14, 15, 16[3], 17, 18, 20, 4:13[2], 14, 19, 22, 23, 5:6[2], 7[3], 8, 9, 10[2], 11, 12, 13, 14[2], 15, 16, 18, 19, 6:1[2], 3[4], 4, 8, 10, 11[4], 12, 13, 7:1, 2, 3, 5, 7, 9:8, 12:31, 38, 40, 13:6[3], 7, 8, 9[2], 10, 11[2], 13, 14, 15[2], 17, 19[2], 21[2], 22, 23, 25, 28, 30, **ESTHER** 3:9, 4:11, 16[4], 5:4, 8[3], 12, 13

ESTHER 7:3, 4[2], 8:5[2], 6[2], 7, **JOB** 1:15, 16, 17, 19, 21[2], 3:3, 11[3], 12, 13[3], 16, 24, 25[2], 26[3], 4:7, 8, 16[2], 5:3[2], 8[2], 6:8[2], 10[3], 11[2], 22, 24[2], 28, 29, 7:3, 4[4], 8, 11[3], 12, 13, 16[2], 19, 20[3], 21[2], 8:8, 18, 9:1, 11[2], 14, 15[3], 16[2], 19, 20[3], 21[3], 22, 27[3], 28[2], 29[2], 30, 32[2], 35, 10:1[2], 2, 7, 9, 13, 14, 15[4], 18, 19[3], 20, 21[2], 11:4, 12:3[2], 4, 13:2[2], 3[2], 13, 14, 15[2], 18[3], 19[2], 20, 22, 14:14, 15, 15:6, 17[3], 16:1, 4[2], 5, 6[3], 12, 15, 22[2], 17:6, 10, 13[2], 14, 19:4, 7[3], 8, 10, 15, 16[2], 17, 18, 19, 20, 25, 26, 27, 20:2, 3, 21:3[2], 6[2], 27, 22:22, 23:3[3]

JOB 23:4, 5, 7, 8[2], 9[2], 10[2], 11, 12[3], 15[4], 17, 27:5[3], 6[7], 11[2], 29:1, 3, 4, 6, 7[2], 12, 13, 14, 15[2], 16[3], 17, 18[3], 24, 25, 30:1[2], 9[2], 19, 20[2], 23, 25, 26[2], 28[3], 29, 31:1[2], 5, 9, 13, 14, 16, 18, 19, 21[2], 23, 24, 25, 26, 28, 29, 30, 32, 33, 34[2], 36, 37[2], 39, 32:6[2], 7, 10[2], 11[2], 12, 14, 16, 17[3], 18, 20[3], 21, 22, 33:2, 2, 6[2], 8, 9[2], 12, 24, 27, 31, 32, 33, 34:5, 6, 31[2], 32[3], 33, 35:3[2], 4, 36:2[2], 3, 37:20, 38:3, 4, 9, 23, 39:6, 40:4[3], 5[3], 7, 14, 15, 41:11, 12, 42:2, 3[3], 4[3], 5, 6, 8[2], **PSALMS** 2:6, 7[2], 8, 3:4, 5[2], 6

PSALMS 4:1[2], 3, 8, 5:2, 3, 7[2], 6:2, 6[3], 7:1, 3, 4[2], 17, 8:3, 9:1[2], 2[2], 13, 14[2], 10:6[2], 11:1, 12:5[2], 13:2, 3, 4[2], 5, 6, 16:1, 4, 6, 7, 8[2], 17:3, 4, 6, 15[3], 18:1, 2, 3[2], 6, 21, 22, 23[2], 29[2], 37[2], 38, 40, 42[2], 43, 49, 19:13[2], 20:6, 22:2, 6, 9, 10, 14, 17, 22[2], 25, 23:1, 4[2], 6, 25:1, 2, 5, 16, 20, 21, 26:1[3], 3, 4[2], 5, 6[2], 7, 8, 11, 12, 27:1[2], 3, 4[3], 6[3], 7, 8, 13[2], 14, 28:1[2], 2[2], 7[2], 30:1, 2, 3, 6[2], 7, 8[2], 9, 12, 31:1, 5, 6[2], 7, 9, 11, 12[2], 13, 14[2], 17, 22[3], 32:3, 5[4], 8[2], 34:1, 4, 11, 35:3, 11, 13, 14[2], 15

PSALMS 35:18[2], 37:25[2], 35, 36, 38:6[3], 8[2], 13[2], 14, 15, 16, 17, 18[2], 20, 39:1[4], 2[2], 3[2], 4[2], 7, 9[2], 10, 12, 13[2], 40:1, 5, 7[2], 8, 9[2], 10[3], 12, 17, 41:4[2], 9, 10, 11, 42:2, 4[4], 5, 6, 9[2], 11, 43:2, 4[2], 5, 44:6, 45:1[2], 17, 46:10[3], 49:4[2], 5, 50:7[3], 8, 9, 11, 12[2], 13, 15, 21[3], 22, 23, 51:3, 4, 5, 7[2], 13, 16, 52:8[2], 9[2], 54:6[2], 55:2, 6[3], 7, 8, 9, 12[2], 16, 17, 23, 56:3[2], 4[3], 9[2], 10[2], 11[2], 12, 13, 57:1, 2, 4, 7, 8, 9[2], 59:8, 16[2], 17, 60:6[2], 8, 61:2[2], 4[2], 8[2], 62:2, 6, 11, 63:1, 2, 4[3], 6, 7, 66:13[2], 14, 15[2], 16, 17, 18, 68:22[2], 69:2[2], 3[2], 4[2], 7

PSALMS 69:8, 10, 11[2], 12, 17, 20[3], 29, 30, 70:5, 71:1, 3, 6, 7, 14, 15, 16[2], 17, 18[2], 22[2], 23, 73:3[2], 13, 14, 15[3], 16, 17[2], 21, 22[2], 23, 25[2], 28[2], 75:2[2], 3, 4, 9[2], 10, 77:1, 2, 3[2], 4[2], 5, 6[2], 10[2], 11[2], 12, 78:2[2], 81:5[2], 6, 7[3], 8, 10[2], 12, 14, 16, 82:6, 84:10, 85:8, 86:1, 2, 3, 4, 7, 11, 12[2], 87:4, 88:1, 4[2], 8[2], 9[2], 13, 15[3], 89:1[2], 2, 3[2], 4, 19[2], 20[2], 23, 25, 27, 28, 29, 32, 33, 34, 35[2], 50, 91:2[2], 14[2], 15[3], 16, 92:4, 10, 94:18, 95:10, 11, 101:1[2], 2[2], 3[2], 4, 5[2], 8[2], 102:2[2], 4, 6[2], 7, 9, 11, 24, 104:33[4], 34, 105:11, 106:5[3], 108:1, 2, 3[2], 7[2]

PSALMS 108:9[2], 109:4, 22, 23[2], 25, 30[2], 110:1, 2, 3[2], 5, 7, 111:1, 116:1, 2[2], 3, 4[2], 6, 9, 10[3], 11, 12, 13, 14, 16[2], 17, 18, 118:5, 6, 7, 10, 11, 12, 13, 17, 19[2], 21, 25[2], 28[2], 119:6[2], 7[2], 8, 10, 11[2], 13, 14, 15, 16[2], 17, 18, 19, 22, 26, 27, 30[2], 31, 32, 33, 34[2], 35, 39, 40, 42[2], 43, 44, 45[2], 46, 47[2], 48[3], 51, 52, 55, 56[2], 57[2], 58, 59, 60, 61, 62, 63, 66, 67[3], 69, 70, 71[2], 73, 74, 75, 76, 77, 78, 80, 81, 83[2], 87, 88, 92, 93, 94[2], 95, 96, 97, 99, 100[2], 101[2], 102, 104[2], 106[3], 107, 108, 109, 110, 111, 112, 113[2], 114, 115, 116

PSALMS
119:117[2]
119
120
121
125[2]
127
128[2]
131[2]
134
141[2]
144
145[2]
146[2]
147[2]
148
152
153
157
158
159
162
163[2]
164
166
167
168
173
174
176[2]
120:1
5[2]
7[2]
121:1
122:1
8
9
123:1
130:1
5[2]
6
131:1
2
132:3
4
5
11
12
14[2]
15[2]
16
17[2]
18
135:5
137:5
6[2]
138:1[2]
2
3
7
139:6
7[2]
8
9
11
14[2]
15
18[3]
21[2]
22[2]
140:6
12
141:1[2]
10
142:1[2]
2[2]
3
4
5[2]
6[2]
7
143:5[3]
6
7
8[3]
9
12
144:2
9[2]
145:1[2]
2[2]
5
6
146:2[4]

PROV.
1:23[2]
24[2]
26[2]
28
3:28
4:2
3
11[2]
5:12
14
7:6
7
14[2]
15[2]
16
17
8:4
6
12
13
14[2]
17

PROV.
8:20
21[2]
23
24
25
27
30[2]
9:5
20:9[2]
22
22:13
19
20
21
23:35[4]
24:29[2]
30
32
26:19
27:11
30:2
3
7[2]
9[2]
18
20

ECCL.
1:12
13
14
16[2]
17[2]
2:1[2]
2
3[2]
4[3]
5[2]
6
7[2]
8[2]
9
10[2]
11[2]
12
13
14
15[3]
17
18[3]
19[2]
20[2]
24
25
3:10
12
14
16
17
18
22
4:1
2
4
7[2]
8
15
5:13
18
6:1
3
7:15
23[3]
25
26
27
28[3]
29
8:2
9
10
12
14
15
16
17
9:1
11
13
16
10:5
7
12:1

CANT.
1:5
6[2]
7
9
2:1
3
5
7
16
3:1[3]
2[4]
3
4[4]
5
4:6
5:1[4]
2
3[4]
5
6[4]
8[2]
6:3

CANT.
6:11
12
7:8[3]
10
12
13
8:1[3]
2[2]
4
5
10[2]

ISAIAH
1:2
11[2]
13
14
15[2]
24
25
26
3:4
7
5:1
2
3
4[2]
5[3]
6[2]
6:1
5[4]
8[4]
11
8:2
3
17[2]
18
10:6[2]
11[2]
12
13[4]
14
12:1
2
13:3[2]
11[2]
12
13
17
14:13[2]
14[2]
22
23[2]
24[2]
25
30
15:9
16:9[2]
10
18:4[2]
19:2
3
4
11
21:2
3[2]
8[2]
10[2]
22:4[2]
19
20
21[2]
22
23
23:4[2]
24:16
25:1[2]
26:9[2]
27:3[3]
4[2]
28:16
17
22
29:2
3[2]
11[2]
12[2]
14
30:7
33:10[3]
13
24
36:5[2]
8[2]
10
11
17
37:7[2]
24[3]
25[2]
26[3]
28
29[2]
35
38:3[2]
5[3]
6[2]
8
10[3]
11[3]
12
13
14[3]
15[2]
17
19
22

ISAIAH
39:4
40:6
25
41:4[2]
8
9[2]
10[5]
13[2]
14
15
17[2]
18[2]
19[2]
25
27
28[2]
42:1[2]
6
8[2]
9[2]
14[4]
15[3]
16[4]
19
43:1[2]
2
3[2]
4[2]
5[2]
6
7[3]
10[2]
11[2]
12[3]
13[2]
14
15
19[2]
20
21
23
25
28
44:1
2
3[2]
5
6[2]
7[2]
8[2]
16[2]
19[5]
21
22[2]
24
26
27
45:1[2]
2[2]
3[2]
4[2]
5[2]
6
7[3]
8
12[3]
13[2]
18
19[4]
21
22
23
24
46:4[5]
9[2]
10
11[4]
13[2]
47:3[2]
6[2]
7
8[3]
10
48:3[2]
4
5[2]
6
7
8
9[3]
10[2]
11[2]
12[3]
13
15[4]
16[2]
17
49:3
4[3]
5
6
8[3]
11
15
16
18
20
21[2]
22
23
25[2]
26[2]
50:1[2]
2[5]
3[2]
4
5

ISAIAH
50:6[2]
7[4]
51:2
4
12[2]
15
16[3]
19
22
23
52:5
6[2]
53:12
54:7[2]
8[2]
9[3]
11
12
16[2]
55:3
4
11[2]
56:3
5[2]
7
8
12
57:6
11
12
15
16[3]
17[2]
18[2]
19[2]
58:5
6
9
14
59:21
60:7
10[2]
13
15
16
17[3]
21
22
61:8[4]
10
62:1[2]
6
8
63:1
3[3]
5[2]
6[2]
7
65:1[3]
2[2]
5
6
7
8[2]
9
12[4]
17
18[2]
19
24[2]
66:2
4[4]
9[2]
12
13
18[2]
19[2]
21
22

JER.
1:5[4]
6[3]
7[3]
8
9
10
11[2]
12
13[2]
15
16
17[2]
18
19
2:2
7
9[2]
20[2]
21
23[2]
25[2]
30
31
34
35[3]
3:7
8[2]
12
14[3]
15
18
19[3]
22
4:6
10

JER.
4:12
19[2]
21
23
24
25
26
27
28[3]
31
5:1
4
5
7[2]
9
14
15
29
6:2
8
10
11[3]
12
15
17
19
21
27
7:3
7[2]
11
12[2]
13[2]
14[3]
15[2]
16
22[2]
23[3]
25
31
34
8:6[2]
10
13
17
18
21[2]
9:1
2[2]
7[2]
9
10
11
13
15
16[3]
24[2]
25
10:18
19[2]
23
11:4[4]
5[3]
7[2]
8[2]
10
11[2]
14
18
19[2]
20
22
23
12:1
7[3]
8
14[2]
15[2]
17
13:2
5
6
7[2]
9
11
13
14[2]
24
26
27
14:12[3]
13[2]
14[2]
15
16
18[2]
15:3
4
6[2]
7[3]
8[2]
9
10
11
13
14
15
16[2]
17
19
20[2]
21[2]
16:5
9
13[2]
15[2]
16[2]

JER.
16:18
21[2]
17:3
4[2]
10[2]
14[2]
16[2]
22
27
18:2
3
6
7
8[3]
9
10[3]
11
17[2]
20
19:2
3
5
7[3]
8
9
11
12
15[2]
20:4[2]
5[2]
7[3]
8[3]
9[4]
10
12
14
18
21:2
4[2]
5
6
7
8
10
13
14[2]
22:5
6
7
14
21[2]
24[2]
25
26
23:2
3[2]
4
5
6
8
9
11
12
13
14
15
21[2]
23
24[2]
25[3]
30
31
32[2]
33
34
38
39[4]
40
24:3
5[2]
6[4]
7[3]
8
9[2]
10[2]
25:3
6
9
10
12
13[2]
14
15
16
17
27
29[2]
26:2
3[2]
4
5
6
14
27:5
6[2]
8[2]
10
11
12
15[2]
16
22[2]
28:2
3
4[2]
7
11

JER.
28:14[2]
16
29:4
7
8
10
11[2]
12
14[6]
17
18[2]
19
20
21
23[2]
31
32[2]
30:2
3[3]
6
8
9
10
11[5]
14
15
16
17[2]
18
19[2]
20
21
22
31:1
2
3[2]
4
8
9[3]
13
14
18[3]
19[6]
20[3]
25[2]
26
27
28[2]
31
32[3]
33[2]
34[2]
37
32:3
5
8[2]
9
10
11
12
13
16[2]
27
28
31
33
35
37[3]
38
39
40[3]
41[2]
42[3]
44
33:3
5[2]
6[2]
7
8[2]
9[2]
11
14[2]
15
22
25
26[3]
34:2
5
13[2]
17[2]
18
20
21
22[2]
35:3
4
5[2]
14
15[2]
17[4]
36:2[2]
3[2]
5[2]
18
31[3]
37:14
18
20[3]
38:14
15[2]
16[2]
19
20[2]
25
26
39:16
17

JER.
39:18
40:4[2]
10
15[2]
42:4[4]
10[4]
11
12
17
19
21
43:10[2]
12
44:2
4[2]
10
11
12
13[2]
26
27
29
30[2]
45:3[2]
4[4]
5[2]
46:5
8[2]
18
25
26
27
28[5]
48:12
30
31[2]
32
33
35
38
44
47
49:2
5
6
8[2]
10[2]
11
13
14
15
16
19[2]
27
32[2]
35
36
37[4]
38
39
50:9
18[2]
19
20[2]
21
24
31[2]
32
44[2]
51:1
14
20[2]
21[2]
22[3]
23[3]
24
25[2]
36[2]
39[2]
40
44[2]
47
52
57
64

LAM.
1:11
14
16
18[2]
19
20[2]
21
2:13[4]
22
3:1
7
8
14
17
18
21[2]
24
54[2]
55
57
63

EZEKIEL
1:1[2]
4
15
24
27[2]
28[3]

EZEKIEL
2:1
2
3
4
8[2]
9
3:2
3[2]
6
8
9
10
12
13
14
15[2]
17
18[2]
20[2]
22
23[3]
26
27[2]
4:5
6
8
13
14[2]
15
16
5:2
5
8[2]
9[3]
10[2]
11[3]
12[2]
13[4]
14
15[2]
16[3]
17[3]
6:3[3]
4
5[2]
7
8
9
10[3]
12
13
14[2]
7:3
4[3]
8[2]
9[3]
20
21
22
24[2]
27[3]
8:1
2
4
5
6
7
8
10
18[3]
9:8[2]
10[2]
11
10:1
9
15
20[2]
22
11:1
5
7
8
9
10[2]
11
12
13[2]
16[3]
17[2]
19[3]
20
21
24
25
12:6
7[6]
11[2]
13[2]
14[2]
15[2]
16[2]
20
23
25[4]
28
13:7
8
9
13
14[2]
15
20[2]
21[2]
22
23[2]
14:3
4

EZEKIEL
14:5
7
8[3]
9[2]
11
13
15
16
17[2]
18
19
20
21
22[2]
23[2]
15:6[2]
7[3]
8
16:3
6[3]
7
8[3]
9[3]
10[3]
11[2]
12
14
17
19[2]
27
37[2]
38[2]
39
41
42[2]
43
48
50[2]
53[2]
59
60[2]
61
62[2]
63
17:16
19[2]
20[2]
21
22[2]
23
24[2]
18:3
23
30
32
20:3[2]
5[3]
6[2]
7[2]
8[2]
9[2]
10
11
12[2]
13[2]
14[2]
15[3]
17
18
19
20
21[2]
22[2]
23[2]
25
26[3]
28[2]
29
31[3]
33[2]
34
35[2]
36[2]
37[2]
38[3]
40[2]
41[3]
42[3]
44[2]
47
48
49
21:3
4
5
15
17[3]
24
27[2]
30[2]
31[2]
32
22:4
13
14[2]
15
16[2]
19
20[2]
21
22
26
30[3]
31[3]
23:9
13
22[2]

EZEKIEL
23:24
25
27
28
30
31
34
43
46
48
49
24:8
9
13[2]
14[5]
16
18[3]
20
21
22
24
25
27
25:4
5[2]
7[5]
9
11[2]
13[2]
14
16[2]
17[3]
26:2
3
4
5
6
7
13
14[2]
19[2]
20[2]
21
27:3
28:2[2]
7
9
10
14
16[2]
17[2]
18[2]
22[4]
23[2]
24
25[2]
26[2]
29:3[2]
4[3]
5
6
8
9[2]
10[2]
12[2]
13
14
15
16
19
20
21[3]
30:8[2]
10
12[3]
13[3]
14
15[2]
16
18
19[2]
21
22[2]
23
24
25[3]
26[2]
31:9
11[2]
15[4]
16[2]
32:3
4[3]
5
6
7[3]
8
9[2]
10[2]
12
13
14
15[3]
32
33:2
6
7
8[2]
11[2]
13
14
20
22
27[2]
28
29[2]
30

EZEKIEL
34:8
10[3]
11[2]
12
13
14
15[2]
16[3]
17
20[2]
22[2]
23
24[2]
25
26[2]
27[2]
29
30
31
35:3[3]
4[2]
6[2]
7
8
9[2]
11[4]
12[2]
13
14
15[2]
36:5
6
7
9[2]
10
11[3]
12
15
18
19[2]
21
22
23[3]
24
25[2]
26[4]
27
28[2]
29[2]
30
32
33[2]
36[3]
37[2]
38
37:3
5
6[2]
7[3]
8
10
12
13[2]
14[2]
19
21
22
23[2]
25
26[2]
27
28
38:3
4[2]
11[2]
16[2]
17[2]
19
21
22[2]
23[3]
39:1
2
3
4
5
6[2]
7[3]
8
11
13
17
19
21[3]
22
23
24
25
27
28[2]
29[2]
40:4[2]
41:8
43:3[5]
6
7
8
9
27
44:4
5
12
14
28[2]
47:5
7
14

DANIEL
1:10
12
2:3
8
9
23
24
25
26
30
3:14
15
25
29
4:2
4
5
6
7
8
9[2]
10
13
30
34[3]
36
37
5:11
14
16
17
6:22
26
7:2
4
6
7
8
9
11[2]
13
15
16
19
21
28
8:2[5]
3
4
5
6
7
13
15[2]
16
17[2]
18
19
27[3]
9:2
3
4
16
20
21[2]
22
23
10:2[2]
4
5
7
8[2]
9[3]
11[3]
12
13
14
15[2]
16[2]
19
20[3]
21
11:1[2]
2
12:5
7
8[3]

HOSEA
1:4
5
6[2]
7
9
2:2
3
4
5
6
7
8
9
10
11
12[2]
13
14
15
17
18[2]
19[2]
20
21[2]
23[3]
3:2
3[2]
4:5

HOSEA
4:6[2]
7
9
14
5:2
3
9
10
11
12
14[4]
15
6:4[2]
5[2]
6
10
11
7:1
2
12[3]
13
15
8:4
10
12
14
9:10[2]
12[2]
13
15[3]
16
10:10
11[2]
11:1
3[2]
4[3]
8[4]
9[4]
11
12:8[2]
9
10[2]
11
13:5
7[2]
8[2]
10
11
14[4]
14:4[2]
5
8[3]

JOEL
1:19
2:19
20
25[2]
27[2]
28
29
30
3:1
2
4
7
8
10
12
17
21[2]

AMOS
1:3
4
5
6
7
8[2]
9
10
11
12
13
14
2:1
2
3
4
5
6
9[2]
10
11
13
3:1
2[2]
14[2]
15
4:6
7[2]
9
10[3]
11
12[2]
5:1
17
21[3]
22[2]
23
27
6:8[2]
14
7:2[2]
5[2]
8[3]
9

AMOS
7:14[3]
15
8:2
7
9[2]
10[3]
11
9:1[2]
2
3[2]
4[2]
7
8[2]
9[2]
11[3]
14
15[2]

OBADIAH
2
4
8

JONAH
1:9[2]
12
2:2[2]
4[3]
6
7
9[3]
3:2
4:2[4]
3
9
11

MICAH
1:6[3]
7
8[3]
15
2:3
11
12[3]
3:1[2]
8
9
4:6[3]
7
13[3]
5:10[2]
11
12
13
14[2]
15
6:3[2]
4[2]
6[2]
7
11
13
14
16
7:1
7[2]
8[3]
9[3]
15

NAHUM
1:12[2]
13
14[2]
2:13[3]
3:5[3]
6
7

HABAK.
1:2
5
6
2:1[3]
3:2
7
16[3]
18[2]

ZEPH.
1:2
3[3]
4[2]
8
9
10
12
17
2:5
8
9
15
3:6[2]
7[2]
8[2]
9
11
12
18
19[3]
20[4]

HAGGAI
1:8[2]
9
11

HAGGAI
1:13
2:4
5
6
7[2]
9
15
17
19
21
22[3]
23[2]

ZECH.
1:3
6
8
9[2]
14
15[2]
16
18
19
21
2:1
2
5
6
9
10[2]
11
3:4[2]
5
7
8
9[3]
4:2[2]
4
5
11
12
13
5:1
2[2]
4
6
9
10
6:1
4
7:3[2]
13
14
8:2[2]
3
7
8[2]
10
11
12
13
14[2]
15
17
21
9:6
7
8[2]
10
11
12[2]
13
10:3
6[6]
8[2]
9
10[2]
12
11:5
6[3]
7[5]
8
9[2]
10[3]
12
13[2]
14[2]
16
12:2
3
4[2]
6
9
10
13:2[2]
5[2]
6
7
9[3]
14:2

MALACHI
1:2[2]
3
4
6[2]
9
10[2]
13
14
2:2[3]
3
4
5
9
3:1
5[2]

MALACHI
3:6[2]
7
10
11
17[2]
4:3
4
5
6

MATT.
2:8
13
15
3:9
11[3]
14
17
4:9
19
5:17[2]
18
20
22
26
28
32
34
39
44
6:2
5
16
25
29
7:23[3]
24
8:3
7
8
9[2]
10[3]
11
19
9:13[2]
21[2]
28
10:15
16
23
27
32
33
34[2]
35
42
11:9
10
11
16
22
24
25
28
29
12:6
7
18[2]
27
28
31
36
44[2]
13:13
15
17
30
35[2]
14:27
15:24
32[2]
16:11
13
15
18[2]
19
28
17:5
12
16
17[2]
20
18:3
10
13
18
19
20
21
22
26
29
32
33
19:9
16[2]
20[2]
23
24
28
20:4
13
14
15[2]
22[2]
23
32

MATT. 21:21, 24[3], 27[2], 29, 30, 31, 43, 22:4, 32, 44, 23:34, 36, 37, 39, 24:2, 5, 25, 34, 47, 25:12[2], 20, 22, 23, 24, 25, 26[2], 27, 35[3], 36[2], 40, 42[2], 43, 45, 26:13, 15, 18, 21, 22, 25, 29[3], 31, 32[2], 33, 34, 35[2], 36, 39, 42, 48, 53, 55, 61, 63, 64, 70, 72, 74, 27:4[2], 17, 19, 21, 22, 24, 43, 63, 28:5, 7, 20[2]

MARK 1:7[2], 8, 11, 17, 24, 38[2], 41, 2:11, 17, 3:28, 5:7[2]

MARK 5:23, 28[2], 41, 6:11, 16, 22, 23, 24, 25, 50, 8:2, 3, 12, 19, 24, 27, 29, 9:1, 13, 17, 18, 19[2], 24, 25, 41, 10:15, 17[2], 20, 29, 36, 38[2], 39[2], 51[2], 11:23, 24, 29[3], 33[2], 12:15, 26, 36, 43, 13:6, 23, 30, 37[2], 14:9, 14, 18, 19[2], 25[3], 27, 28[2], 29, 30, 31[2], 32, 36, 44, 49, 58[2], 62, 68[2], 71, 15:9, 12

LUKE 1:18[2], 19, 34, 2:10, 48, 49, 3:8, 16[3], 22, 4:6[3], 24, 25, 34, 43[2]

LUKE 5:5, 8, 13, 24, 32, 6:9, 27, 46, 47, 7:6, 7, 8[2], 9[2], 14, 26, 27, 28, 31, 40, 43, 44, 45, 47, 8:28[2], 46, 9:9, 18, 20, 27, 38, 40, 41, 57, 61, 10:3, 12, 18, 19, 21, 24, 25, 35[2], 11:6, 7, 8, 9, 18, 19, 20, 24[2], 49, 51, 12:4, 5[2], 8, 17[2], 18[3], 19, 22, 37, 44, 49[2], 50[2], 51[2], 59, 13:3, 5, 8, 18, 20, 24, 25, 27[2], 32[3], 33, 34, 35, 14:18[3], 19[3], 20[2], 24

LUKE 15:6, 7, 9[2], 10, 17, 18[2], 21, 29[3], 31, 16:2, 3[3], 4[2], 9, 24, 27, 28, 17:4, 8[2], 9, 34, 18:4, 5, 8, 11[2], 12[3], 14, 17, 18, 21, 29, 41[2], 19:5, 8[3], 13, 20, 21, 22[4], 23, 26, 27, 40, 20:3, 8[2], 13[2], 43, 21:3, 8, 15, 32, 22:11, 15[2], 16[2], 18[2], 29, 32, 33, 34, 35, 37, 53, 57, 58, 60, 67, 68, 70, 23:4, 14, 15, 16, 22[2], 43, 46, 24:39, 44[2], 49

JOHN 1:15, 20, 21

JOHN 1:23, 26, 27, 30, 31[2], 32, 33, 34, 48, 50[2], 51, 2:4, 19, 3:3, 5, 7, 11, 12[2], 28[3], 30, 4:14[2], 15, 17[2], 19, 25, 26, 29, 32, 35, 38, 39, 5:7[2], 17, 19, 24, 25, 30[4], 31, 32, 34[2], 36[2], 41, 42, 43, 45, 6:20, 26, 32, 35, 36, 37, 38, 39, 40, 41, 42, 44, 47, 48, 51[3], 53, 54, 56, 57, 63, 65, 70, 7:7, 8, 17, 21, 23, 28[2], 29[2], 33[2], 34, 36, 8:11, 12, 14[6], 15

JOHN 8:16[3], 18, 21[2], 22, 23[2], 24[2], 25, 26[3], 28[3], 29, 34, 37, 38[2], 40, 42[2], 45, 46, 49[2], 50, 51, 54, 55[5], 58[2], 9:4, 5[2], 7, 9, 11[2], 12, 15, 25[4], 27, 36, 38, 39, 10:1, 7[2], 9, 10, 11, 14, 15[2], 16[2], 17[2], 18[4], 25[2], 26, 27, 28, 30, 32, 34, 36[2], 37, 38[2], 11:11[2], 15[2], 22, 24, 25, 27, 40, 41, 42[2], 12:24, 26, 27[2], 28, 32[2], 40, 46, 47[2], 48, 49[3], 50[3], 13:7, 8, 12, 13, 14, 15[2]

JOHN 13:16, 18[2], 19[2], 20[2], 21, 26, 33[4], 34[2], 36, 37, 38, 14:2[2], 3[3], 4, 6, 9, 10[3], 11, 12[3], 13, 14, 16, 18[2], 19, 20[2], 21, 25, 26, 27[3], 28[5], 29, 30, 31[2], 15:1, 3, 4, 5[2], 9, 10, 11, 12, 14, 15[4], 16, 17, 19, 20, 22, 24, 26, 16:1, 4[4], 5, 6, 7[5], 10, 12, 15, 16, 17, 19, 20, 22, 23, 25[2], 26[2], 27, 28[2], 32, 33[2], 17:4[2], 5, 6, 8[2], 9[2], 10, 11[2], 12[3], 13[2], 14[2], 15

JOHN 17:16, 18, 19, 20, 21, 22, 23, 24[2], 25, 26, 18:5, 6, 8[2], 9, 11, 17, 20[3], 21[2], 23, 25, 26, 35, 36, 37[4], 38, 39[2], 19:4[2], 6, 10, 15, 21, 22[2], 28, 20:13, 15, 17[2], 21, 25[2], 21:3, 15, 16, 17, 18, 22[2], 23[2], 25

ACTS 1:1, 2:17, 18, 19, 25[2], 35, 3:6[3], 17, 5:38, 7:3, 7, 32, 34[4], 43, 56, 8:19, 23, 31, 34, 37, 9:5, 10, 13, 16, 10:14, 20, 21, 26, 28, 29[3], 30[2], 33, 34

ACTS 10:37, 11:5[2], 6[2], 7, 8, 11, 15, 16, 17[2], 12:11, 13:2, 22, 25[3], 33, 34, 41, 46, 47, 15:16[3], 16:18, 30, 17:3, 22, 23[3], 18:6[2], 10[2], 14, 15, 21[2], 19:15[2], 21[2], 20:18[2], 20, 22, 24[3], 25[2], 26[2], 27, 29, 31, 32, 33, 35, 21:13, 37, 39[2], 22:1, 3, 4, 5, 6, 7, 8[2], 10[2], 11[2], 13, 17[3], 19[2], 20, 21, 28[2], 23:1, 5, 6[2], 27, 28[2], 29, 30, 35, 24:4[2], 10[2], 11, 14[2], 16, 17, 20, 21[2], 22, 25[2], 25:8, 10[3]

ACTS 25:11[3], 15, 16, 17, 18, 20[2], 21[2], 22, 25[2], 26[3], 26:2[3], 3[2], 5, 6, 7, 9[2], 10[3], 11[2], 12, 13, 14, 15[2], 16[2], 17, 19, 22, 25, 26[2], 27, 29[2], 27:10, 22, 23[2], 25, 34, 28:17[2], 19[2], 20[2], 27

ROMANS 1:8, 9[2], 10, 11[2], 12, 13[3], 14, 15, 16, 3:5, 7, 26, 4:17, 6:19, 7:1, 7[2], 9[2], 10, 14, 15[6], 16[3], 17, 18[2], 19[4], 20[3], 21[2], 22, 23, 24, 25[2], 8:18, 38, 9:1[2], 2, 3, 9, 13[2], 15[4], 17[2], 25

ROMANS 9:33, 10:18, 19[3], 20[2], 21, 11:1[2], 3, 4, 11, 13[3], 14, 19, 25, 27, 12:1, 3, 19, 14:11, 14, 15:8, 9, 14, 15, 16, 17[2], 18, 19, 20[2], 22, 24[4], 25, 28[2], 29[3], 30, 31[2], 32, 16:1, 4, 17, 19[2], 22

1 COR. 1:4, 10, 12[5], 14[2], 15, 16[3], 19, 2:1[2], 2, 3, 3:1, 2, 4[2], 6, 10, 4:3[2], 4[2], 6, 8, 9, 14[2], 15, 16, 17[2], 18, 19, 21, 5:3[2], 9, 11, 12, 6:5, 12, 15, 7:6, 7[2], 8[2], 10[2]

1 COR. 7:12, 17, 25[2], 26[2], 28, 29, 32, 35[2], 40[2], 8:13[2], 9:1[3], 2[2], 6, 8, 15[2], 16[3], 17, 18[3], 19[3], 20[3], 21, 22[4], 23[2], 26[2], 27[3], 10:1, 15[2], 19, 20[2], 29, 30[3], 33, 11:1, 2[2], 3, 17[2], 18[2], 22[3], 23[2], 34[2], 12:1, 3, 15[2], 16[2], 21[2], 31, 13:1[2], 2[4], 3[2], 11[6], 12[3], 14:5, 6[3], 11[2], 14, 15[4], 18[2], 19[2], 21, 37, 15:1[2], 2, 3[2], 9[2], 10[4], 11, 31[3], 32, 34, 50, 51, 16:1, 2, 3[2], 4, 5[3], 6[2], 7[2], 8, 10, 11

1 COR. 16:12, 15, 17

2 COR. 1:13, 15, 17[4], 23[2], 2:1[2], 2, 3[4], 4[2], 5, 8, 9[2], 10[4], 12, 13[3], 4:13[2], 5:8, 11, 6:2[2], 13, 16[2], 17, 7:3[2], 4[2], 7, 8[4], 9, 12[2], 14[3], 16[2], 8:3, 8, 10, 13, 22, 9:2[2], 3[2], 5, 6, 10:1, 2[4], 8[2], 9[2], 11:2[3], 3, 5[2], 6, 7[2], 8, 9[4], 11, 12[3], 16[2], 17[2], 18, 21[3], 22[3], 23[2], 24, 25[4], 29[2], 30[2], 31, 33, 12:1, 2[3], 3[2], 5[2], 6[4], 7[2], 8, 9, 10[3], 11[4], 13, 14[3], 15[3]

2 COR. 12:16[2], 17[2], 18[2], 20[5], 21[2], 13:1, 2[5], 6, 7, 10[2]

GAL. 1:6, 9, 10[4], 11, 12[2], 13, 16[2], 17[2], 18, 19, 20[2], 21, 2:1, 2[3], 10, 11, 14[2], 18[3], 19[2], 20[5], 21, 3:2, 15, 17, 4:1, 11, 12[3], 13, 15, 16[2], 18, 19, 20[2], 5:2, 3, 17, 11[3], 12, 16, 21[2], 6:11, 14[2], 17

EPHES. 1:15[2], 3:1, 3, 7, 8, 13, 14, 4:1, 17, 5:32, 6:19, 20[3], 21, 22

PHIL. 1:3, 7, 8, 9, 12, 17, 18, 19, 20

PHIL. 1:21, 22[2], 23, 25[2], 27[2], 2:16[2], 17[2], 19[3], 20, 23[2], 24[2], 25, 27, 28[2], 3:4[2], 7, 8[3], 10, 11, 12[4], 13[2], 14, 18, 4:2, 3, 4, 10, 11[3], 12[3], 13, 15, 17[2], 18[2]

COLOS. 1:2, 20, 23, 25, 29, 2:1[2], 4, 5[2], 4:3, 4[2], 8, 13

1 THESS. 2:18, 3:5[2], 4:9, 13, 5:1, 23, 27

2 THESS. 2:5[2], 3:17

1 TIM. 1:3[2], 12, 13, 15, 16, 18, 20, 2:1, 7[2], 8, 12, 3:14, 15, 4:13, 5:14, 21, 6:13

2 TIM. 1:3, 4

2 TIM. 1:5, 11, 12[5], 2:7, 9, 10, 3:11, 4::1, 6, 7[3], 12, 13, 16, 17, 20

TITUS 1:5[2], 3:8, 12[2]

PHILE. 4, 8, 9, 10[2], 12, 13, 14, 19[3], 21[2], 22[2]

HEB. 1:5[2], 13, 2:12[2], 13[2], 3:10, 11, 4:3, 5:5, 6:14[2], 7:9, 8:8, 9[3], 10[3], 12[2], 10:7[2], 9, 16[3], 17, 30, 11:32, 12:21, 26, 13:5, 6, 19[2], 22[2], 23

JAMES 1:13, 2:18[2]

1 PETER 1:16, 2:6, 11, 5:1, 12[2]

2 PETER 1:12, 13[2], 14, 15, 17, 3:1[2]

1 JOHN 2:1, 4, 7

1 JOHN 8, 12, 13[3], 14[2], 21, 26, 4:20, 5:13, 16

2 JOHN 1[2], 4[2], 5[2], 12[2]

3 JOHN 1, 2, 3, 4, 9, 10[2], 13[2], 14[2]

JUDE 3, 5

REV. 1:8, 9, 10, 11, 12[2], 17[3], 18[2], 2:2, 4, 5, 6, 7, 9[2], 10, 13, 14, 15, 16, 17, 19, 20, 21, 22, 23[3], 24[2]1, 25, 26, 27, 28, 3:1, 2, 3[2], 5[2], 8[2], 9[3], 10, 11, 12[3], 15[2], 16, 17, 18, 19[2], 20[2], 21[2], 4:1[3], 2, 4, 5:1, 2, 4

REV. 5:6, 11[2], 13, 6:1[2], 2, 3, 5[2], 6, 7, 8, 9, 12, 7:1, 2, 4, 9, 14, 8:2, 13, 9:1, 13, 16, 17, 10:1, 4[2], 5, 8, 9, 10[3], 11:3, 12:10, 13:1, 2, 3, 11, 14:1, 2[2], 6, 13, 14, 15:1, 2, 5, 16:1, 5, 7, 13, 15, 17:1, 3, 6[3], 7, 18:1, 4, 7, 19:1, 6, 10[2], 11, 17, 19, 20:1, 4, 11, 12, 21:1, 2, 3, 5, 6[2], 7, 9, 22, 22:7, 8[3], 9, 12, 13, 16[2], 18, 20

in

1722

GEN. 1:1, 6, 11, 12, 14, 15, 17, 20, 22[2], 26, 27[2], 29, 2:3, 4, 5, 8, 9, 17, 3:3, 5, 8, 10, 16, 19, 4:3, 8, 12, 14, 16, 20, 21

GEN. 5:1, 2, 3, 6:4[2], 5, 8, 9, 14, 16[2], 17, 7:1, 7, 9, 11, 12, 15, 16[2], 22[2], 23, 8:1, 4, 5, 9, 11, 13, 14, 17, 21, 9:6, 7, 13

GEN. 9:14, 16, 27, 10:5[2], 8, 10, 20, 25, 32, 11:2, 28, 31, 32, 12:3, 5, 6, 10[2], 13:2, 7, 12, 17, 18, 14:1, 3, 4, 5[3], 6, 7, 8, 12, 13

GEN. 14:14, 15:1, 3, 6, 10, 13, 15, 16, 18, 16:2, 3[2], 4, 5, 6, 7, 12, 17:7, 9, 12, 13[2], 17, 21, 23[2], 24, 25, 26, 27, 18:1[2], 3, 9, 10

GEN. 18:11, 18, 26, 19:1, 2[2], 3, 5, 8, 12[2], 14[2], 15, 17, 19, 27, 29, 30[2], 31, 33, 34, 20:1, 3, 5, 6[2], 8[2], 11, 21:2, 7, 11, 12[3], 14[2], 15

GEN 21:18, 20, 21, 22, 33, 34, 22:3, 6, 9, 13[2], 14, 17, 18, 23:2, 6, 9, 10[2], 11, 13, 16, 17, 18[2], 19[2], 24:1[2], 10, 23, 25, 27, 31, 37, 45

GEN. 24:48, 54, 62, 63, 65, 25:8, 9, 18, 23, 24, 27, 26:1, 2, 3, 4, 6, 12, 15, 17, 18, 19, 22, 29, 31[2], 27:15, 30, 41, 45, 28:11, 14, 15

GEN. 28:16, 18, 20, 21, 29:2, 3, 21, 23[2], 25, 26, 30, 30:2, 3, 4, 14[2], 16[2], 27, 33, 35, 37[2], 38, 40, 41, 42, 31:10, 11, 14, 18[2], 20, 23, 24

GEN. 31:25[2], 28, 29, 34, 40, 41, 54, 55, 32:5, 21, 32, 33:8, 10, 15, 18, 34:5, 7[2], 11, 15, 19, 21, 28[2], 29, 30, 35:3[2], 4[2], 6, 13, 14, 17, 18

GEN. 35:19, 22, 26, 36:5, 6, 8, 9, 16, 17, 21, 24, 30, 31, 32, 33, 34, 35[2], 36, 37, 38, 39, 43, 37:1[2], 7, 12, 13, 15, 17, 22, 24, 29

GEN. 37:31, 33, 38:1, 2, 7, 8, 9, 11[2], 12, 13, 14, 16[3], 18[2], 21, 22, 24, 25, 27[2], 39:2, 3, 4, 5[3], 6, 8, 9, 12, 13, 14[2], 17, 20, 21

GEN. 39:22, 40:3[2], 4, 5[2], 6[2], 7, 9, 10, 11, 16, 17, 41:2, 8, 10[2], 11, 14, 16, 17, 18, 19, 22[2], 30, 31, 34, 35, 36, 37[2], 38, 40, 42, 43

GEN. 41:44, 47, 48[3], 52, 53, 54[2], 56, 57, 42:1, 2, 3, 5, 13, 16[2], 19, 21, 27[2], 28, 32, 34, 35, 38, 43:1, 11[2], 12[3], 15, 18[2], 21[3], 22[2], 23, 26

GEN. 43:28, 44:1, 2, 5[2], 8, 12, 17[2], 18, 28, 30, 45:6[2], 7, 10, 13, 16, 46:2, 5, 6, 12, 15, 20, 27, 31, 34, 47:1, 4[3], 6[2], 7, 9, 11[3], 13

GEN. 47:14[2], 15[3], 17, 18, 24, 25, 27[2], 28, 29[2], 30, 48:3, 5, 6, 7[3], 9, 13[2], 16, 20, 49:1, 5, 6[2], 7[2], 8, 11[2], 17, 24, 27, 29[2], 30[3], 50:4[2], 5[2]

GEN. 50:8, 11, 13, 19, 22, 26[2]

EXOD. 1:5, 14[4], 19, 2:3, 11, 12, 15, 22, 23, 3:1, 2, 7, 16, 20, 21, 22, 4:2, 4, 14, 15, 17, 18[3], 19

EXOD. 4:20, 21, 24, 27, 30, 5:1[2], 14, 16, 19, 20, 21[3], 23, 6:5, 8, 11, 28, 7:3, 10, 11, 15[2], 16, 17[3], 18, 19[2], 20[4], 21, 8:9, 11, 17[2], 20, 22[3]

EXOD. 8:25, 28, 29, 9:1, 3, 5, 8, 9, 13, 14, 16[2], 18, 19[2], 21, 22, 24, 25, 26, 31, 10:1, 2[2], 3, 14, 15, 16, 19, 22, 23, 28, 11:2, 3[4]

EXOD. 11:5, 8, 9, 12:1, 3, 6, 8, 11[2], 12, 16[2], 17[2], 18, 19[2], 20, 22[3], 23, 27, 29[2], 30[2], 33, 34, 36, 40, 42, 46, 48, 13:3, 4, 5, 6, 7, 8, 9, 10, 14, 15, 20[2], 21[2], 14:3[2], 11[2], 12[2], 23, 24, 27, 29, 15:4, 6[2], 7, 8, 10, 11[2], 13[2], 17[5], 19[2], 20, 22, 26, 16:2, 3, 4, 5, 7, 8[2], 10, 12, 13, 16, 25, 26, 29, 32, 17:1, 5, 6[2], 8, 9, 14[2], 18:1, 2, 3, 5, 6, 7, 8, 11, 12[2], 14, 15, 17, 23, 24, 27, 19:1, 2, 9, 11, 16[2], 18, 20:4[2], 7[2], 10, 11, 24, 21:2, 3, 13, 16, 29[2], 36[2], 22:4, 5[2], 6, 13, 21, 23, 31, 23:2

EXOD. 23:3, 6, 9, 10, 11, 13, 14, 15[2], 16[3], 17, 19, 20, 21, 23, 26, 29, 33, 24:4, 6, 7, 10, 17, 18, 25:7[2], 12[3], 15, 18, 21, 22, 26, 33[3], 34, 40, 26:4[3], 5[3], 10[2], 13, 17[2], 23, 28, 30, 33, 34, 27:4, 8, 11, 19, 21, 28:1, 3, 4, 11[2], 17, 20[2], 24, 25, 26[2], 29[2], 30[2], 32[2], 35, 38, 41, 43[2], 29:1, 3, 17, 24[2], 29, 30[2], 31, 32, 39, 44, 30:10[2], 30, 36, 31:3[4], 4[3], 5[3], 6, 10, 15[2], 17, 32:2, 3, 12, 15, 17, 20, 26, 27, 34, 33:3[2], 5, 10, 12, 13[2], 16, 17, 22, 34:1, 2[3], 4[2], 5, 6, 9, 10[2], 12, 18[2], 21[2], 23, 24, 26, 29, 32[2], 34

EXOD. 34:35, 35:15, 19[2], 26, 31[4], 32[3], 34, 35[4], 36:1, 2, 11[3], 12[3], 17, 28, 29, 37:13, 19[2], 20, 38:18, 23[3], 24, 39:1, 3[4], 6, 10, 13[2], 16, 17, 18, 23, 26, 37, 41[2], 40:4[4], 13, 15, 17[2], 18, 22, 23, 24, 26, 36, 38

LEVIT. 1:7, 8, 9, 12, 2:4, 5, 6, 7, 11, 4:6, 7, 17, 18, 29, 33, 5:4, 5[2], 13, 15, 16, 24, 6:2[3], 3, 5[2], 7, 9, 12[2], 16[2], 18, 20[2], 21[2], 22, 25, 26[2], 27, 28[2], 30[2], 7:2, 6, 9[3], 24[2], 26, 35[2], 36, 38[3], 8:8, 21, 31, 33, 9:9, 10:3, 5, 13, 14, 17, 18[2], 19, 11:9[4], 10[4], 11, 12, 13, 33, 34, 46, 12:8, 4, 5[2], 13:2[2], 3[3], 4[2]

LEVIT. 13:5[2], 6, 7, 8, 9, 10[2], 11, 12, 14, 18[2], 19, 20, 22, 23, 24, 25[2], 26, 27, 28[2], 30[2], 31[2], 32[3], 34[3], 35, 36, 37, 38, 39[2], 42[2], 43[3], 44, 45, 46, 47, 48[3], 49[5], 51[5], 52[3], 53[4], 55, 57[4], 59[2], 14:2, 3, 5, 6, 8, 9, 13[2], 16[2], 17, 18, 27, 28, 29, 32, 34, 35, 36[2], 37[2], 39, 40, 42, 43, 44[2], 47[2], 48[2], 50, 51[2], 15:3, 5, 6, 7, 8, 10, 11[2], 12, 13, 16, 18, 19, 20, 21, 22, 27, 31, 16:2, 4, 16[2], 17[3], 21, 22, 24, 26, 27[3], 28, 29, 32, 17:3, 5, 11, 15, 18:3, 5, 15, 18, 24[2], 19:6, 15[2], 17[2], 24, 25, 28, 33, 34, 35[4], 20:2

LEVIT. 20:12, 17, 23, 21:5, 11, 13, 17, 20, 23, 22:2, 11, 13, 18, 21, 23, 24, 25[2], 28, 23:3, 4, 5, 7, 8, 14, 21, 24[2], 28, 29, 30, 31, 32, 39[2], 41[3], 42[2], 43, 24:3[2], 5, 6, 8, 9, 10, 12, 16, 19, 20, 25:1, 3, 4, 7, 9, 11[2], 13, 18[2], 19, 20, 21, 22, 24, 28[2], 29, 30[2], 31, 33, 35, 45, 53, 54[2], 26:1, 3, 4, 5, 6, 16, 20, 22, 26, 28, 34, 35, 36, 39[3], 44, 45, 46, 27:21, 23, 24, 34

NUM. 1:1[3], 3, 16, 19, 45, 2:9, 16[2], 17[2], 24, 31, 3:1[2], 3, 4[3], 13[2], 14, 25, 28, 4:3, 4, 6, 8, 12[2], 15, 16[2], 19, 20, 23[2]

NUM. 4:27[3], 28, 31, 33, 35, 37, 39, 41, 43, 47, 5:3, 17[2], 18[2], 23, 6:5, 9, 18, 7:10, 84, 8:15, 17, 19, 22[2], 24, 26, 9:1[2], 3[2], 5, 7, 10, 13[2], 14, 17, 18, 20, 21, 22, 23, 10:9, 10[3], 11, 12, 14, 29, 33, 11:1, 5, 8[3], 9, 10, 11, 12, 15, 18[2], 25, 26[2], 27, 31, 12:5[2], 6[2], 7, 8, 14[2], 15, 16, 19[4], 22, 28, 29[2], 32, 33[2], 14:2[2], 8, 10, 13, 14[2], 16, 22[2], 25, 28, 29, 31, 32, 33[2], 34, 35, 40, 45, 15:3[3], 8, 13, 14, 15, 21, 26, 30, 32, 34, 38, 16:2, 7, 13, 17, 18[2], 21, 26, 27, 45, 49, 17:4, 7, 18:10, 11, 13[2], 14, 15, 20

NUM. 18:21, 31[2], 19:5, 7, 8[2], 9, 14[2], 16[2], 17, 18, 19, 20:1[2], 5, 12, 13, 15, 16[2], 23, 27, 28, 21:1, 5, 10, 11, 12, 13, 14[2], 20[2], 25[3], 27, 31, 22:1, 7, 13, 21, 22, 23[2], 24, 26, 29, 31[2], 34, 36[2], 38, 23:5, 12, 16, 21[2], 24:2, 7, 14, 21, 25:1, 6[2], 7, 9, 11, 15, 18[3], 26:2, 3, 9, 19, 59, 63, 64, 65, 27:3[4], 14[4], 17[2], 18, 19, 21, 28:2, 4, 6, 7, 11, 16, 17, 18, 23, 26, 29:1, 39, 30:3[2], 5, 7, 10, 14, 16[2], 31:6, 10, 16, 35, 36, 32:5, 13[2], 14, 15, 17, 26, 30, 33, 39, 33:3[2], 5, 6[2], 8[2], 9, 11, 12, 13, 15, 18, 20, 22

NUM. 33:23, 24, 25, 28, 29, 31, 33, 36, 37, 38[2], 39, 40[2], 41, 42, 43, 44[2], 45, 46, 47, 48, 49, 50, 54, 55[3], 34:29, 35:1, 2, 3, 5, 12, 14, 21, 25, 28, 29, 32, 36:8, 12, 13

DEU. 1:1[2], 3[3], 4[2], 5, 6[2], 7[4], 8, 17, 25, 27, 30, 31[2], 32, 33[4], 37, 38, 39[2], 44[2], 46, 2:4, 7, 8, 9, 10, 12[2], 14, 20, 21, 22[2], 23[2], 24, 25, 29[2], 37, 3:4, 10, 11, 19, 24[2], 29, 4:1, 5, 6, 7, 10, 14, 15, 17, 18, 19, 21, 22, 25[2], 27, 30[2], 34, 37, 38, 39[2], 42, 43[4], 46[2], 5:1, 2, 4, 8[3], 11[2], 14, 15, 16, 22[2], 29, 31, 33[2], 6:1

DEU. 6:3, 6, 7, 16, 18[2], 20, 21, 23, 7:7, 13, 17, 8:1, 2[2], 5, 6, 9, 11, 16, 17, 9:1, 4[2], 7, 8, 9, 10[2], 15, 18[2], 28, 10:2[2], 3, 4[2], 5, 6[2], 8, 10, 11, 12, 15, 18, 19, 11:3, 5, 6[2], 8, 9, 10, 14[2], 15, 18[2], 19, 21, 22, 29, 30[2], 31, 12:1, 7, 8, 10[2], 13, 14[2], 15, 18[2], 21, 25, 28, 29, 31, 13:5, 12, 18, 14:9, 21[2], 23, 25, 29, 15:4, 7, 8, 9, 10[2], 11, 12, 15, 18[2], 20, 16:1, 2, 3, 4, 6, 7[2], 11, 12, 13, 14, 15[3], 16[5], 18, 17:2, 4, 8, 9, 15, 18, 20[2], 18:5, 7, 16[2], 18, 19, 20[2], 21, 22, 19:1[2], 2, 4

DEU. 19:6, 9, 10, 11, 14[2], 15, 17, 20:5, 6, 7, 14, 19[2], 21:1[2], 3, 4, 5, 6, 9, 13[2], 14, 23, 22:1, 3, 6[2], 7, 13, 15, 19, 21[2], 23, 24, 25, 26, 27, 23:1, 4, 7, 8, 14[2], 16[2], 20[2], 21, 22, 24, 24:1[3], 3, 8, 13[2], 14, 18, 19[3], 22, 25:5, 6, 7, 9[2], 10, 13, 14, 15, 19, 26:1, 2, 3, 11, 14, 17, 19[3], 27:3, 4, 15, 23, 28:3, 6, 8[3], 9, 11[5], 12, 16[2], 19, 20, 29[2], 32, 35[2], 38, 48[4], 52[2], 53[2], 55[3], 57[2], 58, 61, 62, 66, 67, 29:1[2], 2, 5, 9, 11, 16, 19, 20, 21, 23[2], 27, 28[3], 30:9[4], 10, 12, 14[2], 16[3], 19, 20, 31:2, 7, 10[2]

DEU. 31:11[2], 13, 14[2], 15[2], 17[2], 18[2], 19, 24, 26, 28, 29[2], 30, 32:10[2], 20, 22, 28, 34, 35, 37, 44, 47, 49, 50[2], 51[2], 33:3, 5, 12, 16, 18[2], 19, 21, 24, 26[2], 28, 34:5, 6[2], 8, 10, 11[2], 12[3]

JOSH. 1:11, 14, 17, 18, 2:2, 6, 11[3], 18, 19, 21, 3:1, 7, 8, 13, 15, 17, 4:3, 6, 9[2], 10, 11, 14, 19[2], 20, 21, 5:1, 4, 5, 6, 7, 8[2], 10[2], 11, 13, 6:1, 11, 12, 17, 18, 21, 23, 25, 26[2], 7:1, 5, 13, 14, 15, 16, 21[2], 22, 8:4, 9, 10, 12, 13, 14, 16, 17, 18[2], 22, 24[2], 30, 31, 32, 34, 9:1[3], 9, 25, 27, 10:6, 11, 12[3], 13[2], 16

JOSH. 10:17, 21, 27, 30, 11:2[2], 3[2], 4, 13, 17, 19, 20, 22[4], 12:2, 5[3], 7, 8[6], 23, 13:1[2], 9, 10, 12[3], 16, 17, 19, 21[2], 27, 30, 31, 32, 14:1, 4[2], 6[2], 7, 10, 11[2], 12[2], 15:5, 33, 48, 61, 16:10, 17:10[2], 11[2], 12, 15, 16, 18:5[2], 8, 9, 10, 16, 19:2, 14, 50, 51, 20:4, 6[2], 7[4], 8[3], 21:2[2], 6, 11, 21, 27, 32, 38, 39, 22:2, 5, 7, 9, 10, 11, 16, 17, 19, 20[2], 22[2], 24, 25, 27, 28, 33, 23:1, 2, 6, 12[2], 13[2], 14[2], 24:2, 7[2], 13, 14[3], 15, 17[2], 18, 25, 26, 30[3], 32[2], 33[2]

JUD. 1:4, 5, 9[3], 10, 16[2], 21, 27, 29[2], 35[3], 2:8[2], 9[3], 11, 17, 19

JUD. 3:3[2], 7, 12[2], 20, 22, 24, 27, 4:1, 2[3], 5, 11, 14, 18[3], 20, 21, 22, 5:6[2], 7[2], 8[2], 10, 11[2], 17[2], 18, 19, 20, 24, 25, 28, 31, 6:1, 2, 10, 11, 14, 15[2], 17, 19[3], 21, 24, 26, 28, 33, 37, 7:1, 3, 8[2], 12, 16, 19[2], 20[2], 21, 22, 8:2, 3, 6, 9, 10, 11, 15, 27[2], 28[2], 29, 31, 32[3], 9:2, 3, 6, 7, 15[2], 16, 19[2], 24, 25[2], 26, 32[2], 33, 34, 35[2], 41, 43, 44[2], 48, 56, 10:1[2], 2, 4, 5, 6, 8[3], 14, 17[2], 11:2, 3, 4, 7, 11, 12, 17[2], 20, 26[3], 31, 39, 40, 12:3, 7, 9, 12[3], 15[3], 13:1, 9, 20, 25, 14:1, 2, 6, 8, 9

JUD. 14:14, 15:1[3], 4, 6, 8, 9[2], 19[2], 20, 16:1, 2[3], 4, 9[2], 12[2], 18, 21, 30, 31, 17:2, 4, 6[3], 10, 12, 18:1[4], 3[2], 6, 7[2], 10, 12[2], 14, 17[2], 19, 20, 22, 28, 31, 19:1[2], 4, 5[2], 7, 8, 9, 11[2], 13[2], 15[4], 16, 17, 20, 26, 27, 20:1, 2, 6[2], 10, 13, 19, 20, 22[3], 27, 28, 29, 30, 31[2], 33[2], 36, 37[2], 38, 39[2], 42, 45, 47, 21:1, 3[2], 12, 13, 15, 19[2], 20[2], 21, 22, 23, 25[3]

RUTH 1:1[3], 6[3], 7, 8, 9, 11, 14, 15[2], 22[2], 2:2, 3, 7, 8, 10, 11, 13, 14, 17, 18, 19[2], 20, 22[2], 23, 3:1, 2, 4, 6, 10, 13, 16, 17, 18, 4:7[3], 11[3]

RUTH 4:13, 14, 15, 16

1 SAM. 1:3, 9, 10, 13, 17, 18, 19, 24, 2:1[3], 9, 13, 14, 26, 27[2], 29, 31, 32[3], 33, 34, 35[2], 36, 3:2, 3, 9, 11, 12, 21[2], 4:1, 2[2], 6, 8, 14, 19[2], 21, 5:3, 5, 9, 6:1, 3, 8, 13, 18, 7:1, 2, 6, 16[2], 8:2, 3, 5, 7, 18[2], 21, 9:6, 7, 9, 11, 12, 15, 18, 19, 22, 10:2, 25, 11:4, 7, 8, 11[2], 13, 15, 12:1, 5, 8, 17[2], 23, 24, 13:2[3], 3, 4, 5[2], 6[6], 7, 16[2], 17, 22[2], 14:2[3], 3, 7, 9, 15[2], 16, 19, 22, 27[2], 33, 34, 39, 43, 45, 15:2, 4, 5, 12[2], 14, 17, 19, 21, 22[2], 33[2], 16:12, 13, 22

1 SAM. 17:1, 2, 8, 12, 19, 20, 21, 22, 25, 28, 40[4], 45, 46, 49[2], 50, 54, 55, 56, 57, 18:5[2], 10[2], 13, 14, 16, 18[2], 21[2], 22[2], 23[2], 26, 27[2], 19:2[2], 3, 5, 7[2], 9[2], 11, 13, 15, 16[2], 18, 19, 22[2], 23[2], 24, 20:1, 3, 5, 8, 13, 19, 24, 29[2], 34, 35, 42[2], 21:3, 5[2], 6, 9[2], 11, 12, 13, 15, 22:2[2], 4, 5, 6[3], 8, 11, 13[2], 14[2], 23, 23:3, 6, 7, 14[4], 15[2], 16, 18, 19[3], 23, 24[2], 25[2], 29, 24:1, 3[2], 10, 11[3], 20, 25:1, 2[3], 3, 4, 5, 6, 7, 8[2], 9, 15, 21[2], 24, 28, 29, 34, 35, 36, 37, 26:1, 2, 3[2], 7, 15[2], 18, 19, 20, 21, 24[2]

1 SAM. 27:1[2], 5[4], 7, 11, 28:1, 3[2], 4[2], 20, 21, 24, 29:1, 2, 3, 4, 5, 6[4], 7, 8, 9, 10[2], 11, 30:6, 11, 24, 27[3], 28[3], 29[3], 30[3], 31, 31:1, 7, 8, 9

2 SAM. 1:9, 10, 18, 20[2], 23[2], 24, 25[2], 2:3, 11, 16[2], 19, 23, 26, 27, 32[2], 3:2, 5, 6, 7, 17, 19[3], 21, 22[2], 23, 25, 27, 30, 32, 38, 4:1, 7, 10, 11, 12[3], 5:2[2], 3, 5[2], 6[2], 9, 14, 18, 22, 24, 6:3, 11, 16, 17[3], 18, 20, 22[2], 7:1, 2, 3, 5, 6[3], 7, 9, 10, 18, 19, 23, 27, 8:6, 13, 14, 9:4[2], 10, 12, 13, 10:1, 4, 8[3], 9, 10, 17, 11:2, 4, 11[2], 12, 14, 15[2], 21

2 SAM. 12:1, 9, 11, 16, 24, 30, 13:5, 6, 8, 12, 13, 16, 20, 23, 30, 14:3, 6, 13, 19[2], 20, 22[2], 25[2], 28, 32, 15:4, 7, 8, 9, 10, 11, 17, 21[2], 25, 26, 27, 28, 16:2, 4, 8[2], 19[3], 22, 23, 17:3, 8[2], 9[2], 11, 12, 16, 18[2], 23[2], 25, 26, 29, 18:6, 10, 12[2], 14[2], 17, 18[3], 25, 19:3, 6, 8[2], 10, 13, 22, 24, 27, 30, 33, 37, 43[3], 20:1[2], 3[2], 8[2], 9, 10[2], 12[2], 15[2], 18, 19[3], 22, 21:1, 2, 4, 5, 6, 9[4], 12, 14[3], 16, 19, 20[2], 22:1, 3, 7, 19, 20, 25, 31, 23:2, 3, 5, 7, 8, 12, 13[2], 14[2], 17, 20[2], 21, 39, 24:3, 5[2], 10, 11

2 SAM. 24:13^2 14 18

1 KINGS 1:1 2 6 13 14 15 22 25 30 35 41 42 45 52 2:3^3 4 5^2 6 8 10 11^2 26 27 34 35^2 36 38 39 3:2 3^2 5^2 6^3 7 8 14 17^2 18^2 19 20^2 21^2 25 26 27 28 4:7 8 9^2 10 11 13^3 15 16^2 17 18 19^3 20 27 31 33 5:1 5 9^2 14 15 16 6:1^3 6 7^3 12 19 20^4 27 37^2 38^3 7:3 4^2 5 14^2 19 20 24^2 35 46^2 51 8:1 2 4 6 9 12 13 17 18 20 22 23 25 30 31 32 33 34 36 37^2 39 40 43 45 47^2 48 52 58

1 KINGS 8:61 65 9:4^2 11 16 18^2 19^3 21 23 25 26^2 27 10:2 5 6 9 11 14 17 20 21 22 24 26 27^2 11:2^3 6 7 12 14 15^2 16 19 20^2 21 22 24 29^2 30 33^2 36 38^2 40 41 42 43^2 12:2^2 16^2 17 25 26 27 29^2 32^4 33^2 13:2 4^2 8^2 11^2 16^2 19 22 24 25^2 28 30 31 32^2 14:5 6^2 8 10 11^2 13^2 15 19 20 21^2 22 24 25 27 29 31^2 15:1 2 3 4 5^2 7 8^2 9 10 11 13 15 17 18 21 23^3 24^2 25 26^3 28^2 31 33^2 34^3 16:2 4^2 5 6^2 7^3 8^2 9^3 10^3 13 14

1 KINGS 16:15^2 16 19^5 20 23^2 25 26^2 27 28^2 29^2 30 31 32^2 34^3 17:6^2 7 10 11 12^3 17 24 18:1 2 4 7 13 18 23 27 32 33^2 36 38 45 19:8 11^3 12 13^3 16 18 20:6^2 12^3 16 23 24 25 29^2 34^2 35 37 21:1 2 8^2 9 11^2 13^2 18^2 19 20 21 24^2 25 26 27 29^2 22:2 3 10^2 16 17 22 23 25 27^2 28 35 37 38 39 40 41 42 43^3 45 46 47 49 50^2 51 52^4

2 KINGS 1:2^2 3 6 13 14 16 17^2 18 2:12 21 24 3:1^2 2 18 20 21 22 23 24 25 27 4:2^2 4 8 10

2 KINGS 4:15 29 33 35 36 37 38 40 41 42 5:1 3 4 8 10 12^2 14 15^2 18^4 19 20 23 24 25 6:6 8 12^2 13 20 25 32 7:1 2 3 4 5 7 12^2 13^2 15 17 18 19 20 8:2 8 15^2 16 17 18^2 20 23 24^2 25 26 27^3 28 29^2 9:1 2 8 10 15^2 16 17 21^2 24 25 26 27 28^3 29 31 34 36 37 10:1 5 7 8^2 9 11 12 16 17 19 24 25 29^2 30^3 31 32^2 34 35^2 36 11:2 3 4 5 8^2 9 10 11 15 18 20 12:1^2 2^2 8 6 9 10^3 18^2 19 20 21^2 13:1^2

2 KINGS 13:2 5 6 8 9^2 10^2 11 12 13 17 20 24 14:1 2 3 5 6 7 8 9^3 11 14^2 15 16^2 18 19 20 23^2 24 28 29 15:1 2 3 5 6 7^2 8^2 9 10 11 13^2 14^2 15 17^2 18 19 20 21 22 23^2 24 25^3 26 27^2 28 29 30^2 31 32 33 34 35 36 37 38^2 16:1 2^2 3 4 8^2 18 19 20^2 17:1^2 2 4^2 6^4 8 9 10 11 14 17 19 22 24^2 26 28 29^2 31 32 18:1 2 3 4 5 9 10 11^3 13 15 17 22^2 26^3 28 30 19:7 10 12 27 28^2 29^2 35^2 37^2 20:1^2 3^2

2 KINGS 20:11 13^3 15^2 17^2 18 19 20 21 21:1 2 4^2 5 6 7^3 12 15 16^2 17 18^3 19 20 21^2 22 23 24 25 26^3 22:1 2^2 3 5 8 9 14^2 20 23:2^2 3 4 5^3 8^2 9 10 11^2 12 14 16 19^2 21 22 23^2 24^4 28 29 30^3 31 32 33^3 34 36 37 24:1 5 6 8 9 12 13^2 17 18 19 20 25:1^3 3 5 8 11 13^3 15^2 19^3 21 22 24 27^3 28

1 CHRON. 1:19 43 44 45 46^2 47 48 49 50 2:3 4 6 7 21 22 24 3:1 4^2 5 4:22 38 41^2 5:8 9^2 10^2 11 12 16^4 17^2 18 20^2

1 CHRON. 5:22 23 6:10^2 31 32 54 55 62 67 71 76 78 80 7:2^2 5 21 23 29 8:8 28 32 9:1 2^2 3 9 16 18^2 20 22^3 24 25 26 28 31 33^2 35 10:1 7^2 8 10^2 12 11:2^2 3 7 10 14 15 16 19 22^2 23 12:2 15 17 21 33 35 36 40 13:2^2 3 4 7 14 14:4 9 11 13 15 15:1 29 16:1 2 10 14 19 27^2 29 35 39 40 17:1^2 2 4 5 8 9 14^2 17 19 21 25 18:6 12 13 19:1 4 9^2 10 11 13 17^2 18 20:2 3 21:12 13 16^2 18 19 23 28 29^2 22:2 3^2 4 7

1 CHRON. 22:8 9 14^2 15 23:11 13 25 28^3 29 31^2 32 24:3 19 31 25:5 6 7 26:12 27 30^2 31 27:1^2 2 4 5 6 7 8 9 10 11 12 13 14 15 21 24 25^4 28 29^2 28:2 8^2 13 19 29:2 11^2 12^2 17^2 18 21 25^2 27^2 28^2 29^3

2 CHRON. 1:1 2 3 7 8 9 10 11 14 15 2:2 7^7 8 9 11 14^{10} 16 17 18 3:1^3 2^2 4 10 16 4:2 3 6^3 7 8 17^2 18 5:1 3^2 5 7 10 12 13 6:1 5 7 8^3 10 11 12 13 14^2 16^2 18 22 24 28^2 29 31^2 32 37^2 38 40 41 7:8 9

2 CHRON. 7:10 11^2 15 18 8:4^2 6^2 8 11 13^4 17 9:1^2 4 5 8 11 13 16 19 20 22 23 25 27^3 29^3 30 31^2 10:2 16^2 17 11:3 5^2 10^2 11 12 13 17 23 12:2 5 12 13^2 15 16^2 13:1 2 3^2 4 8 11 20 22 14:1^3 2 6^2 10^2 11 14 15 15:3 5^2 9 10^2 16 16:1^2 9 10^2 11 12^3 13 14^3 17:1 2^3 3 4 5^2 6 7^2 9 12 13^3 19 18:1 2 3 9^3 15 16 21 22 26^2 27 34 19:1 3^2 5 6 8 9 10 11 20:2 5^2 6^3 9^3 14 17 20^2 24 25^2 26 27 31 32^2 34^2 36 21:1^2 3

2 CHRON. 21:5 6^2 8 9 11 12^2 13 17 18 19 20^3 22:1 2 3 4 6 9 11 12 23:1 2 3 5 6 7^2 8 9 10 13 14 17 18^2 19^2 24:1 2 6 9^2 10 11 13 14 16^2 21 25^3 27^2 25:1 2 4^2 10 12 17 18^3 21 24 26 27 28 26:1 3 4 5^2 7 8 9 10^5 15 17 19^3 20 21 23^2 27:1 2 4^2 7 8 9^2 28:1^2 2 3^2 4 6^2 9 13 22 24^2 25 26 27^3 29:1 2 3^2 4 6 7 9 10 17^2 18 19^2 25 31 34 35^2 30:2^2 5 12 13 14 15 16 17 25 26^2 31:1^2 2 3

2 CHRON. 31:4^2 5^2 6^2 7^2 11 12 15^2 16 17 18^2 19^2 21^4 32:5^2 6 10^2 18 21 23 24 26 29 30 31^3 32^2 33^2 33:1 2 4^2 5 6^2 7^3 12 14^3 15 17 18^2 20^2 21 22 24 25 34:1 2^2 3^2 4^2 6 8 10^2 13 15 17 21^3 22^2 24 28 30^2 31^2 32 33 35:1 2 3 5 10^2 12 13^3 14 15 18 19 22 24^2 25^3 26 27 36:1^2 2 3 5^2 6 7 8^3 9^2 11 12 14 17 22^2 23^2

EZRA 1:1^2 2 3^2 4^2 5 7 2:42 68 70^2 3:1 2 8^2 6 10 11 4:4 6^2 7^3 8 10 15^2 17 23 5:1^2 8^2 13

EZRA 5:14 15^2 16^2 17 6:1^2 2^2 3 5 7 15 18^3 22 7:1 6 7 8^2 10 13 14 15 16^2 17 25 27^2 8:1 15 22 29 31 33 9:2 7 8^2 9^4 14 15 10:2 9 13 14 16

NEH. 1:1^3 3^2 11 2:1^3 5 12^2 15 17 20 3:17 26 4:2 4 11 13 16 17 20 21 22 5:5 9 14 16 18 6:2^2 5^2 7 10^2 11 14 15^2 16 17 18^2 19 7:3 73^2 8:5 7 8^2 14^3 15^2 16^4 18 9:1 3^2 9 12^3 15 17 19^3 21 23 24 25^2 27 28 29 30 33 35^3 36 37 10:29 34 36^2 37 11:1^2 3^4 17 18 20^2 21

NEH. 11:24 25^3 27 28 30^2 31 36^2 12:7 9 12 22 23 26^2 39 40 46 47^2 13:1^2 6^2 7^2 11 15^5 16 19 23 24^2 27 28 30

ESTHER 1:1 2^2 3 5^2 7^2 9 10 12 14 16 17^2 22 2:3 5 12 14^3 15^2 16^2 17 19 21^2 22 23 3:2 3 7^2 8 12 13 14 15 4:3^2 8 11 13 16^2 5:1^2 2^3 8 9 12 14 6:4 5^2 6^2 7:3 5 7 8 9 8:5^3 8^2 9 10 11 12 13 15 17^2 9:1^3 2 4 6 11 12^2 13 15 16 19 20 31 32 10:2

JOB 1:1 4 5^2 7^2 8 10 12 13 18 22 2:2^2

JOB 2:3 6 10 3:3 20^2 23 26 4:13 18 19^3 21 5:4 13 14^3 19^2 20^2 23 24 26^3 6:2 4 6 10 13 29 30 7:11^2 21^2 8:12 16 9:4^2 5 29 31 32 10:1 3 13 11:4 14^2 18 12:5 9 10 12 24 25 13:14^2 15 27 14:8^2 13 17 15:9 15^2 21^2 28^2 31 16:4 8 9 15 17 19 17:2 3 13 16 18:3 4 6 10^2 15 17 19 19:2 8 15^2 23 24 26 28 20:11 12 14 20 22^2 26^2 28 21:7 8 13^2 16 17 21^2 23 25 26 32 34^2 22:8 12 14 22 26 23:6 13 24:5 6 7 13 14 16^2 17 18 23 25:2

JOB 25:5 26:8 27:3^2 10 15 20 28:13 14 29:2^2 4 7 18 20^2 25 30:1 2 3 6^3 10 14^2 17^2 24 25 28 31:6 15^2 21 26 32 33 32:1 5 8 22 33:2 5 6 8 9 11 12 15^3 34:8 20 24^2 25 26 35:10 14 15^2 16 36:4 5 8^2 11^2 13 14 15^2 20 31 37:8 12 16 20 23^3 38:16 32 33 36 37 40^3 39:4 10 14^2 16 21^2 40:12 13^2 16^2 21 41:9 22 23 42:6 11 15

PSALMS 1:1^3 2^2 3 5^2 2:4^2 5^2 9 12 3:2 4:1 4 5 7^2 8^2 5:3^2 4 5 7^2 8 9 10 11^2 6:1^2 5^2 7:1 2 3 5 6

PSALMS 7:8 10 8:1 9 9:2 4 8^2 9 10 11 14^2 15^2 16 19 20 10:1 2^2 4 6^2 8^2 9^3 13 11:1 2 4^2 12:5 6 13:2^2 5^2 14:1 5^2 15:1^2 2 4 16:1 3^2 6 7 9 10 11 17:3 5 7 10 11 12 14 15 18 *title* 2 6 13 18 19 24 30 42 19:4 11 14 20:1 5^2 7^2 21:1^2 5 7 9^2 13 22:2^2 4 5 8 14 22 25 23:2 3 5 6 24:3 7 8 9 25:2 5 8 9 12 20 26:1^2 3 4 6 10 11 12^2 27:3 4^2 5^3 6 9 11 13 28:3 7 29:2 9 30:5^2 6 9 31:1^2 6 7^2 8 9 14

PSALMS 31:15 17 19 20^2 21 22 24 32:2 6^2 8 9 10 11^2 33:1 4 7 8 18 19 21^2 22 34:1 2 8 22 35:7 9^2 15 16 18 20 25 27 36:2 4 5 9 10 37:3^2 4 5 7^2 8 11 19^2 23 31 33 35 39 40 38:1^2 2 3^2 7 14 15 39:6^2 7 40:3^2 5 7 9 16 41:1 3 9 12 42:4 5^2 8^2 10 11 43:5 44:1^2 3 6 8 17 19 45:4 5 9 14 16 17 46:1 5 8 9^2 10 48:1^2 3 6 8^2 9 49:5 6^2 12 14^3 20 50:15 16 21 22 51 *title* 4 5^2 6^2 10 16 18 52:1 7^2 8^2 53:1 5

PSALMS 54:5 55:2 3 7 9 10 11 14 15 18 21 23 56 *title* 3 4^2 7 8 10^2 11 13 57 *title* 1^2 58:2^2 6 7 9 10 11 59:3 7 8 12 13^2 16^2 60 *title* 6 61:4^2 62:4 7^2 8 9 10^2 63 *title* 1 2 4 6 7 11 64:1 4 5 10^3 65:1 4 5 8 66:3 5 6 9 14 18 68:5 6^2 14^2 16^2 17^2 21 23^2 24 26 30 34 69:1 2 12 13^3 17 21 25 35 70:4 71:1 2 9 16 72:4 7 9 14 16 17 73:4 5 11 12^2 13^2 19 21 25 28 74:3 4 8^2 12 13 14 75:8 76:1^2 2^2 7 77:2^2 6 9 13 18

PSALMS
77:19^{2}
78:2
5^{2}
7
9
10
12^{3}
14
15
17
18
19
22^{2}
26^{2}
28
30
33^{2}
37
40^{2}
43^{2}
51^{2}
52
55
66
79:10
80:5
81:3^{2}
5
7^{2}
9
12
13
82:1
5
83:4
12
84:4
5^{2}
7
10^{3}
12
85:6
9
13
86:2
5
7
11
15
87:1
5
7
88:5
6^{3}
11^{2}
12^{2}
13
89:2
5
6
7^{2}
10
12
15
16^{2}
17
19
24
25^{2}
30
37
43
47
49
50
90:1
4^{2}
5
6^{2}
8
9
91:1
2
6
11
12
15
92:2
4
12
13^{2}
14
15
94:5
15
17
19
23
95:4
8^{3}
10
11
96:6
9
97:11
12
98:2
99:2
4
7
101:2
6
7
102:2^{3}
14
16
21^{3}

PSALMS
102:23
24
103:8
19
22
104:3
22
24
27
31
34
105:7
12^{2}
18
23
27
30^{2}
31
32
35
36
39
41
106:5
7
14^{2}
16
18
19
21
22
23
25
26
27
29
47
107:4^{2}
5
6
10^{3}
13
14
16
19
23^{2}
24
26
28
32^{2}
40
108:7
109:13
17
111:1^{2}
8
112:1
3
4
6
7
113:6^{2}
115:3
8
9
10
11
116:9
11
14
15
18
19^{2}
118:5^{2}
8^{2}
9^{2}
10
11
12
15
23
24
26
119:1^{2}
3
11
14^{2}
15
16
19
23
35
37
40
42
43
47
48
50
51
54
55
70
74
75
78
80
81
83
89
92
109
114
133
147
148
161

PSALMS
120:1
5^{2}
121:8
123:1
124:8
125:1
4
126:4
5^{2}
127:1^{2}
4
5
128:1
129:8
130:5
7
131:1^{2}
3
132:6
11
133:1
134:1
2
135:2^{2}
6^{3}
17
18
136:10
15
23
137:2
4
7
138:3^{2}
5
7
139:4
8
9
15^{2}
16^{2}
18
20
24^{2}
140:2
7
11
13
141:5
6
8
142 *title*
3
5
143:1^{2}
2
3
8^{2}
144:2
12
13
14^{2}
15
145:15
17^{2}
18
146:3^{3}
4
5
147:3
10^{2}
11^{3}
14
148:1
149:1
2^{2}
3
4
5
6^{2}
150:1^{2}

PROV.
1:14
15
17^{2}
20
21^{3}
22
2:13
14
15
20
21^{2}
3:4
5
6
7
12
16^{2}
23
27
33
4:3
11^{2}
14
21
5:10
14^{2}
16
23
6:8^{2}
14
18
25
27
29

PROV.
6:34
7:9^{3}
11
12^{2}
25
8:2^{2}
3
8^{2}
20^{2}
22
31
9:4
6
9
14
16
17
18
10:5^{2}
8
13
17
19
11:4
6
8
14
20
21
22
28
31
12:4
6
15
20
25
27
28^{2}
13:6
23
14:2^{2}
3
7
13
14
23
26
28^{2}
32^{2}
33^{2}
15:3
4
6^{2}
22
23
16:1
2
5^{2}
10^{2}
15
20
21
27
31
17:8
12
16
18
24
18:2
5
9
11
17
21
19:1^{2}
20
21
24
20:4
5
7
8
20
21:1
2
9^{2}
10
14^{2}
16
19
20
24
22:5^{2}
6
13
15
18
19
20
22
29
23:7
9
17
19
28
32
34
24:6
7
10
23
27
25:5
6^{2}

PROV.
25:7
8
11
13
19^{2}
20
24^{2}
26:1^{2}
5
7
8
9
12
13^{2}
15
16
19
25
27:10
14
15
19
22
28:6^{2}
10^{2}
11
18
25
26
29:2
6
11
20
22
23
25
27
30:4^{2}
5
9
12
19^{2}
25
26
28
29
32
31:8
11
23
25
26
31

ECCL.
1:1
12
16
18
2:1
3
5
7^{2}
9
10
14^{2}
15^{2}
16
21^{3}
23
24
26
3:9
10
11^{2}
12^{2}
17
18
22
4:14
15
16
5:2
4
7
8
14
15
16
17
19
20
6:4^{2}
12
7:4^{2}
8^{2}
9^{2}
14^{2}
15^{3}
19
8:2
3
8^{2}
10
11
9:1^{2}
3
6
9^{2}
10
12^{3}
15
17
10:1
6^{2}
16
17

ECCL.
10:20^{2}
11:3
5
6^{2}
8
9^{4}
12:1^{2}
3
4
5
9

CANT.
1:4
9
14
2:12
14^{2}
3:2^{2}
8^{2}
11^{2}
4:7
5:4
6:2
13
7:4
5
11
8:8
9:10
13

ISAIAH
1:1
6
7
8^{2}
11
21
2:2^{2}
3
5
6
10
11
17
20
22
3:7
14
18
25
4:1
2
3^{3}
6
5:1
2
4
8
9
11
12
16^{2}
21^{2}
25
30^{2}
6:1
5
6
12
13^{2}
7:1
3
6
11^{2}
13^{3}
19^{2}
20
21
22
23
8:1
6
9^{3}
11
18^{2}
20
9:1^{2}
2^{3}
3
4
5
9
14
17
18
10:3^{2}
5
7
17
20^{2}
23
24
25
27
11:3
9
10
11
15
16
12:1
4
5
6
13:3

ISAIAH
13:4
8
10
13^{2}
17
20
22^{2}
14:1
2
3
6
13^{2}
18^{2}
20
25
28
30
31
32
15:1^{2}
4^{2}
5
16:3
5^{3}
10^{2}
17:4
5
6^{3}
9
11^{3}
18:2
4^{2}
5
7
19:1
3
9
10
14^{2}
16
17
18^{2}
19^{2}
20^{2}
21
23
24^{2}
20:1
6
21:1
5
8^{2}
13^{2}
22:2
3
5
7
8
12
14
16
20
23
25^{2}
23:1
13
15
24:11
12
13
15^{2}
18
21
22^{2}
23^{2}
25:4
5
6
7
8
9^{2}
10
11
26:1^{2}
2
3^{2}
4^{2}
8
9^{2}
10^{2}
12
16
17^{3}
18^{2}
19
27:1^{2}
2
4^{2}
8^{2}
9
12
13^{4}
28:4
5
6
7^{2}
14
16
20
21^{2}
25^{2}
29^{2}
29:15
18
19^{2}
21
23

ISAIAH
29:24
30:2^{2}
3
7
8^{2}
12
13
14^{2}
15^{3}
19
21
23^{2}
25
26
28
29
32^{2}
31:1^{2}
7
9^{2}
32:1^{2}
2^{2}
13
16^{2}
18^{3}
19
33:2
12
14
17
34:5
6^{2}
11
13^{2}
35:6^{2}
7
36:1
2
6^{2}
7
11^{3}
13
15
37:7
10
12
28
29^{2}
30
36^{2}
38^{2}
38:1^{2}
3^{2}
8
10
11
15
16
17
20
39:2^{3}
4^{2}
6^{2}
7
8
40:3^{2}
11
12^{4}
14
22
24
26
41:16^{2}
18^{2}
19^{2}
42:1
2
4
6
7
12
16
17
22^{2}
24
43:4
14
16^{2}
19^{2}
20^{2}
26
44:7
12
13
16
19
20
23
45:2^{2}
13
14^{2}
17
18
19^{3}
23
24
25
46:6
7
13
47:1
8
9^{3}
10^{2}
13
48:1
10

ISAIAH
48:16
49:2^{2}
3
4^{2}
5
8^{2}
9^{3}
20
21
22
50:4
10^{2}
11^{3}
51:6
7
9^{2}
14
16^{2}
20
52:6
10
53:9^{2}
10
54:6
8
14
16
17
55:2
11
56:5
7
9
57:2^{2}
5
6
10
13
15
17
58:2
3
10
11
12
14
59:4
6
7
8
9
10^{2}
13
14
19
20
21
60:10^{2}
18
22
61:3
6
7^{2}
8
10^{2}
11
62:2^{2}
4
7
9
63:1^{3}
2^{2}
3^{2}
4
6^{2}
9^{3}
13
64:5^{2}
65:2
3
4^{2}
5
8^{2}
10
16^{3}
18
19^{3}
23
25
66:3
4
8
13
17^{2}
20^{3}

JER.
1:1^{2}
2^{2}
3^{2}
5
9
2:2^{3}
5
17
18^{2}
19
23
24^{2}
27
28
30
34
37
3:2^{2}
6
16^{2}

JER.
3:18
23^{2}
25
4:2^{5}
5^{3}
11
19
20
30
31
5:1
6
7
8
13
14
18
19^{2}
20^{2}
24^{2}
30
31
6:1^{2}
3
6
7
10
11
16
23
24
26
29
7:2^{2}
3
4
6
7^{2}
8
10
11
12
17^{2}
22
23
24^{2}
30^{2}
31^{2}
32
8:3
7
8^{2}
9
12
16
18
19^{3}
22
9:2
4
6
8
23^{3}
24^{3}
26^{3}
10:5
6
7
13
14^{2}
15
23^{2}
24
11:4
6^{2}
7
8
12
14
15
17
21
12:2
5^{2}
8
16
13:1
4
10
17
21
22
25
27
14:4
5
6
8^{2}
9
13
14
15^{2}
16
15:4
7
11^{2}
13
14
15
17^{2}
16:2
3^{2}
6
7
9^{2}
19
17:3

JER.
17:4^{2}
5
6^{3}
7
8
11
13
17
19^{3}
20
21
24
25
29^{2}
18:4
6^{2}
10
15^{3}
17
21
23
19:4
7
9
10
11
14
20:1
2^{2}
6
7
9^{3}
16
21:4
5^{3}
7
9
12
14
22:2
3
4^{2}
12
15
20
21
23^{2}
30^{2}
23:5
8
11
12
13^{2}
14^{2}
18
19
20
22
24
25
26
29
24:8^{2}
9
25:1
5
13
23
24
34
26:1
2^{2}
4
7
9^{2}
10
14
15
16
18
20
27:1
11
15
18^{2}
19
21^{2}
28:1^{5}
5^{3}
7^{2}
11
15
17
29:5
7
8
9
10
15
16
21
22^{2}
23^{2}
25
26^{4}
28^{2}
29
31
30:2
6
8
10
11
24
31:2
4
9

JER.
31:10
12
13
15
17
22
23^{2}
24^{2}
29
32
33^{2}
32:1
2^{2}
7
8^{3}
9
10
12^{3}
14
15
19^{2}
20^{2}
23^{2}
34
35
37^{3}
40
41
43
44^{6}
33:1
5^{2}
10^{3}
12^{2}
13^{6}
15^{3}
16
20
34:5
6
13
15^{3}
17
18
35:1
7^{2}
8
9
10
15
36:1
6^{4}
8^{2}
9^{3}
10^{5}
13
14^{3}
15^{2}
18
20^{3}
21^{2}
22^{3}
23
28^{2}
30^{2}
32
37:1
4
10
12
13
15^{2}
17
18
21^{2}
38:2
4^{2}
5
6^{3}
7^{3}
9^{3}
13
14
22^{2}
28
39:1^{2}
2^{2}
3^{2}
5^{2}
6
9
10
15
16
17
18
40:1
6
7^{2}
9
10^{2}
11^{3}
13
15^{3}
41:1^{2}
6
8
10^{2}
12
17
18
42:10
13
16
20
22
43:4

JER.
43:5
8
9^{5}
12^{2}
13
44:1^{2}
3
6^{2}
8^{2}
9^{2}
10^{2}
12
13
15^{2}
16
17^{2}
21^{2}
23^{3}
24
26^{3}
27
29
45:1^{2}
3
5
46:2^{2}
10
11
14^{4}
19
21
25
26
27
28
48:2
5^{2}
6
7^{2}
11
18
20
26^{2}
28^{3}
35^{2}
38
41^{2}
44
47
49:1
2
4^{2}
7
11
16
18^{2}
21
22
24
26^{2}
27
32
33
34
38
39
50:2^{2}
4^{2}
5
9^{2}
14
16
20^{2}
22
25
28
30^{2}
32
37
39
42
43
51:1
2
3
4^{2}
6
7
10
13
16
17
18
20
21^{2}
22^{3}
23^{3}
24^{2}
27
30
39
44
46^{3}
47
58^{2}
59
60
62
52:1
2
3
4^{3}
6^{3}
8
9
10
11^{2}

JER.
52:12^{2}
15
17^{2}
19^{2}
20
25^{2}
27^{2}
28
29
31^{4}
32

LAM.
1:2
4
7
9
12
15^{2}
19
20
2:1^{2}
2
3
4
5
6^{2}
7^{2}
11
12
17
19^{3}
20
21^{2}
22^{2}
3:6
10^{2}
11
20^{2}
24
27
29
36
41
45
53
57
66
4:1
3
5^{2}
6
7
8
10
11
13
14
17
18
19
20
21
5:11^{2}

EZEKIEL
1:1^{3}
2
3
16
20
21
28^{2}
3:3
10
14^{2}
18
19
20
4:9
12
14
16
5:2^{2}
3^{2}
4
5
6
7
8^{2}
9
10^{2}
12
13^{2}
14
15^{4}
6:6
7
9
10
13
14
7:4
7
9
13
15^{2}
19^{2}
20
8:1^{4}
3
4
5
7
8^{2}
9
10

EZEKIEL
8:11^{2}
12^{2}
18^{2}
9:1^{2}
2^{2}
4
5
7
8
10:1
2^{3}
3
6
8
10
13
17
19
11:2
6
7
10
11^{2}
12
16
20
24
12:2
3^{2}
4^{2}
5
6^{2}
7^{3}
8
10
11
12
13
15
22
23
25
13:4
5^{2}
9^{2}
13^{3}
14
21
14:3
4
5
7^{2}
14
16
18
19
20
23
16:4^{2}
5^{2}
6^{3}
12
15
22^{2}
24
29
31^{4}
34^{3}
38
41
43
47
49^{2}
51
52
53
54^{2}
56
59
60
17:5
8
9
10
15
16^{2}
17
20
23^{2}
18:3
9
17
18
22
24^{3}
26
32
19:4
8
9^{2}
10
11
12
13^{2}
20:1^{2}
5^{2}
6
8
9^{2}
11
13^{4}
14
15
16
17
18^{3}
19

EZEKIEL
20:21^{3}
22^{2}
23
26^{2}
27^{2}
36
40^{3}
41
43
47^{2}
21:20
21
22
23
24^{2}
30^{2}
31
32
22:3
4^{2}
6
7^{3}
9^{3}
10^{2}
11^{2}
12
13
14
15
16
18
20^{2}
21^{2}
22^{2}
24
25^{2}
27
30
23:3^{2}
8
11^{3}
15
19^{2}
21
31
32
37
38
39
43
44^{3}
45
24:1^{3}
7
11
12
13
18^{2}
25
26
27
25:4^{2}
6
10
14
26:1^{2}
5
6
8
12
15
17
18^{2}
20^{3}
27:4
8
9^{2}
10^{2}
11
12
13
14
16
17
18^{2}
19^{2}
20
21^{3}
22
24^{3}
25^{2}
26
27^{4}
30
32
34^{2}
35
28:2^{2}
8
9
12
13^{3}
14
15^{2}
18
22^{3}
23
25^{3}
29:1^{3}
3
4
12
17^{3}
21^{2}
30:4^{2}
5
6

EZEKIEL
30:7^{2}
8
9^{3}
13
14^{2}
16
18
19
20^{3}
24
31:1^{3}
2
3
6
7^{2}
8^{3}
9
10^{2}
12
14^{2}
15
16
17
18^{3}
32:1^{3}
2
3
10
17^{2}
19
20
23^{2}
24
25^{3}
26
27
28
32^{2}
33:6
8
9
10
11
12^{3}
15
21^{3}
22^{2}
27^{4}
30
34:12^{2}
13
14^{3}
25^{2}
26
27
29
35:5^{2}
8^{3}
36:2
3
5
6^{2}
15
17
23^{2}
27
28
31
33^{2}
34
38
37:1^{2}
2
6
8
14^{2}
17
19^{2}
20
22
24
25
26
28
38:8
12
14
16^{2}
17^{2}
18
23
39:6
7^{2}
9
11^{2}
15
26
27^{2}
40:1^{4}
2
3^{2}
5
25^{2}
27
29^{2}
33
39
44
41:6^{2}
42:3
6
8
10
12
43:7^{2}
8^{2}
9

EZEKIEL
43:11^{2}
16
17
18
21
44:2^{2}
3
5
7^{4}
8
9^{2}
11
13
17^{2}
19
24^{3}
27^{2}
28
29
30
45:1
2^{2}
3
8^{2}
16
17^{4}
18^{2}
21^{2}
25^{3}
46:1
3^{2}
4
6
8
9^{3}
10^{2}
11^{2}
21
22
23
47:3
5
19
22
23
48:8^{3}
9^{2}
10^{5}
13^{2}
15^{2}
18
21
22
28

DANIEL
1:1
4^{5}
8
14
15
17^{2}
18^{2}
20^{2}
2:1
4
5
16
19
22
24^{2}
25^{2}
27
28^{2}
40
41
44^{2}
45
49
3:1^{2}
13
16
20
21
24
25
28
29
30
4:1
4^{2}
6
7
8^{2}
9
10^{2}
12^{2}
13
15^{3}
17
18^{2}
21
23^{2}
25
29
31
32
35
36
37
5:2
3
5
7^{2}
8
9

DANIEL 5:11^4 12 13 14^2 15 16 20 21 23^2 27 29 30 6:3 4 10 19^2 22 23 24 25 26 27^2 28^2 7:1 2 5 7^2 8 13 15^2 19 21 23 28^2 8:1 2^4 6 7 18 22 23 25^2 9:1 2^2 6 10 11 13 14 21^2 24 25 27 10:1 2 3 4 5 6 8^2 9 14 17^2 21^2 11:1 2 6^2 7 14 16 20^4 21^2 38 39 45 12:1 2 6 7 13

HOSEA 1:1^2 5 10 2:3 9^2 10 15^2 18 19^4 20 21 23 3:5 4:1 5^2 16 19 5:4 5 8^2 9 11 15 6:2^2 9 10 7:1 2 5 6^2 16 8:6 9:2 3^2 5^2

HOSEA 9:6 8^2 9 10^2 13 15 10:4^2 9 10^2 12^2 13^2 14^2 15 11:9 11 12:3 4 7 8^2 9^2 10^3 13:1^2 5 9 10 11^2 13 16 14:3 9

JOEL 1:2^2 13 2:1^2 5 8 9^2 15 23^2 26 27 29 30^2 32^2 3:1^2 13 14^2 17 18 19 21

AMOS 1:1^2 14^3 2:7 8 16 3:4 5 6^2 9^5 10 12^4 13 14 4:1 6^2 5:6^2 7 10 11 12 13 15 16^2 17 20 21 25 6:1^2 6 9 13 14 7:1 7 8 10 17^2 8:3^2 9^2 11 13 9:1 3^2 6^2 9 11^2

OBADIAH 1 3^2 7 8 11^2 12^3 13^3 14^2 18 20

JONAH 1:4 5 17

JONAH 2:3 7 3:6 8 4:2 5 8 10^2

MICAH 1:1 10^2 11 13 2:1 4 5 11 12 3:2 4 4:1^2 2 5^2 6 7 9^2 10^3 13 5:1 2 4^2 5 6 7 8^2 10 15 6:10 12 13^2 14 16 7:2 5^3 6^2 8 11^2 12 14^4 18

NAHUM 1:3^3 6 7^2 13 2:1 3^2 2:4^2 5 10 12 13 3:10^2 13 17^2 18

HABAK. 1:5 15^2 2:4 13 19 20 3:2^3 7 11 12^2 16^2 17^2 18^2

ZEPH. 1:1 9 10 11 18^2 2:3 7^2 14^4 15^2 3:2 5 11^2 12 13 15 16 17^2 19 20

HAGGAI 1:1^3 4 6 8 13 14 15^2 2.1^2 3^3 9 10^2

HAGGAI 2:12 15 17 19 20 22 23

ZECH. 1:1^2 7 8 16 2:1 5 10 11^2 12 3:7 9 10 4:10 5:4 7 9 11 6:2^2 3^2 8 14 15 7:1^3 3^2 5 7 10 12 8:3 4^2 5 6^3 8^3 9^2 10 11 15 16 17 22 23 9:1 4 6 7 16 10:1^2 2 3 5^2 9 11 12^2 11:8 11 13 16^2 12:2 3^2 4 5^2 6^4 8 9 10^2 11^3 13:1 2 3 4 6^2 8 14:1 3 4^2 5 6 8^3 9 10 11 12^2 13 14 15 20^2 21^4

MALACHI 1:7 10 11 12 14 2:6^3 9 11^2 17^2 3:1 3 4^2 5 8 10 11 17 4:2 3 4

MATT. 1:20^2 2:1^2 2 5 6 9 12 13 16^2 18 19^2 22^3 23 3:1^2 3 6 12 17 4:6 13^2 16^2 21 23 5:3 8 11 15 16 18 19^2 20 21 22^3 25 28 45 48 6:1 2^2 4^2 5^2 6^2 9 10^2 18^2 20 23 29 7:3^2 4 11 13^2 15 21 22^4 8:10 11 13 24 32 9:4 10 16 25 31 33 35 10:9 11 15 16 17 19 20 23 27^3 28 32 33 35^2 41^2 42^2 11:1 2 6 8^2 11 16 21^3 23^2 24 26 29 12:5^2 6 18 19 21 32^2 36 40^2 41 42 50 13:3 10 13 14 19 21 24 27 30^2 31 32 33 34

MATT. 13:35 40^2 43 44 54 57^3 14:2 3 8 10 11 24 25 33 15:9 17 32 33 16:3 17 19^2 26 27 28 17:5 22 18:1 2 4 5 6^2 10^2 14 16 18^2 19 20^2 19:21 28^2 20:1 3 17 21 21:8^2 9^2 12 14 15 18 19 22 24 28 32 33 41 42^2 22:11 12 15 16 28 30^3 36 43 23:2 6 7 9 13^2 30^2 34 39 24:5 7 14 15 16 18 19 20 26^2 30^2 38^2 40 43 44 45 48 50^2 25:4 10 18 25 31 35 36 38 39 43^2 44 26:6^2 12 13 23 29 55^2 58 61 64 67 69 27:4 5 7 19 29

MATT. 27:40 43 44 51 59 60^2 28:1 18^2 19

MARK 1:2 3 4 5 9^2 11 13 14 19 20 23 35 39 45 2:1 6 8^2 15 20 26 3:23 29 4:2 11 15 17 19 28 29 31^2 36 38 5:4 5^2 13 14^2 15 20 27 29 30^2 33 34 39 40 6:2 4^2 8 10 11 14 17 22 25^2 27 28 29 40 47 48 51 55 56 7:7 32 8:1 4 12 14 26 37 38^2 9:33 36^2 37 38 39 41 42 50 10:10 16 21 24 30^2 32 37 52 11:4 8^2 9 10^2 15 20 22 23 25 26 27 12:4 11 13 14 23 25^2 26^2

MARK 12:35 38^3 39 41 42 43 44^2 13:6 8 9 11 14 16 17 18 19 24 25 26 29 32 35 14:3^2 14 17 20 25 30 31 49 60 62 66 15:1 7 29 38 41 43 46^2 16:2 7 12 17

LUKE 1:1^2 3 5 6 7 8 15 17 18 19 20 21 22 25 26 28 29 31 36 39 41 44^2 47 51 54 66 69 75 79^2 80^2 2:1 7^3 8^2 11 12^2 14 16 19 21 23 24 25 27 28 29 34 38^2 40 43 44 46^2 51 52 3:1 2 4^2 15^2 17 18 20 22^2 4:2 5 11 14 15 20 21 23^2 24 25^2

LUKE 4:27^2 28 33 35 44 5:7 12 18^2 19 22 29 35 6:1 8 12^2 17 23^3 41^2 42^3 7:1 7 9 21 23 25^2 28 32 37^2 45 50 8:10 13 15 16 23 27^2 29 34 35 48 51 9:12 14 26^2 31 36 48 49 57 10:7 12 13^3 20^2 21^3 26 34 11:1 2^3 6 7 21 26 31 32 33^2 35 37 43^2 52^2 12:1 3^4 12 15 27 28 33 38^2 42 45 46^2 52 53^4 58 13:4^2 6 7 10 11 14^2 19 21 24^2 26^2 28 29 35 14:8 10^2 15 21 23 15:4 7 10 14^2 21 25 28 16:8 10^4 11 12 15 19 23^3 24^3 25

LUKE 17:4^2 6 24 26^2 27 28 30 31^3 34^2 36 18:2 3 9 12 17 22 30^2 19:17 20 30 36 38^3 42 43 44 47 20:1 31 33 34 35 42 45 46^3 21:2 3 4^2 6 8 11 14 19 21^3 23^2 25^3 27 37^3 38^2 22:6 10 16 19 20 28 30 37 44 53 55 23:4 9 11 14 19 22 29 31^2 38 40 43 45 53^3 24:1 3 4 6 12 18^2 19 27 29 35^2 36 38 44^3 47 49 53

JOHN 1:1 2 4 5 10 18 23 28 45 47 2:1 11 14 19 20^2 23^3 25 3:13 14 15 16 18 21 23 4:14 18 20^2

JOHN 4:21 23^2 24^2 31 44 53 5:2 3 4 6 13 14 26^2 28^2 35 38 39 42 43^2 45 6:10^2 31 37 45 49 53 56^2 59^2 61 63 7:1^2 4 5 9 10 18 28 37 8:2 3^2 4^2 5 9 12 17 20^2 21 24^2 31 33 35 37 44^2 9:3 5 34 10:2 9^2 23^2 25 34 38^2 11:6 9^2 10^2 13 17 20 24 25 26 30 31 33 38 52 56 12:25 35 36 46 48 13:1 21 31 32^2 14:1^2 2 10^3 11^2 13^2 14 17 20^3 26 30 15:2 4^4 5^2 6 7^2 9 10^2 11 16 25 16:21 23^2 24 25^2 26 33^2 17:10 11^2 12^2 13^2 21^3

JOHN 17:23^3 26^2 18:13 15 16 20^3 26 38 19:4 6 13^3 17 18 20 40 41^2 20:5^2 7 8 12 19 25 26 30^2 21:2 8

ACTS 1:2 7 8^3 10 11 13 14 15^2 18 19 20 21 2:1 6 8 9^3 10^2 11 12 17 18 19^2 22 26 27 31 37 38 42^3 46 3:6 11 13 16^2 22 25 26 4:3 7 12 16 17 18 19 24 5:4^2 7 10 12 18 20 21 22 25^2 28 34^2 37 40 42^2 6:1^2 7 15 7:2^2 4 5 6 7^2 10 12 16 17 20^2 22^3 29 30^3 34 35 36^2 38^3 39 41^2 42^2 44 45 48 51 8:8 9 16

ACTS 8:21^2 23^2 25 28 33 40 9:10 11 12^2 17 20 21 22 25 27^2 28 29 31^2 37^2 42 43 10:1 3^2 17 23 25 27 30^2 31^2 32 35 39^2 42 43 48 11:1 3 5^2 13 22 26 27 28 29 12:4 5 7 14 21 13:1 5 13 14 17 18 19 27 28 29 33^2 35 40 41^2 43 14:1 3 8 11^2 14 16^2 17 22 23 25 15:21^2 23 33 35 36 16:3 5^2 6 9 12 18 24 29 32 34 36 17:2 11^2 16 17^2 21 22^2 24 28 31^3 18:2 4 5 9 10 18 21 23 24 25^2 26 19:5 9 10 16 21 22 27

ACTS 19:29 30 39 40^2 29:6 8 9 10 13 14 16 19 22 23 29 21:8 27 29 31 39 40 22:2 3^3 17^2 19 23:1 6^2 9 10 11 16 21 35 24:3 12^3 14^2 18 20 21 24 25:3 5 14 26:3 10^2 11 13 14 16 18 21 26 27:12 20 21 27 31 35 37^2 39 28:7 8 9 11^2 18 30^2

ROMANS 1:2 7 9^2 15 18 19 21 27^2 28 32 2:7 12 14 15 16 17 19 20 28 29^2 3:4 9 16 20 24 25 26 4:10^4 12 18 19 20 5:2 3 5 6 8 11 13 17 6:1 4 5^2 10^2 12^2 21 7:5^2 6^2 8

ROMANS 7:13 17 18^2 20 22 23^2 8:1 2 3^3 4 8 9^3 10 11^2 18 20 22 37 39 9:1^2 2 7 17 25 26 28 33 10:6 8^2 9 14^2 11:17 19 22 23^3 25^3 30 32 12:4 5 10 11^2 12^3 16 17 18 20 13:4 9 13^4 14:1 5 13 17 18 22 15:12 13^2 15^2 17 23 24 27 29 30 31 16:2^2 3 5 7 8 9 10 11 12^2 13 22

1 COR. 1:2^2 5^3 6 7 8 10^2 13 15 21 29 30 31 2:3^3 4 5^2 7 11 13 3:1 16 18 19 21 4:2 6^2 10 15^2 17^3 20^2 21^2 5:3^2 4 5 9 6:4 11 19 20^2

1 COR. 7:15 17 18 20 22 28 34^2 37^2 38^2 39 8:4^2 5^2 6 7 10 9:1 2 9 10^2 18 24 25 10:2^2 5 8 19 25 28 33 11:2 11 13 17 18 21 22^2 23 24 25^2 34 12:6 18 25 27 28 13:6^2 9^2 10 12 14:2^2 4 7 10 13 14 19^2 20^3 21 23 24 25 27 28 33 34 35 40 15:2^2 10 17 18 19^2 22^2 23 28 30 31 41 42^2 43^4 52^2 54 58^3 16:2 11 13 19^2 24

2 COR. 1:1 4^2 5 6 8 9^3 10 12^2 14^2 15 19 20^2 21 22 2:1 3 5 9 10 13 14^2 15^2 17^2 3:2 3^2 7 9

2 COR. 3:10 14^2 18 4:2^2 4 6^2 7 8 10^2 11 12^2 5:1 2 4 6 10 11 12^2 17 19 20 21 6:1 2^2 3^2 4^5 5^6 12^2 13 16^2 7:1 3 4 7 9 11^3 12 13 14 16^2 8:2 6 7^5 18 20 21^2 22^2 9:3 4 7 8 11 14 10:1 3 6 11^2 14 16^2 17 11:1 3 6^3 7 9 10^2 17 23^4 25 26^2 27^5 32 33 12:2^9 3 5 7 9^2 10^5 11^2 12^2 18^2 19 13:1 3^2 4 5^2 11

GAL. 1:13^2 14^2 16 22 23 24 2:2 4^3 6 8^2 16 20^2 21 3:3 4^2 8 10^2 11^2 12 17 18 26 28 4:3 9 14 18

GAL. 4:19^2 20 25^2 5:1 6 10 14^2 16 21 25^2 6:1^2 4^2 6^2 9^2 12 13 14 15 17

EPHES. 1:1 3^2 4^2 6 7 8 9 10^5 11 12 18^2 15 16 17 18 20^2 21^2 23 2:1 2^2 3^2 4 5 6^2 7^2 10^2 11^3 12 13 15^3 16 21^2 22 3:3 4 5 6 9 10 11 12 15 16 17 20 21 4:2 3 4 6 13 14 15^2 16^2 17^2 18 21 23 24 5:2 5 8 9 12 19^2 20 21 24 33 6:1 4 5 9 10^2 12 13 18 20 21 24

PHIL. 1:1 4 5 6 7^3 8 9^2 13^3 14 18^2 20^2 22 23 24

PHIL. 1:26 27 28 29 30[2] 2:1 3 5[2] 6 7 8 10[2] 12[2] 13 15[2] 16[3] 19 22 24 25 29[2] 3:1 3[3] 4[2] 6 9 14 15 19 20 4:1 2 3[2] 4 6

PHIL. 4:9 10 11[2] 12 15 16 19 21 COLOS. 1:2 4 5[2] 6[3] 8 9 10[2] 12 14 16[2] 18 19 20 21 22[2] 23 24[2] 27 28[2] 29 2:1 2 3 5[3] 6 7[2]

COLOS. 2:9 10 11 12 13 15 16[3] 18 20 23[2] 3:3 4 7[2] 10 11 15 16[4] 17[2] 18 20 22[2] 4:1 2 3 5 7 12[2] 13[2] 15[2] 16 17 1 THESS. 1:1[2] 2

1 THESS. 1:3[2] 5[4] 6 7 8[2] 9 2:1[2] 2 3 4 13[2] 14[2] 17[2] 19 3:2 5 7 8 10 12 13 4:4 5 6 10 14 16 17[2] 5:2 4 7[2] 12 13 18[2]

2 THESS. 1:1 4[3] 8 10[3] 12[2] 2:2 6 10 12 17 3:4 6 13 17 1 TIM. 1:2 4 13 14 16 2:2[2] 3 6 7[2] 9[2] 11 12 14 15[2] 3:4 9 11 13[2] 15

1 TIM. 3:16[3] 4:1 2 6[2] 10 12[6] 14 16[2] 5:5[2] 6 7 17 6:9 13 15 16 17[3] 18 19 2 TIM. 1:1 3 5[3] 6[2] 9 13[2] 14 15 17 18[2] 2:1[2] 7 10 14

2 TIM. 2:20 25 3:1 12 14 15 16 4:2 5 TITUS 1:2 3 5[3] 13 16 2:2[3] 3 7[2] 9 10 12 3:1 3 8 15 PHILE. 2 4 6[2] 7 8 10 11 13[2]

PHILE 16[2] 20[2] 21 23 HEB. 1:1[2] 2 6 10 2:5 6 8[3] 10 12 13 17[2] 18 3:2 5 8[3] 10 11 12[2] 15 17 19 4:2 3 4 5 6 7 13 15

HEB. 4:16 5:1 6 7[2] 13 6:7 10 18 7:9 10 19 8:1 5 9[2] 10 13 9:9 10 12 24 26 10:3 6 7 16 22 32 34[3] 38 11:9[3] 12 13 19 26 34

HEB. 11:37 38[3] 12:3 9 23 13:3[2] 4 18 21[3] 22 JAMES 1:6 8 9 10 11 23 25 27 2:2[3] 3 4 5 10 16 3:2[2] 3 7 14 18 4:1 5[2] 10 16

JAMES 5:5[2] 10 14 1 PETER 1:4 5 6 8 11 14 15 17 20 21[2] 22 2:6[2] 10 12 24 3:1 4[2] 5[3] 15 16 18 19 20 4:1[2] 2 3 6[2] 11 15 19

1 PETER 5:6 9[3] 14 2 PETER 1:4 8[2] 12 13[2] 15 17 18 19[2] 21 2:1 5 8 10 11 12 13 18 19 22 3:1 3 5 7 10[2] 11 14 16[3] 18[2] 1 JOHN 1:5

1 JOHN 1:6 7[2] 8 10 2:4 5[2] 6 8[2] 9[2] 10[2] 11[2] 14 15[2] 16 24[2] 27[2] 28 3:3 5 6 9 10 14 15 17 18[4] 22 24[3] 4:2 3[2] 4[2] 9 12[2] 13[2] 15[2]

1 JOHN 4:16[3] 17[2] 18[2] 5:7 8[2] 10 11 14 19 20[2] 2 JOHN 1 2 3 4 6 7 9[2] 3 JOHN 1 2 3[2] 4 JUDE 1 4 5 6 7 10 11[2] 12 16

JUDE 18 20 21 REV. 1:4 5 9[3] 10 11[2] 13 16[2] 20 2:1[2] 7 8 12 13 17 18 24 3:1 4[2] 5 7 12 18 20 21[2] 4:1 2[2] 3 4 6 5:1

REV. 5:3[2] 6[2] 13[3] 6:5 6 15[2] 7:3 9 13 14 15 17 8:1 9 9:4 6 10 11[2] 14 17 19[2] 10:2 7 8 9 10 11:3 5 6 8 9 12 13 15 19[2]

REV. 12:1 2 3 7 8 10 12 13:6[2] 8 13 14 16[2] 14:1 5 6 9[2] 10[2] 13 14 15 16 17 18 19 15:1[2] 5 6 16:3 16 19 17:3 4[2] 8 17 18:6

REV. 18:7 8 10 16 17 19[2] 22[3] 23[2] 24 19:1 8 11 13 14[2] 17[2] 20:1 4 6 8 12 13[2] 15 21:8 10 14 23 24 27[2] 22:2 3 4 14 16 18 19

is

1961, *2076*

GEN. 1:11 29[2] 30 2:9 11[3] 12[2] 13[2] 14[3] 18 23 3:3 13 17 22 4:6 9 13 5:1 6:3 13 14 17[2] 21 7:15 8:17 21 9:4 10 12[2] 15 16 17[2] 18 10:9 12 6 11:9 12:12 18 19 13:9 18 14:2 3 6 7 8 15 17 23 15:2 3 13 16 16:6 14 17:4 10 12[3] 13 14 17 18:9 14 20 21 19:8 13 19 20 31 37 38 20:2 3 5[2] 7

GEN. 20:11 12 13[2] 15 16 21:13 17 22 22:7 14 17 23:2 9[2] 11 15 19 20 24:23 35 51 65[2] 25:9 18 26:7 9 10 20 27:11 20 22 27 33 36 28:16 17[2] 29:6 7 19 25 30:15 30 33 31:5 14 16 29 32 35 36 43 48 50[2] 32:2 8 18[2] 20 27 29 30 32 33:11 17 18 34:14 21 35:6[2] 10 19 20 27 36:1 8 19 43 37:10 22 26

GEN. 37:27 30 33[2] 38:14 18 21 24 39:8 9 40:8 12 18 41:15 16 25[2] 26 28[2] 32[2] 38[2] 39 42:2 13[2] 14 21 22 28[3] 30 32[2] 36[2] 38[2] 43:7 27[2] 28[2] 29 32 44:5 10 15 16 17 20[2] 28 30 31 45:12 20 26[2] 28[2] 46:33 34 47:3 4 6 18[2] 23 48:1 7 18 49:9 14 21 22 24 28 29 30 32 50:10 11[2] 20 EXOD. 1:22 2:6 14 18 20[2]

EXOD. 3:3 5 9 13 15[2] 16 4:2 14 22 5:2 16[2] 22 7:14 17 18 8:10 19 26 9:3[2] 4 14 27 28 29 10:5 7 10 11:5 12:11 19 22[2] 27 42[2] 43 44 48 49 13:2 8 14 14:12 15:2[3] 3[2] 6 11[2] 26 16:12 15 16 23[2] 25 26 32 36 17:3 7 18:11 14 17 18[2] 19:5 20:4[3] 10[2] 11 17 20 21:21 30 22:16 25 27[2] 31 23:16 21 25:3 26:5 10

EXOD. 27:21 28:8 26 29:1 13[2] 14 18 21 22[2] 23 25 27[4] 28 30 32 34 38 30:6[2] 10 13 32 31:7 13 14 15 17 32:1 5 9 17 18[2] 23 26 33:13 16 21 34:9 10 14[2] 19[2] 35:4 5 36:25 38:21 26 40:9 LEVIT. 1:5 8[2] 12[2] 13 17[2] 2:3 6 8[2] 9 10[2] 15 16 3:3 4[2] 5[3] 9 10[2] 11 14 15[2] 16[2] 4:3 5 7[2] 8 9[2] 14 16 18[3]

LEVIT. 4:21 22 24 31 35 5:1 8 9 11 12 17 19 6:4 9[2] 14 15 17[2] 20[2] 21 22[2] 25[3] 27 28 29 30 7:1[2] 4[3] 5 6 7[3] 9[2] 11 15 24 35 37 8:5 28 31 9:6 10:3 7 12 13 17 11:3 4 5 6 7 10 26 32 33 36 37 46 12:7 13:3[2] 6 8 9 11[2] 13 15[2] 17 18 20 22 23 24 25[2] 27 28[2] 30 31 36

LEVIT. 13:37[3] 39[2] 40[3] 41[2] 42 44[3] 45 46 47 49 51[3] 52[2] 54 55[3] 57[2] 59 14:4 7 8 11 13[3] 14 16 17[2] 18[2] 19 22 25 27 28[2] 29[2] 31[2] 32[3] 35 36 40 43 44[2] 46 48 54 57[3] 15:2 3 4 8 13 17 31 32[2] 33[2] 16:2 6 11[2] 13 15 18 17:2 11[2] 14[3] 18:6 7 8 10 11 12 13 14 15 16 17 19 22 23 25 27 19:7

LEVIT. 19:13 20 20:14 17 21 27 21:2[2] 3 7[2] 10[2] 12 19 22:4[2] 7[2] 8 11 13 24 25 27 23:3[2] 5 6 8 28 36 24:9 16 25:5 12 23 28 29 30 34 48 49 27:22 26 28 30[2] NUM. 1:51 3:26 47 48 4:15 16 24 25 26[2] 28 31 33 5:2 15 17 18 29[2] 6:4 7 8 13 18 19 20 21 8:24 9:13[2] 10:7 11:6[2] 14 17 20 23

NUM. 12:7[2] 12 13:18 19 20 27 32 14:7 9[2] 18 42 15:25 29 16:3 5 11 13 40 46 18:11[2] 13[2] 16 19 31 19:2[2] 9[2] 13[2] 14[2] 15 16 20 20:5[2] 13 21:5[2] 8 11 13[2] 14 16 20 28 30 22:5[2] 6[2] 11 32 36[2] 23:19 21[2] 23[2] 24:9[2] 21 26:9 27:11 14 18 28:3 6 10 14 16 17 23 29:1 30:1 9 20 21 32:4 19 33:6 7 36 34:2 13 35:16 17

NUM. 35:18 21 31 32 33 36:6 DEU. 1:14 16 17[2] 25 28 36[2] 3:11 12 16 18 24 25 4:6[2] 7[2] 8 17 18 24 31 32 35[2] 38 39[2] 44 48[2] 5:8[3] 14[2] 21 26 6:4 15 18 24 7:9 21 25[2] 26 8:13[2] 18[2] 9:3 13 10:9 14[2] 15 17 21[2] 11:10[2] 11 12:8 12 18 22 23 25 28 13:6 11 14 15 18 14:8 10 19 21 27 15:2[2] 3 9 16

DEU. 16:11 17 20 17:1[2] 4 6 15 18 18:2 22 19:4 6[2] 16 17 20:1 4 5 6 7 8[2] 11 14 19 21:2 3 4 6 9 16 17[2] 20[2] 23[2] 22:23 26[2] 28[2] 23:1 7 10 11 15 19 23 24:2 4[2] 14 15 25:6 26:11 12 28:23[2] 43 54 61 29:5 11 15 23[2] 28 30:11[2] 12 13 14 20 31:6 8 11 12 17 32:4[3] 5 6 9[2] 20 21 22 27 28

DEU. 32:31 32 33 34 35 36[2] 39[2] 47[2] 49[2] 33:1 7 17 22 26 27 29[2] 34:1 4 JOSH. 1:2 8 9 2:9 11 3:10 16 4:24 5:4 9 15 6:7 7:2 13 15 8:18 31 34 9:12[2] 10:13 11:4 12:2[2] 9 13:2 3[2] 4 9[2] 16[2] 25 28 14:11 15:7[2] 8[2] 9 10 12 13 20 25 49 54 60 16:8 17:10 16 18 18:7 13 14 16 17 28[2] 19:8 11 16 23 31

JOSH. 19:39 48 20:7 21:11 22:9 16 17 28 29 31 34 23:3 6 10 24:17 18 19[2] 30 JUD. 1:26 4:11 14[2] 20 5:9 28 6:12 13 15 24 25 31 7:1 3 14 8:2 21[2] 9:2 3 18 28[3] 32 33[2] 38[3] 10:8 18 13:17 18 14:3 15 18[2] 15:2 11 19 16:2[2] 3 9 15 17:2 18:6 9 10[2] 12 14 19 24 19:10 12 18 19[4] 23 24 20:5 12[2] 21:3 5 6

JUD. 21:8 11 12 19[2] RUTH 1:13 15 19 2:5 6 19 20 22 3:2 12[2] 4:3 4 11 15 17[2] 1 SAM. 1:8 2:1[2] 2[3] 3 5 20 24 35 36 3:17 18 4:7 16 17[2] 21 22[2] 5:7 6:3 9 20 9:6[2] 7[2] 9 11 12[3] 16 18 19 20[2] 24 10:1 5 7 11[3] 12[2] 24 11:12 12:5[3] 6 17[2] 13:5 14:1 2 6 7 17 15:7 11 22 23 28[2] 29 32 16:6

1 SAM. 16:12 16[2] 18[2] 19 17:25[2] 26 29 46 47 18:18 19:14 17 19 22 24 20:1[2] 2 3 5 6 7[2] 18 21 26[2] 37 21:3[2] 4[2] 5 8 9[3] 11 14 22:8[3] 14[3] 17 23:7 19 22[2] 24:1 6 10 11 14 16 25:10[2] 17[2] 25[4] 29 26:1 3 4 5 11 15 16[2] 17[2] 18 20 27:1 28:7 14[2] 15 16[2] 29:1 3 5 6 30:20 24 2 SAM. 1:9[2] 18 19 21 2:7 16

2 SAM. 3:12 13 23 24[2] 29 38 4:10 5:7 6:2 7:3[2] 18 19 22 23 26 10:1[2] 2 3[2] 4[2] 8 11:3 21 24 12:14 18 19 21 23 13:16[2] 20 23 28 30 32 33 35 14:5 7[2] 13 15 17 19 20 30 15:2 3 31 16:3 17 17:2 3 7 8 9 10[2] 11 14 20 29 18:3 13 18 20 25 27[2] 28 29 32[2] 19:9 10 11 26 27[2] 30 42 20:11 21

2 SAM. 21:1 22:2 3 4 31[3] 32 33 35 48 51 23:5 15 17 24:16 21 1 KINGS 1:9 25 26 41 45 2:3 15[2] 22 29 35 38 42 43 44 3:6 8 9 22 27 4:12 13 20 29 33 5:4 6 6:1 17 38 8:1 2 21 23 24 35 41 46 60[2] 9:14 26 11:7 11 33 38 12:24 28 32 13:3 26 31 14:2 5 10 13 15 15:19 17:3 5 24 18:8

1 KINGS 18:10[2] 11 14 24 27[4] 39[2] 41 43 19:4 7 20:3 6 28[2] 32[2] 21:2 5 14[2] 15 18[3] 21 22:3 7 8 13 16 32 2 KINGS 1:3[2] 6[2] 8 16[2] 2:14 19[2] 3:11[2] 12 18 4:1[2] 4 6 9 13 14[2] 23 25 26[4] 27 31 40 5:3 4 6 8 15 21 22 26 6:1 11 12 13[2] 19[2] 32 33 7:4 9 8:5[2] 7 13 9:8 11 12 18 17 18 19 20

2 KINGS
9:22 23 27 32 34 36 37 10:5 15[3] 30 33 11:5 12:4[2] 14:6 18:10 17 19 21 22 19:3[2] 9 13 21 28 30 20:3 10 15 17 19[2] 22:4 5 13[4] 23:10 17[2] 21 25:4 8

1 CHRON.
1:27 5:1 6:10 7:31 11:4 5 11 17 12:17 13:6[2] 11 14:15 16:14 25[2] 32 34 40 17:2[2] 16 20[2] 21 24 19:13 21:15 17[2] 23 24 22:1[2] 5[2] 14 16 18[2] 19 23:29[2] 27:6 29:1[3] 5 11[3] 12[2] 14 15 16

2 CHRON.
1:10 12 2:4 5[2] 6 5:2 9 13 6:11 14 15 26[2] 32[2] 33 36 40 7:3 15 21 11:4 12:6 13:4 6 10 12 14:7 11 15:2 16:3 7 9 18:6 7[2]

2 CHRON.
18:31 19:2 6 7 11 20:2 6[2] 9 15 22:9 23:4 18 25:4 7 9 26:23 28:11 13[2] 22 29:10 30:9 31:3 10 32:7 8[2] 34:21[4] 35:12 21 36:23[2]

EZRA.
1:2 3[4] 4 5 9 2:68 3:2 4 11 4:11 15 19 24 5:2 8[2] 15 16[2] 17 6:2 5[2] 12 18[2] 7:11 14 15 16 17 23 25 27 8:1 22[2] 9:6 7 11 13 15 10:2 13[2] 23

NEH.
1:3 2:2[2] 19 4:10[2] 14 19 5:5[2] 9 14 6:6 7 11 8:9[2] 10[3] 11 15 9:5 6 10 18 33 10:34 36 13:11 17

ESTHER
1:1 19 20 2:7 16[2] 3:7[3] 8[2] 11 13 4:11[2] 16 5:3 6[2] 7 6:3 4 8

ESTHER
7:2[2] 5[2] 6 8:8 9 12 9:1 12[2] 24

JOB
1:8 10 12 16 2:3 6 3:3 19 20[2] 23[2] 25[2] 4:5 6 19 21 5:4 7 13 17 27 6:6[2] 11[2] 12[2] 13[2] 14 16 17 26 28 29 30 7:1 5[2] 7 9 17 8:12 16 19 9:1 4 19 22 24[2] 32 33 35 10:1 3 7 13 22 11:4 6 8 9 18 12:4 5[3] 10 12 13 16 24 13:9 19 28 14:1[2] 2 7 10 17 18 15:9 11 14[2] 16 20 21 22 23[2] 31 16:6 8 16[2] 17 19[2] 17:1 3 7 12 13 15 16 18:8 10 15 21 19:7 17 28 29 20:5 7 14[2] 23[2]

JOB
20:25 26 29 21:4 8 9 15 16[2] 17 21 28 30 22:2 3[2] 5 12 18 20 29 30 23:2[2] 8 13 14 24:14 17 18[2] 22 25:3 4 6[2] 26:2 3 6 8 14 27:3[2] 8 11 13 14 19 28:1 2[2] 5 7 11 12 13 14[2] 18 20 21 28[2] 30:16 18 30 31 31:2 3 11[2] 12 28 35 32:8 19[2] 33:9 12 19 21 24 34:4 6 7 17 18 22 31 36 35:2 10 14 15 36:4[2] 5[2] 14 16 18 26 37:1 4 10[2] 12 16 18 20 22 23 38:2 14 15 19[2] 21 24 26[2] 30 39:8 11 16[2] 20 22 24 30 40:11 12 16[2] 19

JOB
41:9 10[2] 11[2] 16 22 24 33[2] 34 42:3 7[2] 8

PSALMS
1:1 2 2:12 3:2 8 4:3 5:9[3] 6:3 5 7 7:2 4 8 10 11 15 8:1 4 9 9:6 15 16[2] 10:4 7[2] 11 16 11:4[2] 12:4 14:1[2] 3 5 6 15:4 16:3 5 8 9 11 17:12 13 18:2 3 30[3] 31[2] 32 34 47 19:3[3] 4 5 6[2] 7[2] 8 9 11[2] 21:5 22:11[2] 14[2] 15 28[2] 23:1 24:1 6 8 10[2] 25:8 11 12 14 26:3 10[2] 27:1[2] 28:3 7 8[2] 29:3[2] 4[2] 30:5 9 31:9 10 19 32:1[3] 2[2] 4 6 33:1 4 5 12[2] 16[2] 17 18 20 34:8[2] 9 12 16 18 20 35:10[2] 36:1 4 5

PSALMS
36:6 7 9 37:13 16 26[2] 31 33 37 39[2] 38:3[2] 7 9[2] 10 17 20 39:1 4 5[2] 7 11 40:4 7 8 41:1 42:3 6 10 11 43:5 44:15 17 18 25 45:1[2] 2 6[2] 11 13[2] 46:1 4 5 7[2] 11[2] 47:2[2] 5 7 9 48:1 2 3 10[2] 14 49:8 11 12 13 16[2] 20[2] 50:6 10 12 51:3 52 *title* 7 9 53:1[2] 3[2] 54:4[2] 6 55:4 11 15 56:9 57:4 6 7[2] 10 58:4 11[2] 59:8 17 60:7[4] 8 11 12 61:2[2] 62:2[2] 5 6[2] 7[2] 8 63:1 3 64:6 65:4 9 66:5 10 68:2 5 15 16 17 20[2] 27 34[2] 35 69:2 3 13 16 71:11 18 19[2] 73:1 4

PSALMS
73:11 25 26 28 74:9[2] 12 16[2] 75:1 7 8[3] 76:1[2] 2 12 77:8 10 13[2] 19 79:10[2] 80:16[2] 83:8 18 84:5[2] 10 11 12 85:9 12 86:8 13 87:1 88:3 89:7 8 10 11 13[2] 15 18[2] 19 34 41 47 48 90:4 6 9 10[2] 11 91:2 9 92:1 7 15[3] 93:1[3] 2 4 94:12 22[2] 95:3 4 5 7 10 96:4[2] 12 97:11 99:2[2] 3 5 9 100:3[2] 5[2] 102 *title* 4 13 103:1 5 8 11[2] 12 16 17 20 104:13 20 24 25 26 105:7 106:1 107:1 40 43 108:1 4 8[4] 9 12 13 109:19 21 22 27 111:3 4 9 10 112:1 4 7 8 113:3 4 5 115:2 3 8

PSALMS
115:9 10 11 116:5[2] 15 117:2 118:1 6 8 9 14[2] 15 16 22 23[2] 24 27 29 119:38 50 64 70 71 72 77 89 90 96 97 105 109 118 126 140 142[2] 144 155 160 174 120:5 121:5[2] 122:3[2] 123:4 124:7[2] 8 125:2 127:2 3 5 128:1 129:4 130:4 7[2] 131:1 2[2] 132:14 133:1 2 135:3[2] 5[2] 17 18 136:1 138:5 139:4 6 17 140:3 143:4[2] 10 144:3 4 8 10 11 15[4] 145:3[2] 8 9 13 17 18 146:3 5[2] 6 147:1[3] 5[2] 148:13[2]

PROV.
1:7 17 19 2:7 10 3:13 14 15 16 18[2] 19 27[2] 32[2] 33 4:7 13 16 18 19 5:3 4 6:14 23[2] 26 30 34 7:11

PROV.
7:12 19 23 27 8:4 7 8 11 13 14 19 34 9:4 10[2] 13[2] 16 17 10:1 5[2] 7 11 13[3] 14 15[2] 17 18 19 20[2] 23 25[2] 26 29 32 11:1[2] 2 8 10 11[2] 12 13 14[2] 15[2] 17 22[2] 23[2] 24[3] 30[2] 12:1 4[2] 8 9[2] 11 13 15[2] 16 18[2] 19 20[2] 26 27 28[2] 13:5 6 7[2] 10 12 14 15 17 19[2] 22 23[3] 14:2 3 4[2] 6 8[2] 9 12 13[2] 16 17[2] 20 21 23 24[2] 26 27 28[2] 29[3] 30 32 33[2] 34 35[2] 15:4[2] 5 6[2] 8[2] 9 10 13 15 16 17[2] 18 19[2] 21[2] 23 24 27 29 33[2] 16:1 5[2] 6 8

PROV.
16:10 12 14 15[2] 16 17 19 20 22 25 27 29 31 32[2] 33[3] 17:1 3 5 8 14 16 17 24 25 26 27 28[2] 18:5 7 9[3] 10[2] 11 12[2] 13 17 19 24 19:1[3] 2 4 6 10 11 12[2] 13 14 18 22[2] 26 20:1[4] 2 3 5 11 14[3] 15 16 17 18 23 25[2] 27 28 29[2] 21:1 2 3 4 5 6 8[2] 9 11[3] 15 19 20 24 27 30 31[2] 22:1 2 6 7 13 14[2] 15 18 22 23:1 5 7[2] 11 18 22 27[2] 31 24:3[2] 5 6 7 9[2] 10 13[2] 23 25:2[2] 3 7 11 12 13 14 15 16 18 19 20

PROV.
25:24 25 26 27[2] 28[2] 26:1 7 8 9 12 13[2] 16 17 19 20[2] 21 26 27:3[2] 4[3] 5 7 8 10[2] 13 21 28:3 6[2] 7[2] 11 12[2] 14 15 16 18 21 24[2] 25 26 29:6 9 18[2] 20[2] 24 27[3] 30:4[2] 5[2] 9 11 12[2] 13 14 15 16[2] 20 21 22 23[2] 28 30 31 31:4[2] 6 10 14 15 18 21 22 23 26 30[2]

ECCL.
1:2 7 8 9[4] 10 11 14 15[2] 17 18 2:1 2 15 16[2] 17[3] 19 21[3] 23 24 26[3] 3:1 2 12 13 15[3] 17 19 22[2] 4:3[2] 4[2] 6 8[6] 10 12 13 14 16[2] 5:2 3 5 8 9[2] 10 11

ECCL.
5:12 13 14 16 18[2] 19 6:1[2] 2[2] 3 7[2] 9[2] 10[4] 11 12 7:1 2[2] 3[2] 4[2] 5 6[2] 8[2] 10 11[2] 12[3] 15[2] 18 20 24 26 8:1 4[2] 6[2] 8[2] 9[2] 10 11[2] 14[3] 16[2] 17 9:1 2[3] 3[4] 4[3] 5 6[2] 9 10 11 16[2] 18 10:1 2 3[2] 5 6 10 11 13[2] 14 16 17 19 11:5[2] 7[2] 8 12:4 5 8 12[2] 13

CANT.
1:1 2 3 13 14 16 2:2 3 6 9 11[2] 12[2] 14[2] 16 3:6 7 4:1 2 3 4 7 10[2] 11 12 5:2[2] 9[2] 10 11 14 15 16[4] 6:1[2] 2 3 5 6 9[2] 10 7:2[2] 4[2] 5[2] 7 10 8:5 6[2]

CANT.
8:12[2]

ISAIAH
1:5 6 7[2] 8 11 13[2] 21 22 2:7[4] 8 12[2] 22[2] 3:7 8[2] 14 4:3[2] 5:7 16 25[3] 30 6:3[2] 5 7 7:2 8[2] 9[2] 13 18[2] 20 22 8:10 20[2] 9:5 6[2] 12[2] 15 17[3] 19 21[2] 10:4[2] 5 7 9[3] 28[2] 29[2] 32 12:1 2[3] 4 5 6 13:6 15[2] 22 14:6 7[2] 8 9 11[2] 16 26[4] 27 29 15:1[2] 2 6[2] 8 16:4 6 9 10 12[2] 13 17:1 14[2] 18:1 5[2] 19:11 20:6 21:2 9[2] 22:5 15 25 23:1[3] 3[2] 7[2] 10 14 24:5 10[2] 11[3] 12[2] 13 19[3] 25:4 7 9[2] 10 26:3 4 7 8 11 17 19 27:1 4 7 9 11 28:1 4[2] 8

ISAIAH
28:12[2] 14 20 27 28 29 29:8[2] 11[4] 12[2] 13 17 20[2] 30:7 9 14 18 21 27 29 33[3] 31:2 3 4 9 33:5 6 9[2] 17 18[3] 22[3] 23 34:1[2] 9[2] 8 36:4 6 7 37:3[2] 4 9 13 21 29 31 38:3 8 12[2] 16 22 39:4[2] 6 8 40:2[2] 6[2] 7 10 16 20 22 26 27[2] 28[2] 41:7 17 24 26[4] 42:8 10 19[3] 21 22 43:7 9 11 13 14 44:3 6 8[2] 10 12[2] 16 19 20 28 45:5[2] 6[2] 14[3] 18 21[2] 22 23 46:9[2] 47:1 4 48:2 4 22 49:4 6 7 20 50:1[3] 2[2] 4 8[2] 9 10 51:5[2] 7 13 15 18[2] 52:5[2] 6 53:1 2

ISAIAH
53:3 7[2] 54:5[2] 9 17[3] 55:2[2] 6 56:1 2 57:1 6 10 15[2] 19[2] 21 58:5[2] 6 7 59:1 5 6 8 9 11[2] 14[2] 21[2] 60:1[2] 61:1 62:11 63:1[2] 4[2] 11[2] 15 16 64:5 7 10 11 65:4 6 8[2] 66:1[4] 2 3

JER.
1:13 2:6 8 14[3] 19[2] 22 25 26[3] 34 3:6 23[2] 4:7[3] 8 18[2] 20[2] 22 31[2] 5:12 13 15[2] 16 19 27 30 6:6[2] 7[2] 10[2] 11 13 14 16 18 25 29 7:10 11[2] 14 28[3] 30 31 8:5 8[2] 9 10 11 16 18 19 20[2] 22[3] 9:6 8 12[3] 19 21[2] 10:5 6[2] 7 8 9[2] 10[2] 13 14[4] 16[4] 19[3] 20[2] 22 23[2] 11:5 9 15

JER.
11:19 12:8 9 11 13:4 10 17 20 25 14:2 4 17[2] 19[2] 15:9 10 14 18 16:10[2] 17 19 21 17:1[2] 7[2] 9 12 15 18:6 12 19:2 20:11 15 21:12 22:14 28[3] 23:6 9 10[3] 15 19 28 29 33 25:3 13 18 29 38 26:11 16 28:6 29:26 28 30:7[3] 12[2] 13 15 17 21 31:9 17 20[2] 35 32:7[2] 8[4] 14 17 18 24[2] 25 27 34 43[2] 33:2 5 11 12 16 34:8 15 36:7 37:7 14 17[2] 38:5 9[3] 14 21 40:3 4 41:17 43:9 13 44:22 23 45:3 46:7 10 17 18[2] 20 47:2 5[2] 48:1[3] 4 11 15[2] 16 17 19 20[3] 21 25[2] 29 32 33 38 39

JER.
48:41 47 49:3 7[3] 10[2] 14 19[3] 21 23[2] 24 25 29 50:2[3] 15 17 22 23[2] 25 27 31 34[2] 35 36[2] 37[2] 38[2] 44[3] 46[2] 51:6 8 9[2] 11[2] 13 16 17[4] 19[4] 31 33[2] 41[3] 42[2] 48 55 56[2] 57 52:28

LAM.
1:1 3 4 6 8 9 12[2] 14 16 17[2] 18 20[2] 21 22 2:9 11 12 13 15 16 2:3 18 20 22 23 24 25 26 27 30 37 47 4:1[2] 3 6 8[3] 15 18[2] 22 5:1 2 4 8 15[2] 16 17 18

EZEKIEL.
1:28 3:21 4:14 5:5 6:12[3] 7:2 3 5 6[3] 10[2] 11 12[2] 13[2] 14 15[3] 19 23[2] 8:17 9:6 9[2] 10:15 20

EZEKIEL
11:3[2] 7 15 23 12:12 19 22 23 27 13:12[2] 15 16 15:2[2] 4[3] 5 16:7 20 30 34[2] 44[2] 46[2] 17:12 18:4 5 9 10 18 19 21 25[2] 27 29 19:2 10 13 14[2] 20:6 15 29[2] 21:9 10[2] 11[2] 13 14 15[2] 16 25 26[2] 27 28[2] 29 22:18 22 24 25 23:4 20[2] 22 28 37 45 24:6[2] 7 13 24 27 25:8 26:2[3] 10 15 28:5 29:3 9 30:3[2] 5 12 31:10 18 32:16 20 22 23 24 25 26 29 33:6 14 16 17[2] 19 20 21 24 27 30 34:5 12 36:35 37:11 19 38:8[3] 39:4 8[3] 40:45[2] 46[2] 41:4 22[2] 42:13 15 43:4 12[2] 13 44:3 9 22 26

EZEKIEL
44:31
45:13
14
20
46:11
20
47:16[2]
17
18
19
20
48:12
14
22
29
35

DANIEL
2:5
8
9
10[2]
11[3]
15
22
28
30
36
43
45
47[2]
3:4
14
15
17
25
29
4:3[2]
8
9
17
18
22[2]
24[3]
30
31[2]
34[2]
37
5:11[2]
14[2]
23
25
26
28
6:12
13
15
20
26
7:14
27
28
8:2
21[3]
26
9:11[2]
13[2]
14
17
18
10:4
14
17
21[2]
11:35
36
12:12

HOSEA
2:2
4:1
13
17
18
5:1
3[2]
4
6:3
4
8[2]
10[2]
7:7
8
11
8:3
5
6
8[2]
9:7[2]
8
13
15
16[2]
10:1
2
5
7
10
11[2]
12
11:8
12
12:1
5
7
13:3
4

HOSEA
13:8
9
10
12[2]
13
14:4
8
9

JOEL
1:5
6
9
10[3]
11
12[2]
13
15
16
17[2]
2:1
3
4
11[3]
13
17
3:13[3]
14

AMOS
2:11
13[2]
15
16
3:5
4:3
13[2]
5:2[3]
8
11
12
13
18[2]
27
6:8
10[2]
7:2
5
10
13[2]
8:2
9:5
6[2]
9
11

OBADIAH
1
3
7
15
20

JONAH
1:2
7
8[3]
12
2:9
3:8
4:3
8

MICAH
1:2
5[3]
9[3]
13
2:1[2]
3
7
8
10[2]
13
3:1
8
11
4:6
9[2]
5:2
6:8
10
12
7:1[2]
2[2]
4[2]
10[2]
18

NAHUM
1:2[2]
3
5
6
7
11
15
2:1
3
8
9
10[2]
11
3:1
3[2]
7
17

NAHUM
3:18
19[2]

HABAK.
1:4
13
16
2:3
4[2]
5[2]
6
13
19
20
3:19

ZEPH.
1:7
8
14[2]
15
2:5
15[3]
3:1
5
6[2]
8
15
17

HAGGAI
1:2
4
6
9
10[2]
2:3[2]
6
8[2]
13
14[4]
19

ZECH.
1:7
11
2:2[2]
13
3:2
4:1
6
5:2
3
5
6[3]
7
8
6:12
7:13
8:23[2]
9:9
11
17[2]
10:5
7
11:2[2]
3[3]
9
16
12:8
10
13:7
8
9[4]
14:4
16

MALACHI
1:6[2]
7
8[2]
10
12[2]
13
14
2:1
7
11
14
17[2]
3:2
14[2]

MATT.
1:16
20[2]
23
2:2[2]
5
3:2
3
9
10[2]
11
12
17
4:4
6
7
10
13
16
17
5:3
10
12
13

MATT.
5:14
16
22
29
30
32
34
35[2]
37
45
48[2]
6:1
6
10
13
18
21
22
23[2]
25
30[2]
34
7:3[2]
4
6
9
11
12
13
14[2]
19
21
8:27
9:5
15
16[2]
18
24
37
10:2
7
10
11
20
24
25
26
28
32
35
37[2]
38
11:6
10[2]
11[2]
14
16
19
30[2]
12:2
6
8
10
12[2]
18
23
25
26
28
30[2]
33
41
42
43
44
45
48
50[2]
13:11[2]
14
15
19
20
21
22
23
24
31
32[3]
33
37
38
39[2]
44
45
47
52[3]
55[2]
57
14:2[2]
4
15[2]
26
27
15:5
8
17
22
26
28
16:2[2]
3
7
11
17
26
17:4

MATT.
17:5
12
15
18:1
4
8
9
10
11
12
14[2]
19
23
19:3
9
10
11
12
14
17[2]
24
26
20:1[2]
4
7
14
15[2]
23[2]
21:9
10
11
13
20
21
38
42[3]
22:2
8
17
20
23
32
36
38
39
42
45
23:8
9[2]
10
11
15
16[2]
17
18[2]
19
26
38
39
24:6
17
18
23
26[2]
28
32[2]
33
45
46
50
25:14
25
26:2[2]
8
18
22
24[2]
25
26
28[2]
31
38
41[2]
45[2]
46
48
62
66
68
27:4
6[2]
17
22
33
37
46
64
28:6[2]
7
15
18

MARK
1:2
15[2]
27[2]
2:9
16
19
21
22
24
26
28
3:4
17
21

MARK
3:29
33
35
4:11
15
21
22
26
29[2]
31[3]
32
40
41
5:9[2]
35
39
41
6:2[2]
3
4
15[2]
16[2]
18
35[2]
50
7:2
6[2]
11[2]
15
27
29
34
8:16
21
9:5
7
12
13[2]
21
26
31[2]
39
40[2]
42
43
44
45
46
47
48
50
10:2
14
18[2]
24
25
27
29
40[2]
11:9
17
21
25
26
12:7
10
11
14
16
18
27
28
29[2]
30
31[2]
32[2]
33
35
37
13:11
15
16
21[2]
28[2]
29
33
34
14:8
14
19[2]
20
21[2]
22
24[2]
27
34
38[2]
41[3]
42
44
58
60
69
15:22
34
42
16:6[2]
16

LUKE
1:13
28
36
42
43
45
49[2]

LUKE
1:50
61[2]
63
2:4
11[2]
15
23
24
34
49
3:4
8
9[2]
13
17
4:4
6
8
10
12
18
21
22
24
36
5:21
23
34
39
6:2
4
5
9
20
23
35
36
40[2]
41[2]
42[3]
44
45[2]
47
48
49
7:16
22
23
27
28[3]
34
35
39[2]
47
49
8:10
11[2]
17
25[2]
26
30
46
49
52
9:9
19
25
33
35
38
48
50[2]
56
62
10:2
7
9
11
22[2]
26
29
42
11:4
6
7
8
11
17
20
23[2]
24
26
27
29
31
32
34[5]
35
39
40[2]
12:1
2
6
21[2]
23[2]
26
27
28[2]
32
34
42
43
46
48
54
56
57

LUKE
13:18
19
21
25
35[2]
14:3
15
22[2]
29
32
34
35
15:4
10
24[2]
27
31
32[2]
16:2
10[5]
12[2]
15[2]
16
17
18
25
26
17:1
7
21
30
31
37
18:16
19[2]
25
29
19:7
9[2]
10
20
46[2]
20:2
14
17[3]
22
27
33
38
41
44
21:9
20
30
31
37
22:1
11
19[2]
20[2]
21
22
26[2]
27[2]
37
38
53
59
64
23:2
15
33
38
24:6[2]
21
29[2]
34
39
46

JOHN
1:15
18
19
27
30[2]
33
34
38
41
42
47
2:4
10
3:4
6[4]
8[2]
13
18[3]
19[2]
29[2]
31[4]
33
4:5
9
10
11
18
20
22
23
24
25[2]
29
34
37
42

JOHN
4:54
5:2[2]
7
10[2]
12
24
25[2]
27
28
30
31
32[2]
45
6:1
7
9
14
20
29
31
33
39
40
42[2]
45
46
50
51
55[2]
58
60
70
7:4
6[2]
8
11
12
16
18[2]
22
25
26
27[2]
28
36
40
41
8:7
13
14
16
17[2]
19
26
29
34
39
44[2]
47
50
52
53
54[3]
9:4
7
8
9[2]
11
12
16[2]
17
19
20
21
23
24
29
30[2]
36
37
10:1
2
12
13
20
29[2]
34
38
11:3
4
10
14
16
28
50
12:13
14
19
23
27
31
34
35
50
13:10[2]
16[2]
19
25
26
31[2]
14:21
22
24
26
28
29
15:1

JOHN
15:6[2]
8
12
20
25
26
16:7
8
11
13
17
18
21[4]
32
17:1
3
12
17
18:31
36[2]
37
38
19:13
17
30
35
40
20:16
31
21:7
14
20
22
23
24[2]

ACTS
1:7
8
11
12
19[2]
20
2:15
16
25
29[2]
34
39
3:2
11
16
4:9
11[2]
12[2]
16
24
36
5:9
17
32
6:2
9
7:33
34
37
38
40
42
49[3]
8:10
21
26
33
36
37
9:5
11
15
20
21
22
36
10:4
5
6
14
21
28[2]
30
32[2]
34
35
36
11:13
12:15
22
13:8
9
11
26
33
38
40
15:15
16
17
19
16:12
17:3
7
19
24
25
29
10:4
27

ACTS
19:28
34
35[2]
38
20:10
32
35
21:22
28
22:22
25
26
23:5
8
19
25:14
16[2]
26:14
18
27:8
12
16
33
34
28:4
22
27
28

ROMANS
1:8
9
12
15
16
17[2]
18
19
25
26
27
2:2
11
24[2]
25
27
28[4]
29[4]
3:1
4
5
8
10[2]
11[2]
12
13[2]
14
18
20
21
22[2]
24
27[2]
28
29[2]
30
4:4
5
8
14
15[2]
16[4]
17
5:5[2]
13[2]
14
15
16[2]
6:6
7[2]
21
23[2]
7:2[2]
3[2]
4
7
12
13
14
16
17
18[3]
20
21
23
8:1
6[2]
7[2]
9
10[2]
24[2]
27
33
34[4]
36
39
9:5
8
9
13
14
16
30
33
10:1
2
4

ROMANS
10:5
6[2]
7
8[2]
10
12[2]
15
20
11:5
6[4]
8
11
16
24
25
26
27
12:1
2
3
6
9[2]
19[2]
13:1
3
4[3]
7
9
10
11[2]
12[2]
14:1
2
4
11
14[2]
17
18
20
21[3]
22
23[3]
15:3
9
15
21
27
16:1[2]
5[2]
19[2]
25
26

1 COR.
1:2
4
9
13
18[2]
19
20[3]
25[2]
30
31
2:9
11
12
15[2]
3:3
5[2]
7
10
11[2]
13
17
19[2]
23
4:2
3
4
6
17
20
5:1[3]
6
7
11
6:5
7
13
16[2]
17
18
19[2]
7:1
8
9
14[2]
15
18[2]
19[2]
22[4]
24
26[2]
29
32
33
34[2]
35
39[2]
40
8:3
4[2]
6
7[2]
10
9:3

1 COR.
9:9
10
11
16
17
18
25
10:7
13[2]
16[2]
19[3]
25
26
27
28[2]
29
11:3[3]
5
7[2]
8
11
12[2]
13
14
15[2]
20
21[2]
24[2]
25
12:3
6
7
8
12[2]
14
15
16
13:4[2]
5
10[3]
13
14:5
7
9
10
14
15
17
21
24[2]
25
26
33
34
35
15:12
13
14[2]
16
17
20
26
27[2]
36
39[2]
40[2]
41
42[3]
43[4]
44[4]
45
46[3]
47[2]
48[2]
54[2]
55[2]
56[2]
58
16:9
15
19

2 COR.
1:1
6[3]
7
12
18
21
2:2
3
6
16
3:5
11[2]
13
14
15[2]
17[3]
4:3
4
13
16
17
5:2
5
13[2]
17
6:2[2]
11[2]
7:4[2]
14
15
8:10
12
15
18

2 COR.
8:19
20
23
9:1
8
9
12
10:6
7[2]
10
15[2]
18
11:3
10
14
15
21
29[2]
31
12:1
4
9[2]
13
13:1
3[2]
5
7

GAL.
1:7
11
2:16
17
21
3:10[2]
11[2]
12
13[2]
16
18
20[2]
21
25
28[2]
4:1
2
15
18
22
24
25[3]
26[3]
27
29
5:3[2]
4
11
14
22
23
6:3
6
7
14

EPHES.
1:14
18
19
21[2]
23
2:4
8
11
14
3:2
5
8
9
13
15
18
20
4:4
6
7
9
10
15
18
21
22
24
28
29
5:5
9
10
12
13
17
18
23[3]
24
6:1
2
9[2]
17

PHIL.
1:7
8
18
21[2]
22
23
24
28

PHIL.
1:29
2:9
11
13
3:1[2]
6
9[3]
19[3]
20
21
4:5

COLOS.
1:5
6[2]
7
15
17
18[2]
23
24[2]
25
26
27[2]
2:10
17
3:3
4
5
10
11[2]
14
18
20
25
4:1
7
9
11
12
15
16

1 THESS.
1:1
8
2:5
13
16
19
3:10
4:3
6
5:15
18
21
24

2 THESS.
1:3
5
6
2:2
4[3]
9
3:1
3
17

1 TIM.
1:1
4
5
8
9
10
14
15
20
2:3
5
3:1
13
15
16
4:4
5
8[3]
9
10
14
5:4
5
6
8
18
6:3
4
5
6
7
10
15
20
subscr.

2 TIM.
1:1
5
6
10
12
13
2:1
5

2 TIM.
2:9
10
11
17
18
3:15
16[2]
4:6
8
10
11[2]

TITUS
1:1
3
13
15[2]
2:8
3:8
10
11[2]

PHILE.
6
8
12

HEB.
1:8[2]
2:6
8
11
14
18
3:4[2]
13
15
4:7
10
12[2]
13[2]
14
5:1
2
4
13[2]
6:4
7
8[3]
10
16
20
7:2
5
6
7
8
12
14
15
16
18
25
26
28
8:1[2]
3[2]
6
10
13
9:2
3
11
15
16
17[2]
20
22
23
24
27
10:3
4
7
15
16
18[2]
20
23
25
31
11:1
6[3]
7
10
12
16[2]
18
27
12:1
2
7
13
29
13:4
6
9
11
15
16
17
21
23

JAMES
1:6
8
9

JAMES
1:10
11
12[2]
13
14[2]
15
17[2]
21
23
26
27
2:10
17
19
20
24
26[2]
3:2
5
6[3]
7
8
13
15
16[2]
17[2]
18
4:4[2]
12[2]
14[2]
16
17
5:3
4
11
13[2]
14

1 PETER
1:13
15
16
24
25[2]
2:3
6
7[2]
15
19
20[2]
22
3:4[2]
12
13[2]
15
17
20
22[2]
4:5
7
12
14[2]
17
5:2
12
13

2 PETER
1:4
9
17
20
2:17
19[2]
20
22[2]
3:4
8
9[2]
15

1 JOHN
1:3
5[3]
7
8
9
10
2:2
4[2]
5
7
8[2]
9[2]
10
11
13
14
15
16[3]
18[2]
21
22[3]
25
27[2]
29[2]
3:2
3
4
5
7[2]
8
9[3]
10
11
15
20

1 JOHN
3:23
4:2[2]
3[4]
4[3]
6
7[2]
8
10
12
15
16
17[2]
18[2]
20
5:1[3]
3
4[2]
5[2]
6[3]
9[2]
11[2]
14
16[2]
17[2]
18[2]
20[4]

2 JOHN
6[2]
7
11

3 JOHN
3
11[3]
12

JUDE
13
24

REV.
1:3[2]
4[2]
5
8[2]
9
2:7
8
13
3:7[2]
12
4:8[2]
5:2
12
13
6:13
14
17
7:17
8:11
9:11[2]
12
13
19
10:8
11:2[2]
8
14
18
12:10[2]
12
14
13:4[2]
10
18[3]
14:7
8[2]
10
12
15[2]
17
15:1
16:15
17
17:8[3]
9
10[2]
11[3]
14
18
18:2[3]
8
10
17
18
19
19:7
8
10
13
20:2
5
6
8
12
14
21:3
6[2]
8
16
17
23
22:7
10
11[4]
12
17

it 846

GEN.
1:4 6 7 9 10 11 12 15 18 21 24 25 28 29 30 31 $2:3^2$ 5^3 10 11 13 14 15 17 18 3:3 6 15 17^2 18 19 4:3 8 12 14 6:1 6^2 7 12 14 15^2 16^2 21 7:4 10 17 8:6 13 9:5 13 14 16 23 10:9 11:2 9 12:11 12 13 14 13:10 15 17 14:1 15:6 7 8 17 16:2 6 10 14 17:11 18:6 7 8 10 11 21 28 29 30 31 32 19:13 17 20^2 29 34 20:13 15 21:12 14 16 22 26 22:1 6 14 20 23:8 9 11^2 13^2 24:14 15 22 30 43 52 65 25:11 22 26:8

GEN.
26:21 22 32 33 27:1 4 5 10 20^2 25^2 30 31 33 40 $28:12^2$ 13^2 16 18 29:2 7 10 13 19 23 25 26 30:15 25 28 30 33 34 35 41 31:2 5 10 22 29 32 35 37 39 44 45 47^2 48 32:8 18 29 33:11 15 20 34:7 21 25 35:8 12 17 18 22^2 37:5 9 10 14 21 23 24 25 26 32^2 33^2 38:1 9^2 13 17 18 23 24^2 27 28 29 39:5 7 10 11 13 15 18 19 22 23 40:1 8 10^2 12 14 20 41:1 7 8 13^2 15^2 16 21 24 31 32^2 42 49 42:6 14 27 28

GEN.
42:35 42:2 11 12^2 21^2 44:5 9 10^2 24 31 45:8 12 16 28 46:33 47:18 24 26 48:1 14 17^2 19^2 49:4 7^2 15 28 50:9 11 20^2

EXOD.
1:10 16^2 21 $2:3^2$ 5 6 9^2 11 18 20 23 3:21 $4:3^4$ 4^3 6 7^2 8 9^2 24 25 5:11 19 22 $6:8^2$ 28 $7:9^2$ 10 8:10 16 17 26 9:8 9 10^2 18 24^2 28 10:10 13 $11:6^2$ 12:2 4 5 6^2 7^2 8 9 10^2 11^3 14^2 22 25 26 27 29 34 39 41^2 42 46 47 48 51 13:2 5 9 11^2 13 14 15 16 17 14:2 5 12 16 20^3 24 27 15:23 $16:5^2$ 10 13

EXOD.
$16:15^3$ 16 18 19 20^2 21^2 22 24^2 25 26^2 27 31^2 32 33 34 17:6 11 12 14 15 18:13 18 22 19:12 13^3 16 18 23 20:8 10 11 18 25^3 21:26 29 31 33 34 35 36 $22:1^2$ 4 7 9 10^2 11^2 12 13^2 14^3 15^4 26 27^2 30^2 31 23:4 11 13 15 23 24:6 8 10^2 16 25:2 9 11^3 12^3 15 24 25 26 32 36 37 39 26:6 11 13^2 24^2 31 32 $27:2^2$ 4 5 7 8^3 21^2 $28:7^2$ 8 15^2 16 17 25 28 32^5 33 35 36 37^3 38^2 43 29:7 12 14 16 18^2 20 21 22 25 26^2 28^3 34^2 36^3

EXOD.
$29:37^2$ 30:1 2 3^2 4^5 6 7 8 10^3 16^2 18 21 25^2 32^5 33^2 35 36^3 37 31:13 14^2 17 $32:4^2$ 5^2 8 9 13 18^2 19 20^4 24^3 30 33:1 7^3 8 9 16^2 22 34:9 10 12 29 35:5 24 36:2 3 6 7 13 18 35 38 $37:1^3$ 2^2 3^4 11 13 21 22 24 25^4 26^4 27^3 38:1 2^2 4 7 8 21 30 $39:3^2$ 4^3 5 9 10 18 19 20 21 23 30 31^2 43^2 40:4 9^2 10 11 17 19 23 29 37 38

LEVIT.
1:3 4 6 10 11 12 13^3 15^2 16 17^4 2:1 2^2 3 4 5 6^2 7 8^2 9^2 10

LEVIT.
$2:15^2$ 16^2 $3:1^3$ 2 4 5^2 6 7 8 9 10 11^2 12 13^2 15 16 17 4:5 8 9 10 14 17 19 20 21 24^2 25 26 30 31^2 32 33 34 35 $5:1^2$ 2^2 3^3 4^3 5 8 9 10 11^2 12^4 13 16^2 17 18^2 19 6:3 4 5^3 7 9^2 12^4 13 14 15^3 16^2 17 18^2 20 21^3 22^3 23 25 26^3 27 28^3 29 30 7:1 3 4 5 6^2 7 9 12 14^2 15^2 16^2 18^5 19 24 25 26 27 30 8:7 15^4 16 19 21 23^3 28 29^2 30 31^2 9:1 9 15^2 16 17 10:3 9 12^2 13^2 15^2 16 17^2 18^2 19

LEVIT.
$11:32^6$ 33^2 35 37 38 40^2 41 12:7 13:2 3 6 8 10 11 13 15 19 20^3 21^2 22^2 23 25^4 26^2 27^2 28^3 30^3 31^2 32 39 42 43 47 48 49 50 51 52^2 54 55^5 56 57^2 58^2 59^2 14:6 9 13 14 15 25 35^2 36 43 44^2 45 46 48 53 57^2 15:3 23^2 25 16:12 14 15 18^2 19^3 29 31 17:3 4 9^2 11^2 13 14^3 15 18:8 16 17 22 23 25 28^2 19:5 6^3 7^3 8 23^2 25 20:14 17 21 24^2 21:24 22:7 9^2 11 14^2 20 21 23 27^2 28^2 29 30^2 23:3 11 14 21^2 27 28 29 30 31 32

LEVIT.
23:36 41^3 $24:3^2$ 7 8 9^3 18 19 20 21 25:5 10 11^2 12^2 16 21 25 26^2 27 28^3 29^3 30^3 34 50 26:1 16 32 34 35^4 37 27:4 5 6 7^2 9 10^3 11 12^4 13 14^4 15^3 17 18 19^3 20 21 24 26^3 27^5 30 33^5

NUM.
$1:50^2$ 51^2 3:26 4:5 6 9 10^2 11 14^4 15 25 $5:7^2$ 10 13 15^2 17 25 26 27 6:9 18 $7:1^3$ 5 10 84 88 8:24 $9:3^3$ 11^2 12^3 15 16 20 21^2 22^2 10:11 29 32^2 35 36 $11:1^2$ 8^6 9 14 17^2 18 20^2 25^2 31^3 33 12:2 13:18 19 20 23 27^2 30^2 32^2 14:3 7 8

NUM.
14:11 13 14 23 24 35 41 15:11 19 20 24 25^2 26 28 34 39^2 16:4 7 9 13 31 42^2 17:5 8 $18:10^3$ 11 13 15 19 23 26 27 29 30^2 31^2 32^3 19:6 9^2 10 12 15 18^2 21 22 20:5 8 19 $21:8^3$ 9^2 14 17 18 28 34 41 $23:19^2$ 20 22 23 27 24:1 8 25:7 13 26:1 $27:11^2$ 13 28:6 24 29:1 11 $30:7^2$ 8 11 13^2 $31:23^3$ 29^2 54 $32:39^2$ 42 33:53 55 56 34:5 12 35:23 25 33^2 36:3 9

DEU.
1:3 17^2 21 24 25^2 36 39^2 2:16 19 24 3:9 11^2 26 27 4:2 5 14 26^2 32 35 38 39

DEU.
4:40 5:12 14 16 23 27^2 29 31 33 6:1 3^2 10 18 24 6:25 7:1 12 25^2 26^4 8:9 18^2 19 9:6 11 13 21^4 10:15 8 11:10 11 12 13 29^2 31 12:1 16 24^2 25 28 32^2 13:14 15 16^3 $14:8^2$ 10 21^3 24 25 28 $15:2^3$ 3 4 9 16 17 18 20 21^2 22^2 23 16:3 7 $17:4^3$ 14 18 19 18:3 19 22 19:2 13 14 20:2 5^2 6^2 9 10^2 11^3 12^2 13 19^2 20 $21:1^2$ 3 7 14 16 $22:2^4$ 7 23:11 13 16 20 21^3 22 $24:1^2$ 3 13 15^3 19 20 21^2 25:2 6 8 9 19^3 $26:1^2$ 2 4 10 12 27:2 4

DEU.
27:15 28:1 15 21 24 38 63^2 67^2 68 29:8 19 22 23 27 28 30:1 5 11^2 12^4 13^4 14 16 18 31:6 7 8 9 13 19^2 21^2 22 24 26^2 32:19 27 47^3 $34:4^2$

JOSH.
1:1 7 11 15 2:2 5^2 14 19 21 3:2 3^2 4^2 13 34 4:1 7 11 18 24 5:1 8 13 6:5 8 11 15 16 17 18 20 26 7:9 11 14 15 19 21 22^2 8:2 5 7 8 14^2 18 19 24^2 25 28 29 31 9:1 12^2 16 24 25 $10:1^2$ 2 4 5 11 14^2 17 18 20 24 27 28 30^3 31^2 32^2 34^2 35^2 36 37^3 38

JOSH.
10:39 11:1 20 23 12:6 13:6 14:7 15:3 4 16 17 18 16:6 7 17:9 10^2 13 18^3 18:4 5 8 9 20 19:14 47^3 21:11 12 18 22 23 24 27 28^2 30 34 43 23:1 10 15 24:4 15 17 26 27^2 29 32

JUD.
1:1 8^2 12 13 14 17 28 2:4 18 19 22 3:16 21 27 4:20 21 6:3 5 7 11 18 19^2 24^2 25^2 27^3 28 30 31 37 38 39 40 7:4 9^2 13^3 15 17 $8:27^2$ 33 9:7 25 33 42 45 47 48^2 50 51 52^2 11:4 5 23 31^2 35 39^2 12:5 6 13:16 18 19 20^2 14:4 11 12^2 13^2 15^2

JUD.
$14:16^3$ 17 15:1 15 17 $16:2^2$ 4 9 14 16 25 29 17:2 3 18:2 9 10 12 19 28^2 19:1 5 11 26 30^3 20:9 28 21:4 22

RUTH
1:1 13 19 2:6 11 17 18 22 3:1 4 8 12 13 14 15^3 $4:4^6$ 5 6^2 7 8 16^2 17

1 SAM.
1:12 20 2:14 16^2 19 24 30 36 3:2 9 11 17 18 $4:3^2$ 13 18 20 5:1 2^2 7 9^2 10 11^2 6:2 3^2 8^3 9^3 13 15 16 21 7:1 2^2 6 7 9 12^2 8:1 9:20 23 24^4 26 $10:1^2$ 5 7 9 11 12 25^2 11:2 7 9 11^2 12:3 6 15 17 22 13:3

1 SAM.
13:10 22 14:1 6 14 15 19 27 39 $15:11^2$ 12 27 28 16:2 6 16 18^2 23 17:25 27 35 39 48 49 51 54 18:1 4 6 10 11 19 23 26 30 19:5 13^2 19 21 $20:2^2$ 4 7 9^2 12 13^2 16 27 33 35 $21:5^3$ 6 9^3 22:1 15 17 22 23:6 7 13 22 23 $24:1^2$ 4 5 11 16 25:11 20 27 30 37 38 $26:12^2$ 17 22 27:4 28:1 14 17 24^2 25 29:4 $30:1^2$ 8 25^2 31:4 8 9

2 SAM.
1:1 2^2 18 20^2 2:1 23 26^2 3:18 24 26 28 29 35 36^2 37 4:4 12 5:9 24 6:3 4 6^2 10 12

2 SAM.
6:13 17^2 21 7:1 4 15 25 29^3 8:1 $10:3^2$ 5 7 17 11:1 2 14 16 25 $12:3^2$ 4 12 15 18 21 28 29^2 30 13:1 2 5^2 8 23 30 35 36 $14:15^2$ 26^3 30 32 15:1 2 5 7 25 32 35^2 16:11 12 16 $17:9^3$ 13 21 27 18:3 10 18 29 19:1 6 19 25 36 $20:8^2$ 15 20^2 22 21:1 10 11 18 22:9 48 23:5 12 16^3 17^2 24:3 12 16^2 24

1 KINGS
1:11 18 21 27 41 48 51 2:3 15 29 37 39 41 3:6 15 18 19 20 21^3 26^3 27 5:7 6:1 7 9 14 16 17 20 21 38 7:3

1 KINGS
7:7 23^2 24^3 25 26^2 27 31^2 8:10 15 17 18 24^2 54 9:1 8 10 16^2 28 10:6 7 18 21 11:4 11 12^2 15 29 30 35 38 $12:2^2$ 10 20 28 13:3 4^2 6 9 17 20 23 24 25 26 29^2 31 34^2 14:5 6 8 10 11 25 28 15:13 21 29 16:11 18 31^2 17:4 7 11 12^2 13 17 18:1 4 6 12 13 17 23^3 24 25 26 27 29 33 34^4 36^2 39 44 45 19:4 10 13^2 14 17 20:1 6^3 11 12 13 26 29 33 40 21:1 2^6 3 6^2 11 15 16^2 18 27 22:2 3 6 12 15 32^2 33^2

1 KINGS
22:43

2 KINGS
1:3 6 8 16 2:1 3 5 8 9 10^2 11 12 20 3:5 14 15 20 25^3 4:6 8^2 10 11 18 23^2 25 26^4 27 40 41 44 5:7 8 13 16 26 6:5 6^2 7^2 13 20 24 25 30 7:2 7 8^2 11 13 18 19 20 8:1 3 5 7 15^3 9:3 12 13 15^3 17 18 19 22^2 30 10:7 9 15^2 19 20 25 27 11:6 18 12:5 6 7 9^2 10 11 12 16 17 18 13:16 17 19 21 14:5 17 22 26 15:12 16 16:8 9^2 10 11 14 15 17^2 17:5 7 25 18:1 4^2 9^2 10 16 21^2 25^2

2 KINGS
18:26 $19:1^2$ 4 14^2 25^3 26 32^2 34 35 37 20:4 7 10 11 19 21:12 13^2 22:3 5^2 8 9 10 11 $23:6^2$ 15 16 17 21 35 24:2 11 20 $25:1^3$ 17 24 25 27

1 CHRON.
4:10 6:10 55 7:23 9:32 10:4 8 13 11:7 14 18^4 19^3 12:15 17 22 $13:2^2$ 3 6 13 14:8 15 15:1 3 12 13 26 29 $16:1^2$ 19 30 17:3 11 13 24 27^3 18:1 19:1 8 17 $20:1^2$ 2^3 3 4 8 21:2 10 15^2 17^2 22 23^2 24 30 22:5 7 14 23:26 26:28 27:24 28:8 10 20 29:12

2 CHRON.
$1:4^2$ 5 6 2:4 16^2 $3:4^2$ 8 4:2 3^3 4

LUKE 18:15 25 26 35 36 43 19:7 15 24 29 41 46[2] 20:1 4 7 9 13 16 18[2] 22 24 21:5 13 14 21 35 22:16 17 19 22 23 36 38 44 64 66 23:3 24 26

LUKE 23:44 53[3] 24:4 10 15 21 24 29 30[2] 39 43 46[2] 51 **JOHN** 1:5 27[2] 32 39 2:5 8 9 17 19 20 3:8[3] 27 4:6 9 10 53 5:10[2] 13 15 6:17 20 31 39 42

JOHN 6:45 60 61 63 65 71 7:7[2] 10 17 22 51 8:9 17 44 54 56 9:4 14 27 32 37 10:10 17 18[4] 22[2] 34 11:2 22 38[2] 42 50 57 12:13 14 24[3] 25 28[2] 29[2] 13:19[2]

JOHN 13:24 25 26[3] 30 14:2 8 14 17 21 22 27 29[2] 15:2[2] 4 7 16 18[2] 16:7 14 15 23 26 18:10 11 14 18 25 28 31 34 19:2 11 14 19 20 24[3] 29[2] 30 31

JOHN 19:35 40 20:1 14 27 21:4 6 7[2] 8 12 **ACTS** 1:7 19 20 2:2 3 15 17 21 24[2] 3:10 12 17 23 4:3 5 10 14 16 17 19 37[2] 5:2[2] 4[4] 7 9 38 39[2]

ACTS 6:12 15 7:5[2] 23 31[2] 42 44 53 9:5 6 18 32 37 42 43 10:4 11 28 42 11:4 5[2] 26 30 12:3 9 15[2] 18 22 13:17 33 38 41 46 14:1 6 15:5 15 16 22

ACTS 15:25 28 34 16:16 35 17:14 18:14 15[2] 19:1 19 39 20:16 35 21:1 3 20 22 35 22:6 10 17 22 25 23:5 12 30 31 24:3 21 25:16 27 26:8 14 27:1 8 14 25[2] 28[2] 35

ACTS 27:39[2] 44 28:8 17 19 22 28[2] **ROMANS** 1:16 17 19 2:24 27 3:4 10 19 27 30 4:3 10 16[2] 17 22 23[2] 24 5:16 6:12 7:11 12 16 17[2] 20[2] 8:3 7 25 33 34 36

ROMANS 9:12 13 16 20 26[2] 28 32[2] 33 10:8 15 11:6[3] 7 8 26 35 12:8 16 19 13:9 11 14:6[2] 11 14 20 21 22 15:3 9 21 26 27 **1 COR.** 1:11 18 19 21 31

1 COR. 2:8 9 3:2 13[3] 19 4:2 3 7[2] 9 12 5:1 6:5 13 7:1 5 8 9 21[2] 26 29 31 8:7 9:9 10 11 15 25 27 10:7 13 16[2] 28 11:6 13 14 15 18 24 25

1 COR. 12:6 15 16 18 26[2] 13:3 8 14:7 9 10 15 21 26 27 34 35 36 15:11 27 32 36 37 38[2] 42[2] 43[4] 44[2] 45 16:4 6 15 **2 COR.** 1:6[2] 2:10[2] 3:16 4:3 13 5:10 13[2]

2 COR. 7:8 11 12 8:11 12 15 9:1 5 9 11:15 17[2] 12:1 4 8 13 16 **GAL.** 1:12[2] 13 15 2:6 3:4 5 6 10 11 13 15[2] 17 18[2] 19[2] 4:15 18 22 27 29

EPHES. 2:8 3:5 4:9 29 5:3 12 25 26 27[2] 29 32 6:3 **PHIL.** 1:6 7 20 27 29 2:6 13 23 25 3:1 21 *subscr.* **COLOS.** 1:6[3] 9 19 2:14 15 3:18 23 4:4 16 17

1 THESS. 2:1 13[2] 3:1 4 4:10 5:24 **2 THESS.** 1:3 6 3:1 **1 TIM.** 1:8 13 4:4 5 5:16 6:7 **2 TIM.** 2:11 4:16 **TITUS** *subscr.* **PHILE.** 14 19[2] **HEB.** 2:10 17

HEB. 3:13 15 17 4:1 2 6[2] 7 6:4 7[2] 17 18 7:8 11 14 15 8:3 9:5 17 23 27 10:4 7 31 11:2 4 6 18 12:11 13 17 20 13:9 17 **JAMES** 1:2 5 11[2] 15[2]

JAMES 2:14 16 17 23 3:6[2] 8 4:3 14 17[2] 5:3 7 17[2] **1 PETER** 1:7 11 12 16 2:6 13 20[4] 3:3 4 11 17 4:4 11 12 17 **2 PETER** 1:13 2:13 21[2] 22

1 JOHN 1:2 2:18[2] 21 27 3:1 2 4:3[2] 5:6 16 **2 JOHN** 6 **JUDE** 3 **REV.** 1:9 11 2:17 3:8 4:1 5:6 6:1 11 14 7:2 8:3 5[2] 8 10[2] 12 9:4 5 6

REV. 9:7 9 10:1 9[4] 10[3] 11:2[2] 6 12:4 13:3 7 18 14:3 19 15:2 16:3 17 18:21 19:6 10 15 20:11 13 21:6 16 18 21 22 23[2] 24[2] 25 26 27 22:2 3 9

me

1691 or 3165

GEN. 3:12 13 4:10 14[2] 25 6:7 13 7:1 9:12 13 15 17 12:12 13 18[2] 19 13:8 9 14:21 24 15:2 3 9 16:2 5 13[2] 17:1 2 4 7 10 11 18:21 27 31 19:8 19[2] 20 20:5 6 9[2] 11 13[3] 21:6 16 23[3] 26 30 22:12 23:4 8 9[2] 11 13[2] 15[2] 24:5 7[2] 12 17 23 27 30 37 39 40 43 44 45 48[2] 49[2] 54 56[2] 25:30

GEN. 25:31 32 33 26:7 27 27:3 4 7 9 12[2] 13[2] 19[2] 20 25 26 31 33 34 36[2] 38 46 28:20[2] 22 29:15 19 21 25[2] 27 32 33 34 30:1 6[2] 13 14 16 18 20[2] 24 25 26[2] 27 28 29 31[2] 33[2] 31:5[2] 7[2] 9 11 13 26 27 28 29 31 32 35 36 40 42[2] 44 48 49 50 51 52 32:9 11[2] 16 20[2] 26[2] 29

GEN. 33:10 11 13 14 15[3] 34:4 11[2] 12[3] 30[4] 35:3[2] 37:9 14 16 38:16[2] 17 39:7 8 9 12 14[2] 15 17[2] 18 19 40:8 9 14[4] 15 41:10[2] 13 16 24 51 52 42:20 33 34 36[2] 43:6 8 9 16 29 44:21 27 28 29 34 45:1 4 5[2] 7 8[2] 9[2] 10 18 46:30 31 47:29[2] 30[2] 31 48:3[2] 4 7[2] 9[2] 15 16 29 50:5[4] 20 **EXOD.** 2:9

EXOD. 2:14 3:9 13[2] 14 15 16 4:1 18 23 25 5:1 22 6:7 12[2] 30 7:16[2] 8:1 8 9 20 28 9:1 13 14 10:3[2] 17 28 11:8 12:32 13:2 8 14:15 17 18 17:2 4 18:4 15 16 19:5 6 20:5 6 23 24 25 22:23 27 29 30 31 23:14 15 33 24:12 25:2 8 30 28:1 3 4 41 29:1 44 30:30 31 31:13 17 32:2 10 23 24 26

EXOD. 32:32 33 33:12[3] 13 15 18 20 21 34:2 20 40:13 15 **LEVIT.** 10:3 19 14:35 20:26 22:2 25:23 26:14 18 21[2] 23[2] 27[2] 40[2] **NUM.** 3:13 41 8:16[2] 11:11 12 13 14 15[5] 16 14:11[2] 22 23 24 27[2] 29 35 16:28 29 17:5 10 18:9 20:12[2] 18 21:22 22:5 6 8 10 11 13 16 17[2] 18 19 28 29 32 33[3] 34[2] 37 23:1[2] 3[2] 7[2] 10 11

NUM. 23:13[2] 18 27 29[2] 24:12 13 27:14 28:2[2] 32:11 **DEU.** 1:14 17 21 23 37 41 42 2:1 2 9 17 27 28[2] 29 31 3:2 25 26[4] 4:5 10[3] 14 21 5:7 9 10 22 23 28[2] 29 31 7:4 8:17 9:4 10 11 12 13 14 19 10:1[2] 4 5 10 11 17:14[2] 18:15 16[2] 17 26:10 13 14 28:20 31:2 16 19 20 28 32:21[2] 34 35 39 41

DEU. 32:51[2] **JOSH.** 2:4 12[2] 7:19[2] 8:5 10:4[2] 22 14:6 7 8 10 11 12[2] 15:19[3] 17:14[2] 18:4 6 8 24:15 **JUD.** 1:3 7 15[3] 3:28 4:8[2] 18 19 5:13 6:17[2] 39[2] 7:2[3] 17 18 8:5 15 24 9:7 9 15 48 54[2] 10:12 13 11:7[illegible] 9[2] 12[2] 17 27[2] 31 35[2] 36 37[2] 12:2 3[3] 5 13:6[2] 7 10[2] 16 14:2 3[2] 12 13[2] 16[3] 15:11 12[2] 16:6 7 10[3] 11

JUD. 16:13[3] 15[3] 17 18 26 28[2] 30 17:2 10[2] 13 18:4[2] 24 19:18 19 20 20:5[3] **RUTH** 1:8 11 13[2] 16 17[2] 20[3] 21[4] 2:2 7 10 11 13[2] 21 3:5 17[2] 4:4 **1 SAM.** 1:11 27 2:16 28 29 30[4] 35 36 3:5 6 8 17[2] 8:7 8 9:16 18 19[2] 21 10:2 8 15 12:1 3 12 23 13:9 11 12 14:12 33 34 42 43 15:1 11[2] 16 20

1 SAM. 15:25 30[2] 32 16:1 2 3 5 17[2] 19 22 17:8 9[2] 10 35 37[2] 43 44 45 18:8 17 19:15 17[3] 20:2[2] 3 5 6[2] 8[3] 10 14 23 28 29[3] 31 42 21:2[2] 3 8 9 14 22:3 8[5] 13[2] 15 17 23[2] 23:11 12 21 22 23 24:10 12[2] 15[2] 17 18[3] 19 21[2] 25:19 21 24[2] 32 33 34[2] 26:6 7 19[2] 24 27:1[3] 5 28:1 7 8[2] 9

1 SAM. 28:11 12 15[6] 16 17 19 21 22 29:3[2] 6[2] 30:7 13 15[4] 31:4[3] **2 SAM.** 1:4 7[2] 8 9[5] 26[2] 2:7 22 3:8 12 14[2] 35 39 4:10 5:20 6:9 21[2] 7:5[2] 7 18 10:2 11[2] 11:6 12:10 22 23 13:4 5 6 9 11 12 13 16[2] 17 14:9 10 15 17 18 14:32[4] 15:4 7 8 25[2] 26 28 33[2] 34 36 16:3 9 12 17:1 18:13 19 22 23

2 SAM. 18:29 19:13[2] 19 22 25 26 33[2] 36 38[2] 20:4 20 22:3 5[2] 6[2] 17[2] 18[3] 19 20[3] 21[2] 23 25 34 36[2] 37 40[3] 41 44[3] 45[2] 48 49[4] 23:2 3 5 15 17 24:13 14 17 24 **1 KINGS** 1:12 13 17 24 26[2] 30 51 2:4[2] 5 7 8[2] 15 16 17 20 23 24[3] 28 30 31 32 42 3:20 24 5:4 6 8 9 8:25[2] 9:3 4 6

1 KINGS 9:13 10:7 11:21 22[2] 33 36[2] 12:5 9 12 24 27 13:6[2] 7 8 9 13 15 17 18 27 31 14:2 8 9[2] 15:19[2] 16:2 17:10 11 12 13[2] 18 19 18:9 12 14 19 30 37[2] 19:2 18 20 20:5 7 10[2] 32 35 36 37 39 21:2 3 6 20 22 29[2] 22:4 8 14 16 18 24 28 34 **2 KINGS** 2:2 4 6 9 10 20 3:7[2] 15

2 KINGS 4:2 6 22 24 27[2] 28 5:7[2] 8 11 22[2] 6:11 19 28 31 8:4 10 13 14 9:12 18 19 10:6 15 16 19 16:7[2] 15 18:14[2] 20 22 25 27[2] 31[2] 19:6 20 27 28 20:8 21:15 22:10 13 15 17[2] 19 **1 CHRON.** 4:10[4] 10:4[2] 11:17 19 12:17[3] 13:12 17:4 6 12 16 17 19:2 12[3] 21:2 12 13[2] 17 22[2] 22:7 8 28:2[3] 8 4[3] 5 6 19[2] 29:17

2 CHRON 1:8 9 10 2:3 7[2] 8 9 6:16 7:17 9:6 10:5 6 9 12 11:4 12:5 13:4 15:2 16:3[2] 18:3 7 15 17 23 27 33 20:20 28:11 23 29:5 34:18 21 23 25[2] 27 35:21[2] 23 36:23[2] **EZRA.** 1:2[2] 4:18 21 7:28[3] 8:1 9:1 4 **NEH.** 1:3 9 2:2 4 5 6[2] 7[2] 8[3] 9 12[2] 14 18[2] 4:18 23 5:15 18[2] 19 6:2[2] 4 5 12 13 14 19[2]

NEH. 12:40 13:8 14 22 28 31 **ESTHER** 4:16 5:13 7:3 8 **JOB** 2:3 3:12 25[2] 4:12 14 6:4 8 9[2] 13[2] 22[2] 23[2] 24[2] 28 7:3 8 12 13 14[2] 16 19[2] 20 21 9:11 16 17 18[2] 19 20[2] 28 31[2] 34[2] 35 10:2[3] 8[3] 9[2] 10[2] 11[2] 12 14[2] 15 16[2] 17[3] 18[2] 20 13:18[2] 15 19 20 21[2] 22[2] 23 24 26[2] 14:3 13[4] 15:17 16:7 8[2] 9[4]

JOB 16:10[3] 11[2] 12[4] 13 14[2] 20 17:1 2 3[2] 6 19:2 3[2] 5[2] 6[2] 9 10 11[2] 12 13[2] 14 15 16 18[2] 19[2] 21[3] 22 27 28 20:2 3 21:3 4 5 16 27 34 22:18 23:5[2] 6[2] 10 14 16 24:15 25 27:3 5 6 7 28:14[2] 29:2 5[2] 6 8 11[4] 13 14 20 21 23 30:1 2 10[2] 11[2] 12 14[2] 15 16[3] 17 18 19 20[2] 21[2] 22[2]

JOB 30:23 26 27 30 31:6 8 13 15 18 20 23 29 34 35 36 38 32:10 14 18[2] 21[2] 22 33:4[2] 5[2] 9 10[2] 27 31 32 33 34:2 10 32 34[2] 36:2 38:3 40:7 8 41:10 11 42:3 4 7 8 **PSALMS** 2:7 8 3:1[2] 3 4 5[2] 6 7 4:1[3] 8[2] 5:7 8 6:1[2] 2[2] 4 8 7:1[3] 4 6 8[2] 9:13[3] 13:1[2] 2 3 4 6 16:1

PSALMS 16:6 7[2] 8 11 17:3[2] 4 6[2] 8[2] 9[2] 15 18:4[2] 5[2] 16[2] 17[3] 18 19[3] 20[2] 22[2] 24 32 33 35[3] 36 39[2] 40[2] 43[3] 44[3] 47[2] 48[4] 19:12 13 22:1[2] 7[2] 9[2] 11 12[2] 13 15 16[2] 17 19[2] 21[2] 23:2[2] 3 4[2] 5 6 25:2 4[2] 5[2] 7 16[2] 17 19 20[3] 21 26:1 2[3] 11[3] 27:2 3[2] 5[3] 6 7[2] 9[3] 10[2] 11[2] 12[2] 28:1[2] 3 30:1[2] 2 3

PSALMS
30:10
11[2]
31:1[2]
2[3]
3[2]
4[2]
5
8
9
13[2]
13
15[2]
16
17
21
32:4
7[2]
34:3
4[2]
11
35:1[2]
3
7
12
13
15[2]
16
19[2]
21
22
24[2]
26
36:11[2]
38:1[2]
2[2]
4
10[2]
12
16[3]
17
19
21[2]
22
39:1
3
4
8[2]
10
13
40:1
2
7
11[2]
12[3]
13[2]
14
15
17
41:4
5
6
7[3]
9
10[2]
11[2]
12[3]
42:3
4
5
6
7
8
9
10[2]
11
43:1[2]
2
3[2]
5
44:6
15[2]
49:5
15
50:5[2]
8
15[2]
23
51:1
2[2]
3
5
6
7[2]
8
10[2]
11[2]
12
14
54:1[2]
3
7
55:2[2]
3[2]
4[2]

PSALMS
55:5[2]
12[3]
16[2]
18[2]
56:1[3]
2[2]
4
5
9
11
12
57:1[2]
2
3[2]
5
59:1[3]
2
3
4
10[2]
60:5
8
9[2]
61:2
3
5
63:8
64:2
65:3
18
19
20
69:1
2
4[2]
9[2]
12
13[2]
14[4]
15[3]
16[2]
17
18
21[2]
29
70:1[2]
5
71:1
2[4]
3
4
6
9[2]
10
12
17
18
20[3]
21
73:2
16
23
24[2]
28
77:1
81:8
11
13
86:1
3
7
11
13
14
16[2]
17[4]
87:4
88:6
7[2]
8[2]
14
16[2]
17[2]
18
89:26
36
91:14
15
92:4
11
94:16[2]
18
19
95:9[2]
101:2
3
4
6[2]
102:2[3]
8[3]
10[2]
24
103:1
106:4[2]

PSALMS
108:6
10[2]
109:2[2]
3[2]
5
21[2]
22
25
26[2]
116:2
3[2]
6
12
118:5[2]
6
7[2]
10
11[2]
12
13[2]
18[2]
19
21
119:8
10[2]
12
19
22
23
25
26[2]
27
28
29[2]
30
31
33
34
35
36
37
40
41
42
49
50
51
53
58
61
64
66
68
69
71
72
73[3]
74
75
77
78
79
82
84
85
86[2]
87
88
93
94
95[2]
98[2]
102
107
108
110
115
116[2]
117
121
122
124
125
132[2]
133
134
135
139
143
144
145
146
149
153
154[2]
156
159
161
169
170
171
173
175
120:1

PSALMS
120:5
122:1
129:1
2[2]
131:1
138:3[2]
7[2]
8
139:1[2]
5[2]
6
10[2]
11[2]
13
17
19
23[2]
24
140:1[2]
4[2]
5[2]
9
141:1
4
5[2]
9
142:3[2]
4[2]
6
7
143:1
3
4[2]
7[2]
8[2]
9[2]
10[2]
11
144:2
7[2]
11[2]

PROV.
1:28[3]
33
4:4[2]
5:7
13
7:14
24
8:15
16
17[3]
18
21
22
32
34
35
36[2]
9:11
22:26
35[2]
24:29
27:11
30:7
8[4]
18

ECCL.
1:16
2:4[3]
5
6
7[2]
8[2]
9[2]
15
17
18
7:23
9:13

CANT.
1:2
4[2]
6[4]
7
13
14
2:4[2]
5[2]
6
10
14[2]
3:3
4
4:6
8[2]
5:2
6
7[4]
6:5
12

CANT.
7:10
8:2
3
6
12
13

ISAIAH
1:2
11
12
13
14
24[2]
3:7
5:3
6:5
6
8
8:1
2
3
5
11[2]
18
10:4
12:1
21:2
3
4[2]
6
11
16
22:4[2]
24:16
26:9
27:4[2]
5[2]
29:2
13[3]
16
30:1
31:4
36:5
7
10
12[2]
16[2]
37:6
21
28
29
38:12[3]
13
14
15
16[2]
20
39:3
40:25
41:1
43:10[3]
11
20
22[2]
23[2]
24[4]
26
27
44:6
7
8
17
21
22
45:4
5[2]
6
11[2]
19
21[2]
22
23
46:3[2]
5[3]
9
12
47:8
10[2]
48:12
16[2]
19
49:1[2]
2[3]
3
5
14[2]
16
20[2]
21
23
50:4
7
8[3]

ISAIAH
50:9[2]
51:1
4[3]
5
7
54:9
15
17
55:3
11
56:3
4
11
57:8
11[2]
13
16
17
58:2[2]
59:21
60:9
61:1[3]
10[2]
63:3
5[2]
15
65:1[4]
3
5
6
7
10
66:1
22
23
24

JER.
1:4
7
9
11
12
13
14
16
2:1
2
5[2]
8[2]
13
21
22
27[2]
29[2]
32
35
3:1
4
6
7
10
11
19[2]
20
4:1
12
17
19
22
31
5:5
7
11
19
22
6:7
20[2]
7:10
16
18
19
26
8:18
19
21
9:3
6
24
10:19
20
24[2]
11:6
9
11
14
17
18[2]
19
20
12:1
3[2]
8[2]
9

JER.
12:11
13:1
3
5
6
8
11[2]
22
25[2]
14:11
14
15:1[2]
6
8
10[4]
15[4]
16
17
18
19
16:1
11[2]
12
17:13
14[2]
15
16
17
18[3]
19
24
27
18:5
15
19[2]
22
23[2]
19:4
20:7[2]
8
11
12
14
17[2]
22:6
14
16
23:9
14
17
24:1
3
4
7[2]
25:3
6
7[2]
15
17
26:3
4
12
14[2]
15[2]
27:2
5
28:1
8
29:12[2]
13[2]
30:20
21[2]
31:3
18[2]
26
34
36[2]
32:6
8[2]
25
27
29
30[2]
31
32
33
39
40
33:3
8[2]
9
18
22
34:14
15
17
18
35:14
15
16
19
36:18
37:7[2]
18

JER.
37:20
38:14
15[2]
19[2]
21
26
39:18
40:4[2]
10
15
42:9
10
20
21
44:3
8
45:3
49:4
11
19[3]
50:44[3]
51:1
34[5]
35
53

LAM.
1:12[2]
13[2]
14
15[2]
16
19
20
21[2]
22
3:2[2]
3[2]
5[2]
6
7
10
11[2]
12
15[2]
16
20
52
53
60
61
62[2]

EZEKIEL
2:1
2[4]
3[3]
9
10
3:1
2
3
4
7
10
12[2]
14[3]
16
17
22[2]
24[4]
4:15
16
6:1
9[2]
7:1
8:1[2]
3[3]
5
6
7
8
9
12
13
14
15
16
17[2]
9:9
10
11
11:1[2]
2
5[2]
14
24[3]
25
12:1
8
17
21
26
13:1

EZEKIEL
13:19
14:1[2]
2
5
7[2]
11
12
13
15:1
16:1
20
26
43
50
17:1
11
20
18:1
20:1
2
3
8[2]
12
13
20
21
27[2]
38
39
40
45
49
21:1
8
18
22:1
12
17
18
23
30
23:1
35[2]
36
37
38
24:1
15
19
20
25:1
26:1
2
27:1
28:1
11
20
29:1
17
20
30:1
9
20
31:1
32:1
17
33:1
7
21
22[2]
23
34:1
35:1
13[2]
36:16
17
37:1[3]
2
3
4
9
10
11
15
38:1
16
39:23
26
40:1[2]
2[2]
3
4
17
24
28
32
35
45
48
49
41:1
4
22
42:1[2]

EZEKIEL
42:13
15
43:1
5[2]
6[2]
7
8
9
18
19[2]
44:1
2
4
5
10[2]
13[2]
15[5]
16
46:19
20
21[2]
24
47:1
2[2]
3
4[2]
6[3]
8

DANIEL
1:10
2:5[2]
6[2]
8
9[4]
23[2]
24
26
30[2]
4:1
5[2]
6[2]
7
8
9
18
34
36[4]
5:7
15[2]
16
6:22[2]
7:15
18[2]
28[3]
8:1[3]
14
15
17
18[3]
9:21
22[2]
10:7
8[2]
10[2]
11[2]
12
13[2]
15
16[2]
17[3]
18[2]
19[2]
21

HOSEA
2:5
7
12
13
16[2]
19[2]
20
23
3:1
2
3
4:6
7
5:3
15
6:7
7:7
13[3]
14[2]
15
8:2
4
11:7
8
12
12:8[2]
13:4[2]
6

HOSEA
13:9
10
14:8

JOEL
2:12
3:4[3]

AMOS
4:6
8
9
10
11
5:4
22
23
25
7:1
4
7
8
15[2]
8:1
2
9:7

OBADIAH
4

JONAH
1:2
12[2]
2:2
3[3]
5[2]
6
7
4:3
8

MICAH
2:4
5:2
6:1
7:1
7
8[2]
9[2]
10

HABAK.
1:3[3]
2:1[2]
2
3:14
19

ZEPH.
2:15
3:7
8
11

HAGGAI
2:14
17

ZECH.
1:3
4
9[2]
13
14[2]
19[2]
20
2:2
3
8
9
11
3:1
4:1[2]
2
4
5[2]
6
8
9
13
5:2
3
5[2]
10
11
6:4
5
8[2]
9
15
7:4
5[2]
8:1
14

ZECH.
8:18
9:13
10:9
11:7
8
11
12
13
15
12:10
13:5

MALACHI
2:5
6
3:1
5
7
8
9
10
13

MATT.
2:8
3:11
14
4:9
19
7:4
21
22
23
8:2
9
21
22
9:9
10:32
33
37[4]
38[2]
40[3]
11:6
27
28
29
12:30[3]
14:8
18
28
30
15:5
8[3]
9
22
25
32
16:23[2]
24[2]
17:17
27
18:5
6
21
26
28
29
32
19:14
17
21
28
20:13
15
21:2
24
22:18
19
23:39
25:20
22
35[2]
36[3]
40
41
42[2]
43[3]
45
26:10
11
15
21
23[2]
31
34
38
39
40
42
46
53
55[2]
75

MATT.
27:10
46
28:10
18

MARK
1:7
17
40
2:14
5:7
31
6:22
23
25
7:6[2]
7
11
14
8:2
33
34[2]
38
9:19
37[4]
39
42
10:14
18
21
47
48
11:29
30
12:15[2]
14:6
7
18[2]
20
27
30
36
42
48
49
72
15:34

LUKE
1:3
25[2]
38
43[2]
48
49
2:49
4:6
7
8
18[3]
23
5:6
12
27
6:42
46
47
7:8
23
42
44
45
8:28
45[2]
46[2]
9:23[2]
26
48[3]
59[2]
61
10:16[4]
22
40[2]
11:5
6
7[2]
23[3]
12:8
9
13
14
13:27
35
14:18
19
26
27
15:6
9
12[2]
19
29
31
16:3

LUKE
16:4
24
17:8
18:3
5[2]
13
16
19
22
38
39
19:27
20:3
23
24
22:19
21[2]
28
29
34
37[2]
42
53
61
68[2]
23:14
28
42
43
24:39[2]
44

JOHN
1:15[3]
27[2]
30[3]
33[2]
43
48
2:17
3:28
4:7
9
10
15
21
29
34
39
5:7[2]
11[2]
24
30
32[2]
36[3]
37[2]
39
40
43
46[2]
6:26
35[2]
36
37[3]
38
39[2]
40
44[2]
45
47
56
57[2]
65
7:7
16
19
23
28[2]
29
33
34[2]
36[2]
37
38
8:12
16
18[2]
19[2]
21
26
28
29[3]
37
40
42[2]
45
46[2]
49
54
9:4
11
10:8
9
15

JOHN
10:17
18
25
27
29
32
37
38[2]
11:25
26
41
42[2]
12:8
26[3]
27
30
32
44[3]
45[2]
46
47
48
49[2]
50
13:8
13
18[2]
20[3]
21
33
36[2]
38
14:1
7
9[2]
10[2]
11[3]
12
15
19[2]
20
21[2]
23[2]
24[2]
28
30
31
15:2
4[2]
5[2]
6
7
9
16
18
20
21
23
24
25
26
27
16:3
5[2]
9
10
14
16[2]
17[2]
19[2]
23
27
32[2]
33
17:4
5
6[2]
7
8[2]
9
11
12
18
20
21[2]
22
23[3]
24[4]
25
26
18:8
9
11
21[2]
23
34
35
19:10
11[2]
20:15
17
21
29
21:15

JOHN
21:16
17[2]
19
22

ACTS
1:4
8
2:28[2]
29
3:22
5:8
7:7
28
37
42
49
8:19
24[2]
31
36
9:4
6
15
17
10:28
29
30
11:5
7
9
11
12[2]
12:8
11
13:2
25
15:13
16:15
20:19
22
23
24
34
21:39
22:5
6
7[2]
8
9[2]
10
11
13[2]
18[2]
21
27
23:3[2]
11
18[2]
19
22
30
24:12
13
18
19
20
25:5
9
11[2]
15
24
27
26:3
5
13[2]
14[2]
18
21[2]
28
29
27:21
23
25
28:18[2]

ROMANS
1:12
15
7:8
11[2]
13[2]
17
18[2]
20
21
23
24
8:2
9:1
19
20
10:20[2]
14:11

ROMANS
15:3
15
18
30[2]
16:7

1 COR.
1:11
17
3:10
4:3
4
16
6:12[2]
7:1
9:3
15[2]
16[2]
17
10:23[2]
11:1
2
24
25
13:3
14:11
21
15:8
12[2]
32
16:4
6
9
11
21

2 COR.
1:17
19
2:2[2]
5
12
7:7
9:1
4
11:2
9
10[2]
16[2]
28
32
12:1
6[3]
7[2]
8
9[2]
11
18
21
13:3
10

GAL.
1:2
11
15[2]
16
17
24
2:1
3
6[2]
7
8
9[2]
20[3]
4:12
14
15
21
6:14
17

EPHES.
3:2
3
7
8
6:19[2]

PHIL.
1:7
12
26
30[2]
2:18
22
23
27
30
3:1
7
17
4:9

PHIL.
4:10
13
15
21

COLOS.
1:25
29
4:11
18

1 TIM.
1:12[3]
16

2 TIM.
1:8
13
15
16
17[2]
18
2:2
3:11[2]
4:8[2]
9
10
11[2]
14
16[2]
17[2]
18[2]

TITUS
1:3
3:12
15

PHILE.
11
13[2]
16
17
19
20
22

HEB.
1:5
2:13
3:9[2]
8:10
11
10:5
7
30
34
11:32
13:6

JAMES
2:18

2 PETER
1:14

JUDE
3

REV.
1:10
12
17[2]
3:4
18
20
21
4:1
5:5
7:13
14
10:4
8
9[2]
11
11:1
14:13
17:1[2]
3
7
15
19:9[2]
10
21:5
6
9[2]
10[2]
15
22:1
6
8
9
10
12

my

1700 or 3456

GEN.
2:23
4:9
13
23[3]
6:2
18
9:9
11

GEN.
9:13
15
12:13[2]
19
13:8
15:2
3
16:2

GEN.
16:5[2]
8
17:2
4
7
9
10
18

GEN.
17:14
19
21
18:3
12
19:2
8
18

GEN.
19:19
20
34
20:2
5[3]
9
11
12[2]

GEN.
20:13[2]
15
21:10
23
30
22:7
8
18

GEN.
23:4
6
8
11[2]
13
15
24:2
3

GEN.
24:4
6
7[3]
8
12[2]
14
27[3]
35

GEN.
24:36
37[2]
38[2]
39
40
41[2]
42
44

GEN.
24:48[3]
49
54
56
65
26:5[2]
7
9

GEN.
26:24
27:1
2
4
7
8
11
12

GEN.
27:13
18[2]
19
20
21
24
25
26

GEN.
27:27
31
34
36
37
38[2]
41
43

GEN.
27:46[2]
28:21
29:4
14
15
21
32[2]
34

GEN.
30:3[2]
6
8
15[2]
16
18[2]
20
23

GEN.
30:25
26[2]
30
32
33[2]
31:5
6
7

GEN.
31:26
28
29
30
35
36
37[2]
39

GEN.
31:40
41
42[2]
43[2]
50[2]
32:4
5
9[2]

GEN. 32:10, 11, 17, 18, 29, 30, 33:8, 9, 10[2], 11, 13, 14[2], 15, 34:8, 30, 35:3, 37:7[2], 16, 33, 35, 38:11, 26, 39:8[2], 15, 18, 40:9, 11, 16[2], 17, 41:9, 17, 22, 40[2], 51[2], 52, 42:10, 28[2], 36, 37[2], 38[2], 43:3, 5, 9, 14, 29, 44:2, 5, 7, 9, 10, 16[2], 17, 18[2], 19, 20, 22, 23, 24[2], 27[2], 29, 30, 32[2], 33, 34[2], 45:3, 9, 12[2], 13[3], 28, 46:31[2], 47:1[2], 6, 9[3], 18[3], 25, 29, 30, 48:9, 11, 15[2], 16[2], 18, 19, 22[2], 49:3[3], 4, 6, 9, 26, 29[2], 50:5[3], 25

EXOD. 3:7, 10, 15[2], 20[2], 4:1, 10, 13, 18, 22[2], 23, 5:1, 6:3, 4, 5, 7:3[2], 4, 16, 8:1, 8, 20, 21, 22, 23, 9:1, 13, 14, 15, 16[2], 17, 27, 29, 10:1, 2, 3, 4, 17, 28[2], 11:9, 12:31, 13:15, 19, 15:2[4], 9[3], 16:4, 28[2], 18:4, 19, 19:5[2], 20:6, 24, 21:5[3], 22:24, 25, 23:18[2], 21, 27, 25:2, 29:43, 31:13, 32:10, 22, 33, 33:12, 14, 17, 19, 20, 22[2], 23[2], 34:9, 25

LEVIT. 6:17, 15:31, 17:10, 18:4, 5[2], 26[2], 19:3, 12, 19, 30[2], 37[2], 20:3[3], 5, 6, 8, 22[2], 21:23, 22:2, 3, 31, 32, 23:2, 25:18[2], 21, 42, 55, 26:2[2], 3[2], 9, 11[2], 12, 15[4], 17, 25, 30, 42[3], 43[2], 44

NUM. 6:27, 10:30, 11:15, 23, 28, 29, 12:6, 7, 8, 11, 17, 14:22[3], 24, 34, 15:40, 20:19[2], 24, 21:2, 22:18, 38, 23:10, 12, 24:14, 25:11[3], 12, 27:14, 28:2[3], 32:25, 27, 36:2[2]

DEU. 2:28, 4:5, 10, 5:10, 29, 8:17, 9:4, 15, 17, 11:13, 18, 18:16, 18, 19[2], 20, 22:16, 17, 25:7[2], 26:5, 14[2], 31:16, 17[2], 18, 20, 27, 29, 32:1, 2[2], 20, 34, 39, 40, 41, 42

JOSH. 1:2, 7, 2:12, 13[4], 5:14, 7:11, 19, 21, 9:23, 14:8[2], 9, 11[2], 15:16, 22:2, 24:15

JUD. 1:3, 7, 12, 2:1, 2, 20[2], 4:18, 5:9, 21, 6:10, 13, 15[3], 18, 8:19[2], 23, 9:9, 11[2], 13, 15, 17, 18, 29, 11:7, 12, 13, 19, 31, 35[2], 36, 37[2], 12:2, 3[3], 13:8, 18, 14:3, 16[3], 18[2], 15:1, 16:13, 17[2], 28, 17:2, 3[2], 13, 18:24, 19:23, 24, 20:4, 5, 6, 23, 28

RUTH 1:11[3], 12, 13, 16[2], 2:2, 2:8[2], 13, 21[2], 22, 3:1, 10, 11[2], 16, 18, 4:4, 6, 10

1 SAM. 1:15[2], 16, 26[2], 27, 2:1[2], 24, 28, 29[3], 32, 35, 3:6, 16, 4:16, 9:5, 16[3], 17, 21, 10:2, 12:2[2], 5, 14:29, 39, 40, 42, 15:11, 25, 30, 16:22, 18:17, 18[2], 21, 19:2, 3[2], 20:1[2], 2[2], 9, 12, 13[2], 15, 29[2], 42, 21:2, 8[2], 15[2], 22:3[2], 8[3], 12, 15, 23, 23:10, 12, 17[2], 24:6, 8, 10, 11[3], 15, 16, 21[3], 25:5, 11[4], 24, 25[2], 26[2], 27[2], 28[2], 29, 30, 31[3], 39, 41, 26:17[3], 18, 19, 20, 21[2], 23, 24, 25, 27:12, 28:9, 21[2], 29:6, 8, 9, 30:13, 15, 23

2 SAM. 1:9, 10, 26, 2:22, 3:7, 12, 13[2], 14, 18[3], 21, 28, 4:8, 9, 5:2, 7:5, 7, 8[2], 10, 11, 13, 14, 15, 18, 9:7, 10, 11[2], 11:11[3], 12:28, 13:4, 5[2], 6[2], 11, 12, 13, 20, 25, 26, 32, 33, 14:7[2], 9[2], 11, 12, 15, 16, 17[2], 18, 19[2], 20, 22, 24, 31, 15:7, 15, 21[2], 16:3, 4, 9, 11[3], 18:5, 18, 22, 28, 31, 32, 33[5], 19:4, 12[3], 13[2], 19[2], 20, 26[2], 27[2], 28[2], 30, 35, 37[3], 20:9, 22:2[3], 3[6], 7[4], 18, 19[2], 21[2], 22, 25[2], 29[2], 30, 33[2], 34[2], 35, 37, 39, 44, 47[2], 23:2, 5[3], 24:3[2], 17, 21, 22, 24

1 KINGS 1:2[3], 13[2], 17[2], 18, 20[2], 21[2], 24[2], 27[2], 29, 30[2], 31, 33, 35, 36, 37[2], 48, 2:15, 20, 24, 26[2], 31, 32, 38, 44, 3:6, 7, 3:14[3], 17, 20[2], 21, 22[2], 23[2], 26, 5:3, 4, 5[3], 6, 9[3], 12[4], 13, 8:15, 16[3], 17, 18[2], 19, 20, 24, 25[2], 26, 28, 29, 59, 9:3, 4[2], 7[2], 13, 11:11[2], 13, 32, 33[3], 34[3], 36[2], 38[5], 12:10[2], 11[2], 14[2], 13:6, 30, 31, 14:7, 8[2], 15:19, 16:2[2], 17:1, 12, 18[2], 20, 21, 18:7, 10, 12, 13, 19:4[2], 10, 14, 20[2], 20:4, 6, 7[4], 9, 32, 34[2], 21:2, 3, 4, 6, 22:4[2], 49

2 KINGS 1:13, 14, 2:12[2], 19, 3:7[2], 4:1[2], 16, 19[2], 28, 29[2], 5:3, 6, 13, 18[2], 20, 22, 6:8, 12, 15, 21, 26, 28, 29, 8:5, 9, 12, 9:7, 32, 10:6, 9, 15, 16, 13:14[2], 14:9, 17:13[3], 18:23, 24, 27, 19:12, 23, 24, 28[2], 34, 20:5, 6, 15, 19, 21:4, 7, 8, 15, 22:17, 23:27[2]

1 CHRON. 4:10, 11:2[2], 19, 16:22, 17:4, 6, 7[2], 9, 10, 13[2], 14, 25, 21:3[3], 17[2], 23, 22:5, 7[3], 8[2], 10[2], 11, 14, 28:2[2], 3, 4[3], 5[2], 6[3], 7[2], 9, 20, 29:1, 2[2], 3[3], 14, 17, 19

2 CHRON. 1:8, 9, 11, 2:3, 4, 7, 8, 13, 14, 15, 6:4, 5[3], 6[2], 7, 8[2], 9, 10, 15, 16[3], 19, 40, 7:13, 14[3], 16, 17[2], 19[2], 20[3], 8:11, 10:10[2], 11[2], 14[2], 12:7, 8, 16:3, 18:3, 13, 25:16, 18, 29:11, 32:13, 14, 15, 33:4, 7, 34:25

EZRA 7:13, 28, 9:3[4], 5[6], 6[3], 10:3

NEH. 1:2, 6, 9, 2:3[2], 5, 8, 12[2], 18, 4:16, 23[2], 5:10[2], 13, 14, 5:16, 17, 19, 6:9, 14, 19, 7:2, 5, 13:14[3], 19, 22, 29, 31

ESTHER 4:16, 5:7[2], 8[2], 7:3[4], 4[2], 8:6[2]

JOB 1:5, 8, 21, 2:3, 3:10, 24, 4:14, 15[2], 5:8, 6:2[2], 3, 4, 7[2], 8, 11[2], 12[2], 13, 15, 21, 24, 29, 30[2], 7:5[2], 6, 7, 11[3], 13[3], 15[2], 16, 19, 21, 9:14, 15, 16, 17, 18, 21[2], 25, 27[2], 28, 30, 10:1[4], 6, 12, 15, 20, 11:4, 13:6[2], 14[3], 16, 17[2], 18, 19, 23[3], 26, 27[3], 14:14[2], 16[2], 17, 16:4, 5[2], 6, 7, 8[2], 12, 13[2], 15[2], 16[2], 17, 18[2], 19[2], 20, 17:1[2], 7, 11[3], 13, 14[3], 14[2], 19:2, 5, 8[2], 9[2], 12, 13, 14[2], 15, 16[2], 17[2], 19, 20[4], 21, 22, 23, 25

ESTHER 19:26[2], 27, 20:2, 3[2], 21:2, 4[2], 6, 23:2[3], 4[2], 7, 11, 12, 16, 17, 24:25, 27:2[2], 3[2], 4[2], 6[2], 29:3, 4[2], 5, 6, 7, 14, 18[2], 19[2], 20[3], 21, 22[2], 24, 30:1, 10, 11, 12[2], 13[2], 15[2], 16, 17[2], 18[3], 22, 25, 27, 30[2], 31[2], 31:4[2], 5, 7, 8, 9, 10, 13[2], 17, 18[2], 20, 21[2], 22, 24[2], 25, 27[3], 30, 31, 32, 33[2], 35, 36, 37, 38, 32:17, 19, 20, 22, 33:1[2], 2[3], 3[2], 7[2], 11[2], 34:2, 5, 6[2], 16, 36, 35:2, 3, 10, 36:3[2], 4, 37:1, 38:10, 40:4, 8, 7[2], 42:8[3]

PSALMS 2:6[2], 7, 3:2, 3, 4, 7, 4:1[2], 2, 7, 5:1[2], 2[3], 3[2], 8, 6:2, 3, 4, 6[4], 8, 9[2], 7:1[2], 2, 3[2]

PSALMS 7:5[2], 8, 10, 9:1, 4[2], 13, 11:1[2], 13:2[2], 3, 5, 14:4, 16:1, 2[3], 3, 4, 5[2], 7, 8, 9[3], 10, 17:1[2], 2, 3, 5[2], 6, 9, 13, 18:1, 2[8], 6[4], 17, 18[2], 20[2], 21, 24[2], 28[3], 29, 32, 33[2], 34, 36[2], 38, 46[2], 19:14[4], 22:1[3], 2, 9, 10[2], 14[3], 15[3], 16[2], 17, 18[2], 19, 20[2], 22, 25[2], 23:1, 3, 5[2], 6, 25:1, 2, 5, 7[2], 15, 17[2], 18[2], 20, 26:2[2], 9[2], 11, 27:1[3], 2[2], 3, 4, 7, 8[2], 9[2], 10[2], 28:1, 2[2], 6, 7[5], 30:1, 2, 3, 6, 7, 9, 10, 11[2], 12[2], 31:1, 2, 3[2], 4, 5, 7[2], 8, 9[2], 10[4], 11, 13, 14, 15, 22[2], 32:3[2], 4, 5[3], 7, 34:1, 2, 4, 35:1, 3, 4[2]

PSALMS 35:7, 9, 10, 11, 12, 13[3], 14, 17[2], 23[4], 24, 27, 28, 36:1, 38:3[3], 5[2], 7[2], 8, 9[2], 10[2], 11[4], 12[2], 15, 16, 17, 18, 21, 22, 39:1[3], 2[2], 3[2], 4, 5, 7, 8, 9, 12[4], 40:1, 2[2], 3, 5, 8[2], 9, 10, 12, 14, 17[3], 41:4, 7, 9, 42:1, 2, 3[2], 4, 5, 6[2], 8[2], 9, 10, 11[3], 43:1, 2, 4[2], 5[2], 44:4, 6[2], 15[2], 45:1[2], 49:3[2], 4, 5, 15, 50:5, 7, 16[2], 17, 51:1, 2, 3[2], 5, 9, 14[2], 15[2], 53:4, 54:2[2], 3, 4, 55:1[2], 2, 4, 8, 13, 17, 18, 56:4, 5, 6[2], 8[2], 11, 13[2], 57:1[2], 4, 6[2], 7[2], 8, 59:1, 3[3], 4, 9, 10[2], 11, 16[2], 17[3], 60:7, 8[2], 61:1[2], 2, 5

PSALMS 61:8, 62:1[2], 2[3], 5[2], 6[3], 7[4], 63:1[3], 3, 4, 5[2], 6, 7, 8, 9, 64:1[3], 66:13, 14[2], 16, 17[2], 18, 19, 20, 68:22, 24[2], 69:1, 3[3], 5[2], 6[2], 7, 8[2], 10[2], 11, 13, 18, 19[3], 20, 21[2], 70:2[2], 5[2], 71:1, 3[3], 4, 5[3], 6[2], 7, 8, 9, 10, 12[2], 13[2], 15, 17, 21, 22, 23[2], 24[2], 73:2[2], 13[2], 21[2], 23, 26[4], 28, 74:12, 77:1[2], 2[3], 3, 6[2], 10, 78:1[3], 2, 81:8, 11[2], 13[2], 14, 83:13, 84:2[3], 3[2], 8, 10, 86:2[2], 4, 6[2], 7, 11, 12[2], 13, 14, 87:7, 88:1, 2[2], 3[2], 9, 13, 14, 15, 89:1, 3[2], 20[2], 21, 24[3], 26[3], 27, 28[2], 30[2], 31[2], 33[2], 34[2], 35, 47, 50, 91:2[3], 9, 14, 16, 92:10, 11[2], 15

PSALMS 94:17[2], 18, 19[2], 22[3], 95:9, 10, 11[2], 101:2, 7[2], 102:1[3], 3[2], 4[2], 5[3], 9, 11, 23[2], 24[2], 103:1, 2, 22, 104:1[2], 33[2], 34, 35, 105:15, 108:1[2], 8, 9[2], 109:1, 4[2], 5, 20, 22, 24[2], 26, 30, 110:1[2], 111:1, 116:1[2], 4, 7, 8[2], 11, 14, 16, 18, 118:6, 7[2], 14[2], 21, 28[2], 119:5, 13, 20, 24[2], 25, 26, 28, 32, 34, 39, 43, 48, 50[2], 54[2], 57, 58, 59[2], 69, 76, 77, 80, 81, 92, 97, 99[2], 101, 103[2], 105[2], 108, 109[2], 111, 114[2], 115, 116, 120, 129, 131, 133, 139, 143, 145, 149, 154, 157, 161, 167, 168, 169, 170, 171, 172, 174, 175, 120:1, 2, 6, 121:1, 2, 122:8, 129:1, 2, 3, 130:2[2], 5, 6, 131:1

PSALMS 131:2, 3[2], 132:12[2], 14, 137:5, 6, 138:1, 3, 139:2[2], 3[3], 4, 8, 13[2], 14, 15, 16[2], 23[2], 140:4, 6[2], 7[2], 141:1, 2[2], 3[2], 4, 5[2], 6, 8[2], 142:1[3], 2[2], 3[2], 4[2], 5[2], 6[2], 7, 143:1[2], 3[2], 4[2], 6[2], 7, 8, 10, 11, 12, 144:1[3], 2[6], 145:1, 21, 146:1, 2

PROV. 1:8, 10, 15, 23[3], 24, 25[2], 30[2], 2:1[3], 3:1[3], 11, 21, 4:2, 3[2], 4[2], 5, 10[2], 20[3], 5:1[3], 7, 12, 13, 20, 6:1, 8, 20, 7:1[3], 2[2], 4, 6[2], 14, 16, 17, 24, 8:4, 6, 7[2], 8, 10, 19[2], 31, 32, 34[2], 9:5, 19:27, 20:9[2], 22:17, 23:15[2], 16, 19, 26[2], 24:13, 21, 27:11[2], 30:9, 31:2[3]

ECCL. 1:13, 16, 17, 2:7, 9, 10[6], 11, 15[2], 18, 2:19, 20, 4:8, 7:15, 28, 8:9, 9:1, 12:12

CANT. 1:6, 7, 9, 12, 13[2], 14, 15, 16, 2:2, 3[2], 6, 7, 8, 9, 10[3], 13[2], 14, 16, 17, 3:1[2], 2, 3, 4[2], 5, 4:1, 7, 8, 9[4], 10[2], 11, 12[2], 16[2], 5:1[9], 2[8], 3[2], 4[2], 5[3], 6[3], 7, 8, 10, 16[2], 6:2, 3[2], 4, 9[2], 12, 7:9, 10, 11, 12, 13, 8:1[2], 2[2], 3, 4, 10, 12, 14

ISAIAH 1:3, 12, 14, 25, 3:7, 12[2], 15, 5:1[3], 3[2], 4, 5, 13, 6:7, 7:13, 8:4[2], 16, 10:2, 6, 8, 10, 13[2], 14, 24, 11:9, 12:2[4], 13:3[3], 14:13, 25[2], 15:5, 16:9, 11, 18:4[2], 19:25[2], 20:3, 21:3, 4[2], 8[2], 10[2], 22:4, 20, 24:16[2], 25:1, 26:9[2], 19, 20, 27:5

ISAIAH 28:23[2], 29:23, 30:1, 2, 32:9[2], 13, 18, 33:13, 34:5[2], 16, 36:8, 9, 12, 19, 20[2], 37:12, 24, 29[2], 35, 38:10[2], 12, 13, 15[2], 16, 17[2], 20, 39:4, 8, 40:1, 27[3], 41:8[2], 9, 10, 25, 42:1[3], 8[3], 14, 19[2], 43:4, 6[2], 7[2], 10[2], 12, 13, 20[2], 21, 44:1, 2, 3[2], 8, 17, 20, 21[2], 28[2], 45:4, 11[2], 12, 13[2], 23, 46:10[2], 11, 13[3], 47:6, 48:3, 5[2], 9[2], 11[2], 12, 13, 18, 49:1[2], 2, 3, 4[4], 5[2], 6[2], 11[2], 14, 16, 21, 22, 50:1, 2[2], 6[3], 7, 51:4[3], 5[2], 6[2], 7, 8[2], 16[2], 22, 52:4, 5[2], 6[2], 13, 53:8, 11, 54:8, 10[2], 55:8[2], 9[2], 11[2], 56:1[2], 4[2], 5, 6, 7[2], 57:11, 13, 14, 21, 58:1, 2, 13, 59:21[3], 60:7

ISAIAH 60:10[2], 13[2], 21[2], 61:10[2], 62:1, 9, 63:3[3], 4, 5, 6, 8, 65:1, 2, 3, 5, 8, 9[2], 10, 11, 13[3], 14, 15, 19, 22, 25, 66:1[3], 2, 5, 18, 19[3], 20

JER. 1:9[2], 12, 16, 2:7, 11, 13, 19, 27, 31, 32, 3:4[2], 13, 19, 4:1, 4, 11, 19[6], 20[2], 22, 31, 5:9, 14, 22, 26, 29, 31, 6:8, 12, 14, 19[2], 26, 27, 7:10, 11, 12[3], 14, 15, 20, 23[2], 25, 30[2], 31, 8:7, 11, 18, 19, 20, 21, 9:1[2], 2, 7, 9, 13[2], 10:19[2], 20[5], 11:4[2], 7[2], 15, 20, 12:7, 10[3], 14, 16[4], 13:2, 10, 17, 14:14, 15, 17, 15:1[2], 6, 7, 10, 15, 18[2], 19, 16:5, 11, 17[2], 18, 19[3], 21[2], 17:3, 14

JER. 17:16, 17, 18:2, 10[2], 15, 20, 22, 19:5, 15, 20:9, 10[2], 11, 12, 14, 15, 17[2], 18, 21:10, 12, 22:18, 21, 24, 23:1, 2[2], 3, 9, 11, 13, 22[3], 25, 27[3], 28[2], 29, 30, 32, 39, 24:7, 25:8, 9, 13, 15, 29, 26:4, 5, 27:5[2], 6, 15, 29:9, 10, 19[2], 21, 23, 32, 30:3, 10, 22, 31:1, 9, 14[2], 18, 19[2], 20[2], 26, 32, 33[2], 32:7, 8, 9, 31[2], 34, 35, 37, 38, 40, 41[2], 33:5[2], 20[2], 21[3], 22, 24, 25, 26, 34:15[2], 16, 18, 35:13, 36:6, 37:20[2], 38:9, 26, 39:16, 42:18[2], 43:10, 44:4, 6, 10[2], 11, 26[2], 29, 45:3[2], 46:10, 27, 28, 49:25, 37, 38, 50:6, 51:20, 34, 35[2], 45

LAM. 1:9, 12, 13[2], 14[5]

LAM. 1:15[2] 16[2] 18[3] 19[2] 20 21 22[3] 2:11[3] 21[2] 22 3:4[3] 7 8 9[2] 11 13 14 16 17 18[2] 19 20 21 24[2] 48 51 53 56[3] 58[2] 59[2] 4:3 6 10 **EZEKIEL** 1:28 2:2 7 3:2 3 4 10 14 17 23 24 4:14[3] 5:6[3] 7[2] 11 12 13[3]

EZEKIEL 5:14 7:8 14 22 8:6 9:6 8 10:2 13 19 11:12[2] 13 20[2] 12:7[2] 13[2] 28 13:9 10 13[2] 15 18 19[2] 21 23 14:8[2] 9[2] 11 19 21 15:7[2] 16:8 14 17[2] 19 21 27 42[2] 60 62 17:9[2] 19 20[2] 18:17[2] 19 21 25 29 20:8[2] 9 11[2] 12 13[4]

EZEKIEL 20:14 15 16[3] 19[2] 20 21[5] 22 24[3] 39 44 21:3 4 5 10 12[2] 17 31 22:8 20 22 26[2] 31 23:18[2] 25 38[2] 39 24:13 18 21 25:3 14[4] 17 28:25 29:3 30:15 24 25 32:3 10 32 33:7 22[2] 31 34:6[2] 8[5] 10[3] 11 12 15 17 19 22

EZEKIEL 34:23 24 26 30 31[2] 36:5[2] 6[2] 8 12 18 20 23 27[3] 28 37:12 13 14 23 24[3] 25[2] 26 27[2] 28 38:16[2] 14 17 18[2] 19[2] 20 21 39:7[3] 17 19 20 21[3] 23 24 25 29[2] 43:3 7[3] 8[3] 44:4 7[5] 8[2] 9 11 13 15 16[3] 23 24[4]

EZEKIEL 45:8[2] 9 46:18 48:11 **DANIEL** 1:10[2] 2:3 23 3:14 15 4:4 5[2] 8 9 10 13[2] 18 19 24 27 30[2] 36[5] 5:13 6:22 26 7:2 15[2] 28[3] 8:17 18 9:3 4[2] 18 19 20[5] 10:3 8 9[2] 10[2] 15 16[4] 17[2] 19 12:8 **HOSEA** 1:9 10 2:2 5[6] 7

HOSEA 2:9[4] 12[2] 23[3] 4:6 8 12 5:10 15[2] 6:5 11 7:2 12 8:1[2] 2 12 9:8 17 10:10 11:1 7 8 12:8 13:11 **JOEL** 1:6 7[2] 13 2:1 25 26 27 28 29 3:2[2] 3 5[3] 17 **AMOS** 2:7 7:8 15 8:2 9:3 10 12 14 **OBADIAH** 13 16

JONAH 1:12 2:2 5 6[2] 7[2] 4:2[2] 3 **MICAH** 1:9 2:4 7 8 9[2] 3:3 5 6:1 5 7[4] 16 7:1 7[2] 9 **HABAK.** 1:12 2:1 3:16[3] 18 19[3] **ZEPH.** 2:8 9[2] 12 3:8[3] 10[2] 11 **HAGGAI** 2:5 23 **ZECH.** 1:6[3] 9 16 17 2:11 3:7[4] 8 4:4

ZECH. 4:5 6 13 5:4 6:4 8 8:7 8 11:4 8 10[2] 12[2] 12:5 13:5 6 7[2] 9[3] 14:5 **MALACHI** 1:6[2] 11[3] 14 2:2 4 5[2] 9 3:1 17 4:2 4 **MATT.** 2:6 15 3:17 5:11 7:21 8:6 8 9[2] 21 9:18 10:18 22 32 33 39 11:10 27 29 30[2]

MATT. 12:18[4] 44 48[2] 49[2] 50[2] 13:30 35 15:13 22 16:17 18 25 17:5 15 18:5 10 19 20 21 35 19:20 29 20:21 23[4] 21:13 28 37 22:4[3] 44 24:5 9 35 37 48 25:27[2] 34 40 26:12[2] 18[2] 26 28 29 38 39 42 53 27:35[2] 46[2] 28:10 **MARK** 1:2

MARK 1:11 3:33[2] 34[2] 35[2] 5:9 23 31 6:23 8:35 38 9:7 17 37 39 41 10:20 29 40[2] 51 11:17 12:6 36[2] 13:6 9 13 31 14:8 14 22 24 34 15:34[2] 16:17 **LUKE** 1:18 20 25 43 44 46 47[2] 2:49 3:22 6:47 7:6 7 8 27 44[2] 45 46[2]

LUKE 8:21[2] 9:24 26 35 38 48 59 61 10:22 29 40 11:7 24 12:4 13 17 18[3] 19 45 14:23 24 26 27 33 15:6 17 18 24 29 16:3 5 21 24 27 18:41 19:8 23[2] 46 20:13 42[2] 21:8 12 17 33 22:11 19 20 28 29 30[2] 42 23:46

LUKE 24:39[2] 49 **JOHN** 2:16 3:29 4:34 49 5:17 24 30 31 43 47 6:32 51 54[2] 55[2] 56[2] 65 7:6 8 8:14 16 19[2] 21 28 31[2] 37 38 43[2] 49 51 52 54[2] 56 10:14 15 16 17[2] 18 25 26 27[2] 28 29[2] 30 32 37 11:21 32 12:7

JOHN 12:26[2] 27 48 13:6 8 9[3] 35 37 38 14:2 7 12 13 14 15 20 21[2] 23 24 26 27 28 15:1 7 8[2] 9 10[3] 11 12 14 15 16 20 21 23 24 16:5 10 23 24 26 17:13 24 18:11 36[4] 37 19:24[2] 20:13 17[4] 21 25[2]

JOHN 20:27[2] 28[2] 21:15 16 17 **ACTS** 2:14 17 18[3] 25[2] 26[3] 27 34[2] 7:34 49[3] 50 59 9:15 16 10:30 11:8 13:22 33 15:7 17 19 16:15 20:24[2] 25 29 34 22:1 6 24:14 17 25:26 26:4[2] 10 28:19 **ROMANS** 1:8 9[3] 2:16 3:7 7:4 18 23[3] 9:1 2 3[2]

ROMANS 9:17[2] 25[2] 26 10:1 21 11:3 14 27 12:3 15:14 24[3] 31 16:3 4 5 7[2] 8 9 11 21[2] 25 **1 COR.** 1:4 11 2:4[2] 4:14 17[2] 5:4 7:25 40 8:13[2] 9:1 15 17 18[2] 27 10:14 29 11:24 25 33 13:3[2] 14:14[2] 18 19[2] 58 6:6 18 24 **2 COR.** 1:16

2 COR. 1:23 2:3 13[2] 6:13 16 18 7:4[2] 8:10 23 11:1 12:9[3] 21 **GAL.** 1:13 14[2] 15 4:14[2] 19 20 6:17 **EPHES.** 1:16 3:4 13 14 6:10 19 21 **PHIL.** 1:3 7[3] 8 13 14 16 19 20[3] 21 22 26 2:2 12[3] 25[2] 3:1 8 4:1[3] 3[2] 14 16

PHIL. 4:19 **COLOS.** 1:24[2] 2:1 4:7 10 11 18 **1 TIM.** 1:2 11 **2 TIM.** 1:2 3[2] 6 16 2:1 8 3:10 4:6 7 16 **PHILE.** 4[2] 10[2] 20 23 24 **HEB.** 1:5 13 2:12 13 3:9 10 11[2] 4:3[2] 5 5:5 8:9 10 10:16 34 38 12:5 13:6

JAMES 1:2 16 19 2:1 3 5 14 18[2] 3:1 10 12 5:10 12 **1 PETER** 5:13 **2 PETER** 1:14 15 17 **1 JOHN** 2:1 3:13 18 **3 JOHN** 4 **REV.** 1:20 2:3 13[3] 16 20 26 27 3:5 8[2] 10 12[5] 16 20 21[2] 10:10[2] 11:3 18:4 21:7 22:12

not

3808, *3756*

GEN. 2:5[2] 16 18 20 25 3:1 3 4 11 17 4:5 7[2] 9 12 5:24 6:3 7:2 8 8:12 21 22 9:4 23 11:7 12:18 13:6[3] 9 14:23[2] 15:1 4 10 13 16 16:10 17:12 14 15 18:3 15 21 24 25 28 29 30[2] 31 32[2] 19:7 8 17 18 20 21 31 33 35 20:4 5 6 7

GEN. 20:9 11 12 21:10 12 16 17 23 26 22:12[2] 16 24:3 5 6 8[2] 21 27 33 37 39 41 49 56 26:2 22 24 29 27:1 2 12 21 23 36[2] 28:1 6 8 15 16 29:25 26 30:31 33 40 42 31:2 5 7 15 20 24 27 28 29 32[2] 33 34 35[2] 38[2] 39 52[3]

GEN. 32:10 25 26 32 34:7 17 19 23 35:5 10 17 36:7 37:4 13 21 27 29 30 38:9 14 16 20 23 26 39:6 8 10 23 40:8 23 41:16 21 31 36 42:2 4 8 13 15 20 21 22[3] 23 32 36[2] 37 38 43:3 5[3] 8 9 23 32 44:4 5 15 18 26 28 30

GEN. 44:31 32 34 45:1 3 5 8 9 20 24 26 46:3 47:9 18[2] 19[2] 22[2] 26 29 48:10 11 18 49:4 6 10 50:19 21 **EXOD.** 1:8 17 19 2:3 3:2 3 5 19[2] 21 4:1[3] 8 9 10 11 14 21 5:2 8 9 10 11 14 19 6:3 9 12 7:4 13 16 24 8:15 18

EXOD. 8:19 21 26[2] 28 29[2] 31 9:6 7[2] 11 12 17 18 19 21 30 32[2] 33 10:7 11 15 19 20 23 26[2] 27 11:7 9 10 12:9 13 23 30[2] 39[2] 45 46 13:13 17 22 14:12 13 20 28 15:23 16:8 15 20 24 25 17:7 17 18 19:12 13[2] 15 24 20:4 5 7[2] 10 13

EXOD. 20:14 15 16 17[2] 19 20[2] 23 25 26 21:5 7 8 10 11 13 18 21 28 29 33 36 22:8 11[2] 13 14 15 16 18 22 25 28 29 23:1[2] 2 6 7[2] 9 18 19 21[2] 24 29 33 24:2 11 25:15 28:28 32 35 43 29:33 34 30:15[2] 20 21 32 37 32:1 18 22

EXOD. 32:23 32 33:3 11 12 15[2] 16 20 23 34:10 20 25 26 29 39:21 23 40:35 37[2] **LEVIT.** 1:17 2:12 4:1 13 22 27 5:1 7 8 11 17 18 6:12 17 23 7:15 18 19 8:33 35 10:1 6 7 9 17 18 11:4[2] 5 6 7 8[2] 10 11 13 26 41 42 43 47 12:8

LEVIT. 13:4[2] 5 6 11 21 23 28 31 32[2] 33 34 36 53 55[2] 14:32 36 48 15:11 31 16:2[2] 13 22 17:4 9 16 18:3[2] 7[2] 8 9 10 11 12 13 14[2] 15[2] 16 17 19 20 21 22 24 26 28 30[2] 19:4 7 9 10 11 12 13[2] 14 15 16 17[2] 18 19[2] 20[3] 23

LEVIT. 19:26 27 28 29 31 33 20:4 19 22 23 25 21:4 5 6 7 10 14 17 18 21 23[2] 22:2 4 6 8 10 12 15 20[2] 22 23 24 25 28 23:22 29 25:5 11 14 17 20 23 28 30[2] 34 37 39 42 43 46 53 54 26:11 13 14[2] 15 18 20 21 23

LEVIT. 26:26 27 31 35 44 27:10 11 20[2] 22 27 33[2] **NUM.** 1:47 49 2:33 4:15 18 19 20 5:3 14 19 28 6:7 9:6 7 13[2] 19 22 10:7 30 31 11:11 14 15 17 19 23 25 26 12:2 7 8[2] 11 12 14 15 20 13:31 14:3 9[2] 16 22 23 30 41 42[3] 43 44

NUM. 15:22 34 39 16:12 14[2] 15[2] 28 29 40[2] 17:10 18:3 4 17 19:12[2] 13[2] 20[2] 20:12[2] 17[2] 18 20 24 21:22[2] 23 34 22:12[2] 30 34 37[3] 23:8[2] 9 12 13 19[3] 21 24 26 24:1 12 17[2] 25:11 26:11 62 64 65 27:3 17 29:7 30:2 5 11 12 31:18 23 35 49 32:5 9 11 18 19

NUM. 32:23 30 33:55 35:12 23[2] 27 30 33 34 36:7 **DEU.** 1:9 17[2] 21 26 29 32 35 37 42[2] 43 45 2:5[3] 9[2] 19[2] 30 36 37 3:2 4[2] 11 22 26 27 4:2 21[2] 22 26 31 42 5:3 5 8 9 11[2] 14 17 32 6:10 11[3] 14 16 7:3 7 10 14 18 21 22

DEU. 7:25 8:3[2] 4 9 11[2] 16 20 9:4 5 6 7 23 26 27 28 10:10 17 11:2[3] 10 16 17 28[2] 30 12:4 8 9 13 16 17 19 23[2] 24 25 30[2] 31 32 13:2 3 6 8 13 16 14:1 3 7[2] 8[2] 10[2] 12 19 21[2] 24 27 15:2 6[2] 7 9 10 13 16 18

DEU. 15:21 23 16:5 16 19[2] 21 17:1 3 7 11 12 15[2] 16 17 20[2] 18:9 10 14 16[2] 19 20 21 22[3] 19:4 6[2] 10 13 14 15 21 20:1 3[3] 5 6 7 15 18 19[2] 20 21:1 3[2] 7 8 14[2] 16 18[2] 20 23[2] 22:1 2[2] 3 4 5 6 8 9 10 11 14 17

DEU. 22:19 20 24 28 29 30 23:1 2[2] 3[2] 4 5 6 7[2] 10[2] 15 16 18 19 20 21 24 25 24:4[2] 5 10 12 14 16 17 19 20 21 25:3 4 5 6 7[2] 8 9 12 13 14 18 19 26:13 14 27:5 26 28:12 18[2] 14 15 27 29 30[2] 31[2] 33 40 41 44

DEU. 28:45 47 49 50 51 55 56 58 61 62 29:4 5[2] 6 15 20 23 26[2] 30:11 12 17 18 31:2 6[2] 8[2] 13 17[2] 21 32:5 6[2] 17[3] 21[2] 27[2] 31 34 47 51 52 33:6[2] 9 11 34:4 7 10 **JOSH.** 1:5[2] 7 8 9[2] 18 2:4 5 14 22 3:4[2] 5:5 6[2] 7 6:10 7:3[2]

JOSH. 7:12 13 19 8:1 4 14 17[2] 26 35[2] 9:14 18 19 26 10:6 8[2] 13[2] 19[2] 25 11:6 11 19 13:13 33 15:63 16:10 17:12 13 16 17 18:2 20:5[2] 9 21:44 45 22:3 17 19 20[2] 22 24 26 27 28 31 33 23:6 7 14[2] 24:10 12 13[3] 19 **JUD.** 1:19 21 28 32 34 2:2

JUD. 2:3 10 14 17[2] 19 20 21 23 3:1 22 25 28 29 4:6 8[2] 9 14 16 18 5:23 30[2] 6:10[2] 13 14 18 23[2] 27 39 7:4[2] 8:1 2 19 20 23 34 9:15 20 28 38 41 54 10:6 11 11:2 7 10 15 17[2] 18 20 24 26 27 28 12:1 2 3 6 13:2 3

JUD.
13:4[2]
6
9
14
16[2]
23
14:4
6
9
14
15
16[3]
18[2]
15:1
2
11
12
13
16:8
9
15[2]
17
20
18:1
9
25
19:10
12[2]
20
23[2]
24
25
20:8
13
16
34
21:1
5[2]
7
8
14
17
18
22[2]
RUTH
1:16
20
2:8[2]
9[2]
11
13
15
16
20
22
3:1
2
3
10
11
13
14
17
18
4:4
10
14
1 SAM.
1:7
8[2]
11
13
16
22[2]
2:3
12
15
16[2]
25
31
32
33
3:2
5
6
7
13
14
17
4:7
9
15
20[2]
5:7
11
12
6:3[2]
6
9[2]
10
7:8
8:3
5
7[2]
18
9:2
4[2]
7
13
20[2]
21
10:1
16
21
11:7

1 SAM.
11:11
13
12:4
5
14
15
17
19
20[2]
21
22
13:8
11
12
13
14[2]
14:1
8
9
17
27
31
34
36
37
39
45[2]
15:3
9
11
17
19
26
29[2]
16:7[2]
10
11
17:8
29
33
39[2]
47
18:17
25
26
19:4[2]
6
11
20:2[2]
3
5
9
12
14[2]
15[2]
26[3]
27
29
30
31
37
38
39
21:8
11[2]
22:5
15
17[2]
23
23:14
17[2]
19
24:7
10
11[2]
12
13
18
21[2]
25:7
11
15
19
25[2]
28
34
26:1
8
9
14
15[2]
16[2]
20
23
28:6
13
18
23
29:3
4[2]
5
6[2]
7
8
9
30:2
10
17
21
22[2]
23
31:4
2 SAM.
1:10
14
20[2]

2 SAM.
1:21
22[2]
23
2:19
21
26
3:8
11
13
22
26
29
34
37
38
4:11
5:6
8
23
6:10
7:6
7
15
9:3
7
10:3
11:3
9
10[3]
11
13
20
21
25
12:13
17
18
23
13:4
12[2]
13
14
16
20
25[2]
26
28[2]
30
32
33
14:2
7
10
11[2]
13
14
18
19
24[2]
28
29[2]
15:11
14
27
35
16:17
19
17:6
7
8
12
13
16
17
19
20
22
23
18:3[2]
11
12
14
20
29
19:7[2]
10
13[2]
19
21
22
23
25
43
20:3
10
21
21:2
17
22:22
23
37
38
39
42
44
23:5[2]
16
17[2]
19[2]
23
24:14
1 KINGS
1:4
6
8
10

1 KINGS
1:11
18
19
26
27
51
52
2:4
6
8
9
16
17
20[2]
23
26
28
32
36
42
43
3:7
11
13[2]
21
5:3
6
6:6
13
7:31
8:5
8
11
19
25
41
46
56
57
9:5
6
12
20
21
10:3[2]
7[2]
20
11:2
4
6
10[2]
11
12
13
33
34
39
41
12:15
16
24
31
13:4
8
10
16
21
22
28
33
14:2
4
8
29
15:3
5
7
14
17
23
29
31
16:11
14
15
20
27
17:1
12
13
14
16
18:5
10[3]
12
13
18
21
40
44
19:2
4
11[2]
12
18[2]
20:7
8
9
11
28
36
21:4
6
15
29
22:3
7

1 KINGS
22:8[2]
17
18
28
33
39
43[2]
45
48
49
2 KINGS
1:3[2]
4
6[3]
15
16[2]
18
2:2
4
6
10[2]
16
17
18[2]
21
3:2
3
11
14[2]
17
26
4:2
3
6
16
24
27
28[2]
29[2]
30
31
39
40
5:12[2]
13
17
20
26
6:9
10
11
16
19
22
27
32
7:2
9
19
8:19
23
9:3
18
20
37
10:4
5
19
21[2]
29
31
34
11:2
6
15
12:3
6
7
13
15
16
19
13:2
6
8
11
12
23
14:3
4
6[2]
11
15
18
24
26
27
28
15:4
6
9
16
18
20
21
24
28
35
36
16:2
5
19
17:2
9
12
14[2]

2 KINGS
17:15
19[2]
22
25
26[2]
34
35
37
38
40
18:6
7
12[2]
22
26
27
29[2]
30
31
32[2]
36[2]
19:3
6
10[2]
25
32
33
20:1
13
15
19
20
21:9
17
22
25
22:2
13
17
20
23:9
22
26
28
33
24:4
5
7
25:24
1 CHRON.
4:10
27
5:1
10:4
13
14
11:5
18
19
21
25
12:19
33
13:3
13
14:14
15:13[2]
16:22
30
17:4
5
6
13
19:3
21:3
6
13
17[2]
24
30
22:8
13
18[2]
23:11
26:10
27:23
24
28:3
20[2]
29:1
25
2 CHRON.
1:11
4:18
5:6
9
11
14
6:9
16
32
36
42
7:2
7
18
8:7
8
11
15
9:2
6[2]
19
20
29

2 CHRON.
10:15
16
11:4
12:7[2]
12
14
15
13:5
7
9
10
12[2]
14:11
13
15:7
13
17
16:7
8
12
17:3
4
18:6
7
17[2]
27
30
32
19:6
10[2]
20:6[3]
7
10[2]
12
15[2]
17[2]
32
33[2]
37
21:7
12
20
22:11
23:8
14
24:5
6
19
22
25
25:2
4[2]
7[2]
13
15
16
20
26
26:18
27:2
28:1
10
13
20
21
27
29:7
11
34
30:3[2]
5
7
8
9
17[2]
18
19
26
32:7
11
12
13
15
17[2]
25
26
33:10
23
34:21
25
33
35:3
15
21[2]
22[2]
36:12
EZRA
2:59
62
63
3:6
13
4:13
14
21
22
5:5
16
6:8
7:24
25
26
9:1
9
12
14

EZRA
10:8
13
NEH.
1:7
2:1
2
3
16
3:5
4:5[2]
10
11
14
5:9[2]
13
14
15
18
6:1
9
11
12
7:3
4
61
64
65
8:9
17
9:16
17
19[2]
20
21[2]
29[2]
30
31
32
35
10:30
31
39
13:1
2
6
10
14
18[2]
19
24
25
26
ESTHER
1:15
16
17
19
2:10[2]
20
3:2
4
5
8
4:4
11[2]
13
16
5:9
6:1
13
7:4
9:10
15
16
27
28
10:2
JOB
1:10
12
22
2:10[2]
12
3:4
6[2]
10
11[2]
16
18
21
26
4:6
16
21
5:6
17
24
6:10[2]
13
29
7:1[2]
8
11
16
19
21[2]
8:10
12
15[2]
18
20
9:5
7
11[2]

JOB
9:13
15
16
18
21
24
28
32
34
35[2]
10:2
7
10
14
15
19
20
21
11:2
11
14
15
20
12:3[2]
9
11
13:2
11
16
20[2]
21
14:2
4
6
7
12[2]
21[2]
15:6
9[2]
15
18
22
29
30
31
32
16:6
13
17
18
22
17:2[2]
4
18:5
21
19:3
7
22
27
20:4
8
13
17
18[2]
19
20[2]
26
21:4
10[2]
14
16
29[2]
22:5
7
11
12
14
20
23:8
11
17
24:1[2]
12
13
16
18
21[2]
25
25:3
5[2]
26:8
27:4
5
6[2]
11
14
15
19[2]
22
28:7
8
13
14[2]
17
19
29:16
22
24[2]
30:10
20[2]
24
25[2]
27
31:3
4
15[2]
17

JOB
31:20[2]
23
31[2]
32
34
32:6
9
13
14
16
21
22
33:7
12
13
14
21
27
33
34:12
19
23
27
30
31
32
33
35:13
14
15[2]
36:4
5
6
7
12
13
19
20
21
26
32
37:4
21
23
24
39:4
16
22
40:5
23
41:9
12
33
42:3[2]
7
8
PSALMS
1:1
3
4
5
3:6
4:4
5:4
5
6:1
7:12
9:10
12
18[2]
19
10:4[2]
6
12
13
14:3
4
15:3
4
5
16:2
4
8
10
17:1
3
5
18:21
22
36
38
41
43
19:3
13
21:2
7
11
22:2[2]
5
11
19
24
23:1
24:4
25:2[2]
7
20
26:1
4
5
9
27:3
9[3]
12
28:1

PSALMS
28:3
5[2]
30:1
3
12
31:8
17
32:2
5
6
9
33:16
34:5
10
20
35:11
15[2]
19
20
22[2]
24
25[2]
36:4[2]
11[2]
12
37:1
7
8
10[2]
19
21
24
25
28
33
36[2]
38:1
9
13[2]
14
21[2]
39:1
6
8
9
12
40:4
6[2]
9
10[2]
11
12
41:2
11
44:3
6
9
12
17
18
21
23
46:2
5
49:9
12
16
17
20
50:3
8
12
51:11[2]
16[2]
17
52:7
53:3
4
54 *title*
3
55:1
11
12
19
23
56:4
8
11
13
58:5
8
59:3
5
11
13
15
60:10[2]
62:2
6
10[3]
64:4
66:7
9
18
20
69:4
5
6[2]
14
15[2]
17
23
27
28
33
71:9[2]
12

PSALMS
71:15
18
73:5
74:9
19[2]
21
23
75:4[2]
5[2]
77:2
19
78:4
7
8[3]
10
22[2]
30
32
37
38
39
42
44
50
53
56
63
67
79:6[2]
8
80:18
81:5
11
82:5
83:1[3]
85:6
8
86:14
89:22
30
31
33
34
35
43
48
91:5
7
92:6
94:7
9[2]
10[2]
14
95:8
10
11
96:10
100:3
101:3
4
5
7[2]
102:2
17
24
103:2
9
10
104:5
9[2]
105:15
28
37
106:7[2]
11
13
23
24
25
34
107:38
108:11[2]
109:1
14
16
17
110:4
112:6
7
8
115:1[2]
5[2]
6[2]
7[2]
17
118:6
17
18
119:6
8
10
11
16
19
31
36
43
46
51
60
61
80
83
85
87
102
109

PSALMS
119:110
116
121
122
133
136
141
153
155
157
158
176
121:3[2]
6
124:1
2
6
125:3
127:5
129:2
7
131:1
132:3
4
10
11
135:16[2]
17
137:6[2]
138:8
139:4
12
15
21[2]
140:8[2]
10
11
141:4[2]
5
8
143:2
7
146:3
147:10[2]
20[2]
148:6
PROV.
1:8
10
15
28[2]
29
3:1
3
5
7
11
15
21
23
24
25
27
28
29
30
31
4:2
5
6
12[2]
13
14[2]
15
16
19
21
27
5:6
7
8
13
17
6:4
20
25
27
28
29
30
33
34
35
7:11
19
23
25[2]
8:1
10
11
26
29
33
9:8
18
10:3
19
30
11:4
21
12:3[2]
7
27
13:1
8

PROV.
14:5
6
7
10
22
15:7
12
16:5
10
25
17:5
7
13
26
18:5
19:2
5[2]
9
10
18
23
24
20:1
4
13
19
21
22
23
21:13
17
26
22:6
20
22
24
26
28
29
23:3
4
5
6
7
9
10[2]
13[2]
17
18
20
22
23
31
35[2]
24:1
7
12[4]
14
15[2]
17[2]
19
21
23
28[2]
29
25:6[2]
8[2]
9
10
27[2]
26:1
2
4
7
17
19
25
27:1[2]
2[2]
10
22
24
28:5
13
20
21
22
27
29:7
19[2]
24
30:2
6
7
10
11
12
15
16[2]
18
25
30
31:3
4[2]
12
18
21
27
ECCL.
1:7
8
2:10[2]
21
23
4:3

ECCL.
4:8
10
12
16
5:1
2[2]
4
5[2]
6
8
10
12
20
6:2
3
5
6
7
7:9
10[2]
16
17
18
20[2]
28[2]
8:3[2]
7
11
13[2]
17[2]
9:2
5
11
12
16
10:4
10
15
17
20[3]
11:2
4[2]
5[2]
6[2]
12:1
2
CANT.
1:6[2]
8
2:7
3:1
2
4
5
5:6
6:6
7:2
8:1
4
ISAIAH
1:3[2]
6
11
15
23
2:4
9
3:7
9
5:4
6
12
25
6:9[2]
7:1
4
7
8
9[2]
12
17
25
8:10
11
12
19
20
9:1
3
12
13
17
20
21
10:4
7[2]
8
9[3]
11
24
11:3
9
13[2]
12:2
13:17[2]
18
22
14:17
20
21
29
16:3
6
12
17:8

ISAIAH
17:10
14
22:2
4
11
14
23:4
13
18
24:9
20
26:10[2]
11
14[2]
18
27:4
9
11
28:12
15
16
18
22
25
27
28
29:9[2]
12[2]
16
17
22
30:1[2]
2
5
6
9
10[2]
14[2]
15
20
31:1
2
3[2]
4
8[2]
32:3
10
33:1[2]
19[2]
20[2]
23[2]
24
34:10
35:4
8[2]
9
36:7
11
12
14[2]
15
16
21[2]
37:3
6
10[2]
26
33
34
38:1
11
39:2
4
40:9
16
20[2]
21[4]
24[3]
26
28[3]
31[2]
41:3
7
9
10[2]
12
13
14
17
42:2
3[2]
4
8
16[3]
20[2]
24[2]
25[2]
43:1
2[2]
5
6
17
18
19
22
23[2]
25
44:2
8[3]
9[2]
18
20
21
45:1
4
5
13

ISAIAH
45:17
18
19[2]
21
23
46:2
7[2]
10
13[2]
47:3
7
8
11[3]
14[2]
48:1
6[2]
7[2]
8[3]
9
10
11
16
19
21
49:5
10
15[2]
23
50:5
6
7[2]
51:6
7
9
10
14
21
52:12
15[2]
53:3
7[2]
54:1[2]
2
4[4]
9
10
11
14[2]
15
55:2[2]
5[2]
8
10
11
13
56:5
57:4
10[2]
11[3]
12
16
58:1
2
3
4
6
7[2]
11
13
59:1
2
6
8[2]
21
60:11
12
62:1[2]
6
8
12
63:8
13
16
19
64:3
4
9
65:1[3]
2
5
6
8[2]
12[3]
17
20
22[2]
23
25
66:4[2]
9
19
24
JER.
1:7
8
17
19
2:2
8[3]
11
17
19
20
23[2]
24
27

JER.
2:34
35
37
3:1
2
4
5
8
10
12[2]
13
19
25
4:1
3
6
8
11
22
27
28
29
5:3[2]
4
9[2]
10[2]
12
13
15
18
19
21[2]
22[4]
28[2]
29[2]
6:8
15
16
17
19
20
25
29
7:4
6[2]
9
13[2]
16[2]
17
19
20
22
24[2]
26
27[2]
28
31
8:2
4[2]
6
7
12
17
19[2]
20
22
9:3[2]
4
5
9[2]
13
23[2]
10:2[2]
4
5[2]
7
10
11
16
20
21[2]
23[2]
24
25[2]
11:3
8[2]
11[2]
12
14[2]
19
21[2]
12:4
6
13
17
13:1
11
12
14
15
17
21
27
14:9
10[2]
11
12[2]
13
14
15[2]
17
18
21[3]
22
15:1
7
14

JER. 15:15, 17, 19, 20, 16:2, 4, 5, 6, 8, 11, 12, 13^2, 17, 17:4, 6^2, 8^2, 11^2, 16, 17, 18^2, 23^2, 27^3, 18:10, 15, 17, 18^2, 23, 19:5, 15, 20:3, 9^2, 11^2, 14, 16, 17, 21:7, 10, 22:5, 6, 10, 11, 13, 15, 16, 17, 18^2, 21^2, 26, 27, 28, 30, 23:2, 10, 16^2, 20, 21^2, 23, 24^2, 29, 32^2, 38, 40, 24:2, 6^2, 25:3, 4, 6^2, 7, 8, 29, 33, 26:2, 4, 5, 16, 19, 24, 27:8^2, 9^2, 13, 14^2, 15, 16, 17, 18, 20, 28:15, 29:6, 8, 9, 11, 16, 19^2, 23, 27, 31, 32, 30:5, 10, 11^2, 14, 19^2, 24, 31:9, 12, 15, 32, 40, 32:4, 5, 23, 33^2, 35, 40^2, 33:3, 20, 21

JER. 33:24, 25^2, 26, 34:3, 4, 14, 17, 18, 35:13, 14^2, 15^2, 16, 17^2, 19, 36:24, 25^2, 31, 37:4, 9^2, 14^2, 19, 20, 38:4, 5, 15^2, 16, 17, 18^2, 20, 23, 24, 25^2, 26, 27, 39:16, 17, 18, 40:3, 5, 7, 9, 14, 16, 41:8^2, 42:5, 10^2, 11^2, 13, 19, 21, 43:2^2, 4, 7, 44:3, 4, 5, 10, 16, 21^2, 23, 27, 45:5, 46:5, 6, 11, 15, 21, 27^2, 28^3, 47:3, 48:11^2, 27, 30^2, 49:9, 10^2, 12^2, 25, 36, 50:2, 5, 7, 13, 20, 24, 42, 51:3, 5, 6, 9, 19, 26, 39, 44, 50, 57, 63

LAM. 1:9, 10, 14, 2:1, 2, 8, 14, 17, 18, 21, 3:2, 22^2, 31, 33, 36, 37, 38, 42, 43

LAM. 3:44, 49, 56, 57, 4:8, 12, 14, 15, 16^2, 17, 5:7, 12

EZEKIEL 1:9, 12, 17, 2:6^2, 8, 3:5, 6^2, 7^2, 9, 18, 19, 20^2, 21^2, 25, 26, 4:8, 14^2, 5:6, 7, 9^2, 6:10, 7:4, 7, 9, 12, 13^2, 19^2, 8:12, 18^2, 9:5, 6, 9, 10, 10:11^2, 16, 11:3, 11, 12, 12:2^2, 6, 9, 12, 13, 13:5, 6, 7^3, 9, 12, 19^2, 22^2, 14:23, 16:4^2, 16, 22, 28, 29, 31, 43^2, 47, 48, 56, 61, 17:9, 10, 12, 14, 18, 18:3, 6, 7, 8, 11, 12, 13, 14, 15^2, 16, 17^2, 18, 19, 20, 21, 22, 23, 24, 25^3, 28, 29^3, 30, 20:3, 7, 8^2, 9, 13, 14, 15, 16, 18, 21, 22, 24, 25^2, 31

EZEKIEL 20:32, 38, 39, 44, 47, 48, 49, 21:5, 26, 22:24, 28, 30, 23:27, 48, 24:6, 7, 8, 12, 13^2, 14, 17^2, 19, 22, 23, 25, 25:10, 26:15, 19, 20, 28:2, 29:5, 30:21, 31:8^3, 32:7, 9, 27, 33:4, 5, 6^2, 8, 9, 12^2, 13, 15, 17^2, 20, 31, 32, 34:2, 3, 4, 8, 10, 35:6, 9, 36:22, 31, 32, 37:18, 38:14, 39:7, 41:6, 42:6, 14, 44:2, 8, 13, 18, 19, 31, 46:2, 9, 18^2, 20, 47:5^2, 11, 12, 48:11, 14

DANIEL 1:8^2, 2:5, 9, 10, 11, 18, 24, 30, 43^2, 44, 3:6, 11, 12^2, 14, 15, 16, 18^2, 24, 28, 4:7, 18, 19, 30, 5:8, 10, 15, 22, 23^2, 6:5, 8^2, 12^2, 13, 17, 22, 26, 7:14^2

DANIEL 8:5, 22, 24, 9:11, 12, 13, 14, 18, 19, 26, 10:7, 12, 19, 11:4, 6, 12, 15, 17, 19, 21, 24, 25, 27, 29, 38, 42, 12:8

HOSEA 1:7, 9^2, 10, 2:2, 4, 6, 7^2, 8, 23^2, 3:3^2, 4:10^2, 14^2, 15^2, 5:3, 4^2, 6, 13, 6:6, 7:2, 8, 9^2, 10, 14, 16, 8:4^2, 6, 13, 9:1, 2, 3, 4^2, 12, 17, 10:3, 9, 11:3, 5, 9^4, 13:13, 14:3^2

JOEL 1:16, 2:2, 7, 8, 13, 17, 21, 22, 3:21

AMOS 1:3, 6, 9^2, 11, 13, 2:1, 4^2, 6, 11, 12, 14, 15, 3:6^2, 8, 10, 4:6, 7^2, 8^2, 9, 10, 11, 5:5^2, 11^2, 14, 18, 20^2, 21, 22, 23, 6:6, 10, 13, 7:3, 6, 8

AMOS 7:10, 13, 16^2, 8:2, 8, 11, 12, 9:1^2, 4, 7^2, 8, 9, 10

OBADIAH 5^2, 8, 12, 13^2, 16, 18

JONAH 1:6, 13, 14^2, 3:7, 9, 10, 4:2, 10, 11

MICAH 1:5^2, 10^2, 11, 2:3, 6^2, 7, 10, 3:1, 4, 5, 6^2, 11, 4:3, 12, 5:7, 15, 6:14^2, 15^3, 7:5^2, 8, 18

NAHUM 1:3, 9, 3:1, 17, 19

HABAK. 1:2^2, 5, 6, 12^2, 13, 17, 2:3^2, 4, 6^2, 7, 13, 3:17

ZEPH. 1:6, 12, 13^2, 2:1, 3:2^4, 3, 5^2, 7, 11, 13, 15, 16^2

HAGGAI 1:2, 6^2, 2:3, 5, 17, 19

ZECH. 1:4^2, 6, 12, 3:2, 4:5, 6, 13, 7:6, 7, 10, 11, 13^3, 14, 8:11, 13, 14, 15

ZECH. 9:5, 10:6, 10, 11:5^2, 6, 9, 12, 16, 12:7, 13:3, 14:2, 6, 7, 17, 18^3, 19

MALACHI 1:2, 8^2, 2:2^3, 6, 9, 10^2, 13, 15, 16, 3:5, 6^2, 7, 10^2, 11, 18

MATT. 1:19, 20, 25, 2:6, 12, 18^2, 3:9, 10, 11, 4:4, 7, 5:17^2, 21, 27, 29, 30, 33, 34, 36, 39, 42, 46, 47, 6:1, 2, 3, 5, 7, 8, 13, 15, 16, 18, 19, 20, 25, 26^2, 28, 29, 30, 7:1^2, 3, 6, 19, 21, 22, 25, 26, 29, 8:8, 10^2, 20, 9:12, 13^3, 14, 24, 10:5^2, 13, 14, 20, 23, 24, 26^3, 28^2, 29^2, 31, 34^3, 37^2, 38^2, 11:6, 11, 17^3, 20, 12:2, 3, 4, 5, 7^2, 11, 16, 19, 20^2

MATT. 12:23, 24, 25, 30^2, 31, 32, 13:5, 11, 12, 13^2, 14^2, 17^2, 19, 21, 27, 34, 55^2, 56, 57, 58, 14:4, 16, 27, 15:2, 6, 11, 13, 17, 20, 23, 24, 26, 32, 16:3, 9, 11^2, 12, 17, 18, 22, 23, 28, 17:7, 12, 16, 19, 21, 24, 18:3, 10, 12, 13, 14, 16, 22, 25, 30, 33, 35, 19:4, 6, 8, 10, 14, 18^3, 20:13, 15, 22, 23, 26, 28, 21:21^2, 25, 29, 30, 32^2, 22:3, 8, 11, 12, 16, 17, 29, 31, 32, 23:3^2, 4, 8, 23, 30, 37, 39, 24:2^3, 6^2, 17, 20, 21, 23, 26^2, 29, 34, 35, 36, 39, 42, 43, 44, 50^2, 25:9^2, 12, 24^2, 26^2, 29, 43^3, 44, 45^2, 26:5

MATT. 26:11, 24, 29, 35, 39, 40, 41, 42, 70, 72, 74, 27:6, 13, 34, 28:5, 6, 10

MARK 1:7, 22, 35, 2:2, 4, 17, 18, 24, 26, 27, 3:12, 20, 4:5, 12^2, 13, 21, 22, 25, 27, 34, 38, 5:3, 7, 10, 19, 36, 39, 6:3^2, 4, 9, 11, 18, 19, 26, 34, 50, 52, 7:3, 4, 5, 18, 19, 24, 27, 8:17, 18^2, 21, 33, 9:1, 6, 18, 28, 30, 32, 37, 38^2, 39, 40, 41, 44^2, 46^2, 48^2, 10:9, 14, 15^2, 19^4, 27, 38, 40, 43, 45, 11:13, 16, 17, 23, 26, 31, 12:10, 14^2, 15, 24^2, 26, 27, 34, 13:2^2, 7^2, 11, 14, 15, 16, 18, 19, 21, 24, 30, 31, 32, 33

MARK 13:35, 14:2, 7, 29, 31, 36, 37, 49, 56, 68, 71, 15:23, 16:6^2, 11, 14, 16, 18

LUKE 1:13, 20^2, 22, 30, 34, 60, 2:10, 26, 37, 43, 45, 49, 50, 3:8, 9, 15, 16, 4:4, 12, 22, 35, 41, 42, 5:10, 19, 31, 32, 36, 6:2, 3, 4, 29, 30, 37^4, 39, 40, 41, 42, 43, 44, 46, 48, 49, 7:6^3, 9^2, 13, 23, 28, 30, 32^2, 45, 46, 8:10^2, 17^2, 18, 19, 28, 31, 47, 49, 50, 52^2, 9:5, 27, 33, 40, 45^2, 49, 50^2, 53, 55, 56, 58, 10:6, 7, 10, 20, 24^2, 40, 42, 11:4, 7, 8, 23^2, 35, 38, 40, 42, 44^2, 46, 52, 12:2^2, 4, 6^2, 7, 10, 15, 21

LUKE 12:26, 27^3, 29, 32, 33^2, 39, 40, 46^2, 47, 48, 56, 57, 59, 13:9, 14, 15, 16, 24, 25, 27, 34, 35, 14:5, 6, 8, 12, 26, 27, 28, 29, 30, 31, 33, 15:4, 8, 13, 28, 16:11, 12, 31, 17:8, 9, 17, 18, 20, 22, 23, 31^2, 18:1, 2, 4^2, 7, 11, 13, 16, 17, 20^4, 30, 19:3, 14, 21^2, 22^2, 23, 26, 27, 44^2, 48, 20:5, 7, 26, 38, 40, 21:6^2, 8^2, 9^2, 14, 15, 18, 21, 32, 33, 22:16, 18, 26, 27, 32, 34, 40, 42, 57, 58, 60, 67, 68, 23:28, 34, 40, 51, 24:3, 6, 11, 16, 18, 23, 24, 26, 32, 39, 41

JOHN 1:3, 5, 8, 10, 11, 13

JOHN 1:20^2, 21, 25, 26, 27, 31, 33, 2:4, 9, 12, 16, 24, 25, 3:7, 8, 10, 11, 12, 15, 16, 17, 18^3, 24, 28, 34, 36^2, 4:2, 15, 18, 22, 29, 32, 35, 42, 48, 5:10, 13, 18, 23^2, 24, 28, 30, 31, 34, 38^2, 40, 41, 42, 43, 44, 45, 47, 6:7, 17, 20, 22, 24, 26, 27, 32, 36, 38, 42, 43, 46, 50, 58, 64^2, 70, 7:1, 6, 8^2, 10, 16, 19, 22, 23, 24, 25, 28^2, 30, 34, 35, 36, 39^2, 42, 45, 49, 8:6, 12, 13, 16, 20, 23, 24, 27, 29, 35, 40, 41, 43, 44, 45, 46, 47^2, 48, 49, 50, 55^3, 57, 9:8, 12, 16^2, 18, 21^2, 25, 27

JOHN 9:29, 30, 31, 32, 33, 39, 10:1, 5^2, 6, 8, 10, 12^2, 13, 16, 21, 25, 26^2, 33, 34, 37^2, 38, 11:4, 9^2, 15, 21, 30, 32, 37^2, 40, 50, 51, 52, 56, 12:5, 6, 8, 9, 15, 16, 30, 35, 37, 39, 40, 42, 44, 46, 47^3, 48, 49, 13:7, 8, 9, 10^2, 11, 16, 18, 36, 38, 14:1, 2, 5, 9, 10^2, 17, 18, 22^2, 24^3, 27^2, 30, 15:2, 6, 15^2, 16, 19, 20, 21, 22^2, 24^2, 16:1, 3, 4, 7^2, 9, 13, 16, 17, 19, 26, 30, 32, 17:9, 14^2, 15, 16^2, 25, 18:1, 17^2, 25^2, 26, 28, 30^2, 31, 36^3, 40, 19:10^2, 12, 21, 24, 31, 33, 36, 20:2, 5, 7, 9, 13

JOHN 20:14, 17^2, 24, 25, 27, 29, 30, 21:4, 6, 8, 11, 18, 23^3, 25

ACTS 1:4, 5, 7, 2:7, 15, 24, 25, 27, 31, 34, 3:23, 4:18, 5:4^3, 7, 22, 28^2, 40, 42, 6:2, 10, 13, 7:5, 18, 19, 25, 32, 39, 40, 48, 50, 52, 53, 60, 8:21, 32, 9:21, 26, 38, 10:14, 15, 28, 41, 47, 11:8, 9, 12:9, 14, 19, 22, 23, 13:10, 11, 25^2, 27, 35, 39, 14:17, 18, 15:19, 38^2, 16:7, 21, 17:4, 5, 6, 12, 24, 27, 29, 18:9^2, 20, 19:2, 9, 26, 27, 30, 31, 32, 35, 20:10, 12, 16, 22, 27, 29, 31, 21:4, 12, 13, 14, 21, 34, 38, 22:9, 11, 18, 22, 23:5^2, 9, 21, 24:4

ACTS 25:7, 11, 16, 24, 27, 26:19, 25, 26, 29, 32, 27:7, 10, 12, 14, 15, 21, 24, 34, 39, 28:4, 19, 24, 25, 26^2

ROMANS 1:13, 16, 21, 28^2, 32, 2:4, 8, 13, 14^2, 21^2, 22, 26, 27, 28, 29^2, 3:3, 8, 10, 12, 17, 29, 4:2, 4, 5, 8, 10, 11, 12, 13, 16, 17, 19^2, 20, 23, 5:3, 5, 11, 13, 14, 15, 16, 6:3, 6, 12, 14^2, 15, 16, 7:1, 6, 7^3, 15^2, 16, 18, 19^2, 20, 8:1, 3, 4, 7, 9^2, 12, 15, 18, 20, 23, 24, 25, 26, 32^2, 9:1, 6^2, 8, 10, 11^2, 16, 21, 24, 25^2, 26, 30, 31, 32, 33, 10:2, 3, 6, 11, 14^2, 16, 18, 19

ROMANS 10:20^2, 11:2^2, 4, 7, 8^2, 10, 18^2, 20, 21^2, 23, 25, 30, 31, 12:2, 3, 4, 11, 14, 16^2, 19, 21, 13:3^2, 4, 5, 9^5, 13^3, 14, 14:1, 3^4, 6^4, 13, 15^2, 16, 17, 20, 22, 23^2, 15:1, 3, 18^2, 20, 21^2, 31, 16:4, 18

1 COR. 1:16, 17^2, 20, 21, 26^3, 27, 28, 2:1, 2, 4, 5, 6, 8, 9, 12, 13, 14, 3:1, 2^2, 3, 4, 16, 4:3, 4, 6, 7^2, 14, 15, 18, 19, 20, 5:1, 2, 6^2, 8, 9, 10, 11^2, 12, 6:1, 2, 3, 5^2, 7^2, 9^3, 12^2, 13, 15, 16, 19^2, 7:1, 4^2, 5^2, 6, 10^2, 11, 12^3, 13^2, 15, 18^2, 21, 23, 27^2, 28^2, 30^3, 31, 35, 36, 38, 8:7

1 COR. 8:8^2, 10, 9:1^4, 2, 4, 5, 6, 7^2, 8, 9, 12^2, 13, 16, 18, 21, 24, 26^2, 10:1, 5, 6, 13, 16^2, 18, 20^2, 23, 27, 28, 29, 33, 11:6, 7, 8, 14, 17^2, 20, 22^3, 29, 31, 32, 34, 12:1, 14, 15^3, 16^3, 13:1, 2, 3, 4^3, 5^3, 6, 14:2, 11, 16, 17, 20, 21, 22^4, 23, 24, 33, 34, 39, 15:9, 10^2, 13, 14, 15^2, 16^2, 17, 29, 32, 33, 34^2, 36, 37, 39, 46, 51, 58, 16:7, 12, 22

2 COR. 1:8, 9, 12, 18, 19, 23, 24, 2:1, 4, 5^2, 11, 13, 17, 3:3^2, 5, 6, 7, 8, 13^2, 4:1, 2, 4, 5, 7, 8^2, 9^2, 16, 18^3, 5:1, 3, 4, 7, 12^2

2 COR. 5:15, 19, 6:1, 3, 9, 12, 14, 17, 7:3, 7, 8, 9, 10, 12, 14, 8:5, 8, 10, 12^2, 13, 19, 21, 9:4, 5, 7, 12, 10:2, 3, 4, 8^2, 9, 12^2, 13, 14^2, 15, 16, 18, 11:4^3, 5, 6, 11, 17, 29^2, 31, 12:1, 4, 5, 6, 13, 14^2, 16, 18^2, 20^2, 21, 13:2, 3, 5, 6, 7, 10

GAL. 1:1, 7, 10, 11, 16, 20, 2:5, 14, 15, 16^2, 20, 21, 3:1, 10, 12, 16, 20, 4:8, 12, 14, 17, 18, 21, 27^2, 30, 31, 5:1, 7, 8, 13, 15, 16, 18, 21, 26, 6:4, 7^2, 9^2

EPHES 1:16, 21, 2:8, 9, 3:5, 13, 4:17, 20, 26^2, 30, 5:3, 4, 7, 15, 17

EPHES. 5:18, 27, 6:4, 6, 7, 12; PHIL. 1:16, 21, 29, 2:4, 6, 12, 16, 21, 27, 30, 3:1, 9, 12, 13, 4:11, 17

COLOS. 1:9, 23, 2:1, 8, 18, 19, 21^{3}, 23, 3:2, 9, 19, 21, 22, 23; 1 THESS. 1:5, 8, 2:1, 3, 4, 8, 9

1 THESS. 2:13, 15, 17, 19, 4:5^{2}, 7, 8, 9, 13^{2}, 15, 5:3, 4, 5, 6, 9, 19, 20; 2 THESS. 1:8, 2, 3, 5

2 THESS. 2:10, 12, 3:2, 6, 7, 8, 9, 10, 11, 13, 14, 15; 1 TIM. 1:9, 20, 2:7, 9, 12, 14, 3:3^{4}, 5, 6

1 TIM. 3:8^{3}, 11, 4:14, 5:1, 8, 9, 13^{2}, 16, 18, 19, 6:1, 2, 3, 17; 2 TIM. 1:7, 8, 9, 12, 16, 2:5, 9

2 TIM. 2:13, 14, 15, 20, 24, 4:3, 8, 16; TITUS 1:6, 7^{4}, 11, 14, 2:3^{2}, 5, 9, 10, 3:5, 14; PHILE. 14

PHILE. 16, 19; HEB. 1:12, 14, 2:5, 8^{2}, 11, 16, 3:8, 10, 11, 15, 16, 17, 18^{2}, 19, 4:2^{2}, 6, 7, 8, 13

HEB. 4:15, 5:5, 12, 6:1, 10, 12, 7:6, 11, 16, 20, 21, 23, 27, 8:2, 4, 9^{3}, 11, 9:7, 8, 9, 11^{2}, 24, 10:1

HEB. 10:2, 4, 5, 8, 25, 35, 37, 39, 11:1, 3, 5^{2}, 7, 8, 13, 16, 23, 27, 31^{2}, 35, 38, 39, 40, 12:4

HEB. 12:5, 7, 8, 9, 18, 19, 20, 25^{3}, 26, 13:2, 6, 9^{3}, 16, 17; JAMES 1:5, 7, 16, 20, 22, 23, 25

JAMES 1:26, 2:1, 4, 5, 6, 7, 11^{2}, 14, 16, 17, 21, 24, 25, 3:1, 2, 10, 14^{2}, 15, 4:1, 2^{3}, 3, 4, 11^{2}

JAMES 4:14, 17, 5:6, 9, 12, 17^{2}; 1 PETER 1:4, 8^{2}, 12, 14, 18, 23, 2:6, 10^{2}, 16, 18, 23^{2}, 3:1, 3, 4, 6

1 PETER 3:7, 9, 14, 21, 4:4, 12, 16, 17, 5:2^{2}, 4; 2 PETER 1:12, 16, 21, 2:3^{2}, 4, 5, 10, 11, 12, 21, 3:8, 9^{2}

1 JOHN 1:6, 8, 10^{2}, 2:1, 2, 4^{2}, 11, 15^{2}, 16, 19^{2}, 21^{2}, 23, 27, 28, 3:1^{2}, 2, 6^{2}, 9, 10^{3}, 12, 13, 14, 18

1 JOHN 3:21, 4:1, 3^{2}, 6^{2}, 8^{2}, 10, 18, 20^{2}, 5:3, 6, 10^{2}, 12^{2}, 16^{3}, 17, 18^{2}; 2 JOHN 1, 5, 7, 8, 9^{2}, 10^{2}, 12

3 JOHN 9, 10, 11^{2}, 13; JUDE 5, 6, 9, 10, 19; REV. 1:17, 2:2^{2}, 3, 9, 11, 13, 21, 24^{2}

REV. 3:2, 3^{2}, 4, 5, 8, 9, 17, 18, 4:8, 5:5, 6:6, 10, 7:1, 3, 8:12, 9:4^{2}, 5, 6, 20^{3}, 10:4, 11:2, 6, 9

REV. 12:8, 11, 13:8, 15, 14:4, 15:4, 16:9, 11, 18, 20, 17:8^{3}, 10, 11, 18:4^{2}, 19:10, 20:4, 5, 15, 21:25, 22:9, 10

O

5599

GEN. 17:18, 27:34, 38, 32:9, 43:20, 49:6, 18; EXOD. 4:10, 13, 15:6^{2}, 11, 16, 17^{2}, 32:4, 8, 34:9; NUM. 10:36, 12:13, 16:22, 21:17, 29, 24:5^{2}; DEU. 3:24, 4:1, 5:1, 29, 6:3, 4, 9:1, 26, 20:3, 21:8, 26:10, 27:9, 32:1^{2}, 6, 29, 43, 33:23, 29^{2}; JOSH. 7:7, 8, 13; JUD. 3:19, 5:3^{2}, 21, 31, 6:22

JUD. 13:8, 16:28^{2}, 21:3; 1 SAM. 1:11, 4:9, 17:55, 20:12, 23:10, 11, 20, 26:17; 2 SAM. 1:25, 7:18, 19^{2}, 22, 25, 27, 28, 29, 14:4, 9, 22, 15:31, 34, 16:4, 18:33^{2}, 19:4, 26, 20:1, 22:29, 50, 23:17, 24:10; 1 KINGS 1:13, 20, 24, 3:7, 17, 26, 8:28, 53, 12:16, 28, 13:2, 17:18, 20, 21, 18:26, 37, 19:4, 20:4, 21:20, 22:28

2 KINGS 1:11, 13, 4:40, 6:12, 26, 8:5, 9:5^{2}, 23, 13:14, 19:15, 19, 20:3; 1 CHRON. 16:13, 34, 35, 17:16, 17^{2}, 19, 20, 25, 27, 21:17, 29:11^{2}, 16, 18; 2 CHRON. 1:9, 6:14, 16, 17, 19, 41^{2}, 42, 10:16, 13:12, 14:11^{2}, 20:6, 12, 17, 20, 25:7; EZRA 9:6, 10, 15; NEH. 1:5, 11, 4:4, 6:9, 13:14, 22, 29, 31

ESTHER 7:3; JOB 7:7, 20, 13:5, 14:13, 16:18, 21, 19:21, 33:31, 34:2, 37:14; PSALMS 2:10, 3:3, 7^{2}, 4:1, 2, 5:1, 3, 8, 10, 6:1, 2^{2}, 3, 4, 7:1, 3, 6, 8, 8:1, 9, 9:1, 2, 6, 13, 19, 10:1, 12^{2}, 12:7, 13:1, 3, 16:1, 2, 17:1, 6, 7, 13, 14, 18:1, 15, 49, 19:14, 21:1, 22:2, 3, 19^{2}

PSALMS 24:6, 7, 9, 25:1, 2, 4, 6, 7, 11, 17, 22, 25, 26:1, 2, 6, 27:7, 9, 11, 28:1, 29:1, 30:1, 2, 3, 4, 8, 10, 12, 31:1, 5, 9, 14, 17, 23, 33:1, 22, 34:3, 8, 9, 35:1, 22^{2}, 24, 36:6, 7, 10, 38:1, 15^{2}, 21^{2}, 22, 39:12, 13, 40:5, 8, 9, 11, 13^{2}, 17, 41:10, 42:1

PSALMS 42:5, 6, 11, 43:1^{2}, 3, 4, 5, 44:1, 4, 23, 45:3, 6, 10, 47:1, 48:9, 10, 50:7^{2}, 51:1, 10, 14, 15, 17, 52:1, 4, 54:1, 2, 6, 55:1, 9, 23, 56:1, 2, 7, 12, 57:1, 5, 7, 9, 11, 58:1^{2}, 6^{2}, 59:1, 3, 5, 8, 11, 17, 60:1^{2}, 10^{2}, 61:1, 5, 7, 62:12, 63:1, 64:1, 65:1, 2, 5

PSALMS 66:8, 10, 67:3, 4, 5, 68:7, 9, 10, 24, 28, 32, 35, 69:1, 5, 6^{2}, 13^{2}, 16, 29, 70:1^{2}, 5^{2}, 71:1, 4, 5, 12^{2}, 17, 18, 19^{2}, 22^{2}, 72:1, 73:20, 74:1, 10, 18, 19, 21, 22, 75:1, 76:6, 77:13, 16, 78:1, 79:8, 9, 12, 80:1, 3, 4, 7, 14, 19, 81:8^{2}, 82:8, 83:1^{2}, 13, 16, 84:1, 3, 8^{2}

PSALMS 84:9, 12, 85:4, 7, 86:1, 2, 3, 4, 6, 8, 9, 11, 12, 14, 15, 16, 87:3, 88:1, 13, 89:5, 8, 15, 51, 90:13, 14, 92:1, 5, 9, 93:3, 5, 94:1^{2}, 5, 12, 18, 95:1, 6, 96:1, 7, 9, 97:8, 98:1, 99:8, 101:1, 2, 102:1, 12, 24, 103:1, 2, 22, 104:1^{2}, 24, 35, 105:1, 6, 106:1, 4^{2}, 47

PSALMS 107:1, 108:1, 3, 5, 11^{2}, 109:1, 21, 26^{2}, 113:1, 114:5, 115:1, 9, 10, 116:4, 7, 16, 19, 117:1, 118:1, 25^{2}, 29, 119:5, 8, 10, 12, 31, 33, 41, 52, 55, 57, 64, 65, 75, 89, 97, 107, 108, 137, 145, 149, 151, 156, 159, 169, 174, 120:2, 122:2, 123:1, 3, 125:4, 126:4, 130:1, 3, 132:8, 135:1, 9, 13^{2}

PSALMS 135:19^{2}, 20, 136:1, 2, 3, 26, 137:7, 8, 139:4, 19, 21, 23, 140:4, 6, 7, 8, 141:3, 7, 8, 142:5, 143:7, 9, 11, 144:5, 9, 145:1, 10, 146:1, 147:12^{2}; PROV. 4:10, 5:7, 6:9, 7:24, 8:4, 5, 32, 30:13, 31:4; ECCL. 10:16, 17, 11:9; CANT. 1:5, 7, 8, 9, 2:7, 14, 3:5, 11, 4:11, 16

CANT. 5:1, 8, 9, 16, 6:1, 4, 13, 7:1, 6, 13, 8:1, 4, 12; ISAIAH 1:2^{2}, 2:5, 5:3, 8:8, 9, 10:5, 24, 30^{2}, 12:12, 14:12, 31^{2}, 16:9, 21:2^{2}, 10, 13, 23:4, 10, 12, 24:17, 26:8, 13, 15, 27:12, 33:2, 37:16, 17^{2}, 20, 38:3, 14, 16, 40:9^{2}, 27^{2}, 41:1, 43:1^{2}, 22, 44:1, 2, 21^{2}, 23^{2}, 45:15, 46:3, 8, 47:1^{2}

ISAIAH 47:5, 48:1, 12, 18, 49:1, 3, 13^{3}, 51:4, 9, 17, 52:1^{2}, 2^{2}, 54:1, 11, 62:6, 63:16, 17, 64:4, 8, 9; JER. 2:4, 12, 28, 31, 3:20, 4:1, 14, 19, 5:3, 15, 21, 6:8, 18, 19, 23, 26, 7:29, 9:20, 10:1, 6, 7, 17, 23, 24, 11:5, 13, 20, 12:1, 3, 13:27, 14:7, 8, 9, 20, 22, 15:5

JER. 15:15, 16, 16:19, 17:3, 12, 13, 14, 18:6^{2}, 19, 19:3, 20:7, 12, 21:12, 13, 22:2, 23, 29, 30:10^{2}, 31:4, 7, 10, 21, 22, 23, 32:25, 34:4, 37:20, 42:19, 45:2, 46:11, 19, 27^{2}, 28, 47:6, 48:2, 19, 28, 32, 43, 46, 49:3, 4, 8, 16, 30, 50:11, 24, 31, 42, 51:13, 25, 62; LAM. 1:9, 11, 20, 2:13^{2}

LAM. 2:18, 20, 3:55, 58, 59, 61, 64, 4:21, 22, 5:1, 19, 21; EZEKIEL 3:25, 7:7, 8:15, 17, 10:13, 11:4, 5, 12:25, 13:4, 11, 16:35, 18:25, 29, 30, 31, 20:31, 39, 44, 23:22, 26:3, 27:3^{2}, 8, 28:16, 22, 33:7, 8, 10, 11, 20, 34:9, 17, 35:3, 15, 36:8, 22, 32, 37:3, 4, 9, 12, 13, 38:3, 16, 39:1

EZEKIEL 44:6, 45:9; DANIEL 2:4, 23, 29, 31, 37, 3:4, 9, 10, 12, 14, 16, 17, 18, 24, 4:9, 18, 22, 24, 27, 31, 5:10, 18, 22, 6:7, 8, 12, 13, 15, 20, 21, 22, 8:17, 9:4, 7, 8, 15, 16, 17, 18, 19^{4}, 22, 10:11, 16, 19, 12:4, 8; HOSEA 5:1^{2}, 3, 8, 6:4^{2}, 11, 8:5

HOSEA 9:1, 14, 10:9, 13:9, 14^{2}, 14:1; JOEL 1:11^{2}, 19, 2:17, 21, 3:4, 11; AMOS 2:11, 3:1, 4:5, 12^{2}, 5:1, 25, 6:14, 7:2, 5, 12, 8:4, 14, 9:7; OBADIAH 9; JONAH 1:6, 14^{2}, 2:6, 4:2, 3; MICAH 1:2, 13, 15, 2:7, 12, 3:1, 4:8, 10, 13, 5:1, 6:2, 3, 5, 8, 7:8; NAHUM 1:15, 3:18

HABAK. 1:2, 12^{3}, 3:2^{2}; ZEPH. 2:1, 5, 3:14^{3}; HAGGAI 1:4, 2:4^{2}, 23; ZECH. 1:9, 12, 2:7, 10, 13, 3:2, 8, 4:7, 8:13, 9:9^{2}, 13^{2}, 11:1, 2, 7, 13:7; MALACHI 1:6, 2:1; MATT. 3:7, 6:30, 8:26, 11:25, 12:34, 14:31, 15:22, 28, 16:3, 8, 17:17, 18:32, 20:30, 31, 23:37, 26:39, 42; MARK 9:19, 12:29

LUKE 3:7, 5:8, 9:41, 10:21, 12:28, 13:34, 24:25; JOHN 17:5, 25; ACTS 1:1, 7:42, 13:10, 18:14, 25:26, 26:13, 19; ROMANS 2:1, 3, 7:24, 9:20, 11:33; 1 COR. 7:16^{2}, 15:55^{2}; 2 COR. 6:11; GAL. 3:1; 1 TIM. 6:11, 20; HEB. 1:8, 10:7, 9; JAMES 2:20; REV. 4:11, 6:10, 11:17, 15:4, 16:5

of

GEN. 1:2^{3}, 6, 10, 14, 15, 17, 20, 24, 25, 26^{2}, 27, 28^{2}, 29^{2}, 30^{2}, 2:1, 4^{2}, 5^{2}, 6, 7^{3}, 9^{5}, 10, 11^{2}, 12, 13^{2}, 14^{2}, 17^{4}, 19^{3}

GEN. 2:20^{2}, 21, 23^{2}, 3:1^{3}, 2^{3}, 3^{4}, 6, 7, 8^{4}, 11, 12, 14^{2}, 17^{6}, 18, 19^{2}, 20, 21, 22^{3}, 23, 24^{4}, 4:2^{2}, 3^{3}, 4^{3}, 10, 14, 16^{3}, 17^{3}

GEN. 4:19^{2}, 20^{2}, 21, 22^{2}, 23, 25, 26, 5:1^{3}, 4, 8, 11, 14, 17, 20, 23, 27, 29^{2}, 31, 6:1, 2^{2}, 4^{4}, 5^{3}, 7^{2}, 8, 9, 14^{2}, 15^{4}

GEN. 6:16, 17^{2}, 19^{3}, 20^{5}, 21, 7:2^{2}, 3^{3}, 4, 6, 7^{3}, 8^{4}, 10, 11^{4}, 13^{2}, 14, 15^{2}, 16, 18, 21^{4}, 22^{2}, 23^{3}, 8:2^{2}, 3, 4^{2}, 5^{2}, 6^{2}, 8

GEN. 8:9^{2}, 10, 13^{3}, 14, 16, 17^{4}, 19, 20^{2}, 21, 9:2^{5}, 5^{5}, 6, 10^{6}, 11, 12, 13, 15, 16, 17, 18^{3}, 19^{2}, 21, 22^{2}, 23, 25, 26, 27

GEN. 9:29, 10:1^{2}, 2, 3, 4, 5, 6, 7^{2}, 10^{2}, 11, 14, 18, 19, 20, 21^{3}, 22, 23, 30, 31, 32, 11:1^{2}, 2, 4, 5, 8, 9^{3}, 10

GEN. 11:27, 28^{2}, 29^{5}, 31^{3}, 32, 12:1, 2, 3, 4, 5^{2}, 6^{2}, 8^{2}, 13, 15, 17, 13:1, 4^{2}, 7^{2}, 10^{3}, 11, 12^{2}, 13, 16^{2}, 17^{2}, 18, 14:1^{5}, 2^{5}

GEN. 14:3, 7, 8^{6}, 9^{4}, 10^{3}, 11, 13^{3}, 15, 17^{4}, 18^{2}, 19^{2}, 20, 21, 22^{2}, 24, 15:1, 2^{2}, 4^{2}, 7^{2}, 9^{3}, 12, 13, 16, 18, 16:2, 3, 7^{2}

GEN. 16:8, 9, 10, 11, 12, 13, 17:4, 5, 6^{2}, 8, 11^{2}, 12^{2}, 14, 16^{4}, 23^{2}, 24, 25, 27^{2}, 18:1^{2}, 5, 6, 10, 11, 13, 14, 18, 19^{2}

GEN. 18:20, 21, 25, 28^{2}, 19:1, 4^{2}, 8, 11, 12, 13^{2}, 14, 15, 16^{2}, 22, 24, 25, 26, 28^{3}, 29^{3}, 30, 31, 32, 34, 36, 37, 38^{2}, 20:2^{2}

GEN. 20:5^{2}, 6, 11, 12^{2}, 13, 16^{2}, 18^{3}, 21:2, 3, 9, 10, 11, 12^{2}, 13^{2}, 14^{2}, 15, 16, 17^{4}, 19, 21^{3}, 22, 25^{2}, 26, 27, 28, 30, 31

GEN. 21:32^{2}, 33, 22:2^{3}, 3, 6^{2}, 8, 9, 11^{2}, 13, 14^{2}, 15^{2}, 17^{2}, 18, 21, 23:1^{2}, 2, 3, 4^{2}, 5, 6^{2}, 7^{2}, 8^{2}, 9^{3}, 10^{5}, 11^{2}, 12, 13^{3}

GEN. 23:15, 16^{3}, 17, 18^{3}, 19^{3}, 20^{2}, 24:2, 3^{4}, 7^{2}, 9, 10^{4}, 11^{2}, 12, 13^{3}, 15^{2}, 17, 22^{3}, 24^{2}, 27^{3}, 28, 30, 31, 37^{2}, 40^{2}, 42, 43^{2}, 47

GEN. 24:48, 53^{2}, 60^{3}, 62, 25:3, 4^{2}, 6, 7^{2}, 8, 9^{3}, 10^{2}, 11, 12, 13^{3}, 16, 17^{2}, 18, 19, 20^{2}, 21, 22, 23, 27, 28, 34, 26:1^{2}, 2

GEN. 26:4^{2}, 7^{3}, 8, 9, 10, 14^{3}, 15, 17, 18^{3}, 19, 20^{2}, 21, 22, 24, 25, 26^{2}, 29, 33, 34^{2}, 35, 27:2, 9, 15, 16^{3}, 17, 19, 22

GEN. 27:25, 27^{3}, 28^{4}, 30^{2}, 31, 33, 34, 39^{3}, 41^{2}, 42, 45, 46^{7}, 28:1^{2}, 2^{3}, 3, 4, 5^{2}, 6^{2}, 8, 9^{2}, 11^{2}, 12^{2}, 13^{2}, 14^{2}, 15, 16, 17^{2}

GEN. 28:18, 19^{2}, 22, 29:1^{2}, 2^{2}, 4, 5, 10^{3}, 13, 14, 16^{2}, 22, 30:2, 14^{2}, 16, 32, 35, 36, 37^{2}, 40^{2}, 41, 31:1^{2}, 2, 3, 5, 9, 11

GEN. 31:13, 15, 18^{2}, 25, 29^{2}, 33, 35, 37, 38, 39^{3}, 42^{4}, 48, 53^{4}, 32:1, 2, 3^{2}, 9^{2}, 10^{3}, 11^{2}, 12, 13, 16, 20, 24, 25^{3}, 30, 32^{3}

GEN. 33:8, 10, 15[2], 17, 18[2], 19[4], 34:1[2], 2[2], 3, 6, 7[2], 8, 13, 15, 19, 20[2], 23, 24[4], 25[2], 26[2], 27, 30, 35:1, 3, 5[2], 6, 7, 8, 9, 11[3], 14, 15, 20, 21, 22, 23, 24, 25, 26[2], 27, 28, 29, 36:1, 2[5], 3, 5[2], 6[3], 7, 9[2], 10[5], 11, 12, 13[2], 14[3], 15[4], 16[3], 17[4], 18[3], 19, 20, 21[3], 22, 23, 24[2], 25[2], 26, 27, 28, 29, 30[2], 31[2], 32[2], 33[2], 34[2], 35[3], 36, 37, 38, 39[4], 40[2], 43[3], 37:1, 2[2], 3[2], 14[2], 20, 21, 22, 23[2], 25, 28[2], 31, 32, 36[2], 38:2, 7, 12[2], 19, 20, 21, 22, 27, 39:1[4], 2, 5, 11[2], 14, 19, 21[2], 22[2], 23, 40:1[3], 2[3], 3[2], 4, 5[4], 7

GEN. 40:8, 12, 14[2], 15[2], 17[3], 20[2], 41:1, 2, 3[2], 5, 8, 10, 11, 12, 14, 15, 16, 17, 18, 19, 25, 27, 29[2], 30[2], 31, 33, 34[2], 35[2], 36[2], 37[2], 38, 41, 42, 43, 44, 45[3], 46[3], 48[3], 49, 50[3], 51, 52[2], 53[2], 54[2], 55, 56[2], 42:5[2], 6, 7, 9[2], 12, 13[2], 15, 16[2], 19[3], 21, 27, 29, 30[2], 32[2], 33[3], 35[2], 36, 43:2, 7[3], 9, 11, 12, 14, 16, 18, 19[2], 21, 23, 27[2], 29, 34, 44:1, 2, 4, 8[3], 9, 16, 20, 24, 31, 33, 45:2, 8[2], 9, 10, 11, 12, 13[2], 17, 18[2], 19[2], 20, 21[2], 22[4], 23, 25, 26, 27[2], 46:1, 2, 3, 6, 8, 9, 10[2], 11, 12[3], 13, 14, 15[2], 16

GEN. 46:17[2], 18, 19, 20[3], 21, 22, 23, 24, 25, 26, 27[3], 28, 31, 34, 47:1, 2, 4[2], 6[4], 9[3], 11[3], 13, 14, 15[2], 17, 18[2], 20, 21[2], 22[2], 24[2], 25, 26[2], 27[2], 28[2], 30, 48:3, 4, 5, 6, 7[2], 10, 16[2], 17, 19, 21, 22[2], 49:2, 3[3], 5, 8, 10, 11, 13[2], 16[2], 20, 24[4], 25[5], 26[6], 28, 29, 30[4], 32[3], 50:3, 4[3], 5, 7[4], 8[2], 10, 11[2], 13[5], 17[4], 19, 23[3], 24, 25[2]

EXOD. 1:1[2], 5[2], 7, 9[2], 10, 12[2], 13, 14, 15[4], 16, 17, 18, 2:1[3], 3, 5, 6, 7, 10, 11, 13, 15[2], 16, 19[2], 23[5], 25, 3:1[4], 2[4], 4[2], 6[4], 7[2], 8[4], 9[2], 10[2], 11[2], 12, 13, 14, 15[5], 16[5], 17[3]

EXOD. 3:18[3], 19, 21, 22[4], 4:5[4], 7, 8[2], 9[3], 10[2], 13, 14, 16[2], 20[2], 25, 26, 27, 28, 29, 30, 5:1, 3, 4, 5, 6, 8, 10, 11, 12[2], 14[2], 15[2], 18, 19[3], 21[2], 6:1, 3, 4[2], 5[2], 6[3], 7, 9[2], 11[3], 12[2], 13[5], 14[4], 15[3], 16[4], 17, 18[3], 19[2], 20[2], 21, 22, 23[2], 24[2], 25[4], 26[2], 27[2], 28, 29, 30, 7:2[2], 3, 4[3], 5, 11, 16, 18[2], 19[5], 20[2], 21[3], 24[2], 8:3, 5, 6[2], 7, 12, 13[4], 16[2], 17[3], 19, 21[4], 22[3], 24[5], 26[2], 29, 31[2], 9:1, 3, 4[4], 6[4], 7[3], 8[3], 9[2], 10, 11, 12, 13, 20[2], 21, 22[3], 23, 24, 25[3], 26[2], 29, 33, 35[2], 10:1, 2, 3, 5[3], 6[2], 12[3], 13, 14[2], 15[5], 19

EXOD. 10:20, 21, 22, 23, 11:2[5], 3[4], 4, 5[4], 6, 7[2], 9, 10[2], 12:1, 2[2], 3[3], 4, 5, 6[3], 7[2], 9, 10[2], 12[3], 13, 15, 16, 17[3], 18[2], 19, 21, 22[3], 27[3], 28, 29[4], 31, 33, 35[5], 36, 37, 39[3], 40[2], 41[3], 42[4], 43, 46[2], 47, 50, 51[3], 13:2[3], 3[3], 5, 8[2], 9, 11, 12, 13[2], 14[2], 15[4], 16[2], 17[2], 18[5], 19[2], 20, 21[2], 22[2], 14:2, 3[2], 5[3], 7[2], 8[4], 9, 10[2], 11, 13, 15, 16[2], 17, 19[3], 20[2], 22[2], 23, 24[4], 25, 27, 28[2], 29[2], 30[2], 15:1, 3, 7, 8[2], 14, 15[3], 16, 17, 19[4], 20, 22, 23[3], 26[2], 27, 16:1[6], 2[2], 3[3], 6[2], 7, 9[2], 10[3], 12[2], 14, 15, 16[2], 17, 19, 20[2], 22, 23, 27

EXOD. 16:29[2], 31[2], 32[2], 33, 35[3], 36, 17:1[4], 3, 5[2], 6[3], 7[4], 9[2], 10, 12, 13, 14[2], 15, 18:1[3], 3[2], 4[3], 5, 7, 9[2], 10[5], 12, 15, 16, 21[6], 24, 25[5], 19:1[4], 2, 3[3], 6[2], 7, 8, 9, 11, 12, 16, 17[2], 18, 19, 20[2], 21, 20:2[4], 4, 5[2], 6, 7, 10, 18, 22, 23[2], 24, 25[2], 21:9, 10, 19, 26[2], 28, 30[2], 32, 34[2], 35, 22:5[4], 6, 7, 8, 9[2], 11[2], 14, 17, 21, 25, 28, 29[3], 31, 23:5, 8, 9[2], 11[2], 12, 13[3], 15[2], 16[5], 18[2], 19[3], 21, 25, 26, 29, 31[2], 24:1[2], 3, 4[2], 5[3], 6[2], 7[2], 8, 9, 10[3], 11[2], 12, 18, 16[3], 17[5], 18, 25:2[2], 3, 9[2], 10, 11, 12[3], 13, 14, 15

EXOD. 25:17, 18[3], 19, 20, 22[2], 23, 24, 25, 26, 27, 28, 29, 31[3], 32[6], 33, 35[4], 36[3], 38, 39[2], 26:1[2], 2[3], 4[4], 5, 6, 7, 8[3], 9, 10[2], 11, 12[3], 13[4], 14[2], 15, 16[2], 17, 19, 20, 21, 22, 23, 24, 25, 26[3], 27[4], 28, 29, 31[2], 32[2], 33, 34, 35, 36[2], 37[3], 27:1, 2[2], 3, 4[2], 5[2], 6, 7, 9[3], 10[3], 11[4], 12[2], 13, 14[2], 16[3], 17[2], 18[3], 19[3], 20, 21[3], 28:1, 3, 6[4], 8[4], 9[2], 10[2], 11[5], 12[3], 13, 14[2], 15[7], 17[2], 21[3], 22[2], 23[2], 24[2], 25[2], 26[3], 27[3], 28[3], 29[3], 30[3], 31[2], 32[4], 33[5], 34, 36[2], 37, 38[2], 39[3], 43, 29:2, 4, 5[2], 10[2], 11[2], 12[4], 14, 15, 17, 19, 20[7], 21[3], 22[2], 23[4]

EXOD. 29:24, 25, 26[2], 27[6], 28[4], 29, 30, 31, 32[3], 34[3], 38, 40[5], 41, 42[2], 43, 44, 45, 46[2], 30:1, 2, 3, 4[2], 5, 6, 10[3], 12[2], 13[2], 16[5], 18[3], 20, 22[3], 24[3], 25[2], 26[2], 27, 28, 31, 32, 33, 34, 35, 36[3], 31:2[4], 3[2], 5[3], 6[4], 7[3], 8, 9, 10[2], 13, 15, 16, 17, 18[4], 32:1[4], 2[3], 4[2], 7[2], 8[2], 10, 11[2], 12[2], 13[2], 14, 15, 16[2], 17[2], 18[3], 19, 20[2], 22, 23[3], 26[2], 27, 28[3], 31, 32, 33, 34, 33:1[2], 3, 5[2], 6[2], 7[2], 9, 11[2], 16, 19, 22, 34:1, 2, 4[2], 5, 7, 10, 12, 15[2], 16, 18[2], 20[2], 22[4], 23, 25[3], 26[3], 27, 28, 29, 30[2], 31, 32, 34, 35[3], 35:1[2], 2, 4[2], 5[2]

EXOD. 35:12, 15, 16, 17[2], 18[2], 19[2], 20[3], 21[2], 22[2], 23, 24[2], 25[4], 29[3], 30[5], 31[2], 33[3], 34[3], 35[8], 36:1[2], 3[4], 4, 5, 6, 8[3], 9[3], 11[4], 12[2], 13, 14, 15[3], 17[2], 18, 19[2], 20, 21[2], 22, 24, 25, 26, 27, 28, 29, 30, 31[3], 32[3], 34, 35[2], 36[3], 37[2], 38[2], 37:1[4], 2, 3[4], 4, 5, 6, 7[3], 8, 9, 10, 11, 12[2], 13, 16, 17[3], 18[5], 19[2], 21[4], 22[3], 23, 24[2], 25[5], 26[3], 27[2], 28, 29, 38:1[2], 2, 3[2], 4[2], 5, 6, 7, 8[7], 9[2], 10[2], 11[3], 12[3], 14[2], 15[2], 16[2], 17[6], 18[3], 19[4], 20[3], 21[6], 22[4], 23[3], 24[3], 25[3], 26, 27[5], 28, 29, 30[3], 31[4], 39:1[2], 2, 5[3], 6[3], 7[2], 8[3], 10, 13, 14[3], 15[2], 16[2]

EXOD. 39:17[2], 18[2], 19[4], 20[3], 21[3], 22[3], 23[2], 24[2], 25[2], 26, 27[2], 28[3], 29[2], 30[3], 31, 32[4], 34[3], 35, 39, 40[4], 41, 42, 40:2[3], 3, 5[3], 6[4], 8, 10, 12[2], 17, 19, 21[2], 22[2], 24[2], 26, 28, 29[4], 30, 32, 33, 34[2], 35[2], 36, 38[3]

LEVIT. 1:1[2], 2[5], 3[4], 4, 5[2], 7, 9, 10[3], 11, 13, 14[3], 15, 16, 17, 2:1, 2[4], 3[3], 4[2], 5, 7, 8, 9, 10[2], 11, 12, 13[3], 14[4], 16[4], 3:1[2], 2[3], 3[2], 5, 6[2], 8[2], 9[2], 11, 13[3], 16, 4:2[4], 3, 4[2], 5[2], 6[2], 7[9], 8, 10[3], 11, 13[4], 14, 15[2], 16[2], 17, 18[7], 22[2], 23, 24, 25[6], 26[2], 27[3], 28, 29[2], 30[4], 31, 33, 34[5], 35[2], 5:1[3], 2[3], 3[2], 4[2], 5

LEVIT. 5:9[6], 11[2], 12, 13, 15[4], 16, 17[2], 18, 6:3, 5, 6, 7, 9[3], 12, 14[2], 15[5], 16[2], 17, 18[3], 20[5], 21[2], 22, 23, 26[2], 27, 30, 7:1, 3, 8, 10, 11[2], 12[2], 13[2], 14[3], 15[3], 16[2], 17[2], 18[4], 20[3], 21[4], 23[5], 24[4], 25[2], 26[4], 27, 29[4], 30, 32[2], 33[2], 34[4], 35[6], 36[2], 37[7], 38[2], 8:2, 3[2], 4[2], 7, 12, 14, 15[2], 18, 22[2], 23[5], 24[4], 26[3], 29[2], 30[2], 31[3], 32[2], 33[4], 35[3], 36, 9:1, 3[3], 5, 6, 7, 8, 9[3], 10, 17, 18, 19[2], 22, 23[2], 10:1[2], 4[3], 5, 6, 7[3], 9, 11[2], 12[2], 13[2], 14[4], 15, 16[2], 17, 18, 11:2, 4[2], 8, 9, 10[2], 11, 21, 22, 25, 26, 27, 28, 32[2], 33, 34, 35, 36

LEVIT. 11:37, 38, 39, 40[3], 44, 45[2], 46[4], 12:2[2], 3, 4[2], 5, 6[4], 13:2[4], 3[3], 4, 7[2], 9, 11, 12, 19, 20[2], 25[2], 27, 28[2], 31[2], 38, 39, 41, 43[2], 47, 48[3], 49[2], 51, 52, 53, 56[5], 57, 58, 59[4], 14:2[2], 3[2], 5, 6, 8, 10[3], 11[2], 14[6], 15[3], 16, 17[7], 18[2], 21[2], 23[2], 24[2], 25[7], 26[2], 27, 28[7], 29[2], 30[2], 32[2], 34[4], 37, 38[2], 39, 42, 45[3], 50, 51, 52, 53, 54[2], 55[2], 57, 15:2[3], 7, 10, 12[2], 13, 14[2], 16, 17, 18, 25[7], 26[3], 28, 29[2], 30, 31, 32[2], 33[6], 16:1[2], 5[4], 6, 7[2], 11[2], 12[3], 13, 14[3], 15[2], 16[6], 17[2], 18[5], 19[3], 20[2], 21[5], 23, 24, 25, 29[2], 31, 33[2], 34, 17:2, 3[3], 4[3], 5[3]

LEVIT. 17:6[3], 8[3], 9[2], 10[4], 11, 12[2], 13[3], 14[6], 15[2], 18:2, 3[4], 6[2], 7[2], 8, 9[3], 10[2], 11[2], 12, 13, 14, 15, 16, 17, 21[2], 24, 26[2], 27, 29, 30, 19:2[2], 5, 8, 9[3], 10, 12, 13, 15[2], 16, 18, 19, 21[2], 22, 23[2], 25, 27[2], 29, 32, 34, 36[2], 20:2[6], 3, 4[2], 11, 12, 13, 17, 18[2], 19[2], 23, 25, 21:1, 5, 6[3], 8, 9, 12[4], 14, 17[2], 21[4], 22[3], 24, 22:2[2], 3[2], 4[3], 5, 6, 7, 8, 10[3], 11[2], 12[2], 13, 14, 15[2], 16, 18[4], 19[3], 21, 22, 25[3], 29, 30, 32, 33[2], 23:2[2], 3[2], 4, 5, 6[2], 10[3], 12, 13[3], 15, 17[3], 18[2], 19[3], 20, 22[4], 24[4], 27[2], 28, 31, 32[2], 34[3], 37, 38, 39[2]

LEVIT. 23:40[4], 43[3], 44[2], 24:2, 3[2], 8, 9[2], 10[4], 11[4], 12, 15, 16[2], 22[2], 23[3], 25:2, 4, 5[4], 6, 8[3], 9[3], 11[2], 12, 13, 14, 15[4], 16[5], 22[2], 24, 25[2], 27, 28[2], 30, 31[2], 32[3], 33[6], 34[2], 36, 38[3], 40, 41, 42[2], 44[2], 45[4], 46, 47, 48, 49[2], 50[4], 51[2], 52[2], 54, 55[3], 26:1, 4, 6, 8[2], 10, 13[3], 16, 19, 20, 22, 25[2], 26, 29[2], 30, 31, 36[3], 38, 39[2], 40, 41[3], 43[3], 44, 45[4], 46[2], 27:2, 3[3], 5, 6[3], 9, 11, 15[2], 16[4], 17, 18, 19[2], 22[2], 23[2], 24[3], 25, 26, 27[2], 28[4], 29, 30[5], 31, 32[3], 34

NUM. 1:1[5], 2[5], 4[3], 5[4], 6[2], 7[2], 8[2], 9[2], 10[6], 11[2], 12[2], 13[2], 14[2], 15[2], 16[4], 18[3]

NUM. 1:19, 20[3], 21[3], 22[5], 23[3], 24[4], 25[3], 26[4], 27[3], 28[4], 29[3], 30[4], 31[3], 32[6], 33[3], 34[4], 35[3], 36[4], 37[3], 38[4], 39[3], 40[4], 41[3], 42[4], 43[3], 44[2], 45[3], 47, 49[3], 50, 52, 53[5], 54, 2:2[4], 3[7], 4, 5[4], 7[4], 9, 10[5], 12[4], 13, 14[4], 15, 16, 17[3], 18[5], 19, 20[4], 21, 22[4], 23, 24[2], 25[5], 26, 27[4], 28, 29[4], 30, 31, 32[4], 33, 34[2], 3:1, 2[2], 3, 4[2], 6, 7[3], 8[5], 9[2], 12[3], 13, 14, 15[2], 16, 17, 18[2], 19, 20[3], 21[4], 22[3], 23, 24[4], 25[5], 26[3], 27[6], 28[2], 29[3], 30[5], 31, 32[4], 33[4], 34[2], 35[6], 36[3], 37, 38[4], 39[2], 40[4], 41[6], 42, 43[3], 45[4], 46[4], 47, 48, 49, 50[4], 51[2], 4:2[4], 3, 4[3], 5, 6[2], 7[2], 8[2]

NUM. 4:9[2], 10, 11[2], 12[3], 14[3], 15[6], 16[4], 18[2], 22[3], 23, 24[2], 25[5], 26[4], 27[3], 28[6], 29[2], 30[2], 31[3], 32[3], 33[6], 34[3], 35, 36, 37[5], 38[3], 39, 40[2], 41[6], 42[4], 43, 44, 45[5], 46[3], 47[3], 48, 49[3], 5:2[2], 4[2], 6, 8, 9[3], 12, 13, 14[4], 15[4], 17[2], 18, 19, 20, 21, 25, 26, 29[2], 30, 6:2[2], 3[3], 4[2], 5[4], 7, 8, 9[2], 10[2], 12[2], 13[4], 14[2], 15[3], 17[2], 18[6], 19[4], 21[3], 23, 27, 7:2[4], 3, 5[3], 7, 8[3], 9[2], 10, 11, 12[3], 13[4], 14[3], 15, 16, 17[4], 18[2], 19[4], 20[2], 21, 22, 23[4], 24[3], 25[4], 26[2], 27, 28, 29[4], 30[3], 31[5], 32[2], 33, 34, 35[4], 36[3], 37[4], 38[2], 39, 40, 41[4], 42[3], 43[5], 44[2], 45, 46, 47[4], 48[3]

NUM. 7:49[4], 50[2], 51, 52, 53[4], 54[3], 55[6], 56[2], 57, 58, 59[4], 60[3], 61[4], 62[2], 63, 64, 65[4], 66[3], 67[4], 68[2], 69, 70, 71[4], 72[3], 73[4], 74[2], 75, 76, 77[4], 78[3], 79[4], 80[2], 81, 82, 83[4], 84[4], 85[2], 86[3], 87[2], 88[3], 89[3], 8:4[2], 6, 7, 9[3], 10, 11[3], 12, 14, 15[2], 16[5], 17[3], 18[2], 19[7], 20[3], 22, 24[2], 25, 26, 9:1[4], 2, 3[2], 4, 5[3], 6, 7[3], 10[4], 11, 12[3], 13, 14, 15[2], 16, 17[2], 18[3], 19[2], 20[2], 22, 23[5], 10:2[4], 3[2], 4[2], 8, 10[3], 11[2], 12[4], 13[2], 14[4], 15[4], 16[4], 17[2], 18[2], 19[4], 20[4], 22[4], 23[4], 24[4], 25[5], 26[4], 27[4], 28[2], 29[2], 31, 33[3], 34[2], 36, 11:1[2], 3[2], 4, 7, 8[3], 10[2], 11, 15, 16[4], 17[2], 18

NUM. 11:20, 22, 24[3], 25, 26[4], 28[3], 30, 31, 33, 34, 12:1, 3, 4, 5[2], 8, 12[2], 16, 13:2[4], 3[4], 4[3], 5[3], 6[3], 7[3], 8[3], 9[3], 10[3], 11[5], 12[3], 13[3], 14[3], 15[3], 16[2], 17, 20[4], 21, 22, 23[4], 24[3], 25, 26[4], 27, 28, 29[2], 32[3], 33[2], 14:2[2], 5[3], 6[3], 7[2], 9, 10[6], 12, 14[3], 15, 17, 18[2], 19[2], 21, 23, 25, 27[2], 29, 30[2], 34[2], 38[3], 39, 40, 41, 44[3], 15:2[2], 3[2], 4[3], 5[2], 6[3], 7[2], 9[3], 10[2], 13[2], 14, 15, 18, 19[2], 20[3], 21[2], 23, 24[2], 25[2], 26[2], 27, 29, 31, 32, 38[4], 39, 41[2], 16:1[6], 2[4], 3, 7, 8[2], 9[4], 10, 12, 13, 14[2], 15, 17, 18[2], 19[3], 22[2], 24, 25, 26[2], 27[2], 28, 29[2], 31

NUM. 16:34, 37[2], 38[3], 39, 40[4], 41[3], 42[2], 43, 47, 49, 50[2], 17:2[6], 3[3], 4, 5[2], 6[3], 7, 8[3], 9, 12, 13, 18:1[2], 2[4], 3[2], 4[3], 5[3], 6[3], 7[2], 8[5], 9[5], 11[4], 12[4], 13, 15[3], 16[2], 17[3], 18, 19[3], 20, 21[3], 22[2], 23[3], 24[3], 26[4], 27[2], 28[3], 29[4], 30[2], 31, 32[4], 19:2[2], 4[3], 6[2], 9[4], 10[2], 11, 13[3], 16, 17[3], 20[2], 21[2], 20:1[2], 4, 5[5], 6[4], 8, 10, 12[2], 13[2], 14, 16[2], 17[2], 19[2], 22, 23[2], 24[2], 26, 27, 28[2], 29, 21:1[2], 3[2], 4[4], 5, 6, 9[2], 10, 12, 13[4], 14[3], 15[3], 18[2], 20[2], 21, 22[2], 24[4], 25, 26[4], 27, 28[5], 29[2], 31, 33[2], 34, 22:1[2], 2, 3[3], 4[4], 5[6], 6, 7[4], 8, 10[3], 11[3], 13, 14, 16

NUM. 22:18[2], 21, 22, 23[2], 24[2], 25, 26, 27, 28, 31[2], 32, 34, 35[2], 36[2], 41[2], 23:6, 7[3], 9, 10[4], 13, 14[3], 17, 18, 19, 21, 22[2], 23[2], 24[2], 28, 24:2, 3, 4[2], 6, 7, 8[2], 13[3], 15, 16[3], 17[4], 19[2], 20, 24, 25:1, 2, 3, 4[2], 5, 6[3], 7[2], 8[4], 11[4], 12, 13[2], 14[3], 15[3], 18[5], 26:1, 2[3], 3, 4[4], 5[6], 6[4], 7[2], 8, 9[2], 11, 12[7], 13[4], 14, 15[7], 16[4], 17[4], 18[3], 19[2], 20[7], 21[5], 22[2], 23[6], 24[4], 25[2], 26[8], 27[2], 28, 29[6], 30[5], 31[4], 32[4], 33[3], 34[2], 35[7], 36[3], 37[4], 38[7], 39[4], 40[5], 41[2], 42[4], 43[2], 44[8], 45[6], 46[2], 47[3], 48[6], 49[4], 50[2], 51[2], 53, 54, 55[2], 57[7], 58[6], 59[2], 62[3], 63[2], 64[3], 65[3], 27:1[9]

NUM. 27:2[2], 3[2], 4[2], 7[3], 8, 11[3], 12, 14[4], 16[2], 17, 18, 20[3], 21[2], 23, 28:2, 3, 5, 7, 8[2], 9[2], 10, 11[2], 12[2], 13[2], 14[5], 15, 16[2], 17, 18, 19, 20, 24[2], 26, 27, 28, 30, 29:1[2], 2, 3, 5, 6, 7, 8, 9, 11[3], 12, 13[2], 14[3], 15, 16, 17, 19, 20, 23, 25, 26, 29, 32, 36[2], 40, 30:1[2], 2, 5[2], 6, 8, 9[2], 12[2], 31:2[2], 3[2], 4[2], 5[3], 6[2], 8[4], 9[3], 11[2], 12[3], 13, 14[2], 16[4], 20[3], 21[2], 23, 26[4], 28[7], 29[2], 30[11], 32[2], 35, 36, 37, 38, 39, 40, 42[2], 47[7], 48[3], 49[3], 50[2], 51, 52[5], 53, 54[5], 32:1[5], 2[3], 4, 6[2], 7[2], 9[3], 11[2], 12[3], 13, 14, 17[3], 18, 21, 24, 25[2]

NUM. 32:25, 28[4], 29[3], 30, 31[2], 32[2], 33[5], 34, 37, 39[2], 40, 41, 33:1[5], 2, 3[3], 5, 6, 8[2], 9, 11, 12[2], 15, 16, 36, 37[2], 38[5], 40[4], 44, 47, 48[2], 49, 50, 51[2], 52, 53, 54, 55[2], 34:2[3], 3[3], 4, 5[2], 8[2], 9, 11[3], 12, 13, 14[7], 17[2], 18, 19[4], 20[4], 21[3], 22[4], 23[5], 24[4], 25[4], 26[4], 27[4], 28[4], 29[2], 35:1, 2[3], 3, 4[2], 5, 8[4], 10[2], 11, 13, 14[2], 15, 16, 18, 19, 20[2], 21, 22, 24, 25[5], 26[2], 27[5], 28[4], 29, 30, 31[2], 32[2], 33[2], 34, 36:1[10], 2[2], 3[7], 4[5], 5[4], 6[3], 7[6], 8[7], 9[3], 10, 11, 12[5], 13[3]

DEU. 1:2, 3[2], 4[2], 5, 7[2], 10, 11, 15, 17[2], 19[2], 20, 21, 22, 23[2]

DEU. 1:24, 25[2], 26, 27[3], 28, 29, 34, 35[2], 36, 38, 40, 41, 43, 2:1, 4[3], 5, 6[2], 7, 8[4], 9[2], 12[2], 14[2], 15, 16, 18, 19[5], 20, 22, 23, 24, 25[4], 26[4], 29, 30, 34, 35, 36[2], 37[3], 3:1, 2, 3, 4[2], 6[2], 7, 8[4], 10[3], 11[8], 13[5], 14[3], 16[2], 17, 18, 26, 27, 4:1, 2, 3, 4, 6, 9, 11, 12[3], 13, 15[3], 16[2], 17[2], 18[2], 19, 20[3], 23[2], 25[2], 28, 31, 32[2], 33[3], 34, 36[3], 37, 42, 43[3], 44, 45[2], 46[4], 47[3], 48, 49[2], 5:3, 4[2], 5[2], 6[3], 8, 9[2], 10, 11, 14[2], 15, 22[5], 23[3], 24[2], 25, 26[4], 28[3], 6:2, 3, 7, 9, 11, 12[3], 14[2], 15[2], 17, 18, 21, 7:4, 6, 7, 8[4]

DEU. 7:13[4], 15[2], 18, 19, 22, 25, 8:3[2], 6, 7[4], 8[2], 9, 14[3], 15[2], 20, 9:2[3], 4, 5[2], 7[2], 9[2], 10[5], 11[3], 12[2], 14, 15, 16, 17, 18[2], 19, 21, 23, 26, 27, 10:1[2], 3[2], 4[3], 6[3], 7[2], 8[3], 12, 13, 14, 16, 17[2], 18, 19, 22, 11:2, 3[2], 4[2], 6[3], 7, 10[2], 11[3], 12[3], 14, 19, 20, 21[2], 24, 25[2], 27, 28[2], 30[2], 12:1, 3[3], 5, 6[3], 11, 14, 15[3], 17[7], 21[2], 22, 25, 27[3], 28, 13:1, 3[2], 5[7], 6[2], 7[4], 9, 10[3], 12, 13[2], 15[3], 16[2], 17[2], 18[2], 14:1, 7[2], 8, 9, 11, 12, 20, 21[2], 22, 23[5], 28[2], 29, 15:1, 2[3], 3, 5, 7[3], 9, 11, 14[4], 15, 19[4], 16:1[3], 2, 3[6], 4, 5, 6[2]

DEU. 16:10[3], 13, 15, 16[3], 17, 19[2], 21[2], 17:2[2], 3[2], 4, 6[3], 7[2], 8, 9, 10, 11, 18[3], 19[2], 20, 18:1[2], 4[5], 5[2], 6[3], 7, 8[2], 9, 12, 14, 15[2], 16[3], 19, 20, 22[2], 19:2, 3, 4, 5, 6[2], 11, 12[3], 13, 14, 15[2], 20:1[3], 3, 6[2], 9[2], 11, 13, 14, 15[2], 16[2], 19[2], 21:3, 4, 5[2], 6, 8, 9[2], 13, 14, 16[2], 17[4], 18[2], 19[2], 20, 21, 22, 23, 22:3, 9[2], 11[2], 12, 14, 15[3], 17[3], 18, 19[3], 20, 21[2], 22, 24, 26, 29, 23:1, 2[2], 3[2], 4[4], 8[2], 10[2], 14, 16, 17[4], 18[3], 19[3], 21, 23, 25, 24:1, 2, 3[2], 7[3], 8, 9, 14[2], 17[2], 19, 21, 22, 25:5[3], 6[2], 7, 8, 9, 10, 11[3], 17

DEU. 25:18, 19, 26:1, 2[4], 4[2], 7, 8, 10, 12[3], 13, 14, 27:1, 3[2], 5, 6[2], 8, 9, 10, 14, 15[2], 18, 19, 21, 22[2], 26, 28:1[2], 2, 4[5], 9, 10[3], 11[3], 12, 13, 14, 15, 18[4], 20, 24, 25, 26, 27, 28, 33, 34, 35[2], 39, 42, 45, 47[2], 48[2], 49, 50[2], 51[4], 53[3], 54[2], 55[3], 56[2], 57, 58, 59[3], 60[2], 61, 62[2], 64, 65[3], 66, 67[2], 29:1[3], 2, 7[2], 8, 9, 10[3], 11[2], 16, 18, 19[2], 20, 21[4], 22[2], 23, 24, 25[4], 27, 28, 29, 30:4[2], 6, 8, 9[4], 10[2], 20, 31:4[2], 6[2], 7[2], 9[4], 10[4], 12, 14[2], 15[3], 16[2], 19[2], 21[2], 22, 23[3], 24[2], 25[2], 26[4], 28, 29[2], 30[3], 32:1, 3, 4, 5, 7[2], 8[4]

DEU. 32:9, 10, 13[4], 14[8], 15, 18, 19[3], 22, 24[3], 25, 26, 27, 28, 32[5], 33[2], 35, 38[2], 39, 42[3], 43, 44[3], 45, 46, 49[3], 51[5], 52, 33:1[2], 2, 3, 4[2], 5[2], 7[2], 8[2], 11[3], 12[2], 13[3], 15[2], 16[5], 17[5], 18, 19[4], 20[2], 21[3], 22, 23[2], 24, 26, 28[2], 29, 34:1[4], 2[2], 3[3], 5[3], 6[2], 8[3], 9[4], 11, 12

JOSH. 1:1[3], 2, 3, 4[2], 5, 6, 8[2], 9, 10, 12, 13, 14, 15, 18, 2:1[2], 2[3], 3, 5[2], 6[2], 9[2], 10[3], 11, 17, 18, 19[2], 20, 23, 24[2], 3:1, 3[2], 6[2], 7, 8[3], 9[2], 11[3], 12[3], 13[6], 14, 15[3], 16, 17[3], 4:2[2], 3[3], 4[3], 5[6], 7[5], 8[6], 9[3], 10, 11[2], 12[4], 13, 14[2], 16[2], 17, 18[6], 19[3]

JOSH. 4:20, 21, 23, 24[2], 5:1[7], 2, 3[2], 4[3], 5, 6[4], 9[2], 10[3], 11[2], 12[6], 14[2], 15, 6:1[2], 2, 3, 4, 5[2], 6[3], 7, 8[3], 10, 11, 12, 13[3], 15, 18[2], 19[2], 20, 21, 23, 24[4], 26, 7:1[9], 2, 4[2], 5[3], 6[2], 7, 9[2], 11, 12, 13[2], 15, 16, 17[3], 18[5], 19, 20, 21[4], 23[3], 24[3], 26[4], 8:1[2], 3[2], 8, 9, 10, 11[2], 12, 13[3], 14[2], 15, 19, 20[2], 21[2], 22[3], 23, 24[4], 25[2], 26, 27[2], 29[4], 30, 31[5], 32[4], 33[6], 34[2], 35[2], 9:1, 3, 5, 6, 7, 9[3], 10[3], 11, 12, 13[2], 14[2], 15, 16, 17, 18[3], 19, 20, 21[2], 23[4], 24[3], 26[3], 27[3], 10:1[2], 2, 3[8], 4, 5[6], 6[2], 7[3], 8, 11, 12[3], 13[2], 14, 18

JOSH. 10:19, 20[3], 21[2], 22[2], 23[6], 24[5], 25, 27[2], 28[3], 30[3], 32[2], 33, 35, 37, 39, 40[5], 41, 42, 11:1[4], 2[4], 3, 5, 6, 7[2], 8[2], 10, 11, 12[4], 13, 14[3], 15, 16[3], 17, 19[2], 20, 21[2], 22[3], 12:1[3], 2[5], 3[2], 4[4], 5[3], 6[4], 7[4], 9[2], 10[2], 11[2], 12[2], 13[2], 14[2], 15[2], 16[2], 17[2], 18[2], 19[2], 20[2], 21[2], 22[2], 23[4], 24, 13:2, 3[2], 4[2], 5, 6[2], 7, 8, 9[3], 10[4], 11, 12[3], 13, 14[3], 15[2], 16[2], 19, 21[5], 22[2], 23[4], 24, 25[3], 26, 27[5], 28[2], 29[4], 30[3], 31[6], 32, 33[2], 14:1[7], 2, 3, 4, 5, 6[3], 7, 8, 10, 13, 14[3], 15:1[6], 2, 4, 5[3], 6[3], 7[3], 8[7], 9[4], 10, 11[2], 12[2], 13[5], 14[2], 15[2], 17[2], 18, 19

JOSH. 15:20[3], 21[4], 47, 62, 63[3], 16:1[3], 2, 3[2], 4, 5[3], 8[3], 9[3], 17:1[5], 2[10], 3[5], 4[3], 5, 6[3], 7[2], 8[3], 9[6], 11[4], 12[2], 13, 14, 15[2], 16[6], 17, 18, 18:1[3], 2, 3[2], 4, 5, 7[3], 10, 11[6], 12[2], 13[2], 14[3], 15[3], 16[6], 17[3], 19[4], 20[3], 21[4], 28[2], 19:1[4], 8[4], 9[9], 10[2], 12, 14, 16[2], 17, 22, 23[3], 24[2], 27[2], 31[3], 32[2], 39[3], 40[2], 41, 47[5], 48[3], 49[3], 50, 51[8], 20:2[3], 3, 4[5], 5, 6, 7, 8[6], 9[3], 21:1[7], 2[2], 3[3], 4[8], 5[9], 6[10], 7[7], 8[2], 9[6], 10[5], 11[3], 12[2], 13[2], 16, 17[2], 19[2], 20[7], 21, 23[2], 25[2], 26[2], 27[6], 28[2], 30[2], 32[3], 33, 34[5], 36[2], 38[3], 40[3], 41[3], 44, 45[2], 22:1, 2, 3[2], 4[2], 5, 7[2], 8

JOSH. 22:9[10], 10[5], 11[8], 12[4], 13[6], 14[5], 15[4], 16[2], 17[2], 18, 19[4], 20[2], 21[5], 22[2], 24[2], 25[2], 27, 28[2], 29, 30[6], 31[7], 32[7], 33[3], 34[2], 23:3, 5, 6[2], 7[2], 10, 12, 13, 14[2], 16[2], 24:1[2], 2[4], 3[2], 6, 8, 9[3], 10, 11, 12, 13, 14, 15[2], 17[3], 23, 26[3], 27, 29[2], 30[3], 31[3], 32[10], 33

JUD. 1:1[2], 4, 8[2], 9, 10, 11[2], 13, 14, 15, 16[6], 17, 19[3], 20, 21[2], 22, 23[2], 24, 25, 26, 27[4], 30[2], 31[7], 32, 33[5], 34, 35[2], 36, 2:1[2], 2, 4[2], 5, 6, 7[3], 8[2], 9[3], 11[2], 12[5], 14[3], 15, 16[2], 17[2], 18[5], 20, 21, 22, 23, 3:1[2], 2[2], 3[2], 4[2], 5, 7[2], 8[4], 9[3], 10[2], 11, 12[4], 13[2], 14[2], 15[4], 16

JUD. 3:17, 20, 22, 23, 24, 25, 27[2], 28, 29[2], 30, 31[2], 4:1[2], 2[4], 3[3], 4, 5[2], 6[7], 7, 9, 11[4], 12, 13[3], 15, 16[3], 17[4], 19, 20[2], 21, 23[2], 24[4], 5:1, 2, 3, 4[3], 5, 6[3], 7, 9, 11[5], 12, 14[5], 15[3], 16[3], 18, 19[3], 21, 22[2], 23[3], 24, 28[2], 30[6], 6:1[3], 2[3], 3, 4, 6[2], 7[3], 8[4], 9[4], 10, 11, 12[2], 13[2], 14, 19[2], 20, 21[5], 22[2], 24, 25[2], 26[2], 27[2], 28[2], 29, 30[2], 33[2], 34, 37, 38[2], 7:1[4], 3[2], 4[2], 5, 6[2], 8[2], 11, 12, 13[2], 14[3], 15[3], 17, 18[3], 19[2], 20[2], 22, 23[4], 24, 25[3], 8:1, 2[4], 3[2], 5[3], 6[2], 7, 8[2], 9, 10[3], 11[2], 12, 13, 14[4], 15[2], 16[3], 17[2], 18[2], 19, 22[2]

JUD. 8:24[2], 25, 26[3], 28[2], 29, 30, 32[3], 33, 34[3], 35, 9:1[3], 2[3], 3[3], 4[3], 5[2], 6[3], 7[2], 15[2], 16, 17[2], 18[2], 20[4], 21, 23[2], 24[3], 25[2], 26[2], 27, 28[4], 30[3], 31, 35[3], 36[2], 37[2], 39, 40, 43, 44[2], 46[4], 47[2], 49[2], 51[2], 52, 53, 54, 55, 56, 57[4], 10:1[3], 4, 6[8], 7[4], 8[3], 9[2], 10, 11[2], 12, 14, 15, 16, 17[2], 18[3], 11:1[2], 2, 3, 4[2], 5[4], 6, 7[2], 8[3], 9[2], 10, 11, 12[2], 13[4], 14[2], 15[3], 17[3], 18[7], 19[2], 21[4], 22, 23, 25[2], 26, 27[2], 28[3], 29[4], 30, 31[2], 32, 33[3], 35, 36[4], 39, 40[2], 12:1[2], 2[2], 3, 4[3], 5[2], 6[2], 7[2], 8, 12, 13, 15[3], 13:1[3], 2[3], 3, 5[2], 6[3], 7, 8, 9[2], 13[2], 14[2]

JUD. 13:15, 16[3], 17, 18, 20[2], 21[2], 25[2], 14:1[2], 2[2], 3[2], 4, 5, 6, 8[3], 9[2], 12[2], 13, 14[2], 16, 17, 18, 19[3], 15:1, 2, 5, 6, 7, 8, 10, 11[2], 12, 14, 15, 16[2], 17[2], 18[2], 20, 16:2, 3[3], 4, 5[2], 8, 9, 13, 14[2], 18[2], 19, 20, 21, 22, 23, 24[2], 25, 27[2], 28, 29[3], 31[2], 17:1, 2[3], 3, 4[2], 5[2], 7[3], 8[2], 9, 10[2], 11, 12, 18:1[2], 2[4], 3[2], 5, 7, 10, 11[5], 13, 14, 15[2], 16[4], 17[2], 19, 20, 22[2], 23, 25[2], 26, 27, 29[3], 30[6], 31, 19:1[2], 3[2], 5, 6, 8, 11, 12[3], 13, 15, 16[3], 17, 18[2], 19, 22[3], 23, 26[2], 27[2], 29, 30[4], 20:1[2], 2[5], 3[3], 4, 5, 6[2], 7, 8[2]

JUD. 20:10[5], 11, 12[2], 13[4], 14[3], 15[3], 17[2], 18[5], 19, 20[2], 21[3], 22, 23[3], 24[2], 25[3], 26[2], 27[4], 28[3], 30[2], 31[5], 32[2], 33[6], 34, 35[2], 36[2], 37, 38[2], 39[3], 40[3], 41[2], 42[4], 44[2], 45[3], 46[2], 48[4], 21:1[2], 2, 3, 5[2], 6, 7, 8[2], 9[2], 10[3], 12[3], 13, 14[2], 15, 16[2], 17[2], 18[2], 19[4], 20, 21[5], 23[2], 24

RUTH 1:1[2], 2[5], 4[4], 5[2], 6[2], 7[2], 9[2], 13, 22[3], 2:1[4], 2, 3[3], 6[2], 9, 10, 11, 12[2], 13, 14, 16[2], 17, 19, 20[3], 23[3], 3:2, 7[2], 10, 11, 13[3], 15, 17, 4:1, 2[2], 3[3], 4, 5[6], 9[2], 10[4], 11[2], 12[3], 15[2], 17[2], 18

1 SAM. 1:1[6], 2[2], 3[4], 7, 9[2], 10, 11[3], 15, 16[3], 17[2], 20, 24[3], 27

1 SAM. 2:3[2], 4, 8[3], 9, 10[4], 12[2], 13, 15, 17, 20, 22[2], 23, 25, 27[2], 28[5], 29[2], 30[2], 31, 33[3], 34, 36[4], 3:1, 3[3], 7, 11, 14[2], 15[2], 17, 19, 20, 21, 4:1, 2, 3[5], 4[6], 5[2], 6[4], 8[2], 10, 11[2], 12[2], 13, 14[2], 16[2], 17, 18[3], 19, 20, 21[2], 22, 5:1, 2[2], 3[2], 4[4], 5[2], 6[2], 7[3], 8[7], 9[2], 10[4], 11[4], 12, 6:1[2], 2, 3, 4[2], 5[3], 8[2], 9, 11[2], 12[3], 13, 14[2], 15[8], 16, 18[7], 19[4], 20, 21[2], 7:1[4], 2, 3[3], 4, 6, 7[4], 8[3], 11[2], 12, 13[3], 14[2], 15, 8:2[2], 4, 7, 8, 9, 10[2], 11, 12[2], 14, 15[2], 17, 18, 19, 21[2], 22, 9:1[6], 2[2], 3[2], 4[3], 5, 6, 7, 8[3], 9, 10, 12

1 SAM.
9:16[4] 17 20 21[6] 23 25 26[3] 27[2] 10:1 2[2] 3[3] 4[2] 5[3] 6 8 10[2] 11 12 13 16[2] 18[3] 19 20[2] 21[3] 22 23 25 26 27 11:1 3[2] 4[2] 5[3] 6 7[4] 8[2] 9[2] 10 11[3] 15[2] 12:3 4 6[2] 7[2] 8 9[6] 10[2] 11[2] 12[2] 14 15[3] 17 13:2[3] 3[2] 4 6 7[2] 10 13 15 16 17[3] 18[2] 19 22[3] 23[2] 14:1 2 3[3] 4[2] 5 6 11[3] 12[2] 14[2] 16[2] 18[3] 19 22 24[2] 25 27 28 29 30[2] 36 37[2] 38 41 43 45 47[2] 48[2] 49[4] 50[5] 51[3] 52 15:1[2] 2 4 5 6[2] 8[2] 9[3] 10 13[2] 14[2] 15[2] 17[2] 19[2] 20[2] 21[2] 22[2] 23[2] 24 26 27

1 SAM.
15:28[2] 29 30 32[2] 34 35 16:4 7 10 12 13[3] 14 18[3] 20 17:2[2] 4[3] 5[4] 6[2] 7[2] 8 10 11 12[3] 13[2] 17 18 19[2] 22[2] 23[3] 24 25 26 28 32 33 34 35 36[2] 37[6] 38[2] 40 42 44[2] 45[4] 46[2] 50 51 52[4] 53 54 55 57[2] 58 18:1[3] 4 5[3] 6[4] 10 11 12 15 17 21[2] 23 24 25[3] 27 29 30[2] 19:3 4 6 10 13 16 20[3] 23 20:6 8 11 12 14 15[2] 16[2] 21 23 27[2] 28 30[3] 31 33 34 37 41 42[2] 21:1 2 3 5[2] 7[3] 9[2] 10[2] 11[3] 12[2] 13 15 22:3[2] 4 6[2] 7[4] 8[3] 9[3] 10[2] 11[2] 12 13[2] 15[3]

1 SAM.
22:17[3] 19[3] 20[3] 22[2] 23:2 3 4 5 6 10 11[2] 12[2] 13 14 15 17 19[4] 20 21 23[2] 24[2] 25[2] 26[3] 24:1 2[2] 3 4[3] 6 7 8 11[2] 12 13 14 15 16 20 21 25:1 3[6] 9 10 14[2] 17 18[4] 20 21 22 24 25[2] 28[2] 29[5] 31 32 34 35 36 37 39[3] 40 41[2] 42[2] 43[2] 44[2] 26:1 2[3] 3 5[2] 6 11 12 13 14 15 16 19[3] 20[2] 22 24[2] 27:1[5] 2[2] 6 7 8[3] 10[3] 11 28:2 3 5 6 7 9 13 14 16 17 18 19[3] 20[2] 22[2] 29:1 3[4] 4[3] 5 6 7 8 9[2] 11 30:5 6[2] 12[3] 13 14[2] 15 16[5] 17[2]

1 SAM.
30:22[3] 26[5] 29[2] 31:1 3 7[3] 9[2] 10 11[2] 12[3]

2 SAM.
1:1[2] 2 3[2] 4 12[2] 13 15 18[3] 19 20[3] 21[4] 22[4] 24[2] 25 26 27 2:1[3] 3 4[3] 5[2] 7 8[3] 10 11 12[3] 13[5] 15[4] 17[2] 18[2] 21[2] 23 24[3] 25[2] 30 31[3] 32[2] 3:1[3] 2 3[5] 4[2] 6[3] 7 8[2] 9 10[2] 13 14 15 17 18[6] 19[3] 22 23 25 26 27 28[2] 29[2] 32 36 37[2] 39[2] 4:2[6] 4[3] 5[3] 6 8[5] 9[2] 10 11 12[2] 5:1 3 6 7[2] 8 9 10 11 13 14 17 18 19 20[2] 22 23 24[3] 6:1 2[4] 3[4] 4[3] 5[3] 6[2] 7[2] 8 9[2] 10[3] 11[2] 12[6] 13 15[3] 16[2] 17[2] 18[3]

2 SAM.
6:19[4] 20[5] 21 22[3] 23[2] 7:2[2] 4 6[2] 7[4] 8 9[2] 10[2] 12 13 14[3] 19[2] 26[2] 27[2] 29[2] 8:1[2] 3[2] 4 5[3] 6 7[2] 8 9[2] 10[3] 11 12[10] 13[2] 14 16[2] 17[2] 18 9:1[2] 2[2] 3[3] 4[2] 5[3] 6[2] 7 11 12 10:1[2] 2[4] 3[2] 4 6[6] 7[2] 8[4] 9[3] 10[3] 11 12[2] 14[2] 16[2] 18[3] 19 11:1 2 3 7 8[2] 9[2] 11 13 14 15 17[4] 19[2] 21[2] 23 24 26 12:3[2] 4[2] 7[3] 8[2] 9[3] 10 11[2] 14 17 18 20 25[2] 26 27 28 30[2] 31[4] 13:1 3 6 10 11 13 18 19 21 29 30 32[3] 34 36 37 39 14:1 4 9 11[2] 13 16[4] 17[2] 19[2]

2 SAM.
14:20[3] 22 25 26 27 15:2[5] 3 6[2] 10[2] 11 13[2] 14 23 24[4] 25[2] 27 28 29 31 32 34 35 16:1[7] 3[2] 5[4] 6 7 8[3] 10 11 15 18 19 21[2] 22[2] 23[3] 17:4 8[2] 9 10 12 14[5] 15 16 18 20 21 22 23 24 25[3] 26 27[7] 29 18:1 2[5] 3[3] 6 7[3] 8 9[3] 11 12 14 17 19[2] 22 23 27[3] 31 32 19:5[5] 9[6] 10 11[2] 13[4] 14[3] 16[3] 17[3] 18 19 20[2] 21 22 24 27 28 29 32 35 37[2] 38 40 41[2] 42[4] 43[5] 20:1[3] 2[3] 3 4 5 6 7[2] 10 11 12[2] 13[2] 14 15 16 17 19[2] 21[2] 22[2] 23[2] 24 21:1[2]

2 SAM.
21:2[6] 3 4[2] 5[2] 6[2] 7[4] 8[5] 9[3] 10[6] 11[2] 12[4] 13[3] 14[3] 16[4] 17[3] 18[2] 19[3] 20 21[2] 22[2] 22:1[5] 3[2] 5[2] 6[2] 7 8 9[2] 11 12 13 16[5] 17 19 21 22 31 35 36 41 43[2] 44[2] 46 47[2] 51 23:1[5] 2 3[3] 4[2] 6[2] 7 8 9[3] 11[2] 12 13[4] 14 15[3] 16[3] 17[2] 18[2] 20[6] 21 22 24 29[5] 30[2] 32[2] 33 34[3] 36[2] 37 24:1 2[3] 3 4[4] 5[3] 6 7[4] 8 9[3] 10 11 12 13 14[2] 15 16[3] 18 19 21 22 24[3]

1 KINGS
1:3 5 7 8 9[2] 11[2] 12 19[2] 20[2] 25 26 27 29 30 32 33 36[2] 37 38 39[2] 40 41[3] 42

1 KINGS
1:44 46 47 48 50[2] 51 52 2:1 2 3[2] 4 5[7] 7[3] 8[2] 10 12 13[2] 16 20 22 24 25[2] 26[2] 27[2] 28[2] 29[2] 30 31 32[6] 33[2] 34 35[2] 39[5] 43 45 46 3:1[5] 3 6 7 8 11 15 17 28 4:2 3[2] 4 5 6 8 9 10 11[2] 12 13[4] 14 15 16 17 18 19[6] 21[3] 22[2] 23 25 26 29 30[3] 31 33[6] 34[4] 5:1[3] 3[2] 5 6 7 8[2] 11 13 16 17 6:1[4] 3[2] 4 5[4] 6[2] 7[2] 8[2] 9 10 11 13 15[6] 16[2] 18 19[2] 20 21 23 24[4] 25 26[2] 27[4] 29[2] 30 31[3] 32[2] 33[3] 34[3] 36[2] 37[2] 38 7:2[3] 7[2] 8 9[2]

1 KINGS
7:10[3] 11 12[5] 13 14[3] 15[4] 16[4] 17[3] 19[2] 21 22[2] 23 24 26[2] 27[3] 28 29 30[2] 31[3] 32[2] 33[2] 34[2] 35[4] 36[2] 37 38[2] 39[3] 40[2] 41[4] 42[2] 43[2] 46 47 48[3] 49[2] 50[5] 51[3] 8:1[9] 2 3 4[2] 5 6[4] 7 8 9[4] 10[2] 11[3] 14[2] 15 16[3] 17[3] 18 19 20[4] 21[3] 22[3] 23 25[2] 26 27 28 29 30[2] 34 36[2] 37 38 39[2] 41 42[3] 43 46 47 51[3] 52[2] 53[3] 54[2] 55 56[2] 59[2] 60 63[3] 64[4] 65 66 9:1[2] 4 5[2] 7[2] 9[2] 10[2] 11[2] 13 14[3] 15 19[2] 20[3] 21[2] 22[4] 23 24[2] 26[3] 27[2] 10:1[4] 2 4 5[4] 6[2] 9 10[4] 11[2] 12[2] 13[2] 14[2] 15[7] 16[2]

1 KINGS
10:17[4] 18 19[2] 21[8] 22[3] 23 25[2] 28 29[4] 11:1 2[2] 4 5[2] 6 7[3] 9 11 12[2] 14 15 17 18[3] 19[3] 20[2] 21 23[2] 24 25 26[2] 27[2] 28[3] 29 31[3] 32[2] 33[4] 34[2] 35 39 40[2] 41[4] 43 12:2[3] 3 4 8 14 15 16 17[2] 19 20[2] 21[4] 22[2] 23[4] 24[3] 26 27[4] 28[3] 31[4] 32[3] 33[3] 13:1[3] 2[3] 4[2] 5[2] 6[3] 7 8 9 11 12 14[2] 17 18 20 21[2] 22[2] 26[3] 29[2] 31 32[3] 33[5] 34[2] 14:1 2 3[2] 4[2] 5[2] 6[2] 7 8 10[3] 11[2] 13[3] 14 15 16[2] 17 18[2] 19[5] 21[3] 22 24[2] 25[2] 26[4] 27[3] 28 29[5] 31 15:1[2] 2 3[2] 5[3] 6 7[5] 8 9[2]

1 KINGS
15:10 11 12 15 16 17[2] 18[7] 19[2] 20[3] 21 22[2] 23[6] 24 25[3] 26[2] 27[3] 28[2] 29[2] 30[3] 31[5] 32 33[3] 34[2] 16:1[2] 2[2] 3[4] 4[3] 5[6] 7[6] 8[3] 9[3] 10[2] 11[3] 12[2] 13[3] 14[5] 15[2] 16 18 19[2] 20[5] 21[3] 22 23[2] 24[5] 25 26[3] 27[5] 29[4] 30[2] 31[4] 32 33[2] 34[2] 17:1[3] 2 4 5 6 8 10[2] 11 12 14[3] 15 16[3] 17[2] 18 19 22[2] 23 24[2] 18:1 3 4 5 9 10 12 13[2] 15 18 19[2] 20 22 24[2] 25[2] 26 29[2] 30 31[4] 32[2] 36[4] 38 40[2] 41[2] 42 44 46[2] 19:2[2] 6 7 8[2] 9 10[2] 13 14[2] 15 16[3] 17[2] 19[2] 21[2] 20:1 2 4 6 7[2]

1 KINGS
20:9 10 11 13 14[2] 15[3] 17[3] 19[3] 20 21 22[3] 23[3] 24 26 27[3] 28[4] 29[2] 30 31[3] 32 35[3] 36 39[2] 40 41[2] 42 43 21:1[2] 2[2] 3 4[2] 7[2] 10 11 13[4] 15[2] 16[2] 17 18[2] 19 20 22[4] 23[2] 24[2] 25 26 28 22:2[2] 3[4] 4 5[2] 6[2] 7[2] 8[3] 9[2] 10[3] 11[2] 13[3] 15 16 18 19[2] 22 23 24[2] 26[2] 27[2] 28 29[2] 30[2] 31[2] 32[2] 33[2] 34[4] 35[2] 36 38[2] 39[5] 41[3] 42 43[2] 44 45[5] 46[3] 48 49 50 51[3] 52[5] 53

2 KINGS
1:1 2[3] 3[5] 6[2] 7 8 9[3] 10[2] 11[2] 12[2] 13[4] 14 15[2] 16[3] 17[4] 18[5] 2:3 5 7[2] 9 11[2] 12[2] 13[2] 14[2] 15[2]

2 KINGS
2:16 19[2] 21 22 23 24[3] 3:1[3] 2[2] 3[2] 4[2] 5[2] 6 7[2] 8 9[4] 10[2] 11[6] 12[3] 13[5] 14[3] 15 16 18 19[2] 20 24 25[2] 26[2] 4:1[3] 2 3 7[2] 9 13 16[2] 17 21[2] 22[3] 25[2] 27[2] 28 29 30 31 34 38[2] 39 40[2] 42[4] 44 5:1[3] 2[2] 3 4[2] 5[5] 6[2] 7[2] 8[2] 9[2] 11 12[2] 14[3] 15[2] 17 18[3] 20[2] 22[4] 23[3] 27 6:1 6 8 9[2] 10[3] 11[4] 12 15[2] 17[3] 18 20[2] 21 23[2] 24 25[4] 26 27[2] 30 31[2] 32[2] 33 7:1[4] 2 3 4 5[3] 6[7] 8 9 10[3] 12[2] 13[4] 14 15 16[4] 17[2] 18[4] 19 8:2[3] 3[2] 4[2] 6 7[2] 8[3] 9[4] 11 12 16[4]

2 KINGS
8:18[5] 20 21 22 23[5] 24 25[5] 26[2] 27[6] 28[2] 29[5] 9:1[3] 2[2] 3 5[2] 6[2] 7[5] 8 9[4] 10 11 13 14[4] 15[3] 16 17 20[2] 21[3] 22 25[2] 26[4] 27[2] 28 29[2] 30 33 35[2] 36[3] 37[3] 10:1 3 5 6[2] 8[2] 10[3] 11[3] 13[5] 14[2] 15 17 19[2] 21[3] 22 23[6] 24[2] 25[4] 26[2] 27[2] 28 29[2] 30[3] 31[3] 32 33 34[5] 11:1 2[3] 3 4[3] 5[3] 6[2] 7[3] 10 11[2] 13[3] 14 15[3] 18[4] 19[6] 20 12:1[2] 2 4[4] 5[2] 6[2] 7[3] 8[2] 9[3] 10 11[4] 12[3] 13[6] 14 16 17 18[6] 19[5] 20 21[3] 13:1[4] 2[3] 3[5] 4[2] 5[2] 6[2] 7[2] 8[5] 10[3] 11[3] 12[6] 13 14[3] 16 17[2] 18 19 20[2]

2 KINGS
13:21[3] 22[3] 23 24 25[7] 14:1[5] 2 3 6[3] 7[3] 8[3] 9[2] 10 11[2] 13[6] 14[2] 15[6] 16 17[5] 18[5] 20 21[2] 23[5] 24[3] 25[6] 26 27[3] 28[5] 29 15:1[4] 2 3 5[2] 6[5] 7 8[3] 9[3] 10 11[5] 12[2] 13[3] 14[2] 15[5] 17[3] 18[3] 19[2] 20[7] 21[5] 23[3] 24[3] 25[4] 26[5] 27[3] 28[3] 29[4] 30[4] 31[5] 32[5] 33 34 35[2] 36[5] 37[2] 38 16:1[4] 2 3[4] 5[3] 6 7[7] 8[3] 9[3] 10[3] 13 14[3] 15[4] 17[2] 18[2] 19[5] 20 17:1[3] 2[2] 3 4[4] 5 6[4] 7[5] 8[4] 9[2] 14 16[2] 17 18[2] 19[2] 20[3] 21[2] 22[2] 23[2] 24[4] 25[2] 26[6] 27[4] 28 29[2] 30[3] 31 32[4] 33 34 36[2] 39[2] 18:1[5] 2 3 4 5[2] 7

2 KINGS
18:8 9[6] 10[4] 11[3] 12[2] 13[3] 14[6] 15[2] 16[4] 17 18[2] 19 21[2] 23 24[3] 26[2] 28 29 30[2] 31[4] 32[3] 33[5] 34[4] 35[3] 37[3] 19:1 2 3[2] 4[2] 5 6[3] 8 9[2] 10[3] 11 12[2] 13[5] 14[3] 15[3] 16 17[2] 18 19 20[3] 21[2] 22 23[5] 24[2] 25 26[2] 29[2] 30[2] 31[4] 32 35[2] 36 37[2] 20:1 4 5[3] 6[3] 7 8 9 11 12[2] 13[2] 16 18[3] 19 20[5] 21:2[3] 3[2] 4[2] 5[3] 6 7[4] 8[2] 9 11 12[2] 13[2] 14[2] 15 16 17[5] 18[2] 19[2] 20 22[2] 23 24[2] 25[5] 26 22:1[2] 2[2] 3[4] 4[3] 5[7] 7 8[2] 9[3] 11[2] 12[3] 13[4] 14[4] 15 16 17 18[3] 23:1[2] 2[6] 3 4[7] 5[3] 6[3] 7[2]

2 KINGS
23:8[7] 9[3] 10[2] 11[5] 12[6] 13[7] 14 15 16[3] 17[4] 18[2] 19[3] 20 21 22[5] 23 24[3] 25 26[2] 27[2] 28[5] 29[2] 30[2] 31[2] 32 33[4] 34 35[4] 36[2] 37 24:1 2[6] 3[2] 5[6] 7[5] 8[2] 9 10[2] 11 12[4] 13[6] 14[3] 15 16[2] 17 18[2] 19 20[2] 25:1[3] 2 3[2] 4[2] 5[2] 6 7[3] 8[6] 9[2] 10[3] 11[4] 12[3] 13[4] 14 15[3] 16[2] 17[3] 18[2] 19[7] 20[2] 21[3] 22[4] 23[6] 24[2] 25[3] 26[2] 27[5] 28 29 30[2]

1 CHRON.
1:5 6 7 8 9[2] 12 17 19 23 28 29 31 32[3] 33[2] 34 35 36 37 38 39 40[2] 41[2] 42[2] 43[4] 44[2] 45[2] 46[3] 47 48 49 50[3] 51 54 2:1 3[5] 4 5

1 CHRON.
2:6[2] 7[2] 8 9 10[2] 16 17 18[3] 21[2] 22 23[3] 24 25[2] 26 27[2] 28[2] 29[2] 30 31[3] 32[2] 33[2] 42[5] 43 44 45[2] 47 49[4] 50[4] 51[2] 52[2] 53[2] 54[3] 55[4] 3:1[3] 2[4] 3 5[2] 9[2] 15 16 17 19[2] 21[5] 22[2] 23 24 4:1 2 3[2] 4[5] 5 6 7 8[2] 10 11[2] 12[2] 13[2] 14[2] 15[2] 16 17[2] 18[5] 19[3] 20[2] 21[5] 22 24 26 27 31 34 35[3] 37[3] 38 39[2] 40[2] 41[2] 42[4] 43 5:1[4] 2 3[2] 4 6[2] 7 8[3] 9[2] 10[2] 11[2] 13[2] 14[8] 15[4] 16 17[4] 18[3] 20 21[4] 22 23[2] 24[5] 25[2] 26[6] 6:1 2 3[2] 15 16 17[2] 18 19[2] 20 22 25 26 28 29

JOB 35:8, 9[4], 11[2], 12[2], 36:6, 8, 16[2], 17, 19, 26, 27, 29[2], 30, 37:1, 2[2], 3, 4, 6, 7, 9[2], 10[2], 12, 14, 15, 16[2], 19, 22, 23, 24, 38:1, 3, 4, 7, 8, 13[3], 16[2], 17[3], 18, 21, 22[2], 23[2], 24[2], 25[2], 26[2], 27, 28, 29[2], 30, 31[2], 32, 34, 37, 39, 41, 39:1, 5, 7[2], 8, 17, 20, 24, 25, 28, 40:6, 7, 11, 16, 17, 18[2], 19[2], 20, 21, 22, 41:6, 9[2], 13, 14, 18, 19[2], 20[2], 21, 23, 24, 25, 26, 29, 31, 34, 42:4, 5, 7, 8, 10, 11[3], 12[2], 14[3], 15, 17

PSALMS 1:1[3], 2, 3, 5, 6[2], 2:2, 6, 8[2], 9, 10, 3:2, 3, 4, 6[2], 7, 4 *title*, 1

PSALMS 4:2, 5, 6, 5 *title*, 2, 5, 7, 8, 10, 6 *title*, 5, 7[2], 8[2], 7 *title*, 6[2], 7, 9, 10, 13, 17, 8 *title*, 2[3], 3, 4[2], 6, 7, 8[3], 9 *title*, 9, 12, 13[2], 14[2], 16, 18, 20, 10:1, 3, 4, 5, 7, 8, 14, 15, 16, 17, 18, 11 *title*, 4, 6, 12 *title*, 1, 5[2], 6[2], 13 *title*, 3, 14 *title*, 2, 4, 5, 6, 7[3], 15 *title*, 16 *title*, 4, 5[2], 11[2], 17 *title*, 1, 4[3], 8[2], 12, 14[3], 18 *title*[5], 2, 4[2], 5[2], 6, 7, 8[2], 10, 11, 12, 13, 15[4], 16, 18, 20, 21, 24, 30, 34, 35, 40, 43[2], 44, 45, 46, 19 *title*, 1, 4, 5, 6[2], 7[2], 8[2], 9[2], 11, 14[2], 20 *title*, 1[3], 2, 5, 6, 7, 21 *title*, 2, 3[2], 4[2]

PSALMS 21:7, 9, 10, 12, 22 *title*, 1, 3, 6[2], 9, 12, 14[2], 15, 16, 20, 21, 22, 23[2], 24, 25, 27[2], 23 *title*, 3, 4[2], 5, 6[2], 24 *title*, 3, 5, 6, 7, 8, 9, 10[3], 25 *title*, 5, 6, 7, 10, 14, 15, 17[2], 22, 26 *title*, 5, 7[2], 8, 10, 27 *title*, 1[2], 4[4], 5[2], 6, 9, 11, 12, 13[2], 14, 28 *title*, 2, 3, 4[2], 5[2], 6, 8, 29 *title*, 2, 3[2], 4[3], 5[2], 7[2], 8[2], 9[2], 30 *title*[2], 4[2], 31 *title*, 2, 4, 5, 8, 10, 12, 13, 15, 19, 20[3], 22, 24, 32 *title*, 4, 5, 6, 7, 33:2, 4, 5[2], 6[3], 7, 8[2], 10[3], 11[2], 13, 14[2], 16, 18, 34 *title*, 6, 7, 11, 15, 16[2], 17, 18[2], 19[2], 20, 22[2], 35 *title*, 2

PSALMS 35:5, 6, 12, 27, 28[2], 36 *title*[2], 1[2], 3, 7[2], 8[3], 9, 11[2], 12, 37 *title*, 1[2], 4, 7[2], 11, 14, 16, 17, 18, 19, 20[2], 22[2], 23, 28, 30[2], 31[2], 37, 38, 39[3], 38 *title*, 3[2], 5, 8[2], 10, 39 *title*, 4, 8, 10, 40 *title*, 2[2], 5, 7[2], 12, 15, 41 *title*, 1, 2, 3, 5, 9, 13, 42 *title*, 4[2], 5, 6[2], 7, 8, 9[2], 11, 43:2[3], 4, 5, 44 *title*, 1, 3, 14, 15, 16[2], 19[2], 20, 21, 45 *title*[2], 1[2], 2, 4, 5, 6, 7, 8[2], 9, 12, 13, 14, 16, 46 *title*, 2, 4[3], 5, 7[2], 8, 9, 11[2], 47 *title*, 1, 4, 5, 7, 8, 9[4], 48 *title*, 1[2], 2[3], 6, 7, 8[3], 9[2], 10[2], 11[2], 49 *title*, 1, 3[3], 5[2], 6, 7

PSALMS 49:8, 15, 16, 19, 50 *title*, 1, 2[2], 9[2], 10, 11[2], 13[2], 15, 23, 51 *title*, 1, 12, 14[2], 17, 18, 19, 52 *title*, 1, 5[3], 7, 8[2], 53 *title*, 2, 3, 4, 5, 6[3], 54 *title*, 2, 7, 55 *title*, 3[4], 4, 10, 14, 19, 21, 23, 56 *title*, 13, 57 *title*, 1, 3, 4, 58 *title*, 1, 2, 4, 5, 6, 8[2], 10, 59 *title*, 2, 5[2], 9, 10, 12[2], 13, 16[3], 17, 60 *title*[3], 3, 4, 6, 7, 8, 11, 61 *title*, 2, 4, 5, 62 *title*, 3, 7, 8[2], 63 *title*[2], 7, 9, 11, 64 *title*, 1, 2[3], 5, 6[2], 9[2], 65 *title*, 4[2], 5[4], 7[3], 8, 9[2], 12, 66:2, 3, 5[2], 8, 15[2], 19, 67:7, 68 *title*, 2, 5[2], 8[3], 10, 11, 12, 13, 15[3], 17[2], 19, 20, 21[2]

PSALMS 68:22, 23[2], 24, 26, 27[3], 29, 30[4], 31, 32, 33[2], 35[2], 69 *title*, 3, 4, 6[2], 9[2], 12, 13[2], 14[2], 16, 18, 20, 24, 26, 28[2], 30, 35, 36, 70 *title*, 3, 4[4], 6[2], 9, 16[3], 20, 22, 24, 72:4[2], 7, 8, 10[3], 13, 15[2], 16[4], 18, 20[2], 73 *title*, 1, 3, 10, 15, 17, 26, 74 *title*, 1, 2[2], 4, 7, 8, 11, 12[2], 13, 14, 17, 19[3], 20[3], 23[2], 75 *title*, 3, 8[4], 9, 10[2], 76 *title*, 3, 4, 5[2], 6, 9, 10[2], 12[2], 77 *title*, 2, 5, 10[2], 11[2], 12[2], 15, 18, 20, 78 *title*, 1, 2, 4, 7, 9[2], 10, 12[3], 14, 15, 16, 23, 24[2], 27, 28, 31[3], 38, 41, 43, 45, 49, 51[2], 54, 55, 60, 65[2], 67[2], 68

PSALMS 78:72[2], 79 *title*, 2[4], 9[2], 10[2], 11[2], 13, 80 *title*, 1, 4[2], 5, 7, 8, 10, 13[2], 14, 16, 17[2], 19, 81 *title*, 1, 4[2], 5, 7[2], 10[2], 11, 15, 16[2], 82 *title*, 1, 2, 4[2], 5[2], 6[2], 7, 83 *title*, 4, 6[2], 7, 8, 9, 12, 84 *title*, 1, 2, 3, 5, 6, 7, 8[2], 9, 10[2], 12, 85 *title*, 1, 2, 3, 4, 11, 13, 86 *title*, 4, 6, 7, 14, 15, 16, 87 *title*, 2, 3[2], 4, 5, 88 *title*[2], 1, 3, 9, 12, 89 *title*, 1[2], 5, 6, 7[2], 8, 9, 14, 15, 17, 18, 19, 22, 26, 27, 29, 34, 39, 42, 43, 45, 48, 50[2], 51, 90 *title*[2], 3, 8, 10, 11, 17[3], 91:1[2], 2, 3, 8, 92:3, 4, 7, 9, 10, 11

PSALMS 92:13[2], 93:2, 4[2], 94:2, 4, 7, 11, 12, 13, 16, 19, 20, 21, 22, 95:1, 4, 7[2], 8, 96:5, 7, 9, 12, 97:1, 2, 5[3], 7, 8[2], 10[3], 12, 98:2, 3[3], 5, 6, 8, 100 *title*, 3, 101 *title*, 1, 3, 6, 8[2], 102 *title*, 5[2], 6[2], 10, 15[2], 17, 19, 20, 21, 24, 25[3], 26, 28, 103 *title*, 7, 15, 17, 20, 21, 22, 104:3[2], 5, 7, 11, 12, 13, 14[2], 15, 16[3], 20, 24, 30, 31, 34, 35, 105:2, 3, 5, 6[2], 11[2], 16, 19, 20, 21[2], 23, 27, 30, 31, 33, 35, 36, 38, 40, 44[2], 106:2, 5[2], 7, 10[2], 11, 16, 17, 20, 22, 25, 28, 32, 38[3], 40, 41, 45, 46, 48, 107:2[2], 3, 6, 7

PSALMS 107:8, 10, 11[2], 13, 14, 15, 16[2], 17[2], 18[2], 19, 21, 22, 24, 26, 28, 31, 32[2], 34, 37, 43, 108 *title*, 7, 8, 12, 109 *title*, 1, 2[2], 3, 10, 14[2], 15, 20[2], 24, 31, 110 *title*, 2[3], 3[4], 4, 5, 7, 111:1, 2[2], 4, 5, 6[2], 7, 10[2], 112:2, 4, 7, 10, 113:1[2], 2, 3[2], 7[2], 8, 9, 114:1[3], 7[3], 8, 115:4, 10, 12[3], 15, 16, 116:3[2], 4, 9, 13[2], 14, 15[2], 16, 17[2], 18, 19[2], 117:2, 118:3, 10, 11, 12[2], 15[3], 16[2], 17, 19, 20, 22, 26[3], 27, 119:1, 7, 13, 14, 18, 27[2], 29, 30, 32, 33, 35, 43[2], 46, 52, 53, 54, 61, 62, 63[2], 64, 72[2], 84, 88, 96, 108, 111, 115, 116, 119

PSALMS 119:120[2], 123, 130, 134, 136, 144, 147, 152, 160, 161, 164, 172, 120 *title*, 4[2], 5, 121 *title*, 122 *title*[2], 1, 4[3], 5[3], 6, 9[2], 123 *title*, 2[4], 4[2], 124 *title*[2], 7[2], 8, 125 *title*, 3[2], 5, 126 *title*, 1, 127 *title*, 2, 3[2], 4[2], 5, 128 *title*, 2, 3, 5[3], 129 *title*, 4, 8[2], 130 *title*, 1, 2, 131 *title*[2], 2, 132 *title*, 2, 3, 5, 6[2], 8, 10, 11[2], 17, 133 *title*, 2, 3[2], 134 *title*, 1[2], 3, 135:1[2], 2[3], 7[2], 8[2], 9, 11[3], 15[2], 19[2], 20, 21, 136:2, 3, 14, 19, 20, 26, 137:1, 3[4], 6, 7[2], 8, 138 *title*, 4[2], 5[2], 7[2], 8, 139 *title*, 9[2], 15, 16, 17, 140 *title*, 4, 6, 7[2], 8, 9[2], 12[2], 141 *title*, 2, 3, 4, 9[2], 142 *title*, 5, 7, 143 *title*, 5[2], 10, 11, 12, 144 *title*

PSALMS 144:3[3], 7[2], 8, 9, 11[2], 12, 13, 145 *title*, 5[3], 6[2], 7[2], 8[2], 11[3], 12[2], 15, 16, 19, 21, 146:3, 8, 9, 147:2, 4, 5, 10[2], 13, 14, 148:3, 4, 5, 11[2], 13, 14[2], 149:1, 2, 6, 8, 150:1, 3

PROV. 1:1[3], 2, 3, 5, 6, 7[2], 8[2], 9, 17, 19[3], 21[2], 25, 29, 30, 31, 32[2], 33, 2:5[2], 6, 8[2], 12, 13[2], 14, 17[2], 19[2], 20[2], 22, 3:2, 3, 4, 9, 11[2], 14[2], 16, 17, 18, 25[3], 27, 31, 33[3], 35, 4:1, 3, 5, 9[2], 10, 11, 13, 14[2], 17[2], 18, 19, 21, 23[2], 26, 5:3, 6, 7, 8, 10, 13, 14, 15[2], 16, 18, 20, 21[2], 22, 23, 6:2[2], 3, 5[2], 9, 10, 20, 23[2]

PROV. 6:24[2], 26[2], 31, 34[2], 7:2, 3, 6, 7, 10[2], 16[2], 18, 20, 21, 22, 24, 27, 8:2[2], 3, 4, 5, 6[2], 8, 12, 13, 16, 20[3], 22[2], 26[2], 27, 28, 29, 31[2], 34, 35, 9:3, 5[2], 6, 10[2], 11, 14[2], 18, 10:1[2], 2, 3[2], 4, 6[2], 7[2], 11[3], 13[3], 14, 15, 16[2], 17, 19, 20[2], 21[2], 22, 23, 24[2], 27[2], 28[2], 29[2], 31, 32[2], 11:3[2], 4, 5, 6, 7, 8, 11[2], 12[2], 13, 14, 20, 21, 22, 23[2], 26, 29, 30[2], 12:2[2], 3, 5[2], 6[2], 7, 8, 10[2], 11, 12[2], 13[2], 14[2], 15, 18[2], 19, 20[2], 23, 24, 25, 26, 27, 28, 13:2[2], 4[2], 8, 9[2], 12, 14[3], 15, 20, 22, 23[2], 25[2], 14:3[3], 4, 7[2], 8[2]

PROV. 14:11[2], 12, 13, 17, 19, 20, 23, 24[2], 26[2], 27[3], 28[3], 29[2], 30[2], 33[2], 15:2[2], 3, 4, 6[2], 7[2], 8[2], 9, 11[2], 13, 14[2], 15[2], 16, 17, 19[3], 21[2], 22, 23, 24, 25[2], 26[2], 27, 28[2], 29, 30, 31, 33[2], 16:1[2], 2, 4, 6, 10, 11, 13, 14[2], 15[2], 17, 19, 21, 22[2], 23, 25, 26, 31[2], 33, 17:1, 2, 6[2], 8, 12, 14, 16, 18[2], 21, 23[2], 24[2], 27[2], 28, 18:4[2], 5, 7, 8[2], 10, 12, 14, 15[2], 19, 20[2], 21, 22, 19:3, 6, 7, 11, 12, 13[2], 14, 19, 21, 22, 23, 27, 28, 29, 20:2[2], 4, 5[2], 8, 10, 12, 15[2], 16, 17, 24, 27[3], 29[2], 30[2], 21:1[2], 2, 4, 5[2], 6[2], 7, 8

PROV. 21:9, 10, 12, 13, 15, 16[3], 20, 22[2], 25, 27, 31[2], 22:2, 4, 5, 8, 9, 11[2], 12[2], 14[2], 15[2], 17, 21[3], 23, 26[2], 23:3, 6, 9[2], 10, 12, 17, 20, 24[2], 29, 34[2], 24:2, 5, 6, 9, 10, 14, 15, 19, 20, 22, 23, 30[3], 33, 25:1[3], 2[2], 3, 6[2], 7, 11[2], 12[2], 13[3], 14, 17, 19[2], 22, 24, 26:6, 7[2], 9[2], 12[2], 22[2], 27:1, 6[2], 9, 10, 13, 16, 17, 19, 20, 23, 25, 26, 27, 28:2[2], 7, 17, 19, 21[2], 24, 25, 29:6, 7, 20[2], 25, 30:1[2], 2, 3, 4, 5, 7, 9, 17, 19[5], 20, 27, 33[3], 31:1, 2[2], 5, 6[2], 8, 9, 11[2], 12, 16, 21, 22, 23, 26, 27[2], 31[2]

ECCL. 1:1[2], 2[2], 3, 8, 10, 11[2], 13, 14, 16, 17, 2:2[2], 3[2], 5[2], 6, 7, 8[5], 10, 11, 16[2], 17, 20, 22[3], 24, 26, 3:8[2], 10, 13[2], 16[2], 18[2], 19, 20, 21[2], 4:1[2], 4[2], 6, 8[2], 14, 16[3], 5:1[2], 3[2], 6, 7, 8[2], 9, 11, 12[2], 15[2], 18[2], 19, 20[2], 6:2, 3, 7, 9[3], 12, 7:1[2], 2[3], 3, 4[4], 5[2], 6[2], 8, 9, 12, 13, 14[2], 15, 18[2], 25[3], 8:1[2], 2[2], 3, 4, 6, 8, 10, 11[2], 14[2], 15[2], 17, 9:1, 3[3], 5, 9[3], 11[2], 12, 17[2], 18, 10:1, 4, 12[2], 13[3], 14, 15[2], 17, 18, 20, 11:3, 5[3], 8, 9[3], 12:1, 3[2], 4[3], 5, 8, 10, 11[2], 12[2], 13[2]

CANT. 1:1, 2, 3[2], 5[3], 6

CANT. 1:7, 8, 9, 10[2], 11[2], 13, 14[2], 17[2], 2:1[2], 3, 5, 7[2], 8, 12[3], 14[2], 17, 3:4, 5[2], 6[3], 7, 8, 9[2], 10[5], 11[4], 4:1, 2, 3[2], 4[2], 6[2], 8[3], 9[2], 10, 11[2], 13, 14, 15[2], 5:2[2], 4, 5, 7, 8[2], 12[2], 13, 15[2], 16, 6:2, 5, 6, 7, 9[2], 11[2], 12, 13, 7:1[3], 2, 4[3], 5, 7, 8[3], 9[2], 13, 8:1, 2[3], 4, 6, 7, 9[2], 11, 14

ISAIAH 1:1[4], 4[2], 6, 8[2], 9, 10[4], 11[7], 13, 15, 16, 19, 20, 21, 23[2], 24[4], 26, 28[2], 29, 31, 2:1, 2[2], 3[6], 5[2], 6[2], 7[4], 8[2], 10[2], 11[2], 12[2], 13[2], 16, 17[2], 19[4], 20[2], 21[4], 22, 3:1[3], 2, 3, 6[3], 7, 8, 9, 10, 11, 12

ISAIAH 3:14[2], 15[2], 16, 17[3], 18, 20, 22, 24[6], 4:1, 2[3], 4[5], 5[2], 6, 5:1, 2, 3, 7[4], 8, 9[2], 10[2], 12[2], 15, 16, 17, 18, 19[2], 22, 23, 24[4], 25[2], 26, 27[2], 29, 30, 6:3[2], 4[2], 5[4], 6, 8, 10, 12, 7:1[7], 2[3], 3[3], 4[4], 5, 6[2], 8[2], 9[2], 11, 13, 16, 17, 18[3], 19[2], 20[2], 22, 25[3], 8:2, 4[3], 6, 7[2], 8[2], 9, 11, 13, 14[4], 17, 18, 22, 9:1[4], 2[2], 4[4], 5[2], 6, 7[5], 9[2], 11, 13, 16[2], 18[2], 19[3], 20, 10:2, 3, 5, 6[2], 10[3], 12[4], 13[2], 14, 16[2], 17, 18[2], 19[2], 20[4], 21, 22[2], 23[2], 24[3], 26[4], 27, 29, 30, 31, 32[3], 33[2], 34, 11:1[3], 2[6], 3[4], 4[3], 5[2], 8, 9[2], 10[2], 11[2]

ISAIAH 11:12[3], 13[2], 14[3], 15, 16[3], 12:3[2], 6[3], 13:1[2], 2, 4[6], 5[2], 6, 8, 9[2], 10, 11[2], 12, 13[4], 18, 19[2], 21[2], 22, 14:1, 2[2], 4, 5[2], 8, 9[2], 11, 12, 13[3], 14, 15, 17, 18[2], 19[3], 20, 21[2], 22, 23[3], 24, 27, 29[2], 30, 32[2], 15:1[3], 3, 4, 5[4], 6, 7, 8, 9[4], 16:1[3], 2[3], 3, 4[2], 5, 6[3], 7, 8[3], 9[2], 10, 14[2], 17:1, 2, 3[4], 4[2], 5, 6[3], 7, 8, 9[2], 10[3], 11[2], 12[4], 13[2], 14[2], 18:1, 2, 3, 4[2], 6[3], 7[5], 19:1[4], 3, 4[2], 6, 7, 11[5], 12, 13[3], 16[4], 17[4], 18[4], 19[2], 20[3], 22, 23, 24, 25[2], 20:1, 2, 4[2], 5[2], 6[2], 21:1[2], 3[3], 4, 7[3], 9[3], 10[4], 11[4], 13, 14[2], 15, 16[2]

ISAIAH 21:17[5], 22:1[2], 2, 4[3], 5[6], 6, 7, 8[3], 9[3], 10, 11, 12, 14[2], 15, 18[2], 20, 21[2], 22[2], 24[4], 25, 23:1[3], 2[2], 3[3], 4, 5, 6, 7, 8, 9[3], 10, 12, 13, 14, 15[2], 17[3], 24:2[2], 4, 6, 8[3], 10, 11, 13[2], 15[3], 16, 17, 18[4], 21[2], 23, 25:1, 2[3], 3, 4, 5[3], 6[6], 7, 8, 10, 11[2], 12[2], 26:1, 6[2], 7[2], 8[3], 9, 10[2], 11, 13, 15, 17, 18, 19, 21[2], 27:2, 5, 6[2], 7, 8, 9[2], 11, 12[3], 13[2], 28:1[4], 2[2], 3[2], 4, 5[4], 6, 7[3], 8, 13, 14, 17, 21, 22, 24, 28, 29, 29:4[3], 5[2], 6[3], 7[2], 8, 10, 11[2], 13, 14[2], 16[3], 18[4], 19, 21, 22, 23[4], 30:1[2], 2[2], 3[2], 5, 6[5]

ISAIAH 30:9, 11[3], 12, 14[3], 15, 17[3], 18, 19, 20[2], 22[4], 23[3], 25[2], 26[6], 27[2], 28[3], 29[3], 30[3], 31, 32, 33[3], 31:1, 2[2], 4[4], 5, 6, 7[2], 8[2], 9, 32:2[2], 3[2], 4[2], 6[2], 7, 13[2], 14[3], 17[2], 20, 33:2, 3[2], 4[2], 6[3], 7, 12, 15[3], 16[2], 19[2], 20[3], 21, 23, 34:1, 2, 3, 4, 5, 6[5], 8[3], 11[2], 13, 14[3], 16[3], 35:2[4], 4, 5[2], 6, 7[2], 8, 10, 36:1[3], 2[3], 4, 6[2], 8, 9[3], 11, 13[2], 15[2], 16[4], 17[2], 18[5], 19[3], 20[3], 22[3], 37:1, 2[2], 3[3], 4[2], 5, 6[3], 8, 9, 10[3], 11, 12[2], 13[4], 14[2], 16[4], 17, 18[2], 19, 20, 21[3], 22[2], 23, 24[5], 25[2], 26, 27[2], 30[2], 31[2], 32[6], 33, 36[2], 37, 38[2], 38:1, 4, 5

ISAIAH 38:6[3], 8[2], 9[3], 10[4], 11[2], 12, 13, 15, 16, 17, 20[2], 21, 22, 39:1[2], 2[3], 5[2], 7[3], 8, 40:2, 3[2], 5[2], 6, 7, 8, 9, 12[2], 13, 14[2], 15[2], 21, 22, 23, 26, 28[3], 41:5, 6, 8, 9, 10, 12, 14[2], 16, 17, 18[3], 20[2], 21, 22, 24[2], 25, 28, 42:5, 6[2], 7, 9, 10, 11[2], 13, 22, 25[2], 43:3, 6, 13, 14, 15, 18, 20, 22, 23, 24, 28, 44:5[2], 6[2], 9, 11, 12, 13[2], 14, 19[2], 21, 23, 25, 26[3], 28, 45:1, 2[2], 3[3], 6, 9, 11[3], 13, 14[4], 15, 16[2], 19[2], 20[2], 22, 23, 25, 46:3[2], 6, 7, 9, 47:1[2], 4[2], 5[2], 7, 8, 9[3], 12, 13, 14, 48:1[7], 2[3], 3, 10, 13, 17

ISAIAH 48:18, 19, 20[3], 21, 49:1[2], 2, 5, 6[3], 7[3], 8[2], 9, 10, 12, 15, 16, 17, 19[2], 23, 25[2], 26, 50:1[2], 4, 10[2], 11[2], 51:1, 3[2], 4, 7[2], 9[2], 10[2], 11, 12[3], 13[4], 15, 16[2], 17[4], 18, 20[4], 22[5], 23, 52:2[2], 7[2], 9, 10[3], 11[3], 12, 14, 53:1, 2, 3[2], 4, 5, 6, 8[3], 10, 11[2], 12, 54:1[2], 2[2], 4[2], 5[3], 6, 9[2], 10, 12[3], 13[2], 17[3], 55:3, 5[2], 11, 12, 13[2], 56:2, 3, 4, 5[2], 6[3], 7[2], 8, 9, 57:3[2], 4[2], 5, 6, 10[2], 11[2], 14[2], 15[3], 17[2], 19, 58:1, 2[3], 3, 4, 6, 8, 9[2], 11, 12[4], 13, 14[3], 59:5, 6[2], 7, 8, 13, 17[2], 19[3], 21[5], 60:1, 3, 5[2], 6[3], 7[3], 9[3], 10, 11

ISAIAH 60:13[3], 14[5], 15, 16[3], 20, 21[2], 61:1[2], 2[3], 3[5], 4, 5, 6[3], 10[2], 62:2, 3[3], 6, 8[2], 9, 10, 11[3], 12, 63:1, 3, 4[2], 7[4], 9[2], 11[2], 12, 14, 15[4], 16, 17, 18, 64:4, 7[2], 8, 65:1[2], 3, 4, 7, 9[3], 10[2], 14[3], 16[2], 19[2], 20, 21, 22[3], 23[2], 66:1, 2, 5, 6[2], 7, 11[2], 12, 14, 15, 16, 19, 20[3], 21, 24

JER. 1:1[4], 2[5], 3[8], 4, 5, 8, 11[2], 13, 14[2], 15[5], 16, 18[2], 2:1, 2[3], 3, 4[4], 6[7], 10, 13, 16[2], 18[4], 19, 20, 21, 26, 27, 28[2], 31[2], 34[2], 36[2], 3:4, 6, 8, 9, 14[2], 16[2], 17[3], 18[4], 19[2], 20, 21[2], 23[2], 24, 25, 4:1, 3, 4[5], 7, 8, 9[2], 11[2], 16

JER. 4:17, 19[2], 21, 26, 29, 30, 31[5], 5:1, 4[2], 5[2], 6[2], 11[2], 14, 15, 20, 22, 24, 27[2], 28[3], 6:1[5], 2, 4, 6[2], 9[2], 10, 11[4], 12, 13[3], 14[2], 17, 19, 22, 23, 24, 25, 26, 29, 7:2[3], 3[2], 4[3], 12, 15[2], 17[2], 18, 19, 20[2], 21[2], 22[2], 24, 25[2], 28, 29, 30, 31[3], 32[3], 33[3], 34[6], 8:1[8], 2[2], 3[3], 5, 6, 7[2], 8[2], 9, 11[2], 12, 14, 15, 16[3], 19[4], 21[2], 22[2], 9:1[3], 2[2], 4, 6, 7[2], 10[4], 11[2], 12, 14, 15[3], 17, 19[2], 20[2], 22, 26[2], 10:1, 2[2], 3[4], 5, 7[2], 8, 9[4], 13[3], 15[2], 16[4], 17[2], 18, 20, 22[3], 23, 11:2[3], 3[2], 4[2], 6[3], 7[2], 8[2], 9[2], 10[3], 12[3], 13[3], 16[3], 17[5], 18, 19

JER. 11:20, 21[3], 22, 23[2], 12:1[2], 3, 4[2], 5[2], 6, 7[2], 9, 12[3], 13[3], 14[2], 16[2], 13:2, 3, 4, 8, 9[2], 10, 11[3], 12, 13[2], 16, 18, 19[2], 22, 24, 25, 27, 14:1, 2, 8[2], 9, 14[2], 16[2], 17, 19, 30, 21, 22, 15:1, 3[2], 4[4], 7[2], 8[2], 9, 10[3], 11[2], 15, 16[2], 17[2], 21[4], 16:1, 4[4], 5, 7, 8, 9[7], 12, 13, 14[3], 15[2], 16[2], 18, 19[2], 17:1[5], 8, 10, 11, 12, 13[2], 15, 16, 17, 18, 19[4], 20[3], 21, 22, 24, 25[4], 26[4], 27[2], 18:4[2], 5, 6[2], 8, 10, 11[2], 12, 13, 14[2], 17, 18, 21[2], 23, 19:1[4], 2[3], 3[5], 4[2], 5, 6[3], 7[4], 8, 9[3], 10, 11, 13[6], 14, 15[2], 20:1[2], 2[2], 3, 4[3], 5[4]

JER. 20:8, 9, 10, 12, 13[2], 18, 21:1[2], 2[2], 4[4], 6[2], 7[6], 8[2], 10[2], 11[3], 12[5], 13[2], 14, 22:1[2], 2[3], 3[2], 4[2], 6[2], 9, 11[4], 16, 18[2], 19[2], 23[2], 24[2], 25[5], 29, 30[2], 23:1, 2[2], 3[2], 7[3], 8[3], 9[4], 10[3], 12, 13, 14[3], 15[3], 16[5], 17, 18, 19[2], 20[2], 22, 26[3], 33, 34, 36[4], 38[3], 39, 24:1[6], 4, 5[4], 8[3], 9, 25:1[6], 2[2], 3[4], 5, 6, 7, 8, 9[2], 10[6], 11, 12[2], 14[2], 15[2], 16, 18, 19, 20[5], 21, 22[3], 24[2], 25[3], 26[4], 27[3], 28, 29[2], 30, 31, 32[2], 33[3], 34[3], 35, 36[4], 37[2], 38[3], 26:1[4], 2[2], 3[3], 5, 6, 7, 8, 9[2], 10[4], 13[2], 15, 16, 17[3], 18[6], 19[2], 20[4], 22, 23[2], 24[3], 27:1[4], 3[7], 4[3], 6[3]

JER. 27:7[2], 8[3], 9, 11[2], 12[3], 13, 14[2], 16[2], 17, 18[5], 19[2], 20[4], 21[6], 28:1[8], 2[4], 3[2], 4[5], 5[3], 6, 7, 8[4], 9[2], 11[5], 12[2], 13[2], 14[6], 16, 29:1[2], 2, 3[5], 4[2], 5, 7, 8[3], 11[2], 14, 16[4], 17, 18, 20, 21[8], 22[3], 25[3], 26[2], 27, 28, 29, 30, 31, 30:2, 3, 5[3], 7[2], 8[2], 10, 11[2], 14[3], 15, 16, 17, 18, 19[2], 21[2], 23[2], 24[2], 31:1[2], 2, 3, 4, 5, 7[2], 8, 9, 10, 11, 12[4], 14, 16, 19, 21, 23[5], 27[4], 31[2], 32[2], 33, 34[2], 35[3], 36, 37[2], 38[2], 40[4], 32:1[3], 2[3], 3[3], 4[5], 6, 7[2], 8[5], 9[2], 11, 12[7], 14[3], 15[2], 16[2], 18[3], 19[3], 20, 21[2], 23, 24[4], 25, 26, 27, 28[3], 30[4], 31[3], 32[7]

JER. 32:35[3], 36[3], 37, 39[2], 43, 44[5], 33:1[2], 4[4], 5, 6, 7[2], 9[2], 10[2], 11[10], 12[2], 13[6], 14[2], 15, 17[2], 19, 20[2], 22[3], 23, 25, 26[3], 34:1[3], 2[4], 3[3], 4[3], 5, 6, 7[4], 9[2], 10, 12, 13[5], 14, 17, 18, 19[4], 20[4], 21[5], 22, 35:1[3], 2[3], 3[3], 4[9], 5[3], 6, 8[2], 11[5], 12, 13[4], 14[2], 16[3], 17[3], 18[4], 19[3], 36:1[3], 2[2], 3, 4[4], 5, 6[4], 8[2], 9[4], 10[7], 11[4], 12[4], 13, 14[5], 16, 20[2], 21[3], 24, 26[3], 27[2], 28, 29[2], 30[3], 31[2], 32[4], 37:1[5], 2[2], 3[2], 5[2], 6, 7[3], 10, 11[2], 12[2], 13[4], 15, 17[2], 19, 20, 21[4], 38:1[4], 3[2], 4[4], 6[3], 7[2], 8, 10, 11, 13[2], 14, 16, 17[3], 18[3], 19, 20, 22[2], 23[3], 24, 28, 39:1[3]

JER. 39:2[2], 3[5], 4[5], 5[3], 6[4], 8[2], 9[3], 10[4], 11[2], 13[2], 14[4], 15[2], 16[2], 17[2], 40:1[2], 2, 5[5], 6, 7[6], 8[5], 9[4], 11[4], 12[2], 13[2], 14[3], 15[2], 16[3], 41:1[5], 2[4], 3, 5, 6[2], 7[3], 8[4], 9[5], 10[4], 11[4], 12, 13[2], 14, 15, 16[6], 17, 18[5], 42:1[3], 2, 6[2], 7, 8[2], 9, 10, 11[4], 13, 14[3], 15[4], 16, 17, 18[3], 19, 21, 43:1[2], 2[2], 3[2], 4[4], 5[4], 6[4], 7[2], 8, 9[3], 10[3], 11, 12[3], 13[4], 44:1[2], 2[3], 3, 6[2], 7[3], 8[3], 9[7], 11[2], 12[3], 13, 14[4], 15, 16, 17[5], 18, 19, 21[3], 22[3], 23, 24[2], 25[3], 26[5], 27[3], 28[5], 30[6], 45:1[5], 2, 46:1, 2[6], 10[5], 11, 12, 13[2], 16, 17, 18, 20, 21[3], 22, 24[3], 25[3], 26[5], 27, 28[3]

JER. 47:1, 2[2], 3[6], 4[3], 5, 6, 48:1[2], 2, 3, 5[3], 10, 13[3], 15[2], 16, 18, 19, 24[2], 25, 27, 28, 29[2], 31, 32[3], 33, 34[3], 36, 38, 41, 43, 44[2], 45[7], 46, 47[2], 49:2[2], 3, 6[2], 7, 8[2], 12[2], 16[3], 18[2], 19[2], 20[3], 21[2], 22[3], 25[2], 26[2], 27[2], 28[3], 30[2], 32, 33, 34[4], 35[3], 36[2], 39, 50:1, 3, 4[2], 7[2], 8[4], 9[2], 11, 12, 13[2], 15, 16[2], 17[2], 18[4], 20[2], 21[2], 22[2], 23, 25[4], 26, 27, 28[5], 29, 30, 31, 33[2], 34[2], 35, 37, 38, 39[2], 40, 41, 42, 43[4], 44[2], 45[3], 46[2], 51:1, 2, 4, 5[4], 6[3], 7, 10, 11[4], 12[2], 13, 14, 16[3], 18[2], 19[4], 20, 23, 24, 26, 27, 28[2], 29[2], 30, 31, 32

JER. 51:33[4], 34, 35, 41, 42, 43, 44[2], 45[3], 47[2], 49[2], 51, 53, 54[2], 55[2], 56[2], 57, 58[2], 59[4], 63[2], 64, 52:1[2], 2, 3[2], 4[3], 5, 6[2], 7[4], 8[2], 9[2], 10[3], 11[3], 12[5], 13[3], 14[3], 15[6], 16[3], 17[4], 18, 19[3], 20[2], 21[2], 22[3], 24[2], 25[9], 26[2], 27[3], 29, 30[3], 31[8], 32, 33, 34[4]

LAM. 1:1, 3[2], 4, 5, 6, 7[4], 12, 14, 15[2], 21, 2:1[3], 2[3], 3, 4[2], 5, 6[3], 7[4], 8[2], 10[3], 11[3], 12, 13[2], 14, 15[3], 17[2], 18[3], 19[4], 20[2], 21, 22, 3:1, 6, 13, 22, 26, 32, 33, 34, 35[2], 38[2], 39, 45, 48[3], 51[2], 55, 58, 62, 64, 65, 66, 4:1[2], 2[3], 3, 4[2], 6[5], 7, 9[2], 10[3], 12[3], 13[4], 16[2], 19, 20[3]

LAM. 4:21[2], 22[3], 5:8, 9[3], 10, 11, 12, 15, 18[2], 21

EZEKIEL 1:1[3], 2[2], 3[4], 4[5], 5[3], 7[3], 8, 10[5], 11, 13[4], 14[2], 16[3], 18, 20, 21, 22[3], 24[5], 26[4], 27[5], 28[7], 2:2, 3[2], 6[4], 8, 9, 3:1[2], 3, 4[2], 5[3], 6[2], 7[2], 10, 11[2], 12[2], 13[4], 14[8], 15[2], 16[2], 17[2], 22, 23[2], 25, 26, 4:1, 3[2], 4[3], 5[4], 6[2], 7, 8, 9, 11, 12, 13, 14[2], 16[2], 5:1, 2[2], 4[3], 5, 7, 8[2], 9, 10[2], 12[2], 14, 16[2], 6:1, 2[2], 3[2], 5[2], 7, 9, 11[2], 12, 13, 7:1, 2[3], 4, 7[2], 9, 11[5], 13, 16[3], 19[3], 20[3], 21[2], 23[2], 24[2], 26, 27[2], 8:1[3], 2[4], 3[6], 4[2], 5[3], 6[2], 7, 8, 10[3], 11[6], 12[4], 14[2], 15, 16[4]

EZEKIEL 8:17[2], 9:2, 3[3], 4[3], 8[2], 9[4], 10:1[3], 2, 3, 4[4], 5[2], 7, 8, 9[2], 10, 12, 14[4], 15, 17, 18[2], 19[4], 20[2], 21[2], 22[2], 11:1[5], 2, 4, 5[3], 7[3], 9[2], 10, 11, 12, 13[3], 14, 15[4], 17[2], 19[2], 21, 22[2], 23[3], 24[2], 25, 12:1, 2[2], 3, 6, 8, 9[2], 10, 13, 16, 17, 18, 19[7], 21, 22[2], 23, 24, 26, 27[4], 28, 13:1, 2[4], 5[2], 9[4], 16[2], 17[3], 18[2], 19[2], 21, 22[2], 23, 14:1[2], 2, 3[3], 4[4], 5, 6, 7[5], 8, 9, 10[3], 11, 12, 13[2], 15, 15:1, 2[2], 3, 4[2], 6[2], 16:1, 2, 3[2], 5, 7, 8, 13, 15, 16, 17[2], 20, 22, 25, 26, 27[3], 29, 30, 31, 32, 35, 36[2], 39, 41, 43, 45

EZEKIEL 16:49[4], 51, 53[4], 56, 57[4], 60, 63, 17:1, 2[2], 3[2], 4[3], 5[2], 6, 7, 9, 11, 12, 13[3], 14, 16, 22[3], 23[4], 24, 18:1, 2, 4[2], 6[2], 10[2], 11, 15[2], 17, 19, 20[4], 25[2], 29[3], 30, 31, 32, 19:1, 3, 4, 5, 7, 9[2], 10, 11[2], 14[2], 20:1[4], 2, 3[4], 4[2], 5[3], 6[3], 7[2], 8[4], 9[2], 10[2], 13, 15, 17, 18, 22, 27[2], 28, 30[2], 31[3], 32, 34, 35, 36[2], 37, 38[2], 39, 40[5], 41, 42, 44, 45, 46[2], 47[2], 49, 21:1, 2[2], 3[2], 4, 5, 6[2], 8, 9, 10, 11, 12[3], 14[3], 15, 18, 19[5], 20, 21[3], 25, 28[2], 29[2], 30, 31[2], 32, 22:1, 2, 3, 6, 7, 9, 12, 13, 15, 16, 17, 18[4], 19

EZEKIEL 22:20, 21, 22, 23, 24[2], 25, 29, 31, 23:1, 2[2], 3, 4, 6, 7, 8, 9[2], 12, 14, 15[4], 17, 19[2], 20[2], 21[2], 23[2], 24, 26, 27, 28[2], 29, 31, 32, 33[2], 36, 39, 42[2], 46[2], 48, 49, 24:1[2], 2[4], 5[2], 6, 7[2], 11[3], 12, 15, 16[2], 17[2], 20, 21[3], 22, 25[3], 25:1, 2, 3[3], 4, 6, 7, 8, 9[2], 10, 12, 13, 14, 16, 26:1[2], 2[2], 4[2], 5[2], 7[2], 9, 10[5], 11, 12[3], 13[2], 14, 15[2], 16, 17, 18, 20[4], 27:1, 2, 3[3], 4, 5[2], 6[6], 7, 8, 9[2], 10[4], 11, 12[3], 13[2], 14[2], 15[3], 16[3], 17[2], 18[4], 21, 22[2], 23, 24[3], 25[3], 26, 27[5], 28[2], 29, 31, 32, 33[4], 34[2], 35, 28:1, 2[8], 5, 6

EZEKIEL 28:7[2], 8[2], 9, 10[2], 11, 12[3], 13[3], 14[3], 16[6], 17[2], 18[2], 20, 21, 22, 23, 24[2], 25[2], 29:1[2], 2[2], 3[2], 4[4], 5[3], 6[3], 7, 8, 9, 10[3], 11[2], 12[2], 13, 14[3], 15, 16[2], 17[2], 18[2], 19[2], 20, 21[4], 30:1, 2, 3[2], 5, 6[2], 7[2], 9, 10[3], 11, 12[2], 13[4], 15[2], 17[2], 18[2], 20, 21[3], 22[2], 24[3], 25[6], 31:1[2], 2[2], 3, 4, 5[3], 6[2], 7, 8[2], 9[3], 11[2], 12[3], 13[2], 14[4], 15, 16[4], 17, 18[4], 32:1[2], 2[3], 3, 4[2], 6, 8, 9, 10, 11[2], 12[4], 13[2], 15[2], 16, 17[2], 18[4], 20[2], 21[2], 22, 23[3], 24[3], 25[4], 26[2], 27[4], 28, 30[3], 32[2], 33:2[4], 4, 5, 7[2], 9, 10[2], 11[2], 12[5], 15, 16, 17[2], 20[2], 21[3], 22, 23, 24[3], 27

EZEKIEL 33:28^{2}, 29, 30^{3}, 32, 34:1, 2^{3}, 5, 6, 7, 8, 9, 12, 13^{2}, 14^{2}, 18^{2}, 25^{2}, 26, 27^{5}, 28, 29^{2}, 30, 31, 35:1, 2, 5^{4}, 11, 12, 15^{3}, 36:1^{4}, 3^{3}, 4^{3}, 5^{3}, 6^{2}, 8^{2}, 10^{2}, 12, 15^{2}, 16, 17^{3}, 20^{2}, 21, 22^{2}, 23, 24, 26^{2}, 30^{3}, 32, 34, 35, 37^{2}, 38^{2}, 37:1^{4}, 3, 4, 8, 9, 11^{2}, 12^{2}, 13, 15, 16^{4}, 18, 19^{4}, 21, 22, 23^{2}, 26^{2}, 28, 38:1, 2^{3}, 3, 4^{3}, 5, 6^{2}, 8^{4}, 11, 12^{2}, 13, 14^{2}, 15^{2}, 16, 17^{2}, 18, 19^{2}, 20^{4}, 23, 39:1^{2}, 2^{2}, 3^{2}, 4^{3}, 7, 9, 10^{2}, 11^{5}, 12^{2}, 13, 14^{3}, 15, 16, 17^{3}, 18^{9}, 19, 20, 22, 23^{2}, 25^{2}, 27^{2}, 28, 29, 40:1^{4}, 2^{3}, 3^{2}, 4^{2}, 5^{3}, 6^{2}, 7^{2}, 8

EZEKIEL 40:9^{2}, 10^{2}, 11^{3}, 13^{2}, 14^{2}, 15^{4}, 18^{2}, 19^{2}, 20, 21, 22, 23, 38, 39, 40^{2}, 41, 42^{2}, 43, 44^{3}, 45^{2}, 46^{4}, 48^{3}, 49, 41:1, 2^{2}, 3^{2}, 5^{2}, 6^{2}, 7^{2}, 8^{3}, 9^{2}, 10, 11^{2}, 12, 14^{3}, 15^{2}, 19^{2}, 20, 21^{4}, 22^{2}, 25^{2}, 26^{2}, 42:2, 4^{2}, 5, 6, 7, 8, 10^{2}, 11, 12^{2}, 14, 15, 43:2^{4}, 3, 4^{2}, 5, 6, 7^{8}, 8, 9^{2}, 10^{3}, 11^{2}, 12^{3}, 13^{2}, 18^{2}, 19^{2}, 20^{3}, 21^{2}, 22, 23, 25, 44:1^{2}, 2, 3^{3}, 4^{3}, 5^{5}, 6^{3}, 7, 8^{2}, 9^{2}, 11, 12, 13^{2}, 14^{2}, 15^{3}, 17^{2}, 22^{3}, 30^{6}, 31^{2}, 45:1^{2}, 2, 3^{3}, 4^{2}, 5^{3}, 6^{5}, 7^{7}, 8^{2}, 9, 11^{3}, 13^{6}, 14^{5}, 15^{4}, 16, 17^{3}, 18, 19^{7}, 20, 21^{2}, 22, 23^{2}, 24^{2}, 25^{2}, 46:1^{2}, 2^{4}, 3^{2}, 5

EZEKIEL 46:6, 7, 8^{2}, 9^{6}, 10, 11, 13^{2}, 14^{3}, 16, 17^{3}, 18^{3}, 19^{2}, 21^{2}, 22^{3}, 23, 24^{3}, 47:1^{5}, 2^{2}, 6^{2}, 7, 9, 10, 12, 13, 15^{2}, 16^{3}, 17^{2}, 18, 19, 21, 22^{2}, 48:1^{5}, 2, 3, 4, 5, 6, 7, 8^{4}, 9^{2}, 10, 11^{3}, 12^{2}, 13, 14^{2}, 17, 18^{2}, 19^{2}, 20, 21^{5}, 22^{5}, 23, 24, 25, 26, 27, 28^{2}, 29, 30, 31^{6}, 32^{3}, 33^{3}, 34^{3}, 35

DANIEL 1:1^{4}, 2^{7}, 3^{5}, 4, 5^{2}, 6^{2}, 7^{5}, 8^{3}, 9, 10^{2}, 11, 13^{3}, 15^{2}, 16, 18^{2}, 20^{2}, 21, 2:1^{2}, 6, 7, 8, 12, 14^{2}, 16, 18^{4}, 19, 20, 23^{2}, 24^{2}, 25^{2}, 27, 28, 30, 32^{3}, 33^{3}, 34, 35, 37^{2}, 38^{4}, 39, 41^{4}, 42^{3}, 43, 44^{2}, 45, 47^{4}, 48^{3}, 49^{4}, 3:1^{3}, 2^{2}, 3^{2}

DANIEL 3:5^{2}, 6, 7^{2}, 10^{2}, 11, 12^{2}, 15^{4}, 17, 19^{2}, 21, 22, 23, 24, 25^{3}, 26^{4}, 27^{2}, 28, 29, 30, 4:5, 6^{2}, 8^{2}, 9^{3}, 10^{2}, 11, 12^{3}, 13, 15^{5}, 17^{4}, 18^{2}, 21^{2}, 22, 23^{5}, 24, 25^{3}, 26, 27, 29^{3}, 30^{3}, 32^{2}, 33, 34, 35^{3}, 36, 37, 5:1, 2, 3^{3}, 4^{6}, 5^{4}, 6, 7^{2}, 10^{2}, 11^{4}, 12^{3}, 13^{4}, 14^{2}, 15, 16^{2}, 21^{3}, 23^{4}, 24, 26, 29, 30, 6:2, 5, 7^{4}, 8, 12^{4}, 13^{3}, 14, 15, 16, 17^{2}, 18, 19, 20, 23^{3}, 24^{3}, 26^{2}, 27, 28^{2}, 7:1^{4}, 2, 5^{2}, 6^{2}, 7, 8^{2}, 9^{2}, 11^{2}, 12, 13^{3}, 15^{2}, 16^{3}, 17, 18, 19^{3}, 20^{3}, 22^{2}, 24, 25^{2}, 27^{3}, 28, 8:1^{2}, 2^{2}, 4, 5, 6, 7, 8, 9^{2}, 10^{3}, 11^{2}, 12, 13, 15

DANIEL 8:16, 17^{2}, 19, 20, 21, 22, 23, 25, 26, 9:1^{5}, 2^{4}, 6, 7^{4}, 8, 10, 11^{2}, 13, 15, 16, 17, 20^{2}, 21, 23, 24, 25, 26^{2}, 27^{2}, 10:1^{3}, 4^{3}, 5, 6^{4}, 9^{2}, 10, 13^{4}, 16^{2}, 17, 18, 20^{2}, 21, 11:1, 2, 4, 5^{2}, 6^{4}, 7^{4}, 8^{3}, 9, 10, 11^{2}, 13, 14^{2}, 15^{2}, 17^{2}, 19, 20^{2}, 21, 22^{2}, 24, 25^{2}, 26^{2}, 30, 31, 35^{3}, 36, 37^{2}, 38, 40^{3}, 41^{3}, 42, 43^{3}, 44^{2}, 45, 12:1^{2}, 2^{2}, 3, 4, 5^{4}, 6^{2}, 7^{2}, 8, 9, 10, 13

HOSEA 1:1^{7}, 2^{4}, 3, 4^{4}, 5^{2}, 6, 7, 10^{4}, 11^{4}, 2:2, 4, 10^{2}, 12, 13, 15^{5}, 17^{2}, 18^{4}, 3:1^{4}, 2^{3}, 4, 5, 4:1^{4}, 3^{3}, 6^{2}, 8, 12, 13, 19, 5:1^{2}, 2, 4^{2}, 5

HOSEA 5:9^{2}, 10, 12, 13, 14, 6:5, 6, 8, 9^{2}, 10^{2}, 11, 7:1^{3}, 5^{2}, 10, 12, 16^{2}, 8:1, 4, 6, 10^{2}, 12, 13, 9:4^{2}, 5^{2}, 6, 7^{3}, 8^{3}, 9, 15^{2}, 16, 10:1^{2}, 4, 5^{3}, 6, 8^{2}, 9^{2}, 13^{2}, 14, 15^{2}, 11:1, 4^{2}, 5, 6, 9^{2}, 11^{3}, 12, 12:5, 7, 9^{2}, 10, 11, 12, 13, 13:2^{4}, 3^{2}, 4, 5, 8^{2}, 10, 12, 13^{3}, 14, 15^{2}, 14:2, 3, 7, 9

JOEL 1:1^{2}, 2^{2}, 3, 5^{2}, 6^{2}, 8, 9, 11, 12^{2}, 13^{3}, 14^{2}, 15, 16, 18^{2}, 19^{2}, 20^{3}, 2:1^{2}, 2^{5}, 3, 4^{2}, 5^{4}, 7, 11, 13^{2}, 16^{2}, 17, 22^{2}, 23, 24, 26, 27, 30, 31, 32, 3:1, 2, 4, 6, 7, 8^{2}, 9, 12, 14^{3}, 16^{4}, 18^{4}, 19

AMOS 1:1^{7}, 2^{2}, 3^{2}, 4^{2}, 5^{4}, 6, 7, 8, 9, 10, 11, 12, 13^{3}, 14^{3}, 2:1^{3}, 2^{2}, 4^{2}, 5, 6^{2}, 7^{3}, 8^{2}, 9, 10^{2}, 11^{3}, 13, 15, 3:1^{2}, 2^{2}, 4, 9^{2}, 12^{5}, 13^{2}, 14^{3}, 15, 4:1^{2}, 5^{2}, 6^{2}, 10^{2}, 11^{2}, 13^{2}, 5:1, 2, 3, 4, 6, 8^{3}, 11^{3}, 14, 15^{2}, 16^{2}, 18^{2}, 20, 22, 23^{2}, 25, 26^{2}, 27, 6:1^{3}, 2, 3, 4^{4}, 5^{2}, 6, 7, 8^{2}, 10^{4}, 12, 13, 14^{4}, 7:1^{2}, 2^{2}, 8, 9^{3}, 10^{4}, 11, 12, 14, 16^{2}, 17, 8:1, 2^{2}, 3, 4, 5^{2}, 6^{2}, 8, 10, 11^{3}, 12, 14^{2}, 9:1^{5}, 3^{2}, 5^{2}, 6^{2}, 7^{4}, 8^{3}, 9, 10, 11^{2}, 12^{2}, 13, 14^{3}, 15

OBADIAH 1, 3^{2}, 6, 7, 8^{3}, 9^{2}, 11, 12^{4}, 13^{4}, 14^{3}, 15, 17

OBADIAH 18^{5}, 19^{5}, 20^{6}, 21

JONAH 1:1^{2}, 3^{2}, 5^{2}, 8, 9, 10, 17, 2:1, 2^{3}, 3, 4, 6, 9^{2}, 3:1, 3^{2}, 5^{3}, 6, 7, 10, 4:2^{2}, 5^{3}, 6, 8

MICAH 1:1^{3}, 3^{2}, 5^{5}, 6^{2}, 7^{3}, 9, 10, 11^{4}, 12^{2}, 13^{4}, 14^{2}, 15^{2}, 2:1, 4, 5, 7^{2}, 8, 9, 11^{2}, 12^{6}, 13, 3:1^{3}, 3, 7, 8^{4}, 9^{4}, 12^{2}, 4:1^{3}, 2^{6}, 4^{2}, 5^{2}, 8^{4}, 10^{3}, 12, 13^{2}, 5:1^{2}, 2^{3}, 3^{2}, 4^{4}, 6^{2}, 7^{3}, 8^{4}, 10, 11, 12, 13^{3}, 14, 6:2, 4^{4}, 5^{3}, 6, 7^{5}, 8, 9, 10^{2}, 11, 12, 13, 14, 16^{4}, 7:1, 2, 4^{2}, 5, 6, 7, 9, 10, 13^{2}, 14^{3}, 15^{3}, 17^{4}, 18^{2}, 19, 20

NAHUM 1:1^{3}, 3, 4, 6, 7, 8, 11, 14^{3}, 15

NAHUM 2:2^{2}, 3^{2}, 6, 7, 8^{2}, 9^{4}, 10, 11^{2}, 13^{2}, 3:1, 2^{5}, 3^{3}, 4^{4}, 5, 10, 11, 12, 13^{2}, 16, 18, 19^{2}

HABAK. 1:2, 6, 7, 13, 14, 15, 2:8^{5}, 9, 11^{2}, 13^{2}, 14^{2}, 16, 17^{6}, 18^{2}, 19, 3:1, 2^{2}, 3, 4^{2}, 7^{3}, 8, 9, 10, 11^{2}, 13^{3}, 14, 15, 16, 17, 18

ZEPH. 1:1^{8}, 3^{2}, 4^{3}, 5, 7^{2}, 8, 10, 11, 14^{3}, 15^{5}, 16, 18^{3}, 2:2^{2}, 3^{2}, 5^{4}, 7^{3}, 8^{3}, 9^{6}, 10^{2}, 11^{2}, 14^{3}, 3:8, 9, 10^{2}, 11^{3}, 12^{2}, 13, 14^{2}, 15^{2}, 17, 18^{2}, 20

HAGGAI 1:1^{6}, 2, 3, 5, 7, 9^{2}, 11, 12^{5}, 14^{9}, 15^{2}, 2:1^{2}, 2^{4}, 3, 4^{3}, 5, 6, 7^{2}, 8, 9^{4}, 10^{3}, 11, 12, 13, 14, 15, 16^{2}, 17

HAGGAI 2:18^{2}, 20^{2}, 21, 22^{4}, 23^{3}

ZECH. 1:1^{4}, 3^{3}, 4, 6^{2}, 7^{5}, 11, 12^{3}, 14, 16, 17, 21^{2}, 2:4, 5^{2}, 6^{2}, 7, 8^{2}, 9, 10^{2}, 11^{2}, 13, 3:1, 2, 4, 5, 6, 7, 9^{2}, 10, 4:1, 2^{2}, 3, 6^{2}, 8, 9^{3}, 10^{3}, 11, 12, 14, 5:3, 4^{4}, 7^{2}, 8^{2}, 9, 11, 6:1, 5^{2}, 9, 10^{7}, 11^{2}, 12^{3}, 13^{2}, 14^{2}, 15^{3}, 7:1^{3}, 2, 3^{2}, 4^{2}, 5, 8, 9, 10, 12^{2}, 13, 8:1^{2}, 2, 3^{4}, 4^{2}, 5^{2}, 6^{4}, 7, 8, 9^{6}, 10, 11^{2}, 12, 13^{2}, 14^{2}, 15, 16, 17, 18^{2}, 19^{6}, 20^{2}, 21^{2}, 22, 23^{5}, 9:1^{6}, 3, 6, 7, 8^{3}, 9^{3}, 10, 11^{2}, 12, 13, 14, 15^{2}, 16^{2}, 10:1^{3}, 3^{2}, 4^{4}, 5, 6^{2}, 7, 10^{4}, 11^{3}, 11:2^{2}, 3^{5}, 4

ZECH. 11:6^{3}, 7^{2}, 9, 11^{2}, 12, 13^{3}, 15, 16, 12:1^{4}, 2, 3, 4^{2}, 5^{3}, 6^{3}, 7^{5}, 8^{3}, 10^{4}, 11^{2}, 12^{4}, 13^{3}, 13:1^{2}, 2^{4}, 3, 4, 6, 7, 14:1^{2}, 2^{2}, 3, 4^{4}, 5^{4}, 8^{2}, 10^{3}, 13^{2}, 14, 15^{5}, 16^{3}, 17^{3}, 18^{2}, 19^{3}, 20, 21^{4}

MALACHI 1:1^{2}, 3, 4^{2}, 5, 6, 7, 8, 9, 10, 11^{3}, 12, 13^{2}, 14, 2:2, 3, 4, 5, 6, 7^{2}, 8^{3}, 10, 11^{2}, 12^{3}, 13, 14^{2}, 15^{2}, 16^{2}, 17^{2}, 3:1^{2}, 2, 3^{2}, 4^{2}, 5, 6, 7^{2}, 10^{2}, 11^{2}, 12, 14, 16, 17, 4:1, 1^{2}, 2^{2}, 4, 5^{2}, 6^{2}

MATT. 1:1^{4}, 3, 5^{2}, 6^{2}, 16^{2}, 18^{2}, 20^{3}, 22, 24, 2:1^{2}, 2, 4^{2}, 5, 6^{3}, 7, 12, 13, 15^{3}, 16^{2}, 19, 20, 21, 22^{3}, 3:1

MATT. 3:2, 3^{3}, 4, 6, 7^{2}, 9, 10, 13, 14, 16^{2}, 4:1^{2}, 3, 4^{2}, 5, 6, 8^{2}, 13, 15^{4}, 16, 17, 18, 19, 21, 23^{3}, 25, 5:3, 9, 10, 11, 13^{2}, 14, 19^{3}, 20^{2}, 21^{2}, 22^{3}, 27, 29, 30, 31, 32, 33, 35, 37, 42, 45, 6:1^{2}, 2, 5^{2}, 8, 16, 22^{2}, 23, 26, 27, 28, 29, 30^{2}, 32, 33, 34, 7:4, 5^{2}, 9, 15, 16^{2}, 21^{2}, 24, 26, 27, 8:6, 11, 12^{2}, 14, 20^{2}, 21, 26, 27, 28^{2}, 29, 30, 31, 32^{2}, 33, 34, 9:2^{3}, 3, 6^{2}, 9, 14, 15, 16, 20^{2}, 22, 27, 34, 35, 38, 10:1^{2}, 2^{2}, 3, 5^{2}, 6^{2}, 7, 10, 14^{2}, 15^{2}, 16, 17, 20, 22, 23^{2}, 25^{2}, 29, 30, 31, 36, 37^{2}

MATT. 10:38, 41^{2}, 42^{3}, 11:1, 2^{2}, 10, 11^{2}, 12^{2}, 19^{3}, 20, 22, 24^{2}, 25, 27, 29, 12:1, 4, 8^{2}, 23, 24, 28^{2}, 31, 32, 34^{3}, 35^{3}, 36, 38^{2}, 39, 40^{2}, 41^{2}, 42^{3}, 43, 45, 50, 13:1, 5, 11^{2}, 14, 15, 18, 19, 21, 22^{2}, 24, 27, 30, 31^{2}, 32^{2}, 33^{2}, 35, 36^{2}, 37, 38^{2}, 39, 40, 41^{2}, 42^{2}, 43, 44, 45, 46, 47^{2}, 49, 50^{2}, 52^{2}, 58, 14:1^{2}, 6, 8, 13^{2}, 20, 24, 25, 27, 29, 31, 33^{2}, 34, 35^{2}, 36, 15:1, 2, 3, 6^{2}, 7, 9, 11, 14, 18, 19, 21, 22^{3}, 24^{2}, 27, 29, 31, 37, 39, 16:3^{2}, 4, 6^{3}, 8, 9, 10, 11^{3}, 12^{5}, 13^{2}, 14, 16, 18, 19^{2}, 21, 23^{2}, 27^{2}, 28^{2}, 17:5, 9

MATT. 17:12^{2}, 13, 18, 20^{2}, 22^{2}, 25^{4}, 26, 27, 18:1, 2, 3, 4, 6, 7, 10^{2}, 11, 12, 13^{2}, 14^{2}, 16, 19^{2}, 20, 23^{2}, 27, 28, 19:1, 7, 8^{2}, 10, 12^{2}, 14^{2}, 23, 24^{2}, 28^{3}, 20:1, 8, 11, 12, 13, 18, 20^{2}, 22^{2}, 23^{2}, 25, 28, 30, 31, 21:1, 3, 5^{2}, 9^{2}, 11^{2}, 12^{3}, 13^{2}, 15, 16^{2}, 17, 23, 25^{2}, 26, 31^{3}, 32, 34^{2}, 37, 39, 40, 42, 43, 45, 22:2, 5, 13, 16^{2}, 27, 28, 29, 30, 31, 32^{5}, 35, 42^{2}, 23:4, 5^{2}, 7, 13, 15, 16, 22, 23^{2}, 25^{3}, 26, 27^{2}, 28, 29^{2}, 30^{2}, 31, 32, 33^{2}, 34^{2}, 35^{3}, 39, 24:1, 3^{4}, 6^{2}, 8, 9, 12, 14, 15^{2}, 17, 21, 27^{3}, 29^{2}, 30^{5}, 31^{2}, 32, 36^{2}

MATT. 24:37^{2}, 39^{2}, 43, 44, 50^{2}, 51, 25:1, 2, 8, 13, 14, 19, 21, 23, 30, 31^{2}, 34^{2}, 40, 45^{2}, 26:2^{2}, 3^{2}, 6, 7, 13, 14, 15, 17^{2}, 21, 22, 24^{3}, 27, 28^{2}, 29^{2}, 30, 31^{2}, 33, 37, 45^{2}, 47^{2}, 51^{2}, 53, 56, 61, 63, 64^{3}, 65, 66, 67, 69, 71, 73, 75, 27:1, 3, 5, 6, 8, 9^{4}, 11, 12, 19, 21, 24^{2}, 27^{2}, 29^{2}, 32, 33, 37, 40, 42, 43, 47, 48, 51, 52, 53, 54, 56^{2}, 57, 58, 60, 62, 28:1^{2}, 2, 4, 11, 19^{3}, 20

MARK 1:1^{3}, 3^{2}, 4^{2}, 5^{4}, 6, 7, 9^{2}, 10, 13, 14^{2}, 15, 16, 17, 19, 24^{2}, 25, 26, 29^{2}, 30^{2}, 34, 2:3^{2}, 4, 5, 6, 9, 10^{2}, 14^{2}

MARK 2:17, 18^{4}, 19, 21, 23, 26^{2}, 28^{2}, 3:5, 9, 11, 17^{3}, 18, 21, 22, 28, 29, 35, 4:4, 5, 10, 11^{2}, 19^{3}, 26, 28, 30, 31, 32^{2}, 37, 38, 41, 5:1^{2}, 2^{2}, 7, 8, 10, 11, 17, 22^{2}, 23, 25, 26, 27, 29^{2}, 30, 34, 35, 36, 37, 38^{2}, 40, 42^{2}, 6:3^{3}, 6, 11, 14, 15, 21, 22^{2}, 23^{2}, 24, 25, 29, 33, 37, 43^{2}, 44, 47, 48, 50, 52, 53, 54, 56, 7:1, 2, 3, 4^{2}, 5, 6, 7, 8^{3}, 9, 13^{2}, 14, 15, 20, 21^{2}, 24, 25, 26, 28, 29, 31^{4}, 35, 8:3, 8, 10, 11, 15^{4}, 19, 20, 23, 27, 28, 30, 31^{3}, 33^{2}, 38^{5}, 9:1^{3}, 7, 9, 12^{2}, 13, 17, 21, 24, 25

MARK 9:26, 31^{2}, 35^{2}, 36, 37, 39, 41, 42, 47, 10:1^{2}, 4, 5, 6, 10, 14^{2}, 15, 23, 24, 25^{2}, 26, 33, 35, 38^{2}, 39^{2}, 44^{2}, 45, 46^{3}, 47^{2}, 48, 49, 11:1^{2}, 3, 5, 9, 10^{2}, 13, 14, 15^{2}, 17^{3}, 19, 29, 30^{2}, 32, 12:2^{2}, 8, 9, 10, 13^{2}, 14^{2}, 22, 23, 24, 26^{4}, 27^{2}, 28^{2}, 29, 34, 35, 38, 44^{2}, 13:1^{3}, 3, 7^{2}, 8, 13, 14^{2}, 15, 19, 25, 26, 27^{2}, 28, 32, 34, 35, 14:1^{2}, 2, 3^{3}, 4, 9^{2}, 10, 12, 13^{2}, 14, 18, 20, 21^{3}, 23, 24, 25^{3}, 26, 27, 41^{2}, 43, 47^{2}, 54, 61, 62^{3}, 64, 65, 66^{2}, 67, 69, 70, 71, 15:2, 3, 9, 12, 17, 18, 21^{2}, 22, 26^{2}, 32, 35, 36

MARK 15:38, 39, 40^{2}, 43^{3}, 45, 46^{2}, 47, 16:1, 2^{2}, 3, 6, 9^{2}, 11, 12, 14, 19

LUKE 1:1, 2, 3, 4, 5^{6}, 6, 8, 9^{2}, 10^{2}, 11^{3}, 15, 16^{2}, 17^{3}, 19, 23, 26, 27, 29, 32^{2}, 33^{2}, 35^{3}, 38, 39, 40, 41, 42, 43, 44, 45, 48, 51, 52, 54, 59, 61, 65, 66^{2}, 68, 69^{2}, 70, 71, 74^{2}, 75, 76^{2}, 77^{2}, 78, 79^{2}, 80, 2:2, 4^{5}, 9^{2}, 10, 11, 13, 21^{2}, 22^{2}, 23, 24^{2}, 25, 27, 31, 32, 33, 34, 35, 36^{4}, 37, 38, 39, 40, 41, 42, 43, 46, 3:1^{8}, 2^{2}, 3^{2}, 4^{4}, 6, 7^{2}, 8^{2}, 9, 14, 15, 16, 23^{3}, 24^{5}, 25^{4}, 26^{5}, 27^{5}, 28^{5}, 29^{5}, 30^{5}, 31^{5}, 32^{5}, 33^{5}, 34^{5}, 35^{5}, 36^{5}

LUKE
3:37[5] 38[4] 4:1 2 3 4 5[2] 6 9[2] 14[2] 15 17 18[2] 19 20 22 25[2] 26[2] 27[2] 29[2] 30 31 33 34[2] 35[2] 37 38 40 41[2] 43 44 5:1[2] 2 3[2] 6 9 10 12 15 17[4] 19 24[2] 27 29[2] 33[2] 34 36[2] 6:1 2 4 5[2] 13 15 16 17[5] 19 20 22 26 30[2] 34 35 42 44[2] 45[6] 49 7:1 3[2] 7 11 12[3] 18[2] 19 21 24 27 28[2] 29 30[2] 31 34[2] 35 36 37 38 39 42 44 8:1[2] 2[2] 4 5 10[2] 11 12 13 14 21 22 23 24 25 26 27 28 29[2] 32 33 35[2] 36 37[2] 38 41 42 43[2] 44[2] 46

LUKE
8:48 49 51 9:2 5 7[2] 8[3] 9 11[3] 17 19 20 22[2] 26[5] 27[3] 29 31 35 36 38 43 44[2] 45 46 47 52 55[2] 56 58[2] 60 62 10:2 6 7 9 10 11[3] 19 21 22 30 34 35 36 11:1 5 6 8 11[2] 15[2] 16 20[2] 24 26 27 28 29 30 31[4] 32[2] 34[3] 36[3] 39[2] 41 42[2] 44 45 46 47 48 49[2] 50[3] 51[3] 52 53 54 12:1[4] 4 6 7 8[2] 9 10 13 15[2] 16 20 25 27 28 29 30[2] 31 39 40 42 44 46 48[3] 51 56[2] 57 13:1 7 10 11 14 15 16 18 19[3] 20 21 25 27 28[2] 29

LUKE
13:31 33 35 14:1[2] 5 8[2] 10 14 15[2] 18 19 21[2] 24[2] 28 32 33 15:4[2] 8 10[2] 12[2] 15 17 19 26 16:2 4 5 6 7 8[2] 9[2] 15 16 17 20 24 28 17:2 6 7 11 15 20[3] 21 22[3] 24[2] 25 26[3] 28 29 30 18:3 8 12 16[2] 17 24 25 29 31 34 37 38 39 19:3 8 9 10 11 22 29[2] 31 34 37[3] 38 39 44 46[2] 47 20:1 4[2] 6 10[2] 13 15[2] 17 20[2] 21[2] 26 27 32 33 34 36[2] 37[3] 38[2] 39 42 45 46 21:3 4[3] 5 9 16 17 18 21 22 24[3] 25 26 27 30 31 34 35

LUKE
21:36 37 22:1 3[2] 6 7 10 11 16 18[2] 19 21 22 23 24 25 30 39 44 47 48 50[2] 52 53 55 58 59[2] 61 66 69[3] 70 71 23:1 3 6 8[2] 11 15 17 22 23[2] 26 27[2] 28 35 37 38[2] 39 41 45 51[4] 52 24:1 3 7[2] 10 13 14 17 18 19 22 23 24 25 31 35[2] 36 42[2] 44 47 48 49[2]

JOHN
1:4 7 8 12 13[6] 14[3] 15[2] 16 18 19 22 23[2] 24 29[2] 30 34 35 36 40 42 44[2] 45[3] 46 47 49[2] 51[2] 2:1[2] 3 6[3] 8 9[2] 11[2] 14 15[2] 16 17 21[2] 25 3:1[2] 3 5[3] 6[2]

JOHN
3:8 10 12 13 14 18[2] 22 25 29[2] 31[2] 34 36 4:5[2] 7 9[3] 10[2] 13 14[2] 22 30 32 34 39[3] 42[2] 46 47[2] 52 54 5:1 3[3] 4[2] 19 25[2] 27 29[2] 30[2] 31 32[2] 36[2] 37 39 42 44 46 6:1[2] 4 7[2] 8 11 13 14 18 22 25 26 27 28 29 33 35 38 39 40 42 45[2] 46 48 51[2] 53[2] 58 60 62 64 65 66 68 69 70 71[3] 7:2 7 13[2] 14 17[3] 18 19 22[2] 23 25 28 31 36 37 38[2] 39 40[2] 41 42[4] 43 44 48[2] 50 52[2] 8:1 12[2] 13 14 17 18[2] 23[2] 26[2] 27 28[2] 34 39 40 41[2]

JOHN
8:42 44[4] 46[2] 47[2] 52 54 59[2] 9:3 4 5 6[2] 7 11 16[2] 17 18 21 22 23 31 32 33 35 40 10:2 5 7 14 16 18[2] 20 21[2] 22 25 26 28 29 32 35 36[2] 37 39 41 11:1[2] 4[2] 8 9 11 13[3] 19 22 27 37[2] 39 40 42 45 46 49 51 52 55 12:2 3[4] 4 7 9 11[2] 13[3] 15 16 17 21[2] 23 24 30 31[2] 34[3] 36 38[2] 41 42[2] 43[2] 49 13:1[2] 2 18 21 22 23 24 26 29[2] 31 14:10 17 21 30 15:4 15 16 19[3] 26[2] 16:2 4 5 8[3] 9 10 11[2] 13[2] 14 15 17 19 21 25

JOHN
16:33 17:6 7 12[2] 14[2] 15 16[2] 24 18:3 5 7 9 12 15 17 18 19[2] 22[2] 23 25 26[2] 28 32 33 34 36[2] 37 39 19:2 3 5 7 14 17 19[2] 20 21[3] 25[2] 29 32[2] 34 36 38[5] 39 40[2] 42 20:1 2 12 19[2] 24 25[2] 30 31 21:1 2[3] 6[2] 9 10 11 12 15 16 17 24

ACTS
1:1 3[3] 4[2] 6 8 9 11 13[2] 14 15[2] 16 17 18 19 20 21 22[2] 24[2] 25 2:1 2 3[2] 5 10[2] 11 13 14 15 17 18 19 20 21 22[4] 23 24[2] 28[2] 29 30[2] 31[2] 33[3] 36 37 38[4] 42 46 3:1 2[2] 5 6[2]

ACTS
3:10 12 13[5] 15 16 18 19[2] 21[3] 22 24 25[3] 26 4:1 4[2] 6[2] 8[2] 9 10[3] 11[2] 13[2] 15 18 19 21 22 25 26 27[2] 30 31 32[5] 33[2] 34[2] 36[3] 5:2 3[2] 7 9[2] 12 13 14 15 16 17 19 20 21[2] 24[2] 30 31 32 34 35 36 37[2] 38 39 40 41 6:1[2] 2[2] 3[2] 4 5[3] 7[3] 8 9[5] 14 15 7:2 3 4[2] 8 10[3] 11 16[4] 17 22 23 24 29 30[3] 31 32[4] 34 35 36 37[2] 40[3] 41 42[4] 43[2] 44 45[3] 46 49 52[4] 53 55[3] 56[2] 58 8:1 3 5 7 9 10 11 12[2] 14 16[2] 18 20 21 22[2] 23[2] 24

ACTS
8:25[2] 26 27[4] 32 34[3] 37 39[2] 9:1 2[2] 11[2] 13 15 20 24 26 27 29 31[2] 33 36 10:1 3[2] 7[2] 12[3] 22[3] 28 31 32 33 34[2] 36[2] 38[2] 39[2] 41 42[2] 43 45[2] 48 11:1 2 5 6[2] 16 20[2] 21 22[2] 23[2] 24[2] 28[2] 30 12:1 2 3 4 5 7 10 11[5] 12[2] 13 17 18 20 22[2] 23[2] 24 13:1 5[2] 7[2] 10[4] 11 12 15[3] 16 17[4] 18 19 20 21[4] 22 23 24[2] 25 26[3] 27 28 29 31 34 36 38 39 40 42 43[2] 44 46[2] 47[2] 48 49 50[2] 51 14:1[3] 3 4 5[2] 6[2] 11[2] 13 14 15 19 22[2] 26 27 15:1 2

ACTS
15:3 4[2] 5[3] 6 7 10 11 14 15 16 17 18 20 21 22 23 26 35 36 40 16:1 2 3 4 6[2] 9 12[2] 13 14[4] 16 17[2] 18[2] 19 26 27[2] 32 33 36 39 40[2] 17:1 2 4[3] 5[2] 6 7 8 9[2] 10 11 12[3] 13[3] 18[3] 22[2] 24 26[4] 27 28 29 30 32[3] 18:3 8[2] 11 12 14 15[3] 17[2] 18 23 25[3] 26 19:4 5 8[2] 9[2] 10[2] 11 12 13[2] 14[2] 16 17 19[3] 20 22 25 27 28[2] 29 31[2] 33 34[2] 35[4] 37[2] 40 20:4[4] 6 7 11 16 17 19[2] 24[4] 25 26 27 28 30 31 32 35 38 21:5 6 8[3] 11

ACTS
21:12 13 14 16[3] 20[2] 21 26[3] 27 28 30 31 32 35[2] 36 39[2] 22:3[3] 5 8 9 10 11[2] 12 14[2] 15 16 18 20[2] 30 23:5[2] 6[2] 9 10 11[2] 12 16 17 20 21 23 27[2] 29[4] 34[2] 24:4 5[3] 7 8[2] 10 14 15[2] 16 21 22[2] 23 25 26 25:2 8 9 11[2] 15 16 18 19[2] 20[3] 21 23[3] 24 25 26 26:2 4 5 6[2] 7 9[2] 10 13 16[2] 18[2] 20[2] 22 25 26[2] 31[2] 27:1 2[3] 5[2] 6 8 10[2] 11 12 19 21 22[3] 23 25 29 30[2] 32 34[2] 35 36 41 42 44 28:2[2] 3[2] 7[2] 8[3] 11 15 16 17[3] 18 19 20

ACTS
28:21[3] 22 23[3] 27[2] 28 31

ROMANS
1:1[2] 3[2] 4[2] 6 7 8 9[2] 10 12 16[3] 17 18[2] 19 20[2] 23 24 25 27[2] 29 30[2] 32[2] 2:2 3 4[2] 5[3] 9[2] 11 13[2] 15 16 17 18 19[2] 20[4] 23 24 25 26 29[3] 3:1 2 3 5 7 12 13 14 17 18 20[2] 21 22[2] 23[2] 25[2] 26 27[2] 28 29[3] 4:4[2] 6 11[4] 12[4] 13[2] 14[2] 16[5] 17 18 19 20 5:2[2] 5 10 14[2] 15[2] 16 17[3] 18[3] 19 6:3 4[2] 5[2] 6 13[2] 16[2] 17[2] 18 19[3] 20 21 23[2] 7:2 4 5 6[2] 8 22 23[2] 24 25[2] 8:2[3] 3 4 5[2] 7 9[3] 10[2] 11 13 14[2]

ROMANS
8:15[2] 16 17 18 19[3] 20 21[3] 23[2] 27[2] 29 33 34 35 39 9:4[2] 5 6[2] 7 8[3] 9 11[3] 16[3] 21 22 23[2] 24[2] 26 27[3] 29 30 31[2] 32 33 10:2 3[2] 4 5 6 8 13 14 15[3] 17 18 20 11:1[4] 2 4[2] 5 6[2] 8 12[4] 13 14 15[3] 17[3] 20 22 24 25[2] 26 29 33[3] 34 36 12:1 2[2] 3[2] 5 6 13 16[2] 17 20 21 13:1[2] 2 3[2] 4[2] 10 11 12[2] 14:7 9 10 12[2] 14 16 17 18 20 23[2] 15:1 2 3 4 5 6 7 8[2] 12 13[2] 14[2] 15[2] 16[3] 18[2] 19[3] 21 26 27 29[3] 30 31 32 33 16:1 2[3]

ROMANS
16:4 5 7 10 11[2] 16 18 20[2] 23[2] 24 25[3] 26[3]

1 COR.
1:1[2] 2[2] 4 6 7 8 9 10 11[3] 12[5] 13 14 16 17[3] 18[2] 19[2] 20[2] 21[2] 24[2] 25[2] 27[2] 28 30[2] 2:1[3] 4[3] 5[2] 6[3] 7 8[3] 9 10 11[4] 12[3] 14[2] 15 16[2] 3:4[2] 10 13 16[2] 17[2] 19 20 4:1[5] 3[2] 5[3] 6[2] 13[2] 16 17 19 20 21 5:4[2] 5[2] 8[2] 10[2] 6:1 4 9[2] 10 11[3] 12 15[3] 19[2] 7:4[2] 6 7 19[2] 23 25[2] 31 33 34[2] 36 40 8:3 4 6 7 9 10 9:2 5 7[3] 9[2] 10 12[2] 13[2] 14 15 16 17 18 10:4 5 7 8 9[2] 10[2] 11 16[5]

1 COR.
10:17 18[2] 21[5] 27 29[2] 30 31 32 33 11:1[2] 3[3] 7[2] 8[2] 10 12[2] 16 18 22 23 24 25 27[3] 28[2] 32 12:3 4 5 6 7 8[2] 9 10[4] 12 15[2] 16[2] 18 21[2] 22 23 27 28[2] 29 30 13:1[2] 2 13 14:10[2] 11 12[2] 16[2] 21 24[2] 25[2] 26 32 33[3] 36 37 15:3 5[2] 6[2] 7[2] 8[4] 9[2] 10[2] 12 13 15[2] 19 20 21 32 34 37[2] 39[5] 40[2] 41[3] 42 47 49[2] 50 52 56[2] 58 16:1 2[2] 10 15[3] 17[2] 19 21 23

2 COR.
1:1[3] 3[3] 4 5 6 7[3] 8[3] 9 11 12[2] 14 16[2] 19 20[2] 22 24 2:3[2] 4[2] 6 9 10 11[2]

2 COR.
2:12 13 14 15 16[2] 17[4] 3:1[2] 2 3[4] 5[3] 6[3] 7[4] 8 9[2] 10 12 13[2] 14 17 18[2] 4:2[4] 4[5] 6[5] 7[3] 10[2] 11 13 15[2] 17 5:1[2] 4 5 9 10 11 14 18[2] 19 21 6:1 2[2] 4 7[3] 16[2] 7:1[2] 4[2] 6 10[2] 11 12 13 14 15 8:1[3] 2[3] 3 4 5 8[3] 9 11[2] 16 17 19[3] 21[2] 23[4] 24[2] 9:2[3] 3 4 5[2] 7 10 12[2] 13[2] 14 10:1 2 4[2] 5[2] 7 8 12 13[2] 14 15[2] 16 11:7 8 10[3] 13 14 15 17 20 22 23 24 26[2] 28 30 31 32 12:1 2 3 5[2] 6[2] 7[2] 9 11 12 17[2] 18 21 13:1 3

2 COR.
13:4[2] 11[3] 14[3]

GAL.
1:1 2 4 6 7 10 11 12[2] 13[2] 14[2] 19 21 22 2:2 4 5 6 7[2] 8 9 12 14[2] 15 16[5] 17 20[2] 21 3:2[3] 5[2] 9 10[3] 11 12 13 14[2] 15 16[2] 17[2] 18[2] 19[2] 20 21 22 26 27 4:1 2 3 4[2] 5 6 7 9 11 13 14 15 19 20 23[2] 26 28 30[2] 31[2] 5:1 4[2] 5 8 11 15 16 18 19 21[2] 22 26 6:1 2 8[2] 10[2] 12 14 16 17 18

EPHES.
1:1[2] 3 4 5[2] 6[2] 7[2] 9 10[2] 11[2] 12 13[3] 14[3] 15 16 17[4] 18[4] 19[2] 23 2:2[4] 3[4] 7 8[2] 9 12[2] 13

EPHES.
2:14 15[2] 19[2] 20 22 3:1 2[3] 4 5 6[2] 7[3] 8[2] 9[2] 10 12 14 15 16 19[2] 4:1[2] 3[2] 4 6 7[3] 9 12[4] 13[7] 14[2] 16[3] 17 18[3] 23 25 29 30[2] 5:1 4 5[2] 6[3] 8 9 11 12[2] 17 20 21 23[3] 26 30[3] 33 6:4 5 6[2] 8 9 10 11[2] 12[2] 13 14 15[2] 16[2] 17[3] 19

PHIL.
1:1 3 4 6[2] 7[3] 8 10 11[2] 12 14 15[2] 16 17[2] 19[2] 22 25 27[3] 28[3] 29 2:1[2] 2[2] 3 4 6 7[3] 8 10[2] 11 13 15 16 17 19 22 26 30 3:2[3] 5[5] 8 9[3] 10[2] 11 12 14[2] 17 18[3] 4:2 3 7 8 9

PHIL. 4:10, 11, 15, 18^2, 22, 23

COLOS. 1:1^2, 3, 4^2, 5^2, 6^2, 7^2, 9, 10^2, 12^2, 13^2, 14, 15^2, 18, 20, 22, 23, 24^2, 25^2, 27^3, 2:2^6, 3, 5, 8^2, 9, 10, 11^3, 12^2, 13, 14^2, 15, 16^3, 17^2, 18^2, 19, 20, 22, 23^3, 3:1, 6^2, 8, 10, 12^3, 14, 15, 16, 17, 22, 24, 25, 4:3^2, 9, 11, 12^3, 16, 18

1 THESS. 1:1, 2, 3^4, 4, 5, 6^3, 8, 9^2, 2:2, 3^2, 4, 5, 6^4, 8^2, 9^2, 11, 12, 13^4, 14^3, 19^2, 3:2^2, 6, 13, 4:1, 3, 4, 5, 6, 9, 12, 15^2, 16^2, 5:1, 2, 5^4, 8^3, 18, 22, 23^2, 28

2 THESS. 1:1, 3, 4, 5^4, 8, 9^2, 11^3, 12^2, 2:1, 2, 3^2, 4, 7^2, 8^2, 9, 10^2, 13^3, 14^2, 3:1, 5, 6^2, 8, 16, 17, 18

1 TIM. 1:1^2, 5^4, 7, 9^2, 11, 14, 15^2, 20, 2:1^2, 3, 4, 7, 3:1, 2^2, 3, 5^2, 6, 7^2, 8, 9, 10, 12, 13, 15^3, 16^2, 4:1, 3, 4, 5, 6^4, 8^2, 9, 10^2, 12, 14^2, 5:8, 9, 10, 17, 18, 22, 25, 6:1^2, 2, 3, 4, 5^3, 10^2, 11, 12, 13, 14, 15, 20

2 TIM. 1:1^3, 3, 4, 6^2, 7^4, 8^6, 10, 11, 13^2, 15, 16^2, 18, 2:2, 3, 4, 6, 8^2, 9, 14^2, 15, 17, 18, 19^2, 20^4, 22, 24, 25, 26^2, 3:2, 3, 4^2, 5, 6, 7, 8, 10, 11, 14^2, 16, 17, 4:2, 5, 6, 8, 15, 17^2, 18

TITUS 1:1^4, 2, 3, 6^2, 7, 8^2, 10, 12^2, 14, 2:3, 5, 7, 8^2, 10, 11, 13, 14, 3:2, 4, 5^3, 7, 11

PHILE. 1, 4, 5, 6^2, 7, 9, 13, 14, 20, 25

HEB. 1:2, 3^4, 5, 6, 7^2, 8^2, 9, 10^2, 13, 14, 2:2, 4, 6^2, 7, 9^2, 10, 11, 12, 14^3, 15, 16^2, 17, 3:1^2, 3, 5, 6, 8, 12, 13^2, 14^2, 16, 19, 4:1^3, 3, 4, 6, 8, 9, 11, 12^5, 13, 14, 15, 16^2, 5:2, 4, 6, 7, 9, 10^2, 11^2, 12^4, 13, 14^2, 6:1^4, 2^7, 4^2, 5^2, 6, 9, 10, 11^2, 12, 16, 17^2, 19, 20, 7:1^3, 2^4, 3^3, 4, 5^7, 6, 7, 8, 10, 11^2, 12^2, 13^2, 14^2, 15, 16^2, 17, 18, 19, 21, 22, 23, 28, 8:1^3, 2^2, 3, 5^2, 6, 8^2, 9^2, 10, 9:1, 3, 4^2, 5^2, 6, 7, 8, 10, 11^2, 12, 13^4, 14, 15^4, 16^2, 17^2, 19^2, 20, 21, 22, 23, 24^2, 25, 26^3, 28, 10:1^2, 2, 3, 4^2, 7^2, 10^2, 12, 18, 19, 21, 22, 23, 25^2, 26, 27, 29^4, 31, 32, 33, 34^2, 35, 36^2, 39^3, 11:1^2, 3^2, 4, 6, 7^4, 9^2, 11, 12, 13, 15, 18, 21^2, 22^3, 23^2, 24, 25^2, 26^2, 27, 28, 30, 32^6, 33, 34^4, 36^2, 38^2, 12:1, 2^3, 3, 5^2, 9^2, 10, 11, 13, 15^3, 16, 17, 19^2, 22^2, 23^3, 24^3, 27^2, 13:7^2, 11, 15^2, 20^3, 22, 24

JAMES 1:1^2, 3, 5^2, 6, 7, 9, 10, 11^2, 12, 13, 14, 17^2, 18^4, 20^2, 21, 22, 23, 24, 25^2, 2:1^3, 4, 5^2, 9, 10, 11, 12, 15, 16, 23, 3:4, 6^3, 7^5, 8, 9, 10, 13^2, 17, 18^2, 4:1, 4^3, 10, 11^4, 5:3, 4^5, 5, 7^2, 8, 10^3, 11^4, 14^2, 15, 16, 17, 19, 20^2

1 PETER 1:1, 2^4, 3^2, 5, 7^3, 8, 9^2, 10^2, 11^3, 13^2, 15, 17^2, 19^2, 20, 22, 23^3, 24^2, 25, 2:2, 4^2, 7, 8^2, 9^2, 10, 12, 13, 14^2, 15^2, 16^2, 25, 3:1, 3^5, 4^4, 7^2, 8^2, 12^2, 13, 14, 15, 16^2, 17, 20^2, 21^4, 22, 4:2^3, 3^3, 4^2, 7, 8, 10^2, 11^2, 13, 14^4, 15, 17^3, 19^2, 5:1^3, 2^2, 4, 5, 6, 10, 12, 14

2 PETER 1:1^2, 2^2, 3, 4, 8, 11, 12, 16^2, 19, 20^2, 21^2, 2:2^2, 3^2, 4, 5^2, 6, 7, 9^2, 10^2, 12, 13, 14, 15^3, 16, 17, 18^2, 19^3, 20, 21, 3:1, 2^4, 4^2, 5^4, 7^2, 8, 10, 11, 12^2, 14, 15, 16, 17, 18

1 JOHN 1:1^2, 5, 7, 2:2, 5, 10, 14, 15, 16^5, 17, 19^3, 21, 27^2, 29, 3:1^2, 2, 4, 8^3, 9^2, 10^3, 12, 16, 19, 22, 23, 4:1, 2^2, 3^2, 4, 5^2, 6^4, 7^2, 9, 13, 14, 15, 17, 5:1^2, 2, 3, 4, 5, 9^4, 10^2, 12, 13^4, 15, 18^2, 19, 20

2 JOHN 3, 4, 9^2, 11, 13

3 JOHN 3, 6, 7, 10, 11, 12^2

JUDE 1^2, 3, 4^2, 5^2, 6, 7, 8, 9, 10, 11^3, 12^2, 13^2, 14^2, 15^2, 16, 17^2, 21^2, 22, 23, 24

REV. 1:1, 2^5, 3, 5^3, 7^2, 9^3, 10, 13^2, 14, 15, 16, 18^2, 20^2, 2:1^3, 5, 6, 7^4, 8, 9^2, 10^3, 11, 12, 14^2, 15, 16, 17, 18^3, 21, 22, 23, 24, 27^3, 3:1^2, 5^2, 7^2, 9^2, 10^2, 12^5, 14^4, 16, 17, 18^2, 4:1, 4, 5^3, 6^3, 8^2, 5:1, 5^4, 6^4, 7^2, 8^3, 9, 11^3, 6:1^3, 5, 6^3, 7, 8^2, 9^2, 11, 12, 13^2, 14, 15^2, 16^2, 17, 7:1^2, 2, 3, 4^4, 5^6, 6^6, 7^6, 8^6, 9, 13, 14^2, 15, 17^2, 8:1, 3, 4^3, 5, 7, 8, 9^2, 10^2, 11^2, 12^5, 13^5, 9:1, 2^4, 3^2, 4^2, 5, 7^2, 8^2, 9^4, 11, 13, 15, 16^3, 17^5, 18^2, 20^5, 21^4, 10:1, 7^3, 8, 10, 11:1, 4, 5, 6, 7, 8, 9, 11, 13^3, 15^3, 18, 19^2, 12:1, 4^2, 5, 6, 10^3, 11^2, 12^2, 14^2, 15^2, 16, 17^3, 13:1^3, 2^2, 3, 8^3, 10, 11, 12, 13, 14^2, 15^3, 17^2, 18^2, 14:2^3, 5, 6, 7^2, 8^3, 10^6, 11^2, 12^3, 14, 15^2, 17, 18^2, 19^3, 20^2, 15:1, 2^4, 3^4, 5^2, 6, 7^3, 8^2, 16:1^3, 2, 3, 4, 5, 6, 7, 9, 10^2, 11^3, 12^2, 13^6, 14^5, 17^2, 19^4, 21^4, 17:1^2, 2^3, 3^2, 4^2, 5^2, 6^3, 7^2, 8^3, 12, 14^2, 17, 18, 18:2^3, 3^6, 4^3, 9^2, 10, 11, 12^5, 13, 15^2, 18, 19, 22^4, 23^4, 24^3, 19:1, 2, 5, 6^3, 7, 8, 9^2, 10^4, 12, 13, 15^4, 16^2, 17^2, 18^6, 19, 20^2, 21^2, 20:1, 4^3, 5, 6^2, 7, 8^3, 9^3, 10, 12^2, 14, 15^2, 21:2, 3^2, 6^3, 9^2, 10, 11, 12^3, 14^3, 16, 17^2, 18^3, 19^3, 21^2, 22, 23^3, 24^3, 25, 26, 27, 22:1^5, 2^7, 3^2, 5, 6, 7^2, 8, 9^3, 10^2, 14, 16, 17, 18^2, 19^5, 21

our

2257

GEN. 1:26^2, 5:29^2, 19:31, 32^2, 34, 23:6, 24:60, 29:26, 31:1^2, 14, 15, 16^2, 32, 33:12, 34:9, 14, 16, 17, 21, 31, 37:26, 27^3, 41:12, 42:13, 21, 32^2, 43:4, 7^2, 8, 18^2, 21^3, 22^3, 28, 44:8, 25, 26^2, 31, 46:34^2, 47:3, 18^4, 19^3, 25

EXOD. 1:10, 3:18, 5:3, 8, 21, 8:10, 27, 10:9^6, 25, 26^2, 12:27, 17:3^2, 34:9^2

LEVIT. 25:20

NUM. 11:6^2, 13:33, 14:3^2, 20:3, 4, 15^2, 16, 21:5, 27:3, 4^2, 31:49, 50, 32:16^2, 17, 18, 19, 26^4, 32, 36:2, 3^2, 4

DEU. 1:6, 19, 20, 25, 28^2, 41, 2:1, 8, 29, 33, 36, 37, 3:3^2, 4:7, 5:2, 3, 24, 25, 27^2, 6:4, 20, 22, 23, 24^2, 25^2, 21:7^2, 20^2, 26:3, 7^5, 15, 29:15, 18, 29^2, 31:17, 32:3, 27, 31^2

JOSH. 2:11, 13, 14^2, 19, 20, 24, 5:13, 7:9, 9:11^2, 12^3, 13^2, 24, 17:4, 18:6, 21:2, 22:19, 24, 25, 27^5, 28^2, 29, 24:17^3, 18, 24

JUD. 6:13, 9:3, 10:10, 11:2, 6, 8, 24, 13:23, 16:23^3, 24^4, 18:5, 19:19, 21:7, 18, 22

RUTH 2:20, 3:2, 4:3

1 SAM. 2:2, 4:3, 5:7, 10, 11, 7:8, 20^2, 9:6, 7, 8, 12:10, 19, 14:9, 10, 16:16, 17:9, 46, 20:29, 23:20, 25:14, 17, 30:23

2 SAM. 7:22, 10:12, 12:18, 18:12, 19:9, 43, 22:32

1 KINGS 1:11, 43, 47, 8:21, 40, 53, 57^2, 58^2, 59, 61, 65, 12:4, 10, 20:31^2

2 KINGS 7:9, 18:22, 19:19, 22:13

1 CHRON. 12:17, 19, 13:2^2, 3, 15:13, 16:14, 35, 17:20, 19:13^2, 28:2, 8, 29:10, 13, 15^2, 16, 18

2 CHRON. 2:4, 5, 6:31, 10:4, 10, 13:10, 11, 12, 14:7, 11, 19:7, 20:6, 7, 9, 12^2, 28:13^3, 29:6^2, 9^4, 32:8^2, 11, 34:21

EZRA 4:3, 5:12, 7:27, 8:17, 18, 21^3, 22, 23, 25, 30, 31, 33, 9:6^3, 7^4, 8^4, 9^3, 10, 13^4, 15, 10:2, 3^2, 14^3

NEH. 4:4, 9^2, 11, 15, 20, 23, 5:2^2, 3, 4, 5^3, 8^2, 9^2, 6:1, 16^2, 18^4, 8:10, 9:9, 16, 32^6, 34^4, 36, 37^3, 38, 10:29, 30^2, 32, 33, 34^3, 35, 36^6, 37^5, 38, 39, 13:2, 4, 18, 27

JOB 8:9, 17:16, 22:20, 28:22, 37:19

PSALMS 8:1, 9, 12:4^3, 17:11, 18:31, 20:5^2, 7, 22:4, 33:20^3, 21, 35:21, 40:3, 44:1^2, 5, 7, 9, 13, 18^2, 20^2, 24^2, 25^2, 26, 46:1, 7, 11, 47:3, 4, 6, 48:1, 8, 14^2, 50:3, 59:11, 60:10, 12, 65:3, 5, 66:8, 9^2, 11, 12, 67:6, 68:19, 20, 74:9, 77:13, 78:3, 5, 79:4, 9^2, 10, 12, 80:6^2, 81:1, 3, 84:9, 85:4, 9, 12, 89:17, 18^2, 90:1, 8^2, 9^2, 10, 12^2, 14, 17^3, 92:13, 23, 95:1, 6, 7, 98:3, 99:5, 8, 9^2, 103:10^2, 12, 14, 105:7, 106:6, 7, 47, 108:11, 13, 113:5, 115:3, 116:5, 118:23, 122:2, 9, 123:2^2, 4, 124:1, 2, 4, 5, 7, 8, 126:2^2, 4, 135:2, 136:23, 137:2, 141:7, 144:12^2, 13^3, 14^2, 147:1, 5, 7

PROV. 1:13, 7:18

CANT. 1:16, 17^2, 2:9, 12, 15, 7:13, 8:8

ISAIAH 1:10, 3:6, 4:1^3, 20:6, 25:9, 26:8, 12, 13, 28:15, 33:2, 20, 22^3, 35:2, 36:7, 37:20, 38:20, 40:3, 8, 42:17, 47:4, 52:10, 53:1, 3, 4^2, 5^3, 55:7, 58:3, 59:12^4, 13, 61:2, 6, 63:16^3, 17, 18, 64:6^2, 7, 8^2, 11^4

JER. 3:22, 23, 24^2, 25^6, 5:19, 24, 6:24, 8:14, 9:18^2, 19, 21^2, 11:21, 12:4, 14:7^2, 20^2, 22, 16:10^3, 19, 17:12, 18:12, 20:10, 21:13, 23:6, 36, 26:16, 19, 31:6, 33:16, 35:6, 8^5, 10, 36:15, 37:3, 42:2, 6^2, 20^2, 43:2, 44:17^4, 19, 25, 46:16, 50:28, 51:10^2, 51

LAM. 3:40, 41^2, 44, 46, 4:17^3, 18^5, 19, 20, 5:1, 2^2, 3, 4^2, 5, 7, 9^2, 10, 15^2, 16, 17^2, 21

EZEKIEL 33:10^2, 21, 37:11^3, 40:1

DANIEL 1:13, 3:17, 9:6^3, 8^3, 9, 10, 12, 13^3, 14, 15, 16^2, 17, 18^3

HOSEA 7:5, 14:2, 3^2

JOEL 1:16

AMOS 6:13

MICAH 2:4, 4:5, 11, 5:5^2, 6^2, 7:17, 19, 20

ZECH. 1:6^2, 9:7

MALACHI 2:10

MATT. 3:9, 6:9, 11, 12, 8:17, 20:33, 21:42, 23:30, 25:8, 27:25

MARK 9:40, 11:10, 12:11, 29

LUKE 1:55, 71, 72, 73, 74, 75, 78, 79, 3:8, 7:5, 11:2, 3, 4, 13:26, 17:5, 10, 23:41, 24:20, 22, 32

JOHN 3:11, 4:12, 20, 6:31, 7:51, 8:39, 53, 9:20, 11:11, 48, 12:38, 14:23, 19:7

ACTS 2:8, 11, 39, 3:12, 13, 25, 5:30, 7:2, 11, 12, 15, 19^2, 38, 39, 44, 45^2, 13:17, 14:17, 15:10, 25, 26, 36, 16:20, 17:20, 28, 19:25, 27, 20:21, 21:5^2, 6, 7, 15, 22:14, 24:6, 7, 26:5, 6, 7, 27:10, 19, 28:17, 25

ROMANS 1:3, 7, 3:5, 4:1, 12, 24, 25^2, 5:1, 5, 11, 21, 6:6, 11, 23, 7:5, 25, 8:16, 23, 26, 39, 9:10, 10:16, 12:7, 13:11, 15:4, 6, 16:1, 9, 18, 20, 24

1 COR. 1:1, 2, 3, 7, 8, 9, 10, 2:7, 4:12, 5:4^2, 7, 6:11, 9:1, 10^2, 10:1, 6, 11, 12:23, 24, 15:3, 14, 31, 57, 16:12, 23

2 COR. 1:1, 2, 3, 4, 5, 7, 8, 11, 12, 15, 18, 22, 3:2^2, 5, 4:3, 6, 10, 11, 16, 17, 5:1, 2, 12, 6:11^2, 7:3, 4, 5, 12, 14, 8:9, 22, 23, 24, 9:3, 10:4, 8, 13, 14, 15^2, 16, 11:31

GAL. 1:3, 4^2, 2:4, 3:24, 6:14, 18

EPHES. 1:2, 3, 14, 17, 2:3^2, 14, 3:11, 14, 5:20, 6:22, 24

PHIL. 1:2, 3:20, 21, 4:20, 23

COLOS. 1:1, 2, 3, 7, 3:4

1 THESS. 1:1, 2, 3, 5, 2:1, 2, 3, 4, 8, 9, 19^2, 20, 3:2^2, 5, 7, 9, 11^3, 13^2, 5:9, 23, 28

2 THESS. 1:1, 2, 8, 10, 11, 12^2, 2:1^2, 14^2, 15, 16^2, 3:6, 12, 14, 18

1 TIM. 1:1^2, 2, 12, 14, 2:3, 6:3, 14

2 TIM. 1:2, 8, 9, 10, 4:15

TITUS 1:3, 4, 2:10, 13, 3:4, 6

PHILE. 1^2, 2^2, 3, 25

HEB. 1:3, 3:1, 14, 4:14, 15, 7:14, 10:22^2, 23, 12:2, 9, 10, 29, 13:15, 20, 23

JAMES 2:1, 2:21, 3:6

1 PETER 1:3, 2:24, 4:3

2 PETER 1:1, 2, 8, 11, 14, 16, 3:15^2, 18

1 JOHN 1:1^2, 3, 9^2, 2:2, 3:5, 16, 17^2, 19, 20^2, 21, 4:10, 17, 5:4

2 JOHN 12

3 JOHN 12, 14

JUDE 4^2, 17, 21, 25

REV. 1:5, 5:10, 6:10, 7:3, 10, 12, 11:8, 15, 12:10^3, 19:1, 5, 22:21

out 4480, *1537*

GEN. 2:9, 10, 19, 23, 3:19, 24, 4:14, 16, 8:10, 19, 9:10, 10:11, 14, 12:1, 4, 13:1, 14:8, 17, 15:4, 7, 14, 17:6, 19:5, 6, 8, 12, 14[2], 24, 29, 30, 21:10, 17, 21, 22:11, 15, 23:4, 8, 24:11, 13, 15, 29, 44, 63, 25:25, 26, 26:8, 27:3, 30, 28:10, 16, 29:2, 30:16[2], 31:13, 33, 32:25, 34:1, 6, 7, 24[2], 26[2], 35:9, 11, 37:14, 21, 22, 23, 28, 38:28[2], 29, 30, 39:12, 15, 18, 40:14, 15, 17, 41:2, 3, 14, 18, 33, 45, 46, 42:2, 43:23, 31, 44:4, 8[2], 16, 28, 45:1, 19, 24, 25, 46:26, 47:1, 10, 30, 48:12, 14, 22, 49:20, 50:24

EXOD. 1:5, 10[2], 2:10, 11, 13, 19, 3:2, 4, 8[2], 3:10, 11, 12, 17, 20, 4:7, 9, 5:10, 6:1, 6[3], 7, 11, 13, 26, 27, 7:2, 4, 5, 15, 19, 8:6, 12, 13[3], 16, 17, 29, 30, 9:15, 29, 33, 10:5, 6, 11, 12, 18, 21, 11:1, 4, 6, 8[3], 10, 12:5, 15, 17, 21, 22, 33, 39[2], 41, 42, 46, 51, 13:3[3], 4, 8, 9, 14, 16, 18, 14:8, 10, 11, 16, 21, 26, 30, 45, 53, 15:12, 20, 22, 16:1, 4, 6, 27, 29, 17:3, 6, 9, 14, 18:1, 7, 9[2], 10[2], 21, 25, 19:1, 3, 17, 20:2[2], 21:2, 3[2], 4, 5, 7, 11, 27, 22:6, 7, 23:13, 15, 16, 28, 29, 30, 31, 24:16, 25:32[3], 33, 35, 28:35, 29:23, 46, 32:1[2]

EXOD. 32:4, 7, 8[2], 11, 12, 19, 23, 24, 27, 32, 33, 33:1, 2, 7, 8, 11, 34:11, 18, 24, 34[2], 37:7, 8, 9, 18[3], 19, 21

LEVIT. 1:1, 15, 2:14, 4:12[2], 18, 25, 30, 34, 5:9, 15, 18, 6:6, 12, 13, 7:14, 35, 8:26, 33, 9:9, 23, 24, 10:2, 4, 5, 7, 14, 11:45, 13:12, 20, 25, 56[4], 14:3, 8, 38, 41, 43, 45, 53, 15:2, 16, 25, 16:17, 18, 17:3, 13, 18:24, 25, 28[2], 19:36, 20:22, 23, 21:12, 22:33, 23:17, 43, 24:10, 23, 25:12, 28, 30, 31, 33, 38, 42, 51, 54, 55, 26:6, 13, 33, 45, 27:21

NUM. 1:1, 3:9, 5:2, 3, 4, 23, 25, 6:19, 9:1, 10:12, 33, 34, 11:15, 20[2], 24, 26, 12:4[2], 12, 14, 15, 13:16, 17, 14:44, 15:41, 16:13, 14, 27, 35, 37, 46, 17:9, 18:29[2], 20:5, 8, 10, 11, 16, 18, 20, 21:5, 13, 23, 26, 28, 32[2], 33, 22:5[2], 11[2], 23, 32, 36, 23:7, 22, 24:7, 8, 17[3], 19, 26:4, 27:17[2], 21, 28:26, 30:2, 6, 12, 31:5, 27, 28, 36, 32:11, 21, 23, 24, 33:1, 2[2], 3, 12, 38, 52, 55, 34:5, 7, 8, 9, 10, 12, 25

DEU. 1:22, 24, 27, 33, 44, 2:14, 23, 26, 32, 3:1, 8, 4:12, 15, 20[2], 33, 34, 36[2], 37[2], 38, 45, 46, 5:4, 6, 15[2], 22, 23, 24, 26, 6:12, 19, 21, 23, 7:1, 8[2], 19[2], 22, 8:3, 7, 8:9, 14, 15, 9:3, 4[2], 5, 7, 10, 12[2], 14, 16, 17, 21, 26, 28[2], 29[2], 10:4, 11:10, 23, 28, 12:3, 5, 27, 13:5[3], 10, 13, 15:11, 13, 14[3], 16:1, 3[2], 6, 17:18, 18:5, 6, 12, 20:1[2], 21:19, 22:21, 24, 23:4, 10, 23, 24:1, 2, 3, 5, 9, 11, 25:4, 6, 11, 17, 19, 26:4, 8, 13, 27:18, 28:6, 7, 19, 25, 38, 57, 29:7, 20, 21, 25, 28, 30:4, 31:2, 21, 32:13, 39, 33:18, 27

JOSH. 1:8, 2:1, 2, 3, 5, 7, 10, 19, 3:10, 12[2], 4:2[2], 3, 4, 8, 16, 17, 18, 19, 20, 5:4[2], 5[2], 6, 6:1, 10, 22[2], 23[2], 25, 7:23[2], 8:3, 5, 6, 14, 17, 18[2], 19[2], 22, 8:26, 9:12, 26, 10:22[2], 23, 24, 11:4, 13:6, 12, 14:7, 11, 12, 15:3, 4, 7, 9, 11[3], 63, 16:2, 3, 6, 7, 8[2], 10, 17:12, 13, 18, 18:4, 12, 14, 15[2], 19:9, 12, 13, 17, 24, 27, 32, 34, 40, 47, 20:2, 8[3], 21:3, 4[4], 5[3], 6[4], 7[3], 9[2], 16, 17, 20, 23, 25, 27, 28, 30, 32, 34, 36, 38, 22:9, 31, 32, 23:5, 9, 13, 24:5, 6, 10, 12, 17, 18, 32

JUD. 1:16, 19[2], 21, 24, 27, 28, 29, 30, 31, 32, 33, 2:1, 3, 12, 15, 16, 17, 18, 21, 23, 3:10, 19, 20, 22[2], 24, 4:6, 14, 18, 22, 5:4[2], 14[3], 28, 6:8, 9[3], 19, 20, 21[2], 30, 6:38, 7:23[3], 8:34, 9:4, 15, 17, 20[2], 27, 29, 33, 35, 38, 39, 41, 42, 43, 10:12, 11:2, 3, 5, 7, 13, 24, 34, 36, 12:2, 13:5, 14:9, 12, 14[2], 18, 15:17, 16:14, 20[2], 21, 25, 17:7, 8, 18:2, 11[2], 14, 17, 19:1, 16, 23, 24, 27, 30, 20:1, 10, 14, 15, 20, 21, 25, 28, 31, 33[3], 34, 38, 40, 42, 21:16, 21[2], 24

RUTH 1:7, 13, 21, 22, 2:6, 17, 22, 4:3

1 SAM. 1:3, 15, 16, 2:3, 5, 8, 10, 28, 3:3, 4:1, 3[2], 8, 12, 13, 16[2], 5:10, 7:3, 6, 8, 11, 14, 8:8, 18, 20, 9:11, 14, 16[2], 26, 10:18[3], 19, 11:2, 3, 5, 7, 10, 12:6, 8, 12:10, 11, 13:10, 17, 23, 14:11, 48, 15:6, 16:16, 17:4[2], 8, 23, 34, 35[2], 37[3], 40, 51, 18:5, 6, 11, 13, 16, 19:3, 8, 10, 20:11[2], 21, 35, 36, 41, 21:5, 23:13, 15, 23, 24:2, 7, 8, 14, 15, 21, 25:5, 14, 29[2], 37, 26:4, 19, 20, 24, 27:1, 28:1, 3, 9, 13, 17, 29:6, 30:16[2]

2 SAM. 1:2, 3, 2:12, 13, 23, 3:18[2], 25, 26, 4:4, 9, 5:2, 13, 24, 6:3, 4, 20, 7:6, 9, 12, 8:1, 9:5, 10:3, 8, 16, 11:8, 13, 17, 23, 12:7, 11, 13:9[3], 17, 14:16[2], 15:11, 24, 35, 16:5, 7, 17:1, 21, 18:3, 4, 6, 19:9[3], 19, 20:7[2], 8, 10, 12, 13, 16, 22, 21:10, 17, 22:1[2], 7, 22:9, 15, 17, 46, 23:4, 16[2], 21, 29, 24:4, 7, 16, 20

1 KINGS 1:29, 39, 2:27, 37, 42, 46, 3:7, 4:23, 33, 5:6, 12, 6:1, 8, 7:13, 47, 8:1, 8, 9, 10, 16[2], 19, 21, 41, 42, 44, 51, 53, 9:7[2], 9, 12, 24, 10:28, 29[2], 11:12, 18[2], 29, 31, 32, 34, 35, 12:25, 28, 13:1, 3, 5, 14:15, 21, 24, 15:12, 17, 16:2, 17:19, 23, 18:28, 44, 19:13, 20:16, 17[3], 18[2], 19, 21, 24, 31, 39, 42, 21:10, 13, 26, 22:3, 32, 34, 35, 46

2 KINGS 2:23, 24, 3:6, 4:4, 5, 18, 21, 37, 39, 40[2], 41, 5:2[2], 11, 27, 6:7, 27[2], 7:12[2], 16, 20, 8:3, 9:2, 15, 19, 21[2], 24, 9:30, 32, 10:3, 9, 25, 26, 28, 11:8, 9, 12:11[4], 12, 13:5, 25[2], 14:27, 16:3, 7[2], 17:7, 8, 18, 20, 23[2], 36[2], 39, 18:18, 29, 31, 33, 34, 35[2], 19:9, 19, 27, 31[2], 35, 20:4, 6, 21:2, 7, 8, 15, 23:4, 6, 8, 16, 18, 27, 24:3, 7, 12, 13, 20, 25:7, 19, 21, 27

1 CHRON. 5:18, 6:60, 61[2], 62[3], 63[3], 65[3], 66, 70, 71, 72, 74, 76, 77, 78, 80, 7:11, 9:28, 11:2, 18[2], 23, 12:2, 17, 13:7, 14:8, 15, 17, 15:25, 29, 16:33, 17:21[2], 18:1, 19:3, 6[3], 9, 10, 20:1, 2, 3, 21:16, 21, 26:14, 27, 27:1, 28:18

2 CHRON. 1:10, 16, 17[2], 2:2, 8, 14, 16, 4:18, 5:2, 9, 10, 5:11, 6:5, 9, 32, 34, 7:20[2], 22, 8:11, 9:28[2], 10:2, 11:13, 16, 12:3, 7, 13, 13:9, 14:5, 8[2], 9, 10, 15:2, 5, 8[2], 9[3], 17, 16:1, 2, 7, 17:6, 18:20, 21[2], 31, 33, 19:2, 3, 4, 20:4, 7, 10, 11, 17, 21, 21:15, 19, 22:7, 23:2, 7, 8, 11, 14, 24:5, 6, 25:6, 10, 15, 26:11, 18, 20[2], 28:3, 9, 21[2], 29:5, 7, 16[2], 30:6, 25, 31:1[2], 32:11, 13, 14[2], 15[2], 17[2], 33:2, 8, 15[2], 34:14, 21, 25, 33, 35:20, 24

EZRA 1:7, 2:1, 3:8, 5:14[2], 6:4, 5, 21, 7:20, 28, 8:35, 9:5, 10:1

NEH. 1:9, 2:13, 3:25, 26, 27, 4:2, 5, 5:13[2], 6:8, 7:6, 8:17, 9:7, 15, 18, 27, 12:27, 28, 12:29, 44, 13:8, 14

ESTHER 2:9, 13, 23, 3:15, 4:1, 11, 5:2, 7:8[2], 8:4, 14, 15, 9:4

JOB 1:17, 21, 3:11, 24, 5:5, 6, 6:17, 8:10, 19, 9:6, 8, 10, 14, 10:7, 10, 18, 11:7[2], 13, 12:15, 22, 13:9, 14:4, 12, 18, 19, 15:13, 22, 25, 30, 16:13, 20, 18:4, 5, 6, 18, 19:7, 20:15, 25[2], 21:17, 22:16, 24:4, 12[2], 24, 26:7, 27:21, 22, 23, 28:2[2], 3, 4, 5, 10, 27, 29:6, 7, 16, 17, 19, 25, 30:16, 24, 31:7, 8, 12, 34, 32:11, 13, 33:6, 21, 35:9, 36:16, 26, 37:1, 2, 9[2], 18, 22, 23, 38:1, 8, 13, 29, 39:3, 5, 40:6, 41:1, 19[2], 20[2], 21

PSALMS 3:4, 5:10, 8:2, 9:5, 10:5, 16, 14:7, 15:5, 17:1, 18:6, 8[2], 14[2], 16, 42, 45, 19:4, 5, 20:2, 21:8[2], 22:7, 9, 14[2], 25:15, 17, 22, 27:12, 31:4, 12, 34:6, 17, 19, 35:3, 37:14, 40:2[2], 42:4, 43:3, 44:2[2], 20, 21, 45:8[2], 50:2, 9[2], 51:1, 9, 52:5[2], 53:6, 54:7, 55:23, 58:6, 59:7, 60:6, 8, 10, 62:8, 64:6, 66:12, 68:6, 31[2], 33, 35, 69:14[2], 24, 28, 71:4[2], 6, 73:7, 10, 74:11, 75:8[2], 77:17[2], 78:15, 16, 20, 55, 65, 79:6, 80:8[2], 11, 13, 81:5, 10, 16, 82:4, 5, 84:2, 85:5, 11, 88:9, 89:19, 34, 94:12, 97:10, 102 *title*, 104:2, 14, 35, 105:41, 107:3, 6, 13, 14, 19, 28, 108:7, 9, 109:10, 13, 14, 110:2, 111:2, 113:7[2], 114:1, 118:26, 119:18, 43, 121:8, 124:7, 128:5, 130:1, 132:5, 134:3, 135:7, 136:6, 142:2, 7, 143:11, 144:6, 7, 14, 147:18

PROV. 1:23, 24, 2:6, 22, 3:10, 4:23, 5:15[2], 6:9, 8:12, 9:1, 10:31, 11:8, 12:13, 13:9, 15:2, 28, 17:14, 23, 20:5, 20, 21:16, 22:10[2], 24:20, 25:1, 2, 19, 26:20, 28:11, 30:17, 31:18, 20

ECCL. 1:13, 3:11, 4:14, 7:24, 25, 27, 29, 8:3, 17[2], 12:3, 9, 10

CANT. 3:6, 4:16, 8:11

ISAIAH 2:3, 5:2, 25, 8:8, 9:12, 17, 21, 10:4, 11:1[2], 16, 12:3, 6, 13:9, 13, 14:19, 26, 27, 29, 15:4, 5, 16:2, 4, 8, 10[2], 18:2, 7, 19:23, 21:11, 22:16[2], 23:11, 24:18, 26:16, 17, 19, 21, 28:7[2], 27, 29:4[4], 9, 10, 18[2], 30:11[2], 13, 14, 31:3, 34:3[2], 11, 34:16, 35:6, 36:16, 18, 19, 20[2], 37:28, 32[2], 38:6, 40:12, 22[2], 26, 42:5[2], 7[2], 43:13, 25, 44:13[3], 22, 45:12, 23, 46:6, 7, 48:1, 3, 21[2], 51:17, 22, 52:11[2], 12, 53:2, 8, 12, 55:11, 12, 57:4, 14, 58:7, 10, 59:5, 21[3], 62:10, 12, 63:11, 65:2, 9[2], 66:5, 11, 20

JER. 1:5, 10, 14, 2:6, 13, 3:18, 4:1, 16, 5:6[2], 6:1[2], 4, 7[2], 11, 12, 7:15[2], 18, 20, 22, 25, 8:1[2], 9:8, 18, 19[2], 10:3, 12, 13, 17, 18, 22, 25, 11:4, 7, 12:3, 8, 14[2], 15, 14:16, 15:1, 6, 21[2], 16:9, 13, 14, 16, 17:8, 16, 19, 22, 18:21, 23, 19:13, 20:3, 8, 18, 21:9, 12[2], 22:3, 11, 14, 26, 28, 23:3, 7, 8, 23:16, 39, 24:5, 26:23, 27:10, 15, 30:7, 19, 31:32, 37, 32:4, 17, 21[2], 29, 37, 43, 34:3, 13[2], 36:6, 11, 21, 30, 37:4, 5, 12, 17, 21, 38:8, 10, 13, 18, 23[2], 39:4[2], 7, 14, 40:12, 44:7, 17[2], 18, 19[2], 25, 28, 46:20, 47:2, 48:15, 31, 44, 45, 49:5, 20, 50:3, 8[2], 28, 45, 51:6, 15, 16, 25, 34, 44, 45, 55, 52:3, 7, 11, 25, 27, 31

LAM. 1:10, 2:4, 8, 12, 19[2], 3:7, 8, 38, 55, 4:1, 3, 11, 5:8

EZEKIEL 1:4[3], 5, 13, 3:25, 4:12, 5:2, 8, 12, 14, 9:8, 10:7, 19, 11:7, 9, 17, 19, 12:5, 12, 14, 13:2, 17, 21, 23, 14:9, 13, 19, 15:7, 16:5, 15, 27, 16:36, 19:14, 20:8, 9, 10, 13, 14, 21, 28, 32[2], 34[4], 38[2], 41[2], 21:3, 4, 5, 19, 31, 22:15, 22, 31, 23:26, 34, 48, 24:6[2], 12, 25:7[2], 13, 16, 27:6, 33, 28:16, 29:4, 7, 30:13, 22, 25, 31:4, 11, 32:3, 7, 21, 33:21, 34:11, 12[3], 13, 25, 27, 35:3, 7, 11, 36:5, 20, 24, 26, 37:1, 12, 13, 23, 38:8, 12, 15, 39:3[2], 10[2], 14, 27, 29, 42:11, 14, 43:6, 11, 23, 25, 44:3, 45:14, 15[3], 46:9, 18[2], 20, 47:1, 2[2], 8, 12, 48:19, 30

DANIEL 2:34, 45, 3:15, 17, 5:2, 3, 13, 6:23[2], 7:17, 24, 25, 8:4, 7, 9, 22, 9:15, 11:7, 41, 44[2]

HOSEA 1:11, 2:2, 10, 15, 17, 18, 4:2, 5:10, 7:5, 9:15, 10:11, 11:1, 11[2], 12:8, 13, 13:3[2]

JOEL 1:16, 2:28, 29, 3:7, 16

AMOS 3:4, 12[2], 4:3, 11, 5:3, 6, 8, 6:4[2], 10[2], 7:11, 8:8, 9:3, 6, 7, 15

OBADIAH 6, 8[2]

JONAH 1:4, 2:1, 2, 4, 10, 5:3

MICAH 1:3, 2:9, 13, 4:6, 9, 10, 5:2, 10, 12, 13, 14, 6:4[2], 7:2, 15, 17

NAHUM 1:6, 11, 14, 2:2, 9

HABAK. 1:2, 2:11[2], 3:4, 13, 14

ZEPH. 1:4, 17, 2:4, 13, 3:11, 15, 19

HAGGAI 2:5, 16[2]

ZECH. 1:21, 2:3, 13, 3:2, 4:1, 12, 5:9, 6:1, 12, 8:10, 23, 9:4, 7, 11, 10:4[4], 10[2], 11:6, 13:2[2], 14:8

MALACHI 2:8, 12, 13, 3:10, MATT. 2:6, 15, 3:5, 16, 4:4, 5:13, 26, 29, 7:4[2], 5[4], 22, 8:12, 16, 28, 29, 31, 32, 34[2], 9:17, 32, 33, 34, 10:1

MATT. 10:8, 14, 11:7, 8, 9, 12:11, 14, 24, 26, 27[2], 28, 34, 35[2], 43, 44, 13:1, 41, 52, 14:13, 26, 29, 35, 15:11, 17, 18, 19, 22, 17:5, 18

MATT. 17:19, 21, 18:9, 28, 20:1, 3, 5, 6, 30, 21:12, 16, 17, 33, 39, 41, 22:10, 16, 24:1, 17, 27, 25:6, 8, 26:30, 51, 55, 71, 75, 27:23, 32

MATT. 27:53, 60, MARK 1:5, 10, 23, 25, 26, 29, 34, 35, 39, 45, 3:5, 15, 21, 22, 23, 31, 4:3, 32, 5:2[2], 8, 10, 13, 14, 17, 30

MARK 5:40, 6:1, 12, 13, 33, 34, 49, 54, 7:12, 15, 19, 20, 21, 26, 29, 30, 8:23, 27, 9:7, 18, 24, 25, 26, 28, 38, 47, 10:21, 46, 47

MARK 11:11, 15, 19, 12:1, 8, 13:1, 15, 14:26, 48, 68, 15:13, 14, 20, 21, 39, 46, 16:8, 9, 17, LUKE 1:22, 42, 74, 2:1, 4, 4:14, 22, 29

LUKE 4:33, 35[2], 36, 37, 38, 41[2], 5:2, 3[2], 4, 17, 36, 6:12, 17, 19, 22, 42[4], 45[2], 7:24, 25, 26, 8:2, 3[3], 4, 5, 12, 27, 28, 29, 31

LUKE 8:33, 35[2], 38, 46, 54, 9:5, 35, 38, 39, 40, 49, 10:10, 35, 11:14[2], 15, 18, 19[2], 20, 24[2], 54, 12:54, 13:28, 31, 32, 33, 14:5, 7, 21, 23

LUKE 14:35, 15:28, 16:4, 17:24, 29, 19:22, 40, 45, 20:12, 15, 21:21, 37, 22:39, 52, 62, 23:18, 26, 24:31, 50, JOHN 1:46, 2:8, 15[2], 4:30, 47, 54, 6:37, 7:38

JOHN 7:41, 42, 52, 8:9, 59, 9:22, 34, 35, 10:3, 9, 28, 29, 39, 11:11, 31, 55, 12:17, 31, 34, 42, 13:1, 30, 31, 15:19, 16:2, 27, 17:6, 8, 15

JOHN 18:16, 29, 38, 19:6, 12, 15, 34, 20:2, ACTS 1:9, 18, 21, 2:5, 17, 18, 3:19, 4:15, 5:6, 9, 16, 6:3, 7:3, 4, 10, 12, 19, 21, 36

ACTS 7:40, 45, 57, 58, 8:7, 9, 39, 9:1, 28, 10:45, 12:9, 10, 11, 17, 13:17, 42, 50, 14:14, 19, 15:14, 24, 16:13, 18[2], 27[2], 30, 37[2], 39[2], 40, 17:2

ACTS 17:5, 19:12, 16, 28, 33, 34, 21:5, 28, 30, 38, 22:18, 23, 23:6, 24:7, 27:19, 29, 30[2], 38, 42, 28:3, 21, 23[2], ROMANS 2:18, 3:12, 11:24, 26, 33

ROMANS 13:11, 1 COR. 5:7, 10, 9:9, 14:36, 15:8, 2 COR. 1:8, 16, 2:4, 4:6, 6:17, 8:11, 12:2, 3, GAL. 2:4, 4:15, 30, EPHES. 4:29, PHIL. 1:12, 2:12

COLOS. 2:14, 3:8, 1 THESS. 1:8, 2 THESS. 2:7, 1 TIM. 1:5, 5:18, 6:7, 2 TIM. 1:17, 2:22, 26, 3:11, 4:2, 17, HEB. 3:16, 5:2, 7:5, 14, 8:9, 11:8[2]

HEB. 11:15, 34, 12:13, JAMES 2:25, 3:10, 13, 1 PETER 2:9, 2 PETER 2:9, 3:5, 1 JOHN 2:19[2], 4:1, 18, 3 JOHN 10, JUDE 5, 13

JUDE 23, REV. 1:16, 2:5, 3:5, 12[2], 16, 4:5, 5:7, 9, 6:4, 14, 7:14, 8:4, 9:2, 3, 17, 18, 10:10, 11:2, 5, 7, 12:9[3], 15, 16, 13:1, 11, 14:10

REV. 14:15, 17, 18, 20, 16:1[2], 2, 3, 4, 7, 8, 10, 12, 13[3], 17[2], 21, 17:8, 18:4, 19:5, 15, 21, 20:7, 8, 9, 12, 21:2, 3, 10, 22:1, 19[2]

shall

GEN. 1:29, 2:23, 24[2], 3:1, 3, 4, 5, 15, 16, 18, 4:7, 12, 14[2], 15, 24, 5:29, 6:3[2], 15, 17, 19, 20, 21, 8:22, 9:2, 3, 4, 6, 11[2], 13, 14[2], 15, 16, 25, 26, 27[2], 12:3, 12[2], 13, 13:16, 15:4[2], 5, 8, 13[2], 14, 16, 16:10, 12, 17:5[2], 6, 10[2], 11, 12, 13, 14, 15, 16, 17[2], 19, 20, 21, 18:5, 10, 12, 13, 14, 17, 18[2], 19, 25, 27, 29, 30, 31, 32, 19:2, 20, 20:7, 13, 21:10, 12, 22:14, 17, 18

GEN. 23:6, 9, 24:7, 14[3], 43, 55, 25:23[3], 32, 26:2, 4, 11, 22, 27:12, 33, 37, 39, 40, 46, 28:14[2], 21, 22, 29:15, 30:3, 15, 24, 30, 31, 32, 33[3], 31:8[2], 32:4, 8, 19, 28, 34:10[2], 11, 12, 23, 30[2], 35:10[2], 11[2], 37:10, 20, 30, 38:18, 40:13, 14, 19[3], 41:16, 27, 30[3], 31[2], 36[2], 40, 44, 42:15[2], 16, 20[2], 33, 34[2], 38[2], 43:3, 5, 16, 44:10[2], 16[3], 17, 23, 29, 31[2], 32, 34[2], 45:6, 13[2], 18, 46:4, 33[3], 34, 47:19, 23, 24[3], 48:5, 6[2]

GEN. 48:19[4], 20, 21, 49:1, 8[3], 9, 10[2], 12, 13[3], 16, 17[2], 19[2], 20[2], 25[2], 26, 27[3], 50:17, 25, EXOD. 1:16[2], 22[2], 2.7, 3:12[2], 13[3], 18[2], 21[2], 22[3], 4:8, 9[2], 15, 16[3], 21, 5:7, 8[2], 11, 18[2], 19, 6:1[2], 7, 12, 30, 7:1, 2, 4, 5, 9[2], 17, 18[3], 8:3[2], 4, 9, 11[2], 21, 22, 23, 26[2], 27, 28, 9:3, 4[2], 5, 9[2], 19[4], 29[2], 10:5[3], 6, 7, 8, 14, 26[2], 11:1[2], 5, 6[2], 7, 8, 9, 12:2[2], 3, 4, 5[2], 6[2], 7[2]

EXOD. 12:8[2], 10[2], 11[2], 13[2], 14[3], 15[3], 16[3], 17[2], 18, 19[2], 20[2], 22[2], 24, 25[2], 26[2], 27, 43, 44, 45, 46[2], 47, 48[3], 49, 13:3, 5[2], 6, 7[3], 9, 11[3], 12, 14, 16, 19, 14:2, 4, 13, 14[2], 16, 17, 18, 15:9[2], 14[2], 15[3], 16[2], 18, 24, 16:4, 5[3], 6, 7, 8[2], 12[3], 25, 26[2], 17:4, 6, 18:19, 22[5], 23, 19:5, 6, 12, 13[4], 20:23[2], 21:2[2], 3[2], 4[2], 5, 6[4], 7, 8[2], 9, 10, 11, 12, 13, 15, 16, 17, 19[3], 20, 21, 22[2]

EXOD. 21:26, 27, 28[3], 29[2], 30, 31, 32[3], 33[2], 34[2], 35[2], 36[2], 22:1[2], 2, 3[2], 4, 5[4], 6, 7, 8, 9[3], 11[3], 12, 13, 14, 15, 16, 17, 19, 20, 22, 24[2], 27[2], 30, 31[3], 23:11, 15, 17, 18, 23, 25[2], 26, 28, 33, 24:2[3], 25:2, 3, 9, 10[2], 12, 15[2], 16, 17, 19, 20[3], 21, 23, 27, 31[2], 32, 34, 35, 36[2], 37, 38, 39, 26:2[2], 3[2], 6, 8[2], 12, 13, 16[2], 17, 20, 24[4], 25, 28, 31, 32, 33, 37, 27:1[2], 2

EXOD. 27:7[2], 8, 9, 10[2], 11, 12, 13, 14, 15, 16[2], 17, 18, 19, 21[2], 28:4[2], 5, 6, 7[2], 8, 12, 16[3], 17[2], 18, 20, 21[2], 28, 29, 30[2], 32[2], 35[2], 37, 38[3], 42, 43[2], 29:9, 10, 15, 19, 21, 26, 28[2], 29, 30, 32, 33[2], 34, 37[2], 42, 43, 46, 30:2[4], 4, 7[2], 8, 9[2], 10[2], 12, 13[2], 14, 15[2], 19, 20, 21[2], 25, 29, 31, 32[3], 33, 34, 36, 37[2], 38[2], 31:11, 13, 14[3], 15, 16, 32:1, 13, 23, 30, 34, 33:14

EXOD. 33:16[2], 20, 22, 23, 34:3, 10, 13, 20, 23, 24, 25, 35:2[3], 3, 10, 40:9, 10, 15, LEVIT. 1:2, 3, 4[2], 5[2], 6, 7, 8, 9[2], 10, 11[2], 12[2], 13[2], 14, 15[2], 16, 17[3], 2:1[2], 2[3], 3, 4, 5, 7, 8, 9[2], 10, 11[3], 12[2], 16, 3:1, 2[2], 3, 4, 5, 6, 7, 8[2], 9[2], 10, 11, 12, 13[2], 14, 15, 16, 17, 4:2[2], 4[2], 5, 6, 7[2], 8, 9, 10, 12[2], 14, 15[2], 16, 17, 18[2], 19, 20[4], 21, 23, 24

LEVIT. 4:25[2], 26[3], 28, 29, 30[2], 31[4], 32, 33, 34[2], 35[4], 5:1, 2, 3[2], 4[2], 5[3], 6[2], 7, 8[3], 9[2], 10[3], 11[3], 12[2], 13[3], 15, 16[4], 17, 18[3], 6:4[2], 5[2], 6, 7[2], 9, 10[3], 11, 12[4], 13[2], 14, 15[2], 16[3], 17, 18[3], 20, 21, 22[2], 23[2], 25, 26[2], 27[2], 28[2], 29, 30[2], 7:2[2], 4, 5, 6, 7, 8, 9, 10, 11, 12, 13, 14[2], 15[2], 16[2], 17, 18[4], 19[3], 20, 21[2], 23, 24, 25, 26, 27, 29, 30[2], 31[2], 32, 33, 8:31, 32, 33[2]

LEVIT. 8:35, 9:6, 10:7, 9, 13, 14, 15[2], 11:2, 3, 4, 8[2], 9[2], 10, 11[3], 12, 13[2], 20, 23, 24[2], 25, 26, 27, 28, 29, 31, 32[3], 33[2], 34[2], 35[3], 36[2], 37, 38, 39, 40[2], 41[2], 42, 43[2], 44[3], 45, 12:2[2], 3, 4[2], 5[2], 6, 7[2], 8[3], 13:2[2], 3[2], 4, 5[2], 6[3], 7, 8, 9, 10, 11[2], 13[2], 14, 15, 16, 17[2], 20, 21, 22, 23, 25[2], 26, 27[2], 28, 30[2], 31, 32, 33[3], 34[3], 36[2], 37, 39, 43, 44, 45[3], 46[4], 49, 50

LEVIT. 13:51, 52[2], 53, 54[2], 55, 56, 58[2], 14:2[2], 3[2], 4, 5, 6[2], 7[3], 8[3], 9[6], 10, 11, 12, 13[2], 14[2], 15, 16[2], 17, 18[2], 19[2], 20[3], 21, 22, 23, 24[2], 25[2], 26, 27, 28, 29, 30, 31, 35, 36[2], 37, 38, 39[2], 40[2], 41[2], 42[3], 44, 45[2], 46, 47[2], 48[2], 49, 50, 51, 52, 53[2], 15:3, 4, 5, 6, 7, 8, 9, 10[2], 11, 12[2], 13[2], 14, 15[2], 16, 17, 18[2], 19[2], 20[2], 21, 22, 23, 24[2], 25[2], 26[2], 27[2], 28[2], 29, 30[2]

LEVIT. 15:31, 16:3, 4[5], 5, 6, 7, 8, 9, 10, 11[3], 12, 13, 14[2], 15, 16[2], 17, 18[2], 19, 20, 21[2], 22[2], 23[3], 24, 25, 26, 27[2], 28[2], 29[2], 30, 31[2], 32[4], 33[3], 34, 17:4[2], 6, 7[2], 9, 12[2], 13, 14[2], 15[2], 16, 18:3[2], 4, 5[2], 6, 23, 26[2], 29[2], 30, 19:2, 3, 5, 6[2], 7, 8[2], 11, 12, 13, 15, 19[2], 20[2], 21, 22[2], 23[5], 24, 25, 26[2], 27, 28, 30, 33, 34, 35, 36, 37, 20:2[2], 8, 9[2], 10, 11[2], 12[2], 13[2]

LEVIT. 20:14, 15[2], 16[2], 17[3], 18[3], 19, 20[3], 21[2], 22, 23, 24, 25[2], 26, 27[3], 21:1, 4, 5[2], 6[2], 7[2], 8, 9, 10, 11, 12, 13, 14[2], 15, 18, 21[2], 22, 23, 22:3, 4, 6[2], 7[2], 8, 9, 10[2], 11[2], 13[2], 14[2], 15, 19, 20[2], 21[2], 22, 23, 24[2], 25[2], 27[2], 28, 30[2], 31, 32, 23:2, 3[2], 4, 7, 8[2], 10[2], 11[2], 12, 13[2], 14[2], 15[2], 16[2], 17[3], 18[2], 19, 20[2], 21[3], 24, 25[2], 27[3], 28, 29[2], 31[2], 32[3], 34, 35[2], 36[4], 37, 39[3]

LEVIT. 23:40[2], 41[3], 42[2], 24:3[2], 4, 5, 8, 9[2], 15, 16[3], 17, 18, 19, 20, 21[2], 22, 25:2, 4, 6, 7, 8, 9, 10[4], 11[2], 12[2], 13, 14, 15, 17, 18[2], 19[2], 20[3], 21, 22[2], 23, 24, 25, 28[3], 30[2], 31[2], 33, 40[2], 41[3], 42, 44[2], 45[2], 46[3], 50[3], 51[2], 52[2], 53[2], 54, 26:1[2], 2, 4[2], 5[3], 6[3], 7[2], 8[3], 10, 11, 12, 15, 16[3], 17[3], 20[3], 22[2], 25[2], 26[3], 29[2], 30, 32, 33, 34[2], 35, 36[3], 37[2], 38[2], 39[2], 40, 43[3], 27:2[2], 3[2]

LEVIT. 27:4, 5, 6[2], 7, 8[3], 9, 10[3], 11, 12[2], 13, 14[4], 15[2], 16[3], 17, 18[2], 19[2], 20, 21[2], 23[2], 24, 25[2], 26, 27[4], 28[2], 29[3], 31, 32, 33[4], NUM. 1:3, 4, 5, 50[3], 51[3], 52, 53[2], 2:2[2], 3[2], 5[2], 7, 9, 10[2], 12[2], 14, 16, 17[2], 18[2], 20[2], 22, 24, 25[2], 27[2], 29, 31, 3:7, 8, 10[2], 12, 13, 23, 24, 25, 29, 30, 31, 32, 35, 36, 38[2], 45, 4:4, 5[2], 6[3], 7[2], 8[2], 9, 10[2], 11[2], 12[2], 13, 14[2], 15[2]

NUM. 4:19, 20, 25, 26, 27[2], 28, 32, 5:3[2], 6, 7[2], 8, 9, 10[2], 15[3], 16, 17[2], 18[2], 19, 21[2], 22[2], 23, 24[2], 25[2], 26[2], 27[5], 28[2], 30[2], 31[2], 6:2, 3[3], 4, 5[3], 6, 7, 9[2], 10, 11[2], 12[3], 13, 14, 16[2], 17[2], 18[2], 19[2], 20, 21, 23, 27, 7:11, 8:2, 10, 11, 12, 14, 15, 24, 25[2], 26[2], 9:3[2], 10[2], 11, 12[2], 13[2], 14[3], 10:3, 4, 5, 6[2], 7[2], 8[2], 9[3], 10, 32[3], 11:4, 17, 18[3], 19, 22[2], 23, 12:8, 13:2, 14:13, 21

NUM. 14:23[2], 24, 27, 29, 30, 31, 32, 33, 34[2], 35[2], 41, 43, 15:4, 9, 11, 12[2], 13, 14, 15[2], 16, 19[2], 20[2], 21, 24[2], 25[3], 26, 27, 28[2], 29, 30, 31[2], 35[2], 39, 16:7[2], 22, 28, 30, 38, 17:3, 5[3], 13[2], 18:1[2], 2, 3[2], 4[2], 5, 7[3], 9[3], 10[2], 11, 12, 13[3], 14, 15, 18, 23[3], 24, 26, 27, 28, 29, 30, 31, 32[2], 19:3[2], 4, 5[2], 6, 7[4], 8[2], 9[2], 10[2], 11, 12[3], 13[2], 14, 16, 17[2], 18, 19[3], 20[3], 21[3], 22[2]

NUM. 20:8, 12, 24[2], 26[2], 21:8[2], 22:4, 6, 8, 11, 20, 35, 38, 23:8[2], 9[2], 19[2], 23, 24[2], 24:7[4], 8[2], 9, 14, 17[5], 18[3], 19[3], 20, 22[2], 23, 24[4], 25:13, 26:53, 54, 55[2], 56, 65, 27:8, 9, 10, 11[3], 21[4], 28:2, 3, 7, 11, 14, 15, 17, 18[2], 19[2], 20[2], 23, 24[2], 25[2], 26[2], 27, 31[2], 29:1[2], 2, 3, 7[3], 8[2], 9, 12[3], 13[2], 14, 17, 18, 21, 24, 27, 30, 33, 35[2], 36, 37, 39, 30:2[2], 4[3], 5[2], 7[2], 8[2], 9, 11[2], 12[2]

NUM. 30:15[2], 31:4, 23[4], 24[3], 32:6[2], 11, 15, 17, 22[2], 26, 29[2], 30, 33:52, 53, 54[5], 55[3], 56[2], 34:2, 3[2], 4[3], 5[2], 6[2], 7[2], 8[2], 9[3], 10, 11[3], 12[3], 13, 17, 18, 35:2, 3[2], 4[2], 5[3], 6[4], 7[3], 8[5], 11, 12, 13[2], 14[3], 15, 16, 17, 18, 19[2], 21[2], 24, 25[3], 26, 27, 28, 29, 30[2], 31[2], 32, 33, 34, 36:3[3], 4[3], 6, 7[2], 8, 9[3], DEU. 1:17[3], 22[2], 28, 30, 35, 36, 38[2], 39[2], 2:4, 6[2], 25[2], 29, 3:18, 19, 20, 21

SHALL—*continued.*

DEU. 3:22[2], 28[2], 4:2[2], 6, 10, 22, 25[3], 26[3], 27[3], 28, 5:25, 27[2], 32[2], 33[2], 6:6, 8, 10[2], 14, 16, 17, 25, 7:1, 2, 5[2], 12[2], 14, 16[2], 19, 23[2], 24[2], 25, 8:1, 19[2], 20, 9:3[2], 11:8, 13[2], 18, 19, 22, 23, 24[3], 25[3], 29, 31[2], 32, 12:1, 2[2], 3[2], 4, 5[2], 6, 7[2], 8, 11[3], 12, 14, 16[2], 18, 20, 22, 26, 27, 29, 13:4[2], 5, 8, 9, 11[2], 16[2], 17, 14:1, 4, 6, 7, 8, 9[2], 11, 12, 19, 21, 23, 24, 25, 29[2], 15:2[2], 3, 4[2], 6, 10[2], 11, 16, 17, 18[2], 20, 22, 16:2, 4[2], 6, 7, 8, 15[2], 16[3], 17, 18, 7:6[2], 7, 8, 9[2], 10[2], 11[3], 12, 13, 15, 16[2], 17[2], 18[2]

DEU. 17:19[2], 18:1[2], 2, 3[2], 6, 7, 8, 10, 15, 18[2], 19[2], 20[3], 21, 19:4, 5, 12, 13, 15[2], 17[2], 18, 19, 20[2], 21[2], 20:2[2], 3, 5, 8[2], 9[2], 11[4], 21:2[2], 3[2], 4[2], 5[2], 6, 7, 8, 12, 13[3], 14, 16, 17, 19, 20, 21[2], 23, 22:2, 5[2], 15, 16, 17, 18, 19[2], 21[2], 22, 24[2], 25, 29[2], 30, 23:1, 2[2], 3[2], 8, 10[2], 11[3], 13, 14, 16[2], 17, 22, 24:5[4], 6, 7, 8[2], 11, 13, 15, 16[3], 19, 20, 21, 25:1, 2[2], 5[2], 6[2], 8, 9[3], 10, 12, 19, 26:1, 2, 3, 4, 27:2, 4[2], 12, 13, 14, 15, 16, 17, 18, 19, 20, 21, 22, 23, 24, 25, 27, 28:1, 2, 4, 5, 7[2], 8[2], 9

DEU. 28:10[2], 11, 12, 13, 15[2], 17, 18, 20, 21, 22[2], 23[2], 24[2], 25, 26[2], 28, 29, 30, 31[4], 32[3], 33, 35, 36, 37, 38, 39, 40, 41, 42, 43, 44[2], 45[2], 46, 48[2], 49, 50, 51[2], 52[2], 53, 54[2], 55[2], 56, 57[3], 60, 62, 63[2], 64, 65[2], 66, 68[3], 29:19, 20[3], 21, 22[3], 24, 25, 30:1, 12, 13, 16, 18[2], 31:3, 4, 5, 11, 17[3], 18, 20[2], 21[3], 32:2[2], 20, 22[2], 24, 25, 35[2], 36, 37, 42, 46, 47, 33:3, 10[2], 12[3], 17, 19[3], 22, 25[2], 27[2], 28[3], 29

JOSH. 1:3, 4, 5, 8, 11, 14[2], 15, 18, 2:5, 14, 19[5], 3:3, 4, 8, 10, 13[4], 4:3[2], 7[2], 21, 22, 6:3, 4[3], 5[4], 10[3], 17[2], 19

JOSH. 6:26[2], 7:8, 9[2], 14[7], 15[2], 25, 8:2, 4, 5, 7, 8[3], 9:7, 23, 10:8, 25, 14:9, 12, 15:4, 17:18[2], 18:4[2], 5[3], 6, 20:3, 4[3], 5, 6[3], 22:22, 25, 28, 34, 23:5[2], 10, 12, 13, 15[2], 16[2], 24:27[2]

JUD. 1:1, 2, 2:2[2], 3[2], 4:9[2], 20, 5:11[2], 24[2], 6:15, 37, 7:4[5], 11, 17[2], 8:23[2], 9:33, 10:18, 11:9, 24, 31[2], 13:5[3], 7, 8[2], 12[2], 15, 22, 14:16, 15:3, 18, 16:2, 7, 11, 17, 18:5, 10, 20:9, 18[2], 23, 28[2], 21:1, 5, 7, 11[2], 16, 22

RUTH 1:16, 2:2, 9, 3:1, 3, 4[2], 13, 4:12, 15

1 SAM. 1:11, 28, 2:9[2], 10[4], 25[2], 30, 31, 32[2], 33[3], 34[3], 35[2], 36[3], 3:9, 11, 14, 4:8, 5:7, 8, 6:2[2], 3[2], 4[2]

1 SAM. 6:5[2], 9, 20, 8:9, 11[2], 17, 18[2], 9:7, 13[2], 17, 19, 10:2, 3, 5[2], 27, 11:7, 9[2], 10, 12, 13, 12:12, 14, 15, 17, 25[2], 13:14, 14:10, 37, 39, 45[2], 15:33, 16:16[2], 17:9, 25, 26, 27, 36, 47, 18:25, 19:6, 20:7, 10, 31, 32, 21:15, 23:2, 17, 20, 23, 24:4, 12, 13, 20, 25:6, 11, 29[2], 30[3], 31[2], 26:10[3], 27:1[3], 12, 28:8, 10, 11, 15, 19, 29:9, 30:8[2], 23, 24[2]

2 SAM. 2:1[2], 26[2], 3:12, 39, 4:11, 5:8[2], 19, 24, 6:9, 22, 7:10, 12, 13, 14, 15, 16, 9:10[2], 11[2], 11:11, 12:5, 6, 10, 11, 14, 23[2], 13:13, 14:7[2], 10, 17, 18, 15:8, 10, 14, 15, 21, 25, 35, 36, 16:3, 10, 20, 21[2], 17:2, 3, 6

2 SAM. 17:10, 12[3], 13, 21, 22, 19:37, 38[2], 20:6, 18, 21, 21:2[2], 4, 17, 22:4, 44, 45[2], 46[2], 23:4, 6, 7, 24:13[2]

1 KINGS 1:13[2], 17[2], 20, 21[3], 24[2], 30, 33[2], 52[3], 2:4, 24, 32, 33[2], 37[2], 44, 45[2], 3:5, 12, 13, 5:5, 6, 9, 8:19[2], 25, 29, 30, 33, 38, 42[2], 44, 47, 59, 9:3, 5, 6, 7, 8[3], 9, 11:2[2], 32, 38, 12:10, 24, 26, 27[2], 13:2[3], 3[2], 22, 32, 14:3[2], 5[2], 11[2], 12, 13[2], 14[2], 15[3], 16, 16:4[2], 17:1, 4, 14[2], 18:12[3], 24, 31, 19:17[3], 20:6[3], 10, 14, 23, 25, 28, 36, 39, 40, 42, 21:19, 23, 24[2], 22:6[3], 12, 15[3], 16, 20

2 KINGS 1:2, 2:9, 10[2], 16, 21, 3:8, 17[3], 19[2], 4:2, 10[2]

2 KINGS 4:23, 43[2], 5:8, 10, 17, 27, 6:8, 15, 21[2], 27, 31, 7:1, 4[3], 12, 18, 8:1, 8, 9, 10, 9:8, 10[2], 36, 37[2], 10:4, 10, 18, 19[2], 24, 30, 11:5[2], 6[2], 7, 8, 12:5, 14:6[2], 15:12, 16:15, 17:12, 35, 36[3], 37[2], 38[2], 39[2], 18:22, 29, 30, 19:6, 7[2], 10[2], 29[3], 30, 31[2], 32, 33[2], 20:8[2], 9, 17[2], 18[3], 21:12, 14, 22:17[2], 18, 20, 23:27, 25:24

1 CHRON. 11:6, 19, 12:17, 13:12, 14:10, 15, 16:30, 33, 17:9[3], 11[2], 12, 13, 14, 27, 21:12, 22:9[3], 10[2], 23:26, 28:6, 21[2]

2 CHRON. 1:7, 12, 2:8, 9, 14, 6:9[2], 16, 21, 24, 29[3], 7:14, 15, 16, 18, 19, 21[2], 22, 8:11, 10:10, 11:4, 12:7, 8, 13:12, 15:7, 18:5[2], 11, 14[3], 15

2 CHRON. 18:19, 19:9, 10[3], 11[2], 20:16, 17, 20[2], 23:3, 4[2], 5[2], 6[2], 7[2], 25:4[3], 8, 9, 26:18, 28:13, 30:9[2], 32:11, 12, 15, 17, 33:4, 34:25[2], 26, 28, 35:3

EZRA 4:21, 6:8, 11, 12, 7:18, 20, 21, 24, 9:10

NEH. 2:6, 8, 4:3, 11, 12, 20, 5:8, 6:7, 9, 9:29, 10:38[2], 39, 13:25, 27

ESTHER 1:15, 17[3], 18[2], 20[3], 4:11[2], 14[2], 5:3, 6[2], 8, 6:6, 9, 11, 7:2[2], 8:6, 9:12[2]

JOB 1:21, 2:10[2], 4:17[2], 5:19[2], 20, 23, 24, 25, 7:4, 7, 8, 9, 10[2], 13[2], 20, 21[2], 8:2, 10, 13, 14[2], 15[4], 18, 19, 22[2], 9:14, 19, 20[2], 31[2], 10:21, 11:3, 17, 19[2], 20[3], 12:2, 7[2], 8[2], 13:11, 16[2], 18, 19, 14:6, 12, 14, 22[2]

JOB 15:21, 22, 24[2], 29[3], 30[3], 31, 32[2], 33[2], 34[2], 16:3, 22[2], 17:5, 8[2], 9[2], 15, 16, 18:4[2], 5[2], 6[2], 7[2], 9[2], 11[2], 12[2], 13[2], 14[2], 15[2], 16[2], 17[2], 18, 19, 20, 19:25, 26, 27[2], 20:7[2], 8[3], 9[2], 10[2], 11, 15[2], 16[2], 17, 18[4], 20[2], 21[2], 22[2], 23[2], 24[2], 26[3], 27[2], 28[2], 21:19, 20[2], 22, 26[2], 30, 31[2], 32[2], 33[2], 22:21, 25, 27, 28[2], 29, 30, 23:10, 24:15, 20[4], 27:4, 6, 13, 14, 15[2], 17[2], 19[2], 22, 23, 28:12, 15, 17, 18, 19[2], 29:18[2], 31:14[2], 33:3[2], 7[2], 25[2], 26[2], 28, 33, 34:11, 15[2], 17, 20[3], 24, 36:4, 11, 12[2], 37:19, 20[2], 38:11, 15, 40:2, 4, 41:6[2], 9, 42:8

PSALMS 1:3[3], 5, 6, 2:4[2], 5, 8, 5:4, 5

PSALMS 6:5, 7:7, 8, 16[2], 9:3, 7, 8[2], 17, 18[2], 10:6[2], 11:6[2], 12:3, 13:2[2], 5, 14:7[2], 15:1[2], 5, 16:4, 8, 9, 17:3, 15, 18:3, 43, 44[2], 45, 19:13[2], 21:1[2], 7, 8[2], 9[2], 22:25, 26[3], 27[2], 29[2], 30[2], 31[2], 23:1, 6, 24:3[2], 5, 7, 9, 25:12[2], 13[2], 15, 26:1, 27:1[2], 3, 5[3], 6, 14, 28:5, 30:6, 9[2], 31:24, 32:6[2], 10[2], 33:17, 21, 34:1, 2[2], 10, 21[2], 22, 35:9[2], 10, 28, 36:8, 9, 12, 37:2, 4, 5, 6, 9[2], 10[2], 11[2], 13, 15[2], 17, 18, 19[2], 20[4], 22[2], 24, 28, 29, 31, 34, 38[2], 40[2], 39:6, 40:3[2], 41:2, 5, 8, 42:2, 5, 8, 11, 43:5, 44:6, 21, 45:4, 11, 12[2], 14[2], 15[2], 16, 17, 46:4, 5[2], 47:3, 4, 49:3[2], 5

PSALMS 49:11, 14[3], 15, 17[2], 19[2], 50:3[4], 4, 6, 51:7[2], 13, 14, 15, 19, 52:5[2], 6[2], 53:6[2], 54:5, 55:16, 17, 19, 22[2], 23, 56:7, 9, 57:3[2], 58:9, 10[2], 11, 59:10[2], 60:12[2], 61:7, 62:2, 3[2], 6, 63:3, 5[2], 9, 10[2], 11[3], 64:5, 7[2], 8[2], 9[3], 10[3], 65:1, 2, 4, 66:3, 4[3], 67:6[2], 7[2], 68:13, 21, 29, 31[2], 69:31, 32[2], 36[2], 71:6, 15, 23, 24, 72:2, 3, 4[3], 5, 6, 7, 8, 9[2], 10[2], 11[2], 12, 13[2], 14[2], 15[4], 16[3], 17[4], 73:27, 74:10[2], 75:2, 8, 10, 76:10, 12, 79:5, 80:3, 7, 19, 81:9, 82:7, 85:11[2], 12[2], 13[2], 86:9, 87:5[2], 6, 7, 88:10, 11, 12, 13, 89:2, 5, 12, 14, 15, 16[2], 17, 21[2], 22, 24[2], 26, 28, 36, 37, 46

PSALMS 89:48[2], 91:1, 3, 4[2], 7[2], 10[2], 11, 12, 15, 92:7, 9[2], 10, 11[2], 12[2], 13, 14[2], 94:3[2], 4, 7[2], 9[2], 10[2], 15[2], 20, 23[3], 96:10[2], 12, 13, 98:9, 101:3, 4, 6[2], 7[2], 102:15, 16[2], 18[3], 26[3], 28[2], 103:16, 104:12, 31[2], 34, 107:42[2], 43, 108:13[2], 109:7, 110:2, 3, 5, 6[3], 7[2], 112:2[2], 3, 6[2], 7, 8, 132:12[2], 16, 18, 137:4, 8, 9, 138:4, 5, 7, 139:7[2], 10[2], 11[2], 140:11, 13[2], 141:5[4], 6, 142:7, 143:2, 144:5, 145:4[2], 6, 7[2], 10[2], 11, 21, 146:9, 148:6

PROV. 1:5, 9, 13[2], 28[3], 31, 32[2], 33[3], 2:11[2], 21[2], 22[2], 3:2, 6, 8, 10[2], 22, 23, 24, 26[2], 35[2], 4:6[2], 8[2], 9[2], 10, 12, 5:22[2], 23[2], 6:11, 15[2], 22[3], 29, 31[2], 33[2], 8:6

PROV. 8:7, 17, 35, 9:11[2], 10:7, 8, 9, 10, 24[2], 27, 28[2], 29, 30[2], 31, 11:3[2], 5[2], 6[2], 7, 9, 15, 18, 21[2], 25[2], 26[2], 27, 28[2], 29[2], 31, 12:3[2], 6, 7, 8[2], 11, 13, 14[2], 19, 21[2], 24[2], 13:2[2], 3, 4, 9, 11[2], 13, 18[2], 20[2], 21, 25, 14:3, 11[2], 14[2], 22, 26, 15:10, 27, 16:3, 5, 20, 21, 17:2[2], 5, 11, 13, 18:20, 21, 19:5[2], 9[2], 15, 16, 19, 21, 23[2], 20:4, 17, 20, 21, 22, 21:7, 13[2], 15, 16, 17[2], 18, 28, 22:5, 8[2], 9, 10[2], 11, 13, 14, 15, 16, 18, 29[2], 23:11, 13, 15, 16, 18, 21[2], 24[2], 25[2], 33[2], 35, 24:4, 8, 12, 14[2], 16, 20[2], 22, 24[2], 25[2], 26, 34, 25:4

PROV. 25:5, 22, 26:2, 26, 27, 27:14, 18[2], 28:2, 8, 9, 10[2], 13[2], 14, 16, 17, 18[2], 19[2], 20[2], 22, 23, 25, 26, 27[2], 29:1, 14, 16, 17[2], 21, 23[2], 25, 30:17[2], 31:11, 25, 30

ECCL. 1:9[2], 11[2], 2:16, 18, 19[2], 21, 3:14, 17, 22[2], 4:12, 15, 16, 5:10, 15[2], 16, 20, 6:4, 12, 7:18, 26[2], 8:1, 5, 7[2], 8, 12, 13[2], 15, 17[2], 9:5, 10:8[2], 9[2], 14[2], 20[2], 11:2, 3, 4[2], 6[2], 8, 12:3[2], 4[3], 5[5], 7[2], 14

CANT. 1:13, 5:3[2], 7:8[2], 8:8[2]

ISAIAH 1:18[2], 19, 20, 27, 28[2], 29[2], 30, 31[3], 2:2[4], 3[2], 4[5], 11[3], 12[2], 17[3], 18, 19, 20, 3:4, 5[2], 6, 7, 10[2], 11[2], 24[2], 25, 26[2], 4:1, 2[2], 3[2], 4[2]

ISAIAH 4:5, 6, 5:5[2], 6[2], 9, 10[2], 14, 15[3], 16[2], 17[2], 24[2], 26, 27[3], 28, 29[5], 30, 6:8, 13[4], 7:7[2], 8, 9, 14[3], 15, 16[2], 17, 18[2], 19[2], 20[2], 21[2], 22[4], 23[3], 24[2], 25[3], 8:4[2], 7, 8[4], 9[3], 10[2], 12, 14, 15, 19, 21[4], 22[2], 9:1, 5, 6[2], 7, 9, 11, 12, 17[2], 18[3], 19[2], 20[4], 21, 10:3, 4[2], 11, 15[2], 16[2], 17[2], 18[2], 19, 20[3], 21, 22, 23, 24[2], 25, 26[2], 27[3], 32[2], 33[3], 34[2], 11:1[2], 2, 3[2], 4[3], 5, 6[3], 7[3], 8[2], 9[2], 10[4], 11[3], 12[2], 13[4], 14[4], 15[3], 16[2], 12:3, 4, 13:6, 7[2], 8[5], 9, 10[3], 13, 14[2], 15[2], 16[2], 17[2], 18[3], 19, 20[4], 21[4], 22[2], 14:1[2], 2[4], 3[2], 10, 16, 20, 24[2], 25, 27[2]

ISAIAH 14:29[2], 30[3], 31[2], 32[2], 15:2[2], 3[2], 4[4], 5[4], 6, 7, 9, 16:2[2], 5[2], 6, 7[3], 10[3], 11, 12[3], 14, 17:1, 2[3], 3[2], 4[3], 5[2], 6, 7[2], 8[2], 9[2], 11, 13[4], 18:5, 6[3], 7, 19:1[3], 2, 3[2], 4, 5[2], 6[3], 7, 8[3], 9, 10, 15, 16[2], 17[2], 18[2], 19, 20[4], 21[4], 22[5], 23[3], 24, 25, 20:4, 5, 6[2], 21:13, 16, 17, 22:7[3], 13, 14, 18, 19, 20, 21, 22[4], 23, 24, 25[2], 23:5, 7, 15[3], 17[3], 18[3], 24:2, 3, 9[2], 13[2], 14[3], 18[3], 20[4], 21[2], 22[3], 23[2], 25:2, 3[2], 5, 6, 8, 9, 10[2], 11[2], 12, 26:1, 6, 11[2], 14[2], 19[3], 21[2], 27:1[2], 5, 6[2], 9[2], 10[3], 11, 12[3], 13[4], 28:2, 3, 4, 5, 9[2], 15[2], 16, 17[2]

ISAIAH 28:18[4], 19[3], 21[2], 29:2[2], 4[3], 5[3], 7, 8[2], 14[2], 16[3], 17[2], 18[2], 19[2], 22[2], 23[2], 24[2], 30:2, 6, 7, 13, 14[3], 15[2], 16[2], 17[2], 19[2], 20[2], 21, 22, 23[3], 24, 25, 26[2], 28[2], 29, 30[2], 31, 32[3], 31:3, 4, 7, 8[4], 9[2], 32:1[2], 2, 3[2], 4[2], 5, 8, 10[3], 12, 13, 14[3], 16, 17, 18, 19[2], 33:1, 4[2], 6, 7[2], 11[3], 12[2], 14[2], 16[4], 17[2], 18, 20[4], 21[2], 24[2], 34:3[3], 4[3], 5[2], 7[2], 9[2], 10[4], 11[3], 12[3], 13[2], 14[3], 15[2], 16[2], 17[2], 35:1, 2[3], 5[2], 6[2], 7[2], 8[5], 9[4], 10[3], 36:7, 14, 15, 37:6, 7, 10[2], 30[2], 31, 32[2], 33, 34[2], 38:7, 10, 11[2], 15[2], 19[2], 21, 22, 39:6[2], 7[3], 8, 40:4[3], 5[2], 6, 8, 10, 11[3]

ISAIAH 41:20, 24[6], 25, 30[2], 31[4], 41:11[3], 12, 16[2], 22, 25[3], 27, 42:1, 2, 3[3], 4[2], 13[4], 17[2], 43:2[2], 10, 13, 17[2], 19[2], 20, 21, 44:4, 5[3], 7[3], 9, 11[3], 15, 19[2], 26, 28[2], 45:1, 9, 13[2], 14[6], 16[2], 17[2], 23[3], 24[3], 25[2], 46:7[2], 10, 13[2], 47:3[2], 7, 8[2], 9[2], 11[3], 13, 14[4], 15[3], 48:14, 15, 49:5[2], 7, 9[4], 10[4], 11, 12, 17[2], 19[2], 20, 22[2], 23[3], 24, 25[2], 26[2], 50:7[2], 9[3], 11[2], 51:3[2], 4, 5[3], 6[3], 8[3], 11[4], 12[2], 19[2], 52:1, 3, 6[2], 8[4], 10, 12, 13[2], 15[4], 53:2[2], 8, 10[3], 11[4], 12, 54:3, 5, 10[3], 13[2], 14, 15[3], 17[2], 55:3, 5, 11[4], 12[3], 13[4], 56:5, 7[2], 12, 57:2, 12, 13[4], 14, 58:4, 8[4], 9[2], 10, 11

ISAIAH 58:12[2], 59:6[2], 8, 19[3], 20, 21, 60:2[3], 3, 4[2], 5[3], 6[4], 7[3], 9, 10[2], 11[2], 12[2], 13, 14[3], 18, 19[3], 20[4], 21[2], 22, 61:4[3], 5[2], 6[4], 7[4], 9[2], 10, 62:2[2], 4[2], 5[2], 6, 8, 9[2], 12, 63:3, 64:5, 65:9[2], 10, 12, 13[6], 14[3], 15[2], 16[2], 17, 19, 20[3], 21[2], 22[3], 23, 24, 25[4], 66:5[2], 8[2], 9[2], 12[2], 13, 14[3], 16, 17, 18[2], 19, 20, 22[2], 23[2], 24[4]

JER. 1:7, 14, 15[2], 19[2], 2:3[2], 19[2], 24, 35, 3:1[2], 15, 16[6], 17[3], 18[2], 19, 4:2[2], 7, 9[4], 10, 11, 12, 13[2], 14, 21, 27, 28, 29[3], 5:6[4], 7, 9[2], 12[2], 13[2], 14, 17[4], 19[3], 29[2], 6:3[3], 9, 10, 11, 12, 15[2], 16, 21[2], 22, 23, 26, 30, 7:20[3]

JER. 7:23, 32[2], 33[2], 34, 8:1, 2[3], 3, 4[2], 10, 12[2], 13[3], 17, 9:7, 9[2], 22[2], 10:10[2], 11[2], 15, 21[2], 11:4, 11[2], 12[2], 22[2], 23, 12:4[2], 12[2], 13[3], 15, 16[2], 13:10, 12[3], 17[2], 18, 19[4], 21[2], 27, 14:13[2], 15[2], 16[2], 15:2[2], 5[3], 11, 12, 14, 20[2], 16:4[6], 6[3], 7[2], 10[2], 13, 14, 16[2], 19[2], 20, 21, 17:4, 6[3], 8[5], 11[2], 13[2], 14[2], 24, 25[2], 26, 27[2], 18:7, 9, 14, 16, 18, 20, 19:2, 3, 6, 8, 9[2], 11, 13, 20:4[4], 5, 6, 10[2], 11[5], 21:3, 6, 7[2], 9[3], 10[2], 13[2], 14, 22:4, 5, 7, 8[2], 9, 10, 11, 12[2], 18[2], 19, 22[2], 26, 27, 30[2], 23:3, 4[3], 5[2], 6[3], 7, 8, 12[2], 17[2], 19, 20[2], 24, 26, 32

JER. 23:33, 34, 35, 36[2], 38, 40, 24:7[2], 9, 25:11[2], 12, 14, 16, 26, 28[2], 29, 30[3], 31, 32[2], 33[3], 34, 35, 36, 26:9[2], 15, 18[2], 27:4, 7[2], 8, 9, 11, 14, 16, 22[2], 28:9, 14, 29:7, 12[2], 13[2], 21, 22, 32[2], 30:3, 7, 8[2], 9, 10[3], 16[3], 18[2], 19[3], 20[2], 21[3], 22, 23, 24[2], 31:1, 5[2], 6[2], 8, 9[2], 12[4], 13, 14, 16[2], 17, 18, 22, 23[2], 24, 28, 29, 30[2], 33[2], 34[2], 36, 38, 39[2], 40[2], 32:3, 4[4], 5[3], 7, 15, 28, 29, 36, 38, 40, 43, 44, 33:9[3], 10[2], 11[2], 12, 13, 15, 16[3], 17, 18, 34:2, 3[2], 5, 20, 22, 35:6, 7[2], 15, 19, 36:29[2], 30[2], 37:7[2], 8, 9[2], 19, 38:2[4], 3[2], 17[2], 18[2]

JER. 38:20[3], 22[2], 23, 39:12, 16, 18, 40:9, 15, 42:4[2], 5, 14, 16[4], 17[3], 18[4], 20, 22, 43:10, 11, 12[3], 13[2], 44:12[4], 14[3], 26, 27, 28[3], 29[2], 46:6, 10[2], 14, 18, 19, 22[2], 23, 24[2], 26, 27[2], 47:2[4], 3, 48:2, 3, 5, 7, 8[4], 9, 12[2], 13, 18[2], 26[2], 30[2], 31, 33[2], 34, 36[2], 37[2], 38, 39[2], 40[2], 41, 42, 43, 44[2], 45[2], 49:2[3], 3, 4, 5[2], 10, 12, 13[2], 17[3], 18[2], 19, 20[2], 22[2], 26[2], 27, 28, 29[3], 32, 33[2], 36[2], 39, 50:3[4], 4[2], 5[2], 9[4], 10[2], 12[3], 13[3], 16[2], 19[2], 20[3], 30[2], 32[3], 34, 36[2], 37[2], 38, 39[4], 40[2], 41[2], 42[3], 44, 45[2], 51:2[3], 4, 14, 18, 26, 29[2], 31, 33, 35[2], 37, 38[2], 44[2], 46[3]

JER. 51:47[2], 48[2], 49, 52, 53, 56, 57, 58[4], 62[2], 63, 64[3]

LAM. 1:21, 2:13[3], 20[2], 4:15, 20, 21, 5:21

EZEKIEL 2:5, 3:18, 19, 20[3], 21, 25[2], 4:3[2], 7, 13, 16[2], 5:4, 10[2], 11, 12[3], 13[2], 15[2], 16[2], 17[2], 6:2, 4[2], 6[2], 7[2], 8[2], 9[3], 10, 11, 12[3], 13[2], 14, 7:4[3], 9[2], 11[2], 13[3], 15[2], 16[2], 17[2], 18[3], 19[4], 21, 22[2], 24[2], 25[2], 26[4], 27[4], 8:18, 9:10, 11:10[2], 11[2], 12, 16, 18[2], 20, 12:11[2], 12[4], 13[3], 15[2], 16, 19, 20[3], 23, 24, 25[3], 28[2], 13:9[5], 11[4], 12, 13, 14[4], 21[2], 23[2], 14:8, 10[2], 16[3], 18[2], 20[2], 22[5], 23[2], 15:3, 5, 7[3], 16:16[2], 39[4], 40, 41, 42, 44, 53, 55[3], 17:9[3], 10[3], 15[3], 16, 17, 18, 20

EZEKIEL 17:21[3], 23[3], 24, 18:3, 4, 9, 13[4], 17[2], 18, 19, 20[5], 21[2], 22[2], 24[3], 26, 27, 28[2], 30, 19:14, 20:11, 13, 20, 21, 31, 32, 38[2], 40, 42[2], 43[2], 44, 47[3], 48[2], 21:4, 5, 7[6], 12[3], 13, 19, 23, 24, 25, 26, 27, 29, 30, 22:5, 14, 21, 22[2], 23:24[3], 25[5], 26, 29[4], 45, 47[2], 49[3], 24:12, 14[2], 16, 21, 22[2], 23[3], 24[2], 25, 26, 27[2], 25:4[3], 5, 11, 13, 14[2], 17[2], 26:2, 4, 5[2], 6[2], 8[2], 9, 10[3], 11[3], 12[3], 13, 15, 16[4], 17, 18[2], 19[3], 20[3], 27:27, 28, 29[2], 30[4], 31[2], 32, 34, 35[3], 36, 28:7[2], 8, 18, 19, 22[3], 23[2], 24[2], 25[3], 26[4], 29:4, 6, 9[2], 11[3], 12, 14, 15[3], 16[3], 19[2], 21, 30:3

EZEKIEL 30:4[5], 5, 6[3], 7[2], 8[2], 9[2], 11[2], 13, 16[3], 17[2], 18[5], 19, 21, 24, 25[4], 26, 31:11, 13[2], 16, 32:3, 6, 7[2], 9, 10[3], 11, 12[2], 13, 15[4], 16[3], 20, 21, 27[2], 29, 31[2], 32, 33:4, 5[2], 8, 9, 12[3], 13[4], 15[2], 16[2], 18, 19, 25, 26, 27[2], 28[3], 29, 33, 34:10, 14[3], 22, 23[3], 25, 26, 27[4], 28[4], 29, 30, 35:6[2], 8, 9[2], 10, 15, 36:7, 8, 9, 10[2], 11[2], 12, 23[2], 25, 27, 28[2], 30, 31[2], 33[2], 34, 35, 36, 38[2], 37:5, 6[2], 13, 14[4], 17, 18, 19, 20, 22[3], 23[2], 24[3], 25[3], 26, 27[2], 28[2], 38:8, 10[2], 13, 16[2], 18[3], 19, 20[4], 21, 23, 39:6, 7, 9[3], 10[3], 11[4], 12, 13[3], 14[2], 15, 16[2]

EZEKIEL 39:18, 19, 20, 21, 22, 23, 28, 40:4, 42:13[2], 14[4], 43:7, 12, 13[3], 14[2], 15[2], 16, 17[4], 18, 21, 22, 24[2], 25, 26[2], 27[2], 44:2[4], 3[3], 9, 10, 11[3], 12, 13[2], 14, 15[2], 16[3], 17[3], 18[3], 19[3], 20[2], 21, 22[2], 23, 24[4], 25, 26, 27, 28[2], 29[2], 30[2], 31, 45:1[5], 2, 3, 4[3], 5, 6[2], 7[2], 8[3], 10, 11[2], 12[2], 13[2], 14, 16, 17[2], 19, 20, 21[2], 22, 23, 24, 25, 46:1[3], 2[6], 3, 4[2], 5[2], 6[2], 7[2], 8[3], 9[5], 10[2], 11, 12[5], 15, 16[2], 17[3], 18, 20[2], 24, 47:8, 9[7], 10[4], 11[2], 12[5], 13[3], 14[2], 15, 17, 18, 20, 21, 22[5], 23[2], 48:8[3], 9[2], 10[2], 11, 12, 13[2], 14, 15[2], 16, 17, 18[3], 19, 20[2], 21[3]

EZEKIEL 48:22, 23, 24, 28, 29, 31, 35

DANIEL 1:10, 2:5[2], 6, 9, 28, 29, 30, 39[2], 40[2], 41[2], 42, 43[2], 44[5], 45, 3:6, 10[2], 15[2], 29[2], 4:25[5], 26, 32[4], 5:7[3], 6:5, 7[2], 12[2], 26[2], 7:14[2], 17, 18, 23[4], 24[4], 25[3], 26[2], 27[2], 8:13, 14, 17, 19[2], 22, 23, 24[4], 25[5], 26, 9:25[2], 26[4], 27[2], 10:14, 20, 11:2[3], 3[2], 4[4], 5[3], 6[5], 7[5], 8[2], 9[2], 10[4], 11[4], 12[3], 13[3], 14[3], 15[3], 16[4], 17[4], 18[4], 19[2], 20[2], 21[3], 22[2], 23[3], 24[4], 25[4], 26[3], 27[4], 28[3], 29[2], 30[4], 31[4], 32[2], 33[2], 34[3], 35, 36[5], 37[2], 38[2], 39[4], 40[4], 41[3], 42[3], 43[2], 44[2], 45[2], 12:1[4], 2, 3, 4[2], 6, 7[3], 8, 10[4], 11[2]

HOSEA 1:5, 10[3], 11[3], 2:6, 7[5]

HOSEA 2:10, 12, 15, 16, 17, 21[2], 22[2], 23, 3:4, 5[2], 4:3[3], 5, 9, 10[3], 13[2], 14, 19, 5:5[2], 6[2], 7, 9[2], 14, 6:2, 3[2], 4[2], 7:12, 16[2], 8:1, 2, 3, 6, 7[3], 8, 10, 11, 13, 14, 9:2[2], 3[3], 4[5], 6[4], 7, 11, 12, 13, 16, 17, 10:2[3], 3, 5[2], 6[3], 8[3], 10[2], 11[2], 14[2], 15[2], 11:5[2], 6[2], 8[4], 10[4], 11, 12:8, 14[2], 13:3, 8, 13, 14, 15[5], 16[4], 14:3, 5, 6[2], 7[3], 8, 9[4]

JOEL 1:15, 2:2, 3, 4, 5, 6[2], 7[4], 8[3], 9[4], 10[4], 11, 19, 20[2], 24[2], 26[2], 27[2], 28[4], 31, 32[5], 3:1, 8, 15[2], 16[2], 17[3], 18[6], 19[2], 20

AMOS 1:2[2], 4, 5, 7, 8, 10, 12, 14, 15, 2:2[2], 5

AMOS 2:14[3], 15[3], 16, 3:5, 6[2], 11[3], 12, 14[2], 15[2], 4:2, 3[2], 5:2, 3[2], 4, 5[2], 6, 9, 11[2], 13, 14, 16[3], 17, 20, 6:7[2], 9[2], 10[4], 12, 14, 7:2, 3, 5, 6, 9[2], 11[2], 17[4], 8:3[4], 8[3], 9, 12[3], 13, 14, 9:1[2], 2, 3, 4, 5[4], 9, 10[2], 13[3], 14[3], 15

OBADIAH 3, 8, 9, 10, 15[2], 16[4], 17[3], 18[3], 19[3], 20[2], 21[2]

JONAH 1:11, 12, 3:4

MICAH 1:4[2], 7[3], 14, 15, 2:3[2], 4, 5, 6[2], 10, 11, 12, 13, 3:4, 6[6], 7[2], 12[2], 4:1[4], 2[2], 3[4], 4[2], 7, 8[2], 10, 12, 5:1, 2, 3, 4[3], 5[4], 6[2], 7, 8, 9[2], 10, 6:6[2], 7, 9, 11, 14, 16, 7:4, 8[2], 9, 10[4], 11, 12

MICAH 7:13, 16[3], 17[4]

NAHUM 1:8, 9, 10, 12[2], 15, 2:3[2], 4[4], 5[4], 6[2], 7[3], 8[3], 13[2], 3:7[3], 12[2], 13[2], 15[3], 18, 19

HABAK. 1:2, 6, 7, 8[3], 9[3], 10[4], 11[2], 12, 17, 2:1, 3, 4, 6, 7[3], 8, 11[2], 13[2], 14, 16[2], 17, 19, 3:17[6]

ZEPH. 1:8, 10[2], 12, 13[3], 14, 17[2], 18[3], 2:3, 4[3], 5, 6, 7[4], 9[3], 10, 11, 12, 14[5], 3:8, 10, 12, 13[4], 16

HAGGAI 2:7, 9, 12, 13[2], 15, 22

ZECH. 1:16[2], 17[3], 2:4, 9[2], 11[2], 12[2], 3:9, 10, 4:7, 9, 10[2], 5:3[2], 4[3], 11, 6:12[2], 13[5], 14, 15[3], 8:3, 4, 5, 8[2], 12[4], 13[2], 16, 19, 20[2], 21, 22, 23[3], 9:1[2], 2, 4, 5[5], 6, 7[2]

ZECH. 9:8, 10[3], 14[4], 15[4], 16[2], 17, 10:1, 5[3], 6, 7[4], 8, 9[2], 10, 11[5], 12, 11:6, 16[3], 17[3], 12:2, 3, 5[2], 6[2], 7, 8[3], 9, 10[3], 11, 12, 13:1, 2[2], 3[4], 4[3], 5, 6[2], 7, 8[3], 9[2], 14:1, 2[3], 3, 4[4], 5[4], 6[2], 7[4], 8[3], 9[2], 10[2], 11[3], 12[4], 13[4], 14[2], 15[2], 16[2], 17[2], 18, 19, 20[2], 21[3]

MALACHI 1:4[2], 5[2], 11[3], 2:2, 4, 3:1[3], 2, 3[2], 4, 7, 10, 11[2], 12[2], 17, 18, 4:1[4], 2[2], 3[3], 6

MATT. 1:21[2], 23[3], 2:6[2], 23, 3:11, 4:4, 6[2], 5:4, 5, 6, 7, 8, 9, 11[2], 13, 18, 19[5], 20[2], 21[2], 22[5], 31, 32[2], 39, 41, 6:4, 6, 7, 18, 22, 23, 25[3], 30, 31[3], 33, 34

MATT. 7:2[2], 7[3], 8, 11, 16, 20, 21, 26, 8:8, 11[2], 12[2], 9:15[2], 18, 21, 10:11, 14, 15, 18, 19[3], 21[2], 22[2], 23, 25, 26[2], 29, 32, 33, 36, 39[2], 41[2], 42[2], 11:6, 10, 16, 22, 24, 29, 12:11[2], 18, 19[2], 20[2], 21, 25, 26, 27, 31[2], 32[2], 36[2], 39, 40, 41[2], 42[2], 45, 50, 13:12[3], 14[4], 40, 41[2], 42[2], 43, 49[2], 50[2], 15:5, 6, 13, 14, 16:4, 18, 19[2], 22, 25[2], 26[2], 27[2], 28, 17:11, 12, 17[2], 20[3], 22, 23[2], 18:3, 4, 5, 6, 15[2], 17, 18[4], 19[3], 21, 35, 19:5[3], 9[2], 16, 23, 27, 28[2], 29[2], 30[2], 20:7, 16, 18[2], 19[2], 22, 23[2], 26, 32, 21:2, 3, 13, 21[3], 22[2], 25, 26, 41, 43, 44[3], 22:9

MATT. 22:13, 24, 28, 23:11, 12[4], 14, 16[2], 18, 20, 21, 22, 34[2], 36, 39[2], 24:2[2], 3[2], 5[2], 6, 7[2], 9[3], 10[3], 11[2], 12[2], 13[2], 14[2], 15, 21[2], 22, 23, 24[3], 26, 27, 29[4], 30[3], 31[2], 33, 34, 35[2], 37, 39, 40[2], 41[2], 46, 47, 48, 49, 50, 51[2], 25:1, 29[3], 30, 31[2], 32[2], 33, 34, 37, 40, 41, 44, 45, 46, 26:13[2], 21, 23, 31[2], 33, 48, 52, 53, 54, 64, 27:22, 64, 28:7, 10

MARK 1:2, 8, 2:20[2], 3:28[2], 29, 35, 4:22, 24[2], 25[2], 30[2], 5:23, 28, 6:11[2], 24, 37, 7:11[2], 8:12, 35[2], 36[2], 37, 38[2], 9:1, 19[2], 31[2], 35, 37[2], 39, 41[2], 42, 43, 45, 49[2], 10:7, 8, 11, 12, 15[2], 17, 23, 30

MARK 10:31, 33[2], 34[5], 35, 39[2], 40, 43[2], 44, 11:2, 17, 23[5], 24, 31, 32, 12:7, 9, 15[2], 23[2], 25, 40, 13:2[2], 4[3], 6[2], 7[2], 8[3], 9[3], 11[3], 12[3], 13[3], 14, 19[2], 21, 22[2], 24[2], 25[2], 26, 27[2], 29, 30, 31[2], 14:9[2], 13, 14[2], 18, 27[2], 29, 32, 44, 62, 15:12, 16:3, 7, 16[2], 17[3], 18[4]

LUKE 1:13, 14, 15[3], 16, 17, 18, 20[2], 32[3], 33[2], 34, 35[4], 37, 45, 48, 60, 66, 2:10, 12[2], 23, 34, 35, 3:5[4], 6, 10, 12, 14, 16, 4:4, 7, 10, 11, 5:35[2], 37, 6:21[2], 22[3], 25[2], 26, 35[2], 37[3], 38[3], 39, 40, 7:7, 23, 27, 31, 8:17[2], 18[2], 50, 9:24[2], 26[3], 27, 41, 44, 48[3], 10:6[2], 12, 14, 19, 25

LUKE 10:42, 11:5[2], 7, 9[3], 10, 11, 12, 13, 18, 19, 22, 29, 30, 31, 32[2], 36, 49, 51, 12:2[2], 3[2], 5, 8[2], 9, 10[3], 11[2], 12, 17, 20[2], 22[2], 29[2], 31, 37[2], 38, 42, 43, 45, 47, 48[2], 52, 53, 13:3, 5, 8, 18, 20, 24, 25, 26, 27, 28[2], 29, 30[2], 32, 35[2], 14:5, 11[2], 15, 24, 34, 15:7, 16:3, 12, 17:10, 21, 22[2], 23, 24, 26, 30, 31, 33[4], 34[3], 35[2], 36[2], 18:7, 8, 14[2], 17[2], 18, 24, 30, 31, 32[2], 33[2], 41, 19:26[2], 30, 31, 43[2], 44[2], 20:5, 13, 15, 16[2], 18[3], 35, 47, 21:6[2], 7[2], 8, 9, 10, 11[2], 12, 13, 14, 15, 16[2], 17, 18, 20, 23, 24[3], 25, 26, 27, 32

LUKE 21:33, 35, 36, 22:10, 11[2], 12, 18, 26, 34, 49, 69, 23:29, 30, 31

JOHN 1:51, 3.12, 36, 4:13, 14[4], 21, 23, 24, 25[2], 28, 29, 43, 47, 6:5, 27, 28, 35[2], 37, 45, 51, 57, 58, 62, 68, 7:17, 34[2], 35, 36[2], 38, 41, 8:12, 21[2], 24[2], 28, 32[2], 33, 36[2], 51, 52, 55, 9:21, 10:9[2], 16[2], 28[2], 11:12, 23, 24, 25, 26, 48, 12:25[2], 26, 27, 31, 48, 13:21, 26, 32[2], 33, 35, 38, 14:12[2], 13, 14, 16, 17, 19, 20, 21, 26, 15:7[2], 8, 10, 16, 26, 27, 16:2, 4, 13[3], 14[3], 15[2], 16[2], 17[2], 19[2], 20[4], 22, 23[2], 24, 25[2], 26, 32[2], 33, 17:20, 18:11, 19:15, 24, 36, 37, 20:25, 21:6, 18

JOHN 21:21, 23 ACTS 1:5, 8[2], 11, 2:17[4], 18, 20, 21[3], 26, 37, 38, 39, 3:19, 20, 22[3], 23[2], 25, 4:16, 5:9, 6:14[2], 7:3

ACTS 7:7[2], 37[2], 8:33, 9:6, 10:6, 32, 43, 11:14[2], 16, 13:22, 41, 15:11, 27, 29, 18:10, 19:39, 20:22, 25, 29, 30, 21:11[2], 22:10[2], 23:3, 24:15

ACTS 24:22, 26:2, 27:22, 25, 34, 28:26[3] ROMANS 1:17, 2:12[2], 13, 16, 26, 27, 3:3, 5, 6, 20, 30, 4:1, 18, 24, 5:9, 10

ROMANS 5:17, 19, 6:1[2], 2, 5, 8, 14, 15, 7:3, 7, 24, 8:11, 13[2], 18, 21, 31, 32, 33, 35[2], 39, 9:7, 9, 12, 14

ROMANS 9:20, 26[2], 27, 30, 33, 10:5, 6, 7, 11, 13[2], 14[3], 15, 11:15, 22, 24, 26[3], 27, 35, 13:2, 14:4, 10, 11[2], 12, 15:12[3]

ROMANS 15:21[2], 29, 16:20 1 COR. 1:8, 3:8, 13[4], 14, 15[3], 17, 4:5, 17, 21, 6:2[2], 3, 5, 9, 10, 13, 15, 16, 7:28, 8:10

1 COR. 8:11, 9:11, 11:22[2], 27[2], 12:15, 16, 13:8[3], 10, 12, 14:6[2], 7, 8, 9[2], 11[2], 16, 15:22, 24[2], 26, 28[2], 29, 37, 49, 51[2], 52[3]

1 COR. 15:54[3], 16:3, 4, 5, 12 2 COR. 1:7, 13, 3:8, 16[2], 4:14[2], 5:3, 6:16, 18, 9:6[2], 10:15, 11:10, 15, 12:6, 20[2], 13:1, 4

2 COR. 13:6, 11 GAL. 2:16, 3:8, 11, 12, 4:30, 5:2, 10, 16, 21, 6:4, 5, 7, 8[2], 9 EPHES. 5:14, 31[3], 6:8, 16, 21

PHIL. 1:19, 20[2], 22, 25, 2:23, 24, 3:15, 21, 4:7, 9, 19 COLOS. 3:4[2], 24, 25, 4:7, 9 1 THESS. 4:15, 16[2], 17[2], 5:3

2 THESS. 1:7, 9, 10, 2:3, 8[3], 11, 3:3 1 TIM. 2:15, 3:5, 4:1, 6:15 2 TIM. 2:2, 11, 12, 21, 3:1, 2, 9[2], 12, 13

2 TIM. 4:1, 3, 4[2], 8, 18 TITUS 3:12 PHILE. 22 HEB. 1:5, 11[2], 12[2], 14, 2:3, 3:11, 4:3, 5, 6:6, 8:10, 11[2]

HEB. 9:14, 28, 10:27, 29, 30, 37, 38[2], 11:18, 32, 12:9, 14, 20, 25, 13:6 JAMES 1:5, 7, 10, 11, 12, 25, 2:10, 12

JAMES 2:13, 3:1, 4:10, 14, 15, 5:1, 3[2], 15[3], 20[2] 1 PETER 2:6, 12, 20, 4:5, 8, 13, 17, 18, 5:1, 4[2]

2 PETER 1:8, 10, 11, 2:1[2], 2[2], 3, 12, 13, 3:3, 10[3], 11, 12[2] 1 JOHN 2:18, 24[2], 27, 28, 3:2[4], 19, 4:15, 5:16[3]

2 JOHN 2 3 JOHN 14 REV. 1:7[2], 19, 2:10[2], 11, 23, 27[2], 3:4, 5, 10, 12, 5:10, 6:17, 7:15, 16[2], 17[3], 9:6[4]

REV. 10:7, 9[2], 11:2, 3, 7[3], 8, 9[2], 10[2], 15, 13:8, 10, 14:10[2], 15:4[2], 17:8[2], 13, 14[2], 16[3], 17, 18:7, 8[2], 9[2], 11, 15, 21[2]

REV. 18:22[3], 23[2], 19:15, 20:6[2], 7, 8, 10, 21:3[2], 4[3], 7[2], 8, 24, 25[2], 26, 27, 22:3[3], 4[2], 5[2], 12, 18[2], 19[2]

shalt

GEN 2:17[2], 3:14, 15, 16, 17[2], 18, 19[2], 4:7[2], 12, 6:14, 15, 16[3], 18, 19, 21, 7:2, 12:2, 15:15, 16:11, 17:4, 9, 15, 19, 20:7[2], 13, 21:23, 30, 24:3, 4, 7, 8, 37, 38, 40, 41[2], 27:10, 40[2], 28:1, 6, 14, 22, 27, 31, 50[2], 52, 32:18, 35:17, 37:8[2], 40:13, 41:40, 43:9, 45:10[2], 47:30, 49:4, 50:5 EXOD. 3:14, 15, 18, 4:9, 12, 15, 16, 17[2], 22, 6:1, 7:2, 9, 15[2], 16, 17, 9:15, 28

EXOD. 12:46, 13:5, 6, 8, 10, 12, 13[3], 14, 15:17, 17:6, 18:20[2], 21, 23, 19:3, 6, 12, 24, 20:3, 4, 5, 7, 9, 10, 13, 14, 15, 16, 17[2], 22, 24[2], 25, 26, 21:1, 14, 23, 22:18, 21, 25[2], 26, 28, 29[2], 30[2], 23:1, 2[2], 3, 4, 5, 6, 8, 9, 10[2], 11[2], 12[2], 14, 15[2], 18, 19[2], 22, 24[2], 27, 31, 32, 25:11[3], 11, 13, 14, 16, 17, 18[2], 21[2], 23, 24, 25[2], 26

EXOD. 25:28, 29[2], 30, 31, 37, 26:1[2], 4[2], 5[2], 6, 7[2], 9[2], 10, 11, 14, 15, 17, 18, 19, 22, 23, 26, 29[2], 30, 31, 32, 33, 34, 35[2], 36, 37[2], 27:1, 2[2], 3[2], 4[2], 5, 6, 8, 9, 20, 28:2, 3, 9, 11[2], 12, 13, 14, 15[3], 17, 22, 23[2], 24, 25, 26[2], 27[2], 30, 31, 33, 36, 37, 39[3], 40[3], 41[2], 42, 29:1, 2, 3, 4[2], 5, 6, 7, 8, 9[2], 10, 11

EXOD. 29:12, 13, 14, 15, 16[2], 17, 18, 19, 20, 21, 22, 24[2], 25, 26, 27, 31, 34, 35[2], 36[3], 37, 38, 39[2], 41[2], 30:1[2], 3[2], 4, 5, 6, 16[2], 18[3], 25, 26, 29, 30, 31, 35, 36, 37, 33:21, 23, 34:14, 17, 18[2], 20[3], 21[3], 22, 24, 25, 26[2], 40:2, 3, 4[2], 5, 6, 7[2], 8, 9[2], 10, 11, 12, 13, 14, 15 LEVIT. 2:6, 8, 13[3], 14, 15, 6:21[2], 27, 9:3, 13:55

LEVIT. 13:57, 58, 17:8, 18:7[2], 8, 9, 10, 11, 12, 13, 14[2], 15[2], 16, 17[2], 18, 19, 20, 21[2], 22, 23, 19:9[2], 10[3], 12, 13, 14[2], 15[2], 16[2], 17[2], 18[2], 19[2], 27, 32, 34, 20:2, 16, 19, 21:8, 23:22[3], 24:5, 6, 7, 15, 25:3[2], 4, 5, 8, 9, 15, 16[2], 17, 35, 37, 39, 43[2], 44 NUM. 1:49, 50, 3:9, 10, 15, 41, 46[2], 48, 4:23, 29, 30, 7:5, 8:7, 8, 9[2], 10, 12

NUM. 8:13, 14, 15, 26, 10:2, 11:23, 14:15, 15:5, 6, 7, 10, 17:3, 4, 10, 18:10, 15[2], 16, 17[3], 20[2], 30, 20:8[2], 18, 20, 34, 21:12[2], 20, 22:35, 23:5, 13[2], 26:54[2], 27:7[2], 8, 13, 20, 28:3, 4[2], 7, 8[2], 21, 31:2, 30 DEU. 1:37, 2:28, 3:2, 27, 28, 4:25, 29[2], 30, 40, 5:7, 8, 9, 11, 13, 14, 17, 18, 19, 20, 21[2], 31, 6:5, 7[2], 8, 9, 11, 13[2], 18, 21, 7:2[2], 3[3]

DEU. 7:11, 14, 16[2], 17, 18[2], 21, 24, 25, 26[3], 8:2, 5, 6, 9[2], 10, 18, 9:3, 10:2, 20[3], 11:1, 20, 29, 12:5, 14[2], 18, 20, 21[2], 22, 24[2], 25[2], 26, 27[2], 31, 32, 13:3, 5, 8[3], 9, 10, 12, 14, 15, 16[2], 18, 14:3, 21[2], 22, 23, 25[2], 26[3], 27, 28[2], 15:1, 6[3], 7, 8[2], 10, 11, 12, 13, 14[2], 15, 17[2], 19[2], 20, 21, 22, 23[2], 16:2, 3[2], 6, 7[2], 8[2], 9, 10[2]

DEU. 16:11, 12[2], 13, 14, 15[2], 18, 19[2], 20, 21[2], 22, 17:1, 5[2], 7, 8, 9, 10[2], 11[2], 12, 14[3], 15[2], 18:4, 9, 13, 14, 22, 19:2, 3, 7, 9[2], 13, 14[2], 19, 20:12, 13, 14[2], 15, 16, 17, 19[3], 20[2], 21:9[2], 12, 13, 14[3], 21, 23, 22:1[2], 2[2], 3[3], 4[2], 6, 7, 8, 9, 10, 11, 12, 21, 22, 24, 26, 23:6, 7[2], 12[2], 13[3], 15, 16, 18, 19, 20, 21[2], 22, 23, 24

DEU. 23:25, 24:4, 7, 10, 11, 12, 13, 14, 15, 17, 18, 19, 20, 21, 22, 25:4, 12, 13, 14, 15[2], 19[2], 26:2[4], 3, 5, 10, 11, 13, 16, 27:2, 3, 4, 5[2], 6[2], 7[2], 8, 10, 28:1, 2, 3[2], 6[2], 9, 12[2], 13[2], 14, 16[2], 19[2], 25[2], 29[3], 30[5], 31[2], 33, 34[2], 36[2], 37, 38[2], 39[2], 40[2], 41[2], 43, 44[2], 48, 49, 53, 64, 65, 66[2], 67[4], 68, 30:1, 2[2], 5, 8, 10, 17

DEU. 31:2, 3, 7, 11, 16, 23, 32:52[2], 33:29, 34:4 JOSH. 1:6, 8[3], 2:18[2], 3:8, 6:3, 8:2, 11:6, 17:17, 18[2] JUD. 4:20, 6:14, 16, 23, 26, 7:5, 11, 9:33[2], 11:2, 30, 13:3, 5, 7 RUTH 2:21, 3:4[3] 1 SAM. 2:16, 32, 3:9, 9:16, 10:2, 3[2], 4, 5[2], 6[2], 8[3], 14:44, 16:3[2], 16, 18:21, 19:11, 20:2, 8, 14, 15, 18, 19[2], 31, 22:16, 23, 23:17, 24:20, 26:25[2], 28:1, 2, 19, 30:8 2 SAM. 3:13

2 SAM. 5:2[2], 6, 23, 24, 7:5, 8, 12, 9:7, 10, 10:11, 11:25, 12:13, 13:13, 15:33, 35, 18:3, 20[3], 19:23, 38 1 KINGS 2:37[2], 42, 5:6, 9[3], 8:19, 44, 11:37[2], 12:10[2], 13:17, 14:5, 17:4, 19:16[2], 20:5, 13, 34, 39, 21:19[2], 22:11, 22, 25[2] 2 KINGS 1:4[2], 6[2], 2:16[2], 4:4[3], 16, 5:10, 6:22, 7:2[2], 19[2], 8:13, 9:7, 10:5, 13:18, 19, 19:11, 20:1, 5, 9, 18, 22:20 1 CHRON. 11:2[2], 5, 14:15[2], 17:4, 7, 19:12, 21:22, 22:8, 13, 28:3

2 CHRON. 2:16[2], 6:9, 34, 7:17, 10:10[2], 16:9, 18:10, 21[2], 24[2], 21:15, 34:28 EZRA 4:13, 15, 16, 7:20 ESTHER 4:13, 6:13[2] JOB 5:21[2], 22[2], 23, 24[3], 25, 26, 7:21, 11:15[3], 16, 17[2], 18[3], 19, 14:15, 17:4, 22:23[2], 24, 25, 26[2], 27[2], 28, 29, 35:14, 38:11 PSALMS 2:9[2], 5:3, 6, 12:7[2], 17:3, 21:9, 10, 12[2], 31:20[2], 32:7[2], 8, 36:8, 37:3[2], 10, 34, 50:15, 51:6, 19, 55:23, 59:8[2], 65:3, 67:4, 71:20[2], 21, 73:20, 24

PSALMS 76:10, 81:9, 82:8, 89:2, 91:4, 5, 8, 13[2], 92:10, 102:12, 13, 26[2], 27, 112:9, 10[3], 115:14, 116:12, 118:7, 17, 20, 119:6, 7, 9, 27, 32, 33, 34[2], 42, 44, 88, 117, 144, 146, 165, 171, 172, 175, 120:3[2], 121:4, 6, 7[2], 8, 122:2, 6, 125:1, 3, 5[2], 126:5, 6, 127:5[2], 128:2[2], 5, 6, 130:3, 8, 138:7, 142:7 PROV. 2:5, 9, 3:4, 23, 24[2], 4:12, 9:12[2], 20:13, 22:24, 23:8, 14[2], 34, 35, 24:6

PROV. 25:22, 27:27 ECCL. 11:1, 12:1 ISAIAH 1:26, 12:1, 14:4, 15, 20, 17:10, 11, 22:18, 23:12[2], 25:5, 29:4[2], 6, 30:19, 22[2], 23, 33:1[3], 19, 37:11, 38:1, 39:7, 41:12[2], 15[2], 16[3], 43:2, 44:21, 26, 28, 47:1, 5, 11[3], 12, 49:18, 20, 21, 23, 51:22, 53:10, 54:3, 4[4], 14[3], 17, 55:5, 58:9[2], 11, 12[2], 13, 14, 60:5, 16[3], 18, 62:2, 3, 4[2], 12 JER. 1:7[2], 2:36, 37[2], 3:19[2], 4:1, 2, 30, 5:19

JER. 7:27[2], 28, 8:4, 13:12, 13, 14:17, 15:2, 19[2], 16:2[2], 8, 10, 11, 17:4, 18:22, 19:10, 11, 20:6[3], 21:8, 22:15, 22, 23, 23:33, 37, 25:27, 28, 26:4, 8, 28:13, 16, 29:24, 31:4[3], 5, 34:3[3], 4, 5, 14, 36:6, 29, 37:17, 38:17, 18, 23[3], 24, 26, 39:17, 18, 40:16, 45:4, 46:11[2], 48:2, 7, 49:12[2], 51:26, 61[2], 62, 63, 64 LAM. 4:21[2] EZEKIEL 2:4, 7, 3:18, 25, 26[2], 27, 4:3, 4[2], 5, 6, 7[2], 8

EZEKIEL 4:9[2], 10[3], 11[2], 12[2], 15, 5:2[3], 3, 8:6, 13, 15, 12:3, 4[2], 6[2], 16:41, 43, 61[2], 62, 21:7, 32[3], 22:2, 16[2], 23:32[2], 33, 34[2], 24:13, 16, 27[2], 25:7, 26:14[2], 21[2], 27:34, 36[2], 28:8, 9, 10, 19[2], 29:5[2], 31:18[2], 32:28[2], 33:7, 8, 14, 35:4[2], 12, 15, 36:12[2], 14, 15[2], 38:8, 9[2], 10, 11, 14, 15, 16, 39:4, 5, 43:19, 20[2], 21, 22, 23, 24, 25, 44:6, 45:3, 18, 20, 46:13[2], 14 DANIEL 4:26, 5:16[2], 12:13

HOSEA 2:16[2], 20, 3:3[3], 4:5, 6, 13:4 AMOS 7:17 OBADIAH 10 MICAH 1:14, 2:5, 4:10[4], 13, 5:12, 13, 6:14[3], 15[5] NAHUM 3:11[3] HABAK. 2:7 ZEPH. 3:11[2], 15 ZECH. 2:11, 3:7[2], 4:7, 9, 13:3 MATT. 1:21, 4:7, 10[2], 5:21, 26, 27, 33[2], 36, 43, 6:5, 7:5, 11:23, 12:37[2], 16:19[2], 17:27, 19:18[4], 19, 21, 22:37, 39, 26:34, 75 MARK 6:23, 10:21, 12:30, 31, 14:30, 72

LUKE 1:13, 14, 20, 31[2], 76[2], 4:8[2], 12, 5:10, 6:42, 10:15, 27, 28, 12:59, 13:9, 14:10, 14[2], 17:4, 8, 18:22, 22:34, 61, 23:43 JOHN 1:33, 42, 50, 13:7, 8, 36, 21:18[2] ACTS 2:28, 13:11, 35, 16:31, 22:15, 23:5, 25:12, 22 ROMANS 2:3, 7:7, 10:9[3], 11:22, 12:20, 13:3, 9[6] 1 COR. 7:16[2], 9:9, 14:16 GAL. 5:14 1 TIM. 4:6, 16, 5:18 HEB. 1:12 JAMES 2:8 3 JOHN 6 REV. 2:10, 3:3[2], 16:5, 18:14

she

1931, *846*

GEN. 2:23, 3:6, 12, 20, 4:1, 2, 17, 22, 25[2], 8:9

GEN. 11:30, 12:14, 16, 18, 19, 15:9, 16:1, 4[2], 5, 6

GEN. 16:8, 13[2], 16, 18:15, 19:26, 33, 35, 38, 20:2, 3

GEN. 20:5, 12[2], 16, 21:7, 9, 10, 14, 15, 16[3], 19

GEN. 22:20, 24, 24:14[2], 16, 18, 19, 20, 24[2], 25, 36

GEN. 24:44, 45, 46[2], 47, 55, 58, 64, 65[2], 67, 25:2

GEN. 25:21, 22[2], 26, 26:7[3], 9, 27:16, 17, 42, 29:9, 12

GEN. 29:32, 33[2], 34, 35[2], 30:1, 3[2], 4, 6, 8, 9

GEN. 30:11, 13, 15, 17, 18, 20, 21, 23, 24, 35

GEN. 31:38, 32:14, 15, 34:1, 35:8, 16, 17, 18[2], 36:12, 14

GEN. 38:3, 4[2], 5[2], 14[3], 15, 16[2], 17, 18[2], 19, 24

GEN. 38:25[3], 26, 28, 29, 39:7, 10, 12, 13, 14, 16

GEN. 39:17, 19, 45:23, 46:25, 18 EXOD. 1:16, 2:2[2], 3[3]

EXOD. 2:5[2], 6[3], 7, 10[3], 22, 26, 6:20, 23, 25, 21:4

EXOD. 21:7, 8, 11 LEVIT. 12:2[2], 4[2], 5[3], 6, 7

LEVIT. 12:8[3], 15:19, 20[2], 22, 23, 25, 26[2], 28[3], 29, 18:7

LEVIT. 18:9, 11, 12, 13, 14, 15, 19, 19:20[2], 20:17, 18

LEVIT. 21:9[3], 22:12, 13, 26:43 NUM. 5:13[2], 14[2], 27, 28

NUM.	JOSH.	JUD.	RUTH	1 SAM.	1 KINGS	2 KINGS	1 CHRON.	ESTHER	PROV.	CANT.	JER.	EZEKIEL	MICAH	MATT.	LUKE	JOHN	1 COR.
12:10	6:17	16:16	3:18	28:24	2:20	4:16	4:17	4:4	8:2	6:9[2]	51:8	25:13	1:7	20:21	1:57[2]	11:31[2]	7:36
14	22	18	4:13[2]	25	21	21	7:14	8	3	10	9	14[2]	11	22:28	2:6	32	39[2]
22:25	23	19[4]	1 SAM.	2 SAM.	3:19	22	16	5:2	9:1	8:4	42	16[2]	13	26:10	7	12:7	40[2]
27	25[3]	20	1:7[3]	4:4	20	23	23	12	2[3]	5	53	17	5:3	12[2]	36	16:21[3]	11:5
28	15:18[3]	19:3	10	6:16	26	24	15:29	JOB	3[2]	8[2]	LAM.	18	7:10	MARK	37	20:2	GAL.
33	JUD.	20:5	11	11:4[3]	27	25	2 CHRON.	1:3	4	9[2]	1:1[3]	19[2]	NAHUM	1:31	38	11[3]	4:27
26:59	1:14[3]	RUTH	12	26	10:1	26	9:1[3]	39:16	13	ISAIAH	2[2]	20	2:7	5:23[2]	4:39	13	EPHES.
30:4[2]	15	1:3	13[2]	27	2[3]	27[2]	5	18[2]	14	3:26	3[2]	43	10[2]	26	7:12	14[2]	5:33
5	4:4	6[3]	18	12:24	6	28	9	28	16	8:3	4	24:7[2]	3:10[2]	27	37	15	1 TIM.
6[3]	5	7[2]	20	13:2	10	36	12[4]	29	12:4	28:3	7	12	ZEPH.	28	39	16	2:15
7	6	9	22	8	13[3]	37	15:16	30	23:22	17	8[2]	26:2[3]	2:15	29[2]	44	18	5:5
8[3]	9	15	23	9	14:5[2]	5:2	22:10	42:12	25	40:2	9[3]	17	3:2[4]	42	47	ACTS	6[2]
10	18	18[3]	24[2]	10	6	3	11[2]	PSALMS	28	49:15	10	32:20	ZECH.	6:19	8:42	5:8	10[5]
11	19	20	26	11	17	6:28	23:12	45:14	30:20	51:18[2]	EZEKIEL	DANIEL	9:4	24[2]	47[5]	10	HEB.
DEU.	5:24	2:2	2:5	12	15:13	29	13[3]	46:5	23	66:7[3]	5:6	11:6[2]	MALACHI	25	50	9:36	11:31
21:12	25[2]	3	19	14	17:11	8:2	15	68:12	31:12	8	16:46	17	2:14	7:26	52	37	JAMES
13[2]	26[4]	7[3]	21	16	12	3	34:22	80:11	13	JER.	48	HOSEA	MATT.	28	53	39	2:25
14	29	10	4:19[2]	18	15[2]	6[2]	23	84:3	14[2]	2:1	49	1:6	1:18	30[2]	55	40[3]	REV.
22:19	8:31	13	20[2]	14:4	18	9:30	36:21[2]	PROV.	15	3:6	19:2[2]	8[2]	21	10:12	10:39	12:14[2]	2:21
21[2]	11:34	14[2]	21	5	21:8	31	ESTHER	1:20	16[2]	7[2]	3	2:2	25	12:23	40	15	6:13
24	36	15	22	11	9	34	1:15	21[2]	17	9	5[3]	3	8:15	42	11:31	16:14	12:2
29	37	16	18:19	27	11	11:1	17	3:15	18	4:17	10	5[2]	9:18	44[2]	13:13	15[3]	5
24:2[2]	38	17[2]	21	20:17	2 KINGS	13	19	18	19	6:6	11[2]	6	21	14:3	15:8[2]	18	6
4	39[2]	18[5]	19:14	18	2:24	14	2:1	4:6[2]	20[2]	7	12[2]	7[4]	12:42	6	9[2]	ROMANS	14[2]
25:6	13:9	19[2]	25:3	21:8[2]	4:2	16[2]	7	8[2]	21	11:15	13	8	14:7	8[3]	18:3	7:2	14:8
57[2]	14	23	19[2]	1 KINGS	5[2]	22:14	9	9[2]	22	15:9[3]	14	12	8	9	5	3[5]	18:6[2]
JOSH.	14:3	3:5	20[3]	1:17	6	15	10	13	24	33:16	25:5[2]	13[3]	11	67[2]	20:33	16:2[2]	7[2]
2:6[2]	6	6	23	22	7	1 CHRON.	12	7:11	25	46:24	7[3]	15[2]	15:23	16:10	21:4[2]	1 COR.	8
8	17[3]	7	35	28	8	1:32	13	12	26	50:9	8	13:16	25	LUKE	JOHN	7:11	19
9	15:2	9	36	2:13	9	2:21	14[4]	13	27	12	9	AMOS	27	1:29[2]	8:11	12	19:8
15[2]	16:8	14[2]	41	14	12	26	15	21[2]	30	14	10	5:2[3]		36	11:20	28	
16	9	15[2]	42	16	13	29	17	26	CANT.	15[2]	11			42	27	34[3]	
21[3]	14	16[3]	28:12	19	14	35	20		2:7	29[2]	12			45	28[2]		
	15	17	14		15	49			3:5						29[2]		

that 834 or 2088 or 3588, *1565* or *3754*

GEN.	GEN.	GEN.	GEN.	GEN.	GEN.	EXOD.	EXOD.	EXOD.	EXOD.	LEVIT.	LEVIT.	LEVIT.	LEVIT.	NUM.	NUM.	NUM.	NUM.
1:4	13:14	24:9	30:38	38:26	46:34	7:20[2]	14:5[2]	22:16	32:30	5:11	13:13	18:29	25:50[2]	3:6	10:6	17:10	26:37
10	16	11	41[2]	27	47:1	21	12[3]	20	33:5	13	17	30[2]	51	12	9	18:2	41
12	14:2	14[4]	31:1[2]	28	13	25	15	25	7	16	24	19:8[2]	26:13	13	10	3	43
18	5	15	5	29	14	8:1	18	26	8	6:2	31[2]	13	15[2]	22[2]	11	5	47
20[2]	7	22	6	30	17	8[2]	20	27[2]	13[3]	3[2]	33	20	16	32	32	7	50
21[2]	10	30	10[2]	39:3[3]	18[2]	9	21	31	16[3]	4[3]	37	25	17	34	35[2]	11	54
25[2]	13	32	12	4	19[2]	10[2]	24	23:5	17	5	39	31	25	36	11:1	13	57
26	14	36	16	5[4]	24	15	25[2]	11	22	7	41	34	36	38[2]	4	15	62
28	17	43	19	6	26	16	26	12	34:1	18	47	20:2[2]	39	39	11	16	63
30	23[3]	49	20[2]	7	29	20	28	13	3	22	50	3	40	43	12	23	27:3
31	24	52	21	8	48:1	22[2]	30	22	7	26	51	5[2]	41	46	13	19:2	11
2:3	15:4	54	22	10	10	28	31	24:12	10	27	52	6[2]	44	49[2]	16	3	14
4[2]	7	55	24	11	17	29	15:7	25:2[2]	11	7:3	54	9	45	51	17	8	17
9	8	56	26	13	20	9:1	26[2]	8	19[2]	4[2]	55	10[2]	27:8	4:3	20	9	20
11	13[2]	65	27	14	49:1[2]	4	16:4	9	29[2]	7	57	11	9	15	21	10[2]	29:40
12	14	66	29	15[2]	15[2]	6	5[2]	14	32	8	14:4	14	15	16	25[2]	11	30:2
13	17[2]	25:5	32	18	17[2]	13	6	21	34	9[3]	5	22	18	19	26	13[2]	5
14[2]	16:2	11	35	19	25	14[2]	7[2]	26	35	14	6	24	19	23	29[2]	14[2]	7
17	4	18	36	22	26	15	8	28	35:1	15	7	25	23	25	32[3]	16	8[2]
19	5	26	37	23[2]	28	16	10	33	10	16	8[3]	26	28[2]	26	34[2]	18[2]	9
3:5	10	30	39	40:1	29	17	12	35	22	18[2]	9	27[2]		30	12:14	20[2]	14
6	13[2]	26:1	43	7	30	19	13	37	24	19[2]	11[2]	21:2[2]	NUM.	35	13:2	21[3]	15
7	17:12[2]	5	52[2]	15	32	20	14	40	25[2]	20[3]	14	3	1:3	36	18	22	31:8
11	13	8	32:2	16	50:14	21	18	26:5	34	21[2]	16	7	5	37[2]	19[2]	20:3	17
13[2]	14	11	5	20	15	22	22	10	35[2]	24[2]	17[2]	10[2]	20	38	28	4	18
14	17[2]	12	7	41:1		28	23[4]	11	36:1	25	18[2]	17	21	39	31	14	20
4:3	18	21	13[2]	8[2]	EXOD.	29	25	12[2]	4	27[2]	19	18[2]	22[2]	40	32[2]	29	23[2]
8	23	22	19	15[2]	1:5	30	27	13[2]	8	29	25	19	23	41[2]	14:1	21:1	26
14	24	28	20	21	6	34	29	33	18	30	27	20	24	42	2	7	27
5:1	18:17	29[2]	21	24	10	10:1	32	27:5	19	33	28[2]	21	25	43	3	8[2]	35
5	18	32	22	27	21	2[3]	17:2	20	37:8	36	29[2]	23	26	44	6	9	36
6:2	19[3]	27:1	23	31	22	3	3	28:1	13	8:10	31	22:2[2]	27	45	14[4]	13	42
3	25[3]	4	25	32	2:2	5[2]	6	3[3]	38:15	16	32	3[2]	28	46	23	15	43
4	19:5[2]	7	29	35	7	6	11	4	22	25	35	4	29	47	29	16	52
5[2]	11[2]	8	32	36[2]	11	7[2]	16	28[2]	24	26	36[2]	8	30	48	35	20	32:1
6	14	10	33:9	53	12[2]	8	18:1[2]	32	25	31	40	11	31	5:2[2]	37	27	9
7	17	19	11	57	13	11[2]	8[2]	35	26[2]	32	41	18	32	3	38	29	11
17	21	20	13	42:1	18	12	11	37	39:5	35	43	20	33	6[2]	42	32	13
21	25	21	14	2[2]	20[2]	13	13	38[2]	7	36	46[2]	23[2]	34	17	45	22:2	24
22	29	25	15	5	23	15	14[2]	41	21[2]	9:1	47[2]	24	35	18	15:12	4[2]	32
7:2	32	30	16	6	3:8	17	17	43	28	5	15:4	33	36	19	13	6[3]	33:55
4	33	31	34:5[5]	14[2]	10	20	18	29:1	32	6	6[2]	23:12	37	22	15	19	56
5	34[2]	33	14[2]	16	11[2]	21	19	13[3]	42	19	7[2]	14	38	24[2]	16	20	34:2
8	35	40	15	21	12	25	20	21	40:4	10:3[2]	8[2]	15	39	27[2]	19	24	35:2
10	20:6	45	24[2]	23	16	28	22	22[2]	9	10	9	21	40	6:4	23[2]	28	6
14	7[2]	28:3	25	28	18	11:5[2]	24	23	13	11	10[2]	23	41	6	24	34	8[2]
16	9[2]	4	28[2]	29	19	7[2]	19:8	27	15	12[2]	11	28	42	11[2]	26	35[2]	11
19	10	6[2]	29	33	20	8[2]	9	30[2]	16	20	12	29[2]	43	12	28	36	12
21[2]	13	7	35:1	34[2]	21	9	12	32	17	11:2	13	30[2]	44	20	29[3]	38[2]	15[2]
22	16	8	2[2]	35	22	10	16[3]	38	37	3	20[2]	42	45[2]	21[2]	30[2]	40	16
23	21:3	11[2]	5	43:7	4:2	12:8	20:4[3]	46[3]		4[3]	22	43[2]	46	7:1	31	41[2]	20
8:1	6[2]	15	6	8	5[2]	10	5	30:6	LEVIT.	9	28	24:2	50	2[2]	32	23:12	21[2]
11	7[2]	18	17	12	8	15	6	12	1:5	10[2]	31[2]	7	51	5	33	19[2]	23
17[2]	12	19[2]	18	14	9	16	7	13[2]	8	12	32	12	53	9	38[2]	26[2]	32[2]
9:2	22[3]	20	20	15	14	19[2]	10	14[2]	12	20	33	14[2]	54	10	39[2]	27	33[2]
3	23[2]	21	22[2]	18[2]	21[2]	22[2]	11	16	17	21	16:2[7]	16[2]	2:4	12	40	28	36:8[2]
10[2]	30	22	36:7	21	23	25	12	20	2:8	26	13[3]	17	5	88	16:7	24:1	
12	31	29:2	16	25	24	27	17	21	10	27	15[2]	18	6	89	9	9[2]	DEU.
14	22:4	7	17	44:2	31[2]	29[3]	20[2]	29	3:3[2]	28	16	21[2]	8	8:11	11	13	1:3[2]
16[2]	6	10	18	7	5:1	33	22	30	4	29	18	23	9	15	13[2]	19[2]	9
17	8	12	24[2]	15[2]	2	36	26	38	5	31	26	25:5	10	17	14	20	16[2]
18	9	13	29	17	9	37	21:12[2]	31:6[3]	9[2]	34[2]	28	6	11	19	21	25:4	17
10:11	14	19	30	21	19	41	14	7	10	36	29[2]	7	13	20	28	5	18
11:2	23:4	21	31	30	22	42	15	11	14[2]	39	30[2]	11[2]	15	22	30[2]	9	19
7	6	23	40	31[2]	6:7	44	16	13[3]	15	40[2]	17:3[2]	25	16	24	31[2]	11	30
12:1	8	25	37:4	34	11	48	17	14[2]	17	41	4[2]	27	19	9:4	32	14[2]	31[2]
3	9	31	10	45:1	26	49[2]	19	32:1[2]	4:3	42	5[2]	28[2]	21	5	33	15	35
5[2]	10	33	22[2]	8	27	51	22	10[2]	5	43[2]	8	30[2]	23	6[3]	34	26:1	36
11	11	30:1	23[2]	10	29[2]	13:5	26	13	8[2]	44	9	33	24	7	35	2	39
12	15	8	38:1[2]	11	7:2[2]	8	28	18[3]	9	45	10[4]	35	26	13[2]	37	7	41
13	17	9	9[3]	12[2]	4	9	29	19	16	46[2]	11	36	27	14	39	9	44
14[2]	18	15	14	13	5	12[3]	35	21	18	47[2]	12	39	28	15	40[2]	10	46
18	20	16	16[2]	15	13	14	36	22	35	12:7	13[2]	44	30	17	42	18	2:6[2]
20	24:2	25[2]	18	24	16	15[2]	22:2	23	5:3	13:4	15[3]	45[2]	31	21[2]	45	22	17
13:1	3	27	21[2]	46:1	17	17[2]	6[2]	25	4	7	18:6	47	32	22	49[2]	25	20
6[2]	6	33[2]	22	26	18	14:2	11	28	5[2]	8	26	48	34	10:2	17:5	27	25
10	7	35	24	32	19[2]	4[3]	13	29	8	12	28[3]	49	3:1	5	8	34	28[2]

DEU.
2:30
31
34
36
3:4
8
9
12
18^2
19
21^2
23
24
25^2
4:1
2
3
4
5
7
8
10^4
14^2
15
17
18^2
21^2
22^3
26
32^2
34
35^2
36
39
40^2
42^2
5:1
5
8^3
9
10
11
14^2
15^2
16^2
21
23
24
26
27^2
28^2
29^3
31
33^3
6:1
2^2
3^3
18^3
23
24
7:4
6
9^2
10^2
12
15
16
20
25
8:1
3^3
5
7
11
13
15
16^2
18^2
19
9:3
4
5
6
7
8
11
14
19
21
24
10:1
2
8
10
11
14
21
11:6
8
9^2
14^2
15
16
17^2
18
21
25
29
12:1
3
7
8
10
11
12
13^2
14

DEU.
12:18^2
19
23
25^2
28^2
30^3
13:3^2
5^2
10
14
15^2
17
18
14:2
6^2
7^2
9^2
19
21^3
22
23
24
26
27
29
15:2
3
8
9
10^2
14
15
18
19
16:3
6
11^2
12
13
14
20^2
17:1
2
4
5^5
6
9
10^2
12^3
14
16^2
17
18^2
19
20^3
18:3
8
10^2
12
16^2
17
18
19
20^2
22
19:3
4
5
10
11
12
13
14
15
16
20:4
5
6
7
8
9
11^2
14
16
18
20^2
21:2
3^2
4
6^3
9
11
13
15
16^2
17
18
21
23^3
22:5^2
7^2
8
18^2
21
22
23
24^2
25
28
29
23:1
8
10^2
13
14
16
19

DEU.
23:20^2
23
24:1
4^2
7
8^2
9
13
14^2
18
19
22
25:1
2
6^2
9^2
10
11
15
16^2
18
19
26:2^2
3^2
9
11
12
14
15
18
19
27:2
3^2
4
15
16
17
18
19
20
21
22
23
24
25
26
28:1
7
8
10
13
15
20
23^2
34
35
43
54
55
57
58^2
63
29:2
6^2
9^2
11
12
13^2
15^2
18
19
20^2
21
22^4
23^2
27
29
30:2
3
6
7
12^2
13^2
14
16^2
17
18^2
19^2
20^4
31:5
6
8
12^3
13
14^2
17^3
18^2
19
20
21
25
26
28
29
32:6
13
17
18^2
21
27
29^3
35
36
39^2
41
42
48

DEU.
32:49
33:11^3
13
16^2
20
34:1
12
JOSH.
1:1
3^2
7^2
8^2
16
18^2
2:3
5
9^3
10
12
13^2
14
19
23
3:2
4
7^2
8
10^2
13^3
15^2
16^3
17
4:1
6^2
7
10^2
11
14
16^2
18^2
24^3
5:1^2
2
4^2
5^2
6^4
8
12
13
6:5
7
8
9
15^2
17^3
20^2
21
22^2
23^2
24
25
26^2
7:14
15^3
24
26
8:5^2
8
9
11
13^2
14^2
16
17
18^2
20^2
21^2
22^2
24
25^3
27
29^2
33^3
34
35^2
9:2
9
10^2
16^3
24
26
27
10:1
4
6
10
11
14^2
20
24
27
28^2
30
32^2
35^4
37^3
39
40
11:1
2
4
10
11
13^2
15
16

JOSH.
11:17
19
20^3
21
23
26
12:4
6
7
13:2
4
9^2
16^2
17
22
25
14:4
6
8
9
11
12^2
14
15:2
4
7^2
8
16
17
18
46
16:1
10
17:7
12
13
16
18:6
8^2
13
14
16
19:8
10
11
21
20:3^2
4^3
6^2
9^2
21:26
44
22:2^2
10
16^3
18^2
20
23
27^3
28^2
29^2
30
31
34
23:1^2
3^2
4^2
6^2
7^2
10
11
12
13
14
15
24:5
8
15
16
17
20
22
25
26
29
31^2
33
JUD.
1:1
3
9
10
12
14
17
21
28
29
35
2:4
5
7^2
10
12
14^2
16
18
19
20
22
3:2
3
18
19^2
22
24

JUD.
3:27
29
30
4:2
4
9
12
13
15
20
23
5:1
5
7^2
9
10^2
13
14
18
21
30
31
6:3
8
9
11
17
21
22
25^3
27^2
28^2
30^2
31^2
32
37
40
7:1^2
2
4
5^2
6
7
9
11
13^3
15
17
18
19^2
8:1
3
4
5
6
10^2
11
15^2
21
24
26^3
28
31
33
9:2^3
6
7
16
24
25^2
28
32
33^2
34
35
38^2
41
42
44^2
45^2
46
47
48^2
49
54
55
10:4
8^2
9
18
11:4
5
6
8
12
21
24
26^2
31
35^2
36
37
39
40
12:3
5^2
6
14
13:8
10
11
13
14^2
16
17
20
21

JUD.
14:3
4^3
9
11
13
15^3
17
15:1
2
7
11^2
12^2
14^2
17^2
19
16:3
4
5
7
11
16
17
18
20
25^2
26^3
27
28
30
17:2
6
13
18:1
5
7^2
9
10
12
14^2
17^2
19
22
23
24
26
27
28
31
19:1
5
6
9^2
10
12
15
18
22^2
23
30^3
20:2
3
4^2
5
10^2
12
13
15^2
17
21
26
34
35
26
38
41
46^3
48^2
21:3
4
5^2
7^2
8
11^2
12
13
15
16
17^2
18
19
22^2
23
24
RUTH
1:1
6^2
9
11
13
18
19
2:5
6^2
7
9^3
10
11
13^2
16
17
18
19
22^2
35
3:1
2

RUTH
3:4
5
6
8
11^2
12^2
13
14
15
16
4:3
4
9^3
10
11^2
14
1 SAM.
1:4
12
17
20
22
26
2:4
5^4
13
14^2
15
21
22^2
24
30^3
31^2
34
35
36^3
3:2
4
8
9
11
13
14
17^2
20
4:3
4
5
6
8
9
15
16
18
19^2
20
5:5
7
9
10
11
12
6:5
8
9^3
15
7:2
6
7
8
10
8:1
7^2
8
9
10
11
18
20^2
9:5
6^2
8
9
13
16
19
20
22
24^3
26^2
27
10:5^2
7
9^2
11^3
14
16
18
24
11:2
3
9^2
10
11^3
12^2
12:1
5
6^2
7
12
14
17^2
18
19
23
13:3

1 SAM.
13:4^2
6
8
10^2
11^3
14
15
16
17
18
22^2
14:1^3
2
3
6^2
7
14
17
18
19^2
20
21^3
22
23
24^2
27
28
31
33
34
37
39
43
45
48
15:2
3
7
9^3
11
25
28
29
30
35
16:4
6
13
16
17
18
23
17:10
12^2
25^2
26^3
27
28
37
41
43
46^2
47
48
49
18:1
2
3
4
6
9
10
15
18
19
21^2
23
27
28^2
30^2
19:1
10
15
17
18
22
24
20:1
2
3
5
6
7
9
13
14
26
27
30
33
35
21:6
7^2
9^3
10
15
22:2^3
4
6^2
7
8^5
11
13^2
17
18^2
21
22^2

1 SAM.
22:23
25
26
28
35
23:6
7^2
9
10
13
15
22
23
24:1
4
5
6
10
11^2
16
18
19
20^2
21^2
25:4
6^2
7
10
11
17
20
21^3
22^2
26
27
30
31^3
34
37
38^2
39^2
42
26:3
4
11^2
16^2
27:1
2
4
5
6
7
28:1^2
3
7^3
9
14
15
21
22
25
29:4
7
8
9
10
30:1
2
4
9^2
10
15
16
18
19
21^2
22^3
23^2
24^2
25^2
31:5
6
7^4
8
11
2 SAM.
1:2^2
4
5^2
6
10^4
11
13
15
2:1
3
4^2
5
11
16
17
23
26
29
31
3:6
8
13
19^2
20
21^3
23
24
25
27

2 SAM.
3:29^5
31
37
38
4:1
2
4^2
10
12^2
5:2
8^2
14
17
20
24
6:2^2
3
9
12
13
17
7:2
3
4^2
6
9
10
11^2
18
22
25
28
29
8:1
7
9
11
9:1^2
3
8
9
10
11
12
10:1
3^2
6
9
10
12^2
14
15
16
19^2
11:2
12
14
15
16^2
20
21
22
26
27
12:4^2
5
8
14
15
18^3
19^2
21
22
31
13:1
2
5
6
10
15
16
17
18
19
23
24^2
27
30
32^2
33
34
36
14:1
2
7^2
11
13
14
15^2
16
18
19
20
22^2
26
32
15:1
2^2
4
5
6
7
11
14
17
22
30

2 SAM.
15:32
35
36
16:2
4
12^2
14
16
21^2
17:2
7
8
9
10^2
11^3
12
13
14
16
21
22^3
25
28
29
18:1
3
7
8
9
11
12
15
19
22
28
31
32^2
19:2^2
3
6^3
7^2
14
19^2
20
22
25
26
28
34
37
38^2
43
20:8
10
11^2
12^3
15
19
20
21:3
5
17
18
22:1
18
28
31
35
37
39
40
41^2
48
49^2
23:3
7
8
9
10
15
16
17^2
18
24:2
3
5
9
10
12
13
16
17
21
24
1 KINGS
1:2
11
12
20
21
29
35
40
41
45^2
49
51
2:1
3^2
4
5^2
7
11
15^3
17
27

1 KINGS
2:29
31
37^2
39
41
42^2
43
44
46
3:4^2
6
8
9
10
12
13^2
16
18^2
23
27
65
4:12
29
33
5:1
3
4
6^4
7
9
15
16
6:1
6
7
17
21
27
7:3
18
19
29
40
41
42
48
51
8:1
4
5^2
8
10
11
12
16^2
18
19
20
23
24
25^3
27
29^2
36
40^2
41
43^4
46^2
47
50^2
52^2
54
56
58
59
60
64
66
9:2
3
4
8
11
16
19
20
21
23^2
25
27
10:2^2
4
6
8
11
13
14
15
27
11:4
7
10^2
17
19
21^3
22
25
27
28
29^2
30
33^2
36
37
38^3
41
42

1 KINGS
12:3
6^2
8
9
10^2
13
15
16
18
20
22^2
13:2
3
4^2
6
9
10
11^2
14
17
18
20^2
21
23
26
31
14:1
2^2
5
6
8
9
10^2
11^2
14
22
25
28
29
15:5^2
7
11
12
17
18^2
19
21
23
29^2
31
16:4
7
11^2
14
16^2
18^2
20
22^2
25
27
30
31
33
17:3
4
5
7
10
12^2
14
17^2
24^2
18:1
4
5
7
9
10
12
17^2
18
24
26
27
29^2
30
36^4
37^3
38
44^2
45
19:1
3
4
8
13
17^3
20:4
6
9
10
11^2
12
13
16
25
26
28
29
30
31
37
41
21:1
2
3
5

1 KINGS
21:8
10
13
14^2
16^2
21^2
24^2
27
22:2
3
7
13^2
14
16^2
17
18
20^2
25
31
32
33^2
35
39^2
43
45
53
2 KINGS
1:2
3
4
6^3
2:1
3^2
5^2
8
9
11
13
14
16
3:2
5
9
10
11
14
15
17^2
20
21^2
24
26^2
27
4:1
4
6
8^2
9
10
11
17^2
18
22
25^2
40
41
42
43
5:3
4
6
7^2
8^3
15
18
20
6:9
12^2
13
16^2
17
20^2
22
24
28
29
30
7:9
12
13^2
19
8:3
4
5
6^2
10
12
13^2
14
15^2
23
9:7
8
22
25
37
10:1
3
5^2
7
9
10^2
11
17
19
21^2

2 KINGS
10:22
24
25
29^2
30^2
34
36
11:1
2
5^2
6
7
8
9^3
10
15
17
12:2
4^4
6
9^2
10^3
12
13
14
18^2
19
13:2
5
8
11
12
21
14:3
5
6
9^3
10
14
22
24
26
27
28
15:3
4^3
5
6
9
16^2
18
19
21
24
26
28
31
34^2
36
16:2
6
8
10
11
16
17
18
17:2^2
9
14
15^3
25
38
18:1
3^2
4
5^2
9
10
12
14
15
16
20
21
22
26
27^2
32
35^2
19:1
4
8
19^2
20
21
25^2
29
30
31
33
35^2
37
20:3
4
8^2
9^2
12^2
13^2
15^2
17^3
18
21:2
8^2
11
12
15

2 KINGS
21:16
17^2
20
21^2
24
22:2
3
4
5
7
9^3
11
13^3
15
17
19
23:3
4
5
7
8
10
11
12
13
15^2
16
17^3
18
19^2
20
22
24^3
25
26
28
32^2
33
37^2
24:3
4
5
7
9^2
10
16
19^2
20
25:1
10
11^2
13^2
19^2
22
23
25^4
27^2
28
1 CHRON.
1:43
2:9
24
55
4:10^5
21
23
33
43
5:18
20
6:10^2
31
33
49
61
7:21^2
40
9:1
16
28
31
33
10:5
7^3
8
11
13
14
17
19
31
12:1
8
15
20
22
24
32
38
13:2^3
4
6
11
12
14
14:2
8
11
15
15:12^2
13
26^2
27
29
16:1
7

1 CHRON.
16:10
12
30
32
35
39
40
41
42
17:1
2
3
5
7
8
10^2
11^2
16
24
25
27
18:1
7
11
19:1
3^2
6
9
10
13
14
15
16^2
19
20:1^2
3
4^2
21:2
5^2
10
12^2
15
17^3
18
22^2
23
24
28^2
29
22:2
5
12
13
19
23:13
24
25
29^2
32
25:7^2
26:6
28
27:1
6
26
28
29^2
28:1
8
9
12
14
17
18
29:3
9
11
14
16
17
21
22
27
30
2 CHRON.
1:3
5
7
10^2
11
12
13
15
2:6
7^2
10
12^2
17
3:1
4
15
17^2
4:11
19
20
21
5:1^3
5
6
9
11
13
14
6:1
4
5^2

2 CHRON. 6:6 8 10 11 14 15 16^{2} 20^{2} 31 33^{3} 34 40 7:7 10 11 13 15 16 17 21^{2} 8:2 6^{2} 7 10 11 18 9:1^{2} 3 6 12 13 14 23 27 10:2 4 6 8^{2} 9^{2} 10^{2} 15 16 17 18^{2} 11:1 13 12:2 3 5 7 8 10 12 13:5 9^{2} 15 18 14:2 8^{2} 11 13^{2} 15:5^{2} 8 9 13 18^{2} 16:1 2 3 5 7 17:10^{2} 18:2 6 12 13 15 16 17 19^{2} 24 30 31 32^{2} 33 34 19:2 3 10^{2} 20:1 2 6 12 21 29 32 37 21:6 7 16 17^{2} 19 22:1 8^{2} 10 11^{2} 23:4 6 8^{3} 9 14 16 19 21 24:2 4 5

2 CHRON. 24:7 9 11^{2} 20 23 26 25:2 3^{2} 5 10 12 25:13 14^{2} 16^{2} 18^{3} 19 20 24 27 26:2 4 7 11 13 17 18 27:2^{2} 28:1 7 9^{2} 12 15 16 22 23 29:2^{2} 6 10 11 16 24 29 34 36 30:1 3 5 6 8 9^{2} 14 17^{2} 19 21 22 25^{3} 31:1 4^{2} 6 10 16 19^{2} 20 21 32:2 4 5 7 9 10 14^{3} 18^{2} 21 23 26 31^{3} 33:2 8^{2} 13 15 18 19 22 25 34:2 4^{2} 9^{2} 10^{2} 12 13 14 16 17 21^{4} 22^{2} 23 24 25 28 30 32 33^{2} 35:3 6 7 12 17^{2} 18^{2} 21 22 24^{2} 26 36:5 8 9 12 17

2 CHRON. 36:20 22^{2} **EZRA** 1:1 4 6^{2} 11 2:1 62 63 3:5^{2} 7 8 12 13 4:1 10 11 12 13 15^{2} 16 17 19^{2} 21 22 5:1 4 5 6 8 10^{2} 11 12 14 15 16 17 6:2 8^{2} 9 10 11 12 7:11 13^{2} 16 17 18 19 21 24 25^{3} 8:1 15 17 21 22^{2} 34 35 9:2 4^{2} 8 12 13^{2} 14 10:3 5 6 7 8^{2} 13 17 18 19 **NEH.** 1:2^{2} 3 4 5^{2} 6 8 9 2:1 5^{2} 7 8^{2} 10 12 14 16 17^{2} 18 19 3:15 16 25 26 27 4:1^{2} 3 7^{3} 10 12 15^{2} 16^{2} 17^{2} 18 22 23 5:2^{2} 3^{2} 4^{2} 9 11

NEH. 5:12 13 14^{2} 15 17^{2} 18 19 6:1^{3} 2 3 6^{2} 9 11 12^{2} 13^{3} 14 16^{3} 7:2 5 6^{2} 64 65 72 8:1 2 3^{2} 9 12 14 15 17^{2} 9:6^{2} 10 11 15 17 18 21 23 24 28 29 32 33 35 36 10:1 28 30 31^{2} 36 37^{2} 39 11:2 3 6 12 19 23 12:1 31 38 40 43^{2} 44^{2} 13:1^{2} 2 3 7 10^{2} 14 17 19^{4} 21 22^{4} 23 **ESTHER** 1:2 5 8 10 13 16 17 19^{2} 22^{2} 2:2 3 7 8 10 12 14 15 17 3:1 2 4^{2} 5 6 7^{4} 9^{2} 12^{2} 14^{2} 4:1 7^{2} 8^{2} 11 13 16 17 5:1 2^{2} 4 5^{2} 8

ESTHER 5:9^{2} 12 14 6:1 2^{2} 3 4 8^{3} 9 10 13 14 7:5 7 10 8:1 3 6 9^{3} 11 13^{2} 14 9:1^{4} 5 11^{2} 15 16^{2} 18 19 20 21 22 24 25^{2} 26 27 28^{2} **JOB** 1:1^{2} 3 5^{2} 8^{2} 10 11 12 2:3^{2} 4 11 13 3:4 6 7 8 12 15 20 25 4:4 8 19 5:1 11^{2} 12 24 25 6:2 6 7 8^{3} 9^{2} 11^{2} 14 26 7:7 8 9 12 8:13 15 17^{2} 18 20 22 9:16 26 28 32 33 10:3^{2} 6^{2} 7^{2} 9 13 18 20 11:5 6^{3} 16 12:5^{2} 6 9 13:5 9 13 18 19 28 14:1 5 6 7^{2} 13^{2} 15:7 9^{2} 14^{2} 17

JOB 15:22 23 31 16:3 21 17:3 5 9 18:20^{2} 21 19:3 4 6 8 15 23^{2} 24 25^{2} 20:5 18 20 26 29 21:13^{2} 15 18 22 29 30 22:2 3^{2} 23:10 11 13 14^{2} 24:1 7 13 21 25:4 6 26:2^{2} 3 27:5 7 11 15 18 28:11 28 29:2 12^{2} 13 25 30:1 23 25 31 31:6 12 15 28 29 31 34 35^{3} 38 32:5 12^{2} 20 33:12 17 20 21^{2} 27 34:2 9 10 17^{2} 19 23 25 28 30 32 36 35:2 36:2 4 9 10 16 24 32 37:2 7 12 20 24 34 38:2 13^{2} 20^{2} 35 39:2 12 15^{2} 24 40:2^{2} 8 11 12 14 19 23 41:10 11

JOB 41:16 17^{2} 26 42:2 3^{2} 7^{2} 8 11^{2} 46:5 **PSALMS** 1:1 3 2:4 12 3:1^{2} 6 4:3^{2} 6 7 5:4 6 11^{2} 7:1 4^{2} 6 8 8:2 4^{2} 9:10^{2} 13^{2} 14 15 17 20 10:2 10 18 11:2 5 12:3 5 13:4 14:1 2 3 7 15:2 3 4^{2} 5^{2} 16:3 4 17:1 2 3 5 7^{2} 9 12 18 *title* 12 30 32 34 36 38 39 40^{2} 47 48 20:6 21:8 22:3 7 8 9 23 25 26 29^{2} 31^{2} 24:1 4 6^{2} 25:3 12^{2} 14 26:7 27:4^{2} 28:1 30:3 12 31:4 6 11 15 19^{2} 24 32:6 10 11 33:18^{2} 34:7 8^{2} 9 10 12^{2} 16 18 21 22 35:1^{2} 3 4^{2} 8^{2} 10^{2}

PSALMS 35:11 14 19^{2} 20 26^{2} 27 28 36:4 10 37:9 13 16 22 37 38:12^{2} 13 14 19 20^{2} 39:1 4 13 40:4^{2} 12 14^{2} 15 16 41:1 7 8 10 11 42:4 44:5 7 13 16 45:14 46:10 48:13 49:6 9 10 11 12 20^{2} 50:4 5 16 21 22 23 51:4 8 52:7 53:1 2^{2} 3 5 6 54:4 55:6 12^{3} 18 19 56:1 2 13 57:2 3 4 58:4 8 11^{2} 59:1 13^{2} 60:4^{2} 5 12 61:2 5 8 62:11 63:9 11^{2} 64:4 8 65:2 4 5 8 66:16 67:2 68:1 4 11 12 18 20 23 28 30 33^{2} 35 69:4^{3} 6^{2} 9 10 12 14 22 23 31 32 34 35 36

PSALMS 70:2^{2} 3 4 6 10 13^{2} 18 24 72:6 9 12 73:25 27^{2} 28 74:3 9 18^{2} 23 75:1 76:11^{2} 77:4 14 78:4 5 6 7 8 11 20 35 39^{2} 44 53 60 65 79:4 6^{2} 11 80:1^{2} 12 13 15 81:5 13 83:2 4 16 18^{2} 84:4 11 12 85:6 9^{2} 12 86:2 5 17 87:4 5 6 88:4^{2} 5 89:7 10 15 19 23 34 35 41 48 90:9 12 14 91:1 5 6^{2} 92:7 11 13 15 93:1 94:9^{2} 10^{2} 11 13 95:10 11 96:10^{2} 12 97:7^{2} 10 98:8 99:6 7 8 100:3^{2} 101:3 5 6^{2} 7^{2} 8 102:4 8 11 20 103:1 5 6 11 13 14 17 18 20^{2} 21 104:5

PSALMS 104:9^{2} 14 15 26 27 28 105:3 5 19 34 45 106:3^{2} 4 5^{3} 8 10 20 25 31 32 33 40 41 46 107:7 8 15 21 23^{2} 29 31 34 36 38 108:6 13 109:11 15 16^{2} 20 27^{3} 31 111:2 5 6 10 112:1^{2} 113:6 8 114:5^{2} 6 115:8^{2} 11 13 17 118:2 3 4^{2} 7^{2} 13 26 119:2^{2} 5 11 17 18 20 21 42 53 57 63^{2} 71^{2} 73 74 75^{2} 77 79^{2} 80 84 101 106 116 118 125 132 138 148 150 152 162 120:5^{2} 6 121:3 4 122:3 6 123:1 2 4 125:1 4^{2} 126:1 5 6 127:1 5 128:1^{2} 4^{2} 129:5 7 130:4 6^{2} 131:2 132:12 133:2^{2} 3

PSALMS 134:3 135:2 5^{3} 6 18^{2} 20 136:5 6 7 10 137:3^{2} 8 9 138:8 139:14 21^{2} 140:9 10^{2} 12^{2} 141:4 10 142:4 7^{2} 143:3 7 12 144:3^{2} 4 10 12^{2} 13^{2} 14^{2} 15^{3} 145:14^{2} 18^{2} 19 20 146:4 5 6 8 147:11^{2} 148:4 149:2 6 **PROV.** 1:12 19 29 2:2 7 12 19 20 27 3:13^{2} 18^{2} 4:18 22 5:2^{2} 6 13 6:11 17 18^{2} 19^{2} 29 32 7:5 23 8:9^{2} 11 17^{2} 21^{2} 29 32 34 36^{2} 9:4 7^{2} 16 18^{2} 10:4 5^{3} 9^{2} 10 13^{2} 17^{2} 18^{2} 19 26 11:12 13 15^{2} 17 18 19 20 24^{2} 25 26^{2} 27^{2} 28 29 30 12:1 4 8 9^{2} 11^{2} 15 17 18 20 22 13:3^{2}

PROV. 13:6 7^{2} 11 13 18^{2} 20 23 24^{2} 14:2^{2} 6 13 17 21^{2} 22^{2} 29^{2} 31^{2} 33^{2} 35 15:5 9 10^{2} 12 14 15 18 21 24 27^{2} 31 32^{2} 16:5 13 17 20 22 25 26 29 32^{3} 17:2 5 8 9^{2} 15^{2} 19^{2} 20^{2} 21 24 25 27 28 18:2 9^{2} 13 17 21 24^{2} 19:1^{2} 2^{2} 5 6 8^{2} 9 16^{2} 17^{2} 20 21 23 25 26^{2} 27 20:8 16 19^{2} 25 21:5 6 16 17^{2} 21 28 22:5 8 9 11 14 16^{2} 19 21^{3} 26^{2} 23:5 6 22 24 25 30^{2} 34^{2} 24:8 11^{2} 12^{2} 21 24 25 26 34 25:7^{2} 10 13 18 20^{2} 28^{2} 26:6 8^{2} 10 16 17^{2} 19

PROV. 26:24 27 28 27:8^{2} 10 11^{2} 13 14 18 28:3 4 5 6^{2} 7 8^{2} 9 11 13 14^{2} 16^{2} 17 18 19^{2} 20 21 22^{2} 23^{2} 25^{2} 26 27^{2} 29:1^{2} 3 4 5 14 18 20 21 27 30:5 11 12 15 16^{2} 17 23 31:1 3 6^{2} 11 18 30 **ECCL.** 1:9^{3} 11^{2} 13 14 15^{2} 16 17 18 2:3 6 7 8 9 11^{3} 12 13 14 15 16 17 18 21 24^{3} 26^{3} 3:2 9^{2} 11^{2} 12 13 14 15 16^{2} 18^{3} 19^{2} 21^{2} 22^{3} 4:1 3 4 10 14 15 16^{2} 5:1 4 5^{2} 6 8 10^{2} 11 16^{2} 18^{2} 6:2^{2} 3^{3} 8 10^{3} 11 7:2 10 11 12 13 14

ECCL. 7:15^{2} 18^{2} 20 21 22 24 29 8:2 7 8^{3} 9 12^{2} 14^{2} 15 16^{2} 17^{2} 9:1^{2} 2^{4} 3^{2} 4 5 6 9 11 12^{2} 15 17 10:1 3^{2} 8 9 20 11:4^{2} 5 6 8 9 12:3 5 10 **CANT.** 1:7 2:7 14 15 3:3 4^{2} 5 6 4:1 2 5 16 5:2 7 8^{2} 9 6:1 5 9 10 13 7:3 9^{2} 8:1 4 5^{2} 10 12 13 **ISAIAH** 1:4 28 29 30 2:1 2 8 11 12^{2} 13 14 17 20 3:7 10 15 18 24 4:1 2 3 5:2 4 6 8^{3} 11^{3} 14 16 18 19^{2} 20^{3} 21 22 30 6:1 4 7:1 8 15 16 17^{2} 18^{3} 20 21

ISAIAH 7:22^{2} 23 25 8:6 11 17 19^{3} 21 9:2^{2} 9 13 15 16 10:1^{2} 2^{2} 12 14 15^{3} 19 20^{2} 24 27^{2} 32^{2} 11:10 11^{2} 16 12:1 4^{2} 21 25 32 13:3 8 14 15^{2} 14:3 6 16^{3} 17^{2} 19^{2} 26^{2} 28 29 15:7 9 16:2 3 12^{2} 13^{2} 14 17:4^{2} 5 7 8 9 12 14^{2} 18:2 19:3 7 8^{2} 9^{2} 10 13 16 17 18 19 21 23 24 20:1 6^{2} 21:3 10 14^{2} 22:1 2 3 7 8 9 11 12 16^{3} 20^{2} 25^{2} 23:1 2 13 15^{2} 16^{2} 17 18 24:6 8 9 10 18^{2} 21^{3} 25:7 9 11 26:1 2 5 17 20 27:1^{2} 2 5 6 7^{2} 9 11^{2} 12^{2} 13^{2}

ISAIAH 28:1 4 5 6^{2} 8 9 13 14 16 19 20^{2} 21 29:4 5 7^{3} 8 11^{2} 12 15 16^{2} 18 20 21^{2} 24^{2} 30:1^{3} 2 5 6 8 9^{2} 14^{2} 16 18^{2} 23^{2} 26 31:1 2 3^{2} 7 32:3^{2} 9 11 20^{2} 33:1 13^{2} 15^{4} 17 18 19 20 24 34:1^{2} 35:4 36:1 5 6 11 12^{2} 20^{2} 22 37:1 4 6 8 16 20^{2} 26^{2} 30 31 32 34 38 38:3 7^{2} 13 18 22 39:1 2^{2} 4^{2} 6^{3} 7 40:2^{2} 3 9^{2} 11 20^{4} 22^{2} 23 26^{2} 28 29 31 41:3 7^{3} 11^{2} 12^{2} 20^{2} 23^{2} 24 26^{3} 27 28 42:5^{5} 7 8 10^{2} 11 16^{2} 17^{2} 18 19^{2} 43:1^{2} 7 8^{2} 9 10^{2}

ISAIAH 43:12 13 25 26 44:2 3 7 8 9^{2} 10 13 18^{2} 20 24^{4} 25^{2} 26^{2} 27 28 45:3^{2} 6^{2} 9^{2} 10 15 16 18^{2} 19 20^{3} 21 23 24 46:5 10 11 12 47:7 8^{3} 13 48:4 8^{3} 9 16 17 18 49:5 6^{2} 9^{3} 10 15 17 19 20 23^{2} 25 26^{2} 50:2 4^{2} 6 7 8 9 10^{3} 11^{3} 51:1^{2} 2 6 7 9 10 12^{3} 13 14^{3} 15 16 18^{2} 22 23^{3} 52:5^{2} 6^{3} 7^{5} 11 53:2 15 54:1^{2} 9^{2} 10 16^{2} 17^{2} 55:1^{2} 2^{3} 5^{2} 10 11^{2} 13 56:2^{3} 3 4^{2} 5 6^{2} 8 11 57:1 11 13 15^{2} 19^{2} 58:2 5 6^{2} 7^{4} 12 59:1 2 5^{2} 15^{2} 16^{2} 20 21

ISAIAH 60:8 11 12 14^{2} 15 16 21 61:1 2 3^{3} 9^{2} 11 62:1 6 9^{2} 63:1^{3} 2 5 7 8 11^{2} 12 13^{2} 64:1 2 4 5^{2} 7^{2} 65:1^{3} 2 3^{2} 5 8 10 11^{6} 12 16^{2} 18 20 24 66:1 2 3^{4} 4 5^{3} 6 10^{2} 11^{2} 17 18 19^{3} 23 24 **JER.** 1:1 7 17 2:2 3 5 6^{3} 8^{2} 11 13 17 19^{2} 24^{2} 28 3:1 6 9 13 16 17 18 4:4 9^{2} 11 14 16 31^{3} 5:1^{2} 6 7 19 22 24 26 6:10 11 15^{2} 27 7:1^{2} 2 7 8 18 22 23^{2} 25 28 32 8:3 10 12 13 16^{2} 19 9:1^{2} 2^{2} 10 12^{3} 17^{3} 18 24^{3} 25

JER. 9:26[2], 10:4, 11, 18, 23[2], 25[2], 11:1, 3, 4, 5, 7, 13, 14, 17, 19[2], 20[2], 21[2], 12:1, 4, 14, 17, 13:4, 6, 11, 12, 13, 15, 20[2], 23, 24, 26, 14:1, 8, 9, 15, 18[2], 22, 15:4, 9, 10, 13, 15, 18, 16:3[3], 10, 12, 13, 14, 15[2], 21, 17:4, 5, 7, 8, 11, 13[2], 16, 18, 20, 23, 18:4, 8[2], 10, 14, 16, 19, 20, 19:2, 6, 7, 8, 9, 10, 11, 15[2], 20:1, 2, 3, 6, 12, 16, 17, 18, 21:2, 4, 7, 9[3], 12[2], 22:2[2], 5, 10, 13[2], 14, 21, 23, 25, 26, 30, 23:1, 2, 5, 7, 14, 16, 17[2], 24, 25, 26, 28[2], 29, 30, 31, 32, 34[2], 39, 24:2, 3

JER. 24:5, 7, 8[2], 10, 25:1[2], 3, 5, 7, 12[2], 13[2], 16, 23, 24, 30, 31, 33, 26:2, 3, 8[2], 12, 13, 15, 20, 24, 27:5, 8[3], 10, 11, 13, 14, 15[2], 16, 18, 19, 21, 22, 28:1, 3, 4, 5, 6, 7, 8, 9, 12, 14, 29:1, 2, 4, 6[2], 8, 10, 11, 16[4], 17, 25, 26[3], 31, 32, 30:1, 2, 3[2], 4, 7[2], 8[2], 13, 16[3], 19, 20, 21, 31:4, 6, 8, 10, 11, 17, 19[2], 24, 27, 28, 30, 31, 32[2], 33, 37, 38, 32:1, 7, 8[2], 9, 11[2], 12[2], 14, 23, 24, 29, 31[2], 35, 39, 40[2], 42, 33:2, 9[2], 10, 11[2], 13, 14[2], 15, 20, 21, 22, 24, 26, 34:7, 8[2], 9[2], 10[2]

JER. 34:13, 18, 20, 21, 35:7, 8, 10, 11, 14, 17, 18, 36:1, 2, 3[3], 6, 7, 8, 9[2], 13, 23[3], 24, 25, 27, 28, 31, 37:5, 7, 10, 11, 15, 18, 20, 21[2], 38:1, 2[2], 4, 5, 6, 7, 9, 14, 16[2], 19, 21, 22, 25, 26, 27, 28, 39:4, 9[4], 14, 16, 17, 40:1[2], 6, 7[2], 10, 11[4], 13, 14, 15, 41:1, 2, 3[2], 5, 7[2], 8, 9, 10[2], 11[2], 12, 13[2], 14, 16[2], 42:3[2], 10, 12, 16, 17[2], 19, 20, 22, 43:1, 3, 5, 6, 10, 13, 44:1, 2, 3[2], 4, 8[4], 10, 12, 13, 14[2], 15[3], 16, 20, 21, 22, 24, 25, 26[2], 27, 28[2], 29[3], 30[2], 45:1, 4[2], 46:7, 9[2], 10, 13, 25

JER. 46:26, 47:1[2], 2[2], 4[2], 48:9, 10[2], 12[2], 17[2], 18, 19[2], 20, 28[2], 35[2], 36, 41, 44[2], 45, 49:2[2], 4, 5[2], 8, 12, 13, 16[2], 17, 19[2], 20[2], 22, 26, 31, 32, 34, 37, 39, 50:1, 4, 5, 7, 10, 12, 13, 14, 16, 20, 21, 28, 29[2], 30, 31, 33, 34, 37, 44[3], 45[2], 51:1[2], 2, 3[2], 4, 7, 12, 13, 24, 31, 32, 39, 44, 46[2], 47, 48, 50, 52, 60[2], 62[2], 63, 64, 52:2[2], 3, 4, 14, 15[3], 17[2], 19, 20, 25[2], 31, 32

LAM. 1:1[2], 6, 7, 8, 10[2], 12, 16, 17, 21[3], 2:4, 13, 15[2], 16, 17[2], 19, 22[2], 3:1, 6, 7, 22, 25[2], 26, 27, 30, 37, 44, 57, 62, 4:5[2]

LAM. 4:6, 9[2], 12, 13, 14, 17, 18, 21, 5:8, 16

EZEKIEL 1:18, 23, 25, 26, 28[2], 2:2[2], 3, 5, 8, 3:1, 2, 3, 8, 10, 13, 15, 16, 21, 26, 27[2], 4:4, 9, 12, 14, 17, 5:5, 6, 7[2], 9, 13, 14[2], 15, 6:6, 7, 8[2], 9, 10[2], 12[3], 13, 14, 7:4, 7, 9[3], 13, 15[2], 16, 27, 8:1, 3, 4, 6[2], 9, 13, 17, 9:1, 4[3], 8, 10:1, 6, 7[2], 12, 15, 20[2], 11:2, 5, 10, 12[2], 13, 20, 24, 25, 12:4, 6, 10, 12[2], 14, 15, 16[2], 19[3], 20[2], 22[2], 25, 27[2], 13:2[2], 3, 6, 9[3], 11, 14[3], 15[2], 18[2], 19[3], 21, 22, 23[2], 14:4[2], 5, 7, 8[2], 9, 10, 11[2], 15[2], 17[2], 19

EZEKIEL 14:22[3], 23[2], 15:7, 16:5[2], 15, 21, 24, 25, 27, 31[2], 32, 33, 34, 37[3], 38, 44, 45, 46[2], 47, 52[2], 54[3], 57, 62, 63[2], 17:7, 8[3], 9, 14[2], 15[2], 16, 19[2], 20, 21[2], 24, 18:2, 4, 5, 8[2], 10[2], 11, 14, 15, 17[2], 18, 19, 20, 21[2], 22[2], 23[2], 24[4], 26, 27[2], 28, 32, 19:5, 9, 11, 14, 20:1, 6[2], 9, 12[3], 14, 15, 20[2], 22, 23, 24[3], 25, 26[5], 27, 32[2], 38[2], 42, 43, 44, 48, 21:4, 5[2], 7, 10, 11, 14, 15, 19, 20, 23[2], 26[2], 29, 22:3, 4, 5[2], 9, 10, 14, 16, 22, 24, 30[2], 23:7, 13, 14, 37, 40, 43, 44, 45, 48, 49, 24:8, 11[3], 19, 21, 24[2], 26[3], 27[2], 25:5

EZEKIEL 25:7, 10, 11, 12, 17, 26:1, 2[2], 6, 17[2], 18, 19, 20[3], 27:3, 7[2], 8, 27, 29, 28:3, 8, 9[2], 13, 14, 15, 17, 18, 19, 22, 23, 24[3], 25, 26[2], 29:3, 6, 9, 12[2], 15, 16, 18, 21[2], 30:5, 6, 7[2], 8, 9, 12, 20, 22, 25, 26, 31:1, 9[2], 14[3], 16[2], 17[3], 18, 32:1, 8, 15[3], 17, 18, 20, 21, 24, 25[2], 27, 28, 29[2], 30[2], 32, 33:5, 11, 12[2], 13, 14, 15, 16[2], 19, 21[2], 22, 24, 27[3], 28, 29, 30, 32, 33, 34:2, 3, 4[4], 10, 12[2], 16[4], 19[2], 27[2], 30[2], 35:4, 5, 7[2], 8, 9, 12, 15, 36:3, 4[2], 7, 11, 18, 23, 28, 30, 31, 33, 34, 35, 36[3], 38, 37:6

EZEKIEL 37:9, 13, 14, 25, 28, 38:7, 8, 10, 11[2], 12[3], 14, 16, 17, 18, 19, 20[3], 22, 23, 39:4, 6[2], 7, 9, 10[3], 11, 12, 13, 14, 15, 17[2], 21[2], 22[2], 26, 28, 40:1, 4[2], 6, 10[2], 12[2], 20, 21, 22, 24, 34, 37, 39, 41, 47, 48[2], 49, 41:6, 9[2], 11[2], 12, 17, 18, 19, 22, 42:1, 7, 8, 12, 13, 43:1, 3[2], 8, 10, 11[2], 19, 21, 44:3, 5, 7, 8, 9, 10, 14, 15, 17, 18, 22[2], 25, 27, 30, 31, 45:11, 13, 20[2], 22, 46:1, 2, 4, 8, 9[2], 12, 18, 20, 24, 47:2, 3, 5[2], 9, 12, 22[2], 48:9, 10, 11, 12, 15, 18, 19, 22, 23, 35

DANIEL 1:3, 5

DANIEL 1:8[2], 13, 16, 18, 20[2], 2:8, 9, 10[2], 11[2], 13, 16, 18[2], 21, 25, 28, 29, 30[3], 34[2], 35[2], 40, 45[2], 46, 47, 3:3[2], 5[2], 7[2], 8, 10[2], 11, 15[2], 17, 18, 19, 20, 28[2], 29[2], 4:1, 2, 6, 9[2], 17[2], 19, 20, 22, 25[2], 26[2], 30, 32, 34, 37, 5:2, 3, 5, 6, 13, 14[2], 15, 16, 17[3], 19, 21[2], 25, 29, 6:2, 7, 8, 10, 12[2], 13, 15[2], 17, 21, 22, 23, 25, 26, 7:7, 14[2], 16, 20[3], 22, 24, 8:1, 2, 4[2], 6, 7, 13, 21, 22, 9:2, 4[2], 7[3], 11[2], 12, 13, 15, 16, 17, 25, 26, 27, 10:1, 7, 11, 12, 16, 21[2], 11:3, 6[3], 16, 24, 26, 30, 31, 32, 33

DANIEL 11:36[2], 12:1[5], 2, 3[2], 5[2], 7[2], 11[2], 12

HOSEA 1:1, 2:3, 5[2], 6, 8, 10, 12, 16[2], 18, 21, 23, 4:3, 4, 6, 14, 5:9, 10, 6:5, 8, 7:2, 7, 8:3, 4, 9:4, 10, 12, 10:5, 10, 11, 11:3, 4, 12:8, 9, 13:2, 3[2], 8, 10, 14:7

JOEL 1:1, 4[3], 2:5, 11, 16, 17, 25, 26, 27[2], 28, 38, 3:1, 3, 6, 17, 18[2], 21

AMOS 1:5, 8, 13, 2:7, 13, 15[3], 16[2], 3:1, 12, 14[2], 4:1, 2[2], 13[2], 5:3[2], 8[2], 9[2], 10[2], 13, 14, 15, 18, 6:1, 3, 4, 5, 6, 7[2], 8, 9, 10[2], 7:2, 8:3[2], 4, 5, 8, 9[2], 11, 13, 14, 9:1[3], 5[2], 6[2], 8, 11[2], 12[2], 13[2]

OBADIAH 3[2], 7[2], 8, 9, 11[2], 12, 14[2], 20

JONAH 1:2, 4, 5, 6, 7, 10, 11, 12, 2:8, 9[2], 3:2[2], 8, 9, 10[3], 4:2, 6, 7, 8[2], 11

MICAH 1:1, 2, 4, 2:1, 4, 5, 6[2], 7[2], 8, 3:4, 5[3], 6, 9, 4:1, 6, 7[2], 11, 5:2, 3, 7, 10[2], 6:5, 10, 16, 7:3, 5, 10, 11[2], 12, 13, 18

NAHUM 1:5, 7, 11, 14, 15[2], 2:1, 3:4, 7[2], 8[2], 19

HABAK. 1:3, 6[2], 8, 13[2], 14, 2:2[2], 6[3], 7[2], 8, 9[3], 12, 13, 15[3], 17, 18[2], 19, 3:8, 16

ZEPH. 1:5[4], 6[2], 8, 9, 10[2], 11, 12, 15, 17, 18, 2:5, 15[3], 3:1, 6[3], 8[2], 9, 11[2], 16, 18, 19[4], 20[2]

HAGGAI 1:2, 6, 9, 11, 2:3, 5, 13, 14, 18, 22, 23

ZECH. 1:8, 9, 10, 11, 13, 14, 15, 19, 21, 2:3, 7, 8, 9, 11[2], 3:2, 4, 7, 8, 9[2], 10, 4:1[2], 4, 5, 9, 14, 5:3[4], 4, 5[2], 6, 7, 10, 6:4, 7, 8, 15[2], 7:1, 11, 13, 14, 8:9[3], 10, 13[2], 16, 17, 20, 23[3], 9:7, 8[2], 12, 16, 11:1, 5, 9[4], 10, 11[3], 13, 14, 16[5], 17, 12:3[2], 4, 6, 7, 8[3], 9[3], 10, 11, 14, 13:1, 2[2], 3[3], 4[2], 7, 8, 14:4, 6, 7, 8[2], 9, 12, 13[2], 15, 16[2], 17, 18[2], 19, 20, 21[2]

MALACHI 1:6, 7, 9, 10, 12, 2:4[2], 12[2], 13, 15, 16[2], 17, 3:3, 5[2], 10[2]

MALACHI 3:14[2], 15[2], 16[3], 17[2], 18[2], 4:1[3], 2, 3

MATT. 1:6, 20, 22, 2:2, 6, 8, 12, 15, 16[2], 17, 22, 23, 3:3, 9, 11, 4:3, 4, 12, 14, 17, 24[2], 5:4, 14, 15, 16, 17, 21, 22, 23, 27, 28, 29[2], 30[2], 32[2], 33, 38, 39, 42[2], 43, 44[2], 45, 6:1, 2, 4, 5, 7, 16, 18, 23[2], 29, 32, 7:1, 3[2], 6, 8[3], 11, 12, 13, 14, 19, 21[3], 23, 25, 26, 27, 8:4, 8, 10, 11, 16[2], 17, 24, 27, 28[2], 33, 34, 9:6[2], 12[3], 13, 16, 22, 26, 28, 30, 31, 38, 10:14, 15, 19, 20, 22, 25[2], 26[2], 27[2], 34, 37[2], 38, 39[2], 40[3], 41[2], 11:3, 8, 11[2], 15, 24, 28, 12:1

MATT. 12:2, 3, 5, 6, 10, 11, 16, 17, 22, 30[2], 36[2], 45, 48, 13:2, 12, 17, 19, 20[2], 22[2], 23[2], 28, 32, 35, 37, 39, 41, 44[2], 46, 47, 52, 53, 54, 14:1, 15, 20, 21, 33, 35[3], 36, 15:4, 11[2], 12, 17, 28, 30, 31, 37, 38, 16:1, 11, 12, 13, 14, 15, 18, 20[2], 21[2], 23[2], 17:10, 12, 13, 18, 24, 27[2], 18:6, 7[2], 10[2], 11, 12, 13[2], 14, 16, 19[2], 25, 27, 28, 31, 32[2], 34, 19:1, 4, 12, 13, 16, 17, 21, 22, 23, 28, 29, 30, 20:1, 7, 9, 10, 14, 21, 22[2], 23, 25[2], 30, 32, 33, 21:4, 9[3], 12[2], 15, 31, 32, 34, 45, 22:3, 16, 21, 23, 31, 34

MATT. 22:46, 23:3, 12, 13, 17, 18, 19, 21[2], 22[2], 26[2], 31, 35, 37, 39, 24:2, 4, 6, 13, 19[2], 20, 24, 32, 33, 36, 38[2], 43, 46, 47, 48, 50[2], 25:3, 9, 10, 16, 17, 18, 20, 22, 24, 25, 26, 29[3], 26:2, 4, 12, 13, 16[2], 17, 21, 23, 24[2], 29, 41, 46, 48[2], 52, 54, 55, 56, 57, 63, 68, 71, 73, 27:3, 4[2], 8, 9[2], 14, 15, 17, 18, 19, 20, 21, 24[2], 31, 33, 35, 39, 40, 46, 47, 54[2], 62, 63[2], 64, 28:2, 7, 10, 11

MARK 1:9, 14, 22, 27, 32[2], 34, 36, 38, 45, 2:1, 2, 8, 10[2], 11, 12, 15, 16, 17[2], 21, 23, 24, 25, 3:2, 9

MARK 3:10, 12, 14[2], 20, 24, 25, 29, 4:1, 8, 9, 10, 11, 12, 15, 22, 24, 25[3], 28, 31, 32, 37, 38, 40, 41, 5:4, 7, 10, 12, 14[2], 15, 16[2], 18[2], 23, 26, 29[2], 30, 32, 36, 38, 40, 43[2], 6:2, 5, 8, 10, 11, 12, 13, 14, 15[2], 20, 21, 22, 25, 36, 44, 55[2], 56, 7:2, 9, 11, 15[2], 18, 20[2], 26, 32, 34, 36, 8:8, 9, 21, 25, 27, 29, 30, 31, 32, 33[2], 9:1[2], 7, 9, 10, 11, 12, 13, 18, 23, 25, 26, 30, 31, 32, 33, 37, 39, 40, 42[2], 43, 45, 10:13[2], 17, 18, 22, 23, 24, 29, 31, 35, 36, 37, 38[2], 39[2], 42, 47, 48, 52[2], 11:3

MARK 11:5, 9[3], 10, 16, 23[2], 24, 25, 32, 12:2, 12, 14, 15, 17[2], 19, 26, 28, 34[2], 35, 41, 43, 44, 13:2, 11[3], 13, 14[2], 15, 16, 17[2], 18, 20, 24, 25, 28, 29, 30, 32, 14:4, 9, 12, 20, 21[2], 25[2], 28, 35, 42, 44[2], 47, 58, 69, 70, 72, 15:5, 6, 7, 9, 10, 11, 12, 29[2], 32[2], 35, 39, 42, 16:1, 4, 7, 10, 11, 12, 16[2], 17

LUKE 1:4, 7, 8, 19, 20, 21, 22, 23, 35, 41, 45, 49, 50, 57, 59, 61, 65, 66, 71[2], 74[2], 79, 2:1[2], 6[2], 18, 20, 23, 24, 26, 35, 38[2], 46, 47, 49[2], 3:7, 8, 11[3], 13, 20, 21, 4:3, 4, 6, 18, 20

LUKE 4:25, 29, 40, 41, 42, 45[2], 5:1, 3, 7[2], 9, 24[2], 29, 31[2], 36, 6:1, 4, 5, 6, 7, 12, 18, 21[2], 23, 24, 25[2], 28, 29[2], 30[2], 31, 32, 38, 40, 41[2], 42[3], 48, 49[3], 7:3, 4, 6, 9, 10[2], 11, 14, 15, 16[2], 19, 20, 21[2], 22, 28[2], 29, 36, 37, 39, 43, 49[2], 8:1, 8, 10, 12, 14, 15, 16, 17[2], 18, 22, 31, 34, 36, 38, 40, 41, 45, 46, 47, 53, 9:5[2], 7[3], 8[2], 10, 11, 12, 17, 18, 19, 20, 21, 32[2], 37, 39, 45[2], 48[2], 50, 51, 54, 57, 10:2, 9, 11, 12[3], 16[4], 20, 21[2], 23, 24, 31, 36, 37, 38, 40[2], 42, 11:1, 4, 10[3], 11, 13, 18

LUKE 11:23^2, 26, 27, 28, 33, 35, 38, 40^3, 44, 48, 50, 52, 54, 12:1, 2^2, 3, 4^3, 9, 10, 13, 26, 27, 30, 33^2, 36^2, 37, 39, 42, 43, 44^2, 45, 46, 47, 58, 51, 56, 58, 13:1^2, 2, 4^2, 9, 14, 17, 23, 32, 33, 34, 35, 14:1, 9, 10^3, 11, 12, 15^2, 17, 21, 23, 24, 29, 31, 32^2, 35, 15:4, 7^2, 10, 12, 14, 15, 16, 29, 31, 32, 16:1, 2, 4, 9, 10^3, 12^2, 15, 16, 18, 22, 24, 25, 26^2, 27, 28, 17:1, 2^2, 9^2, 10, 11, 12, 14, 15, 18, 24, 27, 29, 31^2, 34, 18:1, 3, 8, 9, 11, 12, 14^2, 15, 19, 22, 24^2, 26, 29, 31, 35, 37

LUKE 18:39, 41^2, 19:4^2, 7^2, 10, 11, 15^2, 21^2, 22^3, 23, 24^2, 26^3, 27, 32, 37, 38, 40, 43, 45^2, 20:1, 6, 7, 10, 14, 17, 18^2, 19, 20^2, 21, 27, 28, 35, 37, 40, 41, 21:3, 4, 6, 8, 20, 21, 22, 23^2, 30, 31, 34, 35, 36^2, 37^2, 22:8, 9, 21, 22, 23, 25, 26^3, 27^4, 30, 31, 32, 34^2, 36^2, 37^2, 40, 47, 63, 64, 70, 23:2, 7^2, 14, 23, 24, 25, 26, 29, 48^2, 49, 53, 54, 24:10, 12, 13, 15, 16, 17, 21, 23^2, 25, 33, 37, 39, 44, 45, 47

JOHN 1:3, 7, 8^2, 9^2, 12, 15, 21, 22^2, 25, 31, 33, 34, 39, 48, 2:9, 10, 14, 16, 17, 18

JOHN 2:20, 25, 3:2^2, 6^2, 7, 8, 11^2, 13, 15, 16^2, 17, 18^2, 19, 20, 21^3, 26, 28^2, 29, 31^3, 32, 33^2, 36^2, 4:1, 5, 9, 10, 11, 14^2, 15, 18, 19, 20, 24, 25, 26, 27, 29, 32, 34, 36^4, 37, 38, 39^2, 40, 42, 44, 45, 47^2, 50, 53, 54, 5:6^2, 10, 11, 12, 13^2, 15, 18, 20^2, 23^2, 24^2, 25, 28, 29^2, 32^2, 34, 36^3, 40, 42, 44, 45^2, 6:2^2, 5, 7, 11, 12, 13, 14^3, 15, 18, 22^2, 23, 24, 27, 28, 29, 30, 32, 35^2, 36, 37^2, 38, 39, 40^2, 42, 45, 46, 47, 48, 50, 51, 56, 57, 58^2, 61, 63^2, 64^2, 65, 66, 69^2, 71, 7:3^2, 4, 7, 16, 18^3, 23

JOHN 7:26, 28, 32, 33, 35, 36, 37, 38, 39^2, 42, 50, 8:5, 6, 7, 12, 16, 17, 18^2, 24^2, 25, 26, 27, 28^2, 29^2, 37, 38^2, 40, 47, 48, 50, 52, 54^2, 9:2, 3, 4, 8^2, 11, 13, 16, 17, 18^2, 22^2, 24^2, 25, 29, 30, 31, 32^2, 35, 36, 37, 39^2, 40, 10:1, 2, 8, 10^2, 12, 17, 21, 25, 33, 38^2, 41, 11:2, 4^2, 6, 7, 11^2, 13, 15, 16, 17, 20, 22, 24, 25, 27, 29, 30, 31, 37, 39, 40, 41, 42^3, 44, 49, 50^3, 51^3, 52^3, 56, 57^2, 12:2, 6, 9^2, 10, 11, 12^2, 13, 16^2, 17, 18^2, 20, 23, 25^2, 29^2, 34, 35, 36, 38, 39, 40, 44^2, 45^2, 46, 48^3

JOHN 12:50, 13:1, 3^2, 5, 10, 15, 16^2, 18^2, 19^2, 20^3, 21, 24, 27, 29^3, 34, 35, 14:3, 9, 10^3, 11, 12^2, 13^2, 16, 20^2, 21^3, 22, 24, 29, 31^2, 15:2^3, 5, 8, 11^2, 12, 13, 15, 16^3, 17, 18, 20, 21, 23, 25^2, 16:1, 2^2, 4^2, 5, 7, 13, 15^2, 17, 18, 19^2, 20, 21, 23, 24, 26^2, 27, 30^3, 32, 33, 17:1, 2, 3, 7, 8^2, 11, 12^2, 13, 15^2, 19, 21^4, 22, 23^3, 24^2, 25, 26, 18:4, 8, 9, 13, 14^2, 15, 16, 17, 28, 32, 36, 37^3, 39^2, 19:4^2, 8, 10, 11, 13^2, 21, 24, 27, 28^2, 31^4, 33, 35^3, 36, 38, 20:3, 7, 8, 9, 14, 18^2, 29, 31^3, 21:3, 4, 7^2, 12

JOHN 21:14^2, 15, 16, 17, 20, 22^2, 23, 24, 25^2

ACTS 1:1, 2, 4, 8, 16, 19^2, 21, 22^2, 25^2, 2:6, 14, 16, 20, 21, 24, 25, 29, 30^2, 31, 36^2, 39, 41, 44, 3:2, 10^2, 11, 17, 18, 19, 23^2, 24, 4:2, 5, 10, 13^2, 16^2, 17^2, 21, 23, 24^2, 29, 30, 32^2, 34^2, 5:5, 9, 15^2, 17, 21^2, 28, 32, 33, 40, 41, 6:2, 14, 15, 7:5, 6^2, 7, 12, 16, 19, 24, 25, 27, 36, 37, 38, 44^2, 45, 8:1, 4, 7^2, 8, 9, 11, 14, 15, 18, 19, 20, 24, 26, 31, 37, 39, 9:2, 12, 14, 17^2, 20, 21^4, 22, 23, 26, 27, 35, 37, 38^2, 43, 10:2, 7, 14, 15, 22

ACTS 10:27, 28^3, 33^2, 34, 35, 37, 38, 43^2, 45, 47, 11:1^2, 2, 9, 16, 17, 19, 22, 23, 26, 28, 12:1, 9, 10, 11, 15, 19, 25, 13:1^2, 16, 20, 27, 28, 29, 32, 33, 34, 38, 39, 40, 42, 46, 47, 14:1, 6, 9, 15^2, 17, 18, 21, 22, 27, 15:2, 4, 5, 7^2, 11, 17, 19, 20^2, 21, 24, 26, 29, 39, 16:2, 3, 4, 10, 12^2, 14, 19, 26, 27, 32, 38, 17:3^2, 6, 7, 11, 13, 22, 24^2, 27, 29, 31^2, 18:2, 5, 7, 14, 21, 28^2, 19:1, 4^2, 9, 10, 12, 16^2, 18, 22, 23, 25, 26^2, 27^2, 31, 34, 35^2, 36, 20:18, 20, 22, 23^2, 24, 25, 26, 29, 31, 34^2

ACTS 20:35, 38, 21:1, 4, 8, 11, 12, 21^2, 22, 23, 24^3, 25^2, 26, 28, 29, 31, 35, 38^2, 22:2, 6, 9^2, 11^2, 14^2, 17, 19^2, 20, 22, 24^2, 25^2, 26, 29, 23:2, 4, 5, 6, 8, 9, 12, 14, 15, 19, 20, 21, 22, 24, 27, 30, 34, 24:2^2, 4^2, 9, 10^2, 11^2, 14, 15, 21, 22, 23, 26^2, 25:3, 4^2, 16, 24, 25^2, 26, 26:5, 8, 9, 18^2, 20, 23^3, 26, 27, 29^2, 30, 27:1, 10, 13, 20, 24, 25, 27, 33, 43, 44, 28:1, 6, 8, 16, 17, 19, 20, 21, 22, 25, 28^2, 30

ROMANS 1:7, 8, 9, 11, 12^2, 13^2, 15, 16, 19, 20^2, 21, 26, 27^2, 32^2, 2:1^2, 2, 3^2, 4

ROMANS 2:8, 9, 10, 18, 19, 21^2, 22^2, 23, 28, 29, 3:2, 4, 8^2, 9, 11^2, 12, 19^2, 22, 24, 25, 26, 28, 4:1, 4, 5^2, 9, 11^3, 12, 13, 16^3, 18^2, 21, 23, 24, 5:3, 8, 12, 14^2, 16, 20, 21, 6:1, 2, 3, 4, 6^3, 7, 8, 9, 10^2, 12, 13, 16, 17^2, 7:1^2, 3^2, 4^2, 6^2, 13^3, 14, 15^3, 16^2, 17^2, 18^3, 19^2, 20^3, 21, 24, 8:3, 4, 5^2, 8, 9, 11^3, 16, 17^2, 18, 22, 24, 25, 27, 28^2, 29, 32, 33, 34^3, 37, 38, 9:2, 3, 8, 11^2, 16^3, 17^2, 20^2, 23, 26, 30, 32, 10:1, 2, 4, 6, 7, 8, 9^2, 12, 15, 19, 20^2, 11:7, 8^2, 10, 11, 19, 25^2, 31

ROMANS 11:32, 33^3, 34^2, 12:1, 2^2, 3^3, 6, 7, 8^4, 9, 15^2, 13:1, 2, 3, 4^2, 8, 11^2, 14:1, 2, 3^3, 4, 6^4, 9, 13, 14^2, 18, 22, 23, 15:1, 3, 4, 6, 8, 9, 12, 13, 14, 15, 16^2, 19, 21, 29, 30, 31^3, 32, 16:2^2, 5, 11, 18, 25

1 COR. 1:2^2, 5, 7, 8, 10^3, 11, 12, 14, 15, 18, 21^2, 26, 28, 29, 31^2, 2:5, 6^2, 9, 12^2, 15, 16, 3:7^3, 8^2, 11, 16, 18, 20, 4:2, 3, 4, 6^3, 7, 8, 9, 5:1^2, 2^2, 3, 5, 6, 7, 11, 12^2, 13, 6:2, 3^2, 5^2, 6, 8, 9, 15, 16, 17, 18^2, 19, 7:5^2, 7^2, 12, 13, 22^2, 25, 26, 29^2, 30^3, 31, 32^2

1 COR. 7:33^2, 34^2, 35^3, 36, 37^2, 38^2, 40, 8:1, 2, 4^3, 5, 9, 9:3, 9, 10^4, 13, 14, 15^2, 18^2, 19, 20^4, 21^3, 22^2, 23, 24^2, 25, 26^2, 10:1, 4, 12, 13^2, 19^2, 20^2, 25, 27, 28, 30, 33, 11:2, 3, 5^2, 13, 14, 17^2, 18, 19, 22, 23^2, 29, 32, 34, 12:2, 3^3, 11, 25^2, 28, 13:2, 10^2, 14:1, 2, 3, 4^2, 5^5, 11^3, 13^3, 16, 21, 22^3, 23^2, 24, 25, 27, 30, 31, 37^2, 15:3^2, 4^2, 5^2, 6, 7, 9, 12^2, 15^2, 20, 23, 26, 27, 28^2, 36, 37^2, 46^3, 48^2, 50, 54, 58, 16:2, 4, 6^2, 10, 11, 15^2, 16^2, 17, 18, 19

2 COR. 1:4, 7, 8, 9, 10, 11, 12, 14, 15, 17^2

2 COR. 1:23, 24, 2:1, 2, 3, 4^2, 5, 7, 8, 9, 15^2, 3:5, 7, 10^2, 11^2, 12, 13^2, 4:7, 10, 11, 14, 15, 5:1, 3, 4^3, 5, 6, 9, 10^2, 12, 14, 15^2, 19, 21, 6:1, 3, 15, 7:3, 6^2, 7, 8, 9^3, 11, 12^3, 16, 8:2, 4, 6^2, 7, 9^2, 11^2, 12^2, 13^2, 14^3, 15, 20, 9:2, 3, 4, 5^2, 8, 10, 10:2, 5, 7^2, 9, 11, 12, 15, 17^2, 18, 11:2, 3, 4, 7, 9, 12^3, 16, 17, 18, 28^2, 31, 12:4, 8, 9, 13, 19, 20, 21, 13:2, 5, 6^2, 7^3

GAL. 1:4, 6^2, 7, 8, 9, 11, 13, 16, 23, 2:2, 4^2, 5, 7, 8, 9^2, 10, 12, 13, 14, 16^2, 19, 3:1

GAL. 3:5, 7, 8, 10, 11, 12, 13, 14^2, 17^3, 22^2, 24, 25^2, 4:1, 5^2, 9, 15, 17, 21, 22, 27^2, 29^2, 5:2, 3^2, 7, 8, 10^2, 15, 17^2, 21, 24, 6:6^2, 7, 8^2, 13, 14

EPHES. 1:4, 10, 12, 13^2, 17, 18, 21^2, 23, 2:2, 7, 8, 10, 11^2, 12, 16, 17, 18, 3:3, 6, 8, 10, 13, 16, 17^2, 19, 20^3, 4:1, 9^2, 10^3, 14, 16, 17, 18, 21, 22, 24, 28^3, 29^2, 5:5, 13, 14, 15, 26, 27^2, 28, 33, 6:3, 5, 8, 9, 11, 12, 19^2, 20, 21, 22^2, 24

PHIL. 1:6, 9, 10^3, 12, 13, 17, 19, 20^2, 25, 26, 27^2, 28, 2:2, 10, 11^2, 15, 16^2, 19, 22, 24, 25

PHIL. 2:26, 28^2, 3:4, 8, 9, 10, 12^2, 18, 21, 4:2, 10, 11, 14, 15, 17, 22

COLOS. 1:9, 10, 16^2, 18, 19, 21, 24, 28, 2:1, 2, 14, 3:9, 10, 24, 25, 4:1^2, 3, 4, 5, 6, 8, 12, 13^2, 16^2, 17

1 THESS. 1:7^2, 8, 2:1, 2, 10, 12, 13, 16, 3:3^2, 4, 6, 10^2, 4:1, 3, 4, 6^2, 8, 9, 10, 11, 12^3, 13, 14, 15, 5:1, 2, 4^2, 7, 10, 14, 15, 21, 24, 27

2 THESS. 1:3, 4^2, 5, 6, 8^2, 10^2, 11, 12, 2:2^2, 3^2, 4^4, 5, 6, 8, 10^2, 11, 12, 3:1, 2, 4, 6^2, 8, 10, 11, 12^2, 14^2

1 TIM. 1:3^2, 8, 9, 10^2, 12, 15, 16, 18

1 TIM. 1:20, 2:1, 2^2, 8, 9, 3:4, 13, 15, 4:1, 8^2, 10, 14, 15, 16, 5:3, 4, 5, 6, 7, 14, 16^3, 17, 18, 20^2, 21, 25, 6:1, 2, 5, 9, 14, 17^2, 18^2, 19, 20

2 TIM. 1:3, 4, 5^2, 6, 12^3, 14, 15, 18^2, 2:1, 2, 4^2, 6, 8, 10, 14, 15, 18, 19^2, 22, 23, 25, 26, 3:1, 3, 8, 12, 15, 17, 4:8, 13, 16, 17^2

TITUS 1:2, 5^2, 9, 13, 14, 15, 16, 2:2, 3, 4, 5, 8^3, 10, 11, 12, 13, 14, 3:4, 7, 8^2, 10, 11^2, 13, 14, 15^2

PHILE. 6, 8, 12, 13, 14, 15, 18, 21, 22

HEB. 2:3, 6^2, 8^2, 9, 11, 14^3, 17

HEB. 2:18^2, 3:2, 4, 10, 16, 17, 18^2, 19, 4:2, 6, 10, 11, 13, 14^2, 16, 5:1, 2^2, 4, 5, 7^2, 9, 12, 13, 14, 6:7, 8, 9, 10, 11, 12, 18, 19, 7:2, 5^2, 6, 8^2, 11, 14, 15, 21, 25, 8:3, 4^2, 5, 7, 9, 10, 13^2, 9:4^2, 8, 9^2, 11, 15^2, 23, 25, 28, 10:2, 4, 9, 14, 15, 16, 20, 23, 26, 28, 30, 33, 34, 36, 37, 39, 11:3^2, 4, 5^2, 6^4, 13, 14^2, 15, 16, 17, 18, 19, 28, 31, 35, 40, 12:1, 2, 3, 10, 13, 17, 18^2, 19^2, 20, 21, 24^2, 25^4, 27^3, 13:3, 6, 9^2, 12, 15, 17^4, 19, 20^2, 21, 23, 24

JAMES 1:3, 4, 5, 6

JAMES 1:7^2, 9, 10, 12^2, 18, 2:3, 5, 7, 11, 12, 13, 19, 20, 24, 3:1, 3, 6, 17, 18, 4:1, 3, 4, 5^2, 17, 5:1, 11^2, 12, 13, 14, 16, 17^2, 20

1 PETER 1:4, 7, 10, 11, 12^2, 13, 18, 21^2, 22, 2:2, 3, 6, 9, 12, 14^2, 15, 21, 23, 24, 3:1, 3, 7, 9^2, 10^2, 12, 13, 15^2, 16^2, 17, 18, 20, 4:1, 2, 4, 5, 6^2, 11, 13, 15^2, 17^2, 19, 5:1, 4, 6, 9^2, 10, 12, 13, 14

2 PETER 1:1, 3^2, 4^2, 8, 9^2, 14, 15, 19^2, 20, 2:1, 4, 6, 8, 10, 12, 13, 14, 17, 18, 22, 3:2, 3, 4, 5, 6, 8, 9^2, 10^3, 11, 13, 14^2, 15

2 PETER 3:16^2

1 JOHN 1:1, 2, 3^2, 4, 5, 6, 8, 10, 2:1, 3, 4, 5, 6, 9, 10, 11^2, 13^2, 14, 15, 16, 17, 19^2, 21, 22^3, 23, 24, 25, 26, 27, 28, 29^2, 3:1, 2, 3, 5, 7, 8^2, 10, 11^2, 12, 14^2, 15, 19, 22, 23, 24^2, 4:2^2, 3^4, 4^2, 6^2, 7, 8, 9^2, 10^2, 13, 14, 15, 16^2, 17, 18, 20, 21, 5:1^4, 2, 3, 4, 5^3, 6^2, 7, 8, 10^3, 11, 12^2, 13^4, 14^2, 15^2, 16^2, 18^3, 19, 20^4

2 JOHN 1, 4, 5^2, 6^2, 7, 8^2, 9, 11, 12

3 JOHN 2, 3, 4, 7, 8, 10, 11^2, 12

JUDE 1, 3, 5^2, 15, 18, 24

REV. 1:2, 3^2, 5

REV.
1:9
12
18
2:1
6
7^2
10
11^2

REV.
2:14
15
17^3
20
22
23
25
26

REV.
2:29
3:1^3
2
5
6
7^4
9
10

REV.
3:11^2
12
13
15
17
18^4
21
22

REV.
4:3
9
10^2
5:1
7
12
13^2
14

REV.
6:2
4^3
5
8
9
10
11^2
16

REV.
7:1
15
8:3
9:4
5^2
17
20

REV.
10:6^4
11:1
6
7
10^2
18^3
12:6

REV.
12:9
12^2
13
14
15
13:6
8

REV.
13:10^2
13
14^3
15^2
17^2
18
14:3

REV.
14:6
7
8
12
13
15
16

REV.
14:18
15:2
4
16:12
14
15
17:1

REV.
17:7
8^3
11
14
18
18:4^2
10

REV.
18:14
16^2
19^2
21
24
19:4
5

REV.
19:8
10
11
12
15
17
18^2

REV.
19:19
20^3
21
20:2
3^2
4
6

REV.
20:10
11
21:5
6
7
10
15

REV.
21:17
27
22:7
11^3
14^2
17^2
18^2

the

3588

GEN.
1:1^3
2^6
4^3
5^5
6^4
7^5
8^4
9^3
10^3
11^4
12^2
13^2
14^4
15^3
16^5
17^3
18^4
19^3
20^4
21
22^3
23^3
24^3
25^3
26^7
27
28^6
29^4
30^3
31^3
2:1^3
2^2
3
4^7
5^6
6^3
7^4
8^2
9^7
10
11^3
12^2
13^4
14^4
15^3
16^3
17^3
18^2
19^5
20^3
21^2
22^3
25
3:1^5
2^5
3^4
4^2
5
6^4
7
8^9
9
10
11
12^3
13^4
14^4
15
16
17^4
18^2
19^2
20
21
22^3
23^3
24^5
4:1
2
3^3
4^3
6
7
8
9
10^2
11
12^2
13
14^3
15^2
16^4
17^3
19^4
20
21^2
22
26^2
5:1^4
2
4
5
8
11
14

GEN.
5:17
20
23
27
29^2
31
6:1^2
2^2
3
4^4
5^3
6^2
7^6
8^2
9
11^2
12^2
13^3
14^2
15^5
16^4
17^3
18
19
20
7:1^2
2^2
3^5
4^3
5
6^2
7^3
8
9^3
10^3
11^8
12^2
13^4
14^2
15^2
16
17^6
18^4
19^4
20^2
21^2
22^2
23^7
24^2
8:1^4
2^4
3^5
4^5
5^7
6^3
7^2
8^3
9^7
10^2
11^4
12
13^{10}
14^4
16
17^3
19^2
20^2
21^4
22
9:1
2^7
3
4^2
5^4
6
7
10^5
11^2
12^2
13^2
14^3
15
16^4
17^3
18^3
19^2
21
22^2
23
26
27
28
29
10:1^3
2
3
4
5^2
6
7^2
8
9^3
10^2
11
12

GEN.
10:16^3
17^3
18^5
19^2
20
21^4
22
23
25^2
29
30
31
32^5
11:1
2^2
4^2
5^4
6^2
8^4
9^6
10^2
27
28^2
29^5
31^3
32
12:1
3
4
5^3
6^5
7^2
8^6
9
10^2
12
14^2
15^2
17
13:1
3^3
4^5
6
7^5
9^5
10^5
11^3
12^3
13^2
14
15
16^4
17^3
18
14:1
2
3^2
4
5^5
6^2
7^3
8^7
9
10^3
11
13^3
15
16^3
17^5
18^2
19
20
21^3
22^4
24^3
15:1^2
2
4^2
5
6
7^2
10^2
11^2
12
16^3
17
18^5
19^3
20^3
21^4
16:2^2
3^2
5
7^5
8
9^2
10^2
11^3
12
13^2
14
17:1^2
8^2
11^2
12

GEN.
17:14
21
23^3
24
25
26
27^3
18:1^5
2^2
4
6^2
7
8^2
9
10^2
11
13
14^3
16^2
17
18^2
19^3
20^2
21
22^2
23^2
24^3
25^6
26^3
27
28^2
30
31
32
33
19:1^2
2
4^5
5
6^2
8
9^2
10^3
11^4
12^2
13^3
14
15^4
16^5
17^2
19
21
22^2
23^2
24^2
25^4
27^3
28^5
29^6
30
31^5
33
34^3
35
36
37^2
38^4
20:1
3
5
6
7
8^2
11
12^2
16
18^3
21:1^2
2
3
8^2
9^2
10
11
12
13^2
14^3
15^4
16^2
17^5
18
19^2
20^2
21^2
22
23^2
28
32^3
33^3
34
22:2^2
3^4
4^2
5^2
6^3

GEN.
22:9^4
10
11^2
12
13^2
14^3
15^3
16^2
17^5
18^2
21
23:1^2
2^2
3
5
6
7^3
8
9^2
10^5
11^4
12^2
13^4
15
16^4
17^6
18^3
19^4
20^8
24:1
3^6
5^3
7^2
8
9^2
10^4
11^4
13^4
14^2
15
16^2
17
20^2
21^2
22^2
24^2
26^2
27^4
28
29^2
30^6
31^3
32^4
35
37^2
39
40
42
43^2
44^3
45
46
47^3
48^3
49^2
50^2
51
52^2
53
54^2
55^2
56
57
60^2
61^3
62^3
63^3
64
65^3
66
25:3
4^2
6^3
7^2
8
9^4
10^2
11^2
12^2
13^3
16
17^3
18
19
20^4
21^2
22^2
23^5
25
27^2
29
32
26:1^4
2^2
3

GEN.
26:4^3
7^4
8
10
12^2
13
14
15^3
17
18^5
19
20^4
21
22^3
24^3
25^2
26
28
29^2
31
32^2
33^2
34^4
27:2
3
5
7
9^2
15
16^4
17^3
20
22^3
27^4
28^3
30
34
39^3
40
41^2
46^4
28:1
2^2
4^2
5^2
6
8
9^3
11^2
12^3
13^4
14^3
16
17^2
18^3
19^3
21
22
29:1^3
2^3
3^6
5
6
7^2
8^4
10^5
13
14
16^4
20
22^2
23
25
26^2
27
31
32
33
35
30:2^2
13
14^2
16^2
17
19
24
27
30
32^5
33^2
35^5
36
37^3
38^5
39^2
40^6
41^6
42^3
43
31:1
2
3^2
4
5
8^4

GEN.
31:9
10^4
11
12^2
13^3
16
18^2
19
20
21^2
22
23
24
25^2
26
29^2
33
34^3
35^2
38
39
40^3
42^4
46
48
49
53^4
54^2
55
32:1
2
3^2
6
7^3
8^2
9
10^3
11^4
12^2
16
17
19^3
20
21^2
22
23
24^2
25^2
26
30^2
31
32^6
33:1^2
2
3
5^3
6
8
10
13^3
14^2
15^2
17^2
18^2
19^2
34:1^3
2^3
3^3
5
6
7^3
8
10
12
13
19^3
20^2
21^2
22
24^2
25^4
26^2
27^3
28^2
29
30^4
35:1
2
3^2
4^2
5^3
6^2
7^2
8
12^2
13
14
15^2
17
19
20
21
22
23
24

GEN.
35:25
26^2
27
28
29
36:1
2^6
5^2
6^4
7
9^3
10^5
11
12
13^2
14^3
15^3
16^3
17^4
18^3
19
20^3
21^4
22
23
24^4
25^2
26
27
28
29^2
30^2
31^3
32^2
33
34
35^3
37
38
39^4
40^2
43^4
37:1^2
2^5
3
5
7
8
9^3
10
11
13
14^2
15^2
17
22
24
27
28^2
29^2
30
31^3
32
35
36^2
38:7^3
9^2
10^2
12^2
14
16
17
19
20^4
21^3
22^2
24
25^2
27
28^2
30
39:1^3
2^3
3^2
5^7
6
8
11^3
14
17
19
20^3
21^4
22^5
23^4
40:1^3
2^4
3^5
4^2
5^5
6
7
9
10^2
11^2

GEN.
40:12^2
13
15^3
16^2
17^3
18^2
19
20^4
21^2
22
23
41:1^2
2
3^4
4^2
5
6
7^2
8^3
9
10^3
11
12^2
14
17^2
18
19
20^3
21
23
24^3
25
26^3
27^3
28
29
30^4
31^2
32^2
33
34^4
35^3
36^5
37^3
38
40
41
43^3
44
45^2
46^2
47^2
48^8
49^2
50^2
51^2
52^3
53^2
54^3
55^3
56^7
57
42:5^3
6^5
7
9^3
12^2
13^3
15
16
18
19^2
21
22
25
26
27
29
30^4
32^2
33^4
34
35
38^3
43:1^2
2
3
5
6
7^2
8
9
11^3
12^2
13
14
15
16
17^3
18^3
19^3
20
21^2
23
24^2

GEN.
43:25
26^3
27
32^3
33^3
44:1^2
2^4
3^2
4^2
8^2
11
12^2
13
14
16^2
17^2
22
24
26
28
29
30^2
31^3
32^2
33^2
34^2
45:2^2
6^3
7
8
10
12
16
17
18^4
19
20^2
21^3
23^2
24
25
26
27^3
46:1
2^2
3
5^2
6
8^2
9
10^2
11
12^3
13
14
15^2
16
17^2
18
19
20^2
21
22^2
23
24
25^2
26^2
27^3
28
31
32
34^2
47:1^2
4^4
6^4
9^8
11^4
13^5
14^5
15^4
17^4
18^2
19
20^4
21^3
22^3
23^2
24^3
25
26^4
27^2
28^2
29
31
48:2
3
5
6
7^4
10
12
14^2
15
16^5
17

GEN.
48:18
21
22^2
49:1
3^3
8
9
10^3
11^3
13^2
16
17^3
19
22
24^5
25^5
26^7
27^3
28
29^3
30^5
32^4
33^2
50:2^2
3^2
4^2
5
7^4
8^2
10
11^6
13^5
15
17^4
19
23^3
24
25

EXOD.
1:1^2
5^2
7^2
9^2
10
12^3
13^2
14
15^6
16^3
17^3
18^3
19^4
20^2
21
22
2:1
2
3^3
5^5
6^3
7^2
8^2
9^2
10^2
12^2
13^3
14
15^2
16^2
17
19^3
20
21
23^4
25
3:1^6
2^5
3
4^3
5
6^4
7^2
8^9
9^4
10
11
12
13^2
14
15^5
16^3
17^8
18^5
19
20
21^2
22
4:1
2
3^2
4^2
5^4
6
8^4

EXOD.
4:9^7
10
11^5
13
14^3
16
19^2
20^2
21^2
22
24^3
25
26
27^3
28^3
29^2
30^5
31^3
5:1^2
2^2
3^5
4^2
5^2
6^3
7
8
9
10^3
12^2
13
14^2
15
16
17
18
19^2
20
21^3
22
6:1
2
3
4^2
5^3
6^4
7^3
8^3
9
10
11
12^2
13^4
14^4
15^3
16^4
17
18^3
19^2
20^2
21
22
24^3
25^4
26^3
27
28^3
29^2
30
7:1
2
3
4^2
5^3
6
8
10
11^3
13
14^2
15^4
16^3
17^5
18^6
19^3
20^8
21^7
22^2
24^4
25^2
8:1^2
3^2
4
5^5
6^3
7^2
8^4
9^2
10
11
12^2
13^6
15
16^4
17^5
18

EXOD.
8:19^3
20^4
21^3
22^5
24^5
25
26^5
27^2
28^2
29^4
30
31
32
9:1^3
3^6
4^4
5^3
6^5
7^4
8^4
9^2
10
11^5
12^3
13^4
14
15
16
18
19^3
20^4
21^3
22^4
23^5
24^2
25^6
26^2
27
28
29^5
30
31^5
32^2
33^5
34^3
35^3
10:1^2
2^2
3^2
4
5^6
6^5
7^2
8
9
10
11
12^6
13^5
14^3
15^{11}
16
17
18
19^4
20^2
21^2
22
23
24
25
26^2
27
11:1
2^2
3^9
4^2
5^7
6
7^3
8
9^2
10^2
12:1^2
2^3
3^3
4^5
5^3
6^5
7^4
8
9
10^2
11
12^5
13^5
14
15^3
16^2
17^2
18^5
19^2
21^2
22^8
23^8

EXOD.
12:25^2
27^7
28^2
29^8
30^2
31^2
33^3
34
35^3
36^5
37
39
40^2
41^6
42^4
43^3
46^2
47
48^3
49
50^2
51^4
13:1
2^3
3^3
4
5^7
6^2
8
9^2
11^3
12^4
13
14^2
15^8
16
17^5
18^6
19^2
20^2
21^2
22^4
14:1
2^3
3^3
4^2
5^4
7
8^4
9^3
10^4
11
12^4
13^4
14
15^2
16^4
17^2
18^2
19^4
20^6
21^5
22^5
23^3
24^8
25^4
26^4
27^8
28^5
29^4
30^5
31^5
15:1^5
2
3^2
4^2
5^2
6
7
8^6
9^2
10^2
11
12
13
14^2
15^3
16^2
17^3
18
19^8
20^3
21^3
22^3
23^2
24
25^4
26^4
27
16:1^6
2^3
3^6
4^2
5
6^3

EXOD.
16:7^4
8^6
9^3
10^6
11
12^4
13^5
14^5
15^3
16^3
17
19
20
21
22^3
23^5
24
25^2
26^2
27^2
28
29^5
30^2
31^3
32^5
33
34^2
35^3
36
17:1^6
2^2
3^2
4
5^4
6^5
7^6
9^3
10^2
12^6
13^2
14^3
15
16^2
18:1^2
3^2
4^4
5^2
7
8^5
9^4
10^7
11^2
12
13^5
14^3
15
16
17
19^2
20^2
21
22^2
24
25
26^2
19:1^5
2^3
3^4
4
5
6^2
7^3
8^5
9^5
10^2
11^5
12^4
13^2
14^3
15^2
16^7
17^4
18^4
19^2
20^6
21^3
22^3
23^3
24^4
25
20:2^3
4^3
5^5
7^3
8
10^3
11^5
12^2
18^7
20
21^2
22^2
21:1
2
4

EXOD.
21:5
6^2
7
9
19
22^2
26^2
28^3
29^2
30
32^2
34^4
35^3
36^2
22:3
4
5^2
6^4
7^2
8^4
9^3
11^2
12
14
15
17
20
21
24
26
28^2
29^2
30
31^2
23:1
5
6
7^2
8^4
9^2
10
11^4
12^3
13
14
15^3
16^7
17^2
18^3
19^4
20^2
23^6
25^2
26
27
28^3
29^3
30
31^7
24:1^2
2^2
3^7
4^5
5^2
6^3
7^5
8^5
9
10^2
11^2
12^2
13
14
15^2
16^6
17^7
18^4
25:1
2
3
6
7^2
9^4
10^3
12^3
14^5
15^3
16
17^2
18^2
19^6
20^5
21^4
22^5
23^3
25
26^3
27^4
28^2
29
30
31^2
32^5
33^3
34

EXOD.
25:35^5
36
37
38^2
40
26:1
2^3
3
4^7
5^6
6^2
7
8^3
9^3
10^6
11^3
12^6
13^7
14
15
16
17^2
18^3
19
20^3
22^2
23^3
24^2
26^3
27^7
28^3
29^3
30^3
32
33^8
34^4
35^9
36^2
37
27:1^2
2^3
3
4^2
5^5
6
7^5
8
9^4
10^3
11^3
12^3
13^3
14^2
15
16^2
17^2
18^4
19^6
20^3
21^7
28:1^2
3^2
4^2
6
7^2
8^4
9^2
10^3
11^5
12^5
14^3
15^3
16^2
17^2
18
19
20
21^5
22^2
23^4
24^4
25^5
26^5
27^6
28^8
29^5
30^7
31^2
32^4
33^2
34^2
35^2
36^2
37^2
38^4
39^3
41
42^2
43^4
29:1^2
3^3
4^3
5^8
6^3
7

EXOD.
29:9^2
10^4
11^5
12^7
13^7
14^3
15^2
16^2
17^3
18^4
19^3
20^3
21^4
22^{10}
23^3
24^3
25^3
26^3
27^6
28^4
29
30^3
31^3
32^7
33
34^5
36
37^2
38^2
39^3
40^3
41^5
42^4
43^2
44^4
45
46^3
30:2^5
3^3
4^4
5
6^5
7
8^2
10^5
11
12^3
13^4
14
15^3
16^7
17
18^3
20^4
22
24^2
25^2
26^4
27^3
28^2
30
31
32
34
35^2
36^3
37^3
31:1
2^3
3
6^3
7^7
8^3
9^2
10^6
11^2
12
13^2
14
15^4
16^3
17^3
18
32:1^5
2^2
3^2
4
5
6^2
7^2
8^2
11^2
12^4
13
14^2
15^6
16^5
17^3
18^3
19^5
20^4
22^2
23^2
24
25

EXOD.
32:26[4], 27[2], 28[3], 29, 30[3], 31, 33, 34[3], 35[3], 33:1[4], 2[6], 3[2], 4, 5[3], 6[2], 7[9], 8[3], 9[5], 10[4], 11[4], 12, 16[3], 17, 19[2], 21, 22, 34:1[4], 2[4], 3[2], 4[4], 5[4], 6[3], 7[7], 8, 10[4], 11[6], 12[3], 14, 15[2], 18[4], 19, 20[2], 21, 22[4], 23[3], 24[3], 25[5], 26[4], 27[2], 28[5], 29[3], 30[2], 31[2], 32[2], 34[3], 35[4], 35:1[4], 2[2], 3, 4[4], 5[2], 8[2], 9[2], 10, 11, 12[5], 13[2], 14[4], 15[7], 16, 17[5], 18[4], 19[6], 20[3], 21[5], 22, 24[2], 25, 26, 27[3], 28[3], 29[4], 30[5], 31, 32, 33, 34[2], 35[4], 36:1[4], 2[2], 3[5], 4[3], 5[4], 6[4], 7[2], 8[2], 9[3], 10, 11[4], 12[5], 13[2], 14[2], 15[3], 17[6], 18, 19, 20, 21[2], 22[2], 23[2], 24, 25[3], 27[2], 28[3], 29[2], 31[3], 32[6]

EXOD.
36:33[4], 34[3], 37, 38, 37:1[4], 3[3], 5[5], 6[3], 7[2], 8[5], 9[5], 10[4], 12, 13[3], 14[5], 15[2], 16[2], 17[3], 18[5], 19[3], 20, 21[4], 22, 24, 25[6], 26[3], 27[4], 28, 29[4], 38:1[4], 2[4], 3[8], 4[2], 5[3], 6, 7[5], 8[7], 9[4], 10[2], 11[4], 12[3], 13, 14[3], 15[2], 16[2], 17[7], 18[8], 19, 20[3], 21[8], 22[4], 23, 24[8], 25[4], 26[2], 27[5], 28[2], 29[2], 30[8], 31[8], 39:1[4], 2, 3[5], 4, 5[4], 6, 7[4], 8[3], 9[3], 10[2], 11, 12, 13, 14[5], 15[2], 16[3], 17[4], 18[5], 19[5], 20[6], 21[8], 22[2], 23[4], 24[2], 25[5], 26[3], 29, 30[4], 31[2], 32[6], 33[2], 34[4], 35[4], 36[3], 37[5], 38[5], 39[2], 40[9], 41[5], 42[3], 43[2], 40:1, 2[5], 3[4], 4[4], 5[7], 6[6], 7[4], 8[3], 9[3], 10[3], 11, 12[3], 13[2], 15, 16, 17[5]

EXOD.
40:18[3], 19[5], 20[6], 21[7], 22[6], 23[3], 24[5], 25[3], 26[4], 27, 28[3], 29[8], 30[4], 32[4], 33[6], 34[5], 35[6], 36[3], 37[2], 38[5]

LEVIT.
1:1[3], 2[5], 3[5], 4[2], 5[9], 6, 7[5], 8[7], 9[3], 10[3], 11[5], 12[4], 13[5], 14[2], 15[6], 16[4], 17[6], 2:1, 2[8], 3[4], 4, 7, 8[4], 9[4], 10[3], 11, 12[4], 13[2], 14[2], 16[6], 3:1[2], 2[7], 3[6], 4[6], 5[5], 6[2], 7, 8[5], 9[10], 10[6], 11[5], 12, 13[6], 14[5], 15[6], 16[6], 17, 4:1, 2[3], 3[4], 4[8], 5[4], 6[6], 7[15], 8[7], 9[6], 10[5], 11[2], 12[4], 13[6], 14[5], 15[7], 16[5], 17[4], 18[13], 19, 20[3], 21[4], 22[2], 23, 24[5], 25[7], 26[4], 27[3], 28, 29[5], 30[7], 31[7], 32, 33[4], 34[8], 35[10], 5:1, 2, 3, 6[4], 7[2], 8[2], 9[8], 10[3], 11, 12[5], 13[3], 14, 15[6]

LEVIT.
5:16[7], 17[2], 18[4], 19, 6:1, 2, 4, 5[3], 6[3], 7[2], 8, 9[8], 10[6], 11[2], 12[6], 13[2], 14[5], 15[8], 16[5], 17[2], 18[4], 19, 20[5], 21[3], 22[2], 23, 24, 25[6], 26[5], 27[3], 28, 29[2], 30[5], 7:1[2], 2[5], 3[4], 4[6], 5[3], 6[2], 7[3], 8[4], 9[5], 10, 11[3], 12, 13[2], 14[5], 15[4], 16[4], 17[4], 18[4], 19[2], 20[4], 21[5], 22, 23, 24[3], 25[4], 28, 29[5], 30[6], 31[4], 32[3], 33[5], 34[6], 35[8], 36[3], 37[8], 38[5], 8:1, 2[3], 3[4], 4[5], 5[3], 7[6], 8[4], 9[5], 10[2], 11[3], 12, 13, 14[5], 15[7], 16[6], 17[3], 18[4], 19[2], 20[4], 21[6], 22[3], 23[4], 24[6], 25[8], 26[4], 27, 28[3], 29[4], 30[3], 31[6], 32[2], 33[4], 34, 35[5], 36[2], 9:1[2], 2, 3[3], 4[2], 5[4], 6[4], 7[5], 8[3], 9[8], 10[7], 11[3], 12[3], 13[4]

LEVIT.
9:14[4], 15[5], 16[2], 17[4], 18[5], 19[8], 20[4], 21[3], 22[3], 23[6], 24[5], 10:1, 2[2], 3[2], 4[4], 5, 6[4], 7[6], 8, 9[2], 11[4], 12[4], 13[3], 14[3], 15[6], 16[3], 17[5], 18[3], 19[4], 11:2[4], 3[3], 4[5], 5[3], 6[3], 7[3], 9[4], 10[4], 12, 13[4], 14[2], 16[4], 17[3], 18[3], 19[4], 20, 22[4], 24[2], 25[2], 26[3], 27, 28[2], 29[5], 30[5], 31, 32, 38, 39[2], 40[4], 41, 42[2], 44[2], 45[2], 46[5], 47[3], 12:1, 2[3], 3[2], 4[3], 5, 6[6], 7[3], 8[4], 13:1, 2[5], 3[9], 4[6], 5[6], 6[6], 7[4], 8[4], 9[2], 10[5], 11[2], 12[5], 13[3], 15[3], 16[2], 17[4], 18[2], 19[3], 20[5], 21[3], 22[2], 23[2], 24[2], 25[7], 26[4], 27[5], 28[5], 29[2], 30[5], 31[7], 32[6], 33[3], 34[7], 35[2], 36[4], 37[3], 38, 39[4], 40, 41, 42, 43, 44, 45[2], 46[3]

LEVIT.
13:47[2], 48, 49[6], 50[3], 51[7], 52[2], 53[5], 54[3], 55[5], 56[7], 57[4], 58[3], 59[3], 14:1, 2[4], 3[5], 4, 5[2], 6[8], 7[3], 8, 9, 10[2], 11[6], 12[3], 13[8], 14[8], 15[3], 16[4], 17[9], 18[6], 19[3], 20[5], 22[2], 23[6], 24[6], 25[9], 26[3], 27[3], 28[9], 29[5], 30[3], 31[5], 32[2], 33, 34[3], 35[3], 36[7], 37[5], 38[5], 39[5], 40[4], 41[3], 42[2], 43[4], 44[4], 45[6], 46[3], 47[2], 48[7], 49, 50[2], 51[8], 52[8], 53[4], 54, 55, 57, 15:1, 2, 4, 5, 6[2], 7[3], 8[2], 9, 10[2], 11[2], 12[2], 14[6], 15[5], 16, 17[2], 18[2], 19, 21, 22, 23, 24, 25[5], 26[3], 27, 29[5], 30[6], 31, 32, 33[2], 16:1[4], 2[7], 3, 4[3], 5[3], 6, 7[5], 8[4], 9[2], 10[5], 11[4], 12[3], 13[7], 14[5], 15[8], 16[6], 17[4], 18[8], 19[3], 20[5]

LEVIT.
16:21[8], 22[3], 23[4], 24[4], 25[3], 26[3], 27[7], 28, 29[3], 30, 32[5], 33[7], 34[2], 17:1, 2[3], 3[3], 4[6], 5[9], 6[9], 8[2], 9[3], 10[2], 11[6], 12, 13[3], 14[7], 15, 18:1, 2[2], 3[4], 4, 5, 6, 7[2], 8, 9[2], 10, 11, 12, 13, 14, 15, 16, 17, 18, 21[3], 24, 25[3], 27[3], 28[2], 29, 30, 19:1, 2[3], 3, 4, 5, 6[4], 7, 8[2], 9[3], 10[2], 12[2], 13[2], 14[3], 15[4], 16[2], 18[2], 21[4], 22[5], 23[2], 24[3], 25[4], 26, 27[2], 28[2], 29[2], 30, 31, 32[4], 34[3], 36[2], 37, 20:1, 2[5], 4[3], 6, 7, 8, 10[3], 11, 15, 16[2], 17, 18, 19, 22, 23[2], 24, 25, 26, 21:1[4], 5, 6[4], 8[2], 9[2], 10[3], 12[5], 15, 16, 17, 21[5], 22[3], 23[3], 24, 22:1, 2[3]

LEVIT.
21:3[4], 4[3], 6[2], 7[2], 8, 9, 10[3], 11, 12[2], 13, 14[4], 15[3], 16[2], 17, 18[4], 19[3], 21, 22[3], 24, 25, 26, 27[3], 29, 30[3], 31, 32[2], 33[2], 23:1, 2[3], 3[4], 4[2], 5[3], 6[4], 7, 8[2], 9, 10[5], 11[5], 12[3], 13[4], 14, 15[5], 16[3], 17[2], 18[4], 19[2], 20[7], 21, 22[5], 23, 24[4], 25, 26, 27[2], 28, 30, 32[2], 33, 34[4], 35, 36[3], 37[3], 38[3], 39[7], 40[5], 41[3], 43[3], 44[3], 24:1, 2[3], 3[7], 4[3], 6[2], 7[2], 8[2], 9[3], 10[4], 11[5], 12[2], 13, 14[2], 15, 16[7], 22[2], 23[4], 25:1, 2[4], 3, 4[3], 5[2], 6[2], 7[2], 8[2], 9[6], 10[3], 11, 12[3], 13, 15[4], 16[7], 17, 18, 19, 20, 21, 22[3], 23[2], 24[2], 26, 27[4], 28[3], 30[4], 31[5], 32[5], 33[8], 34[2], 38[3]

LEVIT.
25:40, 41, 42, 44, 45[2], 46, 47[3], 50[5], 51[2], 52[2], 53, 54, 55[3], 26:1, 2, 4[3], 5[4], 6[3], 7, 8, 10[2], 13[3], 16[2], 19, 20[2], 25[4], 26, 29[2], 30, 31, 32, 33, 34[2], 36[2], 38[2], 39, 40, 41[2], 42, 43[2], 44[2], 45[5], 46[4], 27:1, 2[3], 3[3], 5[2], 6[2], 7, 8[3], 9[2], 10, 11[2], 12[2], 14[3], 15[2], 16[2], 17, 18[6], 19[3], 20[2], 21[5], 22[2], 23[6], 24[5], 25[3], 26[4], 28[3], 30[8], 31, 32[6], 33, 34[3]

NUM.
1:1[8], 2[5], 4, 5[4], 6, 7, 8, 9, 10[3], 11, 12, 13, 14, 15, 16[3], 18[6], 19[2], 20[4], 21, 22[4], 23, 24[4], 25, 26[4], 27, 28[4], 29, 30[4], 31, 32[4], 33, 34[4], 35, 36[4], 37, 38[4], 39, 40[4], 41, 42[4], 43, 44[2]

NUM.
1:45[2], 47[2], 48, 49[3], 50[6], 51[5], 52, 53[7], 54[2], 2:1, 2[4], 3[7], 5[3], 7[3], 9, 10[6], 12[4], 14[4], 16[2], 17[6], 18[6], 20[4], 22[4], 24[2], 25[6], 27[4], 29[4], 31, 32[3], 33[3], 34[3], 3:1[3], 2[3], 3[4], 4[5], 5, 6[2], 7[6], 8[7], 9[2], 10, 11, 12[6], 13[6], 14[2], 15[2], 16[2], 17, 18[2], 19, 20[4], 21[6], 22[2], 23[3], 24[5], 25[11], 26[9], 27[10], 28[4], 29[4], 30[6], 31[8], 32[7], 33[5], 34[2], 35[7], 36[5], 37[2], 38[9], 39[4], 40[5], 41[9], 42[3], 43[2], 44, 45[7], 46[4], 47[4], 48[4], 49[2], 50[5], 51[4], 4:1, 2[4], 3[4], 4[5], 5[3], 6[2], 7[5], 8[2], 9[3], 10, 11[2], 12[2], 13[2], 14[8], 15[9], 16[12], 17, 18[4], 19, 20, 21, 22[3], 23[4], 24[3], 25[10], 26[9], 27[4], 28[8], 29[2], 30[4], 31[7], 32[4], 33[8], 34[5], 35[4]

NUM.
4:37[7], 38[2], 39[4], 40, 41[6], 42[3], 43[4], 45[5], 46[3], 47[6], 49[4], 5:1, 2[3], 3[2], 4[4], 5, 6[2], 7[2], 8[7], 9[3], 10, 11, 12, 13[2], 14[2], 15[2], 16[2], 17[6], 18[9], 19[3], 21[6], 22[2], 23[2], 24[5], 25[6], 26[6], 27[4], 28, 29, 30[4], 31, 6:1, 2[2], 4[4], 5[7], 6[2], 7, 8[2], 9[3], 10[5], 11[4], 12[4], 13[6], 14[3], 16[2], 17[4], 18[10], 19[7], 20[5], 21[5], 22, 23, 24, 25, 26, 27, 7:1[5], 2[4], 3[3], 4, 5[4], 6[3], 7, 8[4], 9[3], 10[5], 11[3], 12[3], 13[3], 15, 16, 17[3], 18[2], 19[3], 21, 22, 23[3], 24[3], 25[3], 27, 28, 29[3], 30[3], 31[3], 33, 34, 35[3], 36[3], 37[3], 39, 40, 41[3], 42[3], 43[3], 45, 46, 47[3], 48[3], 49[3], 51, 52, 53[3], 54[3], 55[3], 57, 58, 59[3]

NUM.
7:60[3], 61[3], 63, 64, 65[3], 66[3], 67[3], 69, 70, 71[3], 72[3], 73[3], 75, 76, 77[3], 78[3], 79[3], 81, 82, 83[3], 84[4], 85[3], 86[5], 87[7], 88[9], 89[6], 8:1, 2[3], 3[3], 4[6], 5, 6[2], 9[5], 10[4], 11[5], 12[7], 13[2], 14[3], 15[4], 16[3], 17[4], 18[3], 19[10], 20[6], 21[2], 22[5], 23, 24[4], 25[2], 26[4], 9:1[5], 2[2], 3[3], 4[2], 5[6], 6[2], 7[3], 8, 9, 10[3], 11[2], 12[3], 13[5], 14[7], 15[9], 16[2], 17[6], 18[7], 19[5], 20[6], 21[5], 22[3], 23[9], 10:1, 2[4], 3[4], 4[2], 5[2], 6[3], 7, 8[3], 9[3], 10[5], 11[6], 12[4], 13[3], 14[5], 15[4], 16[4], 17[4], 18[3], 19[4], 20[4], 21[4], 22[4], 23[4], 24[4], 25[6], 26[4], 27[4], 28[2], 29[5], 31, 32[2], 33[6], 34[3], 35, 36, 11:1[7], 2[3], 3[4], 4[2], 5[6], 7[3], 8[3], 9[4], 10[4]

NUM.
11:11[2], 12[2], 16[6], 17[3], 18[3], 20, 21, 22[4], 23[2], 24[7], 25[4], 26[9], 27, 28[2], 29[2], 30[2], 31[7], 32[4], 33[6], 34[2], 35, 12:1, 2[2], 3[4], 4[3], 5[5], 6, 8[2], 9[2], 10[2], 11, 12, 13, 14[2], 15[2], 16[2], 13:1, 2[2], 3[4], 4[2], 5[2], 6[2], 7[2], 8[2], 9[2], 10[2], 11[3], 12[2], 13[2], 14[2], 15[2], 16[4], 17[2], 18[2], 19, 20[6], 21[2], 22[2], 23[3], 24[4], 25, 26[6], 27[2], 28[4], 29[10], 30, 31[2], 32[5], 33[3], 14:1[2], 2[3], 3[2], 5[3], 6[3], 7[3], 8, 9[4], 10[6], 11[2], 12, 13[2], 14, 15[2], 16[3], 17, 18[6], 19[2], 20, 21[3], 22, 23, 24, 25[6], 26, 27[2], 28, 30[3], 31, 33[2], 34[3], 35, 36[4], 37[4], 38[4], 39[2], 40[5], 41[2], 42, 43[5], 44[5], 45[2], 15:1, 2[2], 3[4], 4[2], 5[2], 6

NUM.
15:7[2], 8, 10, 12, 13[2], 14, 15[4], 16, 17, 18[2], 19[3], 20[3], 21[2], 22, 23[4], 24[6], 25[5], 26[4], 27, 28[3], 29[2], 30[4], 31[2], 32[3], 33, 35[4], 36[3], 37, 38[4], 39[2], 41[3], 16:1[5], 2[3], 3[4], 5, 7[3], 9[6], 10[2], 11, 12, 13, 14, 15, 16, 17, 18[3], 19[7], 20, 22[3], 23, 24[2], 25, 26[2], 27[2], 28, 29[3], 30[4], 31, 32[2], 33[3], 34[2], 35[2], 36, 37[5], 38[4], 39[3], 40[5], 41[5], 42[6], 43[2], 44, 46[4], 47[5], 48[3], 49[2], 50[4], 17:1, 2[3], 3[3], 4[3], 5[3], 6[2], 7[3], 8[4], 9[3], 10[3], 11, 12, 13[2], 18:1[4], 2[3], 3[5], 4[5], 5[5], 6[6], 7[3], 8[5], 9, 10, 11[3], 12[7], 13[2], 15[4], 16[3], 17[5], 18[3], 19[5], 20[2], 21[5], 22[3], 23[5], 24[5], 25, 26[5], 27[4], 28[4], 29[3]

NUM.
18:30[6], 31[2], 32[3], 19:1, 2[4], 3[2], 4[3], 5, 6[4], 7[4], 8, 9[5], 10[5], 11, 12[4], 13[4], 14[3], 16, 17[2], 18[4], 19[5], 20[5], 21[2], 22[2], 20:1[5], 2, 3[2], 4[2], 6[7], 7, 8[5], 9[2], 10[2], 11[3], 12[4], 13[3], 14[2], 15, 16[2], 17[7], 18, 19, 22[2], 23[3], 24[3], 27[3], 28[3], 29[2], 21:1[4], 2, 3[5], 4[6], 5[2], 6[3], 7[5], 8, 9, 10, 11[2], 12, 13[6], 14[5], 15[4], 16[3], 18[7], 20[3], 21, 22[5], 23, 24[5], 25[3], 26[4], 27, 28[3], 29, 31[2], 32[2], 33[3], 34[2], 22:1[2], 2[2], 3[2], 4[6], 5[6], 6, 7[4], 8[2], 10, 11[2], 12, 13[3], 14, 16, 18[3], 19, 20[2], 21[2], 22[3], 23[9], 24[3], 25[5], 26[4], 27[4], 28[3], 29, 30, 31[5], 32[2], 33, 34[3], 35[5], 36[2], 38, 40, 41[4], 23:3, 5

NUM.
23:6, 7[3], 8, 9[5], 10[5], 12, 13, 14[2], 15, 16, 17[2], 19, 21[2], 22, 24[4], 26, 28, 24:1[2], 2, 3[2], 4[3], 6[5], 7, 8[2], 11, 13[3], 14, 15[2], 16[5], 17[2], 19, 20[2], 21, 22, 24, 25:1[2], 2[3], 3[2], 4[7], 5, 6[8], 7[4], 8[6], 9, 10, 11[4], 13[2], 14[5], 15[3], 16, 17, 18[5], 26:1[4], 2[3], 3[2], 4[5], 5[6], 6[4], 7[2], 8, 9[4], 10[2], 11, 12[7], 13[4], 14[2], 15[7], 16[3], 17[4], 18[2], 19[2], 20[7], 21[5], 22, 23[5], 24[4], 25, 26[7], 27[2], 28, 29[5], 30[5], 31[4], 32[4], 33[3], 34, 35[7], 36[3], 37[3], 38[7], 39[4], 40[5], 41, 42[4], 43[2], 44[7], 45[5], 46, 47[2], 48[5], 49[4], 50, 51[2], 52, 53[2], 54[2], 55[3], 56[2], 57[7], 58[12], 59[2], 61, 62[2], 63[3], 64[3], 65[4], 27:1[8]

NUM.
27:2[6], 3[4], 4[2], 5, 6, 7[2], 8, 11[2], 12[3], 14[6], 15, 16[4], 17[2], 18[3], 19[2], 20[2], 21[5], 22[3], 23[2], 28:1, 2, 3[3], 4[3], 5, 6, 7[6], 8[5], 9[3], 10[2], 11[3], 13, 14[4], 15[3], 16[4], 17[2], 18, 19[2], 21, 23[2], 24[5], 25, 26[3], 27[3], 29, 30, 31, 29:1[4], 2[2], 4, 5, 6[4], 7, 8[2], 10, 11[4], 12[3], 13[2], 14[2], 15, 16[2], 17[2], 18[4], 19[3], 20[2], 21[4], 22, 23[2], 24[4], 25[2], 26[2], 27[4], 28, 29[2], 30[4], 31, 32[2], 33[4], 34, 35, 36[2], 37[4], 38, 39, 40[2], 30:1[5], 2, 3, 5[2], 7, 8[2], 12[3], 13, 14, 16[3], 31:1, 2[2], 3[4], 4[2], 5, 6[6], 7[3], 8[4], 9[3], 11[2], 12[8], 13[4], 14[4], 15, 16[6], 17, 18, 19[3], 21[6], 22[6], 23[5], 24[2], 25

NUM.
31:26[5], 27[3], 28[6], 29[2], 30[9], 31[2], 32[4], 36[2], 37[2], 38[2], 39[2], 40[2], 41[4], 42[2], 43[2], 47[5], 48[3], 49[2], 50[2], 51[2], 52[5], 53, 54[7], 32:1[5], 2[5], 4[3], 6[2], 7[4], 8, 9[6], 10[2], 11[2], 12[4], 13[5], 14[2], 15, 17[4], 18, 20, 21, 22[4], 23, 25[2], 26, 27, 28[5], 29[5], 30, 31[3], 32[3], 33[12], 34, 37, 38, 39[3], 40, 41[2], 42, 33:1[4], 2[2], 3[8], 4[3], 5, 6[2], 8[4], 10, 11[2], 12, 14, 15, 16, 36, 37[2], 38[8], 40[5], 44, 47, 48[2], 49, 50[2], 51[2], 52[2], 53[8], 54[7], 55[3], 34:1, 2[5], 3[4], 4[4], 5[4], 6[2], 7, 8[5], 9[2], 11[5], 12[4], 13[5], 14[7], 15[8], 16, 17[5], 18, 19[4], 20[3], 21[2], 22[3], 23[5], 24[4], 25[4], 26[4], 27[4], 28[4], 29[4], 35:1[2], 2[5], 3[2], 4[5]

NUM.
35:5[9] 6[3] 7[2] 8[4] 9 10[2] 11 12[3] 14 15[3] 16 17 18 19[2] 21[2] 24[3] 25[9] 26[3] 27[5] 28[7] 30[2] 31 32[4] 33[5] 34[3] 36:1[10] 2[5] 3[7] 4[6] 5[5] 6[5] 7[5] 8[5] 9[3] 10[2] 11 12[5] 13[6]

DEU.
1:1[4] 2 3[6] 4[3] 5 6 7[12] 8[3] 10[2] 11 14 15 16[2] 17[5] 18 19[4] 20[3] 21[3] 22 23 24[2] 25[3] 26[2] 27[4] 28[4] 30 31[3] 32 33 34[2] 36[3] 37 38 40[3] 41[3] 42 43[3] 44 45[2] 46 2:1[4] 2 4[3] 7[3] 8[5] 9[3] 10[2] 11[2] 12[4] 13[2] 14[6] 15[3] 16[2] 17 18 19[4] 20 21[2] 22[2] 23[2] 24[2] 25[4] 26 27[3] 29[4] 30 31 33 34[3] 35[3] 36[5] 37[6] 3:1[2] 2[2] 3[2] 4[2] 6

DEU.
3:7[3] 8[4] 9[2] 10[3] 11[5] 12[4] 13[5] 14[3] 16[8] 17[5] 18[3] 20[3] 21[3] 22 23 25 26[2] 27 28 29 4:1[4] 2[3] 3[3] 4 5[2] 6[2] 7 9[2] 10[6] 11[3] 12[5] 14[2] 15[4] 16[2] 17[4] 18[5] 19[6] 20[2] 21[2] 23[4] 24 25[4] 26 27[4] 28 29 30[2] 31[2] 32[5] 33[3] 34[2] 35 36[2] 39[2] 40[2] 41 42 43[5] 44[2] 45[4] 46[4] 47[3] 48[2] 49[4] 5:1 2 3 4[4] 5[5] 6[3] 8[3] 9[5] 11[3] 12[2] 14[3] 15[4] 16[3] 22[7] 23[5] 24[3] 25[2] 26[4] 27[2] 28[5] 31[4] 32[3] 33[3] 6:1[5] 2[2] 3[2] 4 5 7 9 10[2] 12[3] 13 14[2] 15[5] 16 17[2] 18[4] 19 20[4] 21 22 23 24[2] 25 7:1[9] 2 4[2] 6[4] 7[2] 8[5] 9[2] 11[3]

DEU.
7:12[3] 13[5] 15[2] 16[2] 18 19[8] 20[2] 21 22[3] 23 25[3] 8:1[3] 2[3] 3[2] 5 6[2] 7 10[2] 11 14[3] 15 16 17 18 19 20[4] 9:2[3] 3[2] 4[4] 5[5] 6 7[5] 8[2] 9[6] 10[9] 11[5] 12[2] 13 15[4] 16[3] 17 18[4] 19[3] 20[2] 21[4] 22 23[4] 24[2] 25[3] 26 27 28[4] 10:1[3] 2[4] 3[3] 4[10] 5[4] 6[3] 8[6] 9[2] 10[4] 11[3] 12[3] 13[2] 14[4] 15 16 17 18[3] 19[2] 20 22[2] 11:1 2 3[2] 4[4] 5 6[5] 7[2] 8[2] 9[2] 10[2] 11[2] 12[7] 13 14[3] 17[5] 19 20 21[5] 22 23 24[5] 25[4] 27[2] 28[3] 29[4] 30[7] 31[2] 32 12:1[4] 2[4] 3[2] 4 5[2] 6 7[2] 8 9[3] 10[2] 11[3] 12[2] 14[2] 15[6] 16 17[2] 18[5]

DEU.
12:19[2] 20 21[3] 22[4] 23[5] 24 25[2] 26[2] 27[8] 28[2] 29[2] 31[3] 13:2[2] 3[3] 4 5[7] 6[2] 7[6] 9[2] 10[3] 12 13[2] 14 15[6] 16[6] 17[3] 18[4] 14:1[3] 2[4] 4[4] 5[7] 6[4] 7[7] 8[3] 9 12[3] 13[3] 15[4] 16[3] 17[3] 18[4] 21[2] 22[2] 23[5] 24[4] 25[3] 26 27 28[3] 29[6] 15:1 2[3] 4[3] 5[2] 6 7 9[3] 10 11[2] 12 14 15[2] 17 18 19[4] 20[3] 21 22[4] 23[2] 16:1[5] 2[6] 3[5] 4[3] 5[2] 6[6] 7[3] 8[2] 9[3] 10[4] 11[7] 13 14[4] 15[5] 16[6] 17[2] 18[2] 19[4] 20[2] 21[2] 22 17:1[2] 2[3] 3[2] 4 6[2] 7[5] 8[2] 9[4] 10[2] 11[6] 12[5] 13 14[3] 15 16[3] 18[3] 19[3] 20[5] 18:1[5] 2 3[6] 4[3] 5[3] 6[3] 7[4] 8 9[3]

DEU.
18:10 12[2] 13 14 15[2] 16[5] 17 20[2] 21[2] 22[6] 19:1[3] 2[2] 3[2] 4[2] 5[5] 6[4] 8[2] 9 10 12[3] 13 14[2] 15[3] 17[5] 18[2] 19 20:1[2] 2[3] 4 5[3] 6 7 8[2] 9[4] 11 13[3] 14[7] 15[2] 16[2] 17[7] 18 19[4] 20[2] 21:1[3] 2 3[4] 4[4] 5[5] 6[4] 8 9[3] 10 11 13 15[3] 16[5] 17[6] 18[2] 19[2] 20 21 23[2] 22:4 5[2] 6[7] 7[2] 9[2] 12 15[7] 16[2] 17[4] 18 19[2] 20[2] 21[4] 22[3] 23 24[4] 25[3] 26[2] 27[2] 29[2] 23:1[3] 2[4] 3[4] 4[2] 5[4] 8[3] 9 10[2] 11[2] 12 14[2] 15 17[2] 18[5] 20[2] 21[2] 23 25[2] 24:3[2] 4[3] 6[2] 7 8[3] 9[2] 11[2] 12 13[3] 15[2] 16[4] 17[3] 18 19[6] 20[4] 21[4] 22

DEU.
25:1[3] 2[2] 4[2] 5[3] 6[2] 7[4] 8 9[2] 10 11[4] 15[2] 16 17 18[2] 19[4] 26:1[2] 2[6] 3[4] 4[4] 5 6 7[2] 8 10[4] 11[3] 12[7] 13[6] 14[3] 15 16 17 18 19 27:1[3] 2[3] 3[4] 5 6[3] 7 8[2] 9[4] 10[2] 11[2] 12 14[2] 15[6] 16 17 18[3] 19[3] 20 21 22[3] 23 24 25 26[2] 28:1[4] 2[2] 3[2] 4[5] 7 8[4] 9[3] 10[3] 11[6] 12[4] 13[5] 14[3] 15[2] 16[2] 18[4] 20[2] 21[3] 22[2] 23 24[2] 25[3] 26[3] 27[5] 28 29 30 32 33 34 35[5] 36 37 38[2] 39[3] 40 42 43 44[2] 45[2] 47[2] 48 49[4] 50[3] 51[3] 52 53[3] 54[3] 55[3] 56[4] 57 58[2] 59[2] 60 61[2] 62[3] 63[3] 64[4] 65[2] 67[3] 68[2]

DEU.
29:1[6] 2[2] 3[2] 4 5 6 7[2] 8[3] 9 10[2] 11[2] 12[2] 15 16[2] 18[2] 19[2] 20[5] 21[5] 22[5] 23[3] 24[2] 25[3] 27[3] 28 29[3] 30:1[4] 2 3[3] 4[2] 5[2] 6[3] 7 8[2] 9[5] 10[4] 13[2] 14 16[3] 18 20[4] 31:2 3[2] 4[3] 5[2] 6 7[3] 8 9[6] 10[4] 11[2] 12[3] 13[2] 14[5] 15[6] 16[4] 18 19[2] 20 21[2] 22[2] 23[4] 24 25[4] 26[5] 27 28 29[5] 30[3] 32:1 2[6] 3[2] 4 5 6 7[2] 8[7] 9[2] 10[2] 12 13[6] 14[4] 15 18 19[2] 22[4] 24[3] 25[5] 26 27[3] 30 32[2] 23[2] 35[2] 36 38[2] 42[5] 43 44[4] 46[2] 47 48 49[3] 50 51[5] 52[2] 33:1[3] 3 4[2] 5[3] 7[2] 8 11[2] 12[4] 13[4] 14[4] 15[4] 16[8]

DEU.
33:17[7] 19[5] 20[3] 21[6] 23[4] 26[3] 27[3] 28 29[3] 34:1[5] 2[3] 3[4] 4[2] 5[5] 6 8[3] 9[4] 10 11[4] 12[2]

JOSH.
1:1[5] 2[2] 3 4[8] 5 6 7[3] 8 9 10[2] 11[4] 12[3] 13[4] 14[2] 15[6] 17 2:1[2] 2[3] 3[3] 4[2] 5[4] 6[4] 7[4] 8 9[5] 10[6] 11 12 14[3] 15[3] 16[3] 17 18[2] 19[3] 21[2] 22[4] 23[3] 24[4] 3:1[2] 2[2] 3[6] 4 5[2] 6[7] 7[2] 8[5] 9[3] 10[8] 11[4] 12 13[10] 14[5] 15[7] 16[6] 17[7] 4:1[2] 2 3[4] 4[2] 5[6] 7[6] 8[8] 9[6] 10[6] 11[6] 12[4] 13[2] 14[3] 15 16[3] 17 18[9] 19[4] 21 23[4] 24[5] 5:1[10] 2[3] 3[3] 4[5] 5[4] 6[8] 7 8[2] 9[4] 10[5] 11[5] 12[7] 14[3] 15[3] 6:1 2[3] 3[2] 4[5] 5[7]

JOSH.
6:6[6] 7[4] 8[8] 9[7] 10[2] 11[5] 12[4] 13[9] 14[3] 15[6] 16[6] 17[5] 18[3] 19[4] 20[11] 21[3] 22[4] 23[2] 24[7] 25[2] 26[4] 27[2] 7:1[10] 2[3] 3[2] 4[2] 5[5] 6[5] 7[3] 9[4] 10 11 12[2] 13[4] 14[8] 15[3] 16[2] 17[5] 18[4] 19 20 21[4] 22[2] 23[4] 24[5] 25 26[4] 8:1[3] 2[3] 3 4[3] 5[3] 6[2] 7[3] 8[4] 9[2] 10[4] 11[4] 12[2] 13[8] 14[5] 15[2] 16[2] 17 18[4] 19[3] 20[6] 21[5] 22[3] 23 24[8] 25 26[2] 27[4] 29[6] 30 31[6] 32[4] 33[10] 34[5] 35[4] 9:1[11] 3 5 6[2] 7[2] 9[3] 10[2] 11[2] 12 13 14[3] 15[2] 16 17[2] 18[6] 19[3] 20 21[3] 23 24[4] 26[2] 27[4] 10:1 2[2] 4 5[7] 6[5] 7[2] 8 10[2] 11[4] 12[7] 13[6] 14[3] 15 17

JOSH.
10:18[2] 19[2] 20[2] 21[3] 22[3] 23[6] 24[5] 25 26[2] 27[6] 28[6] 30[8] 32[6] 35[3] 37[6] 39[6] 40[6] 41 42 43 11:1[2] 2[7] 3[10] 4[2] 5 6 7[2] 8[3] 9 10[3] 11[3] 12[6] 13 14[5] 15[2] 16[8] 17[2] 19[3] 20[2] 21 22[3] 23[3] 12:1[9] 2[8] 3[9] 4[3] 5[4] 6[8] 7[7] 8[12] 9[2] 10[2] 11[2] 12[2] 13[2] 14[2] 15[2] 16[2] 17[2] 18[2] 19[2] 20[2] 21[2] 22[2] 23[4] 24[2] 13:1 2[8] 3[9] 4[6] 5[4] 6[8] 7[2] 8[4] 9[6] 10[4] 11[2] 12[3] 13[6] 14[3] 15[2] 16[6] 17 19[2] 21[6] 22[4] 23[7] 24[2] 25[3] 26 27[6] 28[3] 29[4] 30[2] 31[5] 32[3] 33[2] 14:1[9] 2[4] 3[3] 4[3] 5[3] 6[6] 7[3] 8[3] 9[2] 10 11 12[5] 13 14[4] 15[3] 15:1[7] 2[3] 3[2] 4[3] 5[7]

JOSH.
15:6[5] 7[8] 8[13] 9[7] 10[3] 11[6] 12[5] 13[6] 14[2] 15[2] 17[2] 19[2] 20[3] 21[4] 32 33 46 47[3] 48 61 62 63[5] 16:1[5] 2 3[5] 4 5[5] 6[5] 8[7] 9[5] 10[3] 17:1[4] 2[10] 3[5] 4[7] 5[2] 6[3] 7[4] 8[3] 9[9] 10[3] 11[4] 12[3] 13[2] 14[2] 15[4] 16[6] 17 18[3] 18:1[5] 2 3[3] 4[2] 5[3] 6[3] 7[7] 8[4] 9[3] 10[3] 11[6] 12[7] 13[6] 14[7] 15[5] 16[11] 17[4] 18 19[8] 20[5] 21[4] 28[2] 19:1[5] 8[5] 9[8] 10[3] 11[2] 12[2] 13 14[4] 16[2] 17[2] 22[2] 23[4] 24[3] 27[4] 29[6] 31[3] 32[3] 33 34[4] 35 39[4] 40[3] 41 46 47[6] 48[3] 49[3] 50[4] 51[12] 20:1 2[2] 3[2] 4[6] 5[2] 6[5] 7 8[6] 9[6] 21:1[9] 2[4] 3[4] 4[9] 5[6] 6[6] 7[4] 8[4]

JOSH.
21:9[4] 10[5] 11[4] 12[4] 13[3] 17 19[3] 20[6] 21 23 25 26[3] 27[5] 28 30 32[2] 33[2] 34[5] 36 38[2] 40[4] 41[4] 43[2] 44[2] 45[2] 22:1[3] 2[2] 3[3] 4[5] 5[5] 7[3] 8 9[10] 10[5] 11[8] 12[3] 13[7] 14[3] 15[4] 16[5] 17[3] 18[3] 19[8] 20[3] 21[5] 22[3] 23[2] 24 25[3] 27[3] 28[3] 29[4] 30[8] 31[10] 32[8] 33[5] 34[4] 23:1 3[2] 4[2] 5[2] 6[4] 7 8 9 10 11 12 13[2] 14[4] 15[3] 16[5] 24:1[2] 2[6] 3[3] 6[3] 7[4] 8[3] 9[2] 11[8] 12[3] 13 14[5] 15[7] 16[2] 17[5] 18[5] 19[2] 20 21[2] 22[2] 23[2] 24[2] 25 26[4] 27[3] 28 29[3] 30[3] 31[6] 32[6] 33

JUD.
1:1[4] 2[2] 3 4[3] 5[2] 8[4] 9[5] 10[2] 11[2] 13 15[2] 16[7] 17[3]

JUD.
1:18[3] 19[5] 20 21[4] 22[2] 23[3] 24[4] 25[6] 26[5] 27[5] 28 29[2] 30[3] 31[2] 32[4] 33[6] 34[4] 35[3] 36[4] 2:1[2] 2 4[4] 5 6[3] 7[7] 8[3] 9[4] 10[2] 11[3] 12[5] 13 14[4] 15[4] 16[2] 17[3] 18[7] 19 20[2] 21 22[2] 23[2] 3:1[3] 2[3] 3[5] 4[3] 5[2] 7[5] 8[4] 9[5] 10[3] 11[2] 12[7] 13[2] 14[2] 15[6] 17 18[3] 19 21 22[6] 23[3] 24[2] 25[3] 26 27[3] 28[3] 30[2] 31[2] 4:1[3] 2[4] 3[3] 4 5[2] 6[4] 7[2] 9[3] 11[5] 12 13[3] 14[3] 15[3] 16[6] 17[6] 18 20[2] 21[3] 22[2] 23[2] 24[3] 5:1 2[3] 3[2] 4[4] 5[3] 6[5] 7[2] 8 9[3] 10 11[9] 13[4] 14[2] 15[3] 16[4] 17 18[3] 19[3] 20 21[2] 22[4] 23[8] 24[3] 26[3] 28[3] 30[3] 31[2] 6:1[3]

JUD.
6:2[5] 3[4] 4[2] 5 6[3] 7[3] 8[4] 9[3] 10[3] 11[4] 12[3] 13[5] 14[3] 15 16[2] 19[3] 20[4] 21[11] 22[2] 23 24[2] 25[5] 26[6] 27[3] 28[7] 29 30[4] 33[5] 34[2] 37[4] 38[4] 39[3] 40[2] 7:1[7] 2[3] 3[3] 4[5] 5[4] 6[3] 7[4] 8[4] 9[3] 10 11[4] 12[7] 13[2] 14[3] 15[6] 16[2] 17[2] 18[4] 19[8] 20[7] 21 22[6] 23[2] 24[4] 25[5] 8:1[2] 2[8] 3 4 5[2] 6[2] 7[3] 8[2] 9 10[3] 11[4] 12[2] 13[2] 14[3] 15[2] 16[4] 17[3] 18 19[2] 20 21[2] 22[2] 23 24 25 26[4] 28[3] 29 32[3] 33 34[3] 35[2] 9:1[3] 2[3] 3[2] 4 5[2] 6[4] 7 8[2] 9[2] 10[2] 11[2] 12[2] 13[2] 14[2] 15[4] 16 17 18[2] 20[4] 23[2] 24[4] 25[3] 26[2] 27[3] 28[4] 30[4] 31[2]

JUD.
9:32[2] 33[4] 34 35[5] 36[5] 37[3] 38 39 40[2] 42[3] 43[4] 44[7] 45[4] 46[4] 47[2] 48[3] 49[5] 51[5] 52[3] 53 55 56 57[4] 10:1[2] 4 6[11] 7[6] 8[5] 9[2] 10[2] 11[6] 12[3] 14[2] 15[2] 16[3] 17[2] 18[3] 11:1[2] 2 3 4 5[3] 6 7 8[3] 9[3] 10[2] 11[3] 12[2] 13[3] 14[2] 15[3] 16[2] 17[3] 18[8] 19[2] 21[5] 22[8] 23[2] 24 25 26[2] 27[4] 28[3] 29[3] 30[2] 31[3] 32[2] 33[4] 35 36[3] 37 38 39 40[8] 12:1[2] 2 3[2] 4[4] 5[4] 6[2] 7[2] 12[2] 13 15[5] 13:1[6] 2[2] 3[3] 5[4] 6[2] 7[3] 8[3] 9[4] 10[3] 11[3] 12 13[3] 14 15[2] 16[4] 17[2] 18[2] 19[2] 20[7] 21[3] 23 24[3] 25[3] 14:1[2] 2[2] 3[2] 4[3] 5 6[2] 7 8[4] 9[3]

JUD.
14:10[2] 12[2] 14[4] 15[3] 16 17[4] 18[4] 19[3] 15:1[2] 3 4 5[6] 6[4] 8[2] 9 10 11[3] 12[2] 13 14[4] 16[2] 17 18[4] 19[2] 20[2] 16:2[5] 3[5] 4 5[3] 8[2] 9[4] 12[2] 13[2] 14[5] 18[3] 19 20[2] 21[2] 22 23[2] 24[2] 25[2] 26[4] 27[4] 28[2] 29[4] 30[5] 31[2] 17:2[2] 3[3] 4[3] 5 7 8[3] 10[2] 11[3] 12[3] 13 18:1[3] 2[4] 3[4] 6[2] 7[6] 9[2] 10 11 13[2] 14[2] 15[4] 16[4] 17[10] 18[5] 19 20[6] 21[3] 22[4] 23 24 25[2] 26 27[5] 28 29[6] 30[8] 31[2] 19:1 2 3[2] 4 5[3] 6[2] 7 8[3] 9[4] 10 11[3] 12[2] 14 15 16[3] 17[3] 18[3] 19 20[2] 21 22[8] 23[3] 25[5] 26[5] 27[7] 28[2] 29 30[3] 20:1[4] 2[5] 3[3] 4[3]

JUD.
20:5[2] 6[2] 8 9 10[3] 11[2] 12[2] 13[5] 14[3] 15[3] 17 18[5] 19[2] 20[2] 21[3] 22[4] 23[5] 24[3] 25[4] 26[5] 27[4] 28[4] 30[3] 31[8] 32[5] 33[3] 34 35[4] 36[4] 37[5] 38[3] 39[4] 40[5] 41[2] 42[6] 43[2] 45[3] 46 47[3] 48[7] 21:1 2[2] 4[2] 5[6] 6 7 8[4] 9[2] 10[7] 11 12[3] 13[3] 14 15[3] 16[3] 18 19[5] 20[2] 21[4] 22 23[2] 24

RUTH
1:1[4] 2[5] 4[5] 5 6[3] 7[3] 8[2] 9[2] 13[2] 17 19 20 21[3] 22[3] 2:1 2[2] 3[4] 4[3] 5 6[4] 7[4] 9[4] 10 11[2] 12[2] 14[3] 15 16 17 18 19 20[4] 21 23[2] 3:2 3[2] 4 6 7[2] 8 10[3] 11 13[6] 14[2] 15[2] 16 18[3] 4:1[2] 2[2] 3[2] 4[2] 5[7] 6

RUTH
4:7 8 9[3] 10[7] 11[6] 12[3] 13 14[2] 16 17[3] 18

1 SAM.
1:1[4] 2[4] 3[4] 4 5 6 7[2] 9[3] 10 11[2] 12 15 16 17 18 19[3] 20[2] 21[3] 22[2] 23[2] 24[3] 25 26[2] 27 28[3] 2:1[2] 2 3 4[2] 5 6[2] 7 8[9] 9[2] 10[6] 11[3] 12[2] 13[4] 14[4] 15[4] 16 17[5] 18 19 20[3] 21[3] 22[4] 24 25[4] 26[2] 27[2] 28[4] 29[2] 30[3] 31[2] 32 33[3] 36 3:1[4] 3[4] 4 6 7[3] 8[4] 10 11[2] 13 14[2] 15[9] 17[3] 18 19[2] 20 21[4] 4:1[3] 2[4] 3[9] 4[8] 5[5] 6[9] 7[2] 8[5] 9 10 11[2] 12[2] 13[5] 14[4] 16[3] 17[4] 18[4] 19[2] 20[2] 21[3] 22[2] 5:1[2] 2[3] 3[4] 4[8] 5[2] 6[3] 7[3] 8[8] 9[5]

1 SAM. 5:10[5] 11[6] 12[4] 6:1[4] 2[5] 3[2] 4[4] 5[2] 6[2] 7[2] 8[5] 9 10[2] 11[6] 12[9] 13[2] 14[6] 15[9] 16[3] 17[3] 18[10] 19[7] 20 21[4] 7:1[7] 2[4] 3[6] 4[2] 5 6[3] 7[6] 8[4] 9[3] 10[4] 11[2] 12[2] 13[6] 14[6] 15 17 8:2[2] 4 5 6[2] 7[3] 8[2] 9[2] 10[3] 11[2] 14 15 17 18 19[2] 20 21[4] 22[2] 9:1[4] 2[2] 3[3] 4[4] 5[2] 7[3] 8[3] 9 10[2] 11[3] 12[3] 13[4] 14[3] 15 16[3] 17[2] 18[2] 19[2] 20 21[5] 22[2] 23[2] 24[3] 25[4] 26[4] 27[4] 10:1 2[4] 3 5[4] 6[2] 10[2] 11[4] 12[2] 13 14 16[3] 17[2] 18[5] 19 20[2] 21[3] 22[4] 23[2] 24[3] 25[5] 27 11:1[2] 2 3[2] 4[5] 5[5] 6 7[5] 8[2] 9[5] 10 11[8] 12[3] 13

1 SAM. 11:14[2] 15[4] 12:2 3 5 6[3] 7[3] 8[2] 9[7] 10[3] 11[2] 12[3] 13[2] 14[5] 15[6] 16 17[3] 18[4] 19[2] 20[3] 22[2] 23[3] 24 13:2[2] 3[6] 4[3] 5[3] 6[3] 7[3] 8[2] 9 10 11[3] 12 13[3] 14[3] 15 16[2] 17[5] 18[5] 19[3] 20[2] 21[5] 22[3] 23[3] 14:4[4] 2[2] 3[5] 4[7] 5[3] 6[4] 10 11[5] 12[4] 15[6] 16[2] 17 18[3] 19[5] 20[2] 21[5] 22[3] 23[2] 24[4] 25[2] 26[5] 27[4] 28[4] 29 30[3] 31[2] 32[5] 33[3] 34[4] 35[4] 36[3] 37[2] 38[2] 39[2] 40[2] 41[2] 43[2] 45[4] 46[2] 47[4] 48[2] 49[6] 50[5] 51[3] 52[2] 15:1[4] 2[2] 4 5 6[5] 7 8[5] 9[6] 10[2] 11 12 13[3] 14[3] 15[7] 16 17[3] 18[3] 19[5] 20[6] 21[5] 22[4] 23[3] 24[3] 25 26[3] 27 28[2]

1 SAM. 15:29 30[2] 31 32[3] 33 35 16:1[2] 2[2] 3 4[3] 5[3] 6 7[6] 8 9 10 11[2] 12 13[4] 14[3] 16 18[3] 19 23[2] 17:1 2[4] 3[3] 4[2] 5[2] 7 8 10[2] 11 12[3] 13[6] 14[2] 16 17 18 19[3] 20[6] 21[2] 22[4] 23[5] 24[2] 25[3] 26[5] 27[2] 28[4] 30[3] 31 34 36[4] 37[6] 40[2] 41[3] 42 43[2] 44[5] 45[4] 46[9] 47[3] 48[3] 49[3] 50[3] 51[3] 52[7] 53[2] 54[2] 55[3] 56[2] 57[4] 58[2] 18:1[2] 4 5[4] 6[3] 7 8[2] 10[4] 11[2] 12 13 14 17[3] 18 19[2] 20 21[4] 22[2] 23 24 25[5] 26[2] 27[3] 28 29 30[3] 19:2 3 4 5[2] 6[2] 8 9[2] 10[4] 11 13 15[2] 16[2] 20[4] 21 23 24 20:3 5[4] 6

1 SAM. 20:8 11[2] 12 13[2] 14[2] 15[4] 16[3] 18 19[3] 20 21[4] 22[3] 23[2] 24[3] 25[2] 27[4] 29[2] 30[3] 31[2] 34[3] 35[3] 36[2] 37[5] 38[2] 39[2] 40 41[3] 42[4] 21:1[2] 2[3] 4[2] 5[5] 6[4] 7[4] 8 9[5] 10 11[3] 12 13[2] 14 15 22:1 3 4[3] 5[4] 6 7 8 9[4] 10[3] 11[5] 13 14[2] 15[2] 16 17[8] 18[4] 19[6] 20[2] 21 22[3] 23:1[2] 2[3] 3[2] 4[3] 5[2] 6 8 9[2] 10 11[2] 12[3] 14[2] 15 16 17 18[2] 19[4] 20[2] 21 23[4] 24[3] 25[2] 26[2] 27[2] 28 24:1[2] 2[2] 3[4] 4[4] 6[4] 7 8[3] 10[3] 11[2] 12[2] 13[3] 14 15 18 19 20 21 22 25:1[2] 2 3[5] 4 5 7 8 9 10 13 14[2] 15[2]

1 SAM. 25:16[2] 20[3] 21 22[3] 23[2] 24 25 26[2] 27 28[4] 29[5] 30[2] 31 32 34[3] 36[2] 37[2] 38 39[5] 40 41[3] 42 44 26:1[2] 2[2] 3[4] 5[3] 6[3] 7[4] 8[3] 9 10[2] 11[4] 12[3] 13[2] 14[3] 15[3] 16[4] 19[7] 20[5] 21 22[2] 23[3] 24[2] 27:1[3] 2[2] 3[2] 5[2] 6 7[3] 8[6] 9[5] 10[6] 11[3] 28:1 3[2] 4 5[2] 6[2] 8[2] 9[3] 10[2] 11 12[2] 13[3] 14 15 16 17[3] 18[3] 19[7] 20[4] 21 22 23[3] 24[2] 29:1[2] 2[3] 3[6] 4[6] 6[4] 7[2] 8[2] 9[3] 10[2] 11[4] 30:1[3] 2 3 4 5[3] 6[4] 7[3] 8 9[2] 10 11 14[4] 15 16[5] 17[3] 18 20[2] 21[4] 22[2] 23[2] 24[2] 26[5] 29[4] 31 31:1[3] 2[2] 3[3] 7[7] 8[3] 9[4] 10[2]

1 SAM. 31:11[2] 12[4]

2 SAM. 1:1[2] 2[3] 3 4[4] 5 6[2] 10[2] 11 12[4] 13[2] 14 15 16 18[4] 20[5] 21[3] 22[6] 25[3] 26 27[2] 2:1[3] 2[2] 3 4[3] 5[2] 6 7 8[2] 9 10 11[2] 12[3] 13[9] 14 15[2] 16 17[2] 19[2] 21 22 23[6] 24[4] 25[2] 26[3] 27[2] 28 29 30 31 32 3:1[3] 2 3[5] 4[4] 5 6[3] 7 8[3] 9 10[3] 12 14 15 17 18[5] 19[3] 20 21 22 23[3] 24 25 26 27[3] 28[3] 29[3] 30 31[2] 32[3] 33 34 35[2] 36[3] 37[3] 38 39[3] 4:2[6] 3 4 5[5] 6[3] 7[2] 8[6] 9[3] 11 12[3] 5:1 2[2] 3[3] 6[6] 7[3] 8[7] 9[2] 10 12 14 17[3] 18[2] 19[4] 20[3] 22[2] 23[2] 24[6]

2 SAM. 5:25[2] 6:1 2[5] 3[4] 4[3] 5[2] 6[2] 7[3] 8[3] 9[3] 10[5] 11[5] 12[6] 13[2] 14 15[5] 16[4] 17[5] 18[3] 19[4] 20[5] 21[4] 22 23[2] 7:1[2] 2[3] 3[2] 4[2] 5 6[2] 7[3] 8[3] 9[3] 10 11[2] 13 14 18 19 23[2] 25 26[3] 29[2] 8:1[3] 2[2] 3[2] 4 5[2] 6[2] 7[2] 9 11 12[3] 13[2] 14 16[3] 17[4] 18[3] 9:1 2[2] 3[4] 4[4] 5[2] 6[2] 7 9 10[2] 11[4] 12 13 10:1[2] 2[4] 3[3] 4[2] 5[2] 6[4] 7[2] 8[6] 9[4] 10[4] 11[2] 12[3] 13[3] 14[4] 15 16[4] 17 18[4] 19[3] 11:1[3] 2[4] 3[4] 5 6 7[2] 8[2] 9[3] 11[3] 12 13 14[2] 15[3] 16 17[5] 18[2] 19[4] 20[3] 21[4] 22 23[5] 24[4] 25[3] 26 27[3] 12:1[3] 2 4[4]

2 SAM. 12:5[3] 6 7[3] 8 9[6] 10[3] 11[2] 12 13[2] 14[3] 15[2] 16 17[2] 18[6] 19[2] 20[3] 21[2] 22[2] 24 25[3] 26[2] 27 28[4] 29 30[4] 31[5] 13:1[2] 3 4 5 6[2] 8 10[4] 13[2] 15 16 17 18[2] 23 25 26 27 29[2] 30[2] 31[2] 32[5] 33[3] 34[4] 35[2] 36[2] 37 39 14:1[2] 2 3[2] 4[3] 5 6[3] 7[4] 8[2] 9[4] 10 11[5] 12[2] 13[4] 14 15[5] 16[4] 17[4] 18[5] 19[8] 20[2] 21[2] 22[4] 24[2] 25[2] 26[3] 28 29[2] 30 32[2] 33[5] 15:2[4] 3 4 6[3] 7[2] 8[2] 9 10[3] 12[3] 13[2] 14[3] 15[3] 16[3] 17[2] 18[4] 19[3] 21[4] 22[2] 23[7] 24[6] 25[5] 27[4] 28[2] 29 30[2] 31 32[3] 34[2] 35[3] 37 16:1[3] 2[7] 3[4] 4 5[3]

2 SAM. 16:6[3] 8[6] 9[3] 10[2] 11 12[2] 13 14[2] 15[2] 16[3] 18[2] 19 21[2] 22[3] 23[3] 17:2[2] 3[3] 4[2] 5 7 8[2] 9[2] 10 11[2] 12[3] 13 14[8] 15[2] 16[4] 17 19[2] 20[4] 21[2] 22[2] 23 24 25[2] 26 27[4] 29[5] 18:1 2[8] 3[2] 4[4] 5[5] 6[4] 7[2] 8[5] 9[7] 11[2] 12[4] 13 14[3] 16[3] 17 18[2] 19[3] 20 21 22 23[2] 24[5] 25[3] 26[4] 27[6] 28[6] 29[3] 30 31[2] 32[4] 33[3] 19:1 2[4] 3[2] 4[2] 5[6] 7[2] 8[7] 9[7] 10 11[6] 12[2] 13[2] 14[4] 15[3] 16[2] 17[3] 18[3] 19[4] 20[3] 22[2] 24[5] 25[2] 26 27[2] 28[2] 29[2] 30[2] 31 32 33 34[2] 35[2] 36[2] 38 39[3] 40[4] 41[5] 42[4] 43[7] 20:1[2] 2[2] 3[4] 4[2] 5[2] 6 7[4]

2 SAM. 20:8[2] 9[2] 10[4] 12[6] 13[3] 14[2] 15[4] 16 17[2] 18 19[2] 21[6] 22[6] 23[4] 24[2] 25 26 21:1[4] 2[8] 3[4] 4 5[3] 6[3] 7[5] 8[7] 9[7] 10[5] 11[2] 12[6] 13[3] 14[4] 15[2] 16[3] 17[4] 18[4] 19[5] 20 21[2] 22[3] 22:1[6] 2 3[2] 4 5[2] 6[2] 7 8[2] 10 11[2] 12 13 14[2] 16[8] 19[2] 21[2] 22[2] 25 26[2] 27[2] 28[2] 29 31[2] 32 36 41 42 43[4] 44[2] 47[2] 48 49 50 51 23:1[6] 2[2] 3[3] 4[5] 6 7[3] 8[7] 9[5] 10[4] 11[5] 12[4] 13[6] 14[2] 15[3] 16[6] 17[2] 18[3] 19 20[3] 21[3] 22[2] 23[2] 24[3] 25[2] 26[3] 27[2] 28[2] 29[3] 30[2] 31[2] 32[2] 33[3] 34[5] 35[2] 36[2] 37[3] 39 24:2[7] 3[6] 4[8] 5[4] 6 7[5] 8[2]

2 SAM. 24:9[6] 10[3] 11[4] 12 14[3] 15[4] 16[9] 17[3] 18[3] 19[2] 20[3] 21[5] 22[2] 23[3] 24[4] 25[4]

1 KINGS 1:2[3] 3[2] 4[3] 5 7[2] 8[4] 9[4] 10[2] 11[2] 12 14 15[5] 16[2] 17 18 19[5] 20[3] 21 22[2] 23[5] 25[4] 26[2] 27[3] 28[2] 29[2] 30 31[2] 32[4] 33[2] 34[3] 36[4] 37[3] 38[5] 39[4] 40[4] 41[4] 42[2] 44[7] 45[4] 46[2] 47[3] 48[2] 49 50[2] 51[3] 52 53 2:1 2[2] 3[3] 4[2] 5[7] 6 7[2] 8[4] 9 10 11 12 13[2] 15[3] 17[2] 18 19[2] 20 21 22[4] 23 24[2] 25[2] 26[4] 27[4] 28[4] 29[4] 30[4] 31[3] 32[6] 33[3] 34[2] 35[5] 36 37[2] 38[3] 39[2] 42[4] 43[3] 44[3] 45[2] 46[4] 3:1[4] 2[3] 3[2] 4[2] 5 8 10[2] 11 13 15[3]

1 KINGS 3:16 17[2] 18[3] 19 21[2] 22[6] 23[6] 24[2] 25[4] 26[5] 27[3] 28[4] 4:2[3] 3[3] 4[3] 5[4] 6[3] 7 8 9 10[2] 11[3] 12[2] 13[4] 14 15 16 17 18 19[6] 20[2] 21[5] 23 24[4] 25 28[3] 29[2] 30[4] 31[2] 33[3] 34[2] 5:1 3[5] 4 5[3] 6 7[2] 8 9[2] 12 13 14 15 16[4] 17[3] 18[2] 6:1[8] 2[5] 3[8] 4 5[6] 6[8] 7[2] 8[7] 9[2] 10[2] 11[2] 13 14 15[8] 16[6] 17[2] 18[2] 19[5] 20[4] 21[3] 22[4] 23 24[8] 25[2] 26[3] 27[12] 28 29[2] 30[2] 31[4] 32[3] 33[3] 34[5] 35 36 37[5] 38[6] 7:2[6] 3 5[2] 6[5] 7[4] 8[2] 9[5] 10 11 12[6] 14 16[6] 17[5] 18[5] 19[4] 20[6] 21[7] 22[4] 23[2] 24[3] 25[5] 26[2] 27[3] 28[4]

1 KINGS 7:29[4] 30[3] 31[6] 32[5] 33[3] 34[3] 35[7] 36[4] 37 38 39[8] 40[6] 41[10] 42[4] 43 44 45[5] 46[3] 47[3] 48[6] 49[7] 50[12] 51[10] 8:1[10] 2[4] 3[3] 4[8] 6[9] 7[6] 8[5] 9[5] 10[5] 11[6] 12[2] 14[3] 15 16[2] 17[3] 18 19[2] 20[6] 21[4] 22[4] 25 27[2] 28[3] 29[2] 30 31 32[2] 33 34[2] 36[2] 37[2] 38 39[2] 40[2] 43[2] 44[3] 46[3] 47[2] 48[3] 51 52[2] 53[3] 54[3] 55 56[2] 57 59[5] 60[3] 61 62 63[5] 64[13] 65[3] 66[5] 9:1[4] 2[2] 3 5[2] 7 8 9[3] 10[5] 11[2] 12 13 14 15[5] 16[2] 17 18[2] 19[2] 20[3] 21[2] 22 23[4] 24 25[5] 26[3] 27[3] 10:1[4] 3 4[2] 5[5] 6 7[3] 9[3] 10[2] 11 12[5] 13 14 15[6] 17[3] 18[2]

1 KINGS 10:19[6] 20[4] 21[4] 22[3] 23[2] 24 26[2] 27[3] 28[2] 29[3] 11:1[2] 2[3] 4[2] 5[4] 6[3] 7[4] 9[2] 10 11[2] 12 13 14[3] 15[3] 19[4] 20[2] 21[2] 23 25[2] 26[2] 27[4] 28[4] 29[4] 30 31[4] 32[2] 33[6] 34[2] 35 36 39 40 41[4] 42 43 12:2[2] 3 4 5 6 8[3] 9 10 12[4] 13[3] 14[2] 15[7] 16[4] 17[2] 18 19 20[3] 21[5] 22 23[4] 24[6] 25 27[3] 28[2] 29[2] 30[2] 31[3] 32[8] 33[6] 13:1[3] 2[7] 3[5] 4[4] 5[7] 6[7] 7[2] 8[2] 9[3] 10 11[4] 12 13[2] 14[2] 17[3] 18[2] 20[4] 21[6] 22[4] 23[2] 24[5] 25[6] 26[9] 27 28[7] 29[6] 31[2] 32[7] 33[5] 34[3] 14:1 2[2] 3 4 5[2] 6[2] 7[2] 8[2] 10[4] 11[6] 12[2] 13[3] 14[2] 15[4]

1 KINGS 14:16 17[3] 18[4] 19[5] 20 21[4] 22[2] 24[5] 25 26[6] 27[5] 28[5] 29[5] 31 15:1[2] 2 3[3] 4 5[5] 6 7[5] 8 9 10 11[2] 12[3] 13 14[2] 15[4] 18[10] 20[4] 22[2] 23[7] 24 25[2] 26[3] 27[3] 28 29[4] 30[2] 31[5] 33[2] 34[3] 16:1[3] 2[2] 3[4] 4[5] 5[5] 7[10] 8[2] 9 10 11 12[4] 13[3] 14[5] 15[3] 16[5] 18[4] 19[3] 20[5] 21[3] 22[3] 23 24[6] 25[2] 26[3] 27[5] 29[3] 30[3] 31[4] 32 33[2] 34[6] 17:1[3] 2[2] 3 4[2] 5[3] 6[4] 7[2] 8[2] 10[3] 12 14[6] 15 16[4] 17[4] 20[2] 21[2] 22[4] 23[3] 24[3] 18:1[4] 3[2] 4[2] 5[3] 6 7 9 10[2] 12[3] 13[3] 15 18[2] 19[3] 20[2] 21[3] 22[2] 23 24[5] 25[2] 26[3] 28 29[3] 30[4] 31[5]

1 KINGS 18:32[4] 33[5] 34[4] 35[3] 36[4] 37 38[8] 39[5] 40 42[2] 43 44[3] 45[2] 46[3] 19:1[2] 2[2] 4 6 7[4] 8[2] 9[2] 10[3] 11[11] 12[4] 13[2] 14[3] 15[2] 16[2] 17[2] 18 19[2] 20 21[3] 20:1 2 3 4 5 6 7[3] 8[2] 9[4] 10[3] 11 12[3] 13[2] 14[5] 15[5] 16[3] 17[3] 19[4] 20[3] 21[3] 22[5] 23[4] 24 25[2] 26[3] 27[4] 28[7] 29[5] 30[4] 31[3] 32 33[2] 34 35[5] 36[2] 37 38[3] 39[4] 40 41[3] 42 43 21:1[2] 2 3[2] 4[3] 6 7[3] 8[8] 9[2] 10 11[5] 12 13[5] 15[2] 16[2] 17[3] 18 19[4] 20[2] 21 22[5] 23[3] 24[5] 25[2] 26[3] 28[3] 29[2] 22:2[3] 3[3] 4 5[3] 6[5] 7 8[4] 9[2] 10[5] 11[8] 12[3] 13[5] 14[2] 15[5] 16[3] 17[2]

1 KINGS 22:18 19[4] 20 21 22[2] 23[3] 24[4] 26[4] 27[2] 28 29[2] 30[4] 31[2] 32[3] 33[3] 34[5] 35[7] 36[3] 37[2] 38[5] 39[7] 41[2] 42 43[6] 44 45[5] 46[4] 48 49[2] 50 51[2] 52[6] 53

2 KINGS 1:1 2 3[6] 4 5 6[3] 8 9[3] 10 11 12 13[3] 14[2] 15[3] 16[2] 17[4] 18[5] 2:1 2[2] 3[3] 4[2] 5[3] 6[2] 7[2] 8 12[2] 13[2] 14[4] 15[4] 16[2] 19[5] 21[4] 22[2] 23[2] 24[3] 3:1[2] 2[3] 3[2] 4[2] 5[2] 6 7[2] 8[2] 9[5] 10[3] 11[5] 12[4] 13[6] 14[8] 15[3] 16 17 18[3] 20[4] 21[3] 22[6] 23[2] 24[4] 25[5] 26[3] 27 4:1[5] 2[2] 4 5[2] 6[2] 7[3] 10 11 13[3] 15 16 17[2] 18[2] 21[3] 22[3] 25[2] 26 27[5] 29[2] 30[3] 31[4]

2 KINGS 4:32[2] 33[2] 34[4] 35[3] 37 38[6] 39[2] 40[3] 41[3] 42[4] 43[2] 44[2] 5:1[3] 2[2] 3[5] 4[2] 5[5] 6[7] 7[2] 8[3] 9[2] 11[4] 12 13 14[3] 15[2] 16 17 18[5] 20[3] 21 22[2] 24[3] 26 27 6:1[3] 5[2] 6[3] 8 9[3] 10[3] 11[3] 12[3] 14 15[3] 17[4] 18[2] 19[3] 20[3] 21 23[2] 25 26[2] 27[3] 28 29 30[5] 31[2] 32[8] 33[3] 7:1[4] 2[3] 3[2] 4[5] 5[5] 6[9] 7[2] 8[2] 9[2] 10[5] 11[2] 12[7] 13[5] 14[3] 15[4] 16[5] 17[3] 18[3] 19[2] 20[2] 8:1[3] 2[5] 3[5] 4[4] 5[4] 6[7] 7[2] 8[3] 10 11 12[3] 13 15 16[3] 18[6] 19 20 21[5] 22[2] 23[5] 24 25[3] 26 27[7] 28[3] 29[4] 9:1[3] 2[2] 3[3] 4[3] 5[2] 6[6] 7[7] 8[2] 9[5] 10[3] 11[2]

2 KINGS 9:12, 13[2], 14[2], 15[3], 17[2], 18[3], 19, 20[4], 21[2], 22, 24, 25[4], 26[7], 27[5], 28, 29[2], 31, 32, 33[2], 35[3], 36[5], 37[4], 10:1[2], 3, 5[5], 6[6], 7[2], 8[5], 9, 10[6], 11, 12[2], 13[6], 14[2], 15[2], 16, 17[2], 18, 19[4], 21[3], 22[2], 23[6], 24[2], 25[9], 26[2], 27[2], 29[3], 30[4], 31[3], 32[2], 33[5], 34[5], 36, 11:1[2], 2[4], 3[3], 4[10], 5[4], 6[5], 7[5], 8[3], 9[6], 10[4], 11[8], 12[4], 13[6], 14[7], 15[10], 16[4], 17[6], 18[8], 19[14], 20[5], 12:1, 2[3], 3[3], 4[11], 5[3], 6[4], 7[6], 8[4], 9[11], 10[6], 11[9], 12[4], 13[5], 14[3], 15[2], 16[4], 18[6], 19[5], 20, 21[3], 13:1[3], 2[4], 3[5], 4[4], 5[4], 6[3], 7[3], 8[5], 10[2], 11[4], 12[5], 13, 14[3], 16[3], 17[5], 18[3], 19, 20[5], 21[4], 22, 23, 25[6], 14:1[2], 3[2]

2 KINGS 14:4[3], 5[2], 6[9], 7[2], 8[2], 9[4], 11, 12, 13[5], 14[6], 15[5], 16, 17[2], 18[5], 20, 21, 22, 23[3], 24[4], 25[9], 26[2], 27[4], 28[5], 29, 15:1, 3[2], 4[3], 5[7], 6[5], 7, 8[2], 9[4], 10[2], 11[5], 12[4], 13[2], 14[2], 15[5], 16[2], 17[2], 18[4], 19[3], 20[5], 21[5], 23[2], 24[4], 25[4], 26[5], 27[2], 28[4], 29[2], 30[4], 31[5], 32[3], 33, 34[2], 35[6], 36[5], 37[3], 38, 16:1[3], 2[2], 3[7], 4[2], 6[2], 7[4], 8[6], 9[3], 10[5], 11[2], 12[5], 13[2], 14[9], 15[13], 16, 17[5], 18[7], 19[5], 20, 17:1[2], 2[3], 4[3], 5[2], 6[5], 7[4], 8[6], 9[5], 11[4], 12, 13[5], 14[2], 15[2], 16[3], 17[3], 18[2], 19[3], 20[3], 21[3], 22[2], 23[2], 24[4], 25[3], 26[9], 27[5], 28[2], 29[3], 30[3], 31[3], 32[5], 33[3], 34[5], 35, 36[2], 37[4], 38, 39[2], 41

2 KINGS 18:1[2], 2, 3[2], 4[5], 5[2], 6[2], 7[2], 8[5], 9[2], 10[3], 11[4], 12[4], 13[2], 14[2], 15[5], 16[6], 17[5], 18[6], 19[2], 20, 21, 22, 23, 24[2], 25[2], 26[6], 27[2], 28[4], 29, 30[4], 31[2], 32, 33[4], 34[2], 35[3], 36[2], 37[6], 19:1[2], 2[6], 3[2], 4[7], 5, 6[4], 7, 8, 10[2], 11, 12[3], 13[4], 14[6], 15[5], 16[2], 17[2], 18[2], 19[3], 20[2], 21[5], 22, 23[9], 24[2], 26[5], 28, 29[4], 30[2], 31[2], 32[2], 33[3], 35[5], 37[3], 20:1[3], 2[2], 4[3], 5[6], 6[2], 7, 8[5], 9[4], 10[2], 11[4], 12, 13[6], 14, 15, 16[2], 17[2], 18[3], 19[2], 20[6], 21:2[6], 3[2], 4[3], 5[4], 6[3], 7[4], 8[3], 9[3], 10[2], 11, 12, 13[3], 14[2], 15, 16[2], 17[5], 18[2], 19, 20[2], 21[2], 22[3], 23[2], 24[4], 25[5], 26, 22:1, 2[5], 3[7], 4[7]

2 KINGS 22:5[12], 6, 7, 8[7], 9[10], 10[4], 11[4], 12[6], 13[6], 14[7], 15[2], 16[5], 17, 18[4], 19[3], 20[2], 23:1[2], 2[13], 3[6], 4[13], 5[9], 6[9], 7[6], 8[12], 9[5], 10[3], 11[11], 12[11], 13[11], 14[3], 15[6], 16[8], 17[5], 18[2], 19[6], 20[3], 21[5], 22[5], 23[2], 24[12], 25[2], 26[3], 27[2], 28[5], 29[2], 30[3], 31, 32[2], 33[2], 34[2], 35[9], 36, 37[2], 24:2[8], 3[3], 4[2], 5[5], 7[5], 8, 9[2], 10[2], 11, 12[4], 13[9], 14[6], 15[4], 16[2], 17, 18, 19[2], 20[3], 25:1[4], 2[2], 3[6], 4[10], 5[4], 6[2], 7[2], 8[6], 9[4], 10[5], 11[9], 12[4], 13[9], 14[5], 15[4], 16[5], 17[8], 18[6], 19[11], 20[2], 21[2], 22[4], 23[8], 24[4], 25[6], 26[4], 27[7], 28[2], 29, 30[2]

1 CHRON. 1:5, 6, 7, 8, 9[2], 10, 12, 14[3], 15[3], 16[3], 17, 19[3], 23, 27

1 CHRON. 1:28, 29, 31, 32[2], 33[2], 34, 35, 36, 37, 38, 39, 40[2], 41[2], 42[2], 43[5], 44, 45[2], 46[3], 48, 49, 50[3], 51, 54, 2:1, 3[6], 4, 5, 6, 7[3], 8, 9, 10, 13[2], 14[2], 15[2], 16, 17[2], 18, 21[2], 22, 23[4], 24, 25[3], 26, 27[2], 28[2], 29[2], 30, 31[3], 32[2], 33[2], 42[5], 43, 44, 45[2], 47, 49[4], 50[4], 51[2], 52[2], 53[7], 54[5], 55[7], 3:1[5], 2[5], 3[2], 5, 9[3], 15[5], 16, 17, 19[2], 21[5], 22[2], 23, 24, 4:1, 2[3], 3[2], 4[5], 5, 6, 7, 8[2], 10, 11[2], 12[2], 13[2], 14[2], 15[3], 16, 17[2], 18[5], 19[5], 20[2], 21[7], 22[2], 23[2], 24, 26, 27, 31, 33, 34, 35[3], 37[5], 38, 39[3], 40, 41[2], 42[2], 43[2], 5:1[7], 3[2], 4, 6, 7[2]

1 CHRON. 5:8[3], 9[4], 10[4], 11[2], 12[2], 13, 14[4], 15[3], 16, 17[2], 18[4], 19, 20[2], 22[2], 23[3], 24[3], 25[4], 26[7], 6:1, 2, 3[2], 10[2], 15[2], 16, 17[2], 18, 19[3], 22, 25, 26, 28[2], 29, 31[4], 32[5], 33[4], 34[4], 35[4], 36[4], 37[4], 38[4], 39[2], 40[3], 41[3], 42[3], 43[3], 44[5], 45[3], 46[3], 47[4], 48[3], 49[6], 50, 54[4], 55[2], 56[4], 57[2], 60, 61[4], 62[5], 63[4], 64[2], 65[6], 66[3], 67, 70[4], 71[3], 72, 74, 76, 77[3], 78[4], 80, 7:1, 2[2], 3[2], 4, 5, 6, 7[2], 8[2], 9[2], 10[2], 11[2], 12[2], 13[2], 14[3], 15[3], 16[2], 17[4], 19, 20, 21, 24[2], 28[4], 29[3], 30, 31[2], 33[2], 34, 35, 36, 38, 39, 40[5], 8:1[2], 2[2], 3, 6[4], 8, 10, 12[2], 13[3], 16, 18, 21, 25, 27

1 CHRON. 8:28, 29, 34, 35, 38, 39[3], 40[2], 9:1[2], 2[4], 3[3], 4[6], 5[2], 6, 7[4], 8[6], 9[2], 10, 11[7], 12[8], 13[4], 14[5], 15[3], 16[7], 17[2], 18[3], 19[12], 20[3], 21[4], 22[2], 23[6], 24[2], 26[3], 27[3], 28[2], 29[8], 30[4], 31[6], 32[3], 33[4], 34, 35, 40, 41, 44, 10:1[3], 2[3], 3[3], 5, 7[3], 8[3], 9[5], 10[2], 11, 12[4], 13[2], 14[3], 11:2, 3[5], 4[3], 5[3], 6[2], 7[2], 8[3], 9, 10[4], 11[4], 12[3], 13[3], 14[3], 16[6], 16[2], 17[3], 18[6], 19[2], 20[3], 21[3], 22[2], 23[3], 24[3], 25[2], 26[4], 27[2], 28[3], 29[2], 30[3], 31[3], 32[2], 33[2], 34[4], 35[3], 36[2], 37[2], 38[2], 39[4], 40[2], 41[2], 42[3], 43[2], 44[3], 45[2], 46[3], 47, 12:1[3], 2[2], 3[5], 4[4], 5, 6, 7, 8[7], 9[3], 10[2], 11[2], 12[2], 13[2], 14[4], 15[4]

1 CHRON. 12:16[2], 17, 18[2], 19[4], 20, 21[3], 22, 23[6], 24[2], 25[2], 26, 27[2], 29[5], 30[2], 31, 32[3], 35, 37[5], 38, 13:1, 2[4], 3[2], 4[4], 5[2], 6[3], 7[3], 9[3], 10[3], 11, 12, 13[4], 14[4], 14:2, 4, 8[2], 9[2], 10[2], 11[2], 13[2], 14, 15[4], 16[2], 17[3], 15:1[2], 2[5], 3[2], 4[2], 5[2], 6[2], 7[2], 8[2], 9[2], 10[2], 11[2], 12[6], 13[3], 14[4], 15[6], 16[4], 17[5], 18[2], 19, 21, 22[2], 23, 24[4], 25[6], 26[4], 27[6], 28[4], 29[5], 16:1[3], 2[5], 4[4], 5, 6[3], 7[2], 8[2], 10[2], 11, 12, 14[2], 15, 16, 17, 18[2], 23[2], 24, 25, 26[4], 28[3], 29[4], 30[2], 31[4], 32[3], 33[5], 34, 35, 36[3], 37[4], 38, 39[5], 40[5], 41[2], 42, 43, 17:1[4], 3[2], 4, 5, 6, 7[3], 8[3], 9[2], 10[3], 16[2], 17

1 CHRON. 17:18, 21, 23, 24[3], 27, 18:1[3], 2, 3, 4, 5[2], 6[2], 7[2], 8[3], 9, 11[5], 12[3], 13[2], 15[3], 16[3], 17[5], 19:1[2], 2[5], 3[3], 4, 5[3], 6[2], 7[2], 8[2], 9[6], 10[3], 11[4], 12[2], 13[2], 14[3], 15[3], 16[6], 17[3], 18[4], 19[4], 20:1[6], 2[2], 3[4], 4[4], 5[4], 6[2], 7, 8[3], 21:2[3], 3[2], 4, 5[3], 6, 8, 9, 10, 11, 12[8], 13[3], 14, 15[7], 16[5], 17, 18[5], 19[3], 20, 21[2], 22[5], 23[5], 24[2], 25, 26[3], 27[3], 28[3], 29[6], 30[3], 22:1[4], 2[3], 3[4], 4, 5[2], 6, 7[2], 8[3], 10, 11[3], 12[3], 13[2], 14[2], 16[5], 17, 18[5], 19[10], 23:2[3], 3[2], 4[3], 5[2], 6, 7, 8[2], 9[3], 10[2], 11[2], 12, 13[3], 14[2], 15, 16[2], 17[3], 18[2], 19[5], 20[3], 21[2], 22, 33, 24[9], 25, 26[3]

1 CHRON. 23:27[2], 28[10], 29[4], 30, 31[6], 32[10], 24:1[3], 2, 3[2], 4[6], 5[5], 6[10], 7[2], 8[2], 9[2], 10[2], 11[2], 12[2], 13[2], 14[2], 15[2], 16[2], 17[2], 18[2], 19[6], 20[4], 21[2], 22[2], 23[5], 24[2], 25[2], 26[2], 27, 29, 30[4], 31[7], 25:1[6], 2[5], 3[3], 4, 5[4], 6[6], 7[3], 8[4], 9[2], 10, 11, 12, 13, 14, 15, 16, 17, 18, 19, 20, 21, 22, 23, 24, 25, 26, 27, 28, 29, 30, 31, 26:1[5], 2[5], 3[3], 4[6], 5[3], 6, 7, 8[2], 10[4], 11[4], 12[5], 13[3], 14, 15, 16[4], 18, 19[4], 20[5], 21[4], 22[4], 23[4], 24[2], 26[7], 27[3], 28[5], 29[2], 30[5], 31[6], 32[4], 27:1[6], 2[3], 3[5], 4[3], 5[4], 6[2], 7[3], 8[3], 9[4], 10[4], 11[4], 12[4], 13[4], 14[4], 15[3], 16[6], 17[2], 18[2], 19[2], 20[4], 21[3]

1 CHRON. 27:22[3], 23[4], 24[4], 25[8], 26[4], 27[6], 28[5], 29[5], 30[4], 31[4], 32[2], 33[3], 34[3], 28:1[15], 2[6], 4[6], 5[4], 8[6], 9[4], 10[2], 11[8], 12[10], 13[10], 15[7], 16[2], 17[4], 18[7], 19[2], 20[5], 21[7], 29:1[5], 2[5], 3[3], 4[3], 5[4], 6[6], 7[2], 8[5], 9[3], 10[2], 11[8], 15, 17[2], 18[3], 19[2], 20[6], 21[3], 22[5], 23[2], 24[4], 25[2], 26, 27, 29[8], 30[3]

2 CHRON. 1:1[2], 2[4], 3[7], 4[2], 5[6], 6[4], 9[2], 11, 12[2], 13[3], 14[2], 15[3], 16[2], 17[3], 2:1[2], 2, 3, 4[8], 5, 6, 7, 9, 10, 11[2], 12[3], 14[3], 15[4], 17[3], 18, 3:1[6], 2[3], 3[6], 4[7], 5, 6[2], 7[6], 8[5], 9[3], 10, 11[8], 12[6], 13, 14, 15[3], 16[4], 17[9], 4:1[3], 2, 3[2], 4[5], 5[4], 6[5], 7[3], 8[3], 9[5], 10[4], 11[5], 12[10], 13[4], 14

2 CHRON. 4:16[5], 17[3], 18[2], 19[5], 20[3], 21[3], 22[11], 5:1[9], 2[10], 3[4], 4[3], 5[7], 6[2], 7[9], 8[6], 9[6], 10[4], 11[3], 12[4], 13[7], 14[5], 6:1[2], 3[3], 4, 5[3], 7[3], 8, 9[2], 10[7], 11[4], 12[4], 13[3], 14[2], 16, 18[2], 19[3], 20[2], 21, 22, 23[2], 24[2], 25[3], 26, 27[2], 28[2], 30[2], 31, 32, 33[3], 34[2], 35, 37[2], 38[3], 39, 40, 41, 42[2], 7:1[6], 2[6], 3[8], 4[3], 5[3], 6[6], 7[10], 8[4], 9[4], 10[5], 11[5], 12, 13[2], 15, 18, 20, 21, 22[2], 8:1[3], 2[2], 4[2], 5[2], 6[5], 7[6], 8[2], 9, 10[2], 11[7], 12[4], 13[8], 14[8], 15[4], 16[7], 17[2], 18[3], 9:1[2], 3[3], 4[5], 5, 6[3], 8[2], 9[2], 10[2], 11[6], 12[2], 13, 14[2], 15, 16[2], 17, 18[4], 19[4], 20[5], 21[3], 22[2], 23[3], 25[2], 26[5], 27[3], 29[9]

2 CHRON. 9:31, 10:2[3], 4, 5, 6, 8[3], 9, 10[2], 12[4], 13[3], 14[2], 15[7], 16[4], 17[2], 18[2], 19, 11:1[2], 2[3], 3, 4[3], 11, 13[2], 14[3], 15[3], 16[3], 17[3], 18[4], 20, 21, 22[2], 23, 12:1[3], 2[2], 3[4], 4, 5[4], 6[3], 7[4], 8[3], 9[6], 10[5], 11[5], 12[2], 13[3], 14, 15[4], 16, 13:1, 2, 3[2], 5[2], 6[3], 7[2], 8[4], 9[7], 10[5], 11[7], 12, 13, 14[4], 15[2], 16, 18[3], 19[3], 20[2], 22[4], 14:1[2], 2[2], 3[5], 4[3], 5[4], 6[2], 7[2], 9, 10[2], 11, 12[3], 13[3], 14[4], 15, 15:1[2], 2, 3, 4, 5[2], 8[9], 9[2], 10[3], 11[3], 12, 13, 14, 15[2], 16[3], 17[2], 18[2], 19[2], 16:1[3], 2[4], 4[3], 6[3], 7[5], 8[3], 9[4], 10[3], 11[3], 12[3], 13, 14[3], 17:2[3], 3[2], 4[2], 5[2], 6[3], 7[2], 9[5], 10[4]

2 CHRON. 17:11[2], 13[2], 14[4], 15, 16[2], 18, 19[3], 18:2, 3, 4[3], 5[2], 6, 7[5], 8[2], 9[4], 10[2], 11[4], 12[4], 13, 14[2], 15[4], 16[2], 17, 18[4], 19, 20[2], 21[2], 22[3], 23[4], 25[4], 26[2], 27, 28[2], 29[4], 30[4], 31[4], 32[3], 33[4], 34[6], 19:1, 2[5], 3[2], 4[2], 5[2], 6[3], 7[3], 8[6], 9[2], 10, 11[9], 20:1[3], 2, 3, 4[3], 5[4], 6[2], 7[2], 9, 10[2], 13, 14[9], 15[2], 16[4], 17[3], 18[4], 19[6], 20[3], 21[5], 22[2], 23[3], 24[4], 25[3], 26[6], 27[2], 28[2], 29[4], 30, 31, 32[3], 33[3], 34[6], 36, 37[3], 21:1, 2[2], 3[2], 4[3], 6[6], 7[3], 8[2], 9[3], 10[4], 11[2], 12[4], 13[5], 14, 15, 16[5], 17[3], 18, 19[2], 20[3], 22:1[6], 2, 3[2], 4[4], 5[2], 6[3], 7[4], 8[4], 9[4], 10[3], 11[8], 12[2], 23:1[7], 2[4], 3[6]

2 CHRON. 23:4[5], 5[7], 6[7], 7[4], 8[6], 9[3], 10[8], 11[4], 12[6], 13[8], 14[8], 15[3], 16[3], 17[4], 18[11], 19[4], 20[14], 21[4], 24:2[4], 4, 5[6], 6[9], 7[5], 8[4], 9[4], 10[3], 11[7], 12[7], 13[3], 14[8], 16[2], 17[4], 18[2], 19, 20[7], 21[5], 22[3], 23[8], 24[4], 25[6], 26[2], 27[7], 25:2[2], 3[2], 4[7], 5, 7[3], 8[2], 9[5], 10, 11[2], 12[5], 13[3], 14[4], 15[4], 16[3], 17[3], 18[3], 19, 20[2], 21[2], 22, 23[6], 24[7], 25[2], 26[4], 27[2], 28, 26:1[2], 2, 4[2], 5[3], 6[5], 7[3], 8[2], 9[4], 10[4], 11[6], 12[4], 13[2], 14, 15[2], 16[4], 17[2], 18[6], 19[6], 20[3], 21[7], 22[4], 23[3], 27:1, 2[5], 3[4], 4[2], 5[7], 6, 7[4], 9, 28:1[2], 2[2], 3[7], 4[2], 5[5], 6[2], 7[4], 8[2], 9[3], 10[2], 11[3], 12[7], 13[2], 14[5], 15[5], 16, 17, 18[7], 19[2]

2 CHRON. 28:21[6], 22[2], 23[4], 24[7], 25, 26[3], 27[3], 29:1, 2[2], 3[5], 4[3], 5[4], 6[4], 7[5], 8[2], 9, 10, 11, 12[11], 13[2], 14[2], 15[6], 16[12], 17[10], 18[7], 19[3], 20[5], 21[6], 22[10], 23[4], 24[5], 25[8], 26[4], 27[7], 28[4], 29, 30[6], 31[4], 32[4], 33, 34[7], 35[7], 36[3], 30:1[4], 2[4], 3[2], 4[3], 5[2], 6[9], 7, 8[3], 9[2], 10[2], 12[6], 13[2], 14[3], 15[8], 16[6], 17[6], 18[3], 19[3], 20[2], 21[6], 22[5], 23, 24[3], 25[6], 26[3], 27[3], 31:1[6], 2[7], 3[9], 4[6], 5[6], 6[5], 7[4], 8[3], 9[3], 10[7], 11[2], 12[5], 13[5], 14[8], 15[4], 16[2], 17[4], 18[2], 19[8], 20, 21[4], 32:1[2], 3[3], 4[5], 5[3], 6[4], 7[2], 8[3], 10, 11[3], 12, 13[3], 14, 15, 16, 17[4], 18[4], 19[6], 20[3], 21[7], 22[5], 23[2], 24[2], 25, 26[5], 28, 30[3], 31[5]

2 CHRON. 32:32[7], 33[4], 33:2[6], 3[2], 4[3], 5[4], 6[5], 7[3], 8[6], 9[4], 10, 11[5], 12[2], 13, 14[6], 15[9], 16[3], 17[3], 18[8], 19[3], 22[3], 23, 25[4], 34:2[5], 3[7], 4[6], 5[2], 6, 7[5], 8[10], 9[7], 10[9], 11[3], 12[8], 13[3], 14[6], 15[6], 16[3], 17[7], 18[4], 19[3], 20[5], 21[7], 22[7], 23[2], 24[5], 25, 26[4], 27[2], 28[4], 29[2], 30[13], 31[5], 32[3], 33[6], 35:1[4], 2[4], 3[6], 4[3], 5[8], 6[4], 7[5], 8[6], 9[2], 10[4], 11[4], 12[7], 13[4], 14[7], 15[6], 16[6], 17[3], 18[6], 19[2], 20, 21, 22[3], 23[2], 24[2], 25[3], 26[4], 27[2], 36:1[3], 3[2], 4, 5[2], 7[3], 8[4], 9[2], 10[4], 12[5], 13, 14[7], 15, 16[3], 17[4], 18[7], 19[4], 20[3], 21[4], 22[6], 23[4]

EZRA 1:1[6], 2[3], 3[3], 4[3], 5[6], 7[5], 8[3], 9, 11[2], 2:1[4], 2[3], 3, 4

EZRA 2:5, 6[2], 7, 8, 9, 10, 11, 12, 13, 14, 15, 16, 17, 18, 19, 20, 21, 22, 23, 24, 25, 26, 27, 28, 29, 30, 31[2], 32, 33, 34, 35, 36[3], 37, 38, 39, 40[3], 41[2], 42[8], 43[4], 44[3], 45[3], 46[3], 47[3], 48[3], 49[3], 50[3], 51[3], 52[3], 53[3], 54[2], 55[4], 56[3], 57[4], 58[2], 60[3], 61[7], 62, 63[2], 64, 68[5], 69[2], 70[6], 3:1[4], 2[7], 3[3], 4[4], 5[5], 6[6], 7[4], 8[13], 9[5], 10[9], 11[6], 12[4], 13[8], 4:1[5], 2[3], 3[5], 4[4], 5[2], 6[3], 7[6], 8[3], 9[12], 10[6], 11[5], 12[6], 13[4], 14[3], 15[5], 16[3], 17[6], 18, 20, 22[2], 23[3], 24[4], 5:1[6], 2[4], 3[2], 4[2], 5[4], 6[6], 7, 8[5], 10[8], 11[3], 12[5], 13[3], 14[6], 15[2], 16[3], 17[4], 6:1[4], 2[3], 3[10], 4[2]

EZRA	EZRA	NEH.	NEH.	ESTHER	ESTHER	JOB	JOB	JOB	JOB	JOB	PSALMS	PSALMS	PSALMS	PSALMS	PSALMS	PSALMS	PSALMS
7:5[5]	10:33	7:1[5]	10:14[2]	1:17[3]	9:14[2]	7:2[2]	17:11	25:5[2]	31:40	39:5[3]	8:5	19:8[6]	31:21	40:2	51:6[2]	66:5[2]	74:20[4]
6[3]	34	2[2]	28[10]	18[4]	15[4]	4[3]	12[2]	6	32:2[4]	6[2]	6	9[4]	22	3	8	6[2]	21[2]
7[5]	43	3[4]	29[3]	19[5]	16[3]	8	13[2]	26:2	5	7[4]	7[2]	10	23[4]	4[2]	12	7[2]	22
8[5]		4[3]	30[2]	20[2]	17[4]	9[2]	14	3	6[2]	8[2]	8[6]	13	24	7[2]	17	8	23[2]
9[4]	NEH.	5[5]	31[7]	21[5]	18[5]	11[2]	16[3]	5[2]	8[2]	9	9	14[2]	32:2[2]	9	18	11	75 *title*
10[3]	1:1[5]	6[4]	32[3]	22[3]	19[5]	21[2]	18:1	7[3]	9	10[3]	9 *title*	20 *title*	3	10	19	15	2
12	2[5]	7[2]	33[10]	2:1	20[3]	8:1	4[2]	8[2]	18	13[3]	4	1[4]	4	12	52 *title*[3]	18	3[3]
13[2]	3[5]	8	34[10]	2[2]	21[4]	2	5[3]	9	33:3	14[2]	5[2]	2	5[2]	16	1	19	4[3]
14[8]	4	9	35[4]	3[9]	22[4]	3	6	10[2]	4[3]	15[2]	7	5[2]	6	17	5[2]	67 *title*	6[3]
15[5]	5	10	36[6]	4[4]	23	5	7	11	6	18	8[2]	6[2]	8	41 *title*	6	3[2]	7
19[7]	6[4]	11[2]	37[10]	5[4]	24[6]	6	9[3]	12[2]	8	19	9[2]	7[2]	9[2]	1[2]	7[2]	4[3]	8[7]
17[3]	7[3]	12	38[10]	6[2]	25[3]	8[2]	10[2]	13[2]	11	20	11[2]	9	10[2]	2[3]	8[2]	5[2]	9
18[4]	8[2]	13	39[13]	7	26[2]	11[2]	13[2]	14	15[2]	21[2]	12[2]	21 *title*	11	3[2]	53 *title*	6	10[4]
19[5]	9[3]	14	11:1[5]	8[6]	27	13[2]	14	27:2	16	22	13	1	33:1[2]	13	1	7[2]	76 *title*
20[6]	11[4]	15	2[2]	9[5]	28[2]	16	17[2]	3[2]	18[2]	23[3]	14[2]	2	2[2]	42 *title*[2]	2	68 *title*	3[5]
21[5]	2:1[5]	16	3[7]	11[2]	29[3]	17[2]	18	7[2]	19	24[3]	15[3]	3	4[2]	1[2]	4	2[3]	4
22[7]	2	17	4[9]	12[5]	30[4]	19[2]	21[3]	8[2]	22[2]	25[5]	16[4]	7[4]	5[3]	2	5	3	5[2]
7:1[4]	3[5]	18	5[7]	13[4]	31[4]	20	19:9	10	24	26[2]	17[2]	9[3]	6[5]	4[3]	6[2]	4	6
2[3]	4[2]	19	6	14[9]	32[2]	22[2]	17	11[2]	25	27	18[3]	10[2]	7[3]	5	54 *title*[2]	5[2]	8
3[3]	5[3]	20	7[8]	15[8]	10:1[4]	9:5	20	13[3]	28[2]	28[4]	19	12	8[4]	6[3]	2	6[2]	9[2]
4[3]	6[3]	21	9[3]	16[3]	2[7]	6[2]	21	14	30[3]	29	20	22 *title*	10[5]	7	4	7	10[2]
5[5]	7[4]	22	10[2]	17[4]	3[4]	7[2]	24	16[2]	34:3[2]	30	10:2[3]	1	11[3]	8[4]	55 *title*	8[5]	11
6[5]	8[9]	23	11[7]	18[4]		8[3]	25[2]	17[3]	8	40:1	3[3]	2[2]	12[3]	9[2]	3[4]	10	12[3]
7[8]	9[5]	24	12[8]	19[3]	JOB	9[2]	28[2]	18	10	2	4[2]	3	13[2]	11	4	11[3]	77 *title*
8[3]	10[5]	25	13[5]	20	1:1	13	29[3]	19	11	3	8[5]	6	14[3]	43:1	7	12	2[3]
9[5]	12[2]	26	14[2]	21[4]	3[3]	22[2]	20:1	20	12	6[2]	9[2]	7[2]	16	2[3]	8	13[2]	5[2]
10[2]	13[6]	27	15[5]	22[3]	5[3]	23[3]	3[2]	21	13[2]	11	10	8	18[2]	4[2]	9	14	6
11[8]	14[4]	28	16[5]	23[4]	6[2]	24[5]	5[4]	28:1	16	12	12	9	20	5	10[2]	15[3]	7
12[3]	15[5]	29	17[9]	3:1[3]	7[3]	26[3]	6[2]	2[2]	19[4]	13	13	10	34:1	44 *title*[2]	11	16[2]	10[3]
13	16[7]	30	18[2]	2[3]	8[2]	31	8	3[2]	20[2]	16	14[3]	14	2[2]	1	14	17[3]	11[2]
14	17[3]	31	19[2]	3[3]	9	10:1	9	4[4]	21	17	15[3]	15	3	2	16	18[2]	13
15[3]	18[2]	32	20[4]	6[4]	10[2]	3[3]	10	5	22	19[2]	16[2]	16[2]	4	3[2]	18	19[2]	14[2]
16[6]	19[5]	33[2]	21[2]	7[6]	12[3]	5	11[2]	6[2]	25	20[3]	17[2]	20[3]	6	8	21	20[3]	15
17[2]	20	34[2]	22[10]	8[4]	14[2]	9	14	7	26	21[3]	18[4]	21[3]	7[2]	10	22[2]	21[2]	16[3]
18[4]	3:1[6]	35	23[2]	9[5]	15[4]	18[2]	16[2]	8[2]	28[4]	22[3]	11 *title*	22[2]	8[2]	11	23	22[3]	17[2]
19[2]	2[2]	36	24[5]	10[4]	16[3]	19[2]	17[3]	9[3]	30[2]	41:6[2]	1	23[3]	9	14[3]	56 *title*[2]	23[3]	18[5]
20[2]	3[6]	37	25[5]	11[3]	17[5]	21[2]	18	10	36	8	2[3]	24[2]	10[2]	15	7	24[2]	19
21[7]	4[5]	38	27	12[9]	19[4]	22[2]	19	11[2]	35:5[2]	9[2]	3[2]	25	11[2]	16[2]	10	25[3]	20
23[6]	5[2]	39[3]	28	13[6]	20	11:1	22[2]	12	8	11	4[3]	26[2]	15[3]	19[2]	13[2]	26[3]	78:1
24	6[7]	40	30[3]	14[2]	21[4]	2	23	13[3]	9[4]	13	5[3]	27[5]	16[4]	20	57 *title*[2]	27[3]	4[3]
25[4]	7[6]	41	31	15[6]	2:1[3]	6	24[2]	14[2]	10	14	6[2]	28[4]	17[2]	21[2]	1	30[6]	6[2]
26[3]	8[5]	42	35	4:1[2]	2[3]	7	25[2]	15	11[3]	18[2]	7[2]	29	18	22[2]	3	32[2]	7
27[4]	9[3]	43[3]	36	2[2]	3[2]	9[3]	27[2]	16[3]	12	23	12 *title*	30	19[3]	25[2]	4	33	9[2]
28[4]	10[2]	44[2]	12:1[4]	3[2]	4	17[2]	28[2]	17[3]	13	24	1[3]	23:1	21[2]	45 *title*[2]	5[2]	34	10
8:1[4]	11[5]	45[7]	7[3]	4	6	20[4]	29[2]	18	36:6[3]	25	3[2]	2	22[2]	1[3]	6	35	12[3]
2[3]	12[3]	46[4]	8[2]	5	7[3]	12:2	21:7	19	7[2]	26[4]	5[5]	3	35:3[2]	2	9[2]	69 *title*	13[2]
3[3]	13[7]	47[3]	9	6[3]	8	4	9	20	12	28	6[2]	4[2]	5[3]	5[3]	10[2]	1	14[2]
4[2]	14[6]	48[3]	12[3]	7[4]	10[2]	5	12[3]	21[3]	13	29	8[2]	5	6[2]	6	11[2]	2	15[3]
5[2]	15[12]	49[3]	22[6]	8[4]	11[3]	6	13	22	14	30	13 *title*	6[3]	9	7	58 *title*	4	16
6[2]	16[8]	50[3]	23[7]	9	13	7[3]	14	23[2]	15	31[2]	3	24:1[4]	10[3]	8	2	9[2]	17[2]
7[2]	17[4]	51[3]	24[5]	11[8]	3:3[2]	8[3]	15	24[3]	16	32	6	2[2]	12	9	3[2]	12[3]	19
8[2]	18[3]	52[3]	25[3]	13[2]	4	9[2]	16[2]	25[3]	17[2]	34	14 *title*	3[2]	15	11	4[2]	13[2]	20[3]
9[2]	19[6]	53[3]	26[7]	14[2]	5[3]	10[2]	17[2]	26[3]	19	42:1	1	5[3]	17	12[3]	5	14[2]	21
10[2]	20[7]	54[3]	27[4]	16[3]	6[4]	11[2]	18[2]	28[2]	20	5[2]	2[2]	6	18	13	6[2]	15[3]	23[2]
11[2]	21[6]	55[3]	28[4]	5:1[8]	8	12	20[2]	29:2	26	7[4]	4[2]	7	19	14[2]	8[2]	16	24
12[2]	22[3]	56[2]	29[3]	2[7]	9[4]	15[2]	21[2]	4[2]	27[2]	8	5[2]	8[2]	20	15	9	26	25
13	23[2]	57[4]	30[5]	3[3]	10	16[2]	25	5	28	9[5]	6[3]	9	27[2]	16	10[4]	28[3]	26[2]
14	24[5]	58[3]	31[5]	4[3]	11[3]	17	26[2]	6	29[3]	10[3]	7[3]	10[2]	28	17	11[2]	30	27[2]
15[4]	25[8]	59[4]	32	5[3]	12[2]	18	27	7[3]	30[2]	11[2]	15:2	25:5[2]	36 *title*[3]	46 *title*[2]	59 *title*[2]	31	28
17[5]	26[5]	60[2]	35[7]	6[4]	14	19	28[4]	8[2]	31	12[2]	4	7	1[2]	2[4]	2	32	31[3]
18[4]	27[3]	62[3]	36[3]	8[6]	17[2]	20[4]	29	9	32[2]	14[6]	5	8[2]	3	3[3]	3	33[2]	35
19	28[2]	63[6]	37[7]	9	18[3]	21[2]	30[3]	10[2]	33[3]	15[2]	16:2	9[2]	5[2]	4[5]	5[2]	34[2]	40[2]
20[4]	29[4]	64	38[7]	11[6]	19[2]	22	32[2]	11[2]	37:2[2]		3[3]	11[2]	6	5	6	35	41
21	30[3]	65[2]	39[7]	12[4]	20	23[2]	33[2]	12[2]	3[3]	PSALMS	5[2]	12[2]	7[2]	6[3]	8	36	42[2]
22[5]	31[7]	66	40[4]	13[2]	22	24[4]	22:1	13[2]	4	1:1[6]	6	13	8[2]	7[2]	10	70 *title*	43
24[2]	32[5]	70[5]	41	14[5]	24	25	3	15[2]	6[4]	2[2]	7[2]	14[2]	9	8[3]	12[2]	71:4[4]	46[2]
25[6]	4:1[2]	71[4]	42	6:1[4]	25	13:2	6	16[2]	7	3	8	15[2]	10	9[6]	13[2]	6	48
28[5]	2[4]	72[2]	43[3]	2[4]	4:1	3	7[2]	17[3]	8	4[3]	11	17	11[2]	10[2]	14	8	49
29[7]	3	73[8]	44[12]	3[2]	3	6	8[3]	18	9[3]	5[4]	17:1	26:1	12	11[2]	16[2]	9	50
30[7]	4	8:1[7]	45[6]	4[6]	4	19	9[2]	19[2]	10[3]	6[5]	2	5[2]	37:1	47 *title*[2]	17	15[2]	51[3]
31[7]	5	2[5]	46[2]	5[3]	6	25	12[3]	23[2]	11	2:1[2]	3	7	2[2]	1	60 *title*[2]	16[2]	52
33[11]	6[4]	3[5]	47[8]	6[4]	7	26	13	24	12[3]	2[4]	4[4]	8[2]	3[2]	2[2]	2[2]	20[2]	53
34	7[5]	4[2]	13:1[6]	7[3]	8	27[2]	14	25[2]	14	4[2]	8[3]	12[2]	4[2]	3[2]	3	22[2]	54
35[4]	10[3]	5[5]	2[2]	8[5]	9[2]	14:5	15	30:1	15	7[2]	9	27:1[3]	5	4	4	24	55[2]
36[6]	11[2]	6[5]	3[2]	9[8]	10[6]	7	17	2	16[3]	8[3]	11	2	6[2]	5[2]	6	72:1[2]	56
9:1[14]	12	7[4]	4[4]	10[5]	11[2]	8[4]	18[2]	3	17[2]	10	13	4[6]	7[2]	7[2]	7	3[3]	60[2]
2[4]	13[4]	8[4]	5[12]	11[6]	13[2]	9	19[2]	4	18	11	14[2]	5[2]	9[2]	8[2]	9	4[5]	61
3	14[5]	9[10]	6[3]	12	15	10	20[2]	6[4]	21[3]	12[2]	18 *title*[9]	6	10	9[6]	11	5	62
4[4]	15	10[4]	7[3]	13[2]	16	11[3]	22	7[2]	22	3:3	2[2]	10	11[3]	48 *title*	61 *title*	6[2]	63
5[2]	16[9]	11[3]	8[2]	14[2]	19[2]	12	23	8	23	4	3	12	12[2]	1[3]	2[3]	7[2]	64
6	17[3]	12[2]	9[5]	7:1[2]	5:1	13	24[3]	11	38:1[2]	5	4[2]	13[4]	13	2[6]	3	8[3]	65
7[5]	18[2]	13[9]	10[5]	2[5]	2[2]	14	25	12[2]	4[2]	7[3]	5[2]	14[2]	14[3]	4	4	9[2]	66
8	19[6]	14[5]	11[2]	3[2]	3	15	26	14	5[2]	8	6	28:1	16	7	5	10[3]	67[2]
9[4]	20[2]	15	12[5]	4[2]	4	18[2]	28	15	6[2]	4 *title*	7[3]	2	17[4]	8[3]	6	12[2]	68[2]
11[5]	21[5]	16[8]	13[6]	5[2]	5[3]	19[6]	29	16	7[2]	3[2]	9	3[2]	18[3]	9	62 *title*	13[3]	69
12[2]	22[4]	17[6]	14[2]	6[3]	6[2]	15:1	30[3]	17	8[2]	5[2]	10[2]	4[2]	19[2]	10[2]	7	15	70
14	23[2]	18[7]	15[3]	7[5]	7	2	23:5	18[2]	9[2]	6	11	5[3]	20[4]	11	9	16[6]	71
10:1[2]	5:1[2]	9:1[2]	16[2]	8[10]	10[2]	5[2]	7	19	12[2]	7	12	6[2]	21[2]	12	63 *title*	17	72[2]
2[4]	3	2[2]	17[2]	9[6]	12[2]	7[2]	9[2]	22	13[3]	5 *title*	13[3]	7	22	13	2	18[2]	79:1
3[4]	4	3[5]	18	10[2]	13[3]	8	10	23	14	2	15[5]	8[2]	23	49 *title*[2]	6	19	2[6]
5[2]	5	4[3]	19[6]	8:1[5]	14[3]	10	12[2]	24	15[2]	3[2]	18[2]	29:1[2]	24	1	7	20[2]	6[2]
6[4]	7[2]	5[2]	20	2[2]	15[4]	11	14	25	16[4]	5	20[2]	2[4]	25	3	9[2]	73:3[3]	9
7[2]	8[2]	9[4]	21[2]	3[4]	16	15	16	27	17[3]	6[2]	21[2]	3[5]	28[3]	4	10	9[2]	10[4]
8[4]	9[3]	7[4]	22[4]	4[2]	17[3]	19	17[2]	28[2]	18[2]	7	24[2]	4[4]	29[2]	5[2]	11[2]	11	11[3]
9[8]	11[5]	8[7]	24[3]	5[8]	20[2]	20[3]	24:1	31	19[2]	10	25	5[5]	30[2]	6	64 *title*	12[2]	80 *title*
10[2]	12	9[2]	28[4]	6[2]	21[2]	21	2	31:2	20[3]	12	26[2]	7[3]	31	8	1	14	1
11[4]	13[3]	10	29[4]	7[6]	22[2]	22	3[2]	3[2]	21	6 *title*	27	8[5]	32[2]	10[2]	2[4]	15	4
12	14[7]	11[6]	30[3]	8[6]	23[4]	23	4[4]	7	22[4]	5	28	9[4]	33	12	4	17	5
13	15[4]	12[3]	31[2]	9[10]	25[2]	24	5[2]	11	23[2]	6	30[2]	10[3]	34[3]	14[4]	6[2]	26	8
14[4]	16[2]	14		10[2]	6:2	25	6[3]	13	24[3]	8[2]	31	11[2]	35	15[2]	9	28	9
15[3]	17[2]	15[2]	ESTHER	11[5]	3[2]	26	7[2]	15[2]	25[2]	9[2]	35	30 *title*[2]	37[3]	16	10[3]	74:1	10[6]
16[8]	18[3]	19[6]	1:1	12[4]	4[4]	29[2]	8[3]	16[3]	26[2]	7 *title*[3]	39	3[2]	38[3]	19	65 *title*	2	11[2]
17[3]	6:1[5]	21	2[3]	13[3]	5[2]	30[2]	9[3]	17	27[3]	5[3]	40	4[2]	39[4]	20	1	3[3]	12
18[4]	2[2]	22[4]	3[4]	14[4]	6	33[2]	10[2]	20	28[2]	6[2]	41	5	40[2]	50:1[6]	4[2]	4	13[4]
19	3	23[2]	4[2]	15[3]	7	34[2]	12[3]	21[2]	29[2]	7[2]	42[4]	8	38:6	2	5[4]	5	15[2]
20	4	24[7]	5[6]	16	8	16:5	13[3]	22	30[3]	8[2]	43[4]	9[2]	8	4[2]	6	6	16
21	5	27[3]	6	17[6]	10[2]	10	14[4]	24	31[2]	9[5]	44	12	10	6	7[5]	7[2]	17[2]
22	6[3]	28[2]	7[3]	9:1[10]	12	11[3]	15[3]	26[2]	33[3]	10	45	31 *title*	12	10[2]	8[3]	8[2]	81 *title*
23[2]	7	29	8[4]	2[4]	14[2]	13	16[3]	28[2]	34	11[2]	46[2]	4	20	11[4]	9[2]	10[2]	1
24[2]	9	30[3]	9[3]	3[7]	15	15	17[4]	29	36[2]	13[2]	47	6	39 *title*	12[2]	10[3]	12[2]	2[3]
25	10[8]	32[6]	10[6]	4[2]	16[2]	16	18[4]	31	37[2]	15	48	8[2]	1	13[2]	11	13[4]	3[3]
26	11	35	11[5]	5[3]	18	22	19[2]	32[3]	38[2]	17[3]	49	13	3	14	12[3]	14[3]	4
27	14[5]	36[3]	12[3]	6[2]	19[2]	17:1	20[2]	34[2]	39[4]	8 *title*	19 *title*	15	4	15	13[2]	15[2]	5
28	15[3]	37	13[4]	10[5]	23[3]	5	21[2]	35	40	1[2]	1[3]	17[2]	8[2]	16	66 *title*	16[4]	6[2]
29	16	10:1[2]	14[5]	11[3]	26	6	22	37	41	2[3]	4[4]	18[2]	10	23	2	17[2]	7[2]
30	17[2]	8	15[4]	12[7]	27	8[2]	24[3]	38	39:1[4]	3[3]	6[4]	19	40 *title*	51 *title*[2]	3	18[2]	10[2]
31	18[4]	9[3]	16[8]	13[3]	7:1	9	25:1	39[2]	2[2]	4	7[6]	20[3]	1	1	4	19[4]	15[7]

ISAIAH
34:5 6[7] 7[3] 8[4] 9[3] 10 11[6] 12[2] 13 14[6] 15[2] 16[2] 17 35:1[4] 2[5] 3[2] 5[4] 6[5] 7[3] 8[3] 9 10[2] 36:1[2] 2[5] 3[3] 4[2] 6 7 8 9[2] 10[2] 11[5] 12[2] 13[4] 14 15[4] 16[2] 18[5] 19[2] 20[2] 21 22[6] 37:1[2] 2[6] 3[2] 4[7] 5 6[4] 7 8 10[2] 11 12[3] 13[4] 14[6] 15 16[4] 17[2] 18[2] 19[2] 20[3] 21[2] 22[5] 23 24[9] 25[3] 27[5] 29 30[4] 31[2] 32[2] 33[2] 34[3] 36[5] 38[3] 38:1[3] 2[2] 4[2] 5[2] 6[2] 7[2] 8[4] 9 10[4] 11[6] 15 16 17 18[2] 19[4] 20[5] 21 22[3] 39:1 2[6] 3 5[2] 6[2] 7[2] 8[2] 40:2 3[5] 4[2] 5[4] 6[4] 7[5] 8[3] 9[2] 10 11 12[7] 13[2] 14[2] 15[4] 16 19[2] 21[3]

ISAIAH
40:22[4] 23[3] 24[2] 25 26 27 28[5] 29 30[2] 31 41:1 2[4] 3 4[5] 5[3] 7[5] 8 9[3] 10 13 14[2] 15[2] 16[4] 17[3] 18[4] 19[9] 20[3] 21[2] 22[2] 23 25[4] 26 27 42:1 2 3 4[2] 5[4] 6[3] 7[4] 8 9 10[6] 11[7] 12[2] 13 15[2] 16 17 19 20 21[2] 23 24[2] 25[2] 43:1 2[4] 3[2] 5[2] 6[4] 8[2] 9[2] 10 11 12 13 14[4] 15[2] 16[3] 17[3] 18[2] 19[2] 20[6] 23 24 28[3] 44:2[2] 3 4[2] 5[4] 6[5] 7[2] 11 12[3] 13[5] 14[5] 16[2] 17 19[4] 23[3] 24[5] 25[2] 26[4] 27 28 45:1[4] 2[3] 3[3] 5 6[4] 7[2] 8[3] 9[4] 10 11[3] 12[2] 13 14[3] 15 17 18[4] 19[3] 20[2] 21 22[2] 23 24

ISAIAH
45:25[2] 46:1[3] 2 3[4] 6[2] 7 9 10[3] 11[2] 47:1[3] 2[4] 4[2] 5[2] 6 7 8 9[3] 12 13[4] 14[3] 48:1[5] 2[3] 3[2] 5 7[2] 8 10 12[2] 13[3] 14[2] 16[3] 17[4] 18[2] 19[3] 20[4] 21[5] 22[2] 49:1[3] 2 4 5[4] 6[5] 7[5] 8[3] 9[2] 10[2] 12[3] 13 14 15 16 18 19[3] 20[3] 22[3] 23[3] 24[3] 25[5] 26[2] 50:1[2] 2[2] 3 4[4] 5 6[2] 7 9[2] 10[4] 11[2] 51:1[4] 3[4] 4 5[2] 6[4] 7[2] 8[2] 9[4] 10[6] 11[2] 12 13[8] 14[2] 15[3] 16[4] 17[5] 18[3] 19[2] 20[5] 22[5] 23[3] 52:1[3] 2[2] 3 4[2] 5[2] 7[2] 8[3] 9 10[6] 11[3] 12[2] 14 15 53:1[2] 5 6[2] 7 8[3] 9[2] 10[3] 11 12[6] 54:1[5] 2[2] 3[4] 5[4] 6

ISAIAH
54:8 9[3] 10[4] 13[2] 16[4] 17[4] 55:1 3 4[2] 5[2] 6 7[3] 8 9[2] 10[5] 11 12[4] 13[5] 56:1 2[3] 3[5] 4[3] 6[6] 8[2] 9[2] 57:1[3] 3[4] 4 5[4] 6[2] 8[2] 9 10[2] 13[2] 14[3] 15[6] 16[2] 17[2] 19[3] 20[2] 21 58:1 2[2] 3 4 5 6[4] 7[3] 8[3] 9[5] 10[3] 11 12[5] 13[4] 14[6] 59:1 5 6 8 10[3] 13[2] 14 15 17 18 19[6] 20[2] 21[4] 60:1[2] 2[4] 3[2] 5[4] 6[4] 7[3] 8 9[5] 10 11[2] 12 13[6] 14[6] 16[5] 19[3] 20[2] 21[3] 22 61:1[7] 2[3] 3[5] 4[4] 5[2] 6[5] 7 8 9[4] 10[3] 11[5] 62:1[2] 2[3] 3[3] 4 5[2] 6 7 8[3] 9[2] 10[6] 11[4] 12[3] 63:1 2 3[2] 4[2] 6[2] 7[8] 9[2] 11[3]

ISAIAH
63:12[2] 13[2] 14[3] 15[2] 17 18 64:1[2] 2[4] 3 4[4] 6 8[2] 65:2 4[2] 5 7[4] 8[3] 10[2] 11[2] 12[2] 13 15 16[5] 17 19[2] 20[2] 21 22[3] 23[3] 25[6] 66:1[5] 2 5[3] 6[3] 8 9[3] 11[2] 12[3] 14[2] 15 16[3] 17[5] 19[4] 20[5] 21 22[3] 23 24[2]

JER.
1:1[4] 2[5] 3[7] 4[2] 5[3] 7 8 9[2] 10[2] 11[2] 12 13[5] 14[4] 15[8] 16 18[6] 19 2:1[2] 2[5] 3[3] 4[4] 5 6[4] 7[2] 8[5] 9 10 12 13 15 16[2] 17[2] 18[5] 19[2] 20 21 22 23 24[2] 26[2] 27 28[2] 29 31[2] 33 34[3] 37 3:1[2] 2[5] 3 4 5 6[4] 8[2] 9[2] 10 11[2] 12[3] 13[3] 14 16[5] 17[6] 18[5] 19[2] 20 21[3] 22

JER.
3:23[4] 24 25[3] 4:1[2] 2[2] 3[2] 4[3] 5[3] 6[2] 7[3] 8[2] 9[7] 10[2] 11[3] 16[2] 17 19[3] 20 21[3] 23[2] 24[2] 25[2] 26[4] 27[2] 28[2] 29[4] 31[3] 5:1[3] 2 3 4[3] 5[6] 6[2] 7[2] 8 9 10 11[4] 12 13[2] 14 15 17 18 19 20 22[5] 24[5] 28[7] 29 30 31[3] 6:1[3] 2 3 4[3] 6[3] 9[3] 10[2] 11[7] 12[8] 13[3] 14[2] 15[2] 16[4] 17[2] 19 20 21[4] 22[4] 23 24 25[4] 26 29[5] 30 7:1[2] 2[5] 3[2] 4[6] 6[3] 7 11 12[2] 13 14 15 17[2] 18[5] 19[2] 20[5] 21[2] 22[2] 23 24[2] 25[3] 28[2] 29[2] 30[3] 31[4] 32[5] 33[5] 34[9] 8:1[10] 2[5] 3[3] 4 6[2] 7[8] 8[4] 9[3] 10[4] 11[2] 12[2] 13[5] 14[3] 16[6]

JER.
8:17 19[4] 20[2] 21[2] 22[2] 9:1[2] 2 3[3] 5 6[2] 7[2] 9 10[8] 11 12[4] 13 14 15[2] 16 17[2] 19 20[3] 21[3] 22[5] 23[4] 24[3] 25[3] 26[5] 10:1[2] 2[5] 3[7] 5 7[2] 8 9[5] 10[5] 11[4] 12[3] 13[5] 14 15[2] 16[4] 17[2] 18[3] 21[2] 22[4] 23 25[2] 11:1[2] 2[3] 3[3] 4[3] 5 6[4] 7[2] 8[2] 9[3] 10[3] 11 12[3] 13[3] 14 15 16[3] 17[4] 18 19[4] 20[2] 21[4] 22[3] 23[2] 12:1[2] 3[2] 4[5] 5[3] 6 7[2] 8 9[3] 11 12[8] 13[2] 14[3] 16[3] 17 13:1 2[2] 3[3] 4[2] 5 6[2] 7[4] 8[2] 9[3] 10 11[5] 12 13[6] 14[3] 15 16[3] 17 18[3] 19[2] 20[2] 22 23[2] 24[3] 25[2] 27[3] 14:1[3] 2[3] 3[2] 4[3] 5[2] 6[3] 8[3]

JER.
14:9 10[2] 11 12[3] 13[2] 14[3] 15[2] 16[4] 17 18[6] 19 20 21 22[3] 15:1 2[7] 3[7] 4[2] 6 7[2] 8[6] 9[4] 10 11[4] 12[2] 13 16 17[2] 19[3] 20 21[4] 16:1[2] 3[3] 4[6] 5[3] 6[2] 7[2] 8 9[6] 10[2] 11 12 14[5] 15[5] 16[3] 18 19[4] 21 17:1[4] 2[2] 3[2] 4 5[3] 6[4] 7[3] 8[3] 9 10[4] 11[2] 12[2] 13[4] 15[2] 16 17 18 19[7] 20[3] 21[3] 22[2] 24[4] 25[4] 26[8] 27[5] 18:1[2] 2 3[2] 4[4] 5[2] 6[3] 8 10 11[3] 12 13[3] 14[4] 15 17[4] 18[6] 19 21[4] 23 19:1[5] 2[5] 3[5] 4[2] 5 6[5] 7[7] 8 9[4] 10[3] 11 12[2] 13[6] 14[4] 15[3] 20:1[4] 2[5] 3[3] 4[5] 5[6] 8[2] 10 11 12[3] 13[5] 14[2]

JER.
20:15 16[5] 17 18 21:1[5] 2[2] 4[6] 6 7[10] 8[3] 9[4] 10[3] 11[4] 12[5] 13[3] 14[3] 22:1[3] 2[3] 3[7] 4[2] 5 6[3] 7 8 9[2] 10 11[2] 12 16[3] 18[2] 19[2] 20 22 23[2] 24[3] 25[5] 27 29[2] 30[2] 23:1[3] 2[4] 3 4 5[3] 6 7[5] 8[4] 9[3] 10[4] 11 12[3] 13 14[3] 15[5] 16[5] 17[2] 18[2] 19[3] 20[4] 22 23 24[2] 25 26[3] 28[4] 29[2] 30[2] 31[2] 32[2] 33[4] 34[5] 35[2] 36[5] 37[3] 38[7] 39 24:1[6] 2[2] 3[3] 4[2] 5[4] 7 8[5] 9[2] 10[4] 25:1[5] 2[4] 3[5] 4[2] 5[3] 6 7[2] 8 9[5] 10[10] 11 12[4] 13 14 15[3] 16 17[4] 18[3] 20[7] 21 22[5] 23 24[4] 25[4] 26[7] 27[3] 28[2] 29[4] 30[4] 31[6] 32[3] 33[6]

JER.
25:34[3] 35[3] 36[5] 37[3] 38[3] 26:1[4] 2[6] 3[2] 4 5[2] 6[2] 7[5] 8[5] 9[5] 10[7] 11[4] 12[4] 13[4] 15[2] 16[6] 17[4] 18[7] 19[4] 20[4] 21[3] 22[2] 23[4] 24[4] 27:1[4] 2 3[8] 4[2] 5[4] 6[4] 7 8[9] 9 11[4] 12[2] 13[6] 14[3] 15[2] 16[5] 17 18[8] 19[6] 20[2] 21[7] 22[2] 28:1[12] 2[4] 3[2] 4[5] 5[8] 6[5] 7[2] 8 9[5] 10[3] 11[7] 12[7] 13[2] 14[5] 15[3] 16[4] 17[3] 29:1[8] 2[6] 3[3] 4[2] 5 7[4] 8[3] 9 10 11[2] 14[5] 15 16[5] 17[4] 18[6] 19[3] 20[3] 21[5] 22[4] 23 24 25[6] 26[6] 28 29[3] 30[2] 31[3] 32[5] 30:1[2] 2[2] 3[5] 4[2] 5 7 8 9 10[2] 11 12 14[3] 15 17 18[5] 19 21[2] 23[4] 24[4] 31:1[4] 2[4] 3 4

JER.
31:5[2] 6[3] 7[4] 8[6] 9 10[3] 11[2] 12[6] 13[2] 14[3] 15 16[4] 17 18[2] 19 20 21[2] 22[2] 23[5] 24 25 27[6] 28 29[2] 30 31[4] 32[5] 33[3] 34[4] 35[8] 36[2] 37[5] 38[7] 39[2] 40[9] 32:1[4] 2[5] 3[3] 4[4] 5[2] 6[2] 7[2] 8[9] 9[2] 10[3] 11[3] 12[12] 14[3] 15[2] 16[4] 17[2] 18[6] 19[3] 20 21 24[8] 25[4] 26[2] 27[2] 28[4] 29[2] 30[5] 31 32[5] 33[2] 34 35[4] 36[7] 39 42[2] 43[2] 44[10] 33:1[5] 2[4] 4[7] 5[2] 6 7[3] 9[5] 10[3] 11[16] 12[2] 13[12] 14[4] 15[2] 16[2] 17[3] 18[2] 19[2] 20[3] 21[2] 22[5] 23[2] 24[2] 25[2] 26[2] 34:1[6] 2[5] 3[2] 4[4] 5[4] 6 7[3] 8[4] 10[3] 11[2] 12[3] 13[5] 14 15 16[2] 17[7] 18[5] 19[8] 20[6] 21[4] 22[2]

JER.
35:1[4] 2[5] 3[4] 4[11] 5[3] 6 7 8[2] 11[5] 12[2] 13[5] 14[2] 15[2] 16[3] 17[4] 18[5] 19[3] 36:1[3] 2[4] 3[2] 4[4] 5[2] 6[8] 7[4] 8[6] 9[7] 10[13] 11[5] 12[9] 13[4] 14[9] 16[2] 18 19 20[8] 21[8] 22[4] 23[6] 24 25[2] 26[7] 27[6] 28[3] 29[2] 30[6] 31[3] 32[6] 37:1[3] 2[5] 3[6] 4 5 6[3] 7[3] 8 9[2] 10[2] 11[2] 12[3] 13[6] 14[2] 15[4] 16[2] 17[5] 19 20[3] 21[8] 38:1[6] 2[5] 3[3] 4[8] 5[2] 6[6] 7[6] 8[2] 9[5] 10[4] 11[5] 12[2] 13[3] 14[6] 16[3] 17[4] 18[3] 19[3] 20[2] 21[2] 22[4] 23[8] 25[3] 26 27[3] 28[3] 39:1[2] 2[5] 3[6] 4[9] 5[3] 6[4] 8[5] 9[7] 10[6] 11[2] 13[3] 14[5] 15[4] 16[3] 17[3] 18[2] 40:1[4] 2[3] 3[2] 4[2] 5[7] 6[2] 7[7] 8[6]

JER.
40:9[5] 10 11[6] 12[2] 13[4] 14[4] 15[4] 16[2] 41:1[7] 2[7] 3[3] 4 5[2] 6[2] 7[6] 8 9[5] 10[9] 11[5] 12[3] 13[4] 14[2] 15[2] 16[10] 17 18[5] 42:1[7] 2[2] 3[3] 4[3] 5[3] 6[4] 7[2] 8[6] 9[2] 10 11[2] 13[2] 14[3] 15[4] 16[3] 17[5] 18[3] 19 20[3] 21[3] 22[4] 43:1[4] 2[4] 3[2] 4[7] 5[5] 6[7] 7[3] 8[2] 9[5] 10[3] 11[3] 12[3] 13[5] 44:1[4] 2[4] 4 6[2] 7 8[4] 9[7] 11[2] 12[9] 13[4] 14[4] 15[4] 16[3] 17[3] 18[3] 19 20[4] 21[6] 22[3] 23[3] 24[5] 25[3] 26[7] 27[4] 28[5] 29 30[4] 45:1[6] 2[2] 3 4 5 46:1[4] 2[4] 3 4[8] 5 6[4] 7 8[4] 9[6] 10[6] 11 12[4] 13[4] 14 15 16[3] 17 18[4] 20 21[3] 22 23[2] 24[4] 25[3] 26[5]

JER.
46:27[6] 28[2] 47:1[4] 2[7] 3[5] 4[6] 5 6 7[2] 48:1[2] 2 5[3] 6[2] 8[4] 9 10[2] 12[2] 13 14 15[3] 16 17[2] 18 19 21 24[2] 25[2] 26 28[5] 29[2] 30 31 32[4] 33[3] 34[2] 35[2] 36[2] 37[2] 38[3] 39 40 41[3] 42 43[3] 44[6] 45[7] 46 47[4] 49:1[2] 2[4] 3 4 5 6[3] 7[2] 8[2] 12[2] 13[2] 14[3] 15 16[7] 17 18[3] 19[4] 20[5] 21[5] 22[3] 23 25[2] 26[2] 27[2] 28[4] 29 31[2] 32[3] 34[5] 35[3] 36[3] 37[2] 38[3] 39[3] 50:1[5] 2 3 4[4] 5[2] 6 7[4] 8[5] 9 10 11 12[2] 13[2] 14[2] 15[2] 16[4] 17[2] 18[4] 20[3] 21[3] 22 23[3] 24 25[6] 26 27[2] 28[5] 29[4] 30[2] 31[2] 32 33[3] 34[2] 35[3] 36 37[2]

JER.
50:38 39[5] 40[2] 41[3] 42[4] 43[2] 44[4] 45[6] 46[4] 51:1[2] 2 3 4[3] 5[2] 6[3] 7[4] 9 10[3] 11[9] 12[7] 13 14 15[3] 16[5] 17 18[2] 19[4] 20 21[2] 22[2] 23[2] 24[2] 25[3] 26 27[7] 28[6] 29[3] 30 31 32[3] 33[4] 34 35[3] 36 39 40 41[3] 42[3] 44[2] 45[3] 46[3] 47[3] 48[5] 49[3] 50[2] 51[2] 52[3] 53[2] 54[2] 55[2] 56[2] 57[2] 58[5] 59[6] 60 63 64[2] 52:1 2[2] 3[3] 4[4] 5[2] 6[7] 7[11] 8[4] 9[3] 10[3] 11[2] 12[6] 13[6] 14[5] 15[10] 16[4] 17[9] 18[6] 19[9] 20[4] 21[3] 22[4] 23[2] 24[6] 25[13] 26[3] 27[2] 28[2] 29 30[5] 31[7] 32[2] 33 34[3]

LAM.
1:1[3] 2 3[2] 4[2] 5[4] 6[2] 7[4] 9 10[2] 11 12[2] 13 14[2] 15[5]

LAM.
1:16[2] 17 18 19[2] 20 2:1[5] 2[7] 3[2] 4[2] 5[2] 6[6] 7[7] 8[5] 9[4] 10[5] 11[7] 12[3] 13 15[4] 16[2] 17[3] 18[3] 19[7] 20[5] 21[6] 22[2] 3:3 12 13 24 25[2] 26[2] 27 29 31 32 33 34[2] 35[3] 36 37 38[2] 39 40 41 45 48[2] 50 51 53 58 64 66[2] 4:1[5] 2[4] 3[5] 4[3] 5 6[5] 8 9[3] 10[4] 11[2] 12[7] 13[5] 14 15 16[5] 19[4] 20[4] 21[2] 22 5:6[2] 9[2] 10 11[3] 12 13[3] 14[3] 15 16 18[2]

EZEKIEL
1:1[7] 2[3] 3[8] 4[5] 5[3] 7[3] 8 10[7] 12 13[6] 14[2] 15[3] 16[4] 19[5] 20[5] 21[5] 22[6] 23[3] 24[6] 25 26[7] 27[5] 28[10] 2:2 3 3:1 4 5 11[3] 12[3] 13[5] 14[4] 15[2]

EZEKIEL
3:16[3] 17[2] 18[3] 19 21[2] 22[3] 23[5] 24 26 27 4:1 2 3[2] 4[4] 5[5] 6[2] 7 8 9[2] 13[3] 16 5:1 2[5] 4[4] 5[3] 6[2] 7[4] 8[4] 9 10[6] 11 12[4] 13 14[2] 15[2] 16[2] 17[2] 6:1[2] 2 3[7] 5[2] 6[2] 7[3] 8[3] 9[2] 10 11[6] 12[3] 13[4] 14[3] 7:1[2] 2[5] 3 4[2] 5 6 7[6] 9[2] 10[3] 12[5] 13[4] 14[3] 15[6] 16[2] 19[5] 20[2] 21[4] 22 23[2] 24[4] 26[4] 27[6] 8:1[7] 2[4] 3[10] 4[4] 5[7] 6[2] 7[3] 8[2] 9 10[3] 11[4] 12[7] 14[4] 16[12] 17[4] 9:1 2[4] 3[7] 4[8] 5[2] 6[3] 7[4] 8 9[7] 11[3] 10:1[5] 2[5] 3[6] 4[10] 5[5] 6[4] 7[4] 8[2] 9[5] 10 11[2] 12[2] 13 14[8] 15[3] 16[5] 17[2] 18[5] 19[8] 20[4]

EZEKIEL
10:21[2] 22[3] 11:1[8] 2 3[2] 5[4] 6[2] 7[5] 8[2] 9[2] 10[3] 11[3] 12[3] 13[2] 14[2] 15[4] 16[4] 17[4] 18[2] 19 21[2] 22[4] 23[7] 24[4] 25[8] 12:1[2] 2 5 6[3] 7[3] 8[3] 9[2] 10[3] 12[4] 13[2] 14 15[3] 16[5] 17[2] 19[6] 20[3] 21[2] 22[2] 23[3] 24 25[4] 26[2] 27[3] 28[3] 13:1[2] 2[3] 3[2] 4[2] 5[6] 6[3] 7 8[2] 9[6] 12[2] 13 14[5] 15[2] 16[2] 17 18[5] 19[2] 20[4] 21 22[4] 23 14:1 2[2] 3 4[6] 5 6[2] 7[4] 8[2] 9[3] 10[4] 11[2] 12[2] 13[3] 14 15[2] 16[2] 17 18 20 21[5] 22 23 15:1[2] 2[3] 4[4] 5 6[6] 7 8[2] 16:1[2] 3[2] 4 5[3] 7[2] 8[2] 14[2] 15 16[2] 19 21 22 23 25 26 27[9] 28[8] 29

EZEKIEL
16:30^{2} 31 34 35^{2} 36^{3} 41^{2} 43^{2} 44 45 48 49^{3} 53^{4} 56 57^{4} 58 59^{3} 60 62 63
17:1^{2} 2 3^{3} 4 5^{2} 6 7 9^{5} 10^{2} 11^{2} 12^{4} 13^{3} 14 15 16^{4} 17 18^{2} 19 21^{2} 22^{4} 23^{4} 24^{8}
18:1^{2} 2^{3} 3 4^{5} 6^{3} 7^{3} 9 10 11 12^{3} 15^{3} 16^{3} 17^{2} 19^{4} 20^{11} 21 23^{2} 24^{3} 25^{2} 27 29^{3} 30 32^{2}
19:1 3 4^{2} 6^{2} 7^{3} 8^{2} 9^{2} 10 11^{3} 12^{3} 13 14
20:1^{6} 2^{2} 3^{3} 4 5^{4} 6^{3} 7^{3} 8^{4} 9^{2} 10^{2} 12 13^{3} 14 15^{3} 17 18^{2} 19 20 21^{2} 22^{2} 23^{3} 26^{4} 27^{2} 28^{4} 29^{2} 30^{3} 31^{2} 32^{3} 33 34^{2} 35^{2} 36^{3} 37^{3} 38^{4} 39 40^{6} 41^{3} 42^{4} 44^{2} 45^{2} 46^{4}

EZEKIEL
20:47^{8} 48
21:1^{2} 2^{2} 3^{4} 4^{4} 5 6 7^{2} 8^{2} 9 10 11^{2} 12^{3} 13^{3} 14^{6} 15^{3} 16^{2} 17 18^{2} 19^{5} 20^{3} 21^{6} 22^{5} 23 24^{2} 26^{4} 28^{6} 29^{2} 30^{2} 31^{2} 32^{4}
22:1^{2} 2 3^{3} 4 6 7^{4} 9^{2} 12 13 14^{2} 15^{2} 16^{3} 17 18^{4} 19^{2} 20^{3} 21^{2} 22^{4} 23^{2} 24^{2} 25^{4} 26^{3} 27^{2} 28^{2} 29^{4} 30^{3} 31^{2}
23:1^{2} 2 3 4^{2} 5^{2} 7 8 9^{3} 10 12 14^{3} 15^{2} 17^{2} 19^{3} 20^{2} 21^{3} 22 23^{3} 25^{2} 27 28^{3} 29 30 31 32 33^{2} 34^{2} 35 36 37 38 39^{2} 42^{2} 44^{2} 45^{3} 46 47 48 49^{2}
24:1^{6} 2^{3} 3^{2} 4^{4} 5^{4} 6^{3} 7^{3} 8 9^{3} 10^{3} 11^{4} 12 14^{2} 15^{2} 16 17^{3} 18^{3} 19 20^{2}

EZEKIEL
25:21^{5} 22 24 25^{3} 27
25:1^{2} 2 3^{6} 4^{2} 5^{2} 6^{3} 7^{4} 8^{3} 9^{4} 10^{5} 11 12^{2} 13^{2} 14^{2} 15^{3} 16^{5} 17
26:1^{5} 2^{2} 3^{2} 4^{2} 5^{5} 6^{3} 7^{2} 8^{3} 10^{5} 11^{3} 12^{2} 13^{2} 14^{3} 15^{6} 16^{3} 17 18^{4} 19^{3} 20^{7} 21
27:1^{2} 3^{4} 4^{2} 6^{4} 7 8 9^{4} 10 11^{2} 12 13 14 15^{2} 16^{2} 17 18^{4} 21 22 23 25^{3} 26^{3} 27^{5} 28^{3} 29^{5} 30 32^{3} 33^{4} 34^{5} 35^{2} 36^{2}
28:1^{2} 2^{6} 6^{2} 7^{3} 8^{4} 9 10^{4} 11^{2} 12^{3} 13^{11} 14^{4} 15 16^{4} 17 18^{5} 19 20^{2} 22^{3} 23^{4} 24^{2} 25^{2} 26^{4}
29:1^{6} 3^{3} 4^{3} 5^{7} 6 8 9^{3} 10^{3} 12^{7} 13^{4} 14^{3} 15^{4} 16^{3} 17^{6} 18^{3} 19^{3} 20 21^{6}
30:1^{2} 2 3^{5} 4^{2} 5^{4}

EZEKIEL
30:6^{5} 7^{4} 8 9^{2} 10^{3} 11^{5} 12^{7} 13^{4} 15^{2} 17^{2} 18^{3} 19 20^{6} 21^{2} 22^{3} 23^{3} 24^{3} 25^{7} 26^{4}
31:1^{6} 3^{2} 4^{4} 5^{3} 6^{3} 7 8^{5} 9^{3} 10^{2} 11^{3} 12^{8} 13^{4} 14^{8} 15^{8} 16^{7} 17^{3} 18^{8}
32:1^{6} 2^{3} 3 4^{6} 5^{2} 6^{3} 7^{4} 8^{2} 9^{3} 10 11^{3} 12^{6} 13^{4} 14 15^{3} 16^{4} 17^{5} 18^{6} 19 20^{3} 21^{4} 22 23^{5} 24^{6} 25^{7} 26^{3} 27^{6} 28^{3} 29^{3} 30^{6} 31^{3} 32^{6}
33:1^{2} 2^{4} 3^{4} 4^{4} 5^{2} 6^{3} 7^{2} 8^{2} 9 10 11^{4} 12^{9} 13 14 15^{3} 17^{3} 18 19 20^{2} 21^{5} 22^{4} 23^{2} 24^{3} 25^{3} 26 27^{8} 28^{3} 29^{2} 30^{6} 31 32
34:1^{2} 2^{6} 3^{6} 4 5^{2} 6^{2} 7^{3} 8^{3} 9^{2} 10^{4} 11 12^{2} 13^{6} 14^{2} 15 16^{2} 17^{3} 18^{4} 20^{3}

EZEKIEL
34:21 24^{2} 25^{4} 26^{2} 27^{5} 28^{3} 29^{3} 30^{3} 31^{2}
35:1^{2} 3 4 5^{6} 6 8 9 10 11 12^{2} 14^{2} 15^{3}
36:1^{3} 2^{3} 3^{5} 4^{11} 5^{4} 6^{8} 7^{2} 10^{3} 11 13 14 15^{5} 16^{2} 17^{2} 18^{2} 19^{2} 20^{3} 21^{2} 22^{3} 23^{5} 24 28 29 30^{5} 32 33^{3} 34^{2} 35^{2} 36^{4} 37^{2} 38^{4}
37:1^{6} 2 4^{2} 5 6 7 8^{3} 9^{4} 10 11 12^{2} 13 14^{2} 15^{2} 16^{3} 18 19^{5} 20 21^{3} 22^{2} 25 26 28^{3}
38:1^{2} 2^{2} 3^{2} 6^{2} 8^{5} 9 10^{2} 12^{5} 13^{2} 14 15 16^{3} 17^{2} 18^{3} 19^{2} 20^{13} 21 22 23^{2}
39:1^{2} 2^{3} 4^{5} 5^{2} 6^{2} 7^{4} 8^{2} 9^{8} 10^{4} 11^{7} 12^{2} 13^{4} 14^{5} 15^{4} 16^{3} 17^{3} 18^{5} 20 21^{2} 22^{2} 23^{4} 25^{3} 27^{2}

EZEKIEL
39:28 29^{2}
40:1^{10} 2^{4} 3^{2} 4^{3} 5^{7} 6^{7} 7^{5} 8^{2} 9^{5} 10^{3} 11^{5} 12^{4} 13^{4} 14^{3} 15^{6} 16^{3} 17^{3} 18^{6} 19 20^{5} 21^{7} 22^{4} 23^{5} 24^{4} 25^{3} 26^{2} 27^{3} 28^{3} 29^{4} 30 31^{4} 32^{3} 33^{4} 34^{4} 35 36^{6} 37^{4} 38^{5} 39^{5} 40^{6} 41^{2} 42^{5} 43^{3} 44^{11} 45^{5} 46^{9} 47^{3} 48^{5} 49^{5}
41:1^{6} 2^{8} 3^{5} 4^{4} 5^{4} 6^{6} 7^{9} 8^{4} 9^{5} 10^{3} 11^{7} 12^{7} 13^{4} 14^{5} 15^{9} 16^{7} 17^{3} 19^{7} 20^{4} 21^{8} 22^{7} 23^{2} 24^{3} 25^{5} 26^{6}
42:1^{7} 2^{3} 3^{4} 4^{2} 5^{5} 6^{6} 7^{6} 8^{4} 9^{3} 10^{7} 11^{4} 12^{8} 13^{11} 14^{4} 15^{3} 16^{3} 17^{2} 18^{2} 19^{2} 20^{3}
43:1^{3} 2^{5} 3^{7} 4^{6} 5^{5} 6^{2} 7^{7} 8 9^{2} 10^{3} 11^{11} 12^{7} 13^{10} 14^{7} 15^{2} 16^{2} 17^{4} 18^{4} 19^{4} 20^{5} 21^{5}

EZEKIEL
43:22^{4} 23 24^{3} 25 26 27^{4}
44:1^{4} 2^{3} 3^{7} 4^{7} 5^{8} 6^{3} 7^{2} 8 9^{2} 10 11^{6} 12^{3} 13^{2} 14^{3} 15^{8} 17^{4} 19^{5} 21 22^{2} 23^{4} 27^{5} 29^{3} 30^{6} 31
45:1^{7} 2^{2} 3^{4} 4^{7} 5^{5} 6^{5} 7^{17} 8^{4} 9^{2} 11^{8} 12 13^{2} 14^{4} 15^{3} 16^{3} 17^{10} 18^{5} 19^{11} 20^{3} 21^{2} 22^{3} 23^{3} 25^{10}
46:1^{8} 2^{10} 3^{6} 4^{4} 5^{3} 6^{2} 7 8^{4} 9^{14} 10^{2} 11^{4} 12^{6} 13^{2} 14^{4} 15^{3} 16^{3} 17^{2} 18^{2} 19^{7} 20^{7} 21^{4} 22^{2} 23 24^{3}
47:1^{12} 2^{6} 3^{5} 4^{5} 5 6^{2} 7^{4} 8^{5} 9^{2} 10^{3} 11^{2} 12^{6} 13^{4} 14 15^{5} 16^{3} 17^{6} 18^{5} 19^{5} 20^{4} 21 22^{4} 23^{2}
48:1^{7} 2^{3} 3^{3} 4^{3} 5^{3} 6^{3} 7^{3} 8^{9} 9^{2} 10^{8} 11^{4} 12^{3} 13^{5} 14^{3} 15^{6} 16^{5} 17^{6}

EZEKIEL
48:18^{7} 19^{2} 20^{4} 21^{18} 22^{9} 23^{4} 24^{3} 25^{3} 26^{3} 27^{3} 28^{6} 29^{3} 30^{3} 31^{4} 32 33 34 35^{3}

DANIEL
1:1^{2} 2^{7} 3^{5} 4^{4} 5^{5} 6 7^{3} 8^{5} 9^{2} 10^{5} 11^{2} 13^{4} 15^{4} 16^{2} 18^{5} 19^{2} 20^{2} 21
2:1^{2} 2^{7} 3^{2} 4^{4} 5^{5} 6^{4} 7^{3} 8^{3} 9^{4} 10^{4} 11^{3} 12^{2} 13^{2} 14^{3} 15^{4} 16^{3} 17 18^{3} 19^{2} 20 21^{3} 22^{3} 23 24^{6} 25^{4} 26^{3} 27^{9} 28^{3} 30^{3} 31 34 35^{11} 36^{3} 37 38^{5} 39 40 41^{5} 42^{3} 43 44^{3} 45^{11} 46 47 48^{4} 49^{5}
3:1^{4} 2^{3} 3^{12} 5^{4} 6^{2} 7^{8} 8 9 10^{3} 11 12^{3} 13 14 15^{5} 16 17 18 19^{3} 20^{2} 21^{2} 22^{4} 23^{2} 24^{4} 25^{5} 26^{5} 27^{4} 28^{2} 29 30^{2}
4:1^{2} 2^{2} 5^{2} 6^{3}

DANIEL
4:7^{6} 8^{5} 9^{5} 10^{4} 11^{5} 12^{7} 13 14^{3} 15^{8} 17^{10} 18^{5} 19^{5} 20^{4} 21^{5} 22^{2} 23^{10} 24^{4} 25^{5} 26^{3} 27 28 29^{3} 30^{5} 31^{3} 32^{4} 33^{3} 34^{3} 35^{5} 36^{2} 37
5:1^{2} 2^{4} 3^{4} 4 5^{8} 6^{2} 7^{9} 8^{4} 10^{5} 11^{8} 12^{8} 13^{5} 14^{2} 15^{5} 16^{4} 17^{4} 18 19 21^{6} 23^{4} 24^{2} 25 26^{2} 27 28 29^{2} 30^{2} 31^{2}
6:1^{2} 2^{2} 3^{3} 4^{2} 5 6 7^{7} 8^{4} 9^{2} 10 12^{7} 13^{4} 14^{3} 15^{5} 16^{3} 17^{5} 18^{2} 19^{3} 20^{4} 21 22 23^{3} 24^{6} 25 26^{3} 27^{2} 28^{3}
7:1^{4} 2^{3} 3 4^{4} 5^{3} 6^{3} 7^{4} 8^{4} 9^{5} 10^{2} 11^{5} 12^{2} 13^{4} 15^{2} 16^{3} 17 18^{4} 19^{4} 20^{2} 21^{2} 22^{6} 23^{3} 24^{2} 25^{4} 26^{2} 27^{7} 28^{3}
8:1^{3} 2^{3} 3^{4} 4 5^{5}

DANIEL
8:6^{3} 7^{5} 8^{3} 9^{3} 10^{4} 11^{4} 12^{3} 13^{5} 14 15^{3} 16^{2} 17^{3} 18 19^{4} 20^{2} 21^{4} 22 23^{3} 24^{2} 25 26^{4} 27^{2}
9:1^{6} 2^{7} 3 4^{3} 6^{3} 7^{3} 9 10^{3} 11^{4} 12 13^{2} 14^{3} 15 16 17^{2} 18 20^{3} 21^{5} 23^{4} 24^{3} 25^{6} 26^{7} 27^{8}
10:1^{5} 4^{4} 6^{4} 7^{3} 9^{3} 10 11 12 13^{4} 14^{2} 15 16^{3} 17 18 20^{2} 21
11:1^{2} 2^{3} 4 5^{2} 6^{7} 7^{3} 8^{2} 9^{2} 11^{5} 12 13^{3} 14^{4} 15^{5} 16 17^{2} 18^{3} 19 20^{2} 21^{3} 22^{3} 23 24^{4} 25^{4} 26 27^{2} 28 29^{4} 30^{3} 31^{3} 32^{2} 33^{2} 35^{2} 36^{3} 37^{2} 38 39^{2} 40^{7} 41^{3} 42^{3} 43^{4} 44^{2} 45^{3}
12:1^{3} 2^{2} 3^{3} 4^{4} 5^{6} 6^{4} 7^{5} 8 9^{3} 10^{3} 11^{3} 12 13^{3}

HOSEA
1:1^{6} 2^{6} 3 4^{5} 5^{3} 6 7^{3} 10^{7} 11^{4}
2:3 4 5 9^{2} 10 12^{3} 13^{2} 14 15^{4} 16 17 18^{9} 20 21^{3} 22^{4} 23
3:1^{4} 3 4 5^{4}
4:1^{6} 3^{6} 4 5^{3} 6 8 10 11 12 13^{4} 14 15^{2} 16 19
5:1 2 4^{3} 5 6 7 8^{2} 9^{2} 10^{2} 11 12 13 14
6:1 2 3^{5} 4 5^{3} 6 7 9^{2} 10^{2} 11
7:1^{4} 3^{2} 4^{2} 5^{2} 6^{2} 8 10^{2} 12^{2} 16^{4}
8:1^{3} 3^{2} 6^{2} 7^{4} 8 10^{3} 12 13^{2} 14
9:2^{3} 3 4^{3} 5^{4} 6 7^{6} 8^{3} 9 10^{3} 11^{3} 13 15 16 17
10:1^{3} 3 4^{2} 5^{5} 7^{2} 8^{6} 9^{3} 10 11 12 13^{2} 14^{2} 15
11:4 5^{2} 6 7 9^{4} 10^{3}

HOSEA
11:11^{2} 12^{2}
12:1^{2} 2 3^{2} 4 5^{2} 7 9^{4} 10^{3} 11^{2} 12 13
13:2^{4} 3^{7} 4^{2} 5^{2} 7 8^{2} 12 13^{3} 14^{2} 15^{4} 16
14:1 2^{2} 3^{2} 5^{2} 6 7^{4} 9^{4}

JOEL
1:1^{3} 2^{2} 4^{6} 5 6^{2} 7 8 9^{6} 10^{5} 11^{4} 12^{8} 13^{4} 14^{6} 15^{4} 16^{2} 17^{4} 18^{3} 19^{6} 20^{6}
2:1^{5} 2^{4} 3^{2} 4^{2} 5^{4} 6 7 8 9^{4} 10^{5} 11^{3} 12 13^{2} 14 15 16^{7} 17^{7} 18 19^{2} 20^{3} 21 22^{6} 23^{6} 24^{2} 25^{5} 26^{2} 27^{2} 29^{2} 30^{2} 31^{5} 32^{5}
3:1 2^{2} 4 6^{3} 7 8^{4} 9^{3} 10 12^{3} 13^{4} 14^{3} 15^{3} 16^{7} 17 18^{6} 19^{2} 21

AMOS
1:1^{6} 2^{4} 3^{2} 4^{2} 5^{7} 6^{3} 7^{2} 8^{5} 9^{4} 10^{2} 11^{3} 12 13^{4} 14^{5} 15

AMOS
2:1^{4} 2^{3} 3^{4} 4^{5} 5 6^{4} 7^{7} 8^{3} 9^{4} 10^{4} 11 12^{2} 14^{4} 15^{2} 16^{2}
3:1^{3} 2^{2} 4 5^{2} 6^{3} 7^{2} 8^{2} 9^{8} 10 11^{2} 12^{6} 13^{3} 14^{6} 15^{5}
4:1^{3} 2^{2} 3^{3} 5^{2} 6 7^{3} 8 9^{2} 10^{5} 11^{2} 13^{7}
5:2 3^{3} 4^{2} 6^{2} 7 8^{9} 9^{4} 10 11 12^{3} 13 14^{2} 15^{5} 16^{5} 17 18^{4} 19^{2} 20^{2} 22 23^{2} 25 26^{2} 27^{2}
6:1^{3} 2^{2} 3^{2} 4^{5} 5^{2} 6^{2} 7^{2} 8^{5} 10^{6} 11^{3} 12^{2} 14^{5}
7:1^{6} 2^{2} 3^{2} 4^{3} 6^{2} 7 8^{3} 9^{4} 10^{4} 11 12 13^{2} 15^{3} 16^{3} 17^{3}
8:1 2^{2} 3^{3} 4^{3} 5^{5} 6^{4} 7^{3} 8^{2} 9^{4} 10^{2} 11^{5} 12^{4} 13 14^{2}
9:1^{8} 3^{4} 4 5^{3} 6^{7} 7^{5} 8^{7} 9^{3} 10^{3} 11^{3} 12^{3} 13^{7} 14^{4}

AMOS
9:15

OBADIAH
1^{4} 2 3^{4} 4^{3} 5 6 7^{3} 8^{3} 9^{2} 11^{4} 12^{6} 13^{4} 14^{2} 15^{3} 16 17 18^{5} 19^{6} 20^{6} 21^{3}

JONAH
1:1^{3} 3^{5} 4^{4} 5^{6} 6 7 9^{4} 10^{4} 11^{2} 12^{2} 13^{3} 14 15^{2} 16^{3} 17^{3}
2:1^{2} 2^{2} 3^{4} 5^{4} 6^{3} 7 9^{2} 10^{3}
3:1^{3} 2 3^{2} 4 5^{3} 6 7^{2} 8 10
4:2^{3} 4 5^{5} 6^{3} 7^{3} 8^{3} 9 10^{3}

MICAH
1:1^{4} 2^{2} 3^{3} 4^{4} 5^{5} 6^{4} 7^{6} 8^{2} 9 10^{2} 11^{2} 12^{3} 13^{6} 14^{2} 15 16
2:1^{2} 3 4 5^{2} 7^{3} 8^{2} 9 11^{2} 12^{5} 13^{4}
3:1 2 3^{3} 4 5^{2} 6^{3} 7^{2} 8^{2} 9 11^{5} 12^{4}
4:1^{7} 2^{7} 4^{2} 5^{3} 6 7 8^{6} 10^{4} 12^{4} 13^{3}
5:1^{2} 2 3^{3}

MICAH
5:4^{7} 5^{2} 6^{5} 7^{6} 8^{6} 10^{2} 11 13^{2} 14 15
6:1^{3} 2^{3} 4^{2} 5^{3} 6^{2} 7^{3} 8 9^{4} 10^{4} 11^{2} 12^{2} 14^{2} 15 16^{6}
7:1^{4} 2^{2} 3^{3} 4^{3} 5 6^{5} 7^{2} 8 9^{3} 10^{3} 11^{2} 12^{3} 13^{2} 14^{4} 15^{2} 16 17^{3} 18^{2} 19^{2} 20^{3}

NAHUM
1:1^{4} 2^{3} 3^{7} 4^{3} 5^{4} 6^{2} 7^{2} 8 9^{2} 11 12 14^{4} 15^{3}
2:1^{2} 2^{4} 3^{5} 4^{4} 5^{2} 6^{3} 7 9^{4} 10^{3} 11^{7} 12 13^{5}
3:1^{2} 2^{6} 3^{3} 4^{4} 5^{3} 8^{4} 10^{2} 11 12^{3} 13^{3} 14^{3} 15^{6} 16^{3} 17^{5} 18^{2} 19^{2}

HABAK.
1:1^{2} 4^{3} 5 6^{4} 8^{3} 9^{3} 10^{2} 13^{2} 14^{3} 15 17
2:1 2^{2} 3^{2} 4 8^{5} 9 11^{4} 13^{4} 14^{6} 16^{3} 17^{5} 18^{4} 19^{3} 20^{2}
3:1 2^{4} 3^{3}

HABAK.
3:4^{2} 5 6^{4} 7^{3} 8^{4} 9^{3} 10^{4} 11^{3} 12^{2} 13^{6} 14^{2} 15^{2} 16^{3} 17^{8} 18^{3} 19^{2}

ZEPH.
1:1^{6} 2^{2} 3^{8} 4^{5} 5^{3} 6^{2} 7^{5} 8^{4} 9^{2} 10^{5} 11 12^{2} 13 14^{6} 16^{3} 17^{2} 18^{5}
2:2^{7} 3^{4} 4 5^{8} 6 7^{6} 8^{3} 9^{6} 10^{2} 11^{5} 13 14^{9} 15
3:1 2^{2} 3^{2} 4^{2} 5^{3} 6 8^{7} 9^{3} 10^{2} 11 12^{8} 13 14 15^{4} 17^{2} 18^{2} 20^{3}

HAGGAI
1:1^{11} 2^{4} 3^{2} 5 7 8^{3} 9 10^{2} 11^{8} 12^{12} 13^{4} 14^{11} 15^{4}
2:1^{6} 2^{5} 4^{5} 5 6^{5} 7^{2} 8^{3} 9^{4} 10^{6} 11^{3} 12^{2} 13 14 15^{2} 16^{2} 17^{2} 18^{5} 19^{6} 20^{4} 21^{2} 22^{7} 23^{4}

ZECH.
1:1^{7} 2 3^{3} 4^{3} 5 6^{2} 7^{9} 8^{2} 9 10^{4} 11^{5} 12^{3} 13^{2}

ZECH.
1:14^{3} 15^{2} 16^{2} 17^{2} 19^{2} 20 21^{4}
2:2^{3} 3 4 5^{3} 6^{6} 7 8^{4} 9 10^{2} 11^{3} 12^{2} 13
3:1^{3} 2^{4} 3 4 5^{2} 6^{3} 7 8^{2} 9^{4} 10^{3}
4:1 2^{3} 3^{4} 4 5 6^{3} 7 8^{2} 9^{3} 10^{6} 11^{3} 12^{2} 14^{3}
5:2^{2} 3^{4} 4^{7} 5 6 7^{2} 8^{4} 9^{5} 10^{2} 11
6:1 2^{2} 3^{2} 4 5^{6} 6^{5} 7^{4} 8^{2} 9^{2} 10^{4} 11^{3} 12^{5} 13^{4} 14^{4} 15^{5}
7:1^{5} 2^{2} 3^{5} 4^{2} 5^{4} 7^{6} 8^{2} 9 10^{4} 11 12^{5} 13 14^{3}
8:1^{2} 2 3^{5} 4^{2} 5^{3} 6^{4} 7^{3} 8 9^{8} 10 11^{2} 12^{5} 13 14^{2} 15 16^{3} 17 18^{2} 19^{11} 20^{2} 21^{3} 22^{2} 23^{3}
9:1^{6} 3^{3} 4^{2} 5 6^{2} 8 9 10^{7} 11^{2} 12 13^{2} 14^{5} 15^{3} 16^{3}

ZECH.
9:17^{2}
10:1^{4} 2^{2} 3^{5} 4^{3} 5^{5} 6^{3} 7 9 10^{2} 11^{7} 12^{3}
11:1 2^{4} 3^{4} 4^{3} 5 6^{6} 7^{5} 9^{2} 10 11^{4} 13^{6} 14 15^{2} 16^{4} 17^{3}
12:1^{5} 2^{2} 3^{2} 4^{3} 5^{3} 6^{5} 7^{6} 8^{5} 9 10^{3} 11^{3} 12^{5} 13^{3} 14
13:1^{2} 2^{7} 3^{2} 4 6 7^{5} 8^{3} 9^{3}
14:1^{3} 2^{7} 3^{2} 4^{9} 5^{8} 6 7 8^{2} 9^{2} 10^{6} 12^{3} 13^{3} 14^{2} 15^{6} 16^{4} 17^{4} 18^{5} 19^{3} 20^{7} 21^{4}

MALACHI
1:1^{3} 2^{2} 3^{2} 4^{6} 5^{2} 6 7^{2} 8^{3} 9 10^{2} 11^{7} 12^{8} 13^{4} 14^{4}
2:2 3 4 5 6 7^{4} 8^{4} 9^{3} 10 11^{3} 12^{6} 13^{3} 14^{3} 15^{3} 16^{3} 17^{4}
3:1^{5} 2 3^{2} 4^{2} 5^{7} 6 7^{3} 10^{4} 11^{5} 12 13 14 15 16^{3} 17 18^{2}

MALACHI
4:1[4] 2[2] 3[4] 4[2] 5[4] 6[6]

MATT.
1:1[4] 6[3] 11 16 17[3] 18[2] 20[3] 22[2] 24[2]
2:1[3] 2[2] 3 4[2] 5 6[3] 7[2] 8 9[4] 10 11[2] 13[4] 14 15[3] 16[5] 17 19 20[3] 21[2] 22[2] 23
3:1[2] 2 3[5] 4 5 7[2] 10[4] 11 12[2] 16[3]
4:1[3] 3[2] 4 5[3] 6 7 8[4] 10 11 13[2] 14 15[5] 16[2] 17 18[2] 21 22 23[3] 24
5:1 3[2] 5[2] 7 8 9[2] 10 12 13[3] 14[2] 15 17[2] 18 19[4] 20[3] 21 22[2] 23 24 25[5] 26 32 33 35[3] 39 40 45[5] 46[2] 47
6:2[3] 5[4] 7 13[3] 16 22[3] 23 24[4] 25[2] 26[2] 28[2] 30[3] 32 33 34[5]
7:3[2] 4 5[2] 6 12[2] 13[3]

MATT.
7:14[2] 19 21[2] 25[3] 26 27[4] 28 29
8:1 4[2] 6 8[2] 11[2] 12[2] 13[2] 15 16[2] 17 18 20[4] 22 24[3] 26[2] 27[3] 28[4] 29 31[2] 32[4] 33[3] 34
9:2[3] 3 6[3] 8 9 10 11 13 14[2] 15[5] 16[2] 17[3] 20 22 23[3] 24 25[3] 26 28[2] 33[3] 34[3] 35[4] 37[2] 38[2]
10:2[4] 3[2] 4 5[3] 6[2] 7 8[3] 10 13 14 15[2] 16 17 18 20 21[5] 22 23[2] 24[2] 25[4] 27[2] 28[2] 29 30 35[2] 41[2] 42
11:2[2] 5[7] 7[3] 11[2] 12[4] 13[2] 16 19 20 21 22 23 24[2] 25 27[5]
12:1[3] 2[2] 4[3] 5[5] 6 7 8[2] 10 11 12 13[2] 14 17 18 19 21 22 23 24[3] 28[2] 29

MATT.
12:31[2] 32[3] 33[3] 34[3] 35[3] 36 38[2] 39[2] 40[4] 41[3] 42[6] 43 45[2] 46 50[2]
13:1[3] 2[2] 4[2] 6 7 10 11[2] 14 18[2] 19[4] 20[3] 21 22[5] 23[2] 24 25 26[3] 27[2] 28 29[2] 30[5] 31 32[5] 33[2] 34 35[3] 36[5] 37[2] 38[8] 39[7] 40[3] 41 43[3] 44[2] 45 47[2] 48[2] 49[5] 50 52 55
14:1[2] 2[2] 5 6 8 9[2] 10 11 12 13[2] 15[3] 19[7] 20 22[2] 23[2] 24[4] 25[3] 26[2] 28 29[2] 30 32[2] 33[2] 34 35 36
15:2[2] 3 4 6 9 10 11[2] 12 14[4] 17[3] 18[3] 19 20 21 22 24[2] 26 27[2] 29 31[6] 32[2] 33 35[2] 36[4] 37 39[2]
16:1[2] 2 3[6] 4[2] 5 6[3] 9[2] 10[2] 11[3]

MATT.
16:12[4] 13[2] 14[2] 16[3] 18 19[2] 20 21[2] 23 26 27[2] 28
17:2[2] 5 6 9[4] 10 12 13[2] 14 15[2] 18[2] 19 22 23 25[3] 26 27[2]
18:1[4] 2 3 4[2] 6[2] 7[2] 10 11 12 13 14 16 17[2] 20 23 26 27[2] 28[2] 30 34
19:1 3 4 8[2] 10[2] 12 13 14 17 20 21 22 23 24[2] 28[4] 30
20:1[2] 2 3[2] 4 5 6[2] 7 8[5] 9 10 11[2] 12[2] 16[2] 17[2] 18[3] 19[2] 20 21[3] 22[2] 23 24[2] 25[2] 28 30 31[2]
21:1 2 3 4 5[2] 6 7[2] 8[3] 9[5] 10 11[2] 12[5] 13 14[3] 15[5] 16 17 18[2] 19[2] 20[2] 21[2] 23[4] 25 26 28 30 31[5] 32[3]

MATT.
21:34[4] 35 36 38[3] 39 40[2] 41 42[7] 43[2] 45 46
22:2 3 4 6 7 8 9[2] 10[2] 11[2] 13[2] 15 16[3] 19 21[2] 23[2] 25 26[3] 27 28[2] 29[2] 30[2] 31[2] 32[6] 33 34[2] 36[2] 37 38 39 40[2] 41 42 44
23:1 2[2] 5 6[3] 7 9 13 14 15 16[3] 17[3] 18[2] 19[3] 20 21 22 23[3] 25[3] 26[2] 29[4] 30[3] 31[2] 32 33 35[6] 37 39[2]
24:1[3] 3[5] 6 8 12 13[2] 14[3] 15[3] 16 17 18 20[2] 21[2] 22 24 26[2] 27[5] 28[2] 29[6] 30[6] 31[2] 32 33 36 37[3] 38[4] 39[3] 40[3] 41[3] 43[3] 44 49 50 51
25:1[2] 4 5 6 8[2] 9 10[3] 11 13[3] 14 16[2] 18

MATT.
25:19 21 23 24 25 27 28 30 31[3] 32 33[3] 34[4] 37 40[2] 41[2] 45 46
26:2[2] 3[6] 5[2] 6[2] 9 10 11 13 14[2] 17[4] 18[3] 19[2] 20 23[2] 24[2] 26 27 28[2] 29 30 31[3] 34 35 36 37 40 41[2] 42 44[2] 45[3] 47[3] 51 52[2] 54 55[2] 56[3] 57[3] 58[3] 59[2] 60 61 62 63[4] 64[3] 65 67 69 71 72 74[2] 75[2]
27:1[3] 2[3] 3[2] 4 5[2] 6[4] 7 8 9[4] 10[2] 11[4] 12 14 15[2] 19 20[2] 21[2] 23[2] 24[2] 25 27[4] 29[2] 30[2] 31 35 37[2] 38[2] 40[3] 41[2] 42[2] 43 44[2] 45[3] 46 49 50 51[6] 52[2] 53[2] 54[3] 56[2] 57 58[2] 59 60[3] 61[2] 62[4] 64[6] 66[2]

MATT.
28:1[5] 2[4] 4 5[2] 6[2] 7 8 9 11[4] 12[2] 14 15[2] 16 19[4] 20[2]

MARK
1:1[3] 2 3[4] 4[3] 5[2] 7 8 10[3] 12[2] 13[3] 14[2] 15[3] 16[2] 19[2] 20[2] 21[2] 22 24 26 27 28 29[2] 31[2] 33[2] 34 35 38 42 44 45
2:1 2[2] 3 4[5] 5[2] 6 9[2] 10[3] 12 13[2] 14[2] 16 17[2] 18[4] 19[4] 20[2] 21[3] 22[4] 23[3] 24[2] 26[5] 27[2] 28[2]
3:1 2 3[2] 4 5[3] 6[2] 7 9 11 17[3] 18[2] 20 22[3] 27 28 29 32 35[2]
4:1[5] 4[3] 6 7 10[2] 11[2] 14[2] 15[3] 16 17 18 19[4] 20 26[2] 27 28[5] 29[3] 30 31[3] 32[3] 33 35[3] 36[2] 37[2] 38[2] 39[3] 41[2]
5:1[4] 2[2]

MARK
5:3 4[2] 5[2] 7 8 10 11 12[2] 13[5] 14[3] 15[2] 16[2] 18[2] 19 21[2] 22[2] 23 27 29 30 31 33[2] 35[3] 36[3] 37 38[4] 39 40[4] 41[2] 42[2]
6:2[2] 3[3] 6 7 11[2] 14[2] 15 16 22[4] 23 24[2] 25[3] 26 27[2] 28[2] 30 33 35[2] 36[2] 39 41[4] 43[2] 44 45[3] 47[4] 48[4] 49 51[2] 52[2] 53[2] 54 56[3]
7:1[2] 3[4] 4[2] 5[3] 7 8[3] 9 10 13 14 15[2] 17[3] 18 19[2] 20[2] 21 23 24 26[2] 27[3] 28[3] 29 30[2] 31[4] 33 35 36[2] 37[2]
8:1 2 3 4 6[4] 8 10 11 13[2] 14[2] 15[3] 19 20 23[3] 26[2] 27[2] 28[2] 29 31[3] 33[2] 34 35[2] 36 38[3]
9:1 7 9[3]

MARK
9:10[2] 11 12 14 15 16 17 20[2] 22[2] 24[2] 25[2] 26 27 28 31[3] 33[2] 34[2] 35[2] 36 42 43 44 45 46 47 48 50
10:2 5 6[2] 10[2] 14[2] 15 17 19 21[2] 23 24[2] 25[2] 29 30 31 32[2] 33[4] 34 35 37 38[2] 39[2] 41 42 44 45 46[2] 48 49 51 52
11:1 2 3 4[2] 5 7 8[3] 9[2] 10[4] 11[3] 12 13 15[5] 16 17 18[2] 19 20[3] 21 23 27[4] 30 32
12:1 2[5] 4 7[2] 8 9[4] 10[4] 11 12[2] 13[2] 14[2] 17[2] 18 20 21[2] 22[2] 23[2] 24[2] 25[2] 26[6] 27[4] 28[2] 29[3] 30[2] 31 32[2] 33[4] 34 35[3] 36 37 38[2] 39[3] 41[3] 43
13:1

MARK
13:3[2] 4 7 8 9 10 11 12[4] 13[2] 14[3] 15[2] 16 18 19[2] 20[3] 22 24[2] 25[2] 26[2] 27[4] 28 29 32[3] 33 34[2] 35[4]
14:1[4] 2[2] 3[3] 4 5 7 8 9 10[2] 12[3] 13 14[5] 16[2] 17[2] 20[2] 21[2] 23 24 25[3] 26 27[2] 30 31 35[2] 38[2] 39 41[4] 43[4] 47 49[2] 51 52 53[4] 54[4] 55[2] 60[2] 61[4] 62[3] 63 64 65[2] 66[3] 68[2] 72[4]
15:1[4] 2[2] 3 7 8 9[2] 10 11[2] 12[2] 14 15 16[3] 18 19 20 21 22[2] 25 26[3] 27[2] 28[2] 29 30 31[2] 32[2] 33[3] 34 37 38[4] 39[3] 40[2] 42[4] 43[2] 44 45[2] 46[3] 47
16:1[2] 2[6] 4 5[2] 6 8 9[2] 12 13 14

MARK
16:15[2] 16[3] 18 19[2] 20[2]

LUKE
1:2[2] 3 4 5[4] 6[2] 8[2] 9[4] 10[3] 11[3] 13 15[3] 16[2] 17[8] 18 19[2] 20 21[2] 22 23 25[2] 26[2] 27[2] 28[2] 30 32[4] 33 34 35[5] 36 38[3] 39 40 41[3] 42 43 44[2] 45 46 48 51[2] 52 53[2] 58 59[3] 65 66[2] 67 68 69 70[2] 71 72 73 74 75 76[4] 77 78[2] 79[2] 80[3]
2:1 4[3] 6 7 8[2] 9[4] 10 11[2] 12 13[2] 14 15[3] 16 17 18 20[2] 21[4] 22[3] 23[4] 24[2] 25[3] 26[2] 27[6] 31 32[2] 34 35 36[2] 37 39[2] 40[2] 41[2] 42[2] 43[2] 44 46[3] 50
3:1[4] 2[4] 3[3] 4[7] 5[2] 6 7[2] 9[4] 10 14 15[2] 16[2] 17[2]

LUKE
3:18 19[2] 21[2] 22 23[2] 24[5] 25[5] 26[5] 27[5] 28[5] 29[5] 30[5] 31[5] 32[5] 33[5] 34[5] 35[5] 36[5] 37[5] 38[4]
4:1[3] 2 3[2] 5[3] 6[2] 8 9[2] 12 13[2] 14[3] 16[2] 17[4] 18[7] 19[2] 20[4] 22 25[3] 27[3] 28 29[3] 30 31 33 34 35[2] 36 37[2] 38 39 40 41 42 43 44
5:1[3] 2[2] 3[4] 4 5[2] 7[2] 9[2] 10 13 14 15 16 17[3] 19[4] 21[2] 24[3] 27 32 33[3] 34[3] 35[2] 36[4] 37[3] 39
6:1[4] 2[2] 4[3] 5[2] 6 7[2] 8[3] 9 10[2] 15 16[2] 17[3] 19 20 22 23[2] 26 29[2] 33 35[4] 38 39[3] 40 41[2] 42[4] 45[4] 46 48[3] 49[3]
7:1[2] 3[2] 6[2] 9 10[2] 11 12[4] 13 14 17

LUKE
7:18 20 22[7] 24[4] 28[2] 29[3] 30[2] 31 32 33 34 36[2] 37[2] 38[2] 39 41[2] 44[2] 45 47 50
8:1[3] 3 5[3] 7 10[2] 11[3] 12[3] 13[2] 15[2] 16 19 21 22[2] 23 24[3] 25 26[2] 27[2] 29[5] 31 32 33[5] 34 35[3] 36 37[4] 38[2] 39 40 41 42 44 45 47[2] 49[3] 51[4] 54
9:2[2] 5 6[2] 7[2] 8 10[2] 11[2] 12[4] 16[4] 18 19[2] 20 22[3] 24 25 26[2] 27 29 32 34 35 36 37[2] 38 42[3] 43 44[2] 47 48 51 52 56 57 58[2] 60[2] 62[2]
10:1 2[4] 4 6 7[2] 9[2] 10[2] 11[2] 13 14 17[2] 19[2] 20 21 22[5] 23[2] 26 27 31 32[2] 35[2] 36
11:7 13

LUKE
11:14[3] 15[2] 20[2] 24 26[2] 27[3] 28 29[3] 30[2] 31[7] 32[3] 33 34[3] 35 36[2] 38 39[4] 42[2] 43[3] 44 45 46 47[2] 48 49 50[4] 51[4] 52 53[2]
12:1[3] 3[3] 4 7 8[2] 9 10[2] 11 12[2] 13[2] 15[2] 16 22 23[2] 24[2] 26 27 28[3] 30[2] 31 32 33 36 37 38[2] 39[3] 40 42 45 46[2] 48 49 53[10] 54[2] 55 56[3] 58[6] 59
13:1 2 4 7[2] 10[2] 14[5] 15[3] 16 17[2] 18 19[3] 20 21 22 24 25[4] 28[2] 29[5] 31[2] 32 33 34 35[3]
14:1[3] 2 3[2] 5 7 8 9 10[2] 13[4] 14[2] 15 18 21[8] 22 23[3] 28 29 32 34 35[2]
15:1 2 4[2] 8 9 10[2] 12[2]

LUKE
15:13 16[2] 21 22[2] 23 25[2] 26 27 30
16:3[2] 4 5 8[4] 9 10 11[2] 13[4] 14 15 16[3] 17 21[3] 22[3] 24 29 30 31[2]
17:1 2 5[2] 6[3] 7 9 11 14 17 20[3] 21 22[4] 24[4] 26[3] 27[3] 28 29 30[2] 31[3] 34[2] 35[2] 36[3] 37[2]
18:6[2] 8[2] 10[3] 11 12 13 14 16 17 20 22 24 25 27 29 30 31[3] 32 33 34 35 36 39 43
19:2[2] 3 5 8[3] 10 11 15[2] 16 18 23 24 29[2] 30[2] 31 33[3] 34 35 36 37[5] 38[4] 39[2] 40 41 42 43 44[2] 45 46 47[5] 48
20:1[6] 2 4 6 9 10[5] 13[2] 14[3] 15[3] 16 17[4] 19[4] 20[2]

LUKE
20:21[2] 25[2] 26 27 29 30 31[2] 32 33 34 35[2] 36[4] 37[6] 38[2] 39 42[2] 45[2] 46[5] 47
21:1[2] 4[2] 5 6[2] 8 9 12 20 21[3] 22 23 24[5] 25[6] 26[2] 27 29[2] 31 35[2] 36 37 38[3]
22:1[2] 2[2] 3[2] 4 6[2] 7[2] 8 10[2] 11[5] 13 14[2] 16 17 18[3] 20[2] 21[2] 22 24 25[2] 26 30 31 34 37[2] 39 40 44 47 48 49 50[2] 53[2] 54 55[2] 56 59 60 61[4] 63 64 66[4] 67 69[3] 70
23:1 2 3[2] 4[2] 5[2] 6 10 12 13[3] 14 17 19 22 23[2] 26[2] 29[5] 30[2] 31 33[5] 35[3] 36 37[2] 38[2] 39 40[2] 41 44[3] 45[4] 46 47 48[2] 49 51[4]

LUKE
23:52 54[2] 55[2] 56[2]
24:1[5] 2[2] 3[2] 5[3] 7[3] 9[3] 10[2] 12[2] 18[2] 19 20 21 22 24[2] 25 27[3] 28 29 32[2] 33[2] 35 36 44[4] 45 46[2] 49[2] 53

JOHN
1:1[4] 2 4[2] 5[2] 7[2] 9[2] 10[3] 12 13[3] 14[4] 17 18[3] 19[2] 20 23[5] 24 29[4] 32 33[4] 34 35 36 37 39 40 41[2] 42 43 44 45[3] 48 49[2] 50 51[2]
2:1[2] 2 3 5 6[3] 7[2] 8[2] 9[6] 10[2] 13 14[2] 15[5] 17 18 20 21 22[3] 23[3]
3:1[2] 2 3 4 5[2] 6[2] 8[3] 13 14[3] 16 17[3] 18[2] 19[2] 20[2] 21 22 25 26 28 29[5] 31[2] 34[2] 35[2] 36[3]
4:1[2] 5 6[2] 8 9[3] 10 11[2] 12

JOHN
4:14[2] 15 17 19 20 21[2] 22 23[4] 25 27 28[3] 29 30 31 33 34 35 39[3] 40 42[4] 45[4] 46 47 49 50[2] 52[3] 53[3] 54
5:1 2[2] 3[2] 4[5] 7[3] 9[3] 10[3] 11 14 15[2] 16[2] 18[3] 19[3] 20[2] 21[3] 22[2] 23[4] 25[3] 26[2] 27 28[3] 29[2] 30[3] 32 33 36[4] 37 39 42 44 45
6:1[2] 4[3] 10[3] 11[4] 12 13[2] 14[2] 16 17 18 19[2] 21[5] 22[5] 23[2] 24 25[2] 26[2] 27[3] 28 29 31 32 33[2] 35 37 38 39[2] 40[3] 41[2] 42 44[2] 45[2] 46[2] 49 50 51[4] 52 53[2] 54 57[2] 59 62 63[3] 64 67 68 69[2] 71[2]
7:1 2 3 4 7[2] 10 11[2] 12[2] 13 14[3]

JOHN 7:15, 17, 18, 19^{2}, 20, 22^{2}, 23^{3}, 24, 26^{2}, 28, 31, 32^{4}, 35^{4}, 37^{2}, 38, 39^{2}, 40^{2}, 41, 42^{3}, 43, 45^{2}, 46, 47, 48^{2}, 49, 8:1, 2^{3}, 3^{2}, 4, 5, 6, 8, 9^{4}, 10, 12^{3}, 13, 15, 16, 17, 18, 20^{2}, 22, 25^{2}, 26^{2}, 27, 28, 29, 32^{2}, 34, 35^{3}, 36, 39, 40, 41, 44^{5}, 45, 46, 48, 52^{2}, 53, 57, 59^{2}, 9:3, 4^{2}, 5^{3}, 6^{5}, 7, 8, 11, 13, 14^{2}, 15, 16^{2}, 17, 18^{2}, 22^{3}, 24^{2}, 30, 32^{2}, 35, 10:1^{3}, 2^{3}, 3^{2}, 4, 5, 7^{2}, 8, 9, 10, 11^{3}, 12^{6}, 13^{2}, 14, 15^{3}, 19, 21^{3}, 22^{2}, 23, 24^{2}, 25, 31, 33, 35^{2}, 36^{3}, 37, 38^{2}, 40, 11:1, 2, 4^{2}, 6, 8, 9^{3}, 10, 15, 17, 19

JOHN 11:20, 24^{2}, 25^{2}, 27^{3}, 28, 30, 31^{3}, 33^{2}, 36, 37^{2}, 38, 39^{2}, 40, 41^{3}, 42, 45^{2}, 46, 47^{2}, 48, 49, 50^{2}, 52, 54^{2}, 55^{3}, 56^{2}, 57^{2}, 12:1^{2}, 2, 3^{4}, 5, 6^{2}, 7, 8, 9^{2}, 10, 11, 12^{2}, 13^{3}, 16, 17^{2}, 18, 19^{2}, 20, 21, 23^{2}, 24, 29, 31^{2}, 32, 34^{3}, 35^{2}, 36^{2}, 38^{4}, 42^{3}, 43^{2}, 46, 47^{2}, 48^{3}, 49, 50, 13:1^{5}, 2^{2}, 3, 5^{2}, 16, 18, 22, 26^{2}, 27, 28, 29^{3}, 30, 31, 33, 38, 14:4, 5, 6^{4}, 8, 9^{2}, 10^{5}, 11^{3}, 12, 13^{2}, 16, 17^{2}, 19, 22, 24^{2}, 26^{3}, 27, 28, 30, 31^{3}, 15:1^{2}, 3, 4^{2}, 5^{3}, 6, 9, 15, 16, 18, 19^{5}, 20^{2}, 24, 25, 26^{4}, 27, 16:2^{2}, 3, 4^{2}, 7^{2}, 8, 11, 13, 15

JOHN 16:16, 17, 20, 21^{3}, 23, 24^{2}, 26, 27, 28^{4}, 32^{2}, 33^{2}, 17:1, 3, 4^{2}, 5^{2}, 6^{2}, 8, 9, 11^{2}, 12^{3}, 13, 14^{4}, 15^{2}, 16^{2}, 18^{2}, 19, 21, 22, 23, 24^{2}, 25, 26, 18:1^{2}, 2, 3, 6, 9, 10^{2}, 11^{2}, 12^{3}, 13, 14^{2}, 15^{3}, 16^{3}, 17^{2}, 18, 19, 20^{4}, 22^{3}, 23, 24, 26^{3}, 27, 28^{3}, 31, 32, 33^{4}, 35, 36, 37^{3}, 38, 39^{3}, 19:2, 3, 5^{3}, 6, 7^{2}, 8, 9, 11, 12, 13^{3}, 14^{4}, 15, 17^{2}, 18, 19^{4}, 20^{3}, 21^{5}, 23^{3}, 24^{2}, 25^{2}, 26, 27, 28, 30^{2}, 31^{5}, 32^{4}, 34, 36, 38^{3}, 39, 40^{4}, 41^{2}, 42^{2}, 20:1^{5}, 2^{3}, 3, 4^{2}, 5, 6^{2}, 7^{2}, 8, 9^{2}, 10, 11^{2}, 12^{5}, 15, 18^{2}, 19^{7}, 20^{2}, 22, 24, 25^{6}, 26^{2}, 30, 31^{2}

JOHN 21:1^{2}, 2, 4^{3}, 6^{4}, 7^{3}, 8^{2}, 10, 11^{2}, 12^{2}, 14^{2}, 16, 17^{2}, 20, 23, 24, 25^{3}

ACTS 1:1, 2^{3}, 3^{2}, 4^{2}, 5, 6, 7^{3}, 8^{3}, 12, 13^{2}, 14^{2}, 15^{3}, 16^{2}, 18^{2}, 19^{2}, 20, 21^{2}, 22, 24, 26^{2}, 2:1, 2, 4^{2}, 6, 9, 10, 11, 14, 15^{2}, 16, 17, 19, 20^{3}, 21^{2}, 22, 23, 24, 25, 28, 29, 30^{2}, 31, 33^{4}, 34^{2}, 36, 37^{2}, 39^{2}, 41, 42, 43, 46, 47^{3}, 3:1^{3}, 2^{3}, 3, 6, 7, 8, 9, 10^{2}, 11^{3}, 12, 13^{3}, 14^{2}, 15^{2}, 16^{2}, 18, 19^{3}, 21^{4}, 22^{2}, 23, 24, 25^{5}, 4:1^{5}, 2^{3}, 3, 4^{3}, 5, 6^{3}, 7, 8^{2}, 9^{2}, 10^{3}, 11^{3}, 13, 14, 15, 17, 18, 19, 20, 21, 22, 23, 24, 25^{3}, 26^{4}, 27^{2}, 30

ACTS 4:31^{3}, 32^{2}, 33^{3}, 34^{2}, 35, 36^{3}, 37^{2}, 5:2^{2}, 3^{3}, 5, 6, 7, 8, 9^{4}, 10^{2}, 11, 12^{3}, 13^{2}, 14^{2}, 15^{4}, 16, 17^{3}, 18^{2}, 19^{3}, 20^{3}, 21^{7}, 22^{2}, 23^{3}, 24^{4}, 25^{3}, 26^{3}, 27^{2}, 29, 30, 32, 33, 34^{4}, 37^{2}, 40^{2}, 41^{2}, 42, 6:1^{5}, 2^{4}, 3, 4^{2}, 5^{3}, 6, 7^{5}, 8, 9^{3}, 10^{2}, 12^{4}, 13, 14, 15^{2}, 7:1, 2, 3, 4^{2}, 7, 8^{3}, 9, 10, 11, 13, 16^{3}, 17^{3}, 19^{2}, 22^{2}, 23, 24, 26, 28, 29, 30^{2}, 31^{3}, 32^{4}, 33^{2}, 34, 35^{4}, 36^{3}, 37^{2}, 38^{5}, 40, 41^{2}, 42^{5}, 43^{2}, 44^{3}, 45^{4}, 46, 48^{2}, 49^{2}, 51, 52^{4}, 53^{2}, 54, 55^{3}, 56^{3}, 58^{2}, 8:1^{3}, 3, 4, 5, 6^{2}, 9^{2}, 10^{3}, 12^{3}, 13, 14^{2}, 15, 16^{2}, 17, 18^{2}, 19, 20, 21, 22

ACTS 8:23^{2}, 24, 25^{4}, 26^{4}, 27^{2}, 28, 29, 30, 32^{3}, 33, 34^{2}, 35, 36, 37, 38^{3}, 39^{4}, 40, 9:1^{3}, 2, 4, 5^{2}, 6^{2}, 7, 8^{2}, 10, 11^{3}, 14, 15^{3}, 17^{4}, 19, 20^{2}, 21, 22^{2}, 23, 24, 25^{2}, 26, 27^{4}, 29^{3}, 30, 31^{5}, 32, 33, 35, 38, 39^{3}, 40, 41, 42, 10:1^{2}, 2, 3^{2}, 6, 7, 9^{4}, 11^{2}, 12^{2}, 15^{2}, 16, 17^{2}, 19^{2}, 21^{2}, 22^{3}, 23, 24, 30, 31, 32^{2}, 36^{2}, 37, 38^{2}, 39^{2}, 40, 41^{2}, 42^{2}, 43, 44^{2}, 45^{4}, 47, 48^{2}, 11:1^{3}, 2, 4^{2}, 5, 6^{3}, 9, 11, 12^{2}, 15^{2}, 16^{3}, 17^{2}, 18, 19^{3}, 20^{2}, 21^{3}, 22^{2}, 23^{2}, 24^{2}, 26^{2}, 28^{3}, 29^{2}, 30^{2}, 12:1^{2}, 2^{2}, 3^{2}, 4, 5, 6^{4}, 7^{4}, 8, 9, 10^{5}, 11^{5}, 12^{3}, 13^{2}, 14^{2}, 16

ACTS 12:17^{4}, 18, 19, 20^{2}, 22^{2}, 23^{4}, 24, 13:1^{2}, 2^{3}, 4, 5^{3}, 6, 7^{3}, 8^{3}, 9, 10^{3}, 11^{4}, 12^{3}, 14^{2}, 15^{6}, 17^{3}, 18^{2}, 19, 20^{2}, 21^{3}, 22, 24^{2}, 26^{2}, 27^{2}, 29, 30, 31, 32^{2}, 33^{2}, 34^{2}, 36, 38, 39, 40, 42^{4}, 43^{3}, 44^{3}, 45^{2}, 46^{2}, 47^{4}, 48^{3}, 49^{3}, 50^{4}, 51, 52^{2}, 14:1^{4}, 2^{3}, 3^{2}, 4^{4}, 5^{2}, 6, 7, 9, 11^{4}, 12, 13^{3}, 14^{2}, 15^{2}, 18, 19^{2}, 20^{3}, 21, 22^{4}, 23, 25, 26^{2}, 27^{3}, 28, 15:1^{2}, 2, 3^{4}, 4^{2}, 5^{3}, 6, 7^{3}, 8^{2}, 10^{2}, 11^{2}, 12^{2}, 14^{2}, 15^{2}, 16^{2}, 17^{4}, 18^{2}, 19, 21, 22^{3}, 23^{3}, 24, 26, 27, 28, 30^{2}, 31, 32, 33^{2}, 35^{2}, 36^{2}, 38, 39^{2}, 40^{2}, 41, 16:1, 2, 3, 4^{3}, 5^{2}, 6^{3}, 7, 9, 10^{3}, 11

ACTS 16:12, 13^{3}, 14^{3}, 15, 17^{4}, 18^{3}, 19^{3}, 20, 22^{2}, 23, 24^{2}, 25, 26^{3}, 27^{4}, 31, 32^{2}, 33^{2}, 35^{2}, 36^{3}, 38^{2}, 39, 40^{3}, 17:1, 2, 3, 4^{2}, 5^{5}, 6^{3}, 7, 8^{3}, 9, 10^{2}, 11^{2}, 13^{3}, 14^{2}, 15, 16, 17^{4}, 18^{3}, 21, 22, 23, 24, 26^{4}, 27, 29^{2}, 30, 31^{3}, 32^{2}, 34^{2}, 18:3, 4^{3}, 5^{2}, 6, 7, 8^{4}, 9^{2}, 11, 12^{3}, 13, 14, 16, 17^{4}, 18, 19^{2}, 22, 23^{2}, 24, 25^{6}, 26^{2}, 27^{2}, 28^{2}, 19:1, 2, 4^{2}, 5^{2}, 6, 7, 8^{4}, 9^{3}, 10^{3}, 11, 12^{3}, 13^{3}, 14, 15, 16^{2}, 17^{3}, 19, 20, 21, 23, 24, 25, 27^{3}, 28, 29^{2}, 30^{2}, 31^{2}, 32^{2}, 33^{4}, 34^{2}, 35^{6}, 38^{2}, 41, 20:1^{2}, 3, 4, 6, 7^{4}, 8, 9, 12, 15^{3}, 16^{2}, 17^{2}, 18

ACTS 20:19^{3}, 21^{2}, 22^{2}, 23, 24^{4}, 25, 26, 27, 28^{4}, 29, 31, 32, 35^{3}, 38^{2}, 21:1, 3^{2}, 4, 5^{2}, 7, 8^{4}, 9, 11^{5}, 13^{2}, 14^{2}, 16, 17, 18^{2}, 19, 20^{2}, 21^{3}, 22, 24, 25, 26^{5}, 27^{4}, 28^{4}, 29^{2}, 30^{4}, 31^{2}, 32^{2}, 33, 34^{4}, 35^{4}, 36^{2}, 37^{2}, 38, 39, 40^{4}, 22:2^{2}, 3^{4}, 4, 5^{4}, 7, 9^{2}, 10, 11^{2}, 12^{2}, 13, 14^{2}, 16^{2}, 17, 20^{2}, 21, 22, 23, 24^{2}, 25, 26^{2}, 27, 28, 29, 30^{4}, 23:1, 2^{2}, 3^{2}, 5^{2}, 6^{6}, 7^{3}, 8^{2}, 9^{2}, 10^{3}, 11^{2}, 12, 14, 15^{2}, 16, 17^{2}, 18^{2}, 19^{2}, 20^{2}, 22^{2}, 23^{2}, 24, 26, 27, 28, 30^{2}, 31, 32^{3}, 33^{2}, 34^{2}, 24:1^{3}, 5^{4}, 6, 7, 9, 10^{2}, 12^{4}, 13, 14^{4}, 15^{2}, 18, 20, 21^{2}, 22^{2}, 24, 26

ACTS 24:27, 25:1, 2^{3}, 3, 6^{2}, 7, 8^{3}, 9, 10, 12, 14, 15^{3}, 16^{4}, 17^{3}, 18, 21, 22, 23^{4}, 24^{2}, 27, 26:1, 2^{2}, 3, 4^{2}, 5^{2}, 6^{2}, 7, 8, 9, 10^{2}, 12, 13^{3}, 14^{3}, 16, 17^{2}, 18, 19, 20^{2}, 21^{2}, 22, 23^{4}, 25, 26, 27, 30^{2}, 27:2, 3, 4, 5, 6, 7, 8^{2}, 9, 10, 11^{4}, 12^{3}, 13, 15^{2}, 16, 17^{2}, 18^{2}, 19^{3}, 21, 22, 23, 27^{2}, 29^{2}, 30^{5}, 31^{3}, 32^{3}, 33^{2}, 34, 37, 38^{3}, 39^{3}, 40^{5}, 41^{5}, 42, 43^{2}, 44^{2}, 28:1, 2^{3}, 3^{2}, 4^{3}, 5^{2}, 7^{3}, 8, 9, 11, 13^{2}, 15^{2}, 16^{4}, 17^{5}, 19, 20, 21, 23^{3}, 24, 25^{2}, 27, 28^{2}, 29, 31^{2}

ROMANS 1:1, 2, 3^{2}, 4^{4}, 5, 6, 7, 8, 9, 10, 11, 12

ROMANS 1:14^{4}, 15, 16^{4}, 17^{2}, 18^{2}, 20^{4}, 23^{2}, 24, 25^{3}, 26, 27^{3}, 32^{2}, 2:1, 2, 3^{2}, 4^{2}, 5^{2}, 8, 9^{2}, 10^{2}, 12^{2}, 13^{4}, 14^{5}, 15^{3}, 16^{2}, 17, 18^{2}, 19, 20^{4}, 23^{2}, 24^{2}, 25^{2}, 26^{3}, 27^{3}, 28, 29^{3}, 3:1, 2, 3, 5, 6, 7, 12, 13, 17, 19^{3}, 20^{4}, 21^{4}, 22, 23, 24, 25^{2}, 26, 27, 28^{2}, 29^{4}, 30, 31^{2}, 4:1, 3, 4, 5, 6^{2}, 8^{2}, 9^{2}, 11^{3}, 12^{3}, 13^{5}, 14^{2}, 15, 16^{6}, 17, 18, 19, 20, 24, 5:2, 5^{2}, 6, 10, 11, 12, 13^{2}, 14^{2}, 15^{5}, 16^{3}, 17, 18^{3}, 19, 20^{2}, 6:4^{3}, 5^{2}, 6, 9, 12, 13, 14, 15, 17, 18, 19^{2}, 20, 21, 22, 23^{2}, 7:1^{2}, 2^{4}, 4^{3}, 5^{3}, 6^{3}, 7^{3}, 8^{2}, 9^{2}, 10, 11, 12^{2}, 13

ROMANS 7:14, 16, 19^{2}, 22^{2}, 23^{2}, 24, 25^{4}, 8:1^{2}, 2^{3}, 3^{4}, 4^{4}, 5^{6}, 7^{2}, 8, 9^{4}, 10^{2}, 11^{3}, 12^{2}, 13^{4}, 14^{2}, 15^{2}, 16^{2}, 18^{2}, 19^{4}, 20^{2}, 21^{4}, 22, 23^{4}, 26^{2}, 27^{5}, 28, 29^{2}, 33, 34, 35, 36^{2}, 39, 9:1^{2}, 3, 4^{7}, 5^{2}, 6, 7, 8^{6}, 9, 11^{2}, 12^{2}, 17^{2}, 20, 21^{3}, 22, 23^{2}, 24^{2}, 26^{3}, 27^{4}, 28^{3}, 29, 30^{2}, 31^{2}, 32^{2}, 10:3, 4^{2}, 5^{3}, 6, 7^{2}, 8^{2}, 9^{2}, 10^{2}, 11, 12^{3}, 13^{2}, 15^{2}, 16, 17, 18^{3}, 11:1^{2}, 2, 4^{3}, 5, 7^{2}, 8, 11, 12^{6}, 13^{2}, 15^{5}, 16^{4}, 17^{3}, 18^{3}, 19, 21, 22, 24^{2}, 25^{2}, 26, 28^{3}, 29, 12:1, 2, 4, 6^{2}, 11, 13, 16, 17, 19, 13:1^{2}, 2^{2}, 3^{3}, 4^{2}, 8, 10^{2}, 11, 12^{4}, 13, 14^{3}, 14:1, 6^{6}

ROMANS 14:8^{3}, 9, 10, 11, 14, 17^{2}, 19, 20, 15:1^{2}, 3, 4, 5, 6, 7, 8^{4}, 9^{2}, 11, 12^{2}, 13^{3}, 15^{2}, 16^{6}, 18, 19^{3}, 20, 25, 26, 27, 29^{3}, 30^{3}, 31, 32, 33, 16:1, 2, 4^{2}, 5^{2}, 7, 8, 11^{2}, 12^{3}, 13, 14, 15, 16, 17, 18^{2}, 20^{2}, 22, 23^{3}, 24, 25^{4}, 26^{5}, *subscr.*^{2}

1 COR. 1:1, 2^{2}, 3, 4, 6, 7, 8^{2}, 9, 10^{4}, 11, 13, 16, 17^{2}, 18^{3}, 19^{4}, 20^{4}, 21^{3}, 22^{2}, 23^{2}, 24^{2}, 25^{2}, 26, 27^{6}, 28, 31, 2:1, 4, 5^{2}, 6^{2}, 7^{3}, 8^{2}, 9^{2}, 10^{2}, 11^{4}, 12^{4}, 13^{2}, 14^{3}, 16^{3}, 3:5, 6, 7, 10^{2}, 13^{2}, 16^{2}, 17^{2}, 19^{2}, 20^{3}, 22, 4:1^{2}, 4, 5^{5}, 9^{2}, 13^{3}, 15, 17, 19^{3}, 20, 21, 5:1, 4^{2}, 5^{5}, 6

1 COR. 5:7, 8^{3}, 10^{3}, 6:1^{2}, 2^{4}, 4, 6, 9^{2}, 10, 11^{3}, 12, 13^{6}, 14, 15^{3}, 17, 18, 19^{2}, 7:1, 3^{4}, 4^{4}, 5, 8, 10^{3}, 11, 12^{2}, 13, 14^{4}, 15, 17, 19^{2}, 20, 22^{2}, 23, 25^{2}, 26, 28, 29, 31, 32^{3}, 33^{2}, 34^{5}, 35, 36, 39^{3}, 40, 8:3, 4^{2}, 6, 7, 8^{2}, 10^{2}, 11, 12, 13, 9:1, 2^{2}, 5^{2}, 7^{3}, 8^{2}, 9^{4}, 12, 13^{4}, 14^{3}, 16^{2}, 17, 18^{3}, 19, 20^{5}, 21, 22^{2}, 23, 24, 25, 26, 10:1^{2}, 2^{2}, 3, 4, 5, 6, 7, 10, 11^{2}, 13, 16^{5}, 18^{3}, 19, 20^{2}, 21^{5}, 22, 25, 26^{3}, 28, 29, 31, 32^{3}, 33, 11:2, 3^{5}, 6, 7^{4}, 8^{4}, 9^{4}, 10^{2}, 11^{5}, 12^{4}, 16, 17^{2}, 18, 20, 22, 23^{3}, 25^{3}, 26, 27^{3}, 29, 32^{2}

1 COR. 11:34, 12:3^{3}, 4, 5, 6, 7^{2}, 8^{4}, 9^{3}, 10^{2}, 11, 12^{2}, 14, 15^{4}, 16^{4}, 17^{4}, 18^{2}, 19, 21^{4}, 22, 23, 24, 25^{3}, 26, 27, 28, 30, 31, 13:1, 2, 3, 6, 13, 14:2, 4, 5, 7, 8^{2}, 9^{2}, 10, 11^{2}, 12^{2}, 15^{4}, 16^{3}, 17, 19, 21^{2}, 23, 25, 27, 28, 29^{2}, 30, 32^{3}, 33^{2}, 34^{2}, 35, 36, 37^{3}, 15:1, 3, 4^{2}, 5, 6, 7, 9^{3}, 10^{2}, 12^{2}, 13, 15, 16, 20^{2}, 21^{2}, 23, 24^{3}, 26, 28, 29^{3}, 32^{2}, 34, 35, 39, 40^{4}, 41^{3}, 42^{2}, 45^{2}, 47^{4}, 48^{2}, 49^{4}, 50, 52^{4}, 54, 56^{3}, 57, 58^{3}, 16:1^{3}, 2^{2}, 7^{2}, 10^{2}, 11, 12, 13, 15^{4}, 17, 19^{3}, 20, 21, 22, 23, *subscr.*^{2}

2 COR. 1:1^{3}, 2, 3^{2}, 4, 5, 6^{2}

2 COR. 1:7^{2}, 9^{2}, 11^{2}, 12^{3}, 13, 14^{2}, 17^{2}, 19, 20^{2}, 22^{2}, 2:2, 3, 4, 9, 10, 12, 14, 16^{4}, 17^{2}, 3:3^{4}, 6^{5}, 7^{4}, 8^{2}, 9^{2}, 10, 13^{2}, 14^{3}, 15, 16^{2}, 17^{3}, 18^{5}, 4:2^{4}, 4^{5}, 5, 6^{5}, 7^{2}, 10^{4}, 11, 13, 14, 15^{3}, 16, 18^{4}, 5:1, 5^{3}, 6^{2}, 8^{2}, 10^{2}, 11^{2}, 14, 16^{2}, 18, 19^{2}, 21, 6:1, 2^{3}, 3, 4, 6, 7^{5}, 13, 16^{3}, 17^{2}, 18, 7:1^{2}, 6, 7^{2}, 8, 10^{2}, 12^{2}, 13^{2}, 15, 8:1^{2}, 2^{2}, 4^{4}, 5^{2}, 6, 8^{2}, 9, 11, 16^{2}, 17, 18^{3}, 19^{3}, 21^{3}, 22, 23^{3}, 24^{2}, 9:1^{2}, 2, 3, 5^{2}, 9, 10^{2}, 12^{3}, 13^{2}, 14, 10:1, 2, 3^{2}, 4^{2}, 5^{2}, 7, 8, 12, 13^{2}, 14, 16^{2}, 17, 18, 11:3^{2}, 5, 7, 9, 10^{2}, 13, 15

2 COR. 11:17, 18, 20, 22, 24, 25, 26^{4}, 28^{2}, 30, 31, 32^{4}, 33, 12:1, 2^{3}, 3^{2}, 6, 7^{4}, 8, 9, 11, 12, 14^{5}, 15^{2}, 18^{2}, 21, 13:1^{2}, 2, 4^{2}, 5, 8^{2}, 10^{2}, 11, 13, 14^{5}, *subscr.*^{2}

GAL. 1:1^{2}, 2^{2}, 3, 4, 6, 7, 10, 11, 12, 13^{2}, 14^{2}, 16, 19^{2}, 20, 21, 22, 23, 2:2, 5^{2}, 7^{4}, 8^{4}, 9^{4}, 10^{2}, 11, 12^{2}, 13, 14^{6}, 15, 16^{8}, 17, 18, 19^{2}, 20^{4}, 21^{2}, 3:1, 2^{4}, 3^{2}, 5^{4}, 7^{2}, 8^{3}, 10^{5}, 11^{3}, 12^{2}, 13^{2}, 14^{4}, 15, 16, 17^{3}, 18^{2}, 19^{4}, 21^{3}, 22^{2}, 23^{2}, 24, 26, 29, 4:1, 2^{2}, 3^{2}, 4^{3}, 5^{2}, 6, 9, 13^{3}, 15, 16, 21^{2}, 22^{2}, 23^{3}, 24^{3}, 26, 27, 28, 29^{2}, 30^{6}, 31^{2}, 5:1^{2}, 3, 4, 5^{2}

GAL. 5:7, 9, 10, 11^{2}, 13, 14, 16^{3}, 17^{7}, 18^{2}, 19^{2}, 21^{2}, 22^{2}, 24^{2}, 25^{2}, 6:1, 2, 6, 8^{3}, 10, 12^{2}, 13, 14^{3}, 16, 17^{2}, 18, *subscr.*

EPHES. 1:1^{3}, 2, 3, 4^{2}, 5^{2}, 6^{3}, 7^{2}, 9, 10^{2}, 11^{2}, 12, 13^{2}, 14^{4}, 15^{2}, 17^{4}, 18^{5}, 19^{2}, 20^{2}, 22^{2}, 23, 2:2^{6}, 3^{5}, 7^{2}, 8, 11^{3}, 12^{3}, 13, 14, 15^{2}, 16^{2}, 18, 19^{2}, 20^{3}, 21^{2}, 22, 3:1, 2^{2}, 3, 4, 5^{2}, 6^{3}, 7^{3}, 8^{3}, 9^{4}, 10^{4}, 11, 12, 14, 15, 16^{2}, 18, 19^{2}, 20, 21, 4:1^{3}, 3^{3}, 7^{2}, 9, 10, 12^{6}, 13^{7}, 14, 15^{2}, 16^{5}, 17^{2}, 18^{4}, 21, 22^{3}, 23, 24, 26, 27, 28, 29^{2}, 30^{2}, 5:5, 6^{2}, 8, 9^{2}, 10, 11, 13, 14, 16^{2}, 17^{2}, 18, 19, 20^{2}, 21

EPHES. 5:22, 23^7, 24^2, 25, 26^2, 29^2, 32, 33, 6:1, 2, 3, 4^2, 5, 6^3, 7, 8^2, 9, 10^2, 11^3, 12^2, 13^2, 14, 15^2, 16^3, 17^4, 18, 19^2, 21, 22, 23^3, *subscr.*

PHIL. 1:1^3, 2, 5^2, 6, 7^2, 8, 10, 11^2, 12^3, 13, 14^3, 16, 17^3, 19^2, 22^2, 27^3, 29, 30, 2:1, 2, 4, 6, 7^2, 8^2, 10^2, 11^2, 15^3, 16^2, 17, 18, 19, 21, 22^3, 24, 28^2, 29, 30, 3:1^2, 2

PHIL. 3:3^3, 4^2, 5^5, 6^3, 8^3, 9^3, 10^2, 11^2, 14^3, 16^2, 18^2, 20^2, 21, 4:1, 2^2, 3^2, 4, 5, 7, 9, 10^2, 15^2, 18, 21, 22, 23, *subscr.*

COLOS. 1:1, 2^2, 3, 4^2, 5^4, 6^3, 8, 9^2, 10^2, 12^3, 13^2, 14, 15^3, 18^7, 19, 22, 23, 24^2, 25^2, 26, 27^4, 2:1, 2^4, 3, 5^3, 6, 7, 8^3, 9, 10, 11^5, 12^3, 13, 14^2, 16^2, 17, 19^3, 20^3, 22^2, 23^3, 3:1, 2, 5, 6^2

COLOS. 3:7, 9, 10^2, 12, 14, 15^2, 16^2, 17^3, 18, 20, 22, 23, 24^4, 25, 4:2, 3, 5, 7, 8, 11^2, 12, 14, 15^2, 16^3, 17^2, 18^2, *subscr.*

1 THESS. 1:1^4, 3, 5, 6^3, 8^2, 9, 10^2, 2:2, 4, 6, 8, 9, 13^3, 14^2, 15, 16^3, 17, 3:2, 5, 8, 9, 12, 13^2, 4:1, 2, 3, 5^2, 6^2, 10, 15^3, 16^5, 17^4, 5:1^2, 2^3, 5^4, 7^2, 8^3, 12, 14^2, 18, 19, 23^2, 26

1 THESS. 5:27^2, 28, *subscr.*

2 THESS. 1:1^3, 2, 3, 4, 5^2, 7, 8, 9^3, 11^2, 12^3, 2:1, 2, 3, 4, 7^2, 8^3, 9, 10^2, 12, 13^4, 14^2, 15, 3:1, 3, 4^2, 5^3, 6^2, 16^2, 17^2, 18, *subscr.*^{2}

1 TIM. 1:1, 2, 5^2, 7, 8, 9^3, 11, 12, 14, 15, 17^2, 18, 2:3, 4^2, 5, 7^2, 11, 12, 14^2, 3:1, 2, 5, 6^2, 7^2, 8, 9^2, 10, 12^2, 13^2, 15^5, 16^5, 4:1^3, 3

1 TIM. 4:5, 6^2, 8, 10^2, 12, 14^4, 16, 5:1, 2^2, 8, 9^2, 10^2, 11, 14^3, 16, 17^2, 18^4, 21^2, 25, 6:1^2, 2, 3^2, 5, 10^3, 12, 13, 14, 15^2, 16, 17, 19, 21, *subscr.*^{2}

2 TIM. 1:1, 2, 5, 6^2, 7, 8^4, 10^2, 11, 12, 13, 14, 16^2, 18^2, 2:1, 2^2, 4, 6^2, 7, 8^2, 9, 10^2, 14^2, 15, 18^3, 19^4, 21, 22, 24^2, 25^2, 26^2, 3:1, 5, 7^2, 8^2, 11, 14

2 TIM. 4:1^3, 2, 3, 4, 5, 6, 7, 8^2, 11, 13^3, 14^2, 17^5, 18, 19, 21, 22, *subscr.*^{5}

TITUS 1:1^3, 2, 3, 4^3, 5, 6, 7, 9, 10, 12, 13, 14, 15, 2:1, 2, 3, 4, 5, 8, 10, 11, 13^2, 3:4, 5, 7, 9, 10, 13, 15, *subscr.*^{2}

PHILE. 2, 3, 5, 6^2, 7^2, 9, 13^2, 16^2, 20^2, 25

HEB. 1:1, 2, 3^5, 4, 5, 6^3, 7, 8^2, 9

HEB. 1:10^5, 12, 13, 2:1^2, 2, 3^2, 4, 5^2, 6, 7^2, 9^3, 10, 12^2, 13, 14^4, 16^2, 17^2, 3:1^2, 3^2, 6^4, 7, 8^3, 12, 13, 14^2, 15, 17, 4:2^2, 3^3, 4^2, 9, 11, 12^5, 13, 14^2, 15, 16, 5:2^2, 3, 6, 7, 8, 9, 10, 12^3, 13, 6:1^3, 2^3, 4^2, 5^3, 6, 7^2, 10, 11^3, 12, 15, 16, 17^2, 18, 19^2, 20^2, 7:1^3, 3, 4^3, 5^6, 6, 7^2, 10, 11^5, 12^2, 13, 15, 16^2

HEB. 7:17, 18^2, 19^3, 21^2, 25, 26, 27, 28^5, 8:1^6, 2^3, 4, 5^4, 6, 7, 8^4, 9^5, 10^3, 11^3, 13, 9:1, 2^5, 3^3, 4^6, 5^2, 6^3, 7^4, 8^4, 9^3, 10, 12^2, 13^5, 14^3, 15^5, 16^2, 17, 18, 19^5, 20^2, 21^3, 22, 23^3, 24^4, 25, 26^5, 27, 28^2, 10:1^4, 2, 4, 5, 7^2, 8, 9^2, 10^3, 11, 12, 15, 16^2, 19^2, 20, 21, 23, 25^4, 26^2, 27, 29^4, 30^2, 31^2, 32, 34, 36^2, 38, 39^2

HEB. 11:1^2, 2, 3^2, 7^4, 9^3, 12^4, 13^2, 17, 19, 21^2, 22^2, 23, 24, 25^2, 26^4, 27^2, 28^3, 29^2, 30, 31^2, 32^2, 33, 34^5, 37, 38^2, 39, 12:1^2, 2^6, 5^3, 6, 7, 9, 11^2, 12^2, 13, 14, 15, 17, 18, 19^3, 20, 21, 22^3, 23^4, 24^3, 26^2, 27, 13:3, 4, 6, 7^3, 8, 9, 10, 11^4, 12^2, 13, 15^2, 17, 19^2, 20^5, 22, 24^2, *subscr.*

JAMES 1:1^2, 3, 6^2, 7, 9, 10^3, 11^6

JAMES 1:12^3, 17, 18, 20^2, 21, 22, 23, 25^2, 27^3, 2:1^2, 3^2, 5^2, 6^2, 7, 8^2, 9, 10, 11, 12, 16, 19, 21, 23^2, 25^2, 26^2, 3:1, 2^2, 3, 4^2, 5, 6^4, 7, 8, 9^2, 10, 11, 12, 14, 17, 18, 4:4^4, 5^2, 6^2, 7, 10^3, 11^4, 14, 15, 5:3^2, 4^5, 5, 6, 7^6, 8^2, 9^2, 10^3, 11^4, 12, 14^4, 15^3, 16, 17^2, 18^3, 19, 20^2

1 PETER 1:1, 2^4, 3^3, 5^2, 7^2, 9^2

1 PETER 1:10^2, 11^3, 12^4, 13^4, 17^2, 19, 20^2, 21, 22^3, 23, 24^4, 25^4, 2:2^2, 3, 6, 7^5, 8, 9, 10, 11, 12^2, 13^2, 14^2, 15^2, 16, 17^2, 18^2, 24, 25, 3:1^4, 3, 4^4, 5^2, 7^3, 12^5, 15^2, 17, 18^4, 19, 20^3, 21^6, 22, 4:1^3, 2^4, 3^3, 4, 5^2, 6^3, 7, 8, 10^3, 11, 12, 14^2, 17^4, 18^3, 19^2, 5:1^3, 2^2, 3, 4, 5^3, 6, 8, 9^3, 10, 12, 13

2 PETER 1:1, 2, 3

2 PETER 1:4^3, 8, 10, 11, 12, 16, 17^2, 18, 19^2, 20, 21^3, 2:1^2, 2, 4, 5^5, 6, 7^2, 9^4, 10^2, 11, 12, 13^2, 15^4, 16^3, 17, 18^2, 19^2, 20^6, 21^2, 22^4, 3:2^5, 3, 4^4, 5^5, 6, 7^4, 8, 9, 10^8, 12^4, 15, 16, 17^2, 18

1 JOHN 1:1^2, 2^2, 3, 5, 6, 7^3, 8, 2:1^2, 2^3, 4, 5, 7^4, 8^2, 9, 10, 13^3, 14^3, 15^6, 16^8, 17^3, 18^2, 20, 21^2, 22^3, 23^5, 24^4

1 JOHN 2:25, 27^2, 3:1^3, 2, 4^3, 8^6, 10^3, 11^2, 13, 14, 16^2, 17, 19, 23, 24, 4:1^2, 2^2, 3^2, 4, 5^3, 6^2, 9^2, 10, 14^4, 15, 16, 17, 5:1, 2, 3, 4^3, 5^2, 6^2, 7^3, 8^3, 9^3, 10^3, 11, 12^2, 13^4, 14, 15, 19, 20^2

2 JOHN 1^4, 2, 3^4, 4, 5, 6^2, 7^2, 9^4, 13

3 JOHN 1^3, 3^3, 5, 6, 7, 8, 9^2, 10^2, 12, 14

JUDE 1^2, 3^3

JUDE. 4^2, 5^3, 6^3, 7^2, 8, 9^4, 11^3, 12, 13^2, 14^2, 17^2, 18, 19, 20, 21^2, 23^3, 24, 25

REV. 1:1, 2^2, 3^2, 4^2, 5^6, 7, 8^4, 9^4, 10^2, 11^3, 12, 13^5, 15, 16, 17^2, 18, 19^3, 20^8, 2:1^5, 5, 6^2, 7^5, 8^4, 9^2, 10, 11^3, 12^3, 14^2, 15^2, 16, 17^4, 18^3, 19^2, 23^2, 24^2, 26^2, 27, 28, 29^2, 3:1^4, 2, 5^2, 6^2, 7^3, 9, 10^4, 12^4, 13^2, 14^7, 18^2, 20^2, 22^2

REV. 4:1, 2^2, 3, 4^2, 5^3, 6^4, 7^4, 8, 9, 10^3, 5:1^3, 2^2, 3^2, 4, 5^6, 6^7, 7^3, 8^4, 9^2, 10, 11^5, 12, 13^5, 14^2, 6:1^4, 3^2, 4, 5^2, 6^4, 7^3, 8^4, 9^4, 10, 12^3, 13^2, 14, 15^9, 16^5, 17, 7:1^7, 2^6, 3^4, 4^3, 5^3, 6^3, 7^3, 8^3, 9^2, 10^2, 11^5, 13, 14^2, 15^2, 16^3, 17^3, 8:1^2, 2, 3^4, 4^5, 5^4, 6^2, 7^3, 8^4, 9^5, 10^4, 11^5, 12^{10}, 13^6, 9:1^4, 2^7, 3^4, 4^3, 5

REV. 9:7^3, 8^2, 9^2, 11^4, 13^3, 14^4, 15^2, 16^4, 17^5, 18^4, 20^3, 10:1, 2^2, 4^2, 5^3, 6^5, 7^5, 8^6, 9^2, 10^2, 11:1^3, 2^4, 4^4, 6^2, 7^2, 8^2, 9, 10^2, 11, 13^6, 14^2, 15^3, 16, 18^6, 19^2, 12:1^2, 4^5, 6^2, 7^2, 9^4, 10^3, 11^4, 12^4, 13^4, 14^4, 15^3, 16^5, 17^5, 13:1^4, 2^4, 3^2, 4^4, 7, 8^5, 10^5, 11, 12^4, 13^2, 14^7, 15^6, 18^3, 14:1, 2^3, 3^5, 4^3, 5, 6^3, 7^3, 8^2, 9^2, 10^8, 11^3, 12^4

REV. 14:13^3, 14^2, 15^5, 16^3, 17, 18^5, 19^6, 20^5, 15:1^2, 2^5, 3^4, 5^3, 6^3, 7^3, 8^5, 16:1^5, 2^5, 3^4, 4^2, 5^2, 6, 7, 8, 9, 10^3, 11, 12^6, 13^6, 14^5, 16, 17^4, 18, 19^6, 20, 21^4, 17:1^4, 2^5, 3^2, 4, 5^3, 6^5, 7^5, 8^7, 9^3, 10, 11^3, 12^2, 13, 14^2, 15^2, 16^3, 17^2, 18^3, 18:1, 2^3, 3^7, 6, 8, 9^3, 10, 11^2, 12, 14, 15^2, 17, 18, 19, 21, 22^2, 23^6, 24^2, 19:1, 2^3

REV. 19:4^3, 5, 6^4, 7^2, 8^2, 9^3, 10^3, 13, 14, 15^3, 17^5, 18^5, 19^4, 20^4, 21^4, 20:1^2, 2^2, 3^3, 4^4, 5^4, 6^2, 7, 8^6, 9^5, 10^4, 11^2, 12^5, 13^3, 14^2, 15^2, 21:1^2, 2, 3, 4, 5, 6^4, 8^4, 9^5, 10^2, 11, 12^4, 13^4, 14^5, 15^3, 16^8, 17^3, 18^3, 19^7, 20^8, 21^3, 22^3, 23^6, 24^4, 25, 26^2, 27, 22:1^2, 2^8, 3^2, 5^2, 6^3, 7^2, 8^2, 9^2, 10^3, 13^4, 14^3, 16^4, 17^3, 18^3, 19^5, 21

thee

4571

GEN. 3:11^2, 15, 16, 17, 18, 4:7, 12, 6:14, 18^2, 19, 20, 21^2, 7:1, 2, 8:16, 17, 12:1^2, 2, 3^2, 12^2, 13^2, 13:8, 9, 15, 17, 15:7, 16:2, 5^3, 6, 17:2, 4, 5, 6^2, 7^4, 8, 9, 10, 16, 18

GEN. 17:19, 20, 21, 18:3, 10, 14, 25^2, 19:5, 9, 17, 21, 22, 20:6^2, 7, 9, 15, 16, 21:12, 17, 22, 23, 22:2^2, 17, 23:6, 11^2, 13, 15, 24:2, 3, 7, 8, 12, 14, 17, 23, 40, 41, 43, 45

GEN. 24:50, 51, 25:30, 26:2, 3, 24, 28^2, 29^2, 27:3, 4, 7, 8, 10, 19, 21, 25, 28, 29^3, 37, 42, 45^2, 28:2, 3, 4^2, 13, 14, 15^3, 22, 29:18, 19, 25, 27, 30:2, 14, 15, 16, 26^2, 27, 29

GEN. 30:30, 31, 31:3, 12, 13, 16, 27, 32, 35, 38, 39, 41, 42, 44, 48, 49, 50, 51, 52, 32:6, 9, 11, 12, 17^3, 26, 29, 33:5, 10, 11^2, 12, 14, 15, 35:1, 11, 12^2, 37:10, 13, 14, 16

GEN. 38:16^2, 17, 18, 25, 29, 39:9, 40:13, 14^2, 19^3, 41:15, 39, 41, 44, 42:37^2, 43:4, 9^2, 29, 44:8, 18, 32, 33, 45:11, 46:3, 4^2, 47:4, 5, 6, 29^2, 48:2, 4^4, 5^2, 9, 20^2, 22, 49:8, 25^2, 50:5, 6, 17^3

EXOD. 2:7^2, 9, 14, 3:10, 12^3, 18, 4:1, 5, 8, 12, 13, 14^2, 16, 18, 23, 5:3, 6:29, 7:1, 2, 15, 16, 8:4, 9^2, 11, 21, 29, 9:15, 16^2, 30, 10:17, 28, 11:8^2, 12:24, 48, 13:5^2, 7^2, 9^2, 11^3, 14

EXOD. 14:12, 15:7, 11^2, 17, 26^2, 17:5, 6, 18:6, 14, 18^2, 19^2, 22^2, 23, 19:9^3, 24^2, 20:2, 4, 12, 24^2, 21:13, 22:25, 23:5, 7, 15, 20^3, 23^2, 25, 27^2, 28^2, 29^2, 30, 31, 33^2, 24:12, 25:9, 16, 21, 22^3, 40

EXOD. 26:30, 27:8, 20, 28:1, 29:35, 42, 30:6, 23, 34, 36, 37, 31:6, 11, 32:4, 7, 8, 10, 21, 32, 34^2, 33:2, 3^2, 5^4, 12, 13^2, 14^2, 17, 18, 19^2, 22^2, 34:1, 3, 9, 10, 11^2, 12, 15, 17, 18

EXOD. 34:24, 27

LEVIT. 9:2, 10:9, 14, 15, 19:13, 19, 33, 21:8, 24:2, 25:6^2, 8^2, 15, 35^2, 36, 39^2, 40^2, 41, 47^2

NUM. 5:19, 20, 21, 6:24^2, 25^2, 26^2, 10:2, 3, 4, 29, 31, 32, 35^2, 11:15, 16

NUM. 11:17^3, 23, 12:11, 13, 14:12, 15, 17, 19, 16:10^2, 18:1^2, 2^4, 4, 7, 8, 9, 10, 11^2, 12, 19^4, 19:2, 20:17, 21:7, 29, 22:6, 8, 9, 16^2, 17^2, 20^2, 28, 29, 30, 32, 33, 34, 35, 37^3, 38, 23:3

NUM. 23:11, 13, 26, 27^2, 24:9^2, 10, 11^2, 14, 22, 27:12, 18

DEU. 1:21^2, 31, 38, 2:7^2, 9, 19, 25^4, 31, 3:25, 26, 27, 4:21, 23, 30, 31^2, 32, 35, 36^3, 37, 38^3, 40^4, 5:6, 8, 12, 15^2, 16^3

DEU. 5:27, 28, 31^2, 6:2, 3^2, 6, 10^2, 12, 15^2, 17, 18, 19, 20, 7:1^2, 2, 4, 6, 11, 12, 13^4, 15^3, 16^2, 19, 20, 22^2, 23, 24, 25, 8:1, 2^3, 3^4, 4, 5, 7, 10, 11, 14, 15^2, 16^4

DEU. 8:18, 9:3^2, 4^2, 5, 6, 12, 14, 10:1^2, 10, 12, 13, 21, 22, 11:29, 12:1, 7, 14, 15, 20, 21^3, 25^2, 28^3, 29, 30, 13:1, 2, 5^3, 6, 7^2, 10^2, 12, 17^3, 18, 14:2, 24^3, 27, 29^2, 15:4^2, 5

DEU. 15:6^3, 7, 9^2, 10, 11, 12^3, 13, 14, 15^2, 16^4, 18^5, 16:1, 4, 5, 9, 10, 15, 17, 18^2, 20, 21^2, 22, 17:2, 4, 8^2, 9, 10^2, 11^3, 14, 15^3, 18:9, 12, 14^2, 15^2, 18, 19:1, 2^2, 3^2, 7

DEU. 19:8, 9^2, 10^2, 13, 14, 20:1^2, 11^4, 12^2, 14, 15, 16, 17, 20, 21:1, 23, 22:2^2, 6, 7^2, 12, 23:4, 5^2, 9, 13, 14^4, 15, 16, 20, 21^2, 22, 24:4, 11, 13^2, 15^2, 18^2, 19, 22, 25:3, 15, 17

DEU. 25:18^3, 19^2, 26:1, 2, 11, 16, 18^2, 19, 27:2^2, 3^2, 10, 28:1^2, 2^2, 7^2, 8^3, 9^2, 10, 11^2, 12, 13^2, 14, 15^3, 20, 21^2, 22^2, 23, 24, 25, 27, 28, 29, 31, 35, 36^2, 37, 43^2, 44, 45^4, 46

DEU. 28:48^2, 49, 51^2, 52^3, 53^2, 55, 57, 60^2, 61, 64, 65, 66, 68^2, 29:12, 13^3, 30:1^3, 2^3, 3^2, 4^2, 5^3, 7^2, 8, 9^2, 11^2, 14, 15, 16^2, 31:3, 6^3, 8^4, 23, 26, 32:6^3, 7^2, 18^2, 49, 52, 33:10, 27

DEU. 33:29^2, 34:4

JOSH. 1:5^4, 7, 9^2, 17^2, 2:3, 14, 18, 19, 3:7^2, 5:2, 7:10, 13, 19, 25, 8:1, 2, 9:25, 10:8, 13:6, 14:6, 17:15^2

JUD. 1:3, 24^2, 3:19, 20, 4:6, 7, 9, 14, 19, 20, 22, 5:14

JUD. 6:12 14 16 18^3 23 39 7:2 4^6 9 9:31 32 33 10:10 15^2 11:8 17 19 24 27 36 12:1^2 13:4 15^3 17 14:15 16 15:2 12^2 13^3 16:5 6^2 9 10 12 14 15 20 28^2 17:2 3 10 18:3 5 19 23 24 25 19:6 8 11 20

RUTH 1:10 16^2 17 2:4 9 12 19 22 3:1^2 3^3 4^2 11 13^3 15 4:4^3 8 12 14 15^3

1 SAM. 1:8 14 17 23 26 2:2 15 20 34 36 3:9 17^4 8:7^2 8 9:3 16 17 18 19^2 20 23^3 24^2 26 27 10:1 2 3 4^2 6 7^3 8^2 15 11:1 3 5 10 13:13 14 14:7^2 36 40 15:1 16 17 18 15:23 25 26^2 28 30 16:1 2 3^2 15 16^2 22 17:37 45 46^3 18:17 22^2 19:2^2 3^2 4 17 20:4 8 9^3 10 12^2 13^4 21^2 22^2 23 29^2 37 42 21:1 2^2 22:3 5 23:11 12 17^2 27 24:4^2 10^3 11^2 12^3 13 15 17 19 25:6 8^2 24 25 26 28^2 29 30^2 31 32 34 40^2 26:6 8 11 15 19^2 21 23 27:5 28:2 8^2 10 11 15 16 18 19 22^2 29:6^2 8 10 30:7 15

2 SAM. 1:4 9 16 26 2:21^3 22^2 3:12^2 13^2 21 24 25 5:2 24 7:3 8 9^2 11^3 12 15 16 20 22^2 23 24 26 27^2 29^2 9:7^2 10:3^2 11^2 11:12 20 25 12:7^2 8^2 12:11 12 14 13:5^3 6 13^3 20 24 25 26^2 14:2 5 8 10^2 11 12 17 18^2 19 32^2 15:3 7 20^2 26 31 35 16:4 8 9 21 17:3 11 18:11 12 14 22 31 32 33 19:6 7^3 21^2 33 37^2 38^2 41 20:16 21 30 50 24:10 12^3 13^2 17 21 23 24

1 KINGS 1:12^2 13 14 30 2:4 8^2 14 16 17^2 18 20^3 26^2 36 42^2 43 3:5 6^2 12^5 13^2 5:6 6:12 26 8:13^2 23 25 27 28 33^3 35 40 43^2 46 47 48^2 50^2 52 9:4 5 10:8 9^3 11^2 31^2 35 37 38^4 12:4 10 28 13:2^3 7 8 16^3 18 21 22 14:2^2 3^2 5 6 7^2 14:8 9^2 12 15:19^2 16:2^2 17:3^2 4 9^2 10 11 13 18 21 18:10^2 12^3 41 44^2 19:7 20^3 20:5 6 22 25 31 32 34^2 35 36 37 21:2^3 3 4 6^3 7 14 20 21 22:5 13 16 18 23 24

2 KINGS 1:10 12 13 2:2^2 4^2 6^2 9^3 10^2 16 19 3:13^2 14^2 4:2 3 4 10 13 22 24 26^2 29 30 5:6^2 10 13^2 15 17 22 26^2 27 6:1 2 3 7 17 18 27^2 28 7:13 8:4 9 14 9:3^2 5^2 6 11 12 18 19 26 14:10^2 18:23^2 26 27 19:9 10 19 21^3 28 29 20:3^2 5 6 14 18 22:19 20

1 CHRON. 11:2 12:18^2 14:15 16:18 17:2 17:7 8^3 10^2 11 13 18 20^2 21 24 25 27^2 19:3^2 12^2 21:8 10^3 11 12 17 23^2 22:9 11^2 12^2 15 16 28:9^2 10 20^3 21^2 29:12 13 14^2 15 16 17 18

2 CHRON. 1:7 11 12^4 2:11 16 6:2 14^2 16 18 19 24^2 26 31 33^2 34 36 37 38 39 40 7:17^2 18 9:7 8^3 10:4 5 10 14:11^3 16:3^2 18:3 4 12 15 17 22 23 19:2 3 20:2 6 8 9 12 25:7 8 9 16 19^2 26:18 34:27 28 35:21^4

EZRA 4:12 5:10 7:13 18 19 9:6 15^2 10:4^2

NEH. 1:5 6^2 7 8 11^2 4:5^2 6:7 10^2 9:6 8 10 18 26^2 27 28^3 32 35

ESTHER 3:11^2 5:3 6 7:2 9:12

JOB 1:11 15 16 17 19 2:5 4:2 5^2 7 5:1 19^2 20 23 7:20^2 8:6 8 10^2 18 22 10:3 9 13 11:3 5 6^2 18 19^2 12:7^2 8^3 13:20 14:3 5 15 15:6^2 11^2 12 17 16:3 17:3 18:4 22:4^3 10^2 11 21 22 27 28 26:3 30:20 33:1 7^2 12 32 33 35:3 4^2 36:2 4 16 17 18^2 38:3 17 34 35 39:9 10 40:4 7 14^2 15 41:3^2 4 42:2 4^2 5^2 7

PSALMS 2:7 8 5:2 3 4 10 11^2 6:5^2 7:1 7 9:1 2 10^2 10:14 16:1 2 17:6 7 18:1 29 49 20:1^2 2^2 4 21:4 8 11 22:4 5^2 10 19 22 25 22:27 25:1 2 3 5 16 20 21 27:8 28:1 2 30:1 2 8 9 12^2 31:1 14 17 19^2 22 32:5 6 8^3 9 33:22 35:10 18^2 36:9 10 37:4 34 38:9^2 15 39:5 7 12 40:5 16^2 41:4 42:1 6 43:4 44:5 17 45:2 4 5 7 8 14 17 49:18 50:7 8 12 15 17 21 51:4^2 13 52:5^4 9 53:5 54:6 55:22 23 56:3 9 12 57:1 9^2 59:9 17 60:4 61:2 62:12 63:1^3 2 3 4 5 6^2 8 65:1^2 2 4 66:3 4^2 13 15 67:3^2 5^2 68:29 69:5 6^2 9 13 19 70:4^2 71:1 6^2 14 19 22^2 23 72:5 73:22 23 25^2 27^2 74:22 23 75:1^2 76:10 77:16^2 79:6 11 12 79:13 80:14 18 81:7^3 8 9 10 16 83:2 5 84:4 5 12 85:6 86:2 3 4 5 7 8 9 12 14 87:3 7 88:1 2 9^2 10 13^2 89:8^2 90:8 13 91:3 4 7 10 11^2 12 94:20 101:1 102:1 28 103:4 104:27 105:11 108:3^2 114:5 116:4 7 17 19 118:21 25^2 28^2 119:7 10 11 62 63 74 76 79 108 120 126 146 164 168 169 170 175 120:3^2 121:3 6 7 122:6 8 123:1 128:2 5 130:1 4 134:4 135:9 137:5 6 8 138:1^2 4 139:12^2 14 15 18 20 21^2 141:1 2 8^2 142:5 143:6^2 8^2 9 144:9^2 145:1 2 10 15 147:13 14

PROV. 1:10 2:1 11^2 12 16 3:2 3 3:28 29 30 4:6^2 8^2 9 11^2 24^2 25 5:17 19 6:22^3 24 25 7:1 5 15^2 9:8^2 20:22 22:18 19^2 20 21^2 27 23:1 7^2 11 22 25 25:7 8 10 16 17^2 22 27:2 29:17 30:6 7 9 10

ECCL. 2:1 7:21 8:2 9:9 10:4 16 11:9

CANT. 1:3 4^3 9 11 4:7 6:1 13 7:5 12 13 8:1^2 2^3 5^4

ISAIAH 1:25 2:10 3:12^2 7:5 11 17 8:1 9:3 10:24^2 12:1 6 14:3 8 9^3 10 11^2 16^3 29 16:4 9^3 19:12 22:1 3 15 16 17^2 18 19^2 24:17 25:1 3^2 26:3^2 8^2 9^2 13^2 16 20 29:3^3 11 12 30:19^2 21 22 33:1^3 2 36:8^2 11 12 37:9 10 22^3 29 37:30 38:3^2 6 7 18^2 19 39:3 7 40:9 41:9^4 10^4 11^2 12^2 14 15 42:5^3 43:1^4 2^3 3 4^2 5^2 23^2 44:2^3 8 21 22 24 45:2 3^2 4^2 5 14^5 47:3 5 9^2 10 11^3 13^2 15^2 48:5^2 6 9^2 10^2 17^2 49:6 7 8^4 15 16 17^2 18^3 19 23 25 26 51:16 19^3 23 52:1 14 54:6 7^2 8^2 9^2 10^2 14 15 17^2 55:5^3 57:8 12 13 58:8 9 11 12 14^2 59:12 21 60:1 2^2 4 5^2 6 7^2 9 10^3 11 12 13 14^4 15^2 19^2 62:4 5^2 64:4 5 7 9 11 65:15

JER. 1:5^4 7^2 8^2 10 17^2 18 19^4 2:2 17 19^3 21 22^2 28^2 31 35 3:19^2 3:22 4:14 18 30^2 5:7 6:8^2 23 26^2 27 7:16 27^2 10:6 7^3 25 11:15 17^2 20 12:1^2 3 5^2 6^3 13:1 6 12 20 21^3 27 14:7 20 22 15:2 5^2 6^2 11 14 19^2 20^6 21^2 16:2 10 19 17:4^2 13 16^2 18:2 20 23 19:2 10 20:4 12 15 21:2 13 22:6 7 21 23 24 25 26^2 23:33 37 25:15 26:2 27:2 28:8 15 16 29:22 26 30:2^2 10 11^6 14^3 15 16^3 17^3 31:3^2 4 21^2 23 32:7^2 8 17 20 25 33:3^2 34:3 4 5^3 14^3 36:2^3 19 28 37:18 20^3 38:4 10 14 15^2 16^2 20^4 22 25^5 39:12 16 17 18^2 40:4^6 5 14 15^3 42:2^2 5 43:2 3 44:16 45:2 45:5 46:14^2 27 28^5 48:2 18 27 32 43 46 49:5^2 9 15 16^2 50:21 24 31^2 42 51:14^2 20^2 21^2 22^3 23^3 25^4 26 36

LAM. 1:22 2:13^5 14^2 15 16 17 3:57 4:21 22 5:21

EZEKIEL 2:2 3 4 6 8^2 3:3 4 6^2 7 10 11 17 22 25^2 27 4:1 3^2 5 6 8^2 9^2 15 5:1^3 8^2 9 10^3 11 12^3 14^2 15^2 17^3 7:3^4 4^3 6 7 8^4 9^2 8:6 13 15 12:3 6 9 16:4 5^3 6^4 7 8^5 9^3 10^3 11 14 17 19^2 23 24^2 27^3 33 34^3 37 38^2 39^3 40^3 41^2 42^2 44 57 59 60^2 61 62 63 20:47^2 21:3^2 4 7 16 19 29^3 21:30 31^3 22:4 5^2 6 7^3 9^3 10^2 11 12 13 14 15^3 23:22^2 24^3 25^2 26 27 28 29 30 24:2 13^2 14 16 17 26^2 25:4^3 7^5 26:3^2 8^3 10 14 15 16 17^2 19^3 20^2 21 27:5 7 8 9^2 10 15 21 25 26^2 27^2 30 31^2 32^2 34 35 36 28:3 4 7 8 9^2 13 14 15 16^3 17^3 18^4 19^2 22^2 29:3 4 5^3 7^2 8^2 10 21 32:3^2 4^4 6 7 8 10^2 11 33:7 30 31^2 35:3^3 6^3 9 11 14 15 36:12 15 37:16 18 38:3 4^2 6 7 9 13 15 16^2 17 39:1 2^4 4^2 40:4 44:5

DANIEL 1:12 13 2:23^3 29^2 31 37 38 39^2 3:12 16 18 4:9^2 18 19^2 25^4 26 27 31^2 32^3 5:10 14^2 16 23 6:7 12 13 16 20 22 8:19 9:7^2 8 15 9:16 18 22 23 10:11^2 14 19 20 21 11:2

HOSEA 1:2 2:19^2 20 3:3 4:5 6 5:8 6:4^2 11 8:2 5 11:8^4 9 12:9 13:5 10 11 14:3

JOEL 1:19 20 3:11 4:12^2 5:17

AMOS 6:10 7:2 5 10 12

OBADIAH 2 3 4 5^2 7^5 10 15

JONAH 1:8 11 14^3 2:7 9 3:2 4:2^2 3

MICAH 1:13 15 16^3 2:11 12 4:8 9^2 10 11 5:2 10 13 14 6:3^2 4^3 8^2 13^3 14 15 16 7:12 17 18

NAHUM 1:11 12^2 13 14 15 2:13 3:5 6^3 7^3 13 14 15^3 19^2

HABAK. 1:2 2:7^2 8 16 17 3·10

ZEPH. 2:5 3:11 12 15 17^3 18 19

HAGGAI 2:23^3

ZECH. 1:9 2:10 11^2 3:2^2 4^2 7 8 9:9 11 12 13 11:15 14:1 5

MALACHI 1:7 8 2:14 3:8 13

MATT. 1:20 2:6 13 3:14 4:6^2 9 10 5:23 25^2 26 29^3 30^3 39 40 41 42^2 6:2 4 6 18 23 8:13 19 29 9:2 5 22 11:10 21^2 23 24 25 12:38 47 14:4 28 15:28 16:17 18 19 22^2 23 17:4 27 18:8^3 9^3 15^3 16^2 17 22 26 29 32 33 27 20:13 14 21:5 19 23 23:37 25:21 23 24 37^3 38^3 39^2 44^2 26:17 33 34 35^2 62 63 68 73 27:13

MARK 1:2 24^2 37 2:5 9 3:32 5:7^2 19^2 23 31 34 41 6:18 22 23 8:33 9:5 17 25 34 43^2 45^2 47^2 10:28 49 51 52 11:14 28 14:30 31^2 36 60 15:4

LUKE 1:3 13 19^2 28 35^3 48 4:6 8 10^2 11 34^2 5:20 23 24 6:29 30 7:7 14 20 27 40 47 50 8:20 28^2 39 45^2 48 9:33 38 57 61 10:13^2 21 35 11:7 27 35 36 12:20 58^3 59 13:31^2 34 14:9^2 10^3 12^2 14 18 19 15:18 29 16:2 27 17:3 4^2 19 18:11 28 41 42 19:21 22 43^4 44^3 20:2 22:11 32 33 34 64 23:43 23:48

JOHN 1:48^2 50^2 2:4 3:3 5 7 11 26 4:10^2 26 5:10 12 14 6:30 7:20 8:10 11 9:21 37 10:33 11:8 22 28 40 41 13:8 37 38 16:30 17:1 3 4 5 7 8 11 13 21 25^2 18:26 30 34 35 19:10^2 11^2 21:3 15 16 17 18^3 20 22 23

ACTS 3:6 5:9 7:3^2 27 34 35 8:20 22 34 9:5 6 17 34 10:6 19 20 22^2 32 33^2 11:14 12:9 13:11 33 47 16:18 17:32 18:10^3 21:21 23 24 37 39 22:10^2 14 18 19 21 23:3 18^2 20 21 30^2 35 24:2 4^2 8 14 19 25 25:26 26:2 3^2 14 16^3 17^2 24 27:24 28:21^2

ROMANS 2:4 2:27 4:17 9:17^2 10:8 11:21 22 13:4 15:3 9

1 COR. 4:7 8:10 12:21

2 COR. 6:2^2 12:9

GAL. 3:8

EPHES. 5:14 6:3

PHIL. 4:3

1 TIM. 1:3 18^2 3:14^2 4:14^2 16 5:21 6:13 21

2 TIM. 1:3 4 5^2 6^2 14 2:7 3:15 17 4:1 11 13 21

TITUS 1:5^2 2:15 3:12 15

PHILE. 4 7 8 9 10 11^2 16 18^2 19 20 21 23

HEB. 1:5 9 2:12 5:5 6:14^2 8:5 13:5^2

JAMES 2:18

2 JOHN 5^2 13

3 JOHN 3 13 14^2

JUDE 9

REV. 2:4 5 10 14 16 20 3:3^2 8 9 10 16 18 4:1 11:17^2 14:15 15:4^2 17:1 7 18:14^2 22^3 23^2 21:9

their

846

GEN. 1:21 25 5:2 6:20 7:14 8:19 9:23^3 10:5^2 20^2 30 31^2 32 11:7 12:5 13:6 14:6 11 24 17:7 8 9 23 18:20 22 26 19:10 33 34 36 20:8 24:52 59 25:13 16^2 26:18 31:43 53 32:15 33:2 6 34:13 18 20^2 21 23^2 27 28^3 29^3 35:4^3 36:7^2 19 30 40^3 43^2 37:2 4 12 16 21 22 25^2 32 40:1 42:6 24 25 26 28 29 35^2 36 43:2 11 15 24^2 26 27 28 44:3 11 13 45:25 27 46:5^3 6^2 32^3 47:1^2 4 9 12 17^2 22^2 30 48:6^2 49:5 6^4 7^2 28 50:8^3 15 17

EXOD. 1:11 14^2 2:11 16 17 18 23 24 3:7^3 4:5 31^2

EXOD. 5:4 5 6 10 21 6:4 6 14 16 17 19 25 26 7:11 12 19^4 22 8:7 18 26 10:7 23 12:3 34^4 42 51 13:20 14:10 22^2 25 26^2 29^2 16:1^2 17:1 18:7 23 19:7 10 14 21:32 22:23 23:24^3 26 27 32 33 25:20^3 34^2 36^2 40 26:21 25 29 32 37 27:10^2 11^2 12^2 14^2 15^2 16^2 17^2 18 21 28:10^2 12 20 21 38 42 29:10 15 19 20^2 25 28^2 45 46^2 30:12 19^2 21^3 31:16 32:3 4 15 25^2 32 34 33:6 34:13^3 15^2 16^4 35:17 18 25 36:26 30 34 36 38^4 37:9^3 22^2 38:10^3 11^3 12^3 14^2 15^2 17^2 19^2 28 39:13 14 15^3 40:31^2

EXOD. 40:36 38

LEVIT. 4:15 6:17 7:34 36 38 8:14 16 18 22 24^3 25 28 9:24 10:5 19^2 11:8^2 11^2 21 27 35 36 37 38 13:38 39 15:31^2 16:16^3 21^2 22 27^3 34 17:5 7^2 18:3 6 9 10 29 20:4 5 11 12 13 16 17 18 19 20 24 27 21:5^3 6^3 17 22:16 25 23:4 18^2 24:14 25:32 33 34^2 45 26:4 13 20 36^2 39^2 40^2 41^3 43^2 44^2 45^3

NUM. 1:2^4 3 16 17 18^4 20^4 22^4 24^3 26^3 28^3 30^3 32^3 34^3 36^3 38^3 40^3 42^3 45 47 52^2 2:2 3 4 9 10 16 17 18 24 25 31 32^2 34^3 3:10 15^2 17

NUM. 3:18 19 20^2 31 37^3 39 40 45 4:2^2 22^2 26^2 27^3 28 29^2 31^2 32^6 33 34^2 36 38^2 40^2 42^2 44 46^2 5:3 7 6:15^2 7:2 3 7 8 9 10 11 87 8:7^2 10 12 21 22 26^2 9:17 18 20 22 23 10:6^2 12 13 14 18 22 25 28 11:10 12 33 13:2 4 33 14:1 5 6 9 23 15:25^3 38^2 16:15 22 26 27^2 32^2 38 45 17:2^3 3 6^3 10 18:11 17^2 20 21 23 20:6 8^2 11 18 21:2 3 18 22:7 24:2 8 25:2^2 18 26:2 12 15 20 23 26 28 35 37 38 41 42^2 44 48 50 55 57 59 27:5

NUM. 27:7^2 14 19 28:2 14 20 28 31 29:3 6^2 9 11 14 18^3 19 21^3 24^3 27^3 30^3 33^3 37^3 30:9 31:9^4 10^2 29 32:17 38 33:1 2^4 4^2 12 52^3 34:14^4 15 35:2 3^3 7 36:3 4^2 6 11 12^2

DEU. 1:8 25 2:5 9 12 21 22 23 4:10 37 38 5:29 7:5^4 10 16 24^2 25 9:5 14 27^2 10:6 11 15 11:4^2 6^3 9 12:2 3^4 29 30^2 31^4 13:13 14:8^2 18:2^2 18 19:1^2 20:18^2 21:5 6 23:3 6^2 8 29:8 17^2 25 28 7 11 13 19 20 21^2 28 32:5 8 20 21 27 29 30 31 32^3 33 35^2 36 37^2 38^2 33:29

JOSH. 1:6 3:14 4:6 18 21 5:1 6 7^2 8 7:6 8^2 11 12^3 16 8:13 19 33^2 9:4 5^2 14 16 17^2 10:5 13 19 24 40 42 11:4 6^2 9^2 13 17 20 21 23^2 12:1 7 13:8 14 15 16 23 24 25 28^2 29 30 31 33 14:2 4^3 15:1 2 5 12 20 32 36 41 44 46 51 54 57 59 60 62 16:4 5^2 8 9 17:2^2 4 18:2 5^2 7^2 10 11^2 12 20 21 24 28^2 19:1^2 2 6 7 8 9 10^2 11 15 16^2 17 18 22^2 23^2 24 25 30 31^2 32 33 38 39^2 40 41 47 48^2 49 21:3^2 7 8

JOSH. 21:19 20 26 33^2 40^2 41 42 43 44^4 22:6 7^2 9 14 23:1 2^4 5 7 24:1^3 8

JUD. 1:4 7^3 2:2 3 4 10 12 14^2 17^2 18^2 19^3 20 22 3:4 6^5 7 25 5:18 20 22 6:5^3 9 7:2 6^3 8^2 12 19 20^2 8:3 10 21 26 28 33 34^2 9:3 24^2 26 27^2 57 10:12 12:2 13:20 14:17 19 15:13 16:18 23 24 25 18:1 2^2 8^2 14 16 23 26 29 19:14 21 22 20:13 22 33^2 42 21:2 6 22^2 23^2

RUTH 1:9 14

1 SAM. 1:19 2:20 26 33 5:9 6:6 7 10 11 13^2 8:9 22 9:16 10:4 12 21 11:4 12:9

1 SAM. 14:30 46 15:24 17:1 18^2 51 53 18:27 21:13 22:17^2 23:5 25:12 28:1 23 29:1 30:2 3^3 4 31:9 13

2 SAM. 1:23^2 2:26 3:18 30 4:12^2 5:21 7:10 23 24 10:3 4^3 18 12:30 13:31 36 15:11 36 16:8 18:28 20:2 3 22:46 23:17 19

1 KINGS 2:4^2 15 33 4:8 27 7:26 31 33^4 8:7 23 25 35 37^2 44 45^3 48^5 49^3 50 66 9:9 21 10:5 29 11:2 8 12:16 27 13:11 12 14:15^2 22^2 27 30 15:16 32 16:2 13 26 18:28 37 39 19:21 20:6 23 24 25 32^2 22:10

2 KINGS 1:14 3:24 27 5:24 6:20 22 23 7:7^4 15 8:12^4 21 10:7 11:12 13:3 5 14:12

2 KINGS 16:15^2 17:7 9^2 14^3 15 16 17^2 19 23 25 29^2 31 33 34^2 40 41^4 18:12 27^2 35 36 37 19:17 18 26 21:8 14^2 15 22:7 17 23:2 3^2 9 14 25:21 23^2 24

1 CHRON. 1:29 3:9 19 4:1 27 31 32 33^3 38^3 39 41^3 42 5:7^2 9 10^2 13^2 15 16 20^2 21^2 22 24^2 25 6:19 32^2 33 44 48 54^3 57 60^2 62 63 64 65 66 7:2^2 4^2 5^2 7^2 9^3 11 21 22 28 30 32 40 8:28 32 9:1 2^2 6 9^3 13^2 17 19 22^3 23 25^2 26 32 34 38^2 10:7 9 10 12 11:19^2 21 12:30 32^2 39 13:2 8 14:12

1 CHRON. 15:15 16 17 18 16:21 38 17:9 22 19:4^2 7 20:2 21:16 23:3^2 11 22 24^2 28 32 24:2 3^2 4^2 19^3 30 31^2 25:1 3 6 7 26:6 8^2 13 27:1^2 28:15 19 29:18 20^2 21

2 CHRON. 1:17 3:13^2 4:4 7 16 20 5:8 12^2 13 6:14 16 25 26 28^2 34 35^3 36 37 38^5 39^3 7:3 6^2 10 14^3 22 8:8 14^3 9:4^2 6 10:16 11:13 14^2 16^2 13:10 16 18 14:4 15:4 12^3 15^2 17:14 18:9 19:4 10 20:13^3 27 33^3 21:3 22:5 24:18^2 24^2 25:4 5 10 15 20 26:11 13 28:6 8 15 29:6^2 15 23 24 30 34 30:7 16^2 22 27^2 31:1 2 6 15^2

2 CHRON. 31:16^4 17^3 18^5 19 32:13 17 33:17 34:5 6 25 30 32 33^2 35:2 10^2 11 15^2 25 36:15 17^2

EZRA 1:6 2:59^2 61 62 65^2 66^2 67^2 69 70^2 3:8^2 9^2 10 12 4:5 7 9 17 23 5:3 5 8 10 6:12 13 18^2 20 22 7:13 16 17^2 8:1 19 24 26 9:1 2^2 11^2 12^4 10:16^2 19^3

NEH. 2:18 3:5^3 18 23 4:3 4^2 5^2 13^4 15 5:1^2 5 6 8 11^4 14 15 6:6 9 14 16 7:61^2 63 64 67^2 68^2 69 73^2 8:6^3 7 12 15 16 9:2^2 3^3 4 6 9 11 15^2 16 17^3 20^2 21^2 23^2 24^2 26 27^3 28 29 35^2

NEH. 9:37 10:10 28^3 29^2 30 11:3 9 12 14^2 19 25 30 31 12:7 9 24 27 42 45 13:11 13^2 24 25^3

ESTHER 1:17^2 20 22 2:3 12 3:8 12 8:9^3 11 13 9:2^2 5 10 15 16^4 22 27^3 28 31^3

JOB 1:4^2 5^2 13 18 2:12^3 3:8 15 4:21 5:5 12^2 13 15 6:17 18 8:4 8 10 11:3 20 12:18 14:12 15:18 35 16:10 17:2 4 19:12 15 20:10 21:8^4 9 10^2 11^2 13 16^2 17 29 22:6 18 24:5^2 11^2 18 23 27:23 29:9^2 10^3 23 25 30:2 4 9^2 12 31:16 39 33:16 34:24 25 36:9^2 10 11^2 14 15 20 37:8 38:15 40 39:3^2 4

JOB 40:12 13 22 42:15^2

PSALMS 2:3^2 12 4:7^2 5:9^4 10^2 11 7:7 9:5 6 10 15 10:17 11:2^2 6 16:4^3 17:7 10^2 11 14^3 18:45 19:3 4^2 21:10^2 12 22:13 26:10 28:3 4^4 8 33:15^2 19 34:5 15 17 35:6 7 16 17 21 25 36:7 37:14 15^3 18 39 40:15 44:1 3^2 12 49:6^2 8 10 11^5 13^4 14^2 55:9 15 23 56:5 57:4 58.4 6^2 59:7^2 12^3 62:4 64:3^3 8 65:7 68:27^2 69:22^2 23^2 25^2 27 70:3 72:14^2 73:4^2 7^2 9^2 17 20 74:4 8 76:5^2 78:4 5 6 7 8^2 12 18^2 28^2 29 30^3 33^2 35^2 36^2 37 38 44^2 46^2 47 48^2 50^2 51 53 55 57 58^2

PSALMS 78:63^2 64^2 79:3 10 12^2 81:12^2 14^2 15 83:11^2 16 85:2 89:17 32^2 90:10 16 91:12 93:3^2 94:23^2 95:10 98:8 99:8 102:17 28 104:11 12 17 21^2 22 27 29^2 105:14 24 25 29^2 30^2 31 32 33^3 35^2 36^2 37 106:11 15^2 18 20 21 25 27 29 32 35 36 37^2 38^2 39^2 42^2 43^2 44^2 107:5 6^2 12 13^2 14 17^2 18 19^2 20 26 27 28^2 30 38 109:10^2 13 25 29 115:2 4 7 9^2 10^2 11^2 119:70 118 123:2 124:3 6 125:3 4 5 129:3 132:12 135:12 17 136:21 140:2 3^2 9 141:4 5 6 10 144:8 11 12 145:15 19 147:3 4 149:2 5 6^2 8^2

PROV. 1:6 15 16 18^2 22 31^2 2:15 4:16 22 8:21 9:15 10:15 11:6 20 14:24 17:6 18:19 20:29 21:12 22:23 23:11 24:2^2 22 25:27 29:13 16 30:5 11^2 12^2 13^2 14 25 26

ECCL. 2:3 3:11 4:1 9 5:11 13 9:3 6^3

ISAIAH 2:4^2 7^4 8^3 3:4 8^2 9^3 10 12 16 17 18^4 5:12 13^2 14^3 17 21^2 24^2 25 27^2 28^3 29 6:10^5 13 8:12 19 21^2 9:17^2 10:2 5 13 25 29 11:7 14 13:8 10 11^2 16^4 18^2 20 21 22^2 14:1 2^2 9 21 25 15:2 3^2 4 16:10^2 18:2 7 20:4 5^2 21:14 24:14 25:11^2 26:11 14 21 28:25 29:13^4 14^2 15^2 19 30:6^2 7 26

ISAIAH 31:3 4 33:2 7 9 23 24 34:2 3^4 4 7^2 35:10 36:12^2 20 21 22 37:18 19 27 40:24 26 31 41:1 17 29^2 42:11 15 43:9 14 44:9^2 18^2 25 45:12 20 46:1 47:9 49:9 22^2 23^2 26^2 50:2 3 51:7 11 52:15 53:11 54:17 55:12 56:7^2 11 57:2 8 58:1^2 2 59:5 6^4 7^3 8 18 60:8 9^2 10 11 61:6 7^2 8 9^2 62:6 63:3 6 8 9 10 65:2 4 6 7^2 22 23 66:3^3 5^2 18^2 24^2

JER. 1:8 16^2 17 2:11^2 26^4 27^3 3:17 21^2 24^4 4:16 5:3 4 5 6^3 16 24 27 31 6:3^2 10 12^2 19 23 27 7:18 19 24^2 26^3 28^2

JER. 7:30 31^2 8:1 7 10^2 12 19 9:3^2 5 8 14^2 16 10:7 9 15 21 11:8^2 10^2 12 14 18 22^2 23 12:2^2 14 13:10 14:3^4 4 6 10^3 11 12 14 16^4 15:7 8 9 16:3^2 4 7^2 15^2 17^2 18^3 17:1 2^3 23^2 25 18:8 15 16 17 21^6 22 23^3 19:4 5 7^3 9^4 15 20:4 5 11 21:7^2 22:9 23:3 8 10^2 11 12^2 16 22^2 26 27 31 32^2 24:5 7^2 9 10 25:12 14^2 36 38 26:3 27:4 8 11^2 29:23 30:3 9^2 10 20^2 21^2 31:12 13^2 17 23 32 33^3 34^2 32:18 22 30^2 32^4 34 35^2 38 39 40 44 33:8^2 12 20 26

JER. 34:14 16 20^3 21^2 35:14 16 36:3^2 6 7 15 36:24 31 37:7 38:18 19 23 40:7 8 9 41:5^3 8 42:17 43:1^2 44:3 5^2 9 12 15 46:5 10 21^2 25^2 26 27 47:3 5 48:12 13 33 34 44 49:1 3 7 20 21 29^5 32^3 35 37^2 50:4 5 6^2 7^2 9 27^2 34^2 37^2 38 42 45 51:5 18 24 30^2 39^2 55 56

LAM. 1:11 14 19^2 22 2:10^2 12^3 15^2 16 18 20 3:14 46 60^2 61^2 62 63^3 64 65 4:3 7 8^3 10^2 14 20 5:7 8 12 14

EZEKIEL 1:5 7^2 8^4 9 10 11^3 13 16^3 17 18^2 20 22 23^2

EZEKIEL
1:24[2] 25[2] 26 2:3 6[3] 7[2] 3:8[2] 9 4:4 5 12 13 17 5:10 16 6:5 9[4] 13[4] 14 7:11 18 19[7] 20[2] 24[2] 27[2] 8:16[2] 17 9:10[2] 10:8 10 11 12[4] 16 19 21 22[2] 11:19 20 21[4] 22 12:3[2] 4[2] 5 6 7 16 19[2]

EZEKIEL
13:2 3 17 14:3[4] 5[2] 10 11[2] 14[2] 20[2] 22 23[2] 16:39 40 45[2] 47[2] 53 55[2] 19:4 7[2] 8[2] 20:4 8 16[2] 18[3] 24[2] 26 28[4] 30 21:6 14 15[3] 28 29 22:6 10 26 31[2] 23:3[3] 4 7 8 15[3] 17 20 24 30 36

EZEKIEL
23:37[3] 39[2] 42[2] 45 47[4] 24:25[5] 25:4[2] 26:10 16[3] 17 27:9 11 29 30[2] 32 35[2] 28:7 25 26 29:7[2] 14 16 30:11 13 31:6[2] 14[4] 32:2 10 14[2] 24[2] 25[2] 26 27[5] 29 30[3] 33:2[2] 17 29 31[3] 34:10[2] 13 14 23 24 27[2] 30 35:5[2]

EZEKIEL
36:5[2] 7 12 17[4] 18 19[2] 23 37:10 20 21 23[5] 25[3] 27 38:16 39:22 23[2] 24[2] 26[3] 27 28[2] 40:16 22[3] 41 44 41:16 42:4 11[3] 14 43:7[4] 8[4] 9[2] 10 11 44:10[2] 12[2] 13[2] 18[2] 19[2] 20[3] 22 28[2] 45:4 8 46:16 18 47:10[2] 12

EZEKIEL
48:29 34

DANIEL
1:15 16 2:30 3:21[4] 27[2] 28[2] 29 4:21 6:24[3] 7:12[2] 8:23 9:7 11:8[3] 32

HOSEA
1:7 2:5 17 3:5[2] 4:7 8[2] 9[2] 12[3] 18 19 5:4[2] 5 6[2] 7 15[2] 7:2[3] 3[2] 6[2] 7[2] 10 12 14[2] 15 16[3] 8:4[2] 13[2] 9:4[3]

HOSEA
9:6[2] 9[2] 10 11 12 15[3] 16[2] 10:2[3] 8 10 11:3 4 6 11 12:11 13:2[2] 6[2] 8 16[2] 14:4

JOEL
1:3[2] 17 2:6 7 10 17 22 3:6 13 15 19 21

AMOS
1:13 15 2:4[2] 8 3:10 4:1 5:12 6:2 4 7:11 8:7

AMOS
9:4 15[2]

OBADIAH
12 13[5] 17

JONAH
1:2 2:8 3:8 10[2] 4:11[2]

MICAH
2:1[2] 9[2] 12 13 3:2[3] 3[2] 4 5[2] 7 4:3[2] 13[2] 6:12[2] 16 7:4 13 16[4] 17 19

NAHUM
2:2 5 7 3:3[2] 17

HABAK.
1:7[2] 8[3] 9 15[2]

HABAK.
1:16[4] 17 2:15 3:11 14

ZEPH.
1:9 12[2] 13[2] 17[2] 18[2] 2:7[2] 8 10 14 3:6[3] 7[2] 13

HAGGAI
1:12[2] 14 2:14 22

ZECH.
1:21 2:9 5:6 9 7:2 11 12 8:8 12 9:16 10:2 5 6 7[3] 9 11:3 5 6 8 16

ZECH.
12:5[2] 12[2] 13[2] 14 14:12[6]

MALACHI
4:6

MATT.
1:21 2:11 12 3:6 4:6 20 21[2] 22 23 6:2 5 7 14 15 16 7:6 16 20 8:22 33 34 9:2 4 29 30 35 10:17 21 11:1 5 16 12:9 25 13:15[5] 43 54 58

MATT.
14:14 15:2 8[3] 27 17:6 8 25 18:10 31 35 19:12 20:4 8 31 34[2] 21:7 8 41 22:5 7 16 18 22 23:3 4 5[3] 25:1 3 4[2] 7 26:43 67 27:39

MARK
1:5 18 19 20 23 39 2:5 6 3:4 5 4:12 15

MARK
5:17 6:6 8[2] 26 52 7:3 6[2] 8:3 9:44 46 48 10:42 11:4 7 8 12:12 15 44 13:12 14:40 46 56 59 65 15:19 29 16:14

LUKE
1:16 20 51 52 66 77 2:8 39 44 3:15 4:11 15 29 5:2 6 7 11 15

LUKE
5:20 22 30 6:1 8 17 22 23 26 7:21 8:3 12 25 9:47 60 11:17 48 12:36 42 13:1 14:4 16:4 8 17:13 19:32 35 36 40 20:23 26 21:1 4 12 22:66 23:25 24:5 11 16 31 45

JOHN
3:19 4:38 8:9 10:39 11:19

JOHN
11:46 12:40[4] 13:12 15:22 25 17:19 20 18:8 19:3 31 20:10

ACTS
1:9 19 26 2:37 45 46 4:5 23 24 29 5:18 6:1 6 7:19 34 39 41 54 57 58 60 8:17 36 9:24 10:9 11:18 12:17 20[2] 25 13:3 5 18 19

ACTS
13:22 27 33 50 51 14:2 3 5 11 13 14 16 15:3 9 13 22 26 16:19 22 24 33 17:21 26 18:3 19:18 19 21:21 24 22:22 23 30 23:16 28 29 25:19 26:18 27:13 43 28:6 27[5]

ROMANS
1:21[2] 24[2] 26 27[2] 28

ROMANS
2:15[3] 3:3 13[3] 15 16 18 10:3 18[2] 11:9 10[2] 11 12 18 24 27 30 13:7 15:27[3] 16:4 5 18

1 COR.
3:19 8:7 12 14:35 16:19

2 COR.
3:14 15 5:19 6:16 8:2[3] 3[2] 5 14[2] 9:14 11:15

GAL.
2:13

EPHES.
4:17 18

EPHES.
5:24[2] 28[2]

PHIL.
2:21 3:19[2]

COLOS.
2:2

1 THESS.
2:15 16 5:13

2 THESS.
3:12

1 TIM.
3:11 12[2] 4:2 5:4 12 6:1

2 TIM.
2:3 17 3:8 4:3 4 16

TITUS
1:12 15 2:4[2] 5 9 3:13

HEB.
2:10 15 3:10 5:14 7:5 8:9 10[2]

HEB.
8:12[3] 10:16[2] 17 11:16 35 12:10 13:7

JAMES
1:27 3:3

1 PETER
3:5 12 14 4:14 19

2 PETER
2:2 3 8 12 13 3:3 16

3 JOHN
6

JUDE
6[2] 13 15[2] 16[2] 18

REV.
2:22 3:4 4:4 10 6:11[2] 14 7:3 9 11 14

REV.
7:17 9:4 5 7[2] 8 9 10[2] 17 18 19[4] 20 21[4] 10:3 4 11:5[2] 6 7 8 9[2] 11 12 16[2] 12:8 11[2] 13:16[2] 14:1 2 5 11 13[2] 15:6 16:10 11[3] 17:13 17[2] 18:11 19 19:19 21 20:4[2] 12 13 21:3 4 8 24 22:4

them

846

GEN.
1:14 15 17 22 26 27 28 2:1 19[2] 3:7 21 5:2 6:1 2 4 7 13[2] 19 20 21 7:3 9:1 19 10:1 11:3 6 8 9 29 31 12:3 13:6 14:8 14 15[2] 24 15:5 10 11 13 18:2 8 16 19:1 3[2] 5 6 8[2] 9 10 12 13 17 18 20:14 21:27 31 22:6 8 23:8 24:28 53 56 60 25:6

GEN.
25:26 26:15 18[2] 27 30 31 27:9 13 14 15 28:11 29:4 5 6 7 9[2] 30:14 35 37 40 42 31:5 9 32 33 34[2] 55 32:2 4 16 23[2] 33:3 13 34:14 21[3] 23 35:4 5 36:7 37:6 13 17[2] 18 22 26 39:14 40:3 4[2] 5 6[2] 8[2] 11 17 22 41:3 6 8[2] 19 21[2] 23 27 30 35[2] 42:7[4] 9[2]

GEN.
42:12 14 17 18 22 23[2] 24[4] 25[2] 27 28 29 36 43:2 11 16 23 24 27 32 34 44:4[2] 6[2] 15 45:1 15 21[2] 22 24 26 27 47:2 6[3] 11 17[2] 20 21 22[2] 24 48:6 9[2] 10[3] 12 13[2] 16[2] 20 49:7[2] 28[3] 29[2] 50:12 19 21[2]

EXOD.
1:7 10[2] 11[2] 12 14 16 17 18 19 21 2:17[2] 25

EXOD.
3:8[2] 9 13[2] 16 22 4:20 5:4 5 7 8 9 13 14 21 6:1[2] 3 4[2] 13 7:5 6 13 22 8:2 14 15 19 9:2[2] 12 17 19 27 10:2 8 10 14[2] 19 27 12:3 16 21 33 36 38 42 13:17 31[3] 14:3 4 7 9[2] 10 13 17 19[2] 20 22 23 25[2] 28[2] 29 15:5 7[2] 9[2] 10 12

EXOD.
15:13 15 16 17[2] 19 21 25[2] 16:3 4 12 15 16 20[2] 23 17:2 8[2] 11 16 18:20[2] 21 22 25 19:10[2] 21 22 24 25 20:5[3] 6 11 21:1 34 22:11 23 23:23 24[2] 29 30 31 32 24:12 14 25:3 8[2] 12 13 14 18 28[2] 29 40 26:1 24 37[2] 27:6 28:9 11 14 25 26 27 33 40[2] 41[4] 42

EXOD.
29:1[2] 2 3[2] 4 8 9[2] 13[2] 17 22 24 25[2] 29 30 33 35 46[2] 30:5 12[3] 13 14 21 29[2] 30 31:5 32:2[2] 3 4 8[2] 10[2] 12[3] 13 18[3] 19 21 24[2] 25 27 31 34 34:31[2] 32 33 35:1[2] 23 26 29 33 35[2] 36:8[2] 14 29 36[2] 37:4 7 15 28 38:6 25 28 39:7 18 19 20 43 40:12

EXOD.
40:14 15

LEVIT.
1:12 2:12 3:4 10 15 16 4:2 9 10 20[2] 35 5:8 6:10 17 18 7:4 5 7 34 35 36[2] 8:6 10 11 13[3] 26 27 28[2] 9:2 7 13 14 22 10:1[2] 2 3 4 5 11 17 11:1 4[2] 9 22 24 25 26 28 31 32 33 42 43 13:58 14:6 12 23 24 40 42 45

LEVIT.
14:51 15:2 14 15 29 31 16:4 7 16 21 23 28 17:2 5[2] 7 8 16 18:2 5 29 19:2 10 31[2] 37 20:6 8 11[2] 12[2] 13[2] 16 18 22 23 27[2] 21:1 23 22:3 9 16[2] 18 22 25 31 23:2 10 20 22 43 24:6 12 25:2 18 31 44 45 46[2] 51 26:3 36[2] 39 41[2] 43[2] 44[4] 27:2

NUM.
1:3 19 21 22 23 25 27 29 31 33 35 37 39 41 43 47 49 2:4 13 15 19 21 23 26 28 30 3:6 15 16 22[2] 32 34 43 47 48 49[2] 51 4:8 12[3] 19[2] 23 26 27 29 30 36 40 44 48 5:3 4 12 23 6:2 16 19 20 23 27 7:1[2] 2 3 5[2] 6 9

NUM.
7:13 19 25 31 37 43 49 55 61 67 73 79 8:6 7[5] 8 13 15[2] 16 17 20 21[3] 22 9:8 10:2[2] 3 33[2] 34 35 11:1[2] 3 4 12[2] 16[2] 17 21 22[4] 24 25 26[2] 28 29 31 32 12:9 13:2 8 17[2] 26[2] 14:2 6 9[2] 10 11 12[2] 13 14[2] 16[2] 23 28 31 40 45[2] 15:2 18 25

NUM.
15:26 29 38[2] 39 16:3[3] 7 9 15[2] 17 18 19 21 28 30[2] 31 32 33[2] 34[2] 38[3] 45 46 49 17:2 4 8 11 12[2] 18 20 24 26[2] 30 19:9 10 20:6 8 10 12 13 21 25 26 28 21:1 3 16 30[2] 33 22:6[2] 8 11[3] 12 20 23:11 13[4] 21 22 25[2] 27 24:8 10 25:4 8 11 17

NUM.
26:3 7 10 18 22 25 27 34 37 41 43 47 50 62[2] 64 65[2] 27:3 7[2] 17[4] 28:2 3 31 30:12[3] 14[2] 15[2] 31:3 6[2] 8 13 15 27[2] 30 36 47 51 32:7 8 9 13 15 17 19 20 28 29[2] 33 41 33:4 51 55 56 34:2 35:2 3 5 6 7 8[2] 10 15 36:6

DEU.
1:3 8[2]

DEU.
1:13 15 29 39 42 2:5 6[2] 9 11 12[4] 14 15[2] 19[2] 20 21[3] 22[2] 23 3:4 6 14 20 22 28 4:1 3 6 7 9 10 13 14 19[2] 31 37 5:1[3] 9[3] 10 22[2] 29[2] 30 31[3] 6:1 7[2] 8 9 7:2[5] 3 5 9 10[2] 11 12 15[2] 16 17 18 20 21 22 23 24 25 8:19[2] 9:3[4] 4[2]

DEU.
9:5 10 12[2] 14 17[2] 28[5] 10:2 4 11 15[2] 11:4[2] 6 9 16 18 19[2] 20 21 22 12:3 18 22[2] 29[2] 30 13:2 17 14:7[2] 17:3 5 19 18:2 8 12 18[2] 19:1 9 20:1[2] 3[2] 17 19[4] 20 21:5 8 10[2] 18 22:1[2] 4[2] 19 22 24[2] 23:8 24:8 25:1 5 13 16 26:13 27:2 3 4 5 26 28:13 14 25[2]

DEU.
28:26 31 32 39[2] 41 55 57 61 29:1 2 7 9 17 25[2] 26[2] 28[2] 30:1 7 17 20 31:2 3 4[2] 5[2] 6 7[2] 10 16[3] 17[4] 20[2] 21[3] 23 28 32:11 19 20 21[2] 23[2] 24 26[2] 28 30[2] 35 38 41 46 33:2[2] 11[2] 17 27

JOSH.
1:2 6 14 15 2:4 5[2] 6[2] 7[2] 8 15 16 21 22[2]

JOSH.
2:23 4:3[3] 5 7 8[3] 12 5:1 5 6 7[2] 6:6 8 13 23 26 7:2 5[3] 11 21[2] 23[3] 24 25[2] 8:3 4 5 6[2] 9 11 12 15 16 20 22[3] 24 33[3] 35 9:5 8 11[2] 15[4] 16[2] 18[2] 19[2] 20[3] 21[4] 22[2] 26[3] 27 10:1 8[3] 9 10[4] 11 18 19[3] 20[2] 24 25 26[3] 27[2] 28 39 41 11:4 6[2]

JOSH.
11:7[2] 8[5] 9 11 12[3] 13 14 17 20[2] 21 12:6 13:6 8[2] 12 14 22[2] 33 14:1 3 12 15:63 17:4 13 15 18:1 4[2] 7 8 10 19:9[2] 47 49 20:4[2] 9 21:2 11 21 42 44[2] 22:2 4 6[2] 7[2] 8 12 15 30 32 33 23:2 5[2] 7[3] 12[2] 16 24:5 7[2] 8[2] 11 12 13 25

JUD.
1:1 4

JUD.
1:22 25 28 29 30 32 33 34 2:3 10 12[3] 14[3] 15[2] 16[2] 17 18[5] 19[2] 21 22 23[2] 3:1 2 4 8 9 15 23 25 27 28 4:2 5:14 21 30 31 6:1 2 3 4 8 9 20 35 7:1 4[2] 6 17 24 8:2 4 8 10 11 12 16 19 20 23 24 25 34 9:1 7 8 9

JUD.	1 SAM.	2 SAM.	1 KINGS	2 KINGS	2 CHRON.	2 CHRON.	NEH.	JOB	PSALMS	PSALMS	PROV.	ISAIAH	ISAIAH	JER.	JER.	LAM.	EZEKIEL
9:11	8:7	7:21	15:18^2	18:13	2:2	30:7	4:23	12:24	40:14^2	94:23^3	1:12	11:6	52:5^2	13:20	31:8^3	1:22	20:9^2
13	8	8:1	22	19	11	9^2	5:2	25	15	97:10	15	14^2	15	21	9^2	2:2	10^2
24	9^3	2^2	18:4^2	23	17	10^2	5	14:21	41:10	99:3	32^2	13:2	54:2	24	13^2	17	11^3
25	11	4	6	27	18	12	7^2	15:19	42:4	6^2	2:7	3	56:5^2	14:10	28^2	21	12^3
33	12	7	13	19:6	3:10	14	8	17:4	43:3^2	7^2	3:3^2	8	7^2	12^2	32^3	3:20	13^3
38	14^2	10:4	23^2	11	15	17	10	20:15^2	44:2^2	8^2	18	15	57:6	13	34^2	25	14
43^3	16	5	26	12	16^2	18	11^2	21:8	3^2	101:3	21	17	8	14^3	32:13	64	15^3
44	21	9	27	18	4:4	31:1	12^3	9	5	102:26^2	27	14:1^2	13^2	15	14	65^2	17^3
49^2	22	10	28	20:13^3	6^2	6	15	17	7	103:11	4:21^2	2^4	59:8	16^3	18	66	19
51^2	9:4^2	16	40^5	15	7	7	6:3	26	13	13	22	18	12	17^2	22^2	4:4	21^4
57	11	19	19:2	21:3	8	11	4	29	48:6	17	5:6	20	20	18	23^2	15	22
10:7	12	11:23	21	8^2	9	32:1	8	22:17	49:7	18	13	22	21	15:1^2	33^2	16^2	23^3
16	14	12:11	20:15	9	17	6^2	17	19	14^2	104:8	17	25	60:9	2	37^4		25
11:9	20	17	18^2	14	5:12^2	18^2	7:3^3	20	50:21	12	6:21^2	16:4	14	3	39^3	EZEKIEL	26^2
11	22^3	31	19	21	6:25^2	22	5	24:5	53:3	22	7:3^2	17:2	61:1	4	40^3	1:18	27
14	26	13:9	20	24	26	26	65	12	5^2	24	8:8	13	3^2	7^2	41^3	19	28^2
21	10:5	10	23	22:5^2	27	33:3	8:8	17^2	54:3	27	9	14^2	7	8	42^2	20	29
24	6	11	25	7	28	8	10^2	26:8	4	28	17	18:6^2	8	9	44	21	38^2
25	10	30	27^2	9	34	11	12	29:22	5	105:3	10:26	19:3	9^2	10	33:5	2:4^2	40^2
26	18	14:6	21:8	15	36^3	15	16	24	55:15^3	14	11:3^2	4	62:12	16	6^2	5	21:23
32^2	11:2	36^2	11^2	23:4^2	38	22	17	30:5	19	24	6	12^2	63:3^2	19^2	7	6	29
33	7^2	16:1	22:6	5	7:6	25	9:1	31	23	27	12:6	20^2	6	16:3^2	8	7	22:26
35	8	17:9	10	12^2	19	34:4^4	6	32:8	57:4	32	20	22^2	7	5	9	3:4	28^2
12:2	11	17	11	16	20^2	12	10	34:25	58:7^2	37	26	23:1	9^4	6^2	11^2	6	30
3	12	18	13	19	22^4	21	11	26	8	38^2	14:3	13	10	7^3	13	9	31^2
13:1	12:5	20^2	17	20	8:2	23	12^2	36:7	9	40	22	18	11	8	24^2	11^3	23:4
14:9^2	8	22		24:2	8^2	35:2	13^2	9	59:1	44	19:7	24:8	12^2	11^3	26	13	6
12	9^2	18:1	2 KINGS	3	18	11	14^2	13	8	106:8	20:10	9	13	15^2	34:8	15^2	7^2
14	13:16	4	1:2	16	9:8^2	13	15^4	31	11^3	9	12	25:11	19	16^2	9	17	12
18	19	14	3	20	16	15	17^2	37:4	12	10^3	26	26:5	65:1^2	21^2	10^2	25^2	15
19^2	14:8	31	5	25:13	10:7^2	25	18	12	13^3	11	21:6	11	8	17:11^2	11	26	16^2
15:3^2	9	19:3	7	19	9	36:7	19^4	15	14^2	15	7	14	21^2	18^4	13	27	17^2
5	10	28	12	20	10	15	20^2	21	15	25^2	22:2	16	23	20	16	4:6	22
7	11	20:3^3	2:11	21^2	13	17^2	21	39:4	60:4	26^2	5	27:4^2	66:4	18:8	20^2	9	23^3
8	12	8	12	22	14	20	22^2	14	62:10	27	18	5	19^2	10	21	13	27
11^2	21	19	16	24^2	16		23	15^2	63:11	29	21	6	21	15	22	5:2	28^2
12	22	21:2^3	18		17	EZRA	24^3	40:13	64:5	34	23	11^5		17^2	35:2^3	3	36
16:3^3	32^2	6^2	24^3	1 CHRON.	11:11	1:5	26^2	41:16	6	36	26^2	28:1	JER.	19	4	4^3	37^2
8	34^3	7	3:9	2:6	12	6	27^5	42:9	7	41^3	24:1	6	1:16	20^2	5	6	43
12	36^2	9^2	10	23	14	7	28^4	15	8	42	11	9	17^2	22	15^2	12	45
23	37	10^2	13	53	16	8	29^3		65:3	43	21	13	2:3	23^2	16	13^2	46^2
25	47	12^2	21	4:21	23	9	30^3	PSALMS	5	45	22	29:1	13	19:7^2	17^3	16	47^2
26	48^2	13	24	41	12:5	11	31^2		9	46^2	25^2	15	25	9^2	36:3	6:2	24:3
17:4	15:3	22:15^2	4:31	42	7^2	2:63	34	2:4	68:1	107:3	25:13	30:5	28	11^2	6	10	5
18:1^2	4	18	33	5:11	10	65	35^2	5^2	2	5	27:3	6	37	20:4^2	13	12	20
2	6	23	39^2	20^3	11^2	3:3	10:31	9^2	3^2	6	28:4	8	3:2	5^3	14	14	25
4	9	28	44	25	13:7	7^2	11:23	5:6	17	7	13	22	4:12	12	18^2	7:11^2	27
6	15	31	5:12	26^2	9	4:2	12:9	10^3	18	13	30:5	28	5:3^2	21:3	25	16^2	25:2
7	18	38^2	22	6:55	13^2	3	24	11^3	25	14	7	31:1	5	4	26	18	10
8	16:5	39^2	23^2	67	16	4	27	6:10	69:6	19	27	2	6^2	7^2	31^2	19	12
9	20	40	24^2	78	17	5	29	7:1	9	20^2	31:29	4	7^2	22:7	32	20	17^2
18	17:3	41	6:4	7:3	14:7	20	31	9:6	11	22		32:3^2	13^2	9	37:5	22	26:20^2
21	8	42	11	4	9	23	32	10	14	28	ECCL.	33:4	14	25^2	10	27^2	27:31
27	23^2	43^3	16	9	11	5:1	36	12	22	30	2:5	34:2^2	19	23:2^2	38:4	8:11^2	28:8
31	24	49	18	40	13	2^2	37	13	24^2	32	10	7	6:10	3^2	11	18	18
19:6	31	23:6	19^2	8:6	14^2	3^2	38^3	20	27	34	14	16	13^2	4^2	26	9:1	24
8	36	7	21^3	7	15:4	4	40	10:2	28	38	3:12	17^2	15^2	8	27	2	25
14	39^2	18	22^2	8	6	5	43	5	70:2^2	40	18	35:1	18	12^2	39:4	7	26^2
15	40	24:1	23^2	32	9	9	44	12:7^2	3	109:10	19	4	21	14	5	8	29:12
23^2	18:16	12	33	9:20	15^2	10	47	15:4	71:13^2	15^2	4:16	36:1	30^2	15^2	10	10:1	14
24^3	27		7:10	25	16:8	12	13:2^2	17:7^2	73:6^2	20	5:11^2	4	7:16	17	40:7	2	15
25	19:8	1 KINGS	12	27^2	9	14	10	18:14^2	10	25	7:11	8	22^2	21	9	13	16
20:13	20	1:20	9:11	28^2	17:8^2	15	11^2	17	18^2	28^2	12	37:6	23	22	10	16^2	21
20	20:11	33	15	29	9	6:5	13	37	27	29	8:11	11	25	32^4	14	17	30:5
25	21	40	17	10:7	14	9	15	38	74:8	111:2	12	12	27^2	33	41:5	19^2	9
28	40	2:7	18	12	18:5	20	17	40	75:8^2	5	9:1	19	28	24:1	6^3	11:4	23
32	21:13	32	19	11:3	9^2	21	21^2	41^2	78:4	6	5	38:21	31	5	7^2	5	26
34	22:2	5:3	20	14	16	22^2	25^4	42^2	5	115:8^3	11	39:2^3	33	6^6	8^2	16^3	31:14
40	4	9^4	10:1	20	31	7:17	29	19:4	6^2	13	12	4	8:2	7	9	19^2	16
41	11	14	6^2	12:15	19:2	24	30	11^2	11	118:4	10:15	40:11	3^2	8	10	20	17
42^3	23:5	18	7^2	17^2	4	25^2		13	13	7^2	11:8	22	4	9^2	18	21	18
43^2	26	6:12	8	18^2	9	8:1	ESTHER	21:9^3	14	10	12:1	24^2	9	10^2	42:17^2	22^2	32:10
45^3	24:7	15	14^4	19	10	13	1:7	12^2	15	11		26	10^2	25:4	43:1	24	12
48	22	16	18	29	20:1	14	2:3	22:4	24^2	12	CANT.	29	12	6^2	9	25	13^2
21:6	25:7^2	32^2	22	32	10^2	15	15	18	25	19	3:4	41:1^2	13^3	9^3	10^2	12:10^2	15
7^2	14	34	25^3	34	12	17^2	3:4^2	25	27	119:63^2	4:2	2	19	10	12^2	11	18^2
10	15	7:6^2	26	39	16^2	20	8	24:6	29	84	5:3	3	9:2	14^2	44:4	12	20
12	16	15	29	40	17	22^2	11	9	31^2	93	6:6	12^3	7^2	16	13	14	21
13	18	25	32	13:2	23	24	13	25:3	34	118		15	9	18	21	15^2	22
14^2	20	37	11:4^4	14:8	25^2	25	4:7	14^2	38	129	ISAIAH	16^3	10	26	27^2	16	23
15	43	46	5	10^2	27^2	28	8	28:1	42	152	1:14	17^2	13	27	30	19	24^2
16	26:12^2	8:21	9	11	21:3	29^2	15	4^3	45^3	165	23	22^5	14	28	45:5	23^2	25^3
17	13	34	15	14^3	22:8	30	5:8	5^2	49^2	167	31	27	15^2	30^2	46:5	28	26
18	14	35	12:5^2	15:2	12	33	11	9^2	52	125:4	2:9	28^2	16^3	31	15	13:2	28
19	27:5	36	7	12	23:3	10:3	8:11^2	29:6	53	5	3:4	42:5^2	18	26:2	21	6	29^2
22^3	30:2	37	11	18	8	6	17	31:6	54	126:1	9	7	22	3	25	11	30^3
23^3	8^2	44	13:3	16:10	14	10	9:1^3	15	55^2	2	12	9	25	4	26	15	31
	17^2	46^3	4	21	24:5	14^2	2^2	17	66	127:5	4:2	11	10:2	5	47.2	17	32
RUTH	19^2	47^2	7^2	41	13	15	3	19^2	72^2	129:5	5:8	12	5^2	19	48:39	20^3	33:2
1:4	21	48	17	42	17	16	5	20^2	79:3	6	11^2	16^4	11	27:2	49:2	14:3	6
5	22^2	50^4	18	17:9^2	19^3	44	21	33:6	4	132:12	18	22	14	3	11	4^2	7
6	27^3	52	23^5	18:1	20		22^2	18^2	80:5^2	135:18^3	20	43:9^3	16	4	20^2	15:7^3	10
9	28^3	53	14:27	4	23	NEH.	23	19	81:12	136:11	21	44:7^2	18	8	32	16:17	21
13^2	29^3	9:6	15:29	7	25:5^3	1:2	24^3	34:7^2	16	139:16	22	9	11:3	15	36	18^2	17
19	30^3	7	16:17	11	10	5	26	9	82:4	17	25^2	11^2	4^2	17	37^4	19	25
20	31	9^3	17:6	19:4^2	12^2	9^3	27^2	16^2	83:4	18	26	45:8	5	18^2	50:6^2	20	27
2:9	31:7	13	7	5	13	2:9	28	17	8	21	27^2	16	6	22^3	7^2	21^3	31
16^2	12	21	9	6	14^3	10	31	18	9	22^2	30	22^2	7	28:3	20	27	32^2
	13	10:17	10	10	20	17		19	13	140:9	6:13	47:6^2	8^2	13	21	28	33
1 SAM.		29	11	16	26:9	18	JOB	20	15^2	10^2	7:19	14	10	29:5^2	27^2	33	34:2
2:8^3	2 SAM.	11:2	12	17^2	14	20^2	1:4	22	17^2	143:7	20	48:3^2	11^2	9	28	36	3
10	1:10	18	15^4	20:3	27:5	3:2	5^2	35:1^2	84:5	12	8:7	5^2	12	17^2	33^3	37^4	4
16	11	24	16	21:2	28:5^2	4^3	6	3	7	144:6^2	12	6	14^2	18^3	43	50	6
23	18	12:5	18	6	8	5	14	4^2	11	145:15	15	7^2	20	19^2	45^2	53	10^2
26	2:5	7^3	20^3	10	9^3	7	15^2	5^2	85:8	18	19	13	22	21^2	51:1^2	54	11
30	7	9	21	23:6	12	9	16	6	9	19^2	20	14	23	22	17	61	12
34	14	10	22	22	13	10	17	19^2	86:5	20	9:2	21^2	12:2	23	19	17:12^2	13^4
3:13	36	14	24	31	15^7	27	2:1	20	14	146:8	10	49:9	3^2	28^2	39	18:19	14
5:6^3	4:7	16	25^2	24:3	23^2	29	3:8	24	87:4	147:11	13	10^4	4	31	40	24	15
8	9	17	26^2	6	29:3	4:4	4:19	25^2	88:4	18	16^2	18^2	6	30:3	52:3	26	16
6:6	12^2	28	27^2	19	4	8	21	26^2	8	20	10:1	26	14^2	9	17	19:12	20
7	5:3	13:11	17:28	25:7	5	9^2	5:4	27^2	89:7	148:5	6	50:6	15^3	16	25	20:3	21
10	19	12	29	26:30	8	11^2	6:19	36:8	9	6	10	9	13:10^2	19^4	26^2	4^3	23^3
12	21	14:15	32^2	31	21	12	8:4	10	11	13	15	51:8^2	12	20	27^2	5^3	24
15	23^2	23	35^4	27:23	23	14	9:5	37:40^4	12	149:3^2	18	17	13	21		6^3	25
7:10	6:22	27	18:11	26	24	16	12:15	39:6	23	5	20	23^2	14^2	31:4	LAM.	7	26
11	7:10^2	28^2	12^2	29:8	34	21	23^2	40:5	90:5	9	22	52:4	19	5	1:13	8^2	27^2

EZEKIEL
34:28^{2}
29
30
35:11^{2}
12
13
36:18
19^{2}
20
23
27
37^{2}
37:2
4
8^{3}
10
12
17
19^{3}
21^{3}
22^{2}
23^{2}
24^{2}
26^{5}
27
28
38:4^{2}
5^{2}
7
8
11^{2}
15
17
39:6
7
9
10^{2}
12
13^{2}
18
21
23^{2}
24^{2}
26
27^{3}
28^{3}
29
40:4
22
26
41:25
42:9
11
12
43:8^{2}
10
11^{2}
24^{3}
44:11^{2}
12^{2}
14
17
19
23
28^{2}
45:15
46:10
17
18
20
23^{2}
24
48:10
12
18

DANIEL
1:4
5^{2}
12
14^{2}
16
17
18^{2}
19^{2}
20^{2}
2:3
21
34
35^{2}
38
3:14
20
27
4:7
19
5:3
23
6:2
6:24^{3}
7:8
16
21
24
8:9
10
9:4^{2}
7
10:7
11:7
24
30
34
35^{3}
39
12:2

HOSEA
1:6
7^{2}
10^{2}
2:5
7^{3}
12^{2}
13
18^{2}
23
4:9^{2}
12^{2}
16
5:2
4
5
6
7
10^{2}
6:5^{2}
8
7:2
7
12^{3}
13^{3}
8:4
5
10
13
9:2
4
6^{3}
12^{3}
14^{2}
15^{3}
17
10:9
10^{2}
11:2^{2}
3^{2}
4^{3}
6
7
11
13:2^{2}
7^{2}
8^{3}
14^{2}
14:4
9^{2}

JOEL
2:3^{5}
4
10
17^{2}
3:2^{2}
6
7^{2}
8
9

AMOS
1:6
2:4
9
4:3
9
5:8
11^{2}
22
6:1
7
7:8
8:2
3
9:1^{5}
2^{2}
3^{2}
4^{2}
6
9:14^{2}
15^{2}

OBADIAH
11
18^{2}

JONAH
1:3
5
9
10
12
13
3:5^{2}
7
8
10

MICAH
2:1
2^{2}
6^{2}
8
12
13^{3}
3:2
3^{2}
4^{2}
6
4:4
7
12
5:3
6:11
7:13
14

NAHUM
1:7
2:2
10
11
3:18

HABAK.
1:10
12^{2}
13
14
15^{3}
16
2:7
17
3:16

ZEPH.
1:5^{2}
6
13
18^{2}
2:7
9^{2}
11
3:7
8
11
13
18
19

HAGGAI
2:22

ZECH.
1:3
21
2:9
3:5
6:6
10
11
13
7:14^{2}
8:8
9:8
14
15
16
10:1
3
5
6^{5}
8^{3}
9
10^{4}
12
11:5^{3}
6
11:8
12
13^{2}
12:8^{2}
13:9^{3}
14:8^{2}
13
17
21

MALACHI
1:4
2:2
5
17
3:3
7
16
17
4:1^{2}

MATT.
2:4
7
8
9
3:7
4:16
19
21
24
5:2
19
21
27
33
44^{3}
46
6:1
8
26
7:6
11
12
16
20
23
24
26
29
8:4
10
15
26
30
32
33
9:12
15^{3}
18
24
28
30
36
10:1^{2}
5
18
21
25
26
28
29
11:4
5
11
25
12:3
4
11
15
16
25
27
39
13:3
4
7
10
11
13
14
15
17^{2}
24
28^{2}
29
30^{2}
31
33
13:34
37
39
41
42
51
52
54
57
14:6
9
14
16^{2}
18
25
27
15:3
10
14
30^{3}
32
34
36
16:1
2
4
6
8
12
15
17:1
2
3
5
7
9
11
12
13
20
22
27^{2}
18:2
8^{2}
12
17
19
20
19:2
4^{3}
8
11
13^{2}
14
15
26^{2}
28
20:2
4
6
7
8
12
13
17
23^{2}
25^{3}
31
32
34
21:2^{3}
3^{2}
6
7
8
12^{2}
13
14
16
17
21
24
27
31^{2}
36
37
42
45
22:1
3
4
6^{2}
20
21
29
35
41
43
23:4^{2}
23:13
26
30
31
34^{3}
37
24:2
4
16
19^{2}
39
45
25:2
3
9
14
16
19
20
22
32
34
40
41
45
26:10
15
19
22
27
31
36
38
40
43
44
45
48
51
70
71
73
27:6
7
10
17
21
22
26
35
47
48
65
28:9
10
16
18
19
20

MARK
1:17
20
22
31
32
38
44
2:2^{2}
8
12
14
17
19^{3}
20
25
26
27
3:4
5
12
14
17
23^{2}
33
34
4:2^{2}
9
11^{2}
12
13
21
24
33
34
35
40
5:10
12
5:13
16
19^{2}
38
39
40^{2}
43
6:4
5
7^{2}
8
10
11
13
22
31
33^{2}
34^{2}
36
37^{3}
38
39
41^{3}
46
48^{4}
50^{2}
51
7:6
9
14
18
36^{2}
8:1
3^{2}
5
6^{2}
7^{2}
9
13
14
15
17
21
27
29
30
31
34
9:1^{2}
2^{2}
3
4
7
9
12
14^{2}
16
29
31
33
35
36^{2}
10:1
3
5
6
11
13^{2}
14^{2}
16^{3}
24^{2}
27
32^{2}
36
38
39
40
42^{4}
11:2
5^{2}
6^{2}
8
16^{2}
17
22
24^{2}
29
33
12:1
4
6
12
15
16
17
23
24
28^{2}
38
12:43
13:5
9
12
14
17^{2}
14:10
13
16
20
22
23
24
27
34
37
40
41
44
47
48
52
69^{2}
70
15:6
7
8
9
11
12
14
15
24
35
16:6
10
12
13
14^{2}
15
17
18
19
20

LUKE
1:2
22^{2}
50
52
65
66^{2}
79
2:7
9^{2}
10
15
17
18
19
20
34
38
46^{2}
49
50
51^{2}
3:11
13
14
16
4:6
18
20
21
22
23
26
27
30
31
39
40^{3}
41^{2}
42
43
5:2
7
14
17
22
25
29
31
34^{2}
35
36
6:1
2
6:3
4
5
9
10
13
17
19
27
28^{2}
30
31
32^{2}
33
34
39
47
7:6
19
22
38^{2}
42^{2}
44
8:21
22
31
32^{3}
34
36
37
54
56
9:1
2
3
5
10
11^{3}
13^{2}
14
15
16
17
18
20
21^{2}
23
34
45
46^{2}
48
54
55
56
61
10:1
2
9
18
21
24^{2}
35
11:2
5
13
15
17
19
31
44^{2}
47
48
49^{2}
52
53
12:4
6
15
16
24
37^{2}
38
42
13:2
4
14
23
32
34
14:5
7
10
15
17
19
23
25
15:1
3
15:4
6
12^{2}
16:15
28
29^{2}
30
17:14^{2}
15
20
23^{2}
27
29
37
18:1
7
8
15^{2}
16^{2}
29
31
34
19:13^{2}
24
27^{2}
32
33
40
45^{2}
46
20:3
8
15
17
19
23
25
33
34
41
21:8
10
21^{3}
23^{2}
26
29
35
22:4
6
10
13
15
19
23
24^{2}
25^{3}
35
36
38
40
41
45
46
47
50
52^{3}
55
58
67
70
23:1
14
17
20
22
23
25
28
34
35
51
24:1
4
5
10
11^{2}
13
15
17
18
19
24
25
27
29
30^{2}
33^{2}
34
35
24:36^{2}
38
40
41
43
44
46
50^{2}
51^{2}

JOHN
1:12^{2}
22
26
38^{2}
39
2:7^{2}
8
15
16
19
20
24
3:22
4:32
34
40
52
5:11
17
19
21
39
6:2
7^{2}
11
13^{2}
17
20
26
29
31
32
35
43
53
61
70
7:6
9
16
21
25
33
44
45
47
50^{2}
8:2
6
7
12
14
21
23
25
27
28
34
39
42
47
58
59
9:15
16
19
20
27
30
41
10:1
4
6^{2}
7
8
12
16
20
25
27
28^{2}
29^{2}
32
34
35
11:11
14
19
11:37
44
46^{2}
49^{2}
12:2
20
23
35
36
37
40
13:1
5
12
17
29
14:21
15:6^{2}
22
24
16:4
12
19
31
17:6
8^{2}
9^{2}
10
12^{3}
14^{2}
15^{2}
17
18
20
22
23^{2}
26^{3}
18:4
5^{2}
6
7
9
18
21^{2}
29
31
38
19:4
5
6
15
16
24
20:2
13
17
19
20
21
22^{2}
23
24
25
26
21:3
5
6
10
12
13

ACTS
1:3
4^{2}
7
10
16
2:3^{2}
4
6
11
14
38
41
45
3:2
5^{2}
8
11
4:1
3^{2}
4
7
8
13
14
15
16^{2}
17
4:18^{2}
19
21^{3}
23
24
32^{2}
33
34^{2}
35
5:5
9
13^{2}
15^{2}
16
18
19
21
22
24
25
26
27^{3}
32
33
35
38
40^{2}
6:2
6
9
7:6^{2}
24
25
26^{2}
34
36
39
42
43
52
8:3
5
7
11
14
15
16
17
18
25^{2}
9:2
21^{2}
27
28
38
39^{2}
40
10:7
8^{2}
20^{2}
23^{3}
24
28
44
46
48
11:3
4
12
15
17
20
21
23
28
12:10
17^{2}
20
21
25
13:2
3^{2}
8
13
15
17
19
20
21
22
27
31
42
43^{2}
50
51
14:5^{2}
18
22
14:23^{2}
27
15:2^{2}
4
5^{2}
7
8^{2}
9
12
14
19
20
21
23
32
37
38^{3}
39
16:4
7
10
19
20
22^{2}
23^{3}
24
25
30
33
34^{2}
37^{2}
39^{3}
40
17:2^{2}
4
5^{2}
6
9
12
16
17
18
33
34
18:2
3
6
11
16
19
20
21
26
27
19:2
3
6^{2}
9
12^{2}
13^{2}
16^{3}
17
19^{3}
22
38
20:1
2
6
7
18
30
32
34
36
21:1
7
16
19
23
24^{3}
26^{2}
32
40
22:2
5
11
19
20
30
23:2
10^{2}
21^{2}
24
27
31
24:21
22
25:5
6
25:11
26:10
11^{4}
13
18^{2}
20
30
27:9
10
21
24
33
35
42
43
28:3
14
17
23
27

ROMANS
1:19^{2}
24
26
28
32^{2}
2:2
3
7
8
19
3:2
19
22
4:11^{2}
12
5:14
7:1
8:1
28^{2}
30^{3}
9:25
26
10:2
5
15
19
20^{2}
11:8
9
11
12^{2}
14^{2}
15^{2}
17^{2}
22
23
27
32
12:14
15^{2}
15:3
26
27^{2}
28
31
16:10
11
14
15
17^{2}

1 COR.
1:2
11
18
21
24
2:6
9
10
14
4:19
5:12^{2}
13
6:4
13
15
7:8
9
36
8:9
9:3
20^{2}
21^{2}
10:4
5
7
8
10:9
10
11
27
11:2
22
12:18
14:10
22^{4}
34
35
15:20
16:3
18

2 COR.
1:4
2:3
13
15^{2}
4:3
4^{2}
5:12
15
19
6:16^{2}
17
8:22
24
9:2
13
11:8
12
12:17
13:2

GAL.
1:17
2:2^{2}
12
14
3:10
12^{2}
22
4:5
8
15
17
6:10
16

EPHES.
2:10
17
4:18
5:7
11
12
6:4
5
9
24

PHIL.
1:28
2:1
3:8
17

COLOS.
2:15
3:7
19
4:5
13^{2}

1 THESS.
2:16
4:12
13
14
15
17
5:3
12
13
14

2 THESS.
1:6
8
10
2:10
11
3:12

1 TIM.
1:10
16
18
3:7
10
4:3
15
16^{2}
5:4
16^{3}
20
6:2^{3}
17

2 TIM.
2:14^{2}
19
22
25
3:11
14
4:8

TITUS
1:13
15
2:9
3:1
13
15

HEB.
1:12
14
2:1
3
4
11
15
18
3:17
18
4:2^{3}
8
5:2
9
14
6:6
7
12
16
7:6
8
25^{2}
8:8
9^{3}
10^{2}
9:10
28
10:14
16^{2}
33
39^{2}
11:6
13^{3}
16
28
31
12:9
11
19
13:3^{3}
7
9
17
24

JAMES
1:12
2:5
16^{2}
25
3:18
5:3
4
11
14

1 PETER
1:11
12
2:7
8
14^{2}
3:7
12
4:4
6
17
19

2 PETER
1:1
12
2:1
4^{2}
6^{2}
8

1 PETER
2:10
11
18
19
20
21^{2}
22
3:16

1 JOHN
2:26
4:4
5
5:16

3 JOHN
9
10^{2}

JUDE
1
5
7
11
15
23

REV.
2:2^{3}
9
14
15
16
22
27
3:9^{2}
10
4:8
5:8
11
13
6:8
9
10
11^{2}
7:4
14
15
16
17^{2}
8:2
12
9:3
4
5^{2}
6
11
16
17^{2}
19
10:4
11:1
5^{2}
6
7^{3}
10^{2}
11^{3}
12^{2}
18^{2}
12:4
10
12
13:6
7
12
14^{2}
14:6
9
13
15:1
2
16:2
6
14
16
17:14
18:14
19:15
18^{2}
20^{2}
20:4^{3}
8
9
10
11
13
21:3^{2}
14
24
22:5
8
9

they

1992, *846*

GEN.
2:4
24
25
3:7
8
4:8
5:2
6:2^{2}
4
19
7:14
15
16
7:23^{2}
8:17
9:2
23
11:2^{2}
3^{2}
4
6^{2}
7
8
31^{2}
12:5^{3}
12^{2}
12:20
13:6^{2}
11
14:4
7
8
10
11
12
15:13
14^{2}
16
18:5
18:8
9
19
21
19:2
3^{2}
4
5
8
9^{2}
11^{2}
16
17
19:33
35
20:11
17
21:30
31
32^{2}
22:6
8
9
19
24:19
41
24:54^{2}
57
58
59
60
61
25:18
25
26:18
20
21
22
28
26:30
31^{2}
32
29:2
3
4
5
6
8^{2}
20
30:38
41
31:23
31:37
43
46^{2}
54
32:18
33:4
6^{2}
7
34:5
7^{2}
8
14
22
34:23
25
26
27
28
29
30
31
35:4
5^{2}
16
36:7^{2}
37:4
37:5
8
16
17
18^{2}
19
23
24
25^{2}
28^{2}
31
32^{2}
38:21
39:22
40:4
5
6
8
15
41:2
14
18
21^{3}
43
42:7
8
42:10
13
20
21
23
26
28
29
35^{3}
43:2^{2}
7
15
18^{2}
43:19^{2}
24
25^{3}
26
28^{2}
32
33
34
44:1
4
7
13
14
45:3
4
24
25
27
46:6^{2}
28
32^{2}
47:1^{2}
2
4
14
17
47:18
22
25
27
48:5
9
49:6^{2}
26
31^{2}
50:8
10^{2}
11
15
50:16
17^{2}
18
26

EXOD.
1:10^{2}
11^{2}
12^{3}
14^{2}
19
2:16
18
2:19
23
3:13
18
4:1^{2}
5
8^{2}
9
18
31^{2}
5:1
3
8^{3}
5:9
10
16
19
20^{2}
21
6:4
9
27
7:6
7
10
11

EXOD.
7:12[2], 16, 17, 19, 24, 8:1, 8, 9, 11, 14, 17, 18, 20, 21, 9:1, 10, 13, 19, 32, 10:3, 5[2], 6[2], 7, 8, 11, 12, 14[2], 15[2], 23, 12:3, 7[2], 8[2], 28, 33[2], 35, 36[3], 39[4], 50, 13:17, 20, 14:2, 3, 4, 5, 10, 11, 15, 17, 25, 15:5, 10, 16, 22[2], 23[3], 27[2], 16:1, 4, 5[3], 10, 15, 18[2], 20, 21, 22, 24, 27, 32, 35[3], 17:4, 7, 12, 18:7[2], 11, 16[2], 20[2], 22[3], 26[3], 19:1, 2, 13, 14, 17, 21, 20:18, 19, 21:28, 35, 23:11, 33[2], 24:2, 7, 10, 11, 25:2, 10, 15, 37[2], 26:24[3], 25, 27:8, 20, 28:3, 4[2], 5, 6, 20, 21, 28, 30, 38, 41, 42, 43[4], 29:33[2], 46, 30:4, 12

EXOD.
30:13, 15, 20[4], 21[2], 29, 30, 31:6, 11, 32:4, 6, 8[2], 13, 15, 17, 20, 22, 23, 24, 35, 33:4, 34:15, 30, 35:21[2], 22, 25, 36:3[2], 4, 5, 6, 7, 29, 39:1, 3, 4, 6, 7, 9, 10, 13, 15, 16, 17, 18, 19, 20, 21, 24, 25, 27, 30, 31, 32, 33, 43[2], 40:15, 32[3], 37

LEVIT.
2:12, 4:13, 14, 24, 33, 6:16, 20, 7:2[2], 8:28, 9:5, 13, 20, 24, 10:2, 5, 7, 14, 15, 19, 11:8, 10, 11, 13[3], 28, 31, 32, 35, 42, 13:54, 14:36, 40[2], 41[2], 42, 15:18, 31[2], 16:1, 27, 17:5[2], 7[2], 18:17, 19:20, 20:12, 13, 14[2], 16, 17, 19, 20[2], 21, 23, 27, 21:5[2], 6[3], 7[2], 22:2[3], 9[3], 11, 15[2]

LEVIT.
22:16, 18, 25, 23:17[3], 18, 20, 24:2, 9, 11, 12, 23, 31[2], 25:42[2], 45[2], 46, 55, 26:7, 17, 26, 36, 37[2], 39[2], 40[3], 41, 43[2], 44, 27:11

NUM.
1:1, 18[2], 46, 50[2], 54, 2:2, 3, 16, 17[2], 24, 31[2], 34[2], 3:4[2], 6, 7, 8, 9, 10, 13, 31, 4:5, 7, 8, 9[2], 10, 11, 12[2], 13, 14[3], 15[2], 19[2], 20[2], 25, 26, 37, 41, 49[2], 5:2, 3, 7, 9, 6:7, 27, 7:3[2], 5, 9, 11, 8:11, 16, 21, 22, 24, 25, 9:1, 4, 5, 6[2], 11, 12[2], 18[2], 20[2], 21[2], 22, 23[3], 10:3, 4, 6, 8, 10, 13, 21, 28, 33, 34, 11:13, 16, 17, 21, 25, 26[2], 32[2], 34, 12:2, 4, 5, 13:2, 18, 19[3]

NUM.
13:21, 22, 23[3], 25, 26, 27, 31, 32[2], 14:4, 7, 9, 11, 12, 14[2], 23, 27, 31, 32, 35[2], 40, 44, 15:25, 32, 33, 34, 38[2], 16:2, 3, 16, 18, 22, 27, 29, 30, 33[2], 34, 37, 38[3], 39[2], 42, 45, 49, 17:5, 9, 10, 18:2, 3[3], 4, 6, 9, 12, 13, 15, 17, 21, 22, 23[2], 24[2], 19:2, 17, 20:2, 6, 27, 29, 21:3, 4, 6, 11, 12, 13, 16, 18, 27, 32, 33, 35[2], 22:3, 5[2], 6, 7, 12, 14, 15, 16, 39, 24:6, 25:2, 18[2], 26:9, 10, 41, 50, 55, 57, 61, 62, 63, 64, 65, 27:2, 21[2], 28:19, 31, 29:8, 13, 30:9, 31:7[2], 8[2], 10[2], 11, 12, 49, 52, 32:1, 5, 9[3], 11

NUM.
32:12, 16, 30[2], 38, 33:3, 6, 7[2], 8, 9[2], 10, 11, 12, 13, 14, 15, 16, 17, 18, 19, 20, 21, 22, 23, 24, 25, 26, 27, 28, 29, 30, 31, 32, 33, 34, 35, 36, 37, 41, 42, 43, 44, 45, 46, 47, 48, 49, 34:29, 35:2, 3, 12, 36:2, 3[2], 4, 6[2], 12

DEU.
1:22, 24, 25, 39[2], 2:4, 12, 15, 21, 22, 3:20, 4:9, 10[3], 45, 46, 47, 5:28[3], 29, 31, 6:8, 7:4[2], 20, 23, 9:12[2], 14, 29, 10:5, 7, 11, 11:4, 18, 30, 12:30, 31[2], 14:7[2], 12, 19, 15:6, 16:16, 18, 17:5, 9, 10[2], 11[3], 18:1, 2, 3, 8, 17[2], 19:14, 20:8, 9, 11, 18[2], 20, 21:2, 6, 7, 15, 18, 20

DEU.
22:17, 19, 21, 22, 24, 28, 23:3, 4[2], 25:1[2], 12, 28:7, 10, 22, 41, 46, 60, 29:22, 25, 26[2], 31:12[2], 16, 17[2], 18[2], 20[2], 21, 24, 30, 32:5[2], 7, 16[2], 17[2], 20, 21[2], 24, 27, 28, 29[3], 37, 33:3, 9, 10[2], 11, 17[2], 19[3]

JOSH.
1:15, 16, 2:1, 3, 4, 7[2], 8, 13, 21, 22, 24, 3:1[2], 3, 6, 7, 13, 15, 4:8, 9, 14[2], 16, 18, 20, 5:4, 5, 6, 7[2], 8[3], 11, 12[2], 6:5, 11, 14[2], 15[2], 19, 20, 21, 23, 24[2], 7:3[2], 4, 5, 11[3], 12, 21, 22, 23, 24, 25, 26, 8:5, 6[3], 9, 13, 14, 15, 16, 17, 19[2], 20[2], 21, 22[3], 23, 24[3], 29, 31, 33, 9:2, 4[2], 6, 8

JOSH.
9:9, 13, 16[4], 24, 26, 10:2, 5, 11[4], 20, 23, 24[2], 26, 27[2], 34, 35, 36, 37, 39, 11:4, 5, 7, 8[2], 11, 14[3], 19, 20[2], 14:4, 5, 16:10, 17:4, 10, 13, 16[2], 18[2], 18:4[2], 5, 19:2, 49, 50, 51, 20:2, 4, 5, 7, 8, 21:2, 9, 11, 12, 13, 20, 21, 27, 43, 22:6, 9, 10, 15[2], 28, 23:12, 13, 24:1, 2, 7, 8, 22, 30, 32, 33

JUD.
1:4, 5[3], 6, 7, 10, 16, 17, 19, 20, 22, 24, 25[2], 28, 32, 34, 35, 2:3, 5[2], 9, 12, 13, 14, 15[2], 17[4], 19[2], 22, 3:4, 6, 12, 24[2], 25[3], 26, 28, 29, 4:12, 24, 5:7, 8, 11[2], 14, 19, 20, 23, 30[2], 6:3, 4

JUD.
6:5[4], 29[3], 35, 7:11, 19[2], 20, 21, 25[3], 8:1, 5, 18[3], 19, 24[2], 25[2], 28, 35, 9:3, 4, 7, 8, 9, 25, 27, 31, 34, 36, 41, 42, 46, 51, 55, 10:4, 8, 16, 11:2, 6, 13, 17, 18, 21, 22, 12:4, 6[2], 14:9, 11[2], 13, 14, 15, 15:6, 10, 11, 12, 13[2], 16:2, 7, 11, 23, 24[2], 25[3], 30, 17:4, 18:2[3], 3[3], 5, 7[2], 8, 9, 12[2], 13, 15, 19, 21, 22, 23[2], 26, 27[2], 28[2], 29, 31, 19:4, 5, 8[2], 11, 14[2], 15, 21, 22, 25[2], 20:5, 6, 10[3], 22, 31, 32, 34, 36[3], 38, 39[2], 41, 42[2], 43, 45[2], 48[2], 21:5, 8, 12[2], 14[3], 17, 19, 20, 23[2], 24

RUTH
1:2, 4[2], 7

RUTH
1:9, 10, 11, 13, 14, 19[4], 22, 2:4, 9[2], 21, 22, 4:2, 17

1 SAM.
1:9[2], 19, 25, 2:4, 5[2], 12, 14, 15, 20, 22, 26, 27, 30, 34, 4:2[2], 4, 6[2], 7[2], 9, 10, 5:2, 3[2], 4, 7, 8[3], 9[2], 10[2], 11, 6:4[2], 6[2], 11, 12, 13[2], 14, 16, 18, 19, 21, 7:6, 7, 10, 11, 13, 8:2, 6, 7[3], 8[3], 19, 9:4[4], 5, 10, 11[2], 12, 13, 14[2], 20, 25, 26[2], 27, 10:2, 4, 5, 10, 14, 21, 22, 23, 27, 11:5[2], 7, 9[2], 11[2], 15[2], 12:4, 5, 9[2], 10, 21, 13:5, 6, 21, 14:9, 10, 11, 13, 15, 16, 17, 20, 21, 22[2], 25, 30, 31, 33[2], 35, 36, 15:3, 6, 9, 15, 18

1 SAM.
16:6, 17:11, 19, 31, 51, 53, 18:6, 7, 8[2], 20, 27, 30, 19:1, 8, 20[2], 21[2], 22, 24, 20:11, 41, 21:11, 22:1, 4, 11, 17, 23:1[2], 12, 13, 18, 24, 25, 28, 25:7, 8, 9, 11, 13, 16, 26, 29, 41, 43, 26:12[2], 19[3], 27:10, 28:4, 8, 25[2], 29:5, 30:2, 4, 10, 11[2], 12, 16[2], 19, 20, 21[3], 22[2], 24, 31:7[2], 8, 9, 10[2], 13

2 SAM.
1:12[2], 23[3], 2:3, 4[3], 13, 16[2], 24, 28, 29, 32[2], 3:11, 21, 23, 32, 4:6[3], 7[2], 8, 12[2], 5:3, 8, 17, 21, 6:3, 4, 6, 13, 17, 7:10, 8:14, 9:2, 10:5, 6, 13, 14, 15, 16, 19[2], 11:10, 20, 12:18, 19, 20, 13:9, 30, 32, 14:6, 7[2], 11[2], 15:24

2 SAM.
15:29, 30, 36, 16:22, 17:8[2], 10, 17[2], 18[2], 20[4], 21[2], 22, 29, 18:3[2], 17, 19:3, 8, 14, 17, 20:3, 7, 8, 14, 15[2], 18[3], 22[2], 21:5, 9[2], 13, 14[2], 18, 19, 22:39[2], 42, 45, 46, 23:6, 7, 9, 24:3, 5, 6[2], 7, 8[2], 13, 17

1 KINGS
1:1, 3, 7, 23, 25, 32, 39, 41, 44, 45, 53, 2:7, 39, 3:22, 24, 28[2], 4:21, 27, 28, 5:1, 6, 12, 14, 17, 18, 6:8, 10, 27, 7:28, 47, 8:1, 4, 8[3], 9, 25, 26, 30, 33, 35[2], 36, 40[2], 42, 43, 46[2], 47[2], 50[2], 51, 52, 66, 9:8, 9[2], 12, 22, 28, 10:25, 29, 11:2[2], 18[3], 24, 29, 33, 41, 12:3, 7[2], 8, 13, 20, 24, 27, 13:11

1 KINGS
13:13, 20, 25, 27, 30, 14:15, 18, 19, 22[2], 23, 24, 29, 15:7, 8, 22, 23, 31, 16:5, 13[2], 14, 17, 20, 27, 18:6, 10[2], 26[3], 28, 29, 34[2], 39[2], 40, 19:10, 14, 21, 20:6[2], 12, 15, 16, 17, 18[2], 20, 23[2], 25, 29, 32, 33, 21:12, 13, 14, 22:1, 6, 32[2], 33, 37, 38, 39, 45, 48

2 KINGS
1:6, 8, 18, 2:2, 4, 6, 7, 8[2], 9, 11, 14, 15[2], 16, 17[3], 18, 20, 3:9, 21, 22, 23[2], 24[3], 25[3], 26, 27, 4:39, 40[4], 42, 43[2], 44, 5:23, 24, 6:4[2], 14, 16[2], 18, 20[4], 22, 23[2], 25, 7:3, 4[2], 5[2], 6, 7, 8, 9, 10[3], 11, 12[3], 13[2], 14, 15, 8:23, 9:12, 13, 21, 27

2 KINGS
9:33, 35[2], 36, 37, 10:4, 7, 8, 13, 14, 16, 20, 21, 24, 25, 26, 27, 34, 35, 11:2, 7, 9, 12[2], 16, 17, 18, 19, 20, 12:10[2], 11[2], 14, 15[3], 19, 21, 13:5, 6, 8, 9, 12, 20, 21[3], 14:12, 15, 18, 19[2], 20, 28, 15:6, 7, 11, 15, 16, 21, 26, 31, 36, 16:5, 18, 19, 17:8, 9, 10, 11, 12, 14, 15[3], 16, 17, 19, 21, 22, 24, 25, 26[3], 28[2], 29, 32, 33[2], 34[3], 40[2], 41, 18:10, 12, 17[3], 18, 20, 27, 34, 35, 19:3, 18[2], 26[2], 31, 35[2], 37, 20:7, 14[2], 15[2], 18[2], 20, 21:8, 9, 14, 15, 17, 25, 22:7, 14, 17[2], 19, 20, 23:1, 8, 9, 28, 24:5, 25:1, 6[2]

2 KINGS
25:7, 14[2], 23[2], 26

1 CHRON.
4:14, 23, 28, 39, 40[2], 43, 5:10[2], 16, 19, 20[3], 21, 22, 23, 25, 6:31, 32[2], 33, 55, 56, 57, 65, 67[2], 7:2, 4, 21, 8:6, 9:1, 18, 23, 27, 28, 33, 38, 10:7[2], 8, 9[2], 10, 12, 11:3, 7, 14, 19, 12:1[2], 2, 15[2], 19, 21[2], 33, 39, 40, 13:2, 4, 7, 9, 14:11[2], 12[2], 16, 15:26, 16:1[2], 20, 17:9, 19:6, 7, 11, 14, 15, 16[2], 17, 19[2], 20:4, 8, 21:3[2], 5, 17[2], 23:11, 24, 25, 26, 32, 24:4, 5, 25:8, 26:6, 8, 13, 14, 27, 31, 28:21, 29:8, 9[2], 21, 22, 29

2 CHRON.
1:17[2], 2:17, 3:13, 4:6[2], 20, 5:5, 9[2], 10, 13, 6:21, 24, 26[2], 27, 31[2], 32

2 CHRON.
6:34, 36[2], 37[2], 38[2], 7:3, 9[2], 22, 8:9, 15, 18, 9:24, 28, 29, 10:3, 7[2], 11:4, 17[2], 12:2, 6, 7[2], 8[2], 15, 13:11[2], 13, 14, 18, 14:1, 7, 10, 13[3], 14[2], 15, 15:4, 9[2], 10, 11[2], 12, 14, 15, 16:4, 6, 11, 14[2], 17:9, 10, 18:5, 9, 10, 14, 29, 31[2], 32, 19:8, 10, 20:2, 4, 8, 10[2], 11, 16, 20[2], 21, 22[2], 23, 24[2], 25[4], 26[2], 27, 28, 29, 34, 36, 37, 21:17, 20, 22:4, 9[4], 23:2[2], 6[3], 11, 15[2], 16, 20, 21, 24:7, 8, 9, 10, 11[2], 13, 14[3], 16, 18, 19[2], 21, 23, 24[2], 25[4], 26, 27, 25:10, 12, 13, 20, 21, 22, 26, 27[2], 28, 26:18, 20, 23[2], 27:7, 9, 28:5, 6, 15

2 CHRON.
28:18, 23[2], 26, 27[2], 29:7, 15, 16, 17[4], 18, 19, 21, 22[5], 23[2], 24, 29, 30[2], 34, 30:1, 3, 5[3], 9, 10, 14[2], 15, 16[2], 18, 22, 23, 31:1, 4, 5, 6, 7, 8, 11, 18, 32:3, 18[2], 19, 21, 32, 33, 33:8, 10, 18, 19, 20, 34:4, 9[3], 10[2], 11, 13, 14, 16, 17, 22[2], 24, 25[2], 28, 33, 35:1, 6, 11, 12[3], 13[2], 14, 15, 24, 25, 27, 36:8, 16, 19, 20

EZRA
1:6, 2:59[3], 62[2], 63, 68, 69, 3:3[2], 4, 6, 7[2], 8, 10, 11[2], 4:2, 6, 11, 13, 15, 23, 5:5[2], 7, 11, 14, 6:3, 8, 9, 10, 13, 14[2], 18, 7:13, 8:17[2], 18, 36[2], 9:2, 10:5[2], 7[2], 17, 19[3], 44

NEH.
1:3, 2:7, 18[2], 19, 3:1[3], 6, 8, 13, 4:2[4], 3, 5, 7, 11, 12[2], 17[2], 22, 5:8[2], 12[2], 6:2, 4, 9, 10[2], 13[2], 16[2], 19, 7:3, 5, 61[3], 64, 65, 67, 8:1, 4, 6, 8, 9, 12, 14, 15, 18, 9:3[2], 10, 11, 12, 15, 16, 18, 19, 21, 22, 23, 24[2], 25[2], 26[2], 27, 28[4], 29, 30, 35[2], 37, 10:28, 29, 11:30, 12:27, 37, 39, 43, 44, 13:1, 2, 3[2], 5, 9, 13, 15[2], 19, 21, 29

ESTHER
1:7, 8, 17, 2:3, 23, 3:4[2], 6, 8, 9, 14, 4:12, 6:1, 9, 14, 7:8, 10, 8:7, 9:5, 10[2], 12, 14, 15, 16, 17, 18, 21, 22, 23, 26[2], 27, 31, 10:2

JOB
1:15, 19, 2:11[2]

JOB
2:12[3], 13[2], 3:18, 22, 4:8, 9[2], 20[2], 21, 5:4, 14, 6:15, 17[3], 18, 20[3], 8:10, 22, 9:5, 25[2], 26, 11:6, 20, 12:6, 7[2], 15[2], 25, 14:12, 21, 15:24, 35, 16:10[3], 17:12, 16, 18:20[2], 19:15, 18, 19, 23, 24, 20:7, 21:11, 12, 13, 14, 18, 26, 30, 22:12, 26[2], 24:1, 2, 3[2], 4, 5, 6[2], 7[2], 8, 9, 10[2], 13[2], 16[3], 17, 24[2], 27:13, 28:1, 4[2], 29:22, 23[2], 24[2], 30:1, 3, 5[2], 7[2], 8[2], 10[2], 11, 12[2], 13[3], 14[2], 15, 24, 31:13, 32:3, 4, 15[3], 16, 34:19, 20, 25, 27, 28, 35:9[2], 12, 36:7[2], 8, 9, 10, 11[2], 12[3], 13, 14, 27, 37:12, 38:14, 35, 40, 41, 39:22, 3[3], 4[2], 16, 41:6, 17[3], 23[2], 25, 42:11[2]

PSALMS
2:12, 3:1^{2}, 5:9, 10, 9:3, 10, 15^{2}, 10:2, 11:2^{2}, 12:2^{2}, 14:1^{2}, 3^{2}, 4, 5, 17:10^{2}, 11^{2}, 14, 18:17, 18, 37, 38^{2}, 41, 44^{2}, 19:10, 20:8, 21:11^{3}, 22:4, 5^{2}, 7^{3}, 13, 16, 17, 18, 26, 29^{2}, 31, 23:4, 24:1, 25:6, 19^{2}, 27:2, 28:5, 31:4, 11, 13^{2}, 32:6, 9, 34:5, 10, 21, 35:7^{2}, 11, 12, 13, 15^{2}, 16, 20^{2}, 21, 36:8, 12, 37:2, 3^{2}, 9, 19^{2}, 20^{2}, 22, 28, 40, 38:4, 12^{2}, 16^{2}, 19^{2}, 20, 39:6, 40:5^{2}, 12, 41:7, 8, 42:3, 10, 44:3, 10, 45:8, 15^{2}, 48:4, 5^{3}, 49:6, 11, 14, 19, 51:19, 53:1, 3, 4^{2}, 5, 54:3, 55:3^{2}, 10, 19^{2}, 21, 56:2, 5, 6^{4}, 7, 8, 57:6^{3}, 58:3^{2}, 4, 8, 59 *title*, 3, 4, 6^{2}, 7^{2}, 12, 13, 15

PSALMS
62:4^{4}, 9, 63:10^{2}, 64:4^{2}, 5^{3}, 6^{2}, 7, 8, 9, 65:8, 12, 13^{2}, 66:4, 6, 68:24, 69:4^{2}, 12, 21^{2}, 23, 26^{2}, 35, 36, 71:10, 24^{2}, 72:5, 9, 16, 73:5^{2}, 8^{2}, 9, 11, 12, 19^{2}, 27, 74:4, 6, 7^{2}, 8^{2}, 76:5, 77:16, 78:5, 7, 10, 17, 18, 19^{2}, 22, 29, 30, 32, 34^{2}, 35, 36^{2}, 37, 39, 40, 41, 42, 44, 53, 56, 57, 58, 79:1^{2}, 2, 3, 7, 12, 80:12, 16, 81:12, 82:5^{3}, 83:2, 3, 4, 5^{2}, 8, 10, 16, 84:4^{2}, 7, 86:17, 88:5, 17^{2}, 89:15, 16^{2}, 31, 51, 90:5^{2}, 10, 91:12, 92:7, 14^{2}, 94:4, 5, 6, 7, 11, 21, 95:10, 11, 97:7, 98:8, 99:6, 7, 101:6, 102:8, 26^{2}, 104:7^{2}, 8^{2}, 9^{2}, 11, 22, 28^{2}, 29^{2}, 30, 32

PSALMS
105:12, 13, 18, 27, 28, 38, 41, 44, 45, 106:3, 7, 12^{2}, 13^{2}, 16, 19, 20, 21, 24^{2}, 28, 29, 32, 33, 34, 36, 37, 38, 39, 41, 42, 43, 107:4^{2}, 6, 7, 11, 12, 13, 18, 19, 23, 26^{2}, 27, 28, 30^{2}, 36, 38, 39, 43, 109:2, 3, 4, 5, 25^{2}, 27, 28, 111:8, 10, 115:5^{4}, 6^{4}, 7^{5}, 8, 118:11^{2}, 12^{2}, 119:2, 3^{2}, 74^{2}, 78, 86, 87, 91, 98, 111, 126, 136, 150^{2}, 155, 158, 165, 120:7, 122:1, 6, 124:3, 125:1, 126:2, 5, 127:1, 5^{2}, 129:1, 2^{2}, 3, 8, 130:6^{2}, 135:16^{4}, 17^{2}, 18, 137:3^{2}, 138:4, 5, 139:18, 20, 140:2, 3, 5^{2}, 8, 10, 141:6^{2}, 9, 142:3, 6, 144:5, 145:7, 11, 147:20, 148:5

PROV.
1:9, 11

PROV.
1:18^{2}, 28^{3}, 29, 30^{2}, 31, 2:15, 19, 3:2, 22, 4:16^{3}, 17, 19^{2}, 22, 7:5, 8:9, 32, 36, 11:20, 12:22, 14:22, 15:22, 16:13, 17:15, 18:8, 21, 19:7, 21:7, 22:18, 23:3, 5, 30^{2}, 35^{2}, 26:22, 28:4, 5, 28, 30:24, 25, 26, 27, 31:5

ECCL.
1:7, 16, 2:3, 3:18^{2}, 19, 4:1^{2}, 3, 9, 10, 11, 16, 5:1^{2}, 8, 11, 7:29, 8:10^{2}, 9:3^{2}, 5^{2}, 6, 11:3, 6, 8, 12:3, 5

CANT.
1:6, 3:8, 5:7^{2}, 6:5, 9

ISAIAH
1:2, 4^{3}, 6, 14, 18^{3}, 23, 28, 29, 31, 2:4^{2}, 6^{2}, 8, 19, 20, 3:9^{3}, 10, 12, 16, 5:6, 8, 12, 13, 24, 26, 29^{2}, 30, 6:10, 13, 7:19, 22, 8:19, 20, 21^{3}, 22^{2}, 9:2, 3^{2}, 12, 13, 16, 18, 20^{2}

ISAIAH
9:21, 10:1, 2, 4^{2}, 18, 29^{2}, 11:9, 14^{3}, 13:2, 5, 8^{3}, 14, 17, 18, 14:1, 2^{3}, 7, 10, 16, 21, 15:3, 5^{2}, 7^{3}, 16:7, 8^{3}, 17:2, 3, 9, 13, 18:6, 19:3, 6, 8^{2}, 9^{2}, 10, 12, 13^{2}, 14, 20, 21, 22, 20:5, 21:14, 15, 22:3, 9, 24, 23:5, 13^{2}, 24:5, 6, 9, 14^{3}, 22^{2}, 26:11^{2}, 14^{4}, 16^{2}, 19, 27:11, 13, 28:7^{5}, 12, 13, 29:9^{2}, 15, 23, 24^{2}, 30:1, 5, 6, 16, 18, 31:1^{3}, 3, 32:12, 33:1^{2}, 12, 17, 23^{2}, 34:12, 17^{2}, 35:2, 10, 36:5, 12, 19, 20, 21, 37:3, 19^{2}, 27^{2}, 32, 36^{2}, 38, 38:18, 39:3^{2}, 4^{2}, 7^{2}, 40:17, 24^{3}, 31^{4}, 41:6, 11^{3}, 12, 22, 29, 42:9, 16^{2}, 17^{2}, 22^{3}, 24^{2}, 43:2, 9, 17^{4}, 21, 44:4, 9^{4}

ISAIAH
44:11^{3}, 18^{3}, 45:6, 14^{5}, 16^{2}, 20, 46:1, 2^{3}, 6^{3}, 7^{2}, 47:9, 14^{2}, 15^{2}, 48:2, 3^{2}, 7, 13, 21, 49:9, 10, 15, 17, 19, 21, 22, 23^{2}, 26, 50:9, 51:5, 6, 11, 20^{2}, 52:5, 6, 8^{2}, 15^{3}, 54:15, 56:10^{3}, 11^{3}, 12, 57:2, 6^{2}, 12, 58:2^{3}, 3, 12, 59:4^{2}, 5, 6, 7, 8^{2}, 19, 60:4^{2}, 6^{3}, 7, 11, 14^{2}, 21, 61:3, 4^{3}, 7^{2}, 9, 62:9^{2}, 12, 63:8, 10, 12, 15, 19, 65:11, 16, 21^{2}, 22^{2}, 23^{2}, 24^{2}, 25, 66:3, 4^{2}, 5, 17, 18, 19, 20, 24^{2}

JER.
1:15^{2}, 19^{2}, 2:5, 6, 8, 13, 15, 24^{2}, 26, 27^{2}, 28, 30, 3:1, 16^{3}, 17^{2}, 18, 21^{2}, 4:2, 17, 22^{5}, 23, 24, 29, 30, 5:2^{3}, 3^{4}, 4^{2}, 5, 7, 8, 10

JER.
5:12, 15, 16, 17^{4}, 22^{3}, 23, 24, 26^{3}, 27, 28^{6}, 6:3^{2}, 9, 10^{3}, 14, 15^{6}, 16, 17, 19, 23^{3}, 28^{3}, 7:17, 18, 19^{2}, 24, 26^{2}, 27^{2}, 30, 31, 32, 8:1, 2^{8}, 4, 5^{2}, 6, 9^{2}, 11, 12^{6}, 16, 17, 19, 9:2, 3^{4}, 5^{2}, 6, 10^{2}, 13, 16, 17^{2}, 10:4^{2}, 5^{4}, 8, 9, 11, 15^{2}, 18, 20, 21, 25, 11:8^{2}, 10^{2}, 11^{2}, 12^{2}, 14, 17, 19, 12:1, 2^{3}, 4, 5^{2}, 6^{3}, 10^{2}, 11, 13^{3}, 16^{3}, 17, 13:11^{2}, 12, 14:2, 3^{3}, 4, 6, 10^{2}, 12^{2}, 14, 15, 16^{2}, 18, 15:2, 7, 20, 16:4^{5}, 6, 10, 12, 16^{2}, 17, 18^{2}, 20, 21, 17:13^{2}, 15, 19, 23^{2}, 25, 26, 18:12, 15^{2}, 18, 20, 22, 19:4^{2}, 5, 9^{2}, 11, 13, 15^{2}, 20:4

JER.
20:10, 11^{3}, 21:6, 22:7, 8, 9^{2}, 12, 18^{2}, 27^{2}, 28^{2}, 23:3, 4^{2}, 7, 8, 12, 13, 14^{3}, 16^{2}, 17^{2}, 21^{2}, 22^{2}, 26, 27, 32, 24:2, 3, 7^{2}, 8, 10, 25:5, 16, 28, 30, 33^{2}, 26:3, 10, 23, 24, 27:10, 11, 14, 15, 16, 18, 22^{2}, 28:14^{2}, 29:6, 9, 17, 19, 23, 30:3, 9, 14, 16^{2}, 17, 19^{2}, 31:1, 9^{2}, 12^{2}, 15, 16, 23, 24, 29, 32, 33, 34^{2}, 37, 32:14, 22^{3}, 24, 29, 31, 32^{2}, 33^{2}, 34, 35^{2}, 38, 39, 40, 33:5, 8^{3}, 9, 24^{2}, 34:5^{2}, 10, 11^{2}, 18^{2}, 22, 35:6, 14, 17^{2}, 36:3, 7, 9, 15, 16^{2}, 17, 20^{2}, 24, 31, 37:4, 5, 9, 10, 15, 21^{2}, 38:6^{2}, 7, 9^{2}, 13, 18, 19, 20, 22, 23

JER.
38:25, 27, 39:1, 4, 5^{2}, 14, 16, 40:7, 8^{2}, 12, 41:1, 7, 12, 13, 17, 18, 42:5, 17, 43:3, 5, 7^{3}, 44:2, 3^{4}, 5, 6, 9, 10^{2}, 12^{4}, 14^{2}, 46:6, 12, 15, 16, 17, 21^{2}, 22, 23^{2}, 48:2, 32, 34, 39, 45, 49:9^{3}, 12, 23^{2}, 29^{3}, 50:3^{2}, 4^{2}, 5, 6^{3}, 7, 9, 16^{2}, 20, 33, 36^{2}, 37^{2}, 38^{2}, 42^{3}, 51:2, 4, 14, 18^{2}, 24, 26, 30^{3}, 32, 38^{2}, 39, 57, 58, 64, 52:7, 9, 18^{2}

LAM.
1:2, 6, 8, 10, 11^{2}, 14, 19^{2}, 21^{3}, 2:7, 8, 10^{2}, 12^{2}, 14, 15, 16^{2}, 19^{2}, 3:6, 23, 53, 4:2, 3, 5^{2}, 7^{2}, 8, 9^{2}, 10, 14^{2}, 15^{4}, 16^{2}, 18, 19^{2}, 5:11, 13

EZEKIEL
1:5, 7, 8^{2}, 9^{3}

EZEKIEL
1:10^{3}, 12^{4}, 16, 17^{4}, 18^{2}, 20, 24^{3}, 25, 2:3, 4, 5^{4}, 6, 7^{3}, 3:6, 7, 9, 11^{2}, 15, 25, 26, 27, 4:16, 17, 5:6^{2}, 12, 13, 17, 6:9^{4}, 10, 11, 13, 14, 7:13, 14, 16, 18, 19^{2}, 20, 21, 22, 24, 25, 26, 27, 8:6, 9, 12, 13, 16, 17^{4}, 18, 9:2, 6, 7, 8, 9, 10:10, 11^{7}, 12, 17^{2}, 19, 20, 22, 11:7, 15, 16, 18^{2}, 20^{2}, 12:2^{2}, 3^{2}, 4, 11, 12, 15, 16^{3}, 19, 23, 27, 13:6^{3}, 9^{3}, 10, 15, 21, 14:5, 10, 11, 14, 15, 16^{2}, 18^{2}, 20^{2}, 22, 23, 15:7, 8, 16:33^{2}, 37, 39^{2}, 40^{2}, 41, 47, 50, 51, 52^{2}, 17:15, 21, 23, 18:22, 19:4, 9^{2}, 20:8^{3}, 9, 12, 13^{3}, 16, 20, 21^{2}

EZEKIEL
20:24, 25, 26^{2}, 27, 28^{4}, 38^{2}, 49, 21:7, 23, 29^{2}, 22:7^{3}, 9^{2}, 10^{2}, 12, 18^{2}, 20, 25^{3}, 26^{2}, 29, 23:3^{3}, 4^{2}, 8^{2}, 10^{2}, 13, 17, 24^{2}, 25^{3}, 26, 29, 37^{3}, 38^{2}, 39^{3}, 40, 43, 44^{3}, 45^{2}, 47, 49, 24:14, 25, 27, 25:3, 4^{3}, 11, 13, 14^{2}, 17, 26:4, 6, 12^{3}, 16^{2}, 17, 27:5^{2}, 6, 10^{3}, 11^{2}, 12, 13^{2}, 14, 15, 16, 17^{2}, 21^{2}, 22^{2}, 29, 30, 31^{2}, 32, 35, 28:3, 7^{2}, 8, 16, 17, 19, 22, 23, 24, 25^{2}, 26^{3}, 29:6, 7^{2}, 9, 13, 14, 15, 16^{2}, 20, 21, 30:4, 6^{2}, 7, 8, 11, 19, 25, 26, 31:14, 17^{2}, 32:3, 10, 12, 15, 16^{2}, 20, 21^{2}, 24, 25^{2}, 26, 27^{3}, 29, 30^{2}, 33:24, 27^{2}, 29^{2}, 31^{5}, 32^{2}

EZEKIEL
33:33, 34:5^{3}, 10, 12, 14^{2}, 19^{2}, 22, 25, 27, 28^{2}, 29, 30^{2}, 35:8, 12^{2}, 15, 36:3, 7, 8, 11, 12, 13, 17, 18^{2}, 19, 20^{4}, 21, 35, 38, 37:2, 9, 10, 11, 17, 19, 21, 22^{2}, 23^{3}, 24^{2}, 25^{3}, 26, 27, 38:8, 23, 39:6, 9^{2}, 10^{3}, 11^{2}, 12, 14^{2}, 16, 23^{2}, 26^{3}, 28, 40:10, 22, 38, 41, 42^{2}, 49, 41:6^{3}, 42:6, 11^{2}, 13^{2}, 14^{4}, 43:7, 8^{2}, 9^{2}, 10, 11^{3}, 18, 22^{2}, 24, 25, 26^{2}, 44:7, 10, 11^{3}, 12^{2}, 13^{3}, 15^{2}, 16^{3}, 17^{3}, 18^{2}, 19^{5}, 20^{2}, 21, 22^{2}, 23, 24^{4}, 25^{2}, 26, 29, 45:8, 46:6, 10^{2}, 15, 20^{2}, 47:9, 10, 11, 12, 22^{2}, 48:14, 19

DANIEL
1:4, 5, 16, 19, 2:2, 7, 13, 18, 43^{2}, 46, 3:3

DANIEL
3:9, 12, 13, 19, 24, 25, 28, 4:6, 7, 25^{3}, 26, 32^{2}, 5:3, 4, 8, 15^{2}, 20, 21, 23, 29, 6:4, 12, 13, 16, 22, 23, 24^{3}, 7:5, 12, 13, 25, 26, 9:7, 11, 10:7, 11:2, 6^{2}, 14, 21, 22, 25, 26, 27, 31^{2}, 33^{2}, 34^{2}, 12:3^{2}

HOSEA
1:11, 2:4, 8, 17, 21, 22, 23, 4:2, 4, 7^{2}, 8^{2}, 10^{3}, 12, 13, 14^{3}, 18, 19, 5:4^{2}, 6^{2}, 7^{2}, 15^{2}, 6:7^{2}, 9, 7:1, 2^{2}, 3, 4, 6^{2}, 7, 10, 11^{2}, 12, 13^{3}, 14^{4}, 15, 16^{2}, 8:1, 4^{4}, 5, 7^{2}, 8, 9, 10^{2}, 12, 13^{2}, 9:3^{2}, 4^{2}, 6, 9, 10^{2}, 12, 16^{2}, 17^{2}, 10:1, 2, 3, 4, 8, 9, 10, 11:2^{3}, 3, 4, 5, 7, 10, 11, 12:1

HOSEA
12:8, 11^{2}, 13:2^{2}, 3, 6^{3}, 16, 14:7^{2}

JOEL
1:18, 2:4, 5, 7^{4}, 8^{3}, 9^{4}, 17, 3:2, 3^{2}, 8, 19

AMOS
1:3, 6, 9, 13^{2}, 2:4, 6, 8^{2}, 3:3, 10, 4:8, 5:10^{2}, 12^{3}, 16^{2}, 6:2, 6, 7, 9, 14, 7:2, 8:3, 12^{2}, 14^{2}, 9:2^{2}, 3^{2}, 4, 12, 14^{3}, 15

OBADIAH
5^{3}, 7, 16^{4}, 18, 19^{3}

JONAH
1:7^{2}, 8, 11, 13, 14, 15, 2:8, 3:10

MICAH
1:5, 7, 16, 2:1, 2^{2}, 6^{3}, 12, 13, 3:3, 4^{2}, 5, 7, 10, 11, 4:3^{2}, 4, 12^{2}, 5:1, 4, 6, 15, 7:1, 2^{2}, 3^{2}, 4, 16, 17^{3}

NAHUM
1:10^{3}, 12^{2}, 2:4^{3}, 5^{2}, 8^{2}, 3:3, 7, 10, 12^{2}, 17^{2}

HABAK.
1:7, 8, 9^{2}, 10^{3}, 15^{3}, 16, 17

HABAK.
2:7, 3:10, 11, 14

ZEPH.
1:11, 13^{2}, 17^{2}, 2:4, 7^{2}, 8, 10^{2}, 3:3, 4, 7, 9, 12, 13, 19

HAGGAI
1:14, 2:14

ZECH.
1:4, 5^{2}, 6^{2}, 10, 11, 15, 2:9, 3:5, 8, 4:10^{2}, 5:9^{2}, 6:7^{2}, 15, 7:2, 11^{2}, 12^{2}, 13^{2}, 14^{2}, 8:8^{2}, 9:15^{3}, 16, 10:2^{3}, 5^{2}, 6, 7, 8^{2}, 9^{2}, 12, 11:5, 6, 12, 12:2, 6, 10^{3}, 13:2, 4, 9^{2}, 14:12, 13, 21

MALACHI
1:4^{2}, 7, 3:3, 15^{2}, 16, 17, 4:3

MATT.
1:11, 12, 18, 23, 2:5, 9^{3}, 10^{2}, 11^{4}, 12^{2}, 13, 18, 20, 4:6, 18, 20, 22, 24, 5:4^{2}, 5, 6^{2}, 7, 8, 9, 10, 12, 16, 6:2^{2}, 5^{3}, 7^{2}, 16^{3}, 26^{3}, 28^{3}, 7:6, 15, 8:16, 29, 32^{2}, 33, 34^{2}, 9:2

MATT.
9:8, 11, 12^{2}, 15, 17, 24, 28, 31^{2}, 32^{2}, 36, 10:17^{2}, 19, 23, 25^{2}, 36, 11:7, 8, 18, 19, 20, 21, 12:2, 3, 10^{2}, 14, 16, 24, 27, 36, 41, 45, 13:5^{3}, 6^{3}, 13^{3}, 15^{2}, 16^{2}, 41, 48, 51, 54, 56, 57, 14:5, 13, 15, 16, 17, 20^{2}, 21, 26^{2}, 32, 33, 34^{2}, 35, 36, 15:2^{2}, 9, 12, 14, 18, 31^{2}, 32^{2}, 34, 37^{2}, 38, 16:5, 7, 12, 14, 20, 28, 17:6, 8^{2}, 9, 12^{2}, 14, 16, 22, 23^{2}, 24^{2}, 18:19, 31, 19:5, 6, 7, 11, 25, 20:4, 7, 9^{2}, 10^{3}, 11^{2}, 18, 22, 24, 25, 29, 30, 31^{2}, 33, 34, 21:1, 7, 15, 20, 25, 27, 31, 34, 36, 37, 38, 39, 41, 45, 46^{3}, 22:3

MATT.
22:5, 8, 10, 15, 16, 19, 21, 22^{2}, 28, 30, 33, 34, 42, 23:3^{2}, 4^{2}, 5^{2}, 25, 24:9, 24, 26, 30, 31, 38, 25:3, 5, 10^{2}, 44, 26:4, 5, 8, 15, 19, 21, 22, 26, 30^{2}, 50, 52, 57, 60, 66, 67, 73, 27:4, 7, 9^{2}, 13, 15, 16, 17, 18, 20, 21, 22, 23, 28, 29^{3}, 30, 31^{2}, 32^{3}, 33, 34, 35^{3}, 36, 39, 47, 54^{2}, 66, 28:8, 9^{2}, 10^{2}, 11, 12^{2}, 15^{2}, 17^{2}

MARK
1:5, 16, 18, 20, 21, 22, 27^{3}, 29^{2}, 30, 32, 34, 36, 37^{2}, 45, 2:3, 4^{4}, 8, 12, 15, 16, 17^{2}, 18, 19^{2}, 20, 23, 24, 25, 3:2^{2}, 4, 6, 8^{2}, 9, 10, 11, 12, 13, 14, 19, 20, 21^{2}

MARK
3:28, 30, 32, 4:10, 12^{3}, 15^{2}, 16^{2}, 17, 18, 20, 33, 34, 36^{2}, 38, 41, 5:1, 13, 14^{2}, 15^{2}, 16, 17, 40, 42, 6:3, 8, 12, 13, 29, 30^{2}, 31, 32, 34, 36^{2}, 37, 38^{2}, 40, 42, 43, 44, 49^{2}, 50, 51, 52, 53^{2}, 54^{2}, 55, 56^{2}, 7:2^{2}, 3, 4^{4}, 7, 15, 32, 36^{2}, 8:2, 3, 5, 6, 7, 8^{2}, 9, 14, 16, 19, 20, 22, 28, 30, 9:1, 4, 6, 8^{2}, 9^{3}, 10, 11, 13^{2}, 15, 18^{2}, 20, 30, 31, 32, 34^{2}, 10:4, 8^{2}, 13, 23, 26, 32^{4}, 33, 34, 37, 39, 41, 42, 46, 49, 11:1, 4^{2}, 6^{2}, 7, 9^{2}, 12, 15, 18^{2}, 20^{2}, 27, 31, 32, 33, 12:3, 4, 5, 6, 8, 12^{3}, 13

MARK 12:14[2], 16[2], 17, 18, 23, 25[2], 26, 43, 44, 13:9, 11, 26, 14:1, 2, 5, 11[2], 12, 16, 18, 19, 22, 23, 26[2], 31, 32, 40, 46, 50, 53, 64, 70, 15:4, 6, 13, 14, 16, 17, 19, 20[2], 21, 22, 23, 24[2], 25, 27, 29, 32, 35, 16:1, 2, 3, 4[2], 5[2], 6, 8[4], 10, 11[2], 12, 13[2], 14[2], 17[2], 18[4], 20

LUKE 1:2, 6, 7[2], 22, 58, 59[2], 61, 62, 63, 66, 2:6, 9, 16, 17[2], 18, 20, 22, 39[2], 42, 43[2], 44[2], 45[2], 46, 48[2], 50, 4:2, 11, 28[2], 29, 32, 36[2], 38, 40, 41, 5:6[2], 7[4], 9, 11[2], 18, 19[3], 26[2], 31[2], 33, 35, 6:3, 7, 11[2], 18[2], 22, 39, 44, 7:4[2], 10, 14, 16, 20, 25, 31, 32, 42, 49, 8:10[2], 12[2]

LUKE 8:13[3], 14[2], 15, 16, 22, 23[2], 24[2], 25[2], 26, 31, 32, 34[2], 35[2], 36, 37, 40, 45, 53, 56, 9:6, 10[2], 11, 12, 13, 14, 15, 17, 19, 27, 32[3], 33, 34[2], 36[2], 37, 40, 43[2], 45[3], 52, 53, 54, 56, 57, 10:7, 8, 10, 13, 38, 11:19, 26, 28, 29, 32, 33, 48, 49, 54, 12:1, 4, 11, 24, 27[3], 36, 48

LUKE 13:2, 4, 29, 14:1, 4, 6, 7, 12, 14, 18, 15:25, 16:4, 9, 14, 15, 26[2], 28, 29, 30, 31[2], 17:1, 13, 14[2], 21, 23, 27[4], 28[6], 37, 18:9, 15[2], 24, 26, 33, 34[2], 37, 39, 43, 19:7[2], 11[2], 25, 32, 33, 34, 35[3], 36, 37, 42, 44, 48, 20:5, 6, 7[2], 10, 11, 12, 13[2], 14, 15, 16[2], 19[2], 20[3], 21, 24

LUKE 20:26[2], 27, 31, 35, 36[2], 40, 41, 21:3, 7, 12, 16, 24, 27, 30, 22:2[2], 5, 9, 13[2], 23, 25, 28, 35, 38, 49[2], 54, 55, 64[2], 65, 70, 71, 23:2, 5, 12, 18, 21, 23, 24, 25, 26[3], 29, 30, 31, 33[2], 34[3], 56, 24:1[2], 2, 3, 4, 5[2], 8, 11, 14, 15, 16, 19, 23[3], 24, 28[2], 29, 31[2], 32, 33

LUKE 24:35, 36, 37[2], 41, 42, 45, 52

JOHN 1:21, 22, 24, 25, 37, 38, 39, 2:3[2], 7, 8, 12, 20, 23, 3:21, 23, 26, 4:24, 30, 35, 40, 45, 52, 5:12, 23, 25, 29[2], 39[2], 6:2, 9, 11, 12, 13, 14, 15, 19[3], 21[2], 23, 24, 25[2], 28, 30, 34, 42, 45, 60, 63[2], 64, 7:25, 26, 30, 39, 40, 45, 52

JOHN 8:3, 4, 6[2], 7, 9, 19, 25, 27, 33, 39, 41, 59, 9:8, 10, 12, 13, 17, 18, 19, 22, 24, 26, 28, 34[2], 35, 39[2], 10:4, 5[2], 6[2], 10[2], 16, 25, 27, 28, 39, 11:13, 31, 34, 41, 42, 53, 56[2], 57, 12:2, 9[2], 10, 12[2], 16[2], 18, 37, 39, 40, 42[2], 43, 15:6, 20[4], 21[2], 22[2], 24[2], 25, 16:2, 3[2], 9

JOHN 16:18, 19, 17:3, 6[2], 7, 8[2], 9, 11, 13, 14, 15[2], 16, 19, 21[2], 22, 23, 24[2], 18:5, 6, 7, 18, 21, 25, 28[4], 30, 40, 19:2, 3, 6, 15, 16, 18, 23, 24[3], 29, 31, 33[2], 37[2], 40, 42, 20:2[2], 4, 9, 13[3], 20, 23[2], 29, 21:3[3], 5, 6[2], 8, 9[2], 15, 25

ACTS 1:4, 6[2], 9, 10, 12, 13[2], 23

ACTS 1:24, 26, 2:1, 2, 4, 7, 18, 37[2], 41, 42, 46, 3:2, 10[2], 4:1, 2, 3, 7[2], 13[5], 14, 15[2], 17, 18, 21[3], 23, 24[2], 29, 31[4], 32, 5:12, 15, 16, 17, 21[3], 22, 24, 26[2], 27[2], 33[2], 40[4], 41[2], 42, 6:5, 6[3], 10, 11, 12, 7:6, 7[2], 19[2], 25, 26, 35, 41, 52, 54[3], 57, 59, 8:1, 4, 10, 11, 12[2], 14

ACTS 8:15[2], 16, 17[2], 36[2], 38, 39, 9:2, 8, 24, 26, 27, 30, 37[2], 38, 39, 10:9, 10, 22, 24, 39, 45, 46, 48, 11:2, 18[2], 19, 20, 22, 23, 26, 30, 12:10[3], 15[2], 16[2], 19, 20, 25, 13:2, 3[2], 4[2], 5[3], 6[2], 13, 14[2], 17, 27[3], 28[2], 29[2], 45, 48, 51, 14:1, 3, 6, 7, 11, 12, 14, 18[2], 21[2], 23[3], 24[2], 25[2]

ACTS 14:26[2], 27[2], 28, 15:2, 3[2], 4[3], 11, 13, 20, 23, 30[4], 31[2], 33[2], 36, 39, 16:3, 4[2], 6, 7[2], 8, 19, 23[2], 31, 32, 37[2], 38[3], 39, 40[3], 17:1[2], 6[2], 8[2], 9[2], 11, 13, 15[2], 19, 27[2], 32, 18:3, 6, 20, 26, 19:2, 3, 4, 5[2], 6, 10, 16, 19, 26, 28[2], 29, 32, 33, 34, 20:8, 12, 18, 37, 38[2], 21:5, 6

ACTS 21:12, 20[3], 21[2], 22, 24[2], 25[2], 27, 29[2], 30, 31, 32[2], 22:2[2], 9[2], 18, 19, 22, 23, 24, 25, 29, 23:4, 12[2], 13, 14, 20, 21[3], 24, 28, 30, 32, 33, 24:12, 13[2], 14, 15, 19, 20, 25:7, 14, 17, 18, 26:5, 10, 18, 20, 30, 31[2], 27:1, 12, 13[2], 17[3], 18, 27, 28[2], 29, 30[2], 36[2], 38[2], 39[3], 40[2], 41, 43, 44

ACTS 28:1[2], 2, 4, 6[3], 10, 15, 17, 18, 21, 23, 25[2], 27[2], 28

ROMANS 1:20, 21[2], 22, 28, 32, 3:9[2], 12[2], 13, 17, 4:7, 11, 14, 17, 5:17, 8:5[2], 8, 14, 23, 9:6, 7[2], 8, 26, 32[2], 10:1, 2, 3, 14[5], 15[2], 16, 18, 11:3[2], 8[2], 10, 11[2], 20, 23[2], 28[2], 31, 13:2, 6, 15:21[2], 27, 16:18

1 COR. 2:8[2], 14[2], 3:20

1 COR. 7:8, 9, 14, 29[2], 30[6], 31, 8:11, 9:13[2], 14, 24, 25, 10:4, 5, 6, 11, 18, 20, 33, 11:19, 12:19, 20, 13:8[2], 14:7, 21, 23, 34, 35, 15:10, 11, 18, 23, 29[2], 35, 48[2], 16:4, 15, 17, 18

2 COR. 5:15, 6:16, 8:3, 5, 23, 9:4, 5, 13, 10:10, 12, 11:12[2], 22[3], 23, 12:21

GAL. 1:23, 24, 2:4, 6[2], 7, 9[2], 10

GAL. 2:12, 14, 3:7, 9, 4:17[2], 5:12, 21, 24, 6:12[2], 13[2]

EPHES. 4:14, 5:31

PHIL. 3:18, 4:2, 22

COLOS. 1:16, 20, 3:21, 4:9

1 THESS. 1:9, 2:14, 15, 16, 5:3[2], 7[2]

2 THESS. 2:10[2], 11, 12, 3:12

1 TIM. 1:3, 7[2], 20, 2:15, 3:13, 5:7, 11[2], 12, 13[2], 17, 24, 25, 6:2[3], 9, 10, 17, 18[2], 19

2 TIM. 1:15, 2:10, 14, 16

2 TIM. 2:23, 26, 3:6, 8, 4:3[2], 4

TITUS 1:10, 11, 13, 16[3], 2:3, 4, 10, 3:8, 9, 14

HEB. 1:4, 11[2], 14, 2:11, 3:10, 11, 16, 18, 19, 4:3, 5, 6, 6:6[2], 7:5[2], 23[2], 8:9, 10, 11, 9:15, 10:1, 2, 11:13, 14[2], 15[3], 16, 23, 29, 30, 35, 37[3], 38, 40, 12:10, 19, 20, 25, 13:10, 17[3], 24

JAMES 2:7, 12

JAMES 3:3, 4[2], 4:1, 5:15

1 PETER 1:12, 2:8, 12[3], 3:1, 2, 10, 16[2], 4:4, 6

2 PETER 1:8, 21, 2:3, 10[2], 12, 13[3], 14, 18[2], 19[2], 20[2], 21, 3:4, 5, 16[2]

1 JOHN 2:19[7], 4:1, 5[2]

2 JOHN 1

3 JOHN 7

JUDE 10[3], 11, 12[2], 15, 18, 19

REV. 1:3, 7, 15, 2:2, 9, 22, 24, 27, 3:4[2], 9, 4:4, 8[2], 11

REV. 5:9, 6:4, 9, 10, 11[2], 7:13, 14, 15, 16, 8:7, 11, 9:4, 5[2], 8, 9, 10, 11, 19, 20, 21, 11:2, 3, 6, 7, 9, 10, 11, 12[2], 18, 12:6, 11[2], 13:4[2], 14, 14:3, 4[3], 5, 11, 12, 13, 15:3, 16:4, 6[2], 9, 10, 14, 15, 17:8[2], 14, 18:9, 18, 19, 19:3, 9, 20:4[2], 6, 9, 13, 21:3, 26, 27, 22:4, 5[2], 14[2]

thou

859, *477*

GEN. 2:16, 17[2], 3:9, 11[3], 12, 13, 14[2], 15, 16, 17[3], 18, 19[2], 4:6, 7[3], 10, 11, 12[2], 14, 6:14, 15, 16[3], 18, 19, 21[2], 7:1, 2, 8:16, 10:19, 30, 12:2, 11, 13, 18, 19, 13:9[2], 10, 14, 15, 14:23, 15:2, 3, 5, 15, 16:8, 11, 13, 17:1, 4, 8

GEN. 17:9, 15, 19, 18:5, 15, 23, 24, 28, 19:12[2], 15, 17[2], 19, 21, 22, 34, 20:3, 4, 6, 7[2], 9[3], 10, 13, 21:22, 23[2], 26, 29, 30, 22:2, 12[2], 16, 18, 23:6[2], 13, 24:3, 4, 5, 6, 7, 8, 14[2], 23, 31[2], 37, 38, 40, 41[2], 42, 44, 47

GEN. 24:58, 60, 25:18, 26:9, 10[2], 16, 29[2], 27:10, 18, 19, 20, 21, 24, 32, 33, 36, 38, 40[2], 43, 45, 28:1, 3, 4, 6, 13, 14, 15, 22, 29:14, 15, 25[2], 27, 30:15[2], 16, 26, 29, 30, 31, 31:13[2], 24, 26, 27, 28, 29, 30[2], 31, 32[2], 36, 37

GEN. 31:39, 41, 42, 43, 44[2], 50[2], 52, 32:10, 12, 17[2], 18, 26, 28, 29, 33:8, 9, 10, 35:1, 17, 37:8[2], 10, 15, 38:16[2], 17[2], 23, 29, 39:9, 17, 40:13[2], 41:15, 39, 40[2], 43:4, 5, 8, 9, 44:3, 4, 18, 21, 23, 45:10[4], 11[2], 19, 30, 47:6, 8, 25, 30[2]

GEN. 48:6, 49:3, 4[3], 6[2], 8, 9, 50:5

EXOD. 2:13, 14[2], 3:5, 10, 12, 14, 15, 18[2], 4:9[2], 10, 12, 13, 15, 16, 17[2], 21[2], 22, 23, 25, 26, 5:15, 22[2], 23, 6:1, 29, 7:2, 9, 15[2], 16[2], 17, 8:2, 10, 21, 22, 9:2, 14, 15, 17[2], 19, 29

EXOD. 10:2, 3, 4, 7, 25, 28[2], 29, 44, 46, 13:5, 6, 8, 10, 12[2], 13[4], 14, 14:11[2], 15, 16, 15:7[2], 10, 12, 13[3], 16, 17[2], 26, 17:3, 5, 6, 18:14, 17, 18[3], 19[2], 20, 21, 23[2], 19:3, 6, 12, 23, 24[2], 20:3, 4, 5, 7, 9, 10[2], 13, 14

EXOD. 20:15, 16, 17[2], 19, 22, 24, 25[4], 26, 21:1, 2, 14, 23, 22:18, 21, 23, 25[3], 26[2], 28, 29[2], 30[2], 23:1, 2[2], 3, 4[2], 5[2], 6, 7, 8, 9, 10, 11[2], 12[2], 14, 15[3], 16[2], 18, 19[2], 22, 24[2], 27, 30, 31, 32, 33, 24:1, 12, 25:11[2], 12, 13

EXOD. 25:14, 16, 17, 18[2], 21[2], 23, 24, 25[2], 26, 28, 29[2], 30, 31, 37, 40, 26:1[2], 4[2], 5[2], 6, 7[2], 9, 10, 11, 14, 15, 17, 18, 19, 22, 23, 26, 29[2], 30, 31, 32, 33[2], 34, 35[2], 36, 37[2], 27:1, 2[2], 3[2], 4[2], 5, 6, 8, 9, 20

EXOD. 28:1, 2, 3, 9, 11[2], 12, 13, 14, 15[3], 17, 22, 23, 24, 25, 26[2], 27, 30, 31, 33, 36, 37, 39[3], 40[3], 41, 42, 29:1, 2, 3, 4, 5, 6, 7, 8, 9[2], 10, 11, 12, 13, 14, 15, 16[2], 17, 18, 19, 20, 21, 22, 24, 25

EXOD. 29:26, 27, 31, 34, 35[2], 36[4], 37, 38, 39[2], 41, 30:1[2], 3[2], 4[2], 5, 6, 12[3], 16, 18[3], 23, 25, 26, 29, 30, 31, 35, 36, 37, 31:13, 32:7, 11, 13, 21, 22, 32[2], 33:1[2], 3, 12[5], 16, 17[2], 20, 21, 23, 34:1, 10, 11, 12[2], 14, 15[2], 16

EXOD. 34:17, 18[3], 20[4], 21[3], 22, 24, 25, 26[2], 27, 40:2, 3, 4[2], 5, 6, 7, 8, 9, 10, 11, 12, 13, 14, 15[2]

LEVIT. 1:2, 2:4, 6, 8, 13[3], 14[2], 15, 6:21[2], 27, 8:3, 9:3, 10:9, 14, 13:55, 57, 58, 17:8, 18:7[2], 8, 9, 10, 11, 12, 13

LEVIT. 18:14[2], 15[2], 16, 17[2], 18, 19, 20, 21[2], 22, 23, 19:9[2], 10[3], 12, 13, 14, 15[2], 16[2], 17[2], 18[2], 19[2], 27, 32, 34, 20:2, 16, 21:8, 22:23, 23:22[4], 24:5, 6, 7, 15, 25:3[2], 4, 5, 8, 9, 14, 15, 16[2], 17, 35, 36, 37, 39, 43, 44, 27:12

NUM. 1:3, 49, 50, 3:9, 10, 15, 41, 47[2], 48, 4:23, 29, 30, 5:19[2], 20[2], 7:5, 8:2, 7, 8, 9[2], 10, 12, 13, 14, 15, 26, 10:2[2], 29, 31[2], 32, 11:11[2], 12[2], 15, 16, 17, 18, 21, 23, 29, 13:2, 27, 14:13, 14[3], 15, 17, 19, 15:5, 6, 7, 8

NUM. 15:10, 16:11, 13[2], 14[2], 15, 16[2], 17, 22, 37, 17:2, 3, 4, 10, 18:1[2], 2[2], 7, 10, 15[2], 16, 17[2], 20[2], 30, 20:8[4], 14, 18, 20, 21:2, 29, 34[2], 22:6[2], 12[2], 17, 20, 28, 29, 30, 32, 34, 35, 37, 23:5, 11[2], 13[2], 18, 27, 24:10, 11, 12, 21

NUM. 26:54[2], 27:7[2], 8, 13[2], 20, 28:3, 4[2], 7, 8, 21, 31:2, 26, 30

DEU. 1:14, 31, 37, 2:4, 7, 18, 19, 28, 31, 37, 3:2[2], 21, 24, 27, 28, 4:9, 10, 19[2], 25, 29[3], 33, 35, 36, 33, 40[2], 5:7, 8, 9, 11, 13, 14[3], 15, 17, 18

DEU. 5:19, 20, 21[2], 27[2], 31[2], 6:2[2], 5, 7[5], 8, 9, 10, 11[4], 12, 13, 18[2], 21, 7:1[2], 2[2], 3[3], 6, 11, 14, 15, 16[2], 17, 18, 19, 21, 22, 24[2], 25[2], 26[4], 8:2[2], 3, 5, 6, 9[3], 10[2], 11, 12, 13, 14, 17, 18, 19, 9:1, 2[2], 3, 4

DEU. 9:5, 6, 7[2], 12, 26[2], 28, 29, 10:2[2], 20[3], 11:1, 10[2], 14, 15, 19[4], 20, 29[2], 12:5, 13[2], 14[2], 15, 17[2], 18[4], 19[2], 20[2], 21[2], 22, 23[2], 24[2], 25[2], 26[2], 27[2], 28, 29[2], 30[2], 31, 32, 13:2, 3, 5, 6[2], 8[3], 9, 10, 12, 14, 15, 16, 18, 14:2

DEU. 14:3, 21[4], 22, 23[2], 24, 25, 26[4], 27, 28, 29, 15:1, 3, 5, 6[3], 7, 8, 9, 10[3], 11, 12, 13[2], 14[2], 15[2], 17[2], 18[2], 19[2], 20[2], 21, 22, 23[2], 16:2, 3[5], 4, 5, 6[2], 7[2], 8[2], 9[2], 10[2], 11[2], 12[3], 13[2], 14[2], 15[2], 18, 19[2], 20[2], 21[2], 22

DEU.
17:1
4
5
7
8
9
10[2]
11[2]
12
14
15[3]
18:4
9[2]
13
14
16
21
22
19:1
2
3
7
9[2]
13
14[2]
19
20:1[2]
10
12
13
14[2]
15
16
17
19[4]
20[3]
21:8
9[2]
10[2]
11
12
13
14[5]
21
22
22:1[2]
2[3]
3[5]
4[2]
6[2]
8[3]
9[2]
10
11
12[2]
21
22
24
26
23:6
7[3]
12[2]
13[3]
15
16
18
19
20[3]
21[2]
22
23[3]
24[3]
25[3]
24:4
7
8
10[2]
11[2]
12
13
14
15
17
18[2]
19[2]
20[2]
21
22[2]
25:4
12
13
14
15[2]
18
19[2]
26:1
2[3]
3
5
10[2]
11[2]
12
13[2]
14
15[2]
16
17
18
19
27:2
3[3]
4
5[2]
6[3]
7
8
9

DEU.
27:10
28:1
2
3[2]
6[4]
8
9
10
12[2]
13[3]
14
15
16[2]
19[4]
20[4]
21
22
24
25
27
29[3]
30[4]
31[2]
33[2]
34[2]
36[3]
37
38
39
40[2]
41[2]
43
44[2]
45[2]
47
48
49
51
52
53
58[2]
60
61
62
63
64[2]
65
66
67[4]
68
29:12
30:1
2
5
6
8
10[2]
12
13
14
16[2]
17
18
19
20[4]
31:2
3
7[2]
11
14
16
23
32:14
15[3]
18
50
52[2]
33:7
8[2]
23
29[2]
34:4
JOSH.
1:2
6
7[4]
8[4]
9[2]
16[2]
18
2:17
18[3]
20[2]
3:8
13
5:15
6:3
7:7
9
10
13
19
25
8:1
2[2]
10:12[2]
11:6
13:1
6
14:6
9
12
15:18
19
17:14
15

JOSH.
17:17[2]
18[2]
JUD.
1:14
15
4:8[2]
9
20
22
5:4[2]
12
16
21
6:4
12
14
16
17
18
23
26
36[2]
37[2]
7:5
10[2]
11
8:1[3]
18
21
22[3]
9:8
10
12
14
32
33[3]
36
38[2]
10:15
11:2[2]
8
12[2]
23
24
25
27
30
31
32
33
35[2]
36
12:1
5
13:3[2]
5
7
8
11
16[3]
18
14:3
16[2]
15:2
11[2]
18
16:6
10[2]
13[3]
15[2]
17:2[2]
9
18:3[2]
19
23
25
19:9
17[2]
RUTH
1:15
16[2]
17
2:8
9[2]
10
11[3]
12
13[2]
14
19[2]
21
22
3:1
4[3]
5
9[2]
10[3]
11[2]
15
16
18
4:4[2]
5[2]
6
11
1 SAM.
1:8[2]
11
14
17
23
2:16
32
3:5

1 SAM.
3:6
8
9
17
4:20
8:5
9:16
21
27
10:2[3]
3[2]
4
5[3]
6
7
8[3]
12:4[2]
13:11[2]
13[2]
14
14:37
43
44
15:1
7
13
17[2]
19
23
26
28
16:1
3[2]
4
16
17:29[4]
33[2]
43
45[2]
52
56
58[2]
18:17
21
19:3
5[2]
11[2]
17
20:2
8[3]
13
14
15
18
19[3]
21
23
30[2]
31
21:1
9[2]
22:12
13[2]
16[2]
18
23[2]
23:17
24:4
9
11[2]
14
17[2]
18[3]
19
20
21[2]
25:6
7
17
25
31
33
34
26:11
14[2]
15[2]
16
25[2]
27:8
28:1[3]
2
9[2]
12[2]
13
15[2]
16
18
19
21
22[3]
29:4
6
7
8
9
30:8
13[2]
15[2]
2 SAM.
1:3
5
8
13
14
25
26

2 SAM.
2:20
26[2]
27
3:7
8
13[3]
21
24[2]
25[2]
34
5:2
6[2]
19
22
23
24[2]
25
7:5
8
9
12
18
19
20
21
22
23
24[2]
25[2]
27
28[2]
29
9:2
7
8
10[2]
10:3
11
11:10
11
19
21
25[2]
12:7
9[2]
10
12
13
14
21[3]
13:4[3]
12
13
16
14:11
13
15:2
19[2]
20[2]
27
33[2]
34[2]
35[3]
16:2
7[2]
8[3]
10
17
21
17:3
6
8
11
18:3[3]
11[2]
13
20[3]
21
22[2]
19:5
6[3]
7
13[2]
14
19
22
25
28
29[2]
30
38
20:4
6
9
17
19[2]
21:4
17[2]
22:3
26[2]
27[2]
28[2]
29
36
37
40[2]
41
44[2]
49
24:13
1 KINGS
1:6
11
12
13
14

1 KINGS
1:16
17
18
20
24
27
42
2:2
3[3]
5
8
9[3]
13
15
22
26[3]
31
37[3]
42[3]
43
44[2]
3:6[3]
7
8
11
13
14
5:3
6[3]
8
9[3]
6:12[2]
8:18
19
24[2]
25[2]
26
28
29[2]
30[3]
32
33
34[2]
36[3]
39[4]
40
43
44[2]
45
46
48
49
51
53[3]
9:3[2]
4
13
11:11
22[2]
37
38
12:4
7
10[3]
13:8
9
14
17[2]
18
21
14:2
5
6[2]
8
9
12
16:2
17:4
13
18[2]
20
24
18:7
9
11
14
17
18[2]
36
37[2]
19:9
13
15
16[3]
20:5
9
13[2]
14
22
25
34
36[2]
39
42
21:5
7
10
19[3]
20[2]
22
29
22:4[2]
11[2]
16
19
22
25[2]

1 KINGS
22:28
30
2 KINGS
1:4[2]
6[3]
9
16[3]
2:3
5
10[2]
23[2]
3:7[2]
4:1
2
4[3]
7
13[2]
16[2]
23
29
40
5:6
8
10
13
25
6:9
12
22[3]
7:2
19
8:1[2]
10
12[3]
13
14
9:2
7
18
19
25
10:5[2]
30
13:17[2]
19[4]
14:10[4]
17:26
18:14
19
20[3]
21
23
24
19:6
10
11[2]
15[3]
19[3]
20
22[2]
23
25[2]
28
20:1
5
9
18
19
22:18
19[2]
20
23:17
1 CHRON.
4:10[2]
11:2[3]
5
12:18
14:10
15[2]
17:4
7[2]
8
11
16
17
18
19
21
22[2]
23[2]
25[2]
26
27
19:3
12
21:22
22:8[3]
11
12
13[2]
14
28:3[2]
9[4]
20
29:10
11
12
17
2 CHRON.
1:8
9
11[2]
2:3
16[2]

2 CHRON.
6:8
9
15[2]
16[2]
17
20[2]
21[2]
23
25[2]
26
27[3]
30[3]
31
33
34[2]
35
36
38[2]
39
41
7:17
9:6
10:4
7
10[3]
13:4
14:11
16:7
8
9[2]
18:3[2]
10
12
15
21[2]
24[2]
27
29
33
19:2
3
20:6[2]
7
9
10
11
12
15
37
21:12
15
24:6
25:8
15
16[3]
19[5]
26:18
34:26
27[2]
28
35:21
EZRA
4:13
15
16
7:14
16
17
19
20
25
9:11
13
14[2]
15
10:12
NEH.
1:6
7
8
10
2:2
4
5
6
5:12
6:6[3]
7
8
14
9:6[4]
7
8
10[2]
11[2]
12
13
15
17
19
20
21
22
23[2]
24
27[3]
28[3]
29
30[2]
31[2]
33[2]
34
35[2]
36
37

ESTHER
3:3
4:3
14[3]
5:3
14[2]
6:10[2]
13[2]
JOB
1:7
8
10[2]
2:2
3[2]
9
10
4:2
3[2]
4
5[2]
5:6
17
21[2]
22[2]
23
24[2]
25
26
27
7:12
14
17[2]
18
19
20[2]
21[2]
8:2
5
6
9:12
28
31
10:2
3[2]
4[2]
6
7
8
9[2]
10
11
12
13
14[2]
15
16[2]
17
18
11:3
4
7[2]
8[2]
13
15[2]
16
17[2]
18[3]
19
13:22[2]
24
25[2]
26
27[2]
14:3
5
13[3]
15[2]
16[2]
17
19[2]
20[2]
15:4
5
7[2]
8[2]
9[2]
13
16:3
7
8
18
17:4[2]
14[2]
20:4
22:3[2]
6
7[2]
9
11
13
23[3]
24
25
26
27[2]
28
29
26:2[2]
3[2]
4
30:20[2]
21[2]
22[2]
23
31:24
33:5

JOB
33:8
12
13
32
34:16
17
18
32
33[3]
35:2[2]
3
5
6[3]
7[2]
8
14[3]
36:17
21
23
24
37:6
15
16
18
38:3
4[2]
5
11
12
16[2]
17
18[2]
20[2]
21[2]
22[2]
31
32[2]
33[2]
34
35
39
39:1[2]
2[2]
10
11[2]
12
13
19[2]
20
40:7
8[3]
9[2]
41:1[2]
2
4
5[2]
7
42:2
4
PSALMS
2:7
9[2]
3:7[2]
4:1
6
7
8
5:3
4
5
6
10
11
12[2]
6:3
7:6
7
8:2[2]
3
4[2]
5
6[2]
9:2
4[2]
5[3]
6[2]
10
13
10:1[2]
13
14[3]
15[2]
17[3]
12:7[2]
13:1[2]
16:2[2]
5
10[2]
11
17:3[3]
6
7
14
18:25[2]
26[2]
27
28
35
36
39[2]
40
43[2]
48[2]
19:12
21:2
3[2]

PSALMS
21:4
5
6[2]
9
10
12[2]
13
22:1[2]
2
3[2]
4
9[2]
10
15
19
21
23:4
5[2]
25:5
7
17
27:8
9
28:1
30:1
2
3[2]
7[2]
10
11[2]
31:2
3
4
5
7[2]
8
14
19[2]
20[2]
22
32:5
6
7[3]
8
35:17
22
36:6
8
37:1
10
34
38:15
39:5
9
11[2]
40:5
6[3]
9
11
17
41:2
3
10
11
12
42:5[3]
9
11[3]
43:2[3]
5[2]
44:1
2[2]
3
4
7
9
10
11
12
13
14
19
23
24
45:2
7
11
16
48:7
49:16
18
50:15
16[2]
17
18[2]
19
20[2]
21[2]
51:4[3]
6[2]
8
14
15
16[2]
17
18
19
52:1
3
4[2]
9
53:5
55:13
23
56:2
8[2]
13[2]

PSALMS
57:5
11
59:5
8[2]
16
60:1[3]
2[2]
3[2]
4
8
10[2]
61:3
5[2]
6
62:5
12
63:1
7
65:2
3
4
5
8
9[4]
10[4]
11
66:3
10[2]
11[2]
12[2]
67:4
68:7[2]
9[2]
10
18[3]
28
30
35
69:5
19
26[2]
70:5
71:3[2]
5[2]
6
7
17
20
21
22
23
73:18[2]
20[2]
23
24
27
74:1
2[3]
11
13[2]
14
15[2]
16
17[2]
76:4
7[3]
8
10
77:4
14[2]
15
20
79:5
11
80:1[2]
4
5
6
8[2]
9
12
15
17
81:7
8
9
82:8
83:1
18
85:1[2]
2[2]
3[2]
5[2]
6
86:2
5
7
9
10[2]
13
15
17
88:5
6
7
8[2]
10
14[2]
18
89:2
9[2]
10[2]
11
12
13
17
19

PSALMS
89:26
38[2]
39[2]
40[2]
42[2]
43
44
45[2]
46
47
49
90:1
2[2]
3
5
8
15
17[2]
91:4
5
8
9
12
13[2]
92:4
8
10
93:2
94:2
12
13
97:9[2]
99:4[2]
8[3]
101:2
102:10
12
13
25
26[2]
27
104:1[2]
6
8
9
20
24
26
27
28[2]
29[2]
30[2]
35
106:4
108:5
11[2]
109:6
21[2]
27
28
110:1
2
3
4
114:5[4]
7
115:9
116:8
16
118:13
21
28[2]
119:4
12
18
21
25
26
28
32
37
49
57
65
68
75
82
84
86
90
93
98
102
114
117
118
119
132[2]
137
138
151
152
171
120:3
123:1
128:2[2]
5
6
130:3
4
132:8
137:8
138:2
8
7[2]
139:1
2[2]

PSALMS
139:3
4
5
8[2]
13[2]
19
140:6
7
142:3
5
7
143:10
144:3[2]
145:15
16
PROV.
1:10
15
2:1
2
3
4
5
9
20
3:4
15
23
24[3]
28
31
4:8
12[3]
5:2
6[2]
9
11
19
20
6:1[2]
2[2]
3
6
9[2]
22[3]
35
7:4
9:12[4]
14:7
19:19[2]
20
20:13[2]
22
22:18
21
24
25
26
27
29
23:1
2
5
6[2]
8[2]
13
14
17
19
31
34
35
24:1
6
10
11
12
13
14
19
21
24
25:7
8
16[2]
22
26:4
12
27:1
22
23
27
29:20
30:4
6[2]
10
32
31:29
ECCL.
5:1
2
4[2]
5[2]
6
7
8
7:10[2]
16
17[2]
18
21
22
8:4
9:9[2]
10

ECCL.
10:17
11:1
2
5[2]
6
9
12:1
CANT.
1:7[3]
8[2]
15[3]
16
2:17
4:1[3]
7
9[2]
16
5:9[2]
6:1
4
7:6
8:1
12
13
14
ISAIAH
1:26
2:6
3:6[2]
7:3
16
9:3
4
12:1[3]
6
14:3
4
8
10[2]
12[2]
13
15
19
22[2]
29
31
16:4
17:10[2]
11[2]
22:1
2
8
16[3]
18
23:2
4
12[3]
16[2]
25:1[2]
2
4
5
26:3
7
12[2]
14
15[4]
20
27:8
29:4
6
30:19
22[2]
23
32:1[4]
2[2]
19[3]
36:4
5[3]
6
7
8
9
37:6
10
11[2]
16[3]
20[2]
21
23[2]
24
26[2]
29
38:1
12
13
16
17[2]
39:7
8
40:27
28[2]
41:8
9[2]
10
12
14
15
16[2]
42:20
43:1
2[3]
4[2]
22[2]
23[2]

ISAIAH
43:24[4]
26[2]
44:2
17
21[3]
26
28
45:3
4
5
9
10[2]
15
47:1
5[2]
6[2]
7[2]
8
10[3]
11[3]
12[2]
13
16
48:4
5
6[2]
7[2]
8[3]
17
18
49:3
6
9
18
20[2]
21
23
51:9
10
12[2]
16
17
21
22
23
53:10
54:1[2]
3
4[4]
6
11
14[3]
17
55:5[2]
57:6[2]
7[2]
8[5]
9
10[4]
11[3]
13
58:3[2]
5
7[4]
9[3]
10
11
12[2]
13
14
60:5
15
16[2]
18
62:2
3
4[2]
8
12
63:2
14
16[2]
17
19
64:12
3[2]
5[2]
7
8[2]
12[2]
65:5
JER.
1:5
7[2]
11
12
13
17
2:2
17[2]
18[2]
19
20[2]
21
22
23[3]
25
27[2]
28
33[2]
35[2]
36[3]
37[2]
3:1
2[3]
3[2]

JER.
3:4[2]
5[2]
6
7
12
13
19
22
4:1[3]
2
10
14
19
30[6]
5:3[2]
15
17
19
6:8
27
7:16
17
27[2]
28
8:4
10:6
24
11:3
14
15[2]
18
21
12:1
2[2]
3[2]
5[4]
13:4
12
13
21[2]
22
25
27
14:7
8
9[2]
17
19[2]
22[2]
15:2
5
6[2]
10
14
15
17
18
19[5]
16:2[2]
8
10
11
17:4[2]
14
16
17
18:22
23
19:10
20:6[5]
7[2]
21:8
22:2
6
15[2]
21[2]
22
23
25
23:33
37
24:3
25:27
28
30
26:4
8
9
27:13
28:6
7
13[2]
15
16[2]
29:24
25
26
27
30:10
13[2]
15
31:4[2]
5
18[3]
21
22[2]
32:3
17
18
22
23[2]
24[2]
25
33:3
24
34:3[2]
4

JER.
34:5
14
36:6[3]
14
17
19
29[3]
37:18
17
20
38:15[2]
17[2]
18[2]
21
23[2]
24
25
26
39:17[2]
18[2]
40:14
16[2]
43:3
44:16
45:3
4
5[2]
46:11[2]
19
27
28
47:5
6[2]
48:2
7[2]
18
27[2]
49:4
12[3]
16[2]
50:24[4]
31
51:13
20
26
61
62[2]
63[2]
64
LAM.
1:10
21[3]
22
2:20
21[2]
22
3:17
42
43[3]
44
45
56
57[2]
58[2]
59[2]
60
61
4:21
5:19
20
21
22[2]
EZEKIEL
2:4
6[2]
7
8[2]
3:1
5
6
18[2]
19[2]
20
21[2]
25[2]
26
27
4:1
8[2]
4[3]
5
6[2]
7[2]
8[2]
9[3]
10[2]
11[2]
12[2]
15
5:1
2[3]
3
11
7:2
7
8:6[2]
12
13
15[2]
17
9:8
11
11:13
12:2
3[2]

EZEKIEL	EZEKIEL	EZEKIEL	EZEKIEL	HOSEA	MICAH	ZECH.	MATT.	MATT.	MARK	LUKE	LUKE	JOHN	JOHN	ACTS	ROMANS	2 TIM.	JAMES
12:4^2	21:28^2	28:18	43:21	2:16	2:5	4:9	13:28	26:62	14:30	10:26	22:32	8:25	18:9	13:47	9:19	1:6	4:11^2
5	30	19^2	22	20	7	13	14:28	63^2	36	27	34^2	33	17	16:31	20^2	8	12
6^3	32^2	29:5^2	23^2	23^2	4:8	5:2	31^2	64	37^2	28^2	42	48	21	17:19	10:9^2	13	
9	22:2^4	7^2	24	3:3^3	9	6:10	33	68	60	35	48	52^2	22	20	11:17	15	3 JOHN
10	3	31:2	25	4:5	10^4	13:3^2	15:5	69	61	36	58	53^2	23	21:20	18^2	18	2
13:2	4^4	10	44:6	6^3	13		12	70	67	37	60	57^2	25	21	19	2:1	3
17^2	8	18^3	45:3	15	5:2^2	MALACHI	22	73	68	40	61	9:17	33	22	11:20	2^2	5^2
16:4^3	12^2	32:2^3	18	5:3	12	1:2	28	75	70^2	41	67	28	34	24	22^2	3	6^2
5^2	13	6	20	9:1^2	13	2:14	16:14	27:4	72	11:27	70	34^2	35	37	24	3:10	
6^2	16^2	9	46:13^2	14	6:1		16	11^2	15:2^2	45	23:3^2	35	37^2	38	12:20	14^3	REV.
7^3	24	19^2	14	10:9	14^3	MATT.	17	13	4	12:19	37	37	19:9	22:7	13:3^2	15	1:11
8	23:21	28	47:6	13	15^4	1:20	18	19	29	20^2	39	10:24^2	10^2	8^2	4	4:5	19
13^4	28	33:7^2		12:6	7:19	21	19^2	40^2	34	41	40^2	33	11	14	9^6	13	20^2
15	30^2	8^2	DANIEL	13:4	20^2	2:6	23^2	46		58^3	42	36	12^2	15^2	14:4	15	2:2^2
16	31	9^2	1:13	9		13	17:4		LUKE	59^2	43	11:3	20:13	16	10^2		4
17	32^2	10	2:23^2	10	NAHUM	3:14	25	MARK	1:4^2	13:9	24:18	8	15^4	26	15	TITUS	5^2
18	33	12	26	14:1	1:14	4:3	27^3	1:11	13	12		21	29^2	27	22	1:5	6^2
19	34^2	14	30		3:8	6^2	18:15	24^3	14	15	JOHN	22	21:12	23:3^2		2:1	9
20^3	35^2	27	31	AMOS	11^3	7	28	40^2	20^2	26	1:19	26	15^2	4	1 COR.	3:8	10^2
21	36	30	34	5:23	16	9	32^2	41	28^2	14:8^2	21^2	27	16^2	5	4:7^5		13^2
22^2	40	32	37	7:8		10^2	33	44	30	9	22^2	32	17^4	11^2	7:16^4	PHILE.	14
24	41	35:4^2	38	12	HABAK.	5:21	19:17^2	3:11	31	10^2	25^2	40^2	18^6	19	21^2	5	15
25	24:13^2	5	41^2	16^2	1:2^2	22	18^4	4:38	42	12	33	41	22	20	27^2	12	20
26	16	6	43	17	3	23	19	5:7^2	76^2	13	38	42^2		21	28^2	15	3:1^2
28^3	19^2	10	45	8:2	12^3	25^2	21^3	8	2:29	14^2	42^2	12:34	ACTS	22^2	9:9	17	3^3
29^2	25	11	47		13^2	26^2	20:12	31^2	31	22	48^2	13:6	1:6	24:4	14:16^2	19	4
30	27^2	12^2	3:10	OBADIAH	2:7	27	13	35	48	15:29	49^2	7^2	24^2	10	17	21	8
31^2	25:3	15^2	12^2	2	8	33	21	6:22	3:22	30	50^2	8^2	2:27^2	11	15:36^2		10
33	6	36:1	18	3	10	36^2	30	23	4:3	31	2:10	27	28^2	25:9	37^2	HEB.	11
34^2	7	12^2	4:18^2	4^2	15	42	31	25	7	16:2	18^2	36^3	34	10		1:5	15^2
36	26:14^2	13	20	5	16^2	43	21:16^2	7:11	8^2	5	20	38^2	4:24	12^2	GAL.	9	16
37^3	17	14	22	10	3:8	6:2	21^2	8:29	9	7	3:2^2	14:5	27	22	2:14^2	10	17^2
41	20	15^2	25	11^2	9	3	23	33	11	25^2	8	9^2	5:4^2	26:1	4:7	11	18^3
43^2	21^3	37:3	26	12^3	12^2	5^2	22:12	9:22	12	27	10	10	7:28^2	14	27^2	12^2	4:11^2
45^2	27:2	16	32	13^2	13^2	6^3	16^3	23	34^2	17:4	26	22	33	15^2	5:14	2:6^2	5:9^2
47^2	3^2	18^2	35	14^2	14	17^2	17	24	41	6^2	4:9	16:5	8:20	16	6:1	7^2	6:6
48^2	7	20	5:13	15	15	18	37	25	5:10	8	10^2	29	21	24		8	10
51^2	25	38:7^3	16^3			7:3	39	10:18	12^2	18:19	11^2	30^2	23	27^2	EPHES.	5:5	7:14
52^5	33^2	8^2	18	JONAH	ZEPH.	4	44	19	13	20	12	17:2^2	30^2	28	5:14	6	10:11
54^3	34	9^3	22^2	1:6	3:7^2	5^2	23:26	21^3	6:41	22^3	17	3	37^2	29	6:3	7:17	11:17
55	36	10	23^3	8^2	11^3	8:2^2	37	35	42^4	38	18^3	4	9:4	27:24	COLOS.	21	18
58	28:2^3	11	27	10	15	3	25:20	47	7:6	39	19	5	5^2	28:22	4:17^2	8:5	15:3
59	3	13^2	6:12	14	16	4	21^3	48	19	41	27^2	6^2	6^2			10:5^2	4
60	4	14	13	2:2		8	22	51	20	19:17^3	5:6	7	17^2	ROMANS	1 TIM.	6	16:5^2
61^2	5	15^2	16	3	ZECH.	13	23^2	11:21	43	19	14	8^2	10:6	2:1^5	1:3	8	6
62	6	16	20	6	1:3	19	24^3	23^2	44^2	21^4	6:25	9	15	3^2	18	12:5^2	17:7
63	8	17	8:20	4:2	12^2	29	25	28	45	22^2	30^2	11	33^2	4	3:15^2		8
17:9	9^2	39:1	26	4	14	31	26^2	12:14^2	46	23	68	12	11:3	17	4:6^3	JAMES	12
19:1	10	4^2	9:7	9	2:2	9:27	27	30	8:28	42^2	69	18	9	19	12	2:3^2	15
20:4^2	12	5	23	10^2	11	11:3	26:17	31	45	44	7:3	21^2	14	21^4	16	8	16
6	13^2	17	10:12		3:7^3	23	25	32	9:54	20:2	4	22	12:15	22^4	5:18	11^3	18
21:7	14^3	40:4^2	19	MICAH	8	25	34	34	57	21^2	20	23^3	13:10^3	23^2	21	18	18:14
14	15^2	43:10	20	1:11	4:2	12:37^2	39	36	60	39	52	24^3	11	25^2	6:11	19^2	20
19^2	16	19	12:4	13	5	13:10	50	13:2	10:15	42	8:5	25	33	3:4^2	12	20	19:10
25	17	20^2	13^2	14	7^2	27	53	14:12^2	21	22:9	13	26	35	7:7	14	22	22:9

thy

4674 or *4675*

GEN.	GEN.	GEN.	GEN.	EXOD.	EXOD.	LEVIT.	NUM.	DEU.	DEU.	DEU.	DEU.	DEU.	DEU.	JUD.	1 SAM.	1 SAM.	2 SAM.
3:10	22:16	31:33	44:33	8:5	23:16^2	18:16^2	5:21^3	4:21	8:18^2	14:28	19:8^4	26:5	29:11^4	1:3	2:27	24:11^2	11:8^2
14^2	17^2	34	45:9	9^3	17	20	22^3	23	19	29^2	9	10^2	12^2	5:12	28	16	10
15	18	31:3	10^4	10	19^2	21^2	11:11^2	24	9:3^2	15:3	10^2	11	13	14	29	25:7	11
16^2	20	8^2	11	11^3	25^2	19:9^2	12	25	4	4	14^2	12	30:1	6:14	30	8^3	21
17^3	23:6^2	13	46:3	16	26^2	10^2	15	29^3	5^3	5	20:1	13^3	2^3	17	31	26	24^2
19	11	30	30	21^3	31	12	14:13	30	6^2	6	13	15^2	3^3	25^2	34	28	25
4:6	15	31	34	23	33	13	14	31^2	7	7^5	14	16^2	4	26	3:9	29	12:8^3
9	24:2	32	47:3	9:3	28:1	14	19	37	12	9^2	16	17	5^3	30	10	33	9
10	5	37^2	4^2	14	2	15	20	40^3	26^2	10^2	17	19	6^4	7:10	4:17	35^2	10
11	7	38^2	5^2	15	4	16^2	16:10	5:6	27	11^4	21:1	27:2	7	8:15	8:5^2	26:15^2	11^3
14	14^3	41^2	6	19	41	17^2	11	9	29^3	12	2^2	3^2	9^5	22^2	9:20^2	17	13
6:18	17	32:4	15	30	29:12	18^2	16	11	10:9	14^4	6	5	10^3	9:38	10:2	24	13:5^2
7:1	19	5	29^2	10:2^2	26	19^2	18:1^3	12	11	15	8^2	6^2	14^2	54	12:19^2	27:5	7
8:16	23	6	48:1	4	32:4	27	2^3	13	12^5	17^2	10	7	16^2	11:10	13:13^2	28:1	20^3
12:1	40	9^2	2	6^4	7	29	3	14^{10}	13	18	11	9	19	17	14	2	24^2
2	43	10	4	29	8	32	7	15^2	14	19^5	13	10	20^4	19	14:7	17	35
7	44	12	5	11:8	11^2	20:19^2	8	16^5	15	20^2	23^2	28:1^2	31:3	24	28	19	14:6
13	46	18	6	12:24	12^2	21:8	9	20	20	21	22:1^2	2	6	36^2	15:15	21^2	11^2
18	51	20	11^2	13:5	13	17	11^3	21^3	21^2	22	2^2	4^5	11	13:12	21	22	15
19	60	27	18	7	32	23:22^2	19^3	6:2^5	22^2	16:1^2	3	5^2	12^2	16	24	29:6^3	17
13:8	25:23^2	28	22	8	33:1	24:47	20	3	11:1	2	4	7	14	17^2	30	8	19
15	31	29	49:4	9	5	25:3^2	20:8	5^3	10^2	3	5	8^2	16	14:3	33^2	10	20
16^2	26:3^2	33:5	8^3	11	13^4	4^2	14	7	12^2	4	7	9	27^2	13	16:11	31:4	22^2
14:20	4^3	10^2	18	13	15	5^2	16	9^2	14^2	5^2	8	11^4	32:6	15^2	16		31
15:1	9	35:1	25	14	16^3	6^4	17^2	10^2	15^2	6	9^3	12	7^2	15:2	19	2 SAM.	15:2
5	10	10^3	26	14:16	18	7^2	19	13	20	7^2	12	13	50^2	18	17:17^2	1:16^3	3
13	24^2	11	50:6	15:6^2	34:9	11	21:22^2	15^2	29	8	17	15	33:3^3	16:6	18	19	8
15	27:3	12	16	7	10	15	34	18	12:1	10^3	23:5^3	17^2	8^3	15	29	26	15
18	6	37:10^2	17^2	8	16^2	17	22:32	20	7	11^7	6	18^4	9^2	17:10	32	2:21^2	19
16:5	9	13	18	10	19	25	23:3	21	13	13^2	7	20	10^2	18:19^2	34	22	20
6	10	14		12	20	35	15	7:1	14^2	14^6	13	23^2	18^2	25^3	36	3:8	21
9	13	32	EXOD.	13^3	24^3	36^2	24:5^2	2	15^3	15^2	14^3	24	25^3	19:19^2	44	12	27
10	19^2	38:8^2	2:9	16	26^2	37^2	11	3^2	17^8	16^2	16	26	26	20	55	25^2	34^3
11	20	11	13	17		39	12	4	18^8	17	18^2	29	27		58	34^2	16:3
17:5	29	13	3:5^2	26	LEVIT.	43	14	6^2	20^4	18^3	19	31^2	29^2	RUTH	19:11	4:8	4
7^2	31	18^3	6	17:5	2:5	44^2	21^2	9	21^5	20	20^2	32^2	34:4	1:10	20:1	5:1	8^2
8	32	24	18	18:6^2	7	53	27:13^2	12^2	25	21	21^2	33^2		15^2	3^2	6:21	17^5
9	35	39:19	4:6	20:2	13^3	27:2	31:2	13^7	26^2	22	23^3	35^2	JOSH.	16^2	4	7:9	19^2
10	37	40:13	7	5	14^2	3^2	49	16	27^4	17:1^2	24^3	36^2	1:5	2:11^4	6	12^4	21^2
12	39	19^2	9	7	5:15	4	32:4	18	28^2	2^3	25^2	40	8^2	12	7	16^2	17:8^2
13	40^2	41:40	10	9	18	5	5^2	19^2	29	5	24:4	42^2	9	13	8^3	19^2	10
15	42	42:10	12	10^8	6:6	6^2	25	20	31	8^2	9	45	17	14	10	20	18:28
19	44	11	14	12^4	9:7^2	7	27	21	13:5	12	10	46	18^2	3:3	15	21^2	29
18:3	45	13	15	16	10:9	8	31	22	6^7	14	13	47	2:18^4	9	18	23^3	19:5^6
9	28:2^2	43:28	16	17^3	13^2	13		23	10	15^3	14^4	48	19	12	22	24	6
10	4	44:7	19	24^3	14^3	15	DEU.	25	12^2	18:4^3	18	51^4	5:15^2	17	30	25	7^2
19:12	13^2	8	23^2	25	15^4	16	1:21^2	8:2	16	5^2	19^2	52^6	7:9	4:12	31	26^2	14
15	14^2	9	5:15	26	16:2	17	31	3	17	6	21	53^3	10	15^2	42	27^2	19
17	29:15	16	16^2	22:26	18:7^3	18	2:7^4	4^2	18^2	9	25:3	55	8:1		22:14^2	28^2	20
18^2	18	18^2	23^2	28	8^2	19	27	5	14:2	12	13	57	18	1 SAM.	15	29^3	26^2
20:6	30:14	21	7:1^2	29^3	9^3	23	30^2	6	21^2	13	15^2	58	9:8	1:8	16	9:2	27
13	15	23	2	30	10^2	25	3:2	7	22	14	16	59^2	9^2	14	22	7^2	28
16	27	24	9	23:6	11^3	27	24^5	10	23^6	15^2	19^2	62	24^2	17	23	8	29
21:12^3	28	27	19	10	12^2		4:3	11	24^2	16	26:1	64	10:6^2	18	23:10	9	35
13	29	30	8:2	11^3	13^2	NUM.	9^5	13^4	25	19:1^2	2^3	65	14:9^2	26	11^2	10^4	36
22:2	31	31^2	3^5	12^2	14	5:19	10	14	26^3	2^2	3	66^2	24:12^2	2:1	20	11	37^2
12	32	32	4^2	13	15^2	20	19	16^2	27	3^2	4	29:5^2		16	24:9	10:3	20:6

2 SAM.
22:36^2, 50, 24:3, 10, 13^2, 23

1 KINGS
1:2, 13, 14, 17, 19, 26^2, 27, 30, 47^2, 2:3, 4, 6, 7^2, 21, 37, 38, 39, 44, 3:6, 7, 8^2, 9^3, 12, 13, 14^2, 22^2, 23^2, 5:3^2, 6^2, 8, 6:12, 8:19^2, 23, 24^2, 25^2, 26^2, 28, 29, 30^3, 32, 33^2, 34, 35, 36^4, 38, 39, 41^2, 42^3, 43^4, 44^2, 48, 49, 50, 51, 52^2, 53, 9:3^2, 4, 5^2, 10:7, 8^3, 9, 11:11, 12^3, 13, 37, 12:4^2, 7, 9, 10, 28, 13:6, 21, 22^2, 14:9, 12, 15:19^2, 16:3, 17:12, 13, 19, 23, 24, 18:8, 9, 10, 11, 12, 14, 18, 31, 36^2, 44, 19:2, 10^2, 14^2, 15, 16, 20:3^4, 4, 5^4, 6, 9, 31, 32, 33, 34, 39^2, 40^2

1 KINGS
20:42^3, 21:2, 5, 6, 19, 21, 22:4^2, 13, 23, 30, 49

2 KINGS
1:10, 12, 13^2, 14, 2:2, 3^2, 4, 5^2, 6, 9, 16^2, 3:7^2, 13^2, 4:1^2, 3, 4, 7^2, 24, 26, 29^2, 30, 36, 5:8, 10, 15, 17^2, 18^2, 25, 27, 6:3, 12, 22^2, 28, 29, 8:9, 13, 9:1, 7, 22, 10:5, 15, 30, 14:9, 10, 15:12, 16:7^2, 18:23, 24, 26, 27, 19:4^3, 10, 22, 23, 27^4, 28^4, 20:3, 5^3, 6, 17, 18, 22:9, 19, 20^2

1 CHRON.
10:4, 11:1^2, 2, 12:18^2, 16:35^2, 17:11^4, 17, 18^2, 19, 21^2, 22, 23, 24^2, 25^2, 26, 27, 19:3, 21:8, 12, 17, 22:11, 12, 28:6, 9, 21, 29:13, 17, 18, 19^3

2 CHRON.
1:9, 10, 2:8^2, 10, 14^2, 6:2, 9^2, 14, 15^2

2 CHRON.
6:16^2, 17^2, 19^2, 20^2, 21^3, 23, 24^2, 25, 26, 27^4, 29, 30, 31, 32^4, 33^4, 34^2, 38, 39^2, 41^4, 42, 7:12, 17, 18^2, 9:5, 6, 7^3, 8^3, 10:4^2, 7, 9, 10, 14:11, 16:3^2, 7, 18:3, 12, 22, 29, 20:7^2, 8, 9^2, 11, 37, 21:12^2, 13^2, 14^4, 15^2, 25:18, 34:16, 27, 28^2

EZRA
4:11, 15, 7:14, 18, 19, 20, 25^2, 26, 9:10, 11, 14

NEH.
1:6^2, 7, 8, 10^4, 11^4, 2:2, 5^2, 6, 9:5, 8, 14^2, 16, 17, 18, 19, 20^2, 25, 26^2, 27, 28, 29^3, 30^2, 31, 32, 34^3, 35, 13:22

ESTHER
3:8, 4:14^2, 5:3, 6^2, 7:2^2, 3, 9:12^2

JOB
1:11, 12, 18^2, 2:5, 4:4, 6^4, 5:24^2, 25, 26, 27, 8:2, 4, 5, 6, 7^2

JOB
8:21^2, 10:5^2, 12, 17, 11:3, 14, 15, 16, 18, 13:21, 24, 14:13, 15:5, 10, 12, 13^2, 21:14, 22:3, 5, 6, 23, 25, 27^2, 28, 30:21, 33:5, 6, 8, 31, 33, 34:33, 35:4, 6, 8^2, 36:16, 19, 37:17, 38:3, 11, 12, 21, 34, 39:9, 11, 12^2, 26, 27, 40:7, 11, 41:5, 42:7

PSALMS
2:8, 3:8^2, 4:6, 5:5, 7^4, 8^2, 11, 6:1, 4, 8:1^2, 3^2, 6, 9, 9:1, 2, 3, 10, 14^2, 19, 10:5, 14, 13:1, 5^2, 15:1^2, 16:11^2, 17:2, 4, 5, 7^2, 8, 13, 14^2, 15^2, 18:15^2, 35^3, 49, 19:11, 13, 14, 20:3^2, 4, 5^2, 21:1^2, 5, 6, 8, 12, 13, 22:22, 23:4^2, 24:6, 25:4^2, 5, 6^2, 7^2, 11, 26:3^2, 7, 8, 27:8, 9^2, 11, 28:2, 9

PSALMS
30:7^2, 9, 31:1, 3, 7, 15, 16^3, 19, 20, 32:4, 33:22, 34:13^2, 35:3, 24, 28^2, 36:5^2, 6^2, 7^2, 8^2, 9, 10^2, 37:5, 6^2, 38:1^2, 2, 39:10, 12, 40:5^2, 8^2, 10^5, 11^3, 16, 41:12, 42:3, 7^3, 10, 43:3^4, 44:2, 3^2, 5, 8, 12^2, 17, 18, 22, 24, 26, 45:2, 3^4, 4^2, 6^2, 7^2, 8, 9^2, 10, 11^2, 12, 16^2, 17, 48:9, 10^3, 11, 50:7, 8^2, 9^2, 14, 16, 19^2, 20, 51:1^2, 4, 9, 11^2, 12^2, 13, 14, 15, 18, 52:2, 5, 9^2, 54:1^2, 5, 6, 55:22, 56:8^2, 12, 57:1, 5, 10^2, 11, 59:11, 16^2, 60:3, 5^2, 61:4^2, 5, 8, 63:2^2, 3, 4, 7, 8, 65:4^3, 8, 11^2, 66:3^2, 4, 13, 67:2^2, 68:7, 10^2, 23^2, 24, 28^2, 29, 35

PSALMS
69:7, 13^2, 16^2, 17^2, 24, 27, 29, 70:4, 71:2, 8^2, 15^2, 16, 17, 18^2, 19, 22, 24, 72:1^2, 2^2, 73:15, 24, 28, 74:1, 2, 3, 4, 7^2, 10, 11^3, 13, 18, 19^2, 21, 75:1^2, 76:6, 7, 77:11, 12^2, 13, 14, 15, 18, 19^3, 20, 79:1, 2^2, 5, 6, 8, 9^2, 10, 11, 13^3, 80:2, 3, 4, 7, 15, 16, 17^2, 18, 19, 81:10^2, 83:1, 3^2, 15^2, 16, 84:1, 4, 10, 85:1, 2, 3, 6, 7^2, 86:2, 4, 8, 9, 11^3, 12, 13, 16^2, 88:5, 7^2, 11^2, 12^2, 14, 15, 16^2, 89:1, 2, 4^2, 5^2, 8, 10, 12, 13^2, 14^2, 15, 16^2, 17, 19, 39, 46, 49^2, 50, 90:4, 7, 8, 9, 11^2, 13, 14, 16^3, 91:4, 7^2

PSALMS
91:9, 10, 11, 12, 92:1, 2^2, 4^2, 5^2, 93:2, 5, 94:5, 12, 18, 19, 97:8, 99:3, 102:2, 10, 12, 14, 15, 24, 25, 27, 28, 103:3, 4, 5^2, 104:7^2, 13, 24^2, 29, 30, 106:4^2, 5^2, 7^2, 47^2, 108:4^2, 5, 6^2, 109:1, 21^2, 26, 27, 28, 110:1, 2, 3^3, 5, 115:1^3, 116:7, 16^2, 119:4, 5, 6, 7, 8, 9, 10, 11, 12, 13, 14, 15^2, 16^2, 17^2, 18, 19, 20, 21, 22, 23^2, 24, 25, 26, 27^2, 28, 29, 30, 31, 32, 33, 34, 35, 36, 37, 38^3, 39, 40^2, 41^3, 42, 43^2, 44, 45, 47, 47, 48^2, 49, 50, 51, 52, 53, 54, 55^2, 56, 57, 58^2, 59, 60, 61, 62, 63, 64^2, 65^2, 66, 67, 68

PSALMS
119:69, 70, 71, 72, 73^2, 74, 75, 76^3, 77^2, 78^2, 79, 80, 81^2, 82, 83, 84, 85, 86, 87, 88^2, 89, 90, 91, 92, 93, 94, 95, 96, 97, 98, 99, 100, 101, 102, 103, 104, 105, 106, 107, 108, 109, 110, 111, 112, 113, 114, 115, 116, 117, 118, 119, 120, 122, 123^2, 124^3, 125^2, 126, 127, 128, 129, 130, 131, 132, 133, 134, 135^3, 136, 137, 138, 139, 140^2, 141, 142^2, 143, 144^2, 145, 146, 147, 148, 149^2, 150, 151, 152, 153, 154, 155, 156^2, 157, 158, 159^2, 160^2, 161, 162, 163, 164, 165, 166^2, 167, 168^2, 169, 170, 171, 172^2, 173, 174^2, 175, 176^2, 121:3, 5^3, 7, 8^2, 122:2, 7^2, 9, 128:3^3, 5, 6

PSALMS
132:8^2, 9^2, 10, 11^2, 12^2, 135:13^2, 137:9, 138:2^6, 4, 7, 8, 139:7, 10^2, 14, 16, 17, 20, 140:13^2, 142:7, 143:1^2, 2^2, 5^2, 7, 8, 10^2, 11^2, 12^2, 144:5, 145:1, 2, 4^2, 5^2, 6^2, 7^2, 10^2, 11^2, 13^2, 146:10, 147:12, 13^2, 14

PROV.
1:8^2, 9^2, 14, 15, 2:3, 10, 3:3, 6, 8, 9, 10^2, 22^2, 23^2, 24, 26^2, 28, 29, 4:7, 10, 12, 13, 23, 26^2, 27, 5:2, 8, 9, 10^2, 11^2, 16, 18, 6:1^2, 2^2, 3^2, 9, 11^2, 20^2, 21, 7:3, 4, 15, 9:11^2, 16:3^2, 19:18^2, 20, 22:18, 19, 25, 27, 28, 23:2, 8, 9, 16, 22^2, 25^2, 24:6, 10, 12, 13, 14^2, 27, 28^2, 34^2, 25:8, 9^2, 17^2, 27:10^3, 23^2, 26, 27^3, 29:17^2, 30:32, 31:3^2

PROV.
31:8, 9

ECCL.
5:1, 2^2, 6^3, 7:9, 17, 21, 9:7^4, 8^2, 9^4, 10^2, 10:4, 16^2, 17^2, 20^2, 11:1, 6, 9^2, 10^2, 12:1

CANT.
1:2, 3^2, 4, 7^2, 8^2, 10^2, 2:14^4, 4:1^2, 2, 3^4, 4, 5, 9, 10^2, 11^3, 13, 5:9^2, 6:1^2, 5, 6, 7^2, 7:1^2, 2^2, 3, 4^2, 7^2, 8^2, 9, 8:5, 13

ISAIAH
1:22^2, 23, 25^2, 26^2, 2:6, 3:6, 12, 25^2, 4:1, 6:7^2, 7:3, 11, 17^2, 8:8, 10:22, 27^2, 30, 14:3^2, 9, 11^2, 19, 20^2, 30^2, 16:3, 9^2, 17:10^2, 11, 19:12, 20:2^3, 22:2, 3, 7, 18^2, 19^2, 21^3, 23:10, 25:1^2, 12, 26:8^2, 9, 11, 13, 16, 17, 19^2, 20^2, 29:4^3, 5, 30:19, 20^2, 22^2, 23, 33:6, 23, 36:8, 9, 11, 37:4^3, 10, 23, 24

ISAIAH
37:28^4, 29^4, 38:3, 5^4, 17, 18, 19, 39:6, 7, 40:9, 41:10, 13^2, 14, 43:1, 3^2, 4, 5, 23^2, 24^2, 25^2, 27^2, 44:3, 22^2, 24, 27, 28, 45:3, 4, 9, 47:2, 3^2, 6, 7, 9, 10^3, 12^2, 13, 15^2, 48:4^2, 17^2, 18^2, 19^2, 49:16, 17^2, 19^3, 22^2, 23^3, 25, 26^2, 51:13, 15, 16, 22^2, 23^2, 52:1^2, 2, 7, 8, 54:2^3, 3, 4^2, 5^2, 6, 8, 11^2, 12^3, 13^2, 15, 55:5, 57:6^2, 7, 8^2, 9^2, 10, 11, 12^2, 13, 58:1, 7^2, 8^3, 10^3, 11^2, 13^2, 14, 59:21^4, 60:1, 3^2, 4^3, 9^2, 10, 11, 14, 16^2, 17, 18^4, 19^3, 20^3, 21, 62:2^2, 3, 4^3, 5^2, 6, 8^2, 11, 63:2, 14, 15^6, 16, 17^3, 18^2, 19, 64:1, 2^2, 3, 5, 7^2

ISAIAH
64:8, 9, 10, 12, 66:9

JER.
1:9, 17, 2:2, 16, 17, 19^2, 20^2, 23, 25, 28^4, 33^2, 34, 36, 37, 3:2^2, 13^2, 4:7^2, 14, 18^3, 30^3, 5:7, 14, 17^7, 10:6, 17, 25^2, 11:13^2, 16, 20, 21, 12:1, 6^2, 13:1, 4, 20, 22^2, 25^2, 26^3, 27^2, 14:7, 9, 19, 21^3, 15:11, 13^4, 15^2, 16^3, 17, 17:3^4, 18:20, 23, 20:3, 4, 6, 12, 22:2^2, 7, 15, 17, 20^2, 21^3, 22^3, 23, 25, 26, 27:2, 13, 28:6, 29:25, 30:8^2, 10, 12^2, 13, 14^2, 15^2, 17, 31:4, 7, 16^2, 17, 21, 32:17, 21, 23^2, 34:5, 37:18, 38:16, 17, 20, 22^2, 23^2, 39:18^2, 40:2, 42:2, 3, 5, 45:5, 46:12^2, 15, 27, 47:6, 48:7^2, 18^2, 32^3, 46^2, 49:4, 11^2, 16^2, 50:31, 51:13, 36

LAM.
1:10, 2:13, 14^2, 3:23, 55, 4:22, 5:19

EZEKIEL
2:1, 8, 3:3^2, 8^2, 9, 11, 19, 21, 26^2, 27, 4:3, 4, 6, 7, 8, 9, 10, 15, 5:1, 3, 11, 6:2, 11, 7:3, 8, 9, 9:8^2, 11:15^3, 12:3, 4, 6^2, 18^2, 13:4, 17^2, 16:3^4, 4^2, 5, 6^2, 7, 8^2, 9, 11^2, 12, 13, 14^2, 15^2, 16^2, 17, 18, 20^3, 22^3, 23, 25^4, 26^2, 27, 29, 33^3, 34, 36^6, 37^3, 39^3, 43^2, 45, 46^3, 47, 48^2, 49, 51^2, 52^4, 53, 55, 56^3, 57^2, 58, 61^4, 63^2, 19:2, 10^2, 11, 20:46^2, 21:2^2, 6, 12, 16, 30, 32, 22:4^3, 12, 13^2, 15, 23:21^3, 22, 25^5, 26^2, 27^2, 28, 29^4, 31, 32, 33, 35^3, 40, 24:13^2, 14^2, 16, 17^3, 27, 25:1

EZEKIEL
25:4^2, 6, 26:8, 9^2, 10^2, 11^3, 12^7, 13^2, 15, 18^2, 27:4^3, 5, 6, 7, 8^3, 9^2, 10^2, 11^4, 12^2, 13^2, 14, 15, 16^3, 17^2, 18^2, 19^2, 20, 21, 22^2, 23, 24^2, 25, 26, 27^{10}, 28, 33^3, 34^2, 28:4^2, 5^4, 7^2, 13^3, 15, 16, 17^3, 18^2, 21, 29:2, 4^6, 5, 7, 10, 31:2, 32:2^2, 5^2, 6, 8, 9, 10, 12, 33:2, 9, 12, 17, 30, 31, 32, 35:2, 4, 8^3, 9, 11, 12, 36:13, 14, 15, 37:18, 38:2, 4, 7, 9, 10, 13, 15, 39:3^3, 4

DANIEL
1:12, 13, 2:4, 28^3, 29^3, 30, 3:12, 18, 4:22^2, 25, 26, 27^2, 32, 5:10^2, 11^4, 16, 17^2, 18, 23^5, 26, 28, 6:16, 20, 9:5^2, 6^2, 11^2, 13, 15, 16^5, 17^3

DANIEL
9:18^2, 19^3, 23, 24^2, 10:12^3, 14, 11:14, 12:1^2, 9, 13^2

HOSEA
2:6, 4:4, 5, 6^2, 6:5, 8:1, 5, 9:1, 10:13^2, 14^2, 12:6^2, 9, 13:4, 10^3, 14^2, 14:1, 8

JOEL
2:17, 3:11

AMOS
3:11^2, 4:12, 5:23^2, 6:10, 7:16, 17^4, 8:14, 9:15

OBADIAH
1:4, 7^2, 9, 10^2, 12, 15

JONAH
1:6, 8, 2:3^2, 4^2

MICAH
1:11, 16^2, 4:9, 13, 5:10^2, 11^2, 13^2, 14^2, 6:1, 8, 9, 13, 14, 7:4^2, 5^2, 10, 11, 14^2, 15

NAHUM
1:13, 14^3, 15^2, 2:1^3, 13^3, 3:5^4, 9, 12, 13^3, 14, 16, 17^2, 18^3, 19^3

HABAK.
1:13, 2:10^2, 15, 16^2, 3:2^2, 8^2, 9^2, 11, 13

ZEPH.
1:7, 3:11^2, 15, 17

ZECH.
3:8, 9:9, 11^2, 13^2, 11:1^2, 14:1

MALACHI
1:6, 8^2, 2:14^3

MATT.
1:20, 4:6, 7, 10, 5:23^2, 24^4, 29^3, 30^3, 36, 39, 40^2, 43, 6:3^2, 4, 6^4, 9, 10^2, 17, 18^2, 22, 23, 7:3, 4, 5, 22^3, 8:4, 13, 9:2, 5, 6, 14, 18, 22, 11:10^2, 26, 12:2, 37^2, 47^2, 13:27, 15:2, 4, 28, 17:16, 18:8^2, 15^2, 33, 19:19^3, 20:14, 21^2, 21:5, 22:37^4, 39, 44, 23:37, 24:3, 25:21, 23, 25, 26:18, 42, 52, 73

MARK
1:2^2, 25, 44^2, 2:5, 9^2, 11^2, 18, 3:32^2, 5:9, 19, 23, 34^2, 35, 6:18, 7:5, 10^2, 29^2, 9:18, 38, 43, 45, 10:19, 21, 37^3, 52^2, 12:30^5, 31, 36, 14:70

LUKE
1:13, 31, 36, 38, 42, 44, 61, 2:29^2, 30, 32, 35, 48, 4:8, 11, 12, 23, 35

LUKE
5:5, 14, 20, 23, 24, 6:10, 29^2, 30, 41, 42^2, 7:27^2, 48, 50, 8:20^2, 30, 48, 49, 9:40, 41, 49, 10:17, 21, 27^6, 11:2^3, 34^2, 36, 12:20, 13:26, 34, 14:12^4, 15:19^2, 21^2, 27, 29, 30^2, 32, 16:1, 2, 6, 7, 25^2, 17:3, 19^2, 18:20^2, 42^2, 19:5, 16, 18, 20, 39, 42^2, 44^2, 20:43, 22:32^2, 23:42, 46

JOHN
4:16, 18, 42, 50^2, 51, 53, 5:8, 10, 11, 12, 7:3, 8:13, 19, 11:23, 12:15, 28, 13:37, 38, 17:1^3, 2, 6^2, 12, 13, 14, 17^2, 26, 18:11, 19:26, 27, 20:27^2, 21:18

ACTS
2:28, 35^2, 3:25, 4:25, 27, 28^2, 29^2, 30, 5:9, 7:3^2, 32, 33^2, 8:20, 21, 22, 23, 9:13, 14, 15, 17, 34, 10:4, 31, 11:14, 12:8^2, 14:10

ACTS
16:31, 18:9, 22:13, 16, 18, 20, 23:5, 24:2, 4, 25, 26:16

ROMANS
2:5, 17, 23, 25, 3:4, 4:18, 8:36, 9:7, 10:8^2, 9, 11:3, 13:9, 14:10^2, 15^3, 21, 15:9

1 COR.
7:16^2, 14:16, 15:55^2

GAL.
3:16, 5:14

EPHES.
6:2

1 TIM.
4:12, 15, 5:23, 6:20

2 TIM.
1:4, 5^2, 4:5, 9, 21, 22

PHILE.
2, 5, 6, 7, 13, 14^2, 21

HEB.
1:8^2, 9^2, 12, 13, 2:7, 12, 10:7, 9, 11:18

JAMES
2:8, 18^2

2 JOHN
4, 13

3 JOHN
2, 6

REV.
2:2^3, 4, 5, 9, 13, 19^3, 3:1, 2, 8, 9, 11, 15, 18, 4:11, 5:9, 10:9^2, 11:17, 18^3, 14:15, 18, 15:3^2, 4^2, 16:7, 18:10, 14, 23^2, 19:10^2, 22:9^2

to

1510

GEN. 1:14, 16[2], 17, 18[2], 29, 30[3], 2:5, 9[2], 10, 15[2], 19, 20[2], 21, 3:6[2], 7, 12, 16, 18, 21, 22, 23, 24, 4:3, 4, 5, 8, 11, 14, 23, 26[2], 6:1, 4, 16, 17, 19, 20, 21, 22, 7:2, 3, 4, 10, 8:1, 6, 8, 11, 13, 9:8, 10, 11, 14, 15, 20, 10:8, 19, 21, 11:2, 3[2], 4, 5, 6[2], 7, 8, 21, 12:5, 10, 11[2], 12, 14, 19, 13:3, 6, 9[2], 15, 14:1, 7, 10, 17, 21, 22, 23, 15:3, 5, 6, 7, 15, 17, 16:2, 3[3], 6, 7, 9, 16, 17:1, 7[2], 8, 18:2, 5, 7, 10, 11, 14, 16, 19, 21, 25, 27, 31, 19:1[2], 5, 8, 9[3], 10, 11

GEN. 19:13, 17[2], 19, 20, 27, 29, 30, 31, 34, 20:3, 6, 13, 16, 21:2, 3, 6, 17, 22, 23[2], 26, 22:1, 5, 9, 10, 14, 19, 20, 23, 23:2, 7[2], 8, 16, 24:4, 5, 8, 9, 10, 11[2], 13, 14[2], 15[2], 16[2], 17, 20, 21, 22, 23, 25, 27, 30, 32, 33, 36, 37, 38, 41, 43[3], 44, 48, 49, 52[2], 53[3], 56, 63, 65, 25:8, 11, 13, 16, 20[2], 22, 24, 30, 32[2], 33, 26:4, 7[2], 8, 11, 23, 26, 27, 31, 32, 34, 35, 27:1, 3, 4, 5[3], 8, 9, 10, 11, 12, 14, 20, 25[2], 29[2], 30, 37, 40, 42[2], 43, 45, 46, 28:2, 4, 5, 6[2], 7, 9, 11, 12

GEN. 28:13, 14[2], 15, 20, 21, 29:10, 13[3], 14, 19, 20, 23[2], 25[2], 26, 28, 29[2], 30:4, 9, 14, 15, 16, 18, 22, 24, 25[2], 32, 33, 34, 38[2], 41, 31:3, 4, 7, 9, 10, 18[2], 19, 20, 24[2], 26[2], 28, 29[2], 31, 32, 35, 36, 51, 52, 54, 32:3, 5, 6[3], 8, 9, 13, 30, 33:3[2], 4, 8, 11, 14, 17, 18, 34:1, 4, 6, 7, 8, 12, 14[2], 16[2], 17, 19, 21, 22[2], 25, 30[3], 35:1, 2, 3, 6, 12[2], 16[2], 17, 18, 19, 22, 26, 36:4, 12[2], 14, 40, 43, 37:7, 8, 9, 10[5], 12, 13, 14[2], 17, 18, 19, 22[2], 23, 25[3], 27, 28, 32, 35[2], 38:1[2], 8, 9[2], 11, 12

GEN. 38:13[2], 14[2], 15, 16, 20, 22, 23, 24, 25, 26, 27, 28, 29, 39:1, 3, 5, 7, 8, 10[4], 11[2], 13, 14[2], 15, 17[2], 18, 19[2], 22, 23[2], 40:1, 5, 8, 9, 20, 22, 41:1, 8, 11, 12[4], 13[2], 24, 25, 28, 32, 36, 43, 45, 52, 54, 55[2], 57[2], 42:3, 5, 6[2], 7, 9, 10, 12, 21, 24, 25[3], 27, 28, 30, 35, 37[2], 38, 43:2, 6, 7, 15, 16, 19, 20, 21[2], 22, 23, 26[2], 30, 33[2], 44:2, 7, 11, 13, 14, 24, 29, 30, 31[2], 32, 33, 34, 45:1, 4, 5, 7[2], 8, 9, 11, 17, 21, 22[2], 23, 27, 46:1, 3, 5, 18, 22, 28, 29[2], 32, 33, 47:4, 6

GEN. 47:12, 21[2], 24, 48:1, 4, 7, 11, 12, 17, 22, 49:4[2], 15, 28, 29, 50:2, 7, 10, 11, 14, 20[3], 24[3], EXOD. 1:10, 11, 13, 15, 16, 21, 2:1, 4[2], 5[2], 7[2], 8, 11, 13, 14, 15, 16, 18[2], 21, 23, 3:1[3], 4, 6, 8[2], 13, 16, 18[2], 21, 4:8[3], 9, 14, 16[2], 18[2], 20, 21, 23, 24[2], 25, 27[2], 5:2, 7, 8, 10, 12, 14, 16, 17, 21[3], 23[3], 6:1, 3, 4, 7[2], 8[4], 15, 16, 17, 19, 20, 23, 25[2], 26[2], 27[2], 28, 7:1, 14, 15, 17, 18, 20, 23, 24, 8:2, 5, 9, 10[2], 13, 18, 20, 22, 23, 25, 26[2], 27, 28, 29[3], 31, 9:2, 5, 8, 16, 18[2]

EXOD. 10:3, 4[2], 5, 10, 26, 28, 12:2, 3[2], 4[2], 13[2], 14, 16, 21, 23[3], 24[2], 25[2], 26, 29, 35, 37, 41[2], 42[2], 48, 49, 51, 13:5, 6, 10, 11, 14, 15[2], 17[2], 21[2], 14:2[2], 12, 13[3], 20[2], 21, 23, 24, 27, 15:21, 23, 26[2], 27[2], 16:3[3], 5, 8[2], 10, 13, 15[2], 16[2], 18, 21, 22, 23[3], 25[3], 27[2], 28, 32, 33, 34, 35, 17:1[2], 3, 4, 9, 10[2], 11, 16, 18:7, 8, 9, 12, 13[2], 14[2], 15, 18, 19, 21, 23[2], 24, 19:2, 3, 10[2], 12[2], 13, 16, 17, 20, 21, 22, 23, 24, 20:5, 8, 20, 21:6, 7, 8, 12, 14, 15, 16, 17, 19, 29[3], 31, 36, 22:5, 7, 8, 9, 10

EXOD. 22:16, 17[2], 18, 19, 25[2], 26, 27, 29, 31, 23:1, 2[3], 4, 5, 20[2], 24, 27, 24:4, 12, 14, 25:7, 9, 20, 25, 27, 29, 35, 26:3[2], 7, 13, 28, 30, 27:3, 5, 7, 20[2], 21, 28:3, 8, 10, 11, 14, 21[2], 35, 36, 42, 43, 29:1[2], 10, 29[2], 30, 33[2], 35[2], 36, 41[2], 42, 44[2], 30:1, 4, 15, 16, 18, 20[3], 21[3], 37[2], 38, 31:4[2], 5[2], 10, 11, 14, 15[2], 16, 32:1, 5[2], 6[2], 12[2], 13, 14, 19, 20, 27, 28, 29[2], 30, 33:1[2], 5, 7, 8, 9, 11, 19, 22, 34:2, 7, 12, 24, 29, 30, 34, 35, 35:2[3], 9, 19[2], 21, 27, 29[2], 32[2], 33[2], 35, 36:1[3], 2[2], 3, 5, 6

EXOD. 36:7, 12, 18, 29[2], 33[2], 34, 37:2, 3, 5, 9[2], 14, 15, 16, 21, 27[2], 29, 38:5, 7, 18, 21[2], 26, 30, 39:1, 3, 4, 5, 7, 14[3], 26, 30[2], 31, 32, 37, 41[2], 42, 40:4, 5, 16, 17, 30, 35, LEVIT. 1:11, 9, 14, 2:2[4], 13, 4:2, 3, 5, 16, 23, 27, 28, 35, 5:4[2], 7, 10, 11, 12[2], 17, 6:2, 4, 5, 25, 30, 7:8, 35, 36, 38, 8:4, 5, 12, 15, 31, 34[2], 9:1, 4, 16, 10:7, 15, 17[2], 19, 11:1, 7, 8, 21, 31, 37, 45, 47, 12:2, 8, 13:12, 15, 19, 59[2], 14:1, 7, 8, 11, 14, 17, 18, 19, 21[2], 22, 25, 28, 29[2], 31[2], 32[2], 34

LEVIT. 14:35, 36[2], 38, 41, 49, 57, 15:1, 13, 14, 28, 29, 16:10[3], 17, 27, 30, 32, 34, 17:4, 5, 11[2], 18:4, 6[3], 14, 17, 18[3], 19, 20, 21, 23[2], 19:4, 11, 20[2], 24, 29, 31, 32, 20:2[2], 3[2], 5, 6, 9, 10, 11, 12, 13, 15, 16, 22, 24, 27, 21:4, 10, 11, 14, 17, 21[2], 24, 22:2, 8, 16, 18, 21[2], 33, 23:9, 11, 20, 22, 28, 37[2], 43, 24:2[2], 16[2], 17, 19, 20, 21, 23, 25:9, 15, 16[3], 25, 26[2], 27, 28[2], 30, 38[2], 39, 46, 47, 50[2], 26:1, 5, 8, 21, 37, 44[2], 27:8, 14, 16, 17, 18, 19, 20, 24[2], 25, 27[2], 29, NUM. 1:3[2], 18, 20[3], 22[3], 24[3]

NUM. 1:26[3], 28[3], 30[3], 32[3], 34[3], 36[3], 38[3], 40[3], 42[3], 45[2], 50, 51[2], 54, 2:10, 18, 34[2], 3:3, 7, 8, 9, 10, 16, 20, 22, 34, 38, 46, 48[2], 51, 4:3, 7, 11[2], 14[2], 15[2], 16[2], 19[2], 20, 23[2], 24, 30, 31, 33, 37, 41, 45, 47, 49[3], 5:1, 8[2], 15, 19, 20, 21[2], 22[3], 24, 26, 27[2], 29, 6:2[2], 4, 10[2], 21, 7:1, 5[3], 7, 89, 8:1, 12, 15, 19[4], 20, 21, 22, 24, 26, 9:3[2], 5, 12, 13, 14[2], 20[2], 10:3, 7, 8, 9, 10, 11, 13, 14, 18, 22, 28, 30[2], 31[2], 33, 35, 11:4, 13, 14, 16, 18[2], 22[2], 23, 25, 12:8[2], 13:16, 17, 21, 26[4], 30, 31, 32, 14:3[2], 4

NUM. 14:7, 14[2], 16, 20, 22, 25, 28, 29, 30, 36[2], 38, 44, 15:3, 12[3], 24, 28, 34, 35, 39, 41, 16:5[2], 7, 9[4], 10, 12, 13, 16, 28, 31, 33, 40[3], 42, 17:2[2], 5[2], 6, 8, 10, 18:6[2], 7, 8, 11[2], 16[2], 19, 24[2], 28, 20:5[3], 8, 12, 17[2], 21, 21:3, 4, 5, 7, 8, 9, 15, 16, 18, 19[2], 20, 23[2], 29, 32, 33, 34, 22:2, 5[2], 11, 13[2], 14, 16[2], 18, 20, 23, 26, 30, 32, 36, 37[3], 38, 40[2], 41, 23:3[2], 11, 12, 14, 17, 20, 23, 24:1[2], 2, 10, 11[2], 12, 13, 14, 25, 25:1, 2, 26:1, 2[2], 18, 22, 25, 27, 37, 43, 47, 50, 53, 54[4], 55, 56

NUM. 26:59, 27:7, 8, 11, 14, 28:2, 7, 22, 30, 29:5, 9[2], 14, 15, 18, 21, 24, 27, 30, 33, 37, 40, 30:2[2], 13, 14, 31:4, 6[3], 13, 16, 21, 27, 28, 36, 50, 52, 32:2, 6[2], 8, 14, 19, 20, 27, 29, 33[2], 39, 33:2[2], 14, 35, 53, 54[3], 56[2], 34:4[5], 8, 9, 10, 11, 12, 13[2], 14[2], 18, 29, 35:2, 3, 5, 6, 7, 8, 11, 16, 17, 18, 21, 24, 25, 30[2], 31, 32[2], 36:2[3], 3[2], 5, 6[2], 7[2], 9[2], DEU. 1:3, 5, 7[2], 8[2], 9, 14, 19, 27[2], 28, 30, 33[3], 35, 36[2], 38, 41[2], 45, 2:4, 15, 16, 18, 22, 24, 25, 27, 31[2], 32, 34, 3:1[2], 3, 7

DEU. 3:8, 12, 24[3], 28, 4:1, 5, 9, 10, 13, 14[2], 19, 20, 25[2], 26[2], 30, 34[2], 36, 38[3], 5:4, 5, 12, 15, 23, 31, 32[3], 6:1[2], 2, 3, 10[4], 19, 20, 23, 24[2], 25, 7:1, 6, 9, 10[4], 11, 12[2], 13, 24, 25, 8:1, 2[3], 3, 6[2], 16, 18, 9:1[2], 4, 5, 6, 7, 8[2], 9, 10, 11, 18[2], 19, 20, 22, 23, 27[2], 28[2], 10:4, 6, 7, 8[4], 10, 11, 12[4], 13, 15, 20, 11:4[2], 8, 9[2], 10, 11, 13[3]:, 16, 21, 22[4], 25, 28, 29[2], 31[2], 32, 12:1[2], 5, 9[2], 10, 13, 14[2], 15, 19, 20, 21, 29, 30, 31[2], 32, 13:2, 3, 5[3], 9[2], 10, 12, 17, 18[2], 14:23[2], 24[2], 15:4

DEU. 15:5[2], 11[2], 15, 18, 16:2, 6, 8, 9[3], 11, 17, 17:6[2], 7[2], 10[3], 11[4], 12, 16[4], 17[2], 19[3], 20[3], 18:5[2], 8, 9, 10, 14, 16, 19, 20[2], 32, 19:2, 3, 5, 8, 9[3], 14, 16, 19, 20:1, 4[2], 5[2], 9, 10, 18, 19[2], 21:1, 5[2], 10, 11, 12, 16, 22[2], 22:2, 4, 6, 7, 14, 16, 21[2], 22, 27, 23:2, 3, 4, 14[2], 19, 20[2], 21, 22, 24:1, 3, 4[2], 5, 6[2], 8[2], 10, 11, 16[3], 17, 18, 19, 22, 25:2[4], 5, 7[3], 8, 11, 19, 26:2, 3, 5, 8, 13[3], 14[2], 16, 17[4], 18, 19, 27:12, 13, 18, 23, 26, 28:1[3], 7, 11, 12[2], 13[2], 14[4], 15[3], 20, 21, 25, 31[2], 44[2], 45

DEU. 28:50, 55, 56, 58, 63[7], 29:1, 4[3], 8[2], 13[4], 18, 19[3], 21, 22, 27, 29, 30:1[2], 2, 6, 10, 12, 14, 18[2], 19, 20[4], 31:4[2], 7[2], 11, 12, 13[2], 16, 21, 24, 28, 29[2], 32:8[2], 13, 16[2], 17[3], 21[4], 26, 30, 35, 40, 41, 43[2], 45, 46[2], 47, 33:7, 9, 17, 24, 34:1, 4, 5, 10, 11[4], JOSH. 1:1, 2[2], 5, 6, 7[4], 8[2], 11, 12[3], 18, 2:1, 2[2], 3[2], 5, 6, 7, 16, 20, 23, 3:1, 2, 5, 7, 8, 13, 14[2], 4:1, 6, 8, 10[2], 11, 13, 18, 21, 23, 5:1, 8, 13, 14, 6:5, 8, 15, 16, 17, 20, 25, 7:2, 3[2], 6, 7[3], 13, 14[2], 19, 8:1, 2, 3

JOSH. 8:5, 8, 9, 10, 12, 14[2], 16, 20[3], 23, 24, 34, 9:1, 2, 3, 6[2], 10[3], 11[2], 12, 13, 16[2], 20, 24[2], 25, 10:1[3], 6, 10[2], 11[2], 12, 13, 15, 18, 19, 20, 21[2], 24, 25, 27, 28, 32[2], 33, 35[2], 37[2], 38, 39[5], 43, 11:1[4], 2, 3[3], 5, 6, 11, 14, 17, 20, 23[2], 12:3[2], 7[2], 13:1, 3, 4, 15, 24, 31, 14:4, 7, 11[2], 12, 15:1, 3[6], 6[2], 7, 8, 9[2], 10[2], 11[2], 12[2], 13[2], 15, 16[2], 17, 18[2], 20, 16:1, 2[2], 3[2], 5, 6[2], 7[3], 17:1, 4[2], 5, 7, 8, 13[2], 14, 15, 17[2], 18:3, 4[2], 6[2], 8[2], 9[2], 10, 11, 12, 13[2], 15, 16[4], 17[2], 19, 20, 21, 28, 19:1[2]

JOSH. 19:8[2], 10, 11[2], 12[2], 13[4], 14, 16, 17[2], 22, 23, 24, 26[2], 27[4], 29[4], 31, 32[2], 33, 34[5], 39, 40, 47, 48, 49, 50, 20:2, 21:2[2], 12, 13[2], 21, 27, 32, 33, 38, 43, 44, 45, 22:5[6], 7, 9[3], 10, 12[2], 13[2], 15[2], 16, 18[2], 23[3], 24[2], 26, 27[2], 28[3], 29, 31[2], 32, 33[2], 23:1, 4, 6[4], 7, 9, 12, 14, 15, 16, 24:1, 4, 5, 9, 15, 16, 22, 29, 33, JUD. 1:1, 7, 9, 12[2], 13, 14[3], 23, 28[2], 34[2], 36, 2:1[2], 4, 6, 12, 19[3], 22, 3:1, 2, 4[2], 6[2], 9, 10, 18, 27, 28, 4:5, 7, 9, 10, 12, 17, 18[2], 19, 22, 5:3, 11, 16, 23[2], 26[2], 29

JUD. 5:30[2], 6:5, 7, 11, 22, 25, 29, 31, 35, 7:2, 3, 5, 6, 9, 10[2], 11, 17, 20, 22[2], 25, 8:1, 3, 4, 8, 27, 33, 35[2], 9:1, 3, 7, 8, 9, 10, 11, 13, 16, 21, 24, 26, 29[2], 31, 33, 36, 43, 48, 49, 50, 51[2], 52, 53, 10:9, 12, 18[2], 11:3, 4, 5, 8, 9, 10, 12[2], 16, 20, 24, 27, 33, 34[2], 35, 36[2], 39[2], 40, 12:1[2], 3, 5, 13:5, 7[2], 9, 11, 12, 17, 20, 21[2], 23, 25, 14:1, 2, 3, 5[2], 8[2], 9, 10, 11[2], 15[4], 17[2], 19[2], 20, 15:1[3], 2, 4, 6, 10[4], 11[2], 12, 17, 16:1, 3, 4, 5, 6[2], 8, 16, 19, 21, 22, 23[2]

JUD. 16:25 17:3[2] 4 8[3] 9 11 13 18:1 2[4] 7[2] 8 9[3] 10 14[2] 15 17 19[2] 22 30 19:1[2] 2 3[3] 5[2] 7 8 9[3] 12 13[2] 14 15[3] 18[3] 22 25[2] 27 20:1 3 4[2] 5 8 9 10[3] 13[2] 14[2] 18[2] 20[2] 21 23 25 28[2] 31[3] 36 39 40[2] 47 48[3] 21:1 2 3[2] 4 5[3] 7 8[4] 12 13[3] 18 21[2] 22 23 24[3]

RUTH 1:1[2] 7 8 12 16 17 18 19[3] 22 2:2 3 8 10 12 15 17 18 19[2] 20[2] 23 3:2 3 6 7 8 11 13[2] 16[2] 17 4:1 4[2] 5 6 7[2] 10[2] 15 17

1 SAM. 1:3[2] 4[2] 6 7 8[2] 12 19[2] 20

1 SAM. 1:21 25 28[2] 2:6 8[2] 10 11[2] 15[2] 16 19[3] 20 24 28[4] 29 33[2] 35 36[2] 3:2[2] 3 6 8 11 15 17 19 20[2] 21 4:1 3 4 9 12 16 18 19 5:3 4[2] 10[5] 11 12 6:2[2] 3[2] 4[2] 7 9[2] 10 12[3] 13 16 18[2] 20[2] 21[2] 7:1 2 5 6 7 8[2] 10 14 16[2] 17 8:1 4 5 6 8 11 12[3] 13[2] 14 15[2] 16 19 22 9:3 5[2] 6 7[2] 8[2] 9[2] 10 11[2] 12[3] 13[2] 14[2] 16[2] 17 18 19[2] 21 26[2] 27[2] 10:1 2[2] 3[3] 5[3] 8[4] 9[2] 10 11[2] 13 14[3] 17 20 21 24 25 26 11:3[2] 4 9[2] 10 11 12 13[2] 14[2]

1 SAM. 11:15 12:3 7[2] 17 20 22 23 13:2 4 5 7 8[2] 9 10[2] 12 13 14 17 18[3] 20[2] 21 22 23 14:1[2] 4 6[3] 7 9 12 19 20 21 25 26 27 30 31 43 45 46 15:1[2] 2 5 6 7 11 12[3] 13 15 16 21 22[2] 27 28 32 34[3] 35 16:1 2[2] 3 4 5[3] 6 9 10 12[2] 13 16[2] 17 21 22 23 17:1[2] 8[3] 9 13[2] 15 17[2] 20[2] 23 25 26[2] 27 32 33[5] 39 40 43 44[3] 45[3] 46 48[3] 49 52[3] 54 58 18:1 2 4[4] 6[2] 8 10 11 17[2] 18 19[3] 21[2] 23[2] 25[3] 26 27[2] 30 19:1[2] 2[2] 4 5 7

1 SAM. 19:10[2] 11[4] 14 15[2] 18[3] 20 22[2] 23[2] 20:5[2] 6 8 9 10 13[2] 17 18[2] 19 21 24 27[3] 28[2] 29 30 33[2] 35 37 38 40 41 42 21:1[2] 2 6 7 10 11 14 15 22:1[2] 3 8 9[2] 11[2] 13 15[2] 17[2] 18 23:3 4 5 6[3] 7 8[4] 9 10[3] 13 15 16 18 19[2] 20[3] 23[2] 24 25 26[2] 24:1 2 3[2] 4 5 6 7 8 9 10 11 16 17 25:1 5[2] 6[3] 8[2] 9[2] 14 17 22 23 26[2] 29[2] 30[3] 32[2] 33 34 35[2] 36 37 38 39[3] 40[5] 41[2] 44 26:1 2[2] 5 6[5] 7 8[2] 9 10 13 14[3] 15[3] 16 20[2] 23[2] 25[2] 27:1

1 SAM. 27:4 8 9 10 11[2] 12 28:1[2] 2[2] 7[2] 8 9[2] 10[2] 12 14 15[2] 17[3] 19 29:1 4[3] 5 9[2] 11[3] 30:1[2] 3 4 7[2] 9 11 12 13[2] 14 15[3] 19[2] 21[5] 22 24 26[2] 27[3] 28[3] 29[3] 30[3] 31[5] 31:8[2] 9 10 11 12

2 SAM. 1:1 2[3] 14[2] 26 2:1 8 10 12 14 15 19[2] 21[3] 22[2] 23[3] 24 26 29 30 3:5 6 7 8[3] 9[3] 10[3] 12[2] 14[2] 16 17 19[3] 20[2] 23 24 25[3] 27[2] 31[2] 35[3] 37 39 4:2 3 4 5 8[2] 10 5:1 2 3[2] 4 6 8 11 13 17[2] 19 20 24 25 6:2 6[2] 8 9 19[3] 20[3] 21 7:1 3 4 5

2 SAM. 7:6 7 8 11[2] 17[2] 19 21[2] 22 23[5] 24[3] 27[2] 29 8:1 2[3] 3 5 6 7 10[2] 9:9[3] 10 11 10:1 2 3 4 5 14 16 17 19[2] 11:1[2] 2[2] 6 8[2] 9 11[3] 12[2] 13[2] 14[2] 16 27 12:4[3] 5 6 9[3] 10 14[2] 17[2] 18[2] 20 22 23[2] 27 29 13:1 2[2] 4 5 6 7[2] 8[2] 10 11 12 13 23 24 25 30[2] 33[2] 36 37 38 39 14:2[2] 3 4[2] 6 7 8 10 11[2] 15 16 17 19[2] 20[3] 22[2] 23[2] 24[2] 25[2] 29[3] 31 32[3] 33[3] 15:1 2 3 5[2] 6[2] 7 8 9 13 14 15 16 19[2] 22 26 28 29 32[3] 34 35 16:2[2]

2 SAM. 16:3 4 5 10 11[2] 15 16 17[2] 21 17:6 9 11[2] 13 14[2] 15 17 18 20[3] 21 23[2] 24 25[2] 27[2] 29 18:11 17 18 21 22 24 28 32 33 19:5 8 11[6] 12 13[2] 15[5] 16 18 19 20[2] 21 22[2] 25[3] 26 28 31 34 37 38 40 41 42 20:1[2] 2 3 4 5 6 7 9[2] 10[2] 13 14 15 18 19 21 22[2] 21:2[2] 9 10 16 17 18 20 22 22:4 7 21 25[2] 31 35 40 42 44 51[2] 23:5 9 10 13 16 21 23 37 24:1 2[2] 4 6[4] 7[4] 8 13[2] 15 16[2] 18 19 21[2]

1 KINGS 1:3 4 5 8 21 23

1 KINGS 1:31[2] 33[2] 35 38[2] 44 47 48 51 52 53[3] 2:3[2] 4[2] 5[2] 6[2] 7 8[4] 9[2] 13 14 17 19 21[2] 23 24 26[2] 28 30 32 39 40[3] 41 42 44[3] 3:4[2] 5 6 7 9[2] 11 12 14 15[2] 18 21 25 28 4:10 11 12[2] 13[2] 15 24 25 28 34 5:2 5 6[2] 7 8[2] 9 10 11[2] 14 17 18 6:1 3 11 12 19 38 7:7 8 14[3] 16 18 23 32 36 41 42 45 50 8:6 10 11 13 16[2] 17 18 25[2] 28[4] 30 32[3] 33 36 39[2] 43[3] 44 46 52 53 54 56 58 61[2] 64 9:1[3] 3 4[2] 5 8 10 11 12 14

1 KINGS 9:15 19 21 28[2] 10:1 2[2] 6 9[2] 10 13 14 16 17 24[2] 27[2] 11:2 4 11 13 15[2] 17 18[2] 19 21[2] 22[2] 24 25 29 31[4] 33[2] 36 37 38 40 12:1[3] 2 5 7 9 11 12[2] 14[2] 16[2] 18[4] 20 21[4] 23 24[4] 25 27[2] 28[2] 30 13:1 4[2] 5 10 11 17[2] 20 22 23[2] 26 27 29[3] 31[2] 32 34[2] 14:2[3] 3 4[3] 5[2] 6[2] 8 9[2] 12 13 15[2] 16 17[2] 18 21[2] 22 24 25 15:4[2] 17[2] 18 21 25 26 27[2] 29[2] 30 33 34 16:1 2[3] 7 8 11[2] 12 13[2] 15 18[2] 19[2] 21 23 26[3] 29 31[3] 33[2] 34 17:1 4 7 9[3] 10[3]

1 KINGS 17:11[2] 15 16 17 18[4] 24 18:1[2] 2 5 6 9 10 12 15 16[2] 17 19 27 29[2] 31 36 40 42[3] 43 44 45[2] 46 19:2[2] 3[2] 9 10 14 15[2] 16[2] 17 20 20:2 4 6 9 12 22 26[3] 30 31 33[2] 35 42 43[2] 21:1 2 3 4 5 8 10 14 15[3] 16[4] 17 18[2] 20[2] 22[2] 25 26 27 28 22:2[2] 4[3] 5 6 12 13 15[2] 17 24 25 26 29 32[2] 33 36[2] 37 41 42 48[2] 51 52 53[2]

2 KINGS 1:3[3] 6[2] 7 9 10 16[2] 17 2:1 2[2] 3[2] 4[2] 5[2] 6 7 9 11 15[3] 18 20 22 25[2] 3:1 3 5 7[2] 10

2 KINGS 3:12 13[4] 15 20 21[2] 23 24 26 27 4:1 5 6 8[3] 10 12 13[3] 14 16 17 18[2] 19[2] 20 22 23[2] 24 25[3] 26 27[3] 29 31 35 37 38 39 40[2] 44 5:5 6[2] 7 8[2] 10 11 13 14 15 16 17 18 21 22 24 26[3] 6:4 7 10 18[2] 19[2] 20 22 23 24 28[2] 30 31 32[3] 7:1 3 5[2] 6[2] 8 9 10 11 12[2] 16 17[2] 18[3] 8:1 3[2] 5[5] 7 9[2] 14[3] 15 16 17 19[2] 21 25 26 28 29[2] 9:1 2 4 5[2] 10 11[2] 12 15[3] 16[2] 17 18[3] 19[2] 22 23 25 26 27[2] 28 29 30 32[2] 35 10:1[3] 2 5

2 KINGS 10:6[4] 7[3] 9[2] 12 13 15[3] 17[3] 19[3] 21 24 25[4] 29[2] 30 31[2] 32 11:4 9[3] 10 11 13 19 21 12:1 4[2] 5 8[2] 11 12[4] 14 15 17[2] 18 20 13:1 2 7 16 21 14:2 3 5 8 9[4] 10 11 12[2] 13 14 16 19[2] 22 23 24 25 28 15:1 2 3 4 9 12 13 16 17 18 19 20[2] 23 24 27 28 29 32 33 34 37 16:1 2 3[2] 5[2] 6[2] 7 8 9 10[4] 11 12 15 16 17:1 4[2] 5 11[2] 13[2] 14 17 23 26 31 35[2] 17 36 37 18:1[2] 2 3 4 6 8 9 14[2] 16 17[2] 18[2] 19 22 23[2]

2 KINGS 18:25[2] 26 27[4] 29 31[2] 32 37 19:1 2 3[2] 4 5 6 7[2] 9 10 11 16 20[2] 21 23[2] 25[2] 35 37 20:1 2 4[2] 10 21:1 6[2] 7[2] 8[3] 9 11 14 15 16[2] 19 22:1 2[2] 3[2] 4 5[2] 6 8 9 11 13 15 17 18[3] 23:3[2] 4 5[6] 6 8 9 10[2] 11 15[2] 16 19[4] 20 23 25 29 30 31 32 33 34[2] 35[4] 36 37 24:2[2] 3[2] 7 8 9 12 15[2] 16 17 18 19 20 25:1 6[2] 7 11 12 13 20 23[2] 24[3] 25 26 27[2] 28

1 CHRON. 1:10 2:21 23 35 4:27 35 39[2] 42 5:1 2[2] 18[3] 20 26 6:19 32 49[2]

1 CHRON. 6:56 57 62 64 7:2 11 15 21 22 23 40[2] 8:6 9:1 9 22 25[2] 27 29 32[2] 10:4 8 9[2] 11 12 13 11:1 3[3] 4 5 10[2] 13 15[2] 18[2] 21 23 25 31 12:1[2] 8 15 16 17[4] 18 19[4] 20[2] 22[2] 23[6] 24 31 32 36 38[3] 13:2 3 5 6[4] 9 10 11 12 13[2] 14:1[2] 8 11 15 16 15:2[2] 3[2] 14 15[2] 16[3] 19 21 25 26 29[2] 16:3[2] 4 5 7 15 17[2] 20[2] 21 23 25[2] 33 35 37 38 40[3] 41[2] 43[2] 17:1[2] 3[2] 4 5[2] 6[2] 10 11[2] 15[2] 17[2] 18 19 20 21 24 25 27 18:1 3 5 7 10[3] 19:1 2[4] 3[4]

1 CHRON. 19:5 6[2] 7 15 16 19 20:1 2 3 4 21:1 2[4] 3 4 6 11 12[2] 15[2] 17 18[2] 21[3] 22 23 24 25 30 22:2[3] 4 5 6 7[2] 8 9 13 17 19[4] 23:4 5 11 13[3] 28 30[2] 31[2] 24:3 4 7[2] 8[2] 9[2] 10[2] 11[2] 12[2] 13[2] 14[2] 15[2] 16[2] 17[2] 18[2] 19[2] 25:1[2] 2 3[2] 5[2] 6 9[2] 10 11 12 13 14 15 16 17 18 19 20 21 22 23 24 25 26 27 28 29 30 31 26:12 13 14 15[2] 16 27 31 32 27:1 23 24 28:1 2 4[2] 5 6 7 10 11 15 20 29:2[2] 3[2] 4 8 9 20 22

2 CHRON. 1:2[3]

2 CHRON. 1:3 4 6 8 11 13[2] 2:1 2 3[3] 4[5] 6[2] 7[2] 8 9[2] 10 11 12 14[4] 16[3] 18[3] 3:1 2 4 8[2] 11[2] 12[2] 4:2 6 7 11 12[2] 13 16 5:2 7 11 13[3] 14 6:4 5 6 7 8[2] 16[3] 19[3] 20 22 23 24 25[2] 31 33[2] 34 38 7:3 6 7 10[2] 11 12[2] 13 17 18 20 21 8:1 2[2] 3 6 8 13 14[4] 17[2] 18[2] 9:1[2] 5 8[4] 11[2] 12[2] 13 14 16 18[2] 21 23 26 10:1[3] 2 3 6[2] 7[2] 9[2] 11 12[2] 15 16[3] 18[4] 11:1[3] 2 3 4 13 14 16[3] 18 22[2] 12:1 2 4[2] 5[3] 7 10 13[3] 14 13:1 5[4] 8

2 CHRON. 13:9 11 12 13 15 14:4[2] 15 15:2 5[2] 9 12 13 16:1[2] 2 5 7 9[2] 12[2] 17:4 5 7[7] 14 15 18:2[4] 3 4 5[2] 11 12[2] 14[3] 15[2] 16 17 23 24 25[2] 28 29[2] 31[3] 32 33 19:1[2] 2[2] 3 4 6 8 10 20:1[2] 3 4[2] 6 7 11[3] 12 16 17[2] 18 19 21 22[3] 23[2] 24 25 27[3] 28 31 36[3] 37[2] 21:3 4 5 6 7[3] 11 12 13[2] 19 20 22:1 2 3 4 5 6[2] 7[2] 8[2] 9[2] 23:2 7 8[3] 9 10 12 13 15 17 18 24:1 4[2] 5[3] 6[2] 9[2] 11[2] 12[3] 14[2] 17 19[2] 22 23[2] 25:1 3[2] 5[3] 7[2] 8 9[3] 10[3]

2 CHRON. 25:11 13 14[2] 16[2] 17 18[4] 19[2] 21 22[2] 23[2] 24 27[2] 26:2 3 4 5 8[2] 11[2] 13 14 15[2] 16[2] 18[3] 19 20 23 27:1 2 8 28:1 5 7 8 9 10 13[3] 15[5] 16 23 25[2] 29:1 2 8[3] 10 11[2] 15[2] 16[2] 17[2] 18 20 21 24 25 27 30 32 34 30:1[4] 2 3 5[3] 6[2] 7 10[2] 11 13 16 17 19[2] 20 22 23 24[2] 27 31:1[2] 2[4] 3 4 7 10[2] 11 14 15[4] 16 17 18 19[3] 21 32:1 2 3 5 6[2] 8[2] 9 11[2] 13 14 15 17[2] 18[2] 20 21 23[2] 24 25 30 31[2] 33:1 6[3] 7[2] 8[2] 9[2] 10[2] 11 13 14

2 CHRON.
33:16
18
21
34:1
2[2]
3[2]
7
8
9[2]
10[2]
11[3]
15[2]
16[2]
17
19
21
22[3]
23
25
26
28[2]
31[3]
32[3]
33
35:2
4[2]
5
6
7[2]
8[2]
10
12[2]
13
15
16[3]
18
20
21[3]
22
23
24
25
26
36:2
4[2]
5
6[2]
7
9
10
11
15
18
20[2]
21[2]
23

EZRA
1:2
3
5[2]
2:68[2]
3:1
2
4
6
7[4]
8
9
10
4:2[2]
3[2]
5
8
12
14
17[2]
21[2]
22[2]
23[2]
5:2
3[3]
5[2]
8
9[2]
10
13
17[3]
6:5
8
9
12[4]
13
14[2]
17
21
22
7:6
8
9[3]
10[3]
13[2]
14[2]
18[3]
20
21
22[3]
24
26[3]
27
28
8:15[2]
17
21
22[2]
30[2]
31

EZRA
8:32
36
9:1[2]
6[2]
7[4]
8[3]
9[4]
11[2]
12
10:3[3]
5[2]
8
10
13
16

NEH.
1:1
4
9
11[2]
2:1
4
6
7
8[3]
9
10
11
12
13
14[2]
16[5]
19
3:2
5
16
19[2]
21
31
4:1
5
6
7[2]
8[3]
10
11
12
14[2]
15[3]
16
19[2]
22
5:5
8
11
12
13
14
19
6:1
2
3
6[2]
7[7]
10[2]
11
14
16
19[2]
7:1
3
5
6[2]
63
70
71
8:1[2]
6
7
8
12[4]
13
15
9:8
12
15[2]
16
17[5]
19[2]
20
23[2]
26[2]
27
28
36
10:29[3]
31
32
33
34[2]
35
36[2]
37
38
11:1[2]
2
3
17
12:22
24[3]
27[3]
44
45
13:3
5[2]
7

NEH.
13:10
13[2]
19[2]
22[2]
24
26
27[2]
28

ESTHER
1:1
6
7
8[3]
9
11[3]
12
13
15
16[3]
17
20[2]
21
22[3]
2:3
8[3]
9[2]
11
12[4]
13
14
15
18[2]
21
22
3:4[2]
6[2]
7[3]
8
9[2]
11[3]
12[5]
13[5]
14
15
4:4[2]
5[3]
6
7[3]
8[6]
11[4]
12
13
14[2]
16
17
5:1
2
3
5[2]
6
8[3]
12
14[2]
6:1
3
4[2]
6[4]
7
8
9[4]
10[2]
11
12[2]
13
14
7:1
2
4[3]
5
7[2]
8:3
5
6[2]
7
9[6]
11[7]
13[2]
9:1[3]
2
13[3]
14
19
21
22[3]
23
24[3]
27[2]
29
30
31
10:3

JOB
1:4[2]
5
6
7
11
15
16
17
19
2:1[2]
2
3
5

JOB
2:8
11[3]
3:8
20
23
4:2
12
14
20
5:1
4
11[2]
26
6:7
9
14
18
24
26
7:1
3[2]
4
5
9
10
20
8:5[2]
8
22
9:14
15
18
19
26
10:19
21
11:6
12:3
4
5
8
22
24
13:3[2]
6
12
23
25
26
14:15
18
21
15:8
20
24
28
16:8
11
12
17:5
14[2]
16
18:11
14
19:3
17
20[2]
20:2
3
6
10
18
23
21:4
13
30[2]
31
32
22:3[2]
7[2]
14
19
23
23:2
3
24:5
7
10
12
17
21
25:5
26:4
10
28:3
11
24
25
28
29:7
10
11
12
13
15[2]
16
30:1
6
10
21
22[2]
23[2]
24
29[2]
31
31:3[2]
5

JOB
31:7
11
12
16
23
24
28
30[2]
32
36
39
32:1
10
11[2]
19
22
33:1
6
22
23
24
25
30[2]
32[2]
34:4
11[2]
16
18[3]
19
28
31
33
35:2
9
36:2
3
6
10
27
32
37:6[3]
15
38:12
14
20[2]
26[2]
27[3]
34
37
40
39:9
11
17
21
40:19
41:10
13
16
17
31
32[2]
42:7
8

PSALMS
4 *title*
5 *title*
1
6 *title*
6
7:2
6
8[2]
9
17[2]
8 *title*
6
9 *title*
2
6
8
11
20
10:9
14
17
18
11 *title*
1[2]
12 *title*
13 *title*
14 *title*
2
15:3
4
5
16:2
3[2]
10
17:11
14
18 *title*
3
20[2]
24[2]
30
34
38
40
50[4]
19 *title*
4
5
10
20 *title*
4
21 *title*

PSALMS
21:11
22 *title*
7
11
15
19
29
30
23:2
25:7
27:2
4[2]
13
28:1[2]
3
4[3]
29:6
9
30:1
3
7
8
9
12[2]
31 *title*
2[2]
11
32:10
33:10
11
13
16
18
19[2]
34:9
16
35:4[2]
11
12
23
24
26
36 *title*
2
3[2]
10
12
37:5
7
8
14
32
34
38 *title*
17
22
39 *title*
1
4
11
40 *title*
4
5
8
12
13[2]
14
41 *title*
6[2]
13
42 *title*
4
43:3
44 *title*
7
9
10
13[2]
20
25
45 *title*
17
46 *title*
9
47 *title*
6
48:1
10
13
49 *title*
4
7
10
11
18
19
50:4[2]
8
11[2]
19
22
23
51 *title*[2]
1
6
8
52 *title*[2]
3
53 *title*
2
5
54 *title*[2]
2
55 *title*
1
2
56 *title*

PSALMS
57 *title*
58 *title*
5
7
59 *title*[2]
4
5[2]
60 *title*[2]
1
2
3
4
61 *title*
2
62 *title*[2]
4
9
12[2]
63:2
9
64 *title*
3
8
65 *title*
4
8
66 *title*
4
8
9
12
19
67 *title*
1
68 *title*
4
16
33
69 *title*
10
11
16
20
21
23
26
70 *title*[3]
1[2]
2
71:1
2
3
13
18[2]
72:3
8
15
73:1[2]
10
16
24
28[2]
74:7
14[2]
75 *title*
4
9
76 *title*
7
8
9[2]
11
12
77 *title*[2]
2
6
9
78:1[2]
4[2]
5
6[2]
10
13[2]
16
24
25
26
48[2]
50[2]
52
54[2]
55
58[2]
63
66
71
72
79:2
3
4[2]
11[2]
13
80 *title*
3
5
7
9
19
81 *title*
11
82:3
83:9[2]
12
17
84 *title*
7
10

PSALMS
85 *title*
4
5
8[2]
86:5
6
11
87:4
88 *title*
10
15
89:1
4
7[2]
8
19
29
33
39
40
41
42
43
44[2]
90:2
3
11
12
15
91:11
92:1[2]
2
15
94:1[2]
2
95:1
7
96:2
4[2]
13
98:9
100:5
101:3
102:4
5
13
18
20[3]
21
22
103:8
10
17
18[3]
104:9
11
14
15[2]
23
26
29
33
105:8
10
13[2]
14
22
25[2]
39
106:8
23
26
27[2]
29
45
46
47[2]
48
107:4
7
8
12
15
21
23
26[2]
27
31
36
38
40
109 *title*
12
16
26
31
111:4
112:9
113:3
6
9[2]
115:16
116:17
118:8[2]
9[2]
19
119:4
5
9
25
27
31
35
36
38
41
42

PSALMS
119:49
58
60
62
76
91
95
103
112
121
126
128
132
135
149
154
156
159
169
170
121:3
122:4
124:6
125:4
127:2[3]
130:2
132:4[2]
17
133:1
2
135:7
136:3
4
5
6
7
8
9
10
13
14
16
17
25
137:6
7
8
139 *title*
12
140 *title*
4
11
141:4[2]
143:1
3[2]
8[2]
9
10
144:1[2]
4
11
14
145:3
4
8
9
12[2]
18
146:7
147:1
6
9[2]
18
149:7
8
9
150:2

PROV.
1:2[2]
3
4[3]
6
16[2]
2:2
7
12
13
14
16
3:2
8
15
18
22
27[2]
28
32
4:1
8
9[2]
16
20
22
27
5:1
5
13
6:4[2]
6
10
18
24
26
29
30
7:8

PROV.
7:15[2]
21
22[2]
23
24
25
27[2]
8:4
7
9[2]
11[2]
13
21
29
9:4
7
9
15
16
10:3
16[2]
23[2]
26[3]
29[2]
11:1
17
18
19[2]
20
24
29
12:4
6
8
20
21
22
13:5
14
18
19[2]
21
22
25
14:8
15
22
23
27
29
34
15:8
18
21
24
26
28
16:5
7
12[2]
16[3]
17
19[2]
23
24[2]
30[2]
32
17:4[2]
15
16[2]
21
23
25[2]
26
18:5
9
18
19
19:6
7
10
11
23
24
27[2]
20:2
3
10
13
17
25[2]
21:3[2]
5[2]
6
7
9
15[3]
20
25
22:1
7
9
16[3]
19[2]
20
21
25
27
23:1
2[2]
4
7
12
21
30
24:1
8

PROV.
24:9
11[2]
12[2]
13
20
21
23[2]
25
29[4]
33
25:2[2]
8[3]
9
10
13
20
21[2]
24
25
27[2]
26:4
5
8
11
15[2]
17
21[3]
27:1
4
7
14
19[2]
21
23[2]
24
28:10
17[2]
20
21
22
29:7
12
15[2]
27[2]
30:14
17
23
31:3
4
6
8
15[2]
19
20[2]
25
27

ECCL.
1:5
6
11
13[3]
16
17[2]
2:1
3
6
11
12
14
15[2]
16
20[2]
21
26[5]
3:1[2]
2[4]
3[4]
4[4]
5[4]
6[4]
7[4]
8[2]
10[2]
11
12[2]
14
15
20
21
22
4:10[2]
14
5:1[3]
2
4
6[2]
11
12
13
15
18[3]
19[4]
6:2[2]
6
8
7:2[5]
9
11
12
14
25[4]
27
8:1
2
3
6

ECCL.
8:8[2]
9
11
14[2]
15[3]
16[2]
17[3]
9:1
2[3]
3
4[2]
10
11[6]
10:1
3
10[2]
15[2]
16
11:2[2]
7
12:5
7
12

CANT.
1:7
9
2:3
4
3:11
4:6[2]
5:2
5[2]
6
6:2[3]
11[2]
7:7[2]
8
9
12
8:2
11
13[2]
14

ISAIAH
1:11
12
14
16
17
2:2
3[2]
19
20[3]
21[2]
22
3:4
8
10
12
13[2]
15
24
4:1
3
5:1
4
5[2]
8[2]
22[2]
26
7:1[2]
3
7
13
15
16
18
21
22
23
8:2[2]
4
8
10
11
12[2]
14[2]
19
20[3]
21
22
9:2
7[2]
16
10:2[2]
3
6[7]
7
11
12
20
26
27
28[2]
30
31
11:10
11[2]
16
13:5
9
10
11
14
16
18

ISAIAH
13:20
22
14:1
2
3[2]
9
11
12
15[2]
16
19
24
15:1[4]
2[3]
7
16:1[2]
4
10
12[3]
17:4
7[2]
8
11[2]
12[3]
18:1
2
6
7
19:3[4]
14
18
19[2]
21
22
23
20:4
6
21:2
11
14
16
22:1
4
5
7
8
10
12[4]
13
20
21[2]
23
24
23:1
6
7
9[2]
11
12
13
15[2]
17[2]
18[2]
24:2
9
16
18
20
25:2
4[2]
11
12[2]
26:5[2]
8[2]
10
14
21
27:6
7
9
12
13
28:1[2]
2
6[3]
9
11
12[2]
17[2]
19
20
21
24
29:1[3]
11
12
14
15
20
24
30:1[2]
2[3]
4
6
7[2]
8
10[2]
11
13[2]
14[2]
21[2]
28[3]
29[2]
30
31:1[2]
4
9

ISAIAH
32:4
5
6[4]
7
33:1[3]
4
34:1
2
5
10
12
14
17
35:4
10
36:1
2
4
6
7[3]
8[2]
10
11
12[4]
14
16[2]
17
22
37:1
3[2]
4
5
7[2]
9[2]
10
11
17
21
22
24[2]
26[2]
35
38
38:4
5
10
12
13
16
17
19
20[2]
22
39:1
5
6
8
40:2
14
16
17
18
20
22
23
25
29[2]
41:1
2[3]
6
22
23
27[2]
42:1
2
5
7[2]
8[2]
9
10
17
23[2]
24
25
43:6[2]
14
20[2]
23
24
28[2]
44:13
15
19[2]
26[2]
27
28[2]
45:1[4]
9
10
11
16
18
24
46:1[2]
4[2]
5
8
11
47:7
8
9
11
14[2]
15
48:3
5[2]
17

ISAIAH
48:18
20
21
49:5[3]
6[3]
7[3]
8[2]
9[2]
18
20
21
22[2]
23
50:1
2[2]
4[4]
6
8
51:1[2]
4
6
8
10
13
18
23[2]
52:2
5
8
53:1
6
7
10[2]
54:3
4
16
55:1
4[2]
7
10[2]
13
56:3
6[3]
7
8
9
10
11
12
57:1[2]
6
7
8
9
11
15[2]
18
19[2]
21
58:2[2]
4[2]
5[4]
6[3]
7[3]
10
12
14
59:7[2]
18[4]
20
60:3[2]
4
8
9[2]
61:1[5]
2[2]
3[2]
11
62:8
11
63:1
5[2]
6
7[3]
10
12
14[2]
17
64:2[3]
7
65:3[2]
5
10
12[2]
24
66:2[2]
5
6
8
9[3]
12
15
19[3]
20
23[4]

JER.
1:2
7
8
10[2]
12
19
2:1
7
18[4]
24

JER.
2:27[2]
28
33
36
3:1
3
5
9
12
13
3:14
15
16[2]
17[2]
18
4:3
4
7
9
11[3]
16
22[2]
5:1
3[2]
7
19
31
6:1
2
6
10
13
17
19
20[2]
7:1
2
6
7[2]
10
12
14[3]
16
18[4]
19[2]
27
30
31
34
8:5
6
10[2]
14[2]
19
9:3
5
6
8
12
15
21
10:5
7
10
13
20[2]
22
23
24
11:1
2
4
5
8
10[3]
11
13[4]
15
17[2]
19
12:9
11
12
13
14
15[3]
16[3]
13:2
4
6[3]
7
10[3]
11[2]
16
18
21
23
14:1
3[2]
8
10
16[2]
15:2[5]
3[3]
4
5
8[2]
9
10[2]
11
13
14
18
20[2]
16:5
7
8[3]

JER.
16:9
10
21[2]
17:3
4
10[3]
16
21
24[3]
27
18:1
2[3]
3
4[2]
5
7[3]
8
9[2]
11[3]
15[2]
16
18
19[2]
20[2]
21[2]
22
23
19:5
7[2]
9
11
12
14[2]
20:3
4[2]
5
6[2]
15
17
18
21:2
3
9
14
22:1
3
8
16
17[2]
20
27[2]
23:3
13
21
22
27[3]
28
32
35[2]
37
24:1
6
7
9[2]
10
25:1
2
4
5
6[3]
7[2]
12
14[2]
15[2]
17
18[2]
28[2]
29
31[2]
32
35[2]
26:2[2]
3
4[2]
5[2]
6
8[3]
11[2]
12[2]
16[3]
17
18
19
20
21[2]
24[2]
27:2
3[6]
4
6
8
9[5]
10
12[2]
16[3]
18[2]
20
22[2]
28:1
3
4
6
9
15
29:1[4]
3
4

JER.
29:6
7
8[2]
10[2]
11
14
18[3]
19
20
24
25[2]
27
31[3]
32
30:1
3[3]
8
11
13
21[2]
31:2[2]
6
9[2]
12
15[3]
17
18
21
28[3]
32[2]
38
39
32:1
4
5
7
8[2]
11
19[3]
22[2]
23[2]
24[2]
29[3]
30
31
32[2]
33
34
35[4]
37
40
41
44
33:2
5[2]
7
9
11
12
14
15
17
18[3]
21
23
26[2]
34:2
3[2]
8
9
11
12
15
17[6]
20
22[2]
35:2
8
9[2]
10
11[2]
13[2]
14
15[3]
19
36:1
3
8
9[3]
16
20
21
23
25
26
27
29[2]
30[3]
32
37:3
7[4]
11
12[2]
13
14[3]
20[2]
38:2
4
8
9[2]
11
15
16
18
19
21
22

JER.
38:23^{2} 25 26^{3} 27 39:4 5^{2} 7^{2} 9 11 12 40:1 4^{3} 5^{2} 6 7 8^{2} 9^{2} 10 12^{2} 13^{2} 14 15 41:1^{2} 4 5^{2} 6^{3} 10^{3} 12 13 15 17^{2} 42:4^{2} 5^{3} 7 8 9 11^{2} 12^{2} 15^{2} 16 17^{2} 21 22^{2} 43:1^{2} 2^{2} 3^{3} 4 5 7 11^{3} 14 44:1 3^{4} 5^{2} 7^{3} 11 12^{2} 14^{2} 17^{2} 18^{3} 19^{2} 20^{3} 24 25^{2} 28 45:3 46:1 3 13 16^{3} 19 47:1 3 4^{2} 48:4 9 11 12 15 16 32 33 35^{2} 39 49:2 3 9 10^{2} 12 14 24 28 29 34 37 39 50:5^{2} 6 9 16^{2} 19 21 27 28 29^{2} 33 34 39 42 51:9 11 16 24 27 30 31^{3} 32

JER.
51:35^{2} 40 49 53 61^{2} 62 63 52:1 2 3 4 9 11 15 17 26^{2} 27 31

LAM.
1:2 4 11 12 14^{2} 15 17 19 2:2 4 6 8^{2} 10 12 13^{3} 14 17 20 3:13 25 30 32 34 35 36 37 40 64 4:2 3 4 8 5:2^{2} 6^{3} 13 19

EZEKIEL
1:1 9 11^{2} 20^{2} 2:3^{2} 5^{2} 6^{2} 3:2 3 11 15 16 18^{2} 26^{2} 4:3 4 5 8 9 10 11 5:1^{2} 7 13 16 19 6:3^{3} 13 7:3 8 9 13 14^{2} 21 24 27 8:1 3^{3} 4 7 14 17^{3} 9:1 3^{2} 5 8 10:5 6 11 16 11:13 16 24 12:2^{2} 3 12 13^{2} 14

EZEKIEL
12:17 23 25 26 27 13:5 6 13 14 16^{2} 18^{3} 19^{3} 20^{2} 21 14:4^{2} 7^{2} 12 15 19 21 15:3 6 7 16:2 4 5 7 17 20 21^{2} 23 25^{2} 26^{2} 33^{2} 34 41 42 55^{3} 17:3 4 9 12 17 20 24 18:3^{2} 6 7^{2} 9 10 12 15 16 24 30 19:3 6 9 12 14^{2} 26 28 35 42 44^{2} 47^{2} 20:1^{3} 3 4 6 8 10 12 13 21^{2} 26 28 31 32 37 42 21:3 4 7 10 11^{2} 17 19 20^{2} 21 22^{6} 23^{2} 24^{2} 28 29 30 31 32 22:3 4^{2} 6^{2} 9 12 18 20^{2} 27^{3} 23:15^{2} 17 19 21 24 27 32 37^{2} 39^{2} 40 46

EZEKIEL
23:48^{2} 24:6^{2} 7 8^{2} 9 13 14^{3} 17 19 24 26^{2} 27 25:4 7^{2} 14^{2} 15 26:1 3 5 11 13 14 15 17^{2} 20 27:5 7 9 19 30 28:8 17 18 25 29:5^{2} 6 7 14 16 17 18 21 30:9 10 11 13 20 21^{5} 22 31:1 2 14^{3} 15^{2} 16^{2} 18 32:1 4 6 12 14 17 20 21 24 25 27 29 30 33:2 8 9 12 13^{2} 21 22 27^{2} 30^{2} 33 34:2 5 8 10 13 15 18^{2} 25 26 28 35:11^{2} 12 36:4^{7} 5 6^{3} 8^{2} 12 15^{2} 19^{2} 20 27 28 33 37 37:2 5 7 9 12 17 22 38:9 10 11^{2} 12^{3} 13^{4} 16 18 20

EZEKIEL
39:2 3 4^{2} 11 13 14^{2} 17^{2} 24^{2} 28 40:4^{2} 13 16^{3} 23 24 26^{2} 27 28^{2} 29 31 32 33 34 35^{2} 36 37 39 40 46^{2} 48 49 41:1 7 16 17 42:11^{2} 12 14 19 20 43:1 3^{3} 10 14^{2} 18^{2} 19^{2} 44:3 6^{2} 7^{2} 11^{2} 12 13^{3} 15^{3} 16^{2} 17 19 20 23 24 25 27 30 45:4 8^{2} 15 17^{2} 23 25^{4} 46:5^{2} 7 9 11^{5} 14 17^{3} 18 20 21 47:3 4^{2} 5 6^{2} 9 10^{3} 11 12 13 14 15 19^{2} 21 22^{2} 23 48:1^{3} 28

DANIEL
1:2 4 7^{3} 10 11 12^{2} 14 2:2^{2} 3 4 5 9 12 13 14^{2} 15^{2} 17^{2} 21 24 26^{2} 28 29^{3}

DANIEL
2:30^{2} 34 35 39 43 44 45^{2} 3:2^{2} 4 9 13 16^{2} 17 19 20^{2} 26 4:2 3 8 11 17^{2} 18 19^{2} 20 22 25^{2} 26 27 31 32^{2} 34 35 37 5:1 2 7^{2} 8 16 28 6:1 3 4 6 7^{2} 8 12 14^{2} 18 20^{3} 7:4 5 6 11 13 22 25 26 27 8:2 4 6 7^{2} 10^{2} 11 12 13^{2} 15 16 23 25 9:2 3 4^{2} 6^{2} 7^{2} 8^{4} 9 10 16^{2} 17 21 22 23 24^{6} 25 27 10:6 7 12^{2} 13 14 20 11:1 3 4^{2} 6^{2} 10 14 15 16 17 18 21^{2} 25 27^{2} 28 34 35^{2} 36 39 44^{2} 45 12:1^{2} 2 3 4^{2} 6^{2}

DANIEL
12:7 12

HOSEA
1:2 4 5 2:1 7 9 10 11 13 18 21 23 3:1^{2} 2 4:6 10^{2} 12 15 17 5:2 4 5 6 12 13^{2} 14 15 6:3 7:10^{2} 11^{2} 16 8:1 5 9 11^{2} 12 13 9:3 4 10 12 13 10:1^{2} 3 6 8^{2} 11^{2} 12^{2} 11:2 3 4 5 7^{2} 9 12:2^{2} 6 7 9 14 13:2 6 14:2 3 8

JOEL
1:1 19 2:2 9 12 13 17 23 25 28 32 3:4 8^{2} 11 12^{2} 18 20

AMOS
1:6^{2} 9 2:4 7 8 10 12 3:10 14 4:1 4 7^{3} 8 10 12 5:2 3 5^{2} 6 7 16^{2} 18 26 27 6:1^{2} 2^{2} 3 5^{2}

AMOS
6:9 10 13 7:2 4 10^{2} 14 8:4^{2} 9^{2} 12^{4} 9:2

OBADIAH
3 5^{2} 7 9 14 21

JONAH
1:2 3^{4} 4 5 6 7 13^{2} 17 2:5 6 3:3 4 5 7 4:2 3 4 6^{2} 8^{4} 9^{3}

MICAH
1:1 7^{2} 9 13^{2} 14^{2} 2:1 6^{2} 7 3:1 8^{2} 4:1 2^{2} 3 8 10^{2} 5:2 10 6:8^{3} 14 7:1 9 11 12^{4} 15 20^{2}

NAHUM
1:3 2:5 3:1 7

HABAK.
1:3 6 8 13 17 2:1 6^{2} 8 9^{2} 10 12 15 18 19^{2} 3:9 14^{2} 19^{2}

ZEPH.
1:8 10 12 18 2:15 3:1^{2} 2 4 5 8^{3} 9^{2} 16^{2} 18 19

HAGGAI
1:1 4 6 8 9 16^{2}

HAGGAI
2:2^{3} 5 16 17 21

ZECH.
1:6^{3} 10^{2} 11 16 21^{4} 2:2^{2} 3 4 9 11 3:1 4 7 4:2 4 5:3^{2} 10^{2} 11 6:7^{4} 14^{4} 15 7:1 2 3^{2} 5^{2} 9 11 13 8:1 10 12 14^{2} 15^{2} 16 19 20 21^{3} 22^{2} 23 9:10^{2} 12^{2} 10:1 6 11:9 13 17 12:9^{2} 13:1^{2} 2 3 4^{2} 5 8 14:2 5 6 7^{2} 10 13 16^{4} 17 18 19

MALACHI
1:1 2:2^{3} 5 8 15 16 3:1 5^{2} 10 14 16 4:6^{2}

MATT.
1:11 12 17 18 19^{2} 20 2:1 2 8 12 13^{2} 16 19 22 3:5 7^{3} 9^{3} 11 13^{2} 14^{2} 15^{2} 4:1 3 16 17^{2} 5:13^{2} 17^{2} 22 23 24 25^{2}

MATT.
5:28 39 41 42 44 45 6:1^{2} 5 16 18 24 30^{2} 7:2 4 5 8 11^{2} 12^{2} 13 15 18 20 21 22 28 8:4 9^{3} 10 25 28 29^{2} 31 33 34 9:2 5^{2} 6^{2} 7 10 13^{2} 14 16 24 28^{2} 29 32 10:1^{2} 6 13 17 21^{3} 22 28^{2} 34^{2} 35 42 11:1^{3} 5 7^{2} 8 9 14 15 20 23 27 12:1 2 4 10 12 13 18 25 32 39 42 46^{2} 47 13:3 9 11^{2} 12 13 17^{2} 30^{2} 31^{2} 43 48 53 14:4 5 7 9 11^{2} 15 16 18 19^{4} 22^{2} 23 29^{2} 30 15:1 5 20 26^{3} 31^{4} 32 33 35 36^{2} 16:3 5^{2} 11 21 22

MATT.
16:27 17:4 9 14^{2} 16 17 19 20 24^{2} 27 18:7 8^{2} 9^{2} 11 17^{2} 21 24 25^{3} 34 19:1 3 5 7^{2} 8 10 11 12 14 21 24^{2} 20:1 15 18^{2} 19^{4} 20 22^{2} 23^{3} 28^{3} 21:1 9 14 15 19 21 28^{2} 30 33 34 43 44 46 22:3^{2} 5^{2} 8 9 11 13 17 23 34 46 23:1^{2} 4 5 7 13 15 23^{2} 34 24:1 6 9 17 18 19 21 31 43 45 49^{2} 25:1 6 9 10^{2} 11 15^{4} 27^{2} 45 26:1 2 8 9 16 17^{2} 18 22 26 27 45 49 53 55^{2} 57 58 59^{2} 61^{2} 73 74^{2} 27:1^{2} 2 3 4^{2} 6 7 14 15 19

MATT.
27:24 26 31 32 33 34 46 48 49 51 58^{2} 60 28:1^{2} 8 9 14 20

MARK
1:7 9 17 24^{2} 34 40^{2} 44^{2} 45^{3} 2:2 9^{3} 10^{2} 15 17^{2} 18 23^{2} 26^{2} 3:4^{4} 7 9 10 14 15^{3} 21 4:1 3 4 9 11 21^{2} 23 24 25 33 34 41 5:7 14 15 16 17^{2} 19 20 32 37 38 40 43 6:2 7 18 21 27 28^{2} 31 34 36 37^{2} 39 41^{3} 45^{3} 46 53 55 7:2 4 5 11^{2} 12 16 27^{2} 30 32 34 37^{2} 8:1 2 3 6^{3} 7 13 14 22^{2} 26^{2} 31 32 9:5^{2} 6 14 15 18 22 23 32 33 35 41^{2} 43^{2} 45^{2}

MARK
9:47^{2} 10:1^{3} 2^{2} 4^{2} 7 12 13 14 17 21 24 25^{2} 28 30 32^{2} 33^{3} 40^{3} 41 42^{2} 45^{3} 46 47 49 50 11:1 7 13 15^{2} 21 23 27^{2} 28 12:1^{2} 2 12 13 14^{2} 17^{2} 23 33^{2} 36 38 13:5 9^{2} 12^{3} 14 15 16 17^{2} 21 22 27 29 34^{3} 14:1 5 8^{2} 10 11 14 19^{2} 21 22 23 32^{2} 33^{2} 40 45 48 53 55^{2} 64 65^{4} 69^{2} 70 71^{2} 72 15:1 8^{2} 15^{2} 18 20 21 23 36^{2} 38 45 16:8 9

LUKE
1:1 3^{2} 8 9^{2} 16 17^{4} 19^{2} 20 23^{2} 25 27^{2} 38 41 43^{2} 49 50 55^{3} 56 59^{2} 62 72^{3} 73 76 77 79^{3} 2:1

LUKE
2:3 5 10 14 15^{3} 22^{4} 23 24^{2} 27 29 32 38 39^{2} 41 42 44 45 46 51 3:7^{4} 8^{3} 11 12 14 16 21 23 4:6 9 10 16^{2} 18^{7} 19 20 21 31 34^{2} 41 43 5:1 7 11 12 14^{2} 15^{2} 17^{2} 18^{2} 21 23^{2} 24^{2} 26 32^{2} 6:1 2 4^{2} 6 8 9^{4} 11 12^{3} 17 19 26 27 29 30 31^{2} 33^{2} 34^{4} 35 38 42 47^{2} 7:2 4 6 7 8^{2} 10 11 12 15^{2} 19 22 24^{2} 25 26 31 32^{2} 36 38 40 42 43 44 45 47 49 50 8:1 4 10^{2} 14 18^{2} 19 20 22 24 25 27 28 29 31 32 35^{2} 37 39

LUKE
8:40 49 51 53 55 9:1 2^{2} 9 10 12 13 14 16^{3} 17 18 21 23 28^{2} 33^{2} 37 40 42 45 51^{3} 52 53 54 56^{3} 57 58 59 62 10:5 6 7 15^{2} 19 22^{2} 24^{2} 25 29 30 34^{2} 35 38 40^{2} 11:1 4 6^{2} 10 13^{2} 14 17 26 27 29 30 31 37^{2} 42^{2} 46 53 54 12:1 5 12 13 17 19 21 25 26 28 32 37^{2} 39 41 42 45^{3} 47 48 49 50 51 54 55 58^{3} 13:12 14 15 24^{2} 25^{3} 26 32^{2} 33^{2} 14:1^{2} 3 6 7 8 9 17^{2} 18 19 21 23 26 28^{2} 29^{2} 30^{2} 31^{2} 35 15:1 12^{2} 14 15^{3} 17^{2}

LUKE
15:18 19 20 21 22 24 25 29 16:3 4 7 9 11 13 17^{2} 21 22 26^{2} 27 17:3 4 7 11^{2} 14 18^{2} 22 23 31 33 18:1^{3} 10 13 14 16 18 25^{2} 30 31 33 35 40 19:3 4^{2} 5^{2} 7 8 9 10^{2} 11 12^{2} 14 15^{3} 19 24 28 29^{2} 35 37 45 47 48 20:1 9^{3} 10 16 18 19 22 27 30 33 35 46 21:7 9 12 13 14 15 16^{2} 21 23 28^{2} 29 31 34 36^{3} 38^{2} 22:5 6 15 23 31 33^{2} 39 44 45 47 52 23:2^{3} 4^{2} 5 7 8^{2} 12 15 20^{2} 25 30^{3} 32^{2} 33 36 43 48 51 56 24:4

LUKE
24:5 9 11 12 13 15 17 18 20^{2} 21 24 25 26^{2} 29 30^{2} 32^{2} 33 34 46^{2} 50 51 52

JOHN
1:7 8 12^{3} 19 22 27 31 33 38 42 47 2:2 4 7 12 13 3:2 13 17 20 21 23 26^{2} 33 4:5^{3} 7 8 10^{2} 11 15 20 23 28 32 33^{2} 34^{2} 35 38 52 5:1 7 10 16 18 26^{2} 27 35 36 40 45 6:6 11^{2} 15 17 24 31 35 37^{2} 38 44 52 68 7:1 4^{2} 19 20 24 25 30 32 45 50 8:6 26^{3} 27 31 33 37 40 41 56 59 9:11 13 26^{2} 10:3 10 18^{2} 24 29 31 38 11:7

JOHN
11:8 15 19^{2} 31 38 45 46 53^{2} 54 55^{2} 56 12:1 5 10 12^{2} 13 20 21 29 38 47^{2} 13:2 3 5^{2} 6 10^{2} 12 14 15 19 24 26^{2} 29 33 35 14:2 18 21 26 29^{2} 15:25 16:5 10 12^{2} 13 16 17 19 28 32 17:1 4 11 18:6 13^{2} 14 20 31^{3} 36 37 19:4 7 10^{2} 12 16 20 21 23 27 29 33 39 40 20:2^{2} 3 4 8 15 16 17^{3} 21 27 21:1 6 9 11 14 15 16 21 22 23

ACTS
1:1 3^{2} 6 7 16 19 22 25 2:4 7 12 14 17 21 27 28 30^{2} 37 38^{4} 39^{2} 45 46 47

ACTS 3:2, 3, 5, 12, 13, 14, 23, 26, 4:5, 9, 10, 15, 16[2], 17, 18, 19, 23, 24, 28[2], 5:2, 3[3], 9, 13, 14, 20, 21[2], 28, 29, 31[3], 32, 33[2], 34, 35[2], 36[3], 38, 39, 40, 41, 42, 6:4[2], 7, 10, 12, 13, 7:5[3], 7, 13, 14, 17, 19, 23, 26, 30, 31, 33, 34, 35[2], 38[2], 39, 40, 42[2], 43, 44, 46, 54, 60, 8:2, 3, 5, 10[2], 11, 24, 25, 27[2], 29, 30, 32, 36, 38, 40, 9:2[2]

ACTS 9:4, 5, 6, 10, 13, 14, 15, 23, 24, 26[3], 27[2], 29, 30[2], 32[2], 35, 37, 38[3], 40, 43, 10:2[2], 3, 5, 6, 8, 9, 11, 13, 21, 22[2], 28, 32, 33[2], 36, 40[2], 42[3], 43, 48[2], 11:2, 3, 5, 13, 15, 18, 19, 20, 25[2], 26, 28, 29[2], 30, 12:1, 3, 4[4], 10, 11, 12, 13, 17[2], 19[2], 20, 13:2, 4, 5, 7, 8, 10, 11, 13[2], 14, 19, 22[2], 23, 24, 25, 26, 31, 34[2], 35, 42, 43[2], 44

ACTS 13:46[2], 47, 48, 14:1, 3, 5[2], 9, 11, 16, 20, 21[3], 22, 23, 24, 26[2], 15:2, 4, 5, 6, 10[2], 12, 14, 15, 19, 22[2], 24, 25, 28[3], 29, 30, 34, 37, 38[2], 16:1, 3, 4, 6, 7[2], 8, 9, 10[2], 11[2], 12, 13, 15[2], 16[2], 18[2], 20, 21[2], 22, 23, 30, 32, 36[2], 39, 17:1, 5[2], 7, 14[2], 15[2], 16, 18, 20, 21[2], 23, 25, 26, 29, 30, 18:1, 2, 5, 7, 9, 10, 12, 13[2], 14, 15, 19, 20

ACTS 18:22, 24, 26, 27[2], 19:1[2], 13, 17, 21[2], 27, 36[2], 40, 20:1, 3[2], 6, 7[2], 13[2], 14, 15, 16[2], 17, 18, 20, 21[2], 24, 26, 27, 28[2], 30, 31, 32[3], 34, 35[4], 21:1, 3, 4[2], 7, 12[2], 13[4], 15, 17, 21[3], 23, 25, 26, 31, 33, 34, 37, 39, 22:2, 3, 5[3], 6, 9, 10, 12, 17[2], 24, 25, 30, 23:1, 3[3], 9, 10[3], 14, 15[3], 17, 18[3], 19, 20[2], 22, 23[2], 29[3], 30[3], 31, 32[2], 33[2], 35, 24:2, 6[3], 8

ACTS 24:10, 11[2], 16, 17[2], 19, 23[2], 25, 27, 25:1, 3[2], 6, 9[2], 10[2], 11, 13, 15, 16[5], 17, 19, 20, 21[3], 22, 24, 25[2], 26[2], 27[3], 26:1, 3[2], 7, 9[2], 10, 11, 12, 14[2], 16, 18[3], 20[2], 21, 22, 23, 28, 29, 27:2, 3[2], 5, 12[4], 16, 21, 22, 27, 30, 31[2], 33, 34, 35[2], 39, 40, 42, 43[2], 44[2], 28:4, 6, 8[2], 13[2], 14, 15, 16[2], 17, 19[2], 20[2], 22, 23[2]

ROMANS 1:1, 3, 4[2], 5, 7[3], 10

ROMANS 1:11[2], 13, 14[4], 15[2], 16[3], 17, 22, 23[2], 24[2], 28[3], 30, 2:2[2], 4, 6[2], 7, 10[3], 16, 3:15, 19, 25[2], 26, 4:1, 2, 4, 5, 8, 9, 12, 13[2], 16[4], 18, 20, 21, 22, 23, 24, 5:7, 10, 14[2], 16, 18, 6:2, 11, 16[3], 19[3], 22, 7:1, 2, 3[2], 4[3], 5, 10[2], 18, 23, 8:1, 6[2], 7, 12[2], 15, 18, 20, 23, 27, 28[3], 29[2], 31, 33, 38, 39, 9:3, 4, 11, 15, 20, 21, 22[3], 26, 30, 31, 10:1, 2

ROMANS 10:3, 4, 6, 7, 19, 21, 11:1, 2, 4[2], 5, 11, 13, 14, 23, 24, 25, 35, 36[2], 12:2, 3[5], 6[3], 9, 10, 13[2], 16, 17, 13:2, 3[2], 4[2], 7[5], 8, 10, 11, 14, 14:1, 4[2], 6[3], 7[2], 9, 11[2], 12, 13, 14[3], 18, 21[2], 22, 15:1[2], 2, 5[2], 7, 8, 9, 12, 14, 15, 16, 17, 18[2], 20, 21, 22, 23, 24[3], 25, 26, 27, 28, 30, 16:17, 25[4], 26[2], 27, *subscr.*

1 COR. 1:1, 2[2], 17[2], 18, 19

1 COR. 1:21, 27[2], 28[2], 2:1, 2, 6, 12, 3:2, 5, 8, 10, 18, 22, 4:5, 6[3], 7, 8, 9[3], 14, 18, 19, 5:5, 9, 11[2], 12[2], 6:1, 2, 3, 4[2], 5[2], 6, 7[2], 16, 7:1, 2, 5, 8, 9, 11, 12[2], 13, 15, 17, 25, 26, 27, 32, 39[2], 8:2, 6, 8, 9, 10[2], 13[2], 9:2, 3, 4[2], 5, 6, 15, 20, 21[3], 25, 26[2], 27, 10:6, 7[2], 13[3], 15, 19, 20[2], 22, 27[2], 31, 32[3], 11:2, 6, 7, 10, 15, 16

1 COR. 11:20, 22[3], 29, 33, 12:3, 7[2], 8[2], 9[2], 10[5], 11, 13, 21, 22, 23, 24, 13:3[2], 12, 14:3, 6, 8, 9, 12, 22[2], 28[2], 30, 32, 34[2], 35, 37, 39, 15:3, 4, 9, 24, 34[2], 38, 54, 57, 16:1, 3, 7, 12[2], 15, 16, *subscr.*

2 COR. 1:2, 4, 8, 12, 13, 15, 16[3], 17, 23, 2:1, 3, 6, 7, 9, 10[2], 12[2], 14, 16[2], 3:1[2], 3, 4, 5, 7, 13, 16, 18, 4:2, 3, 6[2], 15, 5:2, 8[2], 10

2 COR. 5:12[2], 13, 18[2], 19[2], 20, 21, 7:3[2], 9, 10[2], 11, 14[2], 8:1[2], 3, 4, 5, 7, 8, 10[2], 11, 12[2], 13, 16, 19, 24, 9:1[3], 2, 5, 8[2], 9, 10, 11[2], 10:2[2], 4, 5, 6, 7, 13[3], 14, 15, 16[3], 11:1, 2[2], 7, 8, 9[2], 15, 32, 12:1[2], 2, 4, 6[2], 7[2], 11, 13[2], 14[4], 13:1, 2[2], 3, 7, 10[3], *subscr.*

GAL. 1:3, 4, 5, 10, 16, 17[2], 18[2], 2:1, 2, 3, 4, 5, 6[4], 8, 9[2], 10, 11[3], 14[2]

GAL. 2:17, 19, 3:5, 6, 10, 16[3], 18, 19, 22, 24, 29, 4:5, 9[2], 15, 18, 20[2], 21, 24, 25, 5:3[2], 13, 17, 6:3, 8[2], 12[2], 13, 16

EPHES. 1:1[2], 2, 5[2], 6, 7, 9, 11, 12, 16, 19[2], 21, 22[2], 2:2[2], 7, 15, 17[2], 3:2, 7, 9, 10, 11, 16[2], 18, 19, 20[2], 4:3, 7, 14[2], 16, 19, 22, 27, 28[2], 29, 32, 5:2, 12, 19[2], 21, 24, 27, 28, 6:4, 5[2], 7[2], 11, 13[2], 16, 19, 20, 21

EPHES. 6:23

PHIL. 1:1, 7, 16[2], 19, 20, 21[3], 23, 24, 26, 28[2], 29, 30, 2:6, 11, 13, 19, 23, 25[3], 30, 3:1[3], 7, 13, 21[2], 4:11, 12[6], 17, 18, 19, *subscr.*

COLOS. 1:2, 3, 4, 9[2], 11, 12, 20, 22, 23, 25[3], 26, 27, 29, 2:2, 14[2], 17, 20, 22, 23, 3:9, 15, 16, 17, 21, 22, 33, 4:3, 4, 6, 10, 17[2], *subscr.*

1 THESS. 1:2, 7, 8[2], 9[2], 10[2], 2:2, 4, 8, 15, 16[3], 17

1 THESS. 3:1, 2[2], 4, 5, 6[2], 9, 12, 13, 4:1[2], 4, 9, 11[3], 13, 17, 5:9[2], 12, 13, 15

2 THESS. 1:3, 6[2], 7, 10[2], 12, 2:13[3], 14, 3:7, 8, 9[2], *subscr.*

1 TIM. 1:3, 4, 7, 10, 11, 15, 16[2], 18, 20, 2:4, 6, 12[3], 3:2[2], 3, 5, 8, 13, 14, 15, 4:1, 3[3], 4, 8, 13[3], 15[2], 5:4[2], 11, 13[2], 14[2], 17, 18[2], 19, 24, 6:3[3], 16, 20, *subscr.*

2 TIM. 1:1, 2, 4, 5, 8, 9[2]

2 TIM. 1:10, 12, 2:2[2], 4, 8, 14, 15[2], 20, 24, 25, 3:2, 7[2], 15, 16, 4:3, 6, 8, 9, 10, 11, 12, 14, 16, 18, 21

TITUS 1:1, 3, 4, 7[2], 9[2], 14, 2:3, 4[3], 5[2], 6, 9[2], 11, 3:1[5], 2[2], 5, 7, 8, 12[3], 14, *subscr.*

PHILE. 2[2], 8, 11[3], 13, 16, 19, *subscr.*

HEB. 1:5[2], 13, 14, 2:1[2], 3, 4, 5, 10, 11, 15, 17[3], 18, 3:2, 5, 7, 13, 15, 18[2], 4:1, 6, 7[2], 9

HEB. 4:11, 12, 13, 16, 5:1, 3, 5[2], 7, 11[2], 12, 14[2], 6:5, 6[3], 8, 10[2], 11, 13, 16, 17, 18[2], 7:2, 5[2], 13, 23, 25[3], 27, 8:3[2], 4, 5[3], 9[2], 10[2], 11, 12, 13, 9:9, 11, 13, 14[2], 19[2], 24, 26, 27, 28, 10:1, 2, 7, 9, 15, 19, 20, 24[2], 31, 32, 39, 11:6[2], 7, 8, 11, 15, 16, 19, 20, 24[2], 25[2], 29, 32, 34, 35, 12:11, 19, 22, 23[3], 24[2], 13:2, 8, 10, 14, 15[2], 16[2], 18, 19[2]

HEB. 13:21[2], *subscr.*

JAMES 1:1, 5, 12, 19[3], 21, 26, 27[2], 2:3[2], 5, 8, 9, 16, 3:2, 10, 17, 4:2, 5, 7, 8[2], 9[2], 12[2], 13[2], 15, 17[3], 5:16, 17

1 PETER 1:1, 2, 3, 4, 5, 12, 13[2], 14, 17, 2:4, 5[2], 8, 13[2], 15, 18[3], 23, 24, 3:1, 7, 15[2], 18[2], 4:2[2], 3, 4, 5[2], 6[3], 9, 10, 11, 12, 13, 19[2], 5:1, 3, 5[2], 11

2 PETER 1:1, 3, 5[2], 6[3], 7[2], 10, 12, 13, 15, 17

2 PETER 2:4[2], 8, 9[3], 10, 12, 13, 17, 21[2], 22[3], 3:9[2], 13, 15, 16, 18

1 JOHN 1:9[2], 2:6, 3:5, 16, 4:10, 14, 16, 5:11, 14

2 JOHN 8, 12[3]

3 JOHN 4, 5[2], 8[2], 9, 13, 14[2]

JUDE 1, 3[2], 4, 7, 13, 15[2], 24[2], 25

REV. 1:1[2], 4[2], 6, 8, 12, 13, 2:7[2], 12, 14[3], 17[2], 19, 20[4], 21, 23, 26, 27, 3:2, 7, 9[2], 10, 18, 20, 21[2], 4:3, 8, 9, 11, 5:2[2], 3[2], 4[3]

REV. 5:5[2], 9[3], 12, 6:1, 4[2], 8, 16, 17, 7:2[3], 10, 14, 8:2, 6, 13[2], 9:1, 5, 6, 9, 10, 14, 15, 10:4, 5, 7[2], 11:6[4], 9, 10, 12, 13, 17, 18, 19, 12:2, 4[3], 5[2], 12, 14, 15, 17, 13:3, 4, 5, 6, 7[3], 12, 14[3], 15, 16, 17[3], 14:4, 6[2], 7, 15[2], 18, 15:8, 16:1, 6, 8, 9, 14[2], 19, 17:17[2], 18:6[2], 17, 19:7, 8, 10, 17, 19, 20:8[3], 12, 13, 21:10, 15, 17, 23, 22:6, 8, 12, 14, 16

unto

1519

GEN. 1:9, 28, 2.19, 22, 24, 3:1, 2, 4, 6, 9, 13, 14, 16, 17, 19[2], 21, 4:3, 4, 5, 6, 7, 9, 10, 12, 13, 15, 18, 19, 23[2], 6:1, 4

GEN. 6:13, 20, 21, 7:1, 5, 9, 15, 8:9[2], 12, 13, 20, 9:1, 8, 17, 24, 25, 10:1, 19[2], 21, 25, 30, 11:4, 31, 12:1[2], 4, 6, 7[2], 8[2], 11, 18, 13:3

GEN. 13:4, 8, 10, 14, 17, 18, 14:6, 14, 15, 21, 22, 15:1, 4, 5, 7, 9, 10, 13, 18[2], 16:2[2], 3, 4, 6, 8, 10, 11, 13, 17:1, 7, 8, 9

GEN. 17:15, 17, 18, 21, 23, 18:1, 6, 7[2], 9, 10, 13, 14, 21, 27, 29, 30, 31, 33, 19:3, 5[2], 6, 8[2], 12, 14[2], 16, 18, 19, 20, 21, 31[2], 34

GEN. 19:37, 38, 20:5, 6, 9[2], 10, 13, 14, 16[2], 17, 21:1, 3, 5, 7, 8, 10, 12[2], 14, 17, 22, 23[2], 27, 29, 30, 22:1, 3, 5, 7, 11, 12, 15

GEN. 22:19, 20, 23:3, 5, 13, 14, 15, 16, 18, 20, 24:2, 3, 4, 5[3], 6, 7[3], 10, 12, 14, 20, 24[2], 25, 29, 30, 36, 38[2], 39, 40, 42, 45[2], 47

GEN. 24:48, 50, 54, 56, 58, 60, 65, 25:5, 6[2], 12, 17, 18, 23, 33, 26:1, 2, 3[2], 4, 9, 10, 16, 24, 27, 29, 32, 33, 35, 27:1[2], 6[2], 13, 18

GEN. 27:19, 20, 21, 22, 26, 31, 32, 34, 37[2], 38, 39, 42, 28:1, 4, 5, 9, 22, 29:4, 5, 6, 15, 20, 21[2], 23, 24, 25, 30, 34, 30:1, 3, 4

GEN. 30:14, 15, 16, 17, 25[2], 27, 29, 30, 40, 31:3, 4, 5, 11, 12, 13[2], 14, 16, 24, 29, 39, 43[3], 46, 52, 55, 32:3, 4, 9[2], 10, 16, 18, 19

GEN. 32:27, 32, 33:1[3], 9, 13, 14[2], 16, 34:1, 3[2], 4, 6, 9[2], 11[3], 12, 14[2], 15, 16, 17, 20, 22, 23, 24[2], 35:1[3], 2, 3, 4, 7, 9, 10, 11, 17

GEN. 35:20, 27[3], 29, 36:5, 37:2, 4, 6, 10, 13[2], 18, 22, 23, 26, 29, 30, 35, 36, 38:2, 8[2], 9, 12, 14, 16[3], 18, 39:8, 10, 14[4], 17[3], 19, 40:6, 8[2]

GEN. 40:12, 13, 14[2], 16, 20, 21, 41:8, 9, 13, 14, 15, 17, 24, 25, 28[2], 32, 38, 39, 40, 41, 44, 50[2], 55[2], 56, 42:1, 7[3], 9[2], 10, 12, 14[2], 18

GEN. 42:20, 22, 23, 25, 28[2], 29[3], 31, 33, 34, 36, 37, 43:2, 3[2], 5, 8, 9, 11, 13, 23, 29[2], 32, 34, 44:4[2], 6, 7, 8, 10, 15, 16, 17, 18

GEN. 44:20, 21[2], 22, 23, 24, 27, 32[2], 45:1, 3, 4, 9[2], 10, 12, 17[3], 18, 24, 25, 27, 46:1, 2, 15, 18, 20[2], 25[2], 28[2], 29, 30, 31[4], 34, 47:2, 3[2]

GEN. 47:4, 5[2], 8, 9[2], 15, 17, 18[2], 19, 23, 24, 26, 29, 31[2], 48:2, 3[2], 4, 5[2], 7, 9[2], 10, 11, 13, 15, 17, 18, 21[2], 49:1, 2, 6, 10, 11[2]

GEN. 49:13, 15, 26, 28, 29[2], 50:4, 12, 15, 16, 17[3], 19, 20, 21, 24[2]

EXOD. 1:9, 10, 18, 19[2], 2:9, 10, 11, 20, 23, 25, 3:2, 4, 8[3], 9, 10

EXOD. 3:11[2], 12, 13[4], 14[3], 15[4], 16[2], 17[2], 18, 4:1[2], 2, 4, 5, 6, 9, 10[2], 11, 15, 16, 18[2], 19, 21, 22, 23, 30, 5:1, 3, 4[2], 15, 16, 21, 22

EXOD. 6:1, 2[2], 3[3], 6, 8, 9[2], 10, 11, 12, 13[4], 28, 29[2], 30, 7:1, 2, 4, 7, 8[2], 9[2], 10, 13, 14, 15[2], 16[2], 19[2], 22, 8:1[2], 5, 8, 9, 10

EXOD. 8:12 15 16[2] 19 20[2] 9:1[2] 8[2] 12[2] 13[2] 22 27 29[2] 33 10:1[2] 3[2] 5 6 7[2] 8[2] 9 10 12 21 24 25 28 11:1 5 8[2] 9[2] 12:1 2 3 4 14 21 23 26 29 36 42 43 49 13:1 2 3 5 8 9 11 12 14 14:1 2 10 11 13 15[3] 22 24 26 29 15:1[2] 11 13 25 16:1 3 4 6 9[2] 10 11 12 15 20 23[2] 25 28 33 35 17:2 4[2] 5 9 14 18:5 6[2] 8 13 14 15[2] 16 17 19[2] 22 26 19:3[2] 4[2] 5 6[2] 8 9[3] 10[2] 12 14 15 21[2] 23 24[2] 25[2] 20:4 5 6 19 20 21

EXOD. 20:22[2] 23 24[2] 26 21:6[2] 8 9 11 31 32 34 22:7 8[2] 9 10 11 12 17 20[2] 23 26 27 29 31 23:13 14 22[2] 23 27 31[2] 33 24:1[2] 5 12 14[3] 16 25:1 2 22 25 33 34 26:24 33 27:21 28:1[2] 3[2] 4 12 28 29 35 41 42 43[3] 29:1[2] 4 17[2] 18[2] 25 28 34 35 41 42 30:3 10 11 12 14 15 16 17 20 22 23 30 31[2] 32 34[2] 36 37 38 31:1 12 13 14 18 32:1[2] 2[2] 3 7 9 13[2] 14 17 19 21[2] 23 24 25 26[2] 27 30[2] 31 33 34[2] 33:1[4] 3 5[3] 7 8 11[2] 12[2] 15 17 34:1[2]

EXOD. 34:2 4[2] 7 15 16 25 26 27 31[2] 34 35:1 4 5 22 29 30 36:2 3 5 10[2] 13 37:26 38:4 39:21 31 33 40:1 12 13 15 32

LEVIT. 1:1[2] 2[3] 9 13 15 17 2:1 2 8[3] 9 11 12 14 16 3:3 5 6 9 11 14 4:1 2 3 4 12 31 35 5:6 7 8 12 14 15 16 18 6:1 2 5 6[2] 8 9 11 15 17 19 20 21 22 24 25 7:5 11 14 18 20 21 22 23 25 28 29[3] 32 34[2] 35 38 8:1 3 4 5 7 21 28 31 9:2 3 4 6 7[2] 8 9 12 13 18 23

LEVIT. 10:3 4 6[3] 8 11 12[3] 19 11:1[2] 2 4 5 6 10 11 12 20 23 26 27 28 29 35 38 12:1 2 6[2] 13:1 2 9 16[2] 49 14:1 2 23[2] 33[2] 15:1 2[2] 14[2] 26 29[2] 16:1 2[2] 18 22 29 31 34 17:1 2[4] 4[3] 5[4] 6 7[2] 8 9[2] 12 14 18:1 2[2] 19 19:1 2[2] 4 5 21[2] 23 25 34 20:1 2 3 4 16 24[2] 26 21:1[3] 2[2] 3[2] 6 7 8 16 17 23[2] 24[2] 22:1 2 3[2] 12 13 14[2] 15 17 18[4] 21 22[2] 24 26 27 29 23:1 2[2] 6 8 9 10[4] 12 13 14 15 16[2] 17 18[2] 21 22 23 24

LEVIT. 23:25 26 27[2] 32[2] 33 34[2] 36[3] 37 38 39 41 44 24:1 2 3 7 9 11 13 15 25:1 2[3] 4 5 8[2] 10[4] 11 12 13 14 15[2] 16 27[2] 28 39 40 41[2] 47 49 50[2] 51 52[2] 55 26:1 5[2] 9 14 16 18 21[2] 23 24 27 28 31 40 41 27:1 2[2] 3 5 6 9[2] 11 13 14 15 16 18[2] 19 21 22 23[3] 24 28[2] 30 32

NUM. 1:1 48 50 2:1[2] 5 3:5 6 9[2] 11 13 14 40 44 48 51 4:1[2] 9 17[2] 19[2] 21 27 30 35 39 43 47 5:1 4 5 6 7[2] 8[2] 9 11 12[2] 15 19 21

NUM. 6:1 2[3] 5 6 8 12 13 14 17 21 22 23[3] 25 7:4 5 6 7 8[2] 9[2] 11 89[2] 8:1 2[2] 4[3] 5 7 12 13 16[2] 19 20[2] 22 23 24 26 9:1 4 7 8 9 10[2] 12 14 21 10:1 4 29[2] 30 32[2] 36 11:2[2] 11 12[3] 13[2] 16[3] 18 20 23[2] 25[2] 26 29 35 12:4[4] 6[2] 11 13 14 13:1 2 17 21 22 23 26[3] 27 32 14:2 3 7 11 13 16 18 19 23 26[2] 28 35 39 40 44 45 15:1 2[3] 3 4 7 8 10 13 14 17 18[2] 19 21 22 24 25 33[2] 35 37 38 39 40 16:3 5[3] 8

NUM. 16:9[2] 15 16 19[2] 20[2] 23 24 25 26 30 32 36 37 38 40 44 46[2] 50[2] 17:1 2 6 9 10 12 13 18:1 2[2] 4[2] 7 8[2] 9 10 11 12 13 15 17 19[2] 20 24[2] 25 26 27 28 30[2] 19:1 2 3 10[2] 21 20:5 6[2] 7 8[2] 10 12 14 16 18 19 22 23 24[2] 25 26 21:2 7 8 16 17 21 24[2] 26 29 30[2] 34[2] 22:4 5 7[2] 8[2] 9 10[2] 12 13 14 16 17[2] 18 19 20[3] 25 28[2] 29 30[3] 32 34 35[2] 36 37[3] 38[2] 39 23:1 3 4 5 6 11[2] 13[2] 15 16 17 18 25 26 27[2] 28 29

NUM. 24:10 11 12[2] 14 25:2 3 4 5[2] 6 8 10 12 16 26:1[2] 52 53 59 60 27:4 6 7 8[2] 9 10 11[2] 12[2] 13 15 18 28:1 2[3] 3[2] 6 7 8 11 13[2] 14[3] 15 19[2] 24 26 27 28[2] 29 31 29:1 2 6[2] 8[2] 12 13 14 36 39 30:1 2 3 31:1 2 3[2] 12[3] 15 21 25 28 29 30 41 43 47 48 49 32:2[2] 5 6 9 11[3] 16 17 18 20 25 29 31 33[2] 38 40 33:7 9 49 50 51[2] 56[2] 34:1 2[2] 5 8 11 13 16 17 29 35:1 2[2] 4 6 8 9 10[2] 12 25 29 36:2 4 8 11

NUM. 36:13

DEU. 1:1 2 3[3] 6 7[3] 8[2] 9 17 20[3] 21 22 24 25 29 35 39 41 42[2] 43 44 45 46 2:1 2 4 5 9[2] 12[2] 14 17 19 22 23 26 27 29 31 35 36[2] 37[4] 3:2[3] 6 8 10 12 13 14[2] 15 16[4] 17 20[3] 21[2] 26[2] 4:1[2] 2 4 7 10 11 12 13 15[2] 19[2] 20 21 23 26 30 31 32 35 42 45 48 49 5:1 9[2] 10 22[2] 23 27[2] 28[3] 31 6:7 10 18 21 23 7:2 3[2] 6[2] 8 12[2] 13 16 18[2] 19 23 25 8:1 18 20 9:3 5 7 10 12 13 19 26 27 10:1[3] 3 4[2]

DEU. 10:7 8[2] 10 11[3] 11:3[2] 4[3] 5 6 9[2] 12 13 21 22 24 25 29 12:4 5[2] 7 11 18 26 31[2] 13:2 3 4 7[2] 8[2] 17 14:2[2] 7 8 10 19 21[3] 25 15:2 5 6 8 9[2] 10[2] 11 12 14 16 17[2] 18 19 21 16:1 2 7 9 10[2] 15 21 17:1[2] 5 9[2] 12[2] 14 16 18:2 3 6 12 14[2] 15[3] 17 18[2] 19 19:5 8[2] 19[2] 20:2 3[2] 5 6 7 8[2] 9 10[2] 11[2] 14 15 18 21:2 3 4 5 6 8[2] 11 13 18 19[2] 20 22:1 2[2] 5[2] 13 15[2] 19 23 24 26 29 23:5[2] 15[2] 18 20[2] 21 23 25 24:9 11

DEU. 24:13 15[2] 25:1 3 5[3] 7[2] 8 9[2] 16 17 26:1 2 3[5] 7 11[2] 12 13[2] 15 17 19 27:2 3 5 6 9 14 15 28:1 2 8 9[2] 11 12[3] 13 15 20 21 26[2] 31 32 35 36 45 60 64 68[2] 29:2[5] 4 7[2] 8 11 13[4] 21 24 26 29[2] 30:2 4 10[2] 12 13 14 18 20[2] 31:1 2[2] 4[2] 5[2] 7[4] 9[2] 14 16 18 20[2] 23 28 32:3 17 22 43 46[2] 48 49 50[2] 52 33:2 7 9 19 26 29[2] 34:1[2] 2 3 4[5] 6 9 10

JOSH. 1:1 2 3[2] 4[2] 6[2] 15 17[2] 18 2:3 4 7 8 9 10 12[2] 16 17

JOSH. 2:18 21 22 24 3:4 5 6 7 9 15 4:1 5[2] 7 8[2] 9 10 12 13 15 18[2] 21 5:2 6[2] 9[2] 13[2] 14[2] 15 6:2 6 7 8 16 19 22[2] 25 7:2 3 5 9 10 19[2] 22 23[2] 24 26 8:1[2] 2[2] 5 18 24 27[2] 28 29 30 31 9:3 6[2] 7 8[2] 9 11 12 15 17 18 19[2] 20 21[2] 22 25[2] 26 27 10:3[4] 4 6 8 9 10 11 14 15 22 23 24[2] 25 28 29 30[2] 31 34 36 41[2] 43 11:6 8[3] 9 14 17 23[2] 12:1 2 3 5 6 7[2] 13:1 3 4 5 6[2] 7 9 10 11 14[2] 15 24[2]

JOSH. 13:25 26 27 29 31 33[2] 14:3 4 6[3] 10 13 14 15:3 4 5 8 9 10[2] 11[2] 13 18[2] 46 47 63 16:1 2 3 5 6 8 10 17:7 9 14 17 18:3 10 18 19:10 12 28 33 20:1 2 4[2] 6[3] 21:1[3] 2 3 8 27 34 43[2] 44 45 22:2 3 4[3] 5 6 7[2] 8[2] 9 10 13 15[2] 19 21 24 31 32 23:1 2 3 4[2] 5 7 8[2] 9 11 12[2] 13 14 16 24:2 4[2] 6[2] 7 10 11 15 19 21 22 23 24 27[4] 28

JUD. 1:3 14 20 21 24 25 33 2:1[2] 3 4 5 6 10 12 15 17[2] 19

JUD. 2:20 3:3 4 9 13 15[2] 17 19 20[2] 26 28 4:3 6 7 8 11 13 14 16 18[2] 19 20 21 22 5:3 18 6:4 6 7 8[2] 10 11 12[2] 13 15 16 17 18 19 20 23[2] 24[2] 25 26 27 30 31 35[3] 36 39 7:2 4[4] 5[2] 7[2] 8 9[2] 11[2] 13[2] 17 19 22 24[2] 8:1 2 5[2] 6 8 9 14 15[2] 18 20 22 23 24 27 35 9:1 5 7[3] 8 9 11 12 13 14 15 16 31 36 38 40 48 52[2] 54[2] 55 56 10:4 10 11 14 15[3] 11:2 6 7[2] 8 9 10 12 13[3] 14 15 16 17[2] 19[2] 22[2] 28

JUD. 11:29 30 32 33 34 35 36[2] 37 39 12:1 2 3 5 6 13:3[2] 5 6 7 8[2] 9 10[3] 11[2] 12 13[2] 15 16[2] 17 18 19 22 23 14:3[2] 10 12[2] 13 14 15[2] 16[2] 18[2] 19 15:7 12[3] 13 14 19 16:1 5[2] 7 9 10 11 12 13[2] 14 15 16 17[2] 18 23 26 28 17:2 3[2] 4 9[2] 10[2] 11 18:1[2] 2 3 4 5 6 8[2] 10 12 13[2] 14 15 18[3] 23[2] 24 25 26 27[2] 29 19:2 3 5 6 9 11 12 13 18 21 23[2] 24[2] 25 28[2] 30 20:1 14 26 32 36 42 45[2] 47 21:1 5 12 13 22[4] 23

RUTH 1:7 8 10[2] 14 15[2] 18 20 2:2[2] 3 4 5 8 9 10 11[3] 13[2] 14 19 20[3] 21 22 23 3:1 3 5[2] 6 13 17 4:1 3 8 9[2] 12 13 14 15 16

1 SAM. 1:3 5 10 11[2] 14 21 22 23 24 26 2:10 11 14 16 20 22 23 25 27[3] 28 34 3:1 5 7 9 14 17[2] 4:3 7 8 9 16 20 5:1 5 8[2] 6:5 12 14 15 17 18[2] 7:3[3] 5 8 9[2] 14 17 8:4 5 6 7[3] 8[2] 9[2] 10 22[3] 9:6 10 11 16 17 19 23[2] 24 10:2 7 8 11 14 15 16 17 18 19 11:1 3[2] 7 9[2]

1 SAM. 11:10[2] 12 12:1[3] 2 5 6 8 10 12 17 18 19[3] 20 13:12 15 17[2] 14:1 4 6 7 8[2] 9[2] 10[2] 11 12 17 18 19[2] 23 33 34 35[2] 36[2] 40[3] 41 45 52 15:1[2] 6 10 11 13 15 16[2] 20 21 24 26 28 32 16:1 3[2] 5 7 10 11[2] 15 17 19 20 17:8[2] 13 17 18 28 34 37 39 41 43 44 46 52[2] 55 18:1 8 18 19 19:4[2] 6 11 17[2] 20:2 4 5[2] 11 12[2] 21 22 27 29 30[2] 31 32 36 40[2] 21:1 2[2] 5 8 11 14 22:2 3 5 7 8 13 15 17 22 23:2 3 17[2] 27 24:4[3] 6[2]

1 SAM. 24:16 19 21 22[2] 25:5 6 7 8 11 13 15 16 19 21 22 27[2] 31[2] 34 35 40[2] 26:1 27:2 5 6[2] 8 28:1 7 8[2] 9 11 13[2] 14 15 18 21[4] 22 23 29:3[3] 4[4] 6[3] 8[2] 30:13 15 17 24 25 26 31:1

2 SAM. 1:3[2] 4 5 7 9 10 13 14 16 26 2:1[2] 5[4] 6 3:2 7 8 12 16 21[2] 24 38 4:8 9 5:1 6[2] 14 19 6:10 12 21 23 7:2 4 8 9 17 20 24 27 28 8:10 11 15 9:2[2] 3[2] 4[2] 6 7 9[2] 11 12 10:2 3[3] 5 13 11:4[2] 7 10[3] 11 16 19 20[2] 23[3] 25[2] 12:1[3] 3 4[2]

2 SAM.	2 SAM.	1 KINGS	1 KINGS	2 KINGS	1 CHRON.	2 CHRON.	EZRA	NEH.	JOB	PSALMS	PSALMS	PSALMS	PSALMS	ISAIAH	JER.	JER.	JER.
12:8	21:17	10:13	22:8	13:23^2	18:11	19:4	7:15	12:46	21:15	37:5	88:3	120:3^2	8:14	40:18	6:4	25:33	38:24
11	22:1	11:2^3	13^2	14:6	19:2	20:9	22	47^2	33	39:12	8	121:1	9:3	20	10	26:2^2	25^5
13^2	42	8	14	7	3^2	15	26	13:4	22:2^2	40:1	9	122:1	13	41:9	12	3	26
14	45^2	9	15	13	11	21	28	6	17	3	13	4^2	12:7	13	13^2	4	27
15	50^2	11	16	25	14	24	8:17^3	12	21	5	89:3	123:1		42:3	19	5	39:12
18^2	51	14	18	15:5	20:8	26	22	13	26	15	6^2	2^2	CANT.	5	20	8	14
19	23:10	18	22	12^2	21:5	28	25	16	27	41:2	8	125:3	1:13	10	7:9	10	15
21	13	22	24	16:6	8	33	26	17	28	4	26	4	14	12	12	11	18
31^2	16	24	26	9	9	21:10	28^3	21	23:5	8	35	5	2:10	16	13	12	40:1
13:4^2	19	35	30	17:12	10	23:3	30	25^2	28:28	10	49	130:1	8:11	24	14^2	14	2
5^2	24:3^2	36	34	23	11	14	31	27	29:21	42:3	90:12	132:2^2		44:5	18	15	4^3
6	9	38^2	38	32	13	24:5	35^2		30:20	7	16^2	11	ISAIAH	7	21	16	5
10	10	40	49	34	15	6	36	ESTHER	26	8	92:1^2	135:3	1:4	17^2	22	23	6
11^2	11	12:3		41	17	11	9:4	1:1	31:10	9	94:15	4	6	22	23	27:1	7
13	12^2	5	2 KINGS	18:4	18	17	5	3	37^2	10	95:1	12	9^2	45:9	25^2	3	9
14	13^2	7^2	1:2	8	22	19	6	4	32:12	43:3	2	18	10	10^2	26	4^2	10
15	14	9	3	11	23	20	7	5^2	21	4^2	11	136:1	11	14^3	27^2	5^2	12
16^3	17	10^5	5^2	14	26	23	9	15	33:22	44:3	96:1^2	2	13	19	28	9	14
17	18^2	15^2	6^4	19	22:7	25:12	11	17	23	25	2	22	14	20	8:4	10	15
20	21	16^2	7	21	8	13	12^2	18	24	45:14^2	7^2	26	21	22	10^3	14^3	16
22	22^2	19	9^2	22	9	14	10:1	19	26^3	46:9	8^2	138:1	2:2	23	9:1	15	41:1
25	23^2	20	11^2	26	13	15^2	2	2:2	31	47:1	98:1	6	3:9^2	46:3	6	16^2	6
26	24	22	12	27	25	16^2	4	3^2	33	6	4	139:6	11	7	10:7	17	8
28	25	23^2	13	32	26	26:18^2	7^2	8^2	34:2	9	5	17	5:8	12	11	28:1	14
29		27^2	15^2	19:3	31^2	21	9	9	10	48:10	99:7	140:6	11	47:15	11:2	5	42:1
35	1 KINGS	28	16	6	26:6	27:5	10	13^2	11	14	100:1	13	18	48:11	3	12	2^2
39	1:2	30	2:2^2	9	28:1	28:9^2	11	14	14	50:1	4	141:1^4	20	12	5	15	4^3
14:2	11	32^2	3	29	3	10		15	15	5	101:1	8	21	13	6	29:1	7
3	13^3	33	4	20:1^2	6	13	NEH.	16	23	14^2	2	142:1^2	22	16	7^2	3	9^2
5	15^2	13:1	5	2	29:1	16	1:3	18	28	16	102:1	5	26	22	9	4^2	10
8	16	2	6	5	5	20	9^3	22	31	51 *title*	2	6	30	49:1	11^2	7	12
9	17^2	6	9	8	12	21	2:1	3:3	34	1	12	143:6	6:3	3	12^2	9	20^4
10	27	7	10	11	17	23	2	4^2	36	12	103:7^2	7	6	6	13	12^2	21
12	30	8	16	12	18	25	3	8	37	13	17	8	7:3	51:1^2	14	19	43:1
15^2	33	11	18^2	13	19	29:7	4	10	35:3	18	20	9	4	2	17	21	2
18	42	12	19	14^3	21^2	11	5^3	11	5	52 *title*	104:8	144:9^2	10	4^2	20	25	8
21	51	13	21	16	22	30	6	12	6	54:5	23	10	8:1	7	12:6	28	10^2
27	53	14	22	17^2	24	31	7	14	37:3	6	33	145:18	2	11	8	30	44:2^2
30	2:5^2	15	23^2	19		30:1	8	4:6	14	55:2	105:1	146:2	3	16	9	31	4
31^2	7	18^3	3:3	21:15	2 CHRON.	5	17	7	19	14	2^2	10	5	19	11	30:2	5
32	9	20	4	22:6	1:2	6	18	8^4	38:17	56:1	9	147:1	19^4	52:7	13:1	9	8^2
15:2	14	21	13^2	8	5	8	20	10^2	35	9	10	7^2	22	53:12	3	15	10
3	16	22	26	13^2	7^2	9^2	3:1^2	11^2	41	11	11	19^2	9:6^2	54:9	6	17	12
4	17	26^3	4:1^2	14	8^2	10	2	16	39:4	12	106:1	148:14	13	55:2	8	21^2	15
7^2	18	34	2	15	9	17	4^3	5:3	13^2	57:1^2	4	149:1	10:1	3	11^2	31:3	16^2
9	19^3	14:5^2	6^2	17	12	21	5	4^2	40:6	2^2	25	3	11	6	12^2	6	17^2
14	20	27	9	20	2:15	22	7^2	6	7	9	28		21	7	13	26	18
15	22	15:19	13^2	23:1	3:1	27	8^3	12^2	14	10^2	31^2	PROV.	30	11	18	32	19^2
25	26^2	20	16	4	5:2	31:6	9	14^3	19	59:13	36	1:5	12:6	56:4	27	34	20
26	27	29	17	5	3	16	10^2	6:3	41:3^2	17	37	9	13:2	5	14:2	38	23
27	28	17:1	19	6	6	32:9^2	12	4	42:4	61:1	38	23^2	14:10^2	8	10	40^3	24
33^2	29	2	22	21	7	13	13	5	7	2	47	33	15:4^2	57:9	11	32:6	25
34	30	5	25	25	9	18	15	6^2	8	8	107:1	2:2	5	18	13	7	29
36	31	8	26	35	6:14	23	16^2	11	11	62:11	6	10	8^2	59:16	14^3	8	45:1
16:2	36	13^2	33	24:7	17	24^2	17	13		12	13	18^2	16:1	20	17	12	2
3	38	18^2	36	25:2	19	25	20	14	PSALMS	65:1	18	19	8	60:5^2	15:1	16^2	4
4	39	19	38	8	20	31	24^2	7:2	2:5	2	19	3:5	18:4	7^2	2	18	5
9	42^3	20	42	17	21	33:2	26	5	7	4	28	15	6	9	16	20	48:1
10	3:2	21	5:1	24	25	13	27	8:1^2	3:4	66:1	30	22	7	10	18	24	9
16^2	6	23	3		27	17	31	2^2	8	3^2	108:3	28	19:11	11	19^2	25	12
18	11	18:1	5	1 CHRON.	30^2	18	32	6	4:3	4	4	34	16	13	20	26	27
21^2	12	2	6	1:19	31	22	4:6	7	5:2^2	15	109:4	4:4	17	14	16:1	29	34^3
22	13	5^3	7	2:3	34	34:4	9	9^4	3	17	12	18	20^2	19^2	10	31	46
17:1	16	15	10	9	36	6	12^2	13	7 *title*	67:1	17	20	21	61:1	11	33	49:2
3	26	17	13	19	37	25	14	9:5	4	68:4	19	22	20:1	3^2	12	35	4
6	4:12	19	14	3:1	38	26	15^2	12	10:14	20	25	5:1	21:2	7	15	37	14
7	21	20^2	17^2	4	40	35:1	19	13	13:6	29	110:1	9^2	4	62:11	19	33:1	29
11	27	21	19	5	7:8	3^2	20	20	16:2	31	111:5	6:16	6	63:5	20	3	31
15	28	22	25	4:31	10	8^2	22	22	6	32^2	9	7:4	9	65:1	17:15	6	50:15
20	33	25	26	33	12	9	5:7	23	17:1^2	34	112:4	13	10	2	17	9^2	27
21	5:1	30^3	27^2	39	15	12	8^3	26	6	35	113:3	24	16	11	19	14	29
18:2	3	31	6:1	41	21^2	22	14	27	18 *title*	69:1	5	8:4	22:11^2	15	20	15	44
4	5^3	40	2	43	8:11	36:13	15	30	6	8^2	115:1^3	32	15^2	66:1	24	19	51:2
11	6^2	41	9	5:1	12		16	10:3	39	13	8	11:27	24:16	19	26	22	9
12	7	44	11	8	15	EZRA	17		41	16	116:2	12:14	25:6	20	27	34:1	24
18	9^2	19:2	15	9	16	1:8	6:2	JOB	44	18	7	15	26:15	24	18:8	6	44
20	6:12	5	18	11	9:12	11	3	1:2	49^2	27	12	14:6	27:2		19:2	8^2	48
21	24	8	19	23^2	26	2:1^3	4	7	19:2^2	70:5	14	12	12	JER.	4	14^2	53
23	7:8	9^2	21	26^2	28	69	5	8	6	71:2	18	15:9	28:5	1:3^2	5	16	52:5
24	9	13	26	6:48	10:4^2	3:3	8	12	22:5	3	118:1	10	13	4	11	17	9
26	48	15	28^2	61	7	5	10	14	22	7	6	12	15	5	12	20	22
28	8:1	18	29	63	9	6	17^2	2:2	24	18	18	16:3	29:2	7	13^2	35:1	33
30	2	20	33	67	10^3	7^2	18	3	27	19	27	22	11	9	20:3	2^2	
32	5	21^2	7:4	71	15	8^2	7:3	6	31	22	29	25	15	11	8	5	LAM.
19:2	6	20:2	5	72	16	11	6	7	24:4	23	119:6	18:13	30:10^2	12	12	12	1:12^2
7^2	8	5	10	7:28	19	4:1	65	9	25:1	24	15	19:17	18	13	13	14^3	21
8	15	6	12	10:9	11:3	2^2	70	10	10	72:1	20	20:23	19	14	15	15^2	22^2
11	18^2	7	15	14	14	3^3	8:1	13	16	8	25	22:17	22	16	21:1^2	16	2:1
14	19	8^2	20	11:1	16	6	3	3:6	26:11	74:3	28	21	31:1	17	3	17^2	18
18^2	26	9	8:1	2	23	7	9^2	20	27:6	19	31	23:12	4	2:3	8	18^2	3:10
22	28^2	10^2	3	12:8	12:5	11^2	10^3	25	8	20	33	22	6	10	9	36:1	25
23^2	29	12	6	16	13:7	12^2	12	5:7	12	75:1^2	36	24:11	7	17	22:6^2	2^3	41
25	33	13	8	17^3	10	13	13	8^2	28:1	4	37	14	32:9	21	8	3	64
27	34^2	22	10^2	18	11	15	15	6:22	2	76:11^2	41	24	33:2	27	13	4	65
28	40	23	12	40	14	17^2	17	28	29:1^2	77:1^3	48	25:7	21	31^2	21	9	4:4
29	44	25	22	13:2^4	14:7	18	18^2	7:4	2^2	78:36	49	26:4	34:17	3:1	23:1	13	15
30^2	46	28	9:1	5	9	20	9:4	20	11	46^2	58	28:27	35:2	2	5	14^2	21
33	47	31	5	9	11	23	14	8:5	30:2	62	59	29:17	36:2	4	12	15	5:4
34^2	48^3	34	6	14:10	13	24	27	9:12	4	79:2^2	62	30:1^2	3	6	14	16	16
35	52^4	35	11^2	14	15:2	5:1^2	28	16	8	12	65	5	4	7	16^2	18	21
37	54	36	20	15:2	4	3	29^2	10:2	12	80:6	72	6	10	10	17^2	19	
38	56	39^2	10:1	3	11	4	32	3	31:22	11^2	76	10	11^2	11	33	32	EZEKIEL
39	58	40	6	12^2	14	6	34	15	32:2	81:1^2	77	31:3	37:2	14	38	37:2	1:3
41	59	42	10	16:8	19	7^2	36	11:7	5^2	8^2	79	6^2	3	17	24:3	3	16
20:2	63	21:2^2	17	9^2	16:4	8	37	19	6^2	12	90	24	6^2	18	4	6	2:1^2
3^2	65	3	18	16	7	9	38	12:8	9	13	103		14	22	7	7	2^2
8	66	5	19	18	17:3	12	10:28	13:2	33:2	15	105^2	ECCL.	15	25	10	18	3^2
14	9:2	6^3	22	28^2	16	14	30	12	3	83:9^2	107	1:5	21	4:1	25:2	19	4^2
16	3	7	23	29^2	18:3	15	35	20	34:5	85:1	112	7	30	10	3^3	38:1	7
17^2	8	8	27	34	4	6:5^2	36	27	11	8	116	2:3	38:1^3	12	4	4^2	8
21	13	11^2	30^2	40	5	8	37^2	15:19	15	86:3^2	117	17	2	13	5	12	9
22^2	16	19^2	11:15	17:2	7^2	10	38	21	18	4	124	18	5	18^2	7	14^2	3:1^2
21:2^2	21	25	12:7	5	14	21	39	16:20	35:3	5	130	3:19	7	5:5^2	15	15^3	3
3	24	22:3	13:4	7	17	22	11:30	19:11	10	6	132^2	5:4	15	13	17	16	4^3
4	25	4	14	15	20	7:7	12:37	20:6	23	8^2	146	7:21	39:3^4	19	27	17^2	6
6^2	10:5	5	15^2	26	23	11	38	29	36:5	16^2	149	8:4	40:2	24	28	19	7^2
8	12	6	18	18:3	29	12	39	21:14	10	88:2	120:1	9	9	6:3	30	20^2	10^2

EZEKIEL 3:11[2] 16 17 18 22 24 27 4:3 9 15 16 5:15 6:1 10 7:1 2 7 27 8:5 6 8 9 10 12 13 15 17 9:4 9 10:2 7 13 11:1 2 5 14 15[2] 25 12:1 6 8 9 10 11 19 21 23 28 13:1 2 3 11 12 15 18 14:1 2 4[2] 7 10 22 15:1 16:1 3 5 6[2] 8 20[2] 23 24 27 29 33 34 36 37 54 60 61 17:1 2 3 11 18:1 22 19:4 20:2 3[2] 5[4] 6 7 8 9 15 18 23 27[2] 29[2] 30 31 39 45 21:1 7 8 18 23 29[2] 22:1 4[2] 17 23 24 28 23:1 16 27

EZEKIEL 23:30 36[2] 37 38 40 43 44[4] 24:1 3[2] 15 18 19 20 21 24 26 27 25:1 3 8 9 26:1 2 27:1 3 28:1 2 11 12 20 24 29:1 4[2] 10 17 19 30:1 20 31:1 2 4 8 17 18 32:1 2 17 18 33:1 2 7 8 10 11 12 14 16 21 23 25 27 31 32 34:1 2[2] 18 20 35:1 3 6 15 36:1 3 6 9 11 13 16 22 32 37:3 4[2] 5 9[2] 11 12 15 18 19 21 25 38:1 7[2] 13 14 39:4 11 14 17 24 28 40:4[2] 6 14 15 19 22 45 46 41:4 17 20 22 42:13[2] 43:6 7 18

EZEKIEL 43:19[2] 24 44:2 5[2] 11 12 13[2] 15[2] 16 26 27 28 30 45:1 4 7 46:4 7 12 13 14 16 20 24 47:1 2 6 8 10 14[2] 18 21 22[2] 48:2 3 4 5 6 7 8[2] 9 12 14 18 23 24 25 26 27 28 29 DANIEL 1:1 3 7[2] 10 21 2:3 5 9 19 21 23[2] 24[3] 25[2] 26 27 46 47 3:3 14 18 24[2] 4:1[2] 6 7 11 16 18 20 22 26 27 34[2] 35 36[4] 5:13 15 17 6:2 6 15[2] 16 19 20 21 25[2] 26 7:5 10 16 26 8:1[3] 6 7 13 14[2] 17 9:3 4 6 7[3] 25 26 10:1 11[4]

DANIEL 10:12 15 16 19[2] 20 11:18 12:7 HOSEA 1:1 2 4 6 10[2] 2:1 14 19[2] 20 23 3:1 3 4:12 15 5:4 12 14 6:3[2] 4[2] 7:7 13[2] 14 8:2 11 9:4[2] 10 17 10:1 6 15 11:2 4 12:4 14 13:7 14:1 2 5 JOEL 1:14 20 2:13 14 19 3:3 AMOS 1:5 2:7 3:7 4:6 8[2] 9 10[2] 11 12[2] 13 5:4 15 18 25 6:2 10 14 7:1 4 8 12 15[2] 8:1 2 9:7 OBADIAH 15 20 JONAH 1:1 3[2] 5 6 8 9 10 11[3] 12[2] 14 16 2:1 2 7 9 10 3:1 2[2] 3 6 8 10 4:2[2] 8 9 MICAH 1:9[2] 12

MICAH 1:15[2] 2:11 3:4 6[2] 8 4:1 13[2] 5:2 3 4 6:3 5 9 7:7 8 10 15 18 20 NAHUM 3:13 HABAK. 1:2 10 11 16[2] 2:1 5[2] 7 15[2] 16 19 3:13 16 ZEPH. 1:1 2:5 11 HAGGAI 1:1 9 13 2:20 ZECH. 1:1 3[3] 4[2] 6 7 9 14 19 2:2 4 5 8 11 3:2 4[2] 6 4:2 5 6[2] 7 8 9 11 12 5:2 3 5 11 6:4 5 8 9 12 15 7:1 2 3 4 5[2] 8 8:3 11 15 18 9:9 10 12 11:7 12 13[2] 15[2] 12:2 13:3 6 14:5 10[3] 17 20 21 MALACHI 1:6 8 9 11[2] 14 2:2 4

MALACHI 2:12 3:3 4 7[2] 4:2 4 MATT. 1:17 20[2] 24 2:5 11 3:7 9[2] 10 11 13 15 16 4:6 7 9 10 11 19 24 5:1 15 18 20 22 26 28 32 33 34 39 44 6:2 5 8 16[2] 18[2] 25 27 29 33 34 7:6 7 11 14 21 23 24 26 8:4[2] 5 7 10 11 13[2] 15 16 18 19 20 21 22 26 32 9:2 6 8 9 11 12 15 16 18 24 28[2] 29 37 10:1 15 23 42[2] 11:3 4 7 9 11 16[2] 17 21[2] 22 23 24 25 27 28 29 12:2 3 6 11 20 22 25 28 31[3] 36 39 45 47

MATT. 12:48 13:2 3 10[2] 11[2] 17 24[2] 27 28[2] 31 33[2] 34[2] 36[2] 37 44 45 47 51[2] 52[3] 57 14:2 4 16 17 22 25 27 28 31 35 15:3 8 10 12 15[2] 22 24 28[2] 29 30 32 33 34 16:2 4 6 8 15 17[2] 18 19 21[2] 22 23[2] 24 28 17:3 4 11 12[2] 13 20[4] 22 26[2] 27 18:1 2 3 7 10 13 17[2] 18 19 22[2] 23 24 31 32 34 35 19:3[2] 4 7 8 9 10 11 13 14 16 17 18 20 21 23[3] 24 26 27 28[2] 20:1 4 6 7[2] 8[2] 12 14[2] 17 18[2] 21[2] 22 23 25 28 32 33 21:1[2]

MATT. 21:2[2] 3 5 13 16[2] 19 21[3] 23 24 25 27 31[3] 32 36 37 40 41[2] 42 43 22:1 2 4 12 16 17 19 20 21[4] 24 25 26 29 31 37 39 42 43 44 23:13 14 15 16 23 25 27[2] 28 29 31 34 35 36 37 38 39 24:2 3 4 13 14 19 23 26 27 34 47 25:1 8 12 14 15 20 21 22 23 26 28 29 34 36 39 40[4] 41 44 45 26:1 3 7 10 13 14 15[2] 17 18 21 22 24 25 29 31 33 34[2] 35 36[2] 38[2] 40[2] 45 50 52 58 62 63 64[2] 68 69 71 73 75

MATT. 27:8 11 13 15 17[2] 19 21[2] 22[2] 26 27 33 45 53 55 62 64 65 28:5 10 11 12 18[2] 20 MARK 1:5 13 17 31 32 37 38 40 41 44[2] 2:2 3 4 5 8 11 13 14 16 17 18 19 24 25 27 3:3 4 5 8 13[2] 23[2] 28[2] 31 32 4:1 2 9 11[3] 13 21 24[2] 33 34 35[2] 38 39 40 5:1 8 11 19 21[3] 31 34 36 39 41[2] 6:2 4 7 10 11 18 22 23[2] 24 25 30 31 33 35 37[2] 38 45 48[2] 50 51 7:1 6 9 14[3] 18 27[2] 28 29 31 32 34 8:1[2] 12[2] 17 19

MARK 8:21 22 27 29[2] 34[2] 9:1 4 13[2] 17 19 20 21 23 25 29 31 35 36 41 10:1 3 5 11 14[2] 15 18 20 21 23 24 28 29 32 33[2] 35 36 37[2] 38 39[2] 42 45 49 51[3] 52 11:1 2 3 5 6 11 14 17 21 22 23[2] 24 28 29 33[2] 12:1 4 6 9 13 14 15 16[2] 17 18 19[2] 24 26 32 34 38 43[3] 13:1 2 13 19 30 37[2] 14:9 10[2] 12 13 16 18 19 20 24 25 27 29 30[2] 34[2] 36 37 41 48 61 65 72 15:2 6 8 9 11 12[2] 14 15 22 41[2] 43 44 46 16:2

MARK 16:6 7 12 13 14 15 19 LUKE 1:2 3 11 13 18 19[2] 22[2] 26 28 30 32 34 35 38 61 74 77 80 2:4 10 11 12 15[2] 20 26 34 38 48 49 50 51 3:2 8[2] 9 11 12 13 14 16 18 4:3 5 6[2] 8 9 12 17 21 23[2] 24 26[3] 29 31 40 42 43 5:4 5 7 10 14 20 22 24[2] 27 31 33 34 36 6:2 5 9 10 13 23 24 25[2] 26 27 29 35 38 39 7:2 3 6 7 8 9[2] 13 14 19 20[2] 21 22 24 26 28 32[2] 40[2] 43 44 47 48 8:3 10 21 22[2]

LUKE 8:25 39[2] 47 48 9:3 11 12 13 20 33 43 48 50 57 58 59 60 62 10:2 9[2] 11 12 13[2] 17 18 19 20 21[2] 23 26 28 29 35 36 37 41 11:1 2 5[3] 8 9[2] 13 17 24 27 30 39 41 42 43 44 45 46 47 51[2] 52 53 12:1 4 5 8 10 11[2] 13 14 15 16 20 22[2] 27 31 36[2] 37 41[2] 44 48 13:2 7 8 12 14 18[2] 23[2] 24 25[2] 31 32 34 35[2] 14:3 7 10 14 16 18 23 24 25 15:1 3 6 7 10 15 16 18 21 27 31 16:1[2] 2 5[3] 6 7 9 15 28

LUKE 16:29 30 31 17:1[2] 5 6 7 8 14[2] 19 22 24 37[2] 18:1 3 7 9 13 15 16[2] 17 19 22[2] 29[2] 31[2] 32 35 40 41 42 43 19:5 8 9 13 15 17 22 24 25 26[2] 31 32 33 39 40 42 46 20:2 3 8 15 20 22 23 25[3] 28[2] 34 36 38 41 42 45 21:3 4 10 23 32 22:4 6 9 10 11[2] 13 15 16 18 19 22 25 29[2] 33 35 36 37 38 40 43 46 47 48 49 52 61 67 70 23:1 7 14[2] 15 17 18 22 25 28 42 43[2] 52 24:1[2] 5 6 9 10 12 17 18 19[2]

LUKE 24:25 27 28 36[2] 38 41 44[2] 46 JOHN 1:11 22[2] 25 29 33 38[2] 39 41 43 45 46[2] 48[2] 49 50[2] 51[2] 2:3 4 5[2] 7 8[2] 10 16 18[2] 19 22 24 3:2 3[2] 4 5 7 9 10 11 26[2] 34 4:7 8 9 10 11 13 15 16 17 19 21 25 26[2] 30 32 34 35 36 40 42 45 47 48 49 50[2] 52 53 5:6 8 10 11 12 14[2] 19[2] 22 24[2] 25 29[2] 33[2] 6:5[2] 8 12 13 16 19 20 23 25 26 27[2] 28 29 30 32[2] 33 34 35 36 43 45 47 53[2] 61 63 65[3] 67 7:3 6 8[2] 9 10[2]

JOHN 7:21 22 26 33[2] 35 37 45 50 52 53 8:1 2 3 4 7 9 10 11 12 13 14 19 21 23 24 25[3] 28 34 39[2] 42 48 51 52 55 57 58[2] 9:7 10 11 12 15 17 24 29 30 34 35 37 40 41 10:1 6[2] 7[2] 24 26 28 35 41 11:3 4 8 11 14 15 16 18 21 23 24 25 27 29 31 32 34 39 40[2] 44 49 54 12:16 24 25 27 32 35 50 13:1[2] 6 7 8 9 12 16 20 21 25 27 28 29 33 34 36 37 38 14:3 5 6[2] 8 9 10 12[2] 22[3] 23[2] 25 26 27[2]

JOHN 14:28[3] 15:3 7 11 15 20 21 22 26 16:1 3 4 6 7[2] 12 14 15 17 19 10 23 25 26 29 33 17:6 8 26 18:4 5 6 11 15 16[2] 17 21 24 25 28 29 30[2] 31[2] 33 35 37[2] 38[3] 39[2] 19:4 5 6 9 10[2] 11 14 15 16 26 27 20:1 2 10 13[2] 15[2] 16[2] 17[3] 18 19[2] 20 21 22 23 25[2] 26 28 29 21:3[2] 5 6 7[2] 10 12 15[2] 16[2] 17[4] 18 19 22 23 ACTS 1:2 7 8[2] 12 19 22 2:3 14[2] 29[2] 34 37 38 39 41 3:5 10 11 12 14 20 22[4] 25 26 4:1 3 8 10

ACTS 4:17 19[3] 23 29 35 5:4[2] 8 9 16 35 38 6:2 7:2 3 13 26 31 37[3] 38 40 41 44 46 8:1 5 6 14 20 26[3] 29 35 36 9:1 2 4 6 11 15[2] 17 21 27 34 38 10:3 4 7 8 9 11 15 19 21 28[2] 29 32 36 41 42 11:4 7 11[2] 13 17 18 19 20 21 22 23 24 26 27 29 12:5 8[2] 10[2] 15 17[3] 21 13:4 6 15 20 21 22 23 31 32[2] 33 36 38[2] 41 47 51 14:3 6[2] 13 15[2] 18 27 15:2 3 7 8 13 18 20 23 25[2] 33 36 39 40 16:10 13 14 17

ACTS 16:19 25 32 37 38 17:2 3 5 6 10 15[2] 18 19 23 29 31 34 18:2 6[2] 14 21 26[2] 19:2[2] 3[3] 4 12 22 24 30 31 33 20:1 6 7 13 18 20 22 24 27 28 34 38 21:1[2] 2 8 11 18 20 31 32 37[2] 39 40[2] 22:1 4 5[2] 6 7[2] 8 10 13[2] 15 18 20 21[2] 22 25 27 23:3 15[2] 17[2] 18[2] 21 23 24 26 24:2 4 8 10[2] 14 23 25:6 11[2] 12[2] 13 14 21 22 26 26:1 6 7 11 14 16[2] 17 18 19 20 22 23 28 32[2] 27:1 3 8 10 21 40 28:17 19 21 25 26 28[2]

ACTS 28:30; ROMANS 1:1, 10, 11, 13, 16, 19, 26; 2:5, 8, 14; 3:2, 7, 22; 4:3, 6, 11; 5:4, 15, 16, 18, 21^3; 6:10^2, 11^2, 13^3, 16^2, 19^2, 22; 7:4, 5, 10, 13

ROMANS 7:16; 9:12, 17, 19, 21^2, 23, 26, 29; 10:3, 10^2, 12, 18, 20, 21; 11:4, 8, 9, 11, 27, 35; 12:1, 3, 19; 13:1; 14:6, 8^2; 15:8, 9, 15, 19, 23, 25^2, 27, 29

ROMANS 15:32; 16:1, 4, 5, 19^2; 1 COR. 1:2, 3, 8, 9, 11, 18, 23^2, 24, 30; 2:1, 7, 10, 14; 3:1^4, 10; 4:9, 11, 13, 17, 21; 5:5, 9, 11; 6:12, 17; 7:1, 3

1 COR. 7:10, 27; 8:1, 4, 7; 9:2, 11, 15, 16, 17, 19, 20; 10:2, 11, 28^2; 11:13, 14, 17, 23, 34; 12:2, 21, 31; 14:2, 3, 6, 11^2, 21, 26, 34, 36, 37; 15:1^2, 2

1 COR. 15:3, 6, 28^2; 16:3, 5, 9, 11, 12, 16; 2 COR. 1:1, 13, 15, 16, 20, 23; 2:3, 4^2, 12, 14, 15, 16^2; 3:15; 4:4, 11; 5:5, 11, 12, 15^2, 19^3; 6:11, 13, 18

2 COR. 7:12^2; 8:2, 5, 17; 9:5, 12, 13^3, 15; 10:13, 14; 11:9; 12:9, 17, 19, 20; GAL. 1:2, 6, 8, 9, 17, 20, 22; 2:2, 7^2, 9^3, 14, 19; 3:8, 23, 24; 4:8, 13

GAL. 5:2, 4, 13; 6:6, 10^2, 11, 14^2, *subscr.*; EPHES. 1:5, 9, 14, 15, 17; 2:10, 16, 18, 21; 3:3, 5, 7, 8, 10, 14, 20, 21; 4:7, 8, 13^2, 16, 19, 29, 30

EPHES. 5:10, 20, 22^2, 24, 31; 6:5, 9, 13, 19, 22, *subscr.*; PHIL. 1:2, 11, 12^2, 29; 2:8, 19, 27, 30; 3:10, 11, 13, 15, 21^2; 4:5, 6, 16, 20; COLOS. 1:2, 6

COLOS. 1:8, 10, 11, 12, 20; 2:2; 3:18, 20, 23; 4:3, 7, 8, 9, 10, 11^2; 1 THESS. 1:1^2, 5, 9; 2:1, 2, 8^2, 9^2, 12, 18; 3:6, 11; 4:7^2, 8, 9, 15^2; 5:1, 15

1 THESS. 5:23, 27, *subscr.*; 2 THESS. 1:1, 2; 2:1; 3:9; 1 TIM. 1:2, 6, 17, 18, 20; 2:4; 3:14^2, 16; 4:7, 8, 16^2; 6:16; 2 TIM. 1:12, 14, 16, 18^2; 2:9, 15, 16, 21^2, 24

2 TIM. 3:9, 11, 15, 17; 4:4, 8, 9, 10^2, 18, *subscr.*; TITUS 1:3, 15^2, 16; 2:9, 14; 3:2, 5, 8, 12, 13; PHILE. 1, 13, 16, 19, 21, 22; HEB. 1:1, 2

HEB. 1:5, 8; 2:3, 5, 10, 12, 17; 3:6, 14; 4:2^2, 13, 16; 5:4, 5, 7, 9; 6:1, 6, 7, 8, 11, 17; 7:3, 4, 19, 21, 25; 8:5; 9:20, 27, 28^2; 10:24, 29, 30

HEB. 10:39; 11:4, 26; 12:2, 4, 5^2, 9, 11, 18^2, 22^2; 13:6, 7, 13, 22; JAMES 1:23; 2:2, 3, 16, 23; 4:6; 5:7; 1 PETER 1:2^2, 3, 5, 7, 10, 12^5, 13, 22, 25

1 PETER 2:4, 7^2, 14^2, 24, 25; 3:5, 7^2, 12, 19, 22; 4:7, 12, 19; 5:5, 10, 12; 2 PETER 1:2, 3^2, 4, 11, 16, 19; 2:4, 9, 21, 22; 3:1, 7, 12, 15^2, 16

1 JOHN 1:2^2, 3, 4, 5; 2:1, 7, 8, 12, 13^3, 14^2, 21, 26; 3:14; 5:13, 16^3, 17; 2 JOHN 1, 5, 10, 12^2; 3 JOHN 1, 9, 13; JUDE 2, 3^3, 6, 11, 21, 24

REV. 1:1^3, 4, 5, 6, 11^6, 13, 15, 17; 2:1, 5, 7, 8, 10, 11, 14, 16, 17, 18^2, 20, 23, 24^2, 26, 29; 3:1, 6, 13, 14, 22; 4:3, 6; 5:5, 10, 13^2

REV. 6:2, 4, 8, 11^2, 13; 7:10, 12, 13, 14, 17; 8:3; 9:1, 3, 7^2, 10, 19; 10:4, 8, 9^3, 11; 11:1, 2, 3, 12, 18; 12:5, 11, 12, 13; 13:2, 4^2, 5^2, 7

REV. 13:15; 14:4, 6, 13, 14, 20; 15:7; 16:8, 14, 19; 17:1^2, 7, 13, 15, 17; 18:5, 6, 18; 19:1, 9^3, 10, 17; 20:4; 21:5, 6^2, 9, 11, 18; 22:6^3, 9, 10, 16, 18^2

up

4605, *507*

GEN. 2:6, 21; 4:8; 7:11, 17; 8:7, 13; 13:1, 10, 14; 14:22; 17:22; 18:2, 16; 19:1, 2, 14, 27, 28, 30; 20:18; 21:14, 16, 18, 32; 22:3^2, 4, 13^2, 19; 23:3, 7; 24:16, 54, 63, 65; 25:8, 17, 34; 26:23, 31; 27:38; 28:12, 18^2; 29:11; 31:10, 12, 17, 21, 35, 45, 55; 32:22; 33:1, 5; 35:1, 3, 13, 14, 29; 37:25, 28, 35; 38:8, 12, 13; 39:15, 16, 18; 40:13, 19, 20; 41:2, 3, 4, 5, 6, 18, 19

GEN. 41:20, 21, 22, 23, 27, 34, 35, 44, 48^3; 43:2, 15, 29; 44:4, 17, 24, 30, 33, 34; 45:9, 25; 46:4, 5, 29, 31; 47:14; 48:17; 49:4^2, 9^2, 33^2; 50:5, 6, 7^2, 9, 14, 23, 25; EXOD. 1:8, 10; 2:17, 23; 3:8, 17; 7:12, 20; 8:3, 4, 5, 6, 7, 20; 9:10, 13, 16, 32; 10:12, 14; 12:6, 30, 31, 34, 38; 13:18, 19; 14:10, 16; 15:7; 16:13, 14, 23, 24, 33, 34; 17:3, 10, 11, 12

EXOD. 19:3, 12, 13, 20^2, 23, 24^2; 20:25, 26; 22:2; 24:1, 2, 4, 9, 12, 13^2, 15, 18; 26:15, 30, 33; 29:27; 32:1^2, 4, 6^2, 8, 23, 30; 33:1^2, 3, 5, 8, 10, 12, 15; 34:2, 3, 4^2, 24; 35:21, 26; 36:2, 20; 40:2, 8^2, 17, 18^3, 21, 28, 33^2, 36, 37^2; LEVIT. 6:10; 9:22; 11:45; 13:4, 5, 11, 21, 26, 31, 33, 37, 42, 50, 54; 14:38, 46; 19:32; 20:16; 22:30; 26:1^2; 30:38; NUM. 1:51; 6:26

NUM. 7:1; 9:15, 17, 21^2, 22; 10:11, 21, 35; 11:32; 13:17^2, 21, 30, 31^2, 32^2; 14:1, 13, 36, 37, 40^3, 42, 44; 15:19, 20; 16:2, 3, 12, 13, 14, 24, 25, 27, 30, 32, 34, 37, 45; 17:4, 7; 19:9^2; 20:4, 5, 11, 25, 27; 21:3, 5, 17, 33; 22:4^2, 13, 14, 20, 21, 41; 23:7, 18^2, 24^2; 24:2, 3, 8, 9, 15, 20, 21, 23, 25; 25:4, 7; 26:10; 27:12; 31:52; 32:9, 11, 14; 33:38; DEU. 1:21

DEU. 1:22, 24, 26, 28^2, 41^2, 42, 43; 2:13, 24; 3:1, 27^2; 4:19; 5:5; 6:7; 8:14; 9:1, 9, 23; 10:1, 3; 11:6, 17, 18, 19; 14:25, 28; 16:22; 17:8, 20; 18:15, 18; 19:11, 15, 16; 20:1; 22:4, 14, 19; 23:14; 24:5; 25:7^2, 9; 27:2, 4, 5; 28:7, 33, 43; 29:22; 30:12; 31:5, 16; 32:11, 17, 30, 34^2, 36, 38, 40, 49, 50; 33:2; 34:1; JOSH. 2:6, 8, 10; 3:6^2, 16; 4:5, 8, 9, 16, 17, 18^2, 19, 23^2

JOSH. 5:1, 7; 6:1, 5, 6, 12, 13, 20, 26^2; 7:2^2, 3^2, 4, 10, 13, 16; 8:1, 3, 7, 10^2, 11, 14, 20, 31; 9:4; 10:4, 5, 6, 9, 10, 12, 33, 36; 11:6, 17; 12:7, 8; 15:3^2, 6^2, 7^2, 8^2, 15; 16:1; 17:15; 18:1, 11, 12^2, 17; 19:10, 11, 12, 47; 20:5; 22:12, 33; 24:17, 26, 32; JUD. 1:1, 2, 3, 4, 16, 22, 36; 2:1^2, 4, 16, 18; 3:9, 15; 4:5, 10^2, 12, 14; 6:3^2, 5

JUD. 6:8, 13, 21, 35, 38; 7:1; 8:8, 11, 13, 20, 28; 9:7, 18, 32, 33, 34, 35, 43, 48, 51; 11:2, 13, 16, 31, 37; 12:3; 13:20; 14:2, 19; 15:5, 6, 9, 10^2, 11^4, 13; 16:3, 5, 8, 18^2, 29, 31; 18:9, 12, 17, 30, 31; 19:5, 7, 9, 10, 17, 27, 28^3, 30; 20:3, 9, 18^3, 19, 23^3, 26, 28, 30, 31, 33, 38, 40^2; 21:2, 5^2, 8, 19; RUTH 1:9, 14; 2:15, 18; 3:14; 4:1

RUTH 4:5, 10; 1 SAM. 1:3, 5, 6, 7, 9, 19, 21, 22^2, 24; 2:6, 7, 8^2, 14, 19, 35; 5:12; 6:9, 10, 13, 20, 21; 7:1, 7, 10; 8:8; 9:11, 13^2, 14^2, 19, 24, 26; 10:3, 18, 25; 11:1, 4; 12:6; 13:5, 15; 14:9, 10^2, 12^2, 13, 21, 46; 15:2, 6, 11, 12, 34; 16:13; 17:20, 23, 25^2; 19:15; 20:38; 21:12; 22:8; 23:11, 12, 19, 29; 24:7, 16, 22; 25:5, 13, 35; 26:19; 27:8; 28:8, 11^2, 14, 15

1 SAM. 28:25; 29:9, 10^2, 11^2; 30:4; 2 SAM. 2:1^3, 2, 3, 22, 27, 32; 3:10, 32; 4:4, 12; 5:8, 17, 19^2, 22, 23; 6:2, 12, 15; 7:6, 12; 12:3, 11, 17; 13:29, 34, 36; 14:14; 15:2, 20, 24, 30^4; 17:16, 21; 18:9, 18, 24^2, 28^2, 29, 31, 33; 19:34; 20:2, 3, 15, 19^2, 20, 21; 21:6, 8, 13; 22:9, 49; 23:1, 8, 18; 24:9, 11, 18, 19, 22; 1 KINGS 1:35, 40, 45, 49; 2:19, 33; 3:15; 6:8; 7:21^2

1 KINGS 8:1, 3, 4^2, 20, 35, 54; 9:16, 24; 10:5, 29; 11:14, 15, 23, 26, 27; 12:8, 10, 18, 24, 27, 28^2; 13:4, 29; 14:1, 10, 15, 16, 25; 15:4, 17; 16:17, 32, 34; 17:7, 19; 18:38, 41, 42^2, 43^2, 44, 46; 20:1, 22, 26, 33; 21:16, 21, 25; 22:6, 12, 20, 29, 35, 38; 2 KINGS 1:3, 4, 6^2, 7, 9, 13, 14, 16; 2:1, 11, 13, 16, 23^4; 3:7, 8, 21, 22, 24; 4:21, 29, 34, 35

2 KINGS 4:36, 37; 6:7, 24; 7:5; 8:12; 9:1, 2, 8, 25, 27, 32; 10:1; 12:10^2, 17^2; 13:21; 14:10, 11, 26; 15:4, 16; 16:5, 7^2, 9; 17:3, 4, 5^2, 7, 10, 36; 18:9, 13, 17^2, 25^2; 19:4, 14, 22, 23, 24, 26, 28; 20:5, 6, 8, 17; 21:3^2; 22:4; 23:2, 9, 29; 24:1, 10; 25:4, 6, 27; 1 CHRON 5:; 11:6, 11, 20; 13:6^2; 14:2, 8, 10^2, 11, 14; 15:3, 12, 14, 16, 25, 28; 17:5, 11; 21:1, 16, 18^2

1 CHRON. 21:19, 27; 25:5; 26:16; 28:2; 2 CHRON. 1:4, 6, 17; 2:16; 3:17; 5:2, 4, 5^2, 13; 6:10, 26; 7:13, 20; 8:11; 9:4; 10:8, 10, 18; 11:4; 12:2, 9; 13:4, 6; 16:1; 17:6; 18:2, 5, 11, 14, 19, 28, 34; 20:16, 19, 23; 21:4, 9, 16, 17; 24:7, 23; 25:14, 19, 21; 26:16, 19; 28:9, 12, 15, 24; 29:7, 20; 30:7, 27; 32:5^2, 25; 33:3, 14, 19; 34:30; 35:20; 36:6, 15, 22, 23; EZRA 1:1, 3, 5^2, 11^2

EZRA 2:1, 59, 63, 68; 3:2; 4:2, 12^2, 13, 16, 23; 5:2, 3, 9, 11; 6:1, 11; 7:6, 7, 9, 13, 28; 8:1; 9:5, 6^2, 9; 10:6, 10; NEH. 2:1, 15, 17, 18; 3:1, 3, 6, 13, 14, 15, 19, 31, 32; 4:3, 7, 14; 5:2; 6:1, 10; 7:1, 5, 6, 61, 65; 8:5, 6; 9:3, 4, 5, 18; 10:38; 12:1, 31, 37^2; ESTHER 2:7, 20; 5:9; 7:7; JOB 1:5, 7, 16; 2:2, 12^2; 3:8, 10

JOB 3:11; 4:15; 5:5^2, 11, 18; 6:3, 4; 7:9; 8:11; 9:7; 10:15, 18; 11:10, 15, 20; 12:14, 15; 13:19; 14:10, 11, 17^2; 15:30; 16:4, 8, 12; 17:8; 18:16; 19:8, 12; 20:6, 15, 27; 21:19; 22:22, 23, 24, 26, 29; 24:22; 26:8; 27:7, 16; 28:4, 5; 29:8; 30:4, 12, 20, 22, 28; 31:14, 18, 21, 29; 33:5; 34:7; 36:13; 37:7, 20; 38:3, 8, 10, 34; 39:4, 18, 27, 30; 40:7, 23^2; 41:10, 15, 25; 42:8; PSALMS 3:1, 3; 4:6

PSALMS 5:3; 7:6; 9:13; 10:12; 14:4; 15:3; 16:4; 17:5, 7; 18:8, 35, 39, 48^2; 20:5; 21:9; 22:15; 24:4, 7^2, 9^2; 25:1; 27:2, 5, 6, 10, 12; 28:2, 5, 9; 30:1, 3; 31:8, 19; 33:7; 35:2, 11, 23, 25; 39:6; 40:2, 5, 12; 41:8, 9, 10; 44:5; 47:5; 53:4; 54:3; 56:1, 2; 57:3, 8; 59:1, 15; 63:4; 69:9, 15, 29; 71:6, 20; 74:3, 4, 5, 8, 15, 23; 75:3, 4, 5, 7; 77:9; 78:21, 38, 48; 80:2; 81:3, 12; 83:2

PSALMS 86:4; 87:6; 88:8, 15; 89:2, 4, 42; 90:5, 6; 91:12; 92:11; 93:3^2; 94:2, 16^2, 18; 97:3; 102:10, 16; 104:8; 105:35; 106:9, 17, 18, 26, 30; 107:25, 26; 109:23; 110:7; 113:7; 119:48, 117; 121:1; 122:4; 123:1; 124:2, 3; 127:2^2; 129:6; 132:3; 134:2; 139:8, 21; 140:10; 141:2; 143:8; 144:12; 145:14; 147:2, 3, 6; PROV. 1:12; 2:3, 7; 3:20; 7:1; 8:23, 30; 10:12, 14; 13:22; 15:1, 18; 16:27; 21:20; 22:6; 23:8; 24:16; 25:7; 26:9, 24; 28:25; 29:21, 22; 30:4, 13

PROV. 30:31, 32; 31:28; ECCL. 2:26; 3:2, 3; 4:10^2, 15; 10:4, 12; 12:4; CANT. 2:7, 10; 3:5; 4:2, 12; 5:5; 6:6; 7:8, 12, 13; 8:4, 5^2; ISAIAH 1:2, 6; 2:3, 4, 12, 13, 14; 3:13, 14; 5:5, 6, 11, 13, 24, 26; 6:1; 7:1, 6; 8:7^2, 16; 9:11, 18^2; 10:15^2, 24, 26^2, 28, 29, 30; 11:12, 16; 13:2, 14, 17; 14:4, 8, 9^2, 22; 15:2, 5^3, 7; 18:3; 19:5, 6; 21:2; 22:1; 23:4^2, 13^2, 18; 24:10

ISAIAH 24:14, 18, 22; 25:8; 26:11; 27:9; 28:4, 7, 21; 30:26; 32:9, 13; 33:3, 10, 12; 34:3, 10, 13; 35:9; 36:1, 10^2; 37:4, 14, 23, 24, 25, 27, 29; 38:22; 39:6; 40.9^3, 15, 26, 31; 41:2, 25; 42:2, 11, 13, 15^2; 43:6; 44:4, 11, 26, 27; 45:8, 13, 20; 47:13; 48:13; 49:6, 18, 19, 21, 22^2, 23; 50:2, 9; 51:6, 8, 17, 18; 52:8; 53:2; 55:13^2; 57:7, 8^2, 14^3, 20; 58:1, 12; 59:19; 60:4, 7, 10; 61:1, 4; 62:10^2

ISAIAH	JER.	JER.	EZEKIEL	EZEKIEL	EZEKIEL	DANIEL	AMOS	MICAH	ZECH.	MATT.	MARK	LUKE	JOHN	ACTS	ACTS	1 COR.	HEB.
63:11	23:4	49:5	1:13	23:27	41:16	11:20	2:10	5:9	10:11	15:29	8:24	9:16	4:35	2:32	14:2	5:2	1:12
64:7	7	14	19[2]	46	43:5	21	11	14	12	37	25	17	5:1	3:1	11	6:14[2]	5:7
11	8	19	20	47	24	23	3:1	6:4	11:16	16:9	34	23	8	6	20	8:1	7:27[2]
	10	22	21[2]	26:3[2]	44:12	25[2]	5	14	17	10	9:2	28	9	7	15:2	10:7	11:17[2]
JER.	24:6	28	3:14	8	47:14	12:1	10	7:3	14:10	24	27	51	11	8	5	13:4	19
1:17	25:32	31	4:14	17		4	4:10	6	13	17:1	10:16	10:25	12	13	7	15:15[2]	12:12
2:6	26:5	50:2	7:11	19	DANIEL	7	5:1		16	8	21	34	21	22	16	24	15
24	10	9	8:3	27:2	2:21	9	2	NAHUM	17	27[2]	32	11:27	6:3	26	16:22	35	
3:2	17	21	5[2]	32	44	11	6:8	1:4	18[2]	19:20	33	31	5	4:24	17:13	54	JAMES
6	27:22	26	11	28:2	3:1		10	9	19	20:17	11:20	32	12	26	18:22		4:10
4:3	29:15	32	9:3	5	2	HOSEA	14	2:1		18	12:19	12:19	39	5.5	20:9	2 COR.	5:15
6	19	38	10:4	12[2]	3[2]	1:11	7:1	7	MALACHI	22:7	13:9	21	40	6	11	2:7	1 PETER
7	22	41	15	14	5	2:6	4	3:3	3:15	24	11	13:11	44	10	32	4:14[2]	1:13
13	30:9	44	16[2]	17	7	15	8:4	15	17	23:13	12	25	54	17	21:4	5:4	21
29	13	51:2	17[2]	29:4	12	4:8	8		4:1	32	16	14:10	62	30	12	9:5	2:5[2]
5:10	31:6	3	19[2]	30:21	14	15	10	HABAK.	2	24:9	14:42	16:23	7:8[2]	34	15[2]	12:2	
17[3]	21	9	11:1	31:4	18	19	14	1:3		43	60	17:6	10[2]	36	27	4	2 PETER
6:1	28	11	22	10[2]	22	6:1	9:2	6	MATT.	26:52	15:37	13	14	37	22:3	14	1:13
4	40	12[2]	23	14[2]	24	2	5	9	3:9	27:37	39	18:10	8:7	6:12	13	GAL.	3:1
7:13	32:2	14	24[2]	32:2	4:17	8:4	7	15	12	50	41	13	10	13	22	1:17	10
16	3	27[2]	13:5[2]	3	34	7	11[3]	2:4	16		16:18	21	28	7:20	24:11	18	
25	33	34	10	33:25	5:19	8	15	6	4:1	MARK	19	31	59	21	12	2:1	1 JOHN
29	33:1	36	14:3	34:4	20	9		7	5	1:10		19:4	10:1	37	25:9	2	3:17
9:10[2]	15	42	4	16	23	9:6	OBADIAH	3:10	6	31	LUKE	5	31	42	18	3:23	JUDE
12	34:21	44	7	18	6:23[2]	12	1	16	8	35	1:66	20	11:31	43	26:10	EPHES.	12
18	35:11	53	40	23	7:3	16	6		16	2:4	69	21	41	55	30	2:6	20
21	15	52:7	17:9[2]	29	4	10:4	14	ZEPH.	5:1	9	2:4	22	55	8:31	27:15	4:8	
10:17	36:5	9	14	36:3[2]	5	8	21	2:4	6:19	11	28	28	12:20	39	17	10	REV.
20	20	31	17	7	8[2]	12		3:8	20	12	42	20:28	32	9:40	27	15	4:1
25	37:10		24	13	20	11:8	JONAH		9:6	21	3:5	21:1	34	41	40[2]	6:4	8:4
11:7	11	LAM.	18:6	37:6	8:3[2]	13:12	1:2	HAGGAI	16	3:13	6[2]	12	13:18	10:4		COLOS.	7[2]
13	38:10	1:14[2]	12	8	8	15[2]	3	1:8	10:17	26	8	28[2]	17:1	9	ROMANS	1:5	10:4
14	13[2]	19	15	10	22[2]	16	6	14	19	4:4	20	22:45	18:11	16	1:24	24	5
12:17	39:2	2:2	19:1	12	23		12		21[2]	5	25	23:5	30	26[2]	26	2:7	9
13:19	5	5[2]	3	13	25	JOEL	15	ZECH.	11:5	6	29	46	19:30	40	2:5	18	10
20	15	7	6	38:11	26	1:6	17	1:18	12:42	7	4:11	24:33	21:11	11:2	4:24	1 THESS.	11:12[2]
14:2	42:10	10	12[2]	16	27	10	2:6	21[2]	13:4	8	5:23	50		10	6:4	2:16	12:5
6	45:4	16	20:5[2]	18	9:24	12	4:6	2:1	5	27	24	51	ACTS	28	8:11[2]	4:17	16
15:9	46:4	17	6	39:2	10:5	20	10	13	6	32	25[2]		1:2	12:7[2]	32	1 TIM.	13:1
16:14	7	19	15	15	11:2[2]	2:9		5:1	7	5:29	28	JOHN	9	23	9:17	2:8	11
15	8[2]	22	24	40:6	3	20[2]	MICAH	5	26	6:29	6:8	2:7	10	13:1	10:7	3:6	14:11
18:7	9	3:41	28	22	4[2]	3:9[2]	2:4	7	28	40	20	13	11[2]	16	14:4	16	15:1
15	11	62	42	26	6	12	8	9[2]	29[2]	43	7:15	17	13	22	15:16	4:6	16:12
21	47:2	63	21:15	31	7		13[2]	6:1	14:12	51	16	19	15	31		5:10	18:21
20:9	6	4:5	22	34	10[2]	AMOS	3:10	12	19	7:34	8:6	20	22	33	1 COR.	6:19	19:3
21:2	48:5	5:12	22:30	37	12	1:6	4:2	9:3	20	8:8	7	3:13	2:14[2]	34	4:6	2 TIM.	20:3
22:20[2]	15		23:8	40	14	9	3	13	23	19	8	14[2]	24	43	18	1:6	9
22	44		22	49	15	13	5:8	16	15:13	20	37	4:14	30	50	19	4:8	13[2]

upon

5921, *1909*

GEN.	GEN.	EXOD.	EXOD.	EXOD.	LEVIT.	LEVIT.	NUM.	NUM.	DEU.	JOSH.	JUD.	1 SAM.	1 KINGS	1 KINGS	1 CHRON.	2 CHRON.	NEH.
1:2[2]	24:47	4:9[2]	21:19	34:1	4:31	13:50	4:11	20:28	22:19	10:24[2]	20:5	22:18[2]	1:13	19:19	10:4	24:18	9:10
11	61	20	22	7[2]	33	14:7	14[2]	21:8[2]	23:13	26	37	24:2	17	20:30	12:8	20	13
15	26:7	31	30	28	34	14[3]	25	9	19[2]	11:4	41	12	20	31	18	22	32
17	10	5:3	22:3	35	35	17[4]	5:14[2]	15	20[2]	7	48	13	24	38	19	27	33
25	25	8	25	35:3	5:9	18	15	22:22	24:15[2]	12:2		24[2]	30	21:4	13:11	25:13	10:34
26	27:12	9	24:11	36:17[2]	11	20	25	30	26:6	13:9	RUTH	25:39	33	21	14:11	28	12:31[2]
28	13	21	16	37:3[2]	6:9	25[3]	26	23:4	27:3	19:34	3:3	42	35	27	14	26:15	38
29	15	7:4	25:11	13	10	28[4]	30[2]	24:2	5	20:8	15	26:12	38	29	17	16	13:18[2]
30	16	5	21	16	12[2]	29	6:5	27:18	8	23:15[2]	4:7	28:18	44	22:17	15:13	20	
2:5	28:11	17	22	27	13	48	7	20	12	24:7	10	23	47		15	28:11	ESTHER
21	18	19[5]	30	39:5	15[2]	15:8	19	23	13			30:14[3]	2:5	2 KINGS	27	15	1:6
3:14	29:2	8:3[2]	26:4	15	27	9	25	30:14	28:8	JUD.	1 SAM.	16	12	2:9	16:8	29:8	2:15
4:15	3	4[2]	7	19	7:2	20[2]	26	31:27	15	3:10	1:9	17	25	16	40	22[2]	17
26	32	5	32[2]	24	5	22	27	33:4	20	16	11	31:2	29	3:15	19:17	23	3:13
6:12[2]	30:3	7	34	25	20	24	7:9	35:22	24	22	2:8	4	30	22	20:2	24	4:5
17	31:10	14	27:2	30	31	26	89	23	45	23	10	5	32[2]	27	21:14	27	5:1
7:3	12	18[2]	4	31	8:7[2]	16:2[2]	8:7		46[2]	4:16	28		33[6]	4:4[2]	16	32:8	6:8[2]
4	17	21[3]	7	43	8	4	10	DEU.	48	6:14	34	2 SAM.	34	5[2]	26[2]	12	7:8
6	34	9:3[6]	28:8	40:4	9[3]	8	12	1:36	56	20	4:12	1:2	37	21	22:8	25[2]	8:7[2]
8	35	9[2]	12[2]	13	11	9	24	2:25	60	26	13	6[2]	44	29	28:2	26	12[2]
10	46	10[2]	22	19	12	13[2]	25	4:7	61	28	19	9[2]	46	31	5	33:11	14
12	54	11[2]	23	20	13[2]	14	9:15	10	29:5[2]	34	5:3	10[2]	3:4	32	19	34:4	17
14	32:31[2]	14[3]	26	22	14	15	18	13	20	37	4[2]	15	26	33	29:25	5	9:2
17	32	19[2]	29	23	15[2]	18	19	26	22	39[2]	6	16	5:5	34[5]		21	3
18[2]	34:25	22	30[2]	29	16[2]	19	20	30	27	40	7[2]	19	6:32[3]	35	2 CHRON.	24[2]	13
19	27	23[2]	33	38	18	21[2]	22	32	30:1	7:5	6:8	21	35	5:23	1:6	25	25
21[2]	35:5	33	34		19	22	10:34	36	3	6	11	24	7:2[2]	6:26	4:4[2]	28[2]	27[3]
23	20	10:6	35	LEVIT.	21	25	11:9[2]	39	7	25	7:10	4:11	3	30[2]	13	35:3	10:1[2]
24	37:22	12	36	1:4	22	17:6	11	40	18	8:21	9:16	5:20	16	7:6	14	16	
8:4	27	13	37[2]	5	23[3]	11	17[2]	5:9	31:17	9:5	24	23	17	9	6:13[2]	36:17[2]	JOB
17[2]	34	11:1[2]	38[2]	7[2]	24[4]	18:25	25[2]	6:8	32:2[2]	18	25	6:3	18[2]	17	16		1:12
19	38:28	5	41	8[2]	25	19:17	26	9	23[2]	24[2]	10:1	8	19	20	20[2]	EZRA	15
9:2[3]	29	12:13[2]	43[2]	11	26	19	29	22[3]	24	33	6	9:8	20[2]	8:1	22	3:3[2]	17
16[2]	30	23	29:5	12	27[2]	28	31	7:6	35	44	10	11:2[2]	22	9:25	23	5:5	19
17	39:5	33	6[2]	13	28	20:9	12:3	7	42	49	11:2	21	25[2]	37	27	6:19	20
23	7	34	7	17[3]	30[5]	11	10	15[2]	33:10	53	6	23	29	10:5	7:3[2]	7:6	2:11
11:4	40:6	13:9	8	2:1	9:9	12	11	16	16[2]	57[2]	13:12	24	31	6	22	9[2]	12
8	17	16	10	2	10	13	13:23	22	26	11:29	16	12:16	38	15	9:19	17	13
9	41:3	14:4[2]	12	9	12	16	14:18	8:4	28	37	14:1	18	41	11:12	10:4	24	3:4
12:8	5	17[4]	13[2]	15	13	27	36	11:12	29	38	13[2]	13:29	42	12:11	9	26	5
11	17	18[3]	15	3:2[2]	14	21:5	37	18	34:9	12:1	25	14:7	8:31	13:13	11	28	6
15:11	42	22	16	3	17	10	15:31	20[2]		13:19	32	15:14	32	16[3]	12:7	8:18	25
12	42:1	26[3]	18	5[2]	18	12	32	21	JOSH.	14:6	15:19	32	36	18	13:4	22	4:5
16:5	21	29	19	8[2]	20[2]	22:3	38	25[2]	1:3	17	27	16:1	9:5[2]	16:13	10	31	14
17:17	43:18	30	20[5]	9	24	22	39	29[2]	2:6	19	16:13	8	9	15[2]	11	9:5	5:10[2]
18:6	30	31	21[5]	10	10:6	23:37	16:3	12:1	8	15:12	16	22	25[2]	17	18	13	6:28
19	44:21	15:9	22	11	7	24:4	4	2[2]	9	14[2]	23	17:2	10:20	18:21[2]	14:14		7:1
25	45:14[2]	15	25	13[2]	11:20	6	7	16	15[2]	16	17:5	12[2]	12:4	23	15:1	NEH.	8
31	15	16	38	14	21[2]	7	22	20	19[2]	16:3	6	14	9	19:7	5	2:8	17
19:3	46:4	19	30:1	15	27	14	33	24	3:13	9	38	18:9	32	21:12	17:10	12	8:9
9	47:31	26[2]	4	16	29	25:21	45	27[2]	16	12	39	17	33[2]	22:16[2]	18:16	18	15
16[2]	48:2	16:14	7	4:4	32	37	17:2	13:9	4:5	14	49	28	13:2[3]	20	18	4:4	9:8
23	14[2]	17:6	8	7	37	26:21	3	17	7:6[2]	17	51	20:8	3	23:6	23	12	33
24	17	18:8	10[2]	8	38	25	18:5	14:2	10	19	18:4	12	29	16	19:2	19	10:1
25	18	19:11	32	9	41	30	17	15:23	8:7	20	10	21:10[2]	14:10	20[2]	7	5:4	3
22:2	50:1[2]	16	33	10	42[3]	35	26	17:7	20	26	17[2]	22:7	17:14	24:3	10[2]	18	16
6	23	18	31:18	15	44	36	19:2	18	32	27	19:9	11[2]	19	25:6	20:9	19	17
9		20	32:16	18	46	37	13[2]	19:5	9:4	29	20	28	20	17[2]	12	6:1	12:4
12	EXOD.	22	20	19	13:25		15	10	5[2]	30[2]	23	34	21		14	14	21
17	1:16	24	21	24	27	NUM.	18[4]	21:23	20	18:25	20:9	24:15	18:1	1 CHRON.	22:8	8:2	13:11
24:15	2:25	20:5	29[3]	25	29	1:53	19	22:6[2]	10:11	19:14	25[2]	16	26	1:10	23:11	4	27
16	3:6	12	34	26	30	4:7	20	8	12	20	31	20	28	5:16	20	16	14:3
18	12	25	33:16	29	43	8	20:6	12	13	27	21:13		42	6:49	24:7	9:1	22
30	22[2]	21:14	21	30	45	10	26	14	18	28	22:17		19:11	9:27	9	4	15:26[2]

JOB 15:29, 16:9^{2}, 10^{2}, 13, 14^{2}, 15, 18:8, 15, 19:21^{2}, 25, 20:4, 22, 23^{2}, 25, 21:5, 9, 17, 22:28, 24:23, 25:3, 26:7, 9, 27:9, 10, 22, 28:9, 29:3, 4, 13, 19, 22, 30:12, 14^{2}, 15, 16^{2}, 22, 30, 31:1, 10, 36, 33:7, 15^{2}, 19, 27, 34:14, 21, 23, 36:28, 30, 37:12, 38:5, 24, 39:28, 40:4, 41:8, 30, 33, 42:11, PSALMS 2:6, 3:7, 8, 4:1, 4, 6, 5 *title*, 6 *title*, 2, 7:5, 16^{2}

PSALMS 8 *title*, 9 *title*, 3, 11:2, 6, 12 *title*, 14:2, 4, 17:6, 18:3, 6, 10^{2}, 33, 21:5, 12, 22 *title*, 9, 10, 13, 17, 18, 29, 24:2^{2}, 25:16, 18, 27:2, 5, 7, 29:3^{2}, 10, 30:10, 31:9, 16, 17, 32:4, 33:14, 18^{2}, 22, 34:15, 35:8, 16, 36:4, 37:9, 12, 40:2, 12, 17, 41:2, 8, 43:4, 44:17, 45 *title*, 8, 9, 46 *title*, 47:8, 48:6, 49:4, 50:10, 15, 51:1, 19, 53 *title*, 2, 4, 54:7, 55:3, 4, 5, 10, 15

PSALMS 55:16, 22, 56 *title*, 12, 59:9, 10, 61 *title*, 62:1, 5, 10, 63:6, 64:8, 65:5, 12, 66:11, 67:1, 2, 4, 68:4, 33, 69 *title*, 9, 15, 24, 72:6, 16, 73:25, 74:5, 78:24, 27, 31, 49, 79:6^{3}, 80 *title*, 17^{2}, 18, 81 *title*, 84 *title*, 9, 86:5, 7, 16, 88 *title*, 7, 9, 89:19, 22, 90:17^{2}, 91:13, 14, 15, 92:3^{3}, 94:23, 99:6^{2}, 101:6, 102:7, 13, 103:17, 104:3, 27, 105:1, 16, 38, 106:29, 107:40, 109:25, 112:2, 8, 116:2, 3, 4

PSALMS 116:13, 17, 118:5, 7, 119:49, 53, 87, 132, 135, 121:5, 123:2^{2}, 3^{2}, 125:3, 5, 128:6, 129:3, 6, 8, 132:11, 12, 18, 133:2^{2}, 3, 135:9^{2}, 137:2, 139:5, 140:10, 141:7, 144:9, 145:15, 18^{2}, 147:7, 8, 15, 149:5, 7^{2}, 9, 150:5^{2}, PROV. 1:27, 28, 3:3, 18, 6:21, 28, 7:3^{2}, 8:27, 9:3, 10:6, 24, 11:26, 19:12, 17, 23:5, 31, 34, 24:25, 32, 25:12, 20, 22, 26:14^{2}, 27, 28:22, 30:19, 24, 32, ECCL. 5:2

ECCL. 7:20, 8:6, 14, 9:12, 10:7^{2}, 11:1, 2, 3, CANT. 1:6^{2}, 2:8^{2}, 17, 3:8, 4:16, 5:5, 15, 6:13, 7:5, 8:5, 6^{2}, 9, 14, ISAIAH 1:25, 2:12^{2}, 13^{2}, 14^{2}, 15^{2}, 16^{2}, 3:26, 4:5^{3}, 5:6, 6:1, 7, 7:17^{3}, 19^{2}, 8:7, 17, 9:2, 6, 7^{2}, 8, 10:12, 20^{2}, 26, 11:2, 14^{2}, 12:4, 13:2, 14:13, 16, 25, 26^{2}, 15:9^{3}, 16:5, 18:2, 4, 6^{2}, 19:1, 8, 12, 20:3, 21:3, 8, 13, 22:22, 24, 25, 23:17

ISAIAH 24:17, 20, 21, 26:16, 28:4, 10^{3}, 13^{2}, 22, 27, 29:10, 30:6^{2}, 16^{2}, 17, 18, 25^{2}, 32, 32:11, 13^{2}, 15, 33:4, 20, 34:2^{2}, 5^{2}, 11, 35:10, 36:8, 12, 37:7, 38:21, 40:7, 22, 24, 31, 41:25^{3}, 42:1, 5, 25, 43:2, 22, 44:3^{4}, 19, 45:12, 46:1^{2}, 7, 47:6, 9, 11^{3}, 13, 48:2, 49:13, 16, 22, 50:10, 51:5, 6, 11, 52:7, 53:5, 55:6, 7, 56:7, 57:7, 58:14, 59:17, 21, 60:1, 2^{2}, 61:1, 62:6, 63:3, 64:7

ISAIAH 65:3, 7^{2}, 66:4, 12, 20^{3}, 24, JER. 1:14, 2:3, 15, 20, 34, 37, 3:6, 12, 21, 4:20, 29, 5:3, 10, 12, 15, 6:11^{2}, 12, 19, 21, 23, 26, 7:20^{5}, 8:2, 9:3, 22, 10:25^{2}, 11:8, 11, 16, 23, 12:12, 13:1, 4, 13, 16, 22, 26, 14:16, 22, 15:5, 8^{3}, 14, 16:4, 17, 17:1^{2}, 2, 18, 25, 18:22, 19:3, 13, 15^{2}, 22:2, 4, 23, 24, 30, 23:2, 12, 17, 19, 40, 24:6

JER. 25:13, 26, 29, 30, 33, 26:15^{3}, 27:2, 5, 28:14, 29:12, 16, 17, 30:16, 18, 23, 31:5, 6, 19, 20, 26, 39, 32:19, 23, 29, 42^{2}, 33:17, 21, 35:17^{2}, 36:4, 6, 30, 31^{3}, 39:5, 16, 40:2, 3, 4, 42:12, 17, 18^{2}, 45:5, 46:16, 21, 47:5, 48:8, 18, 21^{4}, 22^{3}, 23^{3}, 24^{3}, 32^{2}, 37^{2}, 38, 43, 44^{2}, 49:5, 8, 36, 37, 50:15, 19, 35^{4}, 36^{2}, 37^{4}, 38^{2}, 42, 51:6, 12, 13, 25, 35^{2}

JER. 51:42, 47, 52, 56^{2}, 60, 64, 52:9, 22^{2}, 23, LAM. 1:10, 14, 2:10^{2}, 11, 3:28, 47, 53, 55, 57, 4:19, 5:1, 18, EZEKIEL 1:3, 15, 17, 22, 26^{2}, 28, 2:1, 2, 3:14, 22, 24, 27, 4:1, 4^{3}, 5, 8, 9, 5:1^{2}, 13, 16^{2}, 17^{2}, 6:3, 12, 13, 14, 7:2, 3^{3}, 4, 8^{2}, 12, 14, 18^{2}, 26^{2}, 8:1, 9:4, 6, 7, 8^{2}, 10, 10:11, 11:5, 8, 13, 21, 23, 12:6

EZEKIEL 12:7, 12, 13, 13:9, 15^{2}, 18, 14:9, 13^{2}, 17, 19, 21, 22^{2}, 16:5, 8, 11, 12, 14, 41, 43, 17:19, 20, 22, 18:6, 8, 11, 13^{2}, 15, 20^{2}, 19:9, 20:8, 13, 21, 21:12^{4}, 29, 31, 22:9, 20, 21, 22, 24, 31^{2}, 23:6, 8, 9, 10, 12^{2}, 14, 15^{2}, 16, 20, 23, 41, 42^{2}, 46, 49, 24:6, 7^{2}, 8, 11, 13, 17^{2}, 22^{3}, 25:7, 11, 12, 13, 14, 16, 17^{2}, 26:7, 14

EZEKIEL 26:16, 19, 27:11^{2}, 29, 30, 28:7, 12, 14, 18, 23, 26, 29:5, 7, 8, 30:4, 9, 15, 25, 31:12, 13^{2}, 14, 32:4^{3}, 5, 8, 11, 27, 33:2, 3, 4, 5, 10, 22, 26, 34:6^{2}, 13, 14^{2}, 36:10, 12, 18^{2}, 20, 25, 29, 37:1, 4, 6^{2}, 8, 9, 10, 16^{2}, 22, 38:12^{2}, 15, 20^{2}, 22^{3}, 39:2, 4, 5, 17, 21, 25, 29, 40:1, 2, 4, 16, 17, 26, 31, 34, 37, 41

EZEKIEL 40:43, 41:25^{2}, 26, 43:3, 12, 14, 20, 24, 27^{2}, 44:4, 17, 18^{2}, 45:19^{3}, 22, 47:10, 12, DANIEL 1:13, 2:10, 28, 29, 34, 46, 3:27, 4:5, 13, 21, 24, 28, 33, 5:5, 6:10, 17, 23, 7:1, 2, 4, 6, 23, 8:7, 10, 17, 9:11, 12^{2}, 13, 14^{2}, 17, 24^{2}, 27, 10:7, 10^{2}, 15, 16, 11:18, 24, 42, 12:6, 7, HOSEA 1:4, 6, 7, 2:4, 13, 23, 4:13^{2}, 5:1

HOSEA 5:10, 7:9, 12, 14, 8:14, 9:1, 10:7, 11, 12, 14, 12:14, 13:13, 14:3, JOEL 1:6, 2:2, 8, 9^{2}, 28, 29^{2}, 3:4, 7, AMOS 1:12, 2:2, 5, 8, 3:5, 9, 14, 4:2, 7^{3}, 13, 5:2, 8, 11, 6:4^{2}, 12, 7:7, 8:2, 10^{2}, 9:1, 4, 6, 8, 9, 15, OBADIAH 11, 15^{2}, 16, 17, JONAH 1:6^{2}, 7^{2}, 8, 12, 14, 2:10, 4:8, MICAH 1:3, 2:1, 3:11^{2}, 4:11, 5:1

MICAH 5:7, 9, 15, 7:16, 19, NAHUM 1:15, 2:7, 3:3, 5, 6, 7, 18, 19, HABAK. 1:13, 2:1^{2}, 2, 3:1, 8, 19, ZEPH. 1:4^{2}, 5, 17, 2:2^{2}, 3:8^{2}, 9, HAGGAI 1:9, 11^{9}, 2:15, ZECH. 1:7, 8, 16, 2:9, 3:5^{2}, 9, 4:2^{2}, 3^{2}, 11^{2}, 5:8, 11, 6:8, 11, 13^{2}, 9:9^{2}, 16, 10:6, 11:11, 17^{2}, 12:4, 10^{3}, 13:7, 14:4, 12, 17, 20, MALACHI 1:7, 2:2, 3, 3:16

MATT. 3:16, 4:13, 6:19, 7:24, 25^{2}, 26, 27, 9:18, 10:13, 27, 11:29, 12:2, 18, 13:5, 16:18, 19:28, 20:25, 23:9, 18, 35^{2}, 36, 24:2, 3, 25:31, 26:10, 27:29, 30, 35, 28:2, MARK 1:10, 2:10, 6:5, 17, 39, 48, 49, 7:30, 32, 8:23, 25, 10:16, 27, 34, 42, 11:7, 11, 13:2, 3, 14:67, 15:19, 24, LUKE 1:12, 35, 58, 2:9, 25, 40, 3:22, 4:18, 5:1, 19, 24, 36, 6:10, 48^{2}, 49

LUKE 8:6, 43, 9:38, 10:6, 11:20, 22, 12:1, 3, 13:4, 17:31, 18:13, 19:35, 43, 44, 20:1, 18, 21:6, 23, 25, 34, 22:25, 56, 61, 23:26, 24:49, JOHN 1:32, 33, 36, 51, 4:27, 9:15, 11:38, 12:35, 18:4, 19:29, 31, ACTS 1:8, 26, 2:3, 17, 43, 3:4, 4:1, 33, 5:11^{2}, 28, 6:12, 7:57, 59, 8:16, 24, 10:9, 11:6, 19, 12:7, 21^{2}, 13:11, 40, 15:10, 17, 28, 16:23, 18:6, 19:6, 13, 20:7

ACTS 21:35, 22:13, 24:7, 26:16, 27:26, 29, ROMANS 2:9, 3:22, 4:9^{2}, 5:12, 18^{2}, 9:28, 10:12, 13, 32, 13:4, 6, 15:20, 1 COR. 1:2, 3:12, 7:35^{2}, 9:16, 10:11, 12:23, 15:10, 16:2, 2 COR. 1:11, 23, 3:15, 5:2, 4, 8:4, 22, 11:28, 12:9, GAL. 4:11, 6:16, EPHES. 2:20, 4:26, 5:6, PHIL. 1:3, 2:7, 17, 27, COLOS. 3:5, 1 THESS. 2:16, 5:3^{2}, 1 TIM. 4:15, HEB. 6:18

HEB. 8:6, 11:21, JAMES 2:21, 4:3, 1 PETER 4:14, 5:7, 2 PETER 2:1, 5, 6, 1 JOHN 1:1, 3:1, JUDE 15, REV. 1:17, 2:24, 3:3, 10^{2}, 12^{2}, 4:3, 4, 5:7, 13, 7:10, 8:3, 7, 10^{2}, 9:3, 10:1, 2, 5^{2}, 8^{2}, 11:10, 11^{2}, 16, 12:1, 3, 13:1^{3}, 8, 14:14, 16:1, 2^{3}, 3, 4, 8, 10, 12, 18, 21, 17:1, 3, 5, 16, 18:24, 19:11, 14, 21, 20:3, 4^{2}, 21:5

US

2248

GEN. 1:26, 3:22, 5:29, 11:3, 4^{4}, 7, 19:5, 13, 31, 32, 34, 20:9, 23:6^{3}, 24:23, 55, 65, 26:10^{2}, 16, 22, 28^{3}, 29, 31:14, 15, 37, 44, 50, 53, 32:18, 20, 33:12, 34:9, 10, 14, 16, 17, 21^{4}, 22^{3}, 23, 35:3, 37:8^{2}, 17

GEN. 37:20, 21, 27, 39:14, 17, 41:12^{2}, 13, 42:2, 21^{2}, 28, 30, 33, 43:2, 3, 4, 7, 18^{3}, 25, 26, 44:26, 27, 30, 31, 47:15, 19^{2}, 25, 50:15^{2}, EXOD. 1:10^{2}, 2:14, 19^{2}, 3:18^{2}, 5:3^{3}, 8, 16, 17, 21, 10:7, 25, 26

EXOD. 13:14, 15, 16, 14:5, 11^{3}, 12, 25, 16:3, 7, 8, 17:2, 3, 7, 9, 19:23, 20:19^{2}, 24:14, 32:1^{3}, 23^{3}, 33:15, 16, 34:9^{2}, NUM. 10:29, 31^{2}, 32^{2}, 11:4, 13, 18^{2}, 12:2, 11, 13:27, 30, 14:3^{2}, 4^{2}, 8^{3}, 9^{2}, 16:13^{3}, 14^{2}, 34

NUM. 20:5^{2}, 14, 15, 16, 17, 21:5, 7, 22:45, 27:4, 31:49, 32:5, 19, DEU. 1:6, 14, 19, 20, 22^{3}, 25^{3}, 27^{4}, 41, 2:29, 30, 32, 33, 36^{2}, 37, 3:1, 5:2, 3^{3}, 24, 25, 27, 6:21, 23^{3}, 24^{2}, 25, 9:28, 13:2^{2}, 6

DEU. 13:13, 26:3, 6^{3}, 8, 9^{2}, 15, 29:29, 30:12^{2}, 13^{2}, 31:17^{2}, 33:4, JOSH. 1:16^{2}, 2:9, 14, 17, 18, 20, 24, 4:23, 5:6, 13, 7:7^{2}, 9, 25, 8:5, 6^{2}, 9:6, 7, 11, 20^{2}, 22^{2}, 25, 10:6^{4}, 17:4, 16, 21:2, 22:17, 19^{2}, 22

JOSH. 22:23, 25, 26^{2}, 27^{2}, 28^{2}, 31, 34, 24:17^{2}, 18, 27^{2}, JUD. 1:1, 24, 6:13^{6}, 8:1^{2}, 21, 22^{2}, 9:8, 10, 12, 14, 11:8, 10, 15^{2}, 19, 24, 12:1, 13:8^{2}, 15, 23^{3}, 14:15^{2}, 15:10^{2}, 11^{2}, 16:5, 24, 25, 18:19^{2}, 25, 19:11, 13

JUD. 19:28, 20:3, 8^{2}, 13, 18, 32^{2}, 39, 21:1, 22, RUTH 2:20, 1 SAM. 4:3^{5}, 7, 8^{2}, 5:7^{2}, 10^{2}, 11, 6:2, 9^{3}, 20, 7:8^{2}, 12, 8:5^{2}, 6, 19, 20^{2}, 9:5^{2}, 6^{2}, 8, 9, 10, 27, 10:16, 19, 27, 11:1, 3^{2}, 10

1 SAM. 11:12, 14, 12:4^{2}, 10, 12, 19, 14:1, 6^{2}, 9, 10^{2}, 12, 17, 36^{3}, 17:9, 20:11, 42, 21:5, 23:19, 25:7, 15, 16, 40, 26:11, 27:11, 29:4^{2}, 9, 30:22, 23^{3}, 2 SAM. 2:14, 5:2, 10:12, 11:23, 13:25, 26, 15:14^{2}, 19, 20, 17:5, 18:3^{5}

2 SAM. 19:9^{2}, 10^{2}, 42^{2}, 43, 20:6^{2}, 21:4, 5^{2}, 6, 17, 24:14, 1 KINGS 3:8, 5:6, 8:57^{3}, 12:4, 9, 10, 18:23, 26, 20:23, 31, 2 KINGS 1:6, 4:9, 10^{3}, 13, 6:1, 2^{3}, 11, 16, 7:4^{3}, 6^{2}, 9, 12, 13, 9:5, 12, 10:5, 14:8

2 KINGS 18:26, 30, 32, 19:19, 22:13^{2}, 1 CHRON. 13:2^{2}, 3^{2}, 15:13, 16:35^{2}, 19:13, 2 CHRON. 10:4, 9, 10, 13:10, 12, 14:7^{2}, 11, 20:9, 11^{3}, 12, 25:17, 29:10, 32:7, 8^{2}, 11, 34:21, EZRA 4:2^{2}, 3^{2}, 12, 14, 18, 5:11, 17, 8:17

EZRA 8:18^{2}, 21, 22, 23, 31^{2}, 9:8^{3}, 9^{4}, 13^{3}, 44^{2}, 10:3, 14, NEH. 2:17, 18, 19^{2}, 20, 4:12^{2}, 15^{2}, 20^{2}, 22, 23, 5:8, 10, 17^{2}, 6:2, 7, 9, 10^{2}, 16, 9:32, 33, 37, 10:32, 13:18, JOB 9:33^{2}, 15:9, 10, 21:14

JOB 22:17, 31:15, 34:4^{3}, 37, 35:11^{2}, 37:19, PSALMS 2:3^{2}, 4:6^{2}, 12:4, 17:11, 19:9, 33:22, 34:3, 44:1, 7^{2}, 9, 10^{2}, 11^{2}, 13^{2}, 14, 17, 19^{2}, 23, 26, 46:7, 11, 47:3, 4, 54 *title*, 60:1^{3}, 3, 10, 11, 62:8, 65:5, 66:10^{2}, 11, 12, 67:1^{2}

PSALMS 67:6, 7, 68:19, 28, 74:1, 8, 9, 78:3, 79:4, 8^{2}, 9^{2}, 80:2, 3, 6, 7, 18, 19, 83:4, 12, 85:4^{2}, 5, 6, 7^{2}, 13, 90:12, 14, 15^{2}, 17^{2}, 95:1^{2}, 2, 6^{2}, 100:3, 103:10^{2}, 12, 106:47^{2}, 108:11, 12, 115:1^{2}, 12^{2}, 117:2, 118:27

PSALMS 119:4, 122:1, 123:2, 3^{2}, 124:2, 3^{2}, 4, 6, 126:3, 136:23, 24, 137:3^{6}, PROV. 1:11, 12, 14, 7:18^{2}, ECCL. 1:10, 12:13, CANT. 2:15, 5:9, 7:11^{2}, 12^{2}, ISAIAH 1:9, 18, 2:3^{2}, 5, 4:1, 6:8, 7:6^{3}, 8:10, 9:6, 14:8, 10

ISAIAH 17:14^{2}, 22:13, 25:9, 26:12^{2}, 13, 28:15, 29:15^{2}, 30:10^{2}, 11, 15, 33:3, 14^{2}, 21, 22, 36:11, 15, 17, 37:20, 40:1, 41:22^{2}, 43:9, 26, 50:8, 53:6, 59:9^{2}, 11, 12^{2}, 63:7, 16^{2}, 17, 64:6, 7^{2}, 12, JER. 2:6^{2}, 27, 3:25, 4:5, 8, 13

JER. 5:12, 19, 24^{2}, 6:4^{2}, 5^{2}, 24, 26, 8:8, 14^{4}, 9:18, 19, 11:19^{2}, 14:7, 9^{2}, 19^{2}, 21^{2}, 16:10, 18:18^{3}, 21:2^{4}, 13, 26:16, 29:15, 28, 31:6, 35:6, 8, 9, 10, 11, 36:17, 37:3, 9, 38:16, 25^{2}, 40:10, 41:8, 42:2^{2}, 3, 5^{2}, 6, 20^{2}

JER. 43:3^{4}, 44:16, 46:16, 48:2, 50:5, 51:9, 10, LAM. 3:40, 41, 43, 45, 46, 47, 4:17^{2}, 19^{2}, 5:1, 4, 8^{2}, 16, 20^{2}, 21, 22^{2}, EZEKIEL 8:12, 11:3, 15, 24:19^{2}, 33:10, 24, 35:12, 37:18, DANIEL 1:12, 2:23, 3:17^{2}, 9:7, 8

DANIEL 9:10, 11, 12^{3}, 13, 14, 16, HOSEA 6:1^{3}, 2^{2}, 3, 10:3, 8^{2}, 12:4, 14:2, 3, AMOS 4:1, 6:13, 9:10, OBADIAH 1, JONAH 1:7, 8^{2}, 11, 14^{2}, MICAH 3:11^{2}, 4:2^{2}, 5:1, 6, 7:19, ZECH. 1:6^{2}, 8:21

MALACHI
1:2
9
2:10
MATT.
1:23
3:15
6:11
12
13[2]
8:25
29
31[2]
9:27
13:36
56
15:15
23
17:4[2]
20:7
12
30
31
21:25
38[2]

MATT.
22:17
25
24:3
25:8
9
11
26:46
63
68
27:4
25
49
MARK
1:24
38
4:35
5:12
6:3
9:5[2]
22[2]
38[2]
40
10:35
37

MARK
12:7
19
13:4
14:15
42
15:36
16:3
LUKE
1:1
2
69
71
74
78
2:15[2]
48
4:34[2]
7:5
16
20
8:22
9:33[2]
49
50[2]

LUKE
10:11
17
11:1
3
4[4]
45
12:41
13:25
15:23
16:26[2]
17:13
19:14
20:2
6
14
22
28
22:8
67
23:18
30[2]
39
24:22
24
29

LUKE
24:32[3]
JOHN
1:14
22
2:18
4:12
25
6:34
52
8:5
9:34
10:24[2]
11:7
15
16
50
14:8[2]
9
22
31
16:17
17:21
18:31
19:24

ACTS
1:17
21[2]
22[2]
2:29
3:4
12
5:28
6:14
7:27
38
40[3]
10:41
42
11:13
15
17
13:33
47
14:11
17
15:7
8
9
24
25

ACTS
15:28
36
16:9
10
14
15[2]
16
17[2]
21
37[4]
17:27
20:5
14
21:5
11
16
17
18
23:9
24:4
7
25:24
27:2
6
7

ACTS
27:20
28:2[2]
7[2]
10[2]
15[2]
ROMANS
3:8
4:16
24
5:5
8[2]
6:3
8:4
18
26
31[2]
32[2]
34
35
37
39
9:24
29
12:6[2]

ROMANS
12:7
13:12[2]
13
14:7
12
13
19
15:2
7
16:6
1 COR.
1:18
30
2:10
12
4:1
6
8
9
5:7
8
6:14
7:15
8:6

1 COR.
8:8
10:8
9
15:32
57
16:16
2 COR.
1:4
5
8
10[2]
11[2]
14
19
20
21[2]
22
2:11
14[2]
3:3
6
4:7
12
14[2]

2 COR.
4:17
5:5[2]
14
18[2]
19
20
21
6:12
7:1
2
6
7
9
8:4[2]
5
7
19[2]
20[2]
9:11
10:2
8
13
GAL.
1:4

GAL.
1:23
2:4
3:13[2]
24
4:26
5:1
25
26
6:9
10
EPHES.
1:3
4
5
6
8
9
2:4
5
6[2]
7
14
3:20
4:7

EPHES.
5:2[2]
PHIL.
3:15
16[2]
17
COLOS.
1:2
8
13[2]
2:14[2]
4:3[2]
1 THESS.
1:6
9
10
2:13
15
16
18
3:6[4]
4:1
7
8

1 THESS.
5:6[2]
8
9
10
25
2 THESS.
1:7
2:2
16[2]
3:1
6
7
9
1 TIM.
6:8
17
2 TIM.
1:7
9[3]
14
2:12

TITUS
2:12
14[2]
3:6
15
HEB.
1:2
2:3
4:1[2]
2
11
14
16
6:1
18
20
7:26
9:12
24
10:15
20
22
23
24

HEB.
11:40[2]
12:1[4]
9
10
28
13:13
15
18
JAMES
1:18
3:3
4:5
1 PETER
1:3
12
2:21[2]
3:18
21
4:1
3
17
5:10

2 PETER
1:1
3[2]
4
3:2
1 JOHN
1:2
3
7
8
9[2]
10
2:19[5]
25
3:1[2]
16
18
20
21
23
24[2]
4:6[2]
7
9
10

1 JOHN
11
12[2]
13[2]
16
19
5:11
14
15
20
2 JOHN
2[2]
3 JOHN
9
10
REV.
1:5[2]
6
5:9
10
6:16[2]
19:7

was

1961, *2258*

GEN.
1:2[2]
3
4
7
9
10
11
12[2]
15
18
21
24
25
30
31
2:5[2]
10
19
20
23
3:1
6
10
20
23
4:2
5
18
19
20
21
22
26
5:24
32
6:5[2]
9
11
12
7:6[2]
12
17[2]
22
23
8:1
2
11
13
9:19
21
10:9
10
19
25[2]
30
11:1
10
29
30
12:4
6
10[2]
11
14[2]
15
18
13:2
6[2]
7
10
14
14:10
14
18
15:12
17
16:1
4
5
14
16
17:1
24
25
26
18:10
15

GEN.
19:22
23
20:16
21:3
5
8[2]
11
15
20
22:20
24
23:1
17[2]
24:1
15
16
29
33
36
67
25:1
8
10
17
20
21
26
27[2]
29
30
26:1[2]
7
8
28
34
27:1
30
28:7
11
17
19
29:2
12
16
17
23
31
33
34
30:2
29
30
37
31:1[2]
2
22
31
36
39
40
48
32:7[2]
24
25
34:19
24
28[2]
29
35:3
4
5
8[2]
16
17
18
19
29
36:12
22
24
32
35
39[2]
37:1
2[2]
3
15

GEN.
37:23[2]
24[2]
29
38:1
2
5
6
7
12
13
14[2]
16
21[2]
22
24
25
29
30
39:1
2[3]
3
5
6
11
13
19
20
21
22
23[2]
40:2
3
9
10
11
15
16[2]
17
20
41:7
8[2]
10
12
13
24
32
37
46
48
49
53
54[2]
55
56
57
42:1
5
6[2]
27
35
43:1
12[2]
18
21
26
34
44:3
12
14
45:8
16
47:13[2]
14
18
28
48:7
14[2]
49:7[2]
15[2]
26
32
33
50:9
11
15
26

EXOD.
1:5
7
14
15
2:2
11
12
21
3:2
6
4:6
7
14
5:13
19
6:3
7:7
15
21[2]
22
8:15
19
24
9:7[2]
11
24[2]
25
26
31[3]
33
35
10:13
15
22
11:3
6
29
30[3]
34
39
40
13:17
14:5[2]
20
15:23
16:14
15
20
24
31[2]
17:1
18:3
4[2]
11
19:16
18
20:21
22:13
24:10
17
18
25:40
26:30
27:8
29:33
31:17
32:16
33:7
8
34:28
34
35:23
24
36:7
9
12
15[2]
21
37:1
6
10
22
25[3]
38:1[2]
18[3]
21
23

EXOD.
38:24[2]
25
29
39:4
5[2]
9[2]
10[2]
19
23
32
40:17
35
36
37
38[2]
LEVIT.
4:10
6:2
3
4
27
8:4
10
16
21
25
26
29
30
9:8
15
18
10:16[2]
18
20
13:18
14:6
48
15:10
16:27
17:15
19:20
21:10
24:10
11
25:33
50
51
27:24
NUM.
1:44
3:16
21
27
33
35
6:12
7:9
10
12
13[2]
17
19
23
25[2]
29
31
35
37[2]
41
43
47
49[2]
53
55
59
61[2]
65
67[2]
71
73
77
79[2]
83
84[2]

NUM.
7:86
88[2]
89[2]
8:4[2]
9:14
15[2]
16
17
20[2]
21[4]
22
10:11
14
15
16
17
18
19
20
22
23
24
25[2]
26
27
34
11:1
2
4
7
8
10[2]
18
25
26
33[3]
12:3
9
10
15[2]
13:20
22
24
14:16
15:34
16:15
31
42
47
48
50
18:6
8
19:13
20:1
2
13
29
21:4
24
26
35
22:3[2]
4
14
22[2]
26
27
30[2]
36
24:10
20
25:3
8
11
13
14[3]
15[3]
18
26:46
59
60
62
64
65
27:3
13

NUM.
28:6
31:14
16
26
32
36[2]
37
38
39
40
41
43
52
32:1
10
13[2]
39
33:14
39
35:23
25
26
36:2
DEU.
1:34
37
2:14
15
20
36
3:3
4
8
11[2]
13
26
4:21
35
8:2
15
9:8
9
10
19[2]
20
21
28
10:6
11:6
20:6
21:15
22:27
26:5
29:7
15[2]
27
32:12
50
33:5
16
21
34:7[2]
9
JOSH.
1:5
17
2:2
5
15
3:7
4:10
5:1
13
6:1
21
24
27[2]
7:1
16
17
18
22
26
8:11
13

JOSH.
8:17
25
29
33
35
9:5
10
24
10:2[2]
14
17
11:10
11
12:4
13:1
16
23[2]
25
29
30
33
14:2
7[2]
11[2]
15[2]
15:1[2]
2
5[2]
9[2]
11
12
15
16:5[2]
17:1[2]
2
7
9
10[2]
18:1
12
14[2]
15
17
19
20[2]
19:1
9[2]
10
18
25
33
41
21:10
22:14
17
24:26
33
JUD.
1:10
11
17
19
22
23
28
36
2:14
15
18
19
20
3:8
17
20
24
25
27
30
31
4:1
2
11
12
16
17
21

JUD.
4:22
5:8[2]
14
15
6:3
6
11
21
22
27
28[5]
30
34
35
38
40[2]
7:8
13[2]
15
8:3[2]
11
13
20
26[2]
28[2]
31
32
33
9:5
6
26
30
44
45
47
51
55
10:2
5
7
9
16
11:1[2]
5
18
34
39
12:5
7
10
12
15
13:2[3]
6[2]
9
16
21
14:4
8
19
20
15:14
18
19
16:2
4
9
16
20
22
27
29
17:1[2]
6[2]
7[2]
11[2]
12
18:1
7
20
28[3]
29[2]
31
19:1[2]
2
10
11

JUD.
19:15
16
26[2]
27
29
30[2]
20:1
3
4
27
34[2]
38
41
21:25[2]
RUTH
1:1
2
3
4
5
7
18
19
2:1
3[2]
5
6
14
15
17
18
3:7
8
4:3
7[2]
9[2]
13
1 SAM.
1:1[2]
2
4
10
13
18
20
24
2:13[2]
17
22
26
3:1[2]
2
3[2]
7
19
20
4:2
6
10[2]
11
15
18
19[2]
21
5:3
4[2]
6
7
9[2]
11[2]
6:1
4
9
14
15
7:2[2]
10
13
14
17[2]
8:1
2
9:1[2]
2[3]
5

1 SAM.
9:9
10
24
10:9
20
21[2]
23
11:6
11
12:8
12
15
13:3
4
7
19
22[2]
14:3
4[2]
5
14
15[2]
18
19
20[2]
25
27
35
39
42
43
50[2]
51[2]
52[2]
15:9[2]
12
16:12
23[3]
17:3
4
5[2]
12[2]
14
20
24
28
40
42
50
51
18:1
4
5
6
8
10
12[3]
14
15
19
28
29
30
19:7
8
9
16
19
20
21
23
20:19
24
26
27[2]
30
33
34
37
41
21:1
6[3]
7[2]
12
22:2[3]
4
6

1 SAM.
22:9
22
23:7[2]
13[2]
15[2]
24:1[2]
3
25:2[3]
3[4]
7
20
21
36[2]
37
39
44
26:4
12
16
21
24
27:4[2]
7
28:3
5
14
20[2]
21
30:3
6[2]
9[2]
10
19
25
31:3
4
5
2 SAM.
1:1
2
10[4]
26
2:10
11[2]
16
17[2]
18
32
3:1
2
6
7
8
22[2]
23
26
27
35
37
4:1
2[2]
4[3]
5:2
4
10
13
6:3
4
7
8
9
12
13
14
20
21
7:9
19
8:16[2]
17
18
9:2[2]
6
12
13
10:9

2 SAM.
10:17
11:1
2
4
7
26
27
12:3
4[2]
5
15
18[2]
19
21
22
30
13:1
2[2]
3[2]
6
8
15
19
21
38
39[2]
14:1
6
25[2]
26[2]
27[2]
15:2
5
12
17
30
32
16:1
5
16
23[2]
17:6
19
22
23[2]
25[2]
27
18:6
7
8
9[2]
14
29
33
19:1
2[2]
16
18
25
32
39
20:1
8
10
13
17
20
23[2]
24[2]
25
26
21:1
7
11
14
16
18[2]
19[2]
20[3]
22:8
10
11
19
24
42
23:1
2

2 SAM.
23:8
9
10
11[2]
14[2]
16
18
19[2]
23
24
24:1
2
11
16
25[2]
1 KINGS
1:1
4
6
15[2]
23
2:10
12
26
29
34
41[2]
46
3:2
4
12
15
17
18[3]
21[2]
26
28
4:1
4
5[2]
6[2]
15
16
19[3]
22
31[2]
5:1
12[2]
14
6:2
3[2]
6[3]
7[3]
8
17
18[3]
20[2]
22
24
25
26
37
38[2]
7:1
2
3
4
5
6[2]
7
8
10
12
14[3]
16[3]
20
22[2]
23[2]
24
25
26[2]
27
28
29
31[2]
32

1 KINGS
7:33
35
38
47
48
51
8:9
17
18[2]
34
37
64[3]
9:1
25
10:2[2]
3
5
6
7
14
19
20
21
11:4[3]
9[2]
14
15[2]
20
21
25
26
27
28[2]
30
40
42
43
12:2[2]
15
18
20[2]
21
13:5
6[2]
9
17
24[2]
26
14:6
8
21[2]
28
30
31[2]
15:2
3
5
6
7
10
11
14
16
22
23
24
32
16:6
9
18
28
17:1
10
11
17[2]
18:2
3
4
7
13
26[3]
29[2]
30
38
45[2]
46
19:6

1 KINGS
19:11[2]
12
13
19
20:12
16
29[2]
36
40[2]
41
21:1
11
15[2]
16
25
22:13
33
35
37
42[2]
43
47[2]
50
2 KINGS
1:2[2]
7
8
2:17
23
3:4
5
9
20[2]
26
27
4:8[2]
18[2]
31
32[2]
36
38
41
5:1[3]
8
11
14
6:5[2]
11
13
15
17
25[2]
26
7:5
7
10
15
16
8:5
6
7[2]
11
17
18
24
26[2]
27
29
9:15
16
21
30
34
10:5[2]
12
15
21[2]
22
30
36
11:1
2
3
14
16
20

2 KINGS
11:21
12:1
2
6
9
10[6]
12
13
16[2]
18
13:2
3
11
13
14
19
21
23
14:2[2]
3
5
9[3]
12
16
20
21
24
25
26[2]
15:2[2]
3
5[2]
9
12
18
24
27
33[2]
34
38
16:2[2]
8
10
12
14
20
17:2
7
18[2]
23
25
18:2[2]
3
5
7
9
10
15
18
36
37
19:2
8
37
20:1
4
18[2]
21:1[3]
2
15
16
18
19[2]
20
26
22:1[2]
2
7[2]
9
19
23:2
3
11
15
22
23
25

2 KINGS
23:26
31[2]
32
36[2]
37
24:8[3]
9
10
18[2]
19
25:2
3
4
13
16
17[2]
19
21
30
1 CHRON.
1:19[2]
39
43
44
45
46[2]
47
48
49
50[2]
2:3
17
19
21
24
26[2]
29
34
42
45[2]
49
3:10
4:3
9
11
40
41
5:1[2]
2
6
7
20
22
6:54
7:2
9
15[2]
16
24
25
40
8:29
34
37
9:17
20[2]
21
27
31
35
40
10:3
4
5
11:2
6
9
12[2]
13[2]
16[2]
18
20
21[2]
23
25
12:3

1 CHRON.
12:14, 18, 22, 27, 40, 13:4, 10, 11, 12, 14:2, 8, 15:22^2, 27, 16:39, 17:13, 17, 18:15, 16, 17, 19:10, 17, 20:1, 2, 4, 5^2, 6^3, 21:5, 6, 7, 15, 20, 30, 22:7, 23:1, 3, 8, 11, 13, 16, 28, 24:21, 25, 29, 25:1, 7, 26:1, 10, 20, 24, 28, 31, 27:2, 3, 4^2, 5, 6^2, 7, 8, 9, 10, 11, 12, 13, 14, 15, 16, 24, 25^2, 26, 27^2, 28^2, 29^2, 30^2, 31^2, 32^2, 33^2, 34^2, 29:27

2 CHRON.
1:1^2, 3^2, 6, 11, 13, 2:14, 3:3^2, 4^3, 6, 8, 9, 11^2, 12^2, 15^2, 4:3^2, 4, 5, 6, 11, 19, 5:1, 3, 10, 13, 6:7, 8^2, 7:7^2, 8:16^3, 9:1^2, 2, 4, 5, 6, 9, 13, 19, 9:20, 31, 10:2, 15, 18, 11:1, 12:13^2, 16, 13:2^2, 7, 13, 14, 14:1, 2, 5, 14, 15:4, 5, 6, 8, 9, 15, 17, 19, 16:3, 6, 10^2, 12^2, 14, 17:3, 6, 15, 16, 18, 18:14, 32, 20:25, 26, 29, 30, 31^2, 32, 21:1, 3, 4, 5, 6, 17^2, 20, 22:2^2, 3, 6, 7^2, 8, 9, 10, 11, 12, 23:15, 18, 19, 21, 24:1^2, 2, 4, 11^2, 13, 15^2, 25:1^2, 2, 3, 10^2, 14, 15, 18^3, 22, 26:1, 3^2, 4, 13, 15^2, 16^2, 19^2, 20, 21^3, 27:1^2, 2, 8, 28:1^2, 5, 7, 9^3, 29:1^2, 2, 6, 8, 25, 28, 32, 34, 35, 36, 30:5, 12, 17, 18, 26^2, 27, 31:1, 12^2, 14, 20, 32:2^2, 4, 5, 14, 15

2 CHRON.
32:21, 23, 24, 25^2, 31^2, 33:1, 2, 12, 13^2, 19^2, 20, 21, 22, 34:1, 2, 3, 9, 14, 16, 17, 27, 30, 35:10, 16, 18, 19, 24, 26, 36:2, 5^2, 8, 9^2, 10, 11, 12, 16

EZRA
1:6, 2:61, 64, 3:1, 3, 6, 11, 12, 13, 4:7, 14, 15, 20, 23, 5:5, 7, 11, 14^2, 17, 6:1, 2^2, 15^2, 7:6, 8, 28^2, 8:22, 23, 31, 33^3, 34, 35, 10:9

NEH.
1:1, 11, 2:1, 2, 10, 11, 12, 14^2, 18, 3:16, 25, 4:1, 3, 6, 15, 18, 5:1, 6, 14, 18^3, 6:1, 6, 10, 13, 15, 16, 18, 7:1, 2, 4, 7, 63, 64, 66, 72, 8:1, 3, 5, 17, 18, 10:29, 11:9^2, 11

NEH.
11:14, 17, 22, 23, 24, 12:8, 37, 43, 13:1, 4, 5, 6, 13^2, 26^2, 28

ESTHER
1:2, 8, 10, 11, 12, 13, 14, 2:1^2, 5^2, 7, 8^7, 12, 13, 15, 16, 20, 22, 23^3, 3:4, 5, 12^2, 14, 15^2, 4:1, 3, 4, 5^2, 6, 8, 5:2^2, 9, 6:2, 4, 7:6, 7, 8^2, 10, 8:1, 9, 13, 14, 15, 9:1, 4, 11, 14, 22, 32, 10:3

JOB
1:1^3, 3^2, 5, 6, 13, 16, 17, 18, 2:1, 11, 13, 3:3^2, 25, 26^2, 4:4, 12, 16^2, 8:7, 15:7, 19, 16:12, 17:6, 20:4, 22:16, 23:17, 29:4^2, 5, 13, 14, 15^2, 16, 19, 20^2, 30:2, 25^2, 31:18, 23, 25, 32:1, 2^2, 3, 5^2, 6, 12, 33:27, 42:7

PSALMS
4:1, 7:4, 18:7, 9, 12, 17, 23, 41, 22:9, 10, 30:7, 31:11, 13, 32:4, 33:9, 35:13, 37:36, 38:13, 14, 39:2, 3^2, 9, 50:21, 51:5, 53:5, 55:12^2, 13, 18, 21, 63 *title*, 66:14, 17, 68:8, 9, 11, 14, 69:10, 12, 20, 73:3, 16, 21^2, 22^2, 74:5, 76:8, 77:3^2, 18, 78:8, 21^2, 30, 35, 37, 59, 62, 79:3, 81:4, 87:4, 5, 6, 95:10, 97:8, 105:17, 18, 37, 38, 106:9, 11, 18, 30, 31, 38, 40, 107:12, 114:2, 3, 116:6, 10, 119:67, 158, 122:1, 124:1, 2, 3, 126:2, 139:15^2, 16, 142 *title*, 3, 4

PROV.
4:3, 5:14, 8:23^2, 24, 25, 27, 30^2, 23:35, 24:31^2

ECCL.
1:10, 12, 2:3, 9, 10, 11^2, 15, 24, 3:16^2, 4:1, 5:6, 7:23, 9:14, 15, 12:7, 9, 12:10^2

CANT.
2:3, 4, 3:4, 5:6, 6:12, 8:10, 11

ISAIAH
1:21, 6:4, 7:2^2, 9:1, 10:14, 26, 11:16, 14:28, 21:3, 14, 22:14, 25, 23:13, 26:16, 28:13, 36:3, 21, 22, 37:2, 8, 38, 38:1, 8, 9, 20, 39:1, 2^3, 41:28^2, 43:10, 12, 13, 47:6, 48:8, 16, 49:20, 50:2^2, 5, 52:14, 53:3, 5^3, 7^2, 8^3, 9, 12, 57:17^2, 59:15, 16^2, 17, 63:3, 5^2, 8, 9, 10, 65:1, 2

JER.
2:2, 3, 3:21, 4:23, 25, 26, 7:12, 8:16, 11:19, 13:7^2, 20, 14:4, 5, 6, 15:9, 16, 17:16, 18:4, 20:1, 2, 7, 8, 9^2, 14, 22:15, 16^2, 25:1, 26:20, 21, 24, 28:1, 31:11, 15, 18, 19^3, 26, 32, 32:1, 2^2, 8, 9, 11^2, 33:1, 35:4^2, 23^3, 37:5, 11, 37:13^3, 16, 38:6^2, 7, 27, 28^3, 39:2, 15, 40:5, 41:7, 9, 44:6^2, 46:2, 5, 21, 48:13, 27^2, 49:12, 21, 51:5, 59, 52:1^2, 2, 5, 6^2, 7^2, 8, 12, 17, 19^2, 20, 21^2, 22^2, 27, 34

LAM.
1:1^2, 2:5, 12, 3:10, 14, 4:6, 7, 20, 5:10

EZEKIEL
1:1, 2, 3, 4, 5, 7, 12, 13^2, 16^2, 20^3, 21, 22, 25^2, 26^3, 28^2, 2:9^2, 10^2, 3:3, 14, 22, 8:3, 4, 14, 9:2, 3^2, 8, 10:1, 4^2, 5, 7^2, 9, 13, 14^2, 17, 19, 21, 22, 11:22, 13:7, 10, 15:5, 16:3, 4, 8, 13, 14, 15, 19, 36, 45, 49, 56, 57, 17:7, 8, 19:4, 5, 7, 8, 10, 11, 12, 21:22, 22:10, 23:5, 11, 13, 17^2, 23:18^2, 40, 42, 43, 24:18, 25:3^2, 26:2, 27:7^2, 12, 16, 18, 20, 28:13^2, 15, 17, 29:18^2, 30:22, 31:3^2, 5, 7^2, 8, 32:15, 25, 33:22^4, 24, 34:4^4, 6, 8, 16^4, 35:10, 15, 36:17, 23, 35, 36, 37:1^2, 7^2, 8, 40:1^2, 2, 3^2, 6^2, 7^2, 9, 12^2, 13, 18, 21, 22^2, 23, 25, 27, 29, 33, 36, 40, 43, 44^2, 47, 48, 49, 41:1, 2, 6, 7^2, 9^4, 10, 11^3, 12^3, 15, 18^2, 19^2, 22, 42:1^2, 2^2, 3^2, 4, 6, 7^2, 8, 9, 11, 12, 43:2, 3, 44:1, 5^3, 46:19^2, 21, 23^2, 47:5, 48:35

DANIEL
1:4, 19, 2:1, 3, 12, 14, 19, 26, 31^2, 32, 34, 35^2, 45, 3:1, 19^3, 22, 24, 27, 4:4, 8, 10, 11, 12^2, 4:19^2, 20, 21, 31, 33^3, 36^2, 5:2, 3, 6, 9^2, 11, 13, 20^2, 21^4, 24^2, 25, 30, 6:2, 3^2, 4^2, 10, 14, 17, 22, 23^3, 7:4^3, 6, 7, 9^2, 10, 11, 14, 15, 19, 20, 22, 8:2^2, 3, 4, 5, 6, 7^3, 8^2, 11^2, 12, 17, 18^2, 26, 27^2, 9:1, 20, 21, 10:1^4, 2, 4, 6, 8^2, 9, 19, 12:1^2, 6, 7

HOSEA
1:10, 2:3, 7, 7:1, 9:8, 10:14, 11:1, 4, 12:13, 13:6

AMOS
1:1, 2:9^2, 4:7, 7:1, 14^3

JONAH
1:4^2, 5^2, 11, 13, 17, 2:6, 3:3, 4:1, 2^2, 6, 7

NAHUM
3:8^3, 9, 10

HABAK.
3:2, 3, 4^2, 8^3, 9, 14

ZEPH.
3:18, 19

HAGGAI
2:15, 18

ZECH.
1:15, 3:3, 5:7, 9, 7:7, 14, 8:2^2, 9, 10^2, 10:2, 3, 11:11^2, 13, 13:6

MALACHI
1:2, 13, 2:5^2, 6^2, 3:16

MATT.
1:16, 18^3, 19, 22^2, 2:1, 3, 9, 15^2, 16^2, 17^2, 18, 19, 22, 23, 3:3, 4, 16, 4:1, 2, 12, 14, 5:1, 21, 27, 6:29, 7:25, 27, 8:1, 3, 5, 13, 14, 16, 17, 23, 24^2, 26, 28, 30, 33, 9:20, 22, 28, 33^2, 36, 10:3, 11:14, 12:3, 4, 9, 10, 13, 17, 22, 40, 13:6, 19, 26, 33, 35, 47, 48, 54, 14:6, 9, 11, 14, 15, 23^2, 24^2, 29, 30, 15:28, 37, 16:20, 17:2^2, 18, 25, 18:11, 24, 27, 31^2, 34^2, 19:8, 20:8, 21:4^2, 10^2, 23^2, 25, 33, 22:7, 10, 12, 31, 22:35, 46, 24:21, 25:6, 10, 25, 35^3, 36^2, 42^2, 43, 26:3, 6, 20, 56, 71^2, 27:1, 3, 8, 9^3, 12, 15, 19, 24, 35, 45, 51, 54, 56, 57^2, 61, 63, 28:2, 3, 5

MARK
1:6, 9, 13^2, 14, 23, 33, 42, 45, 2:1^2, 2, 3, 4, 25, 27, 3:1, 5, 4:1, 6^2, 10, 15, 22, 35, 36, 37, 38, 39, 5:2, 5, 11, 14^2, 15, 16, 18, 21^2, 26, 29^2, 33, 36, 39, 40, 42, 6:2, 14^2, 20, 21, 26, 34, 35, 47^2, 48, 52, 55, 7:17, 26, 30, 32, 35, 8:8, 25, 9:2, 7, 26, 28, 33, 10:1, 14, 17, 22, 47, 11:11, 12, 13, 18, 19, 27, 30, 32, 12:11, 13:19, 14:1, 4, 14:32, 45, 49, 66, 15:7, 25, 26, 28^2, 33^2, 38, 39, 40, 41, 42^2, 46, 47, 16:1, 4^2, 6, 9, 11, 14, 19

LUKE
1:5^3, 7, 9, 12, 26, 27^2, 29, 36, 41, 64, 66, 67, 80, 2:2^2, 4, 6, 7, 13, 17, 20, 21^3, 25^4, 26, 36^2, 37, 40, 42, 51, 3:21, 23^2, 24^5, 25^5, 26^5, 27^5, 28^5, 29^5, 30^5, 31^5, 32^5, 33^5, 34^5, 35^5, 36^5, 37^5, 38^4, 4:1, 16, 17^2, 25^2, 26^2, 27, 29, 32, 33, 38, 40, 41, 42, 5:3, 9, 10, 12, 17^2, 18, 29, 36, 6:3, 6^2, 10, 13, 16, 48, 49, 7:2^2, 4, 6, 12^3, 15, 37, 41, 8:5, 6, 20, 24, 29^2, 32, 34, 35, 36^2, 40, 41, 47^2, 8:53, 56, 9:7^4, 8, 17, 18, 29^2, 36^2, 42, 45, 51, 53, 10:32, 33, 36, 40, 11:1, 14^3, 30, 50, 12:27, 13:10, 11^2, 13, 21, 14:2, 30, 15:6, 20, 24^2, 25, 28, 30, 32^3, 16:1^2, 19^2, 20^2, 22^2, 17:10, 15, 16, 20, 26, 28, 18:2, 3, 23^2, 24, 34, 35, 40, 19:2^3, 3^2, 4, 7, 10, 11, 15, 22, 29, 37, 41, 20:4, 6, 7, 21:5, 37, 22:14, 22, 23, 24, 37, 39, 40, 41, 44, 45, 47, 53, 56, 59, 66, 23:7, 8^2, 19, 25, 38, 44^2, 45^2, 47^2, 50^2, 51, 53^2, 54, 55, 24:6, 10, 12, 13, 18, 19, 23, 35, 44, 51

JOHN
1:1^3, 2, 3^2, 4^2, 6^2, 8^2, 9, 10^2, 14, 15^2, 1:17, 28, 30, 39, 40, 44, 2:1^2, 2, 9^2, 13, 17, 20, 22, 23, 25, 3:1, 23^2, 24, 26, 4:6, 45, 46^2, 47^2, 51, 53, 54, 5:1, 4, 5, 9^2, 10, 13^2, 15, 18, 35, 6:4, 10, 16, 17^2, 21, 22, 24, 62, 71, 7:2, 12, 30, 39^2, 42, 43, 8:4, 9, 20, 44, 56, 58, 9:1, 2, 8, 13, 14, 16, 19, 20, 22, 24, 25, 32^2, 10:19, 22^2, 11:1, 2^2, 6^2, 15, 18, 20, 30^2, 32^2, 33, 38, 39, 41, 44^2, 55, 12:1, 2, 3, 5, 6^2, 9, 12, 16, 17, 21, 13:1, 3, 5, 12, 21, 23, 30, 31, 16:4, 17:5, 12, 18:1, 10, 13^2, 14^2, 15, 16, 18, 28, 37, 40, 19:8, 14

JOHN
19:19, 20^3, 23, 29, 31^2, 32, 33, 41^3, 42, 20:1, 7, 14, 24, 21:4^2, 7^2, 11, 12, 14, 17

ACTS
1:2, 9, 16, 17, 19, 22, 23, 26, 2:1, 6, 16, 24, 26, 31, 3:2, 10, 11, 13, 20, 4:3, 4, 11, 14, 21, 22^2, 31, 33, 34, 35, 36, 5:4^3, 7^2, 36, 6:1, 7:2, 4, 9, 12, 13^2, 20^2, 21, 22^2, 23, 24, 29, 38, 58, 8:1^3, 8, 9^2, 13, 16, 18, 28, 32^2, 33, 40, 9:9, 10, 18, 19^2, 24, 26^2, 28, 33, 36^2, 37, 38^2, 39^2, 42, 10:1, 4, 7, 16^2, 18, 20, 22, 25, 29, 30, 37, 38, 42, 45, 11:2, 5, 10, 11, 17, 21, 22, 23, 24^2, 12:5^2, 6, 12:9^2, 11, 12, 15, 18^2, 20^2, 23, 25, 13:1^2, 6, 7, 12, 29, 31, 32, 36, 43, 46, 49, 14:4, 5, 12, 13, 15:5, 37, 39, 16:1^3, 2, 3, 13, 15, 19, 26, 33, 35, 17:1, 2, 13, 16, 34, 18:3, 5^2, 12, 14, 25, 27^2, 28, 19:1, 16, 17^2, 29, 32, 34, 20:1, 3, 9^2, 11, 14, 20, 21:3, 8, 11, 30, 31, 33, 35^2, 37, 40, 22:3, 6, 17^2, 20^2, 28, 29^2, 30, 23:5, 7, 12, 27^2, 30, 31, 34^2, 24:2, 24, 25:1, 7, 15, 19, 23^3, 26:4, 19, 26, 27, 27:8, 9^3, 12, 15, 20, 25, 27, 33, 39, 41, 42, 28:1, 6, 7, 9, 16, 17, 18, 19

ROMANS
1:3, 13, 1:21, 27, 4:3, 9, 10^2, 13, 18, 19, 20, 21, 22, 23^2, 25^2, 5:13, 14, 16^2, 6:4, 17, 7:8, 9, 10, 13, 8:3, 20, 9:12, 25, 26, 10:20^2, 15:8, 20, 21, 16:25

1 COR.
1:6, 13, 2:3, 4, 7:20, 10:4, 5, 11:9, 29, 13:11, 15:4, 5, 6, 7, 8, 10^3, 45^2, 46, 16:12, 17, *subscr.*

2 COR.
1:15, 17, 18, 19^3, 2:6, 12, 3:7^2, 10, 11, 5:19, 7:7, 13, 8:9, 11, 19, 9:2, 11:5, 9^3, 25^2, 33, 12:4, 7, 13, 13:4, *subscr.*

GAL.
1:11, 12, 22, 2:3^2, 7^2, 8, 9, 10, 11^2, 13, 3:6, 17^2, 19^3, 24, 4:4, 14, 23^3, 28, 29^2

EPHES.
3:5, 7

PHIL.
2:5, 7, 26, 27, 30, *subscr.*

COLOS.
1:23, 2:14^2

1 THESS.
2:1, 3, *subscr.*

2 THESS.
1:10, 2:5, *subscr.*

1 TIM.
1:11, 13, 14, 2:13, 14^2, 3:16, 4:14, *subscr.*

2 TIM.
1:9, 14, 16, 17, 2:8, 3:9, 4:17, *subscr.*^{2}

TITUS
subscr.

PHILE.
11

HEB.
2:2, 3, 9, 3:2^2, 3, 5, 10, 17^2, 4:2, 6, 15, 5:4, 7^2, 6:18, 7:4, 10, 11, 20, 22, 28, 8:5^2, 6, 9:2^2, 4, 8^2, 9, 18, 23, 28, 10:29, 11:4, 5^2, 8, 11^2, 17, 18, 19, 21, 23^3, 24, 38, 12:2, 17, 20, 21

JAMES
1:24, 2:21, 22, 23^3, 25, 5:17

1 PETER
1:11, 12, 20^2, 2:22, 23, 3:20, 4:6

2 PETER
1:9, 2:16, 22, 3:6

1 JOHN
1:1, 2^3, 3:5, 8, 12, 4:9

JUDE 3[2] REV. 1:4 8
REV. 1:9 10 16 18 2:8
REV. 2:13 4:1[2] 2[2] 3[2] 6
REV. 4:7[2] 8 5:3 4 11
REV. 5:12 6:2 4[3] 8[2] 12
REV. 7:2 8:1 3[2] 7[2] 8
REV. 8:12[2] 9:1 3 4 5[2]
REV. 9:9 10 18 10:1[2] 4
REV. 10:10[2] 11:1 8 13 19
REV. 12:4[2] 5[2] 7 8 9[2]
REV. 12:13 17 13:2 3 5[2]
REV. 13:7[2] 12 14:5 16 20
REV. 15:5 8[2] 16:8 10 12
REV. 16:18[2] 19 21 17:4 5
REV. 17:8[2] 11 18:1 16 24
REV. 19:8 11 13 20 20:4
REV. 20:10 11 12 15[2] 21:1
REV. 21:11 18[2] 19 21[2] 22:2

we

587, *2240*

GEN. 3:2 11:4 13:8 19:2 5 9 13 32 34 20:13 24:25 50 57 26:16 22 28 29 32 29:4 5 8[2] 27 31:15 49 32:6 34:14 15 16[4] 17 37:7 20[2] 26 32 38:23 40:8 41:11[2] 12 38 42:2 11 21[3] 31 32 43:4 5 7[2] 8[3] 10 18 20 21[3] 22[2] 44:8[3] 9 16[5] 20 22 24[2] 26[4] 46:34 47:3 4[2] 15 18 19[4] 25 50:15 17 18 EXOD. 1:9 3:18[2] 5:3 8:26 10:9[3] 25 26[3] 12:33

EXOD. 14:5 12[3] 15:24 16:3[2] 7 8 17:2 19:8 20:19[2] 24:3 7 14 32:1 23 33:16 LEVIT. 25:20[2] NUM. 9:7[3] 10:29[2] 31 32 11:5[2] 13 20 12:11[2] 13:27 28 30 31[2] 32[2] 33 14:2 7 40[2] 16:12 14 17:12[3] 13 20:3 4 10 15 16[2] 17[5] 19 21:7[2] 22[4] 30[2] 22:6 31:50 32:5 16 17[2] 18 19 31 32 DEU. 1:19[3] 22[3] 28[3] 41[2] 2:1 2 8[2] 13 14[2] 33 34[2] 35[2] 3:1 3 4[2] 6[2] 7 8

DEU. 3:12 29 4:7 5:24[2] 25[3] 26 27 6:21 25 12:8 18:21 26:7 29:7 8 16[2] 29 30:12 13 JOSH. 1:16[2] 17[2] 2:10 11 14 17 18 19 20 4:23 5:1 6:17 7:7 8:5 6[2] 9:6 7 8 9 11 12[2] 13 19[2] 20[3] 22 24 25 10:4 22:17 23 24 26 27 28[2] 29 31 24:15 16 17[2] 18 21 22 24[2] JUD. 1:3 24[2] 8:6 15 25 9:28[2] 38 10:10[2] 15[2] 11:6 8 10 19 24

JUD. 12:1 13:8 12[2] 15 17 22[2] 14:13 15[2] 15:10 12[2] 13[2] 16:2 5[3] 18:5[3] 9[2] 19:12[2] 18 22 20:8[2] 9[2] 10 13 21:7[3] 16 18 22[2] RUTH 1:10 4:11 1 SAM. 5:8 6:2[2] 4 9 7:6 8:19 20 9:6 7[3] 22[2] 10:14[2] 11:1 3[2] 10 12 12:10[3] 19[2] 14:8[2] 9[2] 10 12 15:15 16:11 17:9 10 20:42 23:3[2] 25:7 8 15[4] 16 30:14[2] 22[2] 2 SAM. 5:1 7:22 11:23 12:18[2] 13:25 14:7[2] 14 15:14 16:20 17:2 6 12[2] 18

2 SAM. 19:6 10 42 43[2] 20:1[2] 21:4 5 6 1 KINGS 3:18[2] 8:47 12:4 9 16[2] 17:12 18:5[2] 20:23[2] 25[2] 31 22:3 7 8 15[2] 2 KINGS 2:16 3:8 11 6:1 2[2] 15 28[2] 29[2] 7:3[2] 4[7] 9[4] 10 12[2] 10:4 5[2] 13[2] 18:22 26 1 CHRON. 11:1 12:18 13:3 15:13 16:35 17:20 29:13 14[2] 15 16 2 CHRON. 2:16[2] 6:37[2] 10:4 9 16[2] 13:10 11 14:7[2] 11[2] 18:3 5 6 7 14 20:9 12[2] 25:9 28:13 29:18 19 31:10

EZRA 4:2[2] 3 14[2] 16 5:4 8 9 10[2] 11 7:24 8:15 21 22 23 31 32 9:7[2] 9 10[2] 14 15[3] 10:2 4 12 13[2] NEH. 1:6 7 2:17[2] 20 4:1 4 6 9 10 11 15 19 21 5:2[3] 3[2] 4 5 8 12[2] 16 9:33 36[2] 37 38 10:30 31[2] 32 34 37 39 13:27 ESTHER 1:15 7:4[2] JOB 2:10[2] 4:2 5:27 8:9 9:32 15:9 18:2 3 19:28 21:14 15[3] 28:23 31:31[2] 32:13 36:26 37:5

JOB 37:19[2] 38:35 PSALMS 12:4 20:5[2] 7 8 9 21:13 33:21 22 35:25[2] 36:9 44:1 5[2] 8 17[2] 20 22[2] 46:2 48:8[2] 9 55:14 60:12 65:4 66:6 12 74:9 75:1[2] 78:3 4 79:4 8 13[2] 80:3 7 14 18[2] 19 90:7[2] 9 10 12 14 15 95:7 100:3[2] 103:14 106:6[3] 108:13 115:18 118:24 26 123:3 124:7 126:1 3 129:8 132:6 137:1 PROV. 1:13[2] 24:12 CANT. 1:4[3] 11 6:1 13 8:8[3] 9[2] ISAIAH 1:9[2] 2:3 4:1 5:19[2] 9:10[2]

ISAIAH 14:10 16:6 20:6[2] 22:13 24:16 25:9[3] 26:1 8 13 17 18[4] 28:15[4] 30:16[2] 33:2 36:7 11 38:20 41:22 23[2] 26[2] 42:24 46:5 51:23 53:2[2] 3[2] 4 5 6[2] 56:12 58:3[2] 59:9[2] 10[5] 11[2] 12 63:19 64:3 5[2] 6[2] 8[2] 9[2] JER. 2:31[2] 3:22 25[3] 4:13 5:12 17 6:24 7:10 8:8 14[2] 15 20 9:19[3] 13:12 14:7 9 19 20[2] 22 15:2 16:10 18:12[2] 20:10[3] 26:19 30:5 35:6 8[2] 9 10 11[2] 36:16 38:4 25 41:8 42:2[2] 3[2] 5

JER. 42:6[3] 13 14[3] 20 44:16 17[4] 18[2] 19[2] 25[2] 48:14 29 50:7 51:9 51[2] LAM. 2:16[4] 3:22 42 4:17 18 20[2] 5:3 4 5 6 7 9 16 21 EZEKIEL 11:3 20:32 21:10 33:10[2] 24 35:10 37:11 DANIEL 2:4 7 23 36 3:16 17 18 24 6:5[2] 9:5 6 8 9 10 11 13[2] 14 15[2] 18 HOSEA 6:2 3[2] 8:2 10:3[2] 14:2 3[2] AMOS 6:10 13 8:5[2] 6 OBADIAH 1 JONAH 1:6

JONAH 1:7 8 11 14[2] 3:9 MICAH 2:4 4:2 5 5:5 HABAK. 1:12 ZECH. 1:11 8:23[2] MALACHI 1:4[2] 6 7 2:10[2] 17 3:7 8 13 14[2] 15 MATT. 2:2 3:9 6:12 31 7:22 8:25 29 9:14 11:3 17 12:38 13:28 14:17 15:33 16:7 17:19 27 19:27[2] 20:18 22 21:25 26[2] 27 22:16 23:30[2] 25:37 38 39 44 26:17 65 27:42 63 28:13 14 MARK 1:24 2:12 4:30[2] 38 5:9 12 6:37 8:16 9:28 38[2] 10:28

MARK 10:33 35[2] 37 39 11:31 32 33 12:14 15[2] 14:12 58 63 15:32 LUKE 1:71 74 3:8 10 12 14 4:23 34 5:5 26 7:19 20 32[2] 8:24 9:12 13[2] 49[2] 54 10:11 11:4 13:26 15:32 17:10[2] 18:28 31 19:14 20:5 6 21 22:8 9 49 71[2] 23:2 41[2] 24:21 JOHN 1:14 16 22 41 45 3:2 11[3] 4:22[2] 42[2] 6:5 28[2] 30 40 68 69 7:27 35 8:33 41[2] 48 52 9:20 21[2] 24 28 29[2]

JOHN 9:31 40 41 10:33 11:16 47 48 12:21 34 13:29 14:5[2] 23 16:18 30[2] 17:11 22 18:30 19:7 15 20:2 25 21:3 24 ACTS 2:8[2] 11 32 37 3:12 15 4:9 12 16[2] 20[2] 5:23[3] 28 29 32 6:2 3 4 11 14 7:40 10:33 39 47 11:12 13:32 46 14:15 22 15:10 11[2] 19 20 24[2] 27 36 16:10 11 12 13[2] 16 28 17:19 20 28[2] 29[2] 32 19:2 13 21 40[2] 20:6[2] 13 14 15[3]

ACTS 21:1[2] 2 3[2] 4 5[4] 6[2] 7[2] 8[2] 10 12[2] 14 15 16 17 23[2] 25 23:9 14[2] 15 24:2 3 5 6 8 26:14 27:1 2 3 4[2] 5[2] 7[2] 15 16 18 19 20 26 27 29 37 28:10 11 12 13[2] 14[2] 16 21 22[2] ROMANS 1:5 2:2 3:5 8[2] 9[2] 19 28 31[2] 4:1 9 24 5:1 2[2] 3 6 8 9 10[3] 11[2] 6:1[2] 2 4[2] 5[2] 6 8[3] 15[2] 7:4 5 6[3]

ROMANS 7:7 14 8:12 15 16 17[2] 22 23 24 25[3] 26[3] 28 31 36[2] 37 9:14 29 30 10:8 12:4 5 13:11 14:8[6] 10 15:1 4 1 COR. 1:22 2:6 7 12[2] 13 16 3:9 4:8 9 10[3] 11 12[2] 13[2] 6:3 8:1[2] 4 6[2] 8[4] 9:4 5 6 11[2] 12[3] 25 10:6 16[2] 17[2] 22[2] 11:16 31[2] 32[3] 12:13[3] 23[2] 13:9[2] 12 15:11 15[2] 19[2] 30 32 49[2] 51[2] 52 2 COR. 1:4[2] 6[3] 8[3] 9[2] 10 12

2 COR. 1:13 14 24 2:11 15 16 17[2] 3:1[2] 4 5 12[2] 18 4:1[3] 5 7 8[2] 11 13[2] 16 18 5:1[2] 2 3 4[2] 6[3] 7 8 9[2] 10 11[2] 12 13[2] 14 16[3] 20[2] 21 6:1 9 7:2[3] 5[2] 13[2] 14 8:1 4 5 6 18 22[2] 9:4 10:2 3[2] 7 11[4] 13 14[3] 15 11:4 6 12 21 12:18[2] 19[3] 13:4[2] 6 7[2] 8 9[3] GAL. 1:8[2] 9 2:4 5 9 10 15 16[2] 17[2] 3:14

GAL. 3:23 24 25 4:3[2] 5 28 31 5:5 25 6:9[2] 10 EPHES. 1:4 7 11 12 2:3 5 10[2] 18 3:12 20 4:13 14 25 5:30 6:12 PHIL. 3:3 16 20 COLOS. 1:3 4 9 14 28[2] 1 THESS. 1:2 5 8 9 2:2[2] 4 5 6 7 8 9[2] 10 11 13 17 18 3:1[2] 3 4[3] 6 7 8 9[2] 10 12 4:1 2 6 10 11 14 15[2] 17[2] 5:5 10[2] 12 14

2 THESS. 1:3 4 11 2:1 13 3:2 4[2] 6 7 8[2] 9 10[2] 11 12 1 TIM. 1:8 2:2 4:10 6:7[2] 2 TIM. 2:11[2] 12[3] 13 TITUS 2:12 3:3 5 7 PHILE. 7 HEB. 2:1[3] 3[2] 5 8 9 3:6[2] 14[2] 19 4:3 13 14 15[2] 16 5:11 6:3 9[2] 11 18 19 7:19 8:1[2] 9:5 10:10 26[2] 30 39 11:3 12:1 9[3] 10 25[2] 28[2] 13:6 10 14[2] 18[2] JAMES 1:18 3:1 2 3[2]

JAMES 3:9[2] 4:13 15 5:11 17 1 PETER 2:24 4:3 2 PETER 1:16[2] 18[2] 19 3:13 1 JOHN 1:1[3] 2 3[2] 4 5 6[3] 7[2] 8[3] 9 10[3] 2:1 3[3] 5[2] 18 28 3:1 2[5] 11 14[3] 16[2] 19[2] 21 22[3] 23 24 4:6[2] 9 10 11 12 13[2] 14 16 17[2] 19 21 5:2[2] 3 9 14[2] 15[5] 18 19[2] 20[3] 2 JOHN 4 5[2] 6 8[3] 3 JOHN 8[2] 12 14 REV. 5:10 7:3 11:17

were

1961, *2258*

GEN. 1:5 7[2] 8 13 19 23 31 2:1 4 25 3:7[2] 4:8 5:4 5 8 11 14 17 20 23 27 31 6:1
GEN. 6:2 4[2] 7:10 11[2] 18 19 20 23[2] 8:2 3 5 7 8 9 11 13 9:18 23 29 10:1 5 18 21
GEN. 10:29 31 11:32 13:13 14:3 5 13 17 17:23 27 18:11 19:11 36 20:8 21:16 23:1 17[2] 20 24:10 32 54 63 25:3
GEN. 25:4 24[2] 26:35 27:1 15 23 42 29:2 3 30:35[2] 42[2] 31:10 19 34:5[2] 7[2] 14 25 35:2 4[2] 5 6 22 26
GEN. 35:28 36:5 7[2] 11 12 13 14 15 16 18 22 23 25 37:7 27 38:27 39:20 22 40:5 6 7 10 41:21
GEN. 41:48 50 53 42:28 35 43:18 34 44:3 4 45:3 46:12 15 20 21 22[2] 25 26 27[3] 31 48:5 10 49:24 50:8
GEN. 50:4 20 EXOD. 1:5 7 12 3:6 5:12 14 19 6:4 16 18 20 7:20[3] 25 8:18 9:26 32[2] 34 10:6 8
EXOD. 10:11 14[2] 12:33 37 39 14:10 11 21 22 29 15:8[2] 23 25 27 17:12[2] 19:1 2[2] 16 21:3 29 22:21 23:9 24:10[2]
EXOD. 28:32 32:3 15[3] 16 25 34:1 30 35:22 25 36:6 9 15 29 30[2] 36 38 37:9 13 14 16 17 20 22
EXOD. 37:25 38:2 9 10[2] 11[2] 12 14 15 16 17[2] 19 20 25 27 39:13 14 40:37 LEVIT. 8:28 10:12 16 14:35
LEVIT. 18:27 28 30 19:34 26:37 NUM. 1:1 16 20 21[2] 22[2] 23[2] 24 25[2] 26 27[2] 28 29[2] 30 31[2] 32 33[2]
NUM. 1:34 35[2] 36 37[2] 38 39[2] 40 41[2] 42 43[2] 44 45[3] 46[2] 47 2:4[2] 6[2] 8[2] 9[2] 11[2] 13[2] 15[2] 16[2] 19[2]
NUM. 2:21[2] 23[2] 24[2] 26[2] 28[2] 30[2] 31[2] 32[3] 33 3:3 17 22[3] 28 34[2] 39[2] 43[2] 49[2] 51 4:36[2] 37[2] 38 40[2] 41
NUM. 4:42 44[2] 45 46 48[2] 49[2] 6:12 7:2[3] 13 86 87 88 8:21 9:1 6[2] 15 22 10:28 11:26[2] 29 31[3] 12:3 8
NUM. 13:3 4 22 33[2] 14:3 6 29 38 15:26 32 16:34 39[2] 49 18:27 19:18 21:32 22:3 22 29 40 23:22 24:8 25:5
NUM. 25:6 9 26:7[2] 9 18 19 20 21 22 25 27 28 33 34 37 40 41[2] 43[2] 47[2] 50[2] 51 54 57
NUM. 26:62[3] 63 31:5 8 38 39 40 48 33:9 38 36:11 12 DEU. 1:41 2:11 14[2] 15 16 3:5 32 4:46 47
DEU. 5:5 29 6:21 7:7[2] 8:15 9:15 10:2 19 24:9 25:17 18 28:62 67[2] 29:17 31:24 30 32:27 29 33:5 34:8 JOSH. 2:4

JOSH.
2:7, 8, 10, 22, 3:15[2], 16, 17, 4:1, 7[2], 11, 18[2], 23[2], 5:1[3], 4, 5[2], 6[2], 7, 8, 6:23, 7:12, 8:7, 11, 14, 15, 16[3], 22, 24[2], 25, 35, 9:1, 10, 13, 16, 17, 24, 10:1, 2, 11[2], 20, 26, 28, 30, 32, 35[2], 39, 11:2, 5, 11, 19, 20, 22, 13:21, 22, 31, 14:4, 12[2], 15:4, 7, 11, 21, 16:8, 9, 17:2, 5, 9, 13, 18:12, 14, 19, 21, 19:8, 22, 33, 20:9, 21:4, 10, 19, 26, 33, 40[2], 41, 42[2], 22:9, 30, 24:15

JUD.
2:10, 12, 15, 3:4, 19, 24, 25, 4:13, 5:6, 15[2], 16, 18, 22, 6:5, 33, 7:1[2], 6, 11, 12, 19[2], 8:4, 10[2], 18[2], 19

JUD.
8:21, 24, 26, 9:29, 34, 35, 36, 40, 43, 44, 47, 48[2], 10:8, 17, 11:3, 33, 12:2, 13:23, 15:14, 16:2, 7, 9, 11, 12, 23, 27[2], 30[2], 17:2, 4, 18:3, 7[2], 16, 17, 22[3], 26, 27, 30, 19:10, 11, 14, 16, 22, 27, 20:3, 11, 15[2], 16, 17[2], 31, 36, 41, 44, 46[2], 21:9[2], 13

RUTH
1:13, 19, 4:11

1 SAM.
1:3, 2:5[2], 12, 27, 4:3, 4, 7, 11, 15, 19, 5:4, 12, 6:13, 15, 7:7[2], 10, 13, 14, 8:2, 9:3, 4, 5, 14, 20, 25, 27, 10:14, 16, 11:8, 9, 11[2], 13:2[2], 4, 6[2], 8, 11, 15, 16, 22, 14:2[2], 14, 17[2], 20, 21[2], 24, 26, 27, 28, 31

1 SAM.
14:41, 49[2], 16:6, 17:1, 2, 11, 13, 19, 31, 18:26, 19:16, 20:9, 21:5, 22:2, 6[2], 11, 23:13, 24, 25:1, 2, 7[2], 15[4], 16[2], 40, 43, 26:12, 27:2, 8, 29:4, 30:1, 2, 3, 4, 5, 16, 21[2], 27[3], 28[3], 29[3], 30[3], 31, 31:7[3]

2 SAM.
1:11, 12, 23[4], 2:3, 4, 18, 24, 3:2, 5, 20, 23, 31, 34, 4:1, 2, 3, 5:13, 14, 6:2, 8:7, 17, 18, 9:12, 21, 10:8, 12, 13, 16, 19, 12:1, 31, 13:18[2], 30, 14:27, 15:4, 11, 14, 16, 21, 22, 24, 16:6, 14, 22, 29, 18:1, 7, 19:9, 17, 28, 43, 20:3, 8, 14, 15, 18, 25, 21:9, 13, 22, 22:9, 13, 16, 18, 23, 24:9[2]

1 KINGS
1:8, 41, 49[2], 2:5, 11, 3:16, 18, 4:2, 4, 20, 28, 32, 5:3, 14, 16, 6:1, 24, 31, 32, 34[3], 7:4, 5, 6, 9, 11, 17, 18, 19[2], 20, 24[2], 25, 28, 29[3], 30, 31, 32[2], 33, 34[2], 41[2], 42, 45, 47, 8:4, 5[2], 8[2], 10, 47, 9:20[2], 21, 22, 23[2], 10:12, 19, 21[3], 11:29, 12:1, 8, 10, 21, 31, 14:4, 9, 20, 24, 15:14, 18, 16:15, 16, 21, 25, 30, 33, 20:1, 15, 23, 27[2], 30, 21:8, 11, 22:43, 48

2 KINGS
2:3, 5, 8, 9, 15, 22, 3:14, 21[2], 4:6, 38, 40, 5:3, 6:20[2], 7:3, 5, 10, 9:5, 10:4, 6, 29[2], 11:2, 9, 10, 12:3, 13, 13:21, 14:4, 14

2 KINGS
15:4, 16[2], 35, 16:17, 17:2, 9, 15, 18:5, 17, 19:12, 18, 26[3], 35, 21:11, 23:4, 7, 8[2], 12, 13[2], 16, 19, 20, 24[2], 24:16, 25:4, 5, 10, 11, 13, 15, 19[3], 25, 26, 28

1 CHRON.
1:19, 23, 51, 2:3, 4, 9, 16, 25, 27, 28, 33, 42, 50, 3:1[2], 4, 5, 9, 15, 19, 24, 4:3, 6, 7, 14, 17, 20[2], 21, 23, 24, 31, 32, 33[2], 38, 41, 43, 5:3, 7, 9, 13, 17, 18, 20[3], 24, 6:18, 48, 49, 60, 61[2], 63, 71, 77, 78, 7:1, 2, 4, 7, 11, 16, 17, 19, 21, 28, 40[2], 8:3, 8, 10, 13, 28, 35, 38, 39, 40, 9:1[3], 2, 9

1 CHRON.
9:17, 18, 19[2], 22[3], 24, 25[2], 26[2], 29, 31, 32, 33[2], 34, 41, 44, 10:7[2], 11:4, 13, 26, 12:1, 2, 8[2], 14, 20, 21[2], 23, 24, 27, 31, 32[3], 33, 38, 39, 40, 14:12, 15:19, 23, 24, 16:19, 41[2], 42, 18:7, 16, 17, 19:5[2], 9[2], 14, 15, 16[2], 19, 20:2, 3, 4, 5, 6, 8, 21:16, 29, 22:2, 23:3, 4[2], 5, 7, 9, 10[2], 11, 14, 15, 17[2], 24[2], 27, 24:4[3], 5[2], 19, 20, 26, 30, 25:5, 6, 7[2], 9, 10, 11, 12, 13, 14, 15, 16, 17, 18, 19, 20, 21, 22, 23, 24, 25, 26, 27, 28, 29, 30, 31, 26:2, 4, 6[2], 7, 8, 11, 12, 17, 21

1 CHRON.
26:22, 26, 29, 30, 31[2], 32, 27:1, 2, 4, 5, 7, 8, 9, 10, 11, 12, 13, 14, 15, 22, 28, 29, 31, 29:8, 15

2 CHRON.
2:17[2], 3:11, 13, 4:3, 4, 12[2], 13, 19, 22, 5:5, 6, 9[2], 11[3], 12, 13, 8:7[2], 8, 9, 10, 9:11, 18[2], 20[3], 10:1, 8, 10, 11:1, 13, 12:3, 5, 15, 13:13, 18, 14:8, 13[2], 15:5, 17, 16:8, 17:10, 13, 18:30, 20:22[2], 24, 25, 33, 37[2], 21:2, 13, 16, 22:4, 6, 11, 23:8[2], 9, 14, 24:14, 25, 25:12, 24, 26:12, 17, 28:6, 15[2], 23, 29:29, 31, 32, 33, 34[2], 35, 30:8, 14, 15, 17[2], 21, 31:1, 6, 13, 15, 19[3], 32:3, 9, 13, 18, 19

2 CHRON.
34:4, 12, 13[3], 32, 33, 35:3, 7[2], 14, 15, 17, 18, 36:20

EZRA
1:6, 11[2], 2:58, 59[2], 62[3], 65[2], 66, 3:1, 5, 8, 12, 5:1, 2, 6, 10, 14, 6:1, 20[2], 21, 8:3, 20, 35, 9:1, 4, 9, 10:15, 16, 18

NEH.
1:2, 9, 2:13[2], 4:7[2], 16, 5:2, 3, 4, 8, 15, 16, 17, 18, 6:16[2], 18, 7:1, 4[2], 60, 61[2], 64[2], 67, 73, 8:3, 12, 13, 17, 9:1, 17, 25, 26, 10:1, 8, 11:6, 12, 18, 19, 20, 21, 22, 36, 12:7, 9, 12, 22, 23, 25, 26, 44, 46, 13:10, 13

ESTHER
1:5[2], 6[2], 2:7, 8, 9, 12, 14, 19, 21, 23, 3:1, 2, 3, 6

ESTHER
3:12[2], 13, 6:1, 14, 8:9, 11, 9:11, 15, 16, 18, 20

JOB
1:2, 5, 13, 14, 18, 4:7, 6:2, 20[2], 9:15, 21, 16:4, 19:20, 23[2], 24, 21:4, 22:16, 28:5, 29:2, 5, 30:3, 5, 7, 8[2], 31:20, 28, 32:4, 15, 33:21, 34:35, 39:16, 42:15

PSALMS
14:2, 5, 7, 17:12, 18:7, 8, 11, 15[2], 17, 22, 27, 38, 22:5[2], 33:6, 34:5[2], 35:13, 39:12, 45:9, 46:6, 48:4, 5, 50:12, 53:2, 5, 6, 55:18, 21[3], 68:25, 33, 73:2, 77:16[2], 78:29, 30, 37, 39, 57, 63, 80:10[2], 81:6, 90:2, 105:12, 106:35, 36, 39, 42, 43, 119:5, 126:1, 139:16[2], 148:5

PROV.
8:24[2], 25, 31

ECCL.
2:7, 9, 4:1, 7:10, 8:10

CANT.
1:6

CANT.
5:4, 6:13

ISAIAH
5:18, 25, 7:23, 10:15, 14:2, 26:18, 20, 27:13, 30:4, 5, 33:3, 37:12, 19, 27[3], 36, 41:5, 11, 42:24, 46:1[2], 51:13, 52:14, 53:3, 63:19

JER.
1:1, 4:25, 26, 5:8, 6:15, 8:12[2], 9:1, 11:13, 14:3, 4, 15:16, 20:2, 22:24, 26, 24:1, 2, 26:9, 29:1, 2, 30:14, 15, 31:2, 15, 34:5, 7, 8, 15, 36:16, 24, 28, 32, 37:15, 21, 40:1[2], 4, 6, 7[2], 11[2], 12, 13, 41:2, 3[2], 7, 8, 9, 10, 11, 13[3], 16, 18, 42:8, 16, 43:5, 44:17, 49:2, 50:11, 33, 52:7, 14, 17, 20, 22, 23[2], 25[2], 30, 32

LAM.
2:4, 6, 4:5, 7[3], 10, 5:12

EZEKIEL
1:1, 7, 9, 11[3], 13, 18[3]

EZEKIEL
1:19[2], 20, 21[2], 23, 27, 7:13, 8:16, 9:6, 8, 10:1, 12, 15, 17, 19, 20, 14:14, 16, 18, 20, 16:47, 50, 17:6, 19:12, 20:9, 24, 25, 22:6, 23:2, 3, 4[3], 6, 7, 42, 27:8[3], 9[2], 10, 11[2], 13, 15[2], 17, 19, 21, 22, 23, 24, 29:13, 31:5, 8[2], 9, 15, 17, 32:27, 29, 34:5[2], 36:19, 31, 37:2[2], 40:7, 10[2], 12, 15, 16[3], 17[2], 21[2], 25, 26[2], 29, 30, 31[2], 33[2], 34[2], 37[2], 38, 39, 40[2], 41, 42, 43, 44, 49, 41:2, 6, 8, 9, 11, 16, 20, 21, 22, 25[3], 26, 42:3, 5[2], 6, 8[2], 10, 11[2], 12, 43:3, 46:22[2], 47:3, 4[2], 5, 7

DANIEL
1:6, 20, 2:34, 42, 3:3

DANIEL
3:20, 21[2], 27, 4:10, 12, 21, 33, 5:3, 6, 9, 12, 6:18, 7:4, 7, 8[2], 9, 10, 12, 19, 20, 8:3, 10:3, 5, 7, 12

HOSEA
2:23, 4:7, 5:10, 8:12, 9:10, 12:8, 13:6[2]

AMOS
4:7, 8, 11

OBADIAH
7

JONAH
1:5[2], 10, 2:5

MICAH
1:13

NAHUM
3:9, 10[2]

HABAK.
3:6

HAGGAI
2:16[3]

ZECH.
1:8[2], 6:1, 2, 7:3, 8:9, 13, 10:2

MATT.
1:11, 12, 2:11, 13, 16, 3:6, 16, 4:18, 24[3], 5:12, 7:28, 8:16[2], 32, 9:25, 30, 31, 36, 11:20, 21, 12:1, 3, 4, 23, 13:2, 6, 54, 57, 14:20, 21, 26, 32, 33, 34, 35, 36, 15:1, 12, 30, 37, 38

MATT.
16:5, 17:6, 14, 23, 24, 18:6[3], 31, 19:12[2], 13, 25, 20:9, 24, 21:1, 15, 22:3, 8[2], 25, 33, 34, 41, 24:24, 37, 38[2], 25:2[2], 3, 10, 26:22, 26, 43, 51, 57, 71, 27:17, 33, 38, 44, 52, 54[2], 55, 28:11[2], 12, 15

MARK
1:5, 16, 19, 22, 27, 29, 32[2], 34, 36, 2:2, 6, 12, 15, 25, 26, 4:10, 33, 34, 36, 5:13[2], 15, 40, 42, 6:2, 3, 13, 31, 34, 42, 44, 50, 51, 54, 55, 56[2], 7:35, 37, 8:8, 9, 9:4, 6, 9, 15, 32, 42[2], 10:24, 26, 32[3], 11:12, 12:14, 20, 41, 13:22, 14:4, 11, 21, 35, 40, 53, 15:32, 40, 44, 16:5, 8[2]

LUKE
1:2

LUKE
1:6, 7, 10, 23, 44, 65, 2:6[2], 8, 9, 15, 18, 21, 22, 33, 47, 48, 3:15[2], 21, 4:2, 20[2], 25, 27, 28, 32, 36, 5:2[2], 7, 9, 10, 17[2], 26[2], 6:3, 4, 11, 18[2], 7:10, 20, 21, 24, 39, 8:1, 4[2], 23, 30, 33, 35[2], 37, 38, 40, 45, 56, 9:10, 14, 17, 18, 30, 32[3], 37, 43, 11:29, 52, 12:1, 13:1, 2, 4, 17[2], 14:7, 17, 24, 16:14, 16, 17:2[2], 9, 12, 14, 17, 27, 18:9, 34, 19:32, 33, 48, 20:29, 22:5, 44, 49, 52, 55, 23:5, 6, 12[2], 23, 32, 33, 39, 48, 24:4, 5, 10, 16, 21, 22, 24, 31, 33, 35, 37, 44, 53

JOHN
1:3, 13, 24[2], 28, 2:6, 3:19, 23, 4:8, 40, 5:35, 6:2, 11, 12, 19, 22[2], 26, 64, 65, 7:10[2], 8:33, 39, 42, 9:10, 33, 40, 41, 10:6, 41, 11:25, 31, 52, 57, 12:12, 16, 20, 13:1, 14:2, 15:19, 16:19, 17:6, 18:30, 36, 19:11, 28, 36[2], 20:19[2], 20, 26, 21:2, 6, 8[2], 9, 11

ACTS
1:6, 13, 15, 2:1, 2, 4, 5, 6, 7, 8, 14[2], 37, 41[2], 43, 44, 3:10, 4:6[2], 13, 26, 27, 31[2], 32, 34[2], 5:12[2], 14, 16[2], 17[2], 21, 33, 36, 37, 41, 6:1, 7, 10, 7:16, 30, 54, 8:1, 4, 7[3], 12, 13, 14, 15, 16, 39, 9:2, 8, 19, 21, 23, 26, 31[2], 10:12, 17

ACTS
10:18, 26, 27, 38, 45, 11:1, 2, 10, 11, 19, 20[2], 26, 12:3, 10, 12, 16, 13:1, 5, 42, 45[2], 48[2], 52, 14:6, 27, 15:4[2], 10, 30, 33, 16:2, 3, 4[2], 5, 6, 7, 12, 14, 26[3], 32, 38, 17:11[2], 12, 14, 21, 18:3, 5, 8, 14, 19:3, 5, 7, 9, 12, 14, 21, 28, 31, 32, 20:8[2], 12, 16, 18, 34, 21:1, 5, 8, 17, 18, 24, 27[2], 30, 38, 22:5, 9[2], 11, 23:6, 9, 13, 24:9, 25:17, 26:10, 14, 29, 31, 27:4, 7, 11, 17, 27, 30, 36, 37, 39[2], 28:1, 7, 9, 10, 14, 17, 24

ROMANS
1:21, 3:2, 4:2, 17, 5:6, 8, 10[2], 19, 6:3[2], 17

ROMANS
6:20[2], 7:5[2], 6, 9:3, 25, 32, 11:7, 19, 20, 15:4[2], 16:7

1 COR.
1:9, 13, 3:2, 4:9, 5:3, 6:11, 7:7, 14, 9:15, 10:1, 2, 5, 6, 7, 9, 10, 11:5, 12:2, 17[4], 19[2], 15:11

2 COR.
1:8, 3:14, 5:1, 14, 7:5[4], 8, 9[2], 13, 8:3, 11:17, 12:12, 13, 13:2

GAL.
1:17, 22, 2:2, 6, 12, 3:16, 23, 4:3[2], 5, 5:12

EPHES.
1:13, 2:1, 3, 5, 12, 13, 17[2], 5:8

PHIL.
3:7, 12, 4:18

COLOS.
1:16[2], 21

1 THESS.
1:5, 7, 2:2[2], 4, 7, 8[2], 3:4, 7

2 THESS.
3:10

TITUS
3:3

PHILE.
14

HEB.
2:15, 3:5, 4:3, 5:8, 6:4[2], 7:11, 21, 23[2], 8:4, 9:6, 9, 15

HEB.
10:32, 33[2], 11:3[2], 13[2], 23, 29, 30, 34, 35, 37[4]

JAMES
5:3

1 PETER
1:18, 2:8, 10, 21, 24, 25, 3:20[2]

2 PETER
1:16, 18, 21, 2:1, 18, 3:2, 4, 5

1 JOHN
2:19[2], 3:12

JUDE
4, 17

REV.
1:14[2], 4:1, 4, 5, 6, 8, 11, 6:1, 9, 11[2], 14, 7:4[2], 5[3], 6[3], 7[3], 8[3], 8:2, 5, 7, 8, 9[2], 10, 11, 9:2, 7[4], 8, 9, 10, 15[2], 16, 17, 19, 20, 10:1, 11:13[2], 15, 18, 19, 12:9, 14, 13:2, 3, 14:3[2], 4[2], 15:2, 8, 16:9, 18[2], 20, 17:8, 18:14, 15, 19, 23[2], 24, 19:6, 12[2], 14, 20, 21[2], 20:4, 5, 12[3], 13[3], 14, 21:1, 19, 21[2], 22:2

with 5973, *4862*

GEN. 3:6, 12, 4:8, 5:22, 24, 6:3, 9, 11, 13[2], 14, 16, 18[2], 19, 7:13, 23, 8:1, 16, 17, 18, 9:3, 8, 9, 10[2], 11, 12, 11:31, 12:4, 13, 17, 13:1, 5, 14:2, 5, 8, 9[2], 13, 17, 24, 15:14, 18, 16:6, 11, 17:3, 4, 12, 13, 19, 21, 22, 23, 27, 18:11, 16, 23, 25, 33, 19:1, 9, 11, 30, 32, 33, 34[2], 35, 36, 20:16, 21:6, 10, 19, 20, 22, 23, 22:3, 5, 23:4[2], 8, 16, 24:15, 32, 40, 45, 49, 54, 55, 58, 25:30, 26:3, 8, 10, 15, 20[2], 24, 28[2], 27:15, 34, 35, 37, 44, 28:4, 15, 20, 29:6, 9, 14, 19, 25, 27, 30, 30:8, 15, 16[2], 20[2], 29, 33

GEN. 31:3, 5, 6, 21, 23, 25, 26, 27, 32[2], 36, 38, 42, 50, 32:4, 6, 7, 9, 10, 11, 15, 20, 24, 25, 28[2], 33:1, 5, 7, 10, 11, 13[2], 15[2], 34:5, 6, 7, 8, 9, 10, 16, 20, 21, 22, 23, 26, 31, 35:2, 3, 6, 13, 14, 15, 22, 37:2[3], 14[2], 25, 38:14, 24, 25, 39:2, 3, 7, 8, 10, 12, 14[2], 18, 21, 23, 40:4, 7, 14, 41:6, 10, 12, 23, 27, 42:4, 6, 13, 24, 25, 26, 32, 33, 38[2], 43:3, 4, 5, 6, 8, 16[2], 19, 32[2], 34, 44:1, 9, 10, 16, 23, 26[2], 29, 30, 31[2], 33, 34, 45:1, 5, 15, 23[2], 46:1, 4, 6, 7[2], 15, 26

GEN. 47:12, 17, 29, 30, 48:1, 12, 21, 22[2], 49:12[2], 25, 29, 30, 50:7, 9, 10, 13, 14

EXOD. 1:1, 7, 10, 11, 13, 14[2], 20, 2:3[2], 21, 24[3], 3:2, 8, 12, 17, 18, 20, 4:12, 15[2], 5:3[3], 15, 6:1[2], 4, 6[2], 7:11, 17, 22, 8:2, 5, 7, 17, 18, 9:9, 10, 15, 24, 10:9[6], 10, 24, 26[2], 12:8[2], 9[4], 10, 11, 22, 38, 48, 13:5, 7[2], 9, 13, 19[2], 14:6, 8, 11, 15:8, 10, 19[2], 20[2], 16:3, 12, 18, 20, 31, 17:2[2], 3, 5, 8, 9[2], 10, 13, 16, 18:5, 6, 12, 18, 19, 22, 19:9, 17, 24, 20:19[2], 22, 23, 21:3, 6, 8, 9, 14, 18[2], 20, 22, 29, 22:14, 15, 16

EXOD. 22:19, 24, 30[3], 23:1, 5, 11[2], 18, 32[2], 24:2, 3, 8, 14, 25:2, 11, 13, 14, 20, 22[2], 24, 28[2], 33[2], 34, 39, 26:1[2], 6, 29[2], 31, 32, 36, 37, 27:2, 6, 8, 16, 17, 28:1, 3, 6, 11[2], 15, 21[2], 28, 41, 29:2[2], 3, 4, 5, 9, 12, 14, 21[2], 34, 40[2], 43, 30:3, 5, 6, 10, 20, 28, 34, 36, 31:3, 6, 8, 9, 18[2], 32:4, 11, 33:3, 9, 12, 14, 15, 16, 22, 34:3, 5, 10, 12, 15, 20, 25, 27[2], 28, 29[2], 31, 32, 33, 34, 35, 35:12, 14, 16, 23, 24, 25, 31, 35, 36:8, 13, 34[2], 35, 36, 38[2], 37:2, 4, 9[2], 11, 15, 26, 28, 38:2, 6

EXOD. 38:7, 17, 23, 39:3, 6, 14, 21, 23, 37[2], 40:3, 12, 14

LEVIT. 1:12, 13, 16, 17, 2:2, 4[2], 5, 7, 11, 13[2], 16, 3:4, 10, 15, 4:9, 11[2], 12, 20[3], 25, 30, 34, 5:4[2], 15, 16, 18, 6:6, 10, 16, 17, 21, 7:4, 10, 12[4], 13, 17, 19, 24, 30, 8:1, 6, 7[3], 13, 15, 17, 30[2], 31, 32, 9:4, 11, 13, 10:9, 14, 15[2], 16, 43[2], 44, 57, 14:10, 16, 21, 27, 31, 37, 52[6], 15:3, 17, 18[2], 24, 33, 16:3, 4[2], 10, 14[2], 15[2], 18, 24, 17:13, 15, 18:20[2], 22[2], 23, 19:13, 19[2], 20, 22, 26, 33, 34, 20:2, 5, 10[2], 11, 12, 13[2], 14, 15, 18, 20, 24, 27

LEVIT. 21:9, 22:6, 8, 11, 14, 23:13, 17, 18[2], 20[2], 23, 25:6, 23, 35[2], 36, 40, 41, 43, 45, 46, 50, 52, 53[2], 54, 26:9, 39, 42[3], 44

NUM. 1:2, 4, 5, 2:2, 17, 31, 3:1, 4:5, 8, 11, 12, 32[2], 5:7, 13[2], 17, 19[2], 20, 21, 23, 6:15[2], 20, 7:13, 19, 25, 31, 37, 43, 49, 55, 61, 67, 73, 79, 87, 89, 8:8[2], 26, 9:11, 10:3, 4, 8, 9, 10, 29, 32, 11:15, 16, 17[2], 18, 33, 12:8, 13:23, 27, 31, 14:8, 9, 10, 12, 21, 24, 27, 43, 15:4, 5, 6, 9[2], 14, 15, 16, 24, 35, 36, 16:2, 10, 13, 14, 18, 22, 30, 17:4, 13, 18:1[2], 2[2], 7, 11[2]

NUM. 18:19[2], 19:4, 5, 12, 16, 20:3, 11, 13, 18, 20[2], 21:18, 24, 22:7, 8, 9, 12, 13, 14, 20, 21, 22, 27, 35[2], 39, 40, 23:13, 17, 21, 24:8, 25:1, 14, 18, 26:3, 10, 27:21, 28:5, 9, 12[2], 13, 20, 28, 29:3, 9, 14, 30:2, 8, 10, 31:6, 8, 10, 14[2], 17, 18, 23, 35, 32:19, 29, 30, 33, 33:1, 3, 34:2, 12, 35:7, 16, 17, 18, 21, 23, 25

DEU. 1:16, 37, 2:5, 7, 9, 19, 24, 26, 3:5, 13, 26, 27, 4:11[2], 21, 23, 29[2], 37, 40[2], 5:2, 3[2], 4, 16, 22, 23, 24, 29[2], 33, 6:3[2], 5[3], 18, 21, 7:2, 3, 5[2], 8, 9, 23, 25, 8:3, 16, 9:8

DEU. 9:10[2], 15, 20, 21, 26, 10:9, 12[2], 14, 22, 11:2, 9, 10, 13[2], 12:3, 12, 23, 25[2], 28[2], 13:3[2], 10, 15[2], 16, 14:27, 29, 15:3, 16, 19, 16:3, 4, 10, 18, 17:5, 19, 18:1, 6, 11, 13, 19:5[2], 13, 20:1, 4, 12, 13, 20, 21:3, 21, 22:2, 3[3], 6, 7, 9, 10, 21, 22[2], 23, 24, 25[2], 28, 29, 23:4[2], 11, 16, 23, 25, 24:5, 12, 25:3, 11, 26:5, 8[5], 9, 15, 16[2], 27:1, 2, 3, 4, 14, 20, 21, 22, 23, 28:22[7], 27[4], 28, 30, 32, 35, 40, 47[2], 68, 29:1[2], 10, 12[2], 14, 15[4], 25, 30:2[2], 6[2], 10[2], 31:6, 7, 8, 16[2], 20, 23, 27, 32:12, 14[2], 15, 16[2], 21[4], 22, 24[4]

DEU. 32:25, 34, 39, 42[2], 43, 33:2, 8[2], 17, 20, 21[2], 23[2], 24, 34:4

JOSH. 1:5[2], 9, 17[2], 2:6, 14, 19, 3:7[2], 4:3, 8, 5:6, 13, 6:4, 5[2], 8, 9[2], 10, 13[2], 16, 17, 20[2], 21, 24, 27, 7:12, 15[2], 24, 25[3], 8:1, 5, 11, 24, 35, 9:2[3], 6, 7, 11[2], 15[2], 16, 10:1, 4[2], 7, 10, 11[2], 15, 20, 24, 28, 29, 30, 31, 32, 34, 35, 36, 37, 38, 39, 43, 11:4, 6:, 7, 9, 10, 11[2], 12, 14, 18, 19, 21, 13:8, 21, 22, 14:4, 8, 12, 15:32, 36, 41, 44, 45, 46, 47[2], 51, 54, 57, 59, 60, 62, 63, 16:9, 18:24, 28, 19:15, 16, 22, 30, 31, 38, 46

JOSH. 19:47, 48, 21:2, 8, 11, 13[2], 14[2], 15[2], 16[3], 17[2], 18[2], 19, 21[2], 22[2], 23[2], 24[2], 25[2], 26, 27[2], 28[2], 29[2], 30[2], 31[2], 32[3], 33, 34[2], 35[2], 36[2], 37[2], 38[2], 39[2], 41, 42, 22:5[2], 8[8], 14, 15, 18, 24, 27[3], 30, 23:4, 12, 24:6, 8, 12[2], 25

JUD. 1:3[3], 8, 16, 17, 18[3], 19, 21, 22, 25, 2:1, 2, 18, 3:27, 31, 4:6, 7, 8[2], 9[2], 10[2], 13, 15, 18, 5:15, 26, 6:5, 12, 13, 16, 17, 26, 39, 7:1, 2, 4[3], 5, 10, 11, 16, 18[2], 19, 8:1[2], 4, 7[2], 10, 15, 16, 9:1[2], 16, 19[2], 23, 26, 32, 33, 34, 35, 38, 39, 44, 45, 48[2], 52, 11:3, 6, 8, 11

JUD. 11:12, 33, 34[2], 38, 39, 12:1[2], 2, 4, 13:9, 19, 14:7, 11, 15, 18, 15:1, 5, 6, 8, 13, 14, 16[2], 16:3, 7, 8, 9, 11, 13, 14[3], 15, 16, 21, 29[2], 30[2], 17:2, 10, 11, 18:4, 7, 11, 16, 17[2], 19, 23, 25, 27[2], 28, 19:3, 4, 5, 10[2], 19, 20, 24, 29, 20:1, 37, 38, 40, 43, 48, 21:5, 10[2], 12

RUTH 1:6, 7, 8[3], 10, 11, 18, 20, 22, 2:4, 6, 19[2], 22, 23, 3:1, 2

1 SAM. 1:24[2], 2:4, 13[2], 18, 19, 22, 26[2], 29, 3:14, 19, 4:4, 5, 8, 12[2], 19, 5:6, 7, 8, 9, 12, 6:11, 15, 19, 7:3, 10, 9:3, 5, 19, 24, 25, 10:5, 6

1 SAM. 10:7, 26, 11:1, 2, 7, 10, 12:2, 7, 20, 24, 13:2[2], 4, 5, 15, 16, 22[3], 14:2, 7, 17, 18, 20, 21[4], 27, 28, 32, 33, 34[2], 43, 45, 15:6, 8, 25, 26, 30, 16:1, 2, 5, 16, 18, 19, 20, 23, 17:5, 7, 9, 19, 20, 23, 25, 28, 32, 33, 37, 38[2], 39, 43, 45[3], 47, 50[2], 57, 18:1, 6[3], 10, 11, 12, 14, 22, 28, 19:3, 8[2], 9[2], 10, 13, 16, 20:5, 8[2], 13[2], 16, 35[2], 41, 21:1, 8, 22:2, 3, 4, 6, 8, 17, 19[2], 23[2], 23:5[2], 6, 19, 23[2], 24:7, 8, 18, 25:7, 15, 16, 25, 26, 29, 31, 33, 39, 42, 26:2, 6[2], 8, 27:2[2], 3[3], 5, 28:1[2]

1 SAM. 28:8, 12, 14[2], 19[2], 23, 29:2, 3, 4[3], 6, 8, 9, 10[2], 30:1, 3, 4, 9, 14, 21, 22[2], 23, 31:5

2 SAM. 1:2, 11, 17, 21, 24, 2:3[2], 23, 3:8, 12[2], 13, 16, 17, 20[2], 21, 22[2], 23, 27, 31[2], 5:3, 10, 6:2[2], 12, 14[2], 15[2], 7:3, 7[2], 9, 12, 14, 22, 29, 8:2[3], 10[2], 11, 10:13, 17, 19, 11:1, 4, 5, 9, 11, 13, 17, 12:3, 9[2], 11, 17, 24, 30, 13:11, 14, 18, 20, 24, 26[2], 27, 28, 31, 14:2, 17, 19, 15:11, 12, 14[2], 19[2], 20[2], 22, 23, 24, 27, 30, 31, 32, 33, 35, 36, 16:1, 10, 14, 15, 17, 18, 21, 23[2], 17:2, 8, 10, 12, 16, 22

2 SAM. 17:24, 29, 18:1, 2, 5[2], 14, 27, 19:4, 7, 17[2], 22, 25, 31, 33[2], 34, 36[2], 37, 38, 40, 41, 20:8, 9, 15, 16, 21:15[2], 16, 17, 18, 19, 26[2], 27[2], 22:40, 23:5[2], 6, 7[2], 9, 21[2], 24:2

1 KINGS 1:1, 7[2], 8, 14, 21, 22, 23, 31, 33, 34, 37[2], 40[3], 41, 44, 49, 51, 2:4[2], 8[3], 9, 10, 32, 43, 3:1, 6, 16, 17, 18, 4:13, 5:6, 6:8, 9, 10, 12, 15[3], 16, 18, 20, 21[2], 22[2], 28, 29, 30, 32, 35, 36, 7:2, 3, 5, 7, 9, 12, 14, 18, 26, 31, 49, 8:5, 9, 15[2], 21, 23[2], 24, 25, 46, 47, 48, 54, 55, 57[2], 61, 62, 65, 9:11, 16

1 KINGS 9:27, 10:1, 2[2], 18, 22, 26, 11:1, 4, 9, 16, 17, 18, 21, 22, 29, 38, 43, 12:6, 8[2], 10, 11[3], 14[2], 18, 21, 13:7, 8, 15, 16[3], 18, 19, 14:3, 6, 8, 20, 22, 31[2], 15:3, 8, 14, 19, 20, 22[2], 24[2], 16:2, 6, 7, 13, 17, 18, 26, 28, 17:18, 20, 18:4, 13, 28, 32, 33, 35, 45, 19:1, 10, 14, 19[2], 21, 20:1, 20, 21, 34[2], 38, 21:8[2], 13, 22:4, 11, 13, 27[2], 31[2], 40, 44, 49, 50[2]

2 KINGS 1:8, 9, 11, 13, 14, 15[2], 2:1, 16, 3:4, 7, 12, 13, 17, 19, 20, 26, 4:13, 26[3], 5:1, 3, 5, 9[2], 23, 26, 6:1, 3, 4, 8, 15, 16[2], 18[2]

2 KINGS 6:22[2], 32, 33, 7:2, 19, 8:2, 4, 9, 12[2], 21, 24[2], 28, 9:13, 15, 18, 19, 24, 28, 10:2[2], 6, 13, 15, 16, 23, 25, 31, 35, 11:3, 4[2], 8[2], 9, 11, 14, 15, 20, 12:15, 21, 13:9, 13[2], 19, 23, 14:10, 15, 16[2], 20, 22, 29[2], 15:7[2], 16, 19, 22, 25[2], 38[2], 16:15, 20[2], 17:15, 18, 35, 36, 38, 18:7, 17, 26, 27, 28, 31, 37, 19:1, 2, 6, 23, 24, 32, 37, 20:3, 21, 21:6, 11, 18, 22:7, 14, 17, 23:2, 3, 11, 14, 18, 24, 25[3], 24:4, 6, 25:7, 9, 10, 11, 17, 24, 25[2], 28

1 CHRON. 2:23[2], 4:9, 10, 23, 5:10, 18, 19[2], 20, 6:32, 33, 57[2], 58[2], 59[2]

1 CHRON. 6:60[3], 64, 67[2], 68[2], 69[2], 70[2], 71[2], 72[2], 73[2], 74[2], 75[2], 76[3], 77[2], 78[2], 79[2], 80[2], 81[2], 7:4, 5, 23, 28, 8:12, 32, 9:20, 25, 38, 11:3, 9, 10[2], 13, 19, 23[2], 42, 12:2, 19, 27, 33, 34[2], 37, 38, 39, 13:1[2], 2, 8[7], 14, 14:1, 12, 15:15, 16[2], 18, 19, 20, 21, 24, 25, 27[2], 28[5], 16:5[3], 6, 16, 38, 41, 42[3], 17:2, 6, 8, 11, 20, 18:10[2], 11, 19:14, 17, 19, 20:3[4], 4, 5, 21:7, 20, 21, 22:11, 13, 15, 16, 18, 23:2, 5, 24:5, 25:1[3], 3, 6, 7, 9, 26:16, 27:32, 28:1[3], 9[2], 20, 21[2], 29:2, 6, 8, 9[2], 17, 21, 22, 30

2 CHRON. 1:1, 3, 14, 2:3[2], 7[2], 8

2 CHRON. 2:12, 13, 14[2], 3:4, 5[2], 6, 7, 8, 9, 10, 4:5, 9, 20, 5:10, 12[3], 13[2], 6:4[2], 11, 14, 15[3], 16, 18, 36, 38[2], 41, 7:3, 6, 8, 18, 8:5, 18, 9:1[3], 17, 18, 21, 25, 31, 10:6, 8[2], 10, 11[2], 14[2], 18, 12:1, 3[2], 16, 13:3[2], 8, 9, 11, 12[2], 14, 17, 19[3], 14:1, 9, 11[3], 13, 15:2[2], 6, 9[2], 12[2], 14[4], 15[2], 16:3, 8, 10[2], 13, 14, 17:3, 8[2], 9, 14, 15, 16, 17[2], 18, 18:1, 2[2], 3[2], 10, 12, 26[2], 30[3], 19:6, 7, 9, 11, 20:1, 13, 17[2], 18, 19, 21, 25, 27, 28, 35, 36, 37, 21:1[2], 3, 4, 7, 9[2], 14, 18, 22:1, 5, 6, 7, 9, 12, 23:1

2 CHRON. 23:3, 7, 8, 13^2, 14, 18^2, 21, 24:21, 24, 25:2, 7^3, 13, 16, 19, 24, 28, 26:2, 13, 17, 19, 23^2, 27:5, 9, 28:5, 9, 10^2, 15, 18^2, 27, 29:8, 10, 18^2, 24, 25^3, 26^2, 27^2, 29, 30^2, 34, 30:6, 21^2, 23, 25, 31:9, 21, 32:3, 7^3, 8^2, 9, 18, 21^2, 33, 33:6^2, 11, 34:6, 25, 31^2, 35:12, 13, 21^3, 22, 36:10, 17, 19, 23

EZRA 1:3, 4^4, 5, 6^6, 11, 2:2, 63^2, 3:9^2, 10^2, 11, 12, 13, 4:2, 3, 5:2, 8, 6:4, 12, 16, 22, 7:13, 16, 17^2, 18, 28, 8:1, 3, 4, 5, 6, 7, 8, 9, 10, 11, 12, 13, 14, 17, 18, 19, 24, 33^2, 9:2, 11^3, 14^2, 10:3, 4, 12, 10:14, 16, 17

NEH. 1:3, 2:3, 9, 12^2, 13, 17, 3:1, 4:13, 17^3, 22, 5:7, 6:5, 7:7, 65, 8:2, 6^2, 9:1^2, 4, 6, 8, 13, 24^2, 10:32, 38, 11:25, 12:1, 24, 27^5, 35, 36, 40, 41, 42, 43, 13:2^2, 9, 11, 17, 25

ESTHER 1:6, 10, 11, 2:6^2, 9, 12^3, 13, 20, 3:1, 11, 12, 4:1^2, 2, 13, 5:9, 12^2, 14, 6:14, 7:1, 8:3, 8^2, 10, 15^2, 9:5, 29, 30

JOB 1:4, 15, 17, 2:7, 10, 11, 13, 3:14, 15^2, 4:2, 18, 5:14, 23^2, 7:5, 14, 8:21^2, 22, 9:2, 3, 14, 17, 18, 30, 35, 10:2, 11^2, 13, 12:2, 5, 12, 13, 16, 18, 13:3, 17, 19, 14:3, 5, 15:2, 3^2, 10, 11^2, 20, 15:27, 16:5, 8, 9, 10, 14, 16, 21, 17:2, 3^2, 18:6, 19:2, 4, 6, 16, 20, 22, 24, 20:11, 26, 21:8, 24, 25, 22:4, 16, 18, 21, 23:4, 6, 7, 14, 24:8, 14, 22, 25:2, 4, 26:10, 12, 27:11, 13, 14, 28:14, 16^2, 19, 22, 29:5, 6, 30:1, 21, 30, 31:1, 5, 13, 18^2, 20, 32:14, 33:19^2, 23, 26, 29, 30, 34:8^2, 9, 23, 35:4, 36:4, 7, 18, 32, 37:4, 5, 18, 22, 23, 38:8, 30, 32, 39:4, 10, 19, 24, 40:2, 9, 10^2, 15, 22, 24, 41:1, 2, 4, 5^2, 7^2, 13, 15, 28, 42:8, 11

PSALMS 2:9, 11^2, 3:4, 4:4, 5:4, 9, 12^2, 6:6^2, 7:4, 11, 14, 8:5, 9:1, 6, 10:14, 12:2^3, 4, 13:6, 15:3, 17:10, 14, 15, 18:25^2, 26^2, 32, 39, 20:6, 21:3, 6, 22:13, 23:4, 5, 25:14, 19, 26:4^2, 5, 7, 9^2, 27:7, 28:3^2, 7, 29:11, 30:11, 31:9, 10^2, 32:7, 8, 9, 33:2^2, 3, 34:3, 35:1^2, 13, 16^2, 19, 26, 36:8, 9, 37:12, 24, 38:7, 39:1^2, 2^2, 3, 11, 12, 42:4^4, 8, 10, 44:1, 2, 9, 19, 45:3, 7, 12, 15, 46:3, 7, 11, 47:1, 5^2, 7, 48:7, 50:5, 18^2, 51:7, 12, 19^2, 54 *title*, 4, 55:18, 20, 58:9, 59:7, 60 *title*^{2}, 5, 10, 62:4, 63:5^2, 64:7, 65:4, 6, 9, 10, 11, 13^2, 66:13, 15^2, 17^2, 68:6, 13^2, 19, 25, 27, 30^2, 69:10, 28, 30^2, 71:8^2, 13, 22^2, 72:2^2, 19, 73:7, 19, 23, 24, 74:6, 75:5, 77:1^2, 6, 15, 78:8, 14^2, 78:36^2, 37, 47^2, 58^2, 62, 71, 80:5, 10, 16, 81:2, 16^2, 83:5, 7, 8, 15^2, 16, 85:5, 86:12, 87:4, 88:4, 7, 89:1, 3, 10, 20, 21, 24, 28, 29, 32^2, 38, 45, 90:5, 14, 91:4, 8, 15, 16, 92:3, 10, 93:1^2, 94:20, 95:2^2, 10, 96:13^2, 98:5^2, 6, 9^2, 100:2^2, 4^2, 101:2, 6, 102:9, 103:4, 5, 10, 104:1, 2^2, 6^2, 13, 28, 105:9, 18, 25, 37, 40, 43^2, 106:4^2, 5, 6, 29, 32, 33, 38, 39^2, 43, 107:9, 12, 22, 108:1, 6, 11, 109:2, 3, 14, 18^2, 29^3, 30, 110:6, 111:1, 112:5, 9, 10, 113:8^2, 116:7, 118:7, 27, 119:2, 7, 10, 13, 17, 34, 58, 65, 69, 78, 93, 98, 124, 145, 120:4, 6, 123:3, 4^2, 125:5, 126:2^2, 126:6^3, 127:5, 128:2, 130:4, 7^2, 132:9, 15, 16, 18, 136:12^2, 138:1, 3, 139:3, 18, 21, 22, 141:4, 142:1^2, 7, 143:2, 147:7, 8, 14, 20, 149:3, 4, 8^2, 150:3^2, 4^2

PROV. 1:11, 13, 15, 31, 2:1, 16, 3:5, 9^2, 10^2, 30, 32, 4:7, 23, 5:10, 17, 18, 19, 20, 22, 6:1, 2^2, 12, 13^3, 22, 25, 32, 7:1, 5, 10, 13, 14, 16^3, 17, 18, 20, 21^2, 8:12, 18, 24, 30, 31, 10:4, 10, 18, 22, 11:2, 9, 12:11, 14, 21, 13:10, 16, 20, 14:1, 10, 14, 18, 15:16, 16:7, 8, 19^2, 17:1, 14, 18:1, 3, 20^2, 19:2, 7, 23, 20:8, 13, 17, 19^2, 21:9, 19, 27, 22:24^2, 23:1, 7, 11, 13, 21, 24:1, 24:4, 21, 28, 31, 25:9, 24, 26:17, 23, 24, 27:14, 22, 28:4, 20, 23, 29:3, 9, 24, 30:8, 16, 19, 22, 28, 31:13, 16, 17, 21, 26

ECCL. 1:8^2, 11, 16, 2:1, 3, 9, 4:6, 8, 15, 5:2, 10^2, 11, 17, 6:3, 4^2, 10, 7:11, 8:12, 13, 15, 16, 9:7^2, 9, 10, 11:5, 12:14

CANT. 1:2, 6, 10^2, 11, 2:3, 5^2, 13, 3:6^2, 10, 11, 4:8^2, 9^2, 13^2, 14^2, 5:1^3, 2^2, 5^2, 12, 14^2, 6:1, 4, 10, 7:1, 2, 8:9

ISAIAH 1:4, 6, 7, 13, 20, 22, 27^2, 3:10, 11, 14, 16^2, 17, 5:2, 13, 18^2, 26, 6:2^3, 4, 6, 10^3, 7:2^2, 4^2, 20, 24^2, 25, 8:1, 10, 11, 9:5^2, 7^2, 10, 12, 10:22, 24, 33, 34, 11:4^4, 6^2, 15, 12:1, 3, 13:9, 14:1, 6, 19, 20, 21, 23, 30, 15:3, 5, 16:4, 9^2, 14, 17:5, 10, 18:1, 5, 19:23, 24^2, 20:4, 21:3, 7^2, 9, 14, 22:2, 6, 12, 17, 21^2, 23:17, 24:21^2, 9, 12, 25:5, 11, 26:9^2, 17, 18, 19, 27:1, 5^2, 6, 8, 28:1, 2, 11, 15^2, 18^2, 27^3, 28^2, 29:2, 6^3, 9^2, 13^2, 30:1, 24^2, 27, 28, 29, 30^3, 31, 32^2, 31:8, 32:7, 33:1^2, 5, 14^2, 21, 34:3, 6^4, 7^4, 14, 15, 35:2, 4^2, 7, 10, 36:2, 12, 13, 16, 22, 37:1, 2, 9, 25, 33, 38, 38:3, 11, 12, 14, 40:9, 10^2, 11^2, 12, 14, 19, 31, 41:3, 4, 7^2, 10^2, 11, 12, 43:2, 5, 23^3, 43:24^4, 44:5, 12^3, 13^3, 16, 45:9^2, 17, 47:6, 12^2, 15, 48:10, 20, 49:4^2, 18^2, 23, 25^2, 26^3, 50:3, 8, 11, 51:11, 21, 52:8, 12, 53:3, 5, 9^2, 12^3, 54:1, 7, 8, 9, 11^3, 55:3, 12^2, 56:12, 57:5, 8, 9, 15, 58:4, 14, 59:3^2, 6, 12, 17, 21, 60:7, 9, 61:8, 10^4, 62:11, 63:1, 3, 11, 12, 64:11, 65:23, 66:10^3, 11^2, 15^4, 16

JER. 1:8, 19, 2:9^2, 22, 29, 35, 3:1, 2^3, 9^2, 10, 15, 18, 20, 4:8, 30^3, 5:17, 18, 6:3, 11^3, 12, 26, 28, 8:8, 19^2, 9:4, 8, 15, 18^2, 25, 10:3, 4^4, 13, 24, 11:5, 10, 15, 16, 19, 12:1^2, 5^2, 6, 13:12^2, 13, 17, 14:3, 17^3, 18^2, 21, 15:6, 7, 11, 14, 17, 15:20, 16:8, 18, 17:1^2, 18, 18:6, 17, 18, 19, 23, 19:4, 5, 10, 20:4, 9, 11, 17, 18, 21:2, 5^2, 7, 10, 22:7, 14^2, 15, 16, 19, 23:15, 24:1, 7, 25:6, 7, 26, 31^2, 26:11, 14, 21, 22, 23, 24, 27:8^3, 18, 28:4, 29:13, 16, 18^3, 23, 30:6^2, 11, 14^2, 23^2, 31:3^2, 4, 7, 8^3, 9^2, 14^2, 24, 27^2, 31^2, 32, 33, 32:4, 5, 21^5, 22, 29, 30, 40, 41^2, 44, 33:5^2, 21^2, 25, 34:2, 3, 5, 8, 13, 22, 36:18^2, 23, 37:8, 10, 15, 38:6, 10, 11, 13, 17, 18, 23, 25, 27, 39:3, 7, 8, 9, 40:4^2, 5, 6, 9, 41:1, 2^2, 3^2, 5, 7, 9, 11, 12, 13^2, 15, 16, 42:6, 8, 11, 43:6, 43:12, 13, 44:8, 25^2, 46:4, 10, 22^2, 25, 28, 47:5, 48:7, 32, 33, 39, 49:2, 3, 20, 50:5, 39, 51:5, 14^2, 16, 20^2, 21^2, 22^3, 23^3, 28, 32, 34, 40, 42, 45, 58, 59, 52:13, 14, 22, 32

LAM. 1:2, 16, 2:1, 4, 10, 11, 3:5, 9, 15^2, 16^2, 30, 41, 43, 44, 48, 4:9^2, 14, 5:6, 9

EZEKIEL 1:15, 2:6, 3:3, 4, 10, 22, 24, 25, 26, 4:12, 16^2, 17, 5:2^2, 11^2, 12^2, 6:9^2, 11^2, 7:15, 18, 27, 8:11, 16, 17, 9:1^2, 2^2, 3, 7, 11, 10:2^2, 4, 6, 7, 11:6, 13, 12:7, 12, 18^3, 19^2, 13:10, 11, 13, 14, 15, 22, 14:11, 16:8, 9^2, 10^4, 11, 12, 13, 16, 17, 26, 28^2, 36^2, 37^2, 16:40^2, 41, 59, 60, 62, 17:3, 7, 12, 13, 16, 17, 20, 21, 18:7, 16, 19:4, 11, 20:6, 7, 15, 18, 31, 33, 34^3, 35, 36^2, 39^2, 40, 41, 44, 21:6^2, 21, 22, 24, 22:7, 11, 14, 28, 31, 23:6, 7^4, 8, 10, 14, 15, 16, 17^2, 23, 24^2, 25, 29, 30, 33^3, 37, 40, 42^2, 43^2, 47^3, 24:4, 7, 12, 16, 26, 25:6^2, 10, 15, 17, 26:7^4, 8, 9, 11, 16, 20^3, 27, 27:9, 11, 12, 14, 16, 21, 22^2, 24, 31^2, 33, 28:4^2, 23, 26, 30:5, 11^2, 24, 31:3^2, 4, 11, 14, 16, 17^2, 18^2, 32:2^2, 3, 4, 5, 6, 7, 18, 19, 21, 24, 25^2, 27^2, 28^2, 29^3, 30^4, 32^2, 33:25, 31, 34:3, 4^2, 34:16, 18^2, 19^2, 21^3, 25, 29, 30, 35:8^2, 13, 36:5^2, 37, 38, 37:6, 19^2, 23^3, 26^2, 27, 38:4^2, 5^2, 6, 9, 13, 15, 22^2, 23, 39:4, 9, 10, 14, 20^3, 40:3, 4^2, 41:13, 15, 16, 18, 42:16^2, 17, 18, 19, 43:2, 22, 44:17, 18, 19, 45:2, 46:14, 23, 47:22, 48:20, 34

DANIEL 1:2, 8^2, 9, 13, 19, 2:5, 11, 14, 18, 22, 41, 43^3, 4:15^3, 23^3, 25^2, 32, 33, 5:7, 16, 21^3, 29, 6:14, 17^2, 20, 7:7, 13, 19, 21, 8:7, 18, 9:3, 15, 22, 26, 27, 10:5, 7, 13, 17, 20, 21, 11:3, 7, 8^2, 11^3, 13^2, 17^2, 22, 23^2, 25^2, 28, 30, 34^2, 38^2, 39^2, 40^2, 44

HOSEA 2:2, 3, 6, 7, 13, 2:18^3, 4:1, 3^2, 4, 5, 14^2, 18, 5:5, 6^2, 7, 6:8, 7:3^2, 5^2, 14, 9:8, 11:4^2, 12^4, 12:1, 2, 3, 4, 13:3, 16, 14:2, 8

JOEL 1:8, 2:12^4, 20, 24, 26, 3:2, 4, 18^2

AMOS 1:3, 11, 13, 14^2, 2:2^3, 3, 3:15, 4:2^2, 5, 9, 10, 5:8, 14, 6:6, 7, 8, 10, 11^2, 12, 7:7, 9, 8:3, 9:1

OBADIAH 7

JONAH 1:3, 2:6, 9, 3:6, 8

MICAH 1:7, 2:4, 8, 10, 3:5, 10^2, 5:1, 6, 6:2^2, 6^2, 7^2, 8, 11^2, 15, 7:2, 3, 14

NAHUM 1:8, 2:3, 7, 12^2, 3:12

HABAK. 1:15, 2:6, 12, 14, 16, 19, 3:9, 13, 14, 15, 16

ZEPH. 1:3, 4, 8, 9, 12, 3:8, 9, 14, 17^2

HAGGAI 1:6^2, 12, 13, 2:4, 5, 7, 12, 17^3

ZECH. 1:2, 6, 9, 13^2, 14^2, 15, 16, 19, 2:1, 3, 7, 3:3, 4, 5, 4:1, 2, 4, 5, 7, 10, 5:4, 5, 10, 6:4, 7:14, 8:2^2, 4, 23^2, 9:4, 8, 13, 14, 15, 10:5, 9, 11, 11:10, 12:3, 4^3, 13:6, 14:5, 18

MALACHI 1:8, 2:3, 4, 5, 6, 13^4, 16, 17, 3:9, 4:2, 4, 6

MATT. 1:18, 23, 2:3, 10, 11, 3:11^3, 12, 4:21, 24^2, 5:22, 25, 28, 41, 7:2^2, 8:11, 16^2, 24, 28, 29, 9:10, 11, 15, 20, 32, 36, 11:7, 12:3, 4, 22, 30, 41, 42, 45, 46, 47, 13:15^3, 20, 29, 56, 14:7, 9, 14, 24, 15:8^2, 20, 22, 30, 32, 16:1, 27, 17:3, 17, 18:9, 16, 26, 27, 29, 19:10, 26^2, 20:2, 13, 15, 20, 22^2, 23^2, 24, 21:2, 25, 22:10, 16, 25, 37^3, 23:4, 30, 24:19, 30, 31, 49, 51, 25:3, 4, 10, 16, 19, 27, 31, 26:11, 15, 18, 20, 23, 29, 35, 36, 37, 38, 40, 47^2, 51, 52, 55^2, 58, 67, 69, 71, 72, 27:7, 19, 22, 34, 38, 41, 44, 46, 48, 50, 54, 28:8, 12, 20

MARK 1:6^2, 8^2, 13, 20, 23, 24, 26, 27, 29, 32, 36, 41, 2:15, 16^2, 19^2, 25, 26, 3:5, 6, 7, 14, 4:10, 16, 24, 30, 33, 36, 5:2, 3, 4, 5, 7^2, 15, 16, 18^2, 24, 40, 42, 6:3, 9, 13, 22, 25, 26, 34, 50, 7:2^2, 5, 6, 8:2, 4, 10, 11, 14, 34, 38, 9:1, 2, 4^2, 8, 10^2, 14, 16, 18, 19, 24, 47, 49^2, 50, 10:27^3, 30, 38^2, 39, 41, 46, 11:11, 31, 12:30^4, 33^4, 13:17, 26, 14:7, 14, 17, 18, 20, 31, 33, 43^2, 48^2, 49, 53, 54, 58, 65, 67, 15:1, 7, 17, 19, 23, 27, 28, 31, 32, 34, 37, 41, 16:10, 14, 17, 20^2

LUKE 1:15, 25, 28, 30, 36, 37, 39, 41, 42, 51, 53, 56, 58, 66, 67, 2:5^2, 13, 16, 36, 37, 40, 48, 51, 52, 3:14, 16^3, 17, 4:28, 32, 33, 34, 36, 38, 40, 5:9, 10, 18, 19, 26, 29, 30, 5:34, 36, 6:3, 4, 11^2, 17, 18, 38, 7:6, 11, 12, 24, 29, 36, 38^3, 44^2, 46^2, 49, 8:1, 7, 13, 14, 15, 16, 22, 23, 28^2, 29, 37, 38, 45, 9:18, 30, 32^3, 41, 49, 10:17, 27^4, 11:7, 20, 23^2, 31, 32, 37, 46^3, 12:13, 25, 46, 47, 48, 50, 58, 13:1, 14, 14:9, 10, 15, 18, 25, 31^2, 15:2, 6, 9, 13, 16, 17, 29, 30, 31, 16:21, 17:15, 20, 18:7, 11, 27^2, 19:7, 23, 37, 44, 20:1, 5, 21:5, 20, 23, 25, 27, 34, 22:4, 11, 14, 15^2, 21, 28, 33, 36, 48, 49, 52, 53, 56, 59, 23:9, 11, 18, 23, 32, 35, 43, 46, 55, 24:1, 10, 15, 24, 29^2, 30, 32, 33

LUKE 24:44 49 52 JOHN 1:1 2 26 31 33[2] 39 2:4 7 3:2 22 26 4:6 9 11 27[2] 40 5:18 6:3 13 22 66 7:33 8:6 29 38[2] 9:6 37 40 11:2[2] 16 31 33 43 44[2] 54 12:2 3[2] 8 17 35 40[2] 13:5

JOHN 13:8 18 33 14:9 16 17 23 25 27 30 15:27 16:4 32 17:5[3] 12 24 18:1 2 3 5 15 18 22 26 19:3 15[2] 18 29 32 34 40 20:7 24 26 21:3 8 ACTS 1:4 5[2] 14[3] 17 18 21 22 26 2:4[2]

ACTS 2:14 28 29 30 40 46[2] 47 3:4 8 10 25 4:8 13 14 24 27 29 31[2] 32 33 5:1 12 16 17[2] 21 23 26 28 31 6:9 7:9[2] 19 38[2] 45 48 54 57[2] 60 8:6 7[3] 11 13 20[3] 31 37 9:7 17

ACTS 9:19 28 39[2] 43 10:2 6 23 27 35 38[3] 41 45 46 11:2 3 12 16[2] 21 23 26 12:2 6 17 20[2] 25 13:1 7 9 16 17 31 45 52[2] 14:4[2] 5 8 13 15 17 18 20 23 27 28 15:2 4 22[2]

ACTS 15:24 25[2] 32 35 37 38[2] 16:3 11 16 28 34 17:2 4 5 11 15 17[4] 23 24 25 34 18:2 3 8 10 12 14 18 19 20 19:4 6 21 26 29[2] 33 34 38 20:9 18 19[2] 24 28 31 34 36 21:1

ACTS 21:5 7 8 16[3] 18 24[2] 26 29 33 36 40 22:9 11 22 25 28 23:15 19 21 27 32 24:1[2] 3 7 12 18[2] 24 26 25:5 12 23[2] 24[2] 26:8 9 12 13 24 30 27:2 10 18 19 24 39 41 28:10[2] 11

ACTS 28:14 16 20[2] 27[3] 31 ROMANS 1:4 9 12 27 29 2:11 3:13 5:1 6:4 6 8[2] 7:18 21 25[2] 8:16 17[2] 18 25 26 32 9:14 22 10:9 10[2] 11:17 12:8[3] 10 15[2] 18 21 14:15[2] 20 15:6 10 13 14 24 30 32[2] 33

ROMANS 16:14 15 16 20 24 1 COR. 1:2 17 2:1 3 4 13 3:2[2] 9 19 4:3 8 12 21 5:4 8[3] 9 10[3] 11 6:6 7 9 20 7:5 12 13 23 24 8:7 9:13 23 10:5 13 20 11:5 32 12:26[2] 30 13:1 14:5[2] 6

1 COR. 14:15[4] 16 18 19 21 23 39 15:10 32 35 16:4 6 7 10 11 12 14 16 19 20 21 23 24 2 COR. 1:1 12 17 21 2:1 4 7 3:3[2] 18 4:14 5:1 2 8 6:1 14[3] 15[2] 16 7:3 4 8 15

2 COR. 8:4 18 19[2] 22 9:4 10:2 12 11:1[2] 2 4 9 25 32 12:16 18 13:4 11 12 14 GAL. 1:2 16 18 2:1[2] 3 5 12 13[2] 20 3:9 4:18 20 25 30 5:1 24 6:11 18 EPHES. 1:3 13 2:5 19

EPHES. 3:12 16 18 19 4:2[2] 14 19 25 28 31 5:6 7 11 18[2] 26 6:2 3 5 6 7 9 14 15 18[2] 23 24 PHIL. 1:1 4 11 20 23 25 27 2:6 12 17 18 22[2] 23 29 4:3[3] 6 9 14 15

PHIL. 4:21 23 COLOS. 1:9 11[2] 2:4 5 7 11 12[2] 13 19 20 22 3:1 3 4 9 16 22 4:2 6[2] 9 18 1 THESS. 1:6 2:2 4 17 3:4 13 4:11 14 16[3] 17[2] 18 5:3 10 26 28 2 THESS. 1:6

2 THESS. 1:7[2] 9 11 2:5 8[2] 9 10 3:1 8 10 12 14 16 17 18 1 TIM. 1:10 14 2:9[2] 10 11 15 3:4 6 4:2 3 4 14 5:2 6:6 10 21 2 TIM. 1:3 4 9 2:4 10 11[2] 12 22 3:6[2] 4:2 11[2]

2 TIM. 4:13 16 17 22 TITUS 2:15 3:15[2] PHILE. 19 13 25 HEB. 1:9 2:4[2] 7 9 3:10 17[2] 4:2 13 15 5:2 7 7:21 8:8[3] 9 10 9:4 11 19 21 22 23[2] 24 25 10:1 16 22[2] 11:7 9[2] 25 31[2] 37

HEB. 12:1[2] 7 14 17 18 20 28 13:3 5 9[3] 12 16 17[2] 23 25 JAMES. 1:6 11 13 17 18 21 2:1 2 22 3:4 13[2] 4:4 5:14 1 PETER 1:7 8 12 18 19 22 2:15 18 20 3:2 6 7 15 4:1

1 PETER 4:4 13 5:5 13 14 2 PETER 1:1 18 2:3 6 7 8 13[2] 14 16 17 20 3:6 8 10[2] 12 17 1 JOHN 1:1 2 3[3] 6 7 2:1 19 2 JOHN 2 3 12 3 JOHN 10 13

JUDE 9 12 14 23 24 REV. 1:7 12 13[2] 2:12 16 22 23 27 3:4 17 18 20[2] 21[2] 4:1 5:1 2 12 6:8[5] 10 11 7:2 9 10 8:3 4 5 7 8 13 9:19 10:1 3 11:6 12:1 2 5 9 17[2]

REV. 13:4 7 10[2] 14:1 2 4 7 9 10 15 18 15:2 6 8 16:8 9 17:1 2[2] 4 6[3] 12 14[2] 16 18:1 2 3 8 9 16 21 19:2 13 15[2] 17 20[3] 21[2] 20:4 6 21:3[3] 8 9 15 16 19 22:12 21

ye

859, *5210*

GEN. 3:1 3 4 5[2] 4:23 9:4 7 17:10 11 18:5[2] 19:2 8 22:5 24:49 26:27 29:4 5 7 31:6 32:4 19 20 34:9 10[2] 11 12 15 17 30 40:7 42:1 7 9[2] 12 14 15[2] 16[2] 19[2] 20 22 33 34[2] 36[2] 38 43:3 5 6[2] 7 27 29 44:4 5 10 15 19 23 27 29[2] 45:4 5 9 13[2] 17 18 19

GEN. 45:24 46:34[2] 47:23 24 49:2 50:17 20 21 25 EXOD. 1:16[2] 18 22[2] 2:18 20 3:12 18 21 22[2] 4:15 5:4 5 7 8[2] 11 14 17[2] 18 19 21 6:7 8:25 28[2] 9:28 30 10:2 11[2] 24 11:7 12:3 5 6 10[2] 11[2] 13 14[2] 15[2] 17[2] 18 20[2] 22 24 25[2] 26 27 31[2] 32 46 13:3 4 19 14:13[3] 14 15:21

EXOD. 16:3 6 7[2] 8 12[3] 16 23[2] 25 26 28 29 17:2[2] 19:4 5[2] 6 12 20:20 22 23[2] 22:21 22 31[3] 23:9[2] 25 24:1 14 25:2 3 9 19 30:9[2] 32 37 31:13[2] 14 32:30 33:5 34:13 35:1 3 5 LEVIT. 1:2 2:11[2] 12 3:17 7:23 24 26 32 8:32 33 35[2] 9:3 6 10:6 7[2] 9[2] 10 11 13 14 17 18

LEVIT. 11:2 3 4 8[2] 9[2] 11[2] 13 21 22 24 33 39 42 43[3] 44[3] 45 14:34 15:31 16:29 30 31 17:14 18:3[4] 4 5 24 26 28 30[3] 19:2 3 4 5[2] 6 9 11 12 15 19 23[2] 25 26[2] 27 28 30 33 34 35 36 37 20:7 8 15 22 23 24 25[2] 26[2] 22:19 20 22 24[2] 25 28 29

LEVIT. 22:30 31 32 23:2 3 4 6 7[2] 8[2] 10[2] 12[2] 14[2] 15[2] 16[2] 17 18 19 21[2] 22 24 25[2] 27 28 31 32[2] 35 36[3] 37 38 39[2] 40[2] 41[2] 42 24:22 25:2 9 10[3] 11 12 13 14 17 18[2] 19 20 22[2] 23 24 44 45 46[2] 26:1[2] 2 3 5 6 7 10 12 13 14 15[3] 16 17[2] 18

LEVIT. 26:21 23 25[2] 26 27 29[2] 34 35 37 38 NUM. 1:2 4:18 27 32 5:3[2] 6:23 9:3[2] 14 10:5 6 7[2] 9[4] 10 11:18[3] 19 20 12:4 8 13:2 20 14:9[2] 28 30 31[2] 34[3] 41 42 43[2] 15:2 12[2] 14 15 18 19[2] 20[3] 21 22 29 39[3] 40 16:3[2] 7[2] 8 10 11 17 26 28 30 41 18:3 5 7

NUM. 18:26[2] 28[3] 29 30 31[2] 32[4] 19:3 20:4 5 8 10 12[2] 24 21:5 17 22:19 25:5 27:8 9 10 11 14 28:2 3 11 18 19 20 23 24 25[2] 26[3] 27 31 29:1[2] 2 7[3] 8 12[3] 13 17 35[2] 36 39 31:4 15 19 23[2] 24[3] 32:6 7 14 15[2] 20[2] 22 23[2] 29 33:51 52 53 54[4] 55[3] 34:2 6 7

NUM. 34:8 10 13 18 35:2 4 5 6[3] 7[2] 8[3] 10 11 13[2] 14[2] 31 32 33[2] 34 DEU. 1:6 10 11 14 17[3] 18 19 20 22 26 27 31[2] 32 33 39 41[3] 42 43 45 46[2] 2:3 4[2] 6[4] 24 3:18 19 20 22 4:1 2[3] 4 5[2] 11 12[2] 14[2] 15[2] 16 20 22 23 25 26[3] 27 28 5:1

DEU. 5:5 23[2] 24 28 32[2] 33[4] 6:1[2] 3 14 16[2] 17 7:5[2] 7[2] 12 25 8:1[2] 19 20[2] 9:7[2] 8 16[2] 18 21 22 23[2] 24 10:19[2] 11:2 5 8[3] 9 10 11 13 16 17 18 19 22 23 25 27 28[2] 31[2] 32 12:1[2] 2[2] 3[2] 4 5 6 7[4] 8 9 10[2] 11[2] 12[2] 16[2] 13:3 4[2] 13 14:1[2] 4 6 7

DEU. 14:8 9[2] 10 11 12 20 21 17:16 18:15 19:19 20:2 3[2] 18 22:24[2] 23:4 24:8 9 25:17 27:2 4[2] 12 28:62[2] 63 68 29:2 6[3] 7 9[2] 10 16[2] 17 18[2] 31:5 13[2] 19 27 29[2] 32:1 3 6 43 46 47[2] 51[2] JOSH. 1:11 14 15 2:5 10[3] 12 13 14 16 3:3[2] 4[3] 8[2] 10 4:3[3] 6 7 17 22 23

JOSH. 4:24 6:3[2] 4 5 10[2] 18[3] 22 7:12 13 14 8:2 4[2] 7 8[3] 9:6 7 8[2] 11 22[2] 23 10:19 25 18:3 6 22:2 3 4 16[3] 18[2] 19 24 25[2] 27 31[2] 23:3 5 6[2] 7 8 11 12 13 14 16[2] 24:6 7 8 11 13[5] 14 15[2] 19 20 22[2] 27 JUD. 2:2[4] 5:2 3[2] 9 10[2] 23[2] 6:10[2] 31[2]

JUD. 7:17 18 8:15 18 19 24 9:7 15 16[3] 18 19[2] 48 10:12 13 14 11:7[3] 9 26 12:2 3[2] 4 14:12 13[2] 15 18[2] 15:7 10 11 18:6 8 9 10[2] 14[2] 18 24[3] 19:24 20:7 11[2] 21:21 22[2] RUTH 1:8 9 11 13[2] 21 4:2 9 10 1 SAM. 2:23 24 29 4:9[2] 6:3[2] 5[2] 6 8 21 7:3 8:17 18[2] 22

1 SAM. 9:13[3] 19 10:14 19[2] 24 11:9[2] 10 12:1 5 11 12[2] 13[2] 14[2] 15 17[2] 20 21[2] 25[3] 14:34 38 40 15:6 32 17:8[2] 9 25 18:25 21:14[2] 15 22:7 13 23:21[2] 23 25:6 13 26:16[2] 27:10 29:10 30:23 2 SAM. 1:21 24 2:5[2] 6 7 3:38 7:7 11:15 20[3] 21 13:28 15:10[2] 36[2] 16:10 19:10 11 12[3] 13 22[2] 42 43[2] 21:3 4 24:2

1 KINGS 1:34 35 45 9:6[2] 11:2 12:6 9 24 18:18 21 24 25 20:28 33 22:3 2 KINGS 1:3 5 2:3 5 16 3:17[4] 19 6:2 17 19 32 7:1 9:11 10:6[3] 8 9 13 11:5 6 8[2] 12:7 17:12 13 27 35 36[3] 37[2] 38[2] 39 18:19 22[2] 31[2] 32 19:6 10 29[2] 22:13 18 1 CHRON. 12:17[2] 15:12[3] 13 16:9 10 13[2] 15 19

1 CHRON. 16:23 28 35 17:6 22:19 28:8 2 CHRON. 7:19 10:6 9 11:4 12:5 13:5 8[2] 9 11 12[2] 15:2[4] 7 18:14 25 27 30 19:6[2] 9 10[2] 20:15[2] 16[2] 17[2] 20[3] 23:4 7 24:6 20[3] 28:9 10 11 13[2] 29:5 8 11 31 30:6 7[2] 8 9[2] 32:10[2] 12 13 34:23 26 EZRA 4:2 3 18 21 22 6:6 8 7:25 8:28 29[2] 9:11

EZRA 9:12 10:10 NEH. 1:8 9 2:17 19[2] 20 4:12 14 20[2] 5:7 8 9[2] 11 8:10 11 13:17 18 21[2] 25 ESTHER 4:16 8:8 JOB 6:21[2] 26 27[2] 12:2 13:2 4[2] 5 7 8[2] 9 10 16:2 4 17:10 18:2 19:2 3[3] 5 21 22 28 29[2] 21:27 28 29[2] 34 27:12[2] 32:6 11 13 34:2[2] 10 18 42:7 8

PSALMS 2:10[2] 12 4:2[3] 6:8 11:1 14:2 22:23[3] 24:7[3] 9[2] 27:8 29:1 30:4 31:23 24 32:9 11[2] 33:1 34:9 11 47:1 7 48:13[2] 49:1[2] 50:22 58:1[3] 2[2] 62:3[3] 8 66:1 8 16 68:13[2] 16[2] 26 32 34 82:2 6 7 90:3 94:8[3] 95:7 96:7 97:7 10 12 99:5 100:1 3 103:20 21[3] 104:35 105:2 3 6[2] 45 106:1 48 111:1 112:1 113:1[2] 9 114:6[3] 115:11 15

PSALMS 116:19 117:1[2] 2 119:115 134:1[2] 135:1[2] 139:19 146:1 10 147:1 20 148:1[2] 2[2] 3[2] 4[2] 7 14 149:1 9 150:1 6 PROV. 1:22 23 24 25 4:1 2 5:7 7:24 8:5[2] 32 CANT. 1:5 2:7[2] 3:3 5[2] 11 5:8[2] 6:13 8:4 ISAIAH 1:5[2] 10[2] 12 15[2] 16 19 20 29[2] 30 2:3 5 22 3:10 14 15 6:9[2] 7:9 13[2] 8:9[4] 12[2]

ISAIAH 10:3^{3} 12:3 4 13:2 6 16:1 7 18:2 3^{3} 19:11 21:5 12^{2} 13^{2} 22:9^{2} 10^{2} 11^{2} 14 23:1 2 6^{2} 14 24:15 25:2 4 19 27:2 12^{2} 28:12 14 15 18 22 23 29:1 9 30:12 15^{2} 16^{2} 17^{2} 21^{3} 22 29 31:6 32:9^{2} 10^{2} 11^{2} 20 33:11^{2} 13^{2} 34:1^{2} 16 35:3 36:4 7 13 16^{2} 37:6 10 30^{2} 40:1^{2} 2 3 18^{2} 21^{3} 25 41:14 23 24 42:10 17 18^{3} 43:10^{2} 12 18 19 44:8^{2} 23^{3} 26 45:8 11 17 19 20 21 22 46:5 8 12 48:1 6 14 16^{2} 20^{4} 49:1 50:1 11^{4} 51:1^{4} 7^{3} 52:3^{2} 9

ISAIAH 52:11^{5} 12 55:1^{2} 2^{2} 6^{2} 12 56:1 9^{2} 12 57:3 4^{3} 14^{2} 58:3 4^{3} 6 61:6^{3} 7 62:6 10 11 65:11 12^{3} 13^{3} 14 15 18 66:1 5 10^{3} 11^{2} 12^{2} 13 14

JER. 2:4 7^{2} 12^{2} 29^{2} 31 3:13 16 20 22 4:4 5^{2} 10 16 5:1^{2} 10 14 19^{3} 22^{2} 31 6:1 4 6 16^{2} 18 7:2 4 5^{2} 6 8 9^{2} 12 13^{3} 14 23^{2} 8:8 9:4^{2} 17 20 10:1 11 11:2 4 6 13 12:9 13:15 16 17 23 14:13^{2} 16:12^{2} 13^{3} 17:4 20^{2} 22^{2} 24 27 18:6 11 13 19:3 20:13 21:3 4 11

JER. 22:3 4 5 10 26^{2} 30 23:2 17 20 35 36^{2} 38^{3} 25:3 4 5 7^{2} 8 27 28 29^{2} 34^{3} 26:4 5 11 12 15^{3} 27:4 9^{2} 10 13 14 15^{2} 29:5 6^{2} 7 8 12^{2} 13^{2} 15 19 20^{2} 26 28 30:6 22 24 31:6 7^{2} 10 32:5^{2} 36 43 33:10 20 34:14 15^{2} 16 17 35:5 6^{2} 7^{4} 13 14 15^{3} 18 36:19 37:7 10 18 40:3 10^{3} 42:9 10 11 13 14^{2} 16^{3} 18^{3} 19^{2} 20 21 22 44:2 3 7 8^{4} 9 20^{2} 22 23^{2} 25^{2} 26 29 46:3 4 9^{2} 14^{2} 48:14 17^{2} 20

JER. 48:26 28 49:3 5 8 14 28 30 50:2 11^{4} 14 29 45 51:3^{2} 27 45^{2} 46 50

LAM. 1:12 4:15

EZEKIEL 5:7 6:3 7 8^{2} 13 7:4 9 9:5^{2} 7 11:5 6^{2} 7 8 10^{2} 11 12^{2} 17 12:20 22 13:2 5 7^{3} 8 9 11 12 14^{3} 18^{2} 19 20^{2} 21 22 23 14:8 22^{2} 23^{2} 15:7 17:12 21 18:2 3 19 25 31^{3} 32 20:3 7 18 20 29 30^{2} 31^{3} 32 34 38 39^{4} 41 42 43^{4} 44^{2} 21:24^{3} 22:19 21 22^{2} 23:40 49^{2} 24:21 22^{2} 23^{2} 24^{2} 25:5 30:2 33:10 11^{3} 20^{2} 25^{2}

EZEKIEL 33:26^{4} 34:3^{4} 4^{6} 7 9 18^{2} 19^{2} 21^{2} 31 35:9 13 36:1 3^{2} 4 6 8^{2} 9 11^{3} 22^{2} 23 25 27 28^{2} 30 31 37:4 5 6^{2} 13 14^{2} 39:17 18 19^{3} 20 44:6 7^{2} 8^{2} 28 30 45:1^{2} 6 10 13 14 20 21 47:13 14 18 21 22 23 48:8 9 20 29

DANIEL 1:10 2:5^{2} 6^{2} 8^{2} 9^{3} 3:5^{2} 14 15^{5} 26

HOSEA 1:9 10 2:1 4:1 15^{2} 18 5:1^{4} 8 9:5 10:13^{3} 14:3

JOEL 1:2^{2} 3 5^{2} 11^{3} 13^{3} 14 2:1 12 19 22 23 26 27 3:4^{3} 5 6^{2} 7 9

JOEL 3:11 13 17

AMOS 2:11 12 3:13 4:1 3^{2} 5 6 8 9 10 11^{2} 5:1 4^{2} 6 7 11^{5} 14^{2} 22 25 26^{2} 6:2^{2} 3 12 13 8:4 9:7

OBADIAH 1 16

MICAH 1:2 10^{2} 11 2:3^{2} 6 8 9^{2} 10 3:1 6^{2} 9 6:1 2^{2} 5 9 16^{2} 7:5^{2}

NAHUM 1:9 2:9

HABAK. 1:5^{2}

ZEPH. 1:11 2:3^{3} 12^{2} 3:8 20^{3}

HAGGAI 1:4 6^{6} 9^{3} 2.3 4 5^{2} 17

ZECH. 1:3 4^{2} 2:9 3:10 6:15^{2} 7:5^{2} 6^{3} 7 8:9 13^{2} 15 16^{2} 9:12 10:1 11:2 12 14:5^{3}

MALACHI 1:2

MALACHI 1:5 6 7^{3} 8^{2} 10 12^{2} 13^{4} 2:1 2^{3} 4 8^{3} 9 13 14 16 17^{3} 3:1^{2} 6 7^{2} 8^{2} 9^{2} 10 12 13 14 18 4:2 3 4

MATT. 2:8 3:2 3 5:11 13 14 20 21 27 33 38 39 43 45 46^{2} 47^{2} 48 6:1^{2} 7 8^{3} 9 14 15 16 24 25^{3} 26 28 30 32 33 7:1 2^{3} 6 7 11 12^{2} 13 16 20 23 8:26^{2} 9:4 6 13 28 38 10:5 7 8 11^{2} 12 14 16 18 19^{2} 20 22 23^{2} 27^{3} 31^{2} 11:4 7 8 9 14 17^{2} 28 29

MATT. 12:3 5 7^{2} 34 13:14^{2} 17^{2} 18 29^{2} 30 51 14:16 15:3 5 6 7 16 17 34 16:2 3^{3} 8^{3} 9^{2} 10 11^{2} 15 17:5 20^{2} 18:3^{2} 10 12 18^{2} 35 19:4 28^{2} 20:4 6 7^{2} 22^{3} 23 25 32 21:2 3 5 13 16 21^{3} 22^{2} 24 25 28 32^{4} 42 22:9^{2} 18^{2} 29 31 42 23:3 8^{2} 10 13^{3} 14^{3} 15^{2} 16 17 19 23^{2} 24 25 27 28^{2} 29 31^{2} 32 33^{3} 34^{2} 35 37 39^{2} 24:2 6^{2} 9 15 20 32 33^{2} 42 44^{2} 25:6 9 13 30 34 35^{3} 36^{3} 40^{2} 41 42^{2} 43^{2}

MATT. 25:45^{2} 26:2 10 11^{2} 15 27 31 36 38 40 41 55^{2} 64 65 66 27:17 21 24 65^{2} 28:5^{2} 13 19

MARK 1:3 15 17 2:8 10 25 4:13^{2} 24^{2} 40^{2} 5:39 6:10^{2} 11 31 37 38 7:8^{2} 9^{2} 11 12 13^{2} 18^{2} 8:5 17^{4} 18^{3} 19 20 21 29 9:16 33 41 50 10:36 38^{3} 39^{2} 42 11:2^{2} 3^{2} 5 17 24^{4} 25^{2} 26 31 12:10 15 24^{2} 26 27 13:7^{2} 9^{2} 11^{4} 13 14 18 23 28 29^{2} 33^{2} 35^{2} 14:6 7^{4} 13 14 27 32 34 38^{2} 48 49 62 64^{2} 71 15:9 12^{2} 16:6

MARK 16:7 15

LUKE 2:12 49 3:4 4:23 5:22 24 30 34 6:2 3 20 21^{4} 22 23 24 25^{2} 31^{2} 32^{2} 33^{2} 34^{3} 35^{2} 36 37^{3} 38 46 7:22 24 25 26 32^{2} 33 34 8:18 9:4 5 13 20 55^{2} 10:2 5 8 10 11 23 24^{2} 11:2 5 9 13 18 39 40 41 42^{2} 43 44 46^{3} 47 48^{3} 52^{3} 12:1 3^{2} 5 7 11^{3} 12 22^{2} 24 26^{2} 28 29^{4} 30 31 33 36 40^{2} 51 54^{2} 55^{2} 56^{3} 57 13:2 3^{2} 4 5^{2} 25^{2} 26 27^{2} 28 32 34 35 16:9 11 12 13

LUKE 16:15 17:6^{2} 10^{2} 22^{2} 19:30^{2} 31^{2} 33 46 20:5 23 21:6 8^{2} 9 14 16 17 20 30 31^{3} 36^{2} 22:10 11 26 28 30 35 40 46^{2} 51 52 53 67 68 70 23:14^{2} 15 24:5 17^{2} 38 39 41 48 49^{2}

JOHN 1:26 38 51 3:7 11 12^{2} 28 4:20 21 22^{2} 32 35 38^{2} 48^{2} 5:20 33 34 35 37 38^{2} 39^{2} 40^{2} 42 43^{2} 44 45 46^{2} 47^{2} 6:26^{3} 29 36 53^{2} 62 67 7:8 19 21 22 23 28^{3} 34^{2} 36^{2} 45 47 8:14 15 19^{3} 21^{2} 22 23^{2} 24^{3} 28^{2} 31^{2} 32 33

JOHN 8:36 37^{2} 38^{2} 39^{2} 40 41 42 43^{2} 44^{2} 45 46 47^{2} 49 54 55 9:19 27^{3} 30 41^{3} 10:20 25 26^{2} 32 34 36 38^{2} 11:15 34 39 49 56 12:8^{2} 19^{2} 35 36^{2} 13:10 11 12 13^{2} 14 15 17^{3} 19 33^{2} 34^{2} 35^{2} 14:1 3 4^{2} 7^{3} 13 14 15 17 19^{2} 20^{2} 24 28^{3} 29 15:3 4^{2} 5^{2} 7^{3} 8^{2} 9 10^{2} 12 14^{2} 16^{3} 17 18 19^{2} 27^{2} 16:1 4 10 12 16^{2} 17^{2} 19^{3} 20^{2} 22 23^{2} 24^{2} 26 27 31 32 33^{2} 18:4 7 8 29 31 39^{2} 19:4 6 35 20:22 23^{2}

JOHN 20:31^{2} 21:5 6 10

ACTS 1:4 5 8^{2} 11^{3} 2:14^{2} 15 22^{2} 23 33 36 38 3:12^{3} 13 14 16 17 19 22 25 4:7 8 10 19 5:8 9 25 28^{2} 30 35^{2} 39^{2} 6:3 7:4 26^{2} 37 42^{2} 43^{2} 49 51^{3} 52 8:24^{2} 10:21^{2} 28 29 37 11:16 13:15^{2} 16 25 39 41^{2} 46 14:15^{2} 15:1^{2} 7 10 24 29^{4} 16:15 17:22^{2} 23 18:14 15 19:2^{2} 3 15 25 26 35 36 37 39 20:18 25 34 35 21:13 22:1 3 23:15^{2} 25:24 27:21 31 33 28:26^{2}

ROMANS 1:6 11 6:3 11 12 13 14 16^{4}

ROMANS 6:17^{2} 18 19 20^{2} 21^{2} 22 7:1 4^{2} 8:9 13^{4} 15^{2} 9:26 11:2 25^{2} 30 12:1 2^{2} 13:5 6 14 14:1 15:6 7 10 11^{2} 13 14 30 16:2^{2} 17

1 COR. 1:5 7 8 9 10^{2} 13 26 30 3:2^{2} 3^{2} 4 5 9^{2} 16^{2} 17 23 4:6 8^{4} 10^{3} 15^{2} 16 21 5:2 4 6 7^{2} 10 12 6:2^{2} 3 4 7^{3} 8 9 11^{3} 15 16 19^{3} 20 7:1 5^{2} 23^{2} 35 8:12^{2} 9:1 2 13 24^{2} 10:1 7 10 13^{2} 15 20 21^{2} 27 31^{2} 11:1 2 17 18 20 22^{2} 25^{2} 26^{2} 33 34 12:2^{3}

1 COR. 12:27 14:1 5^{2} 9^{3} 12^{3} 18 20 23 26 31 15:1^{2} 2^{3} 11 17 58 16:2 3 6 13 15 16 18 20

2 COR. 1:7^{2} 11 13^{2} 14^{2} 15 24 2:4^{2} 7 8 9 10 3:2 3 5:12 20 6:1 11 12^{2} 13 14 16 17 18 7:3 9^{4} 11^{2} 15 8:7^{2} 9^{2} 11 13 24 9:3 4 5 8 10:7 11:1 4^{4} 7 19^{2} 20 12:11 13 19 20 13:3 5^{3} 6 7^{2} 9

GAL. 1:6 9 10 13 3:1 2 3^{2} 4 7 26 28 29^{2} 4:6 8^{2} 9^{3} 10 12^{2} 13 14 15^{2} 17 21^{2}

GAL. 5:2 4 7 10 13 15^{2} 16 17^{2} 18^{2} 6:1 2 11

EPHES. 1:13^{4} 18 2:2 5 8 11 12 13 19 22 3:2 4^{2} 13 17 19 4:1 4 17 20 21 22 24 26 30 32 5:1 5 7 8 15 17 6:4 9 11 13 16 21 22

PHIL. 1:7 10^{2} 12 27 30 2:2^{2} 12 15^{2} 18 22 26 28 3:15 17 4:9 10^{2} 14^{2} 15^{2} 16

COLOS. 1:4 5 6 7 9 10 23^{2} 2:1 6^{2} 7 10 11 12 20^{2} 3:1 3 4 7 8 9 13 15 17 23 24

COLOS. 4:1 6 10 12 16

1 THESS. 1:5 6 7 9 2:2 5 8 9 10 11 12 13^{3} 14^{2} 19 20 3:4 6 8 4:1^{3} 2 3 9^{2} 10^{2} 11 12^{2} 13 5:1 4 5 11

2 THESS. 1:4 5^{2} 12 2:2 5 6 15 3:4 6 7 13

HEB. 3:7 15 4:7 5:11 12^{2} 6:10^{2} 12 10:25 29 32^{2} 33^{2} 34^{2} 36^{3} 12:3 4 5 7 8^{2} 17 18 22 25 13:5 23

JAMES 1:2 4 22 2:3 4 6 7 8^{2} 9^{2} 12 16^{2} 24 3:14 4:2^{5} 3^{3} 4^{2} 5 8^{2} 13 14 15 16

JAMES 5:1 3 5^{2} 6 8 9 11 12 16

1 PETER 1:6^{2} 8^{3} 15 16 17 18^{2} 22 2:2 3 5 9^{2} 15 20^{4} 21^{2} 24 25 3:1 6^{2} 7 8 9^{2} 13 14^{2} 17 4:4 7 13^{2} 14^{2} 5:4 5 10 12 14

2 PETER 1:4 8 10^{2} 12 15 19^{2} 3:1 11 14^{2} 17^{3}

1 JOHN 1:3 2:1 7^{2} 13^{3} 14^{3} 18 20^{2} 21^{2} 24^{3} 27^{3} 29^{2} 3:5 11 15 4:2 3 4 5:13^{3}

2 JOHN 6^{2}

3 JOHN 12

JUDE 3 5 17 20

REV. 2:10^{2} 25 12:12^{2} 18:4^{2} 20 19:5^{2} 18

you

5209

GEN. 1:12 29 9:2 3^{2} 7 9 10^{2} 11 12 15 17:10 11

GEN. 17:12 18:4 19:2 7 8 14 22:5 23:4^{2} 9 26:27 27:45 31:29

GEN. 34:8 9 10^{2} 15^{2} 16^{2} 35:2 37:6 40:8 41:55 42:2 14 16^{2}

GEN. 42:22 34 38 43:3 5 14 23^{2} 44:17 23 45:4 5 7

GEN. 45:8 12 17 18 19 46:33 47:16 23^{2} 48:21 49:1 50:4 20

GEN. 50:21 24 25

EXOD. 3:13 14 15 16^{2} 17 19 20

EXOD. 4:15 5:4 10 11 18 21 6:6^{3} 7^{3} 8^{2} 7:4 9 8:28

EXOD. 9:8 28 10:5^{2} 10^{3} 16 24 11:1^{2} 9 12:2^{2} 13^{5} 14 16^{2}

EXOD. 12:21 22 23 25 26 31 49 13:3 19^{2} 14:13 14 16:4

EXOD. 16:6 8 15 23 29^{2} 32^{2} 18:10 19:4^{2} 20:20 22 23 22:24

EXOD. 23:13 24:8 14^{2} 26:33 29:42 30:36 31:13^{2} 14 29 35:2 5 10

LEVIT. 1:2 8:33 34 9:4 6 10:7 17 11:4 5 6 7 8

LEVIT. 11:10 11 12 20 23 26 27 28 29 31 35 38

LEVIT. 11:45 14:34 16:29^{2} 30^{2} 31 34 17:8 10 11 12^{2} 13 18:3

LEVIT. 18:6 24 26 27 28^{2} 30 19:23 25 28 34^{3} 36 20:8

LEVIT. 20:14 22^{2} 23 24^{3} 25 26 21:8 22:20 25 32 33 23:10

LEVIT. 23:11 15 21 27 28 32 36 40 25:2 6 10 11

LEVIT. 25:12 21 38^{2} 44 45^{2} 46 26:1^{2} 4 6 7 8^{3} 9^{4}

LEVIT. 26:11^2, 12, 13^2, 16^2, 17^4, 18, 21, 22^3, 24^2, 25^2, 26, 28^2, 30, 33^2, 36, 38, 39

NUM. 1:4, 5, 9:8, 10, 14, 10:8, 9, 10, 29, 11:18, 20^2, 12:6, 13:17, 14:25^2, 28, 29, 30, 32, 42, 43^2, 15:2, 14^2, 15^2, 16^2, 18, 23, 39, 41, 16:3, 6, 7, 8, 9^3, 17, 24, 26, 45, 17:4, 5, 18:4, 6, 7, 26, 27, 20:10, 22:8, 13^2, 19, 25:18^2, 28:19, 22, 30, 31, 29:1, 5, 8, 32:21, 23, 24, 29^2, 30^2, 33:52, 53, 55^2, 56, 34:2, 7, 17, 35:11^2, 12, 29

DEU. 1:7, 8, 9^2, 10, 11^3, 13^2, 15, 17, 18, 20, 22, 23, 29, 30^3

DEU. 1:33^2, 40^2, 42, 43, 44^3, 45, 2:3, 4, 5, 13, 3:18^2, 19, 20^2, 22, 4:1^2, 2^2, 3, 4, 5, 8, 12, 13^2, 14, 15, 16, 20^2, 23^2, 26, 27^2, 34, 5:4, 5^2, 30, 32, 33^2, 6:1, 14, 15, 20, 7:4, 7^2, 8^3, 14, 21, 8:19, 9:8^2, 9, 10, 16^2, 19^2, 23^2, 24, 25, 10:4, 15, 11:4, 5, 8, 13, 14, 17^2, 22, 23, 25^4, 26, 27, 28, 31, 32, 12:9, 10^2, 11, 12, 32, 13:1, 3, 5^3, 7, 11, 13, 14, 14:7, 8, 10, 19, 15:4, 7, 16:11, 17:2, 7, 16, 18:10, 19:19, 20, 20:4^2, 18, 21:9, 21, 22:21, 24, 23:4, 10, 16, 24:7, 8, 26:11

DEU. 27:1, 4, 28:54, 55, 63^6, 68, 29:4, 5^2, 10, 14, 18^2, 22, 30:18, 19^2, 31:5, 19, 27, 29^2, 32:38, 46, 47

JOSH. 1:3, 11^2, 13^3, 14, 15^2, 2:9^2, 10, 11, 12^2, 16^2, 3:4, 5, 10^2, 11, 12, 4:2, 3^2, 5^2, 6, 23, 5:9, 6:10, 16, 7:12^2, 13, 8:8, 9:7, 11, 12, 22, 23, 24^3, 18:3, 4, 6, 7, 8, 20:2^2, 22:2^2, 4^2, 5, 16, 19, 25, 27, 28, 23:3^2, 4, 5^2, 7, 9^3, 10^3, 12^2, 13^3, 14^2, 15^5, 16^3, 24:5, 7, 8^3, 9, 10^2, 11, 12^2, 13, 15^2, 20^3, 22, 23, 27

JUD. 2:1^3, 3^2, 6:8^2, 9^4, 10, 7:7, 8:2, 3, 5, 19, 23^3

JUD. 8:24, 9:2^4, 7, 15, 17^2, 19, 10:11, 12^2, 13, 14, 12:2, 14:12^2, 15:7, 19:9^2, 23, 24, 20:12, 21

RUTH 1:8, 9^2, 2:4, 7

1 SAM. 4:9, 6:3^2, 4, 5, 21, 7:3^2, 5, 8:11, 18^2, 9:12, 13, 10:2, 15, 18^2, 19, 11:2, 10^2, 12:1, 2^3, 3, 5, 7^2, 11, 12, 13, 14, 15, 17, 23^2, 24, 14:9, 12, 29, 15:6^2, 17:8^2, 47, 18:23, 22:3, 7^2, 8^2, 23:22, 23, 25:5, 19, 30:24, 26

2 SAM. 1:21, 24, 2:6^2, 3:17, 31, 4:11, 7:23, 13:28^2, 15:27, 28, 16:10, 20, 17:21, 18:2, 4, 22, 20:16, 21:3, 4

1 KINGS 1:33, 9:6, 11:2, 12:11^3, 14^2, 28, 18:25, 20:7, 22:28

2 KINGS 1:6, 7^2, 2:18, 5:7, 6:19, 7:12, 10:2^3, 23, 11:5, 7, 17:13, 36, 37, 38, 39, 18:27, 29^2, 30, 32^2, 22:15, 18, 25:24

1 CHRON. 12:17, 13:2, 22:18^2, 28:8

2 CHRON. 7:19, 10:11^3, 14^2, 12:5, 13:8^2, 9, 12, 15:2^3, 19:6, 7, 10^2, 11, 20:15, 17^2, 23:4, 24:20, 28:10^3, 11, 29:11, 30:6, 8, 9, 32:11, 14, 15^3, 34:23, 26, 36:23

EZRA 1:3, 4:2, 5:3, 9, 7:21, 24

NEH. 1:8, 9, 4:12, 5:10, 11, 6:3, 13:21, 27

ESTHER 8:8

JOB 6:28, 29, 12:2, 3^2, 13:2, 9, 10, 11^2, 16:4^2, 5, 17:10^2, 27:5, 11, 32:6, 12^2, 21, 42:8^3

PSALMS 34:11, 50:22, 62:3, 82:6, 115:14^2, 118:26

PSALMS 127:2, 129:8^2

PROV. 1:23^3, 27, 4:2, 8:4

CANT. 2:7, 3:5, 5:8, 8:4

ISAIAH 1:15, 16, 5:3, 5, 7:13, 14, 8:19, 21:10, 22:14, 28:19, 29:11, 30:11, 13, 16, 18^2, 20, 31:7, 32:11^2, 33:11, 35:4, 36:12, 14^2, 15, 17, 18, 40:21, 41:24, 42:9, 23, 43:12, 46:4^2, 50:1, 10, 51:2, 12, 52:12, 55:3, 12, 59:2^2, 61:6, 65:12, 66:5^2, 13

JER. 2:7, 9, 3:12, 14^3, 15^2, 4:8, 15, 18, 25, 6:17, 7:3, 7, 13^2, 14, 15, 23^2, 25, 8:17^2, 10:1, 11:4, 14:13, 14, 15:14, 16:13^2, 18:6, 11^2, 21:4, 5, 8, 9, 14, 23:2, 16^2, 17, 33, 38, 39^4, 40, 25:3, 4, 5, 6, 27

JER. 26:4, 5, 13, 14, 15, 27:9, 10^3, 14^2, 15^2, 16^2, 29:7, 8^2, 9, 10^3, 11^2, 12, 14^5, 16, 21, 27, 31^2, 34:16, 17^2, 21, 35:14, 15^2, 18, 37:7^2, 10, 19^2, 38:5, 40:3, 9, 42:4^4, 10^5, 11^3, 12^3, 16^2, 18, 19^2, 21^2, 44:4, 7^2, 10, 11, 23, 29^3, 49:3, 30^3, 31, 50:12

LAM. 1:12, 18

EZEKIEL 5:7^2, 16^2, 17, 6:3, 7, 9, 11:7, 8, 9^3, 10, 11, 12, 15, 17^3, 19, 13:8, 12, 15, 18, 14:22, 23, 18:30, 31^2, 20:3, 20, 31^2, 33, 34^2, 35^2, 36, 37^2, 38, 39, 41^4, 42, 44, 22:19, 20^3, 21^2, 22, 23:49, 24:24, 33:20, 30, 34:3, 17, 18, 36:2, 3^2

EZEKIEL 36:7, 9^2, 10, 11^2, 12, 13, 23, 24^3, 25^2, 26^3, 27^2, 29^2, 32, 33^2, 36, 37:5, 6^4, 12^2, 13, 14^2, 39:17, 19, 43:27, 44:6, 45:9, 47:14, 21, 22^5

DANIEL 2:9, 3:4, 15, 4:1, 6:25

HOSEA 5:1, 13^2, 10:12, 15, 14:2

JOEL 2:19^2, 20, 23^2, 25^2, 26, 3:13

AMOS 2:10^2, 13, 3:1, 2^2, 4:2^2, 5, 6, 7, 9, 10, 11, 5:1, 14, 18^2, 27, 6:14^2

JONAH 1:12^2

MICAH 1:2, 11, 2:4, 10, 3:1^2, 6^2, 9

HABAK. 1:5

ZEPH. 2:2^2, 5

HAGGAI 1:4, 6, 10, 13, 2:3, 4, 5^2, 15, 17, 19

ZECH. 1:3, 2:6, 8^2

ZECH. 4:9, 6:7, 15, 7:10, 8:13, 14, 17, 23^2, 9:12, 11:7, 9

MALACHI 1:2, 6, 9, 10^2, 2:1, 2, 3, 4, 9, 3:5, 7, 10^2, 12, 4:2, 5

MATT. 3:7, 9, 11^2, 4:19, 5:11^3, 12, 18, 20, 22, 28, 32, 34, 39, 44^5, 46, 6:2, 5, 14, 16, 25, 27, 29, 30, 33, 7:2, 6, 7^2, 9, 12, 15, 23, 8:10, 11, 9:29, 10:13, 14, 15, 16, 17^2, 19^2, 20, 23^2, 27, 40, 42, 11:9, 11, 17^2, 21, 22^2, 24, 28, 29, 12:6, 11, 28, 31, 36, 13:11, 17, 15:7, 16:11, 28, 17:12, 17^2, 20^2, 18:3, 10, 13, 18, 19^2, 35, 19:8, 9, 23, 24

MATT. 19:28, 20:4, 26^2, 27, 32, 21:2, 3, 21, 24^2, 27, 31^2, 32, 43^2, 22:31, 23:3, 11, 13, 14, 15, 16, 23, 25, 27, 29, 34, 35, 36, 38, 39, 24:2, 4, 9^2, 23, 25, 26, 34, 47, 25:9, 12^2, 34, 40, 45, 26:11, 13, 15, 21^2, 29^2, 32, 55, 64, 27:17, 21, 28:7^2, 14, 20^2

MARK 1:8^2, 17, 3:28, 4:11, 24^2, 6:11^3, 7:6, 14, 8:12, 9:1, 13, 19^2, 41^2, 10:3, 5, 15, 29, 36, 43^2, 44, 11:2, 3, 23, 24, 25, 29^2, 33, 12:43, 13:5, 9, 11^3, 21, 23, 30, 36, 37, 14:7, 9, 13, 15, 18^2, 25, 28, 49, 15:9, 16:7^2

LUKE 2:10, 11, 12, 3:7, 8, 13, 16^2, 4:24, 25, 6:9, 22^3, 24, 25^2, 26^2, 27^2, 28^2, 31, 32, 33, 38^2, 47, 7:9, 26, 28, 32^2, 8:10, 9:5, 27, 41^2, 48, 10:3, 6, 8^2, 9, 10, 11^2, 12, 13, 14, 16^2, 19^2, 20, 24, 11:8, 9^3, 11, 20, 41, 42, 43, 44, 46, 47, 51, 52, 12:4, 5^2, 8, 11, 12, 14, 22, 25, 27, 28, 31, 32, 37, 44, 51, 13:3, 5, 13:15, 24, 25^2, 27^2, 28, 35^2, 14:5, 24, 28, 33, 15:4, 7, 10, 16:9^2, 12, 26^2, 17:6, 7, 10, 21, 23, 34, 18:8, 14, 17, 29, 19:26, 30, 31, 40, 20:3, 8, 21:3, 12^3

LUKE 21:13, 15, 16, 32, 34, 22:10, 12, 15, 16, 18, 19, 20, 26, 27, 29, 31^2, 35, 37, 53, 67, 68, 23:14, 24:6, 36, 44^2, 49

JOHN 1:26, 51, 2:5, 3:12^2, 4:35, 38, 5:19, 24, 25, 38, 42^2, 45^2, 6:26, 27, 32^3, 36, 47, 53^2, 61, 63, 64, 65, 70^2, 7:7, 19^2, 22, 33, 8:7, 24, 25, 26, 32, 34, 36, 37, 40, 45, 46, 51, 58, 9:27, 10:1, 7, 25, 26, 32, 12:8, 24, 35^2, 13:12, 15^2, 16, 18, 19, 20, 21^2, 33^2, 34^2, 14:2^2, 3^2, 9, 10, 12, 16^2, 17^2, 18^2, 20, 25^2, 26^2, 27^3, 28^2, 29, 30, 15:3, 4, 7^2, 9, 11^2

JOHN 15:12, 14, 15^3, 16^3, 17, 18^2, 19^2, 20^2, 21, 26, 16:1, 2^2, 3, 4^4, 5, 6, 7^4, 12, 13^2, 14, 15, 20, 22^2, 23^2, 25^3, 26^2, 27, 33, 18:8, 39^2, 19:4, 20:19, 21^2, 26

ACTS 1:7, 8, 11, 2:14, 22^2, 29, 38, 39, 3:14, 16, 20, 22^2, 26^3, 4:10^2, 11, 19, 5:28, 38, 6:3, 7:37, 43, 10:29, 13:26^2, 32, 34, 38^2, 40, 41, 46^2, 14:15^2, 15:24, 25, 27, 28, 16:36, 17:3, 23, 18:14, 21, 19:13, 20:18, 20^3, 26, 27, 28, 29, 32^3, 35, 22:1, 25, 23:15, 24:21, 25:5, 26, 26:8, 27:22^2, 34^2, 28:20^3, 28

ROMANS 1:7, 8, 9, 10, 11^2, 12^2, 13^3, 15

ROMANS 2:24, 6:14, 17, 8:9, 10, 11^2, 10:19^2, 11:13, 12:1, 3, 14, 18, 15:5, 13, 14, 15^2, 22, 23, 24^3, 28, 29, 30, 32^2, 33, 16:1, 2, 16, 17, 19, 20, 21, 22, 23^2, 24, 25

1 COR. 1:3, 4, 6, 8, 10^2, 11, 12, 13, 14, 2:1^2, 2, 3, 3:1, 2, 3, 16, 18, 4:3, 6, 8, 14^2, 15, 16, 17^2, 18, 19, 21, 5:1, 2, 9, 11, 6:1, 2, 5, 7, 11, 19, 7:5, 28, 32, 35, 9:2, 11, 12, 23, 10:13^2, 27^2, 28, 11:2^2, 3, 14, 17^2, 18, 19^2, 22^3, 23, 24, 30, 12:1, 3, 21, 31, 14:6^3, 25, 26, 36^2, 37, 15:1^2, 2

1 COR. 15:3, 12, 51, 16:2, 5, 6, 7^2, 10, 12, 13, 15, 19^2, 20, 23, 24

2 COR. 1:2, 7, 8, 12, 13, 15, 16^3, 18, 19, 21, 23, 2:1, 2, 3^3, 4^2, 5, 8, 9, 3:1^2, 4:12, 14, 5:12^2, 20^2, 6:1, 11, 17, 18, 7:3^2, 4^2, 7, 8^2, 11, 12^3, 13, 14^2, 15^2, 16, 8:1, 6, 10, 16, 17, 22, 23, 9:1, 2, 3, 4, 5, 8, 14^3, 10:1^3, 2, 9, 13, 14^2, 15, 16, 11:2^3, 6, 7, 8, 9^2, 11, 20^4, 12:11, 12, 13, 14^3, 15^2, 16^2, 17, 18, 19, 20^2, 21, 13:1, 2^2, 3, 4, 5, 11, 13, 14

GAL. 1:3, 6, 7

GAL. 1:8^2, 9, 11, 20, 2:5, 3:1^2, 2, 5^2, 27, 4:11^2, 12, 13, 15, 16, 17^2, 18, 19, 20^2, 5:2^2, 4^2, 7, 8, 10^2, 12, 21^2, 6:11, 12, 13

EPHES. 1:2, 16^2, 17, 2:1, 17, 3:1, 13, 16, 4:1, 6, 31, 32, 5:3, 6, 33, 6:13, 21, 22

PHIL. 1:2, 3, 4, 6, 7^2, 8, 24, 25, 26, 27, 28, 26, 2:5, 13, 17, 19, 25, 26, 3:1, 15, 18, 4:9, 18, 21, 22, 23

COLOS. 1:2, 3, 5, 6^2, 7, 9, 21, 22, 24, 25, 27, 2:1, 4, 5, 8, 13^2, 16, 18, 3:13, 16, 4:7, 8, 9, 10, 12, 13

COLOS. 4:14, 16, 18

1 THESS. 1:1, 2, 5, 8, 9, 2:1, 2, 6, 7, 8^2, 9, 10, 11, 12, 13, 17, 18, 3:2^2, 4^2, 5, 6^2, 7, 9, 11, 12^2, 4:1^2, 2, 4, 6, 9, 10, 11, 13, 15, 5:1, 4, 12^4, 14, 18, 23, 24, 27, 28

2 THESS. 1:2, 3, 4, 6, 7, 10, 11^2, 12, 2:1, 3, 5^2, 13^2, 14, 17, 3:1, 3^2, 4^2, 6, 7, 8, 9, 10^2, 11, 16^2, 18

2 TIM. 4:22

TITUS 2:8, 3:15

PHILE. 3, 6, 22

HEB. 3:12, 13, 4:1, 5:12, 6:9, 11, 9:20, 12:5, 7, 15, 13:7^2, 17^2, 19^2, 21^2, 22^2, 23, 24^2

HEB. 13:25

JAMES 1:5, 26, 2:6^2, 16, 3:13, 4:1, 7, 8, 10, 5:1, 4, 6, 13, 14, 19

1 PETER 1:2, 4, 10, 12^2, 13, 15, 20, 25, 2:7, 9, 11, 12, 3:13, 15^2, 16, 4:4, 12^2, 14, 15, 5:1, 2, 5, 6, 7, 10^2, 12, 13^2, 14

2 PETER 1:2, 8^2, 11, 12, 13^2, 16, 2:1, 3, 13, 3:2, 15

1 JOHN 1:2, 3, 4, 5, 2:1, 8^2, 12^2, 13^3, 14^3, 21, 24^2, 26^2, 27^4, 3:7, 13, 4:4, 5:13

2 JOHN 3, 10, 12^2

JUDE 2, 3^3, 5, 12, 18, 24^2

REV. 1:4, 2:10, 13, 23, 24^2, 12:12, 18:6, 20, 22:16, 21

KEY-WORD COMPARISON

A

KEY-WORD COMPARISON

OF SELECTED WORDS AND PHRASES

IN THE

KING JAMES VERSION

WITH

FIVE LEADING TRANSLATIONS

ABINGDON

PREFACE

The purpose of this new section of *Strong's* is to afford the Bible student and reader with a convenient means of comparing the translation of selected words and phrases in the venerated King James Version with the rendering in several respected modern translations. It replaces the Comparative Concordance that compared the King James Version with the now seldom-used English Revised Version and American Standard Version.

The difficulty in comparing several translations is not only in having to consult several different books or volumes. Even when using one of the parallel printings there is confusion in locating the word or phrase quickly in context because of the variety of printing formats. Usually it is necessary to look back and forth several times to be sure the correct equivalent terms are being noted. By isolating and showing distinctly the compared renderings, this new chart format simplifies the process and encourages the user to seek those comparisons that can enhance the understanding and the meaning of the original.

In every instance, the left-hand column of each page gives the complete verse in the King James Version (KJV) which contains the words or phrases in bold-face type to be compared. To the right in column form are the renderings of the words and phrases in the Revised Standard Version (RSV), the New English Bible (NEB), the Jerusalem Bible (JB), the New American Standard Bible (NAS), and the New International Version (NIV).

The verses from the King James Version are listed in the order in which they appear in the Old and New Testaments. Not every verse is represented, and when a word or phrase is repeated several times in proximity, the comparison of translations is not repeated in every instance.

The reader will find it helpful to use the Dictionaries of Hebrew and Greek in connection with this Key-Word Comparison. Where more information is desired on a particular word, that word should be looked up in the Main Concordance as it appeared in the King James Version. There will be noted the identifying number, regular for the Hebrew and italic for the Greek, that will enable the reader to find the basic word in the appropriate dictionary.

Symbols Used

Brackets [ ] in the KJV column indicate that one or more of the translations have inserted material not appearing in the King James Version.

Deut. 2:14. "until **all the** [ ] generation" (KJV)
"until the entire generation" (RSV)

Ellipses . . . are used when words in a translation correspond to words or phrases of the KJV other than those marked in boldface, indicating that the wording of the translation has been rearranged.

Josh. 6:17. "and the city shall be **accursed**" (KJV)
"devoted . . . for destruction" (RSV)

Parentheses ( ) are used in two ways:

1. When placed around an entire translation, parentheses indicate that the structure of the translation does not correspond to the KJV, making it impossible to make exact comparisons of the words or phrases marked in boldface.

Judg. 8:12. "and took the two kings of Midian, Zebah and Zalmunna, and **discomfited all the host**" (KJV)
"(their whole army melted away)" (NEB)

2. When placed around one word or a group of words within a translation, parentheses indicate that the word (or words) is not a translation of one of the words marked in boldface, but is necessary to understand the translation.

Deut. 22:3. "with **all lost things** of thy brother's, which he hath lost" (KJV)
"anything else (that your fellow-countryman) has lost" (NEB)

OLD TESTAMENT

Genesis

	KJV	RSV	NEB	JB	NAS	NIV
1	**In the beginning God created** the heaven and the earth.	In the beginning God created	In the beginning of creation, when God made	In the beginning God created	In the beginning God created	In the beginning God created
	2 And the earth was without form, and **void;** and darkness was upon the face of the **deep.** And the spirit of God moved upon the face of the waters.	void/deep	void/abyss	void/deep	void/deep	empty/deep
	11 And God said, Let the earth bring forth **grass, the herb yielding seed,** and the fruit tree yielding fruit after his kind, whose seed is in itself, upon the earth: and it was so.	vegetation, plants yielding seed	fresh growth/ plants bearing seed	vegetation: seed bearing plants	vegetation, plants yielding seed	vegetation: seed-bearing plants
	26 And God said, Let us make man in our image, after our likeness: and let them have dominion over the fish of the sea, and over the fowl of the air, and over the cattle, and over all the earth, and over **every creeping thing that creepeth upon the earth.**	every creeping thing that creeps upon the earth	all reptiles that crawl upon the earth	all the reptiles that crawl upon the earth	every creeping thing that creeps on the earth	all the creatures that move along the ground
	28 And God blessed them, and God said unto them, Be fruitful, and **multiply,** and **replenish** the earth, and **subdue** it: and **have dominion** over the fish of the sea, and over the fowl of the air, and over every living thing that moveth upon the earth.	multiply/fill/sub-due/have domin-ion	increase/fill/sub-due/rule over	multiply/fill/con-quer/Be masters	multiply/fill/sub-due/rule over	increase in num-ber/fill/sub-due/rule over
2	18 And the Lord God said, It is not good that the man should be alone; I will make him an **help meet** for him.	helper fit	partner	helpmate	helper suitable	helper suitable
3	21 **Unto Adam also and to his wife did the LORD God make coats** of skins, and clothed them.	for/garments	for/tunics	for/clothes	for/garments	for/garments
4	8 And Cain talked with Abel his brother: **and it came to pass, when they were in the field,** that Cain rose up against Abel his brother, and slew him.	"Let us go out to the field."	'Let us go into the open coun-try.'	'Let us go out'		"Let's go out to the field."
	12 When thou tillest the ground, it shall not henceforth yield unto thee her strength; a **fugitive** and a **vagabond** shalt thou be in the earth.	fugitive/wanderer	vagrant/wanderer	fugitive/wanderer	vagrant/wanderer	(omits)/restless wanderer
7	4 For **yet** seven days, and I will cause it to rain upon the earth forty days and forty nights; and every living **substance** that I have made will I **destroy** from off the face of the **earth.**	in/thing/blot out/ground	In/thing/wipe off/earth	in. . .time/thing /rid/earth	after/thing/blot out/land	from now/crea-ture/ wipe from/earth
8	1 And God remembered Noah, and every living thing, and all the cattle that was with him in the ark: and God made a wind to pass over the earth, and the waters **assuaged;**	subsided	began to subside	subsided	subsided	receded
	16 Go forth **of** the ark, thou, and thy wife, and thy sons, and thy sons' wives with thee.	from	out of	out of	out of	out of
9	1 And God blessed Noah and his sons, and said unto them, Be fruitful, and multiply, and **replenish** the earth.	fill	fill	fill	fill	fill
	20 And Noah **began to be an husbandman,** and he planted a vineyard:	was the first tiller of the soil	began the plant-ing (of vineyards)	a tiller of the soil, was the first	began farming	a man of the soil
10	5 By these were **the isles of the Gentiles** divided in their lands; every one after his tongue, after their families, in their nations.	the coastland peoples	the peoples of the coasts and islands	islands of the nations	coastlands of the nations	maritime peoples

KJV	RSV	NEB	JB	NAS	NIV
11 3 And they said one to another, Go to, let us make brick, and **burn** them **throughly.** And they had brick for stone, and **slime** had they for mortar.	burn/thoroughly/ bitumen	bake/hard/ bitumen	bake/(omits)/ bitumen	burn/thoroughly/ tar	bake/thoroughly/ tar
6 And the LORD said, Behold, the people is one, and they have all one language; and this they begin to do: and now nothing will be **restrained from** them, which they have **imagined** to do.	impossible for/ propose	beyond their reach/have in mind	too hard for/(of their under-takings)	impossible for/ purpose	impossible for/ plan
7 Go to, let us go down, and there **confound** their language, that they may not understand one another's speech.	confuse	confuse	confuse	confuse	confuse
12 6 And Abram passed through the land unto the place of Sichem, unto the **plain** of Moreh. And the Canaanite was then in the land.	oak	terebinth-tree	Oak	oak	great tree
16 And he **entreated Abram well** for her sake: and he had sheep, and oxen, and he asses, and menservants, and maidser-vants, and she asses, and camels.	dealt well with Abram	treated Abram well	treated Abram well	treated Abram well	treated Abram well
14 22 And Abram said to the king of Sodom, I have **lift up mine hand unto the LORD, the most high God,** the possessor of heaven and earth,	sworn to the Lord God Most High	lift my hand and swear by the Lord, God Most High	raise my hand in the presence of Yahweh, God Most High	sworn to the Lord God Most High	raised my hand to the Lord, God Most High
23 That I will not take from a thread **even to a shoelatchet,** and that I will not take any thing that is thine, lest thou shouldest say, I have made Abram rich:	or a sandal-thong	of a shoe-string	not one sandal strap	or a sandal thong	or the thong of a sandal
15 5 And he brought him **forth abroad,** and said, Look now toward heaven, and **tell** the stars, if thou be able to number them: and he said unto him, So shall thy seed be.	outside/number	outside/count	outside/count	outside/count	outside/count
17 21 But my covenant will I establish with Isaac, which Sarah shall bear unto thee at this **set time** in the next year.	season	season	time	season	time
18 1 And the LORD appeared unto him in the **plains** of Mamre: and he sat in the tent door in the heat of the day;	oaks	terebinths	Oak	oaks	great trees
19 3 And he **pressed upon them greatly;** and they turned **in** unto him, and entered into his house; and he made them a feast, and did bake unleavened bread, and they did eat.	urged them strongly/aside	was so insistent/ aside	pressed them so much/(went home with)	urged them strongly/aside	insisted so strongly/(did go with)
9 And they said, Stand back. And they said **again,** This **one fellow** came in to sojourn, and **he will needs be** a judge: now will we deal worse with thee, than with them. And they **pressed sore upon** the man, even Lot, and came near to break the door.	(omits)/fellow/ would play the/ pressed hard against	(omits)/man/ now take it upon himself to (judge)/ pressed close	(omits)/one/would set himself up as/ forced. . . back	(omits)/one/is act-ing like/pressed hard against	(omits)/fellow/ wants to play/ bringing pressure
13 For we will destroy this place, because the **cry of them is waxen** great before the **face of the** LORD; and the LORD hath sent us to destroy it.	outcry/has be-come/(omits)	outcry/has been so/(omits)	outcry/is/ (omits)	outcry/has be-come/(omits)	outcry/is/(omits)
20 6 And God said unto him in a dream, Yea, I know that thou didst this in the integrity of thy heart; for I also withheld thee from sinning against me: therefore **suffered I thee not** to touch her.	I did not let you	I did not let you	I did not let you	I did not let you	I did not let you
21 2 For Sarah conceived, and bare Abraham a son in his old age, at the **set time** of which God had spoken to him.	time	time	time	appointed time	very time
26 And **Abimelech said, I wot not** who hath done this thing: **neither didst thou tell me, neither yet heard I** of it, but today.	do not know/you did not tell me/I have not heard	do not know/You never told me/I have heard nothing	do not know/You yourself never mentioned it to me/I heard nothing	do not know/nei-ther did you tell me/nor did I hear	don't know/You did not tell me/I heard. . .only

	KJV	RSV	NEB	JB	NAS	NIV
22	1 And it came to pass after these things, that God **did tempt** Abraham, and said unto him, Abraham: and he said, Behold, here I am.	tested	put. . .to the test	put. . .to the test	tested	tested
23	8 And he **communed with** them, saying, If it be your mind that I should bury my dead out of my sight; hear me, and entreat for me to Ephron the son of Zohar,	said to	said to	spoke to	spoke with	said to
	10 And Ephron dwelt among the children of Heth: and Ephron the Hittite answered Abraham in the **audience** of the children of Heth, even of all that went in at the gate of his city, saying,	hearing	hearing	sight	hearing	hearing
24	5 And the servant said unto him, **Peradventure** the woman will not be willing to follow me unto this land: must I needs bring thy son again unto the land from whence thou camest?	Perhaps	What if	What if	Suppose	What if
	12 And he said, O LORD God of my master Abraham, I pray thee, **send me good speed** this day, and shew **kindness** unto my master Abraham.	grant me success/steadfast love	give me good fortune/(keep faith)	be with me/kindness	please grant me success/loving-kindness	give me success/kindness
	21 And the man **wondering at her held his peace,** to **wit** whether the LORD had made his journey prosperous or not.	gazed at her in silence/learn	was watching quietly/see	watched in silence/wondering	gazing at her in silence/know	watched her closely/learn
25	8 Then Abraham **gave up the ghost,** and died in a good old age, an old man, and full of years; and was gathered to his people.	breathed his last	breathed his last	dying	died	died
	21 And Isaac **entreated** the LORD for his wife, because she was barren: and the LORD **was entreated of him,** and Rebekah his wife conceived.	prayed to/granted his prayer	appealed to/yielded to his entreaty	prayed to/heard his prayer	prayed/to answered him	prayed to/answered his prayer
	27 And the boys grew: and Esau was a **cunning** hunter, a man **of the field;** and Jacob was a plain man, dwelling in tents.	skilful/quiet	skilful/settled	skilled/quiet	skillful/peaceful	skillful/quiet
	29 And Jacob **sod** pottage: and Esau came from the field, and he was **faint:**	was boiling/famished	prepared/exhausted	had made/exhausted	had cooked/famished	was cooking/famished
26	10 And Abimelech said, What is this thou hast done unto us? one of the people might **lightly** have **lien** with thy wife, and thou shouldest have brought guiltiness upon us.	easily/lain	easily/gone to bed	easily/slept	easily/lain	well/slept
	14 For he had possession of flocks, and possession of herds, and **great store of servants:** and the Philistines envied him.	great household	many slaves	many servants	great household	many. . .servants
	31 And they rose up **betimes** in the morning, and sware one to another: and Isaac sent them away, and they departed from him in peace.	early	early	early	early	Early
27	16 And she put the skins of the kids of the goats upon his hands, and upon the smooth [ ] of his neck:	part	nape	part	part	part
	23 And he **discerned him not,** because his hands were hairy, as his brother Esau's hands: so he blessed him.	did not recognize him	did not recognize him	did not recognize him	did not recognize him	did not recognize him
29	14 And Laban said to him, Surely thou art my bone and my flesh. And he abode with him **the space of a** month.	a	for a whole	for a	a	for a whole
	17 Leah **was tender eyed;** but Rachel was beautiful and **well favoured.**	eyes were weak/lovely	was dull-eyed/graceful	(There was no sparkle in Leah's eyes)/shapely	eyes were weak/(beautiful of form and face)	had weak eyes/lovely in form

KJV	RSV	NEB	JB	NAS	NIV
35 And she conceived again, and bare a son: and she said, Now will I praise the LORD: therefore she called his name Judah; and **left bearing.**	ceased bearing	bore no more children	had no more children	stopped bearing	stopped having children
30 27 And Laban said unto him, I pray thee, if I have found favour in thine eyes, tarry: for I have **learned by experience** that the LORD hath blessed me for thy sake.	learned by divination	become prosperous	learned from the omens	divined	learned by divination
28 And he said, **Appoint** me thy wages, and I will give it.	name	tell	name	Name	Name
35 And he removed that day the he goats that were **ringstraked** and spotted, and all the she goats that were speckled and spotted, and every one that had some white in it, and all the brown among the sheep, and gave them into the hand of his sons.	striped	brindled	striped	striped	streaked
37 And Jacob took him **rods of green poplar, and of the hazel and chestnut tree;** and **pilled white strakes** in them, and made the white appear which was in the rods.	fresh rods of poplar and almond and plane/peeled white streaks	fresh rods of white poplar, almond, and plane trees/peeled off strips of bark	branches in sap. from poplar, almond and plane trees/peeled. . .in white strips	fresh rods of poplar, almond and plane trees/peeled white stripes	fresh-cut branches from poplar, almond and plane trees/made white stripes . . . by peeling the bark
31 32 With whomsoever thou findest thy gods, let him not live: before our brethren **discern** thou what is thine with me, and take it to thee. For Jacob knew not that Rachel had stolen them.	point out	point out	examine	point out	see
34 Now Rachel had taken the **images,** and put them in the camel's **furniture,** and sat upon them. And Laban searched all the tent, but found them not.	household gods/ saddle	household gods/ (camel-) bag	household idols/ litter	household idols/ saddle	household gods/ saddle
37 Whereas thou hast **searched all my stuff,** what hast thou found of all thy household **stuff?** set it here before my brethren and thy brethren, that they may judge betwixt us both.	felt through all my goods/goods	gone through all my possessions/ anything	gone through all my belongings/ anything	felt through all my goods/goods	searched through all my goods/(that belongs to)
32 28 And he said, Thy name shall be called no more Jacob, but Israel: for **as a prince hast thou power** with God and with men, and hast prevailed.	you have striven	you strove	you have been strong (against God, you shall prevail against men)	you have striven	you have struggled
31 And as he passed over **Penuel** the sun rose upon him, and he **halted upon his thigh.**	Penuel/limping because of his thigh	Penuel/limping because of his limp	Peniel/limping because of his hip	Penuel/limping on his thigh	Peniel/limping because of his hip
33 14 Let my lord, **I pray thee, pass over** before his servant: and I will lead on **softly, according as the cattle that goeth before me and the children be able to endure,** until I come unto my lord unto Seir.	(omits)/on/slowly/ according to the pace of the cattle which are before me and according to the pace of the children	I beg you/on/by easy stages/at the pace of the children and of the livestock that I am driving	(omits)/on/at a slower pace/to suit the flock I am driving and the children	Please/on/at my leisure/according to the pace of the cattle that are before me and according to the pace of the children	(omits)/on/slowly/ at the pace of the droves before me and that of the children
34 19 And the young man **deferred not** to do the thing, because he had delight in Jacob's daughter: and he was **more honourable than all the house of his father.**	did not delay/the most honored of all his family.	did not hesitate/ held in respect above anyone in his father's house	did not hesitate/ the most important person in his father's household	did not delay/ more respected than all the household of his father	lost no time/the most honored of all his father's household
27 The sons of Jacob came upon the slain, and **spoiled** the city, because they had defiled their sister.	plundered	plundered	pillaged	looted	looted
35 8 But Deborah Rebekah's nurse died, and she was buried beneath Bethel under an oak: and the name of it was called **Allon-bachuth.**	Allon-bacuth	Allon-bakuth	the Oak of Tears	Allon-bacuth	Allon Bacuth

	KJV	RSV	NEB	JB	NAS	NIV
36	15 These were **dukes** of the sons of Esau: the sons of Eliphaz the firstborn son of Esau; duke Teman, duke Omar, duke Zepho, duke Kenaz,	chiefs	chiefs	chiefs	chiefs	chiefs
37	3 Now Israel loved Joseph more than all his children, because he was the son of his old age: and he made him **a coat of many colours.**	a long robe with sleeves	a long, sleeved robe	a coat with long sleeves	a varicolored tunic	a richly ornamented robe
	22 And Reuben said unto them, Shed no blood, but cast him into this pit that is in the wilderness, and lay no hand upon him; that he might **rid** him out of their hands, to **deliver** him to his father again.	rescue/restore	save/restore	save/restore	rescue/restore	rescue/ take. . .back
	28 Then there passed by Midianites **merchantmen;** and they drew and lifted up Joseph out of the pit, and sold Joseph to the Ishmeelites for twenty pieces of silver: and they brought Joseph into Egypt.	traders	merchants	merchants	traders	merchants
39	6 And he left **all that he had in Joseph's hand;** and he knew not aught he had, save the bread which he did eat. And Joseph was **a goodly person, and well favoured.**	all that he had in Joseph's charge/ handsome and goodlooking	everything he possessed in Joseph's care/handsome and good-looking	Joseph to handle all his possessions/ well built and handsome (vs. 7)	everything he owned in Joseph's charge/ handsome in form and appearance	in Joseph's care everything he had/ well-built and handsome
	8 But he refused, and said unto his master's wife, Behold, my master **wotteth not what** is with me in the house, and he hath **committed** all that he hath to my hand;	has no concern about anything/ put	(He does not know as much as I do about his own house)/entrusted	does not concern himself with what happens/handed over	does not concern himself with anything/put	does not concern himself with anything/entrusted
40	3 And he put them in **ward** in the house of the captain of the guard, into the prison, the place where Joseph was **bound.**	custody/confined	custody/ imprisoned	(under) arrest/ a prisoner	confinement/ imprisoned	custody/confined
41	1 And it came to pass at the end of two full years, that Pharaoh dreamed: and, behold, he **stood by the river.**	was standing by the Nile	was standing by the Nile	was standing by the Nile	was standing by the Nile	was standing by the Nile
	2 And, behold, there came up out of the **river** seven **well favoured kine and fatfleshed;** and they fed in a **meadow.**	Nile/cows sleek and fat/reed grass	Nile/cows, sleek and fat/reeds	Nile/cows, sleek and fat/rushes	Nile/cows, sleek and fat/marsh grass	river/cows, sleek and fat/reeds
	3 And, behold, seven other **kine** came up after them out of the river, **ill favoured and leanfleshed;** and stood by the other kine upon the **brink of the river.**	cows/gaunt and thin/bank of the Nile	cows/gaunt and lean/riverbank	cows/ugly and lean/bank of the Nile	cows/ugly and gaunt/bank of the Nile	cows/ugly and gaunt/riverbank
	24 And the thin ears devoured the seven good ears: and I told this unto the magicians; but there was none that could **declare** it to me.	explain	explain	tell . . . the meaning	explain	explain
	35 And let them gather all the food of those good years that come, and lay up **corn** under the hand of Pharaoh, and let them keep food in the cities.	corn	corn	corn	grain	grain
42	11 We are all one man's sons; we are **true** men, thy servants are no spies.	honest	honest	honest	honest	honest
43	7 And they said, The man **asked us straitly of our state,** and of our kindred, saying, Is your father yet alive? have ye another brother? and we told him according to the tenor of these words: could we certainly know that he would say, Bring your brother down?	questioned us carefully/ourselves	questioned us closely/ourselves	kept questioning us/ourselves	questioned particularly/us	questioned us closely/ourselves
	25 And they made ready the present **against Joseph came** at noon: for they heard that they should eat bread there.	for Joseph's coming	when Joseph arrived	while they waited for Joseph to come	for Joseph's coming	for Joseph's arrival

KJV	RSV	NEB	JB	NAS	NIV
30 And Joseph made haste; for his **bowels** did yearn upon his brother: and he sought where to weep; and he entered into his chamber, and wept there.	heart	feelings	heart	(he was deeply stirred)	(Deeply moved)
44 7 And they said unto him, Wherefore saith my lord these words? **God forbid** that thy servants should do according to this thing:	Far be it	God forbid	(would never think of doing such a thing)	Far be it	Far be it
15 And Joseph said unto them, What deed is this that ye have done? **wot ye not** that such a man as I can **certainly** divine?	Do you not know/ indeed	You might have known/(omits)	Did you not know/ (omits)	Do you not know/ indeed	Don't you know/ (omits)
45 6 For these two years hath the famine been in the land: and yet there are five years, in the which there shall neither be **earing** nor harvest.	plowing	ploughing	ploughing	plowing	plowing
11 And there will I **nourish** thee; for yet there are five years of famine; lest thou, and thy household, and all that thou hast, come to poverty.	provide for	take care of	provide for	provide for	provide for
16 And the **fame** thereof was heard in Pharaoh's house, saying, Joseph's brethren are come: and it pleased Pharaoh well, and his servants.	report	report	news	news	news
20 Also regard not your **stuff;** for the **good** of all the land of Egypt is yours.	goods/best	possessions/best	property/best	goods/beat	belongings/best
49 10 The sceptre shall not depart from Judah, nor a lawgiver from between his feet, **until Shiloh come;** and unto him shall the gathering of the people be.	until he comes to whom it belongs	so long as tribute is brought to him	until he comes to whom it belongs	Until Shiloh comes	until he comes to whom it belongs
23 The archers **have sorely grieved** him, and shot at him, and **hated him:**	fiercely attacked/ harassed him sorely	savagely attacked/ pressed him hard	provoked/assailed him	bitterly attacked/ harassed him	With bitterness. . .attacked/ with hostility

Exodus

KJV	RSV	NEB	JB	NAS	NIV
1 22 And Pharaoh charged all his people, saying, Every son that is born ye shall cast into the **river**, and every daughter ye shall save alive.	Nile	Nile	river	Nile	river
2 3 And when she could not longer hide him, she took for him an **ark** of bulrushes, and daubed it with **slime** and with pitch, and put the child therein; and she laid it in the **flags** by the river's brink.	basket/bitumen/ reeds	basket/clay/reeds	basket/bitumen/ reeds	basket/tar/reeds	basket/tar/reeds
4 And his sister stood **afar off,** to **wit** what would be done to him.	at a distance/ know	at a distance/see	some distance away/see	at a distance/find out	at a distance/see
3 Now Moses kept the flock of Jethro his father in law, the priest of Midian: and he led the flock to the **backside** of the desert, and came to the mountain of God, even to Horeb.	west side	side	far side	west side	far side
22 But every woman shall **borrow** of her neighbour, and of her that sojourneth in her house, jewels of silver, and jewels of gold, and **raiment:** and ye shall put them upon your sons, and upon your daughters; and ye shall **spoil** the Egyptians.	ask/clothing/ despoil	ask/clothing/ plunder	ask/(omits)/ plunder	ask/clothing/ plunder	ask/clothing/ plunder
5 4 And the king of Egypt said unto them, Wherefore do ye, Moses and Aaron, **let** the people from their works? get you unto your burdens.	take. . .away	distracting	taking. . .away	draw. . .away	taking . . . away

KJV	RSV	NEB	JB	NAS	NIV
8 And the **tale** of the bricks, which they did make heretofore, ye shall lay upon them; ye shall **not diminish aught** thereof: for they be idle; therefore they cry, saying, Let us go and [ ] sacrifice to our God.	number/by no means lessen/offer	tally/On no acount reduce/offer	number/not reducing . . . at all/offer	quota/are not to reduce/(no addition)	number/don't reduce/(no addition)
9 Let there more work be laid upon the men, that they may labour therein; and **let them not regard vain words.**	pay no regard to lying words	take no notice of a pack of lies	do not have time to stop and listen to glib speeches	may pay no attention to false words	pay no attention to lies
13 And the **taskmasters hasted them,** saying, Fulfil your works, your daily tasks, as when there was straw.	taskmasters were urgent	overseers kept urging them on	slave-drivers harassed them	taskmasters pressed them	slave drivers kept pressing them
18 Go therefore now, and work; for there shall no straw be given you, yet shall ye deliver the **tale** of bricks.	number	tally	number	quota	quota
6 6 Wherefore say unto the children of Israel, I am the LORD, and I will bring you out from under the burdens of the Egyptians, and I will **rid you out of** their bondage, and I will redeem you with a stretched out arm, and with great judgments:	deliver you from	release you from	release you from	deliver you from	free you from
7 15 Get thee unto Pharaoh in the morning; lo, he goeth out unto the water; and thou shalt stand by the river's brink **against he come;** and the rod which was turned to a serpent shalt thou take in thine hand.	wait for him	wait . . . to meet him	wait for him	to meet him	to meet him
8 26 And Moses said, **It is not meet** so to do; for we shall sacrifice the abomination of the Egyptians to the LORD our God: lo, shall we sacrifice the abomination of the Egyptians before their eyes, and will they not stone us?	would not be right	we cannot do	would not be right	is not right	would not be right
9 3 Behold, the hand of the LORD is upon thy cattle which is in the field, upon the horses, upon the asses, upon the camels, upon the oxen, and upon the sheep: there shall be a very **grievous murrain.**	severe plague	terrible pestilence	deadly plague	severe pestilence	terrible plague
4 And the LORD shall **sever** between the cattle of Israel and the cattle of Egypt: and there shall nothing die of all that is the children's of Israel.	make a distinction	make a distinction	discriminate	make a distinction	make a distinction
22 And the LORD said unto Moses, Stretch forth thine hand toward heaven, that there may be hail in all the land of Egypt, upon man, and upon beast, and upon every **herb** of the field, throughout the land of Egypt.	plant	growing thing	all that grows	plant	everything growing
10 4 Else, if thou refuse to let my people go, behold, to-morrow will I bring the locusts into thy **coast:**	country	country	country	territory	country
12 7 And they shall take of the blood, and **strike** it on the two **side posts** and on the **upper door post** of the houses, wherein they shall eat it.	put/doorposts/lintel	smear/door-posts/lintel	put/doorposts/lintel	put/doorposts/lintel	put/sides/tops of the doorframes
9 Eat not of it raw, nor **sodden at all** with water, but **roast with fire;** his head with his legs, and with **the purtenance thereof.**	boiled/roasted/its inner parts	boiled/roasted/entrails	boiled/roasted over the fire/entrails	boiled/roasted with fire/its entrails	cooked/roast it over the fire/inner parts
13 18 But God led the people about, through the way of the wilderness of **the Red sea:** and the children of Israel went up **harnessed** out of the land of Egypt.	Red Sea/equipped for battle	Red Sea/(omits)	Sea of Reeds/fully armed	Red Sea/in martial array	Red Sea/armed for battle
14 25 And **took off** their chariot wheels, that they drave them heavily: so that the Egyptians said, Let us flee from the face	clogging	clogged	clogged	caused. . .to swerve	make. . .swerve

KJV	RSV	NEB	JB	NAS	NIV
of Israel; for the LORD fighteth for them against the Egyptians.					
15 3 The LORD is **a man of war:** the LORD is his name.	man of war	warrior	warrior	warrior	warrior
13 Thou in thy **mercy** hast led forth the people which thou hast redeemed: thou hast guided them in thy strength unto thy holy **habitation.**	steadfast love/ abode	constant love/ dwelling-place	grace/house	lovingkindness/ habitation	unfailing love/ dwelling
16 15 And when the children of Israel saw it, they said one to another, **It is manna:** for they **wist not** what it was. And Moses said unto them, This is the bread which the LORD hath given you to eat.	"What is it?"/did not know	'What is that?'/ did not know	'What is that?'/ not knowing	"What is it?"/did not know	"What is it?"/did not know
23 And he said unto them, This is that which the LORD hath said, To-morrow is the rest of the holy sabbath unto the LORD: bake that which ye will bake to-day, and **seethe** that ye will **seethe;** and that which remaineth over lay up for you to be kept until the morning.	boil/boil	boil/boil	boil/boil	boil/boil	boil/boil
17 7 And he called the name of the place Massah, and Meribah, because of the **chiding** of the children of Israel, and because they **tempted** the LORD, saying, Is the LORD among us, or not?	faultfinding/ put . . . to the proof	had disputed/challenged	grumbling/ put . . . to the test	quarrel/tested	quarreled/tested
13 And Joshua **discomforted** Amalek and his people with the edge of the sword.	mowed down	defeated	cut down	overwhelmed	overcame
14 And the LORD said unto Moses, Write this for a memorial in a book, and **rehearse** it in the ears of Joshua: for I will utterly **put** out the remembrance of Amalek from under heaven.	recite/blot out	tell/blot out	say/wipe out	recite/blot out	(make sure that Joshua hears it)/ erase
19 5 Now therefore, if ye will obey my voice indeed, and keep my covenant, then ye shall be a **peculiar treasure unto me** above all people: for all the earth is mine:	my own possession	my special possession	my very own	My own possession	my treasured possession
15 And he said unto the people, Be ready against the third day: come not **at your wives.**	near a woman	near a woman	near any woman	near a woman	(Abstain from sexual relations.)
18 And mount Sinai was **altogether on a smoke,** because the LORD descended upon it in fire: and the smoke thereof ascended as the smoke of a **furnace,** and the whole mount quaked greatly.	wrapped in smoke/ kiln	all smoking/kiln	entirely wrapped in smoke/kiln	all in smoke/furnace	covered with smoke/furnace
20 13 Thou shalt not **kill.**	kill	commit murder	kill	murder	murder
22 2 If a thief be found **breaking up,** and be smitten that he die, there shall **no blood be shed** for him.	breaking in/no bloodguilt	in the act/not murder	breaking in/no blood-vengeance	breaking in/no bloodguiltiness	breaking in/not guilty of bloodshed
3 If the **sun be risen upon him,** there shall be blood shed for him; for he should make full restitution; if he have nothing, then he shall be sold for his theft.	sun has risen upon him	after sunrise	it was after dawn (vs. 2)	sun has risen on him	it happens after sunrise
21 Thou shalt neither **vex** a stranger, nor oppress him: for ye were strangers in the land of Egypt.	wrong	wrong	molest	wrong	mistreat
24 And my wrath shall **wax hot,** and I will kill you with the sword; and your wives shall be widows, and your children fatherless.	burn	be roused	flare	be kindled	be aroused
25 If thou lend money to any of my people that is poor by thee, thou shalt not be to him as an **usurer,** neither shalt thou lay upon him **usury.**	creditor/interest	money-lender/interest in advance	usurer/interest	creditor/interest	moneylender/interest
26 If thou **at all** take thy neighbour's **raiment** to pledge, thou shalt **deliver** it unto him **by that** the sun goeth down:	ever/garment/restore/before	(omits)/cloak/return/by	(omits)/cloak/give it back/before	ever/cloak/return/before	(omits)/cloak/return/by

	KJV	RSV	NEB	JB	NAS	NIV
23	2 Thou shalt not follow a multitude to do evil; neither shalt thou **speak** in a **cause to decline after many to wrest judgment:**	bear witness/ cause/turning aside after a multitude so as to pervert justice	give evidence/lawsuit/side with the majority to pervert justice	malicious evidence/ (support a guilty man)/take the side of the greater number in the cause of wrongdoing	testify/dispute/ turn aside after a multitude in order to pervert justice	give testimony/ lawsuit/pervert justice by siding with the crowd
24	13 And Moses rose up, and his **minister** Joshua: and Moses went up into the mount of God.	servant	assistant	servant	servant	aide
25	31 And thou shalt make a **candlestick** of pure gold: of **beaten work** shall the **candlestick** be made: his shaft, and his branches, his **bowls,** his **knops,** and his flowers, shall be of the same.	lampstand/hammered work/lampstand/cups/capitals	lamp-stand/beaten work/lamp-stand/ cups/calyxes	lamp-stand/beaten gold/lamp-stand/ cups/calyx	lampstand/ hammered work/lampstand/cups/bulbs	lampstand/hammer. . .out/ it/cups/buds
26	6 And thou shalt make fifty **taches** of gold, and couple the curtains together with the **taches:** and it shall be one tabernacle.	clasps/clasps	fasteners/them	clasps/(omits)	clasps/clasps	clasps/them
	12 And the remnant that remaineth of the curtains of the tent, the half curtain that remaineth, shall hang over the **backside** of the tabernacle.	back	back	back	back	rear
	30 And thou shalt **rear up** the tabernacle according to the **fashion** thereof which was shewed thee in the mount.	erect/plan	set up/design	erect/model	erect/plan	Set up/plan
28	8 And the **curious girdle** of the ephod, which is upon it, shall be of the same, according to the work thereof; even of gold, of blue, and purple, and scarlet, and fine twined linen.	skilfully woven band	waist-band	woven band	skillfully woven band	skillfully woven waistband
	9 And thou shalt take two onyx stones, and **grave** on them the names of the children of Israel:	engrave	engrave	engrave	engrave	engrave
	11 **With the work of an engraver in stone, like the engravings of a signet,** shalt thou engrave the two stones with the names of the children of Israel: thou shalt make them to be set in **ouches of gold.**	As a jeweler engraves signets/ settings of gold filigree	With the skill of a craftsman, a sealcutter/ gold rosettes	With the art of a jeweller, of an engraver of seals/ settings of gold mesh	As a jeweler engraves a signet/ filigree settings of gold	the way a gem cutter engraves a seal/gold filigree settings
	32 And there shall be an **hole in the top** of it, in the midst thereof: it shall have a binding of woven work round about the hole of it, as it were the hole of an **habergeon,** that it be not rent.	opening for the head/garment	hole for the head/ (omits)	opening for the head/coat of mail	opening at its top/ coat of mail	opening for the head/collar
	36 And thou shalt make a plate of pure gold, and **grave** upon it, like the engravings of a signet, **Holiness** to the Lord.	engrave/Holy	engrave/Holy	engrave/Consecrated	engrave/Holy	engrave/Holy
	40 And for Aaron's sons thou shalt make **coats,** and thou shalt make for them **girdles,** and **bonnets** shalt thou make for them, for **glory** and for **beauty.**	coats/girdles/ caps/glory/beauty	tunics/sashes/ head-dresses/dignity/grandeur	tunic/girdle/head-dress/dignity/ magnificence	tunics/sashes/ caps/glory/beauty	tunics/sashes/ headbands/dignity/honor
29	2 And unleavened bread, and cakes unleavened **tempered** with oil, and wafers unleavened **anointed** with oil: of **wheaten** flour shalt thou make them.	mixed/spread/fine wheat	mixed/smeared/ wheaten	mixed/spread/fine wheat	mixed/spread/fine wheat	mixed/spread/fine wheat
	13 And thou shalt take all the fat that covereth the **inwards,** and the **caul** that is above the liver, and the two kidneys, and the fat that is upon them, and burn them upon the altar.	entrails/appendage	entrails/long lobe	entrails/fatty mass	entrails/lobe	inner parts/ covering
30	25 And thou shalt make it an **oil of holy ointment,** an **ointment compound** after the art of the **apothecary:** it shall be an holy anointing oil.	sacred anointing oil/blended/ perfume	sacred anointing oil/perfume compounded/ perfumer('s)	holy chrism/blend/ perfumer	holy anointing oil/ perfume mixture/ perfumer	sacred anointing oil/ fragrant blend/ perfumer

	KJV	RSV	NEB	JB	NAS	NIV
	35 And thou shalt make it a **perfume, a confection** after the art of the **apothecary, tempered together,** pure and holy:	incense blended/perfumer/seasoned with salt	incense, perfume/perfumer('s)/salted	incense/blend/perfumer/salted	incense, a perfume/perfumer/salted	fragrant blend of incense/perfumer/It is to be salted
	38 Whosoever shall make **like unto that, to smell thereto,** shall even be cut off from his people.	any like it/to use as a perfume	any like it/for his own pleasure	it/for use as perfume	any like it/to use as perfume	any like it/to enjoy its fragrance
33	22 And it shall come to pass, while my glory passeth by, that I will put thee in a **clift** of the rock, and will cover thee with my hand while I pass by:	cleft	crevice	cleft	cleft	cleft
	23 And I will take away mine hand, and thou shalt see my **back parts:** but my face shall not be seen.	back	back	back	back	back
34	21 Six days thou shalt work, but on the seventh day thou shalt rest: in **earing** time and in harvest thou shalt rest.	plowing	ploughing	ploughing	plowing	plowing
35	22 And they came, both men and women, as many as were willing-hearted, and brought **bracelets,** and earrings, and **rings,** and **tablets,** all jewels of gold: and every man that offered offered an offering of gold unto the LORD.	brooches/signet rings/armlets	clasps/finger-rings/pendants	brooches/rings/necklaces, bracelets/(earrings omitted)	brooches/signet rings/bracelets	brooches/rings/ornaments
	32 And to devise **curious works,** to work in gold, and in silver, and in brass,	artistic designs	design	art of designing	designs	artistic designs
	35 Them hath he filled with **wisdom of heart,** to work all manner of work, of the engraver, and of the **cunning workman,** and of the embroiderer, in blue, and in purple, in scarlet, and in fine linen, and of the weaver, even of them that do any work, and of those that devise cunning work.	ability/designer	skill/seamsters	skill/damask weaver	skill/designer	skill/designers
36	8 And **every wise-hearted man** among them that wrought the work of the tabernacle made ten curtains of fine twined linen, and blue, and purple, and scarlet: with cherubims **of cunning work made he them.**	all the able men/skilfully worked	all the craftsmen/worked on them, all made by a seamster	All the most skilled craftsmen/finely brocaded	all the skillful men/the work of a skillful workman	All the skilled men/worked into them by a skilled craftsman
	38 And the five pillars of it with their hooks: and he overlaid their **chapiters** and their fillets with gold: but their five **sockets** were of brass.	capitals/sockets	top of the posets/sockets	capitals/sockets	tops/sockets	tops of the posts/bases
37	9 And the **cherubims** spread out their wings **on high,** and **covered** with their wings over the mercy seat, with their faces one to another; even **to the mercy seatward** were the faces of the cherubims.	cherubim/above/overshadowing/toward the mercy seat	They (cherub)/pointing upwards/screening the cover/inwards over the cover	cherubs/upwards/overshadowed/towards the throne of mercy	cherubim/upward/covering/toward the mercy seat	cherubim/upward/overshadowing/toward the cover
38	23 And with him was Aholiab, son of Ahisamach, of the tribe of Dan, an **engraver,** and a **cunning workman,** and an embroiderer in blue, and in purple, and in scarlet, and fine linen.	craftsman/designer	engraver/seamster	engraver/damask weaver	engraver/skillful workman	craftsman/designer
	24 All the gold that was **occupied** for the work in all the **work of the holy place,** even the gold of the offering, was twenty and nine talents, and seven hundred and thirty shekels, **after the shekel of the sanctuary.**	used/construction of the sanctuary/by the sheckel of the sanctuary	used/work of the sanctuary/by the sacred standard	used/work for the sanctuary/(reckoning by the sanctuary sheckel)	used/work of the sanctuary/according to the sheckel of the sanctuary	used/work on the sanctuary/according to the sanctuary sheckel

Leviticus

	KJV	RSV	NEB	JB	NAS	NIV
1	3 If his offering be a burnt sacrifice of the herd, let him offer a male without blemish: he shall offer it **of his own voluntary will** at the **door of the tabernacle** of the congregation before the LORD.	(omits)/door of the tent of meeting	(omits)/entrance to the Tent of the Presence	(omits)/entrance to the Tent of Meeting	(omits)/doorway of the tent of meeting	(omits)/entrance to the Tent of Meeting

KJV	RSV	NEB	JB	NAS	NIV
2 1 And when any will offer a **meat offering** unto the LORD, his offering shall be of fine flour; and he shall pour oil upon it, and put frankincense thereon:	cereal offering	grain-offering	oblation	grain offering	grain offering
3 1 And if his oblation be **a sacrifice of peace offering,** if he offer it of the herd; whether it be a male or female, he shall offer it without blemish before the LORD.	sacrifice of peace offering	shared-offering	communion sacrifice	sacrifice of peace offerings	fellowship offering
4 16 And the priest that is anointed shall bring **of the bullock's blood** to the **tabernacle of the congregation:**	of the blood of the bull/ tent of meeting	of the blood/Tent of the Presence	of the blood of the bull/ Tent of Meeting	of the blood of the bull/ tent of meeting	of the bull's blood/ Tent of Meeting
6 18 All the males among the children of Aaron shall eat of it. It shall be a statute for ever in your generations concerning the offerings of the LORD made by fire: **every one** that toucheth them shall be holy.	whoever	Whatever	Everything	Whoever	Whatever
28 But the earthen vessel wherein it is **sodden shall be broken: and if it be sodden** in a **brasen pot,** it shall be both scoured, and rinsed in water.	boiled/boiled/ bronze vessel	boiled/boiled/cop-per vessel	cooked/cooking/ bronze vessel	boiled/boiled/ bronze vessel	cooked/cooked/ bronze pot
10 1 And Nadab and Abihu, the sons of Aaron, took **either of them** his censer, and put fire therein, and put incense thereon, and offered **strange** fire before the LORD, which he commanded them not.	each/unholy	(omits)/illicit	each/unlawful	their respective/ strange	(omits)/unau-thorized
6 And Moses said unto Aaron, and unto Eleazar and unto Ithamar, his sons, **Uncover not your heads,** neither rend your clothes; lest ye die, and lest wrath come upon all the people: but let your brethren, the whole house of Israel, bewail the burning which the LORD hath kindled.	"Do not let the hair of your heads hang loose	'You shall not leave your hair dishevelled	'Do not disorder your hair	"Do not uncover your heads	"Do not let your hair become un-kempt
11 19 And the stork, the heron after her kind, and the **lapwing,** and the bat.	hoopoe	hoopoe	hoopoe	hoopoe	hoopoe
35 And every thing whereupon any part of their carcase falleth shall be unclean; whether it be oven, or **ranges for pots,** they shall be broken down: for they are unclean, and shall be unclean unto you.	stove	stove	stove	stove	cooking pot
12 8 And if she be not able to bring a lamb, then she shall bring two **turtles,** or two young pigeons; the one for the burnt offering, and the other for a sin offering: and the priest shall make an atonement for her, and she shall be clean.	turtledoves	turtle-doves	turtledoves	turtledoves	doves
13 2 When a man shall have in the skin of his flesh **a rising, a scab, or bright spot,** and it be in the skin of his flesh like the **plague of leprosy;** then he shall be brought unto Aaron the priest, or unto one of his sons the priests:	a swelling or an eruption or a spot/ leprous disease	a discolora-tion . . . , a pustule or inflammation/ sores of a malig-nant skin-disease	a swelling or scab or shiny spot/case of leprosy	a swelling or a scab or a bright spot/infection of leprosy	a swelling or a rash or a bright spot/infectious skin disease
3 And the priest shall look on the plague in the skin of the flesh: and when the hair in the plague is turned white, and the plague in sight be **deeper than the skin of his flesh,** it is a plague of leprosy: and the priest shall look on him, and pronounce him unclean.	deeper than the skin of his body	deeper than the skin	bites into the skin	deeper than the skin of his body	more than skin deep
10 And the priest shall see him: and, behold, if the rising be white in the skin,					

KJV	RSV	NEB	JB	NAS	NIV
and it have turned the hair white, and there be **quick raw flesh** in the rising;	quick raw flesh	ulceration	ulcer	quick raw flesh	raw flesh
30 Then the priest shall see the plague: and, behold, if it be in sight deeper than the skin; and there be in it a yellow thin hair; then the priest shall pronounce him unclean: it is a **dry scall,** even a leprosy upon the head or beard.	itch	scurf	tinea	scale	itch
14 21 And if he be poor, and cannot **get** so much; then he shall take one lamb for a **trespass** offering to be waved, to make an atonement for him, and one tenth **deal** of fine flour mingled with oil for a meat offering, and a log of oil;	afford/guilt/an ephah	afford/guilt/an ephah	afford/reparation/(omits)	(his means are insufficient)/guilt/an ephah	afford/guilt/an ephah
37 And he shall **look on the plague,** and, behold, if the plague be in the walls of the house with **hollow strakes,** greenish or reddish, which in **sight are lower than the wall;**	examine the disease/spots/appears to be deeper than the surface	(on inspection/depressions/apparently going deeper than the surface	(on examination)/depressions/(pitted)	look at the mark/depressions/appears deeper than the surface	examine the mildew on the walls/depressions/appear to be deeper than the surface
15 29 And on the eighth day she shall take unto her two **turtles,** or two young pigeons, and bring them unto the priest, to the door of the **tabernacle of the congregation.**	turtledoves/tent of meeting	turtle-doves/Tent of the Presence	turtledoves/Tent of Meeting	turtledoves/tent of meeting	doves/Tent of Meeting
16 8 And Aaron shall cast lots upon the two goats; one lot for the LORD, and the other lot for **the scapegoat.**	Azazel	Precipice	Azazel	the scapegoat	the scapegoat
21 And Aaron shall lay both his hands upon the head of the live goat, and confess over him all the iniquities of the children of Israel, and all their transgressions in all their sins, putting them upon the head of the goat, and shall send him away by the hand of a **fit man** into the wilderness:	man who is in readiness	man who is waiting ready	man waiting ready	man who stands in readiness	man appointed for the task
29 And this shall be a statute for ever unto you: that in the seventh month, on the tenth day of the month, ye **shall afflict your souls,** and do no work at all, whether it be one of your own country, or a stranger that sojourneth among you:	shall afflict yourselves	shall mortify yourselves	you must fast	shall humble your souls	must deny yourselves
17 14 For it is the life of all flesh; **the blood of it is for the life thereof:** therefore I said unto the children of Israel, Ye shall eat the blood of no manner of flesh: for the life of all flesh is the blood thereof: whosoever eateth it shall be cut off.	is the blood of it	because the life of every living creature is the blood	for the life of all flesh is in its blood	for the life of all flesh is its blood	because the life of every creature is its blood
18 21 And thou shalt not **let any of thy seed pass through the fire to** Molech, neither shalt thou profane the name of thy God: I am the LORD.	give any of your children to devote them by fire to Molech	surrender any of your children to Molech	hand over any of your children to have them passed to Molech	give any of your offspring to offer them to Molech	give any of your children to be sacrificed to Molech
19 16 Thou shalt not go up and down as a talebearer among thy people: neither shalt thou stand against the **blood** of thy neighbour: I am the LORD.	life	(take sides . . . on a capital life charge)	life	life	life
19 Ye shall keep my statutes. Thou shalt not let thy cattle **gender with a diverse kind: thou shalt not sow thy field with mingled seed:** neither shall a garment **mingled of linen and woollen** come upon thee.	breed/two kinds of seed/made of two kinds of stuff	mate/two kinds of seed/woven with two kinds of yarn	mate/two kinds of grain/made from two kinds of fabric	breed/two kinds of seed/of two kinds of material mixed together	mate/two kinds of seed/woven of two kinds of material
23 And when ye shall come into the land, and shall have planted all manner of trees for food, then ye shall count the fruit thereof as **uncircumcized:** three years shall it be as **uncircumcised** unto you: it shall not be eaten of.	forbidden/forbidden	forbidden/forbidden	its foreskin/uncircumcised	forbidden/forbidden	forbidden/forbidden
20 4 And if the people of the land do **any ways** hide their eyes from the man, when he giveth of his seed unto Molech, and kill him not:	at all	(omits)	(omits)	ever	(omits)

KJV	RSV	NEB	JB	NAS	NIV
8 And ye shall keep my statutes, and do them: I am the LORD which **sanctify** you.	sanctify	hallows	make. . .holy	sanctifies	makes. . .holy
26 And ye shall be holy unto me: for I the LORD am holy, and have **severed you from other people,** that ye should be mine.	separated you from the peoples	made a clear separation between you and the heathen	set you apart from all these peoples	set you apart from the peoples	set you apart from the nations
21 4 But he shall not defile himself, **being a chief man among his people,** to profane himself.	as a husband among his people	for any unmarried woman among his father's kin	If a husband, he must not make himself unclean for his family	as a relative by marriage among his people	for people related to him by marriage
23 38 **Beside the sabbaths of the LORD,** and beside your gifts, and beside all your vows, and beside all your freewill offerings, which ye give unto the LORD.	besides the sabbaths of the Lord	besides the Lord's sabbaths	besides the sabbaths of Yahweh	besides those of the sabbaths of the Lord	in addition to those for the Lord's Sabbaths
25 8 And thou shalt **number seven sabbaths of years** unto thee, seven times seven years; and **the space of the seven sabbaths of years** shall be unto thee forty and nine years.	count seven weeks of years/time of the seven weeks of years	count seven sabbaths of years/ (omits)	count seven weeks of years/a period of seven weeks of years	count off seven sabbaths of years/ the time of seven sabbaths of years	Count off seven sabbaths of years/ the seven sabbaths of years
30 And if it be not redeemed **within the space of a** full year, then the house that is in the walled city shall be **established for ever** to him that bought it throughout his generations: it shall not **go out** in the jubile.	within/made sure in perpetuity/be released	before . . . is out/ vest in perpetuity/ revert	by the end of the/ shall be the property . . . in perpetuity/relinquish	within the space of a/ passes permanently/revert	before. . .has passed/belong permanently/ be returned
34 But the field of the **suburbs** of their cities may not be sold; for it is their perpetual possession.	common land	common land	arable land	pasture fields	pasturelands
36 Take thou no **usury** of him, or increase; but fear thy God; that thy brother may live with thee.	interest	interest	interest	usorious interest	interest
47 And if a sojourner or stranger **wax** rich **by thee,** and thy brother **that dwelleth by him** wax poor, and sell himself unto the stranger or sojourner **by** thee, or to **the stock** of the stranger's family:	becomes/with you/ beside/with/ member	become rich/living with you/(omits)/ member	grows/among you/ (omits)/among/ descendants	becomes/with you/ of yours/with you/ descendants	becomes/among you/of your countrymen/among you/clan
26 25 And I will bring a sword upon you, that shall **avenge the quarrel** of my covenant: and when ye are gathered together within your cities, I will send the pestilence among you; and ye shall be delivered into the hand of the enemy.	execute vengeance	bring war in vengeance	to avenge	execute vengeance	to avenge
30 And I will destroy your high places, and cut down your **images** and cast your **carcases** upon the **carcases** of your idols, and my soul shall abhor you.	incense altars/ dead bodies/dead bodies	incense-altars/ rotting carcasses/ rotting logs	altars of incense/ corpses/corpses	incense altars/remains/remains	incense altars/ dead bodies/lifeless forms

Numbers

KJV	RSV	NEB	JB	NAS	NIV
4 16 And to the office of Eleazar the son of Aaron the priest **pertaineth** the oil for the light, and the **sweet** incense, and the **daily meat** offering, and the anointing oil, and the oversight of all the tabernacle, and of all that therein is, in the sanctuary, and in the vessels thereof.	shall have charge of/fragrant/continual cereal	shall have charge of/fragrant/regular grain	It is to fall. . .to watch over/fragrant/perpetual	the responsibility of/fragrant/continual grain	have charge of/ fragrant/regular grain
5 12 Speak unto the children of Israel, and say unto them, If any man's wife go **aside,** and commit a trespass against him,	astray	astray	astray	astray	astray

	KJV	RSV	NEB	JB	NAS	NIV
	13 And a man lie with her carnally, and it be hid from the eyes of her husband, **and be kept close,** and she be defiled, and there be no witness against her, neither she be taken **with the manner;**	and she is undetected/in the act	and the crime is undetected/in the act	in secret/in the act	and she is undetected/in the act	and her impurity is undetected/in the act
6	3 He shall separate himself from wine and strong drink, and shall drink no vinegar of wine, or vinegar of strong drink, neither shall he drink any **liquor** of grapes, nor eat **moist grapes,** or dried.	juice/fresh	juice/fresh	juice/fresh	juice/fresh	juice/ grapes (as opposed to raisins)
	6 And the days that he separateth himself unto the LORD he shall **come at** no dead body.	go near	go near	go near	go near	go near
	9 And if any man die very suddenly **by him,** and he hath defiled the head of his consecration; then he shall shave his head in the day of his cleansing, on the seventh day shall he shave it.	beside him	by his side	in his presence	beside him	in his presence
	10 And on the eighth day he shall bring two **turtles,** or two young pigeons, to the priest, to the door of the **tabernacle of the congregation:**	turtledoves/tent of meeting	turtle-doves/Tent of the Presence	turtledoves/Tent of Meeting	turtledoves/tent of meeting	doves/Tent of Meeting
	11 And the priest shall offer the one for a sin offering, and the other for a burnt offering, and make an atonement for him, for that he sinned **by** the dead, and shall hallow his head that same day.	by reason of	through contact with	(that he has contracted from)	because of	by being in the presence of
	15 And a basket of unleavened bread, cakes of fine flour **mingled** with oil, and wafers of unleavened bread **anointed** with oil, and their **meat** offering, and their drink offerings.	mixed/spread/cereal	mixed/smeared/grain	mixed/spread/appropriate	mixed/spread/grain	mixed/spread/grain
	19 And the priest shall take the **sodden** shoulder of the ram, and one unleavened cake out of the basket, and one unleavened wafer, and shall put them upon the hands of the Nazarite, after the hair of his **separation** is shaven:	boiled/consecration	boiled/(which had been dedicated)	cooked/(when the nazirite has shaved off his hair)	boiled/dedicated (hair)	boiled/dedication
11	5 We remember the fish, which we did eat in Egypt **freely;** the cucumbers, and the melons, and the leeks, and the onions, and the garlick.	for nothing	for the asking	free	free	at no cost
	12 Have I conceived all this people? have I **begotten them,** that thou shouldest say unto me, Carry them in thy bosom, as **a nursing father** beareth the sucking child, unto the land which thou swarest unto their fathers?	bring them forth/nurse	brought them into the world/nurse	gave them birth/nurse	brought them forth/nurse	give them birth/nurse
	15 And if thou deal thus with me, kill me, I pray thee, **out of hand,** if I have found favour in thy sight; and let me not see my wretchedness.	at once	outright	(omits)	at once	right now
	21 And Moses said, The people, among whom I am, are six hundred thousand **footmen;** and thou hast said, I will give them flesh, that they may eat a whole month.	on foot	on the march	foot soldiers	on foot	on foot
	29 And Moses said unto him, **Enviest thou** for my sake? **would God** that all the LORD'S people were prophets, and that the LORD would put his spirit upon them!	Are you jealous/Would	Are you jealous/I wish	Are you jealous/If only	Are you jealous/Would	Are you jealous/I wish
12	8 With him will I speak **mouth to mouth,** even **apparently,** and not in **dark speeches;** and the similitude of the LORD shall he behold: wherefore then were ye not afraid to speak against my servant Moses?	mouth to mouth/clearly/dark speech	face to face/openly/riddles	face to face/plainly/riddles	mouth to mouth/openly/dark sayings	face to face/clearly/riddles
14	22 **Because all those** men which have	none of the/signs/	one of all those/	Of all the (men)	all of the/signs/	not one of the/

KJV	RSV	NEB	JB	NAS	NIV
seen my glory, and my miracles, which I **did** in Egypt and in the wilderness, and **have tempted me** now these ten times, and have not hearkened to my voice;	wrought/have put me to the proof	signs/wrought/ have challenged me	who/signs/ worked/have put me to the test	performed/have put Me to the test	signs/performed/ tested me
45 Then the Amalekites came down, and the Canaanites which dwelt in that hill, and smote them, and **discomfited** them, even unto Hormah.	pursued	crushed	harried	beat . . . down	beat . . . down
15 38 Speak unto the children of Israel, and bid them that they make them **fringes in the borders** of their garments throughout their generations, and that they put upon the **fringe of the borders** a **ribband** of blue:	tassels on the corners/ tassel of each corner/cord	tassels like flowers/this tassel/ thread	tassels on the hems/this tassel/ cord	tassels on the corners/ tassel of each corner/cord	tassels on the corners/ each tassel/ cord
16 30 But if the LORD make a new thing, and the earth open her mouth, and swallow them up, with all that **appertain** unto them, and they go down **quick** into **the pit;** then ye shall understand that these men have **provoked** the LORD.	belongs/alive/ Sheol/despised	is theirs/alive/ Sheol/held . . . in contempt	belongs/alive/ Sheol/rejected	is theirs/alive/ Sheol/spurned	belongs/alive/ grave/ treated . . . with contempt
21 5 And the people spake against God, and against Moses, Wherefore have ye brought us up out of Egypt to die in the wilderness? for there is no **bread,** neither is there any water; and **our soul** loatheth this **light bread.**	food/we/worth less food	food/we/miserable fare	bread/we/unsatisfying food	food/we/miserable food	bread/we/miserable food
24 And Israel **smote** him with the edge of the sword, and possessed his land from Arnon unto Jabbok, even unto the children of Ammon: for the **border of the children of Ammon was strong.**	slew/Jazer was the boundary of the Ammonites	put . . . to the sword/where the country became difficult	struck . . . down/ Jazer was the Ammonite frontier	struck/the border of the sons of Ammon was Jazer	put . . . to the sword/their border was fortified
23 22 God brought them out of Egypt; he hath as it were the **strength of an unicorn.**	horns of the wild ox	curving horns . . . wild ox	the wild ox's horn	horns of the wild ox	strength of a wild ox
24 14 And now, behold, I go unto my people: come therefore, and I will **advertise thee** what this people shall do to thy people in the latter days.	let you know	warn you	warn you	advise you	warn you
25 17 **Vex** the Midianites, and smite them:	Harass	Make. . .suffer	Harry	Be hostile to	Treat . . . as enemies
26 10 And the earth opened her mouth, and swallowed them up together with Korah, when that company died, **what time** the fire devoured two hundred and fifty men: and they became a **sign.**	when/warning	while/warning sign	when/sign	when/warning	when/warning sign
27 4 Why should the name of our father **be done** away from among his family, because he hath no son? Give unto us therefore a possession among the brethren of our father.	be taken away	should disappear	be lost	be withdrawn	disappear
28 13 And a **several tenth deal** of flour mingled with oil for a meat offering unto one lamb; for a burnt offering of a sweet savour, a sacrifice made by fire unto the LORD.	tenth (see vs. 20—"tenth of an ephah")	one tenth	two-tenths	tenth of an ephah	tenth of an ephah
30 5 But if her father disallow her in the day that he heareth; not any of her vows, or of her bonds wherewith she hath bound her soul, shall stand: and the LORD shall forgive her, because her father **disallowed** her.	opposed	disallowed	expressed his disapproval (vs. 6)	forbidden	forbidden
11 And her husband heard it, and **held his peace** at her, and disallowed her not: then all her vows shall stand, and every bond wherewith she bound her soul shall stand.	said nothing	keeps silence	says nothing	said nothing	says nothing
31 11 And they took all the spoil, and all the **prey,** both of men and of beasts.	booty	plunder	all that they had captured	prey	spoils

KEY-WORD COMPARISON

	KJV	RSV	NEB	JB	NAS	NIV
	23 Every thing that **may abide** the fire, ye shall make it go through the fire, and it shall be clean: nevertheless it shall be purified with the water of separation: and all that abideth not the fire ye shall make go through the water.	can stand	will stand	can withstand	can stand	cannot withstand
32	17 But we ourselves will go ready armed before the children of Israel, until we have brought them unto their place: and our little ones shall dwell in the **fenced** cities because of the inhabitants of the land.	fortified (also vs. 36)	walled (also vs. 36)	fortified (also vs. 36)	fortified (also vs. 36)	fortified (also vs. 36)
33	54 And ye shall divide the land by lot for an inheritance among your families: and to **the more** ye shall give **the more** inheritance, and to **the fewer** ye shall give **the less** inheritance: every man's inheritance shall be in the place where his lot falleth; according to the tribes of your fathers ye shall inherit.	a large tribe/a large/a small tribe/a small	the large family/a large/the small family/a small	a large clan/a greater inheritance/a small clan/ a lesser	the larger/more/ the smaller/less	a larger group/a larger/a smaller group/a smaller
34	5 And the border shall **fetch a compass** from Azmon unto the river of Egypt, and the **goings out** of it shall be at the sea.	turn/termination	turn/limit	turn/end	turn direction/termination	turn/end
35	2 Command the children of Israel, that they give unto the Levites of the inheritance of their possession cities to dwell in; and ye shall give also unto the Levites **suburbs** for the cities round about them.	pasture lands (also vss. 3, 4)	common land (also vs. 3; vs. 4—land)	pasture land (also vss. 3, 4)	pasture lands (also vss. 3, 4)	pasturelands (also vss. 3, 4)
	11 Then ye shall **appoint** you cities to be cities of refuge for you; that the **slayer** may flee thither, which killeth any person at **unawares.**	select/manslayer/ without intent	designate/homicide/by accident	select/man who/ accidentally	select/manslayer/ unintentionally	select/person who/ accidentally
	25 And the congregation shall **deliver the slayer** out of the hand of the **revenger of blood,** and the congregation shall restore him to the city of his refuge, whither he was fled: and he shall abide in it **unto** the death of the high priest, which was anointed with the holy oil.	rescue the manslayer/avenger of blood/until	protect the homicide/vengeance of the kinsman/till	rescue the killer/ avenger of blood/ until	deliver the manslayer/blood avenger/until	accused of murder/ avenger of blood/ until

Deuteronomy

	KJV	RSV	NEB	JB	NAS	NIV
1	5 On this side Jordan, in the land of Moab, **began** Moses to **declare** this law, saying,	undertook/explain	resolved/promulgate	set himself/expound	undertook/expound	began/expound
	12 How can I myself alone bear your **cumbrance,** and your burden, and your strife?	weight	heavy (burden)	heavy (burden)	load	problems
	17 Ye shall not **respect persons** in judgment; but ye shall hear the small as well as the great; ye shall not be **afraid of** the face of man; for the judgment is God's: and the cause that is too hard for you, bring it unto me, and I will hear it.	be partial	must be impartial	must be impartial	show partiality	show partiality
2	14 And the **space in which we came** from Kadeshbarnea, until we **were come over** the brook Zered, was thirty and eight years; until **all the [ ]** generation **of** the men of war **were wasted** out from among the **host,** as the LORD sware unto them.	time from our leaving/crossed/ entire/that is/had perished/camp	journey/crossing/ whole/of/had passed away/ (omits)	our wanderings/ to/whole/of/was lost/camp	time that it took for us to come/ crossed over/ of/perished/camp	time we left/ crossed/entire/of/ had perished/ camp
4	34 Or hath **God assayed** to go and take him a nation from the midst of another nation, by **temptations,** by signs, and by wonders, and by war, and by **a mighty** hand, and by a stretched out arm, and by	any god ever attempted/trials	ever a god attempt/challenge	any god ventured/ ordeals	a god tried/trials	any god ever tried/testings

	KJV	RSV	NEB	JB	NAS	NIV
	great terrors, according to all that the LORD your God did for you in Egypt before your eyes?					
6	5 And thou shalt love the LORD thy God with all thine heart, and with all thy soul, and with all thy **might.**	might	strength	strength	might	strength
8	8 A land of wheat, and barley, and vines, and fig trees, and pomegranates; a land of **oil olive,** and honey;	olive trees	olives, oil	olives, of oil	olive oil	olive oil
	16 Who fed thee in the wilderness with manna, which thy fathers knew not, that he might number thee, and that he might **prove** thee, to do thee good **at thy** latter end;	test/in the	test/in the	test/(your future)	test/in the	test/in the
11	6 And what he did unto Dathan and Abiram, the sons of Eliab, the son of Reuben: how the earth opened her mouth, and swallowed them up, and their households, and their tents, and **all the substance that was in their possession,** in the midst of all Israel:	every living thing that followed them	every living thing in their company	all their retinue	every living thing that followed them	every living thing that belonged to them
	10 For the land, whither thou goest in to possess it, is not as the land of Egypt, from whence ye came out, where thou sowedst thy seed, and wateredst it with thy foot, as a garden of **herbs.**	vegetables	vegetable	vegetable	vegetable	vegetable
	30 Are they not on the other side Jordan, by the way where the sun goeth down, in the land of the Canaanites, which dwell in the champaign over against Gilgal, beside the **plains** of Moreh?	oak	terebinth	Oak	oaks	great trees
12	15 Notwithstanding thou mayest kill and eat flesh in all thy **gates, whatsoever thy soul lusteth after,** according to the blessing of the LORD thy God which he hath given thee: the unclean and the clean may eat thereof, as of the roebuck, and as of the hart.	towns/as much as you desire	settlements/freely	towns/whenever you want	gates/whatever you desire	towns/as you want
14	2 For thou art an holy people unto the LORD thy God, and the LORD hath chosen thee to be a **peculiar people unto himself,** above all the nations that are upon the earth.	people for his own possession	his special possession	his very own people	His own possession	his treasured possession
	15 And the **owl,** and the night hawk, and the **cuckoo,** and the hawk after his kind,	ostrich/sea gull	desert-owl/long-eared owl	ostrich/seagull	ostrich/sea gull	horned owl/any kind of hawk
	16 The little owl, and the great owl, and the **swan,**	water hen	osprey	ibis	white owl	white owl
	17 And the pelican, and the **gier eagle,** and the cormorant,	carrion vulture	fisher-owl	white vulture	carrion vulture	osprey
15	14 Thou shalt furnish him liberally out of thy flock, and out of thy **floor,** and out of thy winepress: of that wherewith the LORD thy God hath blessed thee thou shalt give unto him.	threshing floor	threshing-floor	threshing-floor	threshing floor	threshing floor
16	19 Thou shalt not **wrest judgment;** thou shalt not **respect persons,** neither take a **gift:** for a **gift** doth blind the eyes of the wise, and **pervert the words** of the righteous.	pervert justice/show partiality/bribe/bribe/subverts the cause	pervert the course of justice/show favour/bribe/bribery/makes . . . give a crooked answer	pervert the law/be impartial/bribes/bribe/jeopardises the cause	distort justice/be partial/bribe/bribe/perverts the words	pervert justice/show partiality/bribe/bribe/twists the words
17	1 Thou shalt not sacrifice unto the LORD thy God any bullock, or sheep, wherein is blemish, or any **evilfavouredness:** for that is an abomination unto the LORD thy God.	defect	serious blemish	defect	defect	flaw

KJV	RSV	NEB	JB	NAS	NIV
11 According to the sentence of the law which they shall teach thee, and according to the judgment which they shall tell thee, thou shalt do: thou shalt not **decline** from the sentence which they shall shew thee, to the right hand, nor to the left.	turn aside	swerve	swerving neither right nor left	turn aside	turn aside
19 5 As when a man goeth into the wood with his neighbour to **hew** wood, and his hand **fetcheth a stroke** with the axe to cut down the tree, and the head slippeth from the **helve,** and **lighteth upon** his neighbour, and he die; he shall flee unto one of those cities, and live:	cut/swings/handle/strikes	fell/relaxes his grip/tree/hits	cut/swings/handle/strikes	cut/swings/handle/ strikes	cut/swings/ (omits)/hit
18 And the judges shall **make diligent inquisition:** and, behold, if the witness be a false witness, and hath testified falsely against his brother;	inquire diligently	after careful examination	make a careful inquiry	investigate thoroughly	make a thorough investigation
21 4 And the elders of that city shall bring down the heifer unto a **rough valley,** which is neither **eared** nor sown, and shall **strike off** the heifer's neck there in the valley:	valley with running water/ plowed/break	ravine where there is a stream that never runs dry/ tilled/break	watercourse that is never dry/ ploughed/break	valley with running water/ plowed/break	valley. . .where there is a flowing stream/plowed/ break
22 3 In like manner shalt thou do with his ass; and so shalt thou do with his raiment; and with **all lost thing** of thy brother's, which he hath lost, and thou hast found, shalt thou do likewise: thou mayest not hide thyself.	all lost thing	anything else (that your fellow-countryman) has lost	anything (your brother) loses	anything lost	anything (he) loses
6 If a bird's nest chance to be before thee in the way in any tree, or on the ground, whether they be young ones, or eggs, and the **dam** sitting upon the young, or upon the eggs, thou shalt not take the **dam** with the young:	mother/mother	mother-bird/ mother	mother/mother	mother/mother	mother/mother
14 And **give occasions of speech against her,** and bring up an evil name upon her, and say, I took this woman, and when I came to her, I found **her not a maid:**	charges her with evil conduct/in her the tokens of virginity	brings trumped-up charges against her/proof of virginity in her	taxes her with misconduct/the evidence of her virginity	charges her with shameful deeds/ her a virgin	slanders her/ proof of her virginity
19 And they shall **amerce** him in an hundred shekels of silver, and give them unto the father of the damsel, because he hath brought up an evil name upon a virgin of Israel: and she shall be his wife; he may not put her away all his days.	fine	fine	fine	fine	fine
30 A man shall not take his father's wife, nor **discover his father's skirt.**	uncover her who is his father's.	bring shame on his father.	withdraw the skirt of his father's cloak from her (23:1)	uncover his father's skirt	dishonor his father's bed
23 16 He shall dwell with thee, even among you, in that place which he shall choose in one of thy **gates,** where it **liketh him best: thou shalt not oppress him.**	towns/pleases	settlements/suits	towns/pleases	towns/pleases	town/chooses
24 11 Thou shalt stand **abroad,** and the man to whom thou dost lend shall bring out the pledge **abroad** unto thee.	outside/out	outside/out	outside/out	outside/out	outside/out
25 2 And it shall be, if the **wicked** man **be worthy** to be beaten, that the judge shall cause him to lie down, and to be beaten **before his face, according to his fault, by a certain number.**	guilty/deserves/in his presence/with a number of stripes in proportion to his offense	guilty/is sentenced/in his presence/ the number of strokes shall correspond to the gravity of the offence	who is in the wrong/deserves/ in his presence/ with the number of strokes proportionate to his offence	wicked/deserves/ in his presence/ with the number of stripes according to his guilt	guilty/deserves/in his presence/with the number of lashes his crime deserves
8 Then the elders of his city shall call him, and speak unto him: and if he **stand to it,** and say, **I like not** to take her;	persists/do not wish	still stands his ground/will not	appears before them/refuse	persists/do not desire	persists/do not want
13 Thou shalt not have in thy bag **divers** weights, a great and a small.	two kinds of	unequal	different	differing	differing

KJV	RSV	NEB	JB	NAS	NIV
26 3 And thou shalt go unto the priest **that shall be in those days,** and say unto him, I **profess** this day unto the LORD thy God, that I am come unto the country which the LORD sware unto our fathers for to give us.	who is in office at that time/declare	whoever he shall be in those days/ declare	then in office/ declare	who is in office at that time/declare	in office at the time/declare
6 And the Egyptians **evil entreated us,** and afflicted us, and laid upon us hard bondage:	treated us harshly	ill-treated us	ill-treated us	treated us harshly	mistreated us
27 16 Cursed be he that **setteth light** by his father or his mother. And all the people shall say, Amen.	dishonors	slights	treats . . . dishon-orably	dishonors	dishonors
28 26 And thy carcase shall be meat unto all fowls of the air, and unto the beasts of the earth, and no man shall **fray** them away.	frighten	scare	scare	frighten	frighten
27 The LORD will smite thee with the **botch** of Egypt, and with the **emerods,** and with the **scab,** and with the itch, whereof thou canst not be healed.	boils/ulcers/ scurvy	boils/tumours/ scabs	boils/swellings in the groin/scurvy	boils/tumors/scab	boils/tumors/fes-tering sores
53 And thou shalt eat the **fruit** of thine own body, the flesh of thy sons and of thy daughters, which the LORD thy God hath given thee, in the siege, and in the **straitness,** wherewith thine enemies shall distress thee:	offspring/distress	children/dire straits	fruit/distress	offspring/distress	fruit/suffering
29 19 And it come to pass, when he heareth the words of this **curse,** that he bless himself in his heart, saying, I shall **have peace,** though I walk in the **imagination** of mine heart, **to add drunkenness to thirst:**	sworn covenant/ be safe/stubborn-ness/This would lead to the sweeping away of moist and dry alike	oath/be well/ promptings/but this will bring everything to ruin	sanctions/(may follow the dic-tates of my heart and lack nothing)/much water drives away thirst	curse/have peace/ stubbornness/in order to destroy the watered land with the dry	oath/be safe/ (going my own way)/This will bring disaster on the watered land as well as the dry.
30 18 I **denounce** unto you this day, that ye shall surely perish, and that ye shall not prolong your days upon the land, whither thou passest over Jordan to go to possess it.	declare	tell	tell	declare	declare
32 2 My **doctrine** shall drop as the rain, my speech shall distil as the dew, as the **small rain** upon the tender **herb,** and as the showers upon the **grass:**	teaching/gentle rain/grass/herb	teaching/fine rain/ grass young plants	teaching/showers/ grass/turf	teaching/droplets/ grass/herb	teaching/showers/ grass/tender plants
3 Because I will **publish** the name of the LORD: ascribe ye greatness unto our God.	proclaim	call aloud	proclaim	proclaim	proclaim
8 When the Most High divided to the nations their inheritance, when he sepa-rated the **sons of Adam,** he set the bounds of the people according to the number of the **children of Israel.**	sons of men/sons of God	all mankind/sons of God	sons of men/sons of God	sons of man/sons of Israel	all mankind/sons of Israel
14 Butter of kine, and milk of sheep, with fat of lambs, and rams of the breed of Bashan, and goats, with **the fat of kidneys of wheat;** and thou didst drink the pure blood of the grape.	the finest of wheat	the finest flour of wheat	rich food of the wheat's ear	the finest of the wheat	the finest kernels of wheat
20 And he said, I will hide my face from them, I will see what their end shall be: for they are a **very froward** generation, children in whom is no faith.	perverse	mutinous	deceitful	perverse	perverse
36 For the LORD shall **judge** his people, and **repent himself** for his servants, when he seeth that their power is gone, and **there is none shut up, or left.**	vindicate/have compassion on/ there is none re-maining, bond or free	give. . .justice/ have compassion on/alone, or de-fended by his clan, no one is left	see. . .righted/ take pity on/serf or freeman, there is not one remaining	vindicate/have compassion on/ there is none re-maining, bond or free	judge/have com-passion on/no one is left, slave or free
41 If I whet my glittering sword, and mine hand take hold on judgment; I will					

	KJV	RSV	NEB	JB	NAS	NIV
	render vengeance to mine **enemies,** and will **reward** them that hate me.	adversaries/ requite	adversaries/take vengeance	foes/repay	adversaries/repay	adversaries/repay

Joshua

	KJV	RSV	NEB	JB	NAS	NIV
	4 From the wilderness and this Lebanon even unto the great river, the river Euphrates, all the land of the Hittites, and unto the great sea toward the going down of the sun, shall be your **coast.**	territory	land	territory	territory	territory
2	20 And if thou utter this our business, then we will be **quit of** thine oath which thou hast made us to swear.	guiltless with respect to	quit of	free of	free from	released from
3	15 And as they that bare the ark were come unto Jordan, and the feet of the priests that bare the ark were dipped in the **brim** of the water, (for Jordan overfloweth all his banks all the time of harvest,)	brink	edge	(omits)	edge	edge
	16 That the waters which came down from above stood and rose up upon an heap **very far from the city Adam,** that is beside Zaretan: and those that came down toward the sea of the **plain, even the salt sea, failed, and were cut off:** and the people passed over right against Jericho.	far off, at Adam, the city/Arabah, the Salt Sea, were wholly cut off	a long way back, as far as Adam/ Arabah, the Dead Sea, were completely cut off	a wide space from Adam/Arabah; that is, the Salt Sea, stopped running together	A great distance away at Adam, the city/Arabah, the Salt Sea, were completely cut off	a great distance away, at a town called Adam/Arabah (the Salt Sea) was completely cut off
	17 And the priests that bare the ark of the covenant of the LORD stood firm on dry ground in the midst of Jordan, and all the Israelites passed over on dry ground, until all the **people were passed clean over Jordan.**	nation finished passing over Jordan	the whole nation had crossed the river	the whole nation had finished its crossing of the river	all the nation had finished crossing the Jordan	whole nation had completed the crossing on dry ground
4	1 And it came to pass, when all the people **were clean passed** over Jordan, that the LORD spake unto Joshua, saying,	had finished passing	had finished crossing	had finished crossing	had finished crossing	had finished crossing
	11 And it came to pass, when all the people were **clean passed over,** that the ark of the LORD passed over, and the priests, in the presence of the people.	had finished passing	had finished crossing	were all over	had finished crossing	had crossed
6	1 Now Jericho was **straitly** shut up because of the children of Israel: none went out, and none came in.	from within and from without	(bolted and barred)	carefully (barricaded)	tightly	tightly
	3 And ye shall **compass** the city, all ye men of war, and go round about the city once. Thus shalt thou do six days.	march around	march around	march around	march around	March around
	17 And the city shall be **accursed,** even it, and all that are therein, to the LORD: only Rahab the harlot shall live, she and all that are with her in the house, because she hid the messengers that we sent.	devoted . . . for destruction	under solemn ban	set apart . . . under a ban	under the ban	devoted
	18 And ye, in any wise keep yourselves from the **accursed** thing, lest ye make yourselves **accursed,** when ye take of the **accursed** thing, and make the camp of Israel a **curse,** and trouble it.	devoted to destruction/lest when you have devoted them/ devoted/thing for destruction	forbidden under the ban/you must take none of it for yourselves/under the ban	ban/do not be covetous and take/ that is under the ban/open to the same ban	under the ban/lest you covet them/ under the ban/accursed	devoted/so that you will not bring about your own destruction by taking any of them/ liable to destruction
7	1 But the children of Israel committed a trespass in the **accursed thing:** for Achan, the son of Carmi, the son of Zabdi, the son of Zerah, of the tribe of	devoted things/devoted	ban/forbidden	ban/that fell under the ban	things under the ban/under the ban	devoted things/ (some of them)

KJV	RSV	NEB	JB	NAS	NIV
Judah, took of the **accursed** thing: and the anger of the LORD was kindled against the children of Israel.					
9 For the Canaanites and all the inhabitants of the land shall hear of it, and shall **environ us round,** and cut off our name from the earth: and what wilt thou do unto thy great name?	surround us	come swarming around us	unite against us	surround us	surround us
11 Israel hath sinned, and they have also transgressed my covenant which I commanded them: for they have even taken of the **accursed** thing, and have also stolen, and dissembled also, and they have put it even among their own stuff.	devoted	forbidden	under the ban	under the ban	devoted
12 Therefore the children of Israel could not stand before their enemies, but turned their backs before their enemies, because they **were accursed:** neither will I be with you any more, except ye destroy the **accursed** from among you.	have become a thing for destruction/devoted things	have brought themselves under the ban/every single thing . . . that is forbidden under the ban	have come under the ban/what is under the ban	have become accursed/things under the ban	have been made liable to destruction/whatever . . . is devoted to destruction
13 Up, sanctify the people, and say, Sanctify yourselves against tomorrow: for thus saith the LORD God of Israel, There is an **accursed thing** in the midst of thee, O Israel: thou canst not stand before thine enemies, until ye take away the **accursed thing** from among you.	devoted things/devoted things	forbidden things/them	ban/ban	things under the ban/things under the ban	That which is devoted/it
15 And it shall be, that he that is taken with the **accursed** thing shall be burnt with fire, he and all that he hath: because he hath transgressed the covenant of the LORD, and because he hath wrought folly in Israel.	devoted	forbidden	that is banned	under the ban	devoted
21 When I saw among the spoils a **goodly Babylonish garment,** and two hundred shekels of silver, and a wedge of gold of fifty shekels weight, then I coveted them, and took them; and, behold, they are hid in the earth in the midst of my tent, and the silver under it.	beautiful mantle from Shinar	fine mantle from Shinar	fine robe from Shinar	beautiful mantle from Shinar	beautiful robe from Babylonia
8 2 And thou shalt do to Ai and her king as thou didst unto Jericho and her king: only the spoil thereof, and the cattle thereof, shall ye take for a **prey** unto yourselves: lay thee an ambush for the city behind it.	booty	(omits)	booty	plunder	(omits)
35 There was not a word of all that Moses commanded, which Joshua read not before all the **congregation** of Israel, with the women, and the little ones, and the **strangers** that were **conversant** among them.	assembly/sojourners/lived	congregation/aliens/resident	assembly/strangers/living	assembly/strangers/were living	assembly/aliens/lived
9 4 They did work **wilily,** and went and made **as if they had been ambassadors,** and took old sacks upon their asses, and **wine bottles,** old, and rent, and bound up;	with cunning/ready provisions/wineskins	a ruse/(disguised themselves)/wine-skins	trickery/(set out provided with supplies)/wineskins	craftily/as envoys/wineskins	a ruse/as a delegation/wineskins
5 And **old shoes and clouted** upon their feet, and old garments upon them; and all the bread of their provision was dry and mouldy.	worn-out, patched sandals	old and patched sandals	sandals . . . were worn out and patched	worn-out and patched sandals	worn and patched sandals
13 And these **bottles of wine,** which we filled, were new; and, behold, they be **rent:** and these our garments and our shoes are become old by reason of the very long journey.	wineskins / burst	wine-skins / all rent	wineskins / burst	wineskins / torn	wineskins / cracked
11 6 And the LORD said unto Joshua, Be not afraid because of them: for to-morrow					

KJV	RSV	NEB	JB	NAS	NIV
about this time will I deliver them up all slain before Israel: thou shalt **hock** their horses, and burn their chariots with fire.	hamstring	hamstring	hamstring	hamstring	hamstring
9 And Joshua did unto them as the LORD bade him: he **hocked** their horses, and burnt their chariots with fire.	hamstrung	hamstrung	hamstrung	hamstrung	hamstrung
14 12 Now therefore give me this mountain, whereof the LORD spake in that day; for thou heardest in that day how the Anakims were there, and that the cities were great and **fenced; if so be the** LORD will be with me, then I shall be able to drive them out, as the LORD said.	fortified . . . it may be	well fortified. Perhaps	strong. If	fortified . . . perhaps	fortified, but
15 8 And the border went up by the valley of the son of Hinnom unto the south side of the Jebusite; the same is Jerusalem; and the border went up to the top of the mountain that lieth before the valley of Hinnom westward, which is at the end of the **valley of the giants** northward:	valley of Rephaim (also 18:16)	Vale of Rephaim (also 18:16)	plain of Rephaim (18:16—plain of the Rephaim)	valley of Rephaim (also 18:16)	Valley of Rephaim (also 18:16)
17 9 And the **coast** descended unto the river Kanah, southward of the river: these cities of Ephraim are among the cities of Manasseh: the **coast** of Manasseh also was on the north side of the river, and the **outgoings** of it were at the sea:	boundary/boundary/ends	boundary / boundary / limit	boundary / (omits) / end(ed)	border / border / end(ed)	boundary / boundary / end(ed)
18 But the mountain shall be thine; for t is a wood, and thou shalt cut it down; and the **outgoings** of it shall be thine: for thou shalt drive out the Canaanites, though they have iron chariots, and though they be strong.	its farthest borders	its furthest limits	boundaries	is farthest borders	its farthest limits
20 7 And they appointed Kedesh in Galilee in **mount** Naphtali, and Shechem in **mount** Ephraim, and Kirjatharba, which is Hebron, in the **mountain** of Judah.	the hill country of/ the hill country of/ hill country	the hill-country of/ the hill-country of/ hill-country	the highlands of/ the highlands of/ highlands	the hill country of/ the hill country of/ hill country	the hill country of/ the hill country of/ hill country
9 These were the cities **appointed** for all the children of Israel, and for the stranger that sojourneth among them, that whosoever killeth any person **at unawares** might flee thither, and not die by the hand of the avenger of blood, until he stood before the congregation.	designated/without intent	appointed/ inadvertently	marked out/accidentally	appointed/ unintentionally	designated/accidentally
22 19 Notwithstanding, if the land of your possession be unclean, then pass ye over unto the land of the possession of the LORD, wherein the LORD'S tabernacle dwelleth, and take possession among us: but rebel not against the LORD, nor rebel against us, in building you an altar **beside** the altar of the LORD our God.	other than	apart from	to vie with	besides	other than
20 Did not Achan the son of Zerah commit a trespass in the **accursed thing,** and wrath fell on all the congregation of Israel? and that man perished not alone in his iniquity.	devoted things	ban	ban	things under the ban	devoted things
29 **God forbid** that we should rebel against the LORD, and turn this day from following the LORD, to build an altar for burnt offerings, for **meat** offerings, or for sacrifices, **beside** the altar of the LORD our God that is before his tabernacle.	Far be it/cereal/ other than	God forbid/grain/ in/addition to	(We have no intention)/ oblations/to vie with	Far be it/grain/ besides	Far be it/grain/ other than
24 2 And Joshua said unto all the people, Thus saith the LORD God of Israel, Your fathers dwelt **on the other side of the flood** in old time, even Terah, the father of Abraham, and the father of Nachor: and they served other gods.	beyond the Euphrates (vs. 3—beyond the River, also vs. 15)	beside the Euphrates (also vss. 3, 15)	beyond the River (also vss. 3, 15)	beyond the River (also vss. 3, 15)	beyond the River (also vss. 3, 15)

KJV	RSV	NEB	JB	NAS	NIV
14 Now therefore fear the LORD, and serve him in sincerity and in **truth:** and put away the gods which your fathers served **on the other side of the flood,** and in Egypt; and serve ye the LORD.	faithfulness/beyond the River	truth/beside the Euphrates	perfectly/beyond the River	truth/beyond the River	(with all faithfulness)/beyond the River
31 And Israel served the LORD all the days of Joshua, and all the days of the elders that **overlived** Joshua, and which had known all the works of the LORD, that he had done for Israel.	outlived	outlived	outlived	survived	outlived

Judges

KJV	RSV	NEB	JB	NAS	NIV
1 23 And the house of Joseph sent to **descry** Bethel. (Now the name of the city before was Luz.)	spy out	(sent spies to)	made a reconnaissance of	spied out	spy out
2 23 Therefore the LORD left those nations, without driving them out **hastily;** neither delivered he them into the **hand** of Joshua.	at once/power	(made no haste)/ hands	hurry/hands	quickly/hand	at once/hands
3 21 And Ehud put forth his left hand, and took the dagger from his right thigh, and thrust it into **his** belly.	his	his	the king's	his	the king's
23 Then Ehud went forth through the **porch,** and shut the doors of the parlour upon him, and locked them.	vestibule	porch	porch	vestibule	porch
1 24 When he was gone out, his servants came; and when they saw that, behold, the doors of the parlour were locked, they said, **Surely he covereth his feet in his summer chamber.**	"He is only relieving himself in the closet of the cool chamber."	'He must be relieving himself in the closet of his summer palace.'	'He is probably covering his feet in the inner part of the cool room'.	"He is only relieving himself in the cool room."	"He must be relieving himself in the inner room of the house."
4 11 Now Heber the Kenite, which was of the children of Hobab the father in law of Moses, had severed himself from the Kenites, and pitched his tent unto the **plain** of Zaanaim, which is by Kedesh.	oak	Elon-bezaanannim	Oak	oak	great tree
15 And the LORD **discomfited** Sisera, and all his chariots, and all his **host,** with the edge of the sword before Barak; so that Sisera lighted down off his chariot, and fled away on his feet.	routed/army	put . . . to rout/ army	struck terror into/ troops	routed/army	routed/army
17 **Howbeit** Sisera fled away on his feet to the tent of Jael the wife of Heber the Kenite: for there was peace between Jabin the king of Hazor and the house of Heber the Kenite.	But	Meanwhile	meanwhile	Now	however
5 12 Awake, awake, Deborah: awake, awake, utter a song: arise, Barak, and lead **thy captivity captive,** thou son of Abinoam.	away your captives	Take prisoners in plenty	capture your captors	take away your captives	captive your captives
17 Gilead abode beyond Jordan: and why did Dan remain in ships? Asher continued on the sea shore, and abode in his **breaches.**	landings	creeks	harbours	landings	covers
30 **Have they not sped?** have they not divided the **prey;** to every man a **damsel or two;** to Sisera a prey of divers colours, a **prey of divers colours** of needlework, of divers colours of needlework on both sides, **meet for the necks of them that take the spoil?**	Are they not finding/ prey/ maiden or two/spoil of dyed stuffs/for my neck as spoil	They must be finding/spoil/ wench . . . two wenches/booty of dyed stuffs/to grace the victor's neck	They are gathering, doubtless/ spoil/girl, two girls/garment, two dyed garments/for me	Are they not finding/spoil/ maiden, two maidens/spoil of dyed work/on the neck of the spoiler	Are they not finding/spoils/ girl or two/ colorful garments as spoil/for my neck

	KJV	RSV	NEB	JB	NAS	NIV
6	31 And Joash said unto all that stood against him, Will ye **plead** for Baal? will ye save him? he that will plead for him, let him be put to death whilst it is yet morning: if he be a god, let him plead for himself, because one hath cast down his altar.	contend	pleading	plead	contend	plead
7	13 And when Gideon was come, behold, there was a man that told a dream unto his fellow, and said, Behold, I dreamed a dream, and, lo, a cake of barley bread tumbled into the host of Midian, and came unto a tent, and smote it that it fell, and overturned it, that the tent **lay along.**	lay flat	collapsed	upside down	lay flat	collapsed
8	3 God hath delivered into your hands the princes of Midian, Oreb and Zeeb: and what was I able to do in comparison **of** you? Then their anger was abated toward him, when he had said that.	with	with	with	with	to
	11 And Gideon went up by the **way of them that dwelt in tents** on the east of Nobah and Jogbehah, and **smote the host**: for the **host was secure.**	by the caravan route/attacked the army/army was off its guard	along the track used by the tent-dwellers/attack caught the army/they were off their guard	the nomad's way/routed the army/it thought itself in safety	by the way of those who lived in tents/attacked the camp/camp was unsuspecting	by the route of the Nomads/fell upon/unsuspecting army
	12 And when Zebah and Zalmunna fled, he pursued after them, and took the two kings of Midian, Zebah and Zalmunna, and **discomfited all the host.**	threw all the army into a panic	(their whole army melted away)	destroyed the army	routed the whole army	routing their entire army
9	4 And they gave him threescore and ten pieces of silver out of the house of Baalberith, wherewith Abimelech hired **vain and light persons,** which followed him.	worthless and reckless fellows	idle and reckless men	worthless scoundrels	worthless and reckless fellows	reckless adventurers
	6 And all the men of Shechem gathered together, and all the house of Millo, and went, and made Abimelech king, by **the plain** of the pillar that was in Shechem.	the oak	propped-up terebinth	terebinth	oak	great tree
	37 And Gaal spake again and said, See there come people down by the middle of the land, and another company come along by the **plain of Meonenim.**	Diviners' Oak	Soothsayers' Terebinth	Diviners' Oak	diviners' oak	soothsayers' tree
	46 And when all the men of the tower of Shechem heard that, they entered into an **hold** of the house of **the god Berith.**	hold/El-berith	great hall/El-berith	crypt/El-berith	chamber/El-berith	hold/El-Berith
	53 And a certain woman cast a piece of a millstone upon Abimelech's head, and **all to brake** his skull.	crushed	fractured	crushed	crushing	cracked
11	33 And he smote them from Aroer, even till thou come to Minnith, even twenty cities, and unto **the plain of the vineyards,** with a very great slaughter. Thus the children of Ammon were subdued before the children of Israel.	Abel-keramim	Abel-keramim	Abel-keramim	Abel-keramim	Abel Keramim
12	6 Then said they unto him, Say now Shibboleth: and he said Sibboleth: for he could not **frame to pronounce it right.** Then they took him, and slew him at the **passages** of Jordan: and there fell at that time of the Ephraimites forty and two thousand.	pronounce it right/fords	pronounce the word properly/fords	pronounce the word correctly/fords	pronounce it correctly/fords	pronounce the word correctly/fords
	9 And he had thirty sons, and thirty daughters, whom he **sent abroad,** and took in thirty daughters **from abroad** for **his sons.** And he judged Israel seven **years.**	gave in marriage outside his clan/from outside	gave away . . . in marriage/(omits)	gave . . . in marriage outside his clan/from outside	gave in marriage outside the family/from outside	gave . . . away in marriage to those outside his clan/from outside his clan

KJV	RSV	NEB	JB	NAS	NIV
14 And he had forty sons and thirty **nephews,** that rode on threescore and ten ass colts: and he judged Israel eight years.	grandsons	grandsons	grandsons	grandsons	grandsons
13 12 And Manoah said, Now let thy words come **to pass. How shall we order the child, and how shall we do unto him?**	come true/what is to be the boy's manner of life, and what is he to do	come true/what kind of boy will he be and what will he do?	are fulfilled/what is to be the boy's rule of life? How must he behave?"	come to pass/what shall be the boy's mode of life and vocation	are fulfilled/what is to be the rule for the boy's life and work
14 14 And he said unto them, Out of the eater came **forth meat,** and out of the strong came **forth sweetness.** And they could not in three days expound the riddle.	something to eat/ something sweet	something to eat/ something sweet	what is eaten/ what is sweet	something to eat/ something sweet	something to eat/ something sweet
15 14 And when he came unto Lehi, the Philistines shouted against him: and the spirit of the LORD came mightily upon him, and the cords that were upon his arms became as flax that was burnt with fire, and his **bands loosed** from off his hands.	bonds melted	bonds melted	bonds melted	bonds dropped	bindings dropped
16 And Samson said, With the jawbone of an ass, heaps upon heaps, with the jaw of an ass have I **slain** a thousand men.	slain	slain	struck down	killed	killed
16 9 Now there were men lying in wait, abiding with her in the chamber. And she said unto him, The Philistines be upon thee, Samson. And he **brake the withs,** as a **thread of tow** is broken when it toucheth the fire. So his strength was not known.	snapped the bow-strings/string of tow	snapped the bow-strings/strand of tow	snapped the bow-strings/strand of tow	snapped the cords/ string of tow	snapped the thongs/piece of string
11 And he said unto her, If they bind me fast with new ropes that never were **occupied,** then shall I be weak, and be as another man.	used	used	used	used	used
18 3 When they were by the house of Micah, they **knew** the voice of the young man the Levite: and they turned in thither, and said unto him, Who brought thee hither? and what **makest thou** in this place? and what **hast thou** here?	recognized/are you doing/is your business	recognized/are you doing/is your business	recognized/are you doing/is keep-ing you	recognized/are you doing/do you have	recognized/are you doing/(Why) are you
7 Then the five men departed, and came to Laish, and saw the people that were therein, how they dwelt **careless,** after the manner of the Zidonians, **quiet and secure;** and there was no magistrate in the land, that might put them to shame in any thing; and they were far from the Zidonians, and had no business with any man.	in security/unsus-pecting	carefree/(a quiet, carefree folk)	in security/peace-ful and trusting	in security/quiet and secure	in safety/unsus-pecting and se-cure
11 And there went from thence of the family of the Danites, out of Zorah and out of Eshtaol, six hundred men **ap-pointed with weapons of war.**	armed with weapons of war	armed	armed for war	armed with weapons of war	armed for battle
21 So they turned and departed, and put the little ones and the cattle and the **carriage** before them.	goods	valuables	valuables	valuables	possessions
19 2 And his concubine **played the whore against him,** and went away from him unto her father's house to Bethlehemju-dah, and was there four whole months.	became angry with him	In a fit of anger (she) had left him	In a fit of anger (his concubine) left him	played the harlot against him	was unfaithful to him
6 And they sat down, and did eat and drink both of them together: for the damsel's father had said unto the man, **Be content,** I pray thee, and tarry all night, and let thine heart be merry.	Be pleased	Why not	Come, say you will	Please be willing	Please
20 41 And when the men of Israel turned again, the men of Benjamin were **amazed:** for they saw that **evil** was come upon them.	dismayed/disaster	seized with panic/ disaster	seized with ter-ror/ disaster	terrified/disaster	terrified/disaster

	KJV	RSV	NEB	JB	NAS	NIV
21	2 And the people came to **the house of God,** and **abode** there till **even** before God, and lifted up their voices, **and wept sore;**	Bethel/sat/evening/and wept bitterly	Bethel/remained/sunset/in loud lamentation	Bethel/stayed/evening/and bitter weeping	Bethel/sat/evening/and wept bitterly	Bethel/sat/evening/and weeping bitterly

Ruth

	KJV	RSV	NEB	JB	NAS	NIV
2	2 And Ruth the Moabitess said unto Naomi, Let me now go to the field, and glean ears of **corn** after him in whose sight I shall find **grace.** And she said unto her, Go, my daughter.	grain/favor	corn (fields)/favour	corn/favour	grain/favor	grain/favor
	3 And she went, and came, and gleaned in the field after the reapers: and **her hap was to light** on a part of the field belonging unto Boaz, who was of the **kindred** of Elimelech.	she happened to come/family	As it happened, she was/family	it chanced that she came/clan	she happened to come/family	she found herself/clan
	8 Then said Boaz unto Ruth, **Hearest thou not,** my daughter? Go not to glean in another field, neither go from hence, but abide here **fast by** my maidens:	Now, listen/close to	Listen to me/close to	Listen . . . and understand this/with	Listen carefully/with	listen to me/with
3	18 Then said she, **Sit still,** my daughter, until thou **know** how the matter will **fall:** for the man will not **be in** rest, until he have **finished the thing** this day.	Wait/learn/turns out/(omits)/settle the matter	Wait/see/(what will come of it)/(omits)/settled the matter	Wait/see/go/(omits)/it is settled	Wait/know/turns out/(omits)/has settled it	Wait/find out/(what happens)/(omits)/matter is settled
4	4 And I thought to **advertise thee,** saying, Buy it before the inhabitants, and before the elders of my people. If thou wilt redeem it, redeem it: but if thou wilt not redeem it, then tell me, that I may know: for there is none to redeem it beside thee; and I am after thee. And he said, I will redeem it.	tell you of it	open the matter with you	tell you about this	inform you	bring the matter to your attention
	6 And the kinsman said, I cannot redeem it for myself, lest I **mar** mine own inheritance: redeem thou my right to thyself; for I cannot redeem it.	impair	risk losing	jeopardising	jeopardize	endanger

I Samuel

	KJV	RSV	NEB	JB	NAS	NIV
1	6 And her **adversary also** provoked her **sore, for to make her fret,** because the LORD had **shut up** her womb.	rival used to/sorely/to irritate her/closed her womb	rival used to/(omits)/humiliate her/(she) had no children	rival/(omits)/to annoy her/made her barren	rival/bitterly/to irritate/closed her womb	rival kept/(omits)/in order to irritate her/closed her womb
	24 And when she had weaned him, she took him up with her with **three bullocks,** and one ephah of flour, and a **bottle of wine,** and brought him unto the house of the LORD in Shiloh: and the child was young.	a three-year-old bull/skin of wine	a bull three years old/flagon of wine	a three-year old bull/skin of wine	a three-year-old bull/jug of wine	a three-year-old bull/skin of wine
2	13 And the priests' custom with the people was, that, when any man offered sacrifice, the priest's servant came, while the **flesh** was **in seething,** with a **fleshhook of three teeth** in his hand;	meat/boiling/three-pronged fork	flesh/stewing/three-pronged fork	meat/being cooked/three-pronged fork	meat/boiling/three-pronged fork	meat/being boiled/three-pronged fork
	15 Also before they burnt the fat, the priest's servant came, and said to the man that sacrificed, Give **flesh** to roast for the priest; for he will not have **sodden flesh of thee, but raw.**	meat/boiled meat	meat/what has already been stewed	meat/boiled meat	meat/boiled meat	meat/boiled meat

	KJV	RSV	NEB	JB	NAS	NIV
	16 And if any man said unto him, Let them not fail to burn the fat **presently,** and then take as much as **thy soul desireth;** then he would answer him, Nay; but thou shalt give it me now: and if not, I will take it by force.	first/you wish	first/you want	first/you wish	first/you desire	first/you want
	17 Wherefore the sin of the young men was very great before the LORD: for men **abhorred** the offering of the LORD.	treated . . . with contempt	brought . . . into general contempt	treated . . . with contempt	despised	were treating . . . with contempt
3	1 And the **child** Samuel ministered unto the LORD **before** Eli. And the word of the LORD was **precious** in those days; **there was no open vision.**	boy/under/rare/there was no frequent vision	child/under/seldom heard/no vision was granted	boy/in the presence of/rare/visions were uncommon	boy/before/rare/visions were infrequent	boy/under/rare/there were not many visions
	2 And it came to pass at that time, when Eli was laid down in his place, and his eyes began to **wax** dim, that he could not see;	grow	(were dim)	grow	grow	(becoming so weak)
6	5 Wherefore ye shall make images of your **emerods,** and images of your mice that **mar** the land; and ye shall give glory unto the God of Israel: peradventure he will lighten his hand from off you, and from off your gods, and from off your land.	tumors/ravage	tumours/ravaging	tumours/ravage	tumors/ravage	tumors/are destroying
8	5 And said unto him, Behold, thou art old, and thy sons walk not in thy ways: now **make** us a king to **judge** us like all the nations.	appoint/govern	appoint/govern	give/rule	appoint/judge	appoint/lead
	12 And he will appoint him captains over thousands, and captains over fifties; and will set them to **ear** his ground, and to reap his harvest, and to make his instruments of war, and instruments of his chariots.	plow	plough	plough	do. . .plowing	plow
	13 And he will take your daughters to be **confectionaries,** and to be cooks, and to be bakers.	perfumers	perfumers, (cooks, and confectioners)	perfumers	perfumers	perfumers
	21 And Samuel heard all the words of the people, and he **rehearsed** them in the ears of the LORD.	repeated	told	repeated	repeated	repeated
9	5 And when they were come to the land of Zuph, Saul said to his servant that was with him, Come, and let us **return;** lest my father **leave caring** for the asses, and **take thought** for us.	go back/cease to care/become anxious	turn back/will stop thinking/begin to worry	go back/will stop worrying/start being anxious	return/cease to be concerned/become anxious	go back/will stop thinking/start worrying
	6 And he said unto him, Behold now, there is in this city a man of God, and he is an **honourable man;** all that he saith cometh surely to pass: now let us go thither; peradventure he can shew us **our way that we should go.**	man that is held in honor/about the journey on which we have set out	who has a great reputation/about this errand of ours	man held in honour/on the journey we have undertaken	the man is held in honor/about our journey on which we have set out	highly respected/what way to take
10	3 Then shalt thou go on forward from thence, and thou shalt come to the plain of **Tabor,** and there shall meet thee three men going up to God to Bethel, one carrying three kids, and another carrying three loaves of bread, and another carrying a **bottle of wine:**	oak/skin of wine	terebinth/flagon of wine	Oak/skin of wine	oak/jug of wine	great tree/skin of wine
	22 Therefore they inquired of the LORD further, if the man should yet come thither. And the LORD answered, Behold, he hath hid himself among the **stuff.**	baggage	baggage	baggage	baggage	baggage
13	23 And the garrison of the Philistines went out to the **passage** of Michmash.	pass	pass	Pass	pass	pass

	KJV	RSV	NEB	JB	NAS	NIV
14	8 Then said Jonathan, Behold, we will pass over **unto** these men, and we will **discover ourselves unto them.**	to/show ourselves to them	(omits)/let them see us	to/let ourselves be seen	to/reveal ourselves to them	toward/let them see us
	11 And both of them **discovered** themselves unto the garrison of the Philistines: and the Philistines said, Behold, the Hebrews come forth out of the holes where they had hid themselves.	showed	showed	let themselves be seen	revealed	showed
	20 And Saul and all the people that were with him **assembled themselves,** and they came to the battle: and, behold, every man's sword was against his fellow, and there was a very great **discomfiture.**	rallied/confusion	with shouting/ disorder	formed up/ confusion	rallied/confusion	assembled/ confusion
	41 Therefore Saul said unto the LORD God of Israel, **Give a perfect lot.** And Saul and Jonathan were taken: but the people escaped.	". . . Why has thou not answered thy servant this day. If this guilt is in me or in Jonathan my son . . . give Urim; but if this guilt is in thy people Israel, give Thummin."	'Why hast thou not answered thy servant today? If this guilt lie on me or in my son Jonathan, let the lot be Urim; if it lie in thy people Israel, let it be Thummin.'	'. . . why did you not answer your servant to-day? If the fault lies on me or my son Jonathan . . . , give Urim; if the fault lies on your people Israel, give Thummin.'	"Give a perfect lot."	"Give me the right answer."
15	32 Then said Samuel, Bring ye hither to me Agag the king of the Amalekites. And Agag came unto him **delicately.** And Agag said, Surely the bitterness of death is past.	cheerfully	with faltering step	reluctantly	cheerfully	confidently
	33 And Samuel said, "As thy sword hath made women childless, so shall thy mother be childless among women. And Samuel **hewed Agag in pieces** before the LORD in Gilgal.	hewed Agag in pieces	hewed Agag in pieces	butchered Agag	hewed Agag to pieces	put Agag to death
16	16 Let our lord now command thy servants, which are before thee, to seek out a man, who **is a cunning player on an harp:** and it shall come to pass, when the evil spirit from God is upon thee, that he shall play with his hand, and thou shalt be well.	is skilful in playing the lyre	can play the harp	a skilled harpist	is a skilful player on the harp	can play the harp
	18 Then answered one of the servants, and said, Behold, I have seen a son of Jesse the Bethlehemite, that **is cunning in playing,** and a mighty valiant man, and a man of war, and prudent in matters, and a **comely** person, and the LORD is with him.	is skilful in/man of good presence	can play/handsome	is a skilled player/ man of presence	is a skillful musician/handsome man	knows how to play the harp/fine-looking man
	20 And Jesse took an ass laden with bread, and a **bottle of wine,** and a kid, and sent them by David his son unto Saul.	skin of wine	skin of wine	skin of wine	jug of wine	skin of wine
17	6 And he had greaves of **brass** upon his legs, and a **target of brass** between his shoulders.	bronze/javelin of bronze	bronze/dagger of bronze	bronze/bronze javelin	bronze/bronze javelin	bronze/bronze javelin
	7 And the **staff** of his spear was like a weaver's beam; and his spear's head weighed six hundred shekels of iron: and **one bearing a shield** went before him.	shaft/his shield-bearer	shaft/his shield-bearer	shaft/a shield-bearer	shaft/his shield-carrier	shaft/his shield bearer
	12 Now David was the son of that Ephrathite of Bethlehemjudah, whose name was Jesse; and he had eight sons: and the man **went among men for an old man** in the days of Saul.	was already old and advanced in years	had become a feeble old man	was old and well on in years	was old . . . , advanced in years among men	was old and well-advanced in years
	22 And David left his **carriage** in the hand of the **keeper of the carriage, and** ran into the **army,** and came and **saluted** his brethren.	things/keeper of the baggage/ ranks/greeted	things/quarter-master/line/greet	bundle/baggage guard/battle line/ ask . . . how they were	baggage/baggage keeper/battle line/ greet	things/keeper of supplies/battle lines/greeted

KJV	RSV	NEB	JB	NAS	NIV
28 And Eliab his eldest brother heard when he spake unto the men; and Eliab's anger was kindled against David, and he said, Why camest thou down hither? and with whom hast thou left those few sheep in the wilderness? I know thy **pride,** and the **naughtiness of thine** heart; for thou art come down that thou mightest see the battle.	presumption/evil	(I know you, you impudent young rascal)	insolence/wicked	insolence/wickedness of your	how conceited (you are)/ how wicked (your heart is)
31 And when the words were heard which David spake, they **rehearsed** them before Saul: and he sent for him.	repeated	reported	reported	told	reported
39 And David girded his sword upon his armour, and he **assayed to go;** for he **had not proved it.** And David said unto Saul, I cannot go with these; for I have not proved them. And David put them off him.	tried in vain to go/ was not used to them	hesitated/had not tried them	found he could not walk/not being used to these things	tried to walk/had not tested them	tried walking around/was not used to them
40 And he took his staff in his hand, and chose him five smooth stones out of the brook, and put them in a shepherd's bag which he had, **even in a scrip;** and his sling was in his hand: and he drew near to the Philistine.	or wallet	which served as a pouch	in his pouch	even in his pouch	(the pouch of his shepherd's bag)
18 11 And Saul cast the javelin; for he said, I will smite David even to the wall with it. And David **avoided out of his presence** twice.	evaded him	swerved aside	evaded him	escaped from his presence	eluded him
21 And Saul said, I will give him her, that she may be a snare to him, and that the hand of the Philistines may be against him. Wherefore Saul said to David, Thou shalt this day be my son in law **in the one of the twain.**	a second time	a second time	Twice	"For a second time	("Now you have a second opportunity to become my son-in-law.")
30 Then the princes of the Philistines went forth: and it came to pass, after they **went forth,** that David **behaved himself more wisely** than all the servants of Saul; so that **his name was much set by.**	came out/had more success/his name was highly esteemed	come out/had more success against them/he won a great name for himself	went out/was more successful/ his name was held in great honour	went out/behaved himself more wisely/his name was highly esteemed	go out/met with more success/his name became well known
19 4 And Jonathan spake good of David unto Saul his father, and said unto him, Let not the king sin against his servant, against David; because he hath not sinned against thee, and because his **works have been to thee-ward very good:**	deeds have been of good service to you	conduct towards you has been beyond reproach	what he has done has been greatly to your advantage	deeds have been very beneficial to you	what he has done has benefited you greatly
20 30 Then Saul's anger was kindled against Jonathan, and he said unto him, Thou son of the perverse rebellious woman, do not I know that thou hast chosen the son of Jesse to thine own **confusion,** and unto the **confusion** of thy mother's nakedness?	shame/shame	shame/dishonour	disgrace/disgrace	shame/shame	shame/shame
40 And Jonathan gave his **artillery** unto his lad, and said unto him, Go, carry them to the city.	weapons	weapons	weapons	weapons	weapons
22 4 And he **brought them before** the king of Moab: and they dwelt with him all the while that David was in the **hold.**	left them with/ stronghold	left them at/ stronghold	left them with/ stronghold	left them with/ stronghold	left them with/ stronghold
14 Then Ahimelech answered the king, and said, And who is so faithful among all thy servants as David, which is the king's son in law, and **goeth at thy bidding,** and is honourable in thine house?	captain over your bodyguard	appointed to your staff	captain of your bodyguard	captain over your guard	captain of your bodyguard
23 Abide thou with me, fear not: for he that seeketh my life seeketh thy life: but					

	KJV	RSV	NEB	JB	NAS	NIV
	with me thou shalt be **in safeguard.**	in safekeeping	safe	safe	safe	safe
24	4 And the men of David said unto him, Behold the day of which the LORD said unto thee, Behold, I will deliver thine enemy into thine hand, that thou mayest do to him as it shall seem good unto thee. Then David arose, and cut off the skirt of Saul's robe **privily.**	steathily	stealthily	unobserved	secretly	unnoticed
25	15 But the men were very good unto us, and we were not hurt, neither missed we any thing, as long as we **were conversant with them,** when we were in the fields:	went with them	were going about with them	were in their neighborhood	went about with them	were . . . near them
	24 And fell at his feet, and said, Upon me, my lord, upon me let this iniquity be: and let thine handmaid, I pray thee, speak **in thine audience,** and hear the words of thine handmaid.	in your ears	(let my lord give me a hearing)	in your ear	to you	to you
27	10 And Achish said, **Whither** have ye made a **road** today? And David said, Against the **south** of Judah, and against the **south** of the Jerahmeelites, and against the **south** of the Kenites.	Against whom/raid/ Negeb/Negeb/ Negeb	Where/raid/ Negeb/Negeb/ Negeb	Where/go raid-ing/Negeb/Negeb/ Negeb	Where/raid/ Negev/Negev/ Negev	Where/go raid-ing/Negev/ Negev/Negev
28	7 Then said Saul unto his servants, Seek me a woman **that hath a familiar spirit,** that I may go to her, and inquire of her. And his servants said to him, Behold, there is a woman that hath a familiar spirit at Endor.	who is a medium	who has a familiar spirit	who is a necromancer	who is a medium	who is a medium
	23 But he refused, and said, I will not eat. But his servants, together with the woman, **compelled** him; and he hearkened unto their voice. So he arose from the earth, and sat upon the bed.	urged	pressing	pressed	urged	urging
30	24 For who will **hearken unto** you in this matter? but as his **part** is that goeth down to the battle, so shall his **part** be **that tarrieth by the stuff:** they shall **part** alike.	listen to/share/share/ who stays by the baggage/share	agree to (what you propose)/the same share/who stayed with the stores/share	agree with/ share/share/who stays with the baggage/share	listen to/share/share/ who stays by the baggage/share	listen to/share/same who stayed with the supplies/share
31	9 And they cut off his head, and stripped off his armour, and sent [] into the land of the Philistines round about, to **publish** it in the house of their idols, and among the people.	messengers/carry	messengers/take	it/proclaim	them/carry	messengers/proclaim

II Samuel

	KJV	RSV	NEB	JB	NAS	NIV
1	9 He said unto me again, Stand, I pray thee, **upon** me, and slay me: for **anguish is come upon me, because my life is yet whole in me.**	beside/anguish has seized/yet my life still lingers	over/throes of death have seized/I still live	over/giddiness has come on me/ though my life is wholly in me still	beside/agony has seized/because my life still lingers in me	over/I am in the throes of death/but I'm still alive
	21 Ye mountains of Gilboa, let there be no dew, neither let there be rain, upon you, **nor fields of offerings:** for there the shield of the mighty is vilely cast away, the shield of Saul, as though he had not been anointed with oil.	nor upsurging of the deep	no showers on the uplands	treacherous fields	nor fields of offerings	nor fields that yield offerings of grain
2	21 And Abner said to him, turn thee aside to thy right hand or to thy left, and **lay thee hold on** one of the young men, and take thee his **armour.** But Asahel would not turn aside from following **of** him.	seize/spoil/(omits)	tackle/belt/(omits)	catch/spoil/(omits)	take hold of/spoil/ (omits)	take on/weapons/(omits)
3	10 To **translate** the kingdom from the house of Saul, and to set up the throne of	transfer	bring down	take	transfer	transfer

	KJV	RSV	NEB	JB	NAS	NIV
	David over Israel and over Judah, from Dan even to Beersheba.					
5	23 And when David inquired of the LORD, he said, Thou shalt not go up; but **fetch a compass** behind them, and come upon them over against the **mulberry** trees.	go around/balsam	wheel round/aspens	go round/balsam	circle around/ balsam	circle around/ balsam
6	5 And David and all the house of Israel **played** before the LORD on all manner of instruments made of fir wood, even on harps, and on **psalteries,** and on **timbrels,** and on **cornets,** and on cymbals.	were making merry/lyres/tambourines/ castanets	danced for joy / lutes/ tambourines/ castanets	danced/lyres/ tambourines/ castanets	were celebrating/ lyres/tambourines/castanets	were celebrating/ lyres tambourines/ sistrums
	19 And he **dealt** among all the people, even among the whole multitude of Israel, as well to the women as men, to every one a cake of bread, and a good piece of flesh, and a **flagon of wine.** So all the people departed every one to his house.	distributed/cake of raisins	gave/cake of raisins	distributed/raisin cake	distributed/one (a cake) of raisins	gave/cake of raisins
8	4 And David took from him a **thousand chariots,** and **seven hundred horsemen,** and twenty thousand footmen: and David **hocked** all the chariot horses, but reserved of them for an hundred chariots.	thousand and seven hundred horsemen/hamstrung	seventeen hundred horse/hamstrung	one thousand seven hundred charioteers/hamstrung	1,700 horsemen/ hamstrung	a thousand of his chariots, seven thousand charioteers/hamstrung
	5 And when the Syrians of Damascus came to **succour** Hadadezer king of Zobah, David slew of the Syrians two and twenty thousand men.	help	help	help	help	help
9	3 And the king said, Is there not yet any of the house of Saul, that I may shew the kindness of God unto him? And Ziba said unto the king, Jonathan hath yet a son, **which is lame on his feet.**	he is crippled in his feet	he is a cripple, lame in both feet	a man with crippled feet	who is crippled in both feet	he is crippled in both feet
12	4 And there came a traveller unto the rich man, and he **spared to take of** his own flock and of his own herd, to **dress** for the **wayfaring man** that was come unto him; but took the poor man's lamb, and dressed it for the man that was come to him.	was unwilling to take one of/preparer/wayfarer	too mean to take something from/ serve/guest	refused to take one of/prepare/ wayfarer	unwilling to take from/prepare/ wayfarer	refrained from taking one of/prepare/traveler
	14 **Howbeit,** because by this deed thou hast **given great occasion to the enemies of the LORD to blaspheme,** the child also that is born unto thee shall surely die.	Nevertheless/utterly scorned the Lord	because/shown your contempt for the Lord	Yet/outraged Yahweh	However/given occasion to the enemies of the Lord to blaspheme	But/made the enemies of the Lord show utter contempt
	20 Then David arose from the earth, and washed, and anointed himself, and changed his apparel, and came into the house of the LORD, and worshipped: then he came to his own house; and when **he required,** they set bread before him, and he did eat.	asked	asked	asked	requested	(at his request)
13	6 So Amnon lay down, and **made himself** sick: and when the king was come to see him, Amnon said unto the king, I pray thee, let Tamar my sister come, and make me a couple of cakes in my sight, that I may eat at her hand.	pretended to be	pretended to be	pretended to be	pretended to be	pretended to be
	25 And the king said to Absalom, Nay, my son, let us not all now go, lest we be **chargeable** unto thee. And he pressed him: howbeit he would not go, but blessed him.	burdensome	a burden	a burden	burdensome	a burden
14	20 **To fetch about this form of speech** hath thy servant Joab done this thing: and my lord is wise, according to the wisdom of an angel of God, to know all things that are in the earth.	In order to change the course of affairs	to give a new turn to this affair	to disguise the matter	in order to change the appearance of things	to change the present situation
	26 And when he **polled** his head, (for it was at every year's end that he **polled** it:	cut/cut/cut	cut/(omits)/ (omits)	cut/cut/cut	cut/cut/cut	cut/cut/(omits)

	KJV	RSV	NEB	JB	NAS	NIV
	because the hair was heavy on him, therefore he **polled** it:) he weighed the hair of his head at two hundred shekels after the king's weight.					
16	1 And when David was a little past the top of the hill, behold, Ziba the servant of Mephibosheth met him, with a couple of asses saddled, and upon them two hundred loaves of bread, and an hundred bunches of raisins, and an hundred of summer fruits, and a **bottle of wine.**	skin of wine	flagon of wine	skin of wine	jug of wine	skin of wine
	17 Now Jonathan and Ahimaaz stayed by Enrogel; for they might not be seen to come into the city: and a **wench went** and told them; and they went and told king David.	maidservant used to go	servant girl would go	maidservant was to go	maidservant would go	servant girl was to go
18	3 But the **people answered,** Thou shalt not go **forth:** for if we flee away, they will not care for us; neither if half of us die, will they care for us: but now thou **art** worth ten thousand of us: therefore now it is better that thou **succour** us out of the city.	men said/go out/ help	they said/come out/(remain in the city in support)	troops replied/go /reinforce	people said/go out /help	men said/go out/ support
19	7 Now therefore arise, go forth, and **speak comfortably** unto thy servants: for I swear by the LORD, if thou go not forth, there will not tarry one with thee this night: and that will be worse unto thee than all the evil that befell thee from thy youth until now.	speak kindly	give . . . some encouragement	reassure	speak kindly	encourage
	13 And say ye to Amasa, Art thou not of my bone, and of my flesh? God do so to me, and more also, if thou be not **captain of the host** before me continually in the **room** of Joab.	commander of my army/place	my commander-in-chief/place	my army commander/place	commander of the army/place	commander of my army/place
	32 Now Barzillai was a very aged man, even fourscore years old: and he had **provided the king of sustenance** while he **lay** at Mahanaim; for he was a very **great** man.	provided the king with food/stayed/ wealthy	provided for the king/was/standing	kept the king in provisions/stay/rich	maintained the king/stayed/great	provided for the king/stay/wealthy
	42 And all the men of Judah answered the men of Israel, Because the king is near of kin to us: wherefore then be ye angry for this matter? have we eaten at all of **the king's cost?** or hath he given us any gift?	at the king's expense	at the king's expense	at the king's expense	at the king's expense	at the king's provisions
20	6 And David said to Abishai, Now shall Sheba the son of Bichri do us more harm than did Absalom: take thou thy lord's servants, and pursue after him, lest he get him **fenced** cities, and **escape** us.	fortified/cause us trouble	fortified/escape us	fortified/elude us	fortified/escape from our sight	fortified/escape from us
	15 And they came and besieged him in Abel of Bethmaachah, and they cast up a **bank** against the city, and it stood in the trench: and all the people that were with Joab battered the wall, to throw it down.	mound	siege-ramp	earthworks	mound	siege ramp
21	14 And the bones of Saul and Jonathan his son buried they in the country of Benjamin in Zelah, in the sepulchre of Kish his father; and they performed all that the king commanded. And after that God **was entreated** for the land.	heeded supplications	was entreated to accept prayers	too pity	was moved by entreaty	answered prayer
	17 But Abishai the son of Zeruiah **succoured** him, and **smote** the Philistine, and killed him. Then the men of David **sware unto** him, saying, thou shalt go no more out with us to battle, that thou quench not the **light** of Israel.	came to his aid/ attacked/adjured/lamp	came to David's help/ struck/took an oath/lamp	went to his rescue/ struck down/urged/lamp	helped him/struck/swore to/lamp	came to David's rescue/ struck . . . down/ swore to/lamp
22	6 The **sorrows of hell compassed me about;** the snares of death **prevented me;**	cords of Sheol entangled me/con-	bonds of Sheol tightened about	cords of Sheol girdled me/were	cords of Sheol surrounded	cords of the grave coiled

	KJV	RSV	NEB	JB	NAS	NIV
		fronted me	me/were set to catch me	before me	me/confronted me	around me/con- fronted me
	16 And the channels of the sea appeared, the foundations of the world were **discovered,** at the rebuking of the LORD, at the blast of the breath of his nostrils.	laid bare	laid bare	laid bare	laid bare	laid bare
	19 They **prevented** me in the day of my calamity: but the LORD was my stay.	came upon	confronted me	assailed	confronted	confronted

I Kings

	KJV	RSV	NEB	JB	NAS	NIV
1	6 And his father had not displeased him at any time in saying, Why hast thou done so? and he also was a very **goodly** man; and his mother bare him after Absalom.	handsome	handsome	handsome	handsome	handsome
3	1 And Solomon made **affinity** with Pharaoh king of Egypt, and took Pharaoh's daughter, and brought her into the city of David, until he had made an end of building his own house, and the house of the LORD, and the wall of Jerusalem round about.	a marriage alliance	allied himself . . . by marriage	allied himself by marriage	formed a marriage alliance	made an alliance . . . and married
	19 And this woman's child died in the night; because she **overlaid it.**	lay on it	overlaid it	overlaid him	lay on it	lay on him
	26 Then spake the woman whose the living child was unto the king, for **her bowels yearned upon** her son, and she said, O my lord, give her the living child, and in no wise slay it. But the other said, Let it be neither mine nor thine,	her heart yearned for	the woman . . . moved with love for	she burned with pity for	she was deeply stirred over	The woman . . . was filled with compassion for
4	8 And these are their names: The son of Hur, in **mount** Ephraim:	the hill country of	the hill-country of	the mountain country of	the hill country of	the hill country of
5	1 And Hiram king of Tyre sent his servants unto Solomon; for he had heard that they had anointed him king **in the room of** his father: for Hiram **was ever a lover of** David.	in place of/always loved	in (his father's) place/always been a friend of	in succession to/always been a friend of (vs. 15)	in place/always been a friend of	to succeed/always been on friendly terms with
	4 But now the LORD my God hath given me rest on every side, so that there is neither adversary nor **evil occurrent.**	misfortune	attack	calamities (vs. 18)	misfortune	disaster
	5 And, behold, I purpose to build an house unto the name of the LORD my God, as the LORD spake unto David my father, saying, Thy son, whom I will set upon thy throne in thy **room,** he shall build an house unto my name.	place	place	(to succeed you) (vs. 19)	place	place
	6 Now therefore command thou that they **hew me** cedar trees out of Lebanon; and my servants shall be with thy servants: and unto thee will I give hire for thy servants according to all that thou shalt **appoint:** for thou knowest that there is not among us any that **can skill to hew** timber like unto the Sidonians.	cut for me/set/knows how to cut	be felled/fix/skilled at felling	cut down for me/fix/skilled in felling trees (vs. 20)	cut for me/say/knows how to cut	be cut for me/set/skilled in felling
	18 And Solomon's builders and Hiram's builders did hew them, and the **stone-squarers:** so they prepared timber and stones to build the house.	men of Gebal	Gebalites	Giblites	Gebalites	men of Gebal
6	4 And for the house he made **windows of narrow lights.**	windows with recessed frames	embrasures	windows . . . with frames and latticework	windows with artistic frames	narrow clerestory windows
	7 And the house, when **it was in building,** was built of stone made ready before it was brought thither: so that	the house was built/being built	In the building of the house/being built	The building of the Temple/being built	the house . . . was built/being built	In building the temple/being built

KJV	RSV	NEB	JB	NAS	NIV
there was neither hammer nor axe nor any tool of iron heard in the house, while it was **in building.**					
18 And the cedar of the house within was carved with **knops** and open flowers: all was cedar; there was no stone seen.	gourds	gourds	gourds	gourds	gourds
7 4 And there were **windows** in three rows, and **light was against light** in three **ranks.**	window frames/window opposite window/tiers	window-frames/windows corresponded to each other/levels	architraves/facing one another/sides	artistic window frames/window was opposite window/ranks	windows/facing each other/sets
14 He was a widow's son of the tribe of Naphtali, and his father was a man of Tyre, a worker in brass: and he was filled with wisdom, and understanding, and **cunning** to work all works in brass. And he came to king Solomon, and wrought all his work.	skill	skill	skilled	skill	skilled
16 And he made two **chapiters** of molten brass, to set upon the tops of the pillars: the height of the one **chapiter** was five cubits, and the height of the other **chapiter** was five cubits:	capitals/capital/ capital	capitals/(each) capital	capitals/capital/the other	capitals/capital/ capital	capitals/(each) capital
18 And he made the **pillars,** and two rows round about upon the one network, to cover the **chapiters** that were upon the top, with **pomegranates:** and so did he for the other **chapiter.**	pomegranates/ capital / pomegranates / capital	pomegranates / capital / (did the same) / capital	pomegranates/(omits)/ (omits) / (omits)	pillars/capitals / pomegranates / capital	pomegranates/ capitals / (omits) / capital
19 And the **chapiters** that were upon the top of the pillars were of lily work in the **porch,** four cubits.	capitals/vestibule	capitals/vestibule	capitals/(omits)	capitals/porch	capitals/portico
20 And the **chapiters** upon the two pillars **had pomegranates** also above, over against the **belly** which was by the network: and the pomegranates were two hundred in rows round about upon the other **chapiter.**	capitals/(omits) / rounded projection / capital	capitals/(omits) / cushion / capitals	(omits)/(omits) / raised moulding / capital	capitals/(omits) / rounded projection / capitals	capitals/(omits) / bowlshaped part / (omits)
31 And the mouth of it within the **chapiter** and above was a cubit: but the mouth thereof was round after the work of the base, a cubit and an half: and also upon the mouth of it were **gravings** with their borders, foursquare, not round.	crown/carvings	crown/decorations in relief	(from where the shoulderings met at the top)/engravings	crown/engravings	stand/engraving
36 For on **the plates of the ledges** thereof, and on the **borders** thereof, he **graved** cherubims, lions, and palm trees, according to the **proportion of every one,** and **additions** round about.	surfaces of its stays / panels / carved / space of each / wreaths	plates/panels / carved / blank space / spiral work	(omits)/bands/engraved / scrolls	plates of it stays/ borders/ engraved /wreaths	surfaces of the supports / panels/ engraved / wreaths
8 12 Then spake Solomon, The LORD said that he would dwell in the **thick darkness.**	thick darkness	thick darkness	thick cloud	thick cloud	dark cloud
20 And the LORD hath **performed his word** that he spake, and I am risen up **in the room of** David my father, and sit on the throne of Israel, as the LORD promised, and have built an house for the name of the LORD God of Israel.	fulfilled his promise/in the place of	fulfilled his promise/his place	kept the promise he made (have succeeded)	fulfilled his word/ in place of	kept the promise he made/(have succeeded)
25 Therefore now, LORD God of Israel, keep with thy servant David my father that thou promisedst him, saying, There shall not fail thee a man **in my sight** to sit on the throne of Israel; **so that** thy children take heed to their way, that they walk before me as thou hast walked before me.	before me/if only	appointed by me/if only	before me/if only	(omits)/if only	before me/if only
47 Yet if they shall **bethink themselves** in the land whither they were carried captives, and repent, and make supplication unto thee in the land of them that carried them captives, saying, We have sinned, and have done perversely, we have committed wickedness;	lay it to heart	learn their lesson	come to themselves	take thought	have a change of heart

	KJV	RSV	NEB	JB	NAS	NIV
9	27 And Hiram sent in the **navy** his servants, **shipmen** that **had knowledge of** the sea, with the servants of Solomon.	fleet/seamen/were familiar with	fleet/(experienced seamen)	fleet/sailors/knew	fleet/sailors/knew	fleet/sailors/knew
10	2 And she came to Jerusalem with a very great **train,** with camels that bare spices, and very much gold, and precious stones: and when she was come to Solomon, she **communed with** him of all that was **in her heart.**	retinue/told/on her mind	retinue/told/in her mind	riches/(opened her mind freely to him)	retinue/spoke with/in her heart	caravan/talked with/on her mind
	15 Beside that he had of the **merchantmen,** and of the traffic of the **spice merchants,** and of all the kings of Arabia, and of the governors of the country.	traders/merchants	(tolls levied by the customs officers and profits on foreign trade)	merchants(') / traders(')	traders/merchants	merchants/traders
	16 And king Solomon made two hundred **targets** of beaten gold: six hundred shekels of gold went to **one target.**	shields/each shield	shields/each one	shields/each shield	shields/each large shield	shields/each shield
	21 And all king Solomon's drinking vessels were of gold, and all the vessels of the house of the forest of Lebanon were of pure gold; none were of silver: it was **nothing accounted of** in the days of Solomon.	not considered as anything	reckoned of no value	thought little of	not considered valuable	considered of little value
	26 And Solomon gathered together chariots and horsemen: and he had a thousand and four hundred chariots, and twelve thousand horsemen, whom he **bestowed** in the cities for chariots, and with the king at Jerusalem.	stationed	stabled	stationed	stationed	kept
	28 And Solomon had horses brought out of Egypt, **and linen yarn:** the king's merchants received **the linen yarn** at a price.	and Kue/them from Kue	and Coa/them from Coa	from Cilicia/them from Cilicia	and Kue/them from Kue	and from Kue/them from Kue
	29 And a chariot came up and went out of Egypt for six hundred she-kels of silver, and an horse for an hundred and fifty: and so for all the kings of the Hittites, and for the kings of Syria, did they **bring them out by their means.**	through the king's traders they were exported	in the same way the merchants obtained them for export	were exported through the king's agents . . . in the same way	by the same means they exported them	they exported them
12	6 And king Rehoboam **consulted** with the old men, that stood before Solomon his father while he yet lived, and said, How do ye advise that I may answer this people?	took counsel (also vs. 8)	consulted (also vs. 8)	consulted (also vs. 8)	consulted (also vs. 8)	consulted (also vs. 8)
14	3 And take with thee ten loaves, and **cracknels,** and **a cruse** of honey, and go to him: he shall tell thee what shall become of the child.	some cakes/jar	some raisins/flask	some savoury food/jar	some cakes/jar	some cakes/jar
17	19 And he said unto her, Give me thy son. And he took him out of her bosom, and carried him up into a **loft,** where he abode, and laid him upon his own bed.	upper chamber	roof-chamber	upper room	upper room	upper room
18	21 And Elijah came unto all the people and said, How long **halt ye** between two opinions? if the LORD be God, follow him: but if Baal, then follow him. And the people answered him not a word.	will you go limping	will you sit on the fence	do you mean to hobble	will you hesitate	will you waver
20	11 And the king of Israel answered and said, Tell him, Let not him that girdeth on **his harness** boast himself as he that putteth it off.	armor	("the lame must not think himself a match for the nimble")	armour	armor	armor
	14 And Ahab said, By whom? And he said, Thus saith the LORD, Even by the **young men** of the **princes** of the **provinces.** Then he said, Who shall **order** the battle? And he answered, Thou.	servants/governors/districts/begin	young men/officers/district/draw up	young soldiers/ governors/district/open	young men/rulers/provinces/begin	young offices/commanders/provincial/start

	KJV	RSV	NEB	JB	NAS	NIV
	16 And they went out at noon. But Benhadad was drinking himself drunk in the **pavilions,** he and the kings, the thirty and two kings that helped him.	booths	quarters	awnings	temporary shelters	tents
	24 And do this thing, Take the kings away, every man out of his **place,** and put **captains** in their **rooms:**	post/commanders/places	commands/officers/(other)	posts/commanders / instead	place/captains/place	commands/officers/(other)
	43 And the king of Israel went to his house **heavy and displeased,** and came to Samaria.	resentful and sullen (21:4: vexed and sullen)	sullen and angry (also 21:4)	gloomy and out of temper (also 21:4)	sullen and vexed (also 21:4)	sullen and angry (also 21:4)
22	10 And the king of Israel and Jehoshaphat the king of Judah sat each on his throne, having put on their robes, **in a void place** in the entrance of the gate of Samaria; and all the prophets prophesied before them.	at the threshing floor	(omits)	at the threshing-floor	at the threshing floor	at the threshing floor
	20 And the LORD said, Who shall **persuade** Ahab, that he may go up and fall at Ramothgilead? And one said on this manner, and another said on that manner.	entice	entice	trick	entice	lure
	34 And a certain man drew a bow at a venture, and smote the king of Israel between **the joints of the harness:** wherefore he said unto the driver of his chariot, Turn thine hand, and carry me out of the host; for I am wounded.	the scale armor and the breastplate	where the breastplate joins the plates of the armour	the corslet and the scale-armour of his breastplate	a joint of the armor	the sections of his armor

II Kings

	KJV	RSV	NEB	JB	NAS	NIV
3	4 And Mesha king of Moab was a **sheepmaster,** and **rendered** unto the king of Israel an hundred thousand lambs, and an hundred thousand rams, with the wool.	sheep breeder/had to deliver	sheep-breeder/used to supply	sheep-breeder/used to pay	sheep breeder/used to pay	raised sheep/had to supply
	9 So the king of Israel went, and the king of Judah, and the king of Edom: and they **fetched a compass** of seven days' journey: and there was no water for the **host,** and for the cattle that followed them.	made a circuitous march/army	(When they had been seven days on the march)/army	followed a devious route/troops	made a circuit/army	(After a roundabout march)/army
	19 And ye shall **smite** every **fenced** city, and every choice city, and shall fell every good tree, and stop all **wells** of water, and **mar** every good piece of land with stones.	conquer/fortified/springs/ruin	raze to the ground/fortified/springs/spoil	storm/fortified/waterspring/ruin	strike/fortified/springs/mar	overthrow/fortified/springs/ruin
5	5 And the king of Syria said, **Go to, go,** and I will send a letter unto the king of Israel. And he departed, and took with him ten talents of silver, and six thousand pieces of gold, and ten **changes of raiment.**	Go now/festal garments	you may go/changes of clothing	Go by all means/festal robes	Go now/changes of clothes	By all means, go/sets of clothing
	7 And it came to pass, when the king of Israel had read the letter, that he rent his clothes, and said, Am I God, to kill and to make alive, that this man doth send unto me to **recover** a man of his leprosy? wherefore consider, I pray you, and see how he seeketh a quarrel against me.	cure	cure	cure	cure	to be cured
	11 But Naaman was **wroth,** and went away, and said, Behold, I thought, He will surely come out to me, and stand, and	angry/wave/cure	furious/waved/rid	indignant/wave/cure	furious/wave/cure	angry/wave/cure

KJV	RSV	NEB	JB	NAS	NIV
call on the name of the LORD his God, and **strike** his hand over the place, and **recover** the leper.					
23 And Naaman said, **Be content, take** two talents. And he urged him, and bound two talents of silver in two bags, with two changes of garments, and laid them upon two of his servants; and they bare them before him.	Be pleased to accept	By all means; take	Please accept	Be pleased to take	By all means, take
24 And when he came to the **tower,** he took them from their hand, and **bestowed** them in the house: and he let the men go, and they departed.	hill/put	citadel/deposited	Ophel/put . . . away	hill/deposited	hill/put . . . away
6 1 And the sons of the prophets said unto Elisha, Behold now, the place where we **dwell with thee** is too **strait** for us.	dwell under your charge/small	is living, under you as its head/small	live side by side with you/confined	before you . . . are living/limited	meet with you/small
33 And while he yet talked with them, behold, **the messenger** came down unto him: and he said, Behold, this **evil** is of the LORD; **what** should I wait for the LORD any longer?	king/trouble/why	king/plight/Why	king/misery/why	messenger/ evil/why	messenger/disas-ter/why
8 19 Yet the LORD would not destroy Judah for David his servant's sake, as he promised him to give him **alway a light,** and to his children.	a lamp	a flame	a lamp	a lamp	a lamp
9 27 But when Ahaziah the king of Judah saw this, he fled **by the way of the garden house.** And Jehu followed after him, and said, Smite him also in the chariot. And they did so at the going up to Gur, which is by Ibleam. And he fled to Megiddo, and died there.	in the direction of Beth-haggan	by the road to Beth-haggan	along the Beth-haggan road	by the way of the garden house	up the road to Beth Haggan
30 And when Jehu was come to Jezreel, Jezebel heard of it; and she painted her **face,** and **tired** her head, and looked out **at a** window.	eyes/adorned/of the	eyes/dressed/from a	eyes/adorned/(ap-peared) at the	eyes/adorned/the	eyes/arranged/of a
10 3 Look even out the best and **meetest** of your master's sons, and set him on his father's throne, and fight for your master's house.	fittest	most suitable	worthiest	fittest	most worthy
12 And he arose and departed, and came to Samaria. And as he was at **the shearing house in the way,**	Beth-eked of the Shepherds	a shepherds' shelter	Beth-eked of the Shepherds	Beth-eked of the Shepherds	Beth Eked of the Shepherds
27 And they brake down the image of Baal, and brake down the house of Baal, and made it a **draught house** unto this day.	latrine	privy	latrine	latrine	latrine
11 8 And ye shall **compass** the king round about, every man with his weapons in his hand: and he that cometh within the **ranges,** let him be slain: and be ye with the king as he goeth out and as he cometh in.	surround/ranks	guard round/ranks	surround/ranks	surround/ranks	Station . . . around/ranks
15 But Jehoiada the priest commanded the captains of the hundreds, the officers of the **host,** and said unto them, **Have her forth without the ranges:** and him that followeth her kill with the sword. For the priest had said, Let her not be slain in the house of the LORD.	army/Bring her out between the ranks	troops/Bring her outside the pre-cincts	army/Take her outside the pre-cincts	army/Bring her out between the ranks	troops/Bring her out between the ranks
12 10 And it was so, when they saw that there was much money in the chest, that the king's **scribe** and the high priest came up, and they put up in bags, and **told** the money that was found in the house of the LORD.	secretary/counted	secretary/weighed	secretary/reckon	scribe/counted	secretary/counted
11 And they gave the money, being told, into the hands of them that did the					

	KJV	RSV	NEB	JB	NAS	NIV
	work, that had the oversight of the house of the LORD: and they **laid it out** to the carpenters and builders, that wrought upon the house of the LORD,	paid it out	paid	spent it	paid it out	With it . . . paid
14	12 And Judah **was put to the worse** before Israel; and they fled every man to **their tents.**	was defeated/his home	were routed/their homes	was defeated/his tent	was defeated/his tent	was routed/his home
15	5 And the LORD smote the king, so that he was a leper unto the day of his death, and dwelt in a **several** house. And Jotham the king's son was over the house, judging the people of the land.	separate	his own	(confined to his own room)	separate	separate
16	10 And king Ahaz went to Damascus to meet Tiglathpileser king of Assyria, and saw an altar that was at Damascus: and king Ahaz sent to Urijah the priest the **fashion** of the altar, and the pattern of it, **according to all the workmanship thereof.**	model/exact in all its details	sketch/(omits)	model/(omits)	model/according to all its workmanship	sketch/(omits)
18	13 Now in the fourteenth year of king Hezekiah did Sennacherib king of Assyria come up against all the **fenced** cities of Judah, and took them.	fortified	fortified	fortified	fortified	fortified
	17 And the king of Assyria sent **Tartan** and **Rabsaris** and **Rabshakeh** from Lachish to king Hezekiah with a great host against Jerusalem. And they went up and came to Jerusalem. And when they were come up, they came and stood by the conduit of the upper pool, which is in the highway of the fuller's field.	the Tartan/the Rabsaris/the Rabshakeh	the commander-in-chief/the chief eunuch/the chief officer	the cupbearer-in-chief	Tartan/Rabsaris/Rabshakeh	supreme commander/his chief officer/his field commander
	32 Until I come and take you away to a land like your own land, a land of **corn** and wine, a land of bread and vineyards, a land of **oil olive** and of honey, that ye may live, and not die: and **hearken not** unto Hezekiah, when he **persuadeth** you, saying, The LORD will deliver us.	grain/olive trees/do not listen/misleads	grain/olives/Do not listen/will only mislead	corn/oil/Do not listen/is deluding	grain/olive trees/do not listen/misleads	grain/olive trees/Do not listen/is misleading
20	9 And Isaiah said, This sign shalt thou have of the LORD, that the LORD will do the thing that he hath spoken: shall the shadow go forward ten **degrees,** or go back ten **degrees?**	steps/steps	steps/steps	steps/steps	steps/steps	steps/steps
23	3 And the king stood by a pillar, and made a covenant before the LORD, to walk after the LORD, and to keep his commandments and his testimonies and his statutes with all **their** heart and all **their** soul, to perform the words of this covenant that were written in this book. And all the people **stood to** the covenant.	his/his/joined in	his/(omits)/pledged themselves to	his/(omits)/gave their allegiance to	his/his/entered into	his/his/pledged themselves to
	17 Then he said, What **title** is that that I see? And the men of the city told him, It is the **sepulchre** of the man of God, which came from Judah, and **proclaimed** these things that thou hast done **against** the altar **of** Bethel.	yonder monument/tomb/predicted / at	monument/grave/foretold / at	monument/tomb/foretold / (omits)	monument/grave/proclaimed / of	tombstone/tomb/pronounced / of
	33 And Pharaohnechoh put him in **bands** at Riblah in the land of Hamath, that he might not reign in Jerusalem; and put the land to a tribute of an hundred talents of silver, and a talent of gold.	bonds	(removed him from the throne in Jerusalem)	chains	(imprisoned)	chains
	34 And Pharaohnechoh made Eliakim the son of Josiah king **in the room** of Josiah his father, and **turned** his name to Jehoiakim, and took Jehoahaz away: and he came to Egypt, and died there.	in the place of/changed	in place of/changed	in succession to/changed	in the place of/changed	in place of/changed
25	17 The height of the one pillar was eighteen cubits, and the **chapiter** upon it was brass: and the height of the **chapiter** three cubits; and the **wreathen work,** and pomegranates upon the **chapiter**	capital/capital/network / capital / network	capital/capital/network / (omits) / network	capital/capital/filigree/capital / (so also with the second pillar	capital/capital/network/capital / network	chapiter/(omits) / network / (omits) / network

	KJV	RSV	NEB	JB	NAS	NIV
	round about, all of brass: and like unto these had the second pillar with **wreathen work.**					

I Chronicles

	KJV	RSV	NEB	JB	NAS	NIV
2	7 And the sons of Carmi; Achar, the troubler of Israel, who transgressed in the thing **accursed.**	devoted thing	the sacred ban	the ban	the ban	devoted things
	41 And these **written** by name came in the days of Hezekiah king of Judah, and **smote** their tents, and the **habitations** that were found there, and **destroyed them utterly** unto this day, and **dwelt in their rooms:** because there was pasture there for their flocks.	registered/destroyed/Meunim / exterminated them / settled in their place	written/destroyed/Meunites/annihilated them / occupied the land in their place	registered/overran/dwellings/put them under a ban / settled in their place	recorded/attacked/Meunites/destroyed them utterly / lived in their place	listed/attacked/Meunites/completely destroyed them / settled in their place
5	20 And they were helped against them, and the Hagarites were delivered into their hand, and all that were with them: for they cried to God in the battle, and he **was entreated of them;** because they put their trust in him.	granted their entreaty	listened to their prayer	their prayer was heard	was entreated for them	answered their prayers
9	28 And certain of them had the charge of the **ministering vessels,** that **they should bring them in and out by tale.**	utensils of service / they were required to count them when they were brought in and taken out	vessels used in the service of the temple / keeping count of them as they were brought in and out	furnishings of worship / they counted them whenever they put them away and took them out	utensils of service / they counted them when they brought them in and when they took them out	articles used in the temple service / they counted them when they were brought in and when they were taken out
16	3 And he dealt to every one of Israel, both man and woman, to every one a loaf of bread, and a **good piece of flesh, and a flagon of wine.**	portion of meat, and a cake of raisins	portion of meat, and a cake of raisins	portion of dates, and a raisin cake	portion of meat and a raisin cake	cake of dates and a cake of raisins
18	4 And David took from him a thousand chariots, and seven thousand horsemen, and twenty thousand footmen: David also **houghed** all the chariot horses, but reserved of them an hundred chariots.	hamstrung	hamstrung	hamstrung	hamstrung	hamstrung
19	16 And when the Syrians saw that they **were put to the worse** before Israel, they sent messengers, and drew forth the Syrians that were beyond **the river:** and Shophach the captain of the **host** of Hadarezer **went before them.**	had been defeated/the Euphrates / army / with . . . at their head	had been worsted/Great Bend of the Euphrates / army / (under Shophach)	had been defeated/the river / army / with . . . at their head	had been defeated/the River / army / with . . . leading them	had been routed/the River / army / with . . . leading them
21	12 Either three years' famine; **or three** months to be destroyed before thy foes, while that the sword of thine **enemies** overtaketh thee; **or else** three days **the** sword of the **LORD, even the pestilence,** in the land, and the angel of the **LORD** destroying throughout all the coasts of Israel. Now therefore **advise thyself** what word I shall bring again to him that sent me.	decide	Make your choice	decide	consider	decide
	23 And Ornan said unto David, Take it to thee, and let my lord the king do that which is good in his eyes: lo, I give thee the oxen also for burnt offerings, and the threshing **instruments** for wood, and the wheat for the **meat** offering; I give it all.	sledges/cereal	(threshing-) sledges/ grain	(threshing-)sled / oblation	sledges/grain	sledges/grain
22	15 Moreover there are workmen with thee in abundance, hewers and **workers of stone and timber, and all manner of cunning** men for every manner **of work.**	skilled	skilled	skilled	skillful	skilled
23	29 **Both for the shewbread, and for the fine** flour for **meat** offering, and for the	(omits)/cereal/	(omits)/grain-/	(omits)/obla-	fine/grain/	(omits)/grain/

	KJV	RSV	NEB	JB	NAS	NIV
	unleavened **cakes,** and for that which is baked in the pan, and for **that which is fried,** and for all manner of measure and size;	bread/the offering mixed with oil	wafers/pastry	tion/bread/cakes . . . mixed	wafers/what is well-mixed	wafers/the mixing
25	7 So the number of them, with their brethren that were instructed in the songs of the LORD, even all that were **cunning,** was two hundred fourscore and eight.	skilful	skilled	trained	skillful	skilled
28	7 Moreover I will establish his kingdom for ever, if he **be constant to do** my commandments and my **judgments,** as at this day.	continues resolute / ordinances	steadfastly obeys / commandments	sturdily maintains / commandments	resolutely performs / commandments	unswerving in carrying out / commandments
29	3 Moreover, because I have set my affection to the house of my God, I have **of mine own proper good,** of gold and silver, which I have given to the house of my God, **over and above all that I have prepared for the holy house,**	a treasure of my own / in addition to all that I have provided for the holy house	my own private store / over and above all the store which I have collected for the sanctuary	my own treasure / over and above what I have provided already for the holy Temple	the treasure I have / over and above all that I have already provided for the holy temple	my personal treasures / over and above everything I have provided for this holy temple
	7 And gave for the service of the house of God of gold five thousand talents and ten thousand **drams,** and of silver ten thousand talents, and of brass eighteen thousand talents, and one hundred thousand talents of iron.	darics	darics	darics	darics	darics

II Chronicles

	KJV	RSV	NEB	JB	NAS	NIV
1	16 And Solomon had horses brought out of Egypt, and **linen yarn:** the king's merchants received the **linen yarn** at a price.	and Kue/from Kue	and Coa/from Coa	from Cilicia/from Cilicia	from Kue/from Kue	from Kue/from Kue
2	2 And Solomon **told out** threescore and ten thousand men to bear burdens, and fourscore thousand to **hew in the mountain,** and three thousand and six hundred to oversee them.	assigned/quarry in the hill country	engaged/quarrymen	impressed/quarry in the hill country	assigned/quarry stone in the mountains	conscripted/as stonecutters in the hills
	7 Send me now therefore a man **cunning** to work in gold, and in silver and in brass, and in iron, and in purple, and crimson, and blue, [ ] and that **can skill** to **grave** with the **cunning** men that are with me in Judah and in Jerusalem, whom David my father did provide.	skilled/fabrics/trained . . . in engraving / skilled	skilled/yarn/expert engraver / skilled	skilled/(no insertion)/art of engraving / skilled	skilled/fabrics/knows how to make engravings / skilled	skilled/yarn/experienced in the art of engraving / skilled
	8 Send me also cedar trees, **fir** trees, and algum trees, out of Lebanon: for I know that thy servants **can skill** to cut timber in Lebanon; and, behold, my servants shall be with thy servants,	cypress/know how	pine/are expert at	juniper/know the art of	cypress/know how	pine/are skilled in
	9 Even to prepare me timber in abundance: for the house which I am about to build shall be **wonderful great.**	great and wonderful	great and wonderful	of astounding size	great and wonderful	large and magnificent
	13 And now I have sent a **cunning** man, endued with understanding, of Huram my father's,	skilled	skilful	skilled	skilled	of great skill
	14 The son of a woman of the daughters of Dan, and his father was a man of Tyre, **skilful** to work in gold, and in silver, in brass, in iron, in stone, and in timber, in purple, in blue, and in fine linen, and in crimson; also to **grave any manner of graving,** and to find out every device which shall be put to him, with thy **cunning men,** and with the **cunning men** of my lord David thy father.	trained/to do all sorts of engraving / craftsmen / craftsmen	experienced/trained engraver / craftsmen / those	skilled/in engraving of all kinds / craftsmen / those	knows how to/knows how to execute any design / skilled men / those	trained/is experienced in all kinds of engraving / craftsmen / those

	KJV	RSV	NEB	JB	NAS	NIV
3	5 And the **greater house** he **ceiled** with **fir tree,** which he overlaid with fine gold, and set thereon palm trees and chains.	nave/lined/cypress	large chamber/ panelled/pine	Great Hall/ faced/juniper	main room/over-lain/cypress	main hall/pan-eled/pine
	15 Also he made before the house two pillars of thirty and five cubits high, and the **chapiter** that was on the top of each of them was five cubits.	capital	architrave	capital	capital	capital
4	12 To wit, the two pillars, and the **pommels,** and the **chapiters** which were on the top of the two pillars, and the two **wreaths** to cover the two **pommels** of the **chapiters** which were on the top of the pillars;	bowls/capitals/ networks/bowls / capitals	bowl-shaped capi-tals/networks / bowl-shaped capitals	mouldings/capi-tals/filigree / mouldings / capitals	bowls/capitals/ networks / bowls / capitals	bowl-shaped capi-tals/network / bowl-shaped capitals
	13 And four hundred pomegranates on the two wreaths; two rows of pomegranates on each wreath, to cover the two **pommels** of the **chapiters** which were upon the pillars.	bowls/capitals	bowl-shaped capi-tals	(omits)/(omits)	bowls/capitals	bowl-shaped capi-tals
6	10 The LORD therefore hath **performed his word** that he hath spoken: for I am risen up **in the room of** David my father, and am set on the throne of Israel, as the LORD promised, and have built the house for the name of the LORD God of Israel.	fulfilled his prom-ise/in the place of	fulfilled his prom-ise/his place on	kept the prom-ise/(omits)	fulfilled His word/in the place of	kept the prom-ise/(omits)
	37 Yet if they **bethink themselves** in the land whither they are carried captive, and turn and pray unto thee in the land of their captivity, saying, We have sinned, we have done amiss, and have dealt wickedly;	lay it to heart	learn their lesson	come to them-selves	take thought	have a change of heart
7	7 Moreover Solomon **hallowed** the middle of the court that was before the house of the LORD: for there he offered burnt offerings, and the fat of the peace offerings, because the brasen altar which Solomon had made was not able to **receive** the burnt offerings, and the **meat** offerings, and the fat.	consecrated/could not hold / cereal	consecrated/could not take / grain-	consecrated/could not hold / oblation	consecrated/was not able to con-tain / grain	consecrated/could not hold / grain
9	14 Beside that which **chapmen** and merchants brought. And all the kings of Arabia and governors of the country brought gold and silver to Solomon.	traders	merchants	import agents	traders	traders
	24 And they brought every man his present, **vessels** of silver, and vessels of gold, and **raiment, harness,** and spices, horses, and mules, **a rate** year by year.	articles/garments/ myrrh / so much	vessels/garments/ perfumes / so much	vessels/robes/ armour / this went on	articles/garments/ weapons / so much	articles/robes / weapons / (omits)
11	15 And he ordained him priests for the high places, and for the **devils,** and for the calves which he had made.	satyrs	hill-shrines	satyrs	satyrs	goat . . . idols
14	5 Also he took away out of all the cities of Judah the high places and the **images:** and the kingdom was quiet before him.	incense altars	incense-altars	altars of incense	incense altars	incense altars
18	9 And the king of Israel and Jehoshaphat king of Judah sat **either of them** on his throne, **clothed** in their robes, and they sat **in a void place** at the entering in of the gate of Samaria; and all the prophets prophesied before them.	(omits) / arrayed / at the threshing	(omits)/clothed / (omits)	both/(in full rega-lia) / at the threshing-floor	each/arrayed / at the threshing floor	(omits)/Dressed / at the threshing floor
	33 And a certain man drew a bow at a venture, and **smote** the king of Israel between the **joints of the harness:** therefore he said to his chariot **man,** Turn **thine hand,** that thou mayest carry me out of the **host;** for I am wounded.	struck/scale armor of the breastplate / driver / around / battle	hit/breastplate joins the plates of the armour / driver / around / line	hit/corselet and the scale-armour of his breastplate / charioteer / about / battle	struck/joint of the armor / driver / around / fight	hit/sections of his armor / driver / around / fighting
20	21 And when he had **consulted** with the people, he appointed singers unto the LORD, and that should praise the beauty of holiness, as they went out before the army, and to say, Praise the LORD; for his mercy endureth for ever.	taken counsel	consulting	having held a conference	consulted	consulting

KJV	RSV	NEB	JB	NAS	NIV
21 19 **And it came to pass, that in process of time,** after the end of two years, his bowels **fell out** by reason of **his sickness:** so he died **of sore diseases.** And his people made no burning for him, like the burning of his fathers.	In course of time/ came out / the disease / in great agony	It continued for some time / prolapse / the disease / painful ulceration	it lasted for more than one year / dropped out / disease / in great pain	Now it came about in the course of time / came out / his sickness / in great pain	In the course of time / came out/ the disease / in great pain
20 Thirty and two years old was he when he began to reign, and he reigned in Jerusalem eight years, and departed **without being desired.** Howbeit they buried him in the city of David, but not in the sepulchres of the kings.	with no one's regret	unsung	with no one to regret him	with no one's regret	to no one's regret
23 14 Then Jehoiada the priest brought out the captains of hundreds that were set over the **host,** and said unto them, **Have her forth of the ranges:** and whoso followeth her, let him be slain with the sword. For the priest said, Slay her not in the house of the LORD.	army/Bring her out between the ranks	troops/Bring her outside the precincts	(omits)/Take her outside the precincts	army/Bring her out between the ranks	troops/Bring her out between the ranks
26 10 Also he built towers in the desert, and digged many **wells:** for he had much cattle, both in the low **country,** and in the plains: **husbandmen** also, and vine dressers in the mountains, and **in Carmel:** for he loved **husbandry.**	cisterns/Shephelah/ farmers / in the fertile lands / the soil	cisterns/Shephelah/farmers / in the fertile lands / the soil	cisterns/lowlands/farmers / on the fertile lands / agriculture	cisterns/lowlands/plowmen / fertile fields / the soil	cisterns/foothills/people working his fields / in the fertile lands / the soil
14 And Uzziah prepared for them **throughout all the host** shields, and spears, and helmets, and **habergeons,** and bows, and **slings to cast stones.**	for all the army/coats of mail / stones for slinging	for the whole army/coats of mail / sling-stones	them/coats of mail / sling stones	for all the army/body armor / sling stones	for the entire army/coats of armor / sling-stones
28 25 And in every **several** city of Judah he made high places to burn incense unto other gods, and provoked to anger the LORD God of his fathers.	(omits)	single	(omits)	(omits)	(omits)
30 6 So the **posts** went with the letters from the king and his princes throughout all Israel and Judah, and according to the commandment of the king, saying, Ye children of Israel, turn again unto the LORD God of Abraham, Isaac, and Israel, and he will return to the remnant of you, that are escaped out of the hand of the kings of Assyria.	couriers	Couriers	Couriers	couriers	couriers
22 And Hezekiah spake **comfortably** unto all the Levites that **taught the good knowledge** of the LORD: and they did eat throughout the feast seven days, offering peace offerings, and making confession to the LORD God of their fathers.	encouragingly/showed good skill in the service	encouragingly/had shown true understanding in the service	(words . . . encouraged) / showed how versed they were in the things	encouragingly/showed good insight in the things	encouragingly/showed good understanding of the service
31 19 Also of the sons of Aaron the priests, which were in the fields of **the suburbs of their cities,** in every **several** city, the men that were **expressed** by name, to give portions to all the males among the priests, and to all **that were reckoned by genealogies** among the Levites.	common land belonging to their cities / several / designated / who was enrolled	common lands attached to their cities / (omits) / nominated / who was registered	pasture lands belonging to their towns / (the towns themselves) / expressly named / (Each group was organized by the Levites.)	pasture lands of their cities / (each and every city) / designated genealogically / enrolled	farm lands around their towns / any other / designated / who were recorded in the genealogies
32 5 Also he **strengthened himself,** and built up all the wall that was broken, and raised it up to the towers, and another wall without, and **repaired Millo** in the city of David, and made **darts** and shields in abundance.	set to work resolutely / strengthened the Millo / weapons	acted boldly/strengthened the Millo / weapons	strengthened his defences / strengthened the Millo / missiles	took courage/strengthened the Millo / weapons	worked hard/reinforced the supporting terraces / weapons
9 After this did Sennacherib king of Assyria send his servants to Jerusalem, (but he himself laid siege against Lachish, and all his **power** with him,) unto Hezekiah king of Judah, and unto all Judah that were at Jerusalem, saying,	forces	high command	forces	forces	forces
13 **Know ye not what I and my fathers** have done unto all the people of other					

KJV	RSV	NEB	JB	NAS	NIV
lands? were the gods of the nations of those lands **any ways** able to deliver their lands out of mine hand?	at all	(omits)	ever	at all	ever
33 8 Neither will I any more remove the foot of Israel from out of the land which I have appointed for your fathers; **so that they will take heed** to do all that I have commanded them, according to the whole law and the statutes and the ordinances by the hand of Moses.	if only they will be careful	if only they will be careful	provided they (observe)	if only they will (observe)	if only they will be careful
13 And prayed unto him: and he **was entreated** of him, and heard his supplication, and brought him again to Jerusalem into his kingdom. Then Manasseh knew that the LORD he was God.	received his entreaty	accepted his petition	relented at his prayer	was moved by his entreaty	was moved by his entreaty
34 2 And he did that which was right in the sight of the LORD, and walked in the ways of David his father, and **declined** neither to the right hand, nor to the left.	turn aside	swerving	deviating	turn aside	turning aside
4 And they brake down the altars of Baalim in his presence; and the **images,** that were on high above them, he cut down; and the groves, and the carved images, and the molten images, he brake in pieces, and made dust of them, and strowed it upon the graves of them that had sacrificed unto them.	incense altars	incense-altars	altars of incense	incense altars	incense altars
7 And when he had broken down the altars and the **groves,** and had beaten the graven images into powder, and cut down all the **idols** throughout all the land of Israel, he returned to Jerusalem.	Asherim/incense altars	sacred poles/incense altars	sacred poles/altars of incense	Asherim/incense altars	Asherah poles/incense altars
12 And the men did the work faithfully: and the overseers of them were Jahath and Obadiah, the Levites, of the sons of Merari; and Zechariah and Meshullam, of the sons of the Kohathites, **to set it forward;** and other of the Levites all **that could skill of** instruments of music.	to have oversight/who were skilful with	(under the direction of) / were all skilled	to supervise them/who were all skilled	to supervise/who were skillful with	to direct them/who were skilled in
35 13 And they roasted the passover [] with fire according to the ordinance: but the other holy offerings **sod** they in pots, and in caldrons, and in pans, and **divided them speedily among all the people.**	lamb/boiled/carried them quickly to all the lay people	victim/boiled/served them quickly to all the people	(omits)/(omits)/carrying them speedily to the laity	animals/boiled/carried them speedily to all the lay people	animals/boiled/served them quickly to all the people
15 And the singers the sons of Asaph were in their place, according to the commandment of David, and Asaph, and Heman, and Jeduthun the king's seer; and the porters waited at every gate; they **might not** depart from their service; for their brethren the Levites prepared for them.	did not need to	there was no need for them to	neither . . . had to	did not have to	did not need to
36 3 And the king of Egypt **put him down at** Jerusalem, and **condemned the land in** an hundred talents of silver and a talent of gold.	deposed him in/laid upon the land a tribute of	deposed him/fined the country	carried him off from/imposed a levy of	deposed him at/imposed on the land a fine of	dethroned him in/imposed on Judah a levy of
15 And the LORD God of their fathers sent to them by his messengers, **rising up betimes,** and sending; because he had compassion on his people, and on his dwelling place.	persistently	betimes	tirelessly	again and again	again and again

Ezra

KJV	RSV	NEB	JB	NAS	NIV
4 10 And the rest of the nations whom the great and noble Asnapper brought over, and set in the cities of Samaria, and					

	KJV	RSV	NEB	JB	NAS	NIV
	the rest **that are on this side the river,** and **at such a time.**	of the province Beyond the River (also vs. 11, 6:6, 8, 13; 7:21, 25)/ now	of the province of Beyond-Euphrates (also vss. 11; 6:6, 8, 13; 7:21, 25) / (omits)	of Trans-euphrates/(also vss. 11; 6:6, 8, 13; 7:21, 25) / (omits)	of the region beyond the River (also vss. 11; 6:6, 8, 13; 7:21, 25) / now	in Trans-Euphrates (also vss. 11; 6:6, 8, 13; 7:21, 25) / (omits)
	16 We certify the king that, if this city be builded again, and the walls thereof set up, by this means thou shalt have no **portion on this side the river.**	possession in the province beyond the River	more footing in the province of Beyond-Euphrates	territories left in Transeuphrates	possession in the province beyond the River.	(no)thing in Trans-Euphrates
	20 There have been mighty kings also over Jerusalem, which have ruled over **all countries beyond the river;** and toll, tribute, and custom, was paid unto them.	the whole province Beyond the River	the whole province of Beyond-Euphrates	all Trans-euphrates	all the provinces beyond the River	the whole of Trans-Euphrates
	12 And the God that hath caused his name to dwell there **destroy all** kings and people, that shall **put to their hand** to alter and to destroy this house of God which is at Jerusalem. I Darius have made a decree; let it be done **with speed.**	overthrow/put forth a hand / with all diligence	overthrow/presume / to the letter	overthrow/dares / to the letter	overthrow/attempts / with all diligence	overthrow/lifts a hand / with diligence
8	22 For I was ashamed to **require** of the king a band of soldiers and horsemen to **help** us against the enemy in the way: because we had spoken unto the king, saying, The hand of our God is upon all them for good that seek him; but his power and his wrath is against all them that forsake him.	ask/protect	ask/help	ask/protect	request/protect	ask/protect
	23 So we fasted and besought our God for this: and he **was entreated of us.**	listened to our entreaty	answered our prayer	answered our prayers	listened to our entreaty	answered our prayer
9	5 And at the evening sacrifice I arose up from my **heaviness;** and having rent my garment and my mantle, I fell upon my knees, and spread out my hands unto the LORD my God,	fasting	humiliation	stupor	humiliation	self-abasement
	8 And now for a **little space grace** hath been shewed from the LORD our God, to leave us a remnant **to escape,** and to give us **a nail** in his holy place, that our God **may lighten** our eyes, and **give us a little reviving** in our bondage.	brief moment favor / (omits) / a secure hold / may brighten / grant us a little reviving	brief moment/(the Lord . . .) gracious / (omits) / a foothold / has brought light to / given us some chance to renew our lives	suddenly . . . favour/(omits) / refuge / has cheered / has given us a little respite	brief moment grace/escaped / a peg / may enlighten / grant us a little reviving	brief moment (the Lord . . .) gracious / (omits) a firm place / gives light to / gives . . . a little relief
	12 Now therefore give not your daughters unto their sons, neither take their daughters unto your sons, nor seek their peace or their **wealth** for ever: that ye may be strong, and eat the good of the land, and leave it for an inheritance to your children for ever.	prosperity	prosperity	prosperity	prosperity	prosperity
	14 Should we again break thy commandments, and **join in affinity** with the people of these abominations? wouldest not thou be angry with us till thou hadst consumed us, so that there should be no remnant nor escaping?	intermarry	join in marriage	intermarry	intermarry	intermarry

Nehemiah

	KJV	RSV	NEB	JB	NAS	NIV
4	16 And it came to pass from that time forth, that the half of my servants **wrought in the work,** and the other half of them held both the spears, the shields, and the bows, and the **habergeons;** and the **rulers** were behind all the hourse of Judah.	worked on construction / coats of mail / leaders	engaged in the actual building / coats of mail / officers	continued the work/breastplates / (omits)	carried on the work/breastplates / captains	did the work/armor / officers

	KJV	RSV	NEB	JB	NAS	NIV
5	7 Then I **consulted** with myself, and I rebuked the nobles, and the rulers, and said unto them, Ye exact usury, every one of his brother. And I set a great assembly against them.	took counsel with myself	mastered my feelings	Having turned the matter over in my mind	consulted with myself	pondered them in my mind
7	71 And some of the chief of the fathers gave to the treasure of the work twenty thousand **drams** of gold, and two thousand and two hundred pound of silver.	darics (also vs. 72)	drachmas (also vs. 72)	drachmas	drachmas (also vs. 72)	drachmas (also vs. 72)
9	22 Moreover thou gavest them kingdoms and **nations,** and didst **divide** them into corners: so they possessed the land of Sihon, and the land of the king of Heshbon, and the land of Og king of Bashan.	peoples/allot	peoples/alloting	peoples/alloted	peoples/allot	nations/alloting
10	33 For the shewbread, and for the continual **meat** offering, and for the continual burnt offering, of the sabbaths, of the new moons, for the set feasts, and for the holy things, and for the sin offerings to make an atonement for Israel, and for all the work of the house of our God.	cereal (also 13:9)	grain-(also 13:9)	oblation (also 13:9)	grain (also 13:9)	grain (also 13:9)
13	1 On that day they read in the book of Moses in the **audience of** the people; and therein was found written, that the Ammonite and the Moabite should not come into the congregation of God for ever;	hearing of	(at the public reading)	(were reading . . . to the people)	hearing of	hearing of
	5 And he had prepared for him a great chamber, where aforetime they laid the **meat** offerings, the frankincense, and the vessels, and the tithes of the **corn,** the new wine, and the oil, which was commanded to be given to the Levites, and the singers, and the **porters;** and the offerings of the priests.	cereal/grain/gatekeepers	grain-/corn/doorkeepers	oblations/corn/gatekeepers	grain/grain/gatekeepers	grain/grain/gatekeepers
	26 Did not Solomon king of Israel sin **by these things?** yet among many nations was there no king like him, who was beloved of his God, and God made him king over all Israel: nevertheless even him did **outlandish** women cause to sin.	on account of such women/foreign	for such women/foreign	(Is this not how)/foreign	regarding these things/foreign	because of marriages like these/foreign

Esther

	KJV	RSV	NEB	JB	NAS	NIV
2	9 And the maiden pleased him, and she **obtained kindness** of him; and he speedily gave her **her things for purification, with such things as belonged to her,** and seven maidens, which were **meet** to be given her, out of the king's house: and he **preferred** her and her maids unto the best place **of the house of the women.**	won his favor/her ointments and her portion of food / chosen / advanced / in the harem	received his special favour / her cosmetics and her allowance of food / picked / (gave her privileges) / in the women's quarters	won his favour/all she needed for her dressing room and her meals / special / transferred / of the harem	found favor with him/ her cosmetics and food / choice / transferred / in the harem	won his favor/her beauty treatments and special food / selected / moved / in the harem
	22 And the thing was known to Mordecai, who told it unto Esther the queen; and Esther **certified** the king thereof in Mordecai's name.	told	told	told	informed	reported
	23 And when **inquisition was made of the matter,** it was **found out;** therefore they were both hanged on **a tree:** and it was written in the book of the chronicles before the king.	the affair was investigated/found to be so / on the gallows	the affair was investigated / confirmed / on the gallows	The matter was investigated / proved to be true / to the gallows	the plot was investigated/found to be so / on a gallows	the report was investigated / found to be true / on a gallows
4	14 For if thou altogether holdest thy peace at this time, then shall there **enlargement** and deliverance arise to the Jews from another place; but thou and thy father's house shall be destroyed: and who knoweth whether thou art come to the kingdom for such a time as this?	relief	relief	relief	relief	relief

	KJV	RSV	NEB	JB	NAS	NIV
8	8 Write ye also **for the** Jews, as **it liketh** you, in the king's name, and seal it with the king's ring: for the **writing** which is written in the king's name, and sealed with the king's ring, may no man **reverse.**	with regard to the/you please / edict / revoke(d)	concerning the/think fit / order / revoke(d)	to/judge best /order irrevocable	to the/see fit/ decree / revoked	in behalf of the/seems best / document / revoked
	14 So the **posts** that rode upon **mules and camels** went out, **being hastened and pressed on** by the king's commandment. And the decree was given at Shushan the palace.	couriers/swift horses used in the king's service / in haste, urged	couriers/royal horses / post-haste at the king's urgent command	couriers/the king's horses / in great haste and urgency at the king's command	couriers/royal steeds / hastened and compelled by the king's command	couriers/royal horses / spurred on by the king's command
9	28 And that these days should be remembered and kept throughout every generation, every family, every province, and every city; and that these days of Purim should not **fail from** among the Jews, nor the **memorial** of them **perish from their seed.**	fall into disuse/commemoration / cease among their descendants	(always be observed)/memory / cease among their descendants	be abrogated/ memory / die out among their race	to fail/memory / fade from their descendants	cease to be celebrated/memory /die out among their descendants
10	3 For Mordecai the Jew was next **unto** king Ahasuerus, and great among the Jews, and **accepted** of the multitude of his brethren, seeking the **wealth** of his people, and speaking peace to all **his seed.**	in rank to/popular / welfare / his people	only to/popular / good / their descendants	in rank to/esteemed/good / his entire race	only to/in favor with / good / his whole nation	in rank to/held in high esteem/ good / the Jews

Job

	KJV	RSV	NEB	JB	NAS	NIV
2	7 So went Satan forth from the presence of the LORD, and **smote** Job with **sore boils** from the sole of his foot unto his crown.	afflicted/loathsome sores / of (his) head	smote/running sores / (from head to foot)	struck . . . down/malignant ulcers / of (his) head	smote/sore boils/of (his) head	afflicted/painful sores / of (his) head
3	12 Why did the knees **prevent** me? or why the breasts that I should suck?	receive	(Why was I ever laid on my mother's knees?)	receive	receive	receive
4	2 If we **assay to commune** with thee, wilt thou be grieved? but who can withhold himself from speaking?	ventures a word	ventures to speak	should address a word	ventures a word	ventures a word
6	2 Oh that my **grief** were throughly weighed, and my calamity laid in the balances together!	vexation	resentment	misery	vexation	anguish
	28 Now therefore **be content, look** upon me; for it is evident unto you if I lie.	be pleased to look	I beg you, turn and look	I beg you, look	please look	be so kind as to look
7	11 Therefore I will not **refrain my mouth;** I will speak in the anguish of my spirit; I will complain in the bitterness of my soul.	restrain my mouth	hold my peace	keep silence	restrain my mouth	keep silent
8	11 Can the **rush** grow up without **mire?** can the **flag grow** without water?	papyrus/ marsh/reeds flourish	rushes/marsh/ reeds flourish	papyrus/ marshes/rushes grow	papyrus/ marsh/rushes grow	papyrus/ marsh/reeds thrive
	12 Whilst it is yet in his **greenness,** and not cut down, it withereth before any other **herb.**	flower/plant	flower/green plant	freshest/plants	green/plant	growing/grass
9	25 Now my days are swifter than a **post:** they flee away, they see no good.	runner	runner	(My days run hurrying by)	runner	runner
	33 Neither is there any **daysman** betwixt us, that might lay his hand upon us both.	umpire	one to arbitrate	arbiter	umpire	someone to arbitrate
13	12 Your **remembrances are like unto** ashes, your **bodies to bodies of** clay.	maxims are proverbs of/defenses are defenses of	pompous talk is dust and/defences will crumble like	old maxims are proverbs of/retorts, retorts of	memorable sayings are proverbs of/defenses are defenses of	maxims are proverbs of/defenses are defenses of

KJV	RSV	NEB	JB	NAS	NIV
19 Who is he that will **plead** with me? for now, if I hold my tongue, I shall **give up the ghost.**	contend/be silent and give up the ghost	argue so forcibly/ (reduce me . . . to silence and death)	comes against me/be silenced and die	contend/be silent and die	bring charges (against)/be silent and die
16 3 Shall **vain** words have an end? or what **emboldeneth** thee that thou answerest?	windy/provokes	('Will this windbag never be done?)/makes . . . so stubborn	airy/(What a plague your need to have the last word is!)	windy/plagues	long-winded/ails
13 His archers **compass me round about,** he **cleaveth my reins asunder,** and doth not spare; he poureth out my gall upon the ground.	surround me/slashes open my kidneys	rained upon me from every side/cut deep into my vitals	shooting . . . at me from every side / through the loins . . . pierces me	surround me/splits my kidneys open	surround me/pierces my kidneys
19 Also now, behold, my witness is in heaven, and **my record** is on high.	he that vouches for me	one . . . ready to answer for me	my defender	my advocate	my advocate
17 3 **Lay down now, put me in a surety** with thee; who is he that will **strike hands with** me?	Lay down a pledge for me/give surety for	Be thou my surety/pledge himself for	You . . . must take my own guarantee / clap his hand on	Lay down, now, a pledge for me / be my guarantor	Give me, O God, the pledge you demand / put up security for
18 19 He shall neither have **son** nor **nephew** among his people, **nor any remaining in his dwellings.**	offspring/descendant / no survivor where he used to live	issue/offspring / no survivor in his earthly home	issue/posterity / none to live on where he has lived	offspring/posterity / Nor any survivor where he sojourned	offspring/descendants / no survivor where he once lived
19 19 All my **inward** friends abhorred me: and they whom I loved are turned against me.	intimate	intimate	dearest	associates	intimate
23 Oh that my words were now written! oh that they were **printed in a book!**	inscribed in a book	engraved in an inscription	inscribed on some monument	inscribed in a book	written on a scroll
20 3 I have heard the **check of my reproach,** and the spirit of my understanding causeth me to answer.	censure which insults me	arguments that are a reproach to me	admonitions little to my taste	reproof which insults me	rebuke that dishonors me
21 27 Behold, I know your thoughts, and **the devices which ye wrongfully imagine against me.**	your schemes to wrong me	the arguments you are marshalling against me	the spiteful thought you entertain about me	the plans by which you would wrong me	the schemes by which you would wrong me
22 25 Yea, the Almighty shall be thy **defence,** and **thou shalt have plenty of silver.**	gold/and your precious silver	metal/he will be your silver in double measure	(you will find Shaddai worth bars of gold or silver piled in heaps)	gold/choice silver to you	gold/the choicest silver for you
23 9 On the left hand, **where he doth work,** but I cannot behold him: **he hideth himself** on the right hand, that I cannot see him:	I seek him/I turn to	(omits)/(omits)	If I seek him/(omits)	When He acts/He turns	When he is at work/when he turns
28 1 Surely there is a **vein** for the silver, and a place for gold **where they fine it.**	mine/which they refine	mines/where men refine gold	mines/for refining	mine/where they refine gold	mine/where gold is refined
29 24 **If I laughed** on them, they **believed it not;** and the light of my countenance they cast not down.	I smiled/did not cast down	When I smiled/took heart	If I smiled/(it) was too good to be true	I smiled/did not believe	When I smiled/scarcely believed it
30 10 They abhor me, they **flee far** from me, and **spare not to spit in my face.**	keep aloof/ do not hesitate to spit at the sight of me	shrink/dare to spit in my face	stand aloof/do not scruple to spit in my face	stand aloof/do not refrain from spitting at my face	keep their distance/do not hesitate to spit in my face
13 They **mar** my path, they **set forward** my calamity, **they have no helper.**	break up/promote/no one restrains them	(they tear down my crumbling defences to my undoing) / scramble up against me unhindered	(They have cut me off from all escape) / there is no one to check their attack	break up/profit from / No one restrains them	break up/(succeed in destroying me) / without anyone's helping them
29 I am a brother to **dragons,** and a companion to **owls.**	jackals/ostriches	wolf/owls of the desert	jackal('s)/ ostrich('s)	jackals/ostriches	jackals/owls
31 1 I made a covenant with mine eyes; why then **should I think upon a maid?**	could I look upon a virgin	never to take notice of a girl	not to linger on any virgin	could I gaze at a virgin	not to look lustfully at a girl

KJV	RSV	NEB	JB	NAS	NIV
35 Oh that one would hear me! behold, **my desire is,** that the Almighty would answer me, and that mine adversary had written **a book.**	Here is my signature!/indictment	(omits)/indictment	I have had my say, from A to Z /writ	here is my signature/indictment	I sign now my defense/indictment
32 12 Yea, I attended unto you, and, behold, there was none of you that **convinced** Job, or that answered his words:	confuted	refutes	gave . . . the lie	refuted	proved . . . wrong
19 Behold, my **belly** is as wine which hath no vent; it is ready to burst like new **bottles.**	heart/wineskins	stomach/blacksmith's bellows	heart/wineskin	belly/wineskins	inside/wineskins
36 9 Then he **sheweth** them their work, and their transgressions that they **have exceeded.**	declares/are behaving arrogantly	denounces/(showing how insolence and tyranny was their offence)	shows/have committed	declares/have magnified themselves	tells/sinned arrogantly
10 He openeth also their ear to **discipline,** and commandeth that they return from iniquity.	instruction	warnings	(urging them to amend themselves)	instruction	correction
16 Even so would he have **removed** thee out of **the strait** into a broad place, where there **is no straitness;** and that which should be set on thy table should be full of fatness.	allured/out of distress / was no cramping	(Beware, if you are tempted to exchange hardship for comfort, for unlimited plenty spread before you and a generous table)	(For you, no less, he plans relief from sorrow. Once you lived in luxury unbounded, with food piled high on your table.)	enticed/mouth of distress / with no constraint	is wooing/ jaws of distress / free from restriction
37 4 After it a voice roareth: he thundereth with the **voice of his excellency;** and he will not **stay them** when his voice is heard.	his majestic voice/restrain the lightnings	the voice of majesty/floods of rain pour down unchecked (vs. 6)	God's majestic thunder / check his thunderbolts	His majestic voice / restrain the lightning	his majestic voice / holds nothing back
38 12 Hast thou commanded the morning since thy **days;** and caused the **dayspring** to know his place;	days began/dawn	life/dawn	life/dawn	life/dawn	(Have you ever)/dawn
29 Out of whose womb came the ice? and the hoary frost of heaven, who hath **gendered** it?	given birth to	gave birth to	brings forth	given . . . birth	gives birth to
37 Who can number the clouds in wisdom? or who can **stay the bottles** of heaven,	tilt the waterskins	empty the cisterns	tilts the flasks	tip the water jars	tip over the water jars
39 4 Their young ones **are in good liking,** they grow up **with corn;** they go forth, and return not unto them.	become strong/in the open	grow/in the open forest	are grown and gathered strength / in the open desert (vs. 3)	become strong/in the open field	grow strong/in the wilds
41 18 By his **neesings** a light doth shine, and his eyes are like the eyelids of the morning.	sneezings	sneezing	sneezes (vs. 10)	sneezes	sneezings
20 Out of his nostrils goeth smoke, as out of a **seething** pot **or caldron.**	boiling/and burning rushes	(omits)/on a fire blown to full heat	boiling/on the fire (vss. 11, 12)	boiling/and burning rushes	boiling/over a fire of reeds
26 The sword of him that **layeth** at him cannot hold: the spear, the dart, nor the **habergeon.**	reaches/javelin	touch/javelin	strike/lance (vss. 17, 18)	reaches/javelin	reaches/javelin

Psalms

KJV	RSV	NEB	JB	NAS	NIV
2 1 Why do the **heathen rage,** and the people **imagine a vain thing?**	nations conspire/plot in vain	(are) the nations in turmoil/hatch their futile plots	uproar among the nations/impotent muttering of pagans	nations in an uproar/devising a vain thing	nations rage/peoples plot in vain
5 Then shall he speak unto them in his wrath, and vex them in his **sore displeasure. []**	terrify/in his fury/saying	threatens/in his wrath/(no insert)	strikes . . . with panic/in a rage/(no insert)	terrify/in His fury/(no insert)	terrifies/in his wrath/saying

Ps.	KJV	RSV	NEB	JB	NAS	NIV
	12 **Kiss the Son,** lest he be angry, and ye perish from the way, when his wrath is kindled but a little. Blessed are all they that put their trust in him.	kiss his feet	kiss the king	kiss his feet (vs. 11)	Do homage to the Son	Kiss the Son
4	2 O ye sons of men, how long will ye turn my **glory** into shame? how long will ye **love vanity,** and seek after **leasing?** Selah.	honor / love vain words / lies	honor / set your heart on trifles / lies	(why shut your hearts so long) loving delusions / lies	honor / love what is worthless / deception	glory / love delusions / false gods
5	6 Thou shalt destroy them **that speak leasing:** the LORD will abhor the **bloody** and deceitful man.	who speak lies/bloodthirsty	(thou makest an end of all liars)/men of blood	liars/murderers	who speak falsehood/man of bloodshed	those who tell lies/bloodthirsty . . . men
7	1 O LORD my God, in thee do I **put my trust:** save me from all **them that persecute me,** and deliver me:	take refuge/my pursuers	find refuge/my pursuers	take shelter/who hound me	have taken refuge/who pursue me	take refuge/who pursue me
	9 Oh let the wickedness of the wicked come to an end; but establish the just: for the righteous God trieth the hearts and **reins.**	minds	mind	mind	minds	minds
	13 He hath also prepared for him **the instruments of death;** he **ordaineth** his arrows **against the persecutors.**	his deadly weapons/making/fiery shafts	his deadly shafts/tipped/with fire	weapons/turn/into firebrands	deadly weapons/makes/fiery shafts	his deadly weapons/makes ready/flaming
8	3 When I consider thy heavens, the work of thy fingers, the moon and the stars, which thou hast **ordained;**	established	set in their place	set in place	ordained	set in place
9	6 **O thou enemy, destructions are come to a perpetual end:** and thou hast **destroyed** cities; their **memorial** is perished with them.	The enemy have vanished in everlasting ruins/ rooted out/ very memory	The strongholds of the enemy are thrown down for evermore/laid . . . in ruins/all memory	the enemy is finished, in everlasting ruin / overthrown / memory	The enemy has come to an end in perpetual ruins / (blotted out their name for ever and ever)	Endless ruin has overtaken the enemy / uprooted / memory
	12 When he **maketh inquisition for blood,** he remembereth them: he forgetteth not the cry of the **humble.**	avenges blood / afflicted	(the Avenger of blood) / poor	(the avenger of blood)/wretched	requires blood / afflicted	who avenges blood / afflicted
10	2 The wicked **in his pride doth persecute** the poor: let them be **taken in the devices that they have imagined.**	In arrogance/ hotly pursue/caught in the schemes which they have devised	in his pride/hunts down/his crafty schemes be his own undoing	by the pride/(poor) are devoured/caught in the wiles that the other has devised	In pride/hotly pursue/caught in the plots which they have devised	In his arrogance/hunts down/caught in the schemes he devises
	3 For the wicked boasteth of his heart's desire, **and blesseth the covetous, whom the LORD abhorreth.**	and the man greedy for gain curses and renounces the Lord	and in his greed gives wickedness his blessing	the grasping man blasphemes, the wicked spurns Yahweh	And the greedy man curses and spurns the Lord	he blesses the greedy and reviles the Lord
12	2 They **speak vanity** every one with his neighbour: with flattering lips and with a double heart do they speak.	utters lies	lies	lie	speak falsehood	lies
17	2 Let my **sentence** come forth from thy presence; let thine eyes behold **the things that are equal.**	vindication/the right	judgment in my cause/justice	sentence/what is right	judgment/with equity	vindication/what is right
18	15 Then the channel of **waters** were seen, and the foundations of the world were **discovered** at thy rebuke, O LORD, at the blast of the breath of thy nostrils.	the sea/laid bare	the sea-bed/laid bare	the seas/laid bare	water/laid bare	sea/laid bare
22	17 **I may tell** all my bones: they look and stare upon me.	can count	tell (my tale of misery)	can count	can count	can count
	20 Deliver my soul from the sword; my **darling** from the power of the dog.	life	precious life	dear life	only life	precious life
28	4 Give them according to their deeds, and according to the wickedness of their endeavours: **give** them **after** the work of their hands; render to them their desert.	requite/according to	Reward/for	repay/for	Requite/according to	repay/for

KJV	RSV	NEB	JB	NAS	NIV
29 9 The voice of the LORD maketh the **hinds to calve,** and **discovereth the forests:** and in his temple doth every one speak of his glory.	oaks to whirl/strips the forests bare	hinds calve/brings kids early to birth	the terebinths shuddering/stripping the forests bare	the deer to calve/strips the forests bare	twists the oaks/strips the forests bare
31 8 And hast not **shut me up** into the hand of the enemy: thou hast set my feet **in a large room.**	delivered me / in a broad place	abandoned me / free to range at will	handed me over / space and to spare	given me over / in a large place	handed me over / in a spacious place
33 1 Rejoice in the Lord, O ye righteous: for praise **is comely** for the upright.	befits	comes well (from)	comes well (from)	is becoming	is fitting
34 10 The young lions **do lack, and suffer** hunger: but they that seek the LORD shall not **want** any good thing.	suffer want and / lack	suffer want and go / lack	may go empty and / lack	do lack and suffer / be in want of	may grow weak and / lack
35 8 Let **destruction** come upon **him at unawares;** and let his net that he hath hid **catch** himself: into that very **destruction** let him fall.	ruin / them unawares / ensnare / ruin	destruction / unforeseen . . . him / catch / it (refers to "pit to trap me" in vs.)	Ruin / them unawares / catch / pit	destruction / him unawares / catch / destruction	ruin / them by surprise / entangle / pit
17 Lord, how long wilt thou look on? rescue **my soul** from their **destructions,** my **darling** from the lions.	me / ravages / life	(adds "at those who hate me for no reason" after "look on?") me / cruel grasp / precious life	my soul / onslaughts / dear life	my soul / ravages / only life	life / ravages / precious life
38 8 I am **feeble and sore broken:** I have **roared** by reason of the **disquietness** of my heart.	utterly spent and crushed / groan / tumult	All battered and benumbed / groan / longing	numbed and crushed and overcome / moan aloud / (my heart) moans	benumbed and badly crushed / groan / agitation	feeble and utterly crushed / groan / anguish
11**My lovers** and my **friends** stand aloof from my **sore;** and my kinsmen stand afar off.	My friends / companions / plague	My friends / companions / sickness	My friends / companions / wounds	My loved ones / friends / plague	My friends / companions / wounds
17 For I am ready to **halt,** and my **sorrow** is continually before me.	fall / pain	stumble / suffering	fall / pains	fall / sorrow	fall / pain
39 5 Behold, thou hast made my days as an handbreadth; and mine **age** is as nothing **before thee:** verily every man at his best state is altogether **vanity.** Selah.	lifetime / in thy sight / mere breath	whole life / in thy sight / puff of wind	life-span / to you / puff of wind	lifetime / in Thy sight / mere breath	span of my years / before you / breath
6 Surely every man walketh **in a vain shew:** surely they are **disquieted in vain:** he heapeth up **riches,** and knoweth not who shall gather them.	as a shadow / for nought . . . in turmoil / (omits)	like a shadow / (the riches he piles up are no more than vapour)	only a shadow / (and the wealth he amasses is only a puff of wind)	as a phantom / make an uproar for nothing / riches	(is) a mere phantom / bustles about, but only in vain / wealth
40 5 Many, O LORD my God, are thy wonderful works which thou hast done, and thy thoughts which are **to us-ward: they cannot be reckoned up in order** unto thee: if I would declare and speak of them, they are more than can be numbered.	toward us; none can compare	for our good; none can compare	for us; you have no equal	toward us; There is none to compare	for us no one can recount
7 Then said I, Lo, I come: in the **volume** of the book it is written of me,	roll	(omits phrase beginning "in the volume . . .)	scroll	scroll	scroll
42 1 **As the hart panteth after the water brooks,** so panteth my soul after thee, O God.	As a hart longs for flowing streams	As a hind longs for the running streams	As a doe longs for running streams	As the deer pants for the water brooks	As the deer pants for streams of water
11 Why art thou cast down, O my soul? and why art thou disquieted within me? hope thou in God: for I shall yet praise him, who is the **health of my countenance,** and my God.	my help	my deliverer	my saviour	The help of my countenance	my Savior
44 15 My **confusion** is continually before me, and the shame of my face hath covered me,	disgrace	disgrace	disgrace	dishonor	disgrace

KJV	RSV	NEB	JB	NAS	NIV
18 Our heart is not turned back, neither have our steps **declined** from thy way;	departed	strayed	left	deviated	strayed
19 Though thou hast sore broken us in the place of **dragons,** and covered us with **the shadow of death.**	wild-dogs / the shadow of death	sea-serpent / the darkness of death	jackals / the shadow of death	jackals / the shadow of death	jackals / deep darkness
45 1 My heart **is inditing a good matter:** I speak of the things which I have made touching the king: my tongue is the pen of a ready writer.	overflows with a goodly theme	is stirred by a noble theme	is stirred by a noble theme	overflows with a good theme	stirred by a noble theme
46 2 Therefore will not we fear, though the earth **be removed,** and though the mountains be carried into the midst of the sea;	should change	heaves	gives way	should change	give way
48 12 Walk about Zion, and go round about her: **tell** the towers thereof.	number	count	counting	Count	count
51 2 Wash me **throughly** from mine iniquity, and cleanse me from my sin.	thoroughly	(Wash away all)	clean	thoroughly	(Wash away all)
5 Behold, I was **shapen in** iniquity, and in sin did my mother conceive me.	brought forth	brought to birth	born (guilty)	brought forth	(I have been a sinner from birth)
54 5 He shall **reward** evil unto mine enemies: **cut them off in thy truth.**	requite / in thy faithfulness put an end to them	(May their own malice recoil on my watchful foes) / silence them by thy truth, O Lord	(May their wickedness recoil on themselves) / Yahweh, ever faithful, destroy my enemies	recompense / Destroy them in Thy faithfulness	(Let evil recoil on those who slander me) / in your faithfulness destroy them
55 15 Let death seize upon them, and let them go down **quick into hell: for wickedness is in their dwellings, and among them.**	to Sheol alive; let them go away in terror into their graves	alive into Sheol; for their homes are haunts of evil	still living, to Sheol—since evil shares their homes	alive to Sheol, For evil is in their dwelling, in their midst	alive to the grave, for evil finds lodging among them
56 3 **What time** I am afraid, I will trust in thee.	When	(in my day of fear)	when	When	When
59 15 Let them **wander up and down for meat,** and **grudge** if they be not satisfied.	roam about for food / growl	wandering to and fro in search of food / howling	scavenging for food / growling	wander about for food / growl	wander about for food / howl
62 5 My soul, wait thou only upon God; for my **expectation** is from him.	hope	hope of deliverance	hope	hope	hope
68 19 Blessed be the Lord, who daily **loadeth us with benefits,** even the God of our salvation. Selah.	bears us up	carries us	bears our burdens	bears our burdens	bears our burdens
30 Rebuke **the company of spearmen,** the multitude of the bulls, with the calves of the people, **till every one submit himself with pieces of silver:** scatter thou the people that delight in war.	the beasts that dwell among the reeds / Trample under foot those who lust after tribute	those wild beasts of the reeds / (omits)	the Beast of the Reeds / until, humbled, they bring gold and silver	the beasts in the reeds / Trampling under foot the pieces of silver	the beast among the reeds / Humbled, may it bring bars of silver
69 1 Save me, O God; for the waters are come in unto my **soul.**	neck	neck	neck	life	neck
71 11 Saying, God hath forsaken him: **persecute and take him;** for there is none to deliver him.	pursue and seize him	after him! seize him	Hound him down . . . seize him	Pursue and seize him	pursue him and seize him
63 8 My soul **followeth hard after** thee: thy right hand upholdeth me.	clings to	(I) humbly follow	clings close to	clings to	stay close to
65 13 The pastures are clothed with flocks; the valleys also are covered over with **corn;** they shout for joy, they also sing.	grain	corn	wheat	grain	grain
66 12 Thou **hast caused** men to ride over our heads; we went through fire and through water: but thou broughtest us **out** into **a wealthy place.**	didst let / forth / a spacious place	hast let / out / liberty	let / (you allow us once more to draw breath)	didst make / out / a place of abundance	let / (omits) / a place of abundance

KJV	RSV	NEB	JB	NAS	NIV
67 2 That thy way may be known upon earth, thy **saving health** among all nations.	saving power	saving power	power to save	salvation	salvation
73 5 They are not in trouble as other men; neither are they **plagued** like other men.	stricken	suffer the torments	(no human afflictions for them)	plagued	plagued
77 8 Is his **mercy clean gone** for ever? doth his promise fail for evermore?	steadfast love . . ceased	unfailing love now failed	love over	lovingkindness ceased	unfailing love vanished
78 54 And he brought them to **the border of his sanctuary,** even to this mountain, which his right hand had **purchased.**	to his holy land / won	his holy mountain / won	his sacred frontier / conquered	His holy land / gained	the border of his holy land / taken
79 1 O GOD, the heathen are come into thine inheritance; thy holy temple have they defiled; they have laid Jerusalem **on heaps.**	in ruins	in ruins	to a pile of ruins	in ruins	to rubble
81 3 **Blow up** the trumpet in the new moon, in the time appointed, on our solemn feast day.	Blow	Blow	sound	Blow	Sound
84 1 How **amiable** are thy **tabernacles,** O LORD of hosts!	lovely / dwelling-place	dear / dwelling-place	(I love) / palace	lovely / dwelling places	lovely / dwelling place
4 Blessed are they that dwell in thy house: **they will be still praising thee.** Selah.	ever singing thy praise	they never cease from praising thee	and can praise you all day long	They are ever praising Thee!	they are ever praising you
89 23 And I will **beat down** his foes before **his face,** and **plague** them that hate him.	crush / him / strike down	shatter / him / vanquish	crush / (omits) / strike dead	crush / him / strike	crush / him / strike down
91 3 Surely he shall deliver thee from the snare of the fowler, and from the **noisome** pestilence.	deadly	(raging tempest)	(fowlers hoping to destroy you)	deadly	deadly
105 18 Whose feet they hurt with fetters: **he was laid in** iron:	his neck was put in a collar of	kept . . . an (iron) collar clamped on his neck	they put his neck in	he himself was laid in	his neck was put in
35 And did eat up all the **herbs** in their land, and devoured the fruit of their ground.	vegetation	green thing	greenstuff	vegetation	green thing
109 10 Let his children be **continually vagabonds,** and beg: let them **seek their bread also out of their desolate places.**	wander about / be driven out of the ruins they inhabit	vagabonds / driven from their homes	homeless vagabonds / beggared and hounded from their hovels	wander about / seek sustenance far from their ruined homes	wandering beggars/ be driven from their ruined homes
18 As he clothed himself with cursing like as with his **garment,** so let **it come into his bowels** like water, and like oil into his bones.	coat / soak into his body	garment / seep into his body	cloak / soak right into him	garment / entered into his body	garment / entered into his body
119 50 This is my comfort in my affliction: **for thy word hath quickened me.**	that thy promise gives me life	that thy promise has given me life	that thy promises gives me life	That Thy word has revived me	Your promise renews my life.
101 I **have refrained** my feet from every evil way, that I might keep thy word.	hold back	set no (foot)	refrain	have restrained	have kept
147 I **prevented the dawning of the morning,** and cried: I hoped in thy word.	rise before dawn	rise before dawn	am up before dawn	rise before dawn	rise before dawn
157 Many are my persecutors and mine enemies; yet do I not **decline** from thy testimonies.	swerve	swerved	swerve	turn aside	turned
122 3 Jerusalem is builded as a city that is **compact** together:	bound firmly	(where people come together in unity)	one united	compact	closely compacted

KJV	RSV	NEB	JB	NAS	NIV
123 2 Behold, as the eyes of servants look unto the hand of their masters, and as the eyes of a maiden unto the hand of her mistress; so our eyes **wait upon** the LORD our God, until that he have mercy upon us.	look to	turned to	fixed on	look to	look to
124 3 Then they had swallowed us up **quick,** when their **wrath** was kindled against us:	alive	alive	alive	alive	alive
135 14 For the LORD will judge his people, and he will **repent himself** concerning his servants.	have compassion	have compassion	care(s)	have compassion	have compassion
139 15 My **substance** was not hid from thee, when I was made in secret, and **curiously** wrought in the lowest parts of the earth.	frame / intricately	body / (omits)	bones / (omits)	frame / skillfully	frame / (omits)
144 4 Man is like to **vanity:** his days are as a shadow that passeth away.	breath	puff of wind	mere puff of wind	mere breath	breath

Proverbs

KJV	RSV	NEB	JB	NAS	NIV
1 25 But ye have **set at nought** all my counsel, and **would none of** my reproof:	ignored/would have none of	spurned/would have nothing to do with	ignored/rejected	neglected/did not want	ignored/would not accept
2 14 Who rejoice to do evil, and delight in the **frowardness** of **the wicked;**	perverseness/evil	evil and subversive acts	deceitfulness/(omits)	perversity/evil	perverseness/evil
3 29 **Devise** not evil against thy neighbour, seeing he dwelleth **securely** by thee.	plan/trustingly	Plot/unsuspecting	plot/unsuspecting	devise/insecurity	plot/trustfully
5 16 Let thy fountains **be dispersed abroad,** and **rivers** of waters in the **streets.**	be scattered abroad/streams / streets	overflow/runnels / street	flow to waste/streams / public streets	be dispersed abroad/streams / streets	overflow/streams / public squares
6 2 Thou art snared with the **words of thy mouth,** thou art **taken** with the words of thy mouth.	utterance of your lips/caught	your promise/trapped	your own lips/entrapped	words of your mouth/caught	what you said/ ensnared
12 A **naughty person,** a wicked man, walketh with a **froward mouth.**	worthless person/crooked speech	scoundrel/crooked talk	scoundrel/leer on his lips	worthless person/a false mouth	scoundrel/corrupt mouth
13 He winketh with his eyes, he **speaketh** with his feet, he **teacheth** with his fingers;	scrapes/points	a touch/a sigh	shuffling/ beckoning	signals/points	signals/motions
14 **Frowardness is in his heart, he deviseth mischief** continually; he soweth discord.	with perverted heart devises evil	Subversion is the evil that he is plotting	Deceit in his heart, always scheming evil	Who with perversity in his heart devises evil continually	who plots evil with deceit in his heart
18 An heart that deviseth wicked **imaginations,** feet that **be swift** in running to **mischief,**	plans/make haste/evil	forges/swiftly/evil	weaves/hurry/evil	plans/rapidly/evil	schemes/are quick/evil
8 12 I wisdom dwell **with** prudence, and **find out** knowledge **of witty inventions.**	in/find/and discretion	(I bestow shrewdness and show the way to knowledge and prudence)	(am mistress of discretion)/(the inventor of lucidity of thought)	with/find/and discretion	together with/possess/ and discretion
23 I was set up **from everlasting,** from the beginning, **or ever** the earth was.	Ages ago/before	in times long past/before	From everlasting/before	From everlasting/the earliest times	from eternity/ before
9 15 To call **passengers** who **go right** on their ways:	those who pass by/are going straight	passers-by/hurry	passers-by/pass	those who pass by/are making (their paths) straight	those who pass by/go straight

	KJV	RSV	NEB	JB	NAS	NIV
10	3 The LORD will not **suffer** the **soul of** the righteous **to famish:** but he **casteth away** the **substance** of the wicked.	let/(omits)/to go hungry/thwarts / craving	let/(omits)/to go hungry / disappoints / cravings	leave/(omits) / hungry / thwarts / greed	allow/(omits)/to hunger/thrust aside / craving	let/(omits)/go hungry / thwarts / craving
	9 He that walketh **uprightly** walketh **surely:** but he that perverteth his ways shall be **known.**	in integrity/securely / found out	(A blameless life makes for security)	secure/honourable	in integrity/ securely	(The man) of integrity / securely
	17 He is **in the** way of life that **keepeth** instruction: but he that **refuseth** reproof **erreth.**	on the/heeds/rejects/goes astray	(Correction is the high road to life)/neglect/miss the way	(The path of life is to abide by discipline)/ignores/goes astray	on the/heeds/forsakes/goes astray	(He . . . shows the way to life)/heeds/ignores/leads others astray
	19 In the multitude of words there wanteth not sin: but he that **refraineth** his lips is **wise.**	restrains/prudent	(When men talk too much, sin is never far away; common sense holds its tongue.)	controlled/prudent	restrains/wise	holds/wise
	32 The lips of the righteous know what is acceptable: but the mouth of the wicked **speaketh frowardness.**	what is perverse	know only subversive talk	(drip) with deceit	what is perverted	only what is perverse
11	6 The righteousness of the upright shall deliver them: but transgressors shall be taken in their own **naughtiness.**	lust	greed	desires	greed	evil desires
12	16 A fool's **wrath** is **presently** known: but a prudent man **covereth shame.**	vexation/at once/ignores an insult	ill humour/at once/conceals his feelings	displeasure/right away/overlooks the insult	vexation/at once/conceals dishonor	annoyance/at once/overlooks an insult
	25 **Heaviness** in the heart of man maketh it stoop: but a good word maketh it glad.	Anxiety	(An anxious heart)	Worry	Anxiety	(An anxious heart)
13	23 Much food is in **the tillage** of the poor: but **there is that** is destroyed for **want of judgment.**	The fallow ground/it/injustice	Untilled land/even that/injustice	fallow/there are some/when justice fails	the fallow ground/it/injustice	field/it/injustice
15	4 A **wholesome** tongue is a tree of life: but perverseness therein is a breach in the spirit.	gentle	soothing	that soothes	soothing	that brings healing
16	27 An **ungodly man diggeth up** evil: and in his **lips** there is as a **burning** fire.	worthless man/plots/speech scorching	scoundrel/repeats/lips / scorching	scoundrel/digs deep/lips/that scorches	worthless man/digs up/words/ scorching	scoundrel/plots/speech/ scorching
17	3 The **fining pot** is for silver, and the furnace for gold: but the LORD trieth the hearts.	crucible	melting-pot	crucible	refining pot	crucible
	4 A wicked doer giveth heed to **false** lips; and a liar giveth ear to a **naughty** tongue.	wicked/mischievous	mischievous/(slander)	malicious/slanderous	wicked/destructive	evil/malicious
	8 **A gift** is as a **precious stone** in the eyes of him that **hath** it: whithersoever **it** turneth, **it** prospereth.	bribe/magic stone/he/he gives	bribe/charm/he/he offers	gift/talisman/he/he gives	bribe/charm/he/he (the owner)	bribe/charm/he/he gives
	18 A man **void of understanding striketh hands,** and becometh surety in the presence of his **friend.**	without sense gives a pledge/neighbor	is without sense who gives a guarantee/another	lacks sense who offers guarantees/neighbor	lacking in senses pledges/neighbor	lacking in judgment strikes hand in pledge/neighbor
18	2 A fool hath no **delight** in understanding, but **that his heart may discover itself.**	pleasure/only in expressing his opinion	interest/prefer to display their wit	love/only for airing his opinion	delight/only in revealing his own mind	pleasure/delights in airing his own opinions
	9 He also that is **slothful** in his work is brother to him **that is a great waster.**	slack/who destroys	lazy/who enjoys destruction	idle/the destroyer	slack/him who destroys	slack/one who destroys
21	4 An **high look,** and a proud heart, **and the plowing of the wicked,** is sin.	Haughty eyes/the lamp of the wicked	Haughty looks/(these sins mark a wicked man)	Haughty eye/lamp of the wicked	Haughty eyes/The lamp of the wicked	Haughty eyes/the lamp of the wicked
	15 It is joy to the **just** to do **judgment:** but **destruction** shall be to the **workers of iniquity.**	righteous/justice/dismay/evildoers	good men/justice/ ruin/evildoers	virtuous/justice/dismay/evildoers	righteous/justice/terror/ workers of iniquity	righteous/justice/terror/evildoers

	KJV	RSV	NEB	JB	NAS	NIV
	28 A false witness shall perish: but the **man** that heareth **speaketh constantly.**	word of a man/will endure	he (whose words ring true) / will leave children behind him	obedient/will always be heard	who/will speak forever	whoever (listens to him) / will be destroyed forever
22	8 He that soweth **iniquity** shall reap **vanity:** and the rod of his **anger** shall fail.	in justice/ calamity/fury	injustice/trouble/ (and the end of his work will be the rod)	injustice/disaster/anger	iniquity/vanity/fury	wickedness/trouble/fury
	26 Be not thou one of them that **strike hands,** or of them that are sureties for debts.	give pledges	give guarantees	go surety for debts	give pledges	strikes hands in pledge
	29 Seest thou a man **diligent in his business?** he shall stand before kings; he shall not stand before **mean** men.	skilful in his work/obscure	skilful at his craft/common	sharp at business/obscure	skilled in his work/obscure	skilled in his work/obscure
23	20 Be not among winebibbers; among **riotous** eaters of **flesh:**	gluttonous/meat	greedy/flesh-pots	(those who gorge themselves)/meat	gluttonous/meat	(gorge themselves)/meat
25	18 A man that beareth false witness against his neighbour is a **maul,** and a sword, and a sharp arrow.	war club	club	mace	club	club
26	23 **Burning lips and a wicked heart are like a potsherd covered with silver dross.**	Like the glaze covering an earthen vessel are smooth lips with an evil heart.	Glib speech that covers a spiteful heart is like glaze spread on earthenware.	A glaze applied to an earthen pot: such are smooth lips and wicked heart.	Like an earthen vessel overlaid with silver dross Are burning lips and a wicked heart.	Like a coating of glaze over earthenware are fervent lips with an evil heart.
28	7 Whoso keepeth the law is a wise son: but he that is a companion of **riotous men** shameth his father.	gluttons	riotous company	profligates	gluttons	gluttons
	21 To **have respect of persons** is not good: **for** for a piece of bread that man will **transgress.**	show partiality/but/do wrong	show favour/but /do wrong	show partiality /but/do wrong	show partiality/ Because/transgress	show partiality/ yet/do wrong
29	21 He that **delicately bringeth up** his servant from a child shall have him **become his son at the length.**	pampers/in the end find him his heir	Pamper/in the end he will prove ungrateful	(If . . . slave is pampered)/will prove ungrateful in the end	pampers/in the end find him to be a son	pampers/bring grief in the end
	24 Whoso is partner with a thief hateth his own soul: he heareth cursing, and **bewrayeth** it not.	discloses	give (evidence)	make (no disclosure)	tells	dare not testify
30	8 Remove far from me **vanity** and lies: give me neither poverty nor riches; feed me with **food convenient for me:**	falsehood/food that is needful for me	fraud/food I need	falsehood/my share of bread to eat	deception/food that is my portion	falsehood/my daily bread
31	10 Who can find a **virtuous woman?** for her **price** is far above **rubies.**	good wife/(She is far more precious)/jewels	capable wife/worth/coral	perfect wife/price/pearls	excellent wife/worth / jewels	wife of noble character/worth / rubies

Ecclesiastes

	KJV	RSV	NEB	JB	NAS	NIV
1	2 **Vanity of vanities,** saith the Preacher, vanity of vanities; all is vanity.	Vanity of vanities	Emptiness, emptiness	Vanity of vanities	Vanity of vanities	Meaningless! Meaningless!
	13 And I **gave my heart** to seek and search out by wisdom concerning all things that are done under heaven: this **sore travail** hath God given to the sons of man to be **exercised** therewith.	applied my mind/unhappy business/busy	applied my mind/sorry business/busy themselves	have been at pains/weary task / labour	set my mind/grievous task / exercised	devoted myself/heavy burden / laid upon
5	18 Behold that which I have seen: it is good and **comely** for one to eat and to drink, and to enjoy the good of all his labour that he taketh under the sun all the days of his life, which God giveth him: for it is his portion.	fitting	proper	(the right happiness is)	fitting	proper
7	7 Surely oppression maketh a wise man **mad;** and a gift destroyeth the **heart.**	foolish/mind	crazy/spirit	a fool/heart	mad/heart	into a fool/heart

KJV	RSV	NEB	JB	NAS	NIV
10 1 Dead flies cause the ointment of the **apothecary** to send forth a **stinking savour:** so doth a little folly **him that is in reputation for** wisdom and honour.	perfumer('s)/evil odor / outweighs	perfumer('s)/(turn rancid and ferment) (make wisdom lose its worth)	(bowl of perfumed oil)/ spoil/stronger than	perfumer('s)/stink / weightier than	perfumer('s)/(turn rancid and ferment) / (make wisdom lose its worth)
10 If the iron be blunt, and he do not whet the edge, then must he **put to** more strength: but wisdom **is profitable to direct.**	put forth/helps one to succeed	use	strike (very hard)	exert	use
12 3 In the day when the keepers of the house shall tremble, and the strong men shall bow themselves, and the grinders cease because they are few, and those that look out of the windows **be darkened,**	are dimmed	look no longer	(because day is darkening at the windows)	grow dim	look no longer
5 Also when they shall be afraid of that which is high, and fears shall be in the way, and the almond tree shall flourish, and the **grasshopper shall be a burden,** and desire shall fail: because man goeth to his **long** home, and the mourners go about the streets:	grasshopper drags itself along / eternal	locust's paunch is swollen / everlasting	grasshopper is heavy with food / everlasting	grasshopper drags himself along /	eternal
6 Or ever the silver cord **be loosed,** or the golden bowl be broken, or the pitcher be broken at the fountain, or the wheel broken at the cistern.	is snapped	is snapped	has snapped	is broken	is severed

Song of Solomon

KJV	RSV	NEB	JB	NAS	NIV
2 5 **Stay** me with **flagons, comfort** me with apples: for I am sick **of** love.	Sustain/raisins/refresh / with	refreshed/raisins/revived / with	Feed/raisin cakes/restore / with	Sustain/raisin cakes/ Refresh / (lovesick)	Strengthen/raisins /refresh /with
12 The flowers appear on the earth; the time of **the** singing **of birds** is come, and the voice of the **turtle** is heard in our land;	(omits)/(omits)/ turtledove	(the birds will sing) / turtledove('s)	(glad songs) / (omits) / turtledove	(for pruning the vines) / turtledove	(omits)/(omits) / doves
5 4 My beloved put in his hand **by the hole of the door,** and my **bowels** were moved for him.	to the latch/heart	through the latch-hole / bowels	through the hole in the door / core of my being	through the opening / feelings	through the latch-opening / heart
6 12 **Or ever** I was aware, my soul made me like the chariots of Amminadib.	Before	(omits)	Before	Before	Before
7 1 How beautiful are thy feet with shoes, O prince's daughter! the joints of thy thighs are like jewels, the work of the hands of a **cunning workman.**	master hand	skilled craftsman	master hand	artist	craftsman('s)
5 Thine head upon thee is like Carmel, and the hair of thine head like purple; **the king is held in the galleries.**	a king is held captive in the tresses	your tresses are braided with ribbons	a king is held captive in your tresses	The king is captivated by your tresses	the king is held captive by its tresses

Isaiah

KJV	RSV	NEB	JB	NAS	NIV
1 12 When ye come to appear before me, who hath required this **at your hand, to tread** my courts?	of you/trampling	you/trample	you/to trample	of you/trampling	of you/trampling
13 Bring no more vain oblations; incense is an abomination unto me; the new moons and sabbaths, the calling of assemblies, I cannot **away with;** it is iniquity, even the solemn meeting.	endure	endure	endure	endure	bear

	KJV	RSV	NEB	JB	NAS	NIV
2	9 And the **mean** man **boweth down,** and the **great** man **humbleth** himself: therefore forgive them not.	(omits)/is humbled/(omits)/are brought low	(Mankind)/shall be brought low/ all/shall be humbled	(mortal)/will be humbled/(omits)/ brought low	common/has been humbled/of importance/has been abased	(omits)/will be brought low/ (omits)/humbled
3	2 The mighty man, and the man of war, the judge, and the prophet, and the prudent, and the **ancient,**	elder (also vss. 5, 14)	elder (also vss. 5, 14)	elder (also vss. 5, 14)	elder (also vss. 5, 14)	elder (vs. 5, "the old"; also vs. 14)
	9 **The shew of their countenance** doth witness against them; and they **declare** their sin as Sodom, they hide it not. Woe unto **their soul!** for they have **rewarded** evil unto themselves.	Their partiality/ proclaim/them/ brought	The look on their faces/proclaim/ them/earned	Their insolent airs/ parade/(omits)/ (they are preparing their own downfall)	The expression of their faces/display/them/ brought	The look on their faces/parade/ them/brought
	17 Therefore the Lord will smite with a scab the crown of the head of the daughters of Zion, and the LORD will **discover** their secret parts.	lay bare	(strip the hair from their foreheads)	uncover	make (their foreheads) bare	make (their scalps) bald
	18 In that day the LORD will take away the **bravery** of their **tinkling ornaments about their feet,** and their **cauls,** and their **round tires like the moon,**	finery/anklets/ headbands/crescents	finery/anklets/ discs/crescents	(omits)/ankle ornaments/tiaras/ (omits)	beauty/anklets/ headbands/crescent ornaments	finery/headbands/ crescent necklaces
5	15 And the **mean** man shall be **brought down,** and the **mighty** man shall be **humbled,** and the eyes of the **lofty** shall be humbled:	(omits) / bowed down / (omits) / brought low / haughty/	(mankind) / brought low/(omits)/humbled/(haughty looks)	(mortal)/humbled/ (omits)/brought low/proud	common/humbled/ of importance/ abased/proud	(Both low and high)/humbled/ arrogant
	27 None shall be weary nor stumble among them; none shall slumber nor sleep; neither shall the **girdle of their loins** be loosed, nor the **latchet of their shoes** be broken:	waistcloth/sandal-thong	belt . . . about his waist/ thong to his sandals	belt/sandal-straps	belt at the waist/ sandal strap	belt . . . at the waist/sandal thong
6	10 Make the heart of this people fat, and make their eyes heavy, and shut their eyes; lest they see with their eyes, and hear with their ears, and understand with their heart, and **convert,** and be healed.	turn	turn	be converted	return	turn
7	14 Therefore the LORD himself shall give you a sign; Behold, a **virgin** shall conceive, and bear a son, and shall call his name Immanuel.	young woman	young woman	maiden	virgin	virgin
	15 **Butter** and honey shall he eat, that he may **know to** refuse the evil, and choose the good.	curds/knows how	curds/(has learnt to)	curds/how to	curds/enough to	curds/enough to
	16 For before the child shall know to refuse the evil, and choose the good, the land **that thou abhorrest** shall be forsaken of both her kings.	before whose two kings you are in dread	before whose two kings you cower now	whose two kings terrify you	whose two kings you dread	of the two kings you dread
	21 And it shall come to pass in that day, that a man shall **nourish** a young cow, and two sheep;	keep alive	save alive	raise	keep alive	keep alive
8	6 Forasmuch as this people refuseth the waters of Shiloah that **go softly,** and **rejoice** in Rezin and Remaliah's son;	flow gently/melt in fear before	so softly/gently	in tranquility/trembles before	gently flow(ing)/ rejoice in	gently flow(ing)/ rejoices over
9	1 Nevertheless the **dimness** shall not be such as was in her **vexation,** when at the first he lightly afflicted the land of Zebulun and the land of Naphtali, and afterward did **more grievously afflict** her by the way of the sea, beyond Jordan, in Galilee of the nations.	gloom/anguish/ make glorious	(for there is no escape for an oppressed people)/ dealt heavily with	(The people that walked in darkness has seen a great light)/(on those who live in a land of deep shadow a light has shone)	gloom/anguish/ make it glorious	gloom/distress/ honor

	KJV	RSV	NEB	JB	NAS	NIV
	9 And all the people shall know, even Ephraim and the inhabitant of Samaria, that say in the pride and **stoutness of heart,**	arrogance of heart	arrogance	arrogance of their heart	arrogance of heart	arrogance of heart
10	27 And it shall come to pass in that day, that his burden shall be taken away from off thy shoulder, and his yoke from off thy neck, and the **yoke** shall be destroyed **because of the anointing.**	yoke/from your neck/He has gone up from Rimmon	yoke/from your neck/An invader from Rimmon	yoke/on your neck/He advances from the district of Rimmon	yoke/from your neck/and the yoke will be broken because of fatness	yoke/from your neck/because you have grown so fat
	28 He is come to Aiath, he is passed to Migron; at Michmash he hath **laid up his carriages:**	stores his baggage	left his baggage-train	leaves his baggage train	deposited his baggage	store supplies
11	8 And the sucking child shall play on the hole of the **asp,** and the weaned child shall put his hand on the **cockatrice's** den.	asp/adder's	cobra/viper's	cobra's/viper's	cobra/viper's	cobra/viper's
	15 And the LORD shall utterly destroy the tongue of the Egyptian sea; and **with his mighty wind shall he shake his hand over the river,** and shall smite it in the seven streams, and make men go over dryshod.	will wave his hand over the River with his scorching wind	wave his hand over the River to bring a scorching wind	(dry up the gulf of the Sea of Egypt) with the heat of his breath/and stretch out his hand over the River	And He will wave His hand over the River With His scorching wind	with a scorching wind he will sweep his hand over the Euphrates River
13	2 Lift ye up a **banner** upon the **high mountain, exalt the voice** unto them, **shake the hand,** that they may go into the gates of the nobles.	signal/bare mountain/cry aloud/wave the hand	standard/windy height/roar out your summons/beckon	signal/bare hill/sound the war cry/Beckon	standard/bare hill/Raise your voice/Wave the hand	banner/bare hilltop/shout, beckon
	21 But wild beasts of the desert shall lie there; and their houses shall be full of **doleful creatures;** and **owls** shall dwell there, and satyrs shall dance there.	howling creatures/ostriches	porcupines/desert owls	owls/Ostriches	owls/ostriches	jackals/owls
	22 And the **wild beasts of the islands** shall cry in their **desolate houses,** and **dragons** in their pleasant palaces: and her time is near to come, and her days shall not be prolonged.	wild beasts/there/howling creatures	jackals/mansions/wolves	Hyenas/keeps/jackals	hyenas/fortified towers/jackals	Hyenas/strongholds/jackals
15	5 My heart shall cry out for Moab; his fugitives shall flee unto Zoar, **an heifer of three years old:** for by the **mounting up** of Luhith with weeping shall they **go it up;** for in the way of Horonaim they **shall raise up a cry of** destruction.	to Eglath-shelishiyah/ascent/go up/raise a cry of	(omits)/ascent/go up/there are cries of	(Eglath Shelishiyah)/slopes/climb/(utter heart-rending cries)	and Eglath-shelishiyah/ascent/go up/raise a cry of	as far as Eglath Shelishiyah/way/go up/lament their
16	11 Wherefore my **bowels shall sound like an harp** for Moab, and mine **inward parts** for Kirharesh.	soul moans like a lyre/heart	heart throbs like a harp/very soul	whole being quivers like lyre strings/inmost self	heart intones like a harp/inward feelings	heart laments . . . like a hart/inmost being
17	8 And he shall not look to the **altars,** the work of his hands, neither shall respect that which his fingers have made, either **the groves,** or the **images.**	Asherim/altars of incense (also 27:9)	sacred poles/incense-altars (also 27:9)	sacred poles/solar pillars (also 27:9)	Asherim/incense stands (also 27:9)	Asherah poles/incense altars (also 27:9)
19	6 And they shall turn the rivers far away; and the **brooks of defence** shall be emptied and dried up: the reeds and **flags** shall wither.	branches of Egypt's Nile/rushes	streams of Egypt/rushes	Niles of Egypt/rush	streams of Egypt/rushes	streams of Egypt/rushes
	7 The paper reeds by the **brooks,** by the mouth of the **brooks,** and every thing sown by the brooks, shall wither, be driven away, and be no more.	Nile/Nile	Nile/Nile	Nile/Nile	Nile/Nile	Nile/Nile
	8 The fishers also shall mourn, and all they that **cast angle into the brooks** shall lament, and they that spread nets upon the waters shall languish.	cast hook/Nile	cast their hooks/Nile	cast hook/Nile	cast a line/Nile	cast hooks/Nile

	KJV	RSV	NEB	JB	NAS	NIV
	22 And the LORD shall smite Egypt: he shall smite and heal it: and they shall return even to the LORD, and he shall be **entreated of them,** and shall heal them.	heed their supplications	hear their prayers	listen to them	respond to them	respond to their pleas
21	8 And **he cried, A lion:** My lord, I stand continually upon the watchtower in the daytime, and I am set in my ward whole nights:	he who saw cried	the look-out cried	The look-out shouts	the lookout called	the lookout shouted
22	8 And he **discovered** the covering of Judah, and thou didst look in that day to the **armour** of the house of the forest.	has taken away/weapons	laid open/weapons	falls/armoury	removed/weapons	stripped away/weapons
	25 In that day, saith the LORD of hosts, shall the **nail** that is fastened in the sure place **be removed,** and be cut down, and fall; and the burden that was upon it shall be cut off: for the LORD hath spoken it.	peg/give away	peg/be removed	peg/give way	peg/give way	peg/give way
24	19 The earth is utterly broken down, the earth is **clean dissolved,** the earth is **moved exceedingly.**	rent asunder/violently shaken	convulsed/reels wildly	riven and rent/shiver and shake	split through/shaken violently	is split asunder/is thoroughly shaken
	20 The earth shall **reel to and fro** like a drunkard, and shall **be removed** like a **cottage;** and the transgression thereof shall be heavy upon it; and it shall fall, and not rise again.	staggers/sways/hut	reels to and fro/sways/watchman's shelter	stagger/sway/shanty	reels to and fro/totters/shack	reels/sways/hut
	23 Then the moon shall be confounded, and the sun ashamed, when the LORD of hosts shall reign in mount Zion, and in Jerusalem, and **before his ancients gloriously.**	before his elders he will manifest glory	shows his glory before their elders	his glory will shine in the presence of his elders	His glory will be before His elders	before its elders, gloriously
25	2 For thou hast made of a city an heap; of a **defenced** city a ruin: **a palace of strangers** to be no city; it shall never be built.	fortified/palace of aliens	fortified/mansion	fortified/citadel	fortified/palace of strangers	fortified/stronghold of the foreigners
	5 Thou shalt bring down the noise of **strangers,** as the heat in a dry place; even the heat with the shadow of a cloud: the **branch** of the **terrible ones** shall be **brought low.**	aliens/song/ruthless/stilled	the foe/song/ruthless/dies away	the proud/singing/despots/subdued	aliens/song/ruthless/silenced	foreigners/song/ruthless/stilled
28	7 But they also **have erred through** wine, and through strong drink **are out of the way;** the priest and the prophet **have erred through** strong drink, they are **swallowed up of** wine, they **are out of the way** through strong drink; they err in vision, they stumble in judgment.	reel with/stagger/reel with/are confused with/stagger	are addicted to/clamouring/are addicted to/bemused with/clamouring	reeling with/staggering/are reeling from/muddled with/stagger	reel with/stagger/reel with/confused by/stagger	stagger from/reel/stagger from/befuddled with/stagger
29	**Woe to** Ariel, to Ariel, the city where David dwelt! add ye year to year; **let them kill sacrifices.**	Ho/let the feasts run their round	Alas for/let the pilgrim-feasts run their round	Woe/let the feasts make their full round	Woe, O/observe your feasts on schedule	Woe to/let your cycle of festivals go on
	7 And the multitude of all the nations that fight against Ariel, even all that fight against her and her **munition,** and that distress her, shall be as a dream **of** a night vision.	stronghold/(omits)	siege-works/(omits)	entrenchments besieging her/like	stronghold/(omits)	fortress/with
30	6 The burden of the beasts of the south: into the land of trouble and anguish, from whence come the young and old lion, the viper and fiery flying serpent, they will carry their riches upon the **shoulders** of young asses, and their treasures upon the **bunches** of camels, to a people that shall not profit them.	backs/humps	backs/humps	backs/humps	backs/humps	backs/humps
	14 And he shall break it as the **breaking** of the potter's vessel that is **broken in pieces;** he shall not spare: so that there					

	KJV	RSV	NEB	JB	NAS	NIV
	shall not be found **in the bursting of it** a sherd to take fire from the hearth, or to take water withal out of **the pit.**	among its fragments/cistern	among the fragments/pool	of the fragments/cistern	among its pieces/cistern	among its pieces/cistern
	24 The oxen likewise and the young asses that **ear** the ground shall eat **clean** provender, which hath been winnowed with the shovel and with the **fan.**	till/salted/fork	work/well-seasoned/fork	till/salted/fork	work/salted/fork	work/(fodder and mash)/fork
31	8 Then shall the Assyrian fall with the sword, not of a mighty man; and the sword, not of a mean man, shall devour him: but he shall flee from the sword, and his young men shall be **discomfited.**	put to forced labor	put to forced labour	enslaved	become forced laborers	put to forced labor
32	5 The **vile person** shall be no more called **liberal,** nor the **churl** said to be **bountiful.**	fool/noble/knave/honorable	scoundrel/noble/villain/a prince	fool/noble/villain/honourable	fool/noble/rogue/generous	fool/noble/scoundrel/highly respected
33	16 He shall dwell on **high:** his place of defence shall be the **munitions of rocks:** bread shall be given him; his waters shall be sure.	the heights/fortresses of rocks	the heights/a fastness in the cliffs	the heights/citadel built on rock	the heights/impregnable rock	the heights/mountain fortress
	23 Thy **tacklings are loosed;** they could not **well strengthen** their mast, they could not spread the sail: then is the prey of a great spoil divided; [] the lame take the prey.	tackle hangs loose/ hold/even	rigging is slack/hold/and	tackle hangs loose/ supports/even	tackle hangs slack/ hold/(no insert)	rigging hangs loose/held secure/ and even
34	13 And thorns shall **come up in her palaces,** nettles and **brambles** in the fortresses thereof: and it shall be an **habitation of dragons,** and a **court for owls.**	grow over its strongholds/thistles/haunt of jackals/abode for ostriches	sprout in its palaces/briars/rough land fit for wolves/ haunt of desert-owls	grow in the palaces there/thistles/lair for jackals/lodging for ostriches	come up in its fortified towers/ thistles/haunt of jackals/abode of ostriches	overrun her citadels/brambles/ haunt for jackals/ home for owls
38	8 Behold, I will bring again the shadow of the degrees, which is gone down in the sun dial of Ahaz, ten degrees backward. So the sun returned ten **degrees,** by which degrees it was gone down.	steps	steps	steps	steps	steps
	14 Like a crane or a swallow, **so did I chatter:** I did **mourn** as a dove: mine eyes **fail** with looking upward: O LORD, I am oppressed; **undertake for me.**	I clamor/moan like/are weary/be thou my security	I twitter/moan like/falter/stand surety for me	I am twittering/ moaning like/(turn on the heights)/be my safeguard	so I twitter/moan like/(look wistfully)/be my security	I cried/moaned like/weak/come to my aid
40	2 Speak ye **comfortably** to Jerusalem, and cry unto her, that her warfare **is accomplished,** that her iniquity is pardoned: for she hath received of the LORD'S hand double for all her sins.	tenderly/is ended	tenderly/(she has fulfilled her term of bondage)	to the heart of/is ended	kindly/has ended	tenderly/has been completed
	12 Who hath measured the waters in the hollow of his hand, and **meted out** heaven with **the span,** and **comprehended** the dust of the earth in a **measure,** and weighed the mountains in scales, and the hills in a balance?	marked off/a span/enclosed/ measure	set limits to/its span/held/bushel	calculated/(omits)/ gauged/bushel	marked off/the span/calculated/ measure	marked off/the breadth of his hand/held/basket
	20 He that is so impoverished **that he hath no oblation** chooseth a tree that will not rot; he seeketh unto him a **cunning workman** to prepare a graven image, that shall not be moved.	(omits)/skilful craftsman	(omits)/skilful craftsman	(For it a clever sculptor seeks precious palm wood, selects wood that will not decay to set up a sturdy image.)	for such an offering/skillful craftsmen	to present such an offering/skilled craftsman
41	1 Keep silence before me, **O islands;** and let the people renew their strength: let them come near; then let them speak: let us come near together to judgment.	O coastlands (also 41:5)	all you coasts and islands (also 41:5)	Islands (also 41:5)	Coastlands (also 41:5)	you islands (also 41:5)
	16 Thou shalt **fan** them, and the wind shall carry them away, and the **whirlwind** shall scatter them: and thou shalt rejoice in the LORD, and shalt glory in the Holy One of Israel.	winnow/tempest	winnow/gale	winnow/gale	winnow/storm	winnow/gale
	29 Behold, they are all **vanity;** their	A delusion/empty	empty things/	nothing/wind and	false/wind and	false/wind and

KJV	RSV	NEB	JB	NAS	NIV
works are nothing: their molten images are **wind and confusion.**	wind	wind/mere nothings	emptiness	emptiness	confusion
43 13 **Yea, before the day was** I am he; and there is none that can deliver out of my hand: I will work, and who **shall let it?**	and also henceforth/ can hinder	from this very day/can undo	from eternity/can reverse	Even from eternity/can reverse	and from ancient days/can reverse
20 The beast of the field shall honour me, the **dragons** and the **owls:** because I give waters in the wilderness, and rivers in the desert, to give drink to my people, my chosen.	jackals/ostriches	wolf/ostrich	jackals/ostriches	jackals/ostriches	jackals/owls
44 9 They that make a graven image are all of them **vanity;** and **their delectable things** shall not profit; and they are their own witnesses; they see not, nor know; that they may be ashamed.	nothing/things they delight in	nothing/their cherished images	nothing/works they prize	futile/their precious things	nothing/things they treasure
47 6 I was wroth with my people, I have polluted mine inheritance, and given them into thine hand: thou didst shew them no mercy; upon the **ancient** hast thou very heavily laid thy yoke.	aged	aged	aged	aged	aged
49 20 The children **which thou shalt have, after thou hast lost the other,** shall say again in thine ears, The place is too **strait** for me: give place to me that I may dwell.	born in the time of your bereavement/narrow	born in your bereavement/ narrow	those sons you thought were lost/small	of whom you were bereaved/ cramped	born during your bereavement/ small
23 And kings shall be thy **nursing** fathers, and their queens thy nursing mothers: they shall bow down to thee with their face toward the earth, and lick up the dust of thy feet; and thou shalt know that I am the LORD: for they shall not be ashamed that wait for me.	foster	foster-	foster	guardians	foster
50 10 Who is among you that feareth the LORD, that obeyeth the voice of his servant, that walketh in darkness, and hath no light? **let him** trust in the name of the LORD, and **stay** upon his God.	yet/relies	yet/leans	let/lean	Let/rely	(omits)/rely
52 15 So shall he **sprinkle** many nations; the kings shall shut their mouths at him: for that which had not been told them shall they see; and that which they had not heard shall they consider.	startle	(nations) recoil	will (the crowds) be astonished	sprinkle	sprinkle
53 10 Yet it pleased the LORD to bruise him; he hath put him to grief: when thou shalt make his soul an **offering for sin,** he shall see his seed, he shall prolong his days, and the pleasure of the LORD shall prosper in his hand.	offering for sin	sacrifice for sin	offers . . . in atonement	guilt offering	guilt offering
11 He shall see **of the travail of his soul,** and shall be satisfied: by his knowledge shall my righteous servant justify many; for he shall bear their iniquities.	the fruit of the travail of his soul	all his pains	soul's anguish	of the anguish of His soul	suffering of his soul
54 16 Behold, I have created the smith that bloweth the coals in the fire, and that **bringeth forth an instrument for his work;** and I have created **the waster** to destroy.	produces a weapon for its purpose/ the ravager	forge weapons each for its purpose/the destroyer	from it takes the weapons to work on/the destroyer	brings out a weapon for its work/ the destroyer	forges a weapon fit for its work/ the destroyer
57 4 Against whom **do ye sport yourselves?** against whom make ye a wide mouth, and **draw out** the tongue? are ye not children of transgression, **a seed of falsehood,**	are you making sport/put out/ offspring of deceit	do you open your mouths/wag/ spawn of a lie	are you jeering/ sticking out/children of lies	do you jest/stick out/Offspring of deceit	are you mocking/ stick out/offspring of liars
8 Behind the doors also and the posts hast thou set up thy **remembrance:** for thou hast **discovered thyself** to another than me, and art gone up; thou hast	symbol/uncovered your bed/made it wide/a bargain	sign/stripped and lain down/bed which you have	sign/unroll your bedding/spread it wide/a pact	sign/uncovered yourself/made your bed wide/an	symbols/uncovered your bed/ opened it wide/a

	KJV	RSV	NEB	JB	NAS	NIV
	enlarged thy bed, and made thee **a covenant** with them; thou lovedst their bed where thou sawest it.		made wide/ bargains		agreement	pact
	17 For the iniquity of his covetousness was I **wroth,** and smote him: I hid **me,** and was **wroth,** and he went on **frowardly** in the way of his heart.	angry/my face/ angry/backsliding	angry/my favour/ in anger/wilful	Angered/my face/ in anger/Like a rebel	angry/My face/ angry/turning away	enraged/my face/ in anger/willful
58	4 Behold, ye fast **for strife and debate,** and to smite with the fist of wickedness: ye shall not fast as ye do this day, to make your voice to be heard on high.	only to quarrel and to fight	only to wrangling and strife	quarrel and squabble (when you fast)	for contention and strife	in quarreling and strife
	7 Is it not to **deal** thy bread to the hungry, and that thou bring the poor that are cast out to thy house? when thou seest the naked, that thou cover him; and that thou hide not thyself from thine own flesh?	share	sharing	share	divide	share
59	7 Their feet run to evil, and they make haste to shed innocent blood: their thoughts are thoughts of iniquity; **wasting** and destruction are in their **paths.**	desolation/highways	ruin/trail	havoc/(wherever they go)	Devastation/highways	ruins/ways
60	18 Violence shall no more be heard in thy land, **wasting** nor destruction within thy borders; but thou shalt call thy walls Salvation, and thy gates Praise.	devastation	ruin	devastation	devastation	ruin
63	1 Who is this that cometh from Edom, with **dyed** garments from Bozrah? this that is glorious in his apparel, travelling in the greatness of his strength? I that speak in righteousness, mighty to save.	crimsoned	stained red	stained with crimson	of glowing colors	stained crimson
	2 Wherefore art thou red in thine apparel, and thy garments like him that treadeth in the **winevat?**	wine press	vat	winepress	wine press	winepress
	15 Look down from heaven, and behold from the habitation of thy holiness and of thy glory: where is thy zeal and thy **strength,** the **sounding of thy bowels** and of thy **mercies** toward me? are they restrained?	might/yearning of thy heart/ compassion	valour/thy burning/tender love	might/yearning of your inmost heart/ compassion	mighty deeds/stirrings of Thy heart/ compassion	might/Your tenderness/compassion

Jeremiah

	KJV	RSV	NEB	JB	NAS	NIV
1	12 Then said the LORD unto me, Thou hast well seen: for I **will hasten** my word to perform it.	am watching over	early on the watch	watch over	am watching over	am watching
	17 Thou therefore gird up thy loins, and arise, and speak unto them all that I command thee: be not dismayed at their faces, lest **I confound** thee before them.	dismay	break	make . . . dismayed	dismay	terrify
2	8 The priests said not, Where is the LORD? and they that handle the law knew me not: the **pastors** also transgressed against me, and the prophets prophesied by Baal, and walked after things that do not profit.	rulers	shepherds of the people	shepherds	rulers	leaders
	10 For pass over the **isles of Chittim,** and see; and send unto Kedar, and consider diligently, and see if there be such a thing.	coasts of Cyprus	islands of Kittim	islands of Kittim	coastlands of Kittim	coasts of Kittim
	34 Also in thy skirts is found the **blood of the souls** of the **poor innocents:** I have not found it by secret search, but upon all these.	lifeblood/guiltless poor	life-blood/innocent poor	blood/innocent men	lifeblood/innocent poor	lifeblood/innocent poor

KJV	RSV	NEB	JB	NAS	NIV
37 Yea, thou shalt go forth from him, and thine hands upon thine head: for the LORD hath rejected **thy confidences,** and thou shalt not prosper in them.	those in whom you trust	those in whom you trusted	those that you rely on	those in whom you trust	those you trust
3 15 And I will give you **pastors according** to mine heart, which shall feed you with knowledge and understanding.	shepherds after (also 23:1)	shepherds after (also 23:1)	shepherds after (also 23:1)	shepherds after (also 23:1)	shepherds after (also 23:1)
4 11 At that time shall it be said to this people and to Jerusalem, A dry wind of the high places in the wilderness toward the daughter of my people, not **to fan,** nor to cleanse,	winnow	winnow(ing)	winnow	winnow	winnow
14 O Jerusalem, wash thine heart from wickedness, that thou mayest be saved. How long shall thy **vain** thoughts lodge within thee?	evil	evil	pernicious	wicked	wicked
19 **My bowels,** my bowels! I am pained at my very heart; my heart **maketh a noise in me;** I cannot hold my peace, because thou hast heard, O my soul, the sound of the trumpet, the **alarm of war.**	My anguish/beating wildly/alarm of war	the writhing of my bowels/(the throbbing of my heart)/sound of the battle-cry	I am in anguish!/(My heart is throbbing)/trumpet call	My soul/is pounding in me/alarm of war	my anguish/ pounds within me/battle cry
22 For my people is foolish, they have not known me; they are **sottish** children, and they have none understanding: they are **wise to do** evil, but to do good they have no knowledge.	stupid/skilled in doing	silly/clever only in	slow-witted/clever enough at doing	stupid/shrewd to do	senseless/skilled in doing
5 12 They have **belied** the LORD, and said, It is not he; neither shall evil come upon us; neither shall we see sword nor famine:	spoken falsely of	denied	disowned	lied about	lied about
28 They are **waxen fat, they shine:** yea, they **overpass the** deeds of the wicked: they judge not the cause, the cause of the fatherless, yet they prosper; and the right of the needy do they not **judge.**	grown fat and sleek/know no bounds in/defend	rich and grand, bloated and rancorous/(their thoughts are all of evil)/put right	fat and sleek/ go to any lengths/uphold	fat, they are sleek/excel in/defend	grown fat and sleek/(Their evil deeds) have no limit/defend
6 30 **Reprobate** silver shall men call them, because the LORD hath rejected them.	Refuse	spurned	-reject	rejected	rejected
7 24 But they **hearkened not,** nor inclined their ear, but walked in the counsels and in the **imagination** of their evil heart, and went backward, and not forward.	did not obey / stubbornness	did not listen / stubborn (hearts)	did not listen / (They have grown stubborn)	did not obey / stubbornness	did not obey / stubborn inclinations
33 And the carcases of this people shall be meat for the fowls of the heaven, and for the beasts of the earth; and none shall fray **them** away.	frighten	scare	drive	frighten	frighten
8 7 Yea, the stork in the heaven knoweth her appointed times; and the **turtle** and the crane and the swallow observe the time of their coming; but my people know not the **judgment** of the LORD.	turtledove/ ordinance	dove/ordinances	turtledove/ruling	turtledove/ ordinance	dove/requirements
9 11 And I will make Jerusalem **heaps,** and **a den of dragons;** and I will make the cities of Judah desolate, without an inhabitant.	a heap of ruins/lair of jackals	a heap of ruins/haunt of wolves	a heap of ruins/ a jackal's lair	a heap of ruins/haunt of jackals	a heap of ruins/haunt of jackals
17 Thus saith the LORD of hosts, Consider ye, and call for the mourning women, that they may come; and send for **cunning** women, that they may come.	skilful	skilled in keening	who are best at it	wailing women	most skillful
10 9 Silver **spread into plates** is brought from Tar-shish, and gold from U-phaz, the work of the **workman,** and of the hands of the **founder:** blue and purple is their clothing: they are all the work of **cunning** men.	Beaten / craftsman / goldsmith/skilled	beaten / craftsman / goldsmiths / skilled	leaf / carver / goldsmith('s) / craftsman('s)	Beaten / craftsman / goldsmith / skilled	Hammered / craftsman / goldsmith / skilled
10 But the LORD is the true God, he is the living God, and an everlasting king: at					

KJV	RSV	NEB	JB	NAS	NIV
his wrath the earth shall tremble, and the nations shall not be able to **abide** his indignation.	endure	endure	endure	endure	endure
16 The portion of Jacob is not like them: for he is the **former** of all things; and Israel is the **rod** of his inheritance: The LORD of hosts is his name.	one who formed / tribe	maker / people	maker / tribe	Maker / tribe	Maker / tribe
21 For the **pastors** are become **brutish,** and **have not** sought the LORD: therefore they shall not prosper, and all their flocks **shall be** scattered.	shepherds / stupid / do not / is	shepherds / mere brutes / never / do	shepherds / stupid / have not / have	shepherds / stupid / have not / is	shepherds / senseless / do not / do
22 Behold, the noise of the **bruit** is come, and a great commotion out of the north country, to make the cities of Judah desolate, and a **den of dragons.**	rumor / lair of jackals	rumour / haunt of wolves	(A mighty uproar) / jackal's lair	report / haunt of jackals	report / haunt of jackals
12 2 Thou hast planted them, yea, they have taken root: they grow, yea, they bring forth fruit: thou art near in their mouth, and far from their **reins.**	heart	hearts	hearts	mind	hearts
5 If thou hast run with the **footmen,** and they have wearied thee, then how canst thou **contend** with horses? and if in the **land of peace,** wherein thou trustedst, **they wearied thee,** then how wilt thou do in **the swelling of** Jordan?	footmen / compete / safe land / you fall down / the jungle of the	men / vie / easy country / you fall headlong / in (Jordan's) easy thickets	men on foot / compete / peaceful country / you are not secure / in the thickets along the	footmen / compete / land of peace / you fall down / in the thicket of the	men on foot / compete / safe country / you stumble / the thickets by the
13 9 Thus saith the LORD, **After this manner** will I **mar** the pride of Judah, and the great pride of Jerusalem.	Even so / spoil	Thus / spoil	In the same way / spoil	Just so / destroy	In the same way / ruin
26 Therefore will **I discover** thy skirts **upon** thy face, that thy shame may appear.	lift up / over	stripped off / (omits)	pull . . . up / as high as	stripped . . . off / over	pull up / over
27 I have seen thine adulteries, and thy neighings, the lewdness of thy whoredom, and thine abominations on the hills in the fields. Woe unto thee, O Jerusalem! wilt thou not be made clean? **when shall it once be?**	How long will it be before	How long, how long will	How much longer will	How long will	How long will
14 6 And the wild asses did stand in the **high places,** they **snuffed up the wind like dragons;** their eyes did fail, because there was no **grass.**	bare heights / pant for air like jackals / herbage	high bare places / snuff the wind for moisture, as wolves do / herbage	bare heights / gasp for air like jackals / pasture	bare heights / pant for air like jackals / vegetation	barren heights / pant like jackals / pasture
15 11 **The LORD said,** Verily it shall be well with thy remnant; verily I will cause the enemy to entreat thee well in the time of evil and in the time of affliction.	So let it be, O Lord	The Lord answered	Truthfully, Yahweh	The Lord said	The Lord said
15 O LORD, thou knowest: remember me, and visit me, and **revenge me** of my persecutors; take me not away in thy **longsuffering:** know that for thy sake I have **suffered rebuke.**	take vengeance for me / forbearance / bear reproach	take vengeance for me / (Be patient with me) / what reproaches I endure	avenge me / (Your anger is very slow) / suffer insult	take vengeance for me / patience / endure reproach	Avenge me / long-suffering / suffer reproach
17 8 For he shall be as a tree planted by the waters, and that spreadeth out her roots by the river, and shall not see when heat cometh, but her leaf shall be green; **and shall not be careful** in the year of drought, neither shall cease from yielding fruit.	and is not anxious	it feels no care	it has no worries	And it will not be anxious	It has no worries
16 As for me, I have not **hastened from being a pastor to follow thee:** neither have I desired the woeful day; thou knowest: that which came out of my lips was right before thee.	pressed thee to send evil	(It is not the thought of disaster that makes me press after thee)	urged you to do evil	hurried away from being a shepherd after Thee	run away from being your shepherd
19 Thus said the LORD unto me; Go and stand in the **gate of the children of the people,** whereby the kings of Judah come in, and by the which they go out, and in all the gates of Jerusalem;	Benjamin Gate	Benjamin Gate	Gate of the Sons of the People	public gate	gate of the people

KJV	RSV	NEB	JB	NAS	NIV
18 14 Will a man leave the snow of Lebanon which cometh from **the rock of the field?** or shall the cold flowing waters **that come from another place be forsaken.**	the crags of Sirion / Do the mountain waters run dry	rocky slopes of Lebanon / streaming in torrents ever fail	the lofty crag / Do the proud waters run dry	rock of the open country / from a foreign land ever snatched away	its rocky slopes / from distant sources ever cease to flow
19 1 Thus saith the LORD, Go and get a potter's earthen **bottle,** and take of the **ancients** of the people, and of the **ancients of the priests;**	flask / elders / senior priests	jar / elders / (elders) of the priests	jug / elders / some priests	jug / elders / senior priests	jar / elders / (elders) of the priests
9 And I will cause them to eat the flesh of their sons and the flesh of their daughters, and they shall eat every one the flesh of his friend in the siege and **straitness,** wherewith their enemies, and they that seek their lives, shall **straiten** them.	distress / afflict	dire straits / reduce	shortage / reduce	distress / distress	stress (of the siege) / imposed on
20 7 O LORD, thou hast deceived me, and I was deceived: thou art stronger than I, and hast prevailed: I am **in derision daily,** every one mocketh me.	a laughingstock all the day	a laughing-stock all the day long	a daily laughing-stock	a laughingstock all day long	ridiculed all day long
10 For I heard the defaming of many, fear on every side. Report, say they, and we will report it. All my **familiars** watched for my halting, saying, Peradventure he will be enticed, and we shall prevail against him, and we shall take our revenge on him.	familiar friends	friends	friends	trusted friends	friends
22 14 That saith, I will build me a wide house and large chambers, and cutteth him out windows; and it is **ceiled** with cedar, and painted with vermilion.	paneling	panel	panels	Paneling	panels
22 The wind shall **eat up** all thy **pastors,** and thy lovers shall go into captivity: surely then shalt thou be ashamed and confounded for all thy wickedness.	shepherd/shepherds	carry away/ friends	blow . . . away/ shepherds	sweep away/ shepherds	drive away/shepherds
23 32 Behold, I am against them that prophesy **false** dreams, saith the LORD, and do all them and **cause** my people **to err** by their **lies, and by their lightness;** yet I sent them not, nor commanded them: therefore they shall not profit this people at all, saith the Lord.	lying / lead / astray / lies and their recklessness	(dream lies) / misleading/wild and reckless lies	lying / lead / astray / lies and their pretensions	false / led / astray / falsehoods and reckless boasting	false / lead / astray / with their reckless lies
24 2 One basket had very good figs, even like the figs that are first ripe: and the other basket had very **naughty** figs, which could not be eaten, they were so bad.	bad	bad	bad	bad	poor
31 2 Thus saith the LORD, The people which were left of the sword found grace in the wilderness; **even Israel, when I went to cause him to rest.**	when Israel sought for rest	Israel journeyed to find rest	Israel is marching to his rest	Israel, when it went to find its rest	I will come to give rest to Israel
5 Thou shalt yet plant vines upon the mountains of Samaria: the planters shall plant, and shall **eat them as common things.**	enjoy the fruit	defile(d)	gather the fruit	enjoy them	enjoy their fruit
9 They shall come with weeping, and with **supplications** will I lead them: I will cause them to walk by the rivers of waters in a straight way, wherein they shall not stumble: for I am a father to Israel, and Ephraim is my firstborn.	consolations	comfort	comfort	supplications	(they will pray)
10 Hear the word of the LORD, O ye nations, and declare it in the **isles** afar off, and say, He that scattered Israel will gather him, and keep him, as a shepherd doth his flock.	coastlands	coasts and islands	islands	coastlands	coastlands
12 Therefore they shall come and sing in the height of Zion, and **shall flow together to** the goodness of the LORD,	shall be radiant over	shining with happiness at	will throng towards	shall be radiant over	will rejoice in

KJV	RSV	NEB	JB	NAS	NIV
for wheat, and for wine, and for oil, and for the young of the flock and of the herd: and their soul shall be as a watered garden; and they shall not sorrow any more at all.					
13 Then shall the **virgin** rejoice in the dance, **both young men and old together:** for I will turn their mourning into joy, and will comfort them, and make them rejoice from their sorrow.	maidens / and the young men and the old shall be merry	girl / young men and old shall rejoice	virgin / young men and old will be happy	virgin / And the young men and the old, together	maidens / young men and old as well
17 And there is hope **in thine end,** saith the LORD, that thy children shall come again to their own border.	for your future	(You shall leave descendants after you)	for your descendants	for your future	for your future
20 Is Ephraim my dear son? is he **a pleasant child?** for **since** I spake against him, I do earnestly remember him still: therefore my **bowels are troubled** for him; I will surely have mercy upon him, saith the LORD.	darling child / as often as / heart yearns	child in whom I delight / As often as / heart yearns	child so favoured / that after / tenderness yearn	delightful child / as often as / heart yearns	child in whom I delight / Though . . . often / heart yearns
23 Thus saith the LORD of hosts, the God of Israel; **As yet** they shall use **this speech** in the land of Judah and in the cities thereof, when I shall bring again their captivity; The LORD bless thee, O habitation of justice, and mountain of holiness.	Once more / these words	Once more / these words	again / these words	Once again / this word	once again / these words
32 10 And I **subscribed the evidence,** and sealed it, and took witnesses, and weighed him the money in the balances.	signed the deed	signed . . . the deed	drew up the deed	signed . . . the deed	signed . . . the deed
33 6 Behold, I will bring it health and cure, and I will cure them, and will reveal unto them the abundance of **peace and truth.**	prosperity and security	peace and security	peace and security	peace and truth	peace and security
37 16 When Jeremiah was entered into the dungeon, and into the **cabins,** and Jeremiah had remained there many days;	cells	vaulted pit	underground cell	vaulted cell	dungeon
38 11 So Ebedmelech took the men with him, and went into the house of the king under the treasury, and took thence old **cast clouts** and old **rotten rags,** and let them down by cords into the dungeon to Jeremiah.	rags / worn-out clothes	tattered, cast-off clothes	torn, worn-out rags	worn-out clothes / worn-out rags	old rags / worn-out clothes
12 And Ebedmelech the Ethiopian said unto Jeremiah, Put now these old **cast clouts** and **rotten rags under thine armholes under the cords.** And Jeremiah did so.	rags / clothes / between your armpits and the ropes	old clothes / under your armpits to ease the ropes	torn, worn-out rags / under your armpits to pad the ropes	worn-out clothes / rags / under your armpits under the ropes	old rags / worn-out clothes / under your arms to pad the ropes
19 And Zedekiah the king said unto Jeremiah, I am afraid of the Jews that are fallen to the Chaldeans, lest they deliver me into their hand, and they **mock** me.	abuse	roughly handled	ill-treat	abuse	mistreat
40 4 And now, behold, I loose thee this day from the chains which were upon thine hand. If it seem good unto thee to come with me into Babylon, come; and I will look well unto thee: but if it seem ill unto thee to come with me into Babylon, forbear: behold, all the land is before thee: whither it seemeth good and **convenient** for thee to go, thither go.	right	best	where you please, wherever you choose	right	wherever you please
41 10 Then Ishmael carried away captive all the **residue** of the people that were in Mizpah, even the king's daughters, and all the people that remained in Mizpah, whom Nebuzaradan the captain of the guard had committed to Gedaliah the son of Ahikam: and Ishmael the son of Nethaniah carried them away captive,	rest	rest	remnant	remnant	rest

KJV	RSV	NEB	JB	NAS	NIV
and departed to go over to the Ammonites.					
46 4 Harness the horses; and get up, ye horsemen, and **stand forth** with your helmets; **furbish** the spears, and put on the **brigandines.**	Take your stations / polish / coats of mail	form up / burnished / coats of mail	To your ranks / sharpen / breastplates	take your stand / Polish / scale-armor	Take your positions / Polish / armor
7 Who is this **that cometh up as a flood,** whose waters are moved as the rivers?	rising like the Nile (also vs. 8)	rising like the Nile (also vs. 8)	rose like the Nile (also vs. 8)	that rises like the Nile (also vs. 8)	that rises like the Nile (also vs. 8)
49 19 Behold, he shall come up like a lion from the **swelling** of Jordan against the **habitation of the strong:** but I will suddenly make him run away from her: and who is a chosen man, that I may appoint over her? for who is like me? and who will appoint me the time? and who is that shepherd that will stand before me?	jungle / strong sheepfold (also 50:44)	dense thickets / perennial pastures (also 50:44)	thickets / perennial pasture (also 50:44)	thickets / perennially watered pasture (also 50:44)	thickets / rich pastureland (also 50:44)
31 Arise, **get you up unto the wealthy nation,** that dwelleth **without care,** saith the LORD, which have neither gates nor bars, which dwell alone.	advance against a nation at ease/ securely	let us attack a nation living at peace / fancied security	March on a nation at its ease / in confidence	go up against a nation which is at ease / securely	attack a nation at ease / in confidence
33 And Hazor shall be a **dwelling for dragons,** and a **desolation for ever:** there shall no man abide there, nor any son of man **dwell in it.**	haunt of jackals / everlasting waste / sojourn in her	haunt of wolves / for ever desolate/ make a home in her	lair for jackals / desert for ever / make his home there	haunt of jackals / desolation forever / reside in it	haunt of jackals / desolate place forever / dwell in it
50 36 A sword is upon the **liars;** and they shall **dote:** a sword is upon her **mighty men;** and they shall be **dismayed.**	diviners / become fools / warriors / destroyed	false prophets / made fools / warriors / despair	diviners / lose their wits / men of war / discomfited	oracle priests / become fools / mighty men / shattered	false prophets / become fools / warriors / filled with terror
39 Therefore the wild beasts **of the desert with the wild beasts of the islands shall dwell there,** and the **owls** shall dwell therein: and it shall be no more inhabited for ever; neither shall it be dwelt in from generation to generation.	shall dwell with hyenas in Babylon / ostriches	marmots and jackals shall skulk in it / desert-owls	wild cats and jackals will live there / ostriches	desert creatures will live there along with the jackals / ostriches	desert creatures and hyenas will live there / owl
51 2 And will send unto Babylon **fanners,** that shall **fan** her, and shall empty her land: for in the day of trouble they shall be against her round about.	winnowers / winnow	winnowers / winnow	winnowers / winnow	foreigners / winnow	foreigners / winnow
3 **Against him that bendeth let the archer bend his bow, and against him that lifteth himself up in his brigandine:** and spare ye not her young men; destroy ye utterly all her host.	Let not the archer bend his bow / let him not stand up in his coat of mail	How shall the archer then string his bow / put on his coat of mail	Let no archer bend his bow / Let no man swagger in his coat of mail	Let not him who bends his bow bend it / let him rise up in his scale-armor	Let not the archer string his bow / let him put on his armor
11 **Make bright** the arrows; gather the shields: the LORD hath raised up the spirit of the kings of the Medes: for his **device** is against Babylon, to destroy it; because it is the vengeance of the LORD, the vengeance of his temple.	Sharpen / purpose	Sharpen / purpose	Sharpen / plan	Sharpen / purpose	Sharpen / purpose
19 The portion of Jacob is not like them; for he **is the former of** all things: and Israel is the **rod** of his inheritance: the LORD of hosts is his name.	is the one who formed / tribe	is the maker / people	has formed / tribe	the Maker of all is He / tribe	is the maker / tribe
23 I will also break in pieces with thee the shepherd and his flock; and with thee will I break in pieces the **husbandman** and his **yoke of oxen;** and with thee will I break in pieces **captains** and **rulers.**	farmer / team / governors / commanders	ploughman / team / viceroys / governors	ploughman / team / governors / nobles	farmer / team / governors / prefects	farmer / oxen / governors / officials
32 And that the **passages are stopped,** and the **reeds** they have burned with fire, and the **men of war** are **affrighted.**	fords have been seized / bulwarks / soldiers / in panic	river-crossings are seized / guard-towers / garrison stricken with panic	fords occupied / bastions / fighting men / thrown into panic	fords also have been seized / marshes / men of war / terrified	river crossings seized / marshes / soldiers / terrified
34 Nebuchadrezzar the king of Babylon hath devoured me, he hath crushed me, he hath made me an empty vessel, he					

KJV	RSV	NEB	JB	NAS	NIV
hath swallowed me up like a **dragon,** he hath filled his belly with my **delicates,** he hath **cast** me out.	monster / delicacies / rinsed	dragon / delicate flesh / spewed	dragon / delicacies / (omits)	monster / delicacies / washed	serpent / delicates / spewed
37 And Babylon shall become **heaps,** a **dwellingplace for dragons,** an **astonishment, and an hissing,** without an inhabitant.	a heap of ruins / haunt of jackals / a horror and a hissing	a heap of ruins / haunt of wolves / scene of horror and derision	a heap of stones / lair for jackals / thing of horror and of scorn	a heap of ruins / haunt of jackals / object of horror and hissing	a heap of ruins / haunt of jackals / object of horror and scorn
52 22 And a **chapiter** of brass was upon it; and the height of one **chapiter** was five cubits, with network and pomegranates upon the **chapiters** round about, all of brass. The second pillar also and the pomegranates were like unto these.	capital / capital / capital	capital / (omits) / (omits)	capital / capital / capital	capital / capital / capital	capital / (omits) / (omits)
34 And **for his diet,** there was a **continual diet** given him of the king **of Babylon, every day a portion** until the day of his death, all the days of his life.	allowance / regular allowance / according to his daily need	maintenance / regular daily allowance / of Babylon	upkeep / was ensured / king . . . day after day	for his allowance / regular allowance / of Babylon, a daily portion	(omits) / regular allowance / Day by day

Lamentations

KJV	RSV	NEB	JB	NAS	NIV
1 8 Jerusalem hath grievously sinned; therefore she **is removed:** all that honoured her despise her, because they have seen her nakedness: yea, she **sigheth,** and **turneth backward.**	became filthy/ groans/turns her face away	was treated like a filthy rag/sigh/ turn away	has become a thing unclean/ groans/turns her face away	has become an unclean thing/ groans/turns away	has become unclean/groans/ turns away
9 Her filthiness is in her skirts; she **remembereth not her last end;** therefore **she came down wonderfully:** she had no comforter. O LORD, behold my affliction: for the enemy **hath magnified himself.**	took no thought of her doom/her fall is terrible/has triumphed	gave no thought to her fate/Her fall was beyond belief/ has triumphed	had never thought of ending like this/ sinking as low as this/is triumphant	did not consider her future/she has fallen astonishingly/ has magnified himself	did not consider her future/Her fall was astounding/has triumphed
10 The adversary hath spread out his hand upon all her **pleasant** things: for she hath seen that the **heathen entered** into her sanctuary, whom thou didst command that they should not enter into thy congregation.	precious/nations invade	treasures/Gentiles entering	treasured/pagans enter	precious/nations enter	treasures/pagan nations enter
11 And her people **sigh,** they seek bread; they have given their **pleasant things** for meat to **relieve the soul:** see, O LORD, and consider; for I am **become vile.**	groan/treasures/ revive their strength/despised	groaned/treasures/ give them strength again/accounted cheap	groan/valuables/ keep life in them/ despised	groan/precious things/restore their lives themselves/despised	groan/treasures/ keep themselves alive/despised
13 From above hath he sent fire into my bones, **and it prevaileth against them:** he hath spread a net for my feet, he hath turned me back: he hath made me **desolate** and faint all the day.	he made it descend/stunned	(omits)/an example of desolation	(omits)/deserted	And it prevailed over them/desolate	(omits) / desolate
20 Behold, O LORD; for I am in distress: my **bowels are troubled;** mine heart is **turned** within me; for I have grievously rebelled: **abroad** the sword bereaveth, **at home** there is as death.	soul is in tumult/ wrung/In the street/in the house	bowels writhe in anguish/turns/in the streets/within doors	entrails shudder/ turns over/outside/inside	spirit is greatly troubled/overturned/In the street/In the house	I am in torment within/disturbed/ Outside/inside
2 11 Mine eyes **do fail with tears,** my **bowels are troubled,** my **liver is poured upon the earth,** for the destruction of the daughter of my people; because the **children and the sucklings swoon** in the streets of the city.	are spent with weeping/soul is in tumult/heart is poured out in grief/infants and babies faint	are blinded with tears/bowels writhe in anguish/bile is spilt on the earth/children and infants faint	wasted awaywith weeping/entrails shuddered/liver spilled on the ground/children, mere infants, fainted	fail because of tears/spirit is greatly troubled/ heart is poured out on the earth/ little ones and infants faint	fail from weeping/I am in torment within/ heart is poured out on the ground/children and infants faint
13 What thing shall I take to witness for thee? what thing shall I liken to thee, O daughter of Jerusalem? what shall I equal to thee, that I may comfort thee, O virgin daughter of Zion? for thy **breach** is great like the sea: who can heal thee?	ruin	wound	affliction	ruin	wound

	KJV	RSV	NEB	JB	NAS	NIV
	14 Thy prophets have seen **vain and foolish things** for thee: and they have not **discovered** thine iniquity, to **turn away thy captivity**; but have seen for thee false **burdens and causes of banishment.**	false and deceptive visions/exposed/restore your fortunes/oracles false and misleading	visions . . . were false and painted shams/bring home to you/so reverse your fortunes/visions . . . delusions, false and fraudulent	visions . . . were delusive, tinsel things/pointed out/ward off your exile/visions . . . false, fallacious, misleading	False and foolish visions/exposed/restore you from captivity/false and misleading oracles	visions . . . false and worthless/expose/ward off your captivity/oracles . . . false and misleading
3	60 Thou hast seen all their vengeance and all their **imaginations** against me.	devices	plots	plots	schemes	plots
4	5 They that did **feed delicately** are **desolate** in the streets: they that were **brought up in scarlet embrace dunghills.**	feasted on dainties/perish/brought up in purple lie on ash heaps	fed delicately/desolate/nurtured in purple now grovel on dunghills	used to eat only the best/dying/reared in the purple claw at the rubbish heaps	ate delicacies/desolate/reared in purple Embrace ash pits	once ate delicacies/destitute/nurtured in purple now lie on ash heaps
	10 The hands of the **pitiful** women have **sodden** their own children: they were their **meat** in the destruction of the daughter of my people.	compassionate/boiled/food	Tender-hearted/boiled/food	tender-hearted/boiled/food	compassionate/Boiled/food	compassionate/boiled/food

Ezekiel

	KJV	RSV	NEB	JB	NAS	NIV
4	2 And lay siege against it, and build **a fort** against it, and cast a **mount** against it; set the camp also against it, and set battering rams against it round about.	siege wall / mound	watch-towers / siege-ramp	trench (round it) / earthworks	siege wall / ramp	siege works / ramp
	9 Take thou also unto thee wheat, and barley, and beans, and lentils, and millet, and **fitches**, and put them in one vessel, and make thee bread thereof, according to the number of the days that thou shalt lie upon thy side, three hundred and ninety days shalt thou eat thereof.	spelt	spelt	spelt	spelt	spelt
6	4 And your altars shall be desolate, and your **images** shall be broken: and I will cast down your slain men before your idols.	incense altars (also vs. 6)	incense-altars (vs. 5, "altars")	incense burners (also vs. 5)	incense altars (vs. 5, "altars")	incense altars (vs. 5, "altars")
7	26 Mischief shall come upon mischief, and rumour shall be upon rumour; then shall they seek a vision of the prophet; but the law shall perish from the priest, and counsel from the **ancients.**	elders (also 8:11)	elders (also 8:11)	elders (also 8:11)	elders (also 8:11)	elders (also 8:11)
	12 Then said he unto me, Son of man, hast thou seen what the **ancients** of the house of Israel do in the dark, every man in the **chambers of his imagery?** for they say, The LORD seeth us not; the LORD hath forsaken the earth.	elders / room of pictures	elders / shrine of his own carved image	elders / his painted room	elders / room of his carved images	elders / shrine of his own idol
9	8 And it came to pass, while they were **slaying** them, and I was left, that I fell upon my face, and cried, and said, Ah Lord GOD! wilt thou destroy all **the residue** of Israel in thy pouring out of thy **fury** upon Jerusalem?	smiting / that remains / wrath	did their work / who are left / anger	hacking . . . down / that is left / anger	striking / the whole remnant / wrath	killing / remnant / wrath
12	23 Tell them therefore, Thus saith the Lord GOD; I will make this proverb to cease, and they shall no more use it as a proverb in Israel; but say unto them, The days are at hand, and the **effect** of every vision.	fulfillment	(with all the vision means)	(every vision will come true)	fulfillment	(every vision will be fulfilled)
	25 For I am the LORD: I will speak, and the word that I shall speak shall **come to pass;** it shall be no more **prolonged:** for in your days, O rebellious house, will I say the word, and will perform it, saith the Lord GOD.	be performed / delayed	be done / put off	is said / will soon come true	be performed / delayed	be fulfilled / without delay

KJV	RSV	NEB	JB	NAS	NIV
13 14 So will I break down the wall that ye have daubed with **untempered mortar,** and bring it down to the ground, so that the foundation thereof shall be **discovered,** and it shall fall, and ye shall **be consumed** in the midst thereof: and ye shall know that I am the LORD.	whitewash / laid bare / perish	whitewash / laid bare / be destroyed	plaster / lay bare / perish	whitewash / laid bare / be consumed	whitewash / laid bare / be destroyed
18 And say, Thus saith the Lord GOD; Woe to the women that sew **pillows to all armholes,** and make **kerchiefs** upon the head of every stature to hunt souls! Will ye hunt the souls of my people, and will ye save the souls alive that come unto you?	magic bands upon all wrists / veils	magic bands upon the wrists / veils	frills round wrists / veils	magic bands on all wrists / veils	magic charms on all their wrists / veils
16 4 And as for thy **nativity, in the day** thou wast born thy **navel** was not cut, neither wast thou washed in water to **supple** thee; thou wast not **salted** at all, nor **swaddled** at all.	birth / on the day / navel string / cleanse / rubbed with salt / swathed with bands	birth / when / navel-string / rub(bing) / salted / wrapped in swaddling clothes	birth / the very day / navel-string / cleans(ing) / rub you with salt / wrap you in napkins	birth / on the day / navel cord / cleans(ing) / rubbed with salt / wrapped in cloths	(omits) / On the day / cord / make you clean / rubbed with salt / wrapped in cloth
10 I clothed thee also with broidered work, and shod thee with **badgers' skin,** and I girded thee about with fine linen, and I covered thee with silk.	leather	stout hide	fine leather	porpoise skin	leather
14 And thy renown went forth among the heathen for thy beauty: for it was perfect through **my comeliness,** which I had put upon thee, saith the Lord GOD.	the splendor	the splendour	my own splendour	My splendor	the splendor
24 That thou hast also built unto thee an **eminent place,** and hast made thee an **high** place in every **street.**	vaulted chamber / lofty / square	couch / high-stool / open place	mound / high place / crossroads	shrine / high place / square	mound / lofty shrine / public square
16 34 And **the contrary is in thee from other women** in thy whoredoms, whereas none followeth thee to commit whoredoms: and in that thou givest a reward, and no reward is given unto thee, therefore thou **art contrary.**	you were different from other women / were different	are the very opposite of other women / are the very opposite	you have done the exact opposite from other women / since your behaviour was so outrageous	you are different from those women / are different	you are the opposite of others / are the very opposite
43 Because thou hast not remembered the days of thy youth, but hast **fretted** me in all these things; behold, therefore I also will **recompense thy way** upon thine head, saith the Lord GOD: **and thou shalt not commit this** lewdness **above all** thine abominations.	enraged / requite / Have you not committed / in addition to all your	(you . . . exasperated me) / brought retribution / Did you not commit / as well as all your other	(you . . . provoke me) / bring your conduct down / (Have you not been disgusting with all your filthy practices?)	enraged / bring your conduct down / so that you will not commit this / on top of all your other	enraged / bring down . . . what you have done / Did you not add / to all your other
57 Before thy wickedness was **discovered, as at the time of thy reproach of the daughters of Syria,** and all that are round about her, the daughters of the Philistines, which despise thee round about.	uncovered / Now you have become like her an object of reproach for the daughters of Edom	exposed / in the days when the daughters of Aram with those about her were disgraced	stripped naked / Now the daughters of Edom and all the women around you are jeering at you	uncovered / so now you have become the reproach of the daughters of Edom	uncovered / Even so, you are now scorned by the daughters of Edom
17 3 And say, Thus saith the Lord GOD; A great eagle with great wings, **longwinged, full of feathers,** which had **divers** colours, came unto Lebanon, and took the highest branch of the cedar:	long pinions rich in plummage / many	long pinions, in full plummage / (richly patterned)	and a wide span / (covered with speckled feathers)	long pinions and a full plummage / many	long feathers and full plummage / varied
17 Neither shall Pharaoh with his mighty army and great company **make for** him in the war, by casting up **mounts,** and **building forts,** to cut off many persons:	help / mounds / siege walls built	protect / siege-ramp / watch-tower put up	save / earthworks / trenches dug	help / mounds / build siege walls	help / ramps / siege works erected
22 Thus saith the Lord GOD; I will also take of the highest branch of the high cedar, and will set it; I will crop off from the top of his young twigs a tender one, and will plant it upon an high mountain and **eminent:**	lofty	lofty	(omits)	lofty	lofty
23 In the mountain of the height of Israel will I plant it: and it shall bring forth boughs, and bear fruit, and be a **goodly** cedar: and under it shall dwell all	noble / kinds of	noble / winged	noble / every	stately / birds of	splendid / birds

KJV	RSV	NEB	JB	NAS	NIV
fowl of every wing; in the shadow of the branches thereof **shall they dwell.**	beasts / birds of every sort will nest	birds of very kind / they will roost	kind of bird / every winged creature rest	every kind / they will nest	of every kind / they will find shelter
18 14 Now, lo, if he beget a son, that seeth all his father's sins which he hath done, and **considereth,** and doeth not **such like.**	fears / likewise	(omits) / none of them	(in spite of seeing) / (does not imitate him)	observing / likewise	though he sees them / such things
25 Yet ye say, The way of the Lord is not **equal.** Hear now, O house of Israel; Is **not** my way **equal?** are not your ways **unequal?**	just / not just / not just	without principle / (it is you who act without principle, not I)	unjust / unjust / unjust	right / not right / not right	just / unjust / unjust
20 46 Son of man, set thy face toward the south, and **drop thy word** toward the south, and prophesy against the forest of the south field;	preach against	pour out your words to	utter your words towards	speak out against	preach against
21 19 Also, thou son of man, **appoint** thee two ways, that the sword of the king of Babylon may come: both **twain** shall come forth out of one land: and **choose thou a place, choose** it at the head of the way to **the city.**	mark / of them / make a signpost, make / a	trace out / of them / carve a signpost, carve (at the point where the highway forks)/ (omits)	mark out / of them / Put up a signpost where / a	make / of them / make a signpost; make / the	mark out / (omits) / make a signpost where / the
21 For the king of Babylon stood at the parting of the way, at the head of the two ways, to use divination: he **made his arrows bright,** he **consulted with images,** he looked in the liver.	shakes the arrows / consults the teraphim	casts lots with arrows / consults teraphim	has shaken the arrows / questioned the teraphim	shakes the arrows / consults the household idols	cast lots with arrows / consult his idols
27 **I will overturn, overturn, overturn, it:** and it shall be no more, until he come whose right it is; and I will give it him.	A ruin, ruin, ruin I will make it	Ruin! Ruin! I will bring about such ruin	To ruin, and to ruin on ruin, am I going to bring it	A ruin, a ruin, a ruin, I shall make it	A ruin! A ruin! I will make it a ruin!
22 26 Her priests have violated my law, and have profaned mine holy things: they have put no difference between the holy and **profane,** neither have they shewed difference between the unclean and the clean, and have hid their eyes from my sabbaths, and I am profaned among them.	common	common	profane	profane	unclean
29 The people of the land have **used oppression,** and **exercised** robbery, and have **vexed** the poor and needy: yea, they have **oppressed the stranger wrongfully.**	practiced extortion / committed / oppressed / extorted from the sojourner without redress	(The common people are bullies and robbers; they ill-treat the unfortunate and the poor, they are unjust and cruel to the alien.)	taken to extortion / (omits) / oppressed / ill-treated the settler for no reason	practiced oppression / committed / wronged / oppressed the sojourner without justice	practice extortion / commit / oppress / mistreat the alien, denying them justice
23 10 These **discovered** her nakedness: they took her sons and her daughters, and slew her with the sword: and she became **famous** among women; for they had excuted judgment upon her.	uncovered / a byword	ravished / a byword	uncovered / notorious	uncovered / a byword	stripped / a byword
15 Girded with girdles upon their loins, exceeding in **dyed attire** upon their heads, all of them princes to look to, after the manner of the Babylonians of Chaldea, the land of their nativity:	flowing turbans	turbans with dangling ends	elaborate turbans	flowing turbans	flowing turbans
18 So she **discovered her whoredoms,** and **discovered** her nakedness: then **my mind was alienated from her, like as my mind was alienated from her sister.**	carried on her harlotry so openly / flaunted / I turned in disgust from her, as I had turned from her sister	made no secret that she was a whore / ravished / I was filled with revulsion against her as I was against her sister	flaunted her whoring / stripped / I turned away from her as I had turned away from her sister	uncovered her harlotries / uncovered / I became disgusted with her, as I had become disgusted with her sister	carried on her prostitution openly / exposed / I turned away from her in disgust, just as I had turned away from her sister
29 And they shall deal with thee hatefully, and shall take away all thy labour, and shall leave thee naked and bare: and the nakedness of thy whore-					

KJV	RSV	NEB	JB	NAS	NIV
doms shall be **discovered,** both thy lewdness and thy whoredoms.	uncovered	ravished	exposed	uncovered	exposed
24 17 **Forbear to cry,** make no mourning for the dead, bind **the tire of thine head** upon thee, and put on thy shoes upon thy feet, and cover not thy lips, and eat not the bread of **men.**	Sigh, but not aloud / your turban / mourners	be quiet / (cover your head as usual) / despair	Groan in silence / your turban / (common bread)	Groan silently / your turban / men	Groan quietly / your turban / mourners
23 And your **tires** shall be upon your heads, and your shoes upon your feet: ye shall not mourn nor weep; but ye shall pine away for your iniquities, and **mourn one toward another.**	turbans / groan to one another	(You shall cover your head) / lament to one another	turbans / groan among yourselves	turbans / groan to one another	turbans / groan among yourselves
25 6 For thus saith the Lord GOD; Because thou hast clapped thine hands, and stamped with the feet, and rejoiced in heart with **all thy despite** against the land of Israel;	the malice within you	single-minded scorn	inwardly full of malice	all the scorn of your soul	all the malice of your heart
26 16 Then all the princes of the sea shall come down from their thrones, and **lay away** their robes, and put off their broidered garments; they shall clothe themselves with trembling; they shall sit upon the ground, and shall tremble at every moment, and be **astonished at thee.**	remove / appalled at you	lay aside / horror-struck at your fate	lay aside / terrified at your fate	remove / appalled at you	lay aside / appalled at you.
27 6 Of the oaks of Bashan have they made thine oars; the company of the Ashurites have made thy benches of ivory, brought out of the **isles of Chittim.**	coasts of Cyprus	coasts of Kittim	Kittim isles	coastlands of Cyprus	coasts of Cyprus
9 The **ancients** of Gebal and the **wise men** thereof were in thee thy calkers: all the ships of the sea with their mariners were in thee **to occupy thy merchandise.**	elders / skilled men / barter for your wares	skilled veterans / market your wares	elders / craftsmen / trade with you	elders / wise men / deal in your merchandise	(omits) / Veteran craftsmen / trade for your wares
10 They of Persia and of Lud and of Phut were in thine army, thy men of war: they hanged the shield and helmet in thee; they **set forth thy comeliness.**	made perfect your beauty	gave you your glory	brought you glory	set forth your splendor	bringing you splendor
16 Syria **was thy merchant** by reason of the multitude of the wares of thy making: they **occupied** in thy fairs with emeralds, purple, and broidered work, and fine linen, and coral, and agate.	trafficked with you / exchanged	was a source of your commerce / offering	was your client / exchanged	was your customer / paid for	did business with you / exchanged
17 Judah, and the land of Israel, they **were thy merchants:** they traded in thy market wheat **of Minnith, and pannag,** and **honey, and oil, and balm.**	traded with you / Minnith / olives / and early figs / honey, oil, and balm	dealt with you / from Minnith / meal / syrup, oil, and balsam	also traded with you / from Minnith / wax / honey, tallow and balm	were your traders / of Minnith / cakes / honey, oil, and balm	traded with you / from Minnith / confections / honey, oil and balm
21 Arabia, and all the princes of Kedar, they **occupied with thee** in lambs, and rams, and goats: in these **were they thy merchants.**	were your favored dealers / they trafficked with you	were the source of your commerce / this was your trade with them	were all your clients / they paid	were your customers / they were your customers	were your customers / they did business
27 Thy riches, and thy **fairs,** thy merchandise, thy mariners, and thy pilots, thy calkers, and the **occupiers** of thy merchandise, and all thy men of war, that are in thee, and in all thy **company** which is in the midst of thee, shall fall into the **midst** of the seas in the day of thy ruin.	wares / dealers / company / heart	staple wares / merchants / company / (omits)	goods / commercial agents / host / surrounded (by)	wares / dealers in merchandise / company / heart	merchandise / merchants / everyone else on board / heart
28 13 Thou hast been in Eden the garden of God; every precious stone was thy covering, the **sardius, topaz,** and the **diamond,** the **beryl,** the **onyx,** and the **jasper,** the **sapphire,** the **emerald,** and the **carbuncle,** and gold: the workman-	carnelian, topaz, and jasper / chrysolite, beryl, and onyx / sap-	sardin and chrysolite and jade / topaz, cornelian and green jasper	Sard, topaz, diamond / chrysolite, onyx, jasper / sapphire, car-	The ruby, the topaz, and the diamond / The beryl, the onyx /	ruby, topaz and emerald / chrysolite / onyx and jasper / sapphire

KJV	RSV	NEB	JB	NAS	NIV
ship of thy **tabrets** and of thy **pipes** was prepared in thee in the day that thou wast created.	phire / carbuncle, and emerald / settings / engravings	/ lapis lazuli / purple garnet and green felspar / jingling beads / spangles	buncle, emerald / flutes / tambourines	and the Jasper / The lapis lazuli, the turquoise, and the emerald / settings / sockets	/ turquoise and beryl / settings / mountings
29 3 Speak, and say, Thus saith the Lord GOD; Behold, I am against thee, Pharaoh king of Egypt, the great dragon that lieth in the midst of his rivers, which hath said, My **river** is mine own, and I have made it for myself.	Nile (also vs. 9; 29:3, 9)	Nile (also vs. 9; 29:3, 9)	Nile (also vs. 9; 29: 3, 9)	Nile (also vs. 9; 29:3, 9)	Nile (also vs. 9; 29: 3, 9)
10 Behold, therefore I am against thee, and against thy rivers, and I will make the land of Egypt utterly waste and desolate, from the tower of **Syene** even unto the border of Ethiopia.	Migdol to Syene	Migdol to Syene	Migdol to Syene	Migdol to Syene	Migdol to Aswan
30 2 Son of man, prophesy and say, Thus saith the Lord GOD; **Howl ye, Woe worth** the day!	"Wail, 'Alas for	Woe, Woe for	Howl: Alas	"Wail, 'Alas	" 'Wail and say, "Alas for
6 Thus saith the LORD; They also that uphold Egypt shall fall; and the pride of her power shall come down: **from the tower of Syene** shall they fall in it by the sword, saith the Lord GOD.	from Migdol to Syene	from Migdol to Syene	from Migdol to Syene	From Migdol to Syene	From Migdol to Aswan
15 And I will pour my **fury** upon **Sin,** the **strength** of Egypt; and I will cut off the multitude of **No.**	wrath / Pelusium / stronghold / Thebes	rage / Sin / bastion / Noph	fury / Sin / stronghold / No	wrath / Sin / stronghold / Thebes	wrath / Pelusium / stronghold / Thebes
32 2 Son of man, take up a lamentation for Pharaoh king of Egypt, and say unto him, Thou art like a young lion of the nations, **and** thou art as a **whale** in the seas: and thou **camest** forth **with** thy rivers, and troubledst the waters with thy feet, and fouledst their rivers.	but / dragon / burst / in	you are undone / monster / (scattering the water with its snout)	you have been wiped out / crocodile / (you snorted through your nostrils)	Yet / monster / burst / in	(omits) / monster / thrashing about / in
34 11 For thus saith the Lord GOD; Behold, I, even I, will both search [ ] my sheep, and seek them out.	for	of	after	for	for
36 17 Son of man, when the house of Israel dwelt in their own land, they defiled it by their own way and by their doings: their way was before me as the uncleanness of **a removed woman.**	woman in her impurity	(their ways were foul and disgusting in my sight)	woman's menstruation	uncleanness of a woman in her impurity	woman's monthly uncleanness
38 2 Son of man, set thy face against Gog, the land of Magog, the **chief prince** of Meshech and Tubal, and prophesy against him,	chief prince	prince	prince	prince	chief prince
39 11 And it shall come to pass in that day, that I will give unto Gog a place **there of graves** in Israel, the **valley of the passengers** on the east of the sea: and it shall **stop the noses of the passengers:** and there shall they bury Gog and all his multitude: and they shall call it The valley of Hamongog.	for burial / Valley of the Travelers / block the travelers	burial- / valley of Abarim / (all Abarim will be blocked)	for his grave / valley of the Abarim / turns back the traveller	burial / valley of those who pass / block off the passers-by	burial / valley of those who travel / block the way of travelers
40 16 **And there were narrow windows to the little chambers, and to their posts within the gate round about, and likewise to the arches: and windows were round about inward:** and upon each **post** were palm trees.	And the gateway had windows round about, narrowing inwards into their jambs in the side rooms, and likewise the vestibule had windows round about inside / jambs	Both cells and pilasters had loopholes all round inside the gateway, and the vestibule had windows all round within / pilaster	On each side of the gate there were splayed openings both in the guardrooms and in the spaces between, and there were openings all round inside the porch as well / jambs	And there were shuttered windows looking toward the guardrooms, and toward their side pillars within the gate all around, and likewise for the porches. And there were windows all around inside / pillar	The alcoves and the projecting walls inside the gateway were surmounted by narrow parapet openings all around, as was the portico; the openings all around faced inward / faces
41 16 The door posts, and the narrow windows, and the galleries round about					

KJV	RSV	NEB	JB	NAS	NIV
on their three stories, over against the door, **ceiled** with wood round about, and from the ground up to the windows, and the windows were covered:	paneled	panelled	panelled	paneled	covered
42 13 Then said he unto me, The north chambers and the south chambers, **which are before the separate place,** they be holy chambers, where the priests that approach unto the LORD shall eat the most **holy things:** there shall they lay the most **holy things,** and the **meat offering,** and the sin offering, and the **trespass** offering; for the place is holy.	opposite the yard / holy offerings / holy offerings / cereal offering / guilt	facing the free space / sacred offerings / these offerings / grain-offering / guilt-	giving on to the court / holy things / holy things / oblation / of reparation	opposite the separate area / holy things / holy things / grain offering / guilt	facing the temple courtyard / holy offerings / holy offerings / grain offerings / guilt
43 14 And from the bottom upon the ground even to the lower **settle** shall be two cubits, and the breadth one cubit; and from the lesser **settle** even to the greater **settle** shall be four cubits, and the breadth one cubit.	ledge / ledge / ledge (also vs. 20)	Pedestal-block / pedestal-block / pedestal-block (vs. 20, "pedestal")	plinth / plinth / plinth (also vs. 20)	ledge / ledge / ledge (also vs. 20)	ledge / ledge / ledge (also vs. 20)
17 And the **settle** shall be fourteen cubits long and fourteen broad in the four squares thereof; and the border about it shall be half a cubit; and the bottom thereof shall be a cubit about; and **his stairs shall look toward** the east.	ledge / steps of the altar shall face	pedestal-block / there were steps facing	plinth / The steps were on	ledge / its steps shall face	ledge / The steps of the altar face
44 5 And the LORD said unto me, Son of man, mark well, and behold with thine eyes, and hear with thine ears all that I say unto thee concerning all the ordinances of the **house** of the LORD, and all the laws thereof; and mark well **the entering in of the house, with every going forth of** the sanctuary.	temple / those who may be admitted to the temple and all those who are to be excluded from	house / entrance to the house of the Lord and all the exits from	Temple / which men are admitted to the Temple and which are excluded from	house / the entrance of the house, with all exits of	temple / entrance of the temple and all the exits of
44 20 Neither shall they shave their heads, nor suffer their locks to grow long; they shall only **poll** their heads.	trim the hair of	shave	shave	shave	shave
25 And they shall **come at no** dead person to defile themselves: but for father, or for mother, or for son, or for daughter, for brother, or for sister that hath had no husband, they may defile themselves.	go(ing) near	contact with	not to go near	not go to	go(ing) near
45 2 Of this there shall be for the sanctuary five hundred in length, with five hundred in breadth, square round about; and fifty cubits round about for the **suburbs** thereof.	open space	open land	boundary	open space	open land
19 And the priest shall take of the blood of the sin offering, and put it upon the **posts of the house,** and upon the four corners of the **settle** of the altar, and upon the posts of the gate of the inner court.	doorposts of the temple / ledge	door-posts of the temple / pedestal	doorposts of the Temple / plinth	door posts of the house / ledge	doorposts of the temple / ledge

Daniel

KJV	RSV	NEB	JB	NAS	NIV
1 10 And the prince of the eunuchs said unto Daniel, I fear my lord the king, who hath appointed your meat and your drink: for why should he see **your faces worse liking** than the **children** which are of your **sort?** then shall ye make me endanger my head **to** the king.	that you were in poorer condition / youths / age / with	you looking dejected / young men / age / (omits)	you looking thinner in the face / boys / age / with	your faces looking more haggard / youths / age / to	you looking worse / young men / age / (The king would have my head)
12 Prove thy servants, I beseech thee, ten days; and let them give us **pulse** to eat, and water to drink.	vegetables	vegetables	vegetables	vegetables	vegetables

	KJV	RSV	NEB	JB	NAS	NIV
2	24 Therefore Daniel went in unto Arioch, whom the king had **ordained** to destroy the wise men of Babylon: he went and said thus unto him, Destroy not the wise men of Babylon: bring me in before the king, and I will shew unto the king the interpretation.	appointed	charged	made responsible	appointed	appointed
3	21 Then these men were bound in their **coats, their hosen,** and their hats, and their other garments, and were cast into the midst of the burning fiery furnace.	mantles, their tunics	trousers, their shirts	cloak, hose	trousers, their cloaks	robes, trousers
5	12 Forasmuch as an excellent spirit, and knowledge, and understanding, interpreting of dreams, and **shewing of hard sentences,** and **dissolving of doubts,** were found in the same Daniel, whom the king named Belteshazzar: now let Daniel be called, and he will shew the interpretation.	explain riddles / solve problems	explaining riddles / unbinding spells	solving enigmas / unravelling difficult problems	explanation of enigmas / solving of difficult problems	explain riddles / solve difficult problems
6	3 Then this Daniel **was preferred** above the presidents and princes, because an excellent spirit was in him; and the king **thought** to set him over the whole **realm.**	became distinguished / planned / kingdom	outshone / had it in mind / kingdom	was so evidently superior / considered / kingdom	began distinguishing himself / planned / kingdom	so distinguished himself / planned / kingdom
	24 And the king commanded, and they brought those men which had accused Daniel, and they cast them into the den of lions, them, their children, and their wives; and the lions **had the mastery** of them, and brake all their bones in pieces **or ever** they **came** at the bottom of the den.	overpowered / before / reached	were upon / before / reached	seized / before / reached	overpowered / before / reached	overpowered / before / reached
7	20 And of the ten horns that were **in his** head, and of the other which came up, and before whom three fell; even of that horn that had eyes, and a mouth that spake very great things, **whose look was more stout than his fellows.**	on its / which seemed greater than its fellows	on its / appeared larger	on its / it made a greater show than the other horns	on its / which were larger in appearance than its associates	on its / that looked more imposing than the others
	28 Hitherto is the end of the matter. As for me Daniel, my **cogitations** much **troubled** me, and my **countenance** changed in me: but I kept the matter in my **heart.**	thoughts / alarmed / color / mind	thoughts / dismayed / (I turned pale) / mind	in mind / disturbed / (I grew pale) / (I kept these things to myself)	thoughts / alarming / face / (to myself)	thoughts / troubled / face / (to myself)
8	5 And as I was considering, behold, an he goat came from the west on the face of the whole earth, and touched not the ground: and the goat had **a notable** horn between his eyes.	conspicuous	prominent	majestic	conspicuous	prominent
7	And I saw him come close unto the ram, and he was **moved with choler** against him, and smote the ram, and brake his two horns: and there was no power in the ram to stand before him, but he cast him down to the ground, and stamped upon him: and there was none that could deliver the ram out of his hand.	enraged	working itself into a fury	so enraged	enraged	(I saw him attack the ram furiously)
9	25 Know therefore and understand, that from the going forth of the commandment to restore and to build Jerusalem unto the Messiah the Prince shall be **seven weeks, and threescore and two weeks:** the street shall be built again, and the wall, even in troublous times.	seven weeks. Then for sixty-two weeks	seven weeks . . . then for sixty-two weeks	seven weeks and sixty-two weeks	seven weeks and sixty-two weeks	seven 'sevens,' and sixty-two 'sevens'
	26 And after threescore and two weeks shall **Messiah be cut off, but not for himself:** and the people of the prince that shall come shall destroy the city and the sanctuary; and the end thereof shall be with a flood, and unto the end of the war desolations are determined.	an anointed one shall be cut off, and shall have nothing	one who is anointed shall be removed with no one to take his part	an appointed one will be cut off—and . . . will not be for him (ellipses part of text)	the Messiah will be cut off and have nothing	the Anointed One will be cut off and will have nothing
	27 And he shall confirm the covenant with many for one week: and in the midst					

	KJV	RSV	NEB	JB	NAS	NIV
	of the week he shall cause the sacrifice and the oblation to cease, and for the **overspreading** of abominations he shall make it desolate, even until the consummation, and that determined shall be poured upon the desolate.	wing	train	wing	wing	(abominations) on a wing of the temple
11	21 And **in his estate** shall stand up a **vile** person, to whom **they shall not give the honour of the kingdom:** but he shall come in **peaceably,** and obtain the kingdom by flatteries.	In his place / contemptible / to whom royal majesty has not been given / without warning	will succeed him / contemptible / will not be given recognition as king / by dissimilation	In his place / wretch / he will not be given royal honours / in his own time	in his place / despicable / on whom the honor of kingship has not been conferred / in a time of tranquility	He will be succeeded / contemptible / who has not been given the honor of royalty / when its people feel secure
	24 He shall enter peaceably even upon the **fattest places** of the province; and he shall do that which his fathers have not done, nor his fathers' fathers; he shall scatter among them the **prey,** and spoil, and **riches:** yea, and he shall **forecast his devices** against the strong holds, **even for** a time.	richest parts / plunder / goods / devise plans / but only for	richest districts / booty / property / lay his plans / but only for	richest provinces / plunder / wealth / plotting his strategems / for	richest parts / plunder / possessions / devise his schemes / but only for	richest provinces / plunder / wealth / plot the overthrow / but only for
	30 For the ships of Chittim shall come against him: therefore he shall be **grieved,** and **return,** and **have indignation** against the holy covenant: so shall he do; he shall even return, and **have intelligence with them** that forsake the holy covenant.	afraid / withdraw / take action / give heed to those	receive a rebuff / turn / vent his fury / take due note of those	worsted / retire / take furious action / favour those	disheartened / return / become enraged . . . and take action / show regard for those	lose heart / turn back / vent his fury / show favor to those

Hosea

	KJV	RSV	NEB	JB	NAS	NIV
2	10 And now will I **discover** her lewdness in the sight of her lovers, and none shall **deliver** her out of mine hand.	uncover / rescue	show her up / steal	display / rescue	uncover / rescue	expose / take
	14 Therefore, behold, I will allure her, and bring her into the wilderness, and speak **comfortably** unto her.	tenderly	comfort	(to her heart)	kindly	tenderly
3	1Then said the LORD unto me, Go yet, love a woman beloved of **her friend,** yet an adulteress, according to the love of the LORD toward the children of Israel, who **look** to other gods, and love **flagons of wine.**	of a paramour / turn / cakes of raisins	by another man / resort / raisin-cakes offered to their idols	by her husband / turn / raisin cakes	by her husband / turn / raisin cakes	by another / turn / sacred raisin cakes
8	7 For they have sown the wind, and they shall reap the whirlwind: **it hath no stalk: the bud shall yield no meal: if so be it yield,** the **strangers shall swallow it up.**	The standing grain has no head / it / if it were to / aliens would swallow it up	there are no heads on the standing corn / it / if it / strangers would swallow it up	their wheat will yield no ear / the ear / if it / foreigners will swallow it	The standing grain has no heads / It / Should it / strangers would swallow it up	The stalk has no head / it / Were it to / foreigners would swallow it up
9	2 The **floor** and the **winepress** shall not feed them, and the new wine shall fail **in her.**	Threshing floor / winevat / them	Threshing-floor / winepress / them	floor / vat / them	Threshing floor / wine press / them	Threshing floors / winepresses / the people
10	It is in my desire that I should chastise them; and the people shall be gathered against them, when they shall **bind** themselves in their **two farrows.**	are chastised / double iniquity	bind / two deeds of shame	punish / double crime	bound / double guilt	put them in bonds / double sin
11	6 And the sword shall **abide on** his cities, and shall consume his branches, and devour them, because of their own counsels.	rage against	be swung over	rage through	whirl against	flash in
12	8 And Ephraim said, Yet I am become rich, I have **found me out substance: in all my labours they shall find none iniquity in me that were sin.**	gained wealth for myself"; but all riches can never	made my fortune'; but all his gains will not pay	amassed a fortune.' But he will keep nothing of	found wealth for myself; In all my labors they will	become wealthy. With all my wealth they will

	KJV	RSV	NEB	JB	NAS	NIV
		offset the guilt he has incurred	for the guilt of his sins	all his profites, because of the guilt that he has brought on himself	find in me No iniquity, which would be sin."	not find in me any iniquity or sin."
	11 Is there iniquity in Gilead? surely they **are vanity:** they sacrifice bullocks in Gilgal; yea; their altars are as **heaps** in the furrows of the fields.	come to nought / stone heaps	were worthless / heaps of stones	are falsehood, nothing else / heaps of stones	are worthless / stone heaps	are worthless / piles of stones

Joel

	KJV	RSV	NEB	JB	NAS	NIV
1	6 For a nation is come up upon my land, strong, and without number, whose teeth are the teeth of a lion, and he hath the **cheek teeth** of **a great lion.**	fangs / lioness	fangs / lioness	fangs / lioness	fangs / lioness	fangs / lioness
	7 He hath laid my vine waste, and **barked** my fig tree: he hath made it **clean bare,** and cast it away; the branches thereof are made white.	splintered / stripped off	left . . . broken and leafless / plucked them bare	torn . . . to pieces / stripped . . . clean	splinters / stripped bare	ruined / stripped off their bark
	13 Gird **yourselves,** and lament, ye priests: **howl,** ye ministers of the altar: come, lie all night in sackcloth, ye ministers of my God: for the **meat offering** and the drink offering is withholden from the house of your God.	on sackcloth / wail / cereal offering	on sackcloth /lament / grain-offering	on sackcloth / wail / oblation	with sackcloth / Wail / grain offering	on sackcloth / wail / grain offerings

Amos

	KJV	RSV	NEB	JB	NAS	NIV
3	7 Surely the Lord GOD will do nothing, **but he** revealeth his secret unto his servants the prophets.	without	without	without	Unless	without
5	12 For I know **your manifold** transgressions, and your **mighty** sins: they afflict the **just,** they take a bribe, and they turn aside the poor in the gate from their right.	how many are your / great / righteous	how many your . . . are / countless / guiltless	that . . . are many / enormous / virtuous	your . . . are many / great / righteous	how many are your / great / righteous
	24 But let **judgment** run down as waters, and righteousness as a **mighty** stream.	justice / everflowing	justice / everflowing	justice / unfailing	justice / everflowing	justice / neverfailing
6	13 Ye which rejoice in a **thing of nought,** which say, Have we not taken to us **horns** by our own strength?	Lo-debar/Karnaim	a nothing / power	Lo-debar / Karnaim	Lo-debar / Karnaim	Lo Debar / Karnaim
7	17 Therefore thus saith the LORD; Thy wife shall be an harlot in the city, and thy sons and thy daughters shall fall by the sword, and thy land shall be **divided** by line; and thou shalt die in a **polluted** land: and Israel shall surely go into **captivity forth of his** land.	parceled out / unclean / exile away from its	divided up/heathen / from their (native land and go into) exile	parcelled out/unclean / exile far distant from its	parceled up/unclean / from its (land into) exile	measured and divided up / pagan / exile away from their
9	5 And the Lord GOD of hosts is he that toucheth the land, and it shall melt, and all that dwell therein shall mourn: and it shall rise up **wholly like a flood;** and shall **be drowned,** as by the **flood** of Egypt.	like the Nile/sinks again / Nile	like the Nile/subsides / river	like the Nile/subsides / river	like the Nile/subsides / Nile	like the Nile/sinks/river

Obadiah

	KJV	RSV	NEB	JB	NAS	NIV
1	4 Though thou **exalt** thyself as the eagle, and though thou set thy nest among the stars, thence will I bring thee down, saith the LORD.	soar aloft	soar as high	soared	build high	soar

KJV	RSV	NEB	JB	NAS	NIV
5 If thieves came to thee, if **robbers** by night, (how art thou cut off!) would they not have stolen **till they had enough?** if the grapegatherers came to thee, would they not leave **some grapes?**	thieves/only enough for them-selves / gleanings	robbers/only what they want / gleanings	robbers/to their heart's content / gleanings	robbers/only until they had enough	robbers/only as much as they wanted / few grapes

Jonah

KJV	RSV	NEB	JB	NAS	NIV
1 17 Now the LORD had prepared a **great fish** to swallow up Jonah. And Jonah was in the belly of the fish three days and three nights.	great fish	great fish	great fish	great fish	great fish
3 6 For word came unto the king of Nin-e-veh, and he arose from his throne, and he **laid his robe from him,** and covered him with sackcloth, and sat in ashes.	removed his robe	stripped off his robes of state	took off his robe	laid aside his robe from him	took off his royal robes
4 6 And the LORD God prepared a **gourd,** and made it to come up over Jonah, that it might be a shadow over his head, to deliver him from his grief. So Jonah was exceeding glad of the gourd.	plant	climbing gourd	castor-oil plant	plant	vine
8 And it came to pass, when the sun did arise, that God prepared a **vehement** east wind; and the sun beat upon the head of Jonah, that he **fainted,** and wished in himself to die, and said, It is better for me to die than to live.	sultry/was faint	scorching/grew faint	scorching/was overcome	scorching/became faint	scorching/grew faint

Micah

KJV	RSV	NEB	JB	NAS	NIV
1 6 Therefore I will make Samaria as an heap of the field, and as plantings of a vineyard: and I will pour down the stones thereof into the valley, and I will **discover** the foundations thereof.	uncover	lay . . . bare	lay . . . bare	lay bare	lay bare
8 Therefore I will **wail and howl,** I will go stripped and naked: I will make a **wailing like the dragons,** and mourning as the **owls.**	lament and wail / lamentation like the jackals / ostriches	howl and wail / howl like a wolf / desert-owl	mourn and la-ment / howl like the jackals / ostriches	lament and wail / lament like the jackals / ostriches	weep and wail / howl like a jackal / owl
12 For the inhabitant of Maroth waited **carefully** for good: but evil came down from the LORD unto the **gate** of Jerusa-lem.	anxiously	alarmed	(What hope has she of happiness)	weak	writhe in pain
16 Make thee bald, and **poll thee** for thy **delicate** children; enlarge thy bald-ness as the eagle; for they are gone into **captivity** from thee.	cut off your hair / of your delight / exile	Shave the hair from your head / of your delight / exile	shave your head / that were your joy / exile	cut off your hair / of your delight / exile	Shave your heads in mourning / in whom you delight / exile
3 9 Hear this, I pray you, ye heads of the house of Jacob, and **princes** of the house of Israel, that abhor **judgment,** and pervert all equity.	rulers / justice	rulers / justice	rulers / justice	rulers / justice	rulers / justice
4 12 But they know not the thoughts of the LORD, neither understand they his **counsel:** for he shall gather them as the sheaves **into the floor.**	plan / to the threshing floor	purpose / to the threshing-floor	purpose / on the threshing floor	purpose / to the threshing floor	plan / to the threshing floor
6 5 O my people, remember now what Balak king of Moab **consulted,** and what Balaam the son of Beor answered him from Shittim unto Gilgal; that ye may know the **righteousness** of the LORD.	devised / saving acts	schemed / tri-umph	plot / rightness of the ways	counseled / righ-teous acts	counseled / righ-teous acts

Nahum

	KJV	RSV	NEB	JB	NAS	NIV
1	8 But with an **overrunning** flood he will make an **utter** end of **the place thereof, and darkness shall pursue his enemies.**	overflowing / full end / adversaries / will pursue his enemies into darkness	sweeping / final / all who oppose him / pursues his enemies into darkness	(flood overtakes) / utterly / Those who defy him / pursue his foes into the darkness	overflowing / complete / its site / pursue his enemies into darkness	overwhelming / (omits) / Nineveh / pursue into darkness
2	1 **He that dasheth in pieces** is come up **before thy face:** keep the **munition,** watch the **way,** make thy loins strong, **fortify thy power mightily.**	The Shatterer / against you / ramparts / road / collect all your strength	The battering-ram / against your bastions / road / put forth all your strength	A destroyer / against you / the rampart / road / muster all your forces (vs. 2)	The one who scatters / against you / fortress / road / summon all your strength	An attacker / against you, Nineveh / fortress / road / marshal all your strength
	5 **He shall recount his worthies:** they shall stumble in their walk; they shall make haste to the wall thereof, and the **defence shall be prepared.**	The officers are summoned / mantelet is set up	the leaders display their prowess / mantelets are set in position	The picked troops are called out / mantelet is already in place	He remembers his nobles / mantelet is set up	He summons his picked troops / protective shield is put in place
	7 And **Huzzab shall be led away captive, she shall be brought up,** and her maids shall lead her as with the **voice** of doves, **tabering upon** their breasts.	mistress is stripped, she is carried off / moaning like / beating	train of captives goes into exile / moaning like / beating	The Lady is carried off, taken into exile / like the moaning / beat	She is stripped, she is carried away / moaning like / beating	the city be exiled and carried away / moan like / beat
3	5 Behold, I am against thee, saith the LORD of hosts; and I will **discover** thy skirts **upon** thy face, and I will shew the nations thy nakedness, and the kingdoms thy shame.	lift up / over	uncover / (your breasts to your disgrace)	lift / as high as	lift / over	lift / over
	8 Art thou better than **populous No,** that was **situate among the rivers,** that had the waters round about it, whose rampart was the sea, and her wall was from the sea?	Thebes / sat by the Nile	No-amon / lay by the streams of the Nile	No-amon / beside the river	No-amon / situated by the waters of the Nile	Thebes / situated on the Nile
	19 **There is no healing** of thy **bruise;** thy wound is grievous: all that hear the **bruit** of thee shall clap the hands over thee: for upon whom hath not thy wickedness passed continually?	There is no healing / wound / (omits)	cannot be assuaged / wounds / (have heard about)	There is no remedy / wound / news	There is no relief / breakdown / (hear about you)	Nothing can heal / wound / news

Habakkuk

	KJV	RSV	NEB	JB	NAS	NIV
1	15 They take up all of them with **the angle,** they catch them in their net, and gather them in their drag: therefore they rejoice and are glad.	a hook	hooks	their hook	a hook	hooks
2	2 And the LORD answered me, and said, Write the vision, and make it plain upon **tables,** that he may run that readeth it.	tablets	tablets	tablets	tablets	tablets
3	13 Thou wentest forth for the salvation of thy people, even for salvation **with** thine anointed; thou **woundedst** the head **out of the house** of the wicked by **discovering the foundation unto the neck.** Selah.	of / didst crush / (omits) / laying him bare from thigh to neck	(omits) / dost shatter / house from the roof down / uncovering its foundations to the bare rock	(omits) / have beaten down / house / bared its foundations to the rock	of / didst strike / of the house/ lay him open from thigh to neck	(omits) / crushed / of the land / stripped him from head to foot

Zephaniah

	KJV	RSV	NEB	JB	NAS	NIV
1	**12 And it shall come to pass at that time, that I will search Jerusalem with candles, and punish the men that are settled on their lees:** that say in their	thickening upon	sit in stupor over	stagnating on	stagnant in spirit	complacent

	KJV	RSV	NEB	JB	NAS	NIV
	heart, The LORD will not do good, neither will he do evil.	their lees	the dregs of their wine	their lees		
	15 That day is a day of wrath, a day of **trouble and distress,** a day of **wasteness and desolation,** a day of darkness and gloominess, a day of clouds and thick darkness,	distress and anguish / ruin and devastation	anguish and affliction / destruction and devastation	distress and agony / ruin and devastation	trouble and distress / destruction and desolation	distress and anguish / trouble and ruin
2	9 Therefore as I live, saith the LORD of hosts, the God of Israel, Surely Moab shall be as Sodom, and the children of Ammon as Gomorrah, **even the breeding of** nettles, and saltpits, and a **perpetual desolation:** the **residue** of my people shall **spoil** them, and the remnant of my people shall possess them.	possessed by / waste for ever / remnant / plunder	a pile of / waste land for evermore / survivors / plunder	a realm of / desolation for ever / What is left / plunder	possessed by / perpetual desolation / remnant / plunder	a place of / wasteland forever / remnant / plunder

Haggai

	KJV	RSV	NEB	JB	NAS	NIV
1	4 Is it time for you, O ye, to dwell in your **ceiled** houses, and this house lie waste?	paneled	well-roofed	panelled	paneled	paneled
2	16 **Since those days were,** when one came to an heap of twenty measures, there were but ten: when one came to the **pressfat** for to draw out fifty **vessels** out of the press, there were but twenty.	how did you fare? / winevat / measures	what was your plight / wine-vat / measures	what state were you in / vat / measures	from that time / wine vat / measures	(omits) / wine vat / measures

Zechariah

	KJV	RSV	NEB	JB	NAS	NIV
1	2 The LORD **hath been sore displeased** with your fathers.	was very angry	was very angry	was stirred to anger	was very angry	was very angry
3	5 And I said, Let them set **a fair mitre** upon his head. So they set a fair mitre upon his head, and clothed him with garments. And the angel of the LORD stood by.	clean turban	clean turban	clean turban	clean turban	clean turban
4	7 Who art thou, O great mountain? before Zerubbabel thou shalt become a plain: and he shall bring forth the **headstone** thereof with shoutings, crying, Grace, grace unto it.	top stone	stone called Possession	keystone	top stone	capstone
8	11 But now I will not **be unto the residue** of this people as in the former days, saith the LORD of hosts.	deal with the remnant	am not the same towards the survivors	with the remnant (of this people) I am not as I was	treat the remnant	deal with the remnant
11	3 There is a voice of the howling of the shepherds; for their glory is spoiled: a voice of the roaring of young lions; for **the pride of Jordan is spoiled.**	jungle of the Jordan is laid waste	Jordan's dense thickets are ravaged	thickets of the Jordan have been laid waste	pride of the Jordan is ruined	lush thicket of the Jordan is ruined
13	5 But he shall say, I am no prophet, I am an **husbandman;** for **man taught me to keep cattle** from my youth.	tiller of the soil / the land has been my possession	tiller of the soil / who has been schooled in lust	peasant / the land has been my living	tiller of the ground / a man sold me as a slave	farmer / the land has been my livelihood
	6 And one shall say unto him, What are these wounds **in thine hands?** Then he shall answer, Those with which I was wounded in the house of my friends.	on your back	on your chest	on your body	between your arms	on your body
14	8 And it shall be in that day, that living waters shall go out from Jerusalem; half of them toward the **former** sea, and half of them toward the **hinder** sea: in summer and in winter shall it be.	eastern / western	eastern / western	eastern / western	eastern / western	eastern / western

Malachi

	KJV	RSV	NEB	JB	NAS	NIV
1	3 And I hated Esau, and laid his **mountains** and his heritage waste for the **dragons of the wilderness.**	hill country / jackals of the desert	mountains / lodging in the wilderness	(towns into a wilderness and his heritage into desert pastures)	mountains / jackals of the wilderness	mountains / desert jackals
	13 Ye said also, Behold, what a weariness is it! and ye have **snuffed at it,** saith the LORD of hosts; and ye brought **that which was torn,** and the lame, and the sick; thus ye brought an offering: should I accept this of your hand? saith the LORD.	sniff at it / what has been taken by violence	sniff at it / that are mutilated	sniff disdainfully at me / stolen	disdainfully sniff at it / what was taken by robbery	sniff at it contemptuously / injured
3	2 But who **may abide** the day of his coming? and who shall stand when he appeareth? for he is like a refiner's fire, and like fullers' soap:	can endure	can endure	will be able to resist	can endure	can endure

NEW TESTAMENT

Matthew

KJV	RSV	NEB	JB	NAS	NIV
1 THE book of the **generation** of Jesus Christ, the son of David, the son of Abraham.	genealogy	descent	genealogy	genealogy	genealogy
18 Now the birth of Jesus Christ **was on this wise: When as** his mother Mary was **espoused** to Joseph, before they came together, she was found with child of the Holy **Ghost.**	took place in this way / When / betrothed / Spirit	This is the story of (Omits) / betrothed / Spirit	This is how . . . came to be (Omits) / betrothed / Spirit	was as follows When / betrothed / Spirit	This is how . . . came about (Omits) / pledged / Spirit
19 Then Joseph her husband, being a just man, and not willing to make her a public example, was minded to **put her away privily.**	divorce her quietly	have the marriage contract set aside quietly	divorce her informally	put her away secretly	divorce her quietly
20 But while he thought on these things, behold, the angel of the Lord appeared unto him in a dream, saying, Joseph, thou son of David, fear not to take unto thee Mary thy wife: for that which is conceived in her is of the Holy **Ghost.**	Spirit	Spirit	Spirit	Spirit	Spirit
25 And **knew her not** till she had brought forth her firstborn son: and he called his name JESUS.	knew her not	had no intercourse with her	(though) he had not had intercourse with her	kept her a virgin	had no union with her
2 NOW when Jesus was born in Bethlehem of Judaea in the days of Herod the king, behold, there came **wise men** from the east to Jerusalem,	wise men	astrologers	wise men	magi	Magi
2 Saying, Where is he that is born King of the Jews? for we have seen his star in the east, and are come to **worship** him.	worship	pay (him) homage	do (him) homage	worship	worship
3 When Herod the king had heard these things, he was **troubled,** and all Jerusalem with him.	troubled	greatly perturbed	perturbed	troubled	disturbed
4 And when he had gathered all the chief priests and **scribes of the people** together, he demanded of them where Christ should be born.	scribes of the people	lawyers of the Jewish people	scribes of the people	scribes of the people	teachers of the law
6 And thou Bethlehem, in the land of Juda, art not the least among the **princes** of Juda: for out of thee shall come a **Governor,** that **shall rule** my people Israel.	rulers / ruler / govern	rulers / leader / to be the shepherd of	leaders / leader / will shepherd	leaders / ruler / will shepherd	rulers / ruler / will be the shepherd
7 Then Herod, when he had **privily** called the wise men, inquired of them diligently what time the star appeared.	secretly	to meet him in private	to see him privately	secretly	secretly
8 And he sent them to Bethlehem, and said, Go and **search diligently** for the young child; and when ye have found him, bring me word again, that I may come and **worship** him also.	search diligently / worship	make a careful inquiry / pay (him) homage	find out all about / do (him) homage	make careful search / worship	make a careful search / worship
10 When they saw the star, they **rejoiced with exceeding great joy.**	rejoiced exceedingly with great joy	were overjoyed	(The sight of the star) filled them with great delight	rejoiced exceedingly with great joy	were overjoyed
15 And was there until the death of Herod: that it might be fulfilled **which was spoken of the Lord by the prophet,** saying, Out of Egypt have I called my son.	what the Lord had spoken by the prophet	what the Lord had declared through the prophet	what the Lord had spoken through the prophet	what was spoken by the Lord through the prophet	what the Lord had said through the prophet

KJV	RSV	NEB	JB	NAS	NIV
16 Then Herod, when he saw that he **was mocked** of the wise men **was exceeding wroth,** and sent forth, and slew all the **children** that were in Bethlehem, and in all **the coasts** thereof, from two years old and under, according to the time which he had diligently inquired of the wise men.	had been tricked / was in a furious rage / male children / that region	(astrologers) had tricked him / fell into a passion / children / its neighbourhood	had been tricked / was furious / male children / its surrounding district	had been tricked / became very enraged / male children / its environs	had been outwitted / was furious / boys / its vicinity
17 Then was fulfilled that which was spoken by **Jeremy** the prophet, saying,	Jeremiah	Jeremiah	Jeremiah	Jeremiah	Jeremiah
22 But when he heard that Archelaus did reign in Judaea in **the room** of his father Herod, he was afraid to go thither: notwithstanding, being warned of God in a dream, he turned aside into the **parts** of Galilee:	place / district	region	region	place / regions	place / district
3 4 And the same John had his **raiment** of camel's hair, and a leathern **girdle** about his **loins;** and his **meat** was locusts and wild honey.	garment / girdle / waist / food	coat / belt / waist / food	garment / belt / waist / food	garment / belt / waist / food	clothes / belt / waist / food
7 But when he saw many of the Pharisees and Sadducees come to his baptism, he said unto them, O **generation** of vipers, who hath warned you to flee from the **wrath** to come?	brood / wrath	brood / retribution	brood / retribution (appears as verse *8*)	brood / wrath	brood / wrath
8 Bring forth therefore fruits **meet for** repentance:	that befits	(prove your repentance by the *fruit* it bears)	appropriate	in keeping with	in keeping with
9 And think not to say within yourselves, We have Abraham **to** our father: for I say unto you, that God is able of these stones to raise up children unto Abraham.	as	for	for	for	as
10 And now also the axe is laid unto the root of the trees: therefore every tree which bringeth not forth good fruit is **hewn** down, and cast into the fire.	cut	cut	cut	cut	cut
11 I indeed baptize you with water **unto** repentance: but he that cometh after me is mightier than I, whose **shoes** I am not **worthy** to **bear:** he shall baptize you with the Holy Ghost, and with fire:	for / sandals / worthy / carry	for / shoes / fit / take off	for / sandals / fit / carry	for / sandals / fit / remove	for / sandals / fit / carry
12 Whose **fan** is in his hand, and he will throughly **purge** his **floor,** and gather his wheat into the **garner;** but he will burn up the chaff with unquenchable fire.	winnowing fork / clear / threshing floor / granary	shovel / winnow / threshing floor / granary	winnowing fan / clear / threshing floor / barn	winnowing fork / thoroughly clear / threshing floor / barn	winnowing fork / clear / threshing floor / barn
13 Then cometh Jesus from Galilee to Jordan unto John, to be baptized **of** him.	by	by	by	by	by
14 But John **forbad** him, saying, I have need to be baptized **of** thee, and comest thou to me?	would have prevented / by	tried to dissuade / by	tried to dissuade / from	tried to prevent / by	tried to deter / by
15 And Jesus answering said unto him, **Suffer** it to be so **now:** for thus it becometh us to fulfill all righteousness. Then he suffered him.	Let / now	Let / for the present	Leave (it like this) / for the time being	Permit / at this time	Let / now
16 And **Jesus, when he was baptized,** went up **straightway** out of the water: and, lo, the heavens were opened **unto him,** and he saw the Spirit of God descending like a dove, and lighting upon him:	when Jesus was baptized / immediately / (omits)	After baptism Jesus / at once / (omits)	As soon as Jesus was baptized / (omits) / (omits)	After being baptized, Jesus / immediately / (omits)	As soon as Jesus was baptized / (omits) / (omits)
17 And lo a voice from heaven, saying, This is my beloved Son, **in whom I am well pleased.**	with whom I am well pleased	on whom my favour rests	my favor rests on him	in whom I am well-pleased	with him I am well-pleased
4 THEN was Jesus led up **of** the Spirit into the wilderness to be tempted of the devil.	by	by	by	by	by

KJV	RSV	NEB	JB	NAS	NIV
5 Then the devil taketh him up into the holy city, and setteth him on **a pinnacle** of the temple,	the pinnacle	the parapet	the parapet	the pinnacle	the highest point
7 Jesus said unto him, It is written again, Thou shalt not **tempt** the Lord thy God.	tempt	put . . . to the test	put . . . to the test	put . . . to the test	put . . . to the test
10 Then saith Jesus unto him, **Get thee hence,** Satan: for it is written, Thou shalt worship the Lord thy God, and him only shalt thou serve.	Begone	Begone	Be off	Begone	Away from me
11 Then the devil leaveth him, and, behold, angels came and **ministered unto** him.	ministered to	waited on	looked after	began to minister to	attended
12 Now when Jesus had heard that John **was cast into prison,** he departed into Galilee;	had been arrested	had been arrested	had been arrested	had been taken into custody	had been put in prison
13 And leaving Nazareth, he came and dwelt in Ca-per-na-um, which is **upon the sea coast,** in the **borders** of Zabulon and Nephthalim:	by the sea / territory	on the Sea of Galilee / district	a lakeside town / borders	by the sea / region	by the lake / area
16 The people which sat in darkness saw great light; and to them which sat in the region and shadow of death light **is sprung up.**	has dawned	light dawned	has dawned	dawned	has dawned
20 And they **straightway** left their nets, and followed him.	Immediately	at once	at once	immediately	At once
23 And Jesus went about all Galilee, teaching in their synagogues, and preaching the **gospel** of the kingdom, and healing all manner of sickness and all manner of disease among the people.	gospel	gospel	Good News	gospel	good news
24 And his fame went throughout all Syria: and they brought unto him all sick people that were taken with **divers diseases and torments,** and those which were possessed with devils, and those which were **lunatic,** and those that had the palsy; and he healed them.	various diseases and pains / epileptics	every kind of illness, racked with pain / epileptic	all kinds of diseases and painful complaints of one kind or another / epileptics	various diseases and pains / epileptics	various diseases, those suffering severe pain / epileptics
5 3 **Blessed** are the **poor in spirit:** for theirs is the kingdom of heaven.	blessed / poor in spirit	How blest / those who know their need of God	How happy / poor in spirit	Blessed / poor in spirit	Blessed / poor in spirit
4 **Blessed** are **they that mourn:** for they shall be comforted.	Blessed / those who mourn	How blest / the sorrowful	Happy / those who mourn (appears as verse 5)	Blessed / those who mourn	Blessed / those who mourn
5 **Blessed** are **the meek:** for they shall **inherit the earth.**	Blessed / meek / inherit the earth	How blest / those of a gentle spirit / have the earth for their possession	Happy / the gentle / have the earth for their heritage (appears as verse 4)	Blessed / gentle / inherit the earth	Blessed / meek / inherit the earth
6 **Blessed** are they which do **hunger and thirst after righteousness:** for they shall **be filled.**	Blessed / hunger and thirst for righteousness / be satisfied	How blest / hunger and thirst to see right prevail / be satisfied	Happy / hunger and thirst for what is right / be satisfied	Blessed / hunger and thirst for righteousness / be satisfied	Blessed / hunger and thirst for righteousness / be filled
7 **Blessed** are the **merciful:** for they shall **obtain mercy.**	Blessed / merciful / obtain mercy	How blest / those who show mercy / mercy shall be shown to them	Happy / merciful / have mercy shown them	Blessed / merciful / receive mercy	Blessed / merciful / shown mercy
8 **Blessed** are the pure in heart: for they shall see God.	Blessed	How blest	Happy	Blessed	Blessed
9 **Blessed** are the peacemakers: for they shall be called the children of God.	Blessed	How blest	Happy	Blessed	Blessed
10 **Blessed** are they which are persecuted for righteousness' sake: for theirs is the kingdom of heaven.	Blessed	How blest	Happy	Blessed	Blessed
11 **Blessed** are ye, when men shall **revile** you, and persecute you, and shall	Blessed / revile	How blest / (you) suffer insults	Happy / abuse	Blessed / cast insults at	Blessed / insult

KJV	RSV	NEB	JB	NAS	NIV
say all manner of evil against you falsely, for my sake.					
13 Ye are the salt of the earth: but if the salt have **lost** his **savour,** wherewith shall it be **salted?** it is thenceforth good for nothing, but to be cast out, and to be trodden under foot of men.	lost its taste / restored	becomes tasteless / restored	becomes tasteless / what can make it salty again	become tasteless / made salty again	lost its saltiness / made salty again
15 Neither do men light a **candle,** and put it under a **bushel,** but on a **candlestick;** and it giveth light unto all that are in the house.	lamp / bushel / stand	lamp / meal-tub / lamp-stand	lamp / tub / lampstand	lamp / peck-measure / lampstand	lamp / bowl / stand
18 For **verily** I say unto you, Till heaven and earth pass, one **jot** or one **tittle** shall in no wise pass from the law, till all be fulfilled.	truly / iota / dot	(Omits) / letter / stroke	solemnly / dot / stroke	truly / letter / stroke	(I tell you) the truth / smallest letter / least stroke of a pen
21 Ye have heard that it was said by them of old time, Thou shalt not kill; and whosoever shall kill **shall** be **in danger of** the judgment:	shall be liable to	must be brought to judgment	must answer for it before the court	shall be liable to the court	will be subject to judgment
22 But I say unto you, That whosoever is angry with his brother **without a cause shall be in danger of the judgment:** and **whosoever shall say to his brother, Raca,** shall be in danger of the council: but **whosoever shall** say, **Thou fool, shall** be in danger of hell fire.	(omits) / shall be liable to judgment / insults his brother / whoever says, 'You fool'	(Omits) / must be brought to judgment / abuses his brother / if he sneers at him	(Omits) / will answer for it before the court / Fool / a man calls him 'Renegade'	(Omits) / shall be guilty before the court / whoever shall say to his brother, 'Raca' / whoever shall say, 'You fool'	(Omits) / will be subject to judgment / anyone who says to his brother, 'Raca' / anyone who says 'You fool'
23 Therefore if thou bring thy gift to the altar, and there rememberest that thy brother hath **aught** against thee;	something	a grievance	something	something	something
25 Agree with thine **adversary** quickly, whiles thou art in the way with him; lest at any time the adversary deliver thee to the judge, and the judge deliver thee to the officer, and thou be cast into prison.	accuser	(If) someone sues you	opponent	opponent at law	adversary who is taking you to court
26 Verily I say unto thee, Thou shalt by no means come out thence, till thou hast paid the **uttermost farthing.**	last penny	last farthing	last penny	last cent	last penny
29 And if thy right eye **offend thee,** pluck it out, and cast it from thee: for it is **profitable** for thee that **one of thy members** should perish, and not that thy whole body should be cast into hell.	causes you to sin / pluck / better / one of your members	is your undoing / tear / better / part of your body	should cause you to sin / tear / will do you less harm / one part of you	makes you stumble / tear / better / one of the parts of your body	causes you to sin / gouge / better / one part of your body
32 But I say unto you, That whosoever shall put away his wife, saving for the cause of **fornication,** causeth her to commit adultery: and whosoever shall marry her that is divorced committeth adultery.	unchastity	unchastity	fornication	unchastity	marital unfaithfulness
33 Again, ye have heard that it hath been said by them of old time, Thou shalt not **forswear thyself,** but shalt perform unto the Lord thine oaths:	swear falsely	break your oath	break your oath	make false vows	break your oath
39 But I say unto you, That **ye resist not evil:** but whosoever shall smite thee on thy right cheek, turn to him the other also.	Do not resist one who is evil	Do not set yourself against the man who wrongs you	offer the wicked man no resistance	do not resist him who is evil	Do not resist an evil person
47 And if ye **salute** your brethren only, what do ye more than others? do not even the **publicans** so?	salute / Gentiles	greet / heathen	save your greetings / pagans	greet / Gentiles	greet / pagans
6 1 Take heed that ye do not your **alms** before men, **to be seen of** them: otherwise ye have no reward of your Father **which is in heaven.**	piety / in order to be seen by them	religion / (omits)	good deeds / to attract their notice	righteousness / to be noticed by them	acts of righteousness / to be seen by men
2 Therefore when thou doest thine alms, do not sound a trumpet before thee, as the hypocrites do in the synagogues and in the streets, **that they may**	alms / that they may be praised by men	act of charity / to win admiration from men	alms / to win men's admiration	alms / that they may be honored by men	give to the needy / to be honored by men

KJV	RSV	NEB	JB	NAS	NIV
have glory of men. Verily I say unto you, They have their reward.					
4 That thine alms may be in secret: and thy Father which seeth in secret himself shall reward thee **openly.**	**(omits)**	**(omits)**	**(omits)**	**(omits)**	**(omits)**
6 But thou, when thou prayest, enter into thy **closet, and when thou hast shut thy door, pray to thy Father which is in secret; and thy Father which seeth in** secret shall reward thee **openly.**	**room / (omits)**	**room / (omits)**	**private room / (omits)**	**inner room / (omits)**	**room / (omits)**
7 But when ye pray, use not **vain repetitions,** as the **heathen** do: for they think that they shall be heard for their **much speaking.**	**empty phrases / Gentiles / many words**	**go babbling / heathen / more they say**	**babble / pagans / many words**	**meaningless repetition / Gentiles / many words**	**keep on babbling / pagans / many words**
8 Be not ye therefore **like unto them: for your Father knoweth what things ye** have need of, before ye ask him.	**like**	**imitate**	**like**	**like**	**like**
13 And lead us not into temptation, but deliver us from **evil: For thine is the kingdom, and the power, and the glory, for ever. Amen.**	**evil / (omits)Amen**	**the evil one / (omits)**	**the evil one / (omits)**	**evil / (For Thine is the kingdom, and the power, and the glory, forever. Amen.)**	**the evil one / (omits)**
14 For if ye forgive men their **trespasses,** your heavenly Father will also forgive you:	**trespasses**	**wrongs they have done you**	**failings**	**transgressions**	**(when they) sin against you**
16 Moreover when ye fast, **be not,** as the hypocrites, **of a sad countenance:** for they **disfigure their faces,** that they may appear unto men to fast. Verily I say unto you, They have their reward.	**do not look dismal / disfigure their faces**	**do not look gloomy / make their faces unsightly**	**do not put on a gloomy look / pull long faces**	**do not put on a gloomy face / neglect their appearance**	**do not look somber / disfigure their faces**
17 But thou, when thou fastest, **anoint** thine head, and wash thy face;	**anoint**	**anoint**	**put oil**	**anoint**	**put oil**
18 That thou appear not unto men to fast, but unto thy Father which is in secret: and thy Father, which seeth in secret, shall reward thee **openly.**	**(omits)**	**(omits)**	**(omits)**	**(omits)**	**(omits)**
19 Lay not up for yourselves treasures upon earth, where moth and **rust doth corrupt,** and where thieves break through and steal:	**rust / consume**	**grows *rusty***	**woodworms / destroy**	**rust / destroy**	**rust / destroy**
22 The **light** of the body is the eye: if therefore thine eye be **single,** thy whole body shall be full of light.	**lamp/sound**	**lamp/sound**	**lamp/sound**	**lamp/clear**	**lamp/good**
23 But if thine eye be **evil,** thy whole body shall be full of darkness. If therefore the light that is in thee be darkness, how great is that darkness!	**not sound**	**bad**	**diseased**	**bad**	**bad**
24 No man can serve two masters: for either he will hate the one, and love the other; or else he will hold to the one, and despise the other. Ye cannot serve God and **mammon.**	**mammon**	**Money**	**money**	**mammon**	**Money**
25 Therefore I say unto you, **Take no thought** for your life, what ye shall eat, or what ye shall drink; nor yet for your body, what ye shall put on. Is not the life more than **meat,** and the body than **raiment?**	**do not be anxious / food / clothing**	**put away your anxious thoughts / food / clothes**	**not to worry / food / clothing**	**do not be anxious / food / clothing**	**do not worry / food / clothes**
27 Which of you by **taking thought** can add **one cubit unto his stature?**	**by being anxious / one cubit to his span of life**	**by anxious thought / add a foot to his height**	**for all his worrying / one single cubit to his span of life**	**by being anxious / single cubit to his life's span**	**by worrying / single hour to his life**
29 And yet I say unto you, That even Solomon in all his glory was not **arrayed** like one of these.	**arrayed**	**attired**	**robed**	**(did not) clothe**	**dressed**
30 Wherefore, if God so clothe the grass of the field, which to-day is, and					

KJV	RSV	NEB	JB	NAS	NIV
to-morrow is **cast into the oven,** shall he not much more clothe you, O ye of little faith?	thrown into the oven	thrown on the stove	thrown into the furnace	thrown into the furnace	thrown into the fire
32 (For after all these things do the **Gentiles** seek:) for your heavenly Father knoweth that ye have need of all these things.	Gentiles	heathen	pagan	Gentiles	pagans
33 But seek ye first the kingdom of God, and his righteousness; and all these things shall be **added unto you.**	yours as well	come to you as well	given you as well	added to you	given to you as well
34 **Take** therefore **no thought** for the morrow: for the morrow shall take thought for the things of itself. **Sufficient unto the day is the evil thereof.**	do not be anxious / Let the day's own trouble be sufficient for the day.	do not be anxious / Each day has troubles enough of its own.	do not worry / Each day has enough trouble of its own.	do not be anxious / Each day has enough trouble of its own.	do not worry / Each day has enough trouble of its own.
7 2 For with what judgment ye judge, ye shall be judged: and with what measure ye **mete,** it shall be measured to you again.	give	deal out	measure out	by your standard of measure	use
3 And why beholdest thou the **mote** that is in thy brother's eye, but considerest not the **beam** that is in thine own eye?	speck / log	speck of sawdust / great plank	splinter / plank	speck / log	speck of sawdust / plank
6 Give not that which is holy unto the dogs, neither cast ye your pearls before swine, lest they trample them under their feet, and **turn again and rend you.**	turn to attack you	turn and tear you to pieces	turn on you and tear you to pieces	turn and tear you to pieces	turn and tear you to pieces
13 Enter ye in at the **strait** gate: for wide is the gate, and broad is the way, that leadeth to destruction, and many there be which go in thereat:	narrow	narrow	narrow	narrow	narrow
15 Beware of false prophets, which come to you in sheep's clothing, but inwardly they are **ravening** wolves.	ravenous	savage	ravenous	ravenous	ferocious
20 Wherefore by their fruits ye shall **know** them.	know	recognize	tell	know	recognize
23 And then will I **profess** unto them, I never knew you: depart from me, **ye that work iniquity.**	declare / you evil-doers	tell . . . to their face / you and your wicked ways	tell . . . to their faces / you evil men	declare / you who practice lawlessness	tell . . . plainly / you evildoers
27 And the rain descended, and the floods came, and the winds blew, and beat upon that house; and it fell: and **great was the fall of it.**	great was the fall of it	down it fell with a great crash	what a fall it had	great was its fall	fell with a great crash
28 And it came to pass, when Jesus had ended these sayings, the people were astonished at his **doctrine:**	teaching	teaching	teaching	teaching	teaching
8 WHEN he was come down from the mountain, **great multitudes** followed him.	great crowds	great crowd	large crowds	great multitudes	large crowds
2 And, behold, there came a leper and **worshipped** him, saying, Lord, if thou wilt, thou canst make me clean.	knelt before	bowed low	bowed low in front of	bowed down to	knelt before
4 And Jesus saith unto him, See thou tell no man; but go thy way, shew thyself to the priest, and offer the gift that Moses commanded, for a **testimony unto them.**	proof to the people	that will certify the cure	evidence for them	testimony to them	testimony to them
6 And saying, Lord, my servant lieth at home **sick of the palsy, grievously tormented.**	lying paralyzed at home, in terrible distress	lies at home paralysed and racked with pain	lying at home paralyzed, and in great pain	lying paralyzed at home, suffering great pain	lies at home paralyzed and in terrible suffering
10 When Jesus heard it, **he marvelled,** and said to them that followed, Verily I say unto you, I have not found so great faith, no, not in Israel.	he marveled	with astonishment	he was astonished	He marveled	he was astonished

KJV	RSV	NEB	JB	NAS	NIV
12 But the **children** of the kingdom shall be cast out into outer darkness: there shall be weeping and **gnashing** of teeth.	sons / gnash	those who were born to / grinding	subjects / grinding	sons / gnashing	subjects / grinding
13 And Jesus said unto the centurion, Go thy way; and as thou hast believed, so be it done unto thee. And his servant was healed **in the selfsame hour.**	at that very moment	At that moment	at that moment	that very hour	at that very hour
15 And he touched her hand, and the fever left her: and she arose, and **ministered unto them.**	served him	waited on him	began to wait on him	waited on Him	began to wait on him
25 And his disciples came to him, and awoke him, saying, Lord, save us: **we perish.**	we are perishing	we are sinking	we are going down	we are perishing	We are going to drown!
27 But the men **marvelled,** saying, What **manner** of man is this, that even the winds and the sea obey him!	marveled / sort	were astonished / sort	were astounded / kind	marveled / kind	were amazed / kind
28 And when he was come to the other side into the **country of the Gergesenes,** there met him two possessed with devils, coming out of the tombs, exceeding fierce, so that no man might pass by that way.	country of the Gadarenes	country of the Gadarenes	country of the Gadarenes	counry of the Gadarenes	region of the Gadarenes
29 And, behold, they cried out, saying, What **have we to do with thee,** Jesus, thou Son of God? art thou come hither to torment us before the time?	have you to do with us	do you want with us	do you want with us	do we have to do with you	do you want with us
31 So the devils besought him saying, If thou cast us out, **suffer us to go away** into the herd of swine.	send us away	send us	send us	send us	send us
32 And he said unto them, Go. And when they were come out, they went into the herd of swine: and, behold, the whole herd of swine ran violently down a steep **place** into the sea, and perished in the waters.	bank	over the edge	cliff	bank	bank
34 And, behold, the whole city came out to meet Jesus: and when they saw him, they **besought** him that he would **depart out of their coasts.**	begged / leave their neighborhood	begged / leave the district and go	implored / leave the neighborhood	entreated / depart from their region	pleaded with / leave their region
9 2 And, behold, they brought to him a man sick of the palsy, lying on a **bed:** and Jesus seeing their faith said unto the sick of the palsy; Son, be of good cheer; thy sins be forgiven thee.	bed	bed	bed	bed	mat
8 But when the multitudes saw it, they marvelled, and glorified God, which had given such **power** unto men.	authority	authority	power	authority	authority
9 And as Jesus passed forth from thence, he saw a man, named Matthew, sitting at **the receipt of custom:** and he saith unto him, Follow me. And he arose, and followed him.	at the tax office	in the custom-house	by the customs house	in the tax office	at the tax collector's booth
10 And it came to pass, as Jesus **sat at meat** in the house, behold, many **publicans** and sinners came and sat down with him and his disciples.	sat at table / publicans	was at table / tax-gatherers	at dinner / tax collectors	at the table / tax gatherers	was having dinner / tax collectors
12 But when Jesus heard that, he said unto them, They that be **whole** need not a physician, but they that are sick.	well	healthy	healthy	healthy	healthy
13 But go ye and learn what **that meaneth,** I will have mercy, and not sacrifice: for I am not come to call the righteous, but sinners **to repentance.**	this means / (omits)	that text means / (omits)	the meaning of the words / (omits)	this means / (omits)	this means / (omits)
15 And Jesus said unto them, Can the **children of the bride-chamber** mourn,	wedding guests	bridegroom's	bridegroom's at-	attendants of the	guests of the

KJV	RSV	NEB	JB	NAS	NIV
as long as the bridegroom is with them? but the days will come, when the bridegroom shall be taken from them, and then shall they fast.		friends	tendants	bridegroom	bridegroom
16 No man putteth a piece of **new** cloth unto an old garment, for that which is put in to fill it up taketh from the garment, and the rent is made worse.	unshrunk	unshrunk	unshrunken	unshrunk	unshrunk
17 Neither do men put new wine into old **bottles:** else the **bottles break, and the wine runneth out, and the bottles perish:** but they put new wine into new **bottles,** and both are preserved.	wineskins / skins burst / skins / wine-skins	wine-skins / skins burst / skins / skins	wineskins / skins burst / skins /skins	wineskins / wine-skins burst / wineskins / wine-skins	wineskins / skins will burst / wine-skins / wineskins
18 While he spake these things unto them, behold, there came **a certain ruler,** and **worshipped** him, saying, My daughter **is even now dead:** but come and lay thy hand upon her, and she shall live.	a ruler / knelt before / has just died	a president of the synagogue / bowed low before / has just died	one of the officials / bowed low in front of / has just died	synagogue official / bowed down before / has just died	a ruler of the synagogue / knelt before / is at the point of death
20 And, behold, a woman, which was diseased with an **issue of blood** twelve years, came behind him, and touched the hem of his garment:	hemorrage	haemorrhages	hemorrhage	hemorrhage	bleeding
21 For she said within herself, If I may but touch his garment, I shall be **whole.**	well	cured	well again	well	healed
23 And when Jesus came into the ruler's house, and saw the **minstrels** and the **people making a noise,**	flute players / crowd making a tumult	flute-players / general commotion	flute players / crowd making a commotion	flute-players / crowd in noisy disorder	flute-players / noisy crowd
24 He said unto them, **Give place:** for the **maid** is not dead, but sleepeth. And they laughed him **to scorn.**	Depart / girl / at him	Be off! / girl / at him	Get out of here / little girl / at him	Depart / girl / at Him	Go away / girl / at him
30 And their **eyes were opened;** and Jesus **straitly** charged them, saying, See that no man know it.	eyes were opened / sternly	sight was restored / sternly	sight returned / sternly	eyes were opened / sternly	sight was restored / sternly
10 8 Heal the sick, cleanse the lepers, raise the dead, cast out devils: **freely** ye have received, **freely** give.	without paying / without pay	without cost / without charge	without charge / without charge	freely / freely	Freely / freely
9 Provide neither gold, nor silver, nor brass in your **purses,**	belts	purse	purses	money belts	belts
10 Nor **scrip** for your journey, neither two **coats,** neither **shoes,** nor yet **staves:** for the **workman is worthy of his meat.**	bag / tunics / sandals / laborer deserves his food	pack / coat / shoes / worker earns his keep	haversack / tunic / footwear / workman deserves his keep	bag / tunics / sandals / worker is worthy of his keep	bag / tunic / sandals / worker is worth his keep
16 Behold, I send you forth as sheep in the midst of wolves: be ye therefore **wise** as serpents, and **harmless** as doves.	wise / innocent	wary / innocent	cunning / harmless	shrewd / innocent	shrewd / innocent
17 But beware of men: for they will deliver you up to the councils, and they will **scourge** you in their synagogues;	flog	flog	scourge	scourge	flog
19 But when they deliver you up, **take no thought** how or what ye shall speak: for it shall be given you in that same hour what ye shall speak.	do not be anxious	do not worry	do not worry	do not become anxious	do not worry
22 And ye shall be hated of all men **for my name's sake:** but he that endureth to the end shall be saved.	for my name's sake	for your allegiance to me	on account of my name	on account of My name	because of me
24 The **disciple** is not above his **master,** nor the servant above his lord.	disciple / teacher	pupil / teacher	disciple / teacher	disciple / teacher	student / teacher
25 It is enough for the disciple that he be as his **master,** and the servant as his lord. If they have called the master of the house Beelzebub, how much more shall they call them of his household?	teacher	teacher('s)	teacher	teacher	teacher
26 **Fear them not therefore: for there is** nothing **covered,** that shall not be **re-**	covered / re-	covered up / un-	covered / unco-	covered / re-	concealed / dis-

KJV	RSV	NEB	JB	NAS	NIV
vealed; and hid, that shall not be known.	vealed	covered	vered	vealed	closed
27 What I tell you in darkness, that speak ye in light: and what ye **hear in the ear,** that **preach** ye upon the housetops.	hear whispered / proclaim	hear whispered / shout from the house-tops	hear in whispers / proclaim	hear whispered in your ear / proclaim	whispered in your ear / proclaim
32 Whosoever therefore **shall confess** me before men, him will I **confess** also before my Father which is in heaven.	acknowledges / acknowledge	acknowledge / acknowledge	declares himself for / declare myself for	shall confess / confess	acknowledges / acknowledge
35 For I am come to set a man **at variance** against his father, and the daughter against her mother, and the daughter in law against her mother in law.	(omits)	(omits)	(omits)	(omits)	(omits)
11 2 Now when John had heard in the prison the **works of Christ,** he sent two of his disciples,	deeds of Christ	what Christ was doing	what Christ was doing	works of Christ	what Christ was doing
4 Jesus answered and said unto them, Go and **shew John again** those things which ye do hear and see:	tell John	tell John	tell John	report to John	report to John
6 And blessed is he, whosoever **shall not be offended in me.**	takes no offense at me	does not find me a stumbling-block	does not lose faith in me	keeps from stumbling over me	does not fall away on my account
14 And if ye will **receive** it, this is **Elias,** which **was for** to come.	accept / Elijah / is	accept / Elijah / destined	believe / Elijah / was	accept / Elijah / was	accept / Elijah / was
19 The Son of man came eating and drinking, and they say, Behold a man gluttonous, and a **winebibber,** a friend of **publicans** and sinners. But wisdom is **justified of her children.**	drunkard / tax collector / is justified by her deeds	drinker / tax-gatherer / is proved right by its results	drunkard / tax collectors / has been proved right by her actions	drunkard / tax-gatherer / is vindicated by her deeds	drunkard / tax collectors / is proved right by her actions
20 Then began he to **upbraid** the cities wherein most of his **mighty works** were done, because they repented not:	upbraid / mighty works	spoke of / miracles	reproach / miracles	reproach / miracles	denounce / miracles
23 And thou, Capernaum, which art exalted unto heaven, shalt be brought down to **hell:** for if the mighty works, which have been done in thee, had been done in Sodom, it would have remained until this day.	Hades	the depths	hell	Hades	the depths
25 At that time Jesus answered and said, I thank thee, O Father, Lord of heaven and earth, because thou hast hid these things from the wise and **prudent,** and hast revealed them unto **babes.**	understanding / babes	learned / simple	clever / mere children	intelligent / babes	learned / little children
26 Even so, Father: **for so it seemed good in thy sight.**	for such was thy gracious will	such was thy choice	for that is what it pleased you to do	for thus it was well-pleasing in Thy sight	for this was your good pleasure
29 Take my yoke upon you, and learn of me; for I am **meek and lowly in heart:** and ye shall find rest unto your souls.	gentle and lowly in heart	gentle and humble-hearted	gentle and humble in heart	gentle and humble in heart	gentle and humble in heart
12 1 At that time Jesus went on the sabbath day through the corn; and his disciples were an hungered, and began to pluck the **ears of corn,** and to eat.	heads of grain	ears of corn	ears of corn	heads of grain	heads of grain
4 How he entered into the house of God, and did eat the **shew-bread,** which was not lawful for him to eat, neither for them which were with him, but only for the priests?	bread of the Presence	sacred bread	loaves of offering	consecrated bread	consecrated bread
13 Then saith he to the man, Stretch forth thine hand. And he stretched it forth; and it was restored whole, **like as** the other.	like	like	as	like	as
20 A bruised reed shall he not break, and **smoking flax** shall he not quench, till he **send forth judgment** unto victory.	smoldering flax / brings judgment	smouldering wick / leads justice on	smoldering wick / led the truth	smoldering wick / leads justice	smoldering wick / leads justice

KJV	RSV	NEB	JB	NAS	NIV
22 Then was brought unto him one possessed with a devil, blind and dumb: and he healed him, insomuch that the **blind and dumb** both spake and saw.	dumb man	(omits)	dumb man	dumb man	he
25 And Jesus knew their thoughts, and said unto them, Every kingdom divided against itself **is brought to desolation,** and every city or house divided against itself shall not stand:	is laid waste	goes to ruin	is heading for ruin	is laid waste	will be ruined
29 Or else how can one enter into a strong man's house, and **spoil** his goods, except he first bind the strong man? **and then he will spoil** his house.	plunder / Then indeed he may plunder	goods / before ransacking	property / Only then can he burgle	property / And then he will plunder	possessions / Then he can rob
32 And whosoever speaketh a word against the Son of man, it shall be forgiven him: but whosoever speaketh against the Holy Ghost, it shall not be forgiven him, **neither** in this world, **neither** in the world to come.	either / or	either / or	either / or	either / or	either / or
34 O **generation** of vipers, how can ye, being evil, speak good things? for **out of the abundance of the heart the mouth speaketh.**	brood / out of the abundance of the heart the mouth speaks	brood / the words that the mouth utters come from the overflowing of the heart	Brood / a man's words flow out of what fills his heart	brood / the mouth speaks of that which fills the heart	brood / out of the overflow of the heart the mouth speaks
37 For by thy words thou shalt be **justified,** and by thy words thou shalt be condemned.	justified	acquitted	acquitted	justified	acquitted
40 For as **Jonas** was three days and three nights in the **whale's belly;** so shall the Son of man be three days and three nights in the heart of the earth.	Jonah / belly of the whale	Jonah / sea-monster's belly	Jonah / belly of the sea monster	Jonah / belly of the sea monster	Jonah / belly of a huge fish
41 The men of Nineveh shall rise in judgment with this generation, and shall condemn it: because they repented at the preaching of Jonas; and, behold, **a greater than** Jonas is here.	something greater than	what (is here) is greater than	something greater than	something greater than	one greater than
42 The queen of the south shall rise up in the judgment with this generation, and shall condemn it: for she came from the uttermost parts of the earth to hear the wisdom of Solomon; and, behold, **a greater than** Solomon is here.	something greater than	what (is here) is greater than	something greater than	something greater than	one greater than
44 Then he saith, I will return into my house from whence I came out; and when he is come, he findeth it **empty, swept, and garnished.**	empty, swept, and put in order	unoccupied, swept clean, and tidy	unoccupied, swept, and tidied	unoccupied, swept, and put in order	unoccupied, swept clean, and put in order
47 **Then one said unto him, Behold, thy mother and thy brethren stand without, desiring to speak with thee.**	(omits)	Someone said, "Your mother and brothers are here outside; they want to speak to you."	(omits)	And someone said to Him, "Behold. Your mother and Your brothers are standing outside seeking to speak to You."	Someone told him, "Your mother and brothers are standing outside, wanting to speak to you."
13 4 And when he sowed, some seeds fell **by the way side,** and the fowls came and devoured them up:	along the path / birds	along the footpath / birds	on the edge of the path / birds	beside the road / birds	along the path / birds
5 Some fell upon **stony places,** where they had not much earth: and forthwith they sprung up, because they had no deepness of earth:	rocky ground	rocky ground	patches of rock	rocky places	rocky places
8 But other fell into good ground, and brought forth **fruit,** some an hundredfold, some sixtyfold, some thirtyfold.	grain	fruit	their crop	a crop	a crop
9 **Who** hath ears to hear, let him hear.	He who	If you	anyone who	He who	He who
11 He answered and said unto them, Because it is given unto you to know the **mysteries** of the kingdom of heaven, but to them it is not given.	secrets	secrets	mysteries	mysteries	secrets

KJV	RSV	NEB	JB	NAS	NIV
15 For this people's heart **is waxed gross,** and their ears are **dull** of hearing, and their eyes they have closed; lest at any time they should see with their eyes, and hear with their ears, and should understand with their heart, and **should be converted,** and I should heal them.	has grown dull / heavy / turn for me	has become gross / dulled / might turn again	has grown coarse / dull / and be converted	has become dull / (they)scarcely hear / return	has become calloused / hardly hear / turn
19 When any one heareth the word of the kingdom, and understandeth it not, then cometh the **wicked** one, and **catcheth** away that which was sown in his heart. This is he which received seed by **the way side.**	evil / snatches away / along the path	evil / carries off / along the footpath	evil / carries off / on the edge of the path	evil / snatches away / beside the road	evil / snatches away / along the path
20 But he that received the seed **into stony places,** the same is he that heareth the word, and **anon** with joy receiveth it;	on rocky ground / immediately	on rocky ground / at once	on patches of rock / at once	on the rocky places / immediately	on rocky places / at once
21 Yet hath he not root in himself, but **dureth for a while:** for when tribulation or persecution ariseth because of the word, **by and by** he **is offended.**	endures for a while / immediately / falls away	has no staying-power / at once / falls away	does not last / at once / falls away	is only temporary / immediately / falls away	lasts only a short time / quickly / falls away
22 He also that received seed among the thorns is he that heareth the word; and the care of this world, and the **deceitfulness of riches,** choke the word, and he becometh unfruitful.	delight in riches	false glamour of wealth	lure of riches	deceitfulness of riches	deceitfulness of wealth
25 But while men slept, his enemy came and sowed **tares** among the wheat, and went his way.	weeds	darnel	darnel	tares	weeds
32 Which indeed is the **least** of all seeds: but when it is grown, it is the greatest among **herbs,** and becometh a tree, so that the birds of the air come and **lodge** in the branches thereof.	smallest / shrubs / make nests	smaller / garden-plant / roost	smallest / shrubs / shelter	smaller than / garden plants / nest	smallest / garden plants / perch
36 Then Jesus sent the multitude away, and went into the house: and his disciples came unto him, saying, **Declare** unto us the parable of the **tares** of the field.	Explain / weeds	Explain / darnel	Explain / darnel	Explain / tares	Explain / weeds
45 Again, the kingdom of heaven is like unto a **merchant man,** seeking **goodly** pearls:	merchant / fine	merchant / fine	merchant / fine	merchant / fine	merchant / fine
46 Who, when he had found one pearl of great **price,** went and sold all that he had, and bought it.	value	value	value	value	value
57 And they **were offended in him.** But Jesus said unto them, A prophet is not without honour, save in his own country, and in his own house.	took offense at him	fell foul of him	would not accept him	took offense at Him	took offense at Him
14 5 And when he would have put him to death, he **feared the multitude,** because **they counted** him as a prophet.	feared the people / they held	was afraid of the people / in whose eyes	was afraid of the people / who regarded	feared the multitude / they regarded	was afraid of the people / they considered
8 And she, being before instructed of her mother, said, Give me here John Baptist's head in a **charger.**	platter	dish	dish	platter	platter
15 And when it was evening, his disciples came to him, saying, This is a **desert** place, and the time is now past; send the multitude away, that they may go into the villages, and buy themselves victuals.	lonely	lonely	lonely	desolate	remote
20 And they did all eat, **and were filled:** and they took up of the fragments that remained twelve baskets full.	and were satisfied	to their hearts' content	as much as they wanted	and were satisfied	and were satisfied
24 But the ship was now **in the midst of the sea,** tossed with waves: for the **wind was contrary.**	many furlongs distant from the land / wind was against them	some furlongs from the shore / battling with a headwind	far out on the lake / there was a head-wind	many stadia away from the land / wind was contrary	a considerable distance from the land / wind was against it

KJV	RSV	NEB	JB	NAS	NIV
25 And **in the fourth watch of the night** Jesus went unto them, walking on the sea.	in the fourth watch of the night	Between three and six in the morning	In the fourth watch of the night	in the fourth watch of the night	During the fourth watch of the night
26 And when the disciples saw him walking on the sea, they were **troubled,** saying, It is a **spirit;** and they cried out for fear.	terrified / ghost	shaken / ghost	terrified / ghost	frightened / ghost	terrified / ghost
27 But **straightway** Jesus spake unto them, saying, **Be of good cheer;** it is I; be not afraid.	immediately / Take heart	at once / Take heart	at once / Courage!	immediately / Take courage	immediately / Take courage
36 And **besought** him that they might only touch the hem of his garment: and as many as touched were made **perfectly whole.**	besought / well	was begged to allow / completely cured	begging / completely cured	entreat / cured	begged / healed
15 5 But ye say, Whosoever shall say to his father or his mother, **It is a gift, by whatsoever thou mightest be profited by me;**	What you would have gained from me is given to God,	'Anything of mine which might have been used for your benefit is set apart for God'	Anything I have that I might have used to help you is dedicated to God	"Anything of mine you might have been helped by has been given to God."	'Whatever help you might otherwise have received from me is a gift devoted to God'
6 **And honour not his father or his mother,** he shall be free. Thus have ye made the commandment of God of none effect by your tradition.	he need not honor his father (appears as part of verse 5)	then he must not honour his father or his mother	he is rid of his duty to father or mother	he is not to honor his father or his mother	he is not to honor his father with it
8 This people **draweth nigh unto me with their mouth,** and honoureth me with their lips; but their heart is far from me.	(omits)	(omits)	(omits)	(omits)	(omits)
17 Do not ye yet understand, that whatsoever entereth in at the mouth goeth into the **belly, and is cast out into the draught?**	stomach / so passes on	stomach / so is discharged into the drain	stomach / is discharged into the sewer	stomach / is eliminated	stomach / then out of the body
21 Then Jesus went thence, and departed into the **coasts** of Tyre and Sidon.	district	region	region	district	region
22 And, behold, a woman of Canaan came out of the same coasts, and cried unto him, saying, Have mercy on me, O Lord, thou son of David; my daughter is **grievously vexed** with a devil.	severely possessed	tormented	tormented	cruelly demon-possessed	suffering terribly
30 And great multitudes came unto him, having with them those that were lame, blind, dumb, maimed, and many others, and **cast them down** at Jesus' feet; and he healed them:	put them	threw them down	put down	laid them down	laid them
33 And his disciples say unto him, **Whence should we have so much bread in the wilderness, as to fill so great a multitude?**	"Where are we to get bread enough in the desert to feed so great a crowd?"	'Where in this lonely place can we find bread enough to feed such a crowd?'	"Where could we get enough bread in this deserted place to feed such a crowd?"	"Where would we get so many loaves in a desolate place to satisfy such a great multitude?"	"Where could we get enough bread in this remote place to feed such a crowd?"
37 And they did all eat, and were **filled:** and they took up of the broken **meat** that was left seven baskets full.	were satisfied / broken pieces	ate to their hearts' content / scraps	ate as much as they wanted / scraps	were satisfied / broken pieces	were satisfied / broken pieces
39 And he sent away the multitude, and **took ship, and came** into the coasts of **Magdala.**	got into the boat / Magadan	got into a boat / Magadan	got into the boat / Magadan	got into the boat / Magadan	got into the boat / Magadan
16 1 The Pharisees also with the Sadducees came, and **tempting desired** him that he would shew them a **sign** from heaven.	to test him / asked	to test him / asked	to test him / asked	testing Him / asked	tested him / (by) asking
3 And in the morning, **It will be foul weather** to-day: for the sky is red and **lowering. O ye hypocrites,** ye can **discern the face** of the sky; but can ye not	stormy / threatening / (omits) / interpret the appearance / inter-	(omits entire verse)	stormy weather / overcast / (omits) / read the face / read	a storm / threatening / (omits) / discern the appearance / dis-	stormy / overcast / (omits) / appearance of the sky / interpret

KJV	RSV	NEB	JB	NAS	NIV
discern the signs of the times?	pret			cern	
7 And they **reasoned** among themselves, saying, It is because we have taken no bread.	discussed it	began to say	said	began to discuss	discussed this
8 **Which when Jesus perceived,** he said unto them, O ye of little faith, why **reason** ye among yourselves, because ye have brought no bread?	Jesus, aware of this / discuss	Knowing what was in their minds, Jesus / talk	Jesus knew it / talking	Jesus, aware of this, / discuss	Aware of their discussion, Jesus / talking
12 Then understood they **how that** he bade them not beware of the leaven of bread, but of the **doctrine** of the Pharisees and of the Sadducees.	that / teaching	(omits) / teaching	that / teaching	that / teaching	that / teaching
13 When Jesus came into the **coasts** of Caesarea Philippi, he asked his disciples, saying, **Whom do men say that I the Son of man am?**	"Who do men say that the Son of man is?"	'Who do men say that the Son of Man is?'	"Who do people say the Son of Man is?"	"Who do people say that the Son of Man is?"	"Who do people say the Son of Man is?"
18 And I say also unto thee, That thou art Peter, and upon this rock I will build my church; and the **gates of hell** shall not prevail against it.	powers of death	power of death	gates of the underworld	gates of Hades	gates of Hades
20 Then charged he his disciples that they should tell no man that he was **Jesus the Christ.**	the Christ	the Messiah	the Christ	the Christ	the Christ
22 Then Peter took him and began to rebuke him, saying, **Be it far from thee,** Lord: this shall not be unto thee.	God forbid	"Heaven forbid!"	Heaven preserve you	God forbid it	Perish the thought
23 But he turned, and said unto Peter, Get thee behind me, Satan: thou art an **offence** unto me: for thou **savourest not the things that be** of God, but those that be of men.	hindrance / are not on the side of God	stumbling-block / think as men think	obstacle / the way (you) think is not God's way	stumbling block / are not setting your mind on God's interests	stumbling block / do not have in mind the things of God
26 For what is a man profited, if he shall gain the whole world, and **lose his own soul?** or what shall a man give in **exchange for his soul?**	forfeits his life / return for his life	at the cost of his true self / buy that self back	ruins his life / exchange for his life	forfeits his soul / exchange for his soul	forfeits his soul / exchange for his soul
27 For the Son of man shall come in the glory of his Father with his angels; and then he shall **reward** every man **according to his works.**	repay / for what he has done	give . . . the due reward / for what he has done	reward / according to his behavior	recompense / according to his deeds	reward / according to what he has done
17 2 And was transfigured before them: and his face did shine as the sun, and his **raiment** was white as the light.	garments	clothes	clothes	garments	clothes
4 Then answered Peter, and said unto Jesus, Lord, it is good for us to be here: if thou wilt, **let us make here three tabernacles;** one for thee, and one for Moses, and one for Elias.	I will make three booths here	I will make three shelters here	I will make three tents here	I will make three tabernacles here	I will put up three shelters
9 And as they came down from the mountain, Jesus **charged** them, saying, Tell the vision to no man, until the Son of man be risen again from the dead.	commanded	enjoined	gave . . . this order	commanded	instructed
12 But I say unto you, That Elias is come already, and they knew him not, but have done unto him **whatsoever they listed.** Likewise shall also the Son of man suffer **of them.**	whatever they pleased / at their hands	worked their will upon him / at their hands	as they pleased / at their hands	whatever they wished / at their hands	everything they wished / at their hands
15 Lord, have mercy on my son: for he is **lunatic,** and **sore vexed:** for ofttimes he falleth into the fire, and oft into the water.	an epileptic / suffers terribly	epileptic / has bad fits	lunatic / in a wretched state	lunatic / is very ill	epileptic / is suffering greatly
17 Then Jesus answered and said, O faithless and perverse generation, how long shall I be with you? how long **shall I suffer you?** bring him **hither** to me.	am I to bear with you / here to me	must I endure you / here	must I put up with you / here	shall I put up with you / here	shall I put up with you / here
18 And Jesus rebuked **the devil;** and **he**	him / the demon	the boy / the	it / the devil	him / the demon	the demon / it

KJV	RSV	NEB	JB	NAS	NIV
departed out of him: and the **child** was cured **from that very hour.**	came out of / boy / instantly	devil left / he / from that moment	came out of / who (the boy) / from that moment	came out of / boy / at once	came out of / he / from that moment
19 Then came the disciples to Jesus **apart,** and said, Why could not we cast **him** out?	privately / it	privately / it	privately / it	privately / it	in private / it
20 And Jesus said unto them, Because of your **unbelief:** for verily I say unto you, If ye have faith as a grain of mustard seed, ye shall say unto this mountain, Remove hence to yonder place; and it shall remove; and nothing shall be impossible unto you.	little faith	faith is too small	little faith	littleness of your faith	so little faith
21 **Howbeit this kind goeth not out but by prayer and fasting.**	(omits)	(omits)	(omits)	(But this kind does not go out except by prayer and fasting)	(omits)
22 And while they **abode** in Galilee, Jesus said unto them, The Son of man shall be betrayed into the hands of men:	were gathering	were going about together	were together	were gathering together	came together
23 And they shall kill him, and the third day he shall be raised again. And **they were exceeding sorry.**	they were greatly distressed	they were filled with grief	a great sadness came over them	they were deeply grieved	the disciples were filled with grief
24 And when they were come to Capernaum, **they that received tribute money came** to Peter, and said, Doth not your master pay tribute?	the collectors of the half-sheckel tax	the collectors of the temple-tax	the collectors of the half sheckel	those who collected the two-drachma tax	the collectors of the two-drachma tax
25 He saith, Yes. And when he was come into the house, **Jesus prevented him,** saying, What thinkest thou, Simon? of whom do the kings of the earth take custom or tribute? **of their own children, or of strangers?**	Jesus spoke to him first / From their sons or from others?	Jesus forestalled him / From their own monarchs or from aliens?	But before he could speak, Jesus / From their sons or from foreigners	Jesus spoke to him first / from their sons or from strangers	Jesus was first to speak / from their own sons or from others
26 Peter saith unto him, Of **strangers.** Jesus saith unto him, Then are the **children** free.	others / sons	aliens / their own people	foreigners / sons	strangers / exempt	others / sons
18 3 And said, **Verily** I say unto you, **Except ye be converted,** and become as little children, ye shall not enter into the kingdom of heaven.	Truly / unless you turn	(omits) / unless you turn round	solemnly / unless you change	Truly / unless you are converted	the truth / unless you change
6 But **whoso shall offend** one of these little ones which believe in me, it were better for him that a millstone were hanged about his neck, and that he were drowned in the depth of the sea.	whoever causes . . . to sin	if a man is a cause of stumbling	anyone who is an obstacle to bring down	whoever causes . . . to stumble	if anyone causes . . . to sin
7 Woe unto the world **because of offences!** for it **must needs be that offences come;** but woe to that man by whom the offence cometh!	for temptations to sin / it is necessary that temptations come	that such causes of stumbling arise / Come the must	that there should be such obstacles / Obstacles indeed there must be	because of its stumbling blocks / it is inevitable that stumbling blocks come	because of the things that cause people to sin / Such things must come
8 Wherefore if thy hand or thy foot **offend thee,** cut them off, and cast them from thee: it is better for thee to enter into life **halt** or maimed, rather than having two hands or two feet to be cast into everlasting fire.	causes you to sin / lame	is your undoing / lame	should cause you to sin / lame	causes you to stumble / lame	causes you to sin / crippled
11 **For the son of man is come to save that which was lost.**	(omits)	(omits)	(omits)	(For the Son of Man is come to save that which was lost.)	(omits)
12 **How think ye?** if a man have an hundred sheep, and one of them be gone astray, doth he not leave the ninety and nine, and goeth into the mountains, and seeketh that which is gone astray?	What do you think?	What do you think?	Tell me.	What do you think?	What do you think?
13 And if **so be that** he find it, **verily** I say unto you, he **rejoiceth more of that sheep,** than of the ninety and nine which went not astray.	(omits) / truly / rejoices over it more	(omits) / (omits) / is more delighted over that sheep	(omits) / solemnly / it gives him more joy	it turns out that / truly rejoices over it more than	(omits) / the truth / he is happier about

KJV	RSV	NEB	JB	NAS	NIV
14 Even so it is not the will of **your** Father which is in heaven, that one of these little ones should perish.	my	your	your	your	your
15 Moreover if thy brother shall **trespass** against thee, go and tell him his fault between thee and him alone: if he **shall hear** thee, thou hast gained thy brother.	sins / listens	commits a sin / listens	does something wrong / listens	sins / listens	sins / listens
17 And if he shall neglect to hear them, tell it unto the church: but if he neglect to hear the church, let him be unto thee as an **heathen man and a publican.**	Gentile and a tax collector	pagan or a tax-gatherer	pagan or a tax collector	Gentile and a tax-gatherer	pagan or a tax collector
19 Again I say unto you, That if two of you shall agree on earth **as touching** any thing that they shall ask, it shall be done for them of my Father **which is** in heaven.	about / (omits)	about / (omits)	(omits) / (omits)	about / who is	about / (omits)
23 Therefore is the kingdom of heaven likened unto a certain king, **which would take account of** his servants.	who wished to settle accounts with	who decided to settle accounts with	who decided to settle his accounts with	who wished to settle accounts with	who wanted to settle accounts with
26 The servant therefore **fell down, and worshipped him,** saying, Lord, have patience with me, and I will pay thee all.	fell on his knees, imploring him	fell prostrate at his master's feet	threw himself down at his master's feet	falling down, prostrated himself before him	fell on his knees before him
33 Shouldest not thou also have **had compassion** on thy fellow-servant, even as I **had pity** on thee?	had mercy / had mercy	show . . . the same pity / showed	have pity / had pity	had mercy / had mercy	had mercy / had
34 And his lord **was wroth,** and delivered him to the **tormentors,** till he should pay all that was due **unto him.**	in anger / jailers / (omits)	so angry was / torture / (omits)	in his anger / torturers / (omits)	moved with anger / torturers / him	In anger / jailers / (omits)
19 1 And it came to pass, that when Jesus had finished these sayings, he departed from Galilee, and came into the **coasts** of Judaea beyond **Jordan;**	region / the Jordan	region / Jordan	part / the Jordan	region / the Jordan	region / the Jordan
3 The Pharisees also came unto him, **tempting** him, and saying unto him, Is it lawful for a man to **put away** his wife for every cause?	tested / divorce	tested / divorce	to test / divorce	testing / divorce	test / divorce
5 And said, For this cause shall a man leave father and mother, and shall **cleave** to his wife: and **they twain** shall be one flesh?	be joined / the two	be made one / the two	cling / the two	cleave / the two	be united / the two
8 He saith unto them, Moses because of the hardness of your hearts **suffered** you to put away your wives: but from the beginning it was not so.	allowed	gave . . . permission	allowed	permitted	permitted
9 And I say unto you, Whosoever shall **put away** his wife, except it be for **fornication,** and shall marry another, committeth adultery: **and whoso marrieth her which is put away doth commit adultery.**	divorces / unchastity / (omits)	divorces / unchastity / (omits)	divorces / fornication / (omits)	divorces / immorality / (omits)	divorces / marital unfaithfulness / (omits)
10 His disciples say unto him, If the case of the man be so with his wife, it is **not good** to marry.	not expedient	better not	not advisable	better not	better not
13 Then were there brought unto him little children, that he should put his hands on them, and pray: and the disciples rebuked **them.**	the people	them	them	them	those who brought them
14 But Jesus said, **Suffer** little children, and forbid them not, to come unto me: for **of such is** the kingdom of heaven.	Let / to such	Let / to such	let / to such	let / to such	let / to such
17 And he said unto him, Why **callest thou me good? there is none good but one, that is, God:** but if thou wilt enter	do you ask me about what is good? One there	'Why do you ask me about that? One alone is	"Why do you ask me about what is good? There is	"Why are you asking Me about what is good?	"Why do you ask me about what is good? There is

KJV	RSV	NEB	JB	NAS	NIV
into life, keep the commandments.	is who is good	good.	alone one who is good.	There is only One who is good	only One who is good.
20 The young man saith unto him, All these things have **I kept from my youth up: what lack I yet?**	"All these I have observed; what do I still lack?"	'I have kept all these. Where do I fall short?'	"I have kept all these. What more do I need to do?"	"All these things I have kept; what am I still lacking?"	"All these things I have kept . . . What do I still lack?"
23 Then said Jesus unto his disciples, Verily I say unto you, That a **rich man shall hardly enter** into the kingdom of heaven.	it will be hard for a rich man to enter	a rich man will find it hard to enter	it will be hard for a rich man to enter	it is hard for a rich man to enter	it is hard for a rich man to enter
24 And again I say unto you, It is easier for a **camel** to go through the **eye of a needle,** than for a rich man to enter into the kingdom of God.	camel / eye of a needle	camel / eye of a needle	camel / eye of a needle	camel / eye of a needle	camel / eye of a needle
27 Then answered Peter and said unto him, **Behold,** we have **forsaken all,** and followed thee; what shall we have therefore?	Lo / left everything	(omits) / left everything	(omits) / left everything	Behold / left everything	(omits) / left everything
28 And Jesus said unto them, **Verily** I say unto you, that ye which have followed me, **in the regeneration** when the Son of man shall sit **in the throne of his glory,** ye also shall sit upon twelve thrones, judging the twelve tribes of Israel.	Truly / in the new world / on his glorious throne	(omits) / in the world that is to be / on his throne in heavenly splendour	solemnly / when all is made new / on his throne of glory	Truly / in the regeneration / on His glorious throne	the truth / at the renewal of all things / on his throne in heavenly glory
20 7 They say unto him, Because no man hath hired us. He saith unto them, Go ye also into the vineyard; **and whatsoever is right, that shall ye receive.**	(omits)	(omits)	(omits)	(omits)	(omits)
8 So when even was come, the **lord** of the vineyard saith unto his steward, Call the labourers, and **give them their hire,** beginning from the last unto the first.	owner / pay them their wages	owner / give them their pay	owner / pay them their wages	owner / pay them their wages	owner / pay them their wages
11 And when they had received it, they **murmured against the goodman of the house,**	grumbled at the householder	grumbled at their employer	grumbled at the landowner	grumbled at the landowner	began to grumble against the landowner
14 Take **that thine is,** and go thy way: I **will give unto this last, even as unto thee.**	what belongs to you / choose to give to this last as I give to you	your pay / choose to pay the last man the same as you	your earnings / choose to pay the last comer as much as I pay you	what is yours / wish to give to this last man the same as to you	your pay / want to give the man who was hired last the same as I gave you
15 **Is it not lawful for me to do what I will with mine own? Is thine eye evil, because I am good?**	Am I not allowed to do what I choose with what belongs to me? Or do you begrudge me my curiosity?	Surely I am free to do what I like with my own money. Why be jealous because I am kind?	Have I no right to do what I like with my own? Why be envious because I am generous?	'Is it not lawful for me to do what I wish with what is my own? Or is your eye envious because I am generous?	Don't I have the right to do what I want with my own money? Or are you envious because I am generous?
16 So the last shall be first, and the first last: **for many be called, but few chosen.**	(omits)	(omits)	(omits)	(omits)	(omits)
18 Behold, we go up to Jerusalem; and the Son of man shall be **betrayed** unto the chief priests and unto the scribes, and they shall condemn him to death,	delivered	given up	handed over	delivered	betrayed
20 Then came to him the mother of **Zebedee's children** with her sons, **worshipping** him, and **desiring a certain** thing of him.	sons of Zebedee / kneeling before / asking . . . for something	Zebedee's sons / bowed low / begged a favour	Zebedee's sons / bowed low / to make a request	sons of Zebedee / bowing down / making a request	Zebedee's sons / kneeling down / asked a favor
21 And he said unto her, What **wilt thou?** She saith unto him, **Grant** that these my two sons may sit, the one on thy right hand, and the other on the left, in thy kingdom.	do you want / command	is it you wish / give orders	is it you want / Promise	do you wish / command	is it you want / Grant
22 But Jesus answered and said, Ye know not what ye ask. Are ye able to drink of the cup that I shall drink of, **and to be baptized with the baptism that I**	(omits)	(omits)	(omits)	(omits)	(omits)

KJV	RSV	NEB	JB	NAS	NIV
am baptized with? They say unto him, We are able.					
23 And he saith unto them, Ye shall drink indeed of my cup, **and be baptized with the baptism that I am baptized with:** but to sit on my right hand, and on my left, is not mine to give, but it shall be given to them for whom it is prepared of my Father.	(omits)	(omits)	(omits)	(omits)	(omits)
25 But Jesus called them unto him, and said, Ye know that the **princes** of the **Gentiles exercise dominion** over them, and **they that are great** exercise authority upon them.	rulers / Gentiles / lord it over / their great men	rulers / in the world / lord it over / their great men	rulers / pagans / lord it over / their great men	rulers / Gentiles / lord it over / their great men	rulers / Gentiles / lord it over / their high officials
26 But it shall not be so among you: but whosoever will be great among you, **let him be your minister;**	(omits) / must be your servant	(omits) / must be your servant	(omits) / must be your servant	(omits) / shall be your servant	(omits) / must be your servant
27 And whosoever will be **chief** among you, let him be your **servant:**	first / slave	first / willing slave	first / slave	first / slave	first / slave
28 Even as the Son of man came **not to be ministered unto, but to minister,** and to give his life a ransom for many.	not to be served but to serve	did not come to be served, but to serve	came not to be served but to serve	did not come to be served, but to serve	did not come to be served, but to serve
31 And the **multitude rebuked them, because they should hold their peace:** but they cried the more, saying, Have mercy on us, **O Lord,** thou son of David.	crowd rebuked them telling them to be silent / Lord	people told them sharply to be quiet / Sir	crowd scolded them and told them to keep quiet / Lord	multitude sternly told them to be quiet / Lord	crowd rebuked them and told them to be quiet / Lord
21 2 Saying unto them, Go into the village over against you, and straightway ye shall find an ass tied, and a colt with her: **loose** them, and bring them unto me.	untie	untie	untie	untie	Untie
8 And a very great multitude spread their garments in the way; others cut down branches from the trees, and **strawed them in the way.**	spread them on the road	to spread in his path	spreading them in his path	spreading them in the road	spread them on the road
12 And Jesus went into the temple of God, and **cast** out all them that sold and bought in the temple, and **overthrew** the tables of the moneychangers, and the seats of them that sold **doves,**	drove / overturned / pigeons	drove / upset / pigeons	drove / upset / pigeons	cast / overturned / doves	drove / overturned / doves
13 And said unto them, It is written, My house shall be called the house of prayer; but ye have made it a den of **thieves.**	robbers	robbers' (cave)	robbers' (den)	robbers' (den)	robbers
15 And when the chief priests and scribes saw the wonderful things that he did, and the children crying in the temple, and saying, Hosanna to the son of David; they **were sore displeased,**	were indignant	asked him indignantly	were indignant	became indignant	were indignant
16 And said unto him, Hearest thou what these say? And Jesus saith unto them, Yea; have ye never read, Out of the mouth of babes and sucklings **thou hast perfected praise?**	thou hast brought perfect praise	hast made . . . sound aloud Thy praise	you have made sure of praise	Thou hast prepared praise for thyself	you have raised up praise
19 And when he saw a fig tree in the way, he came to it, and found nothing thereon, but leaves only, and said unto it, Let no fruit grow on thee **henceforward for ever.** And **presently** the fig tree withered away.	ever . . . again / at once	any more / at once	again	No longer . . . ever / at once	again / Immediately
20 And when the disciples saw it, they marvelled, saying, **How soon is the fig tree withered away!**	"How did the fig tree wither at once?"	'How is it . . . that the tree has withered so suddenly?'	"What happened to the tree . . . that it withered there and then?"	"How did the fig tree wither at once?"	"How did the fig tree wither so quickly?"
21 Jesus answered and said unto them, Verily I say unto you, If ye have faith,					

KJV	RSV	NEB	JB	NAS	NIV
and **doubt not,** ye shall not only do this which is done to the fig tree, but also if ye shall say unto this mountain, Be thou **removed,** and be thou cast into the sea; it shall be done.	never doubt / taken up	have no doubts / lifted from your place	do not doubt at all / Get up	do not doubt / taken up	do not doubt / Go
22 And all things, whatsoever ye shall ask in prayer, **believing,** ye shall receive.	if you have faith	in faith	if you have faith	believing	If you believe
24 And Jesus answered and said unto them, I also will ask you **one thing,** which if ye tell me, I in like wise will tell you by what authority I do these things.	a question	a question	a question, only one	one thing	one question
25 The baptism of John, whence was it? from heaven, or of men? **And they reasoned with themselves,** saying, If we shall say, From heaven; he will say unto us, Why did ye not then believe him?	And they argued with one another	This set them arguing among themselves	they argued it out this way among themselves	they began reasoning among themselves	They discussed it among themselves
27 And they answered Jesus, and said, **We cannot tell.** And he said unto them, Neither tell I you by what authority I do these things.	"We do not know."	'We do not know.'	"We do not know."	"We do not know."	"We don't know."
31 **Whether** of them **twain** did the will of his father? They say unto him, The first. Jesus saith unto them, **Verily** I say unto you, That the **publicans** and the harlots go into the kingdom of God before you.	Which of the two / Truly / tax collectors	Which of these two / (omits) / tax-gatherers	Which of the two / solemnly / tax collectors	Which of the two / Truly / tax-gatherers	Which of the two / the truth / tax collectors
33 Hear another parable: There was a certain householder, which planted a vineyard, and hedged it round about, and digged a winepress in it, and built a tower, and **let it out** to **husbandmen,** and went into **a far country:**	let it out / tenants / another country	let it out / vine-growers / abroad	leased it / tenants / abroad	rented it out / vine-growers / journey	rented / some farmers / journey
37 But last of all he sent unto them his son, saying, They will **reverence** my son.	respect	respect	respect	respect	respect
44 **And whosoever shall fall on this stone shall be broken: but on whomsoever it shall fall, it will grind him to powder.**	(omits)	(omits)	(omits)	"And he who falls on this stone will be broken to pieces; but on whomever it falls, it will scatter him like dust."	"He who falls on this stone will be broken to pieces but he on whom it falls will be crushed."
46 But when they **sought to lay hands on** him, they feared the multitude, because they **took him for** a prophet.	tried to arrest / held him to be	wanted to arrest / looked on Jesus as	would have liked to arrest / looked on him as	sought to seize / held Him to be	looked for a way to arrest / held that he was
22 2 The kingdom of heaven **is like unto** a certain king, which **made a marriage** for his son,	may be compared to / gave a marriage feast	is like this / prepared a feast for his son's wedding	may be compared to / gave a feast for his son's wedding	may be compared to / gave a wedding feast	is like / prepared a wedding banquet
3 And sent forth his servants to call them that were **bidden to the wedding:** and they would not come.	invited to the marriage feast	he had invited	had been invited	had been invited to the wedding feast	had been invited to the banquet
4 Again, he sent forth other servants, saying, Tell them **which are bidden,** Behold, I have prepared my dinner: my oxen and my **fatlings** are killed, and all things are ready: come unto the **marriage.**	who are invited / fat calves / marriage feast	the guests / fatted beasts / wedding	who have been invited / fatted calves / wedding	who have been invited / fattened livestock / wedding feast	who have been invited / fattened cattle / wedding banquet
5 But they made light of it, and went their ways, one to his farm, another to his **merchandise:**	business	business	business	business	business
6 And the remnant took his servants, and **entreated them spitefully,** and slew them.	treated them shamefully	attacked them brutally	maltreated them	mistreated them	mistreated them
7 But when the king heard thereof, he was **wroth:** and he sent forth his **armies,**	angry / troops	furious / troops	furious / troops	enraged / armies	enraged / army

KJV	RSV	NEB	JB	NAS	NIV
and destroyed those murderers, and burned up their city.					
8 Then saith he to his servants, The wedding is ready, but **they which were bidden** were not worthy.	those invited	the guests I invited	those who were invited	those who were invited	those I invited
9 Go ye therefore into the **highways,** and as many as ye shall find, **bid to the marriage.**	thoroughfares / invite to the marriage feast	thoroughfares / invite . . . to the wedding	crossroads in the town / invite . . . to the wedding	main highways / invite to the wedding feast	street corners / invite to the banquet
12 And he saith unto him, Friend, how **camest thou in hither not having** a wedding garment? And he was speechless.	did you get in here without	do you come to be here without	did you get in here . . . without	did you come in here without	did you get in here without
16 And they sent out unto him their disciples with the Herodians, saying, Master, we know that thou art true, and teachest the way of God in truth, neither carest thou for any man: **for thou regardest not the person of men.**	for you do not regard the position of men	whoever he may be	because a man's rank means nothing to you	You are not partial to any.	because you pay no attention to who they are
17 Tell us therefore, What thinkest thou? Is it lawful to **give tribute** unto Caesar, or not?	to pay taxes to	to pay taxes to	to pay taxes to	to give a poll-tax to	to pay taxes to
18 But Jesus **perceived their wickedness,** and said, Why **tempt ye me,** ye hypocrites?	aware of their malice / put me to the test	was aware of their malicious intention / are you trying to catch me out	was aware of their malice / do you set this trap for me	perceived their malice / are you testing Me	knowing their evil intent / are you trying to trap me
19 Show me the **tribute money.** And they brought unto him a **penny.**	money for the tax / coin	money in which the tax is paid / silver piece	money you pay the tax with / denarius	coin used for the poll-tax / denarius	coin used for paying the tax / denarius
20 And he saith unto them, Whose **is this image and superscription?**	likeness and inscription is this	head is this, and whose inscription	head is this? Whose name?"	likeness and inscription is this	portrait is this? And whose inscription?"
24 Saying, Master, Moses said, If a man die, having no children, his brother shall marry **his wife, and raise up seed unto his brother.**	the widow, and raise up children for his brother	the widow and carry on the brother's family	the widow, his sister-in-law, to raise children for his brother	his wife, and raise up an offspring to his brother	the widow and have children for him
29 Jesus answered and said unto them, Ye **do err,** not knowing the scriptures, nor the power of God.	are wrong	are mistaken	are wrong	are mistaken	are in error
30 For in the resurrection they neither marry, nor are given in marriage, but are as the angels of **God** in heaven.	(omits)	(omits)	(omits)	(omits)	(omits)
33 And when the **multitude** heard this, they were astonished at his **doctrine.**	crowd / teaching	people / teaching	people / teaching	multitudes / teaching	crowds / teaching
35 Then one of them, which was a lawyer, asked him a question, **tempting** him, and saying,	to test	tested	disconcert	testing	tested
43 He saith unto them, How then doth David **in spirit** call him Lord, saying,	inspired by the Spirit	by inspiration	moved by the Spirit	in the Spirit	speaking by the Spirit
44 The LORD said unto my Lord, Sit thou **on** my right hand, till I **make** thine enemies **thy foot-stool?**	at / put / under thy feet	at / put / under your feet	at / put / under your feet	at / put / beneath Thy feet	at / put / under your feet
46 And no man was able to answer him a word, neither **durst** any man from that day forth ask him any more questions.	did . . . dare	dared	dared	did . . . dare	dared
23 2 Saying, The scribes and the Pharisees **sit in** Moses' seat:	sit on	sit in	occupy	in	in
3 **All therefore whatsoever they bid you observe, that observe and do; but do not ye after their works: for they say, and do not.**	so practice and observe whatever they tell you, but not what they do; for they preach,	therefore do what they tell you; pay attention to their words. But do not follow their	You must therefore do what they tell you and listen to what they say; but do not	therefore, all that they tell you, do and observe, but do not according to their deeds;	So you must obey them and do everything they tell you. But do not do what they

KJV	RSV	NEB	JB	NAS	NIV
	but do not practice.	practice; for they say one thing and do another.	be guided by what they do: since they do not practice what they preach.	for they say things and do not do them.	do, for they do not practice what they preach.
4 For they bind heavy burdens and **grievous to be borne,** and lay them on men's shoulders; but they themselves will not move them **with one of their fingers.**	hard to bear / with their finger	(omits) / raise a finger	(omits) / lift a finger	omits / with so much as a finger	omits / lift a finger
5 But all their works they do for to be seen of men: they make broad their phylacteries, **and enlarge the borders of their garments,**	make . . . their fringes long	go about . . . with large tassels on their robes	wearing . . . longer tassels	lengthen the tassels of their garments	make . . . the tassles of their prayer shawls long
6 And love the **uppermost rooms** at feasts, and the **chief** seats in the synagogues,	place of honor / best	places of honour / chief	place of honor / front	place of honor / chief	place of honor / most important
8 But be not ye called Rabbi: for **one is your Master, even Christ;** and all ye are brethren.	you have one teacher	you have one Rabbi	you have only one Master	One is your Teacher	you have only one Master
10 Neither be ye called masters: for **one is your Master, even Christ.**	you have one master, the Christ	you have one Teacher, the Messiah	you have only one teacher, the Christ	one is your leader, that is, Christ	you have one Teacher, the Christ
12 And whosoever shall exalt himself shall be **abased;** and he that shall humble himself shall be exalted.	humbled	humbled	humbled	humbled	humbled
13 But woe unto you, scribes and Pharisees, hypocrites! for ye shut up the kingdom of heaven against men: for ye neither go in yourselves, **neither suffer ye them that are entering to go in.**	nor allow those who would enter to go in	when others are entering, you stop them	nor allowing others to go in who want to	nor do you allow those who are entering to go in	nor will you let those enter who are trying to
14 Woe unto you, scribes and Pharisees, hypocrites! for ye devour widows' houses, and for a pretence make long prayer: therefore ye shall receive the greater damnation.	(omits)	(omits)	(omits)	("Woe to you, scribes and Pharisees, hypocrites, because you deyour widows' houses, even while for a pretense you make long prayers; therefore you shall receive greater condemnation.)	(omits)
15 Woe unto you, scribes and Pharisees, hypocrites! for ye **compass** sea and land **to make one proselyte,** and when he is made, ye make him **twofold more the child of hell** than yourselves.	traverse / to make a single proselyte / twice as much as child of hell	travel over / to win one convert / twice as fit for hell	travel over / to make a single proselyte / twice as fit for hell	travel about / to make one proselyte / twice as much a son of hell	travel over / to win a single convert / twice as much a son of hell as you are
16 Woe unto you, ye blind guides, which say, Whosoever shall swear by the temple, it is nothing; but whosoever shall swear by the gold of the temple, **he is a debtor!**	he is bound by his oath	he is bound by his oath	he is bound	he is obligated	he is bound by his oath
17 Ye **fools and blind:** for **whether** is greater, the gold, or the temple that **sanctifieth** the gold?	blind fools / which / has made . . . sacred	Blind fools! / Which / sanctifies	Fools and blind! / which makes . . . sacred	fools and blind men / which / sanctified	blind fools / which / makes . . . sacred
18 And, Whosoever shall swear by the altar, it is nothing; but whosoever sweareth by the gift that is upon it, **he is guilty.**	he is bound by his oath	he is bound by his oath	he is bound	he is obligated	he is bound by his oath
23 Woe unto you, scribes and Pharisees, hypocrites! for ye **pay tithe** of mint and **anise** and cummin, and have **omitted** the weightier matters of the law, **judgment,** mercy, and faith: these ought ye to	tithe / dill / neglected / justice	pay tithes / dill / overlooked / justice	pay your tithe / dill / neglected / justice	tithe / dill / neglected / justice	give a tenth / dill / neglected / justice

KJV	RSV	NEB	JB	NAS	NIV
have done, and not to leave the other undone.					
25 Woe unto you, scribes and Pharisees, hypocrites! for ye make clean the outside of the cup and of the **platter,** but within they are full of extortion and **excess.**	plate / rapacity	dish / self-indulgence	dish / intemperance	dish / self-indulgence	dish / self-indulgence
27 Woe unto you, scribes and Pharisees, hypocrites! for ye are like unto **whited sepulchres,** which indeed appear beautiful outward, but are within full of dead men's bones, and of all uncleanness.	whitewashed tombs	tombs covered with whitewash	whitewashed tombs	whitewashed tombs	whitewashed tombs
29 Woe unto you, scribes and Pharisees, hypocrites! because ye build the tombs of the prophets, and **garnish the sepulchres** of the righteous,	adorn the monuments	embellish the monuments	decorate the tombs	adorn the monuments	decorate the graves
30 And say, If we **had been** in the days of our fathers, we would not **have been partakers** with them **in the blood of the prophets.**	had lived / have taken part / in shedding the blood of the prophets	had been alive / have taken part / in the murder of the prophets	had we lived / have joined / in shedding the blood of the prophets	had been living / had been partners / in shedding the blood of the prophets	had lived / taken part / in shedding the blood of the prophets
31 Wherefore ye be witnesses **unto yourselves,** that ye are the **children** of them which **killed** the prophets.	against yourself / sons / murdered	(So you acknowledge) / sons / killed	against you / sons / murdered	against yourselves / sons / murdered	against yourselves / descendants / murdered
33 Ye serpents, ye **generation** of vipers, how can ye escape **the damnation of hell?**	brood / being sentenced to hell	brood / being condemned to hell	brood / being condemned to hell	brood / sentence of hell	brood / condemned to hell
35 That upon you may come all the righteous blood shed upon the earth, from the blood of **righteous** Abel unto the blood of Zacharias son of Barachias, whom ye **slew** between the **temple** and the altar.	innocent / murdered / sanctuary	innocent / murdered / sanctuary	the Holy / murdered / sanctuary	righteous / murdered / temple	righteous / murdered / temple
38 Behold, your house is left unto you **desolate.**	forsaken and desolate	forsaken by God	desolate	desolate	desolate
24 3 And as he sat upon the mount of Olives, the disciples came unto him privately, saying, Tell us, when shall these things be? and what shall be the sign of thy coming, and of the end of the **world?**	age	age	world	age	age
4 And Jesus answered and said unto them, Take heed that no man **deceive you.**	leads you astray	misleads you	deceives you	misleads you	deceives you
5 For many shall come **in** my name, saying, I am **Christ;** and shall deceive many.	in / the Christ	claiming / the Messiah	using / the Christ	in / the Christ	in / the Christ
6 And ye shall hear of wars and rumours of wars: see that ye be not **troubled:** for all these things must come to pass, but the end is not yet.	alarmed	alarmed	alarmed	frightened	alarmed
7 For nation shall rise against nation, and kingdom against kingdom: and there shall be famines, and **pestilences,** and earthquakes, in **divers places.**	(omits) / various places	(omits) / many places	(omits) / here and there	(omits) / various places	(omits) / various places
8 All these are the beginning of **sorrows.**	the birth-pangs	the birth-pangs	the birth pangs	birth pangs	birth pains
9 Then shall they deliver you up **to be afflicted,** and shall **kill** you: and ye shall be hated of all nations **for my name's sake.**	to tribulation, and put you to death / for my name's sake	for punishment and execution / for your allegiance to me	to be tortured and put to death / on account of my name	to tribulation, and to kill your / on account of My name	to be persecuted and put to death / on account of my name
11 And many false prophets shall rise, and shall **deceive many.**	lead many astray	mislead many	deceive many	mislead many	deceive many people
12 And because **iniquity shall abound,** the love of many shall wax cold.	wickedness is multiplied	lawlessness spreads	with the increase of wickedness	lawlessness is increased	the increase of wickedness

KJV	RSV	NEB	JB	NAS	NIV
13 But **he that shall endure** unto the end, the same shall be saved.	who endures	man who holds out	man who stands firm	one who endures	he who stands firm
15 When ye therefore shall see the **abomination of desolation,** spoken of by Daniel the prophet, stand in the holy place, (whoso readeth, let him understand:)	desolating sacrilege	abomination of desolation	disastrous abomination	abomination of desolation	abomination that causes desolation
18 Neither let him which is in the field return back to take his **clothes.**	mantle	coat	cloak	cloak	cloak
21 For then shall be **great tribulation,** such as was not since the beginning of the world to this time, no, nor ever shall be.	great tribulation	time of great distress	(there will be) great distress	great tribulation	great distress
22 And except those days should be shortened, there should no **flesh** be saved: but for the elect's sake those days shall be shortened.	human being	living thing	no one	no life	no one
25 Behold, I have **told you before.**	told you beforehand	forewarned you	forewarned you	told you in advance	told you ahead of time
26 Wherefore if they shall say unto you, Behold, he is in the desert; go not forth: behold, he is in the **secret chambers;** believe it not.	inner rooms	inner room	hiding place	inner rooms	inner rooms
28 For wheresoever the **carcase** is, there will the eagles be gathered together.	body	corpse	corpse	corpse	carcass
29 Immediately after the **tribulation** of those days shall the sun be darkened, and the moon shall not give her light, and the stars shall fall from heaven, and the powers of the heavens shall be shaken:	tribulation	distress	distress	tribulation	distress
32 Now **learn a parable** of the fig tree; When his **branch is yet tender,** and putteth forth leaves, ye know that summer is nigh:	learn its lesson / branch becomes tender	Learn a lesson / tender shoots appear	Take . . . as a parable / twigs grow supple	learn the parable / branch has already become tender	learn this lesson / twigs get tender
33 So likewise ye, when ye shall see all these things, know that **it** is near, even at the **doors.**	he / very gates	the end / very door	he / very gates	He / door	it / door
36 But of that day and hour knoweth no man, no, not the angels of heaven, [ ] but my Father only.	nor the Son	not even the Son	nor the Son	nor the Son	nor the Son
42 Watch therefore: for ye know not what **hour** your Lord **doth come.**	day / is coming	what day / is to come	the day / is coming	which day / is coming	what day / will come
43 But know this, that if the **goodman of the house** had known in what **watch** the thief would come, he would have watched, and would not have **suffered his house to be broken up.**	householder / part of the night / let his house be broken into	householder / time of the night / let his house be broken into	householder / time of the night / allowed anyone to break through the wall of his house	head of the house / time of the night / allowed his house to be broken into	owner of the house / time of the night / let his house be broken into
45 Who then is a faithful and wise servant, whom his **lord hath made ruler** over his household, to give them **meat in due season?**	master has set over / food at the proper time	charged by his master / rations at the proper time	master to place him over / food at the proper time	master put in charge of / food at the proper time	master has put in charge of / food at the proper time
48 **But and if** that evil servant shall say **in his heart,** My lord delayeth his coming:	But if / to himself	But if / to himself	But as for / to himself	But if / in his heart	But suppose / to himself
51 And shall **cut him asunder,** and appoint him his portion with the hypocrites: there shall be weeping and gnashing of teeth.	punish him	cut him in pieces	cut him off	cut him in pieces	cut him to pieces
25 1 Then shall the kingdom of heaven be likened unto ten **virgins,** which took their lamps, and went forth to meet the bridegroom.	maidens	girls	bridesmaids	virgins	virgins

KJV	RSV	NEB	JB	NAS	NIV
4 But the wise took oil in their **vessels** with their lamps.	flasks	flasks	flasks	flasks	jars
5 While the bridegroom **tarried,** they all slumbered and slept.	was delayed	was late in coming	was late	was delaying	was late
8 And the foolish said unto the wise, Give us of your oil; for our lamps are **gone** out.	going	going	going	going	going
10 And while they went to buy, the bridegroom came; and they that were ready went in with him to the **marriage:** and the door was shut.	marriage feast	wedding	wedding hall	wedding feast	wedding banquet
13 Watch therefore, for ye know neither the day nor the hour **wherein the Son of man cometh.**	(omits)	(omits)	(omits)	(omits)	(omits)
14 For **the kingdom of heaven** is as a man **travelling into a far country,** who called his own servants, and **delivered** unto them his goods.	it / going on a journey / entrusted	It / going abroad / put	It / on his way abroad / entrusted	it / about to go on a journey / entrusted	it / going on a journey / entrusted
15 And unto one he gave five talents, to another two, and to another one; to every man according to his **several** ability; and **straightway** took his journey.	according to his ability / Then	according to his capacity / Then	in proportion to his ability / Then	according to his own ability / (omits)	each according to his ability / Then
19 After a long time the lord of those servants cometh, and **reckoneth** with them.	settled accounts	proceeded to settle the accounts	went through his accounts	settled accounts	settled accounts
21 His lord said unto him, Well done, thou good and **faithful** servant: thou hast been **faithful** over a few things, I will **make thee ruler over many things:** enter thou into the **joy of thy lord.**	faithful / faithful / set you over much / joy of your master	trusty / trustworthy / put you in charge of something big / your master's delight	faithful / faithful / trust you with greater / your master's happiness	faithful / faithful / put you in charge of many things / joy of your master	faithful / faithful / put you in charge of many things / your master's happiness
24 Then he which had received the one talent came and said, Lord, I knew thee that thou art an hard man, **reaping** where thou hast not sown, and gathering where thou hast not **strawed:**	reaping / winnow	reap / scattered	reaping / scattered	reaping / scattered no seed	harvesting / gathered seed
27 Thou oughtest therefore to have **put my money to the exchangers,** and then at my coming I should have received mine own with **usury.**	invested my money with the bankers / interest	put my money on deposit / interest	deposited my money with the bankers / interest	put my money in the bank / interest	put my money on deposit with the bankers / interest
30 And cast ye the **unprofitable** servant into outer darkness: there shall be weeping and gnashing of teeth.	worthless	useless	good-for-nothing	worthless	worthless
31 When the Son of man shall come in his glory, and all the **holy** angels with him, then shall he sit **upon the throne of his glory:**	(omits) / on his glorious throne	(omits) / in state on his throne	(omits) / on his throne of glory	(omits) / on His glorious throne	(omits) / on his throne in heavenly glory
35 For I was an **hungered,** and ye gave me **meat:** I was thirsty, and ye gave me drink: I was a stranger, and ye **took me in:**	hungry / food / welcomed me	hungry / food / took me into your home	hungry / food / made me welcome	hungry / something / invited Me in	hungry / something / invited me in
46 And these shall go away into **everlasting** punishment: but the righteous into life eternal.	eternal	eternal	eternal	eternal	eternal
26 2 Ye know that after two days is the feast of the passover, and the Son of man is **betrayed** to be crucified.	will be delivered up	is to be handed over	will be handed over	is to be delivered up	will be handed over
4 And **consulted** that they might **take** Jesus by **subtilty,** and kill him.	took counsel together in order to arrest Jesus by stealth	conferred together to have Jesus arrested by some trick	made plans to arrest Jesus by some trick	plotted together to seize Jesus by stealth	plotted to arrest Jesus in some sly way
7 There came unto him a woman having an **alabaster box of very precious ointment,** and poured it on his head, as	alabaster flask / very expensive	small bottle / fragrant oil, very	alabaster jar / most expensive	alabaster vial / very costly per-	alabaster jar / very expensive

KJV	RSV	NEB	JB	NAS	NIV
he **sat at meat.**	ointment / sat at table	costly / sat at table	ointment / was reclining at the table	fume / reclined at the table	perfume / was reclining at the table
10 When Jesus understood it, he said unto them, Why trouble ye the woman? for **she hath wrought a good work upon me.**	she has done a beautiful thing to me	It is a fine thing she has done for me.	"What she has done for me is one of the good works indeed!	she has done a good deed to Me	She has done a beautiful thing to me
15 And said unto them, What will ye give me, **and I** will deliver him unto you? And they **covenanted with him** for thirty pieces of silver.	if I / paid him	to / weighed him out	if I / paid him	to / weighed out to him	if I / counted out for him
19 And the disciples did as Jesus had **appointed** them; and they **made ready** the passover.	directed / prepared	directed / prepared	told / prepared	directed / prepared	directed / prepared
20 Now when the even was come, he **sat down** with the twelve.	sat at table	sat down	was at table	was reclining at the table	was reclining at the table
25 Then Judas, which betrayed him, answered and said, **Master, is it I?** He said unto him, **Thou hast said.**	"Is it I, Master?" / "You have said so."	'Rabbi, can you mean me?' / 'The words are yours.'	"Not I, Rabbi, surely?" / "They are your own words."	"Surely it is not I, Rabbi?" / "You have said it yourself."	"Surely not I, Rabbi?" / "Yes, it is you."
27 And he took the cup, and gave thanks, and gave it to them, saying, **Drink ye all of it;**	"Drink of it, all of you;	'Drink from it, all of you.	"Drink all of you from this,"	"Drink from it, all of you;	"Drink from it, all of you
28 For this is my blood of the **new testament,** which is **shed** for many for the **remission** of sins.	the covenant / poured out / forgiveness of sins	the covenant / shed / forgiveness of sins	the covenant / poured out / forgiveness of sins	the covenant / poured out / forgiveness of sins	the covenant / poured out / forgiveness of sins
29 But I say unto you, I will not drink **henceforth** of this fruit of the vine, until that day when I drink it new with you in my Father's kingdom.	again	again	From now on	from now on	from now on
31 Then saith Jesus unto them, All ye shall be **offended because of me** this night: for it is written, I will smite the shepherd, and the sheep of the flock shall be scattered abroad.	"You will all fall away because of me	you will all fall from your faith on my account	"You will all lose faith in me	"You will all fall away because of Me	you will all fall away because of Me
34 Jesus said unto him, **Verily** I say unto thee, That this night, before the cock crow, thou shalt **deny** me **thrice.**	Truly / deny me three times	(omits) / disown me three times	solemnly / disowned me three times	Truly / deny Me three times	the truth / disown me three times
35 Peter said unto him, **Though I should die with thee, yet will I not deny thee.** Likewise also said all the disciples.	"Even if I must die with you, I will not deny you."	'Even if I must die with you, I will never disown you.'	"Even if I have to die with you, I will never disown you."	"Even if I have to die with You, I will not deny You."	"Even if I have to die with you, I will never disown you."
37 And he took with him Peter and the two sons of Zebedee, and began to be **sorrowful** and **very heavy.**	sorrowful / troubled	Anguish / dismay (came over him)	sadness / great distress (came over him)	grieved / distressed	sorrowful / troubled
38 Then saith he unto them, My soul is exceeding sorrowful, even unto death: tarry ye here, and **watch with me.**	watch with me	stay awake with me	keep awake with me	keep watch with Me	keep watch with me
41 Watch and pray, that ye **enter not into temptation:** the spirit indeed is willing, but the flesh is weak.	not enter into temptation	be spared the test	not be put to the test	not enter into temptation	will not fall into temptation
45 Then cometh he to his disciples, and saith unto them, **Sleep on now, and take your rest:** behold, the hour is at hand, and the Son of man is betrayed into the hands of sinners.	"Are you still sleeping and taking your rest?	'Still sleeping? Still taking your ease?	"You can sleep on now and take your rest	"Are you still sleeping and taking your rest?	"Are you still sleeping and resting?
50 And Jesus said unto him, **Friend, wherefore art thou come?** Then came they, and laid hands on Jesus, and took him.	"Friend, why are you here?"	'Friend, do what you are here to do.'	"My friend, do what you are here for."	"Friend, do what you have come for."	"Friend, do what you came for."

KJV	RSV	NEB	JB	NAS	NIV
51 And, behold, one of them which were with Jesus stretched out his hand, and drew his sword, and struck a **servant** of the high priest's, and **smote** off his ear.	slave / cut	servant / cut	servant / cut	slave / cut	servant / cutting
53 Thinkest thou that I cannot now pray to my Father, and he shall **presently** give me more than twelve legions of angels?	at once	at once	promptly	at once	at once
55 In that same hour said Jesus to the multitudes, Are ye come out as against a **thief** with swords and **staves** for to take me? I sat daily with you teaching in the temple, and ye laid no hold on me.	robber / clubs	bandit / cudgels	brigand / clubs	robber / clubs	(Am I leading a rebellion) / clubs
58 But Peter followed him afar off unto the high priest's **palace,** and went in, and sat with the **servants,** to see the end.	courtyard / guards	courtyard / attendants	palace / attendants	courtyard / officers	courtyard / guards
59 Now the chief priests, **and elders,** and all the council, sought false witness against Jesus, to put him to death;	the whole council	the whole Council	the whole Sanhedrin	the whole Council	the whole Sanhedrin
66 **What think ye?** They answered and said, **He is guilty of death.**	What is your judgment? / "He deserves death."	What is your opinion?' / 'He is guilty,'	What is your opinion?" / "He deserves to die."	what do you think?" / "He is deserving of death!"	What do you think?" / "He is worthy of death."
69 Now Peter sat without in the **palace:** and a **damsel** came unto him, saying, Thou also wast with Jesus of Galilee.	courtyard / maid	courtyard / serving-maid	courtyard / servant girl	courtyard / servant-girl	courtyard / servant girl
71 And when he was gone out into the porch, another maid saw him, and said **unto them that were there,** This **fellow** was also with Jesus of Nazareth.	to the bystanders / man	to the people there / fellow	to the people there / man	to those who were there / man	to the people there / fellow
73 And after a while **came unto him they that stood by,** and said to Peter, Surely thou also art one of them; for thy **speech betrayeth** thee.	the bystanders came up and said to Peter / accent betrays you	the bystanders came up and said to Peter / accent gives you away	bystanders came up and said to Peter / accent gives you away	bystanders came up and said to Peter / the way you talk gives you away	those standing there went up to Peter and said / your accent gives you away
74 Then **began he to curse and to swear,** saying, I know not the man. And immediately the cock crew.	began to invoke a curse on himself and to swear	broke into curses and declared with an oath	started calling down curses on himself and swearing	began to curse and swear	began to call down curses on himself and he swore to them
27 6 And the chief priests took the silver pieces, and said, It is not lawful for to put them into the treasury, **because it is the price of blood.**	since they are blood money	it is blood-money	it is blood money	since it is the price of blood	since it is blood money
9 Then was fulfilled that which was spoken by Jeremy the prophet, saying, And they took the thirty pieces of silver **the price of him that was valued, whom they of the children of Israel did value;**	the price of him on whom a price had been set by some of the sons of Israel	the price set on a man's head (for that was his price among the Israelites)	the sum at which the precious One was priced by children of Israel	the price of the One whose price had been set by the sons of Israel	the price set on him by the people of Israel
10 And gave them for the potter's field, as the Lord **appointed** me.	directed	directed	directed	directed	commanded
11 And Jesus stood before the governor: and the governor asked him, saying, Art thou the King of the Jews? And Jesus said unto him, **Thou sayest.**	"You have said so."	'The words are yours,'	"It is you who say it."	"It is as you say."	"Yes, it is as you say."
14 And **he answered him to never a word;** insomuch that the governor **marvelled greatly.**	he gave him no answer, not even to a single charge / wondered greatly	he still refused to answer one word / (Governor's) great astonishment	he offered no reply to any of the charges / governor's (complete amazement)	He did not answer him with regard to a single charge / quite amazed	Jesus made no reply, not even to a single charge / great amazement
15 Now at that feast the governor was wont to release unto the **people** a prisoner, **whom they would.**	crowd / whom they wanted	chosen by the people	people / anyone they chose	multitude / whom they wanted	chosen by the crowd
16 And they had then a **notable** prisoner, called Barabbas.	notorious	of some notoriety	notorious	notorious	notorious

KJV	RSV	NEB	JB	NAS	NIV
19 **When** he was set down on the judgment seat, his wife sent unto him, saying, Have thou nothing to do with that **just** man: for I have suffered **many things this day in a dream because of him.**	Besides, while / righteous / much over him today in a dream	While / innocent / on his account in my dreams last night	Now as / (omits) / all day by a dream I had about him	And while / righteous / in a dream because of Him	While / innocent / a great deal today in a dream on account of him
24 When **Pilate saw that he could prevail nothing,** but that rather a **tumult was made,** he took water, and washed his hands before the multitude, saying, I am innocent of **the blood of this just person:** see ye to it.	Pilate saw that he was gaining nothing / riot was beginning / of this man's blood	Pilate could see that nothing was being gained / riot was starting / of this man's blood	Pilate saw that he was making no impression / riot was imminent / of this man's blood	Pilate saw that he was accomplishing nothing / riot was starting / of this Man's blood	Pilate saw that he was getting nowhere / uproar was starting / of this man's blood
27 Then the soldiers of the governor took Jesus into the **common hall,** and gathered unto him the whole band of soldiers.	praetorium	Governor's headquarters	Praetorium	Praetorium	Praetorium
31 And after that they had mocked him, they took the robe off from him, and put his own **raiment** on him, and led him away to crucify him.	clothes	clothes	clothes	garments	clothes
34 They gave him **vinegar** to drink mingled with gall: and when he had tasted thereof, he would not drink.	wine	wine	wine	wine	wine
35 And they crucified him, and parted his garments, casting lots: **that it might be fulfilled which was spoken by the prophet, They parted my garments among them, and upon my vesture did they cast lots.**	(omits)	(omits)	(omits)	(omits)	(omits)
37 And set up over his head **his accusation** written, This is Jesus the King of the Jews.	charge against him	inscription giving the charge	charge against him	charge against Him	charge against him
43 He **trusted** in God; let **him deliver** him now, if he **will have** him: for he said, I am the Son of God.	trusts / God deliver / desires	Did (he) trust / God rescue / wants	puts his trust / God rescue / wants	trusts / Him deliver / takes pleasure	trusts / God rescue/wants
44 The thieves also, which were crucified with him, **cast the same in his teeth.**	also reviled him in the same way	taunted him in the same way	taunted him in the same way	were casting the same insult at Him	also heaped insults on him
51 And, behold, the **veil of** the temple was **rent in twain** from the top to the bottom; and the earth did **quake,** and the **rocks rent;**	curtain / torn in two / shook / rocks were split	curtain / torn in two / (earth)quake / rocks split	veil / torn in two / quaked / rocks were split	veil / torn in two / shook / rocks were split	curtain / torn in two / shook / rocks split
52 And the **graves** were opened; and many bodies of the saints which slept arose,	tombs	graves	tombs	tombs	tombs
54 Now when the centurion, and they that were with him, watching Jesus, saw the earthquake, and those things that were done, they **feared greatly,** saying, Truly this was the Son of God.	were filled with awe	were filled with awe	were terrified	became very frightened	were terrified
56 Among which was Mary Magdalene, and Mary the mother of James and Joses, and the mother of **Zebedee's children.**	sons of Zebedee	sons of Zebedee	Zebedee's sons	sons of Zebedee	Zebedee's sons
60 And laid it in his own new tomb, which he had hewn out in the rock: and he rolled a great stone to the **door of the sepulchre,** and departed.	door of the tomb	entrance	entrance of the tomb	entrance of the tomb	entrance to the tomb
61 And there was Mary Magdalene, and the other Mary, sitting **over against the sepulchre.**	opposite the sepulchre	opposite the grave	opposite the sepulcher	opposite the grave	across from the tomb
63 Saying, Sir, we remember that that **deceiver** said, while he was yet alive, After three days I will rise again.	imposter	imposter	imposter	deceiver	imposter
64 Command therefore that the sepulchre be made sure until the third day, lest his disciples come **by night,** and steal him away, and say unto the people, He is	(omits) / fraud	(omits) / deception	(omits) / piece of fraud	(omits) / deception	(omits) / deception

KJV	RSV	NEB	JB	NAS	NIV
risen from the dead: so the last **error** shall be worse than the first.					
65 Pilate said unto them, **Ye have a watch:** go your way, make it as sure as ye can.	"You have a guard of soldiers	'You may have your guard.'	"You may have your guard."	"You have a guard	"Take a guard;"
28 1 **In the end of the sabbath,** as it began to dawn toward the first day of the week, came Mary Magdalene and the other Mary to see the sepulchre.	Now after the sabbath	The Sabbath was over	After the sabbath,	Now after the Sabbath	After the Sabbath
2 And, behold, there was a great earthquake: for the angel of the Lord descended from heaven, and came and rolled back the stone **from the door,** and sat upon it.	(omits)	(omits)	(omits)	(omits)	(omits)
3 His **countenance** was like lightning, and his **raiment** white as snow:	appearance / raiment	face / garments	face / robe	appearance / garment	appearance / clothes
4 And for fear of him the **keepers** did shake, and became as dead men.	guards	guards	guards	guards	guards
6 He is not here: for he is risen, as he said. Come, see the place where **the Lord** lay.	he	he	he	He	he
10 Then said Jesus unto them, Be not afraid: go tell my brethren **that they go** into Galilee, and there shall they see me.	to go	that they are to leave	that they must leave	to leave	to go
11 Now when they were going, behold, some of the **watch** came into the city, and **shewed** unto the chief priests all the things that were done.	guard / told	guard / reported	guard / to tell	guard / reported	guards / reported
12 And when they were assembled with the elders, and had taken counsel, they gave **large money** unto the soldiers,	a sum of money	a substantial bribe	a considerable sum of money	a large sum of money	a large sum of money
14 And if this come to the governor's ears, we will **persuade him, and secure you.**	satisfy him and keep you out of trouble	put matters right with him and see that you do not suffer	undertake to put things right with him ourselves and to see that you do not get into trouble	win him over and keep you out of trouble	satisfy him and keep you out of trouble
15 So they took the money, and did as they were **taught:** and this **saying is commonly reported** among the Jews until this day.	directed / story has been spread	told / story became widely known, and is current	carried out their instructions / that is the story	instructed / story was widely spread	instructed / story has been widely circulated
18 And Jesus came and spake unto them, saying, All **power** is given unto me in heaven and in earth.	authority	authority	authority	authority	authority
19 Go ye therefore, and **teach** all nations, baptizing them in the name of the Father, and of the Son, and of the Holy Ghost:	make disciples of	make . . . my disciples	make disciples of	make disciples of	make disciples of
20 Teaching them to observe all things whatsoever I have commanded you: **and, lo,** I am with you alway, even unto **the end of the world.** Amen.	and lo / to the close of the age	be assured / to the end of time	and know that / to the end of time	and lo / to the end of the age	And surely / to the very end of the age

Mark

KJV	RSV	NEB	JB	NAS	NIV
1 2 As it is written in **the prophets,** Behold, I send my messenger before thy face, **which** shall prepare thy way before thee.	Isaiah the prophet / who	the prophet Isaiah / whom	the book of the prophet Isaiah / he	Isaiah the prophet / Who	Isaiah the prophet / who
4 John **did baptize** in the wilderness,	the baptizer ap-	the Baptist ap-	the Baptist ap-	the Baptist ap-	John came, bap-

KJV	RSV	NEB	JB	NAS	NIV
and preach the baptism of repentance for the **remission** of sins.	peared / forgiveness	peared / forgiveness	peared / forgiveness	peared / forgiveness	tizing / forgiveness
14 Now after that John was **put in prison,** Jesus came into Galilee, preaching the **gospel of the kingdom of God,**	arrested / gospel of God	arrested / gospel of God	arrested / Good News from God	taken into custody / gospel of God	put in prison / good news of God
20 And straightway he called them: and they left their father Zebedee in the ship with the **hired servants,** and went after him.	hired servants	hired men	men he employed	hired servants	hired men
24 Saying, **Let us alone;** what have **we** to do with **thee,** thou Jesus of Nazareth? art thou come to destroy us? I know thee who thou art, the Holy One of God.	(omits) / you / us	(omits) / you / us	(omits) / you / us	(omits) / we / You	(omits) / you / us
26 And when the unclean spirit **had torn him,** and cried with a loud voice, he came out of him.	convulsing him	threw the man into convulsions	threw the man into convulsions	throwing him into convulsions	shook the man violently
30 But Simon's wife's mother lay sick of a fever, and **anon** they tell him of her.	immediately	at once	straightaway	immediately	(omits)
34 And he healed many that were sick of **divers** diseases, and cast out many devils; and **suffered not** the devils to speak, because they knew him.	various / not permit	various / not let	of one kind or another / not allow	various / not permitting	various / not let
35 And in the morning, rising up a great while before day, he went out, and departed into a **solitary** place, and there prayed.	lonely	lonely	lonely	lonely	solitary
36 And Simon and they that were with him **followed after** him.	pursued	found	set out in search for	hunted for	went to look for
43 And he **straitly** charged him, and forthwith sent him away;	sternly charged	stern warning	sternly ordered	sternly warned	strong warning
45 But he went out, and **began to publish it much,** and **to blaze abroad the matter,** insomuch that Jesus could no more openly enter into the city, but was without in **desert places:** and they came to him from every quarter.	to talk freely about it / to spread the news / the country	made the whole story public / spread it far and wide / open country	started talking about it freely / telling the story everywhere / places where nobody lived	began to proclaim it freely / to spread the news about / unpopulated areas	began to talk freely / spreading the news / lonely places
2 4 And when they could not come nigh unto him for the **press, they uncovered the roof where he was:** and when they had **broken it up,** they let down the bed wherein the **sick of the palsy** lay.	crowd / removed the roof above him / made an opening / paralytic	crowd / opened up the roof over the place where Jesus was / broken through / paralyzed man	crowd / stripped the roof over the place where Jesus was / made an opening / paralytic	crowd / removed the roof above Him / dug an opening / paralytic	crowd / made an opening in the roof above Jesus / dug through / paralyzed man
6 But there were certain of the scribes sitting there, and **reasoning in their hearts,**	questioning in their hearts	thought to themselves	thought to themselves	reasoning in their hearts	thinking to themselves
9 Whether is it easier to say to the sick of the palsy, Thy sins be forgiven thee; or to say, Arise, and take up thy **bed,** and walk?	pallet	bed	stretcher	pallet	mat
11 I say unto thee, Arise, and take up thy **bed,** and **go thy way into thine house.**	pallet / go home	bed / go home	stretcher / go off home	pallet / go home	mat / go home
12 And immediately he arose, took up the bed, and went forth before them all; insomuch that they were all amazed, and glorified God, saying, We never saw it on **this fashion.**	like this	the like	like this	like this	like this
13 And he went forth again by the sea side; and all the multitude **resorted unto him,** and he taught them.	gathered about him	came to him	came to him	were coming to Him	came to him
23 And it came to pass, that he went through the **corn fields** on the sabbath day; and his disciples began, as they went, to pluck the **ears of corn.**	grainfields / heads of grain	cornfields / ears of corn	cornfields / ears of corn	grainfields / heads of grain	grainfields / heads of grain

	KJV	RSV	NEB	JB	NAS	NIV
3	3 And he saith unto the man which had the withered hand, **Stand forth.**	"Come here."	'Come and stand out here.'	"Stand up out in the middle!"	"Rise and come forward!"	"Stand up in front of everyone."
	4 And he saith unto them, Is it lawful to do good on the sabbath days, or to do **evil?** to save life, or to kill? But they **held their peace.**	harm / were silent	evil / had nothing to say	evil / said nothing	harm / kept silent	evil / remained silent
	5 And when he had looked round about on them with anger, being grieved for the hardness of their hearts, he saith unto the man, Stretch forth thine hand. And he stretched it out: and his hand was restored **whole as the other.**	was restored	was restored	was better	was restored	was completely restored
	8 And from Jerusalem, and from Idumaea, and from beyond Jordan; and **they** about Tyre and Sidon, a great multitude, when they had heard what great things he did, came unto him.	from	neighbourhood	region	vicinity	regions
	9 And he spake to his disciples, that a **small ship should wait** on him because of the multitude, lest they should **throng** him.	boat ready / crush	boat ready / crushed	boat ready / crushed	boat . . . ready / crowd	small boat / crowding
	10 For he had healed many; insomuch that they pressed upon him for to touch him, as many as had **plagues.**	all who had diseases	sick people of all kinds	all who were afflicted	all those who had afflictions	those with diseases
	12 And he **straitly charged** them that they should not make him known.	strictly ordered	insisted	warned . . . strongly	earnestly warned	gave . . . strict orders
	14 And he **ordained** twelve, that they should be with him, and that he might send them forth to preach,	appointed	appointed	appointed	appointed	appointed
	15 And to have **power to heal sicknesses,** and to cast out devils:	authority to cast out demons	commission to drive out devils	power to cast out devils	authority to cast out the demons	authority to drive out demons
	19 And Judas Iscariot, which also betrayed him: and **they went into an house.**	(omits)	(omits)	(omits)	(omits)	(omits)
	20 And the multitude cometh together again, so that they could not so much as **eat bread.**	eat	eat	have a meal	eat a meal	eat
	21 And when his **friends** heard of it, they went out to **lay hold** on him: for they said, He is **beside himself.**	family / seize / beside himself	family / take charge / out of his mind	relatives / take charge of / out of his mind	own people / take custody / lost His senses	family / take charge / out of his mind
	26 And if Satan rise up against himself, and be divided, he cannot stand, but **hath an end.**	is coming to an end	that is the end of him	it is the end of him	he is finished	his end has come
	29 But he that shall blaspheme against the Holy Ghost hath never forgiveness, but is **in danger of eternal damnation:**	guilty of an eternal sin	guilty of eternal sin	will never have forgiveness	guilty of an eternal sin	guilty of an eternal sin
4	1 And he began again to teach by the sea side: and there was gathered unto him a great multitude, so that he entered into a ship, and **sat in the sea;** and the whole multitude was by the sea on the land.	sat in it on the sea	there he sat	sat there	sat down	sat in it on the lake
	2 And he taught them many things by parables, and said unto them in his **doctrine,**	in his teaching	as he taught	in the course of his teaching	in His teaching	in his teaching
	7 And some fell among thorns, and the thorns grew up, and choked it, and it yielded no **fruit.**	grain	crop	crop	crop	grain
	10 And when he was alone, they that were about him with the twelve asked **of** him **the parable.**	concerning the parables	about the parables	what the parables meant	about the parables	about the parables

KJV	RSV	NEB	JB	NAS	NIV
12 That seeing they may see, and not perceive; and hearing they may hear, and not understand; lest at any time they **should be converted, and their sins should be forgiven** them.	should turn again, and be forgiven	might turn to God and be forgiven	might turn to God and be forgiven	return and be forgiven	might turn and be forgiven
15 And these are they by the **way side,** where the word is sown; but when they have heard, Satan cometh immediately, and taketh away the word that was sown in their **hearts.**	path / in them	footpath / in them	path / in them	road / in them	path / in them
17 And have no root in themselves, and so endure but for a time: afterward, when **affliction** or persecution ariseth for the word's sake, immediately they **are offended.**	tribulation / fall away	trouble / fall away	trial / fall away	affliction / fall away	trouble / fall away
19 And the cares of this world, and the **deceitfulness of riches,** and the **lusts of other things** entering in, choke the word, and it becometh unfruitful.	delight in riches / desire for other things	false glamour of wealth / all kinds of evil desire	lure of riches / other passions	deceitfulness of riches / desires for other things	deceitfulness of wealth / desires for other things
21 And he said unto them, Is a **candle** brought to be put under a bushel, or under a bed? and not to be set on a **candlestick?**	lamp / stand	lamp / lampstand	lamp / stand	lamp / lampstand	lamp / stand
22 For there is nothing hid, which shall not be manifested; neither was any thing kept secret, but that it should come **abroad.**	to light	into the open	to light	to light	into the open
24 And he said unto them, Take heed what ye hear: with what measure ye **mete,** it shall be measured to you: **and unto you that hear shall more be given.**	give / and still more will be given you	give / with something more besides	measure out / and more besides	(By your) standard (of) / and more shall be given you besides	use / and even more
28 For the earth bringeth forth fruit of herself; first the blade, then the ear, after that the full **corn** in the ear.	grain	corn	grain	grain	kernal
29 But when **the fruit is brought forth,** immediately he putteth in the sickle, because the harvest is come.	the grain is ripe	the crop is ripe	the crop is ready	the crop permits	the grain is ripe
33 And with many such parables spake he the word unto them, as **they were able to hear it.**	were able to hear it	were able to receive it	were capable of understanding it	were able to hear it	could understand
36 And when they had sent away the multitude, they took him **even as he was** in the ship. And there were also with him other **little ships.**	just as / boats	with them / boats	just as he was / boats	along with them, just as He was / boats	along, just as he was / boats
37 And there arose a **great storm of wind,** and the waves beat into the ship, so that it was **now full.**	great storm of wind / already filling	heavy squall / all but swamped	gale / almost swamped	fierce gale of wind / already filling up	furious squall / nearly swamped
38 And he was in the hinder part of the ship, asleep on **a pillow:** and they awake him, and say unto him, Master, carest thou not **that we perish?**	the cushion / if we perish	a cushion / we are sinking	the cushion / We are going down!	the cushion / that we are perishing	a cushion / if we drown
39 And he arose, and rebuked the wind, and said unto the sea, **Peace, be still.** And the wind ceased, and there was a great calm.	"Peace! Be still!"	'Hush! Be still!'	"Quiet now! Be calm!"	"Hush, be still."	"Quiet! Be still!"
40 And he said unto them, Why are ye **so fearful?** how is it that ye have no faith?	afraid	such cowards	so frightened	so timid	so afraid
41 And they **feared exceedingly,** and said one to another, What **manner of man** is this, that even the wind and the sea obey him?	were filled with awe / Who then is this	were awestruck / Who can this be?	filled with awe / "Who can this be?	became very much afraid / Who then is this	were terrified / "Who is this?
5 4 Because that he had been often bound with fetters and chains, and the chains had been **plucked asunder** by him, and	wrenched apart /	snapped / master	snapped / control	torn apart / sub-	tore . . . apart /

KJV	RSV	NEB	JB	NAS	NIV
the fetters broken in pieces: neither could any man **tame him.**	subdue him	him	him	due him	subdue him
5 And always, night and day, he was in the mountains, and in the tombs, crying, and **cutting** himself with stones.	bruising	cut	gash	gashing	cut
7 And cried with a loud voice, and said, **What have I to do with thee,** Jesus, thou Son of the most high God? **I adjure thee by God,** that thou **torment me** not.	What have you to do with me / I adjure you by God / torment me	What do you want with me / In God's name / torment me	What do you want with me / Swear by God / torture me	What do I have to do with You / I implore You by God / torment me	What do you want with me / Swear to God / torture me
11 Now there was there **nigh unto the mountains** a great herd of **swine** feeding.	on the hillside / swine	on the hill-side / swine	on the mountain-side / pigs	on the mountain / swine	on the nearby hillside / pigs
13 And forthwith Jesus gave them leave. And the unclean spirits went out, and entered into the swine: and the herd ran violently down a steep **place** into the sea, (they were about two thousand;) and were **choked** in the sea.	bank / drowned	edge / drowned	cliff / drowned	bank / drowned	bank / drowned
14 And **they that fed the swine** fled, and told it in the city, and in the country. And they went out to see what it was that was done.	herdsmen	the men in charge of them	swineherds	herdsmen	Those tending the pigs
19 Howbeit Jesus **suffered him not,** but saith unto him, Go home to thy friends, and tell them how great things the Lord hath done for thee, and hath had **compassion** on thee.	refused / mercy	would not allow it / mercy	would not let him / mercy	did not let him / mercy	did not let him / mercy
27 When she had heard of Jesus, came in **the press behind,** and touched his garment.	up behind him in the crowd	up from behind in the crowd	up behind him through the crowd	up in the crowd behind Him	up behind him in the crowd
29 And **straightway the fountain of her blood was dried up;** and she felt in her body that she was healed of that **plague.**	immediately the hemorrhage ceased / disease	there and then the source of her hemorrhages dried up / trouble	the source of the bleeding dried up instantly / complaint	immediately the flow of her blood was dried up / affliction	Immediately her bleeding stopped / suffering
30 And Jesus, immediately knowing in himself that **virtue** had gone out of him, turned him about in **the press,** and said, Who touched my **clothes?**	power / the crowd / garments	power / the crowd / clothes	power / the crowd / clothes	power / the crowd / garments	power / the crowd / clothes
34 And he said unto her, Daughter, thy faith **hath made thee whole;** go in peace, and be **whole** of thy **plague.**	has made you well / healed / disease	has cured you / free forever / trouble	has restored you to health / free / complaint	made you well / healed / affliction	has healed you / freed / suffering
35 While he yet spake, there came from **the ruler of the synagogue's house** certain which said, Thy daughter is dead: why troublest thou the **Master** any further?	ruler's house / Teacher	president's house / Rabbi	house of the synagogue official / Master	house of the synagogue official / Teacher	house of Jairus, the synagogue ruler / teacher
36 As soon as Jesus **heard the word that was spoken,** he saith unto the ruler of the synagogue, Be not afraid, only believe.	But ignoring what they said	overhearing the message as it was delivered	had overheard this remark of theirs	overhearing what was being spoken	Ignoring what they said
37 And he **suffered** no man to follow him, save Peter, and James, and John the brother of James.	allowed	allowed	allowed	allowed	did not let
39 And when he was come in, he saith unto them, Why make ye this ado, and weep? the **damsel** is not dead, but sleepeth.	child	child	child	child	child
41 And he took the damsel by the hand, and said unto her, Talitha cumi; which is, being interpreted, **Damsel,** I say unto thee, arise.	Little girl	my child	Little girl	Little girl	Little girl
6 11 And whosoever shall not receive you, nor hear you, when ye depart thence, shake off the dust **under your feet** for a testimony against them. **Verily**	on your feet / (omits)	off your feet / (omits)	from under your feet / (omits)	from the soles of your feet /	off your feet / (omits)

KJV	RSV	NEB	JB	NAS	NIV
I say unto you, It shall be more tolerable for Sodom and Gomorrha in the day of judgment, than for that city.				(omits)	
14 And king Herod heard **of him;** (for **his name was spread abroad:**) and he said, That John the Baptist was risen from the dead, and therefore **mighty works do shew forth themselves in him.**	of it / Jesus' name had become known / these powers are at work in him	of it / the fame of Jesus has spread / these miraculous powers are at work in him	about him / by now his name was well-known / miraculous powers are at work in him	of it / His name had become well known / these miraculous powers are at work in Him	about this / Jesus' name had become well-known / miraculous powers are at work in him
15 Others said, That it is Elias. And others said, That it is a prophet, **or as one of the prophets.**	like one of the prophets of old	like one of the old prophets	like the prophets we used to have	like one of the prophets of old	like one of the prophets of long ago
19 Therefore Herodias **had a quarrel** against him, and would have killed him; but she could not:	had a grudge	nursed a grudge	was furious	had a grudge	nursed a grudge
20 For Herod feared John, knowing that he was a **just man** and an holy, and **observed him;** and when he heard him, he did many things, and heard him gladly.	righteous . . . man / kept him safe	good . . . man / kept him in custody	good . . . man / gave him his protection	righteous man . . . / safe	righteous man . . . / protected him
21 And when a **convenient day** was come, that Herod on his birthday made **a supper** to his **lords, high captains, and chief estates** of Galilee;	an opportunity / banquet / courtiers and officers and the leading men	her opportunity / banquet / chief officials and commanders and the leading men	An opportunity / banquet / nobles of his court, for his army officers and for the leading officers	a strategic day / banquet / lords and military commanders and the leading men	the opportune time / banquet / high officials and military commanders and the leading men
22 And when the daughter of the said Herodias came in, and danced, and pleased Herod and **them that sat with him,** the king said unto the **damsel,** Ask of me whatsoever thou **wilt,** and I will **give it** thee.	his guests / girl / wish / grant it	his guests / girl / like / give it	his guests / girl / like give it	his dinner guests / girl / want / give it	his dinner guests / girl / want / give it
25 And she came in **straightway** with haste unto the king, and asked, saying, I **will** that thou give me **by and by** in a **charger** the head of John the Baptist.	immediately / want / at once / platter	at once / want / here and now / dish	straight back / want / here and now / dish	immediately / want / right away / platter	At once / want / right now / platter
26 And the king was exceeding sorry; yet for his **oath's sake,** and for their **sakes which sat with him,** he would not **reject** her.	because of his oaths and his guests / break his word to	out of regard for his oath and for his guests / refuse	thinking of the oaths he had sworn and of his guests / break his word to	because of his oaths and because of his dinner guests / refuse	because of his oaths and his dinner guests / refuse
27 And immediately the king sent an **executioner,** and commanded his head to be brought: and he went and beheaded him in the prison,	soldier of the guard	soldier of the guard	one of the bodyguard	executioner	executioner
28 And brought his head in a **charger,** and gave it to the **damsel:** and the damsel gave it to her mother.	platter / girl	dish / girl	dish / girl	platter / girl	platter / girl
29 And when his disciples heard of it, they came and took up his **corpse,** and said it in a tomb.	body	body	body	body	body
31 And he said unto them, Come ye yourselves apart into a **desert** place, and rest a while: for there were many coming and going, and they had no leisure so much as to eat.	lonely	lonely	lonely	lonely	quiet
33 And the people saw them departing, and many knew him, and ran afoot thither out of all cities, **and outwent them,** and came together unto him.	and got there ahead of them	arrived there first	reached it before them	got there ahead of them	got there ahead of them
35 And when the **day was now far spent,** his disciples came unto him, and said, This is a **desert** place, and now the **time is far passed:**	it grew late / lonely / hour is now late	the day wore on / lonely / it is getting very late	it was getting late / lonely / it is getting very late	it was already quite late / desolate / it is already quite late	it was late in the day / remote / it's already very late
41 And when he had taken the five loaves and the two fishes, he looked up to heaven, and blessed, and brake the					

KJV	RSV	NEB	JB	NAS	NIV
loaves, and gave them to his disciples to set before **them;** and the two fishes divided he among them all.	the people	(omits)	the people	them	the people
43 And they took up twelve baskets full of the **fragments,** and of the fishes.	broken pieces	scraps	scraps	broken pieces	broken pieces
45 And **straightway** he constrained his disciples to get into the ship, and to go to the other side **before unto** Bethsaida, while he sent away the people.	immediately / before him . . . to	As soon as / to . . . ahead of	Directly after this / go on ahead to	immediately / go ahead of Him to	Immediately / go on ahead of him to
48 And he saw them **toiling in rowing;** for the **wind was contrary unto them:** and about **the fourth watch of the night** he cometh unto them, walking upon the sea, and **would have** passed by them.	making headway painfully / wind was against them / fourth watch of the night / meant to	labouring at the oars / against a head-wind / between three and six in the morning / was going to	worn out with rowing / wind was against them / fourth watch of the night / was going to	straining at the oars / wind was against them / fourth watch of the night / intended to	straining at the oars / wind was against them / fourth watch of the night / was about to
51 And he went up unto them into the ship; and the wind ceased: and they **were sore amazed in themselves beyond measure, and wondered.**	were utterly astounded	were completely dumbfounded	were utterly and completely dumbfounded	were greatly astonished	were completely amazed
52 For they considered not the miracle of the loaves: for their **heart was hardened.**	hearts were hardened	minds were closed	minds were closed	heart was hardened	minds were closed
54 And when they were come out of the ship, **straightway they** knew him,	immediately the people	immediately . . . the people	No sooner had . . . the people	immediately the people	As soon as . . . people
55 And ran through that whole **region** round about, and began to carry about in **beds** those that were sick, where they heard he was.	neighborhood / pallets	country-side / stretchers	countryside / stretchers	country / pallets	region / mats
56 And whithersoever he entered, into villages, or cities, or country, they laid the sick in **the streets,** and besought him that they might touch if it were but the **border** of his garment: and as many as touched him were **made whole.**	the market-places / fringe / made well	market-places / edge / cured	open spaces / fringe / cured	the market places / fringe / being cured	the marketplaces / edge / healed
7 2 And when they saw some of his disciples eat bread with defiled, that is to say, with unwashen, hands, **they found fault.**	(omits)	(omits)	(omits)	(omits)	(omits)
4 And when they come from the market, except **they wash,** they eat not. And many other **things** there be, which they **have received to hold,** as the washing of cups, and pots, brasen vessels, **and of tables.**	they purify themselves / traditions / observe / (omits)	first washing / points / have a traditional rule to maintain / (omits)	first sprinkling themselves / observances / have been handed down to them / (omits)	cleanse themselves / things / have received in order to observe / (omits)	they wash / traditions / observe / (omits)
5 Then the Pharisees and scribes asked him, Why **walk** not thy disciples according to the tradition of the elders, but **eat bread with unwashen hands?**	live / eat with hands defiled	conform / eat their food with defiled hands	respect / eat their food with unclean hands	walk / eat their bread with impure hands	live / eating their food with "unclean" hands
7 Howbeit in vain do they worship me, teaching for doctrines the **commandments** of men.	precepts	commandments	(human) regulations	precepts	rules
8 For laying aside the commandment of God, ye hold the tradition of men, **as the washing of pots and cups: and many other such like things ye do.**	(omits)	(omits)	(omits)	(omits)	(omits)
10 For Moses said, Honour thy father and thy mother; and, Whoso **curseth** father or mother, **let him die the death:**	speaks evil of / let him surely die	curses / must suffer death	curses / must be put to death	speaks evil of / let him be put to death	curses / must be put to death
11 But ye say, If a man shall say to his father or mother, It is Corban, that is to say, a gift, by whatsoever thou mightest be profited by me; **he shall be free.**	(omits)	(omits)	(omits)	(omits)	(omits)
12 And ye **suffer** him no more to do aught for his father or his mother;	permit	permitted	forbidden	permit	let

KJV	RSV	NEB	JB	NAS	NIV
13 Making the word of God of **none effect** through your tradition, which ye have **delivered:** and many **such like** things do ye.	void / hand on / such	null and void / handed down / just like that	null and void / handed down / like this	invalidating / handed down / such as that	nullify / handed down / like that
16 **If any man have ears to hear, let him hear.**	(omits)	(omits)	If anyone has ears to hear, let him listen to this.	("If any man has ears to hear, let him hear.")	(omits)
19 Because it entereth not into his heart, but into the belly, and **goeth out into the draught, purging all meats?**	so passes on?" (Thus he declared all foods clean.)	so passes out into the drain?" Thus he declared all food clean	passes out into the sewer?" (Thus he pronounced all foods clean.)	is eliminated?" (Thus He declared all foods clean.)	then out of his body." (In saying this, Jesus declared all foods "clean.")
22 Thefts, covetousness, wickedness, deceit, lasciviousness, an **evil eye,** blasphemy, pride, foolishness:	envy	envy	envy	envy	envy
24 And from thence he arose, and went into the **borders** of Tyre and Sidon, and entered into an house, and would have no man know it: but he could not be hid.	region	territory	territory	region	vicinity
26 The woman was a **Greek,** a Syrophenician by **nation;** and she **besought** him that he would **cast forth the devil** out of her daughter.	Greek / birth / begged / cast the demon out of	Gentile / nationality / begged / drive the spirit out of	Pagan / birth / begged / cast the devil out of	Gentile / race / kept asking / cast the demon out of	Greek / born in / begged / drive the demon out of
27 But **Jesus** said unto her, Let the children first be filled: for it is not **meet** to take the children's bread, and to **cast** it unto the dogs.	He / right / throw	He / fair / throw	He / fair / throw	He / good / throw	he / right / toss
35 And **straightway** his ears were opened, and the **string of his tongue was loosed,** and he spake plain.	(omits) / his tongue was released	With that / the impediment was removed	(omits) / the ligament of his tongue was loosened	omits / the impediment of his tongue was removed	At this / his tongue was loosened
36 And he charged them that they should tell no man: but the more he charged them, **so much the more a great deal they published it;**	the more zealously they proclaimed it	the more they published it	the more widely they published it	the more widely they continued to proclaim it	the more they kept talking about it
8 3 And if I send them away **fasting** to their own houses, they will faint by the way: for **divers** of them came from **far.**	hungry / some / a long way	unfed / some / a distance	hungry / some / a great distance	hungry / some / a distance	hungry / some / a long distance
4 And his disciples answered him, From **whence** can a **man** satisfy these men with bread here in the **wilderness?**	How / one / desert	How / anyone / lonely place	Where / anyone / deserted place	Where / anyone / desolate place	where / anyone / remote place
10 And **straightway** he entered into a ship with his disciples, and came into **the parts** of Dalmanutha.	immediately / district	without delay / district	immediately / region	immediately / district	(omits) / region
11 And the Pharisees came forth, and **began to question** with him, seeking of him a sign from heaven, **tempting** him.	began to argue with / to test	engaged . . . in discussion / to test	started a discussion with / to test	began to argue with / to test	began to question / to test
25 After that he put his hands again upon his eyes, **and made him look up:** and he was restored, and saw **every man** clearly.	and he looked intently / everything	he looked hard / everything	and he saw clearly / everything	and he looked intently / everything	Then his eyes were opened / everything
26 And he sent him away to his house, saying, **Neither go into the town, nor tell it to any in the town.**	"Do not even enter the village."	'Do not tell anyone in the village.'	"Do not even go into the village."	"Do not even enter the village."	"Don't go into the village."
27 And Jesus went out, and his disciples, into the **towns of** Caesarea Philippi: and **by** the way he asked his disciples, saying unto them, **Whom do men** say that I am?	villages / on / "Who do men	villages / On / 'Who do men	villages / On / "Who do people	villages / on / "Who do people	villages / On / "Who do people
32 And he **spake that saying openly.** And Peter took him, and began to rebuke him.	said this plainly	spoke about it plainly	said all this quite openly	was stating the matter plainly	spoke plainly about this
33 But when he had turned about and looked on his disciples, he rebuked Peter,					

KJV	RSV	NEB	JB	NAS	NIV
saying, Get thee behind me, Satan: **for thou savourest not the things that be of God,** but the things that be of men.	you are not on the side of God	'you think . . . not as God thinks.'	the way you think is not God's way	you are not setting your mind on God's interests	"You do not have in mind the things of God
36 For what shall it profit a man, if he shall gain the whole world, and **lose his own soul?**	forfeit his life	at the cost of his true self	ruin his life	forfeit his soul	forfeit his soul
37 Or what shall a man give **in exchange for his soul?**	in return for his life	to buy that self back	in exchange for his life	in exchange for his soul	in exchange for his soul
9 1 And he said unto them, Verily I say unto you, That there be some of them that stand here, which shall not taste of death, **till** they have seen the kingdom of God **come** with power.	before / has come	before / already come	before / come	until / after it has come	before / come
3 And his **raiment** became **shining, exceeding** white **as snow;** so as no **fuller on earth** can **white** them.	garments / glistening, intensely / (omits) / fuller on earth / bleach	clothes / (omits) dazzling / (omits) / bleacher on earth / equal	clothes / (omits) dazzlingly / (omits) / earthly bleacher / make	garments / radiant and exceedingly white / (omits) / launderer on earth / whiten	clothes / (omits) dazzling / (omits) / anyone in the world / bleach
6 For he **wist not** what to say; for they were **sore** afraid.	did not know / exceedingly	did not know / so	did not know / so	did not know / (omits)	did not know / so
7 And there was a cloud that overshadowed them: and a voice came out of the cloud, **saying,** This is my beloved Son: **hear** him.	(omits) / listen to	(omits) / listen to	(omits) / Listen to	(omits) / listen to	(omits) / Listen to
10 And they kept that **saying with** themselves, questioning one with another what the rising from the dead should mean.	to themselves	among themselves	among themselves	with one another	to themselves
12 And he answered and told them, Elias verily cometh first, and restoreth all things; and how it is written of the Son of man, that he must suffer many things, and be **set at nought.**	treated with contempt	treated with contempt	treated with contempt	treated with contempt	rejected
13 But I say unto you, That Elias is indeed come, and they have **done unto him whatsoever they listed,** as it is written of him.	did to him whatever they pleased	worked their will upon him	treated him as they pleased	did to him whatever they wished	done to him everything they wished
14 And when **he** came to **his** disciples, **he** saw a great multitude about them, and the scribes **questioning** with them.	they / the / they / arguing	they / the / they / arguing	they / the / they / arguing	they / the / they / arguing	they / the other / they / arguing
16 And he asked the scribes, What **question ye** with them?	are you discussing	is this argument about	are you arguing about	are you discussing	are you arguing . . . about
18 And wheresoever **he taketh him, he teareth him:** and he foameth, and **gnasheth** with his teeth, and **pineth away:** and I speak to thy disciples that they should cast **him** out; and they could not.	it seizes him / dashes him down / grinds / becomes rigid / it	it attacks him / it dashes him to the ground / grinds / goes rigid / it	it takes hold of him / it throws him to the ground / grinds / goes rigid / it	it seizes him / it dashes him to the ground / grinds / stiffens out / it	it seizes him / it throws him to the ground / grinds / becomes rigid / the spirit
20 And they brought **him** unto him: and when he saw him, **straightway** the spirit **tare** him; and he fell on the ground, and **wallowed foaming.**	the boy / immediately / convulsed / rolled about, foaming at the mouth	the boy / as soon as / threw . . . into convulsions / rolled about foaming at the mouth	the boy / as soon as / threw . . . into convulsions / writhing there, foaming at the mouth	the boy / immediately / threw . . . into a convulsion / began rolling about and foaming at the mouth	him / immediately / threw into a convulsion / rolled around, foaming at the mouth
21 And he asked his father, How long **is it ago since this came unto him?** And he said, **Of a child.**	has he had this / "From childhood	has he been like this / 'From childhood'	has this been happening to him / "From childhood,"	has this been happening to him / "From childhood	has he been like this / "From childhood,"
23 Jesus said unto him, **If thou canst believe,** all things are possible to him that believeth.	"If you can	'If it is possible!'	"If you can?"	'If you can!'	"What do you mean, 'If you can'?"
24 And straightway the father of the child cried out, and said **with tears,** Lord, I believe; help thou mine unbelief.	(omits)	(omits)	(omits)	(omits)	(omits)

KJV	RSV	NEB	JB	NAS	NIV
25 When Jesus saw that the people came running together, he rebuked the **foul** spirit, saying unto **him,** Thou dumb and deaf spirit, I **charge** thee, come out of him, and enter no more into him.	unclean / it / command	unclean / (omits) / command	unclean / (omits) / command	unclean / it / command	evil / (omits) / command
26 And the spirit cried, and **rent him sore,** and came out of him: and **he was as one dead;** insomuch that many said, He is dead.	convulsing him terribly / the boy was like a corpse	racking him fiercely / boy looked like a corpse	throwing the boy into violent convulsions / boy lay there so like a corpse	throwing him into terrible convulsions / boy became so much like a corpse	convulsed him violently / boy looked so much like a corpse
29 And he said unto them, This kind can come forth by nothing, but by prayer **and fasting.**	(omits)	(omits)	(omits)	(omits)	(omits)
31 For he taught his disciples, and said unto them, The Son of man is delivered into the hands of men, and they shall kill him; and after that he is killed, he shall rise **the third day.**	after three days	three days after being killed	three days after he has been put to death	three days later	after three days
33 And he came to Capernaum: and being in the house he asked them, What was it that ye **disputed among yourselves** by the way?	were . . . discussing	were . . . arguing	were . . . arguing	were . . . discussing	were . . . arguing
34 But they **held their peace:** for by the way they had **disputed among themselves,** who should be the greatest.	were silent / had discussed with one another	were silent / had been discussing	said nothing / had been arguing	kept silent / discussed with one another	kept quiet / had argued
38 And John answered him, saying, Master, we saw one casting out devils in thy name, **and he followeth not us:** and we forbad him, because he followeth not us.	(omits)	(omits)	(omits)	(omits)	(omits)
39 But Jesus said, Forbid him not: for there is no man which shall do **a miracle** in my name, that can **lightly** speak evil of me.	mighty work / soon after	work of divine power / the next moment	miracle / likely	miracle / soon afterward	miracle / in the next moment
40 For he that is not against us is **on our part.**	for us	on our side	for us	for us	for us
41 For whosoever shall give you a cup of water to drink **in my name, because ye belong to Christ,** verily I say unto you, he shall not lose his reward.	because you bear the name of Christ	because you are followers of the Messiah	because you belong to Christ	because of your name as followers of Christ	because you belong to Christ
42 And whosoever **shall offend** one of these little ones that believe in me, it is better for him that a **millstone** were hanged about his neck, and he were **cast** into the sea.	causes . . . to sin / thrown	is a cause of stumbling / thrown	is an obstacle to bring down / thrown	causes . . . to stumble / cast	causes . . . to sin / thrown
43 And if thy hand **offend thee,** cut it off: it is better for thee to enter into life maimed, than having two hands to go into hell, **into the fire that never shall be quenched:**	causes you to sin / into hell, to the unquenchable fire	is your undoing / to hell and the unquenchable fire	should cause you to sin / to hell, into the fire that cannot be put out	causes you to stumble / into hell, into the unquenchable fire	causes you to sin / into hell, where the fire never goes out
44 **Where their worm dieth not, and the fire is not quenched.**	(omits)	(omits)	(omits)	(where their worm does not die, and the fire is not quenched.)	(omits)
45 And if thy foot **offend thee,** cut it off: it is better for thee to enter **halt** into life, than having two feet to be cast into hell, **into the fire that never shall be quenched:**	causes you to sin / lame / into hell	is your undoing / a cripple / into hell	cause you to sin / lame / into hell	causes you to stumble / lame / into hell	causes you to sin / crippled / into hell
46 **Where their worm dieth not, and the fire is not quenched.**	(omits)	(omits)	(omits)	(where their worm does not die, and the fire is not quenched.)	(omits)
48 **Where their worm dieth not, and the fire is not quenched.**	where their worm does not die, and the fire is not quenched	where the devouring worm never dies and the fire is not quenched	where their worm does not die nor fire go out	where their worm does not die, and the fire is not quenched	where 'their worm does not die, and the fire is not put out.'

KJV	RSV	NEB	JB	NAS	NIV
49 For every one shall be salted with fire, **and every sacrifice shall be salted with salt.**	(omits)	(omits)	(omits)	(omits)	(omits)
10 1 And he arose from thence, and cometh into the **coasts** of Judaea **by the farther side of Jordan:** and the **people resort unto him** again; and, **as he was wont,** he taught them again.	region / beyond the Jordan / crowds gathered to him / his custom was	regions / Transjordan / crowd gathered round him / he followed his usual custom	district / far side of the Jordan / crowds gathered around him / as his custom was	region / beyond the Jordan / crowds gathered around Him / according to His custom	region / across the Jordan / crowds of people came to him / as was his custom
4 And they said, Moses **suffered** to write **a bill** of divorcement, and to put her away.	allowed / certificate of divorce	permitted / note of dismissal	allowed / writ of dismissal	permitted / certificate of divorce	permitted / certificate of divorce
5 And Jesus answered and said unto them, For **the hardness of your heart** he wrote you this **precept.**	your hardness of heart / commandment	your minds were closed / rule	you were so unteachable / commandment	your hardness of heart / commandment	your hearts were hard / law
12 And if **a woman** shall **put away** her husband, and be married to another, she committeth adultery.	she (refers to vs. 11) / divorces	she (refers to vs. 11) / divorces	woman / divorces	she herself (refers to vs. 11) divorces	she (refers to vs. 11) / divorces
13 And they brought **young** children to him, that he should touch them: and his disciples rebuked **those that brought them.**	(omits) / them	(omits) / them	little / them	little / them	little / them
14 But when Jesus saw it, he was **much displeased,** and said unto them, **Suffer** the little children to come unto me, and **forbid them not:** for **of** such is the kingdom of God.	indignant / "Let / do not hinder them / to	indignant / 'Let / do not try to stop them / to	indignant / "Let / do not stop them / to	indignant / "Permit / do not hinder them / to	indignant / "Let / do not hinder them / to
18 And Jesus said unto him, why callest thou me good? **there is none good but one, that is, God.**	No one is good but God alone.	No one is good except God alone.	No one is good but God alone.	No one is good except God alone	No one is good—except God alone.
21 Then Jesus beholding him loved him, and said unto him, One thing thou lackest: go thy way, sell whatsoever thou hast, and give to the poor, and thou shalt have treasure in heaven: and come, **take up the cross,** and follow me.	(omits)	(omits)	(omits)	(omits)	(omits)
22 And he was sad at that saying, and went away **grieved:** for he had great possessions.	sorrowful	with a heavy heart	sad	grieved	sad
23 And Jesus looked round about, and saith unto his disciples, How **hardly shall they that have riches** enter into the kingdom of God!	hard it will be for those who have riches	hard it will be for the wealthy	hard it is for those who have riches	hard it will be for those who are wealthy	hard it is for the rich
24 And the disciples were **astonished** at his words. But Jesus answereth again, and saith unto them, Children, how hard is it **for them that trust in riches** to enter into the kingdom of God!	amazed / (omits)	amazed / (omits)	astounded / (omits)	amazed / (omits)	amazed / (omits)
26 And they were astonished **out of measure,** saying **among themselves,** Who then can be saved?	exceedingly / to him	more . . . than ever / to one another	more . . . than ever / to one another	even more / to Him	even more / to each other
30 But he shall receive an hundredfold now in this time, houses, and brethren, and sisters, and mothers, and children, and lands, with persecutions; and in the **world** to come eternal life.	age	age	world	age	age
32 And they were **in the way** going up to Jerusalem; and Jesus **went before** them: and they were amazed; and **as they followed,** they were afraid. And he took again the twelve, and began to tell them what things should happen unto him,	on the road / was walking ahead of / those who followed	on the road / leading the way / those who followed behind	on the road / was walking on ahead of / those who followed	on the road / was walking on ahead of / those who followed	on their way / leading the way / those who followed
34 And they shall mock him, and shall scourge him, and shall spit upon him, and shall kill him: and the **third** day he shall rise again.	after three days	three days afterwards	after three days	three days later	Three days later

KJV	RSV	NEB	JB	NAS	NIV
35 And James and John, the sons of Zebedee, **come unto him,** saying, **Master,** we would that thou shouldest do for us **whatsoever we shall desire.**	**forward to / Teacher / whatever we ask of you**	**approached / 'Master / a favour**	**approached / "Master / a favor**	**came up to / "Teacher / whatever we ask of You**	**came to / Teacher / whatever we ask**
39 **And they said unto him, We can.** And Jesus said unto them, Ye shall indeed drink of the cup that I drink of; and with the baptism that I am baptized withal shall ye be baptized:	"We are able."	'We can'	"We can"	"We are able"	"We can"
41 And when the ten heard it, they began to be **much displeased** with James and John.	indignant	indignant	indignant	indignant	indignant
42 But Jesus called them to him, and saith unto them, Ye know that they which are **accounted** to rule over the Gentiles **exercise lordship** over them; and their great **ones** exercise authority upon them.	those who are supposed to rule / lord it / men	recognized rulers / lord it / men	so-called rulers / lord it / men	those who are recognized as rulers / lord it / men	those who are regarded as rulers / lord it / officials
43 But so shall it not be among you: but whosoever will be great among you, **shall be your minister:**	must be your servant	must be your servant	must be your servant	shall be your servant	must be your servant
44 And whosoever of you will be the **chiefest,** shall be **servant** of all.	first among you / slave	first / willing slave	first among you / slave	first among you / slave	first / slave
45 For even the Son of man came not to **be ministered unto,** but to **minister,** and to give his life a ransom for many.	be served / serve	be served / serve	be served / serve	be served / serve	be served / serve
46 And they came to Jericho: and as he went out of Jericho with his disciples and a great number of people, **blind Bartimaeus,** the son of Timaeus, sat by the **highway** side begging.	Bartimaeus, a blind beggar / roadside	Bartimaeus . . . a blind beggar / roadside	Bartimaeus . . . a blind beggar / road	a blind beggar named Bartimaeus / road	a blind man, Bartimaeus / roadside
48 And many **charged** him that he should **hold his peace:** but he **cried the more a great deal,** Thou son of David, have mercy on me.	rebuked / be silent / cried out all the more	told / hold his tongue / shouted all the more	scolded / keep quiet / shouted all the louder	sternly telling / be quiet / crying out all the more	rebuked / be quiet / shouted all the more
49 And Jesus **stood still,** and **commanded him to be called.** And they call the blind man, saying unto him, **Be of good comfort,** rise; he calleth thee.	stopped / said "Call him." / "Take heart	stopped / said, 'Call him' / 'Take heart	stopped / said, "Call him here / "Courage"	stopped / said, "Call him here." / "Take courage	stopped / said, "Call him." / "Cheer up!
50 And he, casting away his **garment,** rose, and came to Jesus.	mantle	cloak	cloak	cloak	cloak
52 And Jesus said unto him, Go thy way; thy faith hath made thee **whole.** And immediately he received his sight, and followed **Jesus** in the way.	well / him	cured / him	saved / him	well / Him	healed / Jesus
11 4 And they went their way, and found the colt tied by the door **without in a place where two ways met;** and they **loose him.**	out in the open street / untied him	outside in the street / were untying it	in the open street / untied it	outside in the street / untied it	outside in the street / untied it
8 And many spread their garments in the way: and others cut down branches **off the trees,** and **strawed** them in the way.	from the fields / spread	in the fields / spread	in the fields / (omits)	from the fields / spread	in the fields / spread
10 Blessed be the kingdom of our father David, that cometh **in the name of the Lord:** Hosanna in the highest.	(omits)	(omits)	(omits)	(omits)	(omits)
15 And they come to Jerusalem: and Jesus went into the temple, and began to **cast** out them that sold and bought in the temple, and overthrew the tables of the moneychangers, and the seats of them that sold **doves;**	drive / pigeons	driving / pigeons	driving / pigeons	cast / doves	driving / doves
16 And would not **suffer** that any man should carry **any vessel** through the temple.	allow / anything	allow / goods	allow / anything	permit / goods	allow / merchandise

KJV	RSV	NEB	JB	NAS	NIV
18 And the scribes and chief priests heard it, and sought how they might destroy him: for they feared him, because all the people were astonished at his **doctrine.**	teaching	teaching	teaching	teaching	teaching
19 And when even was come, **he** went out of the city.	they	he	he	they	they
23 For verily I say unto you, That whosoever shall say unto this mountain, Be thou **removed,** and be thou cast into the sea; and shall not doubt in his heart, but shall believe that those things which he saith shall come to pass; **he shall have whatsoever he saith.**	taken up / it will be done for him	lifted from your place / it will be done for him	'Get up / it will be done for him	taken up / it shall be granted him	'Go / it will be done for him
24 Therefore I say unto you, What things soever ye **desire,** when ye pray, believe that ye **receive them,** and ye shall have them.	ask / have received it	ask for / have received it	ask . . . for / have it already	ask / have received them	ask for / will receive it
12 3 And they caught him, and beat him, and sent him away **empty.**	empty-handed	empty-handed	empty-handed	empty-handed	empty-handed
4 And again he sent unto them another servant; and **at him they cast stones,** and wounded him in the head, and sent him away **shamefully handled.**	(omits) / treated . . . shamefully	(omits) / treated outrageously	(omits) / treated shamefully	(omits) / treated . . . shamefully	(omits) / treated . . . shamefully
12 And they sought to **lay hold on him,** but feared the **people:** for they **knew** that he had spoken the parable against them: and they left him, and went **their** way.	to arrest him / the multitude / perceived / a(way)	to arrest him / the people / saw / a(way)	to arrest him / the crowds / realized / a(way)	to seize Him / the multitude / understood / a(way)	to arrest him / the crowd / knew / a(way)
13 And they send unto him certain of the Pharisees and of the Herodians, to **catch him in his words.**	entrap him in his talk	trap him with a question	catch him out in what he said	trap Him in a statement	catch him in his words
17 And Jesus answering said unto them, Render to Caesar the things that are Caesar's, and to God the things that are God's. **And they marvelled at him.**	And they were amazed at him	And they heard him with astonishment	This reply took them completely by surprise	And they were amazed at Him	And they were amazed at him.
23 In the resurrection therefore, **when they shall rise,** whose wife shall she be of them? for the seven had her to wife.	(omits)	when they come back to life	when they rise again	when they rise again	(omits)
27 He is not the God of the dead, but the God of the living: ye **therefore do greatly err.**	are quite wrong	are greatly mistaken	are very much mistaken	are greatly mistaken	are badly mistaken
28 And one of the scribes came, and having heard them **reasoning** together, and **perceiving** that he had answered them well, asked him, Which is the first commandment of all?	disputing/seeing	(listening to these) discussions / noted	debating/observed	arguing/recognizing	debating/Noticing
29 And Jesus answered him, The first **of all the commandments** is, Hear, O Israel; The Lord our God **is one Lord:**	(omits)/the Lord is one	(omits)/is the only Lord	(omits)/is the one Lord	(omits)/is one Lord	(omits)/the Lord is one
30 And thou shalt love the Lord thy God with all thy heart, and with all thy soul, and with all thy mind, and with all thy strength: **this is the first commandment.**	(omits)	(omits)	(omits)	(omits)	(omits)
32 And the scribe said unto him, **Well, Master, thou hast said the truth:** for there is one God; and there is none other but he:	"You are right, Teacher	'Well said, Master	"Well spoken, Master	"Right, Teacher	"Well said, Teacher"
33 And to love him with all the heart, and with all the understanding, and with **all the soul,** and with all the strength, and to love his neighbour as himself, is more than all whole burnt offerings and sacrifices.	(omits)	(omits)	(omits)	(omits)	(omits)

KJV	RSV	NEB	JB	NAS	NIV
34 And when Jesus saw that he answered **discreetly,** he said unto him, Thou art not far from the kingdom of God. And no man after that **durst** ask him any question.	wisely/dared	sensibly/ventured	wisely/dared	intelligently/would venture	wisely/dared
35 And Jesus answered and said, while he taught in the temple, **How say** the scribes that Christ is the son of David?	"How can the scribes say	'How can the teachers of the law maintain	"How can the scribes maintain	"How is it that the scribes say	"How is it that the teachers of the law
37 David therefore himself calleth him Lord; and whence is he then his son? And the **common people** heard him gladly.	great throng	great crowd	great majority of the people	great crowd	large crowd
38 And he said unto them **in his doctrine,** Beware of the scribes, which **love** to go in long **clothing,** and love salutations in the marketplaces,	in his teaching/like/robes	as he taught them/love/robes	In his teaching/like/robes	in His teaching/like/robes	As he taught/like/robes
40 Which devour widows' houses, and for a pretence make long prayers: these shall receive greater **damnation.**	condemnation	sentence	sentence	condemnation	(will be punished most severely)
41 And Jesus sat **over against** the treasury, and **beheld how the people cast** money into the treasury: and many that were rich cast in **much.**	opposite/watched the multitudes putting/large sums	opposite/watching as people dropped their/large sums	opposite/watched the people putting/great deal	opposite/began observing how the multitudes were putting/large sums	opposite/watched the crowd putting their/large amounts
42 And there came a certain poor widow, and she threw in two **mites,** which make **a farthing.**	copper coins/penny	tiny coins/farthing	small coins/penny	small copper coins/cent	very small copper coins/fraction of a penny
43 And he called unto him his disciples, and saith unto them, Verily I say unto you, That this poor widow hath **cast** more in, than all they which **have cast** into the treasury:	put/are contributing	given/(omits)	put/have contributed	put/(omits)	put/(omits)
44 For all they did **cast** in of their abundance; but she **of her want did cast** in all that she had, **even** all her living.	contributed/out of her poverty has put / (omits)	have given/with less than enough, has given / (omits)	have . . . put/from the little she had has put / (omits)	put/out of her poverty, put / (omits)	gave/out of her poverty put / (omits)
13 1 And as he went out of the temple, one of his disciples saith unto him, **Master,** see **what manner of** stones and what buildings **are here!**	Teacher/what wonderful/(omits)	Master/what huge/(omits)	Master/(Look at the size of)/(omits)	"Teacher/what wonderful/(omits)	Teacher/what massive/(omits)
3 And as he sat **upon** the mount of Olives **over against** the temple, Peter and James and John and Andrew asked him privately,	on/opposite	on/facing	on/facing	on/opposite	on/opposite
6 For many shall come in my name, saying, I am **Christ;** and **shall deceive many.**	he/lead many astray	he/many will be misled	he/will deceive many	He/will mislead many	he/will deceive many
7 And when ye shall hear of wars and rumours of wars, be ye not **troubled:** for such things must needs be; but the end shall not be yet.	alarmed	alarmed	alarmed	frightened	alarmed
9 But take heed to yourselves: for they shall deliver you up to councils; and in the synagogues ye shall be beaten: and ye shall be brought before **rulers** and kings for my sake, for a testimony against them.	governors	governors	governors	governors	governors
10 And the gospel must first be **published among** all nations.	preached to	proclaimed to	proclaimed to	preached to	preached to
11 But when **they shall lead you,** and deliver you up, **take no thought** beforehand what ye shall speak, neither do ye premeditate: but whatsoever shall be given you in that hour, that speak ye: for **it is not ye that speak, but the Holy Ghost.**	they bring you to trial/do not be anxious	you are arrested/do not worry	they lead you away/do not worry	arrest you/do not be anxious	you are arrested/do not worry

KJV	RSV	NEB	JB	NAS	NIV
12 Now the brother shall betray the brother to death, and the father **the son;** and children shall rise up against their parents, and shall cause them to be put to death.	his child	his child	his child	his child	his child
16 And let him that is in the field not turn back again for to take up his **garment.**	mantle	coat	cloak	cloak	cloak
18 And pray ye that **your flight be not in the winter.**	it may not happen in winter	it may not come in winter	this may not be in winter	that it may not happen in the winter	will not take place in winter
19 For in those days shall be affliction, such as was not from the beginning of the creation which God created unto this time, **neither** shall be.	never	never . . . again	nor ever . . . again	never	never . . . again
20 And except that the Lord had shortened those days, **no flesh** should be saved: but for the elect's sake, whom he hath chosen, he hath shortened the days.	no human being	no living thing	no one	no life	no one
22 For false Christs and false prophets shall rise, and shall shew signs and wonders, **to seduce,** if it were possible, even the elect.	lead astray	mislead	deceive	lead . . . astray	deceive
27 And then shall he send his angels, and shall gather together his elect from the four winds, from the **uttermost** part of the earth to the **uttermost** part of heaven.	ends/ends	farthest bounds/farthest bounds	ends/ends	farthest end/farthest end	ends/ends
29 So ye in like manner, when ye shall see these things **come to pass,** know that **it is nigh,** even at the **doors.**	taking place/he is near/gates	happening/the end is near/door	happening/he is near/gates	happening/He is near/door	happening/it is near/door
33 Take ye heed, watch **and pray:** for ye know not when the time **is.**	(omits)/will come	(omits)/comes	(omits)/will come	(omits)/is	(omits)/will come
34 **For the Son of man** is as a man **taking a far journey,** who left his house, and **gave authority to his servants,** and to every man his work, and commanded the **porter** to watch.	It / going on a journey / puts his servants in charge / doorkeeper	It / away from home / put his servants in charge / doorkeeper	It / traveling / left his servants in charge / doorkeeper	It's / away on a journey / putting slaves in charge / doorkeeper	It's / going away / leaves his house in charge of servants / one at the door
14 3 And being in Bethany in the house of Simon the leper, as he sat **at meat,** there came a woman having an alabaster **box** of ointment of **spikenard** very **precious;** and she brake the box, and poured it on his head.	at table/flask/pure nard/costly	at table/bottle/pure oil of nard/costly	at dinner/jar/pure nard/costly	at the table/vial/pure nard/costly	at the table/jar/pure nard/expensive
4 And there were some that **had indignation within themselves, and said,** Why was this waste of the ointment made?	who said to themselves indignantly	said to one another angrily	said to one another indignantly	were indignantly remarking to one another	were saying indignantly to one another
5 For it might have been sold for more than three hundred pence, and have been given to the poor. And they **murmured against** her.	reproached	turned upon . . . with fury	were angry with	were scolding	rebuked . . . harshly
11 And when they heard it, they were glad, and promised to give him money. And he sought **how he might conveniently** betray him.	an opportunity to betray him	for a good opportunity to betray him	for a way of betraying him when the opportunity should occur	how to betray Him at an opportune time	for an opportunity to hand him over
12 And the first day of unleavened bread, when they **killed the passover,** his disciples said unto him, Where wilt thou that we go and prepare that thou mayest eat the passover?	sacrificied the passover lamb	the Passover lambs were being slaughtered	the Passover lamb was sacrificed	the Passover lamb was being sacrificed	to sacrifice the Passover lamb
13 And he sendeth forth two of his disciples, and saith unto them, Go ye into the city, and there shall meet you **a man** bearing a **pitcher** of water: follow him.	jar	jar	pitcher	pitcher	jar

KJV	RSV	NEB	JB	NAS	NIV
14 And wheresoever he shall go in, say ye to the **goodman of the house,** The **Master** saith, Where is **the guestchamber,** where I shall eat the passover with my disciples?	house-holder/Teacher/my guest room	householder/Master/the room reserved for me	owner of the house/Master/my dining room	owner of the house/Teacher/My guest room	owner of the house/Teacher/my guest room
15 And he will shew you a large upper room furnished and **prepared:** there **make ready** for us.	ready/prepare	set out in readiness/make preparations	all prepared/Make the preparations	ready/prepared	ready/Make preparations
18 And as they **sat** and did eat, Jesus said, **Verily** I say unto you, One of you which eateth with me shall betray me.	were at table/"Truly	sat at supper/(omits)	were at table/solemnly	reclining at the table/"Truly	were reclining at the table/("I tell you) the truth
20 And he answered and said unto them, It is one of the twelve, **that dippeth** with me in the dish.	is dipping bread	is dipping	eating	dips	dips bread
22 And as they did eat, Jesus took bread, and blessed, and brake it, and gave to them, and said, **Take, eat:** this is my body.	"Take	'Take this	"Take it"	"Take it	"Take it
33 And he taketh with him Peter and James and John, and **began to be sore amazed, and to be very heavy;**	began to be greatly distressed and troubled	Horror and dismay came over him	And a sudden fear came over him, and great distress	began to be very distressed and troubled	began to be deeply distressed and troubled
38 Watch ye and **pray, lest ye enter into temptation.** The spirit truly **is ready,** but the flesh is weak.	pray that you may not enter into temptation/is willing	pray that you may be spared the test/is willing	praying not to be put to the test/is willing	praying, that you may not come into temptation/is willing	pray so that you will not fall into temptation/is willing
44 And he that betrayed him had given them a **token,** saying, Whomsoever I shall kiss, that same is he; **take** him, and lead him away **safely.**	sign/seize/under guard	signal/seize/safely	signal/Take . . . in charge/well guarded	signal/seize/under guard	signal/arrest/under guard
65 And some began to spit on him, and to cover his face, and to **buffet** him, and to say unto him, Prophesy: **and the servants did strike him with the palms of their hands.**	strike/And the guards received him with blows	struck . . . with their fists/And the High Priest's men set upon him with blows.	hitting . . . with their fists/And the attendants rained blows on him.	slap . . . with their fists/And the officers received Him with slaps in the face.	struck . . . with their fists/And the guards took him and beat him.
66 And as Peter was **beneath in the palace,** there cometh one of the maids of the high priest:	below in the courtyard	below in the courtyard	down below in the courtyard	below in the courtyard	below in the courtyard
68 But he denied, saying, I know not, neither understand I what thou sayest. And he went out into the **porch; and the cock crew.**	gateway (omits remainder)	porch (omits remainder)	forecourt (omits remainder)	porch (omits remainder)	entryway (omits remainder)
69 And a maid saw him again, and began to say to **them that stood by,** This is one of them.	the bystanders	the bystanders	the bystanders	the bystanders	those standing around
15 3 And the chief priests accused him of many things: **but he answered nothing.**	(omits)	(omits)	(omits)	(omits)	(omits)
7 And there was one named Barabbas, **which lay bound with them that had made insurrection with him,** who had committed murder in the insurrection.	among the rebels in prison	was then in custody with the rebels	was then in prison with the rioters	had been imprisoned with the insurrectionists	was in prison with the insurrectionists
17 And they clothed him with **purple,** and platted a crown of thorns, and put it about his head,	purple cloak	purple	purple	purple	purple robe
19 And they smote him on the head with a reed, and did spit upon him, and bowing their knees **worshipped him.**	knelt down in homage to him	knelt and paid mock homage to him	went down on their knees to do him homage	kneeling and bowing before Him	Falling on their knees, they worshipped him.
21 And they compel one Simon a Cyrenian, who passed by, coming **out of** the country, the father of Alexander and Rufus, to bear his cross.	in from	in from	in from	from	in from
26 And the **superscription of his**	inscription of the	inscription giving	inscription giving	inscription of the	written notice of

KJV	RSV	NEB	JB	NAS	NIV
accusation was written over, The King of the Jews.	charge against him	the charge against him	the charge against him	charge against Him	the charge against him
28 **And the scripture was fulfilled, which saith, And he was numbered with the transgressors.**	(omits)	(omits)	(omits)	(And the Scripture was fulfilled which says, "And He was numbered with transgressors.")	(omits)
29 And they that passed by **railed on** him, wagging their heads, and saying, Ah, thou that destroyest the temple, and buildest it in three days,	derided	hurled abuse at	jeered at	were hurling abuse at	hurled insults at
36 And one ran and filled a sponge full of vinegar, and put it on a reed, and gave him to drink, saying, **Let alone;** let us see whether Elias will come to take him down.	"Wait	(omits)	"Wait	(omits)	"Leave him alone now.
37 And Jesus cried with a loud voice, and **gave up the ghost.**	breathed his last	died	breathed his last	breathed His last	breathed his last
39 And when the centurion, which stood **over against** him, saw that he **so cried out,** and gave up the ghost, he said, Truly this man was the Son of God.	facing/thus breathed his last	opposite/how he died	in front of/how he had died	right in front of/the way He breathed His last	there in front of/how he died
40 There were also women looking on afar off: among whom was Mary Magdalene, and Mary the mother of James the **less** and of Joses, and Salome;	younger	younger	younger	Less	younger
42 And now when the even was come, because it was **the preparation,** that is, the day before the sabbath,	the day of Preparation	Preparation-day	Preparation Day	the preparation day	Preparation Day
43 Joseph of Arimathaea, an **honourable counsellor,** which also waited for the kingdom of God, came, and **went in boldly** unto Pilate, and **craved** the body of Jesus.	respected member of the council/took courage and went to/asked for	respected member of the council/bravely went in/asked for	prominent member of the Council/boldly went/asked for	prominent member of the Council/gathered up courage and went in/asked for	a prominent member of the Council/went boldly/asked for
44 And Pilate **marvelled** if he were already dead: and calling unto him the centurion, he asked him whether **he had been any while dead.**	wondered/he was already dead	was surprised/it was long since he died	astonished/he was already dead	wondered/He was already dead	surprised/if Jesus had already died
45 And when he **knew it of the centurion,** he **gave** the body to Joseph.	learned from the centurion that he was dead/granted	heard the centurion's report/gave	Having been assured of this by the centurion/granted	And ascertaining this from the centurion/granted	learned from the centurion that it was so/gave
46 And he bought fine **linen,** and took him down, and wrapped him in the **linen,** and laid him in a **sepulchre** which was hewn out of a rock, and rolled a stone unto the door of the **sepulchre.**	linen shroud/linen shroud/tomb / tomb	linen sheet/sheet/tomb / (omits)	shroud/shroud / tomb / tomb	linen cloth/linen cloth/tomb / tomb	linen cloth/linen / tomb / tomb
16 5 And entering into the **sepulchre,** they saw a young man sitting on the right side, clothed in a **long** white **garment;** and they were **affrighted.**	tomb / robe / amazed	tomb / robe / dumbfounded	tomb / robe / struck with amazement	tomb / robe / amazed	tomb / robe / alarmed
12 After that he appeared in another form unto two of them, as they **walked, and went into the country.**	were walking into the country	were walking, on their way into the country	were on their way into the country	were walking along on their way into the country	were walking in the country
13 And they went and told it unto the **residue:** neither believed they them.	rest	others	others	others	rest
14 Afterward he appeared unto the eleven as they **sat at meat,** and upbraided them with their unbelief and hardness of heart, because they believed not them which had seen him after he was risen.	sat at table	were at table	were at table	reclining at the table	were eating
16 He that believeth and is baptized shall be saved; but he that believeth not shall be **damned.**	condemned	condemned	condemned	condemned	condemned

KJV	RSV	NEB	JB	NAS	NIV
19 So then after the Lord had spoken unto them, he was **received** up into heaven, and sat **on** the right hand of God.	taken/at	taken/at	taken/at	received/at	taken/at
20 And they went forth, and preached every where, the Lord working with them, and confirming the **word** with **signs following.** Amen.	message/signs that attended it	words/miracles that followed	word/signs that accompanied it	word/signs that followed	word/signs that accompanied it

Luke

KJV	RSV	NEB	JB	NAS	NIV
1 1 Forasmuch as many have taken in hand **to set forth in order a declaration of those things which are most surely believed among us,**	to compile a narrative of the things which have been accomplished among us	to draw up an account of the events that have happened among us	to draw up accounts of the events that have taken place among us	to compile an account of the things accomplished among us	to draw up an account of the things that have been fulfilled among us
3 It seemed good to me also, **having had perfect understanding of all things from the very first,** to write unto thee in order, most excellent Theophilus,	having followed all things closely for some time past	as one who has gone over the whole course of these events in detail	after carefully going over the whole story from the beginning	having investigated everything carefully from the beginning	have carefully investigated everything from the beginning
15 For he shall be great in the sight of the Lord, and shall drink neither wine nor strong drink; and he shall be filled with the Holy Ghost, even **from his mother's womb.**	even from his mother's womb	From his very birth	Even from his mother's womb	while yet in his mother's womb	even from birth
18 And Zacharias said unto the angel, Whereby shall I know this? for I am an old man, and my wife **well stricken** in years.	is advanced	is well on	is getting on	is advanced	is well along
20 And, behold, thou shalt **be dumb,** and not able to speak, until the day that these things shall be performed, because thou believest not my words, which shall be fulfilled in their season.	be silent	remain silent	be silenced	be silent	be silent
21 And the people waited for Zacharias, and **marvelled** that he tarried so long in the temple.	wondered	surprised	were surprised	were wondering	wondering
22 And when he came out, he could not speak unto them: and they perceived that he had seen a vision in the temple: for he beckoned unto them, and remained **speechless.**	dumb	dumb	dumb	mute	unable to speak
25 Thus hath the Lord dealt with me in the days wherein he looked on me, to take away my **reproach among men.**	my reproach among men	my reproach among men	the humiliation I suffered among men	my disgrace among men	my disgrace among the people
27 To a virgin **espoused** to a man whose name was Joseph, of the house of David, and the virgin's name was Mary	betrothed	betrothed	betrothed	engaged	pledged to be married
29 And when she saw him, she was troubled at his saying, and **cast** in her mind what manner of **salutation** this should be.	considered/ greeting	wondered/ greeting	asked/greeting	pondering/ salutation	wondered/ greeting
34 Then said Mary unto the angel, How shall this be, seeing **I know not a man?**	I have no husband	'I am still a virgin.'	I am a virgin	I am a virgin	"I am a virgin
35 And the angel answered and said unto her, The Holy Ghost shall come upon thee, and the power of the Highest shall overshadow thee: therefore also **that holy thing which shall be born of thee** shall be called the Son of God.	the child to be born will be called holy	the holy child to be born	the child will be holy	the holy offspring	the holy one to be born
36 And, behold, thy **cousin** Elisabeth, she hath also conceived a son in her old	kinswoman	kinswoman	kinswoman	relative	relative

KJV	RSV	NEB	JB	NAS	NIV
age; and this is the sixth month with her, who was called barren.					
45 And blessed is she that believed: **for there shall be a performance of those things which were told her from the Lord.**	that there should be a fulfillment of what was spoken to her from the Lord	that the Lord's promise would be fulfilled	that the promise made her by the Lord would be fulfilled	that there would be a fulfillment of what had been spoken to her by the Lord	that what the Lord has said to her will be accomplished
46 And Mary said, **My soul doth magnify the Lord,**	"My soul magnifies the Lord	'Tell out, my soul, the greatness of the Lord	"My soul proclaims the greatness of the Lord	"My soul exalts the Lord	"My soul praises the Lord
55 As he spake to our fathers, to Abraham, and to his **seed** for ever.	posterity	children's children	descendants	offspring	descendants
58 And her neighbours and her **cousins** heard how the Lord had shewed great mercy upon her; and they rejoiced with her.	kinsfolk	relatives	relations	relatives	relatives
63 And he asked for a writing **table,** and wrote, saying, His name is John. And they marvelled all.	tablet	tablet	tablet	tablet	tablet
69 And hath raised up **an horn of salvation** for us in the house of his servant David;	a horn of salvation	a deliverer of victorious power	a power for salvation	a horn of salvation	a horn of salvation
70 As he spake by the mouth of his holy prophets, which have been **since the world began:**	from of old	age after age	from ancient times	from of old	of long ago
78 Through the tender mercy of our God; whereby the **dayspring** from on high hath visited us.	day	morning sun	rising Sun	Sunrise	rising sun
80 And the child grew, and **waxed** strong in spirit, and was in the deserts till the day of his **shewing unto Israel.**	became/manifestation to Israel	became/appeared publicly before Israel	matured/appeared openly to Israel	become/of his public appearance in Israel	became/he appeared publicly to Israel
2 1 And it came to pass in those days, that there went out a decree from Caesar Augustus, that all the world should be **taxed.**	that all the world should be enrolled	for a registration to be made throughout the Roman world	for a census of the whole world to be taken	that a census be taken of all the inhabited earth	that a census should be taken of the entire Roman world
2 (And this **taxing** was first made when **Cyrenius** was governor of Syria.)	enrollment/Quirinius	registration/Quirinius	census/Quirinius	census/Quirinius	census/Quirinius
5 To **be taxed** with Mary his **espoused** wife, **being great with child.**	be enrolled/betrothed / who was with child	register/betrothed/she was expecting a child	to be registered/betrothed / who was with child	register/engaged (to him) / and was with child	register/pledged to be married (to him) / and was expecting a child
7 And she brought forth her firstborn son, and wrapped him in **swaddling clothes,** and laid him in a manger; because there was no room for them in the inn.	swaddling cloths	his swaddling clothes	swaddling clothes	cloths	strips of cloth
8 And there were in the **same country** shepherds **abiding** in the field, keeping watch over their flock by night.	that region/out	this same district/out	the countryside close by/lived	the same region/staying out	nearby/living out
9 And, lo, the angel of the Lord **came upon** them, and the glory of the Lord shone round about them: and they were **sore afraid.**	appeared to/filled with fear	stood before/terror-stricken	appeared to/terrified	stood before/terribly frightened	appeared to/terrified
14 Glory to God in the highest and on earth **peace, good will toward men.**	peace among men with whom he is pleased!"	peace for men on whom his favour rests.'	peace to men who enjoy his favor."	peace among men with whom He is pleased."	peace to men on whom his favor rests."
15 And it came to pass, as the angels were gone away from them into heaven, the shepherds said one to another, Let us now go even unto Bethlehem, and see this thing **which is come to pass,** which the Lord hath made known unto us.	that has happened	that has happened	that has happened	that has happened	that has happened

KJV	RSV	NEB	JB	NAS	NIV
27 **And he came by the Spirit** into the temple: and when the parents brought in the child Jesus, to do for him after the custom of the law,	And inspired by the Spirit he came	Guided by the Spirit he came	Prompted by the Spirit he came	And he came in the Spirit	Moved by the Spirit, he went
31 Which thou hast prepared **before the face of all people;**	in the presence of all peoples	in full view of all the nations	for all the nations to see	in the presence of all peoples	in the sight of all people
32 A light **to lighten** the Gentiles, and the glory of thy people Israel.	for revelation to	that will be a revelation to	a light to enlighten	of revelation to	for revelation to
33 And **Joseph** and his mother marvelled at those things which were spoken of him.	his father	The child's father	the child's father	His father	The child's father
34 And Simeon blessed them, and said unto Mary his mother, Behold, this child is **set for the fall and rising** again of many in Israel; and for a sign which shall be spoken against;	set for the fall and rising	destined . . . will stand Or fall because of him	destined for the fall and for the rising	appointed for the fall and rise	destined to cause the falling and rising
35 (Yea, a sword shall pierce through thy own soul also,) that the thoughts of many hearts **may be revealed.**	may be revealed."	will be laid bare.'	may be laid bare."	may be revealed."	will be revealed
36 And there was one Anna, a prophetess, the daughter of Phanuel, of the tribe of Aser: she was of a great age, and had lived with an husband seven years **from her virginity;**	from her virginity	after she was first married	Her days of girlhood over,	after her marriage	after her marriage
37 **And she was a widow of about fourscore and four years,** which departed not from the temple, but served God with fastings and prayers night and day.	and as a widow till she was eighty-four	and then alone as a widow to the age of eighty-four	before becoming a widow. She was now eighty-four	and then as a widow to the age of eighty-four	and then was a widow until she was eighty-four
38 And she coming in that **instant** gave thanks likewise unto the Lord, and spake of him to all them that looked for redemption in Jerusalem.	very hour	very moment	just at that moment	very moment	very moment
40 And the child grew, and **waxed strong in spirit,** filled with wisdom: and the **grace of God** was upon him.	grew and became strong/favor of God	grew big and strong/God's favour	grew to maturity/God's favor	continued to grow and become strong/grace of God	grew and became strong/grace of God
43 And when **they had fulfilled the days,** as they returned, the **child** Jesus **tarried** behind in Jerusalem; and Joseph and his mother knew not of it.	the feast was ended/boy/stayed	the festive season was over/boy/stayed	after the feast/boy/stayed	after spending the full number of days/boy/stayed	After the feast was over/boy/stayed
46 And it came to pass, that after three days they found him in the temple sitting in the midst of the **doctors,** both hearing them, and asking them questions.	teachers	teachers	doctors	teachers	teachers
48 And when they saw him, they were **amazed:** and his mother said unto him, Son, why **hast thou thus dealt with us?** behold, **thy** father and I have **sought thee sorrowing.**	astonished/have you treated us so/been looking for you anxiously	astonished/have you treated us like this/have been searching for you in great anxiety	overcome/have you done this to us/worried . . . have been, looking for you	astonished/have You treated us this way/have been anxiously looking for You	astonished/have you treated us like this/have been anxiously searching for you
49 And he said unto them, How is it that ye sought me? **wist ye not that I must be about my Father's business?**	Did you know know that I must be in my Father's house?"	'Did you not know that I was bound to be in my Father's house?"	"Did you not know that I must be busy with my Father's affairs?"	Did you not know that I had to be in My Father's house?"	"Didn't you know I had to be in my Father's house?"
51 And he went down with them and came to Nazareth, and **was subject unto them:** but his mother kept all these sayings in her heart.	obedient to them	under their authority	under their authority	(continued) in subjection to them	obedient to them
3 6 And **all flesh** shall see the salvation of God.	all flesh	all mankind	all mankind	all flesh	all mankind
11 He answereth and saith unto them, He that hath two coats, let him **impart to**	share with	share with	share with	share with	share with

KJV	RSV	NEB	JB	NAS	NIV
him that hath none; and he that hath meat, let him do likewise.					
15 And as the people were in expectation, and all men **mused** in their hearts of John, whether he were the Christ, or not;	questioned	wondering about	beginning to think that	wondering	wondering
23 And Jesus himself **began to be about thirty years of age,** being (as was supposed) the son of Joseph, which was the son of Heli,	when he began his ministry, was about thirty years of age	When . . . began his work he was about thirty years old	When he started to teach, . . . was about thirty years old	when He began His ministry . . . was about thirty years of age	was about thirty years old when he began his ministry
4 8 And Jesus answered and said unto him, **Get thee behind me, Satan:** for it is written, Thou shalt worship the Lord thy God, and him only shalt thou serve.	(omits)	(omits)	(omits)	(omits)	(omits)
11 And in their hands they shall bear thee up, lest at any time thou **dash** thy foot against a stone.	strike	strike	hurt	strike	strike
13 And when the devil had ended all the temptation, he departed from him **for a season.**	until an opportune time	biding his time	to return at the appointed time	until an opportune time	until an opportune time
14 And Jesus returned in the power of the Spirit into Galilee: and there went out **a fame of him** through all the region round about.	report concerning him	reports about him	his reputation	news about Him	news about him
15 And he taught in their synagogues, **being glorified of all.**	being glorified of all	all men sang his praises	everyone praised him	was praised by all	everyone praised him
16 And he came to Nazareth, where he had been brought up: and, as his custom was, he went into the synagogue on the sabbath day, and stood up **for** to read.	(omits)	(omits)	(omits)	(omits)	(omits)
17 And there was **delivered** unto him the book of the prophet Esaias. And when he had opened the book, he found the place where it was written,	given	handed	handed	handed	handed
18 The Spirit of the Lord is upon me, because he hath anointed me to preach the **gospel** to the poor; he **hath sent me to heal the brokenhearted,** to **preach** deliverance to the captives, and recovering of sight to the blind, to set at liberty them **that are bruised,**	good news/(omits)/proclaim/who are oppressed	good news/(omits)/proclaim/broken victims	good news/(omits)/proclaim/the downtrodden	gospel/(omits)/proclaim/who are downtrodden	good news/(omits)/proclaim/the oppressed
19 **To preach the acceptable year of the Lord.**	to proclaim the acceptable year of the Lord."	to proclaim the year of the Lord's favour.'	to proclaim the Lord's year of favor	to proclaim the favorable year of the Lord."	to proclaim the year of the Lord's favor."
20 And he closed the book, and he gave it again to the **minister,** and sat down. And the eyes of all them that were in the synagogue were fastened on him.	attendant	attendant	assistant	attendant	attendant
22 **And all bare him witness,** and wondered at the gracious words which proceeded out of his mouth. And they said, Is not this Joseph's son?	And all spoke well of him	There was a general stir of admiration	And he won the approval of all	And all were speaking well of Him	All spoke well of him
37 And the **fame** of him went out into every place of the **country round about.**	reports/surrounding region	news/whole district	reports/surrounding countryside	report/surrounding district	news/surrounding area
41 And devils also came out of many, crying out, and saying, Thou art **Christ** the Son of God. And he rebuking them **suffered them not** to speak: for they knew that he was Christ.	Son of God/would not allow them	Son of God/forbade them	rebuked/would not allow	Son of God/would not allow them	Son of God/would not allow them
42 And when it was day, he departed and went into a **desert place:** and the people sought him, and came unto him, and **stayed him, that he should not depart from them.**	lonely place/kept him from leaving them	lonely spot/pressed him not to leave them	lonely place/prevent him from leaving them	lonely place/tried to keep Him from going away from them	solitary place/tried to keep him from leaving them
43 And he said unto them, I must preach the [ ] kingdom of God to other cities also: for therefore am I sent.	the good news of	the good news of	the Good News of	(no addition)	the good news of

	KJV	RSV	NEB	JB	NAS	NIV
	44 And he **preached** in the synagogues of **Galilee.**	was preaching/Judea	proclaimed the Gospel/Judaea	continued his preaching/Judaea	kept on preaching/Judea	kept on preaching/Judea
5	3 And he entered into one of the ships, which was Simon's, and **prayed** him that he would **thrust** out a little from the land. And he sat down, and taught the people out of the ship.	asked/put	asked/put	asked/put	asked/put	asked/put
	4 Now when he had left speaking, he said unto Simon, **Launch** out into the deep, and let down your nets for a **draught.**	Put/catch	Put/catch	Put/catch	Put/catch	Put/catch
	6 And when they had this done, they enclosed a great **multitude** of fishes: and their **net brake.**	shoal/nets were breaking	haul/nets began to split	number/nets began to tear	quantity/nets began to break	number/nets began to break
	17 And it came to pass on a certain day, as he was teaching, that there were Pharisees and **doctors** of the law sitting by, which were come out of every town of Galilee, and Judaea, and Jerusalem: and the power of the Lord was **present to heal them.**	teachers/with him to heal	teachers/with him to heal the sick	doctors/behind his works of healing	teachers/present for Him to perform healing	teachers/present for him to heal the sick
	24 But that ye may know that the Son of man hath **power** upon earth to forgive sins, (he said unto the **sick of the palsy,**) I say unto thee, Arise, and take up thy couch, and go into thine house.	authority/man who was paralyzed	right/paralysed man	authority/paralyzed man	authority/paralytic	authority/paralyzed man
	26 And they were all amazed, and they glorified God, and were filled with **fear,** saying, We have seen strange things to-day.	amazement	amazement	(were) astounded	fear	(was) amazed
	39 No man also having drunk old wine **straightway** desireth new: for he saith, The old is **better.**	(omits)/good	(omits)/good	(omits)/good	(omits)/good enough	(omits)/better
6	1 And it came to pass **on the second sabbath after the first,** that he went through the **corn fields;** and his disciples plucked the **ears of corn,** and did eat, rubbing them in their hands.	On a sabbath/grainfields/heads of grain	One Sabbath/cornfields/ears of corn	one sabbath/cornfields/ears of corn	on a certain Sabbath/grainfields/heads of grain	One Sabbath/grainfields/heads of grain
	3 And Jesus answering them said, Have ye not read **so much as this,** what David did, when himself was an hungered, and they which were with him;	(omits)	(omits)	(omits)	even	(omits)
	5 And he said unto them, That the Son of man is Lord **also** of the sabbath.	(omits)	even	(omits)	(omits)	(omits)
	8 But he knew their thoughts, and said to the man which had the withered hand, **Rise up, and stand forth in the midst.** And he arose and stood forth.	"Come and stand here."	'Get up and stand out here.'	"Stand up! Come out into the middle."	"Rise and come forward!	"Get up and stand in front of everyone."
	9 Then said Jesus unto them, I will ask you **one thing;** Is it lawful on the sabbath days to do good, or to do **evil?** to save life, or to destroy it?	(omits)/harm	(omits)/evil	(omits)/evil	(omits)/harm	(omits)/evil
	11 And they were **filled with madness; and communed one with another** what they might do to Jesus.	filled with fury and discussed with one another	beside themselves with anger, and began to discuss among themselves	furious, and began to discuss	filled with rage, and discussed together	furious and began to discuss with one another
	17 And he came down with them, and stood **in the plain,** and the company of his disciples, and a great multitude of people out of all Judaea and Jerusalem, and from the sea coast of Tyre and Sidon, which came to hear him, and to be healed of their diseases;	on a level place	on level ground	at a piece of level ground	on a level place	on a level place
	18 And they that were **vexed** with unclean spirits: and they were **healed.**	troubled/cured	troubled/cured	tormented/cured	troubled/cured	troubled/cured

KJV	RSV	NEB	JB	NAS	NIV
19 And the whole multitude sought to touch him: for there went **virtue** out of him, and healed them all.	power	power	power	power	power
22 Blessed are ye, when men shall hate you, and when they shall **separate you from their company,** and shall **reproach** you, and cast out your name as evil, **for the Son of man's sake.**	exclude you/revile/on account of the Son of man	outlaw you/insult/because of the Son of Man	drive you out/abuse/on account of the Son of Man	ostracize you/cast insults at/for the sake of the Son of Man	exclude you/insult/because of the Son of Man
28 Bless them that curse you, and pray for them which **despitefully use** you.	abuse	treat . . . spitefully	treat . . . badly	mistreat	mistreat
29 And unto him that smiteth thee on the one cheek offer also the other; and him that taketh away thy **cloak** forbid not to take thy **coat** also.	coat/shirt	coat/shirt	cloak/tunic	coat/shirt	cloak/tunic
32 For if ye love them which love you, what **thank have ye?** for sinners also love those that love them.	credit is that to you	credit is that to you	thanks can you expect	credit is that to you	credit is that to you
35 But love ye your enemies, and do good, and lend, **hoping for nothing again;** and your reward shall be great, and ye shall be the children of the **Highest:** for he is kind unto the **unthankful** and to the **evil.**	expecting nothing in return/Most High/ungrateful/selfish	without expecting any return/Most High/ungrateful/wicked	without any hope of return/Most High/ungrateful/wicked	expecting nothing in return/Most High/ungrateful/evil men	without expecting to get anything back/Most High/ungrateful/wicked
38 Give, and it shall be given unto you; good measure, pressed down, and shaken together, and running over, shall men give into your **bosom.** For **with the same measure that ye mete** withal it shall be measured to you again.	lap/the measure you give	lap/whatever measure give out	lap/the amount you measure out	lap/by your standard of measure	lap/with the measure you use
40 The **disciple** is not above his **master:** but every one **that is perfect** shall be as his master.	disciple/teacher/when he is fully taught	pupil/teacher/training is complete	disciple/teacher/fully trained	pupil/teacher/after he has been fully trained	student/teacher/who is fully trained
42 **Either** how canst thou say to thy brother, Brother, let me pull out the **mote** that is in thine eye, when thou thyself **beholdest not** the **beam** that is in thine own eye? Thou hypocrite, cast out first the beam out of thine own eye, and then shalt thou see clearly to pull out the mote that is in thy brother's eye.	Or/speck/do not notice/log	(omits)/speck of sawdust/with never a thought/great plank	(omits)/splinter/cannot see/plank	Or/speck/do not see/log	(omits)/speck of sawdust/pay no attention/plank
43 For a good tree bringeth not forth **corrupt** fruit; neither doth a **corrupt** tree bring forth good fruit.	bad/bad	worthless/worthless	rotten/rotten	bad/bad	bad/bad
48 He is like a man which built an house, and digged deep, and laid the foundation on a rock: and when the flood arose, the stream beat vehemently upon that house, and could not shake it: **for it was founded upon a rock.**	because it had been well built	because it had been soundly built	it was so well built	because it had been well built	because it was well built
7 1 Now when he had ended all his sayings in the **audience** of the people, he entered into Capernaum.	hearing	(omits)	(all he wanted the people to hear)	hearing	hearing
2 And a certain centurion's **servant,** who was dear unto him, was sick, and ready to die.	slave	servant	servant	slave	servant
4 And when they came to Jesus, they besought him **instantly,** saying, That he was worthy for whom he should do this:	earnestly	earnestly	earnestly	earnestly	earnestly
11 And it came to pass **the day after,** that he went into a city called Nain; and **many of his disciples** went with him, and much people.	Soon afterward/his disciples	Afterwards/his disciples	soon afterward/his disciples	soon afterwards/His disciples	Soon afterward/his disciples
17 And this **rumour** of him went forth throughout all Judaea, and throughout all the **region round about.**	report/surrounding country	story/whole neighbourhood	opinion/countryside	report/surrounding district	news/surrounding country

KJV	RSV	NEB	JB	NAS	NIV
18 And the disciples of John **shewed** him of all these things.	told	(John) was informed (by)	gave	reported to	told
19 And John calling unto him two of his disciples sent them to **Jesus,** saying, Art thou he that should come? or look we for another?	the Lord	the Lord	the Lord	the Lord	the Lord
25 But what went ye out for to see? A man clothed in soft raiment? Behold, they which are gorgeously apparelled, and live **delicately,** are in kings' courts.	in luxury	(you must look . . . for) luxury	luxuriously	in luxury	in luxury
28 For I say unto you, Among those that are born of women **there is not a greater prophet than John the Baptist:** but he that is least in the kingdom of God is greater than he.	none is greater than John	there is not a mother's son greater than John	there is no one greater than John	there is no one greater than John	there is no one greater than John
30 But the Pharisees and lawyers rejected the **counsel** of God against themselves, being not baptized of him.	purpose	purpose	what God had in mind	purpose	purpose
34 The Son of man is come eating and drinking; and ye say, Behold a gluttonous man, and a **winebibber,** a friend of publicans and sinners!	drunkard	drinker	drunkard	drunkard	drunkard
35 But wisdom is **justified of all her children.**	by all her children	by all who are her children	by all her children	by all her children	by all her children
36 And one of the Pharisees desired him that he would eat with him. And he went into the Pharisee's house, and **sat down to meat.**	took his place at table	took his place at table	took his place at table	reclined at the table	reclined at the table
37 And, behold, a woman in the city, which was a sinner, when she **knew** that Jesus sat at meat in the Pharisee's house, brought an alabaster **box** of ointment,	learned/flask	learned/flask	heard/jar	learned/vial	learned/jar
38 And stood at his feet behind him weeping, and began to **wash** his feet with tears, and did wipe them with the hairs of her head, and kissed his feet, and anointed them with the ointment.	wet	(feet) were wetted	her tears fell on his feet	wet	wet
42 And when they had nothing to pay, he **frankly forgave them both.** Tell me therefore, which of them will love him most?	forgave them both	let them both off	pardoned them both	graciously forgave them both	canceled the debts of both
8 1 And it came to pass afterward, that he went throughout **every city and village,** preaching and **shewing** the **glad tidings** of the kingdom of God: and the twelve were with him,	cities and villages/bringing/good news	town to town and village to village/(omits)/good news	towns and villages/proclaiming/Good News	from one city and village to another/preaching / (omits)	one city and village to another/(omits)/good news
3 And Joanna the wife of Chuza Herod's steward, and Susanna, and many others, which ministered unto him of their **substance.**	means	own resources	own resources	private means	own means
4 And when much people were gathered together, and were come to him out of **every city,** he spake by a parable:	town after town	one town after another	every town	various cities	town after town
9 And his disciples asked him, saying, What **might** this parable **be?**	meant	meant	might mean	might be	meant
12 Those by the **way side** are they that hear; then cometh the devil, and taketh away the word out of their hearts, **lest they should believe** and be saved.	path/that they may not believe	footpath/for fear they should believe	edge of the path/in case they should believe	beside the road/so that they may not believe	path/so that they cannot believe
14 And that which fell among thorns are they, which, when they have heard, go forth, and are choked with cares and riches and pleasures of this life, and bring **no fruit to perfection.**	their fruit does not mature	they bring nothing to maturity	do not reach maturity	bring no fruit to maturity	do not mature

KJV	RSV	NEB	JB	NAS	NIV
17 For nothing is **secret,** that shall not be made manifest; neither any thing **hid,** that shall not be known and come **abroad.**	hid/secret/come to light	hidden/under cover/brought into the open	hidden/secret/brought to light	hidden/secret/come to light	hidden/concealed/brought out into the open
18 Take heed therefore how ye hear: for whosoever hath, to him shall [ ] be given; and whosoever hath not, from him shall be taken even that which he **seemeth to have.**	more/thinks that he has	more/thinks he has	more/thinks he has	more/thinks he has	more/thinks he has
19 Then came to him his mother and his brethren, and could not **come at** him for the press.	reach	get to	get to	get to	get near
20 And it was told him **by certain which said,** Thy mother and thy brethren stand without, desiring to see thee.	(omits)	(omits)	(omits)	(omits)	Someone
23 But as they sailed he fell asleep: and there came down a storm of wind on the lake; and they **were filled with water,** and were in **jeopardy.**	were filling with water/danger	began to ship water/grave danger	started taking in water/danger	began to be swamped/danger	was being swamped/great danger
26 And they arrived at the country of the **Gadarenes,** which is **over against** Galilee.	Gerasenes/opposite	Gergesenes/opposite	Gerasenes/opposite	Gerasenes/opposite	Gerasenes/across the lake
27 And when he went forth to land, there met him out of the city a certain man, which had devils **long time, and ware no clothes,** neither abode in any house, but in the tombs.	for a long time he had worn no clothes	For a long time he had neither worn clothes	for a long time the man had worn no clothes	who had not put on any clothing for a long time	For a long time . . . had not worn clothes
29 (For he had commanded the unclean spirit to come out of the man. For oftentimes it had **caught** him: and he was kept bound with chains and in fetters; and he brake **the bands,** and was driven of the devil into the **wilderness.)**	seized/the bonds/desert	seized/loose/solitary places	seized/the fastenings/wilds	seized/his fetters/desert	seized/his chains/solitary places
31 And they **besought** him that he would not command them to go out into the **deep.**	begged / abyss	begged / Abyss	pleaded with / Abyss	entreating / abyss	begged . . . repeatedly / Abyss
32 And there was there an herd of many swine feeding on the **mountain:** and they **besought** him that he would **suffer** them to enter into them. And he **suffered** them.	hillside / begged / let / gave . . . leave	hill / begged / let / gave . . . leave	mountain / pleaded with / let / gave . . . leave	mountain / entreated / permit / gave . . . permission	hillside / begged / let / gave . . . permission
35 Then **they** went out to see what was done; and came to Jesus, and found the man, out of whom the devils were departed, sitting at the feet of Jesus, clothed, and in his right mind: and they were afraid.	people	the people	the people	the people	the people
39 Return to thine own house, and shew how great things God hath done unto thee. And he went his way, and **published** throughout the whole city how great things Jesus had done unto him.	proclaiming	spreading	spread	proclaiming	told
40 And it came to pass, that, when Jesus was returned, the people **gladly received** him: for they were all waiting for him.	welcomed	welcomed	was welcomed	welcomed	welcomed
42 For he had one only daughter, about twelve years of age, and she lay a-dying. But as he went the people **thronged** him.	pressed round	(he could hardly breathe for the crowds)	(crowds) were almost stifling	were pressing against	almost crushed
43 And a woman having an **issue** of blood twelve years, **which had spent all her living upon physicians,** neither could be healed of any,	flow/(omits)	haemorrhages/(omits)	hemorrhage/(omits)	hemorrhage/(omits)	bleeding/(omits)
44 Came behind him, and touched the **border** of his garment: and immediately her **issue** of blood **stanched.**	fringe/flow/ceased	edge/haemorrhage/stopped	fringe/hemorrhage/stopped	fringe/hemorrhage/stopped	edge/bleeding/stopped

KJV	RSV	NEB	JB	NAS	NIV
46 And Jesus said, Somebody hath touched me: for I perceive that **virtue** is gone **out of** me.	power/forth from	power/out from	power/out from	power/out of	power/out from
48 And he said unto her, Daughter, **be of good comfort:** thy faith hath **made thee whole;** go in peace.	(omits)/made you well	(omits)/cured you	(omits)/restored you to health	(omits)/made you well	(omits)/healed you
51 And when he came into the house, he **suffered** no man to go in, save Peter, and James, and John, and the father and the mother of the **maiden.**	permitted/child	allowed/child('s)	allowed/child('s)	allow/girl('s)	let/child('s)
55 And her spirit came again, and she arose **straightway:** and he **commanded to give her meat.**	at once/directed that something should be given her to eat	immediately/told them to give her something to eat	at once/told them to give her something to eat	immediately/gave orders for something to be given her to eat	at once/told them to give her something to eat
9 1 Then he called **his twelve disciples** together, and gave them power and authority over all **devils,** and to cure diseases.	the twelve/ demons	the Twelve/devils	the Twelve/devils	the twelve/ demons	the Twelve/ demons
2 And he sent them to preach the kingdom of God, and to heal **the sick.**	(omits)	(omits)	(omits)	(omits)	the sick
3 And he said unto them, Take nothing for your journey, neither **staves,** nor **scrip,** neither bread, neither money; neither have **two coats apiece.**	staff/bag/two tunics	stick/pack/second coat	staff/haver-sack/spare tunic	staff/bag/two tunics apiece	staff/bag/extra tunic
7 Now Herod the tetrarch heard of all that was done **by him:** and he was perplexed, because that it was said **of** some, that John was risen from the dead;	(omits)/by	(omits)/(some were saying)	(omits)/(some people were saying)	(omits)/by	(omits)/(some were saying)
9 And Herod said, John have I beheaded: but who is this, of whom I hear such things? And he **desired** to see him.	sought	anxious	anxious	kept trying	tried
10 And the apostles, when they were returned, told him all that they had done. And he took them, and **went aside privately into a desert place belonging to the city called Bethsaida.**	withdrew apart to a city called Bethsaida	withdrew private-ly to a town called Bethsaida	withdrew to a town called Beth-saida where they could be by themselves	withdrew by Himself to a city called Bethsaida	withdrew by themselves to a town called Beth-saida
11 And the people, when they knew it, followed him: and he **received** them, and spake unto them of the kingdom of God, and healed them that had need of healing.	welcomed	welcomed	made . . . wel-come	welcoming	welcomed
12 And when the day began to wear away, then came the twelve, and said unto him, Send the multitude away, that they may go into the towns and country round about, and lodge, and get **victuals:** for we are here in a **desert** place.	provisions/lonely	food/lonely	food/lonely	something to eat/desolate	food/remote
18 And it came to pass, as he was alone praying, his disciples were with him: and he asked them, saying, **Whom** say the people that I am?	Who	Who	Who	Who	Who
25 For what **is** a man **advantaged,** if he gain the whole world, and **lose himself, or be cast away?**	does it profit/ loses or forfeits himself	will . . . gain/at the cost of his true self	gain is it/to have lost or ruined his very self	is . . . profited/ loses or forfeits himself	good is it/yet lose or forfeit his very self
29 And as he prayed, the **fashion** of his countenance was altered, and his raiment was white and **glistering.**	appearance/ dazzling	appearance/ dazzling	aspect/brilliant as lightning (omits "white")	appear-ance/gleaming	appearance/bright as a flash of lightning (omits "white")
31 Who appeared in glory, and spake of his **decease** which he should accomplish at Jerusalem.	departure	departure	passing	departure	departure

KJV	RSV	NEB	JB	NAS	NIV
35 And there came a voice out of the cloud, saying, This is my **beloved Son: hear him.**	Son, my Chosen; listen to him!"	Son, my Chosen; listen to him.'	Son, the Chosen One. Listen to him."	Son, My Chosen One; listen to Him!"	Son whom I have chosen; listen to him."
36 And when the voice **was past,** Jesus was found alone. And they kept **it close,** and told no man in those days any of those things which they had seen.	had spoken/ silence	had spoken/ silence	had spoken/ silence	had spoken/silent	had spoken/kept this to them- selves
38 And, behold, a man **of the company** cried out, saying, **Master,** I **beseech** thee, look upon my son: for he is mine only child.	from the crowd/ Teacher/ beg	in the crowd/ Master/implore	in the crowd / Master / implore	from the multi- tude/ Teacher / beg	in the crowd/ Teacher / beg
39 And, lo, a spirit taketh him and he suddenly crieth out; and it **teareth** him that he foameth again, and **bruising him hardly departeth from him.**	convulses/shatters	throws him into convulsions / mauling	throw . . . into convulsions / leaves the boy worn out	throws . . . into a convulsion / mauls	throws . . . into convulsions / is destroying
42 And as he was yet a-coming, the devil **threw him down, and tare him.** And Jesus rebuked the unclean spirit, and healed the child, and delivered him again to his father.	tore him and con- vulsed him	dashed him into the ground and threw him into convulsions	threw him to the ground in con- vulsions	dashed him to the ground and threw him into a convulsion	threw him to the ground in a con- vulsion
43 And they were all **amazed** at the **mighty power** of God. But while they wondered every one at all things which Jesus did, he said unto his disciples,	astonished / majesty	struck with awe / majesty	awestruck / greatness	amazed / greatness	amazed / greatness
44 **Let these sayings sink down into your ears:** for the Son of man shall be delivered into the hands of men.	"Let these words sink into your ears	'What I now say is for you: ponder my words	"For your part you must have these words con- stantly in your mind:	"Let these words sink into your ears	"Listen carefully to what I am about to tell you:
46 Then there arose a **reasoning** among them, which of them **should be** greatest.	argument / was	dispute / was	argument / was	argument / might be	argument / would be
50 And Jesus said unto him, Forbid him not: for he that is not against **us** is for **us.**	you / you	you / (on) your side	you / you	you / you	you / you
51 And it came to pass, when the time was come that he should be **received up,** he **stedfastly** set his face to go to Jerusalem,	received up / (omits)	taken up to heaven / reso- lutely	taken up to heaven / reso- lutely	His ascension / resolutely	taken up to heaven / reso- lutely
52 And sent messengers **before his face:** and they went, and entered into a village of the Samaritans, to make ready for him.	ahead of him	ahead	ahead of him	on ahead of Him	on ahead
53 **And they did not** receive him, because his face was as though he would go to Jerusalem.	would not receive him	would not have him	would not receive him	did not receive him	did not welcome him
54 And when his disciples James and John saw this, they said, Lord, wilt thou that we command fire to come down from heaven, and consume them, **even as Elias did?**	(omits)	(omits)	(omits)	(omits)	(omits)
55 But he turned, and rebuked them, and said, **Ye known not what manner of spirit ye are of.**	(omits)	(omits)	(omits)	(and said, "You do not know what kind of spirit you are of;	(omits)
56 **For the Son of man is not come to destroy men's lives, but to save them.** And they went to another village.	(omits)	(omits)	(omits)	for the Son of Man did not come to destroy men's lives, but to save them.'	(omits)

KJV	RSV	NEB	JB	NAS	NIV
10 1 After these things the Lord appointed other seventy also, and sent them two and two **before his face** into every city and place, whither he himself would come.	on ahead of him	on ahead	out ahead of him	ahead of Him	ahead of him
6 And if **the** son of peace be there, your peace shall rest upon **it**: if not, it shall turn to you again.	a / him	a / him	a / him	a / him	a / him
7 And in the same house remain, eating and drinking **such things as they give**: for the labourer is worthy of his **hire**. Go not from house to house.	what they provide / wages	(sharing their) food and drink / pay	what food and drink they have to give / wages	what they give you / wages	whatever they give you / wages
13 Woe unto thee, Chorazin! woe unto thee, Bethsaida! for if the **mighty works** had been done in Tyre and Sidon, which have been done in you, they had a great while ago repented, sitting in sackcloth and ashes.	mighty works	miracles	miracles	miracles	miracles
15 And thou, Capernaum, **which art exalted to heaven**, shall be thrust down to hell.	will you be exalted to heaven? / Hades	will you be exalted to the skies? / the depths	did you want to be exalted high as heaven? / hell	will not be exalted to heaven, will you? / Hades	will you be lifted up to the skies? / the depths
16 He that heareth you heareth me; and he that **despiseth** you **despiseth** me; and he that **despiseth** me **despiseth** him that sent me.	rejects / rejects / rejects / rejects	rejects / rejects / rejects / rejects	rejects / rejects / reject / reject	rejects / rejects / rejects / rejects	rejects / rejects / rejects / rejects
19 Behold, I give unto you power to tread on serpents and scorpions, and over all the power of the enemy: and nothing shall **by any means** hurt you.	(omits)	ever	ever	(omits)	(omits)
21 In that hour Jesus rejoiced **in spirit**, and said, I thank thee, O Father, Lord of heaven and earth, that thou hast hid these things from the wise and **prudent**, and hast revealed them unto **babes**: even so, Father; for **so it seemed good in thy sight**.	in the Holy Spirit / understanding / babes / such was thy gracious will	in the Holy Spirit / learned / simple / such was Thy choice	(filled with joy) by the Holy Spirit / clever / mere children / that is what it pleased you to do	in the Holy Spirit / intelligent / babes / thus it was well-pleasing in Thy sight	through the Holy Spirit / learned / little children / this was your good pleasure
22 All things are delivered to me of my Father: and no man knoweth who the Son is, but the Father; and who the Father is, but the Son, and he to whom the Son **will** reveal him.	chooses to	chooses to	chooses to	wills to	chooses to
25 And, behold, a certain lawyer stood up, and **tempted him**, saying, **Master**, what shall I do to inherit eternal life?	to put him to the test / Teacher	to put his test question to him / Master	to disconcert him / Master	put Him to the test / Teacher	to test Jesus / Teacher
29 But he, **willing** to justify himself, said unto Jesus, And who is my neighbour?	desiring	wanted	was anxious	wishing	wanted
30 And Jesus answering said, A certain man went down from Jerusalem to Jericho, and fell among **thieves**, which stripped him **of his raiment**, and **wounded** him, and departed, leaving him half dead.	robbers / (omits) / beat	robbers / (omits) / beat	brigands / all he had / beat	robbers / (omits) / beat	robbers / of his clothes / beat
35 And on the morrow **when he departed**, he took out two **pence**, and gave them to the **host**, and said unto him, Take care of him; and whatsoever thou spendest more, when I come again, I will repay thee.	(omits) / denarii / innkeeper	(omits) / silver pieces / innkeeper	(omits) / silver pieces / innkeeper	(omits) / denarii / innkeeper	(omits) / silver coins / innkeeper
39 And she had a sister called Mary which also sat at Jesus' feet, and **heard his word**.	listened to his teaching	listening to his words	listened to him speaking	listening to the Lord's word	listening to what he said
40 But Martha was **cumbered** about much serving, and came to him, and said, Lord, dost thou not care that my sister hath left me to serve alone? bid her therefore that she help me.	distracted	distracted	distracted	distracted	distracted

KJV	RSV	NEB	JB	NAS	NIV
41 And Jesus answered and said unto her, Martha, Martha, thou art **careful and troubled** about many things.	anxious and troubled	fretting and fussing	worry and fret	worried and bothered	worried and upset
42 But one thing is needful: and Mary hath chosen **that good part,** which shall not be taken away from her.	the good portion	The part . . . is best	the better part	the good part	what is better
11 2 And he said unto them, When ye pray, say, Our Father **which art in heaven,** Hallowed be thy name. Thy kingdom come. **Thy will be done, as in heaven, so in earth.**	(omits) / (omits)	(omits) / (omits)	(omits) / (omits)	(omits) / (omits)	(omits) / (omits)
4 And forgive us our sins; for we also forgive every one that is indebted to us. And lead us not into temptation; **but deliver us from evil.**	(omits)	(omits)	(omits)	(omits)	(omits)
8 I say unto you, Though he will not rise and give him, because he is his friend, yet because of his importunity he will rise and give him **as many as he needeth.**	whatever he needs	what he needs	all he wants	as much as he needs	as much as he needs
11 If a son shall ask **bread of any of you that is a father, will he give him a stone?** or if he ask a fish, will he for a fish give him a serpent?	What father among you / (omits)	a father among you / (omits)	What father among you bread / will hand his son a stone	one of you fathers / (omits)	which of you fathers / (omits)
14 And he was casting out a devil, and it was dumb. And it came to pass, when the devil was gone out, the **dumb** spake; and the people **wondered.**	dumb man / marveled	dumb man / were astonished	dumb man / were amazed	dumb man / marveled	man who had been dumb / were astonished
15 But some of them said, He casteth out devils through **Beelzebub the chief of the devils.**	Beelzebub, the prince of demons	Beelzebub prince of devils	Beelzebub, the prince of devils	Beelzebub, the ruler of the demons	Beelzebub, the prince of demons
17 But he, knowing their thoughts, said unto them, Every kingdom divided against itself is **brought to desolation;** and **a house divided against a house** falleth.	laid waste / divided household	goes to sin / divided household	heading for ruins / household divided against itself	laid waste / house divided against itself	will be ruined / house divided against itself
20 But if I **with** the finger of God cast out devils, **no doubt** the kingdom of God is come upon you.	by / then	by / then be sure	through / then know	by / then	by / then
25 And when he cometh, he findeth it swept and **garnished.**	put in order	tidy	tidied	put in order	put in order
27 And it came to pass, as he spake these things, a certain woman **of the company** lifted up her voice, and said unto him, Blessed is the womb that bare thee, and the **paps** which thou hast sucked.	in the crowd / breasts	in the crowd / breasts	in the crowd / breasts	in the crowd / breasts	in the crowd / (mother who . . . nursed you)
29 And when the people **were gathered thick together,** he began to say, This is an evil generation: they seek a sign; and there shall no sign be given it, but the sign of Jonas **the prophet.**	were increasing / (omits)	swarming round him / (omits)	got even bigger / (omits)	were increasing / (omits)	increased / (omits)
31 The queen of the south shall rise up in the judgment with the men of this generation, and condemn them: for she came from the utmost parts of the earth to hear the wisdom of Solomon; and, behold, a **greater than** Solomon is here.	something greater than	what (is here) is greater than	something greater than	something greater than	one greater than
32 The men of Nineve shall rise up in the judgment with this generation, and shall condemn it: for they repented at the preaching of Jonas; and, behold, a **greater than Jonas** is here.	something greater than Jonah	what (is here) is greater than Jonah	there is something greater than Jonah here	something greater than Jonah	one greater than Jonah

KJV	RSV	NEB	JB	NAS	NIV
39 And the Lord said unto him, Now do ye Pharisees make clean the outside of the cup and the **platter;** but **your inward part is full of ravening and wickedness.**	dish / inside you are full of extortion and wickedness	plate / inside there is nothing but greed and wickedness	plate / inside yourselves you are filled with extortion and wickedness	platter / inside of you, you are full of robbery and wickedness	dish / inside you are full of greed and wickedness
41 But rather give alms **of such things as ye have;** and, behold, all things are clean **unto** you.	those things which are within / for	what is in the cup / (all is clean)	from what you have / for	that which is within / for	what is inside / for
42 But woe unto you, Pharisees! for ye tithe mint and rue and all manner of herbs, and **pass over judgment** and the love of God: these ought ye to have done, and not to leave the other undone.	neglect justice	have no care for justice	overlook justice	disregard justice	neglect justice
46 And he said, Woe unto you also, ye lawyers! for ye **lade** men with burdens **grievous to be borne,** and ye yourselves touch not the burdens with one of your fingers.	load / hard to bear	load / intolerable	load / unendurable	weigh / hard to bear	load / they can hardly carry
47 Woe unto you! for ye build the **sepulchres** of the prophets, and **your fathers killed them.**	tombs / when your fathers killed	tombs / whom your fathers murdered	tombs / the men your ancestors killed	tombs / and it was your fathers who killed them	tombs / and it was your forefathers who killed them
48 Truly ye bear witness that ye **allow** the deeds of your fathers: for they indeed killed them, and ye build their **sepulchres.**	consent / tombs	approve / tombs	approve / (you do the building)	approve / tombs	approve / tombs
51 From the blood of Abel unto the blood of Zacharias, which perished between the altar and **the temple:** verily I say unto you, **It shall be required of** this generation.	sanctuary / it shall be required of	sanctuary / will have to answer for it	sanctuary / will have to answer for it	house of God / it shall be charged against	sanctuary / will be held responsible for it
53 **And as he said these things unto them,** the scribes and the Pharisees began **to urge him vehemently,** and to provoke him to speak of many things:	As he went away from there / press him hard	After he left the house / to assail him fiercely	When he left the house / a furious attack on him	And when He left there / to be very hostile	When Jesus left there / to oppose him fiercely
54 Laying wait for him, and seeking to catch **something out of his mouth, that they might accuse him.**	at something he might say	him with his own words	him out in something he might say	Him in something He might say	him in something he might say
12 1 In the mean time, when there were gathered together **an innumerable multitude of people,** insomuch that they trode one upon another, he began to say unto his disciples first of all, Beware ye of the leaven of the Pharisees, which is hypocrisy.	many thousands of the multitude	crowd of many thousands	people . . . in their thousands	so many thousands of the multitude	crowd of many thousands
3 Therefore whatsoever ye have spoken in darkness shall be heard in the light; and that which ye **have spoken in the ear in closets** shall be proclaimed upon the housetops.	have whispered in private rooms	have whispered behind closed doors	have whispered in hidden places	have whispered in the inner rooms	have whispered in the ear behind closed doors
8 Also I say unto you, Whosoever shall **confess** me before men, him shall the Son of man also confess before the angels of God:	acknowledges	acknowledges	declares himself for	confesses	acknowledges
11 And when they bring you **unto** the synagogues, and unto **magistrates,** and **powers, take ye no thought** how or what thing ye shall answer, or what ye shall say:	before / rulers / authorities / do not be anxious	before / state authorities / do not begin worrying	before / magistrates / authorities / do not worry	before / rulers / authorities / do not become anxious	before / rulers / authorities / do not worry
17 And he thought within himself, saying, What shall I do, because I have **no room** where to **bestow my fruits?**	nowhere / store my crops	not the space / store my produce	not enough room / store my crops	no place / store my crops	no place / store my crops
18 And he said, This will I do: I will pull down my barns, and build **greater;** and there will I **bestow** all my **fruits** and my	bigger ones /	them bigger / col-	bigger ones /	larger ones /	bigger ones /

KJV	RSV	NEB	JB	NAS	NIV
goods.	store / grain / goods	lect / corn / other goods	store / grain / goods	store / grain / goods	store / grain / goods
23 The life is more than **meat,** and the body is more than **raiment.**	food / clothing	food / clothes	food / clothing	food / clothing	food / clothes
29 And seek not ye what ye shall eat, or what ye shall drink, **neither be ye of doubtful mind.**	nor be of anxious mind	you are not to worry	nor must you worry	do not keep worrying	do not worry about it
33 Sell **that ye have,** and give alms; provide yourselves **bags** which **wax** not old, a treasure in the heavens that faileth not, where no thief approacheth, neither moth **corrupteth.**	your possessions / purses that do not grow old / destroys	your possessions / purses that do not wear out / destroy	your possessions / purses that do not wear out / destroy	your possessions / purses which do not wear out / destroys	your possessions / purses . . . that will not wear out / destroys
35 **Let your loins be girded** about, and your **lights** burning;	Let your loins be girded / lamps	Be ready for action, with belts fastened / lamps	See that you are dressed for action / lamps	Be dressed in readiness / lamps	Be dressed for service / lamps
36 And ye yourselves like unto men that wait for their **lord,** when he will return from the **wedding;** that when he cometh and knocketh, they may open unto him immediately.	master / marriage feast	master('s) / wedding-party	master / wedding feast	master / wedding feast	master / wedding banquet
37 Blessed are those servants, whom the lord when he cometh shall find **watching:** verily I say unto you, that he shall gird himself, and make them to sit down to **meat,** and will come forth and serve them.	awake / at table	on the alert / at table	awake / at table	on the alert / at the table	watching / at the table
39 And this know, that if the goodman of the house had known what hour the thief would come, he **would have watched,** and not have suffered his house to be broken through.	(omits)	(omits)	(omits)	(omits)	(omits)
40 Be ye therefore ready also: for the Son of man cometh **at an hour when ye think not.**	at an unexpected hour	at the time you least expect him	at an hour you do not expect	at an hour that you do not expect	at an hour when you do not expect him
48 But he that knew not, **and did commit things worthy of stripes, shall be beaten with few stripes.** For unto whomsoever much is given, of him shall be much required: and to whom men have committed much, of him they will ask the more.	did what deserved a beating / shall receive a light beating	earned a beating / will be flogged less severely	but deserves to be beaten / will receive fewer strokes	committed deeds worthy of a flogging / will receive but few	does things deserving punishment / will be beaten with few blows
49 I am come to send fire on the earth; and **what will I, if it be already kindled?**	would that it were already kindled!	how I wish it were already kindled!	how I wish it were blazing already!	how I wish it were already kindled!	how I wish it were already kindled!
50 But I have a baptism to be baptized with; and **how am I straitened** till it be accomplished!	how I am constrained	what constraint I am under	how great is my distress	how distressed I am	how distressed I am
58 When thou goest with thine **adversary** to the **magistrate,** as thou art in the way, **give diligence that thou mayest be delivered from him;** lest he **hale** thee to the judge, and the judge deliver thee to the officer, and the officer cast thee into prison.	accuser / magistrate / make an effort to settle with him / drag	opponent / court / make an effort to settle with him / drag	opponent / court / try to settle with him / drag	opponent / magistrate / make an effort to settle with him / drag	adversary / magistrate / try hard to be reconciled to him / drag
59 I tell thee, thou shalt not **depart thence,** till thou hast paid the very **last mite.**	get out / last copper	come out / last farthing	get out / last penny	get out of there / last cent	get out / last penny
13 7 Then said he unto the dresser of his vineyard, Behold, these three years I come seeking fruit on this fig tree, and find none: cut it down; why **cumbereth** it the ground?	use up	using up	taking up	use up	use up
11 And behold, there was a woman which had a spirit of infirmity eighteen years, and was **bowed together,** and could in **no wise lift up herself.**	bent over / could not	bent double / quite unable to	bent double / quite unable to	bent double / could not	bent over / could not straighten up

KJV	RSV	NEB	JB	NAS	NIV
	fully straighten herself	stand up straight	stand upright	straighten up at all	at all
18 Then said he, Unto what is the kingdom of God like? and whereunto shall I **resemble** it?	compare	compare	compare	compare	compare
19 It is like a grain of mustard seed, which a man took, and **cast** into his garden; and it grew, and **waxed** a great tree; and the fowls of the air **lodged** in the branches of it.	sowed / became / made nests	sowed / to be / came to roost	threw / became / sheltered	threw / became / nested	planted / became / perched
24 Strive to enter in at the **strait gate:** for many, I say unto you, will seek to enter in, and shall not be able.	narrow door	narrow door	narrow door	narrow door	narrow door
25 When once the master of the house is risen up, and hath shut to the door, and ye begin to stand without, and to knock at the door, saying, Lord, Lord, open unto us; and he shall answer and say unto you, **I know you not whence ye are:**	'I do not know where you come from	"I tell you, I do not know where you come from	I do not know where you come from.'	'I do not know where you are from.'	'I don't know you or where you come from.'
28 There shall be weeping and **gnashing** of teeth, when ye shall see Abraham, and Isaac, and Jacob, and all the prophets, in the kingdom of God, and you yourselves thrust out.	gnash	grinding	grinding	gnashing	grinding
29 And they shall come from the east, and from the west, and from the north, and from the south, **and shall sit down** in the kingdom of God.	and sit at table	for the feast	to take their places at the feast	and will recline at the table	and will take their places at the feast
32 And he said unto them, Go ye, and tell that fox, Behold, I cast out devils, and I do cures today and to-morrow, and the third day **I shall be perfected.**	I finish my course	I reach my goal	attain my end	I reach My goal	I will reach my goal
33 Nevertheless I must **walk** today, and to-morrow, and the day following: for it cannot be that a prophet **perish out of Jerusalem.**	go on my way / perish away from Jerusalem	be on my way / meet his death anywhere but in Jerusalem	go on / die outside Jerusalem	journey on / perish outside of Jerusalem	keep going / die outside Jerusalem
35 Behold, your house is left unto you **desolate:** and verily I say unto you, Ye shall not see me, until the time come when ye shall say, Blessed is he that cometh in the name of the Lord.	forsaken	forsaken by God	(omits)	desolate	desolate
14 1 And it came to pass, as he went into the house of one of the **chief** Pharisees to **eat bread** on the sabbath day, that they watched him.	ruler who belonged to the / to dine	leading / to have a meal	leading / for a meal	leaders of the / to eat bread	prominent / to eat
4 And they **held their peace.** And he took him, and healed him, and let him go;	were silent	said nothing	remained silent	kept silent	remained silent
5 And answered them, saying, Which of you shall have **an ass** or an ox fallen into **a pit,** and will not **straightway** pull him out on the sabbath day?	son / pit / immediately	donkey / well / (will he hesitate)	son / well / without hesitation	son / well / immediately	son / well / immediately
7 And he put forth a parable to **those which were bidden,** when he marked how they chose out the **chief rooms;** saying unto them,	those who were invited / places of honor	them / places of honour	the guests / places of honor	the invited guests / places of honor at the table	the guests / places of honor at the table
8 When thou art bidden **of any man** to a wedding, sit not down in the highest room; lest a more **honourable** man than thou be bidden of him;	by any one / eminent	by someone / distinguished	someone / distinguished	by someone / distinguished	someone / distinguished
10 But when thou art bidden, go and sit down in the lowest **room;** that when he that bade thee cometh, he may say unto thee, Friend, go up higher: then shalt thou **have worship** in the presence of **them that sit at meat** with thee.	place / be honored / all who sit at table	place / the respect in which you are held / all your fellow-guests	place / honored / everyone	place / have honor / all who are at the table	place / be honored / all your fellow guests

KJV	RSV	NEB	JB	NAS	NIV
14 And thou shalt be blessed; for they cannot **recompense** thee: for thou shalt be **recompensed at the resurrection of the just.**	blessed / repaid at the resurrection of the just	repaying / repaid on the day when good men rise from the dead	pay . . . back / repayment will be made to you when the virtuous rise again	blessed / repaid at the resurrection of the righteous	repay / repaid at the resurrection of the righteous
16 Then said he unto him, A certain man made a great **supper,** and **bade** many:	banquet / invited many	dinner party / had sent out many invitations	banquet / invited a large number of people	dinner / invited many	banquet / invited many guests
18 And they all **with one consent** began to make excuse. The first said unto him, I have bought a **piece of ground,** and I must needs go and see it: I pray thee have me excused.	all alike / field	one and all / piece of land	all alike / piece of land	all alike / piece of land	all alike / field
19 And another said, I have bought five yoke of oxen, and I go to **prove** them: I pray thee have me excused.	examine	try . . . out	try . . . out	try . . . out	try . . . out
21 So that servant came, and **shewed** his lord these things. Then the **master of the house** being angry said to his servant, Go out quickly into the streets and lanes of the city, and bring in hither the poor, and the maimed, and the **halt,** and the blind.	reported / householder / lanes / lame	reported / master of the house / alleys / lame	servant / householder / alleys / lame	reported / head of the household / lanes / lame	reported / owner of the house / alleys / lame
32 Or else, while the other is yet a great way off, he sendeth an **ambassage,** and **desireth** conditions of peace.	embassy / asks	envoy / asks	envoys / sue	delegation / asks	delegation / ask
15 12 And the younger of them said to his father, Father, give me **the portion of goods that falleth to me.** And he divided unto them **his living.**	the share of property that falls to me / his living	my share of the property / his estate	the share of the estate that would come to me / the property	the share of the estate that falls to me / his wealth	my share of the estate / his property
13 And not many days after the younger son gathered all together, and took his journey into a far country, and there **wasted his substance** with **riotous** living.	squandered his property / loose	squandered it / reckless	squandered his money / (life of debauchery)	squandered his estate / loose	squandered his wealth / wild
15 And he went and **joined himself** to a citizen of that country; and he sent him into his fields to feed swine.	joined himself	attached himself	hired himself out	attached himself	hired himself out
16 And he would **fain have filled his belly with the husks** that the swine did eat: and no man gave **unto him.**	gladly have fed on the pods / him anything	have been glad to fill his belly with the pods / him anything	willingly have filled his belly with the husks / him anything	longing to fill his stomach with the pods / anything to him	longed to fill his stomach with the pods / him anything
18 I will arise and go to my father, and will say unto him, Father, I have sinned against heaven, and **before thee,**	before you	against you	against you	in your sight	against you
20 And he arose, and came to his father. But when he was yet a great way off, his father saw him, and had compassion, and ran, and **fell on his neck,** and kissed him.	embraced him	flung his arms around him	clasped him in his arms	embraced him	threw his arms around him
29 And he answering said to his father, Lo, these many years do I serve thee, **neither transgressed I** at any time thy commandment: and yet thou never gavest me a kid, that I might make merry with my friends:	I never disobeyed	I never once disobeyed	never once disobeyed	I have never neglected	I've . . . never disobeyed
32 **It was meet** that we should make merry, and be glad: for this thy brother was dead, and is alive again; and was lost, and is found.	It was fitting to	How could we help	it was only right	we had to	we had to
16 4 **I am resolved what to do,** that, **when I am put out of the stewardship,** they may receive me into their houses.	I have decided what to do / when I am put out of the stewardship	What am I to do / now that my employer is dismissing me	I know what I will do / when I am dismissed from office	I know what I shall do / when I am removed from the stewardship	I know what I'll do / when I lose my job

KJV	RSV	NEB	JB	NAS	NIV
8 And the lord commended the **unjust** steward, **because he had done wisely:** for the children of this world are in their generation wiser [ ] than the children of light.	dishonest / for his shrewdness / in dealing with (their own generation)	dishonest / for acting so astutely / in dealing (with their own kind)	dishonest / for his astuteness / in dealing (with their own kind)	unrighteous / because he had acted shrewdly / in relation (to their own kind)	dishonest / because he had acted shrewdly / in dealing (with their own kind)
9 And I say unto you, **Make to yourselves friends of the mammon of unrighteousness;** that, when ye fail, they may receive you into everlasting habitations.	make friends for yourselves by means of unrighteous mammon / it	use your worldly wealth to win friends for yourselves / money	use money, tainted as it is, to win you friends / it	make friends for yourselves by means of the mammon of unrighteousness / it	use worldly wealth to gain friends for yourselves / it
10 He that is faithful in that which is least is faithful also in much: and he that is **unjust** in the least is **unjust** also in much.	dishonest / dishonest	dishonest / dishonest	dishonest / dishonest	unrighteous / unrighteous	dishonest / dishonest
11 If therefore ye have not been faithful in the **unrighteous mammon,** who will commit to your trust the true riches?	unrighteous mammon	wealth of this world	money, that tainted thing	the use of unrighteous mammon	handling worldly wealth
13 No servant can serve two masters: for either he will hate the one, and love the other; or else he will **hold to** the one, and despise the other. Ye cannot serve God and **mammon.**	devoted to / mammon	devoted to / money	treat . . . with respect / money	hold to / mammon	devoted to / money
14 And the Pharisees also, who **were covetous,** heard all these things: and they **derided** him.	were lovers of money / scoffed at	loved money / scoffed at	loved money / laughed at	were lovers of money / were scoffing at	loved money / were sneering at
15 And he said unto them, Ye are they which justify yourselves before men; but God knoweth your hearts: for that which is highly esteemed among men is **abomination** in the sight of God.	abomination	detestable	loathsome	detestable	detestable
16 The law and the prophets were until John: since that time the [ ] kingdom of God is preached, and every man **presseth into it.**	good news of the / enters it violently	good news of the / forces his way in	(no insert) / by violence . . . is getting in	gospel of the / is forcing his way into it	good news of the / is forcing his way into it
17 And it is easier for heaven and earth to pass, than one **tittle** of the law to **fail.**	dot / become void	dot or stroke / lose its force	little stroke / drop out	stroke / fail	stroke of a pen / drop out
19 There was a certain rich man, which was clothed in purple and fine linen, and **fared sumptuously** every day:	feasted sumptuously	feasted in great magnificence	used to . . . feast magnificently	gaily living in splendor	lived in luxury
17 1 Then said he unto the disciples, **It is impossible but that offences will come:** but woe unto him, through whom they come!	"Temptations to sin are sure to come	'Causes of stumbling are bound to arise	"Obstacles are sure to come	"It is inevitable that stumbling blocks should come	"Things that cause people to sin are bound to come
6 And the Lord said, If ye had faith as a grain of mustard seed, ye **might** say unto this sycamine tree, Be thou **plucked up by the root,** and be thou planted in the sea; and it should obey you.	could / 'Be rooted up	could / "Be rooted up	could / 'Be uprooted	would / 'Be uprooted	can / 'Be uprooted
7 But which of you, having a servant plowing or **feeding cattle,** will say unto him **by and by,** when he is come from the field, Go and **sit down to meat?**	keeping sheep / at once / sit down at table	minding sheep / at once / sit down	minding sheep / immediately / have your meal	tending sheep / immediately / sit down to eat	looking after the sheep / now / sit down to eat
8 And will not rather say unto him, **Make ready wherewith I may sup,** and gird thyself, and serve me, till I have eaten and drunken; and afterward thou shalt eat and drink?	'Prepare supper for me	"Prepare my supper	'Get my supper laid	Prepare something for me to eat	'Prepare my supper
9 Doth he thank that servant because he did the things that were commanded him? **I trow not.**	(omits)	(omits)	(omits)	(omits)	(omits)
18 **There are not** found that returned to give glory to God, save this **stranger.**	Was no one found to return / foreigner	Could none be found to come back / foreigner	It seems that no one has come back / foreigner	Was no one found who turned back / foreigner	Was no one found to return / foreigner

KJV	RSV	NEB	JB	NAS	NIV
20 And when he was demanded of the Pharisees, when the kingdom of God should come, he answered them and said, The kingdom of God cometh **not with observation:**	not . . . with signs to be observed	by observation	of observation	with signs to be observed	visibly
21 Neither shall they say, Lo here! or, lo there! for, behold, the kingdom of God is **within you.**	in the midst of you	among you	among you	in your midst	within you
31 In that day, he which shall be upon the housetop, and his **stuff** in the house, let him not come down to take it away: and he that is in the field, let him likewise not return back.	goods	belongings	possessions	goods	goods
36 **Two men shall be in the field; the one shall be taken,** and the other left.	(omits)	(omits)	(omits)	("Two men will be in the field; one will be taken and the other will be left.")	(omits)
18 1 And he spake a parable unto them **to this end,** that men ought always to pray, and not to **faint;**	to the effect / lose heart	to show / lose heart	about (the need) / lose heart	to show / lose heart	to show / give up
3 And there was a widow in that city; and she came unto him, **saying, Avenge me** of mine adversary.	saying, Vindicate me	demanding justice	saying, 'I want justice	saying, 'Give me legal protection	coming . . . with the plea, 'Grant me justice
7 And shall not God avenge his own elect, which cry day and night unto him, **though he bear long with them?**	Will he delay long over them?	while he listens patiently to them	even when he delays to help them	and will He delay long over them	Will he keep putting them off?
12 I fast twice in the week, I give tithes **of all that I possess.**	of all that I get	on all that I get	on all I get	of all that I get	of all my income
32 For he shall be delivered unto the **Gentiles,** and shall be mocked, and **spitefully entreated,** and spitted on.	Gentiles / shamefully treated	Foreign power / maltreated	pagans / maltreated	Gentiles / mistreated	Gentiles / insult (him)
34 And they understood none of these things: and this saying was hid from them, **neither knew** they the things which were spoken.	But they understood none of	But they understood nothing of	But they could make nothing of	And they understood none of	The disciples did not understand any of
19 3 And he sought to see Jesus who he was; and could not for the **press,** because he was **little of stature.**	crowd / small of stature	crowd / a little man	crowd / too short	crowd / small in stature	crowd / a short man
8 And Zacchaeus stood, and said unto the Lord; Behold, Lord, the half of my goods I give to the poor; and if I have taken any thing from any man by **false accusation,** I restore **him** fourfold.	defrauded / it	cheated / him	cheated / him	defrauded / as much	cheated / the amount
13 And he called his ten servants, and delivered them ten pounds, and said unto them, **Occupy** till I come.	'Trade with these	"Trade with this	'Do business with these	'Do business with this	'Put this money to work
14 But his citizens hated him, and sent a **message** after him, saying, We will not have this man to reign over us.	embassy	delegation	delegation . . . with this message	delegation	delegation
17 And he said unto him, Well, [ ] thou good servant: because thou hast been faithful in a very little, have thou authority over ten cities.	done	done	done	done	done
21 For I feared thee, because thou art an **austere** man: thou takest up that thou layedst not down, and reapest that thou didst not sow.	severe	hard	exacting	exacting	hard
22 And he saith unto him, Out of thine own mouth will I **judge** thee, thou wicked servant. Thou knewest that I was an	condemn	judge	condemn	judge	judge

KJV	RSV	NEB	JB	NAS	NIV
austere man, taking up that I laid not down, and reaping that I did not sow.					
23 Wherefore then gavest not thou my money into the bank, that at my coming I might have **required mine own with usury?**	collected it with interest	claimed it with interest	drawn it out with interest	collected it with interest	collected it with interest
36 And as he **went,** they spread their **clothes** in the way.	rode along / garments	went on his way / cloaks	moved off / cloaks	was going / garments	went along / cloaks
42 Saying, If thou hadst known, **even thou, at least in this thy day,** the things **which belong unto** thy peace! but now they are hid from thine eyes.	even today / that make for	on this great day / that leads to	on this day / the message of	in this day, even you / which make for	even you . . . on this day / what would bring you
43 For the days shall come upon thee, that thine enemies shall cast **a trench** about thee, and **compass** thee round, **and keep** thee in on every side,	bank / surround / hem	seige-works / encircle / hem	fortifications / encircle / hem	bank / surround / hem	embankment / encircle / hem
44 And shall **lay thee even with** the ground, and thy children within thee; and they shall not leave in thee one stone upon another; because thou **knewest not the time of thy visitation.**	dash you to / did not know the time of your visitation	bring you to / did not recognize God's moment when it came	dash you . . . to / did not recognize your opportunity when God offered it	level you to / did not recognize the time of your visitation	dash you to / did not recognize the time of God's coming to you
45 And he went into the temple, and began to cast out them that sold therein, **and them that bought;**	(omits)	(omits)	(omits)	(omits)	(omits)
47 And he taught daily in the temple. But the chief priests and the scribes and the **chief** of the people sought to destroy him,	principal men / hung upon his words	leading citizens / hung upon his words	leading citizens	leading men	leaders
48 And could not find what they might do: for all the people **were very attentive to hear him.**	hung upon his words	hung upon his words	hung on his words	were hanging upon His words	hung on his words
20 6 **But and if** we say, Of men; all the people will stone us: for they **be persuaded** that John was a prophet.	But if / are convinced	And if / are convinced	and if / are convinced	But if / are convinced	But if / are persuaded
18 Whosoever shall fall upon that stone shall be broken; [ ] but on whomsoever it shall fall, it will **grind him to powder.**	to pieces / crush him	to pieces / (he) will be crushed (by it)	to pieces / (anyone . . .) will be crushed	to pieces / scatter him like dust	to pieces / (he . . .) will be crushed
20 And they watched him, and sent forth spies, **which should feign themselves just men,** that they might take hold of his words, that so they might deliver him unto the power and authority of the governor.	who pretended to be sincere	in the guise of honest men	to pose as men devoted to the Law	who pretended to be righteous	who pretended to be honest
21 And they asked him, saying, Master, we know that thou sayest and teachest rightly, **neither acceptest thou the person of any,** but teachest the way of God truly:	and show no partiality	you pay deference to no one	you favor no one	and You are not partial to any	and that you do not show partiality
23 But he perceived their **craftiness,** and said unto them, **Why tempt ye me?**	craftiness / (omits)	trick / (omits)	cunning / (omits)	trickery / (omits)	duplicity / (omits)
25 And he said unto them, Render therefore unto Caesar the **things which be** Caesar's, and unto God the **things which be** God's.	things that are / things that are	what is due to / what is due to	what belongs to / what belongs to	things that are / things that are	what is / what is
26 And they **could not take hold of his words** before the people: and they marvelled at his answer, and **held their peace.**	were not able . . . to catch him by what he said / were silent	their attempt to catch him . . . failed / fell silent	were unable to find fault with anything he had to say / were silenced	were unable to catch Him in a saying / became silent	were unable to trap him in what he had said / became silent
30 **And the second took her to wife, and he died childless.**	and the second	then the second married her	The second	and the second	The second
34 And Jesus answering said unto them, The **children** of this world marry, and are given in marriage.	sons	men and women	children	sons	people

KJV	RSV	NEB	JB	NAS	NIV
35 But they which shall be accounted worthy to obtain that **world,** and the resurrection from the dead, neither marry, nor are given in marriage:	age	world	world	age	age
36 Neither can they die any more: for they are equal unto the angels; and are the **children** of God, being the **children** of the resurrection.	sons / sons	sons / they (share in)	sons / children	sons / sons	children / children
37 **Now** that the dead are raised, even Moses shewed at [ ] the bush, when he calleth the Lord the God of Abraham, and the God of Isaac, and the God of Jacob.	in the passage about	(in) the story of	(in) the passage about	(in) the passage about	(in) the account of
45 Then in **the audience of all the people** he said unto his disciples,	in the hearing of all the people	In the hearing of all the people	While all the people were listening	while all the people were listening	While all the people were listening
47 Which devour widows' houses, and for a **shew** make long prayers: the same shall receive greater **damnation.**	pretense / condemnation	appearance' sake / sentence	show / sentence	appearance's sake / condemnation	show / (will be) punished
21 1 And he looked up, and saw the **rich men casting** their gifts into the treasury.	rich putting	rich people dropping	rich people putting	rich putting	rich putting
2 And he saw also a certain poor widow **casting in thither** two **mites.**	put in / copper coins	putting in / tiny coins	putting in / small coins	putting in / small copper coins	put in / very small copper coins
4 For all these have of their abundance **cast in unto the offerings of** God: but she **of her penury** hath cast in all the living that she had.	contributed / out of her poverty	have given / with less than enough	contributed / from the little she had	put into the offering / out of her poverty	gave their gifts / out of her poverty
5 And as some spake of the temple, how it was adorned with **goodly** stones and **gifts,** he said,	noble / gifts	fine / votive offerings	fine / votive offerings	beautiful / votive gifts	beautiful / gifts dedicated to God
8 And he said, Take heed that ye be not **deceived:** for many shall come in my name, saying, I am **Christ;** and the time **draweth near:** go ye not therefore after them.	led astray / he / is at hand	misled / he / is upon us	deceived / he / is near at hand	misled / He / is at hand	deceived / he / is near
9 But when ye shall hear of wars and **commotions,** be not terrified: for these things **must first come to pass;** but the end is not **by and by.**	tumults / must first take place / at once	insurrections / are bound to happen / immediately	revolutions / must happen / so soon	disturbances / must take place first / immediately	revolutions / must happen first / right away
11 And great earthquakes shall be in **divers** places, and famines, and pestilences; and **fearful sights** and great signs shall there be from heaven.	various / terrors	many / terrors	here and there / fearful sights	various / terrors	various / fearful events
13 **And it shall turn to you for a testimony.**	This will be a time for you to bear testimony.	This will be your opportunity to testify	—and that will be your opportunity to bear witness.	"It will lead to an opportunity for your testimony.	This will result in your being witness to them.
14 **Settle it therefore in your hearts,** not to meditate before what ye shall answer:	Settle it therefore in your minds	so make up your minds	Keep this carefully in mind:	"So make up your minds	But make up your mind
15 For I will give you **a mouth** and wisdom, which all your adversaries shall not be able to **gainsay nor resist.**	a mouth / withstand or contradict	power of utterance / resist or refute	an eloquence / resist or contradict	utterance / resist or refute	words / resist or contradict
19 **In your patience possess ye your souls.**	By your endurance you will gain your lives.	By standing firm you will win true life for yourself.	Your endurance will win you your lives.	"By your endurance you will gain your lives.	By standing firm you will save yourselves.
20 And when ye shall see Jerusalem **compassed** with armies, then know that the desolation thereof **is nigh.**	surrounded / has come near	encircled / is near	surrounded / (she) will soon be laid desolate	surrounded / is at hand	surrounded / is near
21 Then let them which are in Judaea flee to the mountains; and let them which **are in the midst of it** depart out; and let not them that are **in the countries enter thereinto.**	inside the city / out in the country enter it	in the city itself / out in the country must not enter	inside the city / in country districts must not take refuge in it	in the midst of the city / in the country enter the city	in the city / in the country not enter the city

KJV	RSV	NEB	JB	NAS	NIV
24 And they shall fall by the edge of the sword, and shall be led away captive **into** all nations: and Jerusalem shall be trodden down of the Gentiles, until the times of the Gentiles be fulfilled.	among	into	to	into	to
25 And there shall be signs in the sun, and in the moon, and in the stars; and upon the earth **distress of nations, with perplexity; the sea and the waves roaring;**	distress of nations in perplexity at the roaring of the sea and the waves	nations will stand helpless, not knowing which way to turn from the roar and surge of the sea	nations in agony, bewildered by the clamor of the ocean and its waves	dismay among nations, in perplexity at the roaring of the sea and the waves	nations will be in anguish and perplexity at the roaring and tossing of the sea
26 **Men's hearts failing them** for fear, **and for looking after those things which are coming on the earth:** for the powers of heaven shall be shaken.	men fainting / and with foreboding of what is coming on the world	men will faint / at the thought of all that is coming upon the world	men dying / as they await what menaces the world	men fainting / and the expectation of the things which are coming upon the world	Men will faint / apprehensive of what is coming on the world
30 When they now **shoot forth,** ye see and know of your own selves that summer is now nigh at hand.	come out in leaf	buds	bud	put forth leaves	sprout leaves
32 Verily I say unto you, This generation shall not pass away, till all **be fulfilled.**	has taken place	(the present generation will live to see it all)	will have taken place	take place	have happened
34 And take heed to yourselves, lest at any time your hearts be **overcharged with surfeiting,** and drunkenness, and cares of this life, and so that day **come upon you unawares.**	weighed down with dissipation / come upon you suddenly like a snare	dulled by dissipation / closes upon you suddenly like a trap	coarsened with debauchery / sprung on you suddenly	weighed down with dissipation / come on you suddenly like a trap	weighed down with dissipation / closes upon you suddenly like a trap
36 Watch ye therefore, and pray always, **that ye may be accounted worthy** to escape all these things that shall come to pass, and to stand before the Son of man.	that you may have strength	for strength	for the strength	in order that you may have strength	that you may be able
22 4 And he went his way, and **communed** with the chief priests and **captains,** how he might betray him unto them.	conferred / officers	went . . . to discuss / officers of the temple police	went . . . to discuss / officers of the guard	discussed / officers	discussed / officers of the temple guard
5 And they were glad, and **covenanted** to give him money.	engaged	undertook	agreed	agreed	agreed
6 And he **promised,** and sought opportunity to betray him unto them in the absence of the multitude.	agreed	agreed	accepted	consented	consented
8 And **he** sent Peter and John, saying, Go and prepare us the passover, that we may eat.	Jesus	Jesus	he	He	Jesus
15 And he said unto them, **With desire** I have desired to eat this passover with you before I suffer.	earnestly	How	(omits)	earnestly	eagerly
16 For I say unto you, **I will not any more eat thereof,** until it be fulfilled in the kingdom of God.	I shall not eat it	never again shall I eat it	I shall not eat it again	I shall never again eat it	I will not eat it again
20 Likewise also the cup after supper, saying, This cup [ ] is the new **testament** in my blood, **which is shed for you.**	which is poured out for you / covenant / (omits)	(omits entire verse)	(no insert) / covenant / which will be poured out for you	which is poured out for you / covenant / (omits)	(no insert) / covenant / which is poured out for you
23 And they began to **inquire among themselves,** which of them it was that should do this thing.	question one another	ask among themselves	ask one another	discuss among themselves	question among themselves
24 And there was also a strife among them, which of them **should be accounted** the greatest.	was to be regarded	should rank	should be reckoned	was regarded to be	was considered to be
28 Ye are they which have continued with me in my **temptations.**	trials	times of trial	trials	trials	trials

KJV	RSV	NEB	JB	NAS	NIV
31 And the Lord said, Simon, Simon, behold, Satan **hath desired** to have you, that he may sift you as wheat:	demanded	been given leave	got his wish	demanded	asked
32 But I have prayed for thee, that thy faith fail not: and when thou **art converted,** strengthen thy brethren.	have turned again	have come to yourself	have recovered	have turned again	have returned to me
37 For I say unto you, that this that is written must yet be accomplished in me, And he was reckoned among the transgressors: for **the things concerning** me have an end.	what is written about me has its fulfillment	all that is written of me is being fulfilled	what scripture says about me is even now reaching its fulfillment	that which refers to Me has its fulfillment	what is written about me is reaching its fulfillment
51 And Jesus answered and said, **Suffer ye thus far.** And he touched his ear, and healed him.	"No more of this!"	'Let them have their way.'	"Leave off!" . . . "That will do!"	"Stop! No more of this!"	"No more of this!"
59 And about the space of one hour **after** another **confidently affirmed,** saying, Of a truth this fellow also was with him: for he is a Galilaean.	After / insisted	(omits) / spoke more strongly	later / insisted	after / began to insist	later / asserted
65 And many other things **blasphemously spake** they against him.	spoke . . . reviling him	went on heaping insults upon him	continued heaping insults on him	saying . . . blaspheming	said many other insulting things to him
68 And if I also ask you, ye will not answer me, **nor let me go.**	(omits)	(omits)	(omits)	(omits)	(omits)
23 4 Then said Pilate to the chief priests and to the people, I find **no fault** in this man.	no crime in	no case for	no case against	no guilt in	no basis for a charge against
5 And they **were the more fierce,** saying, He stirreth up the people, teaching throughout all **Jewry,** beginning from Galilee to this place.	were urgent / Judea	insisted / Judaea	persisted / Judaea	kept on insisting / Judea	insisted / Judea
9 Then he questioned **with him in many words;** but he answered him nothing.	him at some length	him at some length	him at some length	Him at some length	plied him with many questions
11 And Herod with his **men of war set him at nought,** and mocked him, and arrayed him in a gorgeous robe, and sent him again to Pilate.	soldiers treated him with contempt	troops treated him with contempt	guards, treated him with contempt	soldiers, . . . treating Him with contempt	soldiers ridiculed . . . him
14 Said unto them, Ye have brought this man unto me, as one that perverteth the people: and, behold, I, having examined him before you, **have found no fault in this man touching those things whereof ye accuse him:**	did not find this man guilty of your charges against him	found nothing in him to support your charges	found no case against the man in respect of all the charges you bring against him	have found no guilt in this man regarding the charges which you make against Him	have found no basis for your charges against him
15 No, nor yet Herod: **for I sent you to him;** and, lo, **nothing worthy of death is done unto him.**	for he sent him back to us / nothing deserving death has been done by him	for he has referred him back to us / he has done nothing to deserve death	since he has sent him back to us / the man has done nothing that deserves death	for he sent Him back to us / nothing deserving death has been done by Him	for he has sent him back to us / he has done nothing to deserve death
17 **(For of necessity he must release one unto them at the feast.)**	(omits)	(omits)	(omits)	(Now he was obliged to release to them at the feast one prisoner.)	(omits)
23 And they were **instant** with loud voices, requiring that he might be crucified. And the voices of them **and of the chief priests** prevailed.	demanding / (omits)	insisted on their demand / (omits)	kept on shouting / (omits)	were insistent / (omits)	insistently demanded / (omits)
31 For if they do these things **in a green tree,** what shall be done in the dry?	when the wood is green	when the wood is green	(use the) green wood like this	in the green tree	when the tree is green
32 And there were also two other **malefactors,** led with him to be put to death.	criminals	criminals	criminals	criminals	criminals

KJV	RSV	NEB	JB	NAS	NIV
33 And when they were come to the place, which is called **Calvary,** there they crucified him, and the **malefactors,** one on the right hand, and the other on the left.	The Skull / criminals	The Skull / criminals	The Skull / criminals	The Skull / criminals	The Skull / criminals
34 Then said Jesus, Father, forgive them; for they know not what they do. And they **parted his raiment,** and cast lots.	to divide his garments	divided his clothes	to share out his clothing	dividing up His garments	divided up his clothes
38 And a **superscription** also was written over him **in letters of Greek, and Latin, and Hebrew,** This is the King of the Jews.	inscription / (omits)	inscription / (omits)	inscription / (omits)	inscription / (omits)	written notice / (omits)
40 But the other answering rebuked him, saying, Dost not thou fear God, seeing thou art **in the same condemnation?**	under the same sentence of condemnation	under the same sentence as he	the same sentence as he did	under the same sentence of condemnation	under the same sentence
45 And the sun **was darkened,** and the **veil** of the temple was **rent in the midst.**	sun's light failed / curtain / torn in two	sun's light failed / curtain / torn in two	(omits) / veil / torn right down the middle	sun being obscured / veil / torn in two	sun stopped shining / curtain / torn in two
46 And when Jesus had cried with a loud voice, he said, Father, into thy hands I **commend** my spirit: and having said thus, he **gave up the ghost.**	commit / breathed his last	commit / died	commit / breathed his last	commit / breathed His last	commit / breathed his last
47 Now when the centurion saw what was done, he glorified God, saying, Certainly this **was a righteous man.**	man was innocent	man was innocent	was a great and good man	man was innocent	was a righteous man
50 And, behold, there was a man named Joseph, **a counsellor;** and he was a good man, and a **just:**	member of the council / righteous	member of the Council / upright	member of the council / virtuous	member of the Council / righteous	member of the Council / upright
54 And **that day was the preparation,** and the sabbath drew on.	It was the day of Preparation	It was Friday	It was Preparation Day	it was the preparation day	It was Preparation Day
24 1 Now upon the first day of the week, very early in the morning, they came unto the sepulchre, bringing the spices which they had prepared, **and certain others with them.**	(omits)	(omits)	(omits)	(omits)	(omits)
3 And they entered in, and found not the body **of the Lord Jesus.**	(omits)	(omits)	of the Lord Jesus	of the Lord Jesus	of the Lord Jesus
4 And it came to pass, as they were much perplexed thereabout, behold, two men stood by them in **shining garments:**	dazzling apparel	dazzling garments	brilliant clothes	dazzling apparel	clothes that gleamed like lightning
6 **He is not here, but is risen:** remember how he spake unto you when he was yet in Galilee,	(omits)	(omits)	He is not here; he has risen	"He is not here, but He has risen	He is not here; he has risen!
12 **Then arose Peter, and ran unto the sepulchre; and stooping down, he beheld the linen clothes laid by themselves, and departed, wondering in himself at that which was come to pass.**	(omits)	(omits)	Peter, however, went running to the tomb. He bent down and saw the binding cloths but nothing else; he went back home, amazed at what had happened.	(But Peter arose and ran to the tomb; stooping and looking in, he saw the linen wrappings only; and he went away to his home, marveling at that which had happened.)	Peter, however, got up and ran to the tomb. Stooping down, he saw the strips of linen lying by themselves, and he went away, wondering to himself what had happened.
13 And, behold, two of them went that same day to a village called Emmaus, which was from Jerusalem about **threescore furlongs.**	seven miles	seven miles	seven miles	seven miles	seven miles
15 And it came to pass, that, while they **communed together and reasoned,** Jesus himself drew near, and went with them.	were talking and discussing together	talked and discussed it with one another	talked this over	were conversing and discussing	talked and discussed these things with each other

KJV	RSV	NEB	JB	NAS	NIV
16 But their eyes were **holden that they should not know him.**	kept from recognizing	kept them from seeing who it was	prevented them from recognizing	prevented from recognizing Him	kept from recognizing him
17 And he said unto them, What **manner of communications** are these that ye have one to another, as ye walk, [ ] **and are sad?**	this conversation / And they stood still / looking sad	it / They halted / their faces full of gloom	matters / They stopped short / their faces downcast	these words / And they stood still / looking sad	What / They stood still / their faces downcast
18 And the one of them, whose name was Cleopas, answering said unto him, Art thou **only a stranger** in Jerusalem, and hast not known the things which are come to pass there in these days?	the only visitor	the only person	the only person	the only one visiting	the only one living
21 But we **trusted** that it had been he which should have redeemed Israel: and beside all this, to-day is the third day since these things were done.	had hoped	had been hoping	(Our own hope) had been	were hoping	had hoped
26 **Ought not Christ to** have suffered these things, and to enter into his glory?	Was it not necessary that the Christ should	Was the Messiah not bound to	Was it not ordained that the Christ should	Was it not necessary for the Christ to	Did not the Christ have to
28 And they drew nigh unto the village, whither they went: and he **made as though he would have** gone further.	appeared to be	made as if	made as if	acted as though	acted as if
36 And as they thus spake, Jesus himself stood in the midst of them, and saith unto them, **Peace be unto you.**	(omits)	(omits)	"Peace be with you!"	(omits)	"Peace be with you."
38 And he said unto them, Why are ye troubled? and why do **thoughts** arise in your hearts?	questionings	questionings	doubts	doubts	doubts
40 **And when he had thus spoken, he shewed them his hands and his feet.**	(omits)	(omits)	And as he said this he showed them his hands and feet.	(And when he had said this, He showed them His hands and His feet.)	When he had said this, he showed them his hands and feet.
41 And while they yet believed not for joy, and wondered, he said unto them, **Have ye here any meat?**	anything here to eat	anything here to eat	anything here to eat	anything here to eat	anything here to eat
42 And they gave him a piece of a broiled fish, **and of an honeycomb.**	(omits)	(omits)	(omits)	(omits)	(omits)
46 And said unto them, Thus it is written, and **thus it behoved Christ to suffer,** and to rise from the dead the third day:	that the Christ should suffer	that the Messiah is to suffer	that the Christ would suffer	that the Christ should suffer	The Christ will suffer
47 And that repentance **and remission** of sins should be preached in his name among all nations, beginning at Jerusalem.	and forgiveness	bringing forgiveness	for the forgiveness	for forgiveness	and forgiveness

John

KJV	RSV	NEB	JB	NAS	NIV
1 2 **The same** was in the beginning with God.	He	The Word	He	He	He
3 **All things were made by him;** and without him was not any thing made that was made.	all things were made through him	through him all things came to be	Through him all things came to be	All things came into being by Him	Through him all things were made
5 And the light shineth in darkness; and the darkness **comprehended** it not.	has . . . overcome	has . . . mastered	could . . . overpower	did . . . comprehend	has . . . understood

KJV	RSV	NEB	JB	NAS	NIV
9 That was the true Light, which lighteth every man **that cometh** into the world.	was coming	was even then coming	he was coming	which, coming	was coming
10 He was in the world, and the world was made **by** him, and the world knew him not.	through	(though it owed its being to him)	through	through	through
12 But as many as received him, to them gave he power to become the **sons of God,** even to them that believe on his name:	children of God	children of God	children of God	children of God	children of God
13 **Which were born, not of blood, nor of the will of the flesh, nor of the will of man,** but of God.	who were born, not of blood nor of the will of the flesh nor of the will of man	not born of any human stock, or by the fleshly desire of a human father	who was born not out of human stock or urge of the flesh or will of man	who were born not of blood, nor of the will of the flesh, nor of the will of man	children born not of natural descent, nor of human decision or a husband's will
14 And the Word was made flesh, and dwelt among us, (and we beheld his glory, the glory as of the **only begotten of the Father,**) full of grace and truth.	only Son from the Father	Father's only Son	only Son of the Father	only begotten from the Father	one and only (Son), who came from the Father
15 John bare witness of him, and cried, saying, This was he of whom I spake, He that cometh after me **is preferred** before me: for he was before me.	ranks	takes rank	ranks	has a higher rank	has surpassed
16 And of his **fulness** have all we received, and **grace for grace.**	fulness / grace upon grace	full store / grace upon grace	fullness / grace in return for grace	fulness / and grace upon grace	fullness of his grace / one blessing after another
18 No man hath seen God at any time; the only begotten Son, which is in the bosom of the Father, he hath **declared him.**	made him known	made him known	made him known	has explained Him	made him known
38 Then Jesus turned, and saw them following, and saith unto them, What seek ye? They said unto him, Rabbi, (which is to say, being interpreted, **Master,**) where dwellest thou?	Teacher	a teacher	Teacher	Teacher	Teacher
42 And he brought him to Jesus. And when Jesus beheld him, he said, Thou art Simon the son of Jona: thou shalt be called Cephas, which is by interpretation, **A stone.**	Peter	Peter, the Rock	Rock	Peter	Peter
47 Jesus saw Nathanael coming to him, and saith of him, Behold an Israelite indeed, **in whom is no guile!**	in whom is no guile	there is nothing false in him	incapable of deceit	in whom is no guile	in whom there is nothing false
2 3 And **when they wanted wine,** the mother of Jesus saith unto him, They have no wine.	When the wine gave out	The wine gave out	When they ran out of wine	when the wine gave out	When the wine was gone
4 Jesus saith unto her, Woman, **what have I to do with thee?** mine hour is not yet come.	what have you to do with me	Your concern . . . is not mine	why turn to me?	what do I have to do with you	"Why do you involve me?"
6 And there were set there six **waterpots** of stone, **after the manner of** the purifying of the Jews, containing **two or three firkins** apiece.	jars / for / twenty or thirty gallons	water-jars / of the kind used for / twenty to thirty gallons	water jars / meant for / twenty or thirty gallons	waterpots / for / twenty or thirty gallons	water jars / the kind used by / twenty to thirty gallons
8 And he saith unto them, Draw out now, and bear unto the **governor** of the feast. And they bare it.	steward	steward	steward	headwaiter	master
10 And saith unto him, Every man at the beginning doth set forth good wine; and when men **have well drunk,** then **that which is worse:** but thou hast kept the good wine until now.	have drunk freely / the poor wine	have drunk freely / the poorer sort	have had plenty to drink / the cheaper sort	have drunk freely / that which is poorer	have had too much to drink / the cheaper wine
11 This **beginning of miracles** did Jesus in Cana of Galilee, and manifested forth his glory; and his disciples believed on him.	the first of his signs	the first of the signs	the first of the signs	beginning of His signs	the first of his miraculous signs

KJV	RSV	NEB	JB	NAS	NIV
12 After this he went down to Capernaum, he, and his mother, and his brethren, and his disciples: and they continued there **not many days.**	for a few days	not . . . long	only a few days	a few days	for a few days
14 And found in the temple those that sold oxen and sheep and **doves,** and the changers of money **sitting:**	pigeons / at their business	pigeons / seated at their tables	pigeons / sitting at their counters there	doves / seated	doves / sitting at tables
15 And when he had made a **scourge** of small cords, he drove them all out of the temple, and the sheep, and the oxen; and poured out the changers' money, and overthrew the tables;	whip	whip	whip	scourge	whip
17 And his disciples remembered that it was written, The zeal of thine house **hath eaten me up.**	will consume me	will destroy me	will devour me	will consume me	will consume me
23 Now when he was in Jerusalem at the passover, in the feast day, many believed in his name, when they saw the **miracles** which he did.	signs	signs	signs	signs	miraculous signs
24 But Jesus did not **commit** himself unto them, because he knew all men,	trust	trust	trust	entrusting	trust
3 8 The wind bloweth where it **listeth,** and thou hearest the sound thereof, but canst not tell whence it cometh, and whither it goeth: **so is every one** that is born of the Spirit.	wills/so it is with every one	wills/So with everyone	pleases/ That is how it is with all	wishes/so is everyone	pleases/So it is with everyone
10 Jesus answered and said unto him, Art thou **a master** of Israel, and **knowest not** these things?	teacher/not understand	famous teacher/ ignorant of	teacher/not know	teacher/not understand	teacher/not understand
13 And no man hath ascended up to heaven, but he that came down from heaven, even the Son of man **which is in heaven.**	(omits)	whose home is in heaven	who is in heaven	(omits)	(omits)
15 That whosoever believeth in him **should not perish,** but have eternal life.	(omits)	(omits)	(omits)	(omits)	(omits)
16 For God so loved the world, that he gave his **only begotten Son,** that whosoever believeth in him should not perish, but have **everlasting** life.	only Son/eternal	only Son/eternal	only Son/eternal	only begotten Son/eternal	one and only Son/everlasting
19 And this is the **condemnation,** that light is come into the world, and men loved darkness rather than light, because their deeds were evil.	judgment	test	sentence pronounced	judgment	verdict
20 For every one that doeth evil hateth the light, neither cometh to the light, lest his deeds should be **reproved.**	exposed	shown up	exposed	exposed	exposed
25 Then there arose **a question** between some of John's disciples and **the Jews** about **purifying.**	discussion/a Jew/purifying	dispute/Jews/purification	discussion/a Jew/purification	discussion/a Jew/purification	argument/a certain Jew/ceremonial washing
30 He must **increase,** but I must **decrease.**	increase/decrease	grows greater/grow less	grow greater/grow smaller	increase/decrease	become greater/become less important
33 He that hath received his testimony hath **set to his seal** that God is true.	sets his seal	is to attest	are attesting	has set his seal	has certified
34 For he whom God hath sent speaketh the words of God: **for God giveth not the Spirit by measure unto him.**	It is not by measure that he gives the Spirit	so measureless is God's gift of the Spirit	God gives him the Spirit without reserve	for He gives the Spirit without measure	to him God gives the Spirit without limit
4 5 Then cometh he to a city of Samaria, which is called Sychar, near to the **parcel of ground** that Jacob gave to his son Joseph.	field	plot of ground	land	parcel of ground	plot of ground
6 Now Jacob's well was there. Jesus therefore, being wearied with his jour-					

KJV	RSV	NEB	JB	NAS	NIV
ney, sat thus **on** the well: and it was about the sixth hour.	beside	by	by	by	by
15 The woman saith unto him, Sir, give me this water, that **I thirst not,** neither **come hither to draw.**	I may not thirst/come here to draw	I shall not be thirsty/have to come all this way to draw	I may never get thirsty/have to come here again to draw water	I will not be thirsty/come all the way here to draw	I won't get thirsty and have to keep coming here to draw water
20 Our fathers worshipped **in** this mountain; and ye say, that in Jerusalem is the place where men ought to worship.	on	on	on	in	on
24 God is a Spirit: and they that worship him must worship **him** in spirit and in truth.	(omits)	(omits)	(omits)	(omits)	(omits)
27 And upon this came his disciples, and marvelled that he talked with **the** woman: yet no man said, What seekest thou? or, Why talkest thou with her?	a	a	a	a	a
28 The woman then left her waterpot, and went her way into the city, and saith to the **men,**	people	people	people	men	people
29 Come, see a man, which told me all things that ever I did: **is not this** the Christ?	Can this be	Could this be	I wonder if he is	this is not . . . is it	Could this be
32 But he said unto them, I have **meat** to eat that ye know not of.	food	food	food	food	food
34 Jesus saith unto them, My **meat** is to do the will of him that sent me, and to **finish** his work.	food/accomplish	meat and drink/finished	food/complete	food/accomplish	food/finish
36 **And he that reapeth receiveth wages,** and **gathereth fruit** unto life eternal: that both he that soweth and he that reapeth may rejoice together.	He who reaps wages, and gathers fruit	The reaper is drawing his pay and gathering a crop	the reaper is being paid his wages, already he is bringing in the grain	"Already he who reaps is receiving wages, and is gathering fruit	Even now the reaper draws his wages, even now he harvests the crop
38 I sent you to reap that whereon ye bestowed no labour: other men **laboured,** and ye are **entered into** their labours.	labored/entered into	toiled/come in for the harvest of	worked/come into the rewards of	labored/entered into	done the hard work/reaped the benefits of
42 And said unto the woman, Now we believe, not because of thy saying: for we have heard him ourselves, and know that this is indeed **the Christ,** the Saviour of the world.	(omits)	(omits)	(omits)	(omits)	(omits)
52 Then **inquired** he of them the hour when he began **to amend.** And they said unto him, Yesterday at the seventh hour the fever left him.	asked/mend	asked/recover	asked/recover	inquired/get better	inquired/had gotten better
5 2 Now there is at Jerusalem by the sheep **market** a pool, which is called in the **Hebrew** tongue **Bethesda,** having five **porches.**	Gate / Hebrew / Bethzatha / porticoes	Pool / language of the Jews / Bethesda / colonnades	Pool / Hebrew / Bethzatha / porticoes	gate / Hebrew / Bethesda / porticoes	Gate / Aramaci / Bethesda / covered colonnades
3 In these lay a great multitude of **impotent folk,** of blind, **halt, withered, waiting for the moving of the water.**	invalids / lame / paralyzed / (omits)	sick people / lame / paralyzed / (omits)	sick people / lame / paralyzed / waiting for the water to move	those who were sick / lame / withered / (waiting for the moving of the waters	disabled / lame / paralyzed / (omits)
4 **For an angel went down at a certain season into the pool, and troubled the water: whosoever then first after the troubling of the water stepped in was made whole of whatsoever disease he had.**	(omits)	(omits)	for at intervals the angel of the Lord came down into the pool, and the water was disturbed, and the first person to enter the water after the disturbance was cured of any ailment he suffered	for an angel of the Lord went down at certain seasons into the pool, stirred up the water; and whoever then first, after the stirring up of the water, stepped in was made well from whatever	(omits)

KJV	RSV	NEB	JB	NAS	NIV
			from	disease with which he was afflicted.)	
7 The **impotent man** answered him, Sir, I have no man, when the water is troubled, to put me in to the pool: but while I am coming, another steppeth down before me.	sick man	he	sick man	sick man	invalid
8 Jesus saith unto him, Rise, take up thy **bed**, and walk.	pallet	bed	sleeping mat	pallet	mat
13 And he that was healed **wist not** who it was: for Jesus had **conveyed himself away**, a multitude being in that place.	did not know/withdrawn	did not know/slipped away	had no idea/disappeared	did not know/slipped away	had no idea/slipped away
16 And therefore did the Jews persecute Jesus, **and sought to slay him**, because he had done these things on the sabbath day.	(omits)	(omits)	(omits)	(omits)	(omits)
17 But Jesus answered them, My Father worketh **hitherto**, and I work.	is working still	has never yet ceased his work	goes on working	is working until now	is always at his work on this very day
21 For as the Father raiseth up the dead, and **quickeneth them**; even so the Son **quickeneth** whom he will.	gives them life/gives life	gives them life/gives life	gives them life/gives life	gives them life/gives life	gives them life/gives life
24 Verily, verily, I say unto you, He that heareth my word, and believeth on him that sent me, hath everlasting life, and shall not come into **condemnation**; but is passed from death unto life.	judgment	judgment	judgment	judgment	(will not be) condemned
28 **Marvel** not at this: for the hour is coming, in the which all that are in the graves shall hear his voice,	marvel	wonder	be surprised	marvel	be amazed
29 And shall come forth; they that have done good, unto the resurrection of life; and they that have done evil, unto the resurrection of **damnation**.	judgment	doom	condemnation	judgment	(to be) condemned
36 But I have **greater witness** than that of John: for the works which the Father hath **given** me to finish, the same works that I do, bear witness of me, that the Father hath sent me.	testimony . . . greater/granted	testimony higher/gave	testimony . . . greater/given	witness . . . greater/given	testimony weightier/given
41 **I receive not honour** from men.	do not receive glory from men	do not look to men for glory	As for human approval, this means nothing to me.	do not receive glory from men	do not accept praise from men
43 I am come in my Father's name, and ye **receive** me not: if another shall come in his own name, him ye will **receive**.	receive / receive	have . . . welcome / welcome	accept / accept	receive / receive	accept / accept
6 10 And Jesus said, Make the **men** sit down. Now there was much grass in the place. So the **men** sat down, in number about five thousand.	people / men	people / men	people / men	people / men	people / men
11 And Jesus took the loaves; and when he had given thanks, he distributed **to the disciples, and the disciples** to them that were set down; and likewise of the fishes as much as they **would**.	(omits) / wanted	(omits) / wanted	(omits) / wanted	(omits) / wanted	(omits) / wanted
12 When they were filled, he said unto his disciples, Gather up the **fragments** that remain, that nothing be lost.	fragments	pieces	pieces	fragments	pieces
19 So when they had rowed about five and **twenty or thirty furlongs**, they see Jesus walking on the sea, and drawing nigh unto the ship: and they were afraid.	three or four miles	three or four miles	three or four miles	three or four miles	three or four miles
21 Then they **willingly received** him	were glad to take	were ready to	were for taking /	were willing	were willing to

KJV	RSV	NEB	JB	NAS	NIV
into the ship: and immediately the ship was at the land **whither they went.**	/ to which they were going	take / they were making for	they were making for	therefore to receive / to which they were going	take / where they were heading
22 The day following, when the people which **stood** on the **other side** of the sea saw that there was none other boat there, save that one whereinto his disciples were entered, and that Jesus went not with his disciples into the boat, but that his disciples were gone away alone;	remained on the other side	was standing on the opposite shore	had stayed on the other side	stood on the other side	had stayed on the opposite shore
24 When the people therefore saw that Jesus was not there, neither his disciples, they also **took shipping,** and came to Capernaum, seeking for Jesus.	got into the boats	went aboard these boats	got into those boats	got into the small boats	got into the boats
27 Labour not for the **meat which perisheth,** but for that meat which endureth unto everlasting life, which the Son of man shall give unto you: for him hath God the Father **sealed.**	food which perishes / set his seal	perishable food / set the seal of his authority	food that cannot last / set his seal	food which perishes / set His seal	food that spoils / placed his seal of approval
34 Then said they unto him, **Lord, evermore** give us this bread.	Lord . . . always	Sir . . . now and always	Sir / always	Lord, evermore	Sir, from now on
37 All that the Father giveth me shall come to me; and him that cometh to me I will in no wise **cast out.**	cast out	turn away	turn . . . away	cast out	drive away
45 It is written in the prophets, And they shall be all taught of God. Every man therefore that hath heard, and hath learned **of** the Father, cometh unto me.	from	from	from	from	from
47 Verily, verily, I say unto you, He that believeth **on me** hath everlasting life.	(omits)	(omits)	(omits)	(omits)	(omits)
52 The Jews therefore **strove** among themselves, saying, How can this man give us his flesh to eat?	disputed	(This leads to a) fierce dispute	started arguing	began to argue	began to argue
57 As the living Father hath sent me, and I live **by** the Father: so he that eateth me, even he shall live **by** me.	because of / because of	because of / because of	from / from	because of / because of	because of / because of
60 Many therefore of his disciples, when they had heard this, said, **This is an hard saying; who can hear it?**	"This is a hard saying; who can listen to it?"	'This is more than we can stomach! Why listen to such talk?'	"This is intolerable language. How could anyone accept it?"	"This is a difficult statement; who can listen to it?"	"This is a hard teaching. Who can accept it?"
63 It is the spirit that **quickeneth;** the flesh **profiteth nothing:** the words that I speak unto you, they are spirit, and they are life.	gives life / is of no avail	gives life / is of no avail	gives life / has nothing to offer	gives life / profits nothing	gives life / counts for nothing
69 And we believe and are sure that thou art **that Christ, the Son of the living God.**	the Holy One of God	the Holy One of God	the Holy One of God	the Holy One of God	the Holy One of God
7 1 After these things Jesus walked in Galilee: for he **would not walk in Jewry,** because the Jews sought to kill him.	would not go about in Judea	wished to avoid Judaea	could not stay in Judaea	was unwilling to walk in Judea	purposely staying away from Judea
5 For **neither did** his brethren **believe in** him.	even . . . did not believe	even . . . had no faith	Not even . . . had faith	not even . . . were believing	even . . . did not believe
6 Then Jesus said unto them, **My time** is not yet come: but your **time is alway ready.**	My time/your time is always here	The right time for me/any time is right for you	The right time for me/any time is the right time for you	My time/your time is always opportune	The right time/any time is the right time for you
10 But when his brethren were gone up, then went he also up unto the feast, not **openly,** but as it were in **secret.**	publicly/private	publicly/secret	without drawing attention to himself/quite privately	publicly/secret	publicly/secret
12 And there was much murmuring among the people concerning him: for some said, He is a good man: others said,					

KJV	RSV	NEB	JB	NAS	NIV
Nay; but he **deceiveth** the people.	is leading . . . astray	is leading . . . astray	is leading . . . astray	leads . . . astray	deceives
15 And the Jews marvelled, saying, **How knoweth this man letters, having never learned?**	"How is it that this man has learning, when he has never studied?"	'How is it . . . that this untrained man has such learning?'	"How did he learn to read? He had not been taught."	"How has this man become learned, having never been educated?"	"How did this man get such learning without having studied?"
16 Jesus answered them, and said, My **doctrine** is not mine, but his that sent me.	teaching	teaching	teaching	teaching	teaching
18 He that speaketh of himself seeketh his own glory: but he that seeketh his glory that sent him, the same is true, and **no unrighteousness** is in him.	no falsehood	nothing false	(is by no means an imposter)	no unrighteousness	nothing false
19 Did not Moses give you the law, and yet none of you keepeth the law? Why **go ye about** to kill me?	do you seek	are you trying	do you want	do you seek	are you trying
22 Moses therefore gave unto you circumcision; (not because it is of Moses, but of the **fathers;**) and ye on the sabbath day circumcise **a man.**	fathers/a man	patriarchs/(omits)	patriarchs/(omits)	fathers/a man	patriarchs/a child
23 If a man on the sabbath day receive circumcision, that the law of Moses should not be broken; are ye angry at me, because I have made a man **every whit whole** on the sabbath day?	man's whole body well	health . . . the whole of a man's body	man whole and complete	entire man well	healing the whole man
24 Judge not according to the appearance, but judge **righteous judgment.**	right judgment	just . . . judgments	judgment (be according to what is) right	righteous judgment	right judgment
26 But, lo, he speaketh **boldly,** and they say nothing unto him. Do the rulers know indeed that this is the very Christ?	openly	openly	freely	publicly	publicly
27 Howbeit we know this man whence he is: but when Christ cometh, no man **knoweth whence he is.**	will know where he comes from	is to know where he comes from	will know where he comes from	knows where He is from	will know where he is from
35 Then said the Jews among themselves, Whither will he go, that we shall not find him? will he go unto **the dispersed among the Gentiles,** and teach the Gentiles?	the Dispersion among the Greeks	the Dispersion among the Greeks	the people who are dispersed among the Greeks	the Dispersion among the Greeks	where our people live scattered among the Greeks
38 He that believeth on me, as the scripture hath said, **out of his belly** shall flow rivers of living water.	Out of his heart	from within him	From his breast	From his innermost being	from within him
8 6 This they said, **tempting him,** that they might have to accuse him. But Jesus stooped down, and with his finger wrote on the ground, **as though he heard them not.**	to test him/(omits)	as a test/(omits)	as a test/(omits)	testing Him/(omits)	as a trap/(omits)
9 And they which heard it, **being convicted by their own conscience,** went out one by one, beginning at the eldest, even unto the last: and Jesus was left alone, and the woman standing **in the midst.**	(omits)/before him	(omits)/there	(omits)/there	(omits)/where she had been, in the midst	(omits)/there
13 The Pharisees therefore said unto him, Thou **bearest record** of thyself; thy **record** is not true.	are bearing witness/testimony	are witness/testimony	are testifying/testimony	are bearing witness/witness	are, appearing . . . witness/testimony
16 And yet if I judge, my judgment is true: for I am not alone, but I and the **Father** that sent me.	he	he	the one	He	the Father

KJV	RSV	NEB	JB	NAS	NIV
33 They answered him, We be Abraham's **seed,** and were never in bondage to any man: how sayest thou, Ye shall be made free?	descendants	descendants	are descended from	offspring	descendants
41 Ye do the deeds of your father. Then said they to him, We be not **born of fornication;** we have one father, even God.	born of fornication	base-born	born of prostitution	born of fornication	illegitimate children
47 **He that is of God** heareth God's words: ye therefore hear them not, because ye are not of God.	He who is of God	He who has God for his father	A child of God	He who is of God	He who belongs to God
53 Art thou greater than our father Abraham, which is dead? and the prophets are dead: **whom makest thou thyself?**	Who do you claim to be?	What do you claim to be?	Who are you claiming to be?	whom do you make Yourself out to be?	Who do you think you are?
9 3 Jesus answered, Neither hath this man sinned, nor his parents: but that the works of God should be **made manifest in him.**	made manifest in him	be displayed	be displayed	be displayed	be displayed
4 **I** must work the works of him that sent me, while it is day: the night cometh, when no man can work.	We	We	I	We	we
18 But the Jews did not believe **concerning him,** that he had been blind, and received his sight, until they called the parents of him that had received his sight.	(omits)	(omits)	(omits)	it of him	(omits)
34 They answered and said unto him, Thou wast **altogether born in sins,** and dost thou **teach** us? And they cast him out.	born in utter sin/teach	born and bred in sin/give . . . lessons	sinner through and through . . . born	born entirely in sins/teaching	steeped in sin at birth/lecture
35 Jesus heard that they had cast him out; and when he had found him, he said unto him, Dost thou believe **on the Son of God?**	in the Son of man	in the Son of Man	in the Son of Man	in the Son of Man	in the Son of Man
41 Jesus said unto them, If ye were blind, ye should have no **sin:** but now ye say, We see; therefore your **sin remaineth.**	guilt/guilt	(be) guilty/guilt	(be) guilty/guilt	sin/sin	(be) guilty/guilt
10 3 To him the **porter** openeth; and the sheep hear his voice; and he calleth his own sheep by name, and leadeth them out.	gatekeeper	door-keeper	gatekeeper	doorkeeper	watchman
6 This **parable** spake Jesus unto them: but they understood not what things they were which he spake unto them.	figure	parable	parable	figure	figure of speech
9 I am the **door:** by me if any man enter in, he shall be saved, and shall go in and out, and find pasture.	door	door	gate	door	gate
10 The thief cometh not, but for to steal, and to kill, and to destroy: I am come that they might have life, and that they might have it **more abundantly.**	abundantly	in all its fullness	to the full	abundantly	to the full
16 And other sheep I have, which are not of this fold: them also I must bring, and they shall hear my voice; and there shall be **one fold,** and one shepherd.	one flock	one flock	one flock	one flock	one flock
18 No man taketh it from me, but I lay it down of myself. I have **power** to lay it down, and I have **power** to take it again. This **commandment** have I received of my Father.	power/power / charge	right/right / charge	power/power / command	authority/authority / commandment	authority/authority / command
24 Then came the Jews round about him, and said unto him, How long dost thou **make us to doubt?** If thou be the Christ, tell us plainly.	keep us in suspense	keep us in suspense	keep us in suspense	keep us in suspense	keep us in suspense
36 Say ye of him, whom the Father **hath sanctified,** and sent into the world,	consecrated	consecrated	has consecrated	sanctified	set apart as his

KJV	RSV	NEB	JB	NAS	NIV
Thou blasphemest; because I said, I am the Son of God?					very own
11 12 Then said his disciples, Lord, if he sleep, he shall **do well.**	recover	recover	get better	recover	get better
13 Howbeit Jesus spake of his death: but they thought that **he had spoken of taking of rest in sleep.**	he meant taking rest in sleep	he meant natural sleep	that by "rest" he meant "sleep"	He was speaking of literal sleep	he meant natural sleep
15 And I am glad for your sakes that I was not there, **to the intent** ye may believe; nevertheless let us go unto him.	so that	for	because now	so that	so that
16 Then said Thomas, which is called **Didymus,** unto his fellow-disciples, Let us also go, that we may die with him.	the Twin	'the Twin'	the Twin	Didymus	Didymus
18 Now Bethany was nigh unto Jerusalem, about **fifteen furlongs** off:	two miles	two miles	two miles	two miles	two miles
28 And when she had so said, she went her way, and called Mary her sister **secretly,** saying, The Master is come, and calleth for thee.	quietly	taking her aside	in a low voice	secretly	aside
33 When Jesus therefore saw her weeping, and the Jews also weeping which came with her, he **groaned in the spirit, and was troubled,**	he was deeply moved in spirit and troubled	he sighed heavily and was deeply moved	Jesus said in great distress, with a sigh that came straight from the heart	He was deeply moved in spirit, and was troubled	he was deeply moved and troubled
39 Jesus said, Take ye away the stone. Martha, the sister of him that was dead, saith unto him, Lord, by this time **he stinketh:** for he hath been dead four days.	there will be an odor	there will be a stench	he will smell	there will be a stench	there is a bad odor
44 And he that was dead came forth, bound hand and foot with **graveclothes:** and his face was bound about with a **napkin.** Jesus saith unto them, Loose him, and let him go.	bandages/cloth	linen bands/cloth	bands of stuff/cloth	wrappings/cloth	strips of linen/cloth
47 Then gathered the chief priests and the Pharisees a council, and said, **What do we?** for this man doeth many miracles.	"What are we to do?	'What action are we taking?'	what action are we taking?	"What are we doing?	"What are we accomplishing?"
50 Nor consider that it is **expedient for us,** that one man should die for the people, and that the whole nation perish not.	expedient for you	more to your interest	better	expedient for you	better for you
54 Jesus therefore walked no more openly among the Jews; but went thence unto **a country near to the wilderness,** into a city called Ephraim, and there continued with his disciples.	the country near the wilderness	the country bordering on the desert	the country bordering on the desert	the country near the wilderness	a region near the desert
57 Now both the chief priests and the Pharisees had given **a commandment,** that, if any man knew where he were, he should shew it, that they might take him.	orders	orders	orders	orders	orders
12 3 Then took Mary a pound of ointment of **spikenard,** very **costly,** and anointed the feet of Jesus, and wiped his feet with her hair: and the house was filled with the **odour of the ointment.**	pure nard / costly / fragrance of the ointment	pure oil of nard / costly / fragrance	pure nard/costly / scent of the ointment	pure nard / costly / fragrance of the perfume	pure nard / expensive / fragrance of the perfume
6 This he said, not that he cared for the poor; but because he was a thief, **and had the bag, and bare what was put therein.**	and as he had the money box he used to take what was put into it	he used to pilfer the money put into the common purse, which was in his charge	he was in charge of the common fund and used to help himself to the contributions	and as he had the money box, he used to pilfer what was put into it	he was in charge of the common fund and used to help himself to the contributions
7 Then said Jesus, Let her alone: **against the day of my burying hath she kept this.**	let her keep it for the day of my burial	'Let her keep it till the day when she prepares for my burial	she had to keep this scent for the day of my burial	in order that she may keep it for the day of My burial	"It was meant that she should save this perfume for the day of my burial.

KJV	RSV	NEB	JB	NAS	NIV
9 Much people of the Jews therefore **knew** that he was there: and they came not for Jesus' sake only, but that they might see Lazarus also, whom he had raised from the dead.	learned	heard	heard	learned	found out
11 Because that by reason of him many of the Jews **went away, and believed on Jesus.**	were going away and believing in Jesus	were going over to Jesus and putting their faith in him	were leaving them and believing in Jesus	were going away, and were believing in Jesus	were going over to Jesus and putting their faith in him
21 The same came therefore to Philip, which was of Bethsaida of Galilee, and **desired** him, saying, Sir, we would see Jesus.	said to	said to	put this request to	begun to ask	(with a request)
24 Verily, verily, I say unto you, Except a **corn of wheat** fall into the ground and die, it abideth alone: but if it die, it bringeth forth much fruit.	grain of wheat	grain of wheat	wheat grain	grain of wheat	kernel of wheat
27 Now is my soul troubled; and what shall I say? Father, save me from this hour: **but for this cause** came I unto this hour.	No, for this purpose	No, it was for this	But it was for this very reason	But for this purpose	No, it was for this very reason
32 And I, **if I be** lifted up from the earth, will draw all men unto me.	when I am	when I am	when I am	if I be	when I am
33 This he said, **signifying** what death he should die.	to show	to indicate	indicated	to indicate	to show
35 Then Jesus said unto them, **Yet a little while** is the light with you. Walk while ye have the light, lest darkness come upon you: for he that walketh in darkness knoweth not whither he goeth.	for a little longer	still, but not for long	only a little longer now	For a little while longer	just a little while longer
36 While ye have light, **believe in the light,** that ye may be the **children** of light. These things spake Jesus, and departed, and did hide himself from them.	believe in the light/sons	trust to the light/men	believe in the light/sons	believe in the light/sons	Put your trust in the light/sons
40 He hath blinded their eyes, and hardened their heart; that they should not see with their eyes, nor understand with their heart, and **be converted, and I should** heal them.	turn for me to	turn to me to	turn to me for	be converted, and I	turn—and I would
41 These things said Esaias, **when** he saw his glory, and spake of him.	because	because	when	because	because
47 And if any man hear my words, and **believe not,** I judge him not: for I came not to judge the world, but to save the world.	does not come to them	pays no regard to them	does not keep them faithfully	does not keep them	does not keep them
49 For I have not spoken **of myself;** but the Father which sent me, he gave me a commandment, what I should say, and what I should speak.	on my own authority	on my own authority	from myself	on My own initiative	of my own accord
13 7 Jesus answered and said unto him, What I do thou knowest not now; but thou shalt **know hereafter.**	afterward . . . understand	understand . . . one day	later . . . understand	understand hereafter	later . . . understand
8 Peter saith unto him, Thou shalt never wash my feet. Jesus answered him, If I wash thee not, thou hast **no part with me.**	no part in me	not in fellowship with me	nothing in common with me	no part with Me	no part with me
10 Jesus saith to him, He that **is washed** needeth not **save** to wash his feet, but is clean **every whit:** and ye are clean, but not **all.**	has bathed/except/all over/every one of you	has bathed/(omits)/altogether/every one of you	has taken a bath/(omits)/all over/all of you	has bathed/only/completely/all of you	has had a bath/only/whole body/every one of you
19 Now I tell you before **it come,** that, when **it is come to pass,** ye may believe that I am he.	it takes place/it does take place	the event/it happens	it happens/it does happen	it comes to pass/it does occur	it happens/it does happen

KJV	RSV	NEB	JB	NAS	NIV
22 Then the disciples looked one on another, **doubting of whom he spake.**	uncertain of whom he spake	whom could he be speaking of	wondering which he meant	at a loss to know of which one He was speaking	at a loss to know which of them he meant
23 Now there was **leaning on Jesus' bosom** one of his disciples, whom Jesus loved.	lying close to the breast of Jesus	reclining close beside Jesus	reclining next to Jesus	reclining on Jesus' breast	reclining next to him
26 Jesus answered, He it is, to whom I shall give **a sop,** when I have dipped **it.** [ ] And when he had dipped the **sop,** he gave it to Judas Iscariot, the son of Simon.	this morsel / it / (no insert) / morsel	this piece of bread / it / in the dish / it	the piece of bread / piece of bread / in the dish / it	the morsel / it / morsel	piece of bread / it / in the dish / piece of bread
27 And after the sop Satan entered into him. Then said Jesus unto him, **That thou doest,** do quickly.	"What you are going to do	what you have to do	'What you are going to do	"What you do	"What you are about to do
29 For some of them thought, because Judas had **the bag,** that Jesus had said unto him, Buy those things that we have need of against the feast; or, that he should give something to the poor.	the money box	the common purse	the common fund	the money box	the money
14 1 Let not your heart be troubled: ye **believe in** God, **believe** also in me.	believe in/believe	Trust in/trust	Trust in/trust	believe in/believe	Trust in/trust
2 In my Father's house are many **mansions:** if it were not so, I would have told you. I go to prepare a place for you.	rooms	dwelling-places	rooms	dwelling places	rooms
8 Philip saith unto him, Lord, shew us the Father, and **it sufficeth us.**	we shall be satisfied	we ask no more	then we shall be satisfied	it is enough for us	that will be enough for us
16 And I will pray the Father, and he shall give you another **Comforter,** that he may abide with you for ever;	Counselor	Advocate	Advocate	Helper	Counselor
18 I will not leave you **comfortless:** I will come to you.	desolate	bereft	orphans	orphans	orphans
19 Yet a little while, and the world seeth me no more; but ye [ ] see me: because I live, ye shall live also.	will	will	will	will	will
23 Jesus answered and said unto him, If a man love me, he will keep my words: and my Father will love him, and we will come unto him, and make our **abode** with him.	home	dwelling	home	abode	home
25 These things have I spoken unto you, **being yet present** with you.	while I am still	while I am still here	while still	while abiding	while still
30 Hereafter I will not talk much with you: for the prince of this world cometh, and **hath nothing in me.**	has no power over me	has no rights over me	has no power over me	has nothing in Me	has no effect on me
15 1 I am the true vine, and my Father is the **husbandman.**	vinedresser	gardener	vinedresser	vinedresser	gardener
2 Every branch in me that beareth not fruit he taketh away: and every branch that beareth fruit, he **purgeth** it, that it may bring forth more fruit.	prunes	cleans	prunes	prunes	trims clean
8 Herein is my Father glorified, that ye bear much fruit; so **shall ye be** my disciples.	prove to be	so be	will be	prove to be	showing yourselves to be
16 Ye have not chosen me, but I have chosen you, and **ordained** you, that ye should go and bring forth fruit, and that your fruit should remain: that whatsoever ye shall ask of the Father in my name, he may give it you.	appointed	appointed	commissioned	appointed	(omits phrase "and ordained you")
22 If I had not come and spoken unto them, they **had not had** sin: but now they have no **cloak** for their sin.	would not have / excuse	would not be guilty of / excuse	would have been (blameless) / excuse	would not have / excuse	would not be guilty of / excuse

	KJV	RSV	NEB	JB	NAS	NIV
16	1 These things have I spoken unto you, **that ye should not be offended.**	to keep you from falling away	to guard you against the breakdown of your faith	so that your faith may not be shaken	that you may be kept from stumbling	so that you will not go astray
	8 And when he is come, **he will reprove the world of sin,** and of righteousness, and of judgment:	convince the world concerning sin	confute the world	show the world how wrong it was, about sin	convict the world concerning sin	prove the world wrong about sin
	14 He shall glorify me: for he shall **receive of mine,** and shall shew it unto you.	take what is mine	draw from what is mine	be taken from what is mine	take of Mine	(by) taking from what is mine
	21 A woman when she is in travail hath sorrow, because her hour is come: but as soon as she is delivered of the child, she remembereth no more the anguish, for joy that a **man** is born into the world.	child	man	man	child	child
	23 And in that day ye shall ask me nothing. Verily, verily, I say unto you, Whatsoever ye shall ask the Father **in my name,** he will give it you [ ].	(omits)/in my name	in my name/(no insert)	(omits)/in my name	(omits)/in My name	in my name/(no insert)
	25 These things have I spoken unto you **in proverbs:** but the time cometh, when I shall no more speak unto you in proverbs, but I shall shew you plainly of the Father.	in figures	using figures of speech	in metaphors	in figurative language	figuratively
	32 Behold, the hour cometh, yea, is now come, that ye shall be scattered, every man to his **own,** and shall leave me alone: and yet I am not alone, because the Father is with me.	home	home	own way	own home	own home
17	5 And now, O Father, glorify thou me with **thine own self** with the glory which I had with thee before the world was.	in thy own presence	in thy own presence	(omits)	together with Thyself	in your presence
	12 While I was with them in the world, I kept them in thy name: those that thou gavest me I have **kept,** and none of them is lost, but the **son of perdition;** that the scripture might be fulfilled.	guarded/son of perdition	kept . . . safe/man who must be lost	watched over/one who chose to be lost	guarded/son of perdition	kept . . . safe/child of hell
	15 I pray not that thou shouldest take them out of the world, but that thou shouldest keep them from the **evil.**	evil one	evil one	evil one	evil one	evil one
	19 And for their sakes I **sanctify** myself, that they also might be **sanctified** through the truth.	consecrate/consecrated	consecrate/consecrated	consecrate/consecrated	sanctify/sanctified	sanctify/sanctified
	23 I in them, and thou in me, that they may **be made perfect in one;** and that the world may know that thou hast sent me, and hast loved them, as thou hast loved me.	become perfectly one	be perfectly one	be so completely one	be perfected in unity	be brought to complete unity
	24 Father, I **will** that they also, whom thou hast given me, be with me where I am; that they may behold my glory, which thou hast given me: for thou lovedst me before the foundation of the world.	desire	desire	want	desire	want
	26 And I have **declared** unto them thy name, and **will declare it:** that the love wherewith thou hast loved me may be in them, and I in them.	made known/will make it known	made . . . known/will make it known	made . . . known/will continue to make it known	made . . . known/will make it known	revealed/will continue to make you known
18	3 Judas then, **having received a band of men and officers** from the chief priests and Pharisees, cometh thither with lanterns and torches and weapons.	procuring a band of soldiers and some officers	took a detachment of soldiers, and police	brought the cohort . . . together with a detachment of guards	having received the Roman cohort, and officers	guiding a detachment of soldiers and some officials
	6 As soon then as he had said unto them, I am he, they **went backward,** and fell to the ground.	drew back	drew back	moved back	drew back	drew back
	15 And Simon Peter followed Jesus, and so did another disciple: **that** disciple was known unto the high priest, and went	this/court	This/courtyard	This/palace	that/court	this/courtyard

KJV	RSV	NEB	JB	NAS	NIV
in with Jesus into the **palace** of the high priest.					
20 Jesus answered him, I spake openly to the world; I **ever** taught in the synagogue, and in the temple, whither the Jews always **resort;** and in secret have I said nothing.	always/come together	always/congregate	always/meet together	always/come together	always/come together
22 And when he had thus spoken, one of the officers which stood by **struck Jesus with the palm of his hand,** saying, Answerest thou the high priest so?	struck Jesus with his hand	struck him on the face	gave Jesus a slap in the face	gave Jesus a blow	struck him in the face
23 Jesus answered him, If I have spoken **evil,** bear witness of the evil: but **if well,** why smitest thou me?	wrongly/if I have spoken rightly	amiss/if I spoke well	wrong/if there is no offense	wrongly/if rightly	wrong/if I spoke the truth
24 **Now** Annas **had** sent him bound unto Caiaphas the high priest.	Annas then	So Annas	Then Annas	Annas therefore	Then Annas
28 Then led they Jesus from Caiaphas unto the **hall of judgment:** and it was early; and they themselves went not into the judgment hall, lest they should be defiled; but that they might eat the passover.	praetorium	Governor's headquarters	Praetorium	Praetorium	palace of the Roman governor
30 They answered and said unto him, If he were not a **malefactor,** we would not have delivered him up unto thee.	evildoer	criminal	criminal	evildoer	criminal
36 Jesus answered, My kingdom is not of this world: if my kingdom were of this world, then would my servants fight, that I should not be delivered to the Jews: but now **is** my kingdom **not from hence.**	is not from the world	comes from elsewhere	is not of this kind	is not of this realm	is from another place
37 Pilate therefore said unto him, Art thou a king then? Jesus answered, **Thou sayest that** I am a king. To this end was I born, and for this cause came I into the world, that I should bear witness unto the truth. Every one that is of the truth heareth my voice.	"You say that	(' "King" is your word)	"It is you who say it	"You say correctly	'You are right in saying
38 Pilate saith unto him, What is truth? And when he had said this, he went out again unto the Jews, and saith unto them, I find in him no **fault** at all.	crime	case	case	guilt	basis for a charge
40 Then cried they all again, saying, Not this man, but Barabbas. Now Barabbas **was a robber.**	was a robber	was a bandit	was a brigand	was a robber	had taken part in a rebellion
19 1 Then Pilate therefore took Jesus, and **scourged** him.	scourged	flogged	scourged	scourged	flogged
13 When Pilate therefore heard that saying, he brought Jesus forth, and sat down in the judgment seat in a place that is called the Pavement, but in the **Hebrew,** Gabbatha.	Hebrew	language of the Jews	Hebrew	Hebrew	Aramaic
23 Then the soldiers, when they had crucified Jesus, took his garments, and made four parts, to every soldier a part; and also his **coat:** now the **coat** was without seam, woven from the top throughout.	tunic/tunic	tunic/tunic	(omits)/undergarment	tunic/tunic	undergarment/ This garment
24 They said therefore among themselves, Let us not rend it, but cast lots for it, whose it shall be: that the scripture might be fulfilled, which saith, They **parted my raiment** among them, and for my **vesture** they did cast lots. These things therefore the soldiers did.	parted my garments/clothing	shared my garments/clothing	shared out my clothing/clothes	divided My outer garments / clothing	divided my garments/clothing
29 Now there was set a **vessel** full of vinegar and they filled a sponge with	bowl/hyssop	jar/javelin	jar/hyssop stick	jar/branch of hyssop	jar/stalk of the hyssop plant

KJV	RSV	NEB	JB	NAS	NIV
vinegar, and put it upon **hyssop,** and put it to his mouth.					
41 Now in the place where he was crucified there was a garden; and in the garden a new **sepulchre,** wherein was never man yet laid.	tomb	tomb	tomb	tomb	tomb
20 17 Jesus saith unto her, **Touch me not;** for I am not yet ascended to my Father: but go to my brethren, and say unto them, I ascend unto my Father, and your Father; and to my God, and your God.	"Do not hold me	'Do not cling to me	"Do not cling to me	"Stop clinging to Me	"Do not hold on to me
23 Whose soever sins ye **remit,** they are **remitted** unto them; and whose soever sins ye retain, they are retained.	forgive/forgiven	forgive/forgiven	forgive/forgiven	forgive/forgiven	forgive/forgiven
21 1 After these things Jesus **shewed** himself again to the disciples at the sea of Tiberias; and on this wise shewed he himself.	revealed	showed	showed	manifested	appeared
5 Then Jesus saith unto them, **Children,** have ye any **meat?** They answered him, No.	Children/fish	Friends/caught anything	friends/caught anything	Children/fish	friends/(caught any) fish
7 Therefore that disciple whom Jesus loved saith unto Peter, It is the Lord. Now when Simon Peter heard that it was the Lord, he **girt his fisher's coat unto him,** (for he **was naked,**) and did cast himself into the sea.	put on his clothes/stripped for work	wrapped his coat about him/had stripped	wrapped his cloak around him/had practically nothing on	put his outer garment on/was stripped for work	wrapped his outer garment around him/had taken it off
8 And the other disciples came in **a little ship;** (for they were not far from land, but as it were **two hundred cubits,**) dragging the net with fishes.	the boat/a hundred yards	the boat/a hundred yards	the boat/a hundred yards	the little boat/one hundred yards	the boat/hundred yards
11 Simon Peter went up, and drew the net to land full of great fishes, an hundred and fifty and three: and **for all** there were so many, yet was not the net **broken.**	although/torn	yet/torn	in spite of/broken	although/torn	even with/torn
12 Jesus saith unto them, Come **and dine.** And none of the disciples **durst** ask him, Who art thou? knowing that it was the Lord.	have breakfast/dared	have breakfast/dared	have breakfast/was bold enough	have breakfast/ventured	have breakfast/dared
15 **So when they had dined,** Jesus saith to Simon Peter, Simon, son of Jonas, lovest thou me more than these? He saith unto him, Yea, Lord; thou knowest that I love thee. He saith unto him, Feed my lambs.	When they had finished breakfast	After breakfast	After the meal	So when they had finished breakfast	When they had finished eating
16 He saith to him again the second time, Simon, son of Jonas, lovest thou me? He saith unto him, Yea, Lord; thou knowest that I love thee. He saith unto him, **Feed** my sheep.	Tend	tend	Look after	Shepherd	Take care of
18 Verily, verily, I say unto thee, When thou wast young, thou **girdedst** thyself, and walkedst whither thou wouldest: but when thou shalt be old, thou shalt stretch forth thy hands, and another shall **gird** thee, and **carry** thee whither thou wouldest not.	girded/gird/carry	fastened your belt/bind/carry	put on your own belt/put a belt around/take	used to gird/gird/bring	dressed/dress/lead
21 Peter seeing him saith to Jesus, Lord, and what **shall this man do?**	what about this man	what will happen to him	"What about him	what about this man	what about him

Acts

KJV	RSV	NEB	JB	NAS	NIV
1 1 The **former treatise** have I made, O	first book	first part of my	earlier work	first account	former book

KJV	RSV	NEB	JB	NAS	NIV
Theophilus, of all that Jesus began both to do and teach,		work			
2 Until the day in which he was taken up, after that he through the Holy Ghost had given **commandments** unto the apostles whom he had chosen:	commandments	instructions	instructions	orders	instructions
4 And, **being assembled together with them,** commanded them that they should not depart from Jerusalem, but wait for the promise of the Father, which, saith he, ye have heard of me.	while staying with them	While he was in their company	When he had been at table with them	gathering them together	while he was eating with them
14 These all continued with one accord in **prayer and supplication,** with the women, and Mary the mother of Jesus, and with his brethren.	prayer	prayer	prayer	prayer	prayer
15 And in those days Peter stood up in the midst of the **disciples,** and said, (the number of names together were about an hundred and twenty,)	brethren	brotherhood	brothers	brethren	believers
18 Now this man purchased a field with the reward of iniquity; and falling headlong, he burst **asunder in the midst,** and all his **bowels** gushed out.	open in the middle/bowels	open/entrails	open/entrails	open in the middle/bowels	open/intestines
19 And it was known unto all the dwellers at Jerusalem; insomuch as that field is called in their **proper tongue,** Aceldama, that is to say, The field of blood.	language	own language	language	own language	language
20 For it is written in the book of Psalms, Let his habitation be desolate, and let no man dwell therein: and his **bishopric** let another take.	office	charge	office	office	place of leadership
21 Wherefore of these men which have **companied with us** all the time that the Lord Jesus went in and out among us,	accompanied us	bore us company	been with us	accompanied us	been with us
26 And they **gave forth** their lots; and the lot fell upon Matthias; and he was numbered with the eleven apostles.	cast	drew	drew	drew	drew
2 1 And when the day of Pentecost was fully come, they were all **with one accord** in one place.	together	together	met	together	together
3 And there appeared unto them **cloven tongues** like as of fire, and it sat upon each of them.	tongues . . . distributed	tongues . . . dispersed	tongues . . . separated	tongues . . . distributing	tongues . . . separated
6 Now when this was **noised abroad,** the multitude came together, and were **confounded,** because that every man heard them speak in his own language.	at this sound/bewildered	at this sound/bewildered	at this sound/bewildered	when this sound occurred / bewildered	When they heard this sound / (came together) in bewilderment
12 And they were all amazed, and were **in doubt,** saying one to another, What meaneth this?	perplexed	perplexed	unable to explain it	great perplexity	perplexed
15 For these are not drunken, as ye suppose, seeing it is but the **third hour of the day.**	third hour of the day	nine in the morning	third hour of the day	third hour of the day	nine in the morning
23 Him, being delivered by the **determinate counsel** and foreknowledge of God, ye have taken, and by wicked hands have crucified and slain:	definite plan	deliberate will	deliberate intention	predetermined plan	set purpose
24 Whom God hath raised up, having loosed the pains of death: because it was not possible that **he should be holden** of it.	for him to be held	should keep him	for him to be held	for Him to be held	to keep its hold on him
27 Because thou wilt not leave **my soul in hell,** neither wilt thou suffer thine Holy One to see **corruption.**	my soul to Hades/corruption	my soul to death/corruption	my soul to Hades/corruption	my soul to Hades/decay	me to the grave/decay

KJV	RSV	NEB	JB	NAS	NIV
30 Therefore being a prophet, and knowing that God had sworn with an oath to him, that of the **fruit of his loins, according to the flesh, he would raise up Christ to sit** on his throne;	would set one of his descendants	one of his own direct descendants should sit	to make one of his descendants succeed him	to seat one of his descendants	would place one of his descendants
37 Now when they heard this, they were **pricked in** their heart, and said unto Peter and to the rest of the apostles, Men and brethren, what shall we do?	cut to	cut to	cut to	pierced to	cut to
40 And with many other words did he testify and exhort, saying, Save yourselves from this **untoward** generation.	crooked	crooked	perverse	perverse	wicked
42 And they **continued stedfastly** in the apostles' doctrine and fellowship, and in breaking of bread, and in prayers.	devoted themselves	met constantly	remained faithful	were continually devoting themselves	devoted themselves
45 And sold their possessions and goods, and **parted them** to all men, as every man had need.	distributed them	would . . . make a general distribution	shared out the proceeds	were sharing them	gave
46 And they, continuing daily with one accord in the temple, and breaking bread **from house to house, did eat their meat** with gladness and **singleness of heart.**	in their homes/partook of food/generous hearts	in private homes/shared their meals/unaffected joy	in their homes/shared their food/generously	from house to house/were taking their meals together/sincerity of heart	in their homes/ate together/sincere hearts
3 12 And when Peter saw it, he **answered unto** the people, Ye men of Israel, why marvel ye at this? or why look ye so earnestly on us, as though by our own power or holiness we had made this man to walk?	addressed	met . . . with these words	addressed	replied to	said to
13 The God of Abraham, and of Isaac, and of Jacob, the God of our fathers, hath glorified his Son Jesus; whom ye delivered up, and denied him in the presence of Pilate, when he was **determined to** let him go.	decided to	decided to	decided	decided to	decided to
15 And killed the **Prince of** life, whom God hath raised from the dead; whereof we are witnesses.	Author of	him who has led the way to	prince of	Prince of	author of
17 And now, brethren, I **wot** that through ignorance ye did it, as did also your rulers.	know	know quite well	know	know	know
20 And he shall send Jesus Christ, which before was **preached** unto you:	appointed	appointed	predestined	appointed	appointed
22 For Moses truly said unto the fathers, A prophet shall the Lord your God raise up unto you **of** your brethren, like unto me; him shall ye hear in all things whatsoever he shall say unto you.	from	from among	from among	from	from among
26 Unto you first God, having raised up his **Son Jesus,** sent him [ ] to bless you, in turning away every one of you from his iniquities.	servant/first	Servant/first	servant/(no insert)	Servant/(no insert)	servant/first
4 2 Being **grieved** that they taught the people, and preached through Jesus the resurrection from the dead.	annoyed	exasperated	extremely annoyed	greatly disturbed	greatly disturbed
3 And they laid hands on them, and put them in **hold** unto the next day: for it was now eventide.	custody	prison	held (them)	jail	jail
5 And it came to pass on the morrow, that their rulers, and elders, and scribes [ ],	were gathered together in Jerusalem	met in Jerusalem	had a meeting in Jerusalem	were gathered together in Jerusalem	met in Jerusalem
6 And Annas the high priest, and Caiaphas, and John, and Alexander, and as many as were of the kindred of the high					

KJV	RSV	NEB	JB	NAS	NIV
priest, **were gathered together at Jerusalem.**	(omits; see vs. 5)	(omits; see vs. 5)	(omits; see vs. 5)	(omits; see vs. 5)	(omits; see vs. 5)
9 If we this day be examined of the good deed done to the **impotent man,** by what means he is made whole;	cripple	sick man	cripple	sick man	cripple
13 Now when they saw the boldness of Peter and John, and perceived that they were **unlearned and ignorant men,** they marvelled; and they **took knowledge of** them, that they had been with Jesus.	uneducated, common men/ recognized	untrained laymen/recognized	uneducated laymen/recognized	uneducated and untrained men/began to recognize	unschooled, ordinary men/took note
17 But that it spread no further among the people, let us **straitly threaten** them, that they speak henceforth to no man in this name.	warn	caution	caution	warn	warn
27 For of a truth against thy holy **child** Jesus, whom thou hast anointed, both Herod, and Pontius Pilate, with the Gentiles, and the people of Israel, were gathered together,	servant	servant	servant	servant	servant
32 And the multitude of them that believed were of one heart and of one soul: neither said any of them that aught of the things which he possessed was his own; but they had all things **common.**	in common	in common	in common	common property	shared
36 And Joses, who by the apostles was surnamed Barnabas, (which is, being interpreted, The son of **consolation,**) a Levite, and of the country of Cyprus,	encouragement	Exhortation	encouragement	Encouragement	Encouragement
5 2 And kept back part of the price, **his wife also being privy to it,** and brought a certain part, and laid it at the apostles' feet.	with his wife's knowledge	With the full knowledge of his wife	with his wife's connivance	with his wife's full knowledge	With his wife's full knowledge
6 And the young men arose, **wound him up,** and carried him out, and buried him.	wrapped him up	covered his body	wrapped the body in a sheet	covered him up	wrapped up his body
8 And Peter **answered unto her,** Tell me whether ye sold the land for so much? And she said, Yea, for so much.	said to her	turned to her and said	challenged her	responded to her	asked her
13 And of the rest **durst** no man join himself to them: **but the people magnified them.**	dared/but the people held them in high honor	ventured to/But people in general spoke highly of them	ever dared/but the people were loud in their praise	dared/however, the people held them in high esteem	dared/even though they were highly regarded by the people
17 Then the high priest rose up, and all they that were with him, (which is the sect of the Sadducees,) and were filled with **indignation,**	jealousy	jealousy	jealousy	jealousy	jealousy
24 Now when the high priest and the captain of the temple and the chief priests heard these things, they **doubted of them whereunto this would grow.**	were much perplexed about them, wondering what this would come to	were wondering what could have become of them	wondered what this could mean	were greatly perplexed about them as to what would come of this	were puzzled, wondering what would become of this
33 When they heard that, they were **cut to the heart,** and took counsel to slay them.	enraged	touched . . . on the raw	so infuriated (them)	cut to the quick	furious
34 Then stood there up one in the council, a Pharisee named Gamaliel, a **doctor** of the law, **had in reputation** among all the people, and commanded to put the apostles forth a little **space;**	teacher/held in honor/while	teacher/held in high regard/while	doctor/respected/time	teacher/respected/time	teacher/honored/while
6 1 And in those days, when the number of the disciples was multiplied, there arose a murmuring of the **Grecians** against the Hebrews, because their widows were neglected in the daily **ministration.**	Hellenists/distribution	those of them who spoke Greek/distribution	Hellenists/distribution	Hellenistic Jews/serving of food	Grecian Jews/distribution of food

KJV	RSV	NEB	JB	NAS	NIV
2 Then the twelve called the multitude of the disciples unto them, and said, It is not **reason** that we should leave the word of God, and serve tables.	right	(would be) a grave mistake	right	desirable	right
3 Wherefore, brethren, look ye out among you seven men **of honest report,** full of the Holy Ghost and wisdom, whom we may appoint over this business.	of good repute	of good reputation	of good reputation	of good reputation	(omits)
9 Then there arose certain of the synagogue, which is called the synagogue of the **Libertines,** and Cyrenians, and Alexandrians, and of them of Cilicia and of Asia, disputing with Stephen.	Freedmen	Freedmen	Freedmen	Freedmen	Freedmen
11 Then they **suborned** men, which said, We have heard him speak blasphemous words against Moses, and against God.	secretly instigated	put up	procured	secretly induced	secretly persuaded
7 5 And he gave him none inheritance in it, no, not so much as to set his foot on: yet he promised that he would give it to him for a possession, and to his **seed** after him, when as yet he had no child.	posterity	descendants	descendants	offspring	descendants
6 And God spake on this wise, That his **seed** should sojourn in a strange land; and that they should bring them into bondage, and **entreat** them evil four hundred years.	posterity/ill-treat	descendants/(held in) oppression	descendants/oppressed	offspring/mistreated	descendants/mistreated
11 Now there came a **dearth** over all the land of Egypt and Chanaan, and great affliction: and our fathers found **no sustenance.**	famine/no food	famine/nothing to eat	famine/nothing to eat	famine/no food	famine/food
19 The same **dealt subtilly** with our kindred, and evil entreated our fathers, so that they cast out their young children, to the end they might not live.	dealt craftily	made a crafty attack	exploited	took shrewd advantage	dealt treacherously
20 In which time Moses was born, and was **exceeding fair,** and **nourished** up in his father's house three months:	beautiful before God/brought	a fine child, and pleasing to God/nursed	a fine child and favored by God/looked after	lovely in the sight of God/nurtured	no ordinary child/cared for
21 And when he was **cast out,** Pharaoh's daughter **took him up, and nourished him** for her own son.	exposed/adopted him and brought him up	exposed/adopted him and brought him up	exposed/adopted him and brought him up	took him away, and nurtured him	took him and brought him up
26 And the next day he shewed himself unto them as they **strove,** and **would have set them at one** again, saying, Sirs, ye are brethren; why do ye wrong one to another?	quarreling/would have reconciled them	fighting/tried to bring them to make up their quarrel	fighting/tried to reconcile them	fighting together/tried to reconcile them in peace	fighting/tried to reconcile them
38 This is he, that was in **the church** in the wilderness with the angel which spake to him in the mount Sina, and with our fathers: who received the **lively** oracles to give unto us:	the congregation/living	(when they were assembled)/living	the assembly/(words) of life	the congregation/living	the congregation/living
40 Saying unto Aaron, Make us gods to go before us: for as for this Moses, which brought us out of the land of Egypt, we **wot** not what is become of him.	do . . . know	do . . . know	do . . . understand	do . . . know	do(n't) know
45 Which also our fathers that came after brought **in with Jesus** into the **possession of the Gentiles,** whom God drave out before the face of our fathers, unto the days of David;	in with Joshua/when they dispossessed the nations	with Joshua/when they dispossessed the nations	until Joshua/country we had conquered from the nations	in with Joshua/upon dispossessing the nations	under Joshua/when they took the land from the nations
51 Ye **stiffnecked** and uncircumcised in heart and ears, ye do always resist the Holy Ghost: as your fathers did, so do ye.	stiff-necked	stubborn	stubborn	stiff-necked	stubborn
52 Which of the prophets have not your fathers persecuted? and they have slain them which **shewed before** of the coming	announced	foretold	foretold	previously	predicted

KJV	RSV	NEB	JB	NAS	NIV
of the Just One; of whom ye have been now the betrayers and murderers:	beforehand			announced	
53 Who have received the law **by the disposition of angels,** and have not kept it.	as delivered by angels	as God's angels gave it to you	brought to you by angels	as ordained by angels	that was put into effect through angels
54 When they heard these things, they were **cut to the heart,** and they gnashed **on him** with their teeth.	enraged/against him	touched . . . on the raw/with fury	infuriated/at him	cut to the quick/at him	furious/at him
8 3 As for Saul, he made havoc of the church, entering into every house, and **haling** men and women committed them to prison.	dragged off	seizing	arresting	dragging off	dragged off
9 But there was a certain man, called Simon, which beforetime in the same city **used sorcery,** and **bewitched** the people of Samaria, giving out that himself was some great one:	practiced magic/amazed	(with his magical arts)/swept . . . off their feet	practiced magic arts/astounded	was practicing magic/astonishing	had practiced sorcery/amazed
10 To whom they all gave heed, from the least to the greatest, saying, This man is the **great power** of God.	power of God which is called Great	power of God which is called "The Great Power"	divine power that is called Great	what is called the Great Power of God	divine power known as the Great Power
11 And to him they had regard, because that **of long time** he had **bewitched** them with **sorceries.**	for a long time/amazed/magic	for so long/(they . . .) carried away/magic	of the long time/spent working on/magic	for a long time/astonished/magic arts	for a long time/amazed/magic
33 In his humiliation his **judgment** was taken away: and who shall **declare his generation?** for his life is taken from the earth.	justice/describe his generation	redress/speak of his posterity	(no one to defend him) talk about his descendants	judgment/relate His generation	justice/speak of his descendants
37 And Philip said, If thou believest with all thine heart, thou mayest. And he answered and said, I believe that Jesus Christ is the Son of God.	(omits)	(omits)	(omits)	(And Philip said, "If you believe with all your heart, you may." And he answered and said, "I believe that Jesus Christ is the Son of God.")	(omits)
9 2 And desired of him letters to Damascus to the synagogues, that if he found **any of this way,** whether they were men or women, he might bring them bound unto Jerusalem.	any belonging to the Way	anyone . . . who followed the new way	any followers of the Way	any belonging to the Way	any . . . who belonged to the Way
5 And he said, Who art thou, Lord? And the Lord said, I am Jesus whom thou persecutest: **it is hard for thee to kick against the pricks.**	(omits)	(omits)	(omits)	(omits)	(omits)
6 **And he trembling and astonished said, Lord, what wilt thou have me to do? And the Lord said unto him,** Arise, and go into the city, and it shall be told thee what thou must do.	(omits)	(omits)	(omits)	(omits)	(omits)
8 And Saul arose from the earth; and when his eyes were opened, he **saw no man:** but they led him by the hand, and brought him into Damascus.	could see nothing	could not see	could see nothing at all	could see nothing	could see nothing
15 But the Lord said unto him, Go thy way: for he is a chosen **vessel** unto me, to bear my name before the Gentiles, and kings, and the children of Israel:	instrument	instrument	instrument	instrument	instrument
22 But Saul increased the more in strength, and confounded the Jews which dwelt at Damascus, proving that **this is very Christ.**	Jesus was the Christ	Jesus was the Messiah	Jesus was the Christ	Jesus is the Christ	Jesus is the Christ
29 And he spake boldly in the name of the Lord Jesus, and disputed against the **Grecians:** but they **went about** to slay him.	Hellenists/were seeking	Greek-speaking Jews/planned	Hellenists/became determined	Hellenistic Jews/were attempting	Grecian Jews/tried

KJV	RSV	NEB	JB	NAS	NIV
10 1 There was a certain man in Caesarea called Cornelius, a centurion of the band called the Italian **band,**	Cohort	Cohort	cohort	cohort	Regiment
3 He saw in a vision **evidently** about the ninth hour of the day an angel of God coming in to him, and saying unto him, Cornelius.	clearly	clearly	distinctly	clearly	distinctly
11 And saw heaven opened, and **a certain vessel** descending unto him, **as it had been** a great sheet knit at the four corners, and let down to the earth:	something/like	thing/looked like	something/like	certain object/like	something/like
17 Now while Peter **doubted in himself** what this vision which he had seen should mean, behold, the men which were sent from Cornelius had made inquiry for Simon's house, and stood before the gate,	was inwardly perplexed as to	was still puzzling over	was still worrying over	was greatly perplexed in mind as to	was wondering about
20 Arise therefore, and get thee down, and go with them, **doubting nothing:** for I have sent them.	without hesitation	without any misgiving	(do not hesitate)	without misgivings	(Do not hesitate)
22 And they said, Cornelius the centurion, a just man, and one that feareth God, and **of good report** among all the nation of the Jews, was warned from God by an holy angel to send for thee into his house, and to hear words of thee.	well spoken of	acknowledged as such	highly regarded	well spoken of	respected
29 Therefore came I unto you without **gainsaying,** as soon as I was sent for: I ask therefore for what intent ye have sent for me?	objection	demur	objection	objection	objection
31 And said, Cornelius, thy prayer is heard, and thine alms **are had in remembrance** in the sight of God.	have been remembered	remembered	have been accepted as a sacrifice	have been remembered	has . . . remembered
33 Immediately therefore I sent to thee; and **thou hast well done that thou art** come. Now therefore are we all here present before God, to hear all things that are commanded thee of God.	you have been kind enough to	it was kind of you to	you have been kind enough to	you have been kind enough to	it was good of you to
34 Then Peter opened his mouth, and said, Of a truth I perceive that God is **no respecter of persons:**	shows no partiality	has no favorites	does not have favorites	is not one to show partiality	does not show favoritism
42 And he commanded us to preach unto the people, and to testify that it is he which was ordained of God to be the Judge of **quick** and dead.	living	living	living	alive	living
43 To him give all the prophets witness, that through his name whosoever believeth in him shall receive **remission** of sins.	forgiveness	forgiveness	(will have their sins) forgiven	forgiveness	forgiveness
48 And he commanded them to be baptized in the name of the Lord. Then prayed they him to **tarry certain days.**	remain for some days	stay on with them for a while	stay on for some days	stay on for a few days	stay with them for a few days
11 4 But Peter **rehearsed the matter from the beginning, and expounded it by order unto them,** saying,	began and explained to them in order	began by laying before them the facts as they had happened	in reply gave them the details point by point	began speaking and proceeded to explain to them in orderly sequence	began and explained everything to them precisely as it happened
12 And the Spirit bade me go with them, **nothing doubting.** Moreover these six brethren accompanied me, and we entered into the man's house:	making no distinction	(omits)	(omits)	without misgivings	(to have no hesitation about going with them)
20 And some of them were men of Cyprus and Cyrene, which, when they were come to Antioch, spake unto the **Grecians,** preaching the Lord Jesus.	Greeks	Gentiles	Greeks	Greeks	Greeks

	KJV	RSV	NEB	JB	NAS	NIV
	23 Who, when he came, and had seen the grace of God, was glad, and exhorted them all, that with **purpose of heart** they would **cleave unto** the Lord.	steadfast purpose/remain faithful to	resolute hearts/hold fast to	heartfelt devotion/remain faithful to	resolute heart/remain true to	all their hearts, remain true to
	26 And when he had found him, he brought him unto Antioch. And it came to pass, that a whole year they **assembled themselves** with the church, and taught much people. And the disciples were called Christians first in Antioch.	met	lived in fellowship	lived together	met with	met with
	28 And there stood up one of them named Agabus, and signified by the Spirit that there should be great **dearth** throughout all the world: which came to pass in the days of Claudius **Caesar.**	famine/(omits)	famine/(omits)	famine/(omits)	famine/(omits)	famine/(omits)
12	1 Now about that time Herod the king **stretched forth his hands to vex** certain of the church.	laid violent hands upon	attacked	started persecuting	laid hands on . . . in order to mistreat them	arrested . . . intending to persecute them
	4 And when he had apprehended him, he put him in prison, and delivered him to four **quaternions of soldiers** to keep him; intending **after Easter** to bring him forth to the people.	squads of soldiers/after the Passover	squads of four men each/after Passover	squads of four soldiers/after the end of the Passover	squads of soldiers/after the Passover	squads of four soldiers each/after the Passover
	10 When they were past the first and the second **ward,** they came unto the iron gate that leadeth unto the city; which opened to them of his own accord: and they went out, and passed on through one street; and forthwith the angel departed from him.	guard	guard-post	guard posts	guard	guards
	13 And as Peter knocked at the door of the gate, a damsel came to **hearken,** named Rhoda.	answer	answer	answer	answer	answer
	15 And they said unto her, Thou art mad. But she **constantly affirmed** that it was even so. Then said they, It is his angel.	insisted	insisted	insisted	kept insisting	kept insisting
	21 And upon a **set day** Herod, arrayed in royal apparel, sat upon his throne, and made an oration unto them.	appointed day	appointed day	day . . . fixed	appointed day	appointed day
13	7 Which was with the **deputy of the country,** Sergius Paulus, a prudent man; who called for Barnabas and Saul, and desired to hear the word of God.	proconsul	Governor	proconsul	proconsul	proconsul
	13 Now when Paul and his company **loosed** from Paphos, they came to Perga in Pamphylia: and John departing from them returned to Jerusalem.	set sail	went by sea	went by sea	put out to sea	sailed
	16 Then Paul stood up, and beckoning with his hand said, Men of Israel, and ye that fear God, **give audience.**	listen	listen to me	listen	listen	listen to me
	17 The God of this people of Israel chose our fathers, and exalted the people when they dwelt as strangers in the land of Egypt, and with an **high arm** brought he them out of it.	uplifted arm	arm outstretched	divine power	uplifted arm	mighty power
	18 And about the time of forty years **suffered he their manners** in the wilderness.	he bore with them	he bore with their conduct	took care of them	He put up with them	endured their conduct
	36 For David, after he had served his own generation by the will of God, **fell on sleep,** and was **laid unto** his fathers, and saw corruption:	fell asleep/laid with	died/gathered to	died/buried with	fell asleep/laid among	fell asleep/buried with
	49 And the word of the Lord **was published** throughout all the region.	spread	spread	spread	spread	spread

	KJV	RSV	NEB	JB	NAS	NIV
14	2 But the unbelieving Jews stirred up the Gentiles, and **made their minds evil affected** against the brethren.	poisoned their minds	poisoned their minds	poisoned their minds	embittered them	poisoned their minds
	8 And there sat a certain man at Lystra, **impotent in his feet,** being a cripple from his mother's womb, who never had walked:	who could not use his feet	(omits)	(omits)	without strength in his feet	crippled in his feet
	19 And there came thither certain Jews from Antioch and Iconium, who persuaded the people, and, having stoned Paul, **drew** him out of the city, supposing he had been dead.	dragged	dragged	dragged	dragged	dragged
	26 And thence sailed to Antioch, from whence they had been **recommended** to the grace of God for the work which they fulfilled.	where they had been commended	where they had originally been commended	where they had originally been commended	from which they had been commended	where they had been committed
	27 And when they were come, and had gathered the church together, they **rehearsed** all that God had done with them, and how he had opened the door of faith unto the Gentiles.	declared	reported	gave an account	began to report	reported
15	3 And being brought on their way by the **church,** they passed through Phenice and Samaria, declaring the conversion of the Gentiles: and they caused great joy unto all the brethren.	church	congregation	church	church	church
	10 Now therefore why **tempt** ye God, to put a yoke upon the neck of the disciples, which neither our fathers nor we were able to bear?	make trial of	provoke	provoke	put . . . to test	try to test
	19 Wherefore my **sentence** is, that we trouble not them, which from among the Gentiles are turned to God:	judgment	judgment	rule	judgment	judgment
	30 So when they **were dismissed,** they came to Antioch: and when they had gathered the multitude together, they delivered the epistle:	were sent off	were sent off	left	were sent away	were sent off
	37 And Barnabas **determined** to take with them John, whose surname was Mark.	wanted	wanted	suggested	was desirous of	wanted
16	7 After they were come to Mysia, they **assayed** to go into Bithynia: but the Spirit [ ] **suffered them not.**	attempted/of Jesus/did not allow them	tried/of Jesus/would not allow them	thought/of Jesus/would not allow them	were trying/of Jesus/did not permit them	tried/of Jesus/would not allow them to
	10 And after he had seen the vision, immediately we endeavoured to go into Macedonia, **assuredly gathering** that the Lord had called us for to preach the gospel unto them.	concluding	concluding	convinced	concluding	concluding
	11 Therefore **loosing** from Troas, we came with a straight course to Samothracia, and the next day to Neapolis;	Setting sail	sailed	Sailing	putting out to sea	put out to sea
	15 And when she was baptized, and her household, she besought us, saying, If ye have judged me to be faithful to the Lord, come into my house, and abide there. And she **constrained** us.	prevailed upon us	insisted on our going	would take no refusal	prevailed upon us	persuaded us
	35 And when it was day, the magistrates sent the **sergeants,** saying, Let those men go.	police	officers	officers	policemen	officers
	37 But Paul said unto them, They have beaten us openly uncondemned, being Romans, and have cast us into prison; and now do they thrust us out **privily?** nay verily; but let them come themselves and fetch us out.	secretly	privately	on the quiet	secretly	quietly
17	3 **Opening and alleging,** that Christ	explaining and	expounded and	explaining and	explaining and	explaining and

KJV	RSV	NEB	JB	NAS	NIV
must needs have suffered, and risen again from the dead; and that this Jesus, whom I preach unto you, is Christ.	proving	applied	proving	giving evidence	proving
4 And some of them believed, and **consorted with** Paul and Silas; and of the devout Greeks a great multitude, and of the chief women not a few.	joined	joined	joined	joined	joined
5 But the Jews which believed not, moved with envy, took unto them certain **lewd fellows of the baser sort,** and gathered a company, and set all the city on an uproar, and assaulted the house of Jason, and sought to bring them out to the people.	wicked fellows of the rabble	low fellows from the dregs of the populace	gang from the market place	wicked men from the market place	bad characters from the market-place
9 And when they had **taken security** of Jason, and of the other, they let them go.	taken security of	bound over	made . . . give security	had received a pledge	made . . . post bond
14 And then immediately the brethren sent away Paul to go as it were **to the sea:** but Silas and Timotheus abode there still.	to the sea	to the sea	as far as the coast	as far as the sea	to the coast
17 Therefore **disputed** he in the synagogue with the Jews, and with the devout persons, and in the market daily with them that met with him.	argued	argued	held debates	was reasoning	reasoned
22 Then Paul stood in the midst of **Mars' hill,** and said, Ye men of Athens, I perceive that in all things ye are too superstitious.	the Areopagus	the Court of Areopagus	whole Council of the Areopagus	the Areopagus	the Areopagus
23 For as I passed by, and beheld your **devotions,** I found an altar with this inscription, To the Unknown God. Whom therefore ye ignorantly worship, him declare I unto you.	objects of your worship	objects of your worship	sacred monuments	objects of your worship	objects of worship
26 And hath made of one blood all nations of men for to dwell on all the face of the earth, and hath determined **the times before appointed,** and the bounds of their habitation;	allotted periods	the epochs of their history	how long each nation should flourish	their appointed times	the times set for them
30 And the times of this ignorance God **winked at;** but now commandeth all men everywhere to repent:	overlooked	has overlooked	overlooked	overlooked	overlooked
34 Howbeit certain men **clave unto** him, and believed: among the which was Dionysius the Areopagite, and a woman named Damaris, and others with them.	joined	joined	attached themselves to	joined	became followers of
18 3 And because he was of the same craft, he abode with them, and **wrought:** for by their occupation they were tentmakers.	they worked	carried on business together	they worked together	they were working	worked with them
5 And when Silas and Timotheus were come from Macedonia, Paul was **pressed in the spirit,** and testified to the Jews that Jesus was Christ.	occupied with preaching	devoted himself entirely to preaching	devoted all his time to preaching	began devoting himself completely to the word	devoted himself exclusively to preaching
7 And he departed thence, and entered into a certain man's house, named **Justus,** one that worshipped God, whose house **joined hard** to the synagogue.	Titius Justus/was next door	Titius Justus/next door	Justus/next door	Titius Justus, was next to	Titius Justus/next door
10 For I am with thee, and no man shall **set on thee** to hurt thee: for I have much people in this city.	attack you	attempt	attempt	attack you	attack
12 And when Gallio was the **deputy** of Achaia, the Jews made insurrection with one accord against Paul, and brought him to the **judgment seat,**	proconsul/tribunal	proconsul/court	proconsul/tribunal	proconsul/judgment seat	proconsul/court
14 And when Paul was now about to open his mouth, Gallio said unto the Jews, If it were a matter of wrong or **wicked lewdness,** O ye Jews, reason would that I should bear with you:	vicious crime	grave misdemeanor	crime	vicious crime	serious crime

KJV	RSV	NEB	JB	NAS	NIV
16 And he **drave** them from the **judgment seat.**	drove/tribunal	ejected/court	sent/court	drove . . . away/judgment seat	ejected/court
28 For he **mightily convinced** the Jews, and that publicly, shewing by the scriptures that Jesus was Christ.	powerfully confuted	strenuously confuted	(by the energetic way he refuted)	powerfully refuted	vigorously refuted
19 1 And it came to pass, that, while Apollos was at Corinth, Paul having passed through the **upper coasts** came to Ephesus: and finding certain disciples,	upper country	inland regions	overland	upper country	interior
8 And he went into the synagogue, and spake boldly for the space of three months, **disputing and persuading** the things concerning the kingdom of God.	arguing and pleading	(using) argument and persuasion	argued persuasively	reasoning and persuading	arguing persuasively
9 But when **divers were hardened,** and believed not, but spake evil of that way before the multitude, he departed from them, and separated the disciples, disputing daily in the school of one Tyrannus.	some were stubborn	some proved obdurate	attitude of some of the congregation hardened	some were becoming hardened	some of them became obdurate
10 And this continued **by the space** of two years; so that all they which dwelt in Asia heard the word of the Lord Jesus, both Jews and Greeks.	for	for	for	for	for
11 And God wrought **special** miracles by the hands of Paul:	extraordinary	singular	remarkable	extraordinary	extraordinary
13 Then certain of the **vagabond** Jews, exorcists, **took upon them to call over them** which had evil spirits the name of the Lord Jesus, saying, We adjure you by Jesus whom Paul preacheth.	itinerant/undertook to pronounce . . . over those	strolling/tried their hands at using . . . on those	itinerant/tried pronouncing . . . over people who	who went from place to place/attempted to name over those	(Some Jews) who went around/tried to invoke . . . over those
19 Many of them also which used **curious arts** brought their books together, and burned them before all men: and they counted the price of them, and found it fifty thousand pieces of silver.	magic arts	magic	magic	magic	sorcery
23 And the same time there arose no small stir about **that way.**	the Way	the Christian movement	the Way	the Way	the Way
32 Some therefore cried one thing, and some another: for the assembly was confused; and **the more part** knew not wherefore they were come together.	most of them	most of them	most of them	majority	Most of the people
38 Wherefore if Demetrius, and the craftsmen which are with him, have a matter against any man, the **law** is open, and there are **deputies:** let them **implead** one another.	courts/proconsuls/bring charges against one another	assizes/proconsuls/bring their charges and countercharges	assizes/proconsuls/take the case to court	courts/proconsuls/bring charges against one another	courts/proconsuls/press charges
39 But if ye inquire any thing **concerning other matters,** it shall be determined in a lawful assembly.	further	further	any more	beyond this	further
40 For we are in danger to be called in question for this day's uproar, there being no cause whereby we may **give an account of this concourse.**	give to justify this commission	give any explanation of this uproar	give no reason for this gathering	account for this disorderly gathering	account for this commotion
20 9 And there sat in a window a certain young man named Eutychus, being fallen into a deep sleep: and as Paul was long preaching, he sunk down with sleep, and fell down from the third **loft,** and was taken up dead.	story	storey	floor(s)	floor	story
13 And we went **before to** ship, and sailed unto Assos, there intending to take **in** Paul: for so had he appointed, **minding himself** to go afoot.	ahead/aboard/intending himself	ahead/aboard/he was going	on ahead/on board/wanted	ahead/on board/intending himself	on ahead/aboard/he was going
16 For Paul had determined to sail **by**	past	by	wide of	pass	past

KJV	RSV	NEB	JB	NAS	NIV
Ephesus, because he would not spend the time in Asia: for he hasted, if it were possible for him, to be at Jerusalem the day of Pentecost.					
23 Save that the Holy Ghost **witnesseth** in every city, saying that bonds and afflictions **abide** me.	testifies/awaits	assures me/await	made it clear enough/await	testifies/await	warns/are facing
26 Wherefore I **take you to record this day,** that I am pure from the blood of all men.	testify to you this day	here and now declare	here and now I swear	testify to you this day	declare to you today
28 Take heed therefore unto yourselves, and to all the flock, over the which the Holy Ghost hath made you overseers, to feed the church of God, which he hath **purchased with his own blood.**	obtained with the blood of his own Son	won for himself by his own blood	bought with his own blood	purchased with His own blood	bought with his own blood
31 Therefore watch, and remember, that **by the space** of three years I ceased not to warn every one night and day with tears.	for	for	for	for	for
21 3 Now when we **had discovered** Cyprus, we left it on the left hand, and sailed into Syria, and landed at Tyre: for there the ship was to unlade her burden.	had come in sight of	came in sight of	After sighting	had come in sight of	After sighting
6 And when we had taken our leave one of another, we **took ship;** and they returned home again.	went on board the ship	went aboard	went aboard	went on board the ship	went aboard the ship
15 And after those days we **took up our carriages,** and went up to Jerusalem.	made ready	packed our baggage	packed	got ready	got ready
19 And when he had saluted them, he declared **particularly** what things God had wrought among the Gentiles by his ministry.	one by one	in detail	(gave a) detailed account	one by one	in detail
20 And when they heard it, they glorified the Lord, and said unto him, Thou seest, brother, how many thousands of Jews there are which believe; and they are **all zealous of the law:**	all zealous for the law	all of them staunch upholders of the Law	all of them staunch upholders of the Law	all zealous for the Law	all of them are zealous for the law
24 Them take, and purify thyself with them, and **be at charges with them,** that they may shave their heads: and all may know that those things, whereof they were informed concerning thee, are nothing; but that thou thyself also walkest orderly, and keepest the law.	pay their expenses	paying their expenses	pay all the expenses	pay their expenses	pay their expenses
25 As touching the Gentiles which believe, **we have written and concluded** that they observe no such thing, save only that they keep themselves from things offered to idols, and from blood, and from **strangled,** and from fornication.	we have sent a letter with our judgment/what is strangled	we sent them our decision/anything that has been strangled	as we wrote them when we told them our decisions/the meat of strangled animals	we wrote, having decided/what is strangled	we have written to them our decision/the meat of strangled animals
31 And as they went about to kill him, tidings came unto the **chief captain of the band,** that all Jerusalem was in an uproar.	tribune of the cohort	officer commanding the cohort	tribune of the cohort	commander of the Roman cohort	commander of the Roman troops
32 Who immediately took soldiers and centurions, and ran down unto them: and when they saw the chief captain and the soldiers, they **left beating of Paul.**	stopped beating Paul	stopped beating Paul	stopped beating Paul	stopped beating Paul	stopped beating Paul
33 Then the chief captain came near, and took him, and commanded him to be bound with two chains; and **demanded** who he was, and what he had done.	inquired	asked	inquired	began asking	asked

KJV	RSV	NEB	JB	NAS	NIV
34 And some cried one thing, some another, among the multitude: and when he could not know the **certainty** for the tumult, he commanded him to be carried into **the castle.**	facts / the barracks	truth / barracks	positive information / the fortress	facts / the barracks	truth / the barracks
35 And when he came upon the stairs, so it was, that he **was borne of the soldiers** for the violence of the people.	carried by the soldiers	carried by the soldiers	carried by the soldiers	carried by the soldiers	carried by the soldiers
37 And as Paul was to be led into the castle, he said unto the chief captain, May I speak unto thee? **Who** said, Canst thou speak Greek?	he	The commandant	The tribune	he	he
22 5 As also the high priest doth bear me witness, and all the **estate** of the elders: from whom also I received letters unto the brethren, and went to Damascus, to bring them which were there bound unto Jerusalem, for to be punished.	council	Council	councils	Council	council
30 On the morrow, because he would have known the **certainty** wherefore he was accused of the Jews, he loosed him from his bands, and commanded the chief priests and all their council to appear, and brought Paul down, and set him before them.	real reason	what charge	what precise charge	for certain	exactly why
23 1 And Paul, **earnestly beholding** the council, said, Men and brethren, I have lived in all good conscience before God until this day.	looking intently at	fixed his eyes on	looked steadily at	looking intently at	looked straight at
8 For the Sadducees say that there is no resurrection, neither angel, nor spirit: but the Pharisees **confess both.**	acknowledge them all	accept them	accept all three	acknowledge them all	acknowledge them all
12 And when it was day, certain of the Jews banded together and bound themselves under **a curse,** saying that they would neither eat nor drink till they had killed Paul.	an oath	an oath	a vow	an oath	an oath
15 Now therefore ye with the council signify to the chief captain that he bring him down unto you to-morrow, as though ye would inquire something more perfectly concerning him: and we, **or ever he come near,** are ready to kill him.	before he comes near	before he arrives	before he reaches you	before he comes near the place	before he gets here
24 4 Notwithstanding, that I be not further tedious unto thee, I pray thee that thou wouldst hear us of **thy clemency** a few words.	your kindness	your indulgence	(omits)	your kindness	(request that) you be kind enough
8 Commanding his accusers to come unto thee: by examining of whom thyself mayest **take knowledge** of all these things, whereof we accuse him.	will be able to learn	can ascertain	can find out for yourself	will be able to ascertain	will be able to learn
15 And have hope toward God, which they themselves also **allow,** that there shall be a resurrection of the dead, both of the just and unjust.	accept	accept	do (hold)	cherish	(I have the same hope as these men)
16 And herein do **I exercise myself,** to have always a conscience void of offence toward God, and toward men.	take pains	train myself	do my best	do my best	strive always
22 And when Felix heard these things, having more perfect knowledge of that way, he deferred them, and said, When Lysias the chief captain shall come down, I will **know the uttermost of your matter.**	decide your case	go into your case	go into your case	decide your case	decide your case
25 And as he **reasoned** of **righteousness, temperance,** and judgment to come, Felix trembled, and answered, Go	argued/justice/self-control	(the discourse) turned to questions / morals /	began to treat/righteousness / self-control	discussing/righteousness / self-control	discoursed/righteousness / self-control

KJV	RSV	NEB	JB	NAS	NIV
thy way for this time; when I have a convenient season, I will call for thee.		self-control			
26 He hoped also that money should have been given him of Paul, that he might loose him: wherefore he sent for him the oftener, and **communed** with him.	conversed	talked	had talks	converse	talked
27 But after two years **Porcius Festus came into Felix' room:** and Felix, willing to shew the Jews a pleasure, left Paul bound.	Felix was succeeded by Porcius Festus	Felix was succeeded by Porcius Festus	Felix was succeeded by Porcius Festus	Felix was succeeded by Porcius Festus	Felix was succeeded by Porcius Festus
25 1 Now when Festus was come into the province, after three days he **ascended** from Caesarea to Jerusalem.	went up	went up	went up	went up	went up
13 And after certain days king Agrippa and Bernice came unto Caesarea **to salute** Festus.	to welcome	on a courtesy visit to	paid their respects to	paid their respects to	to pay their respects to
19 But had certain questions against him of their **own superstition,** and of one Jesus, which was dead, whom Paul affirmed to be alive.	own superstition	peculiar religion	own religion	own religion	own religion
20 **And because I doubted of such manner of questions,** I asked him whether he would go to Jerusalem, and there be judged of these matters.	Being at a loss how to investigate these questions	Finding myself out of my depth in such discussions	Not feeling qualified to deal with questions of this sort	"And being at a loss how to investigate such matters	I was at a loss how to investigate such matters
26 Of whom I have no certain thing to write unto my lord. Wherefore I have brought him forth before you, and **specially** before thee, O king Agrippa, that, after examination had, I might have somewhat to write.	especially	particularly	in particular	especially	especially
27 For it seemeth to me unreasonable to send a prisoner, and **not withal** to signify the crimes laid against him.	not	without	without	not	without
26 7 Unto which promise our twelve tribes, **instantly** serving God day and night, hope to come. For which hope's sake, king Agrippa, I am accused of the Jews.	earnestly	with intense devotion	constant in	earnestly	earnestly
11 And I punished them oft in every synagogue, and compelled them to blaspheme; and being exceedingly mad against them, I persecuted them even unto **strange** cities.	foreign	foreign	foreign	foreign	foreign
14 And when we were all fallen to the earth, I heard a voice speaking unto me, and saying in the Hebrew tongue, Saul, Saul, why persecutest thou me? it is hard for thee to kick against the **pricks.**	goads	goad	goad	goads	goads
20 But shewed first unto them of Damascus and at Jerusalem, and throughout all the coasts of Judaea, and then to the Gentiles, that they should repent and turn to God, and **do works meet for repentance.**	perform deeds worthy of their repentance	to prove their repentance by deeds	proving their change of heart by their deeds	performing deeds appropriate to repentance	prove their repentance by their deeds
29 And Paul said, I would to God, that not only thou, but also all that hear me this day, **were both almost, and altogether** such as I am, except these bonds.	might become	might become	would come to be	might become	may become
27 1 And when it was determined that we should sail into Italy, they delivered Paul and certain other prisoners unto one named Julius, a centurion of Augustus' **band.**	Cohort	Cohort	cohort	cohort	Regiment
3 And the next day we touched at Sidon. And Julius **courteously entreated** Paul, and gave him liberty to go unto his friends to refresh himself.	treated . . . kindly	considerately (allowed)	was considerate enough	treated . . . with consideration	in kindness to

KJV	RSV	NEB	JB	NAS	NIV
12 And because the haven was commodious to winter in, **the more part** advised to depart thence also, **if by any means they might attain to Phenice, and there to winter;** which is an haven of Crete, and lieth toward the south-west and north-west.	majority/on the chance that somehow they could reach Phoenix . . . and winter there	majority/hoping, if they could get so far, to winter at Phoenix	majority/hoping to reach Phoenix and winter there	majority/if somehow they could reach Phoenix . . . and spend the winter there	majority/hoping to reach Phoenix and winter there
13 And when the south wind blew softly, supposing that they had obtained their purpose, **loosing thence,** they sailed close by Crete.	weighed anchor	weighing anchor	weighed anchor	weighed anchor	weighed anchor
14 But not long after there arose against it a tempestuous wind, called **Euroclydon.**	the northeaster	the 'North-easter'	the "northeaster"	Euraquilo	"northeaster"
15 And when the ship was caught and could not bear up into the wind, we **let her drive.**	gave way to it and were driven	give way and run before it	give way to it and let ourselves be driven	let ourselves be driven along	gave way to it and were driven along
16 And running under a certain island which is called Clauda, we had much work to **come by the boat:**	secure the boat	get the ship's boat under control	bring the ship's boat under control	get the ship's boat under control	make the lifeboat secure
17 Which when they had taken up, they **used helps,** undergirding the ship; and, fearing lest they should **fall into the quicksands, strake sail,** and so were driven.	took measures/run on the Syrtis/lowered the gear	made use of tackle/ running on to the shallows of Syrtis/lowered the mainsail	with the help of tackle/running aground on the Syrtis banks/ floated out the sea anchor	used supporting cables/run aground on the shallows of Syrtis/let down the sea anchor	tied ropes around the ship itself/run aground on the sandbars of Syrtis/lowered the sea anchor
19 And the third day we cast out with our own hands the **tackling** of the ship.	tackle	gear	gear	tackle	tackle
21 But after **long abstinence** Paul stood forth in the midst of them, and said, Sirs, ye should have hearkened unto me, and not have loosed from Crete, and to have gained this harm and loss.	long without food	long time without food	without food for a long time	long time without food	long time without food
27 But when the fourteenth night was come, as we were driven up and down in Adria, about midnight the **shipmen** deemed that they drew near to some **country;**	sailors/land	sailors/land	crew/land of some sort	sailors/land	sailors/land
29 Then fearing lest we should have fallen upon rocks, they cast four anchors out of the stern, and **wished** for the day.	prayed	prayed	prayed	wished	prayed
30 And as the shipmen were about to flee out of the ship, when they had let down the boat into the sea, **under colour as though** they would have cast anchors out of the **foreship,**	under pretense/bow	pretending/bows	as though/bows	on the pretense/bow	pretending/bow
41 And falling into a place where two seas met, they ran the ship aground; and the **forepart** stuck fast, and remained unmoveable, but the hinder part was broken with the violence of the waves.	bow	bow	bows	prow	bow
28 2 And the **barbarous people** shewed us no little kindness: for they kindled a fire, and received us every one, because of the present rain, and because of the cold.	natives	rough islanders	inhabitants	natives	islanders
6 Howbeit they **looked when he should have swollen,** or fallen down dead suddenly: but after they had looked a great while, and saw no harm come to him, they changed their minds, and said that he was a god.	waited, expecting him to swell	still expected that at any moment he would swell up	they were expecting him at any moment to swell up	were expecting that he was about to swell up	expected him to swell up
7 In the **same quarters were possessions** of the chief man of the island, whose name was Publius; who received us, and lodged us three days courteously.	neighborhood of that place were lands	neighbourhood of that place were lands	neighborhood there were estates	neighborhood of that place were lands	There was an estate nearby

KJV	RSV	NEB	JB	NAS	NIV
8 And it came to pass, that the father of Publius lay sick of a fever and of a **bloody flux:** to whom Paul entered in, and prayed, and laid his hands on him, and healed him.	dysentery	dysentery	dysentery	dysentery	dysentery
13 And from thence we **fetched a compass,** and came to Rhegium: and after one day the south wind blew, and we came the next day to Puteoli:	made a circuit	sailed around	followed the coast	sailed around	set sail
23 And when they had appointed him a day, there came many to him into his lodging; to whom he expounded and testified the kingdom of God, **persuading** them concerning Jesus, both out of the law of Moses, and out of the prophets, from morning till evening.	trying to convince	sought to convince	trying to persuade	trying to persuade	tried to convince
29 **And when he had said these words, the Jews departed, and had great reasoning among themselves.**	(omits)	(omits)	(omits)	(And when he had spoken these words, the Jews departed, having a great dispute among themselves.)	(omits)

Romans

KJV	RSV	NEB	JB	NAS	NIV
1 3 Concerning his Son Jesus Christ our Lord, which was **made of the seed of David** according to the flesh;	descended from David	born of David's stock	a descendant of David	was born of a descendant of David	a descendant of David
4 And declared to be the son of God with power, **according to the spirit of holiness, by the resurrection from the dead:** [ ]	according to the Spirit of holiness by his resurrection from the dead/Jesus Christ our Lord	but on the level of the spirit—the Holy Spirit—. . . by a mighty act in that he rose from the dead/it is about Jesus Christ our Lord	in the order of the spirit, the spirit of holiness that was in him . . . through his resurrection from the dead/it is about Jesus Christ our Lord	by the resurrection from the dead, according to the spirit of holiness/Jesus Christ our Lord	through the Spirit of Holiness by . . . his resurrection from the dead/Jesus Christ our Lord
13 Now **I would not have you ignorant,** brethren, that oftentimes I purposed to come unto you, (but was **let** hitherto,) that I might have some fruit among you also, even as among other Gentiles.	want you to know/prevented	should like you to know/without success	want you to know/prevented	do not want you to be unaware/prevented	do not want you to be unaware/prevented
14 **I am debtor** both to the Greeks, and to the Barbarians; both to the wise, and to the unwise.	am under obligation	am under obligation	owe a duty	am under obligation	am obligated
15 So, as much as in me is, **I am ready** to preach the gospel to you that are at Rome also.	I am eager	hence my eagerness	me want	I am eager	I am so eager
17 For therein is the righteousness of God revealed from faith to faith: as it is written, **The just shall live by faith.**	"He who through faith is righteous shall live."	'he shall gain life who is justified through faith.'	The upright man finds life through faith.	"But the righteous man shall live by faith."	"The righteous will live by faith."
21 Because that, when they knew God, they glorified him not as God, neither were thankful; but became **vain in their imaginations,** and their **foolish heart** was darkened.	futile in their thinking/senseless minds	all their thinking has ended in futility/misguided minds	made nonsense out of logic/empty minds	futile in their speculations/foolish heart	their thinking became futile/foolish hearts
23 And changed the glory of the **uncorruptible** God into an image made like to **corruptible** man, and to birds, and fourfooted beasts, and creeping things.	immortal/mortal	immortal/mortal	immortal/mortal	incorruptible/corruptible	immortal/mortal

	KJV	RSV	NEB	JB	NAS	NIV
	25 Who **changed** the truth of God **into** a lie, and worshipped and served the creature more than the Creator, who is blessed for ever. Amen.	exchanged/for	bartered away/for	exchanged/for	exchanged/for	exchanged/for
	28 And even as they did not like to retain God in their knowledge, God gave them over to a reprobate mind, **to do those things which are not convenient;**	and to improper conduct	(omits)	and to their monstrous behavior	to do those things which are not proper	to do what ought not to be done
	29 Being filled with all unrighteousness, fornication, wickedness, covetousness, maliciousness; full of envy, murder, **debate,** deceit, malignity; whisperers,	strife	rivalry	wrangling	strife	strife
	32 Who knowing the judgment of God, that they which commit such things **are worthy of death,** not only do the same, but **have pleasure** in them that do them.	deserve to die/approve	deserve to die/applaud	deserve to die/encourage	are worthy of death/give hearty approval	deserve death/approve
2	11 **For there is no respect of persons with God.**	For God shows no partiality	For God has no favourites	God has no favorites	For there is no partiality with God	For God does not show favoritism
	22 Thou that sayest a man should not commit adultery, dost thou commit adultery? thou that abhorrest idols, dost thou **commit sacrilege?**	rob temples	rob their shrines	rob their temples	rob temples	rob temples
3	4 **God forbid:** yea, let God be true, but every man a liar; as it is written, That thou mightest be justified in thy sayings, and mightest overcome when thou art judged.	By no means!	Certainly not!	That would be absurd	May it never be!	Not at all!
	9 What then? are **we** better than they? No, in no wise: for we have before proved both Jews and Gentiles, that they are all under sin;	we Jews	we Jews	we	we	we
	18 There is no **fear of God before their eyes.**	"There is no fear of God before their eyes."	reverence for God does not enter into their thoughts	there is no fear of God before their eyes.	"There is no fear of God before their eyes."	"There is no fear of God before their eyes."
	25 Whom God hath set forth **to be a propitiation through faith in his blood,** to declare his righteousness for the remission of sins that are past, through the forbearance of God;	as an expiation by his blood, to be received by faith	to be the means of expiating sin by his sacrificial death, effective through faith	to sacrifice his life so as to win reconciliation through faith	as a propitiation in His blood through faith	as a sacrifice of atonement through faith in his blood
4	1 What shall we say then that Abraham our father, as **pertaining to the flesh, hath found?**	according to the flesh / (omits)	our ancestor in the natural line / (omits)	the ancestor from whom we are all descended? / (omits)	our forefather according to the flesh / has found	our forefather / discovered in this matter
	13 For the promise, that he should be the heir of the world, was not to Abraham, or to **his seed,** through the law, but through the righteousness of faith.	his descendants	his posterity	his descendants	his descendants	his offspring
	15 Because the law **worketh** wrath: for where no law is, there is no transgression.	brings	can bring	involves the possibility of	brings about	brings
	16 Therefore it is of faith, that it might be by grace; to the end the promise might be sure to all **the seed;** not to that only which is of the law, but to that also which is of the faith of Abraham; who is the father of us all,	his descendants	Abraham's posterity	Abraham's descendants	the descendants	Abraham's offspring
	18 Who against hope believed in hope, that he might become the father of many nations according to that which was spoken, So shall thy **seed** be.	descendants	descendants	descendants	descendants	offspring
	20 He **staggered not** at the promise of God through unbelief; but was strong in faith, giving glory to God;	No (distrust) made him waver	never doubted	refused either to deny it or even to doubt it	did not waver	did not waver

	KJV	RSV	NEB	JB	NAS	NIV
5	2 By whom also we have access **by faith** into this grace wherein we stand, and rejoice in **hope of the glory of God.**	(omits) / our hope of sharing the glory of God	(omits) / the hope of the divine splendour that is to be ours	by faith and through Jesus / about looking forward to God's glory	by faith / hope of the glory of God	by faith / the hope of the glory of God
	3 And not only so, but we **glory** in **tribulations** also: knowing that **tribulation worketh patience;**	rejoice / sufferings / suffering produces endurance	exult / present sufferings / suffering trains us to endure	boast / sufferings / sufferings bring patience	exult / tribulations / tribulation brings about perseverance	rejoice / sufferings / suffering produces perseverance
	4 And **patience, experience;** and **experience, hope:**	endurance / character / character / hope	endurance / proof that we have stood the test / proof / ground of hope	patience / perseverance / perseverance / hope	perseverance / proven character / proven character / hope	perseverance / character / character / hope
	5 And hope **maketh not ashamed;** because the love of God is shed abroad in our hearts by the Holy Ghost which is given unto us.	does not disappoint	is no mockery	is not deceptive	does not disappoint	does not disappoint
	7 For scarcely for a righteous man will one die: yet peradventure for a good man **some** would even dare to die.	one	one	a man	someone	someone
	11 And not only so, but we also joy in God through our Lord Jesus Christ, by whom we have now received the **atonement.**	reconciliation	reconciliation	reconciliation	reconciliation	reconciliation
	14 Nevertheless death reigned from Adam to Moses, even over them that had not sinned after the **similitude** of Adam's transgression, who **is the figure** of him that was to come.	whose sins were not like / was a type	who had not sinned as / foreshadows	their sin, unlike that of / prefigured	who had not sinned in the likeness of / is a type	who did not sin by breaking a command as did / was a pattern
6	5 For if we have been **planted together in the likeness of his death,** we shall be also in the likeness of his resurrection:	united with him in a death like his	become incorporate with him in a death like his	in union with Christ we have imitated his death	united with Him in the likeness of His death	united with him in his death
	6 Knowing this, that our **old man** is crucified with him, that the body of sin might be destroyed, that henceforth we should not serve sin.	old self	man we once were	former selves	old self	old self
	21 **What fruit** had ye then in those things whereof ye are now ashamed? for the end of those things is death.	what return	what was the gain	what did you get	what benefit	What benefit
7	5 For when we were in the flesh, **the motions** of sins, which were by the law, did work in our members to bring forth fruit unto death.	sinful passions	sinful passions	sinful passions	sinful passions	sinful passions
	6 But now we are delivered from the law, that being dead wherein we were held; that we should serve in newness of spirit, and not in the **oldness of the letter.**	under the old written code	to the old way, the way of a written code	in . . old way of a written law	in oldness of the letter	in the old way of the written code
	8 But sin, taking occasion by the commandment, wrought in me all manner of **concupiscence.** For without the law sin was dead.	covetousness	wrong desires	covetousness	coveting	covetous desire
	15 For that which I do I **allow not:** for what I would, that do I not; but what I hate, that do I.	do not understand	do not even acknowledge	cannot understand	do not understand	do not know
8	1 There is therefore now no condemnation to them which are in Christ Jesus, **who walk not after the flesh,** but after the Spirit.	(omits)	(omits)	(omits)	(omits)	(omits)
	3 For what the law could not do, in that it was weak through the flesh, God sending his own Son in the likeness of					

KJV	RSV	NEB	JB	NAS	NIV
sinful flesh, and for sin, condemned sin in the flesh:	sinful flesh	sinful nature	sinful nature	sinful flesh	sinful man
6 For **to be carnally minded is death;** but to be spiritually minded is life and peace.	To set the mind on the flesh is death	(Those who live on the level of our lower nature have their outlook formed by it, and that spells death)	It is death to limit oneself to what is unspiritual	For the mind set on the flesh is death	The mind of sinful man is death
9 But ye are not in the flesh, but in the Spirit, **if so be that** the Spirit of God dwell in you. Now if any man have not the Spirit of Christ, he is none of his.	if in fact	if only	since	if indeed	if
13 For if ye live after the flesh, ye shall die: but if ye through the Spirit **do mortify** the deeds of the body, ye shall live.	put to death	put to death	put an end to	putting to death	put to death
17 And if children, then heirs; heirs of God, and joint-heirs with Christ; **if so be** that we suffer with him, that we may be also glorified together.	provided	if	(omits)	if indeed	if indeed
18 For I **reckon** that the sufferings of this present time are not worthy to be compared with the glory which shall be revealed in us.	consider	reckon	think	consider	think
19 For the earnest expectation of the **creature** waiteth for the manifestation of the sons of God.	creation	created universe	whole creation	creation	creation
20 For the **creature** was made subject to **vanity,** not willingly, but by reason of him who hath subjected the same in hope,	creation / futility	it / frustration	it / unable (to attain its purpose)	creation / futility	creation / frustration
21 Because the **creature** itself also shall be delivered from the bondage of corruption into the glorious liberty of the children of God.	creation	universe	(omits)	creation	creation
23 And not only they, but ourselves also, which have the first-fruits of the Spirit, even we ourselves groan within ourselves, **waiting for the adoption, to wit, the redemption of our body.**	as we wait for adoption as sons, the redemption of our bodies	while we wait for God to make us his sons and set our whole body free	as we wait for our bodies to be set free	waiting eagerly for our adoption as sons, the redemption of our body	as we wait eagerly for our adoption as sons, the redemption of our bodies
28 And we know that **all things work together for good to them that love God,** to them who are the called according to his purpose.	in everything God works for good with those who love him	in everything . . . he cooperates for good with those who love God	by turning everything to their good God cooperates with all those who love God	God causes all things to work together for good to those who love God	in all things God works for the good of those who love him
38 For I am **persuaded,** that neither death, nor life, nor angels, nor principalities, nor powers, nor things present, nor things to come,	sure	convinced	certain	convinced	convinced
9 5 Whose are the **fathers,** and of **whom** as **concerning the flesh** Christ came, who is over all, God blessed for ever. Amen.	patriarchs / their race / according to the flesh	patriarchs / them / in natural descent	patriarchs / from their flesh and blood	fathers / whom / according to the flesh	patriarchs / from them / (is traced) the human ancestry of
7 Neither, because they are the **seed** of Abraham, are they all children: but, In Isaac shall thy **seed be** called.	descendants / descendants	offspring / descendants	descendants / name	descendants / descendants	children / offspring
16 So then it is not of **him that willeth,** nor of **him that runneth,** but of God that sheweth mercy.	man's will or exertion	man's will or effort	what human beings want or try to do	man who wills or the man who runs	man's desire or effort
18 Therefore hath he mercy on whom he will have mercy, **and whom he will he hardeneth.**	and he hardens the heart of whomever he wills	but also makes men stubborn as he chooses	and when he wants to harden someone's heart he does so	and He hardens whom He desires	and he hardens whom he wants to harden

	KJV	RSV	NEB	JB	NAS	NIV
	21 Hath not the potter power over the clay, of the same lump to make one vessel **unto honour,** and another **unto dishonour?**	for beauty / for menial use	to be treasured / for common use	special / ordinary	for honorable use / for common use	for noble purposes / for common use
	29 And as Esaias said before, Except the Lord of Sabaoth had left us **a seed,** we had been as Sodoma, and been made like unto Gomorrha.	children	the mere germ of a nation	some descendants	a posterity	descendants
10	2 For I bear them record that they have a zeal **of** God, but **not according to knowledge.**	for / it is not enlightened	for / it is an ill-formed zeal	for / their zeal is misguided	for / not in accordance with knowledge	for / their zeal is not based on knowledge
	15 And how shall they preach, except they be sent? as it is written, How beautiful are the feet of them that preach the gospel of peace, **and bring glad tidings of good things!**	(omits)	(omits)	(omits)	(omits)	(omits)
	21 But to Israel he saith, All day long I have stretched forth my hands unto a disobedient and **gainsaying** people.	contrary	defiant	rebellious	obstinate	obstinate
11	3 Lord, they have killed thy prophets, and **digged down** thine altars; and I am left alone, and they seek my life.	demolished	torn down	broken down	torn down	torn down
	7 What then? Israel hath not obtained that which he seeketh for; but **the election** hath obtained it, and the rest were **blinded**	The elect / hardened	the selected few / made blind	the chosen few / not allowed to see	those who were chosen / hardened	the elect / hardened
	8 (According as it is written, God hath given them the spirit of **slumber,** eyes that they should not see, and ears that they should not hear;) unto this day.	stupor	numbness	sluggish (spirit)	stupor	stupor
	20 Well; because of unbelief they were broken off, and thou standest by faith. **Be not highminded,** but fear:	do not become proud	Put away your pride	Rather than making you proud	Do not be conceited	Do not be arrogant
	30 For as ye in times past **have not believed** God, yet have now obtained mercy through **their unbelief:**	were once disobedient to / their disobedience	formerly (you) were disobedient to / their disobedience	being disobedient to / their disobedience	once were disobedient to / their disobedience	were at one time disobedient to / their disobedience
	32 For God hath **concluded them all in unbelief,** that he might have mercy upon all.	consigned all men to disobedience	in making all mankind prisoners to disobedience	imprisoned all men in their own disobedience	shut up all in disobedience	bound all men over to disobedience
12	1 I Beseech you therefore, brethren, by the mercies of God, that ye present your bodies a living sacrifice, holy, acceptable unto God, **which is your reasonable service.**	which is your spiritual worship	the worship offered by mind and heart	in a way that is worthy of thinking beings	which is your spiritual service of worship	which is your spiritual worship
	8 Or he that exhorteth, on exhortation: he that giveth, let him do it **with simplicity;** he that ruleth, with diligence; he that sheweth mercy, with cheerfulness.	in liberality	with all your heart	freely	with liberality	generously
	9 Let love be **without dissimulation.** Abhor that which is evil; cleave to that which is good.	genuine	in all sincerity	(Do not let love be a pretense)	without hypocrisy	sincere
	12 Rejoicing in hope; patient in tribulation; **continuing instant in** prayer;	be constant in	persist in	keep on (praying)	devoted to	faithful in
	13 Distributing to the **necessity** of saints; given to hospitality.	needs	needs	need	needs	need
	16 Be of the same mind one toward another. Mind not high things, but **condescend** to men of low estate. Be not wise in your own conceits.	associate with	go about with	make real friends with	associate with	be willing to associate with
	17 Recompense to no man evil for evil. Provide things **honest** in the sight of all men.	noble	honourable	highest (ideals)	right	right

KJV	RSV	NEB	JB	NAS	NIV
18 If it be possible, **as much as lieth in you,** live peaceably with all men.	so far as it depends upon you	so far as it lies with you	Do all you can	so far as it depends on you	as far as it depends on you
13 1 Let every soul be subject unto the **higher powers.** For there is no power but of God: the powers that be are **ordained** of God.	governing authorities / instituted	supreme authorities / instituted	governing authorities / appointed	governing authorities / established	governing authorities / established
2 Whosoever therefore resisteth the power, resisteth the ordinance of God: and they that resist shall receive to themselves **damnation.**	judgment	punishment	(such an act is bound to be punished)	condemnation	judgment
6 For for this cause pay ye **tribute** also: for they are God's ministers, attending continually upon this very thing.	taxes	taxes	taxes	taxes	taxes
7 Render therefore to all their dues: **tribute** to whom **tribute** is due; **custom** to whom **custom; fear** to whom **fear; honour** to whom **honour.**	taxes / taxes / revenue / revenue / fear / fear / respect / respect	(tax and toll, reverence and respect)	(whether it be direct tax or indirect, fear or honor)	tax / tax / custom / custom / fear / fear / honor / honor	taxes / taxes / revenue / revenue / respect / respect / honor / honor
9 For this, Thou shalt not commit adultery, Thou shalt not kill, Thou shalt not steal, Thou shalt not bear false witness, Thou shalt not covet; and if there be any other commandment, it is **briefly comprehended** in this saying, namely, Thou shalt love they neighbour as thyself.	are summed up	are all summed up	are summed up	is summed up	are summed up
13 Let us walk **honestly,** as in the day; not in **rioting** and drunkenness, not in **chambering** and wantonness, not in strife and envying.	becomingly / reveling / debauchery	with decency / revelling / debauchery	decently / (drunken orgies) / promiscuity	properly / carousing / sexual promiscuity	decently / orgies / sexual immorality
14 1 Him that is weak in the faith receive ye, **but not to doubtful disputations.**	but not for disputes over opinions	without attempting to settle doubtful points	without starting an argument	but not for the purpose of judgment on his opinions	without passing judgment on disputable matters
2 For one believeth that he may eat all things: another, who is weak, eateth **herbs.**	vegetables	vegetables	vegetables	vegetables	vegetables
15 But if thy brother be grieved **with thy meat,** now **walkest thou not charitably.** Destroy not him with thy meat, for whom Christ died.	by what you eat / you are no longer walking in love	by what you eat / your conduct is no longer guided by love	your attitude to food / you are hardly being guided by charity	because of food / you are no longer walking according to love	because of what you eat / you are no longer acting in love
21 It is good neither to eat flesh, nor to drink wine, nor any thing whereby thy brother stumbleth, **or is offended, or is made weak.**	(omits)	(omits)	or fall or weaken in any way	(omits)	(omits)
22 Hast thou faith? have it to thyself before God. Happy is he that condemneth not himself in that thing which he **alloweth.**	approves	(Happy is the man who can make his decision with a clear conscience!)	(consider the man fortunate who can make his decision without going against his conscience)	approves	approves
23 And he that doubteth is **damned** if he eat, because he eateth not of faith: for whatsoever is not of faith is sin.	condemned	guilty	condemned	condemned	condemned
15 15 Nevertheless, brethren, I have written the more boldly unto you **in some sort,** as putting you in mind, because of the grace that is given to me of God,	on some points	at times	some things	on some points	on some points
16 That I should be the minister of Jesus Christ to the Gentiles, **ministering the gospel of God,** that the offering up of the Gentiles might be acceptable, being sanctified by the Holy Ghost.	in the priestly service of the gospel of God	my priestly service is the preaching of the gospel of God	(I am to carry out my priestly duty by bringing the Good News from God)	ministering as a priest the gospel of God	with the priestly duty of proclaiming the gospel of God

	KJV	RSV	NEB	JB	NAS	NIV
	24 Whensoever I take my journey into Spain, I will come to you: for I trust to see you in my journey, and to be **brought on my way thitherward by you,** if first I **be somewhat filled with your company.**	sped on my journey there by you / have enjoyed your company for a little	sent there with your support / having enjoyed your company for a while	complete the rest of my journey with your good wishes / enjoying a little of your company	helped on my way there by you / have first enjoyed your company for a while	have you assist me on my journey there / have enjoyed your company for a while
	27 It hath pleased them verily; and their debtors they are. For if the Gentiles have been made partakers of their spiritual things, their duty is also to minister unto them **in carnal things.**	in material blessings	to their material needs	with temporal possessions	in material things	their material blessings
16	1 I commend unto you Phebe our sister, which is a **servant** of the church which is at Cenchrea:	who is a deaconess	who holds office	a deaconess	who is a servant	a servant
	2 That ye receive her in the Lord, as becometh saints, and that ye assist her in whatsoever business she hath need of you: for she hath been a **succourer** of many, and of myself also.	helper	good friend	(she has looked after a great many people)	helper	great help
	4 Who have for my life **laid down their own necks:** unto whom not only I give thanks, but also all the churches of the Gentiles.	risked their necks	risked their necks	risked death	risked their own necks	risked their lives
	18 For they that are such serve not our Lord Jesus Christ, but their **own belly;** and by good words and fair speeches deceive the hearts of the **simple.**	own appetites / simple-minded	own appetites / innocent people	own appetites / simple-minded	own appetites / unsuspecting	own appetites / naive people
	19 For your obedience is come abroad unto all men. I am glad therefore on your behalf: but yet I would have you wise unto that which is good, and **simple** concerning evil.	guileless	simpletons	innocent	innocent	innocent
	23 Gaius mine host, and of the whole church, saluteth you. Erastus the **chamberlain of the city** saluteth you, and Quartus a brother.	the city treasurer	treasurer of this city	the city treasurer	the city treasurer	the city's director of public works

I Corinthians

	KJV	RSV	NEB	JB	NAS	NIV
1	4 I thank my God always **on your behalf,** for the grace of God which is given you by Jesus Christ;	for you	for you	(omits)	concerning you	for you
	10 Now I beseech you, brethren, by the name of our Lord Jesus Christ, that ye all **speak the same thing,** and that there be no divisions among you; but that ye be perfectly joined together in the same mind and in the same judgment.	that all of you agree	agree among yourselves	to make up the differences between you	that you all agree	that all of you agree
	14 **I thank God** that I baptized none of you, but Crispus and Gaius;	I am thankful	Thank God	I am thankful	I thank God	I am thankful
	17 For Christ sent me not to baptize, but to preach the gospel: not with wisdom of words, lest the cross of Christ should **be made of none effect.**	be emptied of its power	(to do it without relying in the language of worldly wisdom, so that the fact of Christ on his cross might have its full weight)	cannot be expressed	should not be made void	be emptied of its power
	27 But God hath chosen the foolish things of the world to **confound** the wise;	shame/shame	shame/shame	shame/shame	shame/shame	shame/shame

KJV	RSV	NEB	JB	NAS	NIV
and God hath chosen the weak things of the world to **confound** the things which are mighty;					
28 And **base** things of the world, and things which are **despised,** hath God chosen, yea, and things which are not, to bring to nought things that are:	low/despised	low/contemptible	common/contemptible	base/despised	lowly/despised
31 That, according as it is written, He that **glorieth,** let him **glory** in the Lord.	boasts/boast	boast/boast	wants to boast/boast	boasts/boast	boasts/boast
2 4 And my speech and my **preaching** was not with **enticing** words of **man's wisdom,** but in demonstration of the Spirit and of power:	message / plausible words / wisdom	gospel I proclaimed / subtle arguments / (omits)	sermons that I gave / arguments / philosophy	preaching / persuasive words / wisdom	preaching / persuasive words / (wise and persuasive words)
13 Which things also we speak, not in the words which man's wisdom teacheth, but which the Holy Ghost teacheth; **comparing spiritual things with spiritual.**	interpreting spiritual truths to those who interpret the Spirit	because we are interpreting spiritual truths to those who have the Spirit	we teach spiritual things spiritually	combining spiritual thoughts with spiritual words	expressing spiritual truths in spiritual words
3 3 For ye are **yet carnal:** for whereas there is among you envying, and strife, and divisions, are ye not carnal, and walk as men?	still of the flesh	still on the merely natural plane	still unspiritual	still fleshly	still worldly
9 For we are labourers together with God: ye are God's **husbandry,** ye are God's building.	fellow workers	fellow-workers	fellow workers	fellow workers	fellow workers
4 4 For I know nothing **by myself;** yet am I not hereby justified: but he that judgeth me is the Lord.	against myself	on my conscience	(my conscience does not reproach me at all)	against myself	(My conscience is clear)
5 1 It is reported commonly that there is **fornication** among you, and such fornication as is not so much as **named** among the **Gentiles,** that one should have his father's wife.	immorality / found / pagans	sexual immorality / do . . . tolerate / pagans	sexual immorality / unparalleled / pagans	immorality / exist / Gentiles	sexual immorality / occur / pagans
9 I wrote unto you in an epistle not to **company with fornicators:**	associate with immoral men	have nothing to do with loose livers	associate with people living immoral lives	associate with immoral people	associate with sexually immoral people
6 7 Now therefore there is utterly a fault among you, because ye go to law one with another. Why do ye not rather **take wrong?** why do ye not rather suffer yourselves to be defrauded?	suffer wrong	suffer injury	let yourselves be wronged	be wronged	be wronged
12 All things are lawful unto me, but all things are not **expedient:** all things are lawful for me, but I will not be brought under the power of any.	helpful	for my good	good	profitable	beneficial
7 3 Let the husband render unto the wife **due benevolence:** and likewise also the wife unto the husband.	conjugal rights	what is due	what she has the right to expect	his duty	his marital duty
4 The wife hath not **power** of her own body, but the husband: and likewise also the husband hath not **power** of his own body, but the wife.	does not rule over / does not rule over	cannot claim her / cannot claim his	has no rights over / has no rights over	does not have authority over / does not have authority over	does not belong to / does not belong to
5 **Defraud ye not** one the other, except it be with consent for a time, that ye may give yourselves to fasting and prayer; and come together again, that Satan tempt you not for your **incontinency.**	Do not refuse / lack of self-control	Do not deny / lack of self-control	Do not refuse / weakness	Stop depriving / lack of self-control	Do not deprive / lack of self-control
6 But I speak this **by permission,** and not of commandment.	by way of concession	by way of concession	(This is) a concession	by way of concession	as a concession
7 For I would that all men were even as I myself. But every man hath **his proper gift of God,** one after this manner, and another after that.	his own special gift from God	the gift God has granted him	his own particular gifts from God	his own gift from God	his own gift from God

	KJV	RSV	NEB	JB	NAS	NIV
	9 But if they cannot **contain,** let them marry: for it is better to marry than **to burn.**	exercise self-control / to be aflame with passion	control themselves / burn with vain desire	control the sexual urges / to be tortured	self-control / to burn	control themselves / to burn with passion
	19 **Circumcision is nothing, and uncircumcision is nothing,** but the keeping of the commandments of God.	For neither circumcision counts for anything nor uncircumcision.	Circumcision or uncircumcision is neither here nor there	because to be circumcised or uncircumcised means nothing	Circumcision is nothing, and uncircumcision is nothing	Circumcision is nothing and uncircumcision is nothing
	31 And they that use this world, as not abusing it: for the **fashion** of this world passeth away.	form	whole frame	(the world as we know it)	form	present form
	32 But I would have you **without carefulness.** He that is unmarried careth for the things that belong to the Lord, how he may please the Lord:	free from anxieties	free from anxious care	free from all worry	free from concern	free from concern
	36 But if any man think that he behaveth himself **uncomely** toward his **virgin,** if she pass the flower of her age, and need so require, let him do what he will, he sinneth not: let them marry.	not . . . properly / betrothed	not . . . properly / partner in celibacy	(If there is anyone who feels that it would not be fair to his daughter to let her grow too old for marriage)	unbecomingly / virgin daughter	improperly / the virgin he is engaged to
	37 Nevertheless he that standeth stedfast in his heart, having no necessity, but **hath power over his own will,** and hath so decreed in his heart that he will keep **his virgin,** doeth well.	having his desire under control / her as his betrothed	has complete control of his own choice / his partner in her virginity	in complete freedom of choice / his daughter as she is	has authority over his own will / his own virgin daughter	has control over his own will / the virgin
	38 So then he that **giveth her in marriage** doeth well; but he that **giveth her not in marriage** doeth better.	marries his betrothed / refrains from marriage	marries his partner / does not	sees that his daughter is married / keeps his daughter unmarried	gives his own virgin daughter in marriage / does not give her in marriage	marries the virgin / does not marry her
8	6 But to us there is but one God, the Father, **of whom are all things,** and we in him; and one Lord Jesus Christ, by whom are all things, and we by him.	through whom are all things	through whom all things came to exist	through whom all things come	by whom are all things	through whom all things came
	7 Howbeit there is not in every man that knowledge: for some **with conscience** of the idol unto this hour eat it as a thing offered unto an idol; and their conscience being weak is defiled.	being hitherto accustomed to idols	who have been accustomed to idolatry	who have been so long used to idols	being accustomed to the idol until now	are still so accustomed to idols
9	7 Who **goeth a warfare** any time at his own **charges?** who planteth a vineyard, and eateth not of the fruit thereof? or who feedeth a flock, and eateth not of the milk of the flock?	serves as a soldier/expense	serving in the army/expense	to stay in the army/(Nobody ever paid money)	serves as a soldier/expense	serves as a soldier/expense
	17 For if I do this thing willingly, I have a reward: but if against my will, **a dispensation of the gospel is committed unto me.**	I am entrusted with a commission	I am simply discharging a trust	it is a responsibility which has been put into my hands	I have a stewardship entrusted to me	I am simply discharging the trust committed to me
	18 What is my reward then? Verily that, when I preach the gospel, I may make the gospel of Christ **without charge,** that I abuse not my power in the gospel.	free of charge	without expense to anyone	free	without charge	free of charge
	25 And every man that striveth for the mastery is temperate in all things. Now they do it to obtain a **corruptible** crown; but we an **incorruptible.**	perishable wreath / imperishable	fading wreath/never fades	wreath that will wither away / will never wither	perishable wreath / imperishable	crown of laurel that will not last / will last forever
	27 But I keep under my body, and bring it into subjection: lest that by any means, when I have preached to others, I myself should be a **castaway.**	disqualified	rejected	disqualified	disqualified	disqualified for the prize
10	16 The cup of blessing which we bless, is it not the **communion** of the blood of	participation/	means of shar-	communion/	sharing/sharing	participation/

KJV	RSV	NEB	JB	NAS	NIV
Christ? The bread which we break, is it not the **communion** of the body of Christ?	participation	ing/means of sharing	communion		participation
24 Let no man seek his own, but every man another's **wealth.**	good	interests	advantage	good	good
25 Whatsoever is sold in the **shambles,** that eat, asking no question for conscience sake:	meat market	meat-market	butchers' shops	meat market	meat market
11 29 For he that eateth and drinketh unworthily, eateth and drinketh **damnation** to himself, not discerning the Lord's body.	judgment	judgement	condemnation	judgment	judgment
30 For this cause many are weak and sickly among you, and many **sleep.**	have died	have died	have died	sleep	have fallen asleep
32 But when we are judged, we are chastened **of** the Lord, that we should not be condemned with the world.	by	under (the Lord's judgement)	(But when the Lord does punish us like that)	by	by
12 11 But all these worketh that one and the selfsame Spirit, dividing to every man **severally** as he will.	individually	separately	to different people	individually	to each man
23 And those members of the body, which we think to be less honourable, upon these we bestow more abundant honour; and our **uncomely** parts have more abundant **comeliness.**	unpresentable / modesty	unseemly/ seemliness	improper/(get) decorated	unseemly/ seemliness	unpresentable / modesty
24 For our **comely** parts have no need: but God hath tempered the body together, having given more abundant honour to that part which lacked:	more presentable	seemly	more proper	seemly	presentable
25 That there should be no **schism** in the body; but that the members should have the same care one for another.	discord	sense of division	disagreements	division	division
27 Now ye are the body of Christ, and **members in particular.**	individually members of it	each one of you a limb or organ of it	each of you is a different part of it	individually members of it	each one of you is a part of it
28 And God hath set some in the church, first apostles, secondarily prophets, thirdly teachers, after that miracles, then gifts of healings, **helps,** governments, diversities of tongues.	helpers	those who have . . . ability to help others	helpers	helps	those able to help others
31 But **covet earnestly** the best gifts: and yet shew I unto you a more excellent way.	earnestly desire	aim at	Be ambitious for	earnestly desire	eagerly desire
13 1 Though I speak with the tongues of men and of angels, and have not **charity,** I am become as sounding brass, or a tinkling cymbal.	love	love	love	love	love
8 Charity never faileth: but whether there be prophecies, they **shall fail;** whether there be tongues, they shall cease; whether there be knowledge, it shall vanish away.	will pass away	will be over	must fail	will be done away	will cease
10 But when that which is perfect is come, then **that which is in part shall be done away.**	the imperfect will pass away	the partial vanishes	all imperfect things will disappear	the partial will be done away	the imperfect disappears
12 For now we see **through a glass, darkly;** but then face to face: now I know in part; but then shall I know even as also I am known.	in a mirror dimly	only puzzling reflections in a mirror	a dim reflection in a mirror	in a mirror dimly	but a poor reflection
13 And now abideth faith, hope, **charity,** these three; but the **greatest** of these is **charity.**	love / love	love / love	love / love	love / love	love / love

KJV	RSV	NEB	JB	NAS	NIV
14 3 But he that prophesieth speaketh unto men to **edification,** and **exhortation,** and **comfort.**	for their upbuilding and encouragement and consolation	and his words have power to build; they stimulate and they encourage	to their improvement, their encouragement and their consolation	to men for edification and exhortation and consolation	for their strengthening, encouragement and comfort
7 And even things without life giving sound, whether pipe or harp, except they give a distinction in the sounds, how shall it be known what is piped or **harped?**	played	played	played	played	being played
10 There are, it may be, so many kinds of **voices** in the world, and none of them is **without signification.**	languages / without meaning	sound / altogether soundless	languages / meaningless	languages / without meaning	languages / without meaning
11 Therefore if I know not the meaning of the **voice,** I shall be unto him that speaketh a **barbarian,** and he that speaketh shall be a barbarian unto me.	language / foreigner	sound (his words will be gibberish to me, and mine to him)	sounds / savage	language / barbarian	what someone is saying / foreigner
20 Brethren, be not children in understanding: howbeit in malice be ye children, but **in understanding** be men.	in thinking	in your thinking	mentally	in your thinking	in your thinking
24 But if all prophesy, and there come in one that believeth not, or one unlearned, he is **convinced** of all, he is **judged** of all:	convicted / called to account	(the visitor . . . hears from everyone something that searches his conscience and brings conviction)	analyzed / judged	convicted / called to account	convinced / judged
32 And the spirits of the prophets are **subject to the** prophets.	and the spirits of prophets are subject to prophets	It is for prophets to control prophetic inspiration	Prophets can always control their prophetic spirits	and the spirits of prophets are subject to prophets	The spirits of prophets are subject to the control of prophets.
35 And if they will learn any thing, let them ask their husbands at home: for it is **a shame** for women to speak in the church.	is shameful	is a shocking thing	does not seem right	is improper	is disgraceful
15 15 Yea, and we are found false witnesses of God; because we have testified of God that he raised up Christ: whom he raised not up, **if so be that the dead rise not.**	if it is true that the dead are not raised	if the dead are not raised	(omits)	if in fact the dead are not raised	if in fact the dead are not raised
29 Else what shall they do which are baptized **for** the dead if the dead rise not at all? why are they then baptized for the dead?	on behalf of	on behalf of	for	for	for
31 **I protest by your rejoicing which I have in Christ Jesus our Lord,** I die daily.	I protest, brethren, by my pride in you which I have in Christ Jesus our Lord	I swear it by my pride in you, my brothers—for in Christ Jesus our Lord I am proud of you	brothers, and I can swear it by the pride I take in you in Christ Jesus our Lord	I protest, brethren, by the boasting in you, which I have in Christ Jesus our Lord	I mean that, brothers—just as surely as I glory over you in Christ Jesus our Lord
33 Be not deceived: **evil communications** corrupt good manners.	Bad company	Bad company	Bad friends	Bad company	Bad company
36 Thou fool, that which thou sowest **is not quickened,** except it die:	does not come to life	does not come to life	(has to die) before it is given new life	does not come to life	does not come to life
38 But God giveth it a body as it hath pleased him, and to every seed **his** own body.	its	its	its	its	its
42 So also is the resurrection of the dead. **It is sown in corruption; it is raised in incorruption:**	What is sown is perishable, what is raised is imperishable.	What is sown in the earth as a perishable thing is raised imperishable.	the thing that is sown is perishable but what is raised is imperishable	It is sown a perishable body, it is raised an imperishable body	The body that is sown is perishable, it is raised imperishable
44 It is sown a **natural** body; it is raised a spiritual body. **There is a natural body,**	physical / If there is a physical	animal / If there is such a thing as	soul / If the soul has its own em-	natural / If there is a natural body,	natural / If there is a natural body,

	KJV	RSV	NEB	JB	NAS	NIV
	and there is a spiritual body.	body, there is also	an animal body, there is also	bodiment / so does	there is also	there is also
	46 Howbeit that was not first which is spiritual, **but that which is natural;** and afterward that which is spiritual.	but the physical	the animal body comes first	first the one with the soul	but the natural	but the natural
	47 The first man **is of the earth, earthy:** the second man is the Lord from heaven.	was from the earth, a man of dust	was made of the dust of the earth	being from the earth, is earthly by nature	is from the earth, earthy	was of the dust of the earth
16	8 But I will tarry at Ephesus until **Pentecost.**	Pentecost	Whitsuntide	Pentecost	Pentecost	Pentecost
	9 For a great door **and effectual** is opened unto me, and there are many adversaries.	for effective work	for effective work	and important door	for effective service	for effective work
	13 Watch ye, stand fast in the faith, **quit you like men,** be strong.	be courageous	be valiant	be brave	act like men	be men of courage
	15 I beseech you, brethren, (ye know the house of Stephanas, that it is the firstfruits of Achaia, and that they have **addicted themselves** to the ministry of the saints,)	devoted themselves	laid themselves out	really worked hard	devoted themselves	devoted themselves
	22 If any man love not the Lord Jesus Christ, let him be **Anathema Maranatha.**	accursed / Our Lord, come!	outcast / *Maranatha*—Come, O Lord!	a curse on him / *"Maran atha."*	accursed / Maranatha.	a curse be on him / Come, O Lord!

II Corinthians

	KJV	RSV	NEB	JB	NAS	NIV
1	6 And whether we be afflicted, it is for your consolation and salvation, which is effectual in the enduring of the same sufferings which we also suffer: **or whether we be comforted, it is for your consolation and salvation.**	and if we are comforted, it is for your comfort	if our lot be consolation, it is to help us to bring you comfort	you will also share our consolations	if we are comforted, it is for your comfort	if we are comforted, it is for your comfort
	12 For our **rejoicing** is this, the testimony of our conscience, that in simplicity and godly sincerity, not with fleshly wisdom, but by the grace of God, we have had our conversation in the world, and more abundantly **to you-ward.**	boast / toward you	one thing we are proud of / with you	one thing we are proud of / you	confidence / toward you	boast / with you
	13 For we write none other things unto you, than what ye read or **acknowledge;** and I trust ye shall **acknowledge** even to the end;	understand / understand	understand / understand	understand / recognize (vs. 14)	understand / understand	understand / understand (vs. 14)
	15 And in this confidence I was minded to come unto you before, that ye might have a **second benefit;**	double pleasure	benefit of a double visit	(would) benefit doubly	twice . . . blessing	(might) benefit twice
	17 When I therefore was thus minded, **did I use lightness?** or the things that I purpose, do I purpose according to the flesh, that with me there should be yea yea, and nay nay?	Was I vacillating	did I lightly change my mind	Do you think I was not sure of my own intentions	I was not vacillating	did I do it lightly
	22 Who hath also sealed us, and given **the earnest of the Spirit** in our hearts.	his Spirit . . . as a guarantee	as a pledge . . . the Spirit	the pledge, the Spirit	the Spirit . . . as a pledge	his Spirit . . . as a deposit, guaranteeing
	23 Moreover I call God **for a record upon my soul,** that to spare you I came not as yet unto Corinth.	to witness against me	to witness what I am going to say	to witness	as witness to my soul	as my witness
2	1 But I determined this with myself, that I would **not come again to you in**	make you another	my next visit to	not to pay you a	not come to you	make another

	KJV	RSV	NEB	JB	NAS	NIV
	heaviness.	painful visit	you would not be another painful one	second distressing visit	in sorrow again	painful visit to you
	5 But if any have caused grief, he hath not grieved me, but in part: **that I may not overcharge** you all.	not to put it too severely	not to labour the point	not to overstate it	in order not to say too much	not to put it too severely
	7 **So that contrariwise ye ought rather** to forgive him, and comfort him, lest perhaps such a one should be swallowed up with overmuch sorrow.	you should rather turn	Something very different is called for now	the best thing now is	so that on the contrary you should rather	Now instead
	13 **I had no rest in my spirit,** because I found not Titus my brother: but taking my leave of them, I went from thence into Macedonia.	my mind could not rest	I still found no relief of mind	I was so continually uneasy in mind	I had no rest for my spirit	I still had no peace of mind
	17 For we are not as many, **which corrupt the word of God:** but as of sincerity, but as of God, in the sight of God speak we in Christ.	peddlers of God's word	go hawking the word of God about	offering the word of God for sale	peddling the word of God	peddle the word of God for profit
3	2 Ye are our **epistle** written **in our** hearts, **known** and read **of** all men:	letter of recommendation / on your / to be known / by	letter / on our / (any man) can see it for what it is / for	letter / in our / (anybody) can see / (omits)	letter / in our / known / by	letter / on our / known / by
	3 Forasmuch as ye are manifestly declared to be the epistle of Christ ministered by us, written not with ink, but with the Spirit of the living God; not in **tables of** stone, but in **fleshy tables of the heart.**	tablets / tablets of human hearts	tablets / pages of the human heart	tablets / tablets of your living hearts	tablets / tablets of human hearts	tablets / tablets of human hearts
	5 Not that we are **sufficient** of ourselves to think any thing as of ourselves; but our **sufficiency** is of God;	competent / competence	qualified / qualification	qualified / qualifications	adequate / adequacy	competent / competence
	7 But if the **ministration** of death, written and engraven in stones, was glorious, so that the children of Israel could not stedfastly behold the face of Moses for the glory of his countenance; which glory was to be done away:	dispensation	(The law) . . . dispensed	administering	ministry	ministry
	11 For if that which **is done away** was glorious, much more that which remaineth is glorious.	faded away	was soon to fade	was so temporary	fades away	was fading away
	14 But their minds were **blinded:** for until this day remaineth the same veil untaken away in the reading of the old testament; which veil is **done away** in Christ.	hardened / taken away	made insensitive / lifted	dulled / lifted	hardened / unlifted	dull / taken away
	15 But even unto this day, when Moses is read, the veil is upon their **heart.**	minds	minds of the hearers	minds	heart	hearts
	16 Nevertheless when **it** shall turn to the Lord, the veil shall be taken away.	a man	he	they	a man	anyone
	18 But we all, with **open face beholding** as in a glass the glory of the Lord, are changed into the same image from glory to glory, even as by the Spirit of the Lord.	unveiled / beholding	(there is no veil over the face, we all reflect)	unveiled / reflecting	unveiled / beholding	unveiled / reflect
4	2 But have **renounced the hidden things of dishonesty,** not walking in craftiness, nor handling the word of God deceitfully; but by manifestation of the truth commending ourselves to every man's conscience in the sight of God.	renounced disgraceful, underhanded ways	renounced the deeds that men hide for very shame	will have none of the reticence of those who are ashamed	renounced things hidden because of shame	renounced secret and shameful ways
	7 But we have this treasure in earthen vessels, that **the excellency of the** power may be of God, and not of us.	the transcendent	such transcendent	such an overwhelming	the surpassing	this all-surpassing
	14 Knowing that he which raised up the Lord Jesus shall raise up us also by Jesus, and shall present us with you [].	into his presence	to his presence	by his side	(no insert)	in his presence

KJV	RSV	NEB	JB	NAS	NIV
15 For all things are for your sakes, **that the abundant grace might through the thanksgiving of many redound** to the glory of God.	so that as grace extends to more and more people it may increase thanksgiving	so that, as the abounding grace of God is shared by more and more, the greater may be the chorus of thanksgiving that ascends	so that the more grace is multiplied among people, the more thanksgiving there will be	that the grace which is spreading to more and more people may cause the giving of thanks to abound	so that the grace that is reaching more and more people may cause thanksgiving to overflow
16 For which cause we **faint not;** but though our outward man perish, yet the inward man is renewed day by day.	do not lose heart	do not lose heart	there is no weakening on our part	we do not lose heart	do not lose heart
5 1 For we know that if our **earthly house of this tabernacle** were **dissolved,** we have a building of God, an house not made with hands, eternal in the heavens.	earthly tent we live in is destroyed	earthly frame that houses us today should be demolished	tent that we live in on earth is folded up	earthly tent which is our house is torn down	earthly tent we live in is destroyed
4 For we that are in this tabernacle do groan, being burdened: not for that we would be unclothed, but **clothed upon,** that mortality might be swallowed up of life.	further clothed	to have the new body put on over it	to put the second garment over it	to be clothed	to be clothed with our heavenly dwelling
5 Now he that hath wrought us for the selfsame thing is God, who also hath given unto us **the earnest of the Spirit.**	the Spirit as a guarantee	as a pledge . . . the Spirit	the pledge of the Spirit	the Spirit as a pledge	the Spirit as a deposit
13 For whether we be beside ourselves, it is to God: or whether we be **sober,** it is for your cause.	in our right mind	in our right mind	being reasonable	of sound mind	in our right mind
14 For the love of Christ **constraineth** us; because we thus **judge,** that **if** one died for all, then were all dead:	controls / are convinced / (omits)	leaves . . . no choice / have reached the conclusion / (omits)	overwhelms / reflect / if	controls / having concluded / (omits)	compels / are convinced / (omits)
16 Wherefore henceforth know we no man **after the flesh:** yea, though we have known Christ after the flesh, yet now henceforth know we him no more.	from a human point of view	worldly standards (have ceased to count in our estimate of any man)	by the standards of the flesh	according to the flesh	from a worldly point of view
20 Now then we are ambassadors for Christ, as though God did beseech you by us: we pray you **in Christ's stead,** be ye reconciled to God.	on behalf of Christ	in Christ's name	in Christ's name	on behalf of Christ	on Christ's behalf
6 2 (For he saith, I have heard thee in a time accepted, and in the day of salvation have I **succoured** thee: behold, now is the accepted time; behold, now is the day of salvation.)	helped	came to your aid	came to your help	helped	helped
4 But in all things approving ourselves as the ministers of God, in much **patience,** in afflictions, in **necessities,** in distresses,	endurance / necessities	endurance / hardships	fortitude / hardship	endurance / hardships	endurance / hardships
12 Ye are **not straitened in us,** but ye are straitened in **your own bowels.**	not restricted by us / your own affections	On our part . . . no constraint / yourselves	constraint . . . not on our side / your own selves	restrained by us / your own affections	(We are not withholding our affection from you, but you are withholding yours from us)
13 Now for a recompence in the same, (I speak as unto my children,) **be ye also enlarged.**	widen your hearts also	open wide your hearts to us	open your minds in the same way	open wide to us also	open wide your hearts also
15 And what concord hath Christ with Belial? or what part hath he that believeth with an **infidel?**	unbeliever	unbeliever	unbeliever	unbeliever	unbeliever
7 4 **Great is my boldness of speech toward** you, **great is my glorying of** you: I am filled with comfort, I am exceeding joyful in all our tribulation.	have great confidence in / have great pride in	am perfectly frank with / have great pride in	have the very greatest confidence in / am so proud of	Great is my confidence in / great is my boasting on	have great confidence in / take great pride in
8 For though I made you sorry with a letter, I do not **repent,** though I **did repent:** for I perceive that the same	regret / did regret	regret / may have been sorry	regret / did regret	regret / did regret	regret / did regret

KJV	RSV	NEB	JB	NAS	NIV
epistle hath made you sorry, though it were but for a season.					
10 For **godly sorrow worketh** repentance to salvation not to be repented of: but the **sorrow of the world worketh** death.	godly grief produces / worldly grief produces	the wound which is borne in God's way brings / hurt which is borne in the world's way	To suffer in God's way means / to suffer as the world knows suffering brings	the sorrow that is according to the will of God produces / the sorrow of the world produces	Godly sorrow brings / worldly sorrow brings
11 For behold this selfsame thing, that ye **sorrowed after a godly sort,** what **carefulness** it wrought in you, yea, what clearing of yourselves, yea, what indignation, yea, what fear, yea, what vehement desire, yea, what zeal, yea, what revenge! In all things ye have approved yourselves to be clear in this matter.	this godly grief / eagerness	bore your hurt in God's way / (It made you take the matter seriously)	(Just look at what suffering) in God's way / keenness	this godly sorrow / earnestness	this godly sorrow / earnestness
12 Wherefore, though I wrote unto you, I did it not for his cause that had done the wrong, nor for his cause that suffered wrong, **but that our care for you in the sight of God might appear unto you.**	but in order that your zeal for us might be revealed to you in the sight of God	to help to make plain to you, in the sight of God, how truly you are devoted to us	to make you realize, in the sight of God, how truly you are devoted to us	but that your earnestness on our behalf might be made known to you in the sight of God	but rather that before God you could see for yourselves how devoted to us you are
8 Moreover, brethren, we **do you to wit** of the grace of God bestowed on the churches of Macedonia;	want you to know	must tell you	here . . . is the news	wish to make known to you	want you to know
8 I speak not by commandment, but by occasion of the **forwardness** of others, and to prove the sincerity of your love.	earnestness	(how keen others are)	keenness	earnestness	earnestness
19 And not that only, but who was also chosen of the churches to travel with us with this grace, which is administered by us to the glory of the same Lord, **and declaration of your ready mind:**	and to show our good will	and show our own eagerness to serve	to satisfy our impatience to help	and to show our readiness	and to show our eagerness to help
9 2 For I know the **forwardness** of your mind, for which I boast of you to them of Macedonia, that Achaia was ready a year ago; and your zeal hath **provoked very many.**	readiness / stirred up most of them	how eager (you are) / most of them have been fired	how anxious (you are) / been a spur to many more	readiness / stirred up most of them	eagerness / stirred most of them to action
7 Every man according **as he purposeth in his heart,** so let him give, not grudgingly, or of necessity: for God loveth a cheerful giver.	as he has made up his mind	as he has decided for himself	what he has decided in his own mind	as he has purposed in his heart	what he has decided in his heart
10 Now he that **ministereth** seed to the sower both minister bread for your food, and multiply your **seed sown,** and increase the fruits of your righteousness;)	supplies / resources	provides / it	provides / all the seed you want	supplies / seed for sowing	supplies / store of seed
13 Whiles by **the experiment of this ministration they** glorify God for your professed subjection unto the gospel of Christ, and for your liberal distribution unto them, and unto all men;	the test of this service, you	the proof which this affords, many	offering this service, you	the proof given by this ministry they	the service by which you have proved yourselves, men
15 Thanks be unto God for his **unspeakable** gift.	inexpressible	beyond words	inexpressible	indescribable	indescribable
10 1 Now I Paul myself beseech you by the **meekness** and **gentleness** of Christ, who in **presence am base** among you, but being absent am bold toward you:	meekness / gentleness / am humble when face to face	gentleness / magnanimity / so feeble (you say) when I am face to face	gentleness / patience / is so humble when he is facing	meekness / gentleness / am meek when face to face	meekness / gentleness / am "timid" when face to face
2 But I beseech you, that I **may not be bold** when I am present with that confidence, wherewith I think to be bold against some, which think of us as if we walked according to the flesh.	may not have to show boldness	(Spare me . . . the necessity of such bravery)	do not have to bully you	may not be bold	may not have to be as bold (as I expect to be)
5 Casting down **imaginations,** and **every high thing** that exalteth itself against the knowledge of God, and	arguments / every proud argument	sophistries / all that rears its proud head	sophistries (vs. 4) / arrogance	speculations / every lofty thing	arguments / pretension

	KJV	RSV	NEB	JB	NAS	NIV
	bringing into captivity every thought to the obedience of Christ:					
	6 And **having in a readiness to revenge** all disobedience, when your obedience is fulfilled.	being ready to punish	are prepared to punish	are prepared to punish	are ready to punish	will be ready to punish
	10 For his letters, say they, are weighty and powerful; but his bodily presence is weak, and **his speech contemptible.**	his speech of no account	as a speaker he is beneath contempt	no preacher at all	his speech contemptible	his speaking amounts to nothing
	13 But we will not boast of things **without our measure,** but according to the measure of the rule which God hath distributed to us, a measure to reach even unto you.	beyond limit	beyond our proper sphere	without a standard to measure against	beyond our measure	boast beyond proper limits
	14 For we stretch not ourselves beyond our measure, as though we reached not unto you: for we **are come as far as to you also** in preaching the gospel of Christ:	were the first to come all the way to you	were the first to reach Corinth	did come all the way	were the first to come even as far as you	did get as far as you
11	4 For if he that cometh preacheth another Jesus, whom we have not preached, or if ye receive another spirit, which ye have not received, or another gospel, which ye have not accepted, **ye might well bear with him.**	you submit to it readily enough	you manage to put up with that well enough	and you welcome it with open arms	you bear this beautifully	you put up with it easily enough
	9 And when I was present with you, and **wanted, I was chargeable to no man:** for that which was lacking to me the brethren which came from Macedonia supplied: and in all things I have kept myself from being burdensome unto you, and so will I keep myself.	was in want / I did not burden anyone	ran short / I sponged on no one	ran out of money / I was not a burden to anyone	was in need / I was not a burden to anyone	needed something / I was not a burden to anyone
	12 But what I do, that I will do, that I may **cut off occasion** from **them which desire occasion;** that wherein they glory, they may be **found even as we.**	undermine the claim / those who would like to claim / they work on the same terms as we do	cut the ground from under / those who would seize any chance / put their vaunted apostleship on the same level as ours	leaving no opportunity / those people who are looking for an opportunity to claim / equality with us	cut off opportunity / who desire an opportunity / regarded just as we are	cut the ground from under / those who want an opportunity / considered equal with us
	14 And **no marvel;** for Satan himself **is transformed** into an angel of light.	no wonder / disguises himself	nothing surprising about that / masquerades	nothing unexpected about that / goes disguised	no wonder / disguises himself	no wonder / masquerades
	18 Seeing that many **glory after the flesh,** I will glory also.	boast of worldly things	brag of their earthly distinctions	have been boasting of their worldly achievements	boast according to the flesh	are boasting in the way of the world
	19 For ye **suffer** fools gladly, seeing ye yourselves are wise.	bear with	bear with	tolerate	bear with	put up with
	21 **I speak as concerning reproach, as though we had been weak.** Howbeit whereinsoever any is bold, (I speak foolishly,) I am bold also.	To my shame, I must say, we were too weak for that!	And we, you say, have been weak! I admit the reproach.	I hope you are ashamed with us for being weak with you instead!	To my shame I must say that we have been weak by comparison.	To my shame I admit that we were too weak for that!
12	13 For what is it wherein ye were **inferior** to other churches, except it be that I myself was not burdensome to you? forgive me this wrong.	less favored	treated worse	(have) had less	inferior	inferior
	14 Behold, the third time I am ready to come to you; and I will not be burdensome to you: for I seek not yours, but you: for the children ought not to **lay up** for the parents, but the parents for the children.	lay up	make provision	save up	save up	save up
	20 For I fear, lest, when I come, I shall not find you such as I would, and that I shall be found unto you such as ye would not: lest there be **debates,** envyings, wraths, strifes, backbitings, whisperings, **swellings,** tumults:	quarreling / conceit	quarreling / arrogance	wrangling / obstinancies	strife / arrogance	quarreling / arrogance

KJV	RSV	NEB	JB	NAS	NIV
21 And lest, when I come again, my God will humble me among you, and that I shall **bewail** many which have sinned already, and have not repented of the uncleanness and fornication and lasciviousness which they have committed.	mourn over	have tears to shed over	grieving over	mourn over	grieved over
13 2 I told you before, and **foretell you,** as if I were present, the second time; and being absent now I write to them which heretofore have sinned, and to all other, that, if I come again, I will not spare:	warn them	repeat the warning	give warning	say in advance	repeat it
3 Since ye seek a proof of Christ speaking in me, which **to youward** is not weak, but is mighty in you.	in dealing with you	with you	(you have known him not as a weakling)	toward you	in dealing with you
5 Examine yourselves, whether ye be in the faith; prove your own selves. Know ye not your own selves, how that Jesus Christ is in you, except **ye be reprobates?**	you fail to meet the test	you prove unequal to the test	you have failed the test	you fail the test	you fail the test
6 But I trust that ye shall know that we are not **reprobates.**	we have not failed	we are not unequal to it	we . . . have not failed it	we ourselves do not fail the test	we have not failed the test
7 Now I pray to God that ye do no evil; not that we should appear approved, but that ye should do that which is **honest,** though we **be as reprobates.**	right / may seem to have failed	right / even if we should seem to be discredited	well / failed	right / should appear unapproved	right / may seem to have failed
11 Finally, brethren, farewell. **Be perfect, be of good comfort, be of one mind, live in peace;** and the God of love and peace shall be with you.	Mend your ways, heed my appeal, agree with one another, live in peace	Mend your ways; take our appeal to heart; agree with one another; live in peace	try to grow perfect; help one another. Be united; live in peace	be made complete, be comforted, be likeminded, live in peace:	Aim for perfection, listen to my appeal, be of one mind, live in peace.

Galatians

KJV	RSV	NEB	JB	NAS	NIV
1 6 I **marvel** that ye are so soon **removed** from him that called you into the grace of Christ unto another gospel:	am astonished / deserting	am astonished / turning . . . away	am astonished / turned away	am amazed / deserting	am astonished / deserting
10 For do I now **persuade** men, or God? or do I seek to please men? for if I yet pleased men, I should not be the servant of Christ.	seeking the favor of	canvassing for . . . support	looking for . . . approval	seeking the favor of	trying to win the approval of
11 But I **certify you,** brethren, that the gospel which was preached of me is not after man.	would have you know	make it clear to you	want you to realize	would have you know	want you to know
13 For ye have heard **of my conversation in time past** in the Jews' religion, how that beyond measure I persecuted the church of God, and wasted it:	of my former life	what my manner of life	of my career	of my former manner of life	of my previous way of life
14 And **profited** in the Jews' religion **above** many my equals in mine own nation, being more exceedingly zealous of the traditions of my fathers.	advanced . . . beyond	was outstripping	stood out among	was advancing . . . beyond	was advancing . . . beyond
2 5 To whom we **gave place by subjection, no,** not for an hour; that the truth of the gospel might continue with you.	did not yield submission	not for one moment . . . yield	refused even out of deference to yield	did not yield in subjection	did not give in
6 But of these who seemed to be somewhat, (whatsoever they were, it maketh no matter to me: God **accepteth no man's person:**) for they who seemed to be somewhat in conference added nothing to me:	shows no partiality	does not recognize these personal distinctions	has no favorites	shows no partiality	does not judge by external appearance
7 But **contrariwise,** when they saw that the gospel of the uncircumcision was	on the contrary	on the contrary	On the contrary	on the contrary	On the contrary

KJV	RSV	NEB	JB	NAS	NIV
committed unto me, as the gospel of the circumcision was unto Peter;					
10 Only they would that we should remember the poor; the same which I also **was forward** to do.	was eager	made it my business	was anxious	was eager	was eager
21 I **do not frustrate** the grace of God: for if righteousness come by the law, then Christ is dead in vain.	do not nullify	will not nullify	cannot bring myself to give up	do not nullify	do not set aside
3 1 O Foolish Galatians, who hath bewitched you, that ye should not obey the truth, before whose eyes Jesus Christ hath been **evidently set forth,** crucified among you?	publicly portrayed	openly displayed	(in spite of the plain explanation you have had)	publicly portrayed	clearly portrayed
5 **He** therefore that **ministereth** to you the Spirit, and worketh miracles among you, doeth he it by the works of the law, or by the hearing of faith?	he / supplies	God / gives	God / give	He / provides	God / give
11 But that no man is justified by the law in the sight of God, it is evident: for, **The just shall live by faith.**	"He who through faith is righteous shall live"	'he shall gain life who is justified through faith'	the righteous man finds life through faith	"The righteous man shall live by faith."	"The righteous will live by faith."
15 Brethren, I speak after the manner of men; Though it be but a man's covenant, yet if it be confirmed, no man **disannulleth,** or addeth thereto.	annuls	can set . . . aside	is allowed to disregard	sets . . . aside	can set aside
20 Now a mediator **is not** a mediator of one, but God is one.	implies	is not needed for	can only be (between two parties)	is not	does not represent
22 But the scripture hath **concluded all under sin,** that the promise by faith of Jesus Christ might be given to them that believe.	consigned all things to sin	has declared the whole world to be prisoners in subjection to sin	makes no exceptions when it says that sin is master everywhere	has shut up all men under sin	declares that the whole world is a prisoner of sin
4 2 But is under **tutors and governors** until the time appointed of the father.	guardians and trustees	guardians and trustees	guardians and administrators	guardians and managers	guardians and trustees
3 Even so we, when we were children, were in bondage under the **elements** of the world:	elemental spirits	elemental spirits	elemental principles	elemental things	basic principles
9 But now, after that ye have known God, or rather are known of God, how turn ye again to the weak and beggarly **elements,** whereunto ye desire again to be in bondage?	elemental spirits	spirits of the elements	elemental things	elemental things	principles
13 Ye know how through **infirmity of the flesh** I preached the gospel unto you at the first.	bodily ailment	bodily illness	illness	bodily illness	illness
14 And my **temptation** which was in my flesh ye despised not, nor rejected; but received me as an angel of God, even as Christ Jesus.	condition	state	disease	bodily condition	illness
17 They **zealously affect** you, but not well; yea, they would exclude you, that ye might affect them.	make much of	are envious of	have tried to win (you) over	eagerly seek	are zealous to win (you) over
20 I desire to be present with you now, and to change **my voice;** for I stand in doubt of you.	my tone	my tone	what to say	my tone	my tone
24 Which things are an allegory: for these are the two covenants; the one from the mount Sinai, which **gendereth to bondage,** which is **Agar.**	bearing children for slavery / Hagar	bearing children into slavery / Hagar	children are slaves / Hagar	bearing children who are to be slaves / Hagar	is in slavery with her children / Hagar
5 11 And I, brethren, if I yet preach circumcision, why do I yet suffer perse-					

KJV	RSV	NEB	JB	NAS	NIV
cution? then is the **offence** of the cross **ceased.**	stumbling block / removed	stumbling-block / is . . . no more	scandal / (would there be any)	stumbling block / abolished	offense / abolished
12 I would they **were even cut off** which trouble you.	would even mutilate themselves	had better go the whole way and make eunuchs of themselves	(I) would like to see the knife slip	would even mutilate themselves	would go the whole way and emasculate themselves
19 Now the **works of the flesh** are manifest, which are these; Adultery, fornication, uncleanness, lasciviousness,	works of the flesh	kind of behaviour that belongs to the lower nature	self-indulgence	deeds of the flesh	acts of the sinful nature
20 Idolatry, witchcraft, hatred, variance, **emulations,** wrath, strife, seditions, heresies,	jealousy	envy	jealousy	jealousy	jealousy
21 Envyings, murders, drunkenness, revellings, and **such like:** of the which I **tell** you before, as I have also told you in time past, that they which do such things shall not inherit the kingdom of God.	the like / warned	the like / warned	similar things / warned	such things / forewarned	the like / did (warn)
23 Meekness, **temperance:** against such there is no law.	self-control	self-control	self-control	self-control	self-control
24 And they that are Christ's have crucified the flesh with the **affections** and lusts.	passions	passions	passions	passions	passions
26 Let us not be desirous of **vain glory,** provoking one another, envying one another.	have no self-conceit	must not be conceited	must stop being conceited	not become boastful	not become conceited
6 4 But let every man **prove** his own **work,** and then shall he have rejoicing in himself alone, and not in another.	test / work	examine / conduct	examine / conduct	examine / work	test / actions
6 Let him that is taught in the word **communicate** unto him that teacheth in all good things.	share	give . . . a share	contribute	share	share
9 And let us not be weary in well-doing: for in due season we shall reap, if we **faint not.**	do not lose heart	do not slacken our efforts	don't give up the struggle	do not grow weary	do not give up
11 Ye see **how large a letter** I have written unto you with mine own hand.	with what large letters	these big letters	in large letters	with what large letters	what large letters
12 As many as desire to make a fair shew in the flesh, they **constrain** you to be circumcised; **only lest they should** suffer persecution for the cross of Christ.	compel / only in order that they not	trying to force / (their sole object is)	want to force / they want	try to compel / they may not	are trying to compel / (the only reason they do this is to avoid)
14 But God forbid that I should glory, save in the cross of our Lord Jesus Christ, **by whom** the world is crucified unto me, and I unto the world.	by which	through which	through whom	through which	through which
15 For in Christ Jesus neither circumcision availeth any thing, nor uncircumcision, but a new **creature.**	creation	creation	creature	creation	creation

Ephesians

KJV	RSV	NEB	JB	NAS	NIV
1 1 Paul, an apostle of Jesus Christ by the will of God, to the saints **which are at Ephesus, and to the faithful** in Christ Jesus:	who are also faithful	at Ephesus, believers incorporate	who are faithful	who are at Ephesus, and who are faithful	in Ephesus, the faithful
5 Having predestinated **us unto the adoption of children** by Jesus Christ to himself, according to the good pleasure of his will,	us . . . to be his sons	us . . . to be accepted as his sons	that we should become his adopted sons	to adoption as sons	us to be adopted as sons
6 To the praise of the glory of his grace, **wherein he hath made us accepted** in	which he freely	so graciously be-	his free gift to us	which He freely	which he has

KJV	RSV	NEB	JB	NAS	NIV
the beloved.	bestowed on us	stowed on us		bestowed on us	freely given us
8 Wherein he hath **abounded** toward us in all wisdom and prudence;	lavished	lavished	showered	lavished	lavished
9 Having made known unto us the mystery of his will, according to his good pleasure which he hath purposed in **himself:**	Christ	Christ	Christ	Him	Christ
10 **That in the dispensation** of the **fulness of times** he might gather together in one all things in Christ, both which are in heaven, and which are on earth; even in him:	as a plan for the fulness of time	to be put into effect when the time was ripe	to act upon when the times had run their course to the end	with a view to an administration suitable to the fulness of the times	to be put into effect when the times will have reached their fulfillment
14 Which is the **earnest** of our inheritance until the redemption of the purchased possession, unto the praise of his glory.	guarantee	pledge	pledge	pledge	guaranteeing
19 And what is the exceeding greatness of his power **to us-ward** who believe, according to the working of his mighty power,	in us	to us	for us	toward us	for us
22 And hath put all things under his feet, and gave him to be the head over all things **to** the church,	for	to	of	to	for
2 1 And you **hath he quickened,** who were dead in trespasses and sins;	he made alive	(omits)	(omits)	(omits)	(omits)
3 Among whom also we all **had our conversation in times past** in the lusts of our flesh, fulfilling the desires of the flesh and of the mind; and were by nature the children of wrath, even as others.	once lived	were once of their number	were among them too in the past	all formerly lived	also lived among them at one time
13 But now in Christ Jesus ye who **sometimes** were far off **are made nigh** by the blood of Christ.	once / have been brought near	once / have been brought near	used to be / have been brought very close	formerly / have been brought near	once / have been brought near
14 For he is our peace, who hath made both one, and hath broken down the middle wall of **partition between us;**	hostility	enmity . . . between them	barrier which used to keep them apart	barrier	hostility
15 Having abolished in his flesh **the enmity,** even the law of commandments contained in ordinances; for to make in himself **of twain** one new man, so making peace;	(omits) / in place of the two	(omits) / out of the two	the hostility (vs. 14) / out of the two of them	the enmity / the two	(omits) / out of the two
16 And that he might reconcile both unto God in one body by the cross, having **slain the enmity** thereby:	bringing the hostility to an end	on which he killed the enmity	killed the hostility	having put to death the enmity	put to death their hostility
3 2 If ye have heard **of the dispensation** of the grace of God which is given me **to you-ward:**	of the stewardship / for you	how God has assigned / for your benefit	I have been entrusted by God / for you	of the stewardship / for you	about the administration / for you
4 Whereby, when ye read, ye may understand **my knowledge** in the mystery of Christ)	my insight	that I understand	that I see	my insight	my insight
9 And to make all men see **what is the fellowship of the mystery,** which from the beginning of the world hath been hid in God, who created all things by Jesus Christ:	what is the plan of the mystery	(how this hidden purpose was to be put into effect)	how the mystery is to be dispensed	what is the administration of the mystery	my administration of this mystery
13 Wherefore I desire that ye **faint not** at my tribulations for you, which is your glory.	not to lose heart	not to lose heart	never lose confidence	not to lose heart	not to be discouraged
14 For this cause I bow my knees unto the Father **of our Lord Jesus Christ,**	(omits)	(omits)	(omits)	(omits)	(omits)
21 Unto him be glory in the church **by** Christ Jesus throughout all ages, world without end. Amen.	in	in	in	in	in

KJV	RSV	NEB	JB	NAS	NIV
4 1 I Therefore, the prisoner of the Lord, beseech you that ye walk worthy of the **vocation** wherewith ye are called,	calling	calling	vocation	calling	calling
3 **Endeavouring** to keep the unity of the Spirit in the bond of peace.	eager	Spare no effort	Do all you can	being diligent	Do your best
4 There is one body, and one Spirit, even as ye are called **in one hope of your calling;**	to the one hope that belongs to your call	one hope held out in God's call to you	into one and the same hope when you were called	in one hope of your calling	to one hope when you were called
8 Wherefore he saith, When he ascended up on high, **he led captivity captive,** and gave gifts unto men.	he led a host of captives	with captives in his train	he captured prisoners	He led captive a host of captives	he led captives in his train
12 **For the perfecting of** the saints, for the work of the ministry, for the edifying of the body of Christ:	to equip	to equip	so that . . . together make a unity	for the equipping of	to prepare
13 Till we all come in the unity of the faith, and of the knowledge of the Son of God, unto a **perfect man,** unto the measure of the stature of the fulness of Christ:	mature manhood	mature manhood	perfect Man	mature man	(become) mature
14 That we henceforth be no more children, tossed to and fro, and carried about with every wind of doctrine, by the **sleight of men, and cunning craftiness, whereby they lie in wait to deceive:**	by the cunning of men, by their craftiness in deceitful wiles	dupes of crafty rogues and their deceitful schemes	at the mercy of all the tricks men play and their cleverness in practicing deceit	by the trickery of men, by craftiness in deceitful scheming	and by the cunning and craftiness of men in their deceitful scheming
16 From whom the whole body **fitly joined together and compacted** by that which every joint supplieth, according to the effectual working in the measure of every part, maketh increase of the body **unto the edifying of itself** in love.	joined and knit together / and upbuilds itself	Bonded and knit together / and builds itself up	fitted and joined together / has built itself up	being fitted and held together / for the upbuilding of itself	joined and held together / and builds itself up
17 This I say therefore, and testify in the Lord, that ye henceforth walk not as other Gentiles walk, in the **vanity** of their mind,	in the futility of their minds	with their good-for-nothing notions	the aimless kind of life	in the futility of their mind	in the futility of their thinking
19 Who **being past feeling** have given themselves over unto lasciviousness, to work all uncleanness with greediness.	they have become callous	Dead to all feeling	Their sense of right and wrong once dulled	they, having become callous	Having lost all sensitivity
21 **If so be** that ye have heard him, and have been taught by him, as the truth is in Jesus:	assuming	(were you not told of him)	unless	if indeed	Surely
22 That ye put off concerning the former **conversation** the old **man,** which is corrupt according to the deceitful lusts;	manner of life / nature	way of life / human nature	way of life / self	manner of life / self	way of life / self
27 **Neither give place to** the devil.	and give no opportunity to	leave no loop-hole for	or else you will give . . . a foothold	and do not give the devil	and do not give . . . a foothold
32 And be ye kind one to another, tenderhearted, forgiving one another, even as God **for** Christ's **sake** hath forgiven you.	in Christ	in Christ	in Christ	in Christ	in Christ
5 1 **Be ye therefore followers of God,** as dear children;	Therefore be imitators of God	try to be like him	Try, then, to imitate God	Therefore be imitators of God	Be imitators of God, therefore
4 Neither filthiness, nor foolish talking, nor jesting, which are **not convenient:** but rather giving of thanks.	not fitting	out of place	wrong for you	not fitting	out of place
7 **Be not ye** therefore **partakers** with them.	do not associate	have no part or lot	Make sure that you are not included	do not be partakers	do not be partakers
8 For ye were **sometimes** darkness, but now are ye light in the Lord: walk as children of light:	once	once	once	formerly	once
9 (For the fruit of **the Spirit** is in all goodness and righteousness and truth;)	light	light	light	light	light

KJV	RSV	NEB	JB	NAS	NIV
10 **Proving** what is acceptable unto the Lord.	try to learn	Try to find out	Try to discover	trying to learn	find out
11 And have no fellowship with the unfruitful works of darkness, but rather **reprove** them.	expose them	show them up for what they are	exposing them by contrast	expose them	expose them
13 But all things that are **reproved** are made manifest by the light: for whatsoever doth make manifest is light.	exposed	(the light) has shown it up	exposed	exposed	exposed
18 And be not drunk with wine, **wherein is excess;** but be filled with the Spirit;	for that is debauchery	(drunkenness) and the dissipation that goes with it	this is simply dissipation	for that is dissipation	which leads to debauchery
19 Speaking to yourselves in psalms and hymns and spiritual songs, singing and making melody **in your heart** to the Lord;	with all your heart	in your hearts	in your hearts	with your heart	in your heart
21 Submitting yourselves one to another **in the fear of God.**	out of reverence for Christ	out of reverence for Christ	in obedience to Christ	in the fear of Christ	out of reverence for Christ
33 Nevertheless let every one of you in particular so love his wife even as himself; and the wife see that she **reverence** her husband.	respects	pays. . .all respect	respect	respect	respect
6 4 And, ye fathers, provoke not your children to wrath: but bring them up in the **nurture and admonition** of the Lord.	discipline and instruction	instruction, and the correction	(correct them and guide them)	discipline and instruction	training and instruction
9 And, ye masters, do the same things unto them, forbearing threatening: knowing that **your Master also** is in heaven; neither is there **respect of persons** with him.	he who is both their Master and yours / there is no partiality with him	you both have the same Master / he has no favourites	they and you have the same Master / he is not impressed by one person more than by another	both their Master and yours / there is no partiality with Him	he who is both their Master and yours / there is no favoritism with him
16 Above all, taking the shield of faith, wherewith ye shall be able to quench all the fiery darts of the **wicked.**	evil one	evil one	evil one	evil one	evil one
24 Grace be with all them that love our Lord Jesus Christ in **sincerity.** Amen.	with love undying	grace and immortality	(omits)	with a love incorruptible	with an undying love

Philippians

KJV	RSV	NEB	JB	NAS	NIV
1 7 Even as it is meet for me to think this of you all, because I have you in my heart; inasmuch as both in my bonds, and in the defence and confirmation of the gospel, ye all **are partakers of my grace.**	are . . . partakers with me of grace	share in the privilege that is mine	have shared the privileges which have been mine	are partakers of grace with me	share in God's grace with me
8 For God **is my record,** how greatly I long after you all in the **bowels** of Jesus Christ.	is my witness / affection	God knows / deep yearning	God knows / (as Christ Jesus loves you)	is my witness / affection	can testify / affection
12 But I would ye should understand, brethren, that the things which happened unto me have **fallen out** rather unto the furtherance of the gospel;	served	helped on	been a help	turned out	served
13 So that my bonds in Christ are manifest in all the **palace,** and in all other places;	praetorian guard	headquarters	Praetorium	praetorian guard	palace guard
16 The one preach Christ **of contention,** not sincerely, supposing to add affliction to my bonds:	out of partisanship (vs. 17)	in a jealous and quarrelsome spirit	for jealous or selfish motives (vs. 17)	out of selfish ambition (vs. 17)	out of selfish ambition (vs. 17)
20 According to my earnest expectation and my hope, that in nothing I shall					

KJV	RSV	NEB	JB	NAS	NIV
be ashamed, but that with all boldness, as always, so now also Christ **shall be magnified** in my body, whether it be by life, or by death.	will be honored	will shine out clearly	to be glorified	shall . . . be exalted	will be exalted
22 But if I live in the flesh, this is the fruit of my labour: yet what I shall choose I **wot not.**	cannot tell	cannot tell	do not know	do not know	do not know
27 Only let your **conversation** be as it becometh the gospel of Christ: that whether I come and see you, or else be absent, I may hear of your affairs, that ye stand fast in one spirit, with one mind striving together for the faith of the gospel:	manner of life	conduct	anything in your everyday lives	conduct	conduct
2 1 If **there be therefore any consolation** in Christ, **if any comfort of love,** if any fellowship of the Spirit, if **any bowels and mercies,**	there is any encouragement / any incentive of love / any affection and sympathy	our common life . . . yields anything to stir the heart / any loving consolation / any warmth of affection or compassion	our life . . . means anything to you / love can persuade at all / any tenderness and sympathy	there is any encouragement / there is any consolation of love / there is any affection and compassion	you have any encouragement from being united / any comfort from his love / any fellowship with the Spirit
6 Who, being in the form of God, **thought it not robbery to be equal with God:**	did not count equality with God a thing to be grasped	did not think to snatch at equality with God	did not cling to his equality with God	did not regard equality with God a thing to be grasped	did not consider equality with God something to be grasped
7 But **made himself of no reputation,** and took upon him the form of a servant, and was made in the likeness of men:	emptied himself	made himself nothing	emptied himself	emptied Himself	made himself nothing
8 And being **found in fashion as a man,** he humbled himself, and became obedient unto death, even the death of the cross.	found in human form	revealed in human shape	being as all men are (vs. 7)	found in appearance as a man	found in appearance as a man
15 That ye may be blameless and harmless, the sons of God, **without rebuke,** in the midst of a crooked and perverse nation, among whom ye shine as lights in the world;	without blemish	faultless	perfect	above reproach	without fault
16 **Holding forth** the word of life; that I may rejoice in the day of Christ, that I have not run in vain, neither laboured in vain.	holding fast	proffer	offering	holding fast	hold out
28 I sent him therefore **the more carefully,** that, when ye see him again, ye may rejoice, and that I may be the less sorrowful.	the more eager	all the more eager	as promptly as I can	all the more eagerly	all the more eager
29 Receive him therefore in the Lord with all gladness; and **hold such in reputation:**	honor such men	You should honor men like him	people like him are to be honored	hold men like him in high regard	honor men like him
30 Because for the work of Christ he was nigh unto death, not regarding his life, to **supply your lack of service toward me.**	to complete your service to me	to render me the service you could not give	to give me the help that you were not able to give yourselves	to complete what was deficient in your service to me	to make up for the help you could not give me
3 2 Beware of dogs, beware of evil workers, beware of **the concision.**	those who mutilate the flesh	those who insist on mutilation	the cutters	the false circumcision	those mutilators of the flesh
8 Yea doubtless, and I count all things but loss for the **excellency of the knowledge** of Christ Jesus my Lord: for whom I have suffered the loss of all things, and do count them but **dung,** that I may **win** Christ,	surpassing worth of knowing / refuse / gain	gain of knowing / garbage / gaining	supreme advantage of knowing / rubbish / have	surpassing value of knowing / rubbish / gain	surpassing greatness of knowing / rubbish / gain
12 Not as though I had already attained, either were already perfect: but I follow after, if that I may **apprehend** that for which also I am apprehended of Christ Jesus.	make . . . my own	take hold of	capture	laid hold of	take hold of

KJV	RSV	NEB	JB	NAS	NIV
13 Brethren, I count not myself to have apprehended: but this one thing I do, forgetting those things which are behind, and **reaching forth** unto those things which are before,	straining forward	reaching out	strain ahead	reaching forward	straining toward
14 I press toward the **mark** for the prize of the high calling of God in Christ Jesus.	goal	goal	finish	goal	goal
15 Let us therefore, as many as be **perfect,** be thus minded: and if in any thing ye be otherwise minded, God shall reveal even this unto you.	mature	mature	"perfect"	perfect	mature
20 For our **conversation** is in heaven; from whence also we look for the Saviour, the Lord Jesus Christ:	commonwealth	(We . . . are citizens of heaven)	homeland	citizenship	citizenship
21 Who shall change our **vile** body, that it may be fashioned like unto his glorious body, according to the working whereby he is able even to subdue all things unto himself.	lowly	humble	wretched	humble	lowly
4 5 Let your **moderation** be known unto all men. The Lord is at hand.	forbearance	magnanimity	tolerance	forbearing spirit	gentleness
6 **Be careful for nothing;** but in every thing by prayer and supplication with thanksgiving let your requests be made known unto God.	Have no anxiety about anything	have no anxiety	There is no need to worry	Be anxious for nothing	Do not be anxious about anything
7 And the peace of God, which passeth all understanding, shall keep your hearts and minds **through** Jesus Christ.	in	in	in	in	in
8 Finally, brethren, whatsoever things are true, whatsoever things are **honest,** whatsoever things are just, whatsoever things are pure, whatsoever things are lovely, whatsoever things are **of good report;** if there be any **virtue,** and if there be any praise, think on these things.	honorable / gracious / if there is any excellence	noble / gracious / whatever is excellent	noble / (that we . . . honor) / everything that can be thought virtuous	honorable / of good repute / if there is any excellence	noble / admirable/if anything is excellent
14 Notwithstanding ye have well done, that ye did **communicate with** my affliction.	share	share	share	share	share
18 **But I have all, and abound:** I am full, having received of Epaphroditus the things which were sent from you, **an odour of a sweet smell,** a sacrifice acceptable, well-pleasing to God.	I have received full payment, and more / a fragrant offering	However, here I give you my receipt for everything—for more than everything / a fragrant offering	Now for the time being I have everything that I need and more / a sweet fragrance	But I have received everything in full, and have an abundance / a fragrant aroma	I have received full payment and even more / a fragrant offering
23 The grace of our Lord Jesus Christ be **with you all.** Amen.	with your spirit	with your spirit	with your spirit	with your spirit	with your spirit

Colossians

KJV	RSV	NEB	JB	NAS	NIV
1 2 To the saints and faithful brethren in Christ which are at Colosse: Grace be unto you, and peace, from God our Father **and the Lord Jesus Christ.**	(omits)	(omits)	(omits)	(omits)	(omits)
12 Giving thanks unto the Father, which **hath made us meet** to be partakers of the inheritance of the saints in light:	who has qualified us	who has made you fit	who has made it possible for you	who has qualified us	who has qualified you
14 In whom we have redemption **through his blood,** even the forgiveness of sins:	(omits)	(omits)	(omits)	(omits)	(omits)

	KJV	RSV	NEB	JB	NAS	NIV
	17 And he is before all things, and by him all things **consist.**	hold together	are held together	holds . . . in unity	hold together	hold together
	21 And you, that were **sometime alienated** and enemies in your mind by wicked works, yet now hath he reconciled	once . . . estranged	Formerly . . . estranged	Not long ago . . . foreigners	formerly alienated	Once . . . alienated
	25 Whereof I am made a minister, **according to the dispensation of God** which is given to me for you, to fulfil the word of God;	according to the divine office	by virtue of the task	when God (made me responsible for)	according to the stewardship from God	by the commission God (gave me)
	28 Whom we preach, warning every man, and teaching every man in all wisdom; that we may present every man **perfect** in Christ Jesus:	mature	mature	perfect	complete	perfect
2	8 Beware lest any man **spoil** you through philosophy and vain deceit, after the tradition of men, after the rudiments of the world, and not after Christ.	makes a prey of you	(do not let) your minds be captured	traps you	takes you captive	takes you captive
	15 And having **spoiled** principalities and powers, he made a shew of them openly, triumphing over them in it.	disarmed	discarded (like a garment)	got rid of	disarmed	disarmed
	18 Let no man **beguile you of your reward** in a voluntary humility and worshipping of angels, intruding into those things which he hath not seen, vainly puffed up by his fleshly mind,	disqualify you	(You are not) to be disqualified	(Do not be taken in by people who like groveling to angels and worshiping them)	keep defrauding you of your prize	disqualify you for the prize
	23 Which things have indeed a shew of wisdom in **will-worship,** and **humility,** and **neglecting of the body; not in any honour** to the **satisfying of the flesh.**	rigor of devotion / self-abasement / severity to the body / no value in checking the indulgence of the flesh	forced piety / self-mortification / severity to the body / no use at all in combating sensuality	self-imposed devotions / self-abasement / severe treatment of the body / once the flesh starts to protest . . . no use at all	self-made religion / self-abasement / severe treatment of the body / no value against fleshly indulgence	self-imposed worship / false humility / harsh treatment of the body / lack any value in restraining sensual indulgence
3	2 Set your **affection** on things above, not on things on the earth.	minds	thoughts	thoughts	mind	minds
	5 **Mortify** therefore your members which are upon the earth; fornication, uncleanness, inordinate affection, evil **concupiscence,** and covetousness, which is idolatry:	Put to death / desire	put to death / cravings	kill / desires	consider . . . as dead / desire	Put to death / desires
	6 For which things' sake the wrath of God cometh **on the children of disobedience:**	(omits)	(omits)	(omits)	(omits)	(omits)
	7 In the which ye also walked **some time,** when ye lived in them.	once	once	used to	once	used to
	12 Put on therefore, as the elect of God, holy and beloved, **bowels of mercies,** kindness, **humbleness of mind,** meekness, longsuffering;	compassion / lowliness	compassion / humility	compassion / humility	compassion / humility	compassion / humility
	13 Forbearing one another, and forgiving one another, if any man have a **quarrel** against any: even as Christ forgave you, so also do ye.	complaint	complaint	quarrel	complaint	grievances
	14 And above all these things put on **charity,** which is the bond of perfectness.	love	love	love	love	love
	25 But he that doeth wrong shall receive for the wrong which he hath done: and **there is no respect of persons.**	there is no partiality	he has no favourites	he does not favor one person more than another	without partiality	there is no favoritism
4	8 Whom I have sent unto you for the same purpose, that he might know **your estate,** and comfort your hearts;	how we are	all about us	news about us	about our circumstances	about our circumstances
	15 Salute the brethren which are in Laodicea, and Nymphas, and the church which is in **his** house.	her	her	her	her	her

I Thessalonians

	KJV	RSV	NEB	JB	NAS	NIV
1	6 And ye became **followers** of us, and of the Lord, having received the word in much affliction, with joy of the Holy Ghost:	imitators	(you . . . followed the example)	imitators	imitators	imitators
2	1 For yourselves, brethren, know our **entrance** in unto you, that it was not in vain:	visit	visit	visit	coming	visit
	2 But even after that we had suffered before, and were shamefully **entreated,** as ye know, at Philippi, we were bold in our God to speak unto you the gospel of God **with much contention.**	treated/in the face of great opposition	(the injury and outrage which . . . we had suffered)/A hard struggle it was.	insulted/in the face of great opposition	mistreated/amid much opposition	insulted/in spite of strong opposition
	6 Nor of men sought we glory, neither of you, nor yet of others, when we might have **been burdensome,** as the apostles of Christ.	have made demands	have made our weight felt	have imposed ourselves on you (vs. 7)	have asserted our authority	have been a burden to you (vs. 7)
	8 So being affectionately desirous of you, we were willing **to have imparted unto you,** not the gospel of God only, but also our own souls, because ye were dear unto us.	to share with you	to impart to you	to hand over to you	proclaimed to you	to share with you
	9 For ye remember, brethren, our labour and travail: for labouring night and day, because we would not be **chargeable unto any of you,** we preached unto you the gospel of God.	that we might not burden any of you	rather than be a burden to anyone	so as not to be a burden on any one of you	so as not to be a burden to any one of you	in order not to be a burden to anyone
4	4 That every one of you should know how **to possess his vessel in sanctification and honour;**	to take a wife for himself in holiness and honor	to gain mastery over his body, to hallow and honour it	to use the body that belongs to him in a way that is holy and honorable	to possess his own vessel in sanctification and honor	to control his own body in a way that is holy and honorable
	5 Not in the **lust of concupiscence,** even as the Gentiles which know not God:	passion of lust	lust	selfish lust	lustful passion	passionate lust
	6 That no man **go beyond and defraud** his brother in any matter: because that the Lord is the avenger of all such, as we also have forewarned you and testified.	transgress, and wrong	must do . . . wrong . . . or invade	sin by taking advantage of	transgress and defraud	should wrong . . . or take advantage of
	8 He therefore that **despiseth,** despiseth not man, but God, who hath also given unto us his holy Spirit.	disregards	flouts	objects	rejects	rejects
	11 And that ye **study to be quiet,** and to do your own business, and to work with your own hands, as we commanded you;	live quietly	keep calm	living quietly	lead a quiet life	lead a quiet life
	12 That ye may **walk honestly toward them that are without,** and that ye may have lack of nothing.	command the respect of outsiders	command the respect of those outside your own number	are seen to be respectable by those outside the Church	behave properly toward outsiders	win the respect of outsiders
	15 For this we say unto you by the word of the Lord, that we which are alive and remain unto the coming of the Lord shall not **prevent** them which are asleep.	precede	forestall	have any advantage over	precede	precede
5	12 And we beseech you, brethren, to **know** them which labour among you, and are over you in the Lord, and admonish you;	respect	acknowledge	be considerate to	appreciate	respect
	14 Now we exhort you, brethren, warn them that are unruly, comfort the **feebleminded,** support the weak, be patient toward all men.	fainthearted	faint-hearted	those who are apprehensive	fainthearted	timid

	KJV	RSV	NEB	JB	NAS	NIV
	21 **Prove** all things; hold fast that which is good.	test	bring . . . to the test	think (before you do anything)	examine	Test

II Thessalonians

	KJV	RSV	NEB	JB	NAS	NIV
1	22 Abstain from **all appearance of evil.**	every form of evil	the bad of whatever kind	every form of evil	every form of evil	every kind of evil
	3 We are bound to thank God always for you, brethren, as it is **meet,** because that your faith groweth exceedingly, and the **charity** of every one of you all toward each other **aboundeth.**	fitting/love/is increasing	right/love/grows ever greater	quite rightly/ love/never stops increasing	fitting/love/grows ever greater	rightly/love/is increasing
	5 **Which is a manifest token of** the righteous judgment of God, that ye may be counted worthy of the kingdom of God, for which ye also suffer:	This is evidence of	See how this brings out	It all shows that	This is a plain indication of	All this is evidence that
	7 **And to you who are troubled rest with us,** when the Lord Jesus shall be revealed from heaven with his mighty angels,	and to grant rest with us to you who are afflicted	sending . . . relief to you who are troubled, and to us as well	and reward you, who are suffering now, with the same peace as he will give us	and to give relief to you who are afflicted and to us as well	give relief to you who are troubled
	9 Who shall be punished with everlasting **destruction** [ ] from the presence of the Lord, and from the glory of his power;	destruction/and exclusion	ruin/cut off	lost/excluded	destruction/away	destruction/and shut out
	10 When he shall come to be glorified in his saints, and to be **admired in** all themthat believe (because our testimony among you was believed) in that day.	marveled at	adored among	seen in his glory by	glorified in	marveled at
2	3 Let no man deceive you **by any means:** for that day shall not come, **except there come a falling away first,** and that **man of sin** be revealed, the son of perdition;	in any way/unless the rebellion comes first/man of lawlessness	in any way whatever/before the final rebellion against God/wickedness	in this way/until the Great Revolt/the Rebel, the Lost One	in any way/unless the apostasy comes first/man of lawlessness	in any way/until the rebellion occurs/man of lawlessness
	6 And now ye know **what withholdeth** that he might be revealed in his time.	what is restraining him	the restraining hand	what is holding him back	what restrains him	what is holding him back
	7 For the mystery of iniquity doth already work: **only he who now letteth will let, until he be taken out of the way.**	only he who now restrains it will do so until he is out of the way	secret only for the present until the Restrainer disappears from the scene	and the one who is holding it back has first to be removed	only he who now restrains will do so until he is taken out of the way	but the one who now holds it back will continue to do so until he is taken out of the way
	10 And with all **deceivableness** of **unrighteousness** in them that perish; because they received not the love of the truth, that they might be saved.	wicked deception	deception that sinfulness can impose	everything evil that can deceive	deception of wickedness	evil that deceives
3	6 Now we command you, brethren, in the name of our Lord Jesus Christ, that ye withdraw yourselves from every brother that **walketh disorderly,** and not after the tradition which he received of us.	is living in idleness	falls into idle habits	refuses to work	leads an unruly life	is idle
	8 Neither did we eat any man's bread **for nought;** but wrought with labour and travail night and day, that we might not be **chargeable** to any of you:	without paying/that we might not burden any of you	without paying for it/rather than be a burden to any of you	without paying for them/so as not to be a burden on any of you	without paying for it/so that we might not be a burden to any of you	without paying for it/so that we would not become a burden to any of you
	9 Not because we have not **power,** but to make ourselves an ensample unto you to follow us.	that right	the right to maintenance	no right to be	the right to this	the right to such help
	11 For we hear that there are some which **walk among you disorderly,** working not at all, but are busybodies.	are living in idleness	are idling their time away	are living in idleness	are leading an undisciplined life	are idle

	KJV	RSV	NEB	JB	NAS	NIV
	17 The salutation of Paul with mine own hand, which is the **token** in every epistle: so I write.	mark	(This) authenticates	mark	distinguishing mark	distinguishing mark

I Timothy

	KJV	RSV	NEB	JB	NAS	NIV
1	4 Neither give heed to **fables** and endless genealogies, which minister questions, rather than **godly edifying** which is in faith: so do.	myths/divine training	myths/God's plan for us	myths/design of God	myths/administration of God	myths/God's work
	6 From which some having swerved have turned aside unto **vain jangling;**	vain discussion	wilderness of words	empty speculation	fruitless discussion	meaningless talk
	10 For whoremongers, **for them that defile themselves with mankind,** for menstealers, for liars, for perjured persons, and if there be any other thing that is contrary to sound doctrine;	sodomites	perverts	those who are immoral . . . with boys or with men	homosexuals	perverts
	12 And I thank Christ Jesus our Lord, who **hath enabled me, for that** he counted me faithful, putting me into the ministry;	given me strength because	made me equal to the task/for (judging)	given me strength/(omits)	strengthened me/because	given me strength/that
	17 Now unto the King eternal, immortal, invisible, the only **wise** God, be honour and glory for ever and ever. Amen.	(omits)	(omits)	(omits)	(omits)	(omits)
	18 This charge I commit unto thee, son Timothy, according to the prophecies which **went before on thee,** that thou by them mightest war a good warfare;	pointed to you	first pointed you out to me	spoken over you	previously made concerning you	once made about you
2	2 For kings, and for all that are in authority; that we may lead a quiet and peaceable life in all godliness and **honesty.**	godly and respectful in every way	in full observance of religion and high standards	in peace and quiet	in all godliness and dignity	in all godliness and holiness
	7 Whereunto I am ordained a preacher, and an apostle, (I speak the truth **in Christ,** and lie not;) a teacher of the Gentiles in faith and verity.	(omits)	(omits)	(omits)	(omits)	(omits)
	9 In like manner also, that women adorn themselves in modest apparel, **with shamefacedness and sobriety;** not with broided hair, or gold, or pearls, or costly array;	modestly and sensibly	modestly and soberly	quietly and modestly	modestly and discreetly	modestly, with decency and propriety
	11 Let the woman learn in silence with all **subjection.**	submissivenes	submission	(should be) quiet and respectful	submissiveness	submission
3	2 A bishop then must be blameless, the husband of one wife, vigilant, **sober,** of good behaviour, given to hospitality, apt to teach;	sensible	sober	discreet	prudent	self-controlled
	6 Not a **novice,** lest being lifted up with pride he fall into the condemnation of the devil.	recent convert	convert newly baptized	new convert	new convert	recent convert
	8 Likewise must the deacons be grave, not double-tongued, not given to much wine, **not greedy of filthy lucre;**	not greedy for gain	given neither . . . to money-grubbing	with no squalid greed for money	not . . . fond of sordid gain	not pursuing dishonest gain
	10 And let these also first **be proved;** then let them use the office of a deacon, being found blameless.	be tested	undergo a scrutiny	be examined	be tested	be tested
	11 Even so must their **wives** be grave,	women	wives	women	Women	wives

	KJV	RSV	NEB	JB	NAS	NIV
	not slanderers, sober, faithful in all things.					
	13 For they that have used the office of a deacon well **purchase** to themselves a good **degree,** and great boldness in the faith which is in Christ Jesus.	gain/standing	claim/standing	earn/standing	obtain/standing	gain/standing
4	3 Forbidding to marry, and commanding to abstain from **meats,** which God hath created to be received with thanksgiving of them which believe and know the truth.	foods	certain foods	foods	foods	certain foods
	4 For every creature of God is good, and **nothing to be refused,** if it be received with thanksgiving:	nothing is to be rejected	nothing is to be rejected	no food is to be rejected	nothing is to be rejected	nothing is to be rejected
	7 But refuse **profane and old wives' fables,** and **exercise** thyself rather unto godliness.	godless and silly myths/train	godless myths, fit only for old women/Keep . . . in training	godless myths and old wives' tales/Train	worldly fables fit only for old women/discipline	godless myths and old wives' tales/train
	8 For bodily exercise **profiteth** little: but godliness is profitable unto all things, having promise of the life that now is, and of that which is to come.	is of some value	does bring limited benefit	are useful enough	is only of little profit	is of some value
	10 For therefore we both labour and **suffer reproach,** because we trust in the living God, who is the Saviour of all men, **specially** of those that believe.	strive/especially	struggle/above all	battling/particularly	strive/especially	strive/especially
	12 Let no man despise thy youth; but **be thou an example of the believers,** in word, in **conversation,** in **charity,** in spirit, in faith, in purity.	set the believers an example / conduct / love	make yourself an example to believers / behaviour / love	be an example to all the believers / the way you . . . behave / love	show yourself an example of those who believe / conduct / love	set an example for the believers / life / love
	13 Till I come, **give attendance to reading,** to **exhortation,** to **doctrine.**	attend to the public reading of scripture/preaching/teaching	public reading of the scriptures/exhortation/teaching	reading to the people/preaching/teaching	public reading of Scripture/exhortation/teaching	public reading of Scripture / preaching / teaching
	14 Neglect not the gift that is in thee, which was given thee by prophecy, with the laying on of the hands of the **presbytery.**	council of elders	elders as a body	body of elders	presbytery	body of elders
	15 **Meditate** upon these things; give thyself wholly to them; that thy **profiting** may appear to all.	Practice/progress	Make . . . your business/progress	Think hard/how (you are) advancing	Take pains/progress	Be diligent/progress
	16 Take heed unto thyself, and unto the **doctrine;** continue in them: for in doing this thou shalt both save thyself, and them that hear thee.	teaching	teaching	what (you) teach	teaching	doctrine
5	4 But if any widow have children or **nephews,** let them learn first to shew piety at home, and to **requite** their parents: for that is good and acceptable before God.	grandchildren/make some retain to	grandchildren/repay what they owe to	grandchildren/repay their debt to	grandchildren/make some return to	grandchildren/so repaying
	7 And these things **give in charge,** that they may be blameless.	Command this	Add these orders to the rest	remind them of all this, too	Prescribe these things as well	Give the people these instructions, too
	22 **Lay hands suddenly on no man,** neither be partaker of other men's sins: keep thyself pure.	Lay hands suddenly on no man	Do not be hasty in the laying on of hands	Do not be overhasty in laying on hands	Do not lay hands . . . too hastily	Do not be hasty in the laying on of hands
	23 Drink no longer **water,** but use a little wine for thy stomach's sake and thine **often infirmities.**	only water / frequent ailments	water / frequent ailments	only water / frequent bouts of illness	water exclusively / frequent ailments	only water / frequent illnesses
	24 Some men's sins are **open beforehand, going** before to judgment; and some men they follow after.	conspicuous, pointing	so obvious . . . run	obvious (long before anyone makes any complaint about them)	evident, going	obvious, reaching
6	5 Perverse disputings of men of corrupt minds, and destitute of the truth,					

	KJV	RSV	NEB	JB	NAS	NIV
	supposing that gain is godliness: from such withdraw thyself.	imagining that godliness is a means of gain	They think religion should yield dividends	and imagine that religion is a way of making a profit	who suppose that godliness is a means of gain	and who think that godliness is a means to financial gain
	17 Charge them that are rich in this world, that they be not **highminded,** nor trust in uncertain riches, but in the living God, who giveth us richly all things to enjoy;	haughty	proud	look down on	conceited	arrogant
	18 That they do good, that they be rich in good works, ready to distribute, **willing to communicate;**	liberal and generous	to be ready to give away and to share	to be generous and willing to share	to be generous and ready to share	and to be generous and willing to share
	20 O Timothy, keep that which is committed to thy trust, avoiding profane and vain babblings, and oppositions of **science** falsely so called:	knowledge	'knowledge'	knowledge	"knowledge"	knowledge

II Timothy

	KJV	RSV	NEB	JB	NAS	NIV
1	7 For God hath not given us the spirit of fear; but of power, and of love, and of a **sound mind.**	self-control	self-discipline	self-control	discipline	self-discipline
	11 Whereunto I am appointed a preacher, and an apostle, and a teacher **of the Gentiles.**	(omits)	(omits)	(omits)	(omits)	(omits)
2	3 Thou therefore **endure hardness,** as a good soldier of Jesus Christ.	Share in suffering	Take your share of hardship	Put up with your share of difficulties	Suffer hardship with me	Endure hardship with us
	5 **And if a man also strive for masteries, yet is he not crowned, except he strive lawfully.**	An athlete is not crowned unless he competes according to the rules.	Again, no athlete can win a prize unless he has kept the rules.	or take an athlete—he cannot win any crown unless he has kept all the rules of the contest	And also if anyone competes as an athlete, he does not win the prize unless he competes according to the rules.	Similarly, if anyone competes as an athlete, he does not receive the victor's crown unless he competes according to the rules.
	6 The **husbandman** that laboureth must be first partaker of the fruits.	farmer	farmer	farmer	farmer	farmer
	15 **Study** to shew thyself approved unto God, a workman that needeth not to be ashamed, **rightly dividing** the word of truth.	Do your best/ rightly handling	Try hard/be straight forward in your proclamation of	Do all you can/kept a straight course	Be diligent/handling accurately	Do your best/correctly handles
	23 But **foolish and unlearned questions** avoid, knowing that they do **gender strifes.**	stupid, senseless controversies/ breed quarrels	foolish and ignorant speculations/ breed quarrels	futile and silly speculations/give rise to quarrels	foolish and ignorant speculations/produce quarrels	foolish and stupid arguments/produce quarrels
3	3 Without natural affection, trucebreakers, false accusers, **incontinent,** fierce, despisers of those that are good.	profligates	intemperate	profligates	without self-control	without self-control
	4 Traitors, **heady, highminded,** lovers of pleasures more than lovers of God;	reckless/swollen with conceit	adventurers/swollen with self-importance	reckless/demented by pride	reckless/conceited	rash/conceited
	6 For of this sort are they which creep into houses, and lead captive **silly** women laden with sins, led away with **divers lusts,**	weak/various impulses	miserable/all kinds of desires	silly/one craze after another	weak/various impulses	weak-willed/all kinds of evil desires
	7 **Ever learning,** and never able to come to the knowledge of the truth.	who will listen to anybody	who are always wanting to be taught	in the attempt to educate themselves	always learning	always learning
	12 Yea, and all that will **live godly in**	live a godly life	live a godly life	live in devotion	live godly in	live a godly life

	KJV	RSV	NEB	JB	NAS	NIV
	Christ Jesus shall suffer persecution.	in Christ Jesus	as Christians	to Christ	Christ Jesus	in Christ Jesus
4	2 Preach the word; be **instant** in season, out of season; reprove, rebuke, exhort with all longsuffering and doctrine.	be urgent	press it home	insist on it	be ready	be prepared
	7 I have fought a good fight, I have finished **my course,** I have kept the faith:	the race	the course	the race	the course	the race
	14 Alexander the coppersmith did me much evil: the Lord **reward** him according to his works:	requite	(Retribution will fall upon him)	repay	repay	repay
	16 At my first **answer** no man stood with me, out all men forsook me: I pray God that it would not be laid to their charge.	defense	hearing of my case	defense	defense	defense

Titus

	KJV	RSV	NEB	JB	NAS	NIV
1	6 If any be blameless, the husband of one wife, having faithful children not accused **of riot or unruly.**	of being profligate or insubordinate	imputation of loose living, and are . . . out of control	uncontrollable or liable to be charged with disorderly conduct	dissipation or rebellion	being wild and disobedient
	7 For a bishop must be blameless, as the steward of God; not selfwilled, not soon angry, not given to wine, no striker, not **given to filthy lucre;**	greedy for gain	money-grabber	out to make money	fond of sordid gain	pursuing dishonest gain
	9 Holding fast the faithful word as he hath been taught, that he may be able by sound doctrine both to exhort and to convince **the gainsayers.**	those who contradict it	objectors	those who argue against it	those who contradict	those who oppose it
	11 Whose mouths must be stopped, who subvert whole houses, teaching things which they ought not, for **filthy lucre's sake.**	base gain	sordid gain	vile motive of making money	sake of sordid gain	sake of dishonest gain
2	7 In all things shewing thyself a pattern of good works: in doctrine shewing **uncorruptness,** gravity, sincerity,	integrity	integrity	sincerity	purity	integrity
	12 Teaching us that, denying ungodliness and worldly lusts, we should **live** soberly, righteously, and **godly,** in this present world.	live . . . godly lives	live a life of . . . godliness	live . . . religious lives	live . . . godly	live . . . godly lives
	15 These things speak, and exhort, and rebuke with all authority. Let no man **despise** thee.	disregard	slight	question	disregard	despise
3	3 For we ourselves also were **sometimes** foolish, disobedient, deceived, serving divers lusts and pleasures, living in malice and envy, hateful, and hating one another.	once	at one time	there was a time when	once	At one time
	8 This is a faithful saying, and these things **I will** that thou **affirm constantly,** that they which have believed in God might be careful to maintain good works. These things are good and profitable unto men.	desire/insist on	wish/insist on	want/to be uncomprising	want/speak confidently	want/stress
	9 But avoid **foolish questions,** and genealogies, and contentions, and strivings about the law; for they are unprofitable and vain.	stupid controversies	foolish speculations	pointless speculations	foolish controversies	foolish controversies

Philemon

KJV	RSV	NEB	JB	NAS	NIV
6 That the communication of thy faith **may become effectual by the acknowledging** of every good thing which is in you in Christ Jesus.	promote the knowledge	deepen the understanding	give rise to a sense of fellowship that will show	become effective through the knowledge	have a full understanding
7 For we have great joy and consolation in thy love, because the **bowels** of the saints are refreshed by thee, brother.	hearts	(omits)	heart	hearts	hearts
8 Wherefore, though I might be much bold in Christ to enjoin thee **that which is convenient,**	what is required	your duty	whatever is your duty	that which is proper	what you ought to do
9 Yet for love's sake I rather beseech thee, being such an one as Paul **the aged,** and now also a prisoner of Jesus Christ.	an ambassador	ambassador	an old man now	the aged	an old man
12 Whom I have sent again: thou therefore receive him, that is, mine own **bowels:**	heart	part of myself	part of my own self	heart	heart
14 But without **thy mind** would I do nothing; that thy benefit should not be as it were of necessity, but willingly.	your consent	your consent	your consent	your consent	your consent
18 If he hath wronged thee, or oweth thee aught, **put that on mine account;**	charge that to my account	put that down to my account	let me pay for it	charge that to my account	charge it to me
20 Yea, brother, let me have joy of thee in the Lord: **refresh my bowels in the Lord.**	Refresh my heart in Christ	relieve my anxiety . . . in Christ	put new heart into me, in Christ	refresh my heart in Christ	refresh my heart in Christ

Hebrews

KJV	RSV	NEB	JB	NAS	NIV
1 God, who at **sundry** times and in **divers** manners spake in time past unto the fathers by the prophets,	many (ways)/various ways	former times/fragmentary and varied fashion	various times/various different ways	many portions/many ways	many times/various ways
3 Who being the brightness of his glory, and the **express image of his person,** and upholding all things by the word of his power, when he had by himself **purged our sins,** sat down on the right hand of the Majesty on high;	very stamp of his nature/made purification for sins	stamp of God's very being/brought about the purgation of sins	perfect copy of his nature/destroyed the defilement of sin	exact representation of His nature/made purification of sins	exact representation of his being/provided purification for sins
5 For unto which of the angels said **he** at any time, Thou art my Son, this day have I begotten thee? And again, I will be to him a Father, and he shall be to me a Son?	God	God	God	He	God
9 Thou hast loved righteousness, and hated iniquity; therefore God, even thy God, hath anointed thee with the **oil of gladness above thy fellows.**	oil of gladness beyond thy comrades	above thy fellows, (by anointing with the) oil of exultation	oil of gladness, above all your rivals	With the oil of gladness above Thy companions	above your companions (by anointing you with the) oil of joy
2 7 Thou madest him a little lower than the angels; thou crownedst him with glory and honour, **and didst set him over the works of thy hands:**	(omits)	(omits)	(omits)	And hast appointed Him over the works of Thy hands	(omits)
10 For it became him, for whom are all things, and by whom are all things, in					

	KJV	RSV	NEB	JB	NAS	NIV
	bringing many sons unto glory, to make the **captain** of their salvation perfect through sufferings.	pioneer	leader	leader	author	Pioneer
	12 Saying, I will declare thy name unto my brethren, in the midst of the **church** will I sing praise unto thee.	congregation	full assembly	full assembly	congregation	congregation
	17 Wherefore in all things it behoved him to be made like unto his brethren, that he might be a merciful and faithful high priest in things pertaining to God, to **make reconciliation** for the sins of the people.	make expiation	expiate	atone	make propitiation	make atonement
	18 For in that he himself hath suffered being tempted, he is able to **succour** them that are tempted.	help	help	help	come to the aid of	help
3	2 Who was faithful to him that appointed him, as also Moses was faithful **in all his house.**	in God's house	in God's household	in all his house	in all His house	in all God's house
	3 For **this man** was counted worthy of more glory than Moses, inasmuch as he who hath builded the house hath more honour than the house.	Jesus	Jesus	he	He	Jesus
	5 And Moses verily was faithful in **all his house,** as a servant, for a testimony of those things which were to be spoken **after;**	all God's house/later	God's whole household/(omits)	the house of God/later	all His house/later	all God's house/in the future
	6 But Christ as a son **over his own house;** whose house are we, if we hold fast the confidence and the **rejoicing of the hope** firm **unto the end.**	over God's house/pride in our hope/(omits)	set over his household/our hope high/(omits)	as the master in the house/our hope . . . we glory in/(omits)	over His house/boast of our hope/until the end	over God's house/the hope of which we boast/(omits)
	8 Harden not your hearts, as in the **provocation,** in the day of temptation in the wilderness:	rebellion	rebellion	Rebellion	when they provoked Me	rebellion
	10 Wherefore I was **grieved** with that generation, and said, They do alway err in their heart; and they have not known my ways.	provoked	indignant	angry	angry	angry
	16 For some, when they had heard, **did provoke:** howbeit not all that came out of Egypt by Moses.	were rebellious	rebelled	rebelled	provoked	rebelled
4	3 For we which have believed do enter into rest, as he said, As I have sworn in my wrath, **if** they shall [ ] enter into my rest: although the works were finished from the foundation of the world.	(omits)/never	(omits)/never	(omits)/(no one should reach the place of rest)	(omits)/not	(omits)/never
	5 And in this place again, **If** they shall [ ] enter into my rest.	(omits)/never	(omits)/never	(omits)/not	(omits)/not	(omits)/never
	7 Again, he **limiteth** a certain day, saying in David, To-day, after so long a time; as it is said, To-day if ye will hear his voice, harden not your hearts.	sets	fixes	fixed	fixes	set
	8 For if **Jesus** had given them rest, then would he not afterward have spoken of another day.	Joshua	Joshua	Joshua	Joshua	Joshua
	11 Let us labour therefore to enter into that rest, lest any man fall after the same example of **unbelief.**	disobedience	unbelief	disobedience	disobedience	disobedience
	12 For the word of God is **quick,** and powerful, and sharper than any two-edged sword, piercing even to the dividing asunder of soul and spirit, and of the joints and marrow, and is a discerner of the thoughts and intents of the heart.	living	alive	something alive	living	living
5	7 Who in the days of his flesh, when he had offered up prayers and supplications with strong crying and tears unto him that was able to save him from death, and was heard **in that he feared;**	for his godly fear	Because of his humble submission	he submitted so humbly	because of His piety	because of his reverent submission

	KJV	RSV	NEB	JB	NAS	NIV
	14 But strong meat belongeth to them that are of full age, even those who by reason of use have their senses **exercised** to discern both good and evil.	trained	trained	trained	(because of) practice	trained
6	1 Therefore leaving **the principles of the doctrine of Christ,** let us go on unto perfection; not laying again the foundation of repentance from dead works, and of faith toward God,	the elementary doctrine of Christ	the rudiments of Christianity	all the elementary teaching about Christ	the elementary teaching about the Christ	the elementary teachings about Christ
	2 **Of the doctrine of baptisms,** and of laying on of hands, and of resurrection of the dead, and of eternal judgment.	with instruction about ablutions	by instructions about cleansing rites	teaching about baptisms	of instruction about washings	instruction about baptism
	19 Which hope we have as an anchor of the soul, both sure and stedfast, and which entereth into **that within the veil;**	the inner shrine behind the curtain	in through the veil	through beyond the veil	within the veil	the inner sanctity behind the curtain
7	10 For he was yet in the loins of his **father,** when Melchisedec met him.	ancestor	ancestor('s)	ancestor	father	ancestor
	18 **For there is verily a disannulling of the commandment** going before for the weakness and unprofitableness thereof.	commandment is set aside	rules are cancelled	commandment is replaced	there is a setting aside of a . . . commandment	regulation is set aside
	24 But **this man,** because he continueth ever, hath an unchangeable priesthood.	he	Jesus	he	He	he
	28 For the law maketh men high priests which have infirmity; but the word of the oath, which **was since** the law, maketh the Son, who is consecrated for evermore.	came later than	supersedes	came after	came after	came after
8	5 Who **serve unto** the **example** and shadow of **heavenly things,** as Moses was admonished of God when he was about to make the tabernacle: for, See, saith he, that thou make all things according to the pattern shewed to thee in the mount.	serve/copy/heavenly sanctuary	is only/copy/heavenly sanctuary	maintain the service of/model/heavenly realities	serve/copy/heavenly things	serve/copy/what is in heaven
9	1 Then verily the first covenant had also ordinances of divine service, and a **worldly** sanctuary.	earthly	material	on this earth	earthly	earthly
	2 For there was a tabernacle made; **the first,** wherein was the candlestick, and the table, and the shewbread; which is called the **sanctuary.**	the outer one/Holy Place	the first tent/Holy Place	the first/Holy Place	the outer one/holy place	first room/Holy Place
	3 And **after the second veil,** the tabernacle which is called the **Holiest of all;**	Behind the second curtain/Holy of Holies	Beyond the second curtain/Most Holy Place	beyond the second veil/Holy of Holies	behind the second veil/Holy of Holies	Behind the second curtain/Most Holy Place
	5 And over it the cherubims of glory shadowing the mercyseat; of which we cannot now **speak particularly.**	speak in detail	enlarge	go into greater detail	speak in detail	discuss . . . in detail
	8 The Holy Ghost this signifying, that the way into the holiest of all was not yet made manifest, **while as the first tabernacle** was yet standing:	as long as the outer tent	so long as the earlier tent	as long as the outer tent	while the outer tabernacle	as long as the first tabernacle
	11 But Christ **being come** an high priest of good things **to come,** by a greater and more perfect tabernacle, not made with hands, that is to say, not of this **building;**	appeared as/that have come/creation	has come/already in being/created world	has come, as/which were to come/created world	appeared as/to come/creation	came as/that are already here/creation
	22 And almost all things are by the law purged with blood; and without shedding of blood is no **remission.**	forgiveness of sins	forgiveness	remission	forgiveness	forgiveness
	23 It was therefore necessary that the **patterns** of things in the heavens should	copies	copies	copies	copies	copies

KJV	RSV	NEB	JB	NAS	NIV
be purified with these; but the heavenly things themselves with better sacrifices than these.					
24 For Christ is not entered into the holy places made with hands, which are the **figures** of the true; but into heaven itself, now to appear in the presence of God for us:	copy	symbol	copies	mere copy	copy
10 2 For then would they not have ceased to be offered? because that the worshippers once purged should have had no more **conscience** of sins.	consciousness	sense	awareness	consciousness	(would no longer have felt guilty)
7 Then said I, Lo, I come (in the **volume** of the book it is written of me,) to do thy will, O God.	roll	scroll	scroll	roll	scroll
12 But **this man,** after he had offered one sacrifice for sins for ever, sat down on the right hand of God;	Christ	Christ	He	He	this priest
13 From henceforth **expecting** till his enemies be made his footstool.	to wait	waits	is now waiting	waiting	waits
23 Let us hold fast the profession of our **faith** without wavering; (for he is faithful that promised;)	hope	hope	hope	hope	hope
24 And let us consider one another to **provoke** unto love and to good works:	stir up	arouse	stir	stimulate	spur . . . on
29 Of how much **sorer** punishment, suppose ye, shall he be thought worthy, who hath trodden under foot the Son of God, and hath **counted** the blood of the covenant, wherewith he was sanctified, an unholy thing and hath **done despite unto** the Spirit of grace?	worse/profaned/outraged	more severe/profaned/affronted	far severer/treats . . . as if it were not holy / insults	severer/regarded as unclean / insulted	more severely/ treated as an unholy thing / insulted
32 But call to remembrance the former days, in which, after ye were **illuminated,** ye endured a great fight of afflictions;	enlightened	enlightened	received the light	enlightened	received the light
33 Partly, whilst ye **were made a gazingstock** both by reproaches and afflictions; and partly, whilst ye became companions of them that were so used.	being publicly exposed	(were abused and tormented) to make a public show	being . . . publicly espoused	being made a public spectacle	were publicly exposed
34 For ye had compassion **of me in my bonds,** and took joyfully the spoiling of your goods, knowing in yourselves that **ye have in heaven a better and an enduring substance.**	on the prisoners/you yourselves had a better possession and an abiding one	of the prisoners/you possessed something better and more lasting	of those who were in prison/you owned something that was better and lasting	to the prisoners/you have for yourselves a better possession and an abiding one	with those in prison/you yourselves had better and lasting possessions
38 Now **the just** shall live by faith: but if any man draw back, my soul shall have no pleasure in him.	my righteous one	my righteous servant	The righteous man	My righteous one	my righteous one
11 1 Now faith is the **substance** of things hoped for, the **evidence** of things not seen.	assurance/conviction	substance/makes us certain	can guarantee/prove	assurance/conviction	being sure of/certain of
5 By faith Enoch was **translated** that he should not see death; and was not found, because God had **translated** him: for before **his translation** he had this testimony, that he pleased God.	was taken up / taken / he was taken	was carried away / taken / he was taken	was taken up / taken / his assumption	was taken up / took / before his being taken up	was taken from this life / taken / he was taken
17 By faith Abraham, when **he was tried,** offered up Isaac; and he that had received the promises [ ] offered up his only begotten son,	he was tested/was ready to (offer)	the test came/was on the point of (offering)	put to the test/(no insert)	he was tested/(no insert)	God tested him/was about to (sacrifice)
19 Accounting that God was able to raise him up, even from the dead; from whence also he received him **in a figure.**	figuratively speaking	in a sense	figuratively speaking	as a type	figuratively speaking
23 By faith Moses, when he was born, was hid three months of his parents, because they saw **he was a proper child;**	the child was	what a fine child	he was such a	he was a beauti-	he was no ordi-

	KJV	RSV	NEB	JB	NAS	NIV
	and they were not afraid of the king's **commandment.**	beautiful/edict	he was/edict	fine child/edict	ful child/edict	nary child/edict
	30 By faith the walls of Jericho fell down, after they were **compassed about** seven days.	encircled	encircled	(when the people had been around them)	encircled	(the people had marched around them)
	40 **God having provided** some better thing for us, that they without us should not be made perfect.	since God had foreseen	because . . . God had made	Since God had made	because God had provided	God had planned
12	1 Wherefore seeing we also are compassed about with so great a cloud of witnesses, let us lay aside every weight, and the sin which doth so easily beset us, and let us run with **patience** the race that is set before us,	perseverance	resolution	steadily	endurance	perseverance
	2 Looking unto Jesus the **author** and **finisher** of our faith; who for the joy that was set before him endured the cross, despising the shame, and is set down at the right hand of the throne of God.	pioneer/perfecter	(on whom faith depends from start to finish)	(who leads us in our faith and brings it to perfection)	author/perfecter	Pioneer/Perfecter
	11 Now no chastening for the present seemeth to be joyous, but grievous: nevertheless afterward it yieldeth the peaceable fruit of righteousness unto them **which are exercised thereby.**	who have been trained by it	who have been trained by it	on whom it has been used	who have been trained by it	who have been trained by it
13	5 Let your **conversation** be without **covetousness;** and be content with such things as ye have: for he hath said, I will never leave thee, nor forsake thee.	life/love of money	(Do not live for money)	(Put greed out of your lives)	character/love of money	lives/love of money
	7 Remember them which have **the rule** over you, who have spoken unto you the word of God: whose faith **follow,** considering the end of their **conversation.**	imitate/life	life and work/ follow	lives/imitate	conduct/imitate	way of life/ imitate
	8 Jesus Christ [ ] the same yesterday, and to-day, and for ever.	is	is	is	is	is
	16 But to do good and to **communicate** forget not: for with such sacrifices God is well pleased.	share	share	Keep . . . sharing	sharing	share
	18 Pray for us: for we trust we have a good conscience, in all things **willing** to live **honestly.**	desiring to act honorably in all things	our one desire is always to do what is right	we are certainly determined to behave honorably in everything we do	desiring to conduct ourselves honorably in all things	We . . . desire to live honorably in every way

James

	KJV	RSV	NEB	JB	NAS	NIV
1	2 My brethren, count it all joy when ye fall into **divers temptations;**	various trials	trials of many kinds	trials	various trials	trials of many kinds
	6 But let him ask in faith, **nothing wavering.** For **he that wavereth** is like a wave of the sea driven with the wind and tossed.	with no doubting/he who doubts	without a doubt in his mind/the doubter	and no trace of doubts/person who has doubts	without any doubts/one who doubts	and not doubt/he who doubts
	11 For the sun is no sooner risen with a burning heat, but it withereth the grass, and the flower thereof falleth, and the **grace of the fashion of it** perisheth: so also shall the rich man fade away in his ways.	beauty	what was lovely to look at	what looked so beautiful	beauty of its appearance	beauty
	17 Every good gift and every perfect gift is from above, and cometh down from the Father of lights, with whom is no					

	KJV	RSV	NEB	JB	NAS	NIV
	variableness, neither **shadow of turning.**	shadow due to change	play of passing shadows	shadow of a change	shifting shadow	shifting shadows
	21 Wherefore lay apart all filthiness and **superfluity of naughtiness,** and receive with meekness the engrafted word, which is able to save your souls.	rank growth of wickedness	malice that hurries to excess	bad habits that are still left in you	all that remains of wickedness	evil that is so prevalent
2	2 For if there come unto your assembly a man with a gold ring, in **goodly apparel,** and there come in also a poor man **in vile raiment;**	fine clothing/ shabby clothing	(well-dressed man)/shabby clothes	beautifully dressed/shabby clothes	fine clothes/dirty clothes	fine clothes/shabby clothes
	9 But if ye have respect to persons, ye commit sin, and are **convinced of** the law as transgressors.	convicted by	convicted by	under condemnation for	convicted by	convicted by
	20 But wilt thou know, O vain man, that faith without works is **dead?**	barren	barren	useless	useless	useless
3	4 Behold also the ships, which though they be so great, and are driven of fierce winds, yet are they turned about with a very small helm, whithersoever **the governor listeth.**	the will of the pilot directs	the helmsman chooses	the man at the helm . . . anywhere he likes	the inclination of the pilot desires	the pilot wants to go
	6 And the tongue is a fire, a world of iniquity: so is the tongue among our members, that it defileth the whole body, and setteth on fire the course of nature; and it is set on fire **of** hell.	by	by	from	by	by
	13 Who is a wise man and endued with knowledge among you? let him shew out of a good **conversation** his works with meekness of wisdom.	life	conduct	lives	behavior	life
	15 This wisdom descendeth not from above, but is earthly, **sensual,** devilish.	unspiritual	sensual	animal	natural	unspiritual
4	12 There is one lawgiver, [ ] who is able to save and to destroy: who art thou that judgest another?	and judge	and judge	and he is the only judge	and Judge	and Judge
	13 **Go to now,** ye that say, To-day or to-morrow we will go into such a city, and continue there a year, and buy and sell, and get gain:	Come now	A word with you	Here is an answer for	Come now	Now listen
	17 Therefore to him that **knoweth to do good,** and doeth it not, to him it is sin.	knows what is right to do	knows the good he ought to do	knows what is the right thing to do	knows the right thing to do	knows the good he ought to do
5	4 Behold, the hire of the labourers who have **reaped down** your fields, which is of you kept back by fraud, crieth: and the cries of them which have reaped are entered into the ears of the Lord of sabaoth.	mowed	mowed	mowed	mowed	mowed
	5 Ye have lived in pleasure on the earth, and been wanton; ye have **nourished your hearts,** as in a day of slaughter.	fattened your hearts	fattened yourselves	went on eating to your heart's content	fattened your hearts	fattened yourselves
	7 Be patient therefore, brethren, unto the coming of the Lord. Behold, the **husbandman** waiteth for the precious fruit of the earth, and hath long patience for it, until he receive the early and latter rain.	farmer	farmer	farmer	farmer	farmer
	9 **Grudge not one against another,** brethren, lest ye be condemned: behold, the judge standeth before the door.	Do not grumble . . . against one another	do not blame your troubles on one another	Do not make complaints against one another	Do not complain . . . against one another	Don't grumble against each other
	11 Behold, we count them happy which endure. Ye have heard of the patience of Job,and have seen the end of the Lord; that the Lord is **very pitiful,** and of tender mercy.	compassionate	full of pity	kind	full of compassion	full of compassion

	KJV	RSV	NEB	JB	NAS	NIV
	13 Is any among you afflicted? let him pray. Is any merry? let him sing **psalms.**	praise	praises	a psalm	praises	songs of praise
	19 Brethren, **if any** of you do **err** from the truth, and one convert him:	any one/wanders	one/stray	one/strays	any/strays	one/wander

I Peter

	KJV	RSV	NEB	JB	NAS	NIV
1	3 Blessed be the God and Father of our Lord Jesus Christ, which according to his abundant mercy hath begotten us **again** unto a **lively** hope by the resurrection of Jesus Christ from the dead,	living	living	sure	living	living
	6 Wherein ye greatly rejoice, though now for a season, if need be, **ye are in heaviness** through manifold temptations:	you may have to suffer various trials	you smart for a little while under trials of many kinds	you may have to bear . . . being plagued by all sorts of trials	you have been distressed by various trials	you may have suffered grief in all kinds of trials
	15 But as he which hath called you is holy, so be ye holy in all manner of **conversation;**	conduct	behaviour	all you do	behavior	all you do
	18 Forasmuch as ye know that ye were not redeemed with corruptible things, as silver and gold, from your **vain conversation** received by tradition from your fathers;	futile ways	empty folly of your traditional ways	useless way of life	futile way of life	empty way of life
2	2 As newborn babes, desire the **sincere milk of the word,** that ye may grow thereby:	pure spiritual milk	pure milk (spiritual milk, I mean)	nothing but milk—the spiritual honesty	pure milk of the word	pure spiritual milk
	3 **If so be** ye have tasted that the Lord is **gracious.**	for / kindness	surely / good	now that / goodness	if / kindness	now that / good
	4 To whom coming, as unto a living stone, **disallowed** indeed of men, but chosen of God, and precious,	rejected	rejected	rejected	rejected	rejected
	5 Ye also, as **lively** stones, are built up a spiritual house, an holy priesthood, to offer up spiritual sacrifices, acceptable to God by Jesus Christ.	living	living	living	living	living
	6 Wherefore also it is contained in the scripture, Behold, I lay in Sion a chief corner stone, elect, precious: and he that believeth on him shall not be **confounded.**	put to shame	put to shame	disappointed	disappointed	put to shame
	8 And a stone of stumbling, and a **rock of offence,** even to them which stumble at the word, being disobedient: whereunto also they were appointed.	rock that will make them fall	rock to stumble against	rock to bring men down	rock of offense	rock that makes them fall
	9 But ye are a chosen generation, a royal priesthood, an holy nation, **a peculiar people;** that ye should shew forth the praises of him who hath called you out of darkness into his marvellous light:	God's own people	a people claimed by God for his own	a people set apart	a people for God's own possession	a people belonging to God
	16 **As free,** and not using your liberty for a cloak of maliciousness, but as the servants of God.	Live as free men	Live as free men	behave like free men	Act as free men	Live as free men
	18 Servants, be subject to your masters with all **fear;** not only to the good and gentle, but also to the **froward.**	respect / overbearing	submission / perverse	respectful / unfair	respect / unreasonable	respect / harsh
	19 For this is **thankworthy,** if a man **for conscience toward** God endure grief, suffering wrongfully.	approved / mindful of	**a fine thing / because (God) is in his thoughts**	**(there is some merit in) / for the sake of**	**finds favor / for the sake of conscience toward**	commendable / conscious of
	25 For ye were as sheep going astray;					

	KJV	RSV	NEB	JB	NAS	NIV
	but are now returned unto the Shepherd and **Bishop** of your souls.	Guardian	Guardian	guardian	Guardian	Overseer
3	1 Likewise, ye wives, be in subjection to your own husbands; that, if any obey not the word, they also may without the word be won by the **conversation** of the wives;	behavior	reverent behaviour	the way (their wives) behave	behavior	behavior
	6 Even as Sara obeyed Abraham, calling him lord: whose daughters ye are, as long as ye do well, and **are not afraid with any amazement.**	let nothing terrify you	show no fear	give way to fear or worry	without being frightened by any fear	do not give way to fear
	8 Finally, be ye all of one mind, having compassion one of another, love as brethren, **be pitiful,** be courteous:	have . . . sympathy	be . . . kindly	have compassion	be . . . kindhearted	be compassionate
	9 Not rendering evil for evil, or railing for railing: but **contrariwise** blessing; knowing that ye are thereunto called, that ye should inherit a blessing.	on the contrary	on the contrary	instead	instead	but
	11 Let him eschew evil, and do good; let him seek peace, and **ensue** it.	pursue	pursue	pursue	pursue	pursue
	15 But **sanctify the Lord God** in your hearts: and be ready always to give an answer to every man that asketh you a reason of the hope that is in you with meekness and fear:	reverence Christ as Lord	hold the Lord Christ in reverence	reverence the Lord Christ	sanctify Christ as Lord	acknowledge Christ as the holy Lord
	20 Which **sometime** were disobedient, when once the longsuffering of God waited in the days of Noah, while the ark was a-preparing, wherein few, that is, eight souls were saved by water.	formerly	long ago	long ago	once	long ago
4	1 Forasmuch then as Christ hath suffered for us **in the flesh,** arm yourselves likewise with the same **mind:** for **he that** hath suffered in the flesh hath ceased from sin;	in the flesh / thought / whoever	bodily / temper of mind / a man	in this life / resolution / anyone who	in the flesh / purpose / he who	in his body / attitude / he who
	4 Wherein they think it strange that ye run not with them to the same excess of **riot,** speaking evil of you:	wild profligacy	reckless dissipation	flood which is rushing down to ruin	excess of dissipation	flood of dissipation
	14 If ye be reproached for the name of Christ, happy are ye; for the spirit of glory and of God resteth upon you: **on their part he is evil spoken of, but on your part he is glorified.**	(omits)	(omits)	(omits)	(omits)	(omits)
5	2 **Feed** the flock of God **which is among you, taking the oversight thereof,** not by constraint, but willingly; **not for filthy lucre,** but **of a ready mind;**	Tend / that is in your charge / (omits) / not for shameful gain / eagerly	Tend / whose shepherds you are / and do it / gain / out of sheer devotion	Be the shepherds of / that is entrusted to you / watch over it / not for sordid money / because you are eager to do it	shepherd / among you / exercising oversight / not for sordid gain / with eagerness	Be shepherds of / that is under your care / serving as overseers / not greedy for money / eager to serve
	12 By Silvanus, a faithful brother unto you, as I **suppose,** I have written briefly, exhorting, and testifying that this is the true grace of God wherein ye stand.	regard	hold	know	regard	regard

II Peter

	KJV	RSV	NEB	JB	NAS	NIV
1	6 And to knowledge **temperance;** and to temperance patience; and to patience godliness;	self-control	self-control	self-control	self-control	self-control

	KJV	RSV	NEB	JB	NAS	NIV
	7 And to godliness brotherly **kindness;** and to brotherly kindness **charity.**	affection / love	kindness / love	kindness / love	kindness / love	kindness / love
	13 Yea, I think it meet, as long as I am in this **tabernacle,** to stir you up by putting you in remembrance;	body	body	tent	earthly dwelling	tent of this body
	15 Moreover I will **endeavour** that ye may be able after my decease to have these things always in remembrance.	see to it	see to it	take great care	be diligent	make every effort to see
	19 We have also a more sure word of prophecy; whereunto ye do well that ye take heed, as unto a light that shineth in a dark place, until the day dawn, and the **day star** arise in your hearts:	morning star	morning star	morning star	morning star	morning star
	21 For the prophecy came not in old time by the will of man: **but holy men of God spake as they were moved by the Holy Ghost.**	but men moved by the Holy Spirit spoke from God	but, impelled by the Holy Spirit, they spoke the words of God	When men spoke for God it was the Holy Spirit that moved them	but men moved by the Holy Spirit spoke from God	but men spoke from God as they were carried along by the Holy Spirit
2	1 But there were false prophets also among the people, even as there shall be false teachers among you, who privily shall bring in **damnable** heresies, even denying the Lord that bought them, and bring upon themselves swift destruction.	destructive	disastrous	disruptive	destructive	destructive
	13 And shall receive the reward of unrighteousness, as they that count it pleasure to **riot** in the day time. Spots they are and blemishes, **sporting themselves with their own deceivings** while they feast with you;	revel / reveling in their dissipation	carouse / revel in their own deceptions	dissipation / amuse themselves deceiving (you)	revel / reveling in their deceptions	carouse / reveling in their pleasure
	14 Having eyes full of adultery, and that cannot cease from sin; beguiling unstable souls: an heart they have **exercised with covetous practices;** cursed children:	trained in greed	past masters in mercenary greed	Greed is the one lesson their minds have learned	trained in greed	experts in greed
3	9 The Lord is not **slack** concerning his promise, as some men count slackness; but is longsuffering **to us-ward,** not willing that any should perish, but that all should come to repentance.	slow / toward you	slow / with you	slow / with you all	slow / toward you	slow / with you
	10 But the day of the Lord will come as a thief in the night; in the which the heavens shall pass away with a great noise, and the elements shall melt with **fervent heat,** the earth also and the works that are therein shall be burned up.	fire	flames	fire	intense heat	fire
	12 Looking for and hasting unto the coming of the day of God, wherein the heavens being on fire shall be dissolved, and the elements shall melt with **fervent heat?**	fire	flames	heat	intense heat	heat
	16 As also in all his epistles, speaking in them of these things; in which are some things hard to be understood, which they that are unlearned and unstable **wrest,** as they do also the other scriptures, unto their own destruction.	twist	misinterpret	distort	distort	distort

I John

	KJV	RSV	NEB	JB	NAS	NIV
2	2 And he is the **propitiation** for our sins: and not for ours only, but also for the sins of the whole world.	expiation	remedy	sacrifice	propitiation	atoning sacrifice

KJV	RSV	NEB	JB	NAS	NIV
10 He that loveth his brother abideth in the light, and there is none occasion of stumbling **in him.**	in it	(omits)	(omits)	in him	in him
18 Little children, it is the last time: and as ye have heard that antichrist shall come, even now are there many antichrists; whereby we know that it is the last **time.**	hour	hour	days	hour	hour
20 But ye **have an unction** from the Holy One, and ye know all things.	have been anointed	are among the initiated	have been anointed	have an anointing	have an anointing
3 1 Behold, what manner of love the Father hath bestowed upon us, that we should be called the **sons** of God: therefore the world knoweth us not, because it knew him not.	children	children	children	children	children
17 But whoso hath this world's good, and seeth his brother have need, and shutteth up his **bowels of compassion** from him, how dwelleth the love of God in him?	heart	heart	heart	heart	(has no pity on him)
4 9 In this was manifested the love of God toward us, because that God sent his **only begotten Son** into the world, that we might live through him.	only Son	only Son	only Son	only begotten Son	only Son
19 We love **him,** because he first loved us.	(omits)	(omits)	(omits)	(omits)	(omits)
20 If a man say, I love God, and hateth his brother, he is a liar: for he that loveth not his brother whom he hath seen, **how can** he love God whom he hath not seen?	cannot	it cannot be that	cannot	cannot	cannot
5 7 **For there are three that bear record in heaven, the Father, the Word, and the Holy Ghost: and these three are one.**	And the Spirit is the witness, because the Spirit is the truth (vs. 6, KJV; text of vs. 7 omitted)	and there is the Spirit to bear witness, because the Spirit is truth (vs. 6, KJV; text of vs. 7 omitted)	so that there are three witnesses (KJV vss. 7-8 run together.)	And it is the Spirit who bears witness, because the Spirit is the truth (vs. 6, KJV; text of vs. 7 omitted)	For there are three that testify (KJV vss. 7-8 run together.)
8 **And there are three that bear witness in earth, the Spirit, and the water, and the blood: and these three agree in one.**	There are three witnesses, the Spirit, the water, and the blood; and these three agree.	For there are three witnesses, the Spirit, the water, and the blood, and these three are in agreement	the Spirit, the water, and the blood, and all three of them agree	For there are three that bear witness, the Spirit and the water and the blood; and the three are in agreement.	the Spirit, the water, and the blood; and the three are in agreement
13 These things have I written unto you that believe on the name of the Son of God; that ye may know that ye have eternal life, **and that ye may believe on the name of the Son of God.**	(omits)	(omits)	(omits)	(omits)	(omits)

II John

KJV	RSV	NEB	JB	NAS	NIV
8 Look to yourselves, that we lose not those things which **we have wrought,** but that we **receive** a full reward.	you have worked for / win	we worked for / receive	(all our work will be lost) / get	we have accomplished / receive	you have worked for / may be rewarded

III John

KJV	RSV	NEB	JB	NAS	NIV
6 Which have borne witness of thy charity before the church: whom if thou					

KJV	RSV	NEB	JB	NAS	NIV
bring forward on their journey **after a godly sort,** thou shalt do well:	as befits God's service	in a manner worthy of the God we serve	in a way that God would approve	in a manner worthy of God	in a manner worthy of God
14 But I trust I shall shortly see thee, and we shall speak face to face. Peace be to thee. Our friends salute thee. Greet the friends **by name.**	every one of them	one by one	by name	by name	by name

Jude

KJV	RSV	NEB	JB	NAS	NIV
7 Even as Sodom and Gomorrha, and the cities about them in like manner, **giving themselves over to fornication, and going after strange flesh, are set forth** for an example, suffering the vengeance of eternal fire.	acted immorally and indulged in unnatural lust, serve	committed fornication and followed unnatural lusts . . . for all to see	The fornication . . . was equally unnatural, and it is	indulged in gross immorality and went after strange flesh, are exhibited	gave themselves up to sexual immorality and perversion. They serve
11 Woe unto them! for they have gone in the way of Cain, and ran greedily after the error of Balaam for reward, and perished in the **gainsaying** of Core.	rebellion	(rebelled like Korah)	(rebelled just as Korah)	rebellion	rebellion
12 These are spots in your **feasts of charity,** when they feast with you, feeding themselves without fear: clouds they are without water, carried about of winds; trees whose fruit withereth, without fruit, twice dead, plucked up by the roots;	love feasts	love-feasts	community meals	love feasts	love feasts
19 **These be they who separate themselves, sensual, having not the Spirit.**	It is these who set up divisions, worldly people, devoid of the Spirit.	These men draw a line between spiritual and unspiritual persons, although they are themselves wholly-unspiritual.	These unspiritual and selfish people are nothing but mischiefmakers.	These are the ones who cause divisions, worldly-minded, devoid of the Spirit.	These are the men who divide you, who follow mere natural instincts and do not have the Spirit.

Revelation

KJV	RSV	NEB	JB	NAS	NIV
1 7 Behold, he cometh with clouds; and every eye shall see him, and they also which pierced him: and all **kindreds** of the earth shall wail because of him. Even so, Amen.	tribes	peoples	races	tribes	peoples
8 I am Alpha and Omega, **the beginning and the ending,** saith the Lord, which is, and which was, and which is to come, the Almighty.	(omits)	(omits)	(omits)	(omits)	(omits)
9 I John, who also am your brother, and companion in tribulation, and in the kingdom and patience **of Jesus Christ,** was in the isle that is called Patmos, for the word of God, and for the testimony of Jesus Christ.	in Jesus	in Jesus	in Jesus	in Jesus	in Jesus
11 Saying, **I am Alpha and Omega, the first and the last:** and, What thou seest, write in a book, and send it unto the seven churches **which are in Asia;** unto Ephesus, and unto Smyrna, and unto Pergamos, and unto Thyatira, and unto Sardis, and unto Philadelphia, and unto Laodicea.	(omits) / (omits)	(omits) / (omits)	(omits) / (omits)	(omits) / (omits)	(omits) / (omits)
13 And in the midst of the seven candlesticks one like unto the Son of man,					

KJV	RSV	NEB	JB	NAS	NIV
clothed with a garment down to the foot, and girt about the **paps** with a golden girdle.	breast	breast	waist	breast	chest
2 9 I know **thy works,** and tribulation, and poverty, (but thou art rich) and I know the blasphemy of them which say they are Jews, and are not, but are the synagogue of Satan.	(omits)	(omits)	(omits)	(omits)	(omits)
13 I know **thy works** and where thou dwellest, even where Satan's seat is: and thou holdest fast my name, and hast not denied my faith, even in those days wherein Antipas was my faithful martyr, who was slain among you, where Satan dwelleth.	(omits)	(omits)	(omits)	(omits)	(omits)
21 And I gave her **space** to repent of her fornication; and she repented not.	time	time	time	time	time
23 And I will kill her children with death; and all the churches shall know that I am he which searcheth **the reins** and hearts: and I will give unto every one of you according to your works.	mind	thoughts	loins	minds	minds
3 3 Remember therefore how thou hast received and heard, and hold fast, and repent. If therefore thou shalt not **watch,** I will come on thee as a thief, and thou shalt not know what hour I will come upon thee.	awake	wake up	wake up	wake up	wake up
4 3 And he that sat was to look upon like a jasper and **a sardine stone:** and there was a rainbow round about the throne, **in sight like unto an** emerald.	carnelian / looked like an	cornelian / bright as an	ruby / looked like an	sardius / like an . . . in appearance	carnelian / resembling an
4 And round about the throne were four and twenty **seats:** and upon the seats I saw four and twenty elders sitting, clothed in white raiment; and they had on their heads crowns of gold.	thrones	thrones	thrones	thrones	thrones
6 And before the throne there was a sea of glass like unto crystal: and in the midst of the throne, and round about the throne, were four **beasts** full of eyes before and behind.	living creatures	living creatures	animals	living creatures	living creatures
5 1 And I saw in the right hand of him that sat on the throne a **book** written **within and on the backside,** sealed with seven seals.	scroll / within and on the back	scroll / inside and out	scroll / on back and front	book / inside and on the back	scroll / on both sides
6 And I beheld, and, lo, in the midst of the throne and of the four beasts, and in the midst of the elders, stood a Lamb **as it had been slain,** having seven horns and seven eyes, which are the seven Spirits of God sent forth into all the earth.	as though it had been slain	with the marks of slaughter upon him	that seemed to have been sacrificed	as if slain	looking as if it had been slain
8 And when he had taken the book, the four beasts and four and twenty elders fell down before the Lamb, having every one of them harps, and golden **vials** full of **odours,** which are the prayers of saints.	bowls / incense	bowls / incense	bowl / incense	censer / incense	bowls / incense
14 And the four beasts said, Amen. And the four and twenty elders fell down and worshipped **him that liveth for ever and ever.**	(omits)	(omits)	(omits)	(omits)	(omits)
6 1 And I saw when the Lamb opened one of the seals, and I heard, as it were the noise of thunder, one of the four beasts saying, Come **and see.**	(omits)	(omits)	(omits)	(omits)	(omits)
8 And I looked, and behold a pale horse: and his name that sat on him was Death, and **Hell** followed with him. And power was given unto them over the fourth part of the earth, to kill with sword, and with	Hades	Hades	Hades	Hades	Hades

	KJV	RSV	NEB	JB	NAS	NIV
	hunger, and with death, and with the beasts of the earth.					
8	7 The first angel sounded, and there followed hail and fire mingled with blood, [ ] and they were cast upon the earth: and the third part of trees was burnt up, and all green grass was burnt up.	and a third of the earth was burnt up	A third of the earth was burnt	a third of the earth was burned up	and a third of the earth was burned up	A third of the earth was burned up
	12 And the fourth angel sounded, and the third part of the sun was smitten, and the third part of the moon, and the third part of the stars; **so as** the third part of them was darkened, and the day shone not for a third part of it, and the night likewise.	so that	so that	so that	so that	so that
	13 And I beheld, and heard an **angel** flying through the midst of heaven, saying with a loud voice, Woe, woe, woe, to the inhabiters of the earth by reason of the other voices of the trumpet of the three angels, which are yet to sound!	eagle	eagle	eagle	eagle	eagle
9	18 By these three [ ] was the third part of men killed, by the fire, and by the smoke, and by the brimstone, which issued out of their mouths.	plagues	plagues	plagues	plagues	plagues
11	1 And there was given me a **reed like unto a rod:** and the angel stood, saying, Rise, and measure the temple of God, and the altar, and them that worship therein.	measuring rod like a staff	long cane, a kind of measuring-rod	long cane as a measuring rod	measuring rod like a staff	reed like a measuring rod
	8 And their dead bodies shall lie in the street of the great city, which **spiritually** is called Sodom and Egypt, where also our Lord was crucified.	allegorically	in allegory	by the symbolic names	mystically	figuratively
12	4 And his tail **drew the third part of the stars of heaven,** and did cast them to the earth: and the dragon stood before the woman which was ready to be delivered, for to devour her child as soon as it was born.	swept down a third of the stars of heaven	swept down a third of the stars in the sky	dragged a third of the stars from the sky	swept away a third of the stars of heaven	swept a third of the stars out of the sky
	13 And when the dragon saw that he was cast unto the earth, he **persecuted** the woman which brought forth the man child.	pursued	went in pursuit of	sprang in pursuit of	persecuted	pursued
	17 And the dragon was wroth with the woman, and went to make war with the **remnant of her seed,** which keep the commandments of God, and have the testimony of Jesus Christ.	rest of her offspring	rest of her offspring	rest of her children	rest of her offspring	rest of her offspring
13	3 And I saw one of his heads **as it were wounded to death;** and his deadly wound was healed: and all the world wondered after the beast.	seemed to have a mortal wound	appeared to have received a death-blow	seemed to have had a fatal wound	as if it had been slain	seemed to have had a fatal wound
14	2 And I heard a voice from heaven, as the voice of many waters, and as the voice of a great thunder: and I heard the voice of harpers **harping** with their harps:	playing	playing	playing	playing	playing
	5 And in their mouth was found no guile: for they are without fault **before the throne of God.**	(omits)	(omits)	(omits)	(omits)	(omits)
16	6 For they have shed the blood of saints and prophets, and thou hast given them blood to drink; for **they are worthy.**	It is their due!	They have their deserts!	it is what they deserve	They deserve it.	as they deserve
17	6 And I saw the woman drunken with the blood of the saints, and with the blood of the martyrs of Jesus: and when I saw her, I wondered **with great admiration.**	greatly	greatly	completely	greatly	greatly
18	2 And he cried mightily with a strong voice, saying, Babylon the great is fallen, is fallen, and is become the habitation of					

	KJV	RSV	NEB	JB	NAS	NIV
	devils, and the **hold** of every foul spirit, and a **cage** of every unclean and hateful bird.	haunt / haunt	haunt / (haunt)	lodging / (lodging)	prison / prison	haunt / haunt
	3 For all nations have drunk of the wine of the wrath of her fornication, and the kings of the earth have committed fornication with her, and the merchants of the earth are waxed rich through the **abundance of her delicacies.**	wealth of her wantonness	bloated wealth	debauchery	wealth of her sensuality	excessive luxuries
	9 And the kings of the earth, who have committed fornication and **lived deliciously with her,** shall bewail her, and lament for her, when they shall see the smoke of her burning,	were wanton with her	wallowed in her luxury	lived with her in luxury	lived sensuously with her	shared her luxury
	12 The merchandise of gold, and silver, and precious stones, and of pearls, and fine linen, and purple, and silk, and scarlet, and all thyine wood and **all manner vessels** of ivory, and all manner vessels of most precious wood, and of brass, and iron, and marble,	all articles	all kinds	every piece	every kind	every kind
	16 And saying, Alas, alas, that great city, that was clothed in fine linen, and purple, and scarlet, and **decked** with gold, and precious stones, and pearls!	bedecked	bedizened	(for all your finery of gold)	adorned	glittering
21	3 And I heard a great voice **out of heaven** saying, Behold, the **tabernacle** of God is with men, and he will dwell with them, and they shall be his people, and God himself shall be with them, **and be their God.**	from the throne / dwelling / (omits)	from the throne / dwelling / (omits)	from the throne / home / and he will be their God; his name is God-with-them	from the throne / tabernacle / (omits)	from the throne / dwelling / and be their God
22	7 Behold, **I come quickly:** blessed is he that keepeth the sayings of the prophecy of this book.	I am coming soon	I am coming soon	Very soon now, I shall be with you again.	I am coming quickly	I am coming soon
	14 Blessed are they that **do his commandments,** that they may have right to the tree of life, and may enter **in through the gates into the city.**	wash their robes / the city by the gates	wash their robes clean / by the gates of the city	washed their robes clean / through the gates into the city	wash their robes / by the gates into the city	wash their robes / through the gates into the city
	19 And if any man shall take away from the words of the book of this prophecy, God shall take away his part out of the **book of** life, and out of the holy city, and from the things which are written in this book.	tree of	tree of	tree of	tree of	tree of

DICTIONARY

OF

THE HEBREW BIBLE.

A CONCISE

DICTIONARY

OF THE WORDS IN

THE HEBREW BIBLE;

WITH THEIR RENDERINGS

IN THE

AUTHORIZED ENGLISH VERSION.

BY

JAMES STRONG, S.T.D., LL.D.

ABINGDON
NASHVILLE

PREFACE.

THIS work, although prepared as a companion to the Exhaustive Concordance, to which it is specially adapted, is here paged and printed so that it can be bound separately, in the belief that a brief and simple Dictionary of the Biblical Hebrew and Chaldee will be useful to students and others, who do not care at all times to consult a more copious and elaborate Lexicon; and it will be particularly serviceable to many who are unable to turn conveniently and rapidly, amid the perplexities and details of foreign characters with which the pages of Gesenius and Fürst bristle, to the fundamental and essential points of information that they are seeking. Even scholars will find here, not only all of a strictly verbal character which they most frequently want in ordinary consultation of a lexicon, but numerous original suggestions, relations, and distinctions, carefully made and clearly put, which are not unworthy of their attention, especially in the affinities of roots and the classification of meanings. The portable form and moderate cost of the book, it is hoped, will facilitate its use with all classes. The vocabulary is complete as to the ground-forms that actually occur in the biblical text (or *Kethib*), with the pointing that properly belongs to them. Their designation by numbers will especially aid those who are not very familiar with the original language, and the Anglicizing and pronunciation of the words will not come amiss to multitudes who have some acquaintance with it. The addition of the renderings in the common version will greatly contribute to fixing and extending the varied significations and applications of the Hebrew and Chaldee words, as well as to correcting their occasionally wrong translations. On this account, as well as for the sake of precision and to prevent repetition, the use of the same terms in the preceding definitions has been avoided wherever practicable. The design of the volume, being purely *lexical*, does not include grammatical, archæological, or exegetical details, which would have swelled its size and encumbered its plan.

By observing the subjoined directions, in the associated use of the Main Concordance, the reader will have substantially a Concordance-Dictionary of the Authorized Version and the Hebrew Bible.

PLAN OF THE BOOK.

1. All the original words are treated in their alphabetical Hebrew order, and are numbered regularly from the first to the last, each being known throughout by its appropriate number. This renders reference easy without recourse to the Hebrew characters.

2. Immediately after each word is given its exact equivalent in English letters, according to the system of transliteration laid down in the scheme here following, which is substantially that adopted in the Common English Version, only more consistently and uniformly carried out; so that the word could readily be turned back again into Hebrew from the form thus given it.

3. Next follows the precise pronunciation, according to the usual English mode of sounding syllables, so plainly indicated that none can fail to apprehend and apply it. The most approved sounds are adopted, as laid down in the annexed scheme of articulation, and in such a way that any good Hebraist would immediately recognize the word if so pronounced, notwithstanding the minor variations current among scholars in this respect.

4. Then ensues a tracing of the etymology, radical meaning, and applied signification of the word, justly but tersely analyzed and expressed, with any other important peculiarities in this regard.

5. In the case of proper names, the same method is pursued, and at this point the regular mode of Anglicizing it, after the general style of the Common English Version, is given, and a few words of explanation are added to identify it.

6. Finally (after the punctuation-mark :—) are given all the different renderings of the word in the Authorized English Version, arranged in the alphabetical order of the leading terms, and conveniently condensed according to the explanations given below.

By searching out these various renderings in the MAIN CONCORDANCE, to which this Dictionary is designed as a companion, and noting the passages to which the same number corresponding to that of any given Hebrew word is attached in the marginal column, the reader, whether acquainted with the original language or not, will obtain a complete *Hebrew Concordance* also, expressed in the words of the Common English Version. This is an advantage which no other Concordance or Lexicon affords.

HEBREW ARTICULATION.

THE following explanations are sufficient to show the method of transliterating Hebrew words into English adopted in this *Dictionary*.

1. The Hebrew is read *from right to left*. The Alphabet consists of 22 letters (and their variations), which are all regarded as *consonants*, being enunciated by the aid of certain "points" or marks, mostly beneath the letters, and which serve as *vowels*. There is no distinction of *capitals*, *italics*, etc.

2. The letters are as follows:

No.	Form.	Name.		Transliteration and Power.
1.	א	'Aleph	(*aw'-lef*)	**'** unappreciable
2.	בּ	Bêyth	(*bayth*)	**b**
3.	גּ	Gîymel	(*ghee'-mel*)	**g** hard = γ
4.	דּ	Dâleth	(*daw'-leth*)	**d** [cent
5.	ה	Hê'	(*hay*)	**h**, often quies-
6.	ו	Vâv	(*vawv*)	**v**, or **w** quies-
7.	ז	Zayin	(*zah'-yin*)	**z**, as in *zeal* [cent
8.	ח	Chêyth	(*khayth*)	German **ch** = χ [(nearly *kh*)
9.	ט	Têyth	(*tayth*)	**ţ** = תּ [cent
10.	י	Yôwd	(*yode*)	**y**, often quies-
11.	כּ, final ך	Kaph	(*caf*)	**k** = ק
12.	ל	Lâmed	(*law'-med*)	**l**
13.	מ, final ם	Mêm	(*mame*)	**m**
14.	נ, final ן	Nûwn	(*noon*)	**n**
15.	ס	Çâmek	(*saw'-mek*)	**ç** = *s* sharp = שׂ
16.	ע	'Ayin	(*ah'-yin*)	**'** peculiar *
17. {	פ, final ף	Phê'	(*fay*)	**ph** = *f* = φ
	פּ	Pê'	(*pay*)	**p**
18.	צ, final ץ	Tsâdêy	(*tsaw-day'*)	**ts**
19.	ק	Qôwph	(*cofe*)	**q** = *k* = כּ
20.	ר	Rêysh	(*raysh*)	**r**
21. {	שׂ	Sîyn	(*seen*)	**s** sharp = ס = σ
	שׁ	Shîyn	(*sheen*)	**sh**
22. {	ת	Thâv	(*thawv*)	**th**, as in THin
	תּ	Tâv	(*tawv*)	**t** = ט = τ [= ϑ

* The letter *'Ayin*, owing to the difficulty experienced by Occidentals in pronouncing it accurately (it is a deep guttural sound, like that made in *gargling*), is generally neglected (i.e. passed over silently) in reading. We have represented it to the eye (but not exactly to the ear) by the Greek *rough breathing* (for distinctness and typographical convenience, a reversed *apostrophe*) in order to distinguish it from *'Âleph*, which is likewise treated as silent, being similarly represented by the Greek *smooth breathing* (the *apostrophe*).

3. The *vowel-points* are the following:

Form.*	Name.		Representation and Power.
(ָ)	Qâmêts	(*caw-mates'*)	**â**, as in ALL
(ַ)	Pattach	(*pat'-takh*)	**a**, as in *m*A*n*, (*fār*)
(ֲ)	Shᵉvâ'-Pattach	(*she-vaw' pat'-takh*)	**ă**, as in *h*A*t*
(ֵ)	Tsêrêy	(*tsay-ray'*)	**ê**, as in *th*E*y* = η
(ֶ)	Çegôwl	(*seg-ole'*)	{ **e**, as in *th*E*ir*; **e**, as in *m*E*n* = ε
(ֱ)	Shᵉvâ'-Çegôwl	(*she-vaw' seg-ole'*)	**ĕ**, as in *m*E*t*
(ְ)	Shᵉvâ' †	(*she-vaw'*)	{ ᵉ obscure, as in [*av*E*rage*; silent, as *e* in *mad*E
(ִ)	Chîyriq	(*khee'-rik*)	{ **î**, as in *mach*I*ne* ‡; **ĭ**, as in *suppl*I*ant*, [(*mīsery*, *hĭt*)
(ֹ)	Chôwlem §	(*kho'-lem*)	**ô**, as in *no* = ω
(ָ)	Short Qâmêts ‖		**o**, as in *nor* = ο
(ֳ)	Shᵉvà'-Qâmêts	(*she-vaw' caw-mates'*)	**ŏ**, as in *not*
(וּ)	Shûwrêq *	(*shoo-rake'*)	**û**, as in *cr*U*el*
(ֻ)	Qĭbbûts *	(*kib'-boots*)	**u**, as in *f*U*ll*, *rūde*

* The parenthesis-marks ( ) are given here in order to show the place of the vowel-points, whether below, above, or in the middle of the letter.

† *Silent Shᵉvâ'* is not represented by any mark in our method of transliteration, as it is understood whenever there is no other vowel-point.

‡ *Chîyriq* is thus long only when it is followed by a quiescent *yôwd* (either expressed or implied).

§ *Chôwlem* is written *fully* only over *Vâv*, which is then quiescent (*w*); but when used "defectively" (without the *Vâv*) it may be written either over the left-hand corner of the letter to which it belongs, or over the right-hand corner of the following one.

‖ Short *Qâmêts* is found only in *unaccented syllables ending with a consonant sound.*

4. A point in the bosom of a letter is called *Dâgêsh'*, and is of two kinds, which must be carefully distinguished.

a. Dâgêsh *lenè* occurs only in the letters בּ, גּ, דּ, כּ, פּ, תּ, (technically vocalized *Bᵉgad'-Kᵉphath'*,) when they *begin* a clause or sentence, or are preceded by a consonant *sound*; and simply has the effect of removing their aspiration.†

b. Dâgêsh *fortè* may occur in any letter except א, ה, ח, ע or ר; it is equivalent to *doubling* the letter, and at the same time it removes the aspiration of a Bᵉgad-Kᵉphath letter.‡

5. The *Maqqêph'* (־), like a *hyphen*, unites words only for purposes of pronunciation (by removing the primary accent from all except the last of them), but does not affect their meaning or their grammatical construction.

* *Shûwrêq* is written only in the bosom of *Vâv*. Sometimes it is said to be "defectively" written (without the *Vâv*), and then takes the form of *Qibbûts*, which in such cases is called *vicarious*.

† In our system of transliteration Dâgêsh *lenè* is represented only in the letters פּ and תּ, because elsewhere it does not affect the pronunciation (with most Hebraists).

‡ A point in the bosom of הּ is called *Mappîyq* (*map-peek'*). It occurs only in the final vowelless letter of a few words, and we have represented it by *hh*. A Dâgêsh *fortè* in the bosom of וּ may easily be distinguished from the vowel *Shûwrêq* by noticing that in the former case the letter has a proper vowel-point accompanying it.

It should be noted that both kinds of Dâgêsh are often omitted in writing (being then said to be *implied*), but (in the case at least of Dâgêsh *fortè*) the word is (by most Hebraists) pronounced the same as if it were present.

ABBREVIATIONS EMPLOYED.

abb. = abbreviated; abbreviation
absol. = absolute; absolutely
abstr. = abstract; abstractly
act. = active; actively
adj. = adjective; adjectively
adv. = adverb; adverbial; adverbially
aff. = affix; affixed
affin. = affinity
appar. = apparent; apparently
arch. = architecture; architectural; architecturally
art. = article.
artif. = artificial; artificially
Ass. = Assyrian
A. V. = Authorized Version
Bab. = Babylon; Babylonia; Babylonian
caus. = causative; causatively
Chald. = Chaldaism; Chaldee
collat. = collateral; collaterally
collect. = collective; collectively
comp. = compare; comparative; comparatively; comparison
concr. = concrete; concretely
conjec. = conjecture; conjectural; conjecturally
conjug. = conjugation; conjugational; conjugationally
conjunc. = conjunction; conjunctional; conjunctionally
constr. = construct; construction; constructive; constructively
contr. = contracted; contraction
correl. = correlated; correlation; correlative; correlatively
corresp. = corresponding; correspondingly
def. = definite; definitely
denom. = denominative; denominatively
der. = derivation; derivative; derivatively
desc. = descendant; descendants
E. = East; Eastern
e.g. = *exempli gratiâ*; for example
Eg. = Egypt; Egyptian; Egyptians
ellip. = ellipsis; elliptical; elliptically
equiv. = equivalent; equivalently
err. = erroneous; erroneously; error
esp. = especial; especially
etym. = etymology; etymological; etymologically
euphem. = euphemism; euphemistic; euphemistically
euphon. = euphonically; euphonious
extern. = external; externally
infer. = inference; inferential; inferentially
fem. = feminine
fig. = figurative; figuratively
for. = foreign; foreigner
freq. = frequentative; frequentatively
fut. = future
gen. = general; generally; generical; generically
Gr. = Græcism; Greek
gut. = guttural
Heb. = Hebraism; Hebrew
i.e. = *id est*; that is
ident. = identical; identically
immed. = immediate; immediately
imper. = imperative; imperatively
impl. = implication; implied; impliedly
incept. = inceptive; inceptively
incl. = including; inclusive; inclusively
indef. = indefinite; indefinitely
infin. = infinitive
inhab. = inhabitant; inhabitants
ins. = inserted
intens. = intensive; intensively
intern. = internal; internally
interj. = interjection; interjectional; interjectionally
intr. = intransitive; intransitively
Isr. = Israelite; Israelites; Israelitish
Jerus. = Jerusalem
Levit. = Levitical; Levitically
lit. = literal; literally
marg. = margin; marginal (reading)
masc. = masculine
mean. = meaning
ment. = mental; mentally
mid. = middle
modif. = modified; modification
mor. = moral; morally
mus. = musical
nat. = native; natural; naturally; nature
neg. = negative; negatively
obj. = object; objective; objectively
or. = origin; original; originally
orth. = orthography; orthographical; orthographically
Pal. = Palestine
part. = participle
pass. = passive; passively
patron. = patronymic; patronymically
perh. = perhaps
perm. = permutation (of allied letters)
pers. = person; personal; personally
Pers. = Persia; Persian; Persians
phys. = physical; physically
plur. = plural
poet. = poetry; poetical; poetically
pos. = positive; positively
pref. = prefix; prefixed
prep. = preposition; prepositional; prepositionally
prim. = primitive
prob. = probable; probably
prol. = prolonged; prolongation
pron. = pronominal; pronominally; pronoun
prox. = proximate; proximately
rad. = radical
recip. = reciprocal; reciprocally
redupl. = reduplicated; reduplication
refl. = reflexive; reflexively
rel. = relative; relatively
relig. = religion; religious; religiously
second. = secondarily; secondary
signif. = signification; signifying
short. = shortened; shorter
sing. = singular
spec. = specific; specifically
streng. = strengthening
subdiv. = subdivision; subdivisional; subdivisionally
subj. = subject; subjective; subjectively
substit. = substituted.
superl. = superlative; superlatively
symb. = symbolical; symbolically
te . = technical; technically
tran. = transitive; transitively
transc. = transcription
transp. = transposed; transposition
unc. = uncertain; uncertainly
var. = variation.

SIGNS EMPLOYED.

+ (*addition*) denotes a rendering in the A. V. of one or more Heb. words in connection with the one under consideration.

× (*multiplication*) denotes a rendering in the A. V. that results from an idiom peculiar to the Heb.

° (*degree*), appended to a Heb. word, denotes a vowel-pointing corrected from that of the text. (This mark is set in Heb. Bibles over syllables in which the vowels of the marg. have been inserted instead of those properly belonging to the text.)

( ) (*parenthesis*), in the renderings from the A. V., denotes a word or syllable sometimes given in connection with the principal word to which it is annexed.

[ ] (*bracket*), in the rendering from the A. V., denotes the inclusion of an additional word in the Heb.

Italics, at the end of a rendering from the A. V., denote an explanation of the variations from the usual form.

HEBREW AND CHALDEE DICTIONARY

ACCOMPANYING

THE EXHAUSTIVE CONCORDANCE.

א

1. אָב **'âb**, *awb;* a prim. word; *father* in a lit. and immed., or fig. and remote application):—chief, (fore-) father ([-less]), × patrimony, principal. Comp. names in "Abi-".

2. אַב **'ab** (Chald.), *ab;* corresp. to 1:—father.

3. אֵב **'êb**, *abe;* from the same as 24; a *green plant:*—greenness, fruit.

4. אֵב **'êb** (Chald.), *abe;* corresp. to 3:—fruit.

אֹב **'ôb**. See 178.

5. אֲבַגְתָא **'Ăbagthâ'**, *ab-ag-thaw';* of for. or.; *Abagtha*, a eunuch of Xerxes:—Abagtha.

6. אָבַד **'âbad**, *aw-bad';* a prim. root; prop. to *wander* away, i.e. *lose* oneself; by impl. to *perish* (caus. *destroy*):—break, destroy (-uction), + not escape, fail, lose, (cause to, make) perish, spend, × and surely, take, be undone, × utterly, be void of, have no way to flee.

7. אֲבַד **'ăbad** (Chald.), *ab-ad';* corresp. to 6:—destroy, perish.

8. אֹבֵד **'ôbêd**, *o-bade';* act. part. of 6; (concr.) *wretched* or (abstr.) *destruction:*—perish.

9. אֲבֵדָה **'ăbêdâh**, *ab-ay-daw';* from 6; concr. something *lost;* abstr. *destruction*, i.e. Hades:—lost. Comp. 10.

10. אֲבַדֹּה **'ăbaddôh**, *ab-ad-do';* the same as 9, miswritten for 11; a *perishing:*—destruction.

11. אֲבַדּוֹן **'ăbaddôwn**, *ab-ad-done';* intens. from 6; abstr. a *perishing;* concr. Hades:—destruction.

12. אַבְדָן **'abdân**, *ab-dawn';* from 6; a *perishing:*—destruction.

13. אָבְדַן **'obdân**, *ob-dawn';* from 6; a *perishing:*—destruction.

14. אָבָה **'âbâh**, *aw-baw';* a prim. root; to *breathe* after, i.e. (fig.) to *be acquiescent:*—consent, rest content, will, be willing.

15. אָבֶה **'âbeh**, *aw-beh';* from 14; *longing:*—desire.

16. אֵבֶה **'êbeh**, *ay-beh';* from 14 (in the sense of *bending* towards); the *papyrus:*—swift.

17. אֲבוֹי **'ăbôwy**, *ab-o'ee;* from 14 (in the sense of *desiring*); *want:*—sorrow.

18. אֵבוּס **'êbûwç**, *ay-booce';* from 75; a *manger* or *stall:*—crib.

19. אִבְחָה **'ibchâh**, *ib-khaw';* from an unused root (appar. mean. to *turn*); *brandishing* of a sword:—point.

20. אֲבַטִּיחַ **'ăbaṭṭîyach**, *ab-at-tee'-akh;* of uncert. der.; a *melon* (only plur.):—melon.

21. אֲבִי **'Ăbîy**, *ab-ee';* from 1; *fatherly; Abi*, Hezekiah's mother:—Abi.

22. אֲבִיאֵל **'Ăbîy'êl**, *ab-ee-ale';* from 1 and 410; *father* (i.e. *possessor*) *of God; Abiel*, the name of two Isr.:—Abiel.

23. אֲבִיאָסָף **'Ăbîy'âçâph**, *ab-ee-aw-sawf';* from 1 and 622; *father of gathering* (i.e. *gatherer*); *Abiasaph*, an Isr.:—Abiasaph.

24. אָבִיב **'âbîyb**, *aw-beeb';* from an unused root (mean. to *be tender*); *green*, i.e. a young *ear* of grain; hence the name of the month *Abib* or Nisan:—Abib, ear, green ears of corn.

25. אֲבִי גִבְעוֹן **'Ăbîy Gib‘ôwn**, *ab-ee' ghib-one';* from 1 and 1391; *father* (i.e. *founder*) *of Gibon; Abi-Gibon*, perh. an Isr.:—father of Gibeon.

26. אֲבִיגַיִל **'Ăbîygayil**, *ab-ee-gah'-yil*, or shorter אֲבִיגַל **'Ăbîygal**, *ab-ee-gal';* from 1 and 1524; *father* (i.e. *source*) *of joy; Abigail* or *Abigal*, the name of two Israelitesses:—Abigal.

27. אֲבִידָן **'Ăbîydân**, *ab-ee-dawn';* from 1 and 1777; *father of judgment* (i.e. *judge*); *Abidan*, an Isr.:—Abidan.

28. אֲבִידָע **'Ăbîydâ‘**, *ab-ee-daw';* from 1 and 3045; *father of knowledge* (i.e. *knowing*); *Abida*, a son of Abraham by Keturah:—Abida, Abidah.

29. אֲבִיָּה **'Ăbîyâh**, *ab-ee-yaw';* or prol. אֲבִיָּהוּ **'Ăbîyâhûw**, *ab-ee-yaw'-hoo;* from 1 and 3050; *father* (i.e. *worshipper*) *of Jah; Abijah*, the name of several Isr. men and two Israelitesses:—Abiah, Abijah.

30. אֲבִיהוּא **'Ăbîyhûw'**, *ab-ee-hoo';* from 1 and 1931; *father* (i.e. *worshipper*) of *Him* (i.e. *God*); *Abihu*, a son of Aaron:—Abihu.

31. אֲבִיהוּד **'Ăbîyhûwd**, *ab-ee-hood';* from 1 and 1935; *father* (i.e. *possessor*) *of renown; Abihud*, the name of two Isr.:—Abihud.

32. אֲבִיהַיִל **'Ăbîyhayil**, *ab-ee-hah'-yil;* or (more correctly) אֲבִיחַיִל **'Ăbîychayil**, *ab-ee-khah'-yil;* from 1 and 2428; *father* (i.e. *possessor*) *of might; Abihail* or *Abichail*, the name of three Isr. and two Israelitesses:—Abihail.

33. אֲבִי הָעֶזְרִי **'Ăbîy hâ-‘Ezrîy**, *ab-ee'-haw-ez-ree';* from 44 with the art. inserted; *father of the Ezrite;* an *Abiezrite* or descendant of Abiezer:—Abiezrite.

34. אֶבְיוֹן **'ebyôwn**, *eb-yone';* from 14, in the sense of *want* (espec. in feeling); *destitute:*—beggar, needy, poor (man).

35. אֲבִיּוֹנָה **'ăbîyôwnâh**, *ab-ee-yo-naw';* from 14; provocative of *desire;* the *caper* berry (from its *stimulative* taste):—desire.

אֲבִיחַיִל **'Ăbîychayil**. See 32.

36. אֲבִיטוּב **'Ăbîyṭûwb**, *ab-ee-toob';* from 1 and 2898; *father of goodness* (i.e. *good*); *Abitub*, an Isr.:—Abitub.

37. אֲבִיטַל **'Ăbîyṭâl**, *ab-ee-tal';* from 1 and 2919; *father of dew* (i.e. *fresh*); *Abital*, a wife of King David:—Abital.

38. אֲבִיָּם **'Ăbîyâm**, *ab-ee-yawm';* from 1 and 3220; *father of* (the) *sea* (i.e. *seaman*); *Abijam* (or Abijah), a king of Judah:—Abijam.

39. אֲבִימָאֵל **'Ăbîymâ'êl**, *ab-ee-maw-ale';* from 1 and an elsewhere unused (prob. for.) word; *father of Mael* (appar. some Arab tribe); *Abimael*, a son of Joktan:—Abimael.

40. אֲבִימֶלֶךְ **'Ăbîymelek**, *ab-ee-mel'-ek;* from 1 and 4428; *father of* (the) *king; Abimelek*, the name of two Philistine kings and of two Isr.:—Abimelech.

41. אֲבִינָדָב **'Ăbîynâdâb**, *ab-ee-naw-dawb';* from 1 and 5068; *father of generosity* (i.e. *liberal*); *Abinadab*, the name of four Isr.:—Abinadab.

42. אֲבִינֹעַם **'Ăbîynô‘am**, *ab-ee-no'-am;* from 1 and 5278; *father of pleasantness* (i.e. *gracious*); *Abinoam*, an Isr.:—Abinoam.

אֲבִינֵר **'Ăbîynêr**. See 74.

43. אֶבְיָסָף **'Ebyâçâph**, *eb-yaw-sawf';* contr. from 23; *Ebjasaph*, an Isr.:—Ebiasaph.

44. אֲבִיעֶזֶר **'Ăbîy‘ezer**, *ab-ee-ay'-zer;* from 1 and 5829; *father of help* (i.e. *helpful*); *Abiezer*, the name of two Isr.:—Abiezer.

45. אֲבִי־עַלְבוֹן **'Ăbîy-‘albôwn**, *ab-ee-al-bone';* from 1 and an unused root of unc. der.; prob. *father of strength* (i.e. *valiant*); *Abialbon*, an Isr.:—Abialbon.

46. אָבִיר **'âbîyr**, *aw-beer';* from 82; *mighty* (spoken of God):—mighty (one).

47. אַבִּיר **'abbîyr**, *ab-beer';* for 46:—angel, bull, chiefest, mighty (one), stout [-hearted], strong (one), valiant.

48. אֲבִירָם **'Ăbîyrâm**, *ab-ee-rawm';* from 1 and 7311; *father of height* (i.e. *lofty*); *Abiram*, the name of two Isr.:—Abiram.

49. אֲבִישַׁג **'Ăbîyshag**, *ab-ee-shag';* from 1 and 7686; *father of error* (i.e. *blundering*); *Abishag*, a concubine of David:—Abishag.

50. אֲבִישׁוּעַ **'Ăbîyshûwa‘**, *ab-ee-shoo'-ah;* from 1 and 7771; *father of plenty* (i.e. *prosperous*); *Abishua*, the name of two Isr.:—Abishua.

51. אֲבִישׁוּר **'Ăbîyshûwr**, *ab-ee-shoor';* from 1 and 7791; *father of* (the) *wall* (i.e. perh. *mason*); *Abishur*, an Isr.:—Abishur.

52. אֲבִישַׁי **'Ăbîyshay**, *ab-ee-shah'ee;* or (shorter) אַבְשַׁי **'Abshay**, *ab-shah'ee;* from 1 and 7862; *father of a gift* (i.e. prob. *generous*); *Abishai*, an Isr.:—Abishai.

53. אֲבִישָׁלוֹם **'Ăbîyshâlôwm**, *ab-ee-shaw-lome';* or (short.) אַבְשָׁלוֹם **'Abshâlôwm**, *ab-shaw-lome';* from 1 and 7965; *father of peace* (i.e. *friendly*); *Abshalom*, a son of David; also (the fuller form) a later Isr.:—Abishalom, Absalom.

54. אֶבְיָתָר **'Ebyâthâr**, *eb-yaw-thawr';* contr. from 1 and 3498; *father of abundance* (i.e. *liberal*); *Ebjathar*, an Isr.:—Abiathar.

55. אָבַךְ **'âbak**, *aw-bak';* a prim. root; prob. to *coil* upward:—mount up.

56. אָבַל **'âbal**, *aw-bal';* a prim. root; to *bewail:*—lament, mourn.

57. אָבֵל **'âbêl**, *aw-bale';* from 56; *lamenting:*—mourn (-er, -ing).

58. אָבֵל **'âbêl**, *aw-bale';* from an unused root (mean. to *be grassy*); a *meadow:*—plain. Comp. also the prop. names beginning with Abel-.

59. אָבֵל **'Âbêl**, *aw-bale';* from 58; a *meadow; Abel*, the name of two places in Pal.:—Abel.

60. אֵבֶל **'êbel**, *ay'-bel;* from 56; *lamentation:*—mourning.

61. אֲבָל **'ăbâl**, *ab-awl';* appar. from 56 through the idea of *negation; nay*, i.e. *truly* or *yet:*—but, indeed, nevertheless, verily.

62. אָבֵל בֵּית־מַעֲכָה **'Âbêl Bêyth-Ma‘ăkâh**, *aw-bale' bayth ma-a-kaw';* from 58 and 1004 and 4601; *meadow of Beth-Maakah; Abel of Beth-maakah*, a place in Pal.:—Abel-beth-maachah, Abel of Beth-maachah.

63. אָבֵל הַשִּׁטִּים **'Âbêl hash-Shiṭṭîym**, *aw-bale' hash-shit-teem'*; from 58 and the plur. of 7848, with the art. ins.; *meadow of the acacias; Abel hash-Shittim*, a place in Pal.:—Abel-shittim.

64. אָבֵל כְּרָמִים **'Âbêl Kᵉrâmîym**, *aw-bale' ker-aw-meem'*; from 58 and the plur. of 3754; *meadow of vineyards; Abel-Keramim*, a place in Pal.:—plain of the vineyards.

65. אָבֵל מְחוֹלָה **'Âbêl Mᵉchôwlâh**, *aw-bale' mekh-o-law'*; from 58 and 4246; *meadow of dancing; Abel-Mecholah*, a place in Pal.:—Abel-meholah.

66. אַבֵל מַיִם **'Âbêl Mayim**, *aw-bale' mah'-yim*; from 58 and 4325; *meadow of water; Abel-Majim*, a place in Pal.:—Abel-maim.

67. אָבֵל מִצְרַיִם **'Âbêl Mitsrayim**, *aw-bale' mits-rah'-yim*; from 58 and 4714; *meadow of Egypt; Abel-Mitsrajim*, a place in Pal.:—Abel-mizraim.

68. אֶבֶן **'eben**, *eh'-ben*; from the root of 1129 through the mean. to *build; a stone*:—+ carbuncle, + mason, + plummet, [chalk-, hail-, head-, sling-] stone (-ny), (divers) weight (-s).

69. אֶבֶן **'eben** (Chald.), *eh'-ben*; corresp. to 68:—stone.

70. אֹבֶן **'ôben**, *o'-ben*; from the same as 68; *a pair of stones* (only dual); a potter's *wheel* or a midwife's *stool* (consisting alike of two horizontal disks with a support between):—wheel, stool.

71. אֲבָנָה **'Ăbânâh**, *ab-aw-naw'*; perh. fem. of 68; *stony; Abanah*, a river near Damascus:—Abana. Comp. 549.

72. אֶבֶן הָעֵזֶר **'Eben hâ-'êzer**, *eh'-ben haw-e'-zer*; from 68 and 5828 with the art. ins.; *stone of the help; Eben-ha-Ezer*, a place in Pal.:—Ebenezer.

73. אַבְנֵט **'abnêṭ**, *ab-nate'*; of uncert. deriv.; a *belt*:—girdle.

74. אַבְנֵר **'Abnêr**, *ab-nare'*; or (fully) אֲבִינֵר **'Ăbîynêr**, *ab-ee-nare'*; from 1 and 5216; *father of light* (i.e. *enlightening*); *Abner*, an Isr.:—Abner.

75. אָבַס **'âbaç**, *aw-bas'*; a prim. root; to *fodder*:—fatted, stalled.

76. אֲבַעְבֻּעָה **'ăba'bû'âh**, *ab-ah-boo-aw'*; (by redupl.) from an unused root (mean. to *belch* forth); an inflammatory *pustule* (as *eruption*):—blains.

77. אֶבֶץ **'Ebets**, *eh'-bets*; from an unused root prob. mean. to *gleam; conspicuous; Ebets*, a place in Pal.:—Abez.

78. אִבְצָן **'Ibtsân**, *ib-tsawn'*; from the same as 76; *splendid; Ibtsan*, an Isr.:—Ibzan.

79. אָבַק **'âbaq**, *aw-bak'*; a prim. root; prob. to *float* away (as vapor), but used only as denom. from 80; to *bedust*, i.e. *grapple*:—wrestle.

80. אָבָק **'âbâq**, *aw-bawk'*; from root of 79; light *particles* (as *volatile*):—(small) dust, powder.

81. אֲבָקָה **'ăbâqâh**, *ab-aw-kaw'*; fem. of 80:—powder.

82. אָבַר **'âbar**, *aw-bar'*; a prim. root; to *soar*:—fly.

83. אֵבֶר **'êber**, *ay-ber'*; from 82; a *pinion*:—[long-] wing (-ed).

84. אֶבְרָה **'ebrâh**, *eb-raw'*; fem. of 83:—feather, wing.

85. אַבְרָהָם **'Abrâhâm**, *ab-raw-hawm'*; contr. from 1 and an unused root (prob. mean. to *be populous*); *father of a multitude; Abraham*, the later name of Abram:—Abraham.

86. אַבְרֵךְ **'abrêk**, *ab-rake'*; prob. an Eg. word mean. *kneel*:—bow the knee.

87. אַבְרָם **'Abrâm**, *ab-rawm'*; contr. from 48; *high father; Abram*, the original name of Abraham:—Abram.

אַבְשַׁי **'Abshay**. See 52.

אַבְשָׁלוֹם **'Abshâlôwm**. See 53.

88. אֹבֹת **'ôbôth**, *o-both'*; plur. of 178; water-*skins; Oboth*, a place in the Desert:—Oboth.

89. אָגֵא **'Âgê'**, *aw-gay'*; of uncert. der. [comp. 90]; *Agè*, an Isr.:—Agee.

90. אֲגַג **'Ăgag**, *ag-ag'*; or אֲגָג **'Ăgâg**, *ag-awg'*; of uncert. der. [comp. 89]; *flame; Agag*, a title of Amalekitish kings:—Agag.

91. אֲגָגִי **'Ăgâgîy**, *ag-aw-ghee'*; patrial or patron. from 90; an *Agagite* or descendant (subject) of Agag:—Agagite.

92. אֲגֻדָּה **'ăguddâh**, *ag-ood-daw'*; fem. pass. part. of an unused root (mean. to *bind*); a *band, bundle, knot*, or *arch*:—bunch, burden, troop.

93. אֱגוֹז **'ĕgôwz**, *eg-oze'*; prob. of Pers. or.; a *nut*:—nut.

94. אָגוּר **'Âgûwr**, *aw-goor'*; pass. part. of 103; *gathered* (i.e. *received* among the sages); *Agur*, a fanciful name for Solomon:—Agur.

95. אֲגוֹרָה **'ăgôwrâh**, *ag-o-raw'*; from the same as 94; prop. something *gathered*, i.e. perh. a *grain* or *berry*; used only of a small (silver) *coin*:—piece [of] silver.

96. אֶגֶל **'egel**, *eh'-ghel*; from an unused root (mean. to *flow* down or together as drops); a *reservoir*:—drop.

97. אֶגְלַיִם **'Eglayim**, *eg-lah'-yim*; dual of 96; a *double pond; Eglajim*, a place in Moab:—Eglaim.

98. אֲגַם **'ăgam**, *ag-am'*; from an unused root (mean. to *collect* as water); a *marsh*; hence a *rush* (as growing in swamps); hence a *stockade* of reeds:—pond, pool, standing [water].

99. אָגֵם **'âgêm**, *aw-game'*; prob. from the same as 98 (in the sense of *stagnant* water); fig. *sad*:—pond.

100. אַגְמוֹן **'agmôwn**, *ag-mone'*; from the same as 98; a marshy *pool* [others from a different root, a *kettle*]; by impl. a *rush* (as growing there); collect. a *rope* of rushes:—bulrush, caldron, hook, rush.

101. אַגָּן **'aggân**, *ag-gawn'*; prob. from 5059; a *bowl* (as *pounded* out hollow):—basin, cup, goblet.

102. אַגָּף **'aggâph**, *ag-gawf'*; prob. from 5062 (through the idea of *impending*); a *cover* or *heap*; i.e. (only plur.) *wings* of an army, or *crowds* of troops:—bands.

103. אָגַר **'âgar**, *aw-gar'*; a prim. root; to *harvest*:—gather.

104. אִגְּרָא **'iggᵉrâ'** (Chald.), *ig-er-aw'*; of Pers. or.; an *epistle* (as carried by a state courier or postman):—letter.

105. אֲגַרְטָל **'ăgarṭâl**, *ag-ar-tawl'*; of uncert. der.; a *basin*:—charger.

106. אֶגְרֹף **'egrôph**, *eg-rofe'*; from 1640 (in the sense of *grasping*); the *clenched* hand:—fist.

107. אִגֶּרֶת **'iggereth**, *ig-eh'-reth*; fem. of 104; an *epistle*:—letter.

108. אֵד **'êd**, *ade*; from the same as 181 (in the sense of *enveloping*); a *fog*:—mist, vapor.

109. אָדַב **'âdab**, *aw-dab'*; a prim. root; to *languish*:—grieve.

110. אַדְבְּאֵל **'Adbᵉ'êl**, *ad-beh-ale'*; prob. from 109 (in the sense of *chastisement*) and 410; *disciplined of God; Adbeël*, a son of Ishmael:—Adbeel.

111. אֲדַד **'Ădad**, *ad-ad'*; prob. an orth. var. for 2301; *Adad* (or Hadad), an Edomite:—Hadad.

112. אִדּוֹ **'Iddôw**, *id-do*; of uncert. der.; *Iddo*, an Isr.:—Iddo.

אֱדוֹם **'Ĕdôwm**. See 123.

אֱדוֹמִי **'Ĕdôwmîy**. See 30.

113. אָדוֹן **'âdôwn**, *aw-done'*, or (short.) אָדֹן **'âdôn**, *aw-done'*; from an unused root (mean. to *rule*); *sovereign*, i.e. *controller* (human or divine):—lord, master, owner. Comp. also names beginning with "Adoni-".

114. אַדּוֹן **'Addôwn**, *ad-done'*; prob. intens. for 113; *powerful; Addon*, appar. an Isr.:—Addon.

115. אֲדוֹרַיִם **'Ădôwrayim**, *ad-o-rah'-yim*; dual from 142 (in the sense of *eminence*); *double mound; Adorajim*, a place in Pal.:—Adoraim.

116. אֱדַיִן **'ĕdayin** (Chald.), *ed-ah'-yin*; of uncert. der.; *then* (of time):—now, that time, then.

117. אַדִּיר **'addîyr**, *ad-deer'*; from 142; *wide* or (gen.) *large*; fig. *powerful*:—excellent, famous, gallant, glorious, goodly, lordly, mighty (-ier, one), noble, principal, worthy.

118. אֲדַלְיָא **'Ădalyâ'**, *ad-al-yaw'*; of Pers. der.; *Adalja*, a son of Haman:—Adalia.

119. אָדַם **'âdam**, *aw-dam'*; to *show blood* (in the face), i.e. *flush* or turn rosy:—be (dyed, made) red (ruddy).

120. אָדָם **'âdâm**, *aw-dawm'*; from 119; *ruddy*, i.e. a *human being* (an individual or the species, *mankind*, etc.):— × another, + hypocrite, + common sort, × low, man (mean, of low degree), person.

121. אָדָם **'Âdâm**, *aw-dawm'*; the same as 120; *Adam*, the name of the first man, also of a place in Pal.:—Adam.

122. אָדֹם **'âdôm**, *aw-dome'*; from 119; *rosy*:—red, ruddy.

123. אֱדֹם **'Ĕdôm**, *ed-ome'*; or (fully) אֱדוֹם **'Êdôwm**, *ed-ome'*; from 122; *red* [see Gen. 25 : 25]; *Edom*, the elder twin-brother of Jacob; hence the region (Idumæa) occupied by him:—Edom, Edomites, Idumea.

124. אֹדֶם **'ôdem**, *o'-dem*; from 119; *redness*, i.e. the *ruby, garnet*, or some other red gem:—sardius.

125. אֲדַמְדָּם **'ădamdâm**, *ad-am-dawm'*; redupl. from 119; *reddish*:—(somewhat) reddish.

126. אַדְמָה **'Admâh**, *ad-maw'*; contr. for 127; *earthy; Admah*, a place near the Dead Sea:—Admah.

127. אֲדָמָה **'ădâmâh**, *ad-aw-maw'*; from 119; *soil* (from its gen. *redness*):—country, earth, ground, husband [-man] (-ry), land.

128. אֲדָמָה **'Ădâmâh**, *ad-aw-maw'*; the same as 127; *Adamah*, a place in Pal.:—Adamah.

אַדְמוֹנִי **'admôwnîy**. See 132.

129. אֲדָמִי **'Ădâmîy**, *ad-aw-mee'*; from 127; *earthy; Adami*, a place in Pal.:—Adami.

130. אֱדֹמִי **'Ĕdômîy**, *ed-o-mee'*; or (fully) אֱדוֹמִי **'Ĕdôwmîy**, *ed-o-mee'*; patron. from 123; an *Edomite*, or desc. from (or inhab. of) Edom:—Edomite. See 726.

131. אֲדֻמִּים **'Ădummîym**, *ad-oom-meem'*; plur. of 121; *red* spots; *Adummim*, a pass in Pal.:—Adummim.

132. אַדְמֹנִי **'admônîy**, *ad-mo-nee'*, or (fully) אַדְמוֹנִי **'admôwnîy**, *ad-mo-nee'*; from 119; *reddish* (of the hair or the complexion):—red, ruddy.

133. אַדְמָתָא **'Admâthâ'**, *ad-maw-thaw'*; prob. of Pers. der.; *Admatha*, a Pers. nobleman:—Admatha.

134. אֶדֶן **'eden**, *eh'-den*; from the same as 113 (in the sense of *strength*); a *basis* (of a building, a column, etc.):—foundation, socket.

אָדֹן **'âdôn**. See 113.

135. אַדָּן **'Addân**, *ad-dawn'*; intens. from the same as 134; *firm; Addan*, an Isr.:—Addan.

136. אֲדֹנָי **'Ădônây**, *ad-o-noy'*; an emphatic form of 113; the *Lord* (used as a prop. name of God only):—(my) Lord.

137. אֲדֹנִי־בֶזֶק **'Ădônîy-Bezeq**, *ad-o''-nee-beh'-zek*; from 113 and 966; *lord of Bezek; Adoni-Bezek*, a Canaanitish king:—Adoni-bezek.

138. אֲדֹנִיָּה **'Ădônîyâh**, *ad-o-nee-yaw'*; or. (prol.) אֲדֹנִיָּהוּ **'Ădônîyâhûw**, *ad-o-nee-yaw'-hoo*; from 113 and 3050; *lord* (i.e. worshipper) of Jah; *Adonijah*, the name of three Isr.:—Adonijah.

139. אֲדֹנִי־צֶדֶק **'Ădônîy-Tsedeq**, *ad-o''-nee tseh'-dek*; from 113 and 6664; *lord of justice; Adoni-Tsedek*, a Canaanitish king:—Adonizedec.

140. אֲדֹנִיקָם **'Ădônîyqâm**, *ad-o-nee-kawm'*; from 113 and 6965; *lord of rising* (i.e. *high*)' *Adonikam*, the name of one or two Isr.:—Adonikam

141. אֲדֹנִירָם **'Âdônîyrâm**, *ad-o-nee-rawm'*; from 113 and 7311; *lord of height; Adoniram*, an Isr.:—Adoniram.

142. אָדַר **'âdar**, *aw-dar'*; a prim. root; to *expand*, i.e. *be great* or (fig.) *magnificent*:—(become) glorious, honourable.

143. אֲדָר **'Ădâr**, *ad-awr'*; prob. of for. der.; perh. mean. *fire; Adar*, the 12th Heb. month:—Adar.

144. אֲדָר **'Ădâr** (Chald.), *ad-awr'*; corresp. to 143:—Adar.

145. אֶדֶר **'eder**, *eh'-der*; from 142; *amplitude*, i.e. (concr.) a *mantle*; also (fig.) *splendor*:—goodly, robe.

146. אַדָּר **'Addâr**, *ad-dawr'*; intens. from 142; *ample; Addar*, a place in Pal.; also an Isr.:—Addar.

147. אִדַּר **'iddar** (Chald.), *id-dar'*; intens. from a root corresp. to 142; *ample*, i.e. a *threshing-floor*:—threshingfloor.

148. אֲדַרְגָּזֵר **'ădargâzêr** (Chald.), *ad-ar"-gaw-zare'*; from the same as 147, and 1505; a *chief diviner*, or *astrologer*:—judge.

149. אַדְרַזְדָּא **'adrazdâ'** (Chald.), *ad-raz-daw'*; prob. of Pers. or.; *quickly* or *carefully*:—diligently.

150. אֲדַרְכֹּן **'ădarkôn**, *ad-ar-kone'*; of Pers. or.; a *daric* or Pers. coin:—dram.

151. אֲדֹרָם **'Ădôrâm**, *ad-o-rawm'*; contr. for 141; *Adoram* (or Adoniram), an Isr.:—Adoram.

152. אַדְרַמֶּלֶךְ **'Adrammelek**, *ad-ram-meh'-lek*; from 142 and 4428; *splendor of* (the) *king; Adrammelek*, the name of an Assyr. idol, also of a son of Sennacherib:—Adrammelech.

153. אֶדְרָע **'edrâ'** (Chald.), *ed-raw'*; an orth. var. for 1872; an *arm*, i.e. (fig.) *power*:—force.

154. אֶדְרֶעִי **'edre'îy**, *ed-reh'-ee*; from the equivalent of 153; *mighty; Edrei*, the name of two places in Pal.:—Edrei.

155. אַדֶּרֶת **'addereth**, *ad-deh'-reth*; fem. of 117; something *ample* (as a *large* vine, a *wide* dress); also the same as 145:—garment, glory, goodly, mantle, robe.

156. אָדַשׁ **'âdash**, *aw-dash'*; a prim. root; to *tread* out (grain):—thresh.

157. אָהַב **'âhab**, *aw-hab'*; or אָהֵב **'âhêb**, *aw-habe'*; a prim. root; to *have affection* for (sexually or otherwise):—(be-) love (-d, -ly, -r), like, friend.

158. אַהַב **'ahab**, *ah'-hab*; from 157; *affection* (in a good or a bad sense):—love (-r).

159. אֹהַב **'ôhab**, *o'-hab*; from 156; mean. the same as 158:—love.

160. אַהֲבָה **'ahăbâh**, *ă-hab-aw'*; fem. of 158 and mean. the same:—love.

161. אֹהַד **'Ôhad**, *o'-had*; from an unused root mean. to *be united; unity; Ohad*, an Isr.:—Ohad.

162. אֲהָהּ **'ăhâhh**, *ă-haw'*; appar. a prim. word expressing *pain* exclamatorily; *Oh!*:—ah, alas.

163. אַהֲוָא **'Ahăvâ'**, *ă-hav-aw'*; prob. of for. or.; *Ahava*, a river of Babylonia:—Ahava.

164. אֵהוּד **'Êhûwd**, *ay-hood'*; from the same as 161; *united; Ehud*, the name of two or three Isr.:—Ehud.

165. אֱהִי **'ĕhîy**, *e-hee'*; appar. an orth. var. for 346; *where*:—I will be (Hos. 13:10, 14) [*which is often the rendering of the same Heb. form from* 1961].

166. אָהַל **'âhal**, *aw-hal'*; a prim. root; to *be clear*:—shine.

167. אָהַל **'âhal**, *aw-hal'*; a denom. from 168; to *tent*:—pitch (remove) a tent.

168. אֹהֶל **'ôhel**, *o'-hel*; from 166; a *tent* (as *clearly* conspicuous from a distance):—covering, (dwelling) (place), home, tabernacle, tent.

169. אֹהֶל **'Ôhel**, *o'-hel*; the same as 168; *Ohel*, an Isr.:—Ohel.

170. אָהֳלָה **'Ohŏlâh**, *ŏ-hol-aw'*; in form a fem. of 168, but in fact for אָהֳלָהּ **'Ohŏlâhh**, *ŏ-hol-aw'*; from 168; *her tent* (i.e. idolatrous *sanctuary*); *Oholah*, a symbol. name for Samaria:—Aholah.

171. אָהֳלִיאָב **'Ohŏlîy'âb**, *ŏ"-hol-e-awb'*; from 168 and 1; *tent of* (his) *father*; *Oholiab*, an Isr.:—Aholiab.

172. אָהֳלִיבָה **'Ohŏlîybâh**, *ŏ"-hol-ee-baw'*; (similarly with 170) for אָהֳלִיבָהּ **'Ohŏlîybâhh**, *ŏ"-hol-e-baw'*; from 168; *my tent* (is) *in her; Oholibah*, a symbol. name for Judah:—Aholibah.

173. אָהֳלִיבָמָה **'Ohŏlîybâmâh**, *ŏ"-hol-e-baw-maw'*; from 168 and 1116; *tent of* (the) *height; Oholibamah*, a wife of Esau:—Aholibamah.

174. אֲהָלִים **'ăhâlîym**, *ă-haw-leem'*; or (fem.) אֲהָלוֹת **'ăhâlôwth**, *ă-haw-loth'* (only used thus in the plur.); of for. or.; *aloe* wood (i.e. sticks):—(tree of lign-) aloes.

175. אַהֲרוֹן **'Ahărôwn**, *ă-har-one'*; of uncert. deriv.; *Aharon*, the brother of Moses:—Aaron.

176. אוֹ **'ôw**, *o*; presumed to be the "constr." or genitival form of אַו **'av**, *av*, short. for 185; *desire* (and so prob. in Prov. 31:4); hence (by way of alternative) *or*, also *if*:—also, and, either, if, at the least, × nor, or, otherwise, then, whether.

177. אוּאֵל **'Ûw'êl**, *oo-ale'*; from 176 and 410; *wish of God; Uel*, an Isr.:—Uel.

178. אוֹב **'ôwb**, *obe*; from the same as 1 (appar. through the idea of *prattling* a father's name); prop. a *mumble*, i.e. a water-*skin* (from its hollow sound); hence a *necromancer* (ventriloquist, as from a jar):—bottle, familiar spirit.

179. אוֹבִיל **'ôwbîyl**, *o-beel'*; prob. from 56; *mournful; Obil*, an Ishmaelite:—Obil.

180. אוּבָל **'ûwbâl**, *oo-bawl'*; or (short.) אֻבָל **'ûbâl**, *oo-bawl'*; from 2986 (in the sense of 2988); a *stream*:—river.

181. אוּד **'ûwd**, *ood*; from an unused root mean. to *rake* together; a *poker* (for *turning* or *gathering* embers):—(fire-) brand.

182. אוֹדוֹת **'ôwdôwth**, *o-dōth'*; or (short.) אֹדוֹת **'ôdôwth**, *o-dōth'* (only thus in the plur.); from the same as 181; *turnings* (i.e. *occasions*); (adv.) on *account* of:—(be-) cause, concerning, sake.

183. אָוָה **'âvâh**, *aw-vaw'*; a prim. root; to *wish* for:—covet, (greatly) desire, be desirous, long, lust (after).

184. אָוָה **'âvâh**, *aw-vaw'*; a prim. root; to *extend* or *mark* out:—point out.

185. אַוָּה **'avvâh**, *av-vaw'*; from 183; *longing*:—desire, lust after, pleasure.

186. אוּזַי **'Ûwzay**, *oo-zah'ee*; perh. by perm. for 5813, *strong; Uzai*, an Isr.:—Uzai.

187. אוּזָל **'Ûwzâl**, *oo-zawl'*; of uncert. der.; *Uzal*, a son of Joktan:—Uzal.

188. אוֹי **'ôwy**, *ō'ee*; prob. from 183 (in the sense of *crying* out after); *lamentation*; also interj. *Oh!*:—alas, woe.

189. אֱוִי **'Ĕvîy**, *ev-ee'*; prob. from 183; *desirous; Evi*, a Midianitish chief:—Evi.

אוֹיֵב **'ôwyêb**. See 341.

190. אוֹיָה **'ôwyâh**, *o-yaw'*; fem. of 188:—woe.

191. אֱוִיל **'ĕvîyl**, *ev-eel'*; from an unused root (mean. to be *perverse*); (fig.) *silly*:—fool (-ish) (man).

192. אֱוִיל מְרֹדַךְ **'Ĕvîyl Merôdak**, *ev-eel' mer-o-dak'*; of Chald. deriv. and prob. mean. *soldier of Merodak; Evil-Merodak*, a Babylonian king:—Evil-merodach.

193. אוּל **'ûwl**, *ool*; from an unused root mean. to *twist*, i.e. (by impl.) *be strong*; the *body* (as being *rolled* together); also *powerful*:—mighty, strength.

194. אוּלַי **'ûwlay**, *oo-lah'ee*; or (short.) אֻלַי **'ûlay**, *oo-lah'ee*; from 176; *if not*; hence *perhaps*:—if so be, may be, peradventure, unless.

195. אוּלַי **'Ûwlay**, *oo-lah'ee*; of Pers. der.; the *Ulai* (or Eulæus), a river of Persia:—Ulai.

196. אֱוִלִי **'ĕvîlîy**, *ev-ee-lee'*; from 191; *silly, foolish*; hence (mor.) *impious*:—foolish.

197. אוּלָם **'ûwlâm**, *oo-lawm'*; or (short.) אֻלָם **'ûlâm**, *oo-lawm'*; from 481 (in the sense of *tying*); a *vestibule* (as *bound* to the building):—porch.

198. אוּלָם **'Ûwlâm**, *oo-lawm'*; appar. from 481 (in the sense of *dumbness*); *solitary; Ulam*, the name of two Isr.:—Ulam.

199. אוּלָם **'ûwlâm**, *oo-lawm'*; appar. a variation of 194; *however* or *on the contrary*:—as for, but, howbeit, in very deed, surely, truly, wherefore.

200. אִוֶּלֶת **'ivveleth**, *iv-veh'-leth*; from the same as 191; *silliness*:—folly, foolishly (-ness).

201. אוֹמָר **'Ôwmâr**, *o-mawr'*; from 559; *talkative; Omar*, a grandson of Esau:—Omar.

202. אוֹן **'ôwn**, *ōne*; prob. from the same as 205 (in the sense of *effort*, but successful); *ability, power*, (fig.) *wealth*:—force, goods, might, strength, substance.

203. אוֹן **'Ôwn**, *ōne*; the same as 202; *On*, an Isr.:—On.

204. אוֹן **'Ôwn**, *ōne*; or (short.) אֹן **'Ôn**, *ōne*; of Eg. der.; *On*, a city of Egypt:—On.

205. אָוֶן **'âven**, *aw'-ven*; from an unused root perh. mean. prop. to *pant* (hence to *exert* oneself, usually in vain; to *come to naught*); strictly *nothingness*; also *trouble, vanity, wickedness*; spec. an *idol*:—affliction, evil, false, idol, iniquity, mischief, mourners (-ing), naught, sorrow, unjust, unrighteous, vain, vanity, wicked (-ness.) Comp. 369.

206. אָוֶן **'Âven**, *aw'-ven*; the same as 205; *idolatry; Aven*, the contemptuous synonym of three places, one in Cœle-Syria, one in Egypt (On), and one in Pal. (Bethel):—Aven. See also 204, 1007.

207. אוֹנוֹ **'Ôwnôw**, *o-no'*; or (short.) אֹנוֹ **'Ônôw**, *o-no'*; prol. from 202; *strong; Ono*, a place in Pal.:—Ono.

208. אוֹנָם **'Ôwnâm**, *o-nawm'*; a var. of 209; *strong; Onam*, the name of an Edomite and of an Isr.:—Onam.

209. אוֹנָן **'Ôwnân**, *o-nawn'*; a var. of 207; *strong; Onan*, a son of Judah:—Onan.

210. אוּפָז **'Ûwphâz**, *oo-fawz'*; perh. a corruption of 211; *Uphaz*, a famous gold region:—Uphaz.

211. אוֹפִיר **'Ôwphîyr**, *o-feer'*; or (short.) אֹפִיר **'Ôphîyr**, *o-feer'*; and אוֹפִר **'Ôwphîr**, *o-feer'*; of uncert. deriv.; *Ophir*, the name of a son of Joktan, and of a gold region in the East:—Ophir.

212. אוֹפָן **'ôwphân**, *o-fawn'*; or (short.) אֹפָן **'ôphân**, *o-fawn'*; from an unused root mean. to *revolve*; a *wheel*:—wheel.

אוֹפִר **'Ôwphîr**. See 211.

213. אוּץ **'ûwts**, *oots*; a prim. root; to *press*; (by impl.) to *be close, hurry, withdraw*:—(make) haste (-n, -y), labor, be narrow.

214. אוֹצָר **'ôwtsâr**, *o-tsaw'*; from 686; a *depository*:—armory, cellar, garner, store (-house), treasure (-house) (-y).

215. אוֹר **'ôwr**, *ore*; a prim. root; to *be* (caus. *make*) *luminous* (lit. and metaph.):—× break of day, glorious, kindle, (be, en-, give, show) light (-en, -ened), set on fire, shine.

216. אוֹר **'ôwr**, *ore*; from 215; *illumination* or (concr.) *luminary* (in every sense, including *lightning, happiness*, etc.):—bright, clear, + day, light (-ning), morning, sun.

217. אוּר **'ûwr**, *oor*; from 215; *flame*, hence (in the plur.) the *East* (as being the region of light):—fire, light. See also 224.

218. אוּר **'Ûwr**, *oor*; the same as 217; *Ur*, a place in Chaldæa; also an Isr.:—Ur.

219. אוֹרָה **'ôwrâh**, *o-raw'*; fem. of 216; *luminousness*, i.e. (fig.) *prosperity*; also a plant (as being *bright*):—herb light.

220. אֲוֵרָה **'âvêrâh**, *av-ay-raw'*; by transp. for 723; a *stall:*—cote.

221. אוּרִי **'Ûwrîy**, *oo-ree'*; from 217; *fiery; Uri*, the name of three Isr.:—Uri.

222. אוּרִיאֵל **'Ûwrîy'êl**, *oo-ree-ale'*; from 217 and 410; *flame of God; Uriel*, the name of two Isr.:—Uriel.

223. אוּרִיָּה **'Ûwrîyâh**, *oo-ree-yaw'*; or (prol.) אוּרִיָּהוּ **'Ûwrîyâhûw**, *oo-ree-yaw'-hoo;* from 217 and 3050; *flame of Jah; Urijah*, the name of one Hittite and five Isr.:—Uriah, Urijah.

224. אוּרִים **'Ûwrîym**, *oo-reem'*; plur. of 217; *lights; Urim*, the oracular brilliancy of the figures in the high-priest's breastplate:—Urim.

אוֹרְנָה **'Owrenâh**. See 728.

225. אוּת **'ûwth**, *ooth;* a prim. root; prop. to *come*, i.e. (impl.) to *assent:*—consent.

226. אוֹת **'ôwth**, *ōth;* prob. from 225 (in the sense of *appearing*); a *signal* (lit. or fig.), as a *flag, beacon, monument, omen, prodigy, evidence*, etc.:—mark, miracle, (en-) sign, token.

227. אָז **'âz**, *awz;* a demonstrative adv.; *at that time* or *place;* also as a conj., *therefore:*—beginning, for, from, hitherto, now, of old, once, since, then, at which time, yet.

228. אֲזָא **'ăzâ'** (Chald.), *az-aw';* or אֲזָה **'ăzâh** (Chald.), *az-aw';* to *kindle;* (by impl.) to *heat:*—heat, hot.

229. אֶזְבַּי **'Ezbay**, *ez-bah'ee;* prob. from 231; *hyssop-like; Ezbai*, an Isr.:—Ezbai.

230. אֲזַד **'ăzad** (Chald.), *az-awd';* of uncert. der.; *firm:*—be gone.

231. אֵזוֹב **'êzôwb**, *ay-zobe';* prob. of for. der.; *hyssop:*—hyssop.

232. אֵזוֹר **'êzôwr**, *ay-zore';* from 246; something *girt;* a *belt*, also a *band:*—girdle.

233. אֲזַי **'ăzay**, *az-ah'ee;* prob. from 227; *at that time:*—then.

234. אַזְכָּרָה **'azkârâh**, *az-kaw-raw';* from 2142; a *reminder;* spec. *remembrance-offering:*—memorial.

235. אָזַל **'âzal**, *aw-zal';* a prim. root; to *go away*, hence to *disappear:*—fail, gad about, go to and fro [*but in Ezek.* 27 : 19 *the word is rendered by many* "from Uzal," *by others* "yarn"], be gone (spent).

236. אֲזַל **'ăzal** (Chald.), *az-al';* the same as 235; to *depart:*—go (up).

237. אֶזֶל **'ezel**, *eh'-zel;* from 235; *departure; Ezel*, a memorial stone in Pal.:—Ezel.

238. אָזַן **'âzan**, *aw-zan';* a prim. root; prob. to *expand;* but used only as a denom. from 241; to *broaden out the ear* (with the hand), i.e. (by impl.) to *listen:*—give (perceive by the) ear, hear (-ken). See 239.

239. אָזַן **'âzan**, *aw-zan';* a prim. root [rather ident. with 238 through the idea of *scales* as if two ears]; to *weigh*, i.e. (fig.) *ponder:*—give good heed.

240. אָזֵן **'âzên**, *aw-zane';* from 238; a *spade* or *paddle* (as having a *broad* end):—weapon.

241. אֹזֶן **'ôzen**, *o'-zen;* from 238; *broadness*, i.e. (concr.) the *ear* (from its form in man):—+advertise, audience, +displease, ear, hearing, +show.

242. אֻזֵּן שֶׁאֱרָה **'Uzzên She'ĕrâh**, *ooz-zane' sheh-er-aw';* from 238 and 7609; *plat of Sheerah* (i.e. settled by him); *Uzzen-Sheërah*, a place in Pal.:—Uzzen-sherah.

243. אַזְנוֹת תָּבוֹר **'Aznôwth Tâbôwr**, *az-nōth' taw-bore';* from 238 and 8396; *flats* (i.e. *tops*) *of Tabor* (i.e. situated on it); *Aznoth-Tabor*, a place in Pal.:—Aznoth-tabor.

244. אָזְנִי **'Oznîy**, *oz-nee';* from 241; *having* (quick) *ears; Ozni*, an Isr.; also an *Oznite* (collect.), his desc.:—Ozni, Oznites.

245. אֲזַנְיָה **'Ăzanyâh**, *az-an-yaw';* from 238 and 3050; *heard by Jah; Azanjah*, an Isr.:—Azaniah.

246. אֲזִקִּים **'ăziqqîym**, *az-ik-keem';* a var. for 2131; *manacles:*—chains.

247. אָזַר **'âzar**, *aw-zar';* a prim. root; to *belt:*—bind (compass) about, gird (up, with).

248. אֶזְרוֹעַ **'ezrôwa'**, *ez-ro'-ă;* a var. for 2220; the *arm:*—arm.

249. אֶזְרָח **'ezrâch**, *ez-rawkh';* from 2224 (in the sense of *springing up*); a spontaneous *growth*, i.e. *native* (tree or persons):—bay tree, (home-) born (in the land), of the (one's own) country (nation).

250. אֶזְרָחִי **'Ezrâchîy**, *ez-raw-khee';* patron. from 2246; an *Ezrachite* or desc. of Zerach:—Ezrahite.

251. אָח **'âch**, *awkh;* a prim. word; a *brother* (used in the widest sense of literal relationship and metaph. affinity or resemblance [like 1]):—another, brother (-ly), kindred, like, other. Comp. also the prop. names beginning with "Ah-" or "Ahi-".

252. אַח **'ach** (Chald.), *akh;* corresp. to 251:—brother.

253. אָח **'âch**, *awkh;* a var. for 162; *Oh!* (expressive of grief or surprise):—ah, alas.

254. אָח **'âch**, *awkh;* of uncert. der.; a *fire-pot* or *chafing-dish:*—hearth.

255. אֹחַ **'ôach**, *o'-akh;* prob. from 253; a *howler* or lonesome wild animal:—doleful creature.

256. אַחְאָב **'Ach'âb**, *akh-awb';* once (by contr.) אֶחָב **'Echâb** (Jer. 29 : 22), *ekh-awb';* from 251 and 1; *brother* [i.e. *friend*] *of* (his) *father; Achab*, the name of a king of Israel and of a prophet at Babylon:—Ahab.

257. אַחְבָּן **'Achbân**, *akh-bawn';* from 251 and 995; *brother* (i.e. *possessor*) *of understanding; Achban*, an Isr.:—Ahban.

258. אָחַד **'âchad**, *aw-khad';* perh. a prim. root; to *unify*, i.e. (fig.) *collect* (one's thoughts):—go one way or other.

259. אֶחָד **'echâd**, *ekh-awd';* a numeral from 258; prop. *united*, i.e. *one;* or (as an ordinal) *first:*—a, alike, alone, altogether, and, any (-thing), apiece, a certain, [dai-] ly, each (one), + eleven, every, few, first, + highway, a man, once, one, only, other, some, together.

260. אָחוּ **'âchûw**, *aw'-khoo;* of unc. (perh. Eg.) der.; a *bulrush* or any marshy grass (particularly that along the Nile):—flag, meadow.

261. אֵחוּד **'Êchûwd**, *ay-khood';* from 258; *united; Echud*, the name of three Isr.:—Ehud.

262. אַחְוָה **'achvâh**, *akh-vaw';* from 2331 (in the sense of 2324); an *utterance:*—declaration.

263. אַחֲוָה **'achăvâh** (Chald.), *akh-av-aw';* corresp. to 262; *solution* (of riddles):—showing.

264. אַחֲוָה **'achăvâh**, *akh-av-aw';* from 251; *fraternity:*—brotherhood.

265. אֲחוֹחַ **'Ăchôwach**, *akh-o'-akh;* by redupl. from 251; *brotherly; Achoach*, an Isr.:—Ahoah.

266. אֲחוֹחִי **'Ăchôwchîy**, *akh-o-khee';* patron. from 264; an *Achochite* or desc. of Achoach:—Ahohite.

267. אֲחוּמַי **'Ăchûwmay**, *akh-oo-mah'ee;* perh. from 251 and 4325; *brother* (i.e. *neighbour*) *of water; Achumai*, an Isr.:—Ahumai.

268. אָחוֹר **'âchôwr**, *aw-khore';* or (short.) אָחֹר **'âchôr**, *aw-khore';* from 299; the *hinder* part; hence (adv.) *behind, backward;* also (as facing north) the *West:*—after (-ward), back (part, -side, -ward), hereafter, (be-) hind (-er part), time to come, without.

269. אָחוֹת **'achôwth**, *aw-khōth';* irreg. fem. of 251; a *sister* (used very widely [like 250], lit. and fig.):—(an-) other, sister, together.

270. אָחַז **'âchaz**, *aw-khaz';* a prim. root; to *seize* (often with the accessory idea of holding in possession):— + be affrighted, bar, (catch, lay, take) hold (back), come upon, fasten, handle, portion, (get, have or take) possess (-ion).

271. אָחָז **'Âchâz**, *aw-khawz';* from 270; *possessor; Achaz*, the name of a Jewish king and of an Isr.:—Ahaz.

272. אֲחֻזָּה **'ăchuzzâh**, *akh-ooz-zaw';* fem. pass. part. from 270; something *seized*, i.e. a *possession* (esp. of land):—possession.

273. אַחְזַי **'Achzay**, *akh-zah'ee;* from 270; *seizer; Achzai*, an Isr.:—Ahasai.

274. אֲחַזְיָה **'Ăchazyâh**, *akh-az-yaw';* or (prol.) אֲחַזְיָהוּ **'Ăchazyâhûw**, *akh-az-yaw'-hoo;* from 270 and 3050; *Jah has seized; Achazjah*, the name of a Jewish and an Isr. king:—Ahaziah.

275. אֲחֻזָּם **'Ăchuzzâm**, *akh-ooz-zawm';* from 270; *seizure; Achuzzam*, an Isr.:—Ahuzam.

276. אֲחֻזַּת **'Ăchuzzath**, *akh-ooz-zath';* a var. of 272; *possession; Achuzzath*, a Philistine:—Ahuzzath.

277. אֲחִי **'Ăchîy**, *akh-ee';* from 251; *brotherly; Achi*, the name of two Isr.:—Ahi.

278. אֵחִי **'Êchîy**, *ay-khee';* prob. the same as 277; *Echi*, an Isr.:—Ehi.

279. אֲחִיאָם **'Ăchîy'âm**, *akh-ee-awm';* from 251 and 517; *brother of* the *mother* (i.e. *uncle*); *Achiam*, an Isr.:—Ahiam.

280. אֲחִידָה **'achîydâh** (Chald.), *akh-ee-daw';* corresp. to 2420, an *enigma:*—hard sentence.

281. אֲחִיָּה **'Ăchîyâh**, *akh-ee-yaw';* or (prol.) אֲחִיָּהוּ **'Ăchîyâhûw**, *akh-ee-yaw'-hoo;* from 251 and 3050; *brother* (i.e. *worshipper*) *of Jah; Achijah*, the name of nine Isr.:—Ahiah, Ahijah.

282. אֲחִיהוּד **'Ăchîyhûwd**, *akh-ee-hood';* from 251 and 1935; *brother* (i.e. *possessor*) *of renown; Achihud*, an Isr.:—Ahihud.

283. אַחְיוֹ **'Achyôw**, *akh-yo';* prol. from 251; *brotherly; Achio*, the name of three Isr.:—Ahio.

284. אֲחִיחֻד **'Ăchîychûd**, *akh-ee-khood';* from 251 and 2330; *brother of a riddle* (i.e. *mysterious*); *Achichud*, an Isr.:—Ahihud.

285. אֲחִיטוּב **'Ăchîyṭûwb**, *akh-ee-toob';* from 251 and 2898; *brother of goodness; Achitub*, the name of several priests:—Ahitub.

286. אֲחִילוּד **'Ăchîylûwd**, *akh-ee-lood';* from 251 and 3205; *brother of* one *born; Achilud*, an Isr.:—Ahilud.

287. אֲחִימוֹת **'Ăchîymôwth**, *akh-ee-mōth';* from 251 and 4191; *brother of death; Achimoth*, an Isr.:—Ahimoth.

288. אֲחִימֶלֶךְ **'Ăchîymelek**, *akh-ee-meh'-lek;* from 251 and 4428; *brother of* (the) *king; Achimelek*, the name of an Isr. and of a Hittite:—Ahimelech.

289. אֲחִימַן **'Ăchîyman**, *akh-ee-man';* or אֲחִימָן **'Ăchîymân**, *akh-ee-mawn';* from 251 and 4480; *brother of a portion* (i.e. *gift*); *Achiman*, the name of an Anakite and of an Isr.:—Ahiman.

290. אֲחִימַעַץ **'Ăchîyma'ats**, *akh-ee-mah'-ats;* from 251 and the equiv. of 4619; *brother of anger; Achimaats*, the name of three Isr.:—Ahimaaz.

291. אַחְיָן **'Achyân**, *akh-yawn';* from 251; *brotherly; Achjan*, an Isr.:—Ahian.

292. אֲחִינָדָב **'Ăchîynâdâb**, *akh-ee-naw-dawb';* from 251 and 5068; *brother of liberality; Achinadab*, an Isr.:—Ahinadab.

293. אֲחִינֹעַם **'Ăchîynô'am**, *akh-ee-no'-am;* from 251 and 5278; *brother of pleasantness; Achinoam*, the name of two Israelitesses:—Ahinoam.

294. אֲחִיסָמָךְ **'Ăchîyçâmâk**, *akh-ee-saw-mawk';* from 251 and 5564; *brother of support; Achisamak*, an Isr.:—Ahisamach.

295. אֲחִיעֶזֶר **'Ăchîy'ezer**, *akh-ee-eh'-zer;* from 251 and 5828; *brother of help: Achiezer*, the name of two Isr.:—Ahiezer.

296. אֲחִיקָם **'Ăchîyqâm**, *akh-ee-kawm';* from 251 and 6965; *brother of rising* (i.e. *high*); *Achikam*, an Isr.:—Ahikam.

297. אֲחִירָם **'Ăchîyrâm**, *akh-ee-rawm';* from 251 and 7311; *brother of height* (i.e. *high*); *Achiram*, an Isr.:—Ahiram.

298. אֲחִירָמִי **'Achîyrâmîy**, *akh-ee-raw-mee'*; patron. from 297; an *Achiramite* or desc. (collect.) of Achiram:—Ahiramites.

299. אֲחִירַע **'Achîyra'**, *akh-ee-rah'*; from 251 and 7451; *brother of wrong; Achira*, an Isr.:—Ahira.

300. אֲחִישַׁחַר **'Achîyshachar**, *akh-ee-shakh'-ar*; from 251 and 7837; *brother of* (the) *dawn; Achishachar*, an Isr.:—Ahishar.

301. אֲחִישָׁר **'Achîyshâr**, *akh-ee-shawr'*; from 251 and 7891; *brother of* (the) *singer; Achishar*, an Isr.:—Ahishar.

302. אֲחִיתֹפֶל **'Achîythôphel**, *akh-ee-tho'-fel*; from 251 and 8602; *brother of folly; Achithophel*, an Isr.:—Ahithophel.

303. אַחְלָב **'Achlâb**, *akh-lawb'*; from the same root as 2459; *fatness* (i.e. *fertile*); *Achlab*, a place in Pal.:—Ahlab.

304. אַחְלַי **'Achlay**, *akh-lah'ee*; the same as 305; *wishful; Achlai*, the name of an Israelitess and of an Isr.:—Ahlai.

305. אַחֲלַי **'achălay**, *akh-al-ah'ee*; or אַחֲלֵי **'achălêy**, *akh-al-ay'*: prob. from 253 and a var. of 3863; *would that!*:—O that, would God.

306. אַחְלָמָה **'achlâmâh**, *akh-law'-maw*; perh. from 2492 (and thus *dream-stone*); a gem, prob. the *amethyst*:—amethyst.

307. אַחְמְתָא **'Achmᵉthâ'**, *akh-me-thaw'*; of Pers. der.; *Achmetha* (i.e. *Ecbatana*), the summer capital of Persia:—Achmetha.

308. אֲחַסְבַּי **'Achaçbay**, *akh-as-bah'ee*; of uncert. der.; *Achasbai*, an Isr.:—Ahasbai.

309. אָחַר **'âchar**, *aw-khar'*; a prim. root; to *loiter* (i.e. *be behind*); by impl. to *procrastinate*:—continue, defer, delay, hinder, be late (slack), stay (there), tarry (longer).

310. אַחַר **'achar**, *akh-ar'*; from 309; prop. the *hind* part; gen. used as an adv. or conj., *after* (in various senses):—after (that, -ward), again, at, away from, back (from, -side), behind, beside, by, follow (after, -ing), forasmuch, from, hereafter, hinder end, + out (over) live, + persecute, posterity, pursuing, remnant, seeing, since, thence [-forth], when, with.

311. אַחַר **'achar** (Chald.), *akh-ar'*; corresp. to 310; *after*:—[here-] after.

312. אַחֵר **'achêr**, *akh-air'*; from 309; prop. *hinder*; gen. *next, other*, etc.:—(an-) other (man), following, next, strange.

313. אַחֵר **'Achêr**, *akh-air'*; the same as 312; *Acher*, an Isr.:—Aher.

314. אַחֲרוֹן **'achărôwn**, *akh-ar-one'*; or (short.) אַחֲרֹן **'achărôn**, *akh-ar-one'*; from 309; *hinder*; gen. *late* or *last*; spec. (as facing the east) *western*:—after (-ward), to come, following, hind (-er, -ermost, -most), last, latter, rereward, ut(ter)most.

315. אַחְרַח **'Achrach**, *akh-rakh*; from 310 and 251, *after* (his) *brother: Achrach*, an Isr.:—Aharah.

316. אֲחַרְחֵל **'Acharchêl**, *akh-ar-kale'*; from 310 and 2426; *behind* (the) *intrenchment* (i.e. *safe*); *Acharchel*, an Isr.:—Aharhel.

317. אָחֳרִי **'ochŏrîy** (Chald.), *okh-or-ee'*; from 311; *other*:—(an-) other.

318. אָחֳרֵין **'ochŏrêyn** (Chald.), *okh-or-ane'*; or (short.) אָחֳרֵן **'ochŏrên** (Chald.), *okh-or-ane'*; from 317; *last*:—at last.

319. אַחֲרִית **'achărîyth**, *akh-ar-eeth'*; from 310; the *last* or *end*, hence the *future*; also *posterity*:—(last, latter) end (time), hinder (utter) -most, length, posterity, remnant, residue, reward.

320. אַחֲרִית **'achărîyth** (Chald.), *akh-ar-eeth'*; from 311; the same as 319; *later*:—latter.

321. אָחֳרָן **'ochŏrân** (Chald.), *okh-or-awn'*; from 311; the same as 317; *other*:—(an-) other.

אָחֳרֵן **'ochŏrên**. See 318.

322. אֲחֹרַנִּית **'ăchôranniyth**, *akh-o-ran-neeth'*; prol. from 268; *backwards*:—back (-ward, again).

323. אֲחַשְׁדַּרְפַּן **'ăchashdarpan**, *akh-ash-dar-pan'*: of Pers. der.; a *satrap* or governor of a main province (of Persia):—lieutenant.

324. אֲחַשְׁדַּרְפַּן **'ăchashdarpan** (Chald.), *akh-ash-dar-pan'*; corresp. to 323:—prince.

325. אֲחַשְׁוֵרוֹשׁ **'Ăchashvêrôwsh**, *akh-ash-vay-rōsh'*; or (short.) אֲחַשְׁרֹשׁ **'Achashrôsh**, *akh-ash-rōsh'* (Esth. 10 : 1); of Pers. or.; *Achashverosh* (i.e. Ahasuerus or Artaxerxes, but in this case Xerxes), the title (rather than name) of a Pers. king:—Ahasuerus.

326. אֲחַשְׁתָּרִי **'ăchashtârîy**, *akh-ash-taw-ree'*; prob. of Pers. der.; an *achastarite* (i.e. courier); the designation (rather than name) of an Isr.:—Haakashtari [*includ. the art.*].

327. אֲחַשְׁתְּרָן **'ăchastârân**, *akh-ash-taw-rawn'*; of Pers. or.; a *mule*:—camel.

328. אַט **'aṭ**, *at*; from an unused root perh. mean. to *move softly*; (as a noun) a *necromancer* (from their soft incantations), (as an adv.) *gently*:—charmer, gently, secret, softly.

329. אָטָד **'âṭâd**, *aw-tawd'*; from an unused root prob. mean. to *pierce* or *make fast*; a *thorn*-tree (espec. the *buckthorn*):—Atad, bramble, thorn.

330. אֵטוּן **'êṭûwn**, *ay-toon'*; from an unused root (prob. mean. to *bind*); prop. *twisted* (yarn), i.e. *tapestry*:—fine linen.

331. אָטַם **'âṭam**, *aw-tam'*; a prim. root; to *close* (the lips or ears); by anal. to *contract* (a window by bevelled jambs):—narrow, shut, stop.

332. אָטַר **'âṭar**, *aw-tar'*; a prim. root; to *close* up:—shut.

333. אָטֵר **'Âṭêr**, *aw-tare'*; from 332; *maimed*; *Ater*, the name of three Isr.:—Ater.

334. אִטֵּר **'iṭṭêr**, *it-tare'*; from 332; *shut* up, i.e. *impeded* (as to the use of the right hand):— + left-handed.

335. אַי **'ay**, *ah'ee*; perh. from 370; *where?* hence *how?*:—how, what, whence, where, whether, which (way).

336. אִי **'îy**, *ee*; prob. ident. with 335 (through the idea of a *query*); *not*:—island (Job 22 : 30).

337. אִי **'îy**, *ee*; short. from 188; *alas!*:—woe.

338. אִי **'îy**, *ee*; prob. ident. with 337 (through the idea of a *doleful* sound); a *howler* (used only in the plural), i.e. any solitary wild creature:—wild beast of the islands.

339. אִי **'îy**, *ee*; from 183; prop. a *habitable* spot (as *desirable*); dry *land*, a *coast*, an *island*:—country, isle, island.

340. אָיַב **'âyab**, *aw-yab'*; a prim. root; to *hate* (as one of an opposite tribe or party); hence to *be hostile*:—be an enemy.

341. אֹיֵב **'ôyêb**, *o-yabe'*; or (fully) אוֹיֵב **'ôwyêb**, *o-yabe'*; act. part. of 340; *hating*; an *adversary*:—enemy, foe.

342. אֵיבָה **'êybâh**, *ay-baw'*; from 340; *hostility*:—enmity, hatred.

343. אֵיד **'êyd**, *ade*; from the same as 181 (in the sense of *bending* down); *oppression*; by impl. *misfortune, ruin*:—calamity, destruction.

344. אַיָּה **'ayâh**, *ah-yaw'*; perh. from 337; the *screamer*, i.e. a *hawk*:—kite, vulture.

345. אַיָּה **'Ayâh**, *ah-yaw'*; the same as 344; *Ajah*, the name of two Isr.:—Aiah, Ajah.

346. אַיֵּה **'ayêh**, *ah-yay'*; prol. from 335; *where?*:—where.

347. אִיּוֹב **'Îyôwb**, *ee-yobe'*; from 340; *hated* (i.e. *persecuted*); *Ijob*, the patriarch famous for his patience:—Job.

348. אִיזֶבֶל **'Îyzebel**, *ee-zeh'-bel*; from 336 and 2083; *chaste*; *Izebel*, the wife of king Ahab:—Jezebel.

349. אֵיךְ **'êyk**, *ake*; also אֵיכָה **'êykâh**, *ay-kaw'*; and אֵיכָכָה **'êykâkâh**, *ay-kaw'-kah*; prol. from 335; *how?* or *how!*; also *where*:—how, what.

350. אִי־כָבוֹד **Îy-kâbôwd**, *ee-kaw-bode'*; from 336 and 3519; (there is) *no glory*, i.e. *inglorious*; *Ikabod*, a son of Phineas:—I-chabod.

351. אֵיכֹה **'êykôh**, *ay-kō*; prob. a var. for 349, but not as an interrogative; *where*:—where.

אֵיכָה **'êykâh**; אֵיכָכָה **'êykâkâh**. See 349.

352. אַיִל **'ayîl**, *ah'-yil*; from the same as 193; prop. *strength*; hence anything *strong*; spec. a *chief* (politically); also a *ram* (from his strength); a *pilaster* (as a strong support); an *oak* or other strong tree:—mighty (man), lintel, oak, post, ram, tree.

353. אֱיָל **'êyâl**, *eh-yawl'*; a var. of 352; *strength*.—strength.

354. אַיָּל **'ayâl**, *ah-yawl'*; an intens. form of 352 (in the sense of *ram*); a *stag* or male deer:—hart.

355. אַיָּלָה **'ayâlâh**, *ah-yaw-law'*; fem. of 354; a *doe* or female deer:—hind.

356. אֵילוֹן **'Êylôwn**, *ay-lone'*; or (short.) אֵלוֹן **'Êlôwn**, *ay-lone'*; or אֵילֹן **'Êylôn**, *ay-lone'*; from 352; *oak-grove*; *Elon*, the name of a place in Pal., and also of one Hittite, two Isr.:—Elon.

357. אַיָּלוֹן **'Ayâlôwn**, *ah-yaw-lone'*; from 354. *deer-field*; *Ajalon*, the name of five places in Pal.:—Aijalon, Ajalon.

358. אֵילוֹן בֵּית חָנָן **'Êylôwn Bêyth Chânân**, *ay-lone' bayth-chaw-nawn'*; from 356, 1004, and 2603; *oak-grove of* (the) *house of favor*; *Elon of Beth-chanan*, a place in Pal.:—Elon-beth-hanan.

359. אֵילוֹת **'Êylôwth**, *ay-lōth'*, or אֵילַת **'Êylath**, *ay-lath'*; from 352; *trees* or a *grove* (i.e. palms); *Eloth* or *Elath*, a place on the Red Sea:—Elath, Eloth.

360. אֱיָלוּת **'eyâlûwth**, *eh-yaw-looth'*; fem. of 353; *power*; by impl. *protection*:—strength.

361. אֵילָם **'êylâm**, *ay-lawm'*; or (short.) אֵלָם **'êlâm**, *ay-lawm'*; or (fem.) אֵלַמָּה **'êlammâh**, *ay-lam-maw'*; prob. from 352; a *pillar-space* (or colonnade), i.e. a *pale* (or portico):—arch.

362. אֵילִם **'Êylîm**, *ay-leem'*; plur. of 352: *palm-trees*; *Elim*, a place in the Desert:—Elim.

363. אִילָן **'îylân** (Chald.), *ee-lawn'*; corresp. to 356; a *tree*:—tree.

364. אֵיל פָּארָן **'Êyl Pâ'rân**, *ale paw-rawn'*; from 352 and 6290; *oak of Paran*; *El-Paran*, a portion of the district of Paran:—El-paran.

אֵילֹן **'Êylôn**. See 356.

365. אַיֶּלֶת **'ayeleth**, *ah-yeh'-leth*; the same as 355; a *doe*:—hind, Aijeleth.

אַיִם **'ayim**. See 368.

366. אָיֹם **'âyôm**, *aw-yome'*; from an unused root (mean. to *frighten*); *frightful*:—terrible.

367. אֵימָה **'êymâh**, *ay-maw'*; or (short.) אֵמָה **'êmah**, *ay-maw'*; from the same as 366; *fright*; concr. an *idol* (as a bugbear):—dread, fear, horror, idol, terrible, terror.

368. אֵימִים **'Êymîym**, *ay-meem'*; plur. of 367; *terrors*; *Emim*, an early Canaanitish (or Moabitish) tribe:—Emims.

369. אַיִן **'ayin**, *ah'-yin*; as if from a prim. root mean. to *be nothing* or *not exist*; a *non-entity*; gen. used as a neg. particle:—else, except, fail, [father-] less, be gone, in [-curable], neither, never, no (where), none, nor (any, thing), not, nothing, to nought, past, un [-searchable], well-nigh, without. Comp. 370.

370. אַיִן **'ayin**, *ah-yin'*; prob. ident. with 369 in the sense of *query* (comp. 336);—*where?* (only in connection with prep. pref., *whence*):—whence, where.

371. אִין **'îyn**, *een*; appar. a short. form of 369; but (like 370) interrog.; is it *not?*:—not

372. אִיעֶזֶר **'Îy'ezer**, *ee-eh'-zer*; from 336 and 5828; *helpless*; *Iezer*, an Isr.:—Jeezer.

373. אִיעֶזְרִי **'Îy'ezrîy**, *ee-ez-ree'*; patron. from 372; an *Iezrite* or desc. of Iezer:—Jeezerite.

374. אֵיפָה **'êyphâh**, *ay-faw'*; or (short.) אֵפָה **'êphâh**, *ay-faw'*; of Eg. der.; an *ephah* or measure for grain; hence a *measure* in gen.:—ephah, (divers) measure (-s).

375. אֵיפֹה **'êyphôh**, *ay-fō'*; from 335 and 6311; *what place?*; also (of time) *when?*; or (of means) *how?*:—what manner, where.

376. אִישׁ **'îysh**, *eesh*; contr. for 582 [or perh. rather from an unused root mean. to *be extant*]; a *man* as an individual or a male person; often used as an adjunct to a more definite term (and in such cases frequently not expressed in translation):—also, another, any (man), a certain, + champion, consent, each, every (one), fellow, [foot-, husband-] man, (good-, great, mighty) man, he, high (degree), him (that is), husband, man [-kind], + none, one, people, person, + steward, what (man) soever, whoso (-ever), worthy. Comp. 802.

377. אִישׁ **'îysh**, *eesh*; denom. from 376; to *be a man*, i.e. act in a manly way:—show (one) self a man.

378. אִישׁ־בֹּשֶׁת **'Îysh-Bôsheth**, *eesh-bō'-sheth*; from 376 and 1322; *man of shame*; *Ish-Bosheth*, a son of King Saul:—Ish-bosheth.

379. אִישְׁהוֹד **'Îyshhôwd**, *eesh-hode'*; from 376 and 1935; *man of renown*; *Ishod*, an Isr.:—Ishod.

380. אִישׁוֹן **'îyshôwn**, *ee-shone'*; dimin. from 376; the *little man* of the eye; the *pupil* or *ball*; hence the *middle* (of night):—apple [of the eye], black, obscure.

אִישׁ־חַי **'Îysh-Chay**. See 381.

381. אִישׁ־חַיִל **'Îysh-Chayil**, *eesh-khah'-yil*; from 376 and 2428; *man of might*; by defect. transcription (2 Sam. 23 : 20) אִישׁ־חַי **'Îsh-Chay**, *eesh-khah'ee*; as if from 376 and 2416; *living man*; *Ish-chail* (or *Ish-chai*), an Isr.:—a valiant man.

382. אִישׁ־טוֹב **'Îysh-Tôwb**, *eesh-tobe'*; from 376 and 2897; *man of Tob*; *Ish-Tob*, a place in Pal.:—Ish-tob.

אִישַׁי **'Îshay**. See 3448.

אִיתוֹן **'îthôwn**. See 2978.

383. אִיתַי **'îythay** (Chald.), *ee-thah'ee*; corresp. to 3426; prop. *entity*; used only as a particle of affirmation, there *is*:—art thou, can, do ye, have, it be, there is (are), × we will not.

384. אִיתִיאֵל **'Îythîy'êl**, *eeth-ee-ale'*; perh. from 837 and 410; *God has arrived*; *Ithiel*, the name of an Isr., also of a symb. person:—Ithiel.

385. אִיתָמָר **'Îythâmâr**, *eeth-aw-mawr'*; from 339 and 8558; *coast of* the *palm*-tree; *Ithamar*, a son of Aaron:—Ithamar.

386. אֵיתָן **'êythân**, *ay-thawn'*; or (short.) אֵתָן **'êthân**, *ay-thawn'*; from an unused root (mean. to *continue*); *permanence*; hence (concr.) *permanent*; spec. a *chieftain*:—hard, mighty, rough, strength, strong.

387. אֵיתָן **'Êythân**, *ay-thawn'*; the same as 386; *permanent*; *Ethan*, the name of four Isr.:—Ethan.

388. אֵיתָנִים **Êythânîym**, *ay-thaw-neem'*; plur. of 386; always with the art.; the *permanent* brooks; *Ethanim*, the name of a month:—Ethanim.

389. אַךְ **'ak**, *ak*; akin to 403; a particle of affirmation, *surely*; hence (by limitation) *only*:—also, in any wise, at least, but, certainly, even, howbeit, nevertheless, notwithstanding, only, save, surely, of a surety, truly, verily, + wherefore, yet (but).

390. אַכַּד **'Akkad**, *ak-kad'*; from an unused root prob. mean. to *strengthen*; a *fortress*; *Accad*, a place in Bab.:—Accad.

391. אַכְזָב **'akzâb**, *ak-zawb'*; from 3576; *falsehood*; by impl. *treachery*:—liar, lie.

392. אַכְזִיב **'Akzîyb**, *ak-zeeb'*; from 391; *deceitful* (in the sense of a winter-torrent which *fails* in summer); *Akzib*, the name of two places in Pal.:—Achzib.

393. אַכְזָר **'akzâr**, *ak-zawr'*; from an unused root (appar. mean. to *act harshly*); *violent*; by impl. *deadly*; also (in a good sense) *brave*:—cruel, fierce.

394. אַכְזָרִי **'akzârîy**, *ak-zaw-ree'*; from 393; *terrible*:—cruel (one).

395. אַכְזְרִיּוּת **'akzᵉrîyûwth**, *ak-ze-ree-ooth'*; from 394; *fierceness*:—cruel.

396. אֲכִילָה **'ăkîylâh**, *ak-ee-law'*; fem. from 398; something *eatable*, i.e. *food*:—meat.

397. אָכִישׁ **'Âkîysh**, *aw-keesh'*; of uncert. der.; *Akish*, a Philistine king:—Achish.

398. אָכַל **'âkal**, *aw-kal'*; a prim. root; to *eat* (lit. or fig.):—× at all, burn up, consume, devour (-er, up), dine, eat (-er, up), feed (with), food, × freely, × in . . . wise (-deed, plenty), (lay) meat, × quite.

399. אֲכַל **'ăkal** (Chald.), *ak-al'*; corresp. to 398:—+ accuse, devour, eat.

400. אֹכֶל **'ôkel**, *o'-kel*; from 398; *food*:—eating, food, meal [-time], meat, prey, victuals.

401. אֻכָל **'Ûkâl**, *oo-kawl'*; or אֻכָּל **'Ukkâl**, *ook-kawl'*; appar. from 398; *devoured*; *Ucal*, a fancy name:—Ucal.

402. אָכְלָה **'oklâh**, *ok-law'*; fem. of 401; *food*:—consume, devour, eat, food, meat.

403. אָכֵן **'âkên**, *aw-kane'*; from 3559 [comp. 3651]; *firmly*; fig. *surely*; also (advers.) *but*:—but, certainly, nevertheless, surely, truly, verily.

404. אָכַף **'âkaph**, *aw-kaf'*; a prim. root; appar. mean. to *curve* (as with a burden); to *urge*:—crave.

405. אֶכֶף **'ekeph**, *eh'-kef*; from 404; a *load*; by impl. a *stroke* (others *dignity*):—hand.

406. אִכָּר **'ikkâr**, *ik-kawr'*; from an unused root mean. to *dig*; a *farmer*:—husbandman, ploughman.

407. אַכְשָׁף **'Akshâph**, *ak-shawf'*; from 3784; *fascination*; *Acshaph*, a place in Pal.:—Achshaph.

408. אַל **'al**, *al*; a neg. particle [akin to 3808]; *not* (the qualified negation, used as a deprecative); once (Job 24 : 25) as a noun, *nothing*:—nay, neither, + never, no, nor, not, nothing [worth], rather than.

409. אַל **'al** (Chald.), *al*; corresp. to 408:—not.

410. אֵל **'êl**, *ale*; short. from 352; *strength*; as adj. *mighty*; espec. the *Almighty* (but used also of any *deity*):—God (god), × goodly, × great, idol, might (-y one), power, strong. Comp. names in "-el."

411. אֵל **'êl**, *ale*; a demonstr. particle (but only in a plur. sense) *these* or *those*:—these, those. Comp. 428.

412. אֵל **'êl** (Chald.), *ale*; corresp. to 411:—these.

413. אֵל **'êl**, *ale*; (but used only in the shortened constr. form אֶל **'el**, *el*); a prim. particle, prop. denoting motion *towards*, but occasionally used of a quiescent position, i.e. *near*, *with* or *among*; often in general, *to*:—about, according to, after, against, among, as for, at, because (-fore, -side), both . . . and, by, concerning, for, from, × hath, in (-to), near, (out) of, over, through, to (-ward), under, unto, upon, whether, with (-in).

414. אֵלָא **'Êlâ'**, *ay-law'*; a var. of 424; *oak*; *Ela*, an Isr.:—Elah.

415. אֵל אֱלֹהֵי יִשְׂרָאֵל **'Êl 'ĕlôhêy Yisrâ'êl**, *ale el-o-hay' yis-raw-ale'*; from 410 and 430 and 3478; the *mighty God of Jisrael*; *El-Elohi-Jisrael*, the title given to a consecrated spot by Jacob:—El-elohe-israel.

416. אֵל בֵּית־אֵל **'Êl Bêyth-'Êl**, *ale bayth-ale'*; from 410 and 1008; the *God of Bethel*; *El-Bethel*, the title given to a consecrated spot by Jacob:—El-beth-el.

417. אֶלְגָּבִישׁ **'elgâbîysh**, *el-gaw-beesh'*; from 410 and 1378; *hail* (as if a *great pearl*):—great hail [-stones].

418. אַלְגּוּמִּים **'algûwmmîym**, *al-goom-meem'*; by transp. for 484; sticks of *algum* wood:—algum [trees].

419. אֶלְדָּד **'Eldâd**, *el-dâd'*; from 410 and 1730; *God has loved*; *Eldad*, an Isr.:—Eldad.

420. אֶלְדָּעָה **'Eldâ'âh**, *el-daw-aw'*; from 410 and 3045; *God of knowledge*; *Eldaah*, a son of Midian:—Eldaah.

421. אָלָה **'âlâh**, *aw-law'*; a prim. root [rather ident. with 422 through the idea of *invocation*]; to *bewail*:—lament.

422. אָלָה **'âlâh**, *aw-law'*; a prim. root; prop. to *adjure*, i.e. (usually in a bad sense) *imprecate*:—adjure, curse, swear.

423. אָלָה **'âlâh**, *aw-law'*; from 422; an *imprecation*:—curse, cursing, execration, oath, swearing.

424. אֵלָה **'êlâh**, *ay-law'*; fem. of 352; an *oak* or other strong tree:—elm, oak, teil tree

425. אֵלָה **'Êlâh**, *ay-law'*; the same as 424; *Elah*, the name of an Edomite, of four Isr., and also of a place in Pal.:—Elah.

426. אֱלָהּ **'ĕlâhh** (Chald.), *el-aw'*; corresp. to 433; *God*:—God, god.

427. אַלָּה **'allâh**, *al-law'*; a var. of 424:—oak.

428. אֵלֶּה **'êl-leh**, *ale'-leh*; prol. from 411; *these* or *those*:—an- (the) other; one sort, so, some, such, them, these (same), they, this, those, thus, which, who (-m).

429. אֵלֶּה **'êlleh** (Chald.), *ale'-leh*; corresp. to 428:—these.

אֱלֹהַּ **'ĕlôahh**. See 433.

430. אֱלֹהִים **'ĕlôhîym**, *el-o-heem'*; plur. of 433; *gods* in the ordinary sense; but spec. used (in the plur. thus, esp. with the art.) of the supreme *God*; occasionally applied by way of deference to *magistrates*; and sometimes as a superlative:—angels, × exceeding, God (gods) (-dess, -ly), × (very) great, judges, × mighty.

431. אֲלוּ **'ălûw** (Chald.), *al-oo'*; prob. prol. from 412; *lo!*:—behold.

432. אִלּוּ **'illûw**, *il-loo'*; prob. from 408; *nay*, i.e. (softened) *if*:—but if, yea though.

433. אֱלוֹהַּ **'ĕlôwahh**, *el-o'-ah*; rarely (short.) אֱלֹהַּ **'ĕlôahh**, *el-o'-ah*; prob. prol. (emphat.) from 410; a *deity* or the *Deity*:—God, god. See 430.

434. אֱלוּל **'ĕlûwl**, *el-ool'*; for 457; good for *nothing*:—thing of nought.

435. אֱלוּל **'Ĕlûwl**, *el-ool'*; prob. of for. der.; *Elul*, the sixth Jewish month:—Elul.

436. אֵלוֹן **'êlôwn**, *ay-lone'*; prol. from 352; an *oak* or other strong tree:—plain. See also 356.

437. אַלּוֹן **'allôwn**, *al-lone'*; a var. of 436:—oak.

438. אַלּוֹן **'Allôwn**, *al-lone'*; the same as 437; *Allon*, an Isr., also a place in Pal.:—Allon.

439. אַלּוֹן בָּכוּת **'Allôwn Bâkûwth**, *al-lone' baw-kooth'*; from 437 and a var. of 1068; *oak of weeping*; *Allon-Bakuth*, a monumental tree:—Allon-bachuth.

440. אֵלוֹנִי **'Êlôwnîy**, *ay-lo-nee'*; or rather (short.) אֵלֹנִי **'Êlônîy**, *ay-lo-nee'*; patron. from 438; an *Elonite* or desc. (collect.) of Elon:—Elonites.

441. אַלּוּף **'allûwph**, *al-loof'*; or (short.) אַלֻּף **'allûph**, *al-loof'*; from 502; *familiar*; a *friend*, also *gentle*; hence a *bullock* (as being tame; applied, although masc., to a *cow*); and so a *chieftain* (as notable like neat cattle):—captain, duke, (chief) friend, governor, guide, ox.

442. אָלוּשׁ **'Âlûwsh**, *aw-loosh'*; of uncert. der.; *Alush*, a place in the Desert:—Alush.

443. אֶלְזָבָד **'Elzâbâd**, *el-zaw-bawd'*; from 410 and 2064; *God has bestowed*; *Elzabad*, the name of two Isr.:—Elzabad.

444. אָלַח **'âlach**, *aw-lakh'*; a prim. root; to *muddle*, i.e. (fig. and intrans.) to *turn* (morally) *corrupt*:—become filthy.

445. אֶלְחָנָן **'Elchânân**, *el-khaw-nawn'*; from 410 and 2603; *God* (is) *gracious*; *Elchanan*, an Isr.:—Elkanan.

אֵלִי **'Êlîy**. See 1017.

446. אֱלִיאָב **'Ĕlîy'âb**, *el-ee-awb'*; from 410 and 1; *God of* (his) *father; Eliab*, the name of six Isr.:—Eliab.

447. אֱלִיאֵל **'Ĕlîy'êl**, *el-ee-ale'*; from 410 repeated; *God of* (his) *God; Eliel*, the name of nine Isr.:—Eliel.

448. אֱלִיאָתָה **'Ĕlîy'âthâh**, *el-ee-aw-thaw'*; or (contr.) אֱלִיָּתָה **'Ĕlîyâthâh**, *el-ee-yaw-thaw'*; from 410 and 225; *God of* (his) *consent; Eliathah*, an Isr.:—Eliathah.

449. אֱלִידָד **'Ĕlîydâd**, *el-ee-dawd'*; from the same as 419; *God of* (his) *love; Elidad*, an Isr.:—Elidad.

450. אֶלְיָדָע **'Elyâdâ'**, *el-yaw-daw'*; from 410 and 3045; *God* (is) *knowing; Eljada*, the name of two Isr. and of an Aramaean leader:—Eliada.

451. אַלְיָה **'alyâh**, *al-yaw'*; from 422 (in the orig. sense of *strength*); the *stout* part, i.e. the fat *tail* of the Oriental sheep:—rump.

452. אֵלִיָּה **'Êlîyâh**, *ay-lee-yaw'*; or prol. אֵלִיָּהוּ **'Êlîyâhûw**, *ay-lee-yaw'-hoo*; from 410 and 3050; *God of Jehovah; Elijah*, the name of the famous prophet and of two other Isr.:—Elijah, Eliah.

453. אֱלִיהוּ **'Ĕlîyhûw**, *el-ee-hoo'*; or (fully) אֱלִיהוּא **'Ĕlîyhûw'**, *el-ee-hoo'*; from 410 and 1931; *God of him; Elihu*, the name of one of Job's friends, and of three Isr.:—Elihu.

454. אֶלְיְהוֹעֵינַי **'Ely^{e}hôw'êynay**, *el-ye-ho-ay-nah'ee*; or (short.) אֶלְיוֹעֵינַי **'Elyôw'êynay**, *el-yo-ay-nah'ee*; from 413 and 3068 and 5869; *towards Jehovah* (are) *my eyes; Eljehoenai* or *Eljoenai*, the name of seven Isr.:—Elihoenai, Elionai.

455. אֶלְיַחְבָּא **'Elyachbâ'**, *el-yakh-baw'*; from 410 and 2244; *God will hide; Eljachba*, an Isr.:—Eliahbah.

456. אֱלִיחֹרֶף **'Ĕlîychôreph**, *el-ee-kho'-ref*; from 410 and 2779; *God of autumn; Elichoreph*, an Isr.:—Elihoreph.

457. אֱלִיל **'ĕlîyl**, *el-eel'*; appar. from 408; good for *nothing*, by anal. *vain* or *vanity;* spec. an *idol:*—idol, no value, thing of nought.

458. אֱלִימֶלֶךְ **'Ĕlîymelek**, *el-ee-meh'-lek*; from 410 and 4428; *God of* (the) *king; Elimelek*, an Isr.—Elimelech.

459. אִלֵּין **'illêyn** (Chald.), *il-lane'*; or shorter אִלֵּן **'illên**, *il-lane'*; prol. from 412; *these:*—the, these.

460. אֶלְיָסָף **'Elyâçâph**, *el-yaw-sawf'*; from 410 and 3254; *God* (is) *gatherer; Eljasaph*, the name of two Isr.:—Eliasaph.

461. אֱלִיעֶזֶר **'Ĕlîy'ezer**, *el-ee-eh'-zer*; from 410 and 5828; *God of help; Eliezer*, the name of a Damascene and of ten Isr.:—Eliezer.

462. אֱלִיעֵינַי **'Ĕlîy'êynay**, *el-ee-ay-nah'ee*; prob. contr. for 454; *Elienai*, an Isr.:—Elienai.

463. אֱלִיעָם **'Ĕlîy'âm**, *el-ee-awm'*; from 410 and 5971; *God of* (the) *people; Eliam*, an Isr.:—Eliam.

464. אֱלִיפַז **'Ĕlîyphaz**, *el-ee-faz'*; from 410 and 6337; *God of gold; Eliphaz*, the name of one of Job's friends, and of a son of Esau:—Eliphaz.

465. אֱלִיפָל **'Ĕlîyphâl**, *el-ee-fawl'*; from 410 and 6419; *God of judgment; Eliphal*, an Isr.:—Eliphal.

466. אֱלִיפְלֵהוּ **'Ĕlîyph^{e}lêhûw**, *el-ee-fe-lay'-hoo*; from 410 and 6395; *God of his distinction; Eliphelehu*, an Isr.:—Elipheleh.

467. אֱלִיפֶלֶט **'Ĕlîyphelet**, *el-ee-feh'-let*; or (short.) אֶלְפֶּלֶט **'Elpelet**, *el-peh'-let*; from 410 and 6405; *God of deliverance; Eliphelet* or *Elpelet*, the name of six Isr.:—Eliphalet, Eliphelet, Elpalet.

468. אֱלִיצוּר **'Ĕlêytsûwr**, *el-ee-tsoor'*; from 410 and 6697; *God of* (the) *rock; Elitsur*, an Isr.:—Elizur.

469. אֱלִיצָפָן **'Ĕlîytsâphân**, *el-ee-tsaw-fawn'*; or (short.) אֶלְצָפָן **'Eltsâphân**, *el-tsaw-fawn'*; from 410 and 6845; *God of treasure; Elitsaphan* or *Eltsaphan*, an Isr.:—Elizaphan, Elzaphan.

470. אֱלִיקָא **'Ĕlîyqâ'**, *el-ee-kaw'*; from 410 and 6958; *God of rejection; Elika*, an Isr.:—Elika.

471. אֶלְיָקִים **'Elyâqîym**, *el-yaw-keem'*; from 410 and 6965; *God of raising; Eljakim*, the name of four Isr.:—Eliakim.

472. אֱלִישֶׁבַע **'Ĕlîysheba'**, *el-ee-sheh'-bah*; from 410 and 7651 (in the sense of 7650); *God of* (the) *oath; Elisheba*, the wife of Aaron:—Elisheba.

473. אֱלִישָׁה **'Ĕlîyshâh**, *el-ee-shaw'*; prob. of for. der.; *Elishah*, a son of Javan:—Elishah.

474. אֱלִישׁוּעַ **'Ĕlîyshûwa'**, *el-ee-shoo'-ah*; from 410 and 7769; *God of supplication* (or *of riches*); *Elishua*, a son of King David:—Elishua.

475. אֶלְיָשִׁיב **'Elyâshîyb**, *el-yaw-sheeb'*; from 410 and 7725; *God will restore; Eljashib*, the name of six Isr.:—Eliashib.

476. אֱלִישָׁמָע **'Ĕlîyshâmâ'**, *el-ee-shaw-maw'*; from 410 and 8085; *God of hearing; Elishama*, the name of seven Isr.:—Elishama.

477. אֱלִישָׁע **'Ĕlîyshâ'**, *el-ee-shaw'*; contr. for 474; *Elisha*, the famous prophet:—Elisha.

478. אֱלִישָׁפָט **'Ĕlîyshâphât**, *el-ee-shaw-fawt'*; from 410 and 8199; *God of judgment; Elishaphat*, an Isr.:—Elishaphat.

אֱלִיתָה **'Ĕlîyâthâh**. See 448.

479. אִלֵּךְ **'illêk** (Chald.), *il-lake'*; prol. from 412; *these:*—these, those.

480. אַלְלַי **'al^{e}lay**, *al-le-lah'ee*; by redupl. from 421; *alas!:*—woe.

481. אָלַם **'âlam**, *aw-lam'*; a prim. root; to *tie* fast; hence (of the mouth) to be *tongue-tied:*—bind, be dumb, put to silence.

482. אֵלֶם **'êlem**, *ay'-lem*; from 481; *silence* (i.e. mute justice):—congregation. Comp. 3128.

אֵלָם **'êlâm**. See 361.

אֻלָם **'ûlâm**. See 485.

483. אִלֵּם **'illêm**, *il-lame'*; from 481; *speechless:*—dumb (man).

484. אַלְמֻגִּים **'almuggiym**, *al-moog-gheem'*; prob. of for. der. (used thus only in the plur.); *almug* (i.e. prob. sandal-wood) sticks:—almug trees. Comp. 418.

485. אֲלֻמָּה **'ălummâh**, *al-oom-maw'*; or (masc.) אָלֻם **'âlûm**, *aw-loom'*; pass. part. of 481; something *bound;* a *sheaf:*—sheaf.

486. אַלְמוֹדָד **'Almôwdâd**, *al-mo-dawd'*; prob. of for. der.:—*Almodad*, a son of Joktan:—Almodad.

487. אַלַּמֶּלֶךְ **'Allammelek**, *al-lam-meh'-lek*; from 427 and 4428; *oak of* (the) *king; Allammelek*, a place in Pal.:—Alammelech.

488. אַלְמָן **'almân**, *al-mawn'*; prol. from 481 in the sense of *bereavement; discarded* (as a divorced person):—forsaken.

489. אַלְמֹן **'almôn**, *al-mone'*; from 481 as in 488; *bereavement:*—widowhood.

490. אַלְמָנָה **'almânâh**, *al-maw-naw'*; fem. of 488; a *widow;* also a *desolate* place:—desolate house (palace), widow.

491. אַלְמָנוּת **'almânûwth**, *al-maw-nooth'*; fem. of 488; concr. a *widow;* abstr. *widowhood:*—widow, widowhood.

492. אַלְמֹנִי **'almôniy**, *al-mo-nee'*; from 489 in the sense of *concealment; some* one (i.e. *so and so*, without giving the name of the person or place):—one, and such.

אִלֵּן **'illên**. See 459.

אֵלֹנִי **'Êlôniy**. See 440.

493. אֶלְנַעַם **'Elna'am**, *el-nah'-am*; from 410 and 5276; *God* (is his) *delight; Elnaam*, an Isr.:—Elnaam.

494. אֶלְנָתָן **'Elnâthân**, *el-naw-thawn'*; from 410 and 5414; *God* (is the) *giver; Elnathan*, the name of four Isr.:—Elnathan.

495. אֶלָּסָר **'Ellâçâr**, *el-law-sawr'*; prob. of for. der.; *Ellasar*, an early country of Asia:—Ellasar.

496. אֶלְעָד **'El'âd**, *el-awd'*; from 410 and 5749; *God has testified; Elad*, an Isr.:—Elead.

497. אֶלְעָדָה **'El'âdâh**, *el-aw-daw'*; from 410 and 5710; *God has decked; Eladah*, an Isr.:—Eladah.

498. אֶלְעוּזַי **'El'ûwzay**, *el-oo-zah'ee*; from 410 and 5756 (in the sense of 5797); *God* (is) *defensive; Eluzai*, an Isr.:—Eluzai.

499. אֶלְעָזָר **'El'âzâr**, *el-aw-zawr'*; from 410 and 5826; *God* (is) *helper; Elazar*, the name of seven Isr.:—Eleazar.

500. אֶלְעָלֵא **'El'âlê'**, *el-aw-lay'*; or (more properly) אֶלְעָלֵה **'El'âlêh**, *el-aw-lay'*; from 410 and 5927; *God* (is) *going up; Elale* or *Elaleh*, a place east of the Jordan:—Elealeh.

501. אֶלְעָשָׂה **'El'âsâh**, *el-aw-saw'*; from 410 and 6213; *God has made; Elasah*, the name of four Isr.:—Elasah, Eleasah.

502. אָלַף **'âlaph**, *aw-lof'*; a prim. root, to *associate* with; hence to *learn* (and caus. to *teach*):—learn, teach, utter.

503. אָלַף **'âlaph**, *aw-laf'*; denom. from 505; caus. to *make a thousandfold:*—bring forth thousands.

504. אֶלֶף **'eleph**, *eh'-lef*; from 502; a *family;* also (from the sense of *yoking* or *taming*) an *ox* or *cow:*—family, kine, oxen.

505. אֶלֶף **'eleph**, *eh'-lef*; prop. the same as 504; hence (an ox's head being the first letter of the alphabet, and this eventually used as a numeral) a *thousand:*—thousand.

506. אֲלַף **'âlaph** (Chald.), *al-af'*; or אֶלֶף **'eleph**, (Chald.), *eh'-lef*; corresp. to 505:—thousand.

507. אֶלֶף **'Eleph**, *eh'-lef*; the same as 505; *Eleph*, a place in Pal.:—Eleph.

אַלֻּף **'allûph**. See 441.

אֶלְפֶּלֶט **'Elpelet**. See 467.

508. אֶלְפַּעַל **'Elpa'al**, *el-pah'-al*; from 410 and 6466; *God* (is) *act; Elpaal*, an Isr.:—Elpaal.

509. אָלַץ **'âlats**, *aw-lats'*; a prim. root; to *press:*—urge.

אֶלְצָפָן **'Eltsâphân**. See 469.

510. אַלְקוּם **'alqûwm**, *al-koom'*; prob. from 408 and 6965; a *non-rising* (i.e. *resistlessness*):—no rising up.

511. אֶלְקָנָה **'Elqânâh**, *el-kaw-naw'*; from 410 and 7069; *God has obtained; Elkanah*, the name of seven Isr.:—Elkanah.

512. אֶלְקֹשִׁי **'Elqôshîy**, *el-ko-shee'*; patrial from a name of uncert. der.; an *Elkoshite* or native of Elkosh:—Elkoshite.

513. אֶלְתּוֹלַד **'Eltôwlad**, *el-to-lad'*; prob. from 410 and a masc. form of 8435 [comp. 8434]; *God* (is) *generator; Eltolad*, a place in Pal.:—Eltolad.

514. אֶלְתְּקֵא **'Elt^{e}qê**, *el-te-kay'*; or (more prop.) אֶלְתְּקֵה **'Elt^{e}qêh**, *el-te-kay'*; of uncert. der.; *Eltekeh* or *Elteke*, a place in Pal.:—Eltekeh.

515. אֶלְתְּקֹן **'Elt^{e}qôn**, *el-te-kone'*; from 410 and 8626; *God* (is) *straight; Eltekon*, a place in Pal.:—Eltekon.

516. אַל תַּשְׁחֵת **'Al tashchêth**, *al tash-kayth'*; from 408 and 7843; *Thou must not destroy;* prob. the opening words of a popular song:—Al-taschith.

517. אֵם **'êm**, *ame*; a prim. word; a *mother* (as the *bond* of the family); in a wide sense (both lit. and fig.) [like 1]:—dam, mother, × parting.

518. אִם **'im**, *eem;* a prim. particle; used very widely as demonstr., *lo!;* interrog., *whether?;* or conditional, *if, although;* also *Oh that!, when;* hence as a neg., *not:*—(and, can-, doubtless, if, that) (not), + but, either, + except, + more (-over if, than), neither, nevertheless, nor, oh that, or, + save (only, -ing), seeing, since, sith, + surely (no more, none, not), though, + of a truth, + unless, + verily, when, whereas, whether, while, + yet.

519. אָמָה **'âmâh**, *aw-maw';* appar. a prim. word; a *maid-servant* or female slave:—(hand-) bondmaid (-woman,) maid (-servant).

אֵמָה **'êmâh**. See 367.

520. אַמָּה **'ammâh**, *am-maw';* prol. from 517; prop. a *mother* (i.e. *unit*) of measure, or the *fore-arm* (below the elbow), i.e. a *cubit;* also a door-*base* (as a *bond* of the entrance):—cubit, + hundred [*by exchange for* 3967], measure, post.

521. אַמָּה **'ammâh** (Chald.), *am-maw';* corresp. to 520:—cubit.

522. אַמָּה **'Ammâh**, *am-maw';* the same as 520; *Ammah*, a hill in Pal.:—Ammah.

523. אֻמָּה **'ummâh**, *oom-maw';* from the same as 517; a *collection*, i.e. community of persons:—nation, people.

524. אֻמָּה **'ummâh** (Chald.), *oom-maw';* corresp. to 523:—nation.

525. אָמוֹן **'âmôwn**, *aw-mone';* from 539, prob. in the sense of *training; skilled*, i.e. an architect [like 542]:—one brought up.

526. אָמוֹן **'Âmôwn**, *aw-mone';* the same as 525; *Amon*, the name of three Isr.:—Amon.

527. אָמוֹן **'âmôwn**, *aw-mone';* a var. for 1995; a *throng* of people:—multitude.

528. אָמוֹן **'Âmôwn**, *aw-mone';* of Eg. der.; *Amon* (i.e. Ammon or Amn), a deity of Egypt (used only as an adjunct of 4996):—multitude, populous.

529. אֵמוּן **'êmûwn**, *ay-moon';* from 539; *established*, i.e. (fig.) *trusty;* also (abstr.) *trustworthiness:*—faith (-ful), truth.

530. אֱמוּנָה **'ĕmûwnâh**, *em-oo-naw';* or (short.) אֱמֻנָה **'ĕmûnâh**, *em-oo-naw';* fem. of 529; lit. *firmness;* fig. *security;* mor. *fidelity:*—faith (-ful, -ly, -ness, [man]), set office, stability, steady, truly, truth, verily.

531. אָמוֹץ **'Âmôwts**, *aw-mohts';* from 553; *strong; Amots*, an Isr.:—Amoz.

532. אָמִי **'Âmîy**, *aw-mee';* an abbrev. for 526; *Ami*, an Isr.:—Ami.

אֲמִינוֹן **'Ămîynôwn**. See 550.

533. אַמִּיץ **'ammîyts**, *am-meets';* or (short.) אַמִּץ **'ammîts**, *am-meets';* from 553; *strong* or (abstr.) *strength:*—courageous, mighty, strong (one).

534. אָמִיר **'âmîyr**, *aw-meer';* appar. from 559 (in the sense of *self-exaltation*); a *summit* (of a tree or mountain):—bough, branch.

535. אָמַל **'âmal**, *aw-mal';* a prim. root; to *droop;* by impl. to *be sick*, to *mourn:*—languish, be weak, wax feeble.

536. אֻמְלַל **'umlal**, *oom-lal';* from 535; *sick:*—weak.

537. אֲמֵלָל **'ămêlâl**, *am-ay-lawl';* from 535; *languid:*—feeble.

538. אֲמָם **'Ămâm**, *am-awm';* from 517; *gathering*-spot; *Amam*, a place in Pal.:—Amam.

539. אָמַן **'âman**, *aw-man';* a prim. root; prop. to *build up* or *support;* to *foster* as a parent or nurse; fig. to *render* (or *be*) *firm* or faithful, to *trust* or believe, to be *permanent* or quiet; mor. to *be true* or certain; once (Isa. 30 : 21; by interch. for 541) to *go to the right hand:*—hence assurance, believe, bring up, establish, + fail, be faithful (of long continuance, stedfast, sure, surely, trusty, verified), nurse, (-ing father), (put), trust, turn to the right.

540. אֲמַן **'ăman** (Chald.), *am-an';* corresp. to 539:—believe, faithful, sure.

541. אָמַן **'âman**, *aw-man';* denom. from 3225; to take the *right hand* road:—turn to the right. See 539.

542. אָמָּן **'âmân**, *aw-mawn';* from 539 (in the sense of *training*); an *expert:*—cunning workman.

543. אָמֵן **'âmên**, *aw-mane';* from 539; *sure;* abstr. *faithfulness;* adv. *truly:*—Amen, so be it, truth.

544. אֹמֶן **'ômen**, *oh-men';* from 539; *verity:*—truth.

545. אָמְנָה **'omnâh**, *om-naw';* fem. of 544 (in the spec. sense of *training*); *tutelage:*—brought up.

546. אָמְנָה **'omnâh**, *om-naw';* fem. of 544 (in its usual sense); adv. *surely:*—indeed.

547. אֹמְנָה **'ômᵉnâh**, *o-me-naw';* fem. act. part. of 544 (in the orig. sense of *supporting*); a *column:*—pillar.

548. אֲמָנָה **'ămânâh**, *am-aw-naw';* fem. of 543; something *fixed*, i.e. a *covenant*, an *allowance:*—certain portion, sure.

549. אֲמָנָה **'Ămânâh**, *am-aw-naw';* the same as 548; *Amanah*, a mountain near Damascus:—Amana.

אֱמֻנָה **'ĕmûnâh**. See 530.

550. אַמְנוֹן **'Amnôwn**, *am-nohn';* or אֲמִינוֹן **'Ămîynôwn**, *am-ee-nohn';* from 539; *faithful; Amnon* (or Aminon), a son of David:—Amnon.

551. אָמְנָם **'omnâm**, *om-nawm';* adv. from 544; *verily:*—indeed, no doubt, surely, (it is, of a) true (-ly, -th).

552. אֻמְנָם **'umnâm**, *oom-nawm';* an orth. var. of 551:—in (very) deed; of a surety.

553. אָמֵץ **'âmats**, *aw-mats';* a prim. root; to *be alert*, phys. (on foot) or ment. (in courage):—confirm, be courageous (of good courage, stedfastly minded, strong, stronger), establish, fortify, harden, increase, prevail, strengthen (self), make strong (obstinate, speed).

554. אָמֹץ **'âmôts**, *aw-mohts';* prob. from 553; of a *strong* color, i.e. *red* (others *fleet*):—bay.

555. אֹמֶץ **'ômets**, *o'-mets;* from 553; *strength:*—stronger.

אַמִּץ **'ammîts**. See 533.

556. אַמְצָה **'amtsâh**, *am-tsaw';* from 553; *force:*—strength.

557. אַמְצִי **'Amtsîy**, *am-tsee';* from 553; *strong, Amtsi*, an Isr.:—Amzi.

558. אֲמַצְיָה **'Ămatsyâh**, *am-ats-yaw';* or אֲמַצְיָהוּ **'Ămatsyâhûw**, *am-ats-yaw'-hoo;* from 553 and 3050; *strength of Jah; Amatsjah*, the name of four Isr.:—Amaziah.

559. אָמַר **'âmar**, *aw-mar';* a prim. root; to *say* (used with great latitude):—answer, appoint, avouch, bid, boast self, call, certify, challenge, charge, + (at the, give) command (ment), commune, consider, declare, demand, × desire, determine, × expressly, × indeed, × intend, name, × plainly, promise, publish, report, require, say, speak (against, of), × still, × suppose, talk, tell, term, × that is, × think, use [speech], utter, × verily, × yet.

560. אֲמַר **'ămar** (Chald.), *am-ar';* corresp. to 559:—command, declare, say, speak, tell.

561. אֵמֶר **'êmer**, *ay'-mer;* from 559; something *said:*—answer, × appointed unto him, saying, speech, word.

562. אֹמֶר **'ômer**, *o'-mer;* the same as 561:—promise, speech, thing, word.

563. אִמַּר **'immar** (Chald.), *im-mar';* perh. from 560 (in the sense of *bringing forth*); a *lamb:*—lamb.

564. אִמֵּר **'Immêr**, *im-mare';* from 559; *talkative; Immer*, the name of five Isr.:—Immer.

565. אִמְרָה **'imrâh**, *im-raw';* or אֶמְרָה **'emrâh**, *em-raw';* fem. of 561, and mean. the same:—commandment, speech, word.

566. אִמְרִי **'Imrîy**, *im-ree';* from 564; *wordy; Imri*, the name of two Isr.:—Imri.

567. אֱמֹרִי **'Ĕmôrîy**, *em-o-ree';* prob. a patron. from an unused name derived from 559 in the sense of *publicity*, i.e. prominence; thus a *mountaineer;* an *Emorite*, one of the Canaanitish tribes:—Amorite.

568. אֲמַרְיָה **'Ămaryâh**, *am-ar-yaw';* or (prol.) אֲמַרְיָהוּ **'Ămaryâhûw**, *am-ar-yaw'-hoo;* from 559 and 3050; *Jah has said* (i.e. promised); *Amarjah*, the name of nine Isr.:—Amariah.

569. אַמְרָפֶל **'Amrâphel**, *am-raw-fel';* of uncert. (perh. for.) der.; *Amraphel*, a king of Shinar:—Amraphel.

570. אֶמֶשׁ **'emesh**, *eh'-mesh;* time *past*, i.e. *yesterday* or *last night:*—former time, yesterday (-night).

571. אֶמֶת **'emeth**, *eh'-meth;* contr. from 539; *stability;* fig. *certainty, truth, trustworthiness:*—assured (-ly), establishment, faithful, right, sure, true (-ly, -th), verity.

572. אַמְתַּחַת **'amtachath**, *am-takh'-ath;* from 4969; prop. something *expansive*, i.e. a *bag:*—sack.

573. אֲמִתַּי **'Ămittay**, *am-it-tah'ee;* from 571; *veracious; Amittai*, an Isr.:—Amittai.

574. אֵמְתָנִי **'emtânîy** (Chald.), *em-taw-nee';* from a root corresp. to that of 4975; well-*loined* (i.e. burly) or *mighty:*—terrible.

575. אָן **'ân**, *awn;* or אָנָה **'ânâh**, *aw'-naw;* contr. from 370; *where?;* hence *whither?, when?;* also *hither* and *thither:*— + any (no) whither, now, where, whither (-soever).

אֹן **'ôn**. See 204.

576. אֲנָא **'ănâ'** (Chald.), *an-aw';* or אֲנָה **'ănâh** (Chald.), *an-aw';* corresp. to 589; *I:*—I, as for me.

577. אָנָּא **'ânnâ'**, *awn'-naw;* or אָנָּה **'ânnâh**, *awn'-naw;* appar. contr. from 160 and 4994; *oh now!:*—I (me) beseech (pray) thee, O.

אֲנָה **'ănâh**. See 576.

אָנָה **'ânâh**. See 575.

578. אָנָה **'ânâh**, *aw-naw';* a prim. root; to *groan:*—lament, mourn.

579. אָנָה **'ânâh**, *aw-naw';* a prim. root [perh. rather ident. with 578 through the idea of *contraction* in anguish]; to *approach;* hence to *meet* in various senses:—befall, deliver, happen, seek a quarrel.

אָנָּה **'ânnâh**. See 577.

580. אֲנוּ **'ănûw**, *an-oo';* contr. for 587; *we:*—we.

אֹנוֹ **Ônôw**. See 207.

581. אִנּוּן **'innûwn** (Chald.), *in-noon';* or (fem.) אִנִּין **'innîyn** (Chald.), *in-neen';* corresp. to 1992; *they:*— × are, them, these.

582. אֱנוֹשׁ **'ĕnôwsh**, *en-oshe';* from 605; prop. a *mortal* (and thus differing from the more dignified 120); hence a *man* in gen. (singly or collect.):—another, × [blood-] thirsty, certain, chap [-man], divers, fellow, × in the flower of their age, husband, (certain, mortal) man, people, person, servant, some (× of them), + stranger, those, + their trade. It is often unexpressed in the Engl. Version, especially when used in apposition with another word. Comp. 376.

583. אֱנוֹשׁ **'Ĕnôwsh**, *en-ohsh';* the same as 582; *Enosh*, a son of Seth:—Enos.

584. אָנַח **'ânach**, *aw-nakh';* a prim. root; to *sigh:*—groan, mourn, sigh.

585. אֲנָחָה **'ănâchâh**, *an-aw-khaw';* from 585; *sighing:*—groaning, mourn, sigh.

586. אֲנַחְנָא **'ănachnâ'** (Chald.), *an-akh'-naw;* or אֲנַחְנָה **'ănachnâh** (Chald.), *an-akh-naw';* corresp. to 587; *we:*—we.

587. אֲנַחְנוּ **'ănachnûw**, *an-akh'-noo,* appar. from 595; *we:*—ourselves, us, we.

588. אֲנָחֲרָת **'Ănâchărâth**, *an-aw-kha-rawth';* prob. from the same root as 5170; a *gorge* or narrow pass; *Anacharath*, a place in Pal.:—Anaharath.

589. אֲנִי **'ănîy**, *an-ee';* contr. from 595; *I:*—I, (as for) me, mine, myself, we, × which, × who.

590. אֳנִי **'ŏnîy**, *on-ee';* prob. from 579 (in the sense of *conveyance*); a *ship* or (collect.) a *fleet:*—galley, navy (of ships).

591. אֳנִיָּה **'ŏnîyâh**, *on-ee-yaw';* fem. of 590; a *ship:*—ship ([-men]).

592. אֲנִיָּה **'ănîyâh**, *an-ee-yaw';* from 578; *groaning:*—lamentation, sorrow.

אִנִּין **'innîyn**. See 581.

593. אֲנִיעָם **'Ănîy'âm**, *an-ee-awm';* from 578 and 5971; *groaning* of (the) *people; Aniam*, an Isr.:—Aniam.

594. אֲנָךְ **'ănâk**, *an-awk';* prob. from an unused root mean. to *be narrow;* according to most a plumb-*line*, and to others a *hook:*—plumbline.

595. אָנֹכִי **'ânôkîy**, *aw-no-kee'* (sometimes *aw-no'-kee*); a prim. pron.; *I:*—I, me, × which.

596. אָנַן **'ânan**, *aw-nan';* a prim. root; to *mourn*, i.e. *complain:*—complain.

597. אָנַס **'ânaç**, *aw-nas';* to *insist:*—compel.

598. אֲנַס **'ănaç** (Chald.), *an-as';* corresp. to 597; fig. to *distress:*—trouble.

599. אָנַף **'ânaph**, *aw-naf';* a prim. root; to *breathe* hard, i.e. *be enraged:*—be angry (displeased).

600. אֱנַף **'ănaph** (Chald.), *an-af';* corresp. to 639 (only in the plur. as a sing.); the *face:*—face, visage.

601. אֲנָפָה **'ănâphâh**, *an-aw-faw';* from 599; an unclean bird, perh. the *parrot* (from its *irascibility*):—heron.

602. אָנַק **'ânaq**, *aw-nak';* a prim. root; to *shriek:*—cry, groan.

603. אֲנָקָה **'ănâqâh**, *an-aw-kaw'*, from 602; *shrieking:*—crying out, groaning, sighing.

604. אֲנָקָה **'ănâqâh**, *an-aw-kaw';* the same as 603; some kind of lizard, prob. the *gecko* (from its *wail*):—ferret.

605. אָנַשׁ **'ânash**, *aw-nash';* a prim. root; to *be frail, feeble*, or (fig.) *melancholy:*—desperate (-ly wicked), incurable, sick, woeful.

606. אֱנָשׁ **'ĕnâsh** (Chald.), *en-awsh';* or אֱנַשׁ **'ĕnash** (Chald.), *en-ash';* corresp. to 582; a *man:*—man, + whosoever.

אַנְתְּ **'ant**. See 859.

607. אַנְתָּה **'antâh** (Chald.), *an-taw';* corresp. to 859; *thou:*—as for thee, thou.

608. אַנְתּוּן **'antûwn** (Chald.), *an-toon';* plur. of 607; *ye:*—ye.

609. אָסָא **'Âçâ'**, *aw-saw';* of uncert. der.; *Asa*, the name of a king and of a Levite:—Asa.

610. אָסוּךְ **'âçûwk**, *aw-sook';* from 5480; *anointed*, i.e. an oil-*flask:*—pot.

611. אָסוֹן **'âçôwn**, *aw-sone';* of uncert. der.; *hurt:*—mischief.

612. אֵסוּר **'êçûwr**, *ay-soor';* from 631; a *bond* (espec. *manacles* of a prisoner):—band, + prison.

613. אֱסוּר **'ĕçûwr** (Chald.), *es-oor';* corresp. to 612:—band, imprisonment.

614. אָסִיף **'âçîyph**, *aw-seef';* or אָסִף **'âçiph**, *aw-seef';* from 622; *gathered*, i.e. (abstr.) a *gathering* in of crops:—ingathering.

615. אָסִיר **'âçîyr**, *aw-sere';* from 631; *bound*, i.e. a *captive:*—(those which are) bound, prisoner.

616. אַסִּיר **'aççîyr**, *as-sere';* for 615:—prisoner.

617. אַסִּיר **'Aççîyr**, *as-sere';* the same as 616; *prisoner; Assir*, the name of two Isr.:—Assir.

618. אָסָם **'âçâm**, *aw-sawm';* from an unused root mean. to *heap* together; a *storehouse* (only in the plur.):—barn, storehouse.

619. אַסְנָה **'Açnâh**, *as-naw';* of uncert. der.; *Asnah*, one of the Nethinim:—Asnah.

620. אָסְנַפַּר **'Oçnappar**, *os-nap-par';* of for. der.; *Osnappar*, an Assyrian king:—Asnapper.

621. אָסְנַת **'Âçᵉnath**, *aw-se-nath';* of Eg. der.; *Asenath*, the wife of Joseph:—Asenath.

622. אָסַף **'âçaph**, *aw-saf';* a prim. root; to *gather* for any purpose; hence to *receive, take away*, i.e. remove (destroy, leave behind, put up, restore, etc.):—assemble, bring, consume, destroy, fetch, gather (in, together, up again), × generally, get (him), lose, put all together, receive, recover [another from leprosy], (be) rereward, × surely, take (away, into, up), × utterly, withdraw.

623. אָסָף **'Âçâph**, *aw-sawf';* from 622; *collector; Asaph*, the name of three Isr., and of the family of the first:—Asaph.

אָסִף **'âçiph**. See 614.

624. אָסֻף **'âçuph**, *aw-soof';* pass. part. of 622; *collected* (only in the plur.), i.e. a *collection* (of offerings):—threshold, Asuppim.

625. אֹסֶף **'ôçeph**, *o'-sef;* from 622; a *collection* (of fruits):—gathering.

626. אֲסֵפָה **'ăçêphâh**, *as-ay-faw';* from 622; a *collection* of people (only adv.):— × together.

627. אֲסֻפָּה **'ăçuppâh**, *as-up-paw';* fem. of 624; a *collection* of (learned) men (only in the plur.):—assembly.

628. אֲסַפְסֻף **'açpᵉçûph**, *as-pes-oof';* by redupl. from 624; *gathered up together*, i.e. a promiscuous *assemblage* (of people):—mixt multitude.

629. אָסְפַּרְנָא **'ocparnâ'** (Chald.), *os-par-naw';* of Pers. der.; *diligently:*—fast, forthwith, speed (-ily).

630. אַסְפָּתָא **'Açpâthâ'**, *as-paw-thaw';* of Pers. der.; *Aspatha*, a son of Haman:—Aspatha.

631. אָסַר **'âçar**, *aw-sar';* a prim. root; to *yoke* or *hitch;* by anal. to *fasten* in any sense, to *join* battle:—bind, fast, gird, harness, hold, keep, make ready, order, prepare, prison (-er), put in bonds, set in array, tie.

632. אֱסָר **'ĕçâr**, *es-awr';* or אִסָּר **'iççâr**, *is-sawr';* from 631; an *obligation* or *vow* (of abstinence):—binding, bond.

633. אֱסָר **'ĕçâr** (Chald.), *es-awr';* corresp. to 632 in a legal sense; an *interdict:*—decree.

634. אֵסַר־חַדּוֹן **'Êçar-Chaddôwn**, *ay-sar' chad-dohn';* of for. der.; *Esar-chaddon*, an Assyr. king:—Esar-haddon.

635. אֶסְתֵּר **'Eçtêr**, *es-tare';* of Pers. der.; *Ester*, the Jewish heroine:—Esther.

636. אָע **'â'** (Chald.), *aw;* corresp. to 6086; a *tree* or *wood:*—timber, wood.

637. אַף **'aph**, *af;* a prim. particle; mean. *accession* (used as an adv. or conj.); *also* or *yea;* adversatively *though:*—also, + although, and (furthermore, yet), but, even, + how much less (more, rather than), moreover, with, yea.

638. אַף **'aph** (Chald.), *af;* corresp. to 637:—also.

639. אַף **'aph**, *af;* from 599; prop. the *nose* or *nostril;* hence the *face*, and occasionally a *person;* also (from the rapid breathing in passion) *ire:*—anger (-gry), + before, countenance, face, + forbearing, forehead, + [long-] suffering, nose, nostril, snout, × worthy, wrath.

640. אָפַד **'âphad**, *aw-fad';* a prim. root [rather a denom. from 646]; to *gird* on (the ephod):—bind, gird.

אֵפֹד **'êphôd**. See 646.

641. אֵפֹד **'Êphôd**, *ay-fode';* the same as 646 short.; *Ephod*, an Isr.:—Ephod.

642. אֵפֻדָּה **'êphuddâh**, *ay-food-daw';* fem. of 646; a *girding* on (of the ephod); hence gen. a *plating* (of metal):—ephod, ornament.

643. אַפֶּדֶן **'appeden**, *ap-peh'-den;* appar. of for. der.; a *pavilion* or palace-tent:—palace.

644. אָפָה **'âphâh**, *aw-faw';* a prim. root; to *cook*, espec. to *bake:*—bake, (-r, [-meats]).

אֵפָה **'êphâh**. See 374.

645. אֵפוֹ **'êphôw**, *ay-fo';* or אֵפוֹא **'êphôw'**, *ay-fo';* from 6311; strictly a demonstrative particle, *here;* but used of time, *now* or *then:*—here, now, where?

646. אֵפוֹד **'êphôwd**, *ay-fode';* rarely אֵפֹד **'êphôd**, *ay-fode';* prob. of for. der.; a *girdle;* spec. the *ephod* or high-priest's shoulder-piece; also gen. an *image:*—ephod.

647. אֲפִיחַ **'Ăphîyach**, *af-ee'-akh;* perh. from 6315; *breeze; Aphiach*, an Isr.:—Aphiah.

648. אָפִיל **'âphîyl**, *aw-feel';* from the same as 651 (in the sense of *weakness*); *unripe:*—not grown up.

649. אַפַּיִם **'Appayim**, *ap-pah'-yim;* dual of 639; *two nostrils; Appajim*, an Isr.:—Appaim.

650. אָפִיק **'âphîyq**, *aw-feek';* from 622; prop. *containing*, i.e. a *tube;* also a *bed* or *valley* of a stream; also a *strong* thing or a *hero:*—brook, channel, mighty, river, + scale, stream, strong piece.

אֹפִיר **'Ôphîyr**. See 211.

651. אָפֵל **'âphêl**, *aw-fale';* from an unused root mean. to *set* as the sun; *dusky:*—very dark.

652. אֹפֶל **ôphel**, *o'-fel;* from the same as 651; *dusk:*—darkness, obscurity, privily.

653. אֲפֵלָה **'ăphêlâh**, *af-ay-law';* fem. of 651; *duskiness*, fig. *misfortune;* concr. *concealment:*—dark, darkness, gloominess, × thick.

654. אֶפְלָל **'Ephlâl**, *ef-lawl';* from 6419; *judge; Ephlal*, an Isr.:—Ephlal.

655. אֹפֶן **'ôphen**, *o'-fen;* from an unused root mean. to *revolve;* a *turn*, i.e. a *season:*—+ fitly.

אֹפָן **'ôphân**. See 212.

656. אָפֵס **'âphêç**, *aw-face';* a prim. root; to *disappear*, i.e. *cease:*—be clean gone (at an end, brought to nought), fail.

657. אֶפֶס **'epheç**, *eh'-fes;* from 656; *cessation*, i.e. an *end* (espec. of the earth); often used adv. *no further;* also (like 6466) the *ankle* (in the dual), as being the extremity of the leg or foot:—ankle, but (only), end, howbeit, less than nothing, nevertheless (where), no, none (beside), not (any, -withstanding), thing of nought, save (-ing), there, uttermost part, want, without (cause).

658. אֶפֶס דַּמִּים **'Epheç Dammîym**, *eh'-fes dam-meem';* from 657 and the plur. of 1818; *boundary of blood*-drops; *Ephes-Dammim*, a place in Pal.:—Ephes-dammim.

659. אֶפַע **'êpha'**, *eh'-fah;* from an unused root prob. mean. to *breathe;* prop. a *breath*, i.e. *nothing:*—of nought.

660. אֶפְעֶה **'eph'eh**, *ef-eh';* from 659 (in the sense of *hissing*); an *asp* or other venomous serpent:—viper.

661. אָפַף **'âphaph**, *aw-faf';* a prim. root; to *surround:*—compass.

662. אָפַק **'âphaq**, *aw-fak';* a prim. root; to *contain*, i.e. (reflex.) *abstain:*—force (oneself), restrain.

663. אֲפֵק **'Ăphêq**, *af-ake';* or אֲפִיק **'Ăphîyq**, *af-eek';* from 662 (in the sense of *strength*); *fortress; Aphek* (or *Aphik*), the name of three places in Pal.:—Aphek, Aphik.

664. אֲפֵקָה **'Ăphêqâh**, *af-ay-kaw';* fem. of 663; *fortress; Aphekah*, a place in Pal.:—Aphekah.

665. אֵפֶר **'êpher**, *ay'-fer;* from an unused root mean. to *bestrew; ashes:*—ashes.

666. אֲפֵר **'ăphêr**, *af-ayr';* from the same as 665 (in the sense of *covering*); a *turban:*—ashes.

667. אֶפְרֹחַ **'ephrôach**, *ef-ro'-akh;* from 6524 (in the sense of *bursting* the shell); the *brood* of a bird:—young (one).

668. אַפִּרְיוֹן **'appiryôwn**, *ap-pir-yone';* prob. of Eg. der.; a *palanquin:*—chariot.

669. אֶפְרַיִם **'Ephrayim**, *ef-rah'-yim;* dual of a masc. form of 672; *double fruit; Ephrajim*, a son of Joseph; also the tribe descended from him, and its territory:—Ephraim Ephraimites

670. אֲפָרְסָי **'Âphârêçay** (Chald.), *af-aw-re-sah'-ee;* of for. or. (only in the plur.); an *Apharesite* or inhabitant of an unknown region of Assyria:—Apharsite.

671. אֲפַרְסְכַי **'Âpharçᵉkay** (Chald.), *af-ar-sek-ah'ee;* or אֲפַרְסַתְכַי **'Âpharçathkay** (Chald.), *af-ar-sath-kah'ee;* of for. or. (only in the plur.); an *Apharsekite* or *Apharsathkite,* an unknown Assyrian tribe:—Apharsachites, Apharsathchites.

672. אֶפְרָת **'Ephrâth,** *ef-rawth';* or אֶפְרָתָה **'Ephrâthâh,** *ef-raw'-thaw;* from 6509; *fruitfulness; Ephrath,* another name for Bethlehem; once (Psa. 132 : 6) perh. for *Ephraim;* also of an Israelitish woman:—Ephrath, Ephratah.

673. אֶפְרָתִי **'Ephrâthîy,** *ef-rawth-ee';* patrial from 672; an *Ephrathite* or an *Ephraimite:*—Ephraimite, Ephrathite.

674. אַפְּתֹם **'appᵉthôm** (Chald.), *ap-pe-thome';* of Pers. or.; *revenue;* others *at the last:*—revenue.

675. אֶצְבּוֹן **'Etsbôwn,** *ets-bone';* or אֶצְבֹּן **'Etsbôn,** *ets-bone';* of uncert. der.; *Etsbon,* the name of two Isr.:—Ezbon.

676. אֶצְבַּע **'etsba',** *ets-bah';* from the same as 6648 (in the sense of *grasping*); some thing to *seize* with, i.e. a *finger;* by anal. a *toe:*—finger, toe.

677. אֶצְבַּע **'etsba'** (Chald.), *ets-bah';* corresp. to 676:—finger, toe.

678. אָצִיל **'âtsîyl,** *aw-tseel';* from 680 (in its secondary sense of *separation*); an *extremity* (Isa. 41 : 9), also a *noble:*—chief man, noble.

679. אַצִּיל **'atstsîyl,** *ats-tseel';* from 680 (in its primary sense of *uniting*); a *joint* of the hand (i.e. *knuckle*); also (accord. to some) a *party-wall* (Ezek. 41 : 8):—[arm] hole, great.

680. אָצַל **'âtsal,** *aw-tsal';* a prim. root; prop. to *join;* used only as a denom. from 681; to *separate;* hence to *select, refuse, contract:*—keep, reserve, straiten, take.

681. אֵצֶל **'êtsel,** *ay'-tsel;* from 680 (in the sense of *joining*); a *side;* (as a prep.) *near:*—at, (hard) by, (from) (beside), near (unto), toward, with. See also 1018.

682. אָצֵל **'Âtsêl,** *aw-tsale';* from 680; *noble; Atsel,* the name of an Isr., and of a place in Pal.:—Azal, Azel.

683. אֲצַלְיָהוּ **'Âtsalyâhûw,** *ats-al-yaw'-hoo;* from 680 and 3050 prol.; *Jah has reserved; Atsaljah,* an Isr.:—Azaliah.

684. אֹצֶם **'Ôtsem,** *o'-tsem;* from an unused root prob. mean. to *be strong; strength* (i.e. *strong*); *Otsem,* the name of two Isr.:—Ozem.

685. אֶצְעָדָה **'ets'âdâh,** *ets-aw-daw';* a var. from 6807; prop. a *step-chain;* by anal. a *bracelet:*—bracelet, chain.

686. אָצַר **'âtsar,** *aw-tsar;* a prim. root; to *store up:*—(lay up in) store, (make) treasure (-r).

687. אֵצֶר **'Êtser,** *ay'-tser;* from 686; *treasure; Etser,* an Idumæan:—Ezer.

688. אֶקְדָּח **'eqdâch,** *ek-dawkh';* from 6916; *burning,* i.e. a *carbuncle* or other fiery gem:—carbuncle.

689. אַקּוֹ **'aqqôw,** *ak-ko';* prob. from 602; *slender,* i.e. the *ibex:*—wild goat.

690. אֲרָא **'Ărâ',** *ar-aw';* prob. for 738; *lion; Ara,* an Isr.:—Ara.

691. אֶרְאֵל **'er'êl,** *er-ale';* prob. for 739; a h[illegible] (collect.):—valiant one.

692. אַרְאֵלִי **'Ar'êlîy,** *ar-ay-lee';* from 691; *heroic; Areli* (or an *Arelite,* collect.), an Isr. and his desc.:—Areli, Arelites.

693. אָרַב **'ârab,** *aw-rab';* a prim. root; to *lurk:*—(lie in) ambush (-ment), lay (lie in) wait.

694. אֲרָב **'Ărâb,** *ar-awb';* from 693; *ambush; Arab,* a place in Pal.:—Arab.

695. אֶרֶב **'ereb,** *eh'-reb;* from 693; *ambuscade:*—den, lie in wait.

696. [illegible] **'ôreb,** *o'-reb:* the same as 695:—wait.

אַרְבֵּאל **'Arbê'l.** See 1009.

697. אַרְבֶּה **'arbeh,** *ar-beh';* from 7235; a *locust* (from its rapid *increase):*—grasshopper, locust.

698. אָרֳבָה **'orŏbâh,** *or-ob-aw';* fem. of 696 (only in the plur.); *ambuscades:*—spoils.

699. אֲרֻבָּה **'ărubbâh,** *ar-oob-baw';* fem. part. pass. of 693 (as if for *lurking*); a *lattice;* (by impl.) a *window, dove-cot* (because of the pigeon-holes), *chimney* (with its apertures for smoke), *sluice* (with openings for water):—chimney, window.

700. אֲרֻבּוֹת **'Ărubbôwth,** *ar-oob-both;* plur. of 699; *Arubboth,* a place in Pal.:—Aruboth.

701. אַרְבִּי **'Arbîy,** *ar-bee';* patrial from 694; an *Arbite* or native of Arab:—Arbite.

702. אַרְבַּע **'arba',** *ar-bah';* masc. אַרְבָּעָה **'arbâ'âh,** *ar-baw-aw';* from 7251; *four:*—four.

703. אַרְבַּע **'arba'** (Chald.), *ar-bah';* corresp. to 702:—four.

704. אַרְבַּע **'Arba',** *ar-bah';* the same as 702; *Arba,* one of the Anakim:—Arba.

אַרְבָּעָה **'arbâ'âh.** See 702.

705. אַרְבָּעִים **'arbâ'îym,** *ar-baw-eem';* multiple of 702; *forty:*—forty.

706. אַרְבַּעְתַּיִם **'arba'tayim,** *ar-bah-tah'-yim;* dual of 702; *fourfold:*—fourfold.

707. אָרַג **'ârag,** *aw-rag';* a prim. root; to *plait* or *weave:*—weaver (-r).

708. אֶרֶג **'ereg,** *eh'-reg;* from 707; a *weaving;* a *braid;* also a *shuttle:*—beam, weaver's shuttle.

709. אַרְגֹּב **'Argôb,** *ar-gobe';* from the same as 7263; *stony; Argob,* a district of Pal.:—Argob.

710. אַרְגְּוָן **'argᵉvân,** *arg-ev-awn';* a var. for 713; *purple:*—purple.

711. אַרְגְּוָן **'argᵉvân** (Chald.), *arg-ev-awn';* corresp. to 710:—scarlet.

712. אַרְגָּז **'argâz,** *ar-gawz';* perh. from 7264 (in the sense of being *suspended*); a *box* (as a pannier):—coffer.

713. אַרְגָּמָן **'argâmân,** *ar-gaw-mawn';* of for. or.; *purple* (the color or the dyed stuff):—purple.

714. אַרְדְּ **'Ard,** *ard;* from an unused root prob. mean. to *wander; fugitive; Ard,* the name of two Isr.:—Ard.

715. אַרְדּוֹן **'Ardôwn,** *ar-dohn';* from the same as 714; *roaming; Ardon,* an Isr.:—Ardon.

716. אַרְדִּי **'Ardîy,** *ar-dee';* patron. from 714; an *Ardite* (collect.) or desc. of Ard:—Ardites.

717. אָרָה **'ârâh,** *aw-raw';* a prim. root; to *pluck:*—gather, pluck.

718. אֲרוּ **'ărûw** (Chald.), *ar-oo';* prob. akin to 431; *lo!:*—behold, lo.

719. אַרְוַד **'Arvad,** *ar-vad';* prob. from 7300; a refuge for the *roving; Arvad,* an island-city of Pal.:—Arvad.

720. אֲרוֹד **'Ărôwd,** *ar-ode';* an orth. var. of 719; *fugitive; Arod,* an Isr.:—Arod.

721. אַרְוָדִי **'Arvâdîy,** *ar-vaw-dee';* patrial from 719; an *Arvadite* or citizen of Arvad:—Arvadite.

722. אֲרוֹדִי **'Ărôwdîy,** *ar-o-dee';* patron. from 721; an *Arodite* or desc. of Arod:—Arodi, Arodites.

723. אֻרְוָה **'urvâh,** *oor-vaw';* or, אֲרָיָה **'ărâyâh,** *ar-aw-yah';* from 717 (in the sense of *feeding*); a *herding-place* for an animal:—stall.

724. אֲרוּכָה **'ărûwkâh,** *ar-oo-kaw';* or אֲרֻכָה **'ărûkâh,** *ar-oo-kaw';* fem. pass. part. of 748 (in the sense of *restoring* to soundness); *wholeness* (lit. or fig.):—health, made up, perfected.

725. אֲרוּמָה **'Ărûwmâh,** *ar-oo-maw';* a var. of 7316; *height; Arumah,* a place in Pal.:—Arumah.

726. אֲרוֹמִי° **'Ărôwmîy,** *ar-o-mee';* a clerical error for 130; an *Edomite* (as in the marg.):—Syrian.

727. אָרוֹן **'ârôwn,** *aw-rone';* or אָרֹן **'ârôn,** *aw-rone';* from 717 (in the sense of *gathering*); a *box:*—ark, chest, coffin.

728. אֲרַוְנָה **'Ăravnâh,** *ar-av-naw';* or (by transp.) אוֹרְנָה° **'Ôwrnâh,** *ore-naw';* or אַרְנִיָּה° **'Arnîyah,** *ar-nee-yaw';* all by orth. var. for 771; *Aravnah* (or *Arnijah* or *Ornah*), a Jebusite:—Araunah.

729. אָרַז **'âraz,** *aw-raz';* a prim. root; to be *firm;* used only in the pass. participle as a denom. from 730; of *cedar:*—made of cedar.

730. אֶרֶז **'erez,** *eh'-rez;* from 729; a *cedar* tree (from the tenacity of its roots):—cedar (tree).

731. אַרְזָה **'arzâh,** *ar-zaw';* fem. of 730; *cedar wainscoting:*—cedar work.

732. אָרַח **'ârach,** *aw-rakh';* a prim. root; to *travel:*—go, wayfaring (man).

733. אָרַח **'Ârach,** *aw-rakh';* from 732; *way-faring; Arach,* the name of three Isr.:—Arah.

734. אֹרַח **'ôrach,** *o'-rakh;* from 732; a well trodden *road* (lit. or fig.); also a *caravan:*—manner, path, race, rank, traveller, troop, [by-, high-] way.

735. אֹרַח **'ôrach** (Chald.), *o'-rakh;* corresp. to 734; a *road:*—way.

736. אֹרְחָה **'ôrᵉchâh,** *o-rekh-aw';* fem. act. part. of 732; a *caravan:*—(travelling) company.

737. אֲרֻחָה **'ărûchâh,** *ar-oo-khaw';* fem. pass. part. of 732 (in the sense of *appointing*); a *ration* of food:—allowance, diet, dinner, victuals.

738. אֲרִי **'ărîy,** *ar-ee';* or (prol.) אַרְיֵה **'aryêh,** *ar-yay';* from 717 (in the sense of *violence*); a *lion:*—(young) lion, + pierce [*from the marg.*].

739. אֲרִיאֵל **'ărîy'êl,** *ar-ee-ale';* or אֲרִאֵל **'ărî'êl,** *ar-ee-ale';* from 738 and 410; *lion of God,* i.e. *heroic:*—lionlike men.

740. אֲרִיאֵל **'Ărî'êl,** *ar-ee-ale';* the same as 739; *Ariel,* a symb. name for Jerusalem, also the name of an Isr.:—Ariel.

741. אֲרִאֵיל **'ărî'êyl,** *ar-ee-ale';* either by transposition for 739 or, more prob., an orth. var. for 2025; the *altar* of the Temple:—altar.

742. אֲרִידַי **'Ărîyday,** *ar-ee-dah'-ee;* of Pers. or.; *Aridai,* a son of Haman:—Aridai.

743. אֲרִידָתָא **'Ărîydâthâ',** *ar-ee-daw-thaw';* of Pers. or.; *Aridatha,* a son of Haman:—Aridatha.

אַרְיֵה **'aryêh.** See 738.

744. אַרְיֵה **'aryêh** (Chald.), *ar-yay';* corresp. to 738:—lion.

745. אַרְיֵה **'Aryêh,** *ar-yay';* the same as 738; *lion; Arjeh,* an Isr.:—Arieh.

אֲרָיָה **'ărâyâh.** See 723

746. אַרְיוֹךְ **'Aryôwk,** *ar-yoke';* of for. or.; *Arjok,* the name of two Babylonians:—Arioch.

747. אֲרִיסַי **'Ărîyçay,** *ar-ee-sah'-ee;* of Pers. or.; *Arisai,* a son of Haman:—Arisai.

748. אָרַךְ **'ârak,** *aw-rak';* a prim. root; to be (caus. *make*) *long* (lit. or fig.):—defer, draw out, lengthen, (be, become, make, pro-) long, + (out-, over-) live, tarry (long).

749. אֲרַךְ **'ărak** (Chald.), *ar-ak';* prop. corresp. to 748, but used only in the sense of *reaching* to a given point; to *suit:*—be meet.

750. אָרֵךְ **'ârêk** *aw-rake';* from 748; *long:*—long [-suffering, -winged], patient, slow [to anger].

751. אֶרֶךְ **'Erek,** *eh'-rek;* from 748; *length; Erek,* a place in Bab.:—Erech.

75[illegible]. אָרֹךְ **'ârôk,** *aw-roke';* from 748; *long:*—long.

753. אֹרֶךְ **'ôrek,** *o'-rek;* from 748; *length:*—+ for ever, length, long.

754. אַרְכָּא **'arkâ'** (Chald.), *ar-kaw';* or אַרְכָּה **'arkâh** (Chald.), *arkaw';* from 749; *length:*—lengthening, prolonged.

755. אַרְכֻבָה **'arkûbâh** (Chald.), *ar-koo-baw'* from an unused root corresp. to 7392 (in the sense of *bending* the knee); the *knee:*—knee.

אֲרֻכָה **'ărûkâh.** See 724.

756. אַרְכְּוַי **'Ark^evay** (Chald.), *ar-kev-ah'ee;* patrial from 751; an *Arkevite* (collect.) or native of Erek:—Archevite.

757 אַרְכִּי **'Arkîy,** *ar-kee';* patrial from another place (in Pal.) of similar name with 751; an *Arkite* or native of Erek:—Archi, Archite.

758. אֲרָם **'Arâm,** *arawm';* from the same as 759; the *highland; Aram* or Syria, and its inhabitants; also the name of a son of Shem, a grandson of Nahor, and of an Isr.:—Aram, Mesopotamia, Syria, Syrians.

759. אַרְמוֹן **'armôwn,** *ar-mone';* from an unused root (mean. to *be elevated*); a *citadel* (from its *height*):—castle, palace. Comp. 2038.

760. אֲרַם צוֹבָה **'Ăram Tsôbâh,** *ar-am' tsobaw';* from 758 and 6678; *Aram of Tsoba* (or Cœle-Syria):—Aram-zobah.

761. אֲרַמִּי **'Ărammîy,** *ar-am-mee';* patrial from 758; an *Aramite* or Aramæan:—Syrian, Aramitess.

762. אֲרָמִית **'Ărâmîyth,** *ar-aw-meeth';* fem. of 761; (only adv.) *in Aramæan:*—in the Syrian language (tongue), in Syriack.

763. אֲרַם נַהֲרַיִם **'Ăram Nahărayim,** *ar-am' nah-har-ah'-yim;* from 758 and the dual of 5104; *Aram of* (the) *two rivers* (Euphrates and Tigris) or Mesopotamia:—Aham-naharaim, Mesopotamia.

764. אַרְמֹנִי **'Armônîy,** *ar-mo-nee';* from 759; *palatial; Armoni,* an Isr.:—Armoni.

765. אֲרָן **'Ărân,** *ar-awn';* from 7442; *stridulous; Aran,* an Edomite:—Aran.

766. אֹרֶן **'ôren,** *o'-ren;* from the same as 765 (in the sense of *strength*); the *ash* tree (from its toughness):—ash.

767. אֹרֶן **'Ôren,** *o'-ren;* the same as 766; *Oren,* an Isr.:—Oren.

אָרֹן **'ârôn.** See 727.

768. אַרְנֶבֶת **'arnebeth,** *ar-neh'-beth;* of uncert. der.; the *hare:*—hare.

769. אַרְנוֹן **'Arnôwn,** *ar-nohn';* or אַרְנֹן **'Arnôn,** *ar-nohn';* from 7442; a *brawling* stream; the *Arnon,* a river east of the Jordan; also its territory:—Arnon.

אַרְנִיָּה **'Arnîyah.** See 728.

770. אַרְנָן **'Arnân,** *ar-nawn';* prob. from the same as 769; *noisy; Arnan,* an Isr.:—Arnan.

771. אָרְנָן **'Ornân,** *or-nawn';* prob. from 766; *strong; Ornan,* a Jebusite:—Ornan. See 728.

772. אֲרַע **'ăra'** (Chald.), *ar-ah';* corresp. to 776; the *earth;* by impl. (fig.) *low:*—earth, inferior.

773. אַרְעִית **'ar'îyth** (Chald.), *arh-eeth';* fem. of 772; the *bottom:*—bottom.

774. אַרְפָּד **'Arpâd,** *ar-pawd';* from 7502; *spread* out; *Arpad,* a place in Syria:—Arpad, Arphad.

775. אַרְפַּכְשַׁד **'Arpakshad,** *ar-pak-shad';* prob. of for. or.; *Arpakshad,* a son of Noah; also the region settled by him:—Arphaxad.

776. אֶרֶץ **'erets,** *eh'-rets;* from an unused root prob. mean. to *be firm;* the *earth* (at large, or partitively a *land*):— × common, country, earth, field, ground, land, × nations, way, + wilderness, world.

777. אַרְצָא **'artsâ',** *ar-tsaw';* from 776; *earthiness; Artsa,* an Isr.:—Arza.

778. אֲרַק **'ăraq** (Chald.), *ar-ak';* by transmutation for 772; the *earth:*—earth.

779. אָרַר **'ârar,** *aw-rar';* a prim. root; to *execrate:*— × bitterly curse.

780. אֲרָרַט **'Ărâraṭ,** *ar-aw-rat';* of for. or.; *Ararat* (or rather Armenia):—Ararat, Armenia.

781. אָרַשׂ **'âras,** *aw-ras';* a prim. root; to *engage* for matrimony:—betroth, espouse.

782. אֲרֶשֶׁת **'ăresheth,** *ar-eh'-sheth;* from 781 (in the sense of *desiring* to possess); a *longing* for:—request.

783. אַרְתַּחְשַׁשְׁתָּא **'Artachshashtâ',** *ar-takh-shash-taw';* or אַרְתַּחְשַׁשְׁתְּ **'Artachshasht',** *ar-takh-shasht';* or by perm. אַרְתַּחְשַׁסְתְּא **'Artachshaçt',** *ar-takh-shast';* of for. or.; *Artachshasta* (or Artaxerxes), a title (rather than name) of several Pers. kings:—Artaxerxes.

784. אֵשׁ **'êsh,** *aysh;* a prim. word; *fire* (lit. or fig.):—burning, fiery, fire, flaming, hot.

785. אֵשׁ **'êsh** (Chald.), *aysh;* corresp. to 784:—flame.

786. אִשׁ **'ish,** *eesh;* ident. (in or. and formation) with 784; *entity;* used only adv., there *is* or *are:*—are there, none can. Comp. 3426.

787. אֹשׁ **'ôsh** (Chald.), *ohsh;* corresp. (by transp. and abb.) to 803; a *foundation:*—foundation.

788. אַשְׁבֵּל **'Ashbêl,** *ash-bale';* prob. from the same as 7640; *flowing; Ashbel,* an Isr.:—Ashbel.

789. אַשְׁבֵּלִי **'Ashbêlîy,** *ash-bay-lee';* patron. from 788; an *Ashbelite* (collect.) or desc. of Ashbel:—Ashbelites.

790. אֶשְׁבָּן **'Eshbân,** *esh-bawn';* prob. from the same as 7644; *vigorous; Eshban,* an Idumæan:—Eshban.

791. אַשְׁבֵּעַ **'Ashbêa',** *ash-bay'-ah;* from 7650; *adjurer; Asbeä,* an Isr.:—Ashbea.

792. אֶשְׁבַּעַל **'Eshba'al,** *esh-bah'-al;* from 376 and 1168; *man of Baal; Eshbaal* (or Ishbosheth), a son of King Saul:—Eshbaal.

793. אֶשֶׁד **'eshed,** *eh'-shed;* from an unused root mean. to *pour;* an *outpouring:*—stream.

794. אֲשֵׁדָה **'ăshêdâh,** *ash-ay-daw';* fem. of 793; a *ravine:*—springs.

795. אַשְׁדּוֹד **'Ashdôwd,** *ash-dode';* from 7703; *ravager; Ashdod,* a place in Pal.:—Ashdod.

796. אַשְׁדּוֹדִי **'Ashdôwdîy,** *ash-do-dee';* patrial from 795; an *Ashdodite* (often collect.) or inhabitant of Ashdod:—Ashdodites, of Ashdod.

797. אַשְׁדּוֹדִית **'Ashdôwdîyth,** *ash-do-deeth';* fem. of 796; (only adv.) *in the language of Ashdod:*—in the speech of Ashdod.

798. אַשְׁדּוֹת הַפִּסְגָּה **'Ashdôwth hap-Piçgâh,** *ash-doth' hap-pis-gaw';* from the plur. of 794 and 6449 with the art. interposed; *ravines of the Pisgah; Ashdoth-Pisgah,* a place east of the Jordan:—Ashdoth-pisgah.

799. אֶשְׁדָּת **'eshdâth,** *esh-dawth';* from 784 and 1881; a *fire-law:*—fiery law.

800. אֶשָּׁה **'eshshâh,** *esh-shaw';* fem. of 784; *fire:*—fire.

801. אִשָּׁה **'ishshâh,** *ish-shaw';* the same as 800, but used in a liturgical sense; prop. a *burnt-offering;* but occasionally of any *sacrifice:*—(offering, sacrifice), (made) by fire.

802. אִשָּׁה **'ishshâh,** *ish-shaw';* fem. of 376 or 582; irregular plur. נָשִׁים **nâshîym,** *naw-sheem';* a *woman* (used in the same wide sense as 582):—[adulter]ess, each, every, female, × many, + none, one, + together, wife, woman. Often unexpressed in English.

803. אֲשׁוּיָה **'ăshûwyâh,** *ash-oo-yah';* fem. pass. part. from an unused root mean. to *found; foundation:*—foundation.

804. אַשּׁוּר **'Ashshûwr,** *ash-shoor';* or אַשֻּׁר **'Ashshûr,** *ash-shoor';* appar. from 833 (in the sense of *successful*); *Ashshur,* the second son of Shem; also his desc. and the country occupied by them (i.e. Assyria), its region and its empire:—Asshur, Assur, Assyria, Assyrians. See 838.

805. אֲשׁוּרִי **'Ăshûwrîy,** *ash-oo-ree';* or אַשּׁוּרִי **'Ashshûwrîy,** *ash-shoo-ree';* from a patrial word of the same form as 804; an *Ashurite* (collect.) or inhab. of Ashur, a district in Pal.:—Asshurim, Ashurites.

806. אַשְׁחוּר **'Ashchûwr,** *ash-khoor';* prob. from 7835; *black; Ashchur,* an Isr.:—Ashur.

807. אֲשִׁימָא **'Ăshîymâ',** *ash-ee-maw';* of for. or.; *Ashima,* a deity of Hamath:—Ashima.

אֲשֵׁירָה **'ăshêyrah.** See 842.

808. אָשִׁישׁ **'âshîysh,** *aw-sheesh';* from the same as 784 (in the sense of *pressing* down firmly; comp. 803); a (ruined) *foundation:*—foundation.

809. אֲשִׁישָׁה **'ăshîyshâh,** *ash-ee-shaw';* fem. of 808; something closely *pressed* together, i.e. a *cake* of raisins or other comfits:—flagon.

810. אֶשֶׁךְ **'eshek,** *eh'-shek;* from an unused root (prob. mean. to *bunch* together); a *testicle* (as a *lump*):—stone.

811. אֶשְׁכּוֹל **'eshkôwl,** *esh-kole';* or אֶשְׁכֹּל **'eshkôl,** *esh-kole';* prob. prol. from 810; a *bunch of grapes* or other fruit:—cluster (of grapes).

812. אֶשְׁכֹּל **'Eshkôl,** *esh-kole';* the same as 811; *Eshcol,* the name of an Amorite, also of a valley in Pal.:—Eshcol.

813. אַשְׁכְּנַז **'Ashk^enaz,** *ash-ken-az';* of for. or.; *Ashkenaz,* a Japhethite, also his desc.:—Ashkenaz.

814. אֶשְׁכָּר **'eshkâr,** *esh-cawr';* for 7939; a *gratuity:*—gift, present.

815. אֵשֶׁל **'êshel,** *ay'-shel;* from a root of uncert. signif.; a *tamarisk* tree; by extens. a *grove* of any kind:—grove, tree.

816. אָשַׁם **'âsham,** *aw-sham';* or אָשֵׁם **'âshêm,** *aw-shame';* a prim. root; to *be guilty;* by impl. to *be punished* or *perish:*— × certainly, be (-come, made) desolate, destroy, × greatly, be (-come, found, hold) guilty, offend (acknowledge offence), trespass.

817. אָשָׁם **'âshâm,** *aw-shawm';* from 816; *guilt;* by impl. a *fault;* also a *sin-offering:*—guiltiness, (offering for) sin, trespass (offering).

818. אָשֵׁם **'âshêm,** *aw-shame';* from 816; *guilty;* hence *presenting a sin-offering:*—one which is faulty, guilty.

819. אַשְׁמָה **'ashmâh,** *ash-maw';* fem. of 817; *guiltiness,* a *fault,* the *presentation of a sin-offering:*—offend, sin, (cause of) trespass (-ing, offering).

אַשְׁמוּרָה **'ashmûrâh.** See 821.

820. אַשְׁמָן **'ashmân,** *ash-mawn';* prob. from 8081; a *fat* field:—desolate place.

821. אַשְׁמֻרָה **'ashmûrâh,** *ash-moo-raw';* or אַשְׁמוּרָה **'ashmûwrâh,** *ash-moo-raw';* or אַשְׁמֹרֶת **'ashmôreth,** *ash-mo'-reth;* (fem.) from 8104; a night *watch:*—watch.

822. אֶשְׁנָב **'eshnâb,** *esh-nawb';* appar. from an unused root (prob. mean. to *leave interstices*); a latticed *window:*—casement, lattice.

823. אַשְׁנָה **'Ashnâh,** *ash-naw';* prob. a var. for 3466; *Ashnah,* the name of two places in Pal.:—Ashnah.

824. אֶשְׁעָן **'Esh'ân,** *esh-awn';* from 8172; *support; Eshan,* a place in Pal.:—Eshean.

825. אַשָּׁף **'ashshâph,** *ash-shawf';* from an unused root (prob. mean. to *lisp,* i.e. *practise enchantment*); a *conjurer:*—astrologer.

826. אַשָּׁף **'ashshâph** (Chald.), *ash-shawf';* corresp. to 825:—astrologer.

827. אַשְׁפָּה **'ashpâh,** *ash-paw';* perh. (fem.) from the same as 825 (in the sense of *covering*); a *quiver* or arrow-case:—quiver.

828. אַשְׁפְּנַז **'Ashp^enaz,** *ash-pen-az';* of for. or.; *Ashpenaz,* a Bab. eunuch:—Ashpenaz.

829. אֶשְׁפָּר **'eshpâr,** *esh-pawr';* of uncert. der.; a measured *portion:*—good piece (of flesh).

830. אַשְׁפֹּת **'ashpôth**, *ash-pohth'*; or אַשְׁפּוֹת **'ashpôwth**, *ash-pohth'*; or (contr.) שְׁפֹת **sh^ephôth**, *shef-ohth'*; plur. of a noun of the same form as 827, from 8192 (in the sense of *scraping*); a heap of *rubbish* or *filth*:—dung (hill).

831. אַשְׁקְלוֹן **'Ashq^elôwn**, *ash-kel-one'*; prob. from 8254 in the sense of *weighing-place* (i.e. *mart*); *Ashkelon*, a place in Pal.:—Ashkelon, Askalon.

832. אֶשְׁקְלוֹנִי **'Eshq^elôwnîy**, *esh-kel-o-nee'*; patrial from 831; an *Ashkelonite* (collect.) or inhab. of Ashkelon:—Eshkalonites.

833. אָשַׁר **'âshar**, *aw-shar'*; or אָשֵׁר **'âshêr**, *aw-share'*; a prim. root; to *be straight* (used in the widest sense, espec. to *be level*, *right*, *happy*); fig. to *go forward*, *be honest*, *prosper*:—(call, be) bless (-ed, happy), go, guide, lead, relieve.

834. אֲשֶׁר **'ăsher**, *ash-er'*; a prim. rel. pron. (of every gend. and numb.); *who*, *which*, *what*, *that*; also (as adv. and conjunc.) *when*, *where*, *how*, *because*, *in order that*, etc.:— × after, × alike, as (soon as), because, × every, for, + forasmuch, + from whence, + how (-soever), × if, (so) that ([thing] which, wherein), × though, + until, + whatsoever, when, where (+ -as, -in, -of, -on, -soever, -with), which, whilst, + whither (-soever), who (-m, -soever, -se). As it is indeclinable, it is often accompanied by the personal pron. expletively, used to show the connection.

835. אֶשֶׁר **'esher**, *eh'-sher*; from 833; *happiness*; only in masc. plur. constr. as interjec., how *happy!*:—blessed, happy.

836. אָשֵׁר **'Âshêr**, *aw-share'*; from 833; *happy*; *Asher*, a son of Jacob, and the tribe descended from him, with its territory; also a place in Pal.:—Asher.

837. אֹשֶׁר **'ôsher**, *o'-sher*; from 833; *happiness*:—happy.

838. אָשֻׁר **'âshûr**, *aw-shoor'*; or אַשֻּׁר **ashshûr**, *ash-shoor'*; from 833 in the sense of *going*; a *step*:—going, step.

839. אֲשֻׁר **'ăshûr**, *ash-oor'*; contr. for 8391; the *cedar* tree or some other light elastic wood:—Ashurite.

אַשֻּׁר **'Ashshûr**. See 804, 838.

840. אֲשַׂרְאֵל **'Ăsar'êl**, *as-ar-ale'*; by orth. var. from 833 and 410; *right of God*; *Asarel*, an Isr.:—Asareel.

841. אֲשַׂרְאֵלָה **'Ăsar'êlâh**, *as-ar-ale'-aw*; from the same as 840; *right towards God*; *Asarelah*, an Isr.:—Asarelah. Comp. 3480.

842. אֲשֵׁרָה **'ăshêrâh**, *ash-ay-raw'*; or אֲשֵׁירָה **'ăshêyrâh**, *ash-ay-raw'*; from 833; *happy*; *Asherah* (or Astarte) a Phœnician goddess; also an *image* of the same:—grove. Comp. 6253.

843. אָשֵׁרִי **'Âshêrîy**, *aw-shay-ree'*; patron. from 836; an *Asherite* (collect.) or desc. of Asher:—Asherites.

844. אַשְׂרִיאֵל **'Asrîy'êl**, *as-ree-ale'*; an orth. var. for 840; *Asriel*, the name of two Isr.:—Ashriel, Asriel.

845. אַשְׂרִאֵלִי **'Asrî'êlîy**, *as-ree-ale-ee'*; patron. from 844; an *Asrielite* (collect.) or desc. of Asriel:—Asrielites.

846. אֻשַּׁרְנָא **'ushsharnâ'** (Chald.), *oosh-ar-naw'*; from a root corresp. to 833; a *wall* (from its uprightness):—wall.

847. אֶשְׁתָּאֹל **'Eshtâ'ôl**, *esh-taw-ole'*; or אֶשְׁתָּאוֹל **'Eshtâ'ôwl**, *esh-taw-ole'*; prob. from 7592; *intreaty*; *Eshtaol*, a place in Pal.:—Eshtaol.

848. אֶשְׁתָּאֻלִי **'Eshtâ'ûlîy**, *esh-taw-oo-lee'*; patrial from 847; an *Eshtaolite* (collect.) or inhab. of Eshtaol:—Eshtaulites.

849. אֶשְׁתַּדּוּר **'eshtaddûwr** (Chald.), *esh-tad-dure'*; from 7712 (in a bad sense); *rebellion*:—sedition.

850. אֶשְׁתּוֹן **'Eshtôwn**, *esh-tone'*; prob. from the same as 7764; *restful*; *Eshton*, an Isr.:—Eshton.

851. אֶשְׁתְּמֹעַ **'Esht^emôa'**, *esh-tem-o'-ah*; or אֶשְׁתְּמוֹעַ **'Esht^emôwa'**, *esh-tem-o'-ah*; or אֶשְׁתְּמֹה **'Esht^emôh**, *esh-tem-o'*; from 8085 (in the sense of *obedience*); *Eshtemoa* or *Eshtemoh*, a place in Pal.:—Eshtemoa, Eshtemoh.

אַתְּ° **'ath**. See 859.

852. אָת **'âth** (Chald.), *awth*; corresp. to 226; a *portent*:—sign.

853. אֵת **'êth**, *ayth*; appar. contr. from 226 in the demonstr. sense of *entity*; prop. *self* (but gen. used to point out more def. the object of a verb or prep., *even* or *namely*):—[*as such unrepresented in English.*]

854. אֵת **'êth**, *ayth*; prob. from 579; prop. *nearness* (used only as a prep. or adv.), *near*; hence gen. *with*, *by*, *at*, *among*, etc.:—against, among, before, by, for, from, in (-to), (out) of, with. Often with another prep. prefixed.

855. אֵת **'êth**, *ayth*; of uncert. der.; a *hoe* or other digging implement:—coulter, plowshare.

אַתָּ **'attâ**. See 859.

אָתָא **'âthâ'**. See 857.

856. אֶתְבַּעַל **'Ethba'al**, *eth-bah'-al*; from 854 and 1168; *with Baal*; *Ethbaal*, a Phœnician king:—Ethbaal.

857. אָתָה **'âthâh**, *aw-thaw'*; or אָתָא **'âthâ'**, *aw-thaw'*; a prim. root [collat. to 225 contr.]; to *arrive*:—(be-, things to) come (upon), bring.

858. אָתָה **'âthâh** (Chald.), *aw-thaw'*; or אָתָא **'âthâ'** (Chald.), *aw-thaw'*; corresp. to 857:—(be-) come, bring.

859. אַתָּה **'attâh**, *at-taw'*; or (short.) אַתָּ **'attâ**, *at-taw'*; or אַתְּ° **'ath**, *ath*; fem. (irreg.) sometimes אַתִּי **'attîy**, *at-tee'*; plur. masc. אַתֶּם **'attem**, *at-tem'*; fem. אַתֶּן **'atten**, *at-ten'*; or אַתֵּנָה **'attênâh**, *at-tay'-naw*; or אַתֵּנָּה **'attênnâh**, *at-tane'-naw*; a prim. pron. of the sec. pers.; *thou* and *thee*, or (plur.) *ye* and *you*:—thee, thou, ye, you.

860. אָתוֹן **'athôwn**, *aw-thone'*; prob. from the same as 386 (in the sense of *patience*); a female *ass* (from its docility):—(she) ass.

861. אַתּוּן **'attûwn** (Chald.), *at-toon'*; prob. from the corresp. to 784; prob. a *fire-place*, i.e. *furnace*:—furnace.

862. אַתּוּק **'attûwq**, *at-tooke'*; or אַתִּיק **'attîyq**, *at-teek'*; from 5423 in the sense of *decreasing*; a *ledge* or offset in a building:—gallery.

אַתִּי **'attîy**. See 859.

863. אִתַּי **'Ittay**, *it-tah'ee*; or אִיתַי **'Iythay**, *ee-thah'ee*; from 854; *near*; *Ittai* or *Ithai*, the name of a Gittite and of an Isr.:—Ithai, Ittai.

864. אֵתָם **'Êthâm**, *ay-thawm'*; of Eg. der.; *Etham*, a place in the Desert:—Etham.

אַתֶּם **'attem**. See 859.

865. אֶתְמוֹל **'ethmôwl**, *eth-mole'*; or אִתְמוֹל **'ithmôwl**, *ith-mole'*; or אֶתְמוּל **'ethmûwl**, *eth-mool'*; prob. from 853 or 854 and 4136; *heretofore*; def. *yesterday*:— + before (that) time, + heretofore, of late (old), + times past, yester[day].

אַתֶּן **atten**. See 859.

866. אֶתְנָה **'ethnâh**, *eth-naw'*; from 8566; a *present* (as the price of harlotry):—reward.

אַתֵּנָה **'attênâh**, or אַתֵּנָּה **'attênnâh**. See 859.

867. אֶתְנִי **'Ethnîy**, *eth-nee'*; perh. from 866; *munificence*; *Ethni*, an Isr.:—Ethni.

868. אֶתְנַן **'ethnan**, *eth-nan'*; the same as 866; a *gift* (as the price of harlotry or idolatry):—hire, reward.

869. אֶתְנַן **'Ethnan**, *eth-nan'*; the same as 868 in the sense of 867; *Ethnan*, an Isr.:—Ethnan.

870. אֲתַר **'âthar** (Chald.), *ath-ar'*; from a root corresp. to that of 871; a *place*; (adv.) *after*:—after, place.

871. אֲתָרִים **'Âthârîym**, *ath-aw-reem'*; plur. from an unused root (prob. mean. to *step*); *places*; *Atharim*, a place near Pal.:—spies.

ב

872. בְּאָה **b^e'âh**, *bĕ-aw'*; from 935; an *entrance* to a building:—entry.

873. בִּאוּשׁ **bî'ûwsh** (Chald.) *be-oosh'*; from 888; *wicked*:—bad.

874. בָּאַר **bâ'ar**, *baw-ar'*; a prim. root; to *dig*; by anal. to *engrave*; fig. to *explain*:—declare, (make) plain (-ly).

875. בְּאֵר **b^e'êr**, *bĕ-ayr'*; from 874; a *pit*; espec. a *well*:—pit, well.

876. בְּאֵר **B^e'êr**, *bĕ-ayr'*; the same as 875; *Beër*, a place in the Desert, also one in Pal.:—Beer.

877. בֹּאר **bô'r**, *bore*; from 874; a *cistern*:—cistern.

878. בְּאֵרָא **B^e'êrâ'**, *bĕ-ay-raw'*; from 875; a *well*; *Beëra*, an Isr.:—Beera.

879. בְּאֵר אֵלִים **B^e'êr 'Êlîym**, *bĕ-ayr' ay-leem'*; from 875 and the plur. of 410; *well of heroes*; *Beër-Elim*, a place in the Desert:—Beer-elim.

880. בְּאֵרָה **B^e'êrâh**, *bĕ-ay-raw'*; the same as 878; *Beërah*, an Isr.:—Beerah.

881. בְּאֵרוֹת **B^e'êrôwth**, *bĕ-ay-rohth'*; fem. plur. of 875; *wells*; *Beëroth*, a place in Pal.:—Beeroth.

882. בְּאֵרִי **B^e'êrîy**, *bĕ-ay-ree'*; from 875; *fountained*; *Beëri*, the name of a Hittite and of an Isr.:—Beeri.

883. בְּאֵר לַחַי רֹאִי **B^e'êr la-Chay Rô'îy**, *bĕ-ayr' lakh-ah'ee ro-ee'*; from 875 and 2416 (with pref.) and 7203; *well of a living* (One) *my Seer*; *Beër-Lachai-Roï*, a place in the Desert:—Beer-lahai-roi.

884. בְּאֵר שֶׁבַע **B^e'êr Sheba'**, *bĕ-ayr' sheh'-bah*; from 875 and 7651 (in the sense of 7650); *well of an oath*; *Beër-Sheba*, a place in Pal.:—Beer-shebah.

885. בְּאֵרֹת בְּנֵי־יַעֲקָן **B^eêrôth B^enêy-Ya'ăqan**, *bĕ-ay-roth' bĕ-nay' yah-a-can'*; from the fem. plur. of 875, and the plur. contr. of 1121, and 3292; *wells of* (the) *sons of Jaakan*; *Beeroth-Bene-Jaakan*, a place in the Desert:—Beeroth of the children of Jaakan.

886. בְּאֵרֹתִי **B^e'êrôthîy**, *bĕ-ay-ro-thee'*; patrial from 881; a *Beërothite* or inhab. of Beëroth:—Beerothite.

887. בָּאַשׁ **bâ'ash**, *baw-ash'*; a prim. root; to *smell* bad; fig. to *be offensive* morally:—(make to) be abhorred (had in abomination, loathsome, odious), (cause a, make to) stink (-ing savour), × utterly.

888. בְּאֵשׁ **b^e'êsh** (Chald.), *bĕ-aysh'*; corresp. to 887:—displease.

889. בְּאשׁ **b^e'ôsh**, *bĕ-oshe'*; from 877; a *stench*:—stink.

890. בָּאְשָׁה **bo'shâh**, *bosh-aw'*; fem. of 889; *stink-weed* or any other noxious or useless plant:—cockle.

891. בְּאֻשִׁים **b^e'ûshîym**, *bĕ-oo-sheem'*; plur. of 889; *poison-berries*:—wild grapes.

892. בָּבָה **bâbâh**, *baw-baw'*; fem. act. part. of an unused root mean. to *hollow* out; something *hollowed* (as a *gate*), i.e. the *pupil* of the eye:—apple [of the eye].

893. בֵּבַי **Bêbay**, *bay-bah'ee*; prob. of for. or.; *Bebai*, an Isr.:—Bebai.

894. בָּבֶל **Bâbel**, *baw-bel'*; from 1101; *confusion*; *Babel* (i.e. Babylon), including Babylonia and the Bab. empire:—Babel, Babylon.

895. בָּבֶל **Bâbel** (Chald.), *baw-bel'*; corresp. to 894:—Babylon.

896. בַּבְלִי **Bablîy** (Chald.), *bab-lee'*; patrial from 895; a *Babylonian*:—Babylonia.

897. בג **bag**, *bag;* a Pers. word; *food:*—spoil [*from the marg. for* 957.]

898. בגד **bâgad**, *baw-gad';* a prim. root; to *cover* (with a garment); fig. to *act covertly;* by impl. to *pillage:*—deal deceitfully (treacherously, unfaithfully), offend, transgress (-or), (depart), treacherous (dealer, -ly, man), unfaithful (-ly, man), × very.

899. בגד **beged**, *behg'-ed;* from 898; a *covering*, i.e. clothing; also *treachery* or *pillage:*—apparel, cloth (-es, -ing), garment, lap, rag, raiment, robe, × very [treacherously], vesture, wardrobe.

900. בגדות **bôgᵉdôwth**, *bohg-ed-ôhth;* fem. plur. act. part. of 898; *treacheries:*—treacherous.

901. בגוד **bâgôwd**, *baw-gode';* from 898; *treacherous:*—treacherous.

902. בגוי **Bigvay**, *big-vah'ee;* prob. of for. or.; *Bigvai*, an Isr.:—Bigvai.

903. בגתא **Bigthâ'**, *big-thaw';* of Pers. der.; *Bigtha*, a eunuch of Xerxes:—Bigtha.

904. בגתן **Bigthân**, *big-thawn';* or בגתנא **Bigthânâ'**, *big-thaw'-naw;* of similar deriv. to 903; *Bigthan* or *Bigthana*, a eunuch of Xerxes:—Bigthan, Bigthana.

905. בד **bad**, *bad;* from 909; prop. *separation;* by impl. a *part* of the body, *branch* of a tree, *bar* for carrying; fig. *chief* of a city; espec. (with prep. pref.) as adv., *apart, only, besides:*—alone, apart, bar, besides, branch, by self, of each alike, except, only, part, staff, strength.

906. בד **bad**, *bad;* perh. from 909 (in the sense of *divided* fibres); flaxen *thread* or *yarn;* hence a *linen* garment:—linen.

907. בד **bad**, *bad;* from 908; a *brag* or *lie;* also a *liar:*—liar, lie.

908. בדא **bâdâ'**, *baw-daw';* a prim. root; (fig.) to *invent:*—devise, feign.

909. בדד **bâdad**, *baw-dad';* a prim. root; to *divide*, i.e. (reflex.) *be solitary:*—alone.

910. בדד **bâdâd**, *baw-dawd';* from 909; *separate;* adv. *separately:*—alone, desolate, only, solitary.

911. בדד **Bᵉdad**, *bed-ad';* from 909; *separation; Bedad*, an Edomite:—Bedad.

912. בדיה **Bêdᵉyâh**, *bay-dĕ-yaw';* prob. shortened for 5662; *servant of Jehovah; Bedejah*, an Isr.:—Bedeiah.

913. בדיל **bᵉdîyl**, *bed-eel';* from 914; *alloy* (because *removed* by smelting); by anal. *tin:*—+ plummet, tin.

914. בדל **bâdal**, *baw-dal';* a prim. root; to *divide* (in var. senses lit. or fig., *separate, distinguish, differ, select,* etc.):—(make, put) difference, divide (asunder), (make) separate (self, -ation), sever (out), × utterly.

915. בדל **bâdâl**, *baw-dawl';* from 914; a *part:*—piece.

916. בדלח **bᵉdôlach**, *bed-o'-lakh;* prob. from 914; something in *pieces*, i.e. *bdellium*, a (fragrant) gum (perh. *amber*); others a *pearl:*—bdellium.

917. בדן **Bᵉdân**, *bed-awn';* prob. short. for 5658; *servile; Bedan*, the name of two Isr.:—Bedan.

918. בדק **bâdaq**, *baw-dak';* a prim. root; to *gap* open; used only as a denom. from 919; to *mend* a breach:—repair.

919. בדק **bedeq**, *beh'-dek;* from 918; a *gap* or *leak* (in a building or a ship):—breach, + calker.

920. בדקר **Bidqar**, *bid-car';* prob. from 1856 with prep. pref.; *by stabbing*, i.e. *assassin; Bidkar*, an Isr.:—Bidkar.

921. בדר **bᵉdar** (Chald.), *bed-ar';* corresp. (by transp.) to 6504; to *scatter:*—scatter.

922. בהו **bôhûw**, *bo'-hoo;* from an unused root (mean. to *be empty*); a *vacuity*, i.e. (superficially) an undistinguishable *ruin:*—emptiness, void.

923. בהט **bahaṭ**, *bah'-hat;* from an unused root (prob. mean. to *glisten*); white *marble* or perh. *alabaster:*—red [marble].

924. בהילו **bᵉhîylûw** (Chald.), *bĕ-hee-loo';* from 927; a *hurry;* only adv. *hastily:*—in haste.

925. בהיר **bâhîyr**, *baw-here';* from an unused root (mean. to *be bright*); *shining:*—bright.

926. בהל **bâhal**, *baw-hal';* a prim. root; to *tremble* inwardly (or *palpitate*), i.e. (fig.) *be* (caus. *make*) (suddenly) *alarmed* or *agitated;* by impl. to *hasten* anxiously:—be (make) affrighted (afraid, amazed, dismayed, rash), (be, get, make) haste (-n, -y, -ily), (give) speedy (-ily), thrust out, trouble, vex.

927. בהל **bᵉhal** (Chald.), *bĕ-hal';* corresp. to 926; to *terrify, hasten:*—in haste, trouble.

928. בהלה **behâlâh**, *beh-haw-law';* from 926; *panic, destruction:*—terror, trouble.

929. בהמה **bᵉhêmâh**, *bĕ-hay-maw';* from an unused root (prob. mean. to be *mute*); prop. a *dumb* beast; espec. any large quadruped or *animal* (often collect.):—beast, cattle.

930. בהמות **bᵉhêmôwth**, *bĕ-hay-mōhth';* in form a plur. of 929, but really a sing. of Eg. der.; a *water-ox*, i.e. the *hippopotamus* or Nile-horse:—Behemoth.

931. בהן **bôhen**, *bo'-hen;* from an unused root appar. mean. to *be thick;* the *thumb* of the hand or *great toe* of the foot:—thumb, great toe.

932. בהן **Bôhan**, *bo'-han;* an orth. var. of 931; *thumb; Bohan*, an Isr.:—Bohan.

933. בהק **bôhaq**, *bo'-hak;* from an unused root mean. to *be pale;* white *scurf:*—freckled spot.

934. בהרת **bôhereth**, *bo-heh'-reth;* fem. act. part. of the same as 925; a *whitish* spot on the skin:—bright spot.

935. בוא **bôw'**, *bo;* a prim. root; to *go* or *come* (in a wide variety of applications):—abide, apply, attain, × be, befall, + besiege, bring (forth, in, into, to pass), call, carry, × certainly, (cause, let, thing for) to come (against, in, out, upon, to pass), depart, × doubtless again, + eat, + employ, (cause to) enter (in, into, -tering, -trance, -try), be fallen, fetch, + follow, get, give, go (down, in, to war), grant, + have, × indeed, [in-]vade, lead, lift [up], mention, pull in, put, resort, run (down), send, set, × (well) stricken [in age], × surely, take (in), way.

בוב **bûwb.** See 892, 5014.

936. בוז **bûwz**, *booz;* a prim. root; to *disrespect:*—contemn, despise, × utterly.

937. בוז **bûwz**, *booz;* from 936; *disrespect:*—contempt (-uously), despised, shamed.

938. בוז **Bûwz**, *booz;* the same as 937; *Buz*, the name of a son of Nahor, and of an Isr.:—Buz.

939. בוזה **bûwzâh**, *boo-zaw';* fem. pass. part. of 936; something *scorned;* an object of *contempt:*—despised.

940. בוזי **Bûwzîy**, *boo-zee';* patron. from 938; a *Buzite* or desc. of Buz:—Buzite.

941. בוזי **Bûwzîy**, *boo-zee';* the same as 940, *Buzi*, an Isr.:—Buzi.

942. בוי **Bavvay**, *bav-vah'ee;* prob. of Pers. or.; *Bavvai*, an Isr.:—Bavai.

943. בוך **bûwk**, *book;* a prim. root; to *involve* (lit. or fig.):—be entangled (perplexed).

944. בול **bûwl**, *bool;* for 2981; *produce* (of the earth, etc.):—food, stock.

945. בול **Bûwl**, *bool;* the same as 944 (in the sense of *rain*); *Bul*, the eighth Heb. month:—Bul.

בום **bûwm.** See 1116.

946. בונה **Bûwnâh**, *boo-naw';* from 995; *discretion; Bunah*, an Isr.:—Bunah.

בוני **Bûwnîy.** See 1138.

947. בוס **bûwç**, *boos;* a prim. root; to *trample* (lit. or fig.):—loath, tread (down, under [foot]), be polluted.

948. בוץ **bûwts**, *boots;* from an unused root (of the same form) mean. to *bleach*, i.e. (intrans.) *be white;* prob. *cotton* (of some sort):—fine (white) linen.

949. בוצץ **Bôwtsêts**, *bo-tsates';* from the same as 948; *shining; Botsets*, a rock near Michmash:—Bozez.

950. בוקה **bûwqâh**, *boo-kaw';* fem. pass. part. of an unused root (mean. to *be hollow*); *emptiness* (as adj.):—empty.

951. בוקר **bôwkêr**, *bo-kare';* prop. act. part. from 1239 as denom. from 1241; a *cattle-tender:*—herdman.

952. בור **bûwr**, *boor;* a prim. root; to *bore*, i.e. (fig.) *examine:*—declare.

953. בור **bôwr**, *bore;* from 952 (in the sense of 877); a pit *hole* (espec. one used as a *cistern* or *prison*):—cistern, dungeon, fountain, pit, well.

954. בוש **bûwsh**, *boosh;* a prim. root; prop. to *pale*, i.e. by impl. to *be ashamed;* also (by impl.) to *be disappointed*, or *delayed:*—(be, make, bring to, cause, put to, with, a-) shame (-d), be (put to) confounded (-fusion), become dry, delay, be long.

955. בושה **bûwshâh**, *boo-shaw';* fem. part. pass. of 954; *shame:*—shame.

956. בות **bûwth** (Chald.), *booth;* appar. denom. from 1005; to *lodge* over night:—pass the night.

957. בז **baz**, *baz;* from 962; *plunder:*—booty, prey, spoil (-ed).

958. בזא **bâzâ'**, *baw-zaw';* a prim. root; prob. to *cleave:*—spoil.

959. בזה **bâzâh**, *baw-zaw';* a prim. root; to *disesteem:*—despise, disdain, contemn (-ptible), + think to scorn, vile person.

960. בזה **bâzôh**, *baw-zo';* from 959; *scorned:*—despise.

961. בזה **bizzâh**, *biz-zaw';* fem. of 957; *booty:*—prey, spoil.

962. בזז **bâzaz**, *baw-zaz';* a prim. root; to *plunder:*—catch, gather, (take) for a prey, rob (-ber), spoil, take (away, spoil), × utterly.

963. בזיון **bizzâyôwn**, *biz-zaw-yone';* from 959:—*disesteem:*—contempt.

964. בזיותיה **bizyôwthᵉyâh**, *biz-yo-thĕ-yaw';* from 959 and 3050; *contempts of Jah; Bizjothjah*, a place in Pal.:—Bizjothjah.

965. בזק **bâzâq**, *baw-zawk';* from an unused root mean. to *lighten;* a *flash* of lightning:—flash of lightning.

966. בזק **Bezeq**, *beh'-zek;* from 965; *lightning; Bezek*, a place in Pal.:—Bezek.

967. בזר **bâzar**, *baw-zar';* a prim. root; to *disperse:*—scatter.

968. בזתא **Bizthâ'**, *biz-thaw';* of Pers. or.; *Biztha*, a eunuch of Xerxes:—Biztha.

969. בחון **bâchôwn'**, *baw-khone';* from 974; an *assayer* of metals:—tower.

970. בחור **bâchûwr**, *baw-khoor';* or בחר **bâchûr**, *baw-khoor';* part. pass. of 977; prop. *selected*, i.e. a *youth* (often collect.):—(choice) young (man), chosen, × hole.

בחורות **bᵉchûwrôwth.** See 979.

בחורים **Bachûwrîym.** See 980.

971. בחין **bachîyn**, *bakh-een';* another form of 975; a watch-*tower* of besiegers:—tower.

972. בחיר **bâchîyr**, *baw-kheer';* from 977; *select:*—choose, chosen one, elect.

973. בחל **bâchal**, *baw-khal';* a prim. root; to *loathe:*—abhor, get hastily [*from the marg. for* 926].

974. בחן **bâchan**, *baw-khan';* a prim. root; to *test* (espec. metals); gen. and fig. to *investigate:*—examine, prove, tempt, try (trial).

975. בחן **bachan**, *bakh'-an;* from 974 (in the sense of keeping a *look-out*); a watch-*tower:*—tower.

976. בחן **bôchan**, *bo'-khan;* from 974; *trial:*—tried.

977. בחר **bâchar**, *baw-khar';* a prim. root; prop. to *try*, i.e. (by impl.) *select:*—acceptable, appoint, choose (choice), excellent, join, be rather, require.

בחר **bâchûr.** See 970.

978. בחרומי **Bachărûwmîy**, *bakh-ar-oo-mee';* patrial from 980 (by transp.); a *Bacharumite* or inhab. of Bachurim:—Baharumite.

979. בחרות **bᵉchûrôwth**, *bekh-oo-rothe';* or בחורות **bᵉchûwrôwth**, *bekh-oo-roth';* fem. plur. of 970; also (masc. plur.) בחרים **bᵉchûrîym**, *bekh-oo-reem';* *youth* (collect. and abstr.):—young men, youth.

980. בַּחֻרִים **Bachûrîym**, *bakh-oo-reem'*; or בַּחוּרִים **Bachûwrîym**, *bakh-oo-reem'*; masc. plur. of 970; *young men; Bachurim*, a place in Pal.:—Bahurim.

981. בָּטָא **bâṭâʼ**, *baw-taw'*; or בָּטָה **bâṭâh**, *baw-taw'*; a prim. root; to *babble;* hence to *vociferate* angrily:—pronounce, speak (unadvisedly).

982. בָּטַח **bâṭach**, *baw-takh'*; a prim. root; prop. to *hie* for refuge [but not so *precipitately* as 2620]; fig. to *trust*, be *confident* or *sure:*—be bold (confident, secure, sure), careless (one, woman), put confidence, (make to) hope, (put, make to) trust.

983. בֶּטַח **beṭach**, *beh'-takh*; from 982; prop. a place of *refuge;* abstr. *safety*, both the fact (*security*) and the feeling (*trust*); often (adv. with or without prep.) *safely:*—assurance, boldly, (without) care (-less), confidence, hope, safe (-ly, -ty), secure, surely.

984. בֶּטַח **Beṭach**, *beh'-takh;* the same as 983; *Betach*, a place in Syria:—Betah.

985. בִּטְחָה **biṭchâh**, *bit-khaw'*; fem. of 984; *trust:*—confidence.

986. בִּטָּחוֹן **biṭṭâchôwn**, *bit-taw-khone'*; from 982; *trust:*—confidence, hope.

987. בַּטֻּחוֹת **baṭṭûchôwth**, *bat-too-khōth'*; fem. plur. from 982; *security:*—secure.

988. בָּטֵל **bâṭêl**, *baw-tale'*; a prim. root; to *desist* from labor:—cease.

989. בְּטֵל **beṭêl** (Chald.), *bet-ale'*; corresp. to 988; to *stop:*—(cause, make to), cease, hinder.

990. בֶּטֶן **beṭen**, *beh'-ten*; from an unused root prob. mean. to *be hollow;* the *belly*, espec. the *womb;* also the *bosom* or *body* of anything:—belly, body, + as they be born, + within, womb.

991. בֶּטֶן **Beṭen**, *beh'-ten;* the same as 990; *Beten*, a place in Pal.:—Beten.

992. בֹּטֶן **bôṭen**, *bo'-ten;* from 990; (only in plur.) a *pistachio*-nut (from its form):—nut.

993. בְּטֹנִים **Beṭônîym**, *bet-o-neem'*; prob. plur. from 992; *hollows: Betonim*, a place in Pal.:—Betonim.

994. בִּי **bîy**, *bee;* perh. from 1158 (in the sense of *asking*); prop. a *request;* used only adv. (always with "my Lord"); *Oh that!; with leave*, or *if it please:*—alas, O, oh.

995. בִּין **bîyn**, *bene;* a prim. root; to *separate* mentally (or *distinguish*), i.e. (gen.) *understand:*—attend, consider, be cunning, diligently, direct, discern, eloquent, feel, inform, instruct, have intelligence, know, look well to, mark, perceive, be prudent, regard, (can) skill (-ful), teach, think, (cause, make to, get, give, have) understand (-ing), view, (deal) wise (-ly, man).

996. בֵּין **bêyn**, *bane* (sometimes in the plur. masc. or fem.); prop. the constr. contr. form of an otherwise unused noun from 995; a *distinction;* but used only as a prep., *between* (repeated before each noun, often with other particles); also as a conj., *either . . . or:*—among, asunder, at, between (-twixt . . . and), + from (the widest), × in, out of, whether (it be . . . or), within.

997. בֵּין **bêyn** (Chald.), *bane;* corresp. to 996:—among, between.

998. בִּינָה **bîynâh**, *bee-naw'*; from 995; *understanding:*—knowledge, meaning, × perfectly, understanding, wisdom.

999. בִּינָה **bîynâh** (Chald.), *bee-naw'*; corresp. to 998:—knowledge.

1000. בֵּיצָה **bêytsâh**, *bay-tsaw'*; from the same as 948; an *egg* (from its whiteness):—egg.

1001. בִּירָא **bîyrâʼ** (Chald.), *bee-raw'*; corresp. to 1002; a *palace:*—palace.

1002. בִּירָה **bîyrâh**, *bee-raw'*; of for. or.; a *castle* or *palace:*—palace.

1003. בִּירָנִית **bîyrânîyth**, *bee-raw-neeth'*; from 1002; a *fortress:*—castle.

1004. בַּיִת **bayith**, *bah'-yith;* prob. from 1129 abbrev.; a *house* (in the greatest var. of applications, espec. *family*, etc.):—court, daughter, door, + dungeon, family, + forth of, × great as would contain, hangings, home[born], [winter]house (-hold), inside (-ward), palace, place, + prison, + steward, + tablet, temple, web, + within (-out).

1005. בַּיִת **bayith** (Chald.), *bah-yith;* corresp. to 1004:—house.

1006. בַּיִת **Bayith**, *bah'-yith;* the same as 1004; *Bajith*, a place in Pal.:—Bajith.

1007. בֵּית אָוֶן **Bêyth ʼÂven**, *bayth aw'-ven;* from 1004 and 205; *house of vanity; Beth-Aven*, a place in Pal.:—Beth-aven.

1008. בֵּית־אֵל **Bêyth-ʼÊl**, *bayth-ale';* from 1004 and 410; *house of God; Beth-El*, a place in Pal.:—Beth-el.

1009. בֵּית אַרְבֵּאל **Bêyth ʼArbêʼl**, *bayth arbale'*; from 1004 and 695 and 410; *house of God's ambush; Beth-Arbel*, a place in Pal.:—Beth-Arbel.

1010. בֵּית בַּעַל מְעוֹן **Bêyth Baʻal Meʻôwn**, *bayth bah'-al mĕ-own'*; from 1004 and 1168 and 4583; *house of Baal of* (the) *habitation of* [appar. by transp.]; or (shorter) בֵּית מְעוֹן **Bêyth Meʻôwn**, *bayth mĕ-own'*; *house of habitation of* (Baal); *Beth-Baal-Meön*, a place in Pal.:—Beth-baal-meon. Comp. 1186 and 1194.

1011. בֵּית בִּרְאִי **Bêyth Birʼîy**, *bayth bir-ee';* from 1004 and 1254; *house of a creative* one; *Beth-Biri*, a place in Pal.:—Beth-birei.

1012. בֵּית בָּרָה **Bêyth Bârâh**, *bayth baw-raw'*; prob. from 1004 and 5679; *house of* (the) *ford; Beth-Barah*, a place in Pal.:—Beth-barah.

1013. בֵּית־גָּדֵר **Bêyth-Gâdêr**, *bayth-gaw-dare';* from 1004 and 1447; *house of* (the) *wall; Beth-Gader*, a place in Pal.:—Beth-gader.

1014. בֵּית גָּמוּל **Bêyth Gâmûwl**, *bayth gaw-mool';* from 1004 and the pass. part. of 1576; *house of* (the) *weaned; Beth-Gamul*, a place E. of the Jordan:—Beth-gamul.

1015. בֵּית דִּבְלָתַיִם **Bêyth Diblâthayim**, *bayth dib-law-thah'-yim;* from 1004 and the dual of 1690; *house of* (the) *two figcakes; Beth-Diblathajim*, a place E. of the Jordan:—Beth-diblathaim.

1016. בֵּית־דָּגוֹן **Bêyth-Dâgôwn**, *bayth-daw-gohn';* from 1004 and 1712; *house of Dagon; Beth-Dagon*, the name of two places in Pal.:—Beth-dagon.

1017. בֵּית הָאֱלִי **Bêyth hâ-ʼĔlîy**, *bayth haw-el-ee';* patrial from 1008 with the art. interposed; a *Beth-elite*, or inhab. of Bethel:—Bethelite.

1018. בֵּית הָאֵצֶל **Bêyth hâ-ʼêtsel**, *bayth haw-ay'-tsel;* from 1004 and 681 with the art. interposed; *house of the side; Beth-ha-Etsel*, a place in Pal.:—Beth-ezel.

1019. בֵּית הַגִּלְגָּל **Bêyth hag-Gilgâl**, *bayth hag-gil gawl';* from 1004 and 1537 with the article interposed; *house of the Gilgal* (or *rolling*); *Beth-hag-Gilgal*, a place in Pal.:—Beth-gilgal.

1020. בֵּית הַיְשִׁימוֹת **Bêyth ha-Yeshîymôwth**, *bayth hah-yesh-ee-mōth';* from 1004 and the plur. of 3451 with the art. interposed; *house of the deserts; Beth-ha-Jeshimoth*, a town E. of the Jordan:—Beth-jeshimoth.

1021. בֵּית הַכֶּרֶם **Bêyth hak-Kerem**, *bayth hak-keh'-rem;* from 1004 and 3754 with the art. interposed; *house of the vineyard; Beth-hak-Kerem*, a place in Pal.:—Beth-haccerem.

1022. בֵּית הַלַּחְמִי **Bêyth hal-Lachmîy**, *bayth hal-lakh-mee';* patrial from 1035 with the art. ins.; a *Beth-lechemite*, or native of Bethlechem:—Bethlehemite.

1023. בֵּית הַמֶּרְחָק **Bêyth ham-Merchâq**, *bayth ham-mer-khawk';* from 1004 and 4801 with the art. interposed; *house of the breadth; Beth-ham-Merchak*, a place in Pal.:—place that was far off.

1024 בֵּית הַמַּרְכָּבוֹת **Bêyth ham-Markâbôwth**, *bayth ham-mar-kaw-both';* or (short.) בֵּית מַרְכָּבוֹת **Bêyth Markâbôwth**, *bayth mar-kaw-both';* from 1004 and the plur. of 4818 (with or without the art. interposed); *place of* (the) *chariots; Beth-ham-Markaboth* or *Beth-Markaboth*, a place in Pal.:—Beth-marcaboth.

1025. בֵּית הָעֵמֶק **Bêyth hâ-ʻÊmeq**, *bayth haw-Ay'-mek;* from 1004 and 6010 with the art. interposed; *house of the valley; Beth-ha-Emek*, a place in Pal.:—Beth-emek.

1026. בֵּית הָעֲרָבָה **Bêyth hâ-ʻĂrâbâh**, *bayth haw-ar-aw-baw';* from 1004 and 6160 with the art. interposed; *house of the Desert, Beth-ha-Arabah*, a place in Pal.:—Beth-arabah.

1027. בֵּית הָרָם **Bêyth hâ-Râm**, *bayth haw-rawm';* from 1004 and 7311 with the art. interposed; *house of the height; Beth-ha-Ram*, a place E. of the Jordan:—Beth-aram.

1028. בֵּית הָרָן **Bêyth hâ-Rân**, *bayth haw-rawn';* prob. for 1027; *Beth-ha Ran*, a place E. of the Jordan:—Beth-haran.

1029. בֵּית הַשִּׁטָּה **Bêyth hash-Shiṭṭâh**, *bayth hash-shit-taw';* from 1004 and 7848 with the art. interposed; *house of the acacia; Beth-hash-Shittah*, a place in Pal.:—Beth-shittah.

1030. בֵּית הַשִּׁמְשִׁי **Bêyth hash-Shimshîy**, *bayth hash-shim-shee';* patrial from 1053 with the art. inserted; a *Beth-shimshite*, or inhab. of Bethshemesh:—Bethshemite.

1031. בֵּית חָגְלָה **Bêyth Choglâh**, *bayth chog-law';* from 1004 and the same as 2295; *house of a partridge; Beth-Choglah*, a place in Pal.:—Beth-hoglah.

1032. בֵּית חוֹרוֹן **Bêyth Chôwrôwn**, *bayth kho-rone';* from 1004 and 2356; *house of hollowness; Beth-Choron*, the name of two adjoining places in Pal.:—Beth-horon.

בֵּית חָנָן **Bêyth Chânân**. See 358.

1033. בֵּית כַּר **Bêyth Kar**, *bayth kar;* from 1004 and 3733; *house of pasture; Beth-Car*, a place in Pal.:—Beth-car.

1034. בֵּית לְבָאוֹת **Bêyth Lebâʼôwth**, *bayth leb-aw-ōth';* from 1004 and the plur. of 3833; *house of lionesses; Beth-Lebaoth*, a place in Pal.:—Beth-lebaoth. Comp. 3822.

1035. בֵּית לֶחֶם **Bêyth Lechem**, *bayth leh'-khem;* from 1004 and 3899; *house of bread; Beth-Lechem*, a place in Pal.:—Beth-lehem.

1036. בֵּית לְעַפְרָה **Bêyth le-ʻAphrâh**, *bayth lĕ-af-raw';* from 1004 and the fem. of 6083 (with prep. interposed); *house to* (i.e. *of*) *dust; Beth-le-Aphrah*, a place in Pal.:—house of Aphrah.

1037. בֵּית מִלּוֹא **Bêyth Millôwʼ**, *bayth mil-lo';* or בֵּית מִלֹּא **Bêyth Millôʼ**, *bayth mil-lo';* from 1004 and 4407; *house of* (the) *rampart; Beth-Millo*, the name of two citadels:—house of Millo.

1038. בֵּית מַעֲכָה **Bêyth Maʻăkâh**, *bayth mah-ak-aw';* from 1004 and 4601; *house of Maakah; Beth-Maakah*, a place in Pal.:—Beth-maachah.

1039. בֵּית נִמְרָה **Bêyth Nimrâh**, *bayth nim-raw';* from 1004 and the fem. of 5246; *house of* (the) *leopard; Beth-Nimrah*, a place east of the Jordan:—Beth-nimrah. Comp. 5247.

1040. בֵּית עֵדֶן **Bêyth ʻÊden**, *bayth ay'-den;* from 1004 and 5730; *house of pleasure; Beth-Eden*, a place in Syria:—Beth-eden.

1041. בֵּית עַזְמָוֶת **Bêyth ʻAzmâveth**, *bayth az-maw'-veth;* from 1004 and 5820; *house of Azmaveth*, a place in Pal.:—Beth-azmaveth. Comp. 5820.

1042. בֵּית עֲנוֹת **Bêyth ʻĂnôwth**, *bayth an-ōth';* from 1004 and a plur. from 6030; *house of replies; Beth-Anoth*, a place in Pal.:—Beth-anoth.

1043. בֵּית עֲנָת **Bêyth ʻÂnâth**, *bayth an-awth';* an orth. var. for 1042; *Beth-Anath*, a place in Pal.:—Beth-anath.

1044. בֵּית עֵקֶד **Bêyth ʻÊqed**, *bayth ay'-ked;* from 1004 and a deriv. of 6123; *house of* (the) *binding* (for sheep-shearing); *Beth-Eked*, a place in Pal.:—shearing-house.

1045. בֵּית עַשְׁתָּרוֹת **Bêyth** **ʿAshtârôwth,** bayth ash-taw-rōth'; from 1004 and 6252; house of Ashtoreths; Beth-Ashtaroth, a place in Pal.:—house of Ashtaroth. Comp. 1203, 6252.

1046. בֵּית פֶּלֶט **Bêyth Pelet,** bayth peh'-let; from 1004 and 6412; house of escape; Beth-Palet, a place in Pal.:—Beth-palet.

1047. בֵּית פְּעוֹר **Bêyth Peʿôwr,** bayth pĕ-ore'; from 1004 and 6465; house of Peor; Beth-Peor, a place E. of the Jordan:—Beth-peor.

1048. בֵּית פַּצֵּץ **Bêyth Patstsêts,** bayth pats-tsates'; from 1004 and a der. from 6327; house of dispersion; Beth-Patstsets, a place in Pal.:—Beth-pazzez.

1049. בֵּית צוּר **Bêyth Tsûwr,** bayth tsoor'; from 1004 and 6697; house of (the) rock; Beth-Tsur, a place in Pal.:—Beth-zur.

1050. בֵּית רְחוֹב **Bêyth Rᵉchôwb,** bayth rĕ-khobe'; from 1004 and 7339; house of (the) street; Beth-Rechob, a place in Pal.:—Beth-rehob.

1051. בֵּית רָפָא **Bêyth Râphâʾ,** bayth raw-faw'; from 1004 and 7497; house of (the) giant; Beth-Rapha, an Isr.:—Beth-rapha.

1052. בֵּית שְׁאָן **Bêyth Sheʾân,** bayth shĕ-awn'; or בֵּית שָׁן **Bêyth Shân,** bayth shawn'; from 1004 and 7599; house of ease; Beth-Shean or Beth-Shan, a place in Pal.:—Beth-shean, Beth-Shan.

1053. בֵּית שֶׁמֶשׁ **Bêyth Shemesh,** bayth sheh'-mesh; from 1004 and 8121; house of (the) sun; Beth-Shemesh, a place in Pal.:—Beth-shemesh.

1054. בֵּית תַּפּוּחַ **Bêyth Tappûwach,** bayth tap-poo'-akh; from 1004 and 8598; house of (the) apple; Beth-Tappuach, a place in Pal.:—Beth-tappuah.

1055. בִּיתָן **bîythân,** bee-thawn'; prob. from 1004; a palace (i.e. large house):—palace.

1056. בָּכָא **Bâkâʾ,** baw-kaw'; from 1058; weeping; Baca, a valley in Pal.:—Baca.

1057. בָּכָא **bâkâʾ,** baw-kaw'; the same as 1056; the weeping tree (some gum-distilling tree, perh. the balsam):—mulberry tree.

1058. בָּכָה **bâkâh,** baw-kaw'; a prim. root; to weep; gen. to bemoan:—× at all, bewail, complain, make lamentation, × more, mourn, × sore, × with tears, weep.

1059. בֶּכֶה **bekeh,** beh'-keh; from 1058; a weeping:—× sore.

1060. בְּכוֹר **bᵉkôwr,** bek-ore'; from 1069; first-born; hence chief:—eldest (son), firstborn (-ling).

1061. בִּכּוּר **bikkûwr,** bik-koor'; from 1069; the first-fruits of the crop:—first fruit (-ripe [fig.]), hasty fruit.

1062. בְּכוֹרָה **bᵉkôwrâh,** bek-o-raw'; or (short.) בְּכֹרָה **bᵉkôrâh,** bek-o-raw'; fem. of 1060; the firstling of man or beast; abstr. primogeniture:—birthright, firstborn (-ling).

1063. בִּכּוּרָה **bikkûwrâh,** bik-koo-raw'; fem. of 1061; the early fig:—firstripe (fruit).

1064. בְּכוֹרַת **Bᵉkôwrath,** bek-o-rath'; fem. of 1062; primogeniture; Bekorath, an Isr.:—Bechorath.

1065. בְּכִי **bᵉkîy,** bek-ee'; from 1058; a weeping; by analogy, a dripping:—overflowing, × sore, (continual) weeping, wept.

1066. בֹּכִים **Bôkîym,** bo-keem'; plur. act. part. of 1058; (with the art.) the weepers; Bokim, a place in Pal.:—Bochim.

1067. בְּכִירָה **bᵉkîyrâh,** bek-ee-raw'; fem. from 1069; the eldest daughter:—firstborn.

1068. בְּכִית **bᵉkîyth,** bek-eeth'; from 1058; a weeping:—mourning.

1069. בָּכַר **bâkar,** baw-kar'; a prim. root; prop. to burst the womb, i.e. (caus.) bear or make early fruit (of woman or tree); also (as denom. from 1061) to give the birthright:—make firstborn, be firstling, bring forth first child (new fruit).

1070. בֶּכֶר **beker,** beh'-ker; from 1069 (in the sense of youth); a young camel:—dromedary.

1071. בֶּכֶר **Beker,** beh'-ker; the same as 1070; Beker, the name of two Isr.:—Becher.

1072. בִּכְרָה **bikrâh,** bik-raw'; fem. of 1070; a young she-camel:—dromedary.

בְּכֹרָה **bᵉkôrâh.** See 1062.

1073. בַּכֻּרָה **bakkûrâh,** bak-koo-raw'; by orth. var. for 1063; a first-ripe fig:—first-ripe.

1074. בֹּכְרוּ **Bôkᵉrûw,** bo-ker-oo'; from 1069; first-born; Bokeru, an Isr.:—Bocheru.

1075. בִּכְרִי **Bikrîy,** bik-ree'; from 1069; youthful; Bikri, an Isr.:—Bichri.

1076. בַּכְרִי **Bakrîy,** bak-ree'; patron. from 1071; a Bakrite (collect.) or desc. of Beker:—Bachrites.

1077. בַּל **bal,** bal; from 1086; prop. a failure; by impl. nothing; usually (adv.) not at all; also lest:—lest, neither, no, none (that . . .), not (any), nothing.

1078. בֵּל **Bêl,** bale; by contr. for 1168; Bel, the Baal of the Babylonians:—Bel.

1079. בָּל **bâl** (Chald.), bawl; from 1080; prop. anxiety, i.e. (by impl.) the heart (as its seat):—heart.

1080. בְּלָא **bᵉlâ** (Chald.), bel-aw'; corresp. to 1086 (but used only in a mental sense); to afflict:—wear out.

1081. בַּלְאֲדָן **Balʾadân,** bal-ad-awn'; from 1078 and 113 (contr.); Bel (is his) lord; Bal-adan, the name of a Bab. prince:—Baladan.

1082. בָּלַג **bâlag,** baw-lag'; a prim. root; to break off or loose (in a favorable or unfavorable sense), i.e. desist (from grief) or invade (with destruction):—comfort, (recover) strength (-en).

1083. בִּלְגָּה **Bilgâh,** bil-gaw'; from 1082; desistance; Bilgah, the name of two Isr.:—Bilgah.

1084. בִּלְגַּי **Bilgay,** bil-gah'ee; from 1082; desistant; Bilgai, an Isr.:—Bilgai.

1085. בִּלְדַּד **Bildad,** bil-dad'; of uncert. der.; Bildad, one of Job's friends:—Bildad.

1086. בָּלָה **bâlâh,** baw-law'; a prim. root; to fail; by impl. to wear out, decay (caus. consume, spend):—consume, enjoy long, become (make, wax) old, spend, waste.

1087. בָּלֶה **bâleh,** baw-leh'; from 1086; worn out:—old.

1088. בָּלָה **Bâlâh,** baw-law'; fem. of 1087; failure; Balah, a place in Pal.:—Balah.

1089. בָּלַהּ **bâlahh,** baw-lah'; a prim. root [rather by transp. for 926]; to palpitate; hence (caus.) to terrify:—trouble.

1090. בִּלְהָה **Bilhâh,** bil-haw'; from 1089; timid; Bilhah, the name of one of Jacob's concubines; also of a place in Pal.:—Bilhah.

1091. בַּלָּהָה **ballâhâh,** bal-law-haw'; from 1089; alarm; hence destruction:—terror, trouble.

1092. בִּלְהָן **Bilhân,** bil-hawn'; from 1089; timid; Bilhan, the name of an Edomite and of an Isr.:—Bilhan.

1093. בְּלוֹ **bᵉlôw** (Chald.), bel-o'; from a root corresp. to 1086; excise (on articles consumed):—tribute.

1094. בְּלוֹא **bᵉlôwʾ,** bel-o'; or (fully) בְּלוֹי **bᵉlôwy,** bel-o'ee; from 1086; (only in plur. constr.) rags:—old.

1095. בֵּלְטְשַׁאצַּר **Bêlᵉtshaʾtstsar,** bale-tesh-ats-tsar'; of for. der.; Belteshatstsar, the Bab. name of Daniel:—Belteshazzar.

1096. בֵּלְטְשַׁאצַּר **Bêlᵉtshaʾtstsar** (Chald.), bale-tesh-ats-tsar'; corresp. to 1095:—Belteshazzar.

1097. בְּלִי **bᵉlîy,** bel-ee'; from 1086; prop. failure, i.e. nothing or destruction; usually (with prep.) without, not yet, because not, as long as, etc.:—corruption, ig[norantly], for lack of, where no . . . is, so that no, none, not, un[awares], without.

1098. בְּלִיל **belîyl,** bel-eel'; from 1101; mixed, i.e. (spec.) feed (for cattle):—corn, fodder, provender.

1099. בְּלִימָה **bᵉlîymâh,** bel-ee-mah'; from 1097 and 4100; (as indef.) nothing whatever:—nothing.

1100. בְּלִיַּעַל **bᵉlîyaʿal,** bel-e-yah'-al; from 1097 and 3276; without profit, worthlessness; by extens. destruction, wickedness (often in connection with 376, 802, 1121, etc.):—Belial, evil, naughty, ungodly (men), wicked.

1101. בָּלַל **bâlal,** baw-lal'; a prim. root; to overflow (spec. with oil); by impl. to mix; also (denom. from 1098) to fodder:—anoint, confound, × fade, mingle, mix (self), give provender, temper.

1102. בָּלַם **bâlam,** baw-lam'; a prim. root; to muzzle:—be held in.

1103. בָּלַס **bâlac,** baw-las'; a prim. root; to pinch sycamore figs (a process necessary to ripen them):—gatherer.

1104. בָּלַע **bâlaʿ,** baw-lah'; a prim. root; to make away with (spec. by swallowing); gen. to destroy:—cover, destroy, devour, eat up, be at end, spend up, swallow down (up).

1105. בֶּלַע **belaʿ,** beh'-lah; from 1104; a gulp; fig. destruction:—devouring, that which he hath swallowed up.

1106. בֶּלַע **Belaʿ,** beh'-lah; the same as 1105; Bela, the name of a place, also of an Edomite and of two Isr.:—Bela.

1107. בִּלְעֲדֵי **bilʿadêy,** bil-ad-ay'; or בַּלְעֲדֵי **balʿadêy,** bal-ad-ay'; constr. plur. from 1077 and 5703; not till, i.e. (as prep. or adv.) except, without, besides:—beside, not (in), save, without.

1108. בַּלְעִי **Balʿîy,** bel-ee'; patronym. from 1106: a Belaite (collect.) or desc. of Bela:—Belaites.

1109. בִּלְעָם **Bilʿâm,** bil-awm'; prob. from 1077 and 5971; not (of the) people, i.e. foreigner; Bilam, a Mesopotamian prophet; also a place in Pal.:—Balaam, Bileam.

1110. בָּלַק **bâlaq,** baw-lak'; a prim. root; to annihilate:—(make) waste.

1111. בָּלָק **Bâlâq,** baw-lawk'; from 1110; waster; Balak, a Moabitish king:—Balak.

1112. בֵּלְשַׁאצַּר **Bêlshaʾtstsar,** bale-shats-tsar'; or בֵּלְאשַׁצַּר **Bêlʾshatstsar,** bale-shats-tsar'; of for. or. (comp. 1095); Belshatstsar, a Bab. king:—Belshazzar.

1113. בֵּלְשַׁאצַּר **Bêlshaʾtstsar** (Chald.), bale-shats-tsar'; corresp. to 1112:—Belshazzar.

1114. בִּלְשָׁן **Bilshân,** bil-shawn'; of uncert. der.; Bilshan, an Isr.:—Bilshan.

1115. בִּלְתִּי **biltîy,** bil-tee'; constr. fem. of 1086 (equiv. to 1097); prop. a failure of, i.e. (used only as a neg. particle, usually with prep. pref.) not, except, without, unless, besides, because not, until, etc.:—because un[satiable], beside, but, + continual, except, from, lest, neither, no more, none, not, nothing, save, that no, without.

1116. בָּמָה **bâmâh,** baw-maw'; from an unused root (mean. to be high); an elevation:—height, high place, wave.

1117. בָּמָה **Bâmâh,** baw-maw'; the same as 1116; Bamah, a place in Pal.:—Bamah. See also 1120.

1118. בִּמְהָל **Bimhâl,** bim-hawl'; prob. from 4107 with prep. pref.; with pruning; Bimhal, an Isr.:—Bimhal.

1119. בְּמוֹ **bᵉmôw,** bem-o'; prol. for prep. pref.; in, with, by, etc.:—for, in, into, through.

1120. בָּמוֹת **Bâmôwth,** baw-moth'; plur. of 1116; heights; or (fully) בָּמוֹת בַּעַל **Bâmôwth Baʿal,** baw-moth' bah'-al; from the same and 1168; heights of Baal; Bamoth or Bamoth-Baal, a place E. of the Jordan:—Bamoth, Bamoth-baal.

1121. בֵּן **bên,** bane; from 1129; a son (as a builder of the family name), in the widest sense (of lit. and fig. relationship, including grandson, subject, nation, quality or condition, etc.), [like 1, 251, etc.]:—+ afflicted, age, [Ahoh-] [Ammon-] [Hachmon-] [Lev-]ite, [anoint-]ed one, appointed to, (+) ar-

row, [Assyr-] [Babylon-] [Egypt-] [Grec-]ian, one born, bough, branch, breed, + (young) bullock, + (young) calf, × came up in, child, colt, × common, × corn, daughter, × of first, + firstborn, foal, + very fruitful, + postage, × in, + kid, + lamb, (+) man, meet, + mighty, + nephew, old, (+) people, + rebel, + robber, × servant born, × soldier, son, + spark, + steward, + stranger, × surely, them of, + tumultuous one, + valiant[-est], whelp, worthy, young (one), youth.

1122. בֵּן **Bên**, *bane;* the same as 1121; *Ben*, an Isr.:—Ben.

1123. בֵּן **bên** (Chald.), *bane;* corresp. to 1121:—child, son, young.

1124. בְּנָא **bᵉnâʼ** (Chald.), *ben-aw';* or

בְּנָה **bᵉnâh** (Chald.), *ben-aw';* corresp. to 1129; to *build:*—build, make.

1125. בֶּן־אֲבִינָדָב **Ben-ʼĂbîynâdâb**, *ben-ab-ee"-naw-dawb';* from 1121 and 40; (the) *son of Abinadab; Ben-Abinadab*, an Isr.:—the son of Abinadab.

1126. בֶּן־אוֹנִי **Ben-ʼÔwnîy**, *ben-o-nee';* from 1121 and 205; *son of my sorrow; Ben-Oni*, the original name of Benjamin:—Ben-oni.

1127. בֶּן־גֶּבֶר **Ben-Geber**, *ben-gheh'-ber;* from 1121 and 1397; *son of* (the) *hero; Ben-Geber*, an Isr.:—the son of Geber.

1128. בֶּן־דֶּקֶר **Ben-Deqer**, *ben-deh'-ker;* from 1121 and a der. of 1856; *son of piercing* (or *of a lance*); *Ben-Deker*, an Isr.:—the son of Dekar.

1129. בָּנָה **bânâh**, *baw-naw';* a prim. root; to *build* (lit. and fig.):—(begin to) build (-er), obtain children, make, repair, set (up), × surely.

1130. בֶּן־הֲדַד **Ben-Hădad**, *ben-had-ad';* from 1121 and 1908; *son of Hadad; Ben-Hadad*, the name of several Syrian kings:—Ben-hadad.

1131. בִּנּוּי **Binnûwy**, *bin-noo'ee;* from 1129; *built up; Binnui*, an Isr.:—Binnui.

1132. בֶּן־זוֹחֵת **Ben-Zôwchêth**, *ben-zo-khayth';* from 1121 and 2105; *son of Zocheth; Ben-Zocheth*, an Isr.:—Ben-zoketh.

1133. בֶּן־חוּר **Ben-Chûwr**, *ben-khoor';* from 1121 and 2354; *son of Chur; Ben-Chur*, an Isr.:—the son of Hur.

1134. בֶּן־חַיִל **Ben-Chayil**, *ben-khah'-yil;* from 1121 and 2428; *son of might; Ben-Chail*, an Isr.:—Ben-hail.

1135. בֶּן־חָנָן **Ben-Chânân**, *ben-khaw-nawn';* from 1121 and 2605; *son of Chanan; Ben-Chanan*, an Isr.:—Ben-hanan.

1136. בֶּן־חֶסֶד **Ben-Cheçed**, *ben-kheh'-sed;* from 1121 and 2617; *son of kindness; Ben-Chesed*, an Isr.:—the son of Hesed.

1137. בָּנִי **Bânîy**, *baw-nee';* from 1129; *built; Bani*, the name of five Isr.:—Bani.

1138. בֻּנִּי **Bunnîy**, *boon-nee';* or (fuller)

בּוּנִי **Bûwnîy**, *boo-nee';* from 1129; *built; Bunni* or *Buni*, an Isr.:—Bunni.

1139. בְּנֵי־בְרַק **Bᵉnêy-Bᵉraq**, *ben-ay'-ber-ak';* from the plur. constr. of 1121 and 1300; *sons of lightning, Bene-berak*, a place in Pal.:—Bene-barak.

1140. בִּנְיָה **binyâh**, *bin-yaw';* fem. from 1129; a *structure:*—building.

1141. בְּנָיָה **Bᵉnâyâh**, *ben-aw-yaw';* or (prol.)

בְּנָיָהוּ **Bᵉnâyâhûw**, *ben-aw-yaw'-hoo;* from 1129 and 3050; *Jah has built; Benajah*, the name of twelve Isr.:—Benaiah.

1142. בְּנֵי יַעֲקָן **Bᵉnêy Yaʻăqân**, *ben-ay' yah-ak-awn';* from the plur. of 1121 and 3292; *sons of Yaakan; Bene-Jaakan*, a place in the Desert:—Bene-jaakan.

1143. בֵּנַיִם **bênayim**, *bay-nah'-yim;* dual of 996; a *double interval*, i.e. the space between two armies:—+ champion.

1144. בִּנְיָמִין **Binyâmîyn**, *bin-yaw-mene';* from 1121 and 3225; *son of* (the) *right hand; Binjamin*, youngest son of Jacob; also the tribe descended from him, and its territory:—Benjamin.

1145. בֶּן־יְמִינִי **Ben-yᵉmîynîy**, *ben-yem-ee-nee';* sometimes (with the art. ins.)

בֶּן־הַיְמִינִי **Ben-ha-yᵉmînîy**, *ben-hah-yem-ee-nee';* with 376 ins. (1 Sam. 9 : 1)

בֶּן־אִישׁ יְמִינִי **Ben-ʼÎysh Yᵉmîynîy**, *ben-eesh' yem-ee-nee'; son of a man of Jemini;* or short. (1 Sam. 9 : 4; Esth. 2 : 5)

אִישׁ יְמִינִי **ʼÎysh Yᵉmîynîy**, *eesh yem-ee-nee'; a man of Jemini;* or (1 Sam. 20 : 1) simply

יְמִינִי **Yᵉmînîy**, *yem-ee-nee'; a Jeminite;* (plur.

בְּנֵי יְמִינִי **Bᵉnîy Yᵉmîynîy**, *ben-ay' yem-ee-nee';*) patron. from 1144; a *Benjaminite*, or descendant of Benjamin:—Benjamite, of Benjamin.

1146. בִּנְיָן **binyân**, *bin-yawn';* from 1129; an *edifice:*—building.

1147. בִּנְיָן **binyân** (Chald.), *bin-yawn';* corresp. to 1146:—building.

1148. בְּנִינוּ **Bᵉnîynûw**, *ben-ee-noo';* prob. from 1121 with pron. suff.; *our son; Beninu*, an Isr.:—Beninu.

1149. בְּנַס **bᵉnaç** (Chald.), *ben-as';* of uncert. affin.; to *be enraged:*—be angry.

1150. בִּנְעָא **Binʻâʼ**, *bin-aw';* or

בִּנְעָה **Binʻâh**, *bin-aw';* of uncert. der.; *Bina* or *Binah*, an Isr.:—Binea, Bineah.

1151. בֶּן־עַמִּי **Ben-ʻAmmîy**, *ben-am-mee';* from 1121 and 5971 with pron. suff.; *son of my people; Ben-Ammi*, a son of Lot:—Ben-ammi.

1152. בְּסוֹדְיָה **Bᵉçôwdᵉyâh**, *bes-o-deh-yaw';* from 5475 and 3050 with prep. pref.; *in* (the) *counsel of Jehovah; Besodejah*, an Isr.:—Besodeiah.

1153. בְּסַי **Bᵉçay**, *bes-ah'-ee;* from 947; *domineering; Besai*, one of the Nethinim:—Besai.

1154. בֶּסֶר **bêçer**, *beh'-ser;* from an unused root mean. to *be sour;* an *immature* grape:—unripe grape.

1155. בֹּסֶר **bôçer**, *bo'-ser;* from the same as 1154:—sour grape.

1156. בְּעָא **bᵉʻâʼ** (Chald.), *beh-aw';* or

בְּעָה **bᵉʻâh** (Chald.), *beh-aw';* corresp. to 1158; to *seek* or *ask:*—ask, desire, make [petition], pray, request, seek.

1157. בְּעַד **bᵉʻad**, *beh-ad';* from 5704 with prep. pref.; *in up to* or *over against;* gen. *at, beside, among, behind, for*, etc.:—about, at, by (means of), for, over, through, up (-on), within.

1158. בָּעָה **bâʻâh**, *baw-aw';* a prim. root; to *gush* over, i.e. to *swell;* (fig.) to *desire* earnestly; by impl. to *ask:*—cause, inquire, seek up, swell out, boil.

1159. בָּעוּ **bâʻûw** (Chald.), *baw-oo';* from 1156; a *request:*—petition.

1160. בְּעוֹר **Bᵉʻôwr**, *beh-ore';* from 1197 (in the sense of *burning*); a *lamp; Beör*, the name of the father of an Edomitish king; also of that of Balaam:—Beor.

1161. בִּעוּתִים **biʻûwthîym**, *be-oo-theme';* masc. plur. from 1204; *alarms:*—terrors.

1162. בֹּעַז **Bôʻaz**, *bo'-az;* from an unused root of uncert. mean.; *Boaz*, the ancestor of David; also the name of a pillar in front of the temple:—Boaz.

1163. בָּעַט **bâʻaṭ**, *baw-at';* a prim. root; to *trample* down, i.e. (fig.) *despise:*—kick.

1164. בְּעִי **bᵉʻîy**, *beh-ee';* from 1158; a *prayer:*—grave.

1165. בְּעִיר **bᵉʻîyr**, *beh-ere';* from 1197 (in the sense of *eating*): cattle:—beast, cattle.

1166. בָּעַל **bâʻal**, *baw-al';* a prim. root; to *be master;* hence (as denom. from 1167) to *marry:*—Beulah have dominion (over), be husband, marry (-ried, × wife).

1167. בַּעַל **baʻal**, *bah'-al;* from 1166; a *master;* hence a *husband*, or (fig.) *owner* (often used with another noun in modifications of this latter sense):—+ archer, + babbler, + bird, captain, chief man, + confederate, + have to do, + dreamer, those to whom it is due, + furious, those that are given to it, great, + hairy, he that hath it, have, + horseman, husband, lord, man, + married, master, person, + sworn, they of.

1168. בַּעַל **Baʻal**, *bah'-al;* the same as 1167; *Baal*, a Phœnician deity:—Baal, [*plur.*] Baalim.

1169. בְּעֵל **bᵉʻêl** (Chald.), *beh-ale';* corresp. to 1167:—+ chancellor.

1170. בַּעַל בְּרִית **Baʻal Bᵉrîyth**, *bah'-al ber-eeth';* from 1168 and 1285; *Baal of* (the) *covenant; Baal-Berith*, a special deity of the Shechemites:—Baal-berith.

1171. בַּעַל גָּד **Baʻal Gâd**, *bah'-al gawd;* from 1168 and 1409; *Baal of Fortune; Baal-Gad*, a place in Syria:—Baal-gad.

1172. בַּעֲלָה **baʻălâh**, *bah-al-aw';* fem. of 1167; a *mistress:*—that hath, mistress.

1173. בַּעֲלָה **Baʻălâh**, *bah-al-aw';* the same as 1172; *Baalah*, the name of three places in Pal.:—Baalah.

1174. בַּעַל הָמוֹן **Baʻal Hâmôwn**, *bah'-al haw-mone';* from 1167 and 1995; *possessor of a multitude; Baal-Hamon*, a place in Pal.:—Baal-hamon.

1175. בְּעָלוֹת **Bᵉʻâlôwth**, *beh-aw-lōth';* plur. of 1172; *mistresses; Beäloth*, a place in Pal.:—Bealoth, in Aloth [*by mistake for a plur. from* 5927 *with prep. pref.*].

1176. בַּעַל זְבוּב **Baʻal Zᵉbûwb**, *bah'-al zeb-oob';* from 1168 and 2070; *Baal of* (the) *Fly; Baal-Zebub*, a special deity of the Ekronites:—Baal-zebub.

1177. בַּעַל חָנָן **Baʻal Chânân**, *bah'-al khaw-nawn';* from 1167 and 2603; *possessor of grace; Baal-Chanan*, the name of an Edomite, also of an Isr.:—Baal-hanan.

1178. בַּעַל חָצוֹר **Baʻal Châtsôwr**, *bah'-al khaw-tsore';* from 1167 and a modif. of 2691; *possessor of a village; Baal-Chatsor*, a place in Pal.:—Baal-hazor.

1179. בַּעַל חֶרְמוֹן **Baʻal Chermôwn**, *bah'-al kher-mone';* from 1167 and 2768; *possessor of Hermon; Baal-Chermon*, a place in Pal.:—Baal-hermon.

1180. בַּעֲלִי **Baʻălîy**, *bah-al-ee';* from 1167 with pron. suff.; *my master; Baali*, a symbolical name for Jehovah:—Baali.

1181. בַּעֲלֵי בָמוֹת **Baʻălêy Bâmôwth**, *bah-al-ay' baw-mōth';* from the plur. of 1168 and the plur. of 1116; *Baals of* (the) *heights; Baale-Bamoth*, a place E. of the Jordan:—lords of the high places.

1182. בְּעֶלְיָדָע **Bᵉʻelyâdâʻ**, *beh-el-yaw-daw';* from 1168 and 3045; *Baal has known; Beëljada*, an Isr.:—Beeliada.

1183. בְּעַלְיָה **Bᵉʻalyâh**, *beh-al-yaw';* from 1167 and 3050; *Jah* (is) *master; Bealjah*, an Isr.:—Bealiah.

1184. בַּעֲלֵי יְהוּדָה **Baʻălêy Yᵉhûwdâh**, *bah-al-ay' yeh-hoo-daw';* from the plur. of 1167 and 3063; *masters of Judah; Baale-Judah*, a place in Pal.:—Baale of Judah.

1185. בַּעֲלִס **Baʻăliç**, *bah-al-ece';* prob. from a der. of 5965 with prep. pref.; *in exultation; Baalis*, an Ammonitish king:—Baalis.

1186. בַּעַל מְעוֹן **Baʻal Mᵉʻôwn**, *bah-al meh-one';* from 1168 and 4583; *Baal of* (the) *habitation* (of) [comp. 1010]; *Baal-Meön*, a place E. of the Jordan:—Baal-meon.

1187. בַּעַל פְּעוֹר **Baʻal Pᵉʻôwr**, *bah'-al peh-ore';* from 1168 and 6465; *Baal of Peor; Baal-Peör*, a Moabitish deity:—Baal-peor.

1188. בַּעַל פְּרָצִים **Baʻal Pᵉrâtsîym**, *bah'-al per-aw-tseem';* from 1167 and the plur. of 6556; *possessor of breaches; Baal-Peratsim*, a place in Pal.:—Baal-perazim.

1189. בַּעַל צְפוֹן **Baʻal Tsᵉphôwn**, *bah'-al tsef-one';* from 1168 and 6828 (in the sense of *cold*) [according to others an Eg. form of *Typhon*, the destroyer]; *Baal of winter; Baal-Tsephon*, a place in Egypt:—Baal-zephon.

1190. בַּעַל שָׁלִשָׁה **Ba'al Shâlîshâh**, *bah'-al shaw-lee-shaw'*; from 1168 and 8031; *Baal of Shalishah; Baal-Shalishah*, a place in Pal.:—Baal-shalisha.

1191. בַּעֲלָת **Ba'ălâth**, *bah-al-awth'*; a modif. of 1172; *mistressship; Baalath*, a place in Pal.:—Baalath.

1192. בַּעֲלַת בְּאֵר **Ba'ălath Be'êr**, *bah-al-ath' beh-ayr'*; from 1172 and 875; *mistress of a well; Baalath-Beër*, a place in Pal.:—Baalath-beer.

1193. בַּעַל תָּמָר **Ba'al Tâmâr**, *bah'-al taw-mawr'*, from 1167 and 8558; *possessor of* (the) *palm-tree; Baal-Tamar*, a place in Pal.:—Baal-tamar.

1194. בְּעֹן **Be'ôn**, *beh-ohn'*; prob. a contr. of 1010; *Beön*, a place E. of the Jordan:—Beon.

1195. בַּעֲנָא **Ba'ănâ'**, *bah-an-aw'*; the same as 1196; *Baana*, the name of four Isr.:—Baana, Baanah.

1196. בַּעֲנָה **Ba'ănâh**, *bah-an-aw'*; from a der. of 6031 with prep. pref.; *in affliction:—Baanah*, the name of four Isr.:—Baanah.

1197. בָּעַר **bâ'ar**, *baw-ar'*; a prim. root; to *kindle*, i.e. *consume* (by fire or by eating); also (as denom. from 1198) to *be (-come) brutish:*—be brutish, bring (put, take) away, burn, (cause to) eat (up), feed, heat, kindle, set ([on fire]), waste.

1198. בַּעַר **ba'ar**, *bah'-ar*; from 1197; prop. *food* (as *consumed*); i.e. (by exten.) of cattle *brutishness;* (concr.) *stupid:*—brutish (person), foolish.

1199. בַּעֲרָא **Bâ'ărâ'**, *bah-ar-aw'*; from 1198; *brutish; Baara*, an Israelitish woman:—Baara.

1200. בְּעֵרָה **be'êrâh**, *bĕ-ay-raw'*; from 1197; a *burning:*—fire.

1201. בַּעְשָׁא **Ba'shâ'**, *bah-shaw'*; from an unused root mean. to *stink; offensiveness; Basha*, a king of Israel:—Baasha.

1202. בַּעֲשֵׂיָה **Ba'ăsêyâh**, *bah-as-ay-yaw'*; from 6213 and 3050 with prep. pref.; *in* (the) *work of Jah; Baasejah*, an Isr.:—Baaseiah.

1203. בְּעֶשְׁתְּרָה **Be'eshterâh**, *beh-esh-ter-aw'*; from 6251 (as sing. of 6252) with prep. pref.; *with Ashtoreth; Beështerah*, a place E. of the Jordan:—Beeshterah.

1204. בָּעַת **bâ'ath**, *baw-ath'*; a prim. root; to *fear:*—affright, be (make) afraid, terrify, trouble.

1205. בְּעָתָה **be'âthâh**, *beh-aw-thaw'*; from 1204; *fear:*—trouble.

1206. בֹּץ **bôts**, *botse*; prob. the same as 948; *mud* (as *whitish* clay):—mire.

1207. בִּצָּה **bitstsâh**, *bits-tsaw'*; intens. from 1206; a *swamp:*—fen, mire (-ry place).

1208. בָּצוֹר° **bâtsôwr**, *baw-tsore'*; from 1219; *inaccessible*, i.e. *lofty:*—vintage [*by confusion with* 1210].

1209. בֵּצַי **Bêtsay**, *bay-tsah'ee*; perh. the same as 1153; *Betsai*, the name of two Isr.:—Bezai.

1210. בָּצִיר **bâtsîyr**, *baw-tseer'*; from 1219; *clipped*, i.e. the *grape crop:*—vintage.

1211. בְּצֶל **betsel**, *beh'-tsel*; from an unused root appar. mean. to *peel;* an *onion:*—onion.

1212. בְּצַלְאֵל **Betsal'êl**, *bets-al-ale'*; prob. from 6738 and 410 with prep. pref.; *in* (the) *shadow* (i.e. protection) *of God; Betsalel;* the name of two Isr.:—Bezaleel.

1213. בַּצְלוּת **Batslûwth**, *bats-looth'*; or
בַּצְלִית **Batslîyth**, *bats-leeth'*; from the same as 1211; a *peeling; Batsluth* or *Batslith;* an Isr.:—Bazlith, Bazluth.

1214. בָּצַע **bâtsa'**, *baw-tsah'*; a prim. root to *break* off, i.e. (usually) *plunder*; fig. to *finish*, or (intrans.) *stop:*—(be) covet (-ous), cut (off), finish, fulfill, gain (greedily), get, be given to [covetousness], greedy, perform, be wounded.

1215. בֶּצַע **betsa'**, *beh'-tsah*; from 1214; *plunder;* by extens. *gain* (usually unjust):—covetousness, (dishonest) gain, lucre, profit.

1216. בָּצֵק **bâtsêq**, *baw-tsake'*; a prim. root; perh. to *swell* up, i.e. *blister:*—swell.

1217. בָּצֵק **bâtsêq**, *baw-tsake'*; from 1216; *dough* (as *swelling* by fermentation):—dough, flour.

1218. בָּצְקַת **Botsqath**, *bots-cath'*; from 1216; a *swell* of ground; *Botscath*, a place in Pal.:—Bozcath, Boskath.

1219. בָּצַר **bâtsar**, *baw-tsar'*; a prim. root; to *clip* off; spec. (as denom. from 1210) to *gather* grapes; also to *be isolated* (i.e. *inaccessible* by height or fortification):—cut off, (de-) fenced, fortify, (grape) gather (-er), mighty things, restrain, strong, wall (up), withhold.

1220. בֶּצֶר **betser**, *beh'-tser*; from 1219; strictly a *clipping*, i.e. *gold* (as *dug* out):—gold defence.

1221. בֶּצֶר **Betser**, *beh'-tser*; the same as 1220. an *inaccessible* spot; *Betser*, a place in Pal.; also an Isr.:—Bezer.

1222. בְּצַר **betsar**, *bets-ar'*; another form for 1220; *gold:*—gold.

1223. בָּצְרָה **botsrâh**, *bots-raw'*; fem. from 1219; an *enclosure*, i.e. *sheep-fold:*—Bozrah.

1224. בָּצְרָה **Botsrâh**, *bots-raw'*; the same as 1223; *Botsrah*, a place in Edom:—Bozrah.

1225. בִּצָּרוֹן **bitstsârôwn**, *bits-tsaw-rone'*; masc. intens. from 1219; a *fortress:*—stronghold.

1226. בַּצֹּרֶת **batstsôreth**, *bats-tso'-reth*; fem. intens. from 1219; *restraint* (of rain), i.e. *drought:*—dearth, drought.

1227. בַּקְבּוּק **Baqbûwq**, *bak-book'*; the same as 1228; *Bakbuk*, one of the *Nethinim:*—Bakbuk.

1228. בַּקְבֻּק **baqbûk**, *bak-book'*; from 1238; a *bottle* (from the gurgling in *emptying*):—bottle, cruse.

1229. בַּקְבֻּקְיָה **Baqbukyâh**, *bak-book-yaw'*; from 1228 and 3050; *emptying* (i.e. *wasting*) *of Jah; Bakbukjah*, an Isr.:—Bakbukiah.

1230. בַּקְבַּקַּר **Baqbaqqar**, *bak-bak-kar'*; redupl. from 1239; *searcher; Bakbakkar*, an Isr.:—Bakbakkar.

1231. בֻּקִּי **Buqqîy**, *book-kee'*; from 1238; *wasteful; Bukki*, the name of two Isr.:—Bukki.

1232. בֻּקִּיָּהוּ **Buqqîyâh**, *book-kee-yaw'*; from 1238 and 3050; *wasting of Jah; Bukkijah*, an Isr.:—Bukkiah.

1233. בְּקִיעַ **beqîya'**, *bek-ee'-ah*; from 1234; a *fissure:*—breach, cleft.

1234. בָּקַע **bâqa'**, *baw-kah'*; a prim. root; to *cleave;* gen. to *rend, break, rip* or *open:*—make a breach, break forth (into, out, in pieces, through, up), be ready to burst, cleave (asunder), cut out, divide, hatch, rend (asunder), rip up, tear, win.

1235. בֶּקַע **beqa'**, *beh'-kah*; from 1234; a *section* (half) of a shekel, i.e. a *beka* (a weight and a coin):—bekah, half a shekel.

1236. בִּקְעָא **biq'â'** (Chald.), *bik-aw'*; corresp. to 1237:—plain.

1237. בִּקְעָה **biq'âh**, *bik-aw'*; from 1234; prop. a *split*, i.e. a wide level *valley* between mountains:—plain, valley.

1238. בָּקַק **bâqaq**, *baw-kah'*; a prim. root; to *pour* out, i.e. to *empty*, fig. to *depopulate;* by anal. to *spread* out (as a fruitful vine):—(make) empty (out), fail, × utterly, make void.

1239. בָּקַר **bâqar**, *baw-kar'*; a prim. root; prop. to *plough*, or (gen.) *break* forth, i.e. (fig.) to *inspect, admire, care for, consider:*—(make) inquire (-ry), (make) search, seek out.

1240. בְּקַר **beqar** (Chald.), *bek-ar'*; corresp. to 1239:—inquire, make search.

1241. בָּקָר **bâqâr**, *baw-kawr'*; from 1239; a *beeve* or animal of the ox kind of either gender (as used for *ploughing*); collect. a *herd:*—beeve, bull (+ -ock), + calf, + cow, great [cattle], + heifer, herd, kine, ox.

1242. בֹּקֶר **bôqer**, *bo'-ker*; from 1239; prop. *dawn* (as the *break* of day); gen. *morning:*—(+) day, early, morning, morrow.

1243. בַּקָּרָה **baqqârâh**, *bak-kaw-raw'*; intens. from 1239; a *looking after:*—seek out.

1244. בִּקֹּרֶת **biqqôreth**, *bik-ko'-reth*; from 1239; prop. *examination*, i.e. (by impl.) *punishment:*—scourged.

1245. בָּקַשׁ **bâqash**, *baw-kash'*; a prim. root; to *search* out (by any method, spec. in worship or prayer); by impl. to *strive after:*—ask, beg, beseech, desire, enquire, get, make inquisition, procure, (make) request, require, seek (for).

1246. בַּקָּשָׁה **baqqâshâh**, *bak-kaw-shaw'*; from 1245; a *petition:*—request.

1247. בַּר **bar** (Chald.), *bar;* corresp. to 1121; a *son, grandson*, etc.:— × old, son.

1248. בַּר **bar**, *bar;* borrowed (as a title) from 1247; the *heir* (apparent to the throne):—son.

1249. בַּר **bar**, *bar;* from 1305 (in its various senses); *beloved;* also *pure, empty:*—choice, clean, clear, pure.

1250. בָּר **bâr**, *bawr;* or
בַּר **bar**, *bar;* from 1305 (in the sense of *winnowing*): *grain* of any kind (even while standing in the field); by extens. the open *country:*—corn, wheat.

1251. בַּר **bar** (Chald.), *bar;* corresp. to 1250; a *field:*—field.

1252. בֹּר **bôr**, *bore;* from 1305; *purity:*—cleanness, pureness.

1253. בֹּר **bôr**, *bore;* the same as 1252; vegetable *lye* (from its *cleansing*); used as a *soap* for washing, or a *flux* for metals:— × never so, purely.

1254. בָּרָא **bârâ'**, *baw-raw'*; a prim. root; (absol.) to *create;* (qualified) to *cut* down (a wood), *select, feed* (as formative processes):—choose, create (creator), cut down, dispatch, do, make (fat).

1255. בְּרֹאדַךְ בַּלְאֲדָן **Berô'dak Bal'ădân**, *ber-o-dak' bal-ad-awn'*; a var. of 4757; *Berodak-Baladan*, a Bab. king:—Berodach-baladan.

בִּרְאִי **Bir'îy**. See 1011.

1256. בְּרָאיָה **Berâ'yâh**, *ber-aw-yaw'*; from 1254 and 3050; *Jah has created; Berajah*, an Isr.:—Beraiah.

1257. בַּרְבֻּר **barbûr**, *bar-boor'*; by redupl. from 1250; a *fowl* (as fattened on *grain*):—fowl.

1258. בָּרַד **bârad**, *baw-rad'*; a prim. root, to *hail:*—hail.

1259. בָּרָד **bârâd**, *baw-rawd'*; from 1258; *hail:*—hail ([stones]).

1260. בֶּרֶד **Bered**, *beh'-red;* from 1258; *hail; Bered*, the name of a place south of Pal., also of an Isr.:—Bered.

1261. בָּרֹד **bârôd**, *baw-rode'*; from 1258; *spotted* (as if with *hail*):—grisled.

1262. בָּרָה **bârâh**, *baw-raw'*; a prim. root; to *select;* also (as denom. from 1250) to *feed;* also (as equiv. to 1305) to *render clear* (Eccl. 3 : 18):—choose, (cause to) eat, manifest, (give) meat.

1263. בָּרוּךְ **Bârûwk**, *baw-rook'*; pass. part. from 1288; *blessed; Baruk*, the name of three Isr.:—Baruch.

1264. בְּרוֹם **berôwm**, *ber-ome'*; prob. of for. or., *damask* (stuff of variegated thread):—rich apparel.

1265. בְּרוֹשׁ **berôwsh**, *ber-ōsh'*; of uncert. der.; a *cypress* (?) tree; hence a *lance* or a *musical* instrument (as made of that wood):—fir (tree).

1266. בְּרוֹת **berôwth**, *ber-ōth'*; a var. of 1265; the *cypress* (or some elastic tree):—fir.

1267. בָּרוּת **bârûwth**, *baw-rooth'*; from 1262; *food:*—meat.

1268. בֵּרוֹתָה **Bêrôwthâh**, *bay-ro-thaw'*; or
בֵּרֹתַי **Bêrôthay**, *bay-ro-thah'ee;* prob. from 1266; *cypress* or *cypresslike; Berothah* or *Berothai*, a place north of Pal.:—Berothah, Berothai.

1269. בִּרְזוֹת° **Birzôwth**, *beer-zoth'*; prob. fem. plur. from an unused root (appar. mean. to *pierce*); *holes; Birzoth*, an Isr.:– Birzavith [*from the marg.*].

1270. בַּרְזֶל **barzel**, *bar-zel'*; perh. from the root of 1269; *iron* (as *cutting*); by extens. an iron *implement:*—(ax) head, iron.

1271. בַּרְזִלַּי **Barzillay**, *bar-zil-lah'ee;* from 1270; *iron* hearted; *Barzillai*, the name of three Isr.:—Barzillai.

1272. בָּרַח **bârach**, *baw-rakh'*; a prim. root; to *bolt*, i.e. fig. to *flee* suddenly:—chase (away); drive away, fain, flee (away), put to flight, make haste, reach, run away, shoot.

בָּרִחַ **bârîach**. See 1281.

1273. בַּרְחֻמִי **Barchûmîy**, *bar-khoo-mee'*; by transp. for 978; a *Barchumite*, or native of *Bachurim:*—Barhumite.

1274. בְּרִי **b^erîy**, *ber-ee'*; from 1262; *fat:*—fat.

1275. בֵּרִי **Bêrîy**, *bay-ree'*; prob. by contr. from 882; *Beri*, an Isr.:—Beri.

1276. בֵּרִי **Bêrîy**, *bay-ree'*; of uncert. der.; (only in the plur. and with the art.) the *Berites*, a place in Pal.:—Berites.

1277. בָּרִיא **bârîy'**, *baw-ree'*; from 1254 (in the sense of 1262); *fatted* or *plump:*—fat ([fleshed], -ter), fed, firm, plenteous, rank.

1278. בְּרִיאָה **b^erîy'âh**, *ber-ee-aw'*; fem. from 1254; a *creation*, i.e. a *novelty:*—new thing.

1279. בִּרְיָה **biryâh**, *beer-yaw'*; fem. from 1262; *food:*—meat.

1280. בְּרִיחַ **b^erîyach**, *ber-ee'-akh;* from 1272; a *bolt:*—bar, fugitive.

1281. בָּרִיחַ **bârîyach**, *baw-ree'-akh;* or (short.) בָּרִחַ **bâriach**, *baw-ree'-akh;* from 1272; a *fugitive*, i.e. the *serpent* (as *fleeing*), and the constellation by that name:—crooked, noble, piercing.

1282. בָּרִיחַ **Bârîyach**, *baw-ree'-akh;* the same as 1281; *Bariach*, an Isr.:—Bariah.

1283. בְּרִיעָה **B^erîy'âh**, *ber-ee'-aw;* appar. from the fem. of 7451 with prep. pref.; *in trouble; Beriah*, the name of four Isr.:—Beriah.

1284. בְּרִיעִי **B^erîy'îy**, *ber-ee-ee'*; patron. from 1283; a *Beriite* (collect.) or desc. of Beriah:—Beerites.

1285. בְּרִית **b^erîyth**, *ber-eeth':* from 1262 (in the sense of *cutting* [like 1254]); a *compact* (because made by passing between *pieces* of flesh):—confederacy, [con-]feder[-ate], covenant, league.

1286. בְּרִית **B^erîyth**, *ber-eeth'*; the same as 1285; *Berith*, a Shechemitish deity:—Berith.

1287. בֹּרִית **bôrîyth**, *bo-reeth'*; fem. of 1253; vegetable *alkali:*—sope.

1288. בָּרַךְ **bârak**, *baw-rak'*; a prim. root; to *kneel;* by impl. to *bless* God (as an act of adoration), and (vice-versa) man (as a benefit); also (by euphemism) to *curse* (God or the king, as treason):—× abundantly, × altogether, × at all, blaspheme, bless, congratulate, curse, × greatly, × indeed, kneel (down), praise, salute, × still, thank.

1289. בְּרַךְ **b^erak** (Chald.), *ber-ak'*; corresp. to 1288:—bless, kneel.

1290. בֶּרֶךְ **berek**, *beh'-rek;* from 1288; a *knee:*—knee.

1291. בְּרֵךְ **berek** (Chald.), *beh'-rek;* corresp. to 1290:—knee.

1292. בָּרַכְאֵל **Bârak'êl**, *baw-rak-ale';* from 1288 and 410, *God has blessed; Barakel*, the father of one of Job's friends:—Barachel.

1293. בְּרָכָה **B^erâkâh**, *ber-aw-kaw';* from 1288; *benediction;* by impl. *prosperity:*—blessing, liberal, pool, present.

1294. בְּרָכָה **B^erâkâh**, *ber-aw-kaw';* the same as 1293; *Berakah*, the name of an Isr., and also of a valley in Pal.:—Berachah.

1295. בְּרֵכָה **b^erêkâh**, *ber-ay-kaw';* from 1288; a *reservoir* (at which camels *kneel* as a resting-place):—(fish-) pool.

1296. בֶּרֶכְיָה **Berekyâh**, *beh-rek-yaw';* or בֶּרֶכְיָהוּ **Berekyâhûw**, *beh-rek-yaw'-hoo;* from 1290 and 3050; *knee* (i.e. *blessing*) of *Jah; Berekjah*, the name of six Isr.:—Berachiah, Berechiah.

1297. בְּרַם **b^eram**, (Chald.) *ber-am';* perh. from 7313 with prep. pref.; prop. *highly*, i.e. *surely;* but used adversatively, *however:*—but, nevertheless, yet.

1298. בֶּרַע **Bera^c**, *beh'-rah;* of uncert. der.; *Bera*, a Sodomitish king:—Bera.

1299. בָּרַק **bâraq**, *baw-rak';* a prim. root; to *lighten* (lightning):—cast forth.

1300. בָּרָק **bârâq**, *baw-rawk';* from 1299; *lightning;* by anal. a *gleam;* concr. a *flashing* sword:—bright, glitter (-ing, sword), lightning.

1301. בָּרָק **Bârâq**, *baw-rawk';* the same as 1300; *Barak*, an Isr.:—Barak.

1302. בַּרְקוֹס **Barqôwç**, *bar-kose';* of uncert. der.; *Barkos*, one of the Nethimim:—Barkos.

1303. בַּרְקָן **barqân**, *bar-kawn';* from 1300; a *thorn* (perh. as burning *brightly*):—brier.

1304. בָּרֶקֶת **bâreqeth**, *baw-reh'-keth;* or בָּרְקַת **bâr^ekath**, *baw-rek-ath';* from 1300; a gem (as *flashing*), perh. the *emerald:*—carbuncle.

1305. בָּרַר **bârar**, *baw-rar';* a prim. root; to *clarify* (i.e. *brighten*), *examine, select:*—make bright, choice, chosen, cleanse (be clean), clearly, polished, (shew self) pure (-ify), purge (out).

1306. בִּרְשַׁע **Birsha^c**, *beer-shah';* prob. from 7562 with prep. pref.; *with wickedness; Birsha*, a king of Gomorrah:—Birsha.

1307. בֵּרֹתִי **Bêrôthîy**, *bay-ro-thee';* patrial from 1268; a *Berothite*, or inhabitant of Berothai:—Berothite.

1308. בְּשׂוֹר **B^esôwr**, *bes-ore';* from 1319; *cheerful; Besor*, a stream of Pal.:—Besor.

1309. בְּשׂוֹרָה **b^esôwrâh**, *bes-o-raw';* or (short.) בְּשֹׂרָה **b^esôrâh**, *bes-o-raw';* fem. from 1319; glad *tidings;* by impl. *reward for good news:*—reward for tidings.

1310. בָּשַׁל **bâshal**, *baw-shal';* a prim. root; prop. to *boil* up; hence to *be done* in cooking; fig. to *ripen:*—bake, boil, bring forth, is ripe, roast, seethe, sod (be sodden).

1311. בָּשֵׁל **bâshêl**, *baw-shale';* **from 1310**; *boiled:*—× at all, sodden.

1312. בִּשְׁלָם **Bishlâm**, *bish-lawm';* of for. der.; *Bishlam*, a Pers.:—Bishlam.

1313. בָּשָׂם **bâsâm**, *baw-sawm';* from an unused root mean. to *be fragrant;* [comp. 5561] the *balsam* plant:—spice.

1314. בֶּשֶׂם **besem**, *beh'-sem;* or בֹּשֶׂם **bôsem**, *bo'-sem;* from the same as 1313; *fragrance;* by impl. *spicery;* also the *balsam* plant:—smell, spice, sweet (odour).

1315. בָּשְׂמַת **Bosmath**, *bos-math';* fem. of 1314 (the second form); *fragrance; Bosmath*, the name of a wife of Esau, and of a daughter of Solomon:—Bashemath, Basmath.

1316. בָּשָׁן **Bâshân**, *baw-shawn';* of uncert. der.; *Bashan* (often with the art.), a region E. of the Jordan:—Bashan.

1317. בָּשְׁנָה **boshnâh**, *bosh-naw';* fem. from 954; *shamefulness:*—shame.

1318. בָּשַׁס **bâshaç**, *baw-shas';* a prim. root; to *trample* down:—tread.

1319. בָּשַׂר **bâsar**, *baw-sar';* a prim. root; prop. to *be fresh*, i.e. *full* (*rosy*, fig. *cheerful*); to *announce* (glad news):—messenger, preach, publish, shew forth, (bear, bring, carry, preach, good, tell good) tidings.

1320. בָּשָׂר **bâsâr**, *baw-sawr';* from 1319; *flesh* (from its *freshness*); by extens. *body, person;* also (by euphem.) the *pudenda* of a man:—body, [fat, lean] flesh [-ed], kin, [man-] kind, + nakedness, self, skin.

1321. בְּשַׂר **b^esar** (Chald.), *bes-ar';* corresp. to 1320:—flesh.

בְּשֹׂרָה **b^esôrâh**. See 1309.

1322. בֹּשֶׁת **bôsheth**, *bo'-sheth;* from 954; *shame* (the feeling and the condition, as well as its cause); by impl. (spec.) an *idol:*—ashamed, confusion, + greatly, (put to) shame (-ful thing).

1323. בַּת **bath**, *bath;* from 1129 (as fem. of 1121); a *daughter* (used in the same wide sense as other terms of relationship, lit. and fig.):—apple [of the eye], branch, company, daughter, × first, × old, + owl, town, village.

1324. בַּת **bath**, *bath;* prob. from the same as 1327; a *bath* or Heb. measure (as a means of *division*) of liquids:—bath.

1325. בַּת **bath** (Chald.), *bath;* corresp. to 1324:—bath.

1326. בָּתָה **bâthâh**, *baw-thaw';* prob. an orth. var. for 1327; *desolation:*—waste.

1327. בַּתָּה **battâh**, *bat-taw';* fem. from an unused root (mean. to *break* in pieces); *desolation:*—desolate.

1328. בְּתוּאֵל **B^ethûw'êl**, *beth-oo-ale';* appar. from the same as 1326 and 410; *destroyed of God; Bethuel*, the name of a nephew of Abraham, and of a place in Pal.:—Bethuel. Comp. 1329.

1329. בְּתוּל **B^ethûwl**, *beth-ool';* for 1328; *Bethul* (i.e. *Bethuel*), a place in Pal.:—Bethuel.

1330. בְּתוּלָה **b^ethûwlâh**, *beth-oo-law';* fem. pass. part. of an unused root mean. to *separate;* a *virgin* (from her *privacy*); sometimes (by continuation) a *bride;* also (fig.) a *city* or *state:*—maid, virgin.

1331. בְּתוּלִים **b^ethûwlîym**, *beth-oo-leem';* masc. plur. of the same as 1330; (collect. and abstr.) *virginity;* by impl. and concr. the *tokens* of it:—× maid, virginity.

1332. בִּתְיָה **Bithyâh**, *bith-yaw';* from 1323 and 3050; *daughter* (i.e. worshipper) *of Jah; Bithjah*, an Eg. woman:—Bithiah.

1333. בָּתַק **bâthaq**, *baw-thak';* a prim. root; to *cut* in pieces:—thrust through.

1334. בָּתַר **bâthar**, *baw-thar';* a prim. root, to *chop* up:—divide.

1335. בֶּתֶר **bether**, *beh'-ther;* from 1334; a *section:*—part, piece.

1336. בֶּתֶר **Bether**, *beh'-ther;* the same as 1335; *Bether*, a (craggy) place in Pal.:—Bether.

1337. בַּת רַבִּים **Bath Rabbîym**, *bath rab-beem';* from 1323 and a masc. plur. from 7227; the *daughter* (i.e. *city*) *of Rabbah:*—Bath-rabbim.

1338. בִּתְרוֹן **Bithrôwn**, *bith-rone';* from 1334; (with the art.) the *craggy* spot; *Bithron*, a place E. of the Jordan:—Bithron.

1339. בַּת־שֶׁבַע **Bath-Sheba^c**, *bath-sheh'-bah;* from 1323 and 7651 (in the sense of 7650); *daughter of an oath; Bath-Sheba*, the mother of Solomon:—Bath-sheba.

1340. בַּת־שׁוּעַ **Bath-Shûwa^c**, *bath-shoo'-ah;* from 1323 and 7771; *daughter of wealth; Bath-shuä*, the same as 1339:—Bath-shua.

ג

1341. גֵּא **gê'**, *gay';* for 1343; *haughty:*—proud.

1342. גָּאָה **gâ'âh**, *gaw-aw';* a prim. root; to *mount* up; hence in gen. to *rise*, (fig.) be *majestic:*—gloriously, grow up, increase, be risen, triumph.

1343. גֵּאֶה **gê'eh**, *gay-eh';* from 1342; *lofty;* fig. *arrogant:*—proud.

1344. גֵּאָה **gê'âh**, *gay-aw';* fem. from 1342; *arrogance:*—pride.

1345. גְּאוּאֵל **G^e'ûw'êl**, *gheh-oo-ale';* from 1342 and 410; *majesty of God; Geüel*, an Isr.:—Geuel.

1346. גַּאֲוָה **gaʼăvâh**, *gah-av-aw'*; from 1342; *arrogance* or *majesty;* by impl. (concr.) *ornament:*—excellency, haughtiness, highness, pride, proudly, swelling.

1347. גָּאוֹן **gâʼôwn**, *gaw-ohn'*; from 1342; the same as 1346:—arrogancy, excellency (-lent), majesty, pomp, pride, proud, swelling.

1348. גֵּאוּת **gêʼûwth**, *gay-ooth'*; from 1342; the same as 1346:—excellent things, lifting up, majesty, pride, proudly, raging.

1349. גַּאֲיוֹן **gaʼăyôwn**, *gah-ăh-yone'*; from 1342: *haughty:*—proud.

1350. גָּאַל **gâʼal**, *gaw-al'*; a prim. root, to *redeem* (according to the Oriental law of kinship), i.e. to *be the next of kin* (and as such to *buy back* a relative's property, *marry* his widow, etc.):—× in any wise, × at all, avenger, deliver, (do, perform the part of near, next) kinsfolk (-man), purchase, ransom, redeem (-er), revenger.

1351. גָּאַל **gâʼal**, *gaw-al'*; a prim. root, [rather ident. with 1350, through the idea of *freeing*, i.e. *repudiating*]; to *soil* or (fig.) *desecrate:*—defile, pollute, stain.

1352. גֹּאֶל **gôʼel**, *go'-el*; from 1351; *profanation:*—defile.

1353. גְּאֻלָּה **gᵉullâh**, *gheh-ool-law'*; fem. pass. part. of 1350; *redemption* (including the right and the object); by impl. *relationship:*—kindred, redeem, redemption, right.

1354. גַּב **gab**, *gab*; from an unused root mean. to *hollow* or *curve;* the *back* (as *rounded* [comp. 1460 and 1479]; by anal. the *top* or *rim*, a *boss*, a *vault*, *arch* of eye, *bulwarks*, etc.:—back, body, boss, eminent (higher) place, [eye] brows, nave, ring.

1355. גַּב **gab** (Chald.), *gab*; corresp. to 1354:—back.

1356. גֵּב **gêb**, *gabe*; from 1461; a *log* (as *cut* out); also *well* or *cistern* (as *dug*):—beam, ditch, pit.

1357. גֵּב **gêb**, *gabe*; prob. from 1461 [comp. 1462]; a *locust* (from its *cutting*):—locust.

1358. גֹּב **gôb** (Chald.), *gobe*; from a root corresp. to 1461; a *pit* (for wild animals) (as *cut* out):—den.

1359. גֹּב **Gôb**, *gobe*; or (fully)

גּוֹב **Gôwb**, *gobe'*; from 1461; *pit; Gob*, a place in Pal.:—Gob.

1360. גֶּבֶא **gebe**, *geh'-beh*; from an unused root mean. prob. to *collect;* a *reservoir;* by anal. a *marsh:*—marish, pit.

1361. גָּבַהּ **gâbahh**, *gaw-bah'*; a prim. root; to *soar*, i.e. *be lofty;* fig. to *be haughty:*—exalt, be haughty, be (make) high (-er), lift up, mount up, be proud, raise up great height, upward.

1362. גָּבָהּ **gâbâhh**, *gaw-bawh'*; from 1361; *lofty* (lit. or fig.):—high, proud.

1363. גֹּבַהּ **gôbahh**, *go'-bah*; from 1361; *elation, grandeur, arrogance:*—excellency, haughty, height, high, loftiness, pride.

1364. גָּבֹהַּ **gâbôahh**, *gaw-bo'-ah*; or (fully)

גָּבוֹהַּ **gâbôwahh**, *gaw-bo'-ah*; from 1361; *elevated* (or *elated*), *powerful, arrogant:*—haughty, height, high (-er), lofty, proud, × exceeding proudly.

1365. גַּבְהוּת **gabhûwth**, *gab-hooth'*; from 1361; *pride:*—loftiness, lofty.

1366. גְּבוּל **gᵉbûwl**, *gheb-ool'*; or (short.)

גְּבֻל **gᵉbûl**, *gheb-ool'*; from 1379; prop. a *cord* (as *twisted*), i.e. (by impl.) a *boundary;* by extens. the *territory* inclosed:—border, bound, coast, × great, landmark, limit, quarter, space.

1367. גְּבוּלָה **gᵉbûwlâh**, *gheb-oo-law'*; or (short.)

גְּבֻלָה **gᵉbûlâh**, *gheb-oo-law'*; fem. of 1366; a *boundary, region:*—border, bound, coast, landmark, place.

1368. גִּבּוֹר **gibbôwr**, *ghib-bore'*; or (short.)

גִּבֹּר **gibbôr**, *ghib-bore'*; intens. from the same as 1397; *powerful;* by impl. *warrior, tyrant:*—champion, chief, × excel, giant, man, mighty (man, one), strong (man), valiant man.

1369. גְּבוּרָה **gᵉbûwrâh**, *gheb-oo-raw'*; fem. pass. part. from the same as 1368; *force* (lit. or fig.); by impl. *valor, victory:*—force, mastery, might, mighty (act, power), power, strength.

1370. גְּבוּרָה **gᵉbûwrâh** (Chald.), *gheb-oo-raw'*; corresp. to 1369; *power:*—might.

1371. גִּבֵּחַ **gibbêach**, *ghib-bay'-akh*; from an unused root mean. to *be high* (in the forehead); *bald* in the forehead:—forehead bald.

1372. גַּבַּחַת **gabbachath**, *gab-bakh'-ath*; from the same as 1371; *baldness* in the forehead; by anal. a *bare spot* on the right side of cloth:—bald forehead, × without.

1373. גַּבַּי **Gabbay**, *gab-bah'ee*; from the same as 1354; *collective:*—*Gabbai*, an Isr.:—Gabbai.

1374. גֵּבִים **Gêbîym**, *gay-beem'*; plur. of 1356; *cisterns; Gebim*, a place in Pal.:—Gebim.

1375. גְּבִיעַ **gᵉbîyaʻ**, *gheb-ee'-ah*; from an unused root (mean. to *be convex*); a *goblet;* by anal. the *calyx* of a flower:—house, cup, pot.

1376. גְּבִיר **gᵉbîyr**, *gheb-eer'*; from 1396; a *master:*—lord.

1377. גְּבִירָה **gᵉbîyrâh**, *gheb-ee-raw'*; fem. of 1376; a *mistress:*—queen.

1378. גָּבִישׁ **gâbîysh**, *gaw-beesh'*; from an unused root (prob. mean. to *freeze*); *crystal* (from its resemblance to *ice*):—pearl.

1379. גָּבַל **gâbal**, *gaw-bal'*; a prim. root; prop. to *twist* as a rope; only (as a denom. from 1366) to *bound* (as by a line):—be border, set (bounds about).

1380. גְּבַל **Gᵉbal**, *gheb-al'*; from 1379 (in the sense of a *chain* of hills); a *mountain; Gebal*, a place in Phœnicia:—Gebal.

1381. גְּבָל **Gᵉbâl**, *gheb-awl'*; the same as 1380; *Gebal*, a region in Idumæa:—Gebal.

גְּבֻלָה **gᵉbûlâh**. See 1367.

1382. גִּבְלִי **Giblîy**, *ghib-lee'*; patrial from 1380; a *Gebalite*, or inhab. of Gebal:—Giblites, stone-squarer.

1383. גַּבְלֻת **gablûth**, *gab-looth'*; from 1379; a twisted *chain* or *lace:*—end.

1384. גִּבֵּן **gibbên**, *gib-bane'*; from an unused root mean. to be *arched* or *contracted; hunch-backed:*—crookbackt.

1385. גְּבִינָה **gᵉbînah**, *gheb-ee-naw'*; fem. from the same as 1384; *curdled* milk:—cheese.

1386. גַּבְנֹן **gabnôn**, *gab-nohn'*; from the same as 1384; a *hump* or *peak* of hills:—high.

1387. גֶּבַע **Gebaʻ**, *gheh'-bah*; from the same as 1375, a *hillock; Geba*, a place in Pal.:—Gaba, Geba, Gibeah.

1388. גִּבְעָא **Gibʻâʼ**, *ghib-aw'*; by perm. for 1389; a *hill; Giba*, a place in Pal.:—Gibeah.

1389. גִּבְעָה **gibʻâh**, *ghib-aw'*; fem. from the same as 1387; a *hillock:*—hill, little hill.

1390. גִּבְעָה **Gibʻâh**, *ghib-aw'*; the same as 1389; *Gibah;* the name of three places in Pal.:—Gibeah, the hill.

1391. גִּבְעוֹן **Gibʻôwn**, *ghib-ohn'*; from the same as 1387; *hilly; Gibon*, a place in Pal.:—Gibeon.

1392. גִּבְעֹל **gibʻôl**, *ghib-ole'*; prol. from 1375; the *calyx* of a flower:—bolled.

1393. גִּבְעֹנִי **Gibʻônîy**, *ghib-o-nee'*; patrial from 1391; a *Gibonite*, or inhab. of Gibon:—Gibeonite.

1394. גִּבְעַת **Gibʻath**, *ghib-ath'*; from the same as 1375; *hilliness; Gibath:*—Gibeath.

1395. גִּבְעָתִי **Gibʻâthîy**, *ghib-aw-thee'*; patrial from 1390; a *Gibathite*, or inhab. of Gibath:—Gibeathite.

1396. גָּבַר **gâbar**, *gaw-bar'*; a prim. root; to *be strong;* by impl. to *prevail, act insolently:*—exceed, confirm, be great, be mighty, prevail, put to more [strength], strengthen, be stronger, be valiant.

1397. גֶּבֶר **geber**, *gheh'-ber*; from 1396; prop. a *valiant* man or *warrior;* gen. a *person simply:*—every one, man, × mighty.

1398. גֶּבֶר **Geber**, *gheh'-ber*; the same as 1397; *Geber*, the name of two Isr.:—Geber.

1399. גְּבַר **gᵉbar**, *gheb-ar'*; from 1396; the same as 1397; a person:—man.

1400. גְּבַר **gᵉbar** (Chald.), *gheb-ar'*; corresp. to 1399:—certain, man.

1401. גִּבָּר **gibbâr** (Chald.), *ghib-bawr'*; intens. of 1400; *valiant*, or *warrior:*—mighty.

1402. גִּבָּר **Gibbâr**, *ghib-bawr'*; intens. of 1399; *Gibbar*, an Isr.:—Gibbar.

גְּבֻרָה **gᵉbûrâh**. See 1369.

1403. גַּבְרִיאֵל **Gabrîyʼêl**, *gab-ree-ale'*; from 1397 and 410; *man of God; Gabriel*, an archangel:—Gabriel.

1404. גְּבֶרֶת **gᵉbereth**, *gheb-eh'-reth*; fem. of 1376; *mistress:*—lady, mistress.

1405. גִּבְּתוֹן **Gibbᵉthôwn**, *ghib-beth-one'*; intens. from 1389; a *hilly* spot; *Gibbethon*, a place in Pal.:—Gibbethon.

1406. גָּג **gâg**, *gawg*; prob. by redupl. from 1342; a *roof;* by anal. the *top* of an altar:—roof (of the house), (house) top (of the house).

1407. גַּד **gad**, *gad*; from 1413 (in the sense of *cutting*); *coriander* seed (from its furrows):—coriander.

1408. גַּד **Gad**, *gad*; a var. of 1409; *Fortune*, a Bab. deity:—that troop.

1409. גָּד **gâd**, *gawd*; from 1464 (in the sense of *distributing*); *fortune:*—troop.

1410. גָּד **Gâd**, *gawd*; from 1464; *Gad*, a son of Jacob, includ. his tribe and its territory; also a prophet:—Gad.

1411. גְּדָבַר **gᵉdâbâr** (Chald.), *ghed-aw-bawr'*; corresp. to 1489; a *treasurer:*—treasurer.

1412. גֻּדְגֹּדָה **Gudgôdâh**, *gud-go'-daw*; by redupl. from 1413 (in the sense of *cutting*) *cleft; Gudgodah*, a place in the Desert:—Gudgodah.

1413. גָּדַד **gâdad**, *gaw-dad'*; a prim. root [comp. 1464]; to *crowd;* also to *gash* (as if by *pressing* into):—assemble (selves by troops), gather (selves together, self in troops), cut selves.

1414. גְּדַד **gᵉdad** (Chald.), *ghed-ad'*; corresp. to 1413; to *cut* down:—hew down.

גְּדֻדָה **gᵉdûdâh**. See 1417.

1415. גָּדָה **gâdâh**, *gaw-daw'*; from an unused root (mean. to *cut* off); a *border* of a river (as *cut* into by the stream):—bank.

גַּדָּה **Gaddâh**. See 2693.

1416. גְּדוּד **gᵉdûwd**, *ghed-ood'*; from 1413; a *crowd* (espec. of soldiers):—army, band (of men), company, troop (of robbers).

1417. גְּדוּד **gᵉdûwd**, *ghed-ood'*; or (fem.)

גְּדֻדָה **gᵉdûdâh**, *ghed-oo-daw'*; from 1413; a *furrow* (as *cut*):—furrow.

1418. גְּדוּדָה **gᵉdûwdâh**, *ghed-oo-daw'*; fem. part. pass. of 1413; an *incision:*—cutting.

1419. גָּדוֹל **gâdôwl**, *gaw-dole'*; or (short.)

גָּדֹל **gâdôl**, *gaw-dole'*; from 1431; *great* (in any sense); hence *older;* also *insolent:*—+ aloud, elder (-est), + exceeding (-ly), + far, (man of) great (man, matter, thing, -er, -ness), high, long, loud, mighty, more, much, noble, proud thing, × sore, (×) very.

1420. גְּדוּלָה **gᵉdûwlâh**, *ghed-oo-law'*; or (short.) גְּדֻלָּה **gᵉdullâh**, *ghed-ool-law'*; or (less accurately)

גְּדוּלָּה **gᵉdûwllâh**, *ghed-ool-law'*; fem. of 1419; *greatness;* (concr.) *mighty acts:*—dignity, great things (-ness), majesty.

1421. גִּדּוּף **giddûwph**, *ghid-doof'*; or (short.)

גִּדֻּף **giddûph**, *ghid-doof'*; and (fem.)

גִּדּוּפָה **giddûphâh**, *ghid-doo-faw'*; or

גִּדֻּפָה **giddûphâh**, *ghid-doo-faw'*; from 1422; *vilification:*—reproach, reviling.

1422. גְּדוּפָה **gedûwphâh**, *ghed-oo-faw';* fem. pass. part. of 1442; a *revilement:*—taunt.

גְּדוֹר **Gedôwr.** See 1446.

1423. גְּדִי **gedîy**, *ghed-ee';* from the same as 1415; a young *goat* (from *browsing*):—kid.

1424. גָּדִי **Gâdîy**, *gaw-dee';* from 1409; *fortunate; Gadi*, an Isr.:—Gadi.

1425. גָּדִי **Gâdîy**, *gaw-dee';* patron. from 1410; a *Gadite* (collect.) or desc. of Gad:—Gadites, children of Gad.

1426. גַּדִּי **Gaddîy**, *gad-dee';* intens. for 1424; *Gaddi*, an Isr.:—Gaddi.

1427. גַּדִּיאֵל **Gaddîy'êl**, *gad-dee-ale';* from 1409 and 410; *fortune of God; Gaddiel*, an Isr.:—Gaddiel.

1428. גִּדְיָה° **gidyâh**, *ghid-yaw';* or

גַּדְיָה° **gadyâh**, *gad-yaw';* the same as 1415; a river *brink:*—bank.

1429. גְּדִיָּה **gedîyâh**, *ghed-ee-yaw';* fem. of 1423; a young female *goat:*—kid.

1430. גָּדִישׁ **gâdîysh**, *gaw-deesh';* from an unused root (mean. to *heap* up); a *stack* of sheaves; by anal. a *tomb:*—shock (stack) (of corn), tomb.

1431. גָּדַל **gâdal**, *gaw-dal';* a prim. root; prop. to *twist* [comp. 1434], i.e. to *be* (caus. *make*) *large* (in various senses, as in body. mind, estate or honor, also in pride):—advance, boast, bring up, exceed, excellent, be (-come, do, give, make, wax), great (-er, come to . . . estate, + things), grow (up), increase, lift up, magnify (-ifical), be much set by, nourish (up), pass, promote, proudly [spoken], tower.

1432. גָּדֵל **gâdêl**, *gaw-dale';* from 1431; *large* (lit. or fig.):—great, grew.

1433. גֹּדֶל **gôdel**, *go'-del;* from 1431; *magnitude* (lit. or fig.):—greatness, stout (-ness).

1434. גְּדִל **gedîl**, *ghed-eel';* from 1431 (in the sense of *twisting*); *thread*, i.e. a *tassel* or *festoon:*—fringe, wreath.

1435. גִּדֵּל **Giddêl**, *ghid-dale';* from 1431; *stout; Giddel*, the name of one of the Nethinim, also of one of "Solomon's servants":—Giddel.

גָּדֹל **gâdôl.** See 1419.

גְּדֻלָּה **gedullâh.** See 1420.

1436. גְּדַלְיָה **Gedalyâh**, *ghed-al-yaw';* or (prol.)

גְּדַלְיָהוּ **Gedalyâhûw**, *ghed-al-yaw'-hoo;* from 1431 and 3050; *Jah has become great; Gedaljah*, the name of five Isr.:—Gedaliah.

1437. גִּדַּלְתִּי **Giddaltîy**, *ghid-dal'-tee;* from 1431; *I have made great; Giddalti*, an Isr.:—Giddalti.

1438. גָּדַע **gâdaʻ**, *gaw-dah';* a prim. root; to *fell* a tree; gen. to *destroy* anything:—cut (asunder, in sunder, down, off), hew down.

1439. גִּדְעוֹן **Gidʻôwn**, *ghid-ohn';* from 1438; *feller* (i.e. *warrior*); *Gidon*, an Isr.:—Gideon.

1440. גִּדְעֹם **Gidʻôm**, *ghid-ohm';* from 1438; a *cutting* (i.e. *desolation*); *Gidom*, a place in Pal.:—Gidom.

1441. גִּדְעֹנִי **Gidʻônîy**, *ghid-o-nee';* from 1438; *warlike* [comp. 1439]; *Gidoni*, an Isr.:—Gideoni.

1442. גָּדַף **gâdaph**, *gaw-daf';* a prim. root; to *hack* (with words), i.e. *revile:*—blaspheme, reproach.

גִּדֻּף **giddûph**, and

גִּדּוּפָה **giddûphâh.** See 1421.

1443. גָּדַר **gâdar**, *gaw-dar';* a prim. root; to *wall* in or around:—close up, fence up, hedge, inclose, make up [a wall], mason, repairer.

1444. גֶּדֶר **geder**, *gheh'-der;* from 1443; a *circumvallation:*—wall.

1445. גֶּדֶר **Geder**, *gheh'-der;* the same as 1444; *Geder*, a place in Pal.:—Geder.

1446. גְּדֹר **Gedôr**, *ghed-ore';* or (fully)

גְּדוֹר **Gedôwr**, *ghed-ore';* from 1443; *inclosure; Gedor*, a place in Pal.; also the name of three Isr.:—Gedor.

1447. גָּדֵר **gâdêr**, *gaw-dare';* from 1443; a *circumvallation;* by impl. an *inclosure:*—fence, hedge, wall.

1448. גְּדֵרָה **gedêrâh**, *ghed-ay-raw';* fem. of 1447; *inclosure* (espec. for flocks):—[sheep-] cote (fold) hedge, wall.

1449. גְּדֵרָה **Gedêrâh**, *ghed-ay-raw';* the same as 1448; (with the art.) *Gederah*, a place in Pal.:—Gederah, hedges.

1450. גְּדֵרוֹת **Gedêrôwth**, *ghed-ay-rohth';* plur. of 1448; *walls; Gederoth*, a place in Pal.:—Gederoth.

1451. גְּדֵרִי **Gedêrîy**, *ghed-ay-ree';* patrial from 1445; a *Gederite*, or inhab. of Geder:—Gederite.

1452. גְּדֵרָתִי **Gedêrâthîy**, *ghed-ay-raw-thee';* patrial from 1449; a *Gederathite*, or inhab. of Gederah:—Gederathite.

1453. גְּדֵרֹתַיִם **Gedêrôthayim**, *ghed-ay-ro-thah'-yim;* dual of 1448; *double wall; Gederothajim*, a place in Pal.:—Gederothaim.

1454. גֵּה **gêh**, *gay;* prob. a clerical error for 2088; *this:*—this.

1455. גָּהָה **gâhâh**, *gaw-haw';* a prim. root; to *remove* (a bandage from a wound, i.e. *heal* it):—cure.

1456. גֵּהָה **gêhâh**, *gay-haw';* from 1455; a *cure:*—medicine.

1457. גָּהַר **gâhar**, *gaw-har';* a prim. root; to *prostrate* oneself:—cast self down, stretch self.

1458. גַּו **gav**, *gav;* another form for 1460; the *back:*—back.

1459. גַּו **gav** (Chald.), *gav;* corresp. to 1460; the *middle:*—midst, same, there- (where-) in.

1460. גֵּו **gêv** *gave;* from 1342 [corresp. to 1354]; the *back;* by anal. the *middle:*— + among, back, body.

1461. גּוּב **gûwb**, *goob;* a prim. root; to *dig:*—husbandman.

1462. גּוֹב **gôwb**, *gobe;* from 1461; the *locust* (from its *grubbing* as a larve):—grasshopper, × great.

1463. גּוֹג **Gôwg**, *gohg;* of uncert. der.; *Gog*, the name of an Isr., also of some northern nation:—Gog.

1464. גּוּד **gûwd**, *goode;* a prim. root [akin to 1413]; to *crowd* upon, i.e. *attack:*—invade, overcome.

1465. גֵּוָה **gêvâh**, *gay-vaw';* fem. of 1460; the *back*, i.e. (by extens.) the *person:*—body.

1466. גֵּוָה **gêvâh**, *gay-vaw';* the same as 1465; *exaltation;* (fig.) *arrogance:*—lifting up, pride.

1467. גֵּוָה **gêvâh** (Chald.), *gay-vaw';* corresp. to 1466:—pride.

1468. גּוּז **gûwz**, *gooz;* a prim. root [comp. 1494]; prop. to *shear* off; but used only in the (fig.) sense of *passing* rapidly:—bring, cut off.

1469. גּוֹזָל **gôwzâl**, *go-zawl';* or (short.)

גֹּזָל **gôzâl**, *go-zawl';* from 1497; a *nestling* (as being comparatively *nude* of feathers):—young (pigeon).

1470. גּוֹזָן **Gôwzân**, *go-zawn';* prob. from 1468; a *quarry* (as a place of *cutting* stones); *Gozan*, a province of Assyria:—Gozan.

1471. גּוֹי **gôwy**, *go'ee;* rarely (short.)

גֹּי **gôy**, *go'-ee;* appar. from the same root as 1465 (in the sense of *massing*); a foreign *nation;* hence a *Gentile;* also (fig.) a *troop* of animals, or a *flight* of locusts:—Gentile, heathen, nation, people.

1472. גְּוִיָּה **gevîyâh**, *ghev-ee-yaw';* prol. for 1465; a *body*, whether alive or dead:—(dead) body, carcase, corpse.

1473. גּוֹלָה **gôwlâh**, *go-law';* or (short.)

גֹּלָה **gôlah**, *go-law';* act. part. fem. of 1540; *exile;* concr. and coll. *exiles:*—(carried away), captive (-ity), removing.

1474. גּוֹלָן **Gôwlân**, *go-lawn';* from 1473; *captive; Golan*, a place east of the Jordan:—Golan.

1475. גּוּמָּץ **gûwmmâts**, *goom-mawts';* of uncert. der.; a *pit:*—pit.

1476. גּוּנִי **Gûwnîy**, *goo-nee';* prob. from 1598; *protected; Guni*, the name of two Isr.:—Guni.

1477. גּוּנִי **Gûwnîy**, *goo-nee';* patron. from 1476; a *Gunite* (collect. with art. pref.) or desc. of Guni:—Gunites.

1478. גָּוַע **gâvaʻ**, *gaw-vah';* a prim. root; to *breathe* out, i.e. (by impl.) *expire:*—die, be dead, give up the ghost, perish.

1479. גּוּף **gûwph**, *goof;* a prim. root; prop. to *hollow* or *arch*, i.e. (fig.) *close;* to *shut:*—shut.

1480. גּוּפָה **gûwphâh**, *goo-faw';* from 1479; a *corpse* (as *closed* to sense):—body.

1481. גּוּר **gûwr**, *goor;* a prim. root; prop. to *turn* aside from the road (for a lodging or any other purpose), i.e. *sojourn* (as a guest); also to *shrink, fear* (as in a *strange* place); also to *gather* for hostility (as *afraid*):—abide, assemble, be afraid, dwell, fear, gather (together), inhabitant, remain, sojourn, stand in awe, (be) stranger, × surely.

1482. גּוּר **gûwr**, *goor;* or (short.)

גֻּר **gûr**, *goor;* perh. from 1481; a *cub* (as still *abiding* in the lair), espec. of the lion:—whelp, young one.

1483. גּוּר **Gûwr**, *goor;* the same as 1482; *Gur*, a place in Pal.:—Gur.

1484. גּוֹר **gôwr**, *gore;* or (fem.)

גֹּרָה **gôrah**, *go-raw';* a var. of 1482:—whelp.

1485. גּוּר־בַּעַל **Gûwr-Baʻal**, *goor-bah'-al;* from 1481 and 1168; *dwelling of Baal; Gur-Baal*, a place in Arabia:—Gur-baal.

1486. גּוֹרָל **gôwrâl**, *go-rawl';* or (short.)

גֹּרָל **gôral**, *go-ral';* from an unused root mean. to *be rough* (as stone); prop. a *pebble*, i.e. a *lot* (small stones being used for that purpose); fig. a *portion* or *destiny* (as if determined by lot):—lot.

1487. גּוּשׁ **gûwsh**, *goosh;* or rather (by perm.)

גִּישׁ **gîysh**, *gheesh;* of uncert. der.; a *mass* of earth:—clod.

1488. גֵּז **gêz**, *gaze;* from 1494; a *fleece* (as *shorn*); also mown *grass:*—fleece, mowing, mown grass.

1489. גִּזְבָּר **gizbâr**, *ghiz-bawr';* of for. der. *treasurer:*—treasurer.

1490. גִּזְבָּר **gizbâr** (Chald.), *ghiz-bawr';* corresp. to 1489:—treasurer.

1491. גָּזָה **gâzâh**, *gaw-zaw';* a prim. root [akin to 1468]; to *cut* off, i.e. *portion* out:—take.

1492. גַּזָּה **gazzâh**, *gaz-zaw';* fem. from 1494; a *fleece:*—fleece.

1493. גִּזוֹנִי **Gizôwnîy**, *ghee-zo-nee';* patrial from the unused name of a place appar. in Pal.; a *Gizonite* or inhab. of Gizoh:—Gizonite.

1494. גָּזַז **gâzaz**, *gaw-zaz';* a prim. root [akin to 1468]; to *cut* off; spec. to *shear* a flock, or *shave* the hair; fig. to *destroy* an enemy:—cut off (down), poll, shave, ([sheep-]) shear (-er).

1495. גָּזֵז **Gâzêz** *gaw-zaze';* from 1494; *shearer; Gazez*, the name of two Isr.:—Gazez.

1496. גָּזִית **gâzîyth**, *gaw-zeeth';* from 1491; something *cut*, i.e. *dressed* stone:—hewed, hewn stone, wrought.

1497. גָּזַל **gâzal**, *gaw-zal';* a prim. root; to *pluck* off; spec. to *flay, strip* or *rob:*—catch, consume, exercise [robbery], pluck (off), rob, spoil, take away (by force, violence), tear.

1498. גָּזֵל **gâzêl**, *gaw-zale';* from 1497; *robbery*, or (concr.) *plunder:*—robbery, thing taken away by violence.

1499. גֵּזֶל **gêzel**, *ghe'-zel;* from 1497; *plunder*, i.e. *violence:*—violence, violent perverting.

גֹּזָל **gôzâl.** See 1469.

1500. גְּזֵלָה **gᵉzêlâh**, *ghez-ay-law'*; fem. of 1498 and mean. the same:—that (he had robbed) [which he took violently away], spoil, violence.

1501. גָּזָם **gâzâm**, *gaw-zawm'*; from an unused root mean. to *devour*; a kind of *locust*:—palmer-worm.

1502. גַּזָּם **Gazzâm**, *gaz-zawm'*; from the same as 1501; *devourer*:—*Gazzam*, one of the Nethinim:—Gazzam.

1503. גֶּזַע **gezaʻ**, *geh'-zah*; from an unused root mean. to *cut* down (trees); the *trunk* or *stump* of a tree (as felled or as planted):—stem, stock.

1504. גָּזַר **gâzar**, *gaw-zar'*; a prim. root; to *cut* down or off; (fig.) to *destroy, divide, exclude* or *decide*:—cut down (off), decree, divide, snatch.

1505. גְּזַר **gᵉzar** (Chald.), *ghez-ar'*; corresp. to 1504; to *quarry; determine*:—cut out, soothsayer.

1506. גֶּזֶר **gezer**, *gheh'-zer*; from 1504; something *cut* off; a *portion*:—part, piece.

1507. גֶּזֶר **Gezer**, *gheh'-zer*; the same as 1506; *Gezer*, a place in Pal.:—Gazer, Gezer.

1508. גִּזְרָה **gizrâh**, *ghiz-raw'*; fem. of 1506; the *figure* or person (as if *cut* out); also an *inclosure* (as *separated*):—polishing, separate place.

1509. גְּזֵרָה **gᵉzêrâh**, *ghez-ay-raw'*; from 1504; a *desert* (as *separated*):—not inhabited.

1510. גְּזֵרָה **gᵉzêrâh** (Chald.), *ghez-ay-raw'*; from 1505 (as 1504); a *decree*:—decree.

1511. גִּזְרִי **Gizrîy** (in the marg.), *ghiz-ree'*; patrial from 1507; a *Gezerite* (collect.) or inhab. of Gezer; but better (as in the text) by transp.
גִּרְזִי° **Girzîy**, *gher-zee'*; patrial of 1630; a *Girzite* (collect.) or member of a native tribe in Pal.:—Gezrites.

גִּחוֹן **Gîchôwn**. See 1521.

1512. גָּחוֹן **gâchôwn**, *gaw-khone'*; prob. from 1518; the external *abdomen, belly* (as the *source* of the fœtus [comp. 1521]):—belly.

גֵּחֲזִי **Gêchăzîy**. See 1522.

גָּחֹל **gâchol**. See 1513.

1513. גֶּחָל **gechel**, *geh'-khel*; or (fem.)
גַּחֶלֶת **gacheleth**, *gah-kheh'-leth*; from an unused root mean. to *glow* or *kindle*; an *ember*:—(burning) coal.

1514. גַּחַם **Gacham**, *gah'-kham*; from an unused root mean. to *burn; flame*; *Gacham*, a son of Nahor:—Gaham.

1515. גַּחַר **Gachar**, *gah'-khar*; from an unused root mean. to *hide*; *lurker*; *Gachar*, one of the Nethinim:—Gahar.

גֹּי **gôy**. See 1471.

1516. גַּיְא **gayʼ**, *gah'ee*; or (short.)
גַּי **gay**, *gah'ee*; prob. (by transm.) from the same root as 1466 (abbrev.); a *gorge* (from its *lofty* sides; hence narrow, but not a gully or winter-torrent):—valley.

1517. גִּיד **gîyd**, *gheed*; prob. from 1464; a *thong* (as *compressing*); by anal. a *tendon*:—sinew.

1518. גִּיחַ **gîyach**, *ghee'-akh*; or (short.)
גֹּחַ **gôach**, *go'-akh*; a prim. root; to *gush* forth (as water), gen. to *issue*:—break forth, labor to bring forth, come forth, draw up, take out.

1519. גִּיחַ **gîyach** (Chald.), *ghee'-akh*; or (short.)
גּוּחַ **gûwach** (Chald.), *goo'-akh*; corresp. to 1518; to *rush* forth:—strive.

1520. גִּיחַ **Gîyach**, *ghee'-akh*; from 1518; a *fountain*; *Giach*, a place in Pal.:—Giah.

1521. גִּיחוֹן **Gîychôwn**, *ghee-khone'*; or (short.)
גִּחוֹן **Gîchôwn**, *ghee-khone'*; from 1518; *stream*; *Gichon*, a river of Paradise; also a valley (or pool) near Jerusalem:—Gihon.

1522. גֵּיחֲזִי **Gêychăzîy**, *gay-khah-zee'*; or
גֵּחֲזִי **Gêchăzîy**, *gay-khah-zee'*; appar. from 1516 and 2372; *valley of a visionary*; *Gechazi*, the servant of Elisha:—Gehazi.

1523. גִּיל **gîyl**, *gheel*; or (by perm.)
גּוּל° **gûwl**, *gool*; a prim. root; prop. to *spin* round (under the influence of any violent emotion), i.e. usually *rejoice*, or (as *cringing*) *fear*:—be glad, joy, be joyful, rejoice.

1524. גִּיל **gîyl**, *gheel*; from 1523; a *revolution* (of time, i.e. an *age*); also *joy*:—× exceedingly, gladness, × greatly, joy, rejoice (-ing), sort.

1525. גִּילָה **gîylâh**, *ghee-law'*; or
גִּילַת **gîylath**, *ghee-lath'*; fem. of 1524; *joy*:—joy, rejoicing.

גִּילֹה **Gîylôh**. See 1542.

1526. גִּילֹנִי **Gîylônîy**, *ghee-lo-nee'*; patrial from 1542; a *Gilonite* or inhab. of Giloh:—Gilonite.

1527. גִּינַת **Gîynath**, *ghee-nath'*; of uncert. der.; *Ginath*, an Isr.:—Ginath.

1528. גִּיר **gîyr** (Chald.), *gheer*; corresp. to 1615; *lime*:—plaster.

גֵּיר **gêyr**. See 1616.

1529. גֵּישָׁן **Gêyshân**, *gay-shawn'*; from the same as 1487; *lumpish*; *Geshan*, an Isr.:—Geshan.

1530. גַּל **gal**, *gal*; from 1556; something *rolled*, i.e. a *heap* of stone or dung (plur. *ruins*); by anal. a *spring* of water (plur. *waves*):—billow, heap, spring, wave.

1531. גֹּל **gôl**, *gole*; from 1556; a *cup* for oil (as *round*):—bowl.

גְּלָא **gᵉlâʼ**. See 1541.

1532. גַּלָּב **gallâb**, *gal-lawb'*; from an unused root mean. to *shave*; a *barber*:—barber.

1533. גִּלְבֹּעַ **Gilbôaʻ**, *ghil-bo'-ah*; from 1530 and 1158; *fountain of ebullition*; *Gilboa*, a mountain of Pal.:—Gilboa.

1534. גַּלְגַּל **galgal**, *gal-gal'*; by redupl. from 1556; a *wheel*; by anal. a *whirlwind*; also *dust* (as *whirled*):—heaven, rolling thing, wheel.

1535. גַּלְגַּל **galgal** (Chald.), *gal-gal'*; corresp. to 1534; a *wheel*:—wheel.

1536. גִּלְגָּל **gilgâl**, *ghil-gawl'*; a var. of 1534:—wheel.

1537. גִּלְגָּל **Gilgâl**, *ghil-gawl'*; the same as 1536 (with the art. as a prop. noun); *Gilgal*, the name of three places in Pal.:—Gilgal. See also 1019.

1538. גֻּלְגֹּלֶת **gulgôleth**, *gul-go'-leth*; by redupl. from 1556; a *skull* (as *round*); by impl. a *head* (in enumeration of persons):—head, every man, poll, skull.

1539. גֶּלֶד **geled**, *ghe'-led*; from an unused root prob. mean. to *polish*; the (human) *skin* (as *smooth*):—*skin*.

1540. גָּלָה **gâlâh**, *gaw-law'*; a prim. root; to *denude* (espec. in a disgraceful sense); by impl. to *exile* (captives being usually *stripped*); fig. to *reveal*:—+ advertise, appear, bewray, bring, (carry, lead, go) captive (into captivity), depart, disclose, discover, exile, be gone, open, × plainly, publish, remove, reveal, × shamelessly, shew, × surely, tell, uncover.

1541. גְּלָה **gᵉlâh** (Chald.), *ghel-aw'*; or
גְּלָא **gᵉlâʼ** (Chald.), *ghel-aw'*; corresp. to 1540:—bring over, carry away, reveal.

גֹּלָה **gôlâh**. See 1473.

1542. גִּלֹה **Gîlôh**, *ghee-lo'*; or (fully)
גִּילֹה **Gîylôh**, *ghee-lo'*; from 1540; *open*; *Giloh*, a place in Pal.:—Giloh.

1543. גֻּלָּה **gullâh**, *gool-law'*; fem. from 1556; a *fountain, bowl* or *globe* (all as *round*):—bowl, pommel, spring.

1544. גִּלּוּל **gillûwl**, *ghil-lool'*; or (short.)
גִּלֻּל **gillûl**, *ghil-lool'*; from 1556; prop. a *log* (as *round*); by impl. an *idol*:—idol.

1545. גְּלוֹם **gᵉlôwm**, *ghel-ome'*; from 1563; *clothing* (as *wrapped*):—clothes.

1546. גָּלוּת **gâlûwth**, *gaw-looth'*; fem. from 1540; *captivity*; concr. *exiles* (collect.):—(they that are carried away) captives (-ity.)

1547. גָּלוּת **gâlûwth** (Chald.), *gaw-looth'*; corresp. to 1546:—captivity.

1548. גָּלַח **gâlach**, *gaw-lakh'*; a prim. root; prop. to *be bald*, i.e. (caus.) to *shave*; fig. to *lay waste*:—poll, shave (off).

1549. גִּלָּיוֹן **gillâyôwn**, *ghil-law-yone'*; or
גִּלְיוֹן **gilyôwn**, *ghil-yone'*; from 1540; a *tablet* for writing (as *bare*); by anal. a *mirror* (as a *plate*):—glass, roll.

1550. גָּלִיל **gâlîyl**, *gaw-leel'*; from 1556; a *valve* of a folding door (as *turning*); also a *ring* (as *round*):—folding, ring.

1551. גָּלִיל **Gâlîyl**, *gaw-leel'*; or (prol.)
גָּלִילָה **Gâlîylâh**, *gaw-lee-law'*; the same as 1550; a *circle* (with the art.); *Galil* (as a special *circuit*) in the North of Pal.:—Galilee.

1552. גְּלִילָה **gᵉlîylâh**, *ghel-ee-law'*; fem. of 1550; a *circuit* or *region*:—border, coast, country.

1553. גְּלִילוֹת **Gᵉlîylôwth**, *ghel-ee-lowth'*; plur. of 1552; *circles*; *Geliloth*, a place in Pal.:—Geliloth.

1554. גַּלִּים **Gallîym**, *gal-leem'*; plur. of 1530; *springs*; *Gallim*, a place in Pal.:—Gallim.

1555. גָּלְיַת **Golyath**, *gol-yath'*; perh. from 1540; *exile*; *Goljath*, a Philistine:—Goliath.

1556. גָּלַל **gâlal**, *gaw-lal'*; a prim. root; to *roll* (lit. or fig.):—commit, remove, roll (away, down, together), run down, seek occasion, trust, wallow.

1557. גָּלָל **gâlâl**, *gaw-lawl'*; from 1556; *dung* (as in *balls*):—dung.

1558. גָּלָל **gâlâl**, *gaw-lawl'*; from 1556; a *circumstance* (as *rolled* around); only used adv., on *account* of:—because of, for (sake).

1559. גָּלָל **Gâlâl**, *gaw-lawl'*; from 1556, in the sense of 1560; *great*; *Galal*, the name of two Isr.:—Galal.

1560. גְּלָל **gᵉlâl** (Chald.), *ghel-awl'*; from a root corresp. to 1556; *weight* or *size* (as if *rolled*):—great.

1561. גֵּלֶל **gêlel**, *gay'-lel*; a var. of 1557; *dung* (plur. *balls* of dung):—dung.

1562. גִּלֲלַי **Gîlălay**, *ghe-lal-ah'ee*; from 1561; *dungy*; *Gilalai*, an Isr.:—Gilalai.

1563. גָּלַם **gâlam**, *gaw-lam'*; a prim. root; to *fold*:—wrap together.

1564. גֹּלֶם **gôlem**, *go'-lem*; from 1563; a *wrapped* (and unformed *mass*, i.e. as the *embryo*):—substance yet being unperfect.

1565. גַּלְמוּד **galmûwd**, *gal-mood'*; prob. by prol. from 1563; *sterile* (as *wrapped* up too hard); fig. *desolate*:—desolate, solitary.

1566. גָּלַע **gâlaʻ**, *gaw-lah'*; a prim. root; to *be obstinate*:—(inter-) meddle (with).

1567. גַּלְעֵד **Galʻêd**, *gal-ade'*; from 1530 and 5707; *heap of testimony*; *Galed*, a memorial cairn E. of the Jordan:—Galeed.

1568. גִּלְעָד **Gilʻâd**, *ghil-awd'*; prob. from 1567; *Gilad*, a region E. of the Jordan; also the name of three Isr.:—Gilead, Gileadite.

1569. גִּלְעָדִי **Gilʻâdîy**, *ghil-aw-dee'*; patron. from 1568; a *Giladite* or desc. of Gilad:—Gileadite.

1570. גָּלַשׁ **gâlash**, *gaw-lash'*; a prim. root; prob. to *caper* (as a goat):—appear.

1571. גַּם **gam**, *gam*; by contr. from an unused root mean. to *gather*; prop. *assemblage*; used only adv. *also, even, yea, though*; often repeated as correl. *both . . . and*:—again, alike, also, (so much) as (soon), both (so) . . . and, but, either . . . or, even, for all, (in) likewise (manner), moreover, nay . . . neither, one, then (-refore), though, what, with, yea.

1572. גָּמָא **gâmâʼ**, *gaw-maw'*; a prim. root (lit. or fig.) to *absorb*:—swallow, drink.

1573. גֹּמֶא **gômeʼ**, *go'-meh*; from 1572; prop. an *absorbent*, i.e. the *bulrush* (from its *porosity*); spec. the *papyrus*:—(bul-) rush.

1574. גֹּמֶד **gômed**, *go'-med*; from an unused root appar. mean. to *grasp*; prop. a *span*:—cubit.

1575. גַּמָּד **gammâd**, *gam-mawd'*; from the same as 1574; a *warrior* (as grasping weapons):—Gammadims.

1576. גְּמוּל **gᵉmûwl**, *ghem-ool'*; from 1580; *treatment*, i.e. an *act* (of good or ill); by impl. *service* or *requital*:— + as hast served, benefit, desert, deserving, that which he hath given, recompence, reward.

1577. גָּמוּל **gâmûwl**, *gaw-mool'*; pass. part. of 1580; *rewarded*; *Gamul*, an Isr.:—Gamul. See also 1014.

1578. גְּמוּלָה **gᵉmûwlâh**, *ghem-oo-law'*; fem. of 1576; mean. the same:—deed, recompence, such a reward.

1579. גִּמְזוֹ **Gimzôw**, *ghim-zo'*; of uncert. der.; Gimzo, a place in Pal.:—Gimzo.

1580. גָּמַל **gâmal**, *gaw-mal'*; a prim. root; to *treat* a person (well or ill), i.e. *benefit* or *requite*; by impl. (of *toil*) to *ripen*, i.e. (spec.) to *wean*:—bestow on, deal bountifully, do (good), recompense, requite, reward, ripen, + serve, wean, yield.

1581. גָּמָל **gâmâl**, *gaw-mawl'*; appar. from 1580 (in the sense of *labor* or *burden-bearing*): a *camel*:—camel.

1582. גְּמַלִּי **Gᵉmalliy**, *ghem-al-lee'*; prob. from 1581; *camel-driver*; *Gemalli*, an Isr.:—Gemalli.

1583. גַּמְלִיאֵל **Gamliy'êl**, *gam-lee-ale'*; from 1580 and 410; *reward of God*; *Gamliel*, an Isr.:—Gamaliel.

1584. גָּמַר **gâmar**, *gaw-mar'*; a prim. root; to *end* (in the sense of *completion* or *failure*):—cease, come to an end, fail, perfect, perform.

1585. גְּמַר **gᵉmar** (Chald.), *ghem-ar'*; corresp. to 1584:—perfect.

1586. גֹּמֶר **Gômer**, *go'-mer*; from 1584; *completion*; *Gomer*, the name of a son of Japheth and of his desc.; also of a Hebrewess:—Gomer.

1587. גְּמַרְיָה **Gᵉmaryâh**, *ghem-ar-yaw'*; or גְּמַרְיָהוּ **Gᵉmaryâhûw**, *ghem-ar-yaw'-hoo*; from 1584 and 3050; *Jah has perfected*; *Gemarjah*, the name of two Isr.:—Gemariah.

1588. גַּן **gan**, *gan*; from 1598; a *garden* (as *fenced*):—garden.

1589. גָּנַב **gânab**, *gaw-nab'*; a prim. root; to *thieve* (lit. or fig.); by impl. to *deceive*:—carry away, × indeed, secretly bring, steal (away), get by stealth.

1590. גַּנָּב **gannâb**, *gaw-nab'*; from 1589; a *stealer*:—thief.

1591. גְּנֵבָה **gᵉnêbâh**, *ghen-ay-baw'*; from 1589; *stealing*, i.e. (concr.) something *stolen*:—theft.

1592. גְּנֻבַת **Gᵉnûbath**, *ghen-oo-bath'*; from 1589; *theft*; *Genubath*, an Edomitish prince:—Genubath.

1593. גַּנָּה **gannâh**, *gan-naw'*; fem. of 1588; a *garden*:—garden.

1594. גִּנָּה **ginnâh**, *ghin-naw'*; another form for 1593:—garden.

1595. גֶּנֶז **genez**, *gheh'-nez*; from an unused root mean. to *store*; *treasure*; by impl. a *coffer*:—chest, treasury.

1596. גְּנַז **gᵉnaz** (Chald.), *ghen-az'*; corresp. to 1595; *treasure*:—treasure.

1597. גִּנְזַךְ **ginzak**, *ghin-zak'*; prol. from 1595; a *treasury*:—treasury.

1598. גָּנַן **gânan**, *gaw-nan'*; a prim. root; to *hedge* about, i.e. (gen.) *protect*:—defend.

1599. גִּנְּתוֹן **Ginnᵉthôwn**, *ghin-neth-ōne*; or גִּנְּתוֹ **Ginnᵉthôw**, *ghin-neth-o'*; from 1598; *gardener*; *Ginnethon* or *Ginnetho*, an Isr.:—Ginnetho, Ginnethon.

1600. גָּעָה **gâ'âh**, *gaw-aw'*; a prim. root; to *bellow* (as cattle):—low.

1601. גֹּעָה **Gô'âh**, *go-aw'*; fem. act. part. of 1600; *lowing*; *Goah*, a place near Jerus.:—Goath.

1602. גָּעַל **gâ'al**, *gaw-al'*; a prim. root; to *detest*; by impl. to *reject*:—abhor, fail, lothe, vilely cast away.

1603. גַּעַל **Ga'al**, *gah'-al*; from 1602; *loathing*; *Gaal*, an Isr.:—Gaal.

1604. גֹּעַל **gô'al**, *go'-al*; from 1602; *abhorrence*:—loathing.

1605. גָּעַר **gâ'ar**, *gaw-ar'*; a prim. root; to *chide*:—corrupt, rebuke, reprove.

1606. גְּעָרָה **gᵉ'ârâh**, *gheh-aw-raw*; from 1605; a *chiding*:—rebuke (-ing), reproof.

1607. גָּעַשׁ **gâ'ash**, *gaw-ash'*; a prim. root to *agitate* violently:—move, shake, toss, trouble.

1608. גַּעַשׁ **Ga'ash**, *ga'-ash*; from 1607; a *quaking*; *Gaash*, a hill in Pal.:—Gaash.

1609. גַּעְתָּם **Ga'tâm**, *gah-tawm'*; of uncert. der.; *Gatam*, an Edomite:—Gatam.

1610. גַּף **gaph**, *gaf*; from an unused root mean. to *arch*; the *back*; by extens. the *body* or self:— + highest places, himself.

1611. גַּף **gaph** (Chald.), *gaf*; corresp. to 1610:—a *wing*:—wing.

1612. גֶּפֶן **gephen**, *gheh'-fen*; from an unused root mean. to *bend*; a *vine* (as *twining*), esp. the grape:—vine, tree.

1613. גֹּפֶר **gôpher**, *go'-fer*; from an unused root, prob. mean. to *house in*; a kind of tree or wood (as used for *building*), appar. the *cypress*:—gopher.

1614. גָּפְרִית **gophrîyth**, *gof-reeth'*; prob. fem. of 1613; prop. cypress-*resin*; by anal. *sulphur* (as equally inflammable):—brimstone.

1615. גִּר **gîr**, *gheer*; perh. from 3564; *lime* (from being *burned* in a kiln: —chalk [-stone].

1616. גֵּר **gêr**, *gare*; or (fully) גֵּיר **gêyr**, *gare*; from 1481; prop. a *guest*; by impl. a *foreigner*:—alien, sojourner, stranger.

גֻּר **gûr**. See 1482.

1617. גֵּרָא **Gêrâ'**, *gay-raw'*; perh. from 1626; a *grain*; *Gera*, the name of six Isr.:—Gera.

1618. גָּרָב **gârâb**, *gaw-rawb'*; from an unused root mean. to *scratch*; *scurf* (from *itching*):—scab, scurvy.

1619. גָּרֵב **Gârêb**, *gaw-rabe'*; from the same as 1618; *scabby*; *Gareb*, the name of an Isr., also of a hill near Jerus.:—Gareb.

1620. גַּרְגַּר **gargar**, *gar-gar'*; by redupl. from 1641; a *berry* (as if a pellet of *rumination*):—berry.

1621. גַּרְגְּרוֹת **gargᵉrôwth**, *gar-gher-owth'*; fem. plur. from 1641; the *throat* (as used in *rumination*):—neck.

1622. גִּרְגָּשִׁי **Girgâshîy**, *ghir-gaw-shee'*; patrial from an unused name [of uncert. der.]; a *Girgashite*, one of the native tribes of Canaan:—Girgashite, Girgasite.

1623. גָּרַד **gârad**, *gaw-rad'*; a prim. root; to *abrade*:—scrape.

1624. גָּרָה **gârâh**, *gaw-raw'*; a prim. root; prop. to *grate*, i.e. (fig.) to *anger*:—contend, meddle, stir up, strive.

1625. גֵּרָה **gêrâh**, *gay-raw'*; from 1641; the *cud* (as *scraping* the throat):—cud.

1626. גֵּרָה **gêrâh**, *gay-raw'*; from 1641 (as in 1625); prop. (like 1620) a *kernel* (round as if *scraped*), i.e. a *gerah* or small weight (and coin):—gerah.

גֹּרָה **gôrâh**. See 1484.

1627. גָּרוֹן **gârôwn**, *gaw-rone'*; or (short.) גָּרֹן **gârôn**, *gaw-rone'*; from 1641; the *throat* [comp. 1621] (as *roughened* by swallowing):— × aloud, mouth, neck, throat.

1628. גֵּרוּת **gêrûwth**, *gay-rooth'*; from 1481; a (temporary) *residence*:—habitation.

1629. גָּרַז **gâraz**, *gaw-raz'*; a prim. root; to *cut* off:—cut off.

1630. גְּרִזִים **Gᵉrîzîym**, *gher-ee-zeem'*; plur. of an unused noun from 1629 [comp. 1511], *cut* up (i.e. *rocky*); *Gerizim*, a mountain of Pal.:—Gerizim.

1631. גַּרְזֶן **garzen**, *gar-zen'*; from 1629; an *axe*:—ax.

1632. גָּרֹל **gârôl**, *gaw-role'*; from the same as 1486; *harsh*:—man of great [*as in the marg. which reads* 1419].

גֹּרָל **gôrâl**. See 1486.

1633. גָּרַם **gâram**, *gaw-ram'*; a prim. root; to be *spare* or *skeleton-like*; used only as a denom. from 1634; (caus.) to *bone*, i.e. *denude* (by extens. *craunch*) the bones:—gnaw the bones, break.

1634. גֶּרֶם **gerem**, *geh'-rem*; from 1633; a *bone* (as the *skeleton* of the body); hence *self*, i.e. (fig.) *very*:—bone, strong, top.

1635. גֶּרֶם **gerem** (Chald.), *gheh'-rem*; corresp. to 1634; a *bone*:—bone.

1636. גַּרְמִי **Garmîy**, *gar-mee'*; from 1634; *bony*, i.e. *strong*:—Garmite.

1637. גֹּרֶן **gôren**, *go'-ren*; from an unused root mean. to *smooth*; a threshing-*floor* (as made *even*); by anal. any open *area*:—(barn, corn, threshing-) floor, (threshing-, void) place.

גָּרֹן **gârôn**. See 1627.

1638. גָּרַס **gâraç**, *gaw-ras'*; a prim. root; to *crush*; also (intrans. and fig.) to *dissolve*:—break.

1639. גָּרַע **gâra'**, *gaw-rah'*; a prim. root; to *scrape* off; by impl. to *shave*, *remove*, *lessen* or *withhold*:—abate, clip, (di-) minish, do (take) away, keep back, restrain, make small, withdraw.

1640. גָּרַף **gâraph**, *gaw-raf'*; a prim. root; to *bear* off violently:—sweep away.

1641. גָּרַר **gârar**, *gaw-rar'*; a prim. root; to *drag* off roughly; by impl. to *bring up* the cud (i.e. *ruminate*); by anal. to *saw*:—catch, chew, × continuing, destroy, saw.

1642. גְּרָר **Gᵉrâr**, *gher-awr'*; prob. from 1641; a *rolling* country; *Gerar*, a Philistine city:—Gerar.

1643. גֶּרֶשׂ **geres**, *gheh'-res*; from an unused root mean. to *husk*; a *kernel* (collect.), i.e. *grain*:—beaten corn.

1644. גָּרַשׁ **gârash**, *gaw-rash'*; a prim. root; to *drive* out from a possession; espec. to *expatriate* or *divorce*:—cast up (out), divorced (woman), drive away (forth, out), expel, × surely put away, trouble, thrust out.

1645. גֶּרֶשׁ **geresh**, *gheh'-resh*; from 1644; *produce* (as if *expelled*):—put forth.

1646. גְּרֻשָׁה **gᵉrûshâh**, *gher-oo-shaw'*; fem. pass. part. of 1644; (abstr.) *dispossession*:—exaction.

1647. גֵּרְשֹׁם **Gêrᵉshôm**, *gay-resh-ome'*; for 1648; *Gereshom*, the name of four Isr.:—Gershom.

1648. גֵּרְשׁוֹן **Gêrᵉshown**, *gay-resh-one'*; or גֵּרְשׁוֹם **Gêrᵉshôwm**, *gay-resh-ome'*; from 1644; a *refugee*; *Gereshon* or *Gereshom*, an Isr.:—Gershon, Gershom.

1649. גֵּרְשֻׁנִּי **Gerᵉshunnîy**, *gay-resh-oon-nee'*; patron. from 1648; a *Gereshonite* or desc. of Gereshon:—Gershonite, sons of Gershon.

1650. גְּשׁוּר **Gᵉshûwr**, *ghesh-oor'*; from an unused root (mean. to *join*); *bridge*; *Geshur*, a district of Syria:—Geshur, Geshurite.

1651. גְּשׁוּרִי **Gᵉshûwrîy**, *ghe-shoo-ree'*; patrial from 1650; a *Geshurite* (also collect.) or inhab. of Geshur:—Geshuri, Geshurites.

1652. גָּשַׁם **gâsham**, *gaw-sham'*; a prim. root; to *shower* violently:—(cause to) rain.

1653. גֶּשֶׁם **geshem**, *gheh'-shem*; from 1652; a *shower*:—rain, shower.

1654. גֶּשֶׁם **Geshem**, *gheh'-shem*; or (prol.) גַּשְׁמוּ **Gashmûw**, *gash-moo'*; the same as 1653; *Geshem* or *Gashmu*, an Arabian:—Geshem, Gashmu.

1655. גֶּשֶׁם **geshem** (Chald.), *gheh'-shem*; appar. the same as 1653; used in a peculiar sense, the *body* (prob. for the [fig.] idea of a *hard rain*):—body.

1656. גֹּשֶׁם **gôshem**, *go'-shem;* from 1652; equiv. to 1653:—rained upon.

גֻּשְׁמוּ **Gashmûw**. See 1654.

1657. גֹּשֶׁן **Gôshen**, *go'-shen;* prob. of Eg. or.; *Goshen*, the residence of the Isr. in Egypt; also a place in Pal.:—Goshen.

1658. גִּשְׁפָּא **Gishpâ'**, *ghish-paw';* of uncert. der.; *Gishpa*, an Isr.:—Gispa.

1659. גָּשַׁשׁ **gâshash**, *gaw-shash';* a prim. root; appar. to *feel* about:—grope.

1660. גַּת **gath**, *gath;* prob. from 5059 (in the sense of *treading* out grapes); a wine-*press* (or vat for holding the grapes in pressing them):—(wine-) press (fat).

1661. גַּת **Gath**, *gath;* the same as 1660; *Gath*, a Philistine city:—Gath.

1662. גַּת־הַחֵפֶר **Gath-ha-Chêpher**, *gath-hah-khay'-fer;* or (abridged)

גִּתָּה־חֵפֶר **Gittâh-Chêpher**, *ghit-taw-khay'-fer;* from 1660 and 2658 with the art. ins.; *wine-press of (the) well; Gath-Chepher*, a place in Pal.:—Gath-kephr, Gittah-kephr.

1663. גִּתִּי **Gittîy**, *ghit-tee';* patrial from 1661; a *Gittite* or inhab. of Gath:—Gittite.

1664. גִּתַּיִם **Gittayim**, *ghit-tah'-yim;* dual of 1660; *double wine-press; Gittajim*, a place in Pal.:—Gittaim.

1665. גִּתִּית **Gittîyth**, *ghit-teeth';* fem. of 1663; a *Gittite* harp:—Gittith.

1666. גֶּתֶר **Gether**, *gheh'-ther;* of uncert. der.; *Gether*, a son of Aram, and the region settled by him:—Gether.

1667. גַּת־רִמּוֹן **Gath-Rimmôwn**, *gath-rim-mone';* from 1660 and 7416; *wine-press of* (the) *pomegranate; Gath-Rimmon*, a place in Pal.:—Gath-rimmon.

ד

1668. דָּא **dâ'** (Chald.), *daw;* corresp. to 2088; *this:*—one . . . another, this.

1669. דָּאַב **dâ'ab**, *daw-ab';* a prim. root; to *pine:*—mourn, sorrow (-ful).

1670. דְּאָבָה **de'âbâh**, *dĕh-aw-baw';* from 1669; prop. *pining;* by anal. *fear:*—sorrow.

1671. דְּאָבוֹן **de'âbôwn**, *dĕh-aw-bone';* from 1669; *pining:*—sorrow.

1672. דָּאַג **dâ'ag**, *daw-ag';* a prim. root; *be anxious:*—be afraid (careful, sorry), sorrow, take thought.

1673. דֹּאֵג **Dô'êg**, *do-ayg';* or (fully)

דּוֹאֵג **Dôw'êg**, *do-ayg';* act. part. of 1672; *anxious; Doëg*, an Edomite:—Doeg.

1674. דְּאָגָה **de'âgâh**, *dĕh-aw-gaw';* from 1672; *anxiety:*—care (-fulness), fear, heaviness, sorrow.

1675. דָּאָה **dâ'âh**, *daw-aw';* a prim. root; to *dart*, i.e. *fly* rapidly:—fly.

1676. דָּאָה **dâ'âh**, *daw-aw';* from 1675; the *kite* (from its rapid *flight*):—vulture. See 7201.

1677. דֹּב **dôb**, *dobe;* or (fully)

דּוֹב **dôwb**, *dobe;* from 1680; the *bear* (as slow):—bear.

1678. דֹּב **dôb** (Chald.), *dobe;* corresp. to 1677:—bear.

1679. דֹּבֶא **dôbe'**, *do'-beh;* from an unused root (comp. 1680) (prob. mean. to *be sluggish*, i.e. *restful*); *quiet:*—strength.

1680. דָּבַב **dâbab**, *daw-bab';* a prim. root (comp. 1679); to *move* slowly, i.e. *glide:*—cause to speak.

1681. דִּבָּה **dibbâh**, *dib-baw';* from 1680 (in the sense of *furtive* motion); *slander:*—defaming, evil report, infamy, slander.

1682. דְּבוֹרָה **debôwrâh**, *deb-o-raw';* or (short.)

דְּבֹרָה **debôrâh**, *deb-o-raw';* from 1696 (in the sense of *orderly* motion); the *bee* (from its *systematic* instincts):—bee.

1683. דְּבוֹרָה **Debôwrâh**, *deb-o-raw';* or (short.)

דְּבֹרָה **Debôrâh**, *deb-o-raw';* the same as 1682; *Deborah*, the name of two Hebrewesses:—Deborah.

1684. דְּבַח **debach** (Chald.), *deb-akh';* corresp. to 2076; to *sacrifice* (an animal):—offer [sacrifice].

1685. דְּבַח **debach** (Chald.), *deb-akh';* from 1684; a *sacrifice:*—sacrifice.

1686. דִּבְיוֹן **dibyôwn**, *dib-yone';* in the marg. for the textual reading

חֲרְיוֹן° **cheryôwn**, *kher-yone';* both (in the plur. only and) of uncert. der.; prob. some cheap vegetable, perh. a bulbous root:—dove's dung.

1687. דְּבִיר **debîyr**, *deb-eer';* or (short.)

דְּבִר **debîr**, *deb-eer';* from 1696 (appar. in the sense of *oracle*); the *shrine* or innermost part of the sanctuary:—oracle.

1688. דְּבִיר **Debîyr**, *deb-eer';* or (short.)

דְּבִר **Debîr** (Josh. 13 : 26 [but see 3810]), *deb-eer';* the same as 1687; *Debir*, the name of an Amoritish king and of two places in Pal.:—Debir.

1689. דִּבְלָה **Diblâh**, *dib-law';* prob. an orth. err. for 7247; *Diblah*, a place in Syria:—Diblath.

1690. דְּבֵלָה **debêlâh**, *deb-ay-law';* from an unused root (akin to 2082) prob. mean. to *press* together; a *cake* of pressed figs:—cake (lump) of figs.

1691. דִּבְלַיִם **Diblayim**, *dib-lah'-yim;* dual from the masc. of 1690; *two cakes; Diblajim*, a symbol. name:—Diblaim.

דִּבְלָתַיִם **Diblâthayim**. See 1015.

1692. דָּבַק **dâbaq**, *daw-bak';* a prim. root; prop. to *impinge*, i.e. *cling* or *adhere;* fig. to *catch* by pursuit:—abide fast, cleave (fast together), follow close (hard after), be joined (together), keep (fast), overtake, pursue hard, stick, take.

1693. דְּבַק **debaq** (Chald.), *deb-ak';* corresp. to 1692; to *stick* to:—cleave.

1694. דֶּבֶק **debeq**, *deh'-bek;* from 1692; a *joint;* by impl. *solder:*—joint, solder.

1695. דָּבֵק **dâbêq**, *daw-bake';* from 1692; *adhering:*—cleave, joining, stick closer.

1696. דָּבַר **dâbar**, *daw-bar';* a prim. root; perh. prop. to *arrange;* but used fig. (of words) to *speak;* rarely (in a destructive sense) to *subdue:*—answer, appoint, bid, command, commune, declare, destroy, give, name, promise, pronounce, rehearse, say, speak, be spokesman, subdue, talk, teach, tell, think, use [entreaties], utter, × well, × work.

1697. דָּבָר **dâbâr**, *daw-bawr';* from 1696; a *word;* by impl. a *matter* (as *spoken* of) or *thing;* adv. a *cause:*—act, advice, affair, answer, × any such (thing), + because of, book, business, care, case, cause, certain rate, + chronicles, commandment, × commune (-ication), + concern [-ing], + confer, counsel, + dearth, decree, deed, × disease, due, duty, effect, + eloquent, errand, [evil favoured-] ness, + glory, + harm, hurt, + iniquity, + judgment, language, + lying, manner, matter, message, [no] thing, oracle, × ought, × parts, + pertaining, + please, portion, + power, promise, provision, purpose, question, rate, reason, report, request, × (as hast) said, sake, saying, sentence, + sign, + so, some [uncleanness], somewhat to say, + song, speech, × spoken, talk, task, + that, × there done, thing (concerning), thought, + thus, tidings, what [-soever], + wherewith, which, word, work.

1698. דֶּבֶר **deber**, *deh'-ber;* from 1696 (in the sense of *destroying*); a *pestilence:*—murrain, pestilence, plague.

1699. דֹּבֶר **dôber**, *do'-ber;* from 1696 (in its original sense); a *pasture* (from its *arrangement* of the flock):—fold, manner.

דְּבִר **debîr** or **Debîr**. See 1687, 1688.

1699'. דִּבֵּר **dibbêr**, *dib-bare';* for 1697:—word.

1700. דִּבְרָה **dibrâh**, *dib-raw';* fem. of 1697; a *reason, suit* or *style:*—cause, end, estate, order, regard.

1701. דִּבְרָה **dibrâh** (Chald.), *dib-raw';* corresp. to 1700:—intent, sake.

דְּבֹרָה **debôrâh** or **Debôrâh**. See 1682, 1683.

1702. דֹּבְרָה **dôberâh**, *do-ber-aw';* fem. act. part. of 1696 in the sense of *driving* [comp. 1699]; a *raft:*—float.

1703. דַּבָּרָה **dabbârâh**, *dab-baw-raw';* intens. from 1696; a *word:*—word.

1704. דִּבְרִי **Dibrîy**, *dib-ree';* from 1697; *wordy; Dibri*, an Isr.:—Dibri.

1705. דָּבְרַת **Dâberath**, *daw-ber-ath';* from 1697 (perh. in the sense of 1699); *Daberath*, a place in Pal.:—Dabareh, Daberath.

1706. דְּבַשׁ **debash**, *deb-ash';* from an unused root mean. to *be gummy; honey* (from its *stickiness*); by anal. *syrup:*—honey ([-comb]).

1707. דַּבֶּשֶׁת **dabbesheth**, *dab-beh'-sheth;* intens. from the same as 1706; a sticky *mass*, i.e. the *hump* of a camel:—hunch [of a camel].

1708. דַּבֶּשֶׁת **Dabbesheth**, *dab-beh'-sheth;* the same as 1707; *Dabbesheth*, a place in Pal.:—Dabbesheth.

1709. דָּג **dâg**, *dawg;* or (fully)

דָּאג° **dâ'g** (Neh. 13 : 16), *dawg;* from 1711; a *fish* (as *prolific*); or perh. rather from 1672 (as *timid*); but still better from 1672 (in the sense of *squirming*, i.e. moving by the vibratory action of the tail); a *fish* (often used collect.):—fish.

1710. דָּגָה **dâgâh**, *daw-gaw';* fem. of 1709, and mean. the same:—fish.

1711. דָּגָה **dâgâh**, *daw-gaw';* a prim. root; to *move rapidly;* used only as a denom. from 1709; to *spawn*, i.e. *become numerous:*—grow.

1712. דָּגוֹן **Dâgôwn**, *daw-gohn';* from 1709; the *fish-god; Dagon*, a Philistine deity:—Dagon.

1713. דָּגַל **dâgal**, *daw-gal';* a prim. root; to *flaunt*, i.e. *raise a flag;* fig. to *be conspicuous:*—(set up, with) banners, chiefest.

1714. דֶּגֶל **degel**, *deh'-gel;* from 1713; a *flag:*—banner, standard.

1715. דָּגָן **dâgân**, *daw-gawn';* from 1711; prop. *increase*, i.e. *grain:*—corn ([floor]), wheat.

1716. דָּגַר **dâgar**, *daw-gar';* a prim. root; to *brood* over eggs or young:—gather, sit.

1717. דַּד **dad**, *dad;* appar. from the same as 1730; the *breast* (as the seat of *love*, or from its shape):—breast, teat.

1718. דָּדָה **dâdâh**, *daw-daw';* a doubtful root; to *walk gently:*—go (softly, with).

1719. דְּדָן **Dedân**, *ded-awn';* or (prol.)

דְּדָנֶה **Dedâneh** (Ezek. 25 : 13), *deh-daw'-neh;* of uncert. der.; *Dedan*, the name of two Cushites and of their territory:—Dedan.

1720. דְּדָנִים **Dedânîym**, *ded-aw-neem';* plur. of 1719 (as patrial); *Dedanites*, the desc. or inhab. of Dedan:—Dedanim.

1721. דֹּדָנִים **Dôdânîym**, *do-daw-neem';* or (by orth. err.)

רֹדָנִים **Rôdânîym** (1 Chron. 1 : 7), *ro-daw-neem';* a plur. of uncert. der.; *Dodanites*, or desc. of a son of Javan:—Dodanim.

1722. דְּהַב **dehab** (Chald.), *deh-hab';* corresp. to 2091; *gold:*—gold (-en).

1723. דַּהֲוָא° **Dahăvâ'** (Chald.), *dah-hav-aw';* of uncert. der.; *Dahava*, a people colonized in Samaria:—Dehavites.

1724. דָּהַם **dâham**, *daw-ham';* a prim. root (comp. 1740); to *be dumb*, i.e. (fig.) *dumbfounded:*—be astonished.

1725. דָּהַר **dâhar**, *daw-har';* a prim. root; to *curvet* or move irregularly:—pranse.

1726. דַּהֲהַר **dahăhar**, *dah-hah-har';* by redupl. from 1725; a *gallop:*—pransing.

דּוֹאֵג **Dôw'êg**. See 1673.

1727. דּוּב **dûwb**, *doob;* a prim. root; to *mope*, i.e. (fig.) *pine:*—sorrow.

דּוֹב **dôwb**. See 1677.

1728. דַּוָּג **davvâg**, *dav-vawg';* an orth. var. of 1709 as a denom. [1771]; a *fisherman:*—fisher.

1729. דּוּגָה **dûwgâh**, *doo-gaw';* fem. from the same as 1728; prop. *fishery,* i.e. a *hook* for fishing:—fish [hook].

1730. דּוֹד **dôwd**, *dode;* or (short.)
דֹּד **dôd**, *dode;* from an unused root mean. prop. to *boil,* i.e. (fig.) to *love;* by impl. a *love-token, lover, friend;* spec. an *uncle:*—(well-) beloved, father's brother, love, uncle.

1731. דּוּד **dûwd**, *dood;* from the same as 1730; a *pot* (for *boiling*); also (by resemblance of shape) a *basket:*—basket, caldron, kettle, (seething) pot.

1732. דָּוִד **Dâvîd**, *daw-veed';* rarely (fully)
דָּוִיד **Dâvîyd**, *daw-veed';* from the same as 1730; *loving; David,* the youngest son of Jesse.—David.

1733. דּוֹדָה **dôwdâh**, *do-daw';* fem. of 1730; an *aunt:*—aunt, father's sister, uncle's wife.

1734. דּוֹדוֹ **Dôwdôw**, *do-do';* from 1730; *loving; Dodo,* the name of three Isr.:—Dodo.

1735. דּוֹדָוָהוּ **Dôwdâvâhûw**, *do-daw-vaw'-hoo;* from 1730 and 3050; *love of Jah; Dodavah,* an Isr.:—Dodavah.

1736. דּוּדַי **dûwday**, *doo-dah'-ee;* from 1731; a *boiler* or *basket;* also the *mandrake* (as *aphrodisiac*):—basket, mandrake.

1737. דּוֹדַי **Dôwday**, *do-dah'ee;* formed like 1736; *amatory; Dodai,* an Isr.:—Dodai.

1738. דָּוָה **dâvâh**, *daw-vaw';* a prim. root; to *be sick* (as if in menstruation):—infirmity.

1739. דָּוֶה **dâveh**, *daw-veh';* from 1738; *sick* (espec. in menstruation):—faint, menstruous cloth, she that is sick, having sickness.

1740. דּוּחַ **dûwach**, *doo'-akh;* a prim. root; to *thrust* away; fig. to *cleanse:*—cast out, purge, wash.

1741. דְּוַי **d^{e}vay**, *dev-ah'ee;* from 1739; *sickness;* fig. *loathing:*—languishing, sorrowful.

1742. דַּוָּי **davvây**, *dav-voy';* from 1739; *sick;* fig. *troubled:*—faint.

דָּוִיד **Dâvîyd**. See 1732.

1743. דּוּךְ **dûwk**, *dook;* a prim. root; to *bruise* in a mortar:—beat.

1744. דּוּכִיפַת **dûwkîyphath**, *doo-kee-fath';* of uncert. der.; the *hoopoe* or else the *grouse:*—lapwing.

1745. דּוּמָה **dûwmâh**, *doo-maw';* from an unused root mean. to *be dumb* (comp. 1820); *silence;* fig. *death:*—silence.

1746. דּוּמָה **Dûwmâh**, *doo-maw';* the same as 1745; *Dumah,* a tribe and region of Arabia:—Dumah.

1747. דּוּמִיָּה **dûwmîyâh**, *doo-me-yaw';* from 1820; *stillness;* adv. *silently;* abstr. *quiet, trust:*—silence, silent, waiteth.

1748. דּוּמָם **dûwmâm**, *doo-mawm';* from 1826; *still;* adv. *silently:*—dumb, silent, quietly wait.

דּוּמֶשֶׂק° **Dûwmesheq**. See 1833.

1749. דּוֹנַג **dôwnag**, *do-nag';* of uncert. der.; *wax:*—wax.

1750. דּוּץ **dûwts**, *doots;* a prim. root; to *leap:*—be turned.

1751. דּוּק **dûwq** (Chald.), *dook;* corresp. to 1854; to *crumble:*—be broken to pieces.

1752. דּוּר **dûwr**, *dure;* a prim. root; prop. to *gyrate* (or move in a circle), i.e. to *remain:*—dwell.

1753. דּוּר **dûwr** (Chald.), *dure;* corresp. to 1752; to *reside:*—dwell.

1754. דּוּר **dûwr**, *dure;* from 1752; a *circle, ball* or *pile:*—ball, turn, round about.

1755. דּוֹר **dôwr**, *dore;* or (short.)
דֹּר **dôr**, *dore;* from 1752; prop. a *revolution* of time, i.e. an *age* or generation; also a *dwelling:*—age, × evermore, generation, [n-]ever, posterity.

1756. דּוֹר **Dôwr**, *dore;* or (by perm.)
דֹּאר **Dô'r** (Josh. 17 : 11; 1 Kings 4 : 11), *dore;* from 1755; *dwelling; Dor,* a place in Pal.:—Dor.

1757. דּוּרָא **Dûwrâ'** (Chald.), *doo-raw';* prob. from 1753; *circle* or *dwelling; Dura,* a place in Bab.:—Dura.

1758. דּוּשׁ **dûwsh**, *doosh;* or
דּוֹשׁ **dôwsh**, *dōsh;* or
דִּישׁ **dîysh**, *deesh;* a prim. root; to *trample* or *thresh:*—break, tear, thresh, tread out (down), at grass [Jer. 50 : 11, *by mistake for* 1877].

1759. דּוּשׁ **dûwsh** (Chald.), *doosh;* corresp. to 1758; to *trample:*—tread down.

1760. דָּחָה **dâchâh**, *daw-khaw';* or
דָּחַח **dâchach** (Jer. 23 : 12), *daw-khakh';* a prim. root; to *push* down:—chase, drive away (on), overthrow, outcast, × sore, thrust, totter.

1761. דַּחֲוָה **dachăvâh** (Chald.), *dakh-av-aw';* from the equiv. of 1760; prob. a musical *instrument* (as being *struck*):—instrument of music.

1762. דְּחִי **d^{e}chîy**, *deh-khee';* from 1760; a *push,* i.e. (by impl.) a *fall:*—falling.

1763. דְּחַל **d^{e}chal** (Chald.), *deh-khal';* corresp. to 2119; to *slink,* i.e. (by impl.) to *fear,* or (caus.) *be formidable:*—make afraid, dreadful, fear, terrible.

1764. דֹּחַן **dôchan**, *do'-khan;* of uncert. der.; *millet:*—millet.

1765. דָּחַף **dâchaph**, *daw-khaf';* a prim. root; to *urge,* i.e. *hasten:*—(be) haste (-ned), pressed on.

1766. דָּחַק **dâchaq**, *daw-khak';* a prim. root; to *press,* i.e. *oppress:*—thrust, vex.

1767. דַּי **day**, *dahee;* of uncert. der.; *enough* (as noun or adv.), used chiefly with prep. in phrases:—able, according to, after (ability), among, as (oft as), (more than) enough, from, in, since, (much as is) sufficient (-ly), too much, very, when.

1768. דִּי **dîy** (Chald.), *dee;* appar. for 1668; *that,* used as rel., conj., and espec. (with prep.) in adv. phrases; also as a prep. *of:*— × as, but, for (-asmuch +), + now, of, seeing, than, that, therefore, until, + what (-soever), when, which, whom, whose.

1769. דִּיבוֹן **Dîybôwn**, *dee-bone';* or (short.)
דִּיבֹן **Dîybôn**, *dee-bone';* from 1727; *pining:*—Dibon, the name of three places in Pal.:—Dibon. [*Also, with* 1410 *added,* Dibon-gad.]

1770. דִּיג **dîyg**, *deeg;* denom. from 1709; to *fish:*—fish.

1771. דַּיָּג **dayâg**, *dah-yawg';* from 1770; a *fisherman:*—fisher.

1772. דַּיָּה **dayâh**, *dah-yaw';* intens. from 1675; a *falcon* (from its *rapid* flight):—vulture.

1773. דְּיוֹ **d^{e}yôw**, *deh-yo';* of uncert. der.; *ink:*—ink.

1774. דִּי זָהָב **Dîy zâhâb**, *dee zaw-hawb';* as if from 1768 and 2091; *of gold; Dizahab,* a place in the Desert:—Dizahab.

1775. דִּימוֹן **Dîymôwn**, *dee-mone';* perh. for 1769; *Dimon,* a place in Pal.:—Dimon.

1776. דִּימוֹנָה **Dîymôwnâh**, *dee-mo-naw';* fem. of 1775; *Dimonah,* a place in Pal.:—Dimonah.

1777. דִּין **dîyn**, *deen;* or (Gen. 6 : 3)
דּוּן **dûwn**, *doon;* a prim. root [comp. 113]; to *rule;* by impl. to *judge* (as umpire); also to *strive* (as at law):—contend, execute (judgment), judge, minister judgment, plead (the cause), at strife, strive.

1778. דִּין **dîyn** (Chald.), *deen;* corresp. to 1777; to *judge:*—judge.

1779. דִּין **dîyn**, *deen;* or (Job 19 : 29)
דּוּן **dûwn**, *doon;* from 1777; *judgment* (the suit, justice, sentence or tribunal); by impl. also *strife:*—cause, judgment, plea, strife.

1780. דִּין **dîyn** (Chald.), *deen;* corresp. to 1779:—judgment.

1781. דַּיָּן **dayân**, *dah-yawn';* from 1777; a *judge* or *advocate:*—judge.

1782. דַּיָּן **dayân** (Chald.), *dah-yawn';* corresp. to 1781:—judge.

1783. דִּינָה **Dîynâh**, *dee-naw';* fem. of 1779; *justice; Dinah,* the daughter of Jacob:—Dinah.

1784. דִּינַי **Dîynay** (Chald.), *dee-nah'ee;* patrial from an uncert. prim.; a *Dinaite* or inhab. of some unknown Ass. province:—Dinaite.

דִּיפַת **Dîyphath**. See 7384.

1785. דָּיֵק **dâyêq**, *daw-yake';* from a root corresp. to 1751; a *battering*-tower:—fort.

1786. דַּיִשׁ **dayîsh**, *dah'-yish;* from 1758; *threshing*-time:—threshing.

1787. דִּישׁוֹן **Dîyshôwn**,
דִּישֹׁן **Dîyshôn**,
דִּשׁוֹן **Dîshôwn**, or
דִּשֹׁן **Dîshôn**, *dee-shone';* the same as 1788; *Dishon,* the name of two Edomites:—Dishon.

1788. דִּישֹׁן **dîyshôn**, *dee-shone';* from 1758; the *leaper,* i.e. an *antelope:*—pygarg.

1789. דִּישָׁן **Dîyshân**, *dee-shawn';* another form of 1787; *Dishan,* an Edomite:—Dishan, Dishon.

1790. דַּךְ **dak**, *dak;* from an unused root (comp., 1794); *crushed,* i.e. (fig.) *injured:*—afflicted, oppressed.

1791. דֵּךְ **dêk** (Chald.), *dake;* or
דָּךְ **dâk** (Chald.), *dawk;* prol. from 1668; *this:*—the same, this.

1792. דָּכָא **dâkâ'**, *daw-kaw';* a prim. root (comp. 1794); to *crumble;* trans. to *bruise* (lit. or fig.):—beat to pieces, break (in pieces), bruise, contrite, crush, destroy, humble, oppress, smite.

1793. דַּכָּא **dakkâ'**, *dak-kaw';* from 1792; *crushed* (lit. *powder,* or fig. *contrite*):—contrite, destruction.

1794. דָּכָה **dâkâh**, *daw-kaw';* a prim. root (comp. 1790, 1792); to *collapse* (phys. or mentally):—break (sore), contrite, crouch.

1795. דַּכָּה **dakkâh**, *dak-kaw';* from 1794 like 1793; *mutilated:*— + wounded.

1796. דֳּכִי **dŏkîy**, *dok-ee';* from 1794; a *dashing* of surf:—wave.

1797. דִּכֵּן **dikkên** (Chald.), *dik-kane';* prol. from 1791; *this:*—same, that, this.

1798. דְּכַר **d^{e}kar** (Chald.), *dek-ar';* corresp. to 2145; prop. a *male,* i.e. of sheep:—ram.

1799. דִּכְרוֹן **dikrôwn** (Chald.), *dik-rone';* or
דָּכְרָן **dokrân**, *dok-rawn'* (Chald.); corresp. to 2146; a *register:*—record.

1800. דַּל **dal**, *dal;* from 1809; prop. *dangling,* i.e. (by impl.) *weak* or *thin:*—lean, needy, poor (man), weaker.

1801. דָּלַג **dâlag**, *daw-lag';* a prim. root; to *spring:*—leap.

1802. דָּלָה **dâlâh**, *daw-law';* a prim. root (comp. 1809); prop. to *dangle,* i.e. to *let down* a bucket (for *drawing* out water); fig. to *deliver:*—draw (out), × enough, lift up.

1803. דַּלָּה **dallâh**, *dal-law';* from 1802; prop. something *dangling,* i.e. a loose *thread* or *hair;* fig. *indigent:*—hair, pining sickness, poor (-est sort).

1804. דָּלַח **dâlach**, *daw-lakh';* a prim. root; to *roil* water:—trouble.

1805. דְּלִי **d^{e}lîy**, *del-ee';* or
דֳּלִי **dŏlîy**, *dol-ee';* from 1802; a *pail* or *jar* (for *drawing* water):—bucket.

1806. דְּלָיָה **D^{e}lâyâh**, *del-aw-yaw';* or (prol.)
דְּלָיָהוּ **D^{e}lâyâhûw**, *del-aw-yaw'-hoo;* from 1802 and 3050; *Jah has delivered; Delajah,* the name of five Isr.:—Dalaiah, Delaiah.

1807. דְּלִילָה **D^{e}lîylâh**, *del-ee-law';* from 1809; *languishing:*—Delilah, a Philistine woman:—Delilah.

1808. דָּלִיָּה **dâlîyâh**, *daw-lee-yaw';* from 1802; something *dangling,* i.e. a *bough:*—branch.

1809. דָּלַל **dâlal**, *daw-lal';* a prim. root (comp. 1802); to *slacken* or *be feeble;* fig. to *be oppressed:*—bring low, dry up, be emptied, be not equal, fail, be impoverished, be made thin.

1810. דִּלְעָן **Dilʻân**, *dil-awn'*; of uncert. der.; *Dilan*, a place in Pal.:—Dilean.

1811. דָּלַף **dâlaph**, *daw-laf'*; a prim. root; to *drip*; by impl. to *weep*:—drop through, melt, pour out.

1812. דֶּלֶף **deleph**, *deh'-lef*; from 1811; a *dripping*:—dropping.

1813. דַּלְפוֹן **Dalphôwn**, *dal-fone'*; from 1811; *dripping*; *Dalphon*, a son of Haman:—Dalphon.

1814. דָּלַק **dâlaq**, *daw-lak'*; a prim. root; to *flame* (lit. or fig.):—burning, chase, inflame, kindle, persecute (-or), pursue hotly.

1815. דְּלַק **delaq** (Chald.), *del-ak'*; corresp. to 1814:—burn.

1816. דַּלֶּקֶת **dalleqeth**, *dal-lek'-keth*; from 1814; a *burning fever*:—inflammation.

1817. דֶּלֶת **deleth**, *deh'-leth*; from 1802; something *swinging*, i.e. the *valve* of a door:—door (two-leaved), gate, leaf, lid. [In Psa. 141:3, *dâl*, irreg.]

1818. דָּם **dâm**, *dawm*; from 1826 (comp. 119); *blood* (as that which when shed causes *death*) of man or an animal; by anal. the *juice* of the *grape*; fig. (espec. in the plur.) *bloodshed* (i.e. *drops of blood*):—blood (-y, -guiltiness, [-thirsty]), + innocent.

1819. דָּמָה **dâmâh**, *daw-maw'*; a prim. root; to *compare*; by impl. to *resemble*, *liken*, *consider*:—compare, devise, (be) like (-n), mean, think, use similitudes.

1820. דָּמָה **dâmâh**, *daw-maw'*; a prim. root; to *be dumb* or *silent*; hence to *fail* or *perish*; trans. to *destroy*:—cease, be cut down (off), destroy, be brought to silence, be undone, × utterly.

1821. דְּמָה **demâh** (Chald.), *dem-aw'*; corresp. to 1819; to *resemble*:—be like.

1822. דֻּמָּה **dummâh**, *doom-maw'*; from 1820; *desolation*; concr. *desolate*:—destroy.

1823. דְּמוּת **demûwth**, *dem-ooth'*; from 1819; *resemblance*; concr. *model*, *shape*; adv. *like*:—fashion, like (-ness, as), manner, similitude.

1824. דְּמִי **demîy**, *dem-ee'*; or
דֳּמִי **dŏmîy**, *dom-ee'*; from 1820; *quiet*:—cutting off, rest, silence.

1825. דִּמְיוֹן **dimyôwn**, *dim-yone'*; from 1819; *resemblance*:—× like.

1826. דָּמַם **dâmam**, *daw-mam'*; a prim. root [comp. 1724, 1820]; to *be dumb*; by impl. to *be astonished*, to *stop*; also to *perish*:—cease, be cut down (off), forbear, hold peace, quiet self, rest, be silent, keep (put to) silence, be (stand) still, tarry, wait.

1827. דְּמָמָה **demâmâh**, *dem-aw-maw'*; fem. from 1826; *quiet*:—calm, silence, still.

1828. דֹּמֶן **dômen**, *do'-men*; of uncert. der.; *manure*:—dung.

1829. דִּמְנָה **Dimnâh**, *dim-naw'*; fem. from the same as 1828; a *dung-heap*; *Dimnah*, a place in Pal.:—Dimnah.

1830. דָּמַע **dâmaʻ**, *daw-mah'*; a prim. root; to *weep*:—× sore, weep.

1831. דֶּמַע **demaʻ**, *deh'-mah*; from 1830; a *tear*; fig. *juice*:—liquor.

1832. דִּמְעָה **dimʻâh**, *dim-aw'*; fem. of 1831; *weeping*:—tears.

1833. דְּמֶשֶׁק **demesheq**, *dem-eh'-shek*; by orth. var. from 1834; *damask* (as a fabric of Damascus):—in Damascus.

1834. דַּמֶּשֶׂק **Dammeseq**, *dam-meh'-sek*; or
דּוּמֶשֶׂק **Dûwmeseq**, *doo-meh'-sek*; or
דַּרְמֶשֶׂק **Darmeseq**, *dar-meh'-sek*; of for. or.; *Damascus*, a city of Syria:—Damascus.

1835. דָּן **Dân**, *dawn*; from 1777; *judge*; *Dan*, one of the sons of Jacob; also the tribe descended from him, and its territory; likewise a place in Pal. colonized by them:—Dan.

1836. דֵּן **dên** (Chald.), *dane*; an orth. var. of 1791; *this*:—[afore-] time, + after this manner, here [-after], one . . . another, such, there [-fore], these, this (matter), + thus, where [-fore], which.

דָּנִאֵל **Dânîʼêl**. See 1841.

1837. דַּנָּה **Dannâh**, *dan-naw'*; of uncert. der.; *Dannah*, a place in Pal.:—Dannah.

1838. דִּנְהָבָה **Dinhâbâh**, *din-haw-baw'*; of uncert. der.; *Dinhabah*, an Edomitish town:—Dinhaban.

1839. דָּנִי **Dânîy**, *daw-nee'*; patron. from 1835; a *Danite* (often collect.) or desc. (or inhab.) of Dan:—Danites, of Dan.

1840. דָּנִיֵּאל **Dânîyêʼl**, *daw-nee-yale'*; in Ezek.
דָּנִאֵל **Dânîʼêl**, *daw-nee-ale'*; from 1835 and 410; *judge of God*; *Daniel* or *Danijel*, the name of two Isr.:—Daniel.

1841. דָּנִיֵּאל **Dânîyêʼl** (Chald.), *daw-nee-yale'*; corresp. to 1840; *Danijel*, the Heb. prophet:—Daniel.

1842. דָּן יַעַן **Dân Yaʻan**, *dawn yah'-an*; from 1835 and (appar.) 3282; *judge of purpose*; *Dan-Jaan*, a place in Pal.:—Dan-jaan.

1843. דֵּעַ **dêaʻ**, *day'-ah*; from 3045; *knowledge*:—knowledge, opinion.

1844. דֵּעָה **dêʻâh**, *day-aw'*; fem. of 1843; *knowledge*:—knowledge.

1845. דְּעוּאֵל **Deʻûwʼêl**, *deh-oo-ale'*; from 3045 and 410; *known of God*; *Deüel*, an Isr.:—Deuel.

1846. דָּעַךְ **dâʻak**, *daw-ak'*; a prim. root; to *be extinguished*; fig. to *expire* or *be dried up*:—be extinct, consumed, put out, quenched.

1847. דַּעַת **daʻath**, *dah'-ath*; from 3045; *knowledge*:—cunning, [ig-] norantly, know (-ledge), [un-] awares (wittingly).

1848. דֳּפִי **dŏphîy**, *dof'-ee*; from an unused root (mean. to *push* over); a *stumbling-block*:—slanderest.

1849. דָּפַק **dâphaq**, *daw-fak'*; a prim. root; to *knock*; by anal. to *press* severely:—beat, knock, overdrive.

1850. דָּפְקָה **Dophqâh**, *dof-kaw'*; from 1849; a *knock*; *Dophkah*, a place in the Desert:—Dophkah.

1851. דַּק **daq**, *dak*; from 1854; *crushed*, i.e. (by impl.) *small* or *thin*:—dwarf, lean [-fleshed], very little thing, small, thin.

1852. דֹּק **dôq**, *doke*; from 1854; something *crumbling*, i.e. *fine* (as a *thin* cloth):—curtain.

1853. דִּקְלָה **Diqlâh**, *dik-law'*; of for. or.; *Diklah*, a region of Arabia:—Diklah.

1854. דָּקַק **dâqaq**, *daw-kak'*; a prim. root [comp. 1915]; to *crush* (or intrans.) *crumble*:—beat in pieces (small), bruise, make dust, (into) × powder, (be, very) small, stamp (small).

1855. דְּקַק **deqaq** (Chald.), *dek-ak'*; corresp. to 1854; to *crumble* or (trans.) *crush*:—break to pieces.

1856. דָּקַר **dâqar**, *daw-kar'*; a prim. root; to *stab*; by anal. to *starve*; fig. to *revile*:—pierce, strike (thrust) through, wound.

1857. דֶּקֶר **Deqer**, *deh'-ker*; from 1856; a *stab*; *Deker*, an Isr.:—Dekar.

1858. דַּר **dar**, *dar*; appar. from the same as 1865; prop. a *pearl* (from its sheen as rapidly *turned*); by anal. *pearl-stone*, i.e. mother-of-pearl or alabaster:—× white.

1859. דָּר **dâr** (Chald.), *dawr*; corresp. to 1755; an *age*:—generation.

דֹּר **dôr**. See 1755.

1860. דְּרָאוֹן **derâʼôwn**, *der-aw-one'*; or
דֵּרָאוֹן **dêraʼôwn**, *day-raw-one'*; from an unused root (mean. to *repulse*); an object of *aversion*:—abhorring, contempt.

1861. דָּרְבוֹן **dorbôwn**, *dor-bone'* [also *dor-bawn'*]; of uncert. der.; a *goad*:—goad.

1862. דַּרְדַּע **Dardaʻ**, *dar-dah'*; appar. from 1858 and 1843; *pearl of knowledge*; *Darda*, an Isr.:—Darda.

1863. דַּרְדַּר **dardar**, *dar-dar'*; of uncert. der.; a *thorn*:—thistle.

1864. דָּרוֹם **dârôwm**, *daw-rome'*; of uncert. der.; the *south*; poet. the *south wind*:—south.

1865. דְּרוֹר **derôwr**, *der-ore'*; from an unused root (mean. to *move rapidly*); *freedom*; hence *spontaneity* of outflow, and so *clear*:—liberty, pure.

1866. דְּרוֹר **derôwr**, *der-ore'*; the same as 1865, applied to a bird; the *swift*, a kind of swallow:—swallow.

1867. דָּרְיָוֶשׁ **Dârᵉyâvêsh**, *daw-reh-yaw-vaysh'*; of Pers. or.; *Darejavesh*, a title (rather than name) of several Persian kings:—Darius.

1868. דָּרְיָוֶשׁ **Dârᵉyâvêsh** (Chald.), *daw-reh-yaw-vaysh'*; corresp. to 1867:—Darius.

1869. דָּרַךְ **dârak**, *daw-rak'*; a prim. root; to *tread*; by impl. to *walk*; also to *string* a bow (by treading on it in bending):—archer, bend, come, draw, go (over), guide, lead (forth), thresh, tread (down), walk.

1870. דֶּרֶךְ **derek**, *deh'-rek*; from 1869; a *road* (as *trodden*); fig. a *course* of life or *mode* of action, often adv.:—along, away, because of, + by, conversation, custom, [east-] ward, journey, manner, passenger, through, toward, [high-] [path-] way [-side], whither [-soever].

1871. דַּרְכְּמוֹן **darkᵉmôwn**, *dar-kem-one'*; of Pers. or.; a "*drachma*," or coin:—dram.

1872. דְּרָע **derâʻ** (Chald.), *der-aw'*; corresp. to 2220; an *arm*:—arm.

1873. דָּרַע **Dâraʻ**, *daw-rah'*; prob. contr. from 1862; *Dara*, an Isr.:—Dara.

1874. דַּרְקוֹן **Darqôwn**, *dar-kone'*; of uncert. der.; *Darkon*, one of "Solomon's servants":—Darkon.

1875. דָּרַשׁ **dârash**, *daw-rash'*; a prim. root; prop. to *tread* or *frequent*; usually to *follow* (for pursuit or search); by impl. to *seek* or *ask*; spec. to *worship*:—ask, × at all, care for, × diligently, inquire, make inquisition, [necro-] mancer, question, require, search, seek [for, out], × surely.

1876. דָּשָׁא **dâshâ**, *daw-shaw'*; a prim. root; to *sprout*:—bring forth, spring.

1877. דֶּשֶׁא **deshe'**, *deh'-sheh*; from 1876; a *sprout*; by anal. *grass*:—(tender) grass, green, (tender) herb.

1878. דָּשֵׁן **dâshên**, *daw-shane'*; a prim. root; to *be fat*; trans. to *fatten* (or regard as fat); spec. to *anoint*; fig. to *satisfy*; denom. (from 1880) to *remove* (fat) *ashes* (of sacrifices):—accept, anoint, take away the (receive) ashes (from), make (wax) fat.

1879. דָּשֵׁן **dâshên**, *daw-shane'*; from 1878; *fat*; fig. *rich*, *fertile*:—fat.

1880. דֶּשֶׁן **deshen**, *deh'-shen*; from 1878; the *fat*; abstr. *fatness*, i.e. (fig.) *abundance*; spec. the (fatty) *ashes* of sacrifices:—ashes, fatness.

1881. דָּת **dâth**, *dawth*; of uncert. (perh. for.) der.: a royal *edict* or statute:—commandment, commission, decree, law, manner.

1882. דָּת **dâth** (Chald.), *dawth*; corresp. to 1881; decree, law.

1883. דֶּתֶא **dethe'** (Chald.), *deh'-thay*; corresp. to 1877:—tender grass.

1884. דְּתָבָר **dethâbâr** (Chald.), *deth-aw-bawr'*; of Pers. or.; mean. one *skilled in law*; a *judge*:—counsellor.

1885. דָּתָן **Dâthân**, *daw-thawn'*; of uncert. der.; *Dathan*, an Isr.:—Dathan.

1886. דֹּתָן **Dôthân**, *do'-thawn*; or (Chaldaizing dual)
דֹּתַיִן **Dôthayin** (Gen. 37:17), *do-thah'-yin*; of uncert. der.; *Dothan*, a place in Pal.:—Dothan.

ה

1887. הֵא **hê'**, *hay*; a prim. particle; *lo!*:—behold, lo.

1888. הֵא **hê'** (Chald.), *hay*; or
הָא **hâ'** (Chald.), *haw*; corresp. to 1887:—even, lo.

1889. הֶאָח **heâch**, *heh-awkh'*; from 1887 and 253; *aha!*:—ah, aha, ha.

הָאֲרָרִי **Hâ'rârîy**. See 2043.

1890. הַבְהָב **habhâb**, *hab-hawb'*; by redupl. from 3051; *gift* (in sacrifice), i.e. *holocaust*:—offering.

1891. הָבַל **hâbal**, *haw-bal'*; a prim. root; to *be vain* in act, word, or expectation; spec. to *lead astray*:—be (become, make) vain.

1892. הֶבֶל **hebel**, *heh'-bel*; or (rarely in the abs.) הֲבֵל **hăbêl**, *hab-ale'*; from 1891; *emptiness* or *vanity*; fig. something *transitory* and *unsatisfactory*; often used as an adv.:— × altogether, vain, vanity.

1893. הֶבֶל **Hebel**, *heh'-bel*; the same as 1892; *Hebel*, the son of Adam:—Abel.

1894. הֹבֶן **hôben**, *ho'-ben*; only in plur., from an unused root mean. to *be hard*; *ebony*:—ebony.

1895. הָבַר **hâbar**, *haw-bar'*; a prim. root of uncert. (perh. for.) der.; to *be a horoscopist*:— + (astro-) loger.

1896. הֵגֵא **Hêgêʼ**, *hay-gay'*; or (by perm.) הֵגַי **Hêgay**, *hay-gah'ee*; prob. of Pers. or.; *Hege* or *Hegai*, a eunuch of Xerxes:—Hegai, Hege.

1897. הָגָה **hâgâh**, *haw-gaw'*; a prim. root [comp. 1901]; to *murmur* (in pleasure or anger); by impl. to *ponder*:—imagine, meditate, mourn, mutter, roar, × sore, speak, study, talk, utter.

1898. הָגָה **hâgâh**, *haw-gaw'*; a prim. root; to *remove*;—stay, take away.

1899. הֶגֶה **hegeh**, *heh'-geh*; from 1897; a *muttering* (in sighing, thought, or as thunder):—mourning, sound, tale.

1900. הָגוּת **hâgûwth**, *haw-gooth'*; from 1897; *musing*:—meditation.

1901. הָגִיג **hâgîyg**, *haw-gheeg'*; from an unused root akin to 1897; prop. a *murmur*, i.e. *complaint*:—meditation, musing.

1902. הִגָּיוֹן **higgâyôwn**, *hig-gaw-yone'*; intens. from 1897; a *murmuring* sound, i.e. a musical notation (prob. similar to the modern *affettuoso* to indicate solemnity of movement); by impl. a *machination*:—device, Higgaion, meditation, solemn sound.

1903. הָגִין **hâgîyn**, *haw-gheen'*; of uncert. der.; perh. *suitable* or *turning*:—directly.

1904. הָגָר **Hâgâr**, *haw-gawr'*; of uncert. (perh. for.) der.; *Hagar*, the mother of Ishmael:—Hagar.

1905. הַגְרִי **Hagrîy**, *hag-ree'*; or (prol.) הַגְרִיא **Hagrîʼ**, *hag-ree'*; perh. patron. from 1904; a *Hagrite* or member of a certain Arabian clan:—Hagarene, Hagarite, Haggeri.

1906. הֵד **hêd**, *hade*; for 1959; a *shout*:—sounding again.

1907. הַדָּבָר **haddâbâr** (Chald.), *had-daw-bawr'*; prob. of for. or.; a *vizier*:—counsellor.

1908. הֲדַד **Hădad**, *had-ad'*; prob. of for. or. [comp. 111]; *Hadad*, the name of an idol, and of several kings of Edom:—Hadad.

1909. הֲדַדְעֶזֶר **Hădadʻezer**, *had-ad-eh'-zer*; from 1908 and 5828; *Hadad* (is his) *help*; *Hadadezer*, a Syrian king:—Hadadezer. Comp. 1928.

1910. הֲדַדְרִמּוֹן **Hădadrimmôwn**, *had-ad-rim-mone'*; from 1908 and 7417; *Hadad-Rimmon*, a place in Pal.:—Hadad-rimmon.

1911. הָדָה **hâdâh**, *haw-daw'*; a prim. root [comp. 3034]; to *stretch forth* the hand:—put.

1912. הֹדּוּ **Hôdûw**, *ho'-doo*; of for. or.; *Hodu* (i.e. Hindû-stan):—India.

1913. הֲדוֹרָם **Hădôwrâm**, *had-o-rawm'*; or הֲדֹרָם **Hădôrâm**, *had-o-rawm'*; prob. of for. der.; *Hadoram*, a son of Joktan, and the tribe descended from him:—Hadoram.

1914. הִדַּי **Hidday**, *hid-dah'ee*; of uncert. der.; *Hiddai*, an Isr.:—Hiddai.

1915. הָדַךְ **hâdak**, *haw-dak'*; a prim. root [comp. 1854]; to *crush* with the foot:—tread down.

1916. הֲדֹם **hădôm**, *had-ome'*; from an unused root mean. to *stamp* upon; a *footstool*:—[foot-] stool.

1917. הַדָּם **haddâm** (Chald.), *had-dawm'*; from a root corresp. to that of 1916; something *stamped* to pieces, i.e. a *bit*:—piece.

1918. הֲדַס **hădaç**, *had-as'*; of uncert. der.; the *myrtle*:—myrtle (tree).

1919. הֲדַסָּה **Hădaççâh**, *had-as-saw'*; fem. of 1918; *Hadassah* (or Esther):—Hadassah.

1920. הָדַף **hâdaph**, *haw-daf'*; a prim. root; to *push* away or down:—cast away (out), drive, expel, thrust (away).

1921. הָדַר **hâdar**, *haw-dar'*; a prim. root; to *swell* up (lit. or fig., act. or pass.); by impl. to *favor* or *honour*, *be high* or *proud*:—countenance, crooked place, glorious, honour, put forth.

1922. הֲדַר **hădar** (Chald.), *had-ar'*; corresp. to 1921; to *magnify* (fig.):—glorify, honour.

1923. הֲדַר **hădar** (Chald.), *had-ar'*; from 1922; *magnificence*:—honour, majesty.

1924. הֲדַר **Hădar**, *had-ar'*; the same as 1926; *Hadar*, an Edomite:—Hadar.

1925. הֶדֶר **heder**, *heh'-der*; from 1921; *honour*; used (fig.) for the *capital* city (Jerusalem):—glory.

1926. הָדָר **hâdâr**, *haw-dawr'*; from 1921; *magnificence*, i.e. ornament or splendor:—beauty, comeliness, excellency, glorious, glory, goodly, honour, majesty.

1927. הֲדָרָה **hădârâh**, *had-aw-raw'*; fem. of 1926; *decoration*:—beauty, honour.

הֲדֹרָם **Hădôrâm**. See 1913.

1928. הֲדַרְעֶזֶר **Hădarʻezer**, *had-ar-eh'-zer*; from 1924 and 5828; *Hadar* (i.e. *Hadad*, 1908) is his *help*; *Hadarezer* (i.e. Hadadezer, 1909), a Syrian king:—Hadarezer.

1929. הָהּ **hâhh**, *haw*; a short. form of 162; *ah!* expressing grief:—woe worth.

1930. הוֹ **hôw**, *ho*; by perm. from 1929; *oh!*:—alas.

1931. הוּא **hûwʼ**, *hoo*; of which the fem. (beyond the Pentateuch) is הִיא **hîyʼ**, *he*; a prim. word, the third pers. pron. sing., *he* (*she* or *it*); only expressed when emphatic or without a verb; also (intens.) *self*, or (esp. with the art.) the *same*; sometimes (as demonstr.) *this* or *that*; occasionally (instead of copula) *as* or *are*:—he, as for her, him (-self), it, the same, she (herself), such, that (. . . it), these, they, this, those, which (is), who.

1932. הוּא **hûw** (Chald.), *hoo*; or (fem.) הִיא **hîyʼ** (Chald.), *he*; corresp. to 1931:—× are, it, this.

1933. הָוָא **hâvâʼ**, *haw-vaw'*; or הָוָה **hâvâh**, *haw-vaw'*; a prim. root [comp. 183, 1961] supposed to mean prop. to *breathe*; *to be* (in the sense of existence):—be, × have.

1934. הֲוָא **hăvâʼ** (Chald.), *hav-aw'*; or הֲוָה **hăvâh** (Chald.), *hav-aw'*; corresp. to 1933; to *exist*; used in a great variety of applications (especially in connection with other words):—be, become, + behold, + came (to pass), + cease, + cleave, + consider, + do, + give, + have + judge, + keep, + labour, + mingle (self), + put, + see, + seek, + set, + slay, + take heed, tremble, + walk, + would.

1935. הוֹד **hôwd**, *hode*; from an unused root; *grandeur* (i.e. an imposing form and appearance):—beauty, comeliness, excellency, glorious, glory, goodly, honour, majesty.

1936. הוֹד **Hôwd**, *hode*; the same as 1935; *Hod*, an Isr.:—Hod.

1937. הוֹדְוָה **Hôwdᵉvâh**, *ho-dev-aw'*; a form of 1938; *Hodevah* (or Hodevjah), an Isr.:—Hodevah.

1938. הוֹדַוְיָה **Hôwdavyâh**, *ho-dav-yaw'*; from 1935 and 3050; *majesty of Jah*; *Hodavjah*, the name of three Isr.:—Hodaviah.

1939. הוֹדַיְוָהוּ **Howdayᵉvâhûw**, *ho-dah-yeh-vaw'-hoo*; a form of 1938; *Hodajvah*, an Isr.:—Hodaiah.

1940. הוֹדִיָּה **Hôwdîyâh**, *ho-dee-yaw'*; a form for the fem. of 3064; a *Jewess*:—Hodiah.

1941. הוֹדִיָּה **Hôwdîyâh**, *ho-dee-yaw'*; a form of 1938; *Hodijah*, the name of three Isr.:—Hodijah.

הָוָה **hâvâh**. See 1933.

הָוָה **hâvâh**. See 1934.

1942. הַוָּה **havvâh**, *hav-vaw'*; from 1933 (in the sense of eagerly *coveting* and *rushing* upon; by impl. of *falling*); *desire*; also *ruin*:—calamity, iniquity, mischief, mischievous (thing), naughtiness, naughty, noisome, perverse thing, substance, very wickedness.

1943. הֹוָה **hôvâh**, *ho-vaw'*; another form for 1942; *ruin*:—mischief.

1944. הוֹהָם **Hôwhâm**, *ho-hawm'*; of uncert. der.; *Hoham*, a Canaanitish king:—Hoham.

1945. הוֹי **hôwy**, *hoh'ee*; a prol. form of 1930 [akin to 188]; *oh!*:—ah, alas, ho, O, woe.

1946. הוּךְ **hûwk** (Chald.), *hook*; corresp. to 1981; *to go*; caus. to *bring*:—bring again, come, go (up).

1947. הוֹלֵלָה **hôwlêlâh**, *ho-lay-law'*; fem. act. part. of 1984; *folly*:—madness.

1948. הוֹלֵלוּת **hôwlêlûwth**, *ho-lay-looth'*; from act. part. of 1984; *folly*:—madness.

1949. הוּם **hûwm**, *hoom*; a prim. root [comp. 2000]; to *make an uproar*, or *agitate* greatly:—destroy, move, make a noise, put, ring again.

1950. הוֹמָם **Hôwmâm**, *ho-mawm'*; from 2000; *raging*; *Homam*, an Edomitish chieftain:—Homam. Comp. 1967.

1951. הוּן **hûwn**, *hoon*; a prim. root; prop. to *be naught*, i.e. (fig.) to *be* (caus. *act*) *light*:—be ready.

1952. הוֹן **hôwn**, *hone*; from the same as 1951 in the sense of 202; *wealth*; by impl. *enough*:—enough, + for nought, riches, substance, wealth.

1953. הוֹשָׁמָע **Hôwshâmâʻ**, *ho-shaw-maw'*; from 3068 and 8085; *Jehovah has heard*; *Hoshama*, an Isr.:—Hoshama.

1954. הוֹשֵׁעַ **Hôwshêaʻ**, *ho-shay'-ah*; from 3467; *deliverer*; *Hosheă*, the name of five Isr.:—Hosea, Hoshea, Oshea.

1955. הוֹשַׁעְיָה **Hôwshaʻyâh**, *ho-shah-yaw'*; from 3467 and 3050; *Jah has saved*; *Hoshajah*, the name of two Isr.:—Hoshaiah.

1956. הוֹתִיר **Hôwthîyr**, *ho-theer'*; from 3498; *he has caused to remain*; *Hothir*, an Isr.:—Hothir.

1957. הָזָה **hâzâh**, *haw-zaw'*; a prim. root [comp. 2372]; to *dream*:—sleep.

1958. הִי **hîy**, *he*; for 5092; *lamentation*:—woe.

הִיא **hîyʼ**. See 1931, 1932.

1959. הֵידָד **hêydâd**, *hay-dawd'*; from an unused root (mean. to *shout*); *acclamation*:—shout (-ing).

1960. הֻיְּדָה **huyᵉdâh**, *hoo-yed-aw'*; from the same as 1959; prop. an *acclaim*, i.e. a *choir* of singers:—thanksgiving.

1961. הָיָה **hâyâh**, *haw-yaw'*; a prim. root [comp. 1933]; to *exist*, i.e. *be* or *become*, *come to pass* (always emphatic, and not a mere copula or auxiliary):—beacon, × altogether, be (-come, accomplished, committed, like), break, cause, come (to pass), continue, do, faint, fall, + follow, happen, × have, last, pertain, quit (one-) self, require, × use.

1962. הַיָּה **hayâh**, *hah-yaw'*; another form for 1943; *ruin*:—calamity.

1963. הֵיךְ **hêyk**, *hake*; another form for 349; *how?*:—how.

1964. הֵיכָל **hêykâl**, *hay-kawl'*; prob. from 3201 (in the sense of *capacity*); a large public building, such as a *palace* or *temple*:—palace, temple.

1965. הֵיכַל **hêykal** (Chald.), *hay-kal'*; corresp. to 1964:—palace, temple.

1966. הֵילֵל **hêylêl**, *hay-lale'*; from 1984 (in the sense of *brightness*); the *morning-star*:—lucifer.

1967. הֵימָם **Hêymâm**, *hay-mawm'*; another form for 1950; *Hemam*, an Idumæan:—Hemam.

1968. הֵימָן **Hêymân**, *hay-mawn'*; prob. from 539; *faithful; Heman*, the name of at least two Isr.:—Heman.

1969. הִין **hîyn**, *heen*; prob. of Eg. or.; a *hin* or liquid measure:—hin.

1970. הָכַר **hâkar**, *haw-kar'*; a prim. root; appar. to *injure*:—make self strange.

1971. הַכָּרָה **hakkârâh**, *hak-kaw-raw'*; from 5234; *respect*, i.e. partiality:—shew.

הַל **hal**. See 1973.

1972. הָלָא **hâlâʼ**, *haw-law'*; prob. denom. from 1973; to *remove* or be *remote*:—cast far off.

1973. הָלְאָה **hâlᵉâh**, *haw-leh-aw'*; from the prim. form of the art. [הַל **hal**]; *to the distance*, i.e. *far away;* also (of time) *thus far*:—back, beyond, (hence-) forward, hitherto, thenceforth, yonder.

1974. הִלּוּל **hillûwl**, *hil-lool'*; from 1984 (in the sense of *rejoicing*); a *celebration* of thanksgiving for harvest:—merry, praise.

1975. הַלָּז **hallâz**, *hal-lawz'*; from 1976; *this* or *that*:—side, that, this.

1976. הַלָּזֶה **hallâzeh**, *hal-law-zeh'*; from the art. [see 1973] and 2088; *this very*:—this.

1977. הַלֵּזוּ **hallêzûw**, *hal-lay-zoo'*; another form of 1976; *that*:—this.

1978. הָלִיךְ **hâlîyk**, *haw-leek'*; from 1980; a *walk*, i.e. (by impl.) a *step*:—step.

1979. הֲלִיכָה **hălîykâh**, *hal-ee-kaw'*; fem. of 1978; a *walking;* by impl. a *procession* or *march*, a *caravan*:—company, going, walk, way.

1980. הָלַךְ **hâlak**, *haw-lak'*; akin to 3212; a prim. root; to *walk* (in a great variety of applications, lit. and fig.):—(all) along, apace, behave (self), come, (on) continually, be conversant, depart, + be eased, enter, exercise (self), + follow, forth, forward, get, go (about, abroad, along, away, forward, on, out, up and down), + greater, grow, be wont to haunt, lead, march, × more and more, move (self), needs, on, pass (away), be at the point, quite, run (along), + send, speedily, spread, still, surely, + tale-bearer, + travel (-ler), walk (abroad, on, to and fro, up and down, to places), wander, wax, way-] faring man, × be weak, whirl.

1981. הֲלַךְ **hălak** (Chald.), *hal-ak'*; corresp. to 1980 [comp. 1946]; to *walk*:—walk.

1982. הֵלֶךְ **hêlek**, *hay'-lek*; from 1980; prop. a *journey*, i.e. (by impl.) a *wayfarer;* also a *flowing*:— × dropped, traveller.

1983. הֲלָךְ **hălâk** (Chald.), *hal-awk'*; from 1981; prop. a *journey*, i.e. (by impl.) *toll* on goods at a road:—custom.

1984. הָלַל **hâlal**, *haw-lal'*; a prim. root; to *be clear* (orig. of sound, but usually of color); to *shine;* hence to *make a show*, to *boast;* and thus to *be* (clamorously) *foolish;* to *rave;* causat. to *celebrate;* also to *stultify*:—(make) boast (self), celebrate, commend, (deal, make), fool (-ish, -ly), glory, give [light], be (make, feign self) mad (against), give in marriage, [sing, be worthy of] praise, rage, renowned, shine.

1985. הִלֵּל **Hillêl**, *hil-layl'*; from 1984; *praising* (namely God); *Hillel*, an Isr.:—Hillel.

1986. הָלַם **hâlam**, *haw-lam'*; a prim. root; to *strike* down; by impl. to *hammer, stamp, conquer, disband*:—beat (down), break (down), overcome, smite (with the hammer).

1987. הֵלֶם **Hêlem**, *hay'-lem*; from 1986; *smiter; Helem*, the name of two Isr.:—Helem.

1988. הֲלֹם **hălôm**, *hal-ome'*; from the art. [see 1973]; *hither*:—here, hither (-[to]), thither.

1989. הַלְמוּת **halmûwth**, *hal-mooth'*; from 1986; a *hammer* (or *mallet*):—hammer.

1990. הָם **Hâm**, *hawm;* of uncert. der.; *Ham*, a region of Pal.:—Ham.

1991. הֵם **hêm**, *haym;* from 1993; *abundance*, i.e. *wealth*:—any of theirs.

1992. הֵם **hêm**, *haym;* or (prol.)
הֵמָּה **hêmmâh**, *haym'-maw;* masc. plur. from 1931; *they* (only used when emphatic):—it, like, × (how, so) many (soever, more as) they (be), (the) same, × so, × such, their, them, these, they, those, which, who, whom, withal, ye.

1993. הָמָה **hâmâh**, *haw-maw';* a prim. root [comp. 1949]; to *make a loud sound* (like Engl. "hum"); by impl. to *be in great commotion* or *tumult*, to *rage, war, moan, clamor*:—clamorous, concourse, cry aloud, be disquieted, loud, mourn, be moved, make a noise, rage, roar, sound, be troubled, make in tumult, tumultuous, be in an uproar.

1994. הִמּוֹ **himmôw** (Chald.), *him-mo';* or (prol.)
הִמּוֹן **himmôwn** (Chald.) *him-mone';* corresp. to 1992; *they*:— × are, them, those.

1995. הָמוֹן **hâmôwn**, *haw-mone';* or
הָמֹן **hâmôn** (Ezek. 5 : 7), *haw-mone';* from 1993; a *noise, tumult, crowd;* also *disquietude, wealth*:—abundance, company, many, multitude, multiply, noise, riches, rumbling, sounding, store, tumult.

הַמֹּלֶכֶת **ham-môleketh**. See 4447.

1996. הֲמוֹן גּוֹג **Hămôwn Gôwg**, *ham-one' gohg;* from 1995 and 1463; the *multitude of Gog;* the fanciful name of an emblematic place in Pal.:—Hamon-gog.

1997. הֲמוֹנָה **Hămôwnâh**, *ham-o-naw';* fem. of 1995; *multitude; Hamonah*, the same as 1996:—Hamonah.

הֲמוּנֵךְ° **hămûwnêk**. See 2002.

1998. הֶמְיָה **hemyâh**, *hem-yaw';* from 1993; *sound*:—noise.

1999. הֲמֻלָּה **hămullâh**, *ham-ool-law';* or (too fully)
הֲמוּלָּה **hămûwllâh** (Jer. 11 : 16), *ham-ool-law';* fem. pass. part. of an unused root mean. to *rush* (as rain with a windy roar); a *sound*:—speech, tumult.

הַמֶּלֶךְ **ham-melek**. See 4429.

2000. הָמַם **hâmam**, *haw-mam';* a prim. root [comp. 1949, 1993]; prop. to *put in commotion;* by impl. to *disturb, drive, destroy*:—break, consume, crush, destroy, discomfit, trouble, vex.

הָמֹן **hâmôn**. See 1995.

2001. הָמָן **Hâmân**, *haw-mawn';* of for. der.; *Haman*, a Pers. vizier:—Haman.

2002. הַמְנִיךְ **hamnîyk** (Chald.), *ham-neek';* but the text is
הֲמוּנֵךְ° **hămûwnêk**, *ham-oo-nayk';* of for. or.; a *necklace*:—chain.

2003. הָמָס **hâmâç**, *haw-mawce';* from an unused root appar. mean. to *crackle;* a dry *twig* or *brushwood*:—melting.

2004. הֵן **hên**, *hane;* fem. plur. from 1931; *they* (only used when emphatic):— × in, such like, (with) them, thereby, therein, (more than) they, wherein, in which, whom, withal.

2005. הֵן **hên**, *hane;* a prim. particle; *lo!;* also (as expressing surprise) *if*:—behold, if, lo, though.

2006. הֵן **hên** (Chald.), *hane;* corresp. to 2005: *lo!* also *there* [-fore], [un-] *less, whether, but, if*:—(that) if, or, whether.

2007. הֵנָּה **hênnâh**, *hane'-naw;* prol. for 2004; *themselves* (often used emphat. for the copula, also in indirect relation):— × in, × such (and such things), their, (into) them, thence, therein, these, they (had), on this side, those, wherein.

2008. הֵנָּה **hênnâh**, *hane'-naw;* from 2004; *hither* or *thither* (but used both of place and time):—here, hither [-to], now, on this (that) side, + since, this (that) way, thitherward, + thus far, to . . . fro, + yet.

2009. הִנֵּה **hinnêh**, *hin-nay';* prol. for 2005; *lo!*:—behold, lo, see.

2010. הֲנָחָה **hănâchâh**, *han-aw-khaw';* from 5117; *permission* of rest, i.e. *quiet*:—release.

2011. הִנֹּם **Hinnôm**, *hin-nome';* prob. of for. or.; *Hinnom*, appar. a Jebusite:—Hinnom.

2012. הֵנַע **Hênaʻ**, *hay-nah';* prob. of for. der. *Hena*, a place appar. in Mesopotamia:—Hena.

2013. הָסָה **hâçâh**, *haw-saw';* a prim. root; to *hush*:—hold peace (tongue), (keep) silence, be silent, still.

2014. הֲפֻגָה **hăphûgâh**, *haf-oo-gaw';* from 6313; *relaxation*:—intermission.

2015. הָפַךְ **haphak**, *haw-fak';* a prim. root; to *turn* about or over; by impl. to *change, overturn, return, pervert*:— × become, change, come, be converted, give, make [a bed], overthrow (-turn), perverse, retire, tumble, turn (again, aside, back, to the contrary, every way).

2016. הֶפֶךְ **hephek**, *heh'-fek;* or
הֵפֶךְ **hêphek**, *hay'-fek;* from 2015; a *turn*, i.e. the *reverse*:—contrary.

2017. הֹפֶךְ **hôphek**, *ho'-fek;* from 2015; an *upset*, i.e. (abstr.) *perversity*:—turning of things upside down.

2018. הֲפֵכָה **hăphêkâh**, *haf-ay-kaw';* fem. of 2016; *destruction*:—overthrow.

2019. הֲפַכְפַּךְ **hăphakpak**, *haf-ak-pak';* by redupl. from 2015; *very perverse*:—froward.

2020. הַצָּלָה **hatstsâlâh**, *hats-tsaw-law';* from 5337; *rescue*:—deliverance.

2021. הֹצֶן **hôtsen**, *ho'-tsen;* from an unused root mean. appar. to *be sharp* or *strong;* a *weapon* of war:—chariot.

2022. הַר **har**, *har;* a short. form of 2042; a *mountain* or *range* of hills (sometimes used fig.):—hill (country), mount (-ain), × promotion.

2023. הֹר **Hôr**, *hore;* another form for 2022; *mountain; Hor*, the name of a peak in Idumæa and of one in Syria:—Hor.

2024. הָרָא **Hârâʼ**, *haw-raw';* perh. from 2022; *mountainousness; Hara*, a region of Media:—Hara.

2025. הַרְאֵל **harʼêl**, *har-ale';* from 2022 and 410; *mount of God;* fig. the *altar* of burnt-offering:—altar. Comp. 739.

2026. הָרַג **hârag**, *haw-rag';* a prim. root; to *smite* with deadly intent:—destroy, out of hand, kill, murder (-er), put to [death], make [slaughter], slay (-er), × surely.

2027. הֶרֶג **hereg**, *heh'-reg;* from 2026; *slaughter*:—be slain, slaughter.

2028. הֲרֵגָה **hărêgâh**, *har-ay-gaw';* fem. of 2027; *slaughter*:—slaughter.

2029. הָרָה **hârâh**, *haw-raw';* a prim. root; to *be* (or *become*) *pregnant, conceive* (lit. or fig.):—been, be with child, conceive, progenitor.

2030. הָרֶה **hâreh**, *haw-reh';* or
הָרִי **hârîy** (Hos. 14 : 1), *haw-ree';* from 2029; *pregnant*:—(be, woman) with child, conceive, × great.

2031. הַרְהֹר **harhôr** (Chald.), *har-hor';* from a root corresp. to 2029; a mental *conception*:—thought.

2032. הֵרוֹן **hêrôwn**, *hay-rone';* or
הֵרָיוֹן **hêrâyôwn**, *hay-raw-yone';* from 2029; *pregnancy*:—conception.

2033. הֲרוֹרִי **Hărôwrîy**, *har-o-ree';* another form for 2043; a *Harorite* or mountaineer:—Harorite.

2034. הֲרִיסָה **hărîyçâh**, *har-ee-saw';* from 2040; something *demolished*:—ruin.

2035. הֲרִיסוּת **hărîyçûwth**, *har-ee-sooth';* from 2040; *demolition*:—destruction.

2036. הֹרָם **Hôrâm**, *ho-rawm'*; from an unused root (mean. to *tower* up); *high; Horam*, a Canaanitish king:—Horam.

2037. הָרוּם **Hârûm**, *haw-room'*; pass. part. of the same as 2036; *high; Harum*, an Isr.:—Harum.

2038. הַרְמוֹן **harmôwn**, *har-mone'*; from the same as 2036; a *castle* (from its height):—palace.

2039. הָרָן **Hârân**, *haw-rawn'*; perh. from 2022; *mountaineer; Haran*, the name of two men:—Haran.

2040. הָרַס **hâraç**, *haw-ras'*; a prim. root; to *pull* down or in pieces, *break, destroy*:—beat down, break (down, through), destroy, overthrow, pluck down, pull down, ruin, throw down, × utterly.

2041. הֶרֶס **hereç**, *heh'-res*; from 2040; *demolition*:—destruction.

2042. הָרָר **hârâr**, *haw-rawr'*; from an unused root mean. to *loom* up; a *mountain*:—hill, mount (-ain).

2043. הֲרָרִי **Hărârîy** *hah-raw-ree'*; or הָרָרִי **Hârârîy** (2 Sam. 23 : 11), *haw-raw-ree'*; or הָאֲרָרִי **Hâ'rârîy** (2 Sam. 23 : 34, last clause), *haw-raw-ree'*; appar. from 2042; a *mountaineer*:—Hararite.

2044. הָשֵׁם **Hâshêm**, *haw-shame'*; perh. from the same as 2828; *wealthy; Hashem*, an Isr.:—Hashem.

2045. הַשְׁמָעוּת **hashmâ'ûwth**, *hashmaw-ooth'*; from 8085; *announcement*:—to cause to hear.

2046. הִתּוּךְ **hittûwk**, *hit-took'*; from 5413; a *melting*:—is melted.

2047. הֲתָךְ **Hăthâk**, *hath-awk'*; prob. of for. or.; *Hathak*, a Pers. eunuch:—Hatach.

2048. הָתַל **hâthal**, *haw-thal'*; a prim. root; to *deride*; by impl. to *cheat*:—deal deceitfully, deceive, mock.

2049. הָתֹל **hâthôl**, *haw-thole'*; from 2048 (only in plur. collect.); a *derision*:—mocker.

2050. הָתַת **hâthath'**, *haw-thath'*; a prim. root; prop. to *break* in upon, i.e. to *assail*:—imagine mischief.

ו

2051. וְדָן **Vedân**, *ved-awn'*; perh. for 5730; *Vedan* (or Aden), a place in Arabia:—Dan also.

2052. וָהֵב **Vâhêb**, *vaw-habe'*; of uncert. der.; *Vaheb*, a place in Moab:—what he did.

2053. וָו **vâv**, *vaw*; prob. a *hook* (the name of the sixth Heb. letter):—hook.

2054. וָזָר **vâzâr**, *vaw-zawr'*; presumed to be from an unused root mean. to *bear* guilt; *crime*:—× strange.

2055. וַיְזָתָא **Vayezâthâ'**, *vah-yez-aw'-thaw*; of for. or.; *Vajezatha*, a son of Haman:—Vajezatha.

2056. וָלָד **vâlâd**, *vaw-lawd'*; for 3206; a *boy*:—child.

2057. וַנְיָה **Vanyâh**, *van-yaw'*; perh. for 6043; *Vanjah*, an Isr.:—Vaniah.

2058. וׇפְסִי **Vophçîy**, *vof-see'*; prob. from 3254; *additional; Vophsi*, an Isr.:—Vophsi.

2059. וַשְׁנִי **Vashnîy**, *vash-nee'*; prob. from 3461; *weak; Vashni*, an Isr.:—Vashni.

2060. וַשְׁתִּי **Vashtîy**, *vash-tee'*; of Pers. or.; *Vashti*, the queen of Xerxes:—Vashti.

ז

2061. זְאֵב **ze'êb**, *zeh-abe'*; from an unused root mean. to *be yellow*; a *wolf*:—wolf.

2062. זְאֵב **Ze'êb**, *zeh-abe'*; the same as 2061; *Zeëb*, a Midianitish prince:—Zeeb.

2063. זֹאת **zô'th**, *zothe'*; irreg. fem. of 2089; *this* (often used adv.):—hereby (-in, -with), it, likewise, the one (other, same), she, so (much), such (deed), that, therefore, these, this (thing), thus.

2064. זָבַד **zâbad**, *zaw-bad'*; a prim. root; to *confer*:—endure.

2065. זֶבֶד **zebed**, *zeh'-bed*; from 2064; a *gift*:—dowry.

2066. זָבָד **Zâbâd**, *zaw-bawd'*; from 2064; *giver; Zabad*, the name of seven Isr.:—Zabad.

2067. זַבְדִּי **Zabdîy**, *zab-dee'*; from 2065; *giving; Zabdi*, the name of four Isr.:—Zabdi.

2068. זַבְדִּיאֵל **Zabdîy'êl**, *zab-dee-ale'*; from 2065 and 410; *gift of God; Zabdiel*, the name of two Isr.:—Zabdiel.

2069. זְבַדְיָה **Zebadyâh**, *zeb-ad-yaw'*; or זְבַדְיָהוּ **Zebadyâhûw**, *zeb-ad-yaw'-hoo*; from 2064 and 3050; *Jah has given; Zebadjah*, the name of nine Isr.:—Zebadiah.

2070. זְבוּב **zebûwb**, *zeb-oob'*; from an unused root (mean. to *flit*); a *fly* (espec. one of a stinging nature):—fly.

2071. זָבוּד **Zâbûwd**, *zaw-bood'*; from 2064; *given; Zabud*, an Isr.:—Zabud.

2072. זַבּוּד **Zabbûwd**, *zab-bood'*; a form of 2071; *given; Zabbud*, an Isr.:—Zabbud.

2073. זְבוּל **zebûwl**, *ze-bool'*; or זְבֻל **zebûl**, *zeb-ool'*; from 2082; a *residence*:—dwell in, dwelling, habitation.

2074. זְבוּלוּן **Zebûwlûwn**, *zeb-oo-loon'*; or זְבֻלוּן **Zebûlûwn**, *zeb-oo-loon'*; or זְבוּלֻן **Zebûwlûn**, *zeb-oo-loon'*; from 2082; *habitation; Zebulon*, a son of Jacob; also his territory and tribe:—Zebulun.

2075. זְבוּלֹנִי **Zebûwlônîy**, *zeb-oo-lo-nee'*; patron. from 2074; a *Zebulonite* or desc. of Zebulun:—Zebulonite.

2076. זָבַח **zâbach**, *zaw-bakh'*; a prim. root; to *slaughter* an animal (usually in sacrifice):—kill, offer, (do) sacrifice, slay.

2077. זֶבַח **zebach**, *zeh'-bakh*; from 2076; prop. a *slaughter*, i.e. the *flesh* of an animal; by impl. a *sacrifice* (the victim or the act):—offer (-ing), sacrifice.

2078. זֶבַח **Zebach**, *zeh'-bakh*; the same as 2077; *sacrifice; Zebach*, a Midianitish prince:—Zebah.

2079. זַבַּי **Zabbay**, *zab-bah'ee*; prob. by orth. err. for 2140; *Zabbai* (or Zaccai), an Isr.:—Zabbai.

2080. זְבִידָה **Zebîydâh**, *zeb-ee-daw'*; fem. from 2064; *giving; Zebidah*, an Israelitess:—Zebudah.

2081. זְבִינָא **Zebîynâ'**, *zeb-ee-naw'*; from an unused root (mean. to *purchase*); *gainfulness; Zebina*, an Isr.:—Zebina.

2082. זָבַל **zâbal**, *zaw-bal'*; a prim. root; appar. prop. to *inclose*, i.e. to *reside*:—dwell with.

2083. זְבֻל **Zebûl**, *zeb-ool'*; the same as 2073; *dwelling; Zebul*, an Isr.:—Zebul. Comp. 2073.

זְבֻלֻן **Zebûlûwn**. See 2074.

2084. זְבַן **zeban** (Chald.), *zeb-an'*; corresp. to the root of 2081; to *acquire* by purchase:—gain.

2085. זָג **zâg**, *zawg*; from an unused root prob. mean. to *inclose*; the *skin* of a grape:—husk.

2086. זֵד **zêd**, *zade'*; from 2102; *arrogant*:—presumptuous, proud.

2087. זָדוֹן **zâdôwn**, *zaw-done'*; from 2102; *arrogance*:—presumptuously, pride, proud (man).

2088. זֶה **zeh**, *zeh*; a prim. word; the masc. demonst. pron., *this* or *that*:—he, × hence, × here, it (-self), × now, × of him, the one . . . the other, × than the other, (× out of) the (self) same, such (an one) that, these, this (hath, man), on this side . . . on that side, × thus, very, which. Comp. 2063, 2090, 2097, 2098.

2089. זֶה **zeh** (1 Sam. 17 : 34), *zeh*; by perm. for 7716; a *sheep*:—lamb.

2090. זֹה **zôh**, *zo*; for 2088; *this* or *that*:—as well as another, it, this. that, thus and thus.

2091. זָהָב **zâhâb**, *zaw-hawb'*; from an unused root mean. to *shimmer*; *gold*; fig. something *gold-colored* (i.e. *yellow*), as *oil*, a *clear sky*:—gold (-en), fair weather.

2092. זָהַם **zâham**, *zaw-ham'*; a prim. root; to *be rancid*, i.e. (trans.) to *loathe*:—abhor.

2093. זַהַם **Zaham**, *zah'-ham*; from 2092; *loathing; Zaham*, an Isr.:—Zaham.

2094. זָהַר **zâhar**, *zaw-har'*; a prim. root; to *gleam*; fig. to *enlighten* (by caution):—admonish, shine, teach, (give) warn (-ing).

2095. זְהַר **zehar** (Chald.), *zeh-har'*; corresp. to 2094; (pass.) *be admonished*:—take heed.

2096. זֹהַר **zôhar**, *zo'-har*; from 2094; *brilliancy*:—brightness.

2097. זוֹ **zôw**, *zo*; for 2088; *this* or *that*:—that, this.

2098. זוּ **zûw**, *zoo*; for 2088; *this* or *that*:—that this, × wherein, which, whom.

2099. זִו **Zîv**, *zeev'*; prob. from an unused root mean. to *be prominent*; prop. *brightness* [comp. 2122], i.e. (fig.) the month of *flowers; Ziv* (corresp. to Ijar or May):—Zif.

2100. זוּב **zûwb**, *zoob*; a prim. root; to *flow* freely (as water), i.e. (spec.) to *have a* (sexual) *flux*; fig. to *waste* away; also to *overflow*:—flow, gush out, have a (running) issue, pine away, run.

2101. זוֹב **zôwb**, *zobe*; from 2100; a seminal or menstrual *flux*:—issue.

2102. זוּד **zûwd**, *zood*; or (by perm.) זִיד **zîyd**, *zeed*; a prim. root; to *seethe*; fig. to *be insolent*:—be proud, deal proudly, presume, (come) presumptuously, sod.

2103. זוּד **zûwd** (Chald.), *zood*; corresp. to 2102; to *be proud*:—in pride.

2104. זוּזִים **Zûwzîym**, *zoo-zeem'*; plur. prob. from the same as 2123; *prominent; Zuzites*, an aboriginal tribe of Pal.:—Zuzims.

2105. זוֹחֵת **Zôwchêth**, *zo-khayth'*; of uncert. or.; *Zocheth*, an Isr.:—Zoheth.

2106. זָוִית **zâvîyth**, *zaw-veeth'*; appar. from the same root as 2099 (in the sense of *prominence*); an *angle* (as *projecting*), i.e. (by impl.) a *corner-column* (or *anta*):—corner (stone).

2107. זוּל **zûwl**, *zool*; a prim. root [comp. 2151]; prob. to *shake out*, i.e. (by impl.) to *scatter* profusely; fig. to *treat lightly*:—lavish, despise.

2108. זוּלָה **zûwlâh**, *zoo-law'*; from 2107; prop. *scattering*, i.e. *removal*; used adv. *except*:—beside, but, only, save.

2109. זוּן **zûwn**, *zoon*; a prim. root; perh. prop. to *be plump*, i.e. (trans.) to *nourish*:—feed.

2110. זוּן **zûwn** (Chald.), *zoon*; corresp. to 2109:—feed.

2111. זוּעַ **zûwa'**, *zoo'-ah*; a prim. root; prop. to *shake* off, i.e. (fig.) to *agitate* (as with fear):—move, tremble, vex.

2112. זוּעַ **zûwa'** (Chald.), *zoo'-ah*; corresp. to 2111; to *shake* (with fear):—tremble.

2113. זְוָעָה **zevâ'âh**, *zev-aw-aw'*; from 2111; *agitation, fear*:—be removed, trouble, vexation. Comp. 2189.

2114. זוּר **zûwr**, *zoor*; a prim. root; to *turn aside* (espec. for lodging); hence to *be a foreigner, strange, profane*; spec. (act. part.) to *commit adultery*:—(come from) another (man, place), fanner, go away, (e-) strange (-r, thing, woman).

2115. זוּר **zûwr**, *zoor*; a prim. root [comp. 6695]; to *press* together, *tighten*:—close, crush, thrust together.

2116. זוּרֶה **zûwreh**, *zoo-reh'*; from 2115; *trodden* on:—that which is crushed.

2117. זָזָא **zâzâ'**, *zaw-zaw'*; prob. from the root of 2123; *prominent; Zaza*, an Isr.:—Zaza.

2118. זָחַח **zâchach**, *zaw-khakh'*; a prim. root; to *shove* or *displace*:—loose.

2119. זָחַל **zâchal**, *zaw-khal'*; a prim. root; to *crawl*; by impl. to *fear*:—be afraid, serpent, worm.

2120. זֹחֶלֶת **Zôcheleth**, *zo-kheh'-leth*; fem. act. part. of 2119; *crawling* (i.e. *serpent*); *Zocheleth*, a boundary stone in Pal.:—Zoheleth.

2121. זֵידוֹן **zêydôwn**, *zay-dohn'*; from 2102; *boiling* of water, i.e. *wave*:—proud.

2122. זִיו **zîyv** (Chald.), *zeev*; corresp. to 2099; (fig.) *cheerfulness*:—brightness, countenance.

2123. זִיז **zîyz**, *zeez*; from an unused root appar. mean. to *be conspicuous*; *fulness* of the breast; also a moving *creature*:—abundance, wild beast.

2124. זִיזָא **Zîyzâʾ**, *zee-zaw'*; appar. from the same as 2123; *prominence*, *Ziza*, the name of two Isr.:—Ziza.

2125. זִיזָה **Zîyzâh**, *zee-zaw'*; another form for 2124; *Zizah*, an Isr.:—Zizah.

2126. זִינָא **Zîynâʾ**, *zee-naw'*; from 2109; well *fed*; or perh. an orth. err. for 2124; *Zina*, an Isr.:—Zina.

2127. זִיעַ **Zîyaʿ**, *zee'-ah*; from 2111; *agitation*; *Zia*, an Isr.:—Zia.

2128. זִיף **Zîyph**, *zeef*; from the same as 2203; *flowing*; *Ziph*, the name of a place in Pal.; also of an Isr.:—Ziph.

2129. זִיפָה **Zîyphâh**, *zee-faw'*; fem. of 2128; a *flowing*; *Ziphah*, an Isr.:—Ziphah.

2130. זִיפִי **Zîyphîy**, *zee-fee'*; patrial from 2128; a *Ziphite* or inhab. of Ziph:—Ziphim, Ziphite.

2131. זִיקָה **zîyqâh** (Isa. 50 : 11), *zee-kaw'* (fem.); and
זִק **zîq**, *zeek*; or
זֵק **zêq**, *zake*; from 2187; prop. what *leaps* forth, i.e. *flash* of fire, or a burning *arrow*; also (from the orig. sense of the root) a *bond*:—chain, fetter, firebrand, spark.

2132. זַיִת **zayith**, *zah'-yith*; prob. from an unused root [akin to 2099]; an *olive* (as yielding *illuminating* oil), the tree, the branch or the berry:—olive (tree, -yard), Olivet.

2133. זֵיתָן **Zêythân**, *zay-thawn'*; from 2132; *olive* grove; *Zethan*, an Isr.:—Zethan.

2134. זַךְ **zak**, *zak*; from 2141; *clear*:—clean, pure.

2135. זָכָה **zâkâh**, *zaw-kaw'*; a prim. root [comp. 2141]; to *be translucent*; fig. to *be innocent*:—be (make) clean, cleanse, be clear, count pure.

2136. זָכוּ **zâkûw** (Chald.), *zaw-koo'*; from a root corresp. to 2135; *purity*:—innocency.

2137. זְכוּכִית **zᵉkûwkîyth**, *zek-oo-keeth'*; from 2135; prop. *transparency*, i.e. *glass*:—crystal.

2138. זָכוּר **zâkûwr**, *zaw-koor'*; prop. pass. part. of 2142, but used for 2145; a *male* (of man or animals):—males, men-children.

2139. זַכּוּר **Zakkûwr**, *zak-koor'*; from 2142; *mindful*; *Zakkur*, the name of seven Isr.:—Zaccur, Zacchur.

2140. זַכַּי **Zakkay**, *zak-kah'ee*; from 2141; *pure*; *Zakkai*, an Isr.:—Zaccai.

2141. זָכַךְ **zâkak**, *zaw-kak'*; a prim. root [comp. 2135]; to *be transparent* or *clean* (phys. or mor.):—be (make) clean, be pure (-r).

2142. זָכַר **zâkar**, *zaw-kar'*; a prim. root; prop. to *mark* (so as to be recognized), i.e. to *remember*; by impl. to *mention*; also (as denom. from 2145) to *be male*:— × burn [incense], × earnestly, be male, (make) mention (of), be mindful, recount, record (-er), remember, make to be remembered, bring (call, come, keep, put) to (in) remembrance, × still, think on, × well.

2143. זֵכֶר **zêker**, *zay'-ker*; or
זֶכֶר **zeker**, *zeh'-ker*; from 2142; a *memento*, abstr. *recollection* (rarely if ever); by impl. *commemoration*:—memorial, memory, remembrance, scent.

2144. זֶכֶר **Zeker**, *zeh'-ker*; the same as 2143; *Zeker*, an Isr.:—Zeker.

2145. זָכָר **zâkâr**, *zaw-kawr'*; from 2142; prop. *remembered*, i.e. a *male* (of man or animals, as being the most noteworthy sex):— × him, male, man (child, -kind).

2146. זִכְרוֹן **zikrôwn**, *zik-rone'*; from 2142; a *memento* (or memorable thing, day or writing):—memorial, record.

2147. זִכְרִי **Zikrîy**, *zik-ree'*; from 2142; *memorable*; *Zicri*, the name of twelve Isr.:—Zichri.

2148. זְכַרְיָה **Zᵉkaryâh**, *zek-ar-yaw'*; or
זְכַרְיָהוּ **Zᵉkaryâhûw**, *zek-ar-yaw'-hoo*; from 2142 and 3050; *Jah has remembered*; *Zecarjah*, the name of twenty-nine Isr.:—Zachariah, Zechariah.

2149. זֻלּוּת **zullûwth**, *zool-looth'*; from 2151; prop. a *shaking*, i.e. perh. a *tempest*:—vilest.

2150. זַלְזַל **zalzal**, *zal-zal'*; by redupl. from 2151; *tremulous*, i.e. a *twig*:—sprig.

2151. זָלַל **zâlal**, *zaw-lal'*; a prim. root [comp. 2107]; to *shake* (as in the wind), i.e. to *quake*; fig. to *be loose* morally, *worthless* or *prodigal*:—blow down, glutton, riotous (eater), vile.

2152. זַלְעָפָה **zalʿâphâh**, *zal-aw-faw'*; or
זִלְעָפָה **zilʿâphâph**, *zil-aw-faw'*; from 2196; a *glow* (of wind or anger); also a *famine* (as *consuming*):—horrible, horror, terrible.

2153. זִלְפָּה **Zilpâh**, *zil-paw*; from an unused root appar. mean. to *trickle*, as myrrh; fragrant *dropping*; *Zilpah*, Leah's maid:—Zilpah.

2154. זִמָּה **zimmâh**, *zim-maw'*; or
זַמָּה **zammâh**, *zam-maw'*; from 2161; a *plan*, espec. a bad one:—heinous crime, lewd (-ly, -ness), mischief, purpose, thought, wicked (device, mind, -ness).

2155. זִמָּה **Zimmâh**, *zim-maw'*; the same as 2154; *Zimmah*, the name of two Isr.:—Zimmah.

2156. זְמוֹרָה **zᵉmôwrâh**, *zem-o-raw'*; or
זְמֹרָה **zᵉmôrâh**, *zem-o-raw'* (fem.); and
זְמֹר **zᵉmôr**, *zem-ore'* (masc.): from 2168; a *twig* (as *pruned*):—vine, branch, slip.

2157. זַמְזֹם **Zamzôm**, *zam-zome'*; from 2161; *intriguing*; a *Zamzumite*, or native tribe of Pal.:—Zamzummim.

2158. זָמִיר **zâmîyr**, *zaw-meer'*; or
זָמִר **zâmîr**, *zaw-meer'*; and (fem.)
זְמִרָה **zᵉmîrâh**, *zem-ee-raw'*; from 2167; a *song* to be accompanied with instrumental music:—psalm (-ist), singing, song.

2159. זָמִיר **zâmîyr**, *zaw-meer'*; from 2168; a *twig* (as *pruned*):—branch.

2160. זְמִירָה **Zᵉmîyrâh**, *zem-ee-raw'*; fem. of 2158; *song*; *Zemirah*, an Isr.:—Zemira.

2161. זָמַם **zâmam**, *zaw-mam'*; a prim. root; to *plan*, usually in a bad sense:—consider, devise, imagine, plot, purpose, think (evil).

2162. זָמָם **zâmâm**, *zaw-mawm'*; from 2161; a *plot*:—wicked device.

2163. זָמַן **zâman**, *zaw-man'*; a prim. root; to *fix* (a time):—appoint.

2164. זְמַן **zᵉman** (Chald.), *zem-an'*; corresp. to 2163; to *agree* (on a time and place):—prepare.

2165. זְמָן **zᵉmân**, *zem-awn'*; from 2163; an *appointed* occasion:—season, time.

2166. זְמָן **zᵉmân** (Chald.), *zem-awn'*; from 2165; the same as 2165:—season, time.

2167. זָמַר **zâmar**, *zaw-mar'*; a prim. root [perh. ident. with 2168 through the idea of *striking* with the fingers]; prop. to *touch* the strings or parts of a musical instrument, i.e. *play* upon it; to make *music*, accompanied by the voice; hence to *celebrate* in song and music:—give praise, sing forth praises, psalms.

2168. זָמַר **zâmar**, *zaw-mar'*; a prim. root [comp. 2167, 5568, 6785]; to *trim* (a vine):—prune.

2169. זֶמֶר **zemer**, *zeh'-mer*; appar. from 2167 or 2168; a *gazelle* (from its lightly *touching* the ground):—chamois.

2170. זְמָר **zᵉmâr** (Chald.), *zem-awr'*; from a root corresp. to 2167; instrumental *music*:—musick.
זָמִר **zâmîr**. See 2158.
זְמֹר **zᵉmôr**. See 2156.

2171. זַמָּר **zammâr** (Chald.), *zam-mawr'*; from the same as 2170; an instrumental *musician*:—singer.

2172. זִמְרָה **zimrâh**, *zim-raw'*; from 2167; a *musical* piece or *song* to be accompanied by an instrument:—melody, psalm.

2173 זִמְרָה **zimrâh**, *zim-raw'*; from 2168; *pruned* (i.e. *choice*) fruit:—best fruit.
זְמִרָה **zᵉmîrâh**. See 2158.
זְמֹרָה **zᵉmôrâh**. See 2156.

2174. זִמְרִי **Zimrîy**, *zim-ree'*; from 2167; *musical*; *Zimri*, the name of five Isr., and of an Arabian tribe:—Zimri.

2175. זִמְרָן **Zimrân**, *zim-rawn'*; from 2167; *musical*; *Zimran*, a son of Abraham by Keturah:—Zimran.

2176. זִמְרָת **zimrâth**, *zim-rawth'*; from 2167; instrumental *music*; by impl. *praise*:—song.

2177. זַן **zan**, *zan*; from 2109; prop. *nourished* (or fully *developed*), i.e. a *form* or *sort*:—divers kinds, × all manner of store.

2178. זַן **zan** (Chald.), *zan*; corresp. to 2177; *sort*:—kind.

2179. זָנַב **zânab**, *zaw-nab'*; a prim. root mean. to *wag*; used only as a denom. from 2180; to *curtail*, i.e. *cut* off the rear:—smite the hindmost.

2180. זָנָב **zânâb**, *zaw-nawb'*; from 2179 (in the orig. sense of *flapping*); the *tail* (lit. or fig.):—tail.

2181. זָנָה **zânâh**, *zaw-naw'*; a prim. root [highly *fed* and therefore *wanton*]; to *commit adultery* (usually of the female, and less often of simple fornication, rarely of involuntary ravishment); fig. to *commit idolatry* (the Jewish people being regarded as the spouse of Jehovah):—(cause to) commit fornication, × continually, × great, (be an, play the) harlot, (cause to be, play the) whore, (commit, fall to) whoredom, (cause to) go a-whoring, whorish.

2182. זָנוֹחַ **Zânôwach**, *zaw-no'-akh*; from 2186; *rejected*; *Zanoach*, the name of two places in Pal.:—Zanoah.

2183. זָנוּן **zânûwn**, *zaw-noon'*; from 2181; *adultery*; fig. *idolatry*:—whoredom.

2184. זְנוּת **zᵉnûwth**, *zen-ooth'*; from 2181; *adultery*, i.e. (fig.) *infidelity*, *idolatry*:—whoredom.

2185. זֹנוֹת **zônôwth**, *zo-noth'*; regarded by some as if from 2109 or an unused root, and applied to military *equipments*; but evidently the fem. plur. act. part. of 2181; *harlots*:—armour.

2186. זָנַח **zânach**, *zaw-nakh'*; a prim. root mean. to *push* aside, i.e. *reject*, *forsake*, *fail*:—cast away (off), remove far away (off).

2187. זָנַק **zânaq**, *zaw-nak'*; a prim. root; prop. to *draw together* the feet (as an animal about to dart upon its prey), i.e. to *spring* forward:—leap.

2188. זֵעָה **zêʿâh**, *zay-aw'*; from 2111 (in the sense of 3154); *perspiration*:—sweat.

2189. זַעֲוָה **zaʿăvâh**, *zah-av-aw'*; by transp. for 2113; *agitation*, *maltreatment*:— × removed, trouble.

2190. זַעֲוָן **Zaʿăvân**, *zah-av-awn'*; from 2111; *disquiet*; *Zaavan*, an Idumæan:—Zaavan.

2191. זְעֵיר **zᵉʿêyr**, *zeh-ayr'*; from an unused root [akin (by perm.) to 6819], mean. to *dwindle*; *small*:—little.

2192. זְעֵיר **zᵉʿêyr** (Chald.), *zeh-ayr'*; corresp. to 2191:—*little*.

2193. זָעַךְ **zâʿak**, *zaw-ak'*; a prim. root; to *extinguish*:—be extinct.

2194. זָעַם **zâʿam**, *zaw-am'*; a prim. root; prop. to *foam* at the mouth, i.e. to *be enraged*:—abhor, abominable, (be) angry, defy, (have) indignation.

2195. זַעַם **za'am**, *zah'-am;* from 2194; strictly *froth* at the mouth, i.e. (fig.) *fury* (espec. of God's displeasure with sin):—angry, indignation, rage.

2196. זָעַף **zâ'aph**, *zaw-af';* a prim. root; prop. to *boil* up, i.e. (fig.) to *be peevish* or *angry:*—fret, sad, worse liking, be wroth.

2197. זַעַף **za'aph**, *zah'-af;* from 2196; *anger:*—indignation, rage (-ing), wrath.

2198. זָעֵף **zâ'êph**, *zaw-afe';* from 2196; *angry:*—displeased.

2199. זָעַק **zâ'aq**, *zaw-ak';* a prim. root; to *shriek* (from anguish or danger); by anal. (as a herald) to *announce* or *convene* publicly:—assemble, call (together), (make a) cry (out), come with such a company, gather (together), cause to be proclaimed.

2200. זְעִק **ze'îq** (Chald.), *zeh'-eek;* corresp. to 2199; to *make an outcry:*—cry.

2201. זַעַק **za'aq**, *zah'-ak;* and (fem.)

זְעָקָה **ze'âqâh**, *zeh-aw-kaw';* from 2199; a *shriek* or *outcry:*—cry (-ing).

2202. זִפְרֹן **Ziphrôn**, *zi-frone';* from an unused root (mean. to *be fragrant*); *Ziphron*, a place in Pal.:—Ziphron.

2203. זֶפֶת **zepheth**, *zeh'-feth;* from an unused root (mean. to *liquify*); *asphalt* (from its tendency to *soften* in the sun):—pitch.

זִק **zîq**, or זֵק **zêq**. See 2131.

2204. זָקֵן **zâqên**, *zaw-kane';* a prim. root; to *be old:*—aged man, be (wax) old (man).

2205. זָקֵן **zâqên**, *zaw-kane';* from 2204; *old:*—aged, ancient (man), elder (-est), old (man, men and . . . women), senator.

2206. זָקָן **zâqân**, *zaw-kawn';* from 2204; the *beard* (as indicating *age*):—beard.

2207. זֹקֶן **zôqen**, *zo'-ken;* from 2204; old *age:*—age.

2208. זָקֻן **zâqûn**, *zaw-koon';* prop. pass. part. of 2204 (used only in the plur. as a noun); *old* age:—old age.

2209. זִקְנָה **ziqnâh**, *zik-naw';* fem. of 2205; old *age:*—old (age).

2210 זָקַף **zâqaph**, *zaw-kaf';* a prim. root; to *lift*, i.e. (fig.) *comfort:*—raise (up).

2211. זְקַף **zeqaph** (Chald.), *zek-af';* corresp. to 2210; to *hang*, i.e. *impale:*—set up.

2212. זָקַק **zâqaq**, *zaw-kak';* a prim. root; to *strain*, (fig.) *extract, clarify:*—fine, pour down, purge, purify, refine.

2213. זֵר **zêr**, *zare;* from 2237 (in the sense of *scattering*); a *chaplet* (as *spread* around the top), i.e. (spec.) a border *moulding:*—crown.

2214. זָרָא **zârâ'**, *zaw-raw';* from 2114 (in the sense of *estrangement*) [comp. 2219]; *disgust:*—loathsome.

2215. זָרַב **zârab**, *zaw-rab';* a prim. root; to *flow* away:—wax warm.

2216. זְרֻבָּבֶל **Zerubbâbel**, *zer-oob-baw-bel';* from 2215 and 894; *descended of* (i.e. from) *Babylon*, i.e. born there; *Zerubbabel*, an Isr.:—Zerubbabel.

2217. זְרֻבָּבֶל **Zerubbâbel** (Chald.), *zer-oob-baw-bel';* corresp. to 2216:—Zerubbabel.

2218. זֶרֶד **Zered**, *zeh'-red;* from an unused root mean. to *be exuberant* in growth; lined with *shrubbery; Zered*, a brook E. of the Dead Sea:—Zared, Zered.

2219. זָרָה **zârâh**, *zaw-raw';* a prim root [comp. 2114; to *toss* about; by impl. to *diffuse, winnow:*—cast away, compass, disperse, fan, scatter (away), spread, strew, winnow.

2220. זְרוֹעַ **zerôwa'**, *zer-o'-ah;* or (short.)

זְרֹעַ **zerôa'**, *zer-o'-ah;* and (fem.)

זְרוֹעָה **zerôw'âh**, *zer-o-aw';* or

זְרֹעָה **zerô'âh**, *zer-o-aw';* from 2232; the *arm* (as *stretched* out), or (of animals) the *foreleg;* fig. *force:*—arm, + help, mighty, power, shoulder, strength.

2221. זֵרוּעַ **zêrûwa'**, *zay-roo'-ah;* from 2232; something *sown*, i.e. a *plant:*—sowing, thing that is sown.

2222. זַרְזִיף **zarzîyph**, *zar-zeef';* by redupl. from an unused root mean. to *flow;* a *pouring rain:*—water.

זְרוֹעָה **zerôw'âh**. See 2220.

2223. זַרְזִיר **zarzîyr**, *zar-zeer';* by redupl. from 2115; prop. tightly *girt*, i.e. prob. a *racer*, or some fleet animal (as being *slender* in the waist):—+ greyhound.

2224. זָרַח **zârach**, *zaw-rakh';* a prim. root; prop, to *irradiate* (or shoot forth beams), i.e. to *rise* (as the sun); spec. to *appear* (as a symptom of leprosy):—arise, rise (up), as soon as it is up.

2225. זֶרַח **zerach**, *zeh'-rakh;* from 2224; a *rising* of light:—rising.

2226. זֶרַח **Zerach**, *zeh'-rakh;* the same as 2225: *Zerach*, the name of three Isr., also of an Idumæan and an Ethiopian prince:—Zarah, Zerah.

2227. זַרְחִי **Zarchîy**, *zar-khee';* patron. from 2226; a *Zarchite* or desc. of Zerach:—Zarchite.

2228. זְרַחְיָה **Zerachyâh**, *zer-akh-yaw';* from 2225 and 3050; *Jah has risen; Zerachjah*, the name of two Isr.:—Zerahiah.

2229. זָרַם **zâram**, *zaw-ram';* a prim. root; to *gush* (as water):—carry away as with a flood, pour out.

2230. זֶרֶם **zerem**, *zeh'-rem;* from 2229; a *gush* of water:—flood, overflowing, shower, storm, tempest.

2231. זִרְמָה **zirmâh**, *zir-maw';* fem. of 2230; a *gushing* of fluid (semen):—issue.

2232. זָרַע **zâra'**, *zaw-rah';* a prim. root; to *sow;* fig. to *disseminate, plant, fructify:*—bear, conceive seed, set with, sow (-er), yield.

2233. זֶרַע **zera'**, *zeh'-rah;* from 2232; *seed;* fig. *fruit, plant, sowing-time, posterity:*—× carnally, child, fruitful, seed (-time), sowing-time.

2234. זְרַע **zera'** (Chald.), *zer-ah';* corresp. to 2233; *posterity:*—seed.

זְרֹעַ **zerôa'**. See 2220.

2235. זֵרֹעַ **zêrôa'**, *zay-ro'-ah;* or

זֵרָעֹן **zêrâ'ôn**, *zay-raw-ohn';* from 2232; something *sown* (only in the plur.), i.e. a *vegetable* (as food):—pulse.

זְרֹעָה **zer'ôâh**. See 2220.

2236. זָרַק **zâraq**, *zaw-rak';* a prim. root; to *sprinkle* (fluid or solid particles):—be here and there, scatter, sprinkle, strew.

2237. זָרַר **zârar**, *zaw-rar';* a prim. root [comp. 2114]; perh. to *diffuse*, i.e. (spec.) to *sneeze:*—sneeze.

2238. זֶרֶשׁ **Zeresh**, *zeh'-resh;* of Pers. or.; *Zeresh*, Haman's wife:—Zeresh.

2239. זֶרֶת **zereth**, *zeh'-reth;* from 2219; the *spread* of the fingers, i.e. a *span:*—span.

2240. זַתּוּא **Zattûw'**, *zat-too';* of uncert. der.; *Zattu*, an Isr.:—Zattu.

2241. זֵתָם **Zêthâm**, *zay-thawm';* appar. a var. for 2133; *Zetham*, an Isr.:—Zetham.

2242. זֵתַר **Zêthar**, *zay-thar';* of Pers. or.; *Zethar*, a eunuch of Xerxes:—Zethar.

ח

2243. חֹב **chôb**, *khobe;* by contr. from 2245; prop. a *cherisher*, i.e. the *bosom:*—bosom.

2244. חָבָא **châbâ'**, *khaw-baw';* a prim. root [comp. 2245]; to *secrete:*—× held, hide (self), do secretly.

2245. חָבַב **châbab**, *khaw-bab';* a prim. root [comp. 2244, 2247]; prop. to *hide* (as in the bosom), i.e. to *cherish* (with affection):—love.

2246. חֹבָב **Chôbâb**, *kho-bawb';* from 2245; *cherished; Chobab*, father-in-law of Moses:—Hobab.

2247. חָבָה **châbah**, *khaw-bah';* a prim. root [comp. 2245]; to *secrete:*—hide (self).

2248. חֲבוּלָה **chăbûwlâh** (Chald.), *khab-oo-law';* from 2255; prop. *overthrown*, i.e. (morally) *crime:*—hurt.

2249. חָבוֹר **Châbôwr**, *khaw-bore';* from 2266; *united; Chabor*, a river of Assyria:—Habor.

2250. חַבּוּרָה **chabbûwrâh**, *khab-boo-raw';* or

חַבֻּרָה **chabbûrâh**, *khab-boo-raw';* or

חֲבֻרָה **chăbûrâh**, *khab-oo-raw';* from 2266; prop. *bound* (with stripes), i.e. a *weal* (or black-and-blue mark itself):—blueness, bruise, hurt, stripe, wound.

2251. חָבַט **châbaṭ**, *khaw-bat';* a prim. root; to *knock* out or off:—beat (off, out), thresh.

2252. חֲבַיָּה **Chăbayâh**, *khab-ah-yaw';* or

חֲבָיָה **Chăbâyâh**, *khab-aw-yaw';* from 2247 and 3050; *Jah has hidden; Chabajah*, an Isr.:—Habaiah.

2253. חֶבְיוֹן **chebyôwn**, *kheb-yone';* from 2247; a *concealment:*—hiding.

2254. חָבַל **châbal**, *khaw-bal';* a prim. root; to *wind* tightly (as a rope), i.e. to *bind;* spec. by a *pledge;* fig. to *pervert, destroy;* also to *writhe* in pain (espec. of parturition):— × at all, band, bring forth, (deal) corrupt (-ly), destroy, offend, lay to (take a) pledge, spoil, travail, × very, withhold.

2255. חֲבַל **chăbal** (Chald.), *khab-al';* corresp. to 2254; to *ruin:*—destroy, hurt.

2256. חֶבֶל **chebel**, *kheh'-bel;* or

חֵבֶל **chêbel**, *khay'-bel;* from 2254; a *rope* (as *twisted*), espec. a measuring *line;* by impl. a *district* or *inheritance* (as *measured*); or a *noose* (as of *cords*); fig. a *company* (as if *tied* together); also a *throe* (espec. of parturition); also *ruin:*—band, coast, company, cord, country, destruction, line, lot, pain, pang, portion, region, rope, snare, sorrow, tackling.

2257. חֲבַל **chăbal** (Chald.), *khab-al';* from 2255; *harm* (personal or pecuniary):—damage, hurt.

2258. חֲבֹל **chăbôl**, *khab-ole';* or (fem.)

חֲבֹלָה **chăbôlâh**, *khab-o-law';* from 2254; a *pawn* (as security for debt):—pledge.

2259. חֹבֵל **chôbêl**, *kho-bale';* act. part. from 2254 (in the sense of handling *ropes*); a *sailor:*—pilot, shipmaster.

2260. חִבֵּל **chibbêl**, *khib-bale';* from 2254 (in the sense of furnished with *ropes*); a *mast:*—mast.

2261. חֲבַצֶּלֶת **chăbatstseleth**, *khab-ats-tseh'-leth;* of uncert. der.; prob. *meadow-saffron:*—rose.

2262. חֲבַצִּנְיָה **Chăbatstsanyâh**, *khab-ats-tsan-yaw';* of uncert. der.; *Chabatstsanjah*, a Rechabite:—Habazaniah.

2263. חָבַק **châbaq**, *khaw-bak';* a prim. root; to *clasp* (the hands or in embrace):—embrace, fold.

2264. חִבֻּק **chibbûq**, *khib-book';* from 2263; a *clasping* of the hands (in idleness):—fold.

2265. חֲבַקּוּק **Chăbaqqûwq**, *khab-ak-kook';* by redupl. from 2263; *embrace; Chabakkuk*, the prophet:—Habakkuk.

2266. חָבַר **châbar**, *khaw-bar';* a prim. root; to *join* (lit. or fig.); spec. (by means of spells) to *fascinate:*—charm (-er), be compact, couple (together), have fellowship with, heap up, join (self, together), league.

2267. חֶבֶר **cheber**, *kheh'-ber;* from 2266; a *society;* also a *spell:*—+ charmer (-ing), company, enchantment, × wide.

2268. חֶבֶר **Cheber**, *kheh'-ber;* the same as 2267; *community; Cheber*, the name of a Kenite and of three Isr.:—Heber.

2269. חֲבַר **chăbar** (Chald.), *khab-ar';* from a root corresp. to 2266; an *associate:*—companion, fellow.

2270. חָבֵר **châbêr**, *khaw-bare';* from 2266; an *associate:*—companion, fellow, knit together.

2271. חַבָּר **chabbâr**, *khab-bawr';* from 2266; a *partner:*—companion.

2272. חֲבַרְבֻּרָה **chăbarbûrâh**, *khab-ar-boo-raw'*; by redupl. from 2266; a *streak* (like a *line*), as on the tiger:—spot.

2273. חַבְרָה **chabrâh** (Chald.), *khab-raw'*; fem. of 2269; an *associate:*—other.

2274. חֶבְרָה **chebrâh**, *kheb-raw'*; fem. of 2267; *association:*—company.

2275. חֶבְרוֹן **Chebrôwn**, *kheb-rone'*; from 2267; seat of *association; Chebron*, a place in Pal., also the name of two Isr.:—Hebron.

2276. חֶבְרוֹנִי **Chebrôwnîy**, *kheb-ro-nee'*; or

חֶבְרֹנִי **Chebrônîy**, *kheb-ro-nee'*; patron. from 2275; *Chebronite* (collect.), an inhab. of Chebron:—Hebronites.

2277. חֶבְרִי **Chebrîy**, *kheb-ree'*; patron. from 2268; a *Chebrite* (collect.) or desc. of Cheber:—Heberites.

2278. חֲבֶרֶת **chăbereth**, *khab-eh'-reth*; fem. of 2270; a *consort:*—companion.

2279. חֹבֶרֶת **chôbereth**, *kho-beh'-reth*; fem. act. part. of 2266; a *joint:*—which coupleth, coupling.

2280. חָבַשׁ **châbash**, *khaw-bash'*; a prim. root; to *wrap* firmly (espec. a turban, compress, or *saddle*); fig. to *stop*, to *rule:*—bind (up), gird about, govern, healer, put, saddle, wrap about.

2281. חָבֵת **châbêth**, *khaw-bayth'*; from an unused root prob. mean. to *cook* [comp. 4227]; something *fried*, prob. a griddle-*cake:*—pan.

2282. חַג **chag**, *khag*; or

חָג **châg**, *khawg*; from 2287; a *festival*, or a *victim* therefor:—(solemn) feast (day), sacrifice, solemnity.

2283. חָגָא **châgâ'**, *khaw-gaw'*; from an unused root mean. to *revolve* [comp. 2287]; prop. *vertigo*, i.e. (fig.) *fear:*—terror.

2284. חָגָב **châgâb**, *khaw-gawb'*; of uncert. der.; a *locust:*—locust.

2285. חָגָב **Châgâb**, *khaw-gawb'*; the same as 2284; *locust; Chagab*, one of the Nethinim:—Hagab.

2286. חֲגָבָא **Chăgâbâ'**, *khag-aw-baw'*; or

חֲגָבָה **Chăgâbâh**, *khag-aw-baw'*; fem. of 2285; *locust; Chagaba* or *Chagabah*, one of the Nethinim:—Hagaba, Hagabah.

2287. חָגַג **châgag**, *khaw-gag'*; a prim. root [comp. 2283, 2328]; prop. to move in a *circle*, i.e. (spec.) to *march* in a sacred procession, to *observe* a festival; by impl. to *be giddy:*—celebrate, dance, (keep, hold) a (solemn) feast (holiday), reel to and fro.

2288. חֲגָו **chăgâv**, *khag-awv'*; from an unused root mean. to take *refuge*; a *rift* in rocks:—cleft.

2289. חָגוֹר **châgôwr**, *khaw-gore'*; from 2296; *belted:*—girded with.

2290. חֲגוֹר **chăgôwr**, *khag-ore'*; or

חֲגֹר **chăgôr**, *khag-ore'*; and (fem.)

חֲגוֹרָה **chăgôwrâh**, *khag-o-raw'*; or

חֲגֹרָה **chăgôrâh**, *khag-o-raw'*; from 2296; a *belt* (for the waist):—apron, armour, gird (-le).

2291. חַגִּי **Chaggîy**, *khag-ghee'*; from 2287; *festive; Chaggi*, an Isr.; also (patron.) a *Chaggite*, or desc. of the same:—Haggi, Haggites.

2292. חַגַּי **Chaggay**, *khag-gah'ee*; from 2282; *festive; Chaggai*, a Heb. prophet:—Haggai.

2293. חַגִּיָּה **Chaggîyâh**, *khag-ghee-yaw'*; from 2282 and 3050; *festival of Jah; Chaggijah*, an Isr.:—Haggiah.

2294. חַגִּית **Chaggîyth**, *khag-gheeth'*; fem. of 2291; *festive; Chaggith*, a wife of David:—Haggith.

2295. חָגְלָה **Choglâh**, *khog-law'*; of uncert. der.; prob. a *partridge; Choglah*, an Israelitess:—Hoglah. See also 1031.

2296. חָגַר **châgar**, *khaw-gar'*; a prim. root; to *gird* on (as a belt, armor, etc.):—be able to put on, be afraid, appointed, gird, restrain, × on every side.

2297. חַד **chad**, *khad*; abridged from 259; *one:*—one.

2298. חַד **chad** (Chald.), *khad*; corresp. to 2297; as card. *one*; as art. *single*; as ord. *first*; adv. *at once:*—a, first, one, together.

2299. חַד **chad**, *khad*; from 2300; *sharp:*—sharp.

2300. חָדַד **châdad**, *khaw-dad'*; a prim. root; to *be* (caus. *make*) *sharp* or (fig.) *severe:*—be fierce, sharpen.

2301. חֲדַד **Chădad**, *khad-ad'*; from 2300; *fierce; Chadad*, an Ishmaelite:—Hadad.

2302. חָדָה **châdâh**, *khaw-daw'*; a prim. root; to *rejoice:*—make glad, be joined, rejoice.

2303. חַדּוּד **chaddûwd**, *khad-dood'*; from 2300; a *point:*—sharp.

2304. חֶדְוָה **chedvâh**, *khed-vaw'*; from 2302; *rejoicing:*— gladness, joy.

2305. חֶדְוָה **chedvâh** (Chald.), *khed-vaw'*; corresp. to 2304:—*joy*.

2306. חֲדִי **chădîy** (Chald.), *khad-ee'*; corresp. to 2373; a *breast:*—breast.

2307. חָדִיד **Châdîyd**, *khaw-deed'*; from 2300; a *peak; Chadid*, a place in Pal.:—Hadid.

2308. חָדַל **châdal**, *khaw-dal'*; a prim. root; prop. to *be flabby*, i.e. (by impl.) *desist*; (fig.) *be lacking* or *idle:*—cease, end, fail, forbear, forsake, leave (off), let alone, rest, be unoccupied, want.

2309. חֶדֶל **chedel**, *kheh'-del*; from 2308; *rest*, i.e. the state of the *dead:*—world.

2310. חָדֵל **châdêl**, *khaw-dale'*; from 2308; *vacant*, i.e. *ceasing* or *destitute:*—he that forbeareth, frail, rejected.

2311. חַדְלַי **Chadlay**, *khad-lah'ee*; from 2309; *idle; Chadlai*, an Isr.:—Hadlai.

2312. חֵדֶק **chêdeq**, *khay'-dek*; from an unused root mean. to *sting*; a *prickly* plant:—brier, thorn.

2313. חִדֶּקֶל **Chiddeqel**, *khid-deh'-kel*; prob. of for. or.; the *Chiddekel* (or Tigris) river:—Hiddekel.

2314. חָדַר **châdar**, *khaw-dar'*; a prim. root; prop. to *inclose* (as a room), i.e. (by anal.) to *beset* (as in a siege):—enter a privy chamber.

2315. חֶדֶר **cheder**, *kheh'-der*; from 2314; an *apartment* (usually lit.):—([bed] inner) chamber, innermost (-ward) part, parlour, + south, × within.

2316. חֲדַר **Chădar**, *khad-ar'*; another form for 2315; *chamber; Chadar*, an Ishmaelite:—Hadar.

2317. חַדְרָךְ **Chadrâk**, *khad-rawk'*; of uncert. der.; *Chadrak*, a Syrian deity:—Hadrach.

2318. חָדַשׁ **châdash**, *khaw-dash'*; a prim. root; to *be new*; caus. to *rebuild:*—renew, repair.

2319. חָדָשׁ **châdâsh**, *khaw-dawsh'*; from 2318; *new:*—fresh, new thing.

2320. חֹדֶשׁ **chôdesh**, *kho'-desh*; from 2318; the *new* moon; by impl. a *month:*—month (-ly), new moon.

2321. חֹדֶשׁ **Chôdesh**, *kho'-desh*; the same as 2320; *Chodesh*, an Israelitess:—Hodesh.

2322. חֲדָשָׁה **Chădâshâh**, *khad-aw-shaw'*; fem. of 2319; *new; Chadashah*, a place in Pal.:—Hadashah.

2323. חֲדָת **chădath** (Chald.), *khad-ath'*; corresp. to 2319; *new:*—new.

2324. חֲוָא **chăvâ'** (Chald.), *khav-aw'*; corresp. to 2331; to *show:*—shew.

2325. חוּב **chûwb**, *khoob*; also

חָיַב **châyab**, *khaw-yab'*; a prim. root; prop. perh. to *tie*, i.e. (fig. and reflex.) to *owe*, or (by impl.) to *forfeit:*—make endanger.

2326. חוֹב **chôwb**, *khobe*; from 2325; *debt:*—debtor.

2327. חוֹבָה **chôwbâh**, *kho-baw'*; fem. act. part. of 2247; *hiding* place; *Chobah*, a place in Syria:—Hobah.

2328. חוּג **chûwg**, *khoog*; a prim. root [comp. 2287]; to describe a *circle:*—compass.

2329. חוּג **chûwg**, *khoog*; from 2328; a *circle:*—circle, circuit, compass.

2330. חוּד **chûwd**, *khood*; a prim. root; prop. to *tie* a knot, i.e. (fig.) to *propound* a riddle:—put forth.

2331. חָוָה **châvâh**, *khaw-vah'*; a prim. root; [comp. 2324, 2421]; prop. to *live*; by impl. (intens.) to *declare* or *show:*—show.

2332. חַוָּה **Chavvâh**, *khav-vaw'*; causat. from 2331; *life-giver; Chavvah* (or Eve), the first woman:—Eve.

2333. חַוָּה **chavvâh**, *khav-vaw'*; prop. the same as 2332 (*life-giving*, i.e. *living-place*); by impl. an encampment or *village:*—(small) town.

2334. חַוּוֹת יָעִיר **Chavvôwth Yâ'îyr**, *khavvothe' yaw-eer'*; from the plur. of 2333 and a modification of 3265; *hamlets of Jair*, a region of Pal.:—[Bashan-] Havoth-jair.

2335. חוֹזַי **Chôwzay**, *kho-zah'ee*; from 2374; *visionary; Chozai*, an Isr.:—the seers.

2336. חוֹחַ **chôwach**, *kho'-akh*; from an unused root appar. mean. to *pierce*; a *thorn*; by anal. a *ring* for the nose:—bramble, thistle, thorn.

2337. חָוָח **châvâch**, *khaw-vawkh'*; perh. the same as 2336; a *dell* or *crevice* (as if *pierced* in the earth):—thicket.

2338. חוּט **chûwṭ** (Chald.), *khoot*; corresp. to the root of 2339, perh. as a denom.; to *string* together, i.e. (fig.) to *repair:*—join.

2339. חוּט **chûwṭ**, *khoot*; from an unused root prob. mean. to *sew*; a *string*; by impl. a measuring *tape:*—cord, fillet, line, thread.

2340. חִוִּי **Chivvîy**, *khiv-vee'*; perh. from 2333; a *villager*; a *Chivvite*, one of the aboriginal tribes of Pal.:—Hivite.

2341. חֲוִילָה **Chăvîylâh**, *khav-ee-law'*; prob. from 2342; *circular; Chavilah*, the name of two or three eastern regions; also perh. of two men:—Havilah.

2342. חוּל **chûwl**, *khool*; or

חִיל **chîyl**, *kheel*; a prim. root; prop. to *twist* or *whirl* (in a circular or spiral manner), i.e. (spec.) to *dance*, to *writhe* in pain (espec. of parturition) or fear; fig. to *wait*, to *pervert:*—bear, (make to) bring forth, (make to) calve, dance, drive away, fall grievously (with pain), fear, form, great, grieve, (be) grievous, hope, look, make, be in pain, be much (sore) pained, rest, shake, shapen, (be) sorrow (-ful), stay, tarry, travail (with pain), tremble, trust, wait carefully (patiently), be wounded.

2343. חוּל **Chûwl**, *khool*; from 2342; a *circle; Chul*, a son of Aram; also the region settled by him:—Hul.

2344. חוֹל **chôwl**, *khole*; from 2342; *sand* (as *round* or whirling particles):—sand.

2345. חוּם **chûwm**, *khoom*; from an unused root mean. to *be warm*, i.e. (by impl.) *sunburnt* or *swarthy* (blackish):—brown.

2346. חוֹמָה **chôwmâh**, *kho-maw'*; fem. act. part. of an unused root appar. mean. to *join*; a *wall* of protection:—wall, walled.

2347. חוּס **chûwç**, *khoos*; a prim. root; prop. to *cover*, i.e. (fig.) to *compassionate:*—pity, regard, spare.

2348. חוֹף **chôwph**, *khofe*; from an unused root mean. to *cover*; a *cove* (as a *sheltered* bay):—coast [of the sea], haven, shore, [sea-] side.

2349. חוּפָם **Chûwphâm**, *khoo-fawm'*; from the same as 2348; *protection: Chupham*, an Isr.:—Hupham.

2350. חוּפָמִי **Chûwphâmîy**, *khoo-faw-mee'*; patron. from 2349; a *Chuphamite* or desc. of Chupham:—Huphamites.

2351. חוּץ **chûwts**, *khoots*; or (short.)

חֻץ **chûts**, *khoots*; (both forms fem. in the plur.) from an unused root mean. to *sever*; prop. *separate* by a wall, i.e. *outside*, *outdoors:*—abroad, field, forth, highway, more, out (-side, -ward), street, without.

חוֹק **chôwq**. See 2436.

חוּקֹק **Chûwqôq**. See 2712.

2352. חוּר **chûwr**, *khoor;* or (short.)

חֻר **chûr**, *khoor;* from an unused root prob. mean. to *bore;* the *crevice* of a serpent; the *cell* of a prison:—hole.

2353. חוּר **chûwr**, *khoor;* from 2357; *white* linen:—white.

2354. חוּר **Chûwr**, *khoor;* the same as 2353 or 2352; *Chur*, the name of four Isr. and one Midianite:—Hur.

2355. חוֹר **chôwr**, *khore;* the same as 2353; *white* linen:—network. Comp. 2715.

2356. חוֹר **chôwr**, *khore;* or (short.)

חֹר **chôr**, *khore;* the same as 2352; a *cavity, socket, den:*—cave, hole.

2357. חָוַר **châvar**, *khaw-var';* a prim. root; to *blanch* (as with shame):—wax pale.

2358. חִוָּר **chivvâr** (Chald.), *khiv-vawr';* from a root corresp. to 2357; *white:*—white.

חוֹרוֹן **Chôwrôwn**. See 1032.

חוֹרִי **chôwrîy**. See 2753.

2359. חוּרִי **Chûwrîy**, *khoo-ree';* prob. from 2353; *linen*-worker; *Churi*, an Isr.:—Huri.

2360. חוּרַי **Chûwray**, *khoo-rah'ee;* prob. an orth. var. for 2359; *Churai*, an Isr.:—Hurai.

2361. חוּרָם **Chûwrâm**, *khoo-rawm';* prob. from 2353; *whiteness*, i.e. noble; *Churam*, the name of an Isr. and two Syrians:—Huram. Comp. 2438.

2362. חַוְרָן **Chavrân**, *khav-rawn';* appar. from 2357 (in the sense of 2352); *cavernous; Chavran*, a region E. of the Jordan:—Hauran.

2363. חוּשׁ **chûwsh**, *koosh;* a prim. root; to *hurry;* fig. to *be eager* with excitement or enjoyment:—(make) haste (-n), ready.

2364. חוּשָׁה **Chûwshâh**, *khoo-shaw';* from 2363; *haste; Chushah*, an Isr.:—Hushah.

2365. חוּשַׁי **Chûwshay**, *khoo-shah'ee;* from 2363; *hasty; Chushai*, an Isr.:—Hushai.

2366. חוּשִׁים **Chûwshîym**, *khoo-sheem';* or

חֻשִׁים **Chûshîym**, *khoo-shem';* or

חֻשִׁם **Chûshîm**, *khoo-sheem';* plur. from 2363; *hasters; Chushim*, the name of three Isr.:—Hushim.

2367. חוּשָׁם **Chûwshâm**, *khoo-shawm';* or

חֻשָׁם **Chûshâm**, *khoo-shawm';* from 2363; *hastily; Chusham*, an Idumæan:—Husham.

2368. חוֹתָם **chôwthâm**, *kho-thawm';* or

חֹתָם **chôthâm**, *kho-thawm';* from 2856; a *signature*-ring:—seal, signet.

2369. חוֹתָם **Chôwthâm**, *kho-thawm'*, the same as 2368; *seal; Chotham*, the name of two Isr.:—Hotham, Hothan.

2370. חֲזָא **chăzâ'** (Chald.), *khaz-aw';* or

חֲזָה **chăzâh** (Chald.), *khaz-aw';* corresp. to 2372; to *gaze* upon; mentally to *dream, be usual* (i.e. *seem*):—behold, have [a dream], see, be wont.

2371. חֲזָאֵל **Chăzâ'êl**, *khaz-aw-ale';* or

חֲזָהאֵל **Chăzâh'êl**, *khaz-aw-ale';* from 2372 and 410; *God has seen; Chazaël*, a king of Syria:—Hazael.

2372. חָזָה **châzâh**, *khaw-zaw';* a prim. root; to *gaze* at; mentally to *perceive, contemplate* (with pleasure); spec. to *have a vision of:*—behold, look, prophesy, provide, see.

2373. חָזֶה **châzeh**, *khaw-zeh';* from 2372; the *breast* (as most *seen* in front):—breast.

2374. חֹזֶה **chôzeh**, *kho-zeh';* act. part. of 2372; a *beholder* in vision; also a *compact* (as *looked upon* with approval):—agreement, prophet, see that, seer, [star-] gazer.

חֲזָהאֵל **Chăzâh'êl**. See 2371.

2375. חֲזוֹ **Chăzow**, *khaz-o';* from 2372; *seer; Chazo*, a nephew of Abraham:—Hazo.

2376. חֵזֵו **chêzev** (Chald.), *khay'-zev;* from 2370; a *sight:*—look, vision.

2377. חָזוֹן **châzôwn**, *khaw-zone';* from 2372; a *sight* (mentally), i.e. a *dream, revelation*, or *oracle:*—vision.

2378. חָזוֹת **châzôwth**, *khaw-zooth';* from 2372; a *revelation:*—vision.

2379. חֲזוֹת **chăzôwth** (Chald.), *khaz-oth';* from 2370; a *view:*—sight.

2380. חָזוּת **châzûwth**, *khaw-zooth';* from 2372; a *look;* hence (fig.) striking *appearance, revelation*, or (by impl.) *compact:*—agreement, notable (one), vision.

2381. חֲזִיאֵל **Chăzîy'êl**, *khaz-ee-ale';* from 2372 and 410; *seen of God; Chaziel*, a Levite:—Haziel.

2382. חֲזָיָה **Chăzâyâh**, *khaz-aw-yaw';* from 2372 and 3050; *Jah has seen; Chazajah*, an Isr.:—Hazaiah.

2383. חֶזְיוֹן **Chezyôwn**, *khez-yone';* from 2372; *vision; Chezjon*, a Syrian:—Hezion.

2384. חִזָּיוֹן **chizzâyôwn**, *khiz-zaw-yone';* from 2372; a *revelation*, espec. by *dream:*—vision.

2385. חֲזִיז **châzîyz**, *khaw-zeez';* from an unused root mean. to *glare;* a *flash* of lightning:—bright cloud, lightning.

2386. חֲזִיר **chăzîyr**, *khaz-eer';* from an unused root prob. mean. to *inclose;* a *hog* (perh. as *penned*):—boar, swine.

2387. חֵזִיר **Chêzîyr**, *khay-zeer';* from the same as 2386; perh. *protected; Chezir*, the name of two Isr.:—Hezir.

2388. חָזַק **châzaq**, *khaw-zak';* a prim. root; to *fasten* upon; hence to *seize, be strong* (fig. *courageous*, causat. *strengthen, cure, help, repair, fortify*), *obstinate;* to *bind, restrain, conquer:*—aid, amend, × calker, catch, cleave, confirm, be constant, constrain, continue, be of good (take) courage (-ous, -ly), encourage (self), be established, fasten, force, fortify, make hard, harden, help, (lay) hold (fast), lean, maintain, play the man, mend, become (wax) mighty, prevail, be recovered, repair, retain, seize, be (wax) sore, strengthen (self), be stout, be (make, shew, wax) strong (-er), be sure, take (hold), be urgent, behave self valiantly, withstand.

2389. חָזָק **châzâq**, *khaw-zawk';* from 2388; *strong* (usu. in a bad sense, *hard, bold, violent*):—harder, hottest, + impudent, loud, mighty, sore, stiff [-hearted], strong (-er).

2390. חָזֵק **châzêq**, *khaw-zake';* from 2388; *powerful:*— × wax louder. stronger.

2391. חֵזֶק **chêzeq**, *khay'-zek;* from 2388; *help:*—strength.

2392. חֹזֶק **chôzeq**, *kho'-zek;* from 2388; *power:*—strength.

2393. חֶזְקָה **chezqâh**, *khez-kaw';* fem. of 2391; prevailing *power:*—strength (-en self), (was) strong.

2394. חָזְקָה **chozqâh**, *khoz-kaw';* fem. of 2392; *vehemence* (usu. in a bad sense):—force, mightily, repair. sharply.

2395. חִזְקִי **Chizqîy**, *khiz-kee';* from 2388; *strong; Chizki*, an Isr.:—Hezeki.

2396. חִזְקִיָּה **Chizqîyâh**, *khiz-kee-yaw';* or

חִזְקִיָּהוּ **Chizqîyâhûw**, *khiz-kee-yaw'-hoo;* also

יְחִזְקִיָּה **Y^echizqîyâh**, *yekh-iz-kee-yaw';* or

יְחִזְקִיָּהוּ **Y^echizqîyâhûw**, *yekh-iz-kee-yaw'-hoo;* from 2388 and 3050; *strengthened of Jah; Chizkijah*, a king of Judah, also the name of two other Isr.:—Hezekiah, Hizkiah, Hizkijah. Comp. 3169.

2397. חָח **châch**, *khawkh;* once (Ezek. 29 : 4)

חָחִי **châchîy**, *khakh-ee';* from the same as 2336; a *ring* for the nose (or lips):—bracelet, chain, hook.

חָחִי **châchîy**. See 2397.

2398. חָטָא **châṭâ'**, *khaw-taw';* a prim. root; prop. to *miss;* hence (fig. and gen.) to *sin;* by infer. to *forfeit, lack, expiate, repent*, (causat.) *lead astray, condemn:*—bear the blame, cleanse, commit [sin], by fault, harm he hath done, loss, miss, (make) offend (-er), offer for sin, purge, purify (self), make reconciliation, (cause, make) sin (-ful, -ness), trespass.

2399. חֵטְא **chêṭ'**, *khate;* from 2398; a *crime* or its *penalty:*—fault, × grievously, offence, (punishment of) sin.

2400. חַטָּא **chaṭṭâ'**, *khat-taw';* intens. from 2398; a *criminal*, or one accounted *guilty:*—offender, sinful, sinner.

2401. חֲטָאָה **chăṭâ'âh**, *khat-aw-aw';* fem. of 2399; an *offence*, or a *sacrifice* for it:—sin (offering), sinful.

2402. חַטָּאָה **chaṭṭâ'âh** (Chald.), *khat-taw-aw';* corresp. to 2401; an *offence*, and the *penalty* or *sacrifice* for it:—sin (offering).

2403. חַטָּאָה **chaṭṭâ'âh**, *khat-taw-aw';* or

חַטָּאת **chaṭṭâ'th**, *khat-tawth';* from 2398; an *offence* (sometimes habitual *sinfulness*), and its penalty, occasion, sacrifice, or expiation; also (concr.) an *offender:*—punishment (of sin), purifying (-fication for sin), sin (-ner, offering).

2404. חָטַב **châṭab**, *khaw-tab';* a prim. root; to *chop* or *carve* wood:—cut down, hew (-er), polish.

2405. חֲטֻבָה **chăṭûbâh**, *khat-oo-baw';* fem. pass. part. of 2404; prop. a *carving;* hence a *tapestry* (as figured):—carved.

2406. חִטָּה **chiṭṭâh**, *khit-taw';* of uncert. der.; *wheat*, whether the grain or the plant:—wheat (-en).

2407. חַטּוּשׁ **Chaṭṭûwsh**, *khat-toosh';* from an unused root of uncert. signif.; *Chattush*, the name of four or five Isr.:—Hattush.

2408. חֲטִי **chăṭîy** (Chald.), *khat-ee';* from a root corresp. to 2398; an *offence:*—sin.

2409. חַטָּיָא **chaṭṭâyâ'** (Chald.), *khat-taw-yaw';* from the same as 2408; an *expiation:*—sin offering.

2410. חֲטִיטָא **Chăṭîyṭa'**, *khat-ee-taw';* from an unused root appar. mean. to *dig* out; *explorer; Chatita*, a temple porter:—Hatita.

2411. חַטִּיל **Chaṭṭîyl**, *khat-teel';* from an unused root appar. mean. to *wave; fluctuating; Chattil*, one of "Solomon's servants":—Hattil.

2412. חֲטִיפָא **Chăṭîyphâ'**, *khat-ee-faw';* from 2414; *robber; Chatipha*, one of the Nethinim:—Hatipha.

2413. חָטַם **châṭam**, *khaw-tam';* a prim. root; to *stop:*—refrain.

2414. חָטַף **châṭaph**, *khaw-taf';* a prim. root; to *clutch;* hence to *seize* as a prisoner:—catch.

2415. חֹטֶר **chôṭer**, *kho'-ter;* from an unused root of uncert. signif.; a *twig:*—rod.

2416. חַי **chay**, *khah'ee;* from 2421; *alive;* hence *raw* (flesh); *fresh* (plant, water, year), *strong;* also (as noun, espec. in the fem. sing. and masc. plur.) *life* (or living thing), whether lit. or fig.:— + age, alive, appetite, (wild) beast, company, congregation, life (-time), live (-ly), living (creature, thing), maintenance, + merry, multitude, + (be) old, quick, raw, running, springing, troop.

2417. חַי **chay** (Chald.), *khah'ee;* from 2418; *alive;* also (as noun in plur.) *life:*—life, that liveth, living.

2418. חֲיָא **chăyâ'** (Chald.), *khah-yaw';* or

חֲיָה **chăyâh** (Chald.), *khah-yaw';* corresp. to 2421; to *live:*—live, keep alive.

2419. חִיאֵל **Chîy'êl**, *khee-ale';* from 2416 and 410; *living of God; Chiel*, an Isr.:—Hiel.

חָיַב **châyab**. See 2325.

2420. חִידָה **chîydâh**, *khee-daw';* from 2330; a *puzzle;* hence a *trick, conundrum*, sententious *maxim:*—dark saying (sentence, speech), hard question, proverb, riddle.

2421. חָיָה châyâh, *khaw-yaw'*; a prim. root [comp. 2331, 2424]; to *live*, whether lit. or fig.; causat. to *revive:*—keep (leave, make) alive, × certainly, give (promise) life, (let, suffer to) live, nourish up, preserve (alive), quicken, recover, repair, restore (to life), revive, (× God) save (alive, life, lives), × surely, be whole.

2422. חָיֶה châyeh, *khaw-yeh'*; from 2421; *vigorous:*—lively.

2423. חֵיוָא chêyvâʼ (Chald.), *khay-vaw'*; from 2418; an *animal:*—beast.

2424. חַיּוּת chayûwth, *khah-yooth'*; from 2421; *life:*— × living.

2425. חָיַי châyay, *khaw-yah'ee*; a prim. root [comp. 2421]; to *live;* causat. to *revive:*—live, save life.

2426. חֵיל chêyl, *khale;* or (short.)

חֵל chêl, *khale;* a collat. form of 2428; an *army;* also (by anal.) an *intrenchment:*—army, bulwark, host, + poor, rampart, trench, wall.

חַיִל chîyl. See 2342.

2427. חִיל chîyl, *kheel;* and (fem.)

חִילָה chîylâh, *khee-law'*; from 2342; a *throe* (espec. of childbirth):—pain, pang, sorrow.

2428. חַיִל chayil, *khah'-yil;* from 2342; prob. a *force*, whether of men, means or other resources; an *army, wealth, virtue, valor, strength:*—able, activity, (+) army, band of men (soldiers), company, (great) forces, goods, host, might, power, riches, strength, strong, substance, train, (+) valiant (-ly), valour, virtuous (-ly), war, worthy (-ily).

2429. חַיִל chayil (Chald.), *khah'-yil;* corresp. to 2428; an *army*, or *strength:*—aloud, army, × most [mighty], power.

2430. חֵילָה chêylâh, *khay-law'*; fem. of 2428; an *intrenchment:*—bulwark.

2431. חֵילָם Chêylâm, *khay-lawm';* or

חֵלָאם Chêlʼâm, *khay-lawm';* from 2428; *fortress; Chelam*, a place E. of Pal.:—Helam.

2432. חִילֵן Chîylên, *khee-lane';* from 2428; *fortress; Chilen*, a place in Pal.:—Hilen.

2433. חִין chîyn, *kheen;* another form for 2580; *beauty:*—comely.

2434. חַיִץ chayits, *khah'-yits;* another form for 2351; a *wall:*—wall.

2435. חִיצוֹן chîytsôwn, *khee-tsone';* from 2434; prop. the (outer) *wall side;* hence *exterior;* fig. *secular* (as opposed to sacred):—outer, outward, utter, without.

2436. חֵיק chêyq, *khake*, or

חֵק chêq, *khake;* and

חוֹק chôwq, *khoke;* from an unused root, appar. mean. to *inclose;* the *bosom* (lit. or fig.):—bosom, bottom, lap, midst, within.

2437. חִירָה Chîyrâh, *khee-raw';* from 2357 in the sense of *splendor; Chirah*, an Adullamite:—Hirah.

2438. חִירָם Chîyrâm, *khee-rawm'*, or

חִירוֹם Chîyrôwm, *khee-rome';* another form of 2361; *Chiram* or *Chirom*, the name of two Tyrians:—Hiram, Huram.

2439. חִישׁ chîysh, *kheesh;* another form for 2363; to *hurry:*—make haste.

2440. חִישׁ chîysh, *kheesh;* from 2439; prop. a *hurry;* hence (adv.) *quickly:*—soon.

2441. חֵךְ chêk, *khake;* prob. from 2596 in the sense of *tasting;* prop. the *palate* or inside of the mouth; hence the *mouth* itself (as the organ of speech, taste and kissing):—(roof of the) mouth, taste.

2442. חָכָה châkâh, *khaw-kaw';* a prim. root [appar. akin to 2707 through the idea of *piercing*]; prop. to *adhere* to; hence to await:—long, tarry, wait.

2443. חַכָּה chakkâh, *khak-kaw';* prob. from 2442; a *hook* (as *adhering*):—angle, hook.

2444. חֲכִילָה Chakîylâh, *khak-ee-law';* from the same as 2447; *dark; Chakilah*, a hill in Pal.:—Hachilah.

2445. חַכִּים chakkîym (Chald.), *khak-keem';* from a root corresp. to 2449; *wise*, i.e. a *Magian:*—wise.

2446. חֲכַלְיָה Chăkalyâh, *khak-al-yaw';* from the base of 2447 and 3050; *darkness of Jah; Chakaljah*, an Isr.:—Hachaliah.

2447. חַכְלִיל chaklîyl, *khak-leel';* by redupl. from an unused root appar. mean. to *be dark;* darkly *flashing* (only of the eyes); in a good sense, *brilliant* (as stimulated by wine):—red.

2448. חַכְלִלוּת chaklîlûwth, *khak-lee-looth';* from 2447; *flash* (of the eyes); in a bad sense, *blearedness:*—redness.

2449. חָכַם châkam, *khaw-kam';* a prim. root, to *be wise* (in mind, word or act):—× exceeding, teach wisdom, be (make self, shew self) wise, deal (never so) wisely, make wiser.

2450. חָכָם châkâm, *khaw-kawm';* from 2449; *wise*, (i.e. intelligent, skilful or artful):—cunning (man), subtil, ([un-]), wise ([hearted], man).

2451. חָכְמָה chokmâh, *khok-maw';* from 2449; *wisdom* (in a good sense):—skilful, wisdom, wisely, wit.

2452. חָכְמָה chokmâh (Chald.), *khok-maw';* corresp. to 2451; *wisdom:*—wisdom.

2453. חַכְמוֹנִי Chakmôwnîy, *khak-mo-nee';* from 2449; *skilful; Chakmoni*, an Isr.:—Hachmoni, Hachmonite.

2454. חָכְמוֹת chokmôwth, *khok-mōth';* or

חַכְמוֹת chakmôwth, *khak-mōth';* collat. forms of 2451; *wisdom:*—wisdom, every wise [woman].

חֵל chêl. See 2426.

2455. חֹל chôl, *khole;* from 2490; prop. *exposed;* hence *profane:*—common, profane (place), unholy.

2456. חָלָא châlâʼ, *khaw-law';* a prim. root [comp. 2470]; to *be sick:*—be diseased.

2457. חֶלְאָה chelʼâh, *khel-aw';* from 2456; prop. *disease;* hence *rust:*—scum.

2458. חֶלְאָה Chelʼâh, *khel-aw';* the same as 2457; *Chelah*, an Israelitess:—Helah.

2459. חֶלֶב cheleb, *kheh'-leb;* or

חֵלֶב chêleb, *khay'-leb;* from an unused root mean. to *be fat; fat*, whether lit. or fig.; hence the *richest* or *choice* part:— × best, fat (-ness), × finest, grease, marrow.

2460. חֵלֶב Chêleb, *khay'-leb;* the same as 2459; *fatness; Cheleb*, an Isr.:—Heleb.

2461. חָלָב châlâb, *khaw-lawb';* from the same as 2459; *milk* (as the *richness* of kine):—+ cheese, milk, sucking.

2462. חֶלְבָּה Chelbâh, *khel-baw';* fem. of 2459; *fertility: Chelbah*, a place in Pal.:—Helbah.

2463. חֶלְבּוֹן Chelbôwn, *khel-bone';* from 2459; *fruitful; Chelbon*, a place in Syria:—Helbon.

2464. חֶלְבְּנָה chelbᵉnâh, *khel-ben-aw';* from 2459; *galbanam*, an odorous gum (as if *fatty*):—galbanum.

2465. חֶלֶד cheled, *kheh'-led;* from an unused root appar. mean. to *glide* swiftly; *life* (as a *fleeting* portion of time); hence the *world* (as *transient*):—age, short time, world.

2466. חֵלֶד chêled, *khay'-led;* the same as 2465; *Cheled*, an Isr.:—Heled.

2467. חֹלֶד chôled, *kho'-led;* from the same as 2465; a *weasel* (from its *gliding* motion):—weasel.

2468. חֻלְדָּה Chuldâh, *khool-daw';* fem. of 2467; *Chuldah*, an Israelitess:—Huldah.

2469. חֶלְדַּי Chelday, *khel-dah'-ee;* from 2466; *worldliness; Cheldai*, the name of two Isr.:—Heldai.

2470. חָלָה châlâh, *khaw-law';* a prim. root [comp. 2342, 2470, 2490]; prop. to *be rubbed* or *worn;* hence (fig.) to *be weak, sick, afflicted;* or (causat.) to *grieve, make sick;* also to *stroke* (in flattering), *entreat:*—beseech, (be) diseased, (put to) grief, be grieved, (be) grievous, infirmity, intreat, lay to, put to pain, × pray, make prayer, be (fall, make) sick, sore, be sorry, make suit (× supplication), woman in travail, be (become) weak, be wounded.

2471. חַלָּה challâh, *khal-law';* from 2490; a *cake* (as usually *punctured*):—cake.

2472. חֲלוֹם chălôwm, *khal-ome';* or (short.)

חֲלֹם chălôm, *khal-ome';* from 2492; a *dream:*—dream (-er).

2473. חֹלוֹן Chôlôwn, *kho-lone';* or (short.)

חֹלֹן Chôlôn, *kho-lone';* prob. from 2344; *sandy; Cholon*, the name of two places in Pal.:—Holon.

2474. חַלּוֹן challôwn, *khal-lone';* a *window* (as *perforated*):—window.

2475. חֲלוֹף chălôwph, *khal-ofe';* from 2498; prop. *surviving*, by impl. (collect.) *orphans:*— × destruction.

2476. חֲלוּשָׁה chălûwshâh, *khal-oo-shaw';* fem. pass. part. of 2522; *defeat:*—being overcome.

2477. חֲלַח Chălach, *khal-akh';* prob. of for. or.; *Chalach*, a region of Assyria:—Halah.

2478. חַלְחוּל Chalchûwl, *khal-khool';* by redupl. from 2342; *contorted; Chalchul*, a place in Pal.:—Halhul.

2479. חַלְחָלָה chalchâlâh, *khal-khaw-law';* fem. from the same as 2478; *writhing* (in childbirth); by impl. *terror:*—(great, much) pain.

2480. חָלַט châlaṭ, *khaw-lat';* a prim. root; to *snatch* at:—catch.

2481. חֲלִי chălîy, *khal-ee';* from 2470; a *trinket* (as *polished*):—jewel, ornament.

2482. חֲלִי Chălîy, *khal-ee';* the same as 2481; *Chali*, a place in Pal.:—Hali.

2483. חֳלִי chŏlîy, *khol-ee';* from 2470; *malady, anxiety, calamity:*—disease, grief, (is) sick (-ness).

2484. חֶלְיָה chelyâh, *khel-yaw';* fem. of 2481; a *trinket:*—jewel.

2485. חָלִיל châlîyl, *khaw-leel';* from 2490; a *flute* (as *perforated*):—pipe.

2486. חָלִילָה châlîylâh, *khaw-lee'-law;* or

חָלִלָה châlîlâh, *khaw-lee'-law;* a directive from 2490; lit. *for a profaned* thing; used (interj.) *far be it!:*—be far, (× God) forbid.

2487. חֲלִיפָה chălîyphâh, *khal-ee-faw';* from 2498; *alternation:*—change, course.

2488. חֲלִיצָה chălîytsâh, *khal-ee-tsaw';* from 2502; *spoil:*—armour.

2489. חֵלְכָא chêlᵉkâʼ, *khay-lek-aw';* or

חֵלְכָה chêlᵉkâh, *khay-lek-aw';* appar. from an unused root prob. mean. to *be dark* or (fig.) *unhappy;* a *wretch*, i.e. unfortunate:—poor.

2490. חָלַל châlal, *khaw-lal';* a prim. root [comp. 2470]; prop. to *bore*, i.e. (by impl.) to *wound*, to *dissolve;* fig. to *profane* (a person, place or thing), to *break* (one's word), to *begin* (as if by an "opening wedge"); denom. (from 2485) to *play* (the flute):—begin (× men began), defile, × break, defile, × eat (as common things), × first, × gather the grape thereof, × take inheritance, pipe, player on instruments, pollute, (cast as) profane (self), prostitute, slay (slain), sorrow, stain, wound.

2491. חָלָל châlâl, *khaw-lawl';* from 2490; *pierced* (espec. to death); fig. *polluted:*—kill, profane, slain (man), × slew, (deadly) wounded.

חָלִלָה châlîlâh. See 2486.

2492. חָלַם **châlam**, *khaw-lam'*; a prim. root; prop. to *bind* firmly, i.e. (by impl.) to *be* (causat. to *make*) *plump;* also (through the fig. sense of *dumbness*) to *dream:*—(cause to) dream (-er), be in good liking, recover.

2493. חֵלֶם **chêlem** (Chald.), *khay'-lem;* from a root corresp. to 2492; a *dream:*—dream.

2494. חֵלֶם **Chêlem**, *khay'-lem;* from 2492; a *dream; Chelem*, an Isr.:—Helem. Comp. 2469.

2495. חַלָּמוּת **challâmûwth**, *khal-law-mooth';* from 2492 (in the sense of *insipidity*); prob. *purslain:*—egg.

2496. חַלָּמִישׁ **challâmîysh**, *khal-law-meesh';* prob. from 2492 (in the sense of *hardness*); *flint:*—flint (-y), rock.

2497. חֵלֹן **Chêlôn**, *khay-lone';* from 2428; *strong Chelon*, an Isr.:—Helon

2498. חָלַף **châlaph**, *khaw-laf';* a prim. root; prop. to *slide* by, i.e. (by impl.) to *hasten* away, *pass* on, *spring* up, *pierce* or *change:*—abolish, alter change, cut off, go on forward, grow up, be over pass (away, on, through), renew, sprout, strike through.

2499. חֲלַף **chălaph** (Chald.), *khal-af';* corresp. to 2498; to *pass* on (of time):—pass.

2500. חֵלֶף **chêleph**, *khay'-lef;* from 2498; prop. *exchange;* hence (as prep.) *instead* of:—× for.

2501. חֶלֶף **Cheleph**, *kheh'-lef;* the same as 2500; *change; Cheleph*, a place in Pal.:—Heleph.

2502. חָלַץ **châlats**, *khaw-lats';* a prim. root; to *pull* off; hence (intens.) to *strip*, (reflex.) to *depart;* by impl. to *deliver, equip* (for fight); *present, strengthen:*—arm (self), (go, ready) armed (× man, soldier), deliver, draw out, make fat, loose, (ready) prepared, put off, take away, withdraw self.

2503. חֶלֶץ **Chelets**, *kheh'-lets;* or

חֵלֶץ **Chêlets**, *khay'-lets;* from 2502; perh. *strength; Chelets*, the name of two Isr.:—Helez.

2504. חָלָץ **châlâts**, *khaw-lawts';* from 2502 (in the sense of *strength*); only in the dual; the *loins* (as the seat of vigor):—loins, reins.

2505. חָלַק **châlaq**, *khaw-lak';* a prim. root; to *be smooth* (fig.); by impl. (as smooth stones were used for *lots*) to *apportion* or *separate:*—deal, distribute, divide, flatter, give, (have, im-) part (-ner), take away a portion, receive, separate self, (be) smooth (-er).

2506. חֵלֶק **chêleq**, *khay'-lek;* from 2505; prop. *smoothness* (of the tongue); also an *allotment:*—flattery, inheritance, part, × partake, portion.

2507. חֵלֶק **Chêleq**, *khay'-lek;* the same as 2506; *portion; Chelek*, an Isr.:—Helek.

2508. חֲלָק **chălâq** (Chald.), *khal-awk';* from a root corresp. to 2505; a *part:*—portion.

2509. חָלָק **châlâq**, *khaw-lawk';* from 2505; *smooth* (espec. of tongue):—flattering, smooth.

2510. חָלָק **Châlâq**, *khaw-lawk';* the same as 2509; *bare; Chalak*, a mountain of Idumæa:—Halak.

2511. חַלָּק **challâq**, *khal-lawk';* from 2505; *smooth:*—smooth.

2512. חַלֻּק **challûq**, *khal-look';* from 2505; *smooth:*—smooth.

2513. חֶלְקָה **chelqâh**, *khel-kaw';* fem. of 2506; prop. *smoothness;* fig. *flattery;* also an *allotment:*—field, flattering (-ry), ground, parcel, part, piece of land ([ground]), plat, portion, slippery place, smooth (thing).

2514. חֲלַקָּה **chălaqqâh**, *khal-ak-kaw';* fem. from 2505; *flattery:*—flattery.

2515. חֲלֻקָּה **chăluqqâh**, *khal-ook-kaw';* fem. of 2512; a *distribution:*—division.

2516. חֶלְקִי **Chelqîy**, *khel-kee';* patron. from 2507; a *Chelkite* or desc. of Chelek:—Helkites.

2517. חֶלְקַי **Chelqay**, *khel-kah'ee;* from 2505; *apportioned; Chelkai*, an Isr.:—Helkai.

2518. חִלְקִיָּה **Chilqîyâh**, *khil-kee-yaw';* or

חִלְקִיָּהוּ **Chilqîyâhûw**, *khil-kee-yaw'-hoo;* from 2506 and 3050; *portion of Jah; Chilhijah*, the name of eight Isr.:—Hilkiah.

2519. חֲלַקְלַקָּה **chălaqlaqqâh**, *khal-ak-lak-kaw';* by redupl. from 2505; prop. something *very smooth;* i.e. a *treacherous* spot; fig. *blandishment:*—flattery, slippery.

2520. חֶלְקַת **Chelqath**, *khel-kath';* a form of 2513; *smoothness; Chelkath*, a place in Pal.:—Helkath.

2521. חֶלְקַת הַצֻּרִים **Chelqath hats-Tsûrîym**, *khel-kath' hats-tsoo-reem';* from 2520 and the plur. of 6697, with the art. inserted; *smoothness of the rocks; Chelkath Hatstsurim*, a place in Pal.:—Helkath-hazzurim.

2522. חָלַשׁ **châlash**, *khaw-lash';* a prim. root; to *prostrate;* by impl. to *overthrow, decay:*—discomfit, waste away, weaken.

2523. חַלָּשׁ **challâsh**, *khal-lawsh';* from 2522; *frail:*—weak.

2524. חָם **châm**, *khawm;* from the same as 2346; a *father-in-law* (as in *affinity*):—father in law.

2525. חָם **châm**, *khawm;* from 2552; *hot:*—hot, warm.

2526. חָם **Châm**, *khawm;* the same as 2525; *hot* (from the tropical habitat); *Cham*, a son of Noah; also (as a patron.) his desc. or their country:—Ham.

2527. חֹם **chôm**, *khome;* from 2552; *heat:*—heat, to be hot (warm).

2528. חֱמָא **chĕmâ'** (Chald.), *khem-aw';* or

חֲמָה **chămâh** (Chald.), *kham-aw';* corresp. to 2534; *anger:*—fury.

חֵמָא **chêmâ'**. See 2534.

2529. חֶמְאָה **chem'âh**, *khem-aw';* or (short.)

חֵמָה **chêmâh**, *khay-maw';* from the same root as 2346; curdled *milk* or *cheese:*—butter.

2530. חָמַד **châmad**, *khaw-mad';* a prim. root; to *delight* in:—beauty, greatly beloved, covet, delectable thing, (× great) delight, desire, goodly, lust, (be) pleasant (thing), precious (thing).

2531. חֶמֶד **chemed**, *kheh'-med;* from 2530; *delight:*—desirable, pleasant.

2532. חֶמְדָּה **chemdâh**, *khem-daw';* fem. of 2531; *delight:*—desire, goodly, pleasant, precious.

2533. חֶמְדָּן **Chemdân**, *khem-dawn';* from 2531; *pleasant; Chemdan*, an Idumæan:—Hemdan.

2534. חֵמָה **chêmâh**, *khay-maw';* or (Dan. 11:44)

חֵמָא **chêmâ'**, *khay-maw';* from 3179; *heat;* fig. *anger, poison* (from its *fever*):—anger, bottles, hot displeasure, furious (-ly, -ry), heat, indignation, poison, rage, wrath (-ful). See 2529.

2535. חַמָּה **chammâh**, *kham-maw';* from 2525; *heat;* by impl. the *sun:*—heat, sun.

2536. חַמּוּאֵל **Chammûw'êl**, *kham-moo-ale';* from 2535 and 410; *anger of God; Chammuel*, an Isr.:—Hamuel.

2537. חֲמוּטַל **Chămûwṭal**, *kham-oo-tal';* or

חֲמִיטַל **Chămîyṭal**, *kham-ee-tal';* from 2524 and 2919; *father-in-law of dew; Chamutal* or *Chamital*, an Israelitess:—Hamutal.

2538. חָמוּל **Châmûwl**, *khaw-mool';* from 2550; *pitied; Chamul*, an Isr.:—Hamul.

2539. חָמוּלִי **Châmûwlîy**, *khaw-moo-lee';* patron. from 2538; a *Chamulite* (collect.) or desc. of Chamul:—Hamulites.

2540. חַמּוֹן **Chammôwn**, *kham-mone';* from 2552; *warm* spring; *Chammon*, the name of two places in Pal.:—Hammon.

2541. חָמוֹץ **châmôwts**, *khaw-motse';* from 2556; prop. *violent;* by impl. a *robber:*—oppressed.

2542. חַמּוּק **chammûwq**, *kham-mook';* from 2559; a *wrapping*, i.e. *drawers:*—joints.

2543. חֲמוֹר **chămôwr**, *kham-ore';* or (short.)

חֲמֹר **chămôr**, *kham-ore;* from 2560; a male *ass* (from its dun *red*):—(he) ass.

2544. חֲמוֹר **Chămôwr**, *kham-ore';* the same as 2543; *ass; Chamor*, a Canaanite:—Hamor.

2545. חֲמוֹת **chămôwth**, *kham-ōth';* or (short.)

חֲמֹת **chămôth**, *kham-ōth';* fem. of 2524; a *mother-in-law:*—mother in law.

2546. חֹמֶט **chômeṭ**, *kho'-met;* from an unused root prob. mean. to *lie low;* a *lizard* (as *creeping*):—snail.

2547. חֻמְטָה **Chumṭâh**, *khoom-taw';* fem. of 2546; *low; Chumtah*, a place in Pal.:—Humtah.

2548. חָמִיץ **châmîyts**, *khaw-meets';* from 2556; *seasoned*, i.e. *salt* provender:—clean.

2549. חֲמִישִׁי **chămîyshîy**, *kham-ee-shee';* or

חֲמִשִּׁי **chamishshîy**, *kham-ish-shee';* ord. from 2568; *fifth;* also a *fifth:*—fifth (part).

2550. חָמַל **châmal**, *khaw-mal';* a prim. root; to *commiserate;* by impl. to *spare:*—have compassion, (have) pity, spare.

2551. חֶמְלָה **chemlâh**, *khem-law';* from 2550; *commiseration:*—merciful, pity.

2552. חָמַם **châmam**, *khaw-mam';* a prim. root; to *be hot* (lit. or fig.):—enflame self, get (have) heat, be (wax) hot, (be, wax) warm (self, at).

2553. חַמָּן **chammân**, *kham-mawn';* from 2535; a *sun*-pillar:—idol, image.

2554. חָמַס **châmaç**, *khaw-mas';* a prim. root; to *be violent;* by impl. to *maltreat:*—make bare, shake off, violate, do violence, take away violently, wrong, imagine wrongfully.

2555. חָמָס **châmâç**, *khaw-mawce';* from 2554; *violence;* by impl. *wrong;* by meton. unjust *gain:*—cruel (-ty), damage, false, injustice, × oppressor, unrighteous, violence (against, done), violent (dealing), wrong.

2556. חָמֵץ **châmêts**, *khaw-mates';* a prim. root; to *be pungent;* i.e. in taste (*sour*, i.e. lit. *fermented*, or fig. *harsh*), in color (*dazzling*):—cruel (man), dyed, be grieved, leavened.

2557. חָמֵץ **châmêtz**, *khaw-mates';* from 2556; *ferment*, (fig.) *extortion:*—leaven, leavened (bread).

2558. חֹמֶץ **chômets**, *kho'-mets;* from 2556; *vinegar:*—vinegar.

2559. חָמַק **châmaq**, *khaw-mak';* a prim. root; prop. to *enwrap;* hence to *depart* (i.e. turn about):—go about, withdraw self.

2560. חָמַר **châmar**, *khaw-mar';* a prim. root; prop. to *boil* up; hence to *ferment* (with scum); to *glow* (with redness); as denom. (from 2564) to *smear* with pitch:—daub, foul, be red, trouble.

2561. חֶמֶר **chemer**, *kheh'-mer;* from 2560; *wine* (as *fermenting*):—× pure, red wine.

2562. חֲמַר **chămar** (Chald.), *kham-ar';* corresp. to 2561; *wine:*—wine.

חֲמֹר **chămôr**. See 2543.

2563. חֹמֶר **chômer**, *kho'-mer;* from 2560; prop. a *bubbling* up, i.e. of water, a *wave;* of earth, *mire* or *clay* (cement); also a *heap;* hence a *chomer* or dry measure:—clay, heap, homer, mire, motion, mortar.

2564. חֵמָר **chêmâr**, *khay-mawr';* from 2560; *bitumen* (as *rising* to the surface):—slime (-pit).

2565. חֲמֹרָה **chămôrâh**, *kham-o-raw';* from 2560 [comp. 2563]; a *heap:*—heap.

2566. חַמְרָן **Chamrân**, *kham-rawn';* from 2560; *red; Chamran*, an Idumæan:—Amran.

2567. חָמַשׁ **châmash**, *khaw-mash';* a denom. from 2568; to *tax a fifth:*—take up the fifth part.

2568. חָמֵשׁ **châmêsh**, *khaw-maysh'*; masc.

חֲמִשָּׁה **chămishshâh**, *kham-ish-shaw'*; a prim. numeral; *five:*—fif [-teen], fifth, five (× apiece).

2569. חֹמֶשׁ **chômesh**, *kho'-mesh;* from 2567; a *fifth* tax:—fifth part.

2570. חֹמֶשׁ **chômesh**, *kho'-mesh;* from an unused root prob. mean. to *be stout;* the *abdomen* (as *obese*):—fifth [rib].

2571. חָמֻשׁ **châmûsh**, *khaw-moosh'*; pass. part. of the same as 2570; *staunch*, i.e. able bodied *soldiers:*—armed (men), harnessed.

חֲמִשָּׁה **chămishshâh**. See 2568.

חֲמִשִּׁי **chămishshîy**. See 2549.

2572. חֲמִשִּׁים **chămishshîym**, *kham-ish-sheem'*; multiple of 2568; *fifty:*—fifty.

2573. חֵמֶת **chêmeth**, *khay'-meth;* from the same as 2346; a skin *bottle* (as *tied* up):—bottle.

2574. חֲמָת **Chămâth**, *kham-awth'*; from the same as 2346; *walled; Chamath*, a place in Syria:—Hamath, Hemath.

חֲמֹת **chămôth**. See 2545.

2575. חַמַּת **Chammath**, *kham-math';* a var. for the first part of 2576; *hot* springs; *Chammath*, a place in Pal.:—Hammath.

2576. חַמֹּת דֹּאר **Chammôth Dô'r**, *kham-moth' dore;* from the plur. of 2535 and 1756; *hot* springs *of Dor; Chammath-Dor*, a place in Pal.:—Hamath-Dor.

2577. חֲמָתִי **Chămâthîy**, *kham-aw-thee';* patrial from 2574; a *Chamathite* or native of *Chamath:*—Hamathite.

2578. חֲמַת צוֹבָה **Chămath Tsôwbâh**, *kham-ath' tso-baw';* from 2574 and 6678; *Chamath of Tsobah; Chamath-Tsobah;* prob. the same as 2574:—Hamath-Zobah.

2579. חֲמַת רַבָּה **Chămath Rabbâh**, *kham-ath' rab-baw';* from 2574 and 7237; *Chamath of Rabbah; Chamath-Rabbah*, prob. the same as 2574.

2580. חֵן **chên**, *khane;* from 2603; *graciousness*, i.e. subj. (*kindness, favor*) or objective (*beauty*):—favour, grace (-ious), pleasant, precious, [well-] favoured.

2581. חֵן **Chên**, *khane;* the same as 2580; *grace; Chen*, a fig. name for an Isr.:—Hen.

2582. חֵנָדָד **Chênâdâd**, *khay-naw-dawd';* prob. from 2580 and 1908; *favor of Hadad; Chenadad*, an Isr.:—Henadad.

2583. חָנָה **chânâh**, *khaw-naw';* a prim. root [comp. 2603]; prop. to *incline;* by impl. to *decline* (of the slanting rays of evening); spec. to *pitch* a tent; gen. to *encamp* (for abode or siege):—abide (in tents), camp, dwell, encamp, grow to an end, lie, pitch (tent), rest in tent.

2584. חַנָּה **Channâh**, *khan-naw';* from 2603; *favored; Channah*, an Israelitess:—Hannah.

2585. חֲנוֹךְ **Chănôwk**, *khan-oke';* from 2596; *initiated; Chanok*, an antediluvian patriach:—Enoch.

2586. חָנוּן **Chânûwn**, *khaw-noon';* from 2603; *favored; Chanun*, the name of an Ammonite and of two Isr.:—Hanun.

2587. חַנּוּן **channûwn**, *khan-noon';* from 2603; *gracious:*—gracious.

2588. חָנוּת **chânûwth**, *khaw-nooth';* from 2583; prop. a *vault* or *cell* (with an arch); by impl. a *prison:*—cabin.

2589. חַנּוֹת **channôwth**, *khan-nōth';* from 2603 (in the sense of *prayer*); *supplication:*—be gracious, intreated.

2590. חָנַט **chânaṭ**, *khaw-nat';* a prim. root; to *spice;* by impl. to *embalm;* also to *ripen:*—embalm, put forth.

2591. חִנְטָא **chinṭâ'** (Chald.), *khint-taw';* corresp. to 2406; *wheat:*—wheat.

2592. חַנִּיאֵל **Channîy'êl**, *khan-nee-ale';* from 2603 and 410; *favor of God; Channiel*, the name of two Isr.:—Hanniel.

2593. חָנִיךְ **chânîyk**, *kaw-neek';* from 2596; *initiated;* i.e. *practised:*—trained.

2594. חֲנִינָה **chănîynâh**, *khan-ee-naw';* from 2603; *graciousness:*—favour.

2595. חֲנִית **chănîyth**, *khan-eeth';* from 2583; a *lance* (for *thrusting*, like *pitching* a tent):—javelin, spear.

2596. חָנַךְ **chânak**, *khaw-nak';* a prim. root; prop. to *narrow* [comp. 2614]; fig. to *initiate* or *discipline:*—dedicate, train up.

2597. חֲנֻכָּא **chănukkâ'** (Chald.), *chan-ook-kaw';* corresp. to 2598; *consecration:*—dedication.

2598. חֲנֻכָּה **chănukkâh**, *khan-ook-kaw';* from 2596; *initiation*, i.e. *consecration:*—dedicating (-tion).

2599. חֲנֹכִי **Chănôkîy**, *khan-o-kee';* patron. from 2585; a *Chanokite* (collect.) or desc. of Chanok:—Hanochites.

2600. חִנָּם **chinnâm**, *khin-nawm';* from 2580; *gratis*, i.e. devoid of cost, reason or advantage:—without a cause (cost, wages), causeless, to cost nothing, free (-ly), innocent, for nothing (nought), in vain.

2601. חֲנַמְאֵל **Chănam'êl**, *khan-am-ale';* prob. by orth. var. for 2606; *Chanamel*, an Isr.:—Hanameel.

2602. חֲנָמַל **chănâmâl**, *khan-aw-mawl';* of uncert. der.; perh. the *aphis* or plant-louse:—frost.

2603. חָנַן **chânan**, *khaw-nan';* a prim. root [comp. 2583]; prop. to *bend* or stoop in kindness to an inferior; to *favor, bestow;* causat. to *implore* (i.e. move to favor by petition):—beseech, × fair, (be, find, shew) favour (-able), be (deal, give, grant (gracious (-ly), intreat, (be) merciful, have (shew) mercy (on, upon), have pity upon, pray, make supplication, × very.

2604. חֲנַן **chănan** (Chald.), *khan-an';* corresp. to 2603; to *favor* or (causat.) to *entreat:*—shew mercy, make supplication.

2605. חָנָן **Chânân**, *khaw-nawn';* from 2603; *favor; Chanan*, the name of seven Isr.:—Canan.

2606. חֲנַנְאֵל **Chănan'êl**, *khan-an-ale';* from 2603 and 410; *God has favored; Chananel*, prob. an Isr., from whom a tower of Jerusalem was named:—Hananeel.

2607. חֲנָנִי **Chănânîy**, *khan-aw-nee';* from 2603; *gracious; Chanani*, the name of six Isr.:—Hanani.

2608. חֲנַנְיָה **Chănanyâh**, *khan-an-yaw';* or

חֲנַנְיָהוּ **Chănanyâhûw**, *khan-an-yaw'-hoo;* from 2603 and 3050; *Jah has favored; Chananjah*, the name of thirteen Isr.:—Hananiah.

2609. חָנֵס **Chânêç**, *khaw-nace';* of Eg. der.; *Chanes*, a place in Egypt:—Hanes.

2610. חָנֵף **chânêph**, *khaw-nafe';* a prim. root; to *soil*, espec. in a moral sense:—corrupt, defile, × greatly, pollute, profane.

2611. חָנֵף **chânêph**, *khaw-nafe';* from 2610; *soiled* (i.e. with sin), *impious:*—hypocrite (-ical).

2612. חֹנֶף **chôneph**, *kho'-nef;* from 2610; moral *filth*, i.e. *wickedness:*—hypocrisy.

2613. חֲנֻפָּה **chănûphâh**, *khan-oo-faw';* fem. from 2610; *impiety:*—profaneness.

2614. חָנַק **chânaq**, *khaw-nak';* a prim. root [comp. 2596]; to *be narrow;* by impl. to *throttle*, or (reflex.) to *choke* oneself to death (by a rope):—hang self, strangle.

2615. חַנָּתֹן **Channâthôn**, *khan-naw-thone';* prob. from 2603; *favored; Channathon*, a place in Pal.:—Hannathon.

2616. חָסַד **châçad**, *khaw-sad';* a prim. root; prop. perh. to *bow* (the neck only [comp. 2603] in courtesy to an equal), i.e. to *be kind;* also (by euphem. [comp. 1288], but rarely) to *reprove:*—shew self merciful, put to shame.

2617. חֶסֶד **cheçed**, *kheh'-sed;* from 2616; *kindness;* by impl. (towards God) *piety;* rarely (by opp.) *reproof*, or (subject.) *beauty:*—favour, good deed (-liness, -ness), kindly, (loving-) kindness, merciful (kindness), mercy, pity, reproach, wicked thing.

2618. חֶסֶד **Cheçed** *kheh'-sed;* the same as 2617; *favor; Chesed*, an Isr.:—Hesed.

2619. חֲסַדְיָה **Chăçadyâh**, *khas-ad-yaw';* from 2617 and 3050; *Jah has favored; Chasadjah*, an Isr.:—Hasadiah.

2620. חָסָה **châçâh**, *khaw-saw';* a prim. root; to *flee* for protection [comp. 982]; fig. to *confide* in:—have hope, make refuge, (put) trust.

2621. חֹסָה **Chôçâh**, *kho-saw';* from 2620; *hopeful; Chosah*, an Isr.; also a place in Pal.:—Hosah.

2622. חָסוּת **châçûwth**, *khaw-sooth';* from 2620; *confidence:*—trust.

2623. חָסִיד **châçîyd**, *khaw-seed';* from 2616; prop. *kind*, i.e. (religiously) *pious* (a saint):—godly (man), good, holy (one), merciful, saint, [un-] godly.

2624. חֲסִידָה **chăçîydâh**, *khas-ee-daw';* fem. of 2623; the *kind* (maternal) bird, i.e. a *stork:*— × feather, stork.

2625. חָסִיל **châçîyl**, *khaw-seel';* from 2628; the *ravager*, i.e. a *locust:*—caterpillar.

2626. חָסִין **chăçîyn**, *khas-een';* from 2630; prop. *firm*, i.e. (by impl.) *mighty:*—strong.

2627. חַסִּיר **chaççîyr** (Chald.), *khas-seer';* from a root corresp. to 2637; *deficient:*—wanting.

2628. חָסַל **châçal**, *khaw-sal';* a prim. root; to *eat* off:—consume.

2629. חָסַם **châçam**, *khaw-sam';* a prim. root; to *muzzle;* by anal. to *stop* the nose:—muzzle, stop.

2630. חָסַן **châçan**, *khaw-san';* a prim. root; prop. to (*be*) *compact;* by impl. to *hoard:*—lay up.

2631. חֲסַן **chăçan** (Chald.), *khas-an';* corresp. to 2630; to *hold* in occupancy:—possess.

2632. חֵסֶן **chêçen** (Chald.), *khay'-sen;* from 2631; *strength:*—power.

2633. חֹסֶן **chôçen**, *kho'-sen;* from 2630; *wealth:*—riches, strength, treasure.

2634. חָסֹן **châçôn**, *khaw-sone';* from 2630; *powerful:*—strong.

2635. חֲסַף **chăçaph** (Chald.), *khas-af';* from a root corresp. to that of 2636; a *clod:*—clay.

2636. חַסְפַּס **chaçpaç**, *khas-pas';* redupl. from an unused root mean. appar. to *peel;* a *shred* or *scale:*—round thing.

2637. חָסֵר **châçêr**, *khaw-sare';* a prim. root; to *lack;* by impl. to *fail, want, lessen:*—be abated, bereave, decrease, (cause to) fail, (have) lack, make lower, want.

2638. חָסֵר **châçêr**, *khaw-sare';* from 2637; *lacking;* hence *without:*—destitute, fail, lack, have need, void, want.

2639. חֶסֶר **cheçer**, *kheh'-ser;* from 2637; *lack;* hence *destitution:*—poverty, want.

2640. חֹסֶר **chôçer**, *kho'-ser;* from 2637; *poverty:*—in want of.

2641. חַסְרָה **Chaçrâh**, *khas-raw';* from 2637; *want:*—*Chasrah*, an Isr.:—Hasrah.

2642. חֶסְרוֹן **cheçrôwn**, *khes-rone';* from 2637; *deficiency:*—wanting.

2643. חַף **chaph**, *khaf;* from 2653 (in the moral sense of *covered* from soil); *pure:*—innocent.

2644. חָפָא **châphâ'**, *khaw-faw';* an orth. var. of 2645; prop. to *cover*, i.e. (in a sinister sense) to *act covertly:*—do secretly.

2645. חָפָה **châphâh**, *khaw-faw';* a prim. root [comp. 2644, 2653]; to *cover;* by impl. to *veil*, to *incase, protect:*—ceil, cover, overlay.

2646. חֻפָּה **chuppâh**, *khoop-paw';* from 2645; a *canopy:*—chamber, closet, defence.

2647. חֻפָּה **Chuppâh**, *khoop-paw';* the same as 2646; *Chuppah*, an Isr.:—Huppah.

2648. חָפַז **châphaz**, *khaw-faz'*; a prim. root; prop. to *start* up suddenly, i.e. (by impl.) to *hasten* away, to *fear*:—(make) haste (away), tremble.

2649. חִפָּזוֹן **chîppâzôwn**, *khip-paw-zone'*; from 2648; *hasty flight*:—haste.

2650. חֻפִּים **Chuppîym**, *khoop-peem'*; plur. of 2646 [comp. 2349]; *Chuppim*, an Isr.:—Huppim.

2651. חֹפֶן **chôphen**, *kho'-fen*; from an unused root of uncert. signif.; a *fist* (only in the dual):—fists, (both) hands, hand [-ful].

2652. חָפְנִי **Chophnîy**, *khof-nee'*; from 2651; perh. *pugilist*; *Chophni*, an Isr.:—Hophni.

2653. חָפַף **chôphaph**, *khaw-faf'*; a prim. root [comp. 2645, 3182]; to *cover* (in protection):—cover.

2654. חָפֵץ **châphêts**, *khaw-fates'*; a prim. root; prop. to *incline* to; by impl. (lit. but rarely) to *bend*; fig. to *be pleased* with, *desire*:—× any at all, (have, take) delight, desire, favour, like, move, be (well) pleased, have pleasure, will, would.

2655. חָפֵץ **châphêts**, *khaw-fates'*; from 2654; *pleased* with:—delight in, desire, favour, please, have pleasure, whosoever would, willing, wish.

2656. חֵפֶץ **chêphets**, *khay'-fets*; from 2654; *pleasure*; hence (abstr.) *desire*; concr. a *valuable* thing; hence (by extens.) a *matter* (as something in mind):—acceptable, delight (-some), desire, things desired, matter, pleasant (-ure), purpose, willingly.

2657. חֶפְצִי בָהּ **Chephtsîy bâhh**, *khef-tsee' baw*; from 2656 with suffixes; *my delight* (is) *in her*; *Cheptsi-bah*, a fanciful name for Pal.:—Hephzi-bah.

2658. חָפַר **châphar**, *khaw-far'*; a prim. root; prop. to *pry* into; by impl. to *delve*, to *explore*:—dig, paw, search out, seek.

2659. חָפֵר **châphêr**, *khaw-fare'*; a prim. root [perh. rath. the same as 2658 through the idea of *detection*]; to *blush*; fig. to *be ashamed*, *disappointed*; causat. to *shame*, *reproach*:—be ashamed, be confounded, be brought to confusion (unto shame), come (be put to) shame, bring reproach.

2660. חֵפֶר **Chêpher**, *khay'-fer*; from 2658 or 2659; a *pit* or *shame*; *Chepher*, a place in Pal.; also the name of three Isr.:—Hepher.

2661. חֲפֹר **chăphôr**, *khaf-ore'*; from 2658; a *hole*; only in connection with 6512, which ought rather to be joined as one word, thus

חֲפַרְפֵּרָה **chăpharpêrâh**, *khaf-ar-pay-raw'*; by redupl. from 2658; a *burrower*, i.e. prob. a *rat*:—+ mole.

2662. חֶפְרִי **Chephrîy**, *khef-ree'*; patron. from 2660; a *Chephrite* (collect.) or desc. of *Chepher*:—Hepherites.

2663 חֲפָרַיִם **Chăphârayîm**, *khaf-aw-rah'-yim*; dual of 2660; *double pit*; *Chapharajim*, a place in Pal.:—Haphraim.

חֲפַרְפֵּרָה **chăpharpêrâh**. See 2661.

2664. חָפַשׂ **châphas**, *khaw-fas'*; a prim. root; to *seek*; causat. to *conceal* oneself (i.e. let be sought), or *mask*:—change, (make) diligent (search), disguise self, hide, search (for, out).

2665. חֵפֶשׂ **chêphes**, *khay'-fes*; from 2664; something *covert*, i.e. a *trick*:—search.

2666. חָפַשׁ **châphash**, *khaw-fash'*; a prim. root; to *spread* loose, fig. to *manumit*:—be free.

2667. חֹפֶשׁ **Chôphesh**, *kho'-fesh*; from 2666; something *spread* loosely, i.e. a *carpet*:—precious.

2668. חֻפְשָׁה **chuphshâh**, *khoof-shaw'*; from 2666; *liberty* (from slavery):—freedom.

2669. חָפְשׁוּת **chôphshûwth**, *khof-shooth'*; and

חָפְשִׁית **chophshîyth**, *khof-sheeth'*; from 2666; *prostration* by sickness (with 1004, a *hospital*):—several.

2670. חָפְשִׁי **chophshîy**, *khof-shee'*; from 2666; *exempt* (from bondage, tax or care):—free, liberty.

2671. חֵץ **chêts**, *khayts*; from 2686; prop. a *piercer*, i.e. an *arrow*; by impl. a *wound*; fig. (of God) thunder-*bolt*; (by interchange for 6086) the *shaft* of a spear:— + archer, arrow, dart, shaft, staff, wound.

חֻץ **chûts**. See 2351.

2672. חָצַב **châtsab**, *khaw-tsab'*; or

חָצֵב **châtsêb**, *khaw-tsabe'*; a prim. root; to *cut* or carve (wood, stone or other material); by impl. to *hew*, *split*, *square*, *quarry*, *engrave*:—cut, dig, divide, grave, hew (out, -er), make, mason.

2673. חָצָה **châtsâh**, *khaw-tsaw'*; a prim. root [comp. 2686]; to *cut* or *split* in two; to *halve*:—divide, × live out half, reach to the midst, part.

2674. חָצוֹר **Châtsôwr**, *khaw-tsore'*; a collect. form of 2691; *village*; *Chatsor*, the name (thus simply) of two places in Pal. and of one in Arabia:—Hazor.

2675. חָצוֹר חֲדַתָּה **Châtsôwr Chădattâh**, *khaw-tsore' khad-at-taw'*; from 2674 and a Chaldaizing form of the fem. of 2319 [comp. 2323]; *new Chatsor*, a place in Pal.:—Hazor, Hadattah [*as if two places*].

2676. חָצוֹת **châtsôwth**, *khaw-tsoth'*; from 2673; the *middle* (of the night):—mid [-night].

2677. חֵצִי **chêtsîy**, *khay-tsee'*; from 2673; the *half* or *middle*:—half, middle, mid [-night], midst, part, two parts.

2678. חִצִּי **chitstsîy**, *khits-tsee'*; or

חֵצִי **chêtsîy**, *chay-tsee'*; prol. from 2671; an *arrow*:—arrow.

2679. חֲצִי הַמְּנֻחוֹת **Chătsîy ham-M^{e}nûchôwth**, *chat-tsee' ham-men-oo-khoth'*; from 2677 and the plur. of 4496, with the art. interposed; *midst of the resting-places*; *Chatsi-ham-Menuchoth*, an Isr.:—half of the Manahethites.

2680. חֲצִי הַמְּנַחְתִּי **Chătsîy ham-M^{e}nachtîy**, *khat-see' ham-men-akh-tee'*; patron. from 2679; a *Chatsi-ham-Menachtite* or desc. of Chatsi-ham-Menuchoth:—half of the Manahethites.

2681. חָצִיר **châtsîyr**, *khaw-tseer'*; a collat. form of 2691; a *court* or *abode*:—court.

2682. חָצִיר **châtsîyr**, *khaw-tseer'*; perh. orig. the same as 2681, from the *greenness* of a court-yard; *grass*; also a *leek* (collect.):—grass, hay, herb, leek.

2683. חֵצֶן **chêtsen**, *khay'-tsen*; from an unused root mean. to hold *firmly*; the *bosom* (as *comprised* between the arms):—bosom.

2684. חֹצֶן **chôtsen**, *kho'-tsen*; a collat. form of 2683, and mean. the same:—arm, lap.

2685. חֲצַף **chătsaph** (Chald.), *khats-af'*; a prim. root; prop. to *shear* or cut close; fig. to *be severe*:—hasty, be urgent.

2686. חָצַץ **châtsats**, *khaw-tsats'*; a prim. root [comp. 2673]; prop. to *chop* into, pierce or sever; hence to *curtail*, to *distribute* (into ranks); as denom. from 2671, to *shoot* an arrow:—archer, × bands, cut off in the midst.

2687. חָצָץ **châtsâts**, *khaw-tsawts'*; from 2687; prop. something *cutting*; hence *gravel* (as *grit*); also (like 2671) an *arrow*:—arrow, gravel (stone).

2688. חַצְצוֹן תָּמָר **Chats^{e}tsôwn Tâmâr**, *khats-ets-one' taw-mawr'*; or

חַצֲצֹן תָּמָר **Chatsâtsôn Tâmâr**, *khats-ats-one' taw-mawr'*; from 2686 and 8558; *division* [i.e. perh. *row*] *of* (the) *palm-tree*; *Chatsetson-tamar*, a place in Pal.:—Hazezon-tamar.

2689. חֲצֹצְרָה **chătsôts^{e}râh**, *khats-o-tser-aw'*; by redupl. from 2690; a *trumpet* (from its *sundered* or quavering note):—trumpet (-er).

2690. חָצַר **châtsar**, *khaw-tsar'*; a prim. root; prop. to *surround* with a stockade, and thus *separate* from the open country; but used only in the redupl. form

חֲצֹצֵר **chătsôtsêr**, *khast-o-tsare'*; or (2 Chron. 5 : 12)

חֲצֹרֵר **chătsôrêr**, *hhats-o-rare'*; as dem. from 2689; to *trumpet*, i.e. blow on that instrument:—blow, sound, trumpeter.

2691. חָצֵר **châtsêr**, *khaw-tsare'* (masc. and fem.); from 2690 in its original sense; a *yard* (as *inclosed* by a fence); also a *hamlet* (as similarly *surrounded* with walls):—court, tower, village.

2692. חֲצַר אַדָּר **Chătsar Addâr**, *khats-ar' ad-dawr'*; from 2691 and 146; (the) *village of Addar*; *Chatsar-Addar*, a place in Pal.:—Hazar-addar.

2693. חֲצַר גַּדָּה **Chătsar Gaddâh**, *khats-ar' gad-daw'*; from 2691 and a fem. of 1408; (the) *village of* (female) *Fortune*; *Chatsar-Gaddah*, a place in Pal.:—Hazar-gaddah.

2694. חֲצַר הַתִּיכוֹן **Chătsar hat-Tîykôwn**, *khats-ar' hat-tee-kone'*; from 2691 and 8484 with the art. interposed; *village of the middle*; *Chatsar-hat-Tikon*, a place in Pal.:—Hazar-hatticon.

2695. חֶצְרוֹ **Chetsrôw**, *khets-ro'*; by an orth. var. for 2696; *inclosure*; *Chetsro*, an Isr.:—Hezro, Hezrai.

2696. חֶצְרוֹן **Chetsrôwn**, *khets-rone'*; from 2691; *court-yard*; *Chetsron*, the name of a place in Pal.; also of two Isr.:—Hezron.

2697. חֶצְרוֹנִי **Chetsrôwnîy**, *khets-ro-nee'*; patron. from 2696; a *Chetsronite* or (collect.) desc. of Chetsron:—Hezronites.

2698. חֲצֵרוֹת **Chătsêrowth**, *khats-ay-roth'*; fem. plur. of 2691; *yards*; *Chatseroth*, a place in Pal.:—Hazeroth.

2699. חֲצֵרִים **Chătsêrîym**, *khats-ay-reem'*; plur. masc. of 2691; *yards*; *Chatserim*, a place in Pal.:—Hazerim.

2700. חֲצַרְמָוֶת **Chătsarmâveth**, *khats-ar-maw'-veth*; from 2691 and 4194; *village of death*; *Chatsarmaveth*, a place in Arabia:—Hazarmaveth.

2701. חֲצַר סוּסָה **Chătsar Çûwçâh**, *khats-ar' soo-saw'*; from 2691 and 5484; *village of cavalry*; *Chatsar-Susah*, a place in Pal.:—Hazar-susah.

2702. חֲצַר סוּסִים **Chătsar Çûwçîym**, *khats-ar' soo-seem'*; from 2691 and the plur. of 5483; *village of horses*; *Chatsar-Susim*, a place in Pal.:—Hazar-susim.

2703. חֲצַר עֵינוֹן **Chătsar ʽÊynôwn**, *khats-ar' ay-nōne'*; from 2691 and a der. of 5869; *village of springs*; *Chatsar-Enon*, a place in Pal.:—Hazar-enon.

2704. חֲצַר עֵינָן **Chătsar ʽÊynân**, *khats-ar' ay-nawn'*; from 2691 and the same as 5881; *village of springs*; *Chatsar-Enan*, a place in Pal.:—Hazar-enan.

2705. חֲצַר שׁוּעָל **Chătsar Shûwʽâl**, *khats-ar' shoo-awl'*; from 2691 and 7776; *village of* (the) *fox*; *Chatsar-Shual*, a place in Pal.:—Hazar-shual.

חֵק **chêq**. See 2436.

2706. חֹק **chôq**, *khoke*; from 2710; an *enactment*; hence an *appointment* (of time, space, quantity, labor or usage):—appointed, bound, commandment, convenient, custom, decree (-d), due, law, measure, × necessary, ordinance (-nary), portion, set time, statute, task.

2707. חָקָה **châqah**, *khaw-kaw'*; a prim. root; to *carve*; by impl. to *delineate*; also to *intrench*:—carved work, portrayed, set a print.

2708. חֻקָּה **chuqqâh**, *khook-kaw'*; fem. of 2706, and mean. substantially the same:—appointed, custom, manner, ordinance, site, statute.

2709. חֲקוּפָא **Chăqûwphâ'**, *khah-oo-faw'*; from an unused root prob. mean. to *bend*; *crooked*; *Chakupha*, one of the Nethinim:—Hakupha.

2710. חָקַק **châqaq**, *khaw-kak'*; a prim. root; prop. to *hack*, i.e. *engrave* (Judg. 5 : 14, to *be a scribe* simply); by impl. to *enact* (laws being *cut* in stone or metal tablets in primitive times) or (gen.) *prescribe*:—appoint, decree, governor, grave, lawgiver, note, pourtray, print, set.

2711. חֵקֶק **chêqeq**, *khay'-kek*; from 2710; an *enactment*, a *resolution*:—decree, thought.

2712. חֻקֹּק **Chuqqôq**, *khook-koke'*; or (fully) חוּקֹק **Chûwqôq**, *khoo-koke'*; from 2710; *appointed*; *Chukkok* or *Chukok*, a place in Pal.:—Hukkok, Hukok.

2713. חָקַר **châqar**, *khaw-kar'*; a prim. root; prop. to *penetrate*; hence to *examine* intimately:—find out, (make) search (out), seek (out), sound, try.

2714. חֵקֶר **chêqer**, *khay'-ker*; from 2713; *examination*, *enumeration*, *deliberation*:—finding out, number, [un-] search (-able, -ed out, -ing).

2715. חֹר **chôr**, *khore*; or (fully) חוֹר **chôwr**, *khore*; from 2787; prop. *white* or *pure* (from the *cleansing* or *shining* power of fire [comp. 2751]); hence (fig.) *noble* (in rank):—noble.

חֻר **chûr**. See 2352.

2716. חֶרֶא **chereʼ**, *kheh'-reh*; from an unused (and vulg.) root prob. mean. to *evacuate* the bowels; *excrement*:—dung. Also חֲרִי° **chărîy**, *khar-ee'*.

2717. חָרַב **chârab**, *khaw-rab'*; or חָרֵב **chârêb**, *khaw-rabe'*; a prim. root; to *parch* (through drought), i.e. (by anal.) to *desolate*, *destroy*, *kill*:—decay, (be) desolate, destroy (-er), (be) dry (up), slay, × surely, (lay, lie, make) waste.

2718. חֲרַב **chărab** (Chald.), *khar-ab'*; a root corresp. to 2717; to *demolish*:—destroy.

2719. חֶרֶב **chereb**, *kheh'-reb*; from 2717; *drought*; also a *cutting* instrument (from its *destructive* effect), as a *knife*, *sword*, or other sharp implement:—axe, dagger, knife, mattock, sword, tool.

2720. חָרֵב **chârêb**, *khaw-rabe'*; from 2717; *parched* or *ruined*:—desolate, dry, waste.

2721. חֹרֶב **chôreb**, *kho'-reb*; a collat. form of 2719; *drought* or *desolation*:—desolation, drought, dry, heat, × utterly, waste.

2722. חֹרֵב **Chôrêb**, *kho-rabe'*; from 2717; *desolate*; *Choreb*, a (gen.) name for the Sinaitic mountains:—Horeb.

2723. חָרְבָּה **chorbâh**, *khor-baw'*; fem. of 2721; prop. *drought*, i.e. (by impl.) a *desolation*:—decayed place, desolate (place, -tion), destruction, (laid) waste (place).

2724. חָרָבָה **chârâbâh**, *khaw-raw-baw'*; fem. of 2720; a *desert*:—dry (ground, land).

2725. חֲרָבוֹן **chărâbôwn**, *khar-aw-bone'*; from 2717; parching *heat*:—drought.

2726. חַרְבוֹנָא **Charbôwnâʼ**, *khar-bo-naw'*; or חַרְבוֹנָה **Charbôwnâh**, *khar-bo-naw'*; of Pers. or.; *Charbona* or *Charbonah*, a eunuch of Xerxes:—Harbona, Harbonah.

2727. חָרַג **chârag**, *khaw-rag'*; a prim. root; prop. to *leap* suddenly, i.e. (by impl.) to *be dismayed*:—be afraid.

2728. חַרְגֹּל **chargôl**, *khar-gole'*; from 2727; the *leaping* insect, i.e. a *locust*:—beetle.

2729. חָרַד **chârad**, *khaw-rad'*; a prim. root; to *shudder* with terror; hence to *fear*; also to *hasten* (with anxiety):—be (make) afraid, be careful, discomfit, fray (away), quake, tremble.

2730. חָרֵד **chârêd**, *khaw-rade'*; from 2729; *fearful*; also *reverential*:—afraid, trembling.

2731. חֲרָדָה **chărâdâh**, *khar-aw-daw'*; fem. of 2730; *fear*, *anxiety*:—care, × exceedingly, fear, quaking, trembling.

2732. חֲרָדָה **Chărâdâh**, *khar-aw-daw'*; the same as 2731; *Charadah*, a place in the Desert:—Haradah.

2733. חֲרֹדִי **Chărôdîy**, *khar-o-dee'*; patrial from a deriv. of 2729 [comp. 5878]; a *Charodite*, or inhab. of *Charod*:—Harodite.

2734. חָרָה **chârâh**, *khaw-raw'*; a prim. root [comp. 2787]; to *glow* or grow warm; fig. (usually) to *blaze* up, of anger, zeal, jealousy:—be angry, burn, be displeased, × earnestly, fret self, grieve, be (wax) hot, be incensed, kindle, × very, be wroth. See 8474.

2735. חֹר הַגִּדְגָּד **Chôr hag-Gidgâd**, *khore hag-ghid-gawd'*; from 2356 and a collat. (masc.) form of 1412, with the art. interposed; *hole of the cleft*; *Chor-hag-Gidgad*, a place in the Desert:—Hor-hagidgad.

2736. חַרְהֲיָה **Charhăyâh**, *khar-hah-yaw'*; from 2734 and 3050; *fearing Jah*; *Charhajah*, an Isr.:—Harhaiah.

2737. חָרוּז **chârûwz**, *khaw-rooz'*; from an unused root mean. to *perforate*; prop. *pierced*, i.e. a *bead* of pearl, gems or jewels (as strung):—chain.

2738. חָרוּל **chârûwl**, *khaw-rool'*; or (short.) חָרֻל **chârûl**, *khaw-rool'*; appar. pass. part. of an unused root prob. mean. to *be prickly*; prop. *pointed*, i.e. a *bramble* or other thorny weed:—nettle.

חֹרוֹן **chôrôwn**. See 1032, 2772.

2739. חֲרוּמַף **chărûwmaph**, *khar-oo-maf'*; from pass. part. of 2763 and 639; *snub-nosed*; *Charumaph*, an Isr.:—Harumaph.

2740. חָרוֹן **chârôwn**, *khaw-rone'*; or (short.) חָרֹן **chârôn**, *khaw-rone'*; from 2734; a *burning* of anger:—sore displeasure, fierce (-ness), fury, (fierce) wrath (-ful).

2741. חֲרוּפִי **Chărûwphîy**, *khar-oo-fee'*; a patrial from (prob.) a collat. form of 2756; a *Charuphite* or inhab. of Charuph (or Chariph):—Haruphite.

2742. חָרוּץ **chârûwts**, *khaw-roots'*; or חָרֻץ **chârûts**, *khaw-roots'*; pass. part. of 2782; prop. *incised* or (act.) *incisive*; hence (as noun masc. or fem.) a *trench* (as dug), *gold* (as mined), a *threshing-sledge* (having sharp teeth); (fig.) *determination*; also *eager*:—decision, diligent, (fine) gold, pointed things, sharp, threshing instrument, wall.

2743. חָרוּץ **Chârûwts**, *khaw-roots'*; the same as 2742; *earnest*; *Charuts*, an Isr.:—Haruz.

2744. חַרְחוּר **Charchûwr**, *khar-khoor'*; a fuller form of 2746; *inflammation*; *Charchur*, one of the Nethinim:—Harhur.

2745. חַרְחַס **Charchaç**, *khar-khas'*; from the same as 2775; perh. *shining*; *Charchas*, an Isr.:—Harhas.

2746. חַרְחֻר **charchûr**, *khar-khoor'*; from 2787; *fever* (as *hot*):—extreme burning.

2747. חֶרֶט **chereṭ**, *kheh'-ret*; from a prim. root mean. to *engrave*; a *chisel* or *graver*; also a *style* for writing:—graving tool, pen.

חָרִט **chârîṭ**. See 2754.

2748. חַרְטֹם **charṭôm**, *khar-tome'*; from the same as 2747; a *horoscopist* (as *drawing* magical lines or circles):—magician.

2749. חַרְטֹם **charṭôm** (Chald.), *khar-tome'*; the same as 2748:—magician.

2750. חֳרִי **chŏrîy**, *khor-ee'*; from 2734; a *burning* (i.e. intense) anger:—fierce, × great, heat.

חֲרִי° **chărîy**. See 2716.

2751. חֹרִי **chôrîy**, *kho-ree'*; from the same as 2353; *white* bread:—white.

2752. חֹרִי **Chôrîy**, *kho-ree'*; from 2356; *cave-dweller* or troglodyte; a *Chorite* or aboriginal Idumæan:—Horims, Horites.

2753. חֹרִי **Chôrîy**, *kho-ree'*; or חוֹרִי **Chôwrîy**, *kho-ree'*; the same as 2752; *Chori*, the name of two men:—Hori.

2754. חָרִיט **chârîyṭ**, *khaw-reet'*; or חָרִט **chârîṭ**, *khaw-reet'*; from the same as 2747; prop. *cut* out (or *hollow*), i.e. (by impl.) a *pocket*:—bag, crisping pin.

2755. חֲרֵי־יוֹנִים **chărêy-yôwnîym**, *khar-ay'-yo-neem'*; from the plur. of 2716 and the plur. of 3123; *excrements of doves* [or perh. rather the plur. of a single word חֲרָאיוֹן **chârâʼyôwn**, *khar-aw-yone'*; of similar or uncert. deriv.], prob. a kind of vegetable:—doves' dung.

2756. חָרִיף **Chârîyph**, *khaw-reef'*; from 2778; *autumnal*; *Chariph*, the name of two Isr.:—Hariph.

2757. חָרִיץ **chârîyts**, *khaw-reets'*; or חָרִץ **chârîts**, *khaw-reets'*; from 2782; prop. *incisure* or (pass.) *incised* [comp. 2742]; hence a *threshing-sledge* (with *sharp* teeth); also a *slice* (as cut):— + cheese, harrow.

2758. חָרִישׁ **chârîysh**, *khaw-reesh'*; from 2790; *ploughing* or its season:—earing (time), ground.

2759. חֲרִישִׁי **chărîyshîy**, *khar-ee-shee'*; from 2790 in the sense of *silence*; *quiet*, i.e. *sultry* (as noun fem. the *sirocco* or hot east wind):—vehement.

2760. חָרַךְ **chârak**, *khaw-rak'*; a prim. root; to *braid* (i.e. to *entangle* or snare) or *catch* (game) in a net:—roast.

2761. חֲרַךְ **chărak** (Chald.), *khar-ak'*; a root prob. allied to the equiv. of 2787; to *scorch*:—singe.

2762. חֶרֶךְ **cherek**, *kheh'-rek*; from 2760; prop. a *net*, i.e. (by anal.) *lattice*:—lattice.

חָרֻל **chârûl**. See 2738.

2763. חָרַם **charam**, *khaw-ram'*; a prim. root; to *seclude*; spec. (by a ban) to *devote* to relig. uses (espec. destruction); phys. and reflex. to be *blunt* as to the nose:—make accursed, consecrate, (utterly) destroy, devote, forfeit, have a flat nose, utterly (slay, make away).

2734. חֵרֶם **chêrem**, *khay'-rem*; or (Zech. 14 : 11) חֶרֶם **cherem**, *kheh'-rem*; from 2763; phys. (as *shutting in*) a *net* (either lit. or fig.); usually a *doomed* object; abstr. *extermination*:—(ac-) curse (-d, -d thing), dedicated thing, things which should have been utterly destroyed, (appointed to) utter destruction, devoted (thing), net.

2765. חֳרֵם **Chŏrêm**, *khor-ame'*; from 2763; *devoted*; *Chorem*, a place in Pal.:—Horem.

2766. חָרִם **Chârîm**, *khaw-reem'*; from 2763; *snub-nosed*; *Charim*, an Isr.:—Harim.

2767. חָרְמָה **Chormâh**, *khor-maw'*; from 2763; *devoted*; *Chormah*, a place in Pal.:—Hormah.

2768. חֶרְמוֹן **Chermôwn**, *kher-mone'*; from 2763; *abrupt*; *Chermon*, a mount of Pal.:—Hermon.

2769. חֶרְמוֹנִים **Chermôwnîym**, *kher-mo-neem'*; plur. of 2768; *Hermons*, i.e. its peaks:—the Hermonites.

2770. חֶרְמֵשׁ **chermêsh**, *kher-mashe'*; from 2763; a *sickle* (as *cutting*):—sickle.

2771. חָרָן **Chârân**, *kaw-rawn'*; from 2787; *parched*; *Charan*, the name of a man and also of a place:—Haran.

חָרֹן **chârôn**. See 2740.

2772. חֹרֹנִי **Chôrônîy**, *kho-ro-nee'*; patrial from 2773; a *Choronite* or inhab. of Choronaim:—Horonite.

2773. חֹרֹנַיִם **Chôrônayim**, *kho-ro-nah'-yim*; dual of a deriv. from 2356; *double cave-town*; *Choronajim*, a place in Moab:—Horonaim.

2774. חַרְנֶפֶר **Charnepher**, *khar-neh'-fer*; of uncert. der.; *Charnepher*, an Isr.:—Harnepher.

2775. חֶרֶס **chereç**, *kheh'-res*; or (with a directive enclitic) חַרְסָה **charçâh**, *khar'-saw*; from an unused root mean. to *scrape*; the *itch*; also [perh. from the mediating idea of 2777] the *sun*:—itch, sun.

2776. חֶרֶס **Chereç**, *kheh'-res*; the same as 2775; *shining*; *Cheres*, a mount. in Pal.:—Heres.

2777. חַרְסוּת **charçûwth**, *khar-sooth'*; from 2775 (appar. in the sense of a red *tile* used for scraping); a *potsherd*, i.e. (by impl.) a *pottery;* the name of a gate at Jerus.:—east.

2778. חָרַף **châraph**, *khaw-raf';* a prim. root; to *pull* off, i.e. (by impl.) to *expose* (as by *stripping*); spec. to *betroth* (as if a surrender); fig. to carp at, i.e. *defame;* denom. (from 2779) to spend the *winter:*—betroth, blaspheme, defy, jeopard, rail, reproach, upbraid.

2779. חֹרֶף **chôreph**, *kho'-ref;* from 2778; prop. the *crop* gathered, i.e. (by impl.) the *autumn* (and winter) season; fig. *ripeness* of age:—cold, winter ([-house]), youth.

2780. חָרֵף **Chârêph**, *khaw-rafe';* from 2778; *reproachful; Chareph*, an Isr.:—Hareph.

2781. חֶרְפָּה **cherpâh**, *kher-paw';* from 2778; *contumely, disgrace*, the *pudenda:*—rebuke, reproach (-fully), shame.

2782. חָרַץ **chârats**, *khaw-rats';* a prim root; prop. to *point* sharply, i.e. (lit.) to *wound;* fig. to *be alert*, to *decide:*—bestir self, decide, decree, determine, maim, move.

2783. חֲרַץ **chărats** (Chald.), *khar-ats';* from a root corresp. to 2782 in the sense of *vigor;* the *loin* (as the seat of strength):—loin.

חָרוּץ **chârûts**. See 2742.

2784. חַרְצֻבָּה **chartsubbâh**, *khar-tsoob-baw';* of uncert. der.; a *fetter;* fig. a *pain:*—band.

חָרִיץ **chârîts**. See 2757.

2785. חַרְצַן **chartsan**, *khar-tsan';* from 2782; a *sour* grape (as *sharp* in taste):—kernel.

2786. חָרַק **châraq**, *khaw-rak';* a prim. root; to *grate* the teeth:—gnash.

2787. חָרַר **chârar**, *khaw-rar';* a prim. root; to *glow*, i.e. lit. (to *melt, burn, dry* up) or fig. (to *show* or *incite passion:*—be angry, burn, dry, kindle.

2788. חָרֵר **chârêr**, *khaw-rare';* from 2787; *arid:*—parched place.

2789. חֶרֶשׂ **cheres**, *kheh'-res;* a collat. form mediating between 2775 and 2791; a piece of *pottery:*—earth (-en), (pot-) sherd, + stone.

2790. חָרַשׁ **chârash**, *khaw-rash';* a prim. root; to *scratch*, i.e. (by impl.) to *engrave, plough;* hence (from the use of tools) to *fabricate* (of any material); fig. to *devise* (in a bad sense); hence (from the idea of secrecy) to be *silent*, to *let alone;* hence (by impl.) to *be deaf* (as an accompaniment of dumbness):— × altogether, cease, conceal, be deaf, devise, ear, graven, imagine, leave off speaking, hold peace, plow (-er, -man), be quiet, rest, practise secretly, keep silence, be silent, speak not a word, be still, hold tongue, worker.

2791. חֶרֶשׁ **cheresh**, *kheh'-resh;* from 2790; magical *craft;* also *silence:*—cunning, secretly.

2792. חֶרֶשׁ **Cheresh**, *kheh'-resh;* the same as 2791:—*Cheresh*, a Levite:—Heresh.

2793. חֹרֶשׁ **chôresh**, *kho'-resh;* from 2790; a *forest* (perh. as furnishing the material for fabric):—bough, forest, shroud, wood.

2794. חֹרֵשׁ **chôrêsh**, *kho-rashe';* act. part. of 2790; a *fabricator* or mechanic:—artificer.

2795. חֵרֵשׁ **chêrêsh**, *khay-rashe';* from 2790; *deaf* (whether lit. or spir.):—deaf.

2796. חָרָשׁ **chârâsh**, *khaw-rawsh';* from 2790; a *fabricator* of any material:—artificer, (+) carpenter, craftsman, engraver, maker, + mason, skilful, (+) smith, worker, workman, such as wrought.

2797. חַרְשָׁא **Charshâ'**, *khar-shaw';* from 2792; *magician; Charsha*, one of the Nethinim:—Harsha.

2798. חֲרָשִׁים **Chărâshîym**, *khar-aw-sheem';* plur. of 2796; *mechanics*, the name of a valley in Jerus.:—Charashim, craftsmen.

2799. חֲרֹשֶׁת **chărôsheth**, *khar-o'-sheth;* from 2790; mechanical *work:*—carving, cutting.

2800. חֲרֹשֶׁת **Chărôsheth**, *khar-o'-sheth;* the same as 2799; *Charosheth*, a place in Pal.:—Harosheth.

2801. חָרַת **chârath**, *khaw-rath';* a prim. root; to *engrave:*—graven.

2802. חֶרֶת **Chereth**, *kheh'-reth;* from 2801 [but equiv. to 2793]; *forest; Chereth*, a thicket in Pal.:—Hereth.

2803. חָשַׁב **châshab**, *khaw-shab';* a prim. root; prop. to *plait* or interpenetrate, i.e. (lit.) to *weave* or (gen.) to *fabricate;* fig. to *plot* or contrive (usually in a malicious sense); hence (from the mental effort) to *think, regard, value, compute:*—(make) account (of), conceive, consider, count, cunning (man, work, workman), devise, esteem, find out, forecast, hold, imagine, impute, invent, be like, mean, purpose, reckon (-ing be made), regard, think.

2804. חֲשַׁב **chăshab** (Chald.), *khash-ab';* corresp. to 2803; to *regard:*—repute.

2805. חֵשֶׁב **chêsheb**, *khay'-sheb;* from 2803; a *belt* or strap (as being interlaced):—curious girdle.

2806. חַשְׁבַּדָּנָה **Chashbaddânâh**, *khash-bad-daw'-naw;* from 2803 and 1777; *considerate judge; Chasbaddanah*, an Isr.:—Hasbadana.

2807. חֲשֻׁבָה **Chăshûbâh**, *khash-oo-baw';* from 2803; *estimation; Chashubah*, an Isr.:—Hashubah.

2808. חֶשְׁבּוֹן **cheshbôwn**, *khesh-bone';* from 2803; prop. *contrivance;* by impl. *intelligence:*—account, device, reason.

2809. חֶשְׁבּוֹן **Cheshbôwn**, *khesh-bone';* the same as 2808; *Cheshbon*, a place E. of the Jordan:—Heshbon.

2810. חִשָּׁבוֹן **chishshâbôwn**, *khish-shaw-bone';* from 2803; a *contrivance*, i.e. actual (a warlike *machine*) or mental (a *machination*):—engine, invention.

2811. חֲשַׁבְיָה **Chăshabyâh**, *khash-ab-yaw';* or

חֲשַׁבְיָהוּ **Chăshabyâhûw**, *khash-ab-yaw'-hoo;* from 2803 and 3050; *Jah has regarded; Chashabjah*, the name of nine Isr.:—Hashabiah.

2812. חֲשַׁבְנָה **Chăshabnâh**, *khash-ab-naw';* fem. of 2808; *inventiveness; Chashnah*, an Isr.:—Hashabnah.

2813. חֲשַׁבְנְיָה **Chăshabnᵉyâh**, *khash-ab-neh-yaw';* from 2808 and 3050; *thought of Jah; Chashabnejah*, the name of two Isr.:—Hashabniah.

2814. חָשָׁה **châshâh**, *khaw-shaw';* a prim. root; to *hush* or keep quiet:—hold peace, keep silence, be silent, (be) still.

2815. חַשּׁוּב **Chashshûwb**, *khash-shoob';* from 2803; *intelligent; Chashshub*, the name of two or three Isr.:—Hashub, Hasshub.

2816. חֲשׁוֹךְ **chăshôwk** (Chald.), *khash-oke';* from a root corresp. to 2821; the *dark:*—darkness.

2817. חֲשׂוּפָא **Chăsûwphâ'**, *khas-oo-faw';* or

חֲשֻׂפָא **Chăsûphâ'**, *khas-oo-faw';* from 2834; *nakedness; Chasupha*, one of the Nethinim:—Hashupha, Hasupha.

חָשׁוּק **châshûwq**. See 2838.

2818. חֲשַׁח **chăshach** (Chald.), *khash-akh';* a collat. root to one corresp. to 2363 in the sense of *readiness;* to *be necessary* (from the idea of *convenience*) or (transit.) to *need:*—careful, have need of.

2819. חַשְׁחוּת **chashchûwth**, *khash-khooth';* from a root corresp. to 2818; *necessity:*—be needful.

חֲשֵׁיכָה **chăshêykâh**. See 2825.

חֻשִׁים **Chûshîym**. See 2366.

2820. חָשַׂךְ **châsak**, *khaw-sak';* a prim root; to *restrain* or (reflex.) *refrain;* by impl. to *refuse, spare, preserve;* also (by interch. with 2821) to *observe:*—assuage, × darken, forbear, hinder, hold back, keep (back), punish, refrain, reserve, spare, withhold.

2821. חָשַׁךְ **châshak**, *khaw-shak';* a prim. root; to *be dark* (as *withholding* light); transit. to *darken:*—be black, be (make) dark, darken, cause darkness, be dim, hide.

2822. חֹשֶׁךְ **chôshek**, *kho-shek';* from 2821; the *dark;* hence (lit.) *darkness;* fig. *misery, destruction, death, ignorance, sorrow, wickedness:*—dark (-ness), night, obscurity.

2823. חָשֹׁךְ **châshôk**, *khaw-shoke';* from 2821; *dark* (fig. i.e. *obscure*):—mean.

2824. חֶשְׁכָה **cheshkâh**, *khesh-kaw';* from 2821; *darkness:*—dark.

2825. חֲשֵׁכָה **chăshêkâh**, *khash-ay-kaw';* or

חֲשֵׁיכָה **chăshêkâh**, *khash-ay-kaw';* from 2821; *darkness;* fig. *misery:*—darkness.

2826. חָשַׁל **châshal**, *khaw-shal';* a prim. root; to *make* (intrans. *be*) *unsteady*, i.e. *weak:*—feeble.

2827. חֲשַׁל **chăshal** (Chald.), *khash-al';* a root corresp. to 2826; to *weaken*, i.e. *crush:*—subdue.

2828. חָשֻׁם **Châshûm**, *khaw-shoom';* from the same as 2831; *enriched; Chashum*, the name of two or three Isr.:—Hashum.

חֻשָׁם **Chûshâm**. See 2367.

חֻשִׁם **Chûshîm**. See 2366.

2829. חֶשְׁמוֹן **Cheshmôwn**, *khesh-mone';* the same as 2831; *opulent; Cheshmon*, a place in Pal.:—Heshmon.

2830. חַשְׁמַל **chashmal**, *khash-mal';* of uncert. der.; prob. *bronze* or polished spectrum metal:—amber.

2831. חַשְׁמַן **chashman**, *khash-man';* from an unused root (prob. mean. *firm* or *capacious* in resources); appar. *wealthy:*—princes.

2832. חַשְׁמֹנָה **Chashmônâh**, *khash-mo-naw';* fem. of 2831; *fertile; Chasmonah*, a place in the Desert:—Hashmonah.

2833. חֹשֶׁן **chôshen**, *kho'-shen;* from an unused root prob. mean. to *contain* or *sparkle;* perh. a *pocket* (as holding the Urim and Thummim), or *rich* (as containing gems), used only of the *gorget* of the highpriest:—breastplate.

2834. חָשַׂף **châsaph**, *khaw-saf';* a prim. root; to *strip* off, i.e. gen. to *make naked* (for exertion or in disgrace), to *drain* away or *bail up* (a liquid):—make bare, clean, discover, draw out, take, uncover.

2835. חָשִׂף **châsîph**, *khaw-seef';* from 2834; prop. *drawn off*, i.e. separated; hence a small *company* (as divided from the rest):—little flock.

2836. חָשַׁק **châshaq**, *khaw-shak';* a prim. root; to *cling*, i.e. *join*, (fig.) to *love, delight* in; ellipt. (or by interch. for 2820) to *deliver:*—have a delight, (have a) desire, fillet, long, set (in) love.

2837. חֵשֶׁק **chêsheq**, *khay'-shek;* from 2836; *delight:*—desire, pleasure.

2838. חָשֻׁק **châshûq**, *khaw-shook';* or

חָשׁוּק **châshûwq**, *khaw-shook';* pass. part. of 2836; *attached*, i.e. a fence-*rail* or rod connecting the posts or pillars:—fillet.

2839. חִשֻּׁק **chishshûq**, *khish-shook';* from 2836; *conjoined*, i.e. a wheel-*spoke* or rod connecting the hub with the rim:—felloe.

2840. חִשֻּׁר **chishshûr**, *khish-shoor';* from an unused root mean. to *bind* together; *combined*, i.e. the *nave* or hub of a wheel (as holding the spokes together):—spoke.

2841. חַשְׁרָה **chashrâh**, *khash-raw';* from the same as 2840; prop. a *combination* or gathering, i.e. of watery *clouds:*—dark.

חֲשֻׂפָא **Chăsûphâ'**. See 2817.

2842. חָשַׁשׁ **châshash**, *khaw-shash';* by var. for 7179; dry *grass:*—chaff.

2843. חֻשָׁתִי **Chûshâthîy**, *khoo-shaw-thee';* patron. from 2364; a *Chushathite* or desc. of Chushah:—Hushathite.

2844. חַת **chath**, *khath;* from 2865; concr. *crushed;* also *afraid;* abstr. *terror:*—broken, dismayed, dread, fear.

2845. חֵת **Chêth**, *khayth;* from 2865; *terror; Cheth,* an aboriginal Canaanite:—Heth.

2846. חָתָה **châthâh**, *khaw-thaw';* a prim. root; to lay *hold* of; espec. to *pick* up fire:—heap, take (away).

2847. חִתָּה **chittâh**, *khit-taw';* from 2865; *fear:*—terror.

2848. חִתּוּל **chittûwl**, *khit-tool';* from 2853; *swathed,* i.e. a *bandage:*—roller.

2849. חַתְחַת **chathchath**, *khath-khath';* from 2844; *terror:*—fear.

2850. חִתִּי **Chittîy**, *khit-tee';* patron. from 2845; a *Chittite,* or desc. of Cheth:—Hittite, Hittites.

2851. חִתִּית **chittîyth**, *khit-teeth';* from 2865; *fear:*—terror.

2852. חָתַךְ **châthak**, *khaw-thak';* a prim. root; prop. to *cut* off, i.e. (fig.) to *decree:*—determine.

2853. חָתַל **châthal**, *khaw-thal';* a prim. root; to *swathe:*— × at all, swaddle.

2854. חֲתֻלָּה **chăthullâh**, *khath-ool-law';* from 2853; a *swathing* cloth (fig.):—swaddling band.

2855. חֶתְלֹן **Chethlôn**, *kheth-lone';* from 2853; *enswathed; Chethlon,* a place in Pal.:—Hethlon.

2856. חָתַם **châtham**, *khaw-tham';* a prim. root; to *close* up; espec. to *seal:*—make an end, mark, seal (up), stop.

2857. חֲתַם **chătham** (Chald.), *khath-am';* a root corresp. to 2856; to *seal:*—seal.

חֹתָם **chôthâm**. See 2368.

2858. חֹתֶמֶת **chôthemeth**, *kho-the-meth;* fem. act. part. of 2856; a *seal:*—signet.

2859. חָתַן **châthan**, *khaw-than';* a prim. root; to *give* (a daughter) *away* in marriage; hence (gen.) to *contract affinity* by marriage:—join in affinity, father in law, make marriages, mother in law, son in law.

2860. חָתָן **châthân**, *khaw-thawn';* from 2859; a *relative* by marriage (espec. through the bride); fig. a *circumcised* child (as a species of religious espousal):—bridegroom, husband, son in law.

2861. חֲתֻנָּה **chăthunnâh**, *khath-oon-naw';* from 2859; a *wedding:*—espousal.

2862. חָתַף **châthaph**, *khaw-thaf';* a prim. root; to *clutch:*—take away.

2863. חֶתֶף **chetheph**, *kheh'-thef;* from 2862; prop. *rapine;* fig. *robbery:*—prey.

2864. חָתַר **châthar**, *khaw-thar';* a prim. root; to *force* a passage, as by burglary; fig. with oars:—dig (through), row.

2865. חָתַת **châthath**, *khaw-thath';* a prim. root; prop. to *prostrate;* hence to *break* down, either (lit.) by violence, or (fig.) by confusion and fear:—abolish, affright, be (make) afraid, amaze, beat down, discourage, (cause to) dismay, go down, scare, terrify.

2866. חֲתַת **chăthath**, *khath-ath';* from 2865; *dismay:*—casting down.

2867. חֲתַת **Chăthath**, *khath-ath';* the same as 2866; *Chathath,* an Isr.:—Hathath.

ט

2868. טְאֵב **ṭᵉʼêb** (Chald.), *teh-abe';* a prim. root; to *rejoice:*—be glad.

2869. טָב **ṭâb** (Chald.), *tawb;* from 2868; the same as 2896; *good:*—fine, good.

2870. טָבְאֵל **ṭâbᵉʼêl**, *taw-beh-ale';* from 2895 and 410; *pleasing* (to) *God; Tabeël,* the name of a Syrian and of a Persian:—Tabeal, Tabeel.

2871. טָבוּל **ṭâbûwl**, *taw-bool';* pass. part. of 2881; prop. *dyed,* i.e. a *turban* (prob. as of *colored* stuff):—dyed attire.

2872. טַבּוּר **ṭabbûwr**, *tab-boor';* from an unused root mean. to *pile* up; prop. *accumulated;* i.e. (by impl.) a *summit:*—middle, midst.

2873. טָבַח **ṭâbach**, *taw-bakh';* a prim. root; to *slaughter* (animals or men):—kill, (make) slaughter, slay.

2874. טֶבַח **ṭebach**, *teh'-bakh;* from 2873; prop. something *slaughtered;* hence a *beast* (or *meat,* as butchered); abstr. *butchery* (or concr. a place of slaughter):— × beast, slaughter, × slay, × sore.

2875. טֶבַח **Ṭebach**, *teh'-bakh;* the same as 2874; *massacre; Tebach,* the name of a Mesopotamian and of an Isr.:—Tebah.

2876. טַבָּח **ṭabbâch**, *tab-bawkh';* from 2873; prop. a *butcher;* hence a *lifeguardsman* (because acting as executioner); also a *cook* (as usually slaughtering the animal for food):—cook, guard.

2877. טַבָּח **ṭabbâch** (Chald.), *tab-bawkh';* the same as 2876; a *lifeguardsman:*—guard.

2878. טִבְחָה **ṭibchâh**, *tib-khaw';* fem. of 2874 and mean. the same:—flesh, slaughter.

2879. טַבָּחָה **ṭabbâchâh**, *tab-baw-khaw';* fem. of 2876; a female *cook:*—cook.

2880. טִבְחַת **Ṭibchath**, *tib-khath';* from 2878; *slaughter; Tibchath,* a place in Syria:—Tibhath.

2881. טָבַל **ṭâbal**, *taw-bal';* a prim. root; to *dip:*—dip, plunge.

2882. טְבַלְיָהוּ **Ṭᵉbalyâhûw**, *teb-al-yaw'-hoo;* from 2881 and 3050; *Jah has dipped; Tebaljah,* an Isr.:—Tebaliah.

2883. טָבַע **ṭâbaʻ**, *taw-bah';* a prim. root; to *sink:*—drown, fasten, settle, sink.

2884. טַבָּעוֹת **Ṭabbâʻôwth**, *tab-baw-othe';* plur. of 2885; *rings; Tabbaoth,* one of the Nethinim:—Tabbaoth.

2885. טַבַּעַת **ṭabbaʻath**, *tab-bah'-ath;* from 2883; prop. a *seal* (as *sunk* into the wax), i.e. *signet* (for sealing); hence (gen.) a *ring* of any kind:—ring.

2886. טַבְרִמּוֹן **Ṭabrimmôwn**, *tab-rim-mone';* from 2895 and 7417; *pleasing* (to) *Rimmon; Tabrimmon,* a Syrian:—Tabrimmon.

2887. טֵבֵת **Ṭêbeth**, *tay'-beth;* prob. of for. der.; *Tebeth,* the tenth Heb. month:—Tebeth.

2888. טַבַּת **Ṭabbath**, *tab-bath';* of uncert. der.; *Tabbath,* a place E. of the Jordan:—Tabbath.

2889. טָהוֹר **ṭâhôwr**, *taw-hore';* or

טָהֹר **ṭâhôr**, *taw-hore';* from 2891; *pure* (in a phys., chem., cerem. or moral sense):—clean, fair, pure (-ness).

2890. טְהוֹר **ṭᵉhôwr**, *teh-hore';* from 2891; *purity:*—pureness.

2891. טָהֵר **ṭâhêr**, *taw-hare';* a prim. root; prop. to *be bright;* i.e. (by impl.) to *be pure* (phys. *sound, clear, unadulterated;* Levit. *uncontaminated;* mor. *innocent* or *holy*):—be (make, make self, pronounce) clean, cleanse (self), purge, purify (-ier, self).

2892. טֹהַר **ṭôhar**, *to'-har;* from 2891; lit. *brightness;* ceremon. *purification:*—clearness, glory, purifying.

2893. טָהֳרָה **ṭohŏrâh**, *toh-or-aw';* fem. of 2892; cerem. *purification;* moral *purity:*—× is cleansed, cleansing, purification (-fying).

2894. טוּא **ṭûwʼ**, *too;* a prim. root; to *sweep away:*—sweep.

2895. טוֹב **ṭowb**, *tobe;* a prim. root, to *be* (trans. *do* or *make*) *good* (or *well*) in the widest sense:—be (do) better, cheer, be (do, seem) good, (make) goodly, × please, (be, do, go, play) well.

2896. טוֹב **ṭôwb**, *tobe;* from 2895; *good* (as an adj.) in the widest sense; used likewise as a noun, both in the masc. and the fem., the sing. and the plur. (*good,* a *good* or *good* thing, a *good* man or woman; the *good, goods* or *good* things, *good* men or women), also as an adv. (*well*):—beautiful, best, better, bountiful, cheerful, at ease, × fair (word), (be in) favour, fine, glad, good (deed, -lier, liest, -ly, -ness, -s), graciously, joyful, kindly, kindness, liketh (best), loving, merry, × most, pleasant, + pleaseth, pleasure, precious, prosperity, ready, sweet, wealth, welfare, (be) well ([-favoured]).

2897. טוֹב **Ṭôwb**, *tobe;* the same as 2896; *good; Tob,* a region appar. E. of the Jordan:—Tob.

2898. טוּב **ṭûwb**, *toob;* from 2895; *good* (as a noun), in the widest sense, espec. *goodness* (superl. concr. the *best*), *beauty, gladness, welfare:*—fair, gladness, good (-ness, thing, -s), joy, go well with.

2899. טוֹב אֲדֹנִיָּהוּ **Ṭôwb Ădônîyâhûw**, *tobe ado-nee-yah'-hoo;* from 2896 and 138; *pleasing* (to) *Adonijah; Tob-Adonijah,* an Isr.:—Tob-adonijah.

2900. טוֹבִיָּה **Ṭôwbîyâh**, *to-bee-yaw';* or

טוֹבִיָּהוּ **Ṭôwbîyâhûw**, *to-bee-yaw'-hoo;* from 2896 and 3050; *goodness of Jehovah; Tobijah,* the name of three Isr. and of one Samaritan:—Tobiah, Tobijah.

2901. טָוָה **ṭâvâh**, *taw-vaw';* a prim. root; to *spin:*—spin.

2902. טוּחַ **ṭûwach**, *too'-akh;* a prim. root; to *smear,* espec. with lime:—daub, overlay, plaister, smut.

2903. טוֹפָפָה **ṭôwphâphâh**, *to-faw-faw';* from an unused root mean. to *go around* or *bind;* a *fillet* for the forehead:—frontlet.

2904. טוּל **ṭûwl**, *tool;* a prim. root; to *pitch* over or *reel;* hence (transit.) to *cast* down or out:—carry away, (utterly) cast (down, forth, out), send out.

2905. טוּר **ṭûwr**, *toor;* from an unused root mean. to *range* in a reg. manner; a *row;* hence a *wall:*—row.

2906. טוּר **ṭûwr** (Chald.), *toor;* corresp. to 6697; a *rock* or hill:—mountain.

2907. טוּשׂ **ṭûws**, *toos;* a prim. root; to *pounce* as a bird of prey:—haste.

2908. טְוָת **ṭᵉvâth** (Chald.), *tev-awth';* from a root corresp. to 2901; *hunger* (as *twisting*):—fasting.

2909. טָחָה **ṭâchâh**, *taw-khaw';* a prim. root; to *stretch* a bow, as an *archer:*—[bow-] shot.

2910. טֻחָה **ṭûwchâh**, *too-khaw';* from 2909 (or 2902) in the sense of *overlaying;* (in the plur. only) the *kidneys* (as being *covered*); hence (fig.) the inmost *thought:*—inward parts.

2911. טְחוֹן **ṭᵉchôwn**, *tekh-one';* from 2912; a hand *mill;* hence a *millstone:*—to grind.

2912. טָחַן **ṭâchan**, *taw-khan';* a prim. root; to *grind* meal; hence to *be a concubine* (that being their employment):—grind (-er).

2913. טַחֲנָה **ṭachănâh**, *takh-an-aw';* from 2912; a hand *mill;* hence (fig.) *chewing:*—grinding.

2914. טְחֹר **ṭᵉchôr**, *tekh-ore';* from an unused root mean. to *burn;* a *boil* or ulcer (from the inflammation), espec. a tumor in the anus or pudenda (the piles):—emerod.

2915. טִיחַ **ṭîyach**, *tee'-akh;* from (the equiv. of) 2902; mortar or *plaster:*—daubing.

2916. טִיט **ṭîyṭ**, *teet;* from an unused root mean. appar. to *be sticky* [rath. perh. a denom. from 2894, through the idea of dirt to be *swept* away]; *mud* or *clay;* fig. *calamity:*—clay, dirt, mire.

2917. טִין **ṭîyn** (Chald.), *teen;* perh. by interch. for a word corresp. to 2916; *clay:*—miry.

2918. טִירָה **ṭîyrâh**, *tee-raw';* fem. of (an equiv. to) 2905; a *wall;* hence a *fortress* or a *hamlet:*—(goodly) castle, habitation, palace, row.

2919. טַל **ṭal**, *tal;* from 2926; *dew* (as *covering* vegetation):—dew.

2920. טַל **ṭal** (Chald.), *tal;* the same as 2919:—dew.

2921. טָלָא **ṭâlâʼ**, *taw-law';* a prim. root; prop. to *cover* with pieces; i.e. (by impl.) to *spot* or *variegate* (as tapestry):—clouted, with divers colours, spotted.

2922. טְלָא **ṭᵉlâʼ**, *tel-aw';* appar. from 2921 in the (orig.) sense of *covering* (for protection); a *lamb* [comp. 2924]:—lamb.

2923. טְלָאִים **T^{e}lâʼîym**, *tel-aw-eem'*; from the plur. of 2922; *lambs; Telaim,* a place in Pal.:—Telaim.

2924. טָלֶה **ṭâleh**, *taw-leh'*; by var. for 2922; a *lamb:*—lamb.

2925. טַלְטֵלָה **ṭalṭêlâh**, *tal-tay-law'*; from 2904; *overthrow* or *rejection:*—captivity.

2926. טָלַל **ṭâlal**, *taw-lal'*; a prim. root; prop. to *strew* over, i.e. (by impl.) to *cover* in or *plate* (with beams):—cover.

2927. טְלַל **ṭ^{e}lal** (Chald.), *tel-al'*; corresp. to 2926; to *cover* with shade:—have a shadow.

2928. טֶלֶם **Ṭelem**, *teh'-lem*; from an unused root mean. to *break* up or treat violently; *oppression; Telem,* the name of a place in Idumæa, also of a temple doorkeeper:—Telem.

2929. טַלְמוֹן **Ṭalmôwn**, *tal-mone'*; from the same as 2728; *oppressive; Talmon,* a temple doorkeeper:—Talmon.

2930. טָמֵא **ṭâmêʼ**, *taw-may'*; a prim. root; to *be foul,* espec. in a cerem. or mor. sense (*contaminated*):—defile (self), pollute (self), be (make, make self, pronounce) unclean, × utterly.

2931. טָמֵא **ṭâmêʼ**, *taw-may'*; from 2930; *foul* in a relig. sense:—defiled, + infamous, polluted (-tion), unclean.

2932. טֻמְאָה **ṭumʼâh**, *toom-aw'*; from 2930; relig. *impurity:*—filthiness, unclean (-ness).

2933. טָמָה **ṭâmâh**, *taw-maw'*; a collat. form of 2930; to *be impure* in a relig. sense:—be defiled, be reputed vile.

2934. טָמַן **ṭâman**, *taw-man'*; a prim. root; to *hide* (by *covering* over):—hide, lay privily, in secret.

2935. טֶנֶא **ṭeneʼ**, *teh'-neh*; from an unused root prob. mean. to *weave;* a *basket* (of interlaced osiers):—basket.

2936. טָנַף **ṭânaph**, *taw-naf'*; a prim. root; to *soil:*—defile.

2937. טָעָה **ṭâʻâh**, *taw-aw'*; a prim. root; to *wander;* causat. to *lead astray:*—seduce.

2938. טָעַם **ṭâʻam**, *taw-am'*; a prim. root; to *taste;* fig. to *perceive:*— × but, perceive, taste.

2939. טְעַם **ṭ^{e}ʻam** (Chald.), *teh-am'*; corresp. to 2938; to *taste;* causat. to *feed:*—make to eat, feed.

2940. טַעַם **ṭaʻam**, *tah'-am*; from 2938; prop. a *taste,* i.e. (fig.) *perception;* by impl. *intelligence;* transit. a *mandate:*—advice, behaviour, decree, discretion, judgment, reason, taste, understanding.

2941. טַעַם **ṭaʻam** (Chald.), *tah'-am*; from 2939; prop. a *taste,* i.e. (as in 2940) a judicial *sentence:*—account, × to be commanded, commandment, matter.

2942. טְעֵם **ṭ^{e}ʻêm** (Chald.), *teh-ame'*; from 2939, and equiv. to 2941; prop. *flavor;* fig. *judgment* (both subj. and obj.); hence *account* (both subj. and obj.):— + chancellor, + command, commandment, decree, + regard, taste, wisdom.

2943. טָעַן **ṭâʻan**, *taw-an'*; a prim. root; to *load* a beast:—lade.

2944. טָעַן **ṭâʻan**, *taw-an'*; a prim. root; to *stab:*—thrust through.

2945. טַף **ṭaph**, *taf*; from 2952 (perh. referring to the *tripping* gait of children); a *family* (mostly used collect. in the sing.):—(little) children (ones), families.

2946. טָפַח **ṭâphach**, *taw-fakh'*; a prim. root; to *flatten* out or *extend* (as a tent); fig. to *nurse* a child (as *promotive* of growth); or perh. a denom. from 2947, from *dandling* on the palms:—span, swaddle.

2947. טֵפַח **ṭêphach**, *tay'-fakh*; from 2946; a *spread* of the hand, i.e. a *palm-breadth* (not "span" of the fingers); archit. a *corbel* (as a supporting palm):—coping, hand-breadth.

2948. טֹפַח **ṭôphach**, *to'-fakh*; from 2946 (the same as 2947):—hand-breadth (broad).

2949. טִפֻּח **ṭippûch**, *tip-pookh'*; from 2946; *nursing:*—span long.

2950. טָפַל **ṭâphal**, *taw-fal'*; a prim. root; prop. to *stick* on as a patch; fig. to *impute* falsely:—forge (-r), sew up.

2951. טִפְסַר **ṭiphçar**, *tif-sar'*; of for. der.; a military *governor:*—captain.

2952. טָפַף **ṭâphaph**, *taw-faf'*; a prim. root; appar. to *trip* (with short steps) coquettishly:—mince.

2953. טְפַר **ṭ^{e}phar** (Chald.), *tef-ar'*; from a root corresp. to 6852, and mean. the same as 6856; a finger-*nail;* also a *hoof* or *claw:*—nail.

2954. טָפַשׁ **ṭâphash**, *taw-fash'*; a prim. root; prop. appar. to *be thick;* fig. to *be stupid:*—be fat.

2955. טָפַת **Ṭâphath**, *taw-fath'*; prob. from 5197; a *dropping* (of ointment); *Taphath,* an Israelitess:—Taphath.

2956. טָרַד **ṭârad**, *taw-rad'*; a prim. root; to *drive* on; fig. to *follow* close:—continual.

2957. טְרַד **ṭ^{e}rad** (Chald.), *ter-ad'*; corresp. to 2956; to *expel:*—drive.

2958. טְרוֹם **ṭ^{e}rôwm**, *ter-ome'*; a var. of 2962; *not yet:*—before.

2959. טָרַח **ṭârach**, *taw-rakh'*; a prim. root; to *overburden:*—weary.

2960. טֹרַח **ṭôrach**, *to'-rakh*; from 2959; a *burden:*—cumbrance, trouble.

2961. טָרִי **ṭârîy**, *taw-ree'*; from an unused root appar. mean. to *be moist;* prop. *dripping;* hence *fresh* (i.e. recently made such):—new, putrefying.

2962. טֶרֶם **ṭerem**, *teh'-rem*; from an unused root appar. mean. to *interrupt* or *suspend;* prop. *non-occurrence;* used adv. *not yet* or *before:*—before, ere, not yet.

2963. טָרַף **ṭâraph**, *taw-raf'*; a prim. root; to *pluck* off or *pull* to pieces; causat. to *supply* with food (as in morsels):—catch, × without doubt, feed, ravin, rend in pieces, × surely, tear (in pieces).

2964. טֶרֶף **ṭereph**, *teh'-ref*; from 2963; something *torn,* i.e. a fragment, e.g. a *fresh* leaf, *prey, food:*—leaf, meat, prey, spoil.

2965. טָרָף **ṭârâph**, *taw-rawf'*; from 2963; recently *torn* off, i.e. *fresh:*—pluckt off.

2966. טְרֵפָה **ṭ^{e}rêphâh**, *ter-ay-faw'*; fem. (collect.) of 2964; *prey,* i.e. flocks devoured by animals:—ravin, (that which was) torn (of beasts, in pieces).

2967. טַרְפְּלַי **Ṭarp^{e}lay** (Chald.), *tar-pel-ah'ee*; from a name of for. der.; a *Tarpelite* (collect.) or inhab. of Tarpel, a place in Assyria:—Tarpelites.

י

2968. יָאַב **yâʼab**, *yaw-ab'*; a prim. root; to *desire:*—long.

2969. יָאָה **yâʼâh**, *yaw-aw'*; a prim. root; to *be suitable:*—appertain.

יְאֹר **y^{e}ʼôwr**. See 2975.

2970. יַאֲזַנְיָה **Yaʼăzanyâh**, *yah-az-an-yaw'*; or יַאֲזַנְיָהוּ **Yaʼăzanyâhûw**, *yah-az-an-yaw'-hoo*; from 238 and 3050; *heard of Jah; Jaazanjah,* the name of four Isr.:—Jaazaniah. Comp. 3153.

2971. יָאִיר **Yâʼîyr**, *yaw-ere'*; from 215; *enlightener; Jaïr,* the name of four Isr.:—Jair.

2972. יָאִרִי **Yâʼirîy**, *yaw-ee-ree'*; patron. from 2971; a *Jaïrite* or desc. of Jair:—Jairite.

2973. יָאַל **yâʼal**, *yaw-al'*; a prim. root; prop. to *be slack,* i.e. (fig.) to *be foolish:*—dote, be (become, do) foolish (-ly).

2974. יָאַל **yâʼal**, *yaw-al'*; a prim. root [prob. rather the same as 2973 through the idea of mental *weakness*]; prop. to *yield,* espec. *assent;* hence (pos.) to *undertake* as an act of volition:—assay, begin, be content, please, take upon, × willingly, would.

2975. יְאֹר **y^{e}ʼôr**, *yeh-ore'*; of Eg. or.; a *channel,* e.g. a fosse, canal, shaft; spec. the *Nile,* as the one river of Egypt, including its collat. trenches; also the *Tigris,* as the main river of Assyria:—brook, flood, river, stream.

2976. יָאַשׁ **yâʼash**, *yaw-ash'*; a prim. root; to *desist,* i.e. (fig.) to *despond:*—(cause to) despair, one that is desperate, be no hope.

2977. יֹאשִׁיָּה **Yôʼshîyâh**, *yo-shee-yaw'*; or יֹאשִׁיָּהוּ **Yôʼshîyâhûw**, *yo-she-yaw'-hoo*; from the same root as 803 and 3050; *founded of Jah; Joshijah,* the name of two Isr.:—Josiah.

2978. יְאִתוֹן **y^{e}ʼîthôwn**, *yeh-ee-thone'*; from 857; an *entry:*—entrance.

2979. יְאָתְרַי **y^{e}ʼâth^{e}ray**, *yeh-aw-ther-ah'ee*; from the same as 871; *stepping; Jeätherai,* an Isr.:—Jeaterai.

2980. יָבַב **yâbab**, *yaw-bab*; a prim. root; to *bawl:*—cry out.

2981. יְבוּל **y^{e}bûwl**, *yeb-ool'*; from 2986; *produce,* i.e. a *crop* or (fig.) *wealth:*—fruit, increase.

2982. יְבוּס **Y^{e}bûwç**, *yeb-oos'*; from 947; *trodden,* i.e. threshing-place; *Jebus,* the aboriginal name of Jerus.:—Jebus.

2983. יְבוּסִי **Y^{e}bûwçîy**, *yeb-oo-see'*; patrial from 2982; a *Jebusite* or inhab. of Jebus:—Jebusite (-s).

2984. יִבְחַר **Yibchar**, *yib-khar'*; from 977; *choice; Jibchar,* an Isr.:—Ibhar.

2985. יָבִין **Yâbîyn**, *yaw-bene'*; from 995; *intelligent; Jabin,* the name of two Canaanitish kings:—Jabin.

יָבֵישׁ **Yâbêysh**. See 3003.

2986. יָבַל **yâbal**, *yaw-bal'*; a prim. root; prop. to *flow;* causat. to *bring* (espec. with pomp):—bring (forth), carry, lead (forth).

2987. יְבַל **y^{e}bal** (Chald.), *yeb-al'*; corresp. to 2986; to *bring:*—bring, carry.

יֹבֵל **yôbêl**. See 3104.

2988. יָבָל **yâbâl**, *yaw-bawl'*; from 2986; a *stream:*—[water-] course, stream.

2989. יָבָל **Yâbâl**, *yaw-bawl'*; the same as 2988; *Jabal,* an antediluvian:—Jabal.

יֹבֵל **yôbêl**. See 3104.

2990. יַבֵּל **yabbêl**, *yab-bale'*; from 2986; having *running* sores:—wen.

2991. יִבְלְעָם **Yibl^{e}ʻâm**, *yib-leh-awm'*; from 1104 and 5971; *devouring people; Jibleäm,* a place in Pal.:—Ibleam.

2992. יָבַם **yâbam**, *yaw-bam'*; a prim. root of doubtful mean.; used only as a denom. from 2993; to *marry* a (deceased) brother's widow:—perform the duty of a husband's brother, marry.

2993. יָבָם **yâbâm**, *yaw-bawm'*; from (the orig. of) 2992; a *brother-in-law:*—husband's brother.

2994. יְבֵמֶת **y^{e}bêmeth**, *yeb-ay'-meth*; fem. part. of 2992; a *sister-in-law:*—brother's wife, sister in law.

2995. יַבְנְאֵל **Yabn^{e}ʼêl**, *yab-neh-ale'*; from 1129 and 410; *built of God; Jabneël,* the name of two places in Pal.:—Jabneel.

2996. יַבְנֶה **Yabneh**, *yab-neh'*; from 1129; a *building; Jabneh,* a place in Pal.:—Jabneh.

2997. יִבְנְיָה **Yibn^{e}yâh**, *yib-neh-yaw'*; from 1129 and 3050; *built of Jah; Jibnejah,* an Isr.:—Ibneiah.

2998. יִבְנִיָּה **Yibnîyâh**, *yib-nee-yaw'*; from 1129 and 3050; *building of Jah; Jibnijah,* an Isr.:—Ibnijah.

2999. יַבֹּק **Yabbôq**, *yab-boke'*; prob. from 1238; *pouring* forth; *Jabbok,* a river E. of the Jordan:—Jabbok.

3000. יְבֶרֶכְיָהוּ **Y^{e}berekyâhûw**, *yeb-eh-rek-yaw'-hoo*; from 1288 and 3050; *blessed of Jah; Jeberekjah,* an Isr.:—Jeberechiah.

3001. יָבֵשׁ **yâbêsh**, *yaw-bashe'*; a prim. root; to *be ashamed, confused* or *disappointed;* also (as failing) to *dry* up (as water) or *wither* (as herbage):—be ashamed, clean, be confounded, (make) dry (up), (do) shame (-fully), × utterly, wither (away).

3002. יָבֵשׁ **yâbêsh**, *yaw-bashe'*; from 3001: *dry*:—dried (away), dry.

3003. יָבֵשׁ **Yâbêsh**, *yaw-bashe'*; the same as 3002 (also

יָבֵישׁ **Yâbêysh**, *yaw-bashe'*; often with the addition of 1568, i.e. *Jabesh of Gilad*); *Jabesh*, the name of an Isr. and of a place in Pal.:—Jabesh ([-Gilead]).

3004. יַבָּשָׁה **yabbâshâh**, *yab-baw-shaw'*; from 3001; *dry* ground:—dry (ground, land).

3005. יִבְשָׂם **Yibsâm**, *yib-sawm'*; from the same as 1314; *fragrant; Jibsam*, an Isr.:—Jibsam.

3006. יַבֶּשֶׁת **yabbesheth**, *yab-beh'-sheth*; a var. of 3004; *dry* ground:—dry land.

3007. יַבֶּשֶׁת **yabbesheth** (Chald.), *yab-beh'-sheth*; corresp. to 3006; *dry* land:—earth.

3008. יִגְאָל **Yig'âl**, *yig-awl'*; from 1350; *avenger; Jigal*, the name of three Isr.:—Igal, Igeal.

3009. יָגַב **yâgab**, *yaw-gab'*; a prim. root; to *dig* or plough:—husbandman.

3010. יָגֵב **yâgêb**, *yaw-gabe'*; from 3009; a ploughed *field*:—field.

3011. יָגְבְּהָה **Yogbehâh**, *yog-beh-haw'*; fem. from 1361; *hillock; Jogbehah*, a place E. of the Jordan:—Jogbehah.

3012. יִגְדַּלְיָהוּ **Yigdalyâhûw**, *yig-dal-yaw'-hoo*; from 1431 and 3050; *magnified of Jah; Jigdaljah*, an Isr.:—Igdaliah.

3013. יָגָה **yâgâh**, *yaw-gaw'*; a prim. root; to *grieve*:—afflict, cause grief, grieve, sorrowful, vex.

3014. יָגָה **yâgâh**, *yaw-gaw'*; a prim. root [prob. rather the same as 3013 through the common idea of *dissatisfaction*]; to *push* away:—be removed.

3015. יָגוֹן **yâgôwn**, *yaw-gohn'*; from 3013; *affliction*:—grief, sorrow.

3016. יָגוֹר **yâgôwr**, *yaw-gore'*; from 3025; *fearful*:—afraid, fearest.

3017. יָגוּר **Yâgûwr**, *yaw-goor'*; prob. from 1481; a *lodging; Jagur*, a place in Pal.:—Jagur.

3018. יְגִיעַ **yegîya'**, *yeg-ee'-ah*; from 3021; *toil*; hence a *work, produce, property* (as the result of labor):—labour, work.

3019. יָגִיעַ **yâgîya'**, *yaw-ghee'-ah*; from 3021; *tired*:—weary.

3020. יָגְלִי **Yoglîy**, *yog-lee'*; from 1540; *exiled; Jogli*, an Isr.:—Jogli.

3021. יָגַע **yâga'**, *yaw-gah'*; a prim. root; prop. to *gasp*; hence to *be exhausted*, to *tire*, to *toil*:—faint, (make to) labour, (be) weary.

3022. יָגָע **yâgâ'**, *yaw-gaw'*; from 3021; *earnings* (as the product of toil):—that which he laboured for.

3023. יָגֵעַ **yâgêa'**, *yaw-gay'-ah*; from 3021; *tired*; hence (trans.) *tiresome*:—full of labour, weary.

3024. יְגִעָה **yegî'âh**, *yeg-ee-aw'*; fem. of 3019; *fatigue*:—weariness.

3025. יָגֹר **yâgôr**, *yaw-gore'*; a prim. root; to *fear*:—be afraid, fear.

3026. יְגַר שַׂהֲדוּתָא **Yegar Sahădûwthâ'** (Chald.), *yegar' sah-had-oo-thaw'*; from a word derived from an unused root (mean. to *gather*) and a der. of a root corresp. to 7717; *heap of the testimony; Jegar-Sahadutha*, a cairn E. of the Jordan:—Jegar-Sahadutha.

3027. יָד **yâd**, *yawd*; a prim. word; a *hand* (the *open* one [indicating *power, means, direction*, etc.], in distinction from 3709, the *closed* one); used (as noun, adv., etc.) in a great variety of applications, both lit. and fig., both proximate and remote [as follow]:—(+ be) able, × about, + armholes, at, axletree, because of, beside, border, × bounty, + broad, [broken-] handed, × by, charge, coast, + consecrate, + creditor, custody, debt, dominion, × enough, + fellowship, force, × from, hand [-staves, -y work], × he, himself, × in, labour, + large, ledge, [left-] handed, means, × mine, ministry, near, × of, × order, ordinance, × our, parts, pain, power, × presumptuously, service, side, sore, state, stay, draw with strength, stroke, + swear, terror, × thee, × by them, × themselves, × thine own, × thou, through, × throwing, + thumb, times, × to, × under, × us, × wait on, [way-] side, where, + wide, × with (him, me, you), work, + yield, × yourselves.

3028. יַד **yad** (Chald.), *yad*; corresp. to 3027:—hand, power.

3029. יְדָא **yedâ'** (Chald.), *yed-aw'*; corresp. to 3034; to *praise*:—(give) thank (-s).

3030. יִדְאֲלָה **Yidălâh**, *yid-al-aw'*; of uncert. der. *Jidalah*, a place in Pal.:—Idalah.

3031. יִדְבָּשׁ **Yidbâsh**, *yid-bawsh'*; from the same as 1706; perh. *honeyed; Jidbash*, an Isr.:—Idbash.

3032. יָדַד **yâdad**, *yaw-dad'*; a prim. root; prop. to *handle* [comp. 3034], i.e. to *throw*, e.g. lots:—cast.

3033. יְדִדוּת **yedîdûwth**, *yed-ee-dooth'*; from 3039; prop. *affection*; concr. a *darling* object:—dearly beloved.

3034. יָדָה **yâdâh**, *yaw-daw'*; a prim. root; used only as denom. from 3027; lit. to *use* (i.e. hold out) *the hand*; phys. to *throw* (a stone, an arrow) at or away; espec. to *revere* or *worship* (with extended hands); intens. to *bemoan* (by wringing the hands):—cast (out), (make) confess (-ion), praise, shoot, (give) thank (-ful, -s, -sgiving).

3035. יִדּוֹ **Yiddôw**, *yid-do'*; from 3034; *praised; Jiddo*, an Isr.:—Iddo.

3036. יָדוֹן **Yâdôwn**, *yaw-done'*; from 3034; *thankful; Jadon*, an Isr.:—Jadon.

3037. יַדּוּעַ **Yaddûwa'**, *yad-doo'-ah*; from 3045; *knowing; Jaddua*, the name of two Isr.:—Jaddua.

3038. יְדוּתוּן **Yedûwthûwn**, *yed-oo-thoon'*; or

יְדֻתוּן **Yedûthûwn**, *yed-oo-thoon'*; or

יְדִיתוּן **Yedîythûwn**, *yed-ee-thoon'*; prob. from 3034; *laudatory; Jeduthun*, an Isr.:—Jeduthun.

3039. יְדִיד **yedîyd**, *yed-eed'*; from the same as 1730; *loved*:—amiable, (well-) beloved, loves.

3040. יְדִידָה **Yedîydâh**, *yed-ee-daw'*; fem. of 3039; *beloved; Jedidah*, an Israelitess:—Jedidah.

3041. יְדִידְיָה **Yedîydeyâh**, *yed-ee-deh-yaw'*; from 3039 and 3050; *beloved of Jah; Jedidejah*, a name of Solomon:—Jedidiah.

3042. יְדָיָה **Yedâyâh**, *yed-aw-yaw'*; from 3034 and 3050; *praised of Jah; Jedajah*, the name of two Isr.:—Jedaiah.

3043. יְדִיעֲאֵל **Yedîy'ă'êl**, *yed-ee-ah-ale'*; from 3045 and 410; *knowing God; Jediaël*, the name of three Isr.:—Jediael.

3044. יִדְלָף **Yidlâph**, *yid-lawf'*; from 1811; *tearful; Jidlaph*, a Mesopotamian:—Jidlaph.

3045. יָדַע **yâda'**, *yaw-dah'*; a prim. root; to *know* (prop. to ascertain by *seeing*); used in a great variety of senses, fig., lit., euphem. and infer. (including *observation, care, recognition*; and causat. *instruction, designation, punishment*, etc.) [as follow]:—acknowledge, acquaintance (-ted with), advise, answer, appoint, assuredly, be aware, [un-] awares, can [-not], certainly, for a certainty, comprehend, consider, × could they, cunning, declare, be diligent, (can, cause to) discern, discover, endued with, familiar friend, famous, feel, can have, be [ig-] norant, instruct, kinsfolk, kinsman, (cause to, let, make) know, (come to give, have, take) knowledge, have [knowledge], (be, make, make to be, make self) known, + be learned, + lie by man, mark, perceive, privy to, × prognosticator, regard, have respect, skilful, shew, can (man of) skill, be sure, of a surety, teach, (can) tell, understand, have [understanding], × will be, wist, wit, wot.

3046. יְדַע **yeda'** (Chald.), *yed-ah'*; corresp. to 3045:—certify, know, make known, teach.

3047. יָדָע **Yâdâ'**, *yaw-daw'*; from 3045; *knowing; Jada*, an Isr.:—Jada.

3048. יְדַעְיָה **Yeda'yâh**, *yed-ah-yaw'*; from 3045 and 3050; *Jah has known; Jedajah*, the name of two Isr.:—Jedaiah.

3049. יִדְּעֹנִי **yidde'ônîy**, *yid-deh-o-nee'*; from 3045; prop. a *knowing* one; spec. a *conjurer*; (by impl.) a *ghost*:—wizard.

3050. יָהּ **Yâhh**, *yaw*; contr. for 3068, and mean. the same; *Jah*, the sacred name:—Jah, the Lord, most vehement. Cp. names in "-iah," "-jah."

3051. יָהַב **yâhab**, *yaw-hab'*; a prim. root; to *give* (whether lit. or fig.); gen. to *put*; imper. (reflex.) *come*:—ascribe, bring, come on, give, go, set, take.

3052. יְהַב **yehab** (Chald.), *yeh-hab'*; corresp. to 3051:—deliver, give, lay, + prolong, pay, yield.

3053. יְהָב **yehâb**, *yeh-hawb'*; from 3051; prop. what is *given* (by Providence), i.e. a *lot*:—burden.

3054. יָהַד **yâhad**, *yaw-had'*; denom. from a form corresp. to 3061; to *Judaize*, i.e. become Jewish:—become Jews.

3055. יְהֻד **Yehûd**, *yeh-hood'*; a briefer form of one corresp. to 3061; *Jehud*, a place in Pal.:—Jehud.

3056. יֶהְדַּי **Yehday**, *yeh-dah'ee*; perh. from a form corresp. to 3061; *Judaistic; Jehdai*, an Isr.:—Jehdai.

3057. יְהֻדִיָּה **Yehûdîyâh**, *yeh-hoo-dee-yaw'*; fem. of 3064; *Jehudijah*, a Jewess:—Jehudijah.

3058. יֵהוּא **Yêhûw'**, *yay-hoo'*; from 3068 and 1931; *Jehovah (is) He; Jehu*, the name of five Isr.:—Jehu.

3059. יְהוֹאָחָז **Yehôw'âchâz**, *yeh-ho-aw-khawz'*; from 3068 and 270; *Jehovah-seized; Jehoächaz*, the name of three Isr.:—Jehoahaz. Comp. 3099.

3060. יְהוֹאָשׁ **Yehôw'âsh**, *yeh-ho-awsh'*; from 3068 and (perh.) 784; *Jehovah-fired; Jehoäsh*, the name of two Isr. kings:—Jehoash Comp. 3101.

3061. יְהוּד **Yehûwd** (Chald.), *yeh-hood'*; contr. from a form corresp. to 3063; prop. *Judah*, hence *Judæa*:—Jewry, Judah, Judea.

3062. יְהוּדָאִי **Yehûwdâ'îy** (Chald.), *yeh-hoo-daw-ee'*; patrial from 3061; a *Jehudaïte* (or Judaite), i.e. Jew:—Jew.

3063. יְהוּדָה **Yehûwdâh**, *yeh-hoo-daw'*; from 3034; *celebrated; Jehudah* (or Judah), the name of five Isr.; also of the tribe descended from the first, and of its territory:—Judah.

3064. יְהוּדִי **Yehûwdîy**, *yeh-hoo-dee'*; patron. from 3063; a *Jehudite* (i.e. Judaite or Jew), or desc. of Jehudah (i.e. Judah):—Jew.

3065. יְהוּדִי **Yehûwdîy**, *yeh-hoo-dee'*; the same as 3064; *Jehudi*, an Isr.:—Jehudi.

3066. יְהוּדִית **Yehûwdîyth**, *yeh-hoo-deeth'*; fem. of 3064; the *Jewish* (used adv.) language:—in the Jews' language.

3067. יְהוּדִית **Yehûwdîyth**, *yeh-hoo-deeth'*; the same as 3066; *Jewess; Jehudith*, a Canaanitess:—Judith.

3068. יְהֹוָה **Yehôvâh**, *yeh-ho-vaw'*; from 1961; (the) self-*Existent* or Eternal; *Jehovah*, Jewish national name of God:—Jehovah, the Lord. Comp. 3050, 3069.

3069. יְהֹוִה **Yehôvîh**, *yeh-ho-vee'*; a var. of 3068 [used after 136, and pronounced by Jews as 430, in order to prevent the repetition of the same sound, since they elsewhere pronounce 3068 as 136]:—God.

3070. יְהֹוָה יִרְאֶה **Yehôvâh yireh**, *yeh-ho-vaw' yir-eh'*; from 3068 and 7200; *Jehovah will see* (to it); *Jehovah-Jireh*, a symbolical name for Mt. Moriah:—Jehovah-jireh.

3071. יְהֹוָה נִסִּי **Yehôvâh niççîy**, *yeh-ho-vaw' nis-see'*; from 3068 and 5251 with pron. suffix.; *Jehovah (is) my banner; Jehovah-Nissi*, a symbolical name of an altar in the Desert.—Jehovah-nissi.

3072. יְהֹוָה צִדְקֵנוּ **Yehôvâh tsidqênûw**, *yeh-ho-vaw' tsid-kay'-noo*; from 3068 and 6664 with pron. suffix.; *Jehovah (is) our right; Jehovah-Tsidkenu*, a symbolical epithet of the Messiah and of Jerus.:—the Lord our righteousness.

3073. יְהוָֹה שָׁלוֹם **Yᵉhôvâh shâlôwm**, *yeh-ho-vaw' shaw-lome'*; from 3068 and 7965; *Jehovah* (is) *peace*; *Jehovah-Shalom*, a symbolical name of an altar in Pal.:—Jehovah-shalom.

3074. יְהוָֹה שָׁמָּה **Yᵉhôvâh shâmmâh**, *yeh-ho-vaw' shawm'-maw*; from 3068 and 8033 with directive enclitic; *Jehovah* (is) *thither*; *Jehovah-Shammah*, a symbol. title of Jerus.:—Jehovah-shammah.

3075. יְהוֹזָבָד **Yᵉhôwzâbâd**, *yeh-ho-zaw-bawd'*; from 3068 and 2064; *Jehovah-endowed*; *Jehozabad*, the name of three Isr.:—Jehozabad. Comp. 3107.

3076. יְהוֹחָנָן **Yᵉhôwchânân**, *yeh-ho-khaw-nawn'*; from 3068 and 2603; *Jehovah-favored*; *Jehochanan*, the name of eight Isr.:—Jehohanan, Johanan. Comp. 3110.

3077. יְהוֹיָדָע **Yᵉhôwyâdâʻ**, *yeh-ho-yaw-daw'*; from 3068 and 3045; *Jehovah-known*; *Jehojada*, the name of three Isr.:—Jehoiada. Comp. 3111.

3078. יְהוֹיָכִין **Yᵉhôwyâkîyn**, *yeh-ho-yaw-keen'*; from 3068 and 3559; *Jehovah will establish*; *Jehojakin*, a Jewish king:—Jehoiachin. Comp. 3112.

3079. יְהוֹיָקִים **Yᵉhôwyâqîym**, *yeh-ho-yaw-keem'*; from 3068 abbrev. and 6965; *Jehovah will raise*; *Jehojakim*, a Jewish king:—Jehoiakim. Comp. 3113.

3080. יְהוֹיָרִיב **Yᵉhôwyârîyb**, *yeh-ho-yaw-reeb'*; from 3068 and 7378; *Jehovah will contend*; *Jehojarib*, the name of two Isr.:—Jehoiarib. Comp. 3114.

3081. יְהוּכַל **Yᵉhûwkal**, *yeh-hoo-kal'*; from 3201; *potent*; *Jehukal*, an Isr.:—Jehucal. Comp. 3116.

3082. יְהוֹנָדָב **Yᵉhôwnâdâb**, *yeh-ho-naw-dawb'*; from 3068 and 5068; *Jehovah-largessed*; *Jehonadab*, the name of an Isr. and of an Arab:—Jehonadab, Jonadab. Comp. 3122.

3083. יְהוֹנָתָן **Yᵉhôwnâthân**, *yeh-ho-naw-thawn'*; from 3068 and 5414; *Jehovah-given*; *Jehonathan*, the name of four Isr.:—Jonathan. Comp. 3129.

3084. יְהוֹסֵף **Yᵉhôwçêph**, *yeh-ho-safe'*; a fuller form of 3130; *Jehoseph* (i.e. Joseph), a son of Jacob:—Joseph.

3085. יְהוֹעַדָּה **Yᵉhôwʻaddâh**, *yeh-ho-ad-daw'*; from 3068 and 5710; *Jehovah-adorned*; *Jehoäddah*, an Isr.:—Jehoada.

3086. יְהוֹעַדִּין **Yᵉhôwʻaddîyn**, *yeh-ho-ad-deen'*; or
יְהוֹעַדָּן **Yᵉhôwaddân**, *yeh-ho-ad-dawn'*; from 3068 and 5727; *Jehovah-pleased*; *Jehoäddin* or *Jehoäddan*, an Israelitess:—Jehoaddan.

3087. יְהוֹצָדָק **Yᵉhôwtsâdâq**, *yeh-ho-tsaw-dawk'*; from 3068 and 6663; *Jehovah-righted*; *Jehotsadak*, an Isr.:—Jehozadek, Josedech. Comp. 3136.

3088. יְהוֹרָם **Yᵉhôwrâm**, *yeh-ho-rawm'*; from 3068 and 7311; *Jehovah-raised*; *Jehoram*, the name of a Syrian and of three Isr.:—Jehoram, Joram. Comp. 3141.

3089. יְהוֹשֶׁבַע **Yᵉhôwshebaʻ**, *yeh-ho-sheh'-bah*; from 3068 and 7650; *Jehovah-sworn*; *Jehosheba*, an Israelitess:—Jehosheba. Comp. 3090.

3090. יְהוֹשַׁבְעַת **Yᵉhôwshabʻath**, *yeh-ho-shab-ath'*; a form of 3089; *Jehoshabath*, an Israelitess:—Jehoshabeath.

3091. יְהוֹשׁוּעַ **Yᵉhôwshûwaʻ**, *yeh-ho-shoo'-ah*; or
יְהוֹשֻׁעַ **Yᵉhôwshûʻa**, *yeh-ho-shoo'-ah*; from 3068 and 3467; *Jehovah-saved*; *Jehoshuä* (i.e. Joshua), the Jewish leader:—Jehoshua, Jehoshuah, Joshua. Comp. 1954, 3442.

3092. יְהוֹשָׁפָט **Yᵉhôwshâphâṭ**, *yeh-ho-shaw-fawt'*; from 3068 and 8199; *Jehovah-judged*; *Jehoshaphat*, the name of six Isr.; also of a valley near Jerus.:—Jehoshaphat. Comp. 3146.

3093. יָהִיר **yâhîyr**, *yaw-here'*; prob. from the same as 2022; *elated*; hence *arrogant*:—haughty, proud.

3094. יְהַלֶּלְאֵל **Yᵉhallelʼêl**, *yeh-hal-lel-ale'*; from 1984 and 410; *praising God*; *Jehalleiel*, the name of two Isr.:—Jehaleleel, Jehalelel.

3095. יַהֲלֹם **yahălôm**, *yah-hal-ome'*; from 1986 (in the sense of *hardness*); a precious stone, prob. *onyx*:—diamond.

3096. יַהַץ **Yahats**, *yah'-hats*; or
יַהְצָה **Yahtsâh**, *yah'-tsaw*; or (fem.)
יַהְצָה **Yahtsâh**, *yah-tsaw'*; from an unused root mean. to *stamp*; perh. *threshing*-floor; *Jahats* or *Jahtsah*, a place E. of the Jordan:—Jahaz, Jahazah, Jahzah.

3097. יוֹאָב **Yôwʼâb**, *yo-awb'*; from 3068 and 1; *Jehovah-fathered*; *Joäb*, the name of three Isr.:—Joab.

3098. יוֹאָח **Yôwʼâch**, *yo-awkh'*; from 3068 and 251; *Jehovah-brothered*; *Joach*, the name of four Isr.:—Joah.

3099. יוֹאָחָז **Yôwʼâchâz**, *yo-aw-khawz'*; a form of 3059; *Joächaz*, the name of two Isr.:—Jehoahaz, Joahaz.

3100. יוֹאֵל **Yôwʼêl**, *yo-ale'*; from 3068 and 410; *Jehovah* (is his) *God*; *Joël*, the name of twelve Isr.:—Joel.

3101. יוֹאָשׁ **Yôwʼâsh**, *yo-awsh'*; or
יֹאָשׁ **Yôʼâsh** (2 Chron. 24 : 1), *yo-awsh'*; a form of 3060; *Joäsh*, the name of six Isr.:—Joash.

3102. יוֹב **Yôwb**, *yobe*; perh. a form of 3103, but more prob. by err. transc. for 3437; *Job*, an Isr.:—Job.

3103. יוֹבָב **Yôwbâb**, *yo-bawb'*; from 2980; *howler*; *Jobab*, the name of two Isr. and of three foreigners:—Jobab.

3104. יוֹבֵל **yôwbêl**, *yo-bale'*; or
יֹבֵל **yôbêl**, *yo-bale'*; appar. from 2986; the *blast* of a horn (from its *continuous* sound); spec. the *signal* of the silver trumpets; hence the instrument itself and the festival thus introduced:—jubile, ram's horn, trumpet.

3105. יוּבַל **yûwbal**, *yoo-bal'*; from 2986; a *stream*:—river.

3106. יוּבָל **Yûwbâl**, *yoo-bawl'*; from 2986; *stream*; *Jubal*, an antediluvian:—Jubal.

3107. יוֹזָבָד **Yôwzâbâd**, *yo-zaw-bawd'*; a form of 3075; *Jozabad*, the name of ten Isr:—Josabad, Jozabad.

3108. יוֹזָכָר **Yôwzâkâr**, *yo-zaw-kawr'*; from 3068 and 2142; *Jehovah-remembered*; *Jozacar*, an Isr.:—Jozachar.

3109. יוֹחָא **Yôwchâʼ**, *yo-khaw'*; prob. from 3068 and a var. of 2421; *Jehovah-revived*; *Jocha*, the name of two Isr.:—Joha.

3110. יוֹחָנָן **Yôwchânân**, *yo-khaw-nawn'*; a form of 3076; *Jochanan*, the name of nine Isr.:—Johanan.

יוּטָה **Yûwṭâh**. See 3194.

3111. יוֹיָדָע **Yôwyâdâʻ**, *yo-yaw-daw'*; a form of 3077; *Jojada*, the name of two Isr.:—Jehoiada, Joiada.

3112. יוֹיָכִין **Yôwyâkîyn**, *yo-yaw-keen'*; a form of 3078; *Jojakin*, an Isr. king:—Jehoiachin.

3113. יוֹיָקִים **Yôwyâqîym**, *yo-yaw-keem'*; a form of 3079; *Jojakim*, an Isr.:—Joiakim. Comp. 3137.

3114. יוֹיָרִיב **Yôwyârîyb**, *yo-yaw-reeb'*; a form of 3080; *Jojarib*, the name of four Isr.:—Joiarib.

3115. יוֹכֶבֶד **Yôwkebed**, *yo-keh'-bed*; from 3068 contr. and 3513; *Jehovah-gloried*; *Jokebed*, the mother of Moses:—Jochebed.

3116. יוּכַל **Yûwkal**, *yoo-kal'*; a form of 3081; *Jukal*, an Isr.:—Jucal.

3117. יוֹם **yôwm**, *yome*; from an unused root mean. to *be hot*; a *day* (as the *warm* hours), whether lit. (from sunrise to sunset, or from one sunset to the next), or fig. (a space of time defined by an associated term), [often used adv.]:—age, + always, + chronicles, continually (-ance), daily, ([birth-], each, to) day, (now a, two) days (agone), + elder, × end, + evening, + (for) ever (-lasting, -more), × full, life, as (so) long as (. . . live), (even) now, + old, + outlived, + perpetually, presently, + remaineth, × required, season, × since, space, then, (process of) time, + as at other times, + in trouble, weather, (as) when, (a, the, within a) while (that), × whole (+ age), (full) year (-ly), + younger.

3118. יוֹם **yôwm** (Chald.), *yome*; corresp. to 3117; a *day*:—day (by day), time.

3119. יוֹמָם **yôwmâm**, *yo-mawm'*; from 3117; *daily*:—daily, (by, in the) day (-time).

3120. יָוָן **Yâvân**, *yaw-vawn'*; prob. from the same as 3196; *effervescing* (i.e. hot and active); *Javan*, the name of a son of Joktan, and of the race (*Ionians*, i.e. Greeks) descended from him, with their territory; also of a place in Arabia:—Javan.

3121. יָוֵן **yâvên**, *yaw-ven'*; from the same as 3196; prop. *dregs* (as *effervescing*); hence *mud*:—mire, miry.

3122. יוֹנָדָב **Yôwnâdâb**, *yo-naw-dawb'*; a form of 3082; *Jonadab*, the name of an Isr. and of a Rechabite:—Jonadab.

3123. יוֹנָה **yôwnâh**, *yo-naw'*; prob. from the same as 3196; a *dove* (appar. from the *warmth* of their mating):—dove, pigeon.

3124. יוֹנָה **Yônâh**, *yo-naw'*; the same as 3123; *Jonah*, an Isr.:—Jonah.

3125. יְוָנִי **Yᵉvânîy**, *yev-aw-nee'*; patron. from 3121; a *Jevanite*, or desc. of Javan:—Grecian.

3126. יוֹנֵק **yôwnêq**, *yo-nake'*; act. part. of 3243; a *sucker*; hence a *twig* (of a tree felled and sprouting):—tender plant.

3127. יוֹנֶקֶת **yôwneqeth**, *yo-neh'-keth*; fem. of 3126; a *sprout*:—(tender) branch, young twig.

3128. יוֹנַת אֵלֶם רְחֹקִים **yôwnath ʼêlem rᵉchôqîym**, *yo-nath' ay'-lem rekh-o-keem'*; from 3123 and 482 and the plur. of 7350; *dove of* (the) *silence* (i.e. *dumb* Israel) *of* (i.e. among) *distances* (i.e. strangers); the title of a ditty (used for a name of its melody):—Jonath-elem-rechokim.

3129. יוֹנָתָן **Yôwnâthân**, *yo-naw-thawn'*; a form of 3083; *Jonathan*, the name of ten Isr.:—Jonathan.

3130. יוֹסֵף **Yôwçêph**, *yo-safe'*; fut. of 3254; *let him add* (or perh. simply act. part. *adding*); *Joseph*, the name of seven Isr.:—Joseph. Comp. 3084.

3131. יוֹסִפְיָה **Yôwçiphyâh**, *yo-sif-yaw'*; from act. part. of 3254 and 3050; *Jah* (is) *adding*; *Josiphjah*, an Isr.:—Josiphiah.

3132. יוֹעֵאלָה **Yôwʻêʼlâh**, *yo-ay-law'*; perh. fem. act. part. of 3276; *furthermore*; *Joelah*, an Isr.:—Joelah.

3133. יוֹעֵד **Yôwʻêd**, *yo-ade'*; appar. act. part. of 3259; *appointer*; *Joed*, an Isr.:—Joed.

3134. יוֹעֶזֶר **Yôwʻezer**, *yo-eh'-zer*; from 3068 and 5828; *Jehovah* (is his) *help*; *Joezer*, an Isr.:—Joezer.

3135. יוֹעָשׁ **Yôwʻâsh**, *yo-awsh'*; from 3068 and 5789; *Jehovah-hastened*; *Joash*, the name of two Isr.:—Joash.

3136. יוֹצָדָק **Yôwtsâdâq**, *yo-tsaw-dawk'*; a form of 3087; *Jotsadak*, an Isr.:—Jozadak.

3137. יוֹקִים **Yôwqîym**, *yo-keem'*; a form of 3113; *Jokim*, an Isr.:—Jokim.

3138. יוֹרֶה **yôwreh**, *yo-reh'*; act. part. of 3384; *sprinkling*; hence a *sprinkling* (or autumnal showers):—first rain, former [rain].

3139. יוֹרָה **Yôwrâh**, *yo-raw'*; from 3384; *rainy*; *Jorah*, an Isr.:—Jorah.

3140. יוֹרַי **Yôwray**, *yo-rah'-ee*; from 3384; *rainy*; *Jorai*, an Isr.:—Jorai.

3141. יוֹרָם **Yôwrâm**, *yo-rawm'*; a form of 3088; *Joram*, the name of three Isr. and one Syrian:—Joram.

3142. יוּשַׁב חֶסֶד **Yûwshab Cheçed**, *yoo-shab' kheh'-sed*; from 7725 and 2617; *kindness will be returned*; *Jushab-Chesed*, an Isr.:—Jushab-hesed.

3143. יוֹשִׁבְיָה **Yôwshîbyâh**, *yo-shib-yaw'*; from 3427 and 3050; *Jehovah will cause to dwell; Joshibjah*, an Isr.:—Josibiah.

3144. יוֹשָׁה **Yôwshâh**, *yo-shaw'*; prob. a form of 3145; *Joshah*, an Isr.:—Joshah.

3145. יוֹשַׁוְיָה **Yôwshavyâh**, *yo-shav-yaw'*; from 3068 and 7737; *Jehovah-set; Joshavjah*, an Isr.:—Joshaviah. Comp. 3144.

3146. יוֹשָׁפָט **Yôwshâphâṭ**, *yo-shaw-fawt'*; a form of 3092; *Joshaphat*, an Isr.:—Joshaphat.

3147. יוֹתָם **Yôwthâm**, *yo-thawm'*; from 3068 and 8535; *Jehovah* (is) *perfect; Jotham*, the name of three Isr.:—Jotham.

3148. יוֹתֵר **yôwthêr**, *yo-thare'*; act. part. of 3498; prop. *redundant;* hence *over and above*, as adj., noun, adv. or conj. [as follows]:—better, more (-over), over, profit.

3149. °יְזַוְאֵל **Y^{e}zav'êl**, *yez-av-ale'*; from an unused root (mean. to *sprinkle*) and 410; *sprinkled of God; Jezavel*, an Isr.:—Jeziel [*from the marg.*].

3150. יִזִּיָּה **Yizzîyâh**, *yiz-zee-yaw'*; from the same as the first part of 3149 and 3050; *sprinkled of Jah; Jizzijah*, an Isr.:—Jeziah.

3151. יָזִיז **Yâzîyz** *yaw-zeez'*; from the same as 2123; *he will make prominent; Jaziz*, an Isr.:—Jaziz.

3152. יִזְלִיאָה **Yizlîy'ah**, *yiz-lee-aw'*; perh. from an unused root (mean. to *draw up*); *he will draw out; Jizliah*, an Isr.:—Jezliah.

3153. יְזַנְיָה **Y^{e}zanyâh**, *yez-an-yaw'*; or

יְזַנְיָהוּ **Y^{e}zanyâhûw**, *yez-an-yaw'-hoo;* prob. for 2970; *Jezanjah*, an Isr.:—Jezaniah.

3154. יֶזַע **yeza'**, *yeh'-zah;* from an unused root mean to *ooze; sweat*, i.e. (by impl.) a *sweating* dress:—any thing that causeth sweat.

3155. יִזְרָח **Yizrâch**, *yiz-rawkh';* a var. for 250; a *Jizrach* (i.e. Ezrachite or Zarchite) or desc. of Zerach:—Izrahite.

3156. יִזְרַחְיָה **Yizrachyâh**, *yiz-rakh-yaw';* from 2224 and 3050; *Jah will shine; Jizrachjah*, the name of two Isr.:—Izrahiah, Jezrahiah.

3157. יִזְרְעֶאל **Yizr^{e}'ê'l**, *yiz-reh-ale';* from 2232 and 410; *God will sow; Jizreël*, the name of two places in Pal. and of two Isr.:—Jezreel.

3158. יִזְרְעֵאלִי **Yizr^{e}'ê'lîy**, *yiz-reh-ay-lee';* patron. from 3157; a *Jizreëlite* or native of Jizreel:—Jezreelite.

3159. יִזְרְעֵאלִית **Yizr^{e}'ê'lîyth**, *yiz-reh-ay-leeth';* fem. of 3158; a *Jezreëlitess:*—Jezreelitess.

3160. יְחֻבָּה **Y^{e}chubbâh**, *yekh-oob-baw';* from 2247; *hidden; Jechubbah*, an Isr.:—Jehubbah.

3161. יָחַד **yâchad**, *yaw-khad';* a prim. root; to *be* (or become) *one:*—join, unite.

3162. יַחַד **yachad**, *yakh'-ad;* from 3161; prop. a *unit*, i.e. (adv.) *unitedly:*—alike, at all (once), both, likewise, only, (al-) together, withal.

3163. יַחְדוֹ **Yachdôw**, *yakh-doe';* from 3162 with pron. suffix; *his unity*, i.e. (adv.) *together; Jachdo*, an Isr.:—Jahdo.

3164. יַחְדִּיאֵל **Yachdîy'êl**, *yakh-dee-ale';* from 3162 and 410; *unity of God; Jachdiël*, an Isr.:—Jahdiel.

3165. יֶחְדִּיָּהוּ **Yechdîyâhûw**, *yekh-dee-yaw'-hoo;* from 3162 and 3050; *unity of Jah; Jechdijah*, the name of two Isr.:—Jehdeiah.

יְחַוְאֵל **Y^{e}chav'êl**. See 3171.

3166. יַחֲזִיאֵל **Yachăzîy'êl**, *yakh-az-ee-ale';* from 2372 and 410; *beheld of God; Jachaziël*, the name of five Isr.:—Jahaziel, Jahziel.

3167. יַחְזְיָה **Yachz^{e}yâh**, *yakh-zeh-yaw';* from 2372 and 3050; *Jah will behold; Jachzejah*, an Isr.:—Jahaziah.

3168. יְחֶזְקֵאל **Y^{e}chezqê'l**, *yekh-ez-kale';* from 2388 and 410; *God will strengthen; Jechezkel*, the name of two Isr.:—Ezekiel, Jehezekel.

3169. יְחִזְקִיָּה **Y^{e}chizqîyâh**, *yekh-iz-kee-yaw';* or

יְחִזְקִיָּהוּ **Y^{e}chizqîyâhûw**, *yekh-iz-kee-yaw'-hoo;* from 3388 and 3050; *strengthened of Jah; Jechizkijah*, the name of five Isr.:—Hezekiah, Jehizkiah. Comp. 2396.

3170. יַחְזֵרָה **Yachzêrâh**, *yakh-zay-raw';* from the same as 2386; perh. *protection; Jachzerah*, an Isr.:—Jahzerah.

3171. יְחִיאֵל **Y^{e}chîy'êl**, *yekh-ee-ale';* or (2 Chron. 29 : 14)

°יְחַוְאֵל **Y^{e}chav'êl**, *yekh-av-ale';* from 2421 and 410; *God will live; Jechiël* (or *Jechavel*), the name of eight Isr.:—Jehiel.

3172. יְחִיאֵלִי **Y^{e}chîy'êlîy**, *yekh-ee-ay-lee';* patron. from 3171; a *Jechiëlite* or desc. of Jechiel:—Jehieli.

3173. יָחִיד **yâchîyd**, *yaw-kheed';* from 3161; prop. *united*, i.e. *sole;* by impl. *beloved;* also *lonely;* (fem.) the *life* (as not to be replaced):—darling, desolate, only (child, son), solitary.

3174. יְחִיָּה **Y^{e}chîyâh**, *yekh-ee-yaw';* from 2421 and 3050; *Jah will live; Jechijah*, an Isr.:—Jehiah.

3175. יָחִיל **yâchîyl**, *yaw-kheel';* from 3176; *expectant:*—should hope.

3176. יָחַל **yâchal**, *yaw-chal';* a prim. root; to *wait;* by impl. to *be patient, hope:*—(cause to, have, make to) hope, be pained, stay, tarry, trust, wait.

3177. יַחְלְאֵל **Yachl^e'êl**, *yakh-leh-ale';* from 3176 and 410; *expectant of God; Jachleël*, an Isr.:—Jahleel.

3178. יַחְלְאֵלִי **Yachl^e'êlîy**, *yakh-leh-ay-lee';* patron. from 3177; a *Jachleëlite* or desc. of Jachleel.:—Jahleelites.

3179. יָחַם **yâcham**, *yaw-kham';* a prim. root; prob. to *be hot;* fig. to *conceive:*—get heat, be hot, conceive, be warm.

3180. יַחְמוּר **yachmûwr**, *yakh-moor';* from 2560; a kind of *deer* (from the color; comp. 2543):—fallow deer.

3181. יַחְמַי **Yachmay**, *yakh-mah'-ee;* prob. from 3179; *hot; Jachmai*, an Isr.:—Jahmai.

3182. יָחֵף **yâchêph**, *yaw-khafe';* from an unused root mean. to *take off the shoes; unsandalled:*—barefoot, being unshod.

3183. יַחְצְאֵל **Yachts^e'êl**, *yakh-tseh-ale';* from 2673 and 410; *God will allot; Jachtseël*, an Isr.:—Jahzeel. Comp. 3185.

3184. יַחְצְאֵלִי **Yachts^e'êlîy**, *yakh-tseh-ay-lee';* patron. from 3183; a *Jachtseëlite* (collect.) or desc. of Jachtseel:—Jahzeelites.

3185. יַחְצִיאֵל **Yachtsîy'êl**, *yakh-tsee-ale';* from 2673 and 410; *allotted of God; Jachtsiël*, an Isr.:—Jahziel. Comp. 3183.

3186. יָחַר **yâchar**, *yaw-khar';* a prim. root; to *delay:*—tarry longer.

3187. יָחַשׂ **yâchas**, *yaw-khas';* a prim. root; to *sprout;* used only as denom. from 3188; to *enroll* by pedigree:—(number after, number throughout the) genealogy (to be reckoned), be reckoned by genealogies.

3188. יַחַשׂ **yachas**, *yakh'-as;* from 3187; a *pedigree* or family list (as *growing* spontaneously):—genealogy.

3189. יַחַת **Yachath**, *yakh'-ath;* from 3161; *unity; Jachath*, the name of four Isr.:—Jahath.

3190. יָטַב **yâṭab**, *yaw-tab';* a prim. root; to *be* (causat.) *make well*, lit. (*sound, beautiful*) or fig. (*happy, successful, right*):—be accepted, amend, use aright, benefit, be (make) better, seem best, make cheerful, be comely, + be content, diligent (-ly), dress, earnestly, find favour, give, be glad, do (be, make) good ([-ness]), be (make) merry, please (+ well), shew more [kindness], skilfully, × very small, surely, make sweet, thoroughly, tire, trim, very, be (can, deal, entreat, go, have) well [said, seen].

3191. יְטַב **y^{e}ṭab** (Chald.), *yet-ab';* corresp. to 3190:—seem good.

3192. יָטְבָה **Yoṭbâh**, *yot-baw';* from 3190; *pleasantness; Jotbah*, a place in Pal.:—Jotbah.

3193. יָטְבָתָה **Yoṭbâthâh**, *yot-baw'-thaw;* from 3192; *Jotbathah*, a place in the Desert:—Jotbath, Jotbathah.

3194. יֻטָּה **Yuṭṭâh**, *yoot-taw';* or

יוּטָה **Yûwṭâh**, *yoo-taw';* from 5186; *extended; Juttah* (or *Jutah*), a place in Pal.:—Juttah.

3195. יְטוּר **Y^{e}ṭûwr**, *yet-oor';* prob. from the same as 2905; *encircled* (i.e. inclosed); *Jetur*, a son of Ishmael:—Jetur.

3196. יַיִן **yayin**, *yah'-yin;* from an unused root mean. to *effervesce; wine* (as fermented); by impl. *intoxication:*—banqueting, wine, wine [-bibber].

3197. יַךְ **yak**, *yak;* by err. transc. for 3027; a *hand* or *side:*—[way-] side.

יָכוֹל **yâkôwl**. See 3201.

יְכוֹנְיָה **Y^{e}kôwn^{e}yâh**. See 3204.

3198. יָכַח **yâkach**, *yaw-kahh';* a prim. root; to *be right* (i.e. correct); recip. to *argue;* causat. to *decide, justify* or *convict:*—appoint, argue, chasten, convince, correct (-ion), daysman, dispute, judge, maintain, plead, reason (together), rebuke, reprove (-r), surely, in any wise.

יְכִילְיָה **Y^{e}kîyl^{e}yâh**. See 3203.

3199. יָכִין **Yâkîyn**, *yaw-keen';* from 3559; *he* (or *it*) *will establish; Jakin*, the name of three Isr. and of a temple pillar:—Jachin.

3200. יָכִינִי **Yâkîynîy**, *yaw-kee-nee';* patron. from 3199; a *Jakinite* (collect.) or desc. of Jakin:—Jachinites.

3201. יָכֹל **yâkôl**, *yaw-kole';* or (fuller)

יָכוֹל **yâkôwl**, *yaw-kole';* a prim. root; to *be able*, lit. (*can, could*) or mor. (*may, might*):—be able, any at all (ways), attain, can (away with, [-not]), could, endure, might, overcome, have power, prevail, still, suffer.

3202. יְכֵל **y^{e}kêl** (Chald.), *yek-ale';* or

יְכִיל **y^{e}kîyl** (Chald.), *yek-eel';* corresp. to 3201:—be able, can, couldest, prevail.

3203. יְכָלְיָה **Y^{e}kolyâh**, *yek-ol-yaw';* and

יְכָלְיָהוּ **Y^{e}kolyâhûw**, *yek-ol-yaw'-hoo;* or (2 Ch. 26 : 3)

°יְכִילְיָה **Y^{e}kîyl^{e}yâh**, *yek-ee-leh-yaw';* from 3201 and 3050; *Jah will enable; Jekoljah* or *Jekiljah*, an Israelitess:—Jecholiah, Jecoliah.

3204. יְכָנְיָה **Y^{e}konyâh**, *yek-on-yaw';* and

יְכָנְיָהוּ **Y^{e}konyâhûw**, *yek-on-yaw'-hoo;* or (Jer. 27 : 20)

°יְכוֹנְיָה **Y^{e}kôwn^{e}yâh**, *yek-o-neh-yaw';* from 3559 and 3050; *Jah will establish; Jekonjah*, a Jewish king:—Jeconiah. Comp. 3659.

3205. יָלַד **yâlad**, *yaw-lad';* a prim. root; to *bear* young; causat. to *beget;* med. to *act as midwife;* spec. to *show lineage:*—bear, beget, birth ([-day]), born, (make to) bring forth (children, young), bring up, calve, child, come, be delivered (of a child), time of delivery, gender, hatch, labour, (do the office of a) midwife, declare pedigrees, be the son of, (woman in, woman that) travail (-eth, -ing woman).

3206. יֶלֶד **yeled**, *yeh'-led;* from 3205; something *born*, i.e. a *lad* or *offspring:*—boy, child, fruit, son, young man (one).

3207. יַלְדָּה **yaldâh**, *yal-daw';* fem. of 3206; a *lass:*—damsel, girl.

3208. יַלְדוּת **yaldûwth**, *yal-dooth';* abstr. from 3206; *boyhood* (or *girlhood*):—childhood, youth.

3209. יִלּוֹד **yillôwd**, *yil-lode';* pass. from 3205; *born:*—born.

3210. יָלוֹן **Yâlôwn**, *yaw-lone';* from 3885; *lodging; Jalon*, an Isr.:—Jalon.

3211. יָלִיד **yâlîyd**, *yaw-leed';* from 3205; *born:*—([home-]) born, child, son.

3212. יָלַךְ **yâlak**, *yaw-lak';* a prim. root [comp. 1980]; to *walk* (lit. or fig.); causat. to *carry* (in various senses):— × again, away, bear, bring, carry (away), come (away), depart, flow, + follow (-ing), get (away, hence, him), (cause to, make) go (away, -ing, -ne, one's way, out), grow, lead (forth), let down, march, prosper, + pursue, cause to run, spread, take away ([-journey]), vanish, (cause to) walk (-ing), wax, × be weak.

3213. יָלַל **yâlal**, *yaw-lal'*; a prim. root; to *howl* (with a wailing tone) or *yell* (with a boisterous one):—(make to) howl, be howling.

3214. יְלֵל **yᵉlêl**, *yel-ale'*; from 3213; a *howl*;—howling.

3215. יְלָלָה **yᵉlâlâh**, *yel-aw-law'*; fem. of 3214; a *howling*:—howling.

3216. יָלַע **yâlaʻ**, *yaw-lah'*; a prim. root; to *blurt* or utter inconsiderately:—devour.

3217. יַלֶּפֶת **yallepheth**, *yal-leh'-feth*; from an unused root appar. mean. to *stick* or *scrape*; *scurf* or *tetter*:—scabbed.

3218. יֶלֶק **yeleq**, *yeh'-lek*; from an unused root mean. to *lick* up; a *devourer*; spec. the young *locust*:—cankerworm, caterpillar.

3219. יַלְקוּט **yalqûwṭ**, *yal-koot'*; from 3950; a travelling *pouch* (as if for gleanings):—scrip.

3220. יָם **yâm**, *yawm*; from an unused root mean. to *roar*; a *sea* (as breaking in *noisy* surf) or large body of water; spec. (with the art.) the *Mediterranean*; sometimes a large *river*, or an artificial *basin*; locally, the *west*, or (rarely) the *south*:—sea (× -faring man, [-shore]), south, west (-ern, side, -ward).

3221. יָם **yâm** (Chald.), *yawm*; corresp. to 3220:—sea.

3222. יֵם **yêm**, *yame*; from the same as 3117; a *warm* spring:—mule.

3223. יְמוּאֵל **Yᵉmûwʼêl**, *yem-oo-ale'*; from 3117 and 410; *day of God*; *Jemuel*, an Isr.:—Jemuel.

3224. יְמִימָה **Yᵉmîymâh**, *yem-ee-maw'*; perh. from the same as 3117; prop. *warm*, i.e. *affectionate*; hence *dove* [comp. 3123]; *Jemimah*, one of Job's daughters:—Jemimah.

3225. יָמִין **yâmîyn**, *yaw-meen'*; from 3231; the *right* hand or side (leg, eye) of a person or other object (as the *stronger* and more dexterous); locally, the *south*:— + left-handed, right (hand, side), south.

3226. יָמִין **Yâmîyn**, *yaw-meen'*; the same as 3225; *Jamin*, the name of three Isr.:—Jamin. See also 1144.

3227. יְמִינִי **yᵉmîynîy**, *yem-ee-nee'*; for 3225; *right*:—(on the) right (hand).

3228. יְמִינִי **Yᵉmîynîy**, *yem-ee-nee'*; patron. from 3226; a *Jeminite* (collect.) or desc. of Jamin:—Jaminites. See also 1145.

3229. יִמְלָא **Yimlâʼ**, *yeem-law'*; or

יִמְלָה **Yimlâh**, *yim-law'*; from 4390; *full*; *Jimla* or *Jimlah*, an Isr.:—Imla, Imlah.

3230. יַמְלֵךְ **Yamlêk**, *yam-lake'*; from 4427; *he will make king*; *Jamlek*, an Isr.:—Jamlech.

3231. יָמַן **yâman**, *yaw-man'*; a prim. root; to *be* (phys.) *right* (i.e. firm); but used only as denom. from 3225 and transit., to *be right-handed* or *take the right-hand* side:—go (turn) to (on, use) the right hand.

3232. יִמְנָה **Yimnâh**, *yim-naw'*; from 3231; *prosperity* (as betokened by the *right* hand); *Jimnah*, the name of two Isr.; also (with the art.) of the posterity of one of them:—Imna, Imnah, Jimnah, Jimnites.

3233. יְמָנִי **yᵉmânîy**, *yem-aw-nee'*; from 3231; *right* (i.e. at the right hand):—(on the) right (hand).

3234. יִמְנָע **Yimnâʻ**, *yim-naw'*; from 4513; *he will restrain*; *Jimna*, an Isr.:—Imna.

3235. יָמַר **yâmar**, *yaw-mar'*; a prim. root; to *exchange*; by impl. to *change places*:—boast selves, change.

3236. יִמְרָה **Yimrâh**, *yim-raw'*; prob. from 3235; *interchange*; *Jimrah*, an Isr.:—Imrah.

3237. יָמַשׁ **yâmash**, *yaw-mash'*; a prim. root; to *touch*:—feel.

3238. יָנָה **yânâh**, *yaw-naw'*; a prim. root; to *rage* or *be violent*; by impl. to *suppress*, to *maltreat*:—destroy, (thrust out by) oppress (-ing, -ion, -or), proud, vex, do violence.

3239. יָנוֹחַ **Yânôwach**, *yaw-no'-akh*; or (with enclitic)

יָנוֹחָה **Yânôwchâh**, *yaw-no'-khaw*; from 3240; *quiet*; *Janoäch* or *Janochah*, a place in Pal.:—Janoah, Janohah.

יָנוּם **Yânûm**. See 3241.

3240. יָנַח **yânach**, *yaw-nakh'*; a prim. root; to *deposit*; by impl. to *allow to stay*:—bestow, cast down, lay (down, up), leave (off), let alone (remain), pacify, place, put, set (down), suffer, withdraw, withhold. (The Hiphil forms with the *dagesh* are here referred to, in accordance with the older grammarians; but if any distinction of the kind is to be made, these should rather be referred to 5117, and the others here.)

3241. יָנִים **Yânîym**, *yaw-neem'*; from 5123; *asleep*; *Janim*, a place in Pal.:—Janum [*from the marg.*].

3242. יְנִיקָה **yᵉnîyqâh**, *yen-ee-kaw'*; from 3243; a *sucker* or sapling:—young twig.

3243. יָנַק **yânaq**, *yaw-nak'*; a prim. root; to *suck*; causat. to *give milk*:—milch, nurse (-ing mother), (give, make to) suck (-ing child, -ling).

3244. יַנְשׁוּף **yanshûwph**, *yan-shoof'*; or

יַנְשׁוֹף **yanshôwph**, *yan-shofe'*; appar. from 5398; an unclean (aquatic) bird; prob. the *heron* (perh. from its *blowing* cry, or because the *night*-heron is meant [comp. 5399]):—(great) owl.

3245. יָסַד **yâçad**, *yaw-sad'*; a prim. root; to *set* (lit. or fig.); intens. to *found*; reflex. to *sit* down together, i.e. *settle*, *consult*:—appoint, take counsel, establish, (lay the, lay for a) found (-ation), instruct, lay, ordain, set, × sure.

3246. יְסֻד **yᵉçûd**, *yes-ood'*; from 3245; a *foundation* (fig. i.e. *beginning*):— × began.

3247. יְסוֹד **yᵉçôwd**, *yes-ode'*; from 3245; a *foundation* (lit. or fig.):—bottom, foundation, repairing.

3248. יְסוּדָה **yᵉçûwdâh**, *yes-oo-daw'*; fem. of 3246; a *foundation*:—foundation.

3249. יָסוּר **yâçûwr**, *yaw-soor'*; from 5493; *departing*:—they that depart.

3250. יִסּוֹר **yiççôwr**, *yis-sore'*; from 3256; a *reprover*:—instruct.

3251. יָסַךְ **yâçak**, *yaw-sak'*; a prim. root; to *pour* (intrans.):—be poured.

3252. יִסְכָּה **Yiçkâh**, *yis-kaw'*; from an unused root mean. to *watch*; *observant*; *Jiskah*, sister of Lot:—Iscah.

3253. יִסְמַכְיָהוּ **Yiçmakyâhûw**, *yis-mak-yaw-hoo'*; from 5564 and 3050; *Jah will sustain*; *Jismakjah*, an Isr.:—Ismachiah.

3254. יָסַף **yâçaph**, *yaw-saf'*; a prim. root; to *add* or *augment* (often adv. to *continue* to do a thing):—add, × again, × any more, × cease, × come more, + conceive again, continue, exceed, × further, × gather together, get more, give moreover, × henceforth, increase (more and more), join, × longer (bring, do, make, much, put), × (the, much, yet) more (and more), proceed (further), prolong, put, be [strong-] er, × yet, yield.

3255. יְסַף **yᵉçaph** (Chald.), *yes-af'*; corresp. to 3254:—add.

3256. יָסַר **yâçar**, *yaw-sar'*; a prim. root; to *chastise*, lit. (with blows) or fig. (with words); hence to *instruct*:—bind, chasten, chastise, correct, instruct, punish, reform, reprove, sore, teach.

3257. יָע **yâʻ**, *yaw*; from 3261; a *shovel*:—shovel.

3258. יַעְבֵּץ **Yaʻbêts**, *yah-bates'*; from an unused root prob. mean. to *grieve*; *sorrowful*; *Jabets*, the name of an Isr., and also of a place in Pal.:—Jabez.

3259. יָעַד **yâʻad**, *yaw-ad'*; a prim. root; to *fix* upon (by agreement or appointment); by impl. to *meet* (at a stated time), to *summon* (to trial), to *direct* (in a certain quarter or position), to *engage* (for marriage):—agree, (make an) appoint (-ment, a time), assemble (selves), betroth, gather (selves, together), meet (together), set (a time).

יֶעְדּוֹ **Yᵉʻdôw**. See 3260.

3260. יֶעְדִּי **Yᵉʻdîy**, *yed-ee'*; from 3259; *appointed*; *Jedi*, an Isr.:—Iddo [*from the marg.*] See 3035.

3261. יָעָה **yâʻâh**, *yaw-aw'*; a prim. root; appar to *brush* aside:—sweep away.

3262. יְעוּאֵל **Yᵉʻûwʼêl**, *yeh-oo-ale'*; from 3261 and 410; *carried away of God*; *Jeüel*, the name of four Isr.:—Jehiel, Jeiel, Jeuel. Comp. 3273.

3263. יְעוּץ **Yᵉʻûwts**, *yeh-oots'*; from 5779; *counsellor*; *Jeüts*, an Isr.:—Jeuz.

3264. יָעוֹר **yâʻôwr**, *yaw-ore'*; a var. of 3293; a *forest*:—wood.

3265. יָעוּר **Yâʻûwr**, *yaw-oor'*; appar. pass. part of the same as 3293; *wooded*; *Jaür*, an Isr.:—Jair [*from the marg.*].

3266. יְעוּשׁ **Yᵉʻûwsh**, *yeh-oosh'*; from 5789; *hasty*; *Jeüsh*, the name of an Edomite and of four Isr.:—Jehush, Jeush. Comp. 3274.

3267. יָעַז **yâʻaz**, *yaw-az'*; a prim. root; to be *bold* or *obstinate*:—fierce.

3268. יַעֲזִיאֵל **Yaʻăzîyʼêl**, *yah-az-ee-ale'*; from 3267 and 410; *emboldened of God*; *Jaaziël*, an Isr.:—Jaaziel.

3269. יַעֲזִיָּהוּ **Yaʻăzîyâhûw**, *yah-az-ee-yaw'-hoo*; from 3267 and 3050; *emboldened of Jah*; *Jaazijah*, an Isr.:—Jaaziah.

3270. יַעֲזֵיר **Yaʻăzêyr**, *yah-az-ayr'*; or

יַעְזֵר **Yaʻzêr**, *yah-zare'*; from 5826; *helpful*; *Jaazer* or *Jazer*, a place E. of the Jordan:—Jaazer, Jazer.

3271. יָעַט **yâʻaṭ**, *yaw-at'*; a prim. root; to *clothe*:—cover.

3272. יְעַט **yᵉʻaṭ** (Chald.), *yeh-at'*; corresp. to 3289; to *counsel*; reflex. to *consult*:—counsellor, consult together.

3273. יְעִיאֵל **Yᵉʻîyʼêl**, *yeh-ee-ale'*; from 3261 and 410; *carried away of God*; *Jeïel*, the name of six Isr.:—Jeiel, Jehiel. Comp. 3262.

יָעִיר **Yâʻîyr**. See 3265.

3274. יְעִישׁ **Yᵉʻîysh**, *yeh-eesh'*; from 5789; *hasty*; *Jeïsh*, the name of an Edomite and of an Isr.:—Jeush [*from the marg.*]. Comp. 3266.

3275. יַעְכָּן **Yaʻkân**, *yah-kawn'*; from the same as 5912; *troublesome*; *Jakan*, an Isr.:—Jachan.

3276. יָעַל **yâʻal**, *yaw-al'*; a prim. root; prop. to *ascend*; fig. to *be valuable* (obj. *useful*, subj. *benefited*):— × at all, set forward, can do good, (be, have) profit (-able).

3277. יָעֵל **yâʻêl**, *yaw-ale'*; from 3276; an *ibex* (as *climbing*):—wild goat.

3278. יָעֵל **Yâʻêl**, *yaw-ale'*; the same as 3277; *Jaël*, a Canaanite:—Jael.

3279. יַעֲלָא **Yaʻălâʼ**, *yah-al-aw'*; or

יַעֲלָה **Yaʻălâh**, *yah-al-aw'*; the same as 3280 or direct from 3276; *Jaala* or *Jaalah*, one of the Nethinim:—Jaala, Jaalah.

3280. יַעֲלָה **yaʻălâh**, *yah-al-aw'*; fem. of 3277:—roe.

3281. יַעְלָם **Yaʻlâm**, *yah-lawm'*; from 5956; *occult*; *Jalam*, an Edomite:—Jalam.

3282. יַעַן **yaʻan**, *yah'-an*; from an unused root mean. to *pay attention*; prop. *heed*; by impl. *purpose* (sake or account); used adv. to indicate the *reason* or cause:—because (that), forasmuch (+ as), seeing then, + that, + whereas, + why.

3283. יָעֵן **yâʻên**, *yaw-ane'*; from the same as 3282; the *ostrich* (prob. from its *answering* cry:—ostrich.

3284. יַעֲנָה **yaʻănâh**, *yah-an-aw'*; fem. of 3283, and mean. the same:— + owl.

3285. יַעְנַי **Yaʻănay**, *yah-an-ah'ee*; from the same as 3283; *responsive*; *Jaanai*, an Isr.:—Jaanai.

3286. יָעַף **yâʻaph**, *yaw-af'*; a prim. root; to *tire* (as if from wearisome *flight*):—faint, cause to fly, (be) weary (self).

3287. יָעֵף **yâʻêph**, *yaw-afe'*; from 3286; *fatigued*; fig. *exhausted*:—faint, weary.

3288. יְעָף **yᵉʻâph**, *yeh-awf'*; from 3286; *fatigue* (adv. utterly *exhausted*):—swiftly.

3289. יָעַץ **yâʻats**, *yaw-ats'*; a prim. root; to *advise*; reflex. to *deliberate* or *resolve*:—advertise, take advice, advise (well), consult, (give take) counsel (-lor), determine, devise, guide, purpose.

3290. יַעֲקֹב **Yaʻăqôb**, *yah-ak-obe'*; from 6117; *heel*-catcher (i.e. supplanter); *Jaakob*, the Israelitish patriarch:—Jacob.

3291. יַעֲקֹבָה **Yaʻăqôbâh**, *yah-ak-o'-baw*; from 3290; *Jaakobah*, an Isr.:—Jaakobah.

3292. יַעֲקָן **Yaʻăqân**, *yah-ak-awn'*; from the same as 6130; *Jaakan*, an Idumæan:—Jaakan. Comp. 1142.

3293. יַעַר **yaʻar**, *yah'-ar*; from an unused root prob. mean. to *thicken* with verdure; a *copse* of bushes; hence a *forest;* hence *honey* in the *comb* (as hived in trees):—[honey-] comb, forest, wood.

3294. יַעְרָה **Yaʻrâh**, *yah-raw'*; a form of 3295; *Jarah*, an Isr.:—Jarah.

3295. יַעֲרָה **yaʻărâh**, *yah-ar-aw'*; fem. of 3293, and mean. the same:—[honey-] comb, forest.

3296. יַעֲרֵי אֹרְגִים **Yaʻărêy 'Orᵉgîym**, *yah-ar-ay' o-reg-eem'*; from the plur. of 3293 and the masc. plur. part. act. of 707; *woods of weavers; Jaare-Oregim*, an Isr.:—Jaare-oregim.

3297. יְעָרִים **Yᵉʻârîym**, *yeh-aw-reem'*; plur. of 3293; *forests; Jeärim*, a place in Pal.:—Jearim. Comp. 7157.

3298. יַעֲרֶשְׁיָה **Yaʻăreshyâh**, *yah-ar-esh-yaw'*; from an unused root of uncert. signif. and 3050; *Jaareshjah*, an Isr.:—Jaresiah.

3299. יַעֲשׂוּ **Yaʻăsûw**, *yah-as-oo'*; from 6213; *they will do; Jaasu*, an Isr.:—Jaasau.

3300. יַעֲשִׂיאֵל **Yaʻăsîy'êl**, *yah-as-ee-ale'*; from 6213 and 410; *made of God; Jaasiel*, an Isr.:—Jaasiel, Jasiel.

3301. יִפְדְיָה **Yiphdᵉyâh**, *yif-deh-yaw'*; from 6299 and 3050; *Jah will liberate; Jiphdejah*, an Isr.:—Iphedeiah.

3302. יָפָה **yâphâh**, *yaw-faw'*; a prim. root; prop. to *be bright*, i.e. (by impl.) *beautiful:*—be beautiful, be (make self) fair (-r), deck.

3303. יָפֶה **yâpheh**, *yaw-feh'*; from 3302; *beautiful* (lit. or fig.):—+ beautiful, beauty, comely, fair (-est, one), + goodly, pleasant, well.

3304. יְפֵה־פִיָּה **yᵉphêh-phîyâh**, *yef-eh' fee-yaw'*; from 3302 by redupl.; *very beautiful:*—very fair.

3305. יָפוֹ **Yâphô**, *yaw-fo'*; or

יָפוֹא **Yâphôw'** (Ezra 3 : 7), *yaw-fo'*; from 3302; *beautiful; Japho*, a place in Pal.:—Japha, Joppa.

3306. יָפַח **yâphach**, *yaw-fakh'*; a prim. root; prop. to *breathe* hard, i.e. (by impl.) to *sigh:*—bewail self.

3307. יָפֵחַ **yâphêach**, *yaw-fay'-akh*; from 3306; prop. *puffing*, i.e. (fig.) *meditating:*—such as breathe out.

3308. יֳפִי **yŏphîy**, *yof-ee'*; from 3302; *beauty:*—beauty.

3309. יָפִיעַ **Yâphîyaʻ**, *yaw-fee'-ah*; from 3313; *bright; Japhia*, the name of a Canaanite, an Isr., and a place in Pal.:—Japhia.

3310. יַפְלֵט **Yaphlêṭ**, *yaf-late'*; from 6403; *he will deliver; Japhlet*, an Isr.:—Japhlet.

3311. יַפְלֵטִי **Yaphlêṭîy**, *yaf-lay-tee'*; patron. from 3310; a *Japhletite* or desc. of Japhlet:—Japhleti.

3312. יְפֻנֶּה **Yᵉphunneh**, *yef-oon-neh'*; from 6437; *he will be prepared; Jephunneh*, the name of two Isr.:—Jephunneh.

3313. יָפַע **yâphaʻ**, *yaw-fah'*; a prim. root; to *shine:*—be light, shew self, (cause to) shine (forth).

3314. יִפְעָה **yiphʻâh**, *yif-aw'*; from 3313; *splendor* or (fig.) *beauty:*—brightness.

3315. יֶפֶת **Yepheth**, *yeh'-feth*; from 6601; *expansion; Jepheth*, a son of Noah; also his posterity:—Japheth.

3316. יִפְתָּח **Yiphtâch**, *yif-tawkh'*; from 6605; *he will open; Jiphtach*, an Isr.; also a place in Pal.:—Jephthah, Jiphtah.

3317. יִפְתַּח־אֵל **Yiphtach-'êl**, *yif-tach-ale'*; from 6605 and 410; *God will open; Jiphtach-el*, a place in Pal.:—Jiphthah-el.

3318. יָצָא **yâtsâ'**, *yaw-tsaw'*; a prim. root; to *go* (causat. *bring*) *out*, in a great variety of applications, lit. and fig., direct and proxim.:—× after, appear, × assuredly, bear out, × begotten, break out, bring forth (out, up), carry out, come (abroad, out, thereat, without), + be condemned, depart (-ing, -ure), draw forth, in the end, escape, exact, fail, fall (out), fetch forth (out), get away (forth, hence, out), (able to, cause to, let) go abroad (forth, on, out), going out, grow, have forth (out), issue out, lay (lie) out, lead out, pluck out, proceed, pull out, put away, be risen, × scarce, send with commandment, shoot forth, spread, spring out, stand out, × still, × surely, take forth (out), at any time, × to [and fro], utter.

3319. יְצָא **yᵉtsâ'** (Chald.), *yets-aw'*; corresp. to 3318:—finish.

3320. יָצַב **yâtsab**, *yaw-tsab'*; a prim. root; to *place* (any thing so as to stay); reflex. to *station, offer, continue:*—present selves, remaining, resort, set (selves), (be able to, can, with-) stand (fast, forth, -ing, still, up).

3321. יְצֵב **yᵉtsêb** (Chald.), *yets-abe'*; corresp. to 3320; to *be firm;* hence to *speak surely:*—truth.

3322. יָצַג **yâtsag**, *yaw-tsag'*; a prim. root; to *place* permanently:—establish, leave, make, present, put, set, stay.

3323. יִצְהָר **yitshâr**, *yits-hawr'*; from 6671; *oil* (as producing *light*); fig. *anointing:*—+ anointed, oil.

3324. יִצְהָר **Yitshâr**, *yits-hawr'*; the same as 3323; *Jitshar*, an Isr.:—Izhar.

3325. יִצְהָרִי **Yitshârîy**, *yits-haw-ree'*; patron. from 3324; a *Jitsharite* or desc. of Jitshar:—Izeharites, Izharites.

3326. יָצוּעַ **yâtsûwaʻ**, *yaw-tsoo'-ah*; pass. part. of 3331; *spread*, i.e. a *bed;* (arch.) an *extension*, i.e. *wing* or *lean-to* (a single story or collect.):—bed, chamber, couch.

3327. יִצְחָק **Yitschâq**, *yits-khawk'*; from 6711; *laughter* (i.e. *mockery*); *Jitschak* (or Isaac), son of Abraham:—Isaac. Comp. 3446.

3328. יִצְחַר **Yitschar**, *yits-khar'*; from the same as 6713; *he will shine; Jitschar*, an Isr.:—and Zehoar [*from the marg.*].

3329. יָצִיא **yâtsîy'**, *yaw-tsee'*; from 3318; *issue*, i.e. offspring:—those that came forth.

3330. יַצִּיב **yatstsîyb** (Chald.), *yats-tseeb'*; from 3321; *fixed, sure;* concr. *certainty:*—certain (-ty), true, truth.

יָצִיעַ **yâtsîyaʻ**. See 3326.

3331. יָצַע **yâtsaʻ**, *yaw-tsah'*; a prim. root; to *strew* as a surface:—make [one's] bed, × lie, spread.

3332. יָצַק **yâtsaq**, *yaw-tsak'*; a prim. root; prop. to *pour* out (trans. or intrans.); by impl. to *melt* or *cast* as metal; by extens. to *place* firmly, to *stiffen* or grow hard:—cast, cleave fast, be (as) firm, grow, be hard, lay out, molten, overflow, pour (out), run out, set down, stedfast.

3333. יְצֻקָה **yᵉtsûkâh**, *yets-oo-kaw'*; pass. part. fem. of 3332; *poured* out, i.e. *run* into a mould:—when it was cast.

3334. יָצַר **yâtsar**, *yaw-tsar'*; a prim. root; to *press* (intrans.), i.e. *be narrow;* fig. *be in distress:*—be distressed, be narrow, be straitened (in straits), be vexed.

3335. יָצַר **yâtsar**, *yaw-tsar'*; prob. identical with 3334 (through the *squeezing* into shape); ([comp. 3331]); to *mould* into a form; espec. as a *potter;* fig. to *determine* (i.e. form a resolution):—× earthen, fashion, form, frame, make (-r), potter, purpose.

3336. יֵצֶר **yêtser**, *yay'-tser*; from 3335; a *form;* fig. *conception* (i.e. purpose):—frame, thing framed, imagination, mind, work.

3337. יֵצֶר **Yêtser**, *yay'-tser*; the same as 3336; *Jetser*, an Isr.:—Jezer.

3338. יָצֻר **yâtsûr**, *yaw-tsoor'*; pass. part. of 3335; *structure*, i.e. limb or part:—member.

3339. יִצְרִי **Yitsrîy**, *yits-ree'*; from 3335; *formative; Jitsri*, an Isr.:—Isri.

3340. יִצְרִי **Yitsrîy**, *yits-ree'*; patron. from 3337; a *Jitsrite* (collect.) or desc. of Jetser:—Jezerites.

3341. יָצַת **yâtsath**, *yaw-tsath'*; a prim. root; to *burn* or *set on fire;* fig. to *desolate:*—burn (up), be desolate, set (on) fire ([fire]), kindle.

3342. יֶקֶב **yeqeb**, *yeh'-keb*; from an unused root mean. to *excavate;* a *trough* (as dug out); spec. a wine-*vat* (whether the lower one, into which the juice drains; or the upper, in which the grapes are crushed):—fats, presses, press-fat, wine (-press).

3343. יְקַבְצְאֵל **Yᵉqabtsᵉ'êl**, *yek-ab-tseh-ale'*; from 6908 and 410; *God will gather; Jekabtseël*, a place in Pal.:—Jekabzeel. Comp. 6909.

3344. יָקַד **yâqad**, *yaw-kad'*; a prim. root; to *burn:*—(be) burn (-ing), × from the hearth, kindle.

3345. יְקַד **yᵉqad** (Chald.), *yek-ad'*; corresp. to 3344:—burning.

3346. יְקֵדָא **yᵉqêdâ'** (Chald.), *yek-ay-daw'*; from 3345; a *conflagration:*—burning.

3347. יָקְדְעָם **Yoqdᵉʻâm**, *yok-deh-awm'*; from 3344 and 5971; *burning of* (the) *people; Jokdeäm*, a place in Pal.:—Jokdeam.

3348. יָקֶה **Yâqeh**, *yaw-keh'*; from an unused root prob. mean. to *obey; obedient; Jakeh*, a symbolical name (for Solomon):—Jakeh.

3349. יִקָּהָה **yiqqâhâh**, *yik-kaw-haw'*; from the same as 3348; *obedience:*—gathering, to obey.

3350. יְקוֹד **yᵉqôwd**, *yek-ode'*; from 3344; a *burning:*—burning.

3351. יְקוּם **yᵉqûwm**, *yek-oom'*; from 6965; prop. *standing* (extant), i.e. by impl. a *living thing:*—(living) substance.

3352. יָקוֹשׁ **yâqôwsh**, *yaw-koshe'*; from 3369; prop. *entangling;* hence a *snarer:*—fowler.

3353. יָקוּשׁ **yâqûwsh**, *yaw-koosh'*; pass. part. of 3369; prop. *entangled*, i.e. by impl. (intrans.) a *snare*, or (trans.) a *snarer:*—fowler, snare.

3354. יְקוּתִיאֵל **Yᵉqûwthîy'êl**, *yek-ooth-ee'-ale*; from the same as 3348 and 410; *obedience of God; Jekuthiël*, an Isr.:—Jekuthiel.

3355. יָקְטָן **Yoqṭân**, *yok-tawn'*; from 6994; *he will be made little; Joktan*, an Arabian patriarch:—Joktan.

3356. יָקִים **Yâqîym**, *yaw-keem'*; from 6965; *he will raise; Jakim*, the name of two Isr.:—Jakim. Comp. 3079.

3357. יַקִּיר **yaqqîyr**, *yak-keer'*; from 3365; *precious:*—dear.

3358. יַקִּיר **yaqqîyr** (Chald.) *yak-keer'*; corresp. to 3357:—noble, rare.

3359. יְקַמְיָה **Yᵉqamyâh**, *yek-am-yaw'*; from 6965 and 3050; *Jah will rise; Jekamjah*, the name of two Isr.:—Jekamiah. Comp. 3079.

3360. יְקַמְעָם **Yᵉqamʻâm**, *yek-am'-awm*; from 6965 and 5971; (the) *people will rise*, *Jekamam*, an Isr.:—Jekameam. Comp. 3079, 3361.

3361. יָקְמְעָם **Yoqmᵉʻâm**, *yok-meh-awm'*; from 6965 and 5971; (the) *people will be raised; Jokmeäm*, a place in Pal.:—Jokmeam. Comp. 3360, 3362.

3362. יָקְנְעָם **Yoqnᵉʻâm**, *yok-neh-awm'*; from 6969 and 5971; (the) *people will be lamented; Jokneäm*, a place in Pal.:—Jokneam.

3363. יָקַע **yâqaʻ**, *yaw-kah'*; a prim. root; prop. to *sever* oneself, i.e. (by impl.) to *be dislocated;* fig. to *abandon;* causat. to *impale* (and thus allow to drop to pieces by *rotting*):—be alienated, depart, hang (up), be out of joint.

3364. יָקַץ **yâqats**, *yaw-kats'*; a prim. root; to *awake* (intrans.):—(be) awake (-d).

יָקַף **yâqaph**. See 5362.

3365. יָקַר **yâqar**, *yaw-kar'*; a prim. root; prop. appar. to *be heavy*, i.e. (fig.) *valuable;* causat. to *make rare* (fig. to *inhibit*):—be (make) precious, be prized, be set by, withdraw.

3366. יְקָר **yᵉqâr**, *yek-awr'*; from 3365; *value*, i.e. (concr.) *wealth;* abstr. *costliness, dignity:*—honour, precious (things), price.

3367. יְקָר yᵉqâr (Chald.), yek-awr'; corresp. to 3366:—glory, honour.

3368. יָקָר yâqâr, yaw-kawr'; from 3365; valuable (obj. or subj.):—brightness, clear, costly, excellent, fat, honourable women, precious, reputation.

3369. יָקֹשׁ yâqôsh, yaw-koshe'; a prim. root; to ensnare (lit. or fig.):—fowler (lay a) snare.

3370. יָקְשָׁן Yoqshân, yok-shawn'; from 3369; insidious; Jokshan, an Arabian patriarch:—Jokshan.

3371. יָקְתְאֵל Yoqthᵉ'êl, yok-theh-ale'; prob. from the same as 3348 and 410; veneration of God [comp. 3354]; Joktheël, the name of a place in Pal., and of one in Idumæa:—Joktheel.

יָרָא yârâ'. See 3384.

3372. יָרֵא yârê', yaw-ray'; a prim. root; to fear; mor. to revere; caus. to frighten:—affright, be (make) afraid, dread (-ful), (put in) fear (-ful, -fully, -ing), (be had in) reverence (-end), × see, terrible (act, -ness, thing).

3373. יָרֵא yârê', yaw-ray'; from 3372; fearing; mor. reverent:—afraid, fear (-ful).

3374. יִרְאָה yir'âh, yir-aw'; fem. of 3373; fear (also used as infin.); mor. reverence:—× dreadful, × exceedingly, fear (-fulness).

3375. יִרְאוֹן Yirôwn, yir-ohn'; from 3372; fearfulness; Jiron, a place in Pal.:—Iron.

3376. יִרְאִיָּיה Yir'îyâyh, yir-ee-yaw'; from 3373 and 3050; fearful of Jah; Jirijah, an Isr.:—Irijah.

3377. יָרֵב Yârêb, yaw-rabe'; from 7378; he will contend; Jareb, a symbolical name for Assyria:—Jareb. Comp. 3402.

3378. יְרֻבַּעַל Yᵉrubba'al, yer-oob-bah'-al; from 7378 and 1168; Baal will contend; Jerubbaal, a symbol. name of Gideon:—Jerubbaal.

3379. יָרׇבְעָם Yârob'âm, yaw-rob-awm'; from 7378 and 5971; (the) people will contend; Jarobam, the name of two Isr. kings:—Jeroboam.

3380. יְרֻבֶּשֶׁת Yᵉrubbesheth, yer-oob-beh'-sheth; from 7378 and 1322; shame (i.e. the idol) will contend; Jerubbesheth, a symbol. name for Gideon:—Jerubbesheth.

3381. יָרַד yârad, yaw-rad'; a prim. root; to descend (lit. to go downwards; or conventionally to a lower region, as the shore, a boundary, the enemy, etc.; or fig. to fall); causat. to bring down (in all the above applications):—× abundantly, bring down, carry down, cast down, (cause to) come (-ing) down, fall (down), get down, go (-ing) down (-ward), hang down, × indeed, let down, light (down), put down (off), (cause to, let) run down, sink, subdue, take down.

3382. יֶרֶד Yered, yeh'-red; from 3381; a descent; Jered, the name of an antediluvian, and of an Isr.:—Jared.

3383. יַרְדֵּן Yardên, yar-dane'; from 3381; a descender; Jarden, the principal river of Pal.:—Jordan.

3384. יָרָה yârâh, yaw-raw'; or (2 Chr. 26 : 15)

יָרָא yârâ', yaw-raw'; a prim. root; prop. to flow as water (i.e. to rain); trans. to lay or throw (espec. an arrow, i.e. to shoot); fig. to point out (as if by aiming the finger), to teach:—(+) archer, cast, direct, inform, instruct, lay, shew, shoot, teach (-er, -ing), through.

3385. יְרוּאֵל Yᵉrûw'êl, yer-oo-ale'; from 3384 and 410; founded of God; Jeruel, a place in Pal.:—Jeruel

3386. יָרוֹחַ Yârôwach, yaw-ro'-akh; perh. denom. from 3394; (born at the) new moon; Jaroäch, an Isr.:—Jaroah.

3387. יָרוֹק yârôwq, yaw-roke'; from 3417; green, i.e. an herb:—green thing.

3388. יְרוּשָׁא Yᵉrûwshâ', yer-oo-shaw'; or

יְרוּשָׁה Yᵉrûwshâh, yer-oo-shaw'; fem. pass. part. of 3423; possessed; Jerusha or Jerushah, an Israelitess:—Jerusha, Jerushah.

3389. יְרוּשָׁלַםִ Yᵉrûwshâlaim, yer-oo-shaw-lah'-im; rarely

יְרוּשָׁלַיִם Yᵉrûwshâlayim, yer-oo-shaw-lah'-yim; a dual (in allusion to its two main hills [the true pointing, at least of the former reading, seems to be that of 3390]); prob. from (the pass. part. of) 3384 and 7999; founded peaceful; Jerushalaïm or Jerushalem, the capital city of Pal.:—Jerusalem.

3390. יְרוּשְׁלֵם Yᵉrûwshâlêm (Chald.), yer-oo-shaw-lame'; corresp. to 3389:—Jerusalem.

3391. יֶרַח yerach, yeh'-rakh; from an unused root of uncert. signif.; a lunation, i.e. month:—month, moon.

3392. יֶרַח Yerach, yeh'-rakh; the same as 3391; Jerach, an Arabian patriarch:—Jerah.

3393. יְרַח yᵉrach (Chald.), yeh-rakh'; corresp. to 3391; a month:—month.

3394. יָרֵחַ yârêach, yaw-ray'-akh; from the same as 3391; the moon:—moon.

יְרֵחוֹ Yᵉrêchôw. See 3405.

3395. יְרֹחָם Yᵉrôchâm, yer-o-khawm'; from 7355; compassionate; Jerocham, the name of seven or eight Isr.:—Jeroham.

3396. יְרַחְמְאֵל Yᵉrachmᵉ'êl, yer-akh-meh-ale'; from 7355 and 410; God will compassionate; Jerachmeël, the name of three Isr.:—Jerahmeel.

3397. יְרַחְמְאֵלִי Yᵉrachmᵉ'êlîy, yer-akh-meh-ay-lee'; patron. from 3396; a Jerachmeëlite or desc. of Jerachmeel:—Jerahmeelites.

3398. יַרְחָע Yarchâ', yar-khaw'; prob. of Eg. or.; Jarcha, an Eg.:—Jarha.

3399. יָרַט yâraṭ, yaw-rat'; a prim. root; to precipitate or hurl (rush) headlong; (intrans.) to be rash:—be perverse, turn over.

3400. יְרִיאֵל Yᵉrîy'êl, yer-ee-ale'; from 3384 and 410; thrown of God; Jeriël, an Isr.:—Jeriel. Comp. 3385.

3401. יָרִיב yârîyb, yaw-rebe'; from 7378; lit. he will contend; prop. adj. contentious; used as noun, an adversary:—that contend (-eth), that strive.

3402. יָרִיב Yârîyb, yaw-rebe'; the same as 3401; Jarib, the name of three Isr.:—Jarib.

3403. יְרִיבַי Yᵉrîybay, yer-eeb-ah'ee; from 3401; contentious; Jeribai, an Isr.:—Jeribai.

3404. יְרִיָּה Yᵉrîyâh, yer-ee-yaw'; or

יְרִיָּהוּ Yᵉrîyâhûw, yer-ee-yaw'-hoo; from 3384 and 3050; Jah will throw; Jerijah, an Isr.:—Jeriah, Jerijah.

3405. יְרִיחוֹ Yᵉrîychôw, yer-ee-kho'; or

יְרֵחוֹ Yᵉrêchôw yer-ay-kho'; or var. (1 Kings 16 : 34)

יְרִיחֹה Yᵉrîychôh, yer-ee-kho'; perh. from 3394; its month; or else from 7306; fragrant; Jericho or Jerecho, a place in Pal.:—Jericho.

3406. יְרִימוֹת Yᵉrîymôwth, yer-ee-mohth'; or

יְרֵימוֹת Yᵉrêymôwth, yer-ay-mohth'; or

יְרֵמוֹת Yᵉrêmôwth, yer-ay-mohth'; fem. plur. from 7311; elevations; Jerimoth or Jeremoth, the name of twelve Isr.:—Jeremoth, Jerimoth, and Ramoth [from the marg.].

3407. יְרִיעָה yᵉrîy'âh, yer-ee-aw'; from 3415; a hanging (as tremulous):—curtain.

3408. יְרִיעוֹת Yᵉrîy'ôwth, yer-ee-ohth'; plur. of 3407; curtains; Jerioth, an Israelitess:—Jerioth.

3409. יָרֵךְ yârêk, yaw-rake'; from an unused root mean. to be soft; the thigh (from its fleshy softness); by euphem. the generative parts; fig. a shank, flank, side:—× body, loins, shaft, side, thigh.

3410. יַרְכָא yarkâ' (Chald.), yar-kaw'; corresp. to 3411; a thigh:—thigh.

3411. יְרֵכָה yᵉrêkâh, yer-ay-kaw'; fem. of 3409; prop. the flank; but used only fig., the rear or recess:—border, coast, part, quarter, side.

3412. יַרְמוּת Yarmûwth, yar-mooth'; from 7311; elevation; Jarmuth, the name of two places in Pal.:—Jarmuth.

יְרֵמוֹת Yᵉrêmôwth. See 3406.

3413. יְרֵמַי Yᵉrêmay, yer-ay-mah'ee; from 7311; elevated; Jeremai, an Isr.:—Jeremai.

3414. יִרְמְיָה Yirmᵉyâh, yir-meh-yaw'; or

יִרְמְיָהוּ Yirmᵉyâhûw, yir-meh-yaw'-hoo; from 7311 and 3050; Jah will rise; Jirmejah, the name of eight or nine Isr.:—Jeremiah.

3415. יָרַע yâra', yaw-rah'; a prim. root; prop. to be broken up (with any violent action), i.e. (fig.) to fear:—be grievous [only Isa. 15 : 4; the rest belong to 7489].

3416. יִרְפְּאֵל Yirpᵉ'êl, yir-peh-ale'; from 7495 and 410; God will heal; Jirpeël, a place in Pal.:—Irpeel.

3417. יָרַק yâraq, yaw-rak'; a prim. root; to spit:—× but, spit.

3418. יֶרֶק yereq, yeh'-rek; from 3417 (in the sense of vacuity of color); prop. pallor, i.e. hence the yellowish green of young and sickly vegetation; concr. verdure, i.e. grass or vegetation:—grass, green (thing).

3419. יָרָק yârâq, yaw-rawk'; from the same as 3418; prop. green; concr. a vegetable:—green, herbs.

יַרְקוֹן Yarqôwn. See 4313.

3420. יֵרָקוֹן yêrâqôwn, yay-raw-kone'; from 3418; paleness, whether of persons (from fright), or of plants (from drought):—mildew, paleness.

3421. יׇרְקְעָם Yorqᵉ'âm, yor-keh-awm'; from 7324 and 5971; people will be poured forth; Jorkeäm, a place in Pal.:—Jorkeam.

3422. יְרַקְרַק yᵉraqraq, yer-ak-rak'; from the same as 3418; yellowishness:—greenish, yellow.

3423. יָרַשׁ yârash, yaw-rash'; or

יָרֵשׁ yârêsh, yaw-raysh'; a prim. root; to occupy (by driving out previous tenants, and possessing in their place); by impl. to seize, to rob, to inherit; also to expel, to impoverish, to ruin:—cast out, consume, destroy, disinherit, dispossess, drive (-ing) out, enjoy, expel, × without fail, (give to, leave for) inherit (-ance, -or), + magistrate, be (make) poor, come to poverty, (give to, make to) possess, get (have) in (take) possession, seize upon, succeed, × utterly.

3424. יְרֵשָׁה yᵉrêshâh, yer-ay-shaw'; from 3423; occupancy:—possession.

3425. יְרֻשָּׁה yᵉrushshâh, yer-oosh-shaw'; from 3423; something occupied; a conquest; also a patrimony:—heritage, inheritance, possession.

3426. יֵשׁ yêsh, yaysh; perh. from an unused root mean. to stand out, or exist; entity; used adv. or as a copula for the substantive verb (1961); there is or are (or any other form of the verb to be, as may suit the connection):—(there) are, (he, it, shall, there, there may, there shall, there should) be, thou do, had, hast, (which) hath, (I, shalt, that) have, (he, it, there) is, substance, it (there) was, (there) were, ye will, thou wilt, wouldest.

3427. יָשַׁב yâshab, yaw-shab'; a prim. root; prop. to sit down (spec. as judge, in ambush, in quiet); by impl. to dwell, to remain; causat. to settle, to marry:—(make to) abide (-ing), continue, (cause to, make to) dwell (-ing), ease self, endure, establish, × fail, habitation, haunt, (make to) inhabit (-ant), make to keep [house], lurking, × marry (-ing), (bring again to) place, remain, return, seat, set (-tle), (down-) sit (-down, still, -ting down, -ting [place] -uate), take, tarry.

3428. יֶשֶׁבְאָב Yesheb'âb, yeh-sheb-awb'; from 3427 and 1; seat of (his) father; Jeshebab, an Isr.:—Jeshebeab.

3429. יֹשֵׁב בַּשֶּׁבֶת Yôshêb bash-Shebeth, yo-shabe' bash-sheh'-beth; from the act. part. of 3427 and 7674, with a prep. and the art. interposed; sitting in the seat; Josheb-bash-Shebeth, an Isr.:—that sat in the seat.

3430. יִשְׁבּוֹ בְּנֹב° **Yishbôw beNôb**, *yish-bo' beh-nobe;* from 3427 and 5011, with a pron. suffix and a prep. interposed; *his dwelling (is) in Nob; Jishbo-be-Nob*, a Philistine:—Ishbi-benob [*from the marg.*].

3431. יִשְׁבַּח **Yishbach**, *yish-bakh';* from 7623; *he will praise; Jishbach*, an Isr.:—Ishbah.

3432. יָשֻׁבִי **Yâshûbîy**, *yaw-shoo-bee';* patron. from 3437; a *Jashubite*, or desc. of Jashub:—Jashubites.

3433. יָשֻׁבִי לֶחֶם **Yâshûbîy Lechem**, *yaw-shoo'-bee leh'-khem;* from 7725 and 3899; *returner of bread; Jashubi-Lechem*, an Isr.:—Jashubi-lehem. [Prob. the text should be pointed

יֹשְׁבֵי לֶחֶם **Yôshebêy Lechem**, *yo-sheh-bay' leh'-khem*, and rendered "(they were) inhabitants of Lechem," i.e. of Bethlehem (by contraction). Comp. 3902.]

3434. יָשָׁבְעָם **Yâshob'âm**, *yaw-shob-awm';* from 7725 and 5971; *people will return; Jashobam*, the name of two or three Isr.:—Jashobeam.

3435. יִשְׁבָּק **Yishbâq**, *yish-bawk';* from an unused root corresp. to 7662; *he will leave; Jishbak*, a son of Abraham:—Ishbak.

3436. יָשְׁבְּקָשָׁה **Yoshbeqâshâh**, *yosh-bek-aw-shaw';* from 3427 and 7186; *a hard seat; Joshbekashah*, an Isr.:—Joshbekashah.

3437. יָשׁוּב **Yâshûwb**, *yaw-shoob';* or

יָשִׁיב **Yâshîyb**, *yaw-sheeb';* from 7725; *he will return; Jashub*, the name of two Isr.:—Jashub.

3438. יִשְׁוָה **Yishvâh**, *yish-vaw';* from 7737; *he will level; Jishvah*, an Isr.:—Ishvah, Isvah.

3439. יְשׁוֹחָיָה **Yeshôwchâyâh**, *yesh-o-khaw-yaw';* from the same as 3445 and 3050; *Jah will empty; Jeshochajah*, an Isr.:—Jeshoaiah.

3440. יִשְׁוִי **Yishvîy**, *yish-vee';* from 7737; *level; Jishvi*, the name of two Isr.:—Ishuai, Ishvi, Isui, Jesui.

3441. יִשְׁוִי **Yishvîy**, *yish-vee';* patron. from 3440; a *Jishvite* (collect.) or desc. of Jishvi:—Jesuites.

3442. יֵשׁוּעַ **Yêshûwa'**, *yay-shoo'-ah;* for 3091; *he will save; Jeshua*, the name of ten Isr., also of a place in Pal.:—Jeshua.

3443. יֵשׁוּעַ **Yêshûwa'** (Chald.), *yay-shoo'-ah;* corresp. to 3442:—Jeshua.

3444. יְשׁוּעָה **yeshûw'âh**, *yesh-oo'-aw;* fem. pass. part. of 3467; something *saved*, i.e. (abstr.) *deliverance;* hence *aid, victory, prosperity:*—deliverance, health, help (-ing), salvation, save, saving (health), welfare.

3445. יֶשַׁח **yeshach**, *yeh'-shakh;* from an unused root mean. to *gape* (as the empty stomach); *hunger:*—casting down.

3446. יִשְׂחָק **Yischâq**, *yis-khawk';* from 7831; *he will laugh; Jischak*, the heir of Abraham:—Isaac. Comp. 3327.

3447. יָשַׁט **yâshaṭ**, *yaw-shat';* a prim. root; to *extend:*—hold out.

3448. יִשַׁי **Yîshay**, *yee-shah'ee;* by Chald. אִישַׁי **'Îyshay**, *ee-shah'ee;* from the same as 3426; *extant; Jishai*, David's father:—Jesse.

יָשִׁיב **Yâshîyb**. See 3437.

3449. יִשִּׁיָּה **Yishshîyâh**, *yish-shee-yaw';* or

יִשִּׁיָּהוּ **Yishshîyâhûw**, *yish-shee-yaw'-hoo;* from 5383 and 3050; *Jah will lend; Jishshijah*, the name of five Isr.:—Ishiah, Isshiah, Ishijah, Jesiah.

3450. יְשִׂימָאֵל **Yesîymâ'êl**, *yes-eem-aw-ale';* from 7760 and 410; *God will place; Jesimaël*, an Isr.:—Jesimael.

3451. יְשִׁימָה° **yeshîymâh**, *yesh-ee-maw';* from 3456; *desolation:*—let death seize [*from the marg.*].

3452. יְשִׁימוֹן **yeshîymôwn**, *yesh-ee-mone';* from 3456; a *desolation:*—desert, Jeshimon, solitary, wilderness.

יְשִׁימוֹת **yeshîymôwth**. See 1020, 3451.

3453. יָשִׁישׁ **yâshîysh**, *yaw-sheesh';* from 3486; an *old* man:—(very) aged (man), ancient, very old.

3454. יְשִׁישַׁי **Yeshîyshay**, *yesh-ee-shah'ee;* from 3453; *aged; Jeshishai*, an Isr.:—Jeshishai.

3455. יָשַׂם **yâsam**, *yaw-sam';* a prim root; to *place;* intrans. to *be placed:*—be put (set).

3456. יָשַׁם **yâsham**, *yaw-sham';* a prim. root; to *lie waste:*—be desolate.

3457. יִשְׁמָא **Yishmâ'**, *yish-maw';* from 3456; *desolate; Jishma*, an Isr.:—Ishma.

3458. יִשְׁמָעֵאל **Yishmâ'ê'l**, *yish-maw-ale';* from 8085 and 410; *God will hear; Jishmaël*, the name of Abraham's oldest son, and of five Isr.:—Ishmael.

3459. יִשְׁמְעֵאלִי **Yishmâ'ê'lîy**, *yish-maw-ay-lee';* patron. from 3458; a *Jishmaëlite* or desc. of Jishmael:—Ishmaelite.

3460. יִשְׁמַעְיָה **Yishma'yâh**, *yish-mah-yaw';* or

יִשְׁמַעְיָהוּ **Yishma'yâhûw**, *yish-mah-yaw'-hoo;* from 8085 and 3050; *Jah will hear; Jishmajah*, the name of two Isr.:—Ishmaiah.

3461. יִשְׁמְרַי **Yishmeray**, *yish-mer-ah'ee;* from 8104; *preservative; Jishmerai*, an Isr.:—Ishmerai.

3462. יָשֵׁן **yâshên**, *yaw-shane';* a prim. root; prop. to *be slack* or *languid*, i.e. (by impl.) *sleep* (fig. to *die*); also to *grow old, stale* or *inveterate:*—old (store), remain long, (make to) sleep.

3463. יָשֵׁן **yâshên**, *yaw-shane';* from 3462; *sleepy:*—asleep, (one out of) sleep (-eth, -ing), slept.

3464. יָשֵׁן **Yâshên**, *yaw-shane';* the same as 3463; *Jashen*, an Isr.:—Jashen.

3465. יָשָׁן **yâshân**, *yaw-shawn';* from 3462; *old:*—old.

3466. יְשָׁנָה **Yeshânâh**, *yesh-aw-naw';* fem. of 3465; *Jeshanah*, a place in Pal.:—Jeshanah.

3467. יָשַׁע **yâsha'**, *yaw-shah';* a prim. root; prop. to *be open, wide* or *free*, i.e. (by impl.) to *be safe;* causat. to *free* or *succor:*—× at all, avenging, defend, deliver (-er), help, preserve, rescue, be safe, bring (having) salvation, save (-iour), get victory.

3468. יֶשַׁע **yesha'**, *yeh'-shah;* or

יֵשַׁע **yêsha'**, *yay'-shah;* from 3467; *liberty, deliverance, prosperity:*—safety, salvation, saving.

3469. יִשְׁעִי **Yish'îy**, *yish-ee';* from 3467; *saving; Jishi*, the name of four Isr.:—Ishi.

3470. יְשַׁעְיָה **Yesha'yâh**, *yesh-ah-yaw';* or

יְשַׁעְיָהוּ **Yesha'yâhûw**, *yesh-ah-yaw'-hoo;* from 3467 and 3050; *Jah has saved; Jeshajah*, the name of seven Isr.:—Isaiah, Jesaiah, Jeshaiah.

3471. יָשְׁפֵה **yâshephêh**, *yaw-shef-ay';* from an unused root mean. to *polish;* a gem supposed to be *jasper* (from the resemblance in name):—jasper.

3472. יִשְׁפָּה **Yishpâh**, *yish-paw';* perh. from 8192; *he will scratch; Jishpah*, an Isr.:—Ispah.

3473. יִשְׁפָּן **Yishpân**, *yish-pawn';* prob. from the same as 8227; *he will hide; Jishpan*, an Isr.:—Ishpan.

3474. יָשַׁר **yâshar**, *yaw-shar';* a prim. root; to *be straight* or *even;* fig. to *be* (causat. to *make*) *right, pleasant, prosperous:*—direct, fit, seem good (meet), + please (well), be (esteem, go) right (on), bring (look, make, take the) straight (way), be upright (-ly).

3475. יֵשֶׁר **Yêsher**, *yay'-sher;* from 3474; the *right; Jesher*, an Isr.:—Jesher.

3476. יֹשֶׁר **yôsher**, *yo'-sher;* from 3474; the *right:*—equity, meet, right, upright (-ness).

3477. יָשָׁר **yâshâr**, *yaw-shawr';* from 3474; *straight* (lit. or fig.):—convenient, equity, Jasher, just, meet (-est), + pleased well right (-eous), straight, (most) upright (-ly, -ness).

3478. יִשְׂרָאֵל **Yisrâ'êl**, *yis-raw-ale';* from 8280 and 410; *he will rule as God; Jisraël*, a symbolical name of Jacob; also (typically) of his posterity:—Israel.

3479. יִשְׂרָאֵל **Yisrâ'êl** (Chald.), *yis-raw-ale'* corresp. to 3478:—Israel.

3480. יְשַׂרְאֵלָה **Yesar'êlâh**, *yes-ar-ale'-aw;* by var. from 3477 and 410 with directive enclitic; *right towards God; Jesarelah*, an Isr.:—Jesharelah. Comp. 841.

3481. יִשְׂרְאֵלִי **Yisre'êlîy**, *yis-reh-ay-lee';* patron. from 3478; a *Jisreëlite* or desc. of Jisrael:—of Israel, Israelite.

3482. יִשְׂרְאֵלִית **Yisre'êlîyth**, *yis-reh-ay-leeth';* fem. of 3481; a *Jisreëlitess* or female desc. of Jisrael:—Israelitish.

3483. יִשְׁרָה **yishrâh**, *yish-raw';* fem. of 3477; *rectitude:*—uprightness.

3484. יְשֻׁרוּן **Yeshûrûwn**, *yesh-oo-roon';* from 3474; *upright; Jeshurun*, a symbol. name for Israel:—Jeshurun.

3485. יִשָּׂשכָר **Yissâ'kâr**, *yis-saw-kawr'* (strictly *yis-saws-kawr'*); from 5375 and 7939; *he will bring a reward; Jissaskar*, a son of Jacob:—Issachar.

3486. יָשֵׁשׁ **yâshêsh**, *yaw-shaysh';* from an unused root mean. to *blanch; gray-*haired, i.e. an *aged* man:—stoop for age.

3487. יַת **yath** (Chald.), *yath;* corresp. to 853; a sign of the object of a verb: + whom.

3488. יְתִב **yethîyb** (Chald.), *yeth-eeb';* corresp. to 3427; to *sit* or *dwell:*—dwell, (be) set, sit.

3489. יָתֵד **yâthêd**, *yaw-thade';* from an unused root mean. to *pin* through or fast; a *peg:*—nail, paddle, pin, stake.

3490. יָתוֹם **yâthôwm**, *yaw-thome';* from an unused root mean. to *be lonely;* a *bereaved* person:—fatherless (child), orphan.

3491. יָתוּר **yâthûwr**, *yaw-thoor';* pass. part. of 3498; prop. what is *left*, i.e. (by impl.) a *gleaning:*—range.

3492. יַתִּיר **Yattîyr**, *yat-teer';* from 3498; *redundant; Jattir*, a place in Pal.:—Jattir.

3493. יַתִּיר **yattîyr** (Chald.) *yat-teer';* corresp. to 3492; *preeminent;* adv. *very:*—exceeding (-ly), excellent.

3494. יִתְלָה **Yithlâh**, *yith-law';* prob. from 8518; it *will hang*, i.e. be high; *Jithlah*, a place in Pal.:—Jethlah.

3495. יִתְמָה **Yithmâh**, *yith-maw';* from the same as 3490; *orphanage; Jithmah*, an Isr.:—Ithmah.

3496. יַתְנִיאֵל **Yathnîy'êl**, *yath-nee-ale';* from an unused root mean. to *endure*, and 410; *continued of God; Jathniël*, an Isr.:—Jathniel.

3497. יִתְנָן **Yithnân**, *yith-nawn';* from the same as 8577; *extensive; Jithnan*, a place in Pal.:—Ithnan.

3498. יָתַר **yâthar**, *yaw-thar';* a prim. root; to *jut* over or *exceed;* by impl. to *excel;* (intrans.) to *remain* or *be left;* causat. to *leave, cause to abound, preserve:*—excel, leave (a remnant), left behind, too much, make plenteous, preserve, (be, let) remain (-der, -ing, -nant), reserve, residue, rest.

3499. יֶתֶר **yether**, *yeh'-ther;* from 3498; prop. an *overhanging*, i.e. (by impl.) an *excess, superiority, remainder;* also a small *rope* (as hanging free):—+ abundant, cord, exceeding, excellency (-ent), what they leave, that hath left, plentifully, remnant, residue, rest, string, with.

3500. יֶתֶר **Yether**, *yeh'-ther;* the same as 3499 *Jether*, the name of five or six Isr. and of one Midianite:—Jether, Jethro. Comp. 3503.

3501. יִתְרָא **Yithrâ'**, *yith-raw';* by var. for 350[illegible] *Jithra*, an Isr. (or Ishmaelite):—Ithra[illegible]

3502. יִתְרָה **yithrâh**, *yith-raw'*; fem. of 3499; prop. *excellence*, i.e. (by impl.) *wealth:*—abundance, riches.

3503. יִתְרוֹ **Yithrôw**, *yith-ro'*; from 3499 with pron. suffix; *his excellence; Jethro*, Moses' father-in-law:—Jethro. Comp. 3500.

3504. יִתְרוֹן **yithrôwn**, *yith-rone'*; from 3498; *preeminence, gain:*—better, excellency (-leth), profit (-able).

3505. יִתְרִי **Yithrîy**, *yith-ree'*; patron. from 3500; a *Jithrite* or desc. of Jether:—Ithrite.

3506. יִתְרָן **Yithrân**, *yith-rawn'*; from 3498; *excellent; Jithran*, the name of an Edomite and of an Isr.:—Ithran.

3507. יִתְרְעָם **Yithreʿâm**, *yith-reh-awm'*; from 3499 and 5971; *excellence of people; Jithreäm*, a son of David:—Ithream.

3508. יֹתֶרֶת **yôthereth**, *yo-theh'-reth*; fem. act. part. of 3498; the *lobe* or *flap* of the liver (as if redundant or outhanging):—caul.

3509. יְתֵת **Yethêth**, *yeh-thayth'*; of uncert. der.; *Jetheth*, an Edomite:—Jetheth.

כ

3510. כָּאַב **kâʾab**, *kaw-ab'*; a prim. root; prop. to feel *pain*; by impl. to *grieve*; fig. to *spoil:*—grieving, mar, have pain, make sad (sore), (be) sorrowful.

3511. כְּאֵב **keʾêb**, *keh-abe'*; from 3510; *suffering* (phys. or mental), *adversity:*—grief, pain, sorrow.

3512. כָּאָה **kâʾâh**, *kaw-aw'*; a prim. root; to *despond;* causat. to *deject:*—broken, be grieved, make sad.

3513. כָּבַד **kâbad**, *kaw-bad'*; or

כָּבֵד **kâbêd**, *kaw-bade'*; a prim. root; to *be heavy*, i.e. in a bad sense (*burdensome, severe, dull*) or in a good sense (*numerous, rich, honorable*); causat. to *make weighty* (in the same two senses):—abounding with, more grievously afflict, boast, be chargeable, × be dim, glorify, be (make) glorious (things), glory, (very) great, be grievous, harden, be (make) heavy, be heavier, lay heavily, (bring to, come to, do, get, be had in) honour (self), (be) honourable (man), lade, × more be laid, make self many, nobles, prevail, promote (to honour), be rich, be (go) sore, stop.

3514. כֹּבֶד **kôbed**, *ko'-bed*; from 3513; *weight, multitude, vehemence:*—grievousness, heavy, great number.

3515. כָּבֵד **kâbêd**, *kaw-bade'*; from 3513; *heavy;* fig. in a good sense (*numerous*) or in a bad sense (*severe, difficult, stupid*):—(so) great, grievous, hard (-ened), (too) heavy (-ier), laden, much, slow, sore, thick.

3516. כָּבֵד **kâbêd**, *kaw-bade'*; the same as 3515; the *liver* (as the *heaviest* of the viscera):—liver.

כָּבֹד **kâbôd**. See 3519.

3517. כְּבֵדֻת **kebêdûth**, *keb-ay-dooth'*; fem. of 3515; *difficulty:*— × heavily.

3518. כָּבָה **kâbâh**, *kaw-baw'*; a prim. root; to *expire* or (causat.) to *extinguish* (fire, light, anger):—go (put) out, quench.

3519. כָּבוֹד **kâbôwd**, *kaw-bode'*; rarely

כָּבֹד **kâbôd**, *kaw-bode'*; from 3513; prop. *weight;* but only fig. in a good sense, *splendor* or *copiousness:*—glorious (-ly), glory, honour (-able).

3520. כְּבוּדָּה **kebûwddâh**, *keb-ood-daw'*; irreg. fem. pass. part. of 3513; *weightiness*, i.e. *magnificence, wealth:*—carriage, all glorious, stately.

3521. כָּבוּל **Kâbûwl**, *kaw-bool'*; from the same as 3525 in the sense of *limitation; sterile; Cabul*, the name of two places in Pal.:—Cabul.

3522. כַּבּוֹן **Kabbôwn**, *kab-bone'*; from an unused root mean. to *heap up; hilly; Cabbon*, a place in Pal.:—Cabbon.

3523. כְּבִיר **kebîyr**, *keb-eer'*; from 3527 in the orig. sense of *plaiting;* a *matrass* (of intertwined materials):—pillow.

3524. כַּבִּיר **kabbîyr**, *kab-beer'*; from 3527; *vast*, whether in extent (fig. of power, *mighty;* of time, *aged*), or in number, *many:*—+ feeble, mighty, most, much, strong, valiant.

3525. כֶּבֶל **kebel**, *keh'-bel*; from an unused root mean. to *twine* or braid together; a *fetter:*—fetter.

3526. כָּבַס **kâbaç**, *kaw-bas'*; a prim. root; to *trample;* hence to *wash* (prop. by stamping with the feet), whether lit. (including the *fulling* process) or fig.:—fuller, wash (-ing).

3527. כָּבַר **kâbar**, *kaw-bar'*; a prim. root; prop. to *plait* together, i.e. (fig.) to *augment* (espec. in number or quantity, to *accumulate*):—in abundance, multiply.

3528. כְּבָר **kebâr**, *keb-awr'*; from 3527; prop. *extent* of time, i.e. a *great while;* hence *long ago, formerly, hitherto:*—already, (seeing that which), now.

3529. כְּבָר **Kebâr**, *keb-awr'*; the same as 3528; *length; Kebar*, a river of Mesopotamia:—Chebar. Comp. 2249.

3530. כִּבְרָה **kibrâh**, *kib-raw'*; fem. of 3528; prop. *length*, i.e. a *measure* (of uncert. dimension):— × little.

3531. כְּבָרָה **kebârâh**, *keb-aw-raw'*; from 3527 in its orig. sense; a *sieve* (as netted):—sieve.

3532. כֶּבֶשׂ **kebes**, *keh-bes'*; from an unused root mean. to *dominate;* a *ram* (just old enough to *butt*):—lamb, sheep.

3533. כָּבַשׁ **kâbash**, *kaw-bash'*; a prim. root; to *tread* down; hence neg. to *disregard;* pos. to *conquer, subjugate, violate:*—bring into bondage, force, keep under, subdue, bring into subjection.

3534. כֶּבֶשׁ **kebesh**, *keh'-besh*; from 3533; a *footstool* (as trodden upon):—footstool.

3535. כִּבְשָׂה **kibsâh**, *kib-saw'*; or

כַּבְשָׂה **kabsâh**, *kab-saw'*; fem. of 3532; a *ewe:*—(ewe) lamb.

3536. כִּבְשָׁן **kibshân**, *kib-shawn'*; from 3533; a smelting *furnace* (as *reducing* metals):—furnace.

3537. כַּד **kad**, *kad;* from an unused root mean. to *deepen;* prop. a *pail;* but gen. of earthenware; a *jar* for domestic purposes:—barrel, pitcher.

3538. כְּדַב **kedab** (Chald.), *ked-ab'*; from a root corresp. to 3576; *false:*—lying.

3539. כַּדְכֹּד **kadkôd**, *kad-kode'*; from the same as 3537 in the sense of *striking fire* from a metal forged; a *sparkling* gem, prob. the ruby:—agate.

3540. כְּדָרְלָעֹמֶר **Kedorlâʿômer**, *ked-or-law-o'-mer;* of for. or.; *Kedorlaomer*, an early Pers. king:—Chedorlaomer.

3541. כֹּה **kôh**, *ko;* from the prefix *k* and 1931; prop. *like this*, i.e. by impl. (of manner) *thus* (or *so*); also (of place) *here* (or *hither*); or (of time) *now:*—also, here, + hitherto, like, on the other side, so (and much), such, on that manner, (on) this (manner, side, way, way and that way), + mean while, yonder.

3542. כָּה **kâh** (Chald.), *kaw;* corresp. to 3541:—hitherto.

3543. כָּהָה **kâhâh**, *kaw-haw'*; a prim. root; to *be weak*, i.e. (fig.) to *despond* (causat. *rebuke*), or (of light, the eye) to *grow dull:*—darken, be dim, fail, faint, restrain, × utterly.

3544. כֵּהֶה **kêheh**, *kay-heh'*; from 3543; *feeble, obscure:*—somewhat dark, darkish, wax dim, heaviness, smoking.

3545. כֵּהָה **kêhâh**, *kay-haw'*; fem. of 3544; prop. a *weakening;* fig. *alleviation*, i.e. cure:—healing.

3546. כְּהַל **kehal** (Chald.), *keh-hal';* a root corresp. to 3201 and 3557; to *be able:*—be able, could.

3547. כָּהַן **kâhan**, *kaw-han';* a prim. root, appar. mean. to *mediate* in religious services; but used only as denom. from 3548; to *officiate* as a priest; fig. to *put on regalia:*—deck, be (do the office of a, execute the, minister in the) priest ('s office).

3548. כֹּהֵן **kôhên**, *ko-hane';* act. part. of 3547; lit. one *officiating*, a *priest;* also (by courtesy) an *acting priest* (although a layman):—chief ruler, × own, priest, prince, principal officer.

3549. כָּהֵן **kâhên** (Chald.), *kaw-hane';* corresp. to 3548:—priest.

3550. כְּהֻנָּה **kehunnâh**, *keh-hoon-naw';* from 3547; *priesthood:*—priesthood, priest's office.

3551. כַּו **kav** (Chald.), *kav;* from a root corresp. to 3854 in the sense of *piercing;* a *window* (as a perforation):—window.

3552. כּוּב **Kûwb**, *koob;* of for. der.; *Kub*, a country near Egypt:—Chub.

3553. כּוֹבַע **kôwbaʿ**, *ko'-bah;* from an unused root mean. to be *high* or *rounded;* a *helmet* (as *arched*):—helmet. Comp. 6959.

3554. כָּוָה **kâvâh**, *kaw-vaw';* a prim. root; prop. to *prick* or *penetrate;* hence to *blister* (as smarting or eating into):—burn.

כּוֹחַ **kôwach**. See 3581.

3555. כְּוִיָּה **keviyâh**, *kev-ee-yaw';* from 3554; a *branding:*—burning.

3556. כּוֹכָב **kôwkâb**, *ko-kawb';* prob. from the same as 3522 (in the sense of *rolling*) or 3554 (in the sense of *blazing*); a *star* (as *round* or as *shining*); fig. a *prince:*—star ([-gazer]).

3557. כּוּל **kûwl**, *kool;* a prim. root; prop. to *keep in;* hence to *measure;* fig. to *maintain* (in various senses):—(be able to, can) abide, bear, comprehend, contain, feed, forbearing, guide, hold (-ing in), nourish (-er), be present, make provision, receive, sustain, provide sustenance (victuals).

3558. כּוּמָז **kûwmâz**, *koo-mawz';* from an unused root mean. to *store away;* a *jewel* (prob. gold beads):—tablet.

3559. כּוּן **kûwn**, *koon;* a prim. root; prop. to *be erect* (i.e. stand perpendicular); hence (causat.) to *set up*, in a great variety of applications, whether lit. (*establish, fix, prepare, apply*), or fig. (*appoint, render sure, proper* or *prosperous*):—certain (-ty), confirm, direct, faithfulness, fashion, fasten, firm, be fitted, be fixed, frame, be meet, ordain, order, perfect, (make) preparation, prepare (self), provide, make provision, (be, make) ready, right, set (aright, fast, forth), be stable, (e-) stablish, stand, tarry, × very deed.

3560. כּוּן **Kûwn**, *koon;* prob. from 3559; *established; Kun*, a place in Syria:—Chun.

3561. כַּוָּן **kavvân**, *kav-vawn';* from 3559; something *prepared*, i.e. a sacrificial *wafer:*—cake.

3562. כּוֹנַנְיָהוּ **Kôwnanyâhûw**, *ko-nan-yaw'-hoo;* from 3559 and 3050; *Jah has sustained; Conanjah*, the name of two Isr.:—Conaniah, Cononiah. Comp. 3663.

3563. כּוֹס **kôwç**, *koce;* from an unused root mean. to *hold* together; a *cup* (as a container), often fig. a *lot* (as if a potion); also some unclean bird, prob. an *owl* (perh. from the cup-like cavity of its eye):—cup, (small) owl. Comp. 3599.

3564. כּוּר **kûwr**, *koor;* from an unused root mean. prop. to *dig* through; a *pot* or *furnace* (as if excavated):—furnace. Comp. 3600.

כּוֹר **kôwr**. See 3733.

3565. כּוֹר עָשָׁן **Kôwr ʿÂshân**, *kore aw-shawn';* from 3564 and 6227; *furnace of smoke; Cor-Ashan*, a place in Pal.:—Chor-ashan.

3566. כּוֹרֶשׁ **Kôwresh**, *ko'-resh;* or (Ezra 1 : 1 [last time], 2)

כֹּרֶשׁ **Kôresh**, *ko'-resh;* from the Pers.; *Koresh* (or Cyrus), the Pers. king:—Cyrus.

3567. כּוֹרֶשׁ **Kôwresh** (Chald.), *ko'-resh;* corresp. to 3566:—Cyrus.

3568. כּוּשׁ **Kûwsh**, *koosh;* prob. of for. or.; *Cush* (or Ethiopia), the name of a son of Ham, and of his territory; also of an Isr.:—Chush, Cush, Ethiopia.

3569. כּוּשִׁי **Kûwshîy**, *koo-shee';* patron. from 3568; a *Cushite*, or desc. of Cush:—Cushi, Cushite, Ethiopian (-s).

3570. כּוּשִׁי **Kûwshîy**, *koo-shee';* the same as 3569; *Cushi*, the name of two Isr.:—Cushi.

3571. כּוּשִׁית **Kûwshîyth**, *koo-sheeth';* fem. of 3569; a *Cushite woman:*—Ethiopian.

3572. כּוּשָׁן **Kûwshân**, *koo-shawn';* perh. from 3568; *Cushan*, a region of Arabia:—Cushan.

3573. כּוּשַׁן רִשְׁעָתַיִם **Kûwshan Rish'âthâyim**, *koo-shan' rish-aw-thah'-yim;* appar. from 3572 and the dual of 7564; *Cushan of double wickedness; Cushan-Rishathajim*, a Mesopotamian king:—Chushan-rishathayim.

3574. כּוֹשָׁרָה **kôwshârâh**, *ko-shaw-raw';* from 3787; *prosperity;* in plur. *freedom:*—× chain.

3575. כּוּת **Kûwth**, *kooth;* or (fem.)

כּוּתָה **Kûwthâh**, *koo-thaw';* of for. or.; *Cuth* or *Cuthah*, a province of Assyria:—Cuth.

3576. כָּזַב **kâzab**, *kaw-zab';* a prim. root; to *lie* (i.e. *deceive*), lit. or fig.:—fail, (be found a, make a) liar, lie, lying, be in vain.

3577. כָּזָב **kâzâb**, *kaw-zawb';* from 3576; *falsehood;* lit. (*untruth*) or fig. (*idol*):—deceitful, false, leasing, + liar, lie, lying.

3578. כֹּזֵבָא **Kôzebâ'**, *ko-zeb-aw';* from 3576; *fallacious; Cozeba*, a place in Pal.:—Choseba.

3579. כָּזְבִּי **Kozbîy**, *koz-bee';* from 3576; *false; Cozbi*, a Midianitess:—Cozbi.

3580. כְּזִיב **Kezîyb**, *kez-eeb';* from 3576; *falsified; Kezib*, a place in Pal.:—Chezib.

3581. כֹּחַ **kôach**, *ko'-akh;* or (Dan. 11 : 6)

כּוֹחַ **kôwach**, *ko'-akh;* from an unused root mean. to *be firm; vigor*, lit. (*force*, in a good or a bad sense) or fig. (*capacity, means, produce*); also (from its hardiness) a large *lizard:*—ability, able, chameleon, force, fruits, might, power (-ful), strength, substance, wealth.

3582. כָּחַד **kâchad**, *kaw-khad';* a prim. root; to *secrete*, by act or word; hence (intens.) to *destroy:*—conceal, cut down (off), desolate, hide.

3583. כָּחַל **kâchal**, *kaw-khal';* a prim. root; to *paint* (with stibium):—paint.

3584. כָּחַשׁ **kâchash**, *kaw-khash';* a prim. root; to *be untrue*, in word (to *lie, feign, disown*) or deed (to *disappoint, fail, cringe*):—deceive, deny, dissemble, fail, deal falsely, be found liars, (be-) lie, lying, submit selves.

3585. כַּחַשׁ **kachash**, *kakh'-ash;* from 3584; lit. a *failure* of flesh, i.e. *emaciation;* fig. *hypocrisy:*—leanness, lies, lying.

3586. כֶּחָשׁ **kechâsh**, *kekh-awsh';* from 3584; *faithless:*—lying.

3587. כִּי **kîy**, *kee;* from 3554; a *brand* or *scar:*—burning.

3588. כִּי **kîy**, *kee;* a prim. particle [the full form of the prepositional prefix] indicating *causal* relations of all kinds, antecedent or consequent; (by impl.) very widely used as a rel. conj. or adv. [as below]; often largely modified by other particles annexed:—and, + (forasmuch, inasmuch, where-) as, assured [-ly], + but, certainly, doubtless, + else, even, + except, for, how, (because, in, so, than) that, + nevertheless, now, rightly, seeing, since, surely, then, therefore, + (al-) though, + till, truly, + until, when, whether, while, whom, yea, yet.

3589. כִּיד **kîyd**, *keed;* from a prim. root mean. to *strike:* a *crushing;* fig. *calamity:*—destruction.

3590. כִּידוֹד **kîydôwd**, *kee-dode';* from the same as 3589 [comp. 3539]; prop. something *struck* off, i.e. a *spark* (as struck):—spark.

3591. כִּידוֹן **kîydôwn**, *kee-dohn';* from the same as 3589; prop. something to *strike* with, i.e. a *dart* (perh. smaller than 2595):—lance, shield, spear, target.

3592. כִּידוֹן **Kîydôwn**, *kee-dohn';* the same as 3591; *Kidon*, a place in Pal.:—Chidon.

3593. כִּידוֹר **kîydôwr**, *kee-dore';* of uncert. der.; perh. *tumult:*—battle.

3594. כִּיּוּן **Kîyûwn**, *kee-yoon';* from 3559; prop. a *statue*, i.e. idol; but used (by euphemism) for some heathen deity (perh. corresp. to Priapus or Baal-peor):—Chiun.

3595. כִּיּוֹר **kîyôwr**, *kee-yore';* or

כִּיֹּר **kîyôr**, *kee-yore';* from the same as 3564; prop. something *round* (as *excavated* or *bored*), i.e. a chafing-*dish* for coals or a *caldron* for cooking; hence (from similarity of form) a *washbowl;* also (for the same reason) a *pulpit* or platform:—hearth, laver, pan, scaffold.

3596. כִּילַי **kîylay**, *kee-lah'ee;* or

כֵּלַי **kêlay**, *kay-lah'ee;* from 3557 in the sense of *withholding; niggardly:*—churl.

3597. כֵּילַף **kêylaph**, *kay-laf';* from an unused root mean. to *clap* or strike with noise; a *club* or sledge-hammer:—hammer.

3598. כִּימָה **Kîymâh**, *kee-maw';* from the same as 3558; a *cluster* of stars, i.e. the *Pleiades:*—Pleiades, seven stars.

3599. כִּיס **kîyç**, *keece;* a form for 3563; a *cup;* also a *bag* for money or weights:—bag, cup, purse.

3600. כִּיר **kîyr**, *keer;* a form for 3564 (only in the dual); a cooking *range* (consisting of two parallel stones, across which the boiler is set):—ranges for pots.

כִּיֹּר **kîyôr**. See 3595.

3601. כִּישׁוֹר **kîyshôwr**, *kee-shore';* from 3787; lit. a *director*, i.e. the *spindle* or shank of a distaff (6418), by which it is twirled:—spindle.

3602. כָּכָה **kâkâh**, *kaw'-kaw;* from 3541; *just so*, referring to the previous or following context:—after that (this) manner, this matter, (even) so, in such a case, thus.

3603. כִּכָּר **kikkâr**, *kik-kawr';* from 3769; a *circle*, i.e. (by impl.) a circumjacent *tract* or region, espec. the *Ghôr* or valley of the Jordan; also a (round) *loaf;* also a *talent* (or large [round] coin):—loaf, morsel, piece, plain, talent.

3604. כִּכַּר **kikkêr** (Chald.), *kik-kare';* corresp. to 3603; a *talent:*—talent.

3605. כֹּל **kôl**, *kole;* or (Jer. 33 : 8)°

כּוֹל **kôwl**, *kole;* from 3634; prop. the *whole;* hence *all, any* or *every* (in the sing. only, but often in a plur. sense):—(in) all (manner, [ye]), altogether, any (manner), enough, every (one, place, thing), howsoever, as many as, [no-] thing, ought, whatsoever, (the) whole, whoso (-ever).

3606. כֹּל **kôl** (Chald.), *kole;* corresp. to 3605:—all, any, + (forasmuch) as, + be- (for this) cause, every, + no (manner, -ne), + there (where) -fore, + though, what (where, who) -soever, (the) whole.

3607. כָּלָא **kâlâ'**, *kaw-law';* a prim. root; to *restrict*, by act (*hold* back or in) or word (*prohibit*):—finish, forbid, keep (back), refrain, restrain, retain, shut up, be stayed, withhold.

3608. כֶּלֶא **kele'**, *keh'-leh;* from 3607; a *prison:*—prison. Comp. 3610, 3628.

3609. כִּלְאָב **Kil'âb**, *kil-awb';* appar. from 3607 and 1; *restraint of* (his) *father; Kilab*, an Isr.:—Chileab.

3610. כִּלְאַיִם **kil'ayim**, *kil-ah'-yim;* dual of 3608 in the original sense of *separation; two heterogeneities:*—divers seeds (-e kinds), mingled (seed).

3611. כֶּלֶב **keleb**, *keh'-leb;* from an unused root mean. to *yelp*, or else to *attack;* a *dog;* hence (by euphemism) a male *prostitute:*—dog.

3612. כָּלֵב **Kâlêb**, *kaw-labe';* perh. a form of 3611, or else from the same root in the sense of *forcible; Caleb*, the name of three Isr.:—Caleb.

3613. כָּלֵב אֶפְרָתָה **Kâlêb 'Ephrâthâh**, *kaw-labe' ef-raw'-thaw;* from 3612 and 672; *Caleb-Ephrathah*, a place in Eg. (if the text is correct):—Caleb-ephrathah.

3614. כָּלִבּוֹ° **Kâlibbôw**, *kaw-lib-bo';* prob. by err. transc. for

כָּלֵבִי **Kâlêbîy**, *kaw-lay-bee';* patron. from 3612; a *Calebite* or desc. of Caleb:—of the house of Caleb.

3615. כָּלָה **kâlâh**, *kaw-law';* a prim. root; to *end*, whether intrans. (to *cease, be finished, perish*) or trans. (to *complete, prepare, consume*):—accomplish, cease, consume (away), determine, destroy (utterly), be (when . . . were) done, (be an) end (of), expire, (cause to) fail, faint, finish, fulfil, × fully, × have, leave (off), long, bring to pass, wholly reap, make clean riddance, spend, quite take away, waste.

3616. כָּלֶה **kâleh**, *kaw-leh';* from 3615; *pining:*—fail.

3617. כָּלָה **kâlâh**, *kaw-law';* from 3615; a *completion;* adv. *completely;* also *destruction:*—altogether, (be, utterly) consume (-d), consummation (-ption), was determined, (full, utter) end, riddance.

3618. כַּלָּה **kallâh**, *kal-law';* from 3634; a *bride* (as if *perfect*); hence a *son's wife:*—bride, daughter-in-law, spouse.

כְּלוּא **kelûw'**. See 3628.

3619. כְּלוּב **kelûb**, *kel-oob';* from the same as 3611; a bird-*trap* (as furnished with a *clap*-stick or treadle to spring it); hence a *basket* (as resembling a wicker cage):—basket, cage.

3620. כְּלוּב **Kelûwb**, *kel-oob';* the same as 3619; *Kelub*, the name of two Isr.:—Chelub.

3621. כְּלוּבַי **Kelûwbay**, *kel-oo-bay'ee;* a form of 3612; *Kelubai*, an Isr.:—Chelubai.

3622. כְּלוּהַי **Kelûwhay**, *kel-oo-hah'ee;* from 3615; *completed; Keluhai*, an Isr.:—Chelluh.

3623. כְּלוּלָה **kelûwlâh**, *kel-oo-law';* denom pass. part. from 3618; *bridehood* (only in the plur.):—espousal.

3624. כֶּלַח **kelach**, *keh'-lakh;* from an unused root mean. to *be complete; maturity:*—full (old) age.

3625. כֶּלַח **Kelach**, *keh'-lakh;* the same as 3624; *Kelach*, a place in Assyria:—Calah.

3626. כָּל־חֹזֶה **Kol-Chôzeh**, *kol-kho-zeh';* from 3605 and 2374; *every seer; Col-Chozeh*, an Isr.:—Col-hozeh.

3627. כְּלִי **kelîy**, *kel-ee';* from 3615; something *prepared*, i.e. any *apparatus* (as an implement, utensil, dress, vessel or weapon):—armour ([-bearer]), artillery, bag, carriage, + furnish, furniture, instrument, jewel, that is made of, × one from another, that which pertaineth, pot, + psaltery, sack, stuff, thing, tool, vessel, ware, weapon, + whatsoever.

3628. כְּלִיא **kelîy'**, *kel-ee';* or

כְּלוּא **kelûw'**, *kel-oo';* from 3607 [comp. 3608]; a *prison:*—prison.

3629. כִּלְיָה **kilyâh**, *kil-yaw';* fem. of 3627 (only in the plur.); a *kidney* (as an essential *organ*); fig. the *mind* (as the interior self):—kidneys, reins.

3630. כִּלְיוֹן **Kilyôwn**, *kil-yone';* a form of 3631; *Kiljon*, an Isr.:—Chilion.

3631. כִּלָּיוֹן **killâyôwn**, *kil-law-yone';* from 3615; *pining, destruction:*—consumption, failing.

3632. כָּלִיל **kâlîyl**, *kaw-leel';* from 3634; *complete;* as noun, the *whole* (spec. a sacrifice *entirely consumed*); as adv. *fully:*—all, every whit, flame, perfect (-ion), utterly, whole burnt offering (sacrifice), wholly.

3633. כַּלְכֹּל **Kalkôl**, *kal-kole';* from 3557; *sustenance; Calcol*, an Isr.:—Calcol, Chalcol.

3634. כָּלַל **kâlal**, *kaw-lal';* a prim. root; to *complete:*—(make) perfect.

3635. כְּלַל **k^{e}lal** (Chald.), *kel-al';* corresp. to 3634; to *complete:*—finish, make (set) up.

3636. כְּלָל **K^{e}lâl**, *kel-awl';* from 3634; *complete; Kelal*, an Isr.:—Chelal.

3637. כָּלַם **kâlam**, *kaw-lawm';* a prim. root; prop. to *wound;* but only fig., to *taunt* or *insult:*—be (make) ashamed, blush, be confounded, be put to confusion, hurt, reproach, (do, put to) shame.

3638. כִּלְמָד **Kilmâd**, *kil-mawd';* of for. der.; *Kilmad*, a place appar. in the Assyrian empire:—Chilmad.

3639. כְּלִמָּה **k^{e}limmâh**, *kel-im-maw';* from 3637; *disgrace:*—confusion, dishonour, reproach, shame.

3640. כְּלִמּוּת **k^{e}limmûwth**, *kel-im-mooth';* from 3639; *disgrace:*—shame.

3641. כַּלְנֶה **Kalneh**, *kal-neh';* or

כַּלְנֵה **Kalnêh**, *kal-nay';* also

כַּלְנוֹ **Kalnôw**, *kal-no';* of for. der.; *Calneh* or *Calno*, a place in the Assyrian empire:—Calneh, Calno. Comp. 3656.

3642. כָּמַהּ **kâmahh**, *kaw-mah';* a prim. root; to *pine* after:—long.

3643. כִּמְהָם **Kimhâm**, *kim-hawm';* from 3642; *pining; Kimham*, an Isr.:—Chimham.

3644. כְּמוֹ **k^{e}môw**, *kem-o';* or

כָּמוֹ **kâmôw**, *kaw-mo';* a form of the pref. *k*, but used separately [comp. 3651]; *as, thus, so:*—according to, (such) as (it were, well as), in comparison of, like (as, to, unto), thus, when, worth.

3645. כְּמוֹשׁ **K^{e}môwsh**, *kem-oshe';* or (Jer. 48 : 7)

כְּמִישׁ **K^{e}mîysh**, *kem-eesh';* from an unused root mean. to *subdue;* the *powerful; Kemosh*, the god of the Moabites:—Chemosh.

3646. כַּמֹּן **kammôn**, *kam-mone';* from an unused root mean. to *store* up or *preserve;* "*cummin*" (from its use as a *condiment*):—cummin.

3647. כָּמַס **kâmaç**, *kaw-mas';* a prim. root; to *store* away, i.e. (fig.) in the memory:—lay up in store.

3648. כָּמַר **kâmar**, *kaw-mar';* a prim. root; prop. to *intertwine* or *contract*, i.e. (by impl.) to *shrivel* (as with heat); fig. to *be* deeply *affected* with passion (love or pity):—be black, be kindled, yearn.

3649. כָּמָר **kâmâr**, *kaw-mawr';* from 3648; prop. an *ascetic* (as if *shrunk* with self-maceration), i.e. an idolatrous *priest* (only in plur.):—Chemarims, (idolatrous) priests.

3650. כִּמְרִיר **kimrîyr**, *kim-reer';* redupl. from 3648; *obscuration* (as if from *shrinkage* of light), i.e. an *eclipse* (only in plur.):—blackness.

3651. כֵּן **kên**, *kane;* from 3559; prop. *set* upright; hence (fig. as adj.) *just;* but usually (as adv. or conj.) *rightly* or *so* (in various applications to manner, time and relation; often with other particles):— + after that (this, -ward, -wards), as . . . as, + [for-] asmuch as yet, + be (for which) cause, + following, howbeit, in (the) like (manner, -wise), × the more, right, (even) so, state, straightway, such (thing), surely, + there (where) -fore, this, thus, true, well, × you.

3652. כֵּן **kên** (Chald.), *kane;* corresp. to 3651; *so:*—thus.

3653. כֵּן **kên**, *kane;* the same as 3651, used as a noun; a *stand*, i.e. pedestal or station:—base, estate, foot, office, place, well.

3654. כֵּן **kên**, *kane;* from 3661 in the sense of *fastening;* a *gnat* (from infixing its sting; used only in plur. [and irreg. in Exod. 8 : 17, 18; Heb. 13 : 14]):—lice, × manner.

3655. כָּנָה **kânâh**, *kaw-naw';* a prim. root; to *address* by an additional name; hence, to *eulogize:*—give flattering titles, surname (himself).

3656. כַּנֶּה **Kanneh**, *kan-neh';* for 3641; *Canneh*, a place in Assyria:—Canneh.

3657. כַּנָּה **kannâh**, *kan-naw';* from 3661; a *plant* (as *set*):— × vineyard.

3658. כִּנּוֹר **kinnôwr**, *kin-nore';* from an unused root mean. to *twang;* a *harp:*—harp.

3659. כָּנְיָהוּ **Konyâhûw**, *kon-yaw'-hoo;* for 3204; *Conjah*, an Isr. king:—Coniah.

3660. כְּנֵמָא **k^{e}nêmâʼ** (Chald.), *ken-ay-maw';* corresp. to 3644; *so* or *thus:*—so, (in) this manner (sort), thus.

3661. כָּנַן **kânan**, *kaw-nan';* a prim. root; to *set* out, i.e. *plant:*— × vineyard.

3662. כְּנָנִי **K^{e}nânîy**, *ken-aw-nee';* from 3661; *planted; Kenani*, an Isr.:—Chenani.

3663. כְּנַנְיָה **K^{e}nanyâh**, *ken-an-yaw';* or

כְּנַנְיָהוּ **K^{e}nanyâhûw**, *ken-an-yaw'-hoo;* from 3661 and 3050; *Jah has planted; Kenanjah*, an Isr.:—Chenaniah.

3664. כָּנַס **kânaç**, *kaw-nas';* a prim. root; to *collect;* hence, to *enfold:*—gather (together), heap up, wrap self.

3665. כָּנַע **kânaʻ**, *kaw-nah';* a prim. root; prop. to *bend* the knee; hence to *humiliate, vanquish:*—bring down (low), into subjection, under, humble (self), subdue.

3666. כִּנְעָה **kinʻâh**, *kin-aw';* from 3665 in the sense of *folding* [comp. 3664]; a *package:*—wares.

3667. כְּנַעַן **K^{e}naʻan**, *ken-ah'-an;* from 3665; *humiliated; Kenaan*, a son of Ham; also the country inhabited by him:—Canaan, merchant, traffick.

3668. כְּנַעֲנָה **K^{e}naʻănâh**, *ken-ah-an-aw';* fem. of 3667; *Kenaanah*, the name of two Isr.:—Chenaanah.

3669. כְּנַעֲנִי **K^{e}naʻănîy**, *ken-ah-an-ee';* patrial from 3667; a *Kenaanite* or inhabitant of Kenaan; by impl. a *pedlar* (the Canaanites standing for their neighbors the Ishmaelites, who conducted mercantile caravans):—Canaanite, merchant, trafficker.

3670. כָּנַף **kânaph**, *kaw-naf';* a prim. root; prop. to *project* laterally, i.e. prob. (reflex.) to *withdraw:*—be removed.

3671. כָּנָף **kânâph**, *kaw-nawf';* from 3670; an *edge* or *extremity;* spec. (of a bird or army) a *wing*, (of a garment or bed-clothing) a *flap*, (of the earth) a *quarter*, (of a building) a *pinnacle:*— + bird, border, corner, end, feather [-ed], × flying, + (one an-) other, overspreading, × quarters, skirt, × sort, uttermost part, wing ([-ed]).

3672. כִּנְּרוֹת **Kinn^{e}rôwth**, *kin-ner-ôth';* or

כִּנֶּרֶת **Kinnereth**, *kin-neh'-reth;* respectively plur. and sing. fem. from the same as 3658; perh. *harp*-shaped; *Kinneroth* or *Kinnereth*, a place in Pal.:—Chinnereth, Chinneroth, Cinneroth.

3673. כָּנַשׁ **kânash** (Chald.), *kaw-nash';* corresp. to 3664; to *assemble:*—gather together.

3674. כְּנָת **k^{e}nâth**, *ken-awth';* from 3655; a *colleague* (as having the same title):—companion.

3675. כְּנָת **k^{e}nâth** (Chald.), *ken-awth';* corresp. to 3674:—companion.

3676. כֵּס **kêç**, *kace;* appar. a contr. for 3678, but prob. by err. transc. for 5251:—sworn.

3677. כֶּסֶא **keçeʼ**, *keh'-seh;* or

כֶּסֶה **keçeh**, *keh'-seh;* appar. from 3680; prop. *fulness* or the *full moon*, i.e. its festival:—(time) appointed.

3678. כִּסֵּא **kiççêʼ**, *kis-say';* or

כִּסֵּה **kiççêh**, *kis-say';* from 3680; prop. *covered*, i.e. a *throne* (as *canopied*):—seat, stool, throne.

3679. כַּסְדַּי **Kaçday**, *kas-dah'ee;* for 3778:—Chaldean.

3680. כָּסָה **kâçâh**, *kaw-saw';* a prim. root; prop. to *plump*, i.e. *fill up* hollows; by impl. to *cover* (for clothing or secrecy):—clad self, close, clothe, conceal, cover (self), (flee to) hide, overwhelm. Comp. 3780.

כֶּסֶה **keçeh**. See 3677.

כִּסֵּה **kiççêh**. See 3678.

3681. כָּסוּי **kâçûwy**, *kaw-soo'ee;* pass. part. of 3680; prop. *covered*, i.e. (as noun) a *covering:*—covering.

3682. כְּסוּת **k^{e}çûwth**, *kes-ooth';* from 3680; a *cover* (garment); fig. a *veiling:*—covering, raiment, vesture.

3683. כָּסַח **kâçach**, *kaw-sakh';* a prim. root; to *cut off:*—cut down (up).

3684. כְּסִיל **k^{e}çîyl**, *kes-eel';* from 3688; prop. *fat*, i.e. (fig.) stupid or *silly:*—fool (-ish).

3685. כְּסִיל **K^{e}çîyl**, *kes-eel';* the same as 3684; any notable *constellation;* spec. *Orion* (as if a *burly* one):—constellation, Orion.

3686. כְּסִיל **K^{e}çîyl**, *kes-eel';* the same as 3684; *Kesil*, a place in Pal.:—Chesil.

3687. כְּסִילוּת **k^{e}çîylûwth**, *kes-eel-ooth';* from 3684; *silliness:*—foolish.

3688. כָּסַל **kâçal**, *kaw-sal';* a prim. root; prop. to *be fat*, i.e. (fig.) *silly:*—be foolish.

3689. כֶּסֶל **keçel**, *keh'-sel;* from 3688; prop. *fatness*, i.e. by impl. (lit.) the *loin* (as the seat of the leaf *fat*) or (gen.) the *viscera;* also (fig.) *silliness* or (in a good sense) *trust:*—confidence, flank, folly, hope, loin.

3690. כִּסְלָה **kiçlâh**, *kis-law';* fem. of 3689; in a good sense, *trust;* in a bad one, *silliness:*—confidence, folly.

3691. כִּסְלֵו **Kiçlêv**, *kis-lave';* prob. of for. or.; *Kisleu*, the 9th Heb. month:—Chisleu.

3692. כִּסְלוֹן **Kiçlôwn**, *kis-lone';* from 3688; *hopeful; Kislon*, an Isr.:—Chislon.

3693. כְּסָלוֹן **K^{e}çâlôwn**, *kes-aw-lone';* from 3688; *fertile; Kesalon*, a place in Pal.:—Chesalon.

3694. כְּסֻלּוֹת **K^{e}çullôwth**, *kes-ool-lōth';* fem. plur. of pass. part. of 3688; *fattened, Kesulloth*, a place in Pal.:—Chesulloth.

3695. כַּסְלֻחִים **Kaçlûchîym**, *kas-loo'-kheem;* a plur. prob. of for. der.; *Casluchim*, a people cognate to the Eg.:—Casluhim.

3696. כִּסְלֹת תָּבֹר **Kiçlôth Tâbôr**, *kis-lōth' taw-bore';* from the fem. plur. of 3689 and 8396; *flanks of Tabor; Kisloth-Tabor*, a place in Pal.:—Chisloth-tabor.

3697. כָּסַם **kâçam**, *kaw-sam';* a prim. root; to *shear:*— × only, poll. Comp. 3765.

3698. כֻּסֶּמֶת **kuççemeth**, *koos-seh'-meth;* from 3697; *spelt* (from its bristliness as if just *shorn*):—fitches, rie.

3699. כָּסַס **kâçaç**, *kaw-sas';* a prim. root; to *estimate:*—make count.

3700. כָּסַף **kâçaph**, *kaw-saf';* a prim. root; prop. to become *pale*, i.e. (by impl.) to *pine* after; also to *fear:*—[have] desire, be greedy, long, sore.

3701. כֶּסֶף **keçeph**, *keh'-sef;* from 3700; *silver* (from its *pale* color); by impl. *money:*—money, price, silver (-ling).

3702. כְּסַף **k^{e}çaph** (Chald.), *kes-af';* corresp. to 3701:—money, silver.

3703. כָּסִפְיָא **Kâçiphyâʼ**, *kaw-sif-yaw';* perh. from 3701; *silvery; Casiphja*, a place in Bab.:—Casiphia.

3704. כֶּסֶת **keçeth**, *keh'-seth;* from 3680; a *cushion* or pillow (as *covering* a seat or bed):—pillow.

3705. כְּעַן **k^{e}ʻan** (Chald.), *keh-an';* prob. from 3652; *now:*—now.

3706. כְּעֶנֶת **k^{e}ʻeneth** (Chald.), *keh-eh'-neth;* or

כְּעֶת **k^{e}ʻeth** (Chald.), *keh-eth';* fem. of 3705; *thus* (only in the formula "and *so forth*"):—at such a time.

3707. כָּעַס **kâʻaç**, *kaw-as';* a prim. root; to *trouble;* by impl. to *grieve, rage, be indignant:*—be angry, be grieved, take indignation, provoke (to anger, unto wrath), have sorrow, vex, be wroth.

3708. כַּעַס **kaʻaç**, *kah'-as;* or (in Job)

כַּעַשׂ **kaʻas**, *kah'-as;* from 3707; *vexation:*—anger, angry, grief, indignation, provocation, provoking, × sore, sorrow, spite, wrath.

כְּעֶת **k^{e}ʻeth**. See 3706.

3709. כַּף **kaph**, *kaf;* from 3721; the hollow *hand* or palm (so of the *paw* of an animal, of the *sole*, and even of the *bowl* of a dish or sling, the *handle* of a bolt, the *leaves* of a palm-tree); fig. *power:*—branch, + foot, hand ([-ful], -dle, [-led]), hollow, middle, palm, paw, power, sole, spoon.

3710. כֵּף **kêph**, *kafe;* from 3721; a hollow *rock:*—rock.

3711. כָּפָה **kâphâh**, *kaw-faw';* a prim. root; prop. to *bend*, i.e. (fig.) to *tame* or subdue:—pacify.

3712. כִּפָּה **kippâh**, *kip-paw';* fem. of 3709; a *leaf* of a palm-tree:—branch.

3713. כְּפוֹר **kephôwr**, *kef-ore';* from 3722; prop. a *cover*, i.e. (by impl.) a *tankard* (or *covered* goblet); also white *frost* (as *covering* the ground):—bason, hoar (-y) frost.

3714. כָּפִיס **kâphîyç**, *kaw-fece';* from an unused root mean. to *connect;* a *girder:*—beam.

3715. כְּפִיר **kephîyr**, *kef-eer';* from 3722; a *village* (as *covered* in by walls); also a young *lion* (perh. as *covered* with a mane):—(young) lion, village. Comp. 3723.

3716. כְּפִירָה **Kephîyrâh**, *kef-ee-raw';* fem. of 3715; the *village* (always with the art.); *Kephirah*, a place in Pal.:—Chephirah.

3717. כָּפַל **kâphal**, *kaw-fal';* a prim. root; to *fold* together; fig. to *repeat:*—double.

3718. כֶּפֶל **kephel**, *keh'-fel;* from 3717; a *duplicate:*—double.

3719. כָּפַן **kâphan**, *kaw-fan';* a prim. root; to *bend:*—bend.

3720. כָּפָן **kâphân**, *kaw-fawn';* from 3719; *hunger* (as making to *stoop* with emptiness and pain):—famine.

3721. כָּפַף **kâphaph**, *kaw-faf';* a prim. root; to *curve:*—bow down (self).

3722. כָּפַר **kâphar**, *kaw-far';* a prim. root; to *cover* (spec. with bitumen); fig. to *expiate* or *condone*, to *placate* or *cancel:*—appease, make (an) atonement, cleanse, disannul, forgive, be merciful, pacify, pardon, to *pitch*, purge (away), put off, (make) reconcile (-liation).

3723. כָּפָר **kâphâr**, *kaw-fawr';* from 3722; a *village* (as *protected* by walls):—village. Comp. 3715.

3724. כֹּפֶר **kôpher**, *ko'-fer;* from 3722; prop. a *cover*, i.e. (lit.) a *village* (as *covered* in); (spec.) *bitumen* (as used for *coating*), and the *henna* plant (as used for *dyeing*); fig. a *redemption*-price:—bribe, camphire, pitch, ransom, satisfaction, sum of money, village.

3725. כִּפֻּר **kippûr**, *kip-poor';* from 3722; *expiation* (only in plur.):—atonement.

3726. כְּפַר הָעַמּוֹנִי **Kephar hâ-'Ammôwnîy**, *kef-ar' haw-am-mo-nee';* from 3723 and 5984, with the art. interposed; *village of the Ammonite; Kefar-ha-Ammoni*, a place in Pal.:—Chefar-haamonai.

3727. כַּפֹּרֶת **kappôreth**, *kap-po'-reth;* from 3722; a *lid* (used only of the cover of the sacred Ark):—mercy seat.

3728. כָּפַשׁ **kâphash**, *kaw-fash';* a prim. root; to *tread* down; fig. to *humiliate:*—cover.

3729. כְּפַת **kephath** (Chald.), *kef-ath';* a root of uncert. correspondence; to *fetter:*—bind.

3730. כַּפְתֹּר **kaphtôr**, *kaf-tore';* or (Am. 9 : 1)

כַּפְתּוֹר **kaphtôwr**, *kaf-tore';* prob. from an unused root mean. to *encircle;* a *chaplet;* but used only in an architectonic sense, i.e. the *capital* of a column, or a wreath-like *button* or *disk* on the candelabrum:—knop, (upper) lintel.

3731. כַּפְתֹּר **Kaphtôr**, *kaf-tore';* or (Am. 9 : 7)

כַּפְתּוֹר **Kaphtôwr**, *kaf-tore';* appar. the same as 3730; *Caphtor* (i.e. a *wreath*-shaped island), the original seat of the Philistines:—Caphtor.

3732. כַּפְתֹּרִי **Kaphtôrîy**, *kaf-to-ree';* patrial from 3731; a *Caphtorite* (collect.) or native of Caphtor:—Caphthorim, Caphtorim (-s).

3733. כַּר **kar**, *kar;* from 3769 in the sense of *plumpness;* a *ram* (as *full-grown* and *fat*), including a *battering-ram* (as *butting*); hence a *meadow* (as *for sheep*); also a *pad* or camel's saddle (as *puffed out*):—captain, furniture, lamb, (large) pasture, ram. See also 1033, 3746.

3734. כֹּר **kôr**, *kore;* from the same as 3564; prop. a deep round *vessel*, i.e. (spec.) a *cor* or measure for things dry:—cor, measure. Chald. the same.

3735. כָּרָא **kârâ'** (Chald.), *kaw-raw';* prob. corresp. to 3738 in the sense of *piercing* (fig.); to *grieve:*—be grieved.

3736. כַּרְבֵּל **karbêl**, *kar-bale';* from the same as 3525; to *gird* or *clothe:*—clothed.

3737. כַּרְבְּלָא **karbelâ'** (Chald.), *kar-bel-aw';* from a verb corresp. to that of 3736; a *mantle:*—hat.

3738. כָּרָה **kârâh**, *kaw-raw';* a prim. root; prop. to *dig;* fig. to *plot;* gen. to *bore* or open:—dig, × make (a banquet), open.

3739. כָּרָה **kârâh**, *kaw-raw';* usually assigned as a prim. root, but prob. only a special application of 3738 (through the common idea of *planning* implied in a bargain); to *purchase:*—buy, prepare.

3740. כֵּרָה **kêrâh**, *kay-raw';* from 3739; a *purchase:*—provision.

3741. כָּרָה **kârâh**, *kaw-raw';* fem. of 3733; a *meadow:*—cottage.

3742. כְּרוּב **kerûwb**, *ker-oob';* of uncert. der.; a *cherub* or imaginary figure:—cherub, [*plur.*] cherubims.

3743. כְּרוּב **Kerûwb**, *ker-oob';* the same as 3742; *Kerub*, a place in Bab.:—Cherub.

3744. כָּרוֹז **kârôwz** (Chald.), *kaw-roze';* from 3745; a *herald:*—herald.

3745. כְּרַז **keraz** (Chald.), *ker-az';* prob. of Greek or. (κηρύσσω); to *proclaim:*—make a proclamation.

3746. כָּרִי **kârîy**, *kaw-ree';* perh. an abridged plur. of 3733 in the sense of *leader* (of the flock); a *life-guardsman:*—captains, Cherethites [*from the marg.*].

3747. כְּרִית **Kerîyth**, *ker-eeth';* from 3772; a *cut; Kerith*, a brook of Pal.:—Cherith.

3748. כְּרִיתוּת **kerîythûwth**, *ker-ee-thooth';* from 3772; a *cutting* (of the matrimonial bond), i.e. *divorce:*—divorce (-ment).

3749. כַּרְכֹּב **karkôb**, *kar-kobe';* expanded from the same as 3522; a *rim* or top margin:—compass.

3750. כַּרְכֹּם **karkôm**, *kar-kome';* prob. of for. or.; the *crocus:*—saffron.

3751. כַּרְכְּמִישׁ **Karkemîysh**, *kar-kem-eesh';* of for. der.; *Karkemish*, a place in Syria:—Carchemish.

3752. כַּרְכַּס **Karkaç**, *kar-kas';* of Pers. or.; *Karkas*, a eunuch of Xerxes:—Carcas.

3753. כַּרְכָּרָה **karkârâh**, *kar-kaw-raw';* from 3769; a *dromedary* (from its *rapid* motion as if dancing):—swift beast.

3754. כֶּרֶם **kerem**, *keh'-rem;* from an unused root of uncert. mean.; a *garden* or *vineyard:*—vines, (increase of the) vineyard (-s), vintage. See also 1021.

3755. כֹּרֵם **kôrêm**, *ko-rame';* act. part. of an imaginary denom. from 3754; a *vinedresser:*—vine dresser [*as one or two words*].

3756. כַּרְמִי **Karmîy**, *kar-mee';* from 3754; *gardener; Karmi*, the name of three Isr.:—Carmi.

3757. כַּרְמִי **Karmîy**, *kar-mee';* patron. from 3756; a *Karmite* or desc. of *Karmi:*—Carmites.

3758. כַּרְמִיל **karmîyl**, *kar-mele';* prob. of for. or.; *carmine*, a deep red:—crimson.

3759. כַּרְמֶל **karmel**, *kar-mel';* from 3754; a planted *field* (garden, orchard, vineyard or park); by impl. garden *produce:*—full (green) ears (of corn), fruitful field (place), plentiful (field).

3760. כַּרְמֶל **Karmel**, *kar-mel';* the same as 3759; *Karmel*, the name of a hill and of a town in Pal.:—Carmel, fruitful (plentiful) field, (place).

3761. כַּרְמְלִי **Karmelîy**, *kar-mel-ee';* patron from 3760; a *Karmelite* or inhab. of Karmel (the town):—Carmelite.

3762. כַּרְמְלִית **Karmelîyth**, *kar-mel-eeth';* fem of 3761; a *Karmelitess* or female inhab. of Karmel:—Carmelitess.

3763. כְּרָן **Kerân**, *ker-awn';* of uncert. der.: *Keran*, an aboriginal Idumæan:—Cheran.

3764. כָּרְסֵא **korçê'** (Chald.), *kor-say';* corresp. to 3678; a *throne:*—throne.

3765. כִּרְסֵם **kirçêm**, *kir-same';* from 3697; to *lay waste:*—waste.

3766. כָּרַע **kâra'**, *kaw-rah';* a prim. root; to *bend* the knee; by impl. to *sink*, to *prostrate:*—bow (down, self), bring down (low), cast down, couch, fall, feeble, kneeling, sink, smite (stoop) down, subdue, × very.

3767. כָּרָע **kârâ'**, *kaw-raw';* from 3766; the *leg* (from the knee to the ankle) of men or locusts (only in the dual):—leg.

3768. כַּרְפַּס **karpaç**, *kar-pas';* of for. or.; *byssus* or fine vegetable wool:—green.

3769. כָּרַר **kârar**, *kaw-rar';* a prim. root; to *dance* (i.e. *whirl*):—dance (-ing).

3770. כְּרֵשׂ **kerês**, *ker-ace';* by var. from 7164; the *paunch* or belly (as *swelling* out):—belly.

כֹּרֶשׁ **Kôresh.** See 3567.

3771. כַּרְשְׁנָא **Karshenâ'**, *kar-shen-aw';* of for. or.; *Karshena*, a courtier of Xerxes:—Carshena.

3772. כָּרַת **kârath**, *kaw-rath';* a prim. root; to *cut* (off, down or asunder); by impl. to *destroy* or *consume;* spec. to *covenant* (i.e. make an alliance or bargain, orig. by cutting flesh and passing between the pieces):—be chewed, be con- [feder-] ate, covenant, cut (down, off), destroy, fail, feller, be freed, hew (down), make a league ([covenant]), × lose, perish, × utterly, × want.

3773. כָּרֻתָה **kârûthâh**, *kaw-rooth-aw';* pass. part. fem. of 3772; something *cut*, i.e. a hewn *timber:*—beam.

3774. כְּרֵתִי **Kerêthîy**, *ker-ay-thee';* prob. from 3772 in the sense of *executioner;* a *Kerethite* or *life-guardsman* [comp. 2876] (only collect. in the sing. as plur.):—Cherethims, Cherethites.

3775. כֶּשֶׂב **keseb**, *keh'-seb;* appar. by transp. for 3532; a young *sheep:*—lamb, sheep.

3776. כִּשְׂבָּה **kisbâh**, *kis-baw';* fem. of 3775; a young *ewe:*—lamb.

3777. כֶּשֶׂד **Kesed**, *keh'-sed;* from an unused root of uncert. mean.; *Kesed*, a relative of Abraham:—Chesed.

3778. כַּשְׂדִּי **Kasdîy**, *kas-dee'* (occasionally with enclitic

כַּשְׂדִּימָה **Kasdîymâh**, *kas-dee'-maw; towards* the *Kasdites:*—into Chaldea), patron. from 3777 (only in the plur.); a *Kasdite*, or desc. of Kesed; by impl. a *Chaldæan* (as if so descended); also an *astrologer* (as if proverbial of that people:—Chaldeans, Chaldees, inhabitants of Chaldea.

3779. כַּשְׂדַּי **Kasday** (Chald.), *kas-dah'ee;* corresp. to 3778; a *Chaldæan* or inhab. of Chaldæa; by impl. a *Magian* or professional astrologer:—Chaldean.

3780. כָּשָׂה **kâsâh**, *kaw-saw';* a prim. root; to *grow fat* (i.e. be *covered* with flesh):—be covered. Comp. 3680.

3781. כַּשִּׁיל **kashshîyl**, *kash-sheel';* from 3782; prop. a *feller*, i.e. an *axe:*—ax.

3782. כָּשַׁל **kâshal**, *kaw-shal';* a prim. root; to *totter* or *waver* (through weakness of the legs, espec. the ankle); by impl. to *falter*, *stumble*, faint or fall:—bereave [*from the marg.*], cast down, be decayed, (cause to) fail, (cause, make to) fall (down, -ing), feeble, be (the) ruin (-ed, of), (be) overthrown, (cause to) stumble, × utterly, be weak.

3783. כִּשָּׁלוֹן **kishshâlôwn**, *kish-shaw-lone';* from 3782; prop. a *tottering*, i.e. *ruin:*—fall.

3784. כָּשַׁף **kâshaph**, *kaw-shaf'*; a prim. root; prop. to *whisper* a spell, i.e. to *inchant* or practise magic:—sorcerer, (use) witch (-craft).

3785. כֶּשֶׁף **kesheph**, *keh'-shef*; from 3784; *magic:*—sorcery, witchcraft.

3786. כַּשָּׁף **kashshâph**, *kash-shawf'*; from 3784; a *magician:*—sorcerer.

3787. כָּשֵׁר **kâshêr**, *kaw-share'*; a prim. root· prop. to be *straight* or *right;* by impl. to *be acceptable;* also to *succeed* or prosper:—direct, be right, prosper.

3788. כִּשְׁרוֹן **kishrôwn**, *kish-rone'*; from 3787; *success, advantage:*—equity, good, right.

3789. כָּתַב **kâthab**, *kaw-thab'*; a prim. root; to *grave;* by impl. to *write* (describe, inscribe, prescribe, subscribe):—describe, record, prescribe, subscribe, write (-ing, -ten).

3790. כְּתַב **k^{e}thab** (Chald.), *keth-ab'*; corresp. to 3789:—write (-ten).

3791. כָּתָב **kâthâb**, *kaw-thawb'*; from 3789; something *written*, i.e. a *writing, record* or *book:*—register, scripture, writing.

3792. כְּתָב **k^{e}thâb** (Chald.), *keth-awb'*; corresp. to 3791:—prescribing, writing (-ten).

3793. כְּתֹבֶת **k^{e}thôbeth**, *keth-o'-beth*; from 3789; a *letter* or other *mark* branded on the skin:— × any [mark].

3794. כִּתִּי **Kittîy**, *kit-tee'*; or

כִּתִּיִּי **Kittîyîy**, *kit-tee-ee'*; patrial from an unused name denoting Cyprus (only in the plur.); a *Kittite* or Cypriote; hence an *islander* in gen., i.e. the Greeks or Romans on the shores opposite Pal.:—Chittim, Kittim.

3795. כָּתִית **kâthîyth**, *kaw-theeth'*; from 3807; *beaten*, i.e. pure (oil):—beaten.

3796. כֹּתֶל **kôthel**, *ko'-thel;* from an unused root mean. to *compact;* a *wall* (as *gathering* inmates):—wall.

3797. כְּתַל **k^{e}thal** (Chald.), *keth-al'*; corresp. to 3796:—wall.

3798. כִּתְלִישׁ **Kithlîysh**, *kith-leesh'*; from 3796 and 376; *wall of a man; Kithlish*, a place in Pal.:—Kithlish.

3799. כָּתַם **kâtham**, *kaw-tham'*; a prim. root; prop. to *carve* or *engrave*, i.e. (by impl.) to *inscribe* indelibly:—mark.

3800. כֶּתֶם **kethem**, *keh'-them;* from 3799; prop. something *carved* out, i.e. *ore;* hence *gold* (pure as originally mined):—([most] fine, pure) gold (-en wedge).

3801. כְּתֹנֶת **k^{e}thôneth**, *keth-o'-neth;* or

כֻּתֹּנֶת **kuttôneth**, *koot-to'-neth;* from an unused root mean. to *cover* [comp. 3802]; a *shirt:*—coat, garment, robe.

3802. כָּתֵף **kâthêph**, *kaw-thafe'*; from an unused root mean. to *clothe;* the *shoulder* (proper, i.e. upper end of the arm; as being the spot where the garments hang); fig. *side-piece* or lateral projection of anything:—arm, corner, shoulder (-piece), side, undersetter.

3803. כָּתַר **kâthar**, *kaw-thar'*; a prim. root; to *enclose;* hence (in a friendly sense) to *crown*, (in a hostile one) to *besiege;* also to *wait* (as restraining oneself):—beset round, compass about, be crowned inclose round, suffer.

3804. כֶּתֶר **kether**, *keh'-ther;* from 3803; prop. a *circlet*, i.e. a *diadem:*—crown.

3805. כֹתֶרֶת **kôthereth**, *ko-theh'-reth;* fem. act. part. of 3803; the *capital* of a column:—chapiter.

3806. כָּתַשׁ **kâthash**, *kaw-thash';* a prim. root; to *butt* or *pound:*—bray.

3807. כָּתַת **kâthath**, *kaw-thath'*; a prim. root; to *bruise* or violently *strike:*—beat (down, to pieces), break in pieces, crushed, destroy, discomfit, smite, stamp.

ל

3808. לֹא **lô'**, *lo;* or

לוֹא **lôw'**, *lo;* or

לֹה **lôh** (Deut. 3 : 11), *lo;* a prim. particle; *not* (the simple or abs. negation); by impl. *no;* often used with other particles (as follows):— × before, + or else, ere, + except, ig [-norant], much, less, nay, neither, never, no ([-ne], -r, [-thing]), (× as though . . . , [can-], for) not (out of), of nought, otherwise, out of, + surely, + as truly as, + of a truth, + verily, for want, + whether, without.

3809. לָא **lâ'** (Chald.), *law;* or

לָה **lâh** (Chald.) (Dan. 4 : 32), *law;* corresp. to 3808:—or even, neither, no (-ne, -r), ([can-]) not, as nothing, without.

לֻא **lû'**. See 3863.

3810. לֹא דְבַר **Lô' D^{e}bar**, *lo deb-ar';* or

לוֹ דְבַר **Lôw D^{e}bar** (2 Sam. 9 : 4, 5), *lo deb-ar';* or

לִדְבִר **Lidbîr** (Josh. 13 : 26), *lid-beer'* [prob. rather

לֹדְבַר° **Lôd^{e}bar**, *lo-deb-ar'*]; from 3808 and 1699; *pastureless; Lo-Debar*, a place in Pal.:—Debir, Lo-debar.

3811. לָאָה **lâ'âh**, *law-aw';* a prim. root; to *tire;* (fig.) to *be* (or *make*) *disgusted:*—faint, grieve, lothe, (be, make) weary (selves).

3812. לֵאָה **Lê'âh**, *lay-aw';* from 3811; *weary; Leah*, a wife of Jacob:—Leah.

לְאוֹם **l^{e}'owm**. See 3816.

3813. לָאַט **lâ'aṭ**, *law-at';* a prim. root; to *muffle:*—cover.

3814. לָאט **lâ'ṭ**, *lawt;* from 3813 (or perh. for act. part. of 3874); prop. *muffled*, i.e. *silently:*—softly.

3815. לָאֵל **Lâ'êl**, *law-ale';* from the prep. pref. and 410; (belonging) *to God; Laël* an Isr.:—Lael.

3816. לְאֹם **l^{e}ôm**, *leh-ome';* or

לְאוֹם **l^{e}'ôwm**, *leh-ome';* from an unused root mean. to *gather;* a *community:*—nation, people.

3817. לְאֻמִּים **L^{e}'ummîym**, *leh-oom-meem';* plur. of 3816; *communities; Leüm mim*, an Arabian:—Leummim.

3818. לֹא עַמִּי **Lô' 'Ammîy**, *lo am-mee';* from 3808 and 5971 with pron. suffix; *not my people; Lo-Ammi*, the symbol. name of a son of Hosea:—Lo-ammi.

3819. לֹא רֻחָמָה **Lô' Rûchâmâh**, *lo roo-khaw-maw';* from 3808 and 7355; *not pitied; Lo-Ruchamah*, the symbol. name of a daughter of Hosea:—Lo-ruhamah.

3820. לֵב **lêb**, *labe;* a form of 3824; the *heart;* also used (fig.) very widely for the feelings, the will and even the intellect; likewise for the *centre* of anything:— + care for, comfortably, consent, × considered, courag [-eous], friend [-ly], ([broken-], [hard-], [merry-], [stiff-], [stout-], double) heart ([-ed]), × heed, × I, kindly, midst, mind (-ed), × regard ([-ed]), × themselves, × unawares, understanding, × well, willingly, wisdom.

3821. לֵב **lêb** (Chald.), *labe;* corresp. to 3820:—heart.

3822. לְבָאוֹת **L^{e}bâ'ôwth**, *leb-aw-ōth';* plur. of 3833; *lionesses; Lebaoth*, a place in Pal.:—Lebaoth. See also 1034.

3823. לָבַב **lâbab**, *law-bab';* a prim. root; prop. to *be enclosed* (as if with *fat*); by impl. (as denom. from 3824) to *unheart*, i.e. (in a good sense) *transport* (with love), or (in a bad sense) *stultify;* also (as denom. from 3834) to *make cakes:*—make cakes, ravish, be wise.

3824. לֵבָב **lêbâb**, *lay-bawb';* from 3823; the *heart* (as the most interior organ); used also like 3820:— + bethink themselves, breast, comfortably, courage, ([faint], [tender-] heart ([-ed]), midst, mind, × unawares, understanding.

3825. לְבַב **l^{e}bab** (Chald.), *leb-ab';* corresp. to 3824:—heart.

לְבִבָה **l^{e}bîbâh**. See 3834.

3826. לִבָּה **libbâh**, *lib-baw';* fem. of 3820; the *heart:*—heart.

3827. לַבָּה **labbâh**, *lab-baw';* for 3852; *flame:*—flame.

3828. לְבוֹנָה **l^{e}bôwnâh**, *leb-o-naw';* or

לְבֹנָה **l^{e}bônâh**, *leb-o-naw';* from 3836; *frankincense* (from its *whiteness* or perh. that of its smoke):—(frank-) incense.

3829. לְבוֹנָה **L^{e}bôwnâh**, *leb-o-naw';* the same as 3828; *Lebonah*, a place in Pal.:—Lebonah.

3830. לְבוּשׁ **l^{e}bûwsh**, *leb-oosh';* or

לְבֻשׁ **l^{e}bûsh**, *leb-oosh';* from 3847; a *garment* (lit. or fig.); by impl. (euphem.) a *wife:*—apparel, clothed with, clothing, garment, raiment, vestment, vesture.

3831. לְבוּשׁ **l^{e}bûwsh** (Chald.), *leb-oosh';* corresp. to 3830:—garment.

3832. לָבַט **lâbaṭ**, *law-bat';* a prim. root; to *overthrow;* intrans. to *fall:*—fall.

לֻבִּי **Lubbîy**. See 3864.

3833. לָבִיא **lâbîy'**, *law-bee';* or (Ezek. 19 : 2)

לְבִיָּא **l^{e}bîyâ'**, *leb-ee-yaw';* irreg. masc. plur.

לְבָאִים **l^{e}bâ'îym**, *leb-aw-eem';* irreg. fem. plur.

לְבָאוֹת **l^{e}bâ'ôwth**, *leb-aw-ōth';* from an unused root mean. to *roar;* a *lion* (prop. a lioness as the fiercer [although not a *roarer;* comp. 738]):—(great, old, stout) lion, lioness, young [lion].

3834. לְבִיבָה **lâbîybâh**, *law-bee-baw';* or rather

לְבִבָה **l^{e}bîbâh**, *leb-ee-baw';* from 3823 in its orig. sense of *fatness* (or perh. of *folding*); a *cake* (either as *fried* or *turned*):—cake.

3835. לָבַן **lâban**, *law-ban';* a prim. root; to *be* (or *become*) *white;* also (as denom. from 3843) to *make bricks:*—make brick, be (made, make) white (-r).

3836. לָבָן **lâbân**, *law-bawn';* or (Gen. 49 : 12)

לָבֵן **lâbên**, *law-bane';* from 3835; *white:*—white.

3837. לָבָן **Lâbân**, *law-bawn';* the same as 3836; *Laban*, a Mesopotamian; also a place in the Desert:—Laban.

לַבֵּן **Labbên**. See 4192.

3838. לְבָנָא **L^{e}bânâ'**, *leb-aw-naw';* or

לְבָנָה **L^{e}bânâh**, *leb-aw-naw';* the same as 3842; *Lebana* or *Lebanah*, one of the Nethinim:—Lebana, Lebanah.

3839. לִבְנֶה **libneh**, *lib-neh';* from 3835; some sort of *whitish* tree, perh. the *storax:*—poplar.

3840. לִבְנָה **libnâh**, *lib-naw';* from 3835; prop. *whiteness*, i.e. (by impl.) *transparency:*—paved.

3841. לִבְנָה **Libnâh**, *lib-naw';* the same as 3839; *Libnah*, a place in the Desert and one in Pal.:—Libnah.

3842. לְבָנָה **l^{e}bânâh**, *leb-aw-naw';* from 3835; prop. (the) *white*, i.e. the *moon:*—moon. See also 3838.

3843. לְבֵנָה **l^{e}bênâh**, *leb-ay-naw';* from 3835; a *brick* (from the *whiteness* of the clay):—(altar of) brick, tile.

לְבֹנָה **l^{e}bônâh**. See 3828.

3844. לְבָנוֹן **L^{e}bânôwn**, *leb-aw-nohn';* from 3825; (the) *white* mountain (from its snow); *Lebanon*, a mountain range in Pal.:—Lebanon.

3845. לִבְנִי **Libnîy**, *lib-nee';* from 3835; *white; Libni*, an Isr.:—Libni.

3846. לִבְנִי **Libnîy**, *lib-nee';* patron. from 3845; a *Libnite* or desc. of Libni (collect.):—Libnites.

3847. לָבַשׁ **lâbash**, *law-bash';* or

לָבֵשׁ **lâbêsh**, *law-bashe';* a prim. root; prop. *wrap* around, i.e. (by impl.) to *put on* a garment or *clothe* (oneself, or another), lit. or fig.:—(in) apparel, arm, array (self), clothe (self), come upon, put (on, upon), wear.

3848. לְבַשׁ **lᵉbash** (Chald.), *leb-ash'*; corresp. to 3847:—clothe.

לְבוּשׁ **lᵉbûsh**. See 3830.

3849. לֹג **lôg**, *lohg*; from an unused root appar. mean. to *deepen* or *hollow* [like 3537]; a *log* or measure for liquids:—log [of oil].

3850. לֹד **Lôd**, *lode*; from an unused root of uncert. signif.; *Lod*, a place in Pal.:—Lod.

לִדְבִר **Lidbîr**. See 3810.

3851. לַהַב **lahab**, *lah'-hab*; from an unused root mean. to *gleam*; a *flash*; fig. a sharply polished *blade* or *point* of a weapon:—blade, bright, flame, glittering.

3852. לֶהָבָה **lehâbâh**, *leh-aw-baw'*; or

לַהֶבֶת **lahebeth**, *lah-eh'-beth*; fem. of 3851, and mean. the same:—flame (-ming), head [of a spear].

3853. לְהָבִים **Lᵉhâbîym**, *leh-haw-beem'*; plur. of 3851; *flames*; *Lehabim*, a son of Mizrain, and his descend.:—Lehabim.

3854. לַהַג **lahag**, *lah'-hag*; from an unused root mean. to *be eager*; intense mental *application*:—study.

3855. לַהַד **Lahad**, *lah'-had*; from an unused root mean. to *glow* [comp. 3851] or else to *be earnest* [comp. 3854]; *Lahad*, an Isr.:—Lahad.

3856. לָהַהּ **lâhahh**, *law-hah'*; a prim. root mean. prop. to *burn*, i.e. (by impl.) to *be rabid* (fig. *insane*); also (from the *exhaustion* of frenzy) to *languish*:—faint, mad.

3857. לָהַט **lâhaṭ**, *law-hat'*; a prim. root; prop. to *lick*, i.e. (by impl.) to *blaze*:—burn (up), set on fire, flaming, kindle.

3858. לַהַט **lahaṭ**, *lah'-hat*; from 3857; a *blaze*; also (from the idea of *enwrapping*) *magic* (as *covert*):—flaming, enchantment.

3859. לָהַם **lâham**, *law-ham'*; a prim. root; prop. to *burn* in, i.e. (fig.) to *rankle*:—wound.

3860. לָהֵן **lâhên**, *law-hane'*; from the pref. prep. mean. *to* or *for* and 2005; pop. *for if*; hence *therefore*:—for them [*by mistake for prep. suffix*].

3861. לָהֵן **lâwhên** (Chald.), *law-hane'*; corresp. to 3860; *therefore*; also *except*:—but, except, save, therefore, wherefore.

3862. לַהֲקָה **lahăqâh**, *lah-hak-aw'*; prob. from an unused root mean. to *gather*; an *assembly*:—company.

לוֹא **lôwʼ**. See 3808.

3863. לוּא **lûwʼ**, *loo*; or

לֻא **lûʼ**, *loo*; or

לוּ **lûw**, *loo*; a conditional particle; *if*; by impl. (interj. as a wish) *would that!*:—if (haply), peradventure, I pray thee, though, I would, would God (that).

3864. לוּבִי **Lûwbîy**, *loo-bee'*; or

לֻבִּי **Lubbîy** (Dan. 11 : 43), *loob-bee'*; patrial from a name prob. derived from an unused root mean. to *thirst*, i.e. a *dry* region; appar. a *Libyan* or inhab. of interior Africa (only in plur.):—Lubim (-s), Libyans.

3865. לוּד **Lûwd**, *lood*; prob. of for. der.; *Lud*, the name of two nations:—Lud, Lydia.

3866. לוּדִי **Lûwdîy**, *loo-dee'*; or

לוּדִיִּי **Lûwdîyîy**, *loo-dee-ee'*; patrial from 3865; a *Ludite* or inhab. of Lud (only in plur.):—Ludim, Lydians.

3867. לָוָה **lâvâh**, *law-vaw'*; a prim. root; prop. to *twine*, i.e. (by impl.) to *unite*, to *remain*; also to *borrow* (as a form of *obligation*) or (caus.) to *lend*:—abide with, borrow (-er), cleave, join (self), lend (-er).

3868. לוּז **lûwz**, *looz*; a prim. root; to *turn* aside [comp. 3867, 3874 and 3885], i.e. (lit.) to *depart*, (fig.) *be perverse*:—depart, froward, perverse (-ness).

3869. לוּז **lûwz**, *looz*; prob. of for. or; some kind of *nut*-tree, perh. the *almond*:—hazel.

3870. לוּז **Lûwz**, *looz*; prob. from 3869 (as growing there); *Luz*, the name of two places in Pal.:—Luz.

3871. לוּחַ **lûwach**, *loo'-akh*; or

לֻחַ **lûach**, *loo'-akh*; from a prim. root; prob. mean. to *glisten*; a *tablet* (as *polished*), of stone, wood or metal:—board, plate, table.

3872. לוּחִית **Lûwchîyth**, *loo-kheeth'*; or

לֻחוֹת° **Lûchôwth** (Jer. 48 : 5), *loo-khoth'*; from the same as 3871; *floored*; *Luchith*, a place E. of the Jordan:—Luhith.

3873. לוֹחֵשׁ **Lôwchêsh**, *lo-khashe'*; act. part. of 3907; (the) *enchanter*; *Lochesh*, an Isr.:—Hallohesh, Haloshesh [*includ. the art.*].

3874. לוּט **lûwṭ**, *loot*; a prim. root; to *wrap* up:—cast, wrap.

3875. לוֹט **lôwṭ**, *lote*; from 3874; a *veil*:—covering.

3876. לוֹט **Lôwṭ**, *lote*; the same as 3875; *Lot*, Abraham's nephew:—Lot.

3877. לוֹטָן **Lôwṭân**, *lo-tawn'*; from 3875; *covering*; *Lotan*, an Idumæan:—Lotan.

3878. לֵוִי **Lêvîy**, *lay-vee'*; from 3867; *attached*; *Levi*, a son of Jacob:—Levi. See also 3879, 3881.

3879. לֵוִי **Lêvîy** (Chald.), *lay-vee'*; corresp. to 3880:—Levite.

3880. לִוְיָה **livyâh**, *liv-yaw'*; from 3867; something *attached*, i.e. a *wreath*:—ornament.

3881. לֵוִיִּי **Lêvîyîy**, *lay-vee-ee'*; or

לֵוִי **Lêvîy**, *lay-vee'*; patron. from 3878; a *Leviite* or desc. of Levi:—Levite.

3882. לִוְיָתָן **livyâthân**, *liv-yaw-thawn'*; from 3867; a *wreathed* animal, i.e. a *serpent* (espec. the *crocodile* or some other large sea-monster); fig. the constellation of the *dragon*; also as a symbol of *Bab.*:—leviathan, mourning.

3883. לוּל **lûwl**, *lool*; from an unused root mean. to *fold* back; a *spiral* step:—winding stair. Comp. 3924.

3884. לוּלֵא **lûwlêʼ**, *loo-lay'*; or

לוּלֵי **lûwlêy**, *loo lay'*; from 3863 and 3808; *if not*:—except, had not, if (... not), unless, were it not that.

3885. לוּן **lûwn**, *loon*; or

לִין **lîyn**, *leen*; a prim. root; to *stop* (usually over night); by impl. to *stay* permanently; hence (in a bad sense) to be *obstinate* (espec. in words, to *complain*):—abide (all night), continue, dwell, endure, grudge, be left, lie all night, (cause to) lodge (all night, in, -ing, this night), (make to) murmur, remain, tarry (all night, that night).

3886. לוּעַ **lûwaʽ**, *loo'-ah*; a prim. root; to *gulp*; fig. to *be rash*:—swallow down (up).

3887. לוּץ **lûwts**, *loots*; a prim. root; prop. to *make mouths* at, i.e. to *scoff*; hence (from the effort to pronounce a foreign language) to *interpret*, or (gen.) *intercede*:—ambassador, have in derision, interpreter, make a mock, mocker, scorn (-er, -ful), teacher.

3888. לוּשׁ **lûwsh**, *loosh*; a prim. root; to *knead*:—knead.

3889. °לוּשׁ **Lûwsh**, *loosh*; from 3888; *kneading*; *Lush*, a place in Pal.:—Laish [*from the marg.*]. Comp. 3919.

3890. לְוָת **lᵉvâth** (Chald.), *lev-awth'*; from a root corresp. to 3867; prop. *adhesion*, i.e. (as prep.) *with*:—× thee.

לֻחוֹת **Lûchôwth**. See 3872.

לָז **lâz**, and

לָזֶה **lâzeh**. See 1975 and 1976.

3891. לְזוּת **lᵉzûwth**, *lez-ooth'*; from 3868; *perverseness*:—perverse.

3892. לַח **lach**, *lakh*; from an unused root mean. to *be new*; *fresh*, i.e. unused or undried:—green, moist.

3893. לֵחַ **lêach**, *lay'-akh*; from the same as 3892; *freshness*, i.e. vigor:—natural force.

לֻחַ **lûach**. See 3871.

3894. לָחוּם **lâchûwm**, *law-khoom'*; or

לָחֻם **lâchûm**, *law-khoom'*; pass. part. of 3898; prop. *eaten*, i.e. *food*; also *flesh*, i.e. *body*:—while . . . is eating, flesh.

3895. לְחִי **lᵉchîy**, *lekh-ee'*; from an unused root mean. to *be soft*; the *cheek* (from its *fleshiness*); hence the *jaw*-bone:—cheek (bone), jaw (bone).

3896. לֶחִי **Lechîy**, *lekh'-ee*; a form of 3895; *Lechi*, a place in Pal.:—Lehi. Comp. also 7437.

3897. לָחַךְ **lâchak**, *law-khak'*; a prim. root; to *lick*:—lick (up).

3898. לָחַם **lâcham**, *law-kham'*; a prim. root; to *feed* on; fig. to *consume*; by impl. to *battle* (as *destruction*):—devour, eat, × ever, fight (-ing), overcome, prevail, (make) war (-ring).

3899. לֶחֶם **lechem**, *lekh'-em*; from 3898; *food* (for man or beast), espec. *bread*, or *grain* (for making it):—([shew-]) bread, × eat, food, fruit, loaf, meat, victuals. See also 1036.

3900. לְחֶם **lᵉchem** (Chald.), *lekh-em'*; corresp. to 3899:—feast.

3901. לָחֶם **lâchem**, *law-khem'*; from 3898; *battle*:—war.

לָחֻם **lâchûm**. See 3894.

3902. לַחְמִי **Lachmîy**, *lakh-mee'*; from 3899; *foodful*; *Lachmi*, a Philis.; or rather prob. a brief form (or perh. err. transc.) for 1022:—Lahmi. See also 3433.

3903. לַחְמָס **Lachmâç**, *lakh-maws'*; prob. by err. transc. for

°לַחְמָם **Lachmâm**, *lakh-mawm'*; from 3899; *food-like*; *Lachmam* or *Lachmas*, a place in Pal.:—Lahmam.

3904. לְחֵנָה **lᵉchênâh** (Chald.), *lekh-ay-naw'*; from an unused root of uncert. mean.; a *concubine*:—concubine.

3905. לָחַץ **lâchats**, *law-khats'*; a prim. root; prop. to *press*, i.e. (fig.) to *distress*:—afflict, crush, force, hold fast, oppress (-or), thrust self.

3906. לַחַץ **lachats**, *lakh'-ats*; from 3905; *distress*:—affliction, oppression.

3907. לָחַשׁ **lâchash**, *law-khash'*; a prim. root; to *whisper*; by impl. to *mumble* a spell (as a magician):—charmer, whisper (together).

3908. לַחַשׁ **lachash**, *lakh'-ash*; from 3907; prop. a *whisper*, i.e. by impl. (in a good sense) a private *prayer*, (in a bad one) an *incantation*; concr. an *amulet*:—charmed, earring, enchantment, orator, prayer.

3909. לָט **lâṭ**, *lawt*; a form of 3814 or else part. from 3874; prop. *covered*, i.e. *secret*; by impl. *incantation*; also *secrecy* or (adv.) *covertly*:—enchantment, privily, secretly, softly.

3910. לֹט **lôṭ**, *lote*; prob. from 3874; a gum (from its *sticky* nature), prob. *ladanum*:—myrrh.

3911. לְטָאָה **lᵉṭâʼâh**, *let-aw-aw'*; from an unused root mean. to *hide*; a kind of *lizard* (from its *covert* habits):—lizard.

3912. לְטוּשִׁם **Lᵉṭûwshim**, *let-oo-sheem'*; masc. plur. of pass. part. of 3913; *hammered* (i.e. *oppressed*) ones; *Letushim*, an Arabian tribe:—Letushim.

3913. לָטַשׁ **lâṭash**, *law-tash'*; a prim. root; prop. to *hammer* out (an edge), i.e. to *sharpen*:—instructer, sharp (-en), whet.

3914. לֹיָה **lôyâh**, *lo-yaw'*; a form of 3880; a *wreath*:—addition.

3915. לַיִל **layil**, *lah'-yil*; or (Isa. 21 : 11)

לֵיל **lêyl**, *lale*; also

לַיְלָה **layᵉlâh**, *lah'-yel-aw*; from the same as 3883; prop. a *twist* (away of the light), i.e. *night*; fig. *adversity*:—([mid-]) night (season).

3916. לֵילְיָא **leylᵉyâʼ** (Chald.), *lay-leh-yaw'*; corresp. to 3915:—night.

3917. לִילִית **lîylîyth**, *lee-leeth'*; from 3915; a *night* spectre:—screech owl.

3918. לַיִשׁ **layish**, *lah'-yish*; from 3888 in the sense of *crushing*; a lion (from his destructive *blows*):—(old) lion.

3919. לַיִשׁ **Layish**, *lah'-yish*; the same as 3918; *Laïsh*, the name of two places in Pal.:—Laish. Comp. 3889.

3920. לָכַד **lâkad**, *law-kad'*; a prim. root; to *catch* (in a net, trap or pit); gen. to *capture* or occupy; also to *choose* (by lot); fig. to *cohere*:—× at all, catch (self), be frozen, be holden, stick together, take.

3921. לֶכֶד **leked**, *leh'-ked*; from 3920; something to *capture* with, i.e. a *noose*:—being taken.

3922. לֵכָה **lêkâh**, *lay-kaw'*; from 3212; a *journey*; *Lekah*, a place in Pal.:—Lecah.

3923. לָכִישׁ **Lâchîysh**, *law-keesh'*; from an unused root of uncert. mean.; *Lakish*, a place in Pal.:—Lachish.

3924. לֻלָאָה **lûlâ'âh**, *loo-law-aw'*; from the same as 3883; a *loop*:—loop.

3925. לָמַד **lâmad**, *law-mad'*; a prim. root; prop. to *goad*, i.e. (by impl.) to *teach* (the rod being an Oriental *incentive*):—[un-] accustomed, × diligently, expert, instruct, learn, skilful, teach (-er, -ing).

לִמֻּד **limmûd**. See 3928.

3926. לְמוֹ **l^emôw**, *lem-o'*; a prol. and separable form of the pref. prep.; *to* or *for*:—at, for, to, upon.

3927. לְמוּאֵל **L^emûw'êl**, *lem-oo-ale'*; or

לְמוֹאֵל **L^emôw'êl**, *lem-o-ale'*; from 3926 and 410; (belonging) *to God*; *Lemuël* or *Lemoël*, a symbol. name of Solomon:—Lemuel.

3928. לִמּוּד **limmûwd**, *lim-mood'*; or

לִמֻּד **limmûd**, *lim-mood'*; from 3925; *instructed*:—accustomed, disciple, learned, taught, used.

3929. לֶמֶךְ **Lemek**, *leh'-mek*; from an unused root of uncert. mean.; *Lemek*, the name of two antediluvian patriarchs:—Lamech.

3930. לֹעַ **lôa'**, *lo'ah* from 3886; the *gullet*:—throat.

3931. לָעַב **lâ'ab**, *law-ab'*; a prim. root; to *deride*:—mock.

3932. לָעַג **lâ'ag**, *law-ag'*; a prim. root; to *deride*; by impl. (as if imitating a foreigner) to *speak unintelligibly*:—have in derision, laugh (to scorn), mock (on), stammering.

3933. לַעַג **la'ag**, *lah'-ag*; from 3932; *derision*, *scoffing*:—derision, scorn (-ing).

3934. לָעֵג **lâ'êg**, *law-ayg'*; from 3932; a *buffoon*; also a *foreigner*:—mocker, stammering.

3935. לַעְדָּה **La'dâh**, *lah-daw'*; from an unused root of uncert. mean.; *Ladah*, an Isr.:—Laadah.

3936. לַעְדָּן **La'dân**, *lah-dawn'*; from the same as 3935; *Ladan*, the name of two Isr.:—Laadan.

3937. לָעַז **lâ'az**, *law-az'*; a prim. root; to *speak in a foreign tongue*:—strange language.

3938. לָעַט **lâ'aṭ**, *law-at'*; a prim. root; to *swallow* greedily; causat. to *feed*:—feed.

3939. לַעֲנָה **la'ănâh**, *lah-an-aw'*; from an unused root supposed to mean to *curse*; *wormwood* (regarded as *poisonous*, and therefore *accursed*):—hemlock, wormwood.

3940. לַפִּיד **lappîyd**, *lap-peed'*; or

לַפִּד **lappîd**, *lap-peed'*; from an unused root prob. mean. to *shine*; a *flambeau*, *lamp* or *flame*:—(fire-) brand, (burning) lamp, lightning, torch.

3941. לַפִּידוֹת **Lappîydôwth**, *lap-pee-dōth'*; fem. plur. of 3940; *Lappidoth*, the husband of Deborah:—Lappidoth.

3942. לִפְנַי **liphnay**, *lif-nah'ee*; from the pref. prep. (*to* or *for*) and 6440; *anterior*:—before.

3943. לָפַת **lâphath**, *law-fath'*; a prim. root; prop. to *bend*, i.e. (by impl.) to *clasp*; also (reflex.) to *turn* around or aside:—take hold, turn aside (self).

3944. לָצוֹן **lâtsôwn**, *law-tsone'*; from 3887; *derision*:—scornful (-ning).

3945. לָצַץ **lâtsats**, *law-tsats'*; a prim. root; to *deride*:—scorn.

3946. לַקּוּם **Laqqûwm** *lak-koom'*; from an unused root thought to mean to *stop* up by a barricade; perh. *fortification*; *Lakkum*, a place in Pal.:—Lakum.

3947. לָקַח **lâqach**, *law-kakh'*; a prim. root; to *take* (in the widest variety of applications):—accept, bring, buy, carry away, drawn, fetch, get, infold, × many, mingle, place, receive (-ing), reserve, seize, send for, take (away, -ing, up), use, win.

3948. לֶקַח **leqach**, *leh'-kakh*; from 3947; prop. something *received*, i.e. (mentally) *instruction* (whether on the part of the teacher or hearer); also (in an act. and sinister sense) *inveiglement*:—doctrine, learning, fair speech.

3949. לִקְחִי **Liqchîy**, *lik-khee'*; from 3947; *learned*; *Likchi*, an Isr.:—Likhi.

3950. לָקַט **lâqaṭ**, *law-kat'*; a prim. root; prop. to *pick* up, i.e. (gen.) to *gather*; spec. to *glean*:—gather (up), glean.

3951. לֶקֶט **leqeṭ**, *leh'-ket*; from 3950; the *gleaning*:—gleaning.

3952. לָקַק **lâqaq**, *law-kak'*; a prim. root; to *lick* or *lap*:—lap, lick.

3953. לָקַשׁ **lâqash**, *law-kash'*; a prim. root; to *gather* the *after* crop:—gather.

3954. לֶקֶשׁ **leqesh**, *leh'-kesh*; from 3953; the *after crop*:—latter growth.

3955. לְשַׁד **l^eshad**, *lesh-ad'*; from an unused root of uncert. mean.; appar. *juice*, i.e. (fig.) *vigor*; also a sweet or fat *cake*:—fresh, moisture.

3956. לָשׁוֹן **lâshôwn**, *law-shone'*; or

לָשֹׁן **lâshôn**, *law-shone'*; also (in plur.) fem.

לְשֹׁנָה **l^eshônâh**, *lesh-o-naw'*; from 3960; the *tongue* (of man or animals), used lit. (as the instrument of licking, eating, or speech), and fig. (speech, an ingot, a fork of flame, a cove of water):—+ babbler, bay, + evil speaker, language, talker, tongue, wedge.

3957. לִשְׁכָּה **lishkâh**, *lish-kaw'*; from an unused root of uncert. mean.; a *room* in a building (whether for storage, eating, or lodging):—chamber, parlour. Comp. 5393.

3958. לֶשֶׁם **leshem**, *leh'-shem*; from an unused root of uncert. mean.; a *gem*, perh. the *jacinth*:—ligure.

3959. לֶשֶׁם **Leshem**, *leh'-shem*; the same as 3958; *Leshem*, a place in Pal.:—Leshem.

3960. לָשַׁן **lâshan**, *law-shan'*; a prim. root; prop. to *lick*; but used only as a denom. from 3956; to *wag the tongue*, i.e. to *calumniate*:—accuse, slander.

3961. לִשָּׁן **lishshân** (Chald.) *lish-shawn'*; corresp. to 3956; *speech*, i.e. a *nation*:—language.

3962. לֶשַׁע **Lesha'**, *leh'-shah*; from an unused root thought to mean to *break* through; a boiling *spring*; *Lesha*, a place prob. E. of the Jordan:—Lasha.

3963. לֶתֶךְ **lethek**, *leh'-thek*; from an unused root of uncert. mean.; a *measure* for things dry:—half homer.

מ

מַה־ **ma-**, or

מָה־ **mâ-**. See 4100.

3964. מָא **mâ'** (Chald.) *maw*; corresp. to 4100; (as indef.) *that*:—+ what.

3965. מַאֲבוּס **ma'ăbûwç**, *mah-ab-ooce'*; from 75; a *granary*:—storehouse.

3966. מְאֹד **m^e'ôd**, *meh-ode'*; from the same as 181; prop. *vehemence*, i.e. (with or without prep.) *vehemently*; by impl. *wholly*, *speedily*, etc. (often with other words as an intensive or superlative; espec. when repeated):—diligently, especially, exceeding (-ly), far, fast, good, great (-ly), × louder and louder, might (-ily, -y), (so) much, quickly, (so) sore, utterly, very (+ much, sore), well.

3967. מֵאָה **mê'âh**, *may-aw'*; or

מֵאיָה **mê'yâh**, *may-yaw'*; prob. a prim. numeral; a *hundred*; also as a multiplicative and a fraction:—hundred ([-fold], -th), + sixscore.

3968. מֵאָה **Mê'âh**, *may-aw'*; the same as 3967; *Meäh*, a tower in Jerus.:—Meah.

3969. מְאָה **m^e'âh** (Chald.), *meh-aw'*; corresp. to 3967:—hundred.

3970. מַאֲוַי **ma'ăvay**, *mah-av-ah'ee*; from 183; a *desire*:—desire.

מוֹאל **môw'l**. See 4136.

3971. מאוּם **m'ûwm**, *moom*; usually

מוּם **mûwm**, *moom*; as if pass. part. from an unused root prob. mean. to *stain*; a *blemish* (phys. or mor.):—blemish, blot, spot.

3972. מְאוּמָה **m^e'ûwmâh**, *meh-oo'-maw*; appar. a form of 3971; prop. a *speck* or *point*, i.e. (by impl.) *something*; with neg. *nothing*:—fault, + no (-ught), ought, somewhat, any ([no-]) thing.

3973. מָאוֹס **mâ'ôwç**, *maw-oce'*; from 3988; *refuse*:—refuse.

3974. מָאוֹר **mâ'ôwr**, *maw-ore'*; or

מָאֹר **mâ'ôr**, *maw-ore'*; also (in plur.) fem.

מְאוֹרָה **m^e'ôwrâh**, *meh-o-raw'*; or

מְאֹרָה **m^e'ôrâh**, *meh-o-raw'*; from 215; prop. a *luminous* body or *luminary*, i.e. (abstr.) *light* (as an element); fig. *brightness*, i.e. *cheerfulness*; spec. a *chandelier*:—bright, light.

3975. מְאוּרָה **m^e'ûwrâh**, *meh-oo-raw'*; fem. pass. part, of 215; something *lighted*, i.e. an *aperture*; by impl. a *crevice* or *hole* of a serpent):—den.

3976. מֹאזֵן **môzên**, *mo-zane'*; from 239; (only in the dual) a pair of *scales*:—balances.

3977. מֹאזֵן **môzên** (Chald.) *mo-zane'*; corresp. to 3976:—balances.

מֵאיָה **mê'yâh**. See 3967.

3978. מַאֲכָל **ma'ăkâl**, *mah-ak-awl'*; from 398; an *eatable* (includ. provender, flesh and fruit):—food, fruit, ([bake-]) meat (-s), victual.

3979. מַאֲכֶלֶת **ma'ăkeleth**, *mah-ak-eh'-leth*; from 398; something to *eat* with, i.e. a *knife*:—knife.

3980. מַאֲכֹלֶת **ma'ăkôleth**, *mah-ak-o'-leth*; from 398; something *eaten* (by fire), i.e. *fuel*:—fuel.

3981. מַאֲמָץ **ma'ămâts**, *mah-am-awts'*; from 553; *strength*, i.e. (plur.) *resources*:—force.

3982. מַאֲמַר **ma'ămar**, *mah-am-ar'*; from 559; something (authoritatively) *said*, i.e. an *edict*:—commandment, decree.

3983. מֵאמַר **mê'mar** (Chald.), *may-mar'*; corresp. to 3982:—appointment, word.

3984. מָאן **mâ'n** (Chald.), *mawn*; prob. from a root corresp. to 579 in the sense of an *inclosure* by sides; a *utensil*:—vessel.

3985. מָאֵן **mâ'ên**, *maw-ane'*; a prim. root; to *refuse*:—refuse, × utterly.

3986. מָאֵן **mâ'ên**, *maw-ane'*; from 3985; *unwilling*:—refuse.

3987. מֵאֵן **mê'ên**, *may-ane'*; from 3985; *refractory*:—refuse.

3988. מָאַס **mâ'aç**, *maw-as'*; a prim. root; to *spurn*; also (intrans.) to *disappear*:—abhor, cast away (off), contemn, despise, disdain, (become) loathe (-some), melt away, refuse, reject, reprobate, × utterly, vile person.

3989. מַאֲפֶה **ma'ăpheh**, *mah-af-eh'*; from 644; something *baked*, i.e. a *batch*:—baken.

3990. מַאֲפֵל **ma'ăphêl**, *mah-af-ale'*; from the same as 651; something *opaque*:—darkness.

3991. מַאְפֵּלְיָה **ma'phêl^eyâh**, *mah-af-ay-leh-yaw'*; prol. fem. of 3990; *opaqueness*:—darkness.

3992. מָאַר **mâʼar**, *maw-ar'*, a prim. root; to *be bitter* or (causat.) to *embitter*, i.e. *be painful:*—fretting, picking.

מָאֹר **mâʼôr**. See 3974.

3993. מַאֲרָב **maʼărâb**, *mah-ar-awb'*; from 693; an *ambuscade:*—lie in ambush, ambushment, lurking place, lying in wait.

3994. מְאֵרָה **meʼêrâh**, *meh-ay-raw'*; from 779; an *execration:*—curse.

מְאֹרָה **meʼôrâh**. See 3974.

3995. מִבְדָּלָה **mibdâlâh**, *mib-daw-law'*; from 914; a *separation*, i.e. (concr.) a *separate* place:—separate.

3996. מָבוֹא **mâbôwʼ**, *maw-bo'*; from 935; an *entrance* (the place or the act); spec. (with or without 8121) *sunset* or the *west;* also (adv. with prep.) *towards:*—by which came, as cometh, in coming, as men enter into, entering, entrance into, entry, where goeth, going down, + westward. Comp. 4126.

3997. מְבוֹאָה **mebôwâh**, *meb-o-aw'*; fem. of 3996; a *haven:*—entry.

3998. מְבוּכָה **mebûwkâh**, *meb-oo-kaw'*; from 943; *perplexity:*—perplexity,

3999. מַבּוּל **mabbûwl**, *mab-bool'*; from 2986 in the sense of *flowing;* a *deluge:*—flood.

4000. מָבוֹן **mâbôwn**, *maw-bone'*; from 995; *instructing:*—taught.

4001. מְבוּסָה **mebûwçâh**, *meb-oo-saw'*; from 947; a *trampling:*—treading (trodden) down (under foot).

4002. מַבּוּעַ **mabbûwaʻ**, *mab-boo'-ah*; from 5042; a *fountain:*—fountain, spring.

4003. מְבוּקָה **mebûwqâh**, *meb-oo-kah'*; from the same as 950; *emptiness:*—void.

4004. מִבְחוֹר **mibchôwr**, *mib-khore'*; from 977; *select*, i.e. well fortified:—choice.

4005. מִבְחָר **mibchâr**, *mib-khawr'*; from 977; *select*, i.e. best:—choice (-st), chosen.

4006. מִבְחָר **Mibchâr**, *mib-khawr'*; the same as 4005; *Mibchar*, an Isr.:—Mibhar.

4007. מַבָּט **mabbâṭ**, *mab-bawt'*; or

מֶבָּט **mebbâṭ**, *meb-bawt'*; from 5027; something *expected*, i.e. (abstr.) *expectation:*—expectation.

4008. מִבְטָא **mibṭâʼ**, *mib-taw'*; from 981; a rash *utterance* (hasty vow):—(that which . . .) uttered (out of).

4009. מִבְטָח **mibṭâch**, *mib-tawkh'*; from 982; prop. a *refuge*, i.e. (obj.) *security*, or (subj.) *assurance:*—confidence, hope, sure, trust.

4010. מַבְלִיגִית **mablîygîyth**, *mab-leeg-eeth'*; from 1082; *desistance* (or rather *desolation*):—comfort self.

4011. מִבְנֶה **mibneh**, *mib-neh'*; from 1129; a *building:*—frame.

4012. מְבֻנַּי **Mebunnay**, *meb-oon-nah'ee*; from 1129; *built up; Mebunnai*, an Isr.:—Mebunnai,

4013. מִבְצָר **mibtsâr**, *mib-tsawr'*; also (in plur.) fem. (Dan. 11 : 15)

מִבְצָרָה **mibtsârâh**, *mib-tsaw-raw'*; from 1219; a *fortification, castle*, or *fortified* city; fig. a *defender:*—(de-, most) fenced, fortress, (most) strong (hold).

4014. מִבְצָר **Mibtsâr**, *mib-tsawr'*; the same as 4013; *Mibtsar*, an Idumæan:—Mibzar.

מִבְצָרָה **mibtsârâh**. See 4013.

4015. מִבְרָח **mibrâch**, *mib-rawkh'*; from 1272; a *refugee:*—fugitive.

4016. מָבֻשׁ **mâbûsh**, *maw-boosh'*; from 954; (plur.) the (male) *pudenda:*—secrets.

4017. מִבְשָׂם **Mibsâm**, *mib-sawm'*; from the same as 1314; *fragrant; Mibsam*, the name of an Ishmaelite and of an Isr.:—Mibsam.

4018. מְבַשְּׁלָה **mebashshelâh**, *meb-ash-shel-aw'*; from 1310; a cooking *hearth:*—boiling-place.

מָג **Mâg**. See 7248, 7249.

4019. מַגְבִּישׁ **Magbîysh**, *mag-beesh'*; from the same as 1378; *stiffening; Magbish*, an Isr., or a place in Pal.:—Magbish.

4020. מִגְבָּלָה **migbâlâh**, *mig-baw-law'*; from 1379; a *border:*—end.

4021. מִגְבָּעָה **migbâʻâh**, *mig-baw-aw'*; from the same as 1389; a *cap* (as *hemispherical*):—bonnet.

4022. מֶגֶד **meged**, *meh'-ghed*; from an unused root prop. mean. to *be eminent;* prop. a *distinguished* thing; hence something *valuable*, as a product or fruit:—pleasant, precious fruit (thing).

4023. מְגִדּוֹן **Megiddôwn** (Zech. 12 : 11), *meg-id-dōne'*; or

מְגִדּוֹ **Megiddôw**, *meg-id-do'*; from 1413; *rendezvous; Megiddon* or *Megiddo*, a place in Pal.:—Megiddo, Megiddon.

4024. מִגְדּוֹל **Migdôwl**, *mig-dole'*; or

מִגְדֹּל **Migdôl**, *mig-dole'*; prob. of Eg. or.; *Migdol*, a place in Eg.:—Migdol, tower.

4025. מַגְדִּיאֵל **Magdîyʼêl**, *mag-dee-ale'*; from 4022 and 410; *preciousness of God; Magdiël*, an Idumæan:—Magdiel.

4026. מִגְדָּל **migdâl**, *mig-dawl'*; also (in plur.) fem.

מִגְדָּלָה **migdâlâh**, *mig-daw-law'*; from 1431; a *tower* (from its size or height); by anal. a *rostrum;* fig. a (pyramidal) *bed* of flowers:—castle, flower, pulpit, tower. Comp. the names following.

מִגְדֹּל **Migdôl**. See 4024.

מִגְדָּלָה **migdâlâh**. See 4026.

4027. מִגְדַּל־אֵל **Migdal-ʼÊl**, *mig-dal-ale'*; from 4026 and 410; *tower of God; Migdal-El*, a place in Pal.:—Migdal-el.

4028. מִגְדַּל־גָּד **Migdal-Gâd**, *migdal-gawd'*; from 4026 and 1408; *tower of Fortune; Migdal-Gad*, a place in Pal.:—Migdal-gad.

4029. מִגְדַּל־עֵדֶר **Migdal-ʻÊder**, *mig-dal'-ay'-der*; from 4026 and 5739; *tower of a flock; Migdal-Eder*, a place in Pal.:—Migdal-eder, tower of the flock.

4030. מִגְדָּנָה **migdânâh**, *mig-daw-naw'*; from the same as 4022; *preciousness*, i.e. a *gem:*—precious thing, present.

4031. מָגוֹג **Mâgôwg**, *maw-gogue'*; from 1463; *Magog*, a son of Japheth; also a barbarous northern region:—Magog.

4032. מָגוֹר **mâgôwr**, *maw-gore'*; or (Lam. 2 : 22)

מָגוּר **mâgûwr**, *maw-goor'*; from 1481 in the sense of *fearing;* a *fright* (obj. or subj.):—fear, terror. Comp. 4036.

4033. מָגוּר **mâgûwr**, *maw-goor'*; or

מָגֻר **mâgûr**, *maw-goor'*; from 1481 in the sense of *lodging;* a temporary *abode;* by extens. a permanent *residence:*—dwelling, pilgrimage, where sojourn, be a stranger. Comp. 4032.

4034. מְגוֹרָה **megôwrâh**, *meg-o-raw'*; fem. of 4032; *affright:*—fear.

4035. מְגוּרָה **megûwrâh**, *meg-oo-raw'*; fem. of 4032 or of 4033; a *fright;* also a *granary:*—barn, fear.

4036. מָגוֹר מִסָּבִיב **Mâgôwr miç-Çâbîyb**, *maw-gore' mis-saw-beeb'*; from 4032 and 5439 with the prep. inserted; *affright from around; Magor-mis-Sabib*, a symbol. name of Pashur:—Magor-missabib.

4037. מַגְזֵרָה **magzêrâh**, *mag-zay-raw'*; from 1504; a *cutting* implement, i.e. a *blade:*—axe.

4038. מַגָּל **maggâl**, *mag-gawl'*; from an unused root mean. to *reap;* a *sickle:*—sickle.

4039. מְגִלָּה **megillâh**, *meg-il-law'*; from 1556; a *roll:*—roll, volume.

4040. מְגִלָּה **megillâh** (Chald.), *meg-il-law'*; corresp. to 4039:—roll.

4041. מְגַמָּה **megammâh**, *meg-am-maw'*; from the same as 1571; prop. *accumulation*, i.e. *impulse* or *direction:*—sup up.

4042. מָגַן **mâgan**, *maw-gan'*; a denom. from 4043; prop. to *shield; encompass* with; fig. to *rescue*, to *hand* safely *over* (i.e. *surrender*):—deliver.

4043. מָגֵן **mâgên**, *maw-gane'*; also (in plur.) fem.

מְגִנָּה **meginnâh**, *meg-in-naw'*; from 1598; a *shield* (i.e. the small one or *buckler*); fig. a *protector;* also the scaly *hide* of the crocodile:—× armed, buckler, defence, ruler, + scale, shield.

4044. מְגִנָּה **meginnâh**, *meg-in-naw'*; from 4042; a *covering* (in a bad sense), i.e. *blindness* or obduracy:—sorrow. See also 4043.

4045. מִגְעֶרֶת **migʻereth**, *mig-eh'-reth;* from 1605; *reproof* (i.e. curse):—rebuke.

4046. מַגֵּפָה **maggêphâh**, *mag-gay-faw'*; from 5062; a *pestilence;* by anal. *defeat:*—(× be) plague (-d), slaughter, stroke.

4047. מַגְפִּיעָשׁ **Magpîyʻâsh**, *mag-pee-awsh'*; appar. from 1479 or 5062 and 6211; *exterminator of* (the) *moth; Magpiash*, an Isr.:—Magpiash.

4048. מָגַר **mâgar**, *maw-gar'*; a prim. root; to *yield up;* intens. to *precipitate:*—cast down, terror.

4049. מְגַר **megar** (Chald.), *meg-ar'*; corresp. to 4048; to *overthrow:*—destroy.

4050. מְגֵרָה **megêrâh**, *meg-ay-raw'*; from 1641; a *saw:*—axe, saw.

4051. מִגְרוֹן **Migrôwn**, *mig-rone'*; from 4048; *precipice; Migron*, a place in Pal.:—Migron.

4052. מִגְרָעָה **migrâʻâh**, *mig-raw-aw'*; from 1639; a *ledge* or offset:—narrowed rest.

4053. מִגְרָפָה **migrâphâh**, *mig-raw-faw'*; from 1640; something *thrown off* (by the spade), i.e. a *clod:*—clod.

4054. מִגְרָשׁ **migrâsh**, *mig-rawsh'*; also (in plur.) fem. (Ezek. 27 : 28)

מִגְרָשָׁה **migrâshâh**, *mig-raw-shaw'*; from 1644; a *suburb* (i.e. open country whither flocks are *driven* for pasture); hence the *area* around a building, or the *margin* of the sea:—cast out, suburb.

4055. מַד **mad**, *mad;* or

מֵד **mêd**, *made;* from 4058; prop. *extent*, i.e. *height;* also a *measure;* by impl. a *vesture* (as measured); also a *carpet:*—armour, clothes, garment, judgment, measure, raiment, stature.

4056. מַדְבַּח **madbach** (Chald.), *mad-bakh'*; from 1684; a sacrificial *altar:*—altar.

4057. מִדְבָּר **midbâr**, *mid-bawr'*; from 1696 in the sense of *driving;* a *pasture* (i.e. open field, whither cattle are driven); by impl a *desert;* also *speech* (including its organs):—desert, south, speech, wilderness.

4058. מָדַד **mâdad**, *maw-dad'*; a prim. root; prop. to *stretch;* by impl. to *measure* (as if by *stretching* a line); fig. to *be extended:*—measure, mete, stretch self.

4059. מִדַּד **middad**, *mid-dad'*; from 5074; *flight:*—be gone.

4060. מִדָּה **middâh**, *mid-daw'*; fem. of 4055; prop. *extension*, i.e. height or breadth; also a *measure* (including its standard); hence a *portion* (as measured) or a *vestment;* spec. *tribute* (as measured):—garment, measure (-ing, meteyard, piece, size, (great) stature, tribute, wide.

4061. מִדָּה **middâh** (Chald.), *mid-daw'*; or

מִנְדָּה **mindâh** (Chald.), *min-daw'*; corresp. to 4060; *tribute* in money:—toll, tribute.

4062. מַדְהֵבָה **madhêbâh**, *mad-hay-baw'*; perh. from the equiv. of 1722; *gold-making*, i.e. *exactress:*—golden city.

4063. מֶדֶו **medev**, *meh'-dev;* from an unused root mean. to *stretch;* prop. *extent*, i.e. *measure;* by impl. a *dress* (as measured):—garment.

4064. מַדְוֶה **madveh**, *mad-veh'*; from 1738; *sickness:*—disease.

4065. מַדּוּחַ **maddûwach**, *mad-doo'-akh*, from 5080; *seduction:*—cause of banishment.

4066. מָדוֹן **mâdôwn**, *maw-dohn'*; from 1777; a *contest* or quarrel:—brawling, contention (-ous), discord, strife. Comp. 4079, 4090.

4067. מָדוֹן **mâdôwn**, *maw-dohn'*; from the same as 4063; *extensiveness*, i.e. height:—stature.

4068. מָדוֹן **Mâdôwn**, *maw-dohn'*; the same as 4067; *Madon*, a place in Pal.:—Madon.

4069. מַדּוּעַ **maddûwaʻ**, *mad-doo'-ah*; or

מַדֻּעַ **maddûaʻ**, *mad-doo'-ah*; from 4100 and the pass. part. of 3045; *what* (is) *known?*; i.e. (by impl.) (adv.) *why?*:—how, wherefore, why.

4070. מְדוֹר **medôwr** Chald.), *med-ore'*; or

מְדֹר **medôr** (Chald.), *med-ore'*; or

מְדָר **medâr** (Chald.), *med-awr'*; from 1753; a *dwelling*:—dwelling.

4071. מְדוּרָה **medûwrâh**, *med-oo-raw'*; or

מְדֻרָה **medûrâh**, *med-oo-raw'*; from 1752 in the sense of *accumulation*; a *pile* of fuel:—pile (for fire).

4072. מִדְחֶה **midcheh**, *mid-kheh'*; from 1760; *overthrow*:—ruin.

4073. מְדַחְפָה **medachphâh**, *med-akh-faw'*; from 1765; a *push*, i.e. ruin:—overthrow.

4074. מָדַי **Mâday**, *maw-dah'ee*; of for. der.; *Madai*, a country of central Asia:—Madai, Medes, Media.

4075. מָדַי **Mâday**, *maw-dah'ee*; patrial from 4074; a *Madian* or native of Madai:—Mede.

4076. מָדַי **Mâday** (Chald.), *maw-dah'ee*; corresp. to 4074:—Mede (-s).

4077. מָדַי **Mâday** (Chald.), *maw-dah'ee*; corresp. to 4075:—Median.

4078. מַדַּי **madday**, *mad-dah'ee*; from 4100 and 1767; *what* (is) *enough*, i.e. *sufficiently*:—sufficiently.

4079. מִדְיָן **midyân**, *mid-yawn'*; a var. for 4066:—brawling, contention (-ous).

4080. מִדְיָן **Midyân** ,*mid-yawn'*; the same as 4079; *Midjan*, a son of Abraham; also his country and (collect.) his descend.:—Midian, Midianite.

4081. מִדִּין **Middîyn**, *mid-deen'*; a var. for 4080:—Middin.

4082. מְדִינָה **medîynâh**, *med-ee-naw'*; from 1777; prop. a *judgeship*, i.e. *jurisdiction*; by impl. a *district* (as ruled by a judge); gen. a *region*:—(× every) province.

4083. מְדִינָה **medîynâh** (Chald.), *med-ee-naw'*; corresp. to 4082:—province.

4084. מִדְיָנִי **Midyânîy**, *mid-yaw-nee'*; patron. or patrial from 4080; a *Midjanite* or descend. (native) of Midjan:—Midianite. Comp. 4092.

4085. מְדֹכָה **medôkâh**, *med-o-kaw'*; from 1743; a *mortar*:—mortar.

4086. מַדְמֵן **Madmên**, *mad-mane'*; from the same as 1828; *dunghill*; *Madmen*, a place in Pal.:—Madmen.

4087. מַדְמֵנָה **madmênâh**, *mad-may-naw'*; fem. from the same as 1828; a *dunghill*:—dunghill.

4088. מַדְמֵנָה **Madmênâh**. *mad-may-naw'*; the same as 4087; *Madmenah*, a place in Pal.:—Madmenah.

4089. מַדְמַנָּה **Madmannâh**, *mad-man-naw'*; a var. for 4087; *Madmannah*, a place in Pal.:—Madmannah.

4090. מְדָן **medân**, *med-awn'*; a form of 4066:—discord, strife.

4091. מְדָן **Medân**, *med-awn'*; the same as 4090; *Medan*, a son of Abraham:—Medan.

4092. מְדָנִי **Medânîy**, *med-aw-nee'*; a var. of 4084:—Midianite.

4093. מַדָּע **maddâʻ**, *mad-daw'*; or

מַדַּע **maddaʻ**, *mad-dah'*; from 3045; *intelligence* or *consciousness*:—knowledge, science, thought.

מֹדָע **môdâʻ**. See 4129.

מַדֻּעַ **madûaʻ**. See 4069.

4094. מַדְקָרָה **madqârâh**, *mad-kaw-raw'*; from 1856; a *wound*:—piercing.

מְדֹר **medôr**. See 4070.

4095. מַדְרֵגָה **madrêgâh**, *mad-ray-gaw'*; from an unused root mean. to *step*; prop. a *step*; by impl. a *steep* or inaccessible place:—stair, steep place.

מְדֻרָה **medûrâh**. See 4071.

4096. מִדְרָךְ **midrâk**, *mid-rawk'*; from 1869; a *treading*, i.e. a place for stepping on:—[foot-] breadth.

4097. מִדְרָשׁ **midrâsh**, *mid-rawsh'*; from 1875; prop. an *investigation*, i.e. (by impl.) a *treatise* or elaborate compilation:—story.

4098. מְדֻשָּׁה **medushshâh**, *med-oosh-shaw'*; from 1758; a *threshing*, i.e. (concr. and fig.) *down-trodden* people:—threshing.

4099. מְדָתָא **Medâthâ**, *med-aw-thaw'*; of Pers. or.; *Medatha*, the father of Haman:—Hammedatha [*includ. the art.*].

4100. מָה **mâh**, *maw*; or מַה **mah**, *mah*; or

מָ־ **mâ**, *maw*; or מַ־ **ma**, *mah*; also

מֶה **meh**, *meh*; a prim. particle; prop. interrog. *what?* (includ. *how? why? when?*); but also exclam. *what!* (includ. *how!*), or indef. *what* (includ. *whatever*, and even rel. *that which*); often used with prefixes in various adv. or conj. senses:—how (long, oft, [-soever]), [no-] thing, what (end, good, purpose, thing), whereby (-fore, -in, -to, -with), (for) why.

4101. מָה **mâh** (Chald.), *maw*; corresp. to 4100:—how great (mighty), that which, what (-soever), why.

4102. מָהַהּ **mâhahh**, *maw-hah'*; appar. a denom. from 4100; prop. to *question* or hesitate, i.e. (by impl.) to *be reluctant*:—delay, linger, stay selves, tarry.

4103. מְהוּמָה **mehûwmâh**, *meh-hoo-maw'*; from 1949; *confusion* or uproar:—destruction, discomfiture, trouble, tumult, vexation, vexed.

4104. מְהוּמָן **Mehûwmân**, *meh-hoo-mawn'*; of Pers. or.; *Mehuman*, a eunuch of Xerxes:—Mehuman.

4105. מְהֵיטַבְאֵל **Mehêyṭab'êl**, *meh-hay-tab-ale'*; from 3190 (augmented) and 410; *bettered of God*; *Mehetabel*, the name of an Edomitish man and woman:—Mehetabeel, Mehetabel.

4106. מָהִיר **mâhîyr**, *maw-here'*; or

מָהִר **mâhîr**, *maw-here'*; from 4116; *quick*; hence *skilful*:—diligent, hasty, ready.

4107. מָהַל **mâhal**, *maw-hal'*; a prim. root; prop. to *cut down* or *reduce*, i.e. by impl. to *adulterate*:—mixed.

4108. מַהְלֵךְ **mahlêk**, *mah-lake'*; from 1980; a *walking* (plur. collect.), i.e. *access*:—place to walk.

4109. מַהֲלָךְ **mahălâk**, *mah-hal-awk'*; from 1980; a *walk*, i.e. a *passage* or a *distance*:—journey, walk.

4110. מַהֲלָל **mahălâl**, *mah-hal-awl'*; from 1984; *fame*:—praise.

4111. מַהֲלַלְאֵל **Mahălal'êl**, *mah-hal-al-ale'*; from 4110 and 410; *praise of God*; *Mahalalel*, the name of an antediluvian patriarch and of an Isr.:—Mahalaleel.

4112. מַהֲלֻמָּה **mahălummâh**, *mah-hal-oom-maw'*; from 1986; a *blow*:—stripe, stroke.

4113. מַהֲמֹרָה **mahămôrâh**, *mah-ham-o-raw'*; from an unused root of uncert. mean.; perh. an *abyss*:—deep pit.

4114. מַהְפֵּכָה **mahpêkâh**, *mah-pay-kaw'*; from 2015; a *destruction*:—when . . . overthrew, overthrow (-n).

4115. מַהְפֶּכֶת **mahpeketh**, *mah-peh'-keth*; from 2015; a *wrench*, i.e. the *stocks*:—prison, stocks.

4116. מָהַר **mâhar**, *maw-har'*; a prim. root; prop. to *be liquid* or *flow* easily, i.e. (by impl.); to *hurry* (in a good or a bad sense); often used (with another verb) adv. *promptly*:—be carried headlong, fearful, (cause to make, in, make) haste (-n, -ily, (be) hasty, (fetch, make ready) × quickly, rash, × shortly, (be so) × soon, make speed, × speedily, × straightway, × suddenly, swift.

4117. מָהַר **mâhar**, *maw-har'*; a prim. root (perh. rather the same as 4116 through the idea of *readiness* in assent): to *bargain* (for a wife), i.e. to *wed*:—endow, × surely.

4118. מַהֵר **mahêr**, *mah-hare'*; from 4116; prop. *hurrying*; hence (adv.) *in a hurry*:—hasteth, hastily, at once, quickly, soon, speedily, suddenly.

מָהִר **mâhîr**. See 4106.

4119. מֹהַר **môhar**, *mo'-har*; from 4117; a *price* (for a wife):—dowry.

4120. מְהֵרָה **mehêrâh**, *meh-hay-raw'*; fem. of 4118; prop. a *hurry*; hence (adv.) *promptly*:—hastily, quickly, shortly, soon, make (with) speed (-ily), swiftly.

4121. מַהֲרַי **Mahăray**, *mah-har-ah'ee*; from 4116; *hasty*; *Maharai*, an Isr.:—Maharai.

4122. מַהֵר שָׁלָל חָשׁ בַּז **Mahêr Shâlâl Châsh Baz**, *mah-hare' shaw-lawl' khawsh baz*; from 4118 and 7998 and 2363 and 957; *hasting* (is he [the enemy] to the) *booty*, *swift* (to the) *prey*; *Maher-Shalal-Chash-Baz*; the symbol. name of the son of Isaiah:—Maher-shalal-hash-baz.

4123. מַהֲתַלָּה **mahăthallâh**, *mah-hath-al-law'*; from 2048; a *delusion*:—deceit.

4124. מוֹאָב **Môw'âb**, *mo-awb*; from a prol. form of the prep. pref. *m-* and 1; *from* (her [the mother's]) *father*; *Moäb*, an incestuous son of Lot; also his territory and desc.:—Moab.

4125. מוֹאָבִי **Môw'âbîy**, *mo-aw-bee'*; fem.

מוֹאָבִיָּה **Môw'âbîyah**, *mo-aw-bee-yaw'*; or

מוֹאָבִית **Môwâbîyth**, *mo-aw-beeth'*; patron. from 4124; a *Moäbite* or *Moäbitess*, i.e. a desc. from Moab:—(woman) of Moab, Moabite (-ish, -ss).

מוֹאל **môw'l**. See 4136.

4126. מוֹבָא **môwbâ'**, *mo-baw'*; by transp. for 3996; an *entrance*:—coming.

4127. מוּג **mûwg**, *moog*; a prim. root; to *melt*, i.e. lit. (to *soften*, flow down, *disappear*), or fig. (to *fear*, *faint*):—consume, dissolve, (be) faint (-hearted), melt (away), make soft.

4128. מוּד **mûwd**, *mood*; a prim. root; to *shake*:—measure.

4129. מוֹדַע **môwdaʻ**, *mo-dah'*; or rather

מֹדָע **môdâʻ**, *mo-daw'*; from 3045; an *acquaintance*:—kinswoman.

4130. מוֹדַעַת **môwda'ath**, *mo-dah'-ath*; from 3045; *acquaintance*:—kindred.

4131. מוֹט **môwṭ**, *mote*; a prim. root; to *waver*; by impl. to *slip*, *shake*, *fall*:—be carried, cast, be out of course, be fallen in decay, × exceedingly, fall (-ing down), be (re-) moved, be ready, shake, slide, slip.

4132. מוֹט **môwṭ**, *mote*; from 4131; a *wavering*, i.e. *fall*; by impl. a *pole* (as shaking); hence a *yoke* (as essentially a bent pole):—bar, be moved, staff, yoke.

4133. מוֹטָה **môwṭâh**, *mo-taw';* fem. of 4132; a *pole;* by impl. an ox-*bow;* hence a *yoke* (either lit. or fig.):—bands, heavy, staves, yoke.

4134. מוּךְ **mûwk**, *mook;* a prim. root; to *become thin*, i.e. (fig.) *be impoverished:*—be (waxen) poor (-er).

4135. מוּל **mûwl**, *mool;* a prim. root; to *cut short*, i.e. *curtail* (spec. the prepuce, i.e. to *circumcise*); by impl. to *blunt;* fig. to *destroy:*—circumcise (-ing, selves), cut down (in pieces), destroy, × must needs.

4136. מוּל **mûwl**, *mool;* or
מוֹל **môwl** (Deut. 1 : 1), *mole;* or
מוֹאל **môw'l** (Neh. 12 : 38), *mole;* or
מֻל **mûl** (Num. 22 : 5), *mool;* from 4135; prop. *abrupt*, i.e. a *precipice;* by impl. the *front;* used only adv. (with prep. pref.) *opposite:*—(over) against, before, [fore-] front, from, [God-] ward, toward, with.

4137. מוֹלָדָה **Môwlâdâh**, *mo-law-daw';* from 3205; *birth; Moladah*, a place in Pal.:—Moladah.

4138. מוֹלֶדֶת **môwledeth**, *mo-leh'-deth;* from 3205; *nativity* (plur. *birth-place*); by impl. *lineage, native country;* also *offspring, family:*—begotten, born, issue, kindred, native (-ity).

4139. מוּלָה **mûwlâh**, *moo-law';* from 4135; *circumcision:*—circumcision.

4140. מוֹלִיד **Môwlîyd**, *mo-leed';* from 3205; *genitor; Molid*, an Isr.:—Molid.

מוּם **muwm**. See 3971.

מוּמֻכָן **Môwmûkân**. See 4462.

4141. מוּסָב **mûwçâb**, *moo-sawb';* from 5437; a *turn*, i.e. *circuit* (of a building):—winding about.

4142. מוּסַבָּה **mûwçabbâh**, *moo-sab-baw';* or
מֻסַבָּה **mûçabbâh**, *moo-sab-baw';* fem. of 4141; a *reversal*, i.e. the *backside* (of a gem), *fold* (of a double-leaved door), *transmutation* (of a name):—being changed, inclosed, be set, turning.

4143. מוּסָד **mûwçâd**, *moo-sawd';* from 3245; a *foundation:*—foundation.

4144. מוֹסָד **môwçâd**, *mo-sawd';* from 3245; a *foundation:*—foundation.

4145. מוּסָדָה **mûwçâdâh**, *moo-saw-daw';* fem. of 4143; a *foundation;* fig. an *appointment:*—foundation, grounded. Comp. 4328.

4146. מוֹסָדָה **môwçâdâh**, *mo-saw-daw';* or
מֹסָדָה **môçâdâh** *mo-saw-daw';* fem. of 4144; a *foundation:*—foundation.

4147. מוֹסֵר **môwçêr**, *mo-sare';* also (in plur.) fem.
מוֹסֵרָה **môwçêrâh**, *mo-say-raw';* or
מֹסְרָה **môç^{e}râh**, *mo-ser-aw';* from 3256; prop. *chastisement*, i.e. (by impl.) a *halter;* fig. *restraint:*—band, bond.

4148. מוּסָר **mûwçâr**, *moo-sawr';* from 3256; prop. *chastisement;* fig. *reproof, warning* or *instruction;* also *restraint:*—bond, chastening ([-eth]), chastisement, check, correction, discipline, doctrine, instruction, rebuke.

4149. מוֹסֵרָה **Môwçêrâh**, *mo-say-raw';* or (plur.)
מֹסְרוֹת **Môç^{e}rôwth**, *mo-ser-othe';* fem. of 4147; *correction* or *corrections; Moserah* or *Moseroth*, a place in the Desert:—Mosera, Moseroth.

4150. מוֹעֵד **môwʻêd**, *mo-ade';* or
מֹעֵד **môʻêd** *mo-ade';* or (fem.)
מוֹעָדָה **môwʻâdâh** (2 Chron. 8 : 13), *mo-aw-daw';* from 3259; prop. an *appointment*, i.e. a fixed *time* or season; spec. a *festival;* conventionally a *year;* by implication, an *assembly* (as convened for a definite purpose); technically the *congregation;* by extension, the *place of meeting;* also a *signal* (as appointed beforehand):—appointed (sign, time), (place of, solemn) assembly, congregation, (set, solemn) feast, (appointed, due) season, solemn (-ity), synagogue, (set) time (appointed).

4151. מוֹעָד **môwʻâd**, *mo-awd';* from 3259; prop. an *assembly* [as in 4150]; fig. a *troop:*—appointed time.

4152. מוּעָדָה **mûwʻâdâh**, *moo-aw-daw';* from 3259; an *appointed* place, i.e. *asylum:*—appointed.

4153. מוֹעַדְיָה **Môwʻadyâh**, *mo-ad-yaw';* from 4151 and 3050; *assembly of Jah; Moädjah*, an Isr.:—Moadiah. Comp. 4573.

4154. מוּעֶדֶת **mûwʻedeth**, *moo-ay'-deth;* fem. pass. part. of 4571; prop. *made to slip*, i.e. *dislocated:*—out of joint.

4155. מוּעָף **mûwʻâph**, *moo-awf';* from 5774; prop. *covered*, i.e. *dark;* abstr. *obscurity*, i.e. *distress:*—dimness.

4156. מוֹעֵצָה **môwʻêtsâh**, *mo-ay-tsaw';* from 3289; a *purpose:*—counsel, device.

4157. מוּעָקָה **mûwʻâqâh**, *moo-aw-kaw';* from 5781; *pressure*, i.e. (fig.) *distress:*—affliction.

4158. מוֹפַעַת **Môwphaʻath** (Jer. 48 : 21), *mo-fah'-ath;* or
מֵיפַעַת **mêyphaath**, *may-fah'-ath;* or
מֵפַעַת **mêphaath**, *may-fah'-ath;* from 3313; *illuminative; Mophaath* or *Mephaath*, a place in Pal.:—Mephaath.

4159. מוֹפֵת **môwphêth**, *mo-faith';* or
מֹפֵת **môphêth**, *mo-faith';* from 3302 in the sense of *conspicuousness;* a *miracle;* by impl. a *token* or *omen:*—miracle, sign, wonder (-ed at).

4160. מוּץ **mûwts**, *moots;* a prim. root; to *press*, i.e. (fig.) to *oppress:*—extortioner.

4161. מוֹצָא **môwtsâ'**, *mo-tsaw';* or
מֹצָא **môtsâ'**, *mo-tsaw';* from 3318; a *going forth*, i.e. (the act) an *egress*, or (the place) an *exit;* hence a *source* or *product;* spec. *dawn*, the *rising* of the sun (the *East*), *exportation, utterance*, a *gate*, a *fountain*, the *mine*, a *meadow* (as producing grass):—brought out, bud, that which came out, east, going forth, goings out, that which (thing that) is gone out, outgoing, proceeded out, spring, vein, [water-] course [springs].

4162. מוֹצָא **môwtsâ'**, *mo-tsaw';* the same as 4161; *Motsa*, the name of two Isr.:—Moza.

4163. מוֹצָאָה **môwtsâ'âh**, *mo-tsaw-aw';* fem. of 4161; a family *descent;* also a *sewer* [marg.; comp. 6675]:—draught house; going forth.

4164. מוּצַק **mûwtsaq**, *moo-tsak';* or
מוּצָק **mûwtsâq**, *moo-tsawk';* from 3332; *narrowness;* fig. *distress:*—anguish, is straitened, straitness.

4165. מוּצָק **mûwtsâq**, *moo-tsawk';* from 5694; prop. *fusion*, i.e. lit. a *casting* (of metal); fig. a *mass* (of clay):—casting, hardness.

4166. מוּצָקָה **mûwtsâqâh**, *moo-tsaw-kaw';* or
מֻצָקָה **mûtsâqâh**, *moo-tsaw-kaw';* from 3332; prop. something *poured* out, i.e. a *casting* (of metal); by impl. a *tube* (as cast):—when it was cast, pipe.

4167. מוּק **mûwq**, *mook;* a prim. root; to *jeer*, i.e. (intens.) *blaspheme:*—be corrupt.

4168. מוֹקֵד **môwqêd**, *mo-kade';* from 3344; a *fire* or *fuel;* abstr. a *conflagration:*—burning, hearth.

4169. מוֹקְדָה **môwq^{e}dâh**, *mo-ked-aw';* fem. of 4168; *fuel:*—burning.

4170. מוֹקֵשׁ **môwqêsh**, *mo-kashe';* or
מֹקֵשׁ **môqêsh**, *mo-kashe';* from 3369; a *noose* (for catching animals) (lit. or fig.); by impl. a *hook* (for the nose):—be ensnared, gin, (is) snare (-d), trap.

4171. מוּר **mûwr**, *moor;* a prim. root; to *alter;* by impl. to *barter*, to *dispose of:*— × at all, (ex-) change, remove.

4172. מוֹרָא **môwrâ'**, *mo-raw';* or
מֹרָא **môrâ'**, *mo-raw';* or
מוֹרָה **môrâh** (Psa. 9 : 20), *mo-raw';* from 3372; *fear;* by impl. a *fearful* thing or deed:—dread, (that ought to be) fear (-ed), terribleness, terror.

4173. מוֹרַג **môwrag**, *mo-rag';* or
מֹרַג **môrag**, *mo-rag';* from an unused root mean. to *triturate;* a threshing *sledge:*—threshing instrument.

4174. מוֹרָד **môwrâd**, *mo-rawd';* from 3381; a *descent;* arch. an ornamental *appendage*, perh. a *festoon:*—going down, steep place, thin work.

4175. מוֹרֶה **môwreh**, *mo-reh';* from 3384; an *archer;* also *teacher* or *teaching;* also the *early rain* [see 3138]:—(early) rain.

4176. מוֹרֶה **Môwreh**, *mo-reh';* or
מֹרֶה **Môreh**, *mo-reh';* the same as 4175; *Moreh*, a Canaanite; also a hill (perh. named from him):—Moreh.

4177. מוֹרָה **môwrâh**, *mo-raw';* from 4171 in the sense of *shearing;* a *razor:*—razor.

4178. מוֹרָט **môwrâṭ**, *mo-rawt';* from 3399; *obstinate*, i.e. independent:—peeled.

4179. מוֹרִיָּה **Môwrîyâh**, *mo-ree-yaw';* or
מֹרִיָּה **Môrîyâh**, *mo-ree-yaw';* from 7200 and 3050; *seen of Jah; Morijah*, a hill in Pal.:—Moriah.

4180. מוֹרָשׁ **môwrâsh**, *mo-rawsh';* from 3423; a *possession;* fig. *delight:*—possession, thought.

4181. מוֹרָשָׁה **môwrâshâh**, *mo-raw-shaw';* fem. of 4180; a *possession:*—heritage, inheritance, possession.

4182. מוֹרֶשֶׁת גַּת **Môwresheth Gath**, *mo-reh'-sheth gath;* from 3423 and 1661; *possession of Gath; Moresheth-Gath*, a place in Pal.:—Moresheth-gath.

4183. מוֹרַשְׁתִּי **Morashtîy**, *mo-rash-tee';* patrial from 4182; a *Morashtite* or inhab. of Moresheth-Gath:—Morashthite.

4184. מוּשׁ **mûwsh**, *moosh;* a prim. root; to *touch:*—feel, handle.

4185. מוּשׁ **mûwsh**, *moosh;* a prim. root [perh. rather the same as 4184 through the idea of receding by *contact*]; to *withdraw* (both lit. and fig., whether intrans. or trans.):—cease, depart, go back, remove, take away.

4186. מוֹשָׁב **môwshâb**, *mo-shawb';* or
מֹשָׁב **môshâb**, *mo-shawb';* from 3427; a *seat;* fig. a *site;* abstr. a *session;* by extension an *abode* (the place or the time); by impl. *population:*—assembly, dwell in, dwelling (-place), wherein (that) dwelt (in), inhabited place, seat, sitting, situation, sojourning.

4187. מוּשִׁי **Mûwshîy**, *moo-shee';* or
מֻשִּׁי **Mushshîy**, *mush-shee';* from 4184; *sensitive; Mushi*, a Levite:—Mushi.

4188. מוּשִׁי **Mûwshîy**, *moo-shee';* patron. from 4187; a *Mushite* (collect.) or desc. of Mushi:—Mushites.

4189. מוֹשְׁכָה **môwsh^{e}kâh**, *mo-shek-aw';* act part. fem. of 4900; something *drawing*, i.e. (fig.) a *cord:*—band.

4190. מוֹשָׁעָה **môwshâʻâh**, *mo-shaw-aw';* from 3467; *deliverance:*—salvation.

4191. מוּת **mûwth**, *mooth;* a prim. root; to *die* (lit. or fig.); causat. to *kill:*— × at all, × crying, (be) dead (body, man, one), (put to, worthy of) death, destroy (-er), (cause to, be like to, must) die, kill, necro [-mancer], × must needs, slay, × surely, × very suddenly, × in [no] wise.

4192. מוּת **Mûwth** (Psa. 48 : 14), *mooth;* or

מוּת לַבֵּן **Mûwth lab-bên**, *mooth lab-bane';* from 4191 and 1121 with the prep. and art. interposed; "*To die for the son*", prob. the title of a popular song:—death, Muth-labben.

4193. מוֹת **môwth** (Chald.), *mohth;* corresp. to 4194; *death:*—death.

4194. מָוֶת **mâveth**, *maw'-veth;* from 4191; *death* (nat. or violent); concr. the *dead*, their place or state (*hades*); fig. *pestilence, ruin:*—(be) dead ([-ly]), death, die (-d).

מוּת לַבֵּן **Mûwth lab-bên**. See 4192.

4195. מוֹתָר **môwthar**, *mo-thar';* from 3498; lit. *gain;* fig. *superiority:*—plenteousness, preeminence, profit.

4196. מִזְבֵּחַ **mizbêach**, *miz-bay'-akh;* from 2076; an *altar:*—altar.

4197. מֶזֶג **mezeg**, *meh'-zeg;* from an unused root mean. to *mingle* (water with wine); *tempered* wine:—liquor.

4198. מָזֶה **mâzeh**, *maw-zeh';* from an unused root mean. to *suck* out; *exhausted:*—burnt.

4199. מִזָּה **Mizzâh**, *miz-zaw';* prob. from an unused root mean. to *faint* with fear; *terror; Mizzah*, an Edomite:—Mizzah.

4200. מֶזֶו **mezev**, *meh'-zev;* prob. from an unused root mean. to *gather* in; a *granary:*—garner.

4201. מְזוּזָה **m^ezûwzâh**, *mez-oo-zaw';* or

מְזֻזָה **m^ezûzâh**, *mez-oo-zaw';* from the same as 2123; a *door-post* (as *prominent*):—(door, side) post.

4202. מָזוֹן **mâzôwn**, *maw-zone';* from 2109; *food:*—meat, victual.

4203. מָזוֹן **mâzôwn** (Chald.), *maw-zone';* corresp. to 4202:—meat.

4204. מָזוֹר **mâzôwr**, *maw-zore';* from 2114 in the sense of *turning aside* from truth; *treachery*, i.e. a *plot:*—wound.

4205. מָזוֹר **mâzôwr**, *maw-zore';* or

מָזֹר **mâzôr**, *maw-zore';* from 2115 in the sense of *binding* up; a *bandage*, i.e. remedy; hence a *sore* (as needing a compress):—bound up, wound.

מְזֻזָה **m^ezûzâh**. See 4201.

4206. מָזִיחַ **mâzîyach**, *maw-zee'-akh;* or

מֵזַח **mêzach**, *may-zakh';* from 2118; a *belt* (as movable):—girdle, strength.

4207. מַזְלֵג **mazlêg**, *maz-layg';* or (fem.)

מִזְלָגָה **mizlâgâh**, *miz-law-gaw';* from an unused root mean. to *draw* up; a *fork:*—fleshhook.

4208. מַזָּלָה **mazzâlâh**, *maz-zaw-law';* appar. from 5140 in the sense of *raining;* a *constellation*, i.e. Zodiacal sign (perh. as affecting the weather):—planet. Comp. 4216.

4209. מְזִמָּה **m^ezimmâh**, *mez-im-maw';* from 2161; a *plan*, usually evil (*machination*), sometimes good (*sagacity*):—(wicked) device, discretion, intent, witty invention, lewdness, mischievous (device), thought, wickedly.

4210. מִזְמוֹר **mizmôwr**, *miz-more';* from 2167; prop. instrumental *music;* by impl. a *poem* set to notes:—psalm.

4211. מַזְמֵרָה **mazmêrâh**, *maz-may-raw';* from 2168; a *pruning-knife:*—pruning-hook.

4212. מְזַמְּרָה **m^ezamm^erâh**, *mez-am-mer-aw';* from 2168; a *tweezer* (only in the plur.):—snuffers.

4213. מִזְעָר **miz'âr**, *miz-awr';* from the same as 2191; *fewness;* by impl. as superl. *diminutiveness:*—few, × very.

מָזֹר **mâzôr**. See 4205.

4214. מִזְרֶה **mizreh**, *miz-reh';* from 2219; a winnowing *shovel* (as scattering the chaff):—fan.

4215. מְזָרֶה **m^ezâreh**, *mez-aw-reh';* appar. from 2219; prop. a *scatterer*, i.e. the north *wind* (as dispersing clouds; only in plur.):—north.

4216. מַזָּרָה **mazzârâh**, *maz-zaw-raw';* appar. from 5144 in the sense of *distinction;* some noted *constellation* (only in the plur.), perh. collect. the *zodiac:*—Mazzoroth. Comp. 4208.

4217. מִזְרָח **mizrâch**, *miz-rawkh';* from 2224; *sunrise*, i.e. the *east:*—east (side, -ward), (sun-) rising (of the sun).

4218. מִזְרָע **mizrâ'**, *miz-raw';* from 2232; a planted *field:*—thing sown.

4219. מִזְרָק **mizrâq**, *miz-rawk';* from 2236; a *bowl* (as if for sprinkling):—bason, bowl.

4220. מֵחַ **mêach**, *may'-akh;* from 4229 in the sense of *greasing; fat;* fig. *rich:*—fatling (one).

4221. מֹחַ **môach**, *mo'-akh;* from the same as 4220; *fat*, i.e. marrow:—marrow.

4222. מָחָא **mâchâ'**, *maw-khaw';* a prim. root; to *rub* or *strike* the hands together (in exultation):—clap.

4223. מְחָא **m^echâ'** (Chald.), *mekh-aw';* corresp. to 4222; to *strike* in pieces; also to *arrest;* spec. to *impale:*—hang, smite, stay.

4224. מַחֲבֵא **machăbê'**, *makh-ab-ay';* or

מַחֲבֹא **machăbô'**, *makh-ab-o';* from 2244; a *refuge:*—hiding (lurking) place.

4225. מַחְבֶּרֶת **machbereth**, *makh-beh'-reth;* from 2266; a *junction*, i.e. seam or sewed piece:—coupling.

4226. מְחַבְּרָה **m^echabb^erâh**, *mekh-ab-ber-aw';* from 2266; a *joiner*, i.e. brace or cramp:—coupling, joining.

4227. מַחֲבַת **machăbath**, *makh-ab-ath';* from the same as 2281; a *pan* for baking in:—pan.

4228. מַחֲגֹרֶת **machăgôreth**, *makh-ag-o'-reth;* from 2296; a *girdle:*—girding.

4229. מָחָה **mâchâh**, *maw-khaw';* a prim. root; prop. to *stroke* or *rub;* by impl. to *erase;* also to *smooth* (as if with oil), i.e. *grease* or make fat; also to *touch*, i.e. reach to:—abolish, blot out, destroy, full of marrow, put out, reach unto, × utterly, wipe (away, out).

4230. מְחוּגָה **m^echûwgâh**, *mekh-oo-gaw';* from 2328; an instrument for marking a circle, i.e. *compasses:*—compass.

4231. מָחוֹז **mâchôwz**, *maw-khoze';* from an unused root mean. to *enclose;* a *harbor* (as *shut* in by the shore):—haven.

4232. מְחוּיָאֵל **M^echûwyâ'êl**, *mekh-oo-yaw-ale';* or

מְחִיָּיאֵל° **M^echîyyâ'êl**, *mekh-ee-yaw-ale';* from 4229 and 410; *smitten of God; Mechujael* or *Mechijael*, an antediluvian patriarch:—Mehujael.

4233. מַחֲוִים **Machăvîym**, *makh-av-eem';* appar. a patrial, but from an unknown place (in the plur. only for a sing.); a *Machavite* or inhab. of some place named Machaveh:—Mahavite.

4234. מָחוֹל **mâchôwl**, *maw-khole';* from 2342; a (round) *dance:*—dance (-cing).

4235. מָחוֹל **Mâchôwl**, *maw-khole';* the same as 4234; *dancing; Machol*, an Isr.:—Mahol.

מְחוֹלָה **m^echôwlâh**. See 65, 4246.

4236. מַחֲזֶה **machăzeh**, *makh-az-eh';* from 2372; a *vision:*—vision.

4237. מֶחֱזָה **mechĕzâh**, *mekh-ez-aw';* from 2372; a *window:*—light.

4238. מַחֲזִיאוֹת **Machăzîy'ôwth**, *makh-az-ee-oth';* fem. plur. from 2372; *visions; Machazioth*, an Isr.:—Mahazioth.

4239. מְחִי **m^echîy**, *mekh-ee';* from 4229; a *stroke*, i.e. battering-*ram:*—engines.

4240. מְחִידָא **M^echîydâ'**, *mekh-ee-daw';* from 2330; *junction; Mechida*, one of the Nethinim:—Mehida.

4241. מִחְיָה **michyâh**, *mikh-yaw';* from 2421; *preservation of life;* hence *sustenance;* also the live flesh, i.e. the *quick:*—preserve life, quick, recover selves, reviving, sustenance, victuals.

מְחִיָּיאֵל° **M^echîyyâ'êl**. See 4232.

4242. מְחִיר **m^echîyr**, *mekh-eer';* from an unused root mean. to *buy; price, payment, wages:*—gain, hire, price, sold, worth.

4243. מְחִיר **M^echîyr**, *mekh-eer';* the same as 4242; *price; Mechir*, an Isr.:—Mehir.

4244. מַחְלָה **Machlâh**, *makh-law';* from 2470; *sickness; Machlah*, the name appar. of two Israelitesses:—Mahlah.

4245. מַחֲלֶה **machăleh**, *makh-al-eh';* or (fem.)

מַחֲלָה **machălâh**, *makh-al-aw';* from 2470; *sickness:*—disease, infirmity, sickness.

4246. מְחוֹלָה **m^echôwlâh**, *mekh-o-law';* fem. of 4234; a *dance:*—company, dances (-cing).

4247. מְחִלָּה **m^echillâh**, *mekh-il-law';* from 2490; a *cavern* (as if excavated):—cave.

4248. מַחְלוֹן **Machlôwn**, *makh-lone';* from 2470; *sick; Machlon*, an Isr.:—Mahlon.

4249. מַחְלִי **Machlîy**, *makh-lee';* from 2470; *sick; Machli*, the name of two Isr.:—Mahli.

4250. מַחְלִי **Machlîy**, *makh-lee';* patron. from 4249; a *Machlite* or (collect.) desc. of Machli:—Mahlites.

4251. מַחְלֻי **machlûy**, *makh-loo'ee;* from 2470; a *disease:*—disease.

4252. מַחֲלָף **machălâph**, *makh-al-awf';* from 2498; a (sacrificial) *knife* (as *gliding* through the flesh):—knife.

4253. מַחְלָפָה **machlâphâh**, *makh-law-faw';* from 2498; a *ringlet* of hair (as *gliding* over each other):—lock.

4254. מַחֲלָצָה **machălâtsâh**, *makh-al-aw-tsaw';* from 2502; a *mantle* (as easily *drawn off*):—changeable suit of apparel, change of raiment.

4255. מַחְלְקָה **machl^eqâh** (Chald.), *makh-lek-aw';* corresp. to 4256; a *section* (of the Levites):—course.

4256. מַחֲלֹקֶת **machălôqeth**, *makh-al-o'-keth;* from 2505; a *section* (of Levites, people or soldiers):—company, course, division, portion. See also 5555.

4257. מַחֲלַת **machălath**, *makh-al-ath';* from 2470; *sickness; Machalath*, prob. the title (initial word) of a popular song:—Mahalath.

4258. מַחֲלַת **Machălath**, *makh-al-ath';* the same as 4257; *sickness; Machalath*, the name of an Ishmaelitess and of an Israelitess:—Mahalath.

4259. מְחֹלָתִי **M^echôlâthîy**, *mekh-o-law-thee';* patrial from 65; a *Mecholathite* or inhab. of Abel-Mecholah:—Mecholathite.

4260. מַחֲמָאָה **machămâ'âh**, *makh-am-aw-aw';* a denom. from 2529; something *buttery* (i.e. unctuous and pleasant), as (fig.) *flattery:*—× than butter.

4261. מַחְמָד **machmâd**, *makh-mawd';* from 2530; *delightful;* hence a *delight*, i.e. object of affection or desire:—beloved, desire, goodly, lovely, pleasant (thing).

4262. מַחְמֻד **machmûd**, *makh-mood';* or

מַחְמוּד **machmûwd**, *makh-mood';* from 2530; *desired;* hence a *valuable:*—pleasant thing.

4263. מַחְמָל **machmâl**, *makh-mawl';* from 2550; prop. *sympathy;* (by paronomasia with 4261) *delight:*—pitieth.

4264. מַחֲנֶה **machăneh**, *makh-an-eh';* from 2583; an *encampment* (of travellers or troops); hence an *army*, whether lit. (of soldiers) or fig. (of dancers, angels, cattle, locusts, stars; or even the sacred courts):—army, band, battle, camp, company, drove, host, tents.

4265. מַחֲנֵה־דָן **Machănêh-Dân**, *makh-an-ay'-dawn;* from 4264 and 1835; *camp of Dan; Machaneh-Dan*, a place in Pal.:—Mahaneh-dan.

4266. מַחֲנַיִם **Machănayim**, *makh-an-ah'-yim;* dual of 4264; *double camp; Machanajim*, a place in Pal.:—Mahanaim.

4267. מַחֲנַק **machănaq**, *makh-an-ak';* from 2614; *choking:*—strangling.

4268. מַחֲסֶה **machăçeh**, *makh-as-eh';* or

מַחְסֶה **machçeh**, *makh-seh';* from 2620; *a shelter* (lit. or fig.):—hope, (place of) refuge, shelter, trust.

4269. מַחְסוֹם **machçôwm**, *makh-sohm';* from 2629; a *muzzle:*—bridle.

4270. מַחְסוֹר **machçôwr**, *makh-sore';* or

מַחְסֹר **machçôr**, *makh-sore';* from 2637; *deficiency;* hence *impoverishment:*—lack, need, penury, poor, poverty, want.

4271. מַחְסֵיָה **Machçêyâh**, *makh-say-yaw';* from 4268 and 3050; *refuge of* (i.e. *in*) *Jah; Machsejah*, an Isr.:—Maaseiah.

4272. מָחַץ **mâchats**, *maw-khats';* a prim. root; to *dash* asunder; by impl. to *crush, smash* or violently *plunge;* fig. to *subdue* or *destroy:*—dip, pierce (through), smite (through), strike through, wound.

4273. מַחַץ **machats**, *makh'-ats;* from 4272; a *contusion:*—stroke.

4274. מַחְצֵב **machtsêb**, *makh-tsabe';* from 2672; prop. a *hewing;* concr. a *quarry:*—hewed (-n).

4275. מֶחֱצָה **mechĕtsâh**, *mekh-ets-aw';* from 2673; a *halving:*—half.

4276. מַחֲצִית **machătsîyth**, *makh-ats-eeth';* from 2673; a *halving* or the *middle:*—half (so much), mid [-day].

4277. מָחַק **mâchaq**, *maw-khak';* a prim. root; to *crush:*—smite off.

4278. מֶחְקָר **mechqâr**, *mekh-kawr';* from 2713; prop. *scrutinized*, i.e. (by impl.) a *recess:*—deep place.

4279. מָחָר **mâchar**, *maw-khar';* prob. from 309; prop. *deferred*, i.e. the *morrow;* usually (adv.) *tomorrow;* indef. *hereafter:*—time to come, tomorrow.

4280. מַחֲרָאָה **machărâ'âh**, *makh-ar-aw-aw';* from the same as 2716; a *sink:*—draught house.

4281. מַחֲרֵשָׁה **machărêshâh**, *makh-ar-ay-shaw';* from 2790; prob. a *pick-axe:*—mattock.

4282. מַחֲרֶשֶׁת **machăresheth**, *makh-ar-eh'-sheth;* from 2790; prob. a *hoe:*—share.

4283. מָחֳרָת **mochŏrâth**, *mokh-or-awth';* or

מָחֳרָתָם **mochŏrâthâm** (1 Sam. 30 : 17), *mokh-or-aw-thawm';* fem. from the same as 4279; the *morrow* or (adv.) *tomorrow:*—morrow, next day.

4284. מַחֲשָׁבָה **machăshâbâh**, *makh-ash-aw-baw';* or

מַחֲשֶׁבֶת **machăshebeth**, *makh-ash-eh'-beth;* from 2803; a *contrivance*, i.e. (concr.) a *texture, machine*, or (abstr.) *intention, plan* (whether bad, a *plot;* or good, *advice*):—cunning (work), curious work, device (-sed), imagination, invented, means, purpose, thought.

4285. מַחְשָׁךְ **machshâk**, *makh-shawk';* from 2821; *darkness;* concr. a *dark place:*—dark (-ness, place).

4286. מַחְשֹׂף **machsôph**, *makh-sofe';* from 2834; a *peeling:*—made appear.

4287. מַחַת **Machath**, *makh'-ath;* prob. from 4229; *erasure; Machath*, the name of two Isr.:—Mahath.

4288. מְחִתָּה **mᵉchittâh**, *mekh-it-taw';* from 2846; prop. a *dissolution;* concr. a *ruin*, or (abstr.) *consternation:*—destruction, dismaying, ruin, terror.

4289. מַחְתָּה **machtâh**, *makh-taw';* the same as 4288 in the sense of *removal;* a *pan* for live coals:—censer, firepan, snuffdish.

4290. מַחְתֶּרֶת **machtereth**, *makh-teh'-reth;* from 2864; a *burglary;* fig. *unexpected examination:*—breaking up, secret search.

4291. מְטָא **mᵉṭâ'** (Chald.), *met-aw';* or

מְטָה **mᵉṭâh** (Chald.), *met-aw';* appar. corresp. to 4672 in the intrans. sense of being found *present;* to *arrive, extend* or *happen:*—come, reach.

4292. מַטְאֲטֵא **maṭ'ăṭê'**, *mat-at-ay';* appar. a denom. from 2916; a *broom* (as removing *dirt* [comp. Engl. "to dust", i.e. remove dust]):—besom.

4293. מַטְבֵּחַ **maṭbêach**, *mat-bay'-akh;* from 2873; *slaughter:*—slaughter.

4294. מַטֶּה **maṭṭeh**, *mat-teh';* or (fem.)

מַטָּה **maṭṭâh**, *mat-taw';* from 5186; a *branch* (as *extending*); fig. a *tribe;* also a *rod*, whether for chastising (fig. *correction*), ruling (a *sceptre*), throwing (a *lance*), or walking (a *staff;* fig. a *support* of life, e.g. bread):—rod, staff, tribe.

4295. מַטָּה **maṭṭâh**, *mat'-taw;* from 5786 with directive enclitic appended; *downward, below* or *beneath;* often adv. with or without prefixes:—beneath, down (-ward), less, very low, under (-neath).

4296. מִטָּה **miṭṭâh**, *mit-taw';* from 5186; a *bed* (as *extended*) for sleeping or eating; by anal. a *sofa, litter* or *bier:*—bed ([-chamber]), bier.

4297. מֻטֶּה **muṭṭeh**, *moot-teh';* from 5186; a *stretching*, i.e. *distortion* (fig. *iniquity*):—perverseness.

4298. מֻטָּה **muṭṭâh**, *moot-taw';* from 5186; *expansion:*—stretching out.

4299. מַטְוֶה **maṭveh**, *mat-veh';* from 2901; something *spun:*—spun.

4300. מְטִיל **mᵉṭîyl**, *met-eel';* from 2904 in the sense of *hammering* out; an iron *bar* (as *forged*):—bar.

4301. מַטְמוֹן **maṭmôwn**, *mat-mone';* or

מַטְמֹן **maṭmôn**, *mat-mone';* or

מַטְמֻן **maṭmûn**, *mat-moon';* from 2934; a *secret* storehouse; hence a *secreted* valuable (buried); gen. *money:*—hidden riches, (hid) treasure (-s).

4302. מַטָּע **maṭṭâʻ**, *mat-taw';* from 5193; something *planted*, i.e. the place (a *garden* or vineyard), or the thing (a *plant*, fig. of men); by impl. the act, *planting:*—plant (-ation, -ing).

4303. מַטְעַם **maṭʻam**, *mat-am';* or (fem.)

מַטְעַמָּה **maṭʻammâh**, *mat-am-maw';* from 2938; a *delicacy:*—dainty (meat), savoury meat.

4304. מִטְפַּחַת **miṭpachath**, *mit-pakh'-ath;* from 2946; a wide *cloak* (for a woman):—vail, wimple.

4305. מָטַר **mâṭar**, *maw-tar';* a prim. root; to *rain:*—(cause to) rain (upon).

4306. מָטָר **mâṭâr**, *maw-tawr';* from 4305; *rain:*—rain.

4307. מַטָּרָא **maṭṭârâ'**, *mat-taw-raw';* or

מַטָּרָה **maṭṭârâh**, *mat-taw-raw';* from 5201; a *jail* (as a *guard*-house); also an *aim* (as being closely *watched*):—mark, prison.

4308. מַטְרֵד **Maṭrêd**, *mat-rade';* from 2956; *propulsive; Matred*, an Edomitess:—Matred.

4309. מַטְרִי **Maṭrîy**, *mat-ree';* from 4305; *rainy; Matri*, an Isr.:—Matri.

4310. מִי **mîy**, *me;* an interrog. pron. of persons, as 4100 is of things, *who?* (occasionally, by a peculiar idiom, of things); also (indef.) *whoever;* often used in oblique construction with pref. or suff.:—any (man), × he, × him, + O that! what, which, who (-m, -se, -soever), + would to God.

4311. מֵידְבָא **Mêydᵉbâ'**, *may-deb-aw';* from 4325 and 1679; *water of quiet; Medeba*, a place in Pal.:—Medeba.

4312. מֵידָד **Mêydâd**, *may-dawd';* from 3032 in the sense of *loving; affectionate; Medad*, an Isr.:—Medad.

4313. מֵי הַיַּרְקוֹן **Mêy hay-Yarqôwn**, *may hah'-ee-yar-kone';* from 4325 and 3420 with the art. interposed; *water of the yellowness; Me-haj-Jarkon*, a place in Pal.:—Me-jarkon.

4314. מֵי זָהָב **Mêy Zâhâb**, *may zaw-hawb';* from 4325 and 2091, *water of gold; Me-Zahab*, an Edomite:—Mezahab.

4315. מֵיטָב **mêyṭâb**, *may-tawb';* from 3190; the *best* part:—best.

4316. מִיכָא **Mîykâ'**, *mee-kaw';* a var. for 4318; *Mica*, the name of two Isr.:—Micha.

4317. מִיכָאֵל **Mîykâ'êl**, *me-kaw-ale';* from 4310 and (the pref. der. from) 3588 and 410; *who* (is) *like God?; Mikael*, the name of an archangel and of nine Isr.:—Michael.

4318. מִיכָה **Mîykâh**, *mee-kaw';* an abbrev. of 4320; *Micah*, the name of seven Isr.:—Micah, Micaiah, Michah.

4319. מִיכָהוּ **Mîykâhûw**, *me-kaw'-hoo;* a contr. for 4321; *Mikehu*, an Isr. prophet:—Micaiah (2 Chron. 18 : 8).

4320. מִיכָיָה **Mîykâyâh**, *me-kaw-yaw';* from 4310 and (the pref. der. from) 3588 and 3050; *who* (is) *like Jah?; Micajah*, the name of two Isr.:—Micah, Michaiah. Comp. 4318.

4321. מִיכָיְהוּ **Mîykâyᵉhûw**, *me-kaw-yeh-hoo';* or

מִכָיְהוּ **Mîkâyᵉhûw** (Jer. 36 : 11), *me-kaw-yeh-hoo';* abbrev. for 4322; *Mikajah*, the name of three Isr.:—Micah, Micaiah, Michaiah.

4322. מִיכָיָהוּ **Mîykâyâhûw**, *me-kaw-yaw'-hoo;* for 4320; *Mikajah*, the name of an Isr. and an Israelitess:—Michaiah.

4323. מִיכָל **mîykâl**, *me-kawl';* from 3201; prop. a *container*, i.e. a *streamlet:*—brook.

4324. מִיכָל **Mîykâl**, *me-kawl';* appar. the same as 4323; *rivulet; Mikal*, Saul's daughter:—Michal.

4325. מַיִם **mayim**, *mah'-yim;* dual of a prim. noun (but used in a sing. sense); *water;* fig. *juice;* by euphem. *urine, semen:*— + piss, wasting, water (-ing, [-course, -flood, -spring]).

4326. מִיָּמִן **Mîyâmîn**, *me-yaw-meem';* a form for 4509; *Mijamin*, the name of three Isr.:—Miamin, Mijamin.

4327. מִין **mîyn**, *meen;* from an unused root mean. to *portion* out; a *sort*, i.e. *species:*—kind. Comp. 4480.

4328. מְיֻסָּדָה **mᵉyuççâdâh**, *meh-yoos-saw-daw';* prop. fem. pass. part. of 3245; something *founded*, i.e. a *foundation:*—foundation.

4329. מֵיסָךְ **mêyçâk**, *may-sawk';* from 5526; a *portico* (as *covered*):—covert.

מֵיפַעַת **Mêyphaʻath**. See 4158.

4330. מִיץ **mîyts**, *meets;* from 4160; *pressure:*—churning, forcing, wringing.

4331. מֵישָׁא **Mêyshâ'**, *may-shaw';* from 4185; *departure; Mesha*, a place in Arabia; also an Isr.:—Mesha.

4332. מִישָׁאֵל **Mîyshâ'êl**, *mee-shaw-ale';* from 4310 and 410 with the abbrev. insep. rel. [see 834] interposed; *who* (is) *what God* (is)?; *Mishaël*, the name of three Isr.:—Mishael.

4333. מִישָׁאֵל **Mîyshâ'êl** (Chald.), *mee-shaw-ale';* corresp. to 4332; *Mishaël*, an Isr.:—Mishael.

4334. מִישׁוֹר **mîyshôwr**, *mee-shore';* or

מִישֹׁר **mîyshôr**, *mee-shore';* from 3474; a *level*, i.e. a *plain* (often used [with the art. pref.] as a prop. name of certain districts); fig. *concord;* also *straightness*, i.e. (fig.) *justice* (sometimes adv. *justly*):—equity, even place, plain, right (-eously), (made) straight, uprightness.

4335. מֵישַׁךְ **Mêyshak**, *may-shak';* borrowed from 4336; *Meshak*, an Isr.:—Meshak.

4336. מֵישַׁךְ **Mêyshak** (Chald.), *may-shak';* of for. or. and doubtful signif.; *Meshak*, the Bab. name of 4333:—Meshak.

4337. מֵישָׁע **Mêyshâʻ**, *may-shah';* from 3467; *safety; Mesha*, an Isr.:—Mesha.

4338. מֵישַׁע **Mêyshaʻ**, *may-shaw';* a var. for 4337; *safety; Mesha*, a Moabite:—Mesha.

4339. מֵישָׁר **mêyshâr**, *may-shawr';* from 3474; *evenness*, i.e. (fig.) *prosperity* or *con-*

cord; also *straightness,* i.e. (fig.) *rectitude* (only in plur. with sing. sense; often adv.):—agreement, aright, that are equal, equity, (things that are) right (-eously, things), sweetly, upright (-ly, -ness).

4340. מֵיתָר **mêythâr**, *may-thawr';* from 3498; a *cord* (of a tent) [comp. 3499] or the *string* (of a bow):—cord, string.

4341. מַכְאֹב **mak'ôb**, *mak-obe';* sometimes

מַכְאוֹב **mak'ôwb**, *mak-obe';* also (fem. Isa. 53 : 3)

מַכְאֹבָה **mak'ôbâh**, *mak-o-baw';* from 3510; *anguish* or (fig.) *affliction:*—grief, pain, sorrow.

4342. מַכְבִּיר **makbîyr**, *mak-beer';* trans. part. of 3527; *plenty:*—abundance.

4343. מַכְבֵּנָא **Makbênâ'**, *mak-bay-naw';* from the same as 3522; *knoll; Macbena,* a place in Pal. settled by him:—Machbenah.

4344. מַכְבַּנַּי **Makbannay**, *mak-ban-nah'ee;* patrial from 4343; a *Macbannite* or native of Macbena:—Machbanai.

4345. מַכְבֵּר **makbêr**, *mak-bare';* from 3527 in the sense of *covering* [comp. 3531]; a *grate:*—grate.

4346. מַכְבָּר **makbâr**, *mak-bawr';* from 3527 in the sense of *covering;* a cloth (as *netted* [comp. 4345]):—thick cloth.

4347. מַכָּה **makkâh**, *mak-kaw';* or (masc.)

מַכֶּה **makkeh**, *mak-keh';* (plur. only) from 5221; a *blow* (in 2 Chron. 2 : 10, of the *flail);* by impl. a *wound;* fig. *carnage,* also *pestilence:*—beaten, blow, plague, slaughter, smote, × sore, stripe, stroke, wound ([-ed]).

4348. מִכְוָה **mikvâh**, *mik-vaw';* from 3554; a *burn:*—that burneth, burning.

4349. מָכוֹן **mâkôwn**, *maw-kone';* from 3559; prop. a *fixture,* i.e. a *basis;* gen. a *place,* esp. as an *abode:*—foundation, habitation, (dwelling-, settled) place.

4350. מְכוֹנָה **m^ekôwnâh**, *mek-o-naw';* or

מְכֹנָה **m^ekônâh**, *mek-o-naw';* fem. of 4349; a *pedestal,* also a *spot:*—base.

4351. מְכוּרָה **m^ekûwrâh**, *mek-oo-raw';* or

מְכֹרָה **m^ekôrâh**, *mek-o-raw';* from the same as 3564 in the sense of *digging; origin* (as if a mine):—birth, habitation, nativity.

4352. מָכִי **Mâkîy**, *maw-kee';* prob. from 4134; *pining; Maki,* an Isr.:—Machi.

4353. מָכִיר **Mâkîyr**, *maw-keer';* from 4376; *salesman; Makir,* an Isr.:—Machir.

4354. מָכִירִי **Mâkîyrîy**, *maw-kee-ree';* patron. from 4353; a *Makirite* or descend. of Makir:—of Machir.

4355. מָכַךְ **mâkak**, *maw-kak';* a prim. root; to *tumble* (in ruins); fig. to *perish:*—be brought low, decay.

4356. מִכְלָאָה **miklâ'âh**, *mik-law-aw';* or

מִכְלָה **miklâh**, *mik-law';* from 3607; a *pen* (for flocks):—([sheep-]) fold. Comp. 4357.

4357. מִכְלָה **miklâh**, *mik-law';* from 3615; *completion* (in plur. concr. adv. *wholly):*—perfect. Comp. 4356.

4358. מִכְלוֹל **miklôwl**, *mik-lole';* from 3634; *perfection* (i.e. concr. adv. *splendidly):*—most gorgeously, all sorts.

4359. מִכְלָל **miklâl**, *mik-lawl';* from 3634; *perfection* (of beauty):—perfection.

4360. מִכְלֻל **miklûl**, *mik-lool';* from 3634; something *perfect,* i.e. a splendid *garment:*—all sorts.

4361. מַכֹּלֶת **makkôleth**, *mak-ko'-leth;* from 398; *nourishment:*—food.

4362. מִכְמַן **mikman**, *mik-man';* from the same as 3646 in the sense of *hiding; treasure* (as *hidden):*—treasure.

4363. מִכְמָס **Mikmâç** (Ezra 2 : 27; Neh. 7 : 31), *mik-maws';* or

מִכְמָשׁ **Mikmâsh**, *mik-mawsh';* or

מִכְמַשׁ **Mikmash** (Neh. 11 : 31), *mik-mash';* from 3647; *hidden; Mikmas* or *Mikmash,* a place in Pal.:—Mikmas, Mikmash.

4364. מַכְמָר **makmâr**, *mak-mawr';* or

מִכְמֹר **mikmôr**, *mik-more';* from 3648 in the sense of *blackening* by heat; a (hunter's) *net* (as *dark* from concealment):—net.

4365. מִכְמֶרֶת **mikmereth**, *mik-meh'-reth;* or

מִכְמֹרֶת **mikmôreth**, *mik-mo'-reth;* fem. of 4364; a (fisher's) *net:*—drag, net.

מִכְמָשׂ **Mikmâsh**. See 4363.

4366. מִכְמְתָת **Mikm^ethâth**, *mik-meth-awth';* appar. from an unused root mean. to *hide; concealment; Mikmethath,* a place in Pal.:—Michmethath.

4367. מַכְנַדְבַי **Maknadbay**, *mak-nad-bah'ee;* from 4100 and 5068 with a particle interposed; *what* (is) *like* (a) *liberal* (man)?; *Maknadbai,* an Isr.:—Machnadebai.

מְכֹנָה **m^ekônâh**. See 4350.

4368. מְכֹנָה **M^ekônâh**, *mek-o-naw';* the same as 4350; a *base; Mekonah,* a place in Pal.:—Mekonah.

4369. מְכֻנָה **m^ekûnâh**, *mek-oo-naw';* the same as 4350; a *spot:*—base.

4370. מִכְנָס **miknâç**, *mik-nawce';* from 3647 in the sense of *hiding;* (only in dual) *drawers* (from *concealing* the private parts):—breeches.

4371. מֶכֶס **mekeç**, *meh'-kes;* prob. from an unused root mean. to *enumerate;* an *assessment* (as based upon a *census):*—tribute.

4372. מִכְסֶה **mikçeh**, *mik-seh';* from 3680; a *covering,* i.e. weather-*boarding:*—covering.

4373. מִכְסָה **mikçâh**, *mik-saw';* fem. of 4371; an *enumeration;* by impl. a *valuation:*—number, worth.

4374. מְכַסֶּה **m^ekaççeh**, *mek-as-seh';* from 3680; a *covering,* i.e. *garment;* spec. a *coverlet* (for a bed), an *awning* (from the sun); also the *omentum* (as covering the intestines):—clothing, to cover, that which covereth.

4375. מַכְפֵּלָה **Makpêlâh**, *mak-pay-law';* from 3717; a *fold; Makpelah,* a place in Pal.:—Machpelah.

4376. מָכַר **mâkar**, *maw-kar';* a prim. root; to *sell,* lit. (as merchandise, a daughter in marriage, into slavery), or fig. (to *surrender):*— × at all, sell (away, -er, self).

4377. מֶכֶר **meker**, *meh'-ker;* from 4376; *merchandise;* also *value:*—pay, price, ware.

4378. מַכָּר **makkâr**, *mak-kawr';* from 5234; an *acquaintance:*—acquaintance.

4379. מִכְרֶה **mikreh**, *mik-reh';* from 3738; a *pit* (for salt):—[salt-] pit.

4380. מְכֵרָה **m^ekêrâh**, *mek-ay-raw';* prob. from the same as 3564 in the sense of *stabbing;* a *sword:*—habitation.

מְכֹרָה **m^ekôrâh**. See 4351.

4381. מִכְרִי **Mikrîy**, *mik-ree';* from 4376; *salesman; Mikri,* an Isr.:—Michri.

4382. מְכֵרָתִי **M^ekêrâthîy**, *mek-ay-raw-thee';* patrial from an unused name (the same as 4380) of a place in Pal.; a *Mekerathite,* or inhab. of Mekerah:—Mecherathite.

4383. מִכְשׁוֹל **mikshôwl**, *mik-shole';* or

מִכְשֹׁל **mikshôl**, *mik-shole';* masc. from 3782; a *stumbling-block,* lit. or fig. (*obstacle, enticement* [spec. an idol], *scruple):*—caused to fall, offence, × [no-] thing offered, ruin, stumbling-block.

4384. מַכְשֵׁלָה **makshêlâh**, *mak-shay-law';* fem. from 3782; a *stumbling-block,* but only fig. (*fall, enticement* [idol]):—ruin, stumbling-block.

4385. מִכְתָּב **miktâb**, *mik-tawb';* from 3789; a thing *written,* the *characters,* or a *document* (letter, copy, edict, poem):—writing.

4386. מְכִתָּה **m^ekittâh**, *mek-it-taw';* from 3807; a *fracture:*—bursting.

4387. מִכְתָּם **miktâm**, *mik-tawm';* from 3799; an *engraving,* i.e. (techn.) a *poem:*—Michtam.

4388. מַכְתֵּשׁ **maktêsh**, *mak-taysh';* from 3806; a *mortar;* by anal. a *socket* (of a tooth):—hollow place, mortar.

4389. מַכְתֵּשׁ **Maktêsh**, *mak-taysh';* the same as 4388; *dell;* the *Maktesh,* a place in Jerus.:—Maktesh.

מֻל **mûl**. See 4136.

4390. מָלֵא **mâlê'**, *maw-lay';* or

מָלָא **mâlâ'** (Esth. 7 : 5), *maw-law';* a prim. root, to *fill* or (intrans.) *be full* of, in a wide application (lit. and fig.):—accomplish, confirm, + consecrate, be at an end, be expired, be fenced, fill, fulfil, (be, become, × draw, give in, go) full (-ly, -ly set, tale), [over-] flow, fulness, furnish, gather (selves, together), presume, replenish, satisfy, set, space, take a [hand-] full, + have wholly.

4391. מְלָא **m^elâ'** (Chald.), *mel-aw';* corresp. to 4390; to *fill:*—fill, be full.

4392. מָלֵא **mâlê'**, *maw-lay';* from 4390; *full* (lit. or fig.) or *filling* (lit.); also (concr.) *fulness;* adv. *fully:*— × she that was with child, fill (-ed, -ed with), full (-ly), multitude, as is worth.

4393. מְלֹא **m^elô'**, *mel-o';* rarely

מְלוֹא **m^elôw'**, *mel-o';* or

מְלוֹ **m^elôw** (Ezek. 41 : 8), *mel-o';* from 4390; *fulness* (lit. or fig.):— × all along, × all that is (there-) in, fill, (× that whereof . . . was) full, fulness, [hand-] full, multitude.

מִלֹּא **Millô'**. See 4407.

4394. מִלֻּא **millû'**, *mil-loo';* from 4390; a *fulfilling* (only in plur.), i.e. (lit.) a *setting* (of gems), or (techn.) *consecration* (also concr. a dedicatory *sacrifice):*—consecration, be set.

4395. מְלֵאָה **m^elê'âh**, *mel-ay-aw';* fem. of 4392; something *fulfilled,* i.e. *abundance* (of produce):—(first of ripe) fruit, fulness.

4396. מִלֻּאָה **millû'âh**, *mil-loo-aw';* fem. of 4394; a *filling,* i.e. *setting* (of gems):—inclosing, setting.

4397. מַלְאָךְ **mal'âk**, *mal-awk';* from an unused root mean. to *despatch* as a deputy; a *messenger;* spec. of God, i.e. an *angel* (also a prophet, priest or teacher):—ambassador, angel, king, messenger.

4398. מַלְאַךְ **mal'ak** (Chald.), *mal-ak';* corresp. to 4397; an *angel:*—angel.

4399. מְלָאכָה **m^elâ'kâh**, *mel-aw-kaw';* from the same as 4397; prop. *deputyship,* i.e. ministry; gen. *employment* (never servile) or work (abstr. or concr.); also *property* (as the result of *labor):*—business, + cattle, + industrious, occupation, (+ -pied), + officer, thing (made), use, (manner of) work ([-man], -manship).

4400. מַלְאֲכוּת **mal'ăkûwth**, *mal-ak-ooth';* from the same as 4397; a *message:*—message.

4401. מַלְאָכִי **Mal'âkîy**, *mal-aw-kee';* from the same as 4397; *ministrative; Malaki,* a prophet:—Malachi.

4402. מִלֵּאת **millê'th**, *mil-layth';* from 4390; *fulness,* i.e. (concr.) a *plump socket* (of the eye):— × fitly.

4403. מַלְבּוּשׁ **malbûwsh**, *mal-boosh';* or

מַלְבֻּשׁ **malbûsh**, *mal-boosh';* from 3847; a *garment,* or (collect.) *clothing:*—apparel, raiment, vestment.

4404. מַלְבֵּן **malbên**, *mal-bane';* from 3835 (denom.); a *brick-kiln:*—brickwork.

4405. מִלָּה **millâh**, *mil-law';* from 4448 (plur. masc. as if from

מִלֶּה **milleh**, *mil-leh');* a *word;* collect. a *discourse;* fig. a *topic:*— + answer, by-word, matter, any thing (what) to say, to speak (-ing), speak, talking, word.

4406. מִלָּה **millâh** (Chald.), *mil-law'*; corresp. to 4405; a *word, command, discourse,* or *subject:*—commandment, matter, thing, word.

מְלוֹ **m^e^lôw**. See 4393.

מְלוֹא **m^e^lôw'**. See 4393.

4407. מִלּוֹא **millôw'**, *mil-lo'*; or

מִלֹּא **mil-lô'** (2 Kings 12 : 20), *mil-lo'*; from 4390; a *rampart* (as *filled* in), i.e. the *citadel:*—Millo. See also 1037.

4408. מַלּוּחַ **mallûwach**, *mal-loo'-akh;* from 4414; *sea-purslain* (from its *saltness*):—mallows.

4409. מַלּוּךְ **Mallûwk**, *mal-luke';* or

מַלּוּכִי° **Mallûwkîy** (Neh. 12 : 14), *mal-loo-kee';* from 4427; *regnant; Malluk,* the name of five Isr.:—Malluch, Melichu [*from the marg.*].

4410. מְלוּכָה **m^e^lûwkâh**, *mel-oo-kaw';* fem. pass. part. of 4427; something *ruled,* i.e. a *realm:*—kingdom, king's, × royal.

4411. מָלוֹן **mâlôwn**, *maw-lone';* from 3885; a *lodgment,* i.e. *caravanserai* or *encampment:*—inn, place where . . . lodge, lodging (place).

4412. מְלוּנָה **m^e^lûwnâh**, *mel-oo-naw';* fem. from 3885; a *hut,* a *hammock:*—cottage, lodge.

4413. מַלּוֹתִי **Mallôwthîy**, *mal-lo'-thee;* appar. from 4448; *I have talked* (i.e. *loquacious*):—*Mallothi,* an Isr.:—Mallothi.

4414. מָלַח **mâlach**, *maw-lakh';* a prim. root; prop. to *rub* to pieces or pulverize; intrans. to *disappear* as dust; also (as denom. from 4417) to *salt* whether intern. (to *season* with salt) or extern. (to *rub* with salt):— × at all, salt, season, temper together, vanish away.

4415. מְלַח **m^e^lach** (Chald.), *mel-akh';* corresp. to 4414; to *eat* salt, i.e. (gen.) *subsist:*—+ have maintenance.

4416. מְלַח **m^e^lach** (Chald.), *mel-akh';* from 4415; *salt:*—+ maintenance, salt.

4417. מֶלַח **melach**, *meh'-lakh;* from 4414; prop. *powder,* i.e. (spec.) *salt* (as easily pulverized and dissolved:—salt ([-pit]).

4418. מָלָח **mâlâch**, *maw-lawkh';* from 4414 in its orig. sense; a *rag* or old garment:—rotten rag.

4419. מַלָּח **mallâch**, *mal-lawkh';* from 4414 in its second. sense; a *sailor* (as following "the salt"):—mariner.

4420. מְלֵחָה **m^e^lêchâh**, *mel-ay-khaw';* from 4414 (in its denom. sense); prop. *salted* (i.e. land [776 being understood]), i.e. a *desert:*—barren land (-ness), salt [land].

4421. מִלְחָמָה **milchâmâh**, *mil-khaw-maw';* from 3898 (in the sense of *fighting*); a *battle* (i.e. the *engagement*); gen. *war* (i.e. *warfare*):—battle, fight, (-ing), war ([-rior]).

4422. מָלַט **mâlaṭ**, *maw-lat';* a prim. root; prop. to *be smooth,* i.e. (by impl.) to *escape* (as if by *slipperiness*); causat. to *release* or *rescue;* spec. to *bring forth* young, *emit* sparks:—deliver (self), escape, lay, leap out, let alone, let go, preserve, save, × speedily, × surely.

4423. מֶלֶט **meleṭ**, *meh'-let;* from 4422, *cement* (from its plastic *smoothness*):—clay.

4424. מְלַטְיָה **M^e^laṭyâh**, *mel-at-yaw';* from 4423 and 3050; (whom) *Jah has delivered; Melatjah,* a Gibeonite:—Melatiah.

4425. מְלִילָה **m^e^lîylâh**, *mel-ee-law';* from 4449 (in the sense of *cropping* [comp. 4135]); a *head* of grain (as *cut* off):—ear.

4426. מְלִיצָה **m^e^lîytsâh**, *mel-ee-tsaw';* from 3887; an *aphorism;* also a *satire:*—interpretation, taunting.

4427. מָלַךְ **mâlak**, *maw-lak';* a prim. root; to *reign;* incept. to *ascend the throne;* causat. to *induct* into royalty; hence (by impl.) to *take counsel:*—consult, × indeed, be (make, set a, set up) king, be (make) queen, (begin to, make to) reign (-ing), rule. × surely.

4428. מֶלֶךְ **melek**, *meh'-lek;* from 4427; a *king:*—king, royal.

4429. מֶלֶךְ **Melek**, *meh'-lek;* the same as 4428; *king; Melek,* the name of two Isr.:—Melech, Hammelech [*by includ. the art.*].

4430. מֶלֶךְ **melek** (Chald.), *meh'-lek;* corresp. to 4428; a *king:*—king, royal.

4431. מְלַךְ **m^e^lak** (Chald.), *mel-ak';* from a root corresp. to 4427 in the sense of *consultation; advice:*—counsel.

4432. מֹלֶךְ **Môlek**, *mo'-lek;* from 4427; *Molek* (i.e. king), the chief deity of the Ammonites:—Molech. Comp. 4445.

4433. מַלְכָּא **malkâ'** (Chald.), *mal-kaw';* corresp. to 4436; a *queen:*—queen.

4434. מַלְכֹּדֶת **malkôdeth**, *mal-ko'-deth;* from 3920; a *snare:*—trap.

4435. מִלְכָּה **Milkâh**, *mil-kaw';* a form of 4436; *queen; Milcah,* the name of a Hebrewess and of an Isr.:—Milcah.

4436. מַלְכָּה **malkâh**, *mal-kaw';* fem. of 4428; a *queen:*—queen.

4437. מַלְכוּ **malkûw** (Chald.), *mal-koo';* corresp. to 4438; *dominion* (abstr. or concr.):—kingdom, kingly, realm, reign.

4438. מַלְכוּת **malkûwth**, *mal-kooth';* or

מַלְכֻת **malkûth**, *mal-kooth';* or (in plur.)

מַלְכֻיָּה **malkûyâh**, *mal-koo-yâh';* from 4427; a *rule;* concr. a *dominion:*—empire, kingdom, realm, reign, royal.

4439. מַלְכִּיאֵל **Malkîy'êl**, *mal-kee-ale';* from 4428 and 410; *king of* (i.e. appointed by) *God; Malkiël,* an Isr.:—Malchiel.

4440. מַלְכִּיאֵלִי **Malkîy'êlîy**, *mal-kee-ay-lee';* patron. from 4439; a *Malkiëlite* or desc. of Malkiel:—Malchielite.

4441. מַלְכִּיָּה **Malkîyâh**, *mal-kee-yaw';* or

מַלְכִּיָּהוּ **Malkîyâhûw** (Jer. 38 : 6), *mal-kee-yaw'-hoo;* from 4428 and 3050; *king of* (i.e. appointed by) *Jah; Malkijah,* the name of ten Isr.:—Malchiah, Malchijah.

4442. מַלְכִּי־צֶדֶק **Malkîy-Tsedeq**, *mal-kee-tseh'-dek;* from 4428 and 6664; *king of right; Malki-Tsedek,* an early king in Pal.:—Melchizedek.

4443. מַלְכִּירָם **Malkîyrâm**, *mal-kee-rawm';* from 4428 and 7311; *king of a high* one (i.e. of exaltation); *Malkiram,* an Isr.:—Malchiram.

4444. מַלְכִּישׁוּעַ **Malkîyshûwa'**, *mal-kee-shoo'-ah;* from 4428 and 7769; *king of wealth; Malkishua,* an Isr.:—Malchishua.

4445. מַלְכָּם **Malkâm**, *mal-kawm';* or

מִלְכּוֹם **Milkôwm**, *mil-kome';* from 4428 for 4432; *Malcam* or *Milcom,* the national idol of the Ammonites:—Malcham, Milcom.

4446. מְלֶכֶת **m^e^leketh**, *mel-eh'-keth;* from 4427; a *queen:*—queen.

4447. מֹלֶכֶת **Môleketh**, *mo-leh'-keth;* fem. act. part. of 4427; *queen; Moleketh,* an Israelitess:—Hammoleketh [*includ. the art.*].

4448. מָלַל **mâlal**, *maw-lal';* a prim. root; to *speak* (mostly poet.) or *say:*—say, speak, utter.

4449. מְלַל **m^e^lal** (Chald.), *mel-al';* corresp. to 4448; to *speak:*—say, speak (-ing).

4450. מִלֲלַי **Mîlălay**, *mee-lal-ah'ee;* from 4448; *talkative; Milalai,* an Isr.:—Milalai.

4451. מַלְמָד **malmâd**, *mal-mawd';* from 3925; a *goad* for oxen:—goad.

4452. מָלַץ **mâlats**, *maw-lats';* a prim. root; to *be smooth,* i.e. (fig.) *pleasant:*—be sweet.

4453. מֶלְצָר **meltsâr**, *mel-tsawr';* of Pers. der.; the *butler* or other officer in the Bab. court:—Melzar.

4454. מָלַק **mâlaq**, *maw-lak';* a prim. root; to *crack* a joint; by impl. to *wring* the neck of a fowl (without separating it):—wring off.

4455. מַלְקוֹחַ **malqôwach**, *mal-ko'-akh;* from 3947; trans. (in dual) the *jaws* (as taking food); intrans. *spoil* [and captives] (as taken):—booty, jaws, prey.

4456. מַלְקוֹשׁ **malqôwsh**, *mal-koshe';* from 3953; the spring *rain* (comp. 3954); fig. *eloquence:*—latter rain.

4457. מֶלְקָח **melqâch**, *mel-kawkh';* or

מַלְקָח **malqâch**, *mal-kawkh';* from 3947; (only in dual) *tweezers:*—snuffers, tongs.

4458. מֶלְתָּחָה **meltâchâh**, *mel-taw-khaw';* from an unused root mean. to *spread* out; a *wardrobe* (i.e. room where clothing is *spread*):—vestry.

4459. מַלְתָּעָה **maltâ'âh**, *mal-taw-aw';* transp. for 4973; a *grinder,* i.e. back *tooth:*—great tooth.

4460. מַמְּגֻרָה **mamm^e^gûrâh**, *mam-meg-oo-raw';* from 4048 (in the sense of *depositing*); a *granary:*—barn.

4461. מֵמַד **mêmad**, *may-mad';* from 4058; a *measure:*—measure.

4462. מְמוּכָן **M^e^mûwkân**, *mem-oo-kawn';* or (transp.)

מוֹמֻכָן° **Môwmûkân** (Esth. 1 : 16), *mo-moo-kawn';* of Pers. der.; *Memucan* or *Momucan,* a Pers. satrap:—Memucan.

4463. מָמוֹת **mâmôwth**, *maw-mothe';* from 4191; a mortal *disease;* concr. a *corpse:*—death.

4464. מַמְזֵר **mamzêr**, *mam-zare';* from an unused root mean. to *alienate;* a *mongrel,* i.e. born of a Jewish father and a heathen mother:—bastard.

4465. מִמְכָּר **mimkâr**, *mim-kawr';* from 4376; *merchandise;* abstr. a *selling:*— × ought, (that which cometh of) sale, that which . . . sold, ware.

4466. מִמְכֶּרֶת **mimkereth**, *mim-keh'-reth;* fem. of 4465; a *sale:*—+ sold as.

4467. מַמְלָכָה **mamlâkâh**, *mam-law-kaw';* from 4427; *dominion,* i.e. (abstr.) the estate (*rule*) or (concr.) the country (*realm*):—kingdom, king's, reign, royal.

4468. מַמְלָכוּת **mamlâkûwth**, *mam-law-kooth';* a form of 4467 and equiv. to it:—kingdom, reign.

4469. מַמְסָךְ **mamçâk**, *mam-sawk';* from 4537; *mixture,* i.e. (spec.) wine *mixed* (with water or spices):—drink-offering, mixed wine.

4470. מֶמֶר **memer**, *meh'-mer;* from an unused root mean. to *grieve; sorrow:*—bitterness.

4471. מַמְרֵא **Mamrê'**, *mam-ray';* from 4754 (in the sense of *vigor*); *lusty; Mamre,* an Amorite:—Mamre.

4472. מַמְרֹר **mamrôr**, *mam-rore';* from 4843; a *bitterness,* i.e. (fig.) calamity:—bitterness.

4473. מִמְשַׁח **mimshach**, *mim-shakh';* from 4886, in the sense of *expansion; outspread* (i.e. with outstretched wings):—anointed.

4474. מִמְשָׁל **mimshâl**, *mim-shawl';* from 4910; a *ruler* or (abstr.) *rule:*—dominion, that ruled.

4475. מֶמְשָׁלָה **memshâlâh**, *mem-shaw-law';* fem. of 4474; *rule;* also (concr. in plur.) a *realm* or a *ruler:*—dominion, government, power, to rule.

4476. מִמְשָׁק **mimshâq**, *mim-shawk';* from the same as 4943; a *possession:*—breeding.

4477. מַמְתַּק **mamtaq**, *mam-tak';* from 4985; something *sweet* (lit. or fig.):—(most) sweet.

4478. מָן **mân**, *mawn;* from 4100; lit. a *whatness* (so to speak), i.e. *manna* (so called from the question about it):—manna.

4479. מָן **mân** (Chald.), *mawn;* from 4101; *who* or *what* (prop. interrog., hence also indef. and rel.):—what, who (-msoever, + -so).

4480. מִן **min**, *min;* or

מִנִּי **minnîy**, *min-nee';* or

מִנֵּי **minnêy** (constr. plur.), *min-nay'* (Isa. 30 : 11); for 4482; prop. a *part* of; hence

(prep.), *from* or *out of* in many senses (as follows):—above, after, among, at, because of, by (reason of), from (among), in, × neither, × nor, (out) of, over, since, × then, through, × whether, with.

4481. מִן **min** (Chald.), *min;* corresp. to 4480:—according, after, + because, + before, by, for, from, × him, × more than, (out) of, part, since, × these, to, upon, + when.

4482. מֵן **mên**, *mane;* from an unused root mean. to *apportion;* a *part;* hence a musical *chord* (as parted into strings):—in [the same] (Psa. 68 : 23), stringed instrument (Psa. 150 : 4), whereby (Psa. 45 : 8 [*defective plur.*]).

4483. מְנָא **m^enâʼ** (Chald.), *men-aw';* or

מְנָה **m^enâh** (Chald.), *men-aw';* corresp. to 4487; to *count, appoint:*—number, ordain, set.

4484. מְנֵא **menêʼ** (Chald.), *men-ay';* pass. part. of 4483; *numbered:*—Mene.

4485. מַנְגִּינָה **mangîynâh**, *man-ghee-naw';* from 5059; a *satire:*—music.

מִנְדָּה **mindâh.** See 4061.

4486. מַנְדַּע **mandaʻ** (Chald.), *man-dah';* corresp. to 4093; *wisdom* or *intelligence:*—knowledge, reason, understanding.

מְנָה **m^enâh.** See 4483.

4487. מָנָה **mânâh**, *maw-naw';* a prim. root; prop. to *weigh* out; by impl. to *allot* or constitute officially; also to *enumerate* or enroll:—appoint, count, number, prepare, set, tell.

4488. מָנֶה **mâneh**, *maw-neh';* from 4487; prop. a fixed *weight* or measured amount, i.e. (techn.) a *maneh* or mina:—maneh, pound.

4489. מֹנֶה **môneh**, *mo-neh';* from 4487; prop. something *weighed* out, i.e. (fig.) a *portion* of time, i.e. an *instance:*—time.

4490. מָנָה **mânâh**, *maw-naw';* from 4487; prop. something *weighed* out, i.e. (gen.) a *division;* spec. (of food) a *ration;* also a *lot:*—such things as belonged, part, portion.

4491. מִנְהָג **minhâg**, *min-hawg';* from 5090; the *driving* (of a chariot):—driving.

4492. מִנְהָרָה **minhârâh**, *min-haw-raw';* from 5102; prop. a *channel* or fissure, i.e. (by impl.) a *cavern:*—den.

4493. מָנוֹד **mânôwd**, *maw-node';* from 5110; a *nodding* or *toss* (of the head in derision):—shaking.

4494. מָנוֹחַ **mânôwach**, *maw-no'-akh;* from 5117; *quiet,* i.e. (concr.) a *settled spot,* or (fig.) a *home:*—(place of) rest.

4495. מָנוֹחַ **Mânôwach**, *maw-no'-akh;* the same as 4494; *rest; Manoăch,* an Isr.:—Manoah.

4496. מְנוּחָה **menûwchâh**, *men-oo-khaw';* or

מְנֻחָה **m^enûchâh**, *men-oo-khaw';* fem. of 4495; *repose* or (adv.) *peacefully;* fig. *consolation* (spec. *matrimony*); hence (concr.) an *abode:*—comfortable, ease, quiet, rest (-ing place), still.

4497. מָנוֹן **mânôwn**, *maw-nohn';* from 5125; a *continuator,* i.e. *heir:*—son.

4498. מָנוֹס **mânôwç**, *maw-noce';* from 5127; a *retreat* (lit. or fig.); abstr. a *fleeing:*—× apace, escape, way to flee, flight, refuge.

4499. מְנוּסָה **m^enuwçâh**, *men-oo-saw';* or

מְנֻסָה **m^enûçâh**, *men-oo-saw';* fem. of 4498; *retreat:*—fleeing, flight.

4500. מָנוֹר **mânôwr**, *maw-nore';* from 5214; a *yoke* (prop. for *ploughing*), i.e. the *frame* of a loom:—beam.

4501. מְנוֹרָה **m^enôwrâh**, *men-o-raw';* or

מְנֹרָה **m^enôrâh**, *men-o-raw';* fem. of 4500 (in the orig. sense of 5216); a *chandelier:*—candlestick.

4502. מִנְּזָר **minn^ezâr**, *min-ez-awr';* from 5144; a *prince:*—crowned.

4503. מִנְחָה **minchâh**, *min-khaw';* from an unused root mean. to *apportion,* i.e. *bestow;* a *donation;* euphem. *tribute;* spec. a sacrificial *offering* (usually bloodless and voluntary):—gift, oblation, (meat) offering, present, sacrifice.

4504. מִנְחָה **minchâh** (Chald.), *min-khaw';* corresp. to 4503; a sacrificial *offering:*—oblation, meat offering.

מְנֻחָה **m^enûchâh.** See 4496.

מְנֻחוֹת **M^enûchôwth.** See 2679.

4505. מְנַחֵם **M^enachêm**, *men-akh-ame';* from 5162; *comforter; Menachem,* an Isr.:—Menahem.

4506. מָנַחַת **Mânachath**, *maw-nakh'-ath;* from 5117; *rest; Manachath,* the name of an Edomite and of a place in Moab:—Manahath.

מְנַחְתִּי **M^enachtîy.** See 2680.

4507. מְנִי **M^enîy**, *men-ee';* from 4487; the *Apportioner,* i.e. Fate (as an idol):—number.

מִנִּי **minnîy.** See 4480, 4482.

4508. מִנִּי **Minnîy**, *min-nee';* of for. der.; *Minni,* an Armenian province:—Minni.

מְנָיוֹת **m^enâyôwth.** See 4521.

4509. מִנְיָמִין **Minyâmîyn**, *min-yaw-meen';* from 4480 and 3225; *from* (the) *right hand; Minjamin,* the name of two Isr.:—Miniamin. Comp. 4326.

4510. מִנְיָן **minyân** (Chald.), *min-yawn';* from 4483; *enumeration:*—number.

4511. מִנִּית **Minnîyth**, *min-neeth';* from the same as 4482; *enumeration; Minnith,* a place E. of the Jordan:—Minnith.

4512. מִנְלֶה **minleh**, *min-leh';* from 5239; *completion,* i.e. (in produce) *wealth:*—perfection.

מְנֻסָה **m^enûçâh.** See 4499.

4513. מָנַע **mânaʻ**, *maw-nah';* a prim. root; to *debar* (neg. or pos.) from benefit or injury:—deny, keep (back), refrain, restrain, withhold.

4514. מַנְעוּל **manʻûwl**, *man-ool';* or

מַנְעֻל **manʻûl**, *man-ool';* from 5274; a *bolt:*—lock.

4515. מִנְעָל **manʻâl**, *man-awl';* from 5274; a *bolt:*—shoe.

4516. מַנְעַם **manʻam**, *man-am';* from 5276; a *delicacy:*—dainty.

4517. מְנַעְנַע **m^enaʻnaʻ**, *men-ah-ah';* from 5128; a *sistrum* (so called from its *rattling* sound):—cornet.

4518. מְנַקִּית **m^enaqqîyth**, *men-ak-keeth';* from 5352; a *sacrificial basin* (for holding blood):—bowl.

מְנֹרָה **m^enôrâh.** See 4501.

4519. מְנַשֶּׁה **M^enashsheh**, *men-ash-sheh';* from 5382; *causing to forget; Menashsheh,* a grandson of Jacob, also the tribe desc. from him, and its territory:—Manasseh.

4520. מְנַשִּׁי **M^enashshîy**, *men-ash-shee';* from 4519; a *Menashshite* or desc. of Menashsheh:—of Manasseh, Manassites.

4521. מְנָת **m^enâth**, *men-awth';* from 4487; an *allotment* (by courtesy, law or providence):—portion.

4522. מַס **maç**, *mas;* or

מִס **miç**, *mees;* from 4549; prop. a *burden* (as causing to *faint*), i.e. a *tax* in the form of forced *labor:*—discomfited, levy, task [-master], tribute (-tary).

4523. מָס **mâç**, *mawce;* from 4549; *fainting,* i.e. (fig.) *disconsolate:*—is afflicted.

4524. מֵסַב **mêçab**, *may-sab';* plur. masc.

מְסִבִּים **m^eçibbîym**, *mes-ib-beem';* or fem.

מְסִבּוֹת **m^eçibbôwth**, *mes-ib-bohth';* from 5437; a *divan* (as *enclosing* the room); abstr. (adv.) *around:*—that compass about, (place) round about, at table.

מֻסַבָּה **mûçabbâh.** See 4142.

4525. מַסְגֵּר **maçgêr**, *mas-gare';* from 5462; a *fastener,* i.e. (of a person) a *smith,* (of a thing) a *prison:*—prison, smith.

4526. מִסְגֶּרֶת **miçgereth**, *mis-gheh'-reth;* from 5462; something *enclosing,* i.e. a *margin* (of a region, of a panel); concr. a *stronghold:*—border, close place, hole.

4527. מַסַּד **maççad**, *mas-sad';* from 3245; a *foundation:*—foundation.

מוֹסָדָה **môçâdâh.** See 4146.

4528. מִסְדְּרוֹן **miçd^erôwn**, *mis-der-ohn';* from the same as 5468; a *colonnade* or internal portico (from its *rows* of pillars):—porch.

4529. מָסָה **mâçâh**, *maw-saw';* a prim. root; to *dissolve:*—make to consume away, (make to) melt, water.

4530. מִסָּה **miççâh**, *mis-saw';* from 4549 (in the sense of *flowing*); *abundance,* i.e. (adv.) *liberally:*—tribute.

4531. מַסָּה **maççâh**, *mas-saw';* from 5254; a *testing,* of men (judicial) or of God (querulous):—temptation, trial.

4532. מַסָּה **Maççâh**, *mas-saw';* the same as 4531; *Massah,* a place in the Desert:—Massah.

4533. מַסְוֶה **maçveh**, *mas-veh';* appar. from an unused root mean. to *cover;* a *veil:*—vail.

4534. מְסוּכָה **m^eçûwkâh**, *mes-oo-kaw';* for 4881; a *hedge:*—thorn hedge.

4535. מַסָּח **maççâch**, *mas-sawkh';* from 5255 in the sense of *staving* off; a *cordon,* (adv.) or (as a) military *barrier:*—broken down.

4536. מִסְחָר **miçchâr**, *mis-khawr';* from 5503; *trade:*—traffic.

4537. מָסַךְ **mâçak**, *maw-sak';* a prim. root; to *mix,* espec. wine (with spices):—mingle.

4538. מֶסֶךְ **meçek**, *meh'-sek;* from 4537; a *mixture,* i.e. of wine with spices:—mixture.

4539. מָסָךְ **mâçâk**, *maw-sawk';* from 5526; a *cover,* i.e. *veil:*—covering, curtain, hanging.

4540. מְסֻכָּה **m^eçukkâh**, *mes-ook-kaw';* from 5526; a *covering,* i.e. garniture:—covering.

4541. מַסֵּכָה **maççêkâh**, *mas-say-kaw';* from 5258; prop. a *pouring* over, i.e. *fusion* of metal (espec. a *cast* image); by impl. a *libation,* i.e. league; concr. a *coverlet* (as if *poured* out):—covering, molten (image), vail.

4542. מִסְכֵּן **miçkên**, *mis-kane';* from 5531; *indigent:*—poor (man).

4543. מִסְכְּנָה **miçk^enâh**, *mis-ken-aw';* by transp. from 3664; a *magazine:*—store (-house), treasure.

4544. מִסְכֵּנֻת **miçkênûth**, *mis-kay-nooth';* from 4542; *indigence:*—scarceness.

4545. מַסֶּכֶת **maççeketh**, *mas-seh'-keth;* from 5259 in the sense of *spreading* out; something *expanded,* i.e. the *warp* in a loom (as *stretched* out to receive the woof):—web.

4546. מְסִלָּה **m^eçillâh**, *mes-il-law';* from 5549; a *thoroughfare* (as *turnpiked*), lit. or fig.; spec. a *viaduct,* a *staircase:*—causeway, course, highway, path, terrace.

4547. מַסְלוּל **maçlûwl**, *mas-lool';* from 5549; a *thoroughfare* (as turnpiked):—highway.

4548. מַסְמֵר **maçmêr**, *mas-mare';* or

מִסְמֵר **miçmêr**, *mis-mare';* also (fem.)

מַסְמְרָה **maçm^erâh**, *mas-mer-aw';* or

מִסְמְרָה **miçm^erâh**, *mis-mer-aw';* or even

מַשְׂמְרָה **masm^erâh** (Eccles. 12 : 11), *mas-mer-aw';* from 5568; a *peg* (as *bristling* from the surface):—nail.

4549. מָסַס **mâçaç**, *maw-sas'*; a prim. root; to *liquefy*; fig. to *waste* (with disease), to *faint* (with fatigue, fear or grief):—discourage, faint, be loosed, melt (away), refuse, × utterly.

4550. מַסַּע **maççaʻ**, *mas-sah'*; from 5265; a *departure* (from *striking* the tents), i.e. march (not necessarily a single day's travel); by impl. a *station* (or point of *departure*):—journey (-ing).

4551. מַסָּע **maççâʻ**, *mas-saw'*; from 5265 in the sense of *projecting*; a *missile* (spear or arrow); also a *quarry* (whence stones are, as it were, *ejected*):—before it was brought, dart.

4552. מִסְעָד **miçʻâd**, *mis-awd'*; from 5582; a *balustrade* (for stairs):—pillar.

4553. מִסְפֵּד **miçpêd**, *mis-pade'*; from 5594; a *lamentation*:—lamentation, one mourneth, mourning, wailing.

4554. מִסְפּוֹא **miçpôwʼ**, *mis-po'*; from an unused root mean. to *collect*; *fodder*:—provender.

4555. מִסְפָּחָה **miçpâchâh**, *mis-paw-khaw'*; from 5596; a *veil* (as *spread* out):—kerchief.

4556. מִסְפַּחַת **miçpachath**, *mis-pakh'-ath*; from 5596; *scurf* (as *spreading* over the surface):—scab.

4557. מִסְפָּר **miçpâr**, *mis-pawr'*; from 5608; a *number*, def. (arithmetical) or indef. (large, *innumerable*; small, a *few*); also (abstr.) *narration*:— + abundance, account, × all, × few, [in-] finite, (certain) number (-ed), tale, telling, + time.

4558. מִסְפָּר **Miçpâr**, *mis-pawr'*; the same as 4457; *number*; *Mispar*, an Isr.:—Mizpar. Comp. 4559.

מֹסֵרוֹת **Môçerowth**. See 4149.

4559. מִסְפֶּרֶת **Miçpereth**, *mis-peh'-reth*; fem. of 4457; *enumeration*; *Mispereth*, an Isr.:—Mispereth. Comp. 4458.

4560. מָסַר **mâçar**, *maw-sar'*; a prim. root; to *sunder*, i.e. (trans.) *set apart*, or (reflex.) *apostatize*:—commit, deliver.

4561. מֹסָר **môçâr**, *mo-sawr'*; from 3256; *admonition*:—instruction.

4562. מָסֹרֶת **mâçôreth**, *maw-so'-reth*; from 631; a *band*:—bond.

4563. מִסְתּוֹר **miçtôwr**, *mis-tore'*; from 5641; a *refuge*:—covert.

4564. מַסְתֵּר **maçtêr**, *mas-tare'*; from 5641; prop. a *hider*, i.e. (abstr.) a hiding, i.e. *aversion*:—hid.

4565. מִסְתָּר **miçtâr** *mis-tawr'* from 5641 prop. a *concealer*, i.e. a *covert*:—secret (-ly, place).

מְעָא **meʻâʼ**. See 4577.

4566. מַעְבָּד **maʻbâd**, *mah-bawd'*; from 5647; an *act*:—work.

4567. מַעְבָד **maʻbâd** (Chald.), *mah-bawd'*; corresp. to 4566; an *act*:—work.

4568. מַעֲבֶה **maʻăbeh**, *mah-ab-eh'*; from 5666; prop. *compact* (part of soil), i.e. *loam*:—clay.

4569. מַעֲבָר **maʻăbâr**, *mah-ab-awr'*; or fem.

מַעֲבָרָה **maʻăbârâh**, *mah-ab-aw-raw'*; from 5674; a *crossing*-place (of a river, a *ford*; of a mountain, a *pass*); abstr. a *transit*, i.e. (fig.) *overwhelming*:—ford, place where . . . pass, passage.

4570. מַעְגָּל **maʻgâl**, *mah-gawl'*; or fem.

מַעְגָּלָה **maʻgâlâh**, *mah-gaw-law'*; from the same as 5696; a *track* (lit. or fig.); also a *rampart* (as *circular*):—going, path, trench, way ([-side]).

4571. מָעַד **mâʻad**, *maw-ad'*; a prim. root; to *waver*:—make to shake, slide, slip.

מֹעֵד **môʻêd**. See 4150.

4572. מַעֲדַי **Maʻăday**, *mah-ad-ah'ee*; from 5710; *ornamental*; *Maadai*, an Isr.:—Madai.

4573. מַעַדְיָה **Maʻadyâh**, *mah-ad-yaw'*; from 5710 and 3050; *ornament of Jah*; *Maadjah*, an Isr.:—Maadiah. Comp. 4153.

4574. מַעֲדָן **maʻădân**, *mah-ad-awn'*; or (fem.)

מַעֲדַנָּה **maʻădannâh**, *mah-ad-an-naw'*; from 5727; a *delicacy* or (abstr.) *pleasure* (adv. *cheerfully*):—dainty, delicately, delight.

4575. מַעֲדַנָּה **maʻădannâh**, *mah-ad-an-naw'*; by transp. from 6029; a *bond*, i.e. *group*:—influence.

4576. מַעְדֵּר **maʻdêr**, *mah-dare'*; from 5737; a (weeding) *hoe*:—mattock.

4577. מְעָה **meʻâh** (Chald.), *meh-aw'*; or

מְעָא **meʻâʼ** (Chald.), *meh-aw'*; corresp. to 4578; only in plur. the *bowels*:—belly.

4578. מֵעֶה **mêʻâh**, *may-aw'*; from an unused root prob. mean. to *be soft*; used only in plur. the *intestines*, or (collect.) the *abdomen*, fig. *sympathy*; by impl. a *vest*; by extens. the *stomach*, the *uterus* (or of men, the seat of generation), the *heart* (fig.):—belly, bowels, × heart, womb.

4579. מֵעָה **mêʻâh**, *may-aw'*; fem. of 4578; the *belly*, i.e. (fig.) interior:—gravel.

4580. מָעוֹג **mâʻôwg**, *maw-ogue'*; from 5746; a *cake* of bread (with 3934 a *table-buffoon*, i.e. *parasite*):—cake, feast.

4581. מָעוֹז **mâʻôwz**, *maw-oze'* (also

מָעוּז **mâʻûwz**, *maw-ooz'*); or

מָעֹז **mâʻôz**, *maw-oze'* (also

מָעֻז **mâʻûz**, *maw-ooz'*); from 5810; a *fortified* place; fig. a *defence*:—force, fort (-ress), rock, strength (-en), (× most) strong (hold).

4582. מָעוֹךְ **Mâʻôwk**, *maw-oke'*; from 4600; *oppressed*; *Maok*, a Philistine:—Maoch.

4583. מָעוֹן **mâʻôwn**, *maw-ohn'*; or

מָעִין° **mâʻîyn** (1 Chron. 4 : 41), *maw-een'*; from the same as 5772; an *abode*, of God (the Tabernacle or the Temple), men (their home) or animals (their lair); hence a *retreat* (asylum):—den, dwelling ([-] place), habitation.

4584. מָעוֹן **Mâʻôwn**, *maw-ohn'*; the same as 4583; a *residence*; *Maon*, the name of an Isr. and of a place in Pal.:—Maon, Maonites. Comp. 1010, 4586.

4585 מְעוֹנָה **meʻôwnâh**, *meh-o-naw'*; or

מְעֹנָה **meʻônâh**, *meh-o-naw'*; fem. of 4583, and mean. the same:—den, habitation, (dwelling) place, refuge.

4586. מְעוּנִי **Meʻûwnîy**, *meh-oo-nee'*; or

מְעִינִי° **Meʻîynîy**, *meh-ee-nee'*; prob. patrial from 4584; a *Meünite*, or inhab. of Maon (only in plur.):—Mehunim (-s), Meunim.

4587. מְעוֹנֹתַי **Meʻôwnôthay**, *meh-o-no-thah'ee*; plur. of 4585; *habitative*; *Meonothai*, an Isr.:—Meonothai.

4588. מָעוּף **mâʻûwph**, *maw-oof'*; from 5774 in the sense of *covering* with shade [comp. 4155]; *darkness*:—dimness.

4589. מָעוֹר **mâʻôwr**, *maw-ore'*; from 5783; *nakedness*, i.e. (in plur.) the *pudenda*:—nakedness.

מָעֹז **mâʻôz**. See 4583.

מָעֻז **mâʻûz**. See 4583.

4590. מַעַזְיָה **Maʻazyâh**, *mah-az-yaw'*; or

מַעַזְיָהוּ **Maʻazyâhûw**, *mah-az-yaw'-hoo*; prob. from. 5756 (in the sense of *protection*) and 3050; *rescue of Jah*; *Maazjah*, the name of two Isr.:—Maaziah.

4591. מָעַט **mâʻaṭ**, *maw-at'*; a prim. root; prop. to *pare* off, i.e. *lessen*; intrans. to *be* (or caus. to *make*) *small* or *few* (or fig. *ineffective*):—suffer to decrease, diminish, (be, × borrow a, give, make) few (in number, -ness), gather least (little), be (seem) little, (× give the) less, be minished, bring to nothing.

4592. מְעַט **meʻaṭ**, *meh-at'*; or

מְעָט **meʻâṭ**, *meh-awt'*; from 4591; a *little* or *few* (often adv. or compar.):—almost, (some, very) few (-er, -est), lightly, little (while), (very) small (matter, thing), some, soon, × very.

4593. מָעֹט **mâʻôṭ**, *maw-ote'*; pass. adj. of 4591; *thinned* (as to the edge), i.e. *sharp*:—wrapped up.

4594. מַעֲטֶה **maʻăṭeh**, *mah-at-eh'*; from 5844; a *vestment*:—garment.

4595. מַעֲטָפָה **maʻăṭâphâh**, *mah-at-aw-faw'*; from 5848; a *cloak*:—mantle.

4596. מְעִי **meʻîy**, *meh-ee'*; from 5753; a *pile* of rubbish (as *contorted*), i.e. a *ruin* (comp. 5856):—heap.

4597. מָעַי **Mâʻai**, *maw-ah'ee*; prob. from 4578; *sympathetic*; *Maai*, an Isr.:—Maai.

4598. מְעִיל **meʻîyl**, *meh-eel'*; from 4603 in the sense of *covering*; a *robe* (i.e. upper and outer *garment*):—cloke, coat, mantle, robe.

מֵעִים **mêʻîym**. See 4578.

מְעִין **meʻîyn** (Chald.). See 4577.

4599. מַעְיָן **maʻyân**, *mah-yawn'*; or

מַעְיְנוֹ **maʻyenôw** (Psa. 114 : 8), *mah-yen-o'*; or (fem.)

מַעְיָנָה **maʻyânâh**, *mah-yaw-naw'*; from 5869 (as a denom. in the sense of a *spring*); a *fountain* (also collect.), fig. a *source* (of satisfaction):—fountain, spring, well.

מְעִינִי° **Meʻîynîy**. See 4586.

4600. מָעַךְ **mâʻak**, *maw-ak'*; a prim. root; to *press*, i.e. to *pierce*, *emasculate*, *handle*:—bruised, stuck, be pressed.

4601. מַעֲכָה **Maʻăkâh**, *mah-ak-aw'*; or

מַעֲכָת **Maʻăkâth** (Josh. 13 : 13), *mah-ak-awth'*; from 4600; *depression*; *Maakah* (or *Maakath*), the name of a place in Syria, also of a Mesopotamian, of three Isr., and of four Israelitesses and one Syrian woman:—Maachah, Maachathites. See also 1038.

4602. מַעֲכָתִי **Maʻăkâthîy**, *mah-ak-aw-thee'*; patrial from 4601; a *Maakathite*, or inhab. of Maakah:—Maachathite.

4603. מָעַל **mâʻal**, *maw-al'*; a prim. root; prop. to *cover* up; used only fig. to *act covertly*, i.e. *treacherously*:—transgress, (commit, do a) trespass (-ing).

4604. מַעַל **maʻal**, *mah'-al*; from 4603; *treachery*, i.e. sin:—falsehood, grievously, sore, transgression, trespass, × very.

4605. מַעַל **maʻal**, *mah'-al*; from 5927; prop. the *upper* part, used only adv. with pref. *upward*, *above*, *overhead*, *from the top*, etc.:—above, exceeding (-ly), forward, on (× very) high, over, up (-on, -ward), very.

מֵעַל **mêʻal**. See 5921.

4606. מֵעָל **mêʻâl** (Chald.), *may-awl'*; from 5954; (only in plur. as sing.) the *setting* (of the sun):—going down.

4607. מֹעַל **môʻal**, *mo'-al*; from 5927; a *raising* (of the hands):—lifting up.

4608. מַעֲלֶה **maʻăleh**, *mah-al-eh'*; from 5927; an *elevation*, i.e. (concr.) *acclivity* or *platform*; abstr. (the relation or state) a *rise* or (fig.) *priority*:—ascent, before, chiefest, cliff, that goeth up, going up, hill, mounting up, stairs.

4609. מַעֲלָה **maʻălâh**, *mah-al-aw'*; fem. of 4608; *elevation*, i.e. the act (lit. a *journey* to a higher place, fig. a *thought* arising), or (concr.) the condition (lit. a *step* or *grade*-mark, fig. a *superiority* of station); spec. a climactic *progression* (in certain Psalms):—things that come up, (high) degree, deal, go up, stair, step, story.

4610. מַעֲלֵה עַקְרַבִּים **Maʻălêh ʻAqrabbîym,** *mah-al-ay' ak-rab-beem';* from 4608 and (the plur. of) 6137; *Steep of Scorpions,* a place in the Desert:—Maaleh-accrabim, the ascent (going up) of Akrabbim.

4611. מַעֲלָל **maʻălâl,** *mah-al-awl';* from 5953; an *act* (good or bad):—doing, endeavour, invention, work.

4612. מַעֲמָד **maʻămâd,** *mah-am-awd';* from 5975; (fig.) a *position:*—attendance, office, place, state.

4613. מׇעֳמָד **moʻŏmâd,** *moh-om-awd';* from 5975; lit. a *foothold:*—standing.

4614. מַעֲמָסָה **maʻămâçâh,** *mah-am-aw-saw';* from 6006; *burdensomeness:*—burdensome.

4615. מַעֲמָק **maʻămâq,** *mah-am-awk';* from 6009; a *deep:*—deep, depth.

4616. מַעַן **maʻan,** *mah'-an;* from 6030; prop. *heed,* i.e. *purpose;* used only adv., *on account of* (as a motive or an aim), teleologically *in order that:*—because of, to the end (intent) that, for (to, . . . 's sake), + lest, that, to.

4617. מַעֲנֶה **maʻăneh,** *mah-an-eh';* from 6030; a *reply* (favorable or contradictory):—answer, × himself.

4618. מַעֲנָה **maʻănâh,** *mah-an-aw';* from 6031, in the sense of *depression* or *tilling;* a *furrow:*— + acre, furrow.

מְעֹנָה **meʻônâh.** See 4585.

4619. מַעַץ **Maʻats,** *mah'-ats;* from 6095; *closure; Maats,* an Isr.:—Maaz.

4620. מַעֲצֵבָה **maʻătsêbâh,** *mah-ats-ay-baw';* from 6087; *anguish:*—sorrow.

4621. מַעֲצָד **maʻătsâd,** *mah-ats-awd';* from an unused root mean. to *hew;* an *axe:*—ax, tongs.

4622. מַעְצוֹר **maʻtsôwr,** *mah-tsore';* from 6113; obj. a *hindrance:*—restraint.

4623. מַעְצָר **maʻtsâr,** *mah-tsawr';* from 6113; subj. *control:*—rule.

4624. מַעֲקֶה **maʻăqeh,** *mah-ak-eh';* from an unused root mean. to *repress;* a *parapet:*—battlement.

4625. מַעֲקָשׁ **maʻăqâsh,** *mah-ak-awsh';* from 6140; a *crook* (in a road):—crooked thing.

4626. מַעַר **maʻar,** *mah'-ar;* from 6168; a *nude* place, i.e. (lit.) the *pudenda,* or (fig.) a vacant *space:*—nakedness, proportion.

4627. מַעֲרָב **maʻărâb,** *mah-ar-awb';* from 6148, in the sense of *trading; traffic;* by impl. mercantile *goods:*—market, merchandise.

4628. מַעֲרָב **maʻărâb,** *mah-ar-awb';* or (fem.)

מַעֲרָבָה **maʻărâbâh,** *mah-ar-aw-baw';* from 6150, in the sense of *shading;* the *west* (as the region of the *evening* sun):—west.

4629. מַעֲרֶה **maʻăreh,** *mah-ar-eh';* from 6168; a *nude* place, i.e. a *common:*—meadows.

4630. מַעֲרָה° **maʻărâh,** *mah-ar-aw';* fem. of 4629; an *open* spot:—army [*from the marg.*].

4631. מְעָרָה **meʻârâh,** *meh-aw-raw';* from 5783; a *cavern* (as dark):—cave, den, hole.

4632. מְעָרָה **Meʻârâh,** *meh-aw-raw';* the same as 4631; *cave; Meärah,* a place in Pal.:—Mearah.

4633. מַעֲרָךְ **maʻărâk,** *mah-ar-awk';* from 6186; an *arrangement,* i.e. (fig.) mental *disposition:*—preparation.

4634. מַעֲרָכָה **maʻărâkâh,** *mah-ar-aw-kaw';* fem. of 4633; an *arrangement;* concr. a *pile;* spec. a military *array:*—army, fight, be set in order, ordered place, rank, row.

4635. מַעֲרֶכֶת **maʻăreketh,** *mah-ar-eh'-keth;* from 6186; an *arrangement,* i.e. (concr.) a *pile* (of loaves):—row, shewbread.

4636. מַעֲרֹם **maʻărôm,** *mah-ar-ome';* from 6191, in the sense of *stripping; bare:*—naked.

4637. מַעֲרָצָה **maʻărâtsâh,** *mah-ar-aw-tsaw';* from 6206; *violence:*—terror.

4638. מַעֲרָת **Maʻărâth,** *mah-ar-awth';* a form of 4630; *waste; Maarath,* a place in Pal.:—Maarath.

4639. מַעֲשֶׂה **maʻăseh,** *mah-as-eh';* from 6213; an *action* (good or bad); gen. a *transaction;* abstr. *activity;* by impl. a *product* (spec. a *poem*) or (gen.) *property:*—act, art, + bakemeat, business, deed, do (-ing), labour, thing made, ware of making, occupation, thing offered, operation, possession, × well, ([handy-, needle-, net-]) work, (-ing, -manship), wrought.

4640. מַעֲשַׂי **Maʻăsay,** *mah-as-ah'ee;* from 6213; *operative; Maasai,* an Isr.:—Maasiai.

4641. מַעֲשֵׂיָה **Maʻăsêyâh,** *mah-as-ay-yaw';* or

מַעֲשֵׂיָהוּ **Maʻăsêyâhûw,** *mah-as-ay-yaw'-hoo;* from 4639 and 3050; *work of Jah; Maasejah,* the name of sixteen Isr.:—Maaseiah.

4642. מַעֲשַׁקָּה **maʻăshaqqâh,** *mah-ash-ak-kaw';* from 6231; *oppression:*—oppression, × oppressor.

4643. מַעֲשֵׂר **maʻăsêr,** *mah-as-ayr';* or

מַעֲשַׂר **maʻăsar,** *mah-as-ar';* and (in plur.) fem.

מַעַשְׂרָה **maʻasrâh,** *mah-as-raw';* from 6240; a *tenth;* espec. a *tithe:*—tenth (part), tithe (-ing).

4644. מֹף **Môph,** *mofe;* of Eg. or.; *Moph,* the capital of Lower Egypt:—Memphis. Comp. 5297.

מְפִבֹשֶׁת **Mephîbôsheth.** See 4648.

4645. מִפְגָּע **miphgâʻ,** *mif-gaw';* from 6293; an *object of attack:*—mark.

4646. מַפָּח **mappâch,** *map-pawkh';* from 5301; a *breathing out* (of life), i.e. expiring:—giving up.

4647. מַפֻּחַ **mappûach,** *map-poo'-akh;* from 5301; the *bellows* (i.e. *blower*) of a forge:—bellows.

4648. מְפִיבֹשֶׁת **Mephîybôsheth,** *mef-ee-bo'-sheth;* or

מְפִבֹשֶׁת **Mephîbôsheth,** *mef-ee-bo'-sheth;* prob. from 6284 and 1322; *dispeller of shame* (i.e. of Baal); *Mephibosheth,* the name of two Isr.:—Mephibosheth.

4649. מֻפִּים **Muppîym,** *moop-peem';* a plur. appar. from 5130; *wavings; Muppim,* an Isr.:—Muppim. Comp. 8206.

4650. מֵפִיץ **mêphîyts,** *may-feets';* from 6327; a *breaker,* i.e. mallet:—maul.

4651. מַפָּל **mappâl,** *map-pawl';* from 5307; a *falling* off, i.e. chaff; also something *pendulous,* i.e. a flap:—flake, refuse.

4652. מִפְלָאָה **miphlâʼâh,** *mif-law-aw';* from 6381; a *miracle:*—wondrous work.

4653. מִפְלַגָּה **miphlaggâh,** *mif-lag-gaw';* from 6385; a *classification:*—division.

4654. מַפָּלָה **mappâlâh,** *map-paw-law';* or

מַפֵּלָה **mappêlâh,** *map-pay-law';* from 5307; something *fallen,* i.e. a *ruin:*—ruin (-ous).

4655. מִפְלָט **miphlâṭ,** *mif-lawt';* from 6403; an *escape:*—escape.

4656. מִפְלֶצֶת **miphletseth,** *mif-leh'-tseth;* from 6426; a *terror,* i.e. an idol:—idol.

4657. מִפְלָשׂ **miphlâs,** *mif-lawce';* from an unused root mean. to *balance;* a *poising:*—balancing.

4658. מַפֶּלֶת **mappeleth,** *map-peh'-leth;* from 5307; *fall,* i.e. *decadence;* concr. a *ruin;* spec. a *carcase:*—carcase, fall, ruin.

4659. מִפְעָל **miphʻâl,** *mif-awl';* or (fem.)

מִפְעָלָה **miphʻâlâh,** *mif-aw-law';* from 6466; a *performance:*—work.

4660. מַפָּץ **mappâts,** *map-pawts';* from 5310; a *smiting* to pieces:—slaughter.

4661. מַפֵּץ **mappêts,** *map-pates';* from 5310; a *smiter,* i.e. a war *club:*—battle ax.

4662. מִפְקָד **miphqâd,** *mif-kawd';* from 6485; an *appointment,* i.e. *mandate;* concr. a designated *spot;* spec. a *census:*—appointed place, commandment, number.

4663. מִפְקָד **Miphqâd,** *mif-kawd';* the same as 4662; *assignment; Miphkad,* the name of a gate in Jerus.:—Miphkad.

4664. מִפְרָץ **miphrâts,** *mif-rawts';* from 6555; a *break* (in the shore), i.e. a *haven:*—breach.

4665. מִפְרֶקֶת **miphreketh,** *mif-reh'-keth;* from 6561; prop. a *fracture,* i.e. *joint* (*vertebra*) of the neck:—neck.

4666. מִפְרָשׂ **miphrâs,** *mif-rawce';* from 6566; an *expansion:*—that which . . . spreadest forth, spreading.

4667. מִפְשָׂעָה **miphsâʻâh,** *mif-saw-aw';* from 6585; a *stride,* i.e. (by euphem.) the *crotch:*—buttocks.

מֹפֵת **môphêth.** See 4159.

4668. מַפְתֵּחַ **maphtêach,** *maf-tay'-akh;* from 6605; an *opener,* i.e. a *key:*—key.

4669. מִפְתָּח **miphtâch,** *mif-tawkh';* from 6605; an *aperture,* i.e. (fig.) *utterance:*—opening.

4670. מִפְתָּן **miphtân,** *mif-tawn';* from the same as 6620; a *stretcher,* i.e. a *sill:*—threshold.

4671. מֹץ **môts,** *motes;* or

מוֹץ **môwts** (Zeph. 2 : 2), *motes;* from 4160; *chaff* (as *pressed* out, i.e. *winnowed* or [rather] threshed loose):—chaff.

4672. מָצָא **mâtsâʼ,** *maw-tsaw';* a prim. root; prop. to *come* forth to, i.e. *appear* or *exist;* trans. to *attain,* i.e. *find* or *acquire;* fig. to *occur, meet* or *be present:*— + be able, befall, being, catch, × certainly, (cause to) come (on, to, to hand), deliver, be enough (cause to) find (-ing, occasion, out), get (hold upon), × have (here), be here, hit, be left, light (up-) on, meet (with), × occasion serve, (be) present, ready, speed, suffice, take hold on.

מֹצָא **môtsâʼ.** See 4161.

4673. מַצָּב **matstsâb,** *mats-tsawb';* from 5324; a fixed *spot;* fig. an *office,* a military *post:*—garrison, station, place where . . . stood.

4674. מֻצָּב **mutstsâb,** *moots-tsawb';* from 5324; a *station,* i.e. military *post:*—mount.

4675. מַצָּבָה **matstsâbâh,** *mats-tsaw-baw';* or

מִצָּבָה **mitstsâbâh,** *mits-tsaw-baw';* fem. of 4673; a military *guard:*—army, garrison.

4676. מַצֵּבָה **matstsêbâh,** *mats-tsay-baw';* fem. (causat.) part. of 5324; something *stationed,* i.e. a *column* or (memorial *stone*); by anal. an *idol:*—garrison, (standing) image, pillar.

4677. מְצֹבָיָה **Metsôbâyâh,** *mets-o-baw-yaw';* appar. from 4672 and 3050; *found of Jah; Metsobajah,* a place in Pal.:—Mesobaite.

4678. מַצֶּבֶת **matstsebeth,** *mats-tseh'-beth;* from 5324; something *stationary,* i.e. a monumental *stone;* also the *stock* of a tree:—pillar, substance.

4679. מְצַד **metsad,** *mets-ad';* or

מְצָד **metsâd,** *mets-awd';* or (fem.)

מְצָדָה **metsâdâh,** *mets-aw-daw';* from 6679; a *fastness* (as a *covert* of ambush):—castle, fort, (strong) hold, munition.

מְצֻדָה **metsûdâh.** See 4686.

4680. מָצָה **mâtsâh,** *maw-tsaw';* a prim. root; to *suck* out; by impl. to *drain,* to *squeeze* out:—suck, wring (out).

4681. מֹצָה **Môtsâh,** *mo-tsaw';* act. part. fem. of 4680; *drained; Motsah,* a place in Pal.:—Mozah.

4682. מַצָּה **matstsâh,** *mats-tsaw';* from 4711 in the sense of *greedily* devouring for sweetness; prop. *sweetness;* concr. *sweet* (i.e. not soured or bittered with yeast); spec. an *unfermented cake* or loaf, or (ellipt.) the festival of *Passover* (because no leaven was then used):—unleavened (bread, cake), without leaven.

4683. מַצָּה **matstsâh,** *mats-tsaw';* from 5327; a *quarrel:*—contention, debate, strife.

4684. מַצְהָלָה **matshâlâh**, *mats-haw-law';* from 6670; a *whinnying* (through impatience for battle or lust):—neighing.

4685. מָצוֹד **mâtsôwd**, *maw-tsode';* or (fem.)

מְצוֹדָה **metsôwdâh**, *mets-o-daw';* or

מְצֹדָה **metsôdâh**, *mets-o-daw';* from 6679; a *net* (for *capturing* animals or fishes); also (by interch. for 4679) a *fastness* or (besieging) *tower:*—bulwark, hold, munition, net, snare.

4686. מָצוּד **mâtsûwd**, *maw-tsood';* or (fem.)

מְצוּדָה **metsûwdâh**, *mets-oo-daw';* or

מְצֻדָה **metsûdâh**, *mets-oo-daw';* for 4685; a *net*, or (abstr.) *capture;* also a *fastness:*—castle, defence, fort (-ress), (strong) hold, be hunted, net, snare, strong place.

4687. מִצְוָה **mitsvâh**, *mits-vaw';* from 6680; a *command*, whether human or divine (collect. the *Law*):—(which was) commanded (-ment), law, ordinance, precept.

4688. מְצוֹלָה **metsôwlâh**, *mets-o-law';* or

מְצֹלָה **metsôlâh**, *mets-o-law';* also

מְצוּלָה **metsûwlâh**, *mets-oo-law';* or

מְצֻלָה **metsûlâh**, *mets-oo-law';* from the same as 6683; a *deep* place (of water or mud):—bottom, deep, depth.

4689. מָצוֹק **mâtsôwq**, *maw-tsoke';* from 6693; a *narrow* place, i.e. (abstr. and fig.) *confinement* or *disability:*—anguish, distress, straitness.

4690. מָצוּק **mâtsûwq**, *maw-tsook';* or

מָצֻק **mâtsûq**, *maw-tsook';* from 6693; something *narrow*, i.e. a *column* or *hilltop:*—pillar, situate.

4691. מְצוּקָה **metsûwqâh**, *mets-oo-kaw';* or

מְצֻקָה **metsûqâh**, *mets-oo-kaw';* fem. of 4690; *narrowness*, i.e. (fig.) *trouble:*—anguish, distress.

4692. מָצוֹר **mâtsôwr**, *maw-tsore';* or

מָצוּר **mâtsûwr**, *maw-tsoor';* from 6696; something *hemming* in, i.e. (obj.) a *mound* (of besiegers), (abstr.) a *siege*, (fig.) *distress;* or (subj.) a *fastness:*—besieged, bulwark, defence, fenced, fortress, siege, strong (hold), tower.

4693. מָצוֹר **mâtsôwr**, *maw-tsore';* the same as 4692 in the sense of a *limit; Egypt* (as the *border* of Pal.):—besieged places, defence, fortified.

4694. מְצוּרָה **metsûwrâh**, *mets-oo-raw';* or

מְצֻרָה **metsûrâh**, *mets-oo-raw';* fem. of 4692; a *hemming* in, i.e. (obj.) a *mound* (of siege), or (subj.) a *rampart* (of protection), (abstr.) *fortification:*—fenced (city), fort, munition, strong hold.

4695. מַצּוּת **matstsûwth**, *mats-tsooth';* from 5327; a *quarrel:*—that contended.

4696. מֵצַח **mêtsach**, *may'-tsakh;* from an unused root mean. to be *clear*, i.e. *conspicuous;* the *forehead* (as *open* and *prominent*):—brow, forehead, + impudent.

4697. מִצְחָה **mitschâh**, *mits-khaw';* from the same as 4696; a *shin-piece* of armor (as *prominent*), only plur.:—greaves.

מְצֹלָה **metsôlah**. See 4688.

מְצֻלָה **metsûlâh**. See 4688.

4698. מְצִלָּה **metsillâh**, *mets-il-law';* from 6750; a *tinkler*, i.e. a *bell:*—bell.

4699. מְצֻלָּה **metsullâh**, *mets-ool-law';* from 6751; *shade:*—bottom.

4700. מְצֵלֶת **metsêleth**, *mets-ay'-leth;* from 6750; (only dual) double *tinklers*, i.e. cymbals:—cymbals.

4701. מִצְנֶפֶת **mitsnepheth**, *mits-neh'-feth;* from 6801; a *tiara*, i.e. official *turban* (of a king or high priest):—diadem, mitre.

4702. מַצָּע **matstsâʻ**, *mats-tsaw';* from 3331; a *couch:*—bed.

4703. מִצְעָד **mitsʻâd**, *mits-awd';* from 6805; a *step;* fig. *companionship:*—going, step.

4704. מִצְּעִירָה **mitstseʻîyrâh**, *mits-tseh-ee-raw';* fem. of 4705; prop. *littleness:* concr. *diminutive:*—little.

4705. מִצְעָר **mitsʻâr**, *mits-awr';* from 6819; *petty* (in size or number); adv. a *short* (time):—little one (while), small.

4706. מִצְעָר **Mitsʻâr**, *mits-awr';* the same as 4705; *Mitsar*, a peak of Lebanon:—Mizar.

4707. מִצְפֶּה **mitspeh**, *mits-peh';* from 6822; an *observatory*, espec. for military purposes:—watch tower.

4708. מִצְפֶּה **Mitspeh**, *mits-peh';* the same as 4707; *Mitspeh*, the name of five places in Pal.:—Mizpeh, watch tower. Comp. 4709.

4709. מִצְפָּה **Mitspah**, *mits-paw';* fem. of 4708; *Mitspah*, the name of two places in Pal.:—Mitspah. [This seems rather to be only an orth. var. of 4708 when "in pause".]

4710. מִצְפֻּן **mitspûn**, *mits-poon';* from 6845; a *secret* (place or thing, perh. *treasure*):—hidden thing.

4711. מָצַץ **mâtsats**, *maw-tsats';* a prim. root; to *suck:*—milk.

מוּצָקָה **mûtsâqâh**. See 4166.

4712. מֵצַר **mêtsar**, *may-tsar';* from 6896; something *tight*, i.e. (fig.) *trouble:*—distress, pain, strait.

מָצֻק **mâtsûq**. See 4690.

מְצֻקָה **metsûqâh**. See 4691.

מְצֻרָה **metsûrâh**. See 4694.

4713. מִצְרִי **Mitsrîy**, *mits-ree';* from 4714; a *Mitsrite*, or inhab. of Mitsrajim:—Egyptian, of Egypt.

4714. מִצְרַיִם **Mitsrayim**, *mits-rah'-yim;* dual of 4693; *Mitsrajim*, i.e.Upper and Lower Egypt:—Egypt, Egyptians, Mizraim.

4715. מִצְרֵף **mitsrêph**, *mits-rafe';* from 6884; a *crucible:*—fining pot.

4716. מַק **maq**, *mak;* from 4743; prop. a *melting*, i.e. *putridity:*—rottenness, stink.

4717. מַקָּבָה **maqqâbâh**, *mak-kaw-baw';* from 5344; prop. a *perforatrix*, i.e. a *hammer* (as *piercing*):—hammer.

4718. מַקֶּבֶת **maqqebeth**, *mak-keh'-beth;* from 5344; prop. a *perforator*, i.e. a *hammer* (as *piercing*); also (intrans.) a *perforation*, i.e. a *quarry:*—hammer, hole.

4719. מַקֵּדָה **Maqqêdâh**, *mak-kay-daw';* from the same as 5348 in the denom. sense of *herding* (comp. 5349); *fold; Makkedah*, a place in Pal.:—Makkedah.

4720. מִקְדָּשׁ **miqdâsh**, *mik-dawsh';* or

מִקְּדָשׁ **miqqedâsh** (Exod. 15 : 17), *mik-ked-awsh';* from 6942; a *consecrated* thing or place, espec. a *palace*, *sanctuary* (whether of Jehovah or of idols) or *asylum:*—chapel, hallowed part, holy place, sanctuary.

4721. מַקְהֵל **maqhêl**, *mak-hale';* or (fem.)

מַקְהֵלָה **maqhêlâh**, *mak-hay-law';* from 6950; an *assembly:*—congregation.

4722. מַקְהֵלֹת **Maqhêlôth**, *mak-hay-loth';* plur. of 4721 (fem.); *assemblies; Makheloth*, a place in the Desert:—Makheloth.

4723. מִקְוֶה **miqveh**, *mik-veh';* or

מִקְוֵה **miqvêh** (1 Kings 10 : 28), *mik-vay';* or

מִקְוֵא **miqvêʼ** (2 Chron. 1 : 16), *mik-vay';* from 6960; something *waited* for, i.e. *confidence* (obj. or subj.); also a *collection*, i.e. (of water) a *pond*, or (of men and horses) a *caravan* or *drove:*—abiding, gathering together, hope, linen yarn, plenty [of water], pool.

4724. מִקְוָה **miqvâh**, *mik-vaw';* fem. of 4723; a *collection*, i.e. (of water) a *reservoir:*—ditch.

4725. מָקוֹם **mâqôwm**, *maw-kome';* or

מָקֹם **mâqôm**, *maw-kome';* also (fem.)

מְקוֹמָה **meqôwmâh**, *mek-o-mah';* or

מְקֹמָה **meqômâh**, *mek-o-mah';* from 6965; prop. a *standing*, i.e. a *spot;* but used widely of a *locality* (gen. or spec.); also (fig.) of a *condition* (of body or mind):—country, × home, × open, place, room, space, × whither [-soever].

4726. מָקוֹר **mâqôwr**, *maw-kore';* or

מָקֹר **mâqôr**, *maw-kore';* from 6979; prop. something *dug*, i.e. a (gen.) *source* (of water, even when naturally flowing; also of tears, blood [by euphem. of the female *pudenda*]; fig. of happiness, wisdom, progeny):—fountain, issue, spring, well (-spring).

4727. מִקָּח **miqqâch**, *mik-kawkh';* from 3947; *reception:*—taking.

4728. מַקָּחָה **maqqâchâh**, *mak-kaw-khaw';* from 3947; something *received*, i.e. *merchandise* (purchased):—ware.

4729. מִקְטָר **miqṭâr**, *mik-tawr';* from 6999; something to *fume* (incense) on, i.e. a *hearth* place:—to burn . . . upon.

מְקַטְּרָה **meqaṭṭerâh**. See 6999.

4730. מִקְטֶרֶת **miqṭereth**, *mik-teh'-reth;* fem. of 4729; something to *fume* (incense) in, i.e. a *coal-pan:*—censer.

4731. מַקֵּל **maqqêl**, *mak-kale';* or (fem.)

מַקְּלָה **maqqelâh**, *mak-kel-aw';* from an unused root mean. appar. to *germinate;* a *shoot*, i.e. *stick* (with leaves on, or for walking, striking, guiding, divining):—rod, ([hand-]) staff.

4732. מִקְלוֹת **Miqlôwth**, *mik-lohth'* (or perh. *mik-kel-ohth'*); plur. of (fem.) 4731; *rods; Mikloth*, a place in the Desert:—Mikloth.

4733. מִקְלָט **miqlâṭ**, *mik-lawt';* from 7038 in the sense of *taking* in; an *asylum* (as a *receptacle*):—refuge.

4734. מִקְלַעַת **miqlaʻath**, *mik-lah'-ath;* from 7049; a *sculpture* (prob. in bass-relief):—carved (figure), carving, graving.

מָקֹם **mâqôm**. See 4725.

מְקֹמָה **meqômâh**. See 4725.

4735. מִקְנֶה **miqneh**, *mik-neh';* from 7069; something *bought*, i.e. *property*, but only live *stock;* abstr. *acquisition:*—cattle, flock, herd, possession, purchase, substance.

4736. מִקְנָה **miqnâh**, *mik-naw';* fem. of 4735; prop. a *buying*, i.e. *acquisition;* concr. a piece of *property* (land or living); also the *sum* paid:—(he that is) bought, possession, piece, purchase.

4737. מִקְנֵיָהוּ **Miqnêyâhûw**, *mik-nay-yaw'-hoo;* from 4735 and 3050; *possession of Jah; Miknejah*, an Isr.:—Mikneiah.

4738. מִקְסָם **miqçâm**, *mik-sawm';* from 7080; an *augury:*—divination.

4739. מָקַץ **Mâqats**, *maw-kats';* from 7112; *end; Makats*, a place in Pal.:—Makaz.

4740. מַקְצוֹעַ **maqtsôwaʻ**, *mak-tso'-ah;* or

מַקְצֹעַ **maqtsôaʻ**, *mak-tso'-ah;* or (fem.)

מַקְצֹעָה **maqtsôʻâh**, *mak-tso-aw';* from 7106 in the denom. sense of *bending;* an *angle* or recess:—corner, turning.

4741. מַקְצֻעָה **maqtsûʻâh**, *mak-tsoo-aw';* from 7106; a *scraper*, i.e. a carving *chisel:*—plane.

4742. מְקֻצְעָה **mequtsʻâh**, *mek-oots-aw';* from 7106 in the denom. sense of *bending;* an *angle:*—corner.

4743. מָקַק **mâqaq**, *maw-kak';* a prim. root; to *melt;* fig. to *flow*, *dwindle*, *vanish:*—consume away, be corrupt, dissolve, pine away.

מָקֹר **mâqôr**. See 4726.

4744. מִקְרָא **miqrâʼ**, *mik-raw';* from 7121; something *called* out, i.e. a public *meeting* (the act, the persons, or the place); also a *rehearsal:*—assembly, calling, convocation, reading.

4745. מִקְרֶה **miqreh**, *mik-reh';* from 7136; something *met* with, i.e. an *accident* or *fortune:*—something befallen, befalleth, chance, event, hap (-peneth).

4746. מְקָרֶה **meqâreh**, *mek-aw-reh'*; from 7136; prop. something *meeting*, i.e. a *frame* (of timbers):—building.

4747. מְקֵרָה **meqêrâh**, *mek-ay-raw'*; from the same as 7119; a *cooling* off:—× summer.

מֹקֵשׁ **môqêsh**. See 4170.

4748. מִקְשֶׁה **miqsheh**, *mik-sheh'*; from 7185 in the sense of *knotting* up round and hard; something *turned* (rounded), i.e. a *curl* (of tresses):—× well [set] hair.

4749. מִקְשָׁה **miqshâh**, *mik-shaw'*; fem. of 4748; *rounded* work, i.e. moulded by *hammering* (*repoussé*):—beaten (out of one piece, work), upright, whole piece.

4750. מִקְשָׁה **miqshâh**, *mik-shaw'*; denom. from 7180; lit. a *cucumbered* field, i.e. a *cucumber* patch:—garden of cucumbers.

4751. מַר **mar**, *mar*; or (fem.)

מָרָה **mârâh**, *maw-raw'*; from 4843; *bitter* (lit. or fig.); also (as noun) *bitterness*, or (adv.) *bitterly*:—+ angry, bitter (-ly, -ness), chafed, discontented, × great, heavy.

4752. מַר **mar**, *mar*; from 4843 in its orig. sense of *distillation*; a *drop*:—drop.

4753. מֹר **môr**, *more*; or

מוֹר **môwr**, *more*; from 4843; *myrrh* (as *distilling* in drops, and also as *bitter*):—myrrh.

4754. מָרָא **mârâ'**, *maw-raw'*; a prim. root; to *rebel*; hence (through the idea of *maltreating*) to *whip*, i.e. *lash* (self with wings, as the ostrich in running):—be filthy, lift up self.

4755. מָרָא **Mârâ'**, *maw-raw'*; for 4751 fem.; *bitter*; *Mara*, a symbol. name of Naomi:—Mara.

4756. מָרֵא **mârê'** (Chald.), *maw-ray'*; from a root corresp. to 4754 in the sense of *domineering*; a *master*:—lord, Lord.

מֹרָא **môrâ'**. See 4172.

4757. מְרֹאדַךְ בַּלְאֲדָן **Merô'dak Bal'âdân**, *mer-o-dak' bal-aw-dawn'*; of for. der.; *Merodak-Baladan*, a Bab. king:—Merodach-baladan. Comp. 4781.

4758. מַרְאֶה **mar'eh**, *mar-eh'*; from 7200; a *view* (the act of seeing); also an *appearance* (the thing seen), whether (real) a *shape* (espec. if handsome, *comeliness*; often plur. the *looks*), or (mental) a *vision*:—× apparently, appearance (-reth), × as soon as beautiful (-ly), countenance, fair, favoured, form, goodly, to look (up) on (to), look [-eth], pattern, to see, seem, sight, visage, vision.

4759. מַרְאָה **mar'âh**, *mar-aw'*; fem. of 4758; a *vision*; also (causat.) a *mirror*:—looking glass, vision.

4760. מֻרְאָה **mur'âh**, *moor-aw'*; appar. fem. pass. causat. part. of 7200; something *conspicuous*, i.e. the *craw* of a bird (from its *prominence*):—crop.

מֵרֹאוֹן **Mer'ôwn**. See 8112.

4761. מַרְאָשָׁה **mar'âshâh**, *mar-aw-shaw'*; denom. from 7218; prop. *headship*, i.e. (plur. for collect.) *dominion*:—principality.

4762 מַרְאֵשָׁה **Mar'êshâh**, *mar-ay-shaw'*; or

מָרֵשָׁה **Marêshâh**, *mar-ay-shaw'*; formed like 4761; *summit*; *Mareshah*, the name of two Isr. and of a place in Pal.:—Mareshah.

4763. מְרַאֲשָׁה **mera'ăshâh** *mer-ah-ash-aw'*; formed like 4761; prop. a *headpiece*, i.e. (plur. for adv.) *at* (or *as*) the *head-rest* (or pillow):—bolster, head, pillow. Comp. 4772.

4764. מֵרַב **Mêrâb**, *may-rawb'*; from 7231; *increase*; *Merab*, a daughter of Saul:—Merab.

4765. מַרְבַד **marbad**, *mar-bad'*; from 7234; a *coverlet*:—covering of tapestry.

4766. מַרְבֶּה **marbeh**, *mar-beh'*; from 7235; prop. *increasing*; as noun, *greatness*, or (adv.) *greatly*:—great, increase.

4767. מִרְבָּה **mirbâh**, *meer-baw'*; from 7235; *abundance*, i.e. a great quantity:—much.

4768. מַרְבִּית **marbîyth**, *mar-beeth'*; from 7235; a *multitude*; also *offspring*; spec. *interest* (on capital):—greatest part, greatness, increase, multitude.

4769. מַרְבֵּץ **marbêts**, *mar-bates'*; from 7257; a *reclining* place, i.e. *fold* (for flocks):—couching place, place to lie down.

4770. מַרְבֵּק **marbêq**, *mar-bake'*; from an unused root mean. to *tie* up; a *stall* (for cattle):—× fat (-ted), stall.

מֹרַג **môrag**. See 4173.

4771. מַרְגּוֹעַ **margôwa'**, *mar-go'-ah*; from 7280; a *resting* place:—rest.

4772. מַרְגְּלָה **margelâh**, *mar-ghel-aw'*; denom. from 7272; (plur. for collect.) a *footpiece*, i.e. (adv.) *at the foot*, or (direct.) the *foot* itself:—feet. Comp. 4763.

4773. מַרְגֵּמָה **margêmâh**, *mar-gay-maw'*; from 7275; a *stone*-heap:—sling.

4774. מַרְגֵּעָה **margê'âh**, *mar-gay-aw'*; from 7280; *rest*:—refreshing.

4775. מָרַד **mârad**, *maw-rad'*; a prim. root; to *rebel*:—rebel (-lious).

4776. מְרַד **merad** (Chald.), *mer-ad'*; from a root corresp. to 4775; *rebellion*:—rebellion.

4777. מֶרֶד **mered**, *meh'-red*; from 4775; *rebellion*:—rebellion.

4778. מֶרֶד **Mered**, *meh'-red*; the same as 4777; *Mered*, an Isr.:—Mered.

4779. מָרָד **mârâd** (Chald.), *maw-rawd'*; from the same as 4776; *rebellious*:—rebellious.

4780. מַרְדּוּת **mardûwth**, *mar-dooth'*; from 4775; *rebelliousness*:—× rebellious.

4781. מְרֹדָךְ **Merôdâk**, *mer-o-dawk'*; of for. der.; *Merodak*, a Bab. idol:—Merodach. Comp. 4757.

4782. מָרְדֳּכַי **Mordekay**, *mor-dek-ah'ee*; of for. der.; *Mordecai*, an Isr.:—Mordecai.

4783. מֻרְדָּף **murdâph**, *moor-dawf'*; from 7291; *persecuted*:—persecuted.

4784. מָרָה **mârâh**, *maw-raw'*; a prim. root; to *be* (caus. *make*) *bitter* (or unpleasant); (fig.) to *rebel* (or resist; causat. to *provoke*):—bitter, change, be disobedient, disobey, grievously, provocation, provoke (-ing), (be) rebel (against, -lious).

4785. מָרָה **Mârâh**, *maw-raw'*; the same as 4751 fem.; *bitter*; *Marah*, a place in the Desert:—Marah.

מוֹרֶה **Môreh**. See 4175.

4786. מֹרָה **môrâh**, *mo-raw'*; from 4843; *bitterness*, i.e. (fig.) *trouble*:—grief.

4787. מָרָּה **morrâh**, *mor-raw'*; a form of 4786; *trouble*:—bitterness.

4788. מָרוּד **mârûwd**, *maw-rood'*; from 7300 in the sense of *maltreatment*; an *outcast*; (abstr.) *destitution*:—cast out, misery.

4789. מֵרוֹז **Mêrôwz**, *may-roze'*; of uncert. der.; *Meroz*, a place in Pal.:—Meroz.

4790. מְרוֹחַ **merôwach**, *mer-o-akh'*; from 4799; *bruised*, i.e. *emasculated*:—broken.

4791. מָרוֹם **mârôwm**, *maw-rome'*; from 7311; *altitude*, i.e. concr. (an *elevated place*), abstr. (*elevation*), fig. (*elation*), or adv. (*aloft*):—(far) above, dignity, haughty, height, (most, on) high (one, place), loftily, upward.

4792. מֵרוֹם **Mêrôwm**, *may-rome'*; formed like 4791; *height*; *Merom*, a lake in Pal.:—Merom.

4793. מֵרוֹץ **mêrôwts**, *may-rotes'*; from 7323; a *run* (the trial of speed):—race.

4794. מְרוּצָה **merûwtsâh**, *mer-oo-tsaw'*; or

מְרֻצָה **merûtsâh**, *mer-oo-tsaw'*; fem. of 4793; a *race* (the act), whether the manner or the progress:—course, running. Comp. 4835.

4795. מָרוּק **mârûwq**, *maw-rook'*; from 4838; prop. *rubbed*; but used abstr., a *rubbing* (with perfumery):—purification.

מְרוֹר **merôwr**. See 4844.

מְרוֹרָה **merôwrâh**. See 4846.

4796. מָרוֹת **Mârôwth**, *maw-rohth'*; plur. of 4751 fem.; *bitter* springs; *Maroth*, a place in Pal.:—Maroth.

4797. מִרְזַח **mirzach**, *meer-zakh'*; from an unused root mean. to *scream*; a *cry*, i.e. (of joy), a *revel*:—banquet.

4798. מַרְזֵחַ **marzêach**, *mar-zay'-akh*; formed like 4797; a *cry*, i.e. (of grief) a *lamentation*:—mourning.

4799. מָרַח **mârach**, *maw-rakh'*; a prim. root; prop. to *soften* by rubbing or pressure; hence (medicinally) to *apply* as an emollient:—lay for a plaister.

4800. מֶרְחָב **merchâb**, *mer-khawb'*; from 7337; *enlargement*, either lit. (an *open space*, usually in a good sense), or fig. (*liberty*):—breadth, large place (room).

4801. מֶרְחָק **merchâq**, *mer-khawk'*; from 7368; *remoteness*, i.e. (concr.) a *distant* place; often (adv.) *from afar*:—(a-, dwell in, very) far (country, off). See also 1023.

4802. מַרְחֶשֶׁת **marchesheth**, *mar-kheh'-sheth*; from 7370; a *stew*-pan:—fryingpan.

4803. מָרַט **mâraṭ**, *maw-rat'*; a prim. root; to *polish*; by impl. to *make bald* (the head), to *gall* (the shoulder); also, to *sharpen*:—bright, furbish, (have his) hair (be) fallen off, peeled, pluck off (hair).

4804. מְרַט **meraṭ** (Chald.), *mer-at'*; corresp. to 4803; to *pull* off:—be plucked.

4805. מְרִי **merîy**, *mer-ee'*; from 4784; *bitterness*, i.e. (fig.) *rebellion*; concr. *bitter*, or *rebellious*:—bitter, (most) rebel (-lion, -lious).

4806. מְרִיא **merîy'**, *mer-ee'*; from 4754 in the sense of *grossness*, through the idea of *domineering* (comp. 4756); *stall-fed*; often (as noun) a *beeve*:—fat (fed) beast (cattle, -ling).

4807. מְרִיב בַּעַל **Merîyb Ba'al**, *mer-eeb' bah'-al*; from 7378 and 1168; *quarreller of Baal*; *Merib-Baal*, an epithet of Gideon:—Merib-baal. Comp. 4810.

4808. מְרִיבָה **merîybâh**, *mer-ee-baw'*; from 7378; *quarrel*:—provocation, strife.

4809. מְרִיבָה **Merîybâh**, *mer-ee-baw'*; the same as 4808; *Meribah*, the name of two places in the Desert:—Meribah.

4810. מְרִי בַעַל **Merîy Ba'al**, *mer-ee' bah'-al*; from 4805 and 1168; *rebellion of* (i.e. *against*) *Baal*; *Meri-Baal*, an epithet of Gideon:—Meri-baal. Comp. 4807.

4811. מְרָיָה **Merâyâh**, *mer-aw-yaw'*; from 4784; *rebellion*; *Merajah*, an Isr.:—Meraiah. Comp. 3236.

מֹרִיָּה **Môrîyâh**. See 4179.

4812. מְרָיוֹת **Merâyôwth**, *mer-aw-yohth'*; plur. of 4811; *rebellious*; *Merajoth*, the name of two Isr.:—Meraioth.

4813. מִרְיָם **Miryâm**, *meer-yawm'*; from 4805; *rebelliously*; *Mirjam*, the name of two Israelitesses:—Miriam.

4814. מְרִירוּת **merîyrûwth**, *mer-ee-rooth'*; from 4843; *bitterness*, i.e. (fig.) *grief*:—bitterness.

4815. מְרִירִי **merîyrîy**, *mer-ee-ree'*; from 4843; *bitter*, i.e. *poisonous*:—bitter.

4816. מֹרֶךְ **môrek**, *mo'-rek*; perh. from 7401; *softness*, i.e. (fig.) *fear*:—faintness.

4817. מֶרְכָּב **merkâb**, *mer-kawb'*; from 7392; a *chariot*; also a *seat* (in a vehicle):—chariot, covering, saddle.

4818. מֶרְכָּבָה **merkâbâh**, *mer-kaw-baw'*; fem. of 4817; a *chariot*:—chariot. See also 1024.

4819. מַרְכֹּלֶת **markôleth**, *mar-ko'-leth*; from 7402; a *mart*:—merchandise.

4820. מִרְמָה **mirmâh**, *meer-maw'*; from 7411 in the sense of *deceiving; fraud*:—craft, deceit (-ful, -fully), false, feigned, guile, subtilly, treachery.

4821. מִרְמָה **Mirmâh**, *meer-maw'*; the same as 4820; *Mirmah*, an Isr.:—Mirma.

4822. מְרֵמוֹת **Mᵉrêmôwth**, *mer-ay-mohth'*; plur. from 7311; *heights; Meremoth*, the name of two Isr :—Meremoth.

4823. מִרְמָס **mirmâç**, *meer-mawce'*; from 7429; *abasement* (the act or the thing):—tread (down) -ing, (to be) trodden (down) under foot.

4824. מֵרֹנֹתִי **Mêrônôthîy**, *may-ro-no-thee'*; patrial from an unused noun; a *Meronothite*, or inhab. of some (otherwise unknown) Meronoth:—Meronothite.

4825. מֶרֶס **Mereç**, *meh'-res*; of for. der.; *Meres*, a Pers.:—Meres.

4826. מַרְסְנָא **Marçᵉnâ'**, *mar-sen-aw'*; of for. der.; *Marsena*, a Pers.:—Marsena.

4827. מֵרַע **mêra'**, *may-rah'*; from 7489; used as (abstr.) noun, *wickedness*:—do mischief.

4828. מֵרֵעַ **mêrêa'**, *may-ray'-ah*; from 7462 in the sense of *companionship*; a *friend*:—companion, friend.

4829. מִרְעֶה **mir'eh**, *meer-eh'*; from 7462 in the sense of *feeding; pasture* (the place or the act); also the *haunt* of wild animals:—feeding place, pasture.

4830. מִרְעִית **mir'îyth**, *meer-eeth'*; from 7462 in the sense of *feeding; pasturage*; concr. a *flock*:—flock, pasture.

4831. מַרְעֲלָה **Mar'âlâh**, *mar-al-aw'*; from 7477; perh. *earthquake; Maralah*, a place in Pal.:—Maralah.

4832. מַרְפֵּא **marpê'**, *mar-pay'*; from 7495; prop. *curative*, i.e. lit. (concr.) a *medicine*, or (abstr.) a *cure*; fig. (concr.) *deliverance*, or (abstr.) *placidity*:—([in-]) cure (-able), healing (-lth), remedy, sound, wholesome, yielding.

4833. מִרְפָּשׂ **mirpâs**, *meer-paws'*; from 7515; *muddled* water:—that which . . . have fouled.

4834. מָרַץ **mârats**, *maw-rats'*; a prim. root; prop. to *press*, i.e. (fig.) to be *pungent* or vehement; to *irritate*:—embolden, be forcible, grievous, sore.

4835. מְרֻצָה **mᵉrûtsâh**, *mer-oo-tsaw'*; from 7533; *oppression*:—violence. See also 4794.

4836. מַרְצֵעַ **martsêa'**, *mar-tsay'-ah*; from 7527; an *awl*:—aul.

4837. מַרְצֶפֶת **martsepheth**, *mar-tseh'-feth*; from 7528; a *pavement*:—pavement.

4838. מָרַק **mâraq**, *maw-rak'*; a prim. root; to *polish*; by impl. to *sharpen*; also to *rinse*:—bright, furbish, scour.

4839. מָרָק **mârâq**, *maw-rawk'*; from 4838; *soup* (as if a *rinsing*):—broth. See also 6564.

4840. מֶרְקָח **merqâch**, *mer-kawkh'*; from 7543; a *spicy* herb:— × sweet.

4841. מֶרְקָחָה **merqâchâh**, *mer-kaw-khaw'*, fem. of 4840; abstr. a *seasoning* (with spicery); concr. an *unguent-kettle* (for preparing spiced oil):—pot of ointment, × well.

4842. מִרְקַחַת **mirqachath**, *meer-kakh'-ath*; from 7543; an aromatic *unguent*; also an *unguent-pot*:—prepared by the apothecaries' art, compound, ointment.

4843. מָרַר **mârar**, *maw-rar'*; a prim. root; prop. to *trickle* [see 4752]; but used only as a denom. from 4751; to *be* (causat. make) *bitter* (lit. or fig.):—(be, be in, deal, have, make) bitter (-ly, -ness), be moved with choler, (be, have sorely, it) grieved (-eth), provoke, vex.

4844. מְרֹר **mᵉrôr**, *mer-ore'*; or

מְרוֹר **mᵉrôwr**, *mer-ore'*; from 4843; a *bitter* herb:—bitter (-ness).

4845. מְרֵרָה **mᵉrêrâh**, *mer-ay-raw'*; from 4843; *bile* (from its bitterness):—gall.

4846. מְרֹרָה **mᵉrôrâh**, *mer-o-raw'*; or

מְרוֹרָה **mᵉrôwrâh**, *mer-o-raw'*; from 4843; prop. *bitterness*; concr. a *bitter thing*; spec. *bile*; also *venom* (of a serpent):—bitter (thing), gall.

4847. מְרָרִי **Mᵉrârîy**, *mer-aw-ree'*; from 4843; *bitter; Merari*, an Isr.:—Merari. See also 4848.

4848. מְרָרִי **Mᵉrârîy**, *mer-aw-ree'*; from 4847; a *Merarite* (collect.), or desc. of Merari:—Merarites.

מָרֵשָׁה **Mârêshâh**. See 4762.

4849. מִרְשַׁעַת **mirsha'ath**, *meer-shah'-ath*; from 7561; a female *wicked doer*:—wicked woman.

4850. מְרָתַיִם **Mᵉrâthayim**, *mer-aw-thah'-yim*; dual of 4751 fem.; *double bitterness; Merathajim*, an epithet of Babylon:—Merathaim.

4851. מַשׁ **Mash**, *mash*; of for. der.; *Mash*, a son of Aram, and the people desc. from him:—Mash.

4852. מֵשָׁא **Mêshâ'**, *may-shaw'*; of for. der.; *Mesha*, a place in Arabia:—Mesha.

4853. מַשָּׂא **massâ'**, *mas-saw'*; from 5375; a *burden*; spec. *tribute*, or (abstr.) *porterage*; fig. an *utterance*, chiefly a *doom*, espec. *singing*; mental, *desire*:—burden, carry away, prophecy, × they set, song, tribute.

4854. מַשָּׂא **Massâ'**, *mas-saw'*; the same as 4853; *burden; Massa*, a son of Ishmael:—Massa.

4855. מַשָּׁא **mashshâ'**, *mash-shaw'*; from 5383; a *loan*; by impl. *interest* on a debt:—exaction, usury.

4856. מַשֹּׂא **massô'**, *mas-so'*; from 5375; *partiality* (as a *lifting* up):—respect.

4857. מַשְׁאָב **mash'âb**, *mash-awb'*; from 7579; a *trough* for cattle to drink from:—place of drawing water.

מְשֹׁאָה **mᵉshô'âh**. See 4875.

4858. מַשָּׂאָה **massâ'âh**, *mas-saw-aw'*; from 5375; a *conflagration* (from the *rising* of smoke):—burden.

4859. מַשָּׁאָה **mashshâ'âh**, *mash-shaw-aw'*; fem. of 4855; a *loan*:— × any [-thing], debt.

מַשֻּׁאָה **mashshû'âh**. See 4876.

4860. מַשָּׁאוֹן **mashshâ'ôwn**, *mash-shaw-ohn'*; from 5377; *dissimulation*:—deceit.

4861. מִשְׁאָל **Mish'âl**, *mish-awl'*; from 7592; *request; Mishal*, a place in Pal.:—Mishal, Misheal. Comp. 4913.

4862. מִשְׁאָלָה **mish'âlâh**, *mish-aw-law'*; from 7592; a *request*:—desire, petition.

4863. מִשְׁאֶרֶת **mish'ereth**, *mish-eh'-reth*; from 7604 in the orig. sense of *swelling*; a *kneading-trough* (in which the dough *rises*):—kneading trough, store.

4864. מַשְׂאֵת **mas'êth**, *mas-ayth'*; from 5375; prop. (abstr.) a *raising* (as of the hands in prayer), or *rising* (of flame); fig. an *utterance*; concr. a *beacon* (as *raised*); a *present* (as taken), *mess*, or *tribute*; fig. a *reproach* (as a burden):—burden, collection, sign of fire, (great) flame, gift, lifting up, mess, oblation, reward.

מֹשָׁב **môshâb**. See 4186.

מְשֻׁבָה **mᵉshûbâh**. See 4878.

4865. מִשְׁבְּצָה **mishbᵉtsâh**, *mish-bets-aw'*; from 7660; a *brocade*; by anal. a (reticulated) *setting* of a gem:—ouch, wrought.

4866. מִשְׁבֵּר **mishbêr**, *mish-bare'*; from 7665; the *orifice* of the womb (from which the fœtus *breaks* forth):—birth, breaking forth.

4867. מִשְׁבָּר **mishbâr**, *mish-bawr'*; from 7665; a *breaker* (of the sea):—billow, wave.

4868. מִשְׁבָּת **mishbâth**, *mish-bawth'*; from 7673; *cessation*, i.e. destruction:—sabbath.

4869. מִשְׂגָּב **misgâb**, *mis-gawb'*; from 7682; prop. a *cliff* (or other *lofty* or *inaccessible* place); abstr. *altitude*; fig. a *refuge*:—defence, high fort (tower), refuge.

4869; *Misgab*, a place in Moab:—Misgab.

4870'. מִשְׁגֶּה **mishgeh**, *mish-gay'*; from 7686; an *error*:—oversight.

4871. מָשָׁה **mâshâh**, *maw-shaw'*; a prim. root; to *pull* out (lit. or fig.):—draw (out). draw (out).

4872. מֹשֶׁה **Môsheh**, *mo-sheh'*; from 4871; *drawing* out (of the water), i.e. *rescued*; *Mosheh*, the Isr. lawgiver:—Moses.

4873. מֹשֶׁה **Môsheh** (Chald.), *mo-sheh'*; corresp. to 4872:—Moses.

4874. מַשֶּׁה **mashsheh**, *mash-sheh'*; from 5383; a *debt*:— + creditor.

4875. מְשׁוֹאָה **mᵉshôw'âh**, *mesh-o-aw'*; or

מְשֹׁאָה **mᵉshô'âh**, *mesh-o-aw'*; from the same as 7722; (a) *ruin*, abstr. (the act) or concr. (the wreck):—desolation, waste.

4876. מַשּׁוּאָה **mashshûw'âh**, *mash-shoo-aw'*; or

מַשֻּׁאָה **mashshû'âh**, *mash-shoo-aw'*; for 4875; *ruin*:—desolation, destruction.

4877. מְשׁוֹבָב **Mᵉshôwbâb**, *mesh-o-bawb'*; from 7725; *returned*; *Meshobab*, an Isr.:—Meshobab.

4878. מְשׁוּבָה **mᵉshûwbâh**, *mesh-oo-baw'*; or

מְשֻׁבָה **mᵉshûbâh**, *mesh-oo-baw'*; from 7725; *apostasy*:—backsliding, turning away.

4879. מְשׁוּגָה **mᵉshûwgâh**, *mesh-oo-gaw'*; from an unused root mean. to *stray*; *mistake*:—error.

4880. מָשׁוֹט **mâshôwṭ**, *maw-shote'*; or

מִשּׁוֹט **mishshôwṭ**, *mish-shote'*; from 7751; an *oar*:—oar.

4881. מְשׂוּכָה° **mᵉsûwkâh**, *mes-oo-kaw'*; or

מְשֻׂכָה **mesûkâh**, *mes-oo-kaw'*; from 7753; a *hedge*:—hedge.

4882. מְשׁוּסָה° **mᵉshûwçâh**, *mesh-oo-saw'*; from an unused root mean. to *plunder*; *spoliation*:—spoil.

4883. מַשּׂוֹר **massôwr**, *mas-sore'*; from an unused root mean. to *rasp*; a *saw*:—saw.

4884. מְשׂוּרָה **mᵉsûwrâh**, *mes-oo-raw'*; from an unused root mean. appar. to *divide*; a *measure* (for liquids):—measure.

4885. מָשׂוֹשׂ **mâsôws**, *maw-soce'*; from 7797; *delight*, concr. (the cause or object) or abstr. (the feeling):—joy, mirth, rejoice.

4886. מָשַׁח **mâshach**, *maw-shakh'*; a prim. root; to *rub* with oil, i.e. to *anoint*; by impl. to *consecrate*; also to *paint*:—anoint, paint.

4887. מְשַׁח **mᵉshach** (Chald.), *mesh-akh'*; from a root corresp. to 4886; *oil*:—oil.

4888. מִשְׁחָה **mishchâh**, *meesh-khaw'*; or

מָשְׁחָה **moshchâh**, *mosh-khaw'*; from 4886; *unction* (the act); by impl. a consecratory *gift*:—(to be) anointed (-ing), ointment.

4889. מַשְׁחִית **mashchîyth**, *mash-kheeth'*; from 7843; *destructive*, i.e. (as noun) *destruction*, lit. (spec. a *snare*) or fig. (*corruption*):—corruption, (to) destroy (-ing), destruction, trap, × utterly.

4890. מִשְׂחָק **mischâq**, *mis-khawk'*; from 7831; a *laughing-stock*:—scorn.

4891. מִשְׁחָר **mishchâr**, *mish-khawr'*; from 7836 in the sense of day *breaking*; *dawn*:—morning.

4892. מַשְׁחֵת **mashchêth**, *mash-khayth'*; for 4889; *destruction*:—destroying.

4893. מִשְׁחָת **mishchâth**, *mish-khawth'*; or

מָשְׁחָת **moshchâth**, *mosh-khawth'*; from 7843; *disfigurement*:—corruption, marred.

4894. מִשְׁטוֹחַ **mishṭôwach**, *mish-to'-akh*; or

מִשְׁטַח **mishṭach**, *mish-takh'*; from 7849; a *spreading*-place:—(to) spread (forth, -ing, upon).

4895. מַשְׂטֵמָה **masṭêmâh**, *mas-tay-maw'*; from the same as 7850; *enmity*:—hatred.

4896. מִשְׁטָר **mishṭâr**, *mish-tawr'*; from 7860; *jurisdiction:*—dominion.

4897. מֶשִׁי **meshîy**, *meh'-shee*; from 4871; *silk* (as *drawn* from the cocoon):—silk.

מֻשִׁי **Mûshîy**. See 4187.

4898. מְשֵׁיזַבְאֵל **Meshêyzab'êl**, *mesh-ay-zab-ale'*; from an equiv. to 7804 and 410; *delivered of God; Meshezabel*, an Isr.:—Meshezabeel.

4899. מָשִׁיחַ **mâshîyach**, *maw-shee'-akh*; from 4886; *anointed;* usually a *consecrated person* (as a king, priest, or saint); spec. the *Messiah:*—anointed, Messiah.

4900. מָשַׁךְ **mâshak**, *maw-shak'*; a prim. root; to *draw*, used in a great variety of applications (includ. to *sow*, to *sound*, to *prolong*, to *develop*, to *march*, to *remove*, to *delay*, to *be tall*, etc.):—draw (along, out), continue, defer, extend, forbear, × give, handle, make (pro-, sound) long, × sow, scatter, stretch out.

4901. מֶשֶׁךְ **meshek**, *meh'-shek*; from 4900; a *sowing;* also a *possession:*—precious, price.

4902. מֶשֶׁךְ **Meshek**, *meh'-shek;* the same in form as 4901, but prob. of for. der.; *Meshek*, a son of Japheth, and the people desc. from him:—Mesech, Meshech.

4903. מִשְׁכַּב **mishkab** (Chald.), *mish-kab'*; corresp. to 4904; a *bed:*—bed.

4904. מִשְׁכָּב **mishkâb**, *mish-kawb'*; from 7901; a *bed* (fig. a *bier*); abstr. *sleep;* by euphem. carnal *intercourse:*—bed ([-chamber]), couch, lieth (lying) with.

מְשֻׂכָה **mesûkâh**. See 4881.

4905. מַשְׂכִּיל **maskîyl**, *mas-keel'*; from 7919; *instructive*, i.e. a *didactic* poem:—Maschil.

מַשְׁכִּים **mashkiym**. See 7925.

4906. מַשְׂכִּית **maskîyth**, *mas-keeth'*; from the same as 7906; a *figure* (carved on stone, the wall, or any object); fig. *imagination:*—conceit, image (-ry), picture, × wish.

4907. מִשְׁכַּן **mishkan** (Chald.), *mish-kan'*; corresp. to 4908; *residence:*—habitation.

4908. מִשְׁכָּן **mishkân**, *mish-kawn'*; from 7931; a *residence* (includ. a shepherd's *hut*, the *lair* of animals, fig. the *grave;* also the *Temple*); spec. the *Tabernacle* (prop. its wooden walls):—dwelleth, dwelling (place), habitation, tabernacle, tent.

4909. מַשְׂכֹּרֶת **maskôreth**, *mas-koh'-reth;* from 7936; *wages* or a *reward:*—reward, wages.

4910. מָשַׁל **mâshal**, *maw-shal'*; a prim. root; to *rule:*—(have, make to have) dominion, governor, × indeed, reign, (bear, cause to, have) rule (-ing, -r), have power.

4911. משׁל **mâshal**, *maw-shal'*; denom. from 4912; to *liken*, i.e. (trans.) to use figurative language (an allegory, adage, song or the like); intrans. to *resemble:*—be (-come) like, compare, use (as a) proverb, speak (in proverbs), utter.

4912. מָשָׁל **mâshâl**, *maw-shawl'*; appar. from 4910 in some orig. sense of *superiority* in mental action; prop. a pithy *maxim*, usually of a metaphorical nature; hence a *simile* (as an adage, poem, discourse):—byword, like, parable, proverb.

4913. מָשָׁל **Mâshâl**, *maw-shawl'*; for 4861; *Mashal*, a place in Pal.:—Mashal.

4914. מְשׁוֹל **meshôwl**, *mesh-ol'*; from 4911; a *satire:*—byword.

4915. מֹשֶׁל **môshel**, *mo'-shel;* (1) from 4910; *empire;* (2) from 4911; a *parallel:*—dominion, like.

מִשְׁלוֹשׁ **mishlôwsh**. See 7969.

4916. מִשְׁלוֹחַ **mishlôwach**, *mish-lo'-akh;* or

מִשְׁלֹחַ **mishlôach**, *mish-lo'-akh;* also

מִשְׁלָח **mishlâch**, *mish-lawkh'*; from 7971; a *sending* out, i.e. (abstr.) *presentation* (favorable), or *seizure* (unfavorable); also (concr.) a place of *dismissal*, or a *business* to be discharged:—to lay, to put, sending (forth), to set.

4917. מִשְׁלַחַת **mishlachath**, *mish-lakh'-ath;* fem. of 4916; a *mission*, i.e. (abstr. and favorable) *release*, or (concr. and unfavorable) an *army:*—discharge, sending.

4918. מְשֻׁלָּם **Meshullâm**, *mesh-ool-lawm'*; from 7999; *allied; Meshullam*, the name of seventeen Isr.:—Meshullam.

4919. מְשִׁלֵּמוֹת **Meshillêmôwth**, *mesh-il-lay-mohth'*; plur. from 7999; *reconciliations:*—*Meshillemoth*, an Isr.:—Meshillemoth. Comp. 4921.

4920. מְשֶׁלֶמְיָה **Meshelemyâh**, *mesh-eh-lem-yaw'*; or

מְשֶׁלֶמְיָהוּ **Meshelemyâhûw**, *mesh-eh-lem-yaw'-hoo;* from 7999 and 3050; *ally of Jah; Meshelemjah*, an Isr.:—Meshelemiah.

4921. מְשִׁלֵּמִית **Meshillêmîyth**, *mesh-il-lay-meeth'*; from 7999; *reconciliation; Meshillemith*, an Isr.:—Meshillemith. Comp. 4919.

4922. מְשֻׁלֶּמֶת **Meshullemeth**, *mesh-ool-leh'-meth;* fem. of 4918; *Meshullemeth*, an Israelitess:—Meshullemeth.

4923. מְשַׁמָּה **meshammâh**, *mesh-am-maw'*; from 8074; a *waste* or *amazement:*—astonishment, desolate.

4924. מַשְׁמָן **mashmân**, *mash-mawn'*; from 8080; *fat*, i.e. (lit. and abstr.) *fatness;* but usually (fig. and concr.) a *rich* dish, a *fertile* field, a *robust* man:—fat (one, -ness, -test, -test place).

4925. מִשְׁמַנָּה **Mishmannâh**, *mish-man-naw'*; from 8080; *fatness; Mashmannah*, an Isr.:—Mishmannah.

4926. מִשְׁמָע **mishmâ'**, *mish-maw';* from 8085; a *report:*—hearing.

4927. מִשְׁמָע **Mishmâ'**, *mish-maw';* the same as 4926; *Mishma*, the name of a son of Ishmael, and of an Isr.:—Mishma.

4928. מִשְׁמַעַת **mishma'ath**, *mish-mah'-ath;* fem. of 4926; *audience*, i.e. the royal *court;* also *obedience*, i.e. (concr.) a *subject:*—bidding, guard, obey.

4929. מִשְׁמָר **mishmâr**, *mish-mawr'*; from 8104; a *guard* (the man, the post, or the *prison*); fig. a *deposit;* also (as observed) a *usage* (abstr.), or an *example* (concr.):—diligence, guard, office, prison, ward, watch.

4930. מַשְׂמְרָה **masmerâh**, *mas-mer-aw'*; for 4548 fem.; a *peg:*—nail.

4931. מִשְׁמֶרֶת **mishmereth**, *mish-meh'-reth;* fem. of 4929; *watch*, i.e. the act (*custody*) or (concr.) the *sentry*, the *post;* obj. *preservation*, or (concr.) *safe;* fig. *observance*, i.e. (abstr.) *duty*, or (obj.) a *usage* or *party:*—charge, keep, to be kept, office, ordinance, safeguard, ward, watch.

4932. מִשְׁנֶה **mishneh**, *mish-neh';* from 8138; prop. a *repetition*, i.e. a *duplicate* (*copy* of a document), or a *double* (in amount); by impl. a *second* (in order, rank, age, quality or location):—college, copy, double, fatlings, next, second (order), twice as much.

4933. מְשִׁסָּה **mechiççâh**, *mesh-is-saw'*; from 8155; *plunder:*—booty, spoil.

4934. מִשְׁעוֹל **mish'ôwl**, *mish-ole';* from the same as 8168; a *hollow*, i.e. a narrow passage:—path.

4935. מִשְׁעִי **mish'îy**, *mish-ee';* prob. from 8159; *inspection:*—to supple.

4936. מִשְׁעָם **Mish'âm**, *mish-awm';* appar. from 8159; *inspection; Misham*, an Isr.:—Misham.

4937. מִשְׁעֵן **mish'ên**, *mish-ane';* or

מִשְׁעָן **mish'ân**, *mish-awn';* from 8172; a *support* (concr.), i.e. (fig.) a *protector* or *sustenance:*—stay.

4938. מִשְׁעֵנָה **mish'ênâh**, *mish-ay-naw';* or

מִשְׁעֶנֶת **mish'eneth**, *mish-eh'-neth;* fem. of 4937; *support* (abstr.), i.e. (fig.) *sustenance* or (concr.) a *walking-stick:*—staff.

4939. מִשְׂפָּח **mispâch**, *mis-pawkh';* from 5596; *slaughter:*—oppression.

4940. מִשְׁפָּחָה **mishpâchâh**, *mish-paw-khaw';* from 8192 [comp. 8198]; a *family*, i.e. circle of relatives; fig. a *class* (of persons), a *species* (of animals) or *sort* (of things); by extens. a *tribe* or *people:*—family, kind (-red).

4941. מִשְׁפָּט **mishpâṭ**, *mish-pawt';* from 8199; prop. a *verdict* (favorable or unfavorable) pronounced judicially, espec. a *sentence* or formal decree (human or [partic.] divine *law*, individual or collect.), includ. the act, the place, the suit, the crime, and the penalty; abstr. *justice*, includ. a partic. *right*, or *privilege* (statutory or customary), or even a *style:*— + adversary, ceremony, charge, × crime, custom, desert, determination, discretion, disposing, due, fashion, form, to be judged, judgment, just (-ice, -ly), (manner of) law (-ful), manner, measure, (due) order, ordinance, right, sentence, usest, × worthy, + wrong.

4942. מִשְׁפָּת **mishpâth**, *mish-pawth';* from 8192; a *stall* for cattle (only dual):—burden, sheepfold.

4943. מֶשֶׁק **mesheq**, *meh'-shek;* from an unused root mean. to *hold; possession:*— + steward.

4944. מַשָּׁק **mashshâq**, *mash-shawk';* from 8264; a *traversing*, i.e. rapid *motion:*—running to and fro.

4945. מַשְׁקֶה **mashqeh**, *mash-keh';* from 8248; prop. *causing to drink*, i.e. a *butler;* by impl. (intrans.) *drink* (itself); fig. a *well-watered* region:—butler (-ship), cupbearer, drink (-ing), fat pasture, watered.

4946. מִשְׁקוֹל **mishqôwl**, *mish-kole';* from 8254; *weight:*—weight.

4947. מַשְׁקוֹף **mashqôwph**, *mash-kofe';* from 8259 in its orig. sense of *overhanging;* a *lintel:*—lintel, upper door post.

4948. מִשְׁקָל **mishqâl**, *mish-kawl';* from 8254; *weight* (numerically estimated); hence, *weighing* (the act):—(full) weight.

4949. מִשְׁקֶלֶת **mishqeleth**, *mish-keh'-leth;* or

מִשְׁקֹלֶת **mishqôleth**, *mish-ko'-leth;* fem. of 4948 or 4947; a *weight*, i.e. a *plum met* (with line attached):—plummet.

4950. מִשְׁקָע **mishqâ'**, *mish-kaw';* from 8257; a *settling* place (of water), i.e. a pond:—deep.

4951. מִשְׂרָה **misrâh**, *mis-raw';* from 8280; *empire:*—government.

4952. מִשְׁרָה **mishrâh**, *mish-raw';* from 8281 in the sense of *loosening; maceration*, i.e. steeped *juice:*—liquor.

4953. מַשְׁרוֹקִי **mashrôwqîy** (Chald.), *mash-ro-kee';* from a root corresp. to 8319; a (musical) *pipe* (from its *whistling* sound):—flute.

4954. מִשְׁרָעִי **Mishrâ'îy**, *mish-raw-ee';* patrial from an unused noun from an unused root; prob. mean. to *stretch* out; *extension;* a *Mishraite*, or inhab. (collect.) of Mishra:—Mishraites.

4955. מִשְׂרָפָה **misrâphâh**, *mis-raw-faw';* from 8313; *combustion*, i.e. *cremation* (of a corpse), or *calcination* (of lime):—burning.

4956. מִשְׂרְפוֹת מַיִם **Misrephôwth mayim**, *mis-ref-ohth' mah'-yim;* from the plur. of 4955 and 4325; *burnings of water; Misrephoth-Majim*, a place in Pal.:—Misrephoth-mayim.

4957. מַשְׂרֵקָה **Masrêqâh**, *mas-ray-kaw';* a form for 7796 used denom.; *vineyard; Masrekah*, a place in Idumæa:—Masrekah.

4958. מַשְׂרֵת **masrêth**, *mas-rayth';* appar. from an unused root mean. to *perforate*, i.e. hollow out; a *pan:*—pan.

4959. מָשַׁשׁ **mâshash**, *maw-shash';* a prim. root; to *feel* of; by impl. to *grope:*—feel, grope, search.

4960. מִשְׁתֶּה **mishteh**, *mish-teh';* from 8354; *drink;* by impl. *drinking* (the act); also (by impl.), a *banquet* or (gen.) *feast:*—banquet, drank, drink, feast ([-ed], -ing).

4961. מִשְׁתֵּה **mishteh** (Chald.), *mish-teh';* corresp. to 4960; a *banquet:*—banquet.

4962. מַת **math**, *math;* from the same as 4970; prop. an *adult* (as of full length); by impl. a *man* (only in the plur.):— + few, × friends, men, persons, × small.

4963. מַתְבֵּן **mathbên**, *math-bane'*; denom. from 8401; *straw* in the heap:—straw.

4964. מֶתֶג **metheg**, *meh'-theg*; from an unused root mean. to *curb*; a *bit*:—bit, bridle.

4965. מֶתֶג הָאַמָּה **Metheg hâ-'Ammâh**, *meh'-theg haw-am-maw'*; from 4964 and 520 with the art. interposed; *bit of the metropolis*; *Metheg-ha-Ammah*, an epithet of Gath:—Metheg-ammah.

4966. מָתוֹק **mâthôwq**, *maw-thoke'*; or

מָתוּק **mâthûwq**, *maw-thook'*; from 4985; *sweet*:—sweet (-er, -ness).

4967. מְתוּשָׁאֵל **Methûwshâ'êl**, *meth-oo-shaw-ale'*; from 4962 and 410, with the rel. interposed; *man who* (is) *of God*; *Methushaël*, an antediluvian patriarch:—Methusael.

4968. מְתוּשֶׁלַח **Methûwshelach**, *meth-oo-sheh'-lakh*; from 4962 and 7973; *man of a dart*; *Methushelach*, an antediluvian patriarch:—Methuselah.

4969. מָתַח **mâthach**, *maw-thakh'*; a prim. root; to *stretch* out:—spread out.

4970. מָתַי **mâthay**, *maw-thah'ee*; from an unused root mean. to *extend*; prop. *extent* (of time); but used only adv. (espec. with other particles pref.), *when* (either rel. or interrog.):—long, when.

מְתִים **methîym**. See 4962.

4971. מַתְכֹּנֶת **mathkôneth**, *math-ko'-neth*; or

מַתְכֻּנֶת **mathkûneth**, *math-koo'-neth*; from 8505 in the transferred sense of *measuring*; *proportion* (in size, number or ingredients):—composition, measure, state, tale.

4972. מַתְּלָאָה **mattelâ'âh**, *mat-tel-aw-aw'*; from 4100 and 8513; *what a trouble!*:—what a weariness.

4973. מְתַלְּעָה **methalle'âh**, *meth-al-leh-aw'*; contr. from 3216; prop. a *biter*, i.e. a *tooth*:—cheek (jaw) tooth, jaw.

4974. מְתֹם **methôm**, *meth-ohm'*; from 8552; *wholesomeness*; also (adv.) *completely*:—men [*by reading* 4962], soundness.

מֶתֶן **Methen**. See 4981.

4975. מֹתֶן **môthen**, *mo'-then*; from an unused root mean. to *be slender*; prop. the *waist* or small of the back; only in plur. the *loins*:—+ greyhound, loins, side.

4976. מַתָּן **mattân**, *mat-tawn'*; from 5414; a *present*:—gift,[to give, reward.

4977. מַתָּן **Mattân**, *mat-tawn'*; the same as 4976; *Mattan*, the name of a priest of Baal, and of an Isr.:—Mattan.

4978. מַתְּנָא **mattenâ'** (Chald.), *mat-ten-aw'*; corresp. to 4979:—gift.

4979. מַתָּנָה **mattânâh**, *mat-taw-naw'*; fem. of 4976; a *present*; spec. (in a good sense) a sacrificial *offering*, (in a bad sense) a *bribe*:—gift.

4980. מַתָּנָה **Mattânâh**, *mat-taw-naw'*; the same as 4979; *Mattanah*, a place in the Desert:—Mattanah.

4981. מִתְנִי **Mithnîy**, *mith-nee'*; prob. patrial from an unused noun mean. *slenderness*; a *Mithnite*, or inhab. of Methen:—Mithnite.

4982. מַתְּנַי **Mattenay**, *mat-ten-ah'ee*; from 4976; *liberal*; *Mattenai*, the name of three Isr.:—Mattenai.

4983. מַתַּנְיָה **Mattanyâh**, *mat-tan-yaw'*; or

מַתַּנְיָהוּ **Mattanyâhûw**, *mat-tan-yaw'-hoo*; from 4976 and 3050; *gift of Jah*; *Mattanjah*, the name of ten Isr.:—Mattaniah.

מָתְנַיִם **mothnayim**. See 4975.

4984. מִתְנַשֵּׂא **mithnassê'**, *mith-nas-say'*; from 5375; (used as abstr.) supreme *exaltation*:—exalted.

4985. מָתַק **mâthaq**, *maw-thak'*; a prim. root; to *suck*; by impl. to *relish*, or (intrans.) *be sweet*:—be (made, × take) sweet.

4986. מֶתֶק **metheq**, *meh'-thek*; from 4985; fig. *pleasantness* (of discourse):—sweetness.

4987. מֹתֶק **môtheq**, *mo'-thek*; from 4985; *sweetness*:—sweetness.

4988. מָתָק **mâthâq**, *maw-thawk'*; from 4985; a *dainty*, i.e. (gen.) *food*:—feed sweetly.

4989. מִתְקָה **Mithqâh**, *mith-kaw'*; fem. of 4987; *sweetness*; *Mithkah*, a place in the Desert:—Mithcah.

4990. מִתְרְדָת **Mithredâth**, *mith-red-awth'*; of Pers. origin; *Mithredath*, the name of two Persians:—Mithredath.

4991. מַתָּת **mattâth**, *mat-tawth'*; fem. of 4976 abbrev.; a *present*:—gift, reward.

4992. מַתַּתָּה **Mattattâh**, *mat-tat-taw'*; for 4993; *gift of Jah*; *Mattattah*, an Isr.:—Mattathah.

4993. מַתִּתְיָה **Mattithyâh**, *mat-tith-yaw'*; or

מַתִּתְיָהוּ **Mattithyâhûw**, *mat-tith-yaw'-hoo*; from 4991 and 3050; *gift of Jah*; *Mattithjah*, the name of four Isr.:—Mattithiah.

נ

4994. נָא **nâ'**, *naw*; a prim. particle of incitement and entreaty, which may usually be rendered *I pray*, *now* or *then*; added mostly to verbs (in the Imperat. or Fut.), or to interj., occasionally to an adv. or conj.:—I beseech (pray) thee (you), go to, now, oh.

4995. נָא **nâ'**, *naw*; appar. from 5106 in the sense of *harshness* from refusal; prop. *tough*, i.e. *uncooked* (flesh):—raw.

4996. נֹא **Nô'**, *no*; of Eg. origin; *No* (i.e. *Thebes*), the capital of Upper Egypt:—No. Comp. 528.

4997. נֹאד **nô'd**, *node*; or

נֹאוד **nô'wd**, *node*; also (fem.)

נֹאדָה **nô'dâh**, *no-daw'*; from an unused root of uncert. signif.; a (skin or leather) *bag* (for fluids):—bottle.

נֶאְדָּרִי **ne'dârîy**. See 142.

4998. נָאָה **nâ'âh**, *naw-aw'*; a prim. root; prop. to *be at home*, i.e. (by impl.) to be *pleasant* (or *suitable*), i.e. *beautiful*:—be beautiful, become, be comely.

4999. נָאָה **nâ'âh**, *naw-aw'*; from 4998; a *home*; fig. a *pasture*:—habitation, house, pasture, pleasant place.

5000. נָאוֶה **nâveh**, *naw-veh'*; from 4998 or 5116; *suitable*, or *beautiful*:—becometh, comely, seemly.

5001. נָאַם **nâ'am**, *naw-am'*; a prim. root; prop. to *whisper*, i.e. (by impl.) to *utter* as an oracle:—say.

5002. נְאֻם **ne'ûm**, *neh-oom'*; from 5001; an *oracle*:—(hath) said, saith.

5003. נָאַף **nâ'aph**, *naw-af'*; a prim. root; to *commit adultery*; fig. to *apostatize*:—adulterer (-ess), commit (-ing) adultery, woman that breaketh wedlock.

5004. נִאֻף **nî'ûph**, *nee-oof'*; from 5003; *adultery*:—adultery.

5005. נַאֲפוּף **na'aphûwph**, *nah-af-oof'*; from 5003; *adultery*:—adultery.

5006. נָאַץ **nâ'ats**, *naw-ats'*; a prim. root; to *scorn*; or (Eccles. 12 : 5) by interch. for 5132, to *bloom*:—abhor, (give occasion to) blaspheme, contemn, despise, flourish, × great, provoke.

5007. נְאָצָה **ne'âtsâh**, *neh-aw-tsaw'*; or

נֶאָצָה **ne'âtsâh**, *neh-aw-tsaw'*; from 5006; *scorn*:—blasphemy.

5008. נָאַק **nâ'aq**, *naw-ak'*; a prim. root; to *groan*:—groan.

5009. נְאָקָה **ne'âqâh**, *neh-aw-kaw'*; from 5008; a *groan*:—groaning.

5010. נָאַר **nâ'ar**, *naw-ar'*; a prim. root; to *reject*:—abhor, make void.

5011. נֹב **Nôb**, *nobe*; the same as 5108; *fruit*; *Nob*, a place in Pal.:—Nob.

5012. נָבָא **nâbâ'**, *naw-baw'*; a prim. root; to *prophesy*, i.e. speak (or sing) by inspiration (in prediction or simple discourse):—prophesy (-ing), make self a prophet.

5013. נְבָא **nebâ'** (Chald.), *neb-aw'*; corresp. to 5012:—prophesy.

5014. נָבַב **nâbab**, *naw-bab'*; a prim. root; to *pierce*; to *be hollow*, or (fig.) *foolish*:—hollow, vain.

5015. נְבוֹ **Nebôw**, *neb-o'*; prob. of for. der.; *Nebo*, the name of a Bab. deity, also of a mountain in Moab, and of a place in Pal.:—Nebo.

5016. נְבוּאָה **nebûw'âh**, *neb-oo-aw'*; from 5012; a *prediction* (spoken or written):—prophecy.

5017. נְבוּאָה **nebûw'âh** (Chald.), *neb-oo-aw*; corresp. to 5016; inspired *teaching*:—prophesying.

5018. נְבוּזַרְאֲדָן **Nebûwzarădân**, *neb-oo-zar-ad-awn'*; of for. or.; *Nebuzaradan*, a Bab. general:—Nebuzaradan.

5019. נְבוּכַדְנֶאצַּר **Nebûwkadne'tstsar**, *neb-oo-kad-nets-tsar'*; or

נְבֻכַדְנֶאצַּר **Nebûkadne'tstsar** (2 Kings 24 : 1, 10), *neb-oo-kad-nets-tsar'*; or

נְבוּכַדְנֶצַּר **Nebûwkadnetstsar** (Esth. 2 : 6; Dan. 1 : 18), *neb-oo-kad-nets-tsar'*; or

נְבוּכַדְרֶאצַּר **Nebûwkadre'tstsar**, *neb-oo-kad-rets-tsar'*; or

נְבוּכַדְרֶאצּוֹר **Nebûwkadre'tstsôwr** (Ezra 2 : 1; Jer. 49 : 28), *neb-oo-kad-rets-tsore'*; of for. der.; *Nebukadnetstsar* (or *-retstsar*, or *-retstsor*), king of Babylon:—Nebuchadnezzar, Nebuchadrezzar.

5020. נְבוּכַדְנֶצַּר **Nebûwkadnetstsar** (Chald.), *neb-oo-kad-nets-tsar'*; corresp. to 5019:—Nebuchadnezzar.

5021. נְבוּשַׁזְבָּן **Nebûwshazbân**, *neb-oo-shaz-bawn'*; of for. der.; *Nebushazban*, Nebuchadnezzar's chief eunuch:—Nebushazban.

5022. נָבוֹת **Nâbôwth**, *naw-both'*; fem. plur. from the same as 5011; *fruits*; *Naboth*, an Isr.:—Naboth.

5023. נְבִזְבָּה **nebizbâh** (Chald.), *neb-iz-baw'*; of uncert. der.; a *largess*:—reward.

5024. נָבַח **nâbach**, *naw-bakh'*; a prim. root; to *bark* (as a dog):—bark.

5025. נֹבַח **Nôbach**, *no'-bach*; from 5024; a *bark*; *Nobach*, the name of an Isr., and of a place E. of the Jordan:—Nobah.

5026. נִבְחַז **Nibchaz**, *nib-khaz'*; of for. or.; *Nibchaz*, a deity of the Avites:—Nibhaz.

5027. נָבַט **nâbaṭ**, *naw-bat'*; a prim. root; to *scan*, i.e. look intently at; by impl. to *regard* with pleasure, favor or care:—(cause to) behold, consider, look (down), regard, have respect, see.

5028. נְבָט **Nebâṭ**, *neb-awt'*; from 5027; *regard*; *Nebat*, the father of Jeroboam I:—Nebat.

5029. נְבִיא **nebîy'** (Chald.), *neb-ee'*; corresp. to 5030; a *prophet*:—prophet.

5030. נָבִיא **nâbîy'**, *naw-bee'*; from 5012; a *prophet* or (gen.) *inspired* man:—prophecy, that prophesy, prophet.

5031. נְבִיאָה **nebîy'âh**, *neb-ee-yaw'*; fem. of 5030; a *prophetess* or (gen.) *inspired* woman; by impl. a *poetess*; by association a *prophet's wife*:—prophetess.

5032. נְבָיוֹת **Nebâyôwth**, *neb-aw-yoth'*; or

נְבָיֹת **Nebâyôth**, *neb-aw-yoth'*; fem. plur. from 5107; *fruitfulnesses*; *Nebajoth*, a son of Ishmael, and the country settled by him:—Nebaioth, Nebajoth.

5033. נֵבֶךְ **nêbek**, *nay'-bek*; from an unused root mean. to *burst* forth; a *fountain*:—spring.

5034. נָבֵל **nâbêl**, *naw-bale'*; a prim. root; to *wilt*; gen. to *fall away*, *fail*, *faint*; fig. to *be foolish* or (mor.) *wicked*; causat. to *despise*, *disgrace*:—disgrace, dishonour, lightly esteem, fade (away, -ing), fall (down, -ling, off), do foolishly, come to nought, × surely, make vile, wither.

5035. נֶבֶל **nebel**, *neh'-bel*; or

נֵבֶל **nêbel**, *nay'-bel*; from 5034; a *skin-bag* for liquids (from *collapsing* when empty);

hence, a *vase* (as similar in shape when full); also a *lyre* (as having a body of like form):—bottle, pitcher, psaltery, vessel, viol.

5036. נָבָל **nâbâl**, *naw-bawl'*; from 5034; *stupid; wicked* (espec. *impious*):—fool (-ish, -ish man, -ish woman), vile person.

5037. נָבָל **Nâbâl**, *naw-bawl'*; the same as 5036; *dolt; Nabal*, an Isr.:—Nabal.

5038. נְבֵלָה **n^{e}bêlâh**, *neb-ay-law'*; from 5034; a *flabby* thing, i.e. a *carcase* or *carrion* (human or bestial, often collect.); fig. an *idol*:—(dead) body, (dead) carcase, dead of itself, which died, (beast) that (which) dieth of itself.

5039. נְבָלָה **n^{e}bâlâh**, *neb-aw-law'*; fem. of 5036; *foolishness*, i.e. (mor.) *wickedness*; concr. a *crime*; by extens. *punishment*:—folly, vile, villany.

5040. נַבְלוּת **nablûwth**, *nab-looth'*; from 5036; prop. *disgrace*, i.e. the (female) *pudenda*:—lewdness.

5041. נְבַלַּט **N^{e}ballâṭ**, *neb-al-lawt'*; appar. from 5036 and 3909; *foolish secrecy; Neballat*, a place in Pal.:—Neballat.

5042. נָבַע **nâba‘**, *naw-bah'*; a prim. root; to *gush* forth; fig. to *utter* (good or bad words); spec. to *emit* (a foul odor):—belch out, flowing, pour out, send forth, utter (abundantly).

5043. נֶבְרְשָׁא **nebr^{e}shâ'** (Chald.), *neb-reh-shaw'*; from an unused root mean. to *shine*; a *light*; plur. (collect.) a *chandelier*:—candlestick.

5044. נִבְשָׁן **Nibshân**, *nib-shawn'*; of uncert. der.; *Nibshan*, a place in Pal.:—Nibshan.

5045. נֶגֶב **negeb**, *neh'-gheb*; from an unused root mean. to *be parched*; the *south* (from its drought); spec. the *Negeb* or southern district of Judah, occasionally, *Egypt* (as south to Pal.):—south (country, side, -ward).

5046. נָגַד **nâgad**, *naw-gad'*; a prim. root; prop. to *front*, i.e. stand boldly out opposite; by impl. (causat.), to *manifest*; fig. to *announce* (always by word of mouth to one present); spec. to *expose, predict, explain, praise*:—bewray, × certainly, certify, declare (-ing), denounce, expound, × fully, messenger, plainly, profess, rehearse, report, shew (forth), speak, × surely, tell, utter.

5047. נְגַד **n^{e}gad** (Chald.), *neg-ad'*; corresp. to 5046; to *flow* (through the idea of *clearing* the way):—issue.

5048. נֶגֶד **neged**, *neh'-ghed*; from 5046; a *front*, i.e. part opposite; spec. a *counterpart*, or mate; usually (adv., espec. with prep.) *over against* or *before*:—about, (over) against, × aloof, × far (off), × from, over, presence, × other side, sight, × to view.

5049. נֶגֶד **neged** (Chald.), *neh'-ghed*; corresp. to 5048; *opposite*:—toward.

5050. נָגַהּ **nâgahh**, *naw-găh'*; a prim. root; to *glitter*; causat. to *illuminate*:—(en-) lighten, (cause to) shine.

5051. נֹגַהּ **nôgahh**, *no'-găh*; from 5050; *brilliancy* (lit. or fig.):—bright (-ness), light, (clear) shining.

5052. נֹגַהּ **Nôgahh**, *no'-găh*; the same as 5051; *Nogah*, a son of David:—Nogah.

5053. נֹגַהּ **nôgahh** (Chald.), *no'-găh*; corresp. to 5051; *dawn*:—morning.

5054. נְגֹהָה **n^{e}gôhâh**, *neg-o-haw'*; fem. of 5051; *splendor*:—brightness.

5055. נָגַח **nâgach**, *naw-gakh'*; a prim. root; to *but* with the horns; fig. to *war* against:—gore, push (down, -ing).

5056. נַגָּח **naggâch**, *nag-gawkh'*; from 5055; *butting*, i.e. *vicious*:—used (wont) to push.

5057. נָגִיד **nâgîyd**, *naw-gheed'*; or

נָגִד **nâgîd**, *naw-gheed'*; from 5046; a *commander* (as occupying the *front*), civil, military or religious; gen. (abstr. plur.), *honorable* themes:—captain, chief, excellent thing, (chief) governor, leader, noble, prince, (chief) ruler.

5058. נְגִינָה **n^{e}gîynâh**, *neg-ee-naw'*; or

נְגִינַת **n^{e}gîynath** (Psa. 61 : title), *neg-ee-nath'*; from 5059; prop. instrumental *music*; by impl. a stringed *instrument*; by extens. a *poem* set to music; spec. an *epigram*:—stringed instrument, musick, Neginoth [*plur.*], song.

5059. נָגַן **nâgan**, *naw-gan'*; a prim. root; prop. to *thrum*, i.e. *beat* a tune with the fingers; espec. to *play* on a stringed instrument; hence (gen.) to *make music*:—player on instruments, sing to the stringed instruments, melody, ministrel, play (-er, -ing).

5060. נָגַע **nâga‘**, *naw-gah'*; a prim. root; prop. to *touch*, i.e. *lay the hand upon* (for any purpose; euphem., to *lie with* a woman); by impl. to *reach* (fig. to *arrive, acquire*); violently, to *strike* (punish, defeat, destroy, etc.):—beat, (× be able to) bring (down), cast, come (nigh), draw near (nigh), get up, happen, join, near, plague, reach (up), smite, strike, touch.

5061. נֶגַע **nega‘**, *neh'-gah*; from 5060; a *blow* (fig. *infliction*); also (by impl.) a *spot* (concr. a *leprous* person or dress):—plague, sore, stricken, stripe, stroke, wound.

5062. נָגַף **nâgaph**, *naw-gaf'*; a prim. root; to *push, gore, defeat, stub* (the toe), *inflict* (a disease):—beat, dash, hurt, plague, slay, smite (down), strike, stumble, × surely, put to the worse.

5063. נֶגֶף **negeph**, *neh'-ghef*; from 5062; a *trip* (of the foot); fig. an *infliction* (of disease):—plague, stumbling.

5064. נָגַר **nâgar**, *naw-gar'*; a prim. root; to *flow*; fig. to *stretch* out; causat. to *pour* out or down; fig. to *deliver* over:—fall, flow away, pour down (out), run, shed, spilt, trickle down.

5065. נָגַשׂ **nâgas**, *naw-gas'*; a prim. root; to *drive* (an animal, a workman, a debtor, an army); by impl. to *tax, harass, tyrannize*:—distress, driver, exact (-or), oppress (-or), × raiser of taxes, taskmaster.

5066. נָגַשׁ **nâgash**, *naw-gash'*; a prim. root; to *be* or *come* (causat. *bring*) *near* (for any purpose); euphem. to *lie with* a woman; as an enemy, to *attack*; relig. to *worship*; causat. to *present*; fig. to *adduce* an argument; by reversal, to *stand back*:—(make to) approach (nigh), bring (forth, hither, near), (cause to) come (hither, near, nigh), give place, go hard (up), (be, draw, go) near (nigh), offer, overtake, present, put, stand.

5067. נֵד **nêd**, *nade*; from 5110 in the sense of *piling* up; a *mound*, i.e. *wave*:—heap.

5068. נָדַב **nâdab**, *naw-dab'*; a prim. root; to *impel*; hence to *volunteer* (as a soldier), to *present* spontaneously:—offer freely, be (give, make, offer self) willing (-ly).

5069. נְדַב **n^{e}dab** (Chald.), *ned-ab'*; corresp. to 5068; *be* (or *give*) *liberal* (*-ly*):—(be minded of . . . own) freewill (offering), offer freely (willingly).

5070. נָדָב **Nâdâb**, *naw-dawb'*; from 5068; *liberal*; *Nadab*, the name of four Isr.:—Nadab.

5071. נְדָבָה **n^{e}dâbâh**, *ned-aw-baw'*; from 5068; prop. (abstr.) *spontaneity*, or (adj.) *spontaneous*; also (concr.) a *spontaneous* or (by infer., in plur.) *abundant* gift:—free (-will) offering, freely, plentiful, voluntary (-ily, offering), willing (-ly, offering).

5072. נְדַבְיָה **N^{e}dabyâh**, *ned-ab-yaw'*; from 5068 and 3050; *largess of Jah; Nedabjah*, an Isr.:—Nedabiah.

5073. נִדְבָּךְ **nidbâk** (Chald.), *nid-bawk'*; from a root mean. to *stick*; a *layer* (of building materials):—row.

5074. נָדַד **nâdad**, *naw-dad'*; a prim. root; prop. to *wave* to and fro (rarely to *flap* up and down); fig. to *rove, flee*, or (caus.) to *drive* away:—chase (away), × could not, depart, flee (× apace, away), (re-) move, thrust away, wander (abroad, -er, -ing).

5075. נְדַד **n^{e}dad** (Chald.), *ned-ad'*; corresp. to 5074; to *depart*:—go from.

5076. נָדֻד **nâdûd**, *naw-dood'*; pass. part. of 5074; prop. *tossed*; abstr. a *rolling* (on the bed):—tossing to and fro.

5077. נָדָה **nâdâh**, *naw-daw'*; or

נָדָא° **nâdâ'** (2 Kings 17 : 21), *naw-daw'*; a prim. root; prop. to *toss*; fig. to *exclude*, i.e. banish, postpone, prohibit:—cast out, drive, put far away.

5078. נֵדֶה **nêdeh**, *nay'-deh*; from 5077 in the sense of freely *flinging* money; a *bounty* (for prostitution):—gifts.

5079. נִדָּה **niddâh**, *nid-daw'*; from 5074; prop. *rejection*; by impl. *impurity*, espec. personal (menstruation) or moral (idolatry, incest):—× far, filthiness, × flowers, menstruous (woman), put apart, × removed (woman), separation, set apart, unclean (-ness, thing, with filthiness).

5080. נָדַח **nâdach**, *naw-dakh'*; a prim. root; to *push* off; used in a great variety of applications, lit. and fig. (to expel, mislead, strike, inflict, etc.):—banish, bring, cast down (out), chase, compel, draw away, drive (away, out, quite), fetch a stroke, force, go away, outcast, thrust away (out), withdraw.

5081. נָדִיב **nâdîyb**, *naw-deeb'*; from 5068; prop. *voluntary*, i.e. generous; hence, *magnanimous*; as noun, a *grandee* (sometimes a *tyrant*):—free, liberal (things), noble, prince, willing ([hearted]).

5082. נְדִיבָה **n^{e}dîybâh**, *ned-ee-baw'*; fem. of 5081; prop. *nobility*, i.e. reputation:—soul.

5083. נָדָן **nâdân**, *naw-dawn'*; prob. from an unused root mean. to *give*; a *present* (for prostitution):—gift.

5084. נָדָן **nâdân**, *naw-dawn'*; of uncert. der.; a *sheath* (of a sword):—sheath.

5085. נִדְנֶה **nidneh** (Chald.), *nid-neh'*; from the same as 5084; a *sheath*; fig. the *body* (as the receptacle of the soul):—body.

5086. נָדַף **nâdaph**, *naw-daf'*; a prim. root; to *shove* asunder, i.e. *disperse*:—drive (away, to and fro), thrust down, shaken, tossed to and fro.

5087. נָדַר **nâdar**, *naw-dar'*; a prim. root; to *promise* (pos., to do or give something to God):—(make a) vow.

5088. נֶדֶר **neder**, *neh'-der*; or

נֵדֶר **nêder**, *nay'-der*; from 5087; a *promise* (to God); also (concr.) a thing *promised*:—vow ([-ed]).

5089. נֹהַּ **nôahh**, *no'-ăh*; from an unused root mean. to *lament*; *lamentation*:—wailing.

5090. נָהַג **nâhag**, *naw-hag'*; a prim. root; to *drive* forth (a person, an animal or chariot), i.e. *lead, carry away*; reflex. to *proceed* (i.e. impel or guide oneself); also (from the *panting* induced by effort), to *sigh*:—acquaint, bring (away), carry away, drive (away), lead (away, forth), (be) guide, lead (away, forth).

5091. נָהָה **nâhâh**, *naw-haw'*; a prim. root; to *groan*, i.e. *bewail*; hence (through the idea of *crying* aloud) to *assemble* (as if on proclamation):—lament, wail.

5092. נְהִי **n^{e}hîy**, *neh-hee'*; from 5091; an *elegy*:—lamentation, wailing.

5093. נִהְיָה **nihyâh**, *nih-yaw'*; fem. of 5092; *lamentation*:—doleful.

5094. נְהִיר° **n^{e}hîyr** (Chald.), *neh-heere'*; or

נְהִירוּ **nehîyrûw** (Chald.), *neh-hee-roo'*; from the same as 5105; *illumination*, i.e. (fig.) wisdom:—light.

5095. נָהַל **nâhal**, *naw-hal'*; a prim. root; prop. to run with a *sparkle*, i.e. *flow*; hence (trans.) to *conduct*, and (by infer.) to *protect, sustain*:—carry, feed, guide, lead (gently, on).

5096. נַהֲלָל **Nahălâl**, *năh-hal-awl'*; or

נַהֲלֹל **Nahălôl**, *năh-hal-ole'*; the same as 5097; *Nahalal* or *Nahalol*, a place in Pal.:—Nahalal, Nahallal, Nahalol.

5097. נַהֲלֹל **nahălôl**, *năh-hal-ole'*; from 5095; *pasture*:—bush.

5098. נָהַם **nâham**, *naw-ham'*; a prim. root; to *growl*:—mourn, roar (-ing).

5099. נַהַם **naham**, *năh'-ham*; from 5098; a *snarl*:—roaring.

5100. נְהָמָה **n**e**hâmâh**, *neh-haw-maw'*; fem. of 5099; *snarling*:—disquietness, roaring.

5101. נָהַק **nâhaq**, *naw-hak'*; a prim. root; to *bray* (as an ass), *scream* (from hunger):—bray.

5102. נָהַר **nâhar**, *naw-har'*; a prim. root; to *sparkle*, i.e. (fig.) *be cheerful*; hence (from the *sheen* of a running stream) to *flow*, i.e. (fig.) *assemble*:—flow (together), be lightened.

5103. נְהַר **n**e**har** (Chald.), *neh-har'*; from a root corresp. to 5102; a *river*, espec. the Euphrates:—river, stream.

5104. נָהָר **nâhâr**, *naw-hawr'*; from 5102; a *stream* (includ. the *sea*; espec. the Nile, Euphrates, etc.); fig., *prosperity*:—flood, river.

5105. נְהָרָה **n**e**hârâh**, *neh-haw-raw'*; from 5102 in its orig. sense; *daylight*:—light.

5106. נוּא **nûw'**, *noo*; a prim. root; to *refuse*, *forbid*, *dissuade*, or *neutralize*:—break, disallow, discourage, make of none effect.

5107. נוּב **nûwb**, *noob*; a prim. root; to *germinate*, i.e. (fig.) to (causat. *make*) *flourish*; also (of words), to *utter*:—bring forth (fruit), make cheerful, increase.

5108. נוֹב° **nôwb**, *nobe*; or

נֵיב **nêyb**, *nabe*; from 5107; *produce*, lit. or fig.:—fruit.

5109. נוֹבַי° **Nôwbay**, *no-bah'ee*; from 5108; *fruitful*; *Nobai*, an Isr.:—Nebai [*from the marg.*].

5110. נוּד **nûwd**, *nood*; a prim. root; to *nod*, i.e. waver; fig. to *wander*, *flee*, *disappear*; also (from *shaking* the head in sympathy), to *console*, *deplore*, or (from *tossing* the head in scorn) *taunt*:—bemoan, flee, get, mourn, make to move, take pity, remove, shake, skip for joy, be sorry, vagabond, way, wandering.

5111. נוּד **nûwd** (Chald.), *nood*; corresp. to 5116; to *flee*:—get away.

5112. נוֹד **nôwd**, *node* [only defect.

נֹד **nôd**, *node*]; from 5110; *exile*:—wandering.

5113. נוֹד **Nôwd**, *node*; the same as 5112; *vagrancy*; *Nod*, the land of Cain:—Nod.

5114. נוֹדָב **Nôwdâb**, *no-dawb'*; from 5068; *noble*; *Nodab*, an Arab tribe:—Nodab.

5115. נָוָה **nâvâh**, *naw-vaw'*; a prim. root; to *rest* (as at home); causat. (through the implied idea of *beauty* [comp. 5116]), to *celebrate* (with praises):—keep at home, prepare an habitation.

5116. נָוֶה **nâveh**, *naw-veh'*; or (fem.)

נָוָה **nâvâh**, *naw-vaw'*; from 5115; (adj.) *at home*; hence (by impl. of satisfaction) *lovely*; also (noun) a *home*, of God (temple), men (residence), flocks (pasture), or wild animals (*den*):—comely, dwelling (place), fold, habitation, pleasant place, sheepcote, stable, tarried.

5117. נוּחַ **nûwach**, *noo'-akh*; a prim. root; to *rest*, i.e. *settle* down; used in a great variety of applications, lit. and fig., intrans., trans. and causat. (to *dwell*, *stay*, *let fall*, *place*, *let alone*, *withdraw*, *give comfort*, etc.):—cease, be confederate, lay, let down, (be) quiet, remain, (cause to, be at, give, have, make to) rest, set down. Comp. 3241.

5118. נוּחַ **nûwach**, *noo'-akh*; or

נוֹחַ **nôwach**, *no'-akh*; from 5117; *quiet*:—rest (-ed, -ing place).

5119. נוֹחָה **Nôwchâh**, *no-chaw'*; fem. of 5118; *quietude*; *Nochah*, an Isr.:—Nohah.

5120. נוּט **nûwṭ**, *noot*; to *quake*:—be moved.

5121. נָוִית° **Nâvîyth**, *naw-veeth'*; from 5115; *residence*; *Navith*, a place in Pal.:—Naioth [*from the marg.*].

5122. נְוָלוּ **n**e**vâlûw** (Chald.), *nev-aw-loo'*; or

נְוָלִי **n**e**vâlîy** (Chald.), *nev-aw-lee'*; from an unused root prob. mean. to be *foul*; a *sink*:—dunghill.

5123. נוּם **nûwm**, *noom*; a prim. root; to *slumber* (from drowsiness):—sleep, slumber.

5124 נוּמָה **nûwmâh**, *noo-maw'*; from 5123; *sleepiness*:—drowsiness.

5125. נוּן **nûwn**, *noon*; a prim. root; to *resprout*, i.e. propagate by shoots; fig., to *be perpetual*:—be continued.

5126. נוּן **Nûwn**, *noon*; or

נוֹן **Nôwn** (1 Chron. 7 : 27), *nohn*; from 5125; *perpetuity*; *Nun* or *Non*, the father of Joshua:—Non, Nun.

5127. נוּס **nûwç**, *noos*; a prim. root; to *flit*, i.e. *vanish* away (subside, escape; causat. chase, impel, deliver):—× abate, away, be displayed, (make to) flee (away, -ing), put to flight, × hide, lift up a standard.

5128. נוּעַ **nûwaʻ**, *noo'-ah*; a prim. root; to *waver*, in a great variety of applications, lit. and fig. (as subjoined):—continually, fugitive, × make to [go] up and down, be gone away, (be) move (-able, -d), be promoted, reel, remove, scatter, set, shake, sift, stagger, to and fro, be vagabond, wag, (make) wander (up and down).

5129. נוֹעַדְיָה **Nôwʻadyâh**, *no-ad-yaw'*; from 3259 and 3050; *convened of Jah*; *Noädjah*, the name of an Isr., and a false prophetess:—Noadiah.

5130. נוּף **nûwph**, *noof*; a prim. root; to *quiver* (i.e. *vibrate* up and down, or *rock* to and fro); used in a great variety of applications (includ. sprinkling, beckoning, rubbing, bastinadoing, sawing, waving, etc.):—lift up, move, offer, perfume, send, shake, sift, strike, wave.

5131. נוֹף **nôwph**, *nofe*; from 5130; *elevation*:—situation. Comp. 5297.

5132. נוּץ **nûwts**, *noots*; a prim. root; prop. to *flash*; hence, to *blossom* (from the brilliancy of color); also, to *fly* away (from the quickness of motion):—flee away, bud (forth).

5133. נוֹצָה **nôwtsâh**, *no-tsaw'*; or

נֹצָה **nôtsâh**, *no-tsaw'*; fem. act. part. of 5327 in the sense of *flying*; a *pinion* (or wing feather); often (collect.) *plumage*:—feather (-s), ostrich.

5134. נוּק **nûwq**, *nook*; a prim. root; to *suckle*:—nurse.

5135. נוּר **nûwr** (Chald.), *noor*; from an unused root (corresp. to that of 5216) mean. to *shine*; *fire*:—fiery, fire.

5136. נוּשׁ **nûwsh**, *noosh*; a prim. root; to *be sick*, i.e. (fig.) *distressed*:—be full of heaviness.

5137. נָזָה **nâzâh**, *naw-zaw'*; a prim. root; to *spirt*, i.e. *besprinkle* (espec. in expiation):—sprinkle.

5138. נָזִיד **nâzîyd**, *naw-zeed'*; from 2102; something *boiled*, i.e. *soup*:—pottage.

5139. נָזִיר **nâzîyr**, *naw-zeer'*; or

נָזִר **nâzîr**, *naw-zeer'*; from 5144; *separate*, i.e. consecrated (as *prince*, a *Nazirite*); hence (fig. from the latter) an *unpruned* vine (like an unshorn Nazirite):—Nazarite [*by a false alliteration with Nazareth*], separate (-d), vine undressed.

5140. נָזַל **nâzal**, *naw-zal'*; a prim. root; to *drip*, or *shed* by trickling:—distil, drop, flood, (cause to) flow (-ing), gush out, melt, pour (down), running water, stream.

5141. נֶזֶם **nezem**, *neh'-zem*; from an unused root of uncert. mean.; a nose-*ring*:—earring, jewel.

5142. נְזַק **n**e**zaq** (Chald.), *nez-ak'*; corresp. to the root of 5143; to *suffer* (causat. *inflict*) *loss*:—have (en-) damage, hurt (-ful).

5143. נֵזֶק **nêzeq**, *nay'-zek*; from an unused root mean. to *injure*; *loss*:—damage.

5144. נָזַר **nâzar**, *naw-zar'*; a prim. root; to *hold aloof*, i.e. (intrans.) *abstain* (from food and drink, from impurity, and even from divine worship [i.e. *apostatize*]); spec. to *set apart* (to sacred purposes), i.e. *devote*:—consecrate, separate (-ing, self).

5145. נֶזֶר **nezer**, *neh'-zer*; or

נֵזֶר **nêzer**, *nay'-zer*; from 5144; prop. something *set apart*, i.e. (abstr.) *dedication* (of a priest or Nazirite); hence (concr.) unshorn *locks*; also (by impl.) a *chaplet* (espec. of royalty):—consecration, crown, hair, separation.

5146. נֹחַ **Nôach**, *no'-akh*; the same as 5118; *rest*; *Noäch*, the patriarch of the flood:—Noah.

5147. נַחְבִּי **Nachbîy**, *nakh-bee'*; from 2247; *occult*; *Nachbi*, an Isr.:—Nakbi.

5148. נָחָה **nâchâh**, *naw-khaw'*; a prim. root; to *guide*; by impl. to *transport* (into exile, or as colonists):—bestow, bring, govern, guide, lead (forth), put, straiten.

5149. נְחוּם **N**e**chûwm**, *neh-khoom'*; from 5162; *comforted*; *Nechum*, an Isr.:—Nehum.

5150. נִחוּם **nichûwm**, *nee-khoom'*; or

נִחֻם **nichûm**, *nee-khoom'*; from 5162; prop. *consoled*; abstr. *solace*:—comfort (-able), repenting.

5151. נַחוּם **Nachûwm**, *nakh-oom'*; from 5162; *comfortable*; *Nachum*, an Isr. prophet:—Nahum.

5152. נָחוֹר **Nâchôwr**, *naw-khore'*; from the same as 5170; *snorer*; *Nachor*, the name of the grandfather and a brother of Abraham:—Nahor.

5153. נָחוּשׁ **nâchûwsh**, *naw-khoosh'*; appar. pass. part. of 5172 (perh. in the sense of *ringing*, i.e. bell-metal; or from the *red* color of the throat of a serpent [5175, as denom.] when hissing); *coppery*, i.e. (fig.) hard:—of brass.

5154. נְחוּשָׁה **n**e**chûwshâh**, *nekh-oo-shaw'*; or

נְחֻשָׁה **n**e**chûshâh**, *nekh-oo-shaw'*; fem. of 5153; *copper*:—brass, steel. Comp. 5176.

5155. נְחִילָה **n**e**chîylah**, *nekh-ee-law'*; prob. denom. from 2485; a *flute*:—[*plur.*] Nehiloth.

5156. נְחִיר **n**e**chîyr**, *nekh-eer'*; from the same as 5170; a *nostril*:—[*dual*] nostrils.

5157. נָחַל **nâchal**, *naw-khal'*; a prim. root; to *inherit* (as a [*fig.*] mode of descent), or (gen.) to *occupy*; causat. to *bequeath*, or (gen.) *distribute*, *instate*:—divide, have ([inheritance]), take as an heritage, (cause to, give to, make to) inherit, (distribute for, divide [for, for an, by], give for, have, leave for, take [for]) inheritance, (have in, cause to be made to) possess (-ion).

5158. נַחַל **nachal**, *nakh'-al*; or (fem.)

נַחְלָה **nachlâh** (Psa. 124 : 4), *nakh'-law*; or

נַחֲלָה **nachălâh** (Ezek. 47 : 19; 48 : 28), *nakh-al-aw'*; from 5157 in its orig. sense; a *stream*, espec. a winter *torrent*; (by impl.) a (narrow) *valley* (in which a brook runs); also a *shaft* (of a mine):—brook, flood, river, stream, valley.

5159. נַחֲלָה **nachălâh**, *nakh-al-aw'*; from 5157 (in its usual sense); prop. something *inherited*, i.e. (abstr.) *occupancy*, or (concr.) an *heirloom*; gen. an *estate*, *patrimony* or *portion*:—heritage, to inherit, inheritance, possession. Comp. 5158.

5160. נַחֲלִיאֵל **Nachălîy'êl**, *nakh-al-ee-ale'*; from 5158 and 410; *valley of God*; *Nachaliël*, a place in the Desert:—Nahaliel.

5161. נֶחֱלָמִי **Nechĕlâmîy**, *nekh-el-aw-mee'*; appar. a patron. from an unused name (appar. pass. part. of 2492); *dreamed*; a *Nechelamite*, or descend. of Nechlam:—Nehelamite.

5162. נָחַם **nâcham**, *naw-kham'*; a prim. root; prop. to *sigh*, i.e. *breathe* strongly; by impl. to *be sorry*, i.e. (in a favorable sense) to *pity*, *console* or (reflex.) *rue*; or (unfavorably) to *avenge* (oneself):—comfort (self), ease [one's self], repent (-er, -ing, self).

5163. נַחַם **Nacham**, *nakh'-am*; from 5162; *consolation*; *Nacham*, an Isr.:—Naham.

5164. נֹחַם **nôcham**, *no'-kham*; from 5162; *ruefulness*, i.e. desistance:—repentance.

5165. נֶחָמָה **nechâmâh**, *nekh-aw-maw'*; from 5162; *consolation*:—comfort.

5166. נְחֶמְיָה **N**e**chemyâh**, *nekh-em-yaw'*; from 5162 and 3050; *consolation of Jah*; *Nechemjah*, the name of three Isr.:—Nehemiah.

5167. נַחֲמָנִי **Nachămânîy**, *nakh-am-aw-nee'*; from 5162; *consolatory*; *Nachamani*, an Isr.:—Nahamani.

5168. נַחְנוּ **nachnûw**, *nakh-noo'*; for 587; *we*:—we.

5169. נָחַץ **nâchats**, *naw-khats'*; a prim. root; to *be urgent:*—require haste.

5170. נַחַר **nachar**, *nakh'-ar*; and (fem.)

נַחֲרָה **nachărâh**, *nakh-ar-aw'*; from an unused root mean. to *snort* or *snore;* a *snorting:*—nostrils, snorting.

5171. נַחֲרַי **Nachăray**, *nakh-ar-ah'ee;* or

נַחְרַי **Nachray**, *nakh-rah'ee;* from the same as 5170; *snorer; Nacharai* or *Nachrai*, an Isr.:—Naharai, Nahari.

5172. נָחַשׁ **nâchash**, *naw-khash';* a prim. root; prop. to *hiss*, i.e. *whisper* a (magic) spell; gen. to *prognosticate:*— × certainly, divine, enchanter, (use) × enchantment, learn by experience, × indeed, diligently observe.

5173. נַחַשׁ **nachash**, *nakh'-ash;* from 5172; an *incantation* or *augury:*—enchantment.

5174. נְחָשׁ **nᵉchâsh** (Chald.) *nekh-awsh';* corresp. to 5154; *copper:*—brass.

5175. נָחָשׁ **nâchâsh**, *naw-khawsh';* from 5172; a *snake* (from its *hiss*):—serpent.

5176. נָחָשׁ **Nâchâsh**, *naw-khawsh';* the same as 5175; *Nachash*, the name of two persons appar. non-Isr.:—Nahash.

נְחֻשָׁה **nᵉchûshâh**. See 5154.

5177. נַחְשׁוֹן **Nachshôwn**, *nakh-shone';* from 5172; *enchanter; Nachshon*, an Isr.:—Naashon, Nahshon.

5178. נְחֹשֶׁת **nᵉchôsheth**, *nekh-o'-sheth;* for 5154; *copper;* hence, something made of that metal, i.e. *coin*, a *fetter;* fig. *base* (as compared with gold or silver):—brasen, brass, chain, copper, fetter (of brass), filthiness, steel.

5179. נְחֻשְׁתָּא **Nᵉchushtâ'**, *nekh-oosh-taw';* from 5178; *copper; Nechushta*, an Israelitess:—Nehushta.

5180. נְחֻשְׁתָּן **Nᵉchushtân**, *nekh-oosh-tawn';* from 5178; something made *of copper*, i.e. the copper *serpent* of the Desert:—Nehushtan.

5181. נָחַת **nâchath**, *naw-khath';* a prim. root; to *sink*, i.e. *descend;* causat., to *press* or *lead* down:—be broken, (cause to) come down, enter, go down, press sore, settle, stick fast.

5182. נְחַת **nᵉchath** (Chald.), *nekh-ath';* corresp. to 5181; to *descend;* causat., to *bring away, deposit, depose:*—carry, come down, depose, lay up, place.

5183. נַחַת **nachath**, *nakh'-ath;* from 5182; a *descent*, i.e. imposition, unfavorable (*punishment*) or favorable (*food*); also (intrans.; perh. from 5117), *restfulness:*—lighting down, quiet (-ness), to rest, be set on.

5184. נַחַת **Nachath**, *nakh'-ath;* the same as 5183; *quiet; Nachath*, the name of an Edomite and of two Isr.:—Nahath.

5185. נָחֵת **nâchêth**, *naw-khayth';* from 5181; *descending:*—come down.

5186. נָטָה **nâṭâh**, *naw-taw';* a prim. root; to *stretch* or spread out; by impl. to *bend* away (includ. mor. deflection); used in a great variety of application (as follows):— + afternoon, apply, bow (down, -ing), carry aside, decline, deliver, extend, go down, be gone, incline, intend, lay, let down, offer, outstretched, overthrown, pervert, pitch, prolong, put away, shew, spread (out), stretch (forth, out), take (aside), turn (aside, away), wrest, cause to yield.

5187. נְטִיל **nᵉṭîyl**, *net-eel';* from 5190; *laden:*—that bear.

5188. נְטִיפָה **nᵉṭîyphâh**, *net-ee-faw';* from 5197; a *pendant* for the ears (espec. of pearls):—chain, collar.

5189. נְטִישָׁה **nᵉṭîyshâh**, *net-ee-shaw';* from 5203; a *tendril* (as an offshoot):—battlement, branch, plant.

5190. נָטַל **nâṭal**, *naw-tal';* a prim root; to *lift;* by impl. to *impose:*—bear, offer, take up.

5191. נְטַל **nᵉṭal** (Chald.), *net-al';* corresp. to 5190; to *raise:*—take up.

5192. נֵטֶל **nêṭel**, *nay'-tel;* from 5190; a *burden:*—weighty.

5193. נָטַע **nâṭaʻ**, *naw-tah';* a prim. root; prop. to *strike* in, i.e. *fix;* spec. to *plant* (lit. or fig.):—fastened, plant (-er).

5194. נֶטַע **neṭaʻ**, *neh'-tah;* from 5193; a *plant;* collect., a *plantation;* abstr., a *planting:*—plant.

5195. נָטִיעַ **nâṭîaʻ**, *naw-tee'-ah;* from 5193; a *plant:*—plant.

5196. נְטָעִים **Nᵉṭâʻîym**, *net-aw-eem';* plur. of 5194; *Netaïm*, a place in Pal.:—plants.

5197. נָטַף **nâṭaph**, *naw-taf';* a prim. root; to *ooze*, i.e. *distil* gradually; by impl. to *fall in drops;* fig. to *speak* by inspiration:—drop (-ping), prophesy (-et).

5198. נָטָף **nâṭâph**, *naw-tawf';* from 5197; a *drop;* spec., an aromatic *gum* (prob. *stacte*):—drop, stacte.

5199. נְטֹפָה **Nᵉṭôphâh**, *net-o-faw';* from 5197; *distillation; Netophah*, a place in Pal.:—Netophah.

5200. נְטֹפָתִי **Nᵉṭôphâthîy**, *net-o-faw-thee';* patron. from 5199; a *Netophathite*, or inhab. of Netophah:—Netophathite.

5201. נָטַר **nâṭar**, *naw-tar';* a prim. root; to *guard;* fig., to *cherish* (anger):—bear grudge, keep (-er), reserve.

5202. נְטַר **nᵉṭar** (Chald.), *net-ar';* corresp. to 5201; to *retain:*—keep.

5203. נָטַשׁ **nâṭash**, *naw-tash';* a prim. root; prop. to *pound*, i.e. *smite;* by impl. (as if beating out, and thus expanding) to *disperse;* also, to *thrust* off, down, out or upon (includ. *reject, let alone, permit, remit*, etc.):—cast off, drawn, let fall, forsake, join [battle], leave (off), lie still, loose, spread (self) abroad, stretch out, suffer.

5204. נִי **nîy**, *nee;* a doubtful word; appar. from 5091; *lamentation:*—wailing.

5205. נִיד **nîyd**, *need;* from 5110; *motion* (of the lips n speech):—moving.

5206. נִידָה **nîydâh**, *nee-daw';* fem. of 5205; *removal*, i.e. exile:—removed.

5207. נִיחוֹחַ **nîychôwach**, *nee-kho'-akh;* or

נִיחֹחַ **nîychôach**, *nee-kho'-akh;* from 5117; prop. *restful*, i.e. *pleasant;* abstr. *delight:*—sweet (odour).

5208. נִיחוֹחַ **nîychôwach** (Chald.), *nee-kho'-akh;* or (shorter)

נִיחֹחַ **nîychôach** (Chald.), *nee-kho'-akh;* corresp. to 5207; *pleasure:*—sweet odour (savour).

5209. נִין **nîyn**, *neen;* from 5125; *progeny:*—son.

5210. נִינְוֵה **Nîynᵉvêh**, *nee-nev-ay';* of for. or.; *Nineveh*, the capital of Assyria:—Nineveh.

5211. נִיס **nîyç**, *neece;* from 5127; *fugitive:*—that fleeth.

5212. נִיסָן **Nîyçân**, *nee-sawn';* prob. of for. or.; *Nisan*, the first month of the Jewish sacred year:—Nisan.

5213. נִיצוֹץ **nîytsôwts**, *nee-tsotes';* from 5340; a *spark:*—spark.

5214. נִיר **nîyr**, *neer;* a root prob. ident. with that of 5216, through the idea of the *gleam* of a fresh furrow; to *till* the soil:—break up.

5215. נִיר **nîyr**, *neer;* or

נִר **nîr**, *neer;* from 5214; prop. *ploughing*, i.e. (concr.) freshly *ploughed* land:—fallow ground, ploughing, tillage.

5216. נִיר **nîyr**, *neer;* or

נִר **nîr**, *neer;* also

נֵיר **nêyr**, *nare;* or

נֵר **nêr**, *nare;* or (fem.)

נֵרָה **nêrâh**, *nay-raw';* from a prim. root [see 5214; 5135] prop. mean. to *glisten;* a *lamp* (i.e. the burner) or *light* (lit. or fig.):—candle, lamp, light.

5217. נָכָא **nâkâ'**, *naw-kaw';* a prim. root; to *smite*, i.e. *drive away:*—be viler.

5218. נָכֵא **nâkê'**, *naw-kay';* or

נָכָא **nâkâ'**, *naw-kaw';* from 5217; *smitten*, i.e. (fig.) *afflicted:*—broken, stricken, wounded.

5219. נְכֹאת **nᵉkô'th**, *nek-ohth';* from 5218; prop. a *smiting*, i.e. (concr.) an aromatic *gum* [perh. *styrax*] (as *powdered*):—spicery (-ces).

5220. נֶכֶד **neked**, *neh'-ked;* from an unused root mean. to *propagate; offspring:*—nephew, son's son.

5221. נָכָה **nâkâh**, *naw-kaw';* a prim. root; to *strike* (lightly or severely, lit. or fig.):—beat, cast forth, clap, give [wounds], × go forward, × indeed, kill, make [slaughter], murderer, punish, slaughter, slay (-er, -ing), smite (-r, -ing), strike, be stricken, (give) stripes, × surely, wound.

5222. נֵכֶה **nêkeh**, *nay-keh';* from 5221; a *smiter*, i.e. (fig.) *traducer:*—abject.

5223. נָכֶה **nâkeh**, *naw-keh';* *smitten*, i.e. (lit.) maimed, or (fig.) dejected:—contrite, lame.

5224. נְכוֹ **Nᵉkôw**, *nek-o';* prob. of Eg. or.; *Neko* an Eg. king:—Necho. Comp. 6549.

5225. נָכוֹן **Nâkôwn**, *naw-kone';* from 3559; *prepared; Nakon*, prob. an Isr.:—Nachon.

5226. נֵכַח **nêkach**, *nay'-kakh;* from an unused root mean. to *be straightforward;* prop. the *fore* part; used adv., *opposite:*—before, over against.

5227. נֹכַח **nôkach**, *no'-kakh;* from the same as 5226; prop., the *front* part; used adv. (espec. with prep.), *opposite, in front of, forward, in behalf of:*—(over) against, before, direct [-ly], for, right (on).

5228. נָכֹחַ **nâkôach**, *naw-ko'-akh;* from the same as 5226; *straightforward*, i.e. (fig.), *equitable, correct*, or (abstr.), *integrity:*—plain, right, uprightness.

5229. נְכֹחָה **nᵉkôchâh**, *nek-o-khaw';* fem. of 5228; prop. *straightforwardness*, i.e. (fig.) *integrity*, or (concr.) *a truth:*—equity, right (thing), uprightness.

5230. נָכַל **nâkal**, *naw-kal';* a prim root; to *defraud*, i.e. *act treacherously:*—beguile, conspire, deceiver, deal subtilly.

5231. נֵכֶל **nêkel**, *nay'-kel;* from 5230; *deceit:*—wile.

5232. נְכַס **nᵉkaç** (Chald.), *nek-as';* corresp. to 5233:—goods.

5233. נֶכֶס **nekeç**, *neh'-kes;* from an unused root mean. to *accumulate; treasure:*—riches, wealth.

5234. נָכַר **nâkar**, *naw-kar';* a prim. root; prop. to *scrutinize*, i.e. look intently at; hence (with *recognition* implied), to *acknowledge, be acquainted with, care for, respect, revere*, or (with *suspicion* implied), to *disregard, ignore, be strange* toward, *reject, resign, dissimulate* (as if ignorant or disowning):—acknowledge, × could, deliver, discern, dissemble, estrange, feign self to be another, know, take knowledge (notice), perceive, regard, (have) respect, behave (make) self strange (-ly).

5235. נֶכֶר **neker**, *neh'-ker;* or

נֹכֶר **nôker**, *no'-ker;* from 5234; something *strange*, i.e. unexpected *calamity:*—strange.

5236. נֵכָר **nêkâr**, *nay-kawr';* from 5234; *foreign*, or (concr.) a *foreigner*, or (abstr.) *heathendom:*—alien, strange (+ -er).

5237. נָכְרִי **nokrîy**, *nok-ree';* from 5235 (second form); *strange*, in a variety of degrees and applications (*foreign, non-relative, adulterous, different, wonderful*):—alien, foreigner, outlandish, strange (-r, woman).

5238. נְכֹת **nᵉkôth**, *nek-ōth';* prob. for 5219; *spicery*, i.e. (gen.) *valuables:*—precious things.

5239. נָלָה **nâlâh**, *naw-law';* appar. a prim. root; to *complete:*—make an end.

5240. נְמִבְזֶה **nᵉmibzeh**, *nem-ib-zeh';* from 959; *despised:*—vile.

5241. נְמוּאֵל **Nᵉmûwʼêl**, *nem-oo-ale'*; appar. for 3223; *Nemuel*, the name of two Isr.:—Nemuel.

5242. נְמוּאֵלִי **Nᵉmûwʼêlîy**, *nem-oo-ay-lee'*; from 5241; a *Nemuelite*, or desc. of Nemuel:—Nemuelite.

5243. נָמַל **nâmal**, *naw-mal'*; a prim. root; to *become clipped* or (spec.) *circumcised*:—(branch to) be cut down (off), circumcise.

5244. נְמָלָה **nᵉmâlâh**, *nem-aw-law'*; fem. from 5243; an *ant* (prob. from its almost *bisected* form):—ant.

5245. נְמַר **nᵉmar** (Chald.), *nem-ar'*; corresp. to 5246:—leopard.

5246 נָמֵר **nâmêr**, *naw-mare'*; from an unused root mean. prop. to *filtrate*, i.e. *be limpid* [comp. 5247 and 5249]; and thus to *spot* or *stain* as if by dripping; a *leopard* (from its stripes):—leopard.

נִמְרֹד **Nimrôd**. See 5248.

5247. נִמְרָה **Nimrâh**, *nim-raw'*; from the same as 5246; *clear* water; *Nimrah*, a place E. of the Jordan:—Nimrah. See also 1039, 5249.

5248. נִמְרוֹד **Nimrôwd**, *nim-rode'*; or

נִמְרֹד **Nimrôd**, *nim-rode'*; prob. of for. or.; *Nimrod*, a son of Cush:—Nimrod.

5249. נִמְרִים **Nimrîym**, *nim-reem'*; plur. of a masc. corresp. to 5247; *clear* waters; *Nimrim*, a place E. of the Jordan:—Nimrim. Comp. 1039.

5250. נִמְשִׁי **Nimshîy**, *nim-shee'*; prob. from 4871; *extricated*; *Nimshi*, the (grand-) father of Jehu:—Nimshi.

5251. נֵס **nêç**, *nace*; from 5264; a *flag*; also a *sail*; by impl. a *flagstaff*; gen. a *signal*; fig. a *token*:—banner, pole, sail, (en-) sign, standard.

5252. נְסִבָּה **nᵉçibbâh**, *nes-ib-baw'*; fem. part. pass. of 5437; prop. an *environment*, i.e. *circumstance* or *turn* of affairs:—cause.

5253. נָסַג **nâçag**, *naw-sag'*; a prim. root; to *retreat*:—departing away, remove, take (hold), turn away.

נְסָה **nᵉçâh**. See 5375.

5254. נָסָה **nâçâh**, *naw-saw'*; a prim. root; to *test*; by impl. to *attempt*:—adventure, assay, prove, tempt, try.

5255. נָסַח **nâçach**, *naw-sakh'*; a prim. root; to *tear* away:—destroy, pluck, root.

5256. נְסַח **nᵉçach** (Chald.), *nes-akh'*; corresp. to 5255:—pull down.

5257. נְסִיךְ **nᵉçîyk**, *nes-eek'*; from 5258; prop. something *poured* out, i.e. a *libation*; also a molten *image*; by impl. a *prince* (as *anointed*):—drink offering, duke, prince (-ipal).

5258. נָסַךְ **nâçak**, *naw-sak'*; a prim. root; to *pour* out, espec. a libation, or to *cast* (metal); by anal. to *anoint* a king:—cover, melt, offer, (cause to) pour (out), set (up).

5259. נָסַךְ **nâçak**, *naw-sak'*; a prim. root [prob. identical with 5258 through the idea of fusion]; to *interweave*, i.e. (fig.) to *overspread*:—that is spread.

5260. נְסַךְ **nᵉçak** (Chald.), *nes-ak'*; corresp. to 5258; to *pour* out a libation:—offer.

5261. נְסַךְ **nᵉçak** (Chald.), *nes-ak'*; corresp. to 5262; a *libation*:—drink offering.

5262. נֶסֶךְ **neçek**, *neh'-sek*; or

נֵסֶךְ **nêçek**, *nay'-sek*; from 5258; a *libation*; also a *cast idol*:—cover, drink offering, molten image.

נִסְמָן **niçmân**. See 5567.

5263. נָסַס **nâçaç**, *naw-sas'*; a prim. root; to *wane*, i.e. *be sick*.

5264. נָסַס **nâçaç**, *naw-sas'*; a prim. root; to *gleam* from afar, i.e. to *be conspicuous* as a signal; or rather perh. a denom. from 5251 [and ident. with 5263, through the idea of a flag as *fluttering* in the wind]; to *raise a beacon*:—lift up as an ensign, standard bearer.

5265. נָסַע **nâçaʻ**, *naw-sah'*; a prim. root; prop. to *pull* up, espec. the tent-pins, i.e. *start* on a journey:—cause to blow, bring, get, (make to) go (away, forth, forward, onward, out), (take) journey, march, remove, set aside (forward), × still, be on his (go their) way.

5266. נָסַק **nâçaq**, *naw-sak'*; a prim. root; to *go* up:—ascend.

5267. נְסַק **nᵉçaq** (Chald.), *nes-ak'*; corresp. to 5266:—take up.

5268. נִסְרֹךְ **Niçrôk**, *nis-roke'*; of for. or.; *Nisrok*, a Bab. idol:—Nisroch.

5269. נֵעָה **Nêʻâh**, *nay-aw'*; from 5128; *motion*; *Neäh*, a place in Pal.:—Neah.

5270. נֹעָה **Nôʻâh**, *no-aw'*; from 5128; *movement*; *Noäh*, an Israelitess:—Noah.

5271. נָעוּר **nâʻûwr**, *naw-oor'*; or

נָעֻר **nâʻûr**, *naw-oor'*; and (fem.)

נְעֻרָה **nᵉʻûrâh**, *neh-oo-raw'*; prop. pass. part. from 5288 as denom.; (only in plur. collect. or emphat.) *youth*, the state (*juvenility*) or the persons (*young* people):—childhood, youth.

5272. נְעִיאֵל **Nᵉʻîyʼêl**, *neh-ee-ale'*; from 5128 and 410; *moved of God*; *Neïel*, a place in Pal.:—Neiel.

5273. נָעִים **nâʻîym**, *naw-eem'*; from 5276; *delightful* (obj. or subj., lit. or fig.):—pleasant (-ure), sweet.

5274. נָעַל **nâʻal**, *naw-al'*; a prim. root; prop. to *fasten* up, i.e. with a bar or cord; hence (denom. from 5275), to *sandal*, i.e. furnish with slippers:—bolt, inclose, lock, shod, shut up.

5275. נַעַל **naʻal**, *nah'-al*; or (fem.)

נַעֲלָה **naʻălâh**, *nah-al-aw'*; from 5274; prop. a sandal *tongue*; by extens. a *sandal* or slipper (sometimes as a symbol of occupancy, a refusal to marry, or of something valueless):—dryshod, (pair of) shoe ([-latchet], -s).

5276. נָעֵם **nâʻêm**, *naw-ame'*; a prim. root; to *be agreeable* (lit. or fig.):—pass in beauty, be delight, be pleasant, be sweet.

5277. נַעַם **Naʻam**, *nah'-am*; from 5276; *pleasure*; *Naam*, an Isr.:—Naam.

5278. נֹעַם **noʻam**, *no'-am*; from 5276; *agreeableness*, i.e. *delight*, *suitableness*, *splendor* or *grace*:—beauty, pleasant (-ness).

5279. נַעֲמָה **Naʻămâh**, *nah-am-aw'*; fem. of 5277; *pleasantness*; *Naamah*, the name of an antediluvian woman, of an Ammonitess, and of a place in Pal.:—Naamah.

5280. נַעֲמִי **Naʻămîy**, *nah-am-ee'*; patron. from 5283; a *Naamanite*, or desc. of Naaman (collect.):—Naamites.

5281. נָעֳמִי **Noʻŏmîy**, *nō-om-ee'*; from 5278; *pleasant*; *Noömi*, an Israelitess:—Naomi.

5282. נַעֲמָן **naʻămân**, *nah-am-awn'*; from 5276; *pleasantness* (plur. as concr.):—pleasant.

5283. נַעֲמָן **Naʻămân**, *nah-am-awn'*; the same as 5282; *Naaman*, the name of an Isr. and of a Damascene:—Naaman.

5284. נַעֲמָתִי **Naʻămâthîy**, *nah-am-aw-thee'*; patrial from a place corresp. in name (but not ident.) with 5279; a *Naamathite*, or inhab. of Naamah:—Naamathite

5285. נַעֲצוּץ **naʻătsûwts**, *nah-ats-oots'*; from an unused root mean. to *prick*; prob. a *brier*; by impl. a *thicket* of thorny bushes:—thorn.

5286. נָעַר **nâʻar**, *naw-ar'*; a prim. root; to *growl*:—yell.

5287. נָעַר **nâʻar**, *naw-ar'*; a prim. root [prob. ident. with 5286, through the idea of the *rustling* of mane, which usually accompanies the lion's roar]; to *tumble* about:—shake (off, out, self), overthrow, toss up and down.

5288. נַעַר **naʻar**, *nah'-ar*; from 5287; (concr.) a *boy* (as active), from the age of infancy to adolescence; by impl. a *servant*; also (by interch. of sex), a *girl* (of similar latitude in age):—babe, boy, child, damsel [*from the marg.*], lad, servant, young (man).

5289. נַעַר **naʻar**, *nah'-ar*; from 5287 in its der. sense of *tossing* about; a *wanderer*:—young one.

5290. נֹעַר **nôʻar**, *no'-ar*; from 5287; (abstr.) *boyhood* [comp. 5288]:—child, youth.

נָעֻר **nâʻûr**. See 5271.

5291. נַעֲרָה **naʻărâh**, *nah-ar-aw'*; fem. of 5288; a *girl* (from infancy to adolescence):—damsel, maid (-en), young (woman).

5292. נַעֲרָה **Naʻărâh**, *nah-ar-aw'*; the same as 5291; *Naarah*, the name of an Israelitess, and of a place in Pal.:—Naarah, Naarath.

נְעֻרָה **nᵉʻûrâh**. See 5271.

5293. נַעֲרַי **Naʻăray**, *nah-ar-ah'ee*; from 5288; *youthful*; *Naarai*, an Isr.:—Naarai.

5294. נְעַרְיָה **Nᵉʻaryâh**, *neh-ar-yaw'*; from 5288 and 3050; *servant of Jah*; *Neärjah*, the name of two Isr.:—Neariah.

5295. נַעֲרָן **Naʻărân**, *nah-ar-awn'*; from 5288; *juvenile*; *Naaran*, a place in Pal.:—Naaran.

5296. נְעֹרֶת **nᵉʻôreth**, *neh-o'-reth*; from 5287; something *shaken* out, i.e. *tow* (as the refuse of flax):—tow.

נַעֲרָתָה **Naʻărâthâh**. See 5292.

5297. נֹף **Nôph**, *nofe*; a var. of 4644; *Noph*, the capital of Upper Egypt:—Noph.

5298. נֶפֶג **Nepheg**, *neh'-feg*; from an unused root prob. mean. to *spring* forth; a *sprout*; *Nepheg*, the name of two Isr.:—Nepheg.

5299. נָפָה **nâphâh**, *naw-faw'*; from 5130 in the sense of *lifting*; a *height*; also a *sieve*:—border, coast, region, sieve.

5300. נְפוּשְׁסִים° **Nᵉphûwshᵉçîym**, *nef-oo-shes-eem'*; for 5304; *Nephushesim*, a Temple-servant:—Nephisesim [*from the marg.*].

5301. נָפַח **nâphach**, *naw-fakh'*; a prim. root; to *puff*, in various applications (lit., to *inflate*, *blow* hard, *scatter*, *kindle*, *expire*; fig., to *disesteem*):—blow, breath, give up, cause to lose [life], seething, snuff.

5302. נֹפַח **Nôphach**, *no'-fakh*; from 5301; a *gust*; *Nophach*, a place in Moab:—Nophah.

5303. נְפִיל **nᵉphîyl**, *nef-eel'*; or

נְפִל **nᵉphîl**, *nef-eel'*; from 5307; prop., a *feller*, i.e. a *bully* or *tyrant*:—giant.

5304. נְפִיסִים° **Nᵉphîyçîym**, *nef-ee-seem'*; plur. from an unused root mean. to *scatter*; *expansions*; *Nephisim*, a Temple-servant:—Nephusim [*from the marg.*].

5305. נָפִישׁ **Nâphîysh**, *naw-feesh'*; from 5314; *refreshed*; *Naphish*, a son of Ishmael, and his posterity:—Naphish.

5306. נֹפֶךְ **nôphek**, *no'-fek*; from an unused root mean. to *glisten*; *shining*; a gem, prob. the *garnet*:—emerald.

5307. נָפַל **nâphal**, *naw-fal'*; a prim. root; to *fall*, in a great variety of applications (intrans. or causat., lit. or fig.):—be accepted, cast (down, self, [lots], out), cease, die, divide (by lot), (let) fail, (cause to, let, make, ready to) fall (away, down, -en, -ing), fell (-ing), fugitive, have [inheritance], inferior, be judged [*by mistake for* 6419], lay (along), (cause to) lie down, light (down), be (× hast) lost, lying, overthrow, overwhelm, perish, present (-ed, -ing), (make to) rot, slay, smite out, × surely, throw down.

5308. נְפַל **nᵉphal** (Chald.), *nef-al'*; corresp. to 5307:—fall (down), have occasion.

5309. נֶפֶל **nephel**, *neh'-fel*; or

נֵפֶל **nêphel**, *nay'-fel*; from 5307; something *fallen*, i.e. an *abortion*:—untimely birth.

נְפִל **nᵉphîl**. See 5303.

5310. נָפַץ **nâphats**, *naw-fats'*; a prim. root; to *dash* to pieces, or *scatter*:—be beaten in sunder, break (in pieces), broken, dash (in pieces), cause to be discharged, dispersed, be overspread, scatter.

5311. נֶפֶץ **nephets**, *neh'-fets*; from 5310; a *storm* (as dispersing):—scattering.

5312. נְפַק **nᵉphaq** (Chald.), *nef-ak'*; a prim. root; to *issue*; causat., to *bring out*:—come (go, take) forth (out).

5313. נִפְקָא **niphqâʼ** (Chald.), *nif-kaw';* from 5312; an *outgo*, i.e. expense:—expense.

5314. נָפַשׁ **nâphash**, *naw-fash';* a prim. root; to *breathe;* pass., to *be breathed* upon, i.e. (fig.) *refreshed* (as if by a current of air):—(be) refresh selves (-ed).

5315. נֶפֶשׁ **nephesh**, *neh'-fesh;* from 5314; prop. a *breathing* creature, i.e. *animal* or (abstr.) *vitality;* used very widely in a lit., accommodated or fig. sense (bodily or mental):—any, appetite, beast, body, breath, creature, × dead (-ly), desire, × [dis-] contented, × fish, ghost, + greedy, he, heart (-y), (hath, × jeopardy of) life (× in jeopardy), lust, man, me, mind, mortally, one, own, person, pleasure, (her-, him-, my-, thy-) self, them (your) -selves, + slay, soul, + tablet, they, thing, (× she) will, × would have it.

5316. נֶפֶת **nepheth**, *neh'-feth;* for 5299; a *height:*—country.

5317. נֹפֶת **nôpheth**, *no'-feth;* from 5130 in the sense of *shaking* to pieces; a *dripping* i.e. of *honey* (from the comb):—honeycomb.

5318. נֶפְתּוֹחַ **Nephtôwach**, *nef-to'-akh;* from 6605; *opened*, i.e. a *spring; Nephtôach*, a place in Pal.:—Neptoah.

5319. נַפְתּוּל **naphtûwl**, *naf-tool';* from 6617; prop. *wrestled;* but used (in the plur.) trans., a *struggle:*—wrestling.

5320. נַפְתֻּחִים **Naphtûchîym**, *naf-too-kheem ;* plur. of for. or.; *Naphtuchim*, an Eg. tribe:—Naptuhim.

5321. נַפְתָּלִי **Naphtâlîy**, *naf-taw-lee';* from 6617; *my wrestling; Naphtali*, a son of Jacob, with the tribe descended from him, and its territory:—Naphtali.

5322. נֵץ **nêts**, *nayts;* from 5340; a *flower* (from its *brilliancy*); also a *hawk* (from its *flashing* speed):—blossom, hawk.

5323. נָצָא **nâtsâʼ**, *naw-tsaw';* a prim. root; to *go away:*—flee.

5324. נָצַב **nâtsab**, *naw-tsab';* a prim. root; to *station*, in various applications (lit. or fig.):—appointed, deputy, erect, establish, × Huzzah [*by mistake for a prop. name*], lay, officer, pillar, present, rear up, set (over, up), settle, sharpen, stablish, (make to) stand (-ing, still, up, upright), best state.

נְצִב **netsîb**. See 5333.

5325. נִצָּב **nitstsâb**, *nits-tsawb';* pass. part. of 5324; *fixed*, i.e. a *handle:*—haft.

5326. נִצְבָּה **nitsbâh** (Chald.), *nits-baw';* from a root corresp. to 5324; *fixedness*, i.e. *firmness:*—strength.

5327. נָצָה **nâtsâh**, *naw-tsaw';* a prim. root; prop. to *go forth*, i.e. (by impl.) to *be expelled*, and (consequently) *desolate;* causat. to *lay waste;* also (spec.), to *quarrel:*—be laid waste, ruinous, strive (together).

נֹצָה **nôtsâh**. See 5133.

5328. נִצָּה **nitstsâh**, *nits-tsaw';* fem. of 5322; a *blossom:*—flower.

נְצוּרָה **netsûwrâh**. See 5341.

5329. נָצַח **nâtsach**, *naw-tsakh';* a prim. root; prop. to *glitter* from afar, i.e. to be *eminent* (as a superintendent, espec. of the Temple services and its music); also (as denom. from 5331), to *be permanent:*—excel, chief musician (singer), oversee (-r), set forward.

5330. נְצַח **netsach** (Chald.), *nets-akh';* corresp. to 5329; to *become chief:*—be preferred.

5331. נֶצַח **netsach**, *neh'-tsakh;* or

נֵצַח **nêtsach**, *nay'-tsakh;* from 5329; prop. a *goal*, i.e. the bright object at a distance travelled towards; hence (fig.), *splendor*, or (subj.) *truthfulness*, or (obj.) *confidence;* but usually (adv.), *continually* (i.e. to the most distant point of view):—alway (-s), constantly, end, (+ n-) ever (more), perpetual, strength, victory.

5332. נֵצַח **Nêtsach**, *nay'-tsakh;* prob. ident. with 5331, through the idea of *brilliancy* of color; *juice* of the grape (as blood red):—blood, strength.

5333. נְצִיב **netsîyb**, *nets-eeb';* or

נְצִב **netsîb**, *nets-eeb';* from 5324; something *stationary*, i.e. a *prefect*, a military *post*, a *statue:*—garrison, officer, pillar.

5334. נְצִיב **Netsîyb**, *nets-eeb';* the same as 5333; *station; Netsib*, a place in Pal.:—Nezib.

5335. נְצִיחַ **netsîyach**, *nets-ee'-akh;* from 5329; *conspicuous; Netsiach*, a Temple-servant:—Neziah.

5336. נָצִיר° **nâtsîyr**, *naw-tsere';* from 5341; prop. *conservative;* but used pass., *delivered:*—preserved.

5337. נָצַל **nâtsal**, *naw-tsal';* a prim. root; to *snatch* away, whether in a good or a bad sense:— × at all, defend, deliver (self), escape, × without fail, part, pluck, preserve, recover, rescue, rid, save, spoil, strip, × surely, take (out).

5338. נְצַל **netsal** (Chald.), *nets-al';* corresp. to 5337; to *extricate:*—deliver, rescue.

5339. נִצָּן **nitstsân**, *nits-tsawn';* from 5322; a *blossom:*—flower.

5340. נָצַץ **nâtsats**, *naw-tsats';* a prim. root; to *glare*, i.e. *be bright*-colored:—sparkle.

5341. נָצַר **nâtsar**, *naw-tsar';* a prim. root; to *guard*, in a good sense (to *protect, maintain, obey*, etc.) or a bad one (to *conceal*, etc.):—besieged, hidden thing, keep (-er, -ing), monument, observe, preserve (-r), subtil, watcher (-man).

5342. נֵצֶר **nêtser**, *nay'-tser;* from 5341 in the sense of *greenness* as a striking color; a *shoot;* fig., a *descendant:*—branch.

5343. נְקֵא **neqêʼ** (Chald.), *nek-ay';* from a root corresp. to 5352; *clean:*—pure.

5344. נָקַב **nâqab**, *naw-kab';* a prim. root; to *puncture*, lit. (to *perforate*, with more or less violence) or fig. (to *specify, designate, libel*):—appoint, blaspheme, bore, curse, express, with holes, name, pierce, strike through.

5345. נֶקֶב **neqeb**, *neh'-keb;* a *bezel* (for a gem):—pipe.

5346. נֶקֶב **Neqeb**, *neh'-keb;* the same as 5345; *dell; Nekeb*, a place in Pal.:—Nekeb.

5347. נְקֵבָה **neqêbâh**, *nek-ay-baw';* from 5344; *female* (from the sexual form):—female, woman.

5348. נָקֹד **nâqôd**, *naw-kode';* from an unused root mean. to *mark* (by *puncturing* or *branding*); *spotted:*—speckled.

5349. נֹקֵד **nôqêd**, *no-kade';* act. part. from the same as 5348; a *spotter* (of sheep or cattle), i.e. the owner or tender (who thus marks them):—herdman, sheepmaster.

5350. נִקֻּד **niqqud**, *nik-kood';* from the same as 5348; a *crumb* (as *broken* to spots); also a *biscuit* (as *pricked*):—cracknel, mouldy.

5351. נְקֻדָּה **nequddâh**, *nek-ood-daw';* fem. of 5348; a *boss:*—stud.

5352. נָקָה **nâqâh**, *naw-kaw';* a prim. root; to *be* (or *make*) *clean* (lit. or fig.); by impl. (in an adverse sense) to *be bare*, i.e. *extirpated:*—acquit × at all, × altogether, be blameless, cleanse, (be) clear (-ing), cut off, be desolate, be free, be (hold) guiltless, be (hold) innocent, × by no means, be quit, be (leave) unpunished, × utterly, × wholly.

5353. נְקוֹדָא **Neqôwdâʼ**, *nek-o-daw';* fem. of 5348 (in the fig. sense of *marked*); *distinction; Nekoda*, a Temple-servant:—Nekoda.

5354. נָקַט **nâqaṭ**, *naw-kat';* a prim. root; to *loathe:*—weary.

5355. נָקִי **nâqîy**, *naw-kee';* or

נָקִיא **nâqîyʼ** (Joel 4 : 19; Jonah 1 : 14), *naw-kee';* from 5352; *innocent:*—blameless, clean, clear, exempted, free, guiltless, innocent, quit.

5356. נִקָּיוֹן **niqqâyôwn**, *nik-kaw-yone';* or

נִקָּיֹן **niqqâyôn**, *nik-kaw-yone';* from 5352; *clearness* (lit. or fig.):—cleanness, innocency.

5357. נָקִיק **nâqîyq**, *naw-keek';* from an unused root mean. to *bore;* a *cleft:*—hole.

5358. נָקַם **nâqam**, *naw-kam';* a prim. root; to *grudge*, i.e. *avenge* or *punish:*—avenge (-r, self), punish, revenge (self), × surely, take vengeance.

5359. נָקָם **nâqâm**, *naw-kawm';* from 5358; *revenge:*— + avenged, quarrel, vengeance.

5360. נְקָמָה **neqâmâh**, *nek-aw-maw';* fem. of 5359; *avengement*, whether the act or the passion:— + avenge, revenge (-ing), vengeance.

5361. נָקַע **nâqaʻ**, *naw-kah';* a prim. root; to *feel aversion:*—be alienated.

5362. נָקַף **nâqaph**, *naw-kaf';* a prim. root; to *strike* with more or less violence (*beat, fell, corrode*); by impl. (of attack) to *knock together*, i.e. *surround* or *circulate:*—compass (about, -ing), cut down, destroy, go round (about), inclose, round.

5363. נֹקֶף **nôqeph**, *no'-kef;* from 5362; a *threshing* (of olives):—shaking.

5364. נִקְפָּה **niqpâh**, *nik-paw';* from 5362; prob. a *rope* (as *encircling*):—rent.

5365. נָקַר **nâqar**, *naw-kar';* a prim. root; to *bore* (*penetrate, quarry*):—dig, pick out, pierce, put (thrust) out.

5366. נְקָרָה **neqârâh**, *nek-aw-raw';* from 5365; a *fissure:*—cleft, clift.

5367. נָקַשׁ **nâqash**, *naw-kash';* a prim. root; to *entrap* (with a noose), lit. or fig.:—catch. (lay a) snare.

5368. נְקַשׁ **neqash** (Chald.), *nek-ash';* corresp. to 5367; but used in the sense of 5362; to *knock:*—smote.

נֵר **nêr**, נִר **nîr**. See 5215, 5216.

5369. נֵר **Nêr**, *nare;* the same as 5216; *lamp; Ner*, an Isr.:—Ner.

5370. נֵרְגַּל **Nêrgal**, *nare-gal';* of for. or.; *Nergal*, a Cuthite deity:—Nergal.

5371. נֵרְגַּל שַׁרְאֶצֶר **Nêrgal Sharʼetser**, *nare-gal' shar-eh'-tser;* from 5370 and 8272; *Nergal-Sharetser*, the name of two Bab.:—Nergal-sharezer.

5372. נִרְגָּן **nirgân**, *neer-gawn';* from an unused root mean. to *roll* to pieces; a *slanderer:*—talebearer, whisperer.

5373. נֵרְדְּ **nêrd**, *nayrd;* of for. or.; *nard*, an aromatic:—spikenard.

נֵרָה **nêrâh**. See 5216.

5374. נֵרִיָּה **Nêrîyâh**, *nay-ree-yaw';* or

נֵרִיָּהוּ **Nêrîyâhûw**, *nay-ree-yaw'-hoo;* from 5216 and 3050; *light of Jah; Nerijah*, an Isr.:—Neriah.

5375. נָשָׂא **nâsâʼ**, *naw-saw';* or

נָסָה **nâçâh** (Psa. 4 : 6 [7]), *naw-saw';* a prim. root; to *lift*, in a great variety of applications, lit. and fig., absol. and rel. (as follows):—accept, advance, arise, (able to, [armour], suffer to) bear (-er, up), bring (forth), burn, carry (away), cast, contain, desire, ease, exact, exalt (self), extol, fetch, forgive, furnish, further, give, go on, help, high, hold up, honourable (+ man), lade, lay, lift (self) up, lofty, marry, magnify, × needs, obtain, pardon, raise (up), receive, regard, respect, set (up), spare, stir up, + swear, take (away, up), × utterly, wear, yield.

5376. נְשָׂא **nesâʼ** (Chald.), *nes-aw';* corresp. to 5375:—carry away, make insurrection, take.

5377. נָשָׁא **nâshâʼ**, *naw-shaw';* a prim. root; to *lead astray*, i.e. (mentally) to *delude*, or (morally) to *seduce:*—beguile, deceive, × greatly, × utterly.

5378. נָשָׁא **nâshâʼ**, *naw-shaw';* a prim. root [perh. ident. with 5377, through the idea of *imposition*]; to *lend* on interest; by impl. to *dun* for debt:—× debt, exact, giver of usury.

נָשִׂיא **nâsîʼ**. See 5387.

נְשׂוּאָה **nesûʼâh**. See 5385.

5379. נִשֵּׂאת **nissêʼth**, *nis-sayth';* pass. part. fem. of 5375; something *taken*, i.e. a *present:*—gift.

5380. נָשַׁב **nâshab**, *naw-shab';* a prim. root; to *blow;* by impl. to *disperse:*—(cause to) blow, drive away.

5381. נָשַׂג **nâsag**, *naw-sag'*; a prim. root; to *reach* (lit. or fig.):—ability, be able, attain (unto), (be able to, can) get, lay at, put, reach, remove, wax rich, × surely, (over-) take (hold of, on, upon).

5382. נָשָׁה **nâshâh**, *naw-shaw'*; a prim. root; to *forget;* fig., to *neglect;* causat., to *remit, remove:*—forget, deprive, exact.

5383. נָשָׁה **nâshâh**, *naw-shaw'*; a prim. root [rather ident. with 5382, in the sense of 5378]; to *lend* or (by reciprocity) *borrow* on security or interest:—creditor, exact, extortioner, lend, usurer, lend on (taker of) usury.

5384. נָשֶׁה **nâsheh**, *naw-sheh'*; from 5382, in the sense of *failure; rheumatic* or *crippled* (from the incident to Jacob):—which shrank.

5385. נְשׂוּאָה **nᵉsûw'âh**, *nes-oo-aw'*; or rather

נְשֻׂאָה **nᵉsu'âh**, *nes-oo-aw'*; fem. pass. part. of 5375; something *borne*, i.e. a *load:*—carriage.

5386. נְשִׁי **nᵉshîy**, *nesh-ee'*; from 5383; a *debt:*—debt.

5387. נָשִׂיא **nâsîy'**, *naw-see'*; or

נָשִׂא **nâsî'**, *naw-see'*; from 5375; prop. an *exalted* one, i.e. a *king* or *sheik;* also a rising *mist:*—captain, chief, cloud, governor, prince, ruler, vapour.

5388. נְשִׁיָּה **nᵉshîyâh**, *nesh-ee-yaw'*; from 5382; *oblivion:*—forgetfulness.

נָשִׁים **nâshîym**. See 802.

5389. נָשִׁין **nâshîyn** (Chald.), *naw-sheen'*; irreg. plur. fem. of 606:—women.

5390. נְשִׁיקָה **nᵉshîyqâh**, *nesh-ee-kaw'*; from 5401; a *kiss:*—kiss.

5391. נָשַׁךְ **nâshak**, *naw-shak'*; a prim. root; to *strike* with a sting (as a serpent); fig., to *oppress* with interest on a loan:—bite, lend upon usury.

5392. נֶשֶׁךְ **neshek**, *neh'-shek*; from 5391; *interest* on a debt:—usury.

5393. נִשְׁכָּה **nishkâh**, *nish-kaw'*; for 3957; a *cell:*—chamber.

5394. נָשַׁל **nâshal**, *naw-shal'*; a prim. root; to *pluck* off, i.e. *divest, eject*, or *drop:*—cast (out), drive, loose, put off (out), slip.

5395. נָשַׁם **nâsham**, *naw-sham'*; a prim. root; prop. to *blow* away, i.e. *destroy:*—destroy.

5396. נִשְׁמָא **nishmâ'** (Chald.), *nish-maw'*; corresp. to 5397; vital *breath:*—breath.

5397. נְשָׁמָה **nᵉshâmâh**, *nesh-aw-maw'*; fr. 5395; a *puff*, i.e. *wind*, angry or vital *breath*, divine *inspiration, intellect*. or (concr.) an *animal:*—blast, (that) breath (-eth), inspiration, soul, spirit.

5398. נָשַׁף **nâshaph**, *naw-shaf'*; a prim. root; to *breeze*, i.e. *blow* up fresh (as the wind):—blow.

5399. נֶשֶׁף **nesheph**, *neh'-shef*; from 5398; prop. a *breeze*, i.e. (by impl.) *dusk* (when the evening breeze prevails):—dark, dawning of the day (morning), night, twilight.

5400. נָשַׂק **nâsaq**, *naw-sak'*; a prim. root; to *catch* fire:—burn, kindle.

5401. נָשַׁק **nâshaq**, *naw-shak'*; a prim. root [ident. with 5400, through the idea of *fastening up*; comp. 2388, 2836]; to *kiss*, lit. or fig. (*touch*); also (as a mode of *attachment*), to *equip* with weapons:—armed (men), rule, kiss, that touched.

5402. נֶשֶׁק **nesheq**, *neh'-shek*; or

נֵשֶׁק **nêsheq**, *nay'-shek*; from 5401; military *equipment*, i.e. (collect.) *arms* (offensive or defensive), or (concr.) an *arsenal:*—armed men, armour (-y), battle, harness, weapon.

5403. נְשַׁר **nᵉshar** (Chald.), *nesh-ar'*; corresp. to 5404; an *eagle:*—eagle.

5404. נֶשֶׁר **nesher**, *neh'-sher*; from an unused root mean. to *lacerate;* the *eagle* (or other large bird of prey):—eagle.

5405. נָשַׁת **nâshath**, *naw-shath'*; a prim. root; prop. to *eliminate*, i.e. (intrans.) to *dry* up:—fail.

נְתִבָה **nᵉthîbâh**. See 5410.

5406. נִשְׁתְּוָן **nishtᵉvân**, *nish-tev-awn'*; prob. of Pers. or.; an *epistle:*—letter.

5407. נִשְׁתְּוָן **nishtᵉvân** (Chald.), *nish-tev-awn'*; corresp. to 5406:—letter.

נָתוּן° **Nathûwn**. See 5411.

5408. נָתַח **nâthach**, *naw-thakh'*; a prim. root; to *dismember:*—cut (in pieces), divide, hew in pieces.

5409. נֵתַח **nêthach**, *nay'-thakh*; from 5408; a *fragment:*—part, piece.

5410. נָתִיב **nâthîyb**, *naw-theeb'*; or (fem.)

נְתִיבָה **nᵉthîybâh**, *neth-ee-baw'*; or

נְתִבָה **nᵉthîbâh** (Jer. 6 : 16), *neth-ee-baw'*; from an unused root mean. to *tramp;* a (beaten) *track:*—path ([-way]), × travel [-ler], way.

5411. נָתִין **Nâthîyn**, *naw-theen'*; or

נָתוּן° **Nâthûwn** (Ezra 8 : 17), *naw-thoon'* (the prop. form, as pass. part.), from 5414; one *given*, i.e. (in the plur. only) the *Nethinim*, or Temple-servants (as *given* up to that duty):—Nethinims.

5412. נְתִין **Nᵉthîyn** (Chald.), *netheen'*; corresp. to 5411:—Nethinims.

5413. נָתַךְ **nâthak**, *naw-thak'*; a prim. root; to *flow* forth (lit. or fig.); by impl. to *liquefy:*—drop, gather (together), melt, pour (forth, out).

5414. נָתַן **nâthan**, *naw-than'*; a prim. root; to *give*, used with great latitude of application (*put, make*, etc.):—add, apply, appoint, ascribe, assign, × avenge, × be ([healed]), bestow, bring (forth, hither), cast, cause, charge, come, commit consider, count, + cry, deliver (up), direct, distribute do, × doubtless, × without fail, fasten, frame, × get, give (forth, over, up), grant, hang (up), × have, × indeed, lay (unto charge, up), (give) leave, lend, let (out), + lie, lift up, make, + O that, occupy, offer, ordain, pay, perform, place, pour, print, × pull, put (forth), recompense, render, requite, restore, send (out), set (forth), shew, shoot forth (up). + sing, + slander, strike, [sub-] mit, suffer, × surely, × take, thrust, trade, turn, utter, + weep, × willingly, + withdraw, + would (to) God, yield.

5415. נְתַן **nᵉthan** (Chald.), *neth-an'*; corresp. to 5414; *give:*—bestow, give, pay.

5416. נָתָן **Nâthân**, *naw-thawn'*; from 5414; *given; Nathan*, the name of five Isr.:—Nathan.

5417. נְתַנְאֵל **Nᵉthanêl**, *neth-an-ale'*; from 5414 and 410; *given of God; Nethanel*, the name of ten Isr.:—Nethaneel.

5418. נְתַנְיָה **Nᵉthanyâh**, *neth-an-yaw'*; or

נְתַנְיָהוּ **Nᵉthanyâhûw**, *neth-an-yaw'-hoo*; from 5414 and 3050; *given of Jah; Nethanjah*, the name of four Isr.:—Nethaniah.

5419. נְתַן־מֶלֶךְ **Nᵉthan-Melek**, *neth-an' meh'-lek*; from 5414 and 4428; *given of (the) king; Nethan-Melek*, an Isr.:—Nathan-melech.

5420. נָתַס **nâthaç**, *naw-thas'*; a prim. root; to *tear* up:—mar.

5421. נָתַע **nâthaʽ**, *naw-thah'*; for 5422; to *tear* out:—break.

5422. נָתַץ **nâthats**, *naw-thats'*; a prim. root; to *tear* down:—beat down, break down (out), cast down, destroy, overthrow, pull down, throw down.

5423. נָתַק **nâthaq**, *naw-thak'*; a prim. root; to *tear* off:—break (off), burst, draw (away), lift up, pluck (away, off), pull (out), root out.

5424. נֶתֶק **netheq**, *neh'-thek*; from 5423; *scurf:*—(dry) scall.

5425. נָתַר **nâthar**, *naw-thar'*; a prim. root; to *jump*, i.e. be violently *agitated;* causat., to *terrify, shake* off, *untie:*—drive asunder, leap, (let) loose, × make, move, undo.

5426. נְתַר **nᵉthar** (Chald.), *neth-ar'*; corresp. to 5425:—shake off.

5427. נֶתֶר **nether**, *neh'-ther*; from 5425; mineral *potash* (so called from *effervescing* with acid):—nitre.

5428. נָתַשׁ **nâthash**, *naw-thash'*; a prim. root; to *tear* away:—destroy, forsake, pluck (out, up, by the roots), pull up, root out (up), × utterly.

ס

5429. סְאָה **çᵉ'âh**, *seh-aw'*; from an unused root mean. to *define;* a *seäh*, or certain measure (as *determinative*) for grain:—measure.

5430. סְאוֹן **çᵉ'ôwn**, *seh-own'*; from 5431; perh. a military *boot* (as a protection from *mud*):—battle.

5431. סָאַן **çâ'an**, *saw-an'*; a prim. root; to *be miry;* used only as denom. from 5430; to *shoe*, i.e. (act. part.) a *soldier* shod:—warrior.

5432. סַאסְאָה° **ça'çᵉ'âh**, *sah-seh-aw'*; for 5429; *measurement*, i.e. *moderation:*—measure.

5433. סָבָא **çâbâ'**, *saw-baw'*; a prim. root; to *quaff* to satiety, i.e. *become tipsy:*—drunkard, fill self, Sabean, [wine-] bibber.

5434. סְבָא **Çᵉbâ'**, *seb-aw'*; of for. or.; *Seba*, a son of Cush, and the country settled by him:—Seba.

5435. סֹבֶא **çôbe'**, *so'-beh*; from 5433; *potation*, concr. (*wine*), or abstr. (*carousal*):—drink, drunken, wine.

5436. סְבָאִי **Çᵉbâ'îy**, *seb-aw-ee'*; patrial from 5434; a *Sebaite*, or inhab. of Seba:—Sabean.

5437. סָבַב **çâbab**, *saw-bab'*; a prim. root; to *revolve, surround* or *border;* used in various applications, lit. and fig. (as follows):—bring, cast, fetch, lead, make, walk, × whirl, × round about, be about on every side, apply, avoid, beset (about), besiege, bring again, carry (about), change, cause to come about, × circuit, (fetch a) compass (about, round), drive, environ, × on every side, beset (close, come, compass, go, stand) round about, remove, return, set, sit down, turn (self) (about, aside, away, back).

5438. סִבָּה **çibbâh**, *sib-baw'*; from 5437; a (prov-idential) *turn* (of affairs):—cause.

5439. סָבִיב **çâbîyb**, *saw-beeb'*; or (fem.)

סְבִיבָה **çᵉbîybâh**, *seb-ee-baw'*; from 5437; (as noun) a *circle, neighbor*, or *environs;* but chiefly (as adv., with or without prep.) *around:*—(place, round) about, circuit, compass, on every side.

5440. סָבַךְ **çâbak**, *saw-bak'*; a prim. root; to *entwine:*—fold together, wrap.

5441. סְבֹךְ **çôbek**, *so'-bek*; from 5440; a *copse:*—thicket.

5442. סְבָךְ **çᵉbâk**, *seb-awk'*; from 5440; a *copse:*—thick (-et).

5443. סַבְּכָא **çabbᵉkâ'** (Chald.), *sab-bek-aw'*; or

שַׂבְּכָא **sabbᵉkâ'** (Chald.), *sab-bek-aw'*; from a root corresp. to 5440; a *lyre:*—sackbut.

5444. סִבְּכַי **Çibbᵉkay**, *sib-bek-ah'ee*; from 5440; *copse-like; Sibbecai*, an Isr.:—Sibbecai, Sibbechai.

5445. סָבַל **çâbal**, *saw-bal'*; a prim. root; to *carry* (lit. or fig.), or (reflex.) *be burdensome;* spec. to *be gravid:*—bear, be a burden, carry, strong to labour.

5446. סְבַל **çᵉbal** (Chald.), *seb-al'*; corresp. to 5445; to *erect:*—strongly laid.

5447. סֵבֶל **çêbel**, *say'-bel*; from 5445; a *load* (lit. or fig.):—burden, charge.

5448. סֹבֶל **çôbel**, *so'-bel* [only in the form

סֻבָּל **çubbâl**, *soob-bawl'*]; from 5445; a *load* (fig.):—burden.

5449. סַבָּל **çabbâl**, *sab-bawl'*; from 5445; a *porter:*—(to bear, bearer of) burden (-s).

5450. סְבָלָה **çᵉbâlâh**, *seb-aw-law'*; from 5447; *porterage:*—burden.

5451. סִבֹּלֶת **çibbôleth**, *sib-bo'-leth*; for 7641; an *ear* of grain:—Sibboleth.

5452. סְבַר **çᵉbar** (Chald.), *seb-ar'*; a prim. root; to *bear in mind*, i.e. *hope:*—think.

5453. סִבְרַיִם **Çibrayim**, *sib-rah'-yim*; dual from a root corresp. to 5452; *double hope; Sibrajim*, a place in Syria:—Sibraim.

5454. סַבְתָּא **Çabtâʼ**, *sab-taw'*; or

סַבְתָּה **Çabtâh**, *sab-taw'*; prob. of for. der.; *Sabta* or *Sabtah*, the name of a son of Cush, and the country occupied by his posterity:—Sabta, Sabtah.

5455. סַבְתְּכָא **Çabtᵉkâʼ**, *sab-tek-aw'*; prob. of for. der.; *Sabteca*, the name of a son of Cush, and the region settled by him:—Sabtecha, Sabtechah.

5456. סָגַד **çâgad**, *saw-gad'*; a prim. root; to *prostrate* oneself (in homage):—fall down.

5457. סְגִד **çᵉgîd** (Chald.), *seg-eed'*; corresp. to 5456:—worship.

5458. סְגוֹר **çᵉgôwr**, *seg-ore'*; from 5462; prop. *shut up*, i.e. the *breast* (as inclosing the heart); also *gold* (as generally *shut* up safely):—caul, gold.

5459. סְגֻלָּה **çᵉgullâh**, *seg-ool-law'*; fem. pass. part. of an unused root mean. to *shut* up; *wealth* (as closely *shut* up):—jewel, peculiar (treasure), proper good, special.

5460. סְגַן **çᵉgan** (Chald.), *seg-an'*; corresp. to 5461:—governor.

5461. סָגָן **çâgân**, *saw-gawn'*; from an unused root mean. to *superintend*; a *præfect* of a province:—prince, ruler.

5462. סָגַר **çâgar**, *saw-gar'*; a prim. root; to *shut* up; fig. to *surrender*:—close up, deliver (up), give over (up), inclose, × pure, repair, shut (in, self, out, up, up together), stop, × straitly.

5463. סְגַר **çᵉgar** (Chald.), *seg-ar'*; corresp. to 5462:—shut up.

5464. סַגְרִיד **çagrîyd**, *sag-reed'*; prob. from 5462 in the sense of *sweeping* away; a *pouring rain*:—very rainy.

5465. סַד **çad**, *sad*; from an unused root mean. to *estop*; the *stocks*:—stocks.

5466. סָדִין **çâdîyn**, *saw-deen'*; from an unused root mean. to *envelop*; a *wrapper*, i.e. *shirt*:—fine linen, sheet.

5467. סְדֹם **Çᵉdôm**, *sed-ome'*; from an unused root mean. to *scorch*; *burnt* (i.e. *volcanic* or *bituminous*) district; *Sedom*, a place near the Dead Sea:—Sodom.

5468. סֶדֶר **çeder**, *seh'-der*; from an unused root mean. to *arrange*; *order*:—order.

5469. סַהַר **çahar**, *sah'-har*; from an unused root mean. to *be round*; *roundness*:—round.

5470. סֹהַר **çôhar**, *so'-har*; from the same as 5469; a *dungeon* (as *surrounded* by walls):—prison.

5471. סוֹא **Çôwʼ**, *so*; of for. der.; *So*, an Eg. king:—So.

5472. סוּג **çûwg**, *soog*; a prim. root; prop. to *flinch*, i.e. (by impl.) to *go back*, lit. (to *retreat*) or fig. (to *apostatize*):—backslider, drive, go back, turn (away, back).

5473. סוּג **çûwg**, *soog*; a prim. root [prob. rather ident. with 5472 through the idea of *shrinking* from a hedge; comp. 7735]; to *hem* in, i.e. *bind*:—set about.

סוּג° **çûwg**. See 5509.

5474. סוּגַר **çûwgar**, *soo-gar'*; from 5462; an *inclosure*, i.e. *cage* (for an animal):—ward.

5475. סוֹד **çôwd**, *sode*; from 3245; a *session*, i.e. *company* of persons (in close deliberation); by impl. *intimacy*, *consultation*, a *secret*:—assembly, counsel, inward, secret (counsel).

5476. סוֹדִי **Çôwdîy**, *so-dee'*; from 5475; a *confidant*; *Sodi*, an Isr.:—Sodi.

5477. סוּחַ **Çûwach**, *soo'-akh*; from an unused root mean. to *wipe* away; *sweeping*; *Suăch*, an Isr.:—Suah.

5478. סוּחָה **çûwchâh**, *soo-khaw'*; from the same as 5477; something *swept* away, i.e. *filth*:—torn.

סוּט **çûwṭ**. See 7750.

5479. סוֹטַי **Çôwṭay**, *so-tah'ee*; from 7750; *roving*; *Sotai*, one of the Nethinim:—Sotai.

5480. סוּךְ **çûwk**, *sook*; a prim. root; prop. to *smear* over (with oil), i.e. *anoint*:—anoint (self), × at all.

סוֹלְלָה **çôwlᵉlâh**. See 5550.

5481. סוּמְפּוֹנְיָה **çûwmpôwnᵉyâh** (Chald.), *soom-po-neh-yaw'*; or

סוּמְפֹּנְיָה **çûwmpônᵉyâh** (Chald.), *soom-po-neh-yaw'*; or

סִיפֹנְיָא° **çîyphônᵉyâʼ** (Dan. 3 : 10) (Chald.), *see-fo-neh-yaw'*; of Greek origin (συμφωνία); a *bagpipe* (with a double pipe):—dulcimer.

5482. סְוֵנֵה **Çᵉvênêh**, *sev-ay-nay'* [rather to be written

סְוֵנָה **Çᵉvênâh**, *sev-ay'-naw*; for

סְוֵן **Çᵉvên**, *sev-ane'*; i.e. *to Seven*]; of Eg. der.; *Seven*, a place in Upper Eg.:—Syene.

5483. סוּס **çûwç**, *soos*; or

סֻס **çûç**, *soos*; from an unused root mean. to *skip* (prop. for joy); a *horse* (as leaping); also a *swallow* (from its rapid *flight*):—crane, horse ([-back, -hoof]). Comp. 6571.

5484. סוּסָה **çûwçâh**, *soo-saw'*; fem. of 5483; a *mare*:—company of horses.

5485. סוּסִי **Çûwçîy**, *soo-see'*; from 5483; *horse-like*; *Susi*, an Isr.:—Susi.

5486. סוּף **çûwph**, *soof*; a prim. root; to *snatch* away, i.e. *terminate*:—consume, have an end, perish, × be utterly.

5487. סוּף **çûwph** (Chald.), *soof*; corresp. to 5486; to *come to an end*:—consume, fulfil.

5488. סוּף **çûwph**, *soof*; prob. of Eg. or.; a *reed*, espec. the *papyrus*:—flag, Red [sea], weed. Comp. 5489.

5489. סוּף **Çûwph**, *soof*; for 5488 (by ellipsis of 3220); the *Reed* (*Sea*):—Red sea.

5490. סוֹף **çôwph**, *sofe*; from 5486; a *termination*:—conclusion, end, hinder part.

5491. סוֹף **çôwph** (Chald.), *sofe*; corresp. to 5490:—end.

5492. סוּפָה **çûwphâh**, *soo-faw'*; from 5486; a *hurricane*:—Red Sea, storm, tempest, whirlwind, Red sea.

5493. סוּר **çûwr**, *soor*; or

שׂוּר **sûwr** (Hos. 9 : 12), *soor*; a prim. root; to *turn* off (lit. or fig.):—be [-head], bring, call back, decline, depart, eschew, get [you], go (aside), × grievous, lay away (by), leave undone, be past, pluck away, put (away, down), rebel, remove (to and fro), revolt, × be sour, take (away, off), turn (aside, away, in), withdraw, be without.

5494. סוּר **çûwr**, *soor*; prob. pass. part. of 5493; *turned* off, i.e. *deteriorated*:—degenerate.

5495. סוּר **Çûwr**, *soor*; the same as 5494; *Sur*, a gate of the Temple:—Sur.

5496. סוּת **çûwth**, *sooth*; perh. denom. from 7898; prop. to *prick*, i.e. (fig.) stimulate; by impl. to *seduce*:—entice, move, persuade, provoke, remove, set on, stir up, take away.

5497. סוּת **çûwth**, *sooth*; prob. from the same root as 4533; *covering*, i.e. *clothing*:—clothes.

5498. סָחַב **çâchab**, *saw-khab'*; a prim. root; to *trail* along:—draw (out), tear.

5499. סְחָבָה **çᵉchâbâh**, *seh-khaw-baw'*; from 5498; a *rag*:—cast clout.

5500. סָחָה **çâchâh**, *saw-khaw'*; a prim. root; to *sweep* away:—scrape.

5501. סְחִי **çᵉchîy**, *seh-khee'*; from 5500; *refuse* (as *swept* off):—offscouring.

סָחִישׁ **çâchîysh**. See 7823.

5502. סָחַף **çâchaph**, *saw-khaf'*; a prim. root; to *scrape* off:—sweep (away).

5503. סָחַר **çâchar**, *saw-khar'*; a prim. root; to *travel* round (spec. as a *pedlar*); intens. to *palpitate*:—go about, merchant (-man), occupy with, pant, trade, traffick.

5504. סַחַר **çachar**, *sakh'-ar*; from 5503; *profit* (from trade):—merchandise.

5505. סָחַר **çâchar**, *saw-khar'*; from 5503; an *emporium*; abstr. *profit* (from trade):—mart, merchandise.

5506. סְחֹרָה **çᵉchôrâh**, *sekh-o-raw'*; from 5503; *traffic*:—merchandise.

5507. סֹחֵרָה **çôchêrâh**, *so-khay-raw'*; prop. act. part. fem. of 5503; something *surrounding* the person, i.e. a *shield*:—buckler.

5508. סֹחֶרֶת **çôchereth**, *so-kheh'-reth*; similar to 5507; prob. a (black) *tile* (or *tessara*) for laying borders with:—black marble.

סֵט **çêṭ**. See 7750.

5509. סִיג **çîyg**, *seeg*; or

סוּג° **çûwg** (Ezek. 22 : 18), *soog*; from 5472 in the sense of *refuse*; *scoria*:—dross.

5510. סִיוָן **Çîyvân**, *see-vawn'*; prob. of Pers. or.; *Sivan*, the third Heb. month:—Sivan.

5511. סִיחוֹן **Çîychôwn**, *see-khone'*; or

סִיחֹן **Çîychôn**, *see-khone'*; from the same as 5477; *tempestuous*; *Sichon*, an Amoritish king:—Sihon.

5512. סִין **Çîyn**, *seen*; of uncert. der.; *Sin*, the name of an Eg. town and (prob.) desert adjoining:—Sin.

5513. סִינִי **Çîynîy**, *see-nee'*; from an otherwise unknown name of a man; a *Sinite*, or descend. of one of the sons of Canaan:—Sinite.

5514. סִינַי **Çîynay**, *see-nah'ee*; of uncert. der.; *Sinai*, a mountain of Arabia:—Sinai.

5515. סִינִים **Çîynîym**, *see-neem'*; plur. of an otherwise unknown name; *Sinim*, a distant Oriental region:—Sinim.

5516. סִיסְרָא **Çîyçᵉrâʼ**, *see-ser-aw'*; of uncert. der.; *Sisera*, the name of a Canaanitish king and of one of the Nethinim:—Sisera.

5517. סִיעָא **Çîyʻâʼ**, *see-ah'*; or

סִיעֲהָא **Çîyʻăhâʼ**, *see-ah-haw'*; from an unused root mean. to *converse*; *congregation*; *Sia*, or *Siaha*, one of the Nethinim:—Sia, Siaha.

סִיפֹנְיָא° **çîyphônᵉyâʼ**. See 5481.

5518. סִיר **çîyr**, *seer*; or (fem.)

סִירָה **çîyrâh**, *see-raw'*; or

סִרָה **çîrâh** (Jer. 52 : 18), *see-raw'*; from a prim. root mean. to *boil* up; a *pot*; also a *thorn* (as springing up rapidly); by impl. a *hook*:—caldron, fishhook, pan, ([wash-]) pot, thorn.

5519. סָךְ **çâk**, *sawk*; from 5526; prop. a *thicket* of men, i.e. a *crowd*:—multitude.

5520. סֹךְ **çôk**, *soke*; from 5526; a *hut* (as of *entwined* boughs); also a *lair*:—covert, den, pavilion, tabernacle.

5521. סֻכָּה **çukkâh**, *sook-kaw'*; fem. of 5520; a *hut* or *lair*:—booth, cottage, covert, pavilion, tabernacle, tent.

5522. סִכּוּת **çikkûwth**, *sik-kooth'*; fem. of 5519; an (idolatrous) *booth*:—tabernacle.

5523. סֻכּוֹת **Çukkôwth**, *sook-kohth'*; or

סֻכֹּת **Çukkôth**, *sook-kohth'*; plur. of 5521; *booths*; *Succoth*, the name of a place in Egypt and of three in Pal.:—Succoth.

5524. סֻכּוֹת בְּנוֹת **Çukkôwth bᵉnôwth**, *sook-kohth' ben-ohth'*; from 5523 and the (irreg.) plur. of 1323; *booths of* (*the*) *daughters*; *brothels*, i.e. idolatrous *tents* for impure purposes:—Succoth-benoth.

5525. סֻכִּי **Çukkîy**, *sook-kee'*; patrial from an unknown name (perh. 5520); a *Sukkite*, or inhab. of some place near Eg. (i.e. *hut-dwellers*):—Sukkiims.

5526. סָכַךְ **çâkak**, *saw-kak'*; or

שָׂכַךְ **sâkak** (Exod. 33 : 22), *saw-kak'*; a prim. root; prop. to *entwine* as a screen; by impl. to *fence* in, *cover* over, (fig.) *protect*:—cover, defence, defend, hedge in, join together, set, shut up.

5527. סְכָכָה **Çᵉkâkâh**, *sek-aw-kaw'*; from 5526; *inclosure; Secacah*, a place in Pal.:—Secacah.

5528. סָכַל **çâkal**, *saw-kal'*; for 3688; to *be silly:*—do (make, play the, turn into) fool (-ish, -ishly, -ishness).

5529. סֶכֶל **çekel**, *seh'-kel;* from 5528; *silliness;* concr. and collect. *dolts:*—folly.

5530. סָכָל **çâkâl**, *saw-kawl';* from 5528; *silly:*—fool (-ish), sottish.

5531. סִכְלוּת **çiklûwth**, *sik-looth';* or

שִׂכְלוּת **siklûwth** (Eccl. 1 : 17), *sik-looth';* from 5528; *silliness:*—folly, foolishness.

5532. סָכַן **çâkan**, *saw-kan';* a prim. root; to *be familiar* with; by impl. to *minister* to, *be serviceable* to, to *cherish, be customary:*—acquaint (self), be advantage, × ever, (be, [un-]) profit (-able), treasurer, be wont.

5533. סָכַן **çâkan**, *saw-kan';* prob. a denom. from 7915; prop. *to cut*, i.e. *damage;* also to *grow* (caus. *make*) *poor:*—endanger, impoverish.

5534. סָכַר **çâkar**, *saw-kar';* a prim. root; to *shut* up; by impl. to *surrender:*—stop, give over. See also 5462; 7936.

5535. סָכַת **çâkath**, *saw-kath';* a prim. root; to *be silent;* by impl. to *observe* quietly:—take heed.

סֻכֹּת **Çukkôth**. See 5523.

5536. סַל **çal**, *sal;* from 5549; prop. a willow *twig* (as *pendulous*), i.e. an *osier;* but only as woven into a *basket:*—basket.

5537. סָלָא **çâlâʼ**, *saw-law';* a prim. root; to *suspend* in a balance, i.e. *weigh:*—compare.

5538. סִלָּא **Çillâʼ**, *sil-law';* from 5549; an *embankment; Silla*, a place in Jerus.:—Silla.

5539. סָלַד **çâlad**, *saw-lad';* a prim. root; prob. to *leap* (with joy), i.e. *exult:*—harden self.

5540. סֶלֶד **Çeled**, *seh'-led;* from 5539; *exultation; Seled*, an Isr.:—Seled.

5541. סָלָה **çâlâh**, *saw-law';* a prim. root; to *hang* up, i.e. *weigh*, or (fig.) *contemn:*—tread down (under foot), value.

5542. סֶלָה **çelâh**, *seh'-law;* from 5541; *suspension* (of music), i.e. *pause:*—Selah.

5543. סַלּוּ **Çallûw**, *sal-loo';* or

סַלּוּא **Çallûwʼ**, *sal-loo';* or

סָלוּא **Çâlûw**, *saw-loo';* or

סַלַּי **Çallay**, *sal-lah'ee;* from 5541; *weighed; Sallu* or *Sallai*, the name of two Isr.:—Sallai, Sallu, Salu.

5544. סִלּוֹן **çillôwn**, *sil-lone';* or

סַלּוֹן **çallôwn**, *sal-lone';* from 5541; a *prickle* (as if *pendulous*):—brier, thorn.

5545. סָלַח **çâlach**, *saw-lakh';* a prim. root; to *forgive:*—forgive, pardon, spare.

5546. סַלָּח **callâch**, *sal-lawkh';* from 5545; *placable:*—ready to forgive.

סַלַּי **Çallay**. See 5543.

5547. סְלִיחָה **çᵉlîychâh**, *sel-ee-khaw';* from 5545; *pardon:*—forgiveness, pardon.

5548. סַלְכָה **Çalkâh**, *sal-kaw';* from an unused root mean. to *walk; walking; Salcah*, a place E. of the Jordan:—Salcah, Salchah.

5549. סָלַל **çâlal**, *saw-lal';* a prim. root; to *mound* up (espec. a turnpike); fig. to *exalt;* reflex. to *oppose* (as by a dam):—cast up, exalt (self), extol, make plain, raise up.

5550. סֹלְלָה **çôlᵉlâh**, *so-lel-aw';* or

סוֹלְלָה **çôwlᵉlâh**, *so-lel-aw';* act. part. fem. of 5549, but used pass.; a military *mound*, i.e. *rampart* of besiegers:—bank, mount.

5551. סֻלָּם **çullâm**, *sool-lawm';* from 5549; a *stair-case:*—ladder.

5552. סַלְסִלָּה **çalçillâh**, *sal-sil-law';* from 5541; a *twig* (as *pendulous*):—basket.

5553. סֶלַע **çelaʻ**, *seh'-lah;* from an unused root mean. to be *lofty;* a craggy *rock*, lit. or fig. (a *fortress*):—(ragged) rock, stone (-ny), strong hold.

5554. סֶלַע **Çelaʻ**, *seh'-lah;* the same as 5553; *Sela*, the rock-city of Idumæa:—rock, Sela (-h).

5555. סֶלַע הַמַּחְלְקוֹת **Çelaʻ ham-machlᵉqôwth**, *seh'-lah ham-makh-lek-ōth';* from 5553 and the plur. of 4256 with the art. interposed; *rock of the divisions; Sela-ham-Machlekoth*, a place in Pal.:—Sela-hammalekoth.

5556. סָלְעָם **colʻâm**, *sol-awm';* appar. from the same as 5553 in the sense of *crushing* as with a rock, i.e. consuming; a kind of *locust* (from its *destructiveness*):—bald locust.

5557. סָלַף **çâlaph**, *saw-laf';* a prim. root; prop. to *wrench*, i.e. (fig.) to *subvert:*—overthrow, pervert.

5558. סֶלֶף **çeleph**, *seh'-lef;* from 5557; *distortion*, i.e. (fig.) *viciousness:*—perverseness.

5559. סְלִק **çᵉlîq** (Chald.), *sel-eek';* a prim. root; to *ascend:*—come (up).

5560. סֹלֶת **çôleth**, *so'-leth;* from an unused root mean. to *strip; flour* (as *chipped* off):—(fine) flour, meal.

5561. סַם **çam**, *sam;* from an unused root mean. to *smell* sweet; an *aroma:*—sweet (spice).

5562. סַמְגַּר נְבוֹ **Çamgar Nᵉbôw**, *sam-gar' neb-o';* of for. or.; *Samgar-Nebo*, a Bab. general:—Samgar-nebo.

5563. סְמָדַר **çᵉmâdar**, *sem-aw-dar';* of uncert. der.; a vine *blossom;* used also adv. *abloom:*—tender grape.

5564. סָמַךְ **çâmak**, *saw-mak';* a prim. root; to *prop* (lit. or fig.); reflex. to *lean* upon or *take hold* of (in a favorable or unfavorable sense):—bear up, establish, (up-) hold, lay, lean, lie hard, put, rest self, set self, stand fast, stay (self), sustain.

5565. סְמַכְיָהוּ **Çᵉmakyâhûw**, *sem-ak-yaw'-hoo;* from 5564 and 3050; *supported of Jah; Semakjah*, an Isr.:—Semachiah.

5566. סֶמֶל **çemel**, *seh'-mel;* or

סֵמֶל **çêmel**, *say'-mel;* from an unused root mean. to *resemble;* a *likeness:*—figure, idol, image.

5567. סָמַן **çâman**, *saw-man';* a prim. root; to *designate:*—appointed.

5568. סָמַר **çâmar**, *saw-mar';* a prim. root; to *be erect*, i.e. *bristle* as hair:—stand up, tremble.

5569. סָמָר **çâmâr**, *saw-mawr';* from 5568; *bristling*, i.e. *shaggy:*—rough.

5570. סְנָאָה **Çᵉnâʼâh**, *sen-aw-aw';* from an unused root mean. to *prick; thorny; Senaah*, a place in Pal.:—Senaah, Hassenaah [*with the art.*].

סְנֻאָה **çᵉnûʼâh**. See 5574.

5571. סַנְבַלַּט **Çanballaṭ**, *san-bal-lat';* of for. or.; *Sanballat*, a Pers. satrap of Samaria:—Sanballat.

5572. סְנֶה **çᵉneh**, *sen-eh';* from an unused root mean. to *prick;* a *bramble:*—bush.

5573. סֶנֶה **Çeneh**, *seh'-neh;* the same as 5572; *thorn; Seneh*, a crag in Pal.:—Seneh.

סַנָּה **Çannâh**. See 7158.

5574. סְנוּאָה **Çᵉnûwʼâh**, *sen-oo-aw';* or

סְנֻאָה **Çᵉnûʼâh**, *sen-oo-aw';* from the same as 5570; *pointed;* (used with the art. as a prop. name) *Senuah*, the name of two Isr.:—Hasenuah [*includ. the art.*], Senuah.

5575. סַנְוֵר **canvêr**, *san-vare';* of uncert. der.; (in plur.) *blindness:*—blindness.

5576. סַנְחֵרִיב **Çanchêrîyb**, *san-khay-reeb';* of for. or.; *Sancherib*, an Ass. king:—Sennacherib.

5577. סַנְסִן **çançîn**, *san-seen';* from an unused root mean. to be *pointed;* a *twig* (as *tapering*):—bough.

5578. סַנְסַנָּה **Çançannâh**, *san-san-naw';* fem. of a form of 5577; a *bough; Sansannah*, a place in Pal.:—Sansannah.

5579. סְנַפִּיר **çᵉnappîyr**, *sen-ap-peer';* of uncert. der.; a *fin* (collect.):—fins.

5580. סָס **çâç**, *sawce;* from the same as 5483; a *moth* (from the *agility* of the fly):—moth.

סֻס **çûç**. See 5483.

5581. סִסְמַי **Çîçmay**, *sis-mah'ee;* of uncert. der.; *Sismai*, an Isr.:—Sisamai.

5582. סָעַד **çâʻad**, *saw-ad';* a prim. root; to *support* (mostly fig.):—comfort, establish, hold up, refresh self, strengthen, be upholden.

5583. סְעַד **çᵉʻad** (Chald.), *seh-ad';* corresp. to 5582; to *aid:*—helping.

5584. סָעָה **çâʻâh**, *saw-aw';* a prim. root; to *rush:*—storm.

5585. סָעִיף **çâʻîyph**, *saw-eef';* from 5586; a *fissure* (of rocks); also a *bough* (as *subdivided*):—(outmost) branch, clift, top.

5586. סָעַף **çâʻaph**, *saw-af';* a prim. root; prop. to *divide* up; but used only as denom. from 5585, to *disbranch* (a tree):—top.

5587. סָעִף **çâʻiph**, *saw-eef';* or

שָׂעִף **sâʻiph**, *saw-eef';* from 5586; *divided* (in mind), i.e. (abstr.) a *sentiment:*—opinion.

5588. סֵעֵף **çêʻêph**, *say-afe';* from 5586; *divided* (in mind), i.e. (concr.) a *skeptic:*—thought.

5589. סְעַפָּה **çᵉʻappâh**, *seh-ap-paw';* fem. of 5585; a *twig* or *branch:*—bough. Comp. 5634.

5590. סָעַר **çâʻar**, *saw-ar';* a prim. root; to *rush* upon; by impl. to *toss* (trans. or intrans., lit. or fig.):—be (toss with) tempest (-uous), be sore troubled, come out as a (drive with the, scatter with a) whirlwind.

5591. סַעַר **çaʻar**, *sah'-ar;* or (fem.)

סְעָרָה **çᵉʻârâh**, *seh-aw-raw';* from 5590; a *hurricane:*—storm (-y), tempest, whirlwind.

5592. סַף **çaph**, *saf;* from 5605, in its original sense of *containing;* a *vestibule* (as a *limit*); also a *dish* (for holding blood or wine):—bason, bowl, cup, door (post), gate, post, threshold.

5593. סַף **Çaph**, *saf;* the same as 5592; *Saph*, a Philistine:—Saph. Comp. 5598.

5594. סָפַד **çâphad**, *saw-fad';* a prim. root; prop. to *tear* the hair and *beat* the breasts (as Orientals do in grief); gen. to *lament;* by impl. to *wail:*—lament, mourn (-er), wail.

5595. סָפָה **çâphâh**, *saw-faw';* a prim. root; prop. to *scrape* (lit. to *shave;* but usually fig.) together (i.e. to *accumulate* or *increase*) or away (i.e. to *scatter, remove* or *ruin;* intrans. to *perish*):—add, augment, consume, destroy, heap, join, perish, put.

5596. סָפַח **çâphach**, *saw-fakh';* or

שָׂפַח **sâphach** (Isa. 3 : 17), *saw-fakh';* a prim. root; prop. to *scrape* out, but in certain peculiar senses (of *removal* or *association*):—abiding, gather together, cleave, put, smite with a scab.

5597. סַפַּחַת **çappachath**, *sap-pakh'-ath;* from 5596; the *mange* (as making the hair fall off):—scab.

5598. סִפַּי **Çippay**, *sip-pah'ee;* from 5592; *basonlike; Sippai*, a Philistine:—Sippai. Comp. 5593.

5599. סָפִיחַ **çâphîyach**, *saw-fee'-akh;* from 5596; something (spontaneously) *falling* off, i.e. a *self-sown* crop; fig. a *freshet:*—(such) things as (which) grow (of themselves), which groweth of its own accord (itself).

5600. סְפִינָה **çᵉphîynâh**, *sef-ee-naw';* from 5603; a (sea-going) *vessel* (as *ceiled* with a deck):—ship.

5601. סַפִּיר **cappîyr**, *sap-peer';* from 5608; a *gem* (perh. as used for *scratching* other substances), prob. the *sapphire:*—sapphire.

5602. סֵפֶל **çêphel**, *say'-fel;* from an unused root mean. to *depress;* a *basin* (as *deepened* out):—bowl, dish.

5603. סָפַן **çâphan**, *saw-fan'*; a prim. root; to *hide* by covering; spec. to *roof* (pass. part. as noun, a *roof*) or *wainscot*; fig. to *reserve*:—cieled, cover, seated.

5604. סִפֻּן **çippûn**, *sip-poon'*; from 5603; a *wainscot*:—cieling.

5605. סָפַף **çâphaph**, *saw-faf'*; a prim. root; prop. to *snatch* away, i.e. *terminate*; but used only as denom. from 5592 (in the sense of a *vestibule*), to *wait at* the *threshold*:—be a doorkeeper.

5606. סָפַק **çâphaq**, *saw-fak'*; or

שָׂפַק **sâphaq** (1 Kings 20 : 10; Job 27 : 23; Isa. 2 : 6), *saw-fak'*; a prim. root; to *clap* the hands (in token of compact, derision, grief, indignation or punishment); by impl. of satisfaction, to *be enough*; by impl. of excess, to *vomit*:—clap, smite, strike, suffice, wallow.

5607. סֵפֶק **çêpheq**, *say'-fek*; or

שֶׂפֶק **sepheq** (Job 20 : 22; 36 : 18), *seh'-fek*; from 5606; *chastisement*; also *satiety*:—stroke, sufficiency.

5608. סָפַר **çâphar**, *saw-far'*; a prim. root; prop. to *score* with a mark as a tally or record, i.e. (by impl.) to *inscribe*, and also to *enumerate*; intens. to *recount*, i.e. *celebrate*:—commune, (ac-) count, declare, number, + penknife, reckon, scribe, shew forth, speak, talk, tell (out), writer.

5609. סְפַר **çᵉphar** (Chald.), *sef-ar'*; from a root corresp. to 5608; a *book*:—book, roll.

5610. סְפָר **çᵉphâr**, *sef-awr'*; from 5608; a *census*:—numbering.

5611. סְפָר **Çᵉphâr**, *sef-awr'*; the same as 5610; *Sephar*, a place in Arabia:—Sephar.

5612. סֵפֶר **çêpher**, *say'-fer*; or (fem.)

סִפְרָה **çiphrâh** (Psa. 56 : 8 [9]), *sif-raw'*; from 5608; prop. *writing* (the art or a document); by impl. a *book*:—bill, book, evidence, × learn [-ed] (-ing), letter, register, scroll.

5613. סָפֵר **çâphêr** (Chald.), *saw-fare'*; from the same as 5609; a *scribe* (secular or sacred):—scribe.

5614. סְפָרָד **Çᵉphârâd**, *sef-aw-rawd'*; of for. der.; *Sepharad*, a region of Ass.:—Sepharad.

סִפְרָה **çiphrâh**. See 5612.

5615. סְפֹרָה **çᵉphôrâh**, *sef-o-raw'*; from 5608; a *numeration*:—number.

5616. סְפַרְוִי **Çᵉpharvîy**, *sef-ar-vee'*; patrial from 5617; a *Sepharvite* or inhab. of Sepharvain:—Sepharvite.

5617. סְפַרְוַיִם **Çᵉpharvayim** (dual), *sef-ar-vah'-yim*; or

סְפָרִים° **Çᵉphârîym** (plur.), *sef-aw-reem'*; of for. der.; *Sepharvajim* or *Sepharim*, a place in Ass.:—Sepharvaim.

5618. סֹפֶרֶת **Çôphereth**, *so-feh'-reth*; fem. act. part. of 5608; a *scribe* (prop. female); *Sophereth*, a temple servant:—Sophereth.

5619. סָקַל **çâqal**, *saw-kal'*; a prim. root; prop. to *be weighty*; but used only in the sense of *lapidation* or its contrary (as if a *delapidation*):—(cast, gather out, throw) stone (-s), × surely.

5620. סַר **çar**, *sar*; from 5637 contr.; *peevish*:—heavy, sad.

5621. סָרָב **çârâb**, *saw-rawb'*; from an unused root mean. to *sting*; a thistle:—brier.

5622. סַרְבַּל **çarbal** (Chald.), *sar-bal'*; of uncert. der.; a *cloak*:—coat.

5623. סַרְגּוֹן **Çargôwn**, *sar-gōne'*; of for. der.; *Sargon*, an Ass. king:—Sargon.

5624. סֶרֶד **Çered**, *seh'-red*; from a prim. root mean. to *tremble*; *trembling*; *Sered*, an Isr.:—Sered.

5625. סַרְדִּי **Çardîy**, *sar-dee'*; patron. from 5624; a *Seredite* (collect.) or desc. of Sered:—Sardites.

5626. סִרָה **Çîrâh**, *see-raw'*; from 5493; *departure*; *Sirah*, a cistern so-called:—Sirah. See also 5518.

5627. סָרָה **çârâh**, *saw-raw'*; from 5493; *apostasy*, *crime*; fig. *remission*:— × continual, rebellion, revolt ([-ed]), turn away, wrong.

5628. סָרַח **çârach**, *saw-rakh'*; a prim. root; to *extend* (even to *excess*):—exceeding, hand, spread, stretch self, banish.

5629. סֶרַח **çerach**, *seh'-rakh*; from 5628; a *redundancy*:—remnant.

5630. סִרְיֹן **çiryôn**, *sir-yone'*; for 8302; a coat of *mail*:—brigandine.

5631. סָרִיס **çârîyç**, *saw-reece'*; or

סָרִס **çârîç**, *saw-reece'*; from an unused root mean. to *castrate*; a *eunuch*; by impl. *valet* (espec. of the female apartments), and thus a *minister* of state:—chamberlain, eunuch, officer. Comp. 7249.

5632. סָרֵךְ **çârêk** (Chald.), *saw-rake'*; of for. or.; an *emir*:—president.

5633. סֶרֶן **çeren**, *seh'-ren*; from an unused root of unc. mean.; an *axle*; fig. a *peer*:—lord, plate.

5634. סַרְעַפָּה **çarʿappâh**, *sar-ap-paw'*; for 5589; a *twig*:—bough.

5635. סָרַף **çâraph**, *saw-raf'*; a prim. root; to *cremate*, i.e. to *be* (near) *of kin* (such being privileged to kindle the pyre):—burn.

5636. סַרְפָּד **çarpâd**, *sar-pawd'*; from 5635; a *nettle* (as stinging like a *burn*):—brier.

5637. סָרַר **çârar**, *saw-rar'*; a prim. root; to *turn* away, i.e. (morally) *be refractory*:—× away, backsliding, rebellious, revolter (-ing), slide back, stubborn, withdrew.

5638. סְתָו° **çᵉthâv**, *seth-awv'*; from an unused root mean. to *hide*; *winter* (as the dark season):—winter.

5639. סְתוּר **Çᵉthûwr**, *seth-oor'*; from 5641; *hidden*; *Sethur*, an Isr.:—Sethur.

5640. סָתַם **çâtham**, *saw-tham'*; or

שָׂתַם **sâtham** (Num. 24 : 15), *saw-tham'*; a prim. root; to *stop* up; by impl. to *repair*; fig. to *keep secret*:—closed up, hidden, secret, shut out (up), stop.

5641. סָתַר **çâthar**, *saw-thar'*; a prim. root; to *hide* (by covering), lit. or fig.:—be absent, keep close, conceal, hide (self), (keep) secret, × surely.

5642. סְתַר **çᵉthar** (Chald.), *seth-ar'*; corresp. to 5641; to *conceal*; fig. to *demolish*:—destroy, secret thing.

5643. סֵתֶר **çêther**, *say'-ther*; or (fem.)

סִתְרָה **çithrâh** (Deut. 32 : 38), *sith-raw'*; from 5641; a *cover* (in a good or a bad, a lit. or a fig. sense):—backbiting, covering, covert, × disguise [-th], hiding place, privily, protection, secret (-ly, place).

5644. סִתְרִי **Çithrîy**, *sith-ree'*; from 5643; *protective*; *Sithri*, an Isr.:—Zithri.

ע

5645. עָב **ʿâb**, *awb* (masc. and fem.); from 5743; prop. an *envelope*, i.e. *darkness* (or *density*, 2 Chron. 4 : 17); spec. a (scud) *cloud*; also a *copse*:—clay, (thick) cloud, × thick, thicket. Comp. 5672.

5646. עָב **ʿâb**, *awb*; or

עֹב **ʿôb**, *obe*; from an unused root mean. to *cover*; prop. equiv. to 5645; but used only as an arch. term, an *architrave* (as *shading* the pillars):—thick (beam, plant).

5647. עָבַד **ʿâbad**, *aw-bad'*; a prim. root; to *work* (in any sense); by impl. to *serve*, *till*, (caus.) *enslave*, etc.:— × be, keep in bondage, be bondmen, bond-service, compel, do, dress, ear, execute, + husbandman, keep, labour (-ing man), bring to pass, (cause to, make to) serve (-ing, self), (be, become) servant (-s), do (use) service, till (-er), transgress [*from margin*], (set a) work, be wrought, worshipper.

5648. עֲבַד **ʿăbad** (Chald.), *ab-ad'*; corresp. to 5647; to *do*, *make*, *prepare*, *keep*, etc.:—× cut, do, execute, go on, make, move, work.

5649. עֲבַד **ʿăbad** (Chald.), *ab-ad'*; from 5648; a *servant*:—servant.

5650. עֶבֶד **ʿebed**, *eh'-bed*; from 5647; a *servant*:—× bondage, bondman, [bond-] servant, (man-) servant.

5651. עֶבֶד **ʿEbed**, *eh'-bed*; the same as 5650; *Ebed*, the name of two Isr.:—Ebed.

5652. עֲבָד **ʿăbâd**, *ab-awd'*; from 5647; a *deed*:—work.

5653. עַבְדָּא **ʿAbdâʾ**, *ab-daw'*; from 5647; *work*; *Abda*, the name of two Isr.:—Abda.

5654. עֹבֵד אֱדוֹם **ʿObêd ʾĔdôwm**, *o-bade' edome'*; from the act. part. of 5647 and 123; *worker of Edom*; *Obed-Edom*, the name of five Isr.:—Obed-edom.

5655. עַבְדְּאֵל **ʿAbdᵉʾêl**, *ab-deh-ale'*; from 5647 and 410; *serving God*; *Abdeël*, an Isr.:—Abdeel. Comp. 5661.

5656. עֲבֹדָה **ʿăbôdâh**, *ab-o-daw'*; or

עֲבוֹדָה **ʿăbôwdâh**, *ab-o-daw'*; from 5647; *work* of any kind:—act, bondage, + bondservant, effect, labour, ministering (-try), office, service (-ile, -itude), tillage, use, work, × wrought.

5657. עֲבֻדָּה **ʿăbuddâh**, *ab-ood-daw'*; pass. part. of 5647; something *wrought*, i.e. (concr.) *service*:—household, store of servants.

5658. עַבְדוֹן **ʿAbdôwn**, *ab-dohn'*; from 5647; *servitude*; *Abdon*, the name of a place in Pal. and of four Isr.:—Abdon. Comp. 5683.

5659. עַבְדוּת **ʿabdûwth**, *ab-dooth'*; from 5647; *servitude*:—bondage.

5660. עַבְדִּי **ʿAbdîy**, *ab-dee'*; from 5647; *serviceable*; *Abdi*, the name of two Isr.:—Abdi.

5661. עַבְדִיאֵל **ʿAbdîyʾêl**, *ab-dee-ale'*; from 5650 and 410; *servant of God*; *Abdiël*, an Isr.:—Abdiel. Comp. 5655.

5662. עֹבַדְיָה **ʿÔbadyâh**, *o-bad-yaw'*; or

עֹבַדְיָהוּ **ʿÔbadyâhûw**, *o-bad-yaw'-hoo*; act. part. of 5647 and 3050; *serving Jah*; *Obadjah*, the name of thirteen Isr.:—Obadiah.

5663. עֶבֶד מֶלֶךְ **ʿEbed Melek**, *eh'-bed meh'-lek*; from 5650 and 4428; *servant of a king*; *Ebed-Melek*, a eunuch of king Zedekeah:—Ebed-melech.

5664. עֲבֵד נְגוֹ **ʿÂbêd Nᵉgôw**, *ab-ade' neg-o'*; the same as 5665; *Abed-Nego*, the Bab. name of one of Daniel's companions:—Abed-nego.

5665. עֲבֵד נְגוֹא **ʿÂbêd Nᵉgôwʾ** (Chald.), *ab-ade' neg-o'*; of for. or.; *Abed-Nego*, the name of Azariah:—Abed-nego.

5666. עָבָה **ʿâbâh**, *aw-baw'*; a prim. root; to *be dense*:—be (grow) thick (-er).

5667. עֲבוֹט **ʿăbôwṭ**, *ab-ote'*; or

עֲבֹט **ʿăbôṭ**, *ab-ote'*; from 5670; a *pawn*:—pledge.

5668. עָבוּר **ʿâbûwr**, *aw-boor'*; or

עָבֻר **ʿâbûr**, *aw-boor'*; pass. part. of 5674; prop. *crossed*, i.e. (abstr.) *transit*; used only adv. on *account* of, in *order* that:—because of, for (. . . 's sake), (intent) that, to.

5669. עָבוּר **ʻâbûwr**, *aw-boor'*; the same as 5668; *passed*, i.e. *kept* over; used only of *stored* grain:—old corn.

5670. עָבַט **ʻâbaṭ**, *aw-bat'*; a prim. root; to *pawn*; caus. to *lend* (on security); fig. to *entangle*:—borrow, break [*ranks*], fetch [*a pledge*], lend, × surely.

5671. עַבְטִיט **ʻabṭîyṭ**, *ab-teet'*; from 5670; something *pledged*, i.e. (collect.) *pawned* goods:—thick clay [*by a false etym.*].

5672. עֲבִי **ʻăbîy**, *ab-ee'*; or

עֳבִי **ʻŏbîy**, *ob-ee'*; from 5666; *density*, i.e. *depth* or *width*:—thick (-ness). Comp. 5645.

5673. עֲבִידָה **ʻăbîydâh** (Chald.), *ab-ee-daw'*; from 5648; *labor* or *business*:—affairs, service, work.

5674. עָבַר **ʻâbar**, *aw-bar'*; a prim. root; to *cross over*; used very widely of any *transition* (lit. or fig.; trans., intrans., intens. or causat.); spec. to *cover* (in copulation):—alienate, alter, × at all, beyond, bring (over, through), carry over, (over-) come (on, over), conduct (over), convey over, current, deliver, do away, enter, escape, fail, gender, get over, (make) go (away, beyond, by, forth, his way, in, on, over, through), have away (more), lay, meddle, overrun, make partition, (cause to, give, make to, over) pass (-age, along, away, beyond, by, -enger, on, out, over, through), (cause to, make) + proclaim (-amation), perish, provoke to anger, put away, rage, + raiser of taxes, remove, send over, set apart, + shave, cause to (make) sound, × speedily, × sweet smelling, take (away), (make to) transgress (-or), translate, turn away, [way-] faring man, be wrath.

5675. עֲבַר **ʻăbar** (Chald.), *ab-ar'*; corresp. to 5676:—beyond, this side.

5676. עֵבֶר **ʻêber**, *ay'-ber*; from 5674; prop. a region *across*; but used only adv. (with or without a prep.) on the *opposite* side (espec. of the Jordan; usually mean. the *east*):— × against, beyond, by, × from, over, passage, quarter, (other, this) side, straight.

5677. עֵבֶר **ʻÊber**, *ay'-ber*; the same as 5676; *Eber*, the name of two patriarchs and four Isr.:—Eber, Heber.

5678. עֶבְרָה **ʻebrâh**, *eb-raw'*; fem. of 5676; an *outburst* of passion:—anger, rage, wrath.

5679. עֲבָרָה **ʻăbârâh**, *ab-aw-raw'*; from 5674; a *crossing*-place:—ferry, plain [*from the marg.*].

5680. עִבְרִי **ʻIbrîy**, *ib-ree'*; patron. from 5677; an *Eberite* (i.e. Hebrew) or desc. of Eber:—Hebrew (-ess, woman).

5681. עִבְרִי **ʻIbrîy**, *ib-ree'*; the same as 5680; *Ibri*, an Isr.:—Ibri.

5682. עֲבָרִים **ʻĂbârîm**, *ab-aw-reem'*; plur. of 5676; regions *beyond*; *Abarim*, a place in Pal.:—Abarim, passages.

5683. עֶבְרֹן **ʻEbrôn**, *eb-rone'*; from 5676; *transitional*; *Ebron*, a place in Pal.:—Hebron. Perh. a clerical error for 5658.

5684. עֶבְרֹנָה **ʻEbrônâh**, *eb-raw-naw'*; fem. of 5683; *Ebronah*, a place in the Desert:—Ebronah.

5685. עָבַשׁ **ʻâbash**, *aw-bash'*; a prim. root; to *dry* up:—be rotten.

5686. עָבַת **ʻâbath**, *aw-bath'*; a prim. root; to *interlace*, i.e. (fig.) to *pervert*:—wrap up.

5687. עָבֹת **ʻâbôth**, *aw-both'*; or

עָבוֹת **ʻâbôwth**, *aw-both'*; from 5686; *intwined*, i.e. *dense*:—thick.

5688. עֲבֹת **ʻăbôth**, *ab-oth'*; or

עֲבוֹת **ʻăbôwth**, *ab-oth'*; or (fem.)

עֲבֹתָה **ʻăbôthâh**, *ab-oth-aw'*; the same as 5687; something *intwined*, i.e. a *string*, *wreath* or *foliage*:—band, cord, rope, thick bough (branch), wreathen (chain).

5689. עָגַב **ʻâgab**, *aw-gab'*; a prim. root; to *breathe* after, i.e. to *love* (sensually):—dote, lover.

5690. עֶגֶב **ʻegeb**, *eh'-gheb*; from 5689; *love* (concr.), i.e. *amative* words:—much love, very lovely.

5691. עֲגָבָה **ʻăgâbâh**, *ag-aw-baw'*; from 5689; *love* (abstr.), i.e. *amorousness*:—inordinate love.

5692. עֻגָּה **ʻuggâh**, *oog-gaw'*; from 5746; an *ash-cake* (as *round*):—cake (upon the hearth).

עָגֹל **ʻâgôwl**. See 5696.

5693. עָגוּר **ʻâgûwr**, *aw-goor'*; pass. part. [but with act. sense] of an unused root mean. to *twitter*; prob. the *swallow*:—swallow.

5694. עָגִיל **ʻâgîyl**, *aw-gheel'*; from the same as 5696; something *round*, i.e. a *ring* (for the ears):—earring.

5695. עֵגֶל **ʻêgel**, *ay'-ghel*; from the same as 5696; a (male) *calf* (as *frisking* round), espec. one nearly grown (i.e. a *steer*):—bullock, calf.

5696. עָגֹל **ʻâgôl**, *aw-gole'*; or

עָגוֹל **ʻâgôwl**, *aw-gole'*; from an unused root mean. to *revolve*, *circular*:—round.

5697. עֶגְלָה **ʻeglâh**, *eg-law'*; fem. of 5695; a (female) *calf*, espec. one nearly grown (i.e. a *heifer*):—calf, cow, heifer.

5698. עֶגְלָה **ʻEglâh**, *eg-law'*; the same as 5697; *Eglah*, a wife of David:—Eglah.

5699. עֲגָלָה **ʻăgâlâh**, *ag-aw-law'*; from the same as 5696; something *revolving*, i.e. a wheeled *vehicle*:—cart, chariot, wagon.

5700. עֶגְלוֹן **ʻEglôwn**, *eg-lawn'*; from 5695; *vituline*; *Eglon*, the name of a place in Pal. and of a Moabitish king:—Eglon.

5701. עָגַם **ʻâgam**, *aw-gam'*; a prim. root; to *be sad*:—grieve.

5702. עָגַן **ʻâgan**, *aw-gan'*; a prim. root; to *debar*, i.e. from marriage:—stay.

5703. עַד **ʻad**, *ad*; from 5710; prop. a (peremptory) *terminus*, i.e. (by impl.) *duration*, in the sense of *advance* or *perpetuity* (substantially as a noun, either with or without a prep.):—eternity, ever (-lasting, -more), old, perpetually, + world without end.

5704. עַד **ʻad**, *ad*; prop. the same as 5703 (used as a prep., adv. or conj.; especially with a prep.); *as far* (or *long*, or *much*) *as*, whether of space (*even unto*) or time (*during*, *while*, *until*) or degree (*equally with*):—against, and, as, at, before, by (that), even (to), for (-asmuch as), [hither-] to, + how long, into, as long (much) as, (so) that, till, toward, until, when, while, (+ as) yet.

5705. עַד **ʻad** (Chald.), *ad*; corresp. to 5704; × and, at, for, [hither-] to, on, till, (un-) to, until, within.

5706. עַד **ʻad**, *ad*; the same as 5703 in the sense of the *aim* of an attack; *booty*:—prey.

5707. עֵד **ʻêd**, *ayd*; from 5749 contr.; concr. a *witness*; abstr. *testimony*; spec. a *recorder*, i.e. *prince*:—witness.

5708. עֵד **ʻêd**, *ayd*; from an unused root mean. to *set* a period [comp. 5710, 5749]; the *menstrual* flux (as periodical); by impl. (in plur.) *soiling*:—filthy.

עֹד **ʻôd**. See 5750.

5709. עֲדָא **ʻădâʼ** (Chald.), *ad-aw'*; or

עֲדָה **ʻădâh** (Chald.), *ad-aw'*; corresp. to 5710:—alter, depart, pass (away), remove, take (away).

עֹדֵד **ʻÔdêd**. See 5752.

5710. עָדָה **ʻâdâh**, *aw-daw'*; a prim. root; to *advance*, i.e. *pass* on or *continue*; causat. to *remove*; spec. to *bedeck* (i.e. bring an ornament upon):—adorn, deck (self), pass by, take away.

5711. עָדָה **ʻÂdâh**, *aw-daw'*; from 5710; *ornament*; *Adah*, the name of two women:—Adah.

5712. עֵדָה **ʻêdâh**, *ay-daw'*; fem. of 5707 in the orig. sense of *fixture*; a stated *assemblage* (spec. a *concourse*, or gen. a *family* or *crowd*):—assembly, company, congregation, multitude, people, swarm. Comp. 5713.

5713. עֵדָה **ʻêdâh**, *ay-daw'*; fem. of 5707 in its techn. sense; *testimony*:—testimony, witness. Comp. 5712.

5714. עִדּוֹ **ʻIddôw**, *id-do'*; or

עִדּוֹא **ʻIddôwʼ**, *id-do'*; or

עִדִּיא **ʻIddîyʼ**, *id-dee'*; from 5710; *timely*; *Iddo* (or *Iddi*), the name of five Isr.:—Iddo. Comp. 3035, 3260.

5715. עֵדוּת **ʻêdûwth**, *ay-dooth'*; fem. of 5707; *testimony*:—testimony, witness.

5716. עֲדִי **ʻădîy**, *ad-ee'*; from 5710 in the sense of *trappings*; *finery*; gen. an *outfit*; spec. a *headstall*:— × excellent, mouth, ornament.

5717. עֲדִיאֵל **ʻĂdîyʼêl**, *ad-ee-ale'*; from 5716 and 410; *ornament of God*; *Adiël*, the name of three Isr.:—Adiel.

5718. עֲדָיָה **ʻĂdâyâh**, *ad-aw-yaw'*; or

עֲדָיָהוּ **ʻĂdâyâhûw**, *ad-aw-yaw'-hoo*; from 5710 and 3050; *Jah has adorned*; *Adajah*, the name of eight Isr.:—Adaiah.

5719. עָדִין **ʻâdîyn**, *aw-deen'*; from 5727; *voluptuous*:—given to pleasures.

5720. עָדִין **ʻÂdîyn**, *aw-deen'*; the same as 5719; *Adin*, the name of two Isr.:—Adin.

5721. עֲדִינָא **ʻĂdîynâʼ**, *ad-ee-naw'*; from 5719; *effeminacy*; *Adina*, an Isr.:—Adina.

5722. עֲדִינוֹ **ʻădîynôw**, *ad-ee-no'*; prob. from 5719 in the orig. sense of *slender* (i.e. a *spear*); *his spear*:—Adino.

5723. עֲדִיתַיִם **ʻĂdîythayim**, *ad-ee-thah'-yim*; dual of a fem. of 5706; *double prey*; *Adithajim*, a place in Pal.:—Adithaim.

5724. עַדְלַי **ʻAdlay**, *ad-lah'ee*; prob. from an unused root of uncert. mean.; *Adlai*, an Isr.:—Adlai.

5725. עֲדֻלָּם **ʻĂdullâm**, *ad-ool-lawm'*; prob. from the pass. part. of the same as 5724; *Adullam*, a place in Pal.:—Adullam.

5726. עֲדֻלָּמִי **ʻĂdullâmîy**, *ad-ool-law-mee'*; patrial from 5725; an *Adullamite* or native of Adullam:—Adullamite.

5727. עָדַן **ʻâdan**, *aw-dan'*; a prim. root; to be *soft* or *pleasant*; fig. and reflex. to *live voluptuously*:—delight self.

5728. עֲדֶן **ʻăden**, *ad-en'*; or

עֲדֶנָּה **ʻădennâh**, *ad-en'-naw*; from 5704 and 2004; *till now*:—yet.

5729. עֶדֶן **ʻEden**, *eh'-den*; from 5727; *pleasure*; *Eden*, a place in Mesopotamia:—Eden.

5730. עֵדֶן **ʻêden**, *ay'-den*; or (fem.)

עֶדְנָה **ʻednâh**, *ed-naw'*; from 5727; *pleasure*:—delicate, delight, pleasure. See also 1040.

5731. עֵדֶן **ʻÊden**, *ay'-den*; the same as 5730 (masc.); *Eden*, the region of Adam's home:—Eden.

5732. עִדָּן **ʻiddân** (Chald.), *id-dawn'*; from a root corresp. to that of 5708; a set *time*; techn. a *year*:—time.

5733. עַדְנָא **ʻAdnâʼ**, *ad-naw'*; from 5727; *pleasure*; *Adna*, the name of two Isr.:—Adna.

5734. עַדְנָה **ʻAdnâh**, *ad-naw'*; from 5727; *pleasure*; *Adnah*, the name of two Isr.:—Adnah.

5735. עֲדְעָדָה **ʻĂdʻâdâh**, *ad-aw-daw'*; from 5712; *festival*; *Adadah*, a place in Pal.:—Adadah.

5736. עָדַף **ʻâdaph**, *aw-daf'*; a prim. root; to *be* (causat. *have*) *redundant*:—be more, odd number, be (have) over (and above), overplus, remain.

5737. עָדַר **ʻâdar**, *aw-dar'*; a prim. root; to *arrange*, as a battle, a vineyard (to *hoe*); hence to *muster*, and so to *miss* (or find *wanting*):—dig, fail, keep (rank), lack.

5738. עֶדֶר **ʻEder**, *eh'-der*; from 5737; an *arrangement* (i.e. drove); *Eder*, an Isr.:—Ader.

5739. עֵדֶר **ʻêder**, *ay'-der*; from 5737; an *arrangement*, i.e. *muster* (of animals):—drove, flock, herd.

5740. עֵדֶר **ʻÊder**, *ay'-der;* the same as 5739; *Eder*, the name of an Isr. and of two places in Pal.:—Edar, Eder.

5741. עַדְרִיאֵל **ʻAdrîyʼêl**, *ad-ree-ale';* from 5739 and 410; *flock of God; Adriel*, an Isr.:—Adriel.

5742. עָדָשׁ **ʻâdâsh**, *aw-dawsh';* from an unused root of uncert. mean.; a *lentil:*—lentile.

עַוָּא **ʻAvvâʼ**. See 5755.

5743. עוּב **ʻûwb**, *oob;* a prim. root; to be *dense* or *dark*, i.e. to *becloud:*—cover with a cloud.

5744. עוֹבֵד **ʻÔwbêd**, *o-bade';* act. part. of 5647; *serving; Obed*, the name of five Isr.:—Obed.

5745. עוֹבָל **ʻÔwbâl**, *o-bawl';* of for. der.; *Obal*, a son of Joktan:—Obal.

5746. עוּג **ʻûwg**, *oog;* a prim. root; prop. to *gyrate;* but used only as denom. from 5692, to *bake* (round cakes on the hearth):—bake.

5747. עוֹג **ʻÔwg**, *ogue;* prob. from 5746; *round; Og*, a king of Bashan:—Og.

5748. עוּגָב **ʻûwgâb**, *oo-gawb';* or

עֻגָּב **ʻuggâb**, *oog-gawb';* from 5689 in the orig. sense of *breathing;* a *reed*-instrument of music:—organ.

5749. עוּד **ʻûwd**, *ood;* a prim. root; to *duplicate* or *repeat;* by impl. to *protest, testify* (as by reiteration); intens. to *encompass, restore* (as a sort of reduplication):—admonish, charge, earnestly, lift up, protest, call (take) to record, relieve, rob, solemnly, stand upright, testify, give warning, (bear, call to, give, take to) witness.

5750. עוֹד **ʻôwd**, *ode;* or

עֹד **ʻôd**, *ode;* from 5749; prop. *iteration* or *continuance;* used only adv. (with or without prep.), *again, repeatedly, still, more:*—again, × all life long, at all, besides, but, else, further (-more), henceforth, (any) longer, (any) more (-over), × once, since, (be) still, when, (good, the) while (having being), (as, because, whether, while) yet (within).

5751. עוֹד **ʻôwd** (Chald.), *ode;* corresp. to 5750:—while.

5752. עוֹדֵד **ʻÔwdêd**, *o-dade';* or

עֹדֵד **ʻÔdêd**, *o-dade';* from 5749; *reiteration; Oded*, the name of two Isr.:—Oded.

5753. עָוָה **ʻâvâh**, *aw-vaw';* a prim. root; to *crook*, lit. or fig. (as follows):—do amiss, bow down, make crooked, commit iniquity, pervert, (do) perverse (-ly), trouble, × turn, do wickedly, do wrong.

5754. עַוָּה **ʻavvâh**, *av-vaw';* intens. from 5753 abbrev.; *overthrow:*— × overturn.

5755. עִוָּה **ʻIvvâh**, *iv-vaw';* or

עַוָּא **ʻAvvâʼ** (2 Kings 17 : 24), *av-vaw';* for 5754; *Ivvah* or *Avva*, a region of Ass.:—Ava, Ivah.

עָווֹן **ʻâvôwn**. See 5771.

5756. עוּז **ʻûwz**, *ooz;* a prim. root; to *be strong;* causat. to *strengthen*, i.e. (fig.) to *save* (by flight):—gather (self, self to flee), retire.

5757. עַוִּי **ʻAvvîy**, *av-vee';* patrial from 5755; an *Avvite* or native of Avvah (only plur.):—Avims, Avites.

5758. עִוְיָא **ʻivyâʼ** (Chald.), *iv-yaw';* from a root corresp. to 5753; *perverseness:*—iniquity.

5759. עֲוִיל **ʻăvîyl**, *av-eel';* from 5764; a *babe:*—young child, little one.

5760. עֲוִיל **ʻăvîyl**, *av-eel';* from 5765; *perverse* (morally):—ungodly.

5761. עַוִּים **ʻAvvîym**, *av-veem';* plur. of 5757; *Avvim* (as inhabited by Avvites), a place in Pal. (with the art. pref.):—Avim.

5762. עֲוִית **ʻĂvîyth**, *av-veeth';* or [perh.

°עַיּוֹת **ʻAyôwth**, *ah-yōth'*, as if plur. of 5857]

עַיּוּת **ʻAyûwth**, *ah-yōth';* from 5753; *ruin; Avvith* (or *Avvoth*), a place in Pal.:—Avith.

5763. עוּל **ʻûwl**, *ool;* a prim. root; to *suckle*, i.e. *give milk:*—milch, (ewe great) with young.

5764. עוּל **ʻûwl**, *ool;* from 5763; a *babe:*—sucking child, infant.

5765. עָוַל **ʻâval**, *aw-val';* a prim. root; to *distort* (morally):—deal unjustly, unrighteous.

עוֹל **ʻôwl**. See 5923.

5766. עֶוֶל **ʻevel**, *eh'-vel;* or

עָוֶל **ʻâvel**, *aw'-vel;* and (fem.)

עַוְלָה **ʻavlâh**, *av-law';* or

עוֹלָה **ʻôwlâh**, *o-law';* or

עֹלָה **ʻôlâh**, *o-law';* from 5765; (moral) *evil:*—iniquity, perverseness, unjust (-ly), unrighteousness (-ly), wicked (-ness).

5767. עַוָּל **ʻavvâl**, *av-vawl';* intens. from 5765; *evil* (morally):—unjust, unrighteous, wicked.

עוֹלָה **ʻôwlâh**. See 5930.

5768. עוֹלֵל **ʻôwlêl**, *o-lale';* or

עֹלָל **ʻôlâl**, *o-lawl';* from 5763; a *suckling:*—babe, (young) child, infant, little one.

5769. עוֹלָם **ʻôwlâm**, *o-lawm';* or

עֹלָם **ʻôlâm**, *o-lawm';* from 5956; prop. *concealed*, i.e. the *vanishing* point; gen. time *out of mind* (past or fut.), i.e. (practically) *eternity;* freq. adv. (espec. with prep. pref.) *always:*—alway (-s), ancient (time), any more, continuance, eternal, (for, [n-]) ever (-lasting, -more, of old), lasting, long (time), (of) old (time), perpetual, at any time, (beginning of the) world (+ without end). Comp. 5331, 5703.

5770. °עָוַן **ʻâvan**, *aw-van';* denom. from 5869; to *watch* (with jealousy):—eye.

5771. עָוֹן **ʻâvôn**, *aw-vone';* or

עָווֹן **ʻâvôwn** (2 Kings 7 : 9; Psa. 51 : 5 [7]), *aw-vone';* from 5753; *perversity*, i.e. (moral) *evil:*—fault, iniquity, mischief, punishment (of iniquity), sin.

5772. עוֹנָה **ʻôwnâh**, *o-naw';* from an unused root appar. mean. to *dwell* together; (sexual) *cohabitation:*—duty of marriage.

5773. עַוְעֶה **ʻavʻeh**, *av-eh';* from 5753; *perversity:*— × perverse.

5774. עוּף **ʻûwph**, *oof;* a prim root; to *cover* (with wings or obscurity); hence (as denom. from 5775) to *fly;* also (by impl. of dimness) to *faint* (from the darkness of swooning):—brandish, be (wax) faint, flee away, fly (away), × set, shine forth, weary.

5775. עוֹף **ʻôwph**, *ofe;* from 5774; a *bird* (as *covered* with feathers, or rather as *covering* with wings), often collect.:—bird, that flieth, flying, fowl.

5776. עוֹף **ʻôwph** (Chald.), *ofe;* corresp. to 5775:—fowl.

5777. עוֹפֶרֶת **ʻôwphereth**, *o-feh'-reth;* or

עֹפֶרֶת **ʻôphereth**, *o-feh'-reth;* fem. part. act. of 6080; *lead* (from its *dusty* color):—lead.

5778. °עוֹפַי **ʻÔwphay**, *o-fah'-ee;* from 5775; *birdlike; Ephai*, an Isr.:—Ephai [*from marg.*].

5779. עוּץ **ʻûwts**, *oots;* a prim. root; to *consult:*—take advice ([counsel] together).

5780. עוּץ **ʻÛwts**, *oots;* appar. from 5779; *consultation; Uts*, a son of Aram, also a Seirite, and the regions settled by them:—Uz.

5781. עוּק **ʻûwq**, *ook;* a prim. root; to *pack:*—be pressed.

5782. עוּר **ʻûwr**, *oor;* a prim. root [rather ident. with 5783 through the idea of *opening* the eyes]; to *wake* (lit. or fig.):—(a-) wake (-n, up), lift up (self), × master, raise (up), stir up (self).

5783. עוּר **ʻûwr**, *oor;* a prim. root; to (*be*) *bare:*—be made naked.

5784. עוּר **ʻûwr** (Chald.), *oor; chaff* (as the *naked* husk):—chaff.

5785. עוֹר **ʻôwr**, *ore;* from 5783; *skin* (as *naked*); by impl. *hide, leather:*—hide, leather, skin.

5786. עָוַר **ʻâvar**, *aw-var';* a prim. root [rather denom. from 5785 through the idea of a *film* over the eyes]; to *blind:*—blind, put out. See also 5895.

5787. עִוֵּר **ʻivvêr**, *iv-vare';* intens. from 5786; *blind* (lit. or fig.):—blind (men, people).

עוֹרֵב **ʻôwrêb**. See 6159.

5788. עִוָּרוֹן **ʻivvârôwn**, *iv-vaw-rone';* and (fem.)

עַוֶּרֶת **ʻavvereth**, *av-veh'-reth;* from 5787; *blindness:*—blind (-ness).

5789. עוּשׁ **ʻûwsh**, *oosh;* a prim. root; to *hasten:*—assemble self.

5790. עוּת **ʻûwth**, *ooth;* for 5789; to *hasten*, i.e. *succor:*—speak in season.

5791. עָוַת **ʻâvath**, *aw-vath';* a prim. root; to *wrest:*—bow self, (make) crooked, falsifying, overthrow, deal perversely, pervert, subvert, turn upside down.

5792. עַוָּתָה **ʻavvâthâh**, *av-vaw-thaw';* from 5791; *oppression:*—wrong.

5793. עוּתַי **ʻÛwthay**, *oo-thah'-ee;* from 5790; *succoring; Uthai*, the name of two Isr.:—Uthai.

5794. עַז **ʻaz**, *az;* from 5810; *strong, vehement, harsh:*—fierce, + greedy, mighty, power, roughly, strong.

5795. עֵז **ʻêz**, *aze;* from 5810; a she-*goat* (as *strong*), but masc. in plur. (which also is used ellipt. for *goats' hair*):—(she) goat, kid.

5796. עֵז **ʻêz** (Chald.), *aze;* corresp. to 5795:—goat.

5797. עֹז **ʻôz**, *oze;* or (fully)

עוֹז **ʻôwz**, *oze;* from 5810; *strength* in various applications (*force, security, majesty, praise*):—boldness, loud, might, power, strength, strong.

5798. עֻזָּא **ʻUzzâʼ**, *ooz-zaw';* or

עֻזָּה **ʻUzzâh**, *ooz-zaw';* fem. of 5797; *strength; Uzza* or *Uzzah*, the name of five Isr.:—Uzza, Uzzah.

5799. עֲזָאזֵל **ʻăzâʼzêl**, *az-aw-zale';* from 5795 and 235; *goat of departure;* the *scapegoat:*—scapegoat.

5800. עָזַב **ʻâzab**, *aw-zab';* a prim. root; to *loosen*, i.e. *relinquish, permit*, etc.:—commit self, fail, forsake, fortify, help, leave (destitute, off), refuse, × surely.

5801. עִזָּבוֹן **ʻizzâbôwn**, *iz-zaw-bone';* from 5800 in the sense of *letting go* (for a price, i.e. *selling*); *trade*, i.e. the place (*mart*) or the payment (*revenue*):—fair, ware.

5802. עַזְבּוּק **ʻAzbûwq**, *az-book';* from 5794 and the root of 950; *stern depopulator; Azbuk*, an Isr.:—Azbuk.

5803. עַזְגָּד **ʻAzgâd**, *az-gawd';* from 5794 and 1409; *stern troop; Azgad*, an Isr.:—Azgad.

5804. עַזָּה **ʻAzzâh**, *az-zaw';* fem. of 5794; *strong; Azzah*, a place in Pal.:—Azzah, Gaza.

5805. עֲזוּבָה **ʻăzûwbâh**, *az-oo-baw';* fem. pass. part. of 5800; *desertion* (of inhabitants):—forsaking.

5806. עֲזוּבָה **ʻĂzûwbâh**, *az-oo-baw';* the same as 5805; *Azubah*, the name of two Israelitesses:—Azubah.

5807. עֱזוּז **ʻĕzûwz**, *ez-ooz';* from 5810; *forcibleness:*—might, strength.

5808. עִזּוּז **ʻizzûwz**, *iz-zooz';* from 5810; *forcible;* collect. and concr. an *army:*—power, strong.

5809. עַזּוּר **ʻAzzûwr**, *az-zoor';* or

עַזֻּר **ʻAzzûr**, *az-zoor';* from 5826; *helpful; Azzur*, the name of three Isr.:—Azur, Azzur.

5810. עָזַז **ʻâzaz**, *aw-zaz'*; a prim. root; to *be stout* (lit. or fig.):—harden, impudent, prevail, strengthen (self), be strong.

5811. עָזָז **ʻÂzâz**, *aw-zawz'*; from 5810; *strong; Azaz*, an Isr.:—Azaz.

5812. עֲזַזְיָהוּ **ʻĂzazyâhûw**, *az-az-yaw'-hoo*; from 5810 and 3050; *Jah has strengthened; Azazjah*, the name of three Isr.:—Azaziah.

5813. עֻזִּי **ʻUzzîy**, *ooz-zee'*; from 5810; *forceful; Uzzi*, the name of six Isr.:—Uzzi.

5814. עֻזִּיָּא **ʻUzzîyâʼ**, *ooz-zee-yaw'*; perh. for 5818; *Uzzija*, an Isr.:—Uzzia.

5815. עֲזִיאֵל **ʻĂzîyʼêl**, *az-ee-ale'*; from 5756 and 410; *strengthened of God; Aziël*, an Isr.:—Aziel. Comp. 3268.

5816. עֻזִּיאֵל **ʻUzzîyʼêl**, *ooz-zee-ale'*; from 5797 and 410; *strength of God; Uzziël*, the name of six Isr.:—Uzziel.

5817. עָזִּיאֵלִי **ʻOzzîyʼêlîy**, *oz-zee-ay-lee'*; patron. from 5816; an *Uzziëlite* (collect.) or desc. of Uzziel:—Uzzielites.

5818. עֻזִּיָּה **ʻUzzîyâh**, *ooz-zee-yaw'*; or

עֻזִּיָּהוּ **ʻUzzîyâhûw**, *ooz-zee-yaw'-hoo*; from 5797 and 3050; *strength of Jah; Uzzijah*, the name of five Isr.:—Uzziah.

5819. עֲזִיזָא **ʻĂzîyzâʼ**, *az-ee-zaw'*; from 5756; *strengthfulness; Aziza*, an Isr.:—Aziza.

5820. עַזְמָוֶת **ʻAzmâveth**, *az-maw'-veth*; from 5794 and 4194; *strong one of death; Azmaveth*, the name of three Isr. and of a place in Pal.:—Azmaveth. See also 1041.

5821. עַזָּן **ʻAzzân**, *az-zawn'*; from 5794; *strong one; Azzan*, an Isr.:—Azzan.

5822. עָזְנִיָּה **ʻozniyâh**, *oz-nee-yaw'*; prob. fem. of 5797; prob. the *sea-eagle* (from its *strength*):—ospray.

5823. עָזַק **ʻâzaq**, *aw-zak'*; a prim. root; to *grub over*:—fence about.

5824. עִזְקָא **ʻizqâʼ** (Chald.), *iz-kaw'*; from a root corresp. to 5823; a *signet*-ring (as engraved):—signet.

5825. עֲזֵקָה **ʻĂzêqâh**, *az-ay-kaw'*; from 5823; *tilled; Azekah*, a place in Pal.:—Azekah.

5826. עָזַר **ʻâzar**, *aw-zar'*; a prim. root; to *surround*, i.e. *protect* or *aid*:—help, succour.

5827. עֶזֶר **ʻEzer**, *eh'-zer*; from 5826; *help; Ezer*, the name of two Isr.:—Ezer. Comp. 5829.

5828. עֵזֶר **ʻêzer**, *ay'-zer*; from 5826; *aid*:—help.

5829. עֵזֶר **ʻÊzer**, *ay'-zer*; the same as 5828; *Ezer*, the name of four Isr.:—Ezer. Comp. 5827.

עַזֻּר **ʻAzzûr**. See 5809.

5830. עֶזְרָא **ʻEzrâʼ**, *ez-raw'*; a var. of 5833; *Ezra*, an Isr.:—Ezra.

5831. עֶזְרָא **ʻEzrâʼ** (Chald.), *ez-raw'*; corresp. to 5830; *Ezra*, an Isr.:—Ezra.

5832. עֲזַרְאֵל **ʻĂzarʼêl**, *az-ar-ale'*; from 5826 and 410; *God has helped; Azarel*, the name of five Isr.:—Azarael, Azareel.

5833. עֶזְרָה **ʻezrâh**, *ez-raw'*; or

עֶזְרָת **ʻezrâth** (Psa. 60 : 11 [13]; 108 : 12 [13]), *ez-rawth'*; fem. of 5828; *aid*:—help (-ed, -er).

5834. עֶזְרָה **ʻEzrâh**, *ez-raw'*; the same as 5833; *Ezrah*, an Isr.:—Ezrah.

5835. עֲזָרָה **ʻăzârâh**, *az-aw-raw'*; from 5826 in its orig. mean. of *surrounding*; an *inclosure*; also a *border*:—court, settle.

5836. עֶזְרִי **ʻEzrîy**, *ez-ree'*; from 5828; *helpful; Ezri*, an Isr.:—Ezri.

5837. עַזְרִיאֵל **ʻAzrîyʼêl**, *az-ree-ale'*; from 5828 and 410; *help of God; Azriël*, the name of three Isr.:—Azriel.

5838. עֲזַרְיָה **ʻĂzaryâh**, *az-ar-yaw'*; or

עֲזַרְיָהוּ **ʻĂzaryâhûw**, *az-ar-yaw'-hoo*; from 5826 and 3050; *Jah has helped; Azarjah*, the name of nineteen Isr.:—Azariah.

5839. עֲזַרְיָה **ʻĂzaryâh** (Chald.), *az-ar-yaw'*; corresp. to 5838; *Azarjah*, one of Daniel's companions:—Azariah.

5840. עַזְרִיקָם **ʻAzrîyqâm**, *az-ree-kawm'*; from 5828 and act. part. of 6965; *help of an enemy; Azrikam*, the name of four Isr.:—Azrikam.

5841. עַזָּתִי **ʻAzzâthîy**, *az-zaw-thee'*; patrial from 5804; an *Azzathite* or inhab. of Azzah:—Gazathite, Gazite.

5842. עֵט **ʻêṭ**, *ate*; from 5860 (contr.) in the sense of *swooping*, i.e. *side-long stroke*; a *stylus* or marking stick:—pen.

5843. עֵטָא **ʻêṭâʼ** (Chald.), *ay-taw'*; from 3272; *prudence*:—counsel.

5844. עָטָה **ʻâṭâh**, *aw-taw'*; a prim. root; to *wrap*, i.e. *cover, veil, clothe* or *roll*:—array self, be clad, (put a) cover (-ing, self), fill, put on, × surely, turn aside.

5845. עֲטִין **ʻăṭîyn**, *at-een'*; from an unused root mean. appar. to *contain*; a *receptacle* (for milk, i.e. *pail*; fig. *breast*):—breast.

5846. עֲטִישָׁה **ʻăṭîyshâh**, *at-ee-shaw'*; from an unused root mean. to *sneeze*; *sneezing*:—sneezing.

5847. עֲטַלֵּף **ʻăṭallêph**, *at-al-lafe'*; of uncert. der.; a *bat*:—bat.

5848. עָטַף **ʻâṭaph**, *aw-taf'*; a prim. root; to *shroud*, i.e. *clothe* (whether trans. or reflex.); hence (from the idea of *darkness*) to *languish*:—cover (over), fail, faint, feebler, hide self, be overwhelmed, swoon.

5849. עָטַר **ʻâṭar**, *aw-tar'*; a prim. root; to *encircle* (for attack or protection); espec. to *crown* (lit. or fig.):—compass, crown.

5850. עֲטָרָה **ʻăṭârâh**, *at-aw-raw'*; from 5849; a *crown*:—crown.

5851. עֲטָרָה **ʻĂṭârâh**, *at-aw-raw'*; the same as 5850; *Atarah*, an Israelitess:—Atarah.

5852. עֲטָרוֹת **ʻĂṭârôwth**, *at-aw-rōth'*; or

עֲטָרֹת **ʻĂṭârôth**, *at-aw-rōth'*; plur. of 5850; *Ataroth*, the name (thus simply) of two places in Pal.:—Ataroth.

5853. עַטְרוֹת אַדָּר **ʻAṭrôwth ʼAddâr**, *at-rōth' ad-dawr'*; from the same as 5852 and 146; *crowns of Addar; Atroth-Addar*, a place in Pal.:—Ataroth-adar (-addar).

5854. עַטְרוֹת בֵּית יוֹאָב **ʻAṭrôwth bêyth Yôwʼâb**, *at-rōth' bayth yo-awb'*; from the same as 5852 and 1004 and 3097; *crowns of the house of Joäb; Atroth-beth-Joäb*, a place in Pal.:—Ataroth the house of Joab.

5855. עַטְרוֹת שׁוֹפָן **ʻAṭrôwth Shôwphân**, *at-rōth' sho-fawn'*; from the same as 5852 and a name otherwise unused [being from the same as 8226] mean. *hidden; crowns of Shophan; Atroth-Shophan*, a place in Pal.:—Atroth, Shophan [*as if two places*].

5856. עִי **ʻîy**, *ee*; from 5753; a *ruin* (as if overturned):—heap.

5857. עַי **ʻAy**, *ah'ee*; or (fem.)

עַיָּא **ʻAyâʼ** (Neh. 11 : 31), *ah-yaw'*; or

עַיָּת **ʻAyâth** (Isa. 10 : 28), *ah-yawth'*; for 5856; *Ai, Aja* or *Ajath*, a place in Pal.:—Ai, Aija, Aijath, Hai.

5858. עֵיבָל **ʻÊybâl**, *ay-bawl'*; perh. from an unused root prob. mean. to be *bald*; *bare; Ebal*, a mountain of Pal.:—Ebal.

עַיָּה **ʻAyâh**. See 5857.

5859. עִיּוֹן **ʻIyôwn**, *ee-yone'*; from 5856; *ruin; Ijon*, a place in Pal.:—Ijon.

5860. עִיט **ʻîyṭ**, *eet*; a prim. root; to *swoop* down upon (lit. or fig.):—fly, rail.

5861. עַיִט **ʻayiṭ**, *ah'-yit*; from 5860; a *hawk* or other bird of prey:—bird, fowl, ravenous (bird).

5862. עֵיטָם **ʻÊyṭâm**, *ay-tawm'*; from 5861; *hawk-ground; Etam*, a place in Pal.:—Etam.

5863. עִיֵּי הָעֲבָרִים **ʻIyêy hâ-ʻĂbârîym**, *ee-yay' haw-ab-aw-reem'*; from the plur. of 5856 and the plur. of the act. part. of 5674 with the art. interposed; *ruins of the passers; Ije-ha-Abarim*, a place near Pal.:—Ije-abarim.

5864. עִיִּים **ʻIyîym**, *ee-yeem'*; plur. of 5856; *ruins; Ijim*, a place in the Desert:—Iim.

5865. עֵילוֹם **ʻêylôwm**, *ay-lome'*; for 5769:—ever.

5866. עִילַי **ʻÎylay**, *ee-lah'ee*; from 5927; *elevated; Ilai*, an Isr.:—Ilai.

5867. עֵילָם **ʻÊylâm**, *ay-lawm'*; or

עוֹלָם **ʻÔwlâm** (Ezra 10 : 2; Jer. 49 : 36), *o-lawm'*; prob. from 5956; *hidden*, i.e. *distant; Elam*, a son of Shem, and his descend., with their country; also of six Isr.:—Elam.

5868. עֲיָם **ʻăyâm**, *ah-yawm'*; of doubtful or. and authenticity; prob. mean. *strength*:—mighty.

5869. עַיִן **ʻayin**, *ah'-yin*; prob. a prim. word; an *eye* (lit. or fig.); by anal. a *fountain* (as the *eye* of the landscape):—affliction, outward appearance, + before, + think best, colour, conceit, + be content, countenance, + displease, eye ([-brow], [-d], -sight), face, + favour, fountain, furrow [*from the marg.*], × him, + humble, knowledge, look, (+ well), × me, open (-ly), + (not) please, presence, + regard, resemblance, sight, × thee, × them, + think, × us, well, × you (-rselves).

5870. עַיִן **ʻayin** (Chald.), *ah'-yin*; corresp. to 5869; an *eye*:—eye.

5871. עַיִן **ʻAyin**, *ah'-yin*; the same as 5869; *fountain; Ajin*, the name (thus simply) of two places in Pal.:—Ain.

5872. עֵין גֶּדִי **ʻÊyn Gedîy**, *ane geh'-dee*; from 5869 and 1423; *fountain of a kid; En-Gedi*, a place in Pal.:—En-gedi.

5873. עֵין גַּנִּים **ʻÊyn Ganniym**, *ane gan-neem'*; from 5869 and the plur. of 1588; *fountain of gardens; En-Gannim*, a place in Pal.:—En-gannim.

5874. עֵין־דֹּאר **ʻÊyn-Dôʼr**, *ane-dore'*; or

עֵין דּוֹר **ʻÊyn Dôwr**, *ane dore*; or

עֵין־דֹּר **ʻÊyn-Dôr**, *ane-dore'*; from 5869 and 1755; *fountain of dwelling; En-Dor*, a place in Pal.:—En-dor.

5875. עֵין הַקּוֹרֵא **ʻÊyn haq-Qôwrê**, *ane hak-ko-ray'*; from 5869 and the act. part. of 7121; *fountain of One calling; En-hak-Korè*, a place near Pal.:—En-hakhore.

עֵינוֹן **ʻÊynôwn**. See 2703.

5876. עֵין חַדָּה **ʻÊyn Chaddâh**, *ane khad-daw'*; from 5869 and the fem. of a der. from 2300; *fountain of sharpness; En-Chaddah*, a place in Pal.:—En-haddah.

5877. עֵין חָצוֹר **ʻÊyn Châtsôwr**, *ane khaw-tsore'*; from 5869 and the same as 2674; *fountain of a village; En-Chatsor*, a place in Pal.:—En-hazor.

5878. עֵין חֲרֹד **ʻÊyn Chărôd**, *ane khar-ode'*; from 5869 and a der. of 2729; *fountain of trembling; En-Charod*, a place in Pal.:—well of Harod.

5879. עֵינַיִם **ʻÊynayim**, *ay-nah'-yim*; or

עֵינָם **ʻÊynâm**, *ay-nawm'*; dual of 5869; *double fountain; Enajim* or *Enam*, a place in Pal.:—Enaim, openly (Gen. 38 : 21).

5880. עֵין מִשְׁפָּט **ʻÊyn Mishpâṭ**, *ane mish-pawt'*; from 5869 and 4941; *fountain of judgment; En-Mishpat*, a place near Pal.:—En-mishpat.

5881. עֵינָן **ʻÊynân**, *ay-nawn'*; from 5869; *having eyes; Enan*, an Isr.:—Enan. Comp. 2704.

5882. עֵין עֶגְלַיִם **ʻÊyn ʻEglayim**, *ane eg-lah'-yim*; from 5869 and the dual of 5695; *fountain of two calves; En-Eglajim*, a place in Pal.:—En-eglaim.

5883. עֵין רֹגֵל **ʻÊyn Rôgêl**, *ane ro-gale'*; from 5869 and the act. part. of 7270; *fountain of a traveller; En-Rogel*, a place near Jerus.:—En-rogel.

5884. עֵין רִמּוֹן **ʽÊyn Rimmôwn**, *ane rim-mone'*; from 5869 and 7416; *fountain of a pomegranate; En-Rimmon*, a place in Pal.:—En-rimmon.

5885. עֵין שֶׁמֶשׁ **ʽÊyn Shemesh**, *ane sheh'-mesh*; from 5869 and 8121; *fountain of* the *sun; En-Shemesh*, a place in Pal.:—En-shemesh.

5886. עֵין תַּנִּים **ʽÊyn Tannîym**, *ane tan-neem'*; from 5869 and the plur. of 8565; *fountain of jackals; En-Tannim*, a pool near Jerus.:—dragon well.

5887. עֵין תַּפּוּחַ **ʽÊyn Tappûwach**, *ane tap-poo'-akh*; from 5869 and 8598; *fountain of an apple*-tree; *En-Tappuäch*, a place in Pal.:—En-tappuah.

5888. עָיֵף **ʽâyêph**, *aw-yafe'*; a prim. root; to *languish*:—be wearied.

5889. עָיֵף **ʽâyêph**, *aw-yafe'*; from 5888; *languid*:—faint, thirsty, weary.

5890. עֵיפָה **ʽêyphâh**, *ay-faw'*; fem. from 5774; *obscurity* (as if from *covering*):—darkness.

5891. עֵיפָה **ʽÊyphâh**, *ay-faw'*; the same as 5890; *Ephah*, the name of a son of Midian, and of the region settled by him; also of an Isr. and of an Israelitess:—Ephah.

5892. עִיר **ʽîyr**, *eer*; or (in the plur.)
עָר **ʽâr**, *awr*; or
עָיַר **ʽâyar** (Judg. 10 : 4), *aw-yar'*; from 5782 a *city* (a place guarded by *waking* or a watch) in the widest sense (even of a mere *encampment* or *post*):—Ai [*from marg.*], city, court [*from marg.*], town.

5893. עִיר **ʽÎyr**, *eer*; the same as 5892; *Ir*, an Isr.:—Ir.

5894. עִיר **ʽîyr** (Chald.), *eer*; from a root corresp. to 5782; a *watcher*, i.e. an *angel* (as guardian):—watcher.

5895. עַיִר **ʽayir**, *ah'-yeer*; from 5782 in the sense of *raising* (i.e. *bearing* a burden); prop. a young *ass* (as just broken to a load); hence an ass-*colt*:—(ass) colt, foal, young ass.

5896. עִירָא **ʽÎyrâʼ**, *ee-raw'*; from 5782; *wakefulness; Ira*, the name of three Isr.:—Ira.

5897. עִירָד **ʽÎyrâd**, *ee-rawd'*; from the same as 6166; *fugitive; Irad*, an antediluvian:—Irad.

5898. עִיר הַמֶּלַח **ʽÎyr ham-Melach**, *eer ham-meh'-lakh*; from 5892 and 4417 with the art. of substance interp.; *city of* (*the*) *salt; Ir-ham-Melach*, a place near Pal.:—the city of salt.

5899. עִיר הַתְּמָרִים **ʽÎyr hat-Temârîym**, *eer hat-tem-aw-reem'*; from 5892 and the plur. of 8558 with the art. interp.; *city of the palmtrees; Ir-hat-Temarim*, a place in Pal.:—the city of palmtrees.

5900. עִירוּ **ʽÎyrûw**, *ee-roo'*; from 5892; a *citizen; Iru*, an Isr.:—Iru.

5901. עִירִי **ʽÎyrîy**, *ee-ree'*; from 5892; *urbane; Iri*, an Isr.:—Iri.

5902. עִירָם **ʽÎyrâm**, *ee-rawm'*; from 5892; *city-wise; Iram*, an Idumæan:—Iram.

5903. עֵירֹם **ʽêyrôm**, *ay-rome'*; or
עֵרֹם **ʽêrôm**, *ay-rome'*; from 6191; *nudity*:—naked (-ness).

5904. עִיר נָחָשׁ **ʽÎyr Nâchâsh**, *eer naw-khawsh'*; from 5892 and 5175; *city of a serpent; Ir-Nachash*, a place in Pal.:—Ir-nahash.

5905. עִיר שֶׁמֶשׁ **ʽÎyr Shemesh**, *eer sheh'-mesh*; from 5892 and 8121; *city of the sun; Ir-Shemesh*, a place in Pal.:—Ir-shemesh.

5906. עַיִשׁ **ʽAyish**, *ah'-yish*; or
עָשׁ **ʽÂsh**, *awsh*; from 5789; the constellation of the Great *Bear* (perh. from its *migration* through the heavens):—Arcturus.
עַיָּת **ʽAyâth**. See 5857.

5907. עַכְבּוֹר **ʽAkbôwr**, *ak-bore'*; prob. for 5909; *Akbor*, the name of an Idumæan and two Isr.:—Achbor.

5908. עַכָּבִישׁ **ʽakkâbîysh**, *ak-kaw-beesh'*; prob. from an unused root in the lit. sense of *entangling*; a *spider* (as *weaving* a network):—spider.

5909. עַכְבָּר **ʽakbâr**, *ak-bawr'*; prob. from the same as 5908 in the secondary sense of *attacking*; a *mouse* (as *nibbling*):—mouse.

5910. עַכּוֹ **ʽAkkôw**, *ak-ko'*; appar. from an unused root mean. to *hem* in; *Akko* (from its situation on a *bay*):—Accho.

5911. עָכוֹר **ʽÂkôwr**, *aw-kore'*; from 5916; *troubled; Akor*, the name of a place in Pal.:—Achor.

5912. עָכָן **ʽÂkân**, *aw-kawn'*; from an unused root mean. to *trouble; troublesome; Akan*, an Isr.:—Achan. Comp. 5917.

5913. עָכַס **ʽâkaç**, *aw-kas'*; a prim. root; prop. to *tie*, spec. with fetters; but used only as denom. from 5914; to *put on anklets*:—make a tinkling ornament.

5914. עֶכֶס **ʽekeç**, *eh'-kes*; from 5913; a *fetter*; hence an *anklet*:—stocks, tinkling ornament.

5915. עַכְסָה **ʽAkçâh**, *ak-saw'*; fem. of 5914; *anklet; Aksah*, an Israelitess:—Achsah.

5916. עָכַר **ʽâkar**, *aw-kar'*; a prim. root; prop. to *roil* water; fig. to *disturb* or *afflict*:—trouble, stir.

5917. עָכָר **ʽÂkâr**, *aw-kawr'*; from 5916; *troublesome; Akar*, an Isr.:—Achar. Comp. 5912.

5918. עׇכְרָן **ʽOkrân**, *ok-rawn'*; from 5916; *muddler; Okran*, an Isr.:—Ocran.

5919. עַכְשׁוּב **ʽakshûwb**, *ak-shoob'*; prob. from an unused root mean. to *coil*; an *asp* (from lurking *coiled* up):—adder.

5920. עַל **ʽal**, *al*; from 5927; prop. the *top*; spec. the *Highest* (i.e. *God*); also (adv.) *aloft, to Jehovah*:—above, high, most High.

5921. עַל **ʽal**, *al*; prop. the same as 5920 used as a prep. (in the sing. or plur., often with pref., or as conj. with a particle following); *above, over, upon*, or *against* (yet always in this last relation with a downward aspect) in a great variety of applications (as follow):—above, according to (-ly), after, (as) against, among, and, × as, at, because of, beside (the rest of), between, beyond the time, × both and, by (reason of), × had the charge of, concerning for, in (that), (forth, out) of, (from) (off), (up-) on, over, than, through (-out), to, touching, × with.

5922. עַל **ʽal** (Chald.), *al*; corresp. to 5921:—about, against, concerning, for, [there-] fore, from, in, × more, of, (there-, up-) on, (in-) to, + why with.

5923. עֹל **ʽôl**, *ole*; or
עוֹל **ʽôwl**, *ole*; from 5953; a *yoke* (as *imposed* on the neck), lit. or fig.:—yoke.

5924. עֵלָּא **ʽêllâʼ** (Chald.), *ale-law'*; from 5922; *above*:—over.

5925. עֻלָּא **ʽUllâʼ**, *ool-law'*; fem. of 5923; *burden; Ulla*, an Isr.:—Ulla.

5926. עִלֵּג **ʽillêg**, *il-layg'*; from an unused root mean. to *stutter; stuttering*:—stammerer.

5927. עָלָה **ʽâlâh**, *aw-law'*; a prim. root; to *ascend*, intrans. (*be high*) or act. (*mount*); used in a great variety of senses, primary and secondary, lit. and fig. (as follow):—arise (up). (cause to) ascend up, at once, break [*the day*] (up), bring (up), (cause to) burn, carry up, cast up, + shew, climb (up), (cause to, make to) come (up), cut off, dawn, depart, exalt, excel, fall, fetch up, get up, (make to) go (away, up), grow (over), increase, lay, leap, levy, lift (self) up, light, [make] up, × mention, mount up, offer, make to pay, + perfect, prefer, put (on), raise, recover, restore, (make to) rise (up), scale, set (up), shoot forth (up), (begin to) spring (up), stir up, take away (up), work.

5928. עֲלָה **ʽălâh** (Chald.), *al-aw'*; corresp. to 5930; a *holocaust*:—burnt offering.

5929. עָלֶה **ʽâleh**, *aw-leh'*; from 5927; a *leaf* (as *coming up* on a tree); collect. *foliage*:—branch, leaf.

5930. עֹלָה **ʽôlâh**, *o-law'*; or
עוֹלָה **ʽôwlâh**, *o-law'*; fem. act. part. of 5927; a *step* or (collect. *stairs*, as *ascending*); usually a *holocaust* (as *going up* in smoke):—ascent, burnt offering (sacrifice), go up to. See also 5766.

5931. עִלָּה **ʽillâh** (Chald.), *il-law'*; fem. from a root corresp. to 5927; a *pretext* (as *arising* artificially):—occasion.

5932. עַלְוָה **ʽalvâh**, *al-vaw'*; for 5766; moral *perverseness*:—iniquity.

5933. עַלְוָה **ʽAlvâh**, *al-vaw'*; or
עַלְיָה° **ʽAlyâh**, *al-yaw'*; the same as 5932; *Alvah* or *Aljah*, an Idumæan:—Aliah, Alvah.

5934. עָלוּם **ʽâlûwm**, *aw-loom'*; pass. part. of 5956 in the denom. sense of 5958; (only in plur. as abstr.) *adolescence*; fig. *vigor*:—youth.

5935. עַלְוָן **ʽAlvân**, *al-vawn'*; or
עַלְיָן **ʽAlyân**, *al-yawn'*; from 5927; *lofty; Alvan* or *Aljan*, an Idumæan:—Alian, Alvan.

5936. עֲלוּקָה **ʽălûwqâh**, *al-oo-kaw'*; fem. pass. part. of an unused root mean. to *suck*; the *leech*:—horse-leech.

5937. עָלַז **ʽâlaz**, *aw-laz'*; a prim. root; to *jump* for joy, i.e. *exult*:—be joyful, rejoice, triumph.

5938. עָלֵז **ʽâlêz**, *aw-laze'*; from 5937; *exultant*:—that rejoiceth.

5939. עֲלָטָה **ʽălâṭâh**, *al-aw-taw'*; fem. from an unused root mean. to *cover*; *dusk*:—dark, twilight.

5940. עֱלִי **ʽĕlîy**, *el-ee'*; from 5927; a *pestle* (as *lifted*):—pestle.

5941. עֵלִי **ʽÊlîy**, *ay-lee'*; from 5927; *lofty; Eli*, an Isr. high-priest:—Eli.

5942. עִלִּי **ʽillîy**, *il-lee'*; from 5927; *high*, i.e. compar.:—upper.

5943. עִלַּי **ʽillay** (Chald.), *il-lah'ee*; corresp. to 5942; *supreme* (i.e. *God*):—(most) high.
עַלְיָה° **ʽAlyâh**. See 5933.

5944. עֲלִיָּה **ʽălîyâh**, *al-ee-yaw'*; fem. from 5927; something *lofty*, i.e. a *stair-way*; also a *second-story* room (or even one on the roof); fig. the *sky*:—ascent, (upper) chamber, going up, loft, parlour.

5945. עֶלְיוֹן **ʽelyôwn**, *el-yone'*; from 5927; an *elevation*, i.e. (adj.) *lofty* (compar.); as title, the *Supreme*:—(Most, on) high (-er, -est), upper (-most).

5946. עֶלְיוֹן **ʽelyôwn** (Chald.), *el-yone'*; corresp. to 5945; the *Supreme*:—Most high.

5947. עַלִּיז **ʽallîyz**, *al-leez'*; from 5937; *exultant*:—joyous, (that) rejoice (-ing).

5948. עֲלִיל **ʽălîyl**, *al-eel'*; from 5953 in the sense of *completing*; prob. a *crucible* (as *working* over the metal):—furnace.

5949. עֲלִילָה **ʽălîylâh**, *al-ee-law'*; or
עֲלִלָה **ʽălilâh**, *al-ee-law'*; from 5953 in the sense of *effecting*; an *exploit* (of God), or a *performance* (of man, often in a bad sense); by impl. an *opportunity*:—act (-ion), deed, doing, invention, occasion, work.

5950. עֲלִילִיָּה **ʽălîylîyâh**, *al-ee-lee-yaw'*; for 5949; (miraculous) *execution*:—work.
עַלְיָן **ʽAlyân**. See 5935.

5951. עֲלִיצוּת **ʽălîytsûwth**, *al-ee-tsooth'*; from 5970; *exultation*:—rejoicing.

5952. עַלִּית **ʽallîyth**, *al-leeth'*; from 5927; a *second-story* room:—chamber. Comp. 5944.

5953. עָלַל **ʽâlal**, *aw-lal'*; a prim. root; to *effect* thoroughly; spec. to *glean* (also fig.); by impl. (in a bad sense) to *overdo*, i.e. maltreat, be saucy to, pain, impose (also lit.):—abuse, affect, × child, defile, do, glean, mock, practise, throughly, work (wonderfully).

5954. עֲלַל **ʻălal** (Chald.), *al-al'*; corresp. to 5953 (in the sense of *thrusting* oneself in), to *enter;* caus. to *introduce:*—bring in, come in, go in.

עֹלָל **ʻôlâl**. See 5768.

עֲלִלָה **ʻălîlâh**. See 5949.

5955. עֹלֵלָה **ʻôlêlâh**, *o-lay-law';* fem. act. part. of 5953; only in plur. *gleanings;* by extens. *gleaning-time:*—(gleaning) (of the) grapes, grapegleanings.

5956. עָלַם **ʻâlam**, *aw-lam';* a prim. root; to *veil* from sight, i.e. *conceal* (lit. or fig.):—× any ways, blind, dissembler, hide (self), secret (thing).

5957. עָלַם **ʻâlam** (Chald.), *aw-lam';* corresp. to 5769; *remote* time, i.e. the *future* or *past* indefinitely; often adv. *forever:*—for ([n-]) ever (lasting), old.

5958. עֶלֶם **ʻelem**, *eh'-lem;* from 5956; prop. something *kept out of sight* [comp. 5959], i.e. a *lad:*—young man, stripling.

עֹלָם **ʻôlâm**. See 5769.

5959. עַלְמָה **ʻalmâh**, *al-maw';* fem. of 5958; a *lass* (as *veiled* or private):—damsel, maid, virgin.

5960. עַלְמוֹן **ʻAlmôwn**, *al-mone';* from 5956; *hidden; Almon,* a place in Pal. See also 5963.

5961. עֲלָמוֹת **ʻĂlâmôwth**, *al-aw-mōth';* plur. of 5959; prop. *girls,* i.e. the *soprano* or female voice, perh. *falsetto:*—Alamoth.

עַלְמוּת **ʻalmûwth**. See 4192.

5962. עַלְמִי **ʻAlmîy** (Chald.), *al-mee';* patrial from a name corresp. to 5867 contr.; an *Elamite* or inhab. of Elam:—Elamite.

5963. עַלְמֹן דִּבְלָתָיְמָה **ʻAlmôn Diblâthâ-yᵉmâh**, *al-mone' dib-law-thaw'-yem-aw;* from the same as 5960 and the dual of 1690 [comp. 1015] with enclitic of direction; *Almon towards Diblathajim; Almon-Diblathajemah,* a place in Moab:—Almon-dilathaim.

5964. עָלֶמֶת **ʻÂlemeth**, *aw-leh'-meth;* from 5956; a *covering; Alemeth,* the name of a place in Pal. and of two Isr.:—Alameth, Alemeth.

5965. עָלַס **ʻâlaç**, *aw-las';* a prim. root; to *leap* for joy, i.e. *exult, wave* joyously:—× peacock, rejoice, solace self.

5966. עָלַע **ʻâlaʻ**, *aw-lah';* a prim. root; to *sip* up:—suck up.

5967. עֲלַע **ʻălaʻ** (Chald.), *al-ah';* corresp. to 6763; a *rib:*—rib.

5968. עָלַף **ʻâlaph**, *aw-laf';* a prim. root; to *veil* or *cover;* fig. to *be languid:*—faint, overlaid, wrap self.

5969. עֻלְפֶּה **ʻulpeh**, *ool-peh';* from 5968; an *envelope,* i.e. (fig.) *mourning:*—fainted.

5970. עָלַץ **ʻâlats**, *aw-lats';* a prim. root; to *jump* for joy, i.e. *exult:*—be joyful, rejoice, triumph.

5971. עַם **ʻam**, *am;* from 6004; a *people* (as a congregated *unit*); spec. a *tribe* (as those of Israel); hence (collect.) *troops* or *attendants;* fig. a *flock:*—folk, men, nation, people.

5972. עַם **ʻam** (Chald.), *am;* corresp. to 5971:—people.

5973. עִם **ʻîm**, *eem;* from 6004; adv. or prep., *with* (i.e. in *conjunction* with), in varied applications; spec. *equally with;* often with prep. pref. (and then usually unrepresented in English):—accompanying, against, and, as (× long as), before, beside, by (reason of), for all, from (among, between), in, like, more than, of, (un-) to, with (-al).

5974. עִם **ʻîm** (Chald.), *eem;* corresp. to 5973:—by, from, like, to (-ward), with.

5975. עָמַד **ʻâmad**, *aw-mad';* a prim. root; to *stand,* in various relations (lit. and fig., intrans. and trans.):—abide (behind), appoint, arise, cease, confirm, continue, dwell, be employed, endure, establish, leave, make, ordain, be [over], place, (be) present (self), raise up, remain, repair, + serve, set (forth, over, -tle, up), (make to, make to be at a, with-) stand (by, fast, firm, still, up), (be at a) stay (up), tarry.

5976. עָמַד **ʻâmad**, *aw-mad';* for 4571; to *shake:*—be at a stand.

5977. עֹמֶד **ʻômed**, *o'-med;* from 5975; a *spot* (as being *fixed*):—place, (+ where) stood, upright.

5978. עִמָּד **ʻimmâd**, *im-mawd';* prol. for 5973; along *with:*—against, by, from, in, + me, + mine, of, + that I take, unto, upon, with (-in).

עַמֻּד **ʻammûd**. See 5982.

5979. עֶמְדָּה **ʻemdâh**, *em-daw';* from 5975; a *station,* i.e. domicile:—standing.

5980. עֻמָּה **ʻummâh**, *oom-maw';* from 6004; *conjunction,* i.e. *society;* mostly adv. or prep. (with prep. pref.), *near, beside, along with:*—(over) against, at, beside, hard by, in points.

5981. עֻמָּה **ʻUmmâh**, *oom-maw';* the same as 5980; *association; Ummah,* a place in Pal.:—Ummah.

5982. עַמּוּד **ʻammûwd**, *am-mood';* or

עַמֻּד **ʻammûd**, *am-mood';* from 5975; a *column* (as *standing*); also a *stand,* i.e. platform:—× apiece, pillar.

5983. עַמּוֹן **ʻAmmôwn**, *am-mone';* from 5971; *tribal,* i.e. *inbred; Ammon,* a son of Lot; also his posterity and their country:—Ammon, Ammonites.

5984. עַמּוֹנִי **ʻAmmôwnîy**, *am-mo-nee';* patron. from 5983; an *Ammonite* or (adj.) *Ammonitish:*—Ammonite (-s).

5985. עַמּוֹנִית **ʻAmmôwnîyth**, *am-mo-neeth';* fem. of 5984; an *Ammonitess:*—Ammonite (-ss).

5986. עָמוֹס **ʻÂmôwç**, *aw-moce';* from 6006; *burdensome; Amos,* an Isr. prophet:—Amos.

5987. עָמוֹק **ʻÂmôwq**, *aw-moke';* from 6009; *deep; Amok,* an Isr.:—Amok.

5988. עַמִּיאֵל **ʻAmmîyʼêl**, *am-mee-ale';* from 5971 and 410; *people of God; Ammiël,* the name of three or four Isr.:—Ammiel.

5989. עַמִּיהוּד **ʻAmmîyhûwd**, *am-mee-hood';* from 5971 and 1935; *people of splendor; Ammihud,* the name of three Isr.:—Ammihud.

5990. עַמִּיזָבָד **ʻAmmîyzâbâd**, *am-mee-zaw-bawd';* from 5971 and 2064; *people of endowment; Ammizabad,* an Isr.:—Ammizabad.

5991. עַמִּיחוּר **ʻAmmîychûwr**, *am-mee-khoor';* from 5971 and 2353; *people of nobility; Ammichur,* a Syrian prince:—Ammihud [*from the marg.*].

5992. עַמִּינָדָב **ʻAmmîynâdâb**, *am-mee-naw-dawb';* from 5971 and 5068; *people of liberality; Amminadab,* the name of four Isr.:—Amminadab.

5993. עַמִּי נָדִיב **ʻAmmîy Nâdîyb**, *am-mee' naw-deeb';* from 5971 and 5081; *my people* (is) *liberal; Ammi-Nadib,* prob. an Isr.:—Amminadib.

5994. עֲמִיק **ʻămîyq** (Chald.), *am-eek';* corresp. to 6012; *profound,* i.e. unsearchable:—deep.

5995. עָמִיר **ʻâmîyr**, *aw-meer';* from 6014; a *bunch* of grain:—handful, sheaf.

5996. עַמִּישַׁדַּי **ʻAmmîyshadday**, *am-mee-shad-dah'ee;* from 5971 and 7706; *people of* (the) *Almighty; Ammishaddai,* an Isr.:—Ammishaddai.

5997. עָמִית **ʻâmîyth**, *aw-meeth';* from a prim. root mean. to *associate; companionship;* hence (concr.) a *comrade* or kindred man:—another, fellow, neighbour.

5998. עָמַל **ʻâmal**, *aw-mal';* a prim. root; to *toil,* i.e. *work severely* and with irksomeness:—[take] labour (in).

5999. עָמָל **ʻâmâl**, *aw-mawl';* from 5998; *toil,* i.e. *wearing effort;* hence *worry,* wheth. of body or mind:—grievance (-vousness), iniquity, labour, mischief, miserable (-sery), pain (-ful), perverseness, sorrow, toil, travail, trouble, wearisome, wickedness.

6000. עָמָל **ʻÂmâl**, *aw-mawl';* the same as 5999; *Amal,* an Isr.:—Amal.

6001. עָמֵל **ʻâmêl**, *aw-male';* from 5998; *toiling* concr. a *laborer;* fig. *sorrowful:*—that laboureth, that is a misery, had taken [labour], wicked, workman.

6002. עֲמָלֵק **ʻĂmâlêq**, *am-aw-lake';* prob. of for. or.; *Amalek,* a descend. of Esau; also his posterity and their country:—Amalek.

6003. עֲמָלֵקִי **ʻĂmâlêqîy**, *am-aw-lay-kee';* patron. from 6002; an *Amalekite* (or collect. the *Amalekites*) or desc. of Amalek:—Amalekite (-s).

6004. עָמַם **ʻâmam**, *aw-mam';* a prim. root; to *associate;* by impl. to *overshadow* (by *huddling* together):—become dim, hide.

6005. עִמָּנוּאֵל **ʻImmânûwʼêl**, *im-maw-noo-ale';* from 5973 and 410 with suff. pron. ins.; *with us* (is) *God; Immanuel,* a typ. name of Isaiah's son:—Immanuel.

6006. עָמַס **ʻâmaç**, *aw-mas';* or

עָמַשׂ **ʻâmas**, *aw-mas';* a prim. root; to *load,* i.e. *impose* a burden (or fig. infliction):—be borne, (heavy) burden (self), lade, load, put.

6007. עֲמַסְיָה **ʻĂmacyâh**, *am-as-yaw';* from 6006 and 3050; *Jah has loaded; Amasjah,* an Isr.:—Amasiah.

6008. עַמְעָד **ʻAmʻâd**, *am-awd';* from 5971 and 5703; *people of time; Amad,* a place in Pal.:—Amad.

6009. עָמַק **ʻâmaq**, *aw-mak';* a prim. root; to *be* (causat. *make*) *deep* (lit. or fig.):—(be, have, make, seek) deep (-ly), depth, be profound.

6010. עֵמֶק **ʻêmeq**, *ay'-mek;* from 6009; a *vale* (i.e. broad *depression*):—dale, vale, valley [*often used as a part of proper names*]. See also 1025.

6011. עֹמֶק **ʻômeq**, *o'-mek;* from 6009; *depth:*—depth.

6012. עָמֵק **ʻâmêq**, *aw-make';* from 6009; *deep* (lit. or fig.):—deeper, depth, strange.

6013. עָמֹק **ʻâmôq**, *aw-moke';* from 6009; *deep* (lit. or fig.):—(× exceeding) deep (thing)

6014. עָמַר **ʻâmar**, *aw-mar';* a prim. root; prop. appar. to *heap;* fig. to *chastise* (as if *piling* blows); spec. (as denom. from 6016) to *gather* grain:—bind sheaves, make merchandise of.

6015. עֲמַר **ʻămar** (Chald.), *am-ar';* corresp. to 6785; *wool:*—wool.

6016. עֹמֶר **ʻômer**, *o'-mer;* from 6014; prop. a *heap,* i.e. a *sheaf;* also an *omer,* as a dry measure:—omer, sheaf.

6017. עֲמֹרָה **ʻĂmôrâh**, *am-o-raw';* from 6014; a (ruined) *heap; Amorah,* a place in Pal.:—Gomorrah.

6018. עָמְרִי **ʻOmrîy**, *om-ree';* from 6014; *heaping; Omri,* an Isr.:—Omri.

6019. עַמְרָם **ʻAmrâm**, *am-rawm';* prob. from 5971 and 7311; *high people; Amram,* the name of two Isr.:—Amram.

6020. עַמְרָמִי **ʻAmrâmîy**, *am-raw-mee';* patron. from 6019; an *Amramite* or desc. of Amram:—Amramite.

עֲמַשׂ **ʻâmas**. See 6006.

6021. עֲמָשָׂא **ʻĂmâsâʼ**, *am-aw-saw';* from 6006; *burden; Amasa,* the name of two Isr.:—Amasa.

6022. עֲמָשַׂי **ʻĂmâsay**, *am-aw-sah'ee;* from 6006; *burdensome; Amasai,* the name of three Isr.:—Amasai.

6023. עֲמַשְׁסַי **ʻĂmashçay**, *am-ash-sah'ee;* prob. from 6006; *burdensome; Amashsay,* an Isr.:—Amashai.

6024. עֲנָב **ʻĂnâb**, *an-awb';* from the same as 6025; *fruit; Anab,* a place in Pal.:—Anab.

6025. עֵנָב **ʻênâb**, *ay-nawb';* from an unused root prob. mean. to *bear fruit;* a *grape:*—(ripe) grape, wine.

6026. עָנַג **ʻânag**, *aw-nag';* a prim. root; to be *soft* or pliable, i.e. (fig.) *effeminate* or luxurious:—delicate (-ness), (have) delight (self), sport self.

6027. עֹנֶג **ʻôneg**, *o'-neg;* from 6026; *luxury:*—delight, pleasant.

6028. עָנֹג **ʻânôg**, *aw-nogue';* from 6026; *luxurious:*—delicate.

6029. עָנַד **ʻânad**, *aw-nad'*; a prim. root; to *lace* fast:—bind, tie.

6030. עָנָה **ʻânâh**, *aw-naw'*; a prim. root; prop. to *eye* or (gen.) to *heed*, i.e. *pay attention;* by impl. to *respond;* by extens. to *begin* to speak; spec. to *sing, shout, testify, announce:*—give account, afflict [*by mistake for* 6031], (cause to, give) answer, bring low [*by mistake for* 6031], cry, hear, Leannoth, lift up, say, × scholar, (give a) shout, sing (together by course), speak, testify, utter, (bear) witness. See also 1042, 1043.

6031. עָנָה **ʻânâh**, *aw-naw'*; a prim. root [possibly rather ident. with 6030 through the idea of *looking* down or *browbeating*]; to *depress* lit. or fig., trans. or intrans. (in various applications, as follow):—abase self, afflict (-ion, self), answer [*by mistake for* 6030], chasten self, deal hardly with, defile, exercise, force, gentleness, humble (self), hurt, ravish, sing [*by mistake for* 6030], speak [*by mistake for* 6030], submit self, weaken, × in any wise.

6032. עֲנָה **ʻănâh** (Chald.), *an-aw'*; corresp. to 6030:—answer, speak.

6033. עֲנָה **ʻănâh** (Chald.), *an-aw'*; corresp. to 6031:—poor.

6034. עֲנָה **ʻĂnâh**, *an-aw'*; prob. from 6030; an *answer; Anah*, the name of two Edomites and one Edomitess:—Anah.

6035. עָנָו **ʻânâv**, *aw-nawv'*; or [by intermixture with 6041]

עָנָיו **ʻânâyv**, *aw-nawv'*; from 6031; *depressed* (fig.), in mind (*gentle*) or circumstances (*needy*, espec. *saintly*):—humble, lowly, meek, poor°. Comp. 6041.

6036. עָנוּב **ʻÂnûwb**, *aw-noob'*; pass. part. from the same as 6025; *borne* (as fruit); *Anub*, an Isr.:—Anub.

6037. עַנְוָה **ʻanvâh**, *an-vaw'*; fem. of 6035; *mildness* (royal); also (concr.) *oppressed:*—gentleness, meekness.

6038. עֲנָוָה **ʻănâvâh**, *an-aw-vaw'*; from 6035; *condescension*, human and subj. (*modesty*), or divine and obj. (*clemency*):—gentleness, humility, meekness.

6039. עֱנוּת **ʻênûwth**, *en-ooth'*; from 6031; *affliction:*—affliction.

6040. עֳנִי **ʻônîy**, *on-ee'*; from 6031; *depression*, i.e. misery:—afflicted (-ion), trouble.

6041. עָנִי **ʻânîy**, *aw-nee'*; from 6031; *depressed*, in mind or circumstances [practically the same as 6035, although the marg. constantly disputes this, making 6035 subj. and 6041 obj.]:—afflicted, humble°, lowly°, needy, poor.

6042. עֻנִּי **ʻUnnîy**, *oon-nee'*; from 6031; *afflicted; Unni*, the name of two Isr.:—Unni.

6043. עֲנָיָה **ʻĂnâyâh**, *an-aw-yaw'*; from 6030; *Jah has answered; Anajah*, the name of two Isr.:—Anaiah.

עָנָיו **ʻânâyv**. See 6035.

6044. עָנִים **ʻÂnîym**, *aw-neem'*; for plur. of 5869; *fountains; Anim*, a place in Pal.:—Anim.

6045. עִנְיָן **ʻinyân**, *in-yawn'*; from 6031; *ado*, i.e. (gen.) *employment* or (spec.) an *affair:*—business, travail.

6046. עָנֵם **ʻÂnêm**, *aw-name'*; from the dual of 5869; *two fountains; Anem*, a place in Pal.:—Anem.

6047. עֲנָמִים **ʻĂnâmîm**, *an-aw-meem'*; as if plur. of some Eg. word; *Anamim*, a son of Mizraim and his desc., with their country:—Anamim.

6048. עֲנַמֶּלֶךְ **ʻĂnammelek**, *an-am-meh'-lek*; of for. or.; *Anammelek*, an Assyrian deity:—Anammelech.

6049. עָנַן **ʻânan**, *aw-nan'*; a prim. root; to *cover;* used only as denom. from 6051, to *cloud* over; fig. to *act covertly*, i.e. practise magic:—× bring, enchanter, Meonemin, observe (-r of) times, soothsayer, sorcerer.

6050. עֲנַן **ʻănan** (Chald.), *an-an'*; corresp. to 6051:—cloud.

6051. עָנָן **ʻânân**, *aw-nawn'*; from 6049; a *cloud* (as *covering* the sky), i.e. the *nimbus* or thunder-cloud:—cloud (-y).

6052. עָנָן **ʻÂnân**, *aw-nawn'*; the same as 6051; *cloud; Anan*, an Isr.:—Anan.

6053. עֲנָנָה **ʻănânâh**, *an-aw-naw'*; fem. of 6051; *cloudiness:*—cloud.

6054. עָנָנִי **ʻÂnânîy**, *an-aw-nee'*; from 6051; *cloudy; Anani*, an Isr.:—Anani.

6055. עֲנַנְיָה **ʻĂnanyâh**, *an-an-yaw'*; from 6049 and 3050; *Jah has covered; Ananjah*, the name of an Isr. and of a place in Pal.:—Ananiah.

6056. עֲנַף **ʻănaph** (Chald.), *an-af'*; or

עֶנֶף **ʻeneph** (Chald.), *eh'-nef*; corresp. to 6057:—bough, branch.

6057. עָנָף **ʻânâph**, *aw-nawf'*; from an unused root mean. to *cover;* a *twig* (as *covering* the limbs):—bough, branch.

6058. עָנֵף **ʻânêph**, *aw-nafe'*; from the same as 6057; *branching:*—full of branches.

6059. עָנַק **ʻânaq**, *aw-nak'*; a prim. root; prop. to *choke;* used only as denom. from 6060, to *collar*, i.e. adorn with a necklace; fig. to *fit out* with supplies:—compass about as a chain, furnish, liberally.

6060. עָנָק **ʻânâq**, *aw-nawk'*; from 6059; a *necklace* (as if *strangling*):—chain.

6061. עֲנָק **ʻÂnâq**, *aw-nawk'*; the same as 6060; *Anak*, a Canaanite:—Anak.

6062. עֲנָקִי **ʻĂnâqîy**, *an-aw-kee'*; patron. from 6061; an *Anakite* or desc. of Anak:—Anakim.

6063. עָנֵר **ʻÂnêr**, *aw-nare'*; prob. for 5288; *Aner*, an Amorite, also a place in Pal.:—Aner.

6064. עָנַשׁ **ʻânash**, *aw-nash'*; a prim. root; prop. to *urge;* by impl. to *inflict* a penalty, spec. to *fine:*—amerce, condemn, punish, × surely.

6065. עֲנַשׁ **ʻănash** (Chald.), *an-ash'*; corresp. to 6066; a *mulct:*—confiscation.

6066. עֹנֶשׁ **ʻônesh**, *o'-nesh*; from 6064; a *fine:*—punishment, tribute.

עֶנֶת **ʻeneth**. See 3706.

6067. עֲנָת **ʻĂnâth**, *an-awth'*; from 6030; *answer; Anath*, an Isr.:—Anath.

6068. עֲנָתוֹת **ʻĂnâthôwth**, *an-aw-thōth'*; plur. of 6067; *Anathoth*, the name of two Isr., also of a place in Pal.:—Anathoth.

6069. עַנְתֹתִי **ʻAnthôthîy**, *an-tho-thee'*; or

עַנְּתוֹתִי **ʻAnnethôwthîy**, *an-ne-tho-thee'*; patrial from 6068; an *Antothite* or inhab. of Anathoth:—of Anathoth, Anethothite, Anetothite, Antothite.

6070. עַנְתֹתִיָּה **ʻAnthôthîyâh**, *an-tho-thee-yaw'*; from the same as 6068 and 3050; *answers of Jah; Anthothijah*, an Isr.:—Antothijah.

6071. עָסִיס **ʻâçîyç**, *aw-sees'*; from 6072; *must* or fresh grape-juice (as just *trodden* out):—juice, new (sweet) wine.

6072. עָסַס **ʻâçaç**, *aw-sas'*; a prim. root; to *squeeze* out juice; fig. to *trample:*—tread down.

6073. עֳפֶא **ʻôphe'**, *of-eh'*; from an unused root mean. to *cover;* a *bough* (as covering the tree):—branch.

6074. עֳפִי **ʻôphîy** (Chald.), *of-ee'*; corresp. to 6073; a *twig;* bough, i.e. (collect.) *foliage:*—leaves.

6075. עָפַל **ʻâphal**, *aw-fal'*; a prim. root; to *swell;* fig. *be elated:*—be lifted up, presume.

6076. עֹפֶל **ʻôphel**, *o'-fel*; from 6075; a *tumor;* also a *mound*, i.e. fortress:—emerod, fort, strong hold, tower.

6077. עֹפֶל **ʻÔphel**, *o'-fel*; the same as 6076; *Ophel*, a ridge in Jerus.:—Ophel.

6078. עָפְנִי **ʻOphnîy**, *of-nee'*; from an unused noun [denoting a place in Pal.; from an unused root of uncert. mean.]; an *Ophnite* (collect.) or inhab. of Ophen:—Ophni.

6079. עַפְעַף **ʻaphʻaph**, *af-af'*; from 5774; an *eyelash* (as *fluttering*); fig. morning ray:—dawning, eye-lid.

6080. עָפַר **ʻâphar**, *aw-far'*; a prim. root; mean. either to *be gray* or perh. rather to *pulverize;* used only as denom. from 6083, to *be dust:*—cast [dust].

6081. עֵפֶר **ʻÊpher**, *ay'-fer*; prob. a var. of 6082; *gazelle; Epher*, the name of an Arabian and of two Isr.:—Epher.

6082. עֹפֶר **ʻôpher**, *o'-fer*; from 6080; a *fawn* (from the *dusty* color):—young roe [hart].

6083. עָפָר **ʻâphâr**, *aw-fawr'*; from 6080; *dust* (as *powdered* or *gray*); hence *clay, earth, mud:*—ashes, dust, earth, ground, morter, powder, rubbish.

עַפְרָה **ʻAphrâh**. See 1035.

6084. עָפְרָה **ʻOphrâh**, *of-raw'*; fem. of 6082; *female fawn; Ophrah*, the name of an Isr. and of two places in Pal.:—Ophrah.

6085. עֶפְרוֹן **ʻEphrôwn**, *ef-rone'*; from the same as 6081; *fawn-like; Ephron*, the name of a Canaanite and of two places in Pal.:—Ephron, Ephrain [*from the marg.*].

עֹפֶרֶת **ʻôphereth**. See 5777.

6086. עֵץ **ʻêts**, *ates*; from 6095; a *tree* (from its *firmness*); hence *wood* (plur. *sticks*):—+ carpenter, gallows, helve, + pine, plank, staff, stalk, stick, stock, timber, tree, wood.

6087. עָצַב **ʻâtsab**, *aw-tsab'*; a prim. root; prop. to *carve*, i.e. *fabricate* or *fashion;* hence (in a bad sense) to *worry, pain* or *anger:*—displease, grieve, hurt, make, be sorry, vex, worship, wrest.

6088. עֲצַב **ʻătsab** (Chald.), *ats-ab'*; corresp. to 6087; to *afflict:*—lamentable.

6089. עֶצֶב **ʻetseb**, *eh'-tseb*; from 6087; an earthen *vessel;* usually (painful) *toil;* also a *pang* (whether of body or mind):—grievous, idol, labor, sorrow.

6090. עֹצֶב **ʻôtseb**, *o'-tseb*; a var. of 6089; an *idol* (as fashioned); also *pain* (bodily or mental):—idol, sorrow, × wicked.

6091. עָצָב **ʻâtsâb**, *aw-tsawb'*; from 6087; an (idolatrous) *image:*—idol, image.

6092. עָצֵב **ʻâtsêb**, *aw-tsabe'*; from 6087; a (hired) *workman:*—labour.

6093. עִצָּבוֹן **ʻitstsâbôwn**, *its-tsaw-bone'*; from 6087; *worrisomeness*, i.e. *labor* or *pain:*—sorrow, toil.

6094. עַצֶּבֶת **ʻatstsebeth**, *ats-tseh'-beth*; from 6087; an *idol;* also a *pain* or *wound:*—sorrow, wound.

6095. עָצָה **ʻâtsâh**, *aw-tsaw'*; a prim. root; prop. to *fasten* (or *make firm*), i.e. to *close* (the eyes):—shut.

6096. עָצֶה **ʻâtseh**, *aw-tseh'*; from 6095; the *spine* (as giving *firmness* to the body):—back bone.

6097. עֵצָה **ʻêtsâh**, *ay-tsaw'*; fem. of 6086; *timber:*—trees.

6098. עֵצָה **ʻêtsâh**, *ay-tsaw'*; from 3289; *advice;* by impl. *plan;* also *prudence:*—advice, advisement, counsel ([-lor]), purpose.

6099. עָצוּם **ʻâtsûwm**, *aw-tsoom'*; or

עָצֻם **ʻâtsûm**, *aw-tsoom'*; pass. part. of 6105; *powerful* (spec. a *paw*); by impl. *numerous:*—+ feeble, great, mighty, must, strong.

6100. עֶצְיוֹן גֶּבֶר **ʻEtsyôwn** (shorter

עֶצְיֹן **ʻEtsyôn**) **Geber**, *ets-yone' gheh'-ber*; from 6096 and 1397; *backbone-like of a man; Etsjon-Geber*, a place on the Red Sea:—Ezion-gaber, Ezion-geber.

6101. עָצַל **ʻâtsal**, *aw-tsal'*; a prim. root; to *lean* idly, i.e. to be *indolent* or *slack:*—be slothful.

6102. עָצֵל **ʻâtsêl**, *aw-tsale'*; from 6101; *indolent:*—slothful, sluggard.

6103. עַצְלָה **ʻatslâh**, *ats-law'*; fem. of 6102; (as abstr.) *indolence:*—slothfulness.

6104. עַצְלוּת **ʻatslûwth**, *ats-looth'*; from 6101; *indolence:*—idleness.

6105. עָצַם **ʻâtsam**, *aw-tsam'*; a prim. root; to *bind* fast, i.e. *close* (the eyes); intrans.

to be (causat. *make*) *powerful* or *numerous;* denom. (from 6106) to *craunch* the bones:—break the bones, close, be great, be increased, be (wax) mighty (-ier), be more, shut, be (-come, make) strong (-er).

6106. עֶצֶם **ʻetsem**, *eh'-tsem;* from 6105; a *bone* (as *strong*); by extens. the *body;* fig. the *substance*, i.e. (as pron.) *selfsame:*—body, bone, × life, (self-) same, strength, × very.

6107. עֶצֶם **ʻEtsem**, *eh'-tsem;* the same as 6106; *bone; Etsem*, a place in Pal.:—Azem, Ezem.

6108. עֹצֶם **ʻôtsem**, *o'-tsem;* from 6105; *power;* hence *body:*—might, strong, substance.

עָצֻם **ʻâtsûm**. See 6099.

6109. עָצְמָה **ʻotsmâh**, *ots-maw';* fem. of 6108; *powerfulness;* by extens. *numerousness:*—abundance, strength.

6110. עַצֻּמָה **ʻatstsûmâh**, *ats-tsoo-maw';* fem. of 6099; a *bulwark*, i.e. (fig.) *argument:*—strong.

6111. עַצְמוֹן **ʻAtsmôwn**, *ats-mone';* or

עַצְמֹן **ʻAtsmôn**, *ats-mone';* from 6107; *bone-like; Atsmon*, a place near Pal.:—Azmon.

6112. עֵצֶן **ʻêtsen**, *ay'-tsen;* from an unused root mean. to *be sharp* or *strong;* a *spear:*—Eznite [*from the marg.*].

6113. עָצַר **ʻâtsar**, *aw-tsar';* a prim. root; to *inclose;* by anal. to *hold back;* also to *maintain, rule, assemble:*— × be able, close up, detain, fast, keep (self close, still), prevail, recover, refrain, × reign, restrain, retain, shut (up), slack, stay, stop, withhold (self).

6114. עֶצֶר **ʻetser**, *eh'-tser;* from 6113; *restraint:*—+ magistrate.

6115. עֹצֶר **ʻôtser**, *o'-tser;* from 6113; *closure;* also *constraint:*— × barren, oppression, × prison.

6116. עֲצָרָה **ʻătsârâh**, *ats-aw-raw';* or

עֲצֶרֶת **ʻătsereth**, *ats-eh'-reth;* from 6113; an *assembly*, espec. on a *festival* or *holiday:*—(solemn) assembly (meeting).

6117. עָקַב **ʻâqab**, *aw-kab';* a prim. root; prop. to *swell* out or up; used only as denom. from 6119, to *seize by the heel;* fig. to *circumvent* (as if *tripping* up the heels); also to *restrain* (as if holding by the heel):—take by the heel, stay, supplant, × utterly.

6118. עֵקֶב **ʻêqeb**, *ay'-keb;* from 6117 in the sense of 6119; a *heel*, i.e. (fig.) the *last* of anything (used adv. *for ever*); also *result*, i.e. *compensation;* and so (adv. with prep. or rel.) on *account* of:— × because, by, end, for, if, reward.

6119. עָקֵב **ʻâqêb**, *aw-kabe';* or (fem.)

עִקְּבָה **ʻiqqᵉbâh**, *ik-keb-aw';* from 6117; a *heel* (as *protuberant*); hence a *track;* fig. the *rear* (of an army):—heel, [horse-] hoof, last, lier in wait [*by mistake for* 6120], (foot-) step.

6120. עָקֵב **ʻâqêb**, *aw-kabe';* from 6117 in its denom. sense; a *lier in wait:*—heel [*by mistake for* 6119].

6121. עָקֹב **ʻâqôb**, *aw-kobe';* from 6117; in the orig. sense, a *knoll* (as *swelling* up); in the denom. sense (trans.) *fraudulent* or (intrans.) *tracked:*—crooked, deceitful, polluted.

6122. עָקְבָה **ʻoqbâh**, *ok-baw';* fem. of an unused form from 6117 mean. a *trick; trickery:*—subtilty.

6123. עָקַד **ʻâqad**, *aw-kad';* a prim. root; to *tie* with thongs:—bind.

עֵקֶד **ʻÊqed**. See 1044.

6124. עָקֹד **ʻâqôd**, *aw-kode';* from 6123; *striped* (with *bands*):—ring straked.

6125. עָקָה **ʻâqâh**, *aw-kaw';* from 5781; *constraint:*—oppression.

6126. עַקּוּב **ʻAqqûwb**, *ak-koob';* from 6117; *insidious; Akkub*, the name of five Isr.:—Akkub.

6127. עָקַל **ʻâqal**, *aw-kal';* a prim. root; to *wrest:*—wrong.

6128. עֲקַלְקַל **ʻăqalqal**, *ak-al-kal';* from 6127; *winding:*—by [-way], crooked way.

6129. עֲקַלָּתוֹן **ʻăqallâthôwn**, *ak-al-law-thone';* from 6127; *tortuous:*—crooked.

6130. עָקָן **ʻÂqân**, *aw-kawn';* from an unused root mean. to *twist; tortuous; Akan*, an Idumæan:—Akan. Comp. 3292.

6131. עָקַר **ʻâqar**, *aw-kar';* a prim. root; to *pluck* up (espec. by the roots); spec. to *hamstring;* fig. to *exterminate:*—dig down, hough, pluck up, root up.

6132. עֲקַר **ʻăqar** (Chald.), *ak-ar';* corresp. to 6131:—pluck up by the roots.

6133. עֵקֶר **ʻêqer**, *ay'-ker;* from 6131; fig. a *transplanted* person, i.e. naturalized citizen:—stock.

6134. עֵקֶר **ʻÊqer**, *ay'-ker;* the same as 6133; *Eker*, an Isr.:—Eker.

6135. עָקָר **ʻâqâr**, *aw-kawr';* from 6131; *sterile* (as if *extirpated* in the generative organs):—(× male or female) barren (woman).

6136. עִקַּר **ʻiqqar** (Chald.), *ik-kar';* from 6132; a *stock:*—stump.

6137. עַקְרָב **ʻaqrâb**, *ak-rawb';* of uncert. der.; a *scorpion;* fig. a *scourge* or knotted whip:—scorpion.

6138. עֶקְרוֹן **ʻEqrôwn**, *ek-rone';* from 6131; *eradication; Ekron*, a place in Pal.:—Ekron.

6139. עֶקְרוֹנִי **ʻEqrôwnîy**, *ek-ro-nee';* or

עֶקְרֹנִי **ʻEqrônîy**, *ek-ro-nee';* patrial from 6138; an *Ekronite* or inhab. of Ekron:—Ekronite.

6140. עָקַשׁ **ʻâqash**, *aw-kash';* a prim. root; to *knot* or *distort;* fig. to *pervert* (act or declare perverse):—make crooked, (prove, that is) perverse (-rt).

6141. עִקֵּשׁ **ʻiqqêsh**, *ik-kashe';* from 6140; *distorted;* hence *false:*—crooked, froward, perverse.

6142. עִקֵּשׁ **ʻIqqêsh**, *ik-kashe';* the same as 6141; *perverse; Ikkesh*, an Isr.:—Ikkesh.

6143. עִקְּשׁוּת **ʻiqqᵉshûwth**, *ik-kesh-ooth';* from 6141; *perversity:*— × froward.

עָר **ʻâr**. See 5892.

6144. עָר **ʻÂr**, *awr;* the same as 5892; a *city; Ar*, a place in Moab:—Ar.

6145. עָר **ʻâr**, *awr;* from 5782; a *foe* (as *watchful* for mischief):—enemy.

6146. עָר **ʻâr** (Chald.), *awr;* corresp. to 6145:—enemy.

6147. עֵר **ʻÊr**, *ayr;* from 5782; *watchful; Er*, the name of two Isr.:—Er.

6148. עָרַב **ʻârab**, *aw-rab';* a prim. root; to *braid*, i.e. *intermix;* techn. to *traffic* (as if by barter); also to *give* or *be security* (as a kind of exchange):—engage, (inter-) meddle (with), mingle (self), mortgage, occupy, give pledges, be (-come, put in) surety, undertake.

6149. עָרֵב **ʻârêb**, *aw-rabe';* a prim. root [rather identical with 6148 through the idea of close *association*]; to be *agreeable:*—be pleasant (-ing), take pleasure in, be sweet.

6150. עָרַב **ʻârab**, *aw-rab';* a prim. root [rather identical with 6148 through the idea of *covering* with a texture]; to *grow dusky* at sundown: -be darkened, (toward) evening.

6151. עֲרַב **ʻărab** (Chald.), *ar-ab';* corresp. to 6148; to *commingle:*—mingle (self), mix.

6152. עֲרָב **ʻĂrâb**, *ar-awb';* or

עֲרַב **ʻĂrab**, *ar-ab';* from 6150 in the fig. sense of *sterility; Arab* (i.e. *Arabia*), a country E. of Pal.:—Arabia.

6153. עֶרֶב **ʻereb**, *eh'-reb;* from 6150; *dusk:*—+ day, even (-ing, tide), night.

6154. עֵרֶב **ʻêreb**, *ay'-reb;* or

עֶרֶב **ʻereb** (1 Kings 10 : 15), (with the art. pref.), *eh'-reb;* from 6148; the *web* (or transverse threads of cloth); also a *mixture*, (or *mongrel* race):—Arabia, mingled people, mixed (multitude), woof.

6155. עָרָב **ʻârâb**, *aw-rawb';* from 6148; a *willow* (from the use of osiers as wattles):—willow.

6156. עָרֵב **ʻârêb**, *aw-rabe';* from 6149; *pleasant:*—sweet.

6157. עָרֹב **ʻârôb**, *aw-robe';* from 6148; a *mosquito* (from its *swarming*):—divers sorts of flies, swarm.

6158. עֹרֵב **ʻôrêb**, *o-rabe';* or

עוֹרֵב **ʻôwrêb**, *o-rabe';* from 6150; a *raven* (from its *dusky* hue):—raven.

6159. עֹרֵב **ʻÔrêb**, *o-rabe';* or

עוֹרֵב **ʻÔwrêb**, *o-rabe';* the same as 6158; *Oreb*, the name of a Midianite and of a cliff near the Jordan:—Oreb.

6160. עֲרָבָה **ʻărâbâh**, *ar-aw-baw';* from 6150 (in the sense of *sterility*); a *desert;* espec. (with the art. pref.) the (generally) sterile valley of the Jordan and its continuation to the Red Sea:—Arabah, champaign, desert, evening, heaven, plain, wilderness. See also 1026.

6161. עֲרֻבָּה **ʻărubbâh**, *ar-oob-baw';* fem. pass. part. of 6148 in the sense of a *bargain* or *exchange;* something given as *security*, i.e. (lit.) a *token* (of safety) or (metaph.) a *bondsman:*—pledge, surety.

6162. עֲרָבוֹן **ʻărâbôwn**, *ar-aw-bone';* from 6148 (in the sense of *exchange*); a *pawn* (given as security):—pledge.

6163. עֲרָבִי **ʻĂrâbîy**, *ar-aw-bee';* or

עַרְבִי **ʻArbîy**, *ar-bee';* patrial from 6152; an *Arabian* or inhab. of Arab (i.e. Arabia):—Arabian.

6164. עַרְבָתִי **ʻArbâthîy**, *ar-baw-thee';* patrial from 1026; an *Arbathite* or inhab. of (Beth-) Arabah:—Arbathite.

6165. עָרַג **ʻârag**, *aw-rag';* a prim. root; to *long* for:—cry, pant.

6166. עֲרָד **ʻĂrâd**, *ar-awd';* from an unused root mean. to *sequester* itself; *fugitive; Arad*, the name of a place near Pal., also of a Canaanite and an Isr.:—Arad.

6167. עֲרָד **ʻărâd** (Chald.), *ar-awd';* corresp. to 6171; an *onager:*—wild ass.

6168. עָרָה **ʻârâh**, *aw-raw';* a prim. root; to *be* (caus. *make*) *bare;* hence to *empty, pour* out, *demolish:*—leave destitute, discover, empty, make naked, pour (out), rase, spread self, uncover.

6169. עָרָה **ʻârâh**, *aw-raw';* fem. from 6168; a *naked* (i.e. level) plot:—paper reed.

6170. עֲרוּגָה **ʻărûwgâh**, *ar-oo-gaw';* or

עֲרֻגָה **ʻărûgâh**, *ar-oo-gaw';* fem. pass. part. of 6165; something *piled* up (as if [fig.] *raised* by mental aspiration), i.e. a *parterre:*—bed, furrow.

6171. עָרוֹד **ʻârôwd**, *aw-rode';* from the same as 6166; an *onager* (from his *lonesome* habits):—wild ass.

6172. עֶרְוָה **ʻervâh**, *er-vaw';* from 6168; *nudity*, lit. (espec. the *pudenda*) or fig. (*disgrace, blemish*):—nakedness, shame, unclean (-ness).

6173. עַרְוָה **ʻarvâh** (Chald.), *ar-vaw';* corresp. to 6172; *nakedness*, i.e. (fig.) *impoverishment:*—dishonour.

6174. עָרוֹם **ʻârôwm**, *aw-rome';* or

עָרֹם **ʻârôm**, *aw-rome';* from 6191 (in its orig. sense); *nude*, either partially or totally:—naked.

6175. עָרוּם **ʻârûwm**, *aw-room';* pass. part. of 6191; *cunning* (usually in a bad sense):—crafty, prudent, subtil.

6176. עֲרוֹעֵר **ʻărôwʻêr**, *ar-o-ayr';* or

עַרְעָר **ʻarʻâr**, *ar-awr';* from 6209 redupl.; a *juniper* (from its *nudity* of situation):—heath.

6177. עֲרוֹעֵר **ʻĂrôwʻêr**, *ar-o-ayr';* or

עֲרֹעֵר **ʻĂrôʻêr**, *ar-o-ayr';* or

עַרְעוֹר **ʻArʻôwr**, *ar-ore';* the same as 6176; *nudity* of situation; *Aroër*, the name of three places in or near Pal.:—Aroer.

6178. עָרוּץ **ʻârûwts**, *aw-roots'*; pass. part. of 6206; *feared*, i.e. (concr.) a *horrible place* or *chasm*:—cliffs.

6179. עֵרִי **ʻÊrîy**, *ay-ree'*; from 5782; *watchful*; *Eri*, an Isr.:—Eri.

6180. עֵרִי **ʻÊrîy**, *ay-ree'*; patron. of 6179; an *Erite* (collect.) or desc. of Eri:—Erites.

6181. עֶרְיָה **ʻeryâh**, *er-yaw'*; for 6172; *nudity*:—bare, naked, × quite.

6182. עֲרִיסָה **ʻărîyçâh**, *ar-ee-saw'*; from an unused root mean. to *comminute*; *meal*:—dough.

6183. עָרִיף **ʻârîyph**, *aw-reef'*; from 6201; the *sky* (as *drooping* at the horizon):—heaven.

6184. עָרִיץ **ʻârîyts**, *aw-reets'*; from 6206; *fearful*, i.e. *powerful* or *tyrannical*:—mighty, oppressor, in great power, strong, terrible, violent.

6185. עֲרִירִי **ʻărîyrîy**, *ar-e-ree'*; from 6209; *bare*, i.e. destitute (of children):—childless.

6186. עָרַךְ **ʻârak**, *aw-rak'*; a prim. root; to set in a *row*, i.e. *arrange*, put in *order* (in a very wide variety of applications):—put (set) (the battle, self) in array, compare, direct, equal, esteem, estimate, expert [in war], furnish, handle, join [battle], ordain, (lay, put, reckon up, set) (in) order, prepare, tax, value.

6187. עֵרֶךְ **ʻêrek**, *eh'-rek*; from 6186; a *pile*, *equipment*, *estimate*:—equal, estimation, (things that are set in) order, price, proportion, × set at, suit, taxation, × valuest.

6188. עָרֵל **ʻârêl**, *aw-rale'*; a prim. root; prop. to *strip*; but used only as denom. from 6189; to *expose* or *remove* the *prepuce*, whether lit. (to *go naked*) or fig. (to *refrain* from using):—count uncircumcised, foreskin to be uncovered.

6189. עָרֵל **ʻârêl**, *aw-rale'*; from 6188; prop. *exposed*, i.e. projecting loose (as to the prepuce); used only techn. *uncircumcised* (i.e. still having the prepuce uncurtailed):—uncircumcised (person).

6190. עָרְלָה **ʻorlâh**, *or-law'*; fem. of 6189; the *prepuce*:—foreskin, + uncircumcised.

6191. עָרַם **ʻâram**, *aw-ram'*; a prim. root; prop. to *be* (or *make*) *bare*; but used only in the der. sense (through the idea perh. of *smoothness*) to *be cunning* (usually in a bad sense):— × very, beware, take crafty [counsel], be prudent, deal subtilly.

6192. עָרַם **ʻâram**, *aw-ram'*; a prim. root; to *pile* up:—gather together.

6193. עֹרֶם **ʻorem**, *o'-rem*; from 6191; a *stratagem*:—craftiness.

עֵרֹם **ʻÊrôm**. See 5903.

עָרֹם **ʻârôm**. See 6174.

6194. עָרֵם **ʻârêm** (Jer. 50 : 26), *aw-rame'*; or (fem.)

עֲרֵמָה **ʻărêmâh**, *ar-ay-maw'*; from 6192; a *heap*; spec. a *sheaf*:—heap (of corn), sheaf.

6195. עָרְמָה **ʻormâh**, *or-maw'*; fem. of 6193; *trickery*; or (in a good sense) *discretion*:—guile, prudence, subtilty, wilily, wisdom.

עֲרֵמָה **ʻarêmâh**. See 6194.

6196. עַרְמוֹן **ʻarmôwn**, *ar-mone'*; prob. from 6191; the *plane* tree (from its *smooth* and shed bark):—chestnut tree.

6197. עֵרָן **Êrân**, *ay-rawn'*; prob. from 5782; *watchful*; *Eran*, an Isr.:—Eran.

6198. עֵרָנִי **ʻÊrânîy**, *ay-raw-nee'*; patron. from 6197; an *Eranite* or desc. (collect.) of Eran:—Eranites.

עַרְעוֹר **ʻArʻôwr**. See 6177.

6199. עַרְעָר **ʻarʻâr**, *ar-awr'*; from 6209; *naked*, i.e. (fig.) *poor*:—destitute. See also 6176.

עֲרֹעֵר **ʻĂrôʻêr**. See 6177.

6200. עֲרֹעֵרִי **ʻĂrôʻêrîy**, *ar-o-ay-ree'*; patron. from 6177; an *Aroërite* or inhab. of Aroër:—Aroerite.

6201. עָרַף **ʻâraph**, *aw-raf'*; a prim. root; to *droop*; hence to *drip*:—drop (down).

6202. עָרַף **ʻâraph**, *aw-raf'*; a prim. root [rather ident. with 6201 through the idea of *sloping*]; prop. to *bend* downward; but used only as a denom. from 6203, to *break the neck*; hence (fig.) to *destroy*:—that is beheaded, break down, break (cut off, strike off) neck.

6203. עֹרֶף **ʻôreph**, *o-ref'*; from 6202; the *nape* or back of the neck (as *declining*); hence the *back* generally (whether lit. or fig.):—back ([stiff-]) neck ([-ed]).

6204. עָרְפָּה **ʻOrpâh**, *or-paw'*; fem. of 6203; *mane*; *Orpah*, a Moabitess:—Orpah.

6205. עֲרָפֶל **ʻărâphel**, *ar-aw-fel'*; prob. from 6201; *gloom* (as of a *lowering* sky):—(gross, thick) dark (cloud, -ness).

6206. עָרַץ **ʻârats**, *aw-rats'*; a prim. root; to *awe* or (intrans.) to *dread*; hence to *harass*:—be affrighted (afraid, dread, feared, terrified), break, dread, fear, oppress, prevail, shake terribly.

6207. עָרַק **ʻâraq**, *aw-rak'*; a prim. root; to *gnaw*, i.e. (fig.) *eat* (by hyberbole); also (part.) a *pain*:—fleeing, sinew.

6208. עַרְקִי **ʻArqîy**, *ar-kee'*; patrial from an unused name mean. a *tush*; an *Arkite* or inhab. of Erek:—Arkite.

6209. עָרַר **ʻârar**, *aw-rar'*; a prim. root; to *bare*; fig. to *demolish*:—make bare, break, raise up [*perh. by clerical error for* RAZE], × utterly.

6210. עֶרֶשׂ **ʻeres**, *eh'-res*; from an unused root mean. perh. to *arch*; a *couch* (prop. with a *canopy*):—bed (-stead), couch.

6211. עָשׁ **ʻâsh**, *awsh*; from 6244; a *moth*:—moth. See also 5906.

6211'. עֲשַׂב **ʻăsab** (Chald.), *as-ab'*; 6212:—grass.

6212. עֶשֶׂב **ʻeseb**, *eh'-seb*; from an unused root mean. to *glisten* (or *be green*); *grass* (or any tender shoot):—grass, herb.

6213. עָשָׂה **ʻâsâh**, *aw-saw'*; a prim. root; to *do* or *make*, in the broadest sense and widest application (as follows):—accomplish, advance, appoint, apt, be at, become, bear, bestow, bring forth, bruise, be busy, × certainly, have the charge of, commit, deal (with), deck, + displease, do, (ready) dress (-ed), (put in) execute (-ion), exercise, fashion, + feast, [fight-] ing man, + finish, fit, fly, follow, fulfil, furnish, gather, get, go about, govern, grant, great, + hinder, hold ([a feast]), × indeed, + be industrious, + journey, keep, labour, maintain, make, be meet, observe, be occupied, offer, + officer, pare, bring (come) to pass, perform, practise, prepare, procure, provide, put, requite, × sacrifice, serve, set, shew, × sin, spend, × surely, take, × throughly, trim, × very, + vex, be [warr-] ior, work (-man), yield, use.

6214. עֲשָׂהאֵל **ʻĂsâhʼêl**, *as-aw-ale'*; from 6213 and 410; *God has made*; *Asahel*, the name of four Isr.:—Asahel.

6215. עֵשָׂו **ʻÊsâv**, *ay-sawv'*; appar. a form of the pass. part. of 6213 in the orig. sense of *handling*; *rough* (i.e. sensibly *felt*); *Esav*, a son of Isaac, including his posterity:—Esau.

6216. עָשׁוֹק **ʻâshôwq**, *aw-shoke'*; from 6231; *oppressive* (as noun, a *tyrant*):—oppressor.

6217. עָשׁוּק **ʻâshûwq**, *aw-shook'*; or

עָשֻׁק **ʻâshûq**, *aw-shook'*; pass. part. of 6231; used in plur. masc. as abstr. *tyranny*:—oppressed (-ion). [*Doubtful.*]

6218. עָשׂוֹר **ʻâsôwr**, *aw-sore'*; or

עָשֹׂר **ʻâsôr**, *aw-sore'*; from 6235; *ten*; by abbrev. ten *strings*, and so a *decachord*:—(instrument of) ten (strings, -th).

6219. עָשׁוֹת **ʻâshôwth**, *aw-shōth'*; from 6245; *shining*, i.e. polished:—bright.

6220. עַשְׁוָת **ʻAshvâth**, *ash-vawth'*; for 6219; *bright*; *Ashvath*, an Isr.:—Ashvath.

6221. עֲשִׂיאֵל **ʻĂsîyʼêl**, *as-ee-ale'*; from 6213 and 410; *made of God*; *Asiël*, an Isr.:—Asiel.

6222. עֲשָׂיָה **ʻĂsâyâh**, *aw-saw-yaw'*; from 6213 and 3050; *Jah has made*; *Asajah*, the name of three or four Isr.:—Asaiah.

6223. עָשִׁיר **ʻâshîyr**, *aw-sheer'*; from 6238; *rich*, whether lit. or fig. (*noble*):—rich (man)

6224. עֲשִׂירִי **ʻăsîyrîy**, *as-ee-ree'*; from 6235; *tenth*; by abbrev. *tenth month* or (fem.) *part*:—tenth (part).

6225. עָשַׁן **ʻâshan**, *aw-shan'*; a prim. root; to *smoke*, whether lit. or fig.:—be angry (be on a) smoke.

6226. עָשֵׁן **ʻâshên**, *aw-shane'*; from 6225; *smoky*:—smoking.

6227. עָשָׁן **ʻâshân**, *aw-shawn'*; from 6225; *smoke*, lit. or fig. (*vapor, dust, anger*):—smoke (-ing).

6228. עָשָׁן **ʻÂshân**, *aw-shawn'*; the same as 6227; *Ashan*, a place in Pal.:—Ashan.

6229. עָשַׂק **ʻâsaq**, *aw-sak'*; a prim. root (ident. with 6231); to *press upon*, i.e. *quarrel*:—strive with.

6230. עֵשֶׂק **ʻêseq**, *ay'-sek*; from 6229; *strife*:—Esek.

6231. עָשַׁק **ʻâshaq**, *aw-shak'*; a prim. root (comp. 6229); to *press* upon, i.e. *oppress*, *defraud*, *violate*, *overflow*:—get deceitfully, deceive, defraud, drink up, (use) oppress ([-ion], -or), do violence (wrong).

6232. עֵשֶׁק **ʻÊsheq**, *ay-shek'*; from 6231; *oppression*; *Eshek*, an Isr.:—Eshek.

6233. עֹשֶׁק **ʻôsheq**, *o'-shek*; from 6231; *injury*, *fraud*, (subj.) *distress*, (concr.) *unjust gain*:—cruelly, extortion, oppression, thing [deceitfully gotten].

עָשֻׁק **ʻâshûq**. See 6217.

6234. עָשְׁקָה **ʻoshqâh**, *osh-kaw'*; fem. of 6233; *anguish*:—oppressed.

6235. עֶשֶׂר **ʻeser**, *eh'-ser*; masc.

עֲשָׂרָה **ʻăsârâh**, *as-aw-raw'*; from 6237; *ten* (as an *accumulation* to the extent of the digits):—ten, [fif-, seven-] teen.

6236. עֲשַׂר **ʻăsar** (Chald.), *as-ar'*; masc.

עַשְׂרָה **ʻăsrâh** (Chald.), *as-raw'*; corresp. to 6235; *ten*:—ten, + twelve.

6237. עָשַׂר **ʻâsar**, *aw-sar'*; a prim. root (ident. with 6238); to *accumulate*; but used only as denom. from 6235; to *tithe*, i.e. take or give a tenth:— × surely, give (take) the tenth, (have, take) tithe (-ing, -s), × truly.

6238. עָשַׁר **ʻâshar**, *aw-shar'*; a prim. root; prop. to *accumulate*; chiefly (spec.) to *grow* (caus. *make*) *rich*:—be (-come, en-, make, make self, wax) rich, make [1 Kings 22 : 48 *marg.*]. See 6240.

6239. עֹשֶׁר **ʻôsher**, *o'-sher*; from 6238; *wealth*:— × far [richer], riches.

6240. עָשָׂר **ʻâsâr**, *aw-sawr'*; for 6235; *ten* (only in combination), i.e. *-teen*; also (ordinal) *-teenth*:—[eigh-, fif-, four-, nine-, seven-, six-, thir-] teen (-th), + eleven (-th), + sixscore thousand, + twelve (-th).

עָשֹׂר **ʻâsôr**. See 6218.

6241. עִשָּׂרוֹן **ʻissârôwn**, *is-saw-rone'*; or

עִשָּׂרֹן **ʻissârôn**, *is-saw-rone'*; from 6235; (fractional) a *tenth* part:—tenth deal.

6242. עֶשְׂרִים **ʻesrîym**, *es-reem'*; from 6235; *twenty*; also (ordinal) *twentieth*:—[six-] score, twenty (-ieth).

6243. עֶשְׂרִין **ʻesrîyn** (Chald.), *es-reen'*; corresp. to 6242:—twenty.

6244. עָשֵׁשׁ **ʻâshêsh**, *aw-shaysh'*; a prim. root; prob. to *shrink*, i.e. *fail*:—be consumed.

6245. עָשַׁת **ʻâshath**, *aw-shath'*; a prim. root; prob. to be *sleek*, i.e. *glossy*; hence (through the idea of *polishing*) to *excogitate* (as if *forming* in the mind):—shine, think.

6246. עֲשִׁת **ʻăshîth** (Chald.), *ash-eeth'*; corresp. to 6245; to *purpose*:—think.

6247. עֶשֶׁת **ʻesheth**, *eh'-sheth*; from 6245; a *fabric*:—bright.

6248. עַשְׁתּוּת° **ʻashtûwth**, *ash-tooth'*; from 6245; *cogitation*:—thought.

6249. עַשְׁתֵּי **ʻashtêy**, *ash-tay'*; appar. masc. plur. constr. of 6247 in the sense of an *after-*

thought; (used only in connection with 6240 in lieu of 259) *eleven* or (ordinal) *eleventh:*— + eleven (-th).

6250. עֶשְׁתֹּנָה **ʽeshtônâh**, *esh-to-naw';* from 6245; *thinking:*—thought.

6251. עַשְׁתְּרָה **ʽashtᵉrâh**, *ash-ter-aw';* prob. from 6238; *increase:*—flock.

6252. עַשְׁתָּרוֹת **ʽAshtârôwth**, *ash-taw-rōth',* or

עַשְׁתָּרֹת **ʽAshtârôth**, *ash-taw-rōth';* plur. of 6251; *Ashtaroth,* the name of a Sidonian deity, and of a place E. of the Jordan:—Ashtaroth, Astaroth. See also 1045, 6253, 6255.

6253. עַשְׁתֹּרֶת **ʽAshtôreth**, *ash-to'-reth;* prob. for 6251; *Ashtoreth,* the Phœnician goddess of love (and *increase*):—Ashtoreth.

6254. עַשְׁתְּרָתִי **ʽAshtᵉrâthîy**, *ash-ter-aw-thee';* patrial from 6252; an *Ashterathite* or inhab. of Ashtaroth:—Ashterathite.

6255. עַשְׁתְּרֹת קַרְנַיִם **ʽAshtᵉrôth Qarnayim**, *ash-ter-ōth' kar-nah'-yim;* from 6252 and the dual of 7161; *Ashtaroth of* (the) *double horns* (a symbol of the deity); *Ashteroth-Karnaïm,* a place E. of the Jordan:—Ashtoreth Karnaim.

6256. עֵת **ʽêth**, *ayth;* from 5703; *time,* espec. (adv. with prep.) *now, when,* etc.:— + after, [al-] ways, × certain, + continually, + evening, long, (due) season, so [long] as, [even-, evening-, noon-] tide, ([meal-], what) time, when.

6257. עָתַד **ʽâthad**, *aw-thad';* a prim. root; to *prepare:*—make fit, be ready to become.

עַתֻּד **ʽattûd**. See 6260.

6258. עַתָּה **ʽattâh**, *at-taw';* from 6256; at *this time,* whether adv., conj. or expletive:—henceforth, now, straightway, this time, whereas.

6259. עָתוּד **ʽâthûwd**, *aw-thood';* pass. part. of 6257; *prepared:*—ready, treasures.

6260. עַתּוּד **ʽattûwd**, *at-tood';* or

עַתֻּד **ʽattûd**, *at-tood';* from 6257; *prepared,* i.e. *full grown;* spoken only (in plur.) of *he-goats,* or (fig.) *leaders* of the people:—chief one, (he) goat, ram.

6261. עִתִּי **ʽittîy**, *it-tee';* from 6256; *timely:*—fit.

6262. עַתַּי **ʽAttay**, *at-tah'ee;* for 6261; *Attai,* the name of three Isr.:—Attai.

6263. עֲתִיד **ʽăthîyd** (Chald.), *ath-eed';* corresp. to 6264; *prepared:*—ready.

6264. עָתִיד **ʽâthîyd**, *aw-theed';* from 6257; *prepared;* by impl. *skilful;* fem. plur. the *future;* also *treasure:*—things that shall come, ready, treasures.

6265. עֲתָיָה **ʽĂthâyâh**, *ath-aw-yaw';* from 5790 and 3050; *Jah has helped; Athajah,* an Isr.:—Athaiah.

6266. עָתִיק **ʽâthîyq**, *aw-theek';* from 6275; prop. *antique,* i.e. *venerable* or *splendid:*—durable.

6267. עַתִּיק **ʽattîyq**, *at-teek';* from 6275; *removed,* i.e. *weaned;* also *antique:*—ancient, drawn.

6268. עַתִּיק **ʽattîyq** (Chald.), *at-teek';* corresp. to 6267; *venerable:*—ancient.

6269. עֲתָךְ **ʽĂthâk**, *ath-awk';* from an unused root mean. to *sojourn; lodging; Athak,* a place in Pal.:—Athach.

6270. עַתְלַי **ʽAthlay**, *ath-lah'ee;* from an unused root mean. to *compress; constringent; Athlai,* an Isr.:—Athlai.

6271. עֲתַלְיָה **ʽĂthalyâh**, *ath-al-yaw';* or

עֲתַלְיָהוּ **ʽĂthalyâhûw**, *ath-al-yaw'-hoo;* from the same as 6270 and 3050; *Jah has constrained; Athaljah,* the name of an Israelitess and two Isr.:—Athaliah.

6272. עָתַם **ʽâtham**, *aw-tham';* a prim. root; prob. to *glow,* i.e. (fig.) *be desolated:*—be darkened.

6273. עָתְנִי **ʽOthnîy**, *oth-nee';* from an unused root mean. to *force; forcible; Othni,* an Isr.:—Othni.

6274. עָתְנִיאֵל **ʽOthnîyʼêl**, *oth-nee-ale';* from the same as 6273 and 410; *force of God; Othniël,* an Isr.:—Othniel.

6275. עָתַק **ʽâthaq**, *aw-thak';* a prim. root; to *remove* (intrans. or trans.); fig. to *grow old;* spec. to *transcribe:*—copy out, leave off, become (wax) old, remove.

6276. עָתֵק **ʽâthêq**, *aw-thake';* from 6275; *antique,* i.e. *valued:*—durable.

6277. עָתָק **ʽâthâq**, *aw-thawk';* from 6275 in the sense of *license; impudent:*—arrogancy, grievous (hard) things, stiff.

6278. עֵת קָצִין **ʽÊth Qâtsîyn**, *ayth kaw-tseen';* from 6256 and 7011; *time of a judge; Eth-Katsin,* a place in Pal.:—Ittah-kazin [*by includ. directive enclitic*].

6279. עָתַר **ʽâthar**, *aw-thar';* a prim. root [rather denom. from 6281]; to burn *incense* in worship, i.e. *intercede* (recipr. *listen* to prayer):—intreat, (make) pray (-er).

6280. עָתַר **ʽâthar**, *aw-thar';* a prim. root; to *be* (caus. *make*) *abundant:*—deceitful, multiply.

6281. עֶתֶר **ʽEther**, *eh'-ther;* from 6280; *abundance; Ether,* a place in Pal.:—Ether.

6282. עָתָר **ʽâthâr**, *aw-thawr';* from 6280; *incense* (as increasing to a *volume* of smoke); hence (from 6279) a *worshipper:*—suppliant, thick.

6283. עֲתֶרֶת **ʽăthereth**, *ath-eh'-reth;* from 6280; *copiousness:*—abundance.

פ

פֹּא **pôʼ**. See 6311.

6284. פָּאָה **pâʼâh**, *paw-aw';* a prim. root; to *puff,* i.e. *blow* away:—scatter into corners.

6285. פֵּאָה **pêʼâh**, *pay-aw';* fem. of 6311; prop. *mouth* in a fig. sense, i.e. *direction, region, extremity:*—corner, end, quarter, side.

6286. פָּאַר **pâʼar**, *paw-ar';* a prim. root; to *gleam,* i.e. (causat.) *embellish;* fig. to *boast;* also to *explain* (i.e. make clear) oneself; denom. from 6288, to *shake* a tree:—beautify, boast self, go over the boughs, glorify (self), glory, vaunt self.

6287. פְּאֵר **pᵉʼêr**, *peh-ayr';* from 6286; an *embellishment,* i.e. fancy *head-dress:*—beauty, bonnet, goodly, ornament, tire.

6288. פְּאֹרָה **pᵉʼôrâh**, *peh-o-raw';* or

פֹּרָאה **pôrâʼh**, *po-raw';* or

פֻּארָה **pûʼrâh**, *poo-raw';* from 6286; prop. *ornamentation,* i.e. (plur.) *foliage* (includ. the limbs) as *bright* green:—bough, branch, sprig.

6289. פָּארוּר **pâʼrûwr**, *paw-roor';* from 6286; prop. *illuminated,* i.e. a *glow;* as noun, a *flush* (of anxiety):—blackness.

6290. פָּארָן **Pâʼrân**, *paw-rawn';* from 6286; *ornamental; Paran,* a desert of Arabia:—Paran.

6291. פַּג **pag**, *pag;* from an unused root mean. to *be torpid,* i.e. *crude;* an *unripe* fig:—green fig.

6292. פִּגּוּל **piggûwl**, *pig-gool';* or

פִּגֻּל **piggûl**, *pig-gool';* from an unused root mean. to *stink;* prop. *fetid,* i.e. (fig.) *unclean* (ceremonially):—abominable (-tion, thing).

6293. פָּגַע **pâgaʽ**, *paw-gah';* a prim. root; to *impinge,* by accident or violence, or (fig.) by importunity:—come (betwixt), cause to entreat, fall (upon), make intercession, intercessor, intreat, lay, light [upon], meet (together), pray, reach, run.

6294. פֶּגַע **pegaʽ**, *peh'-gah;* from 6293; *impact* (casual):—chance, occurrent.

6295. פַּגְעִיאֵל **Pagʽîyʼêl**, *pag-ee-ale';* from 6294 and 410; *accident of God; Pagiël,* an Isr.:—Pagiel.

6296. פָּגַר **pâgar**, *paw-gar';* a prim. root; to *relax,* i.e. become *exhausted:*—be faint.

6297. פֶּגֶר **peger**, *peh'-gher;* from 6296; a *carcase* (as *limp*), whether of man or beast; fig. an idolatrous *image:*—carcase, corpse, dead body.

6298. פָּגַשׁ **pâgash**, *paw-gash';* a prim. root; to *come in contact with,* whether by accident or violence; fig. to *concur:*—meet (with, together).

6299. פָּדָה **pâdâh**, *paw-daw';* a prim. root; to *sever,* i.e. *ransom;* gener. to *release, preserve:*— × at all, deliver, × by any means, ransom, (that are to be, let be) redeem (-ed), rescue, × surely.

6300. פְּדַהְאֵל **Pᵉdahʼêl**, *ped-ah-ale';* from 6299 and 410; *God has ransomed; Pedahel,* an Isr.:—Pedahel.

6301. פְּדָהצוּר **Pᵉdâhtsûwr**, *ped-aw-tsoor';* from 6299 and 6697; a *rock* (i.e. God) *has ransomed; Pedahtsur,* an Isr.:—Pedahzur.

6302. פָּדוּי **pâdûwy**, *paw-doo'ee;* pass. part. of 6299; *ransomed* (and so occurring under 6299); as abstr. (in plur. masc.) a *ransom:*—(that are) to be (that were) redeemed.

6303. פָּדוֹן **Pâdôwn**, *paw-done';* from 6299; *ransom; Padon,* one of the Nethinim:—Padon.

6304. פְּדוּת **pᵉdûwth**, *ped-ooth';* or

פְּדֻת **pᵉdûth**, *ped-ooth';* from 6929; *distinction;* also *deliverance:*—division, redeem, redemption.

6305. פְּדָיָה **Pᵉdâyâh**, *ped-aw-yaw';* or

פְּדָיָהוּ **Pᵉdâyâhûw**, *ped-aw-yaw'-hoo;* from 6299 and 3050; *Jah has ransomed; Pedajah,* the name of six Isr.:—Pedaiah.

6306. פִּדְיוֹם **pidyôwm**, *pid-yome';* or

פִּדְיֹם **pidyôm**, *pid-yome';* also

פִּדְיוֹן **pidyôwn**, *pid-yone';* or

פִּדְיֹן **pidyôn**, *pid-yone';* from 6299; a *ransom:*—ransom, that were redeemed, redemption.

6307. פַּדָּן **Paddân**, *pad-dawn';* from an unused root mean. to *extend;* a *plateau;* or

פַּדַּן אֲרָם **Paddan ʼĂrâm**, *pad-dan' ar-awm';* from the same and 758; the *table-land of Aram; Paddan* or *Paddan-Aram,* a region of Syria:—Padan, Padan-aram.

6308. פָּדַע **pâdaʽ**, *paw-dah';* a prim. root; to *retrieve:*—deliver.

6309. פֶּדֶר **peder**, *peh'-der;* from an unused root mean. to *be greasy; suet:*—fat.

פְּדֻת **pᵉdûth**. See 6304.

6310. פֶּה **peh**, *peh;* from 6284; the *mouth* (as the means of *blowing*), whether lit. or fig. (particularly *speech*); spec. *edge, portion* or *side;* adv. (with prep.) *according to:*—accord (-ing as, -ing to), after, appointment, assent, collar, command (-ment), × eat, edge, end, entry, + file, hole, × in, mind, mouth, part, portion, × (should) say (-ing), sentence, skirt, sound, speech, × spoken, talk, tenor, × to, + two-edged, wish, word.

6311. פֹּה **pôh**, *po;* or

פֹּא **pôʼ** (Job 38 : 11), *po;* or

פּוֹ **pôw**, *po;* prob. from a prim. insep. particle פ **p** (of demonstrative force) and 1931; *this place* (French *içi*), i.e. *here* or *hence:*—here, hither, the one (other, this, that) side.

פּוֹא **pôwʼ**. See 375.

6312. פּוּאָה **Pûwʼâh**, *poo-aw';* or

פֻּוָּה **Puvvâh**, *poov-vaw';* from 6284; *blast; Puäh* or *Puvvah,* the name of two Isr.:—Phuvah, Pua, Puah.

6313. פּוּג **pûwg**, *poog;* a prim. root; to *be sluggish:*—cease, be feeble, faint, be slacked.

6314. פּוּגָה **pûwgâh**, *poo-gaw';* from 6313; *intermission:*—rest.

פֻּוָּה **Puvvâh**. See 6312.

6315. פּוּחַ **pûwach**, *poo'-akh;* a prim. root; to *puff,* i.e. blow with the breath or air; hence to *fan* (as a breeze), to *utter,* to *kindle* (a fire), to *scoff:*—blow (upon), break, puff, bring into a snare, speak, utter.

6316. פּוּט **Pûwṭ**, *poot;* of for. or.; *Put,* a son of Ham, also the name of his descendants or their region, and of a Persian tribe:—Phut, Put.

6317. פּוּטִיאֵל **Pûwṭîy'êl**, *poo-tee-ale'*; from an unused root (prob. mean. to *disparage*) and 410; *contempt of God; Putiël*, an Isr.:—Putiel.

6318. פּוֹטִיפַר **Pôwṭîyphar**, *po-tee-far'*; of Eg. der.; *Potiphar*, an Eg.:—Potiphar.

6319. פּוֹטִי פֶרַע **Pôwṭîy Phera'**, *po'-tee feh'-rah*; of Eg. der.; *Poti-Phera*, an Eg.:—Poti-pherah.

6320. פּוּךְ **pûwk**, *pook*; from an unused root mean. to *paint; dye* (spec. *stibium* for the eyes):—fair colours, glistering, paint [-ed] (-ing).

6321. פּוֹל **pôwl**, *pole*; from an unused root mean. to *be thick*; a *bean* (as *plump*):—beans.

6322. פּוּל **Pûwl**, *pool*; of for. or.; *Pul*, the name of an Ass. king and of an Ethiopian tribe:—Pul.

6323. פּוּן **pûwn**, *poon*; a prim. root mean. to *turn*, i.e. *be perplexed*:—be distracted.

6324. פּוּנִי **Pûwnîy**, *poo-nee'*; patron. from an unused name mean. a *turn*; a *Punite* (collect.) or desc. of an unknown Pun:—Punites.

6325. פּוּנֹן **Pûwnôn**, *poo-none'*; from 6323; *perplexity; Punon*, a place in the Desert:—Punon.

6326. פּוּעָה **Pûw'âh**, *poo-aw'*; from an unused root mean. to *glitter*; *brilliancy; Puäh*, an Israelitess:—Puah.

6327. פּוּץ **pûwts**, *poots*; a prim. root; to *dash* in pieces, lit. or fig. (espec. to *disperse*):—break (dash, shake) in (to) pieces, cast (abroad), disperse (selves), drive, retire, scatter (abroad), spread abroad.

6328. פּוּק **pûwq**, *pook*; a prim. root; to *waver*:—stumble, move.

6329. פּוּק **pûwq**, *pook*; a prim. root [rather ident. with 6328 through the idea of *dropping* out; comp. 5312]; to *issue*, i.e. *furnish*; causat. to *secure*; fig. to *succeed*:—afford, draw out, further, get, obtain.

6330. פּוּקָה **pûwqâh**, *poo-kaw'*; from 6328; a *stumbling-block*:—grief.

6331. פּוּר **pûwr**, *poor*; a prim. root; to *crush*:—break, bring to nought, × utterly take.

6332. פּוּר **Pûwr**, *poor*; also (plur.)

פּוּרִים **Pûwrîym**, *poo-reem'*; or

פֻּרִים **Pûrîym**, *poo-reem'*; from 6331; a *lot* (as by means of a *broken* piece):—Pur, Purim.

6333. פּוּרָה **pûwrâh**, *poo-raw'*; from 6331; a *wine-press* (as *crushing* the grapes):—winepress.

פּוּרִים **Pûwrîym**. See 6332.

6334. פּוֹרָתָא **Pôwrâthâ'**, *po-raw-thaw'*; of Pers. or.; *Poratha*, a son of Haman:—Poratha.

6335. פּוּשׁ **pûwsh**, *poosh*; a prim. root; to *spread*; fig. *act proudly*:—grow up, be grown fat, spread selves, be scattered.

6336. פּוּתִי **Pûwthîy**, *poo-thee'*; patron. from an unused name mean. a *hinge*; a *Puthite* (collect.) or descend. of an unknown Puth:—Puhites [*as if from* 6312].

6337. פָּז **pâz**, *pawz*; from 6338; *pure* (gold); hence *gold* itself (as refined):—fine (pure) gold.

6338. פָּזַז **pâzaz**, *paw-zaz'*; a prim. root; to *refine* (gold):—best [gold].

6339. פָּזַז **pâzaz**, *paw-zaz'*; a prim. root [rather ident. with 6338]; to *solidify* (as if by *refining*); also to *spring* (as if *separating* the limbs):—leap, be made strong.

6340. פָּזַר **pâzar**, *paw-zar'*; a prim. root; to *scatter*, whether in enmity or bounty:—disperse, scatter (abroad).

6341. פַּח **pach**, *pakh*; from 6351; a (metallic) *sheet* (as *pounded* thin); also a spring *net* (as spread out like a *lamina*):—gin, (thin) plate, snare.

6342. פָּחַד **pâchad**, *paw-kkad'*; a prim. root: to *be startled* (by a sudden alarm); hence to *fear* in general:—be afraid, stand in awe, (be in) fear, make to shake.

6343. פַּחַד **pachad**, *pakh'-ad*; from 6342; a (sudden) *alarm* (prop. the object feared, by impl. the feeling):- -dread (-ful), fear, (thing) great [fear, -ly feared], terror.

6344. פַּחַד **pachad**, *pakh'-ad*; the same as 6343; a *testicle* (as a cause of *shame* akin to fear):—stone.

6345. פַּחְדָּה **pachdâh**, *pakh-daw'*; fem. of 6343; *alarm* (i.e. *awe*):—fear.

6346. פֶּחָה **pechâh**, *peh-khaw'*; of for. or.; a *prefect* (of a city or small district):—captain, deputy, governor.

6347. פֶּחָה **pechâh** (Chald.), *peh-khaw'*; corresp. to 6346:—captain, governor.

6348. פָּחַז **pâchaz**, *paw-khaz'*; a prim. root; to *bubble* up or *froth* (as boiling water), i.e. (fig.) to *be unimportant*:—light.

6349. פַּחַז **pachaz**, *pakh'-az*; from 6348; *ebullition*, i.e. froth (fig. lust):—unstable.

6350. פַּחֲזוּת **pachăzûwth**, *pakh-az-ooth'*; from 6348; *frivolity*:—lightness.

6351. פָּחַח **pâchach**, *paw-khakh'*; a prim. root; to *batter* out; but used only as denom. from 6341, to *spread a net*:—be snared.

6352. פֶּחָם **pechâm**, *peh-khawm'*; perh. from an unused root prob. mean. to *be black*; a *coal*, whether charred or live:—coals.

6353. פֶּחָר **pechâr** (Chald.), *peh-khawr'*; from an unused root prob. mean. to *fashion*; a *potter*:—potter.

6354. פַּחַת **pachath**, *pakh'-ath*; prob. from an unused root appar. mean. to *dig*; a *pit*, espec. for catching animals:—hole, pit, snare.

6355. פַּחַת מוֹאָב **Pachath Môw'âb**, *pakh'-ath mo-awb'*; from 6354 and 4124; *pit of Moäb; Pachath-Moäb*, an Isr.:—Pahath-moab.

6356. פְּחֶתֶת **pechetheth**, *pekh-eh'-theth*; from the same as 6354; a *hole* (by mildew in a garment):—fret inward.

6357. פִּטְדָה **piṭdâh**, *pit-daw'*; of for. der.; a *gem*, prob. the *topaz*:—topaz.

6358. פָּטוּר **pâṭûwr**, *paw-toor'*; pass. part. of 6362; *opened*, i.e. (as noun) a *bud*:—open.

6359. פָּטִיר **pâṭîyr**, *paw-teer'*; from 6362; *open*, i.e. *unoccupied*:—free.

6360. פַּטִּישׁ **paṭṭîysh**, *pat-teesh'*; intens. from an unused root mean. to *pound*; a *hammer*:—hammer.

6361. פַּטִּישׁ **paṭṭîysh** (Chald.), *pat-teesh'*; from a root corresp. to that of 6360; a *gown* (as if *hammered* out wide):—hose.

6362. פָּטַר **pâṭar**, *paw-tar'*; a prim. root; to *cleave* or burst through, i.e. (caus.) to *emit*, whether lit. or fig. (*gape*):—dismiss, free, let (shoot) out, slip away.

6363. פֶּטֶר **peṭer**, *peh'-ter*; or

פִּטְרָה **piṭrâh**, *pit-raw'*; from 6362; a *fissure*, i.e. (concr.) *firstling* (as *opening* the matrix):—firstling, openeth, such as open.

6364. פִּי־בֶסֶת **Pîy-Beceth**, *pee beh'-seth*; of Eg. or.; *Pi-Beseth*, a place in Eg.:—Pi-beseth.

6365. פִּיד **pîyd**, *peed*; from an unused root prob. mean. to *pierce*; (fig.) *misfortune*:—destruction, ruin.

6366. פֵּיָה **pêyâh**, *pay-aw'*; or

פִּיָּה **pîyâh**, *pee-yaw'*; fem. of 6310; an *edge*:—(two-) edge (-d).

6367. פִּי הַחִירֹת **Pî ha-Chîyrôth**, *pee hah-khee-rōth'*; from 6310 and the fem. plur. of a noun (from the same root as 2356), with the art. interp.; *mouth of the gorges; Pi-ha-Chiroth*, a place in Eg.:—Pi-hahiroth. [In Num. 14 ; 19 without Pi-.]

6368. פִּיחַ **pîyach**, *pee'-akh*; from 6315; a *powder* (as easily *puffed* away), i.e. *ashes* or *dust*:—ashes.

6369. פִּיכֹל **Pîykôl**, *pee-kole'*; appar. from 6310 and 3605; *mouth of all; Picol*, a Philistine:—Phichol.

6370. פִּילֶגֶשׁ **pîylegesh**, *pee-leh'-ghesh*; or

פִּלֶגֶשׁ **pîlegesh**, *pee-leh'-ghesh*; of uncert. der.; a *concubine*; also (masc.) a *paramour*:—concubine, paramour.

6371. פִּימָה **pîymâh**, *pee-maw'*; prob. from an unused root mean. to *be plump*; *obesity*:—collops.

6372. פִּינְחָס **Pîynechâç**, *pee-nekh-aws'*; appar. from 6310 and a var. of 5175; *mouth of a serpent; Pinechas*, the name of three Isr.:—Phinehas.

6373. פִּינֹן **pîynôn**, *pee-none'*; prob. the same as 6325; *Pinon*, an Idumæan:—Pinon.

6374. פִּיפִיָּה **pîyphîyâh**, *pee-fee-yaw'*; for 6366, an *edge* or *tooth*:—tooth, × two-edged

6375. פִּיק **pîyq**, *peek*; from 6329; a *tottering*:—smite together.

6376. פִּישׁוֹן **Pîyshôwn**, *pee-shone'*; from 6335; *dispersive; Pishon*, a river of Eden:—Pison.

6377. פִּיתוֹן **Pîythôwn**, *pee-thone'*; prob. from the same as 6596; *expansive; Pithon*, an Isr.:—Pithon.

6378. פַּךְ **pak**, *pak*; from 6379; a *flask* (from which a liquid may *flow*):—box, vial.

6379. פָּכָה **pâkâh**, *paw-kaw'*; a prim. root; to *pour*:—run out.

6380. פֹּכֶרֶת צְבָיִים **Pôkereth Tsebâyîym**, *po-keh'-reth tseb-aw-yeem'*; from the act. part. (of the same form as the first word) fem. of an unused root (mean. to *entrap*) and plur. of 6643; *trap of gazelles; Pokereth-Tsebajim*, one of the "servants of Solomon":—Pochereth of Zebaim.

6381. פָּלָא **pâlâ'**, *paw-law'*; a prim. root; prop. perh. to *separate*, i.e. *distinguish* (lit. or fig.); by impl. to *be* (causat. *make*) *great, difficult, wonderful*:—accomplish, (arise . . . too, be too) hard, hidden, things too high, (be, do, do a, shew) marvellous (-ly, -els, things, work), miracles, perform, separate, make singular, (be, great, make) wonderful (-ers, -ly, things, works), wondrous (things, works, -ly).

6382. פֶּלֶא **pele'**, *peh'-leh*; from 6381; a *miracle*:—marvellous thing, wonder (-ful, -fully).

6383. פִּלְאִי **pil'îy**, *pil-ee'*; or

פָּלִיא **pâlîy'**, *paw-lee'*; from 6381; *remarkable*:—secret, wonderful.

6384. פַּלֻּאִי **Pallû'îy**, *pal-loo-ee'*; patron. from 6396; a *Palluïte* (collect.) or desc. of Pallu:—Palluites.

פְּלָאיָה **Pelâ'yâh**. See 6411.

פִּלְאֶסֶר **Pil'eçer**. See 8407.

6385. פָּלַג **pâlag**, *paw-lag'*; a prim. root; to *split* (lit. or fig.):—divide.

6386. פְּלַג **pelag** (Chald.), *pel-ag'*; corresp. to 6385:—divided.

6387. פְּלַג **pelag** (Chald.), *pel-ag'*; from 6386; a *half*:—dividing.

6388. פֶּלֶג **peleg**, *peh'-leg*; from 6385; a *rill* (i.e. small *channel* of water, as in irrigation):—river, stream.

6389. פֶּלֶג **Peleg**, *peh'-leg*; the same as 6388; *earthquake; Peleg*, a son of Shem:—Peleg.

6390. פְּלַגָּה **pelaggâh**, *pel-ag-gaw'*; from 6385; a *runlet*, i.e. *gully*:—division, river.

6391. פְּלֻגָּה **peluggâh**, *pel-oog-gaw'*; from 6385; a *section*:—division.

6392. פְּלֻגָּה **peluggâh** (Chald.), *pel-oog-gaw'*; corresp. to 6391:—division.

פִּלֶגֶשׁ **pîlegesh**. See 6370.

6393. פְּלָדָה **pelâdâh**, *pel-aw-daw'*; from an unused root mean. to *divide*; a *cleaver*, i.e. iron *armature* (of a chariot):—torch.

6394. פִּלְדָּשׁ **Pildâsh**, *pil-dawsh'*; of uncert. der.; *Pildash*, a relative of Abraham:—Pildash.

6395. פָּלָה **pâlâh**, *paw-law'*; a prim. root; to *distinguish* (lit. or fig.):—put a difference, show marvellous, separate, set apart, sever, make wonderfully.

6396. פַּלּוּא **Pallûw'**, *pal-loo'*; from 6395; *distinguished*; *Pallu*, an Isr.:—Pallu, Phallu.

6397. פְּלוֹנִי **Pelôwnîy**, *pel-o-nee'*; patron. from an unused name (from 6395) mean. *separate*; a *Pelonite* or inhab. of an unknown Palon:—Pelonite.

6398. פָּלַח **pâlach**, *paw-lakh'*; a prim. root; to *slice*, i.e. *break* open or *pierce*:—bring forth, cleave, cut, shred, strike through.

6399. פְּלַח **pelach** (Chald.), *pel-akh'*; corresp. to 6398; to *serve* or worship:—minister, serve.

6400. פֶּלַח **pelach**, *peh'-lakh*; from 6398; a *slice*:—piece.

6401. פִּלְחָא **Pilchâ'**, *pil-khaw'*; from 6400; *slicing*; *Pilcha*, an Isr.:—Pilcha.

6402. פָּלְחָן **polchân** (Chald.), *pol-khawn'*; from 6399; *worship*:—service.

6403. פָּלַט **pâlaṭ**, *paw-lat'*; a prim. root; to *slip* out, i.e. *escape*; causat. to *deliver*:—calve, carry away safe, deliver, (cause to) escape.

6404. פֶּלֶט **Peleṭ**, *peh'-let*; from 6403; *escape*; *Pelet*, the name of two Isr.:—Pelet. See also 1046.

פָּלֵט **pâlêṭ**. See 6412.

6405. פַּלֵּט **pallêṭ**, *pal-late'*; from 6403; *escape*:—deliverance, escape.

פְּלֵטָה **pelêṭâh**. See 6413.

6406. פַּלְטִי **Palṭîy**, *pal-tee'*; from 6403; *delivered*; *Palti*, the name of two Isr.:—Palti, Phalti.

6407. פַּלְטִי **Palṭîy**, *pal-tee'*; patron. from 6406; a *Paltite* or desc. of Palti:—Paltite.

6408. פִּלְטַי **Pilṭay**, *pil-tah'ee*; for 6407; *Piltai*, an Isr.:—Piltai.

6409. פַּלְטִיאֵל **Palṭîy'êl**, *pal-tee-ale'*; from the same as 6404 and 410; *deliverance of God*; *Paltiël*, the name of two Isr.:—Paltiel, Phaltiel.

6410. פְּלַטְיָה **Pelaṭyâh**, *pel-at-yaw'*; or

פְּלַטְיָהוּ **Pelaṭyâhûw**, *pel-at-yaw'-hoo*; from 6403 and 3050; *Jah has delivered*; *Pelatjah*, the name of four Isr.:—Pelatiah.

פָּלִיא **pâlîy'**. See 6383.

6411. פְּלָיָה **Pelâyâh**, *pel-aw-yaw'*; or

פְּלָאיָה **Pelâ'yâh**, *pel-aw-yaw'*; from 6381 and 3050; *Jah has distinguished*; *Pelajah*, the name of three Isr.:—Pelaiah.

6412. פָּלִיט **pâlîyṭ**, *paw-leet'*; or

פָּלֵיט **pâlêyṭ**, *paw-late'*; or

פָּלֵט **pâlêṭ**, *paw-late'*; from 6403; a *refugee*:—(that have) escape (-d, -th), fugitive.

6413. פְּלֵיטָה **pelêyṭâh**, *pel-ay-taw'*; or

פְּלֵטָה **pelêṭâh**, *pel-ay-taw'*; fem. of 6412; *deliverance*; concr. an *escaped* portion:—deliverance, (that is) escape (-d), remnant.

6414. פָּלִיל **pâlîyl**, *paw-leel'*; from 6419; a *magistrate*:—judge.

6415. פְּלִילָה **pelîylâh**, *pel-ee-law'*; fem. of 6414; *justice*:—judgment.

6416. פְּלִילִי **pelîylîy**, *pel-ee-lee'*; from 6414; *judicial*:—judge.

6417. פְּלִילִיָּה **pelîylîyâh**, *pel-ee-lee-yaw'*; fem. of 6416; *judicature*:—judgment.

6418. פֶּלֶךְ **pelek**, *peh'-lek*; from an unused root mean. to *be round*; a *circuit* (i.e. *district*); also a *spindle* (as *whirled*); hence a *crutch*:—(di-) staff, part.

6419. פָּלַל **pâlal**, *paw-lal'*; a prim. root; to *judge* (officially or mentally); by extens. to *intercede*, *pray*:—intreat, judge (-ment), (make) pray (-er, -ing), make supplication.

6420. פָּלָל **Pâlâl**, *paw-lawl'*; from 6419; *judge*; *Palal*, an Isr.:—Palal.

6421. פְּלַלְיָה **Pelalyâh**, *pel-al-yaw'*; from 6419 and 3050; *Jah has judged*; *Pelaljah*, an Isr.:—Pelaliah.

6422. פַּלְמוֹנִי **palmôwnîy**, *pal-mo-nee'*; prob. for 6423; a *certain* one, i.e. so-and-so:—certain.

פִּלְנְאֶסֶר **Pilne'eçer**. See 8407.

6423. פְּלֹנִי **pelônîy**, *pel-o-nee'*; from 6395; *such a* one, i.e. a specified *person*:—such.

פִּלְנֶסֶר **Pilneçer**. See 8407.

6424. פָּלַס **pâlaç**, *paw-las'*; a prim. root; prop. to *roll* flat, i.e. *prepare* (a road); also to *revolve*, i.e. *weigh* (mentally):—make, ponder, weigh.

6425. פֶּלֶס **peleç**, *peh'-les*; from 6424; a *balance*:—scales, weight.

פְּלֶסֶר **Peleçer**. See 8407.

6426. פָּלַץ **pâlats**, *paw-lats'*; a prim. root; prop. perh. to *rend*, i.e. (by impl.) to *quiver*:—tremble.

6427. פַּלָּצוּת **pallâtsûwth**, *pal-law-tsooth'*; from 6426; *affright*:—fearfulness, horror, trembling.

6428. פָּלַשׁ **pâlash**, *paw-lash'*; a prim. root; to *roll* (in dust):—roll (wallow) self.

6429. פְּלֶשֶׁת **Pelesheth**, *pel-eh'-sheth*; from 6428; *rolling*, i.e. *migratory*; *Pelesheth*, a region of Syria:—Palestina, Palestine, Philistia, Philistines.

6430. פְּלִשְׁתִּי **Pelishtîy**, *pel-ish-tee'*; patrial from 6429; a *Pelishtite* or inhab. of Pelesheth:—Philistine.

6431. פֶּלֶת **Peleth**, *peh'-leth*; from an unused root mean. to *flee*; *swiftness*; *Peleth*, the name of two Isr.:—Peleth.

6432. פְּלֵתִי **Pelêthîy**, *pel-ay-thee'*; from the same form as 6431; a *courier* (collect.) or official *messenger*:—Pelethites.

6433. פֻּם **pûm** (Chald.), *poom*; prob. for 6310; the *mouth* (lit. or fig.):—mouth.

6434. פֵּן **pên**, *pane*; from an unused root mean. to *turn*; an *angle* (of a street or wall):—corner.

6435. פֵּן **pên**, *pane*; from 6437; prop. *removal*; used only (in the constr.) adv. as conj. *lest*:—(lest) (peradventure), that . . . not.

6436. פַּנַּג **pannag**, *pan-nag'*; of uncert. der.; prob. *pastry*:—Pannag.

6437. פָּנָה **pânâh**, *paw-naw'*; a prim. root; to *turn*; by impl. to *face*, i.e. *appear*, *look*, etc.:—appear, at [even-] tide, behold, cast out, come on, × corner, dawning, empty, go away, lie, look, mark, pass away, prepare, regard, (have) respect (to), (re-) turn (aside, away, back, face, self), × right [early].

פָּנֶה **pâneh**. See 6440.

6438. פִּנָּה **pinnâh**, *pin-naw'*; fem. of 6434; an *angle*; by impl. a *pinnacle*; fig. a *chieftain*:—bulwark, chief, corner, stay, tower.

6439. פְּנוּאֵל **Penûw'êl**, *pen-oo-ale'*; or (more prop.)

פְּנִיאֵל **Penîy'êl**, *pen-ee-ale'*; from 6437 and 410; *face of God*; *Penuël* or *Peniël*, a place E. of Jordan; also (as Penuel) the name of two Isr.:—Peniel, Penuel.

°פָּנִי **pânîy**. See 6443.

6440. פָּנִים **pânîym**, *paw-neem'*; plur. (but always as sing.) of an unused noun [פָּנֶה **pâneh**, *paw-neh'*; from 6437]; the *face* (as the part that *turns*); used in a great variety of applications (lit. and fig.); also (with prep. pref.) as a prep. (*before*, etc.):— + accept, a- (be-) fore (-time), against, anger, × as (long as), at, + battle, + because (of), + beseech, countenance, edge, + employ, endure, + enquire, face. favour, fear of. for, forefront (-part), form (-er time, -ward), from, front, heaviness, × him (-self), + honourable, + impudent, + in, it, look [-eth] (-s), × me, + meet, × more than, mouth, of, off, (of) old (time), × on, open, + out of, over against, the partial, person, + please, presence, propect, was purposed, by reason, of, + regard, right forth, + serve, × shewbread, sight, state, straight, + street, × thee, × them (-selves), through (+ -out), till, time (-s) past, (un-) to (-ward), + upon, upside (+ down), with (-in, + -stand), × ye, × you.

6441. פְּנִימָה **penîymâh**, *pen-ee'-maw*; from 6440 with directive enclitic; *faceward*, i.e. *indoors*:—(with-) in (-ner part, -ward).

6442. פְּנִימִי **penîymîy**, *pen-ee-mee'*; from 6440; *interior*:—(with-) in (-ner, -ward).

6443. פָּנִין **pânîyn**, *paw-neen'*; or

°פָּנִי **pânîy**, *paw-nee'*; from the same as 6434; prob. a *pearl* (as *round*):—ruby.

6444. פְּנִנָּה **Peninnâh**, *pen-in-naw'*; prob. fem. from 6443 contr.; *Peninnah*, an Israelitess:—Peninnah.

6445. פָּנַק **pânaq**, *paw-nak'*; a prim. root; to *enervate*:—bring up.

6446. פַּס **paç**, *pas*; from 6461; prop. the *palm* (of the hand) or *sole* (of the foot) [comp. 6447]; by impl. (plur.) a *long and sleeved* tunic (perh. simply a *wide* one; from the orig. sense of the root, i.e. of *many breadths*):—(divers) colours.

6447. פַּס **paç** (Chald.), *pas*; from a root corresp. to 6461; the *palm* (of the hand, as being *spread* out):—part.

6448. פָּסַג **pâçag**, *paw-sag'*; a prim. root; to *cut up*, i.e. (fig.) *contemplate*:—consider.

6449. פִּסְגָּה **Piçgâh**, *pis-gaw'*; from 6448; a *cleft*; *Pisgah*, a mt. E. of Jordan:—Pisgah.

6450. פַּס דַּמִּים **Paç Dammîym**, *pas dam-meem'*; from 6446 and the plur. of 1818; *palm* (i.e. *dell*) *of bloodshed*; *Pas-Dammim*, a place in Pal.:—Pas-dammim. Comp. 658.

6451. פִּסָּה **piççâh**, *pis-saw'*; from 6461; *expansion*, i.e. *abundance*:—handful.

6452. פָּסַח **pâçach**, *paw-sakh'*; a prim. root; to *hop*, i.e. (fig.) *skip* over (or *spare*); by impl. to *hesitate*; also (lit.) to *limp*, to *dance*:—halt, become lame, leap, pass over.

6453. פֶּסַח **peçach**, *peh'-sakh*; from 6452; a *pretermission*, i.e. *exemption*; used only tech. of the Jewish *Passover* (the festival or the victim):—passover (offering).

6454. פָּסֵחַ **Pâçêach**, *paw-say'-akh*; from 6452; *limping*; *Paseäch*, the name of two Isr.:—Paseah, Phaseah.

6455. פִּסֵּחַ **piççêach**, *pis-say'-akh*; from 6452; *lame*:—lame.

6456. פְּסִיל **peçîyl**, *pes-eel'*; from 6458; an *idol*:—carved (graven) image, quarry.

6457. פָּסַךְ **Pâçak**, *paw-sak'*; from an unused root mean. to *divide*; *divider*; *Pasak*, an Isr.:—Pasach.

6458. פָּסַל **pâçal**, *paw-sal'*; a prim. root; to *carve*, whether wood or stone:—grave, hew.

6459. פֶּסֶל **peçel**, *peh'-sel*; from 6458; an *idol*:—carved (graven) image.

6460. פְּסַנְטֵרִין **peçanṭêrîyn** (Chald.), *pes-an-tay-reen'*; or

פְּסַנְתֵּרִין **peçantêrîyn**, *pes-an-tay-reen'*; a transliteration of the Gr. ψαλτήριον *psaltēriōn*; a *lyre*:—psaltery.

6461. פָּסַס **pâçaç**, *paw-sas'*; a prim. root; prob. to *disperse*, i.e. (intrans.) *disappear*:—cease.

6462. פִּסְפָּה **Piçpâh**, *pis-paw'*; perh. from 6461; *dispersion*; *Pispah*, an Isr.:—Pispah.

6463. פָּעָה **pâ'âh**, *paw-aw'*; a prim. root; to *scream*:—cry.

6464. פָּעוּ **Pâ'ûw**, *paw-oo'*; or

פָּעִי **Pâ'îy**, *paw-ee'*; from 6463; *screaming*; *Paü* or *Paï*, a place in Edom:—Pai, Pau.

6465. פְּעוֹר **Pᵉʻôwr**, *peh-ore';* from 6473; a *gap; Peör,* a mountain E. of Jordan; also (for 1187) a deity worshipped there:—Peor. See also 1047.

פַּעַי **Pâʻîy.** See 6464.

6466. פָּעַל **pâʻal**, *paw-al';* a prim. root; to *do* or *make* (systematically and habitually), espec. to *practise:*—commit, [evil-] do (-er), make (-r), ordain, work (-er), wrought.

6467. פֹּעַל **pôʻal**, *po'-al;* from 6466; an *act* or *work* (concr.):—act, deed, do, getting, maker, work.

6468. פְּעֻלָּה **pᵉʻullâh**, *peh-ool-law';* fem. pass. part. of 6466; (abstr.) *work:*—labour, reward, wages, work.

6469. פְּעֻלְּתַי **Pᵉʻullᵉthay**, *peh-ool-leh-thah'ee;* from 6468; *laborious; Peüllethai,* an Isr.:—Peulthai.

6470. פָּעַם **pâʻam**, *paw-am';* a prim. root; to *tap,* i.e. beat regularly; hence (gen.) to *impel* or *agitate:*—move, trouble.

6471. פַּעַם **paʻam**, *pah'-am;* or (fem.)

פַּעֲמָה **paʻămâh**, *pah-am-aw';* from 6470; a *stroke,* lit. or fig. (in various applications, as follow):—anvil, corner, foot (-step), going, [hundred-] fold, × now, (this) + once, order, rank, step, + thrice, ([often-], second, this, two) time (-s), twice, wheel.

6472. פַּעֲמֹן **paʻămôn**, *pah-am-one';* from 6471; a *bell* (as *struck*):—bell.

6473. פָּעַר **pâʻar**, *paw-ar';* a prim. root; to *yawn,* i.e. *open* wide (lit. or fig.):—gape, open (wide).

6474. פַּעֲרַי **Paʻăray**, *pah-ar-ah'ee;* from 6473; *yawning; Paarai,* an Isr.:—Paarai.

6475. פָּצָה **pâtsâh**, *paw-tsaw';* a prim. root; to *rend,* i.e. *open* (espec. the mouth):—deliver, gape, open, rid, utter.

6476. פָּצַח **pâtsach**, *paw-tsakh';* a prim. root; to *break* out (in joyful sound):—break (forth, forth into joy), make a loud noise.

6477. פְּצִירָה **pᵉtsîyrâh**, *pets-ee-raw';* from 6484; *bluntness:*— + file.

6478. פָּצַל **pâtsal**, *paw-tsal';* a prim. root; to *peel:*—pill.

6479. פְּצָלָה **pᵉtsâlâh**, *pets-aw-law';* from 6478; a *peeling:*—strake.

6480. פָּצַם **pâtsam**, *paw-tsam';* a prim. root; to *rend* (by earthquake):—break.

6481. פָּצַע **pâtsaʻ**, *paw-tsah';* a prim. root; to *split,* i.e. *wound:*—wound.

6482. פֶּצַע **petsaʻ**, *peh'-tsah;* from 6481; a *wound:*—wound (-ing).

פַּצֵּץ **Patstsets.** See 1048.

6483. פִּצֵּץ **Pitstsêts**, *pits-tsates';* from an unused root mean. to *dissever; dispersive; Pitstsets,* a priest:—Apses [*includ. the art.*].

6484. פָּצַר **pâtsar**, *paw-tsar';* a prim. root; to *peck* at, i.e. (fig.) *stun* or *dull:*—press, urge, stubbornness.

6485. פָּקַד **pâqad**, *paw-kad';* a prim. root; to *visit* (with friendly or hostile intent); by anal. to *oversee, muster, charge, care for, miss, deposit,* etc.:—appoint, × at all, avenge, bestow, (appoint to have the, give a) charge, commit, count, deliver to keep, be empty, enjoin, go see, hurt, do judgment, lack, lay up look, make × by any means, miss, number, officer, (make) overseer have (the) oversight, punish, reckon, (call to) remember (-brance), set (over), sum, × surely, visit, want.

פִּקֻּד **piqqûd.** See 6490.

6486. פְּקֻדָּה **pᵉquddâh**, *pek-ood-daw';* fem. pass. part. of 6485; *visitation* (in many senses, chiefly official):—account, (that have the) charge, custody, that which . . . laid up, numbers, office (-r), ordering, oversight, + prison, reckoning, visitation.

6487. פִּקָּדוֹן **piqqâdôwn**, *pik-kaw-done';* from 6485; a *deposit:*—that which was delivered (to keep), store.

6488. פְּקִדֻת **pᵉqîdûth**, *pek-ee-dooth';* from 6496; *supervision:*—ward.

6489. פְּקוֹד **Pᵉqôwd**, *pek-ode';* from 6485; *punishment; Pekod,* a symbol. name for Bab.:—Pekod.

6490. פִּקּוּד **piqqûwd**, *pik-kood';* or

פִּקֻּד **piqqûd**, *pik-kood';* from 6485; prop. *appointed,* i.e. a *mandate* (of God; plur. only, collect. for the *Law*):—commandment, precept, statute.

6491. פָּקַח **pâqach**, *paw-kakh';* a prim. root; to *open* (the senses, espec. the eyes); fig. to *be observant:*—open.

6492. פֶּקַח **Peqach**, *peh'-kakh;* from 6491; *watch; Pekach,* an Isr. king:—Pekah.

6493. פִּקֵּחַ **piqqêach**, *pik-kay'-akh;* from 6491; *clear-sighted;* fig. *intelligent:*—seeing, wise.

6494. פְּקַחְיָה **Pᵉqachyâh**, *pek-akh-yaw';* from 6491 and 3050; *Jah has observed; Pekachjah,* an Isr. king:—Pekahiah.

6495. פְּקַח־קוֹחַ **pᵉqach-qôwach**, *pek-akh-ko'-akh;* from 6491 redoubled; *opening* (of a dungeon), i.e. *jail-delivery* (fig. *salvation* from sin):—opening of the prison.

6496. פָּקִיד **pâqîyd**, *paw-keed';* from 6485; a *superintendent* (civil, military or religious):—which had the charge, governor, office, overseer, [that] was set.

6497. פֶּקַע **peqaʻ**, *peh'-kah;* from an unused root mean. to *burst;* only used as an architect. term of an ornament similar to 6498, a *semi-globe:*—knop.

6498. פַּקֻּעָה **paqqûʻâh**, *pak-koo-aw';* from the same as 6497; the *wild cucumber* (from *splitting* open to shed its seeds):—gourd.

6499. פַּר **par**, *par;* or

פָּר **pâr**, *pawr;* from 6565; a *bullock* (appar. as *breaking* forth in wild strength, or perh. as *dividing* the hoof):—(+ young) bull (-ock), calf, ox.

6500. פָּרָא **pârâ'**, *paw-raw';* a prim. root; to *bear fruit:*—be fruitful.

6501. פֶּרֶא **pere'**, *peh'-reh;* or

פֶּרֶה **pereh** (Jer. 2 : 24), *peh'-reh;* from 6500 in the secondary sense of *running* wild; the *onager:*—wild (ass).

פֹּרָאה **pôrâ'h.** See 6288.

6502. פִּרְאָם **Pir'âm**, *pir-awm';* from 6501; *wildly; Piram,* a Canaanite:—Piram.

6503. פַּרְבָּר **Parbâr**, *par-bawr';* or

פַּרְוָר **Parvâr**, *par-vawr';* of for or.; *Parbar* or *Parvar,* a quarter of Jerus.:—Parbar, suburb.

6504. פָּרַד **pârad**, *paw-rad';* a prim. root; to *break* through, i.e. *spread* or *separate* (oneself):—disperse, divide, be out of joint, part, scatter (abroad), separate (self), sever self, stretch, sunder.

6505. פֶּרֶד **pered**, *peh'-red;* from 6504; a *mule* (perh. from his *lonely* habits):—mule.

6506. פִּרְדָּה **pirdâh**, *pir-daw';* fem. of 6505; a *she-mule:*—mule.

6507. פְּרֻדָה **pᵉrûdâh**, *per-oo-daw';* fem. pass. part. of 6504; something *separated,* i.e. a *kernel:*—seed.

6508. פַּרְדֵּס **pardêç**, *par-dace';* of for. or.; a *park:*—forest, orchard.

6509. פָּרָה **pârâh**, *paw-raw';* a prim. root; to *bear fruit* (lit. or fig.):—bear, bring forth (fruit), (be, cause to be, make) fruitful, grow, increase.

6510. פָּרָה **pârâh**, *paw-raw';* fem. of 6499; a *heifer:*—cow, heifer, kine.

6511. פָּרָה **Pârâh**, *paw-raw';* the same as 6510; *Parah,* a place in Pal.:—Parah.

פֶּרֶה **pereh.** See 6501.

6512. פֵּרָה **pêrâh**, *pay-raw';* from 6331; a *hole* (as *broken,* i.e. dug):— + mole. Comp. 2661.

6513. פֻּרָה **Pûrâh**, *poo-raw;* for 6288; *foliage; Purah,* an Isr.:—Phurah.

6514. פְּרוּדָא **Pᵉrûwdâ'**, *per-oo-daw';* or

פְּרִידָא **Pᵉrîydâ'**, *per-ee-daw';* from 6504; *dispersion; Peruda* or *Perida,* one of "Solomon's servants":—Perida, Peruda.

פְּרוֹזִי° **pᵉrôwzîy.** See 6521.

6515. פָּרוּחַ **Pârûwach**, *paw-roo'-akh;* pass. part. of 6524; *blossomed; Paruäch,* an Isr.:—Paruah.

6516. פַּרְוַיִם **Parvayim**, *par-vah'-yim;* of for. or.; *Parvajim,* an Oriental region:—Parvaim.

6517. פָּרוּר **pârûwr**, *paw-roor';* pass. part. of 6565 in the sense of *spreading* out [comp. 6524]; a *skillet* (as *flat* or *deep*):—pan, pot.

פַּרְוָר **Parvâr.** See 6503.

6518. פָּרָז **pâraz**, *paw-rawz';* from an unused root mean. to *separate,* i.e. *decide;* a *chieftain:*—village.

6519. פְּרָזָה **pᵉrâzâh**, *per-aw-zaw';* from the same as 6518; an *open* country:—(unwalled) town (without walls), unwalled village.

6520. פְּרָזוֹן **pᵉrâzôwn**, *per-aw-zone';* from the same as 6518; *magistracy,* i.e. *leadership* (also concr. *chieftains*):—village.

6521. פְּרָזִי **pᵉrâzîy**, *per-aw-zee';* or

פְּרוֹזִי° **pᵉrôwzîy**, *per-o-zee';* from 6519; a *rustic:*—village.

6522. פְּרִזִּי **Pᵉrizzîy**, *per-iz-zee';* for 6521; inhab. *of the open country;* a *Perizzite,* one of the Canaanitish tribes:—Perizzite.

6523. פַּרְזֶל **parzel** (Chald.), *par-zel';* corresp. to 1270; *iron:*—iron.

6524. פָּרַח **pârach**, *paw-rakh';* a prim. root; to *break* forth as a bud, i.e. *bloom;* gen. to *spread;* spec. to *fly* (as extending the wings); fig. to *flourish:*— × abroad, × abundantly, blossom, break forth (out), bud, flourish, make fly, grow, spread, spring (up).

6525. פֶּרַח **perach**, *peh'-rakh;* from 6524; a *calyx* (nat. or artif.); gen. *bloom:*—blossom, bud, flower.

6526. פִּרְחַח **pirchach**, *pir-khakh';* from 6524; *progeny,* i.e. a *brood:*—youth.

6527. פָּרַט **pâraṭ**, *paw-rat';* a prim. root; to *scatter* words, i.e. *prate* (or *hum*):—chant.

6528. פֶּרֶט **pereṭ**, *peh'-ret;* from 6527; a *stray* or *single* berry:—grape.

6529. פְּרִי **pᵉrîy**, *per-ee';* from 6509; *fruit* (lit. or fig.):—bough, ([first-]) fruit ([-ful]), reward.

פְּרִידָא **Pᵉrîydâ'.** See 6514.

פֻּרִים **Pûrîym.** See 6332.

6530. פְּרִיץ **pᵉrîyts**, *per-eets';* from 6555; *violent,* i.e. a *tyrant:*—destroyer, ravenous, robber.

6531. פֶּרֶךְ **perek**, *peh'-rek;* from an unused root mean. to *break* apart; *fracture,* i.e. *severity:*—cruelty, rigour.

6532. פֹּרֶכֶת **pôreketh**, *po-reh'-keth;* fem. act. part. of the same as 6531; a *separatrix,* i.e. (the sacred) *screen:*—vail.

6533. פָּרַם **pâram**, *paw-ram';* a prim. root; to *tear:*—rend.

6534. פַּרְמַשְׁתָּא **Parmashtâ'**, *par-mash-taw';* of Pers. or.; *Parmashta,* a son of Haman:—Parmasta.

6535. פַּרְנַךְ **Parnak**, *par-nak';* of uncert. der.; *Parnak,* an Isr.:—Parnach.

6536. פָּרַס **pâraç**, *paw-ras';* a prim. root; to *break* in pieces, i.e. (usually without violence) to *split, distribute:*—deal, divide, have hoofs, part, tear.

6537. פְּרַס **pᵉraç** (Chald.), *per-as';* corresp. to 6536; to *split* up:—divide, [U-] pharsin.

6538. פֶּרֶס **pereç**, *peh'-res;* from 6536; a *claw;* also a kind of *eagle:*—claw, ossifrage.

6539. פָּרַס **Pâraç**, *paw-ras';* of for. or.; *Paras* (i.e. *Persia*), an Eastern country, including its inhab.:—Persia, Persians.

6540. פָּרַס **Pâraç** (Chald.), *paw-ras';* corresp. to 6539:—Persia, Persians.

6541. פַּרְסָה **parçâh**, *par-saw';* fem. of 6538; a *claw* or split *hoof:*—claw, [cloven-] footed, hoof.

6542. פַּרְסִי **Parçîy**, *par-see';* patrial from 6539; a *Parsite* (i.e. *Persian*), or inhab. of Peres:—Persian.

6543. פַּרְסִי **Parçîy** (Chald.), *par-see';* corresp. to 6542:—Persian.

6544. פָּרַע **pâra'**, *paw-rah';* a prim. root; to *loosen;* by impl. to *expose, dismiss;* fig. *absolve, begin:*—avenge, avoid, bare, go back, let, (make) naked, set at nought, perish, refuse, uncover.

6545. פֶּרַע **pera'**, *peh'-rah;* from 6544; the *hair* (as *dishevelled*):—locks.

6546. פַּרְעָה **par'âh**, *par-aw';* fem. of 6545 (in the sense of *beginning*); *leadership* (plur. concr. *leaders*):— + avenging, revenge.

6547. פַּרְעֹה **Par'ôh**, *par-o';* of Eg. der.; *Paroh*, a gen. title of Eg. kings:—Pharaoh.

6548. פַּרְעֹה חָפְרַע **Par'ôh Chophra'**, *par-o' khof-rah';* of Eg. der.; *Paroh-Chophra*, an Eg. king:—Pharaoh-hophra.

6549. פַּרְעֹה נְכֹה **Par'ôh Nekôh**, *par-o' nek-o';* or

פַּרְעֹה נְכוֹ **Par'ôh Nekôw**, *par-o' nek-o';* of Eg. der.; *Paroh-Nekoh* (or *-Neko*), an Eg. king:—Pharaoh-necho, Pharaoh-nechoh.

6550. פַּרְעֹשׁ **par'ôsh**, *par-oshe';* prob. from 6544 and 6211; a *flea* (as the *isolated insect*):—flea.

6551. פַּרְעֹשׁ **Par'ôsh**, *par-oshe';* the same as 6550; *Parosh*, the name of four Isr.:—Parosh, Pharosh.

6552. פִּרְעָתוֹן **Pir'âthôwn**, *pir-aw-thone';* from 6546; *chieftaincy; Pirathon*, a place in Pal.:—Pirathon.

6553. פִּרְעָתוֹנִי **Pir'âthôwnîy**, *pir-aw-tho-nee';* or

פִּרְעָתֹנִי **Pir'âthônîy**, *pir-aw-tho-nee';* patrial from 6552; a *Pirathonite* or inhab. of Pirathon:—Pirathonite.

6554. פַּרְפַּר **Parpar**, *par-par';* prob. from 6565 in the sense of *rushing; rapid; Parpar*, a river of Syria:—Pharpar.

6555. פָּרַץ **pârats**, *paw-rats';* a prim. root; to *break* out (in many applications, direct and indirect, lit. and fig.):—× abroad, (make a) breach, break (away, down, -er, forth, in, up), burst out come (spread) abroad, compel, disperse, grow, increase, open, press, scatter, urge.

6556. פֶּרֶץ **perets**, *peh'-rets;* from 6555; a *break* (lit. or fig.):—breach, breaking forth (in), × forth, gap.

6557. פֶּרֶץ **Perets**, *peh'-rets;* the same as 6556; *Perets*, the name of two Isr.:—Perez, Pharez.

6558. פַּרְצִי **Partsîy**, *par-tsee';* patron. from 6557; a *Partsite* (collect.) or desc. of Perets:—Pharzites.

6559. פְּרָצִים **perâtsîym**, *per-aw-tseem';* plur. of 6556; *breaks; Peratsim*, a mountain in Pal.:—Perazim.

6560. פֶּרֶץ עֻזָּא **Perets 'Uzzâ'**, *peh'-rets ooz-zaw';* from 6556 and 5798; *break of Uzza; Perets-Uzza*, a place in Pal.:—Perez-uzza.

6561. פָּרַק **pâraq**, *paw-rak';* a prim. root; to *break* off or *craunch;* fig. to *deliver:*—break (off), deliver, redeem, rend (in pieces), tear in pieces.

6562. פְּרַק **peraq** (Chald.), *per-ak';* corresp. to 6561; to *discontinue:*—break off.

6563. פֶּרֶק **pereq**, *peh'-rek;* from 6561; *rapine;* also a *fork* (in roads):—crossway, robbery.

6564. פָּרָק° **pârâq**, *paw-rawk';* from 6561; *soup* (as full of *crumbed* meat):—broth. See also 4832.

6565. פָּרַר **pârar**, *paw-rar';* a prim. root; to *break* up (usually fig., i.e. to *violate, frustrate*):— × any ways, break (asunder), cast off, cause to cease, × clean, defeat, disannul, disappoint, dissolve, divide, make of none effect, fail, frustrate, bring (come) to nought, × utterly, make void.

6566. פָּרַשׂ **pâras**, *paw-ras';* a prim. root; to *break* apart, *disperse*, etc.:—break, chop in pieces, lay open, scatter, spread (abroad, forth, selves, out), stretch (forth, out).

6567. פָּרַשׁ **pârash**, *paw-rash';* a prim. root; to *separate*, lit. (to *disperse*) or fig. (to *specify*); also (by impl.) to *wound:*—scatter, declare, distinctly, shew, sting.

6568. פְּרַשׁ **perash** (Chald.), *per-ash';* corresp. to 6567; to *specify:*—distinctly.

6569. פֶּרֶשׁ **peresh**, *peh'-resh;* from 6567; *excrement* (as *eliminated*):—dung.

6570. פֶּרֶשׁ **Peresh**, *peh'-resh;* the same as 6569; *Peresh*, an Isr.:—Peresh.

6571. פָּרָשׁ **pârâsh**, *paw-rawsh';* from 6567; a *steed* (as *stretched* out to a vehicle, not single nor for mounting [comp. 5483]); also (by impl.) a *driver* (in a chariot), i.e. (collect.) cavalry:—horseman.

6572. פַּרְשֶׁגֶן **parshegen**, *par-sheh'-ghen;* or

פַּתְשֶׁגֶן **pathshegen**, *path-sheh'-gen;* of for. or.; a *transcript:*—copy.

6573. פַּרְשֶׁגֶן **parshegen** (Chald.), *par-sheh'-ghen;* corresp. to 6572:—copy.

6574. פַּרְשְׁדֹן **parshedôn**, *par-shed-one';* perh. by compounding 6567 and 6504 (in the sense of *straddling*) [comp. 6576]; the *crotch* (or *anus*):—dirt.

6575. פָּרָשָׁה **pârâshâh**, *paw-raw-shaw';* from 6567; *exposition:*—declaration, sum.

6576. פַּרְשֵׁז **parshêz**, *par-shaze';* a root appar. formed by compounding 6567 and that of 6518 [comp. 6574]; to *expand:*—spread.

6577. פַּרְשַׁנְדָּתָא **Parshandâthâ'**, *par-shan-daw-thaw';* of Pers. or.; *Parshandatha*, a son of Haman:—Parshandatha.

6578. פְּרָת **Perâth**, *per-awth';* from an unused root mean. to *break* forth; *rushing; Perath* (i.e. *Euphrates*), a river of the East:—Euphrates.

פֹּרָת **pôrâth**. See 6509.

6579. פַּרְתַּם **partam**, *par-tam';* of Pers. or.; a *grandee:*—(most) noble, prince.

6580. פַּשׁ **pash**, *pash;* prob. from an unused root mean. to *disintegrate; stupidity* (as a result of *grossness* or of *degeneracy*):—extremity.

6581. פָּשָׂה **pâsâh**, *paw-saw';* a prim. root; to *spread:*—spread.

6582. פָּשַׁח **pâshach**, *paw-shakh';* a prim. root; to *tear* in pieces:—pull in pieces.

6583. פַּשְׁחוּר **Pashchûwr**, *pash-khoor';* prob. from 6582; *liberation; Pashchur*, the name of four Isr.:—Pashur.

6584. פָּשַׁט **pâshaṭ**, *paw-shat';* a prim. root; to *spread* out (i.e. *deploy* in hostile array); by anal. to *strip* (i.e. *unclothe, plunder, flay*, etc.):—fall upon, flay, invade, make an invasion, pull off, put off, make a road, run upon, rush, set, spoil, spread selves (abroad), strip (off, self).

6585. פָּשַׂע **pâsa'**, *paw-sah';* a prim. root; to *stride* (from *spreading* the legs), i.e. *rush* upon:—go.

6586. פָּשַׁע **pâsha'**, *paw-shah';* a prim. root [rather ident. with 6585 through the idea of *expansion*]; to *break* away (from just authority), i.e. *trespass, apostatize, quarrel:*—offend, rebel, revolt, transgress (-ion, -or).

6587. פֶּשַׂע **pesa'**, *peh'-sah;* from 6585; a *stride:*—step.

6588. פֶּשַׁע **pesha'**, *peh'-shah;* from 6586; a *revolt* (national, moral or religious):—rebellion, sin, transgression, trespass.

6589. פָּשַׂק **pâsaq**, *paw-sak';* a prim. root; to *dispart* (the feet or lips), i.e. *become licentious:*—open (wide).

6590. פְּשַׁר **peshar** (Chald.), *pesh-ar';* corresp. to 6622; to *interpret:*—make [interpretations], interpreting.

6591. פְּשַׁר **peshar** (Chald.), *pesh-ar';* from 6590; an *interpretation:*—interpretation.

6592. פֵּשֶׁר **pêsher**, *pay'-sher;* corresp. to 6591:—interpretation.

6593. פִּשְׁתֶּה **pishteh**, *pish-teh';* from the same as 6580 as in the sense of *comminuting; linen* (i.e. the thread, as *carded*):—flax, linen.

6594. פִּשְׁתָּה **pishtâh**, *pish-taw';* fem. of 6593; *flax;* by impl. a *wick:*—flax, tow.

6595. פַּת **path**, *path;* from 6626; a *bit:*—meat, morsel, piece.

6596. פֹּת **pôth**, *pohth;* or

פֹּתָה **pothâh** (Ezek. 13 : 19), *po-thaw';* from an unused root mean. to *open;* a *hole*, i.e. *hinge* or the female *pudenda:*—hinge, secret part.

פְּתָאִי **pethâ'îy**. See 6612.

6597. פִּתְאוֹם **pith'ôwm**, *pith-ome';* or

פִּתְאֹם **pith'ôm**, *pith-ome';* from 6621; *instantly:*—straightway, sudden (-ly).

6598. פַּתְבַּג **pathbag**, *pathbag';* of Pers. or.; a *dainty:*—portion (provision) of meat.

6599. פִּתְגָם **pithgâm**, *pith-gawm';* of Pers. or.; a (judicial) *sentence:*—decree, sentence.

6600. פִּתְגָם **pithgâm** (Chald.), *pith-gawm';* corresp. to 6599; a *word, answer, letter* or *decree:*—answer, letter, matter, word.

6601. פָּתָה **pâthâh**, *paw-thaw';* a prim. root; to *open*, i.e. *be* (causat. *make*) *roomy;* usually fig. (in a mental or moral sense) to *be* (causat. *make*) *simple* or (in a sinister way) *delude:*—allure, deceive, enlarge, entice, flatter, persuade, silly (one).

6602. פְּתוּאֵל **Pethûw'êl**, *peth-oo-ale';* from 6601 and 410; *enlarged of God; Pethuël*, an Isr.:—Pethuel.

6603. פִּתּוּחַ **pittûwach**, *pit-too'-akh;* or

פִּתֻּחַ **pittûach**, *pit-too'-akh;* pass. part. of 6605; *sculpture* (in low or high relief or even intaglio):—carved (work) (are, en-) grave (-ing, -n).

6604. פְּתוֹר **Pethôwr**, *peth-ore';* of for. or.; *Pethor*, a place in Mesopotamia:—Pethor.

6605. פָּתַח **pâthach**, *paw-thakh';* a prim. root; to *open* wide (lit. or fig.); spec. to *loosen, begin, plough, carve:*—appear, break forth, draw (out), let go free, (en-) grave (-n), loose (self), (be, be set) open (-ing), put off, ungird, unstop, have vent.

6606. פְּתַח **pethach** (Chald.), *peth-akh';* corresp to 6605; to *open:*—open.

6607. פֶּתַח **pethach**, *peh'-thakh;* from 6605; an *opening* (lit.), i.e. *door* (*gate*) or *entrance* way:—door, entering (in), entrance (-ry), gate, opening, place.

6608. פֵּתַח **pêthach**, *pay'-thakh;* from 6605; *opening* (fig.) i.e. *disclosure:*—entrance.

פִּתֻּחַ **pathûach**. See 6603.

6609. פְּתִחָה **pethikhâh**, *peth-ee-khaw';* from 6605; something *opened*, i.e. a *drawn* sword:—drawn sword.

6610. פִּתְחוֹן **pithchôwn**, *pith-khone';* from 6605; *opening* (the act):—open (-ing).

6611. פְּתַחְיָה **Pethachyâh**, *peth-akh-yaw';* from 6605 and 3050; *Jah has opened; Pethachjah*, the name of four Isr.:—Pethakiah.

6612. פְּתִי **pethîy**, *peth-ee';* or

פֶּתִי **pethîy**, *peh'-thee;* or

פְּתָאִי **pethâ'îy**, *peth-aw-ee';* from 6601; *silly* (i.e. *seducible*):—foolish, simple (-icity, one).

6613. פְּתַי **pethay** (Chald.), *peth-ah'ee;* from a root corresp. to 6601; *open*, i.e. (as noun) *width:*—breadth.

6614. פְּתִיגִיל **pethîygîyl**, *peth-eeg-eel';* of uncert. der.; prob. a figured *mantle* for holidays:—stomacher.

6615. פְּתַיּוּת **pethayûwth**, *peth-ah-yooth';* from 6612; *silliness* (i.e. *seducibility*):—simple.

6616. פָּתִיל **pâthîyl**, *paw-theel'*; from 6617; *twine:*—bound, bracelet, lace, line, ribband, thread, wire.

6617. פָּתַל **pâthal**, *paw-thal'*; a prim. root; to *twine*, i.e. (lit.) to *struggle* or (fig.) *be* (morally) *tortuous:*—(shew self) froward, shew self unsavoury, wrestle.

6618. פְּתַלְתֹּל **pᵉthaltôl**, *peth-al-tole'*; from 6617; *tortuous* (i.e. crafty):—crooked.

6619. פִּתֹם **Pîthôm**, *pee-thome'*; of Eg. der.; *Pithom*, a place in Eg.:—Pithom.

6620. פֶּתֶן **pethen**, *peh'-then*; from an unused root mean. to *twist*; an *asp* (from its *contortions*):—adder.

6621. פֶּתַע **pethaʿ**, *peh'-thah*; from an unused root mean. to *open* (the eyes); a *wink*, i.e. *moment* [comp. 6597] (used only [with or without prep.] adv. *quickly* or *unexpectedly*):—at an instant suddenly, × very.

6622. פָּתַר **pâthar**, *paw-thar'*; a prim. root; to *open* up, i.e. (fig.) *interpret* (a dream):—interpret (-ation, -er).

6623. פִּתְרוֹן **pithrôwn**, *pith-rone'*; or

פִּתְרֹן **pithrôn**, *pith-rone'*; from 6622; *interpretation* (of a dream):—interpretation.

6624. פַּתְרוֹס **Pathrôwç**, *path-roce'*; of Eg. der.; *Pathros*, a part of Eg.:—Pathros.

6625. פַּתְרֻסִי **Pathrûçîy**, *path-roo-see'*; patrial from 6624; a *Pathrusite*, or inhab. of Pathros:—Pathrusim.

פַּתְשֶׁגֶן **pathshegen**. See 6572.

6626. פָּתַת **pâthath**, *paw-thath'*; a prim. root; to *open*, i.e. *break:*—part.

צ

6627. צָאָה **tsâ'âh**, *tsaw-aw'*; from 3318; *issue*, i.e. (human) *excrement:*—that (which) cometh from (out).

צֹאָה **tsô'âh**. See 6675.

צְאוֹן° **tsᵉ'ôwn**. See 6629.

6628. צֶאֶל **tse'el**, *tseh'-el*; from an unused root mean. to *be slender*; the *lotus* tree:—shady tree.

6629. צֹאן **tsôn**, *tsone*; or

צְאוֹן° **tsᵉ'ôwn** (Psa. 144 : 13), *tseh-one'*; from an unused root mean. to *migrate*; a collect. name for a *flock* (of sheep or goats); also fig. (of men):—(small) cattle, flock (+ -s), lamb (+ -s), sheep ([-cote, -fold, -shearer, -herds]).

6630. צַאֲנָן **Tsa'ănân**, *tsah-an-awn'*; from the same as 6629 used denom.; *sheep pasture*; *Zaanan*, a place in Pal.:—Zaanan.

6631. צֶאֱצָא **tse'ĕtsâ'**, *tseh-ets-aw'*; from 3318; *issue*, i.e. *produce*, *children:*—that which cometh forth (out), offspring.

6632. צָב **tsâb**, *tsawb*; from an unused root mean. to *establish*; a *palanquin* or *canopy* (as a *fixture*); also a species of *lizard* (prob. as clinging *fast*):—covered, litter, tortoise.

6633. צָבָא **tsâbâ'**, *tsaw-baw'*; a prim. root; to *mass* (an army or servants):—assemble, fight, perform, muster, wait upon, war.

6634. צְבָא **tsᵉbâ'** (Chald.), *tseb-aw'*; corresp. to 6633 in the fig. sense of *summoning* one's wishes; to *please:*—will, would.

6635. צָבָא **tsâbâ'**, *tsaw-baw'*; or (fem.)

צְבָאָה **tsᵉbâ'âh**, *tseb-aw-aw'*; from 6633; a *mass* of persons (or fig. things), espec. reg. organized for war (an *army*); by impl. a *campaign*, lit. or fig. (spec. *hardship*, *worship*):—appointed time, (+) army, (+) battle, company, host, service, soldiers, waiting upon, war (-fare).

6636. צְבֹאִים **Tsᵉbô'iym**, *tseb-o-eem'*; or (more correctly)

צְבִיִּים **Tsᵉbîyîym**, *tseb-ee-yeem'*; or

צְבִיִּם **Tsᵉbîyîm**, *tseb-ee-yeem'*; plur. of 6643; *gazelles*; *Tseboïm* or *Tsebijim*, a place in Pal.:—Zeboiim, Zeboim.

6637. צֹבֵבָה **Tsôbêbâh**, *tso-bay-baw'*; fem. act. part. of the same as 6632; the *canopier* (with the art.); *Tsobebah*, an Israelitess:—Zobebah.

6638. צָבָה **tsâbâh**, *tsaw-baw'*; a prim. root; to *amass*, i.e. *grow turgid*; spec. to *array* an army against:—fight, swell.

6639. צָבֶה **tsâbeh**, *tsaw-beh'*; from 6638; *turgid:*—swell.

צֹבָה **Tsôbâh**. See 6678.

6640. צְבוּ **tsᵉbûw** (Chald.), *tseb-oo'*; from 6634; prop. *will*; concr. an *affair* (as a matter of *determination*):—purpose.

6641. צָבוּעַ **tsâbûwaʿ**, *tsaw-boo'-ah*; pass. part. of the same as 6648; *dyed* (in stripes), i.e. the *hyena:*—speckled.

6642. צָבַט **tsâbaṭ**, *tsaw-bat'*; a prim. root; to *grasp*, i.e. *hand* out:—reach.

6643. צְבִי **tsᵉbîy**, *tseb-ee'*; from 6638 in the sense of *prominence*; *splendor* (as *conspicuous*); also a *gazelle* (as *beautiful*):—beautiful (-ty), glorious (-ry), goodly, pleasant, roe (-buck).

6644. צִבְיָא **Tsibyâ'**, *tsib-yaw'*; for 6645; *Tsibja*, an Isr.:—Zibia.

6645. צִבְיָה **Tsibyâh**, *tsib-yaw'*; for 6646; *Tsibjah*, an Israelitess:—Zibiah.

6646. צְבִיָּה **tsᵉbîyâh**, *tseb-ee-yaw'*; fem. of 6643; a *female* gazelle:—roe.

צְבִיִּים° (or צְבִיִּם) **Tsᵉbîyîym**. See 6636.

צְבָיִם° **Tsᵉbâyîm**. See 6380.

6647. צְבַע **tsᵉbaʿ** (Chald.), *tseb-ah'*; a root corresp. to that of 6648; to *dip:*—wet.

6648. צֶבַע **tsebaʿ**, *tseh'-bah*; from an unused root mean. to *dip* (into coloring fluid); a *dye:*—divers, colours.

6649. צִבְעוֹן **Tsibʿôwn**, *tsib-one'*; from the same as 6648; *variegated*; *Tsibon*, an Idumæan:—Zibeon.

6650. צְבֹעִים **Tsᵉbôʿîym**, *tseb-o-eem'*; plur. of 6641; *hyenas*; *Tseboïm*, a place in Pal.:—Zeboim.

6651. צָבַר **tsâbar**, *tsaw-bar'*; a prim. root; to *aggregate:*—gather (together), heap (up), lay up.

6652. צִבֻּר **tsibbûr**, *tsib-boor'*; from 6551; a *pile:*—heap.

6653. צֶבֶת **tsebeth**, *tseh'-beth*; from an unused root appar. mean. to *grip*; a *lock* of stalks:—handful.

6654. צַד **tsad**, *tsad*; contr. from an unused root mean. to *sidle* off; a *side*; fig. an *adversary:*—(be-) side.

6655. צַד **tsad** (Chald.), *tsad*; corresp. to 6654; used adv. (with prep.) at or upon the *side* of:—against, concerning.

6656. צְדָא **tsᵉdâ'** (Chald.), *tsed-aw'*; from an unused root corresp. to 6658 in the sense of *intentness*; a (sinister) *design:*—true.

6657. צְדָד **Tsᵉdâd**, *tsed-awd'*; from the same as 6654; a *siding*; *Tsedad*, a place near Pal.:—Zedad.

6658. צָדָה **tsâdâh**, *tsaw-daw'*; a prim. root; to *chase*; by impl. to *desolate:*—destroy, hunt, lie in wait.

צֵדָה **tsêdâh**. See 6720.

6659. צָדוֹק **Tsâdôwq**, *tsaw-doke'*; from 6663; *just*; *Tsadok*, the name of eight or nine Isr.:—Zadok.

6660. צְדִיָּה **tsᵉdîyâh**, *tsed-ee-yaw'*; from 6658; *design* [comp. 6656]:—lying in wait.

6661. צִדִּים **Tsiddîym**, *tsid-deem'*; plur. of 6654; *sides*; *Tsiddim* (with the art.), a place in Pal.:—Ziddim.

6662. צַדִּיק **tsaddîyq**, *tsad-deek'*; from 6663; *just:*—just, lawful, righteous (man).

צִדֹנִי° **Tsîdônîy**. See 6722.

6663. צָדַק **tsâdaq**, *tsaw-dak'*; a prim. root; to *be* (causat. *make*) *right* (in a moral or forensic sense):—cleanse, clear self, (be, do) just (-ice, -ify, -ify self), (be, turn to) righteous (-ness).

6664. צֶדֶק **tsedeq**, *tseh'-dek*; from 6663; the *right* (nat., mor. or legal); also (abstr.) *equity* or (fig.) *prosperity:*— × even, (× that which is altogether) just (-ice), ([un-]) right (-eous) (cause, -ly, -ness).

6665. צִדְקָה **tsidqâh** (Chald.), *tsid-kaw'*; corresp. to 6666; *beneficence:*—righteousness.

6666. צְדָקָה **tsᵉdâqâh**, *tsed-aw-kaw'*; from 6663; *rightness* (abstr.), subj. (*rectitude*), obj. (*justice*), mor. (*virtue*) or fig. (*prosperity*):—justice, moderately, right (-eous) (act, -ly, -ness).

6667. צִדְקִיָּה **Tsidqîyâh**, *tsid-kee-yaw'*; or

צִדְקִיָּהוּ **Tsidqîyâhûw**, *tsid-kee-yaw'-hoo*; from 6664 and 3050; *right of Jah*; *Tsidkijah*, the name of six Isr.:—Zedekiah, Zidkijah.

6668. צָהַב **tsâhab**, *tsaw-hab'*; a prim. root; to *glitter*, i.e. *be golden* in color:— × fine.

6669. צָהֹב **tsâhôb**, *tsaw-obe'*; from 6668; *golden* in color:—yellow.

6670. צָהַל **tsâhal**, *tsaw-hal'*; a prim. root; to *gleam*, i.e. (fig.) *be cheerful*; by transf. to *sound* clear (of various animal or human expressions):—bellow, cry aloud (out), lift up, neigh, rejoice, make to shine, shout.

6671. צָהַר **tsâhar**, *tsaw-har'*; a prim. root; to *glisten*; used only as denom. from 3323, to *press* out *oil:*—make oil.

6672. צֹהַר **tsôhar**, *tso'-har*; from 6671; a *light* (i.e. *window*); dual *double light*, i.e. *noon:*—midday, noon (-day, -tide), window.

6673. צַו **tsav**, *tsav*; or

צָו **tsâv**, *tsawv*; from 6680; an *injunction:*—commandment, precept.

6674. צוֹא **tsôw'**, *tso*; or

צֹא **tsô'**, *tso*; from an unused root mean. to *issue*; *soiled* (as if *excrementitious*):—filthy.

6675. צוֹאָה **tsôw'âh**, *tso-aw'*; or

צֹאָה **tsô'âh**, *tso-aw'*; fem. of 6674; *excrement*; gen. *dirt*; fig. *pollution:*—dung, filth (-iness). Marg. for 2716.

6676. צַוַּאר **tsavva'r** (Chald.), *tsav-var'*; corresp. to 6677:—neck.

6677. צַוָּאר **tsavvâ'r**, *tsav-vawr'*; or

צַוָּר **tsavvâr** (Neh. 3 : 5), *tsav-vawr'*; or

צַוְּרֹן **tsavvârôn** (Cant. 4 : 9), *tsav-vaw-rone'*; or (fem.)

צַוָּארָה **tsavvâ'râh** (Mic. 2 : 3), *tsav-vaw-raw'*; intens. from 6696 in the sense of *binding*; the back of the *neck* (as that on which burdens are *bound*):—neck.

6678. צוֹבָא **Tsôwbâ'**, *tso-baw'*; or

צוֹבָה **Tsôwbâh**, *tso-baw'*; or

צֹבָה **Tsôbâh**, *tso-baw'*; from an unused root mean. to *station*; a *station*; *Zoba* or *Zobah*, a region of Syria:—Zoba, Zobah.

6679. צוּד **tsûwd**, *tsood*; a prim. root; to *lie* alongside (i.e. in wait); by impl. to *catch* an animal (fig. men); (denom. from. 6718) to *victual* (for a journey):—chase, hunt, sore, take (provision).

6680. צָוָה **tsâvâh**, *tsaw-vaw'*; a prim. root; (intens.) to *constitute*, *enjoin:*—appoint, (for-) bid, (give a) charge, (give a, give in, send with) command (-er, -ment), send a messenger, put, (set) in order.

6681. צָוַח **tsâvach**, *tsaw-vakh'*; a prim. root; to *screech* (exultingly):—shout.

6682. צְוָחָה **tsevâchâh**, *tsev-aw-khaw'*; from 6681; a *screech* (of anguish):—cry (-ing).

6683. צוּלָה **tsûwlâh**, *tsoo-law'*; from an unused root mean. to *sink*; an *abyss* (of the sea):—deep.

6684. צוּם **tsûwm**, *tsoom*; a prim. root; to *cover* over (the mouth), i.e. to *fast:*— × at all, fast.

6685. צוֹם **tsôwm**, *tsome*; or

צֹם **tsôm**, *tsome*; from 6684; a *fast:*—fast (-ing).

6686. צוּעָר **Tsûwʿâr**, *tsoo-awr'*; from 6819; *small; Tsuär*, an Isr.:—Zuar.

6687. צוּף **tsûwph**, *tsoof*; a prim. root; to *overflow:*—(make to over-) flow, swim.

6688. צוּף **tsûwph**, *tsoof*; from 6687; *comb* of honey (from *dripping*):—honeycomb.

6689. צוּף **Tsûwph**, *tsoof*; or

צוֹפַי **Tsôwphay**, *tso-fah'ee*; or

צִיף° **Tsîyph**, *tseef*; from 6688; *honey-comb; Tsuph* or *Tsophai* or *Tsiph*, the name of an Isr. and of a place in Pal.:—Zophai, Zuph.

6690. צוֹפַח **Tsôwphach**, *tso-fakh'*; from an unused root mean. to *expand, breadth; Tsophach*, an Isr.:—Zophah.

צוֹפַי **Tsôwphay.** See 6689.

6691. צוֹפַר **Tsôwphar**, *tso-far'*; from 6852; *departing; Tsophar*, a friend of Job:—Zophar.

6692. צוּץ **tsûwts**, *tsoots*; a prim. root; to *twinkle*, i.e. *glance;* by anal. to *blossom* (fig. *flourish*):—bloom, blossom, flourish, shew self.

6693. צוּק **tsûwq**, *tsook*; a prim. root; to *compress*, i.e. (fig.) *oppress, distress:*—constrain, distress, lie sore, (op-) press (-or), straiten.

6694. צוּק **tsûwq**, *tsook*; a prim. root [rather ident. with 6693 through the idea of *narrowness* (of orifice)]; to *pour out*, i.e. (fig.) *smelt, utter:*—be molten, pour.

6695. צוֹק **tsôwq**, *tsoke*; or (fem.)

צוּקָה **tsûwqâh**, *tsoo-kaw'*; from 6693; a *strait*, i.e. (fig.) *distress:*—anguish, × troublous.

6696. צוּר **tsûwr**, *tsoor*; a prim. root; to *cramp*, i.e. *confine* (in many applications, lit. and fig., formative or hostile):—adversary, assault, beset, besiege, bind (up), cast, distress, fashion, fortify, inclose, lay siege, put up in bags.

6697. צוּר **tsûwr**, *tsoor*; or

צֻר **tsûr**, *tsoor*; from 6696; prop. a *cliff* (or sharp rock, as *compressed*); gen. a *rock* or *boulder;* fig. a *refuge;* also an *edge* (as *precipitous*):—edge, × (mighty) God (one), rock, × sharp, stone, × strength, × strong. See also 1049.

6698. צוּר **Tsûwr**, *tsoor*; the same as 6697; *rock; Tsur*, the name of a Midianite and of an Isr.:—Zur.

צוֹר **Tsôwr.** See 6865.

צַוָּר **tsavvâr.** See 6677.

6699. צוּרָה **tsûwrâh**, *tsoo-raw'*; fem. of 6697; a *rock* (Job 28 : 10); also a *form* (as if *pressed* out):—form, rock.

צַוְּרֹן **tsavvârôn.** See 6677.

6700. צוּרִיאֵל **Tsûwrîyʾêl**, *tsoo-ree-ale'*; from 6697 and 410; *rock of God; Tsuriël*, an Isr.:—Zuriel.

6701. צוּרִישַׁדַּי **Tsûwrîyshadday**, *tsoo-ree-shad-dah'ee*; from 6697 and 7706; *rock of* (the) *Almighty; Tsurishaddai*, an Isr.:—Zurishaddai.

6702. צוּת **tsûwth**, *tsooth*; a prim. root; to *blaze:*—burn.

6703. צַח **tsach**, *tsakh*; from 6705; *dazzling*, i.e. *sunny, bright*, (fig.) *evident:*—clear, dry, plainly, white.

צִחָא **Tsîchâʾ.** See 6727.

6704. צִחֶה **tsicheh**, *tsee-kheh'*; from an unused root mean. to *glow; parched:*—dried up.

6705. צָחַח **tsâchach**, *tsaw-khakh'*; a prim. root; to *glare*, i.e. *be dazzling* white:—be whiter.

6706. צְחִיחַ **tsᵉchîyach**, *tsekh-ee'-akh*; from 6705; *glaring*, i.e. *exposed* to the bright sun:—higher place, top.

6707. צְחִיחָה **tsᵉchîychâh**, *tsekh-ee-khaw'*; fem. of 6706; a *parched* region, i.e. the *desert:*—dry land.

6708. צְחִיחִי° **tsᵉchîychîy**, *tsekh-ee-khee'*; from 6706; *bare spot*, i.e. in the *glaring* sun:—higher place.

6709. צַחֲנָה **tsachănâh**, *tsakh-an-aw'*; from an unused root mean. to *putrefy; stench:*—ill savour.

6710. צַחְצָחָה **tsachtsâchâh**, *tsakh-tsaw-khaw'*; from 6705; a *dry* place, i.e. *desert:*—drought.

6711. צָחַק **tsâchaq**, *tsaw-khak'*; a prim. root; to *laugh* outright (in merriment or scorn); by impl. to *sport:*—laugh, mock, play, make sport.

6712. צְחֹק **tsᵉchôq**, *tsekh-oke'*; from 6711; *laughter* (in pleasure or derision):—laugh (-ed to scorn).

6713. צַחַר **tsachar**, *tsakh'-ar*; from an unused root mean. to *dazzle; sheen*, i.e. *whiteness:*—white.

6714. צֹחַר **Tsôchar**, *tso'-khar*; from the same as 6713; *whiteness; Tsochar*, the name of a Hittite and of an Isr.:—Zohar. Comp. 3328.

6715. צָחֹר **tsâchôr**, *tsaw-khore'*; from the same as 6713; *white:*—white.

6716. צִי **tsîy**, *tsee*; from 6680; a *ship* (as a *fixture*):—ship.

6717. צִיבָא **Tsîybâʾ**, *tsee-baw'*; from the same as 6678; *station; Tsiba*, an Isr.:—Ziba.

6718. צַיִד **tsayid**, *tsah'-yid*; from a form of 6679 and mean. the same; the *chase;* also *game* (thus taken); (gen.) *lunch* (espec. for a journey):—× catcheth, food, × hunter, (that which he took in) hunting, venison, victuals.

6719. צַיָּד **tsayâd**, *tsah'-yawd*; from the same as 6718; a *huntsman:*—hunter.

6720. צֵידָה **tsêydâh**, *tsay-daw'*; or

צֵדָה **tsêdâh**, *tsay-daw'*; fem. of 6718; *food:*—meat, provision, venison, victuals.

6721. צִידוֹן **Tsîydôwn**, *tsee-done'*; or

צִידֹן **Tsîydôn**, *tsee-done'*; from 6679 in the sense of *catching* fish; *fishery; Tsidon*, the name of a son of Canaan, and of a place in Pal.:—Sidon, Zidon.

6722. צִידֹנִי (or צִדֹנִי°) **Tsîydônîy**, *tsee-do-nee'*; patrial from 6721; a *Tsidonian* or inhab. of Tsidon:—Sidonian, of Sidon, Zidonian.

6723. צִיָּה **tsîyâh**, *tsee-yaw'*; from an unused root mean. to *parch; aridity;* concr. a *desert:*—barren, drought, dry (land, place), solitary place, wilderness.

6724. צִיוֹן **tsîyôwn**, *tsee-yone'*; from the same as 6723; a *desert:*—dry place.

6725. צִיּוּן **tsiyûwn**, *tsee-yoon'*; from the same as 6723 in the sense of *conspicuousness* [comp. 5329]; a monumental or guiding *pillar:*—sign, title, waymark.

6726. צִיּוֹן **Tsîyôwn**, *tsee-yone'*; the same (reg.) as 6725; *Tsijon* (as a permanent *capital*), a mountain of Jerus.:—Zion.

6727. צִיחָא **Tsîychâʾ**, *tsee-khaw'*; or

צִחָא **Tsîchâʾ**, *tsee-khaw'*; as if fem. of 6704; *drought; Tsicha*, the name of two Nethinim:—Ziha.

6728. צִיִּי **tsîyîy**, *tsee-ee'*; from the same as 6723; a *desert-dweller*, i.e. *nomad* or wild *beast:*—wild beast of the desert, that dwell in (inhabiting) the wilderness.

6729. צִינֹק **tsîynôq**, *tsee-noke'*; from an unused root mean. to *confine;* the *pillory:*—stocks.

6730. צִיעֹר **Tsîyʿôr**, *tsee-ore'*; from 6819; *small; Tsior*, a place in Pal.:—Zior.

צִיף° **Tsîyph.** See 6689.

6731. צִיץ **tsîyts**, *tseets*; or

צִץ **tsits**, *tseets*; from 6692; prop. *glistening*, i.e. a burnished *plate;* also a *flower* (as *bright* colored); a *wing* (as *gleaming* in the air):—blossom, flower, plate, wing.

6732. צִיץ **Tsîyts**, *tseets*; the same as 6731; *bloom; Tsits*, a place in Pal.:—Ziz.

6733. צִיצָה **tsîytsâh**, *tsee-tsaw'*; fem. of 6731; a *flower:*—flower

6734. צִיצִת **tsîytsîth**, *tsee-tseeth'*; fem. of 6731; a *floral* or *wing*-like projection, i.e. a *fore-lock* of hair, a *tassel:*—fringe, lock.

צִיקְלַג **Tsîyqᵉlag.** See 6860.

6735. צִיר **tsîyr**, *tseer*; from 6696; a *hinge* (as *pressed* in turning); also a *throe* (as a phys. or mental *pressure*); also a *herald* or errand-doer (as *constrained* by the principal):—ambassador, hinge, messenger, pain, pang, sorrow. Comp. 6736.

6736. צִיר **tsîyr**, *tseer*; the same as 6735; a *form* (of beauty; as if *pressed* out, i.e. carved); hence an (idolatrous) *image:*—beauty, idol.

6737. צָיַר **tsâyar**, *tsaw-yar'*; a denom. from 6735 in the sense of *ambassador;* to *make an errand*, i.e. *betake* oneself:—make as if . . . had been ambassador.

6738. צֵל **tsêl**, *tsale*; from 6751; *shade*, whether lit. or fig.:—defence, shade (-ow).

6739. צְלָא **tsᵉlâʾ** (Chald.), *tsel-aw'*; prob. corresp. to 6760 in the sense of *bowing; pray:*—pray.

6740. צָלָה **tsâlâh**, *tsaw-law'*; a prim. root; to *roast:*—roast.

6741. צִלָּה **Tsillâh**, *tsil-law'*; fem. of 6738; *Tsillah*, an antediluvian woman:—Zillah.

6742. צְלוּל **tsᵉlûwl**, *tsel-ool'*; from 6749 in the sense of *rolling;* a (round or flattened) *cake:*—cake.

6743. צָלַח **tsâlach**, *tsaw-lakh'*; or

צָלֵחַ **tsâlêach**, *tsaw-lay'-akh*; a prim. root; to *push* forward, in various senses (lit. or fig., trans. or intrans.):—break out, come (mightily), go over, be good, be meet, be profitable, (cause to, effect, make to, send) prosper (-ity, -ous, -ously).

6744. צְלַח **tsᵉlach** (Chald.), *tsel-akh'*; corresp. to 6743; to *advance* (trans. or intrans.):—promote, prosper.

6745. צֵלָחָה **tsêlâchâh**, *tsay-law-khaw'*; from 6743; something *protracted* or *flattened* out, i.e. a *platter:*—pan.

6746. צְלֹחִית **tsᵉlôchîyth**, *tsel-o-kheeth'*; from 6743; something *prolonged* or tall, i.e. a *vial* or salt-*cellar:*—cruse.

6747. צַלַּחַת **tsallachath**, *tsal-lakh'-ath*; from 6743; something *advanced* or deep, i.e. a *bowl;* fig. the *bosom:*—bosom, dish.

6748. צָלִי **tsâlîy**, *tsaw-lee'*; pass. part. of 6740; *roasted:*—roast.

6749. צָלַל **tsâlal**, *tsaw-lal'*; a prim. root; prop. to *tumble* down, i.e. *settle* by a waving motion:—sink. Comp. 6750, 6751.

6750. צָלַל **tsâlal**, *tsaw-lal'*; a prim. root [rather ident. with 6749 through the idea of *vibration*]; to *tinkle*, i.e. *rattle* together (as the ears in *reddening* with shame, or the teeth in *chattering* with fear):—quiver, tingle.

6751. צָלַל **tsâlal**, *tsaw-lal'*; a prim. root [rather ident. with 6749 through the idea of *hovering* over (comp. 6754)]; to *shade*, as twilight or an opaque object:—begin to be dark, shadowing.

6752. צֵלֶל **tsêlel**, *tsay'-lel*; from 6751; *shade:*—shadow.

6753. צְלֶלְפּוֹנִי **Tsᵉlelpôwnîy**, *tsel-el-po-nee'*; from 6752 and the act. part. of 6437; *shade-facing; Tselelponi*, an Israelitess:—Hazelelponi [*includ. the art.*].

6754. צֶלֶם **tselem**, *tseh'-lem*; from an unused root mean. to *shade;* a *phantom*, i.e. (fig.) *illusion, resemblance;* hence a representative *figure*, espec. an *idol:*—image, vain shew.

6755. צֶלֶם **tselem** (Chald.), *tseh'-lem*; or

צְלֵם **tsᵉlem** (Chald.), *tsel-em'*; corresp. to 6754; an idolatrous *figure:*—form, image.

6756. צַלְמוֹן **Tsalmôwn**, *tsal-mone'*; from 6754; *shady; Tsalmon*, the name of a place in Pal. and of an Isr.:—Zalmon.

6757. צַלְמָוֶת **tsalmâveth**, *tsal-maw'-veth*; from 6738 and 4194; *shade of death*, i.e. the *grave* (fig. *calamity*):—shadow of death.

6758. צַלְמֹנָה **Tsalmônâh**, *tsal-mo-naw'*; fem. of 6757; *shadiness; Tsalmonah*, a place in the Desert:—Zalmonah.

6759. צַלְמֻנָּע **Tsalmunnâʻ,** *tsal-moon-naw'*; from 6738 and 4513; *shade has been denied*; Tsalmunna, a Midianite:—Zalmunna.

6760. צָלַע **tsâlaʻ,** *tsaw-lah'*; a prim. root: prob. to *curve*; used only as denom. from 6763, to *limp* (as if *one-sided*):—halt.

6761. צֶלַע **tselaʻ,** *tseh'-lah*; from 6760; a *limping* or *fall* (fig.):—adversity, halt (-ing).

6762. צֶלַע **Tselaʻ,** *tseh'-lah*; the same as 6761; Tsela, a place in Pal.:—Zelah.

6763. צֵלָע **tsêlâʻ,** *tsay-law'*; or (fem.)

צַלְעָה **tsalʻâh,** *tsal-aw'*; from 6760; a *rib* (as *curved*), lit. (of the body) or fig. (of a door, i.e. *leaf*); hence a *side*, lit. (of a person) or fig. (of an object or the sky, i.e. *quarter*): arch. a (espec. floor or ceiling) *timber* or *plank* (single or collect., i.e. a *flooring*):—beam, board, chamber, corner, leaf, plank, rib, side (chamber).

6764. צָלָף **Tsâlâph,** *tsaw-lawf'*; from an unused root of unknown mean.; Tsalaph, an Isr.:—Zalaph.

6765. צְלָפְחָד **Tseʻlophchâd,** *tsel-of-chawd'*; from the same as 6764 and 259; Tselophchad, an Isr.:—Zelophehad.

6766. צֶלְצַח **Tseltsach,** *tsel-tsakh'*; from 6738 and 6703; *clear shade*; Tseltsach, a place in Pal.:—Zelzah.

6767. צְלָצַל **tseʻlâtsal,** *tsel-aw-tsal'*; from 6750 redupl.; a *clatter*, i.e. (abstr.) *whirring* (of wings); (concr.) a *cricket*; also a *harpoon* (as *rattling*), a *cymbal* (as *clanging*):—cymbal, locust, shadowing, spear.

6768. צֶלֶק **Tseleq,** *tseh'-lek*; from an unused root mean. to *split*; *fissure*; Tselek, an Isr.:—Zelek.

6769. צִלְּתַי **Tsilleʻthay,** *tsil-leth-ah'ee*; from the fem. of 6738; *shady*; Tsillethai, the name of two Isr.:—Zilthai.

צֹם **tsôm.** See 6685.

6770. צָמֵא **tsâmêʼ,** *tsaw-may'*; a prim. root; to *thirst* (lit. or fig.):—(be a-, suffer) thirst (-y).

6771. צָמֵא **tsâmêʼ,** *tsaw-may'*; from 6770; *thirsty* (lit. or fig.):—(that) thirst (-eth, -y).

6772. צָמָא **tsâmâʼ,** *tsaw-maw'*; from 6770; *thirst* (lit. or fig.):—thirst (-y).

6773. צִמְאָה **tsimʼâh,** *tsim-aw'*; fem. of 6772; *thirst* (fig. of *libidinousnes*):—thirst.

6774. צִמָּאוֹן **tsimmâʼôwn,** *tsim-maw-one'*; from 6771; a *thirsty* place, i.e. *desert*:—drought, dry ground, thirsty land.

6775. צָמַד **tsâmad,** *tsaw-mad'*; a prim. root; to *link*, i.e. *gird*; fig. to *serve*, (mentally) *contrive*:—fasten, frame, join (self).

6776. צֶמֶד **tsemed,** *tseh'-med*; a *yoke* or *team* (i.e. *pair*); hence an *acre* (i.e. day's task for a yoke of cattle to plough):—acre, couple, × together, two [asses], yoke (of oxen).

6777. צַמָּה **tsammâh,** *tsam-maw'*; from an unused root mean. to *fasten on*; a *veil*:—locks.

6778. צַמּוּק **tsammûwq,** *tsam-mook'*; from 6784; a cake of *dried* grapes:—bunch (cluster) of raisins.

6779. צָמַח **tsâmach,** *tsaw-makh'*; a prim. root; to *sprout* (trans. or intrans., lit. or fig.):—bear, bring forth, (cause to, make to) bud (forth), (cause to, make to) grow (again, up), (cause to) spring (forth, up).

6780. צֶמַח **tsemach,** *tseh'-makh*; from 6779; a *sprout* (usually concr.), lit. or fig.:—branch, bud, that which (where) grew (upon), spring (-ing).

6781. צָמִיד **tsâmîyd,** *tsaw-meed'*; or

צָמִד **tsâmid,** *tsaw-meed'*; from 6775; a *bracelet* or *arm-clasp*; gen. a *lid*:—bracelet, covering.

6782. צַמִּים **tsammîym,** *tsam-meem'*; from the same as 6777; a *noose* (as *fastening*); fig. *destruction*:—robber.

6783. צְמִתֻת **tseʻmîythûth,** *tsem-ee-thooth'*; or

צְמִתֻת **tseʻmîthûth,** *tsem-ee-thooth'*; from 6789; *excision*, i.e. *destruction*; used only (adv.) with prep. pref. *to extinction*, i.e. *perpetually*:—ever.

6784. צָמַק **tsâmaq,** *tsaw-mak'*; a prim. root; to *dry* up:—dry.

6785. צֶמֶר **tsemer,** *tseh'-mer*; from an unused root prob. mean. to *be shaggy*; *wool*:—wool (-len).

6786. צְמָרִי **Tseʻmâriy,** *tsem-aw-ree'*; patrial from an unused name of a place in Pal.; a Tsemarite or branch of the Canaanites:—Zemarite.

6787. צְמָרַיִם **Tseʻmârayim,** *tsem-aw-rah'-yim*; dual of 6785; *double fleece*; Tsemarajim, a place in Pal.:—Zemaraim.

6788. צַמֶּרֶת **tsammereth,** *tsam-meh'-reth*; from the same as 6785; *fleeciness*, i.e. *foliage*:—highest branch, top.

6789. צָמַת **tsâmath,** *tsaw-math'*; a prim. root; to *extirpate* (lit. or fig.):—consume, cut off, destroy, vanish.

צְמִתֻת **tseʻmîthûth.** See 6783.

6790. צִן **Tsin,** *tseen*; from an unused root mean. to *prick*; a *crag*; Tsin, a part of the Desert:—Zin.

6791. צֵן **tsên,** *tsane*; from an unused root mean. to *be prickly*; a *thorn*; hence a *thorn-hedge*:—thorn.

6792. צֹנֵא **tsônêʼ,** *tso-nay'*; or

צֹנֶה **tsôneh,** *tso-neh'*; for 6629; a *flock*:—sheep.

6793. צִנָּה **tsinnâh,** *tsin-naw'*; fem. of 6791; a *hook* (as *pointed*); also a (large) *shield* (as if *guarding* by *prickliness*); also *cold* (as *piercing*):—buckler, cold, hook, shield, target.

6794. צִנּוֹר **tsinnûwr,** *tsin-noor'*; from an unused root perh. mean. to *be hollow*; a *culvert*:—gutter, water-spout.

6795. צָנַח **tsânach,** *tsaw-nakh'*; a prim. root; to *alight*; (trans.) to *cause to descend*, i.e. *drive down*:—fasten, light [from off].

6796. צָנִין **tsânîyn,** *tsaw-neen'*; or

צָנִן **tsânin,** *tsaw-neen'*; from the same as 6791; a *thorn*:—thorn.

6797. צָנִיף **tsânîyph,** *tsaw-neef'*; or

צָנוֹף **tsânôwph,** *tsaw-nofe'*; or (fem.)

צְנִיפָה **tseʻnîyphâh,** *tsaw-nee-faw'*; from 6801; a *head-dress* (i.e. piece of cloth *wrapped* around):—diadem, hood, mitre.

6798. צָנַם **tsânam,** *tsaw-nam'*; a prim. root; to *blast* or *shrink*:—withered.

6799. צְנָן **Tseʻnân,** *tsen-awn'*; prob. for 6630; Tsenan, a place near Pal.:—Zenan.

צָנִן **tsânin.** See 6796.

6800. צָנַע **tsânaʻ,** *tsaw-nah'*; a prim. root; to *humiliate*:—humbly, lowly.

6801. צָנַף **tsânaph,** *tsaw-naf'*; a prim. root; to *wrap*, i.e. *roll* or *dress*:—be attired, × surely, violently turn.

6802. צְנֵפָה **tseʻnêphâh,** *tsen-ay-faw'*; from 6801; a *ball*:—× toss.

6803. צִנְצֶנֶת **tsintseneth,** *tsin-tseh'-neth*; from the same as 6791; a *vase* (prob. a vial *tapering* at the top):—pot.

6804. צַנְתָּרָה **tsantârâh,** *tsan-taw-raw'*; prob. from the same as 6794; a *tube*:—pipe.

6805. צָעַד **tsâʻad,** *tsaw-ad'*; a prim. root; to *pace*, i.e. *step* regularly; (upward) to *mount*; (along) to *march*; (down and caus.) to *hurl*:—bring, go, march (through), run over.

6806. צַעַד **tsaʻad,** *tsah'-ad*; from 6804; a *pace* or *regular step*:—pace, step.

6807. צְעָדָה **tseʻâdâh,** *tseh-aw-daw'*; fem. of 6806; a *march*; (concr.) an (ornamental) *ankle-chain*:—going, ornament of the legs.

6808. צָעָה **tsâʻâh,** *tsaw-aw'*; a prim. root; to *tip* over (for the purpose of *spilling* or *pouring* out), i.e. (fig.) *depopulate*; by impl. to *impri-*

son or *conquer*; (reflex.) to *lie down* (for coition):—captive exile, travelling, (cause to) wander (-er).

צָעוֹר **tsâʻôwr.** See 6810.

6809. צָעִיף **tsâʻîyph,** *tsaw-eef'*; from an unused root mean. to *wrap* over; a *veil*:—vail.

6810. צָעִיר **tsâʻîyr,** *tsaw-eer'*; or

צָעוֹר **tsâʻôwr,** *tsaw-ore'*; from 6819; *little*; (in number) *few*; (in age) *young*, (in value) *ignoble*:—least, little (one), small (one), + young (-er, -est).

6811. צָעִיר **Tsâʻîyr,** *tsaw-eer'*; the same as 6810; Tsair, a place in Idumæa:—Zair.

6812. צְעִירָה **tseʻîyrâh,** *tseh-ee-raw'*; fem. of 6810; *smallness* (of age), i.e. *juvenility*:—youth.

6813. צָעַן **tsâʻan,** *tsaw-an'*; a prim. root; to *load* up (beasts), i.e. *migrate*:—be taken down.

6814. צֹעַן **Tsôʻan,** *tso'-an*; of Eg. der.; Tsoän, a place in Eg.:—Zoan.

6815. צַעֲנַנִּים **Tsaʻ ănannîym,** *tsah-an-an-neem'*; or (dual)

צַעֲנַיִם **Tsaʻ ănayim,** *tsah-an-ah'-yim*; plur. from 6813; *removals*; Tsaananim or Tsaanajim, a place in Pal.:—Zaannannim, Zaanaim.

6816. צַעְצֻעַ **tsaʻtsûaʻ,** *tsah-tsoo-ah'*; from an unused root mean. to *bestrew* with carvings; *sculpture*:—image [work].

6817. צָעַק **tsâʻaq,** *tsaw-ak'*; a prim. root; to *shriek*; (by impl.) to *proclaim* (an assembly):—× at all, call together, cry (out), gather (selves) (together).

6818. צַעֲקָה **tsaʻ ăqâh,** *tsah-ak-aw'*; from 6817; a *shriek*:—cry (-ing).

6819. צָעַר **tsâʻar,** *tsaw-ar'*; a prim. root; to *be small*, i.e. (fig.) *ignoble*:—be brought low, little one, be small.

6820. צֹעַר **Tsôʻar,** *tso'-ar*; from 6819; *little*; Tsoär, a place E. of the Jordan:—Zoar.

6821. צָפַד **tsâphad,** *tsaw-fad'*; a prim. root; to *adhere*:—cleave.

6822. צָפָה **tsâphâh,** *tsaw-faw'*; a prim. root; prop. to *lean forward*, i.e. to *peer into* the distance; by impl. to *observe*, *await*:—behold, espy, look up (well), wait for, (keep the) watch (-man).

6823. צָפָה **tsâphâh,** *tsaw-faw'*; a prim. root [prob. rather ident. with 6822 through the idea of *expansion* in outlook transf. to *act*]; to *sheet* over (espec. with metal):—cover, overlay.

6824. צָפָה **tsâphâh,** *tsaw-faw'*; from 6823; an *inundation* (as *covering*):—× swimmest.

6825. צְפוֹ **Tsephôw,** *tsef-o'*; or

צְפִי **Tsephîy,** *tsef-ee'*; from 6822; *observant*; Tsepho or Tsephi, an Idumæan:—Zephi, Zepho.

6826. צִפּוּי **tsippûwy,** *tsip-poo'ee*; from 6823; *encasement* (with metal)·—covering, overlaying.

6827. צְפוֹן **Tsephôwn,** *tsef-one'*; prob. for 6837; Tsephon, an Isr.:—Zephon.

6828. צָפוֹן **tsâphôwn,** *tsaw-fone'*; or

צָפֹן **tsâphôn,** *tsaw-fone'*; from 6845; prop. *hidden*, i.e. *dark*; used only of the *north* as a quarter (*gloomy* and *unknown*):—north (-ern, side, -ward, wind).

6829. צָפוֹן **Tsâphôwn,** *tsaw-fone'*; the same as 6828; *boreal*; Tsaphon, a place in Pal.:—Zaphon.

6830. צְפוֹנִי **tseʻphôwnîy,** *tsef-o-nee'*; from 6828; *northern*:—northern.

6831. צְפוֹנִי **Tseʻphôwnîy,** *tsef-o-nee'*; patron. from 6827; a Tsephonite, or (collect.) descend. of Tsephon:—Zephonites.

6832. צְפוּעַ **tseʻphûwaʻ,** *tsef-oo'-ah*; from the same as 6848; *excrement* (as *protruded*):—dung.

6833. צִפּוֹר **tsippôwr,** *tsip-pore'*; or

צִפֹּר **tsippôr,** *tsip-pore'*; from 6852; a little *bird* (as *hopping*):—bird, fowl, sparrow.

6834. צִפּוֹר **Tsippôwr**, *tsip-pore'*; the same as 6833; *Tsippor*, a Moabite:—Zippor.

6835. צַפַּחַת **tsappachath**, *tsap-pakh'-ath*; from an unused root mean. to *expand*; a *saucer* (as *flat*):—cruse.

6836. צְפִיָּה **tsephîyâh**, *tsef-ee-yaw'*; from 6822; *watchfulness*:—watching.

6837. צִפְיוֹן **Tsiphyôwn**, *tsif-yone'*; from 6822; *watch*-tower; *Tsiphjon*, an Isr.:—Ziphion. Comp. 6827.

6838. צַפִּיחִת **tsappîychîth**, *tsap-pee-kheeth'*; from the same as 6835; a flat thin *cake*:—wafer.

6839. צֹפִים **Tsôphîym**, *tso-feem'*; plur. of act. part. of 6822; *watchers*; *Tsophim*, a place E. of the Jordan:—Zophim.

6840. צָפִין° **tsâphîyn**, *tsaw-feen'*; from 6845; a *treasure* (as *hidden*):—hid.

6841. צְפִיר **tsephîyr** (Chald.), *tsef-eer'*; corresp. to 6842; a he-*goat*:—he [goat].

6842. צָפִיר **tsâphîyr**, *tsaw-feer'*; from 6852; a male *goat* (as *prancing*):—(he) goat.

6843. צְפִירָה **tsephîyrâh**, *tsef-ee-raw'*; fem. formed like 6842; a *crown* (as *encircling* the head); also a *turn* of affairs (i.e. *mishap*):—diadem, morning.

6844. צָפִית **tsâphîyth**, *tsaw-feeth'*; from 6822; a *sentry*:—watchtower.

6845. צָפַן **tsâphan**, *tsaw-fan'*; a prim. root; to *hide* (by *covering* over); by impl. to *hoard* or *reserve*; fig. to *deny*; spec. (favorably) to *protect*, (unfavorably) to *lurk*:—esteem, hide (-den one, self), lay up, lurk (be set) privily, (keep) secret (-ly, place).

צָפֹן **tsâphôn**. See 6828.

6846. צְפַנְיָה **Tsephanyâh**, *tsef-an-yaw'*; or

צְפַנְיָהוּ **Tsephanyâhûw**, *tsef-an-yaw'-hoo*; from 6845 and 3050; *Jah has secreted*; *Tsephanjah*, the name of four Isr.:—Zephaniah.

6847. צָפְנַת פַּעְנֵחַ **Tsophnath Paʻnêach**, *tsof-nath' pah-nay'-akh*; of Eg. der.; *Tsophnath-Paneäch*, Joseph's Eg. name:—Zaphnath-paaneah.

6848. צֶפַע **tsephaʻ**, *tseh'-fah*; or

צִפְעֹנִי **tsiphʻônîy**, *tsif-o-nee'*; from an unused root mean. to *extrude*; a *viper* (as *thrusting* out the tongue, i.e. *hissing*):—adder, cockatrice.

6849. צְפִעָה **tsephîʻâh**, *tsef-ee-aw'*; fem. from the same as 6848; an *outcast* thing:—issue.

צִפְעֹנִי **tsiphʻônîy**. See 6848.

6850. צָפַף **tsâphaph**, *tsaw-faf'*; a prim. root; to *coo* or *chirp* (as a bird):—chatter, peep, whisper.

6851. צַפְצָפָה **tsaphtsâphâh**, *tsaf-tsaw-faw'*; from 6687; a *willow* (as growing in *overflowed* places):—willow tree.

6852. צָפַר **tsâphar**, *tsaw-far'*; a prim. root; to *skip* about, i.e. *return*:—depart early.

6853. צְפַר **tsephar** (Chald.), *tsef-ar'*; corresp. to 6833; a *bird*.—bird.

צִפֹּר **tsippôr**. See 6833.

6854. צְפַרְדֵּעַ **tsephardêaʻ**, *tsef-ar-day'-ah*; from 6852 and a word elsewhere unused mean. a *swamp*; a *marsh-leaper*, i.e. *frog*:—frog.

6855. צִפֹּרָה **Tsippôrâh**, *tsip-po-raw'*; fem. of 6833; *bird*; *Tsipporah*, Moses' wife:—Zipporah.

6856. צִפֹּרֶן **tsippôren**, *tsip-po'-ren*; from 6852 (in the denom. sense [from 6833] of *scratching*); prop. a *claw*, i.e. (human) *nail*; also the *point* of a style (or pen, tipped with adamant):—nail, point.

6857. צְפַת **Tsephath**, *tsef-ath'*; from 6822; *watch*-tower; *Tsephath*, a place in Pal.:—Zephath.

6858. צֶפֶת **tsepheth**, *tseh'-feth*; from an unused root mean. to *encircle*; a *capital* of a column:—chapiter.

6859. צְפָתָה **Tsephâthâh**, *tsef-aw'-thaw*; the same as 6857; *Tsephathah*, a place in Pal.:—Zephathah.

צִץ **tsîts**. See 6732.

6860. צִקְלַג **Tsiqlâg**, *tsik-lag'*; or

צִיקְלַג **Tsîyqelag** (1 Chron. 12 : 1, 20), *tsee-kel-ag'*; of uncert. der.; *Tsiklag* or *Tsikelag*, a place in Pal.:—Ziklag.

6861. צִקְלֹן **tsiqlôn**, *tsik-lone'*; from an unused root mean. to *wind*; a *sack* (as *tied* at the mouth):—husk.

6862. צַר **tsar**, *tsar*; or

צָר **tsâr**, *tsawr*; from 6887; *narrow*; (as a noun) a *tight* place (usually fig., i.e. *trouble*); also a *pebble* (as in 6864); (trans.) an *opponent* (as *crowding*):—adversary, afflicted (-tion), anguish, close, distress, enemy, flint, foe, narrow, small, sorrow, strait, tribulation, trouble.

6863. צֵר **Tsêr**, *tsare*; from 6887; *rock*; *Tser*, a place in Pal.:—Zer.

6864. צֹר **tsôr**, *tsore*; from 6696; a *stone* (as if *pressed* hard or to a point); (by impl. of use) a *knife*:—flint, sharp stone.

6865. צֹר **Tsôr**, *tsore*; or

צוֹר **Tsôwr**, *tsore*; the same as 6864; a *rock*; *Tsor*, a place in Pal.:—Tyre, Tyrus.

צֻר **tsûr**. See 6697.

6866. צָרַב **tsârab**, *tsaw-rab'*; a prim. root; to *burn*:—burn.

6867. צָרֶבֶת **tsârebeth**, *tsaw-reh'-beth*; from 6866; *conflagration* (of fire or disease):—burning, inflammation.

6868. צְרֵדָה **Tserêdâh**, *tser-ay-daw'*; or

צְרֵדָתָה **Tserêdâthâh**, *tser-ay-daw'-thaw*; appar. from an unused root mean. to *pierce*; *puncture*; *Tseredah*, a place in Pal.:—Zereda, Zeredathah.

6869. צָרָה **tsârâh**, *tsaw-raw'*; fem. of 6862; *tightness* (i.e. fig. *trouble*); trans. a female *rival*:—adversary, adversity, affliction, anguish, distress, tribulation, trouble.

6870. צְרוּיָה **Tserûwyâh**, *tser-oo-yaw'*; fem. part. pass. from the same as 6875; *wounded*; *Tserujah*, an Israelitess:—Zeruiah.

6871. צְרוּעָה **Tserûwʻâh**, *tser-oo-aw'*; fem. pass. part. of 6879; *leprous*; *Tseruäh*, an Israelitess:—Zeruah.

6872. צְרוֹר **tserôwr**, *tser-ore'*; or (shorter)

צְרֹר **tserôr**, *tser-ore'*; from 6887; a *parcel* (as *packed* up); also a *kernel* or *particle* (as if a *package*):—bag, × bendeth, bundle, least grain, small stone.

6873. צָרַח **tsârach**, *tsaw-rakh'*; a prim. root; to *be clear* (in tone, i.e. *shrill*), i.e. to *whoop*:—cry, roar.

6874. צְרִי **Tserîy**, *tser-ee'*; the same as 6875; *Tseri*, an Isr.:—Zeri. Comp. 3340.

6875. צְרִי **tserîy**, *tser-ee'*; or

צֳרִי **tsŏrîy**, *tsor-ee'*; from an unused root mean. to *crack* [as by *pressure*], hence to *leak*; *distillation*, i.e. *balsam*:—balm.

6876. צֹרִי **Tsôrîy**, *tso-ree'*; patrial from 6865; a *Tsorite* or inhab. of Tsor (i.e. *Syrian*):—(man) of Tyre.

6877. צְרִיחַ **tserîyach**, *tser-ee'-akh*; from 6873 in the sense of *clearness* of vision; a *citadel*:—high place, hold.

6878. צֹרֶךְ **tsôrek**, *tso'-rek*; from an unused root mean. to *need*; *need*:—need.

6879. צָרַע **tsâraʻ**, *tsaw-rah'*; a prim. root; to *scourge*, i.e. (intrans. and fig.) to *be stricken with leprosy*:—leper, leprous.

6880. צִרְעָה **tsirʻâh**, *tsir-aw'*; from 6879; a *wasp* (as *stinging*):—hornet.

6881. צָרְעָה **Tsorʻâh**, *tsor-aw'*; appar. another form for 6880; *Tsorah*, a place in Pal.:—Zareah, Zorah, Zoreah.

6882. צָרְעִי **Tsorʻîy**, *tsor-ee'*; or

צָרְעָתִי **Tsorʻâthîy**, *tsor-aw-thee'*; patrial from 6881; a *Tsorite* or *Tsorathite*, i.e. inhab. of Tsorah:—Zorites, Zareathites, Zorathites.

6883. צָרַעַת **tsâraʻath**, *tsaw-rah'-ath*; from 6879; *leprosy*:—leprosy.

6884. צָרַף **tsâraph**, *tsaw-raf'*; a prim. root; to *fuse* (metal), i.e. *refine* (lit. or fig.):—cast, (re-) fine (-er), founder, goldsmith, melt, pure, purge away, try.

6885. צֹרְפִי **Tsôrephîy**, *tso-ref-ee'*; from 6884; *refiner*; *Tsorephi* (with the art.), an Isr.:—goldsmith's.

6886. צָרְפַת **Tsârephath**, *tsaw-ref-ath'*; from 6884; *refinement*; *Tsarephath*, a place in Pal.:—Zarephath.

6887. צָרַר **tsârar**, *tsaw-rar'*; a prim. root; to *cramp*, lit. or fig., trans. or intrans. (as follows):—adversary, (be in) afflict (-ion), besiege, bind (up), (be in, bring) distress, enemy, narrower, oppress, pangs, shut up, be in a strait (trouble), vex.

6888. צְרֵרָה **Tserêrâh**, *tser-ay-raw'*; appar. by erroneous transcription for 6868; *Tsererah* for *Tseredah*:—Zererath.

6889. צֶרֶת **Tsereth**, *tseh'-reth*; perh. from 6671; *splendor*; *Tsereth*, an Isr.:—Zereth.

6890. צֶרֶת הַשַּׁחַר **Tsereth hash-Shachar**, *tseh'-reth hash-shakh'-ar*; from the same as 6889 and 7837 with the art. interposed; *splendor of the dawn*; *Tsereth-hash-Shachar*, a place in Pal.:—Zareth-shahar.

6891. צָרְתָן **Tsârethân**, *tsaw-reth-awn'*; perh. for 6868; *Tsarethan*, a place in Pal.:—Zarthan.

ק

6892. קֵא **qêʼ**, *kay*; or

קִיא **qîyʼ**, *kee*; from 6958; *vomit*:—vomit.

6893. קָאַת **qâʼath**, *kaw-ath'*; from 6958; prob. the *pelican* (from *vomiting*):—cormorant.

6894. קַב **qab**, *kab*; from 6895; a *hollow*, i.e. vessel used as a (dry) *measure*:—cab.

6895. קָבַב **qâbab**, *kaw-bab'*; a prim. root; to *scoop* out, i.e. (fig.) to *malign* or *execrate* (i.e. *stab* with words):— × at all, curse.

6896. קֵבָה **qêbâh**, *kay-baw'*; from 6895; the *paunch* (as a *cavity*) or first stomach of ruminants:—maw.

6897. קֹבָה **qôbâh**, *ko'-baw*; from 6895; the *abdomen* (as a cavity):—belly.

6898. קֻבָּה **qubbâh**, *koob-baw'*; from 6895; a *pavilion* (as a domed *cavity*):—tent.

6899. קִבּוּץ **qibbûwts**, *kib-boots'*; from 6908; a *throng*:—company.

6900. קְבוּרָה **qebûwrâh**, *keb-oo-raw'*; or

קְבֻרָה **qebûrâh**, *keb-oo-raw'*; fem. pass. part. of 6912; *sepulture*; (concr.) a *sepulchre*:—burial, burying place, grave, sepulchre.

6901. קָבַל **qâbal**, *kaw-bal'*; a prim. root; to *admit*, i.e. *take* (lit. or fig.):—choose, (take) hold, receive, (under-) take.

6902. קְבַל **qebal** (Chald.), *keb-al'*; corresp. to 6901; to *acquire*:—receive, take.

6903. קְבֵל **qebêl** (Chald.), *keb-ale'*; or

קֳבֵל **qŏbêl** (Chald.), *kob-ale'*; corresp. to 6905; (adv.) *in front of*; usually (with other particles) *on account of*, *so as*, *since*, *hence*:—+ according to, + as, + because, before, + for this cause, + forasmuch as, + by this means, over against, by reason of, + that, + therefore, + though, + wherefore.

6904. קֹבֶל **qôbel**, *ko'-bel*; from 6901 in the sense of *confronting* (as standing *opposite* in order to receive); a *battering*-ram:—war.

6905. קָבָל **qâbâl**, *kaw-bawl'*; from 6901 in the sense of *opposite* [see 6904]; the *presence*, i.e. (adv.) *in front of*:—before.

6906. קָבַע **qâbaʻ**, *kaw-bah'*; a prim. root; to *cover*, i.e. (fig.) *defraud*:—rob, spoil.

6907. קֻבַּעַת **qubbaʻath**, *koob-bah'-ath;* from 6906; a *goblet* (as deep like a *cover*):—dregs.

6908. קָבַץ **qâbats**, *kaw-bats';* a prim. root; to *grasp*, i.e. *collect:*—assemble (selves), gather (bring) (together, selves together, up), heap, resort, × surely, take up.

6909. קַבְצְאֵל **Qabtseʼêl**, *kab-tseh-ale';* from 6908 and 410; *God has gathered; Kabtseël*, a place in Pal.:—Kabzeel. Comp. 3343.

6910. קְבֻצָה **qebûtsâh**, *keb-oo-tsaw';* fem. pass. part. of 6908; a *hoard:*— × gather.

6911. קִבְצַיִם **Qibtsayim**, *kib-tsah'-yim;* dual from 6908; a *double heap; Kibtsajim*, a place in Pal.:—Kibzaim.

6912. קָבַר **qâbar**, *kaw-bar';* a prim. root; to *inter:*— × in any wise, bury (-ier).

6913. קֶבֶר **qeber**, *keh'-ber;* or (fem.)

קִבְרָה **qibrâh**, *kib-raw';* from 6912; a *sepulchre:*—burying place, grave, sepulchre.

קְבֻרָה **qebûrâh**. See 6900.

6914. קִבְרוֹת הַתַּאֲוָה **Qibrôwth hat-Taʼăvâh**, *kib-rōth' hat-tah-av-aw';* from the fem. plur. of 6913 and 8378 with the art. interposed; *graves of the longing; Kibroth-hat-Taavh*, a place in the Desert:—Kibroth-hattaavah.

6915. קָדַד **qâdad**, *kaw-dad';* a prim. root; to *shrivel* up, i.e. *contract* or *bend* the body (or neck) in deference:—bow (down) (the) head, stoop.

6916. קִדָּה **qiddâh**, *kid-daw';* from 6915; *cassia* bark (as in *shrivelled* rolls):—cassia.

6917. קָדוּם **qâdûwm**, *kaw-doom';* pass. part. of 6923; a *pristine* hero:—ancient.

6918. קָדוֹשׁ **qâdôwsh**, *kaw-doshe';* or

קָדֹשׁ **qâdôsh**, *kaw-doshe';* from 6942; *sacred* (ceremonially or morally); (as noun) *God* (by eminence), an *angel*, a *saint*, a *sanctuary:*—holy (One), saint.

6919. קָדַח **qâdach**, *kaw-dakh';* a prim. root to *inflame:*—burn, kindle.

6920. קַדַּחַת **qaddachath**, *kad-dakh'-ath;* from 6919; *inflammation*, i.e. febrile disease:—burning ague, fever.

6921. קָדִים **qâdîym**, *kaw-deem';* or

קָדִם **qâdîm**, *kaw-deem';* from 6923; the *fore* or front part; hence (by orientation) the *East* (often adv. *eastward*, for brevity the *east wind*):—east (-ward, wind).

6922. קַדִּישׁ **qaddîysh** (Chald.), *kad-deesh';* corresp. to 6918.—holy (One), saint.

6923. קָדַם **qâdam**, *kaw-dam';* a prim. root; to *project* (one self), i.e. *precede;* hence to *anticipate, hasten, meet* (usually for help):—come (go, [flee]) before, + disappoint, meet, prevent.

6924. קֶדֶם **qedem**, *keh'-dem;* or

קֵדְמָה **qêdmâh**, *kayd'-maw;* from 6923; the *front*, of place (absol. the *fore part*, rel. the *East*) or time (*antiquity*); often used adv. (*before, anciently, eastward*):—aforetime, ancient (time), before, east (end, part, side, -ward), eternal, × ever (-lasting), forward, old, past. Comp. 6926.

6925. קֳדָם **qŏdâm** (Chald.), *kod-awm';* or

קְדָם **qedâm** (Chald.) (Dan. 7 : 13), *ked-awm';* corresp. to 6924; *before:*—before, × from, × I (thought), × me, + of, × it pleased, presence.

קָדִם **qâdîm**. See 6921.

6926. קִדְמָה **qidmâh**, *kid-maw';* fem. of 6924; the *forward* part (or rel.) *East* (often adv. *on the east* or *in front*):—east (-ward).

6927. קַדְמָה **qadmâh**, *kad-maw';* from 6923; *priority* (in time); also used adv. (*before*):—afore, antiquity, former (old) estate.

6928. קַדְמָה **qadmâh** (Chald.), *kad-maw';* corresp. to 6927; *former* time:—afore [-time], ago.

קֵדְמָה **qêdmâh**. See 6924.

6929. קֵדְמָה **Qêdemâh**, *kayd'-maw;* from 6923; *precedence; Kedemah*, a son of Ishmael:—Kedemah.

6930. קַדְמוֹן **qadmôwn**, *kad-mone';* from 6923; *eastern:*—east.

6931. קַדְמוֹנִי **qadmôwnîy**, *kad-mo-nee';* or

קַדְמֹנִי **qadmônîy**, *kad-mo-nee';* from 6930; (of time) *anterior* or (of place) *oriental:*—ancient, they that went before, east, (thing of) old.

6932. קְדֵמוֹת **Qedêmôwth**, *ked-ay-mothe';* from 6923; *beginnings; Kedemoth*, a place in eastern Pal.:—Kedemoth.

6933. קַדְמַי **qadmay** (Chald.), *kad-mah'ee;* from a root corresp. to 6923; *first:*—first.

6934. קַדְמִיאֵל **Qadmîyʼêl**, *kad-mee-ale';* from 6924 and 410; *presence of God; Kadmiël*, the name of three Isr.:—Kadmiel.

קַדְמֹנִי **qadmônîy**. See 6931.

6935. קַדְמֹנִי **Qadmônîy**, *kad-mo-nee';* the same as 6931; *ancient*, i.e. aboriginal; *Kadmonite* (collect.), the name of a tribe in Pal.:—Kadmonites.

6936. קָדְקֹד **qodqôd**, *kod-kode';* from 6915; the *crown* of the head (as the part most *bowed*):—crown (of the head), pate, scalp, top of the head.

6937. קָדַר **qâdar**, *kaw-dar';* a prim. root; to *be ashy*, i.e. *dark*-colored; by impl. to *mourn* (in sackcloth or sordid garments):—be black (-ish), be (make) dark (-en), × heavily, (cause to) mourn.

6938. קֵדָר **Qêdâr**, *kay-dawr';* from 6937; *dusky* (of the skin or the tent); *Kedar*, a son of Ishmael; also (collect.) *bedawin* (as his descendants or representatives):—Kedar.

6939. קִדְרוֹן **Qidrôwn**, *kid-rone';* from 6937; *dusky* place; *Kidron*, a brook near Jerus.:—Kidron.

6940. קַדְרוּת **qadrûwth**, *kad-rooth';* from 6937; *duskiness:*—blackness.

6941. קְדֹרַנִּית **qedôranniyth**, *ked-o-ran-neeth';* adv. from 6937; *blackish ones* (i.e. *in sackcloth*); used adv. in *mourning* weeds:—mournfully.

6942. קָדַשׁ **qâdâsh**, *kaw-dash';* a prim. root; to *be* (causat. *make, pronounce* or *observe* as) *clean* (ceremonially or morally):—appoint, bid, consecrate, dedicate, defile, hallow, (be, keep) holy (-er, place), keep, prepare, proclaim, purify, sanctify (-ied one, self), × wholly.

6943. קֶדֶשׁ **Qedesh**, *keh'-desh;* from 6942; a *sanctum; Kedesh*, the name of four places in Pal.:—Kedesh.

6944. קֹדֶשׁ **qôdesh**, *ko'-desh;* from 6942; a *sacred* place or thing; rarely abstr. *sanctity:*—consecrated (thing), dedicated (thing), hallowed (thing), holiness, (× most) holy (× day, portion, thing), saint, sanctuary.

6945. קָדֵשׁ **qâdêsh**, *kaw-dashe';* from 6942; a (quasi) *sacred* person, i.e. (techn.) a (male) *devotee* (by prostitution) to licentious idolatry:—sodomite, unclean.

6946. קָדֵשׁ **Qâdêsh**, *kaw-dashe';* the same as 6945; *sanctuary; Kadesh*, a place in the Desert:—Kadesh. Comp. 6947.

קָדֹשׁ **qâdôsh**. See 6918.

6947. קָדֵשׁ בַּרְנֵעַ **Qâdêsh Barnêaʻ**, *kaw-dashe' bar-nay'-ah;* from the same as 6946 and an otherwise unused word (appar. compounded of a correspondent to 1251 and a deriv. of 5128) mean. *desert of a fugitive; Kadesh of* (the) *Wilderness of Wandering; Kadesh-Barneä*, a place in the Desert:—Kadesh-barnea.

6948. קְדֵשָׁה **qedêshâh**, *ked-ay-shaw';* fem. of 6945; a female *devotee* (i.e. *prostitute*):—harlot, whore.

6949. קָהָה **qâhâh**, *kaw-haw';* a prim. root; to be *dull:*—be set on edge, be blunt.

6950. קָהַל **qâhal**, *kaw-hal';* a prim. root; to *convoke:*—assemble (selves) (together), gather (selves) (together).

6951. קָהָל **qâhâl**, *kaw-hawl';* from 6950; *assemblage* (usually concr.):—assembly, company, congregation, multitude.

6952. קְהִלָּה **qehillâh**, *keh-hil-law';* from 6950; an *assemblage:*—assembly, congregation.

6953. קֹהֶלֶת **qôheleth**, *ko-heh'-leth;* fem. of act. part. from 6950; a (female) *assembler* (i.e. lecturer); abstr. *preaching* (used as a "nom de plume", *Koheleth*):—preacher.

6954. קְהֵלָתָה **Qehêlâthâh**, *keh-hay-law'-thaw;* from 6950; *convocation; Kehelathah*, a place in the Desert:—Kehelathah.

6955. קְהָת **Qehâth**, *keh-hawth';* from an unused root mean. to *ally* oneself; *allied; Kehath*, an Isr.:—Kohath.

6956. קֳהָתִי **Qŏhâthîy**, *ko-haw-thee';* patron. from 6955; a *Kohathite* (collect.) or desc. of Kehath:—Kohathites.

6957. קַו **qav**, *kav;* or

קָו **qâv**, *kawv;* from 6960 [comp. 6961]; a *cord* (as *connecting*), espec. for measuring; fig. a *rule;* also a *rim*, a musical *string* or *accord:*—line. Comp. 6978.

6958. קוֹא **qôwʼ**, *ko;* or

קָיָה **qâyâh** (Jer. 25 : 27), *kaw-yaw';* a prim. root; to *vomit:*—spue (out), vomit (out, up, up again).

6959. קוֹבַע **qôwbaʻ**, *ko'-bah* or *ko-bah';* a form collat. to 3553; a *helmet:*—helmet.

6960. קָוָה **qâvâh**, *kaw-vaw';* a prim. root; to *bind* together (perh. by *twisting*), i.e. *collect;* (fig.) to *expect:*—gather (together), look, patiently, tarry, wait (for, on, upon).

6961. קָוֶה° **qâveh**, *kaw-veh';* from 6960; a (measuring) *cord* (as if for *binding*):—line.

קוֹחַ **qôwach**. See 6495.

6962. קוּט **qûwṭ**, *koot;* a prim. root; prop. to *cut off*, i.e. (fig.) *detest:*—be grieved, lothe self.

6963. קוֹל **qôwl**, *kole;* or

קֹל **qôl**, *kole;* from an unused root mean. to *call* aloud; a *voice* or *sound:*— + aloud, bleating, crackling, cry (+ out), fame, lightness, lowing, noise, + hold peace, [pro-] claim, proclamation, + sing, sound, + spark, thunder (-ing), voice, + yell.

6964. קוֹלָיָה **Qôwlâyâh**, *ko-law-yaw';* from 6963 and 3050; *voice of Jah; Kolajah*, the name of two Isr.:—Kolaiah.

6965. קוּם **qûwm**, *koom;* a prim. root; to *rise* (in various applications, lit., fig., intens. and caus.):—abide, accomplish, × be clearer, confirm, continue, decree, × be dim, endure, × enemy, enjoin, get up, make good, help, hold, (help to) lift up (again), make, × but newly, ordain, perform, pitch, raise (up), rear (up), remain, (a-) rise (up) (again, against), rouse up, set (up), (e-) stablish, (make to) stand (up), stir up, strengthen, succeed, (as-, make) sure (-ly), (be) up (-hold, -rising).

6966. קוּם **qûwm** (Chald.), *koom;* corresp. to 6965:—appoint, establish, make, raise up self, (a-) rise (up), (make to) stand, set (up).

6967. קוֹמָה **qôwmâh**, *ko-maw';* from 6965; *height:*— × along, height, high, stature, tall.

6968. קוֹמְמִיּוּת **qôwmemîyûwth**, *ko-mem-ee-yooth';* from 6965; *elevation*, i.e. (adv.) *erectly* (fig.):—upright.

6969. קוּן **qûwn**, *koon;* a prim. root; to *strike* a musical note, i.e. *chant* or *wail* (at a funeral):—lament, mourning woman.

6970. קוֹעַ **Qôwaʻ**, *ko'-ah;* prob. from 6972 in the orig. sense of *cutting* off; *curtailment; Koä*, a region of Bab.:—Koa.

6971. קוֹף **qôwph**, *kofe;* or

קֹף **qôph**, *kofe;* prob. of for. or.; a *monkey:*—ape.

6972. קוּץ **qûwts**, *koots;* a prim. root; to *clip* off; used only as denom. from 7019; to *spend the harvest* season:—summer.

6973. קוּץ **qûwts**, *koots;* a prim. root [rather ident. with 6972 through the idea of *severing* oneself from (comp. 6962)]; to be (caus. *make*) *dis-*

gusted or *anxious:*—abhor, be distressed, be grieved, loathe, vex, be weary.

6974. קוּץ **qûwts**, *koots;* a prim. root [rather ident. with 6972 through the idea of *abruptness* in starting up from sleep (comp. 3364)]; to *awake* (lit. or fig.):—arise, (be) (a-) wake, watch.

6975. קוֹץ **qôwts**, *kotse;* or

קֹץ **qôts**, *kotse;* from 6972 (in the sense of *pricking*); a *thorn:*—thorn.

6976. קוֹץ **Qôwts**, *kotse;* the same as 6975; *Kots*, the name of two Isr.:—Koz, Hakkoz [*includ. the art.*].

6977. קְוֻצָּה **qᵉvutstsâh**, *kev-oots-tsaw';* fem. pass. part. of 6972 in its orig. sense; a *forelock* (as *shorn*):—lock.

6978. קַו־קַו **qav-qav**, *kav-kav';* from 6957 (in the sense of a *fastening*); *stalwart:*—× meted out.

6979. קוּר **qûwr**, *koor;* a prim. root; to *trench;* by impl. to *throw forth;* also (denom. from 7023) to *wall up*, whether lit. (to *build* a wall) or fig. (to *estop*):—break down, cast out, destroy, dig.

6980. קוּר **qûwr**, *koor;* from 6979; (only plur.) *trenches*, i.e. a *web* (as if so formed):—web.

6981. קוֹרֵא **Qôwrê'**, *ko-ray';* or

קֹרֵא **Qôrê'** (1 Chron. 26 : 1), *ko-ray';* act. part. of 7121; *crier; Korè*, the name of two Isr.:—Kore.

6982. קוֹרָה **qôwrâh**, *ko-raw';* or

קֹרָה **qôrâh**, *ko-raw';* from 6979; a *rafter* (forming *trenches* as it were); by impl. a *roof:*—beam, roof.

6983. קוֹשׁ **qôwsh**, *koshe;* a prim. root; to *bend;* used only as denom. for 3369, to *set a trap:*—lay a snare.

6984. קוּשָׁיָהוּ **qûwshâyâhûw**, *koo-shaw-yaw'-hoo;* from the pass. part. of 6983 and 3050; *entrapped of Jah; Kushajah*, an Isr.:—Kushaiah.

6985. קַט **qaṭ**, *kat;* from 6990 in the sense of *abbreviation;* a *little*, i.e. (adv.) *merely:*—very.

6986. קֶטֶב **qeṭeb**, *keh'-teb;* from an unused root mean. to *cut* off; *ruin:*—destroying, destruction.

6987. קֹטֶב **qôṭeb**, *ko'-teb;* from the same as 6986; *extermination:*—destruction.

6988. קְטוֹרָה **qᵉṭôwrâh**, *ket-o-raw';* from 6999; *perfume:*—incense.

6989. קְטוּרָה **Qᵉṭûwrâh**, *ket-oo-raw';* fem. pass. part. of 6999; *perfumed; Keturah*, a wife of Abraham:—Keturah.

6990. קָטַט **qâṭaṭ**, *kaw-tat';* a prim. root; to *clip* off, i.e. (fig.) *destroy:*—be cut off.

6991. קָטַל **qâṭal**, *kaw-tal';* a prim. root; prop. to *cut off*, i.e. (fig.) *put to death:*—kill, slay.

6992. קְטַל **qᵉṭal** (Chald.), *ket-al';* corresp. to 6991; to *kill:*—slay.

6993. קֶטֶל **qeṭel**, *keh'-tel;* from 6991; a violent *death:*—slaughter.

6994. קָטֹן **qâṭôn**, *kaw-tone';* a prim. root [rather denom. from 6996]; to *diminish*, i.e. *be* (caus. *make*) *diminutive* or (fig.) *of no account:*—be a (make) small (thing), be not worthy.

6995. קֹטֶן **qôṭen**, *ko'-ten;* from 6994; a *pettiness*, i.e. the *little finger:*—little finger.

6996. קָטָן **qâṭân**, *kaw-tawn';* or

קָטֹן **qâṭôn**, *kaw-tone';* from 6962; *abbreviated*, i.e. *diminutive*, lit. (in quantity, size or number) or fig. (in age or importance):—least, less (-ser), little (one), small (-est, one, quantity, thing), young (-er, -est).

6997. קָטָן **Qâṭân**, *kaw-tawn';* the same as 6996; *small; Katan*, an Isr.:—Hakkatan [*includ. the art.*].

6998. קָטַף **qâṭaph**, *kaw-taf';* a prim. root; to *strip* off:—crop off, cut down (up), pluck.

6999. קָטַר **qâṭar**, *kaw-tar';* a prim. root [rather ident. with 7000 through the idea of fumigation in a *close* place and perh. thus *driving* out the occupants]; to *smoke*, i.e. turn into fragrance by fire (espec. as an act of worship):—burn (incense, sacrifice) (upon), (altar for) incense, kindle, offer (incense, a sacrifice).

7000. קָטַר **qâṭar**, *kaw-tar';* a prim. root; to *inclose:*—join.

7001. קְטַר **qᵉṭar** (Chald.), *ket-ar';* from a root corresp. to 7000; a *knot* (as *tied* up), i.e. (fig.) a *riddle;* also a *vertebra* (as if a knot):—doubt, joint.

7002. קִטֵּר **qiṭṭêr**, *kit-tare';* from 6999; *perfume:*—incense.

7003. קִטְרוֹן **Qiṭrôwn**, *kit-rone';* from 6999; *fumigative; Kitron*, a place in Pal.:—Kitron.

7004. קְטֹרֶת **qᵉṭôreth**, *ket-o'-reth;* from 6999; a *fumigation:*—(sweet) incense, perfume.

7005. קַטָּת **Qaṭṭâth**, *kat-tawth';* from 6996; *littleness, Kattath*, a place in Pal.:—Kattath.

7006. קָיָה **qâyâh**, *kaw-yaw';* a prim. root; to *vomit:*—spue.

7007. קַיִט **qâyiṭ** (Chald.), *kah'-yit;* corresp. to 7019; *harvest:*—summer.

7008. קִיטוֹר **qîyṭôwr**, *kee-tore';* or

קִיטֹר **qîyṭôr**, *kee-tore';* from 6999; a *fume*, i.e. *cloud:*—smoke, vapour.

7009. קִים **qîym**, *keem;* from 6965; an *opponent* (as *rising* against one), i.e. (collect.) enemies:—substance.

7010. קְיָם **qᵉyâm** (Chald.), *keh-yawm';* from 6966; an *edict* (as *arising* in law):—decree, statute.

7011. קַיָּם **qayâm** (Chald.), *kah-yawm';* from 6966; *permanent* (as *rising* firmly):—stedfast, sure.

7012. קִימָה **qîymâh**, *kee-maw';* from 6965; an *arising:*—rising up.

קִימוֹשׁ **Qîymôwsh**. See 7057.

7013. קַיִן **qayin**, *kah'-yin;* from 6969 in the orig. sense of *fixity;* a *lance* (as *striking fast*):—spear.

7014. קַיִן **Qayin**, *kah'-yin;* the same as 7013 (with a play upon the affinity to 7069); *Kajin*, the name of the first child, also of a place in Pal., and of an Oriental tribe:—Cain, Kenite (-s).

7015. קִינָה **qîynâh**, *kee-naw';* from 6969; a *dirge* (as accompanied by *beating* the breasts or on instruments):—lamentation.

7016. קִינָה **Qîynâh**, *kee-naw';* the same as 7015; *Kinah*, a place in Pal.:—Kinah.

7017. קֵינִי **Qêyniy**, *kay-nee';* or

קִינִי **Qîyniy** (1 Chron. 2 : 55), *kee-nee';* patron. from 7014; a *Kenite* or member of the tribe of Kajin:—Kenite.

7018. קֵינָן **Qêynân**, *kay-nawn';* from the same as 7064; *fixed; Kenan*, an antediluvian:—Cainan, Kenan.

7019. קַיִץ **qayits**, *kah'-yits;* from 6972; *harvest* (as the *crop*), whether the product (grain or fruit) or the (dry) season:—summer (fruit, house).

7020. קִיצוֹן **qîytsôwn**, *kee-tsone';* from 6972; *terminal:*—out- (utter-) most.

7021. קִיקָיוֹן **qîyqâyôwn**, *kee-kaw-yone';* perh. from 7006; the *gourd* (as *nauseous*):—gourd.

7022. קִיקָלוֹן **qîyqâlôwn**, *kee-kaw-lone';* from 7036; intense *disgrace:*—shameful spewing.

7023. קִיר **qîyr**, *keer;* or

קִר **qîr** (Isa. 22 : 5), *keer;* or (fem.)

קִירָה **qîyrâh**, *kee-raw';* from 6979; a *wall* (as built in a *trench*):— + mason, side, town, × very, wall.

7024. קִיר **Qîyr**, *keer;* the same as 7023; *fortress; Kir*, a place in Ass.; also one in Moab:—Kir. Comp. 7025.

7025. קִיר חֶרֶשׂ **Qîyr Cheres**, *keer kheh'-res;* or (fem. of the latter word)

קִיר חֲרֶשֶׂת **Qîyr Chăreseth**, *keer khar-eh'-seth;* from 7023 and 2789; *fortress of earthenware; Kir-Cheres* or *Kir-Chareseth*, a place in Moab:—Kir-haraseth, Kir-hareseth, Kir-haresh, Kir-heres.

7026. קֵירֹס **Qêyrôç**, *kay-roce';* or

קֵרֹס **Qêrôç**, *kay-roce';* from the same as 7166; *ankled; Keros*, one of the Nethinim:—Keros.

7027. קִישׁ **Qîysh**, *keesh;* from 6983; a *bow; Kish*, the name of five Isr.:—Kish.

7028. קִישׁוֹן **Qîyshôwn**, *kee-shone';* from 6983; *winding; Kishon*, a river of Pal.:—Kishon, Kison.

7029. קִישִׁי **Qîyshîy**, *kee-shee';* from 6983; *bowed; Kishi*, an Isr.:—Kishi.

7030. קִיתָרֹס° **qîythârôç** (Chald.), *kee-thaw-roce';* of Gr. origin (κίθαρις); a *lyre:*—harp.

7031. קַל **qal**, *kal;* contr. from 7043; *light;* (by impl.) *rapid* (also adv.):—light, swift (-ly).

7032. קָל **qâl** (Chald.), *kawl;* corresp. to 6963:—sound, voice.

קֹל **qôl**. See 6963.

7033. קָלָה **qâlâh**, *kaw-law';* a prim. root [rather ident. with 7034 through the idea of *shrinkage* by heat]; to *toast*, i.e. *scorch* partially or slowly:—dried, loathsome, parch, roast.

7034. קָלָה **qâlâh**, *kaw-law';* a prim. root; to *be light* (as implied in *rapid* motion), but fig. only (*be* [caus. *hold*] *in contempt*):—base, contemn, despise, lightly esteem, set light, seem vile.

7035. קָלַהּ° **qâlahh**, *kaw-lah';* for 6950; to *assemble:*—gather together.

7036. קָלוֹן **qâlôwn**, *kaw-lone';* from 7034; *disgrace;* (by impl.) the *pudenda:*—confusion, dishonour, ignominy, reproach, shame.

7037. קַלַּחַת **qallachath**, *kal-lakh'-ath;* appar. but a form for 6747; a *kettle:*—caldron.

7038. קָלַט **qâlaṭ**, *kaw-lat';* a prim. root; to *maim:*—lacking in his parts.

7039. קָלִי **qâlîy**, *kaw-lee';* or

קָלִיא **qâlîy'**, *kaw-lee';* from 7033; *roasted* ears of grain:—parched corn.

7040. קַלַּי **Qallay**, *kal-lah'ee;* from 7043; *frivolous; Kallai*, an Isr.:—Kallai.

7041. קֵלָיָה **Qêlâyâh**, *kay-law-yaw';* from 7034; *insignificance; Kelajah*, an Isr.:—Kelaiah.

7042. קְלִיטָא **Qᵉlîyṭâ'**, *kel-ee-taw';* from 7038; *maiming; Kelita*, the name of three Isr.:—Kelita.

7043. קָלַל **qâlal**, *kaw-lal';* a prim. root; to *be* (caus. *make*) *light*, lit. (*swift, small, sharp*, etc.) or fig. (*easy, trifling, vile*, etc.):—abate, make bright, bring into contempt, (ac-) curse, despise, (be) ease (-y, -ier), (be a, make, make somewhat, move, seem a, set) light (-en, -er, -ly, -ly afflict, -ly esteem, thing), × slight [-ly], be swift (-er), (be, be more, make, re-) vile, whet.

7044. קָלָל **qâlâl**, *kaw-lawl';* from 7043; *brightened* (as if *sharpened*):—burnished, polished.

7045. קְלָלָה **qᵉlâlâh**, *kel-aw-law';* from 7043; *vilification:*—(ac-) curse (-d, -ing).

7046. קָלַס **qâlaç**, *kaw-las';* a prim. root; to *disparage*, i.e. ridicule:—mock, scoff, scorn.

7047. קֶלֶס **qeleç**, *keh'-les;* from 7046; a *laughing-stock:*—derision.

7048. קַלָּסָה **qallâçâh**, *kal-law-saw';* intens. from 7046; *ridicule:*—mocking.

7049. קָלַע **qâlaʽ**, *kaw-lah';* a prim. root; to *sling;* also to *carve* (as if a *circular* motion, or into *light* forms):—carve, sling (out).

7050. קֶלַע **qelaʽ**, *keh'-lah;* from 7049; a *sling;* also a (door) *screen* (as if *slung* across), or the *valve* (of the door) itself:—hanging, leaf, sling.

7051. קַלָּע **qallâʽ**, *kal-law';* intens. from 7049; a *slinger:*—slinger.

7052. קְלֹקֵל **qᵉlôqêl**, *kel-o-kale'*; from 7043; *insubstantial*:—light.

7053. קִלְּשׁוֹן **qillᵉshôwn**, *kil-lesh-one'*; from an unused root mean. to *prick*; a *prong*, i.e. hay-fork:—fork.

7054. קָמָה **qâmâh**, *kaw-maw'*; fem. of act. part. of 6965; something that *rises*, i.e. a *stalk* of grain:—(standing) corn, grown up, stalk.

7055. קְמוּאֵל **Qᵉmûw'êl**, *kem-oo-ale'*; from 6965 and 410; *raised of God*; *Kemuël*, the name of a relative of Abraham, and of two Isr.:—Kemuel.

7056. קָמוֹן **Qâmôwn**, *kaw-mone'*; from 6965; an *elevation*; *Kamon*, a place E. of the Jordan:—Camon.

7057. קִמּוֹשׁ **qimmôwsh**, *kim-moshe'*; or

קִימוֹשׁ **qîymôwsh**, *kee-moshe'*; from an unused root mean. to *sting*; a *prickly* plant:—nettle. Comp. 7063.

7058. קֶמַח **qemach**, *keh'-makh*; from an unused root prob. mean. to *grind*; *flour*:—flour, meal.

7059. קָמַט **qâmaṭ**, *kaw-mat'*; a prim. root; to *pluck*, i.e. destroy:—cut down, fill with wrinkles.

7060. קָמַל **qâmal**, *kaw-mal'*; a prim. root; to *wither*:—hew down, wither.

7061. קָמַץ **qâmats**, *kaw-mats'*; a prim. root; to *grasp* with the hand:—take an handful

7062. קֹמֶץ **qômets**, *ko'-mets*; from 7061; a *grasp*, i.e. *handful*:—handful.

7063. קִמָּשׁוֹן **qimmâshôwn**, *kim-maw-shone'*; from the same as 7057; a *prickly* plant:—thorn.

7064. קֵן **qên**, *kane*; contr. from 7077; a *nest* (as *fixed*), sometimes includ. the *nestlings*; fig. a *chamber* or *dwelling*:—nest, room.

7065. קָנָא **qânâ'**, *kaw-naw'*; a prim. root; to *be* (caus. *make*) *zealous*, i.e. (in a bad sense) *jealous* or *envious*:—(be) envy (-ious), be (move to, provoke to) jealous (-y), × very, (be) zeal (-ous).

7066. קְנָא **qᵉnâ'** (Chald.), *ken-aw'*; corresp. to 7069; to *purchase*:—buy.

7067. קַנָּא **qannâ'**, *kan-naw'*; from 7065; *jealous*:—jealous. Comp. 7072.

7068. קִנְאָה **qin'âh**, *kin-aw'*; from 7065; *jealousy* or *envy*:—envy (-ied), jealousy, × sake, zeal.

7069. קָנָה **qânâh**, *kaw-naw'*; a prim. root; to *erect*, i.e. *create*; by extens. to *procure*, espec. by purchase (caus. *sell*); by impl. to *own*:—attain, buy (-er), teach to keep cattle, get, provoke to jealousy, possess (-or), purchase, recover, redeem, × surely, × verily.

7070. קָנֶה **qâneh**, *kaw-neh'*; from 7069; a *reed* (as *erect*); by resemblance a *rod* (espec. for measuring), *shaft*, *tube*, *stem*, the *radius* (of the arm), *beam* (of a steelyard):—balance, bone, branch, calamus, cane, reed, × spearman, stalk.

7071. קָנָה **Qânâh**, *kaw-naw'*; fem. of 7070; *reediness*; *Kanah*, the name of a stream and of a place in Pal.:—Kanah.

7072. קַנּוֹא **qannôw'**, *kan-no'*; for 7067; *jealous* or *angry*:—jealous.

7073. קְנַז **Qᵉnaz**, *ken-az'*; prob. from an unused root mean. to *hunt*; *hunter*; *Kenaz*, the name of an Edomite and of two Isr.:—Kenaz.

7074. קְנִזִּי **Qᵉnizzîy**, *ken-iz-zee'*; patron. from 7073; a *Kenizzite* or desc. of Kenaz:—Kenezite, Kenizzites.

7075. קִנְיָן **qinyân**, *kin-yawn'*; from 7069; *creation*, i.e. (concr.) *creatures*; also *acquisition*, *purchase*, *wealth*:—getting, goods, × with money, riches, substance.

7076. קִנָּמוֹן **qinnâmôwn**, *kin-naw-mone'*; from an unused root (mean. to *erect*); *cinnamon* bark (as in *upright* rolls):—cinnamon.

7077. קָנַן **qânan**, *kaw-nan'*; a prim. root; to *erect*; but used only as denom. from 7064; to *nestle*, i.e. *build* or *occupy* as a nest:—make . . . nest.

7078. קֶנֶץ **qenets**, *keh'-nets*; from an unused root prob. mean. to *wrench*; *perversion*:—end.

7079. קְנָת **Qᵉnâth**, *ken-awth'*; from 7069; *possession*; *Kenath*, a place E. of the Jordan:—Kenath.

7080. קָסַם **qâçam**, *kaw-sam'*; a prim. root; prop. to *distribute*, i.e. *determine* by lot or magical scroll; by impl. to *divine*:—divine (-r, -ation), prudent, soothsayer, use [divination].

7081. קֶסֶם **qeçem**, *keh'-sem*; from 7080; a *lot*; also *divination* (includ. its *fee*), *oracle*:—(reward of) divination, divine sentence, witchcraft.

7082. קָסַס **qâçaç**, *kaw-sas'*; a prim. root; to *lop* off:—cut off.

7083. קֶסֶת **qeçeth**, *keh'-seth*; from the same as 3563 (or as 7185); prop. a *cup*, i.e. an *ink-stand*:—inkhorn.

7084. קְעִילָה **Qᵉʻîylâh**, *keh-ee-law'*; perh. from 7049 in the sense of *inclosing*; *citadel*; *Keïlah*, a place in Pal.:—Keilah.

7085. קַעֲקַע **qaʻăqaʻ**, *kah-ak-ah'*; from the same as 6970; an *incision* or gash:—+ mark.

7086. קְעָרָה **qᵉʻârâh**, *keh-aw-raw'*; prob. from 7167; a *bowl* (as *cut* out hollow):—charger, dish.

קֹף **qôph**. See 6971.

7087. קָפָא **qâphâ'**, *kaw-faw'*; a prim. root; to *shrink*, i.e. *thicken* (as unracked wine, curdled milk, clouded sky, frozen water):—congeal, curdle, dark°, settle.

7088. קָפַד **qâphad**, *kaw-fad'*; a prim. root; to *contract*, i.e. roll together:—cut off.

7089. קְפָדָה **qᵉphâdâh**, *kef-aw-daw'*; from 7088; *shrinking*, i.e. terror:—destruction.

7090. קִפּוֹד **qippôwd**, *kip-pode'*; or

קִפֹּד **qippôd**, *kip-pode'*; from 7088; a species of bird, perh. the *bittern* (from its *contracted* form):—bittern.

7091. קִפּוֹז **qippôwz**, *kip-poze'*; from an unused root mean. to *contract*, i.e. *spring* forward; an *arrow-snake* (as *darting* on its prey):—great owl.

7092. קָפַץ **qâphats**, *kaw-fats'*; a prim. root; to *draw together*, i.e. close; by impl. to *leap* (by *contracting* the limbs); spec. to *die* (from *gathering* up the feet):—shut (up), skip, stop, take out of the way.

7093. קֵץ **qêts**, *kates*; contr. from 7112; an *extremity*; adv. (with prep. pref.) *after*:—+ after, (utmost) border, end, [in-] finite, × process.

קֹץ **qôts**. See 6975.

7094. קָצַב **qâtsab**, *kaw-tsab'*; a prim. root; to *clip*, or (gen.) *chop*:—cut down, shorn.

7095. קֶצֶב **qetseb**, *keh'-tseb*; from 7094; *shape* (as if *cut* out); *base* (as if there *cut* off):—bottom, size.

7096. קָצָה **qâtsâh**, *kaw-tsaw'*; a prim. root; to *cut* off; (fig.) to *destroy*; (partially) to *scrape* off:—cut off, cut short, scrape (off).

7097. קָצֶה **qâtseh**, *kaw-tseh'*; or (neg. only)

קֵצֶה **qêtseh**, *kay'-tseh*; from 7096; an *extremity* (used in a great variety of applications and idioms; comp. 7093):—× after, border, brim, brink, edge, end, [in-] finite, frontier, outmost coast, quarter, shore, (out-) side, × some, ut (-ter-) most (part).

7098. קָצָה **qâtsâh**, *kaw-tsaw'*; fem. of 7097; a *termination* (used like 7097):—coast, corner, (selv-) edge, lowest, (uttermost) part.

7099. קֶצֶו **qetsev**, *keh'-tsev*; and (fem.)

קִצְוָה **qitsvâh**, *kits-vaw'*; from 7096; a *limit* (used like 7097, but with less variety):—end, edge, uttermost part.

7100. קֶצַח **qetsach**, *keh'-tsakh*; from an unused root appar. mean. to *incise*; *fennel-flower* (from its *pungency*):—fitches.

7101. קָצִין **qâtsîyn**, *kaw-tseen'*; from 7096 in the sense of *determining*; a *magistrate* (as *deciding*) or other *leader*:—captain, guide, prince, ruler. Comp. 6278.

7102. קְצִיעָה **qᵉtsîyʻâh**, *kets-ee-aw'*; from 7106; *cassia* (as *peeled*; plur. the *bark*):—cassia.

7103. קְצִיעָה **Qᵉtsîyʻâh**, *kets-ee-aw'*; the same as 7102; *Ketsiah*, a daughter of Job:—Kezia.

7104. קְצִיץ **Qᵉtsîyts**, *kets-eets'*; from 7112; *abrupt*; *Keziz*, a valley in Pal.:—Keziz.

7105. קָצִיר **qâtsîyr**, *kaw-tseer'*; from 7114; *severed*, i.e. *harvest* (as *reaped*), the crop, the time, the reaper, or fig.; also a *limb* (of a tree, or simply *foliage*):—bough, branch, harvest (man).

7106. קָצַע **qâtsaʻ**, *kaw-tsah'*; a prim. root; to *strip* off, i.e. (partially) *scrape*; by impl. to *segregate* (as an angle):—cause to scrape, corner.

7107. קָצַף **qâtsaph**, *kaw-tsaf'*; a prim. root; to *crack* off, i.e. (fig.) *burst* out in rage:—(be) anger (-ry), displease, fret self, (provoke to) wrath (come), be wroth.

7108. קְצַף **qᵉtsaph** (Chald.), *kets-af'*; corresp. to 7107; to *become enraged*:—be furious.

7109. קְצַף **qᵉtsaph** (Chald.), *kets-af'*; from 7108; *rage*:—wrath.

7110. קֶצֶף **qetseph**, *keh'-tsef*; from 7107; a *splinter* (as *chipped* off); fig. *rage* or *strife*:—foam, indignation, × sore, wrath.

7111. קְצָפָה **qᵉtsâphâh**, *kets-aw-faw'*; from 7107; a *fragment*:—bark [-ed].

7112. קָצַץ **qâtsats**, *kaw-tsats'*; a prim. root; to *chop* off (lit. or fig.):—cut (asunder, in pieces, in sunder, off), × utmost.

7113. קְצַץ **qᵉtsats** (Chald.), *kets-ats'*; corresp. to 7112:—cut off.

7114. קָצַר **qâtsar**, *kaw-tsar'*; a prim. root; to *dock* off, i.e. *curtail* (trans. or intrans., lit. or fig.); espec. to *harvest* (grass or grain):—× at all, cut down, much discouraged, grieve, harvestman, lothe, mourn, reap (-er), (be, wax) short (-en, -er), straiten, trouble, vex.

7115. קֹצֶר **qôtser**, *ko'-tser*; from 7114; *shortness* (of spirit), i.e. impatience:—anguish.

7116. קָצֵר **qâtsêr**, *kaw-tsare'*; from 7114; *short* (whether in size, number, life, strength or temper):—few, hasty, small, soon.

7117. קְצָת **qᵉtsâth**, *kets-awth'*; from 7096; a *termination* (lit. or fig.); also (by impl.) a *portion*; adv. (with prep. pref.) *after*:—end, part, × some.

7118. קְצָת **qᵉtsâth** (Chald.), *kets-awth'*; corresp. to 7117:—end, partly.

7119. קַר **qar**, *kar*; contr. from an unused root mean. to *chill*; *cool*; fig. *quiet*:—cold, excellent [*from the marg.*].

קִר **qîr**. See 7023.

7120. קֹר **qôr**, *kore*; from the same as 7119; *cold*:—cold.

7121. קָרָא **qârâ'**, *kaw-raw'*; a prim. root [rather ident. with 7122 through the idea of *accosting* a person met]; to *call* out to (i.e. prop. *address* by name, but used in a wide variety of applications):—bewray [self], that are bidden, call (for, forth, self, upon), cry (unto), (be) famous, guest, invite, mention, (give) name, preach, (make) proclaim (-ation), pronounce, publish, read, renowned, say.

7122. קָרָא **qârâ'**, *kaw-raw'*; a prim. root; to *encounter*, whether accidentally or in a hostile manner:—befall, (by) chance, (cause to) come (upon), fall out, happen, meet.

7123. קְרָא **qᵉrâ'** (Chald.), *ker-aw'*; corresp. to 7121:—call, cry, read.

7124. קֹרֵא **qôrê'**, *ko-ray'*; prop. act. part. of 7121; a *caller*, i.e. *partridge* (from its *cry*):—partridge. See also 6981.

7125. קִרְאָה **qîr'âh**, *keer-aw'*; from 7122; an *encountering*, accidental, friendly or hostile (also adv. *opposite*):—× against (he come), help, meet, seek, × to, × in the way.

7126. קָרַב **qârab**, *kaw-rab'*; a prim. root; to *approach* (caus. *bring near*) for whatever purpose:—(cause to) approach, (cause to) bring (forth, near), (cause to) come (near, nigh), (cause to) draw near (nigh), go (near), be at hand, join, be near, offer, present, produce, make ready, stand, take.

7127. קְרֵב **qᵉrêb** (Chald.), *ker-abe';* corresp. to 7126:—approach, come (near, nigh), draw near.

7128. קְרָב **qᵉrâb**, *ker-awb';* from 7126; hostile *encounter:*—battle, war.

7129. קְרָב **qᵉrâb** (Chald.), *ker-awb';* corresp. to 7128:—war.

7130. קֶרֶב **qereb**, *keh'-reb;* from 7126; prop. the *nearest* part, i.e. the *centre*, whether lit., fig. or adv. (espec. with prep.):— × among, × before, bowels, × unto charge, + eat (up), × heart, × him, × in, inward (× -ly, part, -s, thought), midst, + out of, purtenance, × therein, × through, × within self.

7131. קָרֵב **qârêb**, *kaw-rabe';* from 7126; *near:*—approach, come (near, nigh), draw near.

קָרֹב **qârôb**. See 7138.

7132. קְרָבָה **qᵉrâbâh**, *ker-aw-baw';* from 7126; *approach:*—approaching, draw near.

7133. קׇרְבָּן **qorbân**, *kor-bawn';* or

קֻרְבָּן **qurbân**, *koor-bawn';* from 7126; something *brought near* the altar, i.e. a sacrificial *present:*—oblation, that is offered, offering.

7134. קַרְדֹּם **qardôm**, *kar-dome';* perh. from 6923 in the sense of *striking* upon; an *axe:*—ax.

7135. קָרָה **qârâh**, *kaw-raw';* fem. of 7119; *coolness:*—cold.

7136. קָרָה **qârâh**, *kaw-raw';* a prim. root; to *light upon* (chiefly by accident); caus. to *bring about;* spec. to *impose* timbers (for roof or floor):—appoint, lay (make) beams, befall, bring, come (to pass unto), floor, [hap] was, happen (unto), meet, send good speed.

7137. קָרֶה **qâreh**, *kaw-reh';* from 7136; an (unfortunate) *occurrence*, i.e. some accidental (ceremonial) *disqualification:*—uncleanness that chanceth.

קֹרָה **qôrâh**. See 6982.

7138. קָרוֹב **qârôwb**, *kaw-robe';* or

קָרֹב **qârôb**, *kaw-robe';* from 7126; *near* (in place, kindred or time):—allied, approach, at hand, + any of kin, kinsfolk (-sman), (that is) near (of kin), neighbour, (that is) next, (them that come) nigh (at hand), more ready, short (-ly).

7139. קָרַח **qârach**, *kaw-rakh';* a prim. root; to *depilate:*—make (self) bald.

7140. קֶרַח **qerach**, *keh'-rakh;* or

קֹרַח **qôrach**, *ko'-rakh;* from 7139; *ice* (as if bald, i.e. *smooth*); hence, *hail;* by resemblance, rock *crystal:*—crystal, frost, ice.

7141. קֹרַח **Qôrach**, *ko'-rakh;* from 7139; *ice; Korach*, the name of two Edomites and three Isr.:—Korah.

7142. קֵרֵחַ **qêrêach**, *kay-ray'-akh;* from 7139; *bald* (on the back of the head):—bald (head).

7143. קָרֵחַ **Qârêach**, *kaw-ray'-akh;* from 7139; *bald; Kareäch*, an Isr.:—Careah, Kareah.

7144. קׇרְחָה **qorchâh**, *kor-khaw';* or

קׇרְחָא **qorchâ'** (Ezek. 27 : 31), *kor-khaw';* from 7139; *baldness:*—bald (-ness), × utterly.

7145. קׇרְחִי **Qorchîy**, *kor-khee';* patron. from 7141; a *Korchite* (collect.) or desc. of Korach:—Korahite, Korathite, sons of Kore, Korhite.

7146. קָרַחַת **qârachath**, *kaw-rakh'-ath;* from 7139; a *bald* spot (on the back of the head); fig. a *threadbare* spot (on the back side of the cloth):—bald head, bare within.

7147. קְרִי **qᵉrîy**, *ker-ee';* from 7136; hostile *encounter:*—contrary.

7148. קָרִיא **qârîy'**, *kaw-ree';* from 7121; *called*, i.e. *select:*—famous, renowned.

7149. קִרְיָא **qiryâ'** (Chald.), *keer-yaw';* or

קִרְיָה **qiryâh** (Chald.), *keer-yaw';* corresp. to 7151:—city.

7150. קְרִיאָה **qᵉrîy'âh**, *ker-ee-aw';* from 7121; a *proclamation:*—preaching.

7151. קִרְיָה **qiryâh**, *kir-yaw';* from 7136 in the sense of *flooring*, i.e. building; a *city:*—city.

7152. קְרִיּוֹת **Qᵉrîyôwth**, *ker-ee-yōth';* plur. of 7151; *buildings; Kerioth*, the name of two places in Pal.:—Kerioth, Kirioth.

7153. קִרְיַת אַרְבַּע **Qiryath 'Arba'**, *keer-yath' ar-bah';* or (with the art. interposed)

קִרְיַת הָאַרְבַּע **Qiryath hâ-'Arba'** (Neh. 11 : 25), *keer-yath' haw-ar-bah';* from 7151 and 704 or 702; *city of Arba*, or *city of the four* (giants); *Kirjath-Arba* or *Kirjath-ha-Arba*, a place in Pal.:—Kirjath-arba.

7154. קִרְיַת בַּעַל **Qiryath Ba'al**, *keer-yath' bah'-al;* from 7151 and 1168; *city of Baal; Kirjath-Baal*, a place in Pal.:—Kirjath-baal.

7155. קִרְיַת חֻצוֹת **Qiryath Chûtsôwth**, *keer-yath' khoo-tsōth';* from 7151 and the fem. plur. of 2351; *city of streets; Kirjath-Chutsoth*, a place in Moab:—Kirjath-huzoth.

7156. קִרְיָתַיִם **Qiryâthayim**, *keer-yaw-thah'-yim;* dual of 7151; *double city; Kirjathaïm*, the name of two places in Pal.:—Kiriathaim, Kirjathaim.

7157. קִרְיַת יְעָרִים **Qiryath Yᵉ'ârîym**, *keer-yath' yeh-aw-reem';* or (Jer. 26 : 20) with the art. interposed; or (Josh. 18 : 28) simply the former part of the word; or

קִרְיַת עָרִים **Qiryath 'Ârîym**, *keer-yath' aw-reem';* from 7151 and the plur. of 3293 or 5892; *city of forests*, or *city of towns; Kirjath-Jeärim* or *Kirjath-Arim*, a place in Pal.:—Kirjath, Kirjath-jearim, Kirjath-arim.

7158. קִרְיַת סַנָּה **Qiryath Çannâh**, *keer-yath' san-naw';* or

קִרְיַת סֵפֶר **Qiryath Çêpher**, *keer-yath' say'-fer;* from 7151 and a simpler fem. from the same as 5577, or (for the latter name) 5612; *city of branches*, or *of a book; Kirjath-Sannah* or *Kirjath-Sepher*, a place in Pal.:—Kirjath-sannah, Kirjath-sepher.

7159. קָרַם **qâram**, *kaw-ram';* a prim. root; to *cover:*—cover.

7160. קָרַן **qâran**, *kaw-ran';* a prim. root; to *push* or gore; used only as denom. from 7161, to *shoot out horns;* fig. *rays:*—have horns, shine.

7161. קֶרֶן **qeren**, *keh'-ren;* from 7160; a *horn* (as *projecting*); by impl. a *flask*, *cornet;* by resembl. an elephant's *tooth* (i.e. *ivory*), a *corner* (of the altar), a *peak* (of a mountain), a *ray* (of light); fig. *power:*— × hill, horn.

7162. קֶרֶן **qeren** (Chald.), *keh'-ren;* corresp. to 7161; a *horn* (lit. or for sound):—horn, cornet.

7163. קֶרֶן הַפּוּךְ **qeren hap-pûwk**, *keh'-ren hap-pook';* from 7161 and 6320; *horn of cosmetic; Keren-hap-Puk*, one of Job's daughters:—Keren-happuch.

7164. קָרַס **qâraç**, *kaw-ras';* a prim. root; prop. to *protrude;* used only as denom. from 7165 (for alliteration with 7167), to *hunch*, i.e. be hump-backed:—stoop.

7165. קֶרֶס **qereç**, *keh'-res;* from 7164; a *knob* or belaying-pin (from its swelling form):—tache.

קְרֹס **Qᵉrôç**. See 7026.

7166. קַרְסֹל **qarçôl**, *kar-sole';* from 7164; an *ankle* (as a *protuberance* or joint):—foot.

7167. קָרַע **qâra'**, *kaw-rah';* a prim. root; to *rend*, lit. or fig. (*revile*, *paint* the eyes, as if enlarging them):—cut out, rend, × surely, tear.

7168. קֶרַע **qera'**, *keh'-rah;* from 7167; a *rag:*—piece, rag.

7169. קָרַץ **qârats**, *kaw-rats';* a prim. root; to *pinch*, i.e. (partially) to *bite* the lips, *blink* the eyes (as a gesture of malice), or (fully) to *squeeze* off (a piece of clay in order to mould a vessel from it):—form, move, wink.

7170. קְרַץ **qᵉrats** (Chald.), *ker-ats';* corresp. to 7171 in the sense of a *bit* (to "eat the *morsels* of" any one, i.e. *chew* him up [fig.] by *slander*):— + accuse

7171. קֶרֶץ **qerets**, *keh'-rets;* from 7169; *extirpation* (as if by *constriction*):—destruction.

7172. קַרְקַע **qarqa'**, *kar-kah';* from 7167; *floor* (as if a pavement of pieces or *tesseræ*), of a building or the sea:—bottom, (× one side of the) floor.

7173. קַרְקַע **Qarqa'**, *kar-kah';* the same as 7172; *ground-floor; Karka* (with the art. pref.), a place in Pal.:—Karkaa.

7174. קַרְקֹר **Qarqôr**, *kar-kore';* from 6979; *foundation; Karkor*, a place E. of the Jordan:—Karkor.

7175. קֶרֶשׁ **qeresh**, *keh'-resh;* from an unused root mean. to *split* off; a *slab* or plank; by impl. a *deck* of a ship:—bench, board.

7176. קֶרֶת **qereth**, *keh'-reth;* from 7136 in the sense of building; a *city:*—city.

7177. קַרְתָּה **Qartâh**, *kar-taw';* from 7176; *city; Kartah*, a place in Pal.:—Kartah.

7178. קַרְתָּן **Qartân**, *kar-tawn';* from 7176; *city-plot; Kartan*, a place in Pal.:—Kartan.

7179. קַשׁ **qash**, *kash;* from 7197; *straw* (as *dry*):—stubble.

7180. קִשֻּׁא **qishshû'**, *kish-shoo';* from an unused root (mean. to be *hard*); a *cucumber* (from the difficulty of *digestion*):—cucumber.

7181. קָשַׁב **qâshab**, *kaw-shab';* a prim. root; to *prick up* the ears, i.e. *hearken:*—attend, (cause to) hear (-ken), give heed, incline, mark (well), regard.

7182. קֶשֶׁב **qesheb**, *keh'-sheb;* from 7181; a *hearkening:*— × diligently, hearing, much heed, that regarded.

7183. קַשָּׁב **qashshâb**, *kash-shawb';* or

קַשֻּׁב **qashshûb**, *kash-shoob';* from 7181; *hearkening:*—attent (-ive).

7184. קָשָׂה **qâsâh**, *kaw-saw';* or

קַשְׂוָה **qasvâh**, *kas-vaw';* from an unused root mean. to be *round;* a *jug* (from its shape):—cover, cup.

7185. קָשָׁה **qâshâh**, *kaw-shaw';* a prim. root; prop. to *be dense*, i.e. tough or *severe* (in various applications):—be cruel, be fiercer, make grievous, be ([ask a], be in, have, seem, would) hard (-en, [labour], -ly, thing), be sore, (be, make) stiff (-en, [-necked]).

7186. קָשֶׁה **qâsheh**, *kaw-sheh';* from 7185; *severe* (in various applications):—churlish, cruel, grievous, hard ([-hearted], thing), heavy, + impudent, obstinate, prevailed, rough (-ly), sore, sorrowful, stiff ([-necked]), stubborn, + in trouble.

7187. קְשׁוֹט **qᵉshôwṭ** (Chald.), *kesh-ote';* or

קְשֹׁט **qᵉshôṭ** (Chald.), *kesh-ote';* corresp. to 7189; *fidelity:*—truth.

7188. קָשַׁח **qâshach**, *kaw-shakh';* a prim. root; to *be* (caus. *make*) *unfeeling:*—harden

7189. קֹשֶׁט **qôsheṭ**, *ko'-shet;* or

קֹשְׁט **qôshṭ**, *kōsht;* from an unused root mean. to *balance; equity* (as evenly *weighed*), i.e. *reality:*—certainty, truth.

קְשֹׁט **qôshôṭ**. See 7187.

7190. קְשִׁי **qᵉshîy**, *kesh-ee';* from 7185; *obstinacy:*—stubbornness.

7191. קִשְׁיוֹן **Qishyôwn**, *kish-yone';* from 7190; *hard ground; Kishjon*, a place in Pal.:—Kishion, Keshon.

7192. קְשִׂיטָה **qᵉsîyṭah**, *kes-ee-taw';* from an unused root (prob. mean. to *weigh* out); an *ingot* (as definitely *estimated* and stamped for a coin):—piece of money (silver).

7193. קַשְׂקֶשֶׂת **qasqeseth**, *kas-keh'-seth;* by redupl. from an unused root mean. to *shale* off as bark; a *scale* (of a fish); hence a coat of *mail* (as composed of or covered with jointed *plates* of metal):—mail, scale.

7194. קָשַׁר **qâshar**, *kaw-shar';* a prim. root; to *tie*, phys. (*gird*, *confine*, *compact*) or ment. (in *love*, *league*):—bind (up), (make a) conspire (-acy, -ator), join together, knit, stronger, work [treason].

7195. קֶשֶׁר **qesher**, *keh'-sher;* from 7194; an (unlawful) *alliance:*—confederacy, conspiracy, treason.

7196. קִשֻּׁר **qishshûr**, *kish-shoor';* from 7194; an (ornamental) *girdle* (for women):—attire, headband.

7197. קָשַׁשׁ **qâshash**, *kaw-shash';* a prim. root; to *become sapless* through drought; used only as denom. from 7179; to *forage* for straw, stubble or wood; fig. to *assemble:*—gather (selves) (together).

7198. קֶשֶׁת **qesheth**, *keh'-sheth;* from 7185 in the orig. sense (of 6983) of *bending;* a *bow,* for *shooting* (hence fig. *strength*) or the *iris:*—× arch (-er), + arrow, bow ([-man, -shot]).

7199. קַשָּׁת **qashshâth**, *kash-shawth';* intens. (as denom.) from 7198; a *bowman:*—× archer.

ר

7200. רָאָה **râ'âh**, *raw-aw';* a prim. root; to *see,* lit. or fig. (in numerous applications, direct and implied, trans., intrans. and causat.):—advise self, appear, approve, behold, × certainly, consider, discern, (make to) enjoy, have experience, gaze, take heed, × indeed, × joyfully, lo, look (on, one another, one on another, one upon another, out, up, upon), mark, meet, × be near, perceive, present, provide, regard, (have) respect, (fore-, cause to, let) see (-r, -m, one another), shew (self), × sight of others, (e-) spy, stare, × surely, × think, view, visions.

7201. רָאָה **râ'âh**, *raw-aw';* from 7200; a *bird* of prey (prob. the *vulture,* from its sharp *sight*):—glede. Comp. 1676.

7202. רָאֶה **râ'eh**, *raw-eh';* from 7200; *seeing,* i.e. experiencing:—see.

7203. רֹאֶה **rô'eh**, *ro-eh';* act. part. of 7200; a *seer* (as often rendered); but also (abstr.) a *vision:*—vision.

7204. רֹאֵה **Rô'êh**, *ro-ay';* for 7203; *prophet; Roëh,* an Isr.:—Haroeh [*includ. the art.*].

7205. רְאוּבֵן **Re'ûwbên**, *reh-oo-bane';* from the imper. of 7200 and 1121; *see ye a son; Reüben,* a son of Jacob:—Reuben.

7206. רְאוּבֵנִי **Re'ûwbênîy**, *reh-oo-bay-nee';* patron. from 7205; a *Reübenite* or desc. of Reüben:—children of Reuben, Reubenites.

7207. רַאֲוָה **ra'ăvâh**, *rah-av-aw';* from 7200; *sight,* i.e. satisfaction:—behold.

7208. רְאוּמָה **Re'ûwmâh**, *reh-oo-maw';* fem. pass. part. of 7213; *raised; Reümah,* a Syrian woman:—Reumah.

7209. רְאִי **re'îy**, *reh-ee';* from 7200; a *mirror* (as *seen*):—looking glass.

7210. רֳאִי **rô'îy**, *ro-ee';* from 7200; *sight,* whether abstr. (*vision*) or concr. (a *spectacle*):—gazingstock, look to, (that) see (-th).

7211. רְאָיָה **Re'âyâh**, *reh-aw-yaw';* from 7200 and 3050; *Jah has seen; Reäjah,* the name of three Isr.:—Reaia, Reaiah.

7212. רְאִית **re'îyth**, *reh-eeth';* from 7200; *sight:*—beholding.

7213. רָאַם **râ'am**, *raw-am';* a prim. root; to *rise:*—be lifted up.

7214. רְאֵם **re'êm**, *reh-ame';* or

רְאֵים **re'êym**, *reh-ame';* or

רֵים **rêym**, *rame;* or

רֵם **rêm**, *rame;* from 7213; a wild *bull* (from its *conspicuousness*):—unicorn.

7215. רָאמָה **râ'mâh**, *raw-maw';* from 7213; something *high* in value, i.e. perh. *coral:*—coral.

7216. רָאמוֹת **Râ'môwth**, *raw-mōth';* or

רָאמֹת **Râmôth**, *raw-mōth';* plur. of 7215; *heights; Ramoth,* the name of two places in Pal.:—Ramoth.

7217. רֵאשׁ **rê'sh** (Chald.), *raysh;* corresp. to 7218; the *head;* fig. the *sum:*—chief, head, sum.

7218. רֹאשׁ **rô'sh**, *roshe;* from an unused root appar. mean. to *shake;* the *head* (as most easily *shaken*), whether lit. or fig. (in many applications, of place, time, rank, etc.):—band, beginning, captain, chapiter, chief (-est place, man, things), company, end, × every [man], excellent, first, forefront, ([be-]) head, height, (on) high (-est part, [priest]), × lead, × poor, principal, ruler, sum, top.

7219. רֹאשׁ **rô'sh**, *roshe;* or

רוֹשׁ **rôwsh** (Deut. 32 : 32), *roshe;* appar. the same as 7218; a poisonous *plant,* prob. the *poppy* (from its conspicuous *head*); gen. *poison* (even of serpents):—gall, hemlock, poison, venom.

7220. רֹאשׁ **Rô'sh**, *roshe;* prob. the same as 7218; *Rosh,* the name of an Isr. and of a for. nation:—Rosh.

רֵאשׁ **rê'sh**. See 7389.

7221. רִאשָׁה **rî'shâh**, *ree-shaw';* from the same as 7218; a *beginning:*—beginning.

7222. רֹאשָׁה **rô'shâh**, *ro-shaw';* fem. of 7218; the *head:*—head [-stone].

7223. רִאשׁוֹן **rî'shôwn**, *ree-shone';* or

רִאשֹׁן **rî'shôn**, *ree-shone';* from 7221; *first,* in place, time or rank (as adj. or noun):—ancestor, (that were) before (-time), beginning, eldest, first, fore [-father] (-most), former (thing), of old time, past.

7224. רִאשֹׁנִי **rî'shônîy**, *ree-sho-nee';* from 7223; *first:*—first.

7225. רֵאשִׁית **rê'shîyth**, *ray-sheeth';* from the same as 7218; the *first,* in place, time, order or rank (spec. a *firstfruit*):—beginning, chief (-est), first (-fruits, part, time), principal thing.

7226. רַאֲשֹׁת **ra'ăshôth**, *rah-ash-ōth';* from 7218; a *pillow* (being for the *head*):—bolster.

7227. רַב **rab**, *rab;* by contr. from 7231; *abundant* (in quantity, size, age, number, rank, quality):—(in) abound (-undance, -ant, -antly), captain, elder, enough, exceedingly, full, great (-ly, man, one), increase, long (enough, [time]), (do, have) many (-ifold, things, a time), ([ship-]) master, mighty, more, (too, very) much, multiply (-tude), officer, often [-times], plenteous, populous, prince, process [of time], suffice (-ient).

7228. רַב **rab**, *rab;* by contr. from 7232; an *archer* [or perh. the same as 7227]:—archer.

7229. רַב **rab** (Chald.), *rab;* corresp. to 7227:—captain, chief, great, lord, master, stout.

רִב **rîb**. See 7378.

7230. רֹב **rôb**, *robe;* from 7231; *abundance* (in any respect):—abundance (-antly), all, × common [sort], excellent, great (-ly, -ness, number), huge, be increased, long, many, more in number, most, much, multitude, plenty (-ifully), × very [age].

7231. רָבַב **râbab**, *raw-bab';* a prim. root; prop. to *cast* together [comp. 7241], i.e. *increase,* espec. in number; also (as denom. from 7233) to *multiply by the myriad:*—increase, be many (-ifold), be more, multiply, ten thousands.

7232. רָבַב **râbab**, *raw-bab';* a prim. root [rather ident. with 7231 through the idea of *projection*]; to *shoot* an arrow:—shoot.

7233. רְבָבָה **rebâbâh**, *reb-aw-baw';* from 7231; *abundance* (in number), i.e. (spec.) a *myriad* (whether def. or indef.):—many, million, × multiply, ten thousand.

7234. רָבַד **râbad**, *raw-bad';* a prim. root; to *spread:*—deck.

7235. רָבָה **râbâh**, *raw-baw';* a prim. root; to *increase* (in whatever respect):—[bring in] abundance (× -antly), + archer [*by mistake for* 7232], be in authority, bring up, × continue, enlarge, excel, exceeding (-ly), be full of, (be, make) great (-er, -ly, × -ness), grow up, heap, increase, be long, (be, give, have, make, use) many (a time), (any, be, give, give the, have) more (in number), (ask, be, be so, gather, over, take, yield) much (greater, more), (make to) multiply, nourish, plenty (-eous), × process [of time], sore, store, thoroughly, very.

7236. רְבָה **rebâh** (Chald.), *reb-aw';* corresp. to 7235:—make a great man, grow.

7237. רַבָּה **Rabbâh**, *rab-baw';* fem. of 7227: *great; Rabbah,* the name of two places in Pal., E. and W.:—Rabbah, Rabbath.

7238. רְבוּ **rebûw** (Chald.), *reb-oo';* from a root corresp. to 7235; *increase* (of dignity):—greatness, majesty.

7239. רִבּוֹ **ribbôw**, *rib-bo';* from 7231; or

רִבּוֹא **ribbôw'**, *rib-bo';* from 7231; a *myriad,* i.e. indef. *large number:*—great things, ten ([eight] -een, [for] -ty, + sixscore, + threescore, × twenty, [twen] -ty) thousand.

7240. רִבּוֹ **ribbôw** (Chald.), *rib-bo';* corresp. to 7239:—× ten thousand times ten thousand.

7241. רָבִיב **râbîyb**, *raw-beeb';* from 7231; a *rain* (as an *accumulation* of drops):—shower.

7242. רָבִיד **râbîyd**, *raw-beed';* from 7234; a *collar* (as *spread* around the neck):—chain.

7243. רְבִיעִי **rebîyʻîy**, *reb-ee-ee';* or

רְבִעִי **rebiʻîy**, *reb-ee-ee';* from 7251; *fourth;* also (fractionally) a *fourth:*—foursquare, fourth (part).

7244. רְבִיעַי **rebîyʻay** (Chald.), *reb-ee-ah'ee;* corresp. to 7243:—fourth.

7245. רַבִּית **Rabbîyth**, *rab-beeth';* from 7231; *multitude; Rabbith,* a place in Pal.:—Rabbith.

7246. רָבַךְ **râbak**, *raw-bak';* a prim. root; to *soak* (bread in oil):—baken, (that which is) fried.

7247. רִבְלָה **Riblâh**, *rib-law';* from an unused root mean. to *be fruitful; fertile; Riblah,* a place in Syria:—Riblah.

7248. רַב־מָג **Rab-Mâg**, *rab-mawg';* from 7227 and a for. word for a Magian; *chief Magian; Rab-Mag,* a Bab. official:—Rab-mag.

7249. רַב־סָרִיס **Rab-Çârîyç**, *rab-saw-reece';* from 7227 and a for. word for a eunuch; *chief chamberlain; Rab-Saris,* a Bab. official:—Rab-saris.

7250. רָבַע **râbaʻ**, *raw-bah';* a prim. root; to *squat* or *lie* out flat, i.e. (spec.) in copulation:—let gender, lie down.

7251. רָבַע **râbaʻ**, *raw-bah';* a prim. root [rather ident. with 7250 through the idea of *sprawling* "at all fours" (or possibly the reverse is the order of deriv.); comp. 702]; prop. to *be four* (sided); used only as denom. of 7253; to *be quadrate:*—(four-) square (-d).

7252. רֶבַע **rebaʻ**, *reh'-bah;* from 7250; *prostration* (for sleep):—lying down.

7253. רֶבַע **rebaʻ**, *reh'-bah;* from 7251; a *fourth* (part or side):—fourth part, side, square.

7254. רֶבַע **Rebaʻ**, *reh'-bah;* the same as 7253; *Reba,* a Midianite:—Reba.

7255. רֹבַע **rôbaʻ**, *ro'-bah;* from 7251; a *quarter:*—fourth part.

7256. רִבֵּעַ **ribbêaʻ**, *rib-bay'-ah;* from 7251; a descendant of the *fourth* generation, i.e. *great great grandchild:*—fourth.

רִבְעִי **rebîyʻîy**. See 7243.

7257. רָבַץ **râbats**, *raw-bats';* a prim. root; to *crouch* (on all four legs folded, like a recumbent animal); by impl. to *recline, repose, brood, lurk, imbed:*—crouch (down), fall down, make a fold, lay, (cause to, make to) lie (down), make to rest, sit.

7258. רֶבֶץ **rebets**, *reh'-bets;* from 7257; a *couch* or place of repose:—where each lay, lie down in, resting place.

7259. רִבְקָה **Ribqâh**, *rib-kaw'*; from an unused root prob. mean. to *clog* by tying up the fetlock; *fettering* (by beauty); *Ribkah*, the wife of Isaac:—Rebekah.

7260. רַבְרַב **rabrab** (Chald.), *rab-rab'*; from 7229; *huge* (in size); *domineering* (in character):—(very) great (things).

7261. רַבְרְבָן **rabr^ebân** (Chald.), *rab-reb-awn'*; from 7260; a *magnate:*—lord, prince.

7262. רַבְשָׁקֵה **Rabshâqêh**, *rab-shaw-kay'*; from 7227 and 8248; *chief butler; Rabshakeh*, a Bab. official:—Rabshakeh.

7263. רֶגֶב **regeb**, *reh'-gheb*; from an unused root mean. to *pile* together; a *lump* of clay:—clod.

7264. רָגַז **râgaz**, *raw-gaz'*; a prim. root; to *quiver* (with any violent emotion, espec. anger or fear):—be afraid, stand in awe, disquiet, fall out, fret, move, provoke, quake, rage, shake, tremble, trouble, be wroth.

7265. רְגַז **r^egaz** (Chald.), *reg-az'*; corresp. to 7264:—provoke unto wrath.

7266. רְגַז **r^egaz** (Chald.), *reg-az'*; from 7265; violent *anger:*—rage.

7267. רֹגֶז **rôgez**, *ro'-ghez*; from 7264; *commotion, restlessness* (of a horse), *crash* (of thunder), *disquiet, anger:*—fear, noise, rage, trouble (-ing), wrath.

7268. רַגָּז **raggâz**, *rag-gawz'*; intens. from 7264; *timid:*—trembling.

7269. רָגְזָה **rogzâh**, *rog-zaw'*; fem. of 7267; *trepidation:*—trembling.

7270. רָגַל **râgal**, *raw-gal'*; a prim. root; to *walk* along; but only in spec. applications, to *reconnoitre*, to *be a tale-bearer* (i.e. slander); also (as denom. from 7272) to *lead about:*—backbite, search, slander, (e-) spy (out), teach to go, view.

7271. רְגַל **r^egal** (Chald.), *reg-al'*; corresp. to 7272:—foot.

7272. רֶגֶל **regel**, *reh'-gel*; from 7270; a *foot* (as used in *walking*); by impl. a *step*; by euphem. the *pudenda:*— × be able to endure, × according as, × after, × coming, × follow, ([broken-]) foot ([-ed, -stool]), × great toe, × haunt, × journey, leg, + piss, + possession, time.

7273. רַגְלִי **raglîy**, *rag-lee'*; from 7272; a *footman* (soldier):—(on) foot (-man).

7274. רֹגְלִים **Rôg^elîym**, *ro-gel-eem'*; plur. of act. part. of 7270; *fullers* (as *tramping* the cloth in washing); *Rogelim*, a place E. of the Jordan:—Rogelim.

7275. רָגַם **râgam**, *raw-gam'*; a prim. root [comp. 7263, 7321, 7551]; to *cast* together (stones), i.e. to *lapidate:*— × certainly, stone.

7276. רֶגֶם **Regem**, *reh'-gem*; from 7275; stone-*heap; Regem*, an Isr.:—Regem.

7277. רִגְמָה **rigmâh**, *rig-maw'*; fem. of the same as 7276; a *pile* (of stones), i.e. (fig.) a *throng:*—council.

7278. רֶגֶם מֶלֶךְ **Regem Melek**, *reh'-gem meh'-lek*; from 7276 and 4428; *king's heap; Regem-Melek*, an Isr.:—Regem-melech.

7279. רָגַן **râgan**, *raw-gan'*; a prim. root; to *grumble*, i.e. *rebel:*—murmur.

7280. רָגַע **râga^c**, *raw-gah'*; a prim. root; prop. to *toss* violently and suddenly (the sea with waves, the skin with boils); fig. (in a favorable manner) to *settle*, i.e. quiet; spec. to *wink* (from the motion of the eye-lids):—break, divide, find ease, be a moment, (cause, give, make to) rest, make suddenly.

7281. רֶגַע **rega^c**, *reh'-gah*; from 7280; a *wink* (of the eyes), i.e. a very *short space* of time:—instant, moment, space, suddenly.

7282. רָגֵעַ **râgêa^c**, *raw-gay'-ah*; from 7280; *restful*, i.e. peaceable:—that are quiet.

7283. רָגַשׁ **râgash**, *raw-gash'*; a prim. root; to *be tumultuous:*—rage.

7284. רְגַשׁ **r^egash** (Chald.), *reg-ash'*; corresp. to 7283; to *gather* tumultuously:—assemble (together).

7285. רֶגֶשׁ **regesh**, *reh'-ghesh*; or (fem.)

רִגְשָׁה **rigshâh**, *rig-shaw'*; from 7283; a tumultuous *crowd:*—company, insurrection.

7286. רָדַד **râdad**, *raw-dad'*; a prim. root; to *tread* in pieces, i.e. (fig.) to *conquer*, or (spec.) to *overlay:*—spend, spread, subdue.

7287. רָדָה **râdâh**, *raw-daw'*; a prim. root; to *tread* down, i.e. *subjugate*; spec. to *crumble* off:—(come to, make to) have dominion, prevail against, reign, (bear, make to) rule, (-r, over), take.

7288. רַדַּי **Radday**, *rad-dah'ee*; intens. from 7287; *domineering; Raddai*, an Isr.:—Raddai.

7289. רָדִיד **râdîyd**, *raw-deed'*; from 7286 in the sense of *spreading*; a *veil* (as expanded):—vail, veil.

7290. רָדַם **râdam**, *raw-dam'*; a prim. root; to *stun*, i.e. *stupefy* (with sleep or death):—(be fast a-, be in a deep, cast into a dead, that) sleep (-er, -eth).

7291. רָדַף **râdaph**, *raw-daf'*; a prim. root; to *run after* (usually with hostile intent; fig. [of time] *gone by*):—chase, put to flight, follow (after, on), hunt, (be under) persecute (-ion, -or), pursue (-r).

7292. רָהַב **râhab**, *raw-hab'*; a prim. root; to *urge* severely, i.e. (fig.) *importune, embolden, capture, act insolently:*—overcome, behave self proudly, make sure, strengthen.

7293. רַהַב **rahab**, *rah'-hab*; from 7292; *bluster* (-*er*):—proud, strength.

7294. רַהַב **Rahab**, *rah'-hab*; the same as 7293; *Rahab* (i.e. *boaster*), an epithet of Egypt:—Rahab.

7295. רָהָב **râhâb**, *raw-hawb'*; from 7292; *insolent:*—proud.

7296. רֹהַב **rôhab**, *ro'-hab*; from 7292; *pride:*—strength.

7297. רָהָה **râhâh**, *raw-haw'*; a prim. root; to *fear:*—be afraid.

7298. רַהַט **rahaṭ**, *rah'-hat*; from an unused root appar. mean. to *hollow out*; a *channel* or watering-box; by resemblance a *ringlet* of hair (as forming parallel lines):—gallery, gutter, trough.

7299. רֵו **rêv** (Chald.), *rave*; from a root corresp. to 7200; *aspect:*—form.

רוּב° **rûwb**. See 7378.

7300. רוּד **rûwd**, *rood*; a prim. root; to *tramp* about, i.e. *ramble* (free or disconsolate):—have the dominion, be lord, mourn, rule.

7301. רָוָה **râvâh**, *raw-vaw'*; a prim. root; to *slake* the thirst (occasionally of other appetites):—bathe, make drunk, (take the) fill, satiate, (abundantly) satisfy, soak, water (abundantly).

7302. רָוֶה **râveh**, *raw-veh'*; from 7301; *sated* (with drink):—drunkenness, watered.

7303. רוֹהֲגָה° **Rôwhăgâh**, *ro-hag-aw'*; from an unused root prob. mean. to *cry* out; *outcry; Rohagah*, an Isr.:—Rohgah.

7304. רָוַח **râvach**, *raw-vakh'*; a prim. root [rather ident. with 7306]; prop. to *breathe* freely, i.e. *revive*; by impl. to *have ample room:*—be refreshed, large.

7305. רֶוַח **revach**, *reh'-vakh*; from 7304; *room*, lit. (an *interval*) or fig. (*deliverance*):—enlargement, space.

7306. רוּחַ **rûwach**, *roo'-akh*; a prim. root; prop. to *blow*, i.e. *breathe*; only (lit.) to *smell* or (by impl. *perceive* (fig. to *anticipate, enjoy*):—accept, smell, × touch, make of quick understanding.

7307. רוּחַ **rûwach**, *roo'-akh*; from 7306; *wind*; by resemblance *breath*, i.e. a sensible (or even violent) exhalation; fig. *life, anger, unsubstantiality*; by extens. a *region* of the sky; by resemblance *spirit*, but only of a rational being (includ. its expression and functions):—air, anger, blast, breath, × cool, courage, mind, × quarter, × side, spirit ([-ual]), tempest, × vain, ([whirl-]) wind (-y).

7308. רוּחַ **rûwach** (Chald.), *roo'-akh*; corresp. to 7307:—mind, spirit, wind.

7309. רְוָחָה **r^evâchâh**, *rev-aw-khaw'*; fem. of 7305; *relief:*—breathing, respite.

7310. רְוָיָה **r^evâyâh**, *rev-aw-yaw'*; from 7301; *satisfaction:*—runneth over, wealthy.

7311. רוּם **rûwm**, *room*; a prim. root; to *be high* act. to *rise* or *raise* (in various applications, lit. or fig.):—bring up, exalt (self), extol, give, go up, haughty, heave (up), (be, lift up on, make on, set up on, too) high (-er, one), hold up, levy, lift (-er) up, (be) lofty, (× a-) loud, mount up, offer (up), + presumptuously, (be) promote (-ion), proud, set up, tall (-er), take (away, off, up), breed worms.

7312. רוּם **rûwm**, *room*; or

רֻם **rûm**, *room*; from 7311; (lit.) *elevation* or (fig.) *elation:*—haughtiness, height, × high.

7313. רוּם **rûwm** (Chald.), *room*; corresp. to 7311; (fig. only):—extol, lift up (self), set up.

7314. רוּם **rûwm** (Chald.), *room*; from 7313; (lit.) *altitude:*—height.

7315. רוֹם **rôwm**, *rome*; from 7311; *elevation*, i.e. (adv.) *aloft:*—on high.

7316. רוּמָה **Rûwmâh**, *roo-maw'*; from 7311; *height; Rumah*, a place in Pal.:—Rumah.

7317. רוֹמָה **rôwmâh**, *ro-maw'*; fem. of 7315; *elation*, i.e. (adv.) *proudly:*—haughtily.

7318. רוֹמָם **rôwmâm**, *ro-mawm'*; from 7426; *exaltation*, i.e. (fig. and spec.) *praise:*—be extolled.

7319. רוֹמְמָה **rôwm^emâh**, *ro-mem-aw'*; fem. act. part. of 7426; *exaltation*, i.e. *praise:*—high.

7320. רוֹמַמְתִּי עֶזֶר **Rôwmamtîy ^cEzer** (or רֹמַמְתִּי **Rômamtîy**), *ro-mam'-tee eh'-zer*; from 7311 and 5828; *I have raised up a help; Romamti-Ezer*, an Isr.:—Romamti-ezer.

7321. רוּעַ **rûwa^c**, *roo-ah'*; a prim. root; to *mar* (espec. by breaking); fig. to *split* the ears (with sound), i.e. *shout* (for alarm or joy):—blow an alarm, cry (alarm, aloud, out), destroy, make a joyful noise, smart, shout (for joy), sound an alarm, triumph.

7322. רוּף **rûwph**, *roof*; a prim. root; prop. to *triturate* (in a mortar), i.e. (fig.) to *agitate* (by concussion):—tremble.

7323. רוּץ **rûwts**, *roots*; a prim. root; to *run* (for whatever reason, espec. to *rush*):—break down, divide speedily, footman, guard, bring hastily, (make) run (away, through), post, stretch out.

7324. רוּק **rûwq**, *rook*; a prim. root; to *pour* out (lit. or fig.), i.e. *empty:*— × arm, cast out, draw (out), (make) empty, pour forth (out).

7325. רוּר **rûwr**, *roor*; a prim. root; to *slaver* (with spittle), i.e. (by analogy) to *emit* a fluid (ulcerous or natural):—run.

7326. רוּשׁ **rûwsh**, *roosh*; a prim. root; to *be destitute:*—lack, needy, (make self) poor (man).

רוֹשׁ **rôwsh**. See 7219.

7327. רוּת **Rûwth**, *rooth*; prob. for 7468; *friend; Ruth*, a Moabitess:—Ruth.

7328. רָז **râz** (Chald.), *rawz*; from an unused root prob. mean. to *attenuate*, i.e. (fig.) *hide*; a *mystery:*—secret.

7329. רָזָה **râzâh**, *raw-zaw'*; a prim. root; to *emaciate*, i.e. *make* (*become*) *thin* (lit. or fig.):—famish, wax lean.

7330. רָזֶה **râzeh**, *raw-zeh'*; from 7329; *thin:*—lean.

7331. רְזוֹן **R^ezôwn**, *rez-one'*; from 7336; *prince; Rezon*, a Syrian:—Rezon.

7332. רָזוֹן **râzôwn**, *raw-zone'*; from 7329; *thinness:*—leanness, × scant.

7333. רָזוֹן **râzôwn**, *raw-zone'*; from 7336; a *dignitary:*—prince.

7334. רָזִי **râzîy**, *raw-zee'*; from 7329; *thinness:*—leanness.

7335. רָזַם **râzam**, *raw-zam'*; a prim. root; to *twinkle* the eye (in mockery):—wink.

7336. רָזַן **râzan**, *raw-zan'*; a prim. root; prob. to be *heavy*, i.e. (fig.) *honorable*:—prince, ruler.

7337. רָחַב **râchab**, *raw-khab'*; a prim. root; to *broaden* (intrans. or trans., lit. or fig.):—be an en- (make) large (-ing), make room, make (open) wide.

7338. רַחַב **rachab**, *rakh'-ab*; from 7337; a *width*:—breadth, broad place.

7339. רְחֹב **rᵉchôb**, *rekh-obe'*; or

רְחוֹב **rᵉchôwb**, *rekh-obe'*; from 7337; a *width*, i.e. (concr.) *avenue* or *area*:—broad place (way), street. See also 1050.

7340. רְחֹב **Rᵉchôb**, *rekh-obe'*; or

רְחוֹב **Rᵉchôwb**, *rekh-obe'*; the same as 7339; *Rechob*, the name of a place in Syria, also of a Syrian and an Isr.:—Rehob.

7341. רֹחַב **rôchab**, *ro'-khab*; from 7337; *width* (lit. or fig.):—breadth, broad, largeness, thickness, wideness.

7342. רָחָב **râchâb**, *raw-khawb'*; from 7337; *roomy*, in any (or every) direction, lit. or fig.:—broad, large, at liberty, proud, wide.

7343. רָחָב **Râchâb**, *raw-khawb'*; the same as 7342; *proud*; *Rachab*, a Canaanitess:—Rahab.

7344. רְחֹבוֹת **Rᵉchôbôwth**, *rekh-o-bōth'*; or

רְחֹבֹת **Rᵉchôbôth**, *rekh-o-bōth'*; plur. of 7339; *streets*; *Rechoboth*, a place in Assyria and one in Pal.:—Rehoboth.

7345. רְחַבְיָה **Rᵉchabyâh**, *rekh-ab-yaw'*; or

רְחַבְיָהוּ **Rᵉchabyâhûw**, *rekh-ab-yaw'-hoo*; from 7337 and 3050; *Jah has enlarged*; *Rechabjah*, an Isr.:—Rehabiah.

7346. רְחַבְעָם **Rᵉchabʽâm**, *rekh-ab-awm'*; from 7337 and 5971; a *people has enlarged*; *Rechabam*, an Isr. king:—Rehoboam.

רְחֹבֹת **Rᵉchôbôth**. See 7344.

7347. רֵחֶה **rêcheh**, *ray-kheh'*; from an unused root mean. to *pulverize*; a *mill*-stone:—mill (stone).

רְחוֹב **Rᵉchôwb**. See 7339, 7340.

7348. רְחוּם **Rᵉchûwm**, *rekh-oom'*; a form of 7349; *Rechum*, the name of a Pers. and of three Isr.:—Rehum.

7349. רַחוּם **rachûwm**, *rakh-oom'*; from 7355; *compassionate*:—full of compassion, merciful.

7350. רָחוֹק **râchôwq**, *raw-khoke'*; or

רָחֹק **râchôq**, *raw-khoke'*; from 7368; *remote*, lit. or fig., of place or time; spec. *precious*; often used adv. (with prep.):—(a-) far (abroad, off), long ago, of old, space, great while to come.

7351. רְחִיט° **rᵉchîyṭ**, *rekh-eet'*; from the same as 7298; a *panel* (as resembling a *trough*):—rafter.

7352. רַחִיק **rachîyq** (Chald.), *rakh-eek'*; corresp. to 7350:—far.

7353. רָחֵל **râchêl**, *raw-kale'*; from an unused root mean. to *journey*; a *ewe* [the *females* being the predominant element of a flock] (as a good *traveller*):—ewe, sheep.

7354. רָחֵל **Râchêl**, *raw-khale'*; the same as 7353; *Rachel*, a wife of Jacob:—Rachel.

7355. רָחַם **râcham**, *raw-kham'*; a prim. root; to *fondle*; by impl. to *love*, espec. to *compassionate*:—have compassion (on, upon), love, (find, have, obtain, shew) mercy (-iful, on, upon), (have) pity, Ruhamah, × surely.

7356. רַחַם **racham**, *rakh'-am*; from 7355; *compassion* (in the plur.); by extens. the *womb* (as *cherishing* the fœtus); by impl. a *maiden*:—bowels, compassion, damsel, tender love, (great, tender) mercy, pity, womb.

7357. רַחַם **Racham**, *rakh'-am*; the same as 7356; *pity*; *Racham*, an Isr.:—Raham.

7358. רֶחֶם **rechem**, *rekh'-em*; from 7355; the *womb* [comp. 7356]:—matrix, womb.

7359. רְחֵם **rᵉchêm** (Chald.), *rekh-ame'*; corresp. to 7356; (plur.) *pity*:—mercy.

7360. רָחָם **râchâm**, *raw-khawm'*; or (fem.)

רָחָמָה **râchâmâh**, *raw-khaw-maw'*; from 7355; a kind of *vulture* (supposed to be *tender* towards its young):—gier-eagle.

7361. רַחֲמָה **rachămâh**, *rakh-am-aw'*; fem. of 7356; a *maiden*:—damsel.

7362. רַחְמָנִי **rachmânîy**, *rakh-maw-nee'*; from 7355; *compassionate*:—pitiful.

7363. רָחַף **râchaph**, *raw-khaf'*; a prim. root; to *brood*, by impl. to *be relaxed*:—flutter, move, shake.

7364. רָחַץ **râchats**, *raw-khats'*; a prim. root; to *lave* (the whole or a part of a thing):—bathe (self), wash (self).

7365. רְחַץ **rᵉchats** (Chald.), *rekh-ats'*; corresp. to 7364 [prob. through the accessory idea of *ministering* as a servant at the bath]; to *attend* upon:—trust.

7366. רַחַץ **rachats**, *rakh'-ats*; from 7364; a *bath*:—wash[-pot].

7367. רַחְצָה **rachtsâh**, *rakh-tsaw'*; fem. of 7366; a *bathing* place:—washing.

7368. רָחַק **râchaq**, *raw-khak'*; a prim. root; to *widen* (in any [direction), i.e. (intrans.) *recede* or (trans.) *remove* (lit. or fig., of place or relation):—(a-, be, cast, drive, get, go, keep [self], put, remove, be too, [wander], withdraw) far (away, off), loose, × refrain, very, (be) a good way (off).

7369. רָחֵק **râchêq**, *raw-khake'*; from 7368; *remote*:—that are far.

רָחֹק **râchôq**. See 7350.

7370. רָחַשׁ **râchash**, *raw-khash'*; a prim. root; to *gush*:—indite.

7371. רַחַת **rachath**, *rakh'-ath*; from 7306; a *winnowing*-fork (as *blowing* the chaff away):—shovel.

7372. רָטַב **râṭab**, *raw-tab'*; a prim. root; to *be moist*:—be wet.

7373. רָטֹב **râṭôb**, *raw-tobe'*; from 7372; *moist* (with sap):—green.

7374. רֶטֶט **reṭeṭ**, *reh'-tet*; from an unused root mean. to *tremble*; *terror*:—fear.

7375. רֻטֲפַשׁ **rûwṭăphash**, *roo-taf-ash'*; a root compounded from 7373 and 2954; to *be rejuvenated*:—be fresh.

7376. רָטַשׁ **râṭash**, *raw-tash'*; a prim. root; to *dash* down:—dash (in pieces).

7377. רִי **rîy**, *ree*; from 7301; *irrigation*, i.e. a shower:—watering.

7378. רִיב **rîyb**, *reeb*; or

רוּב° **rûwb**, *roob*; a prim. root; prop. to *toss*, i.e. *grapple*; mostly fig. to *wrangle*, i.e. *hold a controversy*; (by impl.) to *defend*:—adversary, chide, complain, contend, debate, × ever, × lay wait, plead, rebuke, strive, × thoroughly.

7379. רִיב **rîyb**, *reeb*; or

רִב **rîb**, *reeb*; from 7378; a *contest* (personal or legal):— + adversary, cause, chiding, contend (-tion), controversy, multitude [*from the marg.*], pleading, strife, strive (-ing), suit.

7380. רִיבַי **Rîybay**, *ree-bah'ee*; from 7378; *contentious*; *Ribai*, an Isr.:—Ribai.

7381. רֵיחַ **rêyach**, *ray'-akh*; from 7306; *odor* (as if *blown*):—savour, scent, smell.

7382. רֵיחַ **rêyach** (Chald.), *ray'-akh*; corresp. to 7381:—smell.

רֵים **rêym**. See 7214.

רֵיעַ **rêyaʽ**. See 7453.

7383. רִיפָה **rîyphâh**, *ree-faw'*; or

רִפָה **rîphâh**, *ree-faw'*; from 7322; (only plur.), *grits* (as *pounded*):—ground corn, wheat.

7384. רִיפַת **Rîyphath**, *ree-fath'*; or (prob. by orth. error)

דִּיפַת **Dîyphath**, *dee-fath'*; of for. or.; *Riphath*, a grandson of Japheth and his desc.:—Riphath.

7385. רִיק **rîyq**, *reek*; from 7324; *emptiness*; fig. a *worthless* thing; adv. *in vain*:—empty, to no purpose, (in) vain (thing), vanity.

7386. רֵיק **rêyq**, *rake*; or (shorter)

רֵק **rêq**, *rake*; from 7324; *empty*; fig. *worthless*:—emptied (-ty), vain (fellow, man).

7387. רֵיקָם **rêyqâm**, *ray-kawm'*; from 7386; *emptily*; fig. (obj.) *ineffectually*, (subj.) *undeservedly*:—without cause, empty, in vain, void.

7388. רִיר **rîyr**, *reer*; from 7325; *saliva*; by resemblance *broth*:—spittle, white [of an egg].

7389. רֵישׁ **rêysh**, *raysh*; or

רֵאשׁ **rêʼsh**, *raysh*; or

רִישׁ **rîysh**, *reesh*; from 7326; *poverty*:—poverty.

7390. רַךְ **rak**, *rak*; from 7401; *tender* (lit. or fig.); by impl. *weak*:—faint [-hearted], soft, tender ([-hearted], one), weak.

7391. רֹךְ **rôk**, *roke*; from 7401; *softness* (fig.):—tenderness.

7392. רָכַב **râkab**, *raw-kab'*; a prim. root; to *ride* (on an animal or in a vehicle); caus. to *place upon* (for riding or gen.), to *despatch*:—bring (on [horse-] back), carry, get [oneself] up, on [horse-] back, put, (cause to, make to) ride (in a chariot, on, -r), set.

7393. רֶכֶב **rekeb**, *reh'-keb*; from 7392; a *vehicle*; by impl. a *team*; by extens. *cavalry*; by analogy a *rider*, i.e. the upper millstone:—chariot, (upper) millstone, multitude [*from the marg.*], wagon.

7394. רֵכָב **Rêkâb**, *ray-kawb'*; from 7392; *rider*; *Rekab*, the name of two Arabs and of two Isr.:—Rechab.

7395. רַכָּב **rakkâb**, *rak-kawb'*; from 7392; a *charioteer*:—chariot man, driver of a chariot, horseman.

7396. רִכְבָּה **rikbâh**, *rik-baw'*; fem. of 7393; a *chariot* (collect.):—chariots.

7397. רֵכָה **Rêkâh**, *ray-kaw'*; prob. fem. from 7401; *softness*; *Rekah*, a place in Pal.:—Rechah.

7398. רְכוּב **rᵉkûwb**, *rek-oob'*; from pass. part. of 7392; a *vehicle* (as *ridden* on):—chariot.

7399. רְכוּשׁ **rᵉkûwsh**, *rek-oosh'*; or

רְכֻשׁ **rᵉkûsh**, *rek-oosh'*; from pass. part. of 7408; *property* (as *gathered*):—good, riches, substance.

7400. רָכִיל **râkîyl**, *raw-keel'*; from 7402; a *scandal-monger* (as *travelling* about):—slander, carry tales, talebearer.

7401. רָכַךְ **râkak**, *raw-kak'*; a prim. root; to *soften* (intrans. or trans.), used fig.:—(be) faint ([-hearted]), mollify, (be, make) soft (-er), be tender.

7402. רָכַל **râkal**, *raw-kal'*; a prim. root; to *travel* for trading:—(spice) merchant.

7403. רָכָל **Râkâl**, *raw-kawl'*; from 7402; *merchant*; *Rakal*, a place in Pal.:—Rachal.

7404. רְכֻלָּה **rᵉkullâh**, *rek-ool-law'*; fem. pass. part. of 7402; *trade* (as *peddled*):—merchandise, traffic.

7405. רָכַס **râkaç**, *raw-kas'*; a prim. root; to *tie*:—bind.

7406. רֶכֶס **rekeç**, *reh'-kes*; from 7405; a mountain *ridge* (as of *tied* summits):—rough place.

7407. רֹכֶס **rôkeç**, *ro'-kes*; from 7405; a *snare* (as of *tied* meshes):—pride.

7408. רָכַשׁ **râkash**, *raw-kash'*; a prim. root; to *lay up*, i.e. collect:—gather, get.

7409. רֶכֶשׁ **rekesh**, *reh'-kesh*; from 7408; a *relay* of animals on a post-route (as *stored* up for that purpose); by impl. a *courser*:—dromedary, mule, swift beast.

רְכֻשׁ **rᵉkûsh**. See 7399.

רֵם **rêm**. See 7214.

7410. רָם **Râm**, *rawm;* act. part. of 7311; *high; Ram*, the name of an Arabian and of an Isr.:—Ram. See also 1027.

רֻם **rûm**. See 7311.

7411. רָמָה **râmâh**, *raw-maw';* a prim. root; to *hurl;* spec. to *shoot;* fig. to *delude* or *betray* (as if causing to fall):—beguile, betray, [bow-] man, carry, deceive, throw.

7412. רְמָה **r^emâh** (Chald.), *rem-aw';* corresp. to 7411; to *throw, set,* (fig.) *assess:*—cast (down), impose.

7413. רָמָה **râmâh**, *raw-maw';* fem. act. part. of 7311; a *height* (as a seat of idolatry):—high place.

7414. רָמָה **Râmâh**, *raw-maw';* the same as 7413; *Ramah*, the name of four places in Pal.:—Ramah.

7415. רִמָּה **rimmâh**, *rim-maw';* from 7426 in the sense of *breeding* [comp. 7311]; a *maggot* (as rapidly *bred*), lit. or fig.:—worm.

7416. רִמּוֹן **rimmôwn**, *rim-mone';* or

רִמֹּן **rimmôn**, *rim-mone';* from 7426; a *pomegranate*, the tree (from its *upright* growth) or the fruit (also an artificial ornament):—pomegranate.

7417. רִמּוֹן **Rimmôwn**, *rim-mone';* or (shorter)

רִמֹּן **Rimmôn**, *rim-mone';* or

רִמּוֹנוֹ **Rimmôwnôw** (1 Chron. 6 : 62 [77]), *rim-mo-no';* the same as 7416; *Rimmon*, the name of a Syrian deity, also of five places in Pal.:—Remmon, Rimmon. The addition "-methoar" (Josh. 19 : 13) is

הַמְּתֹאָר **ham-m^ethô'âr**, *ham-meth-o-awr';* pass. part. of 8388 with the art.; *the* (one) *marked off*, i.e. *which pertains;* mistaken for part of the name.

רָמוֹת **Râmôwth**. See 7418, 7433.

7418. רָמוֹת־נֶגֶב **Râmôwth-Negeb**, *raw-mōth-neh'-gheb;* or

רָמַת נֶגֶב **Râmath Negeb**, *raw'-math neh'-gheb;* from the plur. or construct. of 7413 and 5045; *heights* (or *height*) *of the South; Ramoth-Negeb* or *Ramath-Negeb*, a place in Pal.:—south Ramoth, Ramath of the south.

7419. רָמוּת **râmûwth**, *raw-mooth';* from 7311; a *heap* (of carcases):—height.

7420. רֹמַח **rômach**, *ro'-makh;* from an unused root mean. to *hurl;* a *lance* (as *thrown*); espec. the iron *point:*—buckler, javelin, lancet, spear.

7421. רַמִּי **rammîy**, *ram-mee';* for 761; a *Ramite*, i.e. Aramæan:—Syrian.

7422. רַמְיָה **Ramyâh**, *ram-yaw';* from 7311 and 3050; *Jah has raised; Ramjah*, an Isr.:—Ramiah.

7423. רְמִיָּה **r^emîyâh**, *rem-ee-yaw';* from 7411; *remissness, treachery:*—deceit (-ful, -fully), false, guile, idle, slack, slothful.

7424. רַמָּךְ **rammâk**, *ram-mawk';* of for. or.; a brood *mare:*—dromedary.

7425. רְמַלְיָהוּ **R^emalyâhûw**, *rem-al-yaw'-hoo;* from an unused root and 3050 (perh. mean. to *deck*); *Jah has bedecked; Remaljah*, an Isr.:—Remaliah.

7426. רָמַם **râmam**, *raw-mam';* a prim. root; to *rise* (lit. or fig.):—exalt, get [oneself] up, lift up (self), mount up.

7427. רֹמֵמֻת **rômêmûth**, *ro-may-mooth';* from the act. part. of 7426; *exaltation:*—lifting up of self.

רִמֹּן **rimmôn**. See 7416.

7428. רִמֹּן פֶּרֶץ **Rimmôn Perets**, *rim-mone' peh'-rets;* from 7416 and 6556; *pomegranate of the breach; Rimmon-Perets*, a place in the Desert:—Rimmon-parez.

7429. רָמַס **râmaç**, *raw-mas';* a prim. root; to *tread* upon (as a potter, in walking or abusively):—oppressor, stamp upon, trample (under feet), tread (down, upon).

7430. רָמַשׂ **râmas**, *raw-mas';* a prim. root; prop. to *glide* swiftly, i.e. to *crawl* or *move* with short steps; by analogy to *swarm:*—creep, move.

7431. רֶמֶשׂ **remes**, *reh'-mes;* from 7430; a *reptile* or any other rapidly moving animal:—that creepeth, creeping (moving) thing.

7432. רֶמֶת **Remeth**, *reh'-meth;* from 7411; *height; Remeth*, a place in Pal.:—Remeth.

7433. רָמֹת (or רָאמוֹת **Râmôwth**) גִּלְעָד **Râmôth Gil'âd** (2 Chron. 22 : 5), *raw-mōth' gil-awd';* from the plur. of 7413 and 1568; *heights of Gilad; Ramoth-Gilad*, a place E. of the Jordan:—Ramoth-gilead, Ramoth in Gilead. See also 7216.

7434. רָמַת הַמִּצְפֶּה **Râmath ham-Mits-peh**, *raw-math' ham-mits-peh';* from 7413 and 4707 with the art. interp.; *height of the watch*-tower; *Ramath-ham-Mitspeh*, a place in Pal.:—Ramath-mizpeh.

7435. רָמָתִי **Râmâthîy**, *raw-maw-thee';* patron. of 7414; a *Ramathite* or inhab. of Ramah:—Ramathite.

7436. רָמָתַיִם צוֹפִים **Râmâthayim Tsôw-phîym**, *raw-maw-thah'-yim tso-feem';* from the dual of 7413 and the plur. of the act. part. of 6822; *double height of watchers; Ramathajim-Tsophim*, a place in Pal.:—Ramathaim-zophim.

7437. רָמַת לֶחִי **Râmath Lechîy**, *raw'-math lekh'-ee;* from 7413 and 3895; *height of a jaw-bone; Ramath-Lechi*, a place in Pal.:—Ramath-lehi.

רָן **Rân**. See 1028.

7438. רֹן **rôn**, *rone;* from 7442; a *shout* (of deliverance):—song.

7439. רָנָה **rânâh**, *raw-naw';* a prim. root; to *whiz:*—rattle.

7440. רִנָּה **rinnâh**, *rin-naw';* from 7442; prop. a *creaking* (or shrill sound), i.e. *shout* (of joy or grief):—cry, gladness, joy, proclamation, rejoicing, shouting, sing (-ing), triumph.

7441. רִנָּה **Rinnâh**, *rin-naw';* the same as 7440; *Rinnah*, an Isr.:—Rinnah.

7442. רָנַן **rânan**, *raw-nan';* a prim. root; prop. to *creak* (or emit a stridulous sound), i.e. to *shout* (usually for joy):—aloud for joy, cry out, be joyful, (greatly, make to) rejoice, (cause to) shout (for joy), (cause to) sing (aloud, for joy, out), triumph.

7443. רֶנֶן **renen**, *reh'-nen;* from 7442; an *ostrich* (from its *wail*):—× goodly.

7444. רַנֵּן **rannên**, *ran-nane';* intens. from 7442; *shouting* (for joy):—singing.

7445. רְנָנָה **r^enânâh**, *ren-aw-naw';* from 7442; a *shout* (for joy):—joyful (voice), singing, triumphing.

7446. רִסָּה **Riççâh**, *ris-saw';* from 7450; a *ruin* (as *dripping* to pieces); *Rissah*, a place in the Desert:—Rissah.

7447. רָסִיס **râçîyç**, *raw-sees';* from 7450; prop. *dripping* to pieces, i.e. a *ruin;* also a dew-*drop:*—breach, drop.

7448. רֶסֶן **reçen**, *reh'-sen;* from an unused root mean. to *curb;* a *halter* (as *restraining*); by impl. the *jaw:*—bridle.

7449. רֶסֶן **Reçen**, *reh'-sen;* the same as 7448; *Resen*, a place in Ass.:—Resen.

7450. רָסַס **râçaç**, *raw-sas';* a prim. root; to *comminute;* used only as denom. from 7447, to *moisten* (with drops):—temper.

7451. רַע **ra'**, *rah;* from 7489; *bad* or (as noun) *evil* (nat. or mor.):—adversity, affliction, bad, calamity, + displease (-ure), distress, evil ([-favouredness], man, thing), + exceedingly, × great, grief (-vous), harm, heavy, hurt (-ful), ill (favoured), + mark, mischief (-vous), misery, naught (-ty), noisome, + not please, sad (-ly), sore, sorrow, trouble, vex, wicked (-ly, -ness, one), worse (-st), wretchedness, wrong. [Incl. fem. רָעָה **râ'âh**; as adj. or noun.]

7452. רֵעַ **rêa'**, *ray'-ah;* from 7321; a *crash* (of thunder), *noise* (of war), *shout* (of joy):—× aloud, noise, shouted.

7453. רֵעַ **rêa'**, *ray'-ah;* or

רֵיעַ **rêya'**, *ray'-ah;* from 7462; an *associate* (more or less close):—brother, companion, fellow, friend, husband, lover, neighbour, × (an-) other.

7454. רֵעַ **rêa'**, *ray'-ah;* from 7462; a *thought* (as *association* of ideas):—thought.

7455. רֹעַ **rôa'**, *ro'-ah;* from 7489; *badness* (as *marring*), phys. or mor.:—× be so bad, badness, (× be so) evil, naughtiness, sadness, sorrow, wickedness.

7456. רָעֵב **râ'êb**, *raw-abe';* a prim. root; to *hunger:*—(suffer to) famish, (be, have, suffer, suffer to) hunger (-ry).

7457. רָעֵב **râ'êb**, *raw-abe';* from 7456; *hungry* (more or less intensely):—hunger bitten, hungry.

7458. רָעָב **râ'âb**, *raw-awb';* from 7456; *hunger* (more or less extensive):—dearth, famine, + famished, hunger.

7459. רְעָבוֹן **r^e'âbôwn**, *reh-aw-bone';* from 7456; *famine:*—famine.

7460. רָעַד **râ'ad**, *raw-ad';* a prim. root; to *shudder* (more or less violently):—tremble.

7461. רַעַד **ra'ad**, *rah'-ad;* or (fem.)

רְעָדָה **r^e'âdâh**, *reh-aw-daw';* from 7460; a *shudder:*—fear, trembling.

7462. רָעָה **râ'âh**, *raw-aw';* a prim. root; to *tend* a flock, i.e. *pasture* it; intrans. to *graze* (lit. or fig.); gen. to *rule;* by extens. to *associate* with (as a friend):—× break, companion, keep company with, devour, eat up, evil entreat, feed, use as a friend, make friendship with, herdman, keep [sheep] (-er), pastor, + shearing house, shepherd, wander, waste.

7463. רֵעֶה **rê'eh**, *ray-eh';* from 7462; a (male) *companion:*—friend.

7464. רֵעָה **rê'âh**, *ray'-aw;* fem. of 7453; a female *associate:*—companion, fellow.

7465. רֹעָה **rô'âh**, *ro-aw';* for 7455; *breakage:*—broken, utterly.

7466. רְעוּ **R^e'ûw**, *reh-oo';* for 7471 in the sense of 7453; *friend; Reü*, a postdiluvian patriarch:—Reu.

7467. רְעוּאֵל **R^e'ûw'êl**, *reh-oo-ale';* from the same as 7466 and 410; *friend of God; Reüel*, the name of Moses' father-in-law, also of an Edomite and an Isr.:—Raguel, Reuel.

7468. רְעוּת **r^e'ûwth**, *reh-ooth';* from 7462 in the sense of 7453; a female *associate;* gen. an *additional* one:—+ another, mate, neighbour.

7469. רְעוּת **r^e'ûwth**, *reh-ooth';* prob. from 7462; a *feeding* upon, i.e. grasping after:—vexation.

7470. רְעוּת **r^e'ûwth** (Chald.), *reh-ooth';* corresp. to 7469; *desire:*—pleasure, will.

7471. רְעִי **r^e'îy**, *reh-ee';* from 7462; *pasture:*—pasture.

7472. רֵעִי **Rê'îy**, *ray-ee';* from 7453; *social; Reï*, an Isr.:—Rei.

7473. רֹעִי **rô'îy**, *ro-ee';* from act. part. of 7462; *pastoral;* as noun, a *shepherd:*—shepherd.

7474. רַעְיָה **ra'yâh**, *rah-yaw';* fem. of 7453; a female *associate:*—love.

7475. רַעְיוֹן **ra'yôwn**, *rah-yone';* from 7462 in the sense of 7469; *desire:*—vexation.

7476. רַעְיוֹן **ra'yôwn** (Chald.), *rah-yone';* corresp. to 7475; a *grasp*, i.e. (fig.) mental *conception:*—cogitation, thought.

7477. רָעַל **râ'al**, *raw-al';* a prim. root; to *reel*, i.e. (fig.) to *brandish:*—terribly shake.

7478. רַעַל **ra'al**, *rah'-al;* from 7477; a *reeling* (from intoxication):—trembling.

7479. רַעֲלָה **ra'ălâh**, *rah-al-aw';* fem. of 7478; a long *veil* (as *fluttering*):—muffler.

7480. רְעֵלָיָה **R^e'êlâyâh**, *reh-ay-law-yaw';* from 7477 and 3050; *made to tremble* (i.e. *fearful*) *of Jah; Reëlajah*, an Isr.:—Reeliah.

7481. רָעַם **râ'am**, *raw-am';* a prim. root; to *tumble*, i.e. *be* violently *agitated;* spec.

to *crash* (of thunder); fig. to *irritate* (with anger):—make to fret, roar, thunder, trouble.

7482. רַעַם **raʻam**, *rahʹ-am;* from 7481; a *peal* of thunder:—thunder.

7483. רַעְמָה **raʻmâh**, *rah-mawʹ;* fem. of 7482; the *mane* of a horse (as *quivering* in the wind):—thunder.

7484. רַעְמָה **Raʻmâh**, *rah-mawʹ;* the same as 7483; *Ramah*, the name of a grandson of Ham, and of a place (perh. founded by him):—Raamah.

7485. רַעַמְיָה **Raʻamyâh**, *rah-am-yawʹ;* from 7481 and 3050; *Jah has shaken; Raamjah*, an Isr.:—Raamiah.

7486. רַעְמְסֵס **Raʻmᵉçêç**, *rah-mes-aceʹ;* or

רַעַמְסֵס **Raʻamçêç**, *rah-am-saceʹ;* of Eg. or.; *Rameses* or *Raamses*, a place in Egypt:—Raamses, Rameses.

7487. רַעֲנַן **raʻânan** (Chald.), *rah-aw-nanʹ;* corresp. to 7488; *green*, i.e. (fig.) *prosperous:*—flourishing.

7488. רַעֲנָן **raʻănân**, *rah-an-awnʹ;* from an unused root mean. to *be green; verdant;* by anal. *new;* fig. *prosperous:*—green, flourishing.

7489. רָעַע **râʻaʻ**, *raw-ahʹ;* a prim. root; prop. to *spoil* (lit. by *breaking* to pieces); fig. to *make* (or *be*) *good for nothing*, i.e. *bad* (phys., soc. or mor.):—afflict, associate selves [*by mistake for* 7462], break (down, in pieces), + displease, (be, bring, do) evil (doer, entreat, man), show self friendly [*by mistake for* 7462], do harm, (do) hurt, (behave self, deal) ill, × indeed, do mischief, punish, still, vex, (do) wicked (doer, -ly), be (deal, do) worse.

7490. רְעַע **rᵉʻaʻ** (Chald.), *reh-ahʹ;* corresp. to 7489:—break, bruise.

7491. רָעַף **râʻaph**, *raw-afʹ;* a prim. root; to *drip:*—distil, drop (down).

7492. רָעַץ **râʻats**, *raw-atsʹ;* a prim. root; to *break* in pieces; fig. *harass:*—dash in pieces, vex.

7493. רָעַשׁ **râʻash**, *raw-ash ;* a prim. root; to *undulate* (as the earth, the sky, etc.; also a field of grain), partic. through fear; spec. to *spring* (as a locust):—make afraid, (re-) move, quake, (make to) shake, (make to) tremble.

7494. רַעַשׁ **raʻash**, *rahʹ-ash;* from 7493; *vibration, bounding, uproar:*—commotion, confused noise, earthquake, fierceness, quaking, rattling, rushing, shaking.

7495. רָפָא **râphâʼ**, *raw-fawʹ;* or

רָפָה **râphâh**, *raw-fawʹ;* a prim. root; prop. to *mend* (by stitching), i.e. (fig.) to *cure:*—cure, (cause to) heal, physician, repair, × thoroughly, make whole. See 7503.

7496. רָפָא **râphâʼ**, *raw-fawʹ;* from 7495 in the sense of 7503; prop. *lax*, i.e. (fig.) a *ghost* (as *dead;* in plur. only):—dead, deceased.

7497. רָפָא **râphâʼ**, *raw-fawʹ;* or

רָפָה **râphâh**, *raw-fawʹ;* from 7495 in the sense of *invigorating;* a *giant:*—giant, Rapha, Rephaim (-s). See also 1051.

7498. רָפָא **Râphâʼ**, *raw-fawʹ;* or

רָפָה **Râphâh**, *raw-fawʹ;* prob. the same as 7497; *giant; Rapha* or *Raphah*, the name of two Isr.:—Rapha.

7499. רְפֻאָה **rᵉphûʼâh**, *ref-oo-awʹ;* fem. pass. part. of 7495; a *medicament:*—heal [-ed], medicine.

7500. רִפְאוּת **riphʼûwth**, *rif-oothʹ;* from 7495; a *cure:*—health.

7501. רְפָאֵל **Rᵉphâʼêl**, *ref-aw-aleʹ;* from 7495 and 410; *God has cured; Rephaël*, an Isr.:—Rephael.

7502. רָפַד **râphad**, *raw-fadʹ;* a prim. root; to *spread* (a bed); by impl. to *refresh:*—comfort, make [a bed], spread.

7503. רָפָה **râphâh**, *raw-fawʹ;* a prim. root; to *slacken* (in many applications, lit. or fig.):—abate, cease, consume, draw [toward evening], fail, (be) faint, be (wax) feeble, forsake, idle, leave, let alone (go, down), (be) slack, stay, be still, be slothful, (be) weak (-en). See 7495.

7504. רָפֶה **rapheh**, *raw-fehʹ;* from 7503; *slack* (in body or mind):—weak.

רָפָה **râphâh, Râphâh**. See 7497, 7498.

רִפָּה **riphâh**. See 7383.

7505. רָפוּא **Râphûwʼ**, *raw-fooʹ;* pass. part. of 7495; *cured; Raphu*, an Isr.:—Raphu.

7506. רֶפַח **Rephach**, *rehʹ-fakh;* from an unused root appar. mean. to *sustain; support; Rephach*, an Isr.:—Rephah.

7507. רְפִידָה **rᵉphîydâh**, *ref-ee-dawʹ;* from 7502; a *railing* (as *spread* along):—bottom.

7508. רְפִידִים **Rᵉphîydîym**, *ref-ee-deemʹ;* plur. of the masc. of the same as 7507; *ballusters; Rephidim*, a place in the Desert:—Rephidim.

7509. רְפָיָה **Rᵉphâyâh**, *ref-aw-yawʹ;* from 7495 and 3050; *Jah has cured; Rephajah*, the name of five Isr.:—Rephaiah.

7510. רִפְיוֹן **riphyôwn**, *rif-yoneʹ;* from 7503; *slackness:*—feebleness.

7511. רָפַס **râphaç**, *raw-fasʹ;* a prim. root; to *trample*, i.e. *prostrate:*—humble self, submit self.

7512. רְפַס **rᵉphaç** (Chald.), *ref-asʹ;* corresp. to 7511:—stamp.

7513. רַפְסֹדָה **raphçôdâh**, *raf-so-dawʹ;* from 7511; a *raft* (as *flat* on the water):—flote.

7514. רָפַק **râphaq**, *raw-fakʹ;* a prim. root; to *recline:*—lean.

7515. רָפַשׂ **râphas**, *raw-fasʹ;* a prim. root; to *trample*, i.e. *roil* water:—foul, trouble.

7516. רֶפֶשׁ **rephesh**, *rehʹ-fesh;* from 7515; *mud* (as *roiled*):—mire.

7517. רֶפֶת **repheth**, *rehʹ-feth;* prob. from 7503; a *stall* for cattle (from their *resting* there):—stall.

7518. רַץ **rats**, *rats;* contr. from 7533; a *fragment:*—piece.

7519. רָצָא **râtsâʼ**, *raw-tsawʹ;* a prim. root; to *run;* also to *delight* in:—accept, run.

7520. רָצַד **râtsad**, *raw-tsadʹ;* a prim. root; prob. to *look askant*, i.e. (fig.) *be jealous:*—leap.

7521. רָצָה **râtsâh**, *raw-tsawʹ;* a prim. root; to *be pleased with;* spec. to *satisfy* a debt:—(be) accept (-able), accomplish, set affection, approve, consent with, delight (self), enjoy, (be, have a) favour (-able), like, observe, pardon, (be, have, take) please (-ure), reconcile self.

7522. רָצוֹן **râtsôwn**, *raw-tsoneʹ;* or

רָצֹן **râtsôn**, *raw-tsoneʹ;* from 7521; *delight* (espec. as shown):—(be) acceptable (-ance, -ed), delight, desire, favour, (good) pleasure, (own, self, voluntary) will, as . . . (what) would.

7523. רָצַח **râtsach**, *raw-tsakhʹ;* a prim. root; prop. to *dash* in pieces, i.e. *kill* (a human being), espec. to *murder:*—put to death, kill, (man-) slay (-er), murder (-er).

7524. רֶצַח **retsach**, *rehʹ-tsakh;* from 7523; a *crushing;* spec. a *murder*-cry:—slaughter, sword.

7525. רִצְיָא **Ritsyâʼ**, *rits-yawʹ;* from 7521; *delight; Ritsjah*, an Isr.:—Rezia.

7526. רְצִין **Rᵉtsîyn**, *rets-eenʹ;* prob. for 7522; *Retsin*, the name of a Syrian and of an Isr.:—Rezin.

7527. רָצַע **râtsaʻ**, *raw-tsahʹ;* a prim. root; to *pierce:*—bore.

7528. רָצַף **râtsaph**, *raw-tsafʹ;* a denom. from 7529; to *tessellate*, i.e. embroider (as if with bright stones):—pave.

7529. רֶצֶף **retseph**, *rehʹ-tsef;* for 7565; a red-hot *stone* (for baking):—coal.

7530. רֶצֶף **Retseph**, *rehʹ-tsef;* the same as 7529; *Retseph*, a place in Ass.:—Rezeph.

7531. רִצְפָּה **ritspâh**, *rits-pawʹ;* fem. of 7529; a hot *stone;* also a tessellated *pavement:*—live coal, pavement.

7532. רִצְפָּה **Ritspâh**, *rits-pawʹ;* the same as 7531; *Ritspah*, an Israelitess:—Rizpah.

7533. רָצַץ **râtsats**, *raw-tsatsʹ;* a prim. root; to *crack* in pieces, lit. or fig.:—break, bruise, crush, discourage, oppress, struggle together.

7534. רַק **raq**, *rak;* from 7556 in its orig. sense; *emaciated* (as if *flattened* out):—lean ([-fleshed]), thin.

7535. רַק **raq**, *rak;* the same as 7534 as a noun; prop. *leanness*, i.e. (fig.) limitation; only adv. *merely*, or conj. *although:*—but, even, except, howbeit howsoever, at the least, nevertheless, nothing but, notwithstanding, only, save, so [that], surely, yet (so), in any wise.

7536. רֹק **rôq**, *roke;* from 7556; *spittle:*—spit (-ting, -tle).

7537. רָקַב **râqab**, *raw-kabʹ;* a prim. root; to *decay* (as by worm-eating):—rot.

7538. רָקָב **râqâb**, *raw-kawbʹ;* from 7537; *decay* (by *caries*):—rottenness (thing).

7539. רִקָּבוֹן **riqqâbôwn**, *rik-kaw-boneʹ;* from 7538; *decay* (by *caries*):—rotten.

7540. רָקַד **râqad**, *raw-kadʹ;* a prim. root; prop. to *stamp*, i.e. to *spring* about (wildly or for joy):—dance, jump, leap, skip.

7541. רַקָּה **raqqâh**, *rak-kawʹ;* fem. of 7534; prop. *thinness*, i.e. the *side* of the head:—temple.

7542. רַקּוֹן **Raqqôwn**, *rak-koneʹ;* from 7534 *thinness; Rakkon*, a place in Pal.:—Rakkon.

7543. רָקַח **râqach**, *raw-kakhʹ;* a prim. root; to *perfume:*—apothecary, compound, make [ointment], prepare, spice.

7544. רֶקַח **reqach**, *rehʹ-kakh;* from 7543; prop. *perfumery*, i.e. (by impl.) *spicery* (for flavor):—spiced.

7545. רֹקַח **rôqach**, *roʹ-kakh;* from 7542; an *aromatic:*—confection, ointment.

7546. רַקָּח **raqqâch**, *rak-kawkhʹ;* from 7543; a male *perfumer:*—apothecary.

7547. רִקֻּחַ **raqqûach**, *rak-kooʹ-akh;* from 7543; a *scented* substance:—perfume.

7548. רַקָּחָה **raqqâchâh**, *rak-kaw-khawʹ;* fem. of 7547; a female *perfumer:*—confectioner.

7549. רָקִיעַ **râqîyaʻ**, *raw-keeʹ-ah;* from 7554; prop. an *expanse*, i.e. the *firmament* or (apparently) visible arch of the sky:—firmament.

7550. רָקִיק **râqîyq**, *raw-keekʹ;* from 7556 in its orig. sense; a thin *cake:*—cake, wafer.

7551. רָקַם **râqam**, *raw-kamʹ;* a prim. root; to *variegate* color, i.e. *embroider;* by impl. to *fabricate:*—embroiderer, needlework, curiously work.

7552. רֶקֶם **Reqem**, *rehʹ-kem;* from 7551; *versicolor; Rekem*, the name of a place in Pal., also of a Midianite and an Isr.:—Rekem.

7553. רִקְמָה **riqmâh**, *rik-mawʹ;* from 7551; *variegation* of color; spec. *embroidery:*—broidered (work), divers colours, (raiment of) needlework (on both sides).

7554. רָקַע **râqaʻ**, *raw-kahʹ;* a prim. root; to *pound* the earth (as a sign of passion); by analogy to *expand* (by hammering); by impl. to *overlay* (with thin sheets of metal):—beat, make broad, spread abroad (forth, over, out, into plates), stamp, stretch.

7555. רִקֻּעַ **riqqûaʻ**, *rik-kooʹ-ah;* from 7554; *beaten* out, i.e. a (metallic) *plate:*—broad.

7556. רָקַק **râqaq**, *raw-kakʹ;* a prim. root; to *spit:*—spit.

7557. רַקַּת **Raqqath**, *rak-kathʹ;* from 7556 in its orig. sense of *diffusing;* a *beach* (as *expanded* shingle); *Rakkath*, a place in Pal.:—Rakkath.

7558. רִשְׁיוֹן **rîshyôwn**, *rish-yoneʹ;* from an unused root mean. to *have leave;* a *permit:*—grant.

7559. רָשַׁם **râsham**, *raw-shamʹ;* a prim. root; to *record:*—note.

7560. רְשַׁם **rᵉsham** (Chald.), *resh-amʹ;* corresp. to 7559:—sign, write.

7561. רָשַׁע **râshaʻ**, *raw-shahʹ;* a prim. root; to *be* (caus. *do* or *declare*) *wrong;* by impl to *disturb, violate:*—condemn, make trouble, vex, be (commit, deal, depart, do) wicked (-ly, -ness).

7562. רֶשַׁע **reshaʻ**, *reh'-shah;* from 7561; a *wrong* (espec. moral):—iniquity, wicked (-ness).

7563. רָשָׁע **râshâʻ**, *raw-shaw';* from 7561; morally *wrong;* concr. an (actively) *bad* person:— + condemned, guilty, ungodly, wicked (man), that did wrong.

7564. רִשְׁעָה **rishʻâh**, *rish-aw';* fem. of 7562; *wrong* (espec. moral):—fault, wickedly (-ness).

7565. רֶשֶׁף **resheph**, *reh'-shef;* from 8313; a live *coal;* by analogy *lightning;* fig. an *arrow* (as *flashing* through the air); spec. *fever:*—arrow, (burning) coal, burning heat, + spark, hot thunderbolt.

7566. רֶשֶׁף **Resheph**, *reh'-shef;* the same as 7565; *Resheph,* an Isr.:—Resheph.

7567. רָשַׁשׁ **râshash**, *raw-shash';* a prim. root; to *demolish:*—impoverish.

7568. רֶשֶׁת **resheth**, *reh'-sheth;* from 3423; a *net* (as *catching* animals):—net [-work].

7569. רַתּוֹק **rattôwq** *rat-toke';* from 7576; a *chain:*—chain.

7570. רָתַח **râthach**, *raw-thakh';* a prim. root; to *boil:*—boil.

7571. רֶתַח **rethach**, *reh'-thakh;* from 7570; a *boiling:*— × [boil] well.

7572. רַתִּיקָה° **rattîyqâh**, *rat-tee-kaw';* from 7576; a *chain:*—chain.

7573. רָתַם **râtham**, *raw-tham';* a prim. root: to *yoke* up (to the pole of a vehicle):—bind.

7574. רֶתֶם **rethem**, *reh'-them;* or

רֹתֶם **rôthem**, *ro'-them;* from 7573; the Spanish *broom* (from its pole-like stems):—juniper (tree).

7575. רִתְמָה **Rithmâh**, *rith-maw';* fem. of 7574; *Rithmah,* a place in the Desert:—Rithmah.

7576. רָתַק **râthaq**, *raw-thak';* a prim. root; to *fasten:*—bind.

7577. רְתֻקָה **rethûqâh**, *reth-oo-kaw';* fem. pass. part. of 7576; something *fastened,* i.e. a *chain:*—chain.

7578. רְתֵת **rethêth**, *reth-ayth';* for 7374; *terror:*—trembling.

ש

7579. שָׁאַב **shâ'ab**, *shaw-ab';* a prim. root; to *bale* up water:—(woman to) draw (-er, water).

7580. שָׁאַג **shâ'ag**, *shaw-ag';* a prim. root; to *rumble* or *moan:*— × mightily, roar.

7581. שְׁאָגָה **she'âgâh**, *sheh-aw-gaw';* from 7580; a *rumbling* or *moan:*—roaring.

7582. שָׁאָה **shâ'âh**, *shaw-aw';* a prim. root; to *rush;* by impl. to *desolate:*—be desolate, (make a) rush (-ing), (lay) waste.

7583. שָׁאָה **shâ'âh**, *shaw-aw';* a prim. root [rather ident. with 7582 through the idea of *whirling* to giddiness]; to *stun,* i.e. (intrans.) *be astonished:*—wonder.

7584. שַׁאֲוָה **sha'ǎvâh**, *shah-av-aw';* from 7582; a *tempest* (as *rushing*):—desolation.

7585. שְׁאוֹל **she'ôwl**, *sheh-ole';* or

שְׁאֹל **she'ôl**, *sheh-ole';* from 7592; *hades* or the world of the dead (as if a subterranean *retreat*), includ. its accessories and inmates:—grave, hell, pit.

7586. שָׁאוּל **Shâ'ûwl**, *shaw-ool';* pass. part. of 7592; *asked; Shaül,* the name of an Edomite and two Isr.:—Saul, Shaul.

7587. שָׁאוּלִי **Shâ'ûwlîy**, *shaw-oo-lee';* patron. from 7856; a *Shaülite* or desc. of Shaul:—Shaulites.

7588. שָׁאוֹן **shâ'ôwn**, *shaw-one';* from 7582; *uproar* (as of *rushing*); by impl. *destruction:*— × horrible, noise, pomp, rushing, tumult (× -uous).

7589. שְׁאָט **she'âṭ**, *sheh-awt';* from an unused root mean. to *push* aside; *contempt:*—despite (-ful).

7590. שָׁאט **shâ'ṭ**, *shawt;* for act. part. of 7750 [comp. 7589]; one *contemning:*—that (which) despise (-d).

7591. שְׁאִיָּה **she'îyâh**, *sheh-ee-yaw';* from 7582; *desolation:*—destruction.

7592. שָׁאַל **shâ'al**, *shaw-al';* or

שָׁאֵל **shâ'êl**, *shaw-ale';* a prim. root; to *inquire;* by impl. to *request;* by extens. to *demand:*—ask (counsel, on), beg, borrow, lay to charge, consult, demand, desire, × earnestly, enquire, + greet, obtain leave, lend, pray, request, require, + salute, × straitly, × surely, wish.

7593. שְׁאֵל **she'êl** (Chald.), *sheh-ale';* corresp. to 7592:—ask, demand, require.

7594. שְׁאָל **She'âl**, *sheh-awl';* from 7592; *request; Sheäl,* an Isr.:—Sheal.

שְׁאֹל **she'ôl**. See 7585.

7595. שְׁאֵלָא **she'êlâ'** (Chald.), *sheh-ay-law';* from 7593; prop. a *question* (at law), i.e. judicial *decision* or mandate:—demand.

7596. שְׁאֵלָה **she'êlâh**, *sheh-ay-law';* or

שֵׁלָה **shêlâh** (1 Sam. 1 : 17), *shay-law';* from 7592; a *petition;* by impl. a *loan:*—loan, petition, request.

7597. שְׁאַלְתִּיאֵל **She'altîy'êl**, *sheh-al-tee-ale';* or

שַׁלְתִּיאֵל **Shaltîy'êl**, *shal-tee-ale';* from 7592 and 410; *I have asked God; Sheältiël,* an Isr.:—Shalthiel, Shealtiel.

7598. שְׁאַלְתִּיאֵל **She'altîy'êl** (Chald.), *sheh-al-tee-ale';* corresp. to 7597:—Shealtiel.

7599. שָׁאַן **shâ'an**, *shaw-an';* a prim. root; to *loll,* i.e. *be peaceful:*—be at ease, be quiet rest. See also 1052.

7600. שַׁאֲנָן **sha'ǎnân**, *shah-an-awn';* from 7599; *secure;* in a bad sense, *haughty:*—that is at ease, quiet, tumult. Comp. 7946.

7601 שָׁאַס° **shâ'aç**, *shaw-as';* a prim. root; to *plunder:*—spoil.

7602. שָׁאַף **shâ'aph**, *shaw-af';* a prim. root; to *inhale* eagerly; fig. to *covet;* by impl. to *be angry;* also to *hasten:*—desire (earnestly), devour, haste, pant, snuff up, swallow up.

7603. שְׂאֹר **se'ôr**, *seh-ore';* from 7604; *barm* or yeast-cake (as *swelling* by fermentation):—leaven.

7604. שָׁאַר **shâ'ar**, *shaw-ar';* a prim. root; prop. to *swell* up, i.e. *be* (caus. *make*) *redundant:*—leave, (be) left, let, remain, remnant, reserve, the rest.

7605. שְׁאָר **she'âr**, *sheh-awr';* from 7604; a *remainder:*— × other, remnant, residue, rest.

7606. שְׁאָר **she'âr** (Chald.), *sheh-awr';* corresp. to 7605:— × whatsoever more, residue, rest.

7607. שְׁאֵר **she'êr**, *sheh-ayr';* from 7604; *flesh* (as *swelling* out), as living or for food; gen. *food* of any kind; fig. *kindred* by blood:—body, flesh, food, (near) kin (-sman, -swoman), near (nigh) [of kin]

7608. שַׁאֲרָה **sha'ǎrâh**, *shah-ar-aw';* fem. of 7607; female *kindred* by blood:—near kinswomen.

7609. שֶׁאֱרָה **She'ěrâh**, *sheh-er-aw';* the same as 7608; *Sheërah,* an Israelitess:—Sherah.

7610. שְׁאָר יָשׁוּב **She'âr Yâshûwb**, *sheh-awr' yaw-shoob';* from 7605 and 7725; a *remnant will return; Sheär-Jashub,* the symbol. name of one of Isaiah's sons:—Shear-jashub.

7611. שְׁאֵרִית **she'êrîyth**, *sheh-ay-reeth';* from 7604; a *remainder* or residual (surviving, final) portion:—that had escaped, be left, posterity, remain (-der), remnant, residue, rest.

7612. שֵׁאת **shê'th**, *shayth;* from 7582; *devastation:*—desolation.

7613. שְׂאֵת **se'êth**, *seh-ayth';* from 5375; an *elevation* or leprous scab; fig. *elation* or cheerfulness; *exaltation* in rank or character:—be accepted, dignity, excellency, highness, raise up self, rising.

7614. שְׁבָא **Shebâ'**, *sheb-aw';* of for. or.; *Sheba,* the name of three early progenitors of tribes and of an Ethiopian district:—Sheba, Sabeans.

7615. שְׁבָאִי **Shebâ'îy**, *sheb-aw-ee';* patron. from 7614; a *Shebaïte* or desc. of Sheba:—Sabean.

7616. שָׁבָב **shâbâb**, *shaw-bawb';* from an unused root mean. to *break* up; a *fragment,* i.e. *ruin:*—broken in pieces.

7617. שָׁבָה **shâbâh**, *shaw-baw';* a prim. root; to *transport* into captivity:—(bring away, carry, carry away, lead, lead away, take) captive (-s), drive (take) away.

7618. שְׁבוּ **shebûw**, *sheb-oo';* from an unused root (prob. ident. with that of 7617 through the idea of *subdivision* into flashes or streamers [comp. 7632]) mean. to *flame;* a *gem* (from its sparkle), prob. the *agate:*—agate.

7619. שְׁבוּאֵל **Shebûw'êl**, *sheb-oo-ale';* or

שׁוּבָאֵל **Shûwbâ'êl**, *shoo-baw-ale';* from 7617 (abbrev.) or 7725 and 410; *captive* (or *returned*) *of God; Shebuël* or *Shubaël,* the name of two Isr.:—Shebuel, Shubael.

7620. שָׁבוּעַ **shâbûwaʻ**, *shaw-boo'-ah;* or

שָׁבֻעַ **shâbûaʻ**, *shaw-boo'-ah;* also (fem.)

שְׁבֻעָה **shebûʻâh**, *sheb-oo-aw';* prop. pass. part. of 7650 as a denom. of 7651; lit. *sevened,* i.e. a *week* (spec. of years):—seven, week.

7621. שְׁבוּעָה **shebûwʻâh**, *sheb-oo-aw';* fem. pass. part. of 7650; prop. something *sworn,* i.e. an *oath:*—curse, oath, × sworn.

7622. שְׁבוּת **shebûwth**, *sheb-ooth';* or

שְׁבִית **shebîyth**, *sheb-eeth';* from 7617; *exile:* concr. *prisoners;* fig. a *former state* of prosperity:—captive (-ity).

7623. שָׁבַח **shâbach**, *shaw-bakh';* a prim. root; prop. to *address* in a loud tone, i.e. (spec.) *loud;* fig. to *pacify* (as if by words):—commend, glory, keep in, praise, still, triumph.

7624. שְׁבַח **shebach** (Chald.), *sheb-akh';* corresp. to 7623; to *adulate,* i.e. *adore:*—praise.

7625. שְׁבַט **shebaṭ** (Chald.), *sheb-at';* corresp. to 7626; a *clan:*—tribe.

7626. שֵׁבֶט **shêbeṭ**, *shay'-bet;* from an unused root prob. mean. to *branch* off; a *scion,* i.e. (lit.) a *stick* (for punishing, writing, fighting, ruling, walking, etc.) or (fig.) a *clan:*— × correction, dart, rod, sceptre, staff, tribe.

7627. שְׁבָט **Shebâṭ**, *sheb-awt';* of for. or.; *Shebat,* a Jewish month:—Sebat.

7628. שְׁבִי **shebîy**, *sheb-ee';* from 7618; *exiled; captured;* as noun, *exile* (abstr. or concr. and collect.); by extens. *booty:*—captive (-ity), prisoners, × take away, that was taken.

7629. שֹׁבִי **Shôbîy**, *sho-bee';* from 7617; *captor; Shobi,* an Ammonite:—Shobi.

7630. שֹׁבַי **Shôbay**, *sho-bah'ee;* for 7629; *Shobai,* an Isr.:—Shobai.

7631. שְׂבִיב **sebîyb** (Chald.), *seb-eeb';* corresp. to 7632:—flame.

7632. שָׁבִיב **shâbîyb**, *shaw-beeb';* from the same as 7616; *flame* (as *split* into tongues):—spark.

7633. שִׁבְיָה **shibyâh**, *shib-yaw';* fem. of 7628; *exile* (abstr. or concr. and collect.):—captives (-ity).

7634. שָׁבְיָה **Shobyâh**, *shob-yaw';* fem. of the same as 7629; *captivation; Shobjah,* an Isr.:—Shachia [*from the marg.*].

7635. שָׁבִיל **shâbîyl**, *shaw-beel';* from the same as 7640; a *track* or passage-way (as if *flowing* along):—path.

7636. שָׁבִיס **shâbîyç**, *shaw-beece';* from an unused root mean. to *interweave;* a *netting* for the hair:—caul.

7637. שְׁבִיעִי **shᵉbîʿîy,** sheb-ee-ee'; or

שְׁבִעִי **shᵉbîʿîy,** sheb-ee-ee'; ordinal from 7657; *seventh:*—seventh (time).

שְׁבִית **shᵉbîyth.** See 7622.

7638. שָׂבָךְ **sâbâk,** saw-bawk'; from an unused root mean. to *intwine; a netting* (ornament to the capital of a column):—net.

שַׂבְּכָא **sabbᵉkâʾ.** See 5443.

7639. שְׂבָכָה **sᵉbâkâh,** seb-aw-kaw'; fem. of 7638; *a net-work,* i.e. (in hunting) a *snare,* (in arch.) a *ballustrade;* also a *reticulated* ornament to a pillar:—checker, lattice, network, snare, wreath (-enwork).

7640. שֹׁבֶל **shôbel,** show'-bel; from an unused root mean. to *flow; a lady's train* (as *trailing* after her):—leg.

7641. שִׁבֹּל **shibbôl,** shib-bole; or (fem.)

שִׁבֹּלֶת **shibbôleth,** shib-bo'-leth; from the same as 7640; *a stream* (as *flowing*); also an *ear of grain* (as *growing* out); by anal. a *branch:*—branch, channel, ear (of corn), ([water-]) flood, Shibboleth. Comp. 5451.

7642. שַׁבְלוּל **shablûwl,** shab-lool'; from the same as 7640; *a snail* (as if *floating* in its own slime):—snail.

שִׁבֹּלֶת **shibbôleth.** See 7641.

7643. שְׂבָם **Sᵉbâm,** seb-awm'; or (fem.)

שִׂבְמָה **Sibmâh,** sib-maw'; prob. from 1313; *spice; Sebam* or *Sibmah,* a place in Moab:—Shebam, Shibmah, Sibmah.

7644. שֶׁבְנָא **Shebnâʾ,** sheb-naw'; or

שֶׁבְנָה **Shebnâh,** sheb-naw'; from an unused root mean. to *grow; growth; Shebna* or *Shebnah,* an Isr.:—Shebna, Shebnah.

7645. שְׁבַנְיָה **Shᵉbanyâh,** sheb-an-yaw'; or

שְׁבַנְיָהוּ **Shᵉbanyâhûw,** sheb-an-yaw'-hoo; from the same as 7644 and 3050; *Jah has grown* (i.e. *prospered*); *Shebanjah,* the name of three or four Isr.:—Shebaniah.

7646. שָׂבַע **sâbaʿ,** saw-bah'; or

שָׂבֵעַ **sâbêaʿ,** saw-bay'-ah; a prim. root; to *sate,* i.e. *fill* to satisfaction (lit. or fig.):— have enough, fill (full, self, with), be (to the) full (of), have plenty of, be satiate, satisfy (with), suffice, be weary of.

7647. שָׂבָע **sâbâʿ,** saw-baw'; from 7646; *copiousness:*—abundance, plenteous (-ness, -ly).

7648. שֹׂבַע **sôbaʿ,** so'-bah; from 7646; *satisfaction* (of food or [fig.] *joy*):—fill, full (-ness), satisfying, be satisfied.

7649. שָׂבֵעַ **sâbêaʿ,** saw-bay'-ah; from 7646; *satiated* (in a pleasant or disagreeable sense):—full (of), satisfied (with).

7650. שָׁבַע **shâbaʿ,** shaw-bah'; a prim. root; prop. to *be complete,* but used only as a denom. from 7651; to *seven* oneself, i.e. *swear* (as if by repeating a declaration seven times):—adjure, charge (by an oath, with an oath), feed to the full [by mistake for 7646], take an oath, × straitly, (cause to, make to) swear.

7651. שֶׁבַע **shebaʿ,** sheh'-bah; or (masc.)

שִׁבְעָה **shibʿâh,** shib-aw'; from 7650; a prim. cardinal number; *seven* (as the *sacred* full one); also (adv.) *seven times;* by impl. a *week;* by extens. an *indefinite* number:—(+ by) seven ([-fold], -s, [-teen, -teenth], -th, times). Comp. 7658.

7652. שֶׁבַע **shebaʿ,** sheh'-bah; the same as 7651; *seven; Sheba,* the name of a place in Pal., and of two Isr.:—Sheba.

שָׁבֻעַ **shâbûaʿ.** See 7620.

7653. שִׂבְעָה **sibʿâh,** sib-aw'; fem. of 7647; *satiety:*—fulness.

7654. שָׂבְעָה **sobʿâh,** sob-aw'; fem. of 7648; *satiety:*—(to have) enough, × till . . . be full, [un-] satiable, satisfy, × sufficiently.

שִׁבְעָה **shibʿâh.** See 7651.

7655. שִׁבְעָה **shibʿâh** (Chald.), shib-aw'; corresp. to 7651:—seven (times).

7656. שִׁבְעָה **Shibʿâh,** shib-aw'; masc. of 7651; *seven* (-th); *Shebah,* a well in Pal.:— Shebah.

שְׁבוּעָה **shᵉbûʿâh.** See 7620.

שְׁבִעִי **shᵉbîʿîy.** See 7637.

7657. שִׁבְעִים **shibʿîym,** shib-eem'; multiple of 7651; *seventy:*—seventy, threescore and ten (+ -teen).

7658. שִׁבְעָנָה **shibʿânâh,** shib-aw-naw'; prol. for the masc. of 7651; *seven:*—seven.

7659. שִׁבְעָתַיִם **shibʿâthayim,** shib-aw-thah'-yim; dual (adv.) of 7651; *seven-times:*—seven (-fold, times).

7660. שָׁבַץ **shâbats,** shaw-bats'; a prim. root; to *interweave* (colored) threads in squares; by impl. (of *reticulation*) to *inchase* gems in gold:—embroider, set.

7661. שָׁבָץ **shâbâts,** shaw-bawts'; from 7660; *intanglement,* i.e. (fig.) *perplexity:*—anguish.

7662. שְׁבַק **shᵉbaq** (Chald.), sheb-ak'; corresp. to the root of 7733; to *quit,* i.e. *allow* to remain:—leave, let alone.

7663. שָׂבַר **sâbar,** saw-bar'; erroneously

שָׁבַר **shâbar** (Neh. 2 : 13, 15), shaw-bar'; a prim. root; to *scrutinize;* by impl. (of *watching*) to *expect* (with hope and patience):—hope, tarry, view, wait.

7664. שֵׂבֶר **sêber,** say'-ber; from 7663; *expectation:*—hope.

7665. שָׁבַר **shâbar,** shaw-bar'; a prim. root; to *burst* (lit. or fig.):—break (down, off, in pieces, up), broken ([-hearted]), bring to the birth, crush, destroy, hurt, quench, × quite, tear, view [by mistake for 7663].

7666. שָׁבַר **shâbar,** shaw-bar'; denom. from 7668; to *deal in grain:*—buy, sell.

7667. שֶׁבֶר **sheber,** sheh'-ber; or

שֵׁבֶר **shêber,** shay'-ber; from 7665; a *fracture,* fig. *ruin;* spec. a *solution* (of a dream):—affliction, breach, breaking, broken [-foot-ed, -handed], bruise, crashing, destruction, hurt, interpretation, vexation.

7668. שֶׁבֶר **sheber,** sheh'-ber; the same as 7667; *grain* (as if *broken* into kernels):—corn, victuals.

7669. שֶׁבֶר **Sheber,** sheh'-ber; the same as 7667; *Sheber,* an Isr.:—Sheber.

7670. שִׁבְרוֹן **shibrôwn,** shib-rone'; from 7665; *rupture,* i.e. a *pang;* fig. *ruin:*—breaking, destruction.

7671. שְׁבָרִים **Shᵉbârîym,** sheb-aw-reem'; plur. of 7667; *ruins; Shebarim,* a place in Pal.:—Shebarim.

7672. שְׁבַשׁ **shᵉbash** (Chald.), sheb-ash'; corresp. to 7660; to *intangle,* i.e. *perplex:*—be astonished.

7673. שָׁבַת **shâbath,** shaw-bath'; a prim. root; to *repose,* i.e. *desist* from exertion; used in many impl. relations (caus., fig. or spec.):— (cause to, let, make to) cease, celebrate, cause (make) to fail, keep (sabbath), suffer to be lacking, leave, put away (down), (make to) rest, rid, still, take away.

7674. שֶׁבֶת **shebeth,** sheh'-beth; from 7673; *rest, interruption, cessation:*—cease, sit still, loss of time.

7675. שֶׁבֶת **shebeth,** sheh'-beth; infin. of 3427; prop. *session;* but used also concr. an *abode* or *locality:*—place, seat. Comp. 3429.

7676. שַׁבָּת **shabbâth,** shab-bawth'; intens. from 7673; *intermission,* i.e. (spec.) the *Sabbath:*—(+ every) sabbath.

7677. שַׁבָּתוֹן **shabbâthôwn,** shab-baw-thone'; from 7676; a *sabbatism* or special *holiday:*—rest, sabbath.

7678. שַׁבְּתַי **Shabbᵉthay,** shab-beth-ah'ee; from 7676; *restful; Shabbethai,* the name of three Isr.:—Shabbethai.

7679. שָׂגָא **sâgâʾ,** saw-gaw'; a prim. root; to *grow,* i.e. (caus.) to *enlarge,* (fig.) *laud:*—increase, magnify.

7680. שְׂגָא **sᵉgâʾ** (Chald.), seg-aw'; corresp. to 7679; to *increase:*—grow, be multiplied.

7681. שָׁגֵא **Shâgêʾ,** shaw-gay'; prob. from 7686; *erring; Shage,* an Isr.:—Shage.

7682. שָׂגַב **sâgab,** saw-gab'; a prim. root; to *be* (caus. *make*) *lofty,* espec. *inaccessible;* by impl. *safe, strong;* used lit. and fig.:—defend, exalt, be excellent, (be, set on) high, lofty, be safe, set up (on high), be too strong.

7683. שָׁגַג **shâgag,** shaw-gag'; a prim. root; to *stray,* i.e. (fig.) *sin* (with more or less apology):— × also for that, deceived, err, go astray, sin ignorantly.

7684. שְׁגָגָה **shᵉgâgâh,** sheg-aw-gaw'; from 7683; a *mistake* or inadvertent *transgression:*—error, ignorance, at unawares, unwittingly.

7685. שָׂגָה **sâgâh,** saw-gaw'; a prim. root; to *enlarge* (espec. upward, also fig.):—grow (up), increase.

7686. שָׁגָה **shâgâh,** shaw-gaw'; a prim. root; to *stray* (caus. *mislead*), usually (fig.) to *mistake,* espec. (mor.) to *transgress;* by extens. (through the idea of *intoxication*) to *reel,* (fig.) be *enraptured:*—(cause to) go astray, deceive, err, be ravished, sin through ignorance, (let, make to) wander.

7687. שְׂגוּב **Sᵉgûwb,** seg-oob'; from 7682; *aloft; Segub,* the name of two Isr.:—Segub.

7688. שָׁגַח **shâgach,** shaw-gakh'; a prim. root; to *peep,* i.e. *glance sharply* at:—look (narrowly).

7689. שַׂגִּיא **saggîyʾ,** sag-ghee'; from 7679; (superlatively) *mighty:*—excellent, great.

7690. שַׂגִּיא **saggîyʾ** (Chald.), sag-ghee'; corresp. to 7689; *large* (in size, quantity or number, also adv.):—exceeding, great (-ly), many, much, sore, very.

7691. שְׁגִיאָה **shᵉgîyʾâh,** sheg-ee-aw'; from 7686; a moral *mistake:*—error.

7692. שִׁגָּיוֹן **shiggâyôwn,** shig-gaw-yone'; or

שִׁגָּיֹנָה **shiggâyônâh,** shig-gaw-yo-naw'; from 7686; prop. *aberration,* i.e. (tech.) a *dithyramb* or rambling poem:—Shiggaion, Shigionoth.

7693. שָׁגַל **shâgal,** shaw-gal'; a prim. root; to *copulate* with:—lie with, ravish.

7694. שֵׁגָל **shêgâl,** shay-gawl'; from 7693; a *queen* (from cohabitation):—queen.

7695. שֵׁגָל **shêgâl** (Chald.), shay-gawl'; corresp. to 7694; a (legitimate) *queen:*—wife.

7696. שָׁגַע **shâgaʿ,** shaw-gah'; a prim. root; to *rave through insanity:*—(be, play the) mad (man).

7697. שִׁגָּעוֹן **shiggâʿôwn,** shig-gaw-yone'; from 7696; *craziness:*—furiously, madness.

7698. שֶׁגֶר **sheger,** sheh'-ger; from an unused root prob. mean. to *eject; the fœtus* (as finally *expelled*):—that cometh of, increase.

7699. שַׁד **shad,** shad; or

שֹׁד **shôd,** shode; prob. from 7736 (in its orig. sense) contr.; the *breast* of a woman or animal (as *bulging*):—breast, pap, teat.

7700. שֵׁד **shêd,** shade; from 7736; a *dæmon* (as *malignant*):—devil.

7701. שֹׁד **shôd,** shode; or

שׁוֹד **shôwd** (Job 5 : 21), shode; from 7736; *violence, ravage:*—desolation, destruction, oppression, robbery, spoil (-ed, -er, -ing), wasting.

7702. שָׂדַד **sâdad**, *saw-dad'*; a prim. root; to *abrade*, i.e. *harrow* a field:—break clods, harrow.

7703. שָׁדַד **shâdad**, *shaw-dad'*; a prim. root; prop. to *be burly*, i.e. (fig.) *powerful* (pass. *impregnable*); by impl. to *ravage*:—dead, destroy (-er), oppress, robber, spoil (-er), × utterly, (lay) waste.

7704. שָׂדֶה **sâdeh**, *saw-deh'*; or

שָׂדַי **sâday**, *saw-dah'ee*; from an unused root mean. to *spread* out; a *field* (as *flat*):—country, field, ground, land, soil, × wild.

7705. שִׁדָּה **shiddâh**, *shid-dah'*; from 7703; a *wife* (as *mistress* of the house):—× all sorts, musical instrument.

7706. שַׁדַּי **Shadday**, *shad-dah'ee*; from 7703; the *Almighty*:—Almighty.

7707. שְׁדֵיאוּר **Shᵉdêyʼûwr**, *shed-ay-oor'*; from the same as 7704 and 217; *spreader of light*; *Shedejur*, an Isr.:—Shedeur.

7708. שִׂדִּים **Siddîym**, *sid-deem'*; plur. from the same as 7704; *flats*; *Siddim*, a valley in Pal.:—Siddim.

7709. שְׁדֵמָה **shᵉdêmâh**, *shed-ay-maw'*; appar. from 7704; a cultivated *field*:—blasted, field.

7710. שָׁדַף **shâdaph**, *shaw-daf'*; a prim. root; to *scorch*:—blast.

7711. שְׁדֵפָה **shᵉdêphâh**, *shed-ay-faw'*; or

שִׁדָּפוֹן **shiddâphôwn**, *shid-daw-fone'*; from 7710; *blight*:—blasted (-ing).

7712. שְׁדַר **shᵉdar** (Chald.), *shed-ar'*; a prim. root; to *endeavor*:—labour.

7713. שְׂדֵרָה **sᵉdêrâh**, *sed-ay-raw'*; from an unused root mean. to *regulate*; a *row*, i.e. *rank* (of soldiers), *story* (of rooms):—board, range.

7714. שַׁדְרַךְ **Shadrak**, *shad-rak'*; prob. of for. or.; *Shadrak*, the Bab. name of one of Daniel's companions:—Shadrach.

7715. שַׁדְרַךְ **Shadrak** (Chald.), *shad-rak'*; the same as 7714:—Shadrach.

7716. שֶׂה **seh**, *seh*; or

שֵׂי **sêy**, *say*; prob. from 7582 through the idea of *pushing* out to graze; a member of a flock, i.e. a *sheep* or *goat*:—(lesser, small) cattle, ewe, lamb, sheep.

7717. שָׂהֵד **sâhêd**, *saw-hade'*; from an unused root mean. to *testify*; a *witness*:—record.

7718. שֹׁהַם **shôham**, *sho'-ham*; from an unused root prob. mean. to *blanch*; a gem, prob. the *beryl* (from its *pale* green color):—onyx.

7719. שֹׁהַם **Shôham**, *sho'-ham*; the same as 7718; *Shoham*, an Isr.:—Shoham.

7720. שַׂהֲרֹן **sahărôn**, *sah-har-one'*; from the same as 5469; a round *pendant* for the neck:—ornament, round tire like the moon.

שַׁו° **shav**. See 7723.

7721. שׂוֹא **sôwʼ**, *so*; from an unused root (akin to 5375 and 7722) mean. to *rise*; a *rising*:—arise.

7722. שׁוֹא **shôwʼ**, *sho*; or (fem.)

שׁוֹאָה **shôwʼâh**, *sho-aw'*; or

שֹׁאָה **shôʼâh**, *sho-aw'*; from an unused root mean. to *rush* over; a *tempest*; by impl. *devastation*:—desolate (-ion), destroy, destruction, storm, wasteness.

7723. שָׁוְא **shâvʼ**, *shawv*; or

שַׁו° **shav**, *shav*; from the same as 7722 in the sense of *desolating*; *evil* (as *destructive*), lit. (*ruin*) or mor. (espec. *guile*); fig. *idolatry* (as false, subj.), *uselessness* (as deceptive, obj.; also adv. in *vain*):—false (-ly), lie, lying, vain, vanity.

7724. שְׁוָא **Shᵉvâʼ**, *shev-aw'*; from the same as 7723; *false*; *Sheva*, an Isr.:—Sheva.

7725. שׁוּב **shûwb**, *shoob*; a prim. root; to *turn* back (hence, away) trans. or intrans., lit. or fig. (not necessarily with the idea of *return* to the starting point); gen. to *retreat*; often adv. *again*:—([break, build, circumcise, dig, do anything, do evil, feed, lay down, lie down, lodge, make, rejoice, send, take, weep]) × again, (cause to) answer (+ again), × in any case (wise), × at all, averse, bring (again, back, home again), call [to mind], carry again (back), cease, × certainly, come again (back) × consider, + continually, convert, deliver (again), + deny, draw back, fetch home again, × fro, get [oneself] (back) again, × give (again), go again (back, home), [go] out, hinder, let, [see] more, × needs, be past, × pay, pervert, pull in again, put (again, up again), recall, recompense, recover, refresh, relieve, render (again), × repent, requite, rescue, restore, retrieve, (cause to, make to) return, reverse, reward, + say nay, send back, set again, slide back, still, × surely, take back (off), (cause to, make to) turn (again, self again, away, back, back again, backward, from, off), withdraw.

שׁוּבָאֵל **Shûwbâʼêl**. See 7619.

7726. שׁוֹבָב **shôwbâb**, *sho-bawb'*; from 7725; *apostate*, i.e. idolatrous:—backsliding, frowardly, turn away [*from marg.*].

7727. שׁוֹבָב **Shôwbâb**, *sho-bawb'*; the same as 7726; *rebellious*; *Shobab*, the name of two Isr.:—Shobab.

7728. שׁוֹבֵב **shôwbêb**, *sho-babe'*; from 7725; *apostate*, i.e. heathenish or (actually) heathen:—backsliding.

7729. שׁוּבָה **shûwbâh**, *shoo-baw'*; from 7725; a *return*:—returning.

7730. שׂוֹבֶךְ **sôwbek**, *so'-bek*; for 5441; a *thicket*, i.e. interlaced branches:—thick boughs.

7731. שׁוֹבָךְ **Shôwbâk**, *sho-bawk'*; perh. for 7730; *Shobak*, a Syrian:—Shobach.

7732. שׁוֹבָל **Shôwbâl**, *sho-bawl'*; from the same as 7640; *overflowing*; *Shobal*, the name of an Edomite and two Isr.:—Shobal.

7733. שׁוֹבֵק **Shôwbêq**, *sho-bake'*; act. part. from a prim. root mean. to *leave* (comp. 7662); *forsaking*; *Shobek*, an Isr.:—Shobek.

7734. שׂוּג **sûwg**, *soog*; a prim. root; to *retreat*:—turn back.

7735. שׂוּג **sûwg**, *soog*; a prim. root; to *hedge* in:—make to grow.

7736. שׁוּד **shûwd**, *shood*; a prim. root; prop. to *swell* up, i.e. fig. (by impl. of *insolence*) to *devastate*:—waste.

שׁוֹד **shôwd**. See 7699, 7701.

7737. שָׁוָה **shâvâh**, *shaw-vaw'*; a prim. root; prop. to *level*, i.e. *equalize*; fig. to *resemble*; by impl. to *adjust* (i.e. counterbalance, be suitable, compose, place, yield, etc.):—avail, behave, bring forth, compare, countervail, (be, make) equal, lay, be (make, a-) like, make plain, profit, reckon.

7738. שָׁוָה **shâvâh**, *shaw-vaw'*; a prim. root; to *destroy*:—× substance [*from the marg.*].

7739. שְׁוָה **shᵉvâh** (Chald.), *shev-aw'*; corresp. to 7737; to *resemble*:—make like.

7740. שָׁוֵה **Shâvêh**, *shaw-vay'*; from 7737; *plain*; *Shaveh*, a place in Pal.:—Shaveh.

7741. שָׁוֵה קִרְיָתַיִם **Shâvêh Qiryâthayim**, *shaw-vay' kir-yaw-thah'-yim*; from the same as 7740 and the dual of 7151; *plain of a double city*; *Shaveh-Kirjathajim*, a place E. of the Jordan:—Shaveh Kiriathaim.

7742. שׂוּחַ **sûwach**, *soo'-akh*; a prim. root; to *muse* pensively:—meditate.

7743. שׁוּחַ **shûwach**, *shoo'-akh*; a prim. root; to *sink*, lit. or fig.:—bow down, incline, humble.

7744. שׁוּחַ **Shûwach**, *shoo'-akh*; from 7743; *dell*; *Shuăch*, a son of Abraham:—Shuah.

7745 שׁוּחָה **shûwchâh**, *shoo-khaw'*; from 7743; a *chasm*:—ditch, pit.

7746. שׁוּחָה **Shûwchâh**, *shoo-khaw'*; the same as 7745; *Shuchah*, an Isr.:—Shuah.

7747. שׁוּחִי **Shuchîy**, *shoo-khee'*; patron. from 7744; a *Shuchite* or desc. of Shuach:—Shuhite.

7748. שׁוּחָם **Shûwchâm**, *shoo-khawm'*; from 7743; *humbly*; *Shucham*, an Isr.:—Shuham.

7749. שׁוּחָמִי **Shûwchâmîy**, *shoo-khaw-mee'*; patron. from 7748; a *Shuchamite* (collect.):—Shuhamites.

7750. שׂוּט **sûwṭ**, *soot*; or (by perm.)

סוּט **çûwṭ**, *soot*; a primitive root; to *detrude*, i.e. (intrans. and fig.) *become derelict* (wrongly practise; namely, idolatry):—turn aside to.

7751. שׁוּט **shûwṭ**, *shoot*; a prim. root; prop. to *push* forth; (but used only fig.) to *lash*, i.e. (the sea with oars) to *row*; by impl. to *travel*:—go (about, through, to and fro), mariner, rower, run to and fro.

7752. שׁוֹט **shôwṭ**, *shote*; from 7751; a *lash* (lit. or fig.):—scourge, whip.

7753. שׂוּךְ **sûwk**, *sook*; a prim. root; to *entwine*, i.e. *shut* in (for formation, protection or restraint):—fence, (make an) hedge (up).

7754. שׂוֹךְ **sôwk**, *soke*; or (fem.)

שׂוֹכָה **sôwkâh**, *so-kaw'*; from 7753; a *branch* (as *interleaved*):—bough.

7755. שׂוֹכֹה **Sôwkôh**, *so-ko'*; or

שֹׂכֹה **Sôkôh**, *so-ko'*; or

שׂוֹכוֹ **Sôwkôw**, *so-ko'*; from 7753; *Sokoh* or *Soko*, the name of two places in Pal.:—Shocho, Shochoh, Sochoh, Soco, Socoh.

7756. שׂוּכָתִי **Sûwkâthîy**, *soo-kaw-thee'*; prob. patron. from a name corresp. to 7754 (fem.); a *Sukathite* or desc. of an unknown Isr. named Sukah:—Suchathite.

7757. שׁוּל **shûwl**, *shool*; from an unused root mean. to *hang* down; a *skirt*; by impl. a bottom *edge*:—hem, skirt, train.

7758. שׁוֹלָל **shôwlâl**, *sho-lawl'*; or

שֵׁילָל° **shêylâl** (Mic. 1 : 8), *shay-lawl'*; from 7997; *nude* (espec. bare-foot); by impl. *captive*:—spoiled, stripped.

7759. שׁוּלַמִּית **Shûwlammîyth**, *shoo-lam-meeth'*; from 7999; *peaceful* (with the art. always pref., making it a pet name); the *Shulammith*, an epithet of Solomon's queen:—Shulamite.

7760. שׂוּם **sûwm**, *soom*; or

שִׂים **sîym**, *seem*; a prim. root; to *put* (used in a great variety of applications, lit., fig., infer. and ellip.):—× any wise, appoint, bring, call [a name], care, cast in, change, charge, commit, consider, convey, determine, + disguise, dispose, do, get, give, heap up, hold, impute, lay (down, up), leave, look, make (out), mark, + name, × on, ordain, order, + paint, place, preserve, purpose, put (on), + regard, rehearse, reward, (cause to) set (on, up), shew, + stedfastly, take, × tell, + tread down, ([over-]) turn, × wholly, work.

7761. שׂוּם **sûwm** (Chald.), *soom*; corresp. to 7760:— + command, give, lay, make, + name, + regard, set.

7762. שׁוּם **shûwm**, *shoom*; from an unused root mean. to *exhale*; *garlic* (from its rank odor):—garlic.

7763. שׁוֹמֵר **Shôwmêr**, *sho-mare'*; or

שֹׁמֵר **Shômêr**, *sho-mare'*; act. part. of 8104; *keeper*; *Shomer*, the name of two Isr.:—Shomer.

7764. שׁוּנִי **Shûwnîy**, *shoo-nee'*; from an unused root mean. to *rest*; *quiet*; *Shuni*, an Isr.:—Shuni.

7765. שׁוּנִי **Shûwnîy**, *shoo-nee'*; patron. from 7764; a *Shunite* (collect.) or desc. of Shuni:—Shunites.

7766. שׁוּנֵם **Shûwnêm**, *shoo-name'*; prob. from the same as 7764; *quietly*; *Shunem*, a place in Pal.:—Shunem.

7767. שׁוּנַמִּית **Shûwnammîyth**, *shoo-nam-meeth'*; patrial from 7766; a *Shunammitess*, or female inhab. of Shunem:—Shunamite.

7768. שָׁוַע **shâva'**, *shaw-vah'*; a prim. root; prop. *to be free;* but used only causat. and reflex. to *halloo* (for help, i.e. *freedom* from some trouble):—cry (aloud, out), shout.

7769. שׁוּעַ **shûwa'**, *shoo'-ah;* from 7768; a *halloo:*—cry, riches.

7770. שׁוּעַ **Shûwa'**, *shoo'-ah;* the same as 7769; *Shuä*, a Canaanite:—Shua, Shuah.

7771. שׁוֹעַ **shôwa'**, *sho'-ah;* from 7768 in the orig. sense of *freedom;* a *noble*, i.e. *liberal, opulent;* also (as noun in the derived sense) a *halloo:*—bountiful, crying, rich.

7772. שׁוֹעַ **Shôwa'**, *sho'-ah;* the same as 7771; *rich; Shoä*, an Oriental people:—Shoa.

7773. שֶׁוַע **sheva'**, *sheh'-vah;* from 7768; a *halloo:*—cry.

7774. שׁוּעָא **Shûw'â'**, *shoo-aw';* from 7768; *wealth; Shuä*, an Israelitess:—Shua.

7775. שַׁוְעָה **shav'âh**, *shav-aw';* fem. of 7773; a *hallooing:*—crying.

7776. שׁוּעָל **shûw'âl**, *shoo-awl';* or

שֻׁעָל **shû'âl**, *shoo-awl';* from the same as 8168; a *jackal* (as a *burrower*):—fox.

7777. שׁוּעָל **Shûw'âl**, *shoo-awl';* the same as 7776; *Shuäl*, the name of an Isr. and of a place in Pal.:—Shual.

7778. שׁוֹעֵר **shôw'êr**, *sho-are';* or

שֹׁעֵר **shô'êr**, *sho-are';* act. part. of 8176 (as denom. from 8179); a *janitor:*—door-keeper, porter.

7779. שׁוּף **shûwph**, *shoof;* a prim. root; prop. to *gape*, i.e. *snap* at; fig. to *overwhelm:*—break, bruise, cover.

7780. שׁוֹפָךְ **Shôwphâk**, *sho-fawk';* from 8210; *poured; Shophak*, a Syrian:—Shophach.

7781. שׁוּפָמִי **Shûwphâmîy**, *shoo-faw-mee';* patron. from 8197; a *Shuphamite* (collect.) or desc. of Shephupham:—Shuphamite.

שׁוֹפָן **Shôwphân**. See 5855.

7782. שׁוֹפָר **shôwphâr**, *sho-far';* or

שֹׁפָר **shôphâr**, *sho-far';* from 8231 in the orig. sense of *incising;* a *cornet* (as giving a *clear* sound) or curved horn:—cornet, trumpet.

7783. שׁוּק **shûwq**, *shook;* a prim. root; to *run* after or over, i.e. *overflow:*—overflow, water.

7784. שׁוּק **shûwq**, *shook;* from 7783; a *street* (as *run* over):—street.

7785. שׁוֹק **shôwq**, *shoke;* from 7783; the (lower) *leg* (as a *runner*):—hip, leg, shoulder, thigh.

7786. שׂוּר **sûwr**, *soor;* a prim. root; prop. to *vanquish;* by impl. to *rule* (caus. *crown*):—make princes, have power, reign. See 5493.

7787. שׂוּר **sûwr**, *soor;* a prim. root [rather ident. with 7786 through the idea of *reducing* to pieces; comp. 4883]; to *saw:*—cut.

7788. שׁוּר **shûwr**, *shoor;* a prim. root; prop. to *turn*, i.e. *travel* about (as a harlot or a merchant):—go, sing. See also 7891.

7789. שׁוּר **shûwr**, *shoor;* a prim. root [rather ident. with 7788 through the idea of *going round* for inspection]; to *spy* out, i.e. (gen.) *survey*, (for evil) *lurk for*, (for good) *care for:*—behold, lay wait, look, observe, perceive, regard, see.

7790. שׁוּר **shûwr**, *shoor;* from 7789; a *foe* (as *lying in wait*):—enemy.

7791. שׁוּר **shûwr**, *shoor;* from 7788; a *wall* (as *going about*):—wall.

7792. שׁוּר **shûwr** (Chald.), *shoor;* corresp. to 7791:—wall.

7793. שׁוּר **Shûwr**, *shoor;* the same as 7791; *Shur*, a region of the Desert:—Shur.

7794. שׁוֹר **shôwr**, *shore;* from 7788; a *bullock* (as a *traveller*):—bull (-ock), cow, ox, wall [*by mistake for* 7791].

7795. שׂוֹרָה **sôwrâh**, *so-raw';* from 7786 in the prim. sense of 5493; prop. a *ring*, i.e. (by analogy) a *row* (adv.):—principal.

שׂוֹרֵק **sôwrêq**. See 8321.

7796. שׂוֹרֵק **Sôwrêq**, *so-rake';* the same as 8321; a *vine; Sorek*, a valley in Pal.:—Sorek.

7797. שׂוּשׂ **sûws**, *soos;* or

שִׂישׂ **sîys**, *sece;* a prim. root; to *be bright*, i.e. *cheerful:*—be glad, × greatly, joy, make mirth, rejoice.

7798. שַׁוְשָׁא **Shavshâ'**, *shav-shaw';* from 7797; *joyful; Shavsha*, an Isr.:—Shavsha.

7799. שׁוּשַׁן **shûwshan**, *shoo-shan';* or

שׁוֹשָׁן **shôwshân**, *sho-shawn';* or

שֹׁשָׁן **shôshân**, *sho-shawn';* and (fem.)

שׁוֹשַׁנָּה **shôwshannâh**, *sho-shan-naw';* from 7797; a *lily* (from its *whiteness*), as a flower or arch. ornament; also a (straight) *trumpet* (from the *tubular* shape):—lily, Shoshannim.

7800. שׁוּשַׁן **Shûwshan**, *shoo-shan';* the same as 7799; *Shushan*, a place in Persia:—Shushan.

7801. שׁוּשַׁנְכִי **Shûwshankîy** (Chald.), *shoo-shan-kee';* of for. or.; a *Shushankite* (collect.) or inhab. of some unknown place in Ass.:—Susanchites.

7802. שׁוּשַׁן עֵדוּת **Shûwshan 'Êdûwth**, *shoo-shan' ay-dooth';* or (plur. of former)

שׁוֹשַׁנִּים עֵדוּת **Shôwshannîym 'Êdûwth**, *sho-shan-neem' ay-dooth';* from 7799 and 5715; *lily* (or *trumpet*) *of assemblage; Shushan-Eduth* or *Shoshannim-Eduth*, the title of a popular song:—Shoshannim-Eduth, Shushan-eduth.

שׁוּשַׁק **Shûwshaq**. See 7895.

7803. שׁוּתֶלַח **Shûwthelach**, *shoo-theh'-lakh;* prob. from 7582 and the same as 8520; *crash of breakage; Shuthelach*, the name of two Isr.:—Shuthelah.

7804. שְׁזַב **shᵉzab** (Chald.), *shez-ab';* corresp. to 5800; to *leave*, i.e. (caus.) *free:*—deliver.

7805. שָׁזַף **shâzaph**, *shaw-zaf';* a prim. root; to *tan* (by sun-burning); fig. (as if by a piercing ray) to *scan:*—look up, see.

7806. שָׁזַר **shâzar**, *shaw-zar';* a prim. root; to *twist* (a thread of straw):—twine.

7807. שַׁח **shach**, *shakh;* from 7817; *sunk*, i.e. *downcast:*— + humble.

7808. שֵׂחַ **sêach**, *say'-akh;* for 7879; *communion*, i.e. (reflex.) *meditation:*—thought.

7809. שָׁחַד **shâchad**, *shaw-khad';* a prim. root; to *donate*, i.e. *bribe:*—hire, give a reward.

7810. שַׁחַד **shachad**, *shakh'-ad;* from 7809; a *donation* (venal or redemptive):—bribe (-ry), gift, present, reward.

7811. שָׂחָה **sâchâh**, *saw-khaw';* a prim. root; to *swim;* caus. to *inundate:*—(make to) swim.

7812. שָׁחָה **shâchâh**, *shaw-khaw';* a prim. root; to *depress*, i.e. *prostrate* (espec. reflex. in homage to royalty or God):—bow (self) down, crouch, fall down (flat), humbly beseech, do (make) obeisance, do reverence, make to stoop, worship.

7813. שָׂחוּ **sâchûw**, *saw'-khoo;* from 7811; a *pond* (for *swimming*):—to swim in.

7814. שְׂחוֹק **sᵉchôwq**, *sekh-oke';* or

שְׂחֹק **sᵉchôq**, *sekh-oke';* from 7832; *laughter* (in merriment or defiance):—derision, laughter (-ed to scorn, -ing), mocked, sport.

7815. שְׁחוֹר **shᵉchôwr**, *shekh-ore';* from 7835; *dinginess*, i.e. perh. *soot:*—coal.

שִׁחוֹר **shîchôwr**. See 7883.

שָׁחוֹר **shâchôwr**. See 7838.

7816. שְׁחוּת **shᵉchûwth**, *shekh-ooth';* from 7812; *pit:*—pit.

7817. שָׁחַח **shâchach**, *shaw-khakh';* a prim. root; to *sink* or *depress* (reflex. or caus.):—bend, bow (down), bring (cast) down, couch, humble self, be (bring) low, stoop.

7818. שָׂחַט **sâchaṭ**, *saw-khat';* a prim. root; to *tread* out, i.e. *squeeze* (grapes):—press.

7819. שָׁחַט **shâchaṭ**, *shaw-khat';* a prim. root; to *slaughter* (in sacrifice or massacre):—kill, offer, shoot out, slay, slaughter.

7820. שָׁחַט **shâchaṭ**, *shaw-khat';* a prim. root [rather ident. with 7819 through the idea of *striking*]; to *hammer* out:—beat.

7821. שְׁחִיטָה **shᵉchîyṭâh**, *shekh-ee-taw';* from 7819; *slaughter:*—killing.

7822. שְׁחִין **shᵉchîyn**, *shekh-een';* from an unused root prob. mean. to *burn; inflammation*, i.e. an *ulcer:*—boil, botch.

7823. שָׁחִיס **shâchîyç**, *shaw-khece';* or

סָחִישׁ **çâchîysh**, *saw-kheesh';* from an unused root appar. mean. to *sprout*, *after-growth:*—(that) which springeth of the same.

7824. שָׁחִיף **shâchîyph**, *shaw-kheef';* from the same as 7828; a *board* (as *chipped* thin):—cieled with.

7825. שְׁחִית **shᵉchîyth**, *shekh-eeth';* from 7812; a *pit*-fall (lit. or fig.):—destruction, pit.

7826. שַׁחַל **shachal**, *shakh'-al;* from an unused root prob. mean. to *roar;* a *lion* (from his characteristic *roar*):—(fierce) lion.

7827. שְׁחֵלֶת **shᵉchêleth**, *shekh-ay'-leth;* appar. from the same as 7826 through some obscure idea, perh. that of *peeling* off by concussion of sound; a *scale* or shell, i.e. the aromatic *mussel:*—onycha.

7828. שַׁחַף **shachaph**, *shakh'-af;* from an unused root mean. to *peel*, i.e. *emaciate;* the *gull* (as *thin*):—cuckoo.

7829. שַׁחֶפֶת **shachepheth**, *shakh-eh'-feth;* from the same as 7828; *emaciation:*—consumption.

7830. שַׁחַץ **shachats**, *shakh'-ats;* from an unused root appar. mean. to *strut; haughtiness* (as evinced by the attitude):— × lion, pride.

7831. שַׁחֲצוֹם **Shachatsôwm**, *shakh-ats-ome';* from the same as 7830; *proudly; Shachatsom*, a place in Pal.:—Shahazimah [*from the marg.*].

7832. שָׂחַק **sâchaq**, *saw-khak';* a prim. root; to *laugh* (in pleasure or detraction); by impl. to *play:*—deride, have in derision, laugh, make merry, mock (-er), play, rejoice, (laugh to) scorn, be in (make) sport.

7833. שָׁחַק **shâchaq**, *shaw-khak';* a prim. root; to *comminute* (by trituration or attrition):—beat, wear.

7834. שַׁחַק **shachaq**, *shakh'-ak;* from 7833; a *powder* (as *beaten* small); by anal. a thin *vapor;* by extens. the *firmament:*—cloud, small dust, heaven, sky.

שְׂחֹק **sᵉchôq**. See 7814.

7835. שָׁחַר **shâchar**, *shaw-khar';* a prim. root [rather ident. with 7836 through the idea of the *duskiness* of early dawn]; to *be dim* or dark (in color):—be black.

7836. שָׁחַר **shâchar**, *shaw-khar';* a prim. root; prop. to *dawn*, i.e. (fig.) *be* (up) *early* at any task (with the impl. of earnestness); by extens. to *search* for (with painstaking):—[do something] betimes, enquire early, rise (seek) betimes, seek diligently) early, in the morning).

7837. שַׁחַר **shachar**, *shakh'-ar;* from 7836; *dawn* (lit., fig. or adv.):—day (-spring), early, light, morning, whence riseth.

שִׁחֹר **Shîchôr**. See 7883.

7838. שָׁחֹר **shâchôr**, *shaw-khore';* or

שָׁחוֹר **shâchôwr**, *shaw-khore';* from 7835; prop. *dusky*, but also (absol.) *jetty:*—black.

7839. שַׁחֲרוּת **shachărûwth**, *shakh-ar-ooth'*; from 7836; a *dawning*, i.e. (fig.) *juvenescence*:—youth.

7840. שְׁחַרְחֹרֶת **shᵉcharchôreth**, *shekh-ar-kho'-reth*; from 7835; *swarthy*:—black.

7841. שְׁחַרְיָה **Shᵉcharyâh**, *shekh-ar-yaw'*; from 7836 and 3050; *Jah has sought*; *Shecharjah*, an Isr.:—Shehariah.

7842. שַׁחֲרַיִם **Shachărayim**, *shakh-ar-ah'-yim*; dual of 7837; *double dawn*; *Shacharajim*, an Isr.:—Shaharaim.

7843. שָׁחַת **shâchath**, *shaw-khath'*; a prim. root; to *decay*, i.e. (caus.) *ruin* (lit. or fig.):—batter, cast off, corrupt (-er, thing), destroy (-er, -uction), lose, mar, perish, spill, spoiler, × utterly, waste (-r).

7844. שְׁחַת **shᵉchath** (Chald.), *shekh-ath'*; corresp. to 7843:—corrupt, fault.

7845. שַׁחַת **shachath**, *shakh'-ath*; from 7743; a *pit* (espec. as a trap); fig. *destruction*:—corruption, destruction, ditch, grave, pit.

7846. שֵׂט **sêṭ**, *sayte*; or

סֵט **çêṭ**, *sayt*; from 7750; a *departure* from right, i.e. *sin*:—revolter, that turn aside.

7847. שָׂטָה **sâṭâh**, *saw-taw'*; a prim. root; to *deviate* from duty:—decline, go aside, turn.

7848. שִׁטָּה **shiṭṭâh**, *shit-taw'*; fem. of a deriv. [only in the plur.

שִׁטִּים **shiṭṭîym**, *shit-teem'*, mean. the *sticks* of wood] from the same as 7850; the *acacia* (from its *scourging* thorns):—shittah, shittim. See also 1029.

7849. שָׁטַח **shâṭach**, *shaw-takh'*; a prim. root; to *expand*:—all abroad, enlarge, spread, stretch out.

7850. שֹׁטֵט **shôṭêṭ**, *sho-tate'*; act. part. of an otherwise unused root mean. (prop. to *pierce*; but only as a denom. from 7752) to *flog*; a *goad*:—scourge.

7851. שִׁטִּים **Shiṭṭîym**, *shit-teem'*; the same as the plur. of 7848; *acacia* trees; *Shittim*, a place E. of the Jordan:—Shittim.

7852. שָׂטַם **sâṭam**, *saw-tam'*; a prim. root; prop. to *lurk* for, i.e. *persecute*:—hate, oppose self against.

7853. שָׂטַן **sâṭan**, *saw-tan'*; a prim. root; to *attack*, (fig.) *accuse*:—(be an) adversary, resist.

7854. שָׂטָן **sâṭân**, *saw-tawn'*; from 7853; an *opponent*; espec. (with the art. pref.) *Satan*, the arch-enemy of good:—adversary, Satan, withstand.

7855. שִׂטְנָה **siṭnâh**, *sit-naw'*; from 7853; *opposition* (by letter):—accusation.

7856. שִׂטְנָה **Siṭnâh**, *sit-naw'*; the same as 7855; *Sitnah*, the name of a well in Pal.:—Sitnah.

7857. שָׁטַף **shâṭaph**, *shaw-taf'*; a prim. root; to *gush*; by impl. to *inundate*, *cleanse*; by anal. to *gallop*, *conquer*:—drown, (over-) flow (-whelm), rinse, run, rush, (throughly) wash (away).

7858. שֶׁטֶף **sheṭeph**, *sheh'-tef*; or

שֵׁטֶף **shêṭeph**, *shay'-tef*; from 7857; a *deluge* (lit. or fig.):—flood, outrageous, overflowing.

7859. שְׁטַר **shᵉṭar** (Chald.), *shet-ar'*; of uncert. der.: a *side*:—side.

7860. שֹׁטֵר **shôṭêr**, *sho-tare'*; act. part. of an otherwise unused root prob. mean. to *write*; prop. a *scribe*, i.e. (by anal. or impl.) an official *superintendent* or *magistrate*:—officer, overseer, ruler.

7861. שִׁטְרַי° **Shiṭray**, *shit-rah'ee*; from the same as 7860; *magisterial*; *Shitrai*, an Isr.:—Shitrai.

7862. שַׁי **shay**, *shah'ee*; prob. from 7737; a *gift* (as *available*):—present.

7863. שִׂיא **sîy'**, *see*; from the same as 7721 by perm.; *elevation*:—excellency.

7864. שְׁיָא° **Shᵉyâ'**, *sheh-yaw'*; for 7724; *Sheja*, an Isr.:—Sheva [*from the marg.*].

7865. שִׂיאֹן **Sîy'ôn**, *see-ohn'*; from 7863; *peak*; *Sion*, the summit of Mt. Hermon:—Sion.

7866. שִׁיאוֹן **Shî'yôwn**, *shee-ohn'*; from the same as 7722; *ruin*; *Shijon*, a place in Pal.:—Shihon.

7867. שִׂיב **sîyb**, *seeb*; a prim. root; prop. to *become aged*, i.e. (by impl.) to *grow gray*:—(be) grayheaded.

7868. שִׂיב **sîyb** (Chald.), *seeb*; corresp. to 7867:—elder.

7869. שֵׂיב **sêyb**, *sabe*; from 7867; old *age*:—age.

7870. שִׁיבָה **shîybâh**, *shee-baw'*; by perm. from 7725; a *return* (of property):—captivity.

7871. שִׁיבָה **shîybâh**, *shee-baw'*; from 3427; *residence*:—while . . . lay.

7872. שֵׂיבָה **sêybâh**, *say-baw'*; fem. of 7869; old *age*:—(be) gray (grey, hoar, -y) hairs (head, -ed), old age.

7873. שִׂיג **sîyg**, *seeg*; from 7734; a *withdrawal* (into a private place):—pursuing.

7874. שִׂיד **sîyd**, *seed*; a prim. root prob. mean. to *boil* up (comp. 7736); used only as denom. from 7875; to *plaster*:—plaister.

7875. שִׂיד **sîyd**, *seed*; from 7874; *lime* (as *boiling* when slacked):—lime, plaister.

7876. שָׁיָה **shâyâh**, *shaw-yaw'*; a prim. root; to *keep* in memory:—be unmindful. [Render Deut. 32 : 18, "A Rock bore thee, *thou must recollect*; and (yet) thou hast forgotten," etc.]

7877. שִׁיזָא **Shîyzâ'**, *shee-zaw'*; of unknown der.; *Shiza*, an Isr.:—Shiza.

7878. שִׂיחַ **sîyach**, *see'-akh*; a prim. root; to *ponder*, i.e. (by impl.) *converse* (with oneself, and hence aloud) or (trans.) *utter*:—commune, complain, declare, meditate, muse, pray, speak, talk (with).

7879. שִׂיחַ **sîyach**, *see'-akh*; from 7878; a *contemplation*; by impl. an *utterance*:—babbling, communication, complaint, meditation, prayer, talk.

7880. שִׂיחַ **sîyach**, *see'-akh*; from 7878; a *shoot* (as if *uttered* or put forth), i.e. (gen.) *shrubbery*:—bush, plant, shrub.

7881. שִׂיחָה **sîychâh**, *see-khaw'*; fem. of 7879; *reflection*; by extens. *devotion*:—meditation, prayer.

7882. שִׁיחָה **shîychâh**, *shee-khaw'*; for 7745; a *pit*-fall:—pit.

7883. שִׁיחוֹר **Shîychôwr**, *shee-khore'*; or

שִׁחוֹר **Shîchôwr**, *shee-khore'*; or

שִׁחֹר **Shîchôr**, *shee-khore'*; prob. from 7835; *dark*, i.e. *turbid*; *Shichor*, a stream of Egypt:—Shihor, Sihor.

7884. שִׁיחוֹר לִבְנָת **Shîychôwr Libnâth**, *shee-khore' lib-nawth'*; from the same as 7883 and 3835; *darkish whiteness*; *Shichor-Libnath*, a stream of Pal.:—Shihor-libnath.

7885. שַׁיִט **shayiṭ**, *shah'-yit*; from 7751; an *oar*; also (comp. 7752) a *scourge*° (fig.):—oar, scourge.

7886. שִׁילֹה **Shîylôh**, *shee-lo'*; from 7951; *tranquil*; *Shiloh*, an epithet of the Messiah:—Shiloh.

7887. שִׁילֹה **Shîylôh**, *shee-lo'*; or

שִׁלֹה **Shîlôh**, *shee-lo'*; or

שִׁילוֹ **Shîylôw**, *shee-lo'*; or

שִׁלוֹ **Shîlôw**, *shee-lo'*; from the same as 7886; *Shiloh*, a place in Pal.:—Shiloh.

7888. שִׁילוֹנִי **Shîylôwnîy**, *shee-lo-nee'*; or

שִׁילֹנִי **Shîylônîy**, *shee-lo-nee'*; or

שִׁלֹנִי **Shîlônîy**, *shee-lo-nee'*; from 7887; a *Shilonite* or inhab. of Shiloh:—Shilonite.

שֵׁילָל **shêylâl**. See 7758.

7889. שִׁימוֹן **Shîymôwn**, *shee-mone'*; appar. for 3452; *desert*; *Shimon*, an Isr.:—Shimon.

7890. שַׁיִן **shayin**, *shah'-yin*; from an unused root mean. to *urinate*; *urine*:—piss.

7891. שִׁיר **shîyr**, *sheer*; or (the orig. form)

שׁוּר° **shûwr** (1 Sam. 18 : 6), *shoor*; a prim. root [rather ident. with 7788 through the idea of *strolling* minstrelsy]; to *sing*:—behold [*by mistake for* 7789], sing (-er, -ing man, -ing woman).

7892. שִׁיר **shîyr**, *sheer*; or fem.

שִׁירָה **shîyrâh**, *shee-raw'*; from 7891; a *song*; abstr. *singing*:—musical (-ick), × sing (-er, -ing), song.

שִׂישׁ **sîys**. See 7797.

7893. שַׁיִשׁ **shayish**, *shah'-yish*; from an unused root mean. to *bleach*, i.e. *whiten*; *white*, i.e. *marble*:—marble. See 8336.

7894. שִׁישָׁא **Shîyshâ'**, *shee-shaw'*; from the same as 7893; *whiteness*; *Shisha*, an Isr.:—Shisha.

7895. שִׁישַׁק **Shîyshaq**, *shee-shak'*; or

שׁוּשַׁק° **Shûwshaq**, *shoo-shak'*; of Eg. der.; *Shishak*, an Eg. king:—Shishak.

7896. שִׁית **shîyth**, *sheeth*; a prim. root; to *place* (in a very wide application):—apply, appoint, array, bring, consider, lay (up), let alone, × look, make, mark, put (on), + regard, set, shew, be stayed, × take.

7897. שִׁית **shîyth**, *sheeth*; from 7896; a *dress* (as *put* on):—attire.

7898. שַׁיִת **shayith**, *shah'-yith*; from 7896; *scrub* or *trash*, i.e. wild *growth* of weeds or briers (as if *put* on the field):—thorns.

7899. שֵׂךְ **sêk**, *sake*; from 5526 in the sense of 7753; a *brier* (as of a hedge):—prick.

7900. שֹׂךְ **sôk**, *soke*; from 5526 in the sense of 7753; a *booth* (as *interlaced*):—tabernacle.

7901. שָׁכַב **shâkab**, *shaw-kab'*; a prim. root; to *lie* down (for rest, sexual connection, decease or any other purpose):—× at all, cast down, ([over-]) lay (self) (down), (make to) lie (down, down to sleep, still, with), lodge, ravish, take rest, sleep, stay.

7902. שְׁכָבָה **shᵉkâbâh**, *shek-aw-baw'*; from 7901; a *lying* down (of dew, or for the sexual act):—× carnally, copulation, × lay, seed.

7903. שְׁכֹבֶת **shᵉkôbeth**, *shek-o'-beth*; from 7901; a (sexual) *lying* with:—× lie.

7904. שָׁכָה **shâkâh**, *shaw-kaw'*; a prim. root; to *roam* (through lust):—in the morning [*by mistake for* 7925].

7905. שֻׂכָּה **sukkâh**, *sook-kaw'*; fem. of 7900 in the sense of 7899; a *dart* (as pointed like a *thorn*):—barbed iron.

7906. שֵׂכוּ **Sêkûw**, *say'-koo*; from an unused root appar. mean. to *surmount*; an *observatory* (with the art.); *Seku*, a place in Pal.:—Sechu.

7907. שֶׂכְוִי **sekvîy**, *sek-vee'*; from the same as 7906; *observant*, i.e. (concr.) the *mind*:—heart.

7908. שְׁכוֹל **shᵉkôwl**, *shek-ole'*; infin. of 7921: *bereavement*:—loss of children, spoiling.

7909. שַׁכּוּל **shakkuwl**, *shak-kool'*; or

שַׁכֻּל **shakkul**, *shak-kool'*; from 7921; *bereaved*:—barren, bereaved (robbed) of children (whelps).

7910. שִׁכּוֹר **shikkôwr**, *shik-kore'*; or

שִׁכֹּר **shikkôr**, *shik-kore'*; from 7937; *intoxicated*, as a state or a habit:—drunk (-ard, -en, -en man).

7911. שָׁכַח **shâkach**, *shaw-kakh'*; or

שָׁכֵחַ **shâkêach**, *shaw-kay'-akh*, a prim. root; to *mislay*, i.e. to *be oblivious* of, from want of memory or attention:— × at all, (cause to) forget.

7912. שְׁכַח **sheᵉkach** (Chald.), *shek-akh';* corresp. to 7911 through the idea of disclosure of a *covered* or *forgotten* thing; to *discover* (lit. or fig.):—find.

7913. שָׁכֵחַ **shâkêach**, *shaw-kay'-akh;* from 7911; *oblivious:*—forget.

7914. שְׂכִיָּה **seᵉkîyâh**, *sek-ee-yaw';* fem. from the same as 7906; a *conspicuous* object:—picture.

7915. שַׂכִּין **sakkîyn**, *sak-keen';* intens. perh. from the same as 7906 in the sense of 7753; a *knife* (as *pointed* or edged):—knife.

7916. שָׂכִיר **sâkîyr**, *saw-keer';* from 7936; a man *at wages* by the day or year:—hired (man, servant), hireling.

7917. שְׂכִירָה **sekîyrâh**, *sek-ee-raw';* fem. of 7916; a *hiring:*—that is hired.

7918. שָׁכַךְ **shâkak**, *shaw-kak';* a prim. root; to *weave* (i.e. *lay*) a trap; fig. (through the idea of *secreting*) to *allay* (passions; phys. *abate* a flood):—appease, assuage, make to cease, pacify, set.

7919. שָׂכַל **sâkal**, *saw-kal';* a prim. root; to *be* (caus. *make* or *act*) *circumspect* and hence *intelligent:*—consider, expert, instruct, prosper, (deal) prudent (-ly), (give) skill (-ful), have good success, teach, (have, make to) understand (-ing), wisdom, (be, behave self, consider, make) wise (-ly), guide wittingly.

7920. שְׂכַל **seᵉkal** (Chald.), *sek-al';* corresp. to 7919:—consider.

7921. שָׁכֹל **shâkôl**, *shaw-kole';* a prim. root; prop. to *miscarry*, i.e. *suffer abortion;* by anal. to *bereave* (lit. or fig.):—bereave (of children), barren, cast calf (fruit, young), be (make) childless, deprive, destroy, × expect, lose children, miscarry, rob of children, spoil.

7922. שֶׂכֶל **sekel**, *seh'-kel;* or

שֵׂכֶל **sêkel**, *say'-kel;* from 7919; *intelligence;* by impl. *success:*—discretion, knowledge, policy, prudence, sense, understanding, wisdom, wise.

שַׁכֻּל **shakkûl**. See 7909.

שִׂכְלוּת **siklûwth**. See 5531.

7923. שִׁכֻּלִים **shikkûlîym**, *shik-koo-leem';* plur. from 7921; *childlessness* (by continued bereavements):—to have after loss of others.

7924. שׇׂכְלְתָנוּ **sokleᵉthânûw** (Chald.), *sok-leth-aw-noo';* from 7920; *intelligence:*—understanding.

7925. שָׁכַם **shâkam**, *shaw-kam';* a prim. root; prop. to *incline* (the shoulder to a burden); but used only as denom. from 7926; lit. to *load up* (on the back of man or beast), i.e. to *start early* in the morning:—(arise, be up, get [oneself] up, rise up) early (betimes), morning.

7926. שְׁכֶם **sheᵉkem**, *shek-em';* from 7925; the *neck* (between the shoulders) as the place of burdens; fig. the *spur* of a hill:—back, × consent, portion, shoulder.

7927. שְׁכֶם **Sheᵉkem**, *shek-em';* the same as 7926; *ridge; Shekem*, a place in Pal.:—Shechem.

7928. שֶׁכֶם **Shekem**, *sheh'-kem;* for 7926; *Shekem*, the name of a Hivite and two Isr.:—Shechem.

7929. שִׁכְמָה **shikmâh**, *shik-maw';* fem. of 7926; the *shoulder*-bone:—shoulder blade.

7930. שִׁכְמִי **Shikmîy**, *shik-mee';* patron. from 7928; a *Shikmite* (collect.), or desc. of Shekem:—Shichemites.

7931. שָׁכַן **shâkan**, *shaw-kan';* a prim. root [appar. akin (by transm.) to 7901 through the idea of *lodging;* comp. 5531, 7925]; to *reside* or permanently stay (lit. or fig.):—abide, continue, (cause to, make to) dwell (-er), have habitation, inhabit, lay, place, (cause to) remain, rest, set (up).

7932. שְׁכַן **sheᵉkan** (Chald.), *shek-an';* corresp. to 7931:—cause to dwell, have habitation.

7933. שֶׁכֶן **sheken**, *sheh'-ken;* from 7931; a *residence:*—habitation.

7934. שָׁכֵן **shâkên**, *shaw-kane';* from 7931; a *resident;* by extens. a fellow-*citizen:*—inhabitant, neighbour, nigh.

7935. שְׁכַנְיָה **Sheᵉkanyâh**, *shek-an-yaw';* or (prol.)

שְׁכַנְיָהוּ **Sheᵉkanyâhûw**, *shek-an-yaw'-hoo;* from 7931 and 3050; *Jah has dwelt; Shekanjah*, the name of nine Isr.:—Shecaniah, Shechaniah.

7936. שָׂכַר **sâkar**, *saw-kar';* or (by perm.)

סָכַר **çâkar** (Ezra 4 : 5), *saw-kar';* a prim. root [appar. akin (by prosthesis) to 3739 through the idea of temporary *purchase;* comp. 7937]; to *hire:*—earn wages, hire (out self), reward, × surely.

7937. שָׁכַר **shâkar**, *shaw-kar';* a prim root; to *become tipsy;* in a qualified sense, to *satiate* with a stimulating drink or (fig.) influence:—(be filled with) drink (abundantly), (be, make) drunk (-en), be merry. [Superlative of 8248.]

7938. שֶׂכֶר **seker**, *seh'-ker;* from 7936; *wages:*—reward, sluices.

7939. שָׂכָר **sâkâr**, *saw-kawr';* from 7936; *payment* of contract; concr. *salary, fare, maintenance;* by impl. *compensation, benefit:*—hire, price, reward [-ed], wages, worth.

7940. שָׂכָר **Sâkar**, *saw-kar';* the same as 7939; *recompense; Sakar*, the name of two Isr.:—Sacar.

7941. שֵׁכָר **shêkâr**, *shay-kawr';* from 7937; an *intoxicant*, i.e. intensely alcoholic *liquor:*—strong drink, + drunkard, strong wine.

שִׁכֹּר **shikkôr**. See 7910.

7942. שִׁכְּרוֹן **Shikkeᵉrôwn**, *shik-ker-one';* for 7943; *drunkenness; Shikkeron*, a place in Pal.:—Shicron.

7943. שִׁכָּרוֹן **shikkârôwn**, *shik-kaw-rone';* from 7937; *intoxication:*—(be) drunken (-ness).

7944. שַׁל **shal**, *shal;* from 7952 abbrev.; a *fault:*—error.

7945. שֶׁל **shel**, *shel;* for the rel. 834; used with prep. pref., and often followed by some pron. aff.; on *account* of, *what*soever, *which*soever:—cause, sake.

7946. שַׁלְאֲנָן **shal'ănân**, *shal-an-awn';* for 7600; *tranquil:*—being at ease.

7947. שָׁלַב **shâlab**, *shaw-lab';* a prim. root; to *space* off; intens. (*evenly*) to *make equidistant:*—equally distant, set in order.

7948. שָׁלָב **shâlâb**, *shaw-lawb';* from 7947; a *spacer* or raised *interval*, i.e. the *stile* in a frame or panel:—ledge.

7949. שָׁלַג **shâlag**, *shaw-lag';* a prim. root; prop. mean. to be *white;* used only as denom. from 7950; to be *snow-white* (with the linen clothing of the slain):—be as snow.

7950. שֶׁלֶג **sheleg**, *sheh'-leg;* from 7949; *snow* (prob. from its *whiteness*):—snow (-y).

7951. שָׁלָה **shâlâh**, *shaw-law';* or

שָׁלַו **shâlav** (Job 3 : 26), *shaw-lav';* a prim. root; to be *tranquil*, i.e. *secure* or *successful:*—be happy, prosper, be in safety.

7952. שָׁלָה **shâlâh**, *shaw-law';* a prim. root [prob. rather ident. with 7953 through the idea of *educing*]; to *mislead:*—deceive, be negligent.

7953. שָׁלָה **shâlâh**, *shaw-law';* a prim. root [rather cognate (by contr.) to the base of 5394, 7997 and their congeners through the idea of *extracting*]; to *draw* out or off, i.e. *remove* (the soul by death):—take away.

7954. שְׁלָה **sheᵉlâh** (Chald.), *shel-aw';* corresp. to 7951; to *be secure:*—at rest.

שִׁלֹה **Shîlôh**. See 7887.

7955. שָׁלָה **shâlâh** (Chald.), *shaw-law';* from a root corresp. to 7952; a *wrong:*—thing amiss.

שֵׁלָה **shêlâh**. See 7596.

7956. שֵׁלָה **Shêlâh**, *shay-law';* the same as 7596 (shortened); *request; Shelah*, the name of a postdiluvian patriarch and of an Isr.:—Shelah.

7957. שַׁלְהֶבֶת **shalhebeth**, *shal-heh'-beth;* from the same as 3851 with sibilant pref.; a *flare* of fire:—(flaming) flame.

שָׁלֵו **shâlav**. See 7951.

7958. שְׂלָו **seᵉlâv**, *sel-awv';* or

שְׂלָיו **seᵉlâyv**, *sel-awv';* by orth. var. from 7951 through the idea of *sluggishness;* the *quail* collect. (as *slow* in flight from its weight):—quails.

7959. שֶׁלֶו **shelev**, *sheh'-lev;* from 7951; *security:*—prosperity.

שִׁלוֹ **Shîlôw**. See 7887.

7960. שָׁלוּ **shâlûw** (Chald.), *shaw-loo';* or

שָׁלוּת **shâlûwth** (Chald.), *shaw-looth';* from the same as 7955; a *fault:*—error, × fail, thing amiss.

7961. שָׁלֵו **shâlêv**, *shaw-lave';* or

שָׁלֵיו **shâlêyv**, *shaw-lave';* fem.

שְׁלֵוָה **sheᵉlêvâh**, *shel-ay-vaw';* from 7951; *tranquil;* (in a bad sense) *careless;* abstr. *security:*—(being) at ease, peaceable, (in) prosper (-ity), quiet (-ness), wealthy.

7962. שַׁלְוָה **shalvâh**, *shal-vaw';* from 7951; *security* (genuine or false):—abundance, peace (-ably), prosperity, quietness.

7963. שְׁלֵוָה **sheᵉlêvâh** (Chald.), *shel-ay-vaw';* corresp. to 7962; *safety:*—tranquillity. See also 7961.

7964. שִׁלּוּחַ **shillûwach**, *shil-loo'-akh;* or

שִׁלֻּחַ **shillûach**, *shil-loo'-akh;* from 7971; (only in plur.) a *dismissal*, i.e. (of a wife) *divorce* (espec. the document); also (of a daughter) *dower:*—presents, have sent back.

7965. שָׁלוֹם **shâlôwm**, *shaw-lome';* or

שָׁלֹם **shâlôm**, *shaw-lome';* from 7999; *safe*, i.e. (fig.) *well, happy, friendly;* also (abstr.) *welfare*, i.e. health, prosperity, peace:—× do, familiar, × fare, favour, + friend, × greet, (good) health, (× perfect, such as be at) peace (-able, -ably), prosper (-ity, -ous), rest, safe (-ly), salute, welfare, (× all is, be) well, × wholly.

7966. שִׁלּוּם **shillûwm**, *shil-loom';* or

שִׁלֻּם **shillûm**, *shil-loom';* from 7999; a *requital*, i.e. (secure) *retribution*, (venal) a *fee:*—recompense, reward.

7967. שַׁלּוּם **Shallûwm**, *shal-loom';* or (shorter)

שַׁלֻּם **Shallûm**, *shal-loom';* the same as 7966; *Shallum*, the name of fourteen Isr.:—Shallum.

שְׁלוֹמִית **Sheᵉlôwmîyth**. See 8019.

7968. שַׁלּוּן **Shallûwn**, *shal-loon';* prob. for 7967; *Shallun*, an Isr.:—Shallum.

7969. שָׁלוֹשׁ **shâlôwsh**, *shaw-loshe';* or

שָׁלֹשׁ **shâlôsh**, *shaw-loshe';* masc.

שְׁלוֹשָׁה **sheᵉlôwshâh**, *shel-o-shaw';* or

שְׁלֹשָׁה **sheᵉlôshâh**, *shel-o-shaw';* a prim. number; *three;* occasionally (ordinal) *third*, or (multipl.) *thrice:*— + fork, + often [-times], third, thir [-teen, -teenth], three, + thrice. Comp. 7991.

7970. שְׁלוֹשִׁים **sheᵉlôwshîym**, *shel-o-sheem';* or

שְׁלֹשִׁים **sheᵉlôshîym**, *shel-o-sheem';* multiple of 7969; *thirty;* or (ordinal) *thirtieth:*—thirty, thirtieth. Comp. 7991.

שָׁלוּת **shâlûwth**. See 7960.

7971. שָׁלַח **shâlach**, *shaw-lakh';* a prim. root; to *send* away, for, or out (in a great variety of applications):— × any wise, appoint, bring (on the way), cast (away, out), conduct, × earnestly, forsake, give (up), grow long, lay, leave, let depart (down, go, loose), push away, put (away, forth, in, out), reach forth, send (away, forth, out), set, shoot (forth, out), sow, spread, stretch forth (out).

7972. שְׁלַח **sheᵉlach** (Chald.), *shel-akh';* corresp. to 7971:—put, send.

7973. שֶׁלַח **shelach**, *sheh'-lakh;* from 7971; a *missile* of attack, i.e. *spear;* also (fig.) a *shoot* of growth, i.e. *branch:*—dart, plant, × put off, sword, weapon.

7974. שֶׁלַח **Shelach**, *sheh'-lakh;* the same as 7973; *Shelach,* a postdiluvian patriarch:—Salah, Shelah. Comp. 7975.

7975. שִׁלֹחַ **Shilôach**, *shee-lo'-akh;* or (in imitation of 7974)

שֶׁלַח **Shelach** (Neh. 3 : 15), *sheh'-lakh;* from 7971; *rill; Shiloäch,* a fountain of Jerus.:—Shiloah, Siloah.

שִׁלֻּחַ **shillûach**. See 7964.

7976. שִׁלֻּחָה **shilluchâh**, *shil-loo-khaw';* fem. of 7964; a *shoot:*—branch.

7977. שִׁלְחִי **Shilchîy**, *shil-khee';* from 7973; *missive,* i.e. *armed; Shilchi,* an Isr.:—Shilhi.

7978. שִׁלְחִים **Shilchîym**, *shil-kheem';* plur. of 7973; *javelins* or *sprouts; Shilchim,* a place in Pal.:—Shilhim.

7979. שֻׁלְחָן **shulchân**, *shool-khawn';* from 7971; a *table* (as *spread* out); by impl. a *meal:*—table.

7980. שָׁלַט **shâlaṭ**, *shaw-lat';* a prim. root; to *dominate,* i.e. *govern;* by impl. to *permit:*—(bear, have) rule, have dominion, give (have) power.

7981. שְׁלֵט **shᵉlêṭ** (Chald.), *shel-ate';* corresp. to 7980:—have the mastery, have power, bear rule, be (make) ruler.

7982. שֶׁלֶט **sheleṭ**, *sheh'-let;* from 7980; prob. a *shield* (as *controlling,* i.e. protecting the person):—shield.

7983. שִׁלְטוֹן **shilṭôwn**, *shil-tone';* from 7980; a *potentate:*—power.

7984. שִׁלְטוֹן **shilṭôwn** (Chald.), *shil-tone';* or

שִׁלְטֹן **shilṭôn**, *shil-tone';* corresp. to 7983:—ruler.

7985. שָׁלְטָן **sholṭân** (Chald.), *shol-tawn';* from 7981; *empire* (abstr. or concr.):—dominion.

7986. שַׁלֶּטֶת **shalleṭeth**, *shal-leh'-teth;* fem. from 7980; a *vixen:*—imperious.

7987. שְׁלִי **shᵉlîy**, *shel-ee';* from 7951; *privacy:*—+ quietly.

7988. שִׁלְיָה **shilyâh**, *shil-yaw';* fem. from 7953; a *fœtus* or *babe* (as *extruded* in birth):—young one.

שְׂלָיו **sᵉlâyv**. See 7958.

שְׁלֵיו **shalêyv**. See 7961.

7989. שַׁלִּיט **shallîyṭ**, *shal-leet';* from 7980; *potent;* concr. a *prince* or *warrior:*—governor, mighty, that hath power, ruler.

7990. שַׁלִּיט **shallîyṭ** (Chald.), *shal-leet';* corresp. to 7989; *mighty;* abstr. *permission;* concr. a *premier:*—captain, be lawful, rule (-r).

7991. שָׁלִישׁ **shâlîysh**, *shaw-leesh';* or

שָׁלוֹשׁ **shâlôwsh** (1 Chron. 11 : 11; 12 : 18), *shaw-loshe';* or

שָׁלֹשׁ **shâlôsh** (2 Sam. 23 : 13), *shaw-loshe';* from 7969; a *triple,* i.e. (as a musical instrument) a *triangle* (or perh. rather *three*-stringed lute); also (as an indef. great quantity) a *three*-fold measure (perh. a *treble* ephah); also (as an officer) a general of the *third* rank (upward, i.e. the highest):—captain, instrument of musick, (great) lord, (great) measure, prince, three [*from the marg.*].

7992. שְׁלִישִׁי **shᵉlîyshîy**, *shel-ee-shee';* ordinal from 7969; *third;* fem. a *third* (part); by extens. a *third* (day, year or time); spec. a *third*-story cell):—third (part, rank, time), three (years old).

7993. שָׁלַךְ **shâlak**, *shaw-lak';* a prim. root; to *throw* out, down or away (lit. or fig.):—adventure, cast (away, down, forth, off, out), hurl, pluck, throw.

7994. שָׁלָךְ **shâlâk**, *shaw-lawk';* from 7993; *bird of prey,* usually thought to be the *pelican* (from *casting* itself into the sea):—cormorant.

7995. שַׁלֶּכֶת **shalleketh**, *shal-leh'-keth;* from 7993; a *felling* (of trees):—when cast.

7996. שַׁלֶּכֶת **Shalleketh**, *shal-leh'-keth;* the same as 7995; *Shalleketh,* a gate in Jerus.:—Shalleketh.

7997. שָׁלַל **shâlal**, *shaw-lal';* a prim. root; to *drop* or *strip;* by impl. to *plunder:*—let fall, make self a prey, × of purpose, (make a, [take]) spoil.

7998. שָׁלָל **shâlâl**, *shaw-lawl';* from 7997; *booty:*—prey, spoil.

7999. שָׁלַם **shâlam**, *shaw-lam';* a prim. root; to *be safe* (in mind, body or estate); fig. to *be* (caus. *make*) *completed;* by impl. to *be friendly;* by extens. to *reciprocate* (in various applications):—make amends, (make an) end, finish, full, give again, make good, (re-) pay (again), (make) (to) (be at) peace (-able), that is perfect, perform, (make) prosper (-ous), recompense, render, requite, make restitution, restore, reward, × surely.

8000. שְׁלַם **shᵉlam** (Chald.), *shel-am';* corresp. to 7999; to *complete,* to *restore:*—deliver, finish.

8001. שְׁלָם **shᵉlâm** (Chald.), *shel-awm';* corresp. to 7965; *prosperity:*—peace.

8002. שֶׁלֶם **shelem**, *sheh'-lem;* from 7999; prop. *requital,* i.e. a (voluntary) sacrifice in *thanks:*—peace offering.

8003. שָׁלֵם **shâlêm**, *shaw-lame';* from 7999; *complete* (lit. or fig.); espec. *friendly:*—full, just, made ready, peaceable, perfect (-ed), quiet, Shalem [*by mistake for a name*], whole.

8004. שָׁלֵם **Shâlêm**, *shaw-lame';* the same as 8003; *peaceful; Shalem,* an early name of Jerus.:—Salem.

שָׁלֹם **shâlôm**. See 7965.

8005. שִׁלֵּם **shillêm**, *shil-lame';* from 7999; *requital:*—recompense.

8006. שִׁלֵּם **Shillêm**, *shil-lame';* the same as 8005; *Shillem,* an Isr.:—Shillem.

שִׁלֻּם **shillûm**. See 7966.

שַׁלֻּם **Shallûm**. See 7967.

8007. שַׂלְמָא **Salmâ'**, *sal-maw';* prob. for 8008; *clothing; Salma,* the name of two Isr.:—Salma.

8008. שַׂלְמָה **salmâh**, *sal-maw';* transp. for 8071; a *dress:*—clothes, garment, raiment.

8009. שַׂלְמָה **Salmâh**, *sal-maw';* the same as 8008; *clothing; Salmah,* an Isr.:—Salmon. Comp. 8012.

8010. שְׁלֹמֹה **Shᵉlômôh**, *shel-o-mo';* from 7965; *peaceful; Shelomoh,* David's successor:—Solomon.

8011. שִׁלֻּמָה **shillumâh**, *shil-loo-maw';* fem. of 7966; *retribution:*—reward.

8012. שַׂלְמוֹן **Salmôwn**, *sal-mone';* from 8008; *investiture; Salmon,* an Isr.:—Salmon. Comp. 8009.

8013. שְׁלֹמוֹת **Shᵉlômôwth**, *shel-o-mōth';* fem. plur. of 7965; *pacifications; Shelomoth,* the name of two Isr.:—Shelomith [*from the marg.*], Shelomoth. Comp. 8019.

8014. שַׂלְמַי **Salmay**, *sal-mah'ee;* from 8008; *clothed; Salmai,* an Isr.:—Shalmai.

8015. שְׁלֹמִי **Shᵉlômîy**, *shel-o-mee';* from 7965; *peaceable; Shelomi,* an Isr.:—Shelomi.

8016. שִׁלֵּמִי **Shillêmîy**, *shil-lay-mee';* patron. from 8006; a *Shilemite* (collect.) or desc. of Shillem:—Shillemites.

8017. שְׁלֻמִיאֵל **Shᵉlumîy'êl**, *shel-oo-mee-ale';* from 7965 and 410; *peace of God; Shelumiël,* an Isr.:—Shelumiel.

8018. שֶׁלֶמְיָה **Shelemyâh**, *shel-em-yaw';* or

שֶׁלֶמְיָהוּ **Shelemyâhuw**, *shel-em-yaw'-hoo;* from 8002 and 3050; *thank-offering of Jah; Shelemjah,* the name of nine Isr.:—Shelemiah.

8019. שְׁלֹמִית **Shᵉlômîyth**, *shel-o-meeth';* or

שְׁלוֹמִית **Shᵉlôwmîyth** (Ezra 8 : 10), *shel-o-meeth';* from 7965; *peaceableness; Shelomith,* the name of five Isr. and three Israelitesses:—Shelomith.

8020. שַׁלְמַן **Shalman**, *shal-man';* of for. der.; *Shalman,* a king appar. of Assyria:—Shalman. Comp. 8022.

8021. שַׁלְמֹן **shalmôn**, *shal-mone';* from 7999; a *bribe:*—reward.

8022. שַׁלְמַנְאֶסֶר **Shalman'eçer**, *shal-man-eh'-ser;* of for. der.; *Shalmaneser,* an Ass. king:—Shalmaneser. Comp. 8020.

8023. שִׁלֹנִי **Shilônîy**, *shee-lo-nee';* the same as 7888; *Shiloni,* an Isr.:—Shiloni.

8024. שֵׁלָנִי **Shêlânîy**, *shay-law-nee';* from 7956; a *Shelanite* (collect.), or desc. of Shelah:—Shelanites.

8025. שָׁלַף **shâlaph**, *shaw-laf';* a prim. root; to *pull* out, up or off:—draw (off), grow up, pluck off.

8026. שֶׁלֶף **sheleph**, *sheh'-lef;* from 8025; *extract; Sheleph,* a son of Jokthan:—Sheleph.

8027. שָׁלַשׁ **shâlash**, *shaw-lash';* a prim. root perh. orig. to *intensify,* i.e. *treble;* but appar. used only as denom. from 7969, to *be* (caus. *make*) *triplicate* (by restoration, in portions, strands, days or years):—do the third time, (divide into, stay) three (days, -fold, parts, years old).

8028. שֶׁלֶשׁ **Shelesh**, *sheh'-lesh;* from 8027; *triplet; Shelesh,* an Isr.:—Shelesh.

שָׁלֹשׁ **shâlôsh**. See 7969.

8029. שִׁלֵּשׁ **shillêsh**, *shil-laysh';* from 8027; a desc. of the *third* degree, i.e. *great grandchild:*—third [generation].

8030. שִׁלְשָׁה **Shilshâh**, *shil-shaw';* fem. from the same as 8028; *triplication; Shilshah,* an Isr.:—Shilshah.

8031. שָׁלִשָׁה **Shâlîshâh**, *shaw-lee-shaw';* fem. from 8027; *trebled* land; *Shalishah,* a place in Pal.:—Shalisha.

שְׁלֹשָׁה **shâlôshâh**. See 7969.

8032. שִׁלְשׁוֹם **shilshôwm**, *shil-shome';* or

שִׁלְשֹׁם **shilshôm**, *shil-shome';* from the same as 8028; *trebly,* i.e. (in time) *day before yesterday:*—+ before (that time, -time), excellent things [*from the marg.*], + heretofore, three days, + time past.

שְׁלֹשִׁים **shᵉlôshîym**. See 7970.

שַׁלְתִּיאֵל **Shaltîy'êl**. See 7597.

8033. שָׁם **shâm**, *shawm;* a prim. particle [rather from the rel. 834]; *there* (transf. to time) *then;* often *thither,* or *thence:*—in it, + thence, there (-in, + of, + out), + thither, + whither.

8034. שֵׁם **shêm**, *shame;* a prim. word [perh. rather from 7760 through the idea of definite and conspicuous *position;* comp. 8064]; an *appellation,* as a mark or memorial of individuality; by impl. *honor, authority, character:*—+ base, [in-] fame [-ous], name (-d), renown, report.

8035. שֵׁם **Shêm**, *shame;* the same as 8034; *name; Shem,* a son of Noah (often includ. his posterity):—Sem, Shem.

8036. שֻׁם **shum** (Chald.), *shoom;* corresp. to 8034:—name.

8037. שַׁמָּא **Shammâ'**, *sham-maw';* from 8074; *desolation; Shamma,* an Isr.:—Shamma.

8038. שֶׁמְאֵבֶר **Shem'êber**, *shem-ay'-ber;* appar. from 8034 and 83; *name of pinion,* i.e. *illustrious; Shemeber,* a king of Zeboim:—Shemeber.

8039. שִׁמְאָה **Shim'âh**, *shim-aw';* perh. for 8093; *Shimah,* an Isr.:—Shimah. Comp. 8043.

8040. שְׂמֹאול **sᵉmô'wl**, *sem-ole';* or

שְׂמֹאל **sᵉmôl**, *sem-ole';* a prim. word [rather perh. from the same as 8071 (by insertion of א) through the idea of *wrapping up*]; prop. *dark* (as *enveloped*), i.e. the *north;* hence (by orientation) the *left* hand:—left (hand, side).

8041. שָׂמַאל **sâma'l**, *saw-mal';* a prim. root [rather denom. from 8040]; to use the *left* hand or pass in that direction):—(go, turn) (on the, to the) left.

8042. שְׂמָאלִי **s^e^mâ'lîy**, *sem-aw-lee'*; from 8040; situated on the *left* side:—left.

8043. שִׁמְאָם **Shim'âm**, *shim-awm'*; for 8039 [comp. 38]; *Shimam*, an Isr.:—Shimeam.

8044. שַׁמְגַּר **Shamgar**, *sham-gar'*; of uncert. der.; *Shamgar*, an Isr. judge:—Shamgar.

8045. שָׁמַד **shâmad**, *shaw-mad'*; a prim. root; to *desolate*:—destroy (-uction), bring to nought, overthrow, perish, pluck down, × utterly.

8046. שְׁמַד **sh^e^mad** (Chald.), *shem-ad'*; corresp. to 8045:—consume.

שָׁמֶה **shâmeh**. See 8064.

8047. שַׁמָּה **shammâh**, *sham-maw'*; from 8074; *ruin*; by impl. *consternation*:—astonishment, desolate (-ion), waste, wonderful thing.

8048. שַׁמָּה **Shammâh**, *sham-maw'*; the same as 8047; *Shammah*, the name of an Edomite and four Isr.: -Shammah.

8049. שַׁמְהוּת **Shamhûwth**, *sham-hooth'*; for 8048; *desolation*; *Shamhuth*, an Isr.:—Shamhuth.

8050. שְׁמוּאֵל **Sh^e^mûw'êl**, *shem-oo-ale'*; from the pass. part. of 8085 and 410; *heard of God*; *Shemuël*, the name of three Isr.:—Samuel, Shemuel.

שְׁמוֹנֶה **sh^e^môwneh**. See 8083.

שְׁמוֹנָה **sh^e^môwnâh**. See 8083.

שְׁמוֹנִים **sh^e^môwnîym**. See 8084.

8051. שַׁמּוּעַ **Shammûwa'**, *sham-moo'-ah*; from 8074; *renowned*; *Shammua*, the name of four Isr.:—Shammua, Shammuah.

8052. שְׁמוּעָה **sh^e^mûw'âh**, *shem-oo-aw'*; fem. pass. part. of 8074; something *heard*, i.e. an *announcement*:—bruit, doctrine, fame, mentioned, news, report, rumor, tidings.

8053. שָׁמוּר° **Shâmûwr**, *shaw-moor'*; pass. part. of 8103; *observed*; *Shamur*, an Isr.:—Shamir [*from the marg.*].

8054. שַׁמּוֹת **Shammôwth**, *sham-mōth'*; plur. of 8047; *ruins*; *Shammoth*, an Isr.:—Shamoth.

8055. שָׂמַח **sâmach**, *saw-makh'*; a prim. root; prob. to *brighten* up, i.e. (fig.) *be* (caus. make) *blithe* or *gleesome*:—cheer up, be (make) glad, (have, make) joy (-ful), be (make) merry, (cause to, make to) rejoice, × very.

8056. שָׂמֵחַ **sâmêach**, *saw-may'-akh*; from 8055; *blithe* or *gleeful*:—(be) glad, joyful, (making) merry ([-hearted], -ily), rejoice (-ing).

8057. שִׂמְחָה **simchâh**, *sim-khaw'*; from 8056; *blithesomeness* or *glee*, (religious or festival):—× exceeding (-ly), gladness, joy (-fulness), mirth, pleasure, rejoice (-ing).

8058. שָׁמַט **shâmaṭ**, *shaw-mat'*; a prim. root; to *fling* down; incipiently to *jostle*; fig. to *let alone*, *desist*, *remit*:—discontinue, overthrow, release, let rest, shake, stumble, throw down.

8059. שְׁמִטָּה **sh^e^miṭṭâh**, *shem-it-taw'*; from 8058; *remission* (of debt) or *suspension* of labor):—release.

8060. שַׁמַּי **Shammay**, *sham-mah'ee*; from 8073; *destructive*; *Shammai*, the name of three Isr.:—Shammai.

8061. שְׁמִידָע **Sh^e^mîydâ'**, *shem-ee-daw'*; appar. from 8034 and 3045; *name of knowing*; *Shemida*, an Isr.:—Shemida, Shemidah.

8062. שְׁמִידָעִי **Sh^e^mîydâ'îy**, *shem-ee-daw-ee'*; patron. from 8061; a *Shemidaïte* (collect.) or desc. of Shemida:—Shemidaites.

8063. שְׂמִיכָה **s^e^mîykâh**, *sem-ee-kaw'*; from 5564; a *rug* (as *sustaining* the Oriental sitter):—mantle.

8064. שָׁמַיִם **shâmayim**, *shaw-mah'-yim*; dual of an unused sing.

שָׁמֶה **shâmeh**, *shaw-meh'*; from an unused root mean. to *be lofty*; the *sky* (as *aloft*; the dual perh. alluding to the visible arch in which the clouds move, as well as to the higher ether where the celestial bodies revolve):—air, × astrologer, heaven (-s).

8065. שָׁמַיִן **shâmayin** (Chald.), *shaw-mah'-yin*; corresp. to 8064:—heaven.

8066. שְׁמִינִי **sh^e^mîynîy**, *shem-ee-nee'*; from 8083; *eight*:—eight.

8067. שְׁמִינִית **sh^e^mîynîyth**, *shem-ee-neeth'*; fem. of 8066; prob. an *eight*-stringed lyre:—Sheminith.

8068. שָׁמִיר **shâmîyr**, *shaw-meer'*; from 8104 in the orig. sense of *pricking*; a *thorn*; also (from its *keenness* for scratching) a gem, prob. the *diamond*:—adamant (stone), brier, diamond.

8069. שָׁמִיר **Shâmîyr**, *shaw-meer'*; the same as 8068; *Shamir*, the name of two places in Pal.:—Shamir. Comp. 8053.

8070. שְׁמִירָמוֹת **Sh^e^mîyrâmôwth**, *shem-ee-raw-mōth'*; or

שְׁמָרִימוֹת° **Sh^e^mârîymôwth**, *shem-aw-ree-mōth'*; prob. from 8034 and plur. of 7413; *name of heights*; *Shemiramoth*, the name of two Isr.:—Shemiramoth.

8071. שִׂמְלָה **simlâh**, *sim-law'*; perh. by perm. for the fem. of 5566 (through the idea of a *cover* assuming the shape of the object beneath); a *dress*, espec. a *mantle*:—apparel, cloth (-es, -ing), garment, raiment. Comp. 8008.

8072. שַׂמְלָה **Samlâh**, *sam-law'*; prob. for the same as 8071; *Samlah*, an Edomite:—Samlah.

8073. שַׁמְלַי° **Shamlay**, *sham-lah'ee*; for 8014; *Shamlai*, one of the Nethinim:—Shalmai [*from the marg.*].

8074. שָׁמֵם **shâmêm**, *shaw-mame'*; a prim. root; to *stun* (or intrans. *grow numb*), i.e. *devastate* or (fig.) *stupefy* (both usually in a passive sense):—make amazed, be astonied, (be an) astonish (-ment), (be, bring into, unto, lay, lie, make) desolate (-ion, places), be destitute, destroy (self), (lay, lie, make) waste, wonder.

8075. שְׁמַם **sh^e^mam** (Chald.), *shem-am'*; corresp. to 8074:—be astonied.

8076. שָׁמֵם **shâmêm**, *shaw-mame'*; from 8074; *ruined*:—desolate.

8077. שְׁמָמָה **sh^e^mâmâh**, *shem-aw-maw'*; or

שִׁמָמָה **shîmâmâh**, *shee-mam-aw'*; fem. of 8076; *devastation*; fig. *astonishment*:—(laid, × most) desolate (-ion), waste.

8078. שִׁמָּמוֹן **shimmâmôwn**, *shim-maw-mone'*; from 8074; *stupefaction*:—astonishment.

8079. שְׂמָמִית **s^e^mâmîyth**, *sem-aw-meeth'*; prob. from 8074 (in the sense of *poisoning*); a *lizard* (from the superstition of its *noxiousness*):—spider.

8080. שָׁמַן **shâman**, *shaw-man'*; a prim. root; to *shine*, i.e. (by anal.) *be* (caus. *make*) *oily* or *gross*:—become (make, wax) fat.

8081. שֶׁמֶן **shemen**, *sheh'-men*; from 8080; *grease*, espec. liquid (as from the olive, often perfumed); fig. *richness*:—anointing, × fat (things), × fruitful, oil ([-ed]), ointment, olive, + pine.

8082. שָׁמֵן **shâmên**, *shaw-mane'*; from 8080; *greasy*, i.e. *gross*; fig. *rich*:—fat, lusty, plenteous.

8083. שְׁמֹנֶה **sh^e^môneh**, *shem-o-neh'*; or

שְׁמוֹנֶה **sh^e^môwneh**, *shem-o-neh'*; fem.

שְׁמֹנָה **sh^e^mônâh**, *shem-o-naw'*; or

שְׁמוֹנָה **sh^e^môwnâh**, *shem-o-naw'*; appar. from 8082 through the idea of *plumpness*; a cardinal number, *eight* (as if a *surplus* above the "perfect" seven); also (as ordinal) *eighth*:—eight ([-een, -eenth]), eighth.

8084. שְׁמֹנִים **sh^e^mônîym**, *shem-o-neem'*; or

שְׁמוֹנִים **sh^e^môwnîym**, *shem-o-neem'*; mult. from 8083; *eighty*; also *eightieth*:—eighty (-ieth), fourscore.

8085. שָׁמַע **shâma'**, *shaw-mah'*; a prim. root; to *hear* intelligently (often with impl. of attention, obedience, etc.; caus. to *tell*, etc.):—× attentively, call (gather) together, × carefully, × certainly, consent, consider, be content, declare, × diligently, discern, give ear, (cause to, let, make to) hear (-ken, tell), × indeed, listen, make (a) noise, (be) obedient, obey, perceive, (make a) proclaim (-ation), publish, regard, report, shew (forth), (make a) sound, × surely, tell, understand, whosoever [heareth], witness.

8086. שְׁמַע **sh^e^ma'** (Chald.), *shem-ah'*; corresp. to 8085:—hear, obey.

8087. שֶׁמַע **Shema'**, *sheh'-mah*; for the same as 8088; *Shema*, the name of a place in Pal. and of four Isr.:—Shema.

8088. שֵׁמַע **shêma'**, *shay'-mah*; from 8085; something *heard*, i.e. a *sound*, *rumor*, *announcement*; abstr. *audience*:—bruit, fame, hear (-ing), loud, report, speech, tidings.

8089. שֹׁמַע **shôma'**, *sho'-mah*; from 8085; a *report*:—fame.

8090. שְׁמָע **Sh^e^mâ'**, *shem-aw'*; for 8087; *Shema*, a place in Pal.:—Shema.

8091. שָׁמָע **Shâmâ'**, *shaw-maw'*; from 8085; *obedient*; *Shama*, an Isr.:—Shama.

8092. שִׁמְעָא **Shim'â'**, *shim-aw'*; for 8093; *Shima*, the name of four Isr.:—Shimea, Shimei, Shamma.

8093. שִׁמְעָה **Shim'âh**, *shim-aw'*; fem. of 8088; *annunciation*; *Shimah*, an Isr.:—Shimeah.

8094. שְׁמָעָה **Sh^e^mâ'âh**, *shem-aw-aw'*; for 8093; *Shemaah*, an Isr.:—Shemaah.

8095. שִׁמְעוֹן **Shim'ôwn**, *shim-ōne'*; from 8085; *hearing*; *Shimon*, one of Jacob's sons, also the tribe desc. from him:—Simeon.

8096. שִׁמְעִי **Shim'îy**, *shim-ee'*; from 8088; *famous*; *Shimi*, the name of twenty Isr.:—Shimeah [*from the marg.*], Shimei, Shimhi, Shimi.

8097. שִׁמְעִי **Shim'îy**, *shim-ee'*; patron. from 8096; a *Shimite* (collect.) or desc. of Shimi:—of Shimi, Shimites.

8098. שְׁמַעְיָה **Sh^e^ma'yâh**, *shem-aw-yaw'*; or

שְׁמַעְיָהוּ **Sh^e^ma'yâhûw**, *shem-aw-yaw'-hoo*; from 8085 and 3050; *Jah has heard*; *Shemajah*, the name of twenty-five Isr.:—Shemaiah.

8099. שִׁמְעֹנִי **Shim'ôniy**, *shim-o-nee'*; patron. from 8095; a *Shimonite* (collect.) or desc. of Shimon:—tribe of Simeon, Simeonites.

8100. שִׁמְעָת **Shim'âth**, *shim-awth'*; fem. of 8088; *annunciation*; *Shimath*, an Ammonitess:—Shimath.

8101. שִׁמְעָתִי **Shim'âthîy**, *shim-aw-thee'*; patron. from 8093; a *Shimathite* (collect.) or desc. of Shimah:—Shimeathites.

8102. שֶׁמֶץ **shemets**, *sheh'-mets*; from an unused root mean. to *emit* a sound; an *inkling*:—a little.

8103. שִׁמְצָה **shimtsâh**, *shim-tsaw'*; fem. of 8102; scornful *whispering* (of hostile spectators):—shame.

8104. שָׁמַר **shâmar**, *shaw-mar'*; a prim. root; prop. to *hedge* about (as with thorns), i.e. *guard*; gen. to *protect*, *attend to*, etc.:—beware, be circumspect, take heed (to self), keep (-er, self), mark, look narrowly, observe, preserve, regard, reserve, save (self), sure, (that lay) wait (for), watch (-man).

8105. שֶׁמֶר **shemer**, *sheh'-mer*; from 8104; something *preserved*, i.e. the *settlings* (plur. only) of wine:—dregs, (wines on the) lees.

8106. שֶׁמֶר **Shemer**, *sheh'-mer*; the same as 8105; *Shemer*, the name of three Isr.:—Shamer, Shemer.

8107. שִׁמֻּר **shimmûr**, *shim-moor'*; from 8104; an *observance*:—× be (much) observed.

שֹׁמֵר **Shômêr**. See 7763.

8108. שָׁמְרָה **shomrâh**, *shom-raw'*; fem. of an unused noun from 8104 mean. a *guard*; *watchfulness*:—watch.

8109. שְׁמֻרָה **sh^e^mûrâh**, *shem-oo-raw'*; fem. of pass. part. of 8104; something *guarded*, i.e. an *eye-lid*:—waking.

8110. שִׁמְרוֹן **Shimrôwn**, *shim-rone'*; from 8105 in its orig. sense; *guardianship*; *Shimron*, the name of an Isr. and of a place in Pal.:—Shimron.

8111. שֹׁמְרוֹן **Shômerown**, *sho-mer-one'*; from the act. part. of 8104; *watch-station; Shomeron*, a place in Pal.:—Samaria.

8112. שִׁמְרוֹן מְראוֹן **Shimrôwn Merô'wn**, *shim-rone' mer-one'*; from 8110 and a der. of 4754; *guard of lashing; Shimron-Meron*, a place in Pal.:—Shimon-meron.

8113. שִׁמְרִי **Shimriy**, *shim-ree'*; from 8105 in its orig. sense; *watchful; Shimri*, the name of four Isr.:—Shimri.

8114. שְׁמַרְיָה **Shemaryâh**, *shem-ar-yaw'*; or

שְׁמַרְיָהוּ **Shemaryâhûw**, *shem-ar-yaw'-hoo*; from 8104 and 3050; *Jah has guarded; Shemarjah*, the name of four Isr.:—Shamariah, Shemariah.

שְׁמָרִימוֹת° **Shemârîymôwth**. See 8070.

8115. שָׁמְרַיִן **Shomrayin** (Chald.), *shom-rah'-yin*; corresp. to 8111; *Shomraïn*, a place in Pal.:—Samaria.

8116. שִׁמְרִית **Shimrîyth**, *shim-reeth'*; fem. of 8113; *female guard; Shimrith*, a Moabitess:—Shimrith.

8117. שִׁמְרֹנִי **Shimrônîy**, *shim-ro-nee'*; patron. from 8110; a *Shimronite* (collect.) or desc. of Shimron:—Shimronites.

8118. שֹׁמְרֹנִי **Shômerônîy**, *sho-mer-o-nee'*; patrial from 8111; a *Shomeronite* (collect.) or inhab. of Shomeron:—Samaritans.

8119. שִׁמְרָת **Shimrâth**, *shim-rawth'*; from 8104; *guardship; Shimrath*, an Isr.:—Shimrath.

8120. שְׁמַשׁ **shemash** (Chald.), *shem-ash'*; corresp. to the root of 8121 through the idea of *activity* implied in day-light; to *serve*:—minister.

8121. שֶׁמֶשׁ **shemesh**, *sheh'-mesh*; from an unused root mean. to be *brilliant*; the *sun*; by impl. the *east*; fig. a *ray*, i.e. (arch.) a notched *battlement*:— + east side (-ward), sun ([rising]), + west (-ward), window. See also 1053.

8122. שֶׁמֶשׁ **shemesh** (Chald.), *sheh'-mesh*; corresp. to 8121; the *sun*:—sun.

8123. שִׁמְשׁוֹן **Shimshôwn**, *shim-shone'*; from 8121; *sunlight; Shimshon*, an Isr.:—Samson.

שִׁמְשִׁי **Shimshîy**. See 1030.

8124. שִׁמְשַׁי **Shimshay** (Chald.), *shim-shah'ee*; from 8122; *sunny; Shimshai*, a Samaritan:—Shimshai.

8125. שַׁמְשְׁרַי **Shamsheray**, *sham-sher-ah'ee*; appar. from 8121; *sunlike; Shamsherai*, an Isr.:—Shamsherai.

8126. שֻׁמָתִי **Shûmâthîy**, *shoo-maw-thee'*; patron. from an unused name from 7762 prob. mean. *garlic*-smell; a *Shumathite* (collect.) or desc. of Shumah:—Shumathites.

8127. שֵׁן **shên**, *shane*; from 8150; a *tooth* (as *sharp*); spec. (for 8143) *ivory*; fig. a *cliff*:—crag, × forefront, ivory, × sharp, tooth.

8128. שֵׁן **shên** (Chald.), *shane*; corresp. to 8127; a *tooth*:—tooth.

8129. שֵׁן **Shên**, *shane*; the same as 8127; *crag; Shen*, a place in Pal.:—Shen.

8130. שָׂנֵא **sânê'**, *saw-nay'*; a prim. root; to *hate* (personally):—enemy, foe, (be) hate (-ful, -r), odious, × utterly.

8131. שְׂנֵא **senê'** (Chald.), *sen-ay'*; corresp. to 8130:—hate.

8132. שָׁנָא **shânâ'**, *shaw-naw'*; a prim. root; to *alter*:—change.

8133. שְׁנָא **shenâ'** (Chald.), *shen-aw'*; corresp. to 8132:—alter, change, (be) diverse.

שֵׁנָא **shênâ'**. See 8142.

8134. שִׁנְאָב **Shin'âb**, *shin-awb'*; prob. from 8132 and 1; a *father has turned; Shinab*, a Canaanite:—Shinab.

8135. שִׂנְאָה **sin'âh**, *sin-aw'*; from 8130; *hate*:— + exceedingly, hate (-ful, -red).

8136. שִׁנְאָן **shin'ân**, *shin-awn'*; from 8132; *change*, i.e. *repetition*:— × angels.

8137. שֶׁנַאצַּר **Shenatstsar**, *shen-ats-tsar'*; appar. of Bab. or.; *Shenatstsar*, an Isr.:—Senazar.

8138. שָׁנָה **shânâh**, *shaw-naw'*; a prim. root; to *fold*, i.e. *duplicate* (lit. or fig.); by impl. to *transmute* (trans. or intrans.):—do (speak, strike) again, alter, double, (be given to) change, disguise, (be) diverse, pervert, prefer, repeat, return, do the second time.

8139. שְׁנָה **shenâh** (Chald.), *shen-aw'*; corresp. to 8142:—sleep.

8140. שְׁנָה **shenâh** (Chald.), *shen-aw'*; corresp. to 8141:—year.

8141. שָׁנֶה **shâneh** (in plur. only), *shaw-neh'*; or (fem.)

שָׁנָה **shânâh**, *shaw-naw'*; from 8138; a *year* (as a *revolution* of time):— + whole age, × long, + old, year (× -ly).

8142. שֵׁנָה **shênâh**, *shay-naw'*; or

שֵׁנָא **shênâ'** (Psa. 127 : 2), *shay-naw'*; from 3462; *sleep*:—sleep.

8143. שֶׁנְהַבִּים **shenhabbîym**, *shen-hab-beem'*; from 8127 and the plur. appar. of a for. word; prob. *tooth of elephants*, i.e. *ivory tusk*:—ivory.

8144. שָׁנִי **shânîy**, *shaw-nee'*; of uncert. der.; *crimson*, prop. the insect or its color, also stuff dyed with it:—crimson, scarlet (thread).

8145. שֵׁנִי **shênîy**, *shay-nee'*; from 8138; prop. *double*, i.e. *second*; also adv. *again*:—again, either [of them], (an-) other, second (time).

8146. שָׂנִיא **sânîy'**, *saw-nee'*; from 8130; *hated*:—hated.

8147. שְׁנַיִם **shenayim**, *shen-ah'-yim*; dual of 8145; fem.

שְׁתַּיִם **shettayim**, *shet-tah'-yim*; *two*; also (as ordinal) *twofold*:—both, couple, double, second, twain, + twelfth, + twelve, + twenty (sixscore) thousand, twice, two.

8148. שְׁנִינָה **shenîynâh**, *shen-ee-naw'*; from 8150; something *pointed*, i.e. a *gibe*:—byword, taunt.

8149. שְׁנִיר **Shenîyr**, *shen-eer'*; or

שְׂנִיר **Senîyr**, *sen-eer'*; from an unused root mean. to *be pointed; peak; Shenir* or *Senir*, a summit of Lebanon:—Senir, Shenir.

8150. שָׁנַן **shânan**, *shaw-nan'*; a prim. root; to *point* (trans. or intrans.); intens. to *pierce*; fig. to *inculcate*:—prick, sharp (-en), teach diligently, whet.

8151. שָׁנַס **shânaç**, *shaw-nas'*; a prim. root; to *compress* (with a belt):—gird up.

8152. שִׁנְעָר **Shin'âr**, *shin-awr'*; prob. of for. der.; *Shinar*, a plain in Bab.:—Shinar.

8153. שְׁנָת **shenâth**, *shen-awth'*; from 3462; *sleep*:—sleep.

8154. שָׁסָה **shâçâh**, *shaw-saw'*; or

שָׁשָׂה **shâsâh** (Isa. 10 : 13), *shaw-saw'*; a prim. root; to *plunder*:—destroyer, rob, spoil (-er).

8155. שָׁסַס **shâçaç**, *shaw-sas'*; a prim. root; to *plunder*:—rifle, spoil.

8156. שָׁסַע **shâça'**, *shaw-sah'*; a prim. root; to *split* or *tear*; fig. to *upbraid*:—cleave, (be) cloven ([footed]), rend, stay.

8157. שֶׁסַע **sheça'**, *sheh'-sah*; from 8156; a *fissure*:—cleft, clovenfooted.

8158. שָׁסַף **shâçaph**, *shaw-saf'*; a prim. root; to *cut* in pieces, i.e. slaughter:—hew in pieces.

8159. שָׁעָה **shâ'âh**, *shaw-aw'*; a prim. root; to *gaze* at or about (prop. for help); by impl. to *inspect, consider, compassionate, be nonplussed* (as looking around in amazement) or *bewildered*:—depart, be dim, be dismayed, look (away), regard, have respect, spare, turn.

8160. שְׁעָה **shâ'âh** (Chald.), *shaw-aw'*; from a root corresp. to 8159; prop. a *look*, i.e. a *moment*:—hour.

שְׂעוֹר **se'ôwr**. See 8184.

שְׂעוֹרָה **se'ôwrâh**. See 8184.

8161. שַׁעֲטָה **sha'ăṭâh**, *shah'-at-aw*; fem. from an unused root mean. to *stamp*; a *clatter* (of hoofs):—stamping.

8162. שַׁעַטְנֵז **sha'aṭnêz**, *shah-at-naze'*; prob. of for. der.; *linsey-woolsey*, i.e. cloth of linen and wool carded and spun together:—garment of divers sorts, linen and woollen.

8163. שָׂעִיר **sâ'îyr**, *saw-eer'*; or

שָׂעִר **sâ'ir**, *saw-eer'*; from 8175; *shaggy*; as noun, a *he-goat*; by anal. a *faun*:—devil, goat, hairy, kid, rough, satyr.

8164. שָׂעִיר **sâ'îyr**, *saw-eer'*; formed the same as 8163; a *shower* (as *tempestuous*):—small rain.

8165. שֵׂעִיר **Sê'îyr**, *say-eer'*; formed like 8163; *rough; Seïr*, a mountain of Idumæa and its aboriginal occupants, also one in Pal.:—Seir.

8166. שְׂעִירָה **se'îyrâh**, *seh-ee-raw'*; fem. of 8163; a *she-goat*:—kid.

8167. שְׂעִירָה **Se'îyrâh**, *seh-ee-raw'*; formed as 8166; *roughness; Seïrah*, a place in Pal.:—Seirath.

8168. שֹׁעַל **shô'al**, *sho'-al*; from an unused root mean. to *hollow* out; the *palm*; by extens. a *handful*:—handful, hollow of the hand.

שֻׁעָל **shû'âl**. See 7776.

8169. שַׁעַלְבִים **Sha'albîym**, *shah-al-beem'*; or

שַׁעֲלַבִּין **Sha'ălabbîyn**, *shah-al-ab-been'*; plur. from 7776; *fox-holes; Shaalbim* or *Shaalabbin*, a place in Pal.:—Shaalabbin, Shaalbim.

8170. שַׁעַלְבֹנִי **Sha'albônîy**, *shah-al-bo-nee'*; patrial from 8169; a *Shaalbonite* or inhab. of Shaalbin:—Shaalbonite.

8171. שַׁעֲלִים **Sha'ălîym**, *shah-al-eem'*; plur. of 7776; *foxes; Shaalim*, a place in Pal.:—Shalim.

8172. שָׁעַן **shâ'an**, *shaw-an'*; a prim. root; to *support* one's self:—lean, lie, rely, rest (on, self), stay.

8173. שָׁעַע **shâ'a'**, *shaw-ah'*; a prim. root; (in a good acceptation) to *look* upon (with complacency), i.e. *fondle, please* or *amuse* (self); (in a bad one) to *look* about (in dismay), i.e. *stare*:—cry (out) [*by confusion with* 7768], dandle, delight (self), play, shut.

שָׂעִף **sâ'iph**. See 5587.

8174. שַׁעַף **Sha'aph**, *shah'-af*; from 5586; *fluctuation; Shaaph*, the name of two Isr.:—Shaaph.

8175. שָׂעַר **sâ'ar**, *saw-ar'*; a prim. root; to *storm*; by impl. to *shiver*, i.e. *fear*:—be (horribly) afraid, fear, hurl as a storm, be tempestuous, come like (take away as with) a whirlwind.

8176. שָׁעַר **shâ'ar**, *shaw-ar'*; a prim. root; to *split* or *open*, i.e. (lit., but only as denom. from 8179) to *act as gate-keeper* (see 7778); (fig.) to *estimate*:—think.

8177. שְׂעַר **se'ar** (Chald.), *seh-ar'*; corresp. to 8181; *hair*:—hair.

8178. שַׂעַר **sa'ar**, *sah'-ar*; from 8175; a *tempest*; also a *terror*:—affrighted, × horribly, × sore, storm. See 8181.

8179. שַׁעַר **sha'ar**, *shah'-ar*; from 8176 in its orig. sense; an *opening*, i.e. *door* or *gate*:—city, door, gate, port (× -er).

8180. שַׁעַר **sha'ar**, *shah'-ar*; from 8176; a *measure* (as a *section*):—[hundred-] fold.

שָׂעִר **sâ'ir**. See 8163.

8181. שֵׂעָר **sê'âr**, *say-awr'*; or

שַׂעַר **sa'ar** (Isa. 7 : 20), *sah'-ar*; from 8175 in the sense of *dishevelling*; *hair* (as if *tossed* or *bristling*):—hair (-y), × rough.

שֹׁעֵר **shô'êr**. See 7778.

8182. שֹׁעָר **shô'âr**, *sho-awr'*; from 8176; *harsh* or *horrid*, i.e. *offensive*:—vile.

8183. שְׂעָרָה **se'ârâh**, *seh-aw-raw'*; fem. of 8178; a *hurricane*:—storm, tempest.

8184. שְׂעֹרָה **seʻôrâh**, *seh-o-raw'*; or
שְׂעוֹרָה **seʻôwrâh**, *seh-o-raw'* (fem. mean. the *plant*); and (masc. mean. the *grain*); also
שְׂעֹר **seʻôr**, *seh-ore'*; or
שְׂעוֹר **seʻôwr**, *seh-ore'*; from 8175 in the sense of *roughness*; *barley* (as *villose*):—barley.

8185. שַׂעֲרָה **saʻărâh**, *sah-ar-aw'*; fem. of 8181; *hairiness*:—hair.

8186. שַׁעֲרוּרָה **shaʻărûwrâh**, *shah-ar-oo-raw'*; or
שַׁעֲרִירִיָּה **shaʻărîyrîyâh**, *shah-ar-ee-ree-yaw'*; or
שַׁעֲרֻרִת **shaʻărûrîth**, *shah-ar-oo-reeth'*; fem. from 8176 in the sense of 8175; something *fearful*:—horrible thing.

8187. שְׁעַרְיָה **Sheʻaryâh**, *sheh-ar-yaw'*; from 8176 and 3050; *Jah has stormed*; *Sheărjah*, an Isr.:—Sheariah.

8188. שְׂעֹרִים **Seʻôrîym**, *seh-o-reem'*; masc. plur. of 8184; *barley grains*; *Seörim*, an Isr.:—Seorim.

8189. שַׁעֲרַיִם **Shaʻărayim**, *shah-ar-ah'-yim*; dual of 8179; *double gates*; *Shaarafim*, a place in Pal.:—Shaaraim.

שַׁעֲרִירִיָּה **shaʻărîyrîyâh**. See 8186.

שַׁעֲרֻרִת **shaʻărûrîth**. See 8186.

8190. שַׁעַשְׁגַּז **Shaʻashgaz**, *shah-ash-gaz'*; of Pers. der.; *Shaashgaz*, a eunuch of Xerxes:—Shaashgaz.

8191. שַׁעְשֻׁעַ **shaʻshûaʻ**, *shah-shoo'-ah*; from 8173; *enjoyment*:—delight, pleasure.

8192. שָׁפָה **shâphâh**, *shaw-faw'*; a prim. root; to *abrade*, i.e. *bare*:—high, stick out.

8193. שָׂפָה **sâphâh**, *saw-faw'*; or (in dual and plur.)
שֶׂפֶת **sepheth**, *sef-eth'*; prob. from 5595 or 8192 through the idea of *termination* (comp. 5490); the *lip* (as a natural boundary); by impl. *language*; by anal. a *margin* (of a vessel, water, cloth, etc.):—band, bank, binding, border, brim, brink, edge, language, lip, prating, ([sea-]) shore, side, speech, talk, [vain] words.

8194. שָׁפָה **shâphâh**, *shaw-faw'*; from 8192 in the sense of *clarifying*; a *cheese* (as *strained* from the whey):—cheese.

8195. שְׁפוֹ **Shephôw**, *shef-o'*; or
שְׁפִי **Shephîy**, *shef-ee'*; from 8192; *baldness* [comp. 8205]; *Shepho* or *Shephi*, an Idumæan:—Shephi, Shepho.

8196. שְׁפוֹט **shephôwṭ**, *shef-ote'*; or
שְׁפוּט **shephûwṭ**, *shef-oot'*; from 8199; a judicial *sentence*, i.e. *punishment*:—judgment.

8197. שְׁפוּפָם **Shephûwphâm**, *shef-oo-fawm'*; or
שְׁפוּפָן **Shephûwphân**, *shef-oo-fawn'*; from the same as 8207; *serpent-like*; *Shephupham* or *Shephuphan*, an Isr.:—Shephuphan, Shupham.

8198. שִׁפְחָה **shiphchâh**, *shif-khaw'*; fem. from an unused root mean. to *spread* out (as a *family*; see 4940); a *female slave* (as a member of the *household*):—(bond-, hand-) maid (-en, -servant), wench, bondwoman, womanservant.

8199. שָׁפַט **shâphaṭ**, *shaw-fat'*; a prim. root; to *judge*, i.e. pronounce *sentence* (for or against); by impl. to *vindicate* or *punish*; by extens. to *govern*; pass. to *litigate* (lit. or fig.):— + avenge, × that condemn, contend, defend, execute (judgment), (be a) judge (-ment), × needs, plead, reason, rule.

8200. שְׁפַט **shephaṭ** (Chald.), *shef-at'*; corresp. to 8199; to *judge*:—magistrate.

8201. שֶׁפֶט **shepheṭ**, *sheh'-fet*; from 8199; a *sentence*, i.e. *infliction*:—judgment.

8202. שָׁפָט **Shâphâṭ**, *shaw-fawt'*; from 8199; *judge*; *Shaphat*, the name of four Isr.:—Shaphat.

8203. שְׁפַטְיָה **Shephaṭyâh**, *shef-at-yaw'*; or
שְׁפַטְיָהוּ **Shephaṭyâhûw**, *shef-at-yaw'-hoo*; from 8199 and 3050; *Jah has judged*; *Shephatjah*, the name of ten Isr.:—Shephatiah.

8204. שִׁפְטָן **Shiphṭân**, *shif-tawn'*; from 8199; *judge-like*; *Shiphtan*, an Isr.:—Shiphtan.

8205. שְׁפִי **shephîy**, *shef-ee'*; from 8192; *bareness*; concr. a *bare* hill or plain:—high place, stick out.

8206. שֻׁפִּים **Shuppîym**, *shoop-peem'*; plur. of an unused noun from the same as 8207 and mean. the same; *serpents*; *Shuppim*, an Isr.:—Shuppim.

8207. שְׁפִיפֹן **shephîyphôn**, *shef-ee-fone'*; from an unused root mean. the same as 7779; a kind of *serpent* (as *snapping*), prob. the *cerastes* or horned adder:—adder.

8208. שָׁפִיר **Shaphîyr**, *shaf-eer'*; from 8231; *beautiful*; *Shaphir*, a place in Pal.:—Saphir.

8209. שַׁפִּיר **shappîyr** (Chald.), *shap-peer'*; intens. of a form corresp. to 8208; *beautiful*:—fair.

8210. שָׁפַךְ **shâphak**, *shaw-fak'*; a prim. root; to *spill* forth (blood, a libation, liquid metal; or even a solid, i.e. to *mound* up); also (fig.) to *expend* (life, soul, complaint, money, etc.); intens. to *sprawl* out:—cast (up), gush out, pour (out), shed (-der, out), slip.

8211. שֶׁפֶךְ **shephek**, *sheh'-fek*; from 8210; an *emptying* place, e.g. an ash-*heap*:—are poured out.

8212. שָׁפְכָה **shophkâh**, *shof-kaw'*; fem. of a der. from 8210; a *pipe* (for *pouring* forth, e.g. wine), i.e. the *penis*:—privy member.

8213. שָׁפֵל **shâphêl**, *shaw-fale'*; a prim. root; to *depress* or *sink* (espec. fig. to *humiliate*, intrans. or trans.):—abase, bring (cast, put) down, debase, humble (self), be (bring, lay, make, put) low (-er).

8214. שְׁפַל **shephal** (Chald.), *shef-al'*; corresp. to 8213:—abase, humble, put down, subdue.

8215. שְׁפַל **shephal** (Chald.), *shef-al'*; from 8214; *low*:—basest.

8216. שֵׁפֶל **shêphel**, *shay'-fel*; from 8213; an *humble* rank:—low estate (place).

8217. שָׁפָל **shâphâl**, *shaw-fawl'*; from 8213; *depressed*, lit. or fig.:—base (-st), humble, low (-er, -ly).

8218. שִׁפְלָה **shiphlâh**, *shif-law'*; fem. of 8216; *depression*:—low place.

8219. שְׁפֵלָה **shephêlâh**, *shef-ay-law'*; from 8213; *Lowland*, i.e. (with the art.) the maritime slope of Pal.:—low country, (low) plain, vale (-ley).

8220. שִׁפְלוּת **shiphlûwth**, *shif-looth'*; from 8213; *remissness*:—idleness.

8221. שְׁפָם **Shephâm**, *shef-awm'*; prob. from 8192; *bare* spot; *Shepham*, a place in or near Pal.:—Shepham.

8222. שָׂפָם **sâphâm**, *saw-fawm'*; from 8193; the *beard* (as a *lip-piece*):—beard, (upper) lip.

8223. שָׁפָם **Shâphâm**, *shaw-fawm'*; formed like 8221; *baldly*; *Shapham*, an Isr.:—Shapham.

8224. שִׂפְמוֹת **Siphmôwth**, *sif-mōth'*; fem. plur. of 8221; *Siphmoth*, a place in Pal.:—Siphmoth.

8225. שִׁפְמִי **Shiphmîy**, *shif-mee'*; patrial from 8221; a *Shiphmite* inhab. of Shepham:—Shiphmite.

8226. שָׂפַן **sâphan**, *saw-fan'*; a prim. root; to *conceal* (as a valuable):—treasure.

8227. שָׁפָן **shâphân**, *shaw-fawn'*; from 8226; a species of *rock-rabbit* (from its *hiding*), i.e. prob. the *hyrax*:—coney.

8228. שֶׁפַע **shephaʻ**, *sheh'-fah*; from an unused root mean. to *abound*; *resources*:—abundance.

8229. שִׁפְעָה **shiphʻâh**, *shif-aw'*; fem. of 8228; *copiousness*:—abundance, company, multitude.

8230. שִׁפְעִי **Shiphʻîy**, *shif-ee'*; from 8228; *copious*; *Shiphi*, an Isr.:—Shiphi.

שָׂפַק **sâphaq**. See 5606.

8231. שָׁפַר **shâphar**, *shaw-far'*; a prim. root; to *glisten*, i.e. (fig.) *be* (caus. *make*) *fair*:— × goodly.

8232. שְׁפַר **shephar** (Chald.), *shef-ar'*; corresp. to 8231; to *be beautiful*:—be acceptable, please, + think good.

8233. שֶׁפֶר **shepher**, *sheh'-fer*; from 8231; *beauty*:— × goodly.

8234. שֶׁפֶר **Shepher**, *sheh'-fer*; the same as 8233; *Shepher*, a place in the Desert:—Shapper.

שֹׁפָר **shôphâr**. See 7782.

8235. שִׁפְרָה **shiphrâh**, *shif-raw'*; from 8231; *brightness*:—garnish.

8236. שִׁפְרָה **Shiphrâh**, *shif-raw'*; the same as 8235; *Shiphrah*, an Israelitess:—Shiphrah.

8237. שַׁפְרוּר **shaphrûwr**, *shaf-roor'*; from 8231; *splendid*, i.e. a *tapestry* or *canopy*.—royal pavilion.

8238. שְׁפַרְפָּר **shepharphar** (Chald.), *shef-ar-far'*; from 8231; the *dawn* (as *brilliant* with aurora):— × very early in the morning.

8239. שָׁפַת **shâphath**, *shaw-fath'*; a prim. root; to *locate*, i.e. (gen.) *hang* on or (fig.) *establish*, *reduce*:—bring, ordain, set on.

8240. שָׁפָת **shâphâth**, *shaw-fawth'*; from 8239; a (double) *stall* (for cattle); also a (two-pronged) *hook* (for flaying animals on):—hook, pot.

8241. שֶׁצֶף **shetseph**, *sheh'-tsef*; from 7857 (for alliteration with 7110); an *outburst* (of anger):—little.

8242. שַׂק **saq**, *sak*; from 8264; prop. a *mesh* (as allowing a liquid to *run* through), i.e. coarse loose cloth or *sacking* (used in mourning and for bagging); hence a *bag* (for grain, etc.):—sack (-cloth, -clothes).

8243. שָׁק **shâq** (Chald.), *shawk*; corresp. to 7785; the *leg*:—leg.

8244. שָׂקַד **sâqad**, *saw-kad'*; a prim. root; to *fasten*:—bind.

8245. שָׁקַד **shâqad**, *shaw-kad'*; a prim. root; to *be alert*, i.e. *sleepless*; hence to *be on the lookout* (whether for good or ill):—hasten, remain, wake, watch (for).

8246. שָׁקַד **shâqad**, *shaw-kad'*; a denom. from 8247; to *be* (intens. *make*) *almond-shaped*:—make like (unto, after the fashion of) almonds.

8247. שָׁקֵד **shâqêd**, *shaw-kade'*; from 8245; the *almond* (tree or nut; as being the *earliest* in bloom):—almond (tree).

8248. שָׁקָה **shâqâh**, *shaw-kaw'*; a prim. root; to *quaff*, i.e. (caus.) to *irrigate* or *furnish a potion* to:—cause to (give, give to, let, make to) drink, drown, moisten, water. See 7937, 8354.

8249. שִׁקֻּו **shiqqûv**, *shik-koov'*; from 8248; (plur. collect.) a *draught*:—drink.

8250. שִׁקּוּי **shiqqûwy**, *shik-koo'ee*; from 8248; a *beverage*; *moisture*, i.e. (fig.) *refreshment*:—drink, marrow.

8251. שִׁקּוּץ **shiqqûwts**, *shik-koots'*; or
שִׁקֻּץ **shiqqûts**, *shik-koots'*; from 8262; *disgusting*, i.e. *filthy*; espec. *idolatrous* or (concr.) an *idol*:—abom: iable filth (idol, -ation), detestable (thing).

8252. שָׁקַט **shâqaṭ**, *shaw-kat'*; a prim. root; to *repose* (usually fig.):—appease, idleness, (at, be at, be in, give) quiet (-ness), (be at, be in, give, have, take) rest, settle, be still.

8253. שֶׁקֶט **sheqeṭ**, *sheh'-ket*; from 8252; *tranquility*:—quietness.

8254. שָׁקַל **shâqal**, *shaw-kal'*; a prim. root; to *suspend* or *poise* (espec. in trade):—pay, receive (-r), spend. × throughly, weigh.

8255. שֶׁקֶל **sheqel**, *sheh'-kel;* from 8254; prob. a *weight;* used as a commercial standard:—shekel.

8256. שָׁקָם **shâqâm**, *shaw-kawm';* or (fem.)

שִׁקְמָה **shiqmâh**, *shik-maw';* of uncert. der.; a *sycamore* (usually the tree):—sycamore (fruit, tree).

8257. שָׁקַע **shâqaʻ**, *shaw-kah'* (abbrev. ° Am. 8 : 8); a prim. root; to *subside;* by impl. to *be overflowed, cease;* caus. to *abate, subdue:*—make deep, let down, drown, quench, sink.

8258. שְׁקַעְרוּרָה **sheqaʻrûwrâh**, *shek-ah-roo-raw';* from 8257; a *depression:*—hollow strake.

8259. שָׁקַף **shâqaph**, *shaw-kaf';* a prim. root; prop. to *lean out* (of a window), i.e. (by impl.) *peep* or *gaze* (pass. *be a spectacle*):—appear, look (down, forth, out).

8260. שֶׁקֶף **sheqeph**, *sheh'-kef;* from 8259; a *loophole* (for *looking out*), to admit light and air:—window.

8261. שָׁקֻף **shâqûph**, *shaw-koof';* pass. part. of 8259; an *embrasure* or opening [comp. 8260] with bevelled jam:—light, window.

8262. שָׁקַץ **shâqats**, *shaw-kats';* a prim. root; to *be filthy,* i.e. (intens.) to *loathe, pollute:*—abhor, make abominable, have in abomination, detest, × utterly.

8263. שֶׁקֶץ **sheqets**, *sheh'-kets;* from 8262; *filth,* i.e. (fig. and spec.) an *idolatrous object:*—abominable (-tion).

שִׁקֻּץ **shiqqûts**. See 8251.

8264. שָׁקַק **shâqaq**, *shaw-kak';* a prim. root; to *course* (like a beast of prey); by impl. to *seek greedily:*—have appetite, justle one against another, long, range, run (to and fro).

8265. שָׂקַר **sâqar**, *saw-kar';* a prim. root; to *ogle,* i.e. *blink* coquettishly:—wanton.

8266. שָׁקַר **shâqar**, *shaw-kar';* a prim. root; to *cheat,* i.e. *be untrue* (usually in words):—fail, deal falsely, lie.

8267. שֶׁקֶר **sheqer**, *sheh'-ker;* from 8266; an *untruth;* by impl. a *sham* (often adv.):—without a cause, deceit (-ful), false (-hood, -ly), feignedly, liar, + lie, lying, vain (thing), wrongfully.

8268. שֹׁקֶת **shôqeth**, *sho'-keth;* from 8248; a *trough* (for *watering*):—trough.

8269. שַׂר **sar**, *sar;* from 8323; a *head* person (of any rank or class):—captain (that had rule), chief (captain), general, governor, keeper, lord, ([-task-]) master, prince (-ipal), ruler, steward.

8270. שֹׁר **shôr**, *shore;* from 8324; a *string* (as *twisted* [comp. 8306]), i.e. (spec.) the umbilical cord (also fig. as the centre of strength):—navel.

8271. שְׁרֵא **sherêʼ** (Chald.), *sher-ay';* a root corresp. to that of 8293; to *free, separate;* fig. to *unravel, commence;* by impl. (of unloading beasts) to *reside:*—begin dissolve, dwell, loose.

8272. שַׁרְאֶצֶר **Sharʼetser**, *shar-eh'-tser;* of for. der.; *Sharetser,* the name of an Ass. and an Isr.:—Sharezer.

8273. שָׁרָב **shârâb**, *shaw-rawb';* from an unused root mean. to *glare;* quivering *glow* (of the air), espec. the *mirage:*—heat, parched ground.

8274. שֵׁרֵבְיָה **Shêrêbyâh**, *shay-rayb-yaw';* from 8273 and 3050; *Jah has brought heat; Sherebjah,* the name of two Isr.:—Sherebiah.

8275. שַׁרְבִיט **sharbîyṭ**, *shar-beet';* for 7626; a *rod* of empire:—sceptre.

8276. שָׂרַג **sârag**, *saw-rag';* a prim. root; to *intwine:*—wrap together, wreath.

8277. שָׂרַד **sârad**, *saw-rad';* a prim. root; prop. to *puncture* [comp. 8279], i.e. (fig. through the idea of *slipping* out) to *escape* or survive:—remain.

8278. שְׂרָד **serâd**, *ser-awd';* from 8277; *stitching* (as *pierced* with a needle):—service.

8279. שֶׂרֶד **sered**, *seh'-red;* from 8277; a (carpenter's) *scribing-awl* (for *pricking* or scratching measurements):—line.

8280. שָׂרָה **sârâh**, *saw-raw';* a prim. root; to *prevail:*—have power (as a prince).

8281. שָׁרָה **shârâh**, *shaw-raw';* a prim. root; to *free:*—direct.

8282. שָׂרָה **sârâh**, *saw-raw';* fem. of 8269; a *mistress,* i.e. female noble:—lady, princess, queen.

8283. שָׂרָה **Sârâh**, *saw-raw';* the same as 8282; *Sarah,* Abraham's wife:—Sarah.

8284. שָׁרָה **shârâh**, *shaw-raw';* prob. fem. of 7791; a *fortification* (lit. or fig.):—sing [*by mistake for* 7891], wall.

8285. שֵׁרָה **shêrâh**, *shay-raw';* from 8324 in its orig. sense of *pressing;* a wrist-*band* (as *compact* or *clasping*):—bracelet.

8286. שְׂרוּג **Serûwg**, *ser-oog';* from 8276; *tendril; Serug,* a postdiluvian patriarch:—Serug.

8287. שָׁרוּחֶן **Shârûwchen**, *shaw-roo-khen';* prob. from 8281 (in the sense of *dwelling* [comp. 8271]) and 2580; *abode of pleasure; Sharuchen,* a plac in Pal.:—Sharuhen.

8288. שְׂרוֹךְ **serôwk**, *ser-oke';* from 8308; a *thong* (as *laced* or *tied*):—([shoe-]) latchet.

8289. שָׁרוֹן **Shârôwn**, *shaw-rone';* prob. abridged from 3474; *plain; Sharon,* the name of a place in Pal.:—Lasharon, Sharon.

8290. שָׁרוֹנִי **Shârôwnîy**, *shaw-ro-nee';* patrial from 8289; a *Sharonite* or inhab. of Sharon:—Sharonite.

8291. שַׂרוּק **sarûwq**, *sar-ook';* pass. part. from the same as 8321; a *grapevine:*—principal plant. See 8320, 8321.

8292. שְׁרוּקָה° **sherûwqâh**, *sher-oo-kaw';* or (by perm.)

שְׁרִיקָה **sheriyqâh**, *sher-ee-kaw';* fem. pass. part. of 8319; a *whistling* (in scorn); by anal. a *piping:*—bleating, hissing.

8293. שֵׁרוּת° **shêrûwth**, *shay-rooth';* from 8281 abbrev.; *freedom:*—remnant.

8294. שֶׂרַח **Serach**, *seh'-rakh;* by perm. for 5629; *superfluity; Serach,* an Israelitess:—Sarah, Serah.

8295. שָׂרַט **sâraṭ**, *saw-rat';* a prim. root; to *gash:*—cut in pieces, make [cuttings] pieces.

8296. שֶׂרֶט **sereṭ**, *seh'-ret;* and

שָׂרֶטֶת **sâreṭeth**, *saw-reh'-teth;* from 8295; an *incision:*—cutting.

8297. שָׂרַי **Sâray**, *saw-rah'ee;* from 8269; *dominative; Sarai,* the wife of Abraham:—Sarai.

8298. שָׁרַי **Shâray**, *shaw-rah'ee;* prob. from 8324; *hostile; Sharay,* an Isr.:—Sharai.

8299. שָׂרִיג **sârîyg**, *saw-reeg';* from 8276; a *tendril* (as *intwining*):—branch.

8300. שָׂרִיד **sârîyd**, *saw-reed';* from 8277; a *survivor:*— × alive, left, remain (-ing), remnant, rest.

8301. שָׂרִיד **Sârîyd**, *saw-reed';* the same as 8300; *Sarid,* a place in Pal.:—Sarid.

8302. שִׁרְיוֹן **shiryôwn**, *shir-yone';* or

שִׁרְיֹן **shiryôn**, *shir-yone';* and

שִׁרְיָן **shiryân**, *shir-yawn';* also (fem.)

שִׁרְיָה **shiryâh**, *shir-yaw';* and

שִׁרְיֹנָה **shiryônâh**, *shir-yo-naw';* from 8281 in the orig. sense of *turning;* a *corslet* (as if *twisted*):—breastplate, coat of mail, habergeon, harness. See 5030.

8303. שִׁרְיוֹן **Shiryôwn**, *shir-yone';* and

שִׂרְיֹן **Siryôn**, *sir-yone';* the same as 8302 (i.e. *sheeted* with snow); *Shirjon* or *Sirjon,* a peak of the Lebanon:—Sirion.

8304. שְׂרָיָה **Serâyâh**, *ser-aw-yaw';* or

שְׂרָיָהוּ **Serâyâhûw**, *ser-aw-yaw'-hoo;* from 8280 and 3050; *Jah has prevailed; Serajah,* the name of nine Isr.:—Seraiah.

8305. שְׂרִיקָה **serîyqâh**, *ser-ee-kaw';* from the same as 8321 in the orig. sense of *piercing; hetchelling* (or combing flax), i.e. (concr.) *tow* (by extens. *linen* cloth):—fine.

8306. שָׁרִיר **shârîyr**, *shaw-reer';* from 8324 in the orig. sense as in 8270 (comp. 8326); a *cord,* i.e. (by anal.) *sinew:*—navel.

8307. שְׁרִירוּת **sherîyrûwth**, *sher-ee-rooth';* from 8324 in the sense of *twisted,* i.e. *firm; obstinacy:*—imagination, lust.

8308. שָׂרַךְ **sârak**, *saw-rak';* a prim. root; to *interlace:*—traverse.

8309. שְׁרֵמָה° **sherêmâh**, *sher-ay-maw';* prob. by orth. error for 7709; a *common:*—field.

8310. שַׂרְסְכִים **Sarçekîym**, *sar-seh-keem';* of for. der.; *Sarsekim,* a Bab. general:—Sarsechim.

8311. שָׂרַע **sâraʻ**, *saw-rah';* a prim. root; to *prolong,* i.e. (reflex.) *be deformed* by excess of members:—stretch out self, (have any) superfluous thing.

8312. שַׂרְעַף **sarʻaph**, *sar-af';* for 5587; *cogitation:*—thought.

8313. שָׂרַף **sâraph**, *saw-raf';* a prim. root; to *be* (caus. *set*) *on fire:*—(cause to, make a) burn ([-ing], up), kindle, × utterly.

8314. שָׂרָף **sârâph**, *saw-rawf';* from 8313; *burning,* i.e. (fig.) *poisonous* (serpent); spec. a *saraph* or symbol. creature (from their copper color):—fiery (serpent), seraph.

8315. שָׂרָף **Sâraph**, *saw-raf';* the same as 8314; *Saraph,* an Isr.:—Saraph.

8316. שְׂרֵפָה **serêphâh**, *ser-ay-faw';* from 8313; *cremation:*—burning.

8317. שָׁרַץ **shârats**, *shaw-rats';* a prim. root; to *wriggle,* i.e. (by impl.) *swarm* or *abound:*—breed (bring forth, increase) abundantly (in abundance), creep, move.

8318. שֶׁרֶץ **sherets**, *sheh'-rets;* from 8317; a *swarm,* i.e. active mass of minute animals:—creep (-ing thing), move (-ing creature).

8319. שָׁרַק **shâraq**, *shaw-rak';* a prim. root; prop. to *be shrill,* i.e. to whistle or *hiss* (as a call or in scorn):—hiss.

8320. שָׂרֻק **sâruq**, *saw-rook';* from 8319; *bright red* (as *piercing* to the sight), i.e. *bay:*—speckled. See 8291.

8321. שֹׂרֵק **sôrêq**, *so-rake';* or

שׂוֹרֵק **sôwrêq**, *so-rake';* and (fem.)

שֹׂרֵקָה **sôrêqâh**, *so-ray-kaw';* from 8319 in the sense of *redness* (comp. 8320); a *vine* stock (prop. one yielding *purple* grapes, the richest variety):—choice (-st, noble) wine. Comp. 8291.

8322. שְׁרֵקָה **sherêqâh**, *sher-ay-kaw';* from 8319; a *derision:*—hissing.

8323. שָׂרַר **sârar**, *saw-rar';* a prim. root; to *have* (trans. *exercise;* reflex. *get*) *dominion:*—× altogether, make self a prince, (bear) rule.

8324. שָׁרַר **shârar**, *shaw-rar';* a prim. root; to *be hostile* (only act. part. an *opponent*):—enemy.

8325. שָׁרָר **Shârâr**, *shaw-rawr';* from 8324; *hostile; Sharar,* an Isr.:—Sharar.

8326. שֹׁרֶר **shôrer**, *sho'-rer;* from 8324 in the sense of *twisting* (comp. 8270); the umbilical *cord,* i.e. (by extens.) a *bodice:*—navel.

8327. שָׁרַשׁ **shârash**, *shaw-rash';* a prim. root; to *root,* i.e. strike into the soil, or (by impl.) to pluck from it:—(take, cause to take) root (out).

8328. שֶׁרֶשׁ **sheresh**, *sheh'-resh;* from 8327; a *root* (lit. or fig.):—bottom, deep, heel, root.

8329. שֶׁרֶשׁ **Sheresh**, *sheh'-resh;* the same as 8328; *Sheresh,* an Isr.:—Sharesh.

8330. שֹׁרֶשׁ **shôresh** (Chald.), *sho'-resh;* corresp. to 8328:—root.

8331. שַׁרְשָׁה **sharshâh**, *shar-shaw';* from 8327; a *chain* (as *rooted,* i.e. *linked*):—chain. Comp. 8333.

8332. שְׁרֹשׁוּ° **sherôshûw** (Chald.), *sher-o-shoo';* from a root corresp. to 8327; *eradication,* i.e. (fig.) *exile:*—banishment.

8333. שַׁרְשְׁרָה **sharsh^e râh**, *shar-sher-aw'*; from 8327 [comp. 8331]; a *chain*; (arch.) prob. a *garland*:—chain.

8334. שָׁרַת **shârath**, *shaw-rath'*; a prim. root; to *attend* as a menial or worshipper; fig. to *contribute* to:—minister (unto), (do) serve (-ant, -ice, -itor), wait on.

8335. שָׁרֵת **shârêth**, *shaw-rayth'*; infin. of 8334; *service* (in the Temple):—minister (-ry).

8336. שֵׁשׁ **shêsh**, *shaysh*; or (for alliteration with 4897)

שְׁשִׁי **sh^e shiy**, *shesh-ee'*; for 7893; *bleached* stuff, i.e. *white* linen or (by anal.) marble:—× blue, fine ([twined]) linen, marble, silk.

8337. שֵׁשׁ **shêsh**, *shaysh*; masc.

שִׁשָּׁה **shishshâh**, *shish-shaw'*; a prim. number; *six* (as an overplus [see 7797] beyond five or the fingers of the hand); as ord. *sixth*:—six ([-teen, -teenth]), sixth.

8338. שָׁשָׁא **shâwshâw**, *shaw-shaw'*; a prim. root; appar. to *annihilate*:—leave but the sixth part [*by confusion with* 8341].

8339. שֵׁשְׁבַּצַּר **Shêshbatstsar**, *shaysh-bats-tsar'*; of for. der.; *Sheshbatstsar*, Zerubbabel's Pers. name:—Sheshbazzar.

8340. שֵׁשְׁבַּצַּר **Shêshbatstsar** (Chald.), *shaysh-bats-tsar'*; corresp. to 8339:—Sheshbazzar.

שָׂשָׂה **shâsâh**. See 8154.

8341. שָׁשָׁה **shâshâh**, *shaw-shaw'*; a denom. from 8337; to *sixth* or divide into sixths:—give the sixth part.

8342. שָׂשׂוֹן **sâsôwn**, *saw-sone'*; or

שָׂשֹׂן **sâsôn**, *saw-sone'*; from 7797; *cheerfulness*; spec. *welcome*:—gladness, joy, mirth, rejoicing.

8343. שָׁשַׁי **Shâshay**, *shaw-shah'ee*; perh. from 8336; *whitish*; *Shashai*, an Isr.:—Shashai.

8344. שֵׁשַׁי **Shêshay**, *shay-shah'ee*; prob. for 8343; *Sheshai*, a Canaanite:—Sheshai.

8345. שִׁשִּׁי **shishshîy**, *shish-shee'*; from 8337; *sixth*, ord. or (fem.) fractional:—sixth (part).

8346. שִׁשִּׁים **shishshîym**, *shish-sheem'*; multiple of 8337; *sixty*:—sixty, three score.

8347. שֵׁשַׁךְ **Shêshak**, *shay-shak'*; of for. der.; *Sheshak*, a symbol. name of Bab.:—Sheshach.

8348. שֵׁשָׁן **Shêshân**, *shay-shawn'*; perh. for 7799; *lily*; *Sheshan*, an Isr.:—Sheshan.

שֹׁשָׁן **Shôshân**. See 7799.

8349. שָׁשַׁק **Shâshaq**, *shaw-shak'*; prob. from the base of 7785; *pedestrian*; *Shashak*, an Isr.:—Shashak.

8350. שָׁשַׁר **shâshar**, *shaw-shar'*; perh. from the base of 8324 in the sense of that of 8320; *red* ochre (from its *piercing* color):—vermillion.

8351. שֵׁת **shêth** (Num. 24 : 17), *shayth*; from 7582; *tumult*:—Sheth.

8352. שֵׁת **Shêth**, *shayth*; from 7896; *put*, i.e. *substituted*; *Sheth*, third son of Adam:—Seth, Sheth.

8353. שֵׁת **shêth** (Chald.), *shayth*; or

שִׁת **shith** (Chald.), *sheeth*; corresp. to 8337:—six (-th).

8354. שָׁתָה **shâthâh**, *shaw-thaw'*; a prim. root; to *imbibe* (lit. or fig.):—× assuredly, banquet, × certainly, drink (-er, -ing), drunk (× -ard), surely. [Prop. intensive of 8248.]

8355. שְׁתָה **sh^e thâh** (Chald.), *sheth-aw'*; corresp. to 8354:—drink.

8356. שָׁתָה **shâthâh**, *shaw-thaw'*; from 7896; a *basis*, i.e. (fig.) political or moral *support*:—foundation, purpose.

8357. שֵׁתָה **shêthâh**, *shay-thaw'*; from 7896; the *seat* (of the person):—buttock.

8358. שְׁתִי **sh^e thîy**, *sheth-ee'*; from 8354; *intoxication*:—drunkenness.

8359. שְׁתִי **sh^e thîy**, *sheth-ee'*; from 7896; a *fixture*, i.e. the *warp* in weaving:—warp.

8360. שְׁתִיָּה **sh^e thîyâh**, *sheth-ee-yaw'*; fem. of 8358; *potation*:—drinking.

שְׁתַּיִם **sh^e ttayim**. See 8147.

8361. שִׁתִּין **shittîyn** (Chald.), *shit-teen'*; corresp. to 8346 [comp. 8353]; *sixty*:—threescore.

8362. שָׁתַל **shâthal**, *shaw-thal'*; a prim. root; to *transplant*:—plant.

8363. שְׁתִל **sh^e thîyl**, *sheth-eel'*; from 8362; a *sprig* (as if *transplanted*), i.e. *sucker*:—plant.

8364. שֻׁתַלְחִי **Shûthalchîy**, *shoo-thal-kee'*; patron. from 7803; a *Shuthalchite* (collect.) or desc. of Shuthelach:—Shuthalhites.

שָׂתַם **sâtham**. See 5640.

8365. שָׁתַם **shâtham**, *shaw-tham'*; a prim. root; to *unveil* (fig.):—be open.

8366. שָׁתַן **shâthan**, *shaw-than'*; a prim. root; (caus.) to *make water*, i.e. *urinate*:—piss.

8367. שָׁתַק **shâthaq**, *shaw-thak'*; a prim. root; to *subside*:—be calm, cease, be quiet.

8368. שָׂתַר **sâthar**, *saw-thar'*; a prim. root; to *break* out (as an eruption):—have in [one's] secret parts.

8369. שֵׁתָר **Shêthâr**, *shay-thawr'*; of for. der.; *Shethar*, a Pers. satrap:—Shethar.

8370. שְׁתַר בּוֹזְנַי **Sh^e thar Bôwz^e nay**, *sheth-ar' bo-zen-ah'ee*; of for. der.; *Shethar-Bozenai*, a Pers. officer:—Shethar-boznai.

8371. שָׁתַת **shâthath**, *shaw-thath'*; a prim. root; to *place*, i.e. *array*; reflex. to *lie*:—be laid, set.

ת

8372. תָּא **tâ'**, *taw*; and (fem.)

תָּאָה **tâ'âh** (Ezek. 40 : 12), *taw-aw'*; from (the base of) 8376; a *room* (as *circumscribed*):—(little) chamber.

8373. תָּאַב **tâ'ab**, *taw-ab'*; a prim. root; to *desire*:—long.

8374. תָּאַב **tâ'ab**, *taw-ab'*; a prim. root [prob. rather ident. with 8373 through the idea of *puffing* disdainfully at; comp. 340]; to *loathe* (mor.):—abhor.

8375. תַּאֲבָה **ta'ăbâh**, *tah-ab-aw'*; from 8374 [comp. 15]; *desire*:—longing.

8376. תָּאָה **tâ'âh**, *taw-aw'*; a prim. root; to *mark* off, i.e. (intens.) *designate*:—point out.

8377. תְּאוֹ **t^e 'ôw**, *teh-o'*; and

תּוֹא **tôw'** (the orig. form), *toh*; from 8376; a species of *antelope* (prob. from the white *stripe* on the cheek):—wild bull (ox).

8378. תַּאֲוָה **ta'ăvâh**, *tah-av-aw'*; from 183 (abbrev.); a *longing*; by impl. a *delight* (subj. *satisfaction*, obj. a *charm*):—dainty, desire, × exceedingly, × greedily, lust (ing), pleasant. See also 6914.

8379. תַּאֲוָה **ta'ăvâh**, *tah-av-aw'*; from 8376; a *limit*, i.e. full extent:—utmost bound.

8380. תָּאוֹם **tâ'ôwm**, *taw-ome'*; or

תָּאֹם **tâ'ôm**, *taw-ome'*; from 8382; a *twin* (in plur. only), lit. or fig.:—twins.

8381. תַּאֲלָה **ta'ălâh**, *tah-al-aw'*; from 422; an *imprecation*:—curse.

8382. תָּאַם **tâ'am**, *taw-am'*; a prim. root; to *be complete*; but used only as denom. from 8380, to *be* (caus. *make*) *twinned*, i.e. (fig.) *duplicate* or (arch.) *jointed*:—coupled (together), bear twins.

תְּאֹם **tâ'ôm**. See 8380.

8383. תְּאֻן **t^e 'ûn**, *teh-oon'*; from 205; *naughtiness*, i.e. *toil*:—lie.

8384. תְּאֵן **t^e 'ên**, *teh-ane'*; or (in the sing., fem.)

תְּאֵנָה **t^e 'ênâh**, *teh-ay-naw'*; perh. of for. der.; the *fig* (tree or fruit):—fig (tree).

8385. תַּאֲנָה **ta'ănâh**, *tah-an-aw'*; or

תֹּאֲנָה **tô'ănâh**, *to-an-aw'*; from 579; an *opportunity* or (subj.) *purpose*:—occasion.

8386. תַּאֲנִיָּה **ta'ănîyâh**, *tah-an-ee-yaw'*; from 578; *lamentation*:—heaviness, mourning.

8387. תַּאֲנַת שִׁלֹה **Ta'ănath Shîlôh**, *tah-an-ath' shee-lo'*; from 8385 and 7887; *approach of Shiloh*; *Taanath-Shiloh*, a place in Pal.:—Taanath-shiloh.

8388. תָּאַר **tâ'ar**, *taw-ar'*; a prim. root; to *delineate*; reflex. to *extend*:—be drawn, mark out, [Rimmon-] methoar [*by union with* 7417].

8389. תֹּאַר **tô'ar**, *to'-ar*; from 8388; *outline*, i.e. *figure* or *appearance*:— + beautiful, × comely, countenance, + fair, × favoured, form, × goodly, × resemble, visage.

8390. תַּאֲרֵעַ **Ta'ărêa'**, *tah-ar-ay'-ah*; perh. from 772; *Taareä*, an Isr.:—Tarea. See 8475.

8391. תְּאַשּׁוּר **t^e 'ashshûwr**, *teh-ash-shoor'*; from 833; a species of *cedar* (from its *erectness*):—box (tree).

8392. תֵּבָה **têbâh**, *tay-baw'*; perh. of for. der.; a *box*:—ark.

8393. תְּבוּאָה **t^e bûw'âh**, *teb-oo-aw'*; from 935; *income*, i.e. *produce* (lit. or fig.):—fruit, gain, increase, revenue.

8394. תָּבוּן **tâbûwn**, *taw-boon'*; and (fem.)

תְּבוּנָה **t^e bûwnâh**, *teb-oo-naw'*; or

תּוֹבֻנָה **tôwbûnâh**, *to-boo-naw'*; from 995; *intelligence*; by impl. an *argument*; by extens. *caprice*:—discretion, reason, skilfulness, understanding, wisdom.

8395. תְּבוּסָה **t^e bûwçâh**, *teb-oo-saw'*; from 947; a *treading down*, i.e. *ruin*:—destruction.

8396. תָּבוֹר **Tâbôwr**, *taw-bore'*; from a root corresp. to 8406; *broken region*; *Tabor*, a mountain in Pal., also a city adjacent:—Tabor.

8397. תֶּבֶל **tebel**, *teh'-bel*; appar. from 1101; *mixture*, i.e. *unnatural* bestiality:—confusion.

8398. תֵּבֵל **têbêl**, *tay-bale'*; from 2986; the *earth* (as *moist* and therefore inhabited); by extens. the *globe*; by impl. its *inhabitants*; spec. a partic. *land*, as Babylonia, Pal.:—habitable part, world.

תֻּבַל **Tûbal**. See 8422.

8399. תַּבְלִית **tablîyth**, *tab-leeth'*; from 1086; *consumption*:—destruction.

8400. תְּבַלֻּל **t^e ballûl**, *teb-al-lool'*; from 1101 in the orig. sense of *flowing*; a *cataract* (in the eye):—blemish.

8401. תֶּבֶן **teben**, *teh'-ben*; prob. from 1129; prop. *material*, i.e. (spec.) refuse *haum* or stalks of grain (as *chopped* in threshing and used for fodder):—chaff, straw, stubble.

8402. תִּבְנִי **Tibnî**, *tib-nee'*; from 8401; *strawy*; *Tibni*, an Isr.:—Tibni.

8403. תַּבְנִית **tabnîyth**, *tab-neeth'*; from 1129; *structure*; by impl. a *model*, *resemblance*:—figure, form, likeness, pattern, similitude.

8404. תַּבְעֵרָה **Tab'êrâh**, *tab-ay-raw'*; from 1197; *burning*; *Taberah*, a place in the Desert:—Taberah.

8405. תֵּבֵץ **Têbêts**, *tay-bates'*; from the same as 948; *whiteness*; *Tebets*, a place in Pal.:—Thebez.

8406. תְּבַר **t^e bar** (Chald.), *teb-ar'*; corresp. to 7665; to *be fragile* (fig.):—broken.

8407. תִּגְלַת פִּלְאֶסֶר **Tiglath Pil'eçer**, *tig-lath' pil-eh'-ser*; or

תִּגְלַת פְּלֶסֶר **Tiglath P^e leçer**, *tig-lath pel-eh -ser*; or

תִּלְּגַת פִּלְנְאֶסֶר **Tilgath Piln^e 'eçer**, *til-gath' pil-neh-eh'-ser*; or

תִּלְּגַת פִּלְנֶסֶר **Tilgath Pilneçer**, *til-gath' pil-neh'-ser*; of for. der.; *Tiglath-Pileser* or *Tilgath-pilneser*, an Assyr. king:—Tiglath-pileser, Tilgath-pilneser.

8408. תַּגְמוּל **tagmûwl**, *tag-mool'*; from 1580; a *bestowment:*—benefit.

8409. תִּגְרָה **tigrâh**, *tig-raw'*; from 1624; *strife*, i.e. *infliction:*—blow.

תֹּגַרְמָה **Tôgarmâh**. See 8425.

8410. תִּדְהָר **tidhâr**, *tid-hawr'*; appar. from 1725; *enduring*; a species of hard-wood or *lasting* tree (perh. *oak*):—pine (tree).

8411. תְּדִירָא **tᵉdîyrâ'** (Chald.), *ted-ee-raw'*; from 1753 in the orig. sense of *enduring; permanence*, i.e. (adv.) *constantly:*—continually.

8412. תַּדְמֹר **Tadmôr**, *tad-more'*; or

תַּמֹּר° **Tammôr** (1 Kings 9 : 18), *tam-more'*; appar. from 8558; *palm-city; Tadmor*, a place near Pal.:—Tadmor.

8413. תִּדְעָל **Tidʿâl**, *tid-awl'*; perh. from 1763; *fearfulness; Tidal*, a Canaanite:—Tidal.

8414. תֹּהוּ **tôhûw**, *to'-hoo*; from an unused root mean. to lie *waste*; a *desolation* (of surface), i.e. *desert*; fig. a *worthless* thing; adv. in *vain:*—confusion, empty place, without form, nothing, (thing of) nought, vain, vanity, waste, wilderness.

8415. תְּהוֹם **tᵉhôwm**, *teh-home'*; or

תְּהֹם **tᵉhôm**, *teh-home'*; (usually fem.) from 1949; an *abyss* (as a *surging* mass of water), espec. the *deep* (the *main* sea or the subterranean *water-supply*):—deep (place), depth.

8416. תְּהִלָּה **tᵉhillâh**, *teh-hil-law'*; from 1984; *laudation*; spec. (concr.) a *hymn:*—praise.

8417. תׇּהֳלָה **tohŏlâh**, *to-hol-aw'*; fem. of an unused noun (appar. from 1984) mean. *bluster; braggadocio*, i.e. (by impl.) *fatuity:*—folly.

8418. תַּהֲלֻכָה **tahălûkâh**, *tah-hal-oo-kaw'*; from 1980; a *procession:*— × went.

תְּהֹם **tᵉhôm**. See 8415.

8419. תַּהְפֻּכָה **tahpûkâh**, *tah-poo-kaw'*; from 2015; a *perversity* or *fraud:*—(very) froward (-ness, thing), perverse thing.

8420. תָּו **tâv**, *tawv*; from 8427; a *mark*; by impl. a *signature:*—desire, mark.

8421. תּוּב **tûwb** (Chald.), *toob*; corresp. to 7725; to *come back*; spec. (trans. and ellip.) to *reply:*—answer, restore, return (an answer).

8422. תּוּבַל **Tûwbal**, *too-bal'*; or

תֻּבַל **Tûbal**, *too-bal'*; prob. of for. der.; *Tubal*, a postdiluvian patriarch and his posterity:—Tubal.

8423. תּוּבַל קַיִן **Tûwbal Qayin**, *too-bal' kah'-yin*; appar. from 2986 (comp. 2981) and 7014; *offspring of Cain; Tubal-Kajin*, an antediluvian patriarch:—Tubal-cain.

תּוֹבֻנָה° **tôwbûnâh**. See 8394.

8424. תּוּגָה **tûwgâh**, *too-gaw'*; from 3013; *depression* (of spirits); concr. a *grief:*—heaviness, sorrow.

8425. תּוֹגַרְמָה **Tôwgarmâh**, *to-gar-maw'*; or

תֹּגַרְמָה **Tôgarmâh**, *to-gar-maw'*; prob. of for. der.; *Togarmah*, a son of Gomer and his posterity:—Togarmah.

8426. תּוֹדָה **tôwdâh**, *to-daw'*; from 3034; prop. an *extension* of the hand, i.e. (by impl.) *avowal*, or (usually) *adoration*; spec. a *choir* of worshippers:—confession, (sacrifice of) praise, thanks (-giving, offering).

8427. תָּוָה **tâvâh**, *taw-vaw'*; a prim. root; to *mark* out, i.e. (prim.) *scratch* or (def.) *imprint:*—scrabble, set [a mark].

8428. תָּוָה **tâvâh**, *taw-vaw'*; a prim. root [or perh. ident. with 8427 through a similar idea from *scraping* to pieces]; to *grieve:*—limit [*by confusion with* 8427].

8429. תְּוַהּ **tᵉvahh** (Chald.), *tev-ah'*; corresp. to 8539 or perh. to 7582 through the idea of *sweeping* to ruin [comp. 8428]; to *amaze*, i.e. (reflex. by impl.) *take alarm:*—be astonied.

8430. תּוֹחַ **Tôwach**, *to'-akh*; from an unused root mean. to *depress; humble; Toäch*, an Isr.:—Toah.

8431. תּוֹחֶלֶת **tôwcheleth**, *to-kheh'-leth*; from 3176; *expectation:*—hope.

תּוֹךְ **tôwk**. See 8496.

8432. תָּוֶךְ **tâvek**, *taw'-vek*; from an unused root mean. to *sever*; a *bisection*, i.e. (by impl.) the *centre:*—among (-st), × between, half, × (there-, where-) in (-to), middle, mid [-night], midst (among), × out (of), × through, × with (-in).

8433. תּוֹכֵחָה **tôwkêchâh**, *to-kay-khaw'*; and

תּוֹכַחַת **tôwkachath**, *to-kakh'-ath*; from 3198; *chastisement*; fig. (by words) *correction, refutation, proof* (even in defence):—argument, × chastened, correction, reasoning, rebuke, reproof, × be (often) reproved.

תּוּכִּי **tûwkkîy**. See 8500.

8434. תּוֹלָד **Tôwlâd**, *to-lawd'*; from 3205; *posterity; Tolad*, a place in Pal.:—Tolad. Comp. 513.

8435. תּוֹלְדָה **tôwlᵉdâh**, *to-led-aw'*; or

תֹּלְדָה **tôlᵉdâh**, *to-led-aw'*; from 3205; (plur. only) *descent*, i.e. *family*; (fig.) *history:*—birth, generations.

8436. תּוּלוֹן° **Tûwlôn**, *too-lone'*; from 8524; *suspension; Tulon*, an Isr.:—Tilon [*from the marg.*].

8437. תּוֹלָל **tôwlâl**, *to-lawl'*; from 3213; *causing to howl*, i.e. an *oppressor:*—that wasted.

8438. תּוֹלָע **tôwlâʿ**, *to-law'*; and (fem.)

תּוֹלֵעָה **tôwlêʿâh**, *to-lay-aw'*; or

תּוֹלַעַת **tôwlaʿath**, *to-lah'-ath*; or

תֹּלַעַת **tôlaʿath**, *to-lah'-ath*; from 3216; a *maggot* (as *voracious*); spec. (often with ellips. of 8144) the crimson-*grub*, but used only (in this connection) of the color from it, and cloths dyed therewith:—crimson, scarlet, worm.

8439. תּוֹלָע **Tôwlâʿ**, *to-law'*; the same as 8438; *worm; Tola*, the name of two Isr.:—Tola.

8440. תּוֹלָעִי **Tôwlâʿîy**, *to-law-ee'*; patron. from 8439; a *Tolaïte* (collect.) or desc. of Tola:—Tolaites.

8441. תּוֹעֵבָה **tôwʿêbâh**, *to-ay-baw'*; or

תֹּעֵבָה **tôʿêbâh**, *to-ay-baw'*; fem. act. part. of 8581; prop. something *disgusting* (mor.), i.e. (as noun) an *abhorrence*; espec. *idolatry* or (concr.) an *idol:*—abominable (custom, thing), abomination.

8442. תּוֹעָה **tôwʿâh**, *to-aw'*; fem. act. part. of 8582; *mistake*, i.e. (mor.) *impiety*, or (political) *injury:*—error, hinder.

8443. תּוֹעָפָה **tôwʿâphâh**, *to-aw-faw'*; from 3286; (only in plur. collect.) *weariness*, i.e. (by impl.) *toil* (*treasure* so obtained) or *speed:*—plenty, strength.

8444. תּוֹצָאָה **tôwtsâʾâh**, *to-tsaw-aw'*; or

תֹּצָאָה **tôtsâʾâh**, *to-tsaw-aw'*; from 3318; (only in plur. collect.) *exit*, i.e. (geographical) *boundary*, or (fig.) *deliverance*, (act.) *source:*—border (-s), going (-s) forth (out), issues, outgoings.

8445. תּוֹקַהַת° **Tôwqahath**, *to-kah'-ath*; from the same as 3349; *obedience; Tokahath*, an Isr.:—Tikvath [*by correction for* 8616].

8446. תּוּר **tûwr**, *toor*; a prim. root; to *meander* (caus. *guide*) about, espec. for trade or reconnoitring:—chap [-man], sent to descry, be excellent, merchant [-man], search (out), seek, (e-) spy (out).

8447. תּוֹר **tôwr**, *tore*; or

תֹּר **tôr**, *tore*; from 8446; a *succession*, i.e. a *string* or (abstr.) *order:*—border, row, turn.

8448. תּוֹר **tôwr**, *tore*; prob. the same as 8447; a *manner* (as a sort of *turn*):—estate.

8449. תּוֹר **tôwr**, *tore*; or

תֹּר **tôr**, *tore*; prob. the same as 8447; a *ring-dove*, often (fig.) as a term of endearment:—(turtle) dove.

8450. תּוֹר **tôwr** (Chald.), *tore*; corresp. (by perm.) to 7794; a *bull:*—bullock, ox.

8451. תּוֹרָה **tôwrâh**, *to-raw'*; or

תֹּרָה **tôrâh**, *to-raw'*; from 3384; a *precept* or *statute*, espec. the *Decalogue* or *Pentateuch:*—law.

8452. תּוֹרָה **tôwrâh**, *to-raw'*; prob. fem. of 8448; a *custom:*—manner.

8453. תּוֹשָׁב **tôwshâb**, *to-shawb'*; or

תֹּשָׁב **tôshâb** (1 Kings 17 : 1), *to-shawb'*; from 3427; a *dweller* (but not outlandish [5237]); espec. (as distinguished from a native citizen [act. part. of 3427] and a temporary inmate [1616] or mere lodger [3885]) resident *alien:*—foreigner, inhabitant, sojourner, stranger.

8454. תּוּשִׁיָּה **tûwshîyâh**, *too-shee-yaw'*; or

תֻּשִׁיָּה **tûshîyâh**, *too-shee-yaw'*; from an unused root prob. mean. to *substantiate; support* or (by impl.) *ability*, i.e. (direct) *help*, (in purpose) an *undertaking*, (intellectual) *understanding:*—enterprise, that which (thing as it) is, substance, (sound) wisdom, working.

8455. תּוֹתָח **tôwthâch**, *to-thawkh'*; from an unused root mean. to *smite*; a *club:*—darts.

8456. תָּזַז **tâzaz**, *taw-zaz'*; a prim. root; to *lop* off:—cut down.

8457. תַּזְנוּת **taznûwth**, *taz-nooth'*; or

תַּזְנֻת **taznûth**, *taz-nooth'*; from 2181; *harlotry*, i.e. (fig.) *idolatry:*—fornication, whoredom.

8458. תַּחְבֻּלָה **tachbûlâh**, *takh-boo-law'*; or

תַּחְבּוּלָה **tachbûwlâh**, *takh-boo-law'*; from 2254 as denom. from 2256; (only in plur.) prop. *steerage* (as a management of *ropes*), i.e. (fig.) *guidance* or (by impl.) a *plan:*—good advice, (wise) counsels.

8459. תֹּחוּ **Tôchûw**, *to'-khoo*; from an unused root mean. to *depress; abasement, Tochu*, an Isr.:—Tohu.

8460. תְּחוֹת **tᵉchôwth** (Chald.), *tekh-ōth'*; or

תְּחֹת **tᵉchôth** (Chald.), *tekh-ōth'*; corresp. to 8478; *beneath:*—under.

8461. תַּחְכְּמֹנִי **Tachkᵉmônîy**, *takh-kem-o-nee'*; prob. for 2453; *sagacious; Tachkemoni*, an Isr.:—Tachmonite.

8462. תְּחִלָּה **tᵉchillâh**, *tekh-il-law'*; from 2490 in the sense of *opening*; a *commencement*; rel. *original* (adv. *-ly*):—begin (-ning), first (time).

8463. תַּחֲלוּא **tachălûwʾ**, *takh-al-oo'*; or

תַּחֲלֻא **tachălûʾ**, *takh-al-oo'*; from 2456; a *malady:*—disease, × grievous, (that are) sick (-ness).

8464. תַּחְמָס **tachmâç**, *takh-mawce'*; from 2554; a species of unclean bird (from its *violence*), perh. an *owl:*—night hawk.

8465. תַּחַן **Tachan**, *takh'-an*; prob. from 2583; *station; Tachan*, the name of two Isr.:—Tahan.

8466. תַּחֲנָה **tachănâh**, *takh-an-aw'*; from 2583; (only plur. coll.) an *encampment:*—camp.

8467. תְּחִנָּה **tᵉchinnâh**, *tekh-in-naw'*; from 2603; *graciousness*; caus. *entreaty:*—favour, grace, supplication.

8468. תְּחִנָּה **Tᵉchinnâh**, *tekh-in-naw'*; the same as 8467; *Techinnah*, an Isr.:—Tehinnah.

8469. תַּחֲנוּן **tachănûwn**, *takh-an-oon'*; or (fem.)

תַּחֲנוּנָה **tachănûwnâh**, *takh-an-oo-naw'*; from 2603; earnest *prayer:*—intreaty, supplication.

8470. תַּחֲנִי **Tachănîy**, *takh-an-ee'*; patron. from 8465; a *Tachanite* (collect.) or desc. of Tachan:—Tahanites.

8471. תַּחְפַּנְחֵס **Tachpanchêç**, *takh-pan-khace'*; or
תְּחַפְנְחֵס **T**e**chaphn**e**chêç** (Ezek. 30 : 18), *tekh-af-nekh-ace'*; or
תַּחְפְּנֵס° **Tachp**e**nêç** (Jer. 2 : 16), *takh-pen-ace'*; of Eg. der.; *Tachpanches, Techaphneches* or *Tachpenes*, a place in Egypt:—Tahapanes, Tahpanhes, Tehaphnehes.

8472. תַּחְפְּנֵיס **Tachp**e**nêyç**, *takh-pen-ace'*; of Eg. der.; *Tachpenes*, an Eg. woman:—Tahpenes.

8473. תַּחֲרָא **tachărâ'**, *takh-ar-aw'*; from 2734 in the orig. sense of 2352 or 2353; a linen *corslet* (as *white* or *hollow*):—habergeon.

8474. תַּחָרָה **tachârâh**, *takh-aw-raw'*; a factitious root from 2734 through the idea of the *heat* of jealousy; to *vie* with a rival:—close, contend.

8475. תַּחְרֵעַ **Tachrêa'**, *takh-ray'-ah*; for 8390; *Tachreä*, an Isr.:—Tahrea.

8476. תַּחַשׁ **tachash**, *takh'-ash*; prob. of for. der.; a (clean) animal with fur, prob. a species of *antelope*:—badger.

8477. תַּחַשׁ **Tachash**, *takh'-ash*; the same as 8476; *Tachash*, a relative of Abraham:—Thahash.

8478. תַּחַת **tachath**, *takh'-ath*; from the same as 8430; the *bottom* (as *depressed*); only adv. *below* (often with prep. pref. *underneath*), in *lieu of*, etc.:—as, beneath, × flat, in (-stead), (same) place (where . . . is), room, for . . . sake, stead of, under, × unto, × when . . . was mine, whereas, [where-] fore, with.

8479. תַּחַת **tachath** (Chald.), *takh'-ath*; corresp. to 8478:—under.

8480. תַּחַת **Tachath**, *takh'-ath*; the same as 8478; *Tachath*, the name of a place in the Desert, also of three Isr.:—Tahath.
תְּחֹת **t**e**chôth**. See 8460.

8481. תַּחְתּוֹן **tachtôwn**, *takh-tone'*; or
תַּחְתֹּן **tachtôn**, *takh-tone'*; from 8478; *bottommost*:—lower (-est), nether (-most).

8482. תַּחְתִּי **tachtîy**, *takh-tee'*; from 8478; *lowermost*; as noun (fem. plur.) the *depths* (fig. a *pit*, the *womb*):—low (parts, -er, -er parts, -est), nether (part).

8483. תַּחְתִּים חָדְשִׁי **Tachtîym Chodshîy**, *takh-teem' khod-shee'*; appar. from the plur. masc. of 8482 or 8478 and 2320; *lower* (ones) *monthly*; *Tachtim-Chodshi*, a place in Pal.:—Tahtim-hodshi.

8484. תִּיכוֹן **tîykôwn**, *tee-kone'*; or
תִּיכֹן **tîykôn**, *tee-kone'*; from 8432; *central*:—middle (-most), midst.

8485. תֵּימָא **Têymâ'**, *tay-maw'*; or
תֵּמָא **Têmâ'**, *tay-maw'*; prob. of for. der.; *Tema*, a son of Ishmael, and the region settled by him:—Tema.

8486. תֵּימָן **têymân**, *tay-mawn'*; or
תֵּמָן **têmân**, *tay-mawn'*; denom. from 3225; the *south* (as being on the *right* hand of a person facing the east):—south (side, -ward, wind).

8487. תֵּימָן **Têymân**, *tay-mawn'*; or
תֵּמָן **Têmân**, *tay-mawn'*; the same as 8486; *Teman*, the name of two Edomites, and of the region and desc. of one of them:—south, Teman.

8488. תֵּימְנִי **Têym**e**nîy**, *tay-men-ee'*; prob. for 8489; *Temeni*, an Isr.:—Temeni.

8489. תֵּימָנִי **Têymânîy**, *tay-maw-nee'*; patron. from 8487; a *Temanite* or desc. of Teman:—Temani, Temanite.

8490. תִּימָרָה **tîymârâh**, *tee-maw-raw'*; or
תִּמָרָה **tîmârâh**, *tee-maw-raw'*; from the same as 8558; a *column*, i.e. cloud:—pillar.

8491. תִּיצִי **Tîytsîy**, *tee-tsee'*; patrial or patron. from an unused noun of uncert. mean.; a *Titsite* or desc. or inhab. of an unknown Tits:—Tizite.

8492. תִּירוֹשׁ **tîyrôwsh**, *tee-roshe'*; or
תִּירֹשׁ **tîyrôsh**, *tee-roshe'*; from 3423 in the sense of *expulsion*; *must* or fresh grape-juice (as just *squeezed* out); by impl. (rarely) fermented *wine*:—(new, sweet) wine.

8493. תִּירְיָא **Tîyr**e**yâ'**, *tee-reh-yaw'*; prob. from 3372; *fearful*; *Tirja*, an Isr.:—Tiria.

8494. תִּירָס **Tîyrâç**, *tee-rawce'*; prob. of for. der.; *Tiras*, a son of Japheth:—Tiras.
תִּירשׁ **tîyrôsh**. See 8492.

8495. תַּיִשׁ **tayish**, *tah'-yeesh*; from an unused root mean. to *butt*; a *buck* or he-goat (as given to *butting*):—he goat.

8496. תֹּךְ **tôk**, *toke*; or
תּוֹךְ **tôwk** (Psa. 72 : 14), *toke*; from the same base as 8432 (in the sense of *cutting* to pieces); *oppression*:—deceit, fraud.

8497. תָּכָה **tâkâh**, *taw-kaw'*; a prim. root; to *strew*, i.e. *encamp*:—sit down.

8498. תְּכוּנָה **t**e**kûwnâh**, *tek-oo-naw'*; fem. pass. part. of 8505; *adjustment*, i.e. *structure*; by impl. *equipage*:—fashion, store.

8499. תְּכוּנָה **t**e**kûwnâh**, *tek-oo-naw'*; from 3559; or prob. ident. with 8498; something *arranged* or *fixed*, i.e. a *place*:—seat.

8500. תֻּכִּי **tukkîy**, *took-kee'*; or
תּוּכִּי **tûwkkîy**, *took-kee'*; prob. of for. der.; some imported creature, prob. a *peacock*:—peacock.

8501. תָּכָךְ **tâkâk**, *taw-kawk'*; from an unused root mean. to *dissever*, i.e. *crush*:—deceitful.

8502. תִּכְלָה **tiklâh**, *tik-law'*; from 3615; *completeness*:—perfection.

8503. תַּכְלִית **takliyth**, *tak-leeth'*; from 3615; *completion*; by impl. an *extremity*:—end, perfect (-ion).

8504. תְּכֵלֶת **t**e**kêleth**, *tek-ay'-leth*; prob. for 7827; the cerulean *mussel*, i.e. the color (*violet*) obtained therefrom or stuff dyed therewith:—blue.

8505. תָּכַן **tâkan**, *taw-kan'*; a prim. root; to *balance*, i.e. *measure* out (by weight or dimension); fig. to *arrange*, *equalize*, through the idea of *levelling* (ment. *estimate*, *test*):—bear up, direct, be ([un-]) equal, mete, ponder, tell, weigh.

8506. תֹּכֶן **tôken**, *to'-ken*; from 8505; a fixed *quantity*:—measure, tale.

8507. תֹּכֶן **Tôken**, *to'-ken*; the same as 8506; *Token*, a place in Pal.:—Tochen.

8508. תָּכְנִית **toknîyth**, *tok-neeth'*; from 8506; *admeasurement*, i.e. *consummation*:—pattern, sum.

8509. תַּכְרִיךְ **takrîyk**, *tak-reek'*; appar. from an unused root mean. to *encompass*; a *wrapper* or robe:—garment.

8510. תֵּל **têl**, *tale*; by contr. from 8524; a *mound*:—heap, × strength.

8511. תָּלָא **tâlâ'**, *taw-law'*; a prim. root; to *suspend*; fig. (through *hesitation*) to *be uncertain*; by impl. (of ment. *dependence*) to *habituate*:—be bent, hang (in doubt).

8512. תֵּל אָבִיב **Têl 'Âbîyb**, *tale aw-beeb'*; from 8510 and 24; *mound of green growth*; *Tel-Abib*, a place in Chaldæa:—Tel-abib.

8513. תְּלָאָה **t**e**lâ'âh**, *tel-aw-aw'*; from 3811; *distress*:—travail, travel, trouble.

8514. תַּלְאוּבָה **tal'ûwbâh**, *tal-oo-baw'*; from 3851; *desiccation*:—great drought.

8515. תְּלַאשַּׂר **T**e**la'ssar**, *tel-as-sar'*; or
תְּלַשַּׂר **T**e**lassar**, *tel-as-sar'*; of for. der.; *Telassar*, a region of Assyria:—Telassar.

8516. תַּלְבֹּשֶׁת **talbôsheth**, *tal-bo'-sheth*; from 3847; a *garment*:—clothing.

8517. תְּלַג **t**e**lag** (Chald.), *tel-ag'*; corresp. to 7950; *snow*:—snow.
תִּלְגַת **Tilgath**. See 8407.
תֹּלְדָה **tôl**e**dâh**. See 8435.

8518. תָּלָה **tâlâh**, *taw-law'*; a prim. root; to *suspend* (espec. to *gibbet*):—hang (up).

8519. תְּלוּנָּה **t**e**lûwnâh**, *tel-oo-naw'*; or
תְּלֻנָּה **t**e**lunnâh**, *tel-oon-naw'*; from 3885 in the sense of *obstinacy*; a *grumbling*:—murmuring.

8520. תֶּלַח **Telach**, *teh'-lakh*; prob. from an unused root mean. to *dissever*; *breach*; *Telach*, an Isr.:—Telah.

8521. תֵּל חַרְשָׁא **Têl Charshâ'**, *tale kharshaw'*; from 8510 and the fem. of 2798; *mound of workmanship*; *Tel-Charsha*, a place in Bab.:—Tel-haresha, Tel-harsa.

8522. תְּלִי **t**e**lîy**, *tel-ee'*; prob. from 8518; a *quiver* (as *slung*):—quiver.

8523. תְּלִיתַי **t**e**lîythay** (Chald.), *tel-ee-thah'ee*; or
תַּלְתִּי **taltîy** (Chald.), *tal-tee'*; ordinal from 8532; *third*:—third.

8524. תָּלַל **tâlal**, *taw-lal'*; a prim. root; to *pile* up, i.e. *elevate*:—eminent. Comp. 2048.

8525. תֶּלֶם **telem**, *teh'-lem*; from an unused root mean. to *accumulate*; a *bank* or *terrace*:—furrow, ridge.

8526. תַּלְמַי **Talmay**, *tal-mah'ee*; from 8525; *ridged*; *Talmai*, the name of a Canaanite and a Syrian:—Talmai.

8527. תַּלְמִיד **talmîyd**, *tal-meed'*; from 3925; a *pupil*:—scholar.

8528. תֵּל מֶלַח **Têl Melach**, *tale meh'-lakh*; from 8510 and 4417; *mound of salt*; *Tel-Melach*, a place in Bab.:—Tel-melah.
תְּלֻנָּה **t**e**lunnâh**. See 8519.

8529. תָּלַע **tâla'**, *taw-law'*; a denom. from 8438; to *crimson*, i.e. dye that color:—× scarlet.
תֹּלַעַת **tôla'ath**. See 8438.

8530. תַּלְפִּיָּה **talpîyâh**, *tal-pee-yaw'*; fem. from an unused root mean. to *tower*; something *tall*, i.e. (plur. collect.) *slenderness*:—armoury.
תְּלַשַּׂר **T**e**lassar**. See 8515.

8531. תְּלַת **t**e**lath** (Chald.), *tel-ath'*; from 8532; a *tertiary* rank:—third.

8532. תְּלָת **t**e**lâth** (Chald.), *tel-awth'*; masc.
תְּלָתָה **t**e**lâthâh** (Chald.), *tel-aw-thaw'*; or
תְּלָתָא **t**e**lâthâ'** (Chald.), *tel-aw-thaw'*; corresp. to 7969; *three* or *third*:—third, three.
תַּלְתִּי **tally**. See 8523.

8533. תְּלָתִין **t**e**lâthîyn** (Chald.), *tel-aw-theen'*; mult. of 8532; *ten times three*:—thirty.

8534. תַּלְתַּל **taltal**, *tal-tal'*; by redupl. from 8524 through the idea of *vibration*; a *trailing bough* (as *pendulous*):—bushy.

8535. תָּם **tâm**, *tawm*; from 8552; *complete*; usually (mor.) *pious*; spec. *gentle*, *dear*:—coupled together, perfect, plain, undefiled, upright.

8536. תַּם **tâm** (Chald.), *tawm*; corresp. to 8033; *there*:—× thence, there, × where.

8537. תֹּם **tôm**, *tome*; from 8552; *completeness*; fig. *prosperity*; usually (mor.) *innocence*:—full, integrity, perfect (-ion), simplicity, upright (-ly, -ness), at a venture. See 8550.
תֻּמָּא **Têmâ'**. See 8485.

8538. תֻּמָּה **tummâh**, *toom-maw'*; fem. of 8537; *innocence*:—integrity.

8539. תָּמַהּ **tâmahh**, *taw-mah'*; a prim. root; to *be in consternation*:—be amazed, be astonished, marvel (-lously), wonder.

8540. תְּמַהּ **t**e**mahh** (Chald.), *tem-ah'*; from a root corresp. to 8539; a *miracle*:—wonder.

8541. תִּמָּהוֹן **timmâhôwn**, *tim-maw-hone'*; from 8539; *consternation*:—astonishment.

8542. תַּמּוּז **Tammûwz**, *tam-mooz'*; of uncert. der.; *Tammuz*, a Phœnician deity:—Tammuz.

8543. תְּמוֹל **tᵉmôwl**, *tem-ole'*; or

תְּמֹל **tᵉmôl**, *tem-ole'*; prob. for 865; prop. *ago*, i.e. a (short or long) *time since*; espec. *yesterday*, or (with 8032) *day before yesterday*:— + before (-time), + these [three] days, + heretofore, + time past, yesterday.

8544. תְּמוּנָה **tᵉmûwnâh**, *tem-oo-naw'*; or

תְּמֻנָה **tᵉmûnâh**, *tem-oo-naw'*; from 4327; *something portioned* (i.e. *fashioned*) out, as a *shape*, i.e. (indef.) *phantom*, or (spec.) *embodiment*, or (fig.) *manifestation* (of favor):—image, likeness, similitude.

8545. תְּמוּרָה **tᵉmûwrâh**, *tem-oo-raw'*; from 4171; *barter, compensation*:— (ex-) change (-ing), recompense, restitution.

8546. תְּמוּתָה **tᵉmûwthâh**, *tem-oo-thaw'*; from 4191; *execution* (as a doom):—death, die.

8547. תֶּמַח **Temach**, *teh'-makh*; of uncert. der.; *Temach*, one of the Nethinim:—Tamah, Thamah.

8548. תָּמִיד **tâmîyd**, *taw-meed'*; from an unused root mean. to *stretch*; prop. *continuance* (as indef. *extension*); but used only (attributively as adj.) *constant* (or adv. *constantly*); ellipt. the *regular* (daily) sacrifice:—alway (-s), continual (employment, -ly), daily, ([n-]) ever (-more), perpetual.

8549. תָּמִים **tâmîym**, *taw-meem'*; from 8552; *entire* (lit., fig. or mor.); also (as noun) *integrity, truth*:—without blemish, complete, full, perfect, sincerely (-ity), sound, without spot, undefiled, upright (-ly), whole.

8550. תֻּמִּים **Tummîym**, *toom-meem'*; plur. of 8537; *perfections*, i.e. (techn.) one of the epithets of the objects in the high-priest's breastplate as an emblem of *complete* Truth:—Thummim.

8551. תָּמַךְ **tâmak**, *taw-mak'*; a prim. root; to *sustain*; by impl. to *obtain, keep fast*; fig. to *help, follow close*:—(take, up-) hold (up), maintain, retain, stay (up).

תְּמֹל **tᵉmôl**. See 8543.

8552. תָּמַם **tâmam**, *taw-mam'*; a prim. root; to *complete*, in a good or a bad sense, lit. or fig., trans. or intrans. (as follows):—accomplish, cease, be clean [pass-] ed, consume, have done, (come to an, have an, make an) end, fail, come to the full, be all gone, × be all here, be (make) perfect, be spent, sum, be (shew self) upright, be wasted, whole.

תֵּמָן **têmân, Têmân**. See 8486, 8487.

8553. תִּמְנָה **Timnâh**, *tim-naw'*; from 4487; a *portion* assigned; *Timnah*, the name of two places in Pal.:—Timnah, Timnath, Thimnathah.

תְּמֻנָה **temûnâh**. See 8544.

8554. תִּמְנִי **Timnîy**, *tim-nee'*; patrial from 8553; a *Timnite* or inhab. of Timnah:—Timnite.

8555. תִּמְנָע **Timnâʻ**, *tim-naw'*; from 4513; *restraint*; *Timna*, the name of two Edomites:—Timna, Timnah.

8556. תִּמְנַת חֶרֶס **Timnath Chereç**, *tim-nath kheh'-res*; or

תִּמְנַת סֶרַח **Timnath Çerach**, *tim-nath seh'-rakh*; from 8553 and 2775; *portion of* (the) *sun*; *Timnath-Cheres*, a place in Pal.:—Timnath-heres, Timnath-serah.

8557. תֶּמֶס **temeç**, *teh'-mes*; from 4529; *liquefaction*, i.e. *disappearance*:—melt.

8558. תָּמָר **tâmâr**, *taw-mawr'*; from an unused root mean. to *be erect*; a *palm* tree:—palm (tree).

8559. תָּמָר **Tâmâr**, *taw-mawr'*; the same as 8558; *Tamar*, the name of three women and a place:—Tamar.

8560. תֹּמֶר **tômer**, *to'-mer*; from the same root as 8558; a *palm* trunk:—palm tree.

8561. תִּמֹּר **timmôr** (plur. only), *tim-more'*; or (fem.)

תִּמֹּרָה **timmôrâh** (sing. and plur.), *tim-mo-raw'*; from the same root as 8558; (arch.) a *palm*-like pilaster (i.e. umbellate):—palm tree.

תַּמֹּר **Tammôr**. See 8412.

תִּמָרָה **tîmârâh**. See 8490.

8562. תַּמְרוּק **tamrûwq**, *tam-rook'*; or

תַּמְרֻק **tamrûq**, *tam-rook'*; or

תַּמְרִיק **tamrîyq**, *tam-reek'*; from 4838; prop. a *scouring*, i.e. *soap* or *perfumery* for the bath; fig. a *detergent*:— × cleanse, (thing for) purification (-fying).

8563. תַּמְרוּר **tamrûwr**, *tam-roor'*; from 4843; *bitterness* (plur. as collect.):— × most bitter (-ly).

תַּמְרֻק **tamrûq**, and

תַּמְרִיק **tamrîyq**. See 8562.

8564. תַּמְרוּר **tamrûwr**, *tam-roor'*; from the same root as 8558; an *erection*, i.e. *pillar* (prob. for a guide-board):—high heap.

8565. תַּן **tan**, *tan*; from an unused root prob. mean. to *elongate*; a *monster* (as preternaturally formed), i.e. a *sea-serpent* (or other huge marine animal); also a *jackal* (or other hideous land animal):—dragon, whale. Comp. 8577.

8566. תָּנָה **tânâh**, *taw-naw'*; a prim. root; to *present* (a mercenary inducement), i.e. *bargain* with (a harlot):—hire.

8567. תָּנָה **tânâh**, *taw-naw'*; a prim. root [rather ident. with 8566 through the idea of *attributing* honor]; to *ascribe* (praise), i.e. *celebrate, commemorate*:—lament, rehearse.

8568. תַּנָּה **tannâh**, *tan-naw'*; prob. fem. of 8565; a female *jackal*:—dragon.

8569. תְּנוּאָה **tᵉnûwʼâh**, *ten-oo-aw'*; from 5106; *alienation*; by impl. *enmity*:—breach of promise, occasion.

8570. תְּנוּבָה **tᵉnûwbâh**, *ten-oo-baw'*; from 5107; *produce*:—fruit, increase.

8571. תְּנוּךְ **tᵉnûwk**, *ten-ook'*; perh. from the same as 594 through the idea of *protraction*; a *pinnacle*, i.e. *extremity*:—tip.

8572. תְּנוּמָה **tᵉnûwmâh**, *ten-oo-maw'*; from 5123; *drowsiness*, i.e. *sleep*:—slumber (-ing).

8573. תְּנוּפָה **tᵉnûwphâh**, *ten-oo-faw'*; from 5130; a *brandishing* (in threat); by impl. *tumult*; spec. the official *undulation* of sacrificial offerings:—offering, shaking, wave (offering).

8574. תַּנּוּר **tannûwr**, *tan-noor'*; from 5216; a *fire-pot*:—furnace, oven.

8575. תַּנְחוּם **tanchûwm**, *tan-khoom'*; or

תַּנְחֻם **tanchûm**, *tan-khoom'*; and (fem.)

תַּנְחוּמָה **tanchûwmâh**, *tan-khoo-maw'*; from 5162; *compassion, solace*:—comfort, consolation.

8576. תַּנְחֻמֶת **Tanchûmeth**, *tan-khoo'-meth*; for 8575 (fem.); *Tanchumeth*, an Isr.:—Tanhumeth.

8577. תַּנִּין **tanniyn**, *tan-neen'*; or

תַּנִּים **tannîym** (Ezek. 29 : 3), *tan-neem'*; intens. from the same as 8565; a marine or land *monster*, i.e. *sea-serpent* or *jackal*:—dragon, sea-monster, serpent, whale.

8578. תִּנְיָן **tinyân** (Chald.), *tin-yawn'*; corresp. to 8147; *second*:—second.

8579. תִּנְיָנוּת **tinyânûwth** (Chald.), *tin-yaw-nooth'*; from 8578; a *second time*:—again.

8580. תַּנְשֶׁמֶת **tanshemeth**, *tan-sheh'-meth*; from 5395; prop. a hard *breather*, i.e. the name of two unclean creatures, a lizard and a bird (both perh. from changing color through their *irascibility*), prob. the *tree-toad* and the *water-hen*:—mole, swan.

8581. תָּעַב **tâʻab**, *taw-ab'*; a prim. root; to *loathe*, i.e. (mor.) *detest*:—(make to be) abhor (-red), (be, commit more, do) abominable (-y), × utterly.

תֹּעֵבָה **tôʻêbâh**. See 8441.

8582. תָּעָה **tâʻâh**, *taw-aw'*; a prim. root; to *vacillate*, i.e. *reel* or *stray* (lit. or fig.); also caus. of both:—(cause to) go astray, deceive, dissemble, (cause to, make to) err, pant, seduce, (make to) stagger, (cause to) wander, be out of the way.

8583. תֹּעוּ **Tôʻûw**, *to'-oo*; or

תֹּעִי **Tôʻîy**, *to'-ee*; from 8582; *error*; *Toü* or *Toï*, a Syrian king:—Toi, Tou.

8584. תְּעוּדָה **tᵉʻûwdâh**, *teh-oo-daw'*; from 5749; *attestation*, i.e. a *precept, usage*:—testimony.

8585. תְּעָלָה **tᵉʻâlâh**, *teh-aw-law'*; from 5927; a *channel* (into which water is *raised* for irrigation); also a *bandage* or *plaster* (as placed *upon* a wound):—conduit, cured, healing, little river, trench, watercourse.

8586. תַּעֲלוּל **taʻălûwl**, *tah-al-ool'*; from 5953; *caprice* (as a fit *coming on*), i.e. *vexation*; concr. a *tyrant*:—babe, delusion.

8587. תַּעֲלֻמָּה **taʻălummâh**, *tah-al-oom-maw'*; from 5956; a *secret*:—thing that is hid, secret.

8588. תַּעֲנוּג **taʻănûwg**, *tah-an-oog'*; or

תַּעֲנֻג **taʻănûg**, *tah-an-oog'*; and (fem.)

תַּעֲנֻגָה **taʻănûgâh**, *tah-an-oog-aw'*; from 6026; *luxury*:—delicate, delight, pleasant.

8589. תַּעֲנִית **taʻănîyth**, *tah-an-eeth'*; from 6031; *affliction* (of self), i.e. *fasting*:—heaviness.

8590. תַּעֲנָךְ **Taʻănâk**, *tah-an-awk'*; or

תַּעְנָךְ **Taʻnâk**, *tah-nawk'*; of uncert. der.; *Taanak* or *Tanak*, a place in Pal.:—Taanach, Tanach.

8591. תָּעַע **tâʻaʻ**, *taw-ah'*; a prim. root; to *cheat*; by anal. to *maltreat*:—deceive, misuse.

8592. תַּעֲצֻמָה **taʻătsûmâh**, *tah-ats-oo-maw'*; from 6105; *might* (plur. collect.):—power.

8593. תַּעַר **taʻar**, *tah'-ar*; from 6168; a *knife* or *razor* (as *making* bare); also a *scabbard* (as *being bare*, i.e. empty):—[pen-] knife, rasor, scabbard, shave, sheath.

8594. תַּעֲרֻבָה **taʻărûbâh**, *tah-ar-oo-baw'*; from 6148; *suretyship*, i.e. (concr.) a *pledge*:— + hostage.

8595. תַּעְתֻּעַ **taʻtûaʻ**, *tah-too'-ah*; from 8591; a *fraud*:—error.

8596. תֹּף **tôph**, *tofe*; from 8608 contr.; a *tambourine*:—tabret, timbrel.

8597. תִּפְאָרָה **tiphʼârâh**, *tif-aw-raw'*; or

תִּפְאֶרֶת **tiphʼereth**, *tif-eh'-reth*; from 6286; *ornament* (abstr. or concr., lit. or fig.):—beauty (-iful), bravery, comely, fair, glory (-ious), honour, majesty.

8598. תַּפּוּחַ **tappûwach**, *tap-poo'-akh*; from 5301; an *apple* (from its *fragrance*), i.e. the fruit or the tree (prob. includ. others of the *pome* order, as the quince, the orange, etc.):—apple (tree). See also 1054.

8599. תַּפּוּחַ **Tappûwach**, *tap-poo'-akh*; the same as 8598; *Tappuäch*, the name of two places in Pal., also of an Isr.:—Tappuah.

8600. תְּפוֹצָה **tᵉphôwtsâh**, *tef-o-tsaw'*; from 6327; a *dispersal*:—dispersion.

8601. תֻּפִין **tûphîyn**, *too-feen'*; from 644; *cookery*, i.e. (concr.) a *cake*:—baked piece.

8602. תָּפֵל **tâphêl**, *taw-fale'*; from an unused root mean. to *smear*; *plaster* (as *gummy*) or *slime*; (fig.) *frivolity*:—foolish things, unsavoury, untempered.

8603. תֹּפֶל **Tôphel**, *to'-fel*; from the same as 8602; *quagmire*; *Tophel*, a place near the Desert:—Tophel.

8604. תִּפְלָה **tiphlâh**, *tif-law'*; from the same as 8602; *frivolity*:—folly, foolishly.

8605. תְּפִלָּה **t^{e}phillâh**, *tef-il-law'*; from 6419; *intercession, supplication*; by impl. a *hymn*:—prayer.

8606. תִּפְלֶצֶת **tiphletseth**, *tif-leh'-tseth*; from 6426; *fearfulness*:—terrible.

8607. תִּפְסַח **Tiphçach**, *tif-sakh'*; from 6452; *ford*; *Tiphsach*, a place in Mesopotamia:—Tipsah.

8608. תָּפַף **tâphaph**, *taw-faf'*; a prim. root; to *drum*, i.e. play (as) on the tambourine:—taber, play with timbrels.

8609. תָּפַר **tâphar**, *taw-far'*; a prim. root; to *sew*:—(women that) sew (together).

8610. תָּפַשׂ **tâphas**, *taw-fas'*; a prim. root; to *manipulate*, i.e. *seize*; chiefly to *capture, wield*; spec. to *overlay*; fig. to *use* unwarrantably:—catch, handle, (lay, take) hold (on, over), stop, × surely, surprise, take.

8611. תֹּפֶת **tôpheth**, *to'-feth*; from the base of 8608; a *smiting*, i.e. (fig.) *contempt*:—tabret.

8612. תֹּפֶת **Tôpheth**, *to'-feth*; the same as 8611; *Topheth*, a place near Jerus.:—Tophet, Topheth.

8613. תָּפְתֶּה **Tophteh**, *tof-teh'*; prob. a form of 8612; *Tophteh*, a place of cremation:—Tophet.

8614. תִּפְתָּי **tiphtay** (Chald.), *tif-tah'ee*; perh. from 8199; *judicial*, i.e. a *lawyer*:—sheriff.

תּוֹצָאָה **tôtsâ'âh**. See 8444.

8615. תִּקְוָה **tiqvâh**, *tik-vaw'*; from 6960; lit. a *cord* (as an *attachment* [comp. 6961]); fig. *expectancy*:—expectation ([-ted]), hope, live, thing that I long for.

8616. תִּקְוָה **Tiqvâh**, *tik-vaw'*; the same as 8615; *Tikvah*, the name of two Isr.:—Tikvah.

8617. תְּקוּמָה **t^{e}qûwmâh**, *tek-oo-maw'*; from 6965; *resistfulness*:—power to stand.

8618. תְּקוֹמֵם **t^{e}qôwmêm**, *tek-o-mame'*; from 6965; an *opponent*:—rise up against.

8619. תָּקוֹעַ **tâqôwaʻ**, *taw-ko'-ah*; from 8628 (in the musical sense); a *trumpet*:—trumpet.

8620. תְּקוֹעַ **T^{e}qôwaʻ**, *tek-o'-ah*; a form of 8619; *Tekoä*, a place in Pal.:—Tekoa, Tekoah.

8621. תְּקוֹעִי **T^{e}qôwʻîy**, *tek-o-ee'*; or

תְּקֹעִי **T^{e}qôʻîy**, *tek-o-ee'*; patron. from 8620; a *Tekoïte* or inhab. of Tekoah:—Tekoite.

8622. תְּקוּפָה **t^{e}qûwphâh**, *tek-oo-faw'*; or

תְּקֻפָה **t^{e}qûphâh**, *tek-oo-faw'*; from 5362; a *revolution*, i.e. (of the sun) *course*, (of time) *lapse*:—circuit, come about, end.

8623. תַּקִּיף **taqqîyph**, *tak-keef'*; from 8630; *powerful*:—mightier.

8624. תַּקִּיף **taqqîyph** (Chald.), *tak-keef'*; corresp. to 8623:—mighty, strong.

8625. תְּקַל **t^{e}qal** (Chald.), *tek-al'*; corresp. to 8254; to *balance*:—Tekel, be weighed.

8626. תָּקַן **tâqan**, *taw-kan'*; a prim. root; to *equalize*, i.e. *straighten* (intrans. or trans.); fig. to *compose*:—set in order, make straight.

8627. תְּקַן **t^{e}qan** (Chald.), *tek-an'*; corresp. to 8626; to *straighten* up, i.e. *confirm*:—establish.

8628. תָּקַע **tâqaʻ**, *taw-kah'*; a prim. root; to *clatter*, i.e. *slap* (the hands together), *clang* (an instrument); by anal. to *drive* (a nail or tent-pin, a dart, etc.); by impl. to *become bondsman* (by hand-clasping):—blow ([a trumpet]), cast, clap, fasten, pitch [tent], smite, sound, strike, × suretiship, thrust.

8629. תֵּקַע **têqaʻ**, *tay-kah'*; from 8628; a *blast* of a trumpet:—sound.

תְּקֹעִי **T^{e}qôʻîy**. See 8621.

8630. תָּקַף **tâqaph**, *taw-kaf'*; a prim. root; to *overpower*:—prevail (against).

8631. תְּקֵף **t^{e}qêph** (Chald.), *tek-afe'*; corresp. to 8630; to *become* (caus. *make*) *mighty* or (fig.) *obstinate*:—make firm, harden, be (-come) strong.

8632. תְּקֹף **t^{e}qôph** (Chald.), *tek-ofe'*; corresp. to 8633; *power*:—might, strength.

8633 תֹּקֶף **tôqeph**, *to'-kef*; from 8630; *might* or (fig.) *positiveness*:—authority, power, strength.

תְּקֻפָה **t^{e}qûphâh**. See 8622.

תֹּר **tôr**. See 8447, 8449.

8634. תַּרְאֲלָה **Tar'ălâh**, *tar-al-aw'*; prob. for 8653; a *reeling*; *Taralah*, a place in Pal.:—Taralah.

8635. תַּרְבּוּת **tarbûwth**, *tar-booth'*; from 7235; *multiplication*, i.e. *progeny*:—increase.

8636. תַּרְבִּית **tarbîyth**, *tar-beeth'*; from 7235; *multiplication*, i.e. *percentage* or *bonus* in addition to principal:—increase, unjust gain.

8637. תִּרְגַּל **tirgal**, *teer-gal'*; a denom. from 7270; to *cause to walk*:—teach to go.

8638. תִּרְגַּם **tirgam**, *teer-gam'*; a denom. from 7275 in the sense of *throwing* over; to *transfer*, i.e. *translate*:—interpret.

תֹּרָה **tôrâh**. See 8451.

8639. תַּרְדֵּמָה **tardêmâh**, *tar-day-maw'*; from 7290; a *lethargy* or (by impl.) *trance*:—deep sleep.

8640. תִּרְהָקָה **Tirhâqâh**, *teer-haw'-kaw*; of for. der.; *Tirhakah*, a king of Kush:—Tirhakah.

8641. תְּרוּמָה **t^{e}rûwmâh**, *ter-oo-maw'*; or

תְּרֻמָה **t^{e}rûmâh** (Deut. 12 : 11), *ter-oo-maw'*; from 7311; a *present* (as offered *up*), espec. in *sacrifice* or as *tribute*:—gift, heave offering ([shoulder]), oblation, offered (-ing).

8642. תְּרוּמִיָּה **t^{e}rûwmîyâh**, *ter-oo-mee-yaw'*; formed as 8641; a sacrificial *offering*:—oblation.

8643. תְּרוּעָה **t^{e}rûwʻâh**, *ter-oo-aw'*; from 7321; *clamor*, i.e. *acclamation* of joy or a *battle-cry*; espec. *clangor* of trumpets, as an *alarum*:—alarm, blow (-ing) (of, the) (trumpets), joy, jubile, loud noise, rejoicing, shout (-ing), (high, joyful) sound (-ing).

8644. תְּרוּפָה **t^{e}rûwphâh**, *ter-oo-faw'*; from 7322 in the sense of its congener 7495; a *remedy*:—medicine.

8645. תִּרְזָה **tirzâh**, *teer-zaw'*; prob. from 7329; a species of tree (appar. from its *slenderness*), perh. the *cypress*:—cypress.

8646. תֶּרַח **Terach**, *teh'-rakh*; of uncert. der.; *Terach*, the father of Abraham; also a place in the Desert:—Tarah, Terah.

8647. תִּרְחֲנָה **Tirchănâh**, *teer-khan-aw'*; of uncert. der.; *Tirchanah*, an Isr.:—Tirhanah.

8648. תְּרֵין **t^{e}rêyn** (Chald.), *ter-ane'*; fem.

תַּרְתֵּין **tartêyn**, *tar-tane'*; corresp. to 8147; *two*:—second, + twelve, two.

8649. תָּרְמָה **tormâh**, *tor-maw'*; and

תַּרְמוּת° **tarmûwth**, *tar-mooth'*; or

תַּרְמִית **tarmîyth**, *tar-meeth'*; from 7411; *fraud*:—deceit (-ful), privily.

תְּרֻמָה **t^{e}rûmâh**. See 8641.

8650. תֹּרֶן **tôren**, *to'-ren*; prob. for 766; a *pole* (as a mast or flag-staff):—beacon, mast.

8651. תְּרַע **t^{e}raʻ** (Chald.), *ter-ah'*; corresp. to 8179; a *door*; by impl. a *palace*:—gate mouth.

8652. תָּרָע **târâʻ** (Chald.), *taw-raw'*; from 8651; a *doorkeeper*:—porter.

8653. תַּרְעֵלָה **tarʻêlâh**, *tar-ay-law'*; from 7477; *reeling*:—astonishment, trembling.

8654. תִּרְעָתִי **Tirʻâthîy**, *teer-aw-thee'*; patrial from an unused name mean. *gate*; a *Tirathite* or inhab. of an unknown Tirah:—Tirathite.

8655. תְּרָפִים **t^{e}râphîym**, *ter-aw-feme'*; plur. per. from 7495; a *healer*; *Teraphim* (sing. or plur.) a family idol:—idols (-atry), images, teraphim.

8656. תִּרְצָה **Tirtsâh**, *teer-tsaw'*; from 7521; *delightsomeness*; *Tirtsah*, a place in Pal.; also an Israelitess:—Tirzah.

8657. תֶּרֶשׁ **Teresh**, *teh'-resh*; of for. der.; *Teresh*, a eunuch of Xerxes:—Teresh.

8658. תַּרְשִׁישׁ **tarshîysh**, *tar-sheesh'*; prob. of for. der. [comp. 8659]; a gem, perh. the *topaz*:—beryl.

8659. תַּרְשִׁישׁ **Tarshîysh**, *tar-sheesh'*; prob. the same as 8658 (as the region of the stone, or the reverse); *Tarshish*, a place on the Mediterranean, hence the epithet of a *merchant* vessel (as if for or from that port); also the name of a Persian and of an Isr.:—Tarshish, Tharshish.

8660. תִּרְשָׁתָא **Tirshâthâ'**, *teer-shaw-thaw'*; of for. der.; the title of a Pers. deputy or *governor*:—Tirshatha.

תַּרְתֵּין **tartêyn**. See 8648.

8661. תַּרְתָּן **Tartân**, *tar-tawn'*; of for. der.; *Tartan*, an Assyrian:—Tartan.

8662. תַּרְתָּק **Tartâq**, *tar-tawk'*; of for. der.; *Tartak*, a deity of the Avvites:—Tartak.

8663. תְּשֻׁאָה **t^{e}shûʼâh**, *tesh-oo-aw'*; from 7722; a *crashing* or loud *clamor*:—crying, noise, shouting, stir.

תֹּשָׁב **tôshâb**. See 8453.

8664. תִּשְׁבִּי **Tishbîy**, *tish-bee'*; patrial from an unused name mean. *recourse*; a *Tishbite* or inhab. of Tishbeh (in Gilead):—Tishbite.

8665. תַּשְׁבֵּץ **tashbêts**, *tash-bates'*; from 7660; *checkered* stuff (as *reticulated*):—broidered.

8666. תְּשׁוּבָה **t^{e}shûwbâh**, *tesh-oo-baw'*; or

תְּשֻׁבָה **t^{e}shûbâh**, *tesh-oo-baw'*; from 7725; a *recurrence* (of time or place); a *reply* (as *returned*):—answer, be expired, return.

8667. תְּשׂוּמֶת **t^{e}sûwmeth**, *tes-oo-meth'*; from 7760; a *deposit*, i.e. *pledging*:—+ fellowship.

8668. תְּשׁוּעָה **t^{e}shûwʻâh**, *tesh-oo-aw'*; or

תְּשֻׁעָה **t^{e}shûʻâh**, *tesh-oo-aw'*; from 7768 in the sense of 3467; *rescue* (lit. or fig., pers., national or spir.):—deliverance, help, safety, salvation, victory.

8669. תְּשׁוּקָה **t^{e}shûwqâh**, *tesh-oo-kaw'*; from 7783 in the orig. sense of *stretching* out after; a *longing*:—desire.

8670. תְּשׁוּרָה **t^{e}shûwrâh**, *tesh-oo-raw'*; from 7788 in the sense of *arrival*; a *gift*:—present.

תַּשְׁחֵת **tashchêth**. See 516.

תֻּשִׁיָּה **tûshîyâh**. See 8454.

8671. תְּשִׁיעִי **t^{e}shîyʻîy**, *tesh-ee-ee'*; ord. from 8672; *ninth*:—ninth.

תְּשֻׁעָה **t^{e}shûʻâh**. See 8668.

8672. תֵּשַׁע **têshaʻ**, *tay'-shah*; or (masc.)

תִּשְׁעָה **tishʻâh**, *tish-aw'*; perh. from 8159 through the idea of a *turn* to the next or full number ten; *nine* or (ord.) *ninth*:—nine (+ -teen, + -teenth, -th).

8673. תִּשְׁעִים **tishʻîym**, *tish-eem'*; multiple from 8672; *ninety*:—ninety.

8674. תַּתְּנַי **Tatt^{e}nay**, *tat-ten-ah'ee*; of for. der.; *Tattenai*, a Persian:—Tatnai.

PLACES WHERE THE HEBREW AND THE ENGLISH BIBLES DIFFER IN THE DIVISION OF CHAPTERS AND VERSES.

	English.	*Hebrew.*
Genesis	31:55	32: 1
	32: 1-32	2-33
Exodus	8: 1-4	7:26-29
	5-32	8: 1-28
	22: 1	21:37
	2-31	22: 1-30
Leviticus	6: 1-7	5:20-26
	8-30	6: 1-23
Numbers	16:36-50	17: 1-15
	17: 1-13	16-28
	26: 1 (first clause)	25:19
	29:40	30: 1
	30: 1-16	2-17
Deuteronomy	5:18-33	5:17-30
	12:32	13: 1
	13: 1-18	2-19
	22:30	23: 1
	23: 1-25	2-26
	29: 1	28:69
	2-29	29: 1-28
Joshua	21:36, 37	(not in most copies)
	38-45	21:36-43
1 Samuel	19: 2 (first clause)	19: 1
	20:42	21: 1
	21: 1-15	2-16
	23:29	24: 1
	24: 1-22	2-23
2 Samuel	17:28 (first word)	29 (middle)
	18:33	19: 1
	19: 1-43	2-44
1 Kings	4:21-34	5: 1-14
	5: 1-18	15-32
	18:33 (l. half)	(first half)18:34
	20: 2 (l. half)	(first half)20: 3
	22:22 (f. clause)	(l. cl.)22:21
	43 (last half)	44
	44-53	45-54
2 Kings	11:21	12: 1
	12: 1-21	2-22
1 Chronicles	6: 1-15	5:27-41
	16-81	6: 1-66
2 Chronicles	2: 1	1:18
	2-18	2: 1-17
	14: 1	13:23
	2-15	14: 1-14
Nehemiah	4: 1-6	3:33-38
	7-23	4: 1-17
	9:38	10: 1
	10: 1-39	2-40
Job	41: 1-8	40:25-32
	9-34	41: 1-26
Psalms	3:*title*	3: 1
	1-8	2-9
	4:*title*	4: 1
	1-8	2-9
	5:*title*	5: 1
	1-12	2-13
	6:*title*	6: 1
	1-10	2-11
	7:*title*	7: 1
	1-17	2-18
	8:*title*	8: 1
	1-9	2-10
	9:*title*	9: 1
	1-20	2-21
	11:*title* (first clause)	11: 1
	12:*title*	12: 1
	1-8	2-9
	13:*title*	13: 1
	1-5	2-6
	6 (last half)	6
	14:*title* (first clause)	14: 1
	15:*title* (first clause)	15: 1
	16:*title* (first clause)	16: 1
	17:*title* (first clause)	17: 1
	18:*title*	18:1&(f.c.)2
	1-50	2-51
	19:*title*	19: 1
	1-14	2-15

	English.	*Hebrew.*
Psalms	20:*title*	20: 1
	1-9	2-10
	21:*title*	21: 1
	1-13	2-14
	22:*title*	22: 1
	1-31	2-32
	23:*title* (first clause)	23: 1
	24-28:*title* (first clause)	24-28: 1
	29:*title* (first clause)	29: 1
	30:*title*	30: 1
	1-12	2-13
	31:*title*	31: 1
	1-24	2-25
	32:*title* (first clause)	32: 1
	34:*title*	34: 1
	1-22	2-23
	35&37:*title* (first word)	35&37: 1
	36:*title*	36: 1
	1-12	2-13
	38:*title*	38: 1
	1-22	2-23
	39:*title*	39: 1
	1-13	2-14
	40:*title*	40: 1
	1-17	2-18
	41:*title*	41: 1
	1:13	2-14
	42:*title*	42: 1
	1-11	2-12
	44:*title*	44: 1
	1-26	2-27
	45:*title*	45: 1
	1-17	2-18
	46:*title*	46: 1
	1-11	2-12
	47:*title*	47: 1
	1-9	2-10
	48:*title*	48: 1
	1-14	2-15
	49:*title*	49: 1
	1-20	2-21
	50:*title* (first clause)	50: 1
	51:*title*	51: 1&2
	1-19	2-21
	52:*title* (first clause)	52: 1 & 2
	1-9	2-11
	53:*title*	53: 1
	1-6	2-7
	54:*title*	54: 1 & 2
	1-7	2-9
	55:*title*	55: 1
	1-23	2-24
	56:*title*	56: 1
	1-23	2-24
	57:*title*	57: 1
	1-11	2-12
	58:*title*	58: 1
	1-11	2-12
	59:*title*	59: 1
	1-17	2-18
	60:*title*	60: 1&2
	1-12	3-14
	61:*title*	61: 1
	1-8	2-9
	62:*title*	62: 1
	1-12	2-13
	63:*title*	63: 1
	1-11	2-12
	64:*title*	64: 1
	1-10	2-11
	65:*title*	65: 1
	1-13	2-14
	66:*title* (first clause)	66: 1
	67:*title*	67: 1
	1-7	2-8
	68:*title*	68: 1
	1-35	2-36
	69:*title*	69: 1
	1-36	2-37

	English.	*Hebrew.*
Psalms	70:*title*	70: 1
	1-5	2-6
	72:*title* (first word)	72: 1
	73:*title* (first clause)	73: 1
	74:*title* (first clause)	74: 1
	1-10	2-11
	76:*title*	76: 1
	1-12	2-13
	77:*title*	77: 1
	1-20	2-21
	78 & 79:*title* (f. clause)	78&79: 1
	80:*title*	80: 1
	1-19	2-20
	81:*title*	81: 1
	1-16	2-17
	82:*title* (first clause)	82: 1
	83:*title*	83: 1
	1-18	2-19
	84:*title*	84: 1
	1-12	2-13
	85:*title*	85: 1
	1-13	2-14
	86 & 87:*title* (first cl.)	86&87: 1
	88:*title*	88: 1
	1-18	2-19
	89:*title*	89: 1
	1-52	2-53
	90:*title* (first clause)	90: 1
	92:*title*	92: 1
	11-5	2-16
	98:*title* (first word)	98: 1
	100&101:*title* (1st cl.)	100&101: 1
	102:*title*	102: 1
	1-28	2-29
	103:*title* (first word)	103: 1
	108:*title*	108: 1
	1-13	2-14
	109, 110, 120-134, 138 and 139:*title* (first cl.) same	1
	140:*title*	140: 1
	1-13	2-14
	141:*title* (first clause)	141: 1
	142:*title*	142: 1
	1-6	2-7
	143:*title* (first clause)	143: 1
	144:*title* (first word)	144: 1
	145:*title* (first clause)	145: 1
Ecclesiastes	5: 1	4:17
	2-20	5: 1-19
Canticles	6:13	7: 1
	7: 1-13	2-14
Isaiah	9: 1	8:23
	2-21	9: 1-20
	64: 1	63:19
	2-12	64: 1-11
Jeremiah	9: 1	8:23
	2-26	9: 1-25
Ezekiel	20:45-49	21: 1-5
	21: 1-32	6-37
Daniel	4: 1-3	3:31-33
	4-37	4: 1-34
	5:31	6: 1
	6: 1-28	2-29
Hosea	1:10, 11	2: 1, 2
	2: 1-23	3-25
	11:12	12: 1
	12: 1-14	2-15
	13:16	14: 1
	14: 1-9	2-10
Joel	2:28-32	3: 1-5
	3: 1-21	4: 1-21
Jonah	1:17	2: 1
	2: 1-10	2-11
Micah	5: 1	4:14
	2-15	5: 1-14
Nahum	1:15	2: 1
	2: 1-13	2-14
Zechariah	1:18	2: 1-4
	2: 1-13	2-17
Malachi	4: 1-6	3:19-24

DICTIONARY

OF THE

GREEK TESTAMENT.

A CONCISE

DICTIONARY

OF THE WORDS IN

THE GREEK TESTAMENT;

WITH THEIR RENDERINGS

IN THE

AUTHORIZED ENGLISH VERSION.

BY

JAMES STRONG, S.T.D., LL.D.

ABINGDON
NASHVILLE

PREFACE.

THIS work is entirely similar in origin, method, and design, to the author's HEBREW DICTIONARY, and may be employed separately, for a corresponding purpose and with a like result, namely, to be serviceable to many who have not the wish or the ability to use a more copious Lexicon of New-Testament Greek. In this case also even scholars will find many suggestions and explanations not unworthy their attention.

PLAN OF THE BOOK.

1. All the original words are treated in their alphabetical Greek order, and are numbered regularly from the first to the last, each being known throughout by its appropriate number. This renders reference easy without recourse to the Greek characters.

2. Immediately after each word is given its exact equivalent in English letters, according to the system of transliteration laid down in the scheme here following, which is substantially that adopted in the Common English Version, only more consistently and uniformly carried out; so that the word could readily be turned back again into Greek from the form thus given it.

3. Next follows the precise pronunciation, according to the usual English mode of sounding syllables, so plainly indicated that none can fail to apprehend and apply it. The most approved sounds are adopted, as laid down in the annexed scheme of articulation, and in such a way that any good Græcist would immediately recognise the word if so pronounced, notwithstanding the minor variations current among scholars in this respect.

4. Then ensues a tracing of the etymology, radical meaning, and applied significations of the word, justly but tersely analyzed and expressed, with any other important peculiarities in this regard.

5. In the case of proper names, the same method is pursued, and at this point the regular mode of Anglicizing it, after the general style of the Common English Version, is given, and a few words of explanation are added to identify it.

6. Finally (after the punctuation-mark :—) are given all the different renderings of the word in the Authorized English Version, arranged in the alphabetical order of the leading terms, and conveniently condensed according to the explanations given below.

By searching out these various renderings in the MAIN CONCORDANCE, to which this Dictionary is designed as a companion, and noting the passages to which the same number corresponding to that of any given Greek word is attached in the marginal column, the reader, whether acquainted with the original language or not, will obtain a complete *Greek Concordance* also, expressed in the words of the Common English Version. This is an advantage which no other Concordance or Lexicon affords.

GREEK ARTICULATION.

THE following explanations are sufficient to show the mode of writing and pronouncing Greek words in English adopted in this *Dictionary*.

1. The *Alphabet* is as follows:

No.	Form.		Name.	Transliteration and Power.
1.	Α	α	Alpha (*al'-fah*)	**a**, as in ARM or MAN*
2.	Β	β	Bēta (*bay'-tah*)	**b**
3.	Γ	γ	Gamma (*gam'-mah*)	**g** hard †
4.	Δ	δ	Dĕlta (*del'-tah*)	**d**
5.	Ε	ε	Ĕpsilŏn (*ep'-see-lon*)	**ĕ**, as in MEt
6.	Ζ	ζ	Zēta (*dzay'-tah*)	**z**, as in ADZE‡
7.	Η	η	Ēta (*ay'-tah*)	**ē**, as in thEY
8.	Θ	θ or ϑ	Thēta (*thay'-tah*)	**th**, as in THin§
9.	Ι	ι	Iōta (*ee-o'-tah*)	**i**, as in machIne ‖
10.	Κ	κ or ϰ	Kappa (*cap'-pah*)	**k**
11.	Λ	λ	Lambda (*lamb'-dah*)	**l**
12.	Μ	μ	Mu (*moo*)	**m**
13.	Ν	ν	Nu (*noo*)	**n**
14.	Ξ	ξ	Xi (*ksee*)	**x** = *ks*
15.	Ο	ο	Omikrŏn (*om'-e-cron*)	**ŏ**, as in *not*
16.	Π	π	Pi (*pee*)	**p**
17.	Ρ	ρ	Rhō (*hro*)	**r**
18.	Σ	σ, final ς	Sigma (*sig'-mah*)	**s** sharp
19.	Τ	τ	Tau (*tŏw*)	**t** ¶
20.	Υ	υ	Upsilŏn (*u'-pse-lon*)	**u**, as in *fUll*
21.	Φ	φ	Phi (*fee*)	**ph** = *f*
22.	Χ	χ	Chi (*khee*)	German **ch** *
23.	Ψ	ψ	Psi (*psee*)	**ps**
24.	Ω	ω	Omĕga (*o'-meg-ah*)	**ō**, as in *no*.

2. The mark ʽ, placed over the *initial* vowel of a word, is called the *Rough Breathing*, and is equivalent to the English *h*, by which we have accordingly represented it. Its *absence* over an initial vowel is indicated by the mark ʼ, called the *Smooth Breathing*, which is unappreciable or silent, and is therefore not represented in our method of transliteration.†

3. The following are the Greek *diphthongs*, properly so called :‡

Form.	Transliteration and Power.	Form.	Transliteration and Power.
αι	**ai** (*ah'ee*) [ă + ē]	αυ	**ow**, as in *now*
ει	**ei**, as in hEIght	ευ	**eu**, as in *fEUd*
οι	**oi**, as in OIl	ου	**ou**, as in *thrOUgh*.
υι	**we**, as in sWEet		

4. The *accent* (stress of voice) falls on the syllable where it is written.* It is of three forms: the *acute* (ʹ), which is the only true accent; the *grave* (ˋ) which is its substitute; and the *circumflex* (ˆ or ˜), which is the union of the two. The acute may stand on any one of the last *three* syllables, and in case it occurs on the final syllable, before another word in the same sentence, it is written as a grave. The grave is understood (but never written as such) on every other syllable. The circumflex is written on any syllable (necessarily the last or next to the last one of a word), formed by the contraction of two syllables, of which the *first* would properly have the acute.

5. The following *punctuation*-marks are used: the comma (,), the semicolon (·), the colon or period (.), the interrogation-point (;), and by some editors, also the exclamation-point, parentheses and quotation-marks.

---

* α, when *final*, or before ρ final or followed by any *other* consonant, is sounded like *a* in ARm; elsewhere like *a* in mAn.

† γ, when followed by γ, κ, χ, or ξ, is sounded like *ng* in kING.

‡ ζ is always sounded like *dz*.

§ θ never has the guttural sound, like *th* in THis.

‖ ι has the sound of *ee* when it *ends* an *accented* syllable; in other situations a more obscure sound, like *i* in amIable or ImbecIle.

¶ τ never has a sibilant sound, like *t* in naTion, naTure.

* From the difficulty of producing the true sound of χ, it is generally sounded like *k*.

† These signs are placed over the *second* vowel of a *diphthong*. The same is true of the accents.

The *Rough* Breathing always belongs to υ initial.

The Rough Breathing is always used with ρ, when it begins a word. If this letter be doubled in the middle of a word, the first takes the Smooth, and the second the Rough, Breathing.

As these signs cannot conveniently be written over the first letter of a word, when a *capital*, they are in such cases placed *before* it. This observation applies also to the *accents*. The aspiration *always* begins the syllable.

Occasionally, in consequence of a contraction (*crasis*), the Smooth Breathing is made to stand in the middle of a word, and is then called *Coro'nis*.

‡ The above are combinations of two *short* vowels, and are pronounced like their respective elements, but in more rapid succession than otherwise. Thus αι is midway between *i* in *hIgh*, and *ay* in SAY.

Besides these, there are what are called *improper* diphthongs, in which the former is a *long* vowel. In these,

ᾳ	sounds like α	ηυ	sounds like η + υ
ῃ	" " η	ωυ	" " ω + υ.
ῳ	" " ω		

the second vowel, when ι, is written *under* the first (unless that be a capital), and is *silent;* when υ, it is sounded separately. When the initial is a capital, the ι is placed after it, but does not take the breathing nor accent.

The sign ¨, called *diær'esis*, placed over the *latter* of two vowels, indicates that they do *not* form a diphthong.

* Every word (except a few monosyllables, called *Aton'ics*) must have one accent; several small words (called *Enclit'ics*) throw their accent (always as an acute) on the last syllable of the preceding word (in addition to its own accent, which still has the principal stress), where this is possible.

ABBREVIATIONS EMPLOYED.

abst. = abstract (-ly)
acc. = accusative (case)
adv. = adverb (-ial) (-ly)
aff. = affinity
alt. = alternate (-ly)
anal. = analogy
app. = apparent (-ly)
caus. = causative (-ly)
cer. = { ceremony / ceremonial (-ly) }
Chald. = Chaldee
Chr. = Christian
coll. = collective (-ly)
comp. = { comparative / comparatively / compare / compound (-s) }
concr. = concrete (-ly)
corr. = corresponding
dat. = dative (case)
der. = { derivation / derivative / derived }
dim. = diminutive
dir. = direct (-ly)
E. = East
eccl. = ecclesiastical (-ly)
Eg. = Egypt (-ian)
ell. = { ellipsis / elliptical (-ly) }
eq. = equivalent
esp. = especially
euph. = { euphemism / euphemistic / euphemistically }
ext. = extension
fem. = feminine
fig. = figurative (-ly)
for. = foreign
gen. = genitive (case)
Gr. = Greek
Heb. = { Hebraism / Hebrew }
i.e. = { *id est* / that is }
imper. = imperative
imperf. = imperfect
impers. = impersonal (-ly)
impl. = { implication / implied }
incl. = including
ind. = indicative (-ly)
indiv. = individual (-ly)
inf. = infinitive
inh. = inhabitant (-s)
intens. = intensive (-ly)
intr. = intransitive (-ly)
invol. = { involuntary / involuntarily }
irr. = irregular (-ly)
Isr. = { Israelite (-s) / Israelitish }
Jer. = Jerusalem
Lat. = Latin
lit. = literal (-ly)
mean. = meaning
ment. = mental (-ly)
mid. = middle (voice)
mor. = moral (-ly)
mult. = multiplicative
nat. = natural (-ly)
neg. = negative (-ly)
neut. = neuter
obj. = objective (-ly)
obs. = obsolete
or. = origin (-al) (-ly)
Pal. = Palestine
part. = participle
pass. = passive (-ly)
perh. = perhaps
pers. = person (-al) (-ly)
phys. = physical (-ly)
pl. = plural
pref. = prefix (-ed)
pos. = positive (-ly)
prim. = primary
prob. = probably
prol. = { prolongation / prolonged }
pron. = { pronominal (-ly) / pronoun }
prop. = properly
redupl. = { reduplicated / reduplication }
refl. = reflexive (-ly)
rel. = relative (-ly)
Rom. = Roman
sing. = singular
spec. = special (-ly)
subj. = subjective (-ly)
sup. = superlative (-ly)
tech. = technical (-ly)
term. = termination
trans. = transitive (-ly)
transp. = { transposed / transposition }
typ. = typical (-ly)
unc. = uncertain
var. = { variation / various }
voc. = vocative
vol. = { voluntarily / voluntary }

SIGNS EMPLOYED.

+ (*addition*) denotes a rendering in the A. V. of one or more Gr. words in connection with the one under consideration.

× (*multiplication*) denotes a rendering in the A. V. that results from an idiom peculiar to the Gr.

( ) (*parenthesis*), in the renderings from the A. V., denotes a word or syllable sometimes given in connection with the principal word to which it is annexed.

[ ] (*bracket*), in the rendering from the A. V., denotes the inclusion of an additional word in the Gr.

Italics, at the end of a rendering from the A. V., denote an explanation of the variations from the usual form.

NOTE.

Owing to changes in the enumeration while in progress, there were no words left for Nos. *2717* and *3203–3302*, which were therefore silently dropped out of the vocabulary and references as redundant. This will occasion no practical mistake or inconvenience.

GREEK DICTIONARY OF THE NEW TESTAMENT.

A.

N. B.—The numbers *not in italics* refer to the words in the *Hebrew Dictionary*. Significations within quotation-marks are derivative representatives of the Greek.

1. **Α a**, *al-fah;* of Heb. or.; the first letter of the alphabet; fig. only (from its use as a numeral) the *first:*—Alpha. Often used (usually **ἀν an**, before a vowel) also in composition (as a contraction from *427*) in the sense of *privation;* so in many words beginning with this letter; occasionally in the sense of *union* (as a contraction of *260*).

2. **Ἀαρών Aarōn**, *ah-ar-ohn';* of Heb. or. [175]; *Aaron*, the brother of Moses:—Aaron.

3. **Ἀβαδδών Abaddōn** *ab-ad-dohn';* of Heb. or. [11]; a destroying *angel:*—Abaddon.

4. **ἀβαρής abarēs**, *ab-ar-ace';* from *1* (as a neg. particle) and *922; weightless*, i.e. (fig.) *not burdensome:*—from being burdensome.

5. **Ἀββᾶ Abba**, *ab-bah';* of Chald. or. [2]; *father* (as a voc.):—Abba.

6. **Ἄβελ Abĕl**, *ab'-el;* of Heb. or. [1893]; *Abel*, the son of Adam:—Abel.

7. **Ἀβιά Abia**, *ab-ee-ah';* of Heb. or. [29]; *Abijah*, the name of two Isr.:—Abia.

8. **Ἀβιάθαρ Abiathar**, *ab-ee-ath'-ar;* of Heb. or. [54]; *Abiathar*, an Isr.:—Abiathar.

9. **Ἀβιληνή Abilēnē**, *ab-ee-lay-nay';* of for. or. [comp. 58]; *Abilene*, a region of Syria:—Abilene.

10. **Ἀβιούδ Abiŏud**, *ab-ee-ood';* of Heb. or. [31]; *Abihud*, an Isr.:—Abiud.

11. **Ἀβραάμ Abraam**, *ab-rah-am';* of Heb. or. [85]; *Abraham*, the Heb. patriarch:—Abraham. [In Acts 7 : 16 the text should prob. read *Jacob*.]

12. **ἄβυσσος abussŏs**, *ab'-us-sos;* from *1* (as a neg. particle) and a var. of *1037; depthless*, i.e. (spec.) (infernal) "*abyss*":—deep, (bottomless) pit.

13. **Ἄγαβος Agabŏs**, *ag'-ab-os;* of Heb. or. [comp. 2285]; *Agabus*, an Isr.:—Agabus.

14. **ἀγαθοεργέω agathŏĕrgĕō**, *ag-ath-er-gheh'-o;* from *18* and *2041;* to *work good:*—do good.

15. **ἀγαθοποιέω agathŏpŏiĕō**, *ag-ath-op-oy-eh'-o;* from *17;* to *be a well-doer* (as a favor or a duty):—(when) do good (well).

16. **ἀγαθοποιΐα agathŏpŏiïa**, *ag-ath-op-oy-ee'-ah;* from *17; well-doing*, i.e. *virtue:*—well-doing.

17. **ἀγαθοποιός agathŏpŏiŏs**, *ag-ath-op-oy-os';* from *18* and *4160;* a *well-doer*, i.e. *virtuous:*—them that do well.

18. **ἀγαθός agathŏs**, *ag-ath-os';* a prim. word; "*good*" (in any sense, often as noun):—benefit, good (-s, things), well. Comp. *2570*.

19. **ἀγαθωσύνη agathōsunē**, *ag-ath-o-soo'-nay;* from *18; goodness*, i.e. *virtue* or *beneficence:*—goodness.

20. **ἀγαλλίασις agalliasis**, *ag-al-lee'-as-is;* from *21; exultation;* spec. *welcome:*—gladness, (exceeding) joy.

21. **ἀγαλλιάω agalliaō**, *ag-al-lee-ah'-o;* from **ἄγαν agan** (*much*) and *242;* prop. to *jump for joy*, i.e. *exult:*—be (exceeding) glad, with exceeding joy, rejoice (greatly).

22. **ἄγαμος agamŏs**, *ag'-am-os;* from *1* (as a neg. particle) and *1062; unmarried:*—unmarried.

23. **ἀγανακτέω aganaktĕō**, *ag-an-ak-teh'-o;* from **ἄγαν agan** (*much*) and **ἄχθος achthŏs** (*grief;* akin to the base of *43*); to *be greatly afflicted*, i.e. (fig.) *indignant:*—be much (sore) displeased, have (be moved with, with) indignation.

24. **ἀγανάκτησις aganaktēsis**, *ag-an-ak'-tay-sis;* from *23; indignation:*—indignation.

25. **ἀγαπάω agapaō**, *ag-ap-ah'-o;* perh. from **ἄγαν agan** (*much*) [or comp. 5689]; to *love* (in a social or moral sense):—(be-) love (-ed). Comp. *5368*.

26. **ἀγάπη agapē**, *ag-ah'-pay;* from *25; love*, i.e. *affection* or *benevolence;* spec. (plur.) a *love-feast:*—(feast of) charity ([-ably]), dear, love.

27. **ἀγαπητός agapētŏs**, *ag-ap-ay-tos';* from *25; beloved:*—(dearly, well) beloved, dear.

28. **Ἄγαρ Agar**, *ag'-ar;* of Heb. or. [1904]; *Hagar*, the concubine of Abraham:—Hagar.

29. **ἀγγαρεύω aggarĕuō**, *ang-ar-yew'-o;* of for. or. [comp. 104]; prop. to *be a courier*, i.e., (by impl.) to *press* into public service:—compel (to go).

30. **ἀγγεῖον aggĕiŏn**, *ang-eye'-on;* from **ἄγγος aggŏs** (a *pail*, perh. as *bent;* comp. the base of *43*); a *receptacle:*—vessel.

31. **ἀγγελία aggĕlia**, *ang-el-ee'-ah;* from *32;* an *announcement*, i.e. (by impl.) *precept:*—message.

32. **ἄγγελος aggĕlŏs**, *ang'-el-os;* from **ἀγγέλλω aggĕllō** [prob. der. from *71;* comp. *34*] (to *bring tidings*); a *messenger;* esp. an "*angel*"; by impl. a *pastor:*—angel, messenger.

33. **ἄγε agĕ**, *ag'-eh;* imper. of *71;* prop. *lead*, i.e. *come on:*—go to.

34. **ἀγέλη agĕlē**, *ag-el'-ay;* from *71* [comp. *32*]; a *drove:*—herd.

35. **ἀγενεαλόγητος agĕnĕalŏgētŏs**, *ag-en-eh-al-og'-ay-tos;* from *1* (as neg. particle) and *1075; unregistered* as to birth:—without descent.

36. **ἀγενής agĕnēs**, *ag-en-ace';* from *1* (as neg. particle) and *1085;* prop. *without kin*, i.e. (of unknown descent, and by impl.) *ignoble:*—base things.

37. **ἁγιάζω hagiazō**, *hag-ee-ad'-zo;* from *40;* to *make holy*, i.e. (cer.) *purify* or *consecrate;* (mentally) to *venerate:*—hallow, be holy, sanctify.

38. **ἁγιασμός hagiasmŏs**, *hag-ee-as-mos';* from *37;* prop. *purification*, i.e. (the state) *purity;* concr. (by Hebr.) a *purifier:*—holiness, sanctification.

39. **ἅγιον hagiŏn**, *hag'-ee-on;* neut. of *40;* a *sacred* thing (i.e. spot):—holiest (of all), holy place, sanctuary.

40. **ἅγιος hagiŏs**, *hag'-ee-os;* from **ἅγος hagŏs** (an *awful* thing) [comp. *53*, 2282]; *sacred* (phys. *pure*, mor. *blameless* or *religious*, cer. *consecrated*):—(most) holy (one, thing), saint.

41. **ἁγιότης hagiŏtēs**, *hag-ee-ot'-ace;* from *40; sanctity* (i.e. prop. the state):—holiness.

42. **ἁγιωσύνη hagiōsunē**, *hag-ee-o-soo'-nay;* from *40; sacredness* (i.e. prop. the quality):—holiness.

43. **ἀγκάλη agkalē**, *ang-kal'-ay;* from **ἄγκος agkŏs** (a *bend*, "ache"); an *arm* (as *curved*):—arm.

44. **ἄγκιστρον agkistrŏn**, *ang'-kis-tron;* from the same as *43;* a *hook* (as *bent*):—hook.

45. **ἄγκυρα agkura**, *ang'-koo-rah;* from the same as *43;* an "*anchor*" (as *crooked*):—anchor.

46. **ἄγναφος agnaphŏs**, *ag'-naf-os;* from *1* (as a neg. particle) and the same as *1102;* prop. *unfulled*, i.e. (by impl.) *new* (cloth):—new.

47. **ἁγνεία hagnĕia**, *hag-ni'-ah;* from *53; cleanliness* (the quality), i.e. (spec.) *chastity:*—purity.

48. **ἁγνίζω hagnizō**, *hag-nid'-zo;* from *53;* to *make clean*, i.e. (fig.) *sanctify* (cer. or mor.):—purify (self).

49. **ἁγνισμός hagnismŏs**, *hag-nis-mos';* from *48;* a *cleansing* (the act), i.e. (cer.) *lustration:*—purification.

50. **ἀγνοέω agnŏĕō**, *ag-no-eh'-o;* from *1* (as a neg. particle) and *3539; not to know* (through lack of information or intelligence); by impl. to *ignore* (through disinclination):—(be) ignorant (-ly), not know, not understand, unknown.

51. **ἀγνόημα agnŏēma**, *ag-no'-ay-mah;* from *50;* a thing *ignored*, i.e. *shortcoming:*—error.

52. **ἄγνοια agnŏia**, *ag'-noy-ah;* from *50; ignorance* (prop. the quality):—ignorance.

53. **ἁγνός hagnŏs**, *hag-nos';* from the same as *40;* prop. *clean*, i.e. (fig.) *innocent, modest, perfect:*—chaste, clean, pure.

54. **ἁγνότης hagnŏtēs**, *hag-not'-ace;* from *53; cleanness* (the state), i.e. (fig.) *blamelessness:*—pureness.

55. **ἁγνῶς hagnōs**, *hag-noce';* adv. from *53; purely*, i.e. *honestly:*—sincerely.

56. **ἀγνωσία agnōsia**, *ag-no-see'-ah;* from *1* (as neg. particle) and *1108; ignorance* (prop. the state):—ignorance, not the knowledge.

57. **ἄγνωστος agnōstŏs**, *ag'-noce-tos;* from *1* (as neg. particle) and *1110; unknown:*—unknown.

58. **ἀγορά agŏra**, *ag-or-ah';* from **ἀγείρω agĕirō** (to *gather;* prob. akin to *1453*); prop. the *town-square* (as a place of public resort); by impl. a *market* or *thoroughfare:*—market (-place), street.

59. **ἀγοράζω agŏrazō**, *ag-or-ad'-zo;* from *58;* prop. to *go to market*, i.e. (by impl.) to *purchase;* spec. to *redeem:*—buy, redeem.

60. **ἀγοραῖος agŏraiŏs**, *ag-or-ah'-yos;* from *58; relating to the market-place*, i.e. *forensic* (times); by impl. *vulgar:*—baser sort, low.

61. **ἄγρα agra**, *ag'-rah;* from *71;* (abstr.) a *catching* (of fish); also (concr.) a *haul* (of fish):—draught.

62. **ἀγράμματος agrammatŏs**, *ag-ram-mat-os;* from *1* (as neg. particle) and *1121; unlettered*, i.e. *illiterate:*—unlearned.

63. **ἀγραυλέω agraulĕō**, *ag-row-leh'-o;* from *68* and *832* (in the sense of *833*); to *camp out:*—abide in the field.

64. **ἀγρεύω agrĕuō**, *ag-rew'-o;* from *61;* to *hunt*, i.e. (fig.) to *entrap:*—catch.

65. **ἀγριέλαιος agriĕlaiŏs**, *ag-ree-el'-ah-yos;* from *66* and *1636;* an *oleaster:*—olive tree (which is) wild.

66. **ἄγριος agriŏs**, *ag'-ree-os;* from *68; wild* (as pertaining to the *country*), lit. (*natural*) or fig. (*fierce*):—wild, raging.

67. **Ἀγρίππας Agrippas**, *ag-rip'-pas;* appar. from *66* and *2462; wild-horse* tamer; *Agrippas*, one of the Herods:—Agrippa.

68. **ἀγρός agrŏs**, *ag-ros';* from *71;* a *field* (as a *drive* for cattle); gen. the *country;* spec. a *farm*, i.e. *hamlet:*—country, farm, piece of ground, land.

69. **ἀγρυπνέω agrupnĕō**, *ag-roop-neh'-o;* ultimately from *1* (as neg. particle) and *5258;* to *be sleepless*, i.e. *keep awake:*—watch.

70. **ἀγρυπνία agrupnia**, *ag-roop-nee'-ah;* from *69; sleeplessness*, i.e. a *keeping awake:*—watch.

71. **ἄγω agō**, *ag'-o;* a prim. verb; prop. to *lead;* by impl. to *bring, drive*, (reflex.) *go*, (spec.) *pass* (time), or (fig.) *induce:*—be, bring (forth), carry, (let) go, keep, lead away, be open.

72. **ἀγωγή agōgē**, *ag-o-gay';* redupl. from *71;* a *bringing* up, i.e. *mode of living:*—manner of life.

73. ἀγών **agōn**, *ag-one'*; from *71*; prop. a place of *assembly* (as if *led*), i.e. (by impl.) a *contest* (held there); fig. an *effort* or *anxiety*:—conflict, contention, fight, race.

74. ἀγωνία **agōnia**, *ag-o-nee'-ah*; from *73*; a *struggle* (prop. the state), i.e. (fig.) *anguish*:—agony.

75. ἀγωνίζομαι **agōnizŏmai**, *ag-o-nid'-zom-ahee*; from *73*; to *struggle*, lit. (to *compete* for a prize), fig. (to *contend* with an adversary), or gen. (to *endeavor* to accomplish something):—fight, labor fervently, strive.

76. Ἀδάμ **Adam**, *ad-am'*; of Heb. or. [121]; *Adam*, the first man; typ. (of Jesus) *man* (as his representative):—Adam.

77. ἀδάπανος **adapanŏs**, *ad-ap'-an-os*; from *1* (as neg. particle) and *1160*; *costless*, i.e. *gratuitous*:—without expense.

78. Ἀδδί **Addi**, *ad-dee'*; prob. of Heb. or. [comp. 5716]; *Addi*, an Isr.:—Addi.

79. ἀδελφή **adĕlphē**, *ad-el-fay'*; fem. of *80*; a *sister* (nat. or eccles.):—sister.

80. ἀδελφός **adĕlphŏs**, *ad-el-fos'*; from *1* (as a connective particle) and δελφύς **dĕlphus** (the *womb*); a *brother* (lit. or fig.) near or remote [much like 1]:—brother.

81. ἀδελφότης **adĕlphŏtēs**, *ad-el-fot'-ace*; from *80*; *brotherhood* (prop. the feeling of *brotherliness*), i.e. the (Christian) *fraternity*:—brethren, brotherhood.

82. ἄδηλος **adēlŏs**, *ad'-ay-los*; from *1* (as a neg. particle) and *1212*; *hidden*, fig. *indistinct*:—appear not, uncertain.

83. ἀδηλότης **adēlŏtēs**, *ad-ay-lot'-ace*; from *82*; *uncertainty*:— × uncertain.

84. ἀδήλως **adēlōs**, *ad-ay'-loce*; adv. from *82*; *uncertainly*:—uncertainly.

85. ἀδημονέω **adēmŏnĕō**, *ad-ay-mon-eh'-o*: from a der. of ἀδέω **adĕō**, (to be *sated* to loathing); to *be in distress* (of mind):—be full of heaviness, be very heavy.

86. ᾄδης **haidēs**, *hah'-dace*; from *1* (as a neg. particle) and *1492*; prop. *unseen*, i.e. "*Hades*" or the place (state) of departed souls:—grave, hell.

87. ἀδιάκριτος **adiakritŏs**, *ad-ee-ak'-ree-tos*; from *1* (as a neg. particle) and a der. of *1252*; prop. *undistinguished*, i.e. (act.) *impartial*:—without partiality.

88. ἀδιάλειπτος **adialĕiptŏs**, *ad-ee-al'-ipe-tos*; from *1* (as a neg. particle) and a der. of a compound of *1223* and *3007*; *unintermitted*, i.e. *permanent*:—without ceasing, continual.

89. ἀδιαλείπτως **adialĕiptōs**, *ad-ee-al-ipe'-toce*; adv. from *88*; *uninterruptedly*, i.e. *without omission* (on an appropriate occasion):—without ceasing.

90. ἀδιαφθορία **adiaphthŏria**, *ad-ee-af-thor-ee'-ah*; from a der. of a compound of *1* (as a neg. particle) and a der. of *1311*; *incorruptibleness*, i.e. (fig.) *purity* (of doctrine):—uncorruptness.

91. ἀδικέω **adikĕō**, *ad-ee-keh'-o*; from *94*; to *be unjust*, i.e. (act.) *do wrong* (mor., socially or phys.):—hurt, injure, be an offender, be unjust, (do, suffer, take) wrong.

92. ἀδίκημα **adikēma**, *ad-eek'-ay-mah*; from *91*; a *wrong* done:—evil doing, iniquity, matter of wrong.

93. ἀδικία **adikia**, *ad-ee-kee'-ah*; from *94*; (legal) *injustice* (prop. the quality, by impl. the act); mor. *wrongfulness* (of character, life or act):—iniquity, unjust, unrighteousness, wrong.

94. ἄδικος **adikŏs**, *ad'-ee-kos*; from *1* (as a neg. particle) and *1349*; *unjust*; by extens. *wicked*; by impl. *treacherous*; spec. *heathen*:—unjust, unrighteous.

95. ἀδίκως **adikōs**, *ad-ee'-koce*; adv. from *94*; *unjustly*:—wrongfully.

96. ἀδόκιμος **adŏkimŏs**, *ad-ok'-ee-mos*; from *1* (as a neg. particle) and *1384*; *unapproved*, i.e. *rejected*; by impl. *worthless* (lit. or mor.):—castaway, rejected, reprobate.

97. ἄδολος **adŏlŏs**, *ad'-ol-os*; from *1* (as a neg. particle) and *1388*; *undeceitful*, i.e. (fig.) *unadulterated*:—sincere.

98. Ἀδραμυττηνός **Adramuttēnŏs**, *ad-ram-oot-tay-nos'*; from Ἀδραμύττειον **Adramuttĕiŏn** (a place in Asia Minor); *Adramyttene* or belonging to Adramyttium:—of Adramyttium.

99. Ἀδρίας **Adrias**, *ad-ree'-as*; from Ἀδρία **Adria** (a place near its shore); the *Adriatic* sea (including the Ionian):—Adria.

100. ἁδρότης **hadrŏtēs**, *had-rot'-ace*; from ἁδρός **hadrŏs** (*stout*); *plumpness*, i.e. (fig.) *liberality*:—abundance.

101. ἀδυνατέω **adunatĕō**, *ad-oo-nat-eh'-o*; from *102*; to *be unable*, i.e. (pass.) *impossible*:—be impossible.

102. ἀδύνατος **adunatŏs**, *ad-oo'-nat-os*; from *1* (as a neg. particle) and *1415*; *unable*, i.e. *weak* (lit. or fig.); pass. *impossible*:—could not do, impossible, impotent, not possible, weak.

103. ᾄδω **aidō**, *ad'-o*; a prim. verb; to *sing*:—sing.

104. ἀεί **aĕi**, *ah-eye'*; from an obs. prim. noun (appar. mean. continued *duration*); "*ever*;" by qualification *regularly*; by impl. *earnestly*:—always, ever.

105. ἀετός **aĕtŏs**, *ah-et-os'*; from the same as *109*; an *eagle* (from its *wind*-like flight):—eagle.

106. ἄζυμος **azumŏs**, *ad'-zoo-mos*; from *1* (as a neg. particle) and *2219*; *unleavened*, i.e. (fig.) *uncorrupted*; (in the neut. plur.) spec. (by impl.) the *Passover* week:—unleavened (bread).

107. Ἀζώρ **Azōr**, *ad-zore'*; of Heb. or. [comp. 5809]; *Azor*, an Isr.:—Azor.

108. Ἄζωτος **Azōtŏs**, *ad'-zo-tos*; of Heb. or. [795]; *Azotus* (i.e. Ashdod), a place in Pal.:—Azotus.

109. ἀήρ **aēr**, *ah-ayr'*; from ἄημι **aēmi** (to *breathe* unconsciously, i.e. *respire*; by anal. to *blow*); "*air*" (as naturally *circumambient*):—air. Comp. *5594*.

ἀθά **atha**. See *3134*.

110. ἀθανασία **athanasia**, *ath-an-as-ee'-ah*; from a compound of *1* (as a neg. particle) and *2288*; *deathlessness*:—immortality.

111. ἀθέμιτος **athĕmitŏs**, *ath-em'-ee-tos*; from *1* (as a neg. particle) and a der. of θέμις **thĕmis** (*statute*; from the base of *5087*); *illegal*; by impl. *flagitious*:—abominable, unlawful thing.

112. ἄθεος **athĕŏs**, *ath'-eh-os*; from *1* (as a neg. particle) and *2316*; *godless*:—without God.

113. ἄθεσμος **athĕsmŏs**, *ath'-es-mos*; from *1* (as a neg. particle) and a der. of *5087* (in the sense of *enacting*); *lawless*, i.e. (by impl.) *criminal*:—wicked.

114. ἀθετέω **athĕtĕō**, *ath-et-eh'-o*; from a compound of *1* (as a neg. particle) and a der. of *5087*; to *set aside*, i.e. (by impl.) to *disesteem*, *neutralize* or *violate*:—cast off, despise, disannul, frustrate, bring to nought, reject.

115. ἀθέτησις **athĕtēsis**, *ath-et'-ay-sis*; from *114*; *cancellation* (lit. or fig.):—disannulling, put away.

116. Ἀθῆναι **Athēnai**, *ath-ay'-nahee*; plur. of Ἀθήνη **Athēnē** (the goddess of wisdom, who was reputed to have founded the city); *Athenæ*, the capital of Greece:—Athens.

117. Ἀθηναῖος **Athēnaiŏs**, *ath-ay-nah'-yos*; from *116*; an *Athenæan* or inhab. of Athenæ:—Athenian.

118. ἀθλέω **athlĕō**, *ath-leh'-o*; from ἆθλος **athlŏs** (a *contest* in the public lists); to *contend* in the competitive games:—strive.

119. ἄθλησις **athlēsis**, *ath'-lay-sis*; from *118*; a *struggle* (fig.):—fight.

120. ἀθυμέω **athumĕō**, *ath-oo-meh'-o*; from a comp. of *1* (as a neg. particle) and *2372*; to *be spiritless*, i.e. *disheartened*:—be dismayed.

121. ἀθῶος **athōŏs**, *ath'-o-os*; from *1* (as a neg. particle) and a prob. der. of *5087* (mean. a *penalty*); *not guilty*:—innocent.

122. αἴγειος **aigĕiŏs**, *ah'-ee-ghi-os*; from αἴξ **aix** (a *goat*); belonging to a *goat*:—goat.

123. αἰγιαλός **aigialŏs**, *ahee-ghee-al-os'*; from ἀΐσσω **aïssō** (to *rush*) and *251* (in the sense of the *sea*); a *beach* (on which the *waves dash*):—shore.

124. Αἰγύπτιος **Aiguptiŏs**, *ahee-goop'-tee-os*; from *125*; an *Ægyptian* or inhab. of Ægyptus:—Egyptian.

125. Αἴγυπτος **Aiguptŏs**, *ah'ee-goop-tos*; of uncert. der.; *Ægyptus*, the land of the Nile:—Egypt.

126. ἀΐδιος **aïdiŏs**, *ah-id'-ee-os*; from *104*; *everduring* (forward and backward, or forward only):—eternal, everlasting.

127. αἰδώς **aidōs**, *ahee-doce'*; perh. from *1* (as a neg. particle) and *1492* (through the idea of *downcast* eyes); *bashfulness*, i.e. (towards men), *modesty* or (towards God) *awe*:—reverence, shamefacedness.

128. Αἰθίοψ **Aithiŏps**, *ahee-thee'-ops*; from αἴθω **aithō** (to *scorch*) and ὤψ **ōps** (the *face*, from *3700*); an *Æthiopian* (as a *blackamoor*):—Ethiopian.

129. αἷμα **haima**, *hah'ee-mah*; of uncert. der.; *blood*, lit. (of men or animals), fig. (the *juice* of grapes) or spec. (the atoning *blood* of Christ); by impl. *bloodshed*, also *kindred*:—blood.

130. αἱματεκχυσία **haimatĕkchusia**, *hahee-mat-ek-khoo-see'-ah*; from *129* and a der. of *1632*; an *effusion of blood*:—shedding of blood.

131. αἱμοῤῥέω **haimŏrrhĕō**, *hahee-mor-hreh'-o*; from *129* and *4482*; to *flow blood*, i.e. *have a hæmorrhage*:—diseased with an issue of blood.

132. Αἰνέας **Ainĕas**, *ahee-neh'-as*; of uncert. der.; *Ænĕas*, an Isr.:—Æneas.

133. αἴνεσις **ainĕsis**, *ah'ee-nes-is*; from *134*; a *praising* (the act), i.e. (spec.) a *thank* (-offering):—praise.

134. αἰνέω **ainĕō**, *ahee-neh'-o*; from *136*; to *praise* (God):—praise.

135. αἴνιγμα **ainigma**, *ah'ee-nig-ma*; from a der. of *136* (in its prim. sense); an *obscure* saying ("enigma"), i.e. (abstr.) *obscureness*:— × darkly.

136. αἶνος **ainŏs**, *ah'ee-nos*; appar. a prim. word; prop. a *story*, but used in the sense of *1868*; *praise* (of God):—praise.

137. Αἰνών **Ainōn**, *ahee-nohn'*; of Hebr. or. [a der. of 5869, *place of springs*]; *Ænon*, a place in Pal.:—Ænon.

138. αἱρέομαι **hairĕŏmai**, *hahee-reh'-om-ahee*; prob. akin to *142*; to *take for oneself*, i.e. to *prefer*:—choose. Some of the forms are borrowed from a cognate ἕλλομαι **hellŏmai**, *hel'-lom-ahee*; which is otherwise obsolete.

139. αἵρεσις **hairĕsis**, *hah'ee-res-is*; from *138*; prop. a *choice*, i.e. (spec.) a *party* or (abstr.) *disunion*:—heresy [*which is the Gr. word itself*], sect.

140. αἱρετίζω **hairĕtizō**, *hahee-ret-id'-zo*; from a der. of *138*; to *make a choice*:—choose.

141. αἱρετικός **hairĕtikŏs**, *hahee-ret-ee-kos'*; from the same as *140*; a *schismatic*:—heretic [*the Gr. word itself*].

142. αἴρω **airō**, *ah'ee-ro*; a prim. verb; to *lift*; by impl. to *take up* or *away*; fig. to *raise* (the voice), *keep in suspense* (the mind); spec. to *sail* away (i.e. *weigh anchor*); by Heb. [comp. 5375] to *expiate* sin:—away with, bear (up), carry, lift up, loose, make to doubt, put away, remove, take (away, up).

143. αἰσθάνομαι **aisthanŏmai**, *ahee-sthan'-om-ahee*; of uncert. der.; to *apprehend* (prop. by the senses):—perceive.

144. αἴσθησις **aisthēsis**, *ah'ee-sthay-sis*; from *143*; *perception*, i.e. (fig.) *discernment*:—judgment.

145. αἰσθητήριον **aisthētēriŏn**, *ahee-sthay-tay'-ree-on*; from a der. of *143*; prop. an *organ of perception*, i.e. (fig.) *judgment*:—senses.

146. αἰσχροκερδής **aischrŏkĕrdēs**, *ahee-skhrok-er-dace'*; from *150* and κέρδος **kerdos** (*gain*); *sordid*:—given to (greedy of) filthy lucre.

147. αἰσχροκερδῶς **aischrŏkĕrdōs**, *ahee-skhrok-er-doce'*; adv. from *146*; *sordidly*:—for filthy lucre's sake.

148. αἰσχρολογία **aischrŏlŏgia**, *ahee-skhrol-og-ee'-ah*; from *150* and *3056*; *vile conversation*:—filthy communication.

149. αἰσχρόν **aischrŏn**, *ahee-skhron'*; neut. of *150*; a *shameful* thing, i.e. *indecorum*:—shame.

150. **αἰσχρός aischrŏs**, *ahee-skhros'*; from the same as *153*; *shameful*, i.e. *base* (spec. *venal*):—filthy.

151. **αἰσχρότης aischrŏtēs**, *ahee-skhrot'-ace*; from *150*; *shamefulness*, i.e. *obscenity*:—filthiness.

152. **αἰσχύνη aischunē**, *ahee-skhoo'-nay*; from *153*; *shame* or *disgrace* (abstr. or concr.):—dishonesty, shame.

153. **αἰσχύνομαι aischunŏmai**, *ahee-skhoo'-nom-ahee*; from **αἶσχος aischŏs** (*disfigurement*, i.e.*disgrace*); to *feel shame* (for oneself):—be ashamed.

154. **αἰτέω aitĕō**, *ahee-teh'-o*; of uncert. der.; to *ask* (in gen.):—ask, beg, call for, crave, desire, require. Comp. *4441*.

155. **αἴτημα aitēma**, *ah'ee-tay-mah*; from *154*; a *thing asked* or (abstr.) an *asking*:—petition, request, required.

156. **αἰτία aitia**, *ahee-tee'-a*; from the same as *154*; a *cause* (as if *asked* for), i.e. (logical) *reason* (motive, matter), (legal) *crime* (alleged or proved):—accusation, case, cause, crime, fault, [wh-]ere [-fore].

157. **αἰτίαμα aitiama**, *ahee-tee'-am-ah*; from a der. of *156*; a *thing charged*:—complaint.

158. **αἴτιον aitiŏn**, *ah'ee-tee-on*; neut. of *159*; a *reason* or *crime* [like *156*]:—cause, fault.

159. **αἴτιος aitiŏs**, *ah'ee-tee-os*; from the same as *154*; *causative*, i.e. (concr.) a *causer*:—author.

160. **αἰφνίδιος aiphnidiŏs**, *aheef-nid'-ee-os*; from a comp. of *1* (as a neg. particle) and *5316* [comp. *1810*] (mean. *non-apparent*); *unexpected*, i.e. (adv.) *suddenly*:—sudden, unawares.

161. **αἰχμαλωσία aichmalōsia**, *aheekh-mal-o-see'-ah*; from *164*; *captivity*:—captivity.

162. **αἰχμαλωτεύω aichmalōtĕuō**, *aheekh-mal-o-tew'-o*; from *164*; to *capture* [like *163*]:—lead captive.

163. **αἰχμαλωτίζω aichmalōtizō**, *aheekh-mal-o-tid'-zo*; from *164*: to *make captive*:—lead away captive, bring into captivity.

164. **αἰχμαλωτός aichmalōtŏs**, *aheekh-mal-o-tos'*; from **αἰχμή aichmē** (a *spear*) and a der. of the same as *259*; prop. a *prisoner of war*, i.e. (gen.) a *captive*:—captive.

165. **αἰών aiōn**, *ahee-ohn'*; from the same as *104*; prop. an *age*; by extens. *perpetuity* (also past); by impl. the *world*; spec. (Jewish) a Messianic period (present or future):—age, course, eternal, (for) ever (-more), [n-]ever, (beginning of the, while the) world (began, without end). Comp. *5550*.

166. **αἰώνιος aiōniŏs**, *ahee-o'-nee-os*; from *165*; *perpetual* (also used of past time, or past and future as well):—eternal, for ever, everlasting, world (began).

167. **ἀκαθαρσία akatharsia**, *ak-ath-ar-see'-ah*; from *169*; *impurity* (the quality), phys. or mor.:—uncleanness.

168. **ἀκαθάρτης akathartēs**, *ak-ath-ar'-tace*; from *169*; *impurity* (the state), mor.:—filthiness.

169. **ἀκάθαρτος akathartŏs**, *ak-ath'-ar-tos*; from *1* (as a neg. particle) and a presumed der. of *2508* (mean. *cleansed*); *impure* (cer., mor. [*lewd*] or spec. [*dæmonic*]):—foul, unclean.

170. **ἀκαιρέομαι akairĕŏmai**, *ak-ahee-reh'-om-ahee*; from a comp. of *1* (as a neg. particle) and *2540* (mean. *unseasonable*); to *be inopportune* (for oneself), i.e. to *fail of a proper occasion*:—lack opportunity.

171. **ἀκαίρως akairōs**, *ak-ah'ee-roce*; adv. from the same as *170*; *inopportunely*:—out of season.

172. **ἄκακος akakŏs**, *ak'-ak-os*; from *1* (as a neg. particle) and *2556*; *not bad*, i.e. (obj.) *innocent* or (subj.) *unsuspecting*:—harmless, simple.

173. **ἄκανθα akantha**, *ak'-an-thah*; prob. from the same as *188*; a *thorn*:—thorn.

174. **ἀκάνθινος akanthinŏs**, *ak-an'-thee-nos*; from *173*; *thorny*:—of thorns.

175. **ἄκαρπος akarpŏs**, *ak'-ar-pos*; from *1* (as a neg. particle) and *2590*; *barren* (lit. or fig.):—without fruit, unfruitful.

176. **ἀκατάγνωστος akatagnōstŏs**, *ak-at-ag'-noce-tos*; from *1* (as a neg. particle) and a der. of *2607*; *unblamable*:—that cannot be condemned.

177. **ἀκατακάλυπτος akatakaluptŏs**, *ak-at-ak-al'-oop-tos*; from *1* (as a neg. particle) and a der. of a comp. of *2596* and *2572*; *unveiled*:—uncovered.

178. **ἀκατάκριτος akatakritŏs**, *ak-at-ak'-ree-tos*; from *1* (as a neg. particle) and a der. of *2632*; *without* (legal) *trial*:—uncondemned.

179. **ἀκατάλυτος akatalutŏs**, *ak-at-al'-oo-tos*; from *1* (as a neg. particle) and a der. of *2647*; *indissoluble*, i.e. (fig.) *permanent*:—endless.

180. **ἀκατάπαυστος akatapaustŏs**, *ak-at-ap'-ŏw-stos*; from *1* (as a neg. particle) and a der. of *2664*; *unrefraining*:—that cannot cease.

181. **ἀκαταστασία akatastasia**, *ak-at-as-tah-see'-ah*; from *182*; *instability*, i.e. *disorder*:—commotion, confusion, tumult.

182. **ἀκατάστατος akatastatŏs**, *ak-at-as'-tat-os*; from *1* (as a neg. particle) and a der. of *2525*; *inconstant*:—unstable.

183. **ἀκατάσχετος akataschĕtŏs**, *ak-at-as'-khet-os*; from *1* (as a neg. particle) and a der. of *2722*; *unrestrainable*:—unruly.

184. **Ἀκελδαμά Akeldama**, *ak-el-dam-ah'*; of Chald. or. [mean. *field of blood*; corresp. to 2506 and 1818]; *Akeldama*, a place near Jerus.:—Aceldama.

185. **ἀκέραιος akĕraiŏs**, *ak-er'-ah-yos*; from *1* (as a neg. particle) and a presumed der. of *2767*; *unmixed*, i.e. (fig.) *innocent*:—harmless, simple.

186. **ἀκλινής aklinēs**, *ak-lee-nace'*; from *1* (as a neg. particle) and *2827*; *not leaning*, i.e. (fig.) *firm*:—without wavering.

187. **ἀκμάζω akmazō**, *ak-mad'-zo*; from the same as *188*; to *make a point*, i.e. (fig.) *mature*:—be fully ripe.

188. **ἀκμήν akmēn**, *ak-mane'*; accus. of a noun ("*acme*") akin to **ἀκή akē** (a *point*) and mean. the same; adv. *just* now, i.e. *still*:—yet.

189. **ἀκοή akŏē**, *ak-ŏ-ay'*; from *191*; *hearing* (the act, the sense or the thing heard):—audience, ear, fame, which ye heard, hearing, preached, report, rumor.

190. **ἀκολουθέω akŏlŏuthĕō**, *ak-ol-oo-theh'-o*; from *1* (as a particle of union) and **κέλευθος kĕlĕuthŏs** (a *road*); prop. to *be in the same way with*, i.e. to *accompany* (spec. as a disciple):—follow, reach.

191. **ἀκούω akŏuō**, *ak-oo'-o*; a prim. verb; to *hear* (in various senses):—give (in the) audience (of), come (to the ears), ([shall]) hear (-er, -ken), be noised, be reported, understand.

192. **ἀκρασία akrasia**, *ak-ras-ee'-a*; from *193*; *want of self-restraint*:—excess, incontinency.

193. **ἀκράτης akratēs**, *ak-rat'-ace*; from *1* (as a neg. particle) and *2904*; *powerless*, i.e. *without self-control*:—incontinent.

194. **ἄκρατος akratŏs**, *ak'-rat-os*; from *1* (as a neg. particle) and a presumed der. of *2767*; *undiluted*:—without mixture.

195. **ἀκρίβεια akribĕia**, *ak-ree'-bi-ah*; from the same as *196*; *exactness*:—perfect manner.

196. **ἀκριβέστατος akribĕstatŏs**, *ak-ree-bes'-ta-tos*; superlative of **ἀκριβής akribēs** (a der. of the same as *206*); *most exact*:—most straitest.

197. **ἀκριβέστερον akribĕstĕrŏn**, *ak-ree-bes'-ter-on*; neut. of the comparative of the same as *196*; (adv.) *more exactly*:—more perfect (-ly).

198. **ἀκριβόω akribŏō**, *ak-ree-bŏ'-o*; from the same as *196*; to *be exact*, i.e. *ascertain*:—enquire diligently.

199. **ἀκριβῶς akribōs**, *ak-ree-boce'*; adv. from the same as *196*; *exactly*:—circumspectly, diligently, perfect (-ly).

200. **ἀκρίς akris**, *ak-rece'*; appar. from the same as *206*; a *locust* (as *pointed*, or as *lighting* on the *top* of vegetation):—locust.

201. **ἀκροατήριον akrŏateriŏn**, *ak-rŏ-at-ay'-ree-on*; from *202*; an *audience-room*:—place of hearing.

202. **ἀκροατής akrŏatēs**, *ak-rŏ-at-ace'*; from **ἀκροάομαι akrŏaŏmai** (to *listen*; appar. an intens. of *191*); a *hearer* (merely):—hearer.

203. **ἀκροβυστία akrŏbustia**, *ak-rob-oos-tee'-ah*; from *206* and prob. a modified form of **πόσθη pŏsthē** (the *penis* or male sexual organ); the *prepuce*; by impl. an *uncircumcised* (i.e. *gentile*, fig. *unregenerate*) state or person:—not circumcised, uncircumcised [*with 2192*], uncircumcision.

204. **ἀκρογωνιαῖος akrŏgōniaiŏs**, *ak-rog-o-nee-ah'-yos*; from *206* and *1137*; belonging to the extreme *corner*:—chief corner.

205. **ἀκροθίνιον akrŏthiniŏn**, *ak-roth-in'-ee-on*; from *206* and **θίς this** (a *heap*); prop. (in the plur.) the *top of the heap*, i.e. (by impl.) *best of the booty*:—spoils.

206. **ἄκρον akrŏn**, *ak'-ron*; neut. of an adj. prob. akin to the base of *188*; the *extremity*:—one end . . . other, tip, top, uttermost part.

207. **Ἀκύλας Akulas**, *ak-oo'-las*; prob. for Lat. *aquĭla* (an *eagle*); *Akulas*, an Isr.:—Aquila.

208. **ἀκυρόω akurŏō**, *ak-oo-rŏ'-o*; from *1* (as a neg. particle) and *2964*; to *invalidate*:—disannul, make of none effect.

209. **ἀκωλύτως akōlutōs**, *ak-o-loo'-toce*; adv. from a compound of *1* (as a neg. particle) and a der. of *2967*; in *an unhindered manner*, i.e. *freely*:—no man forbidding him.

210. **ἄκων akōn**, *ak'-ohn*; from *1* (as a neg. particle) and *1635*; *unwilling*:—against the will.

211. **ἀλάβαστρον alabastrŏn**, *al-ab'-as-tron*; neut. of **ἀλάβαστρος alabastrŏs** (of uncert. der.), the name of a stone; prop. an "*alabaster*" box, i.e. (by extens.) a perfume *vase* (of any material):—(alabaster) box.

212. **ἀλαζονεία alazŏnĕia**, *al-ad-zon-i'-a*; from *213*; *braggadocio*, i.e. (by impl.) *self-confidence*:—boasting, pride.

213. **ἀλαζών alazōn**, *al-ad-zone'*; from **ἄλη alē** (*vagrancy*); *braggart*:—boaster.

214. **ἀλαλάζω alalazō**, *al-al-ad'-zo*; from **ἀλαλή alalē** (a *shout*, "*halloo*"); to *vociferate*, i.e. (by impl.) to *wail*; fig. to *clang*:—tinkle, wail.

215. **ἀλάλητος alalētŏs**, *al-al'-ay-tos*; from *1* (as a neg. particle) and a der. of *2980*; *unspeakable*:—unutterable, which cannot be uttered.

216. **ἄλαλος alalŏs**, *al'-al-os*; from *1* (as a neg. particle) and *2980*; *mute*:—dumb.

217. **ἅλας halas**, *hal'-as*; from *251*; *salt*; fig. *prudence*:—salt.

218. **ἀλείφω alĕiphō**, *al-i'-fo*; from *1* (as particle of union) and the base of *3045*; to *oil* (with perfume):—anoint.

219. **ἀλεκτοροφωνία alektŏrŏphōnia**, *al-ek-tor-of-o-nee'-ah*; from *220* and *5456*; *cock-crow*, i.e. the third night-watch:—cockcrowing.

220. **ἀλέκτωρ alĕktōr**, *al-ek'-tore*; from **ἀλέκω** (to *ward off*); a *cock* or male fowl:—cock.

221. **Ἀλεξανδρεύς Alĕxandrĕus**, *al-ex-and-reuce'*; from **Ἀλεξάνδρεια** (the city so called); an *Alexandreian* or inhab. of Alexandria:—of Alexandria, Alexandrian.

222. **Ἀλεξανδρῖνος Alĕxandrinŏs**, *al-ex-an-dree'-nos*; from the same as 221; *Alexandrine*, or belonging to Alexandria:—of Alexandria.

223. **Ἀλέξανδρος Alĕxandrŏs**, *al-ex'-an-dros*; from the same as (the first part of) *220* and *435*; *man-defender*; *Alexander*, the name of three Isr. and one other man:—Alexander.

224. **ἄλευρον alĕurŏn**, *al'-yoo-ron*; from **ἀλέω alĕō** (to *grind*); *flour*:—meal.

225. **ἀλήθεια alēthĕia**, *al-ay'-thi-a*; from *227*; *truth*:—true, × truly, truth, verity.

226. **ἀληθεύω alēthĕuō**, *al-ayth-yoo'-o*; from *227*; to *be true* (in doctrine and profession):—speak (tell) the truth.

227. **ἀληθής alēthēs**, *al-ay-thace'*; from *1* (as a neg. particle) and *2990*; *true* (as *not concealing*):—true, truly, truth.

228. ἀληθινός **alēthinŏs**, *al-ay-thee-nos';* from 227; *truthful:*—true.

229. ἀλήθω **alēthō**, *al-ay'-tho;* from the same as 224; to *grind:*—grind.

230. ἀληθῶς **alēthōs**, *al-ay-thoce';* adv. from 227; *truly:*—indeed, surely, of a surety, truly, of a (in) truth, verily, very.

231. ἁλιεύς **haliĕus**, *hal-ee-yoos';* from 251; a *sailor* (as engaged on the *salt* water), i.e. (by impl.) a *fisher:*—fisher (-man).

232. ἁλιεύω **haliĕuō**, *hal-ee-yoo'-o;* from 231; to *be a fisher*, i.e. (by impl.) to *fish:*—go a-fishing.

233. ἁλίζω **halizō**, *hal-id'-zo;* from 251; to *salt:*—salt.

234. ἀλίσγεμα **alisgĕma**, *al-is'-ghem-ah;* from ἀλισγέω **alisgĕō** (to *soil*); (cer.) *defilement:*—pollution.

235. ἀλλά **alla**, *al-lah';* neut. plur. of 243; prop. *other* things, i.e. (adv.) *contrariwise* (in many relations):—and, but (even), howbeit, indeed, nay, nevertheless, no, notwithstanding, save, therefore, yea, yet.

236. ἀλλάσσω **allassō**, *al-las'-so;* from 243; to *make different:*—change.

237. ἀλλαχόθεν **allachŏthĕn**, *al-lakh-oth'-en;* from 243; *from elsewhere:*—some other way.

238. ἀλληγορέω **allēgŏrĕō**, *al-lay-gor-eh'-o;* from 243 and ἀγορέω **agŏrĕō** (to *harangue* [comp. 58]); to *allegorize:*—be an allegory [*the Gr. word itself*].

239. ἀλληλουϊα **allēlŏuïa**, *al-lay-loo'-ee-ah;* of Heb. or. [imper. of 1984 and 3050]; *praise ye Jah!*, an adoring exclamation:—alleluiah.

240. ἀλλήλων **allēlōn**, *al-lay'-lone;* Gen. plur. from 243 redupl.; *one another:*—each other, mutual, one another, (the other), (them-, your-) selves, (selves) together [*sometimes with 3326 or 4314*].

241. ἀλλογενής **allŏgĕnēs**, *al-log-en-ace';* from 243 and 1085; *foreign*, i.e. not a Jew:—stranger.

242. ἅλλομαι **hallŏmai**, *hal'-lom-ahee;* mid. of appar. a prim. verb; to *jump;* fig. to *gush:*—leap, spring up.

243. ἄλλος **allŏs**, *al'-los;* a prim. word; "*else*," i.e. *different* (in many applications):—more, one (another), (an-, some an-) other (-s, -wise).

244. ἀλλοτριεπίσκοπος **allotriĕpiskŏpŏs**, *al-lot-ree-ep-is'-kop-os;* from 245 and 1985; *overseeing others'* affairs, i.e. a *meddler* (spec. in Gentile customs):—busybody in other men's matters.

245. ἀλλότριος **allŏtriŏs**, *al-lot'-ree-os;* from 243; *another's*, i.e. not one's own; by extens. *foreign, not akin, hostile:*—alien, (an-) other (man's, men's), strange (-r).

246. ἀλλόφυλος **allŏphulŏs**, *al-lof'-oo-los;* from 243 and 5443; *foreign*, i.e. (spec.) *Gentile:*—one of another nation.

247. ἄλλως **allōs**, *al'-loce;* adv. from 243; *differently:*—otherwise.

248. ἀλοάω **alŏaō**, *al-o-ah'-o;* from the same as 257; to *tread* out grain:—thresh, tread out the corn.

249. ἄλογος **alŏgŏs**, *al'-og-os;* from 1 (as a neg. particle) and 3056; *irrational:*—brute, unreasonable.

250. ἀλοή **alŏē**, *al-ŏ-ay';* of for. or. [comp. 174]; *aloes* (the gum):—aloes.

251. ἅλς **hals**, *halce;* a prim. word; "*salt*":—salt.

252. ἁλυκός **halukŏs**, *hal-oo-kos';* from 251; *briny:*—salt.

253. ἀλυπότερος **alupŏtĕrŏs**, *al-oo-pot'-er-os;* compar. of a comp. of 1 (as a neg. particle) and 3077; *more without grief:*—less sorrowful.

254. ἅλυσις **halusis**, *hal'-oo-sis;* of uncert. der.; a *fetter* or *manacle:*—bonds, chain.

255. ἀλυσιτελής **alusitĕlēs**, *al-oo-sit-el-ace';* from 1 (as a neg. particle) and the base of 3081; *gainless*, i.e. (by impl.) *pernicious:*—unprofitable.

256. Ἀλφαῖος **Alphaiŏs**, *al-fah'-yos;* of Heb. or. [comp. 2501]; *Alphœus*, an Isr.:—Alpheus.

257. ἅλων **halōn**, *hal'-ohn;* prob. from the base of 1507; a threshing-*floor* (as *rolled* hard), i.e. (fig.) the *grain* (and chaff, as just threshed):—floor.

258. ἀλώπηξ **alōpĕx**, *al-o'-pakes;* of uncert. der.; a *fox*, i.e. (fig.) a *cunning* person:—fox.

259. ἅλωσις **halōsis**, *hal'-o-sis;* from a collateral form of 138; *capture:*—be taken.

260. ἅμα **hama**, *ham'-ah;* a prim. particle; prop. *at the "same" time*, but freely used as a prep. or adv. denoting close association:—also, and, together, with (-al).

261. ἀμαθής **amathēs**, *am-ath-ace';* from 1 (as a neg. particle) and 3129; *ignorant:*—unlearned.

262. ἀμαράντινος **amarantinŏs**, *am-ar-an'-tee-nos;* from 263; "*amaranthine*", i.e. (by impl.) *fadeless:*—that fadeth not away.

263. ἀμάραντος **amarantŏs**, *am-ar'-an-tos;* from 1 (as a neg. particle) and a presumed der. of 3133; *unfading*, i.e. (by impl.) *perpetual:*—that fadeth not away.

264. ἁμαρτάνω **hamartanō**, *ham-ar-tan'-o;* perh. from 1 (as a neg. particle) and the base of 3313; prop. to *miss* the mark (and so *not share* in the prize), i.e. (fig.) to *err*, esp. (mor.) to *sin.*—for your faults, offend, sin, trespass.

265. ἁμάρτημα **hamartēma**, *ham-ar'-tay-mah;* from 264; a *sin* (prop. concr.):—sin.

266. ἁμαρτία **hamartia**, *ham-ar-tee'-ah;* from 264; *sin* (prop. abstr.):—offence, sin (-ful).

267. ἀμάρτυρος **amarturŏs**, *am-ar'-too-ros;* from 1 (as a neg. particle) and a form of 3144; *unattested:*—without witness.

268. ἁμαρτωλός **hamartōlŏs**, *ham-ar-to-los';* from 264; *sinful*, i.e. a *sinner:*—sinful, sinner.

269. ἄμαχος **amachŏs**, *am'-akh-os;* from 1 (as a neg. particle) and 3163; *peaceable:*—not a brawler.

270. ἀμάω **amaō**, *am-ah'-o;* from 260; prop. to *collect*, i.e. (by impl.) *reap:*—reap down.

271. ἀμέθυστος **amĕthustŏs**, *am-eth'-oos-tos;* from 1 (as a neg. particle) and a der. of 3184; the "*amethyst*" (supposed to *prevent intoxication*):—amethyst.

272. ἀμελέω **amĕlĕō**, *am-el-eh'-o;* from 1 (as a neg. particle) and 3199; to *be careless* of:—make light of, neglect, be negligent, not regard.

273. ἄμεμπτος **amĕmptŏs**, *am'-emp-tos;* from 1 (as a neg. particle) and a der. of 3201; *irreproachable:*—blameless, faultless, unblamable.

274. ἀμέμπτως **amĕmptōs**, *am-emp'-toce;* adv. from 273; *faultlessly:*—blameless, unblamably.

275. ἀμέριμνος **amĕrimnŏs**, *am-er'-im-nos;* from 1 (as a neg. particle) and 3308; *not anxious:*—without care (-fulness), secure.

276. ἀμετάθετος **amĕtathĕtŏs**, *am-et-ath'-et-os;* from 1 (as a neg. particle) and a der. of 3346; *unchangeable*, or (neut. as abstr.) *unchangeability:*—immutable (-ility).

277. ἀμετακίνητος **amĕtakinētŏs**, *am-et-ak-in'-ay-tos;* from 1 (as a neg. particle) and a der. of 3334; *immovable:*—unmovable.

278. ἀμεταμέλητος **amĕtamĕlētŏs**, *am-et-am-el'-ay-tos;* from 1 (as a neg. particle) and a presumed der. of 3338; *irrevocable:*—without repentance, not to be repented of.

279. ἀμετανόητος **amĕtanŏētŏs**, *am-et-an-ŏ'-ay-tos;* from 1 (as a neg. particle) and a presumed der. of 3340; *unrepentant:*—impenitent.

280. ἄμετρος **amĕtrŏs**, *am'-et-ros;* from 1 (as a neg. particle) and 3358; *immoderate:*—(thing) without measure.

281. ἀμήν **amēn**, *am-ane';* of Heb. or. [543]; prop. *firm*, i.e. (fig.) *trustworthy;* adv. *surely* (often as interj. *so be it*):—amen, verily.

282. ἀμήτωρ **amētōr**, *am-ay'-tore;* from 1 (as a neg. particle) and 3384; *motherless*, i.e. *of unknown maternity:*—without mother.

283. ἀμίαντος **amiantŏs**, *am-ee'-an-tos;* from 1 (as a neg. particle) and a der. of 3392; *unsoiled*, i.e. (fig.) *pure:*—undefiled.

284. Ἀμιναδάβ **Aminadab**, *am-ee-nad-ab';* of Heb. or. [5992]; *Aminadab*, an Isr.:—Aminadab.

285. ἄμμος **ammŏs**, *am'-mos;* perh. from 260; *sand* (as *heaped* on the beach):—sand.

286. ἀμνός **amnŏs**, *am-nos';* appar. a prim. word; a *lamb:*—lamb.

287. ἀμοιβή **amŏibē**, *am-oy-bay';* from ἀμείβω **amĕibō** (to *exchange*); *requital:*—requite.

288. ἄμπελος **ampĕlŏs**, *am'-pel-os;* prob. from the base of 297 and that of 257; a *vine* (as *coiling about* a support):—vine.

289. ἀμπελουργός **ampĕlŏurgŏs**, *am-pel-oor-gos';* from 288 and 2041; a *vine-worker*, i.e. *pruner:*—vine-dresser.

290. ἀμπελών **ampĕlōn**, *am-pel-ohn';* from 288; a *vineyard:*—vineyard.

291. Ἀμπλίας **Amplias**, *am-plee'-as;* contr. for Lat. *ampliatus* [*enlarged*]; *Amplias*, a Rom. Chr.:—Amplias.

292. ἀμύνομαι **amunŏmai**, *am-oo'-nom-ahee;* mid. of a prim. verb; to *ward off* (for oneself), i.e. *protect:*—defend.

293. ἀμφίβληστρον **amphiblēstrŏn**, *am-fib'-lace-tron;* from a comp. of the base of 297 and 906; a (fishing) *net* (as *thrown about* the fish):—net.

294. ἀμφιέννυμι **amphiĕnnumi**, *am-fee-en'-noo-mee;* from the base of 297 and ἕννυμι **hĕnnumi** (to *invest*); to *enrobe:*—clothe.

295. Ἀμφίπολις **Amphipŏlis**, *am-fip'-ol-is;* from the base of 297 and 4172; a *city surrounded* by a river; *Amphipolis*, a place in Macedonia:—Amphipolis.

296. ἄμφοδον **amphŏdŏn**, *am'-fod-on;* from the base of 297 and 3598; a *fork* in the road:—where two ways meet.

297. ἀμφότερος **amphŏtĕrŏs**, *am-fot'-er-os;* compar. of ἀμφί **amphi** (*around*); (in plur.) *both:*—both.

298. ἀμώμητος **amōmētŏs**, *am-o'-may-tos;* from 1 (as a neg. particle) and a der. of 3469; *unblameable:*—blameless.

299. ἄμωμος **amōmŏs**, *am'-o-mos;* from 1 (as a neg. particle) and 3470; *unblemished* (lit. or fig.):—without blame (blemish, fault, spot), faultless, unblameable.

300. Ἀμών **Amōn**, *am-one';* of Heb. or. [526]; *Amon*, an Isr.:—Amon.

301. Ἀμώς **Amōs**, *am-oce';* of Heb. or. [531]; *Amos*, an Isr.:—Amos.

302. ἄν **an**, *an;* a prim. particle, denoting a *supposition, wish, possibility* or *uncertainty:*—[what-, where-, whither-, who-]soever. Usually unexpressed except by the subjunctive or potential mood. Also contr. for 1437.

303. ἀνά **ana**, *an-ah';* a prim. prep. and adv.; prop. *up;* but (by extens.) used (distributively) *severally*, or (locally) *at* (etc.):—and, apiece, by, each, every (man), in, through. In compounds (as a prefix) it often means (by impl.) *repetition, intensity, reversal*, etc.

304. ἀναβαθμός **anabathmŏs**, *an-ab-ath-mos';* from 305 [comp. 898]; a *stairway:*—stairs.

305. ἀναβαίνω **anabainō**, *an-ab-ah'ee-no;* from 303 and the base of 939; to *go up* (lit. or fig.):—arise, ascend (up), climb (go, grow, rise, spring) up, come (up).

306. ἀναβάλλομαι **anaballŏmai**, *an-ab-al'-lom-ahee;* mid. from 303 and 906; to *put off* (for oneself):—defer.

307. ἀναβιβάζω **anabibazō**, *an-ab-ee-bad'-zo;* from 303 and a der. of the base of 939; to *cause to go up*, i.e. *haul* (a net):—draw.

308. ἀναβλέπω **anablĕpō**, *an-ab-lep'-o;* from 303 and 991: to *look up;* by impl. to *recover sight:*—look (up), see, receive sight.

309. ἀνάβλεψις **anablĕpsis**, *an-ab'-lep-sis;* from 308; *restoration of sight:*—recovering of sight.

310. ἀναβοάω **anabŏaō**, *an-ab-o-ah'-o;* from 303 and 994; to *halloo:*—cry (aloud, out).

311. ἀναβολή **anabŏlē**, *an-ab-ol-ay';* from 306; a *putting off:*—delay.

312. **ἀναγγέλλω anaggĕllō**, *an-ang-el'-lo;* from 303 and the base of 32; to *announce* (in detail):—declare, rehearse, report, show, speak, tell.

313. **ἀναγεννάω anagĕnnaō**, *an-ag-en-nah'-o;* from 303 and 1080; to *beget* or (by extens.) *bear* (again):—beget, (bear) × again.

314. **ἀναγινώσκω anaginōskō**, *an-ag-in-oce'-ko;* from 303 and 1097; to *know again*, i. e. (by extens.) to *read:*—read.

315. **ἀναγκάζω anagkazō**, *an-ang-kad'-zo;* from 318; to *necessitate;*—compel, constrain.

316. **ἀναγκαῖος anagkaiŏs**, *an-ang-kah'-yos;* from 318; *necessary;* by impl. *close* (of kin):—near, necessary, necessity, needful.

317. **ἀναγκαστῶς anagkastŏs**, *an-ang-kas-toce';* adv. from a der. of 315; *compulsorily:*—by constraint.

318. **ἀναγκή anagkē**, *an-ang-kay';* from 303 and the base of 43; *constraint* (lit. or fig.); by impl. *distress:*—distress, must needs, (of) necessity (-sary), needeth, needful.

319. **ἀναγνωρίζομαι anagnōrizŏmai**, *an-ag-no-rid'-zom-ahee;* mid. from 303 and 1107; to *make* (oneself) *known:*—be made known.

320. **ἀνάγνωσις anagnōsis**, *an-ag'-no-sis;* from 314; (the act of) *reading:*—reading.

321. **ἀνάγω anagō**, *an-ag'-o;* from 303 and 71; to *lead up;* by extens. to *bring out;* spec. to *sail* away:—bring (again, forth, up again), depart, launch (forth), lead (up), loose, offer, sail, set forth, take up.

322. **ἀναδείκνυμι anadĕiknumi**, *an-ad-ike'-noo-mee;* from 303 and 1166; to *exhibit*, i.e. (by impl.) to *indicate, appoint:*—appoint, shew.

323. **ἀνάδειξις anadĕixis**, *an-ad'-ike-sis;* from 322; (the act of) *exhibition:*—shewing.

324. **ἀναδέχομαι anadĕchŏmai**, *an-ad-ekh'-om-ahee;* from 303 and 1209; to *entertain* (as a guest):—receive.

325. **ἀναδίδωμι anadidōmi**, *an-ad-eed'-om-ee;* from 303 and 1325; to *hand over:*—deliver.

326. **ἀναζάω anazaō**, *an-ad-zah'-o;* from 303 and 2198; to *recover life* (lit. or fig.):—(be a-) live again, revive.

327. **ἀναζητέω anazētĕō**, *an-ad-zay-teh'-o;* from 303 and 2212; to *search* out:—seek.

328. **ἀναζώννυμι anazōnnumi**, *an-ad-zone'-noo-mee;* from 303 and 2224; to *gird afresh:*—gird up.

329. **ἀναζωπυρέω anazōpurĕō**, *an-ad-zo-poor-eh'-o;* from 303 and a comp. of the base of 2226 and 4442; to *re-enkindle:*—stir up.

330. **ἀναθάλλω anathallō**, *an-ath-al'-lo;* from 303 and **θάλλω thallō** (to *flourish*); to *revive:*—flourish again.

331. **ἀνάθεμα anathĕma**, *an-ath'-em-ah;* from 394; a (religious) *ban* or (concr.) *excommunicated* (thing or person):—accursed, anathema, curse, × great.

332. **ἀναθεματίζω anathĕmatizō**, *an-ath-em-at-id'-zo;* from 331; to *declare* or *vow* under penalty of execration:—(bind under a) curse, bind with an oath.

333. **ἀναθεωρέω anathĕōrĕō**, *an-ath-eh-o-reh'-o;* from 303 and 2334; to *look again* (i.e. *attentively*) at (lit. or fig.):—behold, consider.

334. **ἀνάθημα anathēma**, *an-ath'-ay-mah;* from 394 [like 331, but in a good sense]; a *votive* offering:—gift.

335. **ἀναίδεια anaidĕia**, *an-ah'ee-die-ah';* from a comp. of 1 (as a neg. particle [comp. 427]) and 127; *impudence*, i.e. (by impl.) *importunity:*—importunity.

336. **ἀναίρεσις anairĕsis**, *an-ah'ee-res-is;* from 337; (the act of) *killing:*—death.

337. **ἀναιρέω anairĕō**, *an-ahee-reh'-o;* from 303 and (the act. of) 138; to *take up*, i.e. *adopt;* by impl. to *take away* (violently), i.e. *abolish, murder:*—put to death, kill, slay, take away, take up.

338. **ἀναίτιος anaitiŏs**, *an-ah'ee-tee-os;* from 1 (as a neg. particle) and 159 (in the sense of 156); *innocent:*—blameless, guiltless.

339. **ἀνακαθίζω anakathizō**, *an-ak-ath-id'-zo;* from 303 and 2523; prop. to *set up*, i.e. (reflex.) to *sit up:*—sit up.

340. **ἀνακαινίζω anakainizō**, *an-ak-ahee-nid'-zo;* from 303 and a der. of 2537; to *restore:*—renew.

341. **ἀνακαινόω anakainŏō**, *an-ak-ahee-nŏ'-o;* from 303 and a der. of 2537; to *renovate:*—renew.

342. **ἀνακαίνωσις anakainōsis**, *an-ak-ah'ee-no-sis;* from 341; *renovation:*—renewing.

343. **ἀνακαλύπτω anakaluptō**, *an-ak-al-oop'-to;* from 303 (in the sense of *reversal*) and 2572; to *unveil:*—open, ([un-]) taken away.

344. **ἀνακάμπτω anakamptō**, *an-ak-amp'-to;* from 303 and 2578; to *turn back:*—(re-) turn.

345. **ἀνακεῖμαι anakĕimai**, *an-ak-i'-mahee;* from 303 and 2749; to *recline* (as a corpse or at a meal):—guest, lean, lie, sit (down, at meat), at the table.

346. **ἀνακεφαλαίομαι anakĕphalaiŏmai**, *an-ak-ef-al-ah'ee-om-ahee;* from 303 and 2775 (in its or. sense); to *sum up:*—briefly comprehend, gather together in one.

347. **ἀνακλίνω anaklinō**, *an-ak-lee'-no;* from 303 and 2827; to *lean back:*—lay, (make) sit down.

348. **ἀνακόπτω anakŏptō**, *an-ak-op'-to;* from 303 and 2875; to *beat back*, i.e. *check:*—hinder.

349. **ἀνακράζω anakrazō**, *an-ak-rad'-zo;* from 303 and 2896; to *scream up* (aloud):—cry out.

350. **ἀνακρίνω anakrinō**, *an-ak-ree'-no;* from 303 and 2919; prop. to *scrutinize*, i.e. (by impl.) *investigate, interrogate, determine:*—ask, question, discern, examine, judge, search.

351. **ἀνάκρισις anakrisis**, *an-ak'-ree-sis;* from 350; a (judicial) *investigation:*—examination.

352. **ἀνακύπτω anakuptō**, *an-ak-oop'-to;* from 303 (in the sense of *reversal*) and 2955; to *unbend*, i.e. *rise;* fig. *be elated;*—lift up, look up.

353. **ἀναλαμβάνω analambanō**, *an-al-am-ban'-o;* from 303 and 2983; to *take up:*—receive up, take (in, unto, up).

354. **ἀνάληψις analēpsis**, *an-al'-ape-sis;* from 353; *ascension:*—taking up.

355. **ἀναλίσκω analiskō**, *an-al-is'-ko;* from 303 and a form of the alternate of 138; prop. to *use up*, i.e. *destroy:*—consume.

356. **ἀναλογία analŏgia**, *an-al-og-ee'-ah;* from a comp. of 303 and 3056; *proportion:*—proportion.

357. **ἀναλογίζομαι analŏgizŏmai**, *an-al-og-id'-zom-ahee;* mid. from 356; to *estimate*, i.e. (fig.) *contemplate:*—consider.

358. **ἄναλος analŏs**, *an'-al-os;* from 1 (as a neg. particle) and 251; *saltless*, i.e. *insipid:*— × lose saltness.

359. **ἀνάλυσις analusis**, *an-al'-oo-sis;* from 360; *departure:*—departure.

360. **ἀναλύω analuō**, *an-al-oo'-o;* from 303 and 3089; to *break up*, i.e. *depart* (lit. or fig.):—depart, return.

361. **ἀναμάρτητος anamartētŏs**, *an-am-ar'-tay-tos;* from 1 (as a neg. particle) and a presumed der. of 264; *sinless:*—that is without sin.

362. **ἀναμένω anemĕnō**, *an-am-en'-o;* from 303 and 3306; to *await:*—wait for.

363. **ἀναμιμνήσκω anamimnēskō**, *an-am-im-nace'-ko;* from 303 and 3403; to *remind;* reflex. to *recollect:*—call to mind, (bring to, call to, put in), remember (-brance).

364. **ἀνάμνησις anamnēsis**, *an-am'-nay-sis;* from 363; *recollection:*—*remembrance* (again).

365. **ἀνανεόω ananĕŏō**, *an-an-neh-ŏ'-o;* from 303 and a der. of 3501; to *renovate*, i.e. *reform:*—renew.

366. **ἀνανήφω ananēphō**, *an-an-ay'-fo;* from 303 and 3525; to become *sober again*, i.e. (fig.) *regain* (one's) *senses:*—recover self.

367. **Ἀνανίας Ananias**, *an-an-ee'-as;* of Heb. or. [2608]; *Ananias*, the name of three Isr.:—Ananias.

368. **ἀναντίῤῥητος anantirrhētŏs**, *an-an-tir'-hray-tos;* from 1 (as a neg. particle) and a presumed der. of a comp. of 473 and 4483; *indisputable:*—cannot be spoken against.

369. **ἀναντιῤῥήτως anantirrhētōs**, *an-an-tir-hray'-toce;* adv. from 368; *promptly:*—without gainsaying.

370. **ἀνάξιος anaxiŏs**, *an-ax'-ee-os;* from 1 (as a neg. particle) and 514; *unfit:*—unworthy.

371. **ἀναξίως anaxiōs**, *an-ax-ee'-oce;* adv. from 370; *irreverently:*—unworthily.

372. **ἀνάπαυσις anapausis**, *an-ap'-ŏw-sis;* from 373; *intermission;* by impl. *recreation:*—rest.

373. **ἀναπαύω anapauō**, *an-ap-ŏw'-o;* from 303 and 3973; (reflex.) to *repose* (lit. or fig. [*be exempt*], *remain*); by impl. to *refresh:*—take ease, refresh, (give, take) rest.

374. **ἀναπείθω anapĕithō**, *an-ap-i'-tho;* from 303 and 3982; to *incite;*—persuade.

375. **ἀναπέμπω anapĕmpō**, *an-ap-em'-po;* from 303 and 3992; to *send up* or *back:*—send (again).

376. **ἀνάπηρος anapĕrŏs**, *an-ap'-ay-ros;* from 303 (in the sense of *intensity*) and **πῆρος pērŏs** (*maimed*); *crippled:*—maimed.

377. **ἀναπίπτω anapipto**, *an-ap-ip'-to;* from 303 and 4098; to *fall back*, i.e. *lie down, lean back:*—lean, sit down (to meat).

378. **ἀναπληρόω anaplērŏō**, *an-ap-lay-rŏ'-o;* from 303 and 4137; to *complete;* by impl. to *occupy, supply;* fig. to *accomplish* (by coincidence or obedience):—fill up, fulfil, occupy, supply.

379. **ἀναπολόγητος anapŏlŏgētŏs**, *an-ap-ol-og'-ay-tos;* from 1 (as a neg. particle) and a presumed der. of 626; *indefensible:*—without excuse, inexcuseable.

380. **ἀναπτύσσω anaptussō**, *an-ap-toos'-so;* from 303 (in the sense of *reversal*) and 4428; to *unroll* (a scroll or volume):—open.

381. **ἀνάπτω anaptō**, *an-ap'-to;* from 303 and 681; to *enkindle:*—kindle, light.

382. **ἀναρίθμητος anarithmētŏs**, *an-ar-ith'-may-tos;* from 1 (as a neg. particle) and a der. of 705; *unnumbered*, i.e. *without number:*—innumerable.

383. **ἀνασείω anasĕiō**, *an-as-i'-o;* from 303 and 4579; fig. to *excite:*—move, stir up.

384. **ἀνασκευάζω anaskĕuazō**, *an-ask-yoo-ad'-zo;* from 303 (in the sense of *reversal*) and a der. of 4632; prop. to *pack up* (baggage), i.e. (by impl. and fig.) to *upset:*—subvert.

385. **ἀνασπάω anaspaō**, *an-as-pah'-o;* from 303 and 4685; to *take up* or *extricate:*—draw up, pull out.

386. **ἀνάστασις anastasis**, *an-as'-tas-is;* from 450; a *standing up* again, i.e. (lit.) a *resurrection* from death (individual, gen. or by impl. [its author]), or (fig.) a (moral) *recovery* (of spiritual truth):—raised to life again, resurrection, rise from the dead, that should rise, rising again.

387. **ἀναστατόω anastatŏō**, *an-as-tat-ŏ'-o;* from a der. of 450 (in the sense of *removal*); prop. to *drive out* of home, i.e. (by impl.) to *disturb* (lit. or fig.):—trouble, turn upside down, make an uproar.

388. **ἀνασταυρόω anastaurŏō**, *an-as-tŏw-rŏ'-o;* from 303 and 4717; to *recrucify* (fig.):—crucify afresh.

389. **ἀναστενάζω anastĕnazō**, *an-as-ten-ad'-zo;* from 303 and 4727; to *sigh deeply:*—sigh deeply.

390. **ἀναστρέφω anastrĕphŏ**, *an-as-tref'-o;* from 303 and 4762; to *overturn;* also to *return;* by impl. to *busy* oneself, i.e. *remain, live:*—abide, behave self, have conversation, live, overthrow, pass, return, be used.

391. **ἀναστροφή anastrŏphē**, *an-as-trof-ay';* from 390; *behavior:*—conversation.

392. **ἀνατάσσομαι anatassŏmai**, *an-at-as'-som-ahee;* from 303 and the mid. of 5021; to *arrange:*—set in order.

393. **ἀνατέλλω anatĕllō**, *an-at-el'-lo;* from 303 and the base of 5056; to (*cause to*) *arise:*—(a-, make to) rise, at the rising of, spring (up), be up.

394. **ἀνατίθεμαι anatithĕmai**, *an-at-ith'-em-ahee;* from 303 and the mid. of 5087; to *set forth* (for oneself), i.e. *propound:*—communicate, declare.

395. ἀνατολή **anatŏlē**, *an-at-ol-ay'*; from *303*; a *rising* of light, i.e. *dawn* (fig.); by impl. the *east* (also in plur.):—dayspring, east, rising.

396. ἀνατρέπω **anatrĕpō**, *an-at-rep'-o*; from *303* and the base of *5157*; to *overturn* (fig.):—overthrow, subvert.

397. ἀνατρέφω **anatrĕphō**, *an-at-ref'-o*; from *303* and *5142*; to *rear* (phys. or ment.):—bring up, nourish (up).

398. ἀναφαίνω **anaphainō**, *an-af-ah'ee-no*; from *303* and *5316*; to *show*, i.e. (reflex.) *appear*, or (pass.) *have pointed* out:—(should) appear, discover.

399. ἀναφέρω **anaphĕrō**, *an-af-er'-o*; from *303* and *5342*; to *take up* (lit. or fig.):—bear, bring (carry, lead) up, offer (up).

400. ἀναφωνέω **anaphōnĕō**, *an-af-o-neh'-o*; from *303* and *5455*; to *exclaim*:—speak out.

401. ἀνάχυσις **anachusis**, *an-akh'-oo-sis*; from a comp. of *303* and χέω **chĕō** (to *pour*); prop. *effusion*, i.e. (fig.) *license*:—excess.

402. ἀναχωρέω **anachōrĕō**, *an-akh-o-reh'-o*; from *303* and *5562*; to *retire*:—depart, give place, go (turn) aside, withdraw self.

403. ἀνάψυξις **anapsuxis**, *an-aps'-ook-sis*; from *404*; prop. a *recovery of breath*, i.e. (fig.) *revival*:—revival.

404. ἀναψύχω **anapsuchō**, *an-aps-oo'-kho*; from *303* and *5594*; prop. to *cool off*, i.e. (fig.) *relieve*:—refresh.

405. ἀνδραποδιστής **andrapŏdistēs**, *an-drap-od-is-tace'*; from a der. of a comp. of *435* and *4228*; an *enslaver* (as bringing *men* to his *feet*):—menstealer.

406. Ἀνδρέας **Andrĕas**, *an-dreh'-as*; from *435*; *manly*; *Andreas*, an Isr.:—Andrew.

407. ἀνδρίζομαι **andrizŏmai**, *an-drid'-zom-ahee*; mid. from *435*; to *act manly*:—quit like men.

408. Ἀνδρόνικος **Andrŏnikŏs**, *an-dron'-ee-kos*; from *435* and *3534*; *man of victory*; *Andronicos*, an Isr.:—Andronicus.

409. ἀνδροφόνος **andrŏphŏnŏs**, *an-drof-on'-os*; from *435* and *5408*; a *murderer*:—manslayer.

410. ἀνέγκλητος **anĕgklētŏs**, *an-eng'-klay-tos*; from *1* (as a neg. particle) and a der. of *1458*; *unaccused*, i.e. (by impl.) *irreproachable*:—blameless.

411. ἀνεκδιήγητος **anĕkdiēgētŏs**, *an-ek-dee-ay'-gay-tos*; from *1* (as a neg. particle) and a presumed der. of *1555*; *not expounded* in full, i.e. *indescribable*:—unspeakable.

412. ἀνεκλάλητος **anĕklalētŏs**, *an-ek-lal'-ay-tos*; from *1* (as a neg. particle) and a presumed der. of *1583*; *not spoken out*, i.e. (by impl.) *unutterable*:—unspeakable.

413. ἀνέκλειπτος **anĕklĕiptŏs**, *an-ek'-lipe-tos*; from *1* (as a neg. particle) and a presumed der. of *1587*; *not left out*, i.e. (by impl.) *inexhaustible*:—that faileth not.

414. ἀνεκτότερος **anĕktŏtĕrŏs**, *an-ek-tot'-er-os*; compar. of a der. of *430*; *more endurable*:—more tolerable.

415. ἀνελεήμων **anĕlĕēmōn**, *an-eleh-ay'-mone*; from *1* (as a neg. particle) and *1655*; *merciless*:—unmerciful.

416. ἀνεμίζω **anemizō**, *an-em-id'-zo*; from *417*; to *toss with the wind*:—drive with the wind.

417. ἄνεμος **anĕmŏs**, *an'-em-os*; from the base of *109*; *wind*; (plur.) by impl. (the four) *quarters* (of the earth):—wind.

418. ἀνένδεκτος **anĕndĕktŏs**, *an-en'-dek-tos*; from *1* (as a neg. particle) and a der. of the same as *1735*; *unadmitted*, i.e. (by impl.) *not supposable*:—impossible.

419. ἀνεξερεύνητος **anĕxĕrĕunētŏs**, *an-ex-er-yoo'-nay-tos*; from *1* (as a neg. particle) and a presumed der. of *1830*; *not searched out*, i.e. (by impl.) *inscrutable*:—unsearchable.

420. ἀνεξίκακος **anĕxikakŏs**, *an-ex-ik'-ak-os*; from *430* and *2556*; *enduring of ill*, i.e. *forbearing*:—patient.

421. ἀνεξιχνίαστος **anĕxichniastŏs**, *an-ex-ikh-nee'-as-tos*; from *1* (as a neg. particle) and a presumed der. of a comp. of *1537* and a der. of *2487*; *not tracked out*, i.e. (by impl.) *untraceable*:—past finding out, unsearchable.

422. ἀνεπαίσχυντος **anĕpaischuntŏs**, *an-ep-ah'ee-skhoon-tos*; from *1* (as a neg. particle) and a presumed der. of a comp. of *1909* and *153*; *not ashamed*, i.e. (by impl.) *irreprehensible*:—that needeth not to be ashamed.

423. ἀνεπίληπτος **anĕpilēptŏs**, *an-ep-eel'-ape-tos*; from *1* (as a neg. particle) and a der. of *1949*; *not arrested*, i.e. (by impl.) *inculpable*:—blameless, unrebukeable.

424. ἀνέρχομαι **anĕrchŏmai**, *an-erkh'-om-ahee*; from *303* and *2064*; to *ascend*:—go up.

425. ἄνεσις **anĕsis**, *an'-es-is*; from *447*; *relaxation* or (fig.) *relief*:—eased, liberty, rest.

426. ἀνετάζω **anĕtazō**, *an-et-ad'-zo*; from *303* and ἐτάζω **ĕtazō** (to *test*); to *investigate* (judicially):—(should have) examine (-d).

427. ἄνευ **anĕu**, *an'-yoo*; a prim. particle; *without*:—without. Comp. *1*.

428. ἀνεύθετος **anĕuthĕtŏs**, *an-yoo'-the-tos*; from *1* (as a neg. particle) and *2111*; *not well set*, i.e. *inconvenient*:—not commodious.

429. ἀνευρίσκω **anĕuriskō**, *an-yoo-ris'-ko*; from *303* and *2147*; to *find out*:—find.

430. ἀνέχομαι **anĕchŏmai**, *an-ekh'-om-ahee*; mid. from *303* and *2192*; to *hold oneself up* against, i.e. (fig.) *put up* with:—bear with, endure, forbear, suffer.

431. ἀνέψιος **anĕpsiŏs**, *an-eps'-ee-os*; from *1* (as a particle of union) and an obsolete νέπος **nĕpŏs** (a *brood*); prop. *akin*, i.e. (spec.) a *cousin*:—sister's son.

432. ἄνηθον **anēthŏn**, *an'-ay-thon*; prob. of for. or.; *dill*:—anise.

433. ἀνήκω **anēkō**, *an-ay'-ko*; from *303* and *2240*; to *attain to*, i.e. (fig.) *be proper*:—convenient, be fit.

434. ἀνήμερος **anēmĕrŏs**, *an-ay'-mer-os*; from *1* (as a neg. particle) and ἥμερος **hēmĕrŏs** (*lame*); *savage*:—fierce.

435. ἀνήρ **anēr**, *an'-ayr*; a prim. word [comp. *444*]; a *man* (prop. as an individual male):—fellow, husband, man, sir.

436. ἀνθίστημι **anthistēmi**, *anth-is'-tay-mee*; from *473* and *2476*; to *stand against*, i.e. *oppose*:—resist, withstand.

437. ἀνθομολογέομαι **anthŏmŏlŏgĕŏmai**, *anth-om-ol-og-eh'-om-ahee*; from *473* and the mid. of *3670*; to *confess in turn*, i.e. *respond* in praise:—give thanks.

438. ἄνθος **anthŏs**, *anth'-os*; a prim. word; a *blossom*:—flower.

439. ἀνθρακιά **anthrakia**, *anth-rak-ee-ah'*; from *440*; a bed of burning *coals*:—fire of coals.

440. ἄνθραξ **anthrax**, *anth'-rax*; of uncert. der.; a live *coal*:—coal of fire.

441. ἀνθρωπάρεσκος **anthrōparĕskŏs**, *anth-ro-par'-es-kos*; from *444* and *700*; *man-courting*, i.e. *fawning*:—men-pleaser.

442. ἀνθρώπινος **anthrōpinŏs**, *anth-ro'-pee-nos*; from *444*; *human*:—human, common to man, man[-kind], [man-]kind, men's, after the manner of men.

443. ἀνθρωποκτόνος **anthrōpŏktŏnŏs**, *anth-ro-pok-ton'-os*; from *444* and κτείνω **ktĕinō** (to *kill*); a *manslayer*:—murderer. Comp. *5406*.

444. ἄνθρωπος **anthrōpŏs**, *anth'-ro-pos*; from *435* and ὤψ **ōps** (the *countenance*; from *3700*); *man-faced*, i.e. a *human* being:—certain, man.

445. ἀνθυπατεύω **anthupatĕuō**, *anth-oo-pat-yoo'-o*; from *446*; to *act as proconsul*:—be the deputy.

446. ἀνθύπατος **anthupatŏs**, *anth-oo'-pat-os*; from *473* and a superlative of *5228*; *instead* of the *highest* officer, i.e. (spec.) a Roman *proconsul*:—deputy.

447. ἀνίημι **aniēmi**, *an-ee'-ay-mee*; from *303* and ἵημι **hiēmi** (to *send*); to *let up*, i.e. (lit.) *slacken*, or (fig.) *desert*, *desist* from:—forbear, leave, loose.

448. ἀνίλεως **anilĕōs**, *an-ee'-leh-oce*; from *1* (as a neg. particle) and *2436*; *inexorable*:—without mercy.

449. ἄνιπτος **aniptŏs**, *an'-ip-tos*; from *1* (as a neg. particle) and a presumed der. of *3538*; *without ablution*:—unwashen.

450. ἀνίστημι **anistēmi**, *an-is'-tay-mee*; from *303* and *2476*; to *stand up* (lit. or fig., trans. or intrans.):—arise, lift up, raise up (again), rise (again), stand up (-right).

451. Ἄννα **Anna**, *an'-nah*; of Heb. or. [2584]; *Anna*, an Israelitess:—Anna.

452. Ἄννας **Annas**, *an'-nas*; of Heb. or. [2608]; *Annas* (i.e. *367*), an Isr.:—Annas.

453. ἀνόητος **anŏētŏs**, *an-ŏ'-ay-tos*; from *1* (as a neg. particle) and a der. of *3539*; *unintelligent*; by impl. *sensual*:—fool (-ish), unwise.

454. ανοια **anŏia**, *an'-oy-ah*; from a comp. of *1* (as a neg. particle) and *3563*; *stupidity*; by impl. *rage*:—folly, madness.

455. ἀνοίγω **anŏigō**, *an-oy'-go*; from *303* and οἴγω **ŏigō** (to *open*); to *open up* (lit. or fig., in various applications):—open.

456. ἀνοικοδομέω **anŏikŏdŏmĕō**, *an-oy-kod-om-eh'-o*; from *303* and *3618*; to *rebuild*:—build again.

457. ἄνοιξις **anŏixis**, *an'-oix-is*; from *455*; *opening* (throat):— × open.

458. ἀνομία **anŏmia**, *an-om-ee'-ah*; from *459*; *illegality*, i.e. *violation of law* or (gen.) *wickedness*:—iniquity, × transgress (-ion of) the law, unrighteousness.

459. ἄνομος **anŏmŏs**, *an'-om-os*; from *1* (as a neg. particle) and *3551*; *lawless*, i.e. (neg.) *not subject to* (the Jewish) *law*; (by impl. a *Gentile*), or (pos.) *wicked*:—without law, lawless, transgressor, unlawful, wicked.

460. ἀνόμως **anŏmōs**, *an-om'-oce*; adv. from *459*; *lawlessly*, i.e. (spec.) *not amenable to* (the Jewish) *law*:—without law.

461. ἀνορθόω **anŏrthŏō**, *an-orth-ŏ'-o*; from *303* and a der. of the base of *3717*; to *straighten up*:—lift (set) up, make straight.

462. ἀνόσιος **anŏsiŏs**, *an-os'-ee-os*; from *1* (as a neg. particle) and *3741*; *wicked*:—unholy.

463. ἀνοχή **anŏchē**, *an-okh-ay'*; from *430*; *self-restraint*, i.e. *tolerance*:—forbearance.

464. ἀνταγωνίζομαι **antagōnizŏmai**, *an-tag-o-nid'-zom-ahee*; from *473* and *75*; to *struggle against* (fig.) ["antagonize"]:—strive against.

465. ἀντάλλαγμα **antallagma**, *an-tal'-ag-mah*; from a comp. of *473* and *236*; an *equivalent* or *ransom*:—in exchange.

466. ἀνταναπληρόω **antanaplērŏō**, *an-tan-ap-lay-rŏ'-o*; from *473* and *378*; to *supplement*:—fill up.

467. ἀνταποδίδωμι **antapŏdidōmi**, *an-tap-od-ee'-do-mee*; from *473* and *591*; to *requite* (good or evil):—recompense, render, repay.

468. ἀνταπόδομα **antapŏdŏma**, *an-tap-od'-om-ah*; from *467*; a *requital* (prop. the thing):—recompense.

469. ἀνταπόδοσις **antapŏdŏsis**, *an-tap-od'-os-is*; from *467*; *requital* (prop. the act):—reward.

470. ἀνταποκρίνομαι **antapŏkrinŏmai**, *an-tap-ok-ree'-nom-ahee*; from *473* and *611*; to *contradict* or *dispute*:—answer again, reply against.

471. ἀντέπω **antĕpō**, *an-tep'-o*; from *473* and *2036*; to *refute* or *deny*:—gainsay, say against.

472. ἀντέχομαι **antĕchŏmai**, *an-tekh'-om-ahee*; from *473* and the mid. of *2192*; to *hold* oneself *opposite* to, i.e. (by impl.) *adhere to*; by extens. to *care for*:—hold fast, hold to, support.

473. ἀντί **anti**, *an-tee'*; a prim. particle; *opposite*, i.e. *instead* or *because* of (rarely *in addition* to):—for, in the room of. Often used in composition to denote *contrast*, *requital*, *substitution*, *correspondence*, etc.

474. **ἀντιβάλλω antiballō**, *an-tee-bal'-lo;* from 473 and 906; to *bandy:*—have.

475. **ἀντιδιατίθεμαι antidiatithĕmai**, *an-tee-dee-at-eeth'-em-ahee;* from 473 and 1303; to *set oneself opposite,* i.e. *be disputatious:*—that oppose themselves.

476. **ἀντίδικος antidikŏs**, *an-tid'-ee-kos;* from 473 and 1349; an *opponent* (in a lawsuit); spec. *Satan* (as the arch-enemy):—adversary.

477. **ἀντίθεσις antithĕsis**, *an-tith'-es-is;* from a comp. of 473 and 5087; *opposition,* i.e. a *conflict* (of theories):—opposition.

478. **ἀντικαθίστημι antikathistēmi**, *an-tee-kath-is'-tay-mee;* from 473 and 2525; to *set down* (troops) *against,* i.e. *withstand:*—resist.

479. **ἀντικαλέω antikalĕō**, *an-tee-kal-eh'-o;* from 473 and 2564; to *invite in return:*—bid again.

480. **ἀντίκειμαι antikĕimai**, *an-tik'-i-mahee;* from 473 and 2749; to *lie opposite,* i.e. *be adverse* (fig. *repugnant*) to:—adversary, be contrary, oppose.

481. **ἀντικρύ antikru**, *an-tee-kroo';* prol. from 473; *opposite:*—over against.

482. **ἀντιλαμβάνομαι antilambanŏmai**, *an-tee-lam-ban'-om-ahee;* from 473 and the mid. of 2983; to *take* hold of *in turn,* i.e. *succor;* also to *participate:*—help, partaker, support.

483. **ἀντίλεγω antilĕgō**, *an-til'-eg-o;* from 473 and 3004; to *dispute, refuse:*—answer again, contradict, deny, gainsay (-er), speak against.

484. **ἀντίληψις antilēpsis**, *an-til'-ape-sis;* from 482; *relief:*—help.

485. **ἀντιλογία antilŏgia**, *an-tee-log-ee'-ah;* from a der. of 483; *dispute, disobedience:*—contradiction, gainsaying, strife.

486. **ἀντιλοιδορέω antilŏidŏrĕō**, *an-tee-loy-dor-eh'-o;* from 473 and 3058; to *rail in reply:*—revile again.

487. **ἀντίλυτρον antilutrŏn**, *an-til'-oo-tron;* from 473 and 3083; a *redemption-price:*—ransom.

488. **ἀντιμετρέω antimĕtrĕō**, *an-tee-met-reh'-o;* from 473 and 3354; to *mete in return:*—measure again.

489. **ἀντιμισθία antimisthia**, *an-tee-mis-thee'-ah;* from a comp. of 473 and 3408; *requital, correspondence:*—recompense.

490. **Ἀντιόχεια Antiŏchĕia**, *an-tee-okh'-i-ah;* from **Ἀντίοχος Antiŏchus** (a Syrian king); *Antiochīa,* a place in Syria:—Antioch.

491. **Ἀντιοχεύς Antiŏchĕus**, *an-tee-okh-yoos';* from 490; an *Antiochian* or inhab. of Antiochia:—of Antioch.

492. **ἀντιπαρέρχομαι antiparĕrchŏmai**, *an-tee-par-er'-khom-ahee;* from 473 and 3928; to *go along opposite:*—pass by on the other side.

493. **Ἀντίπας Antipas**, *an-tee'-pas;* contr. for a comp. of 473 and a der. of 3962; *Antipas,* a Chr.:—Antipas.

494. **Ἀντιπατρίς Antipatris**, *an-tip-at-rece';* from the same as 493; *Antipatris,* a place in Pal.:—Antipatris.

495. **ἀντιπέραν antipĕran**, *an-tee-per'-an;* from 473 and 4008; *on the opposite side:*—over against.

496. **ἀντιπίπτω antipiptō**, *an-tee-pip'-to;* from 473 and 4098 (includ. its alt.); to *oppose:*—resist.

497. **ἀντιστρατεύομαι antistratĕuŏmai**, *an-tee-strat-yoo'-om-ahee;* from 473 and 4754; (fig.) to *attack,* i.e. (by impl.) *destroy:*—war against.

498. **ἀντιτάσσομαι antitassŏmai**, *an-tee-tas'-som-ahee;* from 473 and the mid. of 5021; to *range oneself against,* i.e. *oppose:*—oppose themselves, resist.

499. **ἀντίτυπον antitupŏn**, *an-teet'-oo-pon;* neut. of a comp. of 473 and 5179; *corresponding* ["antitype"], i.e. a *representative, counterpart:*—(like) figure (whereunto).

500. **ἀντίχριστος antichristŏs**, *an-tee'-khris-tos:* from 473 and 5547; an *opponent of the Messiah:*—antichrist.

501. **ἀντλέω antlĕō**, *ant-leh-o;* from **ἄντλος antlŏs** (the *hold* of a ship); to *bale* up (prop. bilge water), i.e. *dip* water (with a bucket, pitcher, etc.):—draw (out).

502. **ἄντλημα antlēma**, *ant'-lay-mah;* from 501; a *baling-vessel:*—thing to draw with.

503. **ἀντοφθαλμέω antŏphthalmĕō**, *ant-of-thal-meh'-o;* from a comp. of 473 and 3788; to *face:*—bear up into.

504. **ἄνυδρος anudrŏs**, *an'-oo-dros;* from 1 (as a neg. particle) and 5204; *waterless,* i.e. *dry:*—dry, without water.

505. **ἀνυπόκριτος anupŏkritŏs**, *an-oo-pok'-ree-tos;* from 1 (as a neg. particle) and a presumed der. of 5271; *undissembled,* i.e. *sincere:*—without dissimulation (hypocrisy), unfeigned.

506. **ἀνυπότακτος anupŏtaktŏs**, *an-oo-pot'-ak-tos;* from 1 (as a neg. particle) and a presumed der. of 5293; *unsubdued,* i.e. *insubordinate* (in fact or temper):—disobedient, that is not put under, unruly.

507. **ἄνω anō**, *an'-o;* adv. from 473; *upward* or *on the top:*—above, brim, high, up.

508. **ἀνώγεον anōgĕōn**, *an-ogue'-eh-on;* from 507 and 1093; *above* the *ground,* i.e. (prop.) the *second floor* of a building; used for a *dome* or a *balcony* on the upper story:—upper room.

509. **ἄνωθεν anōthĕn**, *an'-o-then;* from 507; *from above;* by anal. *from the first;* by impl. *anew:*—from above, again, from the beginning (very first), the top.

510. **ἀνωτερικός anōtĕrikŏs**, *an-o-ter-ee-kos';* from 511; *superior,* i.e. (locally) *more remote:*—upper.

511. **ἀνώτερος anōtĕrŏs**, *an-o'-ter-os;* comp. degree of 507; *upper,* i.e. (neut. as adv.) to a *more conspicuous* place, in a *former* part of the book:—above, higher.

512. **ἀνωφέλες anōphĕlĕs**, *an-o-fel'-ace;* from 1 (as a neg. particle) and the base of 5624; *useless* or (neut.) *inutility:*—unprofitable (-ness).

513. **ἀξίνη axinē**, *ax-ee'-nay;* prob. from **ἄγνυμι agnumi** (to *break;* comp. 4486); an *axe:*—axe.

514. **ἄξιος axiŏs**, *ax'-ee-os;* prob. from 71; *deserving, comparable* or *suitable* (as if *drawing* praise):—due reward, meet, [un-] worthy.

515. **ἀξιόω axiŏō**, *ax-ee-ŏ'-o;* from 514; to *deem entitled* or *fit:*—desire, think good, count (think) worthy.

516. **ἀξίως axiōs**, *ax-ee'-oce;* adv. from 514; *appropriately:*—as becometh, after a godly sort, worthily (-thy).

517. **ἀόρατος aŏratŏs**, *ah-or'-at-os;* from 1 (as a neg. particle) and 3707; *invisible:*—invisible (thing).

518. **ἀπαγγέλλω apaggĕllō**, *ap-ang-el'-lo;* from 575 and the base of 32; to *announce:*—bring word (again), declare, report, shew (again), tell.

519. **ἀπάγχομαι apagchŏmai**, *ap-ang'-khom-ahee;* from 575 and **ἄγχω agchō** (to *choke;* akin to the base of 43); to *strangle oneself off* (i.e. to death):—hang himself.

520. **ἀπάγω apagō**, *ap-ag'-o;* from 575 and 71; to *take off* (in various senses):—bring, carry away, lead (away), put to death, take away.

521. **ἀπαίδευτος apaidĕutŏs**, *ap-ah'ee-dyoo-tos;* from 1 (as a neg. particle) and a der. of 3811; *uninstructed,* i.e. (fig.) *stupid:*—unlearned.

522. **ἀπαίρω apairō**, *ap-ah'ee-ro;* from 575 and 142; to *lift off,* i.e. *remove:*—take (away).

523. **ἀπαιτέω apaitĕō**, *ap-ah'ee-teh-o;* from 575 and 154; to *demand back:*—ask again, require.

524. **ἀπαλγέω apalgĕō**, *ap-alg-eh'-o;* from 575 and **ἀλγέω algĕō** (to *smart*); to *grieve out,* i.e. *become apathetic:*—be past feeling.

525. **ἀπαλλάσσω apallassō**, *ap-al-las'-so;* from 575 and 236; to *change away,* i.e. *release,* (reflex.) *remove:*—deliver, depart.

526. **ἀπαλλοτριόω apallŏtriŏō**, *ap-al-lot-ree-ŏ'-o;* from 575 and a der. of 245; to *estrange away,* i.e. (pass. and fig.) to *be non-participant:*—alienate, be alien.

527. **ἁπαλός apalŏs**, *ap-al-os';* of uncert. der.; *soft:*—tender.

528. **ἀπαντάω apantaō**, *ap-an-tah'-o;* from 575 and a der. of 473; to *meet away,* i.e. *encounter:*—meet.

529. **ἀπάντησις apantēsis**, *ap-an'-tay-sis;* from 528; a (friendly) *encounter:*—meet.

530. **ἅπαξ hapax**, *hap'-ax;* prob. from 537; *one* (or a *single*) *time* (numerically or conclusively):—once.

531. **ἀπαράβατος aparabatŏs**, *ap-ar-ab'-at-os;* from 1 (as a neg. particle) and a der. of 3845; *not passing away,* i.e. *untransferable* (perpetual):—unchangeable.

532. **ἀπαρασκεύαστος aparaskĕuastŏs**, *ap-ar-ask-yoo'-as-tos;* from 1 (as a neg. particle) and a der. of 3903; *unready:*—unprepared.

533. **ἀπαρνέομαι aparnĕŏmai**, *ap-ar-neh'-om-ahee;* from 575 and 720; to *deny utterly,* i.e. *disown, abstain:*—deny.

534. **ἀπάρτι aparti**, *ap-ar'-tee;* from 575 and 737; *from now,* i.e. *henceforth* (*already*):—from henceforth.

535. **ἀπαρτισμός apartismŏs**, *ap-ar-tis-mos';* from a der. of 534; *completion:*—finishing.

536. **ἀπαρχή aparchē**, *ap-ar-khay';* from a comp. of 575 and 756; a *beginning* of sacrifice, i.e. the (Jewish) *first-fruit* (fig.):—first-fruits.

537. **ἅπας hapas**, *hap'-as;* from 1 (as a particle of union) and 3956; absolutely *all* or (sing.) *every* one:—all (things), every (one), whole.

538. **ἀπατάω apataō**, *ap-at-ah'-o;* of uncert. der.; to *cheat,* i.e. *delude:*—deceive.

539. **ἀπάτη apatē**, *ap-at'-ay;* from 538; *delusion:*—deceit (-ful, -fulness), deceivableness (-ving).

540. **ἀπάτωρ apatōr**, *ap-at'-ore;* from 1 (as a neg. particle) and 3962; *fatherless,* i.e. *of unrecorded paternity:*—without father.

541. **ἀπαύγασμα apaugasma**, *ap-ŏw'-gas-mah;* from a comp. of 575 and 826; an *off-flash,* i.e. *effulgence:*—brightness.

542. **ἀπείδω apĕidō**, *ap-i'-do;* from 575 and the same as 1492; to *see* fully:—see.

543. **ἀπείθεια apĕithĕia**, *ap-i'-thi-ah;* from 545; *disbelief* (obstinate and rebellious):—disobedience, unbelief.

544. **ἀπειθέω apĕithĕō**, *ap-i-theh'-o;* from 545; to *disbelieve* (wilfully and perversely):—not believe, disobedient, obey not, unbelieving.

545. **ἀπειθής apĕithēs**, *ap-i-thace';* from 1 (as a neg. particle) and 3982; *unpersuadable,* i.e. *contumacious:*—disobedient.

546. **ἀπειλέω apĕilĕō**, *ap-i-leh'-o;* of uncert. der.; to *menace;* by impl. to *forbid:*—threaten.

547. **ἀπειλή apĕilē**, *ap-i-lay';* from 546; a *menace:*— × straitly, threatening.

548. **ἄπειμι apĕimi**, *ap'-i-mee;* from 575 and 1510; to *be away:*—be absent. Comp. 549.

549. **ἄπειμι apĕimi**, *ap'-i-mee;* from 575 and **εἶμι ĕimi** (to *go*); to *go away:*—go. Comp. 548.

550. **ἀπειπόμην apĕipŏmēn**, *ap-i-pom'-ane;* reflex. past of a comp. of 575 and 2036; to *say off* for oneself, i.e. *disown:*—renounce.

551. **ἀπείραστος apĕirastŏs**, *ap-i'-ras-tos;* from 1 (as a neg. particle) and a presumed der. of 3987; *untried,* i.e. *not temptable:*—not to be tempted.

552. **ἄπειρος apĕirŏs**, *ap'-i-ros;* from 1 (as a neg. particle) and 3984; *inexperienced,* i.e. *ignorant:*—unskilful.

553. **ἀπεκδέχομαι apĕkdĕchŏmai**, *ap-ek-dekh'-om-ahee;* from 575 and 1551; to *expect fully:*—look (wait) for.

554. **ἀπεκδύομαι apĕkduŏmai**, *ap-ek-doo'-om-ahee;* mid. from 575 and 1562; to *divest wholly* oneself, or (for oneself) *despoil:*—put off, spoil.

555. **ἀπέκδυσις apĕkdusis**, *ap-ek'-doo-sis;* from 554; *divestment:*—putting off.

556. **ἀπελαύνω apĕlaunō**, *ap-el-ŏw'-no;* from 575 and 1643; to *dismiss:*—drive.

557. ἀπελεγμός **apĕlĕgmŏs**, *ap-el-eg-mos';* from a comp. of *575* and *1651; refutation,* i.e. (by impl.) *contempt:*—nought.

558. ἀπελεύθερος **apĕlĕuthĕrŏs**, *ap-el-yoo'-ther-os;* from *575* and *1658;* one *freed away,* i.e. a *freedman:*—freeman.

559. Ἀπελλῆς **Apĕllēs**, *ap-el-lace';* of Lat. or.; *Apelles,* a Chr.:—Apelles.

560. ἀπελπίζω **apĕlpizō**, *ap-el-pid'-zo;* from *575* and *1679;* to *hope out,* i.e. *fully expect:*—hope for again.

561. ἀπέναντι **apĕnanti**, *ap-en'-an-tee;* from *575* and *1725; from in front,* i.e. *opposite, before* or *against:*—before, contrary, over against, in the presence of.

ἀπέπω **apĕpō**. See *550*.

562. ἀπέραντος **apĕrantŏs**, *ap-er'-an-tos;* from *1* (as a neg. particle) and a secondary der. of *4008; unfinished,* i.e. (by impl.) *interminable:*—endless.

563. ἀπερισπάστως **apĕrispastōs**, *ap-er-is-pas-toce';* adv. from a comp. of *1* (as a neg. particle) and a presumed der. of *4049; undistractedly,* i.e. *free from* (domestic) *solicitude:*—without distraction.

564. ἀπερίτμητος **apĕritmētŏs**, *ap-er-eet'-may-tos;* from *1* (as a neg. particle) and a presumed der. of *4059; uncircumcised* (fig.):—uncircumcised.

565. ἀπέρχομαι **apĕrchŏmai**, *ap-erkh'-om-ahee;* from *575* and *2064;* to *go off* (i.e. *depart*), *aside* (i.e. *apart*) or *behind* (i.e. *follow*), lit. or fig.:—come, depart, go (aside, away, back, out, . . . ways), pass away, be past.

566. ἀπέχει **apĕchĕi**, *ap-ekh'-i;* 3d pers. sing. pres. indic. act. of *568* used impers.; *it is sufficient:*—it is enough.

567. ἀπέχομαι **apĕchŏmai**, *ap-ekh'-om-ahee;* mid. (reflex.) of *568;* to *hold oneself off,* i.e. *refrain:*—abstain.

568. ἀπέχω **apĕchō**, *ap-ekh'-o;* from *575* and *2192;* (act.) to *have out,* i.e. *receive in full;* (intrans.) to *keep* (oneself) *away,* i.e. *be distant* (lit. or fig.):—be, have, receive.

569. ἀπιστέω **apistĕō**, *ap-is-teh'-o;* from *571;* to *be unbelieving,* i.e. (trans.) *disbelieve,* or (by impl.) *disobey:*—believe not.

570. ἀπιστία **apistia**, *ap-is-tee'-ah;* from *571; faithlessness,* i.e. (neg.) *disbelief* (*want of* Chr. *faith*), or (pos.) *unfaithfulness* (*disobedience*):—unbelief.

571. ἄπιστος **apistŏs**, *ap'-is-tos;* from *1* (as a neg. particle) and *4103;* (act.) *disbelieving,* i.e. *without* Chr. *faith* (spec. a *heathen*); (pass.) *untrustworthy* (person), or *incredible* (thing):—that believeth not, faithless, incredible thing, infidel, unbeliever (-ing).

572. ἁπλότης **haplŏtēs**, *hap-lot'-ace;* from *573; singleness,* i.e. (subj.) *sincerity* (*without dissimulation* or *self-seeking*), or (obj.) *generosity* (*copious bestowal*):—bountifulness, liberal (-ity), simplicity, singleness.

573. ἁπλοῦς **haplŏus**, *hap-looce';* prob. from *1* (as a particle of union) and the base of *4120;* prop. *folded together,* i.e. *single* (fig. *clear*):—single.

574. ἁπλῶς **haplōs**, *hap-loce';* adv. from *573* (in the obj. sense of *572*); *bountifully:*—liberally.

575. ἀπό **apŏ**, *apo';* a prim. particle; "*off,*" i.e. *away* (from something near), in various senses (of place, time, or relation; lit. or fig.):—(× here-) after, ago, at, because of, before, by (the space of), for (-th), from, in, (out) of, off, (up-) on (-ce), since, with. In composition (as a prefix) it usually denotes *separation, departure, cessation, completion, reversal,* etc.

576. ἀποβαίνω **apŏbainō**, *ap-ob-ah'ee-no;* from *575* and the base of *939;* lit. to *disembark;* fig. to *eventuate:*—become, go out, turn.

577. ἀποβάλλω **apŏballō**, *ap-ob-al'-lo;* from *575* and *906;* to *throw off;* fig. to *lose:*—cast away.

578. ἀποβλέπω **apŏblĕpō**, *ap-ob-lep'-o;* from *575* and *991;* to *look away* from everything else, i.e. (fig.) intently *regard:*—have respect.

579. ἀπόβλητος **apŏblētŏs**, *ap-ob'-lay-tos;* from *577; cast off,* i.e. (fig.) such as to *be rejected:*—be refused.

580. ἀποβολή **apŏbŏlē**, *ap-ob-ol-ay';* from *577; rejection;* fig. *loss:*—casting away, loss.

581. ἀπογενόμενος **apŏgĕnŏmĕnŏs**, *ap-og-en-om'-en-os;* past part. of a comp. of *575* and *1096; absent,* i.e. *deceased* (fig. *renounced*):—being dead.

582. ἀπογραφή **apŏgraphē**, *ap-og-raf-ay';* from *583;* an *enrollment;* by impl. an *assessment:*—taxing.

583. ἀπογράφω **apŏgraphō**, *ap-og-raf'-o;* from *575* and *1125;* to *write off* (a copy or list), i.e. *enrol:*—tax, write.

584. ἀποδείκνυμι **apŏdĕiknumi**, *ap-od-ike'-noo-mee;* from *575* and *1166;* to *show off,* i.e. *exhibit;* fig. to *demonstrate,* i.e. *accredit:*—(ap-) prove, set forth, shew.

585. ἀπόδειξις **apŏdĕixis**, *ap-od'-ike-sis;* from *584; manifestation:*—demonstration.

586. ἀποδεκατόω **apŏdĕkatŏō**, *ap-od-ek-at-ŏ'-o;* from *575* and *1183;* to *tithe* (as debtor or creditor):—(give, pay, take) tithe.

587. ἀπόδεκτος **apŏdĕktŏs**, *ap-od'-ek-tos;* from *588; accepted,* i.e. *agreeable:*—acceptable.

588. ἀποδέχομαι **apŏdĕchŏmai**, *ap-od-ekh'-om-ahee;* from *575* and *1209;* to *take fully,* i.e. *welcome* (persons), *approve* (things):—accept, receive (gladly).

589. ἀποδημέω **apŏdēmĕō**, *ap-od-ay-meh'-o;* from *590;* to *go abroad,* i.e. *visit a foreign land:*—go (travel) into a far country, journey.

590. ἀπόδημος **apŏdēmŏs**, *ap-od'-ay-mos;* from *575* and *1218; absent from* one's own *people,* i.e. a *foreign traveller:*—taking a far journey.

591. ἀποδίδωμι **apŏdidōmi**, *ap-od-eed'-o-mee;* from *575* and *1325;* to *give away,* i.e. *up, over, back,* etc. (in various applications):—deliver (again), give (again), (re-) pay (-ment be made), perform, recompense, render, requite, restore, reward, sell, yield.

592. ἀποδιορίζω **apŏdiŏrizō**, *ap-od-ee-or-id'-zo;* from *575* and a comp. of *1223* and *3724;* to *disjoin* (by a boundary, fig. a party):—separate.

593. ἀποδοκιμάζω **apŏdŏkimazō**, *ap-od-ok-ee-mad'-zo;* from *575* and *1381;* to *disapprove,* i.e. (by impl.) to *repudiate:*—disallow, reject.

594. ἀποδοχή **apŏdŏchē**, *ap-od-okh-ay';* from *588; acceptance:*—acceptation.

595. ἀπόθεσις **apŏthĕsis**, *ap-oth'-es-is;* from *659;* a *laying aside* (lit. or fig.):—putting away (off).

596. ἀποθήκη **apŏthēkē**, *ap-oth-ay'-kay;* from *659;* a *repository.* i.e. *granary:*—barn, garner.

597. ἀποθησαυρίζω **apŏthēsaurizō**, *ap-oth-ay-sŏw-rid'-zo;* from *575* and *2343;* to *treasure away:*—lay up in store.

598. ἀποθλίβω **apŏthlibō**, *ap-oth-lee'-bo;* from *575* and *2346;* to *crowd* from (every side):—press.

599. ἀποθνήσκω **apŏthnēskō**, *ap-oth-nace'-ko;* from *575* and *2348;* to *die* off (lit. or fig.):—be dead, death, die, lie a-dying, be slain (× with).

600. ἀποκαθίστημι **apŏkathistēmi**, *ap-ok-ath-is'-tay-mee;* from *575* and *2525;* to *reconstitute* (in health, home or organization):—restore (again).

601. ἀποκαλύπτω **apŏkaluptō**, *ap-ok-al-oop'-to;* from *575* and *2572;* to take *off the cover,* i.e. *disclose:*—reveal.

602. ἀποκάλυψις **apŏkalupsis**, *ap-ok-al'-oop-sis;* from *601; disclosure:*—appearing, coming, lighten, manifestation, be revealed, revelation.

603. ἀποκαραδοκία **apŏkaradŏkia**, *ap-ok-ar-ad-ok-ee'-ah;* from a comp. of *575* and a comp. of κάρα **kara** (the *head*) and *1380* (in the sense of *watching*); *intense anticipation:*—earnest expectation.

604. ἀποκαταλλάσσω **apŏkatallassō**, *ap-ok-at-al-las'-so;* from *575* and *2644;* to *reconcile fully:*—reconcile.

605. ἀποκατάστασις **apŏkatastasis**, *ap-ok-at-as'-tas-is;* from *600; reconstitution:*—restitution.

606. ἀπόκειμαι **apŏkĕimai**, *ap-ok'-i-mahee;* from *575* and *2749;* to *be reserved;* fig. to *await:*—be appointed, (be) laid up.

607. ἀποκεφαλίζω **apŏkĕphalizō**, *ap-ok-ef-al-id'-zo;* from *575* and *2776;* to *decapitate:*—behead.

608. ἀποκλείω **apŏklĕiō**, *ap-ok-li'-o;* from *575* and *2808;* to *close fully:*—shut up.

609. ἀποκόπτω **apŏkŏptō**, *ap-ok-op'-to;* from *575* and *2875;* to *amputate;* reflex. (by irony) to *mutilate* (the privy parts):—cut off. Comp. *2699*.

610. ἀπόκριμα **apŏkrima**, *ap-ok'-ree-mah;* from *611* (in its orig. sense of *judging*); a judicial *decision:*—sentence.

611. ἀποκρίνομαι **apŏkrinŏmai**, *ap-ok-ree'-nom-ahee;* from *575* and κρινω **krino**; to *conclude for oneself,* i.e. (by impl.) to *respond;* by Hebr. [comp. 6030] to *begin to speak* (where an address is expected):—answer.

612. ἀπόκρισις **apŏkrisis**, *ap-ok'-ree-sis;* from *611;* a *response:*—answer.

613. ἀποκρύπτω **apŏkruptō**, *ap-ok-roop'-to;* from *575* and *2928;* to *conceal away* (i.e. *fully*); fig. to *keep secret:*—hide.

614. ἀπόκρυφος **apŏkruphŏs**, *ap-ok'-roo-fos;* from *613; secret;* by impl. *treasured:*—hid, kept secret.

615. ἀποκτείνω **apŏktĕinō**, *ap-ok-ti'-no;* from *575* and κτείνω **ktĕinō** (to *slay*); to *kill* outright; fig. to *destroy:*—put to death, kill, slay.

616. ἀποκυέω **apŏkuĕō**, *ap-ok-oo-eh'o;* from *575* and the base of *2949;* to *breed forth,* i.e. (by transf.) to *generate* (fig.) :—beget, bring forth.

617. ἀποκυλίω **apŏkuliō**, *ap-ok-oo-lee'-o;* from *575* and *2947;* to *roll away:*—roll away (back).

618. ἀπολαμβάνω **apŏlambanō**, *ap-ol-am-ban'-o;* from *575* and *2983;* to *receive* (spec. in *full,* or as a host); also to *take aside:*—receive, take.

619. ἀπόλαυσις **apŏlausis**, *ap-ol'-ŏw-sis;* from a comp. of *575* and λαύω **lauō** (to *enjoy*); full *enjoyment:*—enjoy (-ment).

620. ἀπολείπω **apŏlĕipō**, *ap-ol-ipe'-o;* from *575* and *3007;* to *leave* behind (pass. *remain*); by impl. to *forsake:*—leave, remain.

621. ἀπολείχω **apŏlĕichō**, *ap-ol-i'-kho;* from *575* and λείχω **lĕichō** (to "*lick*"); to *lick* clean:—lick.

622. ἀπόλλυμι **apŏllumi**, *ap-ol'-loo-mee;* from *575* and the base of *3639;* to *destroy* fully (reflex. to *perish,* or *lose*), lit. or fig.:—destroy, die, lose, mar, perish.

623. Ἀπολλύων **Apŏlluōn**, *ap-ol-loo'-ohn;* act. part. of *622;* a *destroyer* (i.e. *Satan*);—Apollyon.

624. Ἀπολλωνία **Apŏllōnia**, *ap-ol-lo-nee'-ah;* from the pagan deity Ἀπόλλων **Apŏllōn** (i.e. the *sun;* from *622*); *Apollonia,* a place in Macedonia:—Apollonia.

625. Ἀπολλώς **Apŏllōs**, *ap-ol-loce';* prob. from the same as *624; Apollos,* an Isr.:—Apollos.

626. ἀπολογέομαι **apŏlŏgĕŏmai**, *ap-ol-og-eh'-om-ahee:* mid. from a comp. of *575* and *3056;* to give an *account* (legal *plea*) of oneself, i.e. *exculpate* (self):—answer (for self), make defence, excuse (self), speak for self.

627. ἀπολογία **apŏlŏgia**, *ap-ol-og-ee'-ah;* from the same as *626;* a *plea* ("apology"):—answer (for self), clearing of self, defence.

628. ἀπολούω **apŏlŏuō**, *ap-ol-oo'-o;* from *575* and *3068;* to *wash* fully, i.e. (fig.) *have remitted* (reflex.):—wash (away).

629. ἀπολύτρωσις **apŏlutrōsis**, *ap-ol-oo'-tro-sis;* from a comp. of *575* and *3083;* (the act) *ransom* in full, i.e. (fig.) *riddance,* or (spec.) Chr. *salvation:*—deliverance, redemption.

630. ἀπολύω **apŏluō**, *ap-ol-oo'-o;* from *575* and *3089;* to *free* fully, i.e. (lit.) *relieve, release, dismiss* (reflex. *depart*), or (fig.) *let die, pardon,* or (spec.) *divorce:*—(let) depart, dismiss, divorce, forgive, let go, loose, put (send) away, release, set at liberty.

631. ἀπομάσσομαι **apŏmassŏmai**, *ap-om-as'-som-ahee;* mid. from *575* and μάσσω **massō** (to *squeeze, knead, smear*); to *scrape away:*—wipe off.

632. ἀπονέμω **apŏnĕmō**, *ap-on-em'-o;* from *575* and the base of *3551;* to *apportion,* i.e. *bestow:*—give.

633. **ἀπονίπτω apŏniptō**, *ap-on-ip'-to;* from *575* and *3538;* to *wash off* (reflex. one's own hands symbolically):—wash.

634. **ἀποπίπτω apŏpiptō**, *ap-op-ip'-to;* from *575* and *4098;* to *fall off:*—fall.

635. **ἀποπλανάω apŏplanaō**, *ap-op-lan-ah'-o;* from *575* and *4105;* to *lead astray* (fig.); pass. to *stray* (from truth):—err, seduce.

636. **ἀποπλέω apŏplĕō**, *ap-op-leh'-o;* from *575* and *4126;* to *set sail:*—sail away.

637. **ἀποπλύνω apŏplunō**, *ap-op-loo'-no;* from *575* and *4150;* to *rinse off:*—wash.

638. **ἀποπνίγω apŏpnigō**, *ap-op-nee'-go;* from *575* and *4155;* to *stifle* (by drowning or overgrowth):—choke.

639. **ἀπορέω apŏrĕō**, *ap-or-eh'-o;* from a comp. of *1* (as a neg. particle) and the base of *4198;* to *have no way* out, i.e. *be at a loss* (mentally):—(stand in) doubt, be perplexed.

640. **ἀπορία apŏria**, *ap-or-ee'-a;* from the same as *639;* a (state of) *quandary:*—perplexity.

641. **ἀποῤῥίπτω apŏrrhiptō**, *ap-or-hrip'-to;* from *575* and *4496;* to *hurl off*, i.e. *precipitate* (oneself):—cast.

642. **ἀπορφανίζω apŏrphanizō**, *ap-or-fan-id'-zo;* from *575* and a der. of *3737;* to *bereave wholly*, i.e. (fig.) *separate* (from intercourse):—take.

643. **ἀποσκευάζω apŏskĕuazō**, *ap-osk-yoo-ad'-zo;* from *575* and a der. of *4632;* to *pack up* (one's) *baggage:*—take up . . . carriages.

644. **ἀποσκίασμα apŏskiasma**, *ap-os-kee'-as-mah;* from a comp. of *575* and a der. of *4639;* a *shading off*, i.e. *obscuration:*—shadow.

645. **ἀποσπάω apŏspaō**, *ap-os-pah'-o;* from *575* and *4685;* to *drag forth*, i.e. (lit.) *unsheathe* (a sword), or rel. (with a degree of force implied) *retire* (pers. or factiously):—(with-) draw (away), after we were gotten from.

646. **ἀποστασία apŏstasia**, *ap-os-tas-ee'-ah;* fem. of the same as *647;* *defection* from truth (prop. the state) ["apostasy"]:—falling away, forsake.

647 **ἀποστάσιον apŏstasiŏn**, *ap-os-tas'-ee-on;* neut. of a (presumed) adj. from a der. of *868;* prop. something *separative*, i.e. (spec.) *divorce:*—(writing of) divorcement.

648. **ἀποστεγάζω apŏstĕgazō**, *ap-os-teg-ad'-zo;* from *575* and a der. of *4721;* to *unroof:*—uncover.

649. **ἀποστέλλω apŏstĕllō**, *ap-os-tel'-lo;* from *575* and *4724;* *set apart*, i.e. (by impl.) to *send out* (prop. on a mission) lit. or fig.:—put in, send (away, forth, out), set [at liberty].

650. **ἀποστερέω apŏstĕrĕō**, *ap-os-ter-eh'-o;* from *575* and **στερέω stĕrĕō** (to *deprive*); to *despoil:*—defraud, destitute, kept back by fraud.

651. **ἀποστολή apŏstŏlē**, *ap-os-tol-ay';* from *649*, *commission*, i.e. (spec.) *apostolate:*—apostleship.

652. **ἀπόστολος apŏstŏlŏs**, *ap-os'-tol-os;* from *649;* a *delegate;* spec. an *ambassador* of the Gospel; officially a *commissioner* of Christ ["*apostle*"] (with miraculous powers):—apostle, messenger, he that is sent.

653. **ἀποστοματίζω apŏstŏmatizō**, *ap-os-tom-at-id'-zo;* from *575* and a (presumed) der. of *4750;* to *speak off-hand* (prop. *dictate*), i.e. to *catechize* (in an invidious manner):—provoke to speak.

654. **ἀποστρέφω apŏstrĕphō**, *ap-os-tref'-o;* from *575* and *4762;* to *turn away* or *back* (lit. or fig.):—bring again, pervert, turn away (from).

655. **ἀποστυγέω apŏstugĕō**, *ap-os-toog-eh'-o;* from *575* and the base of *4767;* to *detest* utterly:—abhor.

656. **ἀποσυνάγωγος apŏsunagōgŏs**, *ap-os-oon-ag'-o-gos;* from *575* and *4864;* *excommunicated:*—(put) out of the synagogue (-s).

657. **ἀποτάσσομαι apŏtassŏmai**, *ap-ot-as'-som-ahee;* mid. from *575* and *5021;* lit. to *say adieu* (by departing or dismissing); fig. to *renounce:*—bid farewell, forsake, take leave, send away.

658. **ἀποτελέω apŏtĕlĕō**, *ap-ot-el-eh'-o;* from *575* and *5055;* to *complete entirely*, i.e. *consummate:*—finish.

659. **ἀποτίθημι apŏtithēmi**, *ap-ot-eeth'-ay-mee;* from *575* and *5087;* to *put away* (lit. or fig.):—cast off, lay apart (aside, down), put away (off).

660. **ἀποτινάσσω apŏtinassō**, *ap-ot-in-as'-so;* from *575* and **τινάσσω tinassō** (to *jostle*); to *brush off:*—shake off.

661. **ἀποτίνω apŏtinō**, *ap-ot-ee'-no;* from *575* and *5099;* to *pay* in full:—repay.

662. **ἀποτολμάω apŏtŏlmaō**, *ap-ot-ol-mah'-o;* from *575* and *5111;* to *venture* plainly:—be very bold.

663. **ἀποτομία apŏtŏmia**, *ap-ot-om-ee'-ah;* from the base of *664;* (fig.) *decisiveness*, i.e. *rigor:*—severity.

664. **ἀποτόμως apŏtŏmōs**, *ap-ot-om'-oce;* adv. from a der. of a comp. of *575* and **τέμνω tĕmnō** (to *cut*); *abruptly*, i.e. *peremptorily:*—sharply (-ness).

665. **ἀποτρέπω apŏtrĕpō**, *ap-ot-rep'-o;* from *575* and the base of *5157;* to *deflect*, i.e. (reflex.) *avoid:*—turn away.

666. **ἀπουσία apŏusia**, *ap-oo-see'-ah;* from the part. of *548;* a *being away:*—absence.

667. **ἀποφέρω appŏhĕrō**, *ap-of-er'-o;* from *575* and *5342;* to *bear off* (lit. or rel.):—bring, carry (away).

668. **ἀποφεύγω apŏphĕugō**, *ap-of-yoo'-go;* from *575* and *5343;* (fig.) to *escape:*—escape.

669. **ἀποφθέγγομαι apŏphthĕggŏmai**, *ap-of-theng'-om-ahee;* from *575* and *5350;* to *enunciate* plainly, i.e. *declare:*—say, speak forth, utterance.

670. **ἀποφορτίζομαι apŏphŏrtizŏmai**, *ap-of-or-tid'-zom-ahee;* from *575* and the mid. of *5412;* to *unload:*—unlade.

671. **ἀπόχρησις apŏchrēsis**, *ap-okh'-ray-sis;* from a comp. of *575* and *5530;* the act of *using up*, i.e. *consumption:*—using.

672. **ἀποχωρέω apŏchōrĕō**, *ap-okh-o-reh'-o;* from *575* and *5562;* to *go away:*—depart.

673. **ἀποχωρίζω apŏchōrizō**, *ap-okh-o-rid'-zo;* from *575* and *5563;* to *rend apart;* reflex. to *separate:*—depart (asunder).

674. **ἀποψύχω apŏpsuchō**, *ap-ops-oo'-kho;* from *575* and *5594;* to *breathe out*, i.e. *faint:*—hearts failing.

675. **Ἄππιος Appiŏs**, *ap'-pee-os;* of Lat. or.; (in the genitive, i.e. possessive case) *of Appius*, the name of a Roman:—Appii.

676. **ἀπρόσιτος aprŏsitŏs**, *ap-ros'-ee-tos;* from *1* (as a neg. particle) and a der. of a comp. of *4314* and **εἶμι ĕimi** (to *go*); *inaccessible:*—which no man can approach.

677. **ἀπρόσκοπος aprŏskŏpŏs**, *ap-ros'-kop-os;* from *1* (as a neg. particle) and a presumed der. of *4350;* act. *inoffensive*, i.e. *not leading into sin;* pass. *faultless*, i.e. *not led into sin:*—none (void of, without) offence.

678. **ἀπροσωπολήπτως aprŏsōpŏlēptōs**, *ap-ros-o-pol-ape'-toce;* adv. from a comp. of *1* (as a neg. particle) and a presumed der. of a presumed comp. of *4383* and *2983* [comp. *4381*]; in a way *not accepting the person*, i.e. *impartially:*—without respect of persons.

679. **ἄπταιστος aptaistŏs**, *ap-tah'ee-stos;* from *1* (as a neg. particle) and a der. of *4417;* *not stumbling*, i.e. (fig.) *without sin:*—from falling.

680. **ἅπτομαι haptŏmai**, *hap'-tom-ahee;* reflex. of *681;* prop. to *attach* oneself to, i.e. to *touch* (in many implied relations):—touch.

681. **ἅπτω haptō**, *hap'-to;* a prim. verb; prop. to *fasten* to, i.e. (spec.) to *set* on fire:—kindle, light.

682. **Ἀπφία Apphia**, *ap-fee'-a;* prob. of for. or.; *Apphia*, a woman of Colossæ:—Apphia.

683. **ἀπωθέομαι apōthĕŏmai**, *ap-o-theh'-om-ahee;* or **ἀπώθομαι apōthŏmai**, *ap-o'-thom-ahee;* from *575* and the mid. of **ὠθέω ōthĕō** or **ὤθω ōthō** (to *shove*); to *push off*, fig. to *reject:*—cast away, put away (from), thrust away (from).

684. **ἀπώλεια apōlĕia**, *ap-o'-li-a;* from a presumed der. of *622;* *ruin* or *loss* (phys., spiritual or eternal):—damnable (-nation), destruction, die, perdition, × perish, pernicious ways, waste.

685. **ἀρά ara**, *ar-ah';* prob. from *142;* prop. *prayer* (as *lifted* to Heaven), i.e. (by impl.) *imprecation:*—curse.

686. **ἄρα ara**, *ar'-ah;* prob. from *142* (through the idea of *drawing* a conclusion); a particle denoting an *inference* more or less decisive (as follows):—haply, (what) manner (of man), no doubt, perhaps, so be, then, therefore, truly, wherefore. Often used in connection with other particles, especially *1065* or *3767* (after) or *1487* (before). Comp. also *687*.

687. **ἆρα ara**, *ar'-ah;* a form of *686*, denoting an *interrogation* to which a negative answer is presumed:—therefore.

688. **Ἀραβία Arabia**, *ar-ab-ee'-ah;* of Heb. or. [6152]; *Arabia*, a region of Asia:—Arabia.

ἄραγε aragĕ. See *686* and *1065*.

689. **Ἀράμ Aram**, *ar-am';* of Heb. or. [7410]; *Aram* (i.e. *Ram*), an Isr.:—Aram.

690. **Ἄραψ Araps**, *ar'-aps;* from *688;* an *Arab* or native of Arabia:—Arabian.

691. **ἀργέω argĕō**, *arg-eh'-o;* from *692;* to *be idle*, i.e. (fig.) to *delay:*—linger.

692. **ἀργός argŏs**, *ar-gos';* from *1* (as a neg. particle) and *2041;* *inactive*, i.e. *unemployed;* (by impl.) *lazy*, *useless:*—barren, idle, slow.

693. **ἀργύρεος argurĕŏs**, *ar-goo'-reh-os;* from *696;* made of *silver:*—(of) silver.

694. **ἀργύριον arguriŏn**, *ar-goo'-ree-on;* neut. of a presumed der. of *696;* *silvery*, i.e. (by impl.) *cash;* spec. a *silverling* (i.e. *drachma* or *shekel*):—money, (piece of) silver (piece).

695. **ἀργυροκόπος argurŏkŏpŏs**, *ar-goo-rok-op'-os;* from *696* and *2875;* a *beater* (i.e. *worker*) *of silver:*—silversmith.

696. **ἄργυρος argurŏs**, *ar'-goo-ros;* from **ἀργός argŏs** (*shining*); *silver* (the metal, in the articles or coin):—silver.

697. **Ἄρειος Πάγος Arĕiŏs Pagŏs**, *ar'-i-os pag'-os;* from **Ἄρης Arēs** (the name of the Greek deity of war) and a der. of *4078;* *rock of Ares*, a place in Athens:—Areopagus, Mars' Hill.

698. **Ἀρεοπαγίτης Arĕŏpagitēs**, *ar-eh-op-ag-ee'-tace;* from *697;* an *Areopagite* or member of the court held on Mars' Hill:—Areopagite.

699. **ἀρέσκεια arĕskĕia**, *ar-es'-ki-ah;* from a der. of *700;* *complaisance:*—pleasing.

700. **ἀρέσκω arĕskō**, *ar-es'-ko;* prob. from *142* (through the idea of *exciting* emotion); to *be agreeable* (or by impl. to seek to be so):—please.

701. **ἀρεστός arĕstŏs**, *ar-es-tos';* from *700;* *agreeable;* by impl. *fit:*—(things that) please (-ing), reason.

702. **Ἀρέτας Arĕtas**, *ar-et'-as;* of for. or.; *Aretas*, an Arabian:—Aretas.

703. **ἀρέτη arĕtē**, *ar-et'-ay;* from the same as *730;* prop. *manliness* (*valor*), i.e. *excellence* (intrinsic or attributed):—praise, virtue.

704. **ἀρήν arēn**, *ar-ane';* perh. the same as *730;* a *lamb* (as a *male*):—lamb.

705. **ἀριθμέω arithmĕō**, *ar-ith-meh'-o;* from *706;* to *enumerate* or *count:*—number.

706. **ἀριθμός arithmŏs**, *ar-ith-mos';* from *142;* a *number* (as reckoned *up*):—number.

707. **Ἀριμαθαία Arimathaia**, *ar-ee-math-ah'ee-ah;* of Heb. or. [7414]; *Arimathæa* (or *Ramah*), a place in Pal.:—Arimathæa.

708. **Ἀρίσταρχος Aristarchŏs**, *ar-is'-tar-khos;* from the same as *712* and *757;* *best ruling;* *Aristarchus*, a Macedonian:—Aristarchus.

709. **ἀριστάω aristaō**, *ar-is-tah'-o;* from *712;* to *take the principal meal:*—dine.

710. **ἀριστερός aristĕrŏs**, *ar-is-ter-os';* appar. a comp. of the same as *712;* the *left* hand (as *second-best*):—left [hand].

711. Ἀριστόβουλος **Aristŏbŏulŏs**, *ar-is-tob'-oo-los;* from the same as *712* and *1012; best counselling; Aristobulus*, a Chr.:—Aristobulus.

712. ἄριστον **aristŏn**, *ar'-is-ton;* appar. neut. of a superlative from the same as *730;* the *best* meal [or *breakfast;* perh. from ἦρι **ēri** ("*early*")], i.e. *luncheon:*—dinner.

713. ἀρκετός **arkĕtŏs**, *ar-ket-os';* from *714; satisfactory:*—enough, suffice (-ient).

714. ἀρκέω **arkĕō**, *ar-keh'-o;* appar. a prim. verb [but prob. akin to *142* through the idea of *raising* a barrier]; prop. to *ward off*, i.e. (by impl.) to *avail* (fig. *be satisfactory*):—be content, be enough, suffice, be sufficient.

715. ἄρκτος **arktŏs**, *ark'-tos;* prob. from *714;* a *bear* (as *obstructing* by ferocity):—bear.

716. ἅρμα **harma**, *har'-mah;* prob. from *142* [perh. with *1* (as a particle of union) prefixed]; a *chariot* (as *raised* or fitted *together* [comp. *719*]):—chariot.

717. Ἀρμαγεδδών **Armagĕddōn**, *ar-mag-ed-dohn';* of Heb. or. [2022 and 4023]; *Armageddon* (or *Har-Megiddon*), a symbol. name:—Armageddon.

718. ἁρμόζω **harmŏzō**, *har-mod'-zo;* from *719;* to *joint*, i.e. (fig.) to *woo* (reflex. to *betroth*):—espouse.

719. ἁρμός **harmŏs**, *har-mos';* from the same as *716;* an *articulation* (of the body):—joint.

720. ἀρνέομαι **arnĕŏmai**, *ar-neh'-om-ahee;* perh. from *1* (as a neg. particle) and the mid. of *4483;* to *contradict*, i.e. *disavow, reject, abnegate:*—deny, refuse.

721. ἀρνίον **arniŏn**, *ar-nee'-on;* diminutive from *704;* a *lambkin:*—lamb.

722. ἀροτριόω **arŏtriŏō**, *ar-ot-ree-ŏ'-o;* from *723;* to *plough:*—plow.

723. ἄροτρον **arŏtrŏn**, *ar'-ot-ron;* from ἀρόω **arŏō** (to *till*); a *plough:*—plow.

724. ἁρπαγή **harpagē**, *har-pag-ay';* from *726; pillage* (prop. abstr.):—extortion, ravening, spoiling.

725. ἁρπαγμός **harpagmŏs**, *har-pag-mos';* from *726; plunder* (prop. concr.):—robbery.

726. ἁρπάζω **harpazō**, *har-pad'-zo;* from a der. of *138;* to *seize* (in various applications):—catch (away, up), pluck, pull, take (by force).

727. ἅρπαξ **harpax**, *har'-pax;* from *726; rapacious:*—extortion, ravening.

728. ἀῤῥαβών **arrhabōn**, *ar-hrab-ohn';* of Heb. or. [6162]; a *pledge*, i.e. part of the purchase-money or property given in advance as *security* for the rest:—earnest.

729. ἄῤῥαφος **arrhaphŏs**, *ar'-hhraf-os;* from *1* (as a neg. particle) and a presumed der. of the same as *4476; unsewed*, i.e. of a single piece:—without seam.

730. ἄῤῥην **arrhēn**, *ar'-hrane;* or
ἄρσην **arsēn**, *ar'-sane;* prob. from *142; male* (as stronger for *lifting*):—male, man.

731. ἄῤῥητος **arrhētŏs**, *ar'-hray-tos;* from *1* (as a neg. particle) and the same as *4490; unsaid*, i.e. (by impl.) *inexpressible:*—unspeakable.

732. ἄῤῥωστος **arrhōstŏs**, *ar'-hroce-tos;* from *1* (as a neg. particle) and a presumed der. of *4517; infirm:*—sick (folk, -ly).

733. ἀρσενοκοίτης **arsĕnŏkŏitēs**, *ar-sen-ok-oy'-tace;* from *730* and *2845;* a *sodomite:*—abuser of (that defile) self with mankind.

734. Ἀρτεμᾶς **Artĕmas**, *ar-tem-as';* contr. from a comp. of *735* and *1435; gift of Artemis; Artemas* (or *Artemidorus*), a Chr.:—Artemas.

735. Ἄρτεμις **Artĕmis**, *ar'-tem-is;* prob. from the same as *736; prompt; Artemis*, the name of a Grecian goddess borrowed by the Asiatics for one of their deities:—Diana.

736. ἀρτέμων **artĕmōn**, *ar-tem'-ohn;* from a der. of *737;* prop. something *ready* [or else more remotely from *142* (comp. *740*); something *hung* up], i.e. (spec.) the *topsail* (rather *foresail* or *jib*) of a vessel:—mainsail.

737. ἄρτι **arti**, *ar'-tee;* adv. from a der. of *142* (comp. *740*) through the idea of *suspension; just now:*—this day (hour), hence [-forth], here [-after], hither [-to], (even) now, (this) present.

738. ἀρτιγέννητος **artigĕnnētŏs**, *ar-teeg-en'-nay-tos;* from *737* and *1084; just born*, i.e. (fig.) a *young convert:*—new born.

739. ἄρτιος **artiŏs**, *ar'-tee-os;* from *737; fresh*, i.e. (by impl.) *complete:*—perfect.

740. ἄρτος **artos**, *ar'-tos;* from *142; bread* (as *raised*) or a *loaf:*—(shew-) bread, loaf.

741. ἀρτύω **artuō**, *ar-too'-o;* from a presumed der. of *142;* to *prepare*, i.e. *spice* (with *stimulating* condiments):—season.

742. Ἀρφαξάδ **Arphaxad**, *ar-fax-ad';* of Heb. or. [775]; *Arphaxad*, a post-diluvian patriarch:—Arphaxad.

743. ἀρχάγγελος **archaggĕlŏs**, *ar-khang'-el-os;* from *757* and *32;* a *chief angel:*—archangel.

744. ἀρχαῖος **archaiŏs**, *ar-khah'-yos;* from *746; original* or *primeval:*—(them of) old (time).

745. Ἀρχέλαος **Archĕlaŏs**, *ar-khel'-ah-os;* from *757* and *2994; people-ruling; Archelaus*, a Jewish king:—Archelaus.

746. ἀρχή **archē**, *ar-khay';* from *756;* (prop. abstr.) a *commencement*, or (concr.) *chief* (in various applications of order, time, place or rank):—beginning, corner, (at the, the) first (estate), magistrate, power, principality, principle, rule.

747. ἀρχηγός **archēgŏs**, *ar-khay-gos';* from *746* and *71;* a *chief leader:*—author, captain, prince.

748. ἀρχιερατικός **archiĕratikŏs**, *ar-khee-er-at-ee-kos';* from *746* and a der. of *2413; high-priestly:*—of the high-priest.

749. ἀρχιερεύς **archiĕrĕus**, *ar-khee-er-yuce';* from *746* and *2409;* the *high-priest* (lit. of the Jews, typ. Christ); by extens. a *chief priest:*—chief (high) priest, chief of the priests.

750. ἀρχιποίμην **archipŏimēn**, *ar-khee-poy'-mane;* from *746* and *4166;* a *head shepherd:*—chief shepherd.

751. Ἄρχιππος **Archippŏs**, *ar'-khip-pos;* from *746* and *2462; horse-ruler; Archippus*, a Chr.:—Archippus.

752. ἀρχισυνάγωγος **archisunagōgŏs**, *ar-khee-soon-ag'-o-gos;* from *746* and *4864; director of the synagogue* services:—(chief) ruler of the synagogue.

753. ἀρχιτέκτων **architĕktōn**, *ar-khee-tek'-tone;* from *746* and *5045;* a *chief constructor*, i.e. "*architect*":—masterbuilder.

754. ἀρχιτελώνης **architĕlōnēs**, *ar-khee-tel-o'-nace;* from *746* and *5057;* a *principal tax-gatherer:*—chief among the publicans.

755. ἀρχιτρίκλινος **architriklinŏs**, *ar-khee-tree'-klee-nos;* from *746* and a comp. of *5140* and *2827* (a *dinner-bed*, because composed of three couches); *director of* the *entertainment:*—governor (ruler) of the feast.

756. ἄρχομαι **archŏmai**, *ar'-khom-ahee;* mid. of *757* (through the impl. of *precedence*); to *commence* (in order of time):—(rehearse from the) begin (-ning).

757. ἄρχω **archō**, *ar'-kho;* a prim. verb; to be *first* (in political rank or power):—reign (rule) over.

758. ἄρχων **archōn**, *ar'-khone;* pres. part. of *757;* a *first* (in rank or power):—chief (ruler), magistrate, prince, ruler.

759. ἄρωμα "**arōma**," *ar'-o-mah;* from *142* (in the sense of *sending* off scent); an *aromatic:*—(sweet) spice.

760. Ἀσά **Asa**, *as-ah';* of Heb. or. [609]; *Asa*, an Isr.:—Asa.

761. ἀσάλευτος **asalĕutŏs**, *as-al'-yoo-tos;* from *1* (as a neg. particle) and a der. of *4531; unshaken*, i.e. (by impl.) *immovable* (fig.):—which cannot be moved, unmovable.

762. ἄσβεστος **asbĕstŏs**, *as'-bes-tos;* from *1* (as a neg. particle) and a der. of *4570; not extinguished*, i.e. (by impl.) *perpetual:*—not to be quenched, unquenchable.

763. ἀσέβεια **asĕbĕia**, *as-eb'-i-ah;* from *765; impiety*, i.e. (by impl.) *wickedness:*—ungodly (-liness).

764. ἀσεβέω **asĕbĕō**, *as-eb-eh'-o;* from *765;* to be (by impl. *act*) *impious* or *wicked:*—commit (live, that after should live) ungodly.

765. ἀσεβής **asĕbēs**, *as-eb-ace';* from *1* (as a neg. particle) and a presumed der. of *4576; irreverent*, i.e. (by extens.) *impious* or *wicked:*—ungodly (man).

766. ἀσέλγεια **asĕlgĕia**, *as-elg'-i-a;* from a comp. of *1* (as a neg. particle) and a presumed σελγής **sĕlgēs** (of uncert. der., but appar. mean. *continent*); *licentiousness* (sometimes including other vices):—filthy, lasciviousness, wantonness.

767. ἄσημος **asēmŏs**, *as'-ay-mos;* from *1* (as a neg. particle) and the base of *4591; unmarked*, i.e. (fig.) *ignoble:*—mean.

768. Ἀσήρ **Asēr**, *as-ayr';* of Heb. or. [836]; *Aser* (i.e. *Asher*), an Isr. tribe:—Aser.

769. ἀσθένεια **asthĕnĕia**, *as-then'-i-ah;* from *772; feebleness* (of body or mind); by impl. *malady;* mor. *frailty:*—disease, infirmity, sickness, weakness.

770. ἀσθενέω **asthĕnĕō**, *as-then-eh'-o;* from *772;* to *be feeble* (in any sense):—be diseased, impotent folk (man), (be) sick, (be, be made) weak.

771. ἀσθένημα **asthĕnēma**, *as-then'-ay-mah;* from *770;* a *scruple* of conscience:—infirmity.

772. ἀσθενής **asthĕnēs**, *as-then-ace';* from *1* (as a neg. particle) and the base of *4599; strengthless* (in various applications, lit., fig. and mor.):—more feeble, impotent, sick, without strength, weak (-er, -ness, thing).

773. Ἀσία **Asia**, *as-ee'-ah;* of uncert. der.; *Asia*, i.e. *Asia Minor*, or (usually) only its western shore:—Asia.

774. Ἀσιανός **Asianŏs**, *as-ee-an-os';* from *773;* an *Asian* (i.e. *Asiatic*) or inhab. of Asia:—of Asia.

775. Ἀσιάρχης **Asiarchēs**, *as-ee ar'-khace;* from *773* and *746;* an *Asiarch* or president of the public festivities in a city of Asia Minor:—chief of Asia.

776. ἀσιτία **asitia**, *as-ee-tee'-ah;* from *777; fasting* (the state):—abstinence.

777. ἄσιτος **asitŏs**, *as'-ee-tos;* from *1* (as a neg. particle) and *4621; without* (taking) *food:*—fasting.

778. ἀσκέω **askĕō**, *as-keh'-o;* prob. from the same as *4632;* to *elaborate*, i.e. (fig.) *train* (by impl. *strive*):—exercise.

779. ἀσκός **askŏs**, *as-kos';* from the same as *778;* a leathern (or skin) *bag* used as a bottle:—bottle.

780. ἀσμένως **asmĕnōs**, *as-men'-oce;* adv. from a der. of the base of *2237; with pleasure:*—gladly.

781. ἄσοφος **asŏphŏs**, *as'-of-os;* from *1* (as a neg. particle) and *4680; unwise:*—fool.

782. ἀσπάζομαι **aspazŏmai**, *as-pad'-zom-ahee;* from *1* (as a particle of union) and a presumed form of *4685;* to *enfold* in the arms, i.e. (by impl.) to *salute*, (fig.) to *welcome:*—embrace, greet, salute, take leave.

783. ἀσπασμός **aspasmŏs**, *as-pas-mos';* from *782;* a *greeting* (in person or by letter):—greeting, salutation.

784. ἄσπιλος **aspilŏs**, *as'-pee-los;* from *1* (as a neg. particle) and *4695; unblemished* (phys. or mor.):—without spot, unspotted.

785. ἀσπίς **aspis**, *as-pece';* of uncert. der.; a *buckler* (or *round* shield); used of a serpent (as *coiling* itself), prob. the "*asp*":—asp.

786. ἄσπονδος **aspŏndŏs**, *as'-pon-dos;* from *1* (as a neg. particle) and a der. of *4689;* lit. *without libation* (which usually accompanied a treaty), i.e. (by impl.) *truceless:*—implacable, truce-breaker.

787. ἀσσάριον **assariŏn**, *as-sar'-ee-on;* of Lat. or.; an *assarius* or *as*, a Roman coin:—farthing.

788. ἆσσον **assŏn**, *as'-son;* neut. comparative of the base of *1451; more nearly*, i.e. *very near:*—close.

789. Ἄσσος **Assŏs**, *as'-sos;* prob. of for. or.; *Assus*, a city of Asia Minor:—Assos.

790. ἀστατέω **astatĕō**, *as-tat-eh'-o;* from *1* (as a neg. particle) and a der. of *2476;* to *be non-stationary*, i.e. (fig.) *homeless:*—have no certain dwelling-place.

791. ἀστεῖος **astĕiŏs**, *as-ti'-os;* from ἄστυ **astu** (a *city*); *urbane*, i.e. (by impl.) *handsome:*—fair.

792. ἀστήρ **astēr**, *as-tare';* prob. from the base of *4766;* a *star* (as *strown* over the sky), lit. or fig.:—star.

793. ἀστήρικτος **astēriktŏs**, *as-tay'-rik-tos;* from *1* (as a neg. particle) and a presumed der. of *4741; unfixed,* i.e. (fig.) *vacillating:*—unstable.

794. ἄστοργος **astŏrgŏs**, *as'-tor-gos;* from *1* (as a neg. particle) and a presumed der. of **στέργω stĕrgō** (to *cherish* affectionately); *hard-hearted* towards kindred:—without natural affection.

795. ἀστοχέω **astŏchĕō**, *as-tokh-eh'-o;* from a comp. of *1* (as a neg. particle) and **στόιχος stŏichŏs** (an *aim*); to *miss* the mark, i.e. (fig.) *deviate* from truth:—err, swerve.

796. ἀστραπή **astrapē**, *as-trap-ay';* from *797; lightning;* by anal. *glare:*—lightning, bright shining.

797. ἀστράπτω **astraptō**, *as-trap'-to;* prob. from *792;* to *flash* as lightning:—lighten, shine.

798. ἄστρον **astrŏn**, *as'-tron;* neut. from *792;* prop. a *constellation;* put for a single *star* (nat. or artificial):—star.

799. Ἀσύγκριτος **Asugkritŏs**, *as-oong'-kree-tos;* from *1* (as a neg. particle) and a der. of *4793; incomparable; Asyncritus,* a Chr.:—Asyncritus.

800. ἀσύμφωνος **asumphōnŏs**, *as-oom'-fo-nos;* from *1* (as a neg. particle) and *4859; inharmonious* (fig.):—agree not.

801. ἀσύνετος **asunĕtŏs**, *as-oon'-ay-tos;* from *1* (as a neg. particle) and *4908; unintelligent;* by impl. *wicked:*—foolish, without understanding.

802. ἀσύνθετος **asunthĕtŏs**, *as-oon'-thet-os;* from *1* (as a neg. particle) and a der. of *4934;* prop. *not agreed,* i.e. *treacherous* to compacts:—covenant-breaker.

803. ἀσφάλεια **asphalĕia**, *as-fal'-i-ah;* from *804; security* (lit. or fig.):—certainty, safety.

804. ἀσφαλής **asphalēs**, *as-fal-ace';* from *1* (as a neg. particle) and **σφάλλω sphallō** (to "*fail*"); *secure* (lit. or fig.):—certain (-ty), safe, sure.

805. ἀσφαλίζω **asphalizō**, *as-fal-id'-zo;* from *804;* to *render secure:*—make fast (sure).

806. ἀσφαλῶς **asphalōs**, *as-fal-oce';* adv. from *804; securely* (lit. or fig.):—assuredly, safely.

807. ἀσχημονέω **aschēmŏnĕō**, *as-kay-mon-eh'-o;* from *809;* to *be* (i.e. *act*) *unbecoming:*—behave self uncomely (unseemly).

808. ἀσχημοσύνη **aschēmŏsunē**, *as-kay-mos-oo'-nay;* from *809;* an *indecency;* by impl. the *pudenda:*—shame, that which is unseemly.

809. ἀσχήμων **askēmōn**, *as-kay'-mone;* from *1* (as a neg. particle) and a presumed der. of *2192* (in the sense of its congener *4976*); prop. *shapeless,* i.e. (fig.) *inelegant:*—uncomely.

810. ἀσωτία **asōtia**, *as-o-tee'-ah;* from a comp. of *1* (as a neg. particle) and a presumed der. of *4982;* prop. *unsavedness,* i.e. (by impl.) *profligacy:*—excess, riot.

811. ἀσώτως **asōtōs**, *as-o'-toce;* adv. from the same as *810; dissolutely:*—riotous.

812. ἀτακτέω **ataktĕō**, *at-ak-teh'-o;* from *813;* to *be* (i.e. *act*) *irregular:*—behave self disorderly.

813. ἄτακτος **ataktŏs**, *at'-ak-tos;* from *1* (as a neg. particle) and a der. of *5021; unarranged,* i.e. (by impl.) *insubordinate* (religiously):—unruly.

814. ἀτάκτως **ataktōs**, *at-ak'-toce;* adv. from *813; irregularly* (mor.):—disorderly.

815. ατεκνος **atĕknŏs**, *at'-ek-nos;* from *1* (as a neg. particle) and *5043; childless:*—childless, without children.

816. ἀτενίζω **atĕnizō**, *at-en-id'-zo;* from a comp. of *1* (as a particle of union) and **τείνω tĕinō** (to *stretch*); to *gaze* intently:—behold earnestly (stedfastly), fasten (eyes), look (earnestly, stedfastly, up stedfastly), set eyes.

817. ἄτερ **atĕr**, *at'-er;* a particle prob. akin to *427; aloof,* i.e. *apart* from (lit. or fig.):—in the absence of, without.

818. ἀτιμάζω **atimazō**, *at-im-ad'-zo;* from *820;* to *render infamous,* i.e. (by impl.) *contemn* or *maltreat:*—despise, dishonour, suffer shame, entreat shamefully.

819. ἀτιμία **atimia**, *at-ee-mee'-ah;* from *820; infamy,* i.e. (subj.) comparative *indignity,* (obj.) *disgrace:*—dishonour, reproach, shame, vile.

820. ἄτιμος **atimŏs**, *at'-ee-mos;* from *1* (as a neg. particle) and *5092;* (neg.) *unhonoured* or (pos.) *dishonoured:*—despised, without honour, less honourable [*comparative degree*].

821. ἀτιμόω **atimŏō**, *at-ee-mŏ'-o;* from *820;* used like *818,* to *maltreat:*—handle shamefully.

822. ἀτμίς **atmis**, *at-mece';* from the same as *109; mist:*—vapour.

823. ἄτομος **atŏmŏs**, *at'-om-os;* from *1* (as a neg. particle) and the base of *5114; uncut,* i.e. (by impl.) *indivisible* [an "*atom*" of time]:—moment.

824. ἄτοπος **atŏpŏs**, *at'-op-os;* from *1* (as a neg. particle) and *5117; out of place,* i.e. (fig.) *improper, injurious, wicked:*—amiss, harm, unreasonable.

825. Ἀττάλεια **Attalĕia**, *at-tal'-i-ah;* from Ἄτταλος **Attalŏs** (a king of Pergamus); *Attaleia,* a place in Pamphylia:—Attalia.

826. αὐγάζω **augazō**, *ŏw-gad'-zo;* from *827;* to *beam* forth (fig.):—shine.

827. αὐγή **augē**, *ŏwg'-ay;* of uncert. der.; a *ray* of light, i.e. (by impl.) *radiance, dawn:*—break of day.

828. Αὔγουστος **Augŏustŏs**, *ŏw'-goos-tos;* from Lat. ["august"]; *Augustus,* a title of the Rom. emperor:—Augustus.

829. αὐθάδης **authadēs**, *ŏw-thad'-ace;* from *846* and the base of *2237; self-pleasing,* i.e. *arrogant:*—self-willed.

830. αὐθαίρετος **authairĕtŏs**, *ŏw-thah'-ee-ret-os;* from *846* and the same as *140; self-chosen,* i.e. (by impl.) *voluntary:*—of own accord, willing of self.

831. αὐθεντέω **authĕntĕō**, *ŏw-then-teh'-o;* from a comp. of *846* and an obsol. **ἕντης hĕntēs** (a *worker*); to *act of oneself,* i.e. (fig.) *dominate:*—usurp authority over.

832. αὐλέω **aulĕō**, *ŏw-leh'-o;* from *836;* to play the *flute:*—pipe.

833. αὐλή **aulē**, *ŏw-lay';* from the same as *109;* a *yard* (as open to the *wind*); by impl. a *mansion:*—court, ([sheep-]) fold, hall, palace.

834. αὐλητής **aulētēs**, *ŏw-lay-tace';* from *832;* a *flute-player:*—minstrel, piper.

835. αὐλίζομαι **aulizŏmai**, *ŏw-lid'-zom-ahee;* mid. from *833;* to *pass the night* (prop. in the open air):—abide, lodge.

836. αὐλός **aulŏs**, *ŏw-los';* from the same as *109,* a *flute* (as *blown*):—pipe.

837. αὐξάνω **auxanō**, *ŏwx-an'-o;* a prolonged form of a prim. verb; to *grow* ("*wax*"), i.e. *enlarge* (lit. or fig., act. or pass.):—grow (up), (give the) increase.

838. αὔξησις **auxēsis**, *ŏwx'-ay-sis;* from *837; growth:*—increase.

839. αὔριον **auriŏn**, *ŏw'-ree-on;* from a der. of the same as *109* (mean. a *breeze,* i.e. the morning *air*); prop. *fresh,* i.e. (adv. with ellipsis of *2250*) *to-morrow:*—(to-) morrow, next day.

840. αὐστηρός **austērŏs**, *ŏw-stay-ros';* from a (presumed) der. of the same as *109* (mean. *blown*); *rough* (prop. as a *gale*), i.e. (fig.) *severe:*—austere.

841. αὐτάρκεια **autarkeia**, *ŏw-tar'-ki-ah;* from *842; self-satisfaction,* i.e. (abstr.) *contentedness,* or (concr.) a *competence:*—contentment, sufficiency.

842. αὐτάρκης **autarkēs**, *ŏw-tar'-kace;* from *846* and *714; self-complacent,* i.e. *contented:*—content.

843. αὐτοκατάκριτος **autŏkatakritŏs**, *ŏw-tok-at-ak'-ree-tos;* from *846* and a der. of *2632; self-condemned:*—condemned of self.

844. αὐτόματος **autŏmatŏs**, *ŏw-tom'-at-os;* from *846* and the same as *3155; self-moved* ["automatic"], i.e. *spontaneous:*—of own accord, of self.

845. αὐτόπτης **autŏptēs**, *ŏw-top'-tace;* from *846* and *3700; self-seeing,* i.e. an *eye-witness:*—eye-witness.

846. αὐτός **autŏs**, *ŏw-tos';* from the particle **αὖ au** [perh. akin to the base of *109* through the idea of a *baffling* wind] (*backward*); the reflex. pron. *self,* used (alone or in the comp. *1438*) of the third pers., and (with the prop. pers. pron.) of the other persons:—her, it (-self), one, the other, (mine) own, said, ([self-], the) same, ([him-, my-, thy-]) self, [your-] selves, she, that, their (-s), them ([-selves]), there [-at, -by, -in, -into, -of, -on, -with], they, (these) things, this (man), those, together, very, which. Comp. *848.*

847. αὐτοῦ **autŏu**, *ŏw-too';* genitive (i.e. possessive) of *846,* used as an adv. of location; prop. belonging to the *same* spot, i.e. *in this* (or *that*) *place:*—(t-) here.

848. αὑτοῦ **hautŏu**, *how-too';* contr. for *1438; self* (in some oblique case or reflex. relation):—her (own), (of) him (-self), his (own), of it, thee, their (own), them (-selves), they.

849. αὐτόχειρ **autŏchĕir**, *ŏw-tokh'-ire;* from *846* and *5495; self-handed,* i.e. doing *personally:*—with . . . own hands.

850. αὐχμηρός **auchmērŏs**, *ŏwkh-may-ros';* from αὐχμός **auchmŏs** [prob. from a base akin to that of *109*] (*dust,* as *dried* by wind); prop. *dirty,* i.e. (by impl.) *obscure:*—dark.

851. ἀφαιρέω **aphairĕō**, *af-ahee-reh'-o;* from *575* and *138;* to *remove* (lit. or fig.):—cut (smite) off, take away.

852. ἀφανής **aphanēs**, *af-an-ace';* from *1* (as a neg. particle) and *5316; non-apparent:*—that is not manifest.

853. ἀφανίζω **aphanizō**, *af-an-id'-zo;* from *852;* to *render unapparent,* i.e. (act.) *consume* (*becloud*), or (pass.) *disappear* (*be destroyed*):—corrupt, disfigure, perish, vanish away.

854. ἀφανισμός **aphanismŏs**, *af-an-is-mos';* from *853; disappearance,* i.e. (fig.) *abrogation:*—vanish away.

855. ἄφαντος **aphantŏs**, *af'-an-tŏs;* from *1* (as a neg. particle) and a der. of *5316; non-manifested,* i.e. *invisible:*—vanished out of sight.

856. ἀφεδρών **aphĕdrōn**, *af-ed-rone';* from a comp. of *575* and the base of *1476;* a place of *sitting apart,* i.e. a *privy:*—draught.

857. ἀφειδία **aphĕidia**, *af-i-dee'-ah;* from a comp. of *1* (as a neg. particle) and *5339; unsparingness,* i.e. *austerity* (*ascetism*):—neglecting.

858. ἀφελότης **aphĕlŏtēs**, *af-el-ot'-ace;* from a comp. of *1* (as a neg. particle) and **φέλλος phĕllŏs** (in the sense of a *stone* as *stubbing* the foot); *smoothness,* i.e. (fig.) *simplicity:*—singleness.

859. ἄφεσις **aphĕsis**, *af'-es-is;* from *863; freedom;* (fig.) *pardon:*—deliverance, forgiveness, liberty, remission.

860. ἁφή **haphē**, *haf-ay';* from *680;* prob. a *ligament* (as *fastening*):—joint.

861. ἀφθαρσία **aphtharsia**, *af-thar-see'-ah;* from *862; incorruptibility;* gen. *unending existence;* (fig.) *genuineness:*—immortality, incorruption, sincerity.

862. ἄφθαρτος **aphthartŏs**, *af'-thar-tos;* from *1* (as a neg. particle) and a der. of *5351; undecaying* (in essence or continuance):—not (in-, un-) corruptible, immortal.

863. ἀφίημι **aphiēmi**, *af-ee'-ay-mee;* from *575* and ἵημι **hiemi** (to *send;* an intens. form of **εἶμι ĕimi,** to *go*); to *send forth,* in various applications (as follow):—cry, forgive, forsake, lay aside, leave, let (alone, be, go, have), omit, put (send) away, remit, suffer, yield up.

864. ἀφικνέομαι **aphiknĕŏmai**, *af-ik-neh'-om-ahee;* from *575* and the base of *2425;* to *go* (i.e. *spread*) *forth* (by rumor):—come abroad.

865. ἀφιλάγαθος **aphilagathŏs**, *af-il-ag'-ath-os;* from *1* (as a neg. particle) and *5358; hostile to virtue:*—despiser of those that are good.

866. ἀφιλάργυρος **aphilargurŏs**, *af-il-ar'-goo-ros;* from *1* (as a neg. particle) and *5366; unavaricious:*—without covetousness, not greedy of filthy lucre.

867. ἄφιξις **aphixis**, *af'-ix-is;* from *864;* prop. *arrival,* i.e. (by impl.) *departure:*—departing.

868. ἀφίστημι **aphistēmi**, *af-is'-tay-mee;* from *575* and *2476;* to *remove,* i.e. (act.) *instigate* to revolt;

usually (reflex.) to *desist, desert*, etc.:—depart, draw (fall) away, refrain, withdraw self.

869. ἄφνω **aphnō**, *af'-no;* adv. from *852* (contr.); *unawares*, i.e. *unexpectedly:*—suddenly.

870. ἀφόβως **aphŏbōs**, *af-ob'-oce;* adv. from a comp. of *1* (as a neg. particle) and *5401*; *fearlessly:*—without fear.

871. ἀφομοιόω **aphŏmŏiŏō**, *af-om-oy-ŏ'-o;* from *575* and *3666*; to *assimilate* closely:—make like.

872. ἀφοράω **aphŏraō**, *af-or-ah'-o;* from *575* and *3708*; to *consider* attentively:—look.

873. ἀφορίζω **aphŏrizō**, *af-or-id'-zo;* from *575* and *3724*; to *set off* by boundary, i.e. (fig.) *limit, exclude, appoint*, etc.:—divide, separate, sever.

874. ἀφορμή **aphŏrmē**, *af-or-may';* from a comp. of *575* and *3729*; a *starting*-point, i.e. (fig.) an *opportunity:*—occasion.

875. ἀφρίζω **aphrizō**, *af-rid'-zo;* from *876*; to *froth* at the mouth (in epilepsy):—foam.

876. ἀφρός **aphrŏs**, *af-ros';* appar. a prim. word; *froth*, i.e. *slaver:*—foaming.

877. ἀφροσύνη **aphrŏsunē**, *af-ros-oo'-nay;* from *878*; *senselessness*, i.e. (euphem.) *egotism;* (mor.) *recklessness:*—folly, foolishly (-ness).

878. ἄφρων **aphrōn**, *af'-rone;* from *1* (as a neg. particle) and *5424*; prop. *mindless*, i.e. *stupid*, (by impl.) *ignorant*, (spec.) *egotistic*, (practically) *rash*, or (mor.) *unbelieving:*—fool (-ish), unwise.

879. ἀφυπνόω **aphupnŏō**, *af-oop-nŏ'-o;* from a comp. of *575* and *5258*; prop. to *become awake*, i.e. (by impl.) to *drop* (off) in slumber:—fall asleep.

880. ἄφωνος **aphōnŏs**, *af'-o-nos;* from *1* (as a neg. particle) and *5456*; *voiceless*, i.e. *mute* (by nature or choice); fig. *unmeaning:*—dumb, without signification.

881. Ἀχάζ **Achaz**, *akh-adz';* of Heb. or. [271]; *Achaz*, an Isr.:—Achaz.

882. Ἀχαΐα **Achaïa**, *ach-ah-ee'-ah;* of uncert. der.; *Achaïa* (i.e. *Greece*), a country of Europe:—Achaia.

883. Ἀχαϊκός **Achaïkŏs**, *ach-ah-ee-kos';* from *882*; an *Achaïan; Achaïcus*, a Chr.:—Achaicus.

884. ἀχάριστος **acharistŏs**, *ach-ar'-is-tos;* from *1* (as a neg. particle) and a presumed der. of *5483*; *thankless*, i.e. *ungrateful:*—unthankful.

885. Ἀχείμ **Achĕim**, *akh-ime';* prob. of Heb. or. [comp. 3137]; *Achim*, an Isr.:—Achim.

886. ἀχειροποίητος **achĕirŏpŏiētŏs**, *akh-i-ropoy'-ay-tos;* from *1* (as a neg. particle) and *5499*; *unmanufactured*, i.e. *inartificial:*—made without (not made with) hands.

887. ἀχλύς **achlus**, *akh-looce';* of uncert. der.; *dimness* of sight, i.e. (prob.) a *cataract:*—mist.

888. ἀχρεῖος **achrĕiŏs**, *akh-ri'-os;* from *1* (as a neg. particle) and a der. of *5534* [comp. *5532*]; *useless*, i.e. (euphem.) *unmeritorious:*—unprofitable.

889. ἀχρειόω **achrĕiŏō**, *akh-ri-ŏ'-o;* from *888*; to *render useless*, i.e. *spoil:*—become unprofitable.

890. ἄχρηστος **achrēstŏs**, *akh'-race-tos;* from *1* (as a neg. particle) and *5543*; *inefficient*, i.e. (by impl.) *detrimental:*—unprofitable.

891. ἄχρι **achri**, *akh'-ree;* or ἄχρις **achris**, *akh'-rece;* akin to *206* (through the idea of a *terminus*); (of time) *until* or (of place) *up to:*—as far as, for, in (-to), till, (even, un-) to, until, while. Comp. *3360*.

892. ἄχυρον **achurŏn**, *akh'-oo-ron;* perh. remotely from χέω **chĕō** (to *shed* forth); *chaff* (as *diffusive*):—chaff.

893. ἀψευδής **apsĕudēs**, *aps-yoo-dace';* from *1* (as a neg. particle) and *5579*; *veracious:*—that cannot lie.

894. ἄψινθος **apsinthŏs**, *ap'-sin-thos;* of uncert. der.; *wormwood* (as a type of *bitterness*, i.e. [fig.] *calamity*):—wormwood.

895. ἄψυχος **apsuchŏs**, *ap'-soo-khos;* from *1* (as a neg. particle) and *5590*; *lifeless*, i.e. *inanimate* (mechanical):—without life.

B

896. Βάαλ **Baal**, *bah'-al;* of Heb. or. [1168]; *Baal*, a Phœnician deity (used as a symbol of idolatry):—Baal.

897. Βαβυλών **Babulōn**, *bab-oo-lone';* of Heb. or. [894]; *Babylon*, the capital of Chaldæa (lit. or fig. [as a type of tyranny]):—Babylon.

898. βαθμός **bathmŏs**, *bath-mos';* from the same as *899*; a *step*, i.e. (fig.) *grade* (of dignity):—degree.

899. βάθος **bathŏs**, *bath'-os;* from the same as *901*; *profundity*, i.e. (by impl.) *extent;* (fig.) *mystery:*—deep (-ness, things), depth.

900. βαθύνω **bathunō**, *bath-oo'-no;* from *901*; to *deepen:*—deep.

901. βαθύς **bathus**, *bath-oos';* from the base of *939*; *profound* (as *going* down), lit. or fig.:—deep, very early.

902. βαΐον **baïŏn**, *bah-ee'-on;* a diminutive of a der. prob. of the base of *939*; a palm *twig* (as *going* out far):—branch.

903. Βαλαάμ **Balaam**, *bal-ah-am';* of Heb. or. [1109]; *Balaam*, a Mesopotamian (symb. of a false teacher):—Balaam.

904. Βαλάκ **Balak**, *bal-ak';* of Heb. or. [1111]; *Balak*, a Moabite:—Balac.

905. βαλάντιον **balantiŏn**, *bal-an'-tee-on;* prob. remotely from *906* (as a *depository*); a *pouch* (for money):—bag, purse.

906. βάλλω **ballō**, *bal'-lo;* a prim. verb; to *throw* (in various applications, more or less violent or intense):—arise, cast (out), × dung, lay, lie, pour, put (up), send, strike, throw (down), thrust. Comp. *4496*.

907. βαπτίζω **baptizō**, *bap-tid'-zo;* from a der. of *911*; to *make whelmed* (i.e. *fully wet*); used only (in the N. T.) of ceremonial *ablution*, espec. (techn.) of the ordinance of Chr. *baptism:*—baptist, baptize, wash.

908. βάπτισμα **baptisma**, *bap'-tis-mah;* from *907*; *baptism* (techn. or fig.):—baptism.

909. βαπτισμός **baptismŏs**, *bap-tis-mos';* from *907*; *ablution* (cerem. or Chr.):—baptism, washing.

910. Βαπτιστής **Baptistēs**, *bap-tis-tace';* from *907*; a *baptizer*, as an epithet of Christ's forerunner:—Baptist.

911. βάπτω **baptō**, *bap'-to;* a prim. verb; to *whelm*, i.e. cover wholly with a fluid; in the N. T. only in a qualified or spec. sense, i.e. (lit.) to *moisten* (a part of one's person), or (by impl.) to *stain* (as with dye):—dip.

912. Βαραββᾶς **Barabbas**, *bar-ab-bas';* of Chald. or. [1347 and *5*]; *son of Abba; Bar-abbas*, an Isr.:—Barabbas.

913. Βαράκ **Barak**, *bar-ak';* of Heb. or. [1301]; *Barak*, an Isr.:—Barak.

914. Βαραχίας **Barachias**, *bar-akh-ee'-as;* of Heb. or. [1296]; *Barachias* (i.e. *Berechijah*), an Isr.:—Barachias.

915. βάρβαρος **barbarŏs**, *bar'-bar-os;* of uncert. der.; a *foreigner* (i.e. *non-Greek*):—barbarian (-rous).

916. βαρέω **barĕō**, *bar-eh'-o;* from *926*; to *weigh* down (fig.):—burden, charge, heavy, press.

917. βαρέως **barĕōs**, *bar-eh'-oce;* adv. from *926*; *heavily* (fig.):—dull.

918. Βαρθολομαῖος **Barthŏlŏmaiŏs**, *bar-thol-om-ah'-yos;* of Chald. or. [1247 and 8526]; *son of Tolmai; Bar-tholomæus*, a Chr. apostle:—Bartholomeus.

919. Βαριησοῦς **Bariēsŏus**, *bar-ee-ay-sooce';* of Chald. or. [1247 and 3091]; *son of Jesus* (or *Joshua*); *Bar-jesus*, an Isr.:—Barjesus.

920. Βαριωνᾶς **Bariōnas**, *bar-ee-oo-nas';* of Chald. or. [1247 and 3124]; *son of Jonas* (or *Jonah*); *Bar-jonas*, an Isr.:—Bar-jona.

921. Βαρνάβας **Barnabas**, *bar-nab'-as;* of Chald. or. [1247 and 5029]; *son of Nabas* (i.e. *prophecy*); *Barnabas*, an Isr.:—Barnabas.

922. βάρος **barŏs**, *bar'-os;* prob. from the same as *939* (through the notion of *going* down; comp. *899*); *weight;* in the N. T. only fig. a *load, abundance, authority:*—burden (-some), weight.

923. Βαρσαβᾶς **Barsabas**, *bar-sab-as';* of Chald. or. [1247 and prob. 6634]; *son of Sabas* (or *Tsaba*); *Bar-sabas*, the name of two Isr.:—Barsabas.

924. Βαρτιμαῖος **Bartimaiŏs**, *bar-tim-ah'-yos;* of Chald. or. [1247 and 2931]; *son of Timæus* (or the *unclean*); *Bar-timæus*, an Isr.:—Bartimæus.

925. βαρύνω **barunō**, *bar-oo'-no;* from *926*; to *burden* (fig.):—overcharge.

926. βαρύς **barus**, *bar-ooce';* from the same as *922*; *weighty*, i.e. (fig.) *burdensome, grave:*—grievous, heavy, weightier.

927. βαρύτιμος **barutimŏs**, *bar-oo'-tim-os;* from *926* and *5092*; highly *valuable:*—very precious.

928. βασανίζω **basanizō**, *bas-an-id'-zo;* from *931*; to *torture:*—pain, toil, torment, toss, vex.

929. βασανισμός **basanismŏs**, *bas-an-is-mos';* from *928*; *torture:*—torment.

930. βασανιστής **basanistēs**, *bas-an-is-tace';* from *928*; a *torturer:*—tormentor.

931. βάσανος **basanŏs**, *bas'-an-os;* perh. remotely from the same as *939* (through the notion of *going* to the bottom); a *touch-stone*, i.e. (by anal.) *torture:*—torment.

932. βασιλεία **basilĕia**, *bas-il-i'-ah;* from *935*; prop. *royalty*, i.e. (abstr.) *rule*, or (concr.) a *realm* (lit. or fig.):—kingdom, + reign.

933. βασίλειον **basilĕiŏn**, *bas-il'-i-on;* neut. of *934*; a *palace:*—king's court.

934. βασίλειος **basilĕiŏs**, *bas-il'-i-os;* from *935*; *kingly* (in nature):—royal.

935. βασιλεύς **basilĕus**, *bas-il-yooce';* prob. from *939* (through the notion of a *foundation* of power); a *sovereign* (abs., rel. or fig.):—king.

936. βασιλεύω **basilĕuō**, *bas-il-yoo'-o;* from *935*; to *rule* (lit. or fig.):—king, reign.

937. βασιλικός **basilikŏs**, *bas-il-ee-kos';* from *935*; *regal* (in relation), i.e. (lit.) belonging to (or befitting) the sovereign (as land, dress, or a *courtier*), or (fig.) *preeminent:*—king's, nobleman, royal.

938. βασίλισσα **basilissa**, *bas-il'-is-sah;* fem. from *936*; a *queen:*—queen.

939. βάσις **basis**, *bas'-ece;* from βαίνω **bainō** (to *walk*); a *pace* ("base"), i.e. (by impl.) the *foot:*—foot.

940. βασκαίνω **baskainō**, *bas-kah'ee-no;* akin to *5335*; to *malign*, i.e. (by extens.) to *fascinate* (by false representations):—bewitch.

941. βαστάζω **bastazō**, *bas-tad'-zo;* perh. remotely der. from the base of *939* (through the idea of *removal*); to *lift*, lit. or fig. (*endure, declare, sustain, receive*, etc.):—bear, carry, take up.

942. βάτος **batŏs**, *bat'-os;* of uncert. der.; a *brier* shrub:—bramble, bush.

943. βάτος **batŏs**, *bat'-os;* of Heb. or. [1324]; a *bath*, or measure for liquids:—measure.

944. βάτραχος **batrachŏs**, *bat'-rakh-os;* of uncert. der.; a *frog:*—frog.

945. βαττολογέω **battŏlŏgĕō**, *bat-tol-og-eh'-o;* from Βάττος **Battŏs** (a proverbial stammerer) and *3056*; to *stutter*, i.e. (by impl.) to *prate* tediously:—use vain repetitions.

946. βδέλυγμα **bdĕlugma**, *bdel'-oog-mah;* from *948*; a *detestation*, i.e. (spec.) *idolatry:*—abomination.

947. βδελυκτός **bdĕluktŏs**, *bdel-ook-tos';* from *948*; *detestable*, i.e. (spec.) *idolatrous:*—abominable.

948. βδελύσσω **bdĕlussō**, *bdel-oos'-so;* from a (presumed) der. of βδέω **bdĕō** (to *stink*); to *be disgusted*, i.e. (by impl.) *detest* (espec. of idolatry):—abhor, abominable.

949. βέβαιος **bĕbaiŏs**, *beb'-ah-yos;* from the base of *939* (through the idea of *basality*); *stable* (lit. or fig.):—firm, of force, stedfast, sure.

950. βεβαιόω **bĕbaiŏō**, *beb-ah-yŏ'-o;* from *949*; to *stabilitate* (fig.):—confirm, (e-) stablish.

951. βεβαίωσις **bĕbaiōsis**, *beb-ah'-yo-sis;* from *950*; *stabiliment:*—confirmation.

952. βέβηλος **bĕbēlŏs**, *beb'-ay-los;* from the base of *939* and βηλός **bēlŏs** (a *threshold*); *accessible* (as by *crossing the door-way*), i.e. (by impl. of Jewish notions) *heathenish, wicked:*—profane (person).

953. **βεβηλόω bĕbēlŏō**, *beb-ay-lŏ'-o;* from *952;* to *desecrate:*—profane.

954. **Βεελζεβούλ Bĕĕlzĕbŏul**, *beh-el-zeb-ool';* of Chald. or. [by parody upon 1176]; *dung-god; Beelzebul*, a name of Satan:—Beelzebub.

955. **Βελίαλ Bĕlial**, *bel-ee'-al;* of Heb. or. [1100]; *worthlessness; Belial*, as an epithet of Satan:—Belial.

956. **βέλος bĕlŏs**, *bel'-os;* from *906;* a *missile*, i.e. *spear* or *arrow:*—dart.

957. **βελτίον bĕltiŏn**, *bel-tee'-on;* neut. of a comp. of a der. of *906* (used for the comp. of *18*); *better:*—very well.

958. **Βενιαμίν Bĕniamin**, *ben-ee-am-een';* of Heb. or. [1144]; *Benjamin*, an Isr.:—Benjamin.

959. **Βερνίκη Bĕrnikē**, *ber-nee'-kay;* from a provincial form of *5342* and *3529;* *victorious; Bernicè*, a member of the Herodian family:—Bernice.

960. **Βέροια Bĕrŏia**, *ber'-oy-ah;* perh. a provincial from a der. of *4008* [*Perœa*, i.e. the region *beyond* the coast-line]; *Berœa*, a place in Macedonia:—Berea.

961. **Βεροιαῖος Bĕrŏiaiŏs**, *ber-oy-ah'-yos;* from *960;* a *Berœæan* or native of Berœa:—of Berea.

962. **Βηθαβαρά Bēthabara**, *bay-thab-ar-ah';* of Heb. or. [1004 and 5679]; *ferry-house; Bethabara* (i.e. *Bethabarah*), a place on the Jordan:—Bethabara.

963. **Βηθανία Bēthania**, *bay-than-ee'-ah;* of Chald. or.; *date-house; Beth-any*, a place in Pal.:—Bethany.

964. **Βηθεσδά Bēthĕsda**, *bay-thes-dah';* of Chald. or. [comp. 1004 and 2617]; *house of kindness; Beth-esda*, a pool in Jerus.:—Bethesda.

965. **Βηθλεέμ Bēthlĕĕm**, *bayth-leh-em';* of Heb. or. [1036]; *Bethleem* (i.e. *Beth-lechem*), a place in Pal.:—Bethlehem.

966. **Βηθσαϊδά Bēthsaïda**, *bayth-sāhee-dah';* of Chald. or. [comp. 1004 and 6719]; *fishing-house; Bethsaïda*, a place in Pal.:—Bethsaida.

967. **Βηθφαγή Bēthphagē**, *bayth-fag-ay';* of Chald. or. [comp. 1004 and 6291]; *fig-house; Bethphagè*, a place in Pal.:—Bethphage.

968. **βῆμα bēma**, *bay'-ma;* from the base of *939;* a *step*, i.e. *foot-breath;* by impl. a *rostrum*, i.e. *tribunal:*—judgment-seat, set [foot] on, throne.

969. **βήρυλλος bērullŏs**, *bay'-rool-los;* of uncert. der.; a "*beryl*":—beryl.

970. **βία bia**, *bee'-ah;* prob. akin to *979* (through the idea of *vital* activity); *force:*—violence.

971. **βιάζω biazō**, *bee-ad'-zo;* from *970;* to *force*, i.e. (reflex.) to *crowd oneself* (into), or (pass.) to *be seized:*—press, suffer violence.

972. **βίαιος biaiŏs**, *bee'-ah-yos;* from *970;* *violent:*—mighty.

973. **βιαστής biastēs**, *bee-as-tace';* from *971;* a *forcer*, i.e. (fig.) *energetic:*—violent.

974. **βιβλιαρίδιον bibliaridiŏn**, *bib-lee-ar-id'-ee-on;* a dimin. of *975;* a *booklet:*—little book.

975. **βιβλίον bibliŏn**, *bib-lee'-on;* a dimin. of *976;* a *roll:*—bill, book, scroll, writing.

976. **βίβλος biblŏs**, *bib'-los;* prop. the inner *bark* of the papyrus plant, i.e. (by impl.) a *sheet* or *scroll* of writing:—book.

977. **βιβρώσκω bibrōskō**, *bib-ro'-sko;* a reduplicated and prolonged form of an obsol. prim. verb [perh. causative of *1006*]; to *eat:*—eat.

978. **Βιθυνία Bithunia**, *bee-thoo-nee'-ah;* of uncert. der.; *Bithynia*, a region of Asia:—Bithynia.

979. **βίος biŏs**, *bee'-os;* a prim. word; *life*, i.e. (lit.) the present state of existence; by impl. the means of *livelihood:*—good, life, living.

980. **βιόω biŏō**, *bee-ŏ'-o;* from *979;* to *spend existence:*—live.

981. **βίωσις biōsis**, *bee'-o-sis;* from *980;* *living* (prop. the act, by impl. the mode):—manner of life.

982. **βιωτικός biōtikŏs**, *bee-o-tee-kos';* from a der. of *980;* *relating to* the present *existence:*—of (pertaining to, things that pertain to) this life.

983. **βλαβερός blabĕrŏs**, *blab-er-os';* from *984;* *injurious:*—hurtful.

984. **βλάπτω blaptō**, *blap'-to;* a prim. verb; prop. to *hinder*, i.e. (by impl.) to *injure:*—hurt.

985. **βλαστάνω blastanō**, *blas-tan'-o;* from **βλαστός blastŏs** (a *sprout*); to *germinate;* by impl. to *yield* fruit:—bring forth, bud, spring (up).

986. **Βλάστος Blastŏs**, *blas'-tos;* perh. the same as the base of *985;* *Blastus*, an officer of Herod Agrippa:—Blastus.

987. **βλασφημέω blasphēmĕō**, *blas-fay-meh'-o;* from *989;* to *vilify;* spec. to *speak impiously:*—(speak) blaspheme (-er, -mously, -my), defame, rail on, revile, speak evil.

988. **βλασφημία blasphēmia**, *blas-fay-me'-ah;* from *989;* *vilification* (espec. against God):—blasphemy, evil speaking, railing.

989. **βλάσφημος blasphēmŏs**, *blas'-fay-mos;* from a der. of *984* and *5345;* *scurrilous*, i.e. *calumnious* (against man), or (spec.) *impious* (against God):—blasphemer (-mous), railing.

990. **βλέμμα blemma**, *blem'-mah;* from *991;* *vision* (prop. concr.; by impl. abstr.):—seeing.

991. **βλέπω blĕpō**, *blep'-o;* a prim. verb; to *look* at (lit. or fig.):—behold, beware, lie, look (on, to), perceive, regard, see, sight, take heed. Comp. *3700*.

992. **βλητέος blētĕŏs**, *blay-teh'-os;* from *906;* fit *to be cast* (i.e. *applied*):—must be put.

993. **Βοανεργές Bŏanĕrgĕs**, *bŏ-an-erg-es';* of Chald. or. [1123 and 7266]; *sons of commotion; Boänerges*, an epithet of two of the Apostles:—Boanerges.

994. **βοάω bŏaō**, *bŏ-ah'-o;* appar. a prol. form of a prim. verb; to *halloo*, i.e. *shout* (for help or in a tumultuous way):—cry.

995. **βοή bŏē**, *bŏ-ay';* from *994;* a *halloo*, i.e. *call* (for aid, etc.):—cry.

996. **βοήθεια bŏēthĕia**, *bŏ-ay'-thi-ah;* from *998;* *aid;* spec. a rope or chain for *frapping* a vessel:—help.

997. **βοηθέω bŏēthĕō**, *bŏ-ay-theh'-o;* from *998;* to *aid* or *relieve:*—help, succour.

998. **βοηθός bŏēthŏs**, *bŏ-ay-thos';* from *995* and **θέω thĕō** (to *run*); a *succorer:*—helper.

999. **βόθυνος bŏthunŏs**, *both'-oo-nos;* akin to *900;* a *hole* (in the ground); spec. a *cistern:*—ditch, pit.

1000. **βολή bŏlē**, *bol-ay';* from *906;* a *throw* (as a measure of distance):—cast.

1001. **βολίζω bŏlizō**, *bol-id'-zo;* from *1002;* to *heave* the lead:—sound.

1002. **βολίς bŏlis**, *bol-ece';* from *906;* a *missile*, i.e. *javelin:*—dart.

1003. **Βοόζ Bŏŏz**, *bŏ-oz';* of Heb. or. [1162]; *Boöz*, (i.e. *Boäz*), an Isr.:—Booz.

1004. **βόρβορος bŏrbŏrŏs**, *bor'-bor-os;* of uncert. der.; *mud:*—mire.

1005. **βοῤῥᾶς borrhas**, *bor-hras';* of uncert. der.; the *north* (prop. wind):—north.

1006. **βόσκω bŏskō**, *bos'-ko;* a prol. form of a prim. verb [comp. *977*, *1016*]; to *pasture;* by extens. to *fodder;* reflex. to *graze:*—feed, keep.

1007. **Βοσόρ Bŏsŏr**, *bos-or';* of Heb. or. [1160]; *Bosor* (i.e. *Beör*), a Moabite:—Bosor.

1008. **βοτάνη bŏtanē**, *bot-an'-ay;* from *1006;* *herbage* (as if for *grazing*):—herb.

1009. **βότρυς bŏtrus**, *bot'-rooce;* of uncert. der.; a *bunch* (of grapes):—(vine) cluster (of the vine).

1010. **βουλευτής bŏulĕutēs**, *bool-yoo-tace';* from *1011;* an *adviser*, i.e. (spec.) a *councillor* or member of the Jewish Sanhedrim:—counsellor.

1011. **βουλεύω bŏulĕuō**, *bool-yoo'-o;* from *1012;* to *advise*, i.e. (reflex.) *deliberate*, or (by impl.) *resolve:*—consult, take counsel, determine, be minded, purpose.

1012. **βουλή bŏulē**, *boo-lay';* from *1014;* *volition*, i.e. (obj.) *advice*, or (by impl.) *purpose:*— + advise, counsel, will.

1013. **βούλημα bŏulēma**, *boo'-lay-mah;* from *1014;* a *resolve:*—purpose, will.

1014. **βούλομαι** *boo'-lom-ahee;* mid. of a prim. verb; to "*will*," i.e. (reflex.) *be willing:*—be disposed, minded, intend, list, (be, of own) will (-ing). Comp. *2309*.

1015. **βουνός bŏunŏs**, *boo-nos';* prob. of for. or.; a *hillock:*—hill.

1016. **βοῦς bŏus**, *booce;* prob. from the base of *1006;* an *ox* (as *grazing*), i.e. an animal of that species ("beef"):—ox.

1017. **βραβεῖον brabĕiŏn**, *brab-i'-on;* from **βραβεύς brabĕus** (an *umpire;* of uncert. der.); an *award* (of arbitration), i.e. (spec.) a *prize* in the public games:—prize.

1018. **βραβεύω brabĕuō**, *brab-yoo'-o;* from the same as *1017;* to *arbitrate*, i.e. (gen.) to *govern* (fig. *prevail*):—rule.

1019. **βραδύνω bradunō**, *brad-oo'-no;* from *1021;* to *delay:*—be slack, tarry.

1020. **βραδυπλοέω bradupiŏĕō**, *brad-oo-plŏ-eh'-o;* from *1021* and a prol. form of *4126;* to *sail slowly:*—sail slowly.

1021. **βραδύς bradus**, *brad-ooce';* of uncert. affin.; *slow;* fig. *dull:*—slow.

1022. **βραδύτης bradutēs**, *brad-oo'-tace;* from *1021;* *tardiness:*—slackness.

1023. **βραχίων brachiōn**, *brakh-ee'-own;* prop. comp. of *1024*, but appar. in the sense of **βράσσω brassō** (to *wield*); the *arm*, i.e. (fig.) *strength:*—arm.

1024. **βραχύς brachus**, *brakh-ooce';* of uncert. affin.; *short* (of time, place, quantity, or number):—few words, little (space, while).

1025. **βρέφος brĕphŏs**, *bref'-os;* of uncert. affin.; an *infant* (prop. unborn) lit. or fig.:—babe, (young) child, infant.

1026. **βρέχω brĕchō**, *brekh'-o;* a prim. verb; to *moisten* (espec. by a shower):—(send) rain, wash.

1027. **βροντή brŏntē**, *bron-tay';* akin to **βρέμω brĕmō** (to *roar*); *thunder:*—thunder (-ing).

1028. **βροχή brŏchē**, *brokh-ay';* from 1026; *rain:*—rain.

1029. **βρόχος brŏchŏs**, *brokh'-os;* of uncert. der.; a *noose:*—snare.

1030. **βρυγμός brugmŏs**, *broog-mos';* from *1031;* a *grating* (of the teeth):—gnashing.

1031. **βρύχω bruchō**, *broo'-kho;* a prim. verb; to *grate* the teeth (in pain or rage):—gnash.

1032. **βρύω bruō**, *broo'-o;* a prim. verb; to *swell* out, i.e. (by impl.) to *gush:*—send forth.

1033. **βρῶμα brōma**, *bro'-mah;* from the base of *977;* *food* (lit. or fig.), espec. (cer.) articles allowed or forbidden by the Jewish law:—meat, victuals.

1034. **βρώσιμος brōsimŏs**, *bro'-sim-os;* from *1035;* *eatable:*—meat.

1035. **βρῶσις brōsis**, *bro'-sis;* from the base of *977;* (abstr.) *eating* (lit. or fig.); by extens. (concr.) *food* (lit. or fig.):—eating, food, meat.

1036. **βυθίζω buthizō**, *boo-thid'-zo;* from *1037;* to *sink;* by impl. to *drown:*—begin to sink, drown.

1037. **βυθός buthŏs**, *boo-thos';* a var. of *899;* *depth*, i.e. (by impl.) the *sea:*—deep.

1038. **βυρσεύς bursĕus**, *boorce-yooce';* from **βύρσα bursa** (a *hide*); a *tanner:*—tanner.

1039. **βύσσινος bussinŏs**, *boos'-see-nos;* from *1040;* made of *linen* (neut. a linen *cloth*):—fine linen.

1040. **βύσσος bussŏs**, *boos'-sos;* of Heb. or. [948]; white *linen:*—fine linen.

1041. **βῶμος bōmŏs**, *bo'-mos;* from the base of *939;* prop. a *stand*, i.e. (spec.) an *altar:*—altar.

Γ

1042. **γαββαθά gabbatha**, *gab-bath-ah';* of Chald. or. [comp. 1355]; *the knoll; gabbatha*, a vernacular term for the Roman tribunal in Jerus.:—Gabbatha.

1043. Γαβριήλ **Gabriēl**, *gab-ree-ale'*; of Heb. or. [1403]; *Gabriel*, an archangel:—Gabriel.

1044. γάγγραινα **gaggraina**, *gang'-grahee-nah*; from γραίνω **grainō** (to *gnaw*); an *ulcer* ("gangrene"):—canker.

1045. Γάδ **Gad**, *gad*; of Heb. or. [1410]; *Gad*, a tribe of Isr.:—Gad.

1046. Γαδαρηνός **Gadarēnŏs**, *gad-ar-ay-nos'*; from Γαδαρά (a town E. of the Jordan); a *Gadarene* or inhab. of Gadara:—Gadarene.

1047. γάζα **gaza**, *gad'-zah*; of for. or.; a *treasure*:—treasure.

1048. Γάζα **Gaza**, *gad'-zah*; of Heb. or. [5804]; *Gazah* (i.e. *'Azzah*), a place in Pal.:—Gaza.

1049. γαζοφυλάκιον **gazŏphulakiŏn**, *gad-zof-oo-lak'-ee-on*; from *1047* and *5438*; a *treasure-house*, i.e. a court in the temple for the collection-boxes:—treasury.

1050. Γάϊος **Gaïŏs**, *gah'-ee-os*; of Lat. or.; *Gaïus* (i.e. *Caius*), a Chr.:—Gaius.

1051. γάλα **gala**, *gal'-ah*; of uncert. affin.; *milk* (fig.):—milk.

1052. Γαλάτης **Galatēs**, *gal-at'-ace*; from *1053*; a *Galatian* or inhab. of Galatia:—Galatian.

1053. Γαλατία **Galatia**, *gal-at-ee'-ah*; of for. or.; *Galatia*, a region of Asia:—Galatia.

1054. Γαλατικός **Galatikŏs**, *gal-at-ee-kos'*; from *1053*; *Galatic* or relating to Galatia:—of Galatia.

1055. γαλήνη **galēnē**, *gal-ay'-nay*; of uncert. der.; *tranquillity*:—calm.

1056. Γαλιλαία **Galilaia**, *gal-il-ah'-yah*; of Heb. or. [1551]; *Galilæa* (i.e. the heathen *circle*), a region of Pal.:—Galilee.

1057. Γαλιλαῖος **Galilaiŏs**, *gal-ee-lah'-yos*; from *1056*; *Galilæan* or belonging to Galilæa:—Galilæan, of Galilee.

1058. Γαλλίων **Galliōn**, *gal-lee'-own*; of Lat. or.; *Gallion* (i.e. *Gallio*), a Roman officer:—Gallio.

1059. Γαμαλιήλ **Gamaliēl**, *gam-al-ee-ale'*; of Heb. or. [1583]; *Gamaliel* (i.e. *Gamliel*), an Isr.:—Gamaliel.

1060. γαμέω **gamĕō**, *gam-eh'-o*; from *1062*; to *wed* (of either sex):—marry (a wife).

1061. γαμίσκω **gamiskō**, *gam-is'-ko*; from *1062*; to *espouse* (a daughter to a husband):—give in marriage.

1062. γάμος **gamŏs**, *gam'-os*; of uncert. affin.; *nuptials*:—marriage, wedding.

1063. γάρ **gar**, *gar*; a prim. particle; prop. assigning a *reason* (used in argument, explanation or intensification; often with other particles):—and, as, because (that), but, even, for, indeed, no doubt, seeing, then, therefore, verily, what, why, yet.

1064. γαστήρ **gastēr**, *gas-tare'*; of uncert. der.; the *stomach*; by anal. the *matrix*; fig. a *gourmand*:—belly, + with child, womb.

1065. γέ **gĕ**, *gheh*; a prim. particle of *emphasis* or *qualification* (often used with other particles prefixed):—and besides, doubtless, at least, yet.

1066. Γεδεών **Gĕdĕōn**, *ghed-eh-own'*; of Heb. or. [1439]; *Gedeon* (i.e. *Gid[e]on*), an Isr.:—Gedeon.

1067. γέεννα **gĕĕnna**, *gheh'-en-nah*; of Heb. or [1516 and 2011]; *valley of* (the son of) *Hinnom*; *gehenna* (or *Ge-Hinnom*), a valley of Jerus., used (fig.) as a name for the place (or state) of everlasting punishment:—hell.

1068. Γεθσημανῆ **Gĕthsēmanē**, *gheth-say-man-ay'*; of Chald. or. [comp. 1660 and 8081]; *oil-press*; *Gethsemane*, a garden near Jerus.:—Gethsemane.

1069. γείτων **gĕitōn**, *ghi'-tone*; from *1093*; a *neighbor* (as adjoining one's *ground*); by impl. a *friend*:—neighbour.

1070. γελάω **gĕlaō**, *ghel-ah'-o*; of uncert. affin.; to *laugh* (as a sign of joy or satisfaction):—laugh.

1071. γέλως **gĕlōs**, *ghel'-oce*; from *1070*; *laughter* (as a mark of gratification):—laughter.

1072. γεμίζω **gĕmizō**, *ghem-id'-zo*; trans. from *1073*, to *fill* entirely:—fill (be) full.

1073. γέμω **gĕmō**, *ghem'-o*; a prim. verb; to *swell* out, i.e. *be full*:—be full.

1074. γενεά **gĕnĕa**, *ghen-eh-ah'*; from (a presumed der. of) *1085*; a *generation*; by impl. an *age* (the period or the persons):—age, generation, nation, time.

1075. γενεαλογέω **gĕnĕalŏgĕō**, *ghen-eh-al-og-eh'-o*; from *1074* and *3056*; to *reckon by generations*, i.e. *trace in genealogy*:—count by descent.

1076. γενεαλογία **gĕnĕalŏgia**, *ghen-eh-al-og-ee'-ah*; from the same as *1075*; *tracing by generations*, i.e. "*genealogy*":—genealogy.

1077. γενέσια **gĕnĕsia**, *ghen-es'-ee-ah*; neut. plur. of a der. of *1078*; *birthday* ceremonies:—birthday.

1078. γένεσις **genesis**, *ghen'-es-is*; from the same as *1074*; *nativity*; fig. *nature*:—generation, nature (-ral).

1079. γενετή **gĕnĕtē**, *ghen-et-ay'*; fem. of a presumed der. of the base of *1074*; *birth*:—birth.

1080. γεννάω **gĕnnaō**, *ghen-nah'-o*; from a var. of *1085*; to *procreate* (prop. of the father, but by extens. of the mother); fig. to *regenerate*:—bear, beget, be born, bring forth, conceive, be delivered of, gender, make, spring.

1081. γέννημα **gĕnnēma**, *ghen'-nay-mah*; from *1080*; *offspring*; by anal. *produce* (lit. or fig.):—fruit, generation.

1082. Γεννησαρέτ **Gĕnnēsarĕt**, *ghen-nay-sar-et'*; of Heb. or. [comp. 3672]; *Gennesaret* (i.e. *Kinnereth*), a lake and plain in Pal.:—Gennesaret.

1083. γέννησις **gĕnnēsis**, *ghen'-nay-sis*; from *1080*; *nativity*:—birth.

1084. γεννητός **gĕnnētŏs**, *ghen-nay-tos'*; from *1080*; *born*:—they that are born.

1085. γένος **gĕnŏs**, *ghen'-os*; from *1096*; "*kin*" (abstr. or concr., lit. or fig., indiv. or coll.):—born, country (-man), diversity, generation, kind (-red), nation, offspring, stock.

1086. Γεργεσηνός **Gĕrgĕsēnŏs**, *gher-ghes-ay-nos'*; of Heb. or. [1622]; a *Gergesene* (i.e. *Girgashite*) or one of the aborigines of Pal.:—Gergesene.

1087. γερουσία **gĕrŏusia**, *gher-oo-see'-ah*; from *1088*; the *eldership*, i.e. (collect.) the Jewish *Sanhedrim*:—senate.

1088. γέρων **gĕrōn**, *gher'-own*; of uncert. affin. [comp. *1094*]; *aged*:—old.

1089. γεύομαι **gĕuŏmai**, *ghyoo'-om-ahee*; a prim. verb; to *taste*; by impl. to *eat*; fig. to *experience* (good or ill):—eat, taste.

1090. γεωργέω **gĕōrgĕō**, *gheh-ore-gheh'-o*; from *1092*; to *till* (the soil):—dress.

1091. γεώργιον **gĕōrgiŏn**, *gheh-ore'-ghee-on*; neut. of a (presumed) der. of *1092*; *cultivable*, i.e. a *farm*:—husbandry.

1092. γεωργός **gĕōrgŏs**, *gheh-ore-gos'*; from *1093* and the base of *2041*; a *land-worker*, i.e. *farmer*:—husbandman.

1093. γῆ **gē**, *ghay*; contr. from a prim. word; *soil*; by extens. a *region*, or the solid part or the whole of the *terrene* globe (includ. the occupants in each application):—country, earth (-ly), ground, land, world.

1094. γῆρας **gēras**, *ghay'-ras*; akin to *1088*; *senility*:—old age.

1095. γηράσκω **gēraskō**, *ghay-ras'-ko*; from *1094*; to *be senescent*:—be (wax) old.

1096. γίνομαι **ginŏmai**, *ghin'-om-ahee*; a prol. and mid. form of a prim. verb; to *cause to be* ("*gen*"-*erate*), i.e. (reflex.) to *become* (*come into being*), used with great latitude (lit., fig., intens., etc.):—arise, be assembled, be (come, -fall, -have self), be brought (to pass), (be) come (to pass), continue, be divided, be done, draw, be ended, fall, be finished, follow, be found, be fulfilled, + God forbid, grow, happen, have, be kept, be made, be married, be ordained to be, partake, pass, be performed, be published, require, seem, be showed, × soon as it was, sound, be taken, be turned, use, wax, will, would, be wrought.

1097. γινώσκω **ginōskō**, *ghin-oce'-ko*; a prol. form of a prim. verb; to "*know*" (absol.), in a great variety of applications and with many impl. (as follow, with others not thus clearly expressed):—allow, be aware (of), feel, (have) know (-ledge), perceive, be resolved, can speak, be sure, understand.

1098. γλεῦκος **glĕukŏs**, *glyoo'-kos*; akin to *1099*; *sweet* wine, i.e. (prop.) *must* (fresh juice), but used of the more saccharine (and therefore highly inebriating) fermented *wine*:—new wine.

1099. γλυκύς **glukus**, *gloo-koos'*; of uncert. affin.; *sweet* (i.e. not bitter nor salt):—sweet, fresh.

1100. γλῶσσα **glōssa**, *gloce-sah'*; of uncert. affin.; the *tongue*; by impl. a *language* (spec. one naturally unacquired):—tongue.

1101. γλωσσόκομον **glōssŏkŏmŏn**, *gloce-sok'-om-on*; from *1100* and the base of *2889*; prop. a *case* (to keep mouthpieces of wind-instruments in), i.e. (by extens.) a *casket* or (spec.) *purse*:—bag.

1102. γναφεύς **gnaphĕus**, *gnaf-yuce'*; by var. for a der. from κνάπτω **knaptō** (to *tease* cloth); a cloth-*dresser*:—fuller.

1103. γνήσιος **gnēsiŏs**, *gnay'-see-os*; from the same as *1077*; *legitimate* (of birth), i.e. *genuine*:—own, sincerity, true.

1104. γνησίως **gnēsiōs**, *gnay-see'-oce*; adv. from *1103*; *genuinely*, i.e. *really*:—naturally.

1105. γνόφος **gnŏphŏs**, *gnof'-os*; akin to *3509*; *gloom* (as of a storm):—blackness.

1106. γνώμη **gnōmē**, *gno'-may*; from *1097*; *cognition*, i.e. (subj.) *opinion*, or (obj.) *resolve* (*counsel*, *consent*, etc.):—advice, + agree, judgment, mind, purpose, will.

1107. γνωρίζω **gnōrizō**, *gno-rid'-zo*; from a der. of *1097*; to *make known*; subj. to *know*:—certify, declare, make known, give to understand, do to wit, wot.

1108. γνῶσις **gnōsis**, *gno'-sis*; from *1097*; *knowing* (the act), i.e. (by impl.) *knowledge*:—knowledge, science.

1109. γνώστης **gnōstēs**, *gnoce'-tace*; from *1097*; a *knower*:—expert.

1110. γνωστός **gnōstŏs**, *gnoce-tos'*; from *1097*; well *known*:—acquaintance, (which may be) known, notable.

1111. γογγύζω **gŏgguzō**, *gong-good'-zo*; of uncert. der.; to *grumble*:—murmur.

1112. γογγυσμός **gŏggusmŏs**, *gong-goos-mos'*; from *1111*; a *grumbling*:—grudging, murmuring.

1113. γογγυστής **gŏggustēs**, *gong-goos-tace'*; from *1111*; a *grumbler*:—murmurer.

1114. γόης **gŏēs**, *gŏ'-ace*; from γοάω **gŏaō** (to *wail*); prop. a *wizard* (as *muttering* spells), i.e. (by impl.) an *impostor*:—seducer.

1115. Γολγοθᾶ **Golgŏtha**, *gol-goth-ah'*; of Chald. or. [comp. 1538]; *the skull*; *Golgotha*, a knoll near Jerus.:—Golgotha.

1116. Γόμοῤῥα **Gŏmŏrrha**, *gom'-or-hrhah*; of Heb. or. [6017]; *Gomorrha* (i.e. *'Amorah*), a place near the Dead Sea:—Gomorrha.

1117. γόμος **gŏmŏs**, *gom'-os*; from *1073*; a *load* (as *filling*), i.e. (spec.) a *cargo*, or (by extens.) *wares*:—burden, merchandise.

1118. γονεύς **gŏnĕus**, *gon-yooce'*; from the base of *1096*; a *parent*:—parent.

1119. γονύ **gŏnu**, *gon-oo'*; of uncert. affin.; the "*knee*":—knee (× -l).

1120. γονυπετέω **gŏnupĕtĕō**, *gon-oo-pet-eh'-o*; from a comp. of *1119* and the alt. of *4098*; to *fall* on the *knee*:—bow the knee, kneel down.

1121. γράμμα **gramma**, *gram'-mah*; from *1125*; a *writing*, i.e. a *letter*, *note*, *epistle*, *book*, etc.; plur. *learning*:—bill, learning, letter, scripture, writing, written.

1122. γραμματεύς **grammatĕus**, *gram-mat-yooce'*; from *1121*; a *writer*, i.e. (professionally) *scribe* or *secretary*:—scribe, town-clerk.

1123. γραπτός **graptŏs**, *grap-tos'*; from *1125*; *inscribed* (fig.):—written.

1124. γραφή **graphē**, *graf-ay'*; from *1125*; a *document*, i.e. holy *Writ* (or its contents or a statement in it):—scripture.

1125. γράφω **graphō**, *graf'-o;* a prim. verb; to "*grave*", espec. to *write;* fig. to *describe:*—describe, write (-ing, -ten).

1126. γραώδης **graōdēs**, *grah-o'-dace;* from γραῦς **graus** (an *old woman*) and *1491; crone-like*, i.e. *silly:*—old wives'.

1127. γρηγορεύω **grēgŏrĕuō**, *gray-gor-yoo'-o;* from *1453;* to *keep awake*, i.e. *watch* (lit. or fig.):—be vigilant, wake, (be) watch (-ful).

1128. γυμνάζω **gumnazō**, *goom-nad'-zo;* from *1131;* to *practise naked* (in the games), i.e. *train* (fig.):—exercise.

1129. γυμνασία **gumnasia**, *goom-nas-ee'-ah;* from *1128; training*, i.e. (fig.) *asceticism:*—exercise.

1130. γυμνητεύω **gumnētĕuō**, *goom-nayt-yoo'-o;* from a der. of *1131;* to *strip*, i.e. (reflex.) *go poorly clad:*—be naked.

1131. γυμνός **gumnŏs**, *goom-nos';* of uncert. affin.; *nude* (absol. or rel., lit. or fig.):—naked.

1132. γυμνότης **gumnŏtēs**, *goom-not'-ace;* from *1131; nudity* (absol. or comp.):—nakedness.

1133. γυναικάριον **gunaikariŏn**, *goo-nahee-kar'-ee-on;* a dimin. from *1135;* a *little* (i.e. *foolish*) *woman:*—silly woman.

1134. γυναικεῖος **gunaikĕiŏs**, *goo-nahee-ki'-os;* from *1135; feminine:*—wife.

1135. γυνή **gunē**, *goo-nay';* prob. from the base of *1096;* a *woman;* spec. a *wife:*—wife, woman.

1136. Γώγ **Gōg**, *gogue;* of Heb. or. [1463]; *Gog*, a symb. name for some future Antichrist:—Gog.

1137. γωνία **gōnia**, *go-nee'-ah;* prob. akin to *1119;* an *angle:*—corner, quarter.

Δ

1138. Δαβίδ **Dabid**, *dab-eed';* of Heb. or. [1732]; *Dabid* (i.e. *David*), the Isr. king:—David.

1139. δαιμονίζομαι **daimŏnizŏmai**, *dahee-mon-id'-zom-ahee;* mid. from *1142;* to *be exercised by a dæmon:*—have a (be vexed with, be possessed with) devil (-s).

1140. δαιμόνιον **daimŏniŏn**, *dahee-mon'-ee-on;* neut. of a der. of *1142;* a *dæmonic being;* by extens. a *deity:*—devil, god.

1141. δαιμονιώδης **daimŏniōdēs**, *dahee-mon-ee-o'-dace;* from *1140* and *1142; dæmon-like:*—devilish.

1142. δαίμων **daimōn**, *dah'ee-mown;* from δαίω **daiō** (to *distribute* fortunes); a *dæmon* or supernatural spirit (of a bad nature):—devil.

1143. δάκνω **daknō**, *dak'-no;* a prol. form of a prim. root: to *bite*, i.e. (fig.) *thwart:*—bite.

1144. δάκρυ **dakru**, *dak'-roo;* or

δάκρυον **dakruŏn**, *dak'-roo-on;* of uncert. affin.; a *tear:*—tear.

1145. δακρύω **dakruō**, *dak-roo'-o;* from 1144; to *shed tears:*—weep. Comp. *2799*.

1146. δακτύλιος **daktuliŏs**, *dak-too'-lee-os;* from *1147;* a *finger*-ring:—ring.

1147. δάκτυλος **daktulŏs**, *dak'-too-los;* prob. from *1176;* a *finger:*—finger.

1148. Δαλμανουθά **Dalmanŏutha**, *dal-man-oo-thah';* prob. of Chald. or.; *Dalmanŭtha*, a place in Pal.:—Dalmanutha.

1149. Δαλματία **Dalmatia**, *dal-mat-ee'-ah;* prob. of for. der.; *Dalmatia*, a region of Europe:—Dalmatia.

1150. δαμάζω **damazō**, *dam-ad'-zo;* a var. of an obs. prim. of the same mean.; to *tame:*—tame.

1151. δάμαλις **damalis**, *dam'-al-is;* prob. from the base of *1150;* a *heifer* (as *tame*):—heifer.

1152. Δάμαρις **Damaris**, *dam'-ar-is;* prob. from the base of *1150;* perh. *gentle; Damaris*, an Athenian woman:—Damaris.

1153. Δαμασκηνός **Damaskēnŏs**, *dam-as-kay-nos';* from *1154;* a *Damascene* or inhab. of Damascus:—Damascene.

1154. Δαμασκός **Damaskŏs**, *dam-as-kos';* of Heb. or. [1834]; *Damascus*, a city of Syria:—Damascus.

1155. δανείζω **danĕizō**, *dan-ide'-zo;* from *1156;* to *loan* on interest; reflex. to *borrow:*—borrow, lend.

1156. δάνειον **danĕiŏn**, *dan'-i-on;* from δάνος **danŏs** (a *gift*); prob. akin to the base of *1325;* a *loan:*—debt.

1157. δανειστής **danĕistēs**, *dan-ice-tace';* from *1155;* a *lender:*—creditor.

1158. Δανιήλ **Daniēl**, *dan-ee-ale';* of Heb. or. [1840]; *Daniel*, an Isr.:—Daniel.

1159. δαπανάω **dapanaō**, *dap-an-ah'-o;* from *1160;* to *expend*, i.e. (in a good sense) to *incur cost*, or (in a bad one) to *waste:*—be at charges, consume, spend.

1160. δαπάνη **dapanē**, *dap-an'-ay;* from δάπτω **daptō** (to *devour*); *expense* (as *consuming*):—cost.

1161. δέ **dĕ**, *deh;* a prim. particle (adversative or continuative); *but, and*, etc.:—also, and, but, moreover, now [*often unexpressed in English*].

1162. δέησις **dĕēsis**, *deh'-ay-sis;* from *1189;* a *petition:*—prayer, request, supplication.

1163. δεῖ **dĕi**, *die;* 3d pers. sing. act. pres. of *1210;* also δεόν **dĕŏn**, *deh-on';* neut. act. part. of the same; both used impers.; *it is* (*was*, etc.) *necessary* (as *binding*):—behoved, be meet, must (needs), (be) need (-ful), ought, should.

1164. δεῖγμα **dĕigma**, *dīgh'-mah;* from the base of *1166;* a *specimen* (as *shown*):—example.

1165. δειγματίζω **dĕigmatizō**, *dīgh-mat-id'-zo;* from *1164;* to *exhibit:*—make a shew.

1166. δεικνύω **dĕiknuō**, *dike-noo'-o;* a prol. form of an obs. prim. of the same mean.; to *show* (lit. or fig.):—shew.

1167. δειλία **dĕilia**, *di-lee'-ah;* from *1169; timidity:*—fear.

1168. δειλιάω **dĕiliaō**, *di-lee-ah'-o;* from *1167;* to *be timid:*—be afraid.

1169. δειλός **dĕilŏs**, *di-los';* from δέος **dĕŏs** (*dread*); *timid*, i.e. (by impl.) *faithless:*—fearful.

1170. δεῖνα **dĕina**, *di'-nah;* prob. from the same as *1171* (through the idea of forgetting the name as *fearful*, i.e. *strange*); *so and so* (when the person is not specified):—such a man.

1171. δεινῶς **dĕinōs**, *di-noce';* adv. from a der. of the same as *1169; terribly*, i.e. *excessively:*—grievously, vehemently.

1172. δειπνέω **dĕipnĕō**, *dipe-neh'-o;* from *1173;* to *dine*, i.e. take the principal (or evening) meal:—sup (× -per).

1173. δεῖπνον **dĕipnŏn**, *dipe'-non;* from the same as *1160; dinner*, i.e. the chief meal (usually in the evening):—feast, supper.

1174. δεισιδαιμονέστερος **dĕisidaimŏnĕstĕrŏs**, *dice-ee-dahee-mon-es'-ter-os;* the comp. of a der. of the base of *1169* and *1142; more religious* than others:—too superstitious.

1175. δεισιδαιμονία **dĕisidaimŏnia**, *dice-ee-dahee-mon-ee'-ah;* from the same as *1174; religion:*—superstition.

1176. δέκα **dĕka**, *dek'-ah;* a prim. number; *ten:*—[eight-] een, ten.

1177. δεκαδύο **dĕkaduŏ**, *dek-ad-oo'-ŏ;* from *1176* and *1417; two* and *ten*, i.e. *twelve:*—twelve.

1178. δεκαπέντε **dĕkapĕntĕ**, *dek-ap-en'-teh;* from *1176* and *4002; ten* and *five*, i.e. *fifteen:*—fifteen.

1179. Δεκάπολις **Dĕkapŏlis**, *dek-ap'-ol-is;* from *1176* and *4172;* the *ten-city* region; the *Decapolis*, a district in Syria:—Decapolis.

1180. δεκατέσσαρες **dĕkatĕssarĕs**, *dek-at-es'-sar-es;* from *1176* and *5064; ten* and *four*, i.e. *fourteen:*—fourteen.

1181. δεκάτη **dĕkatē**, *dek-at'-ay;* fem. of *1182;* a *tenth*, i.e. as a percentage or (tech.) *tithe:*—tenth (part), tithe.

1182. δέκατος **dĕkatŏs**, *dek'-at-os;* ordinal from *1176; tenth:*—tenth.

1183. δεκατόω **dĕkatŏō**, *dek-at-ŏ'-o;* from *1181;* to *tithe*, i.e. to *give* or *take a tenth:*—pay (receive) tithes.

1184. δεκτός **dĕktŏs**, *dek-tos';* from *1209; approved;* (fig.) *propitious:*—accepted (-table).

1185. δελεάζω **dĕlĕazō**, *del-eh-ad'-zo;* from the base of *1388;* to *entrap*, i.e. (fig.) *delude:*—allure, beguile, entice.

1186. δένδρον **dĕndrŏn**, *den'-dron;* prob. from δρύς **drus** (an *oak*); a *tree:*—tree.

1187. δεξιολάβος **dĕxiŏlabŏs**, *dex-ee-ol-ab'-os;* from *1188* and *2983;* a *guardsman* (as if *taking the right*) or light-armed soldier:—spearman.

1188. δεξιός **dĕxiŏs**, *dex-ee-os';* from *1209;* the *right* side or (fem.) hand (as that which usually *takes*):—right (hand, side).

1189. δέομαι **dĕŏmai**, *deh'-om-ahee;* mid. of *1210;* to *beg* (as *binding oneself*), i.e. *petition:*—beseech, pray (to), make request. Comp. 4441.

δεόν **dĕŏn**. See *1163*.

1190. Δερβαῖος **Dĕrbaiŏs**, *der-bah'ee-os;* from *1191;* a *Derbæan* or inhab. of Derbe:—of Derbe.

1191. Δέρβη **Dĕrbē**, *der'-bay;* of for. or.; *Derbê*, a place in Asia Minor:—Derbe.

1192. δέρμα **dĕrma**, *der'-mah;* from 1194; a *hide:*—skin.

1193. δερμάτινος **dĕrmatinŏs**, *der-mat'-ee-nos;* from *1192;* made of *hide:*—leathern, of a skin.

1194. δέρω **dĕrō**, *der'-o;* a prim. verb; prop. to *flay*, i.e. (by impl.) to *scourge*, or (by anal.) to *thrash:*—beat, smite.

1195. δεσμεύω **dĕsmĕuō**, *des-myoo'-o;* from a (presumed) der. of *1196;* to *be a binder* (*captor*), i.e. to *enchain* (a prisoner), to *tie on* (a load):—bind.

1196. δεσμέω **dĕsmĕō**, *des-meh'-o;* from *1199;* to *tie*, i.e. *shackle:*—bind.

1197. δεσμή **dĕsmē**, *des-may';* from *1196;* a *bundle:*—bundle.

1198. δέσμιος **dĕsmiŏs**, *des'-mee-os;* from *1199;* a *captive* (as *bound*):—in bonds, prisoner.

1199. δεσμόν **dĕsmŏn**, *des-mon';* or

δεσμός **dĕsmŏs**, *des-mos';* neut. and masc. respectively from *1210;* a *band*, i.e. *ligament* (of the body) or *shackle* (of a prisoner); fig. an *impediment* or *disability:*—band, bond, chain, string.

1200. δεσμοφύλαξ **dĕsmŏphulax**, *des-mof-oo'-lax;* from *1199* and *5441;* a *jailer* (as *guarding* the *prisoners*):—jailor, keeper of the prison.

1201. δεσμωτήριον **dĕsmōtēriŏn**, *des-mo-tay'-ree-on;* from a der. of *1199* (equiv. to *1196*); a *place of bondage*, i.e. a *dungeon:*—prison.

1202. δεσμώτης **dĕsmōtēs**, *des-mo'-tace;* from the same as *1201;* (pass.) a *captive:*—prisoner.

1203. δεσπότης **dĕspŏtēs**, *des-pot'-ace;* perh. from *1210* and πόσις **pŏsis** (a *husband*); an absolute *ruler* ("despot"):—Lord, master.

1204. δεῦρο **dĕurŏ**, *dyoo'-rŏ;* of uncert. affin.; *here;* used also imper. *hither!;* and of time, *hitherto:*—come (hither), hither [-to].

1205. δεῦτε **dĕutĕ**, *dyoo'-teh;* from *1204* and an imper. form of εἶμι **ĕimi** (to *go*); *come hither!:*—come, × follow.

1206. δευτεραῖος **dĕutĕraiŏs**, *dyoo-ter-ah'-yos;* from *1208; secondary*, i.e. (spec.) on the *second* day:—next day.

1207. δευτερόπρωτος **dĕutĕrŏprōtŏs**, *dyoo-ter-op'-ro-tos;* from *1208* and *4413; second-first*, i.e. (spec.) a designation of the Sabbath immediately after the Paschal week (being the *second* after Passover day, and the *first* of the seven Sabbaths intervening before Pentecost):—second . . . after the first.

1208. δεύτερος **dĕutĕrŏs**, *dyoo'-ter-os;* as the comp. of *1417;* (ordinal) *second* (in time, place or rank; also adv.):—afterward, again, second (-arily, time).

1209. δέχομαι **dĕchŏmai**, *dekh'-om-ahee;* mid. of a prim. verb; to *receive* (in various applications, lit. or fig.):—accept, receive, take. Comp. *2983*.

1210. δέω **dĕō**, *deh'-o;* a prim. verb; to *bind* (in various applications, lit. or fig.):—bind, be in bonds, knit, tie, wind. See also *1163*, *1189*.

1211. **δή dē**, *day;* prob. akin to *1161;* a particle of emphasis or explicitness; *now, then,* etc.:—also, and, doubtless, now, therefore.

1212. **δῆλος dēlŏs**, *day'-los;* of uncert. der.; *clear:*— + bewray, certain, evident, manifest.

1213. **δηλόω dēlŏō**, *day-lŏ'-o;* from *1212;* to *make plain* (by words):—declare, shew, signify.

1214. **Δημᾶς Dēmas**, *day-mas';* prob. for *1216; Demas,* a Chr.:—Demas.

1215. **δημηγορέω dēmēgŏrĕō**, *day-may-gor-eh'-o;* from a comp. of *1218* and *58;* to *be a people-gatherer,* i.e. to *address* a public assembly:—make an oration.

1216. **Δημήτριος Dēmētriŏs**, *day-may'-tree-os;* from **Δημήτηρ Dēmētēr** (*Ceres*); *Demetrius,* the name of an Ephesian and of a Chr.:—Demetrius.

1217. **δημιουργός dēmiŏurgŏs**, *day-me-oor-gos';* from *1218* and *2041;* a *worker* for the *people,* i.e. *mechanic* (spoken of the *Creator*):—maker.

1218. **δῆμος dēmŏs**, *day'-mos;* from *1210;* the *public* (as *bound* together socially):—people.

1219. **δημόσιος dēmŏsiŏs**, *day-mos'-ee-os;* from *1218; public;* (fem. sing. dat. as adv.) *in public:*—common, openly, publickly.

1220. **δηνάριον dēnariŏn**, *day-nar'-ee-on;* of Lat. or.; a *denarius* (or *ten asses*):—pence, penny [-worth].

1221. **δήποτε dēpŏtĕ**, *day'-pot-eh;* from *1211* and *4218;* a particle of generalization; *indeed, at any time:*—(what-) soever.

1222. **δήπου dēpŏu**, *day'-poo;* from *1211* and *4225;* a particle of asseveration; *indeed doubtless:*—verily.

1223. **διά dia**, *dee-ah';* a prim. prep. denoting the *channel* of an act; *through* (in very wide applications, local, causal or occasional):—after, always, among, at, to avoid, because of (that), briefly, by, for (cause) . . . fore, from, in, by occasion of, of, by reason of, for sake, that, thereby, therefore, × though, through (-out), to, wherefore, with (-in). In composition it retains the same general import.

Δία Dia. See *2203.*

1224. **διαβαίνω diabainō**, *dee-ab-ah'ee-no;* from *1223* and the base of *939;* to *cross:*—come over, pass (through).

1225. **διαβάλλω diaballō**, *dee-ab-al'-lo;* from *1223* and *906;* (fig.) to *traduce:*—accuse.

1226. **διαβεβαιόομαι diabĕbaiŏŏmai**, *dee-ab-eb-ahee-ŏ'-om-ahee;* mid. of a comp. of *1223* and *950;* to *confirm thoroughly* (by words), i.e. *asseverate:*—affirm constantly.

1227. **διαβλέπω diablĕpō**, *dee-ab-lep'-o;* from *1223* and *991;* to *look through,* i.e. *recover* full *vision:*—see clearly.

1228. **διάβολος diabŏlŏs**, *dee-ab'-ol-os;* from *1225;* a *traducer;* spec. *Satan* [comp. 7854]:—false accuser, devil, slanderer.

1229. **διαγγέλλω diaggĕllō**, *de-ang-gel'-lo;* from *1223* and the base of *32;* to *herald thoroughly:*—declare, preach, signify.

1230. **διαγίνομαι diaginŏmai**, *dee-ag-in'-om-ahee;* from *1223* and *1096;* to *elapse meanwhile:*—× after, be past, be spent.

1231. **διαγινώσκω diaginōskō**, *dee-ag-in-o'-sko;* from *1223* and *1097;* to *know thoroughly,* i.e. *ascertain exactly:*—(would) enquire, know the uttermost.

1232. **διαγνωρίζω diagnōrizō**, *dee-ag-no-rid'-zo;* from *1123* and *1107;* to *tell abroad:*—make known.

1233. **διάγνωσις diagnōsis**, *dee-ag'-no-sis;* from *1231;* (magisterial) *examination* ("diagnosis"):—hearing.

1234. **διαγογγύζω diagŏgguzō**, *dee-ag-ong-good'-zo;* from *1223* and *1111;* to *complain throughout* a crowd:—murmur.

1235. **διαγρηγορέω diagrēgŏrĕō**, *dee-ag-ray-gor-eh'-o;* from *1223* and *1127;* to *waken thoroughly:*—be awake.

1236. **διάγω diagō**, *dee-ag'-o:* from *1223* and 71; to *pass* time or life:—lead life, living.

1237. **διαδέχομαι diadĕchŏmai**, *dee-ad-ekh'-om-ahee;* from *1223* and *1209;* to *receive in turn,* i.e. (fig.) *succeed to:*—come after.

1238. **διάδημα diadēma**, *dee-ad'-ay-mah;* from a comp. of *1223* and *1210;* a "*diadem*" (as *bound about* the head):—crown. Comp. *4735.*

1239. **διαδίδωμι diadidōmi**, *dee-ad-id'-o-mee;* from *1223* and *1325;* to *give throughout* a crowd, i.e. *deal out;* also to *deliver* over (as to a successor):—(make) distribute (-ion), divide, give.

1240. **διάδοχος diadŏchŏs**, *dee-ad'-okh-os;* from *1237;* a *successor* in office:—room.

1241. **διαζώννυμι diazōnnumi**, *dee-az-own'-noo-mee;* from *1223* and *2224;* to *gird tightly:*—gird.

1242. **διαθήκη diathēkē**, *dee-ath-ay'-kay;* from *1303;* prop. a *disposition,* i.e. (spec.) a *contract* (espec. a devisory *will*):—covenant, testament.

1243. **διαίρεσις diairĕsis**, *dee-ah'ee-res-is;* from *1244;* a *distinction* or (concr.) *variety:*—difference, diversity.

1244. **διαιρέω diairĕō**, *dee-ahee-reh'-o;* from *1223* and *138;* to *separate,* i.e. *distribute:*—divide.

1245. **διακαθαρίζω diakatharizō**, *dee-ak-ath-ar-id'-zo;* from *1223* and *2511;* to *cleanse perfectly,* i.e. (spec.) *winnow:*—throughly purge.

1246. **διακατελέγχομαι diakatĕlĕgchŏmai**, *dee-ak-at-el-eng'-khom-ahee;* mid. from *1223* and a comp. of *2596* and *1651;* to *prove downright,* i.e. *confute:*—convince.

1247. **διακονέω diakŏnĕō**, *dee-ak-on-eh'-o;* from *1249;* to *be an attendant,* i.e. *wait upon* (menially or as a host, friend or [fig.] teacher); techn. to *act as a* Chr. *deacon:*—(ad-) minister (unto), serve, use the office of a deacon.

1248. **διακονία diakŏnia**, *dee-ak-on-ee'-ah;* from *1249; attendance* (as a servant, etc.); fig. (eleemosynary) *aid,* (official) *service* (espec. of the Chr. teacher, or techn. of the *diaconate*):—(ad-) minister (-ing, -tration, -try), office, relief, service (-ing).

1249. **διάκονος diakŏnŏs**, *dee-ak'-on-os;* prob. from an obs. **διάκω diakō** (to *run* on errands; comp. *1377*); an *attendant,* i.e. (gen.) a *waiter* (at table or in other menial duties); spec. a Chr. *teacher* and *pastor* (techn. a *deacon* or *deaconess*):—deacon, minister, servant.

1250. **διακόσιοι diakŏsiŏi**, *dee-ak-os'-ee-oy;* from *1364* and *1540; two hundred:*—two hundred.

1251. **διακούομαι diakŏuŏmai**, *dee-ak-oo'-om-ahee;* mid. from *1223* and *191;* to *hear throughout,* i.e. *patiently listen* (to a prisoner's plea):—hear.

1252. **διακρίνω diakrinō**, *dee-ak-ree'-no;* from *1223* and *2919;* to *separate thoroughly,* i.e. (lit. and reflex.) to *withdraw* from, or (by impl.) *oppose;* fig. to *discriminate* (by impl. *decide*), or (reflex.) *hesitate:*—contend, make (to) differ (-ence), discern, doubt, judge, be partial, stagger, waver.

1253. **διάκρισις diakrisis**, *dee-ak'-ree-sis;* from *1252;* judicial *estimation:*—discern (-ing), disputation.

1254. **διακωλύω diakōluō**, *dee-ak-o-loo'-o;* from *1223* and *2967;* to *hinder altogether,* i.e. *utterly prohibit:*—forbid.

1255. **διαλαλέω dialalĕō**, *dee-al-al-eh'-o;* from *1223* and *2980;* to *talk throughout* a company, i.e. *converse* or (gen.) *publish:*—commune, noise abroad.

1256. **διαλέγομαι dialĕgŏmai**, *dee-al-eg'-om-ahee;* mid. from *1223* and *3004;* to *say thoroughly,* i.e. *discuss* (in argument or exhortation):—dispute, preach (unto), reason (with), speak.

1257. **διαλείπω dialĕipō**, *dee-al-i'-po;* from *1223* and *3007;* to *leave off in the middle,* i.e. *intermit:*—cease.

1258. **διάλεκτος dialĕktŏs**, *dee-al'-ek-tos;* from *1256;* a (mode of) *discourse,* i.e. "*dialect*":—language, tongue.

1259. **διαλλάσσω diallassō**, *dee-al-las'-so;* from *1223* and *236;* to *change thoroughly,* i.e. (ment.) to *conciliate:*—reconcile.

1260. **διαλογίζομαι dialŏgizŏmai**, *dee-al-og-id'-zom-ahee;* from *1223* and *3049;* to *reckon thoroughly,* i.e. (gen.) to *deliberate* (by reflection or discussion):—cast in mind, consider, dispute, muse, reason, think.

1261. **διαλογισμός dialŏgismŏs**, *dee-al-og-is-mos';* from *1260; discussion,* i.e. (internal) *consideration* (by impl. *purpose*), or (external) *debate:*—dispute, doubtful (-ing), imagination, reasoning, thought.

1262. **διαλύω dialuō**, *dee-al-oo'-o;* from *1223* and *3089;* to *dissolve utterly:*—scatter.

1263. **διαμαρτύρομαι diamarturŏmai**, *dee-am-ar-too'-rom-ahee;* from *1223* and *3140;* to *attest* or *protest earnestly,* or (by impl.) *hortatively:*—charge, testify (unto), witness.

1264. **διαμάχομαι diamachŏmai**, *dee-am-akh'-om-ahee;* from *1223* and *3164;* to *fight fiercely* (in altercation):—strive.

1265. **διαμένω diamĕnō**, *dee-am-en'-o;* from *1223* and *3306;* to *stay constantly* (in being or relation):—continue, remain.

1266. **διαμερίζω diamĕrizō**, *dee-am-er-id'-zo;* from *1223* and *3307;* to *partition thoroughly* (lit. in distribution, fig. in dissension):—cloven, divide, part.

1267. **διαμερισμός diamĕrismŏs**, *dee-am-er-is-mos';* from *1266; disunion* (of opinion and conduct):—division.

1268. **διανέμω dianĕmō**, *dee-an-em'-o;* from *1223* and the base of *3551;* to *distribute,* i.e. (of information) to *disseminate:*—spread.

1269. **διανεύω dianĕuō**, *dee-an-yoo'-o;* from *1223* and *3506;* to *nod* (or *express* by signs) *across* an intervening space:—beckon.

1270. **διανόημα dianŏēma**, *dee-an-ŏ'-ay-mah;* from a comp. of *1223* and *3539;* something *thought through,* i.e. a *sentiment:*—thought.

1271. **διάνοια dianŏia**, *dee-an'-oy-ah;* from *1223* and *3563; deep thought,* prop. the faculty (*mind* or its *disposition*), by impl. its exercise:—imagination, mind, understanding.

1272. **διανοίγω dianŏigō**, *dee-an-oy'-go;* from *1223* and *455;* to *open thoroughly,* lit. (as a first-born) or fig. (to *expound*):—open.

1273. **διανυκτερεύω dianuktĕrĕuō**, *dee-an-ook-ter-yoo'-o;* from *1223* and a der. of *3571;* to *sit up the whole night:*—continue all night.

1274. **διανύω dianuō**, *dee-an-oo'-o;* from *1223* and **ἀνύω anuō** (to *effect*); to *accomplish thoroughly:*—finish.

1275. **διαπαντός diapantŏs**, *dee-ap-an-tos';* from *1223* and the genit. of *3956; through all* time, i.e. (adv.) *constantly:*—alway (-s), continually.

1276. **διαπεράω diapĕraō**, *dee-ap-er-ah'-o;* from *1223* and a der. of the base of *4008;* to *cross entirely:*—go over, pass (over), sail over.

1277. **διαπλέω diaplĕō**, *dee-ap-leh'-o;* from *1223* and *4126;* to *sail through:*—sail over.

1278. **διαπονέω diapŏnĕō**, *dee-ap-on-eh'-o;* from *1223* and a der. of *4192;* to *toil through,* i.e. (pass.) *be worried:*—be grieved.

1279. **διαπορεύομαι diapŏrĕuŏmai**, *dee-ap-or-yoo'-om-ahee;* from *1223* and *4198;* to *travel through:*—go through, journey in, pass by.

1280. **διαπορέω diapŏrĕō**, *dee-ap-or-eh'-o;* from *1223* and *639;* to *be thoroughly nonplussed:*—(be in) doubt, be (much) perplexed.

1281. **διαπραγματεύομαι diapragmatĕuŏmai**, *dee-ap-rag-mat-yoo'-om-ahee;* from *1223* and *4231;* to *thoroughly occupy oneself,* i.e. (trans. and by impl.) to *earn* in business:—gain by trading.

1282. **διαπρίω diapriō**, *dee-ap-ree'-o;* from *1223* and the base of *4249;* to *saw asunder,* i.e. (fig.) to *exasperate:*—cut (to the heart).

1283. **διαρπάζω diarpazō**, *dee-ar-pad'-zo;* from *1223* and *726;* to *seize asunder,* i.e. *plunder:*—spoil.

1284. **διαῤῥήσσω diarrhēssō**, *dee-ar-hrayce'-so;* from *1223* and *4486;* to *tear asunder:*—break, rend.

1285. **διασαφέω diasaphĕō**, *dee-as-af-eh'-o;* from *1223* and **σαφής saphēs** (*clear*); to *clear thoroughly,* i.e. (fig.) *declare:*—tell unto.

1286. **διασείω diasĕiō**, *dee-as-i'-o;* from *1223* and *4579;* to *shake thoroughly,* i.e. (fig.) to *intimidate:*—do violence to.

1287. **διασκορπίζω diaskŏrpizō**, *dee-as-kor-pid'-zo;* from *1223* and *4650;* to *dissipate,* i.e. (gen.) to *rout* or *separate;* spec. to *winnow;* fig. to *squander:*—disperse, scatter (abroad), strew, waste.

1288. διασπάω **diaspaō**, *dee-as-pah'-o;* from *1223* and *4685;* to *draw apart*, i.e. *sever* or *dismember:*—pluck asunder, pull in pieces.

1289. διασπείρω **diaspĕirō**, *dee-as-pi'-ro;* from *1223* and *4687;* to *sow throughout*, i.e. (fig.) *distribute* in foreign lands:—scatter abroad.

1290. διασπορά **diaspŏra**, *dee-as-por-ah';* from *1289;* *dispersion*, i.e. (spec. and concr.) the (converted) Isr. *resident* in Gentile countries:—(which are) scattered (abroad).

1291. διαστέλλομαι **diastĕllŏmai**, *dee-as-tel'-lom-ahee;* mid. from *1223* and *4724;* to *set* (oneself) *apart* (fig. *distinguish*), i.e. (by impl.) to *enjoin:*—charge, that which was (give) commanded (-ment).

1292. διάστημα **diastēma**, *dee-as'-tay-mah;* from *1339;* an *interval:*—space.

1293. διαστολή **diastŏlē**, *dee-as-tol-ay';* from *1291;* a *variation:*—difference, distinction.

1294. διαστρέφω **diastrĕphō**, *dee-as-tref'-o;* from *1223* and *4762;* to *distort*, i.e. (fig.) *misinterpret*, or (mor.) *corrupt:*—perverse (-rt), turn away.

1295. διασώζω **diasōzō**, *dee-as-odze'-o;* from *1223* and *4982;* to *save thoroughly*, i.e. (by impl. or anal.) to *cure*, *preserve*, *rescue*, etc.:—bring safe, escape (safe), heal, make perfectly whole, save.

1296. διαταγή **diatagē**, *dee-at-ag-ay';* from *1299;* *arrangement*, i.e. *institution:*—instrumentality.

1297. διάταγμα **diatagma**, *dee-at'-ag-mah;* from *1299;* an *arrangement*, i.e. (authoritative) *edict:*—commandment.

1298. διαταράσσω **diatarassō**, *dee-at-ar-as'-so;* from *1223* and *5015;* to *disturb wholly*, i.e. *agitate* (with alarm):—trouble.

1299. διατάσσω **diatassō**, *dee-at-as'-so;* from *1223* and *5021;* to *arrange thoroughly*, i.e. (spec.) *institute*, *prescribe*, etc.:—appoint, command, give, (set in) order, ordain.

1300. διατελέω **diatĕlĕō**, *dee-at-el-eh'-o;* from *1223* and *5055;* to *accomplish thoroughly*, i.e. (subj.) to *persist:*—continue.

1301. διατηρέω **diatērĕō**, *dee-at-ay-reh'-o;* from *1223* and *5083;* to *watch thoroughly*, i.e. (pos. and trans.) to *observe* strictly, or (neg. and reflex.) to *avoid* wholly:—keep.

1302. διατί **diati**, *dee-at-ee';* from *1223* and *5101;* *through what* cause ?, i.e. *why?:*—wherefore, why.

1303. διατίθεμαι **diatithĕmai**, *dee-at-ith'-em-ahee;* mid. from *1223* and *5087;* to *put apart*, i.e. (fig.) *dispose* (by assignment, compact or bequest):—appoint, make, testator.

1304. διατρίβω **diatribō**, *dee-at-ree'-bo;* from *1223* and the base of *5147;* to *wear through* (time), i.e. *remain:*—abide, be, continue, tarry.

1305. διατροφή **diatrŏphē**, *dee-at-rof-ay';* from a comp. of *1223* and *5142;* *nourishment:*—food.

1306. διαυγάζω **diaugazō**, *dee-ŏw-gad'-zo;* from *1223* and *826;* to *glimmer through*, i.e. *break* (as day):—dawn.

1307. διαφανής **diaphanēs**, *dee-af-an-ace';* from *1223* and *5316;* *appearing through*, i.e. "*diaphanous*":—transparent.

1308. διαφέρω **diaphĕrō**, *dee-af-er'-o;* from *1223* and *5342;* to *bear through*, i.e. (lit.) *transport;* usually to *bear apart*, i.e. (obj.) to *toss about* (fig. *report*); subj. to "*differ*," or (by impl.) *surpass:*—be better, carry, differ from, drive up and down, be (more) excellent, make matter, publish, be of more value.

1309. διαφεύγω **diaphĕugō**, *dee-af-yoo'-go;* from *1223* and *5343;* to *flee through*, i.e. *escape:*—escape.

1310. διαφημίζω **diaphēmizō**, *dee-af-ay-mid'-zo;* from *1223* and a der. of *5345;* to *report thoroughly*, i.e. *divulgate:*—blaze abroad, commonly report, spread abroad, fame.

1311. διαφθείρω **diaphthĕirō**, *dee-af-thi'-ro;* from *1225* and *5351;* to *rot thoroughly*, i.e. (by impl.) to *ruin* (pass. *decay* utterly, fig. *pervert*):—corrupt, destroy, perish.

1312. διαφθορά **diaphthŏra**, *dee-af-thor-ah';* from *1311;* *decay:*—corruption.

1313. διάφορος **diaphŏrŏs**, *dee-af'-or-os;* from *1308;* *varying;* also *surpassing:*—differing, divers, more excellent.

1314. διαφυλάσσω **diaphulassō**, *dee-af-oo-las'-so;* from *1223* and *5442;* to *guard thoroughly*, i.e. *protect:*—keep.

1315. διαχειρίζομαι **diachĕirizŏmai**, *dee-akh-i-rid'-zom-ahee;* from *1223* and a der. of *5495;* to *handle thoroughly*, i.e. *lay* violent *hands* upon:—kill, slay.

1316. διαχωρίζομαι **diachōrizŏmai**, *dee-akh-o-rid'-zom-ahee;* from *1223* and the mid. of *5563;* to *remove* (oneself) *wholly*, i.e. *retire:*—depart.

1317. διδακτικός **didaktikŏs**, *did-ak-tik-os';* from *1318;* *instructive* ("didactic"):—apt to teach.

1318. διδακτός **didaktŏs**, *did-ak-tos';* from *1321;* (subj.) *instructed* or (obj.) *communicated* by teaching:—taught, which . . . teacheth.

1319. διδασκαλία **didaskalia**, *did-as-kal-ee'-ah;* from *1320;* *instruction* (the function or the information):—doctrine, learning, teaching.

1320. διδάσκαλος **didaskalŏs**, *did-as'-kal-os;* from *1321;* an *instructor* (gen. or spec.):—doctor, master, teacher.

1321. διδάσκω **didaskō**, *did-as'-ko;* a prol. (caus.) form of a prim. verb δάω **daō** (to *learn*); to *teach* (in the same broad application):—teach.

1322. διδαχή **didachē**, *did-akh-ay';* from *1321;* *instruction* (the act or the matter):—doctrine, hath been taught.

1323. δίδραχμον **didrachmŏn**, *did'-rakh-mon;* from *1364* and *1406;* a *double drachma* (*didrachm*):—tribute.

1324. Δίδυμος **Didumŏs**, *did'-oo-mos;* prol. from *1364;* *double*, i.e. *twin;* *Didymus*, a Chr.:—Didymus.

1325. δίδωμι **didōmi**, *did'-o-mee;* a prol. form of a prim. verb (which is used as an altern. in most of the tenses); to *give* (used in a very wide application, prop. or by impl., lit. or fig.; greatly modified by the connection):—adventure, bestow, bring forth, commit, deliver (up), give, grant, hinder, make, minister, number, offer, have power, put, receive, set, shew, smite (+ with the hand), strike (+ with the palm of the hand), suffer, take, utter, yield.

1326. διεγείρω **diĕgĕirō**, *dee-eg-i'-ro;* from *1223* and *1453;* to *wake fully*, i.e. *arouse* (lit. or fig.):—arise, awake, raise, stir up.

1327. διέξοδος **diĕxŏdŏs**, *dee-ex'-od-os;* from *1223* and *1841;* an *outlet through*, i.e. prob. an open *square* (from which roads diverge):—highway

1328. διερμηνευτής **diĕrmēnĕutēs**, *dee-er-main-yoo-tace';* from *1329;* an *explainer:*—interpreter.

1329. διερμηνεύω **diĕrmēnĕuō**, *dee-er-main-yoo' o;* from *1223* and *2059;* to *explain thoroughly;* by impl. to *translate:*—expound, interpret (-ation).

1330. διέρχομαι **diĕrchŏmai**, *dee-er'-khom-ahee;* from *1223* and *2064;* to *traverse* (lit.):—come, depart, go (about, abroad, every where, over, through, throughout), pass (by, over, through, throughout), pierce through, travel, walk through.

1331. διερωτάω **diĕrōtaō**, *dee-er-o-tah'-o;* from *1223* and *2065;* to *question throughout*, i.e. *ascertain* by interrogation:—make enquiry for.

1332. διετής **diĕtēs**, *dee-et-ace';* from *1364* and *2094;* *of two years* (in age):—two years old.

1333. διετία **diĕtia**, *dee-et-ee'-a;* from *1332;* a space of *two years* (*biennium*):—two years.

1334. διηγέομαι **diēgĕŏmai**, *dee-ayg-eh'-om-ahee;* from *1223* and *2233;* to *relate fully:*—declare, shew, tell.

1335. διήγεσις **diēgĕsis**, *dee-ayg'-es-is;* from *1334;* a *recital:*—declaration.

1336. διηνεκές **diēnĕkĕs**, *dee-ay-nek-es';* neut. of a comp. of *1223* and a der. of an alt. of *5342;* *carried through*, i.e. (adv. with *1519* and *3588* pref.) *perpetually:*—+ continually, for ever.

1337. διθάλασσος **dithalassŏs**, *dee-thal'-as-sos;* from *1364* and *2281;* *having two seas*, i.e. a *sound* with a double outlet:—where two seas met.

1338. διϊκνέομαι **diïknĕŏmai**, *dee-ik-neh'-om-ahee;* from *1223* and the base of *2425;* to *reach through*, i.e. *penetrate:*—pierce.

1339. διΐστημι **diïstēmi**, *dee-is'-tay-mee;* from *1223* and *2476;* to *stand apart*, i.e. (reflex.) to *remove*, *intervene:*—go further, be parted, after the space of.

1340. διϊσχυρίζομαι **diïschurizŏmai**, *dee-is-khoo-rid'-zom-ahee;* from *1223* and a der. of *2478;* to *stout* it *through*, i.e. *asseverate:*—confidently (constantly) affirm.

1341. δικαιοκρισία **dikaiŏkrisia**, *dik-ah-yok-ris-ee'-ah;* from *1342* and *2920;* a *just sentence:*—righteous judgment.

1342. δίκαιος **dikaiŏs**, *dik'-ah-yos;* from *1349;* *equitable* (in character or act); by impl. *innocent*, *holy* (absol. or rel.):—just, meet, right (-eous).

1343. δικαιοσύνη **dikaiŏsunē**, *dik-ah-yos-oo'-nay;* from *1342;* *equity* (of character or act); spec. (Chr.) *justification:*—righteousness.

1344. δικαιόω **dikaiŏō**, *dik-ah-yŏ'-o;* from *1342;* to *render* (i.e. *show* or *regard* as) *just* or *innocent:*—free, justify (-ier), be righteous.

1345. δικαίωμα **dikaiōma**, *dik-ah'-yo-mah;* from *1344;* an *equitable deed;* by impl. a *statute* or *decision:*—judgment, justification, ordinance, righteousness.

1346. δικαίως **dikaiōs**, *dik-ah'-yoce;* adv. from *1342;* *equitably:*—justly, (to) righteously (-ness).

1347. δικαίωσις **dikaiōsis**, *dik-ah'-yo-sis;* from *1344;* *acquittal* (for Christ's sake):—justification.

1348. δικαστής **dikastēs**, *dik-as-tace';* from a der. of *1349;* a *judger:*—judge.

1349. δίκη **dikē**, *dee'-kay;* prob. from *1166;* *right* (as self-*evident*), i.e. *justice* (the principle, a decision, or its execution):—judgment, punish, vengeance.

1350. δίκτυον **diktuŏn**, *dik'-too-on;* prob. from a prim. verb δίκω **dikō** (to *cast*); a *seine* (for fishing):—net.

1351. δίλογος **dilŏgŏs**, *dil'-og-os;* from *1364* and *3056;* *equivocal*, i.e. telling a different story:—double tongued.

1352. διό **diŏ**, *dee-ŏ';* from *1223* and *3739;* *through which* thing, i.e. *consequently:*—for which cause, therefore, wherefore.

1353. διοδεύω **diŏdĕuō**, *dee-od-yoo'-o;* from *1223* and *3593;* to *travel through:*—go throughout, pass through.

1354. Διονύσιος **Diŏnusiŏs**, *dee-on-oo'-see-os;* from Διόνυσος **Diŏnusŏs** (*Bacchus*); *reveller;* *Dionysius*, an Athenian:—Dionysius.

1355. διόπερ **diŏpĕr**, *dee-op'-er;* from *1352* and *4007;* *on which very account:*—wherefore.

1356. διοπετής **diŏpĕtēs**, *dee-op-et'-ace;* from the alt. of *2203* and the alt. of *4098;* *sky-fallen* (i.e. an *aerolite*):—which fell down from Jupiter.

1357. διόρθωσις **diŏrthōsis**, *dee-or'-tho-sis;* from a comp. of *1223* and a der. of *3717*, mean. to *straighten thoroughly;* *rectification*, i.e. (spec.) the Messianic *restauration:*—reformation.

1358. διορύσσω **diŏrussō**, *dee-or-oos'-so;* from *1223* and *3736;* to *penetrate* burglariously:—break through (up).

Διός **Diŏs**. See *2203*.

1359. Διόσκουροι **Diŏskŏurŏi**, *dee-os'-koo-roy;* from the alt. of *2203* and a form of the base of *2877;* *sons of Jupiter*, i.e. the twins *Dioscuri:*—Castor and Pollux.

1360. διότι **diŏti**, *dee-ot'-ee;* from *1223* and *3754;* *on the very account that*, or *inasmuch as:*—because (that), for, therefore.

1361. Διοτρεφής **Diŏtrĕphēs**, *dee-ot-ref-ace';* from the alt. of *2203* and *5142;* *Jove-nourished;* *Diotrephes*, an opponent of Christianity:—Diotrephes.

1362. διπλοῦς **diplŏus**, *dip-looce';* from *1364* and (prob.) the base of *4119;* *two-fold:*—double, two-fold more.

1363. διπλόω **diplŏō**, *dip-lŏ'-o;* from *1362;* to *render two-fold:*—double.

1364. δίς **dis**, *dece;* adv. from *1417; twice:*—again, twice.

Δίς **Dis**. See *2203*.

1365. διστάζω **distazō**, *dis-tad'-zo;* from *1364;* prop. to *duplicate*, i.e. (ment.) to *waver* (in opinion):—doubt.

1366. δίστομος **distŏmŏs**, *dis'-tom-os;* from *1364* and *4750; double-edged:*—with two edges, two-edged.

1367. δισχίλιοι **dischiliŏi**, *dis-khil'-ee-oy;* from *1364* and *5507: two thousand:*—two thousand.

1368. διϋλίζω **diulizō**, *dee-oo-lid'-zo;* from *1223* and ὑλίζω **hulizō**, *hoo-lid'-zo* (to *filter*); to *strain out:*—strain at [*prob. by misprint*].

1369. διχάζω **dichazō**, *dee-khad'-zo;* from a der. of *1364;* to *make apart*, i.e. *sunder* (fig. *alienate*):—set at variance.

1370. διχοστασία **dichŏstasia**, *dee-khos-tas-ee'-ah;* from a der. of *1364* and *4714; disunion*, i.e. (fig.) *dissension:*—division, sedition.

1371. διχοτομέω **dichŏtŏmĕō**, *dee-khot-om-eh'-o;* from a comp. of a der. of *1364* and a der. of τέμνω **tĕmnō** (to *cut*); to *bisect*, i.e. (by extens.) to *flog* severely:—cut asunder (in sunder).

1372. διψάω **dipsaō**, *dip-sah'-o;* from a var. of *1373;* to *thirst* for (lit. or fig.):—(be, be a-) thirst (-y).

1373. δίψος **dipsŏs**, *dip'-sos;* of uncert. affin.; *thirst:*—thirst.

1374. δίψυχος **dipsuchŏs**, *dip'-soo-khos;* from *1364* and *5590; two-spirited*, i.e. *vacillating* (in opinion or purpose):—double minded.

1375. διωγμός **diōgmŏs**, *dee-ogue-mos';* from *1377; persecution:*—persecution.

1376. διώκτης **diōktēs**, *dee-oke'-tace;* from *1377;* a *persecutor:*—persecutor.

1377. διώκω **diōkō**, *dee-o'-ko;* a prol. (and caus.) form of a prim. verb δίω **diō** (to *flee;* comp. the base of *1169* and *1249*); to *pursue* (lit. or fig.); by impl. to *persecute:*—ensue, follow (after), given to, (suffer) persecute (-ion), press toward.

1378. δόγμα **dŏgma**, *dog'-mah;* from the base of *1380;* a *law* (civil, cer. or eccl.):—decree, ordinance.

1379. δογματίζω **dŏgmatizō**, *dog-mat-id'-zo;* from *1378;* to *prescribe* by statute, i.e. (reflex.) to *submit to* cer. *rule:*—be subject to ordinances.

1380. δοκέω **dŏkĕō**, *dok-eh'-o;* a prol. form of a prim. verb δόκω **dŏkō**, *dok'-o* (used only as an alt. in certain tenses; comp. the base of *1166*) of the same mean.; to *think;* by impl. to *seem* (truthfully or uncertainly):—be accounted, (of own) please (-ure), be of reputation, seem (good), suppose, think, trow.

1381. δοκιμάζω **dŏkimazō**, *dok-im-ad'-zo;* from *1384;* to *test* (lit. or fig.); by impl. to *approve:*—allow, discern, examine, × like, (ap-) prove, try.

1382. δοκιμή **dŏkimē**, *dok-ee-may';* from the same as *1384; test* (abstr. or concr.); by impl. *trustiness:*—experience (-riment), proof, trial.

1383. δοκίμιον **dŏkimiŏn**, *dok-im'-ee-on;* neut. of a presumed der. of *1382;* a *testing;* by impl. *trustworthiness:*—trial, trying.

1384. δόκιμος **dŏkimŏs**, *dok'-ee-mos;* from *1380;* prop. *acceptable* (*current* after assayal), i.e. *approved:*—approved, tried.

1385. δοκός **dŏkŏs**, *dok-os';* from *1209* (through the idea of *holding* up); a *stick* of timber:—beam.

δόκω **dŏkō**. See *1380*.

1386. δόλιος **dŏliŏs**, *dol'-ee-os;* from *1388; guileful:*—deceitful.

1387. δολιόω **dŏliŏō**, *dol-ee-ŏ'-o;* from *1386;* to *be guileful:*—use deceit.

1388. δόλος **dŏlŏs**, *dol'-os;* from an obs. prim. δέλλω **dĕllō** (prob. mean. to *decoy;* comp. *1185*); a *trick* (*bait*), i.e. (fig.) *wile:*—craft, deceit, guile, subtilty.

1389. δολόω **dŏlŏō**, *dol-ŏ'-o;* from *1388;* to *ensnare*, i.e. (fig.) *adulterate:*—handle deceitfully.

1390. δόμα **dŏma**, *dom'-ah;* from the base of *1325;* a *present:*—gift.

1391. δόξα **dŏxa**, *dox'-ah;* from the base of *1380; glory* (as very *apparent*), in a wide application (lit. or fig., obj. or subj.):—dignity, glory (-ious), honour, praise, worship.

1392. δοξάζω **dŏxazō**, *dox-ad'-zo;* from *1391;* to *render* (or *esteem*) *glorious* (in a wide application):—(make) glorify (-ious), full of (have) glory, honour, magnify.

1393. Δορκάς **Dŏrkas**, *dor-kas'; gazelle; Dorcas*, a Chr. woman:—Dorcas.

1394. δόσις **dŏsis**, *dos'-is;* from the base of *1325;* a *giving;* by impl. (concr.) a *gift:*—gift, giving.

1395. δότης **dŏtēs**, *dot'-ace;* from the base of *1325;* a *giver:*—giver.

1396. δουλαγωγέω **dŏulagōgĕō**, *doo-lag-ogue-eh'-o;* from a presumed comp. of *1401* and *71;* to *be a slave-driver*, i.e. to *enslave* (fig. *subdue*):—bring into subjection.

1397. δουλεία **dŏulĕia**, *doo-li'-ah;* from *1398; slavery* (cer. or fig.):—bondage.

1398. δουλεύω **dŏulĕuō**, *dool-yoo'-o;* from *1401;* to *be a slave* to (lit. or fig., invol. or vol.):—be in bondage, (do) serve (-ice).

1399. δούλη **dŏulē**, *doo'-lay;* fem. of *1401;* a *female slave* (invol. or vol.):—handmaid (-en).

1400. δοῦλον **dŏulŏn**, *doo'-lon;* neut. of *1401; subservient:*—servant.

1401. δοῦλος **dŏulŏs**, *doo'-los;* from *1210;* a *slave* (lit. or fig., invol. or vol.; frequently therefore in a qualified sense of *subjection* or *subserviency*):—bond (-man), servant.

1402. δουλόω **dŏulŏō**, *doo-lŏ'-o;* from *1401;* to *enslave* (lit. or fig.):—bring into (be under) bondage, × given, become (make) servant.

1403. δοχή **dŏchē**, *dokh-ay';* from *1209;* a *reception*, i.e. convivial *entertainment:*—feast.

1404. δράκων **drakōn**, *drak'-own;* prob. from an alt. form of δέρκομαι **dĕrkŏmai** (to *look*); a fabulous kind of *serpent* (perh. as supposed to *fascinate*):—dragon.

1405. δράσσομαι **drassŏmai**, *dras'-som-ahee;* perh. akin to the base of *1404* (through the idea of *capturing*); to *grasp*, i.e. (fig.) *entrap:*—take.

1406. δραχμή **drachmē**, *drakh-may';* from *1405;* a *drachma* or (silver) coin (as *handled*):—piece (of silver).

δρέμω **drĕmō**. See *5143*.

1407. δρέπανον **drĕpanŏn**, *drep'-an-on;* from δρέπω **drĕpō** (to *pluck*); a gathering *hook* (espec. for harvesting):—sickle.

1408. δρόμος **drŏmŏs**, *drom'-os;* from the alt. of *5143;* a *race*, i.e. (fig.) *career:*—course.

1409. Δρούσιλλα **Drŏusilla**, *droo'-sil-lah;* a fem. dimin. of *Drusus* (a Rom. name); *Drusilla*, a member of the Herodian family:—Drusilla.

δῦμι **dumi**. See *1416*.

1410. δύναμαι **dunamai**, *doo'-nam-ahee;* of uncert. affin.; to *be able* or *possible:*—be able, can (do, + -not), could, may, might, be possible, be of power.

1411. δύναμις **dunamis**, *doo'-nam-is;* from *1410; force* (lit. or fig.); spec. miraculous *power* (usually by impl. a *miracle* itself):—ability, abundance, meaning, might (-ily, -y, -y deed), (worker of) miracle (-s), power, strength, violence, mighty (wonderful) work.

1412. δυναμόω **dunamŏō**, *doo-nam-ŏ'-o;* from *1411;* to *enable:*—strengthen.

1413. δυνάστης **dunastēs**, *doo-nas'-tace;* from *1410;* a *ruler* or *officer:*—of great authority, mighty, potentate.

1414. δυνατέω **dunatĕō**, *doo-nat-eh'-o;* from *1415;* to *be efficient* (fig.):—be mighty.

1415. δυνατός **dunatŏs**, *doo-nat-os';* from *1410; powerful* or *capable* (lit. or fig.); neut. *possible:*—able, could, (that is) mighty (man), possible, power, strong.

1416. δύνω **dunō**, *doo'-no;* or

δῦμι **dumi**, *doo'-mee;* prol. forms of an obs. prim. δύω **duō**, *doo'-o* (to *sink*); to *go* '*down*":—set.

1417. δύο **duŏ**, *doo'-ŏ;* a prim. numeral; "*two*":—both, twain, two.

1418. δυσ- **dus-**, *doos;* a prim. inseparable particle of uncert. der.; used only in composition as a pref.; *hard*, i.e. *with difficulty:*— + hard, + grievous, *etc.*

1419. δυσβάστακτος **dusbastaktŏs**, *doos-bas'-tak-tos;* from *1418* and a der. of *941; oppressive:*—grievous to be borne.

1420. δυσεντερία **dusĕntĕria**, *doos-en-ter-ee'-ah;* from *1418* and a comp. of *1787* (mean. a *bowel*); a "*dysentery*":—bloody flux.

1421. δυσερμήνευτος **dusĕrmēnĕutŏs**, *doos-er-mane'-yoo-tos;* from *1418* and a presumed der. of *2059; difficult of explanation:*—hard to be uttered.

1422. δύσκολος **duskŏlŏs**, *doos'-kol-os;* from *1418* and κόλον **kŏlŏn** (*food*); prop. *fastidious about eating* (*peevish*), i.e. (gen.) *impracticable:*—hard.

1423. δυσκόλως **duskŏlōs**, *doos-kol'-oce;* adv. from *1422; impracticably:*—hardly.

1424. δυσμή **dusmē**, *doos-may';* from *1416;* the sun-*set*, i.e. (by impl.) the *western* region:—west.

1425. δυσνόητος **dusnŏētŏs**, *doos-nŏ'-ay-tos;* from *1418* and a der. of *3539; difficult of perception:*—hard to be understood.

1426. δυσφημία **dusphēmia**, *doos-fay-mee'-ah;* from a comp. of *1418* and *5345; defamation:*—evil report.

δύω **duō**. See *1416*.

1427. δώδεκα **dōdĕka**, *do'-dek-ah;* from *1417* and *1176; two* and *ten*, i.e. a *dozen:*—twelve.

1428. δωδέκατος **dōdĕkatŏs**, *do-dek'-at-os;* from *1427; twelfth:*—twelfth.

1429. δωδεκάφυλον **dōdĕkaphulŏn**, *do-dek-af'-oo-lon;* from *1427* and *5443;* the *commonwealth* of Israel:—twelve tribes.

1430. δῶμα **dōma**, *do'-mah;* from δέμω **dĕmō** (to *build*); prop. an *edifice*, i.e. (spec.) a *roof:*—housetop.

1431. δωρεά **dōrĕa**, *do-reh-ah';* from *1435;* a *gratuity:*—gift.

1432. δωρεάν **dōrĕan**, *do-reh-an';* acc. of *1431* as adv.; *gratuitously* (lit. or fig.):—without a cause, freely, for naught, in vain.

1433. δωρέομαι **dōrĕŏmai**, *do-reh'-om-ahee;* mid. from *1435;* to *bestow* gratuitously:—give.

1434. δώρημα **dōrēma**, *do'-ray-mah;* from *1433;* a *bestowment:*—gift.

1435. δῶρον **dōrŏn**, *do'-ron;* a *present;* spec. a *sacrifice:*—gift, offering.

E

1436. ἔα **ĕa**, *eh'-ah;* appar. imper. of *1439;* prop. *let it be*, i.e. (as interj.) *aha!:*—let alone.

1437. ἐάν **ĕan**, *eh-an';* from *1487* and *302;* a *conditional* particle; *in case* that, *provided*, etc.; often used in connection with other particles to denote *indefiniteness* or *uncertainty:*—before, but, except, (and) if, (if) so, (what-, whither-) soever, though, when (-soever), whether (or), to whom, [who-] so (-ever). See *3361*.

ἐάν μή **ĕan mē**. See *3361*.

1438. ἑαυτοῦ **hĕautŏu**, *heh-ŏw-too'* (incl. all the other cases); from a reflex. pron. otherwise obsol. and the gen. (dat. or acc.) of *846; him-* (*her-*, *it-*, *them-*, also [in conjunction with the pers. pron. of the other persons] *my-*, *thy-*, *our-*, *your-*) *self* (*selves*), etc.:—alone, her (own, -self), (he) himself, his (own), itself, one (to) another, our (thine) own (-selves), + that she had, their (own, own selves), (of) them (-selves), they, thyself, you, your (own, own conceits, own selves, -selves).

1439. ἐάω **ĕaō**, *eh-ah'-o;* of uncert. affin.; to *let be*, i.e. *permit* or *leave* alone:—commit, leave, let (alone), suffer. See also *1436*.

1440. ἑβδομήκοντα **hĕbdŏmēkŏnta**, *heb-dom-ay'-kon-tah;* from *1442* and a modified form of *1176, seventy:*—seventy, three score and ten.

1441. ἑβδομηκοντακίς **hĕbdŏmēkŏntakis**, *heb-dom-ay-kon-tak-is';* multiple adv. from *1440; seventy times:*—seventy times.

1442. ἕβδομος **hĕbdŏmŏs**, *heb'-dom-os;* ordinal from *2033; seventh:*—seventh.

1443. Ἐβέρ **Ĕbĕr**, *eb-er';* of Heb. or. [5677]; *Eber,* a patriarch:—Eber.

1444. Ἑβραϊκός **Hĕbraïkŏs**, *heb-rah-ee-kos';* from *1443; Hebraïc* or the *Jewish* language:—Hebrew.

1445. Ἑβραῖος **Hĕbraiŏs**, *heb-rah'-yos;* from *1443;* a *Hebræan* (i.e. Hebrew) or *Jew:*—Hebrew.

1446. Ἑβραΐς **Hĕbraïs**, *heb-rah-is';* from *1443;* the *Hebraistic* (i.e. *Hebrew*) or *Jewish* (*Chaldee*) language:—Hebrew.

1447. Ἑβραϊστί **Hĕbraïsti**, *heb-rah-is-tee';* adv. from *1446; Hebraistically* or in the Jewish (Chaldee) language:—in (the) Hebrew (tongue).

1448. ἐγγίζω **ĕggizō**, *eng-id'-zo;* from *1451;* to make *near,* i.e. (reflex.) *approach:*—approach, be at hand, come (draw) near, be (come, draw) nigh.

1449. ἐγγράφω **ĕggraphō**, *eng-graf'-o;* from *1722* and *1125;* to "*engrave*", i.e. *inscribe:*—write (in).

1450. ἔγγυος **ĕgguŏs**, *eng'-goo-os;* from *1722* and γυῖον **guiŏn** (a *limb*); *pledged* (as if *articulated* by a member), i.e. a *bondsman:*—surety.

1451. ἐγγύς **ĕggus**, *eng-goos';* from a prim. verb ἄγχω **agchō** (to *squeeze* or *throttle;* akin to the base of *43*); *near* (lit. or fig., of place or time):—from, at hand, near, nigh (at hand, unto), ready.

1452. ἐγγύτερον **ĕggutĕrŏn**, *eng-goo'-ter-on;* neut. of the comp. of *1451; nearer:*—nearer.

1453. ἐγείρω **ĕgĕirō**, *eg-i'-ro;* prob. akin to the base of *58* (through the idea of *collecting* one's faculties); to *waken* (trans. or intrans.), i.e. *rouse* (lit. from sleep, from sitting or lying, from disease, from death; or fig. from obscurity, inactivity, ruins, nonexistence):—awake, lift (up), raise (again, up), rear up, (a-) rise (again, up), stand, take up.

1454. ἔγερσις **ĕgĕrsis**, *eg'-er-sis;* from *1453;* a *resurgence* (from death):—resurrection.

1455. ἐγκάθετος **ĕgkathĕtŏs**, *eng-kath'-et-os;* from *1722* and a der. of *2524; subinduced,* i.e. surreptitiously *suborned* as a lier-in-wait:—spy.

1456. ἐγκαίνια **ĕgkainia**, *eng-kah'ee-nee-ah;* neut. plur. of a presumed comp. from *1722* and *2537; innovatives,* i.e. (spec.) *renewal* (of religious services after the Antiochian interruption):—dedication.

1457. ἐγκαινίζω **ĕgkainizō**, *eng-kahee-nid'-zo;* from *1456;* to *renew,* i.e. *inaugurate:*—consecrate, dedicate.

1458. ἐγκαλέω **ĕgkalĕō**, *eng-kal-eh'-o;* from *1722* and *2564;* to *call in* (as a debt or demand), i.e. *bring to account* (*charge, criminate,* etc.):—accuse, call in question, implead, lay to the charge.

1459. ἐγκαταλείπω **ĕgkatalĕipō**, *eng-kat-al-i'-po;* from *1722* and *2641;* to *leave behind in* some place, i.e. (in a good sense) *let remain over,* or (in a bad one) to *desert:*—forsake, leave.

1460. ἐγκατοικέω **ĕgkatŏikĕō**, *eng-kat-oy-keh'-o;* from *1722* and *2730;* to *settle down in* a place, i.e. *reside:*—dwell among.

1461. ἐγκεντρίζω **ĕgkĕntrizō**, *eng-ken-trid'-zo;* from *1722* and a der. of *2759;* to *prick in,* i.e. *ingraft:*—graff in (-to).

1462. ἔγκλημα **ĕgklēma**, *eng'-klay-mah;* from *1458;* an *accusation,* i.e. *offence* alleged:—crime laid against, laid to charge.

1463. ἐγκομβόομαι **ĕgkŏmbŏŏmai**, *eng-kom-bŏ'-om-ahee;* mid. from *1722* and κομβόω **kŏmbŏō** (to *gird*); to *engirdle* oneself (for labor), i.e. fig. (the apron being a badge of servitude) to *wear* (in token of mutual deference):—be clothed with.

1464. ἐγκοπή **ĕgkŏpē**, *eng-kop-ay';* from *1465;* a *hindrance:*— × hinder.

1465. ἐγκόπτω **ĕgkŏptō**, *eng-kop'-to;* from *1722* and *2875;* to *cut into,* i.e. (fig.) *impede, detain:*—hinder, be tedious unto.

1466. ἐγκράτεια **ĕgkratĕia**, *eng-krat'-i-ah;* from *1468; self-control* (espec. *continence*):—temperance.

1467. ἐγκρατεύομαι **ĕgkratĕuŏmai**, *eng-krat-yoo' om-ahee;* mid. from *1468;* to *exercise self-restraint* (in diet and chastity):—can ([-not]) contain, be temperate.

1468. ἐγκρατής **ĕgkratēs**, *eng-krat-ace';* from *1722* and *2904; strong in* a thing (*masterful*), i.e. (fig. and reflex.) *self-controlled* (in appetite, etc.):—temperate.

1469. ἐγκρίνω **ĕgkrinō**, *eng-kree'-no;* from *1722* and *2919;* to *judge in,* i.e. *count* among:—make of the number.

1470. ἐγκρύπτω **ĕkgruptō**, *eng-kroop'-to;* from *1722* and *2928;* to *conceal in,* i.e. *incorporate with:*—hid in.

1471. ἔγκυος **ĕgkuŏs**, *eng'-koo-os;* from *1722* and the base of *2949; swelling inside,* i.e. *pregnant:*—great with child.

1472. ἐγχρίω **ĕgchriō**, *eng-khree'-o;* from *1722* and *5548;* to *rub in* (oil), i.e. *besmear:*—anoint.

1473. ἐγώ **ĕgō**, *eg-o';* a prim. pron. of the first pers. *I* (only expressed when emphatic):—I, me. For the other cases and the plur. see *1691, 1698, 1700, 2248, 2249, 2254, 2257,* etc.

1474. ἐδαφίζω **ĕdaphizō**, *ed-af-id'-zo;* from *1475;* to *raze:*—lay even with the ground.

1475. ἔδαφος **ĕdaphŏs**, *ed'-af-os;* from the base of *1476;* a *basis* (*bottom*), i.e. the *soil:*—ground.

1476. ἑδραῖος **hĕdraiŏs**, *hed-rah'-yos;* from a der. of ἕζομαι **hĕzŏmai** (to *sit*); *sedentary,* i.e. (by impl.) *immovable:*—settled, stedfast.

1477. ἑδραίωμα **hĕdraiōma**, *hed-rah'-yo-mah;* from a der. of *1476;* a *support,* i.e. (fig.) *basis:*—ground.

1478. Ἐζεκίας **Ĕzĕkias**, *ed-zek-ee'-as;* of Heb. or. [2396]; *Ezekias* (i.e. *Hezekiah*), an Isr.:—Ezekias.

1479. ἐθελοθρησκεία **ĕthĕlŏthrēskĕia**, *eth-el-oth-race-ki'-ah;* from *2309* and *2356; voluntary* (*arbitrary* and *unwarranted*) *piety,* i.e. *sanctimony:*—will worship.

ἐθέλω **ĕthĕlō**. See *2309*.

1480. ἐθίζω **ĕthizō**, *eth-id'-zo;* from *1485;* to *accustom,* i.e. (neut. pass. part.) *customary:*—custom.

1481. ἐθνάρχης **ĕthnarchēs**, *eth-nar'-khace;* from *1484* and *746;* the *governor* [not king] *of a district:*—ethnarch.

1482. ἐθνικός **ĕthnikŏs**, *eth-nee-kos';* from *1484; national* ("*ethnic*"), i.e. (spec.) a *Gentile:*—heathen (man).

1483. ἐθνικῶς **ĕthnikōs**, *eth-nee-koce';* adv. from *1482;* as a *Gentile:*—after the manner of Gentiles.

1484. ἔθνος **ĕthnŏs**, *eth'-nos;* prob. from *1486;* a *race* (as of the same *habit*), i.e. a *tribe;* spec. a *foreign* (*non-Jewish*) one (usually by impl. *pagan*):—Gentile, heathen, nation, people.

1485. ἔθος **ĕthŏs**, *eth'-os;* from *1486;* a *usage* (prescribed by habit or law):—custom, manner, be wont.

1486. ἔθω **ĕthō**, *eth'-o;* a prim. verb; to *be used* (by habit or conventionality); neut. perf. part. *usage:*—be custom (manner, wont).

1487. εἰ **ĕi**, *i;* a prim. particle of conditionality; *if, whether, that,* etc.:—forasmuch as, if, that, ([al-]) though, whether. Often used in connection or composition with other particles, espec. as in *1489, 1490, 1499, 1508, 1509, 1512, 1513, 1536, 1537.* See also *1437*.

1488. εἶ **ĕi**, *i;* second pers. sing. pres. of *1510;* thou *art:*—art, be.

1489. εἴγε **ĕigĕ**, *i'-gheh;* from *1487* and *1065; if indeed, seeing that, unless,* (with neg.) *otherwise:*—if (so be that, yet).

1490. εἰ δὲ μή(γε) **ĕi dĕ mē**(**gĕ**), *i deh may'-(gheh);* from *1487, 1161* and *3361* (sometimes with *1065* added); *but if not:*—(or) else, if (not, otherwise), otherwise.

1491. εἶδος **ĕidŏs**, *i'-dos,* from *1492;* a *view,* i.e. *form* (lit. or fig.):—appearance, fashion, shape, sight.

1492. εἴδω **ĕidō**, *i'-do;* a prim. verb; used only in certain past tenses, the others being borrowed from the equiv. *3700* and *3708;* prop. to *see* (lit. or fig.); by impl. (in the perf. only) to *know:*—be aware, behold, × can (+ not tell), consider, (have) know (-ledge), look (on), perceive, see, be sure, tell, understand, wist, wot. Comp. *3700*.

1493. εἰδωλεῖον **ĕidōlĕiŏn**, *i-do-li'-on;* neut. of a presumed der. of *1497;* an *image-fane:*—idol's temple.

1494. εἰδωλόθυτον **ĕidōlŏthutŏn**, *i-do-loth'-oo-ton;* neut. of a comp. of *1497* and a presumed der. of *2380;* an *image-sacrifice,* i.e. part of an *idolatrous offering:*—(meat, thing that is) offered (in sacrifice, sacrificed) to (unto) idols.

1495. εἰδωλολατρεία **ĕidōlŏlatrĕia**, *i-do-lol-at-ri'-ah;* from *1497* and *2999; image-worship* (lit. or fig.):—idolatry.

1496. εἰδωλολάτρης **ĕidōlŏlatrēs**, *i-do-lol-at'-race;* from *1497* and the base of *3000;* an *image-* (*servant* or) *worshipper* (lit. or fig.):—idolater.

1497. εἴδωλον **ĕidōlŏn**, *i'-do-lon;* from *1491;* an *image* (i.e. for worship); by impl. a heathen *god,* or (plur.) the *worship* of such:—idol.

1498. εἴην **ĕiēn**, *i'-ane;* optative (i.e. Eng. subjunctive) pres. of *1510* (includ. the other pers.); *might* (*could, would* or *should*) *be:*—mean, + perish, should be, was, were.

1499. εἰ καί **ĕi kai**, *i kahee;* from *1487* and *2532; if also* (or *even*):—if (that), though.

1500. εἰκῆ **ĕikē**, *i-kay';* prob. from *1502* (through the idea of *failure*); *idly,* i.e. *without reason* (or *effect*):—without a cause, (in) vain (-ly).

1501. εἴκοσι **ĕikŏsi**, *i'-kos-ee;* of uncert. affin.; a *score:*—twenty.

1502. εἴκω **ĕikō**, *i'-ko;* appar. a prim. verb; prop. to *be weak,* i.e. *yield:*—give place.

1503. εἴκω **ĕikō**, *i'-ko;* appar. a prim. verb [perh. akin to *1502* through the idea of *faintness* as a copy]; to *resemble:*—be like.

1504. εἰκών **ĕikōn**, *i-kone';* from *1503;* a *likeness,* i.e. (lit.) *statue, profile,* or (fig.) *representation, resemblance:*—image.

1505. εἰλικρίνεια **ĕilikrinĕia**, *i-lik-ree'-ni-ah;* from *1506; clearness,* i.e. (by impl.) *purity* (fig.):—sincerity.

1506. εἰλικρινής **ĕilikrinēs**, *i-lik-ree-nace';* from εἵλη **hĕilē** (the sun's *ray*) and *2919; judged by sunlight,* i.e. tested as *genuine* (fig.):—pure, sincere.

1507. εἱλίσσω **hĕilissō**, *hi-lis'-so;* a prol. form of a prim. but defective verb εἵλω **hĕilō** (of the same mean.); to *coil* or *wrap:*—roll together. See also *1667*.

1508. εἰ μή **ĕi mē**, *i may;* from *1487* and *3361; if not:*—but, except (that), if not, more than, save (only) that, saving, till.

1509. εἰ μή τι **ĕi mē ti**, *i may tee;* from *1508* and the neut. of *5100; if not somewhat:*—except.

1510. εἰμί **ĕimi**, *i-mee';* first pers. sing. pres. indic.; a prol. form of a prim. and defective verb; I *exist* (used only when emphatic):—am, have been, × it is I, was. See also *1488, 1498, 1511, 1527, 2258, 2071, 2070, 2075, 2076, 2771, 2468, 5600*.

1511. εἶναι **ĕinai**, *i'-nahee;* pres. infin. from *1510;* to *exist:*—am, are, come, is, × lust after, × please well, there is, to be, was.

εἵνεκεν **hĕinĕkĕn**. See *1752*.

1512. εἴ περ **ĕi pĕr**, *i per;* from *1487* and *4007; if perhaps:*—if so be (that), seeing, though.

1513. εἴ πως **ĕi pōs**. *i poce;* from *1487* and *4458; if somehow:*—if by any means.

1514. εἰρηνεύω **ĕirēnĕuō**, *i-rane-yoo'-o;* from *1515;* to *be* (*act*) *peaceful:*—be at (have, live in) peace, live peaceably.

1515. εἰρήνη **ĕirēnē**, *i-ray'-nay;* prob. from a prim. verb εἴρω **ĕirō** (to *join*); *peace* (lit. or fig.); by impl. *prosperity:*—one, peace, quietness, rest, + set at one again.

1516. εἰρηνικός **ĕirēnikŏs**, *i-ray-nee-kos';* from *1515; pacific;* by impl. *salutary:*—peaceable.

1517. εἰρηνοποιέω **ĕirēnŏpŏiĕō**, *i-ray-nop-oy-eh'-o;* from *1518;* to *be a peace-maker,* i.e. (fig.) to *harmonize:*—make peace.

1518. εἰρηνοποιός **ĕirēnŏpŏiŏs**, *i-ray-nop-oy-os';* from *1515* and *4160; pacificatory,* i.e. (subj.) *peaceable:*—peacemaker.

εἴρω **ĕirō**. See *1515, 4483, 5346*.

1519. **εἰς ĕis**, *ice;* a prim. prep.; *to* or *into* (indicating the point reached or entered), of place, time, or (fig.) purpose (result, etc.); also in adv. phrases:—[abundant-] ly, against, among, as, at, [back-] ward, before, by, concerning, + continual, + far more exceeding, for [intent, purpose], fore, + forth, in (among, at, unto, -so much that, -to), to the intent that, + of one mind, + never, of, (up-) on, + perish, + set at one again, (so) that, therefore (-unto), throughout, till, to (be, the end, -ward), (here-) until (-to), . . . ward, [where-] fore, with. Often used in composition with the same general import, but only with verbs (etc.) expressing motion (lit. or fig.).

1520. **εἷς hĕis**, *hice;* (includ. the neut. [etc.] **ἕν hĕn**); a prim. numeral; *one:*—a (-n, -ny, certain), + abundantly, man, one (another), only, other, some. See also *1527, 3367, 3391, 3762.*

1521. **εἰσάγω ĕisagō**, *ice-ag'-o;* from *1519* and *71;* to *introduce* (lit. or fig.):—bring in (-to), (+ was to) lead into.

1522. **εἰσακούω ĕisakŏuō**, *ice-ak-oo'-o;* from *1519* and *191;* to *listen* to:—hear.

1523. **εἰσδέχομαι ĕisdĕchŏmai**, *ice-dekh'-om-ahee;* from *1519* and *1209;* to *take into* one's favor:—receive.

1524. **εἴσειμι ĕisĕimi**, *ice'-i-mee;* from *1519* and **εἶμι ĕimi** (to *go*); to *enter:*—enter (go) into.

1525. **εἰσέρχομαι ĕisĕrchŏmai**, *ice-er'-khom-ahee;* from *1519* and *2064;* to *enter* (lit. or fig.):—× arise, come (in, into), enter in (-to), go in (through).

1526. **εἰσί ĕisi**, *i-see';* 3d pers. plur. pres. indic. of *1510;* they *are:*—agree, are, be, dure, × is, were.

1527. **εἷς καθ' εἷς hĕis kath' hĕis**, *hice kath hice;* from *1520* repeated with *2596* inserted; *severally:*—one by one.

1528. **εἰσκαλέω ĕiskalĕō**, *ice-kal-eh'-o;* from *1519* and *2564;* to *invite* in:—call in.

1529. **εἴσοδος ĕisŏdŏs**, *ice'-od-os;* from *1519* and *3598;* an *entrance* (lit. or fig.):—coming, enter (-ing) in (to).

1530. **εἰσπηδάω ĕispēdaō**, *ice-pay-dah'-o;* from *1519* and **πηδάω pēdaō** (to *leap*); to *rush in:*—run (spring) in.

1531. **εἰσπορεύομαι ĕispŏrĕuŏmai**, *ice-por-yoo'-om-ahee;* from *1519* and *4198;* to *enter* (lit. or fig.):—come (enter) in, go into.

1532. **εἰστρέχω ĕistrĕchō**, *ice-trekh'-o;* from *1519* and *5143;* to *hasten inward:*—run in.

1533. **εἰσφέρω ĕisphĕrō**, *ice-fer'-o;* from *1519* and *5342;* to *carry inward* (lit. or fig.):—bring (in), lead into.

1534. **εἶτα ĕita**, *i'-tah;* of uncert. affin.; a particle of *succession* (in time or logical enumeration), *then, moreover:*—after that (-ward), furthermore, then. See also *1899.*

1535. **εἴτε ĕitĕ**, *i'-teh;* from *1487* and *5037; if too:*—if, or, whether.

1536. **εἴ τις ĕi tis**, *i tis;* from *1487* and *5100; if any:*—he that, if a (-ny) man ('s, thing, from any, ought), whether any, whosoever.

1537. **ἐκ ĕk**, *ek;* or

ἐξ ĕx, *ex;* a prim. prep. denoting *origin* (the point *whence* motion or action proceeds), *from, out* (of place, time or cause; lit. or fig.; direct or remote):—after, among, × are, at, betwixt (-yond), by (the means of), exceedingly, (+ abundantly above), for (-th), from (among, forth, up), + grudgingly, + heartily, × heavenly, × hereby, + very highly, in, . . . ly, (because, by reason) of, off (from), on, out among (from, of), over, since, × thenceforth, through, × unto, × vehemently, with (-out). Often used in composition, with the same general import; often of *completion.*

1538. **ἕκαστος hĕkastŏs**, *hek'-as-tos;* as if a superlative of **ἕκας hĕkas** (*afar*); *each* or *every:*—any, both, each (one), every (man, one, woman), particularly.

1539. **ἑκάστοτε hĕkastŏtĕ**, *hek-as'-tot-eh;* as if from *1538* and *5119;* at *every time:*—always.

1540. **ἑκατόν hĕkatŏn**, *hek-at-on';* of uncert. affin.; a *hundred:*—hundred.

1541. **ἑκατονταέτης hĕkatŏntaĕtēs**, *hek-at-on-tah-et'-ace;* from *1540* and *2094; centenarian:*—hundred years old.

1542. **ἑκατονταπλασίων hĕkatŏntaplasiŏn**, *hek-at-on-ta-plah-see'-own;* from *1540* and a presumed der. of *4111;* a *hundred times:*—hundredfold.

1543. **ἑκατοντάρχης hĕkatŏntarchēs**, *hek-at-on-tar'-khace;* or

ἑκατόνταρχος hĕkatŏntarchŏs, *hek-at-on'-tar-khos;* from *1540* and *757;* the *captain of one hundred men:*—centurion.

1544. **ἐκβάλλω ĕkballō**, *ek-bal'-lo;* from *1537* and *906;* to *eject* (lit. or fig.):—bring forth, cast (forth, out), drive (out), expel, leave, pluck (pull, take, thrust) out, put forth (out), send away (forth, out).

1545. **ἔκβασις ĕkbasis**, *ek'-bas-is;* from a comp. of *1537* and the base of *939* (mean. to *go out*); an *exit* (lit. or fig.):—end, way to escape.

1546. **ἐκβολή ĕkbŏlē**, *ek-bol-ay';* from *1544; ejection,* i.e. (spec.) a *throwing overboard* of the cargo:—+ lighten the ship.

1547. **ἐκγαμίζω ĕkgamizō**, *ek-gam-id'-zo;* from *1537* and a form of *1061* [comp. *1548*]; to *marry off* a daughter:—give in marriage.

1548. **ἐκγαμίσκω ĕkgamiskō**, *ek-gam-is'-ko;* from *1537* and *1061;* the same as *1547:*—give in marriage.

1549. **ἔκγονον ĕkgŏnŏn**, *ek'-gon-on;* neut. of a der. of a comp. of *1537* and *1096;* a *descendant,* i.e. (spec.) *grandchild:*—nephew.

1550. **ἐκδαπανάω ĕkdapanaō**, *ek-dap-an-ah'-o;* from *1537* and *1159;* to *expend* (wholly), i.e. (fig.) *exhaust:*—spend.

1551. **ἐκδέχομαι ĕkdĕchŏmai**, *ek-dekh'-om-ahee;* from *1537* and *1209;* to *accept from* some source, i.e. (by impl.) to *await:*—expect, look (tarry) for, wait (for).

1552. **ἔκδηλος ĕkdēlŏs**, *ek'-day-los;* from *1537* and *1212; wholly evident:*—manifest.

1553. **ἐκδημέω ĕkdēmĕō**, *ek-day-meh'-o;* from a comp. of *1537* and *1218;* to *emigrate,* i.e. (fig.) *vacate* or *quit:*—be absent.

1554. **ἐκδίδωμι ĕkdidōmi**, *ek-did-o'-mee;* from *1537* and *1325;* to *give forth,* i.e. (spec.) to *lease:*—let forth (out).

1555. **ἐκδιηγέομαι ĕkdiēgĕŏmai**, *ek-dee-ayg-eh'-om-ahee;* from *1537* and a comp. of *1223* and *2233;* to *narrate* through wholly:—declare.

1556. **ἐκδικέω ĕkdikĕō**, *ek-dik-eh'-o;* from *1558;* to *vindicate, retaliate, punish:*—a (re-) venge.

1557. **ἐκδίκησις ĕkdikēsis**, *ek-dik'-ay-sis;* from *1556; vindication, retribution:*—(a-, re-) venge (-ance), punishment.

1558. **ἔκδικος ĕkdikŏs**, *ek'-dik-os;* from *1537* and *1349;* carrying justice out, i.e. a *punisher:*—a (re-) venger.

1559. **ἐκδιώκω ĕkdiōkō**, *ek-dee-o'-ko;* from *1537* and *1377;* to *pursue out,* i.e. *expel* or *persecute* implacably:—persecute.

1560. **ἔκδοτος ĕkdŏtŏs**, *ek'-dot-os;* from *1537* and a der. of *1325; given out* or *over,* i.e. *surrendered:*—delivered.

1561. **ἐκδοχή ĕkdŏchē**, *ek-dokh-ay';* from *1551; expectation:*—looking for.

1562. **ἐκδύω ĕkduō**, *ek-doo'-o;* from *1537* and the base of *1416;* to cause to *sink out* of, i.e. (spec. as of clothing) to *divest:*—strip, take off from, unclothe.

1563. **ἐκεῖ ĕkĕi**, *ek-i';* of uncert. affin.; *there;* by extens. *thither:*—there, thither (-ward), (to) yonder (place).

1564. **ἐκεῖθεν ĕkĕithĕn**, *ek-i'-then;* from *1563; thence:*—from that place, (from) thence, there.

1565. **ἐκεῖνος ĕkĕinŏs**, *ek-i'-nos;* from *1563; that* one (or [neut.] thing); often intensified by the art. prefixed:—he, it, the other (same), selfsame, that (same, very), × their, × them, they, this, those. See also *3778.*

1566. **ἐκεῖσε ĕkĕisĕ**, *ek-i'-seh;* from *1563; thither:*—there.

1567. **ἐκζητέω ĕkzētĕō**, *ek-zay-teh'-o;* from *1537* and *2212;* to *search out,* i.e. (fig.) *investigate, crave, demand,* (by Hebr.) *worship:*—en- (re-) quire, seek after (carefully, diligently).

1568. **ἐκθαμβέω ĕkthambĕō**, *ek-tham-beh'-o;* from *1569;* to *astonish* utterly:—affright, greatly (sore) amaze.

1569. **ἔκθαμβος ĕkthambŏs**, *ek'-tham-bos;* from *1537* and *2285; utterly astounded:*—greatly wondering.

1570. **ἔκθετος ĕkthĕtŏs**, *ek'-thet-os;* from *1537* and a der. of *5087; put out,* i.e. *exposed* to perish:—cast out.

1571. **ἐκκαθαίρω ĕkkathairō**, *ek-kath-ah'ee-ro;* from *1537* and *2508;* to *cleanse thoroughly:*—purge (out).

1572. **ἐκκαίω ĕkkaiō**, *ek-kah'-yo;* from *1537* and *2545;* to *inflame* deeply:—burn.

1573. **ἐκκακέω ĕkkakĕō**, *ek-kak-eh'-o;* from *1537* and *2556;* to *be* (*bad* or) *weak,* i.e. (by impl.) to *fail* (in heart):—faint, be weary.

1574. **ἐκκεντέω ĕkkĕntĕō**, *ek-ken-teh'-o;* from *1537* and the base of *2759;* to *transfix:*—pierce.

1575. **ἐκκλάω ĕkklaō**, *ek-klah'-o;* from *1537* and *2806;* to *exscind:*—break off.

1576. **ἐκκλείω ĕkklĕiō**, *ek-kli'-o;* from *1537* and *2808;* to *shut out* (lit. or fig.):—exclude.

1577. **ἐκκλησία ĕkklēsia**, *ek-klay-see'-ah;* from a comp. of *1537* and a der. of *2564;* a *calling out,* i.e. (concr.) a popular *meeting,* espec. a religious *congregation* (Jewish *synagogue,* or Chr. community of members on earth or saints in heaven or both):—assembly, church.

1578. **ἐκκλίνω ĕkklinō**, *ek-klee'-no;* from *1537* and *2827;* to *deviate,* i.e. (absol.) to *shun* (lit. or fig.), or (rel.) to *decline* (from piety):—avoid, eschew, go out of the way.

1579. **ἐκκολυμβάω ĕkkŏlumbaō**, *ek-kol-oom-bah'-o;* from *1537* and *2860;* to *escape* by *swimming:*—swim out.

1580. **ἐκκομίζω ĕkkŏmizō**, *ek-kom-id'-zo;* from *1537* and *2865;* to *bear forth* (to burial):—carry out.

1581. **ἐκκόπτω ĕkkŏptō**, *ek-kop'-to;* from *1537* and *2875;* to *exscind;* fig. to *frustrate:*—cut down (off, out), hew down, hinder.

1582. **ἐκκρέμαμαι ĕkkrĕmamai**, *ek-krem'-am-ahee;* mid. from *1537* and *2910;* to *hang upon* the lips of a speaker, i.e. *listen closely:*—be very attentive.

1583. **ἐκλαλέω ĕklalĕō**, *ek-lal-eh'-o;* from *1537* and *2980;* to *divulge:*—tell.

1584. **ἐκλάμπω ĕklampō**, *ek-lam'-po;* from *1537* and *2989;* to *be resplendent:*—shine forth.

1585. **ἐκλανθάνομαι ĕklanthanŏmai**, *ek-lan-than'-om-ahee;* mid. from *1537* and *2990;* to *be* utterly *oblivious* of:—forget.

1586. **ἐκλέγομαι ĕklĕgŏmai**, *ek-leg'-om-ahee;* mid. from *1537* and *3004* (in its prim. sense); to *select;*—make choice, choose (out), chosen.

1587. **ἐκλείπω ĕklĕipō**, *ek-li'-po;* from *1537* and *3007;* to *omit,* i.e. (by impl.) *cease* (*die*):—fail.

1588. **ἐκλεκτός ĕklĕktŏs**, *ek-lek-tos';* from *1586; select;* by impl. *favorite:*—chosen, elect.

1589. **ἐκλογή ĕklŏgē**, *ek-log-ay';* from *1586;* (divine) *selection* (abstr. or concr.):—chosen, election.

1590. **ἐκλύω ĕkluō**, *ek-loo'-o;* from *1537* and *3089;* to *relax* (lit. or fig.):—faint.

1591. **ἐκμάσσω ĕkmassō**, *ek-mas'-so;* from *1537* and the base of *3145;* to *knead out,* i.e. (by anal.) to *wipe dry:*—wipe.

1592. **ἐκμυκτερίζω ĕkmuktĕrizō**, *ek-mook-ter-id'-zo;* from *1537* and *3456;* to *sneer* outright at:—deride.

1593. **ἐκνεύω ĕknĕuō**, *ek-nyoo'-o;* from *1537* and *3506;* (by anal.) to *slip off,* i.e. quietly *withdraw:*—convey self away.

1594. **ἐκνήφω ĕknēphō**, *ek-nay'-fo;* from *1537* and *3525;* (fig.) to *rouse* (oneself) *out* of stupor:—awake.

1595. **ἑκούσιον hĕkŏusiŏn**, *hek-oo'-see-on;* neut. of a der. from *1635; voluntariness:*—willingly.

1596. **ἑκουσίως hĕkŏusiōs**, *hek-oo-see'-oce;* adv. from the same as *1595; voluntarily:*—wilfully, willingly.

1597. **ἔκπαλαι ĕkpalai**, *ek'-pal-ahee;* from *1537* and *3819; long ago, for a long while:*—of a long time, of old.

1598. **ἐκπειράζω ĕkpĕirazō**, *ek-pi-rad'-zo;* from *1537* and *3985; to test thoroughly:*—tempt.

1599. **ἐκπέμπω ĕkpĕmpō**, *ek-pem'-po;* from *1537* and *3992;* to *despatch:*—send away (forth).

ἐκπερισσοῦ ĕkpĕrissŏu. See *1537* and *4053*.

1600. **ἐκπετάννυμι ĕkpĕtannumi**, *ek-pet-an'-noo-mee;* from *1537* and a form of *4072;* to *fly out*, i.e. (by anal.) *extend:*—stretch forth.

1601. **ἐκπίπτω ĕkpiptō**, *ek-pip'-to;* from *1537* and *4098;* to *drop away;* spec. *be driven out* of one's course; fig. to *lose, become inefficient:*—be cast, fail, fall (away, off), take none effect.

1602. **ἐκπλέω ĕkplĕō**, *ek-pleh'-o;* from *1537* and *4126;* to *depart* by ship:—sail (away, thence).

1603. **ἐκπληρόω ĕkplērŏō**, *ek-play-rō'-o;* from *1537* and *4137;* to *accomplish* entirely:—fulfill.

1604. **ἐκπλήρωσις ĕkplērōsis**, *ek-play'-ro-sis;* from *1603; completion:*—accomplishment.

1605. **ἐκπλήσσω ĕkplēssō**, *ek-place'-so;* from *1537* and *4141;* to *strike* with astonishment:—amaze, astonish.

1606. **ἐκπνέω ĕkpnĕō**, *ek-pneh'-o;* from *1537* and *4154;* to *expire:*—give up the ghost.

1607. **ἐκπορεύομαι ĕkpŏrĕuŏmai**, *ek-por-yoo'-om-ahee;* from *1537* and *4198;* to *depart, be discharged, proceed, project:*—come (forth, out of), depart, go (forth, out), issue, proceed (out of).

1608. **ἐκπορνεύω ĕkpŏrnĕuō**, *ek-porn-yoo'-o;* from *1537* and *4203;* to *be utterly unchaste:*—give self over to fornication.

1609. **ἐκπτύω ĕkptuō**, *ek-ptoo'-o;* from *1537* and *4429;* to *spit out*, i.e. (fig.) *spurn:*—reject.

1610. **ἐκριζόω ĕkrizŏō**, *ek-rid-zŏ'-o;* from *1537* and *4492;* to *uproot:*—pluck up by the root, root up.

1611. **ἔκστασις ĕkstasis**, *ek'-stas-is;* from *1839;* a *displacement* of the mind, i.e. *bewilderment*, "*ecstasy*":—+ be amazed, amazement, astonishment, trance.

1612. **ἐκστρέφω ĕkstrĕphō**, *ek-stref'-o;* from *1537* and *4762;* to *pervert* (fig.):—subvert.

1613. **ἐκταράσσω ĕktarassō**, *ek-tar-as'-so;* from *1537* and *5015;* to *disturb wholly:*—exceedingly trouble.

1614. **ἐκτείνω ĕktĕinō**, *ek-ti'-no;* from *1537* and **τείνω tĕinō** (to *stretch*); to *extend:*—cast, put forth, stretch forth (out).

1615. **ἐκτελέω ĕktĕlĕō**, *ek-tel-eh'-o;* from *1537* and *5055;* to *complete* fully:—finish.

1616. **ἐκτένεια ĕktĕnĕia**, *ek-ten'-i-ah;* from *1618; intentness:*—× instantly.

1617. **ἐκτενέστερον ĕktĕnĕstĕrŏn**, *ek-ten-es'-ter-on;* neut. of the comp. of *1618; more intently:*—more earnestly.

1618. **ἐκτενής ĕktĕnēs**, *ek-ten-ace';* from *1614; intent:*—without ceasing, fervent.

1619. **ἐκτενῶς ĕktĕnōs**, *ek-ten-oce';* adv. from *1618; intently:*—fervently.

1620. **ἐκτίθημι ĕktithēmi**, *ek-tith'-ay-mee;* from *1537* and *5087;* to *expose;* fig. to *declare:*—cast out, expound.

1621. **ἐκτινάσσω ĕktinassō**, *ek-tin-as'-so;* from *1537* and **τινάσσω tinassō** (to *swing*); to *shake* violently:—shake (off).

1622. **ἐκτός ĕktŏs**, *ek-tos';* from *1537;* the *exterior;* fig. (as a prep.) *aside from, besides:*—but, except (-ed), other than, out of, outside, unless, without.

1623. **ἕκτος hĕktŏs**, *hek'-tos;* ordinal from *1803; sixth:*—sixth.

1624. **ἐκτρέπω ĕktrĕpō**, *ek-trep'-o;* from *1537* and the base of *5157;* to *deflect*, i.e. *turn away* (lit. or fig.):—avoid, turn (aside, out of the way).

1625. **ἐκτρέφω ĕktrĕphō**, *ek-tref'-o;* from *1537* and *5142;* to *rear up* to maturity, i.e. (gen.) to *cherish* or *train:*—bring up, nourish.

1626. **ἔκτρωμα ĕktrōma**, *ek'-tro-mah;* from a comp. of *1537* and **τιτρώσκω titrōskō** (to *wound*); a *miscarriage* (*abortion*), i.e. (by anal.) *untimely birth:*—born out of due time.

1627. **ἐκφέρω ĕkphĕrō**, *ek-fer'-o;* from *1537* and *5342;* to *bear out* (lit. or fig.):—bear, bring forth, carry forth (out).

1628. **ἐκφεύγω ĕkphĕugō**, *ek-fyoo'-go;* from *1537* and *5343;* to *flee out:*—escape, flee.

1629. **ἐκφοβέω ĕkphŏbĕō**, *ek-fob-eh'-o;* from *1537* and *5399;* to *frighten utterly:*—terrify.

1630. **ἔκφοβος ĕkphŏbŏs**, *ek'-fob-os;* from *1537* and *5401; frightened out* of one's wits:—sore afraid, exceedingly fear.

1631. **ἐκφύω ĕkphuō**, *ek-foo'-o;* from *1537* and *5453;* to *sprout up:*—put forth.

1632. **ἐκχέω ĕkchĕō**, *ek-kheh'-o;* or (by var.)

ἐκχύνω ĕkchunō, *ek-khoo'-no;* from *1537* and **χέω chĕō** (to *pour*); to *pour forth;* fig. to *bestow:*—gush (pour) out, run greedily (out), shed (abroad, forth), spill.

1633. **ἐκχωρέω ĕkchōrĕō**, *ek-kho-reh'-o;* from *1537* and *5562;* to *depart:*—depart out.

1634. **ἐκψύχω ĕkpsuchō**, *ek-psoo'-kho;* from *1537* and *5594;* to *expire:*—give (yield) up the ghost.

1635. **ἑκών hĕkōn**, *hek-own';* of uncert. affin.; *voluntary:*—willingly.

1636. **ἐλαία ĕlaia**, *el-ah'-yah;* fem. of a presumed der. from an obsol. prim.; an *olive* (the tree or the fruit):—olive (berry, tree).

1637. **ἔλαιον ĕlaiŏn**, *el'-ah-yon;* neut. of the same as *1636;* olive *oil:*—oil.

1638. **ἐλαιών ĕlaiōn**, *el-ah-yone';* from *1636;* an *olive-orchard*, i.e. (spec.) the *Mt. of Olives:*—Olivet.

1639. **Ἐλαμίτης Ĕlamitēs**, *el-am-ee'-tace;* of Heb. or. [5867]; an *Elamite* or Persian:—Elamite.

1640. **ἐλάσσων ĕlassōn**, *el-as'-sone;* or

ἐλάττων ĕlattōn, *el-at-tone';* comp. of the same as *1646; smaller* (in size, quantity, age or quality):—less, under, worse, younger.

1641. **ἐλαττονέω ĕlattŏnĕō**, *el-at-ton-eh-o;* from *1640;* to *diminish*, i.e. *fall short:*—have lack.

1642. **ἐλαττόω ĕlattŏō**, *el-at-tŏ'-o;* from *1640;* to *lessen* (in rank or influence):—decrease, make lower.

1643. **ἐλαύνω ĕlaunō**, *el-ŏw'-no;* a prol. form of a prim. verb (obsol. except in certain tenses as an altern. of this) of uncert. affin.; to *push* (as wind, oars or dæmoniacal power):—carry, drive, row.

1644. **ἐλαφρία ĕlaphria**, *el-af-ree'-ah;* from *1645; levity* (fig.), i.e. *fickleness:*—lightness.

1645. **ἐλαφρός ĕlaphrŏs**, *el-af-ros';* prob. akin to *1643* and the base of *1640; light*, i.e. *easy:*—light.

1646. **ἐλάχιστος ĕlachistŏs**, *el-akh'-is-tos;* superl. of **ἔλαχυς ĕlachus** (*short*); used as equiv. to *3398; least* (in size, amount, dignity, etc.):—least, very little (small), smallest.

1647. **ἐλαχιστότερος ĕlachistŏtĕrŏs**, *el-akh-is-tot'-er-os;* comp. of *1646; far less:*—less than the least.

1648. **Ἐλεάζαρ Ĕlĕazar**, *el-eh-ad'-zar;* of Heb. or. [499]; *Eleazar*, an Isr.:—Eleazar.

1649. **ἔλεγξις ĕlĕgxis**, *el'-eng-xis;* from *1651; refutation*, i.e. *reproof:*—rebuke.

1650. **ἔλεγχος ĕlĕgchŏs**, *el'-eng-khos;* from *1651; proof, conviction:*—evidence, reproof.

1651. **ἐλέγχω ĕlĕgchō**, *el-eng'-kho;* of uncert. affin.; to *confute, admonish:*—convict, convince, tell a fault, rebuke, reprove.

1652. **ἐλεεινός ĕlĕĕinŏs**, *el-eh-i-nos';* from *1656; pitiable:*—miserable.

1653. **ἐλεέω ĕlĕĕō**, *el-eh-eh'-o;* from *1656;* to *compassionate* (by word or deed, spec. by divine grace):—have compassion (pity on), have (obtain, receive, shew) mercy (on).

1654. **ἐλεημοσύνη ĕlĕēmŏsunē**, *el-eh-ay-mos-oo'-nay;* from *1656; compassionateness*, i.e. (as exercised towards the poor) *beneficence*, or (concr.) a *benefaction:*—alms (-deeds).

1655. **ἐλεήμων ĕlĕēmōn**, *el-eh-ay'-mone;* from *1653; compassionate* (actively):—merciful.

1656. **ἔλεος ĕlĕŏs**, *el'-eh-os;* of uncert. affin.; *compassion* (human or divine, espec. active):—(+ tender) mercy.

1657. **ἐλευθερία ĕlĕuthĕria**, *el-yoo-ther-ee'-ah;* from *1658; freedom* (legitimate or licentious, chiefly mor. or cer.):—liberty.

1658. **ἐλεύθερος ĕlĕuthĕrŏs**, *el-yoo'-ther-os;* prob. from the alt. of *2064; unrestrained* (to *go* at pleasure), i.e. (as a citizen) *not a slave* (whether *freeborn* or *manumitted*), or (gen.) *exempt* (from obligation or liability):—free (man, woman), at liberty.

1659. **ἐλευθερόω ĕlĕuthĕrŏō**, *el-yoo-ther-ŏ'-o;* from *1658;* to *liberate*, i.e. (fig.) to *exempt* (from mor., cer. or mortal liability):—deliver, make free.

ἐλεύθω ĕlĕuthō. See *2064*.

1660. **ἔλευσις ĕlĕusis**, *el'-yoo-sis;* from the alt. of *2064;* an *advent:*—coming.

1661. **ἐλεφάντινος ĕlĕphantinŏs**, *el-ef-an'-tee-nos;* from **ἔλεφας ĕlĕphas** (an "*elephant*"); *elephantine*, i.e. (by impl.) composed of *ivory:*—of ivory.

1662. **Ἐλιακείμ Ĕliakĕim**, *el-ee-ak-ime';* of Heb. or. [471]; *Eliakim*, an Isr.:—Eliakim.

1663. **Ἐλιέζερ Ĕliĕzĕr**, *el-ee-ed'-zer;* of Heb. or. [461]; *Eliezer*, an Isr.:—Eliezer.

1664. **Ἐλιούδ Ĕliŏud**, *el-ee-ood';* of Heb. or. [410 and 1935]; *God of majesty; Eliud*, an Isr.:—Eliud.

1665. **Ἐλισάβετ Ĕlisabĕt**, *el-ee-sab'-et;* of Heb. or. [472]; *Elisabet*, an Israelitess:—Elisabeth.

1666. **Ἐλισσαῖος Ĕlissaiŏs**, *el-is-sah'-yos;* of Heb. or. [477]; *Elissæus*, an Isr.:—Elissæus.

1667. **ἑλίσσω hĕlissō**, *hel-is'-so;* a form of *1507;* to *coil* or *wrap:*—fold up.

1668. **ἕλκος hĕlkŏs**, *hel'-kos;* prob. from *1670;* an *ulcer* (as if drawn together):—sore.

1669. **ἑλκόω hĕlkŏō**, *hel-kŏ'-o;* from *1668;* to *cause to ulcerate*, i.e. (pass.) *be ulcerous:*—full of sores.

1670. **ἑλκύω hĕlkuō**, *hel-koo'-o;* or

ἕλκω hĕlkō, *hel'-ko;* prob. akin to *138;* to *drag* (lit. or fig.):—draw. Comp. *1667*.

1671. **Ἑλλάς Hĕllas**, *hel-las';* of uncert. affin.; *Hellas* (or *Greece*), a country of Europe:—Greece.

1672. **Ἕλλην Hĕllēn**, *hel'-lane;* from *1671;* a *Hellen* (*Grecian*) or inhab. of Hellas; by extens. a *Greek-speaking* person, espec. a *non-Jew:*—Gentile, Greek.

1673. **Ἑλληνικός Hĕllēnikŏs**, *hel-lay-nee-kos';* from *1672; Hellenic*, i.e. *Grecian* (in language):—Greek.

1674. **Ἑλληνίς Hĕllēnis**, *hel-lay-nis';* fem. of *1672;* a *Grecian* (i.e. *non-Jewish*) woman:—Greek.

1675. **Ἑλληνιστής Hĕllēnistēs**, *hel-lay-nis-tace';* from a der. of *1672;* a *Hellenist* or Greek-speaking Jew:—Grecian.

1676. **Ἑλληνιστί Hĕllēnisti**, *hel-lay-nis-tee';* adv. from the same as *1675; Hellenistically*, i.e. in the Grecian language:—Greek.

1677. **ἐλλογέω ĕllŏgĕō**, *el-log-eh'-o;* from *1722* and *3056* (in the sense of *account*); to *reckon in*, i.e. *attribute:*—impute, put on account.

ἕλλομαι hĕllŏmai. See *138*.

1678. **Ἐλμωδάμ Ĕlmōdam**, *el-mo-dam';* of Heb. or. [perh. for 486]; *Elmodam*, an Isr.:—Elmodam.

1679. **ἐλπίζω ĕlpizō**, *el-pid'-zo;* from *1680;* to *expect* or *confide:*—(have, thing) hope (-d) (for), trust.

1680. **ἐλπίς ĕlpis**, *el-pece';* from a prim. **ἔλπω ĕlpō** (to *anticipate*, usually with pleasure); *expectation* (abstr. or concr.) or *confidence:*—faith, hope.

1681. **Ἐλύμας Ĕlumas**, *el-oo'-mas;* of for. or.; *Elymas*, a wizard:—Elymas.

1682. **ἐλοΐ ĕlŏi**, *el-o-ee';* of Chald. or. [426 with pron. suff.]; *my God:*—Eloi.

1683. ἐμαυτοῦ **ĕmautŏu**, *em-ŏw-too'*; gen. comp. of *1700* and *846*; *of myself* (so likewise the dat.
ἐμαυτῷ **ĕmautōi**, *em-ow-tō'*; and acc.
ἐμαυτόν **ĕmautŏn**, *em-ow-ton'*):—me, mine own (self), myself.

1684. ἐμβαίνω **ĕmbainō**, *em-ba'hee-no;* from *1722* and the base of *939;* to *walk on*, i.e. *embark* (aboard a vessel), *reach* (a pool):—come (get) into, enter (into), go (up) into, step in, take ship.

1685. ἐμβάλλω **ĕmballō**, *em-bal'-lo;* from *1722* and *906;* to *throw on*, i.e. (fig.) *subject to* (eternal punishment):—cast into.

1686. ἐμβάπτω **ĕmbaptō**, *em-bap'-to;* from *1722* and *911;* to *whelm on*, i.e. *wet* (a part of the person, etc.) by contact with a fluid:—dip.

1687. ἐμβατεύω **ĕmbatĕuō**, *em-bat-yoo'-o;* from *1722* and a presumed der. of the base of *939;* equiv. to *1684;* to *intrude on* (fig.):—intrude into.

1688. ἐμβιβάζω **ĕmbibazō**, *em-bib-ad'-zo;* from *1722* and βιβάζω **bibazō** (to *mount;* causat. of *1684*); to *place on*, i.e. *transfer* (aboard a vessel):—put in.

1689. ἐμβλέπω **ĕmblĕpō**, *em-blep'-o;* from *1722* and *991;* to *look on*, i.e. (rel.) to *observe* fixedly, or (absol.) to *discern* clearly:—behold, gaze up, look upon, (could) see.

1690. ἐμβριμάομαι **ĕmbrimaŏmai**, *em-brim-ah'-om-ahee;* from *1722* and βριμάομαι **brimaŏmai** (to *snort* with anger); to have *indignation on*, i.e. (trans.) to *blame*, (intrans.) to *sigh* with chagrin, (spec.) to sternly *enjoin:*—straitly charge, groan, murmur against.

1691. ἐμέ **ĕmĕ**, *em-eh';* a prol. form of *3165; me:*—I, me, my (-self).

1692. ἐμέω **ĕmĕō**, *em-eh'-o;* of uncert. affin.; to *vomit:*—(will) spue.

1693. ἐμμαίνομαι **ĕmmainŏmai**, *em-mah'ee-nom-ahee;* from *1722* and *3105;* to *rave on*, i.e. *rage at:*—be mad against.

1694. Ἐμμανουήλ **Ĕmmanŏuēl**, *em-man-oo-ale';* of Heb. or. [6005]; *God with us; Emmanuel*, a name of Christ:—Emmanuel.

1695. Ἐμμαούς **Ĕmmaŏus**, *em-mah-ooce';* prob. of Heb. or. [comp. 3222]; *Emmaüs*, a place in Pal.:—Emmaus.

1696. ἐμμένω **ĕmmĕnō**, *em-men'-o;* from *1722* and *3306;* to *stay in* the same place, i.e. (fig.) to *persevere:*—continue.

1697. Ἐμμόρ **Ĕmmŏr**, *em-mor';* of Heb. or. [2544]; *Emmor* (i.e. *Chamor*), a Canaanite:—Emmor.

1698. ἐμοί **ĕmŏi**, *em-oy';* a prol. form of *3427; to me:*—I, me, mine, my.

1699. ἐμός **ĕmŏs**, *em-os';* from the oblique cases of *1473* (*1698, 1700, 1691*); *my:*—of me, mine (own), my.

1700. ἐμοῦ **ĕmŏu**, *em-oo';* a prol. form of *3450; of me:*—me, mine, my.

1701. ἐμπαιγμός **ĕmpaigmŏs**, *emp-aheeg-mos';* from *1702; derision:*—mocking.

1702. ἐμπαίζω **ĕmpaizō**, *emp-aheed'-zo;* from *1722* and *3815;* to *jeer at*, i.e. *deride:*—mock.

1703. ἐμπαίκτης **ĕmpaiktēs**, *emp-aheek-tace';* from *1702;* a *derider*, i.e. (by impl.) a *false teacher:*—mocker, scoffer.

1704. ἐμπεριπατέω **ĕmpĕripatĕō**, *em-per-ee-pat-eh'-o;* from *1722* and *4043;* to *perambulate on* a place, i.e. (fig.) to *be occupied among* persons:—walk in.

1705. ἐμπίπλημι **ĕmpiplēmi**, *em-pip'-lay-mee;* or
ἐμπλήθω **ĕmplēthō**, *em-play'-tho;* from *1722* and the base of *4118;* to *fill in* (up), i.e. (by impl.) to *satisfy* (lit. or fig.):—fill.

1706. ἐμπίπτω **ĕmpiptō**, *em-pip'-to;* from *1722* and *4098;* to *fall on*, i.e. (lit.) *be entrapped by*, or (fig.) *be overwhelmed with:*—fall among (into).

1707. ἐμπλέκω **ĕmplĕkō**, *em-plek'-o;* from *1722* and *4120;* to *entwine*, i.e. (fig.) *involve* with:—entangle (in, self with).
ἐμπλήθω **ĕmplēthō**. See *1705*.

1708. ἐμπλοκή **ĕmplŏkē**, *em-plok-ay';* from *1707;* elaborate *braiding* of the hair:—plaiting.

1709. ἐμπνέω **ĕmpnĕō**, *emp-neh'-o;* from *1722* and *4154;* to *inhale*, i.e. (fig.) to *be animated by* (*bent upon*):—breathe.

1710. ἐμπορεύομαι **ĕmpŏrĕuŏmai**, *em-por-yoo'-om-ahee;* from *1722* and *4198;* to *travel in* (a country as a pedlar), i.e. (by impl.) to *trade:*—buy and sell, make merchandise.

1711. ἐμπορία **ĕmpŏria**, *em-por-ee'-ah;* fem. from *1713; traffic:*—merchandise.

1712. ἐμπόριον **ĕmpŏriŏn**, *em-por'-ee-on;* neut. from *1713;* a *mart* ("*emporium*"):—merchandise.

1713. ἔμπορος **ĕmpŏrŏs**, *em'-por-os;* from *1722* and the base of *4198;* a (wholesale) *tradesman:*—merchant.

1714. ἐμπρήθω **ĕmprēthō**, *em-pray'-tho;* from *1722* and πρήθω **prēthō** (to *blow* a flame); to *enkindle*, i.e. *set on fire:*—burn up.

1715. ἔμπροσθεν **ĕmprŏsthĕn**, *em'-pros-then;* from *1722* and *4314; in front of* (in place [lit. or fig.] or time):—against, at, before, (in presence, sight) of.

1716. ἐμπτύω **ĕmptuō**, *emp-too'-o;* from *1722* and *4429;* to *spit at* or *on:*—spit (upon).

1717. ἐμφανής **ĕmphanēs**, *em-fan-ace';* from a comp. of *1722* and *5316; apparent in* self:—manifest, openly.

1718. ἐμφανίζω **ĕmphanizō**, *em-fan-id'-zo;* from *1717;* to *exhibit* (in person) or *disclose* (by words):—appear, declare (plainly), inform, (will) manifest, shew, signify.

1719. ἔμφοβος **ĕmphŏbŏs**, *em'-fob-os;* from *1722* and *5401; in fear*, i.e. *alarmed:*—affrighted, afraid, tremble.

1720. ἐμφυσάω **ĕmphusaō**, *em-foo-sah'-o;* from *1722* and φυσάω **phusaō** (to *puff*) [comp. *5453*]; to *blow at* or *on:*—breathe on.

1721. ἔμφυτος **ĕmphutŏs**, *em'-foo-tos;* from *1722* and a der. of *5453; implanted* (fig.):—engrafted.

1722. ἐν **ĕn**, *en;* a prim. prep. denoting (fixed) *position* (in place, time or state), and (by impl.) *instrumentality* (medially or constructively), i.e. a relation of *rest* (intermediate between *1519* and *1537*); "*in*," *at*, (up-) *on*, *by*, etc.:—about, after, against, + almost, × altogether, among, × as, at, before, between, (here-) by (+ all means), for (. . . sake of), + give self wholly to, (here-) in (-to, -wardly), × mightily, (because) of, (up-) on, [open-] ly, × outwardly, one, × quickly, × shortly, [speedi-] ly, × that, × there (-in, -on), through (-out), (un-) to (-ward), under, when, where (-with), while, with (-in). Often used in compounds, with substantially the same import; rarely with verbs of motion, and then not to indicate direction, except (elliptically) by a separate (and different) prep.

1723. ἐναγκαλίζομαι **ĕnagkalizŏmai**, *en-ang-kal-id'-zom-ahee;* from *1722* and a der. of *43;* to *take in* one's *arms*, i.e. *embrace:*—take up in arms.

1724. ἐνάλιος **ĕnaliŏs**, *en-al'-ee-os;* from *1722* and *251; in the sea*, i.e. *marine:*—thing in the sea.

1725. ἔναντι **ĕnanti**, *en'-an-tee;* from *1722* and *473; in front* (i.e. fig. *presence*) *of:*—before.

1726. ἐναντίον **ĕnantiŏn**, *en-an-tee'-on;* neut. of *1727;* (adv.) *in the presence* (*view*) *of:*—before, in the presence of.

1727. ἐναντίος **ĕnantiŏs**, *en-an-tee'-os;* from *1725; opposite;* fig. *antagonistic:*—(over) against, contrary.

1728. ἐνάρχομαι **ĕnarchŏmai**, *en-ar'-khom-ahee;* from *1722* and *756;* to *commence on:*—rule [*by mistake* for *757*].

1729. ἐνδεής **ĕndĕēs**, *en-deh-ace';* from a comp. of *1722* and *1210* (in the sense of *lacking*); *deficient in:*—lacking.

1730. ἔνδειγμα **ĕndĕigma**, *en'-dighe-mah;* from *1731;* an *indication* (concr.):—manifest token.

1731. ἐνδείκνυμι **ĕndĕiknumi**, *en-dike'-noo-mee;* from *1722* and *1166;* to *indicate* (by word or act):—do, show (forth).

1732. ἔνδειξις **ĕndĕixis**, *en'-dike-sis;* from *1731; indication* (abstr.):—declare, evident token, proof.

1733. ἕνδεκα **hĕndĕka**, *hen'-dek-ah;* from (the neut. of) *1520* and *1176; one* and *ten*, i.e. *eleven:*—eleven.

1734. ἑνδέκατος **hĕndĕkatŏs**, *hen-dek'-at-os*, ord. from *1733; eleventh:*—eleventh.

1735. ἐνδέχεται **ĕndĕchĕtai**, *en-dekh'-et-ahee;* third pers. sing. pres. of a comp. of *1722* and *1209;* (impers.) *it is accepted in*, i.e. *admitted* (*possible*):—can (+ not) be.

1736. ἐνδημέω **ĕndēmĕō**, *en-day-meh'-o;* from a comp. of *1722* and *1218;* to *be in* one's own *country*, i.e. *home* (fig.):—be at home (present).

1737. ἐνδιδύσκω **ĕndiduskō**, *en-did-oos'-ko;* a prol. form of *1746;* to *invest* (with a garment):—clothe in, wear.

1738. ἔνδικος **ĕndikŏs**, *en'-dee-kos;* from *1722* and *1349; in* the *right*, i.e. *equitable:*—just.

1739. ἐνδόμησις **ĕndŏmēsis**, *en-dom'-ay-sis;* from a comp. of *1722* and a der. of the base of *1218;* a *housing in* (*residence*), i.e. *structure:*—building.

1740. ἐνδοξάζω **ĕndŏxazō**, *en-dox-ad'-zo;* from *1741;* to *glorify:*—glorify.

1741. ἔνδοξος **ĕndŏxŏs**, *en'-dox-os;* from *1722* and *1391; in glory*, i.e. *splendid*, (fig.) *noble:*—glorious, gorgeous [-ly], honourable.

1742. ἔνδυμα **ĕnduma**, *en'-doo-mah;* from *1746*, *apparel* (espec. the outer *robe*):—clothing, garment, raiment.

1743. ἐνδυναμόω **ĕndunamŏō**, *en-doo-nam-ŏ'-o;* from *1722* and *1412;* to *empower:*—enable, (increase in) strength (-en), be (make) strong.

1744. ἐνδύνω **ĕndunō**, *en-doo'-no;* from *1772* and *1416;* to *sink* (by impl. *wrap* [comp. *1746*]) *on*, i.e. (fig.) *sneak:*—creep.

1745. ἔνδυσις **ĕndusis**, *en'-doo-sis;* from *1746; investment* with clothing:—putting on.

1746. ἐνδύω **ĕnduō**, *en-doo'-o;* from *1722* and *1416* (in the sense of *sinking* into a garment); to *invest* with clothing (lit. or fig.):—array, clothe (with), endue, have (put) on.
ἐνέγκω **ĕnĕgkō**. See *5342*.

1747. ἐνέδρα **ĕnĕdra**, *en-ed'-rah;* fem. from *1722* and the base of *1476;* an *ambuscade*, i.e. (fig.) murderous *purpose:*—lay wait. See also *1749*.

1748. ἐνεδρεύω **ĕnĕdrĕuō**, *en-ed-ryoo'-o;* from *1747;* to *lurk*, i.e. (fig.) *plot* assassination:—lay wait for.

1749. ἔνεδρον **ĕnĕdrŏn**, *en'-ed-ron;* neut. of the same as *1747;* an *ambush*, i.e. (fig.) murderous *design:*—lying in wait.

1750. ἐνειλέω **ĕnĕilĕō**, *en-i-leh'-o;* from *1772* and the base of *1507;* to *enwrap:*—wrap in.

1751. ἔνειμι **ĕnĕimi**, *en'-i-mee;* from *1772* and *1510;* to *be within* (neut. part. plur.):—such things as . . . have. See also *1762*.

1752. ἕνεκα **hĕnĕka**, *hen'-ek-ah;* or
ἕνεκεν **hĕnĕkĕn**, *hen'-ek-en;* or
εἵνεκεν **hĕinĕkĕn**, *hi'-nek-en;* of uncert. affin.; *on account of:*—because, for (cause, sake), (where-) fore, by reason of, that.

1753. ἐνέργεια **ĕnĕrgĕia**, *en-erg'-i-ah;* from *1756; efficiency* ("*energy*"):—operation, strong, (effectual) working.

1754. ἐνεργέω **ĕnĕrgĕō**, *en-erg-eh'-o;* from *1756;* to *be active, efficient:*—do, (be) effectual (fervent), be mighty in, shew forth self, work (effectually in)

1755. ἐνέργημα **ĕnĕrgēma**, *en-erg'-ay-mah;* from *1754:* an *effect:*—operation, working.

1756. ἐνεργής **ĕnĕrgēs**, *en-er-gace';* from *1722* and *2041: active, operative:*—effectual, powerful.

1757. ἐνευλογέω **ĕnĕulŏgĕō**, *en-yoo-log-eh'-o;* from *1722* and *2127;* to *confer a benefit on:*—bless.

1758. ἐνέχω **ĕnĕchō**, *en-ekh'-o;* from *1722* and *2192;* to *hold in* or *upon,* i.e. *ensnare;* by impl. to *keep a grudge:*—entangle with, have a quarrel against, urge.

1759. ἐνθάδε **ĕnthadĕ**, *en-thad'-eh;* from a prol. form of *1722;* prop. *within,* i.e. (of place) *here, hither:*—(t-) here, hither.

1760. ἐνθυμέομαι **ĕnthumĕŏmai**, *en-thoo-meh'-om-ahee;* from a comp. of *1722* and *2372;* to *be inspirited,* i.e. *ponder:*—think.

1761. ἐνθύμησις **ĕnthumēsis**, *en-thoo'-may-sis;* from *1760; deliberation:*—device, thought.

1762. ἔνι **ĕni**, *en'-ee;* contr. for third pers. sing. pres. indic. of *1751;* impers. *there is* in or among:—be, (there) is.

1763. ἐνιαυτός **ĕniautŏs**, *en-ee-ŏw-tos';* prol. from a prim. ἔνος **ĕnŏs** (a *year*); a *year:*—year.

1764. ἐνίστημι **ĕnistēmi**, *en-is'-tay-mee;* from *1722* and *2476;* to *place on* hand, i.e. (reflex.) *impend,* (part.) be *instant:*—come, be at hand, present.

1765. ἐνισχύω **ĕnischuō**, *en-is-khoo'-o;* from *1722* and *2480;* to *invigorate* (trans. or reflex.):—strengthen.

1766. ἔννατος **ĕnnatŏs**, *en'-nat-os;* ord. from *1767: ninth:*—ninth.

1767. ἐννέα **ĕnnĕa**, *en-neh'-ah;* a prim. number; *nine:*—nine.

1768. ἐννενηκονταεννέα **ĕnnĕnēkŏntaĕnnĕa**, *en-nen-ay-kon-tah-en-neh'-ah;* from a (tenth) multiple of *1767* and *1767* itself; *ninety-nine:*—ninety and nine.

1769. ἐννεός **ĕnnĕŏs**, *en-neh-os';* from *1770; dumb* (as *making signs*), i.e. *silent* from astonishment:—speechless.

1770. ἐννεύω **ĕnnĕuō**, *en-nyoo'-o;* from *1722* and *3506;* to *nod at,* i.e. *beckon* or *communicate by gesture:*—make signs.

1771. ἔννοια **ĕnnŏia**, *en'-noy-ah;* from a comp. of *1722* and *3563; thoughtfulness,* i.e. moral *understanding:*—intent, mind.

1772. ἔννομος **ĕnnŏmŏs**, *en'-nom-os;* from *1722* and *3551;* (subj.) *legal,* or (obj.) *subject* to:—lawful, under law.

1773. ἔννυχον **ĕnnuchŏn**, *en'-noo-khon;* neut. of a comp. of *1722* and *3571;* (adv.) *by night:*—before day.

1774. ἐνοικέω **ĕnŏikĕō**, *en-oy-keh'-o;* from *1722* and *3611;* to *inhabit* (fig.):—dwell in.

1775. ἑνότης **hĕnŏtēs**, *hen-ot'-ace;* from *1520; oneness,* i.e. (fig.) *unanimity:*—unity.

1776. ἐνοχλέω **ĕnŏchlĕō**, *en-okh-leh'-o;* from *1722* and *3791;* to *crowd in,* i.e. (fig.) to *annoy:*—trouble.

1777. ἔνοχος **ĕnŏchŏs**, *en'-okh-os;* from *1758; liable* to (a condition, penalty or imputation):—in danger of, guilty of, subject to.

1778. ἔνταλμα **ĕntalma**, *en'-tal-mah;* from *1781;* an *injunction,* i.e. religious *precept:*—commandment.

1779. ἐνταφιάζω **ĕntaphiazō**, *en-taf-ee-ad'-zo;* from a comp. of *1722* and *5028;* to *inswathe* with cerements for interment:—bury.

1780. ἐνταφιασμός **ĕntaphiasmŏs**, *en-taf-ee-as-mos';* from *1779; preparation* for interment:—burying.

1781. ἐντέλλομαι **ĕntĕllŏmai**, *en-tel'-lom-ahee;* from *1722* and the base of *5056;* to *enjoin:*—(give) charge, (give) command (-ments), injoin.

1782. ἐντεῦθεν **ĕntĕuthĕn**, *ent-yoo'-then;* from the same as *1759; hence* (lit. or fig.); (repeated) *on both sides:*—(from) hence, on either side.

1783. ἔντευξις **ĕntĕuxis**, *ent'-yook-sis;* from *1793;* an *interview,* i.e. (spec.) *supplication:*—intercession, prayer.

1784. ἔντιμος **ĕntimŏs**, *en'-tee-mos;* from *1722* and *5092; valued* (fig.):—dear, more honourable, precious, in reputation.

1785. ἐντολή **ĕntŏlē**, *en-tol-ay';* from *1781; injunction,* i.e. an authoritative *prescription:*—commandment, precept.

1786. ἐντόπιος **ĕntŏpiŏs**, *en-top'-ee-os;* from *1722* and *5117;* a *resident:*—of that place.

1787. ἐντός **ĕntŏs**, *en-tos';* from *1722; inside* (adv. or noun):—within.

1788. ἐντρέπω **ĕntrĕpō**, *en-trep'-o;* from *1722* and the base of *5157;* to *invert,* i.e. (fig. and reflex.) in a good sense, to *respect;* or in a bad one, to *confound:*—regard, (give) reverence, shame.

1789. ἐντρέφω **ĕntrĕphō**, *en-tref'-o;* from *1722* and *5142;* (fig.) to *educate:*—nourish up in.

1790. ἔντρομος **ĕntrŏmŏs**, *en'-trom-os;* from *1722* and *5156; terrified:*— × quake, × trembled.

1791. ἐντροπή **ĕntrŏpē**, *en-trop-ay';* from *1788; confusion:*—shame.

1792. ἐντρυφάω **ĕntruphaō**, *en-troo-fah'-o;* from *1722* and *5171;* to *revel in:*—sporting selves.

1793. ἐντυγχάνω **ĕntugchanō**, *en-toong-khan'-o;* from *1722* and *5177;* to *chance upon,* i.e. (by impl.) *confer with;* by extens. to *entreat* (in favor or against):—deal with, make intercession.

1794. ἐντυλίσσω **ĕntulissō**, *en-too-lis'-so;* from *1722* and τυλίσσω **tulissō** (to *twist;* prob. akin to *1507*); to *entwine,* i.e. *wind* up in:—wrap in (together).

1795. ἐντυπόω **ĕntupŏō**, *en-too-pŏ'-o;* from *1722* and a der. of *5179;* to *enstamp,* i.e. *engrave:*—engrave.

1796. ἐνυβρίζω **ĕnubrizō**, *en-oo-brid'-zo;* from *1722* and *5195;* to *insult:*—do despite unto.

1797. ἐνυπνιάζομαι **ĕnupniazŏmai**, *en-oop-nee-ad'-zom-ahee;* mid. from *1798;* to *dream:*—dream (-er).

1798. ἐνύπνιον **ĕnupniŏn**, *en-oop'-nee-on;* from *1722* and *5258;* something seen *in sleep,* i.e. a *dream* (*vision* in a dream):—dream.

1799. ἐνώπιον **ĕnōpiŏn**, *en-o'-pee-on;* neut. of a comp. of *1722* and a der. of *3700; in the face* of (lit. or fig.):—before, in the presence (sight) of, to.

1800. Ἐνώς **Ĕnōs**, *en-oce';* of Heb. or. [583]; *Enos* (i.e. *Enosh*), a patriarch:—Enos.

1801. ἐνωτίζομαι **ĕnōtizŏmai**, *en-o-tid'-zom-ahee;* mid. from a comp. of *1722* and *3775;* to take *in one's ear,* i.e. to *listen:*—hearken.

1802. Ἐνώχ **Ĕnōk**, *en-oke';* of Heb. or. [2585]; *Enoch* (i.e. *Chanok*), an antediluvian:—Enoch.

ἐξ **ĕx**. See *1537.*

1803. ἕξ **hĕx**, *hex;* a prim. numeral; *six:*—six.

1804. ἐξαγγέλλω **ĕxaggĕllō**, *ex-ang-el'-lo;* from *1537* and the base of *32;* to *publish,* i.e. *celebrate:*—shew forth.

1805. ἐξαγοράζω **ĕxagŏrazō**, *ex-ag-or-ad'-zo;* from *1537* and *59;* to *buy up,* i.e. *ransom;* fig. to *rescue* from loss (*improve* opportunity):—redeem.

1806. ἐξάγω **ĕxagō**, *ex-ag'-o;* from *1537* and *71;* to *lead forth:*—bring forth (out), fetch (lead) out.

1807. ἐξαιρέω **ĕxairĕō**, *ex-ahee-reh'-o;* from *1537* and *138;* act. to *tear out;* mid. to *select;* fig. to *release:*—deliver, pluck out, rescue.

1808. ἐξαίρω **ĕxairō**, *ex-ah'ee-ro;* from *1537* and *142;* to *remove:*—put (take) away.

1809. ἐξαιτέομαι **ĕxaitĕŏmai**, *ex-ahee-teh'-om-ahee;* mid. from *1537* and *154;* to *demand* (for trial):—desire.

1810. ἐξαίφνης **ĕxaiphnēs**, *ex-ah'eef-nace;* from *1537* and the base of *160; of a sudden* (*unexpectedly*):—suddenly. Comp. *1819.*

1811. ἐξακολουθέω **ĕxakŏlŏuthĕō**, *ex-ak-ol-oo-theh'-o;* from *1537* and *190;* to *follow out,* i.e. (fig.) to *imitate, obey,* yield to:—follow.

1812. ἑξακόσιοι **hĕxakŏsiŏi**, *hex-ak-os'-ee-oy;* plur. ordinal from *1803* and *1540; six hundred:*—six hundred.

1813. ἐξαλείφω **ĕxalĕiphō**, *ex-al-i'-fo;* from *1537* and *218;* to *smear out,* i.e. *obliterate* (erase tears, fig. *pardon* sin):—blot out, wipe away.

1814. ἐξάλλομαι **ĕxallŏmai**, *ex-al'-lom-ahee;* from *1537* and *242;* to *spring forth:*—leap up.

1815. ἐξανάστασις **ĕxanastasis**, *ex-an-as'-tas-is;* from *1817;* a *rising from* death:—resurrection.

1816. ἐξανατέλλω **ĕxanatĕllō**, *ex-an-at-el'-lo;* from *1537* and *393;* to *start up out* of the ground, i.e. *germinate:*—spring up.

1817. ἐξανίστημι **ĕxanistēmi**, *ex-an-is'-tay-mee;* from *1537* and *450;* obj. to *produce,* i.e. (fig.) *beget;* subj. to *arise,* i.e. (fig.) *object:*—raise (rise) up.

1818. ἐξαπατάω **ĕxapataō**, *ex-ap-at-ah'-o;* from *1537* and *538;* to *seduce wholly:*—beguile, deceive.

1819. ἐξάπινα **ĕxapina**, *ex-ap'-ee-nah;* from *1537* and a der. of the same as *160; of a sudden,* i.e. *unexpectedly:*—suddenly. Comp. *1810.*

1820. ἐξαπορέομαι **ĕxapŏrĕŏmai**, *ex-ap-or-eh'-om-ahee;* mid. from *1537* and *639;* to *be utterly at a loss,* i.e. *despond:*—(in) despair.

1821. ἐξαποστέλλω **ĕxapŏstĕllō**, *ex-ap-os-tel'-lo;* from *1537* and *649;* to *send away forth,* i.e. (on a mission) to *despatch,* or (peremptorily) to *dismiss:*—send (away, forth, out).

1822. ἐξαρτίζω **ĕxartizō**, *ex-ar-tid'-zo;* from *1537* and a der. of *739;* to *finish out* (time); fig. to *equip fully* (a teacher):—accomplish, thoroughly furnish.

1823. ἐξαστράπτω **ĕxastraptō**, *ex-as-trap'-to;* from *1537* and *797;* to *lighten forth,* i.e. (fig.) to *be radiant* (of very white garments):—glistening.

1824. ἐξαύτης **ĕxautēs**, *ex-ŏw'-tace;* from *1537* and the gen. sing. fem. of *846* (*5610* being understood); *from that* hour, i.e. *instantly:*—by and by, immediately, presently, straightway.

1825. ἐξεγείρω **ĕxĕgĕirō**, *ex-eg-i'-ro;* from *1537* and *1453;* to *rouse fully,* i.e. (fig.) to *resuscitate* (from death), *release* (from infliction):—raise up.

1826. ἔξειμι **ĕxĕimi**, *ex'-i-mee;* from *1537* and εἶμι **ĕimi** (to *go*); to *issue,* i.e. *leave* (a place), *escape* (to the shore):—depart, get [*to land*], go out.

1827. ἐξελέγχω **ĕxĕlĕgchō**, *ex-el-eng'-kho;* from *1537* and *1651;* to *convict fully,* i.e. (by impl.) to *punish:*—convince.

1828. ἐξέλκω **ĕxĕlkō**, *ex-el'-ko;* from *1537* and *1670;* to *drag forth,* i.e. (fig.) to *entice* (to sin):—draw away.

1829. ἐξέραμα **ĕxĕrama**, *ex-er'-am-ah;* from a comp. of *1537* and a presumed ἐράω **ĕraō** (to *spue*); *vomit,* i.e. *food disgorged:*—vomit.

1830. ἐξερευνάω **ĕxĕrĕunaō**, *ex-er-yoo-nah'-o;* from *1537* and *2045;* to *explore* (fig.):—search diligently.

1831. ἐξέρχομαι **ĕxĕrchŏmai**, *ex-er'-khom-ahee;* from *1537* and *2064;* to *issue* (lit. or fig.):—come-(forth, out), depart (out of), escape, get out, go (abroad, away, forth, out, thence), proceed (forth), spread abroad.

1832. ἔξεστι **ĕxĕsti**, *ex'-es-tee;* third pers. sing. pres. indic. of a comp. of *1537* and *1510;* so also ἐξόν **ĕxŏn**, *ex-on';* neut. pres. part. of the same (with or without some form of *1510* expressed); impers. *it is right* (through the fig. idea of *being out* in public):—be lawful, let, × may (-est).

1833. ἐξετάζω **ĕxĕtazō**, *ex-et-ad'-zo;* from *1537* and ἐτάζω **ĕtazō** (to *examine*); to *test thoroughly* (by questions), i.e. *ascertain* or *interrogate:*—ask, enquire, search.

1834. ἐξηγέομαι **ĕxēgĕŏmai**, *ex-ayg-eh'-om-ahee;* from *1537* and *2233;* to *consider out* (aloud), i.e. *rehearse, unfold.*—declare, tell.

1835. ἑξήκοντα **hĕxēkŏnta**, *hex-ay'-kon-tah;* the tenth multiple of *1803*; *sixty:*—sixty [-fold], threescore.

1836. ἑξῆς **hĕxēs**, *hex-ace';* from *2192* (in the sense of *taking hold* of, i.e. *adjoining*); *successive:*—after, following, × morrow, next.

1837. ἐξηχέομαι **ĕxēchĕŏmai**, *ex-ay-kheh'-om-ahee;* mid. from *1537* and *2278*; to "*echo*" *forth*, i.e. *resound* (*be* generally *reported*):—sound forth.

1838. ἕξις **hĕxis**, *hex'-is;* from *2192*; *habit*, i.e. (by impl.) *practice:*—use.

1839. ἐξίστημι **ĕxistēmi**, *ex-is'-tay-mee;* from *1537* and *2476*; to *put* (*stand*) *out* of wits, i.e. *astound*, or (reflex.) *become astounded*, *insane:*—amaze, be (make) astonished, be beside self (selves), bewitch, wonder.

1840. ἐξισχύω **ĕxischuō**, *ex-is-khoo'-o;* from *1537* and *2480*; to *have full strength*, i.e. *be entirely competent:*—be able.

1841. ἔξοδος **ĕxŏdŏs**, *ex'-od-os;* from *1537* and *3598*; an *exit*, i.e. (fig.) *death:*—decease, departing.

1842. ἐξολοθρεύω **ĕxŏlŏthrĕuō**, *ex-ol-oth-ryoo'-o;* from *1537* and *3645*; to *extirpate:*—destroy.

1843. ἐξομολογέω **ĕxŏmŏlŏgĕō**, *ex-om-ol-og-eh'-o;* from *1537* and *3670*; to *acknowledge* or (by impl. of *assent*) *agree fully:*—confess, profess, promise.

ἐξόν **ĕxŏn**. See *1832*.

1844. ἐξορκίζω **ĕxŏrkizō**, *ex-or-kid'-zo;* from *1537* and *3726*; to *exact an oath*, i.e. *conjure:*—adjure.

1845. ἐξορκιστής **ĕxŏrkistēs**, *ex-or-kis-tace';* from *1844*; *one that binds by an oath* (or *spell*), i.e. (by impl.) an "*exorcist*" (*conjurer*):—exorcist.

1846. ἐξορύσσω **ĕxŏrussō**, *ex-or-oos'-so;* from *1537* and *3736*; to *dig out*, i.e. (by extens.) to *extract* (an eye), *remove* (a roofing):—break up, pluck out.

1847. ἐξουδενόω **ĕxŏudĕnŏō**, *ex-oo-den-ŏ'-o;* from *1537* and a der. of the neut. of *3762*; to *make utterly nothing of*, i.e. *despise:*—set at nought. See also *1848*.

1848. ἐξουθενέω **ĕxŏuthĕnĕō**, *ex-oo-then-eh'-o;* a var. of *1847* and mean. the same:—contemptible, despise, least esteemed, set at nought.

1849. ἐξουσία **ĕxŏusia**, *ex-oo-see'-ah;* from *1832* (in the sense of *ability*); *privilege*, i.e. (subj.) *force*, *capacity*, *competency*, *freedom*, or (obj.) *mastery* (concr. *magistrate*, *superhuman*, *potentate*, *token of control*), delegated *influence:*—authority, jurisdiction, liberty, power, right, strength.

1850. ἐξουσιάζω **ĕxŏusiazō**, *ex-oo-see-ad'-zo;* from *1849*; to *control:*—exercise authority upon, bring under the (have) power of.

1851. ἐξοχή **ĕxŏchē**, *ex-okh-ay';* from a comp. of *1537* and *2192* (mean. to *stand out*); *prominence* (fig.):—principal.

1852. ἐξυπνίζω **ĕxupnizō**, *ex-oop-nid'-zo;* from *1853*; to *waken:*—awake out of sleep.

1853. ἔξυπνος **ĕxupnŏs**, *ex'-oop-nos;* from *1537* and *5258*; *awake:*— × out of sleep.

1854. ἔξω **ĕxō**, *ex'-o;* adv. from *1537*; *out* (*-side*, *of doors*), lit. or fig.:—away, forth, (with-) out (of, -ward), strange.

1855. ἔξωθεν **ĕxōthĕn**, *ex'-o-then;* from *1854*; *external* (*-ly*):—out (-side -ward, -wardly), (from) without.

1856. ἐξωθέω **ĕxōthĕō**, *ex-o-theh'-o;* or

ἐξώθω **ĕxōthō**, *ex-o'-tho;* from *1537* and ὠθέω **ōthĕō** (to *push*); to *expel*; by impl. to *propel:*—drive out, thrust in.

1857. ἐξώτερος **ĕxōtĕrŏs**, *ex-o'-ter-os;* comp. of *1854*; *exterior:*—outer.

1858. ἑορτάζω **hĕŏrtazō**, *heh-or-tad'-zo;* from *1859*; to *observe a festival:*—keep the feast.

1859. ἑορτή **hĕŏrtē**, *heh-or-tay';* of uncert. affin.; a *festival:*—feast, holyday.

1860. ἐπαγγελία **ĕpaggĕlia**, *ep-ang-el-ee'-ah;* from *1861*; an *announcement* (for information, assent or pledge; espec. a divine *assurance* of good):—message, promise.

1861. ἐπαγγέλλω **ĕpaggĕllō**, *ep-ang-el'-lo;* from *1909* and the base of *32*; to *announce upon* (reflex.), i.e. (by impl.) to *engage* to do something, to *assert* something respecting oneself:—profess, (make) promise.

1862. ἐπάγγελμα **ĕpaggĕlma**, *ep-ang'-el-mah;* from *1861*; a *self-committal* (by *assurance* of conferring some good):—promise.

1863. ἐπάγω **ĕpagō**, *ep-ag'-o;* from *1909* and *71*; to *superinduce*, i.e. *inflict* (an evil), *charge* (a crime):—bring upon.

1864. ἐπαγωνίζομαι **ĕpagōnizŏmai**, *ep-ag-o-nid'-zom-ahee;* from *1909* and *75*; to *struggle for:*—earnestly contend for.

1865. ἐπαθροίζω **ĕpathrŏizō**, *ep-ath-roid'-zo;* from *1909* and ἀθροίζω **athrŏizō** (to *assemble*); to *accumulate:*—gather thick together.

1866. Ἐπαίνετος **Ĕpainĕtŏs**, *ep-a'hee-net-os;* from *1867*; *praised*; *Epænetus*, a Chr.:—Epenetus.

1867. ἐπαινέω **ĕpainĕō**, *ep-ahee-neh'-o;* from *1909* and *134*; to *applaud:*—commend, laud, praise.

1868. ἔπαινος **ĕpainŏs**, *ep'-ahee-nos;* from *1909* and the base of *134*; *laudation*; concr. a *commendable* thing:—praise.

1869. ἐπαίρω **ĕpairō**, *ep-ahee'-ro;* from *1909* and *142*; to *raise up* (lit. or fig.):—exalt self, poise (lift, take) up.

1870. ἐπαισχύνομαι **ĕpaischunŏmai**, *ep-ahee-skhoo'-nom-ahee;* from *1909* and *153*; to *feel shame for* something:—be ashamed.

1871. ἐπαιτέω **ĕpaitĕō**, *ep-ahee-teh'-o;* from *1909* and *154*; to *ask for:*—beg.

1872. ἐπακολουθέω **ĕpakŏlŏuthĕō**, *ep-ak-ol-oo-theh'-o;* from *1909* and *190*; to *accompany:*—follow (after).

1873. ἐπακούω **ĕpakŏuō**, *ep-ak-oo'-o;* from *1909* and *191*; to *hearken* (favorably) *to:*—hear.

1874. ἐπακροάομαι **ĕpakrŏaŏmai**, *ep-ak-rŏ-ah'-om-ahee;* from *1909* and the base of *202*; to *listen* (intently) *to:*—hear.

1875. ἐπάν **ĕpan**, *ep-an';* from *1909* and *302*; a particle of indef. contemporaneousness; *whenever*, *as soon as:*—when.

1876. ἐπάναγκες **ĕpanagkĕs**, *ep-an'-ang-kes;* neut. of a presumed comp. of *1909* and *318*; (adv.) *on necessity*, i.e. *necessarily:*—necessary.

1877. ἐπανάγω **ĕpanagō**, *ep-an-ag'-o;* from *1909* and *321*; to *lead up on*, i.e. (techn.) to *put out* (to sea); (intrans.) to *return:*—launch (thrust) out, return.

1878. ἐπαναμιμνήσκω **ĕpanamimnēskō**, *ep-an-ah-mim-nace'-ko;* from *1909* and *363*; to *remind of:*—put in mind.

1879. ἐπαναπαύομαι **ĕpanapauŏmai**, *ep-an-ah-pŏw'-om-ahee;* mid. from *1909* and *373*; to *settle on*; lit. (*remain*) or fig. (*rely*):—rest in (upon).

1880. ἐπανέρχομαι **ĕpanĕrchŏmai**, *ep-an-er'-khom-ahee;* from *1909* and *424*; to *come up on*, i.e. *return:*—come again, return.

1881. ἐπανίσταμαι **ĕpanistamai**, *ep-an-is'-tam-ahee;* mid. from *1909* and *450*; to *stand up on*, i.e. (fig.) to *attack:*—rise up against.

1882. ἐπανόρθωσις **ĕpanŏrthōsis**, *ep-an-or'-tho-sis;* from a comp. of *1909* and *461*; a *straightening up again*, i.e. (fig.) *rectification* (*reformation*):—correction.

1883. ἐπάνω **ĕpanō**, *ep-an'-o;* from *1909* and *507*; *up above*, i.e. *over* or *on* (of place, amount, rank, etc.):—above, more than, (up-) on, over.

1884. ἐπαρκέω **ĕparkĕō**, *ep-ar-keh'-o;* from *1909* and *714*; to *avail for*, i.e. *help:*—relieve.

1885. ἐπαρχία **ĕparchia**, *ep-ar-khee'-ah;* from a comp. of *1909* and *757* (mean. a *governor* of a district, "eparch"); a special *region* of government, i.e. a Roman *præfecture:*—province.

1886. ἔπαυλις **ĕpaulis**, *ep'-ŏw-lis;* from *1909* and an equiv. of *833*; a *hut over* the head, i.e. a *dwelling*.

1887. ἐπαύριον **ĕpauriŏn**, *ep-ow'-ree-on;* from *1909* and *839*; occurring *on* the *succeeding* day, i.e. (*2250* being implied) *to-morrow:*—day following, morrow, next day (after).

1888. ἐπαυτοφώρῳ **ĕpautŏphōrō**, *ep-ow-tof-o'-ro;* from *1909* and *846* and (the dat. sing. of) a der. of φώρ **phōr** (a *thief*); *in theft itself*, i.e. (by anal.) *in actual crime:*—in the very act.

1889. Ἐπαφρᾶς **Ĕpaphras**, *ep-af-ras';* contr. from *1891*; *Epaphras*, a Chr.:—Epaphras.

1890. ἐπαφρίζω **ĕpaphrizō**, *ep-af-rid'-zo;* from *1909* and *875*; to *foam upon*, i.e. (fig.) to *exhibit* (a vile passion):—foam out.

1891. Ἐπαφρόδιτος **Ĕpaphrŏditŏs**, *ep-af-rod'-ee-tos;* from *1909* (in the sense of *devoted* to) and Ἀφροδίτη **Aphrŏditē** (*Venus*); *Epaphroditus*, a Chr.:—Epaphroditus. Comp. *1889*.

1892. ἐπεγείρω **ĕpĕgĕirō**, *ep-eg-i'-ro;* from *1909* and *1453*; to *rouse upon*, i.e. (fig.) to *excite* against:—raise, stir up.

1893. ἐπεί **ĕpĕi**, *ep-i';* from *1909* and *1487*; *thereupon*, i.e. *since* (of time or cause):—because, else, for that (then, -asmuch as), otherwise, seeing that, since, when,

1894. ἐπειδή **ĕpĕidē**, *ep-i-day';* from *1893* and *1211*; *since now*, i.e. (of time) *when*, or (of cause) *whereas:*—after that, because, for (that, -asmuch as), seeing, since.

1895. ἐπειδήπερ **ĕpĕidēpĕr**, *ep-i-day'-per;* from *1894* and *4007*; *since indeed* (of cause):—forasmuch.

1896. ἐπεῖδον **ĕpĕidŏn**, *ep-i'-don;* and other moods and persons of the same tense; from *1909* and *1492*; to *regard* (favorably or otherwise):—behold, look upon.

1897. ἐπείπερ **ĕpĕipĕr**, *ep-i'-per;* from *1893* and *4007*; *since* indeed (of cause):—seeing.

1898. ἐπεισαγωγή **ĕpĕisagōgē**, *ep-ice-ag-o-gay';* from a comp. of *1909* and *1521*; a *superintroduction:*—bringing in.

1899. ἔπειτα **ĕpĕita**, *ep'-i-tah;* from *1909* and *1534*; *thereafter:*—after that (-ward), then.

1900. ἐπέκεινα **ĕpĕkĕina**, *ep-ek'-i-nah;* from *1909* and (the acc. plur. neut. of) *1565*; *upon those* parts of, i.e. *on the further side of:*—beyond.

1901. ἐπεκτείνομαι **ĕpĕktĕinŏmai**, *ep-ek-ti'-nom-ahee;* mid. from *1909* and *1614*; to *stretch* (oneself) forward *upon:*—reach forth.

1902. ἐπενδύομαι **ĕpĕnduŏmai**, *ep-en-doo'-om-ahee;* mid. from *1909* and *1746*; to *invest upon* oneself:—be clothed upon.

1903. ἐπενδύτης **ĕpĕndutēs**, *ep-en-doo'-tace;* from *1902*; a *wrapper*, i.e. outer garment:—fisher's coat.

1904. ἐπέρχομαι **ĕpĕrchŏmai**, *ep-er'-khom-ahee;* from *1909* and *2064*; to *supervene*, i.e. *arrive*, *occur*, *impend*, *attack*, (fig.) *influence:*—come (in, upon).

1905. ἐπερωτάω **ĕpĕrōtaō**, *ep-er-o-tah'-o;* from *1909* and *2065*; to *ask for*, i.e. *inquire*, *seek:*—ask (after, questions), demand, desire, question.

1906. ἐπερώτημα **ĕpĕrōtēma**, *ep-er-o'-tay-mah;* from *1905*; an *inquiry:*—answer.

1907. ἐπέχω **ĕpĕchō**, *ep-ekh'-o;* from *1909* and *2192*; to *hold upon*, i.e. (by impl.) to *retain*; (by extens.) to *detain*; (with impl. of *3563*) to *pay attention to:*—give (take) heed unto, hold forth, mark, stay.

1908. ἐπηρεάζω **ĕpērĕazō**, *ep-ay-reh-ad'-zo;* from a comp. of *1909* and (prob.) ἀρειά **arĕia** (*threats*); to *insult*, *slander:*—use despitefully, falsely accuse.

1909. ἐπί **ĕpi**, *ep-ee';* a prim. prep. prop. mean. *superimposition* (of time, place, order, etc.), as a relation of *distribution* [with the gen.], i.e. *over*, *upon*, etc.; of *rest* (with the dat.) *at*, *on*, etc.; of *direction* (with the acc.) *towards*, *upon*, etc.:—about (the times), above, after, against, among, as long as (touching), at, beside, × have charge of, (be-, [where-]) fore, in (a place, as much as, the time of, -to), (because) of, (up-) on (behalf of), over, (by, for) the space of, through (-out), (un-) to (-ward), with. In compounds it retains essentially the same import, *at*, *upon*, etc. (lit. or fig.).

1910. ἐπιβαίνω **ĕpibainō**, *ep-ee-bah'ee-no;* from *1909* and the base of *939*; to *walk upon*, i.e. *mount*, *ascend*, *embark*, *arrive:*—come (into), enter into, go abroad, sit upon, take ship.

1911. ἐπιβάλλω **ĕpiballō**, *ep-ee-bal'-lo;* from *1909* and *906*; to *throw upon* (lit. or fig., trans. or reflex.; usually with more or less force); spec. (with *1438* implied) to *reflect;* impers. to *belong to:*—beat into, cast (up-) on, fall, lay (on), put (unto), stretch forth, think on.

1912. **ἐπιβαρέω ĕpibarĕō**, *ep-ee-bar-eh'-o;* from *1909* and *916;* to *be heavy upon,* i.e. (pecuniarily) to *be expensive to;* fig. to *be severe towards:*—be chargeable to, overcharge.

1913. **ἐπιβιβάζω ĕpibibazō**, *ep-ee-bee-bad'-zo;* from *1909* and a redupl. deriv. of the base of *939* [comp. *307*]; to *cause to mount* (an animal):—set on.

1914. **ἐπιβλέπω ĕpiblĕpō**, *ep-ee-blep'-o;* from *1909* and *991;* to *gaze at* (with favor, pity or partiality):—look upon, regard, have respect to.

1915. **ἐπίβλημα ĕpiblēma**, *ep-ib'-lay-mah;* from *1911;* a *patch:*—piece.

1916. **ἐπιβοάω ĕpibŏaō**, *ep-ee-bo-ah'-o;* from *1909* and *994;* to *exclaim against:*—cry.

1917. **ἐπιβουλή ĕpibŏulē**, *ep-ee-boo-lay';* from a presumed comp. of *1909* and *1014;* a *plan against* someone, i.e. a *plot:*—laying (lying) in wait.

1918. **ἐπιγαμβρεύω ĕpigambrĕuō**, *ep-ee-gam-bryoo'-o;* from *1909* and a der. of *1062;* to *form affinity with,* i.e. (spec.) in a levirate way:—marry.

1919. **ἐπίγειος ĕpigĕiŏs**, *ep-ig'-i-os;* from *1909* and *1093; worldly* (phys. or mor.):—earthly, in earth, terrestrial.

1920. **ἐπιγίνομαι ĕpiginŏmai**, *ep-ig-in'-om-ahee;* from *1909* and *1096;* to *arrive upon,* i.e. *spring up* (as a wind):—blow.

1921. **ἐπιγινώσκω ĕpiginōskō**, *ep-ig-in-oce'-ko;* from *1909* and *1097;* to *know upon* some mark, i.e. *recognise;* by impl. to *become fully acquainted with,* to *acknowledge:*—(ac-, have, take) know (-ledge, well), perceive.

1922. **ἐπίγνωσις epignōsis**, *ep-ig'-no-sis;* from *1921; recognition,* i.e. (by impl.) full *discernment, acknowledgment:*—(ac-) knowledge (-ing, -ment).

1923. **ἐπιγραφή ĕpigraphē**, *ep-ig-raf-ay';* from *1924;* an *inscription:*—superscription.

1924. **ἐπιγράφω ĕpigraphō**, *ep-ee-graf'-o;* from *1909* and *1125;* to *inscribe* (phys. or ment.):—inscription, write in (over, thereon).

1925. **ἐπιδείκνυμι ĕpidĕiknumi**, *ep-ee-dike'-noo-mee;* from *1909* and *1166;* to *exhibit* (phys. or ment.):—shew.

1926. **ἐπιδέχομαι ĕpidĕchŏmai**, *ep-ee-dekh'-om-ahee;* from *1909* and *1209;* to *admit* (as a guest or [fig.] teacher):—receive.

1927. **ἐπιδημέω ĕpidēmĕō**, *ep-ee-day-meh'-o;* from a comp. of *1909* and *1218;* to *make oneself at home,* i.e. (by extens.) to *reside* (in a foreign country):—[be] dwelling (which were) there, stranger.

1928. **ἐπιδιατάσσομαι ĕpidiatassŏmai**, *ep-ee-dee-ah-tas'-som-ahee;* mid. from *1909* and *1299;* to *appoint besides,* i.e. *supplement* (as a codicil):—add to.

1929. **ἐπιδίδωμι ĕpididōmi**, *ep-ee-did'-o-mee;* from *1909* and *1325;* to *give over* (by hand or surrender):—deliver unto, give, let (+ [her drive]), offer.

1930. **ἐπιδιορθόω ĕpidiŏrthŏō**, *ep-ee-dee-or-thŏ'-o;* from *1909* and a der. of *3717;* to *straighten further,* i.e. (fig.) *arrange additionally:*—set in order.

1931. **ἐπιδύω ĕpiduō**, *ep-ee-doo'-o;* from *1909* and *1416;* to *set* fully (as the sun):—go down.

1932. **ἐπιείκεια ĕpiĕikĕia**, *ep-ee-i'-ki-ah;* from *1933; suitableness,* i.e. (by impl.) *equity, mildness:*—clemency, gentleness.

1933. **ἐπιεικής ĕpiĕikēs**, *ep-ee-i-kace';* from *1909* and *1503; appropriate,* i.e. (by impl.) *mild:*—gentle, moderation, patient.

1934. **ἐπιζητέω ĕpizētĕō**, *ep-eed-zay-teh'-o;* from *1909* and *2212;* to *search* (*inquire*) *for;* intens to *demand,* to *crave:*—desire, enquire, seek (after, for).

1935. **ἐπιθανάτιος ĕpithanatiŏs**, *ep-ee-than-at'-ee-os;* from *1909* and *2288;* doomed *to death:*—appointed to death.

1936. **ἐπίθεσις ĕpithĕsis**, *ep-ith'-es-is;* from *2007;* an *imposition* (of hands officially):—laying (putting) on.

1937. **ἐπιθυμέω ĕpithumĕō**, *ep-ee-thoo-meh'-o;* from *1909* and *2372;* to set the *heart upon,* i.e. *long* for (rightfully or otherwise):—covet, desire, would fain, lust (after).

1938. **ἐπιθυμητής ĕpithumētēs**, *ep-ee-thoo-may-tace';* from *1937;* a *craver:*— + lust after.

1939. **ἐπιθυμία ĕpithumia**, *ep-ee-thoo-mee'-ah;* from *1937;* a *longing* (espec. for what is forbidden):—concupiscence, desire, lust (after).

1940. **ἐπικαθίζω ĕpikathizō**, *ep-ee-kath-id'-zo;* from *1909* and *2523;* to *seat upon:*—set on.

1941. **ἐπικαλέομαι ĕpikalĕŏmai**, *ep-ee-kal-eh'-om-ahee;* mid. from *1909* and *2564;* to *entitle;* by impl. to *invoke* (for aid, worship, testimony, decision, etc.):—appeal (unto), call (on, upon), surname.

1942. **ἐπικάλυμα ĕpikaluma**, *ep-ee-kal'-oo-mah;* from *1943;* a *covering,* i.e. (fig.) *pretext:*—cloke.

1943. **ἐπικαλύπτω ĕpikaluptō**, *ep-ee-kal-oop'-to;* from *1909* and *2572;* to *conceal,* i.e. (fig.) *forgive:*—cover.

1944. **ἐπικατάρατος ĕpikataratŏs**, *ep-ee-kat-ar'-at-os;* from *1909* and a der. of *2672; imprecated,* i.e. *execrable:*—accursed.

1945. **ἐπίκειμαι ĕpikĕimai**, *ep-ik'-i-mahee;* from *1909* and *2749;* to *rest upon* (lit. or fig.):—impose, be instant, (be) laid (there-, up-) on, (when) lay (on), lie (on), press upon.

1946. **Ἐπικούρειος Ĕpikŏurĕiŏs**, *ep-ee-koo'-ri-os;* from **Ἐπίκουρος Ĕpikŏurŏs** [comp. *1947*] (a noted philosopher); an *Epicurean* or follower of Epicurus:—Epicurean.

1947. **ἐπικουρία ĕpikŏuria**, *ep-ee-koo-ree'-ah;* from a comp. of *1909* and a (prol.) form of the base of *2877* (in the sense of *servant*); *assistance:*—help.

1948. **ἐπικρίνω ĕpikrinō**, *ep-ee-kree'-no;* from *1909* and *2919;* to *adjudge:*—give sentence.

1949. **ἐπιλαμβάνομαι ĕpilambanŏmai**, *ep-ee-lam-ban'-om-ahee;* mid. from *1909* and *2983;* to *seize* (for help, injury, attainment or any other purpose; lit. or fig.):—catch, lay hold (up-) on, take (by, hold of, on).

1950. **ἐπιλανθάνομαι ĕpilanthanŏmai**, *ep-ee-lan-than'-om-ahee;* mid. from *1909* and *2990;* to *lose out* of mind; by impl. to *neglect:*—(be) forget (-ful of).

1951. **ἐπιλέγομαι ĕpilĕgŏmai**, *ep-ee-leg'-om-ahee;* mid. from *1909* and *3004;* to *surname, select:*—call, choose.

1952. **ἐπιλείπω ĕpilĕipō**, *ep-ee-li'-po;* from *1909* and *3007;* to *leave upon,* i.e. (fig.) to *be insufficient for:*—fail.

1953. **ἐπιλησμονή ĕpilēsmŏnē**, *ep-ee-lace-mon-ay';* from a der. of *1950; negligence:*— × forgetful.

1954. **ἐπίλοιπος ĕpilŏipŏs**, *ep-il'-oy-pos;* from *1909* and *3062; left over,* i.e. *remaining:*—rest.

1955. **ἐπίλυσις ĕpilusis**, *ep-il'-oo-sis;* from *1956; explanation,* i.e. *application:*—interpretation.

1956. **ἐπιλύω ĕpiluō**, *ep-ee-loo'-o;* from *1909* and *3089;* to *solve further,* i.e. (fig.) to *explain, decide:*—determine, expound.

1957. **ἐπιμαρτυρέω ĕpimarturĕō**, *ep-ee-mar-too-reh'-o;* from *1909* and *3140;* to *attest further,* i.e. *corroborate:*—testify.

1958. **ἐπιμέλεια ĕpimĕlĕia**, *ep-ee-mel'-i-ah;* from *1959; carefulness,* i.e. kind *attention* (*hospitality*):— + refresh self.

1959. **ἐπιμελέομαι ĕpimĕlĕŏmai**, *ep-ee-mel-eh'-om-ahee;* mid. from *1909* and the same as *3199;* to *care for* (phys. or otherwise):—take care of.

1960. **ἐπιμελῶς ĕpimĕlōs**, *ep-ee-mel-oce';* adv. from a der. of *1959; carefully:*—diligently.

1961. **ἐπιμένω ĕpimĕnō**, *ep-ee-men'-o;* from *1909* and *3306;* to *stay over,* i.e. *remain* (fig. *persevere*):—abide (in), continue (in), tarry.

1962. **ἐπινεύω ĕpinĕuō**, *ep-een-yoo'-o;* from *1909* and *3506;* to *nod at,* i.e. (by impl.) to *assent:*—consent.

1963. **ἐπίνοια ĕpinŏia**, *ep-in'-oy-ah;* from *1909* and *3563; attention* of the mind, i.e. (by impl.) *purpose:*—thought.

1964. **ἐπιορκέω ĕpiŏrkĕō**, *ep-ee-or-keh'-o;* from *1965;* to *commit perjury:*—forswear self.

1965. **ἐπίορκος ĕpiŏrkŏs**, *ep-ee'-or-kos;* from *1909* and *3727; on oath,* i.e. (falsely) a *forswearer:*—perjured person.

1966. **ἐπιοῦσα ĕpiŏusa**, *ep-ee-oo'-sah;* fem. sing. part. of a comp. of *1909* and **εἶμι hĕimi** (to *go*); *supervening,* i.e. (*2250* or *3571* being expressed or implied) the *ensuing* day or night:—following, next.

1967. **ἐπιούσιος ĕpiŏusiŏs**, *ep-ee-oo'-see-os;* perh. from the same as *1966; to-morrow's;* but more prob. from *1909* and a der. of the pres. part. fem. of *1510; for subsistence,* i.e. *needful:*—daily.

1968. **ἐπιπίπτω ĕpipiptō**, *ep-ee-pip'-to;* from *1909* and *4098;* to *embrace* (with affection) or *seize* (with more or less violence; lit. or fig.):—fall into (on, upon), lie on, press upon.

1969. **ἐπιπλήσσω ĕpiplēssō**, *ep-ee-place'-so;* from *1909* and *4141;* to *chastise,* i.e. (with words) to *upbraid:*—rebuke.

1970. **ἐπιπνίγω ĕpipnigō**, *ep-ee-pnee'-go;* from *1909* and *4155;* to *throttle upon,* i.e. (fig.) *overgrow:*—choke.

1971. **ἐπιποθέω ĕpipŏthĕō**, *ep-ee-poth-eh'-o;* from *1909* and **ποθέω pŏthĕō** (to *yearn*); to *dote upon,* i.e. *intensely crave* possession (lawfully or wrongfully):—(earnestly) desire (greatly), (greatly) long (after), lust.

1972. **ἐπιπόθησις ĕpipŏthēsis**, *ep-ee-poth'-ay-sis;* from *1971;* a *longing for:*—earnest (vehement) desire.

1973. **ἐπιπόθητος ĕpipŏthētŏs**, *ep-ee-poth'-ay-tos;* from *1909* and a der. of the latter part of *1971; yearned upon,* i.e. *greatly loved:*—longed for.

1974. **ἐπιποθία ĕpipŏthia**, *ep-ee-poth-ee'-ah;* from *1971; intense longing:*—great desire.

1975. **ἐπιπορεύομαι ĕpipŏrĕuŏmai**, *ep-ee-por-yoo'-om-ahee;* from *1909* and *4198;* to *journey further,* i.e. *travel on* (*reach*):—come.

1976. **ἐπιῤῥάπτω ĕpirrhaptō**, *ep-ir-hrap'-to;* from *1909* and the base of *4476;* to *stitch upon,* i.e. *fasten* with the needle:—sew on.

1977. **ἐπιῤῥίπτω ĕpirrhiptō**, *ep-ir-hrip'-to;* from *1909* and *4496;* to *throw upon* (lit. or fig.):—cast upon.

1978. **ἐπίσημος ĕpisēmŏs**, *ep-is'-ay-mos;* from *1909* and some form of the base of *4591; remarkable,* i.e. (fig.) *eminent:*—notable, of note.

1979. **ἐπισιτισμός ĕpisitismŏs**, *ep-ee-sit-is-mos';* from a comp. of *1909* and a der. of *4621;* a *provisioning,* i.e. (concr.) *food:*—victuals.

1980. **ἐπισκέπτομαι ĕpiskĕptŏmai**, *ep-ee-skep'-tom-ahee;* mid. from *1909* and the base of *4649;* to *inspect,* i.e. (by impl.) to *select;* by extens. to *go to see, relieve:*—look out, visit.

1981. **ἐπισκηνόω ĕpiskēnŏō**, *ep-ee-skay-nŏ'-o;* from *1909* and *4637;* to *tent upon,* i.e. (fig.) *abide with:*—rest upon.

1982. **ἐπισκιάζω ĕpiskiazō**, *ep-ee-skee-ad'-zo;* from *1909* and a der. of *4639;* to *cast a shade upon,* i.e. (by anal.) to *envelop* in a haze of brilliancy; fig. to *invest* with preternatural influence:—overshadow.

1983. **ἐπισκοπέω ĕpiskŏpĕō**, *ep-ee-skop-eh'-o;* from *1909* and *4648;* to *oversee;* by impl. to *beware:*—look diligently, take the oversight.

1984. **ἐπισκοπή ĕpiskŏpē**, *ep-is-kop-ay';* from *1980; inspection* (for relief); by impl. *superintendence;* spec. the Chr. "*episcopate*":—the office of a "bishop", bishoprick, visitation.

1985. **ἐπίσκοπος ĕpiskŏpŏs**, *ep-is'-kop-os;* from *1909* and *4649* (in the sense of *1983*); a *superintendent,* i.e. Chr. officer in gen. charge of a (or the) church (lit. or fig.):—bishop, overseer.

1986. **ἐπισπάομαι ĕpispaŏmai**, *ep-ee-spah'-om-ahee;* from *1909* and *4685;* to *draw over,* i.e. (with *203* implied) *efface* the mark of *circumcision* (by recovering with the foreskin):—become uncircumcised.

1987. **ἐπίσταμαι ĕpistamai**, *ep-is'-tam-ahee;* appar. a mid. of *2186* (with *3563* implied); to *put* the mind *upon,* i.e. *comprehend,* or *be acquainted with:*—know, understand.

1988. ἐπιστάτης ĕpistatēs, *ep-is-tat'-ace;* from 1909 and a presumed der. of 2476; an *appointee over,* i.e. *commander* (*teacher*):—master.

1989. ἐπιστέλλω ĕpistĕllō, *ep-ee-stel'-lo;* from 1909 and 4724; to *enjoin* (by writing), i.e. (gen.) to *communicate by letter* (for any purpose):—write (a letter, unto).

1990. ἐπιστήμων ĕpistēmōn, *ep-ee-stay'-mone;* from 1987; *intelligent:*—endued with knowledge.

1991. ἐπιστηρίζω ĕpistērizō, *ep-ee-stay-rid'-zo;* from 1909 and 4741; to *support further,* i.e. *reëstablish:*—confirm, strengthen.

1992. ἐπιστολή ĕpistŏlē, *ep-is-tol-ay';* from 1989; a *written message:*—"epistle", letter.

1993. ἐπιστομίζω ĕpistŏmizō, *ep-ee-stom-id'-zo;* from 1909 and 4750; to put something *over* the *mouth,* i.e. (fig.) to *silence:*—stop mouths.

1994. ἐπιστρέφω ĕpistrĕphō, *ep-ee-stref'-o;* from 1909 and 4762; to *revert* (lit., fig. or mor.):—come (go) again, convert, (re-) turn (about, again).

1995. ἐπιστροφή ĕpistrŏphē, *ep-is-trof-ay';* from 1994; *reversion,* i.e. mor. *revolution:*—conversion.

1996. ἐπισυνάγω ĕpisunagō, *ep-ee-soon-ag'-o;* from 1909 and 4863; to *collect upon* the same place:—gather (together).

1997. ἐπισυναγωγή ĕpisunagōgē, *ep-ee-soon-ag-o-gay';* from 1996; a complete *collection;* spec. a Chr. *meeting* (for worship):—assembling (gathering) together.

1998. ἐπισυντρέχω ĕpisuntrĕchō, *ep-ee-soon-trekh'-o;* from 1909 and 4936; to *hasten together upon* one place (or a partic. occasion):—come running together.

1999. ἐπισύστασις ĕpisustasis, *ep-ee-soo'-stas-is;* from the mid. of a comp. of 1909 and 4921; a *conspiracy,* i.e. *concourse* (riotous or friendly):—that which cometh upon, + raising up.

2000. ἐπισφαλής ĕpisphalēs, *ep-ee-sfal-ace';* from a comp. of 1909 and σφάλλω sphallō (to *trip*); fig. *insecure:*—dangerous.

2001. ἐπισχύω ĕpischuō, *ep-is-khoo'-o;* from 1909 and 2480; to *avail further,* i.e. (fig.) *insist stoutly:*—be the more fierce.

2002. ἐπισωρεύω ĕpisōrĕuō, *ep-ee-so-ryoo'-o;* from 1909 and 4987; to *accumulate further,* i.e. (fig.) *seek* additionally:—heap.

2003. ἐπιταγή ĕpitagē, *ep-ee-tag-ay';* from 2004; an *injunction* or *decree;* by impl. *authoritativeness:*—authority, commandment.

2004. ἐπιτάσσω ĕpitassō, *ep-ee-tas'-so;* from 1909 and 5021; to *arrange upon,* i.e. *order:*—charge, command, injoin.

2005. ἐπιτελέω ĕpitĕlĕō, *ep-ee-tel-eh'-o;* from 1909 and 5055; to *fulfill further* (or *completely*), i.e. *execute;* by impl. to *terminate, undergo:*—accomplish, do, finish, (make) (perfect), perform (× -ance).

2006. ἐπιτήδειος ĕpitēdĕiŏs, *ep-ee-tay'-di-os;* from ἐπιτηδές ĕpitēdĕs (*enough*); *serviceable,* i.e. (by impl.) *requisite:*—things which are needful.

2007. ἐπιτίθημι ĕpitithēmi, *ep-ee-tith'-ay-mee;* from 1909 and 5087; to *impose* (in a friendly or hostile sense):—add unto, lade, lay upon, put (up) on, set on (up), + surname, × wound.

2008. ἐπιτιμάω ĕpitimaō, *ep-ee-tee-mah'-o;* from 1909 and 5091; to *tax upon,* i.e. *censure* or *admonish;* by impl. *forbid:*—(straitly) charge, rebuke.

2009. ἐπιτιμία ĕpitimia, *ep-ee-tee-mee'-ah;* from a comp. of 1909 and 5092; prop. *esteem,* i.e. *citizenship;* used (in the sense of 2008) of a *penalty:*—punishment.

2010. ἐπιτρέπω ĕpitrĕpō, *ep-ee-trep'-o;* from 1909 and the base of 5157; to *turn over* (*transfer*), i.e. *allow:*—give leave (liberty, license), let, permit, suffer.

2011. ἐπιτροπή ĕpitrŏpē, *ep-ee-trop-ay';* from 2010; *permission,* i.e. (by impl.) full *power:*—commission.

2012. ἐπίτροπος ĕpitrŏpŏs, *ep-it'-rop-os;* from 1909 and 5158 (in the sense of 2011); a *commissioner,* i.e. domestic *manager, guardian:*—steward, tutor.

2013. ἐπιτυγχάνω ĕpitugchanō, *ep-ee-toong-khan'-o;* from 1909 and 5177; to *chance upon,* i.e. (by impl.) *attain:*—obtain.

2014. ἐπιφαίνω ĕpiphainō, *ep-ee-fah'ee-no;* from 1909 and 5316; to *shine upon,* i.e. *become* (lit.) *visible* or (fig.) *known:*—appear, give light.

2015. ἐπιφάνεια ĕpiphanĕia, *ep-if-an'-i-ah;* from 2016; a *manifestation,* i.e. (spec.) the *advent* of Christ (past or fut.):—appearing, brightness.

2016. ἐπιφανής ĕpiphanēs, *ep-if-an-ace';* from 2014; *conspicuous,* i.e. (fig.) *memorable:*—notable.

2017. ἐπιφαύω ĕpiphauō, *ep-ee-fōw'-o;* a form of 2014; to *illuminate* (fig.):—give light.

2018. ἐπιφέρω ĕpiphĕrō, *ep-ee-fer'-o;* from 1909 and 5342; to *bear upon* (or *further*), i.e. *adduce* (pers. or judicially [*accuse, inflict*]), *superinduce:*—add, bring (against), take.

2019. ἐπιφωνέω ĕpiphōnĕō, *ep-ee-fo-neh'-o;* from 1909 and 5455; to *call at* something, i.e. *exclaim:*—cry (against), give a shout.

2020. ἐπιφώσκω ĕpiphōskō, *ep-ee-foce'-ko;* a form of 2017; to begin to *grow light:*—begin to dawn, × draw on.

2021. ἐπιχειρέω ĕpichĕirĕō, *ep-ee-khi-reh'-o;* from 1909 and 5495; to put the *hand upon,* i.e. *undertake:*—go about, take in hand (upon).

2022. ἐπιχέω ĕpichĕō, *ep-ee-kheh'-o;* from 1909 and χέω chĕō (to *pour*); to *pour upon:*—pour in.

2023. ἐπιχορηγέω ĕpichŏrēgĕō, *ep-ee-khor-ayg-eh'-o;* from 1909 and 5524; to *furnish besides,* i.e. fully *supply,* (fig.) *aid* or *contribute:*—add, minister (nourishment, unto).

2024. ἐπιχορηγία ĕpichŏrēgia, *ep-ee-khor-ayg-ee'-ah;* from 2023; *contribution:*—supply.

2025. ἐπιχρίω ĕpichriō, *ep-ee-khree'-o;* from 1909 and 5548; to *smear over:*—anoint.

2026. ἐποικοδομέω ĕpŏikŏdŏmĕō, *ep-oy-kod-om-eh'-o;* from 1909 and 3618; to *build upon,* i.e. (fig.) to *rear up:*—build thereon (thereupon, on, upon).

2027. ἐποκέλλω ĕpŏkĕllō, *ep-ok-el'-lo;* from 1909 and ὀκέλλω ŏkĕllō (to *urge*); to *drive upon* the shore, i.e. to *beach* a vessel:—run aground.

2028. ἐπονομάζω ĕpŏnŏmazō, *ep-on-om-ad'-zo;* from 1909 and 3687; to *name further,* i.e. *denominate:*—call.

2029. ἐποπτεύω ĕpŏptĕuō, *ep-opt-yoo'-o;* from 1909 and a der. of 3700; to *inspect,* i.e. *watch:*—behold.

2030. ἐπόπτης ĕpŏptēs, *ep-op'-tace;* from 1909 and a presumed der. of 3700; a *looker-on:*—eye-witness.

2031. ἔπος ĕpŏs, *ep'-os;* from 2036; a *word:*—× say.

2032. ἐπουράνιος ĕpŏuraniŏs, *ep-oo-ran'-ee-os;* from 1909 and 3772; *above* the *sky:*—celestial, (in) heaven (-ly), high.

2033. ἑπτά hĕpta, *hep-tah';* a prim. number; *seven:*—seven.

2034. ἑπτακίς hĕptakis, *hep-tak-is';* adv. from 2033; *seven times:*—seven times.

2035. ἑπτακισχίλιοι hĕptakischiliŏi, *hep-tak-is-khil'-ee-oy;* from 2034 and 5507; *seven times a thousand:*—seven thousand.

2036. ἔπω ĕpō, *ep'-o;* a prim. verb (used only in the def. past tense, the others being borrowed from 2046, 4483 and 5346); to *speak* or *say* (by word or writing):—answer, bid, bring word, call, command, grant, say (on), speak, tell. Comp. 3004.

2037. Ἔραστος Ĕrastŏs, *er'-as-tos;* from ἐράω ĕraō (*to love*); *beloved; Erastus,* a Chr.:—Erastus.

2038. ἐργάζομαι ĕrgazŏmai, *er-gad'-zom-ahee;* mid. from 2041; to *toil* (as a task, occupation, etc.), (by impl.) *effect, be engaged in* or *with,* etc.:—commit, do, labor for, minister about, trade (by), work.

2039. ἐργασία ĕrgasia, *er-gas-ee'-ah;* from 2040; *occupation;* by impl. *profit, pains:*—craft, diligence, gain, work.

2040. ἐργάτης ĕrgatēs, *er-gat'-ace;* from 2041; a *toiler;* fig. a *teacher:*—labourer, worker (-men).

2041. ἔργον ĕrgŏn, *er'-gon;* from a prim. (but obsol.) ἔργω ĕrgō (to *work*); *toil* (as an effort or occupation); by impl. an *act:*—deed, doing, labour, work.

2042. ἐρεθίζω ĕrĕthizō, *er-eth-id'-zo;* from a presumed prol. form of 2054; to *stimulate* (espec. to anger):—provoke.

2043. ἐρείδω ĕrĕidō, *er-i'-do;* of obscure affin.; to *prop,* i.e. (reflex.) *get fast:*—stick fast.

2044. ἐρεύγομαι ĕrĕugŏmai, *er-yoog'-om-ahee;* of uncert. affin.; to *belch,* i.e. (fig.) to *speak out:*—utter.

2045. ἐρευνάω ĕrĕunaō, *er-yoo-nah'-o;* appar. from 2046 (through the idea of *inquiry*); to *seek,* i.e. (fig.) to *investigate:*—search.

2046. ἐρέω ĕrĕō, *er-eh'-o;* prob. a fuller form of 4483; an alt. for 2036 in cert. tenses; to *utter,* i.e. *speak* or *say:*—call, say, speak (of), tell.

2047. ἐρημία ĕrēmia, *er-ay-mee'-ah;* from 2048; *solitude* (concr.):—desert, wilderness.

2048. ἔρημος ĕrēmŏs, *er'-ay-mos;* of uncert. affin.; *lonesome,* i.e. (by impl.) *waste* (usually as a noun, 5561 being implied):—desert, desolate, solitary, wilderness.

2049. ἐρημόω ĕrēmŏō, *er-ay-mŏ'-o;* from 2048; to *lay waste* (lit. or fig.):—(bring to, make) desolate (-ion), come to nought.

2050. ἐρήμωσις ĕrēmōsis, *er-ay'-mo-sis;* from 2049; *despoliation:*—desolation.

2051. ἐρίζω ĕrizō, *er-id'-zo;* from 2054; to *wrangle:*—strive.

2052. ἐριθεία ĕrithĕia, *er-ith-i'-ah;* perh. from the same as 2042; prop. *intrigue,* i.e. (by impl.) *faction:*—contention (-ious), strife.

2053. ἔριον ĕriŏn, *er'-ee-on;* of obscure affin.; *wool:*—wool.

2054. ἔρις ĕris, *er'-is;* of uncert. affin.; a *quarrel,* i.e. (by impl.) *wrangling:*—contention, debate, strife, variance.

2055. ἐρίφιον ĕriphiŏn, *er-if'-ee-on;* from 2056; a *kidling,* i.e. (gen.) *goat* (symbol. *wicked* person):—goat.

2056. ἔριφος ĕriphŏs, *er'-if-os;* perh. from the same as 2053 (through the idea of *hairiness*); a *kid* or (gen.) *goat:*—goat, kid.

2057. Ἑρμᾶς Hĕrmas, *her-mas';* prob. from 2060; *Hermas,* a Chr.:—Hermas.

2058. ἑρμηνεία hĕrmēnĕia, *her-may-ni'-ah;* from the same as 2059; *translation:*—interpretation.

2059. ἑρμηνεύω hĕrmēnĕuō, *her-mayn-yoo'-o;* from a presumed der. of 2060 (as the god of language); to *translate:*—interpret.

2060. Ἑρμῆς Hĕrmēs, *her-mace';* perh. from 2046; *Hermes,* the name of the messenger of the Gr. deities; also of a Chr.:—Hermes, Mercury.

2061. Ἑρμογένης Hĕrmŏgĕnēs, *her-mog-en'-ace;* from 2060 and 1096; *born of Hermes; Hermogenes,* an apostate Chr.:—Hermogenes.

2062. ἑρπετόν hĕrpĕtŏn, *her-pet-on';* neut. of a der. of ἕρπω hĕrpō (to *creep*); a *reptile,* i.e. (by Hebr. [comp. 7431]) a small *animal:*—creeping thing, serpent.

2063. ἐρυθρός ĕruthrŏs, *er-oo-thros';* of uncert. affin.; *red,* i.e. (with 2281) the *Red* Sea:—red.

2064. ἔρχομαι ĕrchŏmai, *er'-khom-ahee;* mid. of a prim. verb (used only in the pres. and imperf. tenses, the others being supplied by a kindred [mid.] ἐλεύθομαι ĕlĕuthŏmai, *el-yoo'-thom-ahee;* or [act.] ἔλθω ĕlthō, *el'-tho;* which do not otherwise occur); to *come* or *go* (in a great variety of applications, lit. and fig.):—accompany, appear, bring, come enter, fall out, go, grow, × light, × next, pass, resort, be set.

2065. ἐρωτάω ĕrōtaō, *er-o-tah'-o;* appar. from 2046 [comp. 2045]; to *interrogate;* by impl. to *request:*—ask, beseech, desire, intreat, pray. Comp. 4441.

2066. **ἐσθής ĕsthēs**, *es-thace';* from **ἕννυμι hĕnnumi** (to *clothe*); *dress:*—apparel, clothing, raiment, robe.

2067. **ἔσθησις ĕsthēsis**, *es'-thay-sis;* from a der. of *2066; clothing* (concr.):—garment.

2068. **ἐσθίω ĕsthiō**, *es-thee'-o;* strengthened for a prim. **ἔδω ĕdō** (to *eat*); used only in certain tenses, the rest being supplied by *5315;* to *eat* (usually lit.):—devour, eat, live.

2069. **Ἐσλί Ĕsli**, *es-lee';* of Heb. or. [prob. for 454]; *Esli*, an Isr.:—Esli.

2070. **ἐσμέν ĕsmĕn**, *es-men';* first pers. plur. indic. of *1510;* we *are:*—are, be, have our being, × have hope, + [the gospel] was [preached unto] us.

2071. **ἔσομαι ĕsŏmai**, *es'-om-ahee;* fut. of *1510; will be:*—shall (should) be (have), (shall) come (to pass), × may have, × fall, what would follow, × live long, × sojourn.

2072. **ἔσοπτρον ĕsŏptrŏn**, *es'-op-tron;* from *1519* and a presumed der. of *3700;* a *mirror* (for *looking into*):—glass. Comp. *2734*.

2073. **ἑσπέρα hĕspĕra**, *hes-per'-ah;* fem. of an adj. **ἑσπερός hĕspĕrŏs** (*evening*); the *eve* (*5610* being impl.):—evening (-tide).

2074. **Ἐσρώμ Ĕsrōm**, *es-rome';* of Heb. or. [2696]; *Esrom* (i.e. *Chetsron*), an Isr.:—Esrom.

2075. **ἐστέ ĕstĕ**, *es-teh';* second pers. plur. pres. indic. of *1510;* ye *are:*—be, have been, belong.

2076. **ἐστί ĕsti**, *es-tee';* third pers. sing. pres. indic. of *1510;* he (she or it) *is;* also (with neut. plur.) they *are:*—are, be (-long), call, × can [-not], come, consisteth, × dure for awhile, + follow, × have, (that) is (to say), make, meaneth, × must needs, + profit, + remaineth, + wrestle.

2077. **ἔστω ĕstō**, *es'-to;* second pers. sing. pres. imper. of *1510; be* thou; also

ἔστωσαν ĕstōsan, *es'-to-san;* third pers. of the same; *let* them *be:*—be.

2078. **ἔσχατος ĕschatŏs**, *es'-khat-os;* a superl. prob. from *2192* (in the sense of *contiguity*); *farthest, final* (of place or time):—ends of, last, latter end, lowest, uttermost.

2079. **ἐσχάτως ĕschatōs**, *es-khat'-oce;* adv. from *2078; finally*, i.e. (with *2192*) *at the extremity* of life:—point of death.

2080. **ἔσω ĕsō**, *es'-o;* from *1519; inside* (as prep. or adj.):—(with-) in (-ner, -to, -ward).

2081. **ἔσωθεν ĕsōthĕn**, *es'-o-then;* from *2080; from inside;* also used as equiv to *2080* (*inside*):—inward (-ly), (from) within, without.

2082. **ἐσώτερος ĕsōtĕrŏs**, *es-o'-ter-os;* compar. of *2080; interior:*—inner, within.

2083. **ἑταῖρος hĕtairŏs**, *het-ah'ee-ros;* from **ἔτης ĕtēs** (a *clansman*); a *comrade:*—fellow, friend.

2084. **ἑτερόγλωσσος hĕtĕrŏglōssŏs**, *het-er-og'-loce-sos;* from *2087* and *1100; other-tongued*, i.e. a *foreigner:*—man of other tongue.

2085. **ἑτεροδιδασκαλέω hĕtĕrŏdidaskalĕō**, *het-er-od-id-as-kal-eh'-o;* from *2087* and *1320;* to *instruct differently:*—teach other doctrine (-wise).

2086. **ἑτεροζυγέω hĕtĕrŏzugĕō**, *het-er-od-zoog-eh'-o;* from a comp. of *2087* and *2218;* to *yoke* up *differently*, i.e. (fig.) to *associate discordantly:*—unequally yoke together with.

2087. **ἕτερος hĕtĕrŏs**, *het'-er-os;* of uncert. affin.; (an-, the) *other* or *different:*—altered, else, next (day), one, (an-) other, some, strange.

2088. **ἑτέρως hĕtĕrōs**, *het-er'-oce;* adv. from *2087; differently:*—otherwise.

2089. **ἔτι ĕti**, *et'-ee;* perh. akin to *2094;* "*yet*," *still* (of time or degree):—after that, also, ever, (any) further, (t-) henceforth (more), hereafter, (any) longer, (any) more (-one), now, still, yet.

2090. **ἑτοιμάζω hĕtŏimazō**, *het-oy-mad'-zo;* from *2092;* to *prepare:*—prepare, provide, make ready. Comp. *2680*.

2091. **ἑτοιμασία hĕtŏimasia**, *het-oy-mas-ee'-ah;* from *2090; preparation:*—preparation.

2092. **ἕτοιμος hĕtŏimŏs**, *het-oy'-mos;* from an old noun **ἕτεος hĕtĕŏs** (*fitness*); *adjusted*, i.e. *ready:*—prepared, (made) ready (-iness, to our hand).

2093. **ἑτοίμως hĕtŏimōs**, *het'-oy-moce;* adv. from *2092; in readiness:*—ready.

2094. **ἔτος ĕtŏs**, *et'-os;* appar. a prim. word; a *year:*—year.

2095. **εὖ ĕu**, *yoo;* neut. of a prim. **εὖς ĕus** (*good*); (adv.) *well:*—good, well (done).

2096. **Εὖα Ĕua**, *yoo'-ah;* of Heb. or. [2332]; *Eua* (or *Eva*, i.e. *Chavvah*), the first woman:—Eve.

2097. **εὐαγγελίζω ĕuaggĕlizō**, *yoo-ang-ghel-id'-zo;* from *2095* and *32;* to *announce good* news ("evangelize") espec. the gospel:—declare, bring (declare, show) glad (good) tidings, preach (the gospel).

2098. **εὐαγγέλιον ĕuaggĕliŏn**, *yoo-ang-ghel'-ee-on;* from the same as *2097;* a *good message*, i.e. the *gospel:*—gospel.

2099. **εὐαγγελιστής ĕuaggĕlistēs**, *yoo-ang-ghel-is-tace';* from *2097;* a *preacher* of the gospel:—evangelist.

2100. **εὐαρεστέω ĕuarĕstĕō**, *yoo-ar-es-teh'-o;* from *2101;* to *gratify entirely:*—please (well).

2101. **εὐάρεστος ĕuarĕstŏs**, *yoo-ar'-es-tos;* from *2095* and *701; fully agreeable:*—acceptable (-ted), wellpleasing.

2102. **εὐαρέστως ĕuarĕstōs**, *yoo-ar-es'-toce;* adv. from *2101; quite agreeably:*—acceptably, + please well.

2103. **Εὔβουλος Ĕubŏulŏs**, *yoo'-boo-los;* from *2095* and *1014; good-willer; Eubulus*, a Chr.:—Eubulus.

2104. **εὐγένης ĕugĕnēs**, *yoog-en'-ace;* from *2095* and *1096; well born*, i.e. (lit.) *high* in rank, or (fig.) *generous:*—more noble, nobleman.

2105. **εὐδία ĕudia**, *yoo-dee'-ah;* fem. from *2095* and the alt. of *2203* (as the god of the weather); a *clear sky*, i.e. *fine weather:*—fair weather.

2106. **εὐδοκέω ĕudŏkĕō**, *yoo-dok-eh'-o;* from *2095* and *1380;* to *think well* of, i.e. *approve* (an act); spec. to *approbate* (a person or thing):—think good, (be well) please (-d), be the good (have, take) pleasure, be willing.

2107. **εὐδοκία ĕudŏkia**, *yoo-dok-ee'-ah;* from a presumed comp. of *2095* and the base of *1380; satisfaction*, i.e. (subj.) *delight*, or (obj.) *kindness, wish, purpose:*—desire, good pleasure (will), × seem good.

2108. **εὐεργεσία ĕuĕrgĕsia**, *yoo-erg-es-ee'-ah;* from *2110; beneficence* (gen. or spec.):—benefit, good deed done.

2109. **εὐεργετέω ĕuĕrgĕtĕō**, *yoo-erg-et-eh'-o;* from *2110;* to *be philanthropic:*—do good.

2110. **εὐεργέτης ĕuĕrgĕtēs**, *yoo-erg-et'-ace;* from *2095* and the base of *2041;* a *worker of good*, i.e. (spec.) a *philanthropist:*—benefactor.

2111. **εὔθετος ĕuthĕtŏs**, *yoo'-thet-os;* from *2095* and a der. of *5087; well placed*, i.e. (fig.) *appropriate:*—fit, meet.

2112. **εὐθέως ĕuthĕōs**, *yoo-theh'-oce;* adv. from *2117; directly*, i.e. *at once* or *soon:*—anon, as soon as, forthwith, immediately, shortly, straightway.

2113. **εὐθυδρομέω ĕuthudrŏmĕō**, *yoo-thoo-drom-eh'-o;* from *2117* and *1408;* to *lay a straight course*, i.e. *sail direct:*—(come) with a straight course.

2114. **εὐθυμέω ĕuthumĕō**, *yoo-thoo-meh'-o;* from *2115;* to *cheer up*, i.e. (intrans.) *be cheerful;* neut. comp. (adv.) *more cheerfully:*—be of good cheer (merry).

2115. **εὔθυμος ĕuthumŏs**, *yoo'-thoo-mos;* from *2095* and *2372;* in *fine spirits*, i.e. *cheerful:*—of good cheer, the more cheerfully.

2116. **εὐθύνω ĕuthunō**, *yoo-thoo'-no;* from *2117;* to *straighten* (*level*); tech. to *steer:*—governor, make straight.

2117. **εὐθύς ĕuthus**, *yoo-thoos';* perh. from *2095* and *5087; straight*, i.e. (lit.) *level*, or (fig.) *true;* adv. (of time) *at once:*—anon, by and by, forthwith, immediately, straightway.

2118. **εὐθύτης ĕuthutēs**, *yoo-thoo'-tace;* from *2117; rectitude:*—righteousness.

2119. **εὐκαιρέω ĕukairĕō**, *yoo-kahee-reh'-o;* from *2121;* to *have good time*, i.e. *opportunity* or *leisure:*—have leisure (convenient time), spend time.

2120. **εὐκαιρία ĕukairia**, *yoo-kahee-ree'-ah;* from *2121;* a favorable *occasion:*—opportunity.

2121. **εὔκαιρος ĕukairŏs**, *yoo'-kahee-ros;* from *2095* and *2540; well-timed*, i.e. *opportune:*—convenient, in time of need.

2122. **εὐκαίρως ĕukairōs**, *yoo-kah'ee-roce;* adv. from *2121; opportunely:*—conveniently, in season.

2123. **εὐκοπώτερος ĕukŏpōtĕrŏs**, *yoo-kop-o'-ter-os;* comp. of a comp. of *2095* and *2873; better for toil*, i.e. *more facile:*—easier.

2124. **εὐλάβεια ĕulabĕia**, *yoo-lab'-i-ah;* from *2126;* prop. *caution*, i.e. (religiously) *reverence* (*piety*); by impl. *dread* (concr.):—fear (-ed).

2125. **εὐλαβέομαι ĕulabĕŏmai**, *yoo-lab-eh'-om-ahee;* mid. from *2126;* to *be circumspect*, i.e. (by impl.) to *be apprehensive;* religiously, to *reverence:*—(moved with) fear.

2126. **εὐλαβής ĕulabēs**, *yoo-lab-ace';* from *2095* and *2983; taking well* (*carefully*), i.e. *circumspect* (religiously, *pious*):—devout.

2127. **εὐλογέω ĕulŏgĕō**, *yoo-log-eh'-o;* from a comp. of *2095* and *3056;* to *speak well of*, i.e. (religiously) to *bless* (*thank* or *invoke a benediction upon, prosper*):—bless, praise.

2128. **εὐλογητός ĕulŏgētŏs**, *yoo-log-ay-tos';* from *2127; adorable:*—blessed.

2129. **εὐλογία ĕulŏgia**, *yoo-log-ee'-ah;* from the same as *2127; fine speaking*, i.e. *elegance of language; commendation* ("*eulogy*"), i.e. (reverentially) *adoration;* religiously, *benediction;* by impl. *consecration;* by extens. *benefit* or *largess:*—blessing (a matter of) bounty (× -tifully), fair speech.

2130. **εὐμετάδοτος ĕumĕtadŏtŏs**, *yoo-met-ad'-ot-os;* from *2095* and a presumed der. of *3330; good at imparting*, i.e. *liberal:*—ready to distribute.

2131. **Εὐνίκη Ĕunikē**, *yoo-nee'-kay;* from *2095* and *3529; victorious; Eunice*, a Jewess:—Eunice.

2132. **εὐνόεω ĕunŏĕō**, *yoo-nŏ-eh'-o;* from a comp. of *2095* and *3563;* to *be well-minded*, i.e. *reconcile:*—agree.

2133. **εὔνοια ĕunŏia**, *yoo'-noy-ah;* from the same as *2132; kindness;* euphem. *conjugal duty:*—benevolence, good will.

2134. **εὐνουχίζω ĕunŏuchizō**, *yoo-noo-khid'-zo,* from *2135;* to *castrate* (fig. *live unmarried*):—make . . . eunuch.

2135. **εὐνοῦχος ĕunŏuchŏs**, *yoo-noo'-khos;* from **εὐνή ĕunē** (a *bed*) and *2192;* a *castrated* person (such being employed in Oriental bed-chambers); by extens. an *impotent* or *unmarried* man; by impl. a *chamberlain* (*state-officer*):—eunuch.

2136. **Εὐοδία Ĕuŏdia**, *yoo-od-ee'-ah;* from the same as *2137; fine travelling; Euodia*, a Chr. woman:—Euodias.

2137. **εὐοδόω ĕuŏdŏō**, *yoo-od-ŏ'-o;* from a comp. of *2095* and *3598;* to *help* on the *road*, i.e. (pass.) *succeed in reaching;* fig. to *succeed* in business affairs:—(have a) prosper (-ous journey).

2138. **εὐπειθής ĕupĕithēs**, *yoo-pi-thace';* from *2095* and *3982; good* for *persuasion*, i.e. (intrans.) *compliant:*—easy to be intreated.

2139. **εὐπερίστατος ĕupĕristatŏs**, *yoo-per-is'-tat-os;* from *2095* and a der. of a presumed comp. of *4012* and *2476; well standing around*, i.e. (a *competitor*) *thwarting* (a racer) in every direction (fig. of sin in gen.):—which doth so easily beset.

2140. **εὐποιΐα ĕupŏiia**, *yoo-poy-ee'-ah;* from a comp. of *2095* and *4160; well doing*, i.e. *beneficence:*—to do good.

2141. **εὐπορέω ĕupŏrĕō**, *yoo-por-eh'-o;* from a comp. of *2090* and the base of *4197;* (intrans.) to *be good* for *passing* through, i.e. (fig.) *have* pecuniary *means:*—ability.

2142. **εὐπορία ĕupŏria**, *yoo-por-ee'-ah;* from the same as *2141;* pecuniary *resources:*—wealth.

2143. **εὐπρέπεια ĕuprĕpĕia**, *yoo-prep'-i-ah;* from a comp. of *2095* and *4241;* *good suitableness,* i.e. *gracefulness:*—grace.

2144. **εὐπρόσδεκτος ĕuprŏsdĕktŏs**, *yoo-pros'-dek-tos;* from *2095* and a der. of *4327;* *well-received,* i.e. *approved, favorable:*—acceptable (-ted).

2145. **εὐπρόσεδρος ĕuprŏsĕdrŏs**, *yoo-pros'-ed-ros;* from *2095* and the same as *4332;* *sitting well towards,* i.e. (fig.) *assiduous* (neut. *diligent service*):—× attend upon.

2146. **εὐπροσωπέω ĕuprŏsōpĕō**, *yoo-pros-o-peh'-o;* from a comp. of *2095* and *4383;* *to be of good countenance,* i.e. (fig.) to *make a display:*—make a fair show.

2147. **εὑρίσκω hĕuriskō**, *hyoo-ris'-ko;* a prol. form of a prim.

εὕρω hĕurō, *hyoo'-ro;* which (together with another cognate form

εὑρέω hĕurĕō, *hyoo-reh'-o*) is used for it in all the tenses except the pres. and imperf.; to *find* (lit. or fig.):—find, get, obtain, perceive, see.

2148. **Εὐροκλύδων Ĕurŏkludōn**, *yoo-rok-loo'-dohn;* from **Εὖρος Ĕurŏs** (the *east* wind) and *2830;* a *storm from the East* (or S.E.), i.e. (in modern phrase) a *Levanter:*—Euroklydon.

2149. **εὐρύχωρος ĕuruchōrŏs**, *yoo-roo'-kho-ros;* from **εὐρύς ĕurus** (*wide*) and *5561;* *spacious:*—broad.

2150. **εὐσέβεια ĕusĕbĕia**, *yoo-seb'-i-ah;* from *2152;* *piety;* spec. the *gospel* scheme:—godliness, holiness.

2151. **εὐσεβέω ĕusĕbĕō**, *yoo-seb-eh'-o;* from *2152;* to *be pious,* i.e. (towards God) to *worship,* or (towards parents) to *respect* (*support*):—show piety, worship.

2152. **εὐσεβής ĕusĕbēs**, *yoo-seb-ace';* from *2095* and *4576;* *well-reverent,* i.e. *pious:*—devout, godly.

2153. **εὐσεβῶς ĕusĕbōs**, *yoo-seb-oce';* adv. from *2152;* *piously:*—godly.

2154. **εὔσημος ĕusēmŏs**, *yoo'-say-mos;* from *2095* and the base of *4591;* *well indicated,* i.e. (fig.) *significant:*—easy to be understood.

2155. **εὔσπλαγχνος ĕusplagchnŏs**, *yoo'-splangkh-nos;* from *2095* and *4698;* *well compassioned,* i.e. *sympathetic:*—pitiful, tender-hearted.

2156. **εὐσχημόνως ĕuschēmŏnōs**, *yoo-skhay-mon'-oce;* adv. from *2158;* *decorously:*—decently, honestly.

2157. **εὐσχημοσύνη ĕushēmŏsunē**, *yoo-skhay-mos-oo'-nay;* from *2158;* *decorousness:*—comeliness.

2158. **εὐσχήμων ĕuschēmōn**, *yoo-skhay'-mone;* from *2095* and *4976;* *well-formed,* i.e. (fig.) *decorous, noble* (in rank):—comely, honourable.

2159. **εὐτόνως ĕutŏnōs**, *yoo-ton'-oce;* adv. from a comp. of *2095* and a der. of **τείνω tĕinō** (to *stretch*); *in a well-strung manner,* i.e. (fig.) *intensely* (in a good sense, *cogently*; in a bad one, *fiercely*):—mightily, vehemently.

2160. **εὐτραπελία ĕutrapĕlia**, *yoo-trap-el-ee'-ah;* from a comp. of *2095* and a der. of the base of *5157* (mean. *well-turned,* i.e. *ready at repartee, jocose*); *witticism,* i.e. (in a vulgar sense) *ribaldry:*—jesting.

2161. **Εὔτυχος Ĕutuchŏs**, *yoo'-too-khos;* from *2095* and a der. of *5177;* *well-fated,* i.e. *fortunate;* *Eutychus,* a young man:—Eutychus.

2162. **εὐφημία ĕuphēmia**, *yoo-fay-mee'-ah;* from *2163;* *good language* ("*euphemy*"), i.e. *praise* (*repute*):—good report.

2163. **εὔφημος ĕuphēmŏs**, *yoo'-fay-mos;* from *2095* and *5345;* *well spoken of,* i.e. *reputable:*—of good report.

2164. **εὐφορέω ĕuphŏrĕō**, *yoo-for-eh'-o;* from *2095* and *5409;* to *bear well,* i.e. *be fertile:*—bring forth abundantly.

2165. **εὐφραίνω ĕuphrainō**, *yoo-frah'ee-no;* from *2095* and *5424;* to *put* (mid. or pass. *be*) *in a good* frame of *mind,* i.e. *rejoice:*—fare, make glad, be (make) merry, rejoice.

2166. **Εὐφράτης Ĕuphratēs**, *yoo-frat'-ace;* of for. or. [comp. 6578]; *Euphrates,* a river of Asia:—Euphrates.

2167. **εὐφροσύνη ĕuphrŏsunē**, *yoo-fros-oo'-nay;* from the same as *2165;* *joyfulness:*—gladness, joy.

2168. **εὐχαριστέω ĕucharistĕō**, *yoo-khar-is-teh'-o;* from *2170;* to *be grateful,* i.e. (act.) to *express gratitude* (towards); spec. to *say grace* at a meal:—(give) thank (-ful, -s).

2169. **εὐχαριστία ĕucharistia**, *yoo-khar-is-tee'-ah;* from *2170;* *gratitude;* act. *grateful language* (to God, as an act of worship):—thankfulness, (giving of) thanks (-giving).

2170. **εὐχάριστος ĕucharistŏs**, *yoo-khar'-is-tos;* from *2095* and a der. of *5483;* *well favored,* i.e. (by impl.) *grateful:*—thankful.

2171. **εὐχή ĕuchē**, *yoo-khay';* from *2172;* prop. a *wish,* expressed as a *petition* to God, or in *votive* obligation:—prayer, vow.

2172. **εὔχομαι ĕuchŏmai**, *yoo'-khom-ahee;* mid. of a prim. verb; to *wish;* by impl. to *pray* to God:—pray, will, wish.

2173. **εὔχρηστος ĕuchrēstŏs**, *yoo'-khrays-tos;* from *2095* and *5543;* *easily used,* i.e. *useful:*—profitable, meet for use.

2174. **εὐψυχέω ĕupsuchĕō**, *yoo-psoo-kheh'-o;* from a comp. of *2095* and *5590;* to *be in good spirits,* i.e. *feel encouraged:*—be of good comfort.

2175. **εὐωδία ĕuōdia**, *yoo-o-dee'-ah;* from a comp. of *2095* and a der. of *3605;* *good-scentedness,* i.e. *fragrance:*—sweet savour (smell, -smelling).

2176. **εὐώνυμος ĕuōnumŏs**, *yoo-o'-noo-mos;* from *2095* and *3686;* prop. *well-named* (*good-omened*), i.e. the *left* (which was the *lucky* side among the pagan Greeks); neut. as adv. *at the left* hand:—(on the) left.

2177. **ἐφάλλομαι ĕphallŏmai**, *ef-al'-lom-ahee;* from *1909* and *242;* to *spring upon:*—leap on.

2178. **ἐφάπαξ ĕphapax**, *ef-ap'-ax;* from *1909* and *530;* *upon one occasion* (only):—(at) once (for all).

2179. **Ἐφεσῖνος Ĕphĕsinŏs**, *ef-es-ee'-nos;* from *2181;* *Ephesine,* or situated at Ephesus:—of Ephesus.

2180. **Ἐφέσιος Ĕphĕsiŏs**, *ef-es'-ee-os;* from *2181;* an *Ephesian* or inhab. of Ephesus:—Ephesian, of Ephesus.

2181. **Ἔφεσος Ĕphĕsŏs**, *ef'-es-os;* prob. of for. or.; *Ephesus,* a city of Asia Minor:—Ephesus.

2182. **ἐφευρετής ĕphĕurĕtēs**, *ef-yoo-ret'-ace;* from a comp. of *1909* and *2147;* a *discoverer,* i.e. *contriver:*—inventor.

2183. **ἐφημερία ĕphēmĕria**, *ef-ay-mer-ee'-ah;* from *2184;* *diurnality,* i.e. (spec.) the quotidian *rotation* or *class* of the Jewish priests' service at the Temple, as distributed by families:—course.

2184. **ἐφήμερος ĕphēmĕrŏs**, *ef-ay'-mer-os;* from *1909* and *2250;* *for a day* ("ephemeral"), i.e. *diurnal:*—daily.

2185. **ἐφικνέομαι ĕphiknĕŏmai**, *ef-ik-neh'-om-ahee;* from *1909* and a cognate of *2240;* to *arrive upon,* i.e. *extend to:*—reach.

2186. **ἐφίστημι ĕphistēmi**, *ef-is'-tay-mee;* from *1909* and *2476;* to *stand upon,* i.e. *be present* (in various applications, friendly or otherwise, usually lit.):—assault, come (in, to, unto, upon), be at hand (instant), present, stand (before, by, over).

2187. **Ἐφραΐμ Ĕphraïm**, *ef-rah-im';* of Heb. or. [669 or better 6085]; *Ephraïm,* a place in Pal.:—Ephraim.

2188. **ἐφφαθά ĕphphatha**, *ef-fath-ah';* of Chald. or. [6606]; *be opened!:*—Ephphatha.

2189. **ἔχθρα ĕchthra**, *ekh'-thrah;* fem. of *2190;* *hostility;* by impl. a reason for *opposition:*—enmity, hatred.

2190. **ἐχθρός ĕchthrŏs**, *ekh-thros';* from a prim. **ἔχθω ĕchthō** (to *hate*); *hateful* (pass. *odious,* or act. *hostile*); usually as a noun, an *adversary* (espec. *Satan*):—enemy, foe.

2191. **ἔχιδνα ĕchidna**, *ekh'-id-nah;* of uncert. or.; an *adder* or other poisonous snake (lit. or fig.):—viper.

2192. **ἔχω ĕchō**, *ekh'-o* (includ. an alt. form

σχέω schĕō, *skheh'-o;* used in certain tenses only); a prim. verb; to *hold* (used in very various applications, lit. or fig., direct or remote; such as *possession, ability, contiguity, relation* or *condition*):—be (able, × hold, possessed with), accompany, + begin to amend, can (+ -not), × conceive, count, diseased, do, + eat, + enjoy, + fear, following, have, hold, keep, + lack, + go to law, lie, + must needs, + of necessity, + need, next, + recover, + reign, + rest, return, × sick, take for, + tremble, + uncircumcised, use.

2193. **ἕως hĕōs**, *heh'-oce;* of uncert. affin.; a conj., prep. and adv. of continuance, *until* (of time and place):—even (until, unto), (as) far (as), how long, (un-) til (-l), (hither-, un-, up) to, while (-s).

Z

2194. **Ζαβουλών Zabŏulōn**, *dzab-oo-lone';* of Heb. or. [2074]; *Zabulon* (i.e. *Zebulon*), a region of Pal.:—Zabulon.

2195. **Ζακχαῖος Zakchaiŏs**, *dzak-chah'ee-yos;* of Heb. or. [comp. 2140]; *Zacchæus,* an Isr.:—Zacchæus.

2196. **Ζαρά Zara**, *dzar-ah';* of Heb. or. [2226]; *Zara* (i.e. *Zerach*), an Isr.:—Zara.

2197. **Ζαχαρίας Zacharias**, *dzakh-ar-ee'-as;* of Heb. or. [2148]; *Zacharias* (i.e. *Zechariah*), the name of two Isr.:—Zacharias.

2198. **ζάω zaō**, *dzah'-o;* a prim. verb; to *live* (lit. or fig.):—life (-time), (a-) live (-ly), quick.

2199. **Ζεβεδαῖος Zĕbĕdaiŏs**, *dzeb-ed-ah'-yos;* of Heb. or. [comp. 2067]; *Zebedæus,* an Isr.:—Zebedee.

2200. **ζεστός zĕstŏs**, *dzes-tos';* from *2204;* *boiled,* i.e. (by impl.) *calid* (fig. *fervent*):—hot.

2201. **ζεῦγος zĕugŏs**, *dzyoo'-gos;* from the same as *2218;* a *couple,* i.e. a *team* (of oxen yoked together) or *brace* (of birds tied together):—yoke, pair.

2202. **ζευκτηρία zĕuktēria**, *dzyook-tay-ree'-ah;* fem. of a der. (at the second stage) from the same as *2218;* a *fastening* (*tiller-rope*):—band.

2203. **Ζεύς Zĕus**, *dzyooce;* of uncert. affin.; in the oblique cases there is used instead of it a (prob. cognate) name

Δίς Dis, *deece,* which is otherwise obsolete; *Zeus* or *Dis* (among the Latins *Jupiter* or *Jove*), the supreme deity of the Greeks:—Jupiter.

2204. **ζέω zĕō**, *dzeh'-o;* a prim. verb; to *be hot* (*boil,* of liquids; or *glow,* of solids), i.e. (fig.) *be fervid* (*earnest*):—be fervent.

2205. **ζῆλος zēlŏs**, *dzay'-los;* from *2204;* prop. *heat,* i.e. (fig.) "*zeal*" (in a favorable sense, *ardor;* in an unfavorable one, *jealousy,* as of a husband [fig. of God], or an *enemy, malice*):—emulation, envy (-ing), fervent mind, indignation, jealousy, zeal.

2206. **ζηλόω zēlŏō**, *dzay-lŏ'-o;* from *2205;* to *have warmth* of feeling for or against:—affect, covet (earnestly), (have) desire, (move with) envy, be jealous over, (be) zealous (-ly affect).

2207. **ζηλωτής zēlōtēs**, *dzay-lo-tace';* from *2206;* a "*zealot*":—zealous.

2208. **Ζηλωτής Zēlōtēs**, *dzay-lo-tace';* the same as *2208;* a *Zealot,* i.e. (spec.) *partisan* for Jewish political independence:—Zelotes.

2209. **ζημία zēmia**, *dzay-mee'-ah;* prob. akin to the base of *1150* (through the idea of *violence*); *detriment:*—damage, loss.

2210. **ζημιόω zēmiŏō**, *dzay-mee-ŏ'-o;* from *2209;* to *injure,* i.e. (reflex. or pass.) to *experience detriment:*—be cast away, receive damage, lose, suffer loss.

2211. **Ζηνᾶς Zēnas**, *dzay-nas';* prob. contr. from a poetic form of *2203* and *1435;* *Jove-given;* *Zenas,* a Chr.:—Zenas.

2212. **ζητέω zētĕō**, *dzay-teh'-o;* of uncert. affin.; to *seek* (lit. or fig.); spec. (by Heb.) to *worship* (God), or (in a bad sense) to *plot* (against life):—be (go) about, desire, endeavour, enquire (for), require, (× will) seek (after, for, means). Comp. *4441.*

2213. ζήτημα **zētēma**, *dzay'-tay-mah;* from 2212; a *search* (prop. concr.), i.e. (in words) a *debate:*—question.

2214. ζήτησις **zētēsis**, *dzay'-tay-sis;* from 2212; a *searching* (prop. the act), i.e. a *dispute* or its *theme:*—question.

2215. ζιζάνιον **zizaniŏn**, *dziz-an'-ee-on;* of uncert. or.; *darnel* or false grain:—tares.

2216. Ζοροβάβελ **Zŏrŏbabĕl**, *dzor-ob-ab'-el;* of Heb. or. [2216]; *Zorobabel* (i.e. *Zerubbabel*), an Isr.:—Zorobabel.

2217. ζόφος **zŏphŏs**, *dzof'-os;* akin to the base of 3509; *gloom* (as shrouding like a *cloud*):—blackness, darkness, mist.

2218. ζυγός **zugŏs**, *dzoo-gos';* from the root of ζεύγνυμι **zĕugnumi** (to *join*, espec. by a "yoke"); a *coupling*, i.e. (fig.) *servitude* (a law or *obligation*); also (lit.) the *beam* of the balance (as *connecting* the scales):—pair of balances, yoke.

2219. ζύμη **zumē**, *dzoo'-may;* prob. from 2204; *ferment* (as if *boiling* up):—leaven.

2220. ζυμόω **zumŏō**, *dzoo-mŏ'-o;* from 2219; to *cause to ferment:*—leaven.

2221. ζωγρέω **zōgrĕō**, *dzogue-reh'-o;* from the same as 2226 and 64; to *take alive* (*make a prisoner of war*), i.e. (fig.) to *capture* or *ensnare:*—take captive, catch.

2222. ζωή **zōē**, *dzo-ay';* from 2198; *life* (lit. or fig.):—life (-time). Comp. 5590.

2223. ζώνη **zōnē**, *dzo'-nay;* prob. akin to the base of 2218; a *belt;* by impl. a *pocket:*—girdle, purse.

2224. ζώννυμι **zōnnumi**, *dzone'-noo-mi;* from 2223; to *bind about* (espec. with a belt):—gird.

2225. ζωογονέω **zōŏgŏnĕō**, *dzo-og-on-eh'-o;* from the same as 2226 and a der. of 1096; to *engender alive* i.e. (by anal.) to *rescue* (pass. *be saved*) from death:—live, preserve.

2226. ζῶον **zōŏn**, *dzo'-on;* neut. of a der. of 2198; a *live* thing, i.e. an *animal:*—beast.

2227. ζωοποιέω **zōŏpŏiĕō**, *dzo-op-oy-eh'-o;* from the same as 2226 and 4160; to (*re-*) *vitalize* (lit. or fig.):—make alive, give life, quicken.

H

2228. ἤ **ē**, *ay;* a prim. particle of distinction between two connected terms; disjunctive, *or;* comparative, *than:*—and, but (either), (n-) either, except it be, (n-) or (else), rather, save, than, that, what, yea. Often used in connection with other particles. Comp. especially 2235, 2260, 2273.

2229. ἦ **ē**, *ay;* an adv. of *confirmation;* perh. intens. of 2228; used only (in the N. T.) before 3303; *assuredly:*—surely.

ἡ **hē**. See 3588.

ἧ **hē**. See 3739.

ᾖ $ē_1$. See 5600.

2230. ἡγεμονεύω **hēgĕmŏnĕuō**, *hayg-em-on-yoo'-o;* from 2232; to *act as ruler:*—be governor.

2231. ἡγεμονία **hēgĕmŏnia**, *hayg-em-on-ee'-ah;* from 2232; *government*, i.e. (in time) official *term:*—reign.

2232. ἡγεμών **hēgĕmōn**, *hayg-em-ohn';* from 2233; a *leader*, i.e. *chief* person (or fig. place) of a province:—governor, prince, ruler.

2233. ἡγέομαι **hēgĕŏmai**, *hayg-eh'-om-ahee;* mid. of a (presumed) strengthened form of 71; to *lead*, i.e. *command* (with official authority); fig. to *deem*, i.e. *consider:*—account, (be) chief, count, esteem, governor, judge, have the rule over, suppose, think.

2234. ἡδέως **hēdĕōs**, *hay-deh'-oce;* adv. from a der. of the base of 2237; *sweetly*, i.e. (fig.) *with pleasure:*—gladly.

2235. ἤδη **ēdē**, *ay'-day;* appar. from 2228 (or possibly 2229) and 1211; *even now:*—already, (even) now (already), by this time.

2236. ἥδιστα **hēdista**, *hay'-dis-tah;* neut. plur. of the superl. of the same as 2234; *with great pleasure:*—most (very) gladly.

2237. ἡδονή **hēdŏnē**, *hay-don-ay';* from ἁνδάνω **handanō** (to *please*); sensual *delight;* by impl. *desire:*—lust, pleasure.

2238. ἡδύοσμον **hēduŏsmŏn**, *hay-doo'-os-mon;* neut. of a comp. of the same as 2234 and 3744; a *sweet-scented* plant, i.e. *mint:*—mint.

2239. ἦθος **ēthŏs**, *ay'-thos;* a strengthened form of 1485; *usage*, i.e. (plur.) moral *habits:*—manners.

2240. ἥκω **hēkō**, *hay'-ko;* a prim. verb; to *arrive*, i.e. *be present* (lit. or fig.):—come.

2241. ἠλί **ēli**, *ay-lee';* of Heb. or. [410 with pron. suffix]; *my God:*—Eli.

2242. Ἡλί **Hēli**, *hay-lee';* of Heb. or. [5941]; *Heli* (i.e. *Eli*), an Isr.:—Heli.

2243. Ἡλίας **Hēlias**, *hay-lee'-as;* of Heb. or. [452]; *Helias* (i.e. *Elijah*), an Isr.:—Elias.

2244. ἡλικία **hēlikia**, *hay-lik-ee'-ah;* from the same as 2245; *maturity* (in years or size):—age, stature.

2245. ἡλίκος **hēlikŏs**, *hay-lee'-kos;* from ἧλιξ **hēlix** (a *comrade*, i.e. one of the same age); *as big as*, i.e. (interjectively) *how much:*—how (what) great.

2246. ἥλιος **hēliŏs**, *hay'-lee-os;* from ἕλη **hĕlē** (a *ray;* perh. akin to the alt. of 138); the *sun;* by impl. *light:*—+ east, sun.

2247. ἧλος **hēlŏs**, *hay'-los;* of uncert. affin.; a *stud*, i.e. *spike:*—nail.

2248. ἡμᾶς **hēmas**, *hay-mas';* acc. plur. of 1473; *us:*—our, us, we.

2249. ἡμεῖς **hēmĕis**, *hay-mice';* nom. plur. of 1473; *we* (only used when emphatic):—us, we (ourselves).

2250. ἡμέρα **hēmĕra**, *hay-mer'-ah;* fem. (with 5610 implied) of a der. of ἧμαι **hēmai** (to *sit;* akin to the base of 1476) mean. *tame*, i.e. *gentle; day*, i.e. (lit.) the time space between dawn and dark, or the whole 24 hours (but several days were usually reckoned by the Jews as inclusive of the parts of both extremes); fig. a *period* (always defined more or less clearly by the context):—age, + alway, (mid-) day (by day, [-ly]), + for ever, judgment, (day) time, while, years.

2251. ἡμέτερος **hēmĕtĕrŏs**, *hay-met'-er-os;* from 2349; *our:*—our, your [*by a different reading*].

2252. ἤμην **ēmēn**, *ay'-mane;* a prol. form of 2358; I *was:*—be, was. [*Sometimes unexpressed.*]

2253. ἡμιθανής **hēmithanēs**, *hay-mee-than-ace';* from a presumed comp. of the base of 2255 and 2348; *half dead*, i.e. *entirely exhausted:*—half dead.

2254. ἡμῖν **hēmin**, *hay-meen';* dat. plur. of 1473; *to* (or *for, with, by*) *us:*—our, (for) us, we.

2255. ἥμισυ **hēmisu**, *hay'-mee-soo;* neut. of a der. from an inseparable pref. akin to 260 (through the idea of *partition* involved in *connection*) and mean. *semi-;* (as noun) *half:*—half.

2256. ἡμιώριον **hēmiōriŏn**, *hay-mee-o'-ree-on;* from the base of 2255 and 5610; a *half-hour:*—half an hour.

2257. ἡμῶν **hēmōn**, *hay-mone';* gen. plur. of 1473; *of* (or *from*) *us:*—our (company), us, we.

2258. ἦν **ēn**, *ane;* imperf. of 1510; *I* (*thou*, etc.) *was* (*wast* or *were*):—+ agree, be, × have (+ charge of), hold, use, was (-t), were.

2259. ἡνίκα **hēnika**, *hay-nee'-kah;* of uncert. affin.; *at which time:*—when.

2260. ἤπερ **ēpĕr**, *ay'-per;* from 2228 and 4007; *than at all* (or *than perhaps, than indeed*):—than.

2261. ἤπιος **ēpiŏs**, *ay'-pee-os;* prob. from 2031; prop. *affable*, i.e. *mild* or *kind:*—gentle.

2262. Ἤρ **Ēr**, *ayr;* of Heb. or. [6147]; *Er*, an Isr.:—Er.

2263. ἤρεμος **ērĕmŏs**, *ay'-rem-os;* perh. by transposition from 2048 (through the idea of *stillness*); *tranquil:*—quiet.

2264. Ἡρώδης **Hērōdēs**, *hay-ro'-dace;* comp. of ἥρως **hērōs** (a "*hero*") and 1491; *heroic; Herodes*, the name of four Jewish kings:—Herod.

2265. Ἡρωδιανοί **Hērōdianŏi**, *hay-ro-dee-an-oy';* plur. of a der. of 2264; *Herodians*, i.e. partisans of Herodes:—Herodians.

2266. Ἡρωδιάς **Hērōdias**, *hay-ro-dee-as';* from 2264; *Herodias*, a woman of the Herodian family:—Herodias.

2267. Ἡρωδίων **Hērōdiōn**, *hay-ro-dee'-ohn;* from 2264; *Herodion*, a Chr.:—Herodion.

2268. Ἡσαΐας **Hēsaïas**, *hay-sah-ee'-as;* of Heb. or. [3470]; *Hesaias* (i.e. *Jeshajah*), an Isr.:—Esaias.

2269. Ἠσαῦ **Ēsau**, *ay-sŏw';* of Heb. or. [6215]; *Esau*, an Edomite:—Esau.

2270. ἡσυχάζω **hēsuchazō**, *hay-soo-khad'-zo;* from the same as 2272; to *keep still* (intrans.), i.e. *refrain* from labor, meddlesomeness or speech:—cease, hold peace, be quiet, rest.

2271. ἡσυχία **hēsuchia**, *hay-soo-khee'-ah;* fem. of 2272; (as noun) *stillness*, i.e. desistance from bustle or language:—quietness, silence.

2272. ἡσύχιος **hēsuchiŏs**, *hay-soo'-khee-os;* a prol. form of a comp. prob. of a der. of the base of 1476 and perh. 2192; prop. *keeping* one's *seat* (*sedentary*), i.e. (by impl.) *still* (*undisturbed, undisturbing*):—peaceable, quiet.

2273. ἤτοι **ētŏi**, *ay'-toy;* from 2228 and 5104; *either indeed:*—whether.

2274. ἡττάω **hēttaō**, *hayt-tah'-o;* from the same as 2276; to *make worse*, i.e. *vanquish* (lit. or fig.); by impl. to *rate lower:*—be inferior, overcome.

2275. ἥττημα **hēttēma**, *hayt'-tay-mah;* from 2274; a *deterioration*, i.e. (obj.) *failure* or (subj.) *loss:*—diminishing, fault.

2276. ἧττον **hēttŏn**, *hate'-ton;* neut. of comp. of ἧκα **hēka** (*slightly*) used for that of 2556; *worse* (as noun); by impl. *less* (as adv.):—less, worse.

2277. ἤτω **ētō**, *ay'-to;* third pers. sing. imperative of 1510; *let him* (or *it*) *be:*—let . . . be.

2278. ἠχέω **ēchĕō**, *ay-kheh'-o;* from 2279; to *make* a loud *noise*, i.e. *reverberate:*—roar, sound.

2279. ἦχος **ēchŏs**, *ay'-khos;* of uncert. affin.; a loud or confused *noise* ("*echo*"), i.e. *roar;* fig. a *rumor:*—fame, sound.

Θ

2280. Θαδδαῖος **Thaddaiŏs**, *thad-dah'-yos;* of uncert. or.; *Thaddæus*, one of the Apostles:—Thaddæus.

2281. θάλασσα **thalassa**, *thal'-as-sah;* prob. prol. from 251; the *sea* (gen. or spec.):—sea.

2282. θάλπω **thalpō**, *thal'-po;* prob. akin to θάλλω **thallō** (to *warm*); to *brood*, i.e. (fig.) to *foster:*—cherish.

2283. Θάμαρ **Thamar**, *tham'-ar;* of Heb. or. [8559]; *Thamar* (i.e. *Tamar*), an Israelitess:—Thamar.

2284. θαμβέω **thambĕō**, *tham-beh'-o;* from 2285; to *stupefy* (with surprise), i.e. *astound:*—amaze, astonish.

2285. θάμβος **thambŏs**, *tham'-bos;* akin to an obsol. τάφω **taphō** (to *dumbfound*); *stupefaction* (by surprise), i.e. *astonishment:*—× amazed, + astonished, wonder.

2286. θανάσιμος **thanasimŏs**, *than-as'-ee-mos;* from 2288; *fatal*, i.e. *poisonous:*—deadly.

2287. θανατήφορος **thanatēphŏrŏs**, *than-at-ay'-for-os;* from (the fem. form of) 2288 and 5342; *death-bearing*, i.e. *fatal:*—deadly.

2288. θάνατος **thanatŏs**, *than'-at-os;* from 2348; (prop. an adj. used as a noun) *death* (lit. or fig.):—× deadly, (be . . .) death.

2289. θανατόω **thanatŏō**, *than-at-ŏ'-o;* from 2288; to *kill* (lit. or fig.):—become dead, (cause to be) put to death, kill, mortify.

θάνω **thanō**. See 2348.

2290. θάπτω **thaptō**, *thap'-to;* a prim. verb; to *celebrate funeral rites*, i.e. *inter:*—bury.

2291. Θάρα **Thara**, *thar'-ah;* of Heb. or. [8646]; *Thara* (i.e. *Terach*), the father of Abraham:—Thara.

2292. θαῤῥέω **tharrhĕō**, *thar-hreh'-o;* another form for *2293;* to *exercise courage:*—be bold, × boldly, have confidence, be confident. Comp. *5111.*

2293. θαρσέω **tharsĕō**, *thar-seh'-o;* from *2294;* to *have courage:*—be of good cheer (comfort). Comp. *2292.*

2294. θάρσος **tharsŏs**, *thar'-sos;* akin (by transp.) to θράσος **thrasŏs** (*daring*); *boldness* (subj.):—courage.

2295. θαῦμα **thauma**, *thŏw'-mah;* appar. from a form of *2300;* *wonder* (prop. concr.; but by impl. abstr.):—admiration.

2296. θαυμάζω **thaumazō**, *thŏu-mad'-zo;* from *2295;* to *wonder;* by impl. to *admire:*—admire, have in admiration, marvel, wonder.

2297. θαυμάσιος **thaumasiŏs**, *thŏw-mas'-ee-os;* from *2295;* *wondrous,* i.e. (neut. as noun) a *miracle:*—wonderful thing.

2298. θαυμαστός **thaumastŏs**, *thŏw-mas-tos';* from *2296;* *wondered* at, i.e. (by impl.) *wonderful:*—marvel (-lous).

2299. θεά **thĕa**, *theh-ah';* fem. of *2316;* a female *deity:*—goddess.

2300. θεάομαι **thĕaŏmai**, *theh-ah'-om-ahee;* a prol. form of a prim. verb; to *look* closely at, i.e. (by impl.) to *perceive* (lit. or fig.); by extens. to *visit:*—behold, look (upon), see. Comp. *3700.*

2301. θεατρίζω **thĕatrizō**, *theh-at-rid'-zo;* from *2302;* to *expose as a spectacle:*—make a gazing stock.

2302. θέατρον **thĕatrŏn**, *theh'-at-ron;* from *2300;* *a place for public show* ("theatre"), i.e. general *audience-room;* by impl. a *show* itself (fig.):—spectacle, theatre.

2303. θεῖον **thĕiŏn**, *thi'-on;* prob. neut. of *2304* (in its or. sense of *flashing*); *sulphur:*—brimstone.

2304. θεῖος **thĕiŏs**, *thi'-os;* from *2316;* *godlike* (neut. as noun, *divinity*):—divine, godhead.

2305. θειότης **thĕiŏtēs**, *thi-ot'-ace;* from *2304;* *divinity* (abstr.):—godhead.

2306. θειώδης **thĕiōdēs**, *thi-o'-dace;* from *2303* and *1491;* *sulphur-like,* i.e. *sulphurous:*—brimstone.

θελέω **thĕlĕō**. See *2309.*

2307. θέλημα **thĕlēma**, *thel'-ay-mah;* from the prol. form of *2309;* a *determination* (prop. the thing), i.e. (act.) *choice* (spec. *purpose, decree;* abstr. *volition*) or (pass.) *inclination:*—desire, pleasure, will.

2308. θέλησις **thĕlēsis**, *thel'-ay-sis;* from *2309;* *determination* (prop. the act), i.e. *option:*—will.

2309. θέλω **thĕlō**, *thel'-o;* or ἐθέλω **ĕthĕlō**, *eth-el'-o;* in certain tenses θελέω **thĕlĕō**, *thel-eh'-o;* and ἐθελέω **ĕthĕlĕō**, *eth-el-eh'-o,* which are otherwise obsol.; appar. strengthened from the alt. form of *138;* to *determine* (as an act. *option* from subj. impulse; whereas *1014* prop. denotes rather a pass. *acquiescence* in obj. considerations), i.e., *choose* or *prefer* (lit. or fig.); by impl. to *wish,* i.e. *be inclined* to (sometimes adv. *gladly*); impers. for the fut. tense, to *be about to;* by Heb. to *delight in:*—desire, be disposed (forward), intend, list, love, mean, please, have rather, (be) will (have, -ling, -ling [ly]).

2310. θεμέλιος **thĕmĕliŏs**, *them-el'-ee-os;* from a der. of *5087;* something *put* down, i.e. a *substruction* (of a building, etc.), (lit. or fig.):—foundation.

2311. θεμελιόω **thĕmĕliŏō**, *them-el-ee-ŏ'-o;* from *2310;* to *lay a basis* for, i.e. (lit.) *erect,* or (fig.) *consolidate:*—(lay the) found (-ation), ground, settle.

2312. θεοδίδακτος **thĕŏdidaktŏs**, *theh-od-id'-ak-tos;* from *2316* and *1321;* *divinely instructed:*—taught of God.

2312'. θεολόγος **thĕŏlŏgŏs**, *theh-ol-og'-os;* from *2316* and *3004;* a "*theologian*":—divine.

2313. θεομαχέω **thĕŏmachĕō**, *theh-o-makh-eh'-o;* from *2314;* to *resist deity:*—fight against God.

2314. θεόμαχος **thĕŏmachŏs**, *theh-om'-akh-os;* from *2316* and *3164;* an *opponent of deity:*—to fight against God.

2315. θεόπνευστος **thĕŏpnĕustŏs**, *theh-op'-nyoo-stos;* from *2316* and a presumed der. of *4154;* *divinely breathed* in:—given by inspiration of God.

2316. θεός **thĕŏs**, *theh'-os;* of uncert. affin.; a *deity,* espec. (with *3588*) the supreme *Divinity;* fig. a *magistrate;* by Heb. *very:*— × exceeding, God, god [-ly, -ward].

2317. θεοσέβεια **thĕŏsĕbĕia**, *theh-os-eb'-i-ah;* from *2318;* *devoutness,* i.e. *piety:*—godliness.

2318. θεοσεβής **thĕŏsĕbēs**, *theh-os-eb-ace';* from *2316* and *4576;* *reverent of God,* i.e. *pious:*—worshipper of God.

2319. θεοστυγής **thĕŏstugēs**, *theh-os-too-gace';* from *2316* and the base of *4767;* *hateful to God,* i.e. *impious:*—hater of God.

2320. θεότης **thĕŏtēs**, *theh-ot'-ace;* from *2316;* *divinity* (abstr.):—godhead.

2321. Θεόφιλος **Thĕŏphilŏs**, *theh-of'-il-os;* from *2316* and *5384;* *friend of God;* *Theophilus,* a Chr.:—Theophilus.

2322. θεραπεία **thĕrapĕia**, *ther-ap-i'-ah;* from *2323;* *attendance* (spec. medical, i.e. *cure*); fig. and collec. *domestics:*—healing, household.

2323. θεραπεύω **thĕrapĕuō**, *ther-ap-yoo'-o;* from the same as *2324;* to *wait upon* menially, i.e. (fig.) to *adore* (God), or (spec.) to *relieve* (of disease):—cure, heal, worship.

2324. θεράπων **thĕrapōn**, *ther-ap'-ohn;* appar. a part. from an otherwise obsol. der. of the base of *2330;* a menial *attendant* (as if *cherishing*):—servant.

2325. θερίζω **thĕrizō**, *ther-id'-zo;* from *2330* (in the sense of the *crop*); to *harvest:*—reap.

2326. θερισμός **thĕrismŏs**, *ther-is-mos';* from *2325;* *reaping,* i.e. the *crop:*—harvest.

2327. θεριστής **thĕristēs**, *ther-is-tace';* from *2325;* a *harvester:*—reaper.

2328. θερμαίνω **thĕrmainō**, *ther-mah'ee-no;* from *2329;* to *heat* (oneself):—(be) warm (-ed, self).

2329. θέρμη **thĕrmē**, *ther'-may;* from the base of *2330;* *warmth:*—heat.

2330. θέρος **thĕrŏs**, *ther'-os;* from a prim. θέρω **thĕrō** (to *heat*); prop. *heat,* i.e. *summer:*—summer.

2331. Θεσσαλονικεύς **Thĕssalŏnikĕus**, *thes-sal-on-ik-yoos';* from *2332;* a *Thessalonican,* i.e. inhab. of Thessalonice:—Thessalonian.

2332. Θεσσαλονίκη **Thĕssalŏnikē**, *thes-sal-on-ee'-kay;* from Θεσσαλός **Thĕssalŏs** (a *Thessalian*) and *3529;* *Thessalonice,* a place in Asia Minor:—Thessalonica.

2333. Θευδᾶς **Thĕudas**, *thyoo-das';* of uncert. or.; *Theudas,* an Isr.:—Theudas.

θέω **thĕō**. See *5087.*

2334. θεωρέω **thĕōrĕō**, *theh-o-reh'-o;* from a der. of *2300* (perh. by add. of *3708*); to *be a spectator* of, i.e. *discern,* (lit., fig. [*experience*] or intens. [*acknowledge*]):—behold, consider, look on, perceive, see. Comp. *3700.*

2335. θεωρία **thĕōria**, *theh-o-ree'-ah;* from the same as *2334;* *spectatorship,* i.e. (concr.) a *spectacle:*—sight.

2336. θήκη **thēkē**, *thay'-kay;* from *5087;* a *receptacle,* i.e. *scabbard:*—sheath.

2337. θηλάζω **thēlazō**, *thay-lad'-zo;* from θηλή **thēlē** (the *nipple*); to *suckle;* by impl. to *suck:*—(give) suck (-ling).

2338. θῆλυς **thēlus**, *thay'-loos;* from the same as *2337;* *female:*—female, woman.

2339. θήρα **thēra**, *thay'-rah;* from θήρ **thēr** (a wild *animal,* as *game*); *hunting,* i.e. (fig.) *destruction:*—trap.

2340. θηρεύω **thērĕuō**, *thay-ryoo'-o;* from *2339;* to *hunt* (an animal), i.e. (fig.) to *carp at:*—catch.

2341. θηριομαχέω **thēriŏmachĕō**, *thay-ree-om-akh-eh'-o;* from a comp. of *2342* and *3164;* to *be a beast-fighter* (in the gladiatorial show), i.e. (fig.) to *encounter* (furious men):—fight with wild beasts.

2342. θηρίον **thēriŏn**, *thay-ree'-on;* dimin. from the same as *2339;* a *dangerous animal:*—(venomous, wild) beast.

2343. θησαυρίζω **thēsaurizō**, *thay-sŏw-rid'-zo;* from *2344;* to *amass* or *reserve* (lit. or fig.):—lay up (treasure), (keep) in store, (heap) treasure (together, up).

2344. θησαυρός **thēsaurŏs**, *thay-sow-ros';* from *5087;* a *deposit,* i.e. *wealth* (lit. or fig.):—treasure.

2345. θιγγάνω **thigganō**, *thing-gan'-o;* a prol. form of an obsol. prim. θίγω **thigō** (to *finger*); to *manipulate,* i.e. *have to do with;* by impl. to *injure:*—handle, touch.

2346. θλίβω **thlibō**, *thlee'-bo;* akin to the base of *5147;* to *crowd* (lit. or fig.):—afflict, narrow, throng, suffer tribulation, trouble.

2347. θλίψις **thlipsis**, *thlip'-sis;* from *2346;* *pressure* (lit. or fig.):—afflicted (-tion), anguish, burdened, persecution, tribulation, trouble.

2348. θνήσκω **thnēskō**, *thnay'-sko;* a strengthened form of a simpler prim. θάνω **thanō**, *than'-o* (which is used for it only in certain tenses); to *die* (lit. or fig.):—be dead, die.

2349. θνητός **thnētŏs**, *thnay-tos';* from *2348;* *liable to die:*—mortal (-ity).

2350. θορυβέω **thŏrubĕō**, *thor-oo-beh'-o;* from *2351;* to *be in tumult,* i.e. *disturb, clamor:*—make ado (a noise), trouble self, set on an uproar.

2351. θόρυβος **thŏrubŏs**, *thor'-oo-bos;* from the base of *2360;* a *disturbance:*—tumult, uproar.

2352. θραύω **thrauō**, *thrŏw'-o;* a prim. verb; to *crush:*—bruise. Comp. *4486.*

2353. θρέμμα **thrĕmma**, *threm'-mah;* from *5142;* *stock* (as *raised* on a farm):—cattle.

2354. θρηνέω **thrēnĕō**, *thray-neh'-o;* from *2355;* to *bewail:*—lament, mourn.

2355. θρῆνος **thrēnŏs**, *thray'-nos;* from the base of *2360;* *wailing:*—lamentation.

2356. θρησκεία **thrēskĕia**, *thrace-ki'-ah;* from a der. of *2357;* ceremonial *observance:*—religion, worshipping.

2357. θρῆσκος **thrēskŏs**, *thrace'-kos;* prob. from the base of *2360;* *ceremonious* in worship (as *demonstrative*), i.e. *pious:*—religious.

2358. θριαμβεύω **thriambĕuō**, *three-am-byoo'-o;* from a prol. comp. of the base of *2360* and a der. of *680* (mean. a *noisy iambus,* sung in honor of Bacchus); to *make an acclamatory procession,* i.e. (fig.) to *conquer* or (by Hebr.) to *give victory:*—(cause) to triumph (over).

2359. θρίξ **thrix**, *threeks;* gen. τριχός **trichŏs**, etc.; of uncert. der.; *hair:*—hair. Comp. *2864.*

2360. θροέω **thrŏĕō**, *thrŏ-eh'-o;* from θρέομαι **thrĕŏmai** (to *wail*); to *clamor,* i.e. (by impl.) to *frighten:*—trouble.

2361. θρόμβος **thrŏmbŏs**, *throm'-bos;* perh. from *5142* (in the sense of *thickening*); a *clot:*—great drop.

2362. θρόνος **thrŏnŏs**, *thron'-os;* from θράω **thraō** (to *sit*); a stately *seat* ("*throne*"); by impl. *power* or (concr.) a *potentate:*—seat, throne.

2363. Θυάτειρα **Thuatĕira**, *thoo-at'-i-rah;* of uncert. der.; *Thyatira,* a place in Asia Minor:—Thyatira.

2364. θυγάτηρ **thugatēr**, *thoo-gat'-air;* appar. a prim. word [comp. "daughter"]; a *female child,* or (by Hebr.) *descendant* (or *inhabitant*):—daughter.

2365. θυγάτριον **thugatriŏn**, *thoo-gat'-ree-on;* from *2364;* a *daughterling:*—little (young) daughter.

2366. θύελλα **thuĕlla**, *thoo'-el-lah;* from *2380* (in the sense of *blowing*) a storm:—tempest.

2367. θύϊνος **thuinŏs**, *thoo'-ee-nos;* from a der. of *2380* (in the sense of *blowing;* denoting a certain *fragrant* tree); made of *citron*-wood:—thyine.

2368. θυμίαμα **thumiama**, *thoo-mee'-am-ah;* from *2370;* an *aroma,* i.e. fragrant *powder* burnt in religious service; by impl. the *burning* itself:—incense, odour.

2369. θυμιαστήριον **thumiastēriŏn**, *thoo-mee-as-tay'-ree-on;* from a der. of *2370;* a *place of fumigation,* i.e. the *altar of incense* (in the Temple):—censer.

2370. θυμιάω **thumiaō**, *thoo-mee-ah'-o;* from a der. of *2380* (in the sense of *smoking*); to *fumigate*, i.e. *offer* aromatic *fumes:*—burn incense.

2371. θυμομαχέω **thumŏmachĕō**, *thoo-mom-akh-eh'-o;* from a presumed comp. of *2372* and *3164;* to *be in a furious fight*, i.e. (fig.) to *be exasperated:*—be highly displeased.

2372. θυμός **thumŏs**, *thoo-mos';* from *2380; passion* (as if *breathing* hard):—fierceness, indignation, wrath. Comp. *5590*.

2373. θυμόω **thumŏō**, *thoo-mŏ'-o;* from *2372;* to *put in a passion*, i.e. *enrage:*—be wroth.

2374. θύρα **thura**, *thoo'-rah;* appar. a prim. word [comp. "door"]; a *portal* or entrance (the opening or the closure, lit. or fig.):—door, gate.

2375. θυρεός **thurĕŏs**, *thoo-reh-os';* from *2374;* a large *shield* (as *door*-shaped):—shield.

2376. θυρίς **thuris**, *thoo-rece';* from *2374;* an *aperture*, i.e. *window:*—window.

2377. θυρωρός **thurōrŏs**, *thoo-ro-ros';* from *2374* and οὖρος **ŏurŏs** (a *watcher*); a *gate-warden:*—that kept the door, porter.

2378. θυσία **thusia**, *thoo-see'-ah;* from *2380; sacrifice* (the act or the victim, lit. or fig.):—sacrifice.

2379. θυσιαστήριον **thusiastēriŏn**, *thoo-see-as-tay'-ree-on;* from a der. of *2378;* a *place of sacrifice*, i.e. an *altar* (spec. or gen., lit. or fig.):—altar.

2380. θύω **thuō**, *thoo'-o;* a prim. verb; prop. to *rush* (*breathe* hard, *blow*, *smoke*), i.e. (by impl.) to *sacrifice* (prop. by fire, but gen.); by extens. to *immolate* (*slaughter* for any purpose):—kill, (do) sacrifice, slay.

2381. Θωμᾶς **Thōmas**, *tho-mas';* of Chald. or. [comp. 8380]; *the twin; Thomas*, a Chr.:—Thomas.

2382. θώραξ **thōrax**, *tho'-rax;* of uncert. affin.; the *chest* ("*thorax*"), i.e. (by impl.) a *corslet:*—breastplate.

I

2383. Ἰάειρος **Iaĕirŏs**, *ee-ah'-i-ros;* of Heb. or. [2971]; *Jăïrus* (i.e. *Jair*), an Isr.:—Jairus.

2384. Ἰακώβ **Iakōb**, *ee-ak-obe';* of Heb. or. [3290]; *Jacob* (i.e. *Ja'akob*), the progenitor of the Isr.; also an Isr.:—Jacob.

2385. Ἰάκωβος **Iakōbŏs**, *ee-ak'-o-bos;* the same as *2384* Græcized; *Jacobus*, the name of three Isr.:—James.

2386. ἴαμα **iama**, *ee'-am-ah;* from *2390;* a *cure* (the effect):—healing.

2387. Ἰαμβρῆς **Iambrēs**, *ee-am-brace';* of Eg. or.; *Jambres*, an Eg.:—Jambres.

2388. Ἰαννά **Ianna**, *ee-an-nah';* prob. of Heb. or. [comp. 3238]; *Janna*, an Isr.:—Janna.

2389. Ἰαννῆς **Iannēs**, *ee-an-nace';* of Eg. or.; *Jannes*, an Eg.:—Jannes.

2390. ἰάομαι **iaŏmai**, *ee-ah'-om-ahee;* mid. of appar. a prim. verb; to *cure* (lit. or fig.):—heal, make whole.

2391. Ἰάρεδ **Iarĕd**, *ee-ar'-ed;* of Heb. or. [3382]; *Jared* (i.e. *Jered*), an antediluvian:—Jared.

2392. ἴασις **iasis**, *ee'-as-is;* from *2390; curing* (the act):—cure, heal (-ing).

2393. ἴασπις **iaspis**, *ee'-as-pis;* prob. of for. or. [see 3471]; "*jasper*", a gem:—jasper.

2394. Ἰάσων **Iasōn**, *ee-as'-oan;* fut. act. part. masc. of *2390; about to cure; Jason*, a Chr.:—Jason.

2395. ἰατρός **iatrŏs**, *ee-at-ros';* from *2390;* a *physician:*—physician.

2396. ἴδε **idĕ**, *id'-eh;* second pers. sing. imper. act. of *1492;* used as interj. to denote *surprise; lo!:*—behold, lo, see.

2397. ἰδέα **idĕa**, *id-eh'-ah;* from *1492;* a *sight* [comp. fig. "idea"], i.e. *aspect:*—countenance.

2398. ἴδιος **idiŏs**, *id'-ee-os;* of uncert. affin.; *pertaining to self*, i.e. one's *own;* by impl. *private* or *separate:*— × his acquaintance, when they were alone, apart, aside, due, his (own, proper, several), home, (her, our, thine, your) own (business), private (-ly), proper, severally, their (own).

2399. ἰδιώτης **idiōtēs**, *id-ee-o'-tace;* from *2398;* a *private* person, i.e. (by impl.) an *ignoramus* (comp. "idiot"):—ignorant, rude, unlearned.

2400. ἰδού **idŏu**, *id-oo';* second pers. sing. imper. mid. of *1492;* used as imper. *lo!:*—behold, lo, see.

2401. Ἰδουμαία **Idŏumaia**, *id-oo-mah'-yah;* of Heb. or. [123]; *Idumæa* (i.e. *Edom*), a region E. (and S.) of Pal.:—Idumæa.

2402. ἱδρώς **hidrōs**, *hid-roce';* a strengthened form of a prim. ἴδος **idŏs** (*sweat*); *perspiration:*—sweat.

2403. Ἰεζαβήλ **Iĕzabēl**, *ee-ed-zab-ale';* of Heb. or. [348]; *Jezabel* (i.e. *Jezebel*), a Tyrian woman (used as a synonym of a termagant or false teacher):—Jezabel.

2404. Ἱεράπολις **Hiĕrapŏlis**, *hee-er-ap'-ol-is;* from *2413* and *4172; holy city; Hierapolis*, a place in Asia Minor:—Hierapolis.

2405. ἱερατεία **hiĕratĕia**, *hee-er-at-i'-ah;* from *2407; priestliness*, i.e. the *sacerdotal function:*—office of the priesthood, priest's office.

2406. ἱεράτευμα **hiĕratĕuma**, *hee-er-at'-yoo-mah;* from *2407;* the *priestly fraternity*, i.e. a *sacerdotal order* (fig.):—priesthood.

2407. ἱερατεύω **hiĕratĕuō**, *hee-er-at-yoo'-o;* prol. from *2409;* to *be a priest*, i.e. *perform his functions:*—execute the priest's office.

2408. Ἱερεμίας **Hiĕrĕmias**, *hee-er-em-ee'-as;* of Heb. or. [3414]; *Hieremias* (i.e. *Jermijah*), an Isr.:—Jeremiah.

2409. ἱερεύς **hiĕrĕus**, *hee-er-yooce';* from *2413;* a *priest* (lit. or fig.):—(high) priest.

2410. Ἱεριχώ **Hiĕrichō**, *hee-er-ee-kho';* of Heb. or. [3405]; *Jericho*, a place in Pal.:—Jericho.

2411. ἱερόν **hiĕrŏn**, *hee-er-on';* neut. of *2413;* a *sacred* place, i.e. the entire precincts (whereas *3485* denotes the central *sanctuary* itself) of the *Temple* (at Jerus. or elsewhere):—temple.

2412. ἱεροπρεπής **hiĕrŏprĕpēs**, *hee-er-op-rep-ace';* from *2413* and the same as *4241; reverent:*—as becometh holiness.

2413. ἱερός **hiĕrŏs**, *hee-er-os';* of uncert. affin.; *sacred:*—holy.

2414. Ἱεροσόλυμα **Hiĕrŏsŏluma**, *hee-er-os-ol'-oo-mah;* of Heb. or. [3389]; *Hierosolyma* (i.e. *Jerushalaïm*), the capital of Pal.:—Jerusalem. Comp. *2419*.

2415. Ἱεροσολυμίτης **Hiĕrŏsŏlumitēs**, *hee-er-os-ol-oo-mee'-tace;* from *2414;* a *Hierosolymite*, i.e. inhab. of Hierosolyma:—of Jerusalem.

2416. ἱεροσυλέω **hiĕrŏsulĕō**, *hee-er-os-ool-eh'-o;* from *2417;* to *be a temple-robber* (fig.):—commit sacrilege.

2417. ἱερόσυλος **hiĕrŏsulŏs**, *hee-er-os'-oo-los;* from *2411* and *4813;* a *temple-despoiler:*—robber of churches.

2418. ἱερουργέω **hiĕrŏurgĕō**, *hee-er-oorg-eh'-o;* from a comp. of *2411* and the base of *2041;* to *be a temple-worker*, i.e. *officiate as a priest* (fig.):—minister.

2419. Ἱερουσαλήμ **Hiĕrŏusalēm**, *hee-er-oo-sal-ame';* of Heb. or. [3389]; *Hierusalem* (i.e. *Jerushalem*), the capital of Pal.:—Jerusalem. Comp. *2414*.

2420. ἱερωσύνη **hiĕrōsunē**, *hee-er-o-soo'-nay;* from *2413; sacredness*, i.e. (by impl.) the *priestly office:*—priesthood.

2421. Ἰεσσαί **Iĕssai**, *es-es-sah'ee;* of Heb. or. [3448]; *Jessæ* (i.e. *Jishai*), an Irs.:—Jesse.

2422. Ἰεφθάε **Iĕphthaĕ**, *ee-ef-thah'-eh;* of Heb. or. [3316]; *Jephthaë* (i.e. *Jiphtach*), an Isr.:—Jephthah.

2423. Ἰεχονίας **Iĕchŏnias**, *ee-ekh-on-ee'-as;* of Heb. or. [3204]; *Jechonias* (i.e. *Jekonjah*), an Isr.:—Jechonias.

2424. Ἰησοῦς **Iēsŏus**, *ee-ay-sooce';* of Heb. or. [3091]; *Jesus* (i.e. *Jehoshua*), the name of our Lord and two (three) other Isr.:—Jesus.

2425. ἱκανός **hikanŏs**, *hik-an-os';* from ἵκω **hikō** [ἱκάνω or ἱκνέομαι, akin to *2240*] (to *arrive*): *competent* (as if *coming* in season), i.e. *ample* (in amount) or *fit* (in character):—able, + content, enough, good, great, large, long (while), many, meet, much, security, sore, sufficient, worthy.

2426. ἱκανότης **hikanŏtēs**, *hik-an-ot'-ace;* from *2425; ability:*—sufficiency.

2427. ἱκανόω **hikanŏō**, *hik-an-ŏ'-o;* from *2425;* to *enable*, i.e. *qualify:*—make able (meet).

2428. ἱκετηρία **hikĕtēria**, *hik-et-ay-ree'-ah;* from a der. of the base of *2425* (through the idea of *approaching* for a favor); *intreaty:*—supplication.

2429. ἰκμάς **hikmas**, *hik-mas';* of uncert. affin.; *dampness:*—moisture.

2430. Ἰκόνιον **Ikŏniŏn**, *ee-kon'-ee-on;* perh. from *1504; image-like; Iconium*, a place in Asia Minor:—Iconium.

2431. ἱλαρός **hilarŏs**, *hil-ar-os';* from the same as *2436; propitious* or *merry* ("*hilarious*"), i.e. *prompt* or *willing:*—cheerful.

2432. ἱλαρότης **hilarŏtēs**, *hil-ar-ot'-ace;* from *2431; alacrity:*—cheerfulness.

2433. ἱλάσκομαι **hilaskŏmai**, *hil-as'-kom-ahee;* mid. from the same as *2436;* to *conciliate*, i.e. (trans.) to *atone* for (sin), or (intrans.) *be propitious:*—be merciful, make reconciliation for.

2434. ἱλασμός **hilasmŏs**, *hil-as-mos'; atonement*, i.e. (concr.) an *expiator:*—propitiation.

2435. ἱλαστήριον **hilastēriŏn**, *hil-as-tay'-ree-on;* neut. of a der. of *2433;* an *expiatory* (place or thing), i.e. (concr.) an atoning *victim*, or (spec.) the *lid* of the Ark (in the Temple):—mercyseat, propitiation.

2436. ἵλεως **hilĕōs**, *hil'-eh-oce;* perh. from the alt. form of *138; cheerful* (as *attractive*), i.e. *propitious;* adv. (by Hebr.) God be *gracious!*, i.e. (in averting some calamity) *far* be it:—be it far, merciful.

2437. Ἰλλυρικόν **Illurikŏn**, *il-loo-ree-kon';* neut. of an adj. from a name of uncert. der.; (the) *Illyrican* (shore), i.e. (as a name itself) *Illyricum*, a region of Europe:—Illyricum.

2438. ἱμάς **himas**, *hee-mas';* perh. from the same as *260;* a *strap*, i.e. (spec.) the *tie* (of a sandal) or the *lash* (of a scourge):—latchet, thong.

2439. ἱματίζω **himatizō**, *him-at-id'-zo;* from *2440;* to *dress:*—clothe.

2440. ἱμάτιον **himatiŏn**, *him-at'-ee-on;* neut. of a presumed der. of ἕννυμι **ĕnnumi** (to *put on*); a *dress* (inner or outer):—apparel, cloke, clothes, garment, raiment, robe, vesture.

2441. ἱματισμός **himatismŏs**, *him-at-is-mos';* from *2439; clothing:*—apparel (× -led), array, raiment, vesture.

2442. ἱμείρομαι **himĕirŏmai**, *him-i'-rom-ahee;* mid. from ἵμερος **himĕrŏs** (a *yearning;* of uncert. affin); to *long for:*—be affectionately desirous.

2443. ἵνα **hina**, *hin'-ah;* prob. from the same as the former part of *1438* (through the *demonstrative* idea; comp. *3588*); in order *that* (denoting the *purpose* or the *result*):—albeit, because, to the intent (that), lest, so as, (so) that, (for) to. Comp. *3363*.

ἵνα μή **hina mē**. See *3363*.

2444. ἱνατί **hinati**, *hin-at-ee';* from *2443* and *5101; for what* reason ?, i.e. *why?:*—wherefore, why.

2445. Ἰόππη **Iŏppē**, *ee-op'-pay;* of Heb. or. [3305]; *Joppe* (i.e. *Japho*), a place in Pal.:—Joppa.

2446. Ἰορδάνης **Iŏrdanēs**, *ee-or-dan'-ace;* of Heb. or. [3383]; the *Jordanes* (i.e. *Jarden*), a river of Pal.:—Jordan.

2447. ἰός **iŏs**, *ee-os';* perh. from εἶμι **ĕimi** (to *go*) or ἵημι **hiēmi** (to *send*); *rust* (as if *emitted* by metals); also *venom* (as *emitted* by serpents):—poison, rust.

2448. Ἰουδά **Iŏuda**, *ee-oo-dah'*; of Heb. or. [3063 or perh. 3194]; *Judah* (i.e. *Jehudah* or *Juttah*), a part of (or place in) Pal.:—Judah.

2449. Ἰουδαία **Iŏudaia**, *ee-oo-dah'-yah*; fem. of *2453* (with *1093* impl.); the *Judæan* land (i.e. *Judæa*), a region of Pal.:—Judæa.

2450. Ἰουδαΐζω **Iŏudaizō**, *ee-oo-dah-id'-zo*; from *2453*; *to become a Judæan*, i.e. "*Judaize*":—live as the Jews.

2451. Ἰουδαϊκός **Iŏudaïkŏs**, *ee-oo-dah-ee-kos'*; from *2453*; *Judaïc*, i.e. *resembling a Judæan*:—Jewish.

2452. Ἰουδαϊκῶς **Iŏudaïkōs**, *ee-oo-dah-ee-koce'*; adv. from *2451*; *Judaïcally* or *in a manner resembling a Judæan*:—as do the Jews.

2453. Ἰουδαῖος **Iŏudaiŏs**, *ee-oo-dah'-yos*; from *2448* (in the sense of *2455* as a country); *Judæan*, i.e. belonging to *Jehudah*:—Jew (-ess), of Judæa.

2454. Ἰουδαϊσμός **Iŏudaismŏs**, *ee-oo-dah-is-mos'*; from *2450*; "*Judaïsm*", i.e. the *Jewish faith* and usages:—Jews' religion.

2455. Ἰουδάς **Iŏudas**, *ee-oo-das'*; of Heb. or. [3063]; *Judas* (i.e. *Jehudah*), the name of ten Isr.; also of the posterity of one of them and its region:—Juda (-h, -s); Jude.

2456. Ἰουλία **Iŏulia**, *ee-oo-lee'-ah*; fem. of the same as *2457*; *Julia*, a Chr. woman:—Julia.

2457. Ἰούλιος **Iŏuliŏs**, *ee-oo'-lee-os*; of Lat. or.; *Julius*, a centurion:—Julius.

2458. Ἰουνίας **Iŏunias**, *ee-oo-nee'-as*; of Lat. or.; *Junias*, a Chr.:—Junias.

2459. Ἰοῦστος **Iŏustŏs**, *ee-ooce'-tos*; of Lat. or. ("*just*"); *Justus*, the name of three Chr.:—Justus.

2460. ἱππεύς **hippĕus**, *hip-yooce'*; from *2462*; an *equestrian*, i.e. member of a *cavalry* corps:—horseman.

2461. ἱππικόν **hippikŏn**, *hip-pee-kon'*; neut. of a der. of *2462*; the *cavalry* force:—horse [-men].

2462. ἵππος **hippŏs**, *hip'-pos*; of uncert. affin.; a *horse*:—horse.

2463. ἶρις **iris**, *ee'-ris*; perh. from *2046* (as a symb. of the female *messenger* of the pagan deities); a *rainbow* ("*iris*"):—rainbow.

2464. Ἰσαάκ **Isaak**, *ee-sah-ak'*; of Heb. or. [3327]; *Isaac* (i.e. *Jitschak*), the son of Abraham:—Isaac.

2465. ἰσάγγελος **isaggĕlŏs**, *ee-sang'-el-los*; from *2470* and *32*; *like an angel*, i.e. *angelic*:—equal unto the angels.

2466. Ἰσαχάρ **Isachar**, *ee-sakh-ar'*; of Heb. or. [3485]; *Isachar* (i.e. *Jissaskar*), a son of Jacob (fig. his desc.):—Issachar.

2467. ἴσημι **isēmi**, *is'-ay-mee*; assumed by some as the base of cert. irreg. forms of *1492*; *to know*:—know.

2468. ἴσθι **isthi**, *is'-thee*; sec. pers. imper. pres. of *1510*; *be thou*:—+ agree, be, × give thyself wholly to.

2469. Ἰσκαριώτης **Iskariōtēs**, *is-kar-ee-o'-tace*; of Heb. or. [prob. 377 and 7149]; *inhab. of Kerioth*; *Iscariotes* (i.e. *Keriothite*), an epithet of Judas the traitor:—Iscariot.

2470. ἴσος **isŏs**, *ee'-sos*; prob. from *1492* (through the idea of *seeming*); *similar* (in amount or kind):—+ agree, as much, equal, like.

2471. ἰσότης **isŏtēs**, *ee-sot'-ace*; *likeness* (in condition or proportion); by impl. *equity*:—equal (-ity).

2472. ἰσότιμος **isŏtimŏs**, *ee-sot'-ee-mos*; from *2470* and *5092*; *of equal value* or *honor*:—like precious.

2473. ἰσόψυχος **isŏpsuchŏs**, *ee-sop'-soo-khos*; from *2470* and *5590*; *of similar spirit*:—likeminded.

2474. Ἰσραήλ **Israēl**, *is-rah-ale'*; of Heb. or. [3478]; *Israel* (i.e. *Jisrael*), the adopted name of Jacob, includ. his desc. (lit. or fig.):—Israel.

2475. Ἰσραηλίτης **Israēlitēs**, *is-rah-ale-ee'-tace*; from *2474*; an "*Israelite*", i.e. desc. of Israel (lit. or fig.):—Israelite.

2476. ἵστημι **histēmi**, *his'-tay-mee*; a prol. form of a prim. στάω **staō**, *stah'-o* (of the same mean., and used for it in certain tenses); to *stand* (trans. or intrans.), used in various applications (lit. or fig.):—abide, appoint, bring, continue, covenant, establish, hold up, lay, present, set (up), stanch, stand (by, forth, still, up). Comp. *5087*.

2477. ἱστορέω **histŏrĕō**, *his-tor-eh'-o*; from a der. of *1492*; *to be knowing* (*learned*), i.e. (by impl.) to *visit* for information (*interview*):—see.

2478. ἰσχυρός **ischurŏs**, *is-khoo-ros'*; from *2479*; *forcible* (lit. or fig.):—boisterous, mighty (-ier), powerful, strong (-er, man), valiant.

2479. ἰσχύς **ischus**, *is-khoos'*; from a der. of ἰς **is** (*force*; comp. ἔσχον **ĕschŏn**, a form of *2192*); *forcefulness* (lit. or fig.):—ability, might ([-ily]), power, strength.

2480. ἰσχύω **ischuō**, *is-khoo'-o*; from *2479*; to *have* (or *exercise*) *force* (lit. or fig.):—be able, avail, can do ([-not]), could, be good, might, prevail, be of strength, be whole, + much work.

2481. ἴσως **isōs**, *ee'-soce*; adv. from *2470*; *likely*, i.e. *perhaps*:—it may be.

2482. Ἰταλία **Italia**, *ee-tal-ee'-ah*; prob. of for. or.; *Italia*, a region of Europe:—Italy.

2483. Ἰταλικός **Italikŏs**, *ee-tal-ee-kos'*; from *2482*; *Italic*, i.e. belonging to Italia:—Italian.

2484. Ἰτουραΐα **Itŏuraia**, *ee-too-rah'-yah*; of Heb. or. [3195]; *Ituræa* (i.e. *Jetur*), a region of Pal.:—Ituræa.

2485. ἰχθύδιον **ichthudiŏn**, *ikh-thoo'-dee-on*; dimin. from *2486*; a *petty fish*:—little (small) fish.

2486. ἰχθύς **ichthus**, *ikh-thoos'*; of uncert. affin.; a *fish*:—fish.

2487. ἴχνος **ichnŏs**, *ikh'-nos*; from ἰκνέομαι **iknĕŏmai** (to *arrive*; comp. *2240*); a *track* (fig.):—step.

2488. Ἰωάθαμ **Iōatham**, *ee-o-ath'-am*; of Heb. or. [3147]; *Joatham* (i.e. *Jotham*), an Isr.:—Joatham.

2489. Ἰωάννα **Iōanna**, *ee-o-an'-nah*; fem. of the same as *2491*; *Joanna*, a Chr.:—Joanna.

2490. Ἰωαννᾶς **Iōannas**, *ee-o-an-nas'*; a form of *2491*; *Joannas*, an Isr.:—Joannas.

2491. Ἰωάννης **Iōannēs**, *ee-o-an'-nace*; of Heb. or. [3110]; *Joannes* (i.e. *Jochanan*), the name of four Isr.:—John.

2492. Ἰώβ **Iōb**, *ee-obe'*; of Heb. or. [347]; *Job* (i.e. *Ijob*), a patriarch:—Job.

2493. Ἰωήλ **Iōēl**, *ee-o-ale'*; of Heb. or. [3100]; *Joel*, an Isr.:—Joel.

2494. Ἰωνάν **Iōnan**, *ee-o-nan'*; prob. for *2491* or *2495*; *Jonan*, an Isr.:—Jonan.

2495. Ἰωνᾶς **Iōnas**, *ee-o-nas'*; of Heb. or. [3124]; *Jonas* (i.e. *Jonah*), the name of two Isr.:—Jonas.

2496. Ἰωράμ **Iōram**, *ee-o-ram'*; of Heb. or. [3141]; *Joram*, an Isr.:—Joram.

2497. Ἰωρείμ **Iōrĕim**, *ee-o-rime'*; perh. for *2496*; *Jorim*, an Isr.:—Jorim.

2498. Ἰωσαφάτ **Iōsaphat**, *ee-o-saf-at'*; of Heb. or. [3092]; *Josaphat* (i.e. *Jehoshaphat*), an Isr.:—Josaphat.

2499. Ἰωσῆ **Iōsē**, *ee-o-say'*; gen. of *2500*; *Jose*, an Isr.:—Jose.

2500. Ἰωσῆς **Iōsēs**, *ee-o-sace'*; perh. for *2501*; *Joses*, the name of two Isr.:—Joses. Comp. *2499*.

2501. Ἰωσήφ **Iōsēph**, *ee-o-safe'*; of Heb. or. [3130]; *Joseph*, the name of seven Isr.:—Joseph.

2502. Ἰωσίας **Iōsias**, *ee-o-see'-as*; of Heb. or. [2977]; *Josias* (i.e. *Joshiah*), an Isr.:—Josias.

2503. ἰῶτα **iōta**, *ee-o'-tah*; of Heb. or. [the tenth letter of the Heb. alphabet]; "*iota*", the name of the ninth letter of the Gr. alphabet, put (fig.) for a very small part of anything:—jot.

K

2504. κἀγώ **kagō**, *kag-o'*; from *2532* and *1473* (so also the dat.

κἀμοί **kamŏi**, *kam-oy'*; and acc.

κἀμέ **kamĕ**, *kam-eh'*); *and* (or *also*, *even*, etc.) *I*, (*to*) *me*:—(and, even, even so, so) I (also, in like wise), both me, me also.

2505. καθά **katha**, *kath-ah'*; from *2596* and the neut. plur. of *3739*; *according to which* things, i.e. *just as*:—as.

2506. καθαίρεσις **kathairĕsis**, *kath-ah'ee-res-is*; from *2507*; *demolition*; fig. *extinction*:—destruction, pulling down.

2507. καθαιρέω **kathairĕō**, *kath-ahee-reh'-o*; from *2596* and *138* (includ. its alt.); to *lower* (or with violence) *demolish* (lit. or fig.):—cast (pull, put, take) down, destroy.

2508. καθαίρω **kathairō**, *kath-ah'ee-ro*; from *2513*; to *cleanse*, i.e. (spec.) to *prune*; fig. to *expiate*:—purge.

2509. καθάπερ **kathapĕr**, *kath-ap'-er*; from *2505* and *4007*; *exactly as*:—(even, as well) as.

2510. καθάπτω **kathaptō**, *kath-ap'-to*; from *2596* and *680*; to *seize upon*:—fasten on.

2511. καθαρίζω **katharizō**, *kath-ar-id'-zo*; from *2513*; to *cleanse* (lit. or fig.):—(make) clean (-se), purge, purify.

2512. καθαρισμός **katharismŏs**, *kath-ar-is-mos'*; from *2511*; a *washing* off, i.e. (cer.) *ablution*, (mor.) *expiation*:—cleansing, + purge, purification, (-fying).

2513. καθαρός **katharŏs**, *kath-ar-os'*; of uncert. affin.; *clean* (lit. or fig.):—clean, clear, pure.

2514. καθαρότης **katharŏtēs**, *kath-ar-ot'-ace*; from *2513*; *cleanness* (cer.):—purification.

2515. καθέδρα **kathĕdra**, *kath-ed'-rah*; from *2596* and the same as *1476*; a *bench* (lit. or fig.):—seat.

2516. καθέζομαι **kathĕzŏmai**, *kath-ed'-zom-ahee*; from *2596* and the base of *1476*; to *sit down*:—sit.

2517. καθεξῆς **kathĕxēs**, *kath-ex-ace'*; from *2596* and *1836*; *thereafter*, i.e. *consecutively*; as a noun (by ell. of noun) a *subsequent* person or time:—after (-ward), by (in) order.

2518. καθεύδω **kathĕudō**, *kath-yoo'-do*; from *2596* and εὕδω **hĕudō** (to *sleep*); to lie *down* to *rest*, i.e. (by impl.) to *fall asleep* (lit. or fig.):—(be a-) sleep.

2519. καθηγητής **kathēgētēs**, *kath-ayg-ay-tace'*; from a comp. of *2596* and *2233*; a *guide*, i.e. (fig.) a *teacher*:—master.

2520. καθήκω **kathēkō**, *kath-ay'-ko*; from *2596* and *2240*; to *reach to*, i.e. (neut. of pres. act. part., fig. as adj.) *becoming*:—convenient, fit.

2521. κάθημαι **kathēmai**, *kath'-ay-mahee*; from *2596* and ἧμαι **hēmai** (to *sit*; akin to the base of *1476*); to *sit down*; fig. to *remain*, *reside*:—dwell, sit (by, down).

2522. καθημερινός **kathēmĕrinŏs**, *kath-ay-mer-ee-nos'*; from *2596* and *2250*; *quotidian*:—daily.

2523. καθίζω **kathizō**, *kath-id'-zo*; another (act.) form for *2516*; to *seat down*, i.e. *set* (fig. *appoint*); intrans. to *sit* (down); fig. to *settle* (*hover*, *dwell*):—continue, set, sit (down), tarry.

2524. καθίημι **kathiēmi**, *kath-ee'-ay-mee*; from *2596* and ἵημι **hiēmi** (to *send*); to *lower*:—let down.

2525. καθίστημι **kathistēmi**, *kath-is'-tay-mee*; from *2596* and *2476*; to *place down* (permanently), i.e. (fig.) to *designate*, *constitute*, *convoy*:—appoint, be, conduct, make, ordain, set.

2526. καθό **kathŏ**, *kath-ŏ'*; from *2596* and *3739*; *according to which* thing, i.e. *precisely as*, *in proportion as*:—according to that, (inasmuch) as.

2526'. καθολικός **kathŏlikŏs**, *kath-ol-ee-kos'*; from *2527*; *universal*:—general.

2527. καθόλου **kathŏlŏu**, *kath-ol'-oo*; from *2596* and *3650*; *on the whole*, i.e. *entirely*:—at all.

2528. καθοπλίζω **kathŏplizō**, *kath-op-lid'-zo*; from *2596* and *3695*; to *equip fully* with armor:—arm.

2529. καθοράω **kathŏraō**, *kath-or-ah'-o*; from *2596* and *3708*; to *behold fully*, i.e. (fig.) *distinctly apprehend*:—clearly see.

2530. καθότι **kathŏti**, *kath-ot'-ee*; from *2596* and *3739* and *5100*; *according to which certain* thing, i.e. *as far* (or *inasmuch*) *as*:—(according, forasmuch) as, because (that).

2531. καθώς **kathōs**, *kath-oce'*; from *2596* and *5613*; *just* (or *inasmuch*) *as, that:*—according to, (according, even) as, how, when.

2532. καί **kai**, *kahee;* appar. a prim. particle, having a *copulative* and sometimes also a *cumulative* force; *and, also, even, so, then, too,* etc.; often used in connection (or composition) with other particles or small words:—and, also, both, but, even, for, if, indeed, likewise, moreover, or, so, that, then, therefore, when, yea, yet.

2533. Καϊάφας **Kaïaphas**, *kah-ee-af'-as;* of Chald. or.; *the dell; Caïaphas* (i.e. *Cajepha*), an Isr.:—Caiaphas.

2534. καίγε **kaigĕ**, *ka'hee-gheh;* from *2532* and *1065*; *and at least* (or *even, indeed*):—and, at least.

2535. Κάϊν **Kaïn**, *kah'-in;* of Heb. or. [7014]; *Caïn* (i.e. *Cajin*), the son of Adam:—Cain.

2536. Καϊνάν **Kaïnan**, *kah-ee-nan';* of Heb. or. [7018]; *Caïnan* (i.e. *Kenan*), the name of two patriarchs:—Cainan.

2537. καινός **kainŏs**, *kahee-nos';* of uncert. affin.; *new* (espec. in *freshness;* while *3501* is prop. so with respect to *age*):—new.

2538. καινότης **kainŏtēs**, *kahee-not'-ace;* from *2537*; *renewal* (fig.):—newness.

2539. καίπερ **kaipĕr**, *kah'ee-per;* from *2532* and *4007*; *and indeed,* i.e. *nevertheless* or *notwithstanding:*—and yet, although.

2540. καιρός **kairŏs**, *kahee-ros';* of uncert. affin.; an *occasion,* i.e. *set* or *proper* time:— × always, opportunity, (convenient, due) season, (due, short, while) time, a while. Comp. *5550*.

2541. Καῖσαρ **Kaisar**, *kah'ee-sar;* of Lat. or.; *Cæsar,* a title of the Rom. emperor:—Cæsar.

2542. Καισάρεια **Kaisarĕia**, *kahee-sar'-i-a;* from *2541*; *Cæsaria,* the name of two places in Pal.:—Cæsarea.

2543. καίτοι **kaitŏi**, *kah'ee-toy;* from *2532* and *5104*; *and yet,* i.e. *nevertheless:*—although.

2544. καίτοιγε **kaitŏigĕ**, *kah'ee-toyg-eh;* from *2543* and *1065*; *and yet indeed,* i.e. *although really:*—nevertheless, though.

2545. καίω **kaiō**, *kah'-yo;* appar. a prim. verb; to *set on fire,* i.e. *kindle* or (by impl.) *consume:*—burn, light.

2546. κἀκεῖ **kakĕi**, *kak-i';* from *2532* and *1563*; *likewise in that place:*—and there, there (thither) also.

2547. κἀκεῖθεν **kakĕithĕn**, *kak-i'-then;* from *2532* and *1564*; *likewise from that place* (or *time*):—and afterward (from) (thence), thence also.

2548. κἀκεῖνος **kakĕinŏs**, *kak-i'-nos;* from *2532* and *1565*; *likewise that* (or *those*):—and him (other, them), even he, him also, them (also), (and) they.

2549. κακία **kakia**, *kak-ee'-ah;* from *2556*; *badness,* i.e. (subj.) *depravity,* or (act.) *malignity,* or (pass.) *trouble:*—evil, malice (-iousness), naughtiness, wickedness.

2550. κακοήθεια **kakŏēthĕia**, *kak-ŏ-ay'-thi-ah;* from a comp. of *2556* and *2239*; *bad character,* i.e. (spec.) *mischievousness:*—malignity.

2551. κακολογέω **kakŏlŏgĕō**, *kak-ol-og-eh'-o;* from a comp. of *2556* and *3056*; to *revile:*—curse, speak evil of.

2552. κακοπάθεια **kakŏpathĕia**, *kak-op-ath'-i-ah;* from a comp. of *2556* and *3806*; *hardship:*—suffering affliction.

2553. κακοπαθέω **kakŏpathĕō**, *kak-op-ath-eh'-o;* from the same as *2552*; to *undergo hardship:*—be afflicted, endure afflictions (hardness), suffer trouble.

2554. κακοποιέω **kakŏpŏiĕō**, *kak-op-oy-eh'-o;* from *2555*; to *be a bad-doer,* i.e. (obj.) to *injure,* or (gen.) to *sin:*—do (-ing) evil.

2555. κακοποιός **kakŏpŏiŏs**, *kak-op-oy-os';* from *2556* and *4160*; a *bad-doer;* (spec.) a *criminal:*—evil-doer, malefactor.

2556. κακός **kakŏs**, *kak-os';* appar. a prim. word; *worthless* (*intrinsically* such; whereas *4190* prop. refers to *effects*), i.e. (subj.) *depraved,* or (obj.) *injurious:*—bad, evil, harm, ill, noisome, wicked.

2557. κακοῦργος **kakŏurgŏs**, *kak-oor'-gos;* from *2556* and the base of *2041*; a *wrong-doer,* i.e. *criminal:*—evil-doer, malefactor.

2558. κακουχέω **kakŏuchĕō**, *kak-oo-kheh'-o;* from a presumed comp. of *2556* and *2192*; to *maltreat:*—which suffer adversity, torment.

2559. κακόω **kakŏō**, *kak-ŏ'-o;* from *2556*; to *injure;* fig. to *exasperate:*—make evil affected, entreat evil, harm, hurt, vex.

2560. κακῶς **kakōs**, *kak-oce';* adv. from *2556*; *badly* (phys. or mor.):—amiss, diseased, evil, grievously, miserably, sick, sore.

2561. κάκωσις **kakōsis**, *kak'-o-sis;* from *2559*; *maltreatment:*—affliction.

2562. καλάμη **kalamē**, *kal-am'-ay;* fem. of *2563*; a *stalk* of grain, i.e. (collect.) *stubble:*—stubble.

2563. κάλαμος **kalamŏs**, *kal'-am-os;* of uncert. affin.; a *reed* (the plant or its stem, or that of a similar plant); by impl. a *pen:*—pen, reed.

2564. καλέω **kalĕō**, *kal-eh'-o;* akin to the base of *2753*; to "*call*" (prop. aloud, but used in a variety of applications, dir. or otherwise):—bid, call (forth), (whose, whose sur-) name (was [called]).

2565. καλλιέλαιος **kalliĕlaiŏs**, *kal-le-el'-ah-yos;* from the base of *2566* and *1636*; a *cultivated olive* tree, i.e. a *domesticated* or *improved* one:—good olive tree.

2566. καλλίον **kalliŏn**, *kal-lee'-on;* neut. of the (irreg.) comp. of *2570*; (adv.) *better* than many:—very well.

2567. καλοδιδάσκαλος **kalŏdidaskalŏs**, *kal-od-id-as'-kal-os;* from *2570* and *1320*; a *teacher of* the *right:*—teacher of good things.

2568. Καλοὶ Λιμένες **Kalŏi Limĕnĕs**, *kal-oy' lee-men'-es;* plur. of *2570* and *3040*; *Good Harbors,* i.e. *Fairhaven,* a bay of Crete:—fair havens.

2569. καλοποιέω **kalŏpŏiĕō**, *kal-op-oy-eh'-o;* from *2570* and *4160*; to *do well,* i.e. live virtuously:—well doing.

2570. καλός **kalŏs**, *kal-os';* of uncert. affin.; prop. *beautiful,* but chiefly (fig.) *good* (lit. or mor.), i.e. *valuable* or *virtuous* (for *appearance* or *use,* and thus distinguished from *18*, which is prop. *intrinsic*):— × better, fair, good (-ly), honest, meet, well, worthy.

2571. κάλυμα **kaluma**, *kal'-oo-mah;* from *2572*; a *cover,* i.e. *veil:*—vail.

2572. καλύπτω **kaluptō**, *kal-oop'-to;* akin to *2813* and *2928*; to *cover* up (lit. or fig.):—cover, hide.

2573. καλῶς **kalōs**, *kal-oce';* adv. from *2570*; *well* (usually mor.):—(in a) good (place), honestly, + recover, (full) well.

2574. κάμηλος **kamēlŏs**, *kam'-ay-los;* of Heb. or. [1581]; a "*camel*":—camel.

2575. κάμινος **kaminŏs**, *kam'-ee-nos;* prob. from *2545*; a *furnace:*—furnace.

2576. καμμύω **kammuō**, *kam-moo'-o;* for a comp. of *2596* and the base of *3466*; to *shut down,* i.e. *close* the eyes:—close.

2577. κάμνω **kamnō**, *kam'-no;* appar. a prim. verb; prop. to *toil,* i.e. (by impl.) to *tire* (fig. *faint, sicken*):—faint, sicken, be wearied.

2578. κάμπτω **kamptō**, *kamp'-to;* appar. a prim. verb; to *bend:*—bow.

2579. κἄν **kan**, *kan;* from *2532* and *1437*; *and* (or *even*) *if:*—and (also) if (so much as), if but, at the least, though, yet.

2580. Κανᾶ **Kana**, *kan-ah';* of Heb. or. [comp. 7071]; *Cana,* a place in Pal.:—Cana.

2581. Κανανίτης **Kananitēs**, *kan-an-ee'-tace;* of Chald. or. [comp. 7067]; *zealous; Cananitès,* an epithet:—Canaanite [*by mistake for a der. from 5477*].

2582. Κανδάκη **Kandakē**, *kan-dak'-ay;* of for. or.; *Candacè,* an Eg. queen:—Candace.

2583. κανών **kanōn**, *kan-ohn';* from κάνη **kanē** (a straight *reed,* i.e. *rod*); a *rule* ("*canon*"), i.e. (fig.) a *standard* (of faith and practice); by impl. a *boundary,* i.e. (fig.) a *sphere* (of activity):—line, rule.

2584. Καπερναούμ **Kapĕrnaŏum**, *cap-er-nah-oom';* of Heb. or. [prob. 3723 and 5151]; *Capernaüm* (i.e. *Caphanachum*), a place in Pal.:—Capernaum.

2585. καπηλεύω **kapēlĕuō**, *kap-ale-yoo'-o;* from κάπηλος **kapēlŏs** (a *huckster*); to *retail,* i.e. (by impl.) to *adulterate* (fig.):—corrupt.

2586. καπνός **kapnŏs**, *kap-nos';* of uncert. affin.; *smoke:*—smoke.

2587. Καππαδοκία **Kappadŏkia**, *kap-pad-ok-ee'-ah;* of for. or.; *Cappadocia,* a region of Asia Minor:—Cappadocia.

2588. καρδία **kardia**, *kar-dee'-ah;* prol. from a prim. κάρ **kar** (Lat. *cor,* "*heart*"); the *heart,* i.e. (fig.) the *thoughts* or *feelings* (*mind*); also (by anal.) the *middle:*—(+ broken-) heart (-ed).

2589. καρδιογνώστης **kardiŏgnōstēs**, *kar-dee-og-noce'-tace;* from *2588* and *1097*; a *heart-knower:*—which knowest the hearts.

2590. καρπός **karpŏs**, *kar-pos';* prob. from the base of *726*; *fruit* (as *plucked*), lit. or fig.:—fruit.

2591. Κάρπος **Karpŏs**, *kar'-pos;* perh. for *2590*; *Carpus,* prob. a Chr.:—Carpus.

2592. καρποφορέω **karpŏphŏrĕō**, *kar-pof-or-eh'-o;* from *2593*; to *be fertile* (lit. or fig.):—be (bear, bring forth) fruit (-ful).

2593. καρποφόρος **karpŏphŏrŏs**, *kar-pof-or'-os;* from *2590* and *5342*; *fruitbearing* (fig.):—fruitful.

2594. καρτερέω **kartĕrĕō**, *kar-ter-eh'-o;* from a der. of *2904* (transp.); to *be strong,* i.e. (fig.) *steadfast* (*patient*):—endure.

2595. κάρφος **karphŏs**, *kar'-fos;* from κάρφω **karphō** (to *wither*); a dry *twig* or *straw:*—mote.

2596. κατά **kata**, *kat-ah';* a prim. particle; (prep.) *down* (in place or time), in varied relations (according to the case [gen., dat. or acc.] with which it is joined):—about, according as (to), after, against, (when they were) × alone, among, and, × apart, (even, like) as (concerning, pertaining to, touching), × aside, at, before, beyond, by, to the charge of, [charita-] bly, concerning, + covered, [dai-] ly, down, every, (+ far more) exceeding, × more excellent, for, from . . . to, godly, in (-asmuch, divers, every, -to, respect of), . . . by, after the manner of, + by any means, beyond (out of) measure, × mightily, more, × natural, of (up-) on (× part), out (of every), over against, (+ your) × own, + particularly, so, through (-oughout, -oughout every), thus, (un-) to (-gether, -ward), × uttermost, where (-by), with. In composition it retains many of these applications, and frequently denotes *opposition, distribution* or *intensity.*

2597. καταβαίνω **katabainō**, *kat-ab-ah'ee-no;* from *2596* and the base of *939*; to *descend* (lit. or fig.):—come (get, go, step) down, descend, fall (down).

2598. καταβάλλω **kataballō**, *kat-ab-al'-lo;* from *2596* and *906*; to *throw down:*—cast down, descend, fall (down).

2599. καταβαρέω **katabarĕō**, *kat-ab-ar-eh'-o;* from *2596* and *916*; to *impose upon:*—burden.

2600. κατάβασις **katabasis**, *kat-ab'-as-is;* from *2597*; a *declivity:*—descent.

2601. καταβιβάζω **katabibazō**, *kat-ab-ib-ad'-zo;* from *2596* and a der. of the base of *939*; to *cause to go down,* i.e. *precipitate:*—bring (thrust) down.

2602. καταβολή **katabŏlē**, *kat-ab-ol-ay';* from *2598*; a *deposition,* i.e. *founding;* fig. *conception:*—conceive, foundation.

2603. καταβραβεύω **katabrabĕuō**, *kat-ab-rab-yoo'-o;* from *2596* and *1018* (in its orig. sense); to *award* the price *against,* i.e. (fig.) to *defraud* (of salvation):—beguile of reward.

2604. καταγγελεύς **kataggĕlĕus**, *kat-ang-gel-yooce';* from *2605*; a *proclaimer:*—setter forth.

2605. καταγγέλλω **kataggĕllō**, *kat-ang-gel'-lo;* from *2596* and the base of *32*; to *proclaim, promulgate:*—declare, preach, shew, speak of, teach.

2606. καταγελάω **katagĕlaō**, *kat-ag-el-ah'-o;* to *laugh down,* i.e. *deride:*—laugh to scorn.

2607. καταγινώσκω **kataginōskō**, *kat-ag-in-o'-sko;* from *2596* and *1097*; to *note against,* i.e. *find fault with:*—blame, condemn.

2608. κατάγνυμι **katagnumi**, *kat-ag'-noo-mee;* from *2596* and the base of *4486*; to *rend in pieces,* i.e. *crack apart:*—break.

2609. **κατάγω katagō**, *kat-ag'-o;* from 2596 and 71; to *lead down;* spec. to *moor* a vessel:—bring (down, forth), (bring to) land, touch.

2610. **καταγωνίζομαι katagōnizŏmai**, *kat-ag-o-nid'-zom-ahee;* from 2596 and 75; to *struggle against*, i.e. (by impl.) to *overcome:*—subdue.

2611. **καταδέω katadĕō**, *kat-ad-eh'-o;* from 2596 and 1210; to *tie down*, i.e. *bandage* (a wound):—bind up.

2612. **κατάδηλος katadēlŏs**, *kat-ad'-ay-los;* from 2596 intens. and 1212; *manifest:*—far more evident.

2613. **καταδικάζω katadikazō**, *kat-ad-ik-ad'-zo;* from 2596 and a der. of 1349; to *adjudge against*, i.e. *pronounce guilty:*—condemn.

2614. **καταδιώκω katadiōkō**, *kat-ad-ee-o'-ko;* from 2596 and 1377; to *hunt down*, i.e. *search for:*—follow after.

2615. **καταδουλόω katadŏulŏō**, *kat-ad-oo-lŏ'-o;* from 2596 and 1402; to *enslave utterly:*—bring into bondage.

2616. **καταδυναστεύω katadunastĕuō**, *kat-ad-oo-nas-tyoo'-o;* from 2596 and a der. of 1413; to *exercise dominion against*, i.e. *oppress:*—oppress.

2617. **καταισχύνω kataischunō**, *kat-ahee-skhoo'-no;* from 2596 and 153; to *shame down*, i.e. *disgrace* or (by impl.) *put to the blush:*—confound, dishonour, (be a-, make a-) shame (-d).

2618. **κατακαίω katakaiō**, *kat-ak-ah'ee-o;* from 2596 and 2545; to *burn down* (to the ground), i.e. *consume wholly:*—burn (up, utterly).

2619. **κατακαλύπτω katakaluptō**, *kat-ak-al-oop'-to;* from 2596 and 2572; to *cover wholly*, i.e. *veil:*—cover, hide.

2620. **κατακαυχάομαι katakauchaŏmai**, *kat-ak-ŏw-khah'-om-ahee;* from 2596 and 2744; to *exult against* (i.e. *over*):—boast (against), glory, rejoice against.

2621. **κατάκειμαι katakĕimai**, *kat-ak'-i-mahee;* from 2596 and 2749; to *lie down*, i.e. (by impl.) *be sick;* spec. to *recline* at a meal:—keep, lie, sit at meat (down).

2622. **κατακλάω kataklaō**, *kat-ak-lah'-o;* from 2596 and 2806; to *break down*, i.e. *divide:*—break.

2623. **κατακλείω katakleīō**, *kat-ak-li'-o;* from 2596 and 2808; to *shut down* (in a dungeon), i.e. *incarcerate:*—shut up.

2624. **κατακληροδοτέω kataklērŏdŏtĕō**, *kat-ak-lay-rod-ot-eh'-o;* from 2596 and a der. of a comp. of 2819 and 1325; to *be a giver of lots to each*, i.e. (by impl.) to *apportion an estate:*—divide by lot.

2625. **κατακλίνω kataklinō**, *kat-ak-lee'-no;* from 2596 and 2827; to *recline down*, i.e. (spec.) to *take a place* at table:—(make) sit down (at meat).

2626. **κατακλύζω katakluzō**, *kat-ak-lood'-zo;* from 2596 and the base of 2830; to *dash* (*wash*) *down*, i.e. (by impl.) to *deluge:*—overflow.

2627. **κατακλυσμός kataklusmŏs**, *kat-ak-looce-mos';* from 2626; an *inundation:*—flood.

2628. **κατακολουθέω katakŏlŏuthĕō**, *kat-ak-ol-oo-theh'-o;* from 2596 and 190; to *accompany closely:*—follow (after).

2629. **κατακόπτω katakŏptō**, *kat-ak-op'-to;* from 2596 and 2875; to *chop down*, i.e. *mangle:*—cut.

2630. **κατακρημνίζω katakrēmnizō**, *kat-ak-rame-nid'-zo;* from 2596 and a der. of 2911; to *precipitate down:*—cast down headlong.

2631. **κατάκριμα katakrima**, *kat-ak'-ree-mah;* from 2632; an *adverse sentence* (the verdict):—condemnation.

2632. **κατακρίνω katakrinō**, *kat-ak-ree'-no;* from 2596 and 2919; to *judge against*, i.e. *sentence:*—condemn, damn.

2633. **κατάκρισις katakrisis**, *kat-ak'-ree-sis;* from 2632; *sentencing adversely* (the act):—condemn (-ation).

2634. **κατακυριεύω katakuriĕuō**, *kat-ak-oo-ree-yoo'-o;* from 2596 and 2961; to *lord against*, i.e. *control, subjugate:*—exercise dominion over (lordship), be lord over, overcome.

2635. **καταλαλέω katalalĕō**, *kat-al-al-eh'-o;* from 2637; to *be a traducer*, i.e. to *slander:*—speak against (evil of).

2636. **καταλαλία katalalia**, *kat-al-al-ee'-ah;* from 2637; *defamation:*—backbiting, evil speaking.

2637 **κατάλαλος katalalŏs**, *kat-al'-al-os;* from 2596 and the base of 2980; *talkative against*, i.e. a *slanderer:*—backbiter.

2638. **καταλαμβάνω katalambanō**, *kat-al-am-ban'-o;* from 2596 and 2983; to *take eagerly*, i.e. *seize, possess*, etc. (lit. or fig.):—apprehend, attain, come upon, comprehend, find, obtain, perceive, (over-) take.

2639. **καταλέγω katalĕgō**, *kat-al-eg'-o;* from 2596 and 3004 (in its orig. mean.); to *lay down*, i.e. (fig.) to *enrol:*—take into the number.

2640. **κατάλειμμα katalĕimma**, *kat-al'-ime-mah;* from 2641; a *remainder*, i.e. (by impl.) a *few:*—remnant.

2641. **καταλείπω katalĕipō**, *kat-al-i'-po;* from 2596 and 3007; to *leave down*, i.e. *behind;* by impl. to *abandon, have remaining:*—forsake, leave, reserve.

2642. **καταλιθάζω katalithazō**, *kat-al-ith-ad'-zo;* from 2596 and 3034; to *stone down*, i.e. *to death:*—stone.

2643. **καταλλαγή katallagē**, *kat-al-lag-ay';* from 2644; *exchange* (fig. *adjustment*), i.e. *restoration* to (the divine) favor:—atonement, reconciliation (-ing).

2644. **καταλλάσσω katallassō**, *kat-al-las'-so;* from 2596 and 236; to *change mutually*, i.e. (fig.) to *compound* a difference:—reconcile.

2645. **κατάλοιπος katalŏipŏs**, *kat-al'-oy-pos;* from 2596 and 3062; *left down* (*behind*), i.e. *remaining* (plur. the *rest*):—residue.

2646. **κατάλυμα kataluma**, *kat-al'-oo-mah;* from 2647; prop. a *dissolution* (breaking up of a journey), i.e. (by impl.) a *lodging-place:*—guestchamber, inn.

2647. **καταλύω kataluō**, *kat-al-oo'-o;* from 2596 and 3089; to *loosen down* (*disintegrate*), i.e. (by impl.) to *demolish* (lit. or fig.); spec. [comp. 2646] to *halt* for the night:—destroy, dissolve, be guest, lodge, come to nought, overthrow, throw down.

2648. **καταμανθάνω katamanthanō**, *kat-am-an-than'-o;* from 2596 and 3129; to *learn thoroughly*, i.e. (by impl.) to *note carefully:*—consider.

2649. **καταμαρτυρέω katamarturĕō**, *kat-am-ar-too-reh'-o;* from 2596 and 3140; to *testify against:*—witness against.

2650. **καταμένω katamĕnō**, *kat-am-en'-o;* from 2596 and 3306; to *stay fully*, i.e. *reside:*—abide.

2651. **καταμόνας katamŏnas**, *kat-am-on'-as;* from 2596 and acc. plur. fem. of 3441 (with 5561 impl.); *according to sole* places, i.e. (adv.) *separately:*—alone.

2652. **κατανάθεμα katanathĕma**, *kat-an-ath'-em-ah;* from 2596 (intens.) and 331; an *imprecation:*—curse.

2653. **καταναθεματίζω katanathĕmatizō**, *kat-an-ath-em-at-id'-zo;* from 2596 (intens.) and 332; to *imprecate:*—curse.

2654. **καταναλίσκω katanaliskō**, *kat-an-al-is'-ko;* from 2596 and 355; to *consume utterly:*—consume.

2655. **καταναρκάω katanarkaō**, *kat-an-ar-kah'-o;* from 2596 and **ναρκάω narkaō** (to *be numb*); to *grow utterly torpid*, i.e. (by impl.) *slothful* (fig. *expensive*):—be burdensome (chargeable).

2656. **κατανεύω katanĕuō**, *kat-an-yoo'-o;* from 2596 and 3506; to *nod down* (*towards*), i.e. (by anal.) to *make signs* to:—beckon.

2657. **κατανοέω katanŏĕō**, *kat-an-o-eh'-o;* from 2596 and 3539; to *observe fully:*—behold, consider, discover, perceive.

2658. **καταντάω katantaō**, *kat-an-tah'-o;* from 2596 and a der. of 473; to *meet against*, i.e. *arrive* at (lit. or fig.):—attain, come.

2659. **κατάνυξις katanuxis**, *kat-an'-oox-is;* from 2660; a *prickling* (sensation, as of the limbs *asleep*), i.e. (by impl. [perh. by some confusion with 3506 or even with 3571]) *stupor* (*lethargy*):—slumber.

2660. **κατανύσσω katanussō**, *kat-an-oos'-so;* from 2596 and 3572; to *pierce thoroughly*, i.e. (fig.) to *agitate* violently ("sting to the quick"):—prick.

2661. **καταξιόω kataxiŏō**, *kat-ax-ee-ŏ'-o;* from 2596 and 515; to *deem entirely deserving:*—(ac-) count worthy.

2662. **καταπατέω katapatĕō**, *kat-ap-at-eh'-o;* from 2596 and 3961; to *trample down;* fig. to *reject* with disdain:—trample, tread (down, underfoot).

2663. **κατάπαυσις katapausis**, *kat-ap'-ŏw-sis;* from 2664; *reposing down*, i.e. (by Hebr.) *abode:*—rest.

2664. **καταπαύω katapauō**, *kat-ap-ŏw'-o;* from 2596 and 3973; to *settle down*, i.e. (lit.) to *colonize*, or (fig.) to (*cause to*) *desist:*—cease, (give) rest (-rain).

2665. **καταπέτασμα katapĕtasma**, *kat-ap-et'-as-mah;* from a comp. of 2596 and a congener of 4072; something *spread thoroughly*, i.e. (spec.) the door *screen* (to the Most Holy Place) in the Jewish Temple:—vail.

2666. **καταπίνω katapinō**, *kat-ap-ee'-no;* from 2596 and 4095; to *drink down*, i.e. *gulp entire* (lit. or fig.):—devour, drown, swallow (up).

2667. **καταπίπτω katapiptō**, *kat-ap-ip'-to;* from 2596 and 4098; to *fall down:*—fall (down).

2668. **καταπλέω kataplĕō**, *kat-ap-leh'-o;* from 2596 and 4126; to *sail down* upon a place, i.e. to *land* at:—arrive.

2669. **καταπονέω katapŏnĕō**, *kat-ap-on-eh'-o;* from 2596 and a der. of 4192; to *labor down*, i.e. *wear with toil* (fig. *harass*):—oppress, vex.

2670. **καταποντίζω katapŏntizō**, *kat-ap-on-tid'-zo;* from 2596 and a der. of the same as 4195; to *plunge down*, i.e. *submerge:*—drown, sink.

2671. **κατάρα katara**, *kat-ar'-ah;* from 2596 (intens.) and 685; *imprecation, execration:*—curse (-d, -ing).

2672. **καταράομαι kataraŏmai**, *kat-ar-ah'-om-ahee;* mid. from 2671; to *execrate;* by anal. to *doom:*—curse.

2673. **καταργέω katargĕō**, *kat-arg-eh'-o;* from 2596 and 691; to *be* (*render*) *entirely idle* (*useless*), lit. or fig.:—abolish, cease, cumber, deliver, destroy, do away, become (make) of no (none, without) effect, fail, loose, bring (come) to nought, put away (down), vanish away, make void.

2674. **καταριθμέω katarithmĕō**, *kat-ar-ith-meh'-o;* from 2596 and 705; to *reckon among:*—number with.

2675. **καταρτίζω katartizō**, *kat-ar-tid'-zo;* from 2596 and a der. of 739; to *complete thoroughly*, i.e. *repair* (lit. or fig.) or *adjust:*—fit, frame, mend, (make) perfect (-ly join together), prepare, restore.

2676. **κατάρτισις katartisis**, *kat-ar'-tis-is;* from 2675; *thorough equipment* (subj.):—perfection.

2677. **καταρτισμός katartismŏs**, *kat-ar-tis-mos';* from 2675; *complete furnishing* (obj.):—perfecting.

2678. **κατασείω katasĕiō**, *kat-as-i'-o;* from 2596 and 4579; to *sway downward*, i.e. *make a signal:*—beckon.

2679. **κατασκάπτω kataskaptō**, *kat-as-kap'-to;* from 2596 and 4626; to *undermine*, i.e. (by impl.) *destroy:*—dig down, ruin.

2680. **κατασκευάζω kataskĕuazō**, *kat-ask-yoo-ad'-zo;* from 2596 and a der. of 4632; to *prepare thoroughly* (prop. by external *equipment;* whereas 2090 refers rather to internal *fitness*); by impl. to *construct, create:*—build, make, ordain, prepare.

2681. **κατασκηνόω kataskēnŏō**, *kat-as-kay-nŏ'-o;* from 2596 and 4637; to *camp down*, i.e. *haunt;* fig. to *remain:*—lodge, rest.

2682. **κατασκήνωσις kataskēnōsis**, *kat-as-kay'-no-sis;* from 2681; an *encamping*, i.e. (fig.) a *perch:*—nest.

2683. **κατασκιάζω kataskiazō**, *kat-as-kee-ad'-zo;* from 2596 and a der. of 4639; to *overshade*, i.e. *cover:*—shadow.

2684. κατασκοπέω **kataskŏpĕō**, *kat-as-kop-eh'-o;* from 2685; to *be a sentinel*, i.e. to *inspect insidiously*:—spy out.

2685. κατάσκοπος **kataskŏpŏs**, *kat-as'-kop-os;* from 2596 (intens.) and 4649 (in the sense of a *watcher*); a *reconnoiterer*:—spy.

2686. κατασοφίζομαι **katasŏphizŏmai**, *kat-as-of-id'-zom-ahee;* mid. from 2596 and 4679; to *be crafty against*, i.e. *circumvent*:—deal subtilly with.

2687. καταστέλλω **katastĕllō**, *kat-as-tel'-lo;* from 2596 and 4724; to *put down*, i.e. *quell*:—appease, quiet.

2688. κατάστημα **katastēma**, *kat-as'-tay-mah;* from 2525; prop. a *position* or *condition*, i.e. (subj.) *demeanor*:—behaviour.

2689. καταστολή **katastŏlē**, *kat-as-tol-ay';* from 2687; a *deposit*, i.e. (spec.) *costume*:—apparel.

2690. καταστρέφω **katastrĕphō**, *kat-as-tref'-o;* from 2596 and 4762; to *turn* upside *down*, i.e. *upset*:—overthrow.

2691. καταστρηνιάω **katastrēniaō**, *kat-as-tray-nee-ah'-o;* from 2596 and 4763; to *become voluptuous against*:—begin to wax wanton against.

2692. καταστροφή **katastrŏphē**, *kat-as-trof-ay';* from 2690; an *overturn* ("*catastrophe*"), i.e. *demolition*; fig. *apostasy*:—overthrow, subverting.

2693. καταστρώννυμι **katastrōnnumi**, *kat-as-trone'-noo-mee;* from 2596 and 4766; to *strew down*, i.e. (by impl.) to *prostrate* (*slay*):—overthrow.

2694. κατασύρω **katasurō**, *kat-as-oo'-ro;* from 2596 and 4951; to *drag down*, i.e. *arrest* judicially:—hale.

2695. κατασφάττω **katasphattō**, *kat-as-fat'-to;* from 2596 and 4969; to *kill down*, i.e. *slaughter*:—slay.

2696. κατασφραγίζω **katasphragizō**, *kat-as-frag-id'-zo;* from 2596 and 4972; to *seal closely*:—seal.

2697. κατάσχεσις **kataschĕsis**, *kat-as'-khes-is;* from 2722; a *holding down*, i.e. *occupancy*:—possession.

2698. κατατίθημι **katatithēmi**, *kat-at-ith'-ay-mee;* from 2596 and 5087; to *place down*, i.e. *deposit* (lit. or fig.):—do, lay, shew.

2699. κατατομή **katatŏmē**, *kat-at-om-ay';* from a comp. of 2596 and τέμνω **tĕmnō** (to *cut*); a *cutting down* (*off*), i.e. *mutilation* (ironically):—concision. Comp. 609.

2700. κατατοξεύω **katatŏxĕuō**, *kat-at-ox-yoo'-o;* from 2596 and a der. of 5115; to *shoot down* with an arrow or other missile:—thrust through.

2701. κατατρέχω **katatrĕchō**, *kat-at-rekh'-o;* from 2596 and 5143; to *run down*, i.e. *hasten* from a tower:—run down.

καταφάγω **kataphagō**. See 2719.

2702. καταφέρω **kataphĕrō**, *kat-af-er'-o;* from 2596 and 5342 (includ. its alt.); to *bear down*, i.e. (fig.) *overcome* (with drowsiness); spec. to *cast* a vote:—fall, give, sink down.

2703. καταφεύγω **kataphĕugō**, *kat-af-yoo'-go;* from 2596 and 5343; to *flee down* (*away*):—flee.

2704. καταφθείρω **kataphthĕirō**, *kat-af-thi'-ro;* from 2596 and 5351; to *spoil entirely*, i.e. (lit.) to *destroy*; or (fig.) to *deprave*:—corrupt, utterly perish.

2705. καταφιλέω **kataphilĕō**, *kat-af-ee-leh'-o;* from 2596 and 5368; to *kiss earnestly*:—kiss.

2706. καταφρονέω **kataphrŏnĕō**, *kat-af-ron-eh'-o;* from 2596 and 5426; to *think against*, i.e. *disesteem*:—despise.

2707. καταφροντής **kataphrŏntēs**, *kat-af-ron-tace';* from 2706; a *contemner*:—despiser.

2708. καταχέω **katachĕō**, *kat-akh-eh'-o;* from 2596 and χέω **chĕō** (to *pour*); to *pour down* (*out*):—pour.

2709. καταχθόνιος **katachthŏniŏs**, *kat-akh-thon'-ee-os;* from 2596 and χθών **chthōn** (the *ground*); *subterranean*, i.e. *infernal* (belonging to the world of departed spirits):—under the earth.

2710. καταχράομαι **katachraŏmai**, *kat-akh-rah'-om-ahee;* from 2596 and 5530; to *overuse*, i.e. *misuse*:—abuse.

2711. καταψύχω **katapsuchō**, *kat-ap-soo'-kho;* from 2596 and 5594; to *cool down* (*off*), i.e. *refresh*:—cool.

2712. κατείδωλος **katĕidōlŏs**, *kat-i'-do-los;* from 2596 (intens.) and 1497; *utterly idolatrous*:—wholly given to idolatry.

κατελεύθω **katĕlĕuthō**. See 2718.

2713. κατέναντι **katĕnanti**, *kat-en'-an-tee;* from 2596 and 1725; *directly opposite*:—before, over against.

κατενέγκω **katĕnĕgkō**. See 2702.

2714. κατενώπιον **katĕnōpiŏn**, *kat-en-o'-pee-on;* from 2596 and 1799; *directly in front of*:—before (the presence of), in the sight of.

2715. κατεξουσιάζω **katĕxŏusiazō**, *kat-ex-oo-see-ad'-zo;* from 2596 and 1850; to *have* (*wield*) *full privilege over*:—exercise authority.

2716. κατεργάζομαι **katĕrgazŏmai**, *kat-er-gad'-zom-ahee;* from 2596 and 2038; to *work fully*, i.e. *accomplish*; by impl. to *finish*, *fashion*:—cause, do (deed), perform, work (out).

2718. κατέρχομαι **katĕrchŏmai**, *kat-er'-khom-ahee;* from 2596 and 2064 (includ. its alt.); to *come* (or *go*) *down* (lit. or fig.):—come (down), depart, descend, go down, land.

2719. κατεσθίω **katĕsthiō**, *kat-es-thee'-o;* from 2596 and 2068 (includ. its alt.); to *eat down*, i.e. *devour* (lit. or fig.):—devour.

2720. κατευθύνω **katĕuthunō**, *kat-yoo-thoo'-no;* from 2596 and 2116; to *straighten fully*, i.e. (fig.) *direct*:—guide, direct.

2721. κατεφίστημι **katĕphistēmi**, *kat-ef-is'-tay-mee;* from 2596 and 2186; to *stand over against*, i.e. *rush upon* (*assault*):—make insurrection against.

2722. κατέχω **katĕchō**, *kat-ekh'-o;* from 2596 and 2192; to *hold down* (*fast*), in various applications (lit. or fig.):—have, hold (fast), keep (in memory), let, × make toward, possess, retain, seize on, stay, take, withhold.

2723. κατηγορέω **katēgŏrĕō**, *kat-ay-gor-eh'-o;* from 2725; to *be a plaintiff*, i.e. to *charge* with some offence:—accuse, object.

2724. κατηγορία **katēgŏria**, *kat-ay-gor-ee'-ah;* from 2725; a *complaint* ("*category*"), i.e. criminal *charge*:—accusation (× -ed).

2725. κατήγορος **katēgŏrŏs**, *kat-ay'-gor-os;* from 2596 and 58; *against* one in the *assembly*, i.e. a *complainant* at law; spec. *Satan*:—accuser.

2726. κατήφεια **katēphĕia**, *kat-ay'-fi-ah;* from a comp. of 2596 and perh. a der. of the base of 5316 (mean. *downcast* in look); *demureness*, i.e. (by impl.) *sadness*:—heaviness.

2727. κατηχέω **katēchĕō**, *kat-ay-kheh'-o;* from 2596 and 2279; to *sound down* into the ears, i.e. (by impl.) to *indoctrinate* ("*catechize*") or (gen.) to *apprise of*:—inform, instruct, teach.

2728. κατιόω **katiŏō**, *kat-ee-ŏ'-o;* from 2596 and a der. of 2447; to *rust down*, i.e. *corrode*:—canker.

2729. κατισχύω **katischuō**, *kat-is-khoo'-o;* from 2596 and 2480; to *overpower*:—prevail (against).

2730. κατοικέω **katŏikĕō**, *kat-oy-keh'-o;* from 2596 and 3611; to *house permanently*, i.e. *reside* (lit. or fig.):—dwell (-er), inhabitant (-ter).

2731. κατοίκησις **katŏikēsis**, *kat-oy'-kay-sis;* from 2730; *residence* (prop. the act; but by impl. concr. the mansion):—dwelling.

2732. κατοικητήριον **katŏikētēriŏn**, *kat-oy-kay-tay'-ree-on;* from a der. of 2730; a *dwelling-place*:—habitation.

2733. κατοικία **katŏikia**, *kat-oy-kee'-ah;* *residence* (prop. the condition; but by impl. the abode itself):—habitation.

2734. κατοπτρίζομαι **katŏptrizŏmai**, *kat-op-trid'-zom-ahee;* mid. from a comp. of 2596 and a der. of 3700 [comp. 2072]; to *mirror oneself*, i.e. to *see reflected* (fig.):—behold as in a glass.

2735. κατόρθωμα **katŏrthōma**, *kat-or'-tho-mah;* from a comp. of 2596 and a der. of 3717 [comp. 1357]; something *made fully upright*, i.e. (fig.) *rectification* (spec. *good* public *administration*):—very worthy deed.

2736. κάτω **katō**, *kat'-o;* also (comp.)

κατωτέρω **katōtĕrō**, *kat-o-ter'-o* [comp. 2737]; adv. from 2596; *downwards*:—beneath, bottom, down, under.

2737. κατώτερος **katōtĕrŏs**, *kat-o'-ter-os;* comp. from 2736; *inferior* (locally, of Hades):—lower.

2738. καῦμα **kauma**, *kŏw'-mah;* from 2545; prop. a *burn* (concr.), but used (abstr.) of a *glow*:—heat.

2739. καυματίζω **kaumatizō**, *kŏw-mat-id'-zo;* from 2738; to *burn*:—scorch.

2740. καῦσις **kausis**, *kŏw'-sis;* from 2545; *burning* (the act):—be burned.

2741. καυσόω **kausŏō**, *kŏw-sŏ'-o;* from 2740; to *set on fire*:—with fervent heat.

2742. καύσων **kausōn**, *kŏw'-sone;* from 2741; a *glare*:—(burning) heat.

2743. καυτηριάζω **kautēriazō**, *kŏw-tay-ree-ad'-zo;* from a der. of 2545; to *brand* ("*cauterize*"), i.e. (by impl.) to *render unsensitive* (fig.):—sear with a hot iron.

2744. καυχάομαι **kauchaŏmai**, *kŏw-khah'-om-ahee;* from some (obsol.) base akin to that of αὐχέω **auchĕō** (to *boast*) and 2172; to *vaunt* (in a good or a bad sense):—(make) boast, glory, joy, rejoice.

2745. καύχημα **kauchēma**, *kŏw'-khay-mah;* from 2744; a *boast* (prop. the object; by impl. the act) in a good or a bad sense:—boasting, (whereof) to glory (of), glorying, rejoice (-ing).

2746. καύχησις **kauchēsis**, *kŏw'-khay-sis;* from 2744; *boasting* (prop. the act; by impl. the object), in a good or a bad sense:—boasting, whereof I may glory, glorying, rejoicing.

2747. Κεγχρεαί **Kĕgchrĕai**, *keng-khreh-a'hee;* prob. from κέγχρος **kĕgchrŏs** (*millet*); *Cenchreæ*, a port of Corinth:—Cenchrea.

2748. Κεδρών **Kĕdrōn**, *ked-rone';* of Heb. or. [6939]; *Cedron* (i.e. *Kidron*), a brook near Jerus.:—Cedron.

2749. κεῖμαι **kĕimai**, *ki'-mahee;* mid. of a prim. verb; to *lie* outstretched (lit. or fig.):—be (appointed, laid up, made, set), lay, lie. Comp. 5087.

2750. κειρία **kĕiria**, *ki-ree'-ah;* of uncert. affin.; a *swathe*, i.e. *winding-sheet*:—graveclothes.

2751. κείρω **kĕirō**, *ki'-ro;* a prim. verb; to *shear*:—shear (-er).

2752. κέλευμα **kĕlĕuma**, *kel'-yoo-mah;* from 2753; a *cry* of incitement:—shout.

2753. κελεύω **kĕlĕuō**, *kel-yoo'-o;* from a prim. κέλλω **kĕllō** (to *urge* on); "hail"; to *incite* by word, i.e. *order*:—bid, (at, give) command (-ment).

2754. κενοδοξία **kĕnŏdŏxia**, *ken-od-ox-ee'-ah;* from 2755; *empty glorying*, i.e. *self-conceit*:—vain-glory.

2755. κενόδοξος **kĕnŏdŏxŏs**, *ken-od'-ox-os;* from 2756 and 1391; *vainly glorifying*, i.e. *self-conceited*:—desirous of vain-glory.

2756. κενός **kĕnŏs**, *ken-os';* appar. a prim. word; *empty* (lit. or fig.):—empty, (in) vain.

2757. κενοφωνία **kĕnŏphōnia**, *ken-of-o-nee'-ah;* from a presumed comp. of 2756 and 5456; *empty sounding*, i.e. *fruitless discussion*:—vain.

2758. κενόω **kĕnŏō**, *ken-ŏ'-o;* from 2756; to *make empty*, i.e. (fig.) to *abase*, *neutralize*, *falsify*:—make (of none effect, of no reputation, void), be in vain.

2759. κέντρον **kĕntrŏn**, *ken'-tron;* from κεντέω **kĕntĕō** (to *prick*); a *point* ("centre"), i.e. a *sting* (fig. *poison*) or *goad* (fig. divine *impulse*):—prick, sting.

2760. κεντυρίων **kĕnturiōn**, *ken-too-ree'-ohn;* of Lat. or.; a *centurion*, i.e. *captain* of one hundred soldiers:—centurion.

2761. κενῶς **kĕnōs**, *ken-oce';* adv. from 2756; *vainly*, i.e. *to no purpose*:—in vain.

2762. κεραία **kĕraia**, *ker-ah'-yah;* fem. of a presumed der. of the base of 2768; something *horn-like*, i.e. (spec.) the *apex* of a Heb. letter (fig. the least *particle*):—tittle.

2763. κεραμεύς **kĕramĕus**, *ker-am-yooce';* from 2766; a *potter*:—potter.

2764. **κεραμικός kĕramikŏs**, *ker-am-ik-os';* from *2766; made of clay,* i.e. *earthen:*—of a potter.

2765. **κεράμιον kĕramiŏn**, *ker-am'-ee-on;* neut. of a presumed der. of *2766;* an *earthenware* vessel, i.e. *jar:*—pitcher.

2766. **κέραμος kĕramŏs**, *ker'-am-os;* prob. from the base of *2767* (through the idea of *mixing* clay and water); *earthenware,* i.e. a *tile* (by anal. a thin *roof* or *awning*):—tiling.

2767. **κεράννυμι kĕrannumi**, *ker-an'-noo-mee;* a prol. form of a more prim. **κεράω kĕraō**, *ker-ah'-o* (which is used in certain tenses); to *mingle,* i.e. (by impl.) to *pour* out (for drinking):—fill, pour out. Comp. *3396.*

2768. **κέρας kĕras**, *ker'-as;* from a prim. **κάρ kar** (the *hair* of the head); a *horn* (lit. or fig.):—horn.

2769. **κεράτιον kĕratiŏn**, *ker-at'-ee-on;* neut of a presumed der. of *2768;* something *horned,* i.e. (spec.) the *pod* of the carob-tree:—husk.

κεράω kĕraō. See *2767.*

2770. **κερδαίνω kĕrdainō**, *ker-dah'ee-no;* from *2771;* to *gain* (lit. or fig.):—(get) gain, win.

2771. **κέρδος kĕrdŏs**, *ker'-dos;* of uncert affin.; *gain* (pecuniary or gen.):—gain, lucre.

2772. **κέρμα kĕrma**, *ker'-mah;* from *2751,* a *clipping* (*bit*), i.e. (spec.) a *coin:*—money

2773. **κερματιστής kĕrmatistēs**, *ker-mat-is-tace';* from a der. of *2772;* a *handler of coins,* i.e. *money-broker:*—changer of money.

2774. **κεφάλαιον kĕphalaiŏn**, *kef-al'-ah-yon;* neut. of a der. of *2776;* a *principal* thing, i.e. *main point;* spec. an *amount* (of money):—sum.

2775. **κεφαλαιόω kĕphalaiŏō**, *kef-al-ahee-ŏ'-o;* from the same as *2774;* (spec.) to *strike on the head:*—wound in the head.

2776. **κεφαλή kĕphalē**, *kef-al-ay';* prob. from the prim. **κάπτω kaptō** (in the sense of *seizing*); the *head* (as the part most readily *taken* hold of), lit. or fig.:—head.

2777. **κεφαλίς kĕphalis**, *kef-al-is';* from *2776;* prop. a *knob,* i.e. (by impl.) a *roll* (by extens. from the *end* of a stick on which the MS. was rolled):—volume.

2778. **κῆνσος kēnsŏs**, *kane'-sos;* of Lat. or.; prop. an *enrolment* ("*census*"), i.e. (by impl.) a *tax:*—tribute.

2779. **κῆπος kēpŏs**, *kay'-pos;* of uncert. affin.; a *garden:*—garden.

2780. **κηπουρός kēpŏurŏs**, *kay-poo-ros';* from *2779* and **οὖρος ŏurŏs** (a *warden*); a *garden-keeper,* i.e. *gardener:*—gardener.

2781. **κηρίον kēriŏn**, *kay-ree'-on;* dimin. from **κηός kēŏs** (*wax*); a *cell* for honey, i.e. (collect.) the *comb:*—[honey-] comb.

2782. **κήρυγμα kērugma**, *kay'-roog-mah;* from *2784;* a *proclamation* (espec. of the gospel; by impl. the *gospel* itself):—preaching.

2783. **κήρυξ kērux**, *kay'-roox;* from *2784;* a *herald,* i.e. of divine truth (espec. of the gospel):—preacher.

2784. **κηρύσσω kērussō**, *kay-roos'-so;* of uncert. affin.; to *herald* (as a public *crier*), espec. divine truth (the gospel):—preach (-er), proclaim, publish.

2785. **κῆτος kētŏs**, *kay'-tos;* prob. from the base of *5490;* a huge *fish* (as *gaping* for prey):—whale.

2786. **Κηφᾶς Kēphas**, *kay-fas';* of Chald. or. [comp. 8710]; *the Rock; Cephas* (i.e. *Kepha*), a surname of Peter:—Cephas.

2787. **κιβωτός kibōtŏs**, *kib-o-tos';* of uncert. der.; a *box,* i.e. the sacred *ark* and that of Noah:—ark.

2788. **κιθάρα kithara**, *kith-ar'-ah;* of uncert. affin.; a *lyre:*—harp.

2789. **κιθαρίζω kitharizō**, *kith-ar-id'-zo;* from *2788;* to *play on a lyre:*—harp.

2790. **κιθαρῳδός kitharōidŏs**, *kith-ar-o'-dos;* from *2788* and a der. of the same as *5603;* a *lyre-singer (-player),* i.e. *harpist:*—harper.

2791. **Κιλικία Kilikia**, *kil-ik-ee'-ah;* prob. of for. or.; *Cilicia,* a region of Asia Minor:—Cilicia.

2792. **κινάμωμον kinamōmŏn**, *kin-am'-o-mon;* of for. or. [comp. 7076]; *cinnamon:*—cinnamon.

2793. **κινδυνεύω kinduneuō**, *kin-doon-yoo'-o;* from *2794;* to *undergo peril:*—be in danger, be (stand) in jeopardy.

2794. **κίνδυνος kindunŏs**, *kin'-doo-nos;* of uncert. der.; *danger:*—peril.

2795. **κινέω kinĕō**, *kin-eh'-o;* from **κίω kiō** (poetic for **εἶμι ĕimi**, to *go*); to *stir* (trans.), lit. or fig.:—(re-) move (-r), wag.

2796. **κίνησις kinēsis**, *kin'-ay-sis;* from *2795;* a *stirring:*—moving.

2797. **Κίς Kis**, *kis;* of Heb. or. [7027]; *Cis* (i.e. *Kish*), an Isr.:—Cis.

κίχρημι kichrēmi. See *5531.*

2798. **κλάδος kladŏs**, *klad'-os;* from *2806;* a *twig* or *bough* (as if broken off):—branch.

2799. **κλαίω klaiō**, *klah'-yo;* of uncert. affin.; to *sob,* i.e. *wail* aloud (whereas *1145* is rather to *cry* silently):—bewail, weep.

2800. **κλάσις klasis**, *klas'-is;* from *2806; fracture* (the act):—breaking.

2801. **κλάσμα klasma**, *klas'-mah;* from *2806;* a *piece* (*bit*):—broken, fragment.

2802. **Κλαύδη Klaudē**, *klŏw'-day;* of uncert. der.; *Claude,* an island near Crete:—Clauda.

2803. **Κλαυδία Klaudia**, *klŏw-dee'-ah;* fem. of *2804; Claudia,* a Chr. woman:—Claudia.

2804. **Κλαύδιος Klaudiŏs**, *klŏw'-dee-os;* of Lat. or.; *Claudius,* the name of two Romans:—Claudius.

2805. **κλαυθμός klauthmŏs**, *klŏwth-mos';* from *2799; lamentation:*—wailing, weeping, × wept.

2806. **κλάω klaō**, *klah'-o;* a prim. verb; to *break* (spec. of bread):—break.

2807. **κλείς klĕis**, *klice;* from *2808;* a *key* (as *shutting* a lock), lit. or fig.:—key.

2808. **κλείω klĕiō**, *kli'-o;* a prim. verb; to *close* (lit. or fig.):—shut (up).

2809. **κλέμμα klĕmma**, *klem'-mah;* from *2813; stealing* (prop. the thing stolen, but used of the act):—theft.

2810. **Κλεόπας Klĕŏpas**, *kleh-op'-as;* prob. contr. from **Κλεόπατρος Klĕŏpatrŏs** (comp. of *2811* and *3962*); *Cleopas,* a Chr.:—Cleopas.

2811. **κλέος klĕŏs**, *kleh'-os;* from a shorter form of *2564; renown* (as if *being called*):—glory.

2812. **κλέπτης klĕptēs**, *klep'-tace;* from *2813;* a *stealer* (lit. or fig.):—thief. Comp. *3027.*

2813. **κλέπτω klĕptō**, *klep'-to;* a prim. verb; to *filch:*—steal.

2814. **κλῆμα klēma**, *klay'-mah;* from *2806;* a *limb* or *shoot* (as if *broken* off):—branch.

2815. **Κλήμης Klēmēs**, *klay'-mace;* of Lat. or.; *merciful; Clemes* (i.e. *Clemens*), a Chr.:—Clement.

2816. **κληρονομέω klērŏnŏmĕō**, *klay-ron-om-eh'-o;* from *2818;* to *be* an *heir* to (lit. or fig.):—be heir, (obtain by) inherit (-ance).

2817. **κληρονομία klērŏnŏmia**, *klay-ron-om-ee'-ah;* from *2818; heirship,* i.e. (concr.) a *patrimony* or (gen.) a *possession:*—inheritance.

2818. **κληρονόμος klērŏnŏmŏs**, *klay-ron-om'-os;* from *2819* and the base of *3551* (in its orig. sense of *partitioning,* i.e. [reflex.] *getting* by apportionment); a *sharer by lot,* i.e. an *inheritor* (lit. or fig.); by impl. a *possessor:*—heir.

2819. **κλῆρος klērŏs**, *klay'-ros;* prob. from *2806* (through the idea of using *bits* of wood, etc., for the purpose); a *die* (for drawing chances); by impl. a *portion* (as if so secured); by extens. an *acquisition* (espec. a *patrimony,* fig.):—heritage, inheritance, lot, part.

2820. **κληρόω klērŏō**, *klay-rŏ'-o;* from *2819;* to *allot,* i.e. (fig.) to *assign* (a privilege):—obtain an inheritance.

2821. **κλῆσις klēsis**, *klay'-sis;* from a shorter form of *2564;* an *invitation* (fig.):—calling, vocation.

2822. **κλητός klētŏs**, *klay-tos';* from the same as *2821; invited,* i.e. *appointed,* or (spec.) a *saint:*—called.

2823. **κλίβανος klibanŏs**, *klib'-an-os;* of uncert. der.; an earthen *pot* used for baking in:—oven.

2824. **κλίμα klima**, *klee'-mah;* from *2827;* a *slope,* i.e. (spec.) a "*clime*" or *tract* of country:—part, region.

2825. **κλίνη klinē**, *klee'-nay;* from *2827;* a *couch* (for sleep, sickness, sitting or eating):—bed, table.

2826. **κλινίδιον klinidiŏn**, *klin-id'-ee-on;* neut. of a presumed der. of *2825;* a *pallet* or *little couch:*—bed.

2827. **κλίνω klinō**, *klee'-no;* a prim. verb; to *slant* or *slope,* i.e. *incline* or *recline* (lit. or fig.):—bow (down), be far spent, lay, turn to flight, wear away.

2828. **κλισία klisia**, *klee-see'-ah;* from a der. of *2827;* prop. *reclination,* i.e. (concr. and spec.) a *party* at a meal:—company.

2829. **κλοπή klŏpē**, *klop-ay';* from *2813; stealing:*—theft.

2830. **κλύδων kludōn**, *kloo'-dohn;* from **κλύζω kluzō** (to *billow* or *dash* over); a *surge* of the sea (lit. or fig.):—raging, wave.

2831. **κλυδωνίζομαι kludōnizŏmai**, *kloo-do-nid'-zom-ahee;* mid. from *2830;* to *surge,* i.e. (fig.) to *fluctuate:*—toss to and fro.

2832. **Κλωπᾶς Klōpas**, *klo-pas';* of Chald. or. (corresp. to *256*); *Clopas,* an Isr.:—Clopas.

2833. **κνήθω knēthō**, *knay'-tho;* from a prim. **κνάω knaō** (to *scrape*); to *scratch,* i.e. (by impl.) to *tickle:*— × itching.

2834. **Κνίδος Knidŏs**, *knee'-dos;* prob. of for. or.; *Cnidus,* a place in Asia Minor:—Cnidus.

2835. **κοδράντης kŏdrantēs**, *kod-ran'-tace;* of Lat. or.; a *quadrans,* i.e. the fourth part of an as:—farthing.

2836. **κοιλία kŏilia**, *koy-lee'-ah;* from **κοῖλος kŏilŏs** ("*hollow*"); a *cavity,* i.e. (spec.) the *abdomen;* by impl. the *matrix;* fig. the *heart:*—belly, womb.

2837. **κοιμάω kŏimaō**, *koy-mah'-o;* from *2749;* to *put to sleep,* i.e. (pass. or reflex.) to *slumber;* fig. to *decease:*—(be a-, fall a-, fall on) sleep, be dead.

2838. **κοίμησις kŏimēsis**, *koy'-may-sis;* from *2837; sleeping,* i.e. (by impl.) *repose:*—taking of rest.

2839. **κοινός kŏinŏs**, *koy-nos';* prob. from *4862; common,* i.e. (lit.) shared by all or several, or (cer.) *profane:*—common, defiled, unclean, unholy.

2840. **κοινόω kŏinŏō**, *koy-nŏ'-o;* from *2839;* to *make* (or *consider*) *profane* (cer.):—call common, defile, pollute, unclean.

2841. **κοινωνέω kŏinōnĕō**, *koy-no-neh'-o;* from *2844;* to *share* with others (obj. or subj.):—communicate, distribute, be partaker.

2842. **κοινωνία kŏinōnia**, *koy-nohn-ee'-ah;* from *2844; partnership,* i.e. (lit.) *participation,* or (social) *intercourse,* or (pecuniary) *benefaction:*—(to) communicate (-ation), communion, (contri-) distribution, fellowship.

2843. **κοινωνικός kŏinōnikŏs**, *koy-no-nee-kos';* from *2844; communicative,* i.e. (pecuniarily) *liberal:*—willing to communicate.

2844. **κοινωνός kŏinōnŏs**, *koy-no-nos';* from *2839;* a *sharer,* i.e. *associate:*—companion, × fellowship, partaker, partner.

2845. **κοίτη kŏitē**, *koy'-tay;* from *2749;* a *couch;* by extens. *cohabitation;* by impl. the male *sperm:*—bed, chambering, × conceive.

2846. **κοιτών kŏitōn**, *koy-tone';* from *2845;* a *bedroom:*— + chamberlain.

2847. **κόκκινος kŏkkinŏs**, *kok'-kee-nos;* from *2848* (from the *kernel*-shape of the insect); *crimson-*colored:—scarlet (colour, coloured).

2848. **κόκκος kŏkkŏs**, *kok'-kos;* appar. a prim. word; a *kernel* of seed:—corn, grain.

2849. **κολάζω kŏlazō**, *kol-ad'-zo;* from **κόλος kŏlŏs** (*dwarf*); prop. to *curtail,* i.e. (fig.) to *chastise* (or *reserve* for infliction).—punish.

2850. κολακεία **kŏlakĕia**, *kol-ak-i'-ah;* from a der. of κόλαξ **kŏlax** (a fawner); flattery:— × flattering.

2851. κόλασις **kŏlasis**, *kol'-as-is;* from 2849; penal infliction:—punishment, torment.

2852. κολαφίζω **kŏlaphizō**, *kol-af-id'-zo;* from a der. of the base of 2849; to rap with the fist:—buffet.

2853. κολλάω **kŏllaō**, *kol-lah'-o;* from κόλλα **kŏlla** ("glue"); to glue, i.e. (pass. or reflex.) to stick (fig.):—cleave, join (self), keep company.

2854. κολλούριον **kŏllŏuriŏn**, *kol-loo'-ree-on;* neut. of a presumed der. of κολλύρα **kŏllura** (a cake; prob. akin to the base of 2853); prop. a poultice (as made of or in the form of crackers), i.e. (by anal.) a plaster:—eyesalve.

2855. κολλυβιστής **kŏllubistēs**, *kol-loo-bis-tace';* from a presumed der. of κόλλυβος **kŏllubŏs** (a small coin; prob. akin to 2854); a coin-dealer:—(money-) changer.

2856. κολοβόω **kŏlŏbŏō**, *kol-ob-ŏ'-o;* from a der. of the base of 2849; to dock, i.e. (fig.) abridge:—shorten.

2857. Κολοσσαί **Kŏlŏssai**, *kol-os-sah'ee;* appar. fem. plur. of κολοσσός **kŏlŏssŏs** ("colossal"); Colossæ, a place in Asia Minor:—Colosse.

2858. Κολοσσαεύς **Kŏlŏssaĕus**, *kol-os-sayoos';* fr. 2857; a Colossæan, i.e. inh. of Colossæ:—Colossian.

2859. κόλπος **kŏlpŏs**, *kol'-pos;* appar. a prim. word; the bosom; by anal. a bay:—bosom, creek.

2860. κολυμβάω **kŏlumbaō**, *kol-oom-bah'-o;* from κόλυμβος **kŏlumbŏs** (a diver); to plunge into water:—swim.

2861. κολυμβήθρα **kŏlumbēthra**, *kol-oom-bay'-thrah;* from 2860; a diving-place, i.e. pond for bathing (or swimming):—pool.

2862. κολωνία **kŏlōnia**, *kol-o-nee'-ah;* of Lat. or.; a Roman "colony" for veterans:—colony.

2863. κομάω **kŏmaō**, *kom-ah'-o;* from 2864; to wear tresses of hair:—have long hair.

2864. κόμη **kŏmē**, *kom'-ay;* appar. from the same as 2865; the hair of the head (locks, as ornamental, and thus differing from 2359, which prop. denotes merely the scalp):—hair.

2865. κομίζω **kŏmizō**, *kom-id'-zo;* from a prim. κομέω **kŏmĕō** (to tend, i.e. take care of); prop. to provide for, i.e. (by impl.) to carry off (as if from harm; gen. obtain):—bring, receive.

2866. κομψότερον **kŏmpsŏtĕrŏn**, *komp-sot'-er-on;* neut. compar. of a der. of the base of 2865 (mean. prop. well dressed, i.e. nice); fig. convalescent:—+ began to amend.

2867. κονιάω **kŏniaō**, *kon-ee-ah'-o;* from κονία **kŏnia** (dust; by anal. lime); to whitewash:—whiten.

2868. κονιορτός **kŏniŏrtŏs**, *kon-ee-or-tos';* from the base of 2867 and ὄρνυμι **ŏrnumi** (to "rouse"); pulverulence (as blown about):—dust.

2869. κοπάζω **kŏpazō**, *kop-ad'-zo;* from 2873; to tire, i.e. (fig.) to relax:—cease.

2870. κοπετός **kŏpĕtŏs**, *kop-et-os';* from 2875; mourning (prop. by beating the breast):—lamentation.

2871. κοπή **kŏpē**, *kop-ay';* from 2875; cutting, i.e. carnage:—slaughter.

2872. κοπιάω **kŏpiaō**, *kop-ee-ah'-o;* from a der. of 2873; to feel fatigue; by impl. to work hard:—(bestow) labour, toil, be wearied.

2873. κόπος **kŏpŏs**, *kop'-os;* from 2875; a cut, i.e. (by anal.) toil (as reducing the strength), lit. or fig.; by impl. pains:—labour, + trouble, weariness.

2874. κοπρία **kŏpria**, *kop-ree'-ah;* from κόπρος **kŏprŏs** (ordure; perh. akin to 2875); manure:—dung (-hill).

2875. κόπτω **kŏptō**, *kop'-to;* a prim. verb; to "chop"; spec. to beat the breast in grief:—cut down, lament, mourn, (be-) wail. Comp. the base of 5114.

2876. κόραξ **kŏrax**, *kor'-ax;* perh. from 2880; a crow (from its voracity):—raven.

2877. κοράσιον **kŏrasiŏn**, *kor-as'-ee-on;* neut. of a presumed der. of κόρη **kŏrē** (a maiden); a (little) girl:—damsel, maid.

2878. κορβᾶν **kŏrban**, *kor-ban';* and κορβανᾶς **kŏrbanas**, *kor-ban-as';* of Heb. and Chald. or. respectively [7133]; a votive offering and the offering; a consecrated present (to the Temple fund); by extens. (the latter term) the Treasury itself, i.e. the room where the contribution boxes stood:—Corban, treasury.

2879. Κορέ **Kŏrĕ**, *kor-eh';* of Heb. or. [7141]; Corè (i.e. Korach), an Isr.:—Core.

2880. κορέννυμι **kŏrĕnnumi**, *kor-en'-noo-mee;* a prim. verb; to cram, i.e. glut or sate:—eat enough, full.

2881. Κορίνθιος **Kŏrinthiŏs**, *kor-in'-thee-os;* from 2882; a Corinthian, i.e. inhab. of Corinth:—Corinthian.

2882. Κόρινθος **Kŏrinthŏs**, *kor'-in-thos;* of uncert. der.; Corinthus, a city of Greece:—Corinth.

2883. Κορνήλιος **Kŏrnēliŏs**, *kor-nay'-lee-os;* of Lat. or.; Cornelius, a Roman:—Cornelius.

2884. κόρος **kŏrŏs**, *kor'-os;* of Heb. or. [3734]; a cor, i.e. a specific measure:—measure.

2885. κοσμέω **kŏsmĕō**, *kos-meh'-o;* from 2889; to put in proper order, i.e. decorate (lit. or fig.); spec. to snuff (a wick):—adorn, garnish, trim.

2886. κοσμικός **kŏsmikŏs**, *kos-mee-kos';* from 2889 (in its secondary sense); terrene ("cosmic"), lit. (mundane) or fig. (corrupt):—worldly.

2887. κόσμιος **kŏsmiŏs**, *kos'-mee-os;* from 2889 (in its prim. sense); orderly, i.e. decorous:—of good behaviour, modest.

2888. κοσμοκράτωρ **kŏsmŏkratōr**, *kos-mok-rat'-ore;* from 2889 and 2902; a world-ruler, an epithet of Satan:—ruler.

2889. κόσμος **kŏsmŏs**, *kos'-mos;* prob. from the base of 2865; orderly arrangement, i.e. decoration; by impl. the world (in a wide or narrow sense, includ. its inhab., lit. or fig. [mor.]):—adorning, world.

2890. Κούαρτος **Kŏuartŏs**, *koo'-ar-tos;* of Lat. or. (fourth); Quartus, a Chr.:—Quartus.

2891. κοῦμι **kŏumi**, *koo'-mee;* of Chald. or. [6966]; cumi (i.e. rise!):—cumi.

2892. κουστωδία **kŏustōdia**, *koos-to-dee'-ah;* of Lat. or.; "custody", i.e. a Roman sentry:—watch.

2893. κουφίζω **kŏuphizō**, *koo-fid'-zo;* from κοῦφος **kŏuphŏs** (light in weight); to unload:—lighten.

2894. κόφινος **kŏphinŏs**, *kof'-ee-nos;* of uncert. der.; a (small) basket:—basket.

2895. κράββατος **krabbatŏs**, *krab'-bat-os;* prob. of for. or.; a mattress:—bed.

2896. κράζω **krazō**, *krad'-zo;* a prim. verb; prop. to "croak" (as a raven) or scream, i.e. (gen.) to call aloud (shriek, exclaim, intreat):—cry (out).

2897. κραιπάλη **kraipalē**, *krahee-pal'-ay;* prob. from the same as 726; prop. a headache (as a seizure of pain) from drunkenness, i.e. (by impl.) a debauch (by anal. a glut):—surfeiting.

2898. κρανίον **kraniŏn**, *kran-ee'-on;* dimin. of a der. of the base of 2768; a skull ("cranium"):—Calvary, skull.

2899. κράσπεδον **kraspĕdŏn**, *kras'-ped-on;* of uncert. der.; a margin, i.e. (spec.) a fringe or tassel:—border, hem.

2900. κραταιός **krataiŏs**, *krat-ah-yos';* from 2904; powerful:—mighty.

2901. κραταιόω **krataiŏō**, *krat-ah-yŏ'-o;* from 2900; to empower, i.e. (pass.) increase in vigor:—be strenghtened, be (wax) strong.

2902. κρατέω **kratĕō**, *krat-eh'-o;* from 2904; to use strength, i.e. seize or retain (lit. or fig.):—hold (by, fast), keep, lay hand (hold) on, obtain, retain, take (by).

2903. κράτιστος **kratistŏs**, *krat'-is-tos;* superl. of a der. of 2904; strongest, i.e. (in dignity) very honorable:—most excellent (noble).

2904. κράτος **kratŏs**, *krat'-os;* perh. a prim. word; vigor ["great"] (lit. or fig.):—dominion, might [-ily], power, strength.

2905. κραυγάζω **kraugazō**, *krŏw-gad'-zo;* from 2906; to clamor:—cry out.

2906. κραυγή **kraugē**, *krŏw-gay';* from 2896; an outcry (in notification, tumult or grief):—clamour, cry (-ing).

2907. κρέας **krĕas**, *kreh'-as;* perh. a prim. word; (butcher's) meat:—flesh.

2908. κρεῖσσον **krĕissŏn**, *krice'-son;* neut. of an alt. form of 2909; (as noun) better, i.e. greater advantage:—better.

2909. κρείττων **krĕittōn**, *krite'-tohn;* compar. of a der. of 2904; stronger, i.e. (fig.) better, i.e. nobler:—best, better.

2910. κρεμάννυμι **krĕmannumi**, *krem-an'-noo-mee;* a prol. form of a prim. verb; to hang:—hang.

2911. κρημνός **krēmnŏs**, *krame-nos';* from 2910; overhanging, i.e. a precipice:—steep place.

2912. Κρής **Krēs**, *krace;* from 2914; a Cretan, i.e. inhab. of Crete:—Crete, Cretian.

2913. Κρήσκης **Krēskēs**, *krace'-kace;* of Lat. or.; growing; Cresces (i.e. Crescens), a Chr.:—Crescens.

2914. Κρήτη **Krētē**, *kray'-tay;* of uncert. der.; Cretè, an island in the Mediterranean:—Crete.

2915. κριθή **krithē**, *kree-thay';* of uncert. der.; barley:—barley.

2916. κρίθινος **krithinŏs**, *kree'-thee-nos;* from 2915; consisting of barley:—barley.

2917. κρίμα **krima**, *kree'-mah;* from 2919; a decision (the function or the effect, for or against ["crime"]):—avenge, condemned, condemnation, damnation, + go to law, judgment.

2918. κρίνον **krinŏn**, *kree'-non;* perh. a prim. word; a lily:—lily.

2919. κρίνω **krinō**, *kree'-no;* prop. to distinguish, i.e. decide (mentally or judicially); by impl. to try, condemn, punish:—avenge, conclude, condemn, damn, decree, determine, esteem, judge, go to (sue at the) law, ordain, call in question, sentence to, think.

2920. κρίσις **krisis**, *kree'-sis;* decision (subj. or obj., for or against); by extens. a tribunal; by impl. justice (spec. divine law):—accusation, condemnation, damnation, judgment.

2921. Κρίσπος **Krispŏs**, *kris'-pos;* of Lat. or.; "crisp"; Crispus, a Corinthian:—Crispus.

2922. κριτήριον **kritēriŏn**, *kree-tay'-ree-on;* neut. of a presumed der. of 2923; a rule of judging ("criterion"), i.e. (by impl.) a tribunal:—to judge, judgment (seat).

2923. κριτής **kritēs**, *kree-tace';* from 2919; a judge (gen. or spec.):—judge.

2924. κριτικός **kritikŏs**, *krit-ee-kos';* from 2923; decisive ("critical"), i.e. discriminative:—discerner.

2925. κρούω **krŏuō**, *kroo'-o;* appar. a prim. verb; to rap:—knock.

2926. κρυπτή **kruptē**, *kroop-tay';* fem. of 2927; a hidden place, i.e. cellar ("crypt"):—secret.

2927. κρυπτός **kruptŏs**, *kroop-tos';* from 2928; concealed, i.e. private:—hid (-den), inward [-ly], secret.

2928. κρύπτω **kruptō**, *kroop'-to;* a prim. verb; to conceal (prop. by covering):—hide (self), keep secret, secret [-ly].

2929. κρυσταλλίζω **krustallizō**, *kroos-tal-lid'-zo;* from 2930; to make (i.e. intrans. resemble) ice ("crystallize"):—be clear as crystal.

2930. κρύσταλλος **krustallŏs**, *kroos'-tal-los;* from a der. of κρύος **kruŏs** (frost); ice, i.e. (by anal.) rock "crystal":—crystal.

2931. κρυφῆ **kruphē**, *kroo-fay';* adv. from 2928; privately:—in secret.

2932. κτάομαι **ktaŏmai**, *ktah'-om-ahee;* a prim. verb; to get, i.e. acquire (by any means; own):—obtain, possess, provide, purchase.

2933. κτῆμα **ktēma**, *ktay'-mah;* from *2932;* an *acquirement*, i.e. *estate:*—possession.

2934. κτῆνος **ktēnŏs**, *ktay'-nos;* from *2932; property*, i.e. (spec.) a domestic *animal:*—beast.

2935. κτήτωρ **ktētōr**, *ktay'-tore;* from *2932;* an *owner:*—possessor.

2936. κτίζω **ktizō**, *ktid'-zo;* prob. akin to *2932* (through the idea of the *proprietorship* of the *manufacturer*); to *fabricate*, i.e. *found* (*form* originally):—create, Creator, make.

2937. κτίσις **ktisis**, *ktis'-is;* from *2936;* original *formation* (prop. the act; by impl. the thing, lit. or fig.):—building, creation, creature, ordinance.

2938. κτίσμα **ktisma**, *ktis'-mah;* from *2936;* an original *formation* (concr.), i.e. *product* (created thing):—creature.

2939. κτιστής **ktistēs**, *ktis-tace';* from *2936;* a *founder*, i.e. *God* (as author of all things):—Creator.

2940. κυβεία **kubĕia**, *koo-bi'-ah;* from κύβος **kubŏs** (a "*cube*", i.e. *die* for playing); *gambling*, i.e. (fig.) *artifice* or *fraud:*—sleight.

2941. κυβέρνησις **kubĕrnēsis**, *koo-ber'-nay-sis;* from κυβερνάω **kubĕrnaō** (of Lat. or., to *steer*); *pilotage*, i.e. (fig.) *directorship* (in the church):—government.

2942. κυβερνήτης **kubĕrnētēs**, *koo-ber-nay'-tace;* from the same as *2941; helmsman*, i.e. (by impl.) *captain:*—(ship) master.

2943. κυκλόθεν **kuklŏthĕn**, *koo-kloth'-en;* adv. from the same as *2945; from the circle*, i.e. *all around:*—(round) about.

κυκλός **kuklŏs**. See *2945*.

2944. κυκλόω **kuklŏō**, *koo-klŏ'-o;* from the same as *2945;* to *encircle*, i.e. *surround:*—compass (about), come (stand) round about.

2945. κύκλῳ **kuklōi**, *koo'-klo;* as if dat. of κύκλος **kuklŏs** (a *ring*, "*cycle*"; akin to *2947*); i.e. *in a circle* (by impl. of *1722*), i.e. (adv.) *all around:*—round about.

2946. κύλισμα **kulisma**, *koo'-lis-mah;* from *2947;* a *wallow* (the effect of *rolling*), i.e. *filth:*—wallowing.

2947. κυλιόω **kuliŏō**, *koo-lee-ŏ'-o;* from the base of *2949* (through the idea of *circularity;* comp. *2945*, *1507*); to *roll* about:—wallow.

2948. κυλλός **kullŏs**, *kool-los';* from the same as *2947; rocking* about, i.e. *crippled* (*maimed*, in feet or hands):—maimed.

2949. κῦμα **kuma**, *koo'-mah;* from κύω **kuō** (to *swell* [with young], i.e. *bend, curve*); a *billow* (as *bursting* or *toppling*):—wave.

2950. κύμβαλον **kumbalŏn**, *koom'-bal-on;* from a der. of the base of *2949;* a "*cymbal*" (as *hollow*):—cymbal.

2951. κύμινον **kuminŏn**, *koo'-min-on;* of for. or. [comp. 3646]; *dill* or *fennel* ("cummin"):—cummin.

2952. κυνάριον **kunariŏn**, *koo-nar'-ee-on;* neut. of a presumed der. of *2965;* a *puppy:*—dog.

2953. Κύπριος **Kupriŏs**, *koo'-pree-os;* from *2954;* a *Cyprian* (*Cypriot*), i.e. inhab. of Cyprus:—of Cyprus.

2954. Κύπρος **Kuprŏs**, *koo'-pros;* of uncert. or.; *Cyprus*, an island in the Mediterranean:—Cyprus.

2955. κύπτω **kuptō**, *koop'-to;* prob. from the base of *2949;* to *bend* forward:—stoop (down).

2956. Κυρηναῖος **Kurēnaiŏs**, *koo-ray-nah'-yos;* from *2957;* a *Cyrenæan*, i.e. inhab. of Cyrene:—of Cyrene, Cyrenian.

2957. Κυρήνη **Kurēnē**, *koo-ray'-nay;* of uncert. der.; *Cyrenè*, a region of Africa:—Cyrene.

2958. Κυρήνιος **Kurēniŏs**, *koo-ray'-nee-os;* of Lat. or.; *Cyrenius* (i.e. *Quirinus*), a Roman:—Cyrenius.

2959. Κυρία **Kuria**, *koo-ree'-ah;* fem. of *2962;* *Cyria*, a Chr. woman:—lady.

2960. κυριακός **kuriakŏs**, *koo-ree-ak-os';* from *2962; belonging to* the *Lord* (Jehovah or Jesus):—Lord's.

2961. κυριεύω **kuriĕuō**, *koo-ree-yoo'-o;* from *2962;* to *rule:*—have dominion over, lord, be lord of, exercise lordship over.

2962. κύριος **kuriŏs**, *koo'-ree-os;* from κῦρος **kurŏs** (*supremacy*); *supreme* in authority, i.e. (as noun) *controller;* by impl. *Mr.* (as a respectful title):—God, Lord, master, Sir.

2963. κυριότης **kuriŏtēs**, *koo-ree-ot'-ace;* from *2962; mastery*, i.e. (concr. and coll.) *rulers:*—dominion, government.

2964. κυρόω **kurŏō**, *koo-rŏ'-o;* from the same as *2962;* to *make authoritative*, i.e. *ratify:*—confirm.

2965. κύων **kuōn**, *koo'-ohn;* a prim. word; a *dog* ["*hound*"] (lit. or fig.):—dog.

2966. κῶλον **kōlŏn**, *ko'-lon;* from the base of *2849;* a *limb* of the body (as if *lopped*):—carcase.

2967. κωλύω **kōluō**, *ko-loo'-o;* from the base of *2849;* to *estop*, i.e. *prevent* (by word or act):—forbid, hinder, keep from, let, not suffer, withstand.

2968. κώμη **kōmē**, *ko'-may;* from *2749;* a *hamlet* (as if *laid* down):—town, village.

2969. κωμόπολις **kōmŏpŏlis**, *ko-mop'-ol-is;* from *2968* and *4172;* an unwalled *city:*—town.

2970. κῶμος **kōmŏs**, *ko'-mos;* from *2749;* a *carousal* (as if a *letting loose*):—revelling, rioting.

2971. κώνωψ **kōnōps**, *ko'-nopes;* appar. from a der. of the base of *2759* and a der. of *3700;* a *mosquito* (from its *stinging proboscis*):—gnat.

2972. Κῶς **Kōs**, *koce;* of uncert. or.; *Cos*, an island in the Mediterranean:—Cos.

2973. Κωσάμ **Kōsam**, *ko-sam';* of Heb. or. [comp. 7081]; *Cosam* (i.e. *Kosam*), an Isr.:—Cosam.

2974. κωφός **kōphŏs**, *ko-fos';* from *2875; blunted*, i.e. (fig.) of hearing (*deaf*) or speech (*dumb*):—deaf, dumb, speechless.

Λ

2975. λαγχάνω **lagchanō**, *lang-khan'-o;* a prol. form of a prim. verb, which is only used as an alt. in certain tenses; to *lot*, i.e. *determine* (by impl. *receive*) espec. by lot:—his lot be, cast lots, obtain.

2976. Λάζαρος **Lazarŏs**, *lad'-zar-os;* prob. of Heb. or. [499]; *Lazarus* (i.e. *Elazar*), the name of two Isr. (one imaginary):—Lazarus.

2977. λάθρα **lathra**, *lath'-rah;* adv. from *2990; privately:*—privily, secretly.

2978. λαῖλαψ **lailaps**, *lah'ee-laps;* of uncert. der.; a *whirlwind* (*squall*):—storm, tempest.

2979. λακτίζω **laktizō**, *lak-tid'-zo;* from adv. λάξ **lax** (*heelwise*); to *recalcitrate:*—kick.

2980. λαλέω **lalĕō**, *lal-eh'-o;* a prol. form of an otherwise obsol. verb; to *talk*, i.e. *utter* words:—preach, say, speak (after), talk, tell, utter. Comp. *3004*.

2981. λαλιά **lalia**, *lal-ee-ah';* from *2980; talk:*—saying, speech.

2982. λαμά **lama**, *lam-ah';* or

λαμμᾶ **lamma**, *lam-mah';* of Heb. or. [4100 with prep. pref.]; *lama* (i.e. *why*):—lama.

2983. λαμβάνω **lambanō**, *lam-ban'-o;* a prol. form of a prim. verb, which is used only as an alt. in certain tenses; to *take* (in very many applications, lit. and fig. [prop. obj. or act., to *get hold* of; whereas *1209* is rather subj. or pass., to *have offered* to one; while *138* is more violent, to *seize* or *remove*]):—accept, + be amazed, assay, attain, bring, × when I call, catch, come on (× unto), + forget, have, hold, obtain, receive (× after), take (away, up).

2984. Λάμεχ **Lamĕch**, *lam'-ekh;* of Heb. or. [3929]; *Lamech* (i.e. *Lemek*), a patriarch:—Lamech.

λαμμᾶ **lamma**. See *2982*.

2985. λαμπάς **lampas**, *lam-pas';* from *2989;* a "*lamp*" or *flambeau:*—lamp, light, torch.

2986. λαμπρός **lamprŏs**, *lam-pros';* from the same as *2985; radiant;* by anal. *limpid;* fig. *magnificent* or *sumptuous* (in appearance):—bright, clear, gay, goodly, gorgeous, white.

2987. λαμπρότης **lamprŏtēs**, *lam-prot'-ace;* from *2896; brilliancy:*—brightness.

2988. λαμπρῶς **lamprōs**, *lam-proce';* adv. from *2986; brilliantly*, i.e. (fig.) *luxuriously:*—sumptuously.

2989. λάμπω **lampō**, *lam'-po;* a prim. verb; to *beam*, i.e. *radiate* brilliancy (lit. or fig.):—give light, shine.

2990. λανθάνω **lanthanō**, *lan-than'-o;* a prol. form of a prim. verb, which is used only as an alt. in certain tenses; to *lie hid* (lit. or fig.); often used adv. *unwittingly:*—be hid, be ignorant of, unawares.

2991. λαξευτός **laxĕutŏs**, *lax-yoo-tos';* from a comp. of λᾶς **las** (a *stone*) and the base of *3584* (in its orig. sense of *scraping*); *rock-quarried:*—hewn in stone.

2992. λαός **laŏs**, *lah-os';* appar. a prim. word; a *people* (in gen.; thus differing from *1218*, which denotes one's *own* populace):—people.

2993. Λαοδίκεια **Laŏdikĕia**, *lah-od-ik'-i-ah;* from a comp. of *2992* and *1349;* *Laodicia*, a place in Asia Minor:—Laodicea.

2994. Λαοδικεύς **Laŏdikĕus**, *lah-od-ik-yooce';* from *2993;* a *Laodicean*, i.e. inhab. of Laodicia:—Laodicean.

2995. λάρυγξ **larugx**, *lar'-oongks;* of uncert. der.; the *throat* ("*larynx*"):—throat.

2996. Λασαία **Lasaia**, *las-ah'-yah;* of uncert. or.; *Lasæa*, a place in Crete:—Lasea.

2997. λάσχω **laschō**, *las'-kho;* a strengthened form of a prim. verb, which only occurs in this and another prol. form as alt. in certain tenses; to *crack* open (from a fall):—burst asunder.

2998. λατομέω **latŏmĕō**, *lat-om-eh'-o;* from the same as the first part of *2991* and the base of *5114;* to *quarry:*—hew.

2999. λατρεία **latrĕia**, *lat-ri'-ah;* from *3000; ministration* of God, i.e. *worship:*—(divine) service.

3000. λατρεύω **latrĕuō**, *lat-ryoo'-o;* from λάτρις **latris** (a hired *menial*); to *minister* (to God), i.e. *render* religious *homage:*—serve, do the service, worship (-per).

3001. λάχανον **lachanŏn**, *lakh'-an-on;* from λαχαίνω **lachainō** (to *dig*); a *vegetable:*—herb.

3002. Λεββαῖος **Lĕbbaiŏs**, *leb-bah'-yos;* of uncert. or.; *Lebbæus*, a Chr.:—Lebbæus.

3003. λεγεών **lĕgĕōn**, *leg-eh-ohn';* of Lat. or.; a "*legion*", i.e. Rom. *regiment* (fig.):—legion.

3004. λέγω **lĕgō**, *leg'-o;* a prim. verb; prop. to "*lay*" forth, i.e. (fig.) *relate* (in words [usually of systematic or set *discourse;* whereas *2036* and *5346* generally refer to an *individual* expression or speech respectively; while *4483* is prop. to *break silence* merely, and *2980* means an *extended* or random harangue]); by impl. to *mean:*—ask, bid, boast, call, describe, give out, name, put forth, say (-ing, on), shew, speak, tell, utter.

3005. λεῖμμα **lĕimma**, *lime'-mah;* from *3007;* a *remainder:*—remnant.

3006. λεῖος **lĕiŏs**, *li'-os;* appar. a prim. word; *smooth*, i.e. "*level*":—smooth.

3007. λείπω **lĕipō**, *li'-po;* a prim. verb; to *leave*, i.e. (intrans. or pass.) to *fail* or *be absent:*—be destitute (wanting), lack.

3008. λειτουργέω **lĕitŏurgĕō**, *li-toorg-eh'-o;* from *3011;* to be a *public servant*, i.e. (by anal.) to *perform* religious or charitable *functions* (*worship, obey, relieve*):—minister.

3009. λειτουργία **lĕitŏurgia**, *li-toorg-ee'-ah;* from *3008; public function* (as priest ["*liturgy*"] or almsgiver):—ministration (-try), service.

3010. λειτουργικός **lĕitŏurgikŏs**, *li-toorg-ik-os';* from the same as *3008; functional publicly* ("liturgic"), i.e. *beneficent:*—ministering.

3011. λειτουργός **lĕitŏurgŏs**, *li-toorg-os';* from a der. of *2992* and *2041;* a *public servant*, i.e. a *functionary* in the Temple or Gospel, or (gen.) a *worshipper* (of God) or *benefactor* (of man):—minister (-ed).

3012. λέντιον **lĕntiŏn**, *len'-tee-on;* of Lat. or.; a "*linen*" cloth, i.e. *apron:*—towel.

3013. λεπίς **lĕpis**, *lep-is';* from λέπω **lĕpō** (to *peel*); a *flake:*—scale.

3014. λέπρα **lĕpra**, *lep'-rah;* from the same as 3013; *scaliness*, i.e. "*leprosy*":—leprosy.

3015. λεπρός **lĕprŏs**, *lep-ros';* from the same as 3014; *scaly*, i.e. *leprous* (a *leper*):—leper.

3016. λεπτόν **lĕptŏn**, *lep-ton';* neut. of a der. of the same as 3013; something *scaled* (*light*), i.e. a small *coin:*—mite.

3017. Λευΐ **Lĕuï**, *lyoo-ee';* of Heb. or. [3878]; *Levi*, the name of three Isr.:—Levi. Comp. 3018.

3018. Λευΐς **Lĕuïs**, *lyoo-is';* a form of 3017; *Lewis* (i.e. *Levi*), a Chr.:—Levi.

3019. Λευΐτης **Lĕuïtēs**, *lyoo-ee'-tace;* from 3017; a *Levite*, i.e. desc. of Levi:—Levite.

3020. Λευϊτικός **Lĕuïtikŏs**, *lyoo-it'-ee-kos;* from 3019; *Levitic*, i.e. relating to the Levites:—Levitical.

3021. λευκαίνω **lĕukainō**, *lyoo-kah'ee-no;* from 3022; to *whiten:*—make white, whiten.

3022. λευκός **lĕukŏs**, *lyoo-kos';* from λύκη **lukē** ("*light*"); *white:*—white.

3023. λεών **lĕōn**, *leh-ohn';* a prim. word; a "*lion*":—lion.

3024. λήθη **lēthē**, *lay'-thay;* from 2990; *forgetfulness:*— + forget.

3025. ληνός **lēnŏs**, *lay-nos';* appar. a prim. word; a *trough*, i.e. wine-*vat:*—winepress.

3026. λῆρος **lērŏs**, *lay'-ros;* appar. a prim. word; *twaddle*, i.e. an *incredible* story:—idle tale.

3027. λῃστης **lēstēs**, *lace-tace';* from ληΐζομαι **lēïzŏmai** (to *plunder*); a *brigand:*—robber, thief.

3028. λῆψις **lēpsis**, *lape'-sis;* from 2983; *receipt* (the act):—receiving.

3029. λίαν **lian**, *lee'-an;* of uncert. affin.; *much* (adv.):—exceeding, great (-ly), sore, very (+ chiefest).

3030. λίβανος **libanŏs**, *lib'-an-os;* of for. or. [3828]; the *incense*-tree, i.e. (by impl.) *incense* itself:—frankincense.

3031. λιβανωτός **libanōtŏs**, *lib-an-o-tos';* from 3030; *frankincense*, i.e. (by extens.) a *censer* for burning it:—censer.

3032. Λιβερτῖνος **Libĕrtinŏs**, *lib-er-tee'-nos;* of Lat. or.; a Rom. *freedman:*—Libertine.

3033. Λιβύη **Libuē**, *lib-oo'-ay;* prob. from 3047; *Libye*, a region of Africa:—Libya.

3034. λιθάζω **lithazō**, *lith-ad'-zo;* from 3037; to *lapidate:*—stone.

3035. λίθινος **lithinŏs**, *lith'-ee-nos;* from 3037; *stony*, i.e. made of *stone:*—of stone.

3036. λιθοβολέω **lithŏbŏlĕō**, *lith-ob-ol-eh'-o;* from a comp. of 3037 and 906; to *throw stones*, i.e. *lapidate:*—stone, cast stones.

3037. λίθος **lithŏs**, *lee'-thos;* appar. a prim. word; a *stone* (lit. or fig.):—(mill-, stumbling-) stone.

3038. λιθόστρωτος **lithŏstrōtŏs**, *lith-os'-tro-tos;* from 3037 and a der. of 4766; *stone-strewed*, i.e. a tessellated *mosaic* on which the Rom. tribunal was placed:—Pavement.

3039. λικμάω **likmaō**, *lik-mah'-o;* from λικμός **likmŏs**, the equiv. of λίκνον **liknŏn** (a winnowing *fan* or basket); to *winnow*, i.e. (by anal.) to *triturate:*—grind to powder.

3040. λιμήν **limēn**, *lee-mane';* appar. a prim. word; a *harbor:*—haven. Comp. 2568.

3041. λίμνη **limnē**, *lim'-nay;* prob. from 3040 (through the idea of the nearness of shore); a *pond* (large or small):—lake.

3042. λιμός **limŏs**, *lee-mos';* prob. from 3007 (through the idea of *destitution*); a *scarcity* of food:—dearth, famine, hunger.

3043. λίνον **linŏn**, *lee'-non;* prob. a prim. word; *flax*, i.e. (by impl.) "*linen*":—linen.

3044. Λῖνος **Linŏs**, *lee'-nos;* perh. from 3043; *Linus*, a Chr.:—Linus.

3045. λιπαρός **liparŏs**, *lip-ar-os';* from λίπος **lipŏs** (*grease*); *fat*, i.e. (fig.) *sumptuous:*—dainty.

3046. λίτρα **litra**, *lee'-trah;* of Lat. or. [*libra*]; a *pound* in weight:—pound.

3047. λίψ **lips**, *leeps;* prob. from λείβω **lĕibō** (to *pour* a "*libation*"); the *south* (-west) wind (as bringing rain, i.e. (by extens.) the *south* quarter:—southwest.

3048. λογία **lŏgia**, *log-ee'-ah;* from 3056 (in the commercial sense); a *contribution:*—collection, gathering.

3049. λογίζομαι **lŏgizŏmai**, *log-id'-zom-ahee;* mid. from 3056; to *take an inventory*, i.e. *estimate* (lit. or fig.):—conclude, (ac-) count (of), + despise, esteem, impute, lay, number, reason, reckon, suppose, think (on).

3050. λογικός **lŏgikŏs**, *log-ik-os';* from 3056; *rational* ("*logical*"):—reasonable, of the word.

3051. λόγιον **lŏgiŏn**, *log'-ee-on;* neut. of 3052; an *utterance* (of God):—oracle.

3052. λόγιος **lŏgiŏs**, *log'-ee-os;* from 3056; *fluent*, i.e. an *orator:*—eloquent.

3053. λογισμός **lŏgismŏs**, *log-is-mos';* from 3049; *computation*, i.e. (fig.) *reasoning* (*conscience*, *conceit*):—imagination, thought.

3054. λογομαχέω **lŏgŏmachĕō**, *log-om-akh-eh'-o;* from a comp. of 3056 and 3164; to *be disputatious* (on trifles):—strive about words.

3055. λογομαχία **lŏgŏmachia**, *log-om-akh-ee'-ah;* from the same as 3054; *disputation* about trifles ("*logomachy*"):—strife of words.

3056. λόγος **lŏgŏs**, *log'-os;* from 3004; something *said* (including the *thought*); by impl. a *topic* (subject of discourse), also *reasoning* (the mental faculty) or *motive;* by extens. a *computation;* spec. (with the art. in John) the Divine *Expression* (i.e. *Christ*):—account, cause, communication, × concerning, doctrine, fame, × have to do, intent, matter, mouth, preaching, question, reason, + reckon, remove, say (-ing), shew, × speaker, speech, talk, thing, + none of these things move me, tidings, treatise, utterance, word, work.

3057. λόγχη **lŏgchē**, *long'-khay;* perh. a prim. word; a "*lance*":—spear.

3058. λοιδορέω **lŏidŏrĕō**, *loy-dor-eh'-o;* from 3060; to *reproach*, i.e. *vilify:*—revile.

3059. λοιδορία **lŏidŏria**, *loy-dor-ee'-ah;* from 3060; *slander* or *vituperation:*—railing, reproach [-fully].

3060. λοίδορος **lŏidŏrŏs**, *loy'-dor-os;* from λοιδός **lŏidŏs** (*mischief*); *abusive*, i.e. a *blackguard;*—railer, reviler.

3061. λοιμός **lŏimŏs**, *loy-mos';* of uncert. affin.; a *plague* (lit. the *disease*, or fig. a *pest*):—pestilence (-t).

3062. λοιποί **lŏipŏy**, *loy-poy';* masc. plur. of a der. of 3007; *remaining* ones:—other, which remain, remnant, residue, rest.

3063. λοιπόν **lŏipŏn**, *loy-pon';* neut. sing. of the same as 3062; something *remaining* (adv.):—besides, finally, furthermore, (from) henceforth, moreover, now, + it remaineth, then.

3064. λοιποῦ **lŏipŏu**, *loy-poo';* gen. sing. of the same as 3062; *remaining* time:—from henceforth.

3065. Λουκᾶς **Lŏukas**, *loo-kas';* contr. from Lat. *Lucanus; Lucas*, a Chr.:—Lucas, Luke.

3066. Λούκιος **Lŏukiŏs**, *loo'-kee-os;* of Lat. or.; *illuminative; Lucius*, a Chr.:—Lucius.

3067. λουτρόν **lŏutrŏn**, *loo-tron';* from 3068; a *bath*, i.e. (fig.) *baptism:*—washing.

3068. λούω **lŏuō**, *loo'-o;* a prim. verb; to *bathe* (the *whole* person; whereas 3538 means to wet a *part* only, and 4150 to wash, cleanse *garments* exclusively):—wash.

3069. Λύδδα **Ludda**, *lud'-dah;* of Heb. or. [3850]; *Lydda* (i.e. *Lod*), a place in Pal.:—Lydda.

3070. Λυδία **Ludia**, *loo-dee'-ah;* prop. fem. of Λύδιος **Ludiŏs** [of for. or.] (a *Lydian*, in Asia Minor); *Lydia*, a Chr. woman:—Lydia.

3071. Λυκαονία **Lukaŏnia**, *loo-kah-on-ee'-ah;* perh. remotely from 3074; *Lycaonia*, a region of Asia Minor:—Lycaonia.

3072. Λυκαονιστί **Lukaŏnisti**, *loo-kah-on-is-tee';* adv. from a der. of 3071; *Lycaonistically*, i.e. in the language of the Lycaonians:—in the speech of Lycaonia.

3073. Λυκία **Lukia**, *loo-kee'-ah;* prob. remotely from 3074; *Lycia*, a province of Asia Minor:—Lycia.

3074. λύκος **lukŏs**, *loo'-kos;* perh. akin to the base of 3022 (from the *whitish* hair); a *wolf:*—wolf.

3075. λυμαίνομαι **lumainŏmai**, *loo-mah'ee-nom-ahee;* mid. from a prob. der. of 3089 (mean. *filth*); prop. to *soil*, i.e. (fig.) *insult* (*maltreat*):—make havock of.

3076. λυπέω **lupĕō**, *loo-peh'-o;* from 3077; to *distress;* reflex. or pass. to *be sad:*—cause grief, grieve, be in heaviness, (be) sorrow (-ful), be (make) sorry.

3077. λύπη **lupē**, *loo'-pay;* appar. a prim. word; *sadness:*—grief, grievous, + grudgingly, heaviness, sorrow.

3078. Λυσανίας **Lusanias**, *loo-san-ee'-as;* from 3080 and ἀνία **ania** (*trouble*); *grief-dispelling; Lysanias*, a governor of Abilene:—Lysanias.

3079. Λυσίας **Lusias**, *loo-see'-as;* of uncert. affin.; *Lysias*, a Rom.:—Lysias.

3080. λύσις **lusis**, *loo'-sis;* from 3089; a *loosening*, i.e. (spec.) *divorce:*—to be loosed.

3081. λυσιτελεῖ **lusitĕlĕi**, *loo-sit-el-i';* third pers. sing. pres. indic. act. of a der. of a comp. of 3080 and 5056; impers. it *answers* the *purpose*, i.e. *is advantageous:*—it is better.

3082. Λύστρα **Lustra**, *loos'-trah;* of uncert. or.; *Lystra*, a place in Asia Minor:—Lystra.

3083. λύτρον **lutrŏn**, *loo'-tron;* from 3089; something to *loosen* with, i.e. a redemption *price* (fig. *atonement*):—ransom.

3084. λυτρόω **lutrŏō**, *loo-trŏ'-o;* from 3083; to *ransom* (lit. or fig.):—redeem.

3085. λύτρωσις **lutrōsis**, *loo'-tro-sis;* from 3084; a *ransoming* (fig.):— + redeemed, redemption.

3086. λυτρωτής **lutrōtēs**, *loo-tro-tace';* from 3084; a *redeemer* (fig.):—deliverer.

3087. λυχνία **luchnia**, *lookh-nee'-ah;* from 3088; a *lamp-stand* (lit. or fig.):—candlestick.

3088. λύχνος **luchnŏs**, *lookh'-nos;* from the base of 3022; a portable *lamp* or other *illuminator* (lit. or fig.):—candle, light.

3089. λύω **luō**, *loo'-o;* a prim. verb; to "*loosen*" (lit. or fig.):—break (up), destroy, dissolve, (un-) loose, melt, put off. Comp. 4486.

3090. Λωΐς **Lōïs**, *lo-ece';* of uncert. or.; *Loïs*, a Chr. woman:—Lois.

3091. Λώτ **Lōt**, *lote;* of Heb. or. [3876]; *Lot*, a patriarch:—Lot.

M

3092. Μαάθ **Maath**, *mah-ath';* prob. of Heb. or.; *Maath*, an Isr.:—Maath.

3093. Μαγδαλά **Magdala**, *mag-dal-ah';* of Chald. or. [comp. 4026]; *the tower; Magdala* (i.e *Migdala*), a place in Pal.:—Magdala.

3094. Μαγδαληνή **Magdalēnē**, *mag-dal-ay-nay';* fem. of a der. of 3093; a female *Magdalene*, i.e. inhab. of Magdala:—Magdalene.

3095. μαγεία **magĕia**, *mag-i'-ah;* from 3096; "*magic*":—sorcery.

3096. μαγεύω **magĕuō**, *mag-yoo'-o;* from 3097; to *practice magic:*—use sorcery.

3097. μάγος **magŏs**, *mag'-os;* of for. or. [7248]; a *Magian*, i.e. Oriental *scientist;* by impl. a *magician:*—sorcerer, wise man.

3098. Μαγώγ **Magōg**, *mag-ogue';* of Heb. or. [4031]; *Magog*, a for. nation, i.e. (fig.) an Antichristian party:—Magog.

3099. Μαδιάν **Madian**, *mad-ee-an';* of Heb. or. [4080]; *Madian* (i.e. *Midian*), a region of Arabia:—Madian.

3100. μαθητεύω **mathētĕuō**, *math-ayt-yoo'-o;* from 3101; intrans. to *become a pupil;* trans. to *disciple*, i.e. enrol as scholar:—be disciple, instruct, teach.

3101. μαθητής **mathētēs**, *math-ay-tes';* from 3129; a *learner*, i.e. *pupil:*—disciple.

3102. μαθήτρια **mathētria**, *math-ay'-tree-ah;* fem. from 3101; a female *pupil:*—disciple.

3103. Μαθουσάλα **Mathŏusala**, *math-oo-sal'-ah;* of Heb. or. [4968]; *Mathusala* (i.e. *Methushelach*), an antediluvian:—Mathusala.

3104. Μαϊνάν **Maïnan**, *mahee-nan';* prob. of Heb. or.; *Maïnan*, an Isr.:—Mainan.

3105. μαίνομαι **mainŏmai**, *mah'ee-nom-ahee;* mid. from a prim. μάω **maō** (to *long* for; through the idea of insensate *craving*); to *rave* as a "maniac":—be beside self (mad).

3106. μακαρίζω **makarizō**, *mak-ar-id'-zo;* from *3107;* to *beatify*, i.e. *pronounce* (or *esteem*) *fortunate:*—call blessed, count happy.

3107. μακάριος **makariŏs**, *mak-ar'-ee-os;* a prol. form of the poetical μάκαρ **makar** (mean. the same); supremely *blest;* by extens. *fortunate, well off:*—blessed, happy (× -ier).

3108. μακαρισμός **makarismŏs**, *mak-ar-is-mos';* from *3106;* *beatification*, i.e. *attribution of good fortune:*—blessedness.

3109. Μακεδονία **Makĕdŏnia**, *mak-ed-on-ee'-ah;* from *3110;* *Macedonia*, a region of Greece:—Macedonia.

3110. Μακεδών **Makĕdōn**, *mak-ed'-ohn;* of uncert. der.; a *Macedon* (*Macedonian*), i.e. inhab. of Macedonia:—of Macedonia, Macedonian.

3111. μάκελλον **makĕllŏn**, *mak'-el-lon;* of Lat. or. [*macellum*]; a *butcher's stall, meat market* or *provision-shop:*—shambles.

3112. μακράν **makran**, *mak-ran';* fem. acc. sing. of *3117* (*3598* being implied); *at a distance* (lit. or fig.):—(a-) far (off), good (great) way off.

3113. μακρόθεν **makrŏthĕn**, *mak-roth'-en;* adv. from *3117;* *from a distance* or *afar:*—afar off, from far.

3114. μακροθυμέω **makrŏthumĕō**, *mak-roth-oo-meh'-o;* from the same as *3116;* *to be long-spirited*, i.e. (obj.) *forbearing* or (subj.) *patient:*—bear (suffer) long, be longsuffering, have (long) patience, be patient, patiently endure.

3115. μακροθυμία **makrŏthumia**, *mak-roth-oo-mee'-ah;* from the same as *3116;* *longanimity*, i.e. (obj.) *forbearance* or (subj.) *fortitude:*—longsuffering, patience.

3116. μακροθυμώς **makrŏthumōs**, *mak-roth-oo-moce';* adv. of a comp. of *3117* and *2372;* *with long* (*enduring*) *temper*, i.e. *leniently:*—patiently.

3117. μακρός **makrŏs**, *mak-ros';* from *3372;* *long* (in place [*distant*] or time [neut. plur.]):—far, long.

3118. μακροχρόνιος **makrŏchrŏniŏs**, *mak-rokh-ron'-ee-os;* from *3117* and *5550;* *long-timed*, i.e. *long-lived:*—live long.

3119. μαλακία **malakia**, *mal-ak-ee'-ah;* from *3120;* *softness*, i.e. *enervation* (*debility*):—disease.

3120. μαλακός **malakŏs**, *mal-ak-os';* of uncert. affin.; *soft*, i.e. *fine* (clothing); fig. a *catamite:*—effeminate, soft.

3121. Μαλελεήλ **Malĕlĕēl**, *mal-el-eh-ale';* of Heb. or [4111]; *Maleleël* (i.e. *Mahalalel*), an antediluvian:—Maleleel.

3122. μάλιστα **malista**, *mal'-is-tah;* neut. plur. of the superl. of an appar. prim. adv. μάλα **mala** (*very*); (adv.) *most* (*in the greatest degree*) or *particularly:*—chiefly, most of all, (e-) specially.

3123. μᾶλλον **mallŏn**, *mal'-lon;* neut. of the compar. of the same as *3122;* (adv.) *more* (*in a greater degree*) or *rather:*— + better, × far, (the) more (and more), (so) much (the more), rather.

3124. Μάλχος **Malchŏs**, *mal'-khos;* of Heb. or. [4429]; *Malchus*, an Isr.:—Malchus.

3125. μάμμη **mammē**, *mam'-may;* of nat. or. ["mammy"]; a *grandmother:*—grandmother.

3126. μαμμωνᾶς **mammōnas**, *mam-mo-nas';* of Chald. or. (*confidence*, i.e. fig. *wealth*, personified); *mammonas*, i.e. *avarice* (deified):—mammon.

3127. Μαναήν **Manaēn**, *man-ah-ane';* of uncert. or.; *Manaën*, a Chr.:—Manaen.

3128. Μανασσῆς **Manassēs**, *man-as-sace';* of Heb. or. [4519]; *Manasses* (i.e. *Menashsheh*), an Isr.:—Manasses.

3129. μανθάνω **manthanō**, *man-than'-o;* prol. from a prim. verb, another form of which, μαθέω **mathĕō**, is used as an alt. in cert. tenses; to *learn* (in any way):—learn, understand.

3130. μανία **mania**, *man-ee'-ah;* from *3105;* *craziness:*—[+ make] × mad.

3131. μάννα **manna**, *man'-nah;* of Heb. or. [4478]; *manna* (i.e. *man*), an edible gum:—manna.

3132. μαντεύομαι **mantĕuŏmai**, *mant-yoo'-om-ahee;* from a der. of *3105* (mean. a *prophet*, as supposed to *rave* through *inspiration*); to *divine*, i.e. *utter spells* (under pretence of foretelling):—by soothsaying.

3133. μαραίνω **marainō**, *mar-ah'ee-no;* of uncert. affin.; to *extinguish* (as fire), i.e. (fig. and pass.) to *pass away:*—fade away.

3134. μαρὰν ἀθά **maran atha**, *mar'-an ath'-ah;* of Chald. or. (mean. *our Lord has come*); *maranatha*, i.e. an exclamation of the approaching *divine judgment:*—Maran-atha.

3135. μαργαρίτης **margaritēs**, *mar-gar-ee'-tace;* from μάργαρος **margarŏs** (a pearl-*oyster*); a *pearl:*—pearl.

3136. Μάρθα **Martha**, *mar'-thah;* prob. of Chald. or. (mean. *mistress*); *Martha*, a Chr. woman:—Martha.

3137. Μαρία **Maria**, *mar-ee'-ah;* or
Μαριάμ **Mariam**, *mar-ee-am';* of Heb. or. [4813]; *Maria* or *Mariam* (i.e. *Mirjam*), the name of six Chr. females:—Mary.

3138. Μάρκος **Markŏs**, *mar'-kos;* of Lat. or.; *Marcus*, a Chr.:—Marcus, Mark.

3139. μάρμαρος **marmarŏs**, *mar'-mar-os;* from μαρμαίρω **marmairō** (to *glisten*); *marble* (as sparkling *white*):—marble.

μάρτυρ **martur**. See *3144*.

3140. μαρτυρέω **marturĕō**, *mar-too-reh'-o;* from *3144;* to *be a witness*, i.e. *testify* (lit. or fig.):—charge, give [*evidence*], bear record, have (obtain, of) good (honest) report, be well reported of, testify, give (have) testimony, (be, bear, give, obtain) witness.

3141. μαρτυρία **marturia**, *mar-too-ree'-ah;* from *3144;* *evidence* given (judicially or gen.):—record, report, testimony, witness.

3142. μαρτύριον **marturiŏn**, *mar-too'-ree-on;* neut. of a presumed der. of *3144;* something *evidential*, i.e. (gen.) *evidence* given or (spec.) the *Decalogue* (in the sacred Tabernacle):—to be testified, testimony, witness.

3143. μαρτύρομαι **marturŏmai**, *mar-too'-rom-ahee;* mid. from *3144;* to *be adduced* as a *witness*, i.e. (fig.) to *obtest* (in affirmation or exhortation):—take to record, testify.

3144. μάρτυς **martus**, *mar'-toos;* of uncert. affin.; a *witness* (lit. [judicially] or fig. [gen.]); by anal. a "*martyr*":—martyr, record, witness.

3145. μασσάομαι **massaŏmai**, *mas-sah'-om-ahee;* from a prim. μάσσω **massō** (to *handle* or *squeeze*); to *chew:*—gnaw.

3146. μαστιγόω **mastigŏō**, *mas-tig-ŏ'-o;* from *3148;* to *flog* (lit. or fig.):—scourge.

3147. μαστίζω **mastizō**, *mas-tid'-zo;* from *3149;* to *whip* (lit.):—scourge.

3148. μάστιξ **mastix**, *mas'-tix;* prob. from the base of *3145* (through the idea of *contact*); a *whip* (lit. the Roman *flagellum* for criminals; fig. a *disease*):—plague, scourging.

3149. μαστός **mastŏs**, *mas-tos';* from the base of *3145;* a (prop. female) *breast* (as if *kneaded* up):—pap.

3150. ματαιολογία **mataiŏlŏgia**, *mat-ah-yol-og-ee'-ah;* from *3151;* *random talk*, i.e. *babble:*—vain jangling.

3151. ματαιολόγος **mataiŏlŏgŏs**, *mat-ah-yol-og'-os;* from *3152* and *3004;* an *idle* (i.e. *senseless* or *mischievous*) *talker*, i.e. a *wrangler:*—vain talker.

3152. μάταιος **mataiŏs**, *mat'-ah-yos;* from the base of *3155;* *empty*, i.e. (lit.) *profitless*, or (spec.) an *idol:*—vain, vanity.

3153. ματαιότης **mataiŏtēs**, *mat-ah-yot'-ace;* from *3152;* *inutility;* fig. *transientness;* mor. *depravity:*—vanity.

3154. ματαιόω **mataiŏō**, *mat-ah-yŏ'-o;* from *3152;* to *render* (pass. *become*) *foolish*, i.e. (mor.) *wicked* or (spec.) *idolatrous:*—become vain.

3155. μάτην **matēn**, *mat'-ane;* accus. of a der. of the base of *3145* (through the idea of tentative *manipulation*, i.e. unsuccessful *search*, or else of *punishment*); *folly*, i.e. (adv.) *to no purpose:*—in vain.

3156. Ματθαῖος **Matthaiŏs**, *mat-thah'-yos;* a shorter form of *3161;* *Matthæus* (i.e. *Matthitjah*), an Isr. and Chr.:—Matthew.

3157. Ματθάν **Matthan**, *mat-than';* of Heb. or. [4977]; *Matthan* (i.e. *Mattan*), an Isr.:—Matthan.

3158. Ματθάτ **Matthat**, *mat-that';* prob. a shortened form of *3161;* *Matthat* (i.e. *Mattithjah*), the name of two Isr.:—Mathat.

3159. Ματθίας **Matthias**, *mat-thee'-as;* appar. a shortened form of *3161;* *Matthias* (i.e. *Mattithjah*), an Isr.:—Matthias.

3160. Ματταθά **Mattatha**, *mat-tath-ah';* prob. a shortened form of *3161* [comp. 4992]; *Mattatha* (i.e. *Mattithjah*), an Isr.:—Mattatha.

3161. Ματταθίας **Mattathias**, *mat-tath-ee'-as;* of Heb. or. [4993]; *Mattathias* (i.e. *Mattithjah*), an Isr. and Chr.:—Mattathias.

3162. μάχαιρα **machaira**, *makh'-ahee-rah;* prob. fem. of a presumed der. of *3163;* a *knife*, i.e. *dirk;* fig. *war*, judicial *punishment:*—sword.

3163. μάχη **machē**, *makh'-ay;* from *3164;* a *battle*, i.e. (fig.) *controversy:*—fighting, strive, striving.

3164. μάχομαι **machŏmai**, *makh'-om-ahee;* mid. of an appar. prim. verb; to *war*, i.e. (fig.) to *quarrel, dispute:*—fight, strive.

3165. μέ **mĕ**, *meh;* a shorter (and prob. orig.) form of *1691;* *me:*—I, me, my.

3166. μεγαλαυχέω **mĕgalauchĕō**, *meg-al-ŏw-kheh'-o;* from a comp. of *3173* and αὐχέω **auchĕō** (to *boast;* akin to *837* and *2744*); to *talk big*, i.e. *be grandiloquent* (*arrogant, egotistic*):—boast great things.

3167. μεγαλεῖος **mĕgalĕiŏs**, *meg-al-i'-os;* from *3173;* *magnificent*, i.e. (neut. plur. as noun) a conspicuous *favor*, or (subj.) *perfection:*—great things, wonderful works.

3168. μεγαλειότης **mĕgalĕiŏtēs**, *meg-al-i-ot'-ace;* from *3167;* *superbness*, i.e. *glory* or *splendor:*—magnificence, majesty, mighty power.

3169. μεγαλοπρεπής **mĕgalŏprĕpēs**, *meg-al-op-rep-ace';* from *3173* and *4241;* *befitting greatness* or *magnificence* (*majestic*):—excellent.

3170. μεγαλύνω **mĕgalunō**, *meg-al-oo'-no;* from *3173;* to *make* (or *declare*) *great*, i.e. *increase* or (fig.) *extol:*—enlarge, magnify, shew great.

3171. μεγάλως **mĕgalōs**, *meg-al'-oce;* adv. from *3173;* *much:*—greatly.

3172. μεγαλωσύνη **mĕgalōsunē**, *meg-al-o-soo'-nay;* from *3173;* *greatness*, i.e. (fig.) *divinity* (often God himself):—majesty.

3173. μέγας **mĕgas**, *meg'-as* [includ. the prol. forms, fem. μεγάλη **mĕgalē**, plur. μεγάλοι **mĕgalŏi**, etc.; comp. also *3176*, *3187*]; *big* (lit. or fig., in a very wide application):—(+ fear) exceedingly, great (-est), high, large, loud, mighty, + (be) sore (afraid), strong, × to years.

3174. μέγεθος **mĕgĕthŏs**, *meg'-eth-os;* from *3173;* *magnitude* (fig.):—greatness.

3175. μεγιστᾶνες **mĕgistanĕs**, *meg-is-tan'-es;* plur. from *3176;* *grandees:*—great men, lords.

3176. μέγιστος **mĕgistŏs**, *meg'-is-tos;* superl. of *3173;* *greatest* or *very great:*—exceeding great.

3177. μεθερμηνεύω **mĕthĕrmēnĕuō**, *meth-er-mane-yoo'-o;* from *3326* and *2059;* to *explain over*, i.e. *translate:*—(by) interpret (-ation).

3178. μέθη **mĕthē**, *meth'-ay;* appar. a prim. word; an *intoxicant*, i.e. (by impl.) *intoxication:*—drunkenness.

3179. μεθίστημι **mĕthistēmi**, *meth-is'-tay-mee;* or (1 Cor. 13 : 2)

μεθιστάνω **mĕthistanō**, *meth-is-tan'-o;* from 3326 and 2476; *to transfer*, i.e. *carry away, depose* or (fig.) *exchange, seduce*:—put out, remove, translate, turn away.

3180. μεθοδεία **mĕthŏdĕia**, *meth-od-i'-ah;* from a comp. of 3326 and 3593 [comp. "method"]; *travelling over*, i.e. *travesty* (*trickery*):—wile, lie in wait.

3181. μεθόριος **mĕthŏriŏs**, *meth-or'-ee-os;* from 3326 and 3725; *bounded alongside*, i.e. *contiguous* (neut. plur. as noun, *frontier*):—border.

3182. μεθύσκω **mĕthuskō**, *meth-oos'-ko;* a prol. (trans.) form of 3184; *to intoxicate*:—be drunk (-en).

3183. μέθυσος **mĕthusŏs**, *meth'-oo-sos;* from 3184; *tipsy*, i.e. (as noun) a *sot*:—drunkard.

3184. μεθύω **mĕthuō**, *meth-oo'-o;* from another form of 3178; *to drink to intoxication*, i.e. *get drunk*:—drink well, make (be) drunk (-en).

3185. μεῖζον **mĕizŏn**, *mide'-zon;* neut. of 3187; (adv.) in a *greater* degree:—the more.

3186. μειζότερος **mĕizŏtĕrŏs**, *mide-zot'-er-os;* continued compar. of 3187; *still larger* (fig.):—greater.

3187. μείζων **mĕizōn**, *mide'-zone;* irreg. compar. of 3173; *larger* (lit. or fig., spec. in age):—elder, greater (-est), more.

3188. μέλαν **mĕlan**, *mel'-an;* neut. of 3189 as noun; *ink*:—ink.

3189. μέλας **mĕlas**, *mel'-as;* appar. a prim. word; *black*:—black.

3190. Μελεᾶς **Mĕlĕas**, *mel-eh-as';* of uncert. or.; *Meleas*, an Isr.:—Meleas.

μέλει **mĕlĕi**. See 3199.

3191. μελετάω **mĕlĕtaō**, *mel-et-ah'-o;* from a presumed der. of 3199; *to take care of*, i.e. (by impl.) *revolve* in the mind:—imagine, (pre-) meditate.

3192. μέλι **mĕli**, *mel'-ee;* appar. a prim. word; *honey*:—honey.

3193. μελίσσιος **mĕlissiŏs**, *mel-is'-see-os;* from 3192; *relating to honey*, i.e. *bee* (comb):—honeycomb.

3194. Μελίτη **Mĕlitē**, *mel-ee'-tay;* of uncert. or.; *Melita*, an island in the Mediterranean:—Melita.

3195. μέλλω **mĕllō**, *mel'-lo;* a strengthened form of 3199 (through the idea of *expectation*); *to intend*, i.e. *be about* to be, do, or suffer something (of persons or things, espec. events; in the sense of *purpose, duty, necessity, probability, possibility*, or *hesitation*):—about, after that, be (almost), (that which is, things, + which was for) to come, intend, was to (be), mean, mind, be at the point, (be) ready, + return, shall (begin), (which, that) should (after, afterwards, hereafter) tarry, which was for, will, would, be yet.

3196. μέλος **mĕlŏs**, *mel'-os;* of uncert. affin.; a *limb* or *part* of the body:—member.

3197. Μελχί **Mĕlchi**, *mel-khee';* of Heb. or. [4428 with pron. suf., *my king*]; *Melchi* (i.e. *Malki*), the name of two Isr.:—Melchi.

3198. Μελχισεδέκ **Mĕlchisĕdĕk**, *mel-khis-ed-ek';* of Heb. or. [4442]; *Melchisedek* (i.e. *Malkitsedek*), a patriarch:—Melchisedec.

3199. μέλω **mĕlō**, *mel'-o;* a prim. verb; *to be of interest* to, i.e. *to concern* (only third pers. sing. pres. indic. used impers. *it matters*):—(take) care.

3200. μεμβράνα **mĕmbrana**, *mem-bran'-ah;* of Lat. or. ("*membrane*"); a (written) sheep-*skin*:—parchment.

3201. μέμφομαι **mĕmphŏmai**, *mem'-fom-ahee;* mid. of an appar. prim. verb; *to blame*:—find fault.

3202. μεμψίμοιρος **mĕmpsimŏirŏs**, *mem-psim'-oy-ros;* from a presumed der. of 3201 and μοῖρα **mŏira** (*fate;* akin to the base of 3313); *blaming fate*, i.e. *querulous* (*discontented*):—complainer.

3303. μέν **mĕn**, *men;* a prim. particle; prop. indic. of *affirmation* or *concession* (*in fact*); usually followed by a *contrasted* clause with 1161 (*this* one, the *former*, etc.):—even, indeed, so, some, truly, verily. Often compounded with other particles in an *intensive* or *asseverative* sense.

3304. μενοῦνγε **mĕnŏungĕ**, *men-oon'-geh;* from 3303 and 3767 and 1065; *so then at least*:—nay but, yea doubtless (rather, verily).

3305. μέντοι **mĕntŏi**, *men'-toy;* from 3303 and 5104; *indeed though*, i.e. *however*:—also, but, howbeit, nevertheless, yet.

3306. μένω **mĕnō**, *men'-o;* a prim. verb; *to stay* (in a given place, state, relation or expectancy):—abide, continue, dwell, endure, be present, remain, stand, tarry (for), × thine own.

3307. μερίζω **mĕrizō**, *mer-id'-zo;* from 3313; *to part*, i.e. (lit.) *to apportion, bestow, share*, or (fig.) *to disunite, differ*:—deal, be difference between, distribute, divide, give part.

3308. μέριμνα **mĕrimna**, *mer'-im-nah;* from 3307 (through the idea of *distraction*); *solicitude*:—care.

3309. μεριμνάω **mĕrimnaō**, *mer-im-nah'-o;* from 3308; *to be anxious* about:—(be, have) care (-ful), take thought.

3310. μερίς **mĕris**, *mer-ece';* fem. of 3313; a *portion*, i.e. *province, share* or (abstr.) *participation*:—part (× -akers).

3311. μερισμός **mĕrismŏs**, *mer-is-mos';* from 3307; a *separation* or *distribution*:—dividing asunder, gift.

3312. μεριστής **mĕristēs**, *mer-is-tace';* from 3307; an *apportioner* (*administrator*):—divider.

3313. μέρος **mĕrŏs**, *mer'-os;* from an obsol. but more prim. form of μείρομαι **mĕirŏmai** (to *get* as a *section* or *allotment*); a *division* or *share* (lit. or fig., in a wide application):—behalf, coast, course, craft, particular (+ -ly), part (+ -ly), piece, portion, respect, side, some sort (-what).

3314. μεσημβρία **mĕsēmbria**, *mes-ame-bree'-ah;* from 3319 and 2250; *midday;* by impl. the *south*:—noon, south.

3315. μεσιτεύω **mĕsitĕuō**, *mes-it-yoo'-o;* from 3316; *to interpose* (as arbiter), i.e. (by impl.) *to ratify* (as surety):—confirm.

3316. μεσίτης **mĕsitēs**, *mes-ee'-tace;* from 3319; a *go-between*, i.e. (simply) an *internunciator*, or (by impl.) a *reconciler* (*intercessor*):—mediator.

3317. μεσονύκτιον **mĕsŏnuktiŏn**, *mes-on-ook'-tee-on;* neut. of a comp. of 3319 and 3571; *midnight* (espec. as a watch):—midnight.

3318. Μεσοποταμία **Mĕsŏpŏtamia**, *mes-op-ot-am-ee'-ah;* from 3319 and 4215; *Mesopotamia* (as lying between the Euphrates and the Tigris; comp. 763), a region of Asia:—Mesopotamia.

3319. μέσος **mĕsŏs**, *mes'-os;* from 3326; *middle* (as adj. or [neut.] noun):—among, × before them, between, + forth, mid [-day, -night], midst, way.

3320. μεσότοιχον **mĕsŏtŏichŏn**, *mes-ot'-oy-khon;* from 3319 and 5109; a *partition* (fig.):—middle wall.

3321. μεσουράνημα **mĕsŏuranēma**, *mes-oo-ran'-ay-mah;* from a presumed comp. of 3319 and 3772; *mid-sky*:—midst of heaven.

3322. μεσόω **mĕsŏō**, *mes-ŏ'-o;* from 3319; *to form the middle*, i.e. (in point of time), *to be half-way* over:—be about the midst.

3323. Μεσσίας **Mĕssias**, *mes-see'-as;* of Heb. or. [4899]; the *Messias* (i.e. *Mashiach*), or Christ:—Messias.

3324. μεστός **mĕstŏs**, *mes-tos';* of uncert. der.; *replete* (lit. or fig.):—full.

3325. μεστόω **mĕstŏō**, *mes-tŏ'-o;* from 3324; *to replenish*, i.e. (by impl.) *to intoxicate*:—fill.

3326. μετά **mĕta**, *met-ah';* a prim. prep. (often used adv.); prop. denoting *accompaniment;* "*amid*" (local or causal); modified variously according to the case (gen. *association*, or acc. *succession*) with which it is joined; occupying an intermediate position between 575 or 1537 and 1519 or 4314; less intimate than 1722, and less close than 4862):—after (-ward), × that he again, against, among, × and, + follow, hence, hereafter, in, of, (up-) on, + our, × and setting, since, (un-) to, + together, when, with (+ -out). Often used in composition, in substantially the same relations of *participation* or *proximity*, and *transfer* or *sequence*.

3327. μεταβαίνω **mĕtabainō**, *met-ab-ah'ee-no;* from 3326 and the base of 939; *to change place*:—depart, go, pass, remove.

3328. μεταβάλλω **mĕtaballō**, *met-ab-al'-lo;* from 3326 and 906; *to throw over*, i.e. (mid. fig.) to *turn about* in opinion:—change mind.

3329. μετάγω **mĕtagō**, *met-ag'-o;* from 3326 and 71; *to lead over*, i.e. *transfer* (*direct*):—turn about.

3330. μεταδίδωμι **mĕtadidōmi**, *met-ad-id'-o-mee;* from 3326 and 1325; *to give over*, i.e. *share*:—give, impart.

3331. μετάθεσις **mĕtathĕsis**, *met-ath'-es-is;* from 3346; *transposition*, i.e. *transferral* (to heaven), *disestablishment* (of a law):—change, removing, translation.

3332. μεταίρω **mĕtairō**, *met-ah'ee-ro;* from 3326 and 142; *to betake* oneself, i.e. *remove* (locally):—depart.

3333. μετακαλέω **mĕtakalĕō**, *met-ak-al-eh'-o;* from 3326 and 2564; *to call elsewhere*, i.e. *summon*:—call (for, hither).

3334. μετακινέω **mĕtakinĕō**, *met-ak-ee-neh'-o;* from 3326 and 2795; *to stir* to a place *elsewhere*, i.e. *remove* (fig.):—move away.

3335. μεταλαμβάνω **mĕtalambanō**, *met-al-am-ban'-o;* from 3326 and 2983; *to participate;* gen. to *accept* (and use):—eat, have, be partaker, receive, take.

3336. μετάληψις **mĕtalēpsis**, *met-al'-ape-sis;* from 3335; *participation*:—taking.

3337. μεταλλάσσω **mĕtallassō**, *met-al-las'-so;* from 3326 and 236; *to exchange*:—change.

3338. μεταμέλλομαι **mĕtamĕllŏmai**, *met-am-el'-lom-ahee;* from 3326 and the mid. of 3199; *to care afterwards*, i.e. *regret*:—repent (self).

3339. μεταμορφόω **mĕtamŏrphŏō**, *met-am-or-fŏ'-o;* from 3326 and 3445; *to transform* (lit. or fig. "metamorphose"):—change, transfigure, transform.

3340. μετανοέω **mĕtanŏĕō**, *met-an-ŏ-eh'-o;* from 3326 and 3539; *to think differently* or *afterwards*, i.e. *reconsider* (mor. *feel compunction*):—repent.

3341. μετάνοια **mĕtanŏia**, *met-an'-oy-ah;* from 3340; (subj.) *compunction* (for guilt, includ. *reformation*); by impl. *reversal* (of [another's] decision):—repentance.

3342. μεταξύ **mĕtaxu**, *met-ax-oo';* from 3326 and a form of 4862; *betwixt* (of place or person); (of time) as adj. *intervening*, or (by impl.) *adjoining*:—between, mean while, next.

3343. μεταπέμπω **mĕtapĕmpō**, *met-ap-emp'-o;* from 3326 and 3992; *to send* from *elsewhere*, i.e. (mid.) to *summon* or *invite*:—call (send) for.

3344. μεταστρέφω **mĕtastrĕphō**, *met-as-tref'-o;* from 3326 and 4762; *to turn across*, i.e. *transmute* or (fig.) *corrupt*:—pervert, turn.

3345. μετασχηματίζω **mĕtaschēmatizō**, *met-askh-ay-mat-id'-zo;* from 3326 and a der. of 4976; to *transfigure* or *disguise;* fig. to *apply* (by accommodation) :—transfer, transform (self) ; to *change*.

3346. μετατίθημι **mĕtatithēmi**, *met-at-ith'-ay-mee;* from 3326 and 5087; *to transfer*, i.e. (lit.) *transport*, (by impl.) *exchange*, (reflex.) *change sides*, or (fig.) *pervert*:—carry over, change, remove, translate, turn.

3347. μετέπειτα **mĕtĕpĕita**, *met-ep'-i-tah;* from 3326 and 1899; *thereafter*:—afterward.

3348. μετέχω **mĕtĕchō**, *met-ekh'-o;* from 3326 and 2192; *to share* or *participate;* by impl. *belong* to, *eat* (or *drink*):—be partaker, pertain, take part, use.

3349. μετεωρίζω **mĕtĕōrizō**, *met-eh-o-rid'-zo;* from a comp. of 3326 and a collat. form of 142 or perh. rather of 109 (comp. "meteor"); *to raise in mid-air*, i.e. (fig.) *suspend* (pass. *fluctuate* or *be anxious*):—be of doubtful mind.

3350. μετοικεσία **mĕtŏikĕsia**, *met-oy-kes-ee'-ah;* from a der. of a comp. of 3326 and 3624; *a change of abode*, i.e. (spec.) *expatriation*:— × brought, carried (-ying) away (in-) to.

3351. μετοικίζω **mĕtŏikizō**, *met-oy-kid'-zo;* from the same as *3350;* to *transfer* as a *settler* or *captive*, i.e. *colonize* or *exile:*—carry away, remove into.

3352. μετοχή **mĕtŏchē**, *met-okh-ay';* from *3348;* *participation*, i.e. *intercourse:*—fellowship.

3353. μέτοχος **mĕtŏchŏs**, *met'-okh-os;* from *3348;* *participant*, i.e. (as noun) a *sharer;* by impl. an *associate:*—fellow, partaker, partner.

3354. μετρέω **mĕtrĕō**, *met-reh'-o;* from *3358;* to *measure* (i.e. ascertain in size by a fixed standard); by impl. to *admeasure* (i.e. allot by rule); fig. to *estimate:*—measure, mete.

3355. μετρητής **mĕtrētēs** *met-ray-tace';* from *3354;* a *measurer*, i.e. (spec.) a certain standard *measure* of capacity for liquids:—firkin.

3356. μετριοπαθέω **mĕtriŏpathĕō**, *met-ree-op-ath-eh'-o;* from a comp. of the base of *3357* and *3806;* to *be moderate in passion*, i.e. *gentle* (to *treat indulgently*):—have compassion.

3357. μετρίως **mĕtriōs**, *met-ree'-oce;* adv. from a der. of *3358;* *moderately*, i.e. *slightly:*—a little.

3358. μέτρον **mĕtrŏn**, *met'-ron;* an appar. prim. word; a *measure* ("metre"), lit. or fig.; by impl. a limited *portion* (*degree*):—measure.

3359. μέτωπον **mĕtōpŏn**, *met'-o-pon;* from *3326* and ὤψ **ōps** (the *face*); the *forehead* (as *opposite the countenance*):—forehead.

3360. μέχρι **mĕchri**, *mekh'-ree;* or

μεχρίς **mĕchris**, *mekh-ris';* from *3372;* *as far as*, i.e. *up to* a certain point (as prep. of extent [denoting the *terminus*, whereas *891* refers espec. to the *space* of time or place intervening] or conj.):—till, (un-) to, until.

3361. μή **mē**, *may;* a prim. particle of qualified *negation* (whereas *3756* expresses an absolute denial); (adv.) *not*, (conj.) *lest;* also (as interrog. implying a *neg.* answer [whereas *3756* expects an *affirm.* one]) *whether:*—any, but (that), × forbear, + God forbid, + lack, lest, neither, never, no (× wise in), none, nor, [can-] not, nothing, that not, un [-taken], without. Often used in compounds in substantially the same relations. See also *3362, 3363, 3364, 3372, 3373, 3375, 3378.*

3362. ἐὰν μή **ĕan mē**, *eh-an' may;* i.e. *1437* and *3361;* *if not*, i.e. *unless:*— × before, but, except, if no, (if, + whosoever) not.

3363. ἵνα μή **hina mē**, *hin'-ah may;* i.e. *2443* and *3361;* *in order* (or so) *that not:*—albeit not, lest, that no (-t, [-thing]).

3364. οὐ μή **ŏu mē**, *oo may;* i.e. *3756* and *3361;* a double neg. strengthening the denial; *not at all:*—any more, at all, by any (no) means, neither, never, no (at all), in no case (wise), nor ever, not (at all, in any wise). Comp. *3378*.

3365. μηδαμῶς **mēdamōs**, *may-dam-oce';* adv. from a comp. of *3361* and ἀμός **amŏs** (*somebody*); *by no means:*—not so.

3366. μηδέ **mēdĕ**, *may-deh';* from *3361* and *1161;* *but not, not even;* in a continued negation, *nor:*—neither, nor (yet), (no) not (once, so much as).

3367. μηδείς **mēdĕis**, *may-dice';* includ. the irreg. fem. μηδεμία **mēdĕmia**, *may-dem-ee'-ah*, and the neut. μηδέν **mēdĕn**, *may-den';* from *3361* and *1520;* *not even one* (man, woman, thing):—any (man, thing), no (man), none, not (at all, any man, a whit), nothing, + without delay.

3368. μηδέποτε **mēdĕpŏtĕ**, *may-dep'-ot-eh;* from *3366* and *4218;* *not even ever:*—never.

3369. μηδέπω **mēdĕpō**, *may-dep'-o;* from *3366* and *4452;* *not even yet:*—not yet.

3370. Μῆδος **Mēdŏs**, *may'-dos;* of for. or. [comp. 4074]; a *Median*, or inhab. of Media:—Mede.

3371. μηκέτι **mēkĕti**, *may-ket'-ee;* from *3361* and *2089;* *no further:*—any longer, (not) henceforth, hereafter, no henceforward (longer, more, soon), not any more.

3372. μῆκος **mēkŏs**, *may'-kos;* prob. akin to *3173;* *length* (lit. or fig.):—length.

3373. μηκύνω **mēkunō**, *may-koo'-no;* from *3372;* to *lengthen*, i.e. (mid.) to *enlarge:*—grow up.

3374. μηλωτή **mēlōtē**, *may-lo-tay';* from μῆλον **mēlŏn** (a *sheep*); a *sheep-skin:*—sheepskin.

3375. μήν **mēn**, *mane;* a stronger form of *3303;* a particle of affirmation (only with *2229*); *assuredly:*— + surely.

3376. μήν **mēn**, *mane;* a prim. word; a *month:*—month.

3377. μηνύω **mēnuō**, *may-noo'-o;* prob. from the same base as *3145* and *3415* (i.e. μάω **maō**, to *strive*); to *disclose* (through the idea of mental *effort* and thus calling to *mind*), i.e. *report, declare, intimate:*—shew, tell.

3378. μὴ οὐκ **mē ŏuk**, *may ook;* i.e. *3361* and *3756;* as interrog. and neg. *is it not that?:*—neither (followed by *no*), + never, not. Comp. *3364*.

3379. μήποτε **mēpŏtĕ**, *may'-pot-eh;* or

μή ποτε **mē pŏtĕ**, *may pot'-eh;* from *3361* and *4218;* *not ever;* also *if* (or *lest*) *ever* (or *perhaps*):—if peradventure, lest (at any time, haply), not at all, whether or not.

3380. μήπω **mēpō**, *may'-po;* from *3361* and *4452;* *not yet:*—not yet.

3381. μήπως **mēpōs**, *may'-poce;* or

μή πως **mē pōs**, *may poce;* from *3361* and *4458;* *lest somehow:*—lest (by any means, by some means, haply, perhaps).

3382. μηρός **mērŏs**, *may-ros';* perh. a prim. word; a *thigh:*—thigh.

3383. μήτε **mētĕ**, *may'-teh;* from *3361* and *5037;* *not too*, i.e. (in continued negation) *neither* or *nor;* also, *not even:*—neither, (n-) or, so much as.

3384. μήτηρ **mētēr**, *may'-tare;* appar. a prim. word; a "*mother*" (lit. or fig., immed. or remote):—mother.

3385. μήτι **mēti**, *may'-tee;* from *3361* and the neut. of *5100;* *whether at all:*—not [*the particle usually not expressed, except by the form of the question*].

3386. μήτιγε **mētigĕ**, *may'-tig-eh;* from *3385* and *1065;* *not at all then*, i.e. *not to say* (*the rather still*):—how much more.

3387. μήτις **mētis**, *may'-tis;* or

μή τις **mē tis**, *may tis;* from *3361* and *5100;* *whether any:*—any [*sometimes unexpressed except by the simple interrogative form of the sentence*].

3388. μήτρα **mētra**, *may'-trah;* from *3384;* the *matrix:*—womb.

3389. μητραλῴας **mētralōias**, *may-tral-o'-as;* from *3384* and the base of *257;* a *mother-thresher*, i.e. *matricide:*—murderer of mothers.

3390. μητρόπολις **mētrŏpŏlis**, *may-trop'-ol-is;* from *3384* and *4172;* a *mother city*, i.e. "*metropolis*":—chiefest city.

3391. μία **mia**, *mee'-ah;* irreg. fem. of *1520;* *one* or *first:*—a (certain), + agree, first, one, × other.

3392. μιαίνω **miainō**, *me-ah'ee-no;* perh. a prim. verb; to *sully* or *taint*, i.e. *contaminate* (cer. or mor.):—defile.

3393. μίασμα **miasma**, *mee'-as-mah;* from *3392* ("*miasma*"); (mor.) *foulness* (prop. the effect):—pollution.

3394. μιασμός **miasmŏs**, *mee-as-mos';* from *3392;* (mor.) *contamination* (prop. the act):—uncleanness.

3395. μίγμα **migma**, *mig'-mah;* from *3396;* a *compound:*—mixture.

3396. μίγνυμι **mignumi**, *mig'-noo-mee;* a prim. verb; to *mix:*—mingle.

3397. μικρόν **mikrŏn**, *mik-ron';* masc. or neut. sing. of *3398* (as noun); a *small* space of *time* or *degree:*—a (little) (while).

3398. μικρός **mikrŏs**, *mik-ros';* includ. the comp.

μικρότερος **mikrŏtĕrŏs**, *mik-rot'-er-os;* appar. a prim. word; *small* (in size, quantity, number or (fig.) dignity):—least, less, little, small.

3399. Μίλητος **Milētŏs**, *mil'-ay-tos;* of uncert. or.; *Miletus*, a city of Asia Minor:—Miletus.

3400. μίλιον **miliŏn**, *mil'-ee-on;* of Lat. or.: a *thousand* paces, i.e. a "*mile*":—mile.

3401. μιμέομαι **mimĕŏmai**, *mim-eh'-om-ahee;* mid. from μῖμος **mimŏs** (a "*mimic*"); to *imitate:*—follow.

3402. μιμητής **mimētēs**, *mim-ay-tace';* from *3401;* an *imitator:*—follower.

3403. μιμνήσκω **mimnēskō**, *mim-nace'-ko;* a prol. form of *3415* (from which some of the tenses are borrowed); to *remind*, i.e. (mid.) to *recall to mind:*—be mindful, remember.

3404. μισέω **misĕō**, *mis-eh'-o;* from a prim. μῖσος **misŏs** (*hatred*); to *detest* (espec. to *persecute*); by extens. to *love less:*—hate (-ful).

3405. μισθαποδοσία **misthapŏdŏsia**, *mis-thap-od-os-ee'-ah;* from *3406;* *requital* (good or bad):—recompence of reward.

3406. μισθαποδότης **misthapŏdŏtēs**, *mis-thap-od-ot'-ace;* from *3409* and *591;* a *remunerator:*—rewarder.

3407. μίσθιος **misthiŏs**, *mis'-thee-os;* from *3408;* a *wage-earner:*—hired servant.

3408. μισθός **misthŏs**, *mis-thos';* appar. a prim. word; *pay* for service (lit. or fig.), good or bad:—hire, reward, wages.

3409. μισθόω **misthŏō**, *mis-tho'-o;* from *3408;* to *let* out for wages, i.e. (mid.) to *hire:*—hire.

3410. μίσθωμα **misthōma**, *mis'-tho-mah;* from *3409;* a *rented* building:—hired house.

3411. μισθωτός **misthōtŏs**, *mis-tho-tos';* from *3409;* a *wage-worker* (good or bad):—hired servant, hireling.

3412. Μιτυλήνη **Mitulēnē**, *mit-oo-lay'-nay;* for μυτιλήνη **mutilēnē** (*abounding in shell-fish*); *Mitylene* (or *Mytilene*), a town in the island Lesbos:—Mitylene.

3413. Μιχαήλ **Michaēl**, *mikh-ah-ale';* of Heb. or. [4317]; *Michaël*, an archangel:—Michael.

3414. μνᾶ **mna**, *mnah;* of Lat. or.; a *mna* (i.e. *mina*), a certain *weight:*—pound.

3415. μνάομαι **mnaŏmai**, *mnah'-om-ahee;* mid. of a der. of *3306* or perh. of the base of *3145* (through the idea of *fixture* in the mind or of mental *grasp*); to *bear in mind*, i.e. *recollect;* by impl. to *reward* or *punish:*—be mindful, remember, come (have) in remembrance. Comp. *3403*.

3416. Μνάσων **Mnasōn**, *mnah'-sohn;* of uncert. or.; *Mnason*, a Chr.:—Mnason.

3417. μνεία **mnĕia**, *mni'-ah;* from *3415* or *3403;* *recollection;* by impl. *recital:*—mention, remembrance.

3418. μνῆμα **mnēma**, *mnay'-mah;* from *3415;* a *memorial*, i.e. sepulchral *monument* (*burial-place*):—grave, sepulchre, tomb.

3419. μνημεῖον **mnēmĕiŏn**, *mnay-mi'-on;* from *3420;* a *remembrance*, i.e. *cenotaph* (*place of interment*):—grave, sepulchre, tomb.

3420. μνήμη **mnēmē**, *mnay'-may;* from *3403;* *memory:*—remembrance.

3421. μνημονεύω **mnēmŏnĕuō**, *mnay-mon-yoo'-o;* from a der. of *3420;* to *exercise memory*, i.e. *recollect;* by impl. to *punish;* also to *rehearse:*—make mention, be mindful, remember.

3422. μνημόσυνον **mnēmŏsunŏn**, *mnay-mos'-oo-non;* from *3421;* a *reminder* (*memorandum*), i.e. *record:*—memorial.

3423. μνηστεύω **mnēstĕuō**, *mnace-tyoo'-o;* from a der. of *3415;* to *give a souvenir* (engagement present), i.e. *betroth:*—espouse.

3424. μογιλάλος **mŏgilalŏs**, *mog-il-al'-os;* from *3425* and *2980;* *hardly talking*, i.e. *dumb* (*tongue-tied*):—having an impediment in his speech.

3425. μόγις **mŏgis**, *mog'-is;* adv. from a prim. μόγος **mŏgŏs** (*toil*); *with difficulty:*—hardly.

3426. μόδιος **mŏdiŏs**, *mod'-ee-os;* of Lat. or.; a *modius*, i.e. certain measure for things dry (the quantity or the utensil):—bushel.

3427. μοί **mŏi**, *moy;* the simpler form of *1698;* *to me:*—I, me, mine, my.

3428. μοιχαλίς **mŏichalis**, *moy-khal-is'*; a prol. form of the fem. of *3432*; an *adulteress* (lit. or fig.):—adulteress (-ous, -y).

3429. μοιχάω **mŏichaō**, *moy-khah'-o*; from *3432*; (mid.) to *commit adultery*:—commit adultery.

3430. μοιχεία **mŏichĕia**, *moy-khi'-ah*; from *3431*; *adultery*:—adultery.

3431. μοιχεύω **mŏichĕuō**, *moy-khyoo'-o*; from *3432*; to *commit adultery*:—commit adultery.

3432. μοιχός **mŏichŏs**, *moy-khos'*; perh. a prim. word; a (male) *paramour*; fig. *apostate*:—adulterer.

3433. μόλις **mŏlis**, *mol'-is*; prob. by var. for *3425*; *with difficulty*:—hardly, scarce (-ly), + with much work.

3434. Μολόχ **Mŏlŏch**, *mol-okh'*; of Heb. or. [4432]; *Moloch* (i.e. *Molek*), an idol:—Moloch.

3435. μολύνω **mŏlunō**, *mol-oo'-no*; prob. from *3189*; to *soil* (fig.):—defile.

3436. μολυσμός **mŏlusmŏs**, *mol-oos-mos'*; from *3435*; a *stain*, i.e. (fig.) *immorality*:—filthiness.

3437. μομφή **mŏmphē**, *mom-fay'*; from *3201*; *blame*, i.e. (by impl.) a *fault*:—quarrel.

3438. μονή **mŏnē**, *mon-ay'*; from *3306*; a *staying*, i.e. *residence* (the act or the place):—abode, mansion.

3439. μονογενής **mŏnŏgĕnēs**, *mon-og-en-ace'*; from *3441* and *1096*; *only-born*, i.e. *sole*:—only (begotten, child).

3440. μόνον **mŏnŏn**, *mon'-on*; neut. of *3441* as adv.; *merely*:—alone, but, only.

3441. μόνος **mŏnŏs**, *mon'-os*; prob. from *3306*; *remaining*, i.e. *sole* or *single*; by impl. *mere*:—alone, only, by themselves.

3442. μονόφθαλμος **mŏnŏphthalmŏs**, *mon-of'-thal-mos*; from *3441* and *3788*; *one-eyed*:—with one eye.

3443. μονόω **mŏnŏō**, *mon-ŏ'-o*; from *3441*; to *isolate*, i.e. *bereave*:—be desolate.

3444. μορφή **mŏrphē**, *mor-fay'*; perh. from the base of *3313* (through the idea of *adjustment* of parts); *shape*; fig. *nature*:—form.

3445. μορφόω **mŏrphŏō**, *mor-fŏ'-o*; from the same as *3444*; to *fashion* (fig.):—form.

3446. μόρφωσις **mŏrphōsis**, *mor'-fo-sis*; from *3445*; *formation*, i.e. (by impl.) *appearance* (*semblance* or [concr.] *formula*):—form.

3447. μοσχοποιέω **mŏschŏpŏiĕō**, *mos-khop-oy-eh'-o*; from *3448* and *4160*; to *fabricate* the image of a *bullock*:—make a calf.

3448. μόσχος **mŏschŏs**, *mos'-khos*; prob. strengthened for ὄσχος **ŏschŏs** (a *shoot*); a young *bullock*:—calf.

3449. μόχθος **mŏchthŏs**, *mokh'-thos*; from the base of *3425*; *toil*, i.e. (by impl.) *sadness*:—painfulness, travail.

3450. μοῦ **mŏu**, *moo*; the simpler form of *1700*; *of me*:—I, me, mine (own), my.

3451. μουσικός **mŏusikŏs**, *moo-sik-os'*; from Μοῦσα **Mŏusa** (a *Muse*); "*musical*", i.e. (as noun) a *minstrel*:—musician.

3452. μυελός **muĕlŏs**, *moo-el-os'*; perh. a prim. word; the *marrow*:—marrow.

3453. μυέω **muĕō**, *moo-eh'-o*; from the base of *3466*; to *initiate*, i.e. (by impl.) to *teach*:—instruct.

3454. μῦθος **muthŏs**, *moo'-thos*; perh. from the same as *3453* (through the idea of *tuition*); a *tale*, i.e. *fiction* ("*myth*"):—fable.

3455. μυκάομαι **mukaŏmai**, *moo-kah'-om-ahee*; from a presumed der. of μύζω **muzō** (to "*moo*"); to *bellow* (*roar*):—roar.

3456. μυκτηρίζω **muktērizō**, *mook-tay-rid'-zo*; from a der. of the base of *3455* (mean. *snout*, as that whence *lowing* proceeds); to *make mouths* at, i.e. *ridicule*:—mock.

3457. μυλικός **mulikŏs**, *moo-lee-kos'*; from *3458*; *belonging to a mill*:—mill [-stone].

3458. μύλος **mulŏs**, *moo'-los*; prob. ultimately from the base of *3433* (through the idea of *hardship*); a "*mill*", i.e. (by impl.) a *grinder* (*millstone*):—millstone.

3459. μύλων **mulōn**, *moo'-lone*; from *3458*; a *mill-house*:—mill.

3460. Μύρα **Mura**, *moo'-rah*; of uncert. der.; *Myra*, a place in Asia Minor:—Myra.

3461. μυριάς **murias**, *moo-ree'-as*; from *3463*; a *ten-thousand*; by extens. a "*myriad*" or indefinite number:—ten thousand.

3462. μυρίζω **murizō**, *moo-rid'-zo*; from *3464*; to *apply* (perfumed) *unguent* to:—anoint.

3463. μύριοι **muriŏi**, *moo'-ree-oi*; plur. of an appar. prim. word (prop. mean. *very many*); *ten thousand*; by extens. *innumerably* many:—ten thousand.

3464. μύρον **murŏn**, *moo'-ron*; prob. of for. or. [comp. 4753, *4666*]; "*myrrh*", i.e. (by impl.) *perfumed oil*:—ointment.

3465. Μυσία **Musia**, *moo-see'-ah*; of uncert. or.; *Mysia*, a region of Asia Minor:—Mysia.

3466. μυστήριον **mustēriŏn**, *moos-tay'-ree-on*; from a der. of μύω **muō** (to *shut* the mouth); a *secret* or "*mystery*" (through the idea of *silence* imposed by *initiation* into religious rites):—mystery.

3467. μυωπάζω **muōpazō**, *moo-ope-ad'-zo*; from a comp. of the base of *3466* and ὤψ **ōps** (the *face*; from *3700*); to *shut* the *eyes*, i.e. *blink* (*see indistinctly*):—cannot see afar off.

3468. μώλωψ **mōlōps**, *mo'-lopes*; from μῶλος **mōlŏs** ("*moil*"; prob. akin to the base of *3433*) and prob. ὤψ **ōps** (the *face*; from *3700*); a *mole* ("black eye") or *blow-mark*:—stripe.

3469. μωμάομαι **mōmaŏmai**, *mo-mah'-om-ahee*; from *3470*; to *carp* at, i.e. *censure* (*discredit*):—blame.

3470. μῶμος **mōmŏs**, *mo'-mos*; perh. from *3201*; a *flaw* or *blot*, i.e. (fig.) *disgraceful* person:—blemish.

3471. μωραίνω **mōrainō**, *mo-rah'ee-no*; from *3474*; to *become insipid*; fig. to *make* (pass. *act*) as a *simpleton*:—become fool, make foolish, lose savour.

3472. μωρία **mōria**, *mo-ree'-ah*; from *3474*; *silliness*, i.e. *absurdity*:—foolishness.

3473. μωρολογία **mōrŏlŏgia**, *mo-rol-og-ee'-ah*; from a comp. of *3474* and *3004*; *silly talk*, i.e. *buffoonery*:—foolish talking.

3474. μωρός **mōrŏs**, *mo-ros'*; prob. from the base of *3466*; *dull* or *stupid* (as if *shut* up), i.e. *heedless*, (mor.) *blockhead*, (appar.) *absurd*:—fool (-ish, × -ishness).

3475. Μωσεύς **Mōsĕus**, *moce-yoos'*; or
Μωσῆς **Mōsēs**, *mo-sace'*; or
Μωϋσῆς **Mōüsēs**, *mo-oo-sace'*; of Heb. or.; [4872]; *Moseus*, *Moses* or *Moüses* (i.e. *Mosheh*), the Heb. lawgiver:—Moses.

N

3476. Ναασσών **Naassōn**, *nah-as-sone'*; of Heb. or. [5177]; *Naasson* (i.e. *Nachshon*), an Isr.:—Naasson.

3477. Ναγγαί **Naggai**, *nang-gah'ee*; prob. of Heb. or. [comp. 5052]; *Nangæ* (i.e. perh. *Nogach*), an Isr.:—Nagge.

3478. Ναζαρέθ **Nazarĕth**, *nad-zar-eth'*; or
Ναζαρέτ **Nazarĕt**, *nad-zar-et'*; of uncert. der.; *Nazareth* or *Nazaret*, a place in Pal.:—Nazareth.

3479. Ναζαρηνός **Nazarēnŏs**, *nad-zar-ay-nos'*; from *3478*; a *Nazarene*, i.e. inhab. of Nazareth:—of Nazareth.

3480. Ναζωραῖος **Nazōraiŏs**, *nad-zo-rah'-yos*; from *3478*; a *Nazoræan*, i.e. inhab. of Nazareth; by extens. a *Christian*:—Nazarene, of Nazareth.

3481. Ναθάν **Nathan**, *nath-an'*, of Heb. or. [5416]; *Nathan*, an Isr.:—Nathan.

3482. Ναθαναήλ **Nathanaēl**, *nath-an-ah-ale'*; of Heb. or. [5417]; *Nathanaël* (i.e. *Nathanel*), an Isr. and Chr.:—Nathanael.

3483. ναί **nai**, *nahee*; a prim. particle of strong affirmation; *yes*:—even so, surely, truth, verily, yea, yes.

3484. Ναΐν **Naïn**, *nah-in'*; prob. of Heb. or. [comp. 4999]; *Naïn*, a place in Pal.:—Nain.

3485. ναός **naŏs**, *nah-os'*; from a prim. ναίω **naiō** (to *dwell*); a *fane*, *shrine*, *temple*:—shrine, temple. Comp. *2411*.

3486. Ναούμ **Naŏum**, *nah-oom'*; of Heb. or. [5151]; *Naüm* (i.e. *Nachum*), an Isr.:—Naum.

3487. νάρδος **nardŏs**, *nar'-dos*; of for. or. [comp. 5373]; "*nard*":—[spike-] nard.

3488. Νάρκισσος **Narkissŏs**, *nar'-kis-sos*; a flower of the same name, from ναρκη **narkē** (*stupefaction*, as a "narcotic"); *Narcissus*, a Roman:—Narcissus.

3489. ναυαγέω **nauagĕō**, *nŏw-ag-eh'-o*; from a comp. of *3491* and *71*; to *be shipwrecked* (*stranded*, "navigate"), lit. or fig.:—make (suffer) shipwreck.

3490. ναύκληρος **nauklērŏs**, *nŏw'-klay-ros*; from *3491* and *2819* ("clerk"); a *captain*:—owner of a ship.

3491. ναῦς **naus**, *nŏwce*; from νάω **naō** or νέω **nĕō** (to *float*); a *boat* (of any size):—ship.

3492. ναύτης **nautēs**, *now'-tace*; from *3491*; a *boatman*, i.e. *seaman*:—sailor, shipman.

3493. Ναχώρ **Nachōr**, *nakh-ore'*; of Heb. or. [5152]; *Nachor*, the grandfather of Abraham:—Nachor.

3494. νεανίας **nĕanias**, *neh-an-ee'-as*; from a der. of *3501*; a *youth* (up to about forty years):—young man.

3495. νεανίσκος **nĕaniskŏs**, *neh-an-is'-kos*; from the same as *3494*; a *youth* (under forty):—young man.

3496. Νεάπολις **Nĕapŏlis**, *neh-ap'-ol-is*; from *3501* and *4172*; *new town*; *Neäpolis*, a place in Macedonia:—Neapolis.

3497. Νεεμάν **Nĕĕman**, *neh-eh-man'*; of Heb. or. [5283]; *Neëman* (i.e. *Naaman*), a Syrian:—Naaman.

3498. νεκρός **nĕkrŏs**, *nek-ros'*; from an appar. prim. νέκυς **nĕkus** (a *corpse*); *dead* (lit. or fig.; also as noun):—dead.

3499. νεκρόω **nĕkrŏō**, *nek-rŏ'-o*; from *3498*; to *deaden*, i.e. (fig.) to *subdue*:—be dead, mortify.

3500. νέκρωσις **nĕkrōsis**, *nek'-ro-sis*; from *3499*; *decease*; fig. *impotency*:—deadness, dying.

3501. νέος **nĕŏs**, *neh'-os*; includ. the comp.
νεώτερος **nĕōtĕrŏs**, *neh-o'-ter-os*; a prim. word; "*new*", i.e. (of persons) *youthful*, or (of things) *fresh*; fig. *regenerate*:—new, young.

3502. νεοσσός **nĕŏssŏs**, *neh-os-sos'*; from *3501*; a *youngling* (*nestling*):—young.

3503. νεότης **nĕŏtēs**, *neh-ot'-ace*; from *3501*; *newness*, i.e. *youthfulness*:—youth.

3504. νεόφυτος **nĕŏphutŏs**, *neh-of'-oo-tos*; from *3501* and a der. of *5453*; *newly planted*, i.e. (fig.) a *young convert* ("*neophyte*"):—novice.

3505. Νέρων **Nĕrōn**, *ner'-ohn*; of Lat. or.; *Neron* (i.e. *Nero*), a Rom. emperor:—Nero.

3506. νεύω **nĕuō**, *nyoo'-o*; appar. a prim. verb; to "*nod*", i.e. (by anal.) to *signal*:—beckon.

3507. νεφέλη **nĕphĕlē**, *nef-el'-ay*; from *3509*; prop. *cloudiness*, i.e. (concr.) a *cloud*:—cloud.

3508. Νεφθαλείμ **Nĕphthalĕim**, *nef-thal-ime'*; of Heb. or. [5321]; *Nephthaleim* (i.e. *Naphthali*), a tribe in Pal.:—Nephthalim.

3509. νέφος **nĕphŏs**, *nef'-os*; appar. a prim. word; a *cloud*:—cloud.

3510. νεφρός **nĕphrŏs**, *nef-ros'*; of uncert. affin.; a *kidney* (plur.), i.e. (fig.) the inmost *mind*:—reins.

3511. νεωκόρος **nĕōkŏrŏs**, *neh-o-kor'-os*; from a form of *3485* and κορέω **kŏrĕō** (to *sweep*); a *temple-servant*, i.e. (by impl.) a *votary*:—worshipper.

3512. νεωτερικός **nĕōtĕrikŏs**, *neh-o-ter'-ik-os*; from the comp. of *3501*; *appertaining to younger* persons, i.e. *juvenile*:—youthful.
νεώτερος **nĕōtĕrŏs**. See *3501*.

3513. νή **nē**, *nay*; prob. an intens. form of *3483*; a particle of attestation (accompanied by the object invoked or appealed to in confirmation); *as sure as*:—I protest by.

3514. νήθω **nēthō**, *nay'-tho*; from νέω **nĕō** (of like mean.); to *spin*:—spin.

3515. **νηπιάζω nēpiazō**, *nay-pee-ad'-zo;* from *3516;* to *act* as a *babe*, i.e. (fig.) *innocently:*—be a child.

3516. **νήπιος nēpiŏs**, *nay'-pee-os;* from an obsol. particle **νη- nē-** (implying *negation*) and *2031; not speaking*, i.e. an *infant* (*minor*); fig. a *simple-minded* person, an *immature* Christian:—babe, child (+ -ish).

3517. **Νηρεύς Nērĕus**, *nare-yoos';* appar. from a der. of the base of *3491* (mean. *wet*); *Nereus*, a Chr.:—Nereus.

3518. **Νηρί Nēri**, *nay-ree';* of Heb. or. [5374]; *Neri* (i.e. *Nerijah*), an Isr.:—Neri.

3519. **νησίον nēsiŏn**, *nay-see'-on;* dimin. of *3520;* an *islet:*—island.

3520. **νῆσος nēsŏs**, *nay'-sos;* prob. from the base of *3491;* an *island:*—island, isle.

3521. **νηστεία nēstĕia**, *nace-ti'-ah;* from *3522; abstinence* (from lack of food, or voluntary and religious); spec. the *fast* of the Day of Atonement:—fast (-ing.)

3522. **νηστεύω nēstĕuō**, *nace-tyoo'-o;* from *3523;* to *abstain* from food (religiously):—fast.

3523. **νῆστις nēstis**, *nace'-tis;* from the insep. neg. particle **νη- nē-** (*not*) and *2068; not eating*, i.e. *abstinent* from food (religiously):—fasting.

3524. **νηφάλεος nēphalĕŏs**, *nay-fal'-eh-os;* or **νηφάλιος nēphaliŏs**, *nay-fal'-ee-os;* from *3525; sober*, i.e. (fig.) *circumspect* —sober, vigilant.

3525. **νήφω nēphō**, *nay'-fo;* of uncert. affin.; to *abstain* from wine (*keep sober*), i.e. (fig.) *be discreet:*—be sober, watch.

3526. **Νίγερ Nigĕr**, *neeg'-er;* of Lat. or.; *black; Niger*, a Chr.:—Niger.

3527. **Νικάνωρ Nikanōr**, *nik-an'-ore;* prob. from *3528; victorious; Nicanor*, a Chr.:—Nicanor.

3528. **νικάω nikaō**, *nik-ah'-o;* from *3529;* to *subdue* (lit. or fig.):—conquer, overcome, prevail, get the victory.

3529. **νίκη nikē**, *nee'-kay;* appar. a prim. word; *conquest* (abstr.), i.e. (fig.) the *means of success:*—victory.

3530. **Νικόδημος Nikŏdēmŏs**, *nik-od'-ay-mos;* from *3534* and *1218; victorious* among his *people; Nicodemus*, an Isr.:—Nicodemus.

3531. **Νικολαΐτης Nikŏlaïtēs**, *nik-ol-ah-ee'-tace;* from *3532;* a *Nicolaïte*, i.e. adherent of *Nicolaüs:*—*Nicolaitane.*

3532. **Νικόλαος Nikŏlaŏs**, *nik-ol'-ah-os;* from *3534* and *2992; victorious* over the *people; Nicolaüs*, a heretic:—Nicolaus.

3533. **Νικόπολις Nikŏpŏlis**, *nik-op'-ol-is;* from *3534* and *4172; victorious city; Nicopolis*, a place in Macedonia:—Nicopolis.

3534. **νῖκος nikŏs**, *nee'-kos;* from *3529;* a *conquest* (concr.), i.e. (by impl.) *triumph:*—victory.

3535. **Νινευΐ Ninĕui**, *nin-yoo-ee';* of Heb. or. [5210]; *Ninevi* (i.e. *Nineveh*), the capital of Assyria:—Nineve.

3536. **Νινευΐτης Ninĕuïtēs**, *nin-yoo-ee'-tace;* from *3535;* a *Ninevite*, i.e. inhab. of Nineveh:—of Nineve, Ninevite.

3537. **νιπτήρ niptēr**, *nip-tare';* from *3538;* a *ewer:*—bason.

3538. **νίπτω niptō**, *nip'-to;* to *cleanse* (espec. the hands or the feet or the face); cer. to *perform ablution:*—wash. Comp. *3068.*

3539. **νοιέω nŏiĕō**, *noy-eh'-o;* from *3563;* to *exercise* the *mind* (*observe*), i.e. (fig.) to *comprehend, heed:*—consider, perceive, think, understand.

3540. **νόημα nŏēma**, *nŏ'-ay-mah;* from *3539;* a *perception*, i.e. *purpose*, or (by impl.) the *intellect, disposition*, itself:—device, mind, thought.

3541. **νόθος nŏthŏs**, *noth'-os;* of uncert. affin.; a *spurious* or *illegitimate* son:—bastard.

3542. **νομή nŏmē**, *nom-ay';* fem. from the same as *3551; pasture*, i.e. (the act) *feeding* (fig. *spreading* of a gangrene), or (the food) *pasturage:*— × eat, pasture.

3543. **νομίζω nŏmizō**, *nom-id'-zo;* from *3551;* prop. to *do* by *law* (*usage*), i.e. to *accustom* (pass. *be usual*); by extens. to *deem* or *regard:*—suppose, think, be wont.

3544. **νομικός nŏmikŏs**, *nom-ik-os';* from *3551; according* (or *pertaining*) *to law*, i.e. *legal* (cer.); as noun, an *expert in* the (Mosaic) *law:*—about the law, lawyer.

3545. **νομίμως nŏmimōs**, *nom-im'-oce;* adv. from a der. of *3551; legitimately* (spec. agreeably to the rules of the lists):—lawfully.

3546. **νόμισμα nŏmisma**, *nom'-is-mah;* from *3543; what is reckoned* as of value (after the Lat. *numisma*), i.e. current *coin:*—money.

3547. **νομοδιδάσκαλος nŏmŏdidaskalŏs**, *nom-od-id-as'-kal-os;* from *3551* and *1320;* an *expounder of* the (Jewish) *law*, i.e. a *Rabbi:*—doctor (teacher) of the law.

3548. **νομοθεσία nŏmŏthĕsia**, *nom-oth-es-ee'-ah;* from *3550; legislation* (spec. the *institution of* the Mosaic *code*):—giving of the law.

3549. **νομοθετέω nŏmŏthĕtĕō**, *nom-oth-et-eh'-o;* from *3550;* to *legislate*, i.e. (pass.) to *have* (the Mosaic) *enactments* injoined, *be sanctioned* (by them):—establish, receive the law.

3550. **νομοθέτης nŏmŏthĕtēs**, *nom-oth-et'-ace;* from *3551* and a der. of *5087;* a *legislator:*—lawgiver.

3551. **νόμος nŏmŏs**, *nom'-os;* from a prim. **νέμω nĕmō** (to *parcel* out, espec. *food* or *grazing* to animals); *law* (through the idea of prescriptive *usage*), gen. (*regulation*), spec. (of Moses [includ. the volume]; also of the Gospel), or fig. (a *principle*):—law.

3552. **νοσέω nŏsĕō**, *nos-eh'-o;* from *3554;* to *be sick*, i.e. (by impl. of a diseased appetite) to *hanker* after (fig. to *harp* upon):—dote.

3553. **νόσημα nŏsēma**, *nos'-ay-ma;* from *3552;* an *ailment:*—disease.

3554. **νόσος nŏsŏs**, *nos'-os;* of uncert. affin.; a *malady* (rarely fig. of mor. *disability*):—disease, infirmity, sickness.

3555. **νοσσιά nŏssia**, *nos-see-ah';* from *3502;* a *brood* (of chickens):—brood.

3556. **νοσσίον nŏssiŏn**, *nos-see'-on;* dimin. of *3502;* a *birdling:*—chicken.

3557. **νοσφίζομαι nŏsphizŏmai**, *nos-fid'-zom-ahee;* mid. from **νοσφί nŏsphi** (*apart* or *clandestinely*); to *sequestrate* for oneself, i.e. *embezzle:*—keep back, purloin.

3558. **νότος nŏtŏs**, *not'-os;* of uncert. affin.; the *south* (*-west*) *wind;* by extens. the *southern quarter* itself:—south (wind).

3559. **νουθεσία nŏuthĕsia**, *noo-thes-ee'-ah;* from *3563* and a der. of *5087;* calling *attention* to, i.e. (by impl.) mild *rebuke* or *warning:*—admonition.

3560. **νουθετέω nŏuthĕtĕō**, *noo-thet-eh'-o;* from the same as *3559;* to *put in mind*, i.e. (by impl.) to *caution* or *reprove* gently:—admonish, warn.

3561. **νουμηνία nŏumēnia**, *noo-may-nee'-ah;* fem. of a comp. of *3501* and *3376* (as noun by impl. of *2250*); the festival of *new moon:*—new moon.

3562. **νουνεχῶς nŏunĕchōs**, *noon-ekh-oce';* adv. from a comp. of the acc. of *3563* and *2192;* in a *mind-having* way, i.e. *prudently:*—discreetly.

3563. **νοῦς nŏus**, *nooce;* prob. from the base of *1097;* the *intellect*, i.e. *mind* (divine or human; in thought, feeling, or will); by impl. *meaning:*—mind, understanding. Comp. *5590.*

3564. **Νυμφᾶς Numphas**, *noom-fas';* prob. contr. for a comp. of *3565* and *1435; nymph-given* (i.e. -*born*); *Nymphas*, a Chr.:—Nymphas.

3565. **νύμφη numphē**, *noom-fay';* from a prim. but obsol. verb **νύπτω nuptō** (to *veil* as a bride; comp. Lat. "*nupto*," to *marry*); a young *married* woman (as *veiled*), includ. a *betrothed* girl; by impl. a *son's wife:*—bride, daughter in law.

3566. **νυμφίος numphiŏs**, *noom-fee'-os;* from *3565;* a *bride-groom* (lit. or fig.):—bridegroom.

3567. **νυμφών numphōn**, *noom-fohn';* from *3565;* the *bridal* room:—bridechamber.

3568. **νῦν nun**, *noon;* a prim. particle of present time; "*now*" (as adv. of date, a transition or emphasis); also as noun or adj. *present* or *immediate:*—henceforth, + hereafter, of late, soon, present, this (time). See also *3569, 3570.*

3569. **τανῦν tanun**, *tan-oon';* or **τὰ νῦν ta nun**, *tah noon;* from neut. plur. of *3588* and *3568; the* things *now*, i.e. (adv.) *at present:*—(but) now.

3570. **νυνί nuni**, *noo-nee';* a prol. form of *3568* for emphasis; *just now:*—now.

3571. **νύξ nux**, *noox;* a prim. word; "*night*" (lit. or fig.):—(mid-) night.

3572. **νύσσω nussō**, *noos'-so;* appar. a prim. word; to *prick* ("nudge"):—pierce.

3573. **νυστάζω nustazō**, *noos-tad'-zo;* from a presumed der. of *3506;* to *nod*, i.e. (by impl.) to *fall asleep;* fig. to *delay:*—slumber.

3574. **νυχθήμερον nuchthēmĕrŏn**, *nookh-thay'-mer-on;* from *3571* and *2250;* a *day-and-night*, i.e. full *day* of twenty-four hours:—night and day.

3575. **Νῶε Nōĕ**, *no'-eh;* of Heb. or. [5146]; *Noë*, (i.e. *Noäch*), a patriarch:—Noe.

3576. **νωθρός nōthrŏs**, *no-thros';* from a der. of *3541; sluggish*, i.e. (lit.) *lazy*, or (fig.) *stupid:*—dull, slothful.

3577. **νῶτος nōtŏs**, *no'-tos;* of uncert. affin.; the *back:*—back.

Ξ

3578. **ξενία xĕnia**, *xen-ee'-ah;* from *3581; hospitality*, i.e. (by impl.) a *place of entertainment:*—lodging.

3579. **ξενίζω xĕnizō**, *xen-id'-zo;* from *3581;* to *be a host* (pass. a *guest*); by impl. *be* (*make, appear*) *strange:*—entertain, lodge, (think it) strange.

3580. **ξενοδοχέω xĕnŏdŏchĕō**, *xen-od-okh-eh'-o;* from a comp. of *3581* and *1209;* to *be hospitable:*—lodge strangers.

3581. **ξένος xĕnŏs**, *xen'-os;* appar. a prim. word; *foreign* (lit. *alien*, or fig. *novel*); by impl. a *guest* or (vice-versa) *entertainer:*—host, strange (-r).

3582. **ξέστης xĕstēs**, *xes'-tace;* as if from **ξέω xĕō** (prop. to *smooth;* by impl. [of *friction*] to *boil* or *heat*); a *vessel* (as *fashioned* or for *cooking*) [or perh. by corruption from the Lat. *sextarius*, the *sixth* of a modius, i.e. about a *pint*], i.e. (spec.) a *measure* for liquids or solids, (by anal. a *pitcher*):—pot.

3583. **ξηραίνω xērainō**, *xay-rah'ee-no;* from *3584;* to *desiccate;* by impl. to *shrivel*, to *mature:*—dry up, pine away, be ripe, wither (away).

3584. **ξηρός xērŏs**, *xay-ros';* from the base of *3582* (through the idea of *scorching*); *arid;* by impl. *shrunken, earth* (as opposed to water):—dry, land, withered.

3585. **ξύλινος xulinŏs**, *xoo'-lin-os;* from *3586; wooden:*—of wood.

3586. **ξύλον xulŏn**, *xoo'-lon;* from another form of the base of *3582; timber* (as fuel or material); by impl. a *stick, club* or *tree* or other wooden article or substance:—staff, stocks, tree, wood.

3587. **ξυράω xuraō**, *xoo-rah'-o;* from a der. of the same as *3586* (mean. a *razor*); to *shave* or "*shear*" the hair:—shave.

O

3588. **ὁ hŏ**, *hŏ;* includ. the fem. **ἡ hē**, *hay;* and the neut. **τό tŏ**, *tŏ*, in all their inflections; the def. article; *the* (sometimes to be supplied, at others omitted in English idiom):—the, this, that, one, he, she, it, etc.

ὅ hŏ. See *3739.*

3589. **ὀγδοήκοντα ŏgdŏēkŏnta**, *og-dŏ-ay'-kon-tah;* from *3590; ten times eight:*—fourscore.

3590. **ὄγδοος ŏgdŏŏs**, *og'-dŏ-os;* from *3638;* the *eighth:*—eighth.

3591. **ὄγκος ŏgkŏs**, *ong'-kos;* prob. from the same as *43;* a *mass* (as *bending* or *bulging* by its load), i.e. *burden* (*hindrance*):—weight.

3592. ὅδε **hŏdĕ**, *hod'-eh;* includ. the fem.

ἥδε **hēdĕ**, *hay'-deh;* and the neut.

τόδε **tŏdĕ**, *tod'-e;* from 3588 and 1161; the *same,* i.e. *this* or *that* one (plur. *these* or *those*); often used as pers. pron.:—he, she, such, these, thus.

3593. ὁδεύω **hŏdĕuō**, *hod-yoo'-o;* from 3598; to *travel:*—journey.

3594. ὁδηγέω **hŏdēgĕō**, *hod-ayg-eh'-o;* from 3595; to *show* the *way* (lit. or fig. [*teach*]):—guide, lead.

3595. ὁδηγός **hŏdēgŏs**, *hod-ayg-os';* from 3598 and 2233; a *conductor* (lit. or fig. [*teacher*]):—guide, leader.

3596. ὁδοιπορέω **hŏdŏipŏrĕō**, *hod-oy-por-eh'-o;* from a comp. of 3598 and 4198; to *be a wayfarer,* i.e. *travel:*—go on a journey.

3597. ὁδοιπορία **hŏdŏipŏria**, *hod-oy-por-ee'-ah;* from the same as 3596; *travel:*—journey (-ing).

3598. ὁδός **hŏdŏs**, *hod-os';* appar. a prim. word; a *road;* by impl. a *progress* (the route, act or distance); fig. a *mode* or *means:*—journey, (high-) way.

3599. ὀδούς **ŏdŏus**, *od-ooce ;* perh. from the base of 2068; a "*tooth*":—tooth.

3600. ὀδυνάω **ŏdunaō**, *od-oo-nah'-o;* from 3601; to *grieve:*—sorrow, torment.

3601. ὀδύνη **ŏdunē**, *od-oo'-nay;* from 1416; *grief* (as *dejecting*):—sorrow.

3602. ὀδυρμός **ŏdurmŏs**, *od-oor-mos';* from a der. of the base of 1416; *moaning,* i.e. *lamentation:*—mourning.

3603. ὅ ἐστι **hŏ esti**, *hŏ es-tee';* from the neut. of 3739 and the third pers. sing. pres. ind. of 1510; *which is:*—called, which is (make), that is (to say).

3604. Ὀζίας **Ŏzias**, *od-zee'-as;* of Heb. or. [5818]; *Ozias* (i.e. *Uzzijah*), an Isr.:—Ozias.

3605. ὄζω **ŏzō**, *od'-zo;* a prim. verb (in a strengthened form); to *scent* (usually an ill "odor"):—stink.

3606. ὅθεν **hŏthĕn**, *hoth'-en;* from 3739 with the directive enclitic of source; *from which* place or source or cause (adv. or conj.):—from thence, (from) whence, where (-by, -fore, -upon).

3607. ὀθόνη **ŏthŏnē**, *oth-on'-ay;* of uncert. affin.; a *linen* cloth, i.e. (espec.) a *sail:*—sheet.

3608. ὀθόνιον **ŏthŏniŏn**, *oth-on'-ee-on;* neut. of a presumed der. of 3607; a linen *bandage:*—linen clothes.

3609. οἰκεῖος **ŏikĕiŏs**, *oy-ki'-os;* from 3624; *domestic,* i.e. (as noun), a *relative, adherent:*—(those) of the (his own) house (-hold).

3610. οἰκέτης **ŏikĕtēs**, *oy-ket'-ace;* from 3611; a fellow *resident,* i.e. menial *domestic:*—(household) servant.

3611. οἰκέω **ŏikĕō**, *oy-keh'-o;* from 3624; to *occupy a house,* i.e. *reside* (fig. *inhabit, remain, inhere*); by impl. to *cohabit:*—dwell. See also 3625.

3612. οἴκημα **ŏikēma**, *oy'-kay-mah;* from 3611; a *tenement,* i.e. (spec.) a *jail:*—prison.

3613. οἰκητήριον **ŏikētēriŏn**, *oy-kay-tay'-ree-on;* neut. of a presumed der. of 3611 (equiv. to 3612); a *residence* (lit. or fig.):—habitation, house.

3614. οἰκία **ŏikia**, *oy-kee'-ah;* from 3624; prop. *residence* (abstr.), but usually (concr.) an *abode* (lit. or fig.); by impl. a *family* (espec. *domestics*):—home, house (-hold).

3615. οἰκιακός **ŏikiakŏs**, *oy-kee-ak-os';* from 3614; *familiar,* i.e. (as noun) *relatives:*—they (them) of (his own) household.

3616. οἰκοδεσποτέω **ŏikŏdĕspŏtĕō**, *oy-kod-es-pot-eh'-o;* from 3617; to *be* the *head of* (i.e. *rule*) a *family:*—guide the house.

3617. οἰκοδεσπότης **ŏikŏdĕspŏtēs**, *oy-kod-es-pot'-ace;* from 3624 and 1203; *the head of a family:*—goodman (of the house), householder, master of the house.

3618. οἰκοδομέω **ŏikŏdŏmĕō**, *oy-kod-om-eh'-o;* from the same as 3619; to *be a house-builder,* i.e. *construct* or (fig.) *confirm:*—(be in) build (-er, -ing, up), edify, embolden.

3619. οἰκοδομή **ŏikŏdŏmē**, *oy-kod-om-ay';* fem. (abstr.) of a comp. of 3624 and the base of 1430; *architecture,* i.e. (concr.) a *structure;* fig. *confirmation:*—building, edify (-ication, -ing).

3620. οἰκοδομία **ŏikŏdŏmia**, *oy-kod-om-ee'-ah;* from the same as 3619; *confirmation:*—edifying.

3621. οἰκονομέω **ŏikŏnŏmĕō**, *oy-kon-om-eh'-o;* from 3623; to *manage* (a house, i.e. an estate):—be steward.

3622. οἰκονομία **ŏikŏnŏmia**, *oy-kon-om-ee'-ah;* from 3623; *administration* (of a household or estate); spec. a (religious) "*economy*":—dispensation, stewardship.

3623. οἰκονόμος **ŏikŏnŏmŏs**, *oy-kon-om'-os;* from 3624 and the base of 3551; a *house-distributor* (i.e. *manager*), or *overseer,* i.e. an employee in that capacity; by extens. a fiscal *agent* (*treasurer*); fig. a *preacher* (of the Gospel):—chamberlain, governor, steward.

3624. οἶκος **ŏikŏs**, *oy'-kos;* of uncert. affin.; a *dwelling* (more or less extensive, lit. or fig.); by impl. a *family* (more or less related, lit. or fig.):—home, house (-hold), temple.

3625. οἰκουμένη **ŏikŏumĕnē**, *oy-kou-men'-ay;* fem. part. pres. pass. of 3611 (as noun, by impl. of 1093); *land,* i.e. the (terrene part of the) *globe;* spec. the Roman *empire:*—earth, world.

3626. οἰκουρός **ŏikŏurŏs**, *oy-koo-ros';* from 3624 and οὖρος **ŏurŏs** (a *guard;* be "ware"); a *stayer at home,* i.e. *domestically inclined* (a "good housekeeper"):—keeper at home.

3627. οἰκτείρω **ŏiktĕirō**, *oyk-ti'-ro;* also (in certain tenses) prol.

οἰκτερέω **ŏiktĕrĕō**, *oyk-ter-eh'-o;* from οἶκτος **ŏiktŏs** (*pity*); to *exercise pity:*—have compassion on.

3628. οἰκτιρμός **ŏiktirmŏs**, *oyk-tir-mos';* from 3627; *pity:*—mercy.

3629. οἰκτίρμων **ŏiktirmōn**, *oyk-tir'-mone;* from 3627; *compassionate:*—merciful, of tender mercy.

οἶμαι **ŏimai**. See 3633.

3630. οἰνοπότης **ŏinŏpŏtēs**, *oy-nop-ot'-ace;* from 3631 and a der. of the alt. of 4095; a *tippler:*—winebibber.

3631. οἶνος **ŏinŏs**, *oy'-nos;* a prim. word (or perh. of Heb. or. [3196]); "*wine*" (lit. or fig.):—wine.

3632. οἰνοφλυγία **ŏinŏphlugia**, *oy-nof-loog-ee'-ah;* from 3631 and a form of the base of 5397; an *overflow* (or surplus) of *wine,* i.e. *vinolency* (*drunkenness*):—excess of wine.

3633. οἴομαι **ŏiŏmai**, *oy'-om-ahee;* or (shorter)

οἶμαι **ŏimai**, *oy'-mahee;* mid. appar. from 3634; to *make like* (oneself), i.e. *imagine* (*be of* the *opinion*):—suppose, think.

3634. οἷος **hŏiŏs**, *hoy'-os;* prob. akin to 3588, 3739, and 3745; *such* or *what sort* of (as a correl. or exclamation); espec. the neut. (adv.) with neg. not *so:*—so (as), such as, what (manner of), which.

οἴω **ŏiō**. See 5342.

3635. ὀκνέω **ŏknĕō**, *ok-neh'-o;* from ὄκνος **ŏknŏs** (*hesitation*); to *be slow* (fig. *loath*):—delay.

3636. ὀκνηρός **ŏknērŏs**, *ok-nay-ros';* from 3635; *tardy,* i.e. *indolent;* (fig.) *irksome:*—grievous, slothful.

3637. ὀκταήμερος **ŏktaēmĕrŏs**, *ok-tah-ay'-mer-os;* from 3638 and 2250; an *eight-day* old person or act:—the eighth day.

3638. ὀκτώ **ŏktō**, *ok-to';* a prim. numeral; "*eight*":—eight.

3639. ὄλεθρος **ŏlĕthrŏs**, *ol'-eth-ros;* from a prim. ὄλλυμι **ŏllumi** (to *destroy;* a prol. form); *ruin,* i.e. *death, punishment:*—destruction.

3640. ὀλιγόπιστος **ŏligŏpistŏs**, *ol-ig-op'-is-tos;* from 3641 and 4102; *incredulous,* i.e. *lacking confidence* (in Christ):—of little faith.

3641. ὀλίγος **ŏligŏs**, *ol-ee'-gos;* of uncert. affin.; *puny* (in extent, degree, number, duration or value); espec. neut. (adv.) *somewhat:*— + almost, brief [-ly], few, (a) little, + long, a season, short, small, a while.

3642. ὀλιγόψυχος **ŏligŏpsuchŏs**, *ol-ig-op'-soo-khos;* from 3641 and 5590; *little-spirited,* i.e. *faint-hearted:*—feebleminded.

3643. ὀλιγωρέω **ŏligōrĕō**, *ol-ig-o-reh'-o;* from a comp. of 3641 and ὤρα **ōra** ("*care*"); to *have little regard* for, i.e. to *disesteem:*—despise.

3644. ὀλοθρευτής **ŏlŏthrĕutēs**, *ol-oth-ryoo-tace';* from 3645; a *ruiner,* i.e. (spec.) a venomous *serpent:*—destroyer.

3645. ὀλοθρεύω **ŏlŏthrĕuō**, *ol-oth-ryoo'-o;* from 3639; to *spoil,* i.e. *slay:*—destroy.

3646. ὁλοκαύτωμα **hŏlŏkautōma**, *hol-ok-ŏw'-to-mah;* from a der. of a comp. of 3650 and a der. of 2545; a *wholly-consumed* sacrifice ("holocaust"):—(whole) burnt offering.

3647. ὁλοκληρία **hŏlŏklēria**, *hol-ok-lay-ree'-ah;* from 3648; *integrity,* i.e. physical *wholeness:*—perfect soundness.

3648. ὁλόκληρος **hŏlŏklērŏs**, *hol-ok'-lay-ros;* from 3650 and 2819; *complete* in every *part,* i.e. perfectly *sound* (in body):—entire, whole.

3649. ὀλολύζω **ŏlŏluzō**, *ol-ol-ood'-zo;* a redupl. prim. verb; to "*howl*" or "*halloo*", i.e. *shriek:*—howl.

3650. ὅλος **hŏlŏs**, *hol'-os;* a prim. word; "*whole*" or "*all*", i.e. *complete* (in extent, amount, time or degree), espec. (neut.) as noun or adv.:—all, altogether, every whit, + throughout, whole.

3651. ὁλοτελής **hŏlŏtĕlēs**, *hol-ot-el-ace';* from 3650 and 5056; *complete* to the *end,* i.e. *absolutely perfect:*—wholly.

3652. Ὀλυμπᾶς **Ŏlumpas**, *ol-oom-pas';* prob. a contr. from Ὀλυμπιόδωρος **Ŏlumpiŏdōrŏs** (*Olympian-bestowed,* i.e. *heaven-descended*); *Olympas,* a Chr.:—Olympas.

3653. ὄλυνθος **ŏlunthŏs**, *ol'-oon-thos;* of uncert. der.; an *unripe* (because out of season) *fig:*—untimely fig.

3654. ὅλως **hŏlōs**, *hol'-oce;* adv. from 3650; *completely,* i.e. *altogether;* (by anal.) *everywhere;* (neg.) not *by any means:*—at all, commonly, utterly.

3655. ὄμβρος **ŏmbrŏs**, *om'-bros;* of uncert. affin.; a thunder *storm:*—shower.

3656. ὁμιλέω **hŏmilĕō**, *hom-il-eh'-o;* from 3658; to *be in company* with, i.e. (by impl.) to *converse:*—commune, talk.

3657. ὁμιλία **hŏmilia**, *hom-il-ee'-ah;* from 3658; *companionship* ("homily"), i.e. (by impl.) *intercourse:*—communication.

3658. ὅμιλος **hŏmilŏs**, *hom'-il-os;* from the base of 3674 and a der. of the alt. of 138 (mean. a *crowd*); *association together,* i.e. a *multitude:*—company.

3659. ὄμμα **ŏmma**, *om'-mah;* from 3700; a *sight,* i.e. (by impl.) the *eye:*—eye.

3660. ὀμνύω **ŏmnuō**, *om-noo'-o;* a prol. form of a prim. but obsol. ὄμω **ŏmō**, for which another prol. form (ὀμόω **ŏmŏō**, *om-ŏ'-o*) is used in certain tenses; to *swear,* i.e. *take* (or *declare on*) *oath:*—swear.

3661. ὁμοθυμαδόν **hŏmŏthumadŏn**, *hom-oth-oo-mad-on';* adv. from a comp. of the base of 3674 and 2372; *unanimously:*—with one accord (mind).

3662. ὁμοιάζω **hŏmŏiazō**, *hom-oy-ad'-zo;* from 3664; to *resemble:*—agree.

3663. ὁμοιοπαθής **hŏmŏiŏpathēs**, *hom-oy-op-ath-ace';* from 3664 and the alt. of 3958; *similarly affected:*—of (subject to) like passions.

3664. ὅμοιος **hŏmŏiŏs**, *hom'-oy-os;* from the base of 3674; *similar* (in appearance or character):—like, + manner.

3665. ὁμοιότης **hŏmŏiŏtēs**, *hom-oy-ot'-ace;* from 3664; *resemblance:*—like as, similitude.

3666. ὁμοιόω **hŏmŏiŏō**, *hom-oy-ŏ'-o;* from 3664; to *assimilate,* i.e. *compare;* pass. to *become similar:*—be (make) like, (in the) liken (-ess), resemble.

3667. ὁμοίωμα **hŏmŏiōma**, *hom-oy'-o-mah;* from 3666; a *form;* abstr. *resemblance:*—made like to, likeness, shape, similitude.

3668. ὁμοίως **hŏmŏiōs**, *hom-oy'-oce;* adv. from 3664; *similarly:*—likewise, so.

3669. ὁμοίωσις **hŏmŏiōsis**, *hom-oy'-o-sis;* from 3666; *assimilation*, i.e. *resemblance:*—similitude.

3670. ὁμολογέω **hŏmŏlŏgĕō**, *hom-ol-og-eh'-o;* from a comp. of the base of 3674 and 3056; to *assent*, i.e. *covenant, acknowledge:*—con- (pro-) fess, confession is made, give thanks, promise.

3671. ὁμολογία **hŏmŏlŏgia**, *hom-ol-og-ee'-ah;* from the same as 3670; *acknowledgment:*—con- (pro-) fession, professed.

3672. ὁμολογουμένως **hŏmŏlŏgŏumĕnōs**, *hom-ol-og-ŏw-men'-oce;* adv. of pres. pass. part. of 3670; *confessedly:*—without controversy.

3673. ὁμότεχνος **hŏmŏtĕchnŏs**, *hom-ot'-ekh-nos;* from the base of 3674 and 5078; a *fellow-artificer:*—of the same craft.

3674. ὁμοῦ **hŏmŏu**, *hom-oo';* gen. of ὁμός **hŏmŏs** (the *same;* akin to 260) as adv.; *at the same* place or time:—together.

3675. ὁμόφρων **hŏmŏphrōn**, *hom-of'-rone;* from the base of 3674 and 5424; *like-minded*, i.e. *harmonious:*—of one mind.

ὁμόω **ŏmŏō**. See 3660.

3676. ὅμως **hŏmōs**, *hom'-oce;* adv. from the base of 3674; *at the same* time, i.e. (conj.) *notwithstanding, yet still:*—and even, nevertheless, though but.

3677. ὄναρ **ŏnar**, *on'-ar;* of uncert. der.; a *dream:*—dream.

3678. ὀνάριον **ŏnariŏn**, *on-ar'-ee-on;* neut. of a presumed der. of 3688; a *little ass:*—young ass.

ὀνάω **ŏnaō**. See 3685.

3679. ὀνειδίζω **ŏnĕidizō**, *on-i-did'-zo;* from 3681; to *defame*, i.e. *rail at, chide, taunt:*—cast in teeth, (suffer) reproach, revile, upbraid.

3680. ὀνειδισμός **ŏnĕidismŏs**, *on-i-dis-mos';* from 3679; *contumely:*—reproach.

3681. ὄνειδος **ŏnĕidŏs**, *on'-i-dos;* prob. akin to the base of 3686; *notoriety*, i.e. a *taunt* (*disgrace*):—reproach.

3682. Ὀνήσιμος **Ŏnēsimŏs**, *on-ay'-sim-os;* from 3685; *profitable; Onesimus*, a Chr.:—Onesimus.

3683. Ὀνησίφορος **Ŏnēsiphŏrŏs**, *on-ay-sif'-or-os;* from a der. of 3685 and 5411; *profit-bearer; Onesiphorus*, a Chr.:—Onesiphorus.

3684. ὀνικός **ŏnikŏs**, *on-ik-os';* from 3688; *belonging to* an *ass*, i.e. *large* (so as to be turned by an ass):—millstone.

3685. ὀνίνημι **ŏninēmi**, *on-in'-ay-mee;* a prol. form of an appar. prim. verb

(ὄνομαι **ŏnŏmai**, to *slur*); for which another prol. form (ὀνάω **ŏnaō**) is used as an alt. in some tenses [unless indeed it be identical with the base of 3686 through the idea of *notoriety*]; to *gratify*, i.e. (mid.) to *derive pleasure* or *advantage* from:—have joy.

3686. ὄνομα **ŏnŏma**, *on'-om-ah;* from a presumed der. of the base of 1097 (comp. 3685); a "*name*" (lit. or fig.) [*authority, character*]:—called, (+ sur-) name (-d).

3687. ὀνομάζω **ŏnŏmazō**, *on-om-ad'-zo;* from 3686; to *name*, i.e. *assign an appellation;* by extens. to *utter, mention, profess:*—call, name.

3688. ὄνος **ŏnŏs**, *on'-os;* appar. a prim. word; a *donkey:*—ass.

3689. ὄντως **ŏntōs**, *on'-toce;* adv. of the oblique cases of 5607; *really:*—certainly, clean, indeed, of a truth, verily.

3690. ὄξος **ŏxŏs**, *ox'-os;* from 3691; *vinegar*, i.e. *sour* wine:—vinegar.

3691. ὀξύς **ŏxus**, *ox-oos';* prob. akin to the base of 188 ["*acid*"]; *keen;* by anal. *rapid:*—sharp, swift.

3692. ὀπή **ŏpē**, *op-ay';* prob. from 3700; a *hole* (as if for light), i.e. *cavern;* by anal. a *spring* (of water):—cave, place.

3693. ὄπισθεν **ŏpisthĕn**, *op'-is-then;* from ὄπις **ŏpis** (*regard;* from 3700) with enclitic of source; *from the rear* (as a secure *aspect*), i.e. *at* the *back* (adv. and prep. of place or time):—after, backside, behind.

3694. ὀπίσω **ŏpisō**, *op-is'-o;* from the same as 3693 with enclitic of direction; *to the back*, i.e. *aback* (as adv. or prep. of time or place; or as noun):—after, back (-ward), (+ get) behind, + follow.

3695. ὁπλίζω **hŏplizō**, *hop-lid'-zo;* from 3696; to *equip* (with weapons [mid. and fig.]):—arm self.

3696. ὅπλον **hŏplŏn**, *hop'-lon;* prob. from a prim. ἕπω **hĕpō** (to be *busy* about); an *implement* or *utensil* or *tool* (lit. or fig., espec. offensive for war):—armour, instrument, weapon.

3697. ὁποῖος **hŏpŏiŏs**, *hop-oy'-os;* from 3739 and 4169; of *what* kind *that*, i.e. *how* (*as*) *great* (*excellent*) (spec. as indef. correl. to anteced. def. 5108 of quality):—what manner (sort) of, such as, whatsoever.

3698. ὁπότε **hŏpŏtĕ**, *hop-ot'-eh;* from 3739 and 4218; *what* (-ever) *then*, i.e. (of time) *as soon as:*—when.

3699. ὅπου **hŏpŏu**, *hop'-oo;* from 3739 and 4225; *what* (-ever) *where*, i.e. *at whichever* spot:—in what place, where (-as, -soever), whither (+ soever).

3700. ὀπτάνομαι **ŏptanŏmai**, *op-tan'-om-ahee;* a (mid.) prol. form of the prim. (mid.)

ὄπτομαι **ŏptŏmai**, *op'-tom-ahee*, which is used for it in certain tenses; and both as alt. of 3708; to *gaze* (i.e. with wide-open eyes, as at something remarkable; and thus differing from 991, which denotes simply *voluntary* observation; and from 1492, which expresses merely mechanical, passive or casual vision; while 2300, and still more emphatically its intens. 2334, signifies an earnest but more continued *inspection;* and 4648 a watching *from a distance*):—appear, look, see, shew self.

3701. ὀπτασία **ŏptasia**, *op-tas-ee'-ah;* from a presumed der. of 3700; *visuality*, i.e. (concr.) an *apparition:*—vision.

ὄπτομαι **ŏptŏmai**. See 3700.

3702. ὀπτός **ŏptŏs**, *op-tos';* from an obsol. verb akin to ἕψω **hĕpsō** (to "*steep*"); *cooked*, i.e. *roasted:*—broiled.

3703. ὀπώρα **ŏpōra**, *op-o'-rah;* appar. from the base of 3796 and 5610; prop. *even-tide* of the (summer) season (*dog-days*), i.e. (by impl.) *ripe* fruit:—fruit.

3704. ὅπως **hŏpōs**, *hop'-oce;* from 3739 and 4459; *what* (-ever) *how*, i.e. *in* the *manner that* (as adv. or conj. of coincidence, intentional or actual):—because, how, (so) that, to, when.

3705. ὅραμα **hŏrama**, *hor'-am-ah;* from 3708; *something gazed at*, i.e. a *spectacle* (espec. supernat.):—sight, vision.

3706. ὅρασις **hŏrasis**, *hor'-as-is;* from 3708; the act of *gazing*, i.e. (external) an *aspect* or (intern.) an inspired *appearance:*—sight, vision.

3707. ὁρατός **hŏratŏs**, *hor-at-os';* from 3708; *gazed at*, i.e. (by impl.) *capable of being seen:*—visible.

3708. ὁράω **hŏraō**, *hor-ah'-o;* prop. to *stare* at [comp. 3700], i.e. (by impl.) to *discern* clearly (phys. or ment.); by extens. to *attend* to; by Hebr. to *experience;* pass. to *appear:*—behold, perceive, see, take heed.

3709. ὀργή **ŏrgē**, *or-gay';* from 3713; prop. *desire* (as a *reaching* forth or *excitement* of the mind), i.e. (by anal.) violent *passion* (*ire*, or [justifiable] *abhorrence*); by impl. *punishment:*—anger, indignation, vengeance, wrath.

3710. ὀργίζω **ŏrgizō**, *or-gid'-zo;* from 3709; to *provoke* or *enrage*, i.e. (pass.) *become exasperated:*—be angry (wroth).

3711. ὀργίλος **ŏrgilŏs**, *org-ee'-los;* from 3709; *irascible:*—soon angry.

3712. ὀργυιά **ŏrguia**, *org-wee-ah';* from 3713; a *stretch* of the arms, i.e. a *fathom:*—fathom.

3713. ὀρέγομαι **ŏrĕgŏmai**, *or-eg'-om-ahee;* mid. of appar. a prol. form of an obsol. prim. [comp. 3735]; to *stretch* oneself, i.e. *reach out after* (*long* for):—covet after, desire.

3714. ὀρεινός **ŏrĕinŏs**, *or-i-nos';* from 3735; *mountainous*, i.e. (fem. by impl. of 5561) the *Highlands* (of Judæa):—hill country.

3715. ὄρεξις **ŏrĕxis**, *or'-ex-is;* from 3713; *excitement* of the mind, i.e. *longing* after:—lust.

3716. ὀρθοποδέω **ŏrthŏpŏdĕō**, *or-thop-od-eh'-o;* from a comp. of 3717 and 4228; to *be straight-footed*, i.e. (fig.) to *go directly* forward:—walk uprightly.

3717. ὀρθός **ŏrthŏs**, *or-thos';* prob. from the base of 3735; *right* (as *rising*), i.e. (perpendicularly) *erect* (fig. *honest*), or (horizontally) *level* or *direct:*—straight, upright.

3718. ὀρθοτομέω **ŏrthŏtŏmĕō**, *or-thot-om-eh'-o;* from a comp. of 3717 and the base of 5114; to *make a straight cut*, i.e. (fig.) to *dissect* (*expound*) *correctly* (the divine message):—rightly divide.

3719. ὀρθρίζω **ŏrthrizō**, *or-thrid'-zo;* from 3722; to *use* the *dawn*, i.e. (by impl.) to *repair betimes:*—come early in the morning.

3720. ὀρθρινός **ŏrthrinŏs**, *or-thrin-os';* from 3722; *relating to* the *dawn*, i.e. *matutinal* (as an epithet of Venus, espec. brilliant in the early day):—morning.

3721. ὄρθριος **ŏrthriŏs**, *or'-three-os;* from 3722; *in* the *dawn*, i.e. up *at day-break:*—early.

3722. ὄρθρος **ŏrthrŏs**, *or'-thros;* from the same as 3735; *dawn* (as *sun-rise, rising* of light); by extens. *morn:*—early in the morning.

3723. ὀρθῶς **ŏrthōs**, *or-thoce';* adv. from 3717; *in a straight* manner, i.e. (fig.) *correctly* (also mor.):—plain, right (-ly).

3724. ὁρίζω **hŏrizō**, *hor-id'-zo;* from 3725; to *mark* out or *bound* ("horizon"), i.e. (fig.) to *appoint, decree, specify:*—declare, determine, limit, ordain.

3725. ὅριον **hŏriŏn**, *hor'-ee-on;* neut. of a der. of an appar. prim. ὅρος **hŏrŏs** (a *bound* or *limit*); a *boundary*-line, i.e. (by impl.) a *frontier* (*region*):—border, coast.

3726. ὁρκίζω **hŏrkizō**, *hor-kid'-zo;* from 3727; to *put on oath*, i.e. *make swear;* by anal. to solemnly *enjoin:*—adjure, charge.

3727. ὅρκος **hŏrkŏs**, *hor'-kos;* from ἕρκος **hĕrkŏs** (a *fence;* perh. akin to 3725); a *limit*, i.e. (sacred) *restraint* (spec. *oath*):—oath.

3728. ὁρκωμοσία **hŏrkōmŏsia**, *hor-ko-mos-ee'-ah;* from a comp. of 3727 and a der. of 3660; *asseveration on oath:*—oath.

3729. ὁρμάω **hŏrmaō**, *hor-mah'-o;* from 3730; to *start, spur* or *urge* on, i.e. (reflex.) to *dash* or *plunge:*—run (violently), rush.

3730. ὁρμή **hŏrmē**, *hor-may';* of uncert. affin.; a violent *impulse*, i.e. *onset:*—assault.

3731. ὅρμημα **hŏrmēma**, *hor'-may-mah;* from 3730; an *attack*, i.e. (abstr.) *precipitancy:*—violence.

3732. ὄρνεον **ŏrnĕŏn**, *or'-neh-on;* neut. of a presumed der. of 3733; a *birdling:*—bird, fowl.

3733. ὄρνις **ŏrnis**, *or'-nis;* prob. from a prol. form of the base of 3735; a *bird* (as *rising* in the air), i.e. (spec.) a *hen* (or female domestic fowl):—hen.

3734. ὁροθεσία **hŏrŏthĕsia**, *hor-oth-es-ee'-ah;* from a comp. of the base of 3725 and a der. of 5087; a *limit-placing*, i.e. (concr.) *boundary-line:*—bound.

3735. ὄρος **ŏrŏs**, *or'-os;* prob. from an obsol. ὄρω **ŏrō** (to *rise* or "*rear*"; perh. akin to 142; comp. 3733); a *mountain* (as *lifting* itself above the plain):—hill, mount (-ain).

3736. ὀρύσσω **ŏrussō**, *or-oos'-so;* appar. a prim. verb; to "*burrow*" in the ground, i.e. *dig:*—dig.

3737. ὀρφανός **ŏrphanŏs**, *or-fan-os';* of uncert. affin.; *bereaved* ("*orphan*"), i.e. *parentless:*—comfortless, fatherless.

3738. ὀρχέομαι **ŏrchĕŏmai**, *or-kheh'-om-ahee;* mid. from ὄρχος **ŏrchŏs** (a *row* or *ring*); to *dance* (from the *ranklike* or *regular* motion):—dance.

3739. ὅς **hŏs**, *hos;* includ. fem.

ἥ **hē**, *hay;* and neut.

ὅ **hŏ**, *hŏ;* prob. a prim. word (or perh. a form of the art. 3588); the rel. (sometimes demonstrative) pron., *who, which, what, that:*—one, (an-, the) other, some, that, what, which, who (-m, -se), etc. See also 3757.

3740. ὁσάκις **hŏsakis,** *hos-ak'-is;* multiple adv. from 3739; *how* (i.e. with 302, so) *many times* as:—as oft (-en) as.

3741. ὅσιος **hŏsiŏs,** *hos'-ee-os;* of uncert. affin.; prop. *right* (by intrinsic or divine character; thus distinguished from 1342, which refers rather to *human* statutes and relations; from 2413, which denotes formal *consecration;* and from 40, which relates to *purity* from defilement), i.e. *hallowed* (*pious, sacred, sure*):—holy, mercy, shalt be.

3742. ὁσιότης **hŏsiŏtēs,** *hos-ee-ot'-ace;* from 3741; *piety:*—holiness.

3743. ὁσίως **hŏsiōs,** *hos-ee-oce';* adv. from 3741; *piously:*—holily.

3744. ὀσμή **ŏsmē,** *os-may';* from 3605; *fragrance* (lit. or fig.):—odour, savour.

3745. ὅσος **hŏsŏs,** *hos'-os;* by redupl. from 3739; *as* (*much, great, long,* etc.) *as:*—all (that), as (long, many, much) (as), how great (many, much), [in-] asmuch as, so many as, that (ever), the more, those things, what (great, -soever), wheresoever, wherewithsoever, which, × while, who (-soever).

3746. ὅσπερ **hŏspĕr,** *hos'-per;* from 3739 and 4007; *who especially:*—whomsoever.

3747. ὀστέον **ŏstĕŏn,** *os-teh'-on;* or contr.

ὀστοῦν **ŏstŏun,** *os-toon';* of uncert. affin.; a *bone:*—bone.

3748. ὅστις **hŏstis,** *hos'-tis;* includ. the fem.

ἥτις **hētis,** *hay'-tis;* and the neut.

ὅ,τι **hŏ,ti,** *hot'-ee;* from 3739 and 5100; *which some,* i.e. *any that;* also (def.) *which same:*—× and (they), (such) as, (they) that, in that they, what (-soever), whereas ye, (they) which, who (-soever). Comp. 3754.

3749. ὀστράκινος **ŏstrakinŏs,** *os-tra'-kin-os;* from ὄστρακον **ŏstrakŏn** ["oyster"] (a *tile,* i.e. *terra cotta*); *earthen*-ware, i.e. *clayey;* by impl. *frail:*—of earth, earthen.

3750. ὄσφρησις **ŏsphrēsis,** *os'-fray-sis;* from a der. of 3605; *smell* (the sense):—smelling.

3751. ὀσφύς **ŏsphus,** *os-foos';* of uncert. affin.; the *loin* (extern.), i.e. the *hip;* intern. (by extens.) *procreative power:*—loin.

3752. ὅταν **hŏtan,** *hot'-an;* from 3753 and 302; *whenever* (implying *hypothesis* or more or less *uncertainty*); also caus. (conj.) *inasmuch as:*—as long (soon) as, that, + till, when (-soever), while.

3753. ὅτε **hŏtĕ,** *hot'-eh;* from 3739 and 5037; at *which* (thing) *too,* i.e. *when:*—after (that), as soon as, that, when, while.

ὅ,τε **hŏ,tĕ,** *hŏ,t'-eh;* also fem.

ἥ,τε **hē,tĕ,** *hay'-teh;* and neut.

τό,τε **tŏ,tĕ,** *tot'-eh;* simply the art. 3588 followed by 5037; so written (in some editions) to distinguish them from 3752 and 5119.

3754. ὅτι **hŏti,** *hot'-ee;* neut. of 3748 as conj.; demonst. *that* (sometimes redundant); caus. *because:*—as concerning that, as though, because (that), for (that), how (that), (in) that, though, why.

3755. ὅτου **hŏtŏu,** *hot'-oo;* for the gen. of 3748 (as adv.); during *which same* time, i.e. *whilst:*—whiles.

3756. οὐ **ŏu,** *oo;* also (before a vowel)

οὐκ **ŏuk,** *ook;* and (before an aspirate)

οὐχ **ŏuch,** *ookh;* a prim. word; the absol. neg. [comp. 3361] adv.; *no* or *not:*— + long, nay, neither, never, no (× man), none, [can-] not, + nothing, + special, un ([-worthy]), when, + without, + yet but. See also 3364, 3372.

3757. οὗ **hŏu,** *hoo;* gen. of 3739 as adv.; at *which* place, i.e. *where:*—where (-in), whither ([-soever]).

3758. οὐά **ŏua,** *oo-ah';* a prim. exclamation of surprise; "*ah*":—ah.

3759. οὐαί **ŏuai,** *oo-ah'ee;* a prim. exclamation of grief: "*woe*":—alas, woe.

3760. οὐδαμῶς **ŏudamōs,** *oo-dam-oce';* adv. from (the fem.) of 3762; *by no means:*—not.

3761. οὐδέ **ŏudĕ,** *oo-deh';* from 3756 and 1161; *not however,* i.e. *neither, nor, not even:*—neither (indeed), never, no (more, nor, not), nor (yet), (also, even, then) not (even, so much as), + nothing, so much as.

3762. οὐδείς **ŏudĕis,** *oo-dice';* includ. fem.

οὐδεμία **ŏudĕmia,** *oo-dem-ee'-ah;* and neut.

οὐδέν **ŏudĕn,** *oo-den';* from 3761 and 1520; *not even one* (man, woman or thing), i.e. *none, nobody, nothing:*—any (man), aught, man, neither any (thing), never (man), no (man), none (+ of these things), not (any, at all, -thing), nought.

3763. οὐδέποτε **ŏudĕpŏtĕ,** *oo-dep'-ot-eh;* from 3761 and 4218; *not even at any time,* i.e. *never at all:*—neither at any time, never, nothing at any time.

3764. οὐδέπω **ŏudĕpō,** *oo-dep'-o;* from 3761 and 4452; *not even yet:*—as yet not, never before (yet), (not) yet.

3765. οὐκέτι **ŏukĕti,** *ook-et'-ee;* also (separately)

οὐκ ἔτι **ŏuk ĕti,** *ook et'-ee;* from 3756 and 2089; *not yet, no longer:*—after that (not), (not) any more, henceforth (hereafter) not, no longer (more), not as yet (now), now no more (not), yet (not).

3766. οὐκοῦν **ŏukŏun,** *ook-oon';* from 3756 and 3767; is it *not therefore* that, i.e. (affirm.) *hence* or *so:*—then.

3767. οὖν **ŏun,** *oon;* appar. a prim. word; (adv.) *certainly,* or (conj.) *accordingly:*—and (so, truly), but, now (then), so (likewise then), then, therefore, verily, wherefore.

3768. οὔπω **ŏupō,** *oo'-po;* from 3756 and 4452; *not yet:*—hitherto not, (no . . .) as yet, not yet.

3769. οὐρά **ŏura,** *oo-rah';* appar. a prim. word; a *tail:*—tail.

3770. οὐράνιος **ŏuraniŏs,** *oo-ran'-ee-os;* from 3772; *celestial,* i.e. *belonging to* or *coming from* the *sky:*—heavenly.

3771. οὐρανόθεν **ŏuranŏthĕn,** *oo-ran-oth'-en;* from 3772 and the enclitic of source; *from* the *sky:*—from heaven.

3772. οὐρανός **ŏuranŏs,** *oo-ran-os';* perh. from the same as 3735 (through the idea of *elevation*); the *sky;* by extens. *heaven* (as the abode of God); by impl. *happiness, power, eternity;* spec. the *Gospel* (*Christianity*):—air, heaven ([-ly]), sky.

3773. Οὐρβανός **Ŏurbanŏs,** *oor-ban-os';* of Lat. or.; *Urbanus* (*of* the *city,* "*urbane*"), a Chr.:—Urbanus.

3774. Οὐρίας **Ŏurias,** *oo-ree'-as;* of Heb. or. [223]; *Urias* (i.e. *Urijah*), a Hittite:—Urias.

3775. οὖς **ŏus,** *ooce;* appar. a prim. word; the *ear* (phys. or ment.):—ear.

3776. οὐσία **ŏusia,** *oo-see'-ah;* from the fem. of 5607; *substance,* i.e. *property* (*possessions*):—goods, substance.

3777. οὔτε **ŏutĕ,** *oo'-teh;* from 3756 and 5037; *not too,* i.e. *neither* or *nor;* by anal. *not even:*—neither, none, nor (yet), (no, yet) not, nothing.

3778. οὗτος **hŏutŏs,** *hoo'-tos;* includ. nom. masc. plur.

οὗτοι **hŏutŏi,** *hoo'-toy;* nom. fem. sing.

αὕτη **hautē,** *how'-tay;* and nom. fem. plur.

αὗται **hautai,** *how'-tahee;* from the art. 3588 and 846; *the he* (*she* or it), i.e. *this* or *that* (often with art. repeated):—he (it was that), hereof, it, she, such as, the same, these, they, this (man, same, woman), which, who.

3779. οὕτω **hŏutō,** *hoo'-to;* or (before a vowel)

οὕτως **hŏutōs,** *hoo'-toce;* adv. from 3778; *in this way* (referring to what precedes or follows):—after that, after (in) this manner, as, even (so), for all that, like (-wise), no more, on this fashion (-wise), so (in like manner), thus, what.

3780. οὐχί **ŏuchi,** *oo-khee';* intens. of 3756; *not indeed:*—nay, not.

3781. ὀφειλέτης **ŏphĕilĕtēs,** *of-i-let'-ace;* from 3784; an *ower,* i.e. person *indebted;* fig. a *delinquent;* mor. a *transgressor* (against God):—debtor, which owed, sinner.

3782. ὀφειλή **ŏphĕilē,** *of-i-lay';* from 3784; *indebtedness,* i.e. (concr.) a *sum* owed; fig. *obligation,* i.e. (conjugal) *duty:*—debt, due.

3783. ὀφείλημα **ŏphĕilēma,** *of-i'-lay-mah;* from (the alt. of) 3784; *something owed,* i.e. (fig.) a *due;* mor. a *fault:*—debt.

3784. ὀφείλω **ŏphĕilō,** *of-i'-lo;* or (in cert. tenses) its prol. form

ὀφειλέω **ŏphĕilĕō,** *of-i-leh'-o;* prob. from the base of 3786 (through the idea of *accruing*); to *owe* (pecuniarily); fig. to *be under obligation* (*ought, must, should*); mor. to *fail* in duty:—behove, be bound, (be) debt (-or), (be) due (-ty), be guilty (indebted), (must) need (-s), ought, owe, should. See also 3785.

3785. ὄφελον **ŏphĕlŏn,** *of'-el-on;* first pers. sing. of a past tense of 3784; *I ought* (*wish*), i.e. (interj.) *oh that!:*—would (to God.)

3786. ὄφελος **ŏphĕlŏs,** *of'-el-os;* from ὀφέλλω **ŏphĕllō** (to *heap* up, i.e. *accumulate* or *benefit*); *gain:*—advantageth, profit.

3787. ὀφθαλμοδουλεία **ŏphthalmŏdŏulĕia,** *of-thal-mod-oo-li'-ah;* from 3788 and 1397; *sight-labor,* i.e. that needs watching (*remissness*):—eye-service.

3788. ὀφθαλμός **ŏphthalmŏs,** *of-thal-mos';* from 3700; the *eye* (lit. or fig.); by impl. *vision;* fig. *envy* (from the jealous side-glance):—eye, sight.

3789. ὄφις **ŏphis,** *of'-is;* prob. from 3700 (through the idea of *sharpness* of vision); a *snake,* fig. (as a type of sly cunning) an artful *malicious* person, espec. *Satan:*—serpent.

3790. ὀφρύς **ŏphrus,** *of-roos';* perh. from 3700 (through the idea of the shading or proximity to the organ of *vision*); the eye-"*brow*" or *forehead,* i.e. (fig.) the *brink* of a precipice:—brow.

3791. ὀχλέω **ŏchlĕō,** *okh-leh'-o;* from 3793; to *mob,* i.e. (by impl.) to *harass:*—vex.

3792. ὀχλοποιέω **ŏchlŏpŏiĕō,** *okh-lop-oy-eh'-o;* from 3793 and 4160; to *make a crowd,* i.e. *raise a* public *disturbance:*—gather a company.

3793. ὄχλος **ŏchlŏs,** *okh'-los;* from a der. of 2192 (mean. a *vehicle*); a *throng* (as *borne* along); by impl. the *rabble;* by extens. a *class* of people; fig. a *riot:*—company, multitude, number (of people), people, press.

3794. ὀχύρωμα **ŏchurōma,** *okh-oo'-ro-mah;* from a remote der. of 2192 (mean. to *fortify,* through the idea of *holding* safely); a *castle* (fig. *argument*):—stronghold.

3795. ὀψάριον **ŏpsariŏn,** *op-sar'-ee-on;* neut. of a presumed der. of the base of 3702; a *relish* to other food (as if cooked *sauce*), i.e. (spec.) *fish* (presumably salted and dried as a condiment):—fish.

3796. ὀψέ **ŏpsĕ,** *op-seh';* from the same as 3694 (through the idea of *backwardness*); (adv.) *late* in the day; by extens. *after the close* of the day:—(at) even, in the end.

3797. ὄψιμος **ŏpsimŏs,** *op'-sim-os;* from 3796; *later,* i.e. *vernal* (showering):—latter.

3798. ὄψιος **ŏpsiŏs,** *op'-see-os;* from 3796; *late;* fem. (as noun) *afternoon* (early eve) or *nightfall* (later eve):—even (-ing, [-tide]).

3799. ὄψις **ŏpsis,** *op'-sis;* from 3700; prop. *sight* (the act), i.e. (by impl.) the *visage,* an external *show:*—appearance, countenance, face.

3800. ὀψώνιον **ŏpsōniŏn,** *op-so'-nee-on;* neut. of a presumed der. of the same as 3795; *rations* for a soldier, i.e. (by extens.) his *stipend* or *pay:*—wages.

3801. ὁ ὢν καὶ ὁ ἦν καὶ ὁ ἐρχόμενος **hŏ ōn kai hŏ ēn kai hŏ ĕrchŏmĕnŏs,** *hŏ own kahee hŏ ane kahee hŏ er-khom'-en-os;* a phrase combining 3588 with the pres. part. and imperf. of 1510 and the pres. part. of 2064 by means of 2532; *the* one *being and the* one that *was and the* one *coming,* i.e. *the Eternal,* as a divine epithet of Christ:—which art (is, was), and (which) wast (is, was), and art (is) to come (shalt be).

Π

3802. παγιδεύω **pagidĕuō,** *pag-id-yoo'-o;* from 3803; to *ensnare* (fig.):—entangle.

3803. παγίς **pagis,** *pag-ece';* from 4078; a *trap*

(as *fastened* by a noose or notch); fig. a *trick* or *stratagem* (*temptation*):—snare.

Πάγος **Pagŏs**. See *697*.

3804. πάθημα **pathēma**, *path'-ay-mah;* from a presumed der. of *3806;* something *undergone*, i.e. *hardship* or *pain;* subj. an *emotion* or *influence:*—affection, affliction, motion, suffering.

3805. παθητός **pathētŏs**, *path-ay-tos';* from the same as *3804;* *liable* (i.e. *doomed*) *to experience pain:*—suffer.

3806. πάθος **pathŏs**, *path'-os;* from the alt. of *3958;* prop. *suffering* ("*pathos*"), i.e. (subj.) a *passion* (espec. *concupiscence*):—(inordinate) affection, lust.

πάθω **pathō**. See *3958*.

3807. παιδαγωγός **paidagōgŏs**, *pahee-dag-o-gos';* from *3816* and a redupl. form of *71;* a *boy-leader*, i.e. a servant whose office it was to take the children to school; (by impl. [fig.] a *tutor* ["*pædagogue*"]):—instructor, schoolmaster.

3808. παιδάριον **paidariŏn**, *pahee-dar'-ee-on;* neut. of a presumed der. of *3816;* a *little boy:*—child, lad.

3809. παιδεία **paidĕia**, *pahee-di'-ah;* from *3811;* *tutorage*, i.e. *education* or *training;* by impl. disciplinary *correction:*—chastening, chastisement, instruction, nurture.

3810. παιδευτής **paidĕutēs**, *pahee-dyoo-tace';* from *3811;* a *trainer*, i.e. *teacher* or (by impl.) *discipliner:*—which corrected, instructor.

3811. παιδεύω **paidĕuō**, *pahee-dyoo'-o;* from *3816;* to *train* up a child, i.e. *educate*, or (by impl.) *discipline* (by punishment):—chasten (-ise), instruct, learn, teach.

3812. παιδιόθεν **paidiŏthĕn**, *pahee-dee-oth'-en;* adv. (of *source*) from *3813;* *from infancy:*—of a child.

3813. παιδίον **paidiŏn**, *pahee-dee'-on;* neut. dimin. of *3816;* a *childling* (of either sex), i.e. (prop.) an *infant*, or (by extens.) a half-grown *boy* or girl; fig. an *immature* Christian:—(little, young) child, damsel.

3814. παιδίσκη **paidiskē**, *pahee-dis'-kay;* fem. dimin. of *3816;* a *girl*, i.e. (spec.) a *female slave* or *servant:*—bondmaid (-woman), damsel, maid (-en).

3815. παίζω **paizō**, *paheed'-zo;* from *3816;* to *sport* (as a boy):—play.

3816. παῖς **pais**, *paheece;* perh. from *3817;* a *boy* (as often *beaten* with impunity), or (by anal.) a *girl*, and (gen.) a *child;* spec. a *slave* or *servant* (espec. a *minister* to a king; and by eminence to God):—child, maid (-en), (man) servant, son, young man.

3817. παίω **paiō**, *pah'-yo;* a prim. verb; to *hit* (as if by a single blow and less violently than *5180*); spec. to *sting* (as a scorpion):—smite, strike.

3818. Πακατιανή **Pakatianē**, *pak-at-ee-an-ay';* fem. of an adj. of uncert. der.; *Pacatianian*, a section of Phrygia:—Pacatiana.

3819. πάλαι **palai**, *pal'-ahee;* prob. another form for *3825* (through the idea of *retrocession*); (adv.) *formerly*, or (by rel.) *sometime since;* (ellipt. as adj.) *ancient:*—any while, a great while ago, (of) old, in time past.

3820. παλαιός **palaiŏs**, *pal-ah-yos';* from *3819;* *antique*, i.e. *not recent, worn out:*—old.

3821. παλαιότης **palaiŏtēs**, *pal-ah-yot'-ace;* from *3820;* *antiquatedness:*—oldness.

3822. παλαιόω **palaiŏō**, *pal-ah-yŏ'-o;* from *3820;* to *make* (pass. *become*) *worn out*, or *declare obsolete:*—decay, make (wax) old.

3823. πάλη **palē**, *pal'-ay;* from πάλλω **pallō** (to *vibrate;* another form for *906*); *wrestling:*—+ wrestle.

3824. παλιγγενεσία **paliggĕnĕsia**, *pal-ing-ghen-es-ee'-ah;* from *3825* and *1078;* (spiritual) *rebirth* (the state or the act), i.e. (fig.) spiritual *renovation;* spec. Messianic *restoration:*—regeneration.

3825. πάλιν **palin**, *pal'-in;* prob. from the same as *3823* (through the idea of *oscillatory* repetition); (adv.) *anew*, i.e. (of place) *back*, (of time) *once more*, or (conj.) *furthermore* or *on the other hand:*—again.

3826. παμπληθεί **pamplēthĕi**, *pam-play-thi';* dat. (adv.) of a comp. of *3956* and *4128;* *in full multitude*, i.e. *concertedly* or *simultaneously:*—all at once.

3827. πάμπολυς **pampŏlus**, *pam-pol-ooce;* from *3956* and *4183;* *full many*, i.e. *immense:*—very great.

3828. Παμφυλία **Pamphulia**, *pam-fool-ee'-ah;* from a comp. of *3956* and *5443;* *every-tribal*, i.e. *heterogeneous* (*5561* being impl.); *Pamphylia*, a region of Asia Minor:—Pamphylia.

3829. πανδοχεῖον **pandŏchĕiŏn**, *pan-dokh-i'-on;* neut. of a presumed comp. of *3956* and a der. of *1209;* *all-receptive*, i.e. a public *lodging*-place (*caravanserai* or *khan*):—inn.

3830. πανδοχεύς **pandŏchĕus**, *pan-dokh-yoos';* from the same as *3829;* an *innkeeper* (*warden of a caravanserai*):—host.

3831. πανήγυρις **panēguris**, *pan-ay'-goo-ris;* from *3956* and a der. of *58;* a *mass-meeting*, i.e. (fig.) *universal companionship:*—general assembly.

3832. πανοικί **panŏiki**, *pan-oy-kee';* adv. from *3956* and *3624;* *with* the *whole family:*—with all his house.

3833. πανοπλία **panŏplia**, *pan-op-lee'-ah;* from a comp. of *3956* and *3696;* *full armor* ("*panoply*"):—all (whole) armour.

3834. πανουργία **panŏurgia**, *pan-oorg-ee'-ah;* from *3835;* *adroitness*, i.e. (in a bad sense) *trickery* or *sophistry:*—(cunning) craftiness, subtilty.

3835. πανοῦργος **panŏurgŏs**, *pan-oor'-gos;* from *3956* and *2041;* *all-working*, i.e. *adroit* (*shrewd*):—crafty.

3836. πανταχόθεν **pantachŏthĕn**, *pan-takh-oth'-en;* adv. (of *source*) from *3837;* *from all* directions:—from every quarter.

3837. πανταχοῦ **pantachŏu**, *pan-takh-oo';* gen. (as adv. of *place*) of a presumed der. of *3956;* *universally:*—in all places, everywhere.

3838. παντελής **pantĕlēs**, *pan-tel-ace';* from *3956* and *5056;* *full-ended*, i.e. *entire* (neut. as noun, *completion*):— + in [no] wise, uttermost.

3839. πάντη **pantē**, *pan'-tay;* adv. (of *manner*) from *3956;* *wholly:*—always.

3840. παντόθεν **pantŏthĕn**, *pan-toth'-en;* adv. (of *source*) from *3956;* *from* (i.e. *on*) *all* sides:—on every side, round about.

3841. παντοκράτωρ **pantŏkratōr**, *pan-tok-rat'-ore;* from *3956* and *2904;* the *all-ruling*, i.e. *God* (as absolute and universal *sovereign*):—Almighty, Omnipotent.

3842. πάντοτε **pantŏtĕ**, *pan'-tot-eh;* from *3956* and *3753;* *every when*, i.e. *at all* times:—alway (-s), ever (-more).

3843. πάντως **pantōs**, *pan'-toce;* adv. from *3956;* *entirely;* spec. *at all events*, (with neg. following) *in* no *event:*—by all means, altogether, at all, needs, no doubt, in [no] wise, surely.

3844. παρά **para**, *par-ah';* a prim. prep.; prop. *near*, i.e. (with gen.) *from beside* (lit. or fig.), (with dat.) *at* (or *in*) the *vicinity* of (obj. or subj.), (with acc.) to the *proximity* with (local [espec. *beyond* or *opposed* to] or causal [*on account* of]):—above, against, among, at, before, by, contrary to, × friend, from, + give [such things as they], + that [she] had, × his, in, more than, nigh unto, (out) of, past, save, side . . . by, in the sight of, than, [there-] fore, with. In compounds it retains the same variety of application.

3845. παραβαίνω **parabainō**, *par-ab-ah'ee-no;* from *3844* and the base of *939;* to *go contrary to*, i.e. *violate* a command:—(by) transgress (-ion).

3846. παραβάλλω **paraballō**, *par-ab-al'-lo;* from *3844* and *906;* to *throw alongside*, i.e. (reflex.) to *reach* a place, or (fig.) to *liken:*—arrive, compare.

3847. παράβασις **parabasis**, *par-ab'-as-is;* from *3845;* *violation:*—breaking, transgression.

3848. παραβάτης **parabatēs**, *par-ab-at'-ace;* from *3845;* a *violator:*—breaker, transgress (-or).

3849. παραβιάζομαι **parabiazŏmai**, *par-ab-ee-ad'-zom-ahee;* from *3844* and the mid. of *971;* to *force contrary* to (nature), i.e. *compel* (by entreaty):—constrain.

3850. παραβολή **parabŏlē**, *par-ab-ol-ay';* from *3846;* a *similitude* ("*parable*"), i.e. (symbol.) *fictitious narrative* (of common life conveying a moral), *apothegm* or *adage:*—comparison, figure, parable, proverb.

3851. παραβουλεύομαι **parabŏulĕuŏmai**, *par-ab-ool-yoo'-om-ahee;* from *3844* and the mid. of *1011;* to *misconsult*, i.e. *disregard:*—not (to) regard (-ing).

3852. παραγγελία **paraggĕlia**, *par-ang-gel-ee'-ah;* from *3853;* a *mandate:*—charge, command.

3853. παραγγέλλω **paraggĕllō**, *par-ang-gel'-lo;* from *3844* and the base of *32;* to *transmit a message*, i.e. (by impl.) to *enjoin:*—(give in) charge, (give) command (-ment), declare.

3854. παραγίνομαι **paraginŏmai**, *par-ag-in'-om-ahee;* from *3844* and *1096;* to *become near*, i.e. *approach* (*have arrived*); by impl. to *appear* publicly:—come, go, be present.

3855. παράγω **paragō**, *par-ag'-o;* from *3844* and *71;* to *lead near*, i.e. (reflex. or intrans.) to *go along* or *away:*—depart, pass (away, by, forth).

3856. παραδειγματίζω **paradĕigmatizō**, *par-ad-igue-mat-id'-zo;* from *3844* and *1165;* to *show alongside* (the public), i.e. *expose to infamy:*—make a public example, put to an open shame.

3857. παράδεισος **paradĕisŏs**, *par-ad'-i-sos;* of Oriental or. [comp. 6508]; a *park*, i.e. (spec.) an *Eden* (place of future happiness, "*paradise*"):—paradise.

3858. παραδέχομαι **paradĕchŏmai**, *par-ad-ekh'-om-ahee;* from *3844* and *1209;* to *accept near*, i.e. *admit* or (by impl.) *delight* in:—receive.

3859. παραδιατριβή **paradiatribē**, *par-ad-ee-at-ree-bay';* from a comp. of *3844* and *1304;* *misemployment*, i.e. *meddlesomeness:*—perverse disputing.

3860. παραδίδωμι **paradidōmi**, *par-ad-id'-o-mee;* from *3844* and *1325;* to *surrender*, i.e. *yield up*, *intrust*, *transmit:*—betray, bring forth, cast, commit, deliver (up), give (over, up), hazard, put in prison, recommend.

3861. παράδοξος **paradŏxŏs**, *par-ad'-ox-os;* from *3844* and *1391* (in the sense of *seeming*); *contrary to expectation*, i.e. *extraordinary* ("*paradox*"):—strange.

3862. παράδοσις **paradŏsis**, *par-ad'-os-is;* from *3860;* *transmission*, i.e. (concr.) a *precept;* spec. the Jewish *traditionary law:*—ordinance, tradition.

3863. παραζηλόω **parazēlŏō**, *par-ad-zay-lŏ'-o;* from *3844* and *2206;* to *stimulate alongside*, i.e. *excite to rivalry:*—provoke to emulation (jealousy).

3864. παραθαλάσσιος **parathalassiŏs**, *par-ath-al-as'-see-os;* from *3844* and *2281;* *along* the *sea*, i.e. *maritime* (*lacustrine*):—upon the sea coast.

3865. παραθεωρέω **parathĕōrĕō**, *par-ath-eh-o reh'-o;* from *3844* and *2334;* to *overlook* or *disregard:*—neglect.

3866. παραθήκη **parathēkē**, *par-ath-ay'-kay;* from *3908;* a *deposit*, i.e. (fig.) *trust:*—committed unto.

3867. παραινέω **parainĕō**, *par-ahee-neh'-o;* from *3844* and *134;* to *mispraise*, i.e. *recommend* or *advise* (a different course):—admonish, exhort.

3868. παραιτέομαι **paraitĕŏmai**, *par-ahee-teh'-om-ahee;* from *3844* and the mid. of *154;* to *beg off*, i.e. *deprecate*, *decline*, *shun:*—avoid, (make) excuse, intreat, refuse, reject.

3869. παρακαθίζω **parakathizō**, *par-ak-ath-id'-zo;* from *3844* and *2523;* to *sit down near:*—sit.

3870. παρακαλέω **parakalĕō**, *par-ak-al-eh'-o;* from *3844* and *2564;* to *call near*, i.e. *invite*, *invoke* (by *imploration*, *hortation* or *consolation*):—beseech, call for, (be of good) comfort, desire, (give) exhort (-ation), intreat, pray.

3871. παρακαλύπτω **parakaluptō**, *par-ak-al-oop'-to;* from *3844* and *2572;* to *cover alongside*, i.e. *veil* (fig.):—hide.

3872. παρακαταθήκη **parakatathēkē**, *par-ak-at-ath-ay'-kay;* from a comp. of *3844* and *2698;* something *put down alongside*, i.e. a *deposit* (sacred *trust*):—that (thing) which is committed (un-) to (trust).

3873. παράκειμαι **parakĕimai**, *par-ak'-i-mahee;* from 3844 and 2749; to *lie near*, i.e. *be at hand* (fig. *be prompt* or *easy*):—be present.

3874. παράκλησις **paraklēsis**, *par-ak'-lay-sis;* from 3870; *imploration, hortation, solace:*—comfort, consolation, exhortation, intreaty.

3875. παράκλητος **paraklētŏs**, *par-ak'-lay-tos;* an *intercessor, consoler:*—advocate, comforter.

3876. παρακοή **parakŏē**, *par-ak-ŏ-ay';* from 3878; *inattention*, i.e. (by impl.) *disobedience:*—disobedience.

3877. παρακολουθέω **parakŏlŏuthĕō**, *par-ak-ol-oo-theh'-o;* from 3844 and 190; to *follow near*, i.e. (fig.) *attend* (as a result), *trace out, conform* to:—attain, follow, fully know, have understanding.

3878. παρακούω **parakŏuō**, *par-ak-oo'-o;* from 3844 and 191; to *mishear*, i.e. (by impl.) to *disobey:*—neglect to hear.

3879. παρακύπτω **parakuptō**, *par-ak-oop'-to;* from 3844 and 2955; to *bend beside*, i.e. *lean over* (so as to *peer within*):—look (into), stoop down.

3880. παραλαμβάνω **paralambanō**, *par-al-am-ban'-o;* from 3844 and 2983; to *receive near*, i.e. *associate with* oneself (in any familiar or intimate act or relation); by anal. to *assume* an office; fig. to *learn:*—receive, take (unto, with).

3881. παραλέγομαι **paralĕgŏmai**, *par-al-eg'-om-ahee;* from 3844 and the mid. of 3004 (in its orig. sense); (spec.) to *lay* one's course *near*, i.e. *sail past:*—pass, sail by.

3882. παράλιος **paraliŏs**, *par-al'-ee-os;* from 3844 and 251; *beside* the *salt* (*sea*), i.e. *maritime:*—sea coast.

3883. παραλλαγή **parallagē**, *par-al-lag-ay';* from a comp. of 3844 and 236; *transmutation* (of phase or orbit), i.e. (fig.) *fickleness:*—variableness.

3884. παραλογίζομαι **paralŏgizŏmai**, *par-al-og-id'-zom-ahee;* from 3844 and 3049; to *misreckon*, i.e. *delude:*—beguile, deceive.

3885. παραλυτικός **paralutikŏs**, *par-al-oo-tee-kos';* from a der. of 3886; as if *dissolved*, i.e. "*paralytic*":—that had (sick of) the palsy.

3886. παραλύω **paraluō**, *par-al-oo'-o;* from 3844 and 3089; to *loosen beside*, i.e. *relax* (perf. pas. part. *paralyzed* or *enfeebled*):—feeble, sick of the (taken with) palsy.

3887. παραμένω **paramĕnō**, *par-am-en'-o;* from 3844 and 3306; to *stay near*, i.e. *remain* (lit. *tarry;* or fig. *be permanent, persevere*):—abide, continue.

3888. παραμυθέομαι **paramuthĕŏmai**, *par-am-oo-theh'-om-ahee;* from 3844 and the mid. of a der. of 3454; to *relate near*, i.e. (by impl.) *encourage, console:*—comfort.

3889. παραμυθία **paramuthia**, *par-am-oo-thee'-ah;* from 3888; *consolation* (prop. abstr.):—comfort.

3890. παραμύθιον **paramuthiŏn**, *par-am-oo'-thee-on;* neut. of 3889; *consolation* (prop. concr.):—comfort.

3891. παρανομέω **paranŏmĕō**, *par-an-om-eh'-o;* from a comp. of 3844 and 3551; *to be opposed to law*, i.e. to *transgress:*—contrary to law.

3892. παρανομία **paranŏmia**, *par-an-om-ee'-ah;* from the same as 3891; *transgression:*—iniquity.

3893. παραπικραίνω **parapikrainō**, *par-ap-ik-rah'ee-no;* from 3844 and 4087; to *embitter alongside*, i.e. (fig.) to *exasperate:*—provoke.

3894. παραπικρασμός **parapikrasmŏs**, *par-ap-ik-ras-mos';* from 3893; *irritation:*—provocation.

3895. παραπίπτω **parapiptō**, *par-ap-ip'-to;* from 3844 and 4098; to *fall aside*, i.e. (fig.) to *apostatize:*—fall away.

3896. παραπλέω **paraplĕō**, *par-ap-leh'-o;* from 3844 and 4126; to *sail near:*—sail by.

3897. παραπλήσιον **paraplēsiŏn**, *par-ap-lay'-see-on;* neut. of a comp. of 3844 and the base of 4139 (as adv.); *close by*, i.e. (fig.) *almost:*—nigh unto.

3898. παραπλησίως **paraplēsiōs**, *par-ap-lay-see'-oce;* adv. from the same as 3897; *in a manner near by*, i.e. (fig.) *similarly:*—likewise.

3899. παραπορεύομαι **parapŏrĕuŏmai**, *par-ap-or-yoo'-om-ahee;* from 3844 and 4198; to *travel near:*—go, pass (by).

3900. παράπτωμα **paraptōma**, *par-ap'-to-mah;* from 3895; a *side-slip* (*lapse* or *deviation*), i.e. (unintentional) *error* or (wilful) *transgression:*—fall, fault, offence, sin, trespass.

3901. παραῤῥυέω **pararrhuĕō**, *par-ar-hroo-eh'-o;* from 3844 and the alt. of 4482; to *flow by*, i.e. (fig.) carelessly *pass* (*miss*):—let slip.

3902. παράσημος **parasēmŏs**, *par-as'-ay-mos;* from 3844 and the base of 4591; *side-marked*, i.e. *labelled* (with a *badge* [*figure-head*] of a ship):—sign.

3903. παρασκευάζω **paraskĕuazō**, *par-ask-yoo-ad'-zo;* from 3844 and a der. of 4632; to *furnish aside*, i.e. *get ready:*—prepare self, be (make) ready.

3904. παρασκευή **paraskĕuē**, *par-ask-yoo-ay';* as if from 3903; *readiness:*—preparation.

3905. παρατείνω **paratĕinō**, *par-at-i'-no;* from 3844 and τείνω **tĕinō** (to *stretch*); to *extend along*, i.e. *prolong* (in point of time):—continue.

3906. παρατηρέω **paratērĕō**, *par-at-ay-reh'-o;* from 3844 and 5083; to *inspect alongside*, i.e. *note insidiously* or *scrupulously:*—observe, watch.

3907. παρατήρησις **paratērēsis**, *par-at-ay'-ray-sis;* from 3906; *inspection*, i.e. *ocular evidence:*—observation

3908. παρατίθημι **paratithēmi**, *par-at-ith'-ay-mee;* from 3844 and 5087; to *place alongside*, i.e. *present* (food, truth); by impl. to *deposit* (as a trust or for protection):—allege, commend, commit (the keeping of), put forth, set before.

3909. παρατυγχάνω **paratugchanō**, *par-at-oong-khan'-o;* from 3844 and 5177; to *chance near*, i.e. *fall in with:*—meet with.

3910. παραυτίκα **parautika**, *par-ŏw-tee'-kah;* from 3844 and a der. of 846; *at* the *very* instant, i.e. *momentary:*—but for a moment.

3911. παραφέρω **paraphĕrō**, *par-af-er'-o;* from 3844 and 5342 (includ. its alt. forms); to *bear along* or *aside*, i.e. *carry off* (lit. or fig.); by impl. to *avert:*—remove, take away.

3912. παραφρονέω **paraphrŏnĕō**, *par-af-ron-eh'-o;* from 3844 and 5426; to *misthink*, i.e. *be insane* (*silly*):—as a fool.

3913. παραφρονία **paraphrŏnia**, *par-af-ron-ee'-ah;* from 3912; *insanity*, i.e. *foolhardiness:*—madness.

3914. παραχειμάζω **parachĕimazō**, *par-akh-i-mad'-zo;* from 3844 and 5492; to *winter near*, i.e. *stay* with over the *rainy* season:—winter.

3915. παραχειμασία **parachĕimasia**, *par-akh-i-mas-ee'-ah;* from 3914; a *wintering* over:—winter in.

3916. παραχρῆμα **parachrēma**, *par-akh-ray'-mah;* from 3844 and 5536 (in its orig. sense); *at the thing* itself, i.e. *instantly:*—forthwith, immediately, presently, straightway, soon.

3917. πάρδαλις **pardalis**, *par'-dal-is;* fem. of πάρδος **pardŏs** (a *panther*); a *leopard:*—leopard.

3918. πάρειμι **parĕimi**, *par'-i-mee;* from 3844 and 1510 (includ. its various forms); to *be near*, i.e. *at hand;* neut. pres. part. (sing.) *time being*, or (plur.) *property:*—come, × have, be here, + lack, (be here) present.

3919. παρεισάγω **parĕisagō**, *par-ice-ag'-o;* from 3844 and 1521; to *lead in aside*, i.e. *introduce surreptitiously:*—privily bring in.

3920. παρείσακτος **parĕisaktŏs**, *par-ice'-ak-tos;* from 3919; *smuggled in:*—unawares brought in.

3921. παρεισδύνω **parĕisdunō**, *par-ice-doo'-no;* from 3844 and a comp. of 1519 and 1416; to *settle in alongside*, i.e. *lodge stealthily:*—creep in unawares.

3922. παρεισέρχομαι **parĕisĕrchŏmai**, *par-ice-er'-khom-ahee;* from 3844 and 1525; to *come in alongside*, i.e. *supervene additionally* or *stealthily:*—come in privily, enter.

3923. παρεισφέρω **parĕisphĕrō**, *par-ice-fer'-o;* from 3844 and 1533; to *bear in alongside*, i.e. *introduce simultaneously:*—give.

3924. παρεκτός **parĕktŏs**, *par-ek-tos';* from 3844 and 1622; *near outside*, i.e. *besides:*—except, saving, without.

3925. παρεμβολή **parĕmbŏlē**, *par-em-bol-ay';* from a comp. of 3844 and 1685; a *throwing in beside* (*juxtaposition*), i.e. (spec.) *battle-array, encampment* or *barracks* (tower Antonia):—army, camp, castle.

3926. παρενοχλέω **parĕnŏchlĕō**, *par-en-okh-leh'-o;* from 3844 and 1776; to *harass further*, i.e. *annoy:*—trouble.

3927. παρεπίδημος **parĕpidēmŏs**, *par-ep-id'-ay-mos;* from 3844 and the base of 1927; an *alien alongside*, i.e. a *resident foreigner:*—pilgrim, stranger.

3928. παρέρχομαι **parĕrchŏmai**, *par-er'-khom-ahee;* from 3844 and 2064; to *come near* or *aside*, i.e. to *approach* (*arrive*), *go by* (or *away*), (fig.) *perish* or *neglect*, (caus.) *avert:*—come (forth), go, pass (away, by, over), past, transgress.

3929. πάρεσις **parĕsis**, *par'-es-is;* from 3935; *prætermission*, i.e. *toleration:*—remission.

3930. παρέχω **parĕchō**, *par-ekh'-o;* from 3844 and 2192; to *hold near*, i.e. *present, afford, exhibit, furnish occasion:*—bring, do, give, keep, minister, offer, shew, + trouble.

3931. παρηγορία **parēgŏria**, *par-ay-gor-ee'-ah;* from a comp of 3844 and a der. of 58 (mean. to *harangue* an assembly); an *address alongside*, i.e. (spec.) *consolation:*—comfort.

3932. παρθενία **parthĕnia**, *par-then-ee'-ah;* from 3933; *maidenhood:*—virginity.

3933. παρθένος **parthĕnŏs**, *par-then'-os;* of unknown or.; a *maiden;* by impl. an unmarried *daughter:*—virgin.

3934. Πάρθος **Parthŏs**, *par'-thos;* prob. of for. or.; a *Parthian*, i.e. inhab. of Parthia:—Parthian.

3935. παρίημι **pariēmi**, *par-ee'-ay-mi;* from 3844 and ἵημι **hiēmi** (to *send*); to *let by*, i.e. *relax:*—hang down.

3936. παρίστημι **paristēmi**, *par-is'-tay-mee;* or prol. παριστάνω **paristanō**, *par-is-tan'-o;* from 3844 and 2476; to *stand beside*, i.e. (trans.) to *exhibit, proffer*, (spec.) *recommend*, (fig.) *substantiate;* or (intrans.) to *be at hand* (or *ready*), *aid:*—assist, bring before, command, commend, give presently, present, prove, provide, shew, stand (before, by, here, up, with), yield.

3937. Παρμενᾶς **Parmĕnas**, *par-men-as';* prob. by contr. for Παρμενίδης **Parmĕnidēs** (a der. of a comp. of 3844 and 3306); *constant; Parmenas*, a Chr.:—Parmenas.

3938. πάροδος **parŏdŏs**, *par'-od-os;* from 3844 and 3598; a *by-road*, i.e. (act.) a *route:*—way.

3939. παροικέω **parŏikĕō**, *par-oy-keh'-o;* from 3844 and 3611; to *dwell near*, i.e. *reside* as a *foreigner:*—sojourn in, be a stranger.

3940. παροικία **parŏikia**, *par-oy-kee'-ah;* from 3941; *foreign residence:*—sojourning, × as strangers.

3941. πάροικος **parŏikŏs**, *par'-oy-kos;* from 3844 and 3624; having a *home near*, i.e. (as noun) a *by-dweller* (*alien resident*):—foreigner, sojourn, stranger.

3942. παροιμία **parŏimia**, *par-oy-mee'-ah;* from a comp. of 3844 and perh. a der. of 3633; appar. a state *alongside of supposition*, i.e. (concr.) an *adage;*

spec. an enigmatical or fictitious *illustration:*—parable, proverb.

3943. πάροινος **parŏinŏs**, *par'-oy-nos;* from 3844 and 3631; staying *near wine*, i.e. *tippling* (a *toper*):—given to wine.

3944. παροίχομαι **parŏichŏmai**, *par-oy'-khom-ahee;* from 3844 and οἴχομαι **ŏichŏmai** (to *depart*); to *escape along*, i.e. *be gone:*—past.

3945. παρομοιάζω **parŏmŏiazō**, *par-om-oy-ad'-zo;* from 3946; to *resemble:*—be like unto.

3946. παρόμοιος **parŏmŏiŏs**, *par-om'-oy-os;* from 3844 and 3664; *alike nearly*, i.e. *similar:*—like.

3947. παροξύνω **parŏxunō**, *par-ox-oo'-no;* from 3844 and a der. of 3691; to *sharpen alongside*, i.e. (fig.) to *exasperate:*—easily provoke, stir.

3948. παροξυσμός **parŏxusmŏs**, *par-ox-oos-mos';* from 3947 ("*paroxysm*"); *incitement* (to good), or *dispute* (in anger):—contention, provoke unto.

3949. παροργίζω **parŏrgizō**, *par-org-id'-zo;* from 3844 and 3710; to *anger alongside*, i.e. *enrage:*—anger, provoke to wrath.

3950. παροργισμός **parŏrgismŏs**, *par-org-is-mos';* from 3949; *rage:*—wrath.

3951. παροτρύνω **parŏtrunō**, *par-ot-roo'-no;* from 3844 and ὀτρύνω **ŏtrunō** (to *spur*); to *urge along*, i.e. *stimulate* (to hostility):—stir up.

3952. παρουσία **parŏusia**, *par-oo-see'-ah;* from the pres. part. of 3918; a *being near*, i.e. *advent* (often, *return*; spec. of Christ to punish Jerusalem, or finally the wicked); (by impl.) phys. *aspect:*—coming, presence.

3953. παροψίς **parŏpsis**, *par-op-sis';* from 3844 and the base of 3795; a *side-dish* (the receptacle):—platter.

3954. παῤῥησία **parrhēsia**, *par-rhay-see'-ah;* from 3956 and a der. of 4483; *all out-spokenness*, i.e. *frankness, bluntness, publicity;* by impl. *assurance:*—bold (× -ly, -ness, -ness of speech), confidence, × freely, × openly, × plainly (-ness).

3955. παῤῥησιάζομαι **parrhēsiazŏmai**, *par-hray-see-ad'-zom-ahee;* mid. from 3954; to *be frank* in utterance, or *confident* in spirit and demeanor:—be (wax) bold, (preach, speak) boldly.

3956. πᾶς **pas**, *pas;* includ. all the forms of declension; appar. a prim. word; *all, any, every*, the *whole:*—all (manner of, means), alway (-s), any (one), × daily, + ever, every (one, way), as many as, + no (-thing), × throughly, whatsoever, whole, whosoever.

3957. πάσχα **pascha**, *pas'-khah;* of Chald. or. [comp. 6453]; the *Passover* (the meal, the day, the festival or the special sacrifices connected with it):—Easter, Passover.

3958. πάσχω **paschō**, *pas'-kho;* includ. the forms
πάθω (**pathō**, *path'-o*) and
πένθω (**pĕnthō**, *pen'-tho*), used only in certain tenses for it; appar. a prim. verb; to *experience* a sensation or impression (usually painful):—feel, passion, suffer, vex.

3959. Πάταρα **Patara**, *pat'-ar-ah;* prob. of for. or.; *Patara*, a place in Asia Minor:—Patara.

3960. πατάσσω **patassō**, *pat-as'-so;* prob. prol. from 3817; to *knock* (gently or with a weapon or fatally):—smite, strike. Comp. 5180.

3961. πατέω **patĕō**, *pat-eh'-o;* from a der. prob. of 3817 (mean. a "*path*"); to *trample* (lit. or fig.):—tread (down, under foot).

3962. πατήρ **patēr**, *pat-ayr';* appar. a prim. word; a "*father*" (lit. or fig., near or more remote):—father, parent.

3963. Πάτμος **Patmŏs**, *pat'-mos;* of uncert. der.; *Patmus*, an islet in the Mediterranean:—Patmos.

3964. πατραλῴας **patralō̧as**, *pat-ral-o'-as;* from 3962 and the same as the latter part of 3389; a *parricide:*—murderer of fathers.

3965. πατριά **patria**, *pat-ree-ah';* as if fem. of a der. of 3962; paternal *descent*, i.e. (concr.) a *group* of families or a whole *race* (*nation*):—family, kindred, lineage.

3966. πατριάρχης **patriarchēs**, *pat-ree-arkh'-ace;* from 3965 and 757; a *progenitor* ("patriarch"):—patriarch.

3967. πατρικός **patrikŏs**, *pat-ree-kos';* from 3962; *paternal*, i.e. *ancestral:*—of fathers.

3968. πατρίς **patris**, *pat-rece';* from 3962; a *father-land*, i.e. *native town;* (fig.) heavenly *home:*—(own) country.

3969. Πατρόβας **Patrŏbas**, *pat-rob'-as;* perh. contr. for Πατρόβιος **Patrŏbiŏs** (a comp. of 3962 and 979); *father's life; Patrobas*, a Chr.:—Patrobas.

3970. πατροπαράδοτος **patrŏparadŏtŏs**, *pat-rop-ar-ad'-ot-os;* from 3962 and a der. of 3860 (in the sense of *handing over* or *down*); *traditionary:*—received by tradition from fathers.

3971. πατρῷος **patrō̧ŏs**, *pat-ro'-os;* from 3962; *paternal*, i.e. *hereditary:*—of fathers.

3972. Παῦλος **Paulŏs**, *pŏw'-los;* of Lat. or.; (*little;* but remotely from a der. of 3973, mean. the same); *Paulus*, the name of a Rom. and of an apostle:—Paul, Paulus.

3973. παύω **pauō**, *pŏw'-o;* a prim. verb ("*pause*"); to *stop* (trans. or intrans.), i.e. *restrain, quit, desist, come to an end:*—cease, leave, refrain.

3974. Πάφος **Paphŏs**, *paf'-os;* of uncert. der.; *Paphus*, a place in Cyprus:—Paphos.

3975. παχύνω **pachunō**, *pakh-oo'-no;* from a der. of 4078 (mean. *thick*); to *thicken*, i.e. (by impl.) to *fatten* (fig. *stupefy* or *render callous*):—wax gross.

3976. πέδη **pĕdē**, *ped'-ay;* ultimately from 4228; a *shackle* for the feet:—fetter.

3977. πεδινός **pĕdinŏs**, *ped-ee-nos';* from a der. of 4228 (mean. the *ground*); *level* (as easy for the *feet*):—plain.

3978. πεζεύω **pĕzĕuō**, *ped-zyoo'-o;* from the same as 3979; to *foot* a journey, i.e. *travel* by land:—go afoot.

3979. πεζῇ **pĕzȩ̄**, *ped-zay';* dat. fem. of a der. of 4228 (as adv.); *foot-wise*, i.e. by *walking:*—a- (on) foot.

3980. πειθαρχέω **pĕitharchĕō**, *pi-tharkh-eh'-o;* from a comp. of 3982 and 757; to *be persuaded* by a *ruler*, i.e. (gen.) to *submit* to authority; by anal. to *conform* to advice:—hearken, obey (magistrates).

3981. πειθός **pĕithŏs**, *pi-thos';* from 3982; *persuasive:*—enticing.

3982. πείθω **pĕithō**, *pi'-tho;* a prim. verb; to *convince* (by argument, true or false); by anal. to *pacify* or *conciliate* (by other fair means); reflex. or pass. to *assent* (to evidence or authority), to *rely* (by inward certainty):—agree, assure, believe, have confidence, be (wax) conflent, make friend, obey, persuade, trust, yield.

3983. πεινάω **pĕinaō**, *pi-nah'-o;* from the same as 3993 (through the idea of pinching *toil;* "*pine*"); to *famish* (absol. or comparatively); fig. to *crave:*—be an hungered.

3984. πεῖρα **pĕira**, *pi'-rah;* from the base of 4008 (through the idea of *piercing*); a *test*, i.e. *attempt, experience:*—assaying, trial.

3985. πειράζω **pĕirazō**, *pi-rad'-zo;* from 3984; to *test* (obj.), i.e. *endeavor, scrutinize, entice, discipline:*—assay, examine, go about, prove, tempt (-er), try.

3986. πειρασμός **pĕirasmŏs**, *pi-ras-mos';* from 3985; a putting to *proof* (by experiment [of good], *experience* [of evil], solicitation, discipline or provocation); by impl. *adversity:*—temptation, × try.

3987. πειράω **pĕiraō**, *pi-rah'-o;* from 3984; to *test* (subj.), i.e. (reflex.) to *attempt:*—assay.

3988. πεισμονή **pĕismŏnē**, *pice-mon-ay';* from a presumed der. of 3982; *persuadableness*, i.e. *credulity:*—persuasion.

3989. πέλαγος **pĕlagŏs**, *pel'-ag-os;* of uncert. affin.; deep or open *sea*, i.e. the *main:*—depth, sea.

3990. πελεκίζω **pĕlĕkizō**, *pel-ek-id'-zo;* from a der. of 4141 (mean. an *axe*); to *chop* off (the head), i.e. *truncate:*—behead.

3991. πέμπτος **pĕmptŏs**, *pemp'-tos;* from 4002; *fifth:*—fifth.

3992. πέμπω **pĕmpō**, *pem'-po;* appar. a prim. verb; to *dispatch* (from the subj. view or point of *departure*, whereas ἵημι **hiēmi** [as a stronger form of εἶμι **ĕimi**] refers rather to the obj. point or *terminus ad quem*, and 4724 denotes prop. the *orderly* motion involved), espec. on a temporary errand; also to *transmit, bestow*, or *wield:*—send, thrust in.

3993. πένης **pĕnēs**, *pen'-ace;* from a prim. πένω **pĕnō** (to *toil* for daily subsistence); *starving*, i.e. *indigent:*—poor. Comp. 4434.

3994. πενθερά **pĕnthĕra**, *pen-ther-ah';* fem. of 3995; a *wife's mother:*—mother in law, wife's mother.

3995. πενθερός **pĕnthĕrŏs**, *pen-ther-os';* of uncert. affin.; a *wife's father:*—father in law.

3996. πενθέω **pĕnthĕō**, *pen-theh'-o;* from 3997; to *grieve* (the feeling or the act):—mourn, (be-) wail.

3997. πένθος **pĕnthŏs**, *pen'-thos;* strengthened from the alt. of 3958; *grief:*—mourning, sorrow.

3998. πεντιχρός **pĕntichrŏs**, *pen-tikh-ros';* prol. from the base of 3993; *necessitous:*—poor.

3999. πεντάκις **pĕntakis**, *pen-tak-ece';* mult. adv. from 4002; *five times:*—five times.

4000. πεντακισχίλιοι **pĕntakischiliŏi**, *pen-tak-is-khil'-ee-oy;* from 3999 and 5507; *five times a thousand:*—five thousand.

4001. πεντακόσιοι **pĕntakŏsiŏi**, *pen-tak-os'-ee-oy;* from 4002 and 1540; *five hundred:*—five hundred.

4002. πέντε **pĕntĕ**, *pen'-teh;* a prim. number; "*five*":—five.

4003. πεντεκαιδέκατος **pĕntĕkaidĕkatŏs**, *pen-tek-ahee-dek'-at-os;* from 4002 and 2532 and 1182; *five and tenth:*—fifteenth.

4004. πεντήκοντα **pĕntēkŏnta**, *pen-tay'-kon-tah;* mult. of 4002; *fifty:*—fifty.

4005. πεντηκοστή **pĕntēkŏstē**, *pen-tay-kos-tay';* fem. of the ord. of 4004; *fiftieth* (2250 being implied) from Passover, i.e. the festival of "*Pentecost*":—Pentecost.

4006. πεποίθησις **pĕpŏithēsis**, *pep-oy'-thay-sis;* from the perf. of the alt. of 3958; *reliance:*—confidence, trust.

4007. περ **pĕr**, *per;* from the base of 4008; an enclitic particle significant of *abundance* (*thoroughness*), i.e. *emphasis; much, very* or *ever:*—[whom-] soever.

4008. πέραν **pĕran**, *per'-an;* appar. acc. of an obsol. der. of πείρω **pĕirō** (to "*pierce*"); *through* (as adv. or prep.), i.e. *across:*—beyond, farther (other) side, over.

4009. πέρας **pĕras**, *per'-as;* from the same as 4008; an *extremity:*—end, ut- (ter-) most part.

4010. Πέργαμος **Pĕrgamŏs**, *per'-gam-os;* from 4444; *fortified; Pergamus*, a place in Asia Minor:—Pergamos.

4011. Πέργη **Pĕrgē**, *perg'-ay;* prob. from the same as 4010; a *tower; Perga*, a place in Asia Minor:—Perga.

4012. περί **pĕri**, *per-ee';* from the base of 4008; prop. *through* (all over), i.e. *around;* fig. *with respect* to; used in various applications, of place, cause or time (with the gen. denoting the *subject* or *occasion* or *superlative* point; with the acc. the *locality, circuit, matter, circumstance* or general *period*):—(there-) about, above, against, at, on behalf of, × and

his company, which concern, (as) concerning, for, × how it will go with, ([there-, where-]) of, on, over, pertaining (to), for sake, × (e-) state, (as) touching, [where-] by (in), with. In comp. it retains substantially the same mean. of circuit (*around*), excess (*beyond*), or completeness (*through*).

4013. **περιάγω pĕriagō**, *per-ee-ag'-o;* from *4012* and *71;* to *take around* (as a companion); reflex. to *walk around:*—compass, go (round) about, lead about.

4014. **περιαιρέω pĕriairĕō**, *per-ee-ahee-reh'-o;* from *4012* and *138* (incl. its alt.); to *remove* all *around*, i.e. *unveil, cast off* (anchor); fig. to *expiate:*—take away (up).

4015. **περιαστράπτω pĕriastraptō**, *per-ee-as-trap'-to;* from *4012* and *797;* to *flash* all *around*, i.e. *envelop in light:*—shine round (about).

4016. **περιβάλλω pĕriballō**, *per-ee-bal'-lo;* from *4012* and *906;* to *throw* all *around*, i.e. *invest* (with a palisade or with clothing):—array, cast about, clothe (-d me), put on.

4017. **περιβλέπω pĕriblĕpō**, *per-ee-blep'-o;* from *4012* and *991;* to *look* all *around:*—look (round) about (on).

4018. **περιβόλαιον pĕribŏlaiŏn**, *per-ib-ol'-ah-yon;* neut. of a presumed der. of *4016;* something *thrown around* one, i.e. a *mantle, veil:*—covering, vesture.

4019. **περιδέω pĕridĕō**, *per-ee-deh'-o;* from *4012* and *1210;* to *bind around* one, i.e. *enwrap:*—bind about.

περιδρέμω pĕridrĕmō. See *4063.*

περιέλλω pĕriĕllō. See *4014.*

περιέλθω pĕriĕlthō. See *4022.*

4020. **περιεργάζομαι pĕriĕrgazŏmai**, *per-ee-er-gad'-zom-ahee;* from *4012* and *2038;* to *work* all *around*, i.e. *bustle about* (*meddle*):—be a busybody.

4021. **περίεργος pĕriĕrgŏs**, *per-ee'-er-gos;* from *4012* and *2041;* *working all around*, i.e. *officious* (*meddlesome*, neut. plur. *magic*):—busybody, curious arts.

4022. **περιέρχομαι pĕriĕrchŏmai**, *per-ee-er'-khom-ahee;* from *4012* and *2064* (includ. its alt.); to *come* all *around*, i.e. *stroll, vacillate, veer:*—fetch a compass, vagabond, wandering about.

4023. **περιέχω pĕriĕchō**, *per-ee-ekh'-o;* from *4012* and *2192;* to *hold* all *around*, i.e. *include, clasp* (fig.):— + astonished, contain, after [this manner].

4024. **περιζώννυμι pĕrizōnnumi**, *per-id-zone'-noo-mee;* from *4012* and *2224;* to *gird* all *around*, i.e. (mid. or pass.) to *fasten on one's belt* (lit. or fig.):—gird (about, self).

4025. **περίθεσις pĕrithĕsis**, *per-ith'-es-is;* from *4060;* a *putting* all *around*, i.e. *decorating* oneself with:—wearing.

4026. **περιΐστημι pĕriistēmi**, *per-ee-is'-tay-mee;* from *4012* and *2476;* to *stand* all *around*, i.e. (near) to *be a bystander*, or (aloof) to *keep away* from:—avoid, shun, stand by (round about).

4027. **περικάθαρμα pĕrikatharma**, *per-ee-kath'-ar-mah;* from a comp. of *4012* and *2508;* something *cleaned* off all *around*, i.e. *refuse* (fig.):—filth.

4028. **περικαλύπτω pĕrikaluptō**, *per-ee-kal-oop'-to;* from *4012* and *2572;* to *cover* all *around*, i.e. *entirely* (the face, a surface):—blindfold, cover, overlay.

4029. **περίκειμαι pĕrikĕimai**, *per-ik'-i-mahee;* from *4012* and *2749;* to *lie* all *around*, i.e. *inclose, encircle, hamper* (lit. or fig.):—be bound (compassed) with, hang about.

4030. **περικεφαλαία pĕrikĕphalaia**, *per-ee-kef-al-ah'-yah;* fem. of a comp. of *4012* and *2776;* *encirclement of* the head, i.e. a *helmet:*—helmet.

4031. **περικρατής pĕrikratēs**, *per-ee-krat-ace';* from *4012* and *2904;* *strong* all *around*, i.e. a *master* (*manager*):— + come by.

4032. **περικρύπτω pĕrikruptō**, *per-ee-kroop'-to;* from *4012* and *2928;* to *conceal* all *around*, i.e. *entirely:*—hide.

4033. **περικυκλόω pĕrikuklŏō**, *per-ee-koo-klŏ'-o;* from *4012* and *2944;* to *encircle* all *around*, i.e. *blockade completely:*—compass round.

4034. **περιλάμπω pĕrilampō**, *per-ee-lam'-po;* from *4012* and *2989;* to *illuminate* all *around*, i.e. *invest with a halo:*—shine round about.

4035. **περιλείπω pĕrilĕipō**, *per-ee-li'-po;* from *4012* and *3007;* to *leave* all *around*, i.e. (pass.) *survive:*—remain.

4036. **περίλυπος pĕrilupŏs**, *per-il'-oo-pos;* from *4012* and *3077;* *grieved* all *around*, i.e. *intensely sad:*—exceeding (very) sorry (-owful).

4037. **περιμένω pĕrimĕnō**, *per-ee-men'-o;* from *4012* and *3306;* to *stay around*, i.e. *await:*—wait for.

4038. **πέριξ pĕrix**, *per'-ix;* adv. from *4012;* all *around*, i.e. (as adj.) *circumjacent:*—round about.

4039. **περιοικέω pĕriŏikĕō**, *per-ee-oy-keh'-o;* from *4012* and *3611;* to *reside around*, i.e. *be a neighbor:*—dwell round about.

4040. **περίοικος pĕriŏikŏs**, *per-ee'-oy-kos;* from *4012* and *3624;* *housed around*, i.e. *neighboring* (ellipt. as noun):—neighbour.

4041. **περιούσιος pĕriŏusiŏs**, *per-ee-oo'-see-os;* from the pres. part. fem. of a comp. of *4012* and *1510;* *being beyond* usual, i.e. *special* (one's *own*):—peculiar.

4042. **περιοχή pĕriŏchē**, *per-ee-okh-ay';* from *4023;* a *being held around*, i.e. (concr.) a *passage* (of Scripture, as *circumscribed*):—place.

4043. **περιπατέω pĕripatĕō**, *per-ee-pat-eh'-o;* from *4012* and *3961;* to *tread* all *around*, i.e. *walk* at large (espec. as proof of ability); fig. to *live, deport oneself, follow* (as a companion or votary):—go, be occupied with, walk (about).

4044. **περιπείρω pĕripĕirō**, *per-ee-pi'-ro;* from *4012* and the base of *4008;* to *penetrate entirely*, i.e. *transfix* (fig.):—pierce through.

4045. **περιπίπτω pĕripiptō**, *per-ee-pip'-to;* from *4012* and *4098;* to *fall* into something that is all *around*, i.e. *light among* or *upon, be surrounded with:*—fall among (into).

4046. **περιποιέομαι pĕripŏiĕŏmai**, *per-ee-poy-eh'-om-ahee;* mid. from *4012* and *4160;* to *make around oneself*, i.e. *acquire* (*buy*):—purchase.

4047. **περιποίησις pĕripŏiēsis**, *per-ee-poy'-ay-sis;* from *4046;* *acquisition* (the act or the thing); by extens. *preservation:*—obtain (-ing), peculiar, purchased, possession, saving.

4048. **περιρρήγνυμι pĕrirrhēgnumi**, *per-ir-hrayg'-noo-mee;* from *4012* and *4486;* to *tear* all *around*, i.e. *completely away:*—rend off.

4049. **περισπάω pĕrispaō**, *per-ee-spah'-o;* from *4012* and *4685;* to *drag* all *around*, i.e. (fig.) to *distract* (with care):—cumber.

4050. **περισσεία pĕrissĕia**, *per-is-si'-ah;* from *4052;* *surplusage*, i.e. *superabundance:*—abundance (-ant, [-ly]), superfluity.

4051. **περίσσευμα pĕrissĕuma**, *per-is'-syoo-mah;* from *4052;* a *surplus*, or *superabundance:*—abundance, that was left, over and above.

4052. **περισσεύω pĕrissĕuō**, *per-is-syoo'-o;* from *4053;* to *superabound* (in quantity or quality), *be in excess, be superfluous;* also (trans.) to *cause to superabound* or *excel:*—(make, more) abound, (have, have more) abundance, (be more) abundant, be the better, enough and to spare, exceed, excel, increase, be left, redound, remain (over and above).

4053. **περισσός pĕrissŏs**, *per-is-sos';* from *4012* (in the sense of *beyond*); *superabundant* (in quantity) or *superior* (in quality); by impl. *excessive;* adv. (with *1537*) *violently;* neut. (as noun) *preeminence:*—exceeding abundantly above, more abundantly, advantage, exceedingly, very highly, beyond measure, more, superfluous, vehement [-ly].

4054. **περισσότερον pĕrissŏtĕrŏn**, *per-is-sot'-er-on;* neut. of *4055* (as adv.); in a *more superabundant* way:—more abundantly, a great deal, far more.

4055. **περισσότερος pĕrissŏtĕrŏs**, *per-is-sot'-er-os;* comp. of *4053;* *more superabundant* (in number, degree or character):—more abundant, greater (much) more, overmuch.

4056. **περισσοτέρως pĕrissŏtĕrōs**, *per-is-sot-er'-oce;* adv. from *4055;* *more superabundantly:*—more abundant (-ly), × the more earnest, (more) exceedingly, more frequent, much more, the rather.

4057. **περισσῶς pĕrissōs**, *per-is-soce';* adv. from *4053;* *superabundantly:*—exceedingly, out of measure, the more.

4058. **περιστερά pĕristĕra**, *per-is-ter-ah';* of uncert. der.; a *pigeon:*—dove, pigeon.

4059. **περιτέμνω pĕritĕmnō**, *per-ee-tem'-no;* from *4012* and the base of *5114;* to *cut around*, i.e. (spec.) to *circumcise:*—circumcise.

4060. **περιτίθημι pĕritithēmi**, *per-ee-tith'-ay-mee;* from *4012* and *5087;* to *place around;* by impl. to *present:*—bestow upon, hedge round about, put about (on, upon), set about.

4061. **περιτομή pĕritŏmē**, *per-it-om-ay';* from *4059;* *circumcision* (the rite, the condition or the people, lit. or fig.):— × circumcised, circumcision.

4062. **περιτρέπω pĕritrĕpō**, *per-ee-trep'-o;* from *4012* and the base of *5157;* to *turn around*, i.e. (ment.) to *craze:*— + make mad.

4063. **περιτρέχω pĕritrĕchō**, *per-ee-trekh'-o;* from *4012* and *5143* (includ. its alt.); to *run around*, i.e. *traverse:*—run through.

4064. **περιφέρω pĕriphĕrō**, *per-ee-fer'-o;* from *4012* and *5342;* to *convey around*, i.e. *transport hither and thither:*—bear (carry) about.

4065. **περιφρονέω pĕriphrŏnĕō**, *per-ee-fron-eh'-o;* from *4012* and *5426;* to *think beyond*, i.e. *depreciate* (*contemn*):—despise.

4066. **περίχωρος pĕrichōrŏs**, *per-ikh'-o-ros;* from *4012* and *5561;* *around* the *region*, i.e. *circumjacent* (as noun, with *1093* impl. *vicinity*):—country (round) about, region (that lieth) round about.

4067. **περίψωμα pĕripsōma**, *per-ip'-so-mah;* from a comp. of *4012* and **ψάω psaō** (to *rub*); something *brushed* all *around*, i.e. *off-scrapings* (fig. *scum*):—offscouring.

4068. **περπερεύομαι pĕrpĕrĕuŏmai**, *per-per-yoo'-om-ahee;* mid. from **πέρπερος pĕrpĕrŏs** (*braggart;* perh. by redupl. of the base of *4008*); to *boast:*—vaunt itself.

4069. **Περσίς Pĕrsis**, *per-sece';* a *Persian* woman; *Persis*, a Chr. female:—Persis.

4070. **πέρυσι pĕrusi**, *per'-oo-si;* adv. from *4009;* the *by-gone*, i.e. (as noun) *last year:*— + a year ago.

πετάομαι pĕtaŏmai. See *4072.*

4071. **πετεινόν pĕtĕinŏn**, *pet-i-non';* neut. of a der. of *4072;* a *flying* animal, i.e. *bird:*—bird, fowl.

4072. **πέτομαι pĕtŏmai**, *pet'-om-ahee;* or prol. **πετάομαι pĕtaŏmai**, *pet-ah'-om-ahee;* or contr. **πτάομαι ptaŏmai**, *ptah'-om-ahee;* mid. of a prim. verb; to *fly:*—fly (-ing).

4073. **πέτρα pĕtra**, *pet'-ra;* fem. of the same as *4074;* a (mass of) *rock* (lit. or fig.):—rock.

4074. **Πέτρος Pĕtrŏs**, *pet'-ros;* appar. a prim. word; a (piece of) *rock* (larger than *3037*); as a name, *Petrus*, an apostle:—Peter, rock. Comp. *2786.*

4075. **πετρώδης pĕtrōdēs**, *pet-ro'-dace;* from *4073* and *1491;* *rock-like*, i.e. *rocky:*—stony.

4076. **πήγανον pēganŏn**, *pay'-gan-on;* from *4078;* *rue* (from its *thick* or *fleshy* leaves):—rue.

4077. **πηγή pēgē**, *pay-gay';* prob. from *4078* (through the idea of *gushing* plumply); a *fount* (lit. or fig.), i.e. *source* or *supply* (of water, blood, enjoyment) (not necessarily the original spring):—fountain, well.

4078. **πήγνυμι pēgnumi**, *payg'-noo-mee;* a prol. form of a prim. verb (which in its simpler form occurs only as an alt. in certain tenses); to *fix* ("*peg*"), i.e. (spec.) to *set up* (a tent):—pitch.

4079. **πηδάλιον pēdaliŏn**, *pay-dal'-ee-on;* neut. of a (presumed) der. of **πηδόν pēdŏn** (the *blade* of an oar; from the same as *3976*); a "*pedal*", i.e. *helm:*—rudder.

4080. **πηλίκος pēlikŏs**, *pay-lee'-kos;* a quantitative form (the fem.) of the base of *4225;* *how much* (as indef.), i.e. in size or (fig.) dignity:—how great (large).

4081. **πηλός pēlŏs**, *pay-los';* perh. a prim. word; *clay:*—clay.

4082. **πήρα pēra**, *pay'-rah;* of uncert. affin.; a *wallet* or leather *pouch* for food:—scrip.

4083. **πῆχυς pēchus**, *pay'-khoos;* of uncert. affin.; the *fore-arm*, i.e. (as a measure) a *cubit:*—cubit.

4084. **πιάζω piazō**, *pee-ad'-zo;* prob. another form of *971;* to *squeeze*, i.e. *seize* (gently by the hand [*press*], or officially [*arrest*], or in hunting [*capture*]):—apprehend, catch, lay hand on, take. Comp. *4085.*

4085. **πιέζω piĕzō**, *pee-ed'-zo;* another form for *4084;* to *pack:*—press down.

4086. **πιθανολογία pithanŏlŏgia**, *pith-an-ol-og-ee'-ah;* from a comp. of a der. of *3982* and *3056;* *persuasive language:*—enticing words.

4087. **πικραίνω pikrainō**, *pik-rah'ee-no;* from *4089;* to *embitter* (lit. or fig.):—be (make) bitter.

4088. **πικρία pikria**, *pik-ree'-ah;* from *4089;* *acridity* (espec. *poison*), lit. or fig.:—bitterness.

4089. **πικρός pikrŏs**, *pik-ros';* perh. from *4078* (through the idea of *piercing*); *sharp* (*pungent*), i.e. *acrid* (lit. or fig.):—bitter.

4090. **πικρῶς pikrōs**, *pik-roce';* adv. from *4089;* *bitterly*, i.e. (fig.) *violently:*—bitterly.

4091. **Πιλάτος Pilatŏs**, *pil-at'-os;* of Lat. or.; *close-pressed*, i.e. *firm; Pilatus*, a Rom.:—Pilate.

πίμπλημι pimplēmi. See *4130.*

4092. **πίμπρημι pimprēmi**, *pim'-pray-mee;* a redupl. and prol. form of a prim.

πρέω prĕō, *preh'-o* (which occurs only as an alt. in certain tenses); to *fire*, i.e. *burn* (fig. and pass. *become inflamed* with fever):—be (× should have) swollen.

4093. **πινακίδιον pinakidiŏn**, *pin-ak-id'-ee-on;* dimin. of *4094;* a *tablet* (for writing on):—writing table.

4094. **πίναξ pinax**, *pin'-ax;* appar. a form of *4109;* a *plate:*—charger, platter.

4095. **πίνω pinō**, *pee'-no;* a prol. form of

πίω piō, *pee'-o*, which (together with another form **πόω pŏō**, *pŏ'-o*) occurs only as an alt. in cert. tenses; to *imbibe* (lit. or fig.):—drink.

4096. **πιότης piŏtēs**, *pee-ot'-ace;* from **πίων piōn** (*fat;* perh. akin to the alt. of *4095* through the idea of *repletion*); *plumpness*, i.e. (by impl.) *richness* (*oiliness*):—fatness.

4097. **πιπράσκω pipraskō**, *pip-ras'-ko;* a redupl. and prol. form of

πράω praō, *prah'-o* (which occurs only as an alt. in cert. tenses); contr. from **περάω pĕraō** (to *traverse;* from the base of *4008*); to *traffic* (by *travelling*), i.e. *dispose* of as merchandise or into slavery (lit. or fig.):—sell.

4098. **πίπτω piptō**, *pip'-to;* a redupl. and contr. form of **πέτω pĕtō**, *pet'-o* (which occurs only as an alt. in cert. tenses); prob. akin to *4072* through the idea of *alighting;* to *fall* (lit or fig.):—fail, fall (down), light on.

4099. **Πισιδία Pisidia**, *pis-id-ee'-ah;* prob. of for. or.; *Pisidia*, a region of Asia Minor:—Pisidia.

4100. **πιστεύω pistĕuō**, *pist-yoo'-o;* from *4102;* to *have faith* (in, upon, or with respect to, a person or thing), i.e. *credit;* by impl. to *entrust* (espec. one's spiritual well-being to Christ):—believe (-r), commit (to trust), put in trust with.

4101. **πιστικός pistikŏs**, *pis-tik-os';* from *4102;* *trustworthy*, i.e. *genuine* (*unadulterated*):—spike-[nard].

4102. **πίστις pistis**, *pis'-tis;* from *3982;* *persuasion*, i.e. *credence;* mor. *conviction* (of religious truth, or the truthfulness of God or a religious teacher), espec. *reliance* upon Christ for salvation; abstr. *constancy* in such profession; by extens. the system of religious (Gospel) *truth* itself:—assurance, belief, believe, faith, fidelity.

4103. **πιστός pistŏs**, *pis-tos';* from *3982;* obj. *trustworthy;* subj. *trustful:*—believe (-ing, -r), faithful (-ly), sure, true.

4104. **πιστόω pistŏō**, *pis-tŏ'-o;* from *4103;* to *assure:*—assure of.

4105. **πλανάω planaō**, *plan-ah'-o;* from *4106;* to (prop. *cause* to) *roam* (from safety, truth, or virtue):—go astray, deceive, err, seduce, wander, be out of the way.

4106. **πλάνη planē**, *plan'-ay;* fem. of *4108* (as abstr.); obj. *fraudulence;* subj. a *straying* from orthodoxy or piety:—deceit, to deceive, delusion, error.

4107. **πλανήτης planētēs**, *plan-ay'-tace;* from *4108;* a *rover* ("planet"), i.e. (fig.) an *erratic* teacher:—wandering.

4108. **πλάνος planŏs**, *plan'-os;* of uncert. affin.; *roving* (as a *tramp*), i.e. (by impl.) an *impostor* or *misleader:*—deceiver, seducing.

4109. **πλάξ plax**, *plax;* from *4111;* a *moulding-board*, i.e. *flat* surface ("*plate*", or *tablet*, lit. or fig.):—table.

4110. **πλάσμα plasma**, *plas'-mah;* from *4111;* something *moulded:*—thing formed.

4111. **πλάσσω plassō**, *plas'-so;* a prim. verb; to *mould*, i.e. *shape* or *fabricate:*—form.

4112. **πλαστός plastŏs**, *plas-tos';* from *4111;* *moulded*, i.e. (by impl.) *artificial* or (fig.) *fictitious* (*false*):—feigned.

4113. **πλατεῖα platĕia**, *plat-i'-ah;* fem. of *4116;* a *wide* "*plat*" or "*place*", i.e. open *square:*—street.

4114. **πλάτος platŏs**, *plat'-os;* from *4116;* *width:*—breadth.

4115. **πλατύνω platunō**, *plat-oo'-no;* from *4116;* to *widen* (lit. or fig.):—make broad, enlarge.

4116. **πλατύς platus**, *plat-oos';* from *4111;* spread out "*flat*" ("plot"), i.e. *broad:*—wide.

4117. **πλέγμα plĕgma**, *pleg'-mah;* from *4120;* a *plait* (of hair):—broidered hair.

πλεῖον plĕiŏn. See *4119.*

4118. **πλεῖστος plĕistŏs**, *plice'-tos;* irreg. superl. of *4183;* the *largest number* or *very large:*—very great, most.

4119. **πλείων plĕiōn**, *pli -own;* neut.

πλεῖον plĕiŏn, *pli'-on;* or

πλέον plĕŏn, *pleh'-on;* compar. of *4183;* *more* in quantity, number, or quality; also (in plur.) the *major portion:*— × above, + exceed, more excellent, further, (very) great (-er), long (-er), (very) many, greater (more) part, + yet but.

4120. **πλέκω plĕkō**, *plek'-o;* a prim. word; to *twine* or *braid:*—plait.

πλέον plĕŏn. See 4119.

4121. **πλεονάζω plĕŏnazō**, *pleh-on-ad'-zo;* from *4119;* to *do*, *make* or *be more*, i.e. *increase* (trans. or intrans.); by extens. to *superabound:*—abound, abundant, make to increase, have over.

4122. **πλεονεκτέω plĕŏnĕktĕō**, *pleh-on-ek-teh'-o;* from *4123;* to *be covetous*, i.e. (by impl.) to *overreach:*—get an advantage, defraud, make a gain.

4123. **πλεονέκτης plĕŏnĕktēs**, *pleh-on-ek'-tace;* from *4119* and *2192;* *holding* (*desiring*) *more*, i.e. *eager for gain* (*avaricious*, hence a *defrauder*):—covetous.

4124. **πλεονεξία plĕŏnĕxia**, *pleh-on-ex-ee'-ah;* from *4123;* *avarice*, i.e. (by impl.) *fraudulency*, *extortion:*—covetous (-ness) practices, greediness.

4125. **πλευρά plĕura**, *plyoo-rah';* of uncert. affin.; a *rib*, i.e. (by extens.) *side:*—side.

4126. **πλέω plĕō**, *pleh'-o;* another form for

πλεύω plĕuō, *plyoo'-o*, which is used as an alt. in certain tenses; prob. a form of *4150* (through the idea of *plunging* through the water); to *pass* in a vessel:—sail. See also *4130.*

4127. **πληγή plēgē**, *play-gay';* from *4141;* a *stroke;* by impl. a *wound;* fig. a *calamity:*—plague, stripe, wound (-ed).

4128. **πλῆθος plēthŏs**, *play'-thos;* from *4130;* a *fulness*, i.e. a *large number*, *throng*, *populace:*—bundle, company, multitude.

4129. **πληθύνω plēthunō**, *play-thoo'-no;* from another form of *4128;* to *increase* (trans. or intrans.):—abound, multiply.

4130. **πλήθω plēthō**, *play'-tho;* a prol. form of a prim. **πλέω plĕō**, *pleh'-o* (which appears only as an alt. in certain tenses and in the redupl. form **πίμπλημι pimplēmi**); to "*fill*" (lit. or fig. [*imbue*, *influence*, *supply*]); spec. to *fulfil* (time):—accomplish, full (. . . come), furnish.

4131. **πλήκτης plēktēs**, *plake'-tace;* from *4141;* a *smiter*, i.e. *pugnacious* (*quarrelsome*):—striker.

4132. **πλημμύρα plēmmura**, *plame-moo'-rah;* prol. from *4130;* *flood-tide*, i.e. (by anal.) a *freshet:*—flood.

4133. **πλήν plēn**, *plane;* from *4119;* *moreover* (*besides*), i.e. *albeit*, *save that*, *rather*, *yet:*—but (rather), except, nevertheless, notwithstanding, save, than.

4134. **πλήρης plērēs**, *play'-race;* from *4130;* *replete*, or *covered* over; by anal. *complete:*—full.

4135. **πληροφορέω plērŏphŏrĕō**, *play-rof-or-eh'-o;* from *4134* and *5409;* to *carry* out *fully* (in evidence), i.e. *completely assure* (or *convince*), *entirely accomplish:*—most surely believe, fully know (persuade), make full proof of.

4136. **πληροφορία plērŏphŏria**, *play-rof-or-ee'-ah;* from *4135;* *entire confidence:*—(full) assurance.

4137. **πληρόω plērŏō**, *play-rŏ'-o;* from *4134;* to *make replete*, i.e. (lit.) to *cram* (a net), *level* up (a hollow), or (fig.) to *furnish* (or *imbue*, *diffuse*, *influence*), *satisfy*, *execute* (an office), *finish* (a period or task), *verify* (or *coincide* with a prediction), etc.:—accomplish, × after, (be) complete, end, expire, fill (up), fulfil, (be, make) full (come), fully preach, perfect, supply.

4138. **πλήρωμα plērōma**, *play'-ro-mah;* from *4137;* *repletion* or *completion*, i.e. (subj.) what *fills* (as contents, supplement, copiousness, multitude), or (obj.) what is *filled* (as container, performance, period):—which is put in to fill up, piece that filled up, fulfilling, full, fulness.

4139. **πλησίον plēsiŏn**, *play-see'-on;* neut. of a der. of **πέλας pĕlas** (*near*); (adv.) *close* by; as noun, a *neighbor*, i.e. *fellow* (as man, countryman, Chr. or friend):—near, neighbour.

4140. **πλησμονή plēsmŏnē**, *place-mon-ay';* from a presumed der. of *4130;* a *filling* up, i.e. (fig.) *gratification:*—satisfying.

4141. **πλήσσω plēssō**, *place'-so;* appar. another form of *4111* (through the idea of *flattening* out); to *pound*, i.e. (fig.) to *inflict* with (calamity):—smite. Comp. *5180.*

4142. **πλοιάριον plŏiariŏn**, *ploy-ar'-ee-on;* neut. of a presumed der. of *4143;* a *boat:*—boat, little (small) ship.

4143. **πλοῖον plŏiŏn**, *ploy'-on;* from *4126;* a *sailer*, i.e. *vessel:*—ship (-ping).

4144. **πλόος plŏŏs**, *plŏ'-os;* from *4126;* a *sail*, i.e. *navigation:*—course, sailing, voyage.

4145. **πλούσιος plŏusiŏs**, *ploo'-see-os;* from *4149;* *wealthy;* fig. *abounding* with:—rich.

4146. **πλουσίως plŏusiōs**, *ploo-see'-oce;* adv. from *4145;* *copiously:*—abundantly, richly.

4147. **πλουτέω plŏutĕō**, *ploo-teh'-o;* from *4148;* to *be* (or *become*) *wealthy* (lit. or fig.):—be increased with goods, (be made, wax) rich.

4148. **πλουτίζω plŏutizō**, *ploo-tid'-zo;* from *4149;* to *make wealthy* (fig.):—en- (make) rich.

4149. **πλοῦτος plŏutŏs**, *ploo'-tos;* from the base of *4130;* *wealth* (as *fulness*), i.e. (lit.) *money*, *possessions*, or (fig.) *abundance*, *richness*, (spec.) valuable *bestowment:*—riches.

4150. **πλύνω plunō**, *ploo'-no;* a prol. form of an obsol. **πλύω pluō** (to "*flow*"); to "*plunge*", i.e. *launder* clothing:—wash. Comp. *3068*, *3538.*

4151. **πνεῦμα pnĕuma**, *pnyoo'-mah;* from *4154;* a *current* of air, i.e. *breath* (*blast*) or a *breeze;* by anal. or fig. a *spirit*, i.e. (human) the rational *soul*, (by impl.) *vital principle*, mental *disposition*, etc., or (superhuman) an *angel*, *dæmon*, or (divine) *God*, Christ's *spirit*, the Holy *Spirit:*—ghost, life, spirit (-ual, -ually), mind. Comp. *5590.*

4152. πνευματικός **pnĕumatikŏs**, *pnyoo-mat-ik-os'*; from 4151; *non-carnal*, i.e. (humanly) *ethereal* (as opposed to gross), or (dæmoniacally) a *spirit* (concr.), or (divinely) *supernatural, regenerate, religious*:—spiritual. Comp. 5591.

4153. πνευματικῶς **pnĕumatikōs**, *pnyoo-mat-ik-oce'*; adv. from 4152; *non-physically*, i.e. *divinely, figuratively*:—spiritually.

4154. πνέω **pnĕō**, *pneh'-o*; a prim. word; to *breathe* hard, i.e. *breeze*:—blow. Comp. 5594.

4155. πνίγω **pnigō**, *pnee'-go*; strengthened from 4154; to *wheeze*, i.e. (caus. by impl.) to *throttle* or *strangle* (*drown*):—choke, take by the throat.

4156. πνικτός **pniktŏs**, *pnik-tos'*; from 4155; *throttled*, i.e. (neut. concr.) an animal *choked* to death (*not bled*):—strangled.

4157. πνοή **pnŏē**, *pno-ay'*; from 4154; *respiration*, a *breeze*:—breath, wind.

4158. ποδήρης **pŏdērēs**, *pod-ay'-race*; from 4228 and another element of uncert. affin.; a *dress* (2066 implied) *reaching* the *ankles*:—garment down to the foot.

4159. πόθεν **pŏthĕn**, *poth'-en*; from the base of 4213 with enclitic adv. of origin; *from which* (as interrog.) or *what* (as rel.) place, state, source or cause:—whence.

4160. ποιέω **pŏiĕō**, *poy-eh'-o*; appar. a prol. form of an obsol. prim.; to *make* or *do* (in a very wide application, more or less direct):—abide, + agree, appoint, × avenge, + band together, be, bear, + bewray, bring (forth), cast out, cause, commit, + content, continue, deal, + without any delay, (would) do (-ing), execute, exercise, fulfil, gain, give, have, hold, × journeying, keep, + lay wait, + lighten the ship, make, × mean, + none of these things move me, observe, ordain, perform, provide, + have purged, purpose, put, + raising up, × secure, shew, × shoot out, spend, take, tarry, + transgress the law, work, yield. Comp. 4238.

4161. ποίημα **pŏiēma**, *poy'-ay-mah*; from 4160; a *product*, i.e. *fabric* (lit. or fig.):—thing that is made, workmanship.

4162. ποίησις **pŏiēsis**, *poy'-ay-sis*; from 4160; *action*, i.e. *performance* (of the law):—deed.

4163. ποιητής **pŏiētēs**, *poy-ay-tace'*; from 4160; a *performer*; spec. a "*poet*";—doer, poet.

4164. ποικίλος **pŏikilŏs**, *poy-kee'-los*; of uncert. der.; *motley*, i.e. *various* in character:—divers, manifold.

4165. ποιμαίνω **pŏimainō**, *poy-mah'ee-no*; from 4166; to *tend* as a shepherd (or fig. *superviser*):—feed (cattle), rule.

4166. ποιμήν **pŏimēn**, *poy-mane'*; of uncert. affin.; a *shepherd* (lit. or fig.):—shepherd, pastor.

4167. ποίμνη **pŏimnē**, *poym'-nay*; contr. from 4165; a *flock* (lit. or fig.):—flock, fold.

4168. ποίμνιον **pŏimniŏn**, *poym'-nee-on*; neut. of a presumed der. of 4167; a *flock*, i.e. (fig.) *group* (of believers):—flock.

4169. ποῖος **pŏiŏs**, *poy'-os*; from the base of 4226 and 3634; individualizing interrog. (of character) *what* sort of, or (of number) *which* one:—what (manner of), which.

4170. πολεμέω **pŏlĕmĕō**, *pol-em-eh'-o*; from 4171; to *be* (engaged) in *warfare*, i.e. to *battle* (lit. or fig.):—fight, (make) war.

4171. πόλεμος **pŏlĕmŏs**, *pol'-em-os*; from πέλομαι **pĕlŏmai** (to *bustle*); *warfare* (lit. or fig.; a single encounter or a series):—battle, fight, war.

4172. πόλις **pŏlis**, *pol'-is*; prob. from the same as 4171, or perh. from 4183; a *town* (prop. with walls, of greater or less size):—city.

4173. πολιτάρχης **pŏlitarchēs**, *pol-it-ar'-khace*; from 4172 and 757; a *town-officer*, i.e. *magistrate*:—ruler of the city.

4174. πολιτεία **pŏlitĕia**, *pol-ee-ti'-ah*; from 4177 ("*polity*"); *citizenship*; concr. a *community*:—commonwealth, freedom.

4175. πολίτευμα **pŏlitĕuma**, *pol-it'-yoo-mah*; from 4176; a *community*, i.e. (abstr.) *citizenship* (fig.):—conversation.

4176. πολιτεύομαι **pŏlitĕuŏmai**, *pol-it-yoo'-om-ahee*; mid. of a der. of 4177; to *behave* as a citizen (fig.):—let conversation be, live.

4177. πολίτης **pŏlitēs**, *pol-ee'-tace*; from 4172; a *townsman*:—citizen.

4178. πολλάκις **pŏllakis**, *pol-lak'-is*; mult. adv. from 4183; *many times*, i.e. *frequently*:—oft (-en, -entimes, -times).

4179. πολλαπλασίων **pŏllaplasiōn**, *pol-lap-las-ee'-ohn*; from 4183 and prob. a der. of 4120; *manifold*, i.e. (neut. as noun) *very much more*:—manifold more.

4180. πολυλογία **pŏlulŏgia**, *pol-oo-log-ee'-ah*; from a comp. of 4183 and 3056; *loquacity*, i.e. *prolixity*:—much speaking.

4181. πολυμέρως **pŏlumĕrōs**, *pol-oo-mer'-oce*; adv. from a comp. of 4183 and 3313; *in many portions*, i.e. *variously* as to time and agency (*piecemeal*):—at sundry times.

4182. πολυποίκιλος **pŏlupŏikilŏs**, *pol-oo-poy'-kil-os*; from 4183 and 4164; *much variegated*, i.e. *multifarious*:—manifold.

4183. πολύς **pŏlus**, *pol-oos'*; includ. the forms from the alt. πολλός **pŏllŏs**; (sing.) *much* (in any respect) or (plur.) *many*; neut. (sing.) as adv. *largely*; neut. (plur.) as adv. or noun *often, mostly, largely*:—abundant, + altogether, common, + far (passed, spent), (+ be of a) great (age, deal, -ly, while), long, many, much, oft (-en [-times]), plenteous, sore, straitly. Comp. 4118, 4119.

4184. πολύσπλαγχνος **pŏlusplagchnŏs**, *pol-oo'-splankh-nos*; from 4183 and 4698 (fig.); *extremely compassionate*:—very pitiful.

4185. πολυτελής **pŏlutĕlēs**, *pol-oo-tel-ace'*; from 4183 and 5056; *extremely expensive*:—costly, very precious, of great price.

4186. πολύτιμος **pŏlutimŏs**, *pol-oot'-ee-mos*; from 4183 and 5092; *extremely valuable*:—very costly, of great price.

4187. πολυτρόπως **pŏlutrŏpōs**, *pol-oot-rop'-oce*; adv. from a comp. of 4183 and 5158; *in many ways*, i.e. *variously* as to method or form:—in divers manners.

4188. πόμα **pŏma**, *pom'-ah*; from the alt. of 4095; a *beverage*:—drink.

4189. πονηρία **pŏnēria**, *pon-ay-ree'-ah*; from 4190; *depravity*, i.e. (spec.) *malice*; plur. (concr.) *plots, sins*:—iniquity, wickedness.

4190. πονηρός **pŏnērŏs**, *pon-ay-ros'*; from a der. of 4192; *hurtful*, i.e. *evil* (prop. in effect or influence, and thus differing from 2556, which refers rather to *essential* character, as well as from 4550, which indicates *degeneracy* from original virtue); fig. *calamitous*; also (pass.) *ill*, i.e. *diseased*; but espec. (mor.) *culpable*, i.e. *derelict, vicious, facinorous*; neut. (sing.) *mischief, malice*, or (plur.) *guilt*; masc. (sing.) the *devil*, or (plur.) *sinners*:—bad, evil, grievous, harm, lewd, malicious, wicked (-ness). See also 4191.

4191. πονηρότερος **pŏnērŏtĕrŏs**, *pon-ay-rot'-er-os*; compar. of 4190; *more evil*:—more wicked.

4192. πόνος **pŏnŏs**, *pon'-os*; from the base of 3993; *toil*, i.e. (by impl.) *anguish*:—pain.

4193. Ποντικός **Pŏntikŏs**, *pon-tik-os'*; from 4195; a *Pontican*, i.e. native of Pontus:—born in Pontus.

4194. Πόντιος **Pŏntiŏs**, *pon'-tee-os*; of Lat. or.; appar. *bridged*; *Pontius*, a Rom.:—Pontius.

4195. Πόντος **Pŏntŏs**, *pon'-tos*; *a sea*; *Pontus*, a region of Asia Minor:—Pontus.

4196. Πόπλιος **Pŏpliŏs**, *pop'-lee-os*; of Lat. or.; appar. "*popular*"; *Poplius* (i.e. *Publius*), a Rom.:—Publius.

4197. πορεία **pŏrĕia**, *por-i'-ah*; from 4198; *travel* (by land); fig. (plur.) *proceedings*, i.e. *career*:—journey [-ing], ways.

4198. πορεύομαι **pŏrĕuŏmai**, *por-yoo'-om-ahee*; mid. from a der. of the same as 3984; to *traverse*, i.e. *travel* (lit. or fig.; espec. to *remove* [fig. *die*], *live*, etc.);—depart, go (away, forth, one's way, up), (make a, take a) journey, walk.

4199. πορθέω **pŏrthĕō**, *por-theh'-o*; prol. from πέρθω **pĕrthō** (to *sack*); to *ravage* (fig.):—destroy, waste.

4200. πορισμός **pŏrismŏs**, *por-is-mos'*; from a der. of πόρος **pŏrŏs** (a *way*, i.e. *means*); *furnishing* (*procuring*), i.e. (by impl.) *money-getting* (*acquisition*):—gain.

4201. Πόρκιος **Pŏrkiŏs**, *por'-kee-os*; of Lat. or.; appar. *swinish*; *Porcius*, a Rom.:—Porcius.

4202. πορνεία **pŏrnĕia**, *por-ni'-ah*; from 4203; *harlotry* (includ. *adultery* and *incest*); fig. *idolatry*:—fornication.

4203. πορνεύω **pŏrnĕuō**, *porn-yoo'-o*; from 4204; to *act* the *harlot*, i.e. (lit.) *indulge* unlawful *lust* (of either sex), or (fig.) *practise idolatry*:—commit (fornication).

4204. πόρνη **pŏrnē**, *por'-nay*; fem. of 4205; a *strumpet*; fig. an *idolater*:—harlot, whore.

4205. πόρνος **pŏrnŏs**, *por'-nos*; from πέρνημι **pĕrnēmi** (to *sell*; akin to the base of 4097); a (male) *prostitute* (as *venal*), i.e. (by anal.) a *debauchee* (*libertine*):—fornicator, whoremonger.

4206. πόῤῥω **pŏrrhō**, *por'-rho*; adv. from 4253; *forwards*, i.e. *at a distance*;—far, a great way off. See also 4207.

4207. πόῤῥωθεν **pŏrrhōthĕn**, *por'-rho-then*; from 4206 with adv. enclitic of source; *from far*, or (by impl.) *at a distance*, i.e. *distantly*:—afar off.

4208. ποῤῥωτέρω **pŏrrhōtĕrō**, *por-rho-ter'-o*; adv. compar. of 4206; *farther*, i.e. *a greater distance*:—further.

4209. πορφύρα **pŏrphura**, *por-foo'-rah*; of Lat. or.; the "*purple*" mussel, i.e. (by impl.) the *red-blue* color itself, and finally a garment dyed with it:—purple.

4210. πορφυροῦς **pŏrphurŏus**, *por-foo-rooce'*; from 4209; *purpureal*, i.e. *bluish red*:—purple.

4211. πορφυρόπωλις **pŏrphurŏpōlis**, *por-foo-rop'-o-lis*; fem. of a comp. of 4209 and 4453; a *female trader in purple* cloth:—seller of purple.

4212. ποσάκις **pŏsakis**, *pos-ak'-is*; mult. from 4214; *how many times*:—how oft (-en).

4213. πόσις **pŏsis**, *pos'-is*; from the alt. of 4095; a *drinking* (the act), i.e. (concr.) a *draught*:—drink.

4214. πόσος **pŏsŏs**, *pos'-os*; from an obsol. πός **pŏs** (*who, what*) and 3739; interrog. pron. (of amount) *how much* (*large, long* or [plur.] *many*):—how great (long, many), what.

4215. ποταμός **pŏtamŏs**, *pot-am-os'*; prob. from a der. of the alt. of 4095 (comp. 4224); a *current, brook* or *freshet* (as *drinkable*), i.e. *running water*:—flood, river, stream, water.

4216. ποταμοφόρητος **pŏtamŏphŏrētŏs**, *pot-am-of-or'-ay-tos*; from 4215 and a der. of 5409; *river-borne*, i.e. *overwhelmed by a stream*:—carried away of the flood.

4217. ποταπός **pŏtapŏs**, *pot-ap-os'*; appar. from 4219 and the base of 4226; interrog. *whatever*, i.e. of *what possible* sort:—what (manner of).

4218. ποτέ **pŏtĕ**, *pot-eh'*; from the base of 4225 and 5037; indef. adv., at *some time, ever*:—afore- (any, some-) time (-s), at length (the last), (+ n-) ever, in the old time, in time past, once, when.

4219. πότε **pŏtĕ**, *pot'-eh*; from the base of 4226 and 5037; interrog. adv., at *what time*:— + how long, when.

4220. πότερον **pŏtĕrŏn**, *pot'-er-on*; neut. of a compar. of the base of 4226; interrog. as adv., *which* (of two), i.e. *is it* this or that:—whether.

4221. ποτήριον **pŏtēriŏn**, *pot-ay'-ree-on*; neut. of a der. of the alt. of 4095; a *drinking-vessel*; by extens. the contents thereof, i.e. a *cupful* (*draught*); fig. a *lot* or *fate*:—cup.

4222. ποτίζω **pŏtizō**, *pot-id'-zo*; from a der. of the alt. of 4095; to *furnish drink, irrigate*:—give (make) to drink, feed, water.

4223. Ποτίολοι **Pŏtiŏlŏi**, *pot-ee'-ol-oy;* of Lat. or.; *little wells,* i.e. *mineral springs; Potioli* (i.e. *Puteoli*), a place in Italy:—Puteoli.

4224. **πότος pŏtŏs**, *pot'-os;* from the alt. of *4095; a drinking-bout* or *carousal:*—banqueting.

4225. **πού pŏu**, *poo;* gen. of an indef. pron. **πός pŏs** (*some*) otherwise obsol. (comp. *4214*); as adv. of place, *somewhere,* i.e. *nearly:*—about, a certain place.

4226. **ποῦ pŏu**, *poo;* gen. of an interrog. pron. **πός pŏs** (*what*) otherwise obsol. (perh. the same as *4225* used with the rising slide of inquiry); as adv. of place; *at* (by impl. *to*) *what* locality:—where, whither.

4227. Πούδης **Pŏudēs**, *poo'-dace;* of Lat. or.; *modest; Pudes* (i.e. *Pudens*), a Chr.:—Pudens.

4228. **πούς pŏus**, *pooce;* a prim word; a "*foot*" (fig. or lit.):—foot (-stool).

4229. **πρᾶγμα pragma**, *prag'-mah;* from *4238;* a *deed;* by impl. an *affair;* by extens. an *object* (material):—business, matter, thing, work.

4230. **πραγματεία pragmatĕia**, *prag-mat-i'-ah;* from *4231;* a *transaction,* i.e. *negotiation:*—affair.

4231. **πραγματεύομαι pragmatĕuŏmai**, *prag-mat-yoo'-om-ahee;* from *4229;* to *busy oneself* with, i.e. to *trade:*—occupy.

4232. **πραιτώριον praitōriŏn**, *prahee-to'-ree-on;* of Lat. or.; the *prætorium* or governor's *court-room* (sometimes includ. the whole *edifice* and *camp*):—(common, judgment) hall (of judgment), palace, prætorium.

4233. **πράκτωρ praktōr**, *prak'-tore;* from a der. of *4238;* a *practiser,* i.e. (spec.) an official *collector:*—officer.

4234. **πρᾶξις praxis**, *prax'-is;* from *4238; practice,* i.e. (concr.) an *act;* by extens. a *function:*—deed, office, work.

4235. **πρᾷος praiŏs**, *prah'-os;* a form of *4239,* used in cert. parts; *gentle,* i.e. *humble:*—meek.

4236. **πρᾳότης praiŏtēs**, *prah-ot'-ace;* from *4235; gentleness;* by impl. *humility:*—meekness.

4237. **πρασιά prasia**, *pras-ee-ah';* perh. from **πράσον prasŏn** (a *leek,* and so an *onion-patch*); a garden-*plot,* i.e. (by impl. of regular *beds*) a *row* (repeated in plur. by Hebr. to indicate an arrangement):—in ranks.

4238. **πράσσω prassō**, *pras'-so;* a prim. verb; to "*practise*", i.e. *perform repeatedly* or *habitually* (thus differing from *4160,* which prop. refers to a *single* act); by impl. to *execute, accomplish,* etc.; spec. to *collect* (dues), *fare* (personally):—commit, deeds, do, exact, keep, require, use arts.

4239. **πραΰς praüs**, *prah-ooce';* appar. a prim. word; *mild,* i.e. (by impl.) *humble:*—meek. See also *4235.*

4240. **πραΰτης praütēs**, *prah-oo'-tace;* from *4239; mildness,* i.e. (by impl.) *humility:*—meekness.

4241. **πρέπω prĕpō**, *prep'-o;* appar. a prim. verb; to *tower* up (*be conspicuous*), i.e. (by impl.) to *be suitable* or *proper* (third pers. sing. pres. indic., often used impers., it is *fit* or *right*):—become, comely.

4242. **πρεσβεία prĕsbĕia**, *pres-bi'-ah;* from *4243; seniority* (*eldership*), i.e. (by impl.) an *embassy* (concr. *ambassadors*):—ambassage, message.

4243. **πρεσβεύω prĕsbĕuō**, *pres-byoo'-o;* from the base of *4245;* to be a *senior,* i.e. (by impl.) *act as a representative* (fig. *preacher*):—be an ambassador.

4244. **πρεσβυτέριον prĕsbutĕriŏn**, *pres-boo-ter'-ee-on;* neut. of a presumed der. of *4245;* the *order of elders,* i.e. (spec.) Isr. *Sanhedrim* or Chr. "*presbytery*":—(estate of) elder (-s), presbytery.

4245. **πρεσβύτερος prĕsbutĕrŏs**, *pres-boo'-ter-os;* compar. of **πρέσβυς prĕsbus** (*elderly*); *older;* as noun, a *senior;* spec. an Isr. *Sanhedrist* (also fig. member of the celestial council) or Chr. "*presbyter*":—elder (-est), old.

4246. **πρεσβύτης prĕsbutēs**, *pres-boo'-tace;* from the same as *4245;* an *old man:*—aged (man), old man.

4247. **πρεσβῦτις prĕsbutis**, *pres-boo'-tis;* fem. of *4246;* an *old woman:*—aged woman.

πρήθω prēthō. See *4092.*

4248. **πρηνής prēnēs**, *pray-nace';* from *4253; leaning* (*falling*) *forward* ("*prone*"), i.e. *head foremost:*—headlong.

4249. **πρίζω prizō**, *prid'-zo;* a strengthened form of a prim. **πρίω priō** (to *saw*); to *saw* in two:—saw asunder.

4250. **πρίν prin**, *prin;* adv. from *4253; prior, sooner:*—before (that), ere.

4251. Πρίσκα **Priska**, *pris'-kah;* of Lat. or.; fem. of *Priscus, ancient; Priska,* a Chr. woman:—Prisca. See also *4252.*

4252. Πρίσκιλλα **Priscilla**, *pris'-cil-lah;* dimin. of *4251; Priscilla* (i.e. *little Prisca*), a Chr. woman:—Priscilla.

4253. **πρό prŏ**, *prŏ;* a prim. prep.; "*fore*", i.e. *in front of, prior* (fig. *superior*) *to:*—above, ago, before, or ever. In comp. it retains the same significations.

4254. **προάγω prŏagō**, *prŏ-ag'-o;* from *4253* and *71;* to *lead forward* (magisterially); intrans. to *precede* (in place or time [part. *previous*]):—bring (forth, out), go before.

4255. **προαιρέομαι prŏairĕŏmai**, *prŏ-ahee-reh'-om-ahee;* from *4253* and *138;* to *choose* for oneself *before* another thing (*prefer*), i.e. (by impl.) to *propose* (*intend*):—purpose.

4256. **προαιτιάομαι prŏaitiaŏmai**, *prŏ-ahee-tee-ah'-om-ahee;* from *4253* and a der. of *156;* to *accuse already,* i.e. *previously charge:*—prove before.

4257. **προακούω prŏakŏuō**, *prŏ-ak-oo'-o;* from *4253* and *191;* to *hear already,* i.e. *anticipate:*—hear before.

4258. **προαμαρτάνω prŏamartanō**, *prŏ-am-ar-tan'-o;* from *4253* and *264;* to *sin previously* (to conversion):—sin already, heretofore sin.

4259. **προαύλιον prŏauliŏn**, *prŏ-ŏw'-lee-on;* neut. of a presumed comp. of *4253* and *833;* a *fore-court,* i.e. *vestibule* (*alley-way*):—porch.

4260. **προβαίνω prŏbainō**, *prob-ah'ee-no;* from *4253* and the base of *939;* to *walk forward,* i.e. *advance* (lit. or in years):— + be of a great age, go farther (on), be well stricken.

4261. **προβάλλω prŏballō**, *prob-al'-lo;* from *4253* and *906;* to *throw forward,* i.e. *push to the front, germinate:*—put forward, shoot forth.

4262. **προβατικός prŏbatikŏs**, *prob-at-ik-os';* from *4263; relating to sheep,* i.e. (a *gate*) through which they were led into Jerusalem:—sheep (market).

4263. **πρόβατον prŏbatŏn**, *prob'-at-on;* prop. neut. of a presumed der. of *4260; something that walks forward* (a *quadruped*), i.e. (spec.) a *sheep* (lit. or fig.):—sheep ([-fold]).

4264. **προβιβάζω prŏbibazō**, *prob-ib-ad'-zo;* from *4253* and a redupl. form of *971;* to *force forward,* i.e. *bring to the front, instigate:*—draw, before instruct.

4265. **προβλέπω prŏblĕpō**, *prob-lep'-o;* from *4253* and *991;* to *look* out *beforehand,* i.e. *furnish in advance:*—provide.

4266. **προγίνομαι prŏginŏmai**, *prog-in'-om-ahee;* from *4253* and *1096;* to *be already,* i.e. *have previously transpired:*—be past.

4267. **προγινώσκω prŏginōskō**, *prog-in-oce'-ko;* from *4253* and *1097;* to *know beforehand,* i.e. *foresee:*—foreknow (ordain), know (before).

4268. **πρόγνωσις prŏgnōsis**, *prog'-no-sis;* from *4267; forethought:*—foreknowledge.

4269. **πρόγονος prŏgŏnŏs**, *prog'-on-os;* from *4266;* an *ancestor,* (*grand-*) *parent:*—forefather, parent.

4270. **προγράφω prŏgraphō**, *prog-raf'-o;* from *4253* and *1125;* to *write previously;* fig. to *announce, prescribe:*—before ordain, evidently set forth, write (afore, aforetime).

4271. **πρόδηλος prŏdēlŏs**, *prod'-ay-los;* from *4253* and *1212; plain before* all men, i.e. *obvious:*—evident, manifest (open) beforehand.

4272. **προδίδωμι prŏdidōmi**, *prod-id'-o-mee;* from *4253* and *1325;* to *give before* the other party has given:—first give.

4273. **προδότης prŏdŏtēs**, *prod-ot'-ace;* from *4272* (in the sense of *giving forward* into another's [the enemy's] hands); a *surrender:*—betrayer, traitor.

προδρέμω prŏdrĕmō. See *4390.*

4274. **πρόδρομος prŏdrŏmŏs**, *prod'-rom-os;* from the alt. of *4390;* a *runner ahead,* i.e. *scout* (fig. *precursor*):—forerunner.

4275. **προείδω prŏĕidō**, *pro-i'-do;* from *4253* and *1492; foresee:*—foresee, saw before.

προειρέω prŏĕirĕō. See *4280.*

4276. **προελπίζω prŏĕlpizō**, *prŏ-el-pid'-zo;* from *4253* and *1679;* to *hope in advance* of other confirmation:—first trust.

4277. **προέπω prŏĕpō**, *prŏ-ep'-o;* from *4253* and *2036;* to *say already,* to *predict:*—forewarn, say (speak, tell) before. Comp. *4280.*

4278. **προενάρχομαι prŏĕnarchŏmai**, *prŏ-en-ar'-khom-ahee;* from *4253* and *1728;* to *commence already:*—begin (before).

4279. **προεπαγγέλλομαι prŏĕpaggĕllŏmai**, *prŏ-ep-ang-ghel'-lom-ahee;* mid. from *4253* and *1861;* to *promise of old:*—promise before.

4280. **προερέω prŏĕrĕō**, *prŏ-er-eh'-o;* from *4253* and *2046;* used as alt. of *4277;* to *say already, predict:*—foretell, say (speak, tell) before.

4281. **προέρχομαι prŏĕrchŏmai**, *prŏ-er'-khom-ahee;* from *4253* and *2064* (includ. its alt.); to *go onward, precede* (in place or time):—go before (farther, forward), outgo, pass on.

4282. **προετοιμάζω prŏĕtŏimazō**, *prŏ-et-oy-mad'-zo;* from *4253* and *2090;* to *fit* up *in advance* (lit. or fig.):—ordain before, prepare afore.

4283. **προευαγγελίζομαι prŏĕuaggĕlizŏmai**, *prŏ-yoo-ang-ghel-id'-zom-ahee;* mid. from *4253* and *2097;* to *announce* glad news *in advance:*—preach before the gospel.

4284. **προέχομαι prŏĕchŏmai**, *prŏ-ekh-om-ahee;* mid. from *4253* and *2192;* to *hold* oneself *before* others, i.e. (fig.) to *excel:*—be better.

4285. **προηγέομαι prŏēgĕŏmai**, *prŏ-ay-geh'-om-ahee;* from *4253* and *2233;* to *lead the way* for others, i.e *show deference:*—prefer.

4286. **πρόθεσις prŏthĕsis**, *proth'-es-is;* from *4388;* a *setting forth,* i.e. (fig.) *proposal* (*intention*); spec. the *show*-bread (in the Temple) as *exposed* before God:—purpose, shew [-bread].

4287. **προθέσμιος prŏthĕsmiŏs**, *proth-es'-mee-os;* from *4253* and a der. of *5087; fixed beforehand,* i.e. (fem. with *2250* impl.) a *designated* day:—time appointed.

4288. **προθυμία prŏthumia**, *proth-oo-mee'-ah;* from *4289; predisposition,* i.e. *alacrity:*—forwardness of mind, readiness (of mind), ready (willing) mind.

4289. **πρόθυμος prŏthumŏs**, *proth'-oo-mos;* from *4253* and *2372; forward* in *spirit,* i.e. *predisposed;* neut. (as noun) *alacrity:*—ready, willing.

4290. **προθύμως prŏthumōs**, *proth-oo'-moce;* adv. from *4289; with alacrity:*—willingly.

4291. **προΐστημι prŏïstēmi**, *prŏ-is'-tay-mee;* from *4253* and *2476;* to *stand before,* i.e. (in rank) to *preside,* or (by impl.) to *practise:*—maintain, be over, rule.

4292. **προκαλέομαι prŏkalĕŏmai**, *prok-al-eh'-om-ahee;* mid. from *4253* and *2564;* to *call forth to oneself* (*challenge*), i.e. (by impl.) to *irritate:*—provoke.

4293. **προκαταγγέλλω prŏkataggĕllō**, *prok-at-ang-ghel'-lo;* from *4253* and *2605;* to *announce beforehand,* i.e. *predict, promise:*—foretell, have notice (shew) before.

4294. **προκαταρτίζω prŏkatartizō**, *prok-at-ar-tid'-zo;* from *4253* and *2675;* to *prepare in advance:*—make up beforehand.

4295. **πρόκειμαι prŏkĕimai**, *prok'-i-mahee;* from *4253* and *2749;* to *lie before* the view, i.e. (fig.) to *be present* (to the mind), to *stand forth* (as an example or reward):—be first, set before (forth).

4296. προκηρύσσω **prŏkērussō**, *prok-ay-rooce'-so;* from *4253* and *2784;* to *herald* (i.e. *proclaim*) *in advance:*—before (first) preach.

4297. προκοπή **prŏkŏpē**, *prok-op-ay';* from *4298;* *progress*, i.e. *advancement* (subj. or obj.):—furtherance, profit.

4298. προκόπτω **prŏkŏptō**, *prok-op'-to;* from *4253* and *2875;* to *drive forward* (as if by beating), i.e. (fig. and intrans.) to *advance* (in amount, to *grow;* in time, to *be well along*):—increase, proceed, profit, be far spent, wax.

4299. πρόκριμα **prŏkrima**, *prok'-ree-mah;* from a comp. of *4253* and *2919;* a *prejudgment* (*prejudice*), i.e. *prepossession:*—prefer one before another.

4300. προκυρόω **prŏkurŏō**, *prok-oo-rŏ'-o;* from *4253* and *2964;* to *ratify previously:*—confirm before.

4301. προλαμβάνω **prŏlambanō**, *prol-am-ban'-o;* from *4253* and *2983;* to *take in advance*, i.e. (lit.) *eat before* others have an opportunity; (fig.) to *anticipate, surprise:*—come aforehand, overtake, take before.

4302. προλέγω **prŏlĕgō**, *prol-eg'-o;* from *4253* and *3004;* to *say beforehand*, i.e. *predict, forewarn:*—foretell, tell before.

4303. προμαρτύρομαι **prŏmarturŏmai**, *prom-ar-too'-rom-ahee;* from *4253* and *3143;* to *be a witness in advance*, i.e. *predict:*—testify beforehand.

4304. προμελετάω **prŏmĕlĕtaō**, *prom-el-et-ah'-o;* from *4253* and *3191;* to *premeditate:*—meditate before.

4305. προμεριμνάω **prŏmĕrimnaō**, *prom-er-im-nah'-o;* from *4253* and *3309;* to *care* (anxiously) *in advance:*—take thought beforehand.

4306. προνοέω **prŏnŏĕō**, *pron-ŏ-eh'-o;* from *4253* and *3539;* to *consider in advance*, i.e. *look* out for *beforehand* (act. by way of *maintenance* for others; mid. by way of *circumspection* for oneself):—provide (for).

4307. πρόνοια **prŏnŏia**, *pron'-oy-ah;* from *4306;* *forethought*, i.e. provident *care* or *supply:*—providence, provision.

4308. προοράω **prŏŏraō**, *prŏ-or-ah'-o;* from *4253* and *3708;* to *behold in advance*, i.e. (act.) to *notice* (another) *previously*, or (mid.) to *keep in* (one's own) *view:*—foresee, see before.

4309. προορίζω **prŏŏrizō**, *prŏ-or-id'-zo;* from *4253* and *3724;* to *limit in advance*, i.e. (fig.) *predetermine:*—determine before, ordain, predestinate.

4310. προπάσχω **prŏpaschō**, *prop-as'-kho;* from *4253* and *3958;* to *undergo* hardship *previously:*—suffer before.

4311. προπέμπω **prŏpĕmpō**, *prop-em'-po;* from *4253* and *3992;* to *send forward*, i.e. *escort* or *aid* in travel:—accompany, bring (forward) on journey (way), conduct forth.

4312. προπετής **prŏpĕtēs**, *prop-et-ace';* from a comp. of *4253* and *4098;* *falling forward*, i.e. *headlong* (fig. *precipitate*):—heady, rash [-ly].

4313. προπορεύομαι **prŏpŏrĕuŏmai**, *prop-or-yoo'-om-ahee;* from *4253* and *4198;* to *precede* (as guide or herald):—go before.

4314. πρός **prŏs**, *pros;* a strengthened form of *4253;* a prep. of direction; *forward to*, i.e. *toward* (with the genit. *the side* of, i.e. *pertaining to;* with the dat. *by the side of*, i.e. *near to;* usually with the accus. the place, time, occasion, or respect, which is the *destination* of the relation, i.e. *whither* or *for* which it is predicated):—about, according to, against, among, at, because of, before, between, ([where-]) by, for, × at thy house, in, for intent, nigh unto, of, which pertain to, that, to (the end that), + together, to ([you]) -ward, unto, with (-in). In comp. it denotes essentially the same applications, namely, motion *towards*, accession *to*, or nearness *at.*

4315. προσάββατον **prŏsabbatŏn**, *pros-ab'-bat-on;* from *4253* and *4521;* a *fore-sabbath*, i.e. the *Sabbath-eve:*—day before the sabbath. Comp. *3904.*

4316. προσαγορεύω **prŏsagŏrĕuō**, *pros-ag-or-yoo'-o;* from *4314* and a der. of *58* (mean. to *harangue*); to *address*, i.e. salute by *name:*—call.

4317. προσάγω **prŏsagō**, *pros-ag'-o;* from *4314* and *71;* to *lead towards*, i.e. (trans.) to *conduct near* (*summon, present*), or (intrans.) to *approach:*—bring, draw near.

4318. προσαγωγή **prŏsagōgē**, *pros-ag-ogue-ay';* from *4317* (comp. *72*); *admission:*—access.

4319. προσαιτέω **prŏsaitĕō** *pros-ahee-teh'-o;* from *4314* and *154;* to *ask repeatedly* (*importune*), i.e. *solicit:*—beg.

4320. προσαναβαίνω **prŏsanabainō**, *pros-an-ab-ah'ee-no;* from *4314* and *305;* to *ascend farther*, i.e. *be promoted* (*take an upper* [*more honorable*] *seat*):—go up.

4321. προσαναλίσκω **prŏsanaliskō**, *pros-an-al-is'-ko;* from *4314* and *355;* to *expend further:*—spend.

4322. προσαναπληρόω **prŏsanaplērŏō**, *pros-an-ap-lay-rŏ'-o;* from *4314* and *378;* to *fill up further*, i.e. *furnish fully:*—supply.

4323. προσανατίθημι **prŏsanatithēmi**, *pros-an-at-ith'-ay-mee;* from *4314* and *394;* to *lay up in addition*, i.e. (mid. and fig.) to *impart* or (by impl.) to *consult:*—in conference add, confer.

4324. προσαπειλέω **prŏsapĕilĕō**, *pros-ap-i-leh'-o;* from *4314* and *546;* to *menace additionally:*—threaten further.

4325. προσδαπανάω **prŏsdapanaō**, *pros-dap-an-ah'-o;* from *4314* and *1159;* to *expend additionally:*—spend more.

4326. προσδέομαι **prŏsdĕŏmai**, *pros-deh'-om-ahee;* from *4314* and *1189;* to *require additionally*, i.e. *want further:*—need.

4327. προσδέχομαι **prŏsdĕchŏmai**, *pros-dekh'-om-ahee;* from *4314* and *1209;* to *admit* (to intercourse, hospitality, credence or [fig.] endurance); by impl. to *await* (with confidence or patience):—accept, allow, look (wait) for, take.

4328. προσδοκάω **prŏsdŏkaō**, *pros-dok-ah'-o;* from *4314* and δοκεύω **dŏkĕuō** (to *watch*); to *anticipate* (in thought, hope or fear); by impl. to *await:*—(be in) expect (-ation), look (for), when looked, tarry, wait for.

4329. προσδοκία **prŏsdŏkia**, *pros-dok-ee'-ah;* from *4328;* *apprehension* (of evil); by impl. *infliction* anticipated:—expectation, looking after.

προσδρέμω **prŏsdrĕmō**. See *4370.*

4330. προσεάω **prŏsĕaō**, *pros-eh-ah'-o;* from *4314* and *1439;* to *permit further* progress:—suffer.

4331. προσεγγίζω **prŏsĕggizō**, *pros-eng-ghid'-zo;* from *4314* and *1448;* to *approach near:*—come nigh.

4332. προσεδρεύω **prŏsĕdrĕuō**, *pros-ed-ryoo'-o;* from a comp. of *4314* and the base of *1476;* to *sit near*, i.e. *attend* as a servant:—wait at.

4333. προσεργάζομαι **prŏsĕrgazŏmai**, *pros-er-gad'-zom-ahee;* from *4314* and *2038;* to *work additionally*, i.e. (by impl.) *acquire besides:*—gain.

4334. προσέρχομαι **prŏsĕrchŏmai**, *pros-er'-khom-ahee;* from *4314* and *2064* (includ. its alt.); to *approach*, i.e. (lit.) *come near, visit*, or (fig.) *worship, assent to:*—(as soon as he) come (unto), come thereunto, consent, draw near, go (near, to, unto).

4335. προσευχή **prŏsĕuchē**, *pros-yoo-khay';* from *4336;* *prayer* (*worship*); by impl. an *oratory* (*chapel*):— × pray earnestly, prayer.

4336. προσεύχομαι **prŏsĕuchŏmai**, *pros-yoo'-khom-ahee;* from *4314* and *2172;* to *pray to* God, i.e. *supplicate, worship:*—pray (× earnestly, for), make prayer.

4337. προσέχω **prŏsĕchō**, *pros-ekh'-o;* from *4314* and *2192;* (fig.) to *hold* the mind (*3563* impl.) *towards*, i.e. *pay attention to, be cautious about, apply oneself* to, *adhere to:*—(give) attend (-ance, -ance at, -ance to, unto), beware, be given to, give (take) heed (to, unto) have regard.

4338. προσηλόω **prŏsēlŏō**, *pros-ay-lŏ'-o;* from *4314* and a der. of *2247;* to *peg to*, i.e. *spike* fast:—nail to.

4339. προσήλυτος **prŏsēlutŏs**, *pros-ay'-loo-tos;* from the alt. of *4334;* an *arriver* from a foreign region, i.e. (spec.) an *acceder* (*convert*) to Judaism ("*proselyte*"):—proselyte.

4340. πρόσκαιρος **prŏskairŏs**, *pros'-kahee-ros;* from *4314* and *2540;* *for* the *occasion* only, i.e. *temporary:*—dur- [eth] for awhile, endure for a time, for a season, temporal.

4341. προσκαλέομαι **prŏskalĕŏmai**, *pros-kal-eh'-om-ahee;* mid. from *4314* and *2564;* to *call toward oneself*, i.e. *summon, invite:*—call (for, to, unto).

4342. προσκαρτερέω **prŏskartĕrĕō**, *pros-kar-ter-eh'-o;* from *4314* and *2594;* to *be earnest towards*, i.e. (to a thing) to *persevere, be constantly* diligent, or (in a place) to *attend* assiduously all the exercises, or (to a person) to *adhere* closely *to* (as a servitor):—attend (give self) continually (upon), continue (in, instant in, with), wait on (continually).

4343. προσκαρτέρησις **prŏskartĕrēsis**, *pros-kar-ter'-ay-sis;* from *4342;* *persistency:*—perseverance.

4344. προσκεφάλαιον **prŏskĕphalaiŏn**, *pros-kef-al'-ahee-on;* neut. of a presumed comp. of *4314* and *2776;* something *for* the *head*, i.e. a *cushion:*—pillow.

4345. προσκληρόω **prŏsklērŏō**, *pros-klay-rŏ'-o;* from *4314* and *2820;* to *give* a common *lot to*, i.e. (fig.) to *associate with:*—consort with.

4346. πρόσκλισις **prŏsklisis**, *pros'-klis-is;* from a comp. of *4314* and *2827;* a *leaning towards*, i.e. (fig.) *proclivity* (*favoritism*):—partiality.

4347. προσκολλάω **prŏskŏllaō**, *pros-kol-lah'-o;* from *4314* and *2853;* to *glue to*, i.e. (fig.) to *adhere:*—cleave, join (self).

4348. πρόσκομμα **prŏskŏmma**, *pros'-kom-mah;* from *4350;* a *stub*, i.e. (fig.) *occasion of apostasy:*—offence, stumbling (-block, [-stone]).

4349. προσκοπή **prŏskŏpē**, *pros-kop-ay';* from *4350;* a *stumbling*, i.e. (fig. and concr.) *occasion of sin:*—offence.

4350. προσκόπτω **prŏskŏptō**, *pros-kop'-to;* from *4314* and *2875;* to *strike at*, i.e. *surge against* (as water); spec. to *stub on*, i.e. *trip up* (lit. or fig.):—beat upon, dash, stumble (at).

4351. προσκυλίω **prŏskuliō**, *pros-koo-lee'-o;* from *4314* and *2947;* to *roll towards*, i.e. *block against:*—roll (to).

4352. προσκυνέω **prŏskunĕō**, *pros-koo-neh'-o;* from *4314* and a prob. der. of *2965* (mean. to *kiss*, like a dog *licking* his master's hand); to *fawn* or *crouch* to, i.e. (lit. or fig.) *prostrate* oneself in homage (*do reverence* to, *adore*):—worship.

4353. προσκυνητής **prŏskunētēs**, *pros-koo-nay-tace';* from *4352;* an *adorer:*—worshipper.

4354. προσλαλέω **prŏslalĕō**, *pros-lal-eh'-o;* from *4314* and *2980;* to *talk to*, i.e. *converse with:*—speak to (with).

4355. προσλαμβάνω **prŏslambanō**, *pros-lam-ban'-o;* from *4314* and *2983;* to *take to* oneself, i.e. *use* (food), *lead* (aside), *admit* (to friendship or hospitality):—receive, take (unto).

4356. πρόσληψις **prŏslēpsis**, *pros'-lape-sis;* from *4355;* *admission:*—receiving.

4357. προσμένω **prŏsmĕnō**, *pros-men'-o;* from *4314* and *3306;* to *stay further*, i.e. *remain* in a place, with a person; fig. to *adhere* to, *persevere* in:—abide still, be with, cleave unto, continue in (with).

4358. προσορμίζω **prŏsŏrmizō**, *pros-or-mid'-zo;* from *4314* and a der. of the same as *3730* (mean. to *tie* [*anchor*] or *lull*); to *moor to*, i.e. (by impl.) *land at:*—draw to the shore.

4359. προσοφείλω **prŏsŏphĕilō**, *pros-of-i'-lo;* from *4314* and *3784;* to *be indebted additionally:*—over besides.

4360. προσοχθίζω **prŏsŏchthizō**, *pros-okh-thid'-zo;* from *4314* and a form of ὀχθέω **ŏchthĕō** (to *be vexed* with something irksome); to *feel indignant at:*—be grieved with.

4361. πρόσπεινος **prŏspĕinŏs**, *pros'-pi-nos;* from *4314* and the same as *3983;* *hungering further*, i.e. *intensely hungry:*—very hungry.

4362. **προσπήγνυμι prŏspēgnumi**, *pros-payg'-noo-mee;* from *4314* and *4078;* to *fasten to*, i.e. (spec.) to *impale* (on a cross):—crucify.

4363. **προσπίπτω prŏspiptō**, *pros-pip'-to;* from *4314* and *4098;* to *fall towards*, i.e. (gently) *prostrate* oneself (in supplication or homage), or (violently) to *rush* upon (in storm):—beat upon, fall (down) at (before).

4364. **προσποιέομαι prŏspŏiĕŏmai**, *pros-poy-eh'-om-ahee;* mid. from *4314* and *4160;* to *do forward for oneself*, i.e. *pretend* (as if about to do a thing):—make as though.

4365. **προσπορεύομαι prŏspŏrĕuŏmai**, *pros-por-yoo'-om-ahee;* from *4314* and *4198;* to *journey towards*, i.e. *approach* [not the same as *4313*]:—go before.

4366. **προσρήγνυμι prŏsrēgnumi**, *pros-rayg'-noo-mee;* from *4314* and *4486;* to *tear towards*, i.e. *burst upon* (as a tempest or flood):—beat vehemently against (upon).

4367. **προστάσσω prŏstassō**, *pros-tas'-so;* from *4314* and *5021;* to *arrange towards*, i.e. (fig.) *enjoin:*—bid, command.

4368. **προστάτις prŏstatis**, *pros-tat'-is;* fem. of a der. of *4291;* a *patroness*, i.e. *assistant:*—succourer.

4369. **προστίθημι prŏstithēmi**, *pros-tith'-ay-mee;* from *4314* and *5087;* to *place additionally*, i.e. *lay beside, annex, repeat:*—add, again, give more, increase, lay unto, proceed further, speak to any more.

4370. **προστρέχω prŏstrĕchō**, *pros-trekh'-o;* from *4314* and *5143* (includ. its alt.); to *run towards*, i.e. *hasten* to meet or join:—run (thither to, to).

4371. **προσφάγιον prŏsphagiŏn**, *pros-fag'-ee-on;* neut. of a presumed der. of a comp. of *4314* and *5315;* something *eaten in addition* to bread, i.e. a *relish* (spec. *fish;* comp. *3795*):—meat.

4372. **πρόσφατος prŏsphatŏs**, *pros'-fat-os;* from *4253* and a der. of *4969;* *previously* (recently) *slain* (*fresh*), i.e. (fig.) *lately made:*—new.

4373. **προσφάτως prŏsphatōs**, *pros-fat'-oce;* adv. from *4372;* *recently:*—lately.

4374. **προσφέρω prŏsphĕrō**, *pros-fer'-o;* from *4314* and *5342* (includ. its alt.); to *bear towards*, i.e. *lead to, tender* (espec. to God), *treat:*—bring (to, unto), deal with, do, offer (unto, up), present unto, put to.

4375. **προσφιλής prŏsphilēs**, *pros-fee-lace';* from a presumed comp. of *4314* and *5368;* *friendly towards*, i.e. *acceptable:*—lovely.

4376. **προσφορά prŏsphŏra**, *pros-for-ah';* from *4374;* *presentation;* concr. an *oblation* (bloodless) or *sacrifice:*—offering (up).

4377. **προσφωνέω prŏsphōnĕō**, *pros-fo-neh'-o;* from *4314* and *5455;* to *sound towards*, i.e. *address, exclaim, summon:*—call unto, speak (un-) to.

4378. **πρόσχυσις prŏschusis**, *pros'-khoo-sis;* from a comp. of *4314* and **χέω chĕō** (to *pour*); a *shedding forth*, i.e. *affusion:*—sprinkling.

4379. **προσψαύω prŏspsauō**, *pros-psŏw'-o;* from *4314* and **ψαύω psauō** (to *touch*); to *impinge*, i.e. *lay a finger on* (in order to relieve):—touch.

4380. **προσωποληπτέω prŏsōpŏlēptĕō**, *pros-o-pol-ape-teh'-o;* from *4381;* to *favor an individual*, i.e. *show partiality:*—have respect to persons.

4381. **προσωπολήπτης prŏsōpŏlēptēs**, *pros-o-pol-ape'-tace;* from *4383* and *2983;* an *accepter* of a *face* (*individual*), i.e. (spec.) one *exhibiting partiality:*—respecter of persons.

4382. **προσωποληψία prŏsōpŏlēpsia**, *pros-o-pol-ape-see'-ah;* from *4381;* *partiality*, i.e. *favoritism:*—respect of persons.

4383. **πρόσωπον prŏsōpŏn**, *pros'-o-pon;* from *4314* and **ὤψ ōps** (the *visage;* from *3700*); the *front* (as being *towards view*), i.e. the *countenance, aspect, appearance, surface;* by impl. *presence, person:*—(outward) appearance, × before, countenance, face, fashion, (men's) person, presence.

4384. **προτάσσω prŏtassō**, *prot-as'-so;* from *4253* and *5021;* to *pre-arrange*, i.e. *prescribe:*—before appoint.

4385. **προτείνω prŏtĕinō**, *prot-i'-no;* from *4253* and **τείνω tĕinō** (to *stretch*); to *protend*, i.e. *tie prostrate* (for scourging):—bind.

4386. **πρότερον prŏtĕrŏn**, *prot'-er-on;* neut. of *4387* as adv. (with or without the art.); *previously:*—before, (at the) first, former.

4387. **πρότερος prŏtĕrŏs**, *prot'-er-os;* compar. of *4253;* *prior* or *previous:*—former.

4388. **προτίθεμαι prŏtithĕmai**, *prot-ith'-em-ahee;* mid. from *4253* and *5087;* to *place before*, i.e. (for oneself) to *exhibit;* (to oneself) to *propose* (*determine*):—purpose, set forth.

4389. **προτρέπομαι prŏtrĕpŏmai**, *prot-rep'-om-ahee;* mid. from *4253* and the base of *5157;* to *turn forward* for oneself, i.e. *encourage:*—exhort.

4390. **προτρέχω prŏtrĕchō**, *prot-rekh'-o;* from *4253* and *5143* (includ. its alt.); to *run forward*, i.e. *outstrip, precede:*—outrun, run before.

4391. **προϋπάρχω prŏüparchō**, *prŏ-oop-ar'-kho;* from *4253* and *5225;* to *exist before*, i.e. (adv.) to *be* or *do* something *previously:*—+ be before (-time).

4392. **πρόφασις prŏphasis**, *prof'-as-is;* from a comp. of *4253* and *5316;* an *outward showing*, i.e. *pretext:*—cloke, colour, pretence, show.

4393. **προφέρω prŏphĕrō**, *prof-er'-o;* from *4253* and *5342;* to *bear forward*, i.e. *produce:*—bring forth.

4394. **προφητεία prŏphētĕia**, *prof-ay-ti'-ah;* from *4396* ("*prophecy*"); *prediction* (scriptural or other):—prophecy, prophesying.

4395. **προφητεύω prŏphētĕuō**, *prof-ate-yoo'-o;* from *4396;* to *foretell* events, *divine, speak* under *inspiration, exercise* the prophetic *office:*—prophesy.

4396. **προφήτης prŏphētēs**, *prof-ay'-tace;* from a comp. of *4253* and *5346;* a *foreteller* ("*prophet*"); by anal. an *inspired speaker;* by extens. a *poet:*—prophet.

4397. **προφητικός prŏphētikŏs**, *prof-ay-tik-os';* from *4396;* *pertaining to a foreteller* ("*prophetic*"):—of prophecy, of the prophets.

4398. **προφῆτις prŏphētis**, *prof-ay'-tis;* fem. of *4396;* a *female foreteller* or an *inspired woman:*—prophetess.

4399. **προφθάνω prŏphthanō**, *prof-than'-o;* from *4253* and *5348;* to *get an earlier start of*, i.e. *anticipate:*—prevent.

4400. **προχειρίζομαι prŏchĕirizŏmai**, *prokh-i-rid'-zom-ahee;* mid. from *4253* and a der. of *5495;* to *handle* for oneself *in advance*, i.e. (fig.) to *purpose:*—choose, make.

4401. **προχειροτονέω prŏchĕirŏtŏnĕō**, *prokh-i-rot-on-eh'-o;* from *4253* and *5500;* to *elect in advance:*—choose before.

4402. **Πρόχορος Prŏchŏrŏs**, *prokh'-or-os;* from *4253* and *5525;* *before the dance;* *Prochorus*, a Chr.:—Prochorus.

4403. **πρύμνα prumna**, *proom'-nah;* fem. of **πρυμνύς prumnus** (*hindmost*); the *stern* of a ship:—hinder part, stern.

4404. **πρωΐ prōï**, *pro-ee';* adv. from *4253;* at *dawn;* by impl. the *day-break* watch:—early (in the morning), (in the) morning.

4405. **πρωΐα prōïa**, *pro-ee'-ah;* fem. of a der. of *4404* as noun; *day-dawn:*—early, morning.

4406. **πρώϊμος prōïmŏs**, *pro'-ee-mos;* from *4404;* *dawning*, i.e. (by anal.) *autumnal* (showering, the first of the rainy season):—early.

4407. **πρωϊνός prōïnŏs**, *pro-ee-nos';* from *4404;* pertaining to the *dawn*, i.e. *matutinal:*—morning.

4408. **πρώρα prōra**, *pro'-ra;* fem. of a presumed der. of *4253* as noun; the *prow*, i.e. forward part of a vessel:—forepart (-ship).

4409. **πρωτεύω prōtĕuō**, *prote-yoo'-o;* from *4413;* to *be first* (in rank or influence):—have the preeminence.

4410. **πρωτοκαθεδρία prōtŏkathĕdria**, *pro-tok-ath-ed-ree'-ah;* from *4413* and *2515;* a *sitting first* (in the front row), i.e. *preeminence* in council:—chief (highest, uppermost) seat.

4411. **πρωτοκλισία prōtŏklisia**, *pro-tok-lis-ee'-ah;* from *4413* and *2828;* a *reclining first* (in the place of honor) at the dinner-bed, i.e. *preeminence* at meals:—chief (highest, uppermost) room.

4412. **πρῶτον prōtŏn**, *pro'-ton;* neut. of *4413* as adv. (with or without *3588*); *firstly* (in time, place, order, or importance):—before, at the beginning, chiefly, (at, at the) first (of all).

4413. **πρῶτος prōtŏs**, *pro'-tos;* contr. superl. of *4253;* *foremost* (in time, place, order or importance):—before, beginning, best, chief (-est), first (of all), former.

4414. **πρωτοστάτης prōtŏstatēs**, *pro-tos-tat'-ace;* from *4413* and *2476;* one *standing first* in the ranks, i.e. a *captain* (*champion*):—ringleader.

4415. **πρωτοτόκια prōtŏtŏkia**, *pro-tot-ok'-ee-ah;* from *4416;* *primogeniture* (as a privilege):—birthright.

4416. **πρωτοτόκος prōtŏtŏkŏs**, *pro-tot-ok'-os;* from *4413* and the alt. of *5088;* *first-born* (usually as noun, lit. or fig.):—firstbegotten (-born).

4417. **πταίω ptaiō**, *ptah'-yo;* a form of *4098;* to *trip*, i.e. (fig.) to *err, sin, fail* (of salvation):—fall, offend, stumble.

4418. **πτέρνα ptĕrna**, *pter'-nah;* of uncert. der.; the *heel* (fig.):—heel.

4419. **πτερύγιον ptĕrugiŏn**, *pter-oog'-ee-on;* neut. of a presumed der. of *4420;* a *winglet*, i.e. (fig.) *extremity* (top corner):—pinnacle.

4420. **πτέρυξ ptĕrux**, *pter'-oox;* from a der. of *4072* (mean. a *feather*); a *wing:*—wing.

4421. **πτηνόν ptēnŏn**, *ptay-non';* contr. for *4071;* a *bird:*—bird.

4422. **πτοέω ptŏĕō**, *ptŏ-eh'-o;* prob. akin to the alt. of *4098* (through the idea of causing to *fall*) or to *4072* (through that of causing to *fly* away); to *scare:*—frighten.

4423. **πτόησις ptŏēsis**, *ptŏ'-ay-sis;* from *4422;* *alarm:*—amazement.

4424. **Πτολεμαΐς Ptŏlĕmaïs**, *ptol-em-ah-is';* from **Πτολεμαῖος Ptŏlĕmaiŏs** (*Ptolemy*, after whom it was named); *Ptolemaïs*, a place in Pal.:—Ptolemais.

4425. **πτύον ptuŏn**, *ptoo'-on;* from *4429;* a *winnowing-fork* (as *scattering* like spittle):—fan.

4426. **πτύρω pturō**, *ptoo'-ro;* from a presumed der. of *4429* (and thus akin to *4422*); to *frighten:*—terrify.

4427. **πτύσμα ptusma**, *ptoos'-mah;* from *4429;* *saliva:*—spittle.

4428. **πτύσσω ptussō**, *ptoos'-so;* prob. akin to **πετάννυμι pĕtannumi** (to *spread;* and thus appar. allied to *4072* through the idea of *expansion*, and to *4429* through that of *flattening;* comp. *3961*); to *fold*, i.e. *furl* a scroll:—close.

4429. **πτύω ptuō**, *ptoo'-o;* a prim. verb (comp. *4428*); to *spit:*—spit.

4430. **πτῶμα ptōma**, *pto'-mah;* from the alt. of *4098;* a *ruin*, i.e. (spec.) lifeless *body* (*corpse, carrion*):—dead body, carcase, corpse.

4431. **πτῶσις ptōsis**, *pto'-sis;* from the alt. of *4098;* a *crash*, i.e. *downfall* (lit. or fig.):—fall.

4432. **πτωχεία ptōchĕia**, *pto-khi'-ah;* from *4433;* *beggary*, i.e. *indigence* (lit. or fig.):—poverty.

4433. **πτωχεύω ptōchĕuō**, *pto-khyoo'-o;* from *4434;* to *be a beggar*, i.e. (by impl.) to *become indigent* (fig.):—become poor.

4434. **πτωχός ptōchŏs**, *pto-khos';* from **πτώσσω ptōssō** (to *crouch;* akin to *4422* and the alt. of *4098*); a *beggar* (as *cringing*), i.e. *pauper* (strictly denoting absolute or public *mendicancy*, although also used in a qualified or relative sense; whereas *3993* prop. means only *straitened* circumstances in private), lit. (often as noun) or fig. (*distressed*):—beggar (-ly), poor.

4435. **πυγμή pugmē**, *poog-may';* from a prim. **πύξ pux** (the *fist* as a weapon); the clenched *hand*,

ie. (only in dat. as adv.) *with* the *fist* (hard *scrubbing*):—oft.

4436. **Πύθων Puthōn**, *poo'-thone;* from **Πυθώ Puthō** (the name of the region where Delphi, the seat of the famous *oracle*, was located); a *Python*, i.e. (by anal. with the supposed *diviner* there) *inspiration* (*soothsaying*):—divination.

4437. **πυκνός puknŏs**, *pook-nos';* from the same as *4635; clasped* (*thick*), i.e. (fig.) *frequent;* neut. plur. (as adv.) *frequently:*—often (-er).

4438. **πυκτέω puktĕō**, *pook-teh'-o;* from a der. of the same as *4435;* to *box* (with the fist), i.e. *contend* (as a boxer) at the games (fig.):—fight.

4439. **πύλη pulē**, *poo'-lay;* appar. a prim. word; a *gate*, i.e. the leaf or wing of a folding *entrance* (lit. or fig.):—gate.

4440. **πυλών pulōn**, *poo-lone';* from *4439;* a *gateway, door-way* of a building or city; by impl. a *portal* or *vestibule:*—gate, porch.

4441. **πυνθάνομαι punthanŏmai**, *poon-than'-om-ahee;* mid. prol. from a prim. **πύθω puthō** (which occurs only as an alt. in certain tenses); to *question*, i.e. *ascertain* by inquiry (as a matter of *information* merely; and thus differing from *2065*, which prop. means a *request* as a favor; and from *154*, which is strictly a *demand* of something due; as well as from *2212*, which implies a *search* for something hidden; and from *1189*, which involves the idea of urgent *need*); by impl. to *learn* (by casual intelligence):—ask, demand, enquire, understand.

4442. **πῦρ pur**, *poor;* a prim. word; "*fire*" (lit. or fig., spec. *lightning*):—fiery, fire.

4443. **πυρά pura**, *poo-rah';* from *4442;* a *fire* (concr.):—fire.

4444. **πύργος purgŏs**, *poor'-gos;* appar. a prim. word ("*burgh*"); a *tower* or *castle:*—tower.

4445. **πυρέσσω purĕssō**, *poo-res'-so;* from *4443;* to *be on fire*, i.e. (spec.) to *have a fever:*—be sick of a fever.

4446. **πυρετός purĕtŏs**, *poo-ret-os';* from *4445; inflamed*, i.e. (by impl.) *feverish* (as noun, *fever*):—fever.

4447. **πύρινος purinŏs**, *poo'-ree-nos;* from *4443; fiery*, i.e. (by impl.) *flaming:*—of fire.

4448. **πυρόω purŏō**, *poo-rŏ'-o;* from *4442;* to *kindle*, i.e. (pass.) to *be ignited, glow* (lit.), *be refined* (by impl.), or (fig.) to *be inflamed* (with anger, grief, lust):—burn, fiery, be on fire, try.

4449. **πυρράζω purrhazō**, *poor-hrad'-zo;* from *4450;* to *redden* (intrans.):—be red.

4450. **πυῤῥός purrhŏs**, *poor-hros';* from *4442; fire-like*, i.e. (spec.) *flame-colored:*—red.

4451. **πύρωσις purōsis**, *poo'-ro-sis;* from *4448; ignition*, i.e. (spec.) *smelting* (fig. *conflagration, calamity* as a *test*):—burning, trial.

4452. **-πω -pō**, *po;* another form of the base of *4458;* an enclitic particle of indefiniteness; *yet, even;* used only in comp. See *3369, 3380, 3764, 3768, 4455*.

4453. **πωλέω pōlĕō**, *po-leh'-o;* prob. ultimately from **πέλομαι pĕlŏmai** (to *be busy*, to *trade*); to *barter* (as a *pedlar*), i.e. to *sell:*—sell, whatever is sold.

4454. **πῶλος pōlŏs**, *po'-los;* appar. a prim. word; a "*foal*" or "*filly*", i.e. (spec.) a *young ass:*—colt.

4455. **πώποτε pōpŏtĕ**, *po'-pot-e;* from *4452* and *4218; at any time*, i.e. (with neg. particle) *at no time:*—at any time, + never (. . . to any man), + yet never man.

4456. **πωρόω pōrŏō**, *po-rŏ'-o;* appar. from **πῶρος pōrŏs** (a kind of *stone*); to *petrify*, i.e (fig.) to *indurate* (*render stupid* or *callous*):—blind, harden.

4457. **πώρωσις pōrōsis**, *po'-ro-sis;* from *4456; stupidity* or *callousness:*—blindness, hardness.

4458. **-πώς -pōs**, *poce;* adv. from the base of *4225;* an enclitic particle of indefiniteness of manner; *somehow* or *anyhow;* used only in comp.:—haply, by any (some) means, perhaps. See *1513, 3381*. Comp. *4459*.

4459. **πῶς pōs**, *poce;* adv. from the base of *4226;* an interrog. particle of manner; *in what way?* (sometimes the question is indirect, *how?*); also as exclamation, *how* much!:—how, after (by) what manner (means), that. [*Occasionally unexpressed in English.*]

P

4460. **Ῥαάβ Rhaab**, *hrah-ab';* of Heb. or. [7343]; *Raab* (i.e. *Rachab*), a Canaanitess:—Rahab. See also *4477*.

4461. **ῥαββί rhabbi**, *hrab-bee';* of Heb. or. [7227 with pron. suffix]; *my master*, i.e. *Rabbi*, as an official title of honor:—Master, Rabbi.

4462. **ῥαββονί rhabbŏni**, *hrab-bon-ee';* or

ῥαββουνί rhabbŏuni, *hrab-boo-nee';* of Chald. or.; corresp. to *4461:*—Lord, Rabboni.

4463. **ῥαβδίζω rhabdizō**, *hrab-did'-zo;* from *4464;* to *strike with a stick*, i.e. *bastinado:*—beat (with rods).

4464. **ῥάβδος rhabdŏs**, *hrab'-dos;* from the base of *4474;* a *stick* or *wand* (as a *cudgel*, a *cane* or a *baton* of royalty):—rod, sceptre, staff.

4465. **ῥαβδοῦχος rhabdŏuchŏs**, *hrab-doo'-khos;* from *4464* and *2192;* a *rod-* (the Lat. *fasces*) *holder*, i.e. a Rom. *lictor* (*constable* or *executioner*):—serjeant.

4466. **Ῥαγαῦ Rhagau**, *hrag-ŏw';* of Heb. or. [7466]; *Ragau* (i.e. *Reü*), a patriarch:—Ragau.

4467. **ῥᾳδιούργημα rhaidiŏurgēma**, *hrad-ee-oorg'-ay-mah;* from a comp. of **ῥᾴδιος rhaidiŏs** (*easy*, i.e. *reckless*) and *2041; easy-going behavior*, i.e. (by extens.) a *crime:*—lewdness.

4468. **ῥᾳδιουργία rhaidiŏurgia**, *hrad-ee-oorg-ee'-a;* from the same as *4467; recklessness*, i.e. (by extens.) *malignity:*—mischief.

4469. **ῥακά rhaka**, *rhak-ah';* of Chald. or. [comp. 7386]; O *empty* one, i.e. thou *worthless* (as a term of utter vilification):—Raca.

4470. **ῥάκος rhăkŏs**, *hrak'-os;* from *4486;* a "*rag*," i.e. *piece* of cloth:—cloth.

4471. **Ῥαμᾶ Rhama**, *hram-ah';* of Heb. or. [7414]; *Rama* (i.e. *Ramah*), a place in Pal.:—Rama.

4472. **ῥαντίζω rhantizō**, *hran-tid'-zo;* from a der. of **ῥαίνω rhainō** (to *sprinkle*); to *render besprinkled*, i.e. *asperse* (cer. or fig.):—sprinkle.

4473. **ῥαντισμός rhantismŏs**, *hran-tis-mos';* from *4472; aspersion* (cer. or fig.):—sprinkling.

4474. **ῥαπίζω rhapizō**, *hrap-id'-zo;* from a der. of a prim. **ῥέπω rhĕpō** (to *let fall*, "*rap*"); to *slap:*—smite (with the palm of the hand). Comp. *5180*.

4475. **ῥάπισμα rhapisma**, *hrap'-is-mah;* from *4474;* a *slap:*—(+ strike with the) palm of the hand, smite with the hand.

4476. **ῥαφίς rhaphis**, *hraf-ece';* from a prim. **ῥάπτω rhaptō** (to *sew;* perh. rather akin to the base of *4474* through the idea of *puncturing*); a *needle:*—needle.

4477. **Ῥαχάβ Rhachab**, *hrakh-ab';* from the same as *4460; Rachab*, a Canaanitess:—Rachab.

4478. **Ῥαχήλ Rhachēl**, *hrakh-ale';* of Heb. or. [7354]; *Rachel*, the wife of Jacob:—Rachel.

4479. **Ῥεβέκκα Rhĕbĕkka**, *hreb-bek'-kah;* of Heb. or. [7259]; *Rebecca* (i.e. *Ribkah*), the wife of Isaac:—Rebecca.

4480. **ῥέδα rhĕda**, *hred'-ah;* of Lat. or.; a *rheda*, i.e. four-wheeled *carriage* (*wagon* for riding):—chariot.

4481. **Ῥεμφάν Rhĕmphan**, *hrem-fan';* by incorrect transliteration for a word of Heb. or. [3594]; *Remphan* (i.e. *Kijun*), an Eg. idol:—Remphan.

4482. **ῥέω rhĕō**, *hreh'-o;* a prim. verb; for some tenses of which a prol. form

ῥεύω rhĕuō, *hryoo'-o*, is used; to *flow* ("*run*", as water):—flow.

4483. **ῥέω rhĕō**, *hreh'-o;* for certain tenses of which a prol. form

ἐρέω ĕrĕō, *er-eh'-o*, is used; and both as alt. for *2036;* perh. akin (or ident.) with *4482* (through the idea of *pouring* forth); to *utter*, i.e. *speak* or *say:*—command, make, say, speak (of). Comp. *3004*.

4484. **Ῥήγιον Rhēgiŏn**, *hrayg'-ee-on;* of Lat. or.; *Rhegium*, a place in Italy:—Rhegium.

4485. **ῥῆγμα rhēgma**, *hrayg'-mah;* from *4486;* something *torn*, i.e. a *fragment* (by impl. and abstr. a *fall*):—ruin.

4486. **ῥήγνυμι rhēgnumi**, *hrayg'-noo-mee;* or

ῥήσσω rhēssō, *hrace'-so;* both prol. forms of **ῥήκω rhēkō** (which appears only in certain forms, and is itself prob. a strengthened form of **ἄγνυμι agnumi** [see in *2608*]); to "*break*", "*wreck*" or "*crack*", i.e. (espec.) to *sunder* (by *separation* of the parts; *2608* being its intensive [with the prep. in comp.], and *2352* a *shattering* to minute fragments; but not a *reduction* to the constituent particles, like *3089*) or *disrupt, lacerate;* by impl. to *convulse* (with *spasms*); fig. to *give vent* to joyful emotions:—break (forth), burst, rend, tear.

4487. **ῥῆμα rhēma**, *hray'-mah;* from *4483;* an *utterance* (individ., collect. or spec.); by impl. a *matter* or *topic* (espec. of narration, command or dispute); with a neg. *naught* whatever:— + evil, + nothing, saying, word.

4488. **Ῥησά Rhēsa**, *hray-sah';* prob. of Heb. or. [appar. for 7509]; *Resa* (i.e. *Rephajah*), an Isr.:—Rhesa.

4489. **ῥήτωρ rhētōr**, *hray'-tore;* from *4483;* a *speaker*, i.e. (by impl.) a forensic *advocate:*—orator.

4490. **ῥητῶς rhētōs**, *hray-toce';* adv. from a der. of *4483;* out-*spokenly*, i.e. *distinctly:*—expressly.

4491. **ῥίζα rhiza**, *hrid'-zah;* appar. a prim. word; a "*root*" (lit. or fig.):—root.

4492. **ῥιζόω rhizŏō**, *rhid-zŏ'-o;* from *4491;* to *root* (fig. *become stable*):—root.

4493. **ῥιπή rhipē**, *hree-pay';* from *4496;* a *jerk* (of the eye, i.e. [by anal.] an *instant*):—twinkling.

4494. **ῥιπίζω rhipizō**, *hrip-id'-zo;* from a der. of *4496* (mean. a *fan* or *bellows*); to *breeze up*, i.e. (by anal.) to *agitate* (into waves):—toss.

4495. **ῥιπτέω rhiptĕō**, *hrip-teh'-o;* from a der. of *4496;* to *toss* up:—cast off.

4496. **ῥίπτω rhiptō**, *hrip'-to;* a prim. verb (perh. rather akin to the base of *4474*, through the idea of sudden *motion*); to *fling* (prop. with a quick *toss*, thus differing from *906*, which denotes a *deliberate* hurl; and from **τείνω tĕinō** [see in *1614*], which indicates an *extended* projection); by qualification, to *deposit* (as if a load); by extens. to *disperse:*—cast (down, out), scatter abroad, throw.

4497. **Ῥοβοάμ Rhŏbŏam**, *hrob-ŏ-am';* of Heb. or. [7346]; *Roboäm* (i.e. *Rechabam*), an Isr.:—Roboam.

4498. **Ῥόδη Rhŏdē**, *hrod'-ay;* prob. for **ῥοδή rhŏdē** (a *rose*); *Rodè*, a servant girl:—Rhoda.

4499. **Ῥόδος Rhŏdŏs**, *hrod'-os;* prob. from **ῥόδον rhŏdŏn** (a *rose*); *Rhodus*, an island of the Mediterranean:—Rhodes.

4500. **ῥοιζηδόν rhŏizēdŏn**, *hroyd-zay-don';* adv. from a der. of **ῥοῖζος rhŏizŏs** (a *whir*); *whizzingly*, i.e. *with a crash:*—with a great noise.

4501. **ῥομφαία rhŏmphaia**, *hrom-fah'-yah;* prob. of for. or.; a *sabre*, i.e. a long and broad *cutlass* (any *weapon* of the kind, lit. or fig.):—sword.

4502. **Ῥουβήν Rhŏubēn**, *hroo-bane';* of Heb. or. [7205]; *Ruben* (i.e. *Reuben*), an Isr.:—Reuben.

4503. **Ῥούθ Rhŏuth**, *hrooth;* of Heb. or. [7327]; *Ruth*, a Moabitess:—Ruth.

4504. **Ροῦφος Rhŏuphŏs**, *hroo'-fos;* of Lat. or.; *red; Rufus*, a Chr.:—Rufus.

4505. **ῥύμη rhumē**, *hroo'-may;* prol. from *4506* in its orig. sense; an *alley* or *avenue* (as crowded):—lane, street.

4506. **ῥύομαι rhuŏmai**, *rhoo'-om-ahee;* mid. of an obsol. verb, akin to *4482* (through the idea of a *current;* comp. *4511*); to *rush* or *draw* (for oneself), i.e. *rescue:*—deliver (-er).

4507. **ῥυπαρία rhuparia**, *hroo-par-ee'-ah;* from *4508; dirtiness* (mor.):—filthiness.

4508. **ῥυπαρός rhuparŏs**, *rhoo-par-os'*; from 4509; *dirty*, i.e. (rel.) *cheap* or *shabby*; mor. *wicked*:—vile.

4509. **ῥύπος rhupŏs**, *hroo'-pos*; of uncert. affin.; *dirt*, i.e. (mor.) *depravity*:—filth.

4510. **ῥυπόω rhupŏō**, *rhoo-pŏ'-o*; from 4509; to *soil*, i.e. (intrans.) to *become dirty* (mor.):—be filthy.

4511. **ῥύσις rhusis**, *hroo'-sis*; from 4506 in the sense of its congener 4482; a *flux* (of blood):—issue.

4512. **ῥυτίς rhutis**, *hroo-tece'*; from 4506; a *fold* (as *drawing* together), i.e. a *wrinkle* (espec. on the face):—wrinkle.

4513. **Ῥωμαϊκός Rhōmaïkŏs**, *rho-mah-ee-kos'*; from 4514; *Romaïc*, i.e. *Latin*:—Latin.

4514. **Ῥωμαῖος Rhōmaiŏs**, *hro-mah'-yos*; from 4516; *Romæan*, i.e. *Roman* (as noun):—Roman, of Rome.

4515. **Ῥωμαϊστί Rhōmaïsti**, *hro-mah-is-tee'*; adv. from a presumed der. of 4516; *Romaïstically*, i.e. *in* the *Latin* language:—Latin.

4516. **Ῥώμη Rhōmē**, *hro'-may*; from the base of 4517; *strength*; *Roma*, the capital of Italy:—Rome.

4517. **ῥώννυμι rhōnnumi**, *hrone'-noo-mee*; prol. from **ῥώομαι rhōŏmai** (to *dart*; prob. akin to 4506); to *strengthen*, i.e. (imper. pass.) *have health* (as a parting exclamation, *good-bye*):—farewell.

Σ

4518. **σαβαχθανί sabachthani**, *sab-akh-than-ee'*; of Chald. or. [7662 with pron. suff.]; *thou hast left me*; *sabachthani* (i.e. *shebakthani*), a cry of distress:—sabachthani.

4519. **σαβαώθ sabaōth**, *sab-ah-ōwth'*; of Heb. or. [6635 in fem. plur.]; *armies*; *sabaoth* (i.e. *tsebaoth*), a military epithet of God:—sabaoth.

4520. **σαββατισμός sabbatismŏs**, *sab-bat-is-mos'*; from a der. of 4521; a "*sabbatism*", i.e. (fig.) the *repose* of Christianity (as a type of heaven):—rest.

4521. **σάββατον sabbatŏn**, *sab'-bat-on*; of Heb. or. [7676]; the *Sabbath* (i.e. *Shabbath*), or day of weekly *repose* from secular avocations (also the observance or institution itself); by extens. a *se'nnight*, i.e. the interval between two Sabbaths; likewise the plur. in all the above applications:—sabbath (day), week.

4522. **σαγήνη sagēnē**, *sag-ay'-nay*; from a der. of **σάττω sattō** (to *equip*) mean. *furniture*, espec. a *pack-saddle* (which in the East is merely a bag of *netted* rope); a "*seine*" for fishing:—net.

4523. **Σαδδουκαῖος Saddŏukaiŏs**, *sad-doo-kah'-yos*; prob. from 4524; a *Sadducæan* (i.e. *Tsadokian*), or follower of a certain heretical Isr.:—Sadducee.

4524. **Σαδώκ Sadōk**, *sad-oke'*; of Heb. or. [6659]; *Sadoc* (i.e. *Tsadok*), an Isr.:—Sadoc.

4525. **σαίνω sainō**, *sah'ee-no*; akin to 4579; to *wag* (as a dog its tail fawningly), i.e. (gen.) to *shake* (fig. *disturb*):—move.

4526. **σάκκος sakkŏs**, *sak'-kos*; of Heb. or. [8242]; "*sack*"-cloth, i.e. *mohair* (the material or garments made of it, worn as a sign of grief):—sackcloth.

4527. **Σαλά Sala**, *sal-ah'*; of Heb. or. [7974]; *Sala* (i.e. *Shelach*), a patriarch:—Sala.

4528. **Σαλαθιήλ Salathiēl**, *sal-ath-ee-ale'*; of Heb. or. [7597]; *Salathiël* (i.e. *Sheältiël*), an Isr.:—Salathiel.

4529. **Σαλαμίς Salamis**, *sal-am-ece'*; prob. from 4535 (from the *surge* on the shore); *Salamis*, a place in Cyprus:—Salamis.

4530. **Σαλείμ Salĕim**, *sal-ime'*; prob. from the same as 4531; *Salim*, a place in Pal.:—Salim.

4531. **σαλεύω salĕuō**, *sal-yoo'-o*; from 4535; to *waver*, i.e. *agitate*, *rock*, *topple* or (by impl.) *destroy*; fig. to *disturb*, *incite*:—move, shake (together), which can [-not] be shaken, stir up.

4532. **Σαλήμ Salēm**, *sal-ame'*; of Heb. or. [8004]; *Salem* (i.e. *Shalem*), a place in Pal.:—Salem.

4533. **Σαλμών Salmōn**, *sal-mone'*; of Heb. or. [8012]; *Salmon*, an Isr.:—Salmon.

4534. **Σαλμώνη Salmōnē**, *sal-mo'-nay*; perh. of similar or. to 4529; *Salmone*, a place in Crete:—Salmone.

4535. **σάλος salŏs**, *sal'-os*; prob. from the base of 4525; a *vibration*, i.e. (spec.) *billow*:—wave.

4536. **σάλπιγξ salpigx**, *sal'-pinx*; perh. from 4535 (through the idea of *quavering* or *reverberation*): a *trumpet*:—trump (-et).

4537. **σαλπίζω salpizō**, *sal-pid'-zo*; from 4536; to *trumpet*, i.e. *sound a blast* (lit. or fig.):—(which are yet to) sound (a trumpet).

4538. **σαλπιστής salpistēs**, *sal-pis-tace'*; from 4537; a *trumpeter*:—trumpeter.

4539. **Σαλώμη Salōmē**, *sal-o'-may*; prob. of Heb. or. [fem. from 7965]; *Salomè* (i.e. *Shelomah*), an Israelitess:—Salome.

4540. **Σαμάρεια Samarĕia**, *sam-ar'-i-ah*; of Heb. or. [8111]; *Samaria* (i.e. *Shomeron*), a city and region of Pal.:—Samaria.

4541. **Σαμαρείτης Samarĕitēs**, *sam-ar-i'-tace*; from 4540; a *Samarite*, i.e. inhab. of Samaria:—Samaritan.

4542. **Σαμαρεῖτις Samarĕitis**, *sam-ar-i'-tis*; fem. of 4541; a *Samaritess*, i.e. woman of Samaria:—of Samaria.

4543. **Σαμοθρᾴκη Samŏthrakē**, *sam-oth-rak'-ay*; from 4544 and **Θρᾴκη Thrakē** (*Thrace*); *Samo-thracè* (*Samos of Thrace*), an island in the Mediterranean:—Samothrac'

4544. **Σάμος Samŏs**, *sam'-os*; of uncert. affin.; *Samus*, an island of the Mediterranean:—Samos.

4545. **Σαμουήλ Samŏuēl**, *sam-oo-ale'*; of Heb. or. [8050]; *Samuel* (i.e. *Shemuel*), an Isr.:—Samuel.

4546. **Σαμψών Sampsōn**, *samp-sone'*; of Heb. or. [8123]; *Sampson* (i.e. *Shimshon*), an Isr.:—Samson.

4547. **σανδάλιον sandaliŏn**, *san-dal'-ee-on*; neut. of a der. of **σάνδαλον sandalŏn** (a "*sandal*"; of uncert. or.); a *slipper* or *sole-pad*:—sandal.

4548. **σανίς sanis**, *san-ece'*; of uncert. affin.; a *plank*:—board.

4549. **Σαούλ Saŏul**, *sah-ool'*; of Heb. or. [7586]; *Saül* (i.e. *Shaül*), the Jewish name of *Paul*:—Saul. Comp. 4569.

4550. **σαπρός saprŏs**, *sap-ros'*; from 4595; *rotten*, i.e. *worthless* (lit. or mor.):—bad, corrupt. Comp. 4190.

4551. **Σαπφείρη Sapphĕirē**, *sap-fi'-ray*; fem. of 4552; *Sapphirè*, an Israelitess:—Sapphira.

4552. **σάπφειρος sapphĕirŏs**, *sap'-fi-ros*; of Heb. or. [5601]; a "*sapphire*" or *lapis-lazuli* gem:—sapphire.

4553. **σαργάνη sarganē**, *sar-gan'-ay*; appar. of Heb. or. [8276]; a *basket* (as *interwoven* or *wicker-work*):—basket.

4554. **Σάρδεις Sardĕis**, *sar'-dice*; plur. of uncert. der.; *Sardis*, a place in Asia Minor:—Sardis.

4555. **σάρδινος sardinŏs**, *sar'-dee-nos*; from the same as 4556; *sardine* (3037 being impl.), i.e. a gem, so called:—sardine.

4556. **σάρδιος sardiŏs**, *sar'-dee-os*; prop. adj. from an uncert. base; *sardian* (3037 being impl.), i.e. (as noun) the gem so called:—sardius.

4557. **σαρδόνυξ sardŏnux**, *sar-don'-oox*; from the base of 4556 and **ὄνυξ ŏnux** (the *nail* of a finger; hence the "*onyx*" stone); a "*sardonyx*", i.e. the gem so called:—sardonyx.

4558. **Σάρεπτα Sarĕpta**, *sar'-ep-tah*; of Heb. or. [6886]; *Sarepta* (i.e. *Tsarephath*), a place in Pal.:—Sarepta.

4559. **σαρκικός sarkikŏs**, *sar-kee-kos'*; from 4561; *pertaining to flesh*, i.e. (by extens.) *bodily*, *temporal*, or (by impl.) *animal*, *unregenerate*:—carnal, fleshly.

4560. **σάρκινος sarkinŏs**, *sar'-kee-nos*; from 4561; *similar to flesh*, i.e. (by anal.) *soft*:—fleshly.

4561. **σάρξ sarx**, *sarx*; prob. from the base of 4563; *flesh* (as *stripped* of the skin), i.e. (strictly) the *meat* of an animal (as food), or (by extens.) the *body* (as opposed to the soul [or spirit], or as the symbol of what is external, or as the means of kindred), or (by impl.) *human nature* (with its frailties [phys. or mor.] and passions), or (spec.) a *human being* (as such):—carnal (-ly, + -ly minded), flesh ([-ly]).

4562. **Σαρούχ Sarŏuch**, *sar-ooch'*; of Heb. or. [8286]; *Saruch* (i.e. *Serug*), a patriarch:—Saruch.

4563. **σαρόω sarŏō**, *sar-ŏ'-o*; from a der. of **σαίρω sairō** (to *brush off*; akin to 4951) mean. a *broom*; to *sweep*:—sweep.

4564. **Σάῤῥα Sarrha**, *sar'-hrah*; of Heb. or. [8283]; *Sarra* (i.e. *Sarah*), the wife of Abraham:—Sara, Sarah.

4565. **Σάρων Sarōn**, *sar'-one*; of Heb. or. [8289]; *Saron* (i.e. *Sharon*), a district of Pal.:—Saron.

4566. **Σατᾶν Satan**, *sat-an'*; of Heb. or. [7854]; *Satan*, i.e. the *devil*:—Satan. Comp. 4567.

4567. **Σατανᾶς Satanas**, *sat-an-as'*; of Chald. or. corresp. to 4566 (with the def. affix); *the accuser*, i.e. the *devil*:—Satan.

4568. **σάτον satŏn**, *sat'-on*; of Heb. or. [5429]; a certain *measure* for things dry:—measure.

4569. **Σαῦλος Saulŏs**, *sŏw'-los*; of Heb. or., the same as 4549; *Saulus* (i.e. *Shaül*), the Jewish name of *Paul*:—Saul.

σαυτοῦ sautŏu, etc. See 4572.

4570. **σβέννυμι sbĕnnumi**, *sben'-noo-mee*; a prol. form of an appar. prim. verb; to *extinguish* (lit. or fig.):—go out, quench.

4571. **σέ sĕ**, *seh*; accus. sing. of 4771; *thee*:—thee, thou, × thy house.

4572. **σεαυτοῦ sĕautŏu**, *seh-ŏw-too'*; gen. from 4571 and 846; also dat. of the same, **σεαυτῷ sĕautō**, *seh-ŏw-to'*; and acc. **σεαυτόν sĕautŏn**, *seh-ŏw-ton'*; likewise contr. **σαυτοῦ sautŏu**, *sŏw-too'*; **σαυτῷ sautō**, *sŏw-to'*; and **σαυτόν sautŏn**, *sŏw-ton'*, respectively; *of* (*with*, *to*) *thyself*:—thee, thine own self, (thou) thy (-self).

4573. **σεβάζομαι sĕbazŏmai**, *seb-ad'-zom-ahee*; mid. from a der. of 4576; to *venerate*, i.e. *adore*:—worship.

4574. **σέβασμα sĕbasma**, *seb'-as-mah*; from 4573; something *adored*, i.e. an *object of worship* (god, altar, etc.):—devotion, that is worshipped.

4575. **σεβαστός sĕbastŏs**, *seb-as-tos'*; from 4573; *venerable* (*august*), i.e. (as noun) a title of the Rom. *Emperor*, or (as adj.) *imperial*:—Augustus (-').

4576. **σέβομαι sĕbŏmai**, *seb'-om-ahee*; mid. of an appar. prim. verb; to *revere*, i.e. *adore*:—devout, religious, worship.

4577. **σειρά sĕira**, *si-rah'*; prob. from 4951 through its congener **εἴρω ĕirō** (to *fasten*; akin to 138); a *chain* (as *binding* or *drawing*):—chain.

4578. **σεισμός sĕismŏs**, *sice-mos'*; from 4579; a *commotion*, i.e. (of the air) a *gale*, (of the ground) an *earthquake*:—earthquake, tempest.

4579. **σείω sĕiō**, *si'-o*; appar. a prim. verb; to *rock* (*vibrate*, prop. sideways or to and fro), i.e. (gen.) to *agitate* (in any direction; cause to *tremble*); fig. to throw into a *tremor* (of fear or concern):—move, quake, shake.

4580. **Σεκοῦνδος Sĕkŏundŏs**, *sek-oon'-dos*; of Lat. or.; "*second*"; *Secundus*, a Chr.:—Secundus.

4581. **Σελεύκεια Sĕlĕukĕia**, *sel-yook'-i-ah*; from **Σέλευκος Sĕlĕukŏs** (*Seleucus*, a Syrian king); *Seleuceia*, a place in Syria:—Seleucia.

4582. **σελήνη sĕlēnē**, *sel-ay'-nay*; from **σέλας sĕlas** (*brilliancy*; prob. akin to the alt. of 138, through the idea of *attractiveness*); the *moon*:—moon.

4583. **σεληνιάζομαι sĕlēniazŏmai**, *sel-ay-nee-ad'-zom-ahee*; mid. or pass. from a presumed der. of 4582; to *be moon-struck*, i.e. *crazy*:—be lunatic.

4584. **Σεμεΐ Sĕmĕï**, *sem-eh-ee';* of Heb. or. [8096]; *Semeï* (i.e. *Shimi*), an Isr.:—Semei.

4585. **σεμίδαλις sĕmidalis**, *sem-id'-al-is;* prob. of for. or.; fine wheaten *flour:*—fine flour.

4586. **σεμνός sĕmnŏs**, *sem-nos';* from 4576; *venerable*, i.e. *honorable:*—grave, honest.

4587. **σεμνότης sĕmnŏtēs**, *sem-not'-ace;* from 4586; *venerableness*, i.e. *probity:*—gravity, honesty.

4588. **Σέργιος Sĕrgiŏs**, *serg'-ee-os;* of Lat. or.; *Sergius*, a Rom.:—Sergius.

4589. **Σήθ Sēth**, *sayth;* of Heb. or. [8352]; *Seth* (i.e. *Sheth*), a patriarch:—Seth.

4590. **Σήμ Sēm**, *same;* of Heb. or. [8035]; *Sem* (i.e. *Shem*), a patriarch:—Sem.

4591. **σημαίνω sēmainō**, *say-mah'ee-no;* from **σῆμα sēma** (a *mark;* of uncert. der.); to *indicate:*—signify.

4592. **σημεῖον sēmĕiŏn**, *say-mi'-on;* neut. of a presumed der. of the base of 4591; an *indication*, espec. cer. or supernat.:—miracle, sign, token, wonder.

4593. **σημειόω sēmĕiŏō**, *say-mi-ŏ'-o;* from 4592; to *distinguish*, i.e. *mark* (for avoidance):—note.

4594. **σήμερον sēmĕrŏn**, *say'-mer-on;* neut. (as adv.) of a presumed comp. of the art. 3588 (τ changed to σ) and 2250; on *the* (i.e. *this*) day (or *night* current or just passed); gen. *now* (i.e. at *present*, *hitherto*):—this (to-) day.

4595. **σήπω sēpō**, *say'-po;* appar. a prim. verb; to *putrefy*, i.e. (fig.) *perish:*—be corrupted.

4596. **σηρικός sērikŏs**, *say-ree-kos';* from **Σήρ Sēr** (an Indian tribe from whom *silk* was procured; hence the name of the *silk-worm*); *Seric*, i.e. *silken* (neut. as noun, a *silky* fabric):—silk.

4597. **σής sēs**, *sace;* appar. of Heb. or. [5580]; a *moth:*—moth.

4598. **σητόβρωτος sētŏbrōtŏs**, *say-tob'-ro-tos;* from 4597 and a der. of 977; *moth-eaten:*—motheaten.

4599. **σθενόω sthĕnŏō**, *sthen-ŏ'-o;* from **σθένος sthĕnŏs** (bodily *vigor;* prob. akin to the base of 2476); to *strengthen*, i.e. (fig.) *confirm* (in spiritual knowledge and power):—strengthen.

4600. **σιαγών siagōn**, *see-ag-one';* of uncert. der.; the *jaw*-bone, i.e. (by impl.) the *cheek* or side of the face:—cheek.

4601. **σιγάω sigaō**, *see-gah'-o;* from 4602; to *keep silent* (trans. or intrans.):—keep close (secret, silence), hold peace.

4602. **σιγή sigē**, *see-gay';* appar. from **σίζω sizō** (to *hiss*, i.e. *hist* or *hush*); *silence:*—silence. Comp. 4623.

4603. **σιδήρεος sidērĕŏs**, *sid-ay'-reh-os;* from 4604; made *of iron:*—(of) iron.

4604. **σίδηρος sidērŏs**, *sid'-ay-ros;* of uncert. der.; *iron:*—iron.

4605. **Σιδών Sidōn**, *sid-one';* of Heb. or. [6721]; *Sidon* (i.e. *Tsidon*), a place in Pal.:—Sidon.

4606. **Σιδώνιος Sidōniŏs**, *sid-o'-nee-os;* from 4605; a *Sidonian*, i.e. inhab. of Sidon:—of Sidon.

4607. **σικάριος sikariŏs**, *sik-ar'-ee-os;* of Lat. or.; a *dagger-man* or *assassin;* a *freebooter* (Jewish *fanatic* outlawed by the Romans):—murderer. Comp. 5406.

4608. **σίκερα sikĕra**, *sik'-er-ah;* of Heb. or. [7941]; an *intoxicant*, i.e. intensely fermented *liquor:*—strong drink.

4609. **Σίλας Silas**, *see'-las;* contr. for 4610; *Silas*, a Chr.:—Silas.

4610. **Σιλουανός Silŏuanŏs**, *sil-oo-an-os';* of Lat. or.; "*silvan*"; *Silvanus*, a Chr.:—Silvanus. Comp. 4609.

4611. **Σιλωάμ Silōam**, *sil-o-am';* of Heb. or. [7975]; *Siloäm* (i.e. *Shiloäch*), a pool of Jerus.:—Siloam.

4612. **σιμικίνθιον simikinthiŏn**, *sim-ee-kin'-thee-on;* of Lat. or.; a *semicinctium* or *half-girding*, i.e. narrow covering (*apron*):—apron.

4613. **Σίμων Simōn**, *see'-mone;* of Heb. or. [8095]; *Simon* (i.e. *Shimon*), the name of nine Isr.:—Simon. Comp. 4826.

4614. **Σινᾶ Sina**, *see-nah';* of Heb. or. [5514]; *Sina* (i.e. *Sinai*), a mountain in Arabia:—Sina.

4615. **σίναπι sinapi**, *sin'-ap-ee;* perh. from **σίνομαι sinŏmai** (to *hurt*, i.e. *sting*); *mustard* (the plant):—mustard.

4616. **σινδών sindōn**, *sin-done';* of uncert. (perh. for.) or.; *byssos*, i.e. bleached *linen* (the cloth or a garment of it):—(fine) linen (cloth).

4617. **σινιάζω siniazō**, *sin-ee-ad'-zo;* from **σινίον siniŏn** (a *sieve*); to *riddle* (fig.):—sift.

σῖτα sita. See 4621.

4618. **σιτευτός sitĕutŏs**, *sit-yoo-tos';* from a der. of 4621; *grain-fed*, i.e. *fattened:*—fatted.

4619. **σιτιστός sitistŏs**, *sit-is-tos';* from a der. of 4621; *grained*, i.e. *fatted:*—fatling.

4620. **σιτόμετρον sitŏmĕtrŏn**, *sit-om'-et-ron;* from 4621 and 3358; a *grain-measure*, i.e. (by impl.) *ration* (*allowance* of food):—portion of meat.

4621. **σῖτος sitŏs**, *see'-tos;* plur. irreg. neut.

σῖτα sita, *see'-tah;* of uncert. der.; *grain*, espec. *wheat:*—corn, wheat.

4622. **Σιών Siōn**, *see-own';* of Heb. or. [6726]; *Sion* (i.e. *Tsijon*), a hill of Jerus.; fig. the *Church* (militant or triumphant):—Sion.

4623. **σιωπάω siōpaō**, *see-o-pah'-o;* from **σιωπή siōpē** (*silence*, i.e. a *hush;* prop. *muteness*, i.e. *involuntary* stillness, or *inability* to speak; and thus differing from 4602, which is rather a voluntary *refusal* or *indisposition* to speak, although the terms are often used synonymously); to *be dumb* (but not *deaf* also, like 2974 prop.); fig. to *be calm* (as *quiet* water):—dumb, (hold) peace.

4624. **σκανδαλίζω skandalizō**, *skan-dal-id'-zo* ("scandalize"); from 4625; to *entrap*, i.e. *trip* up (fig. *stumble* [trans.] or *entice* to sin, apostasy or displeasure):—(make to) offend.

4625. **σκάνδαλον skandalŏn**, *skan'-dal-on* ("scandal"); prob. from a der. of 2578; a *trap-stick* (*bent* sapling), i.e. *snare* (fig. *cause* of displeasure or sin):—occasion to fall (of stumbling), offence, thing that offends, stumblingblock.

4626. **σκάπτω skaptō**, *skap'-to;* appar. a prim. verb; to *dig:*—dig.

4627. **σκάφη skaphē**, *skaf'-ay;* a "*skiff*" (as if *dug* out), or *yawl* (carried aboard a large vessel for landing):—boat.

4628. **σκέλος skĕlŏs**, *skel'-os;* appar. from **σκέλλω skĕllō** (to *parch;* through the idea of *leanness*); the *leg* (as *lank*):—leg.

4629. **σκέπασμα skĕpasma**, *skep'-as-mah;* from a der. of **σκέπας skĕpas** (a *covering;* perh. akin to the base of 4649 through the idea of *noticeableness*); *clothing:*—raiment.

4630. **Σκευᾶς Skĕuas**, *skyoo-as';* appar. of Lat. or.; *left-handed; Scevas* (i.e. *Scævus*), an Isr.:—Sceva.

4631. **σκευή skĕuē**, *skyoo-ay';* from 4632; *furniture*, i.e. spare *tackle:*—tackling.

4632. **σκεῦος skĕuŏs**, *skyoo'-os;* of uncert. affin.; a *vessel*, *implement*, *equipment* or *apparatus* (lit. or fig. [spec. a *wife* as contributing to the usefulness of the husband]):—goods, sail, stuff, vessel.

4633. **σκηνή skēnē**, *skay-nay';* appar. akin to 4632 and 4639; a *tent* or cloth hut (lit. or fig.):—habitation, tabernacle.

4634. **σκηνοπηγία skēnŏpēgia**, *skay-nop-ayg-ee'-ah;* from 4636 and 4078; the *Festival of Tabernacles* (so called from the custom of erecting booths for temporary homes):—tabernacles.

4635. **σκηνοποιός skēnŏpŏiŏs**, *skay-nop-oy-os';* from 4633 and 4160; a *manufacturer of tents:*—tentmaker.

4636. **σκῆνος skēnŏs**, *skay'-nos;* from 4633; a *hut* or temporary residence, i.e. (fig.) the human *body* (as the abode of the spirit):—tabernacle.

4637. **σκηνόω skēnŏō**, *skay-nŏ'-o;* from 4636; to *tent* or *encamp*, i.e. (fig.) to *occupy* (as a mansion) or (spec.) to *reside* (as God did in the Tabernacle of old, a symbol of protection and communion):—dwell.

4638. **σκήνωμα skēnōma**, *skay'-no-mah;* from 4637; an *encampment*, i.e. (fig.) the *Temple* (as God's residence), the *body* (as a tenement for the soul):—tabernacle.

4639. **σκία skia**, *skee'-ah;* appar. a prim. word; "*shade*" or a shadow (lit. or fig. [darkness of *error* or an *adumbration*]):—shadow.

4640. **σκιρτάω skirtaō**, *skeer-tah'-o;* akin to **σκαίρω skairō** (to *skip*); to *jump*, i.e. sympathetically *move* (as the *quickening* of a fœtus):—leap (for joy).

4641. **σκληροκαρδία sklērŏkardia**, *sklay-rok-ar-dee'-ah;* fem. of a comp. of 4642 and 2588; *hard-heartedness*, i.e. (spec.) *destitution of* (spiritual) *perception:*—hardness of heart.

4642. **σκληρός sklērŏs**, *sklay-ros';* from the base of 4628; *dry*, i.e. *hard* or *tough* (fig. *harsh*, *severe*):—fierce, hard.

4643. **σκληρότης sklērŏtēs**, *sklay-rot'-ace;* from 4642; *callousness*, i.e. (fig.) *stubbornness:*—hardness.

4644. **σκληροτράχηλος sklērŏtrachēlŏs**, *sklay-rot-rakh'-ay-los;* from 4642 and 5137; *hard-naped*, i.e. (fig.) *obstinate:*—stiffnecked.

4645. **σκληρύνω sklērunō**, *sklay-roo'-no;* from 4642; to *indurate*, i.e. (fig.) *render stubborn:*—harden.

4646. **σκολιός skŏliŏs**, *skol-ee-os';* from the base of 4628; *warped*, i.e. *winding;* fig. *perverse:*—crooked, froward, untoward.

4647. **σκόλοψ skŏlŏps**, *skol'-ops;* perh. from the base of 4628 and 3700; *withered* at the *front*, i.e. a *point* or *prickle* (fig. a bodily *annoyance* or *disability*):—thorn.

4648. **σκοπέω skŏpĕō**, *skop-eh'-o;* from 4649; to take *aim* at (*spy*), i.e. (fig.) *regard:*—consider, take heed, look at (on), mark. Comp. 3700.

4649. **σκοπός skŏpŏs**, *skop-os'* ("scope"); from **σκέπτομαι skĕptŏmai** (to *peer* about ["skeptic"]; perh. akin to 4626 through the idea of *concealment;* comp. 4629); a *watch* (*sentry* or *scout*), i.e. (by impl.) a *goal:*—mark.

4650. **σκορπίζω skŏrpizō**, *skor-pid'-zo;* appar. from the same as 4651 (through the idea of *penetrating*); to *dissipate*, i.e. (fig.) *put to flight*, *waste*, *be liberal:*—disperse abroad, scatter (abroad).

4651. **σκορπίος skŏrpiŏs**, *skor-pee'-os;* prob. from an obsol. **σκέρπω skĕrpō** (perh. strengthened from the base of 4649 and mean. to *pierce*); a "*scorpion*" (from its *sting*):—scorpion.

4652. **σκοτεινός skŏtĕinŏs**, *skot-i-nos';* from 4655; *opaque*, i.e. (fig.) *benighted:*—dark, full of darkness.

4653. **σκοτία skŏtia**, *skot-ee'-ah;* from 4655; *dimness*, *obscurity* (lit. or fig.):—dark (-ness).

4654. **σκοτίζω skŏtizō**, *skot-id'-zo;* from 4655; to *obscure* (lit. or fig.):—darken.

4655. **σκότος skŏtŏs**, *skot'-os;* from the base of 4639; *shadiness*, i.e. *obscurity* (lit. or fig.):—darkness.

4656. **σκοτόω skŏtŏō**, *skot-ŏ'-o;* from 4655; to *obscure* or *blind* (lit. or fig.):—be full of darkness.

4657. **σκύβαλον skubalŏn**, *skoo'-bal-on;* neut. of a presumed der. of 1519 and 2965 and 906; what is *thrown to the dogs*, i.e. *refuse* (*ordure*):—dung.

4658. **Σκύθης Skuthēs**, *skoo'-thace;* prob. of for. or.; a *Scythene* or *Scythian*, i.e. (by impl.) a *savage:*—Scythian.

4659. **σκυθρωπός skuthrōpŏs**, *skoo-thro-pos';* from **σκυθρός skuthrŏs** (*sullen*) and a der. of 3700; *angry-visaged*, i.e. *gloomy* or affecting a *mournful* appearance:—of a sad countenance.

4660. **σκύλλω skullō**, *skool'-lo;* appar. a prim. verb; to *flay*, i.e. (fig.) to *harass:*—trouble (self).

4661. **σκῦλον skulŏn**, *skoo'-lon;* neut. from 4660; something *stripped* (as a *hide*), i.e. *booty:*—spoil.

4662. **σκωληκόβρωτος skōlēkŏbrōtŏs**, *sko-lay-kob'-ro-tos;* from 4663 and a der. of 977; *worm-eaten*, i.e. *diseased with maggots:*—eaten of worms.

4663. σκώληξ **skōlēx**, *sko'-lakes;* of uncert. der.; a *grub, maggot* or *earth-worm:*—worm.

4664. σμαράγδινος **smaragdinŏs**, *smar-ag'-dee-nos;* from 4665; consisting *of emerald:*—emerald.

4665. σμάραγδος **smaragdŏs**, *smar'-ag-dos;* of uncert. der.; the *emerald* or green gem so called:—emerald.

4666. σμύρνα **smurna**, *smoor'-nah;* appar. strengthened for 3464; *myrrh:*—myrrh.

4667. Σμύρνα **Smurna**, *smoor'-nah;* the same as 4666; *Smyrna*, a place in Asia Minor:—Smyrna.

4668. Σμυρναῖος **Smurnaiŏs**, *smoor-nah'-yos;* from 4667; a *Smyrnæan:*—in Smyrna.

4669. σμυρνίζω **smurnizō**, *smoor-nid'-zo;* from 4667; to *tincture with myrrh*, i.e. *embitter* (as a narcotic):—mingle with myrrh.

4670. Σόδομα **Sŏdŏma**, *sod'-om-ah;* plur. of Heb. or. [5467]; *Sodoma* (i.e. *Sedom*), a place in Pal.:—Sodom.

4671. σοί **sŏi**, *soy;* dat. of 4771; *to thee:*—thee, thine own, thou, thy.

4672. Σολομών or Σολομῶν **Sŏlŏmōn**, *sol-om-one';* of Heb. or. [8010]; *Solomon* (i.e. *Shelomoh*), the son of David:—Solomon.

4673. σορός **sŏrŏs**, *sor-os';* prob. akin to the base of 4987; a *funereal receptacle* (*urn, coffin*), i.e. (by anal.) a *bier:*—bier.

4674. σός **sŏs**, *sos;* from 4771; *thine:*—thine (own), thy (friend).

4675. σοῦ **sŏu**, *soo;* gen. of 4771; *of thee, thy:*—× home, thee, thine (own), thou, thy.

4676. σουδάριον **sŏudariŏn**, *soo-dar'-ee-on;* of Lat. or.; a *sudarium* (*sweat-cloth*), i.e. *towel* (for wiping the perspiration from the face, or binding the face of a corpse):—handkerchief, napkin.

4677. Σουσάννα **Sŏusanna**, *soo-san'-nah;* of Heb. or. [7799 fem.]; *lily; Susannah* (i.e. *Shoshannah*), an Israelitess:—Susanna.

4678. σοφία **sŏphia**, *sof-ee'-ah;* from 4680; *wisdom* (higher or lower, worldly or spiritual):—wisdom.

4679. σοφίζω **sŏphizō**, *sof-id'-zo;* from 4680; to *render wise;* in a sinister acceptation, to *form* "*sophisms*", i.e. *continue plausible error:*—cunningly devised, make wise.

4680. σοφός **sŏphŏs**, *sof-os';* akin to σαφής **saphēs** (*clear*); *wise* (in a most gen. application):—wise. Comp. 5429.

4681. Σπανία **Spania**, *span-ee'-ah;* prob. of for. or.; *Spania*, a region of Europe:—Spain.

4682. σπαράσσω **sparassō**, *spar-as'-so;* prol. from σπαίρω **spairō** (to *gasp;* appar. strengthened from 4685 through the idea of *spasmodic* contraction); to *mangle*, i.e. *convulse* with epilepsy:—rend, tear.

4683. σπαργανόω **sparganŏō**, *spar-gan-ŏ'-o;* from σπάργανον **sparganŏn** (a *strip;* from a der. of the base of 4682 mean. to *strap* or *wrap* with strips); to *swathe* (an infant after the Oriental custom):—wrap in swaddling clothes.

4684. σπαταλάω **spatalaō**, *spat-al-ah'-o;* from σπατάλη **spatalē** (*luxury*); to *be voluptuous:*—live in pleasure, be wanton.

4685. σπάω **spaō**, *spah'-o;* a prim. verb; to *draw:*—draw (out).

4686. σπεῖρα **spĕira**, *spi'-rah;* of immed. Lat. or., but ultimately a der. of 138 in the sense of its cogn. 1507; a *coil* (*spira*, "spire"), i.e. (fig.) a *mass* of men (a Rom. military *cohort;* also [by anal.] a *squad* of Levitical janitors):—band.

4687. σπείρω **spĕirō**, *spi'-ro;* prob. strengthened from 4685 (through the idea of *extending*); to *scatter*, i.e. *sow* (lit. or fig.):—sow (-er), receive seed.

4688. σπεκουλάτωρ **spĕkŏulatōr**, *spek-oo-lat'-ore;* of Lat. or.; a *speculator*, i.e. military *scout* (*spy* or [by extens.] *life-guardsman*):—executioner.

4689. σπένδω **spĕndō**, *spen'-do;* appar. a prim. verb; to *pour* out as a libation, i.e. (fig.) to *devote* (one's life or blood, as a sacrifice) ("*spend*"):—(be ready to) be offered.

4690. σπέρμα **spĕrma**, *sper'-mah;* from 4687; something *sown*, i.e. *seed* (includ. the male "*sperm*"); by impl. *offspring;* spec. a *remnant* (fig. as if kept over for planting):—issue, seed.

4691. σπερμολόγος **spĕrmŏlŏgŏs**, *sper-mol-og'-os;* from 4690 and 3004; a *seed-picker* (as the crow), i.e. (fig.) a *sponger, loafer* (spec. a *gossip* or *trifler* in talk):—babbler.

4692. σπεύδω **spĕudō**, *spyoo'-do;* prob. strengthened from 4228; to "*speed*" ("study"), i.e. *urge* on (diligently or earnestly); by impl. to *await* eagerly:—(make, with) haste unto.

4693. σπήλαιον **spēlaiŏn**, *spay'-lah-yon;* neut. of a presumed der. of σπέος **spĕŏs** (a *grotto*); a *cavern;* by impl. a *hiding-place* or *resort:*—cave, den.

4694. σπιλάς **spilas**, *spee-las';* of uncert. der.; a *ledge* or *reef* of rock in the sea:—spot [*by confusion with* 4696].

4695. σπιλόω **spilŏō**, *spee-lŏ'-o;* from 4696; to *stain* or *soil* (lit. or fig.):—defile, spot.

4696. σπίλος **spilŏs**, *spee'-los;* of uncert. der.; a *stain* or *blemish*, i.e. (fig.) *defect, disgrace:*—spot.

4697. σπλαγχνίζομαι **splagchnizŏmai**, *splangkh-nid'-zom-ahee;* mid. from 4698; to have the *bowels* yearn, i.e. (fig.) *feel sympathy*, to *pity:*—have (be moved with) compassion.

4698. σπλάγχνον **splagchnŏn**, *splangkh'-non;* prob. strengthened from σπλήν **splēn** (the "*spleen*"); an *intestine* (plur.); fig. *pity* or *sympathy:*—bowels, inward affection, + tender mercy.

4699. σπόγγος **spŏggŏs**, *spong'-gos;* perh. of for. or.; a "*sponge*":—spunge.

4700. σποδός **spŏdŏs**, *spod-os';* of uncert. der.; *ashes:*—ashes.

4701. σπορά **spŏra**, *spor-ah';* from 4687; a *sowing*, i.e. (by impl.) *parentage:*—seed.

4702. σπόριμος **spŏrimŏs**, *spor'-ee-mos;* from 4703; *sown*, i.e. (neut. plur.) a planted *field:*—corn (-field).

4703. σπόρος **spŏrŏs**, *spor'-os;* from 4687; a *scattering* (of seed), i.e. (concr.) *seed* (as sown):—seed (× sown).

4704. σπουδάζω **spŏudazō**, *spoo-dad'-zo;* from 4710; to *use speed*, i.e. to *make effort, be prompt* or *earnest:*—do (give) diligence, be diligent (forward), endeavour, labour, study.

4705. σπουδαῖος **spŏudaiŏs**, *spoo-dah'-yos;* from 4710; *prompt, energetic, earnest:*—diligent.

4706. σπουδαιότερον **spŏudaiŏtĕrŏn**, *spoo-dah-yot'-er-on;* neut. of 4707 as adv.; *more earnestly* than others), i.e. very *promptly:*—very diligently.

4707. σπουδαιότερος **spŏudaiŏtĕrŏs**, *spoo-dah-yot'-er-os;* compar. of 4705; *more prompt, more earnest:*—more diligent (forward).

4708. σπουδαιοτέρως **spŏudaiŏtĕrōs**, *spoo-dah-yot-er'-oce;* adv. from 4707; *more speedily*, i.e. *sooner* than otherwise:—more carefully.

4709. σπουδαίως **spŏudaiōs**, *spoo-dah'-yoce;* adv. from 4705; *earnestly, promptly:*—diligently, instantly.

4710. σπουδή **spŏudē**, *spoo-day';* from 4692; "*speed*", i.e. (by impl.) *despatch, eagerness, earnestness:*—business, (earnest) care (-fulness), diligence, forwardness, haste.

4711. σπυρίς **spuris**, *spoo-rece';* from 4687 (as *woven*); a *hamper* or *lunch-receptacle:*—basket.

4712. στάδιον **stadiŏn**, *stad'-ee-on;* or masc. (in plur.) στάδιος **stadiŏs**, *stad'-ee-os;* from the base of 2476 (as *fixed*); a *stade* or certain measure of distance; by impl. a *stadium* or *race-course:*—furlong, race.

4713. στάμνος **stamnŏs**, *stam'-nos;* from the base of 2476 (as *stationary*); a *jar* or earthen *tank:*—pot.

4714. στάσις **stasis**, *stas'-is;* from the base of 2476; a *standing* (prop. the act), i.e. (by anal.) *position* (*existence*); by impl. a popular *uprising;* fig. *controversy:*—dissension, insurrection, × standing, uproar.

4715. στατήρ **statēr**, *stat-air';* from the base or 2746; a *stander* (*standard* of value), i.e. (spec.) a *stater* or certain coin:—piece of money.

4716. σταυρός **staurŏs**, *stŏw-ros';* from the base of 2476; a *stake* or *post* (*as set* upright), i.e. (spec.) a *pole* or *cross* (as an instrument of capital punishment); fig. *exposure to death*, i.e. *self-denial;* by impl. the *atonement* of Christ:—cross.

4717. σταυρόω **staurŏō**, *stŏw-rŏ'-o;* from 4716; to *impale* on the cross; fig. to *extinguish* (*subdue*) passion or selfishness:—crucify.

4718. σταφυλή **staphulē**, *staf-oo-lay';* prob. from the base of 4735; a *cluster* of grapes (as if *intertwined*):—grapes.

4719. στάχυς **stachus**, *stakh'-oos;* from the base of 2476; a *head* of grain (as *standing* out from the stalk):—ear (of corn).

4720. Στάχυς **Stachus**, *stakh'-oos;* the same as 4719; *Stachys*, a Chr.:—Stachys.

4721. στέγη **stĕgē**, *steg'-ay;* strengthened from a prim. τέγος **tĕgŏs** (a "*thatch*" or "*deck*" of a building); a *roof:*—roof.

4722. στέγω **stĕgō**, *steg'-o;* from 4721; to *roof* over, i.e. (fig.) to *cover* with silence (*endure* patiently):—(for-) bear, suffer.

4723. στεῖρος **stĕirŏs**, *sti'-ros;* a contr. from 4731 (as *stiff* and *unnatural*); "*sterile*":—barren.

4724. στέλλω **stĕllō**, *stel'-lo;* prob. strengthened from the base of 2476; prop. to *set* fast ("*stall*"), i.e. (fig.) to *repress* (reflex. *abstain* from associating with):—avoid, withdraw self.

4725. στέμμα **stĕmma**, *stem'-mah;* from the base of 4735; a *wreath* for show:—garland.

4726. στεναγμός **stĕnagmŏs**, *sten-ag-mos';* from 4727; a *sigh:*—groaning.

4727. στενάζω **stĕnazō**, *sten-ad'-zo;* from 4728; to *make* (intrans. *be*) *in straits*, i.e. (by impl.) to *sigh, murmur, pray* inaudibly:—with grief, groan, grudge, sigh.

4728. στενός **stĕnŏs**, *sten-os';* prob. from the base of 2476; *narrow* (from obstacles *standing* close about):—strait.

4729. στενοχωρέω **stĕnŏchōrĕō**, *sten-okh-o-reh'-o;* from the same as 4730; to *hem* in closely, i.e. (fig.) *cramp:*—distress, straiten.

4730. στενοχωρία **stĕnŏchōria**, *sten-okh-o-ree'-ah;* from a comp. of 4728 and 5561; *narrowness of room*, i.e. (fig.) *calamity:*—anguish, distress.

4731. στερεός **stĕrĕŏs**, *ster-eh-os';* from 2476; *stiff*, i.e. *solid, stable* (lit. or fig.):—stedfast, strong, sure.

4732. στερεόω **stĕrĕŏō**, *ster-eh-ŏ'-o;* from 4731; to *solidify*, i.e. *confirm* (lit. or fig.):—establish, receive strength, make strong.

4733. στερέωμα **stĕrĕōma**, *ster-eh'-o-mah;* from 4732; something *established*, i.e. (abstr.) *confirmation* (*stability*):—stedfastness.

4734. Στεφανᾶς **Stĕphanas**, *stef-an-as';* prob. contr. for στεφανωτός **stĕphanōtŏs** (*crowned;* from 4737); *Stephanas*, a Chr.:—Stephanas.

4735. στέφανος **stĕphanŏs**, *stef'-an-os;* from an appar. prim. στέφω **stĕphō** (to *twine* or *wreathe*); a *chaplet* (as a badge of royalty, a prize in the public games or a symbol of honor gen.; but more conspicuous and elaborate than the simple *fillet*, 1238), lit. or fig.:—crown.

4736. Στέφανος **Stĕphanŏs**, *stef'-an-os;* the same as 4735; *Stephanus*, a Chr.:—Stephen.

4737. στεφανόω **stephanŏō**, *stef-an-ŏ'-o;* from 4735; to *adorn with* an honorary *wreath* (lit. or fig.):—crown.

4738. στῆθος **stēthŏs**, *stay'-thos;* from 2476 (as *standing* prominently); the (entire extern.) *bosom*, i.e. *chest:*—breast.

4739. στήκω **stēkō**, *stay'-ko;* from the perf. tense of 2476; to *be stationary*, i.e. (fig.) to *persevere:*—stand (fast).

4740. στηριγμός **stērigmŏs**, *stay-rig-mos';* from 4741; *stability* (fig.):—stedfastness.

4741. στηρίζω **stērizō**, *stay-rid'-zo;* from a presumed der. of 2476 (like 4731); to *set fast*, i.e. (lit.) to *turn resolutely* in a certain direction, or (fig.) to *confirm:*—fix, (e-) stablish, stedfastly set, strengthen.

4742. στίγμα **stigma**, *stig'-mah;* from a prim. στίζω **stizō** (to "*stick*", i.e. *prick*); a *mark* incised or punched (for recognition of ownership), i.e. (fig.) *scar* of service:—mark.

4743. στιγμή **stigmē**, *stig-may';* fem. of 4742; a *point* of time, i.e. an *instant:*—moment.

4744. στίλβω **stilbō**, *stil'-bo;* appar. a prim. verb; to *gleam*, i.e. *flash* intensely:—shining.

4745. στοά **stŏa**, *stŏ-ah';* prob. from 2476; a *colonnade* or interior *piazza:*—porch.

4746. στοιβάς **stŏibas**, *stoy-bas';* from a prim. στείβω **stĕibō** (to "*step*" or "*stamp*"); a *spread* (as if *tramped* flat) of loose materials for a couch, i.e. (by impl.) a *bough* of a tree so employed:—branch.

4747. στοιχεῖον **stŏichĕiŏn**, *stoy-khi'-on;* neut. of a presumed der. of the base of 4748; something *orderly* in arrangement, i.e. (by impl.) a *serial* (*basal, fundamental, initial*) constituent (lit.), proposition (fig.):—element, principle, rudiment.

4748. στοιχέω **stŏichĕō**, *stoy-kheh'-o;* from a der. of στείχω **stĕichō** (to *range* in regular line); to *march* in (military) rank (*keep step*), i.e. (fig.) to *conform* to virtue and piety:—walk (orderly).

4749. στολή **stŏlē**, *stol-ay';* from 4724; *equipment*, i.e. (spec.) a "*stole*" or long-fitting *gown* (as a mark of dignity):—long clothing (garment), (long) robe.

4750. στόμα **stŏma**, *stom'-a;* prob. strengthened from a presumed der. of the base of 5114; the *mouth* (as if a *gash* in the face); by impl. *language* (and its relations); fig. an *opening* (in the earth); spec. the *front* or *edge* (of a weapon):—edge, face, mouth.

4751. στόμαχος **stŏmachŏs**, *stom'-akh-os;* from 4750; an *orifice* (the *gullet*), i.e. (spec.) the "*stomach*":—stomach.

4752. στρατεία **stratĕia**, *strat-i'-ah;* from 4754; military *service*, i.e. (fig.) the apostolic *career* (as one of hardship and danger):—warfare.

4753. στράτευμα **stratĕuma**, *strat'-yoo-mah;* from 4754; an *armament*, i.e. (by impl.) a body of *troops* (more or less extensive or systematic):—army, soldier, man of war.

4754. στρατεύομαι **stratĕuŏmai**, *strat-yoo'-om-ahee;* mid. from the base of 4756; to *serve* in a military campaign; fig. to *execute the apostolate* (with its arduous duties and functions), to *contend* with carnal inclinations:—soldier, (go to) war (-fare).

4755. στρατηγός **stratēgŏs**, *strat-ay-gos';* from the base of 4756 and 71 or 2233; a *general*, i.e. (by impl. or anal.) a (military) *governor* (*prætor*), the *chief* (*præfect*) of the (Levitical) temple-wardens:—captain, magistrate.

4756. στρατιά **stratia**, *strat-ee'-ah;* fem. of a der. of στρατός **stratŏs** (an *army;* from the base of 4766, as *encamped*); *camp-likeness*, i.e. an *army*, i.e. (fig.) the *angels*, the celestial *luminaries:*—host.

4757. στρατιώτης **stratiōtēs**, *strat-ee-o'-tace;* from a presumed der. of the same as 4756; a *camper-out*, i.e. a (common) *warrior* (lit. or fig.):—soldier.

4758. στρατολογέω **stratŏlŏgĕō**, *strat-ol-og-eh'-o;* from a comp. of the base of 4756 and 3004 (in its orig. sense); to *gather* (or *select*) as a *warrior*, i.e. *enlist* in the army:—choose to be a soldier.

4759. στρατοπεδάρχης **stratŏpĕdarchēs**, *strat-op-ed-ar'-khace;* from 4760 and 757; a *ruler of an army*, i.e. (spec.) a Prætorian *præfect:*—captain of the guard.

4760. στρατόπεδον **stratŏpĕdŏn**, *strat-op'-ed-on;* from the base of 4756 and the same as 3977; a *camping-ground*, i.e. (by impl.) a body of *troops:*—army.

4761. στρεβλόω **strĕblŏō**, *streb-lŏ'-o;* from a der. of 4762; to *wrench*, i.e. (spec.) to *torture* (by the rack), but only fig. to *pervert:*—wrest.

4762. στρέφω **strĕphō**, *stref'-o;* strengthened from the base of 5157; to *twist*, i.e. *turn* quite around or *reverse* (lit. or fig.):—convert, turn (again, back again, self, self about).

4763. στρηνιάω **strēniaō**, *stray-nee-ah'-o;* from a presumed der. of 4764; to *be luxurious:*—live deliciously.

4764. στρῆνος **strēnŏs**, *stray'-nos;* akin to 4731; a "*straining*", "*strenuousness*" or "strength", i.e. (fig.) *luxury* (*voluptuousness*):—delicacy.

4765. στρουθίον **strŏuthiŏn**, *stroo-thee'-on;* dimin. of στρουθός **strŏuthŏs** (a *sparrow*); a *little sparrow:*—sparrow.

4766. στρώννυμι **strōnnumi**, *strone'-noo-mee;* or simpler

στρωννύω **strōnnuō**, *strone-noo'-o;* prol. from a still simpler

στρόω **strŏō**, *strŏ'-o* (used only as an alt. in certain tenses; prob. akin to 4731 through the idea of *positing*); to "*strew*", i.e. *spread* (as a carpet or couch):—make bed, furnish, spread, strew.

4767. στυγνητός **stugnētŏs**, *stoog-nay-tos';* from a der. of an obsol. appar. prim. στύγω **stugō** (to *hate*); *hated*, i.e. *odious:*—hateful.

4768. στυγνάζω **stugnazō**, *stoog-nad'-zo;* from the same as 4767; to *render gloomy*, i.e. (by impl.) *glower* (*be overcast* with clouds, or *sombreness* of speech):—lower, be sad.

4769. στύλος **stulŏs**, *stoo'-los;* from στύω **stuō** (to *stiffen;* prop. akin to the base of 2476); a *post* ("*style*"), i.e. (fig.) *support:*—pillar.

4770. Στωϊκός **Stōïkŏs**, *sto-ik-os';* from 4745; a "*Stoïc*" (as occupying a particular porch in Athens), i.e. adherent of a certain philosophy:—Stoick.

4771. σύ **su**, *soo;* the pers. pron. of the sec. pers. sing.; *thou:*—thou. See also 4571, 4671, 4675; and for the plur. 5209, 5210, 5213, 5216.

4772. συγγένεια **suggĕnĕia**, *soong-ghen'-i-ah;* from 4773; *relationship*, i.e. (concr.) *relatives:*—kindred.

4773. συγγενής **suggĕnēs**, *soong-ghen-ace';* from 4862 and 1085; a *relative* (by blood); by extens. a fellow *countryman:*—cousin, kin (-sfolk, -sman).

4774. συγγνώμη **suggnōmē**, *soong-gno'-may;* from a comp. of 4862 and 1097; *fellow knowledge*, i.e. *concession:*—permission.

4775. συγκάθημαι **sugkathēmai**, *soong-kath'-ay-mahee;* from 4862 and 2521; to *seat oneself* in company *with:*—sit with.

4776. συγκαθίζω **sugkathizō**, *soong-kath-id'-zo;* from 4862 and 2523; to *give* (or *take*) *a seat* in company *with:*—(make) sit (down) together.

4777. συγκακοπαθέω **sugkakŏpathĕō**, *soong-kak-op-ath-eh'-o;* from 4862 and 2553; to *suffer hardship* in company *with:*—be partaker of afflictions.

4778. συγκακουχέω **sugkakŏuchĕō**, *soong-kak-oo-kheh'-o;* from 4862 and 2558; to *maltreat* in company *with*, i.e. (pass.) *endure persecution together:*—suffer affliction with.

4779. συγκαλέω **sugkalĕō**, *soong-kal-eh'-o;* from 4862 and 2564; to *convoke:*—call together.

4780. συγκαλύπτω **sugkaluptō**, *soong-kal-oop'-to;* from 4862 and 2572; to *conceal altogether:*—cover.

4781. συγκάμπτω **sugkamptō**, *soong-kamp'-to;* from 4862 and 2578; to *bend together*, i.e. (fig.) to *afflict:*—bow down.

4782. συγκαταβαίνω **sugkatabainō**, *soong-kat-ab-ah'ee-no;* from 4862 and 2597; to *descend* in company *with:*—go down with.

4783. συγκατάθεσις **sugkatathĕsis**, *soong-kat-ath'-es-is;* from 4784; a *deposition* (of sentiment) in company *with*, i.e. (fig.) *accord* with:—agreement.

4784. συγκατατίθεμαι **sugkatatithĕmai**, *soong-kat-at-ith'-em-ahee;* mid. from 4862 and 2698; to *deposit* (one's vote or opinion) in company *with*, i.e. (fig.) to *accord* with:—consent.

4785. συγκαταψηφίζω **sugkatapsēphizō**, *soong-kat-aps-ay-fid'-zo;* from 4862 and a comp. of 2596 and 5585; to *count down* in company *with*, i.e. *enroll among:*—number with.

4786. συγκεράννυμι **sugkĕrannumi**, *soong-ker-an'-noo-mee;* from 4862 and 2767; to *commingle*, i.e. (fig.) to *combine* or *assimilate:*—mix with, temper together.

4787. συγκινέω **sugkinĕō**, *soong-kin-eh'-o;* from 4682 and 2795; to *move together*, i.e. (spec.) to *excite* as a mass (to sedition):—stir up.

4788. συγκλείω **sugklĕiō**, *soong-kli'-o;* from 4862 and 2808; to *shut together*, i.e. *include* or (fig.) *embrace* in a common subjection to:—conclude, inclose, shut up.

4789. συγκληρονόμος **sugklērŏnŏmŏs**, *soong-klay-ron-om'-os;* from 4862 and 2818; a *co-heir*, i.e. (by anal.) *participant in common:*—fellow (joint) -heir, heir together, heir with.

4790. συγκοινωνέω **sugkŏinōnĕō**, *soong-koy-no-neh'-o;* from 4862 and 2841; to *share* in company *with*, i.e. *co-participate* in:—communicate (have fellowship) with, be partaker of.

4791. συγκοινωνός **sugkŏinōnŏs**, *soong-koy-no-nos';* from 4862 and 2844; a *co-participant:*—companion, partake (-r, -r with).

4792. συγκομίζω **sugkŏmizō**, *soong-kom-id'-zo;* from 4862 and 2865; to *convey together*, i.e. *collect* or *bear* away in company *with* others:—carry.

4793. συγκρίνω **sugkrinō**, *soong-kree'-no;* from 4862 and 2919; to *judge* of one thing in connection *with* another, i.e. *combine* (spiritual ideas with appropriate expressions) or *collate* (one person with another by way of contrast or resemblance):—compare among (with).

4794. συγκύπτω **sugkuptō**, *soong-koop'-to;* from 4862 and 2955; to *stoop altogether*, i.e. *be completely overcome* by:—bow together.

4795. συγκυρία **sugkuria**, *soong-koo-ree'-ah;* from a comp. of 4862 and κυρέω **kurĕō** (to *light* or *happen;* from the base of 2962); *concurrence*, i.e. *accident:*—chance.

4796. συγχαίρω **sugchairō**, *soong-khah'ee-ro;* from 4862 and 5463; to *sympathize in gladness, congratulate:*—rejoice in (with).

4797. συγχέω **sugchĕō**, *soong-kheh'-o;* or

συγχύνω **sugchunō**, *soong-khoo'-no;* from 4862 and χέω **chĕō** (to *pour*) or its alt.; to *commingle* promiscuously, i.e. (fig.) to *throw* (an assembly) *into disorder*, to *perplex* (the mind):—confound, confuse, stir up, be in an uproar.

4798. συγχράομαι **sugchraŏmai**, *soong-khrah'-om-ahee;* from 4862 and 5530; to *use jointly*, i.e. (by impl.) to *hold intercourse in common:*—have dealings with.

4799. σύγχυσις **sugchusis**, *soong'-khoo-sis;* from 4797; *commixture*, i.e. (fig.) riotous *disturbance:*—confusion.

4800. συζάω **suzaō**, *sood-zah'-o;* from 4862 and 2198; to continue to *live* in common *with*, i.e. *co-survive* (lit. or fig.):—live with.

4801. συζεύγνυμι **suzĕugnumi**, *sood-zyoog'-noo-mee;* from 4862 and the base of 2201; to *yoke together*, i.e. (fig.) *conjoin* (in marriage):—join together.

4802. συζητέω **suzētĕō**, *sood-zay-teh'-o;* from 4862 and 2212; to investigate *jointly*, i.e. *discuss, controvert, cavil:*—dispute (with), enquire, question (with), reason (together).

4803. συζήτησις **suzētēsis**, *sood-zay'-tay-sis;* from 4802; *mutual questioning*, i.e. *discussion:*—disputation (-ting), reasoning.

4804. συζητητής **suzētētēs**, *sood-zay-tay-tace';* from 4802; a *disputant*, i.e. *sophist:*—disputer.

4805. σύζυγος **suzugŏs**, *sood'-zoo-gos;* from 4801; *co-yoked*, i.e. (fig.) as noun, a *colleague;* prob. rather as prop. name; *Syzygus*, a Chr.:—yokefellow.

4806. συζωοποιέω **suzōŏpŏiĕō**, *sood-zo-op-oy-eh'-o;* from 4862 and 2227; to *reanimate conjointly* with (fig.):—quicken together with.

4807. συκάμινος **sukaminŏs**, *soo-kam'-ee-nos;* of Heb. or. [8256] in imitation of 4809; a *sycamore-fig* tree:—sycamine tree.

4808. συκῆ **sukē**, *soo-kay';* from 4810; a *fig-tree:*—fig tree.

4809. συκομωραία **sukŏmōraia**, *soo-kom-o-rah'-yah;* from 4810 and μόρον **mŏrŏn** (the *mul-*

berry); the "*sycamore*"-fig tree:—sycamore tree. Comp. 4807.

4810. **σῦκον sukŏn**, *soo'-kon;* appar. a prim. word; a *fig:*—fig.

4811. **συκοφαντέω sukŏphantĕō**, *soo-kof-an-teh'-o;* from a comp. of 4810 and a der. of 5316; to *be a fig-informer* (reporter of the law forbidding the exportation of figs from Greece), "*sycophant*", i.e. (gen. and by extens.) to *defraud* (*exact* unlawfully, *extort*):—accuse falsely, take by false accusation.

4812. **συλαγωγέω sulagōgĕō**, *soo-lag-ogue-eh'-o;* from the base of 4813 and (the redupl. form of) 71; to *lead* away as *booty*, i.e. (fig.) *seduce:*—spoil.

4813. **συλάω sulaō**, *soo-lah'-o;* from a der. of **σύλλω sullō** (to *strip;* prob. akin to 138; comp. 4661); to *despoil:*—rob.

4814. **συλλαλέω sullalĕō**, *sool-lal-eh'-o;* from 4862 and 2980; to *talk together*, i.e. *converse:*—commune (confer, talk) with, speak among.

4815. **συλλαμβάνω sullambanō**, *sool-lam-ban'-o;* from 4862 and 2983; to *clasp*, i.e. *seize* (*arrest, capture*); spec. to *conceive* (lit. or fig.); by impl. to *aid:*—catch, conceive, help, take.

4816. **συλλέγω sullĕgō**, *sool-leg'-o;* from 4862 and 3004 in its orig. sense; to *collect:*—gather (together, up).

4817. **συλλογίζομαι sullŏgizŏmai**, *sool-log-id'-zom-ahee;* from 4862 and 3049; to *reckon together* (with oneself), i.e. *deliberate:*—reason with.

4818. **συλλυπέω sullupĕō**, *sool-loop-eh'-o;* from 4862 and 3076; to *afflict jointly*, i.e. (pass.) *sorrow at* (on account of) some one:—be grieved.

4819. **συμβαίνω, sumbainō**, *soom-bah'ee-no;* from 4862 and the base of 939; to *walk* (fig. *transpire*) *together*, i.e. *concur* (*take place*):—be (-fall), happen (unto).

4820. **συμβάλλω sumballō**, *soom-bal'-lo;* from 4862 and 906; to *combine*, i.e. (in speaking) to *converse, consult, dispute*, (mentally) to *consider*, (by impl.) to *aid*, (personally) to *join, attack:*—confer, encounter, help, make, meet with, ponder.

4821. **συμβασιλεύω sumbasilĕuō**, *soom-bas-il-yoo'-o;* from 4862 and 936; to *be co-regent* (fig.):—reign with.

4822. **συμβιβάζω sumbibazō**, *soom-bib-ad'-zo;* from 4862 and **βιβάζω bibazō** (to *force;* caus. [by redupl.] of the base of 939); to *drive together*, i.e. *unite* (in association or affection), (mentally) to *infer, show, teach:*—compact, assuredly gather, instruct, knit together, prove.

4823. **συμβουλεύω sumbŏulĕuō**, *soom-bool-yoo'-o;* from 4862 and 1011; to *give* (or *take*) *advice jointly*, i.e. *recommend, deliberate* or *determine:*—consult, (give, take) counsel (together).

4824. **συμβούλιον sumbŏuliŏn**, *soom-boo'-lee-on;* neut. of a presumed der. of 4825; *advisement;* spec. a *deliberative* body, i.e. the provincial *assessors* or lay-court:—consultation, counsel, council.

4825. **σύμβουλος sumbŏulŏs**, *soom'-boo-los;* from 4862 and 1012; a *consultor*, i.e. *adviser:*—counsellor.

4826. **Συμεών Sumĕōn**, *soom-eh-one';* from the same as 4613; *Symeon* (i.e. *Shimon*), the name of five Isr.:—Simeon, Simon.

4827. **συμμαθητής summathētēs**, *soom-math-ay-tace';* from a comp. of 4862 and 3129; a *co-learner* (of Christianity):—fellowdisciple.

4828. **συμμαρτυρέω summarturĕō**, *soom-mar-too-reh'-o;* from 4862 and 3140; to *testify jointly*, i.e. *corroborate* by (concurrent) evidence:—testify unto, (also) bear witness (with).

4829. **συμμερίζομαι summĕrizŏmai**, *soom-mer-id'-zom-ahee;* mid. from 4862 and 3307; to *share jointly*, i.e. *participate* in:—be partaker with.

4830. **συμμέτοχος summĕtŏchŏs**, *soom-met'-okh-os;* from 4862 and 3353; a *co-participant:*—partaker.

4831. **συμμιμητής summimētēs**, *soom-mim-ay-tace';* from a presumed comp. of 4862 and 3401; a *co-imitator*, i.e. *fellow votary:*—follower together.

4832. **συμμορφός summŏrphŏs**, *soom-mor-fos';* from 4862 and 3444; *jointly formed*, i.e. (fig.) *similar:*—conformed to, fashioned like unto.

4833. **συμμορφόω summŏrphŏō**, *soom-mor-fŏ'-o;* from 4832; to *render like*, i.e. (fig.) to *assimilate:*—make conformable unto.

4834. **συμπαθέω sumpathĕō**, *soom-path-eh'-o;* from 4835; to *feel* "*sympathy*" with, i.e. (by impl.) to *commiserate:*—have compassion, be touched with a feeling of.

4835. **συμπαθής sumpathēs**, *soom-path-ace';* from 4841; *having a fellow-feeling* ("*sympathetic*"), i.e. (by impl.) *mutually commiserative;*—having compassion one of another.

4836. **συμπαραγίνομαι sumparaginŏmai**, *soom-par-ag-in'-om-ahee;* from 4862 and 3854; to *be present together*, i.e. to *convene;* by impl. to *appear in aid:*—come together, stand with.

4837. **συμπαρακαλέω sumparakalĕō**, *soom-par-ak-al-eh'-o;* from 4862 and 3870; to *console jointly:*—comfort together.

4838. **συμπαραλαμβάνω sumparalambanō**, *soom-par-al-am-ban'-o;* from 4862 and 3880; to *take along in company:*—take with.

4839. **συμπαραμένω sumparamĕnō**, *soom-par-am-en'-o;* from 4862 and 3887; to *remain in company*, i.e. *still live:*—continue with.

4840. **συμπάρειμι sumparĕimi**, *soom-par'-i-mee;* from 4862 and 3918; to *be at hand together*, i.e. *now present:*—be here present with.

4841. **συμπάσχω sumpaschō**, *soom-pas'-kho;* from 4862 and 3958 (includ. its alt.); to *experience pain jointly* or of the *same kind* (spec. *persecution;* to "*sympathize*"):—suffer with.

4842. **συμπέμπω sumpĕmpō**, *soom-pem'-po;* from 4862 and 3992; to *despatch in company:*—send with.

4843. **συμπεριλαμβάνω sumpĕrilambanō**, *soom-per-ee-lam-ban'-o;* from 4862 and a comp. of 4012 and 2983; to *take by inclosing altogether*, i.e. *earnestly throw the arms about one:*—embrace.

4844. **συμπίνω sumpinō**, *soom-pee'-no;* from 4862 and 4095; to *partake a beverage in company:*—drink with.

4845. **συμπληρόω sumplērŏō**, *soom-play-rŏ'-o;* from 4862 and 4137; to *implenish completely*, i.e. (of space) to *swamp* (a boat), or (of time) to *accomplish* (pass. be *complete*):—(fully) come, fill up.

4846. **συμπνίγω sumpnigō**, *soom-pnee'-go;* from 4862 and 4155; to *strangle completely*, i.e. (lit.) to *drown*, or (fig.) to *crowd:*—choke, throng.

4847. **συμπολίτης sumpŏlitēs**, *soom-pol-ee'-tace;* from 4862 and 4177; a *native of the same town*, i.e. (fig.) *co-religionist* (*fellow-Christian*):—fellow-citizen.

4848. **συμπορεύομαι sumpŏrĕuŏmai**, *soom-por-yoo'-om-ahee;* from 4862 and 4198; to *journey together;* by impl. to *assemble:*—go with, resort.

4849. **συμπόσιον sumpŏsiŏn**, *soom-pos'-ee-on;* neut. of a der. of the alt. of 4844; a *drinking*-party ("*symposium*"), i.e. (by extens.) a *room* of guests:—company.

4850. **συμπρεσβύτερος sumprĕsbutĕrŏs**, *soom-pres-boo'-ter-os;* from 4862 and 4245; a *co-presbyter:*—presbyter, also an elder.

συμφάγω sumphagō. See 4906.

4851. **συμφέρω sumphĕrō**, *soom-fer'-o;* from 4862 and 5342 (includ. its alt.); to *bear together* (*contribute*), i.e. (lit.) to *collect*, or (fig.) to *conduce;* espec. (neut. part. as noun) *advantage:*—be better for, bring together, be expedient (for), be good, (be) profit (-able for).

4852. **σύμφημι sumphēmi**, *soom'-fay-mee;* from 4862 and 5346; to *say jointly*, i.e. *assent to:*—consent unto.

4853. **συμφυλέτης sumphulĕtēs**, *soom-foo-let'-ace;* from 4862 and a der. of 5443; a *co-tribesman*, i.e. *native of the same country:*—countryman.

4854. **σύμφυτος sumphutŏs**, *soom'-foo-tos;* from 4862 and a der. of 5453; *grown* along *with* (*connate*), i.e. (fig.) closely *united* to:—planted together.

4855. **συμφύω sumphuō**, *soom-foo'-o;* from 4862 and 5453; pass. to *grow jointly:*—spring up with.

4856. **συμφωνέω sumphōnĕō**, *soom-fo-neh'-o;* from 4859; to be *harmonious*, i.e. (fig.) to *accord* (*be suitable, concur*) or *stipulate* (by compact):—agree (together, with).

4857. **συμφώνησις sumphōnēsis**, *soom-fo'-nay-sis;* from 4856; *accordance:*—concord.

4858. **συμφωνία sumphōnia**, *soom-fo-nee'-ah;* from 4859; *unison* of sound ("*symphony*"), i.e. a *concert* of instruments (harmonious *note*):—music.

4859. **σύμφωνος sumphōnŏs**, *soom'-fo-nos;* from 4862 and 5456; *sounding together* (*alike*), i.e. (fig.) *accordant* (neut. as noun, *agreement*):—consent.

4860. **συμψηφίζω sumpsēphizō**, *soom-psay-fid'-zo;* from 4862 and 5585; to *compute jointly:*—reckon.

4861. **σύμψυχος sumpsuchŏs**, *soom'-psoo-khos;* from 4862 and 5590; *co-spirited*, i.e. *similar in sentiment:*—like-minded.

4862. **σύν sun**, *soon;* a prim. prep. denoting *union; with* or *together* (but much closer than 3326 or 3844), i.e. by association, companionship, process, resemblance, possession, instrumentality, addition etc.:—beside, with. In comp. it has similar applications, includ. *completeness*.

4863. **συνάγω sunagō**, *soon-ag'-o;* from 4862 and 71; to *lead together*, i.e. *collect* or *convene;* spec. to *entertain* (hospitably):— + accompany, assemble (selves, together), bestow, come together, gather (selves together, up, together), lead into, resort, take in.

4864. **συναγωγή sunagōgē**, *soon-ag-o-gay';* from (the redupl. form of) 4863; an *assemblage* of persons; spec. a Jewish "*synagogue*" (the meeting or the place); by anal. a Christian *church:*—assembly, congregation, synagogue.

4865. **συναγωνίζομαι sunagōnizŏmai**, *soon-ag-o-nid'-zom-ahee;* from 4862 and 75; to *struggle* in company *with*, i.e. (fig.) to *be a partner* (*assistant*):—strive together with.

4866. **συναθλέω sunathlĕō**, *soon-ath-leh'-o;* from 4862 and 118; to *wrestle* in company *with*, i.e. (fig.) to *seek jointly:*—labour with, strive together for.

4867. **συναθροίζω sunathrŏizō**, *soon-ath-royd'-zo;* from 4862 and **ἀθροίζω athrŏizō** (to *hoard*); to *convene:*—call (gather) together.

4868. **συναίρω sunairō**, *soon-ah'ee-ro;* from 4862 and 142; to *make up together*, i.e. (fig.) to *compute* (an account):—reckon, take.

4869. **συναιχμάλωτος sunaichmalōtŏs**, *soon-aheekh-mal'-o-tos;* from 4862 and 164; a *co-captive:*—fellowprisoner.

4870. **συνακολουθέω sunakŏlŏuthĕō**, *soon-ak-ol-oo-theh'-o;* from 4862 and 190; to *accompany:*—follow.

4871. **συναλίζω sunalizō**, *soon-al-id'-zo;* from 4862 and **ἁλίζω halizō** (to *throng*); to *accumulate*, i.e. *convene:*—assemble together.

4872. **συναναβαίνω sunanabainō**, *soon-an-ab-ah'ee-no;* from 4862 and 305; to *ascend* in company *with:*—come up with.

4873. **συνανάκειμαι sunanakĕimai**, *soon-an-ak'-i-mahee;* from 4862 and 345; to *recline* in company *with* (at a meal):—sit (down, at the table, together) with (at meat).

4874. **συναναμίγνυμι sunanamignumi**, *soon-an-am-ig'-noo-mee;* from 4862 and a comp. of 303 and 3396; to *mix up together*, i.e. (fig.) *associate with:*—(have, keep) company (with).

4875. **συναναπαύομαι sunanapauŏmai**, *soon-an-ap-ŏw'-om-ahee;* mid. from 4862 and 373; to *recruit oneself* in company *with:*—refresh with.

4876. **συναντάω sunantaō**, *soon-an-tah'-o;* from 4862 and a der. of 473; to *meet with;* fig. to *occur:*—befall, meet.

4877. **συνάντησις sunantēsis**, *soon-an'-tay-sis;* from *4876;* a *meeting with:*—meet.

4878. **συναντιλαμβάνομαι sunantilambanŏmai**, *soon-an-tee-lam-ban'-om-ahee;* from *4862* and *482;* to *take* hold of *opposite together*, i.e. *co-operate* (*assist*):—help.

4879. **συναπάγω sunapagō**, *soon-ap-ag'-o;* from *4862* and *520;* to *take off together*, i.e. *transport with* (*seduce*, pass. *yield*):—carry (lead) away with, condescend.

4880. **συναποθνήσκω sunapŏthnēskō**, *soon-ap-oth-nace'-ko;* from *4862* and *599;* to *decease* (lit.) in company *with*, or (fig.) similarly *to:*—be dead (die) with.

4881. **συναπόλλυμι sunapŏllumi**, *soon-ap-ol'-loo-mee;* from *4862* and *622;* to *destroy* (mid. or pass. *be slain*) in company *with:*—perish with.

4882. **συναποστέλλω sunapŏstĕllō**, *soon-ap-os-tel'-lo;* from *4862* and *649;* to *despatch* (on an errand) in company *with:*—send with.

4883. **συναρμολογέω sunarmŏlŏgĕō**, *soon-ar-mol-og-eh'-o;* from *4862* and a der. of a comp. of *719* and *3004* (in its orig. sense of *laying*); to *render close-jointed together*, i.e. *organize compactly:*—be fitly framed (joined) together.

4884. **συναρπάζω sunarpazō**, *soon-ar-pad'-zo;* from *4862* and *726;* to *snatch together*, i.e. *seize:*—catch.

4885. **συναυξάνω sunauxanō**, *soon-ŏwx-an'-o;* from *4862* and *837;* to *increase* (*grow up*) *together:*—grow together.

4886. **σύνδεσμος sundĕsmŏs**, *soon'-des-mos;* from *4862* and *1199;* a *joint tie*, i.e. *ligament*, (fig.) *uniting principle, control:*—band, bond.

4887. **συνδέω sundĕō**, *soon-deh'-o;* from *4862* and *1210;* to *bind with*, i.e. (pass.) *be a fellow-prisoner* (fig.):—be bound with.

4888. **συνδοξάζω sundŏxazō**, *soon-dox-ad'-zo;* from *4862* and *1392;* to *exalt* to dignity in company (i.e. *similarly*) *with:*—glorify together.

4889. **σύνδουλος sundŏulŏs**, *soon'-doo-los;* from *4862* and *1401;* a *co-slave*, i.e. *servitor* or *ministrant of the same master* (human or divine):—fellowservant.

συνδρέμω sundrĕmō. See *4936*.

4890. **συνδρομή sundrŏmē**, *soon-drom-ay';* from (the alt. of) *4936;* a *running together*, i.e. (riotous) *concourse:*—run together.

4891. **συνεγείρω sunĕgĕirō**, *soon-eg-i'-ro;* from *4862* and *1453;* to *rouse* (from death) in company *with*, i.e. (fig.) to *revivify* (spiritually) in resemblance to:—raise up together, rise with.

4892. **συνέδριον sunĕdriŏn**, *soon-ed'-ree-on;* neut of a presumed der. of a comp. of *4862* and the base of *1476;* a *joint session*, i.e. (spec.) the Jewish *Sanhedrim;* by anal. a subordinate *tribunal:*—council.

4893. **συνείδησις sunĕidēsis**, *soon-i'-day-sis;* from a prol. form of *4894;* *co-perception*, i.e. moral *consciousness:*—conscience.

4894. **συνείδω sunĕidō**, *soon-i'-do;* from *4862* and *1492;* to *see completely;* used (like its prim.) only in two past tenses, respectively mean. to *understand* or *become aware*, and to *be conscious* or (clandestinely) *informed of:*—consider, know, be privy, be ware of.

4895. **σύνειμι sunĕimi**, *soon'-i-mee;* from *4862* and *1510* (includ. its various inflections); to *be* in company *with*, i.e. *present* at the time:—be with.

4896. **σύνειμι sunĕimi**, *soon'-i-mee;* from *4862* and **εἶμι ĕimi** (to *go*); to *assemble:*—gather together.

4897. **συνεισέρχομαι sunĕisĕrchŏmai**, *soon-ice-er'-khom-ahee;* from *4862* and *1525;* to *enter* in company *with:*—go in with, go with into.

4898. **συνέκδημος sunĕkdēmŏs**, *soon-ek'-day-mos;* from *4862* and the base of *1553;* a *co-absentee* from home, i.e. *fellow-traveller:*—companion in travel, travel with.

4899. **συνεκλεκτός sunĕklĕktŏs**, *soon-ek-lek-tos';* from a comp. of *4862* and *1586;* *chosen* in company *with*, i.e. *co-elect* (*fellow Christian*):—elected together with.

4900. **συνελαύνω sunĕlaunō**, *soon-el-ow'-no;* from *4862* and *1643;* to *drive together*, i.e. (fig.) *exhort* (to reconciliation):— + set at one again.

4901. **συνεπιμαρτυρέω sunĕpimarturĕō**, *soon-ep-ee-mar-too-reh'-o;* from *4862* and *1957;* to *testify further jointly*, i.e. *unite in adding evidence:*—also bear witness.

4902. **συνέπομαι sunĕpŏmai**, *soon-ep'-om-ahee;* mid. from *4862* and a prim. **ἕπω hĕpō** (to *follow*); to *attend* (*travel*) in company *with:*—accompany.

4903. **συνεργέω sunĕrgĕō**, *soon-erg-eh'-o;* from *4904;* to *be a fellow-worker*, i.e. *co-operate:*—help (work) with, work (-er) together.

4904. **συνεργός sunĕrgŏs**, *soon-er-gos';* from a presumed comp. of *4862* and the base of *2041;* a *co-laborer*, i.e. *coadjutor:*—companion in labour, (fellow-) helper (-labourer, -worker), labourer together with, workfellow.

4905. **συνέρχομαι sunĕrchŏmai**, *soon-er'-khom-ahee;* from *4862* and *2064;* to *convene, depart* in company *with, associate* with, or (spec.) *cohabit* (conjugally):—accompany, assemble (with), come (together), come (company, go) with, resort.

4906. **συνεσθίω sunĕsthiō**, *soon-es-thee'-o;* from *4862* and *2068* (includ. its alt.); to *take food* in company *with:*—eat with.

4907. **σύνεσις sunĕsis**, *soon'-es-is;* from *4920;* a mental *putting together*, i.e. *intelligence* or (concr.) the *intellect:*—knowledge, understanding.

4908. **συνετός sunĕtŏs**, *soon-et'-os;* from *4920;* mentally *put* (or *putting*) *together*, i.e. *sagacious:*—prudent. Comp. *5429*.

4909. **συνευδοκέω sunĕudŏkĕō**, *soon-yoo-dok-eh'-o;* from *4862* and *2106;* to *think well of in common*, i.e. *assent to, feel gratified with:*—allow, assent, be pleased, have pleasure.

4910. **συνευωχέω sunĕuōchĕō**, *soon-yoo-o-kheh'-o;* from *4862* and a der. of a presumed comp. of *2095* and a der. of *2192* (mean. to *be in good condition*, i.e. [by impl.] to *fare well*, or *feast*); to *entertain* sumptuously in company *with*, i.e. (mid. or pass.) to *revel together:*—feast with.

4911. **συνεφίστημι sunĕphistēmi**, *soon-ef-is'-tay-mee;* from *4862* and *2186;* to *stand up together*, i.e. to *resist* (or *assault*) *jointly:*—rise up together.

4912. **συνέχω sunĕchō**, *soon-ekh'-o;* from *4862* and *2192;* to *hold together*, i.e. to *compress* (the ears, with a crowd or siege) or *arrest* (a prisoner); fig. to *compel, perplex, afflict, preoccupy:*—constrain, hold, keep in, press, lie sick of, stop, be in a strait, straiten, be taken with, throng.

4913. **συνήδομαι sunēdŏmai**, *soon-ay'-dom-ahee;* mid. from *4862* and the base of *2237;* to *rejoice* in *with* oneself, i.e. *feel satisfaction* concerning:—delight.

4914. **συνήθεια sunēthĕia**, *soon-ay'-thi-ah;* from a comp. of *4862* and *2239;* *mutual habituation*, i.e. *usage:*—custom.

4915. **συνηλικιώτης sunēlikiōtēs**, *soon-ay-lik-ee-o'-tace;* from *4862* and a der. of *2244;* a *co-aged* person, i.e. *alike* in years:—equal,

4916. **συνθάπτω sunthaptō**, *soon-thap'-to;* from *4862* and *2290;* to *inter* in company *with*, i.e. (fig.) to *assimilate* spiritually (to Christ by a sepulture as to sin):—bury with.

4917. **συνθλάω sunthlaō**, *soon-thlah'-o;* from *4862* and **θλάω thlaō** (to *crush*); to *dash together*, i.e. *shatter:*—break.

4918. **συνθλίβω sunthlibō**, *soon-thlee'-bo;* from *4862* and *2346;* to *compress*, i.e. *crowd* on all sides:—throng.

4919. **συνθρύπτω sunthruptō**, *soon-throop'-to;* from *4862* and **θρύπτω thruptō** (to *crumble*); to *crush together*, i.e. (fig.) to *dispirit:*—break.

4920. **συνίημι suniēmi**, *soon-ee'-ay-mee;* from *4862* and **ἵημι hiēmi** (to *send*); to *put together*, i.e. (mentally) to *comprehend;* by impl. to *act piously:*—consider, understand, be wise.

4921. **συνιστάω sunistaō**, *soon-is-tah'-o;* or (strengthened)

συνιστάνω sunistanō, *soon-is-tan'-o;* or

συνίστημι sunistēmi, *soon-is'-tay-mee;* from *4862* and *2476* (includ. its collat. forms); to *set together*, i.e. (by impl.) to *introduce* (favorably), or (fig.) to *exhibit;* intrans. to *stand near*, or (fig.) to *constitute:*—approve, commend, consist, make, stand (with).

4922. **συνοδεύω sunŏdĕuō**, *soon-od-yoo'-o;* from *4862* and *3593;* to *travel* in company *with:*—journey with.

4923. **συνοδία sunŏdia**, *soon-od-ee'-ah;* from a comp. of *4862* and *3598* ("*synod*"); *companionship* on a journey, i.e. (by impl.) a *caravan:*—company.

4924. **συνοικέω sunŏikĕō**, *soon-oy-keh'-o;* from *4862* and *3611;* to *reside together* (as a family):—dwell together.

4925. **συνοικοδομέω sunŏikŏdŏmĕō**, *soon-oy-kod-om-eh'-o;* from *4862* and *3618;* to *construct*, i.e. (pass.) to *compose* (in company with other Christians, fig.):—build together.

4926. **συνομιλέω sunŏmilĕō**, *soon-om-il-eh'-o;* from *4862* and *3656;* to *converse* mutually:—talk with.

4927. **συνομορέω sunŏmŏrĕō**, *soon-om-or-eh'-o;* from *4862* and a der. of a comp. of the base of *3674* and the base of *3725;* to *border together*, i.e. *adjoin:*—join hard.

4928. **συνόχη sunŏchē**, *soon-okh-ay';* from *4912;* *restraint*, i.e. (fig.) *anxiety:*—anguish, distress.

4929. **συντάσσω suntassō**, *soon-tas-so;* from *4862* and *5021;* to *arrange jointly*, i.e. (fig.) to *direct:*—appoint.

4930. **συντέλεια suntĕlĕia**, *soon-tel'-i-ah;* from *4931;* *entire completion*, i.e. *consummation* (of a dispensation):—end.

4931. **συντελέω suntĕlĕō**, *soon-tel-eh'-o;* from *4862* and *5055;* to *complete entirely;* gen. to *execute* (lit. or fig.):—end, finish, fulfil, make.

4932. **συντέμνω suntĕmnō**, *soon-tem'-no;* from *4862* and the base of *5114;* to *contract* by cutting, i.e. (fig.) *do concisely* (*speedily*):—(cut) short.

4933. **συντηρέω suntērĕō**, *soon-tay-reh'-o;* from *4862* and *5083;* to *keep* closely *together*, i.e. (by impl.) to *conserve* (from ruin); ment. to *remember* (and *obey*):—keep, observe, preserve.

4934. **συντίθεμαι suntithĕmai**, *soon-tith'-em-ahee;* mid. from *4862* and *5087;* to *place jointly*, i.e. (fig.) to *consent* (*bargain, stipulate*), *concur:*—agree assent, covenant.

4935. **συντόμως suntŏmōs**, *soon-tom'-oce;* adv. from a der. of *4932;* *concisely* (*briefly*):—a few words.

4936. **συντρέχω suntrĕchō**, *soon-trekh'-o;* from *4862* and *5143* (includ. its alt.); to *rush together* (hastily *assemble*) or *headlong* (fig.):—run (together, with).

4937. **συντρίβω suntribō**, *soon-tree'-bo;* from *4862* and the base of *5147;* to *crush completely*, i.e. to *shatter* (lit. or fig.):—break (in pieces), broken to shivers (+ -hearted), bruise.

4938. **σύντριμμα suntrimma**, *soon-trim'-mah;* from *4937;* *concussion* or utter *fracture* (prop. concr.), i.e. complete *ruin:*—destruction.

4939. **σύντροφος suntrŏphŏs**, *soon'-trof-os;* from *4862* and *5162* (in a pass. sense); a *fellow-nursling*, i.e. *comrade:*—brought up with.

4940. **συντυγχάνω suntugchanō**, *soon-toong-khan'-o;* from *4862* and *5177;* to *chance together*, i.e. *meet* with (*reach*):—come at.

4941. **Συντύχη Suntuchē**, *soon-too'-khay;* from *4940;* an *accident;* *Syntyche*, a Chr. female:—Syntyche.

4942. **συνυποκρίνομαι sunupŏkrinŏmai**, *soon-oo-pok-rin'-om-ahee;* from *4862* and *5271;* to *act hypocritically* in concert *with:*—dissemble with.

4943. **συνυπουργέω sunupŏurgĕō**, *soon-oop-oorg-eh'-o;* from *4862* and a der. of a comp. of *5259* and the base of *2041;* to *be a co-auxiliary*, i.e. *assist:*—help together.

4944. **συνωδίνω sunōdinō**, *soon-o-dee'-no;* from 4862 and 5605; to *have* (parturition) *pangs* in company (concert, simultaneously) *with*, i.e. (fig.) to *sympathize* (in expectation of relief from suffering):—travail in pain together.

4945. **συνωμοσία sunōmŏsia**, *soon-o-mos-ee'-ah,* from a comp. of 4862 and 3660; a *swearing together*, i.e. (by impl.) a *plot:*—conspiracy.

4946. **Συράκουσαι Surakŏusai**, *soo-rak'-oo-sahee;* plur. of uncert. der.; *Syracusæ*, the capital of Sicily:—Syracuse.

4947. **Συρία Suria**, *soo-ree'-ah;* prob. of Heb. or. [6865]; *Syria* (i.e. *Tsyria* or *Tyre*), a region of Asia:—Syria.

4948. **Σύρος Surŏs**, *soo'-ros;* from the same as 4947; a *Syran* (i.e. prob. *Tyrian*), a native of Syria:—Syrian.

4949. **Συροφοίνισσα Surŏphŏinissa**, *soo-rof-oy'-nis-sah;* fem. of a comp. of 4948 and the same as 5403; a *Syro-phœnician* woman, i.e. a female native of Phœnicia in Syria:—Syrophenician.

4950. **σύρτις surtis**, *soor'-tis;* from 4951; a *shoal* (from the sand *drawn* thither by the waves), i.e. the *Syrtis* Major or great bay on the N. coast of Africa:—quicksands.

4951. **σύρω surō**, *soo'-ro;* prob. akin to 138; to *trail:*—drag, draw, hale.

4952. **συσπαράσσω susparassō**, *soos-par-as'-so;* from 4862 and 4682; to *rend completely*, i.e. (by anal.) to *convulse* violently:—throw down.

4953. **σύσσημον sussēmŏn**, *soos'-say-mon;* neut. of a comp. of 4862 and the base of 4591; a *sign in common*, i.e. preconcerted *signal:*—token.

4954. **σύσσωμος sussōmŏs**, *soos'-so-mos;* from 4862 and 4983; *of a joint body*, i.e. (fig.) a *fellow-member* of the Christian community:—of the same body.

4955. **συστασιαστής sustasiastēs**, *soos-tas-ee-as-tace';* from a comp. of 4862 and a der. of 4714; a *fellow-insurgent:*—make insurrection with.

4956. **συστατικός sustatikŏs**, *soos-tat-ee-kos';* from a der. of 4921; *introductory*, i.e. *recommendatory:*—of commendation.

4957. **συσταυρόω sustaurŏō**, *soos-tow-rŏ'-o;* from 4862 and 4717; to *impale* in company *with* (lit. or fig.):—crucify with.

4958. **συστέλλω sustĕllō**, *soos-tel'-lo;* from 4862 and 4724; to *send* (*draw*) *together*, i.e. *enwrap* (*enshroud* a corpse for burial), *contract* (an interval):—short, wind up.

4959. **συστενάζω sustĕnazō**, *soos-ten-ad'-zo;* from 4862 and 4727; to *moan jointly*, i.e. (fig.) *experience a common calamity:*—groan together.

4960. **συστοιχέω sustŏichĕō**, *soos-toy-kheh'-o;* from 4862 and 4748; to *file together* (as soldiers in ranks), i.e. (fig.) to *correspond* to:—answer to.

4961. **συστρατιώτης sustratiōtēs**, *soos-trat-ee-o'-tace;* from 4862 and 4757; a *co-campaigner*, i.e. (fig.) an *associate* in Christian toil:—fellowsoldier.

4962. **συστρέφω sustrĕphō**, *soos-tref'-o;* from 4862 and 4762; to *twist together*, i.e. *collect* (a bundle, a crowd):—gather.

4963. **συστροφή sustrŏphē**, *soos-trof-ay';* from 4962; a *twisting together*, i.e. (fig.) a secret *coalition*, riotous *crowd:*— + band together, concourse.

4964. **συσχηματίζω suschēmatizō**, *soos-khay-mat-id'-zo;* from 4862 and a der. of 4976; to *fashion alike*, i.e. *conform* to the same pattern (fig.):—conform to, fashion self according to.

4965. **Συχάρ Suchar**, *soo-khar';* of Heb. or. [7941]; *Sychar* (i.e. *Shekar*), a place in Pal.:—Sychar.

4966. **Συχέμ Suchĕm**, *soo-khem';* of Heb. or. [7927]; *Sychem* (i.e. *Shekem*), the name of a Canaanite and of a place in Pal.:—Sychem.

4967. **σφαγή sphagē**, *sfag-ay';* from 4969; *butchery* (of animals for food or sacrifice, or [fig.] of men [*destruction*]):—slaughter.

4968. **σφάγιον sphagiŏn**, *sfag'-ee-on;* neut. of a der. of 4967; a *victim* (in sacrifice):—slain beast.

4969. **σφάζω sphazō**, *sfad'-zo;* a prim. verb; to *butcher* (espec. an animal for food or in sacrifice) or (gen.) to *slaughter*, or (spec.) to *maim* (violently):—kill, slay, wound.

4970. **σφόδρα sphŏdra**, *sfod'-rah;* neut. plur. of **σφοδρός sphŏdrŏs** (*violent;* of uncert. der.) as adv.; *vehemently*, i.e. *in a high degree, much:*—exceeding (-ly), greatly, sore, very.

4971. **σφοδρῶς sphŏdrōs**, *sfod-roce';* adv. from the same as 4970; *very much:*—exceedingly.

4972. **σφραγίζω sphragizō**, *sfrag-id'-zo;* from 4973; to *stamp* (with a signet or private mark) for security or preservation (lit. or fig.); by impl. to *keep secret*, to *attest:*—(set a, set to) seal up.

4973. **σφραγίς sphragis**, *sfrag-ece';* prob. strengthened from 5420; a *signet* (as *fencing* in or protecting from misappropriation); by impl. the *stamp* impressed (as a mark of privacy, or genuineness), lit. or fig.:—seal.

4974. **σφυρόν sphurŏn**, *sfoo-ron';* neut. of a presumed der. prob. of the same as **σφαῖρα sphaira** (a *ball*, "*sphere*"; comp. the fem. **σφῦρα sphura**, a *hammer*); the *ankle* (as *globular*):—ancle bone.

4975. **σχεδόν schĕdŏn**, *skhed-on';* neut. of a presumed der. of the alt. of 2192 as adv.; *nigh*, i.e. *nearly:*—almost.

σχέω schĕō. See 2192.

4976. **σχῆμα schēma**, *skhay'-mah;* from the alt. of 2192; a *figure* (as a *mode* or *circumstance*), i.e. (by impl.) external *condition:*—fashion.

4977. **σχίζω schizō**, *skhid'-zo;* appar. a prim. verb; to *split* or *sever* (lit. or fig.):—break, divide, open, rend, make a rent.

4978. **σχίσμα schisma**, *skhis'-mah;* from 4977; a *split* or *gap* ("*schism*"), lit. or fig.:—division, rent, schism.

4979. **σχοινίον schŏiniŏn**, *skhoy-nee'-on;* dimin. of **σχοῖνος schŏinŏs** (a *rush* or *flag*-plant; of uncert. der.); a *rushlet*, i.e. *grass-withe* or *tie* (gen.):—small cord, rope.

4980. **σχολάζω schŏlazō**, *skhol-ad'-zo;* from 4981; to *take a holiday*, i.e. *be at leisure* for (by impl. *devote oneself* wholly to); fig. to *be vacant* (of a house):—empty, give self.

4981. **σχολή schŏlē**, *skhol-ay';* prob. fem. of a presumed der. of the alt. of 2192; prop. *loitering* (as a *withholding* of oneself from work) or *leisure*, i.e. (by impl.) a "*school*" (as *vacation* from phys. employment):—school.

4982. **σώζω sōzō**, *sode'-zo;* from a prim. **σῶς sōs** (contr. for obsol. **σάος saŏs**, "*safe*"); to *save*, i.e. *deliver* or *protect* (lit. or fig.):—heal, preserve, save (self), do well, be (make) whole.

4983. **σῶμα sōma**, *so'-mah;* from 4982; the *body* (as a *sound* whole), used in a very wide application, lit. or fig.:—bodily, body, slave.

4984. **σωματικός sōmatikŏs**, *so-mat-ee-kos';* from 4983; *corporeal* or *physical:*—bodily.

4985. **σωματικῶς sōmatikōs**, *so-mat-ee-koce';* adv. from 4984; *corporeally* or *physically:*—bodily.

4986. **Σώπατρος Sōpatrŏs**, *so'-pat-ros;* from the base of 4982 and 3962; *of a safe father; Sopatrus*, a Chr.:—Sopater. Comp. 4989.

4987. **σωρεύω sōrĕuō**, *sore-yoo'-o;* from another form of 4673; to *pile* up (lit. or fig.):—heap, load.

4988. **Σωσθένης Sōsthĕnēs**, *soce-then'-ace;* from the base of 4982 and that of 4599; *of safe strength; Sosthenes*, a Chr.:—Sosthenes.

4989. **Σωσίπατρος Sōsipatrŏs**, *so-sip'-at-ros;* prol. for 4986; *Sosipatrus*, a Chr.:—Sosipater.

4990. **σωτήρ sōtēr**, *so-tare';* from 4982; a *deliverer*, i.e. God or Christ:—saviour.

4991. **σωτηρία sōtēria**, *so-tay-ree'-ah;* fem. of a der. of 4990 as (prop. abstr.) noun; *rescue* or *safety* (phys. or mor.):—deliver, health, salvation, save, saving.

4992. **σωτήριον sōtēriŏn**, *so-tay'-ree-on;* neut. of the same as 4991 as (prop. concr.) noun; *defender* or (by impl.) *defence:*—salvation.

4993. **σωφρονέω sōphrŏnĕō**, *so-fron-eh'-o;* from 4998; to *be of sound mind*, i.e. *sane*, (fig.) *moderate:*—be in right mind, be sober (minded), soberly.

4994. **σωφρονίζω sōphrŏnizō**, *so-fron-id'-zo;* from 4998; to *make of sound mind*, i.e. (fig.) to *discipline* or *correct:*—teach to be sober.

4995. **σωφρονισμός sōphrŏnismŏs**, *so-fron-is-mos';* from 4994; *discipline*, i.e. *self-control:*—sound mind.

4996. **σωφρόνως sōphrŏnōs**, *so-fron'-oce;* adv. from 4998; *with sound mind*, i.e. *moderately:*—soberly.

4997. **σωφροσύνη sōphrŏsunē**, *so-fros-oo'-nay;* from 4998; *soundness of mind*, i.e. (lit.) *sanity* or (fig.) *self-control:*—soberness, sobriety.

4998. **σώφρων sōphrōn**, *so'-frone;* from the base of 4982 and that of 5424; *safe* (*sound*) *in mind*, i.e. *self-controlled* (*moderate* as to opinion or passion):—discreet, sober, temperate.

T

τά ta. See 3588.

4999. **Ταβέρναι Tabĕrnai**, *tab-er'-nahee;* plur. of Lat. or.; *huts* or *wooden-walled* buildings; *Tabernæ:*—taverns.

5000. **Ταβιθά Tabitha**, *tab-ee-thah';* of Chald. or. [comp. 6646]; *the gazelle; Tabitha* (i.e. *Tabjetha*), a Chr. female:—Tabitha.

5001. **τάγμα tagma**, *tag'-mah;* from 5021; something orderly in *arrangement* (a *troop*), i.e. (fig.) a *series* or *succession:*—order.

5002. **τακτός taktŏs**, *tak-tos';* from 5021; *arranged*, i.e. *appointed* or *stated:*—set.

5003. **ταλαιπωρέω talaipōrĕō**, *tal-ahee-po-reh'-o,* from 5005; to *be wretched*, i.e. *realize* one's own *misery:*—be afflicted.

5004. **ταλαιπωρία talaipōria**, *tal-ahee-po-ree'-ah;* from 5005; *wretchedness*, i.e. *calamity:*—misery.

5005. **ταλαίπωρος talaipōrŏs**, *tal-ah'ee-po-ros;* from the base of 5007 and a der. of the base of 3984; *enduring trial*, i.e. *miserable:*—wretched.

5006. **ταλαντιαῖος talantiaiŏs**, *tal-an-tee-ah'-yos;* from 5007; *talent-like* in weight:—weight of a talent.

5007. **τάλαντον talantŏn**, *tal'-an-ton;* neut. of a presumed der. of the orig. form of **τλάω tlaō** (to *bear;* equiv. to 5342); a *balance* (as *supporting* weights), i.e. (by impl.) a certain *weight* (and thence a *coin* or rather *sum* of money) or "*talent*":—talent.

5008. **ταλιθά talitha**, *tal-ee-thah';* of Chald. or. [comp. 2924]; *the fresh*, i.e. young girl; *talitha* (*O maiden*):—talitha.

5009. **ταμεῖον tamĕiŏn**, *tam-i'-on;* neut. contr. of a presumed der. of **ταμίας tamias** (a *dispenser* or *distributor;* akin to **τέμνω tĕmnō**, to *cut*); a *dispensary* or *magazine*, i.e. a chamber on the ground-floor or interior of an Oriental house (gen. used for *storage* or *privacy*, a spot for retirement):—secret chamber, closet, storehouse.

τανῦν tanun. See 3568.

5010. **τάξις taxis**, *tax'-is;* from 5021; regular *arrangement*, i.e. (in time) fixed *succession* (of rank or character), official *dignity:*—order.

5011. **ταπεινός tapĕinŏs**, *tap-i-nos';* of uncert. der.; *depressed*, i.e. (fig.) *humiliated* (in circumstances or disposition):—base, cast down, humble, of low degree (estate), lowly.

5012. **ταπεινοφροσύνη tapĕinŏphrŏsunē**, *tap-i-nof-ros-oo'-nay;* from a comp. of 5011 and the base of 5424; *humiliation of mind*, i.e. *modesty:*—humbleness of mind, humility (of mind), lowliness (of mind).

5013. **ταπεινόω tapĕinŏō**, *tap-i-nŏ'-o;* from 5011; to *depress;* fig. to *humiliate* (in condition or heart):—abase, bring low, humble (self).

5014. **ταπείνωσις tapĕinōsis**, *tap-i'-no-sis;* from 5013; *depression* (in rank or feeling):—humiliation, be made low, low estate, vile.

5015. **ταράσσω tarassō**, *tar-as'-so;* of uncert. affin.; to *stir* or *agitate* (*roil* water):—trouble.

5016. **ταραχή tarachē**, *tar-akh-ay';* fem. from *5015; disturbance*, i.e. (of water) *roiling*, or (of a mob) *sedition:*—trouble (-ing).

5017. **τάραχος tarachŏs**, *tar'-akh-os;* masc. from *5015*; a *disturbance*, i.e. (popular) *tumult:*—stir.

5018. **Ταρσεύς Tarsĕus**, *tar-syoos';* from *5019*; a *Tarsean*, i.e. native of Tarsus:—of Tarsus.

5019. **Ταρσός Tarsŏs**, *tar-sos';* perh. the same as **ταρσός tarsŏs** (a *flat* basket); *Tarsus*, a place in Asia Minor:—Tarsus.

5020. **ταρταρόω tartarŏō**, *tar-tar-ŏ'-o;* from **Τάρταρος Tartarŏs** (the deepest *abyss* of Hades); to *incarcerate* in eternal torment:—cast down to hell.

5021. **τάσσω tassō**, *tas'-so;* a prol. form of a prim. verb (which latter appears only in certain tenses); to *arrange* in an orderly manner, i.e. *assign* or *dispose* (to a certain position or lot):—addict, appoint, determine, ordain, set.

5022. **ταῦρος taurŏs**, *tŏw'-ros;* appar. a prim. word [comp. 8450, "*steer*"]; a *bullock:*—bull, ox.

5023. **ταῦτα tauta**, *tŏw'-tah;* nom. or acc. neut. plur. of *3778; these* things:— + afterward, follow, + hereafter, × him, the same, so, such, that, then, these, they, this, those, thus.

5024. **ταὐτά tauta**, *tow-tah';* neut. plur. of *3588* and *846* as adv.; in *the same* way:—even thus, (manner) like, so.

5025. **ταύταις tautais**, *tŏw'-taheece;* and **ταύτας tautas**, *tŏw'-tas;* dat. and acc. fem. plur. respectively of *3778*; (*to* or *with* or *by*, etc.) *these:*—hence, that, then, these, those.

5026. **ταύτῃ tautē**, *tŏw'-tay;* and **ταύτην tautēn**, *tŏw'-tane;* and **ταύτης tautēs**, *tŏw'-tace;* dat., acc. and gen. respectively of the fem. sing. of *3778*; (*towards* or *of*) *this:*—her, + hereof, it, that, + thereby, the (same), this (same).

5027. **ταφή taphē**, *taf-ay';* fem. from *2290; burial* (the act):— × bury.

5028. **τάφος taphŏs**, *taf'-os;* masc. from *2290*; a *grave* (the place of interment):—sepulchre, tomb.

5029. **τάχα tacha**, *takh'-ah;* as if neut. plur. of *5036* (adv.); *shortly*, i.e. (fig.) *possibly:*—peradventure (-haps).

5030. **ταχέως tachĕōs**, *takh-eh'-oce;* adv. from *5036; briefly*, i.e. (in time) *speedily*, or (in manner) *rapidly:*—hastily, quickly, shortly, soon, suddenly.

5031. **ταχινός tachinŏs**, *takh-ee-nos';* from *5034; curt*, i.e. *impending:*—shortly, swift.

5032. **τάχιον tachiŏn**, *takh'-ee-on;* neut. sing. of the compar. of *5036* (as adv.); *more swiftly*, i.e. (in manner) *more rapidly*, or (in time) *more speedily:*—out [run], quickly, shortly, sooner.

5033. **τάχιστα tachista**, *takh'-is-tah;* neut. plur. of the superl. of *5036* (as adv.); *most quickly*, i.e. (with *5613* pref.) *as soon* as possible:— + with all speed.

5034. **τάχος tachŏs**, *takh'-os;* from the same as *5036*; a *brief* space (of time), i.e. (with *1722* pref.) in *haste:*— + quickly, + shortly, + speedily.

5035. **ταχύ tachu**, *takh-oo';* neut. sing. of *5036* (as adv.); *shortly*, i.e. *without delay, soon*, or (by surprise) *suddenly*, or (by impl. of ease) *readily:*—lightly, quickly.

5036. **ταχύς tachus**, *takh-oos';* of uncert. affin.; *fleet*, i.e. (fig.) *prompt* or *ready:*—swift.

5037. **τέ tĕ**, *teh;* a prim. particle (enclitic) of connection or addition; *both* or *also* (prop. as correl. of *2532*):—also, and, both, even, then, whether. Often used in comp., usually as the latter part.

5038. **τεῖχος tĕichŏs**, *ti'-khos;* akin to the base of *5088*; a *wall* (as *formative* of a house):—wall.

5039. **τεκμήριον tĕkmēriŏn**, *tek-may'-ree-on;* neut. of a presumed der. of **τεκμάρ tĕkmar** (a *goal* or fixed *limit*); a *token* (as *defining* a fact), i.e. *criterion* of certainty:—infallible proof.

5040. **τεκνίον tĕkniŏn**, *tek-nee'-on;* dimin. of *5043*; an *infant*, i.e. (plur. fig.) *darlings* (Christian *converts*):—little children.

5041. **τεκνογονέω tĕknŏgŏnĕō**, *tek-nog-on-eh'-o;* from a comp. of *5043* and the base of *1096*; to *be a child-bearer*, i.e. *parent* (*mother*):—bear children.

5042. **τεκνογονία tĕknŏgŏnia**, *tek-nog-on-ee'-ah;* from the same as *5041; childbirth* (*parentage*), i.e. (by impl.) *maternity* (the performance of *maternal duties*):—childbearing.

5043. **τέκνον tĕknŏn**, *tek'-non;* from the base of *5088*; a *child* (as *produced*):—child, daughter, son.

5044. **τεκνοτροφέω tĕknŏtrŏphĕō**, *tek-not-rof-eh'-o;* from a comp. of *5043* and *5142*; to *be a child-rearer*, i.e. *fulfil* the duties of *a female parent:*—bring up children.

5045. **τέκτων tĕktōn**, *tek'-tone;* from the base of *5088*; an *artificer* (as *producer* of fabrics), i.e. (spec.) a *craftsman* in wood:—carpenter.

5046. **τέλειος tĕlĕiŏs**, *tel'-i-os;* from *5056; complete* (in various applications of labor, growth, mental and moral character, etc.); neut. (as noun, with *3588*) *completeness:*—of full age, man, perfect.

5047. **τελειότης tĕlĕiŏtēs**, *tel-i-ot'-ace;* from *5046*; (the state) *completeness* (ment. or mor.):—perfection (-ness).

5048. **τελειόω tĕlĕiŏō**, *tel-i-ŏ'-o;* from *5046*; to *complete*, i.e. (lit.) *accomplish*, or (fig.) *consummate* (in character):—consecrate, finish, fulfil, (make) perfect.

5049. **τελείως tĕlĕiōs**, *tel-i'-oce;* adv. from *5046; completely*, i.e. (of hope) *without wavering:*—to the end.

5050. **τελείωσις tĕlĕiōsis**, *tel-i'-o-sis;* from *5448*; (the act) *completion*, i.e. (of prophecy) *verification*, or (of expiation) *absolution:*—perfection, performance.

5051. **τελειωτής tĕlĕiōtēs**, *tel-i-o-tace';* from *5048*; a *completer*, i.e. *consummater:*—finisher.

5052. **τελεσφορέω tĕlĕsphŏrĕō**, *tel-es-for-eh'-o;* from a comp. of *5056* and *5342*; to *be a bearer to completion* (maturity), i.e. to *ripen* fruit (fig.):—bring fruit to perfection.

5053. **τελευτάω tĕlĕutaō**, *tel-yoo-tah'-o;* from a presumed der. of *5055*; to *finish* life (by impl. of *979*), i.e. *expire* (*demise*):—be dead, decease, die.

5054. **τελευτή tĕlĕutē**, *tel-yoo-tay';* from *5053; decease:*—death.

5055. **τελέω tĕlĕō**, *tel-eh'-o;* from *5056*; to *end*, i.e. *complete, execute, conclude, discharge* (a debt):—accomplish, make an end, expire, fill up, finish, go over, pay, perform.

5056. **τέλος tĕlŏs**, *tel'-os;* from a prim. **τέλλω tĕllō** (to *set out* for a definite point or *goal*); prop. the point aimed at as a *limit*, i.e. (by impl.) the *conclusion* of an act or state (*termination* [lit., fig. or indef.], *result* [immed., ultimate or prophetic], *purpose*); spec. an *impost* or *levy* (as *paid*):— + continual, custom, end (-ing), finally, uttermost. Comp. *5411*.

5057. **τελώνης tĕlōnēs**, *tel-o'-nace;* from *5056* and *5608*; a *tax-farmer*, i.e. *collector* of *public revenue:*—publican.

5058. **τελώνιον tĕlōniŏn**, *tel-o'-nee-on;* neut. of a presumed der. of *5057*; a *tax-gatherer's* place of business:—receipt of custom.

5059. **τέρας tĕras**, *ter'-as;* of uncert. affin.; a *prodigy* or *omen:*—wonder.

5060. **Τέρτιος Tĕrtiŏs**, *ter'-tee-os;* of Lat. or.; *third; Tertius*, a Chr.:—Tertius.

5061. **Τέρτυλλος Tĕrtullŏs**, *ter'-tool-los;* of uncert. der.; *Tertullus*, a Rom.:—Tertullus.

τέσσαρα tĕssara. See *5064*.

5062. **τεσσαράκοντα tĕssarakŏnta**, *tes-sar-ak'-on-tah;* the decade of *5064; forty:*—forty.

5063. **τεσσαρακονταετής tĕssarakŏntaĕtēs**, *tes-sar-ak-on-tah-et-ace';* from *5062* and *2094; of forty years* of age:—(+ full, of) forty years (old).

5064. **τέσσαρες tĕssarĕs**, *tes'-sar-es;* neut. **τέσσαρα tĕssara**, *tes'-sar-ah;* a plur. number; *four:*—four.

5065. **τεσσαρεσκαιδέκατος tĕssarĕskaidĕkatŏs**, *tes-sar-es-kahee-dek'-at-os;* from *5064* and *2532* and *1182; fourteenth:*—fourteenth.

5066. **τεταρταῖος tĕtartaiŏs**, *tet-ar-tah'-yos;* from *5064*; pertaining to the *fourth* day:—four days.

5067. **τέταρτος tĕtartŏs**, *tet'-ar-tos;* ord. from *5064; fourth:*—four (-th).

5068. **τετράγωνος tĕtragōnŏs**, *tet-rag'-o-nos;* from *5064* and *1137; four-cornered*, i.e. *square:*—foursquare.

5069. **τετράδιον tĕtradiŏn**, *tet-rad'-ee-on;* neut. of a presumed der. of **τέτρας tĕtras** (a *tetrad*; from *5064*); a *quaternion* or squad (picket) of four Rom. soldiers:—quaternion.

5070. **τετρακισχίλιοι tĕtrakischiliŏi**, *tet-rak-is-khil'-ee-oy;* from the mult. adv. of *5064* and *5507; four times a thousand:*—four thousand.

5071. **τετρακόσιοι tĕtrakŏsiŏi**, *tet-rak-os'-ee-oy;* neut. **τετρακόσια tĕtrakŏsia**, *tet-rak-os'-ee-ah;* plur. from *5064* and *1540; four hundred:*—four hundred.

5072. **τετράμηνον tĕtramēnŏn**, *tet-ram'-ay-non;* neut. of a comp. of *5064* and *3376*; a *four months'* space:—four months.

5073. **τετραπλόος tĕtraplŏŏs**, *tet-rap-lŏ'-os;* from *5064* and a der. of the base of *4118; quadruple:*—fourfold.

5074. **τετράπους tĕtrapŏus**, *tet-rap'-ooce;* from *5064* and *4228*; a *quadruped:*—fourfooted beast.

5075. **τετραρχέω tĕtrarchĕō**, *tet-rar-khch'-o;* from *5076*; to *be a tetrarch:*—(be) tetrarch.

5076. **τετράρχης tĕtrarchēs**, *tet-rar'-khace;* from *5064* and *757*; the *ruler of a fourth* part of a country ("*tetrarch*"):—tetrarch.

τεύχω tĕuchō. See *5177*.

5077. **τεφρόω tĕphrŏō**, *tef-rŏ'-o;* from **τέφρα tephra** (*ashes*); to *incinerate*, i.e. *consume:*—turn to ashes.

5078. **τέχνη tĕchnē**, *tekh'-nay;* from the base of *5088; art* (as *productive*), i.e. (spec.) a *trade*, or (gen.) *skill:*—art, craft, occupation.

5079. **τεχνίτης tĕchnitēs**, *tekh-nee'-tace;* from *5078*; an *artisan*; fig. a *founder* (*Creator*):—builder, craftsman.

5080. **τήκω tēkō**, *tay'-ko;* appar. a prim. verb; to *liquefy:*—melt.

5081. **τηλαυγῶς tēlaugōs**, *tay-lŏw-goce';* adv. from a comp. of a der. of *5056* and *827*; in a *far-shining* manner, i.e. *plainly:*—clearly.

5082. **τηλικοῦτος tēlikŏutŏs**, *tay-lik-oo'-tos;* fem. **τηλικαύτη tēlikautē**, *tay-lik-ŏw'-tay;* from a comp. of *3588* with *2245* and *3778; such as this*, i.e. (in [fig.] magnitude) *so vast:*—so great, so mighty.

5083. **τηρέω tērĕō**, *tay-reh'-o;* from **τηρός tērŏs** (a *watch*; perh. akin to *2334*); to *guard* (from *loss* or *injury*, prop. by keeping *the eye* upon; and thus differing from *5442*, which is prop. to *prevent* escaping; and from *2892*, which implies a *fortress* or full military lines of apparatus), i.e. to *note* (a prophecy; fig. to *fulfil* a command); by impl. to *detain* (in custody; fig. to *maintain*); by extens. to *withhold* (for personal ends; fig. to *keep unmarried*):—hold fast, keep (-er), (ob-, pre-, re) serve, watch.

5084. **τήρησις tērēsis**, *tay'-ray-sis;* from *5083*; a *watching*, i.e. (fig.) *observance*, or (concr.) a *prison:*—hold.

τῇ tē, τήν tēn, τῆς tēs. See *3588*.

5085. **Τιβεριάς Tibĕrias**, *tib-er-ee-as';* from *5086*; *Tiberias*, the name of a town and a lake in Pal.:—Tiberias.

5086. **Τιβέριος Tibĕriŏs**, *tib-er'-ee-os;* of Lat. or.; prob. *pertaining to the* river *Tiberis* or *Tiber*; *Tiberius*, a Rom. emperor:—Tiberius.

5087. **τίθημι tithēmi**, *tith'-ay-mee;* a prol. form of a prim. **θέω thĕō**, *theh'-o* (which is used only as alt. in cert. tenses); to *place* (in the widest application, lit. and fig.; prop. in a passive or horizontal posture, and thus different from *2476*, which prop. denotes an upright and active position, while *2749* is prop. reflexive and utterly prostrate):— + advise, appoint, bow, commit, conceive, give, × kneel down, lay (aside, down, up), make, ordain, purpose, put, set (forth), settle, sink down.

5088. τίκτω **tiktō**, *tik'-to;* a strengthened form of a prim. τέκω **tĕkō**, *tek'-o* (which is used only as alt. in certain tenses); to *produce* (from seed, as a mother, a plant, the earth, etc.), lit. or fig.:—bear, be born, bring forth, be delivered, be in travail.

5089. τίλλω **tillō**, *til'-lo;* perh. akin to the alt. of 138, and thus to 4951; to *pull* off:—pluck.

5090. Τίμαιος **Timaiŏs**, *tim'-ah-yos;* prob. of Chald. or. [comp. 2931]; *Timæus* (i.e. *Timay*), an Isr.:—Timæus.

5091. τιμάω **timaō**, *tim-ah'-o;* from 5093; to *prize*, i.e. *fix* a *valuation* upon; by impl. to *revere:*—honour, value.

5092. τιμή **timē**, *tee-may';* from 5099; a *value*, i.e. *money* paid, or (concr. and collect.) *valuables;* by anal. *esteem* (espec. of the highest degree), or the *dignity* itself:—honour, precious, price, some.

5093. τίμιος **timiŏs**, *tim'-ee-os;* includ. the comp.

τιμιώτερος **timiōtĕrŏs**, *tim-ee-o'-ter-os;* and the superl.

τιμιώτατος **timiōtatŏs**, *tim-ee-o'-tat-os;* from 5092; *valuable*, i.e. (obj.) *costly*, or (subj.) *honored, esteemed*, or (fig.) *beloved:*—dear, honourable, (more, most) precious, had in reputation.

5094. τιμιότης **timiŏtēs**, *tim-ee-ot'-ace;* from 5093; *expensiveness*, i.e. (by impl.) *magnificence:*—costliness.

5095. Τιμόθεος **Timŏthĕŏs**, *tee-moth'-eh-os;* from 5092 and 2316; *dear to God; Timotheus*, a Chr.:—Timotheus, Timothy.

5096. Τίμων **Timōn**, *tee'-mone;* from 5092; *valuable; Timon*, a Chr.:—Timon.

5097. τιμωρέω **timōrĕō**, *tim-o-reh'-o;* from a comp. of 5092 and οὖρος **ŏurŏs** (a *guard*); prop. to *protect* one's *honor*, i.e. to *avenge* (*inflict a penalty*):—punish.

5098. τιμωρία **timōria**, *tee-mo-ree'-ah;* from 5097; *vindication*, i.e. (by impl.) a *penalty:*—punishment.

5099. τίνω **tinō**, *tee'-no;* strengthened for a prim.

τίω **tiō**, *tee'-o* (which is only used as an alt. in certain tenses); to *pay* a price, i.e. as a *penalty:*—be punished with.

5100. τὶς **tis**, *tis;* an enclit. indef. pron.; *some* or *any* person or object:—a (kind of), any (man, thing, thing at all), certain (thing), divers, he (every) man, one (× thing), ought, + partly, some (man, -body, -thing, -what), (+ that no-) thing, what (-soever), × wherewith, whom [-soever], whose ([-soever]).

5101. τίς **tis**, *tis;* prob. emphat. of 5100; an interrog. pron., *who, which* or *what* (in direct or indirect questions):—every man, how (much), + no (-ne, thing), what (manner, thing), where ([-by, -fore, -of, -unto, -with, -withal]), whether, which, who (-m, -se), why.

5102. τίτλος **titlŏs**, *tit'-los;* of Lat. or.; a *titulus* or "*title*" (*placard*):—title.

5103. Τίτος **Titŏs**, *tee'-tos*, of Lat. or. but uncert. signif.; *Titus*, a Chr.:—Titus.

τίω **tiō**. See 5099.

τό **tŏ**. See 3588.

5104. τοί **tŏi**, *toy;* prob. for the dat. of 3588; an enclit. particle of *asseveration* by way of contrast; *in sooth:*—[*used only with other particles in comp.*, *as* 2544, 3305, 5105, 5106, etc.]

5105. τοιγαροῦν **tŏigarŏun**, *toy-gar-oon';* from 5104 and 1063 and 3767; *truly for then*, i.e. *consequently:*—there- (where-) fore.

τοίγε **tŏigĕ**. See 2544.

5106. τοίνυν **tŏinun**, *toy'-noon;* from 5104 and 3568; *truly now*, i.e. *accordingly:*—then, therefore.

5107. τοιόσδε **tŏiŏsdĕ**, *toy-os'-deh* (includ. the other inflections); from a der. of 5104 and 1161; *such-like then*, i.e. *so great:*—such.

5108. τοιοῦτος **tŏiŏutŏs**, *toy-oo'-tos* (includ. the other inflections); from 5104 and 3778; *truly this*, i.e. *of this sort* (to denote character or individuality):—like, such (an one).

5109. τοῖχος **tŏichŏs**, *toy'-khos;* another form of 5038; a *wall:*—wall.

5110. τόκος **tŏkŏs**, *tok'-os;* from the base of 5088; *interest* on money loaned (as a *produce*):—usury.

5111. τολμάω **tŏlmaō**, *tol-mah'-o;* from τόλμα **tŏlma** (*boldness;* prob. itself from the base of 5056 through the idea of *extreme* conduct); to *venture* (obj. or in *act;* while 2292 is rather subj. or in *feeling*); by impl. to be *courageous:*—be bold, boldly, dare, durst.

5112. τολμηρότερον **tŏlmērŏtĕrŏn**, *tol-may-rot'-er-on;* neut. of the comp. of a der. of the base of 5111 (as adv.); *more daringly*, i.e. *with greater confidence* than otherwise:—the more boldly.

5113. τολμητής **tŏlmētēs**, *tol-may-tace';* from 5111; a *daring* (*audacious*) man:—presumptuous.

5114. τομώτερος **tŏmōtĕrŏs**, *tom-o'-ter-os;* comp. of a der. of the prim. τέμνω **tĕmnō** (to *cut;* more comprehensive or decisive than 2875, as if by a *single* stroke; whereas that implies repeated blows, like *hacking*); *more keen:*—sharper.

5115. τόξον **tŏxŏn**, *tox'-on;* from the base of 5088; a *bow* (appar. as the simplest fabric):—bow.

5116. τοπάζιον **tŏpaziŏn**, *top-ad'-zee-on;* neut. of a presumed der. (alt.) of τόπαζος **tŏpazŏs** (a "*topaz*"; of uncert. or.); a gem, prob. the *chrysolite:*—topaz.

5117. τόπος **tŏpŏs**, *top'-os;* appar. a prim. word; a *spot* (gen. in *space*, but limited by occupancy; whereas 5561 is a larger but partic. *locality*), i.e. *location* (as a position, home, tract, etc.); fig. *condition, opportunity;* spec. a *scabbard:*—coast, licence, place, × plain, quarter, + rock, room, where.

5118. τοσοῦτος **tŏsŏutŏs**, *tos-oo'-tos;* from τόσος **tŏsŏs** (*so much;* appar. from 3588 and 3739) and 3778 (includ. its variations); so *vast as this*, i.e. *such* (in quantity, amount, number or space):—as large, so great (long, many, much), these many.

5119. τότε **tŏtĕ**, *tot'-eh;* from (the neut. of) 3588 and 3753; *the when*, i.e. *at the time* that (of the past or future, also in consecution):—that time, then.

5120. τοῦ **tŏu**, *too;* prop. the gen. of 3588; sometimes used for 5127; *of this person:*—his.

5121. τοὐναντίον **tŏunantiŏn**, *too-nan-tee'-on;* contr. for the neut. of 3588 and 1726; *on the contrary:*—contrariwise.

5122. τοὔνομα **tŏunŏma**, *too'-no-mah;* contr. for the neut. of 3588 and 3686; *the name* (is):—named.

5123. τουτέστι **tŏutĕsti**, *toot-es'-tee;* contr. for 5124 and 2076; *that is:*—that is (to say).

5124. τοῦτο **tŏutŏ**, *too'-tŏ;* neut. sing. nom. or acc. of 3778; *that* thing:—here [-unto], it, partly, self [-same], so, that (intent), the same, there [-fore, -unto], this, thus, where [-fore].

5125. τούτοις **tŏutŏis**, *too'-toice;* dat. plur. masc. or neut. of 3778; *to* (*for, in, with* or *by*) *these* (persons or things):—such, them, there [-in, -with], these, this, those.

5126. τοῦτον **tŏutŏn**, *too'-ton;* acc. sing. masc. of 3778; *this* (person, as obj. of verb or prep.):—him, the same, that, this.

5127. τούτου **tŏutŏu**, *too'-too;* gen. sing. masc. or neut. of 3778; *of* (*from* or *concerning*) *this* (person or thing):—here [-by], him, it, + such manner of, that, thence [-forth], thereabout, this, thus.

5128. τούτους **tŏutŏus**, *too'-tooce;* acc. plur. masc. of 3778; *these* (persons, as obj. of verb or prep.):—such, them, these, this.

5129. τούτῳ **tŏutōi**, *too'-to;* dat. sing. masc. or neut. of 3778; *to* (*in, with* or *by*) *this* (person or thing):—here [-by, -in], him, one, the same, there [-in], this.

5130. τούτων **tŏutōn**, *too'-tone;* gen. plur. masc. or neut. of 3778; *of* (*from* or *concerning*) *these* (persons or things):—such, their, these (things), they, this sort, those.

5131. τράγος **tragŏs**, *trag'-os;* from the base of 5176; a *he-goat* (as a *gnawer*):—goat.

5132. τράπεζα **trapĕza**, *trap'-ed-zah;* prob. contr. from 5064 and 3979; a *table* or *stool* (as being *four legged*), usually for food (fig. a *meal*); also a *counter* for money (fig. a broker's *office* for loans at interest):—bank, meat, table.

5133. τραπεζίτης **trapĕzitēs**, *trap-ed-zee'-tace;* from 5132; a money-*broker* or *banker:*—exchanger.

5134. τραῦμα **trauma**, *trŏw'-mah;* from the base of τιτρώσκω **titrōskō** (to *wound;* akin to the base of 2352, 5147, 5149, etc.); a *wound:*—wound.

5135. τραυματίζω **traumatizō**, *trŏw-mat-id'-zo;* from 5134; to *inflict a wound:*—wound.

5136. τραχηλίζω **trachēlizō**, *trakh-ay-lid'-zo;* from 5137; to *seize* by *the throat* or *neck*, i.e. to *expose* the *gullet* of a victim for killing (gen. to *lay bare*):—opened.

5137. τράχηλος **trachēlŏs**, *trakh'-ay-los;* prob. from 5143 (through the idea of *mobility*); the *throat* (*neck*), i.e. (fig.) *life:*—neck.

5138. τραχύς **trachus**, *trakh-oos';* perh. strengthened from the base of 4486 (as if *jagged* by rents); *uneven, rocky* (*reefy*):—rock, rough.

5139. Τραχωνῖτις **Trachōnitis**, *trakh-o-nee'-tis;* from a der. of 5138; *rough* district; *Trachonitis*, a region of Syria:—Trachonitis.

5140. τρεῖς **trĕis**, *trice;* neut.

τρία **tria**, *tree'-ah;* a prim. (plur.) number; "*three*":—three.

5141. τρέμω **trĕmō**, *trem'-o;* strengthened from a prim. τρέω **trĕō** (to "*dread*", "*terrify*"); to "*tremble*" or *fear:*—be afraid, trembling.

5142. τρέφω **trĕphō**, *tref'-o;* a prim. verb (prop. θρέφω **thrĕphō;** but perh. strength. from the base of 5157 through the idea of *convolution*); prop. to *stiffen*, i.e. *fatten* (by impl. to *cherish* [with food, etc.], *pamper, rear*):—bring up, feed, nourish.

5143. τρέχω **trĕchō**, *trekh'-o;* appar. a prim. verb (prop. θρέχω **thrĕchō;** comp. 2359); which uses δρέμω **drĕmō**, *drem'-o* (the base of 1408) as alt. in certain tenses; to *run* or *walk hastily* (lit. or fig.):—have course, run.

5144. τριάκοντα **triakŏnta**, *tree-ak'-on-tah;* the decade of 5140; *thirty:*—thirty.

5145. τριακόσιοι **triakŏsiŏi**, *tree-ak-os'-ee-oy;* plur. from 5140 and 1540; *three hundred:*—three hundred.

5146. τρίβολος **tribŏlŏs**, *trib'-ol-os;* from 5140 and 956; prop. a *crow-foot* (*three-pronged* obstruction in war), i.e. (by anal.) a *thorny* plant (*caltrop*):—brier, thistle.

5147. τρίβος **tribŏs**, *tree'-bos;* from τρίβω **tribō** (to "*rub*"; akin to τείρω **tĕirō**, τρύω **truō**, and the base of 5131, 5134); a *rut* or worn *track:*—path.

5148. τριετία **triĕtia**, *tree-et-ee'-ah;* from a comp. of 5140 and 2094; a *three years' period* (*triennium*):—space of three years.

5149. τρίζω **trizō**, *trid'-zo;* appar. a prim. verb; to *creak* (*squeak*), i.e. (by anal.) to *grate* the teeth (in frenzy):—gnash.

5150. τρίμηνον **trimēnŏn**, *trim'-ay-non;* neut. of a comp. of 5140 and 3376 as noun; a *three months'* space:—three months.

5151. τρίς **tris**, *trece;* adv. from 5140; *three times:*—three times, thrice.

5152. τρίστεγον **tristĕgŏn**, *tris'-teg-on;* neut. of a comp. of 5140 and 4721 as noun; a *third roof* (*story*):—third loft.

5153. τρισχίλιοι **trischiliŏi**, *tris-khil'-ee-oy;* from 5151 and 5507; *three times a thousand:*—three thousand.

5154. τρίτος **tritŏs**, *tree'-tos;* ord. from 5140; *third;* neut. (as noun) a *third part*, or (as adv.) a (or the) *third* time, *thirdly:*—third (-ly).

τρίχες **trichĕs**, etc. See 2359.

5155. τρίχινος **trichinŏs**, *trikh'-ee-nos;* from 2359; *hairy*, i.e. made *of hair* (*mohair*):—of hair.

5156. τρόμος **trŏmŏs**, *trom'-os;* from *5141;* a "*trembling*", i.e. quaking with *fear:*— + tremble (-ing).

5157. τροπή **tropē**, *trop-ay';* from an appar. prim. τρέπω **trĕpō** (to *turn*); a *turn* ("trope"), i.e. *revolution* (fig. *variation*):—turning.

5158. τρόπος **trŏpŏs**, *trop'-os;* from the same as *5157;* a *turn*, i.e. (by impl.) *mode* or *style* (espec. with prep. or rel. pref. as adv. *like*); fig. *deportment* or *character:*—(even) as, conversation, [+ like] manner (+ by any) means, way.

5159. τροποφορέω **trŏpŏphŏrĕō**, *trop-of-or-eh'-o;* from *5158* and *5409;* to *endure* one's *habits:*—suffer the manners.

5160. τροφή **trŏphē**, *trof-ay';* from *5142; nourishment* (lit. or fig.); by impl. *rations* (*wages*):—food, meat.

5161. Τρόφιμος **Trŏphimŏs**, *trof'-ee-mos;* from *5160; nutritive; Trophimus*, a Chr.:—Trophimus.

5162. τροφός **trŏphŏs**, *trof-os';* from *5142;* a *nourisher*, i.e. *nurse:*—nurse.

5163. τροχιά **trŏchia**, *trokh-ee-ah';* from *5164;* a *track* (as a wheel-*rut*), i.e. (fig.) a *course* of conduct:—path.

5164. τροχός **trŏchŏs**, *trokh-os';* from *5143;* a *wheel* (as a *runner*), i.e. (fig.) a *circuit* of phys. effects:—course.

5165. τρύβλιον **trubliŏn**, *troob'-lee-on;* neut. of a presumed der. of uncert. affin.; a *bowl:*—dish.

5166. τρυγάω **trugaō**, *troo-gah'-o;* from a der. of τρύγω **trugō** (to *dry*) mean. ripe *fruit* (as if *dry*); to *collect* the vintage:—gather.

5167. τρυγών **trugōn**, *troo-gone';* from τρύζω **truzō** (to *murmur;* akin to *5149*, but denoting a *duller* sound); a *turtle-dove* (as *cooing*):—turtle-dove.

5168. τρυμαλιά **trumalia**, *troo-mal-ee-ah';* from a der. of τρύω **truō** (to *wear* away; akin to the base of *5134*, *5147* and *5176*); an *orifice*, i.e. a needle's *eye:*—eye. Comp. *5169*.

5169. τρύπημα **trupēma**, *troo'-pay-mah;* from a der. of the base of *5168;* an *aperture*, i.e. a needle's *eye:*—eye.

5170. Τρύφαινα **Truphaina**, *troo'-fahee-nah;* from *5172; luxurious; Tryphæna*, a Chr. woman:—Tryphena.

5171. τρυφάω **truphaō**, *troo-fah'-o;* from *5172;* to *indulge in luxury:*—live in pleasure.

5172. τρυφή **truphē**, *troo-fay';* from θρύπτω **thruptō** (to *break* up or [fig.] *enfeeble*, espec. the mind and body by indulgence); *effeminacy*, i.e. *luxury* or *debauchery:*—delicately, riot.

5173. Τρυφῶσα **Truphōsa**, *troo-fo'-sah;* from *5172; luxuriating; Tryphosa*, a Chr. female:—Tryphosa.

5174. Τρωάς **Trōas**, *tro-as';* from Τρός **Trŏs** (a *Trojan*); the *Troad* (or plain of Troy), i.e. *Troas*, a place in Asia Minor:—Troas.

5175. Τρωγύλλιον **Trōgulliŏn**, *tro-gool'-lee-on;* of uncert. der.; *Trogyllium*, a place in Asia Minor:—Trogyllium.

5176. τρώγω **trōgō**, *tro'-go;* prob. strength. from a collat. form of the base of *5134* and *5147* through the idea of *corrosion* or *wear;* or perh. rather of a base of *5167* and *5149* through the idea of a *craunching* sound; to *gnaw* or *chew*, i.e. (gen.) to *eat:*—eat.

5177. τυγχάνω **tugchanō**, *toong-khan'-o;* prob. for an obsol. τύχω **tuchō** (for which the mid. of another alt. τεύχω **tĕuchō** [to *make ready* or *bring to pass*] is used in cert. tenses; akin to the base of *5088* through the idea of *effecting;* prop. to *affect;* or (spec.) to *hit* or *light upon* (as a mark to be reached), i.e. (trans.) to *attain* or *secure* an object or end, or (intrans.) to *happen* (as if *meeting* with); but in the latter application only impers. (with *1487*), i.e. *perchance;* or (pres. part.) as adj. *usual* (as if commonly *met with*, with *3756*, *extraordinary*), neut. (as adv.) *perhaps;* or (with another verb) as adv. by *accident* (*as it were*):—be, chance, enjoy, little, obtain, × refresh . . . self, + special. Comp. *5180*.

5178. τυμπανίζω **tumpanizō**, *toom-pan-id'-zo;* from a der. of *5180* (mean. a *drum*, "*tympanum*"); to stretch on an instrument of *torture* resembling a drum, and thus *beat* to death:—torture.

5179. τύπος **tupŏs**, *too'-pos;* from *5180;* a *die* (as *struck*), i.e. (by impl.) a *stamp* or *scar;* by anal. a *shape*, i.e. a *statue*, (fig.) *style* or *resemblance;* spec. a *sampler* ("*type*"), i.e. a *model* (for imitation) or *instance* (for warning):—en- (ex-) ample, fashion, figure, form, manner, pattern, print.

5180. τύπτω **tuptō**, *toop'-to;* a prim. verb (in a strength. form); to "*thump*", i.e. *cudgel* or *pummel* (prop. with a stick or *bastinado*), but in any case by *repeated* blows; thus differing from *3817* and *3960*, which denote a [usually single] blow with the hand or any instrument, or *4141* with the *fist* [or a *hammer*], or *4474* with the *palm;* as well as from *5177*, an *accidental* collision); by impl. to *punish;* fig. to *offend* (the conscience):—beat, smite, strike, wound.

5181. Τύραννος **Turannŏs**, *too'-ran-nos;* a provincial form of the der. of the base of *2962;* a "*tyrant*"; *Tyrannus*, an Ephesian:—Tyrannus.

5182. τυρβάζω **turbazō**, *toor-bad'-zo;* from τύρβη **turbē** (Lat. *turba*, a *crowd;* akin to *2351*); to *make* "*turbid*", i.e. *disturb:*—trouble.

5183. Τύριος **Turiŏs**, *too'-ree-os;* from *5184;* a *Tyrian*, i.e. inhab. of Tyrus:—of Tyre.

5184. Τύρος **Turŏs**, *too'-ros;* of Heb. or. [6865]; *Tyrus* (i.e. *Tsor*), a place in Pal.:—Tyre.

5185. τυφλός **tuphlŏs**, *toof-los';* from *5187;* *opaque* (as if *smoky*), i.e. (by anal.) *blind* (phys. or ment.):—blind.

5186. τυφλόω **tuphlŏō**, *toof-lŏ'-o;* from *5185;* to *make blind*, i.e. (fig.) to *obscure:*—blind.

5187. τυφόω **tuphŏō**, *toof-ŏ'-o;* from a der. of *5188;* to envelop with *smoke*, i.e. (fig.) to *inflate* with self-conceit:—high-minded, be lifted up with pride, be proud.

5188. τυφώ **tuphō**, *too'-fo;* appar. a prim. verb; to make a *smoke*, i.e. slowly *consume* without flame:—smoke.

5189. τυφωνικός **tuphōnikŏs**, *too-fo-nee-kos';* from a der. of *5188; stormy* (as if *smoky*):—tempestuous.

5190. Τυχικός **Tuchikŏs**, *too-khee-kos';* from a der. of *5177; fortuitous*, i.e. *fortunate; Tychicus*, a Chr.:—Tychicus.

Υ

5191. ὑακίνθινος **huakinthinŏs**, *hoo-ak-in'-thee-nos;* from *5192;* "*hyacinthine*" or "*jacinthine*", i.e. deep *blue:*—jacinth.

5192. ὑάκινθος **huakinthŏs**, *hoo-ak'-in-thos;* of uncert. der.; the "*hyacinth*" or "*jacinth*", i.e. some gem of a deep *blue* color, prob. the *zirkon:*—jacinth.

5193. ὑάλινος **hualinŏs**, *hoo-al'-ee-nos;* from *5194; glassy*, i.e. *transparent:*—of glass.

5194. ὕαλος **hualŏs**, *hoo'-al-os;* perh. from the same as *5205* (as being transparent like *rain*); *glass:*—glass.

5195. ὑβρίζω **hubrizō**, *hoo-brid'-zo;* from *5196;* to *exercise violence*, i.e. *abuse:*—use despitefully, reproach, entreat shamefully (spitefully).

5196. ὕβρις **hubris**, *hoo'-bris;* from *5228; insolence* (as *over*-bearing), i.e. *insult, injury:*—harm, hurt, reproach.

5197. ὑβριστής **hubristēs**, *hoo-bris-tace';* from *5195;* an *insulter*, i.e. *maltreater:*—despiteful, injurious.

5198. ὑγιαίνω **hugiainō**, *hoog-ee-ah'ee-no;* from *5199;* to *have* sound *health*, i.e. *be well* (in body); fig. to be *uncorrupt* (*true* in doctrine):—be in health, (be safe and) sound, (be) whole (-some).

5199. ὑγιής **hugiēs**, *hoog-ee-ace';* from the base of *837; healthy*, i.e. *well* (in body); fig. *true* (in doctrine):—sound, whole.

5200. ὑγρός **hugrŏs**, *hoo-gros';* from the base of *5205; wet* (as if with *rain*), i.e. (by impl.) *sappy* (*fresh*):—green.

5201. ὑδριά **hudria**, *hoo-dree-ah';* from *5204;* a *water-jar*, i.e. *receptacle* for family supply:—waterpot.

5202. ὑδροποτέω **hudrŏpŏtĕō**, *hoo-drop-ot-eh'-o;* from a comp. of *5204* and a der. of *4095;* to *be a water-drinker*, i.e. to *abstain from vinous beverages:*—drink water.

5203. ὑδρωπικός **hudrōpikŏs**, *hoo-dro-pik-os';* from a comp. of *5204* and a der. of *3700* (as if *looking watery*); to be "*dropsical*":—have the dropsy.

5204. ὕδωρ **hudōr**, *hoo'-dore;* gen.
ὕδατος **hudatŏs**, *hoo'-dat-os*, etc.; from the base of *5205; water* (as if *rainy*) lit. or fig.:—water.

5205. ὑετός **huĕtŏs**, *hoo-et-os';* from a prim. ὕω **huō** (to *rain*); *rain*, espec. a *shower:*—rain.

5206. υἱοθεσία **huiŏthĕsia**, *hwee-oth-es-ee'-ah;* from a presumed comp. of *5207* and a der. of *5087;* the *placing* as a *son*, i.e. *adoption* (fig. Chr. *sonship* in respect to God):—adoption (of children, of sons).

5207. υἱός **huiŏs**, *hwee-os';* appar. a prim. word; a "*son*" (sometimes of animals), used very widely of immed., remote or fig. kinship:—child, foal, son.

5208. ὕλη **hulē**, *hoo-lay';* perh. akin to *3586;* a *forest*, i.e. (by impl.) *fuel:*—matter.

5209. ὑμᾶς **humas**, *hoo-mas';* acc. of *5210; you* (as the obj. of a verb or prep.):—ye, you (+ -ward), your (+ own).

5210. ὑμεῖς **humĕis**, *hoo-mice';* irreg. plur. of *4771; you* (as subj. of verb):—ye (yourselves), you.

5211. Ὑμεναῖος **Humĕnaiŏs**, *hoo-men-ah'-yos;* from Ὑμήν **Humēn** (the god of *weddings*); "*hymenæal*"; *Hymenæus*, an opponent of Christianity:—Hymenæus.

5212. ὑμέτερος **humĕtĕrŏs**, *hoo-met'-er-os;* from *5210; yours*, i.e. *pertaining to you:*—your (own).

5213. ὑμῖν **humin**, *hoo-min';* irreg. dat. of *5210;* to (*with* or *by*) *you:*—ye, you, your (-selves).

5214. ὑμνέω **humnĕō**, *hoom-neh'-o;* from *5215;* to *hymn*, i.e. sing a religious ode; by impl. to *celebrate* (God) in song:—sing an hymn (praise unto).

5215. ὕμνος **humnŏs**, *hoom'-nos;* appar. from a simpler (obsol.) form of ὑδέω **hudĕō** (to *celebrate;* prob. akin to *103;* comp. *5567*); a "*hymn*" or religious ode (one of the Psalms):—hymn.

5216. ὑμῶν **humōn**, *hoo-mone';* gen. of *5210; of* (*from* or *concerning*) *you:*—ye, you, your (own, -selves).

5217. ὑπάγω **hupagō**, *hoop-ag'-o;* from *5259* and *71;* to *lead* (oneself) *under*, i.e. *withdraw* or *retire* (as if *sinking* out of sight), lit. or fig.:—depart, get hence, go (a-) way.

5218. ὑπακοή **hupakŏē**, *hoop-ak-ŏ-ay';* from *5219; attentive hearkening*, i.e. (by impl.) *compliance* or *submission:*—obedience, (make) obedient, obey (-ing).

5219. ὑπακούω **hupakŏuō**, *hoop-ak-oo'-o;* from *5259* and *191;* to *hear under* (as a *subordinate*), i.e. to *listen attentively;* by impl. to *heed* or *conform* to a command or authority:—hearken, be obedient to, obey.

5220. ὕπανδρος **hupandrŏs**, *hoop'-an-dros;* from *5259* and *435;* in subjection *under a man*, i.e. a *married* woman:—which hath an husband.

5221. ὑπαντάω **hupantaō**, *hoop-an-tah'-o;* from *5259* and a der. of *473;* to *go opposite* (*meet*) *under* (*quietly*), i.e. to *encounter, fall in with:*—(go to) meet.

5222. ὑπάντησις **hupantēsis**, *hoop-an'-tay-sis;* from *5221;* an *encounter* or *concurrence* (with *1519* for infin., in order to *fall in with*):—meeting.

5223. ὕπαρξις **huparxis**, *hoop'-arx-is;* from *5225; existency* or *proprietorship*, i.e. (concr.) *property, wealth:*—goods, substance.

5224. ὑπάρχοντα **huparchŏnta**, *hoop-ar'-khon-tah;* neut. plur. of pres. part. act. of *5225* as noun; things *extant* or *in hand*, i.e. *property* or *possessions:*—goods, that which one has, things which (one) possesseth, substance, that hast.

5225. ὑπάρχω **huparchō**, *hoop-ar'-kho;* from *5259* and *756;* to *begin under* (*quietly*), i.e. *come into existence* (*be present* or *at hand*); expletively, to *exist* (as copula or subordinate to an adj., part., adv. or prep., or as auxil. to principal verb):—after, behave, live.

5226. ὑπείκω **hupĕikō**, *hoop-i'-ko;* from *5259* and εἴκω **ĕikō** (to *yield*, be "*weak*"); to *surrender:*—submit self.

5227. ὑπεναντίος **hupĕnantiŏs**, *hoop-en-an-tee'-os;* from *5259* and *1727;* *under* (*covertly*) *contrary* to, i.e. *opposed* or (as noun) an *opponent:*—adversary, against.

5228. ὑπέρ **hupĕr**, *hoop-er';* a prim. prep.; "*over*", i.e. (with the gen.) of place, *above*, *beyond*, *across*, or causal, *for* the sake of, *instead*, *regarding;* with the acc. *superior to*, more *than:*—(+ exceeding abundantly) above, in (on) behalf of, beyond, by, + very chiefest, concerning, exceeding (above, -ly), for, + very highly, more (than), of, over, on the part of, for sake of, in stead, than, to (-ward), very. In comp. it retains many of the above applications.

5229. ὑπεραίρομαι **hupĕrairŏmai**, *hoop-er-ah'ee-rom-ahee;* mid. from *5228* and *142;* to *raise* oneself *over*, i.e. (fig.) to *become haughty:*—exalt self, be exalted above measure.

5230. ὑπέρακμος **hupĕrakmŏs**, *hoop-er'-ak-mos;* from *5228* and the base of *188;* *beyond* the "*acme*", i.e. fig. (of a daughter) *past* the *bloom* (*prime*) of youth:— + pass the flower of (her) age.

5231. ὑπεράνω **hupĕranō**, *hoop-er-an'-o;* from *5228* and *507;* *above upward*, i.e. *greatly higher* (in place or rank):—far above, over.

5232. ὑπεραυξάνω **hupĕrauxanō**, *hoop-er-ŏwx-an'-o;* from *5228* and *837;* to *increase above* ordinary degree:—grow exceedingly.

5233. ὑπερβαίνω **hupĕrbainō**, *hoop-er-bah'ee-no;* from *5228* and the base of *939;* to *transcend*, i.e. (fig.) to *overreach:*—go beyond.

5234. ὑπερβαλλόντως **hupĕrballŏntōs**, *hoop-er-bal-lon'-toce;* adv. from pres. part. act. of *5235;* *excessively:*—beyond measure.

5235. ὑπερβάλλω **hupĕrballō**, *hoop-er-bal'-lo;* from *5228* and *906;* to *throw beyond* the usual mark, i.e. (fig.) to *surpass* (only act. part. *supereminent*):—exceeding, excel, pass.

5236. ὑπερβολή **hupĕrbŏlē**, *hoop-er-bol-ay';* from *5235;* a *throwing beyond* others, i.e. (fig.) *supereminence;* adv. (with *1519* or *2596*) *pre-eminently:*—abundance, (far more) exceeding, excellency, more excellent, beyond (out of) measure.

5237. ὑπερείδω **hupĕrĕidō**, *hoop-er-i'-do;* from *5228* and *1492;* to *overlook*, i.e. *not punish:*—wink at.

5238. ὑπερέκεινα **hupĕrĕkĕina**, *hoop-er-ek'-i-nah;* from *5228* and the neut. plur. of *1565;* *above those* parts, i.e. *still farther:*—beyond.

5239. ὑπερεκτείνω **hupĕrĕktĕinō**, *hoop-er-ek-ti'-no;* from *5228* and *1614;* to *extend inordinately:*—stretch beyond.

5240. ὑπερεκχύνω **hupĕrĕkchunō**, *hoop-er-ek-khoo'-no;* from *5228* and the alt. form of *1632;* to *pour out over*, i.e. (pass.) to *overflow:*—run over.

ὑπερεκπερισσοῦ **hupĕrĕkpĕrissŏu**. See *5228* and *1537* and *4053*.

5241. ὑπερεντυγχάνω **hupĕrĕntugchanō**, *hoop-er-en-toong-khan'-o;* from *5228* and *1793;* to *intercede in behalf of:*—make intercession for.

5242. ὑπερέχω **hupĕrĕchō**, *hoop-er-ekh'-o;* from *5228* and *2192;* to *hold* oneself *above*, i.e. (fig.) to *excel;* part. (as adj., or neut. as noun) *superior*, *superiority:*—better, excellency, higher, pass, supreme.

5243. ὑπερηφανία **hupĕrēphania**, *hoop-er-ay-fan-ee'-ah;* from *5244;* *haughtiness:*—pride.

5244. ὑπερήφανος **hupĕrēphanŏs**, *hoop-er-ay'-fan-os;* from *5228* and *5316;* *appearing above* others (*conspicuous*), i.e. (fig.) *haughty:*—proud.

ὑπερλίαν **hupĕrlian**. See *5228* and *3029*.

5245. ὑπερνικάω **hupĕrnikaō**, *hoop-er-nik-ah'-o;* from *5228* and *3528;* to *vanquish beyond*, i.e. *gain* a decisive *victory:*—more than conquer.

5246. ὑπέρογκος **hupĕrŏgkŏs**, *hoop-er'-ong-kos;* from *5228* and *3591;* *bulging over*, i.e. (fig.) *insolent:*—great swelling.

5247. ὑπεροχή **hupĕrŏchē**, *hoop-er-okh-ay';* from *5242;* *prominence*, i.e. (fig.) *superiority* (in rank or character):—authority, excellency.

5248. ὑπερπερισσεύω **hupĕrpĕrissĕuō**, *hoop-er-per-is-syoo'-o;* from *5228* and *4052;* to *superabound:*—abound much more, exceeding.

5249. ὑπερπερισσῶς **hupĕrpĕrissōs**, *hoop-er-per-is-soce';* from *5228* and *4057;* *superabundantly*, i.e. *exceedingly:*—beyond measure.

5250. ὑπερπλεονάζω **hupĕrplĕŏnazō**, *hoop-er-pleh-on-ad'-zo;* from *5228* and *4121;* to *superabound:*—be exceeding abundant.

5251. ὑπερυψόω **hupĕrupsŏō**, *hoop-er-oop-sŏ'-o;* from *5228* and *5312;* to *elevate above* others, i.e. *raise* to the *highest* position:—highly exalt.

5252. ὑπερφρονέω **hupĕrphrŏnĕō**, *hoop-er-fron-eh'-o;* from *5228* and *5426;* to *esteem* oneself *overmuch*, i.e. *be vain* or *arrogant:*—think more highly.

5253. ὑπερῷον **hupĕrōiŏn**, *hoop-er-o'-on;* neut. of a der. of *5228;* a *higher* part of the house, i.e. apartment in the *third story:*—upper chamber (room).

5254. ὑπέχω **hupĕchō**, *hoop-ekh'-o;* from *5259* and *2192;* to *hold* oneself *under*, i.e. *endure* with patience:—suffer.

5255. ὑπήκοος **hupēkŏŏs**, *hoop-ay'-kŏ-os;* from *5219;* *attentively listening*, i.e. (by impl.) *submissive:*—obedient.

5256. ὑπηρετέω **hupērĕtĕō**, *hoop-ay-ret-eh'-o;* from *5257;* to *be a subordinate*, i.e. (by impl.) *subserve:*—minister (unto), serve.

5257. ὑπηρέτης **hupērĕtēs**, *hoop-ay-ret'-ace;* from *5259* and a der. of ἐρέσσω **ĕrĕssō** (to *row*); an *under-oarsman*, i.e. (gen.) *subordinate* (*assistant*, *sexton*, *constable*):—minister, officer, servant.

5258. ὕπνος **hupnŏs**, *hoop'-nos;* from an obsol. prim. (perh. akin to *5259* through the idea of *subsilience*); *sleep*, i.e. (fig.) spiritual *torpor:*—sleep.

5259. ὑπό **hupŏ**, *hoop-ŏ';* a prim. prep.; *under*, i.e. (with the gen.) of place (*beneath*), or with verbs (the agency or means, *through*); (with the acc.) of place (whither [*underneath*] or where [*below*]) or time (when [*at*]):—among, by, from, in, of, under, with. In comp. it retains the same gen. applications, espec. of *inferior* position or condition, and spec. *covertly* or *moderately*.

5260. ὑποβάλλω **hupŏballō**, *hoop-ob-al'-lo;* from *5259* and *906;* to *throw* in *stealthily*, i.e. *introduce* by collusion:—suborn.

5261. ὑπογραμμός **hupŏgrammŏs**, *hoop-og-ram-mos';* from a comp. of *5259* and *1125;* an *underwriting*, i.e. *copy* for imitation (fig.):—example.

5262. ὑπόδειγμα **hupŏdĕigma**, *hoop-od'-igue-mah;* from *5263;* an *exhibit* for imitation or warning (fig. *specimen*, *adumbration*):—en- (ex-) ample, pattern.

5263. ὑποδείκνυμι **hupŏdĕiknumi**, *hoop-od-ike'-noo-mee;* from *5259* and *1166;* to *exhibit under* the eyes, i.e. (fig.) to *exemplify* (*instruct*, *admonish*):—show, (fore-) warn.

5264. ὑποδέχομαι **hupŏdĕchŏmai**, *hoop-od-ekh'-om-ahee;* from *5259* and *1209;* to *admit under* one's roof, i.e. *entertain* hospitably:—receive.

5265. ὑποδέω **hupŏdĕō**, *hoop-od-eh'-o;* from *5259* and *1210;* to *bind under* one's feet, i.e. *put on* shoes or sandals:—bind on, (be) shod.

5266. ὑπόδημα **hupŏdēma**, *hoop-od'-ay-mah;* from *5265;* something *bound under* the feet, i.e. a *shoe* or *sandal:*—shoe.

5267. ὑπόδικος **hupŏdikŏs**, *hoop-od'-ee-kos;* from *5259* and *1349;* *under sentence*, i.e. (by impl.) *condemned:*—guilty.

5268. ὑποζύγιον **hupŏzugiŏn**, *hoop-od-zoog'-ee-on;* neut. of a comp. of *5259* and *2218;* an animal *under* the *yoke* (*draught-beast*), i.e. (spec.) a *donkey:*—ass.

5269. ὑποζώννυμι **hupŏzōnnumi**, *hoop-od-zone'-noo-mee;* from *5259* and *2224;* to *gird under*, i.e. *frap* (a vessel with cables across the keel, sides and deck):—undergirt.

5270. ὑποκάτω **hupŏkatō**, *hoop-ok-at'-o;* from *5259* and *2736;* *down under*, i.e. *beneath:*—under.

5271. ὑποκρίνομαι **hupŏkrinŏmai**, *hoop-ok-rin'-om-ahee;* mid. from *5259* and *2919;* to *decide* (*speak* or *act*) *under* a false part, i.e. (fig.) *dissemble* (*pretend*):—feign.

5272. ὑπόκρισις **hupŏkrisis**, *hoop-ok'-ree-sis;* from *5271;* *acting under* a feigned part, i.e. (fig.) *deceit* ("*hypocrisy*"):—condemnation, dissimulation, hypocrisy.

5273. ὑποκριτής **hupŏkritēs**, *hoop-ok-ree-tace';* from *5271;* an *actor under* an assumed character (*stage-player*), i.e. (fig.) a *dissembler* ("*hypocrite*"):—hypocrite.

5274. ὑπολαμβάνω **hupŏlambanō**, *hoop-ol-am-ban'-o;* from *5259* and *2983;* to *take* from *below*, i.e. *carry upward;* fig. to *take up*, i.e. *continue* a discourse or topic; ment. to *assume* (*presume*):—answer, receive, suppose.

5275. ὑπολείπω **hupŏlĕipō**, *hoop-ol-i'-po;* from *5295* and *3007;* to *leave under* (*behind*), i.e. (pass.) to *remain* (*survive*):—be left.

5276. ὑπολήνιον **hupŏlēniŏn**, *hoop-ol-ay'-nee-on;* neut. of a presumed comp. of *5259* and *3025;* vessel or receptacle *under* the *press*, i.e. lower *winevat:*—winefat.

5277. ὑπολιμπάνω **hupŏlimpanō**, *hoop-ol-im-pan'-o;* a prol. form for *5275;* to *leave behind*, i.e. *bequeath:*—leave.

5278. ὑπομένω **hupŏmĕnō**, *hoop-om-en'-o;* from *5259* and *3306;* to *stay under* (*behind*), i.e. *remain;* fig. to *undergo*, i.e. *bear* (trials), *have fortitude*, *persevere:*—abide, endure, (take) patient (-ly), suffer, tarry behind.

5279. ὑπομιμνήσκω **hupŏmimnēskō**, *hoop-om-im-nace'-ko;* from *5259* and *3403;* to *remind quietly*, i.e. *suggest* to the (mid. one's own) memory:—put in mind, remember, bring to (put in) remembrance.

5280. ὑπόμνησις **hupŏmnēsis**, *hoop-om'-nay-sis;* from *5279;* a *reminding* or (reflex.) *recollection:*—remembrance.

5281. ὑπομονή **hupŏmŏnē**, *hoop-om-on-ay';* from *5278;* cheerful (or hopeful) *endurance*, *constancy:*—enduring, patience, patient continuance (waiting).

5282. ὑπονοέω **hupŏnŏĕō**, *hoop-on-ŏ-eh'-o;* from *5259* and *3539;* to *think under* (*privately*), i.e. to *surmise* or *conjecture:*—think, suppose, deem.

5283. ὑπόνοια **hupŏnŏia**, *hoop-on'-oy-ah;* from *5282;* *suspicion:*—surmising.

5284. ὑποπλέω **hupŏplĕō**, *hoop-op-leh'-o;* from *5259* and *4126;* to *sail under* the lee of:—sail under.

5285. ὑποπνέω **hupŏpnĕō**, *hoop-op-neh'-o;* from *5259* and *4154;* to *breathe gently*, i.e. *breeze:*—blow softly.

5286. ὑποπόδιον **hupŏpŏdiŏn**, *hoop-op-od'-ee-on;* neut. of a comp. of *5259* and *4228;* something *under* the *feet*, i.e. a *foot-rest* (fig.):—footstool.

5287. ὑπόστασις **hupŏstasis**, *hoop-os'-tas-is;* from a comp. of *5259* and *2476;* a *setting under* (*support*), i.e. (fig.) concr. *essence*, or abstr. *assurance* (obj. or subj.):—confidence, confident, person, substance.

5288. ὑποστέλλω **hupŏstĕllō**, *hoop-os-tel'-lo;* from *5259* and *4724;* to *withhold under* (*out of sight*), i.e. (reflex.) to *cower* or *shrink*, (fig.) to *conceal* (*reserve*):—draw (keep) back, shun, withdraw.

5289. ὑποστολή **hupŏstŏlē**, *hoop-os-tol-ay';* from *5288;* *shrinkage* (*timidity*), i.e. (by impl.) *apostasy:*—draw back.

5290. ὑποστρέφω **hupŏstrĕphō**, *hoop-os-tref'-o;* from *5259* and *4762;* to *turn under* (*behind*), i.e. to *return* (lit. or fig.):—come again, return (again, back again), turn back (again).

5291. ὑποστρώννυμι **hupŏstrōnnumi**, *hoop-os-trone'-noo-mee;* from *5259* and *4766;* to *strew underneath* (the feet as a carpet):—spread.

5292. ὑποταγή **hupŏtagē**, *hoop-ot-ag-ay'*; from *5293*; *subordination*:—subjection.

5293. ὑποτάσσω **hupŏtassō**, *hoop-ot-as'-so*; from *5259* and *5021*; to *subordinate*; reflex. to *obey*:—be under obedience (obedient), put under, subdue unto, (be, make) subject (to, unto), be (put) in subjection (to, under), submit self unto.

5294. ὑποτίθημι **hupŏtithēmi**, *hoop-ot-ith'-ay-mee*; from *5259* and *5087*; to *place underneath*, i.e. (fig.) to *hazard*, (reflex.) to *suggest*:—lay down, put in remembrance.

5295. ὑποτρέχω **hupŏtrĕchō**, *hoop-ot-rekh'-o*; from *5259* and *5143* (includ. its alt.); to *run under*, i.e. (spec.) to *sail past*:—run under.

5296. ὑποτύπωσις **hupŏtupōsis**, *hoop-ot-oop'-o-sis*; from a comp. of *5259* and a der. of *5179*; *typification under* (*after*), i.e. (concr.) a *sketch* (fig.) for imitation:—form, pattern.

5297. ὑποφέρω **hupŏphĕrō**, *hoop-of-er'-o*; from *5259* and *5342*; to *bear* from *underneath*, i.e. (fig.) to *undergo* hardship:—bear, endure.

5298. ὑποχωρέω **hupŏchōrĕō**, *hoop-okh-o-reh'-o*; from *5259* and *5562*; to *vacate down*, i.e. *retire* quietly:—go aside, withdraw self.

5299. ὑπωπιάζω **hupōpiazō**, *hoop-o-pee-ad'-zo*; from a comp. of *5259* and a der. of *3700*; to hit *under* the *eye* (*buffet* or *disable* an antagonist as a pugilist), i.e. (fig.) to *tease* or *annoy* (into compliance), *subdue* (one's passions):—keep under, weary.

5300. ὗς **hus**, *hoos*; appar. a prim. word; a *hog* ("*swine*"):—sow.

5301. ὕσσωπος **hussōpŏs**, *hoos'-so-pos*; of for. or. [231]; "*hyssop*":—hyssop.

5302. ὑστερέω **hustĕrĕō**, *hoos-ter-eh'-o*; from *5306*; to *be later*, i.e. (by impl.) to *be inferior*; gen. to *fall short* (*be deficient*):—come behind (short), be destitute, fail, lack, suffer need, (be in) want, be the worse.

5303. ὑστέρημα **hustĕrēma**, *hoos-ter'-ay-mah*; from *5302*; a *deficit*; spec. *poverty*:—that which is behind, (that which was) lack (-ing), penury, want.

5304. ὑστέρησις **hustĕrēsis**, *hoos-ter'-ay-sis*; from *5302*; a *falling short*, i.e. (spec.) *penury*:—want.

5305. ὕστερον **hustĕrŏn**, *hoos'-ter-on*; neut. of *5306* as adv.; *more lately*, i.e. *eventually*:—afterward, (at the) last (of all).

5306. ὕστερος **hustĕrŏs**, *hoos'-ter-os*; compar. from *5259* (in the sense of *behind*); *later*:—latter.

5307. ὑφαντός **huphantŏs**, *hoo-fan-tos'*; from ὑφαίνω **huphainō** (to *weave*); *woven*, i.e. (perh.) *knitted*:—woven.

5308. ὑψηλός **hupsēlŏs**, *hoop-say-los'*; from *5311*; *lofty* (in place or character):—high (-er, -ly) (esteemed).

5309. ὑψηλοφρονέω **hupsēlŏphrŏnĕō**, *hoop-say-lo-fron-eh'-o*; from a comp. of *5308* and *5424*; to *be lofty in mind*, i.e. *arrogant*:—be highminded.

5310. ὕψιστος **hupsistŏs**, *hoop'-sis-tos*; superl. from the base of *5311*; *highest*, i.e. (masc. sing.) the *Supreme* (God), or (neut. plur.) the *heavens*:—most high, highest.

5311. ὕψος **hupsŏs**, *hoop'-sos*; from a der. of *5228*; *elevation*, i.e. (abstr.) *altitude*, (spec.) the *sky*, or (fig.) *dignity*:—be exalted, height, (on) high.

5312. ὑψόω **hupsŏō**, *hoop-sŏ'-o*; from *5311*; to *elevate* (lit. or fig.):—exalt, lift up.

5313. ὕψωμα **hupsōma**, *hoop'-so-mah*; from *5312*; an *elevated* place or thing, i.e. (abstr.) *altitude*, or (by impl.) a *barrier* (fig.):—height, high thing.

Φ

5314. φάγος **phagŏs**, *fag'-os*; from *5315*; a *glutton*:—gluttonous.

5315. φάγω **phagō**, *fag'-o*; a prim. verb (used as an alt. of *2068* in cert. tenses); to *eat* (lit. or fig.):—eat, meat.

5316. φαίνω **phainō**, *fah'ee-no*; prol. for the base of *5457*; to *lighten* (*shine*), i.e. *show* (trans. or intrans., lit. or fig.):—appear, seem, be seen, shine, × think.

5317. Φάλεκ **Phalĕk**, *fal'-ek*; of Heb. or. [6389]; *Phalek* (i.e. *Peleg*), a patriarch:—Phalec.

5318. φανερός **phanĕrŏs**, *fan-er-os'*; from *5316*; *shining*, i.e. *apparent* (lit. or fig.); neut. (as adv.) *publicly*, *externally*:—abroad, + appear, known, manifest, open [+ -ly], outward ([+ -ly]).

5319. φανερόω **phanĕrŏō**, *fan-er-ŏ'-o*; from *5318*; to *render apparent* (lit. or fig.):—appear, manifestly declare, (make) manifest (forth), shew (self).

5320. φανερῶς **phanĕrōs**, *fan-er-oce'*; adv. from *5318*; *plainly*, i.e. *clearly* or *publicly*:—evidently, openly.

5321. φανέρωσις **phanĕrōsis**, *fan-er'-o-sis*; from *5319*; *exhibition*, i.e. (fig.) *expression*, (by extens.) a *bestowment*:—manifestation.

5322. φανός **phanŏs**, *fan-os'*; from *5316*; a *lightener*, i.e. *light*; *lantern*:—lantern.

5323. Φανουήλ **Phanŏuēl**, *fan-oo-ale'*; of Heb. or. [6439]; *Phanuël* (i.e. *Penuël*), an Isr.:—Phanuel.

5324. φαντάζω **phantazō**, *fan-tad'-zo*; from a der. of *5316*; to *make apparent*, i.e. (pass.) to *appear* (neut. part. as noun, a *spectacle*):—sight.

5325. φαντασία **phantasia**, *fan-tas-ee'-ah*; from a der. of *5324*; (prop. abstr.) a (vain) *show* ("fantasy"):—pomp.

5326. φάντασμα **phantasma**, *fan'-tas-mah*; from *5324*; (prop. concr.) a (mere) *show* ("phantasm"), i.e. *spectre*:—spirit.

5327. φάραγξ **pharagx**, *far'-anx*; prop. strength. from the base of *4008* or rather of *4486*; a *gap* or *chasm*, i.e. *ravine* (*winter-torrent*):—valley.

5328. Φαραώ **Pharaō**, *far-ah-o'*; of for. or. [6547]; *Pharaō* (i.e. *Pharoh*), an Eg. king:—Pharaoh.

5329. Φαρές **Pharĕs**, *far-es'*; of Heb. or. [6557]; *Phares* (i.e. *Perets*), an Isr.:—Phares.

5330. Φαρισαῖος **Pharisaiŏs**, *far-is-ah'-yos*; of Heb. or. [comp. 6567]; a *separatist*, i.e. exclusively *religious*; a *Pharisæan*, i.e. Jewish sectary:—Pharisee.

5331. φαρμακεία **pharmakĕia**, *far-mak-i'-ah*; from *5332*; *medication* ("pharmacy"), i.e. (by extens.) *magic* (lit. or fig.):—sorcery, witchcraft.

5332. φαρμακεύς **pharmakĕus**, *far-mak-yoos'*; from φάρμακον **pharmakŏn** (a *drug*, i.e. spell-giving *potion*); a *druggist* ("pharmacist") or *poisoner*, i.e. (by extens.) a *magician*:—sorcerer.

5333. φαρμακός **pharmakŏs**, *far-mak-os'*; the same as *5332*:—sorcerer.

5334. φάσις **phasis**, *fas'-is*; from *5346* (not the same as "phase", which is from *5316*); a *saying*, i.e. *report*:—tidings.

5335. φάσκω **phaskō**, *fas'-ko*; prol. from the same as *5346*; to *assert*:—affirm, profess, say.

5336. φάτνη **phatnē**, *fat'-nay*; from πατέομαι **patĕŏmai** (to *eat*); a *crib* (for fodder):—manger, stall.

5337. φαῦλος **phaulŏs**, *fŏw'-los*; appar. a prim. word; "*foul*" or "*flawy*", i.e. (fig.) *wicked*:—evil.

5338. φέγγος **phĕggŏs**, *feng'-gos*; prob. akin to the base of *5457* [comp. *5350*]; *brilliancy*:—light.

5339. φείδομαι **phĕidŏmai**, *fi'-dom-ahee*; of uncert. affin.; to *be chary* of, i.e. (subj.) to *abstain* or (obj.) to *treat leniently*:—forbear, spare.

5340. φειδομένως **phĕidŏmĕnōs**, *fi-dom-en'-oce*; adv. from part. of *5339*; *abstemiously*, i.e. *stingily*:—sparingly.

5341. φελόνης **phĕlŏnēs**, *fel-on'-ace*; by transp. for a der. prob. of *5316* (as *showing* outside the other garments); a *mantle* (*surtout*):—cloke.

5342. φέρω **phĕrō**, *fer'-o*; a prim. verb (for which other and appar. not cognate ones are used in certain tenses only; namely,

οἴω **ŏiō**, *oy'-o*; and

ἐνέγκω **ĕnĕgkō**, *en-eng'-ko*); to "*bear*" or *carry* (in a very wide application, lit. and fig., as follows):—be, bear, bring (forth), carry, come, + let her drive, be driven, endure, go on, lay, lead, move, reach, rushing, uphold.

5343. φεύγω **phĕugō**, *fyoo'-go*; appar. a prim. verb; to *run away* (lit. or fig.); by impl. to *shun*; by anal. to *vanish*:—escape, flee (away).

5344. Φῆλιξ **Phēlix**, *fay'-lix*; of Lat. or.; *happy*; *Phelix* (i.e. *Felix*), a Rom.:—Felix.

5345. φήμη **phēmē**, *fay'-may*; from *5346*; a *saying*, i.e. *rumor* ("*fame*"):—fame.

5346. φημί **phēmi**, *fay-mee'*; prop. the same as the base of *5457* and *5316*; to *show* or *make known* one's thoughts, i.e. *speak* or *say*:—affirm, say. Comp. *3004*.

5347. Φῆστος **Phēstŏs**, *face'-tos*; of Lat. der.; *festal*; *Phestus* (i.e. *Festus*), a Rom.:—Festus.

5348. φθάνω **phthanō**, *fthan'-o*; appar. a prim. verb; to *be beforehand*, i.e. *anticipate* or *precede*, by extens. to *have arrived* at:—(already) attain, come, prevent.

5349. φθαρτός **phthartŏs**, *fthar-tos'*; from *5351*; *decayed*, i.e. (by impl.) *perishable*:—corruptible.

5350. φθέγγομαι **phthĕggŏmai**, *ftheng'-gom-ahee*; prob. akin to *5338* and thus to *5346*; to *utter* a clear sound, i.e. (gen.) to *proclaim*:—speak.

5351. φθείρω **phthĕirō**, *fthi'-ro*; prob. strength. from φθίω **phthiō** (to *pine* or *waste*); prop. to *shrivel* or *wither*, i.e. to *spoil* (by any process) or (gen.) to *ruin* (espec. fig. by mor. influences, to *deprave*):—corrupt (self), defile, destroy.

5352. φθινοπωρινός **phthinŏpōrinŏs**, *fthin-op-o-ree-nos'*; from a der. of φθίνω **phthinō** (to *wane*; akin to the base of *5351*) and *3703* (mean. *late autumn*); *autumnal* (as *stripped* of leaves):—whose fruit withereth.

5353. φθόγγος **phthŏggŏs**, *fthong'-gos*; from *5350*; *utterance*, i.e. a *musical* note (vocal or instrumental):—sound.

5354. φθονέω **phthŏnĕō**, *fthon-eh'-o*; from *5355*; to *be jealous* of:—envy.

5355. φθόνος **phthŏnŏs**, *fthon'-os*; prob. akin to the base of *5351*; *ill-will* (as *detraction*), i.e. *jealousy* (*spite*):—envy.

5356. φθορά **phthŏra**, *fthor-ah'*; from *5351*; *decay*, i.e. *ruin* (spontaneous or inflicted, lit. or fig.):—corruption, destroy, perish.

5357. φιάλη **phialē**, *fee-al'-ay*; of uncert. affin.; a broad shallow *cup* ("phial"):—vial.

5358. φιλάγαθος **philagathŏs**, *fil-ag'-ath-os*; from *5384* and *18*; *fond to good*, i.e. a *promoter of virtue*:—love of good men.

5359. Φιλαδέλφεια **Philadĕlphĕia**, *fil-ad-el'-fee-ah*; from Φιλάδελφος **Philadĕlphŏs** (the same as *5361*), a king of Pergamos; *Philadelphia*, a place in Asia Minor:—Philadelphia.

5360. φιλαδελφία **philadĕlphia**, *fil-ad-el-fee'-ah*; from *5361*; *fraternal affection*:—brotherly love (kindness), love of the brethren.

5361. φιλάδελφος **philadĕlphŏs**, *fil-ad'-el-fos*; from *5384* and *80*; *fond of brethren*, i.e. *fraternal*:—love as brethren.

5362. φίλανδρος **philandrŏs**, *fil'-an-dros*; from *5384* and *435*; *fond of man*, i.e. *affectionate* as a wife:—love their husbands.

5363. φιλανθρωπία **philanthrōpia**, *fil-an-thro-pee'-ah*; from the same as *5364*; *fondness of mankind*, i.e. *benevolence* ("*philanthropy*"):—kindness, love towards man.

5364. φιλανθρώπως **philanthrōpōs**, *fil-an-thro'-poce*; adv. from a comp. of *5384* and *444*; *fondly to man* ("philanthropically"), i.e. *humanely*:—courteously.

5365. φιλαργυρία **philarguria**, *fil-ar-goo-ree'-ah*; from *5366*; *avarice*:—love of money.

5366. φιλάργυρος **philargurŏs**, *fil-ar'-goo-ros*; from *5384* and *696*; *fond of silver* (money), i.e. *avaricious*:—covetous.

5367. φίλαυτος **philautŏs**, *fil'-ŏw-tos*; from *5384* and *846*; *fond of self*, i.e. *selfish*:—lover of own self.

5368. φιλέω **philĕō**, *fil-eh'-o*; from *5384*; to be a *friend to* (*fond of* [an individual or an object]), i.e. *have affection* for (denoting *personal* attachment, as a matter of sentiment or feeling; while *25* is wider, embracing espec. the judgment and the *deliberate* assent of the will as a matter of principle, duty and propriety: the two thus stand related very much as *2309* and *1014*, or as *2372* and *3563* respectively; the former being chiefly of the *heart* and the latter of the *head*); spec. to *kiss* (as a mark of tenderness):—kiss, love.

5369. φιλήδονος **philēdŏnŏs,** *fil-ay'-don-os;* from *5384* and *2237*; *fond of pleasure*, i.e. *voluptuous*:—lover of pleasure.

5370. φίλημα **philēma,** *fil'-ay-mah;* from *5368*; a *kiss*:—kiss.

5371. Φιλήμων **Philēmōn,** *fil-ay'-mone;* from *5368*; *friendly*; *Philemon*, a Chr.:—Philemon.

5372. Φιλητός **Philētŏs,** *fil-ay-tos';* from *5368*; *amiable*; *Philetus*, an opposer of Christianity:—Philetus.

5373. φιλία **philia,** *fil-ee'-ah;* from *5384*; *fondness*:—friendship.

5374. Φιλιππήσιος **Philippēsiŏs,** *fil-ip-pay'-see-os;* from *5375*; a *Philippesian* (*Philippian*), i.e. native of Philippi:—Philippian.

5375. Φίλιπποι **Philippŏi,** *fil'-ip-poy;* plur. of *5376*; *Philippi*, a place in Macedonia:—Philippi.

5376. Φίλιππος **Philippŏs,** *fil'-ip-pos;* from *5384* and *2462*; *fond of horses*; *Philippus*, the name of four Isr.:—Philip.

5377. φιλόθεος **philŏthĕŏs,** *fil-oth'-eh-os;* from *5384* and *2316*; *fond of God*, i.e. *pious*:—lover of God.

5378. Φιλόλογος **Philŏlŏgŏs,** *fil-ol'-og-os;* from *5384* and *3056*; *fond of words*, i.e. *talkative* (*argumentative, learned,* "*philological*"); *Philologus*, a Chr.:—Philologus.

5379. φιλονεικία **philŏnĕikia,** *fil-on-i-kee'-ah;* from *5380*; *quarrelsomeness*, i.e. a *dispute*:—strife.

5380. φιλόνεικος **philŏnĕikŏs,** *fil-on'-i-kos;* from *5384* and νεῖκος **nĕikŏs** (a *quarrel*; prob. akin to *3534*); *fond of strife*, i.e. *disputatious*:—contentious.

5381. φιλονεξία **philŏnĕxia,** *fil-on-ex-ee'-ah;* from *5382*; *hospitableness*:—entertain strangers, hospitality.

5382. φιλόξενος **philŏxĕnŏs,** *fil-ox'-en-os;* from *5384* and *3581*; *fond of guests*, i.e. *hospitable*:—given to (lover of, use) hospitality.

5383. φιλοπρωτεύω **philŏprōtĕuō,** *fil-op-rote-yoo'-o;* from a comp. of *5384* and *4413*; to *be fond of being first*, i.e. *ambitious* of distinction:—love to have the preeminence.

5384. φίλος **philŏs,** *fee'-los;* prop. *dear*, i.e. a *friend*; act. *fond*, i.e. *friendly* (still as a noun, an *associate, neighbor*, etc.):—friend.

5385. φιλοσοφία **philŏsŏphia,** *fil-os-of-ee'-ah;* from *5386*; "*philosophy*", i.e. (spec.) Jewish *sophistry*:—philosophy.

5386. φιλόσοφος **philŏsŏphŏs,** *fil-os'-of-os;* from *5384* and *4680*; *fond of wise* things, i.e. a "*philosopher*":—philosopher.

5387. φιλόστοργος **philŏstŏrgŏs,** *fil-os'-tor-gos;* from *5384* and στοργή **stŏrgē** (*cherishing* one's kindred, espec. parents or children); *fond of* natural *relatives*, i.e. *fraternal* towards fellow Chr.:—kindly affectioned.

5388. φιλότεκνος **philŏtĕknŏs,** *fil-ot'-ek-nos;* from *5384* and *5043*; *fond of* one's *children*, i.e. *maternal*:—love their children.

5389. φιλοτιμέομαι **philŏtimĕŏmai,** *fil-ot-im-eh'-om-ahee;* mid. from a comp. of *5384* and *5092*; to be *fond of honor*, i.e. *emulous* (*eager* or *earnest* to do something):—labour, strive, study.

5390. φιλοφρόνως **philŏphrŏnōs,** *fil-of-ron'-oce;* adv. from *5391*; *with friendliness of mind*, i.e. *kindly*:—courteously.

5391. φιλόφρων **philŏphrōn,** *fil-of'-rone;* from *5384* and *5424*; *friendly of mind*, i.e. *kind*:—courteous.

5392. φιμόω **phimŏō,** *fee-mŏ'-o;* from φιμός **phimŏs** (a *muzzle*); to *muzzle*:—muzzle.

5393. Φλέγων **Phlĕgōn,** *fleg'-one;* act. part. of the base of *5395*; *blazing*; *Phlegon*, a Chr.:—Phlegon.

5394. φλογίζω **phlŏgizō,** *flog-id'-zo;* from *5305*; to *cause a blaze*, i.e. *ignite* (fig. to *inflame* with passion):—set on fire.

5395. φλόξ **phlŏx,** *flox;* from a prim. φλέγω **phlĕgō** (to "*flash*" or "*flame*"); a *blaze*:—flame (-ing).

5396. φλυαρέω **phluarĕō,** *floo-ar-eh'-o;* from *5397*; to *be a babbler* or *trifler*, i.e. (by impl.) to *berate* idly or mischievously:—prate against.

5397. φλύαρος **phluarŏs,** *floo'-ar-os;* from φλύω **phluō** (to *bubble*); a *garrulous* person, i.e. *prater*:—tattler.

5398. φοβερός **phŏbĕrŏs,** *fob-er-os';* from *5401*; *frightful*, i.e. (obj.) *formidable*:—fearful, terrible.

5399. φοβέω **phŏbĕō,** *fob-eh'-o;* from *5401*; to *frighten*, i.e. (pass.) to *be alarmed*; by anal. to *be in awe* of, i.e. *revere*:—be (+ sore) afraid, fear (exceedingly), reverence.

5400. φόβητρον **phŏbētrŏn,** *fob'-ay-tron;* neut. of a der. of *5399*; a *frightening* thing, i.e. *terrific* portent:—fearful sight.

5401. φόβος **phŏbŏs,** *fob'-os;* from a prim. φέβομαι **phĕbŏmai** (to *be* put in *fear*); *alarm* or *fright*:—be afraid, + exceedingly, fear, terror.

5402. Φοίβη **Phŏibē,** *foy'-bay;* fem. of φοῖβος **phŏibŏs** (*bright*; prob. akin to the base of *5457*); *Phœbe*, a Chr. woman:—Phebe.

5403. Φοινίκη **Phŏinikē,** *foy-nee'-kay;* from *5404*; *palm*-country; *Phœnice* (or *Phœnicia*), a region of Pal.:—Phenice, Phenicia.

5404. φοῖνιξ **phŏinix,** *foy'-nix;* of uncert. der.; a *palm*-tree:—palm (tree).

5405. Φοῖνιξ **Phŏinix,** *foy'-nix;* prob. the same as *5404*; *Phœnix*, a place in Crete:—Phenice.

5406. φονεύς **phŏnĕus,** *fon-yooce';* from *5408*; a *murderer* (always of *criminal* [or at least *intentional*] homicide; which *443* does not necessarily imply; while *4607* is a spec. term for a *public* bandit):—murderer.

5407. φονεύω **phŏnĕuō,** *fon-yoo'-o;* from *5406*; *to be a murderer* (of):—kill, do murder, slay.

5408. φόνος **phŏnŏs,** *fon'-os;* from an obsol. prim. φένω **phĕnō** (to *slay*); *murder*:—murder, + be slain with, slaughter.

5409. φορέω **phŏrĕō,** *for-eh'-o;* from *5411*; to *have a burden*, i.e. (by anal.) to *wear* as clothing or a constant accompaniment:—bear, wear.

5410. Φόρον **Phŏrŏn,** *for'-on;* of Lat. or.; a *forum* or market-place; only in comp. with *675*; a *station* on the Appian road:—forum.

5411. φόρος **phŏrŏs,** *for'-os;* from *5342*; a *load* (as *borne*), i.e. (fig.) a *tax* (prop. an individ. *assessment* on persons or property; whereas *5056* is usually a gen. *toll* on goods or travel):—tribute.

5412. φορτίζω **phŏrtizō,** *for-tid'-zo;* from *5414*; to *load* up (prop. as a vessel or animal), i.e. (fig.) to *overburden* with ceremony (or spiritual anxiety):—lade, be heavy laden.

5413. φορτίον **phŏrtiŏn,** *for-tee'-on;* dimin. of *5414*; an *invoice* (as part of *freight*), i.e. (fig.) a *task* or *service*:—burden.

5414. φόρτος **phŏrtŏs,** *for'-tos;* from *5342*; something *carried*, i.e. the *cargo* of a ship:—lading.

5415. Φορτουνάτος **Phŏrtŏunatŏs,** *for-too-nat'-os;* of Lat. or.; "*fortunate*"; *Fortunatus*, a Chr.:—Fortunatus.

5416. φραγέλλιον **phragĕlliŏn,** *frag-el'-le-on;* neut. of a der. from the base of *5417*; a *whip*, i.e. Rom. *lash* as a public punishment:—scourge.

5417. φραγελλόω **phragĕllŏō,** *frag-el-lŏ'-o;* from a presumed equiv. of the Lat. *flagellum*; to *whip*, i.e. *lash* as a public punishment:—scourge.

5418. φραγμός **phragmŏs,** *frag-mos';* from *5420*; a *fence*, or inclosing *barrier* (lit. or fig.):—hedge (+ round about), partition.

5419. φράζω **phrazō,** *frad'-zo;* prob. akin to *5420* through the idea of *defining*; to *indicate* (by word or act), i.e. (spec.) to *expound*:—declare.

5420. φράσσω **phrassō,** *fras'-so;* appar. a strength. form of the base of *5424*; to *fence* or inclose, i.e. (spec.) to *block* up (fig. to *silence*):—stop.

5421. φρέαρ **phrĕar,** *freh'-ar;* of uncert. der.; a *hole* in the ground (dug for obtaining or holding water or other purposes), i.e. a *cistern* or *well*; fig. an *abyss* (as a *prison*):—well, pit.

5422. φρεναπατάω **phrĕnapataō,** *fren-ap-at-ah'-o;* from *5423*; to *be a mind-misleader*, i.e. *delude*:—deceive.

5423. φρεναπάτης **phrĕnapatēs,** *fren-ap-at-ace;* from *5424* and *539*; a *mind-misleader*, i.e. *seducer*:—deceiver.

5424. φρήν **phrēn,** *frane;* prob. from an obsol. φράω **phraō** (to *rein* in or *curb*; comp. *5420*); the *midrif* (as a *partition* of the body), i.e. (fig. and by impl. of sympathy) the *feelings* (or sensitive nature; by extens. [also in the plur.] the *mind* or cognitive faculties):—understanding.

5425. φρίσσω **phrissō,** *fris'-so;* appar. a prim. verb; to "*bristle*" or *chill*, i.e. *shudder* (*fear*):—tremble.

5426. φρονέω **phrŏnĕō,** *fron-eh'-o;* from *5424*; to *exercise* the *mind*, i.e. *entertain* or *have a sentiment* or *opinion*; by impl. to *be* (mentally) *disposed* (more or less earnestly in a certain direction); intens. to *interest oneself* in (with concern or obedience):—set the affection on, (be) care (-ful), (be like-, + be of one, + be of the same, + let this) mind (-ed), regard, savour, think.

5427. φρόνημα **phrŏnēma,** *fron'-ay-mah;* from *5426*; (mental) *inclination* or *purpose*:—(be, + be carnally, + be spiritually) mind (-ed).

5428. φρόνησις **phrŏnēsis,** *fron'-ay-sis;* from *5426*; mental *action* or *activity*, i.e. intellectual or mor. *insight*:—prudence, wisdom.

5429. φρόνιμος **phrŏnimŏs,** *fron'-ee-mos;* from *5424*; *thoughtful*, i.e. *sagacious* or *discreet* (implying a *cautious* character; while *4680* denotes *practical* skill or acumen; and *4908* indicates rather *intelligence* or mental acquirement); in a bad sense *conceited* (also in the compar.):—wise (-r).

5430. φρονίμως **phrŏnimōs,** *fron-im'-oce;* adv. from *5429*; *prudently*:—wisely.

5431. φροντίζω **phrŏntizō,** *fron-tid'-zo;* from a der. of *5424*; to *exercise thought*, i.e. *be anxious*:—be careful.

5432. φρουρέω **phrŏurĕō,** *froo-reh'-o;* from a comp. of *4253* and *3708*; to *be a watcher in advance*, i.e. to *mount guard* as a sentinel (*post spies* at gates); fig. to *hem in, protect*:—keep (with a garrison). Comp. *5083*.

5433. φρυάσσω **phruassō,** *froo-as'-so;* akin to *1032, 1031*; to *snort* (as a spirited horse), i.e. (fig.) to *make a tumult*:—rage.

5434. φρύγανον **phruganŏn,** *froo'-gan-on;* neut. of a presumed der. of φρύγω **phrugō** (to *roast* or *parch*; akin to the base of *5395*); something *desiccated*, i.e. a dry *twig*:—stick.

5435. Φρυγία **Phrugia,** *froog-ee'-ah;* prob. of for. or.; *Phrygia*, a region of Asia Minor:—Phrygia.

5436. Φύγελλος **Phugĕllŏs,** *foog'-el-los;* prob. from *5343*; *fugitive*; *Phygellus*, an apostate Chr.:—Phygellus.

5437. φυγή **phugē,** *foog-ay';* from *5343*; a *fleeing*, i.e. *escape*:—flight.

5438. φυλακή **phulakē,** *foo-lak-ay';* from *5442*; a *guarding* or (concr. *guard*), the act, the person; fig. the place, the condition, or (spec.) the time (as a division of day or night), lit. or fig.:—cage, hold, (im-) prison (-ment), ward, watch.

5439. φυλακίζω **phulakizō,** *foo-lak-id'-zo;* from *5441*; to *incarcerate*:—imprison.

5440. φυλακτήριον **phulaktēriŏn,** *foo-lak-tay'-ree-on;* neut. of a der. of *5442*; a *guard-case*, i.e. "*phylactery*" for wearing slips of Scripture texts:—phylactery.

5441. φύλαξ **phulax,** *foo'-lax;* from *5442*; a *watcher* or *sentry*:—keeper.

5442. φυλάσσω **phulassō,** *foo-las'-so;* prob. from *5443* through the idea of *isolation*; to *watch*, i.e.

be on guard (lit. or fig.); by impl. to *preserve, obey, avoid:*—beware, keep (self), observe, save. Comp. *5083*.

5443. **φυλή phulē**, *foo-lay'*; from *5453* (comp. *5444*); an *offshoot*, i.e. *race* or *clan:*—kindred, tribe.

5444. **φύλλον phullŏn**, *fool'-lon;* from the same as *5443*; a *sprout*, i.e. *leaf:*—leaf.

5445. **φύραμα phurama**, *foo'-ram-ah;* from a prol. form of **φύρω phurō** (to *mix* a liquid with a solid; perh. akin to *5453* through the idea of *swelling* in bulk), mean to *knead;* a *mass* of dough:—lump.

5446. **φυσικός phusikŏs**, *foo-see-kos';* from *5449*; "*physical*", i.e. (by impl.) *instinctive:*—natural. Comp. *5591*.

5447. **φυσικῶς phusikōs**, *foo-see-koce';* adv. from *5446*; "*physically*", i.e. (by impl.) *instinctively:*—naturally.

5448. **φυσιόω phusiŏō**, *foo-see-ŏ'-o;* from *5449* in the prim. sense of *blowing;* to *inflate*, i.e. (fig.) *make proud* (*haughty*):—puff up.

5449. **φύσις phusis**, *foo'-sis;* from *5453*; *growth* (by *germination* or *expansion*), i.e. (by impl.) natural *production* (lineal *descent*); by extens. a *genus* or *sort;* fig. native *disposition, constitution* or *usage:*—([man-]) kind, nature ([-al]).

5450. **φυσίωσις phusiōsis**, *foo-see'-o-sis;* from *5448*; *inflation*, i.e. (fig.) *haughtiness:*—swelling.

5451. **φυτεία phutĕia**, *foo-ti'-ah;* from *5452*; trans-*planting*, i.e. (concr.) a *shrub* or *vegetable:*—plant.

5452. **φυτεύω phutĕuō**, *foot-yoo'-o;* from a der. of *5453*; to *set out* in the earth, i.e. *implant;* fig. to *instil* doctrine:—plant.

5453. **φύω phuō**, *foo'-o;* a prim. verb; prob. orig. to "*puff*" or *blow*, i.e. to *swell* up; but only used in the impl. sense, to *germinate* or *grow* (*sprout, produce*), lit. or fig.:—spring (up).

5454. **φωλεός phōlĕŏs**, *fo-leh-os';* of uncert. der.; a *burrow* or *lurking-place:*—hole.

5455. **φωνέω phōnĕō**, *fo-neh'-o;* from *5456*; to emit a *sound* (animal, human or instrumental); by impl. to *address* in words or by name, also in imitation:—call (for), crow, cry.

5456. **φωνή phōnē**, *fo-nay';* prob. akin to *5316* through the idea of *disclosure;* a *tone* (articulate, bestial or artificial); by impl. an *address* (for any purpose), *saying* or *language:*—noise, sound, voice.

5457. **φῶς phōs**, *foce;* from an obsol. **φάω phaō** (to *shine* or make *manifest*, espec. by *rays;* comp. *5316*, *5346*); *luminousness* (in the widest application, nat. or artificial, abstr. or concr., lit. or fig.):—fire, light.

5458. **φωστήρ phōstēr**, *foce-tare';* from *5457*; an *illuminator*, i.e. (concr.) a *luminary*, or (abstr.) *brilliancy:*—light.

5459. **φωσφόρος phōsphŏrŏs**, *foce-for'-os;* from *5457* and *5342*; *light-bearing* ("phosphorus"), i.e. (spec.) the *morning-star* (fig.):—day star.

5460. **φωτεινός phōtĕinŏs**, *fo-ti-nos';* from *5457*; *lustrous*, i.e. *transparent* or *well-illuminated* (fig.):—bright, full of light.

5461. **φωτίζω phōtizō**, *fo-tid'-zo;* from *5457*; to *shed rays*, i.e. to *shine* or (trans.) to *brighten* up (lit. or fig.):—enlighten, illuminate, (bring to, give) light, make to see.

5462. **φωτισμός phōtismŏs**, *fo-tis-mos';* from *5461*; *illumination* (fig.):—light.

X

5463. **χαίρω chairō**, *khah'ee-ro;* a prim. verb; to be "*cheer*"*ful*, i.e. calmly *happy* or well-off; impers. espec. as salutation (on meeting or parting), *be well:*—farewell, be glad, God speed, greeting, hail, joy (-fully), rejoice.

5464. **χάλαζα chalaza**, *khal'-ad-zah;* prob. from *5465*; *hail:*—hail.

5465. **χαλάω chalaō**, *khal-ah'-o;* from the base of *5490*; to *lower* (as into a *void*):—let down, strike.

5466. **Χαλδαῖος Chaldaiŏs**, *khal-dah'-yos;* prob. of Heb. or. [3778]; a *Chaldæan* (i.e. *Kasdi*), or native of the region of the lower Euphrates:—Chaldæan.

5467. **χαλεπός chalĕpŏs**, *khal-ep-os';* perh. from *5465* through the idea of *reducing* the strength; *difficult*, i.e. *dangerous*, or (by impl.) *furious:*—fierce, perilous.

5468. **χαλιναγωγέω chalinagōgĕō**, *khal-in-ag-ogue-eh'-o;* from a comp. of *5469* and the redupl. form of *71*; to *be a bit-leader*, i.e. to *curb* (fig.):—bridle.

5469. **χαλινός chalinŏs**, *khal-ee-nos';* from *5465*; a *curb* or *head-stall* (as *curbing* the spirit):—bit, bridle.

5470. **χάλκεος chalkĕŏs**, *khal'-keh-os;* from *5475*; *coppery:*—brass.

5471. **χαλκεύς chalkĕus**, *khalk-yooce';* from *5475*; a *copper-worker* or *brazier:*—coppersmith.

5472. **χαλκηδών chalkēdōn**, *khal-kay-dōhn';* from *5475* and perh. *1491*; *copper-like*, i.e. "*chalcedony*":—chalcedony.

5473. **χαλκίον chalkiŏn**, *khal-kee'-on;* dimin. from *5475*; a *copper dish:*—brazen vessel.

5474. **χαλκολίβανον chalkŏlibanŏn**, *khal-kol-ib'-an-on;* neut. of a comp. of *5475* and *3030* (in the impl. mean. of *whiteness* or *brilliancy*); *burnished copper*, an alloy of copper (or gold) and silver having a brilliant lustre:—fine brass.

5475. **χαλκός chalkŏs**, *khal-kos';* perh. from *5465* through the idea of *hollowing* out as a vessel (this metal being chiefly used for that purpose); *copper* (the substance, or some implement or coin made of it):—brass, money.

5476. **χαμαί chamai**, *kham-ah'ee;* adv. perh. from the base of *5490* through the idea of a *fissure* in the soil; *earthward*, i.e. *prostrate:*—on (to) the ground.

5477. **Χαναάν Chanaan**, *khan-ah-an';* of Heb. or. [3667]; *Chanaan* (i.e. *Kenaan*), the early name of Pal.:—Chanaan.

5478. **Χαναναῖος Chanaanaiŏs**, *khan-ah-an-ah'-yos;* from *5477*; a *Chanaanæan* (i.e. *Kenaanite*), or native of gentile Pal.:—of Canaan.

5479. **χαρά chara**, *khar-ah';* from *5463*; *cheerfulness*, i.e. calm *delight:*—gladness, × greatly, (× be exceeding) joy (-ful, -fully, -fulness, -ous).

5480. **χάραγμα charagma**, *khar'-ag-mah;* from the same as *5482*; a *scratch* or *etching*, i.e. *stamp* (as a *badge* of servitude), or *sculptured* figure (*statue*):—graven, mark.

5481. **χαρακτήρ charaktēr**, *khar-ak-tare';* from the same as *5482*; a *graver* (the tool or the person), i.e. (by impl.) *engraving* (["*character*"], the *figure* stamped, i.e. an exact *copy* or [fig.] *representation*):—express image.

5482. **χάραξ charax**, *khar'-ax;* from **χαράσσω charassō** (to *sharpen* to a point; akin to *1125* through the idea of *scratching*); a *stake*, i.e. (by impl.) a *palisade* or *rampart* (military *mound* for circumvallation in a siege):—trench.

5483. **χαρίζομαι charizŏmai**, *khar-id'-zom-ahee;* mid. from *5485*; to grant as a *favor*, i.e. gratuitously, in kindness, pardon or rescue:—deliver, (frankly) forgive, (freely) give, grant.

5484. **χάριν charin**, *khar'-in;* acc. of *5485* as prep.; through *favor* of, i.e. *on account* of:—be-(for) cause of, for sake of, + . . . fore, × reproachfully.

5485. **χάρις charis**, *khar'-ece;* from *5463*; *graciousness* (as *gratifying*), of manner or act (abstr. or concr.; lit., fig. or spiritual; espec. the divine influence upon the heart, and its reflection in the life; including *gratitude*):—acceptable, benefit, favour, gift, grace (-ious), joy liberality, pleasure, thank (-s, -worthy).

5486. **χάρισμα charisma**, *khar'-is-mah;* from *5483*; a (divine) *gratuity*, i.e. *deliverance* (from danger or passion); (spec.) a (spiritual) *endowment*, i.e. (subj.) religious *qualification*, or (obj.) miraculous *faculty:*—(free) gift.

5487. **χαριτόω charitŏō**, *khar-ee-tŏ'-o;* from *5485*; to *grace*, i.e. indue with special *honor:*—make accepted, be highly favoured.

5488. **Χαῤῥάν Charrhan**, *khar-hran';* of Heb. or. [2771]; *Charrhan* (i.e. *Charan*), a place in Mesopotamia:—Charran.

5489. **χάρτης chartēs**, *khar'-tace;* from the same as *5482*; a *sheet* ("chart") of writing-material (as to be *scribbled* over):—paper.

5490. **χάσμα chasma**, *khas'-mah;* from a form of an obsol. prim. **χάω chaō** (to "*gape*" or "*yawn*"); a "*chasm*" or *vacancy* (impassable *interval*):—gulf.

5491. **χεῖλος chĕilŏs**, *khi'-los;* from a form of the same as *5490*; a *lip* (as a *pouring* place); fig. a *margin* (of water):—lip, shore.

5492. **χειμάζω chĕimazō**, *khi-mad'-zo;* from the same as *5494*; to *storm*, i.e. (pass.) to *labor under a gale:*—be tossed with tempest.

5493. **χείμαῤῥος chĕimarrhŏs**, *khi'-mar-hros;* from the base of *5494* and *4482*; a *storm-runlet*, i.e. *winter-torrent:*—brook.

5494. **χειμών chĕimōn**, *khi-mone';* from a der. of **χέω chĕō** (to *pour;* akin to the base of *5490* through the idea of a *channel*), mean. a *storm* (as *pouring* rain); by impl. the *rainy* season, i.e. *winter:*—tempest, foul weather, winter.

5495. **χείρ chĕir**, *khire;* perh. from the base of *5494* in the sense of its congener the base of *5490* (through the idea of *hollowness* for grasping); the *hand* (lit. or fig. [*power*]; espec. [by Heb.] a *means* or *instrument*):—hand.

5496. **χειραγωγέω chĕiragōgĕō**, *khi-rag-ogue-eh'-o;* from *5497*; to be a *hand-leader*, i.e. to *guide* (a blind person):—lead by the hand.

5497. **χειραγωγός chĕiragōgŏs**, *khi-rag-o-gos';* from *5495* and a redupl. form of *71*; a *hand-leader*, i.e. personal *conductor* (of a blind person):—some to lead by the hand.

5498. **χειρόγραφον chĕirŏgraphŏn**, *khi-rog'-raf-on;* neut. of a comp. of *5495* and *1125*; something *hand-written* ("*chirograph*"), i.e. a *manuscript* (spec. a legal *document* or *bond* [fig.]):—handwriting.

5499. **χειροποίητος chĕirŏpŏiētŏs**, *khi-rop-oy'-ay-tos;* from *5495* and a der. of *4160*; *manufactured*, i.e. *of human construction:*—made by (make with) hands.

5500. **χειροτονέω chĕirŏtŏnĕō**, *khi-rot-on-eh'-o;* from a comp. of *5495* and **τείνω tĕinō** (to *stretch*); to be a *hand-reacher* or *voter* (by raising the hand), i.e. (gen.) to *select* or *appoint:*—choose, ordain.

5501. **χείρων chĕirōn**, *khi'-rone;* irreg. comp. of *2556*; from an obsol. equiv. **χέρης chĕrēs** (of uncert. der.); *more evil* or *aggravated* (phys., ment. or mor.):—sorer, worse.

5502. **χερουβίμ chĕrŏubim**, *kher-oo-beem';* plur. of Heb. or. [3742]; "*cherubim*" (i.e. *cherubs* or *kerubim*):—cherubims.

5503. **χήρα chēra**, *khay'-rah;* fem. of a presumed der. appar. from the base of *5490* through the idea of *deficiency;* a *widow* (as *lacking* a husband), lit. or fig.:—widow.

5504. **χθές chthĕs**, *khthes;* of uncert. der.; "*yesterday*"; by extens. *in time past* or *hitherto:*—yesterday.

5505. **χιλιάς chilias**, *khil-ee-as';* from *5507*; one *thousand* ("*chiliad*"):—thousand.

5506. **χιλίαρχος chiliarchŏs**, *khil-ee'-ar-khos;* from *5507* and *757*; the *commander of a thousand* soldiers ("*chiliarch*"), i.e. *colonel:*—(chief, high) captain.

5507. **χίλιοι chiliŏi**, *khil'-ee-oy;* plur. of uncert. affin.; a *thousand:*—thousand.

5508. **Χίος Chiŏs**, *khee'-os;* of uncert. der.; *Chios*, an island in the Mediterranean:—Chios.

5509. **χιτών chitōn**, *khee-tone';* of for. or. [3801]; a *tunic* or *shirt:*—clothes, coat, garment.

5510. **χιών chiōn**, *khee-one';* perh. akin to the base of *5490* (*5465*) or *5494* (as *descending* or *empty*); *snow:*—snow.

5511. **χλαμύς chlamus**, *khlam-ooce';* of uncert. der.; a military *cloak:*—robe.

5512. χλευάζω **chlĕuazō**, *khlyoo-ad'-zo;* from a der. prob. of 5491; to *throw out* the *lip*, i.e. *jeer* at:—mock.

5513. χλιαρός **chliarŏs**, *khlee-ar-os';* from χλίω **chliō** (to *warm*); *tepid:*—lukewarm.

5514. Χλόη **Chlŏē**, *khlŏ'-ay;* fem. of appar. a prim. word; "*green*"; *Chloë*, a Chr. female:—Chloe.

5515. χλωρός **chlōrŏs**, *khlo-ros';* from the same as 5514; *greenish*, i.e. *verdant*, *dun-colored:*—green, pale.

5516. χξς **chi xi stigma**, *khee xee stig'-ma;* the 22d, 14th and an obsol. letter (4742 as a *cross*) of the Greek alphabet (intermediate between the 5th and 6th), used as numbers; denoting respectively 600, 60 and 6; 666 as a numeral:—six hundred threescore and six.

5517. χοϊκός **chŏïkŏs**, *khŏ-ik-os';* from 5522; *dusty* or *dirty* (*soil*-like), i.e. (by impl.) *terrene:*—earthy.

5518. χοῖνιξ **chŏinix**, *khoy'-nix;* of uncert. der.; a *chœnix* or cert. dry measure:—measure.

5519. χοῖρος **chŏirŏs**, *khoy'-ros;* of uncert. der.; a *hog:*—swine.

5520. χολάω **chŏlaō**, *khol-ah'-o;* from 5521; to *be bilious*, i.e. (by impl.) *irritable* (*enraged*, "choleric"):—be angry.

5521. χολή **chŏlē**, *khol-ay';* fem. of an equiv. perh. akin to the same as 5514 (from the *greenish* hue); "*gall*" or *bile*, i.e. (by anal.) *poison* or an *anodyne* (wormwood, poppy, etc.):—gall.

5522. χόος **chŏŏs**, *khŏ'-os;* from the base of 5494; a *heap* (as *poured* out), i.e. *rubbish;* loose *dirt:*—dust.

5523. Χοραζίν **Chŏrazin**, *khor-ad-zin';* of uncert. der.; *Chorazin*, a place in Pal.:—Chorazin.

5524. χορηγέω **chŏrēgĕō**, *khor-ayg-eh'-o;* from a comp. of 5525 and 71; to *be a dance-leader*, i.e. (gen.) to *furnish:*—give, minister.

5525. χορός **chŏrŏs**, *khor-os';* of uncert. der.; a *ring*, i.e. round *dance* ("choir"):—dancing.

5526. χορτάζω **chŏrtazō**, *khor-tad'-zo;* from 5528; to *fodder*, i.e. (gen.) to *gorge* (*supply food* in abundance):—feed, fill, satisfy.

5527. χόρτασμα **chŏrtasma**, *khor'-tas-mah;* from 5526; *forage*, i.e. *food:*—sustenance.

5528. χόρτος **chŏrtŏs**, *khor'-tos;* appar. a prim. word; a "*court*" or "*garden*", i.e. (by impl. of *pasture*) *herbage* or *vegetation:*—blade, grass, hay.

5529. Χουζᾶς **Chŏuzas**, *khood-zas';* of uncert. or.; *Chuzas*, an officer of Herod:—Chuza.

5530. χράομαι **chraŏmai**, *khrah'-om-ahee;* mid. of a prim. verb (perh. rather from 5495, to *handle*); to *furnish* what is needed; (give an *oracle*, "*graze*" [touch slightly], *light* upon, etc.), i.e. (by impl.) to *employ* or (by extens.) to *act towards* one in a given manner:—entreat, use. Comp. 5531, 5534.

5531. χράω **chraō**, *khrah'-o;* prob. the same as the base of 5530; to *loan:*—lend.

5532. χρεία **chrĕia**, *khri'-ah;* from the base of 5530 or 5534; *employment*, i.e. an *affair;* also (by impl.) *occasion*, *demand*, *requirement* or *destitution:*—business, lack, necessary (-ity), need (-ful), use, want.

5533. χρεωφειλέτης **chrĕōphĕilĕtēs**, *khreh-o-fi-let'-ace;* from a der. of 5531 and 3781; a *loan-ower*, i.e. *indebted* person:—debtor.

5534. χρή **chrē**, *khray;* third pers. sing. of the same as 5530 or 5531 used impers.; it *needs* (*must* or *should*) be:—ought.

5535. χρῄζω **chrēzō**, *khrade'-zo;* from 5532; to *make* (i.e. *have*) *necessity*, i.e. *be in want* of:—(have) need.

5536. χρῆμα **chrēma**, *khray'-mah;* something *useful* or *needed*, i.e. *wealth*, *price:*—money, riches.

5537. χρηματίζω **chrēmatizō**, *khray-mat-id'-zo;* from 5536; to *utter an oracle* (comp. the orig. sense of 5530), i.e. divinely *intimate;* by impl. (comp. the secular sense of 5532) to constitute a *firm* for business, i.e. (gen.) *bear* as a *title:*—be called, be admonished (warned) of God, reveal, speak.

5538. χρηματισμός **chrēmatismŏs**, *khray-mat-is-mos';* from 5537; a divine *response* or *revelation:*—answer of God.

5539. χρήσιμος **chrēsimŏs**, *khray'-see-mos;* from 5540; *serviceable:*—profit.

5540. χρῆσις **chrēsis**, *khray'-sis;* from 5530; *employment*, i.e. (spec.) sexual *intercourse* (as an *occupation* of the body):—use.

5541. χρηστεύομαι **chrēstĕuŏmai**, *khraste-yoo'-om-ahee;* mid. from 5543; to *show oneself useful*, i.e. *act benevolently:*—be kind.

5542. χρηστολογία **chrēstŏlŏgia**, *khrase-tol-og-ee'-ah;* from a comp. of 5543 and 3004; *fair speech*, i.e. *plausibility:*—good words.

5543. χρηστός **chrēstŏs**, *khrase-tos';* from 5530; *employed*, i.e. (by impl.) *useful* (in manner or morals):—better, easy, good (-ness), gracious, kind.

5544. χρηστότης **chrēstŏtēs**, *khray-stot'-ace;* from 5543; *usefulness*, i.e. mor. *excellence* (in character or demeanor):—gentleness, good (-ness), kindness.

5545. χρίσμα **chrisma**, *khris'-mah;* from 5548; an *unguent* or *smearing*, i.e. (fig.) the spec. *endowment* ("chrism") of the Holy Spirit:—anointing, unction.

5546. Χριστιανός **Christianŏs**, *khris-tee-an-os';* from 5547; a *Christian*, i.e. follower of Christ:—Christian.

5547. Χριστός **Christŏs**, *khris-tos';* from 5548; *anointed*, i.e. the *Messiah*, an epithet of Jesus:—Christ.

5548. χρίω **chriō**, *khree'-o;* prob. akin to 5530 through the idea of *contact;* to *smear* or *rub* with oil, i.e. (by impl.) to *consecrate* to an office or religious service:—anoint.

5549. χρονίζω **chrŏnizō**, *khron-id'-zo;* from 5550; to *take time*, i.e. *linger:*—delay, tarry.

5550. χρόνος **chrŏnŏs**, *khron'-os;* of uncert. der.; a space of *time* (in gen., and thus prop. distinguished from 2540, which designates a *fixed* or special occasion; and from 165, which denotes a particular *period*) or *interval;* by extens. an individ. *opportunity;* by impl. *delay:*— + years old, season, space, (× often-) time (-s), (a) while.

5551. χρονοτριβέω **chrŏnŏtribĕō**, *khron-ot-rib-eh'-o;* from a presumed comp. of 5550 and the base of 5147; to *be a time-wearer*, i.e. to *procrastinate* (*linger*):—spend time.

5552. χρύσεος **chrusĕŏs**, *khroo'-seh-os;* from 5557; made *of gold:*—of gold, golden.

5553. χρυσίον **chrusiŏn**, *khroo-see'-on;* dimin. of 5557; a *golden* article, i.e. gold plating, ornament, or coin:—gold.

5554. χρυσοδακτύλιος **chrusŏdaktuliŏs**, *khroo-sod-ak-too'-lee-os;* from 5557 and 1146; *gold-ringed*, i.e. *wearing* a golden finger-ring or similar *jewelry:*—with a gold ring.

5555. χρυσόλιθος **chrusŏlithŏs**, *khroo-sol'-ee-thos;* from 5557 and 3037; *gold-stone*, i.e. a *yellow gem* ("*chrysolite*"):—chrysolite.

5556. χρυσόπρασος **chrusŏprasŏs**, *khroo-sop'-ras-os;* from 5557 and πράσον **prasŏn** (a *leek*); a *greenish-yellow* gem ("*chrysoprase*"):—chrysoprase.

5557. χρυσός **chrusŏs**, *khroo-sos';* perh. from the base of 5530 (through the idea of the *utility* of the metal); *gold;* by extens. a *golden* article, as an ornament or coin:—gold.

5558. χρυσόω **chrusŏō**, *khroo-sŏ'-o;* from 5557; to *gild*, i.e. *bespangle* with golden ornaments:—deck.

5559. χρώς **chrōs**, *khroce;* prob. akin to the base of 5530 through the idea of *handling;* the *body* (prop. its *surface* or *skin*):—body.

5560. χωλός **chōlŏs**, *kho-los';* appar. a prim. word; "*halt*", i.e. *limping:*—cripple, halt, lame.

5561. χώρα **chōra**, *kho'-rah;* fem. of a der. of the base of 5490 through the idea of *empty expanse;* *room*, i.e. a space of *territory* (more or less extensive; often includ. its inhab.):—coast, county, fields, ground, land, region. Comp. 5117.

5562. χωρέω **chōrĕō**, *kho-reh'-o;* from 5561; to *be in* (*give*) *space*, i.e. (intrans.) to *pass*, *enter*, or (trans.) to *hold*, *admit* (lit. or fig.):—come, contain, go, have place, (can, be room to) receive.

5563. χωρίζω **chōrizō**, *kho-rid'-zo;* from 5561; to *place room* between, i.e. *part;* reflex. to *go away:*—depart, put asunder, separate.

5564. χωρίον **chōriŏn**, *kho-ree'-on;* dimin. of 5561; a *spot* or *plot* of ground:—field, land, parcel of ground, place, possession.

5565. χωρίς **chōris**, *kho-rece';* adv. from 5561; *at a space*, i.e. *separately* or *apart* from (often as prep.):—beside, by itself, without.

5566. χῶρος **chōrŏs**, *kho'-ros;* of Lat. or.; the *north-west* wind:—north west.

Ψ

5567. ψάλλω **psallō**, *psal'-lo;* prob. strengthened from ψάω **psaō** (to *rub* or *touch* the surface; comp. 5597); to *twitch* or *twang*, i.e. to *play* on a stringed instrument (*celebrate* the divine worship *with music* and accompanying odes):—make melody, sing (psalms).

5568. ψαλμός **psalmŏs**, *psal-mos';* from 5567; a set piece of *music*, i.e. a sacred *ode* (accompanied with the voice, harp or other instrument; a "*psalm*"); collect. the book of the *Psalms:*—psalm. Comp. 5603.

5569. ψευδάδελφος **psĕudadĕlphŏs**, *psoo-dad'-el-fos;* from 5571 and 80; a *spurious brother*, i.e. *pretended associate:*—false brethren.

5570. ψευδαπόστολος **psĕudapŏstŏlŏs**, *psoo-dap-os'-tol-os;* from 5571 and 652; a *spurious apostle*, i.e. *pretended preacher:*—false teacher.

5571. ψευδής **psĕudēs**, *psoo-dace';* from 5574; *untrue*, i.e. *erroneous*, *deceitful*, *wicked:*—false, liar.

5572. ψευδοδιδάσκαλος **psĕudŏdidaskalŏs**, *psoo-dod-id-as'-kal-os;* from 5571 and 1320; a *spurious teacher*, i.e. *propagator* of *erroneous* Chr. *doctrine:*—false teacher.

5573. ψευδολόγος **psĕudŏlŏgŏs**, *psoo-dol-og'-os;* from 5571 and 3004; *mendacious*, i.e. *promulgating erroneous* Chr. *doctrine:*—speaking lies.

5574. ψεύδομαι **psĕudŏmai**, *psoo'-dom-ahee;* mid. of an appar. prim. verb; to *utter an untruth* or attempt to *deceive* by falsehood:—falsely, lie.

5575. ψευδομάρτυρ **psĕudŏmartur**, *psoo-dom-ar'-toor;* from 5571 and a kindred form of 3144; a *spurious witness*, i.e. *bearer of untrue testimony:*—false witness.

5576. ψευδομαρτυρέω **psĕudŏmarturĕō**, *psoo-dom-ar-too-reh'-o;* from 5575; to *be an untrue testifier*, i.e. offer *falsehood in evidence:*—be a false witness.

5577. ψευδομαρτυρία **psĕudŏmarturia**, *psoo-dom-ar-too-ree'-ah;* from 5575; *untrue testimony:*—false witness.

5578. ψευδοπροφήτης **psĕudŏprŏphētēs**, *psoo-dop-rof-ay'-tace;* from 5571 and 4396; a *spurious prophet*, i.e. *pretended foreteller* or religious *impostor:*—false prophet.

5579. ψεῦδος **psĕudŏs**, *psoo'-dos;* from 5574; a *falsehood:*—lie, lying.

5580. ψευδόχριστος **psĕudŏchristŏs**, *psoo-dokh'-ris-tos;* from 5571 and 5547; a *spurious Messiah:*—false Christ.

5581. ψευδώνυμος **psĕudōnumŏs**, *psoo-do'-noo-mos;* from 5571 and 3686; *untruly named:*—falsely so called.

5582. ψεῦσμα **psĕusma**, *psoos'-mah;* from 5574; a *fabrication*, i.e. *falsehood:*—lie.

5583. ψεύστης **psĕustēs**, *psoos-tace';* from 5574; a *falsifier:*—liar.

5584. ψηλαφάω **psēlaphaō**, *psay-laf-ah'-o;* from the base of 5567 (comp. 5586); to *manipulate*, i.e. *verify* by contact; fig. to *search* for:—feel after, handle, touch.

5585. ψηφίζω **psēphizō**, *psay-fid'-zo;* from 5586; to *use pebbles* in enumeration, i.e. (gen.) to *compute:*—count.

5586. ψῆφος **psēphŏs**, *psay'-fos;* from the same as 5584; a *pebble* (as worn smooth by *handling*), i.e.

(by impl. of use as a *counter* or *ballot*) a *verdict* (of acquittal) or *ticket* (of admission); a *vote:*—stone, voice.

5587. ψιθυρισμός **psithurismŏs**, *psith-oo-ris-mos';* from a der. of ψίθος **psithŏs** (a *whisper;* by impl. a *slander;* prob. akin to *5574*); *whispering*, i.e. secret *detraction:*—whispering.

5588. ψιθυριστής **psithuristēs**, *psith-oo-ris-tace';* from the same as *5587;* a secret *calumniator:*—whisperer.

5589. ψιχίον **psichiŏn**, *psikh-ee'-on;* dimin. from a der. of the base of *5567* (mean. a *crumb*); a *little bit* or *morsel:*—crumb.

5590. ψυχή **psuchē**, *psoo-khay';* from *5594; breath*, i.e. (by impl.) *spirit*, abstr. or concr. (the *animal* sentient principle only; thus distinguished on the one hand from *4151*, which is the rational and immortal *soul;* and on the other from *2222*, which is mere *vitality*, even of plants: these terms thus exactly correspond respectively to the Heb. 5315, 7307 and 2416):—heart (+ -ily), life, mind, soul, + us, + you.

5591. ψυχικός **psuchikŏs**, *psoo-khee-kos';* from *5590; sensitive*, i.e. *animate* (in distinction on the one hand from *4152*, which is the higher or *renovated* nature; and on the other from *5446*, which is the lower or *bestial* nature):—natural, sensual.

5592. ψύχος **psuchŏs**, *psoo'-khos;* from *5594; coolness:*—cold.

5593. ψυχρός **psuchrŏs**, *psoo-chros';* from *5592; chilly* (lit. or fig.):—cold.

5594. ψύχω **psuchō**, *psoo'-kho;* a prim. verb; to *breathe* (*voluntarily* but *gently;* thus differing on the one hand from *4154*, which denotes prop. a *forcible* respiration; and on the other from the base of *109*, which refers prop. to an inanimate *breeze*), i.e. (by impl. of reduction of temperature by evaporation) to *chill* (fig.):—wax cold.

5595. ψωμίζω **psōmizō**, *pso-mid'-zo;* from the base of *5596;* to *supply* with *bits*, i.e. (gen.) to *nourish:*—(bestow to) feed.

5596. ψωμίον **psōmiŏn**, *pso-mee'-on;* dim. from a der. of the base of *5597;* a *crumb* or *morsel* (as if *rubbed* off), i.e. a *mouthful:*—sop.

5597. ψώχω **psōchō**, *pso'-kho;* prol. from the same base as *5567;* to *triturate*, i.e. (by anal.) to *rub* out (kernels from husks with the fingers or hand):—rub.

Ω

5598. Ω **ō**, i.e. ὦμεγα **ōmĕga**, *o'-meg-ah;* the last letter of the Gr. alphabet, i.e. (fig.) the *finality:*—Omega.

5599. ὦ **ō**, *o;* a prim. interj.; as a sign of the voc. *O;* as a note of exclamation, *oh:*—O.

5600. ὦ **ō**, *o;* includ. the oblique forms, as well as ἦς **ēs**, *ace;* ᾖ **ē**, *ay*, etc.; the subjunctive of *1510;* (*may, might, can, could, would, should, must*, etc.; also with *1487* and its comp., as well as with other particles) *be:*—+ appear, are, (may, might, should) be, × have, is, + pass the flower of her age, should stand, were.

5601. Ὠβήδ **Obēd**, *o-bade';* of Heb. or. [5744]; *Obed*, an Isr.:—Obed.

5602. ὧδε **hōdĕ**, *ho'-deh;* from an adv. form of *3592; in this* same spot, i.e. *here* or *hither:*—here, hither, (in) this place, there.

5603. ᾠδή **ōidē**, *o-day';* from *103;* a *chant* or "*ode*" (the gen. term for any words sung; while *5215* denotes espec. a *religious* metrical composition, and *5568* still more spec. a *Heb.* cantillation):—song.

5604. ὠδίν **ōdin**, *o-deen';* akin to *3601;* a *pang* or *throe*, esp. of childbirth:—pain, sorrow, travail.

5605. ὠδίνω **ōdinō**, *o-dee'-no;* from *5604;* to *experience* the *pains* of parturition (lit. or fig.):—travail in (birth).

5606. ὦμος **ōmŏs**, *o'-mos;* perh. from the alt. of *5342;* the *shoulder* (as that on which burdens are *borne*):—shoulder.

5607. ὤν **ōn**, *oan;* includ. the fem.

ουσα **ŏusa**, *oo'-sah;* and the neut.

ὄν **ŏn**, *on;* pres. part. of *1510; being:*—be, come, have.

5608. ὠνέομαι **ōnĕŏmai**, *o-neh'-om-ahee;* mid. from an appar. prim. ὦνος **ōnŏs** (a *sum* or *price*); to *purchase* (synon. with the earlier *4092*):—buy.

5609. ᾠόν **ōŏn**, *o-on';* appar. a prim. word; an "*egg*":—egg.

5610. ὥρα **hōra**, *ho'-rah;* appar. a prim. word; an "*hour*" (lit. or fig.):—day, hour, instant, season, × short, [even-] tide, (high) time.

5611. ὡραῖος **hōraiŏs**, *ho-rah'-yos;* from *5610; belonging* to the right *hour* or *season* (*timely*), i.e. (by impl.) *flourishing* (*beauteous* [fig.]):—beautiful.

5612. ὠρύομαι **ōruŏmai**, *o-roo'-om-ahee;* mid. of an appar. prim. verb; to "*roar*":—roar.

5613. ὡς **hōs**, *hoce;* prob. adv. of comp. from *3739; which how*, i.e. *in that manner* (very variously used, as follows):—about, after (that), (according) as (it had been, it were), as soon (as), even as (like), for, how (greatly), like (as, unto), since, so (that), that, to wit, unto, when ([-soever]), while, × with all speed.

5614. ὡσαννά **hōsanna**, *ho-san-nah';* of Heb. or. [8467 and 4994]; *oh save!; hosanna* (i.e. *hoshia-na*), an exclamation of adoration:—hosanna.

5615. ὡσαύτως **hōsautōs**, *ho-sŏw'-toce;* from *5613* and an adv. from *846; as thus*, i.e. *in the same way:*—even so, likewise, after the same (in like) manner.

5616. ὡσεί **hōsĕi**, *ho-si';* from *5613* and *1487; as if:*—about, as (it had been, it were), like (as).

5617. Ὡσηέ **Hōsēĕ**, *ho-say-eh';* of Heb. or. [1954]; *Hoseë* (i.e. *Hosheä*), an Isr.:—Osee.

5618. ὥσπερ **hōspĕr**, *hoce'-per;* from *5613* and *4007; just as*, i.e. *exactly like:*—(even, like) as.

5619. ὡσπερεί **hōspĕrĕi**, *hoce-per-i';* from *5618* and *1487; just as if*, i.e. *as it were:*—as.

5620. ὥστε **hōstĕ**, *hoce'-teh;* from *5613* and *5037; so too*, i.e. *thus therefore* (in various relations of *consecution*, as follow):—(insomuch) as, so that (then), (insomuch) that, therefore, to, wherefore.

5621. ὠτίον **ōtiŏn**, *o-tee'-on;* dimin. of *3775;* an *earlet*, i.e. *one* of the ears, or perh. the *lobe* of the ear:—ear.

5622. ὠφέλεια **ōphĕlĕia**, *o-fel'-i-ah;* from a der. of the base of *5624; usefulness*, i.e. *benefit:*—advantage, profit.

5623. ὠφελέω **ōphĕlĕō**, *o-fel-eh'-o;* from the same as *5622;* to *be useful*, i.e. to *benefit:*—advantage, better, prevail, profit.

5624. ὠφέλιμος **ōphĕlimŏs**, *o-fel'-ee-mos;* from a form of *3786; helpful* or *serviceable*, i.e. *advantageous:*—profit (-able).

VARIATIONS

IN THE NUMBERING OF VERSES IN THE GREEK AND ENGLISH NEW TESTAMENT.

English.	Greek.
Mark 13: 8 (last clause) (first clauses)	9
Luke 22: 66 (last word) (first word)	67
John 1: 38 (all after first clause)	39
39	40
40	41
41	42
42	43
John 1: 43	44
44	45
45	46
46	47
47	48
48	49
49	50
John 1: 50	51
51	52
Acts 4: 6 (last clause) (in)	5
13: 33 (former half) (latter half)	32
1 Pet 2: 8 (first two clauses) (last two clauses)	7